GW00787209

THE BIG OFFICIAL UCAS GUIDE TO UNIVERSITY & COLLEGE ENTRANCE

PUBLISHED BY UCAS
IN ASSOCIATION WITH  THE INDEPENDENT STUDY GUIDES **1998**

2

Preface

Publisher's notes

The Official UCAS Guide to University and College Entrance is published for information purposes only and no liability is accepted for its contents. While all reasonable efforts have been made to ensure that the information contained was correct at the time of going to press, the publishers do not accept responsibility for errors or omissions. The Guide should not be regarded as definitive and does not take precedence over the official publications of universities and colleges. Applicants for entry should check with the institutions about the current position on any question of fact.

All rights reserved. No part of this publication may be reproduced, stored in a retrieval system or transmitted in any form or by any means electronic, mechanical, photocopying, recording or otherwise, without the prior permission of the publishers in writing.

Editorial Acknowledgements

Editor:	Tony Higgins
Managing editor:	Irene Finlayson
Technical editor:	David Morgan

Photographic Acknowledgements

The photographs used in this edition of UCE:G are from the Jessop/UCAS/The Independent Student Photographic Competition © UCAS.

Publication details

ISBN:	0 948241 48 9
Edition:	Fifth, 1997
Published by:	Universities and Colleges Admissions Service (UCAS)
Copyright:	UCAS

UCAS Registered in England No. 2839815
Registered Charity No. 1024741
UCAS Ref: UC-0044A/98

The purpose of *The Official UCAS Guide to University and College Entrance 1998* is to help applicants to choose the most appropriate subjects, courses and places of study. It is one of several applicant support resources provided by and through UCAS to help people discover and assess the possibilities open to them.

Ultimately, an applicant's choice must take into account not only the information gained from this and other sources of reference, but also his or her individual preferences, motivations and personal goals.

Finding a good match between an individual's own requirements and those programmes of study on offer will depend initially upon thorough research. This can take time, during a period when a majority of potential applicants are already burdened with sixth form or college studies, and with many other demands made on their time. Nevertheless, it must be given a priority: too many students regret their choices and many ultimately leave higher education, under circumstances and for reasons which could all too easily have been avoided only by a little more prior thought.

In compiling as comprehensive a base of information as is possible, the Guide can help potential applicants to become aware of the wide range of opportunities available, determine where their preferred courses are available and, more important, what the likely grades and qualifications are going to be for entry in 1998. Only official university and college prospectuses will describe what a programme actually contains, and its structure, and all applicants **must** read the prospectuses of their favoured institutions before deciding whether or not to apply. The Guide should help to narrow down the choice initially.

This is the fifth edition of the Guide, and it consolidates changes which arose in response to comments made on behalf of the users by advisers in schools, colleges and careers offices, and from the institutions whose course details are displayed within. This year we are again including with the Guide a multi media CD-ROM entitled *Studylink UK*. This is the official multi media package endorsed not only by UCAS but also by the Committee of Vice-Chancellors and Principals, The Standing Conference of Principals and the British Council. Comments are always welcome and should be addressed to the Editor, Information Services Department, UCAS, Fulton House, Jessop Avenue, Cheltenham, Gloucestershire GL50 3SH.

The editorial team would like to thank those who commented on the drafts, especially Mike Chant of Learning Partnership West, Rosemary Williamson of COSHEP, and colleagues from UCAS and ECCTIS, as well as those representatives from institutions, schools and the careers service who sat on the Consultative Group which drew up the framework for this edition.

UCAS is grateful for the generous support from *The Independent* and BPP Holdings plc (who include in their group Letts Study Guides and MPW).

Price: £18.95
Designed by: The Design Works
Printed by: Linneys ESL
Further copies available from:
Sheed & Ward,
14 Coopers Row,
London EC3N 2BH.

Letts STUDY GUIDES
THE INDEPENDENT

Contents

Section 1

Section 2

Section 3

Photograph: Mark Jarvis

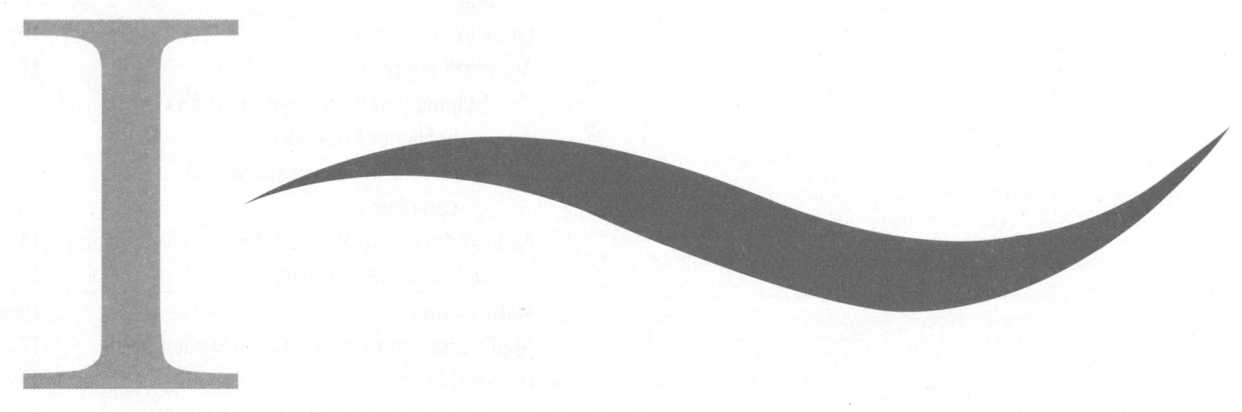

AN INTRODUCTION TO
MAKING THE RIGHT START
TO YOUR FUTURE IN
HIGHER EDUCATION AT A
UNIVERSITY OR COLLEGE

GETTING STARTED

1998

How to get the best out of this Guide

Don't Panic!

Your first impression of this Guide is probably its sheer size and weight - well over 1000 pages, in excess of 30,000 courses and a bulk which makes it an excellent door stop! As the Official Guide to undergraduate entry to Higher Education in the UK, it contains a vast amount of information and presents you with a dazzling array of opportunity. But too much choice can be very daunting.

Don't panic! In practice, as with any other reference book, only some of the information will apply to you. You will also find that the Guide is actually very user-friendly. The secret is to become familiar with how it works, and to use the tips in this section to help you get the best out of it.

When should I use the Guide?

Don't even think about filling in the choices on your UCAS application form without having first consulted both this Guide and the relevant university prospectuses. The Guide should form an important part of your researches, and can be used at various stages. Students commonly start using it six months or more before completing the UCAS form which normally takes place in the autumn of the year before entry to a university or college.

To get the best out of the Guide, you need to have some idea of the types of courses which might interest you, or at least of the broad subject areas. If you have not yet reached that stage, turn to the articles on "Applicant Support" pages 11-13 which will tell you about ways of helping to identify what you are suited for and what you are interested in.

Let's assume that you have reached the stage of wanting to explore the possibilities in one or more subject areas. This is where this Guide comes into its own as the main tool to help you find the right opportunities. Your choice of course in Higher Education will affect the rest of your life, and it is not something to decide in a hurry. You need to do careful research to check that you will have the right qualifications for the course, that it offers what you want, and that you are likely to be happy at the university or college concerned. This process will probably take you several months and will include discussions with teachers, tutors or advisers. You will need to use a number of reference books, consult university and college prospectuses, and look at videos. You will also

want to attend Higher Education fairs, and make visits to universities and colleges. But at the heart of this process you will be able to use the information from this Guide.

What does the Guide offer?

The Guide is quite simple in its layout. Pages 6 to 27 are all about "Getting Started" and give you helpful advice on matters such as entry requirements, interviews, the applications process, etc. You may want to dip into this section first, but you will probably not need to read it all initially.

Section 2 provides a series of half-page data files of each of the Higher Education institutions - this includes universities, colleges, institutes of Higher Education, and specialist institutions such as agricultural colleges and medical schools. The data file gives useful facts and figures about the institution including student numbers and the average cost of accommodation.

Section 3 is the real meat of the Guide containing Tables of courses grouped under alphabetical subject areas. There is a helpful user guide to these Tables on pages 164 to 170 and a bookmark with a key to the abbreviations. The Course Tables show you what courses exist in each subject area, and give you useful information about likely entry requirements. This is the section which it is vital for you to check before applying for any course.

Using the Course Tables

Clearly you will have your own ideas as to what information you want to obtain from the Guide. But the following may be useful to you as an example of how to go about the process:

- Choose a broad subject area which interests you, eg Media Studies, and turn to the index.
- The index will tell you on which Tables the relevant courses appear.
- Turn to the Tables and start scanning through the entries which will be listed under individual universities and colleges in alphabetical order.
- Get a feel of the range of courses offered and the types of institutions providing them.
- Focus in more closely on any course titles which particularly interest you and note which institutions offer them.
- Look at those entries more closely to check how suitable the course is for you

and how suitable you are for the course.
- Check the length of the course, eg three or four years, whether it is full-time or involves a sandwich year, whether it is a degree, Higher National Diploma (HND) or Diploma of Higher Education (DipHE).
- Then check the subject column - the user guide or the bookmark will tell you what subjects are required for entry. If you will not have the relevant qualification, do not include the course on your list. If you are not clear whether you will be suitably qualified, check the prospectus of the university or college concerned. If still in doubt, write direct to the admissions tutor for the course.
- According to whether you are offering GCE A levels/AS, National Diploma or Certificate, Advanced GNVQ or GSVQ Level III, International Baccalaureate, Scottish Highers, or Scottish Qualification Authority (SQA) awards as your main qualification for entry to Higher Education, look up the appropriate column to see what the likely offer level will be for entry in 1998. For example, at GCE A level you might be required to obtain grades BCC, or a points score of 20. Points scores are explained in the user guide.
- If realistically you are unlikely to be able to achieve the expected entry level, it is probably not worthwhile pursuing the course any further, although you might wish to double check in the prospectus. It is important to be realistic when making your choices.
- Remember that substantial areas of Higher Education are very competitive, for example Law and Medicine, and that high grade offers are commonly a way of controlling numbers. The level of the offer does not necessarily reflect the quality of the course.
- When using this information to decide your choices, remember to include at least one institution which is likely to make a lower level offer. You will be able to hold two conditional offers through the UCAS system, one of which should be a lower offer as an insurance.
- Then check out any statistics for 1996 entry which will tell you the number of applications and acceptances for the

course and the average GCE A level/AS points score for those actually admitted. This will give you a measure of the competition and the actual entry standard for the previous intake. Not all institutions display statistics however.

- In those cases where the result of your checks is favourable, make a note of the institution, course name and code. This will help you when doing further research, eg in prospectuses.
- Investigate the possibilities of joint courses, eg Media Studies/European Studies - you will find a substantial number of opportunities of this kind in the Course Tables.
- You may also want to look for general and combined courses under codes beginning with 'Y'.

Using the Data files

Once you have a list of potentially suitable courses, use the data files in Section 2 to find out more about the universities and colleges which offer them.

- Check the type of institution and its size and where it is located.
- Check whether you are likely to be offered accommodation in the first year and what the cost will be.
- Look at the dates of Open Days - for more information ask your school, college or careers office to let you refer to a copy of the UCAS Open Day booklet.
- Use this information to help you decide which of the institutions would be worth researching further - keep a note of those which are still on the list.

What Next?

Clearly this Guide, large though it is, cannot contain all the information you need to know before applying for a course. Once you have arrived at a list of possible institutions and courses, you will then need to look at the individual prospectuses. Most schools, colleges and careers services hold at least one set, and will let you use them on a reference basis. If you are particularly interested in certain universities or colleges, you may wish to write to them to request a personal copy of the prospectus. If you do this, mention what subject area you are interested in as they may have additional literature.

Use the prospectuses to check out in greater depth the entry requirements and any admissions policies which might affect your chances. Look carefully at the course content, methods of assessment, availability of options, and special features. Is the course modular and is there flexibility to take units from other subject areas? What are the facilities like? How much accommodation is there and where is it located? Remember prospectuses are sales documents and tend to show pictures taken on sunny days in summer!

Build on your research in this Guide by using other information sources, eg reference books on specific subjects, alternative prospectuses,

videos, and take the opportunity to visit anywhere you are particularly keen on.

As your researches progress, and your ideas evolve, you may need to go back to this Guide on several occasions to check out other possibilities. There is nothing wrong in changing your mind in the time leading up to filling in your UCAS form. Even after you have applied through UCAS, keep your copy of this Guide because you may need to refer to it in August/September if it is necessary for you to use Clearing.

Suggestions for Advisers - Using the Guide as an Educational Tool

The above gives a basic methodology for student use of the Guide for reference purposes. However careers advisers may wish to consider ways in which the Guide can be used as an educational tool. The Guide is a rich source of information, and can be approached from a number of points of view. The process of conducting research in the Guide can provide students with a deeper understanding of Higher Education, and greater confidence in the use of reference tools.

The following are just a few suggestions about possible avenues of exploration within the Guide:

- Comparisons of grade offers both within a specific subject area and between subject areas, and the relationship between offer levels and the ratio of applicants per place. Do any strong patterns emerge by subject? Are there patterns by regions or by types of institution?
- Investigate the relationship of grade offers to the actual grades achieved by those accepted - where there are differences, what might the explanation be?
- Research interesting combinations of subjects and their availability.
- Student mix - a look at the male/female ratio in individual institutions - why might it differ?
- An analysis of the academic subject spread of a cross-section of types of HEIs.
- A look at the percentage of first year students who can be accommodated by the institution - at what types of institution is it one hundred per cent? If the percentage is much lower, does this matter, or is it perhaps because many of the students are likely to live locally? What about London? Do clear patterns emerge?
- A comparison of accommodation costs - does it depend on the type of institution? Are there regional patterns? Is London really the most expensive? What other factors might affect the cost of living?
- Set a trail based on facts buried within the data files - the students will need to scan them to uncover the answers.

Advisers may wish to draw up a simple course research form for use by students. This could take the form of an A4 single page proforma on which students could record

information about courses/institutions as they pursue in-depth research using the Guide, prospectuses and other reference books. The form might typically include:

- Type of institution
- Course content/opportunities for options/combining subjects
- Grade requirements
- Interview policy
- Date of Open Day
- Availability of first year accommodation
- Cost of living
- Social and recreational facilities
- Distance from home
- Travel costs
- Employment prospects
- What specially appeals to me about this course/institution?

Advisers - staff development

It is essential that all staff advising applicants to Higher Education should be familiar with what the Guide offers and should be adept at using it. Staff development for advisers in schools, colleges and careers offices could usefully include hands-on exploration activities with the Guide.

Many of the points listed above for students could also be adopted for advisers, but at a deeper and more analytical level. Advisers might also want to look at issues such as:

- The acceptability of Advanced GNVQs, eg by GNVQ course title, type of HE course, and type of HE institution - what progression patterns emerge?
- How important is Mathematics and for what subjects in HE? For those subjects, what opportunities are there for those who are not offering it?
- A survey of the HEIs which have the highest percentage of mature students.
- Where is it cheapest to study?
- An analysis of opportunities in the adviser's local region in a particular subject area.
- An investigation of courses coded 'Y'. What opportunities do they offer? How should they be explained to clients?
- An exercise on A level requirements, eg do any HEIs accept students for History degree courses without a History A level? Which Medical schools insist on Chemistry plus one from Physics/Mathematics/Biology?
- Which are the most competitive subject areas in terms of the ratio of applicants to places?

Staff development exploration of the Guide might involve a sheet containing specific questions (eg a client is interested in taking a course in Ceramics - what opportunities are there?) to be answered from the data within the Guide.

Making your choice

Your choice of what to study and where to study has never been wider and it takes time and effort on your part to research the possibilities thoroughly. Institutions offer different programmes of study and facilities and methods of assessment. The extent of your choice and complexity of your decision depend on your starting point and, nowadays, on financial considerations.

I know what I want to do

If you have decided on a particular career which has a clearly defined entry route, eg Dentistry, Architecture, it is easy to identify suitable courses. Where you choose to study may be affected by entry requirements, the type of institution you prefer, local facilities or opportunities for relevant part-time work.

If you have a strong interest in particular subjects whether directly career related or not, again part of the decision is relatively clear and your decision is more focused. It is more satisfying to study something which interests you and at which you are therefore more likely to succeed. Your enthusiasm for what you are doing will make the all-round experience of Higher Education more satisfying than it might be if you study a subject which you or others perceive to be 'useful' but which you find boring. You do need to have some indication of the types of jobs open to graduates in a particular subject but remember that many employers seek graduates with good degrees in any discipline provided they possess the necessary personal qualities and motivation for the job, and can demonstrate how worthwhile their whole educational experience has been.

For example history graduates become merchant bankers, science graduates journalists, and law graduates computer programmers. Where you study a subject of special interest might be affected by the availability of options or subsidiary courses, the flexibility of the programme, the way it is taught and assessed, the facilities offered and links with employers.

Still undecided

You may have no specific career ideas or subject interests but want to continue your education. Do think hard about why you are going into Higher Education and what you will be doing for two, three or four years, or longer. There are several aids available to help you to focus your thinking and crystallise your ideas. The article on "Applicant Support" (pages 11-13) which appears later in this section of the book is a good starting point.

Motivation is a critical factor for successful study. Do not underestimate its importance. One main reason for students discontinuing courses is lack of motivation rather than lack of ability. If you continue with familiar subjects in the hope of making an easy decision, you may find that you don't like the course structure, or that it is too difficult, or that you get bored. If you choose 'new' subjects, try to find out what they involve. Some institutions produce helpful

Photograph: Laura Baxter

Photograph: Laura Baxter

material on a wide range of subjects, professional bodies publish relevant books on their subjects, and there are a number of reference books which will give you an overview of subject areas. These should be available in schools, colleges, libraries and local careers services.

If you decide that you want a qualification to expand your career prospects, look at the effect different courses might have. Some are vocational and lead to specific careers and professional recognition – you may feel happier in a course where you hope to use its content directly at work.

Most university and college careers services produce annual reports with statistics of what happens to their graduates.

Other factors you should look at include the number of students on the course, whether there are any sandwich or practical elements, the assessment arrangements (exam or continuous course work), the difference between doing the same subject as a BA or BSc (eg Geography, Psychology), and the length of the course, especially if postgraduate study may also be required for your eventual career. How does the institution cater for mature students, international students or those with special needs?

Help!

It may all seem bewildering but help and information are readily available. You should read the prospectus carefully and follow this up with enquiries to relevant Admissions Officers and departments. Take advantage of any opportunities to visit institutions to see the work, the accommodation, surroundings and facilities. Talk to students. Staff in institutions are there to help you, as are the local careers services.

Do not be afraid to make direct contact to obtain the information you need to make an informed decision. Admissions staff and course tutors will be happy to talk to you on the telephone and to answer written enquiries. Your first point of contact is given in the institution's data file in the second section of the Guide.

Institutions vary in size, facilities and atmosphere. These matter more to some people than others. Think about where you might be living for the next three, four or five years. Will you be able to continue with a particular interest there, can you afford to live there, will you miss your home life, is it your sort of place? Does the university or college have franchising arrangements at locally-based centres which might be more practical for you? Base your decision on facts and first hand experience, not on misconceptions about a particular town or city.

Money matters

Finance and related costs of accommodation are serious issues for students. While tuition fees for almost all first degree, DipHE and HND courses are likely to be paid automatically, you will still have to find ways of financing your living expenses. You may be awarded a maintenance grant if your parents' combined income is below a certain amount. The maximum maintenance grant at present for students living away from home and staying outside London is around £1,755. For students in London, living away from home, it is £2,160, and for students living at home it is £1,435. This maximum is reduced on a sliding scale according to your parents' income and many families find that they have to provide the full cost of maintenance themselves.

Many student bodies have devised figures to show what an average student needs to cover accommodation, books, travel, clothes and other living costs. The figure consistently quoted is £4 - £5,000 for each year. Student Loans, introduced by the government to top up grants, are a student's main source of income after maintenance grants and parental support. Even with a full maintenance grant and student loan, many students find that they have to work during term time as well as vacations to support themselves.

For some students it may make more sense to live and study at home if there is access to part-time work and cheap digs! The article "Some Useful Publications and Addresses" (pages 26-27) has a section on Student Finance which suggests appropriate publications and provides relevant addresses.

If you do decide to study away from home, most institutions have Accommodation Officers who will provide detailed information and help.

Checklist

READ – Prospectuses, Careers Material, Alternative Student Prospectus, Information on Grants and Loans. See separate article 'Some Useful Publications'.

TALK TO – Admissions Officers, Departments, Students, Careers Advisers, Accommodation Officers, Current Students.

Entry Requirements

Photograph: Kirsty Denholm

Personal qualities, attitudes, skills, values and interests naturally play a large part in an individual's career or educational decisions. Another part of the process of choosing what to study is an understanding of what your education to date will enable you to do. Institutions set academic entry requirements according to what knowledge or skills are needed to study a particular course. The entry standards are often governed by the popularity and demand for their courses. The most difficult courses to enter are therefore not necessarily those which have the most difficult content or which are preferred by employers.

An increasing number of students now enter Higher Education with qualifications other than ones obtained while at school or college and you should check with each institution to find out what is acceptable. Most will allow mature students entry without their having to conform strictly to laid-down requirements, provided they can demonstrate their ability, commitment and motivation. This, however, tends to be more difficult where the course has a highly competitive level of entry. Access courses are a popular route of entry for mature students and it is worth checking with institutions what Access arrangements are in place for their courses.

Minimum Entry Requirements

These are the qualifications which institutions specify for their courses but offers to applicants may well be in excess of the minimum number of passes and specified grades required.

The Course Tables in Section 3 of this book give some indication of these specific requirements but you must check individual prospectuses for detailed information. It is pointless to waste a choice on your UCAS form with an application to a course for which you will not be qualified. Equally, do not be tempted to apply for the wrong course for you just because you have the high academic results needed for entry. You may find the course frustrating because it neither interests nor challenges you sufficiently.

Applicants taking AS qualifications instead of, or in addition to, their third A level will find that these are welcomed where they broaden a student's studies. Institutions' policies on their acceptability for specific courses vary but most accept AS.

The Course Tables assume the acceptability of AS in place of named A levels. It will be indicated if this is not the case. They also contain *expected* entry requirements in terms of Scottish Highers, National Diploma and Certificate and SQA (Scottish Qualification Authority) National Awards, Advanced GNVQ and the International Baccalaureate. The more detailed subject information is given only in terms of GCE but will be helpful as a guide to the general background expected for admission.

Scottish students taking CSYS will find varying attitudes. Many English institutions will specify them as entry requirements but Scottish institutions tend to state their requirements in terms of H grades with CSYS being considered favourably.

Other qualifications which may be acceptable for entry include the International General Certificate of Secondary Education (IGCSE), regarded as equivalent to GCSE, and the Advanced International Certificate of Education (AICE).

Acceptable Subjects

Most subjects studied at school are acceptable for general entrance purposes but occasionally certain ones might not be recognised, or if there is an overlap of two, both together might not be valid, eg Biology and Human Biology, History and Economic History. It cannot be emphasised enough that you should check in the prospectus and with the institutions concerned that you will be qualified for their courses.

General National Vocational Qualifications (GNVQ and GSVQ)

GNVQs are vocational qualifications awarded by Edexcel Foundation (formerly BTEC), City and Guilds and RSA Examination Boards. Rapidly growing numbers of people are achieving these qualifications and HE institutions are becoming more accustomed to them. Some institutions have standard entry conditions for GNVQ applicants but many will treat each application on its merit. The nature of the qualification, however, has to be matched to the course in prospect and, particularly for degree courses, additional performance above the threshold may be sought (as it often is for GCE A level applicants). GSVQs are the Scottish equivalent of GNVQs and are awarded by the SQA.

Applicant Support –

helping you to choose the right course in Higher Education

The UCAS form, on which you can make up to six choices of courses in Higher Education, is a mechanism for making the process of getting into university or college work well for you. The outcome will only be as good as the quality of research and decision-making on your part in the period leading up to form filling in the autumn.

UCAS' mission is to do more than just help you with the process of applying to Higher Education. It is concerned with encouraging you to choose the right course for the right reason – so that you enjoy your studies and come out with a qualification which really suits your needs and interests, and leads to career opportunities. If you are reading this, you are presumably intending to use this book for research. But do you know how to get the best out of it? Which are the most suitable course areas for you to research? How can you avoid making the wrong choice, and perhaps having a false start at a university which could affect your grant entitlement?

To help you with the initial stages of deciding which course areas in Higher Education to research, UCAS recommends that you should use as your starting point a computer-based applicant support programme such as Centigrade. The object of such a programme is to match your interests, abilities and personal qualities with the courses available in Higher Education, using a paper-based questionnaire. It will provide you with a detailed personal report, including a profile of the course areas that are most appropriate for you to research, and a list of universities and colleges which offer suitable courses, as well as a great deal of other helpful information.

It is not intended that the programme will tell you the actual courses to which you should apply. Instead it will focus you on suitable course areas, and stimulate you to get started on some structured research – it will provide you with course analysis forms and an action

plan to help with this process. To get the best out of the programme you need to make some effort to follow it up yourself.

Applicant support programmes are intended to be the starting point for your quest for the right choices, helping you to get the best out of research tools such as this Guide, prospectuses, and ECCTIS and other courses databases. If you really don't know what you want, or you are bewildered by the sheer number of courses on offer, such a programme will help you to focus on a few course areas that are likely to suit you best. If, on the other hand, you have already formed ideas about what you want, such a programme can be useful in raising your awareness of other possiblities, or indeed confirming that you are on the right track.

Applicants normally take Centigrade or other programmes through their school, college or local careers service – you should ask your careers adviser for information. The modest cost of the service is money well spent in view of the risks of making the wrong choices. Let the experts help you to get it right!

UCAS on the Net
(http://www.ucas.ac.uk)

UCAS now has a Web site which will provide information on all aspects of UCAS's work. For applicants there is a wealth of useful information, both for their initial research into which courses and institutions to consider, and for their progress through the applications process.

An interactive course search will help potential applicants with their initial search for courses and institutions, with links to more than 250 university and college Web sites. The UCAS Education Conventions pages give details of the fairs and conventions held throughout the year where all of the universities and colleges within UCAS can provide information and guidance to prospective applicants.

Information from a range of UCAS publications is reproduced giving advice on the application process. Groups such as mature students and international students can obtain advice concerning their special circumstances. There is even advice for parents!

During Clearing the UCAS Web site will also include up-to-the-minute listings of the institutions still offering places.

The site is designed with the computer novice in mind. No mind-boggling graphics or incomprehensible jargon – just plain English and easy to follow screens. You will find us at the following URL: http://www.ucas.ac.uk.

ECCTIS

ECCTIS is the government-supported computerised courses information service. It gives comprehensive information on over 100,000 courses at universities and colleges throughout the UK. It can be found at nearly 5,000 access points – in most secondary schools, careers offices, further education

Photograph: Alan Cullen

Getting Started

Photograph: Elizabeth Palmer

How does ECCTIS+ provide further information on courses, qualifications and careers?

The flexible nature of ECCTIS+ enables a whole range of additional services to be accessed alongside the courses information. Detailed information from professional bodies can be found as well as explanations of vocational qualification structures.

colleges, HE institutions, adult guidance centres, libraries and British Council offices throughout the world.

A typical ECCTIS+ search can be conducted in a matter of minutes. You are asked to specify the subject or subjects that you wish to explore, the level or type of qualification that you wish to pursue, how you want to study – part-time, full-time or sandwich – and any geographical preferences. The system will then generate a comprehensive list detailing all relevant courses. Most records give full information on entry requirements and considerable detail on what the courses actually cover, often telling you what you will be studying each year.

ECCTIS+ is particularly valuable if you are considering combinations of subjects. It is easy to search on two or more subject combinations; it explains different modular schemes and often gives full course details of the individual options themselves.

How does ECCTIS+ relate to admissions information?

ECCTIS+ works closely with UCAS and the information on ECCTIS+ is matched with the course information in the *UCAS Handbook*. The *Handbook*, together with other admissions information, including that from the GATE (GNVQ and Access to Higher Education)

database, is also carried on ECCTIS+.

How can ECCTIS+ help you during Clearing?

ECCTIS+ acts as an agent for UCAS during the Summer Clearing Period – late August until the end of September. Daily updated information on course vacancies is available at a large number of ECCTIS+ access points as well as through a range of telephone helplines which ECCTIS 2000 support. The availability of these helplines is publicised by UCAS through radio, television and certain national newspapers during Clearing.

How can ECCTIS+ help you if you wish to study for a degree but do not have the required entry qualifications?

If you are looking to enter higher education as a mature applicant or to continue further study after a break, ECCTIS+ is designed to inform you of the opportunities available through credit transfer, and carries details of over 800 Access courses, including their location.

Letts STUDY GUIDES
THE INDEPENDENT

Applicant Support –

what your local careers service can offer

Acquiring information and guidance during the period leading up to your UCAS application becomes a way of life. Sometimes your research will be conducted informally and spontaneously, and sometimes with greater structure. There is no one single source of help. Friends, family, school, college, employers, HE institutions and local careers services are all part of a network offering advice and information, opinion and experience. You may need to use all of them, and to be aware throughout that your task is to build up a background of understanding and advice which will enable you to take responsibility for the final decisions. Discussion may cover your initial choices, how to complete your UCAS form and selection of Firm and Insurance offers within the UCAS system.

Professionally trained careers advisers provide client-centred educational and vocational guidance. They offer free, impartial help with the process of decision making, and are in regular contact with HE institutions as well as employers. Whatever your needs, help will be available.

Get to know your local careers service at an early stage in the research process, and try to use it regularly rather than expect to sort everything out during one quick visit just before the closing date for applications to UCAS.

You may have already met your careers adviser at school or college, in which case you should maintain contact with her or him throughout your times of decision making. If you have not yet met your adviser, make a point of doing so now.

It is possible to use the careers centre as a source of information, just as you might use a school careers room or public library. You can visit your local centre without an appointment. If you want to visit but do not know where the nearest one is, look in the telephone book for careers services. Many services provide help and advice for adults and may have a careers adviser who works specifically with adult clients. If not, they can suggest suitable sources of further help.

If you need help with finding or using the information facilities available, a conversation with a member of the guidance staff would be helpful. If you feel that you need a more structured or in-depth discussion with a careers adviser about any aspect of your research or decision making, then you should make an appointment. Centres are open all the year round.

Photograph: Pauline Goy

Examples of resources available in careers offices

Prospectuses
Reference books
Video prospectuses
Careers information
Course leaflets
Computer databases
Computer-assisted guidance
Interest guides
Application forms and handbooks
Clearing information
One to one impartial guidance
  interviews
Information workshops
Employment information
Guide to grants and loans
Links with HE admissions staff
Open day and HE fair information
Sponsorship and sandwich course
  opportunities
Ideas for a year out
Clearing vacancy information

Examples of advisory interview discussion points

The application process
Vocational implications of choice
How to expand subject horizons
Relating interests to courses
Entry requirements

Sponsorship and sandwich
  opportunities
Work experience requirements
Mature applications
Responding to course offers
Applicant's personal statement
  on the UCAS form
Rethink after exam results
Planning a year out
Interview preparation
Use of Records of Achievement
Financial planning
Facilitating links with HE
  admissions staff
Non-degree HE alternatives
Clearing applications

Key Points

Remember, the local careers
service is
  Free
  Available all year
  Staffed by professionally trained
    advisers
  Impartial
  Nationwide

An Introduction to Higher Education in Scotland

Education at all levels has always been extremely important in Scotland – a tradition which continues to this day – and attracts substantial numbers of students (undergraduate and postgraduate) from England, Ireland and Wales, from continental Europe and from overseas.

Higher Education Institutions

There are 22 HEIs in Scotland – 13 Universities:

Aberdeen
Abertay Dundee
Dundee
Edinburgh
Glasgow
Glasgow Caledonian
Heriot-Watt (Edinburgh)
Napier (Edinburgh)
Paisley
The Robert Gordon (Aberdeen)
St Andrews
Stirling, and
Strathclyde (Glasgow)

Two institutions with powers to award their own degrees:

Queen Margaret College (Edinburgh), and
The Royal Scottish Academy of Music and Drama (Glasgow)

Seven Higher Education colleges, all of which offer degree courses which are validated by a university:

Edinburgh College of Art
Glasgow School of Art
Moray House Institute of Education in Edinburgh
Northern College of Education with campuses in Aberdeen and Dundee
St Andrew's College in Glasgow
Scottish College of Textiles in Galashiels, and
Scottish Agricultural College which has campuses in Aberdeen, Ayr and Edinburgh

They vary enormously in size, age and range of subjects offered. Some of the older and larger universities offer a large number of subjects while others specialise in particular areas – the creative arts, engineering, teacher education, etc.

In addition to these there is The Open University whose Scottish Office is at 10 Drumsheugh Gardens, Edinburgh EH3 7QJ.

The Scottish HEIs not only offer the complete range of subjects but also at various levels – undergraduate and postgraduate. Their study facilities are excellent and several institutions are at the leading edge of technology with the latest hardware and software available to help students to enhance their study skills.

Students have a wide selection of venues from which to choose – a city centre or in the countryside – and excellent leisure facilities. Finally, and not least, Scotland offers its students a thoroughly distinctive and strong cultural experience and – whichever institution is chosen – easy access to a land renowned for its great natural beauty.

Academic Tradition

In Scotland there has always been a particular emphasis on breadth of study as well as specialisation. This means that degree courses in arts, in pure sciences, and in social sciences are deliberately flexible and include a large spread of joint (two-subject) honours degrees.

The typical four year honours degree structure – in contrast with the usual three year degree in other parts of the UK – has the added benefit of allowing students to leave open the choice of their ultimate specialisation. This means that students do not have to feel that they are irrevocably committed to the initial choice of specialisation which they put on their UCAS form. As their knowledge and experience widen they may wish to specialise in an area other than their first choice.

However, in the degree courses which lead directly to professional qualifications (for example in medicine, dentistry, veterinary science, accountancy) there is less flexibility as they have to meet the strict subject requirements demanded by the relevant professional bodies. In the area of law, most teaching in Scotland is based on Scots Law and so does not provide the most direct route into practice in England, Wales or Ireland. However, the University of Dundee offers streams in both Scots Law and English Law enabling students to choose to study to practise in Scotland, or England or Northern Ireland (or in some circumstances all three). All Scottish Law degrees do have much to offer those who might like to work in continental Europe, or in European institutions, or wish to use their law training as a gateway to work in other professions.

Entry Qualifications

The majority of applicants to Higher Education in Scotland enter with school qualifications – Scottish Highers or GCE A level or AS. However, a variety of other qualifications is widely recognised and accepted – including SQA awards (including GSVQ) and National Diploma/Certificate qualifications, GNVQ, the Irish Leaving Certificate, the International Baccalaureate and the European Baccalaureate. The expected number, range and level of subjects required appear in the Course Tables. A number of Access courses are also offered.

Application Arrangements

Nearly all the Scottish universities and Higher Education institutions are members of UCAS. The other institutions accept direct applications for some of their courses other than those offered jointly with a university where application will be made to UCAS. For most of the degree courses in Art and Design, offered by The Robert Gordon University (Gray's School of Art), University of Dundee (Duncan of Jordanstone College), Edinburgh College of Art and Glasgow School of Art, there is a common application system. Copies of the forms are available direct from the institutions which also will give full details about the arrangements. Competition for these courses is very keen and students must produce satisfactory evidence of artistic ability.

The Royal Scottish Academy of Music and Drama is not a member of UCAS and applicants must apply direct. Information can be obtained from RSAMD, 100 Renfrew Street, Glasgow G2 3DB (tel: 0141 332 4104).

Grants and Loans

Students studying in Scotland are eligible to apply for the same grants, loans, awards and allowances as for the rest of the United Kingdom. Students who live in Scotland apply to The Student Awards Agency for Scotland (SAAS), Gyleview House, 3 Redheughs Rigg, South Gyle, Edinburgh EH12 9HH direct.

Further Information

The Committee of Scottish Higher Education Principals and UCAS together publish information about all the universities and colleges in Scotland. There is a free leaflet – Signpost (available from COSHEP tel: 0141 353 1880 fax: 0141 353 1881) – and a detailed guide – Entrance Guide to Higher Education in Scotland – which contains the entry requirements (including, in most cases, the "going rates"). See "Some Useful Publications and Addresses" on pages 26 - 27.

 Letts STUDY GUIDES THE INDEPENDENT

Students with Special Needs

Students with special needs start from the same point as anyone else – what do I want to study? – but are advised to contact institutions well in advance of submitting an application. This will establish what is viable and help institutions decide how your needs can be best met.

Think about why you are going into HE. This will narrow down the choice of institution and then you can look at the other factors which are important for your circumstances. Many institutions now devote space in their prospectuses to the facilities they provide for students who have special needs but direct contact is strongly advised.

Another factor is whether or not you want to be close to your home. This may depend on the type of support you need and whether that is available on campus. Not all residential blocks are physically accessible to wheelchair users for example. Teaching rooms may be equally difficult to negotiate and may not have the special aids you need if you have a hearing or visual impairment. Some institutions have learning support units (or a similarly named unit) which are invaluable for help with a variety of needs. Financial help for purchasing special aids, books, audio-equipment and the like is available in many places.

If, having read the prospectus, you need further information, you should contact the institution directly. There may be an adviser for

students with special needs but if not, the Admissions Officer or Student Counsellor should be able to answer some of your queries.

A visit to the place at which you intend studying for the next three or four years is highly desirable.

You can discover for yourself how well designed the site is for your circumstances and what adaptations the institution might be able to make. You could also speak to students, tutors and other staff to solve potential problems. The Students' Union or Association is another useful body to contact.

Do check that, apart from the suitability of the building, the course will be able to accept you. If there is much practical or physical work involved, you may find there is no allowance made for students with a physical disability.

Some applicants wonder if they should mention special needs on the UCAS form. You are strongly advised to do so in order that as much as possible can be done to help you in advance of your starting a course. There is both a simple self-coding question, and additional space on which to expand upon the nature of any special needs that you might have.

Financial help may be available in the form of the disabled students' allowance which comes in three sums – one to cover equipment, one to pay for non-medical personal support and one to pay other disability-related costs of study. This allowance is payable to those eligible for a

mandatory grant. If your parents' income precludes you from a maintenance grant, you may still be able to claim the allowance. In addition, you may be eligible for DSS benefits. You should contact your grant awarding body and local benefit office about these. You will find that a letter of support from your university or college often smooths the way for requests for financial assistance and this is another reason for institutions knowing about your needs as early as possible.

Much useful advice and information can also be obtained from:

SKILL – National Bureau for Students with Disabilities, 366 Brixton Road, London SW9 7AA. Contact information service on 0171 978 9890 (1.30 - 4.30), minicom 0171 738 7722. General telephone number is 0171 274 0565. Fax: 0171 737 7477.

SKILL will also be able to put you in touch with other specialist support bodies, appropriate to your needs, and has produced, with CRAC, a guide to Higher Education for people with disabilities called *Higher Education and Disability*.

Mature Entry

Most institutions are keen to attract mature students and often relax stringent entry requirements if the applicant can demonstrate the necessary motivation and suitability for the course of study. More universities now offer courses on a modular and part-time basis which can be attractive to mature students. Many may give you credit for study you may have undertaken in the past and for the more informal learning you have acquired through work or other experiences (Accreditation of Prior (or Prior Experiential) Learning – APL/APEL).

Apart from considering why you are going into HE and what you want to study, there are other factors which it is important for mature students to consider:

- Find out exactly what the course involves. It may include periods of practical work away from home.
- Plan ahead for your study time. You may have to reduce other commitments and your family will have to expect less of you and more of themselves.
- Look into finance carefully. The Mature Students' Allowance is no longer available and you may find that any grant falls short of your requirements. Remember too that you are unlikely to get a grant for a course if you have had a grant already for a similar course.
- Ensure that the motivation is there to sustain you throughout the course.
- Think through the implications of the very real changes that may take place in your own perspectives, values and growth.
- Prepare for the different experience you will have compared to younger students who may seem to have less to contend with.
- Be realistic about your job prospects if that is a factor in your decision to go into HE. Older graduates in particular do find it more difficult to obtain what they feel is appropriate work and it can take them longer to find such employment. They

may start on a lower rung from the one they expected.

A talk with an appropriate person about all the elements involved in being a mature student should help you feel more confident about your decision. The local careers service may be a good starting point as it may have a careers adviser who works specifically with adult clients. The Careers Adviser, Student Counsellor and Admissions Officer at individual universities should all be good sources of help and information.

If you have been some time away from studying, it is a good idea to consider doing some kind of course beforehand. This may be an evening class, a weekend study course, an Open University module, or an Access course, the last often providing guaranteed entry to a specific undergraduate course. Details of these will be available from HE institutions, FE colleges and from Local Authority Education Departments. This not only provides you with some skills and knowledge, but will demonstrate clear motivation to the course selectors. This is not to say that your previous work and life experiences are not valuable and will not be taken into account – far from it. You

should not underestimate the skills you have but should capitalise on these as a positive asset in your application. Nevertheless, evidence of recent study is very valuable.

Some institutions provide a study skills centre or learning support unit which mature students find a particularly valuable resource. Staff there can help you with issues like taking lecture notes, writing essays, revising, exam techniques. Also look out for institutions which have taken the initiative in understanding the different perspectives and needs which mature students bring to their courses and have set up appropriate mechanisms throughout the whole institution, from admission to the job search at the end.

As many mature students apply to only one institution, you should note that UCAS now charges a reduced fee for a single choice application (£4.00 instead of £12.00).There is a facility for single choice applicants to change their minds and apply subsequently for other choices (up to six in total) on payment of a further £8.00.

UCAS publishes a free booklet *A Mature Student's Guide to Higher Education*.

Photograph: Gordon Jack

Applications from International Students

Section 1 of this guide includes information to help UK applicants decide on the most appropriate choice of course. These articles apply equally to you, as an international applicant, although there are some additional issues of which you need to be aware before you make your decision.

Before You Apply

English Language Proficiency

- Are you sufficiently prepared to understand and participate in lectures, seminars, tutorials and examinations conducted in English?
- Do you have evidence of your written and spoken English language ability? Most institutions accept a number of qualifications as providing evidence of competence, including the British Council IELTS test, the American TOEFL test,

Cambridge Certificate of Proficiency in English, NEAB (formerly JMB) and AEB tests.

If this may be an area of weakness for you, consider pre-sessional courses, English Language Teaching courses in your own country or at one of the many UK language schools. Some universities may offer pre-sessional English language summer courses.

Academic Qualifications

- British Higher Education is selective at the point of entry – do your current or expected qualifications meet the likely requirements?
- Are your qualifications acceptable to all UK institutions?

Your local British Council office may be able to advise you, perhaps by reference to the *International Guide to Qualifications in Education* which it publishes. Other useful publications

are produced by UKCOSA – the Council for International Education. You may need to identify a bridging course or a course with a foundation year to remedy any current or initial weaknesses.

Life in Britain

- Gather information about living in Britain from friends, family, students returning from the UK, institutional information, books and the local British Council office. Although it is a small country, there are considerable variations in climate, surroundings, cost of living, and population. The cultural and social environment will be very different.
- Are there any religious, cultural or social reasons which may inhibit you from studying in the UK?
- Are you prepared to cope with up to three years or more of British weather?

Family

- Are you intending to take any or all of your family with you?
- Have you considered the practicalities of your family accompanying you such as: availability of facilities, extra cost, education provision for dependents, their language proficiency or immigration arrangements?

The British Council strongly advises students to travel alone – initially at least – in order to check provision, possibilities and cost before deciding to bring dependents to Britain. There may be alternatives to doing so.

Cost

- Do you know what the likely costs are?
- Are you able to provide a financial guarantee of your ability to pay your costs for the full duration of the course?
- Did you know that living costs vary from region to region?
- What is the length of your proposed course?

Do you qualify, and have you applied for any scholarships to fund your study? There is little chance of obtaining scholarships from the British Government or universities and colleges, so you must explore other possibilities.

You must be able to finance both your tuition and living costs for the whole course, airfare, initial accommodation cost, appropriate

Photograph: Gail Prentice

seasonal clothing and study expenses –
information is available from the university or
college, your local British Council and recently
returned students (through the alumni
association).

Accommodation

- Can it be provided by the institution or by
  family/friends?
- Is it guaranteed for the duration of the
  course?

Choice of Course, Institution and Qualification

- Obtain current information about the
  course(s) that you are interested in
  (syllabus, teaching and examination
  method etc) from the institution(s),
  prospectuses, reference publications and
  your local British Council office.
- Obtain information about the
  institution(s) where courses are offered
  (region, location, size, facilities etc).

Photograph: Kenneth Dundas

- Obtain information about the qualification
  and continuing education prospects on
  successful completion of the course.
- Is the qualification recognised? By whom?
  Is it recognised at the same level in your
  own country/by future employers?

Much of this information will be available in
prospectuses from the institutions themselves
and the latter may also have an international
office or office of external relations which can
help and advise you.

Prospectuses may be available for reference
in your school, college or local British Council
office.

Making a decision about your preferred
choice of HE course is the first step, and you
are now in a position to make your application.

How to Apply

The application process is described briefly
on page 23. Applications from international
students are welcomed at any time but if you
are considering an application to Oxford or
Cambridge, the closing date will be 15 October
1997.

Applications for popular courses eg Dentistry,
Law, Medicine, Veterinary Science and many
Arts subjects, should be made as early as
possible.

After you Apply

There is a lot to be done, and if your arrival in
Britain is to be trouble-free, you must make
many practical arrangements and preparation
in advance. Seek advice as often as necessary,
and allow plenty of time to make your
arrangements.

Immigration Regulations and Documents

- Request information from the local British
  Government representative and seek
  advice from your local British Council
  office. Find out which documents you
  need to obtain and how and where to get
  them.

- Check what your visa (if you need one)
  allows you to do. Can you work in the UK,
  either during any 'sandwich' element of
  your course or to supplement your
  income while you study?

Accommodation at your chosen institution

- Request accommodation as early as
  possible.
- What is the cost?
- What does this include – food, heating
  and lighting, linen, vacations? If meals are
  provided, does this include weekends?

Travel

- Take advice on how and when to travel to
  Britain, taking into account the start date
  and pre-sessional training if applicable.
- Book tickets, but only once you are sure
  you have a firm place.

Deferred Entry

Deferred entry is known by a variety of names including 'year out', 'year off', 'gap year'. It involves taking a break from full-time study before going on to Higher Education. Lots of students decide to do this and there are many opportunities, both in Britain and abroad.

Do remember that you can expect long vacations to travel or work in when you have entered HE, and those courses which include a year in industry or a period studying or working abroad will also give you the opportunity to have a break from the main routine of studying.

The year out can actually be up to a period of fifteen months, which gives you the opportunity of several options and activities. The key to making it a successful year is to plan – do not end up drifting through just trying to keep busy. In the current economic climate, it would not be wise to assume that 'something will turn up'.

Travelling is an option, although it has to be financed, and remember that once a student you might use part of your vacations to work and travel abroad. Combine your travel, whether abroad or in the UK, with some work. Paid work may be available, whether in offices, bars and restaurants, or au pair work in family homes and you could also look for voluntary work, archaeological digs or work camps. Look for something in which you will be interested, and which leaves you with some free time!

There are books available which may help to give you some ideas. Look at the article "Some Useful Publications and Addresses" (pages 26-27) and try your library or careers library at school or college, or your local careers service. Ask for guidance from a tutor or adviser.

Not all courses consider deferred applications and individual departments may have a quota on the number they will accept in order to be fair to the following year's applicants. If you do decide to apply now, in 1997-98, for deferred entry in 1999, check that deferred entry applications will be considered for your course: it may say in the prospectus, but if not, check with the Admissions Tutor. Do give some thought to what you will do if, for example, you do badly in your current studies, or better than you expect. Allow for the possibility of needing to resit, for example.

It is important that you make your plans known on your UCAS form, in the appropriate section. Admissions Tutors will want to see

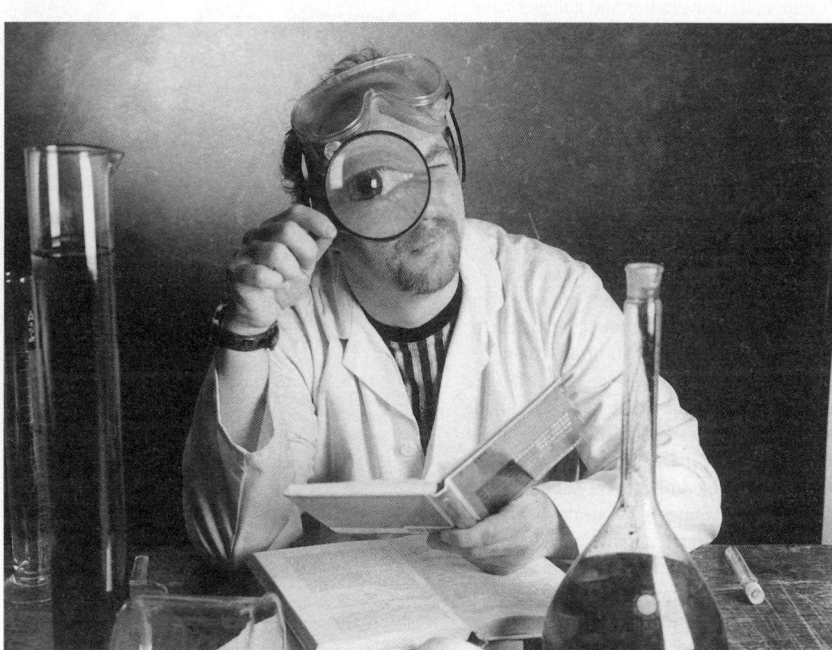

Photograph: Suzanne Scrace

what you are planning to do, particularly if it is relevant in any way to your proposed course. They will, in most cases, expect you to make good use of the year and be able to describe its value.

Why Consider Deferred Entry?
- Acquire experience
- Broaden outlook
- Meet new people
- Improve languages
- Chance to travel
- Break from study
- Earn money
- Sponsorship scheme

Plan and Research
- Finance
- Opportunities
- Application

Seek Advice
- Parents
- Careers advisers
- Tutors
- Books
- Students who deferred

Modular Study and Part-time Programmes

Traditionally, universities and colleges have offered single or joint honours degrees which result in named degrees such as a BSc in Chemistry or a BA in English and Philosophy. Some outside or supporting subjects might be included but usually only for the first year or two. Courses leading to a professional qualification, eg Nursing, Surveying, often had even less flexibility.

Most universities and colleges now offer a great variety of study programmes and, in particular, modular programmes are appealing to a growing number of students. Modular study makes it easier for institutions to offer their courses on both a full-time and part-time basis and enables students to move in and out of study programmes and institutions. Some programmes also offer periods of study off-campus for which credit can be gained.

Modular programmes allow students to build up their degrees from a number of self-contained modules. A minimum number of modules has to be completed successfully for the award of the degree. Such degrees may provide for breadth or specialisation and be particularly attractive to students who have a wide range of interests. They provide a good way to study if you need to have a break in your course for any reason, or wish to change institution, as you may well maintain credit for what you have done. Accumulating credit at a pace which suits individual circumstances is often called Credit Accumulated (CA) and taking credit with you – from one course to another, or one institution to another – is called Credit Transfer (CT); together these are often referred to as CAT schemes.

In most degrees which are modular in spirit there may be core or compulsory modules which have to be completed for the award of a particular qualification. This gives some breadth and flexibility while providing for a named recognisable degree.

If you are applying to an institution which offers modular courses, think about the following:

– Have you decided on a career or profession which stipulates the nature or content of the degree required for progression?
– Will you gain credit for any study already undertaken under a CAT scheme?
– Is there in place a recognition scheme for Accreditation of Prior Learning (APL) or

Photograph: Stevie McBride

Accreditation of Prior Experiential Learning (APEL) – a system whereby your experience can formally be credited towards a degree?
– Does the institution have an established system of academic counselling to guide students through the choice available?
– How large are the classes and are there selection criteria for entry?
– Are all modules effectively of the same value?
– Will you be able to go on to postgraduate study after a particular programme?

Part-time Study

Many of the courses listed are also available by part-time study. Some institutions now offer sufficient part-time courses to be able to publish a part-time prospectus. This guide does not aim to include details of part-time courses (although there may be many features of a course that are common to both full-time and part-time modes of study) and you should contact the universities and colleges direct for information about these.

Part-time study has long been available through the Open University and Birkbeck College of the University of London. The former offers BA and BSc degrees in a wide variety of subjects to adults who wish to study at their own pace, in their own time and, particularly, at home. No formal educational qualifications are required for entry. The success of the OU's

formula and study materials has contributed to the expansion into this way of learning of institutions formerly devoted to full-time study. Credit or Advanced Standing is given to students for qualifications or courses they may have completed. Contact the Open University at Central Enquiry Service, PO Box 200, Milton Keynes MK7 6YZ or at its Regional Centres (see local telephone directories).

Birkbeck College specialises in part-time evening courses for mature adults who wish to attend university without giving up their daytime job. The college is located at Malet Street, London WC1E 7HX.

While the idea of part-time study is very attractive to people who do not wish, or are unable, to study full-time, do not underestimate the size and length of the commitment involved. Work and/or family needs have to be juggled with course work, essays, projects, private study, tutorials, and possibly summer schools. It is a commitment that affects not only you, the potential student, but will spill over into other areas of your life for several years.

Visits and Interviews

Visits

All institutions provide you with the opportunity to visit them. This may be in the form of Open Days when anyone can visit. These give you the chance to find out more about courses, departments, subjects offered, entry requirements, career prospects and the facilities available. Pre-taster courses, where a department lays on activities specific to a course, are other options which may be available. Some institutions offer departmental Open Days, which may be open to anyone or specifically organised for applicants who have been offered a place. These will be held within the appropriate department with staff and students there to answer your questions. Their purpose is to help you to decide if you want to accept an offer.

The institution profiles in Section 2 of this book contain information about Open Days and you should also refer to individual prospectuses and to the UCAS publication *University and College Open Days, Pre-Taster Courses* and *Education Conventions*. Copies of this book are available in schools, colleges and careers offices.

Think ahead

You can prepare for visits by thinking about what is important for you to know about the course, institution and locality before making any further decisions. These might include:

Teaching methods
Assessment
Size
Subject options and degree structure
Accommodation and its cost, ease of access to campus and availability
Laboratory and IT facilities/studio space
Sport and social life
Career destinations of former students
Opportunities for placements or study abroad
Location

Photograph: Vicky Lewis

Additional costs specific to nature of course

If it is impossible for you to attend an Open Day, try to get hold of a video about the institution and the alternative prospectus which may have been written by the students themselves. These are not a substitute for a personal visit but they will give you some idea about the place and its inhabitants!

Interviews and Admissions Practices

The likelihood of your being invited for interview, and the nature of it, will depend to a large extent on the subject area for which you have applied. Institutions' selection policies vary throughout the country and may alter from year to year depending on the number of applications. Not all institutions use interviews as part of the selection procedure and certainly not for every course. This means that some decide on your application form alone and that is why it is so important to complete it as well

as you can. Tutors will look carefully at your exam results, actual and predicted, your referee's statement and your own further information statement. Remember, they are looking for reasons to offer you a place – try to give them every opportunity to do so!

Teacher-training courses require that you must be interviewed in order to gain a place – this is a statutory requirement, and Admissions Tutors for many health-related courses will also want to interview you before making an offer.

If you do get your invitation for interview, it ought to tell you what to expect: if you are not certain, contact the institution and ask for clarification. Being unprepared could cost you your place. Interviews are usually conducted with students individually, but if you are applying for a course where you are expected to work a great deal in groups, it is quite possible that instead of a 'traditional' interview, several of you together may be asked to do a group exercise or hold a discussion. In the case of performance arts, drama, music or the like, an audition may be included.

Getting Started

Treat interviews, open days and visits as two-way activities – you are interviewing them, as much as they are interviewing you. Go prepared with a list of things to find out and ask – tutors will have their own list of things to ask you!

There is a video available on interviewing for HE called *A Two-Way Success*. Check if your school or college has a copy. It comes with (teachers') background notes and exercises and costs £20 from Trotman and Co Ltd.

Before you go

To get the best out of the day, you must prepare. Find out first what type of interview it will be and the programme for the day. Plan your route and make sure you can get there on time – arriving late creates a bad impression. Maps can be misleading, particularly if not to scale. Call and ask how far it is from the station to the site if you are not sure – it could be a very long walk!

You are bound to be nervous on the day, that is expected, but if you are well prepared you will overcome that after the first few minutes. Your application form will provide the agenda for the interview. You could be asked about anything you have written. Looking back at what you put in your further information section will give you some clues as to the questions which an interviewer might ask about you and your reasons for choosing the course.

Practise talking about yourself, your interests and your strengths – if your family and friends get fed up listening, try recording yourself on tape. Be positive in what you say and how you say it.

Before you go, you should review everything you know about the course, and identify what you still have to find out. Have a list of questions ready; write them down if necessary. These may be about some aspect of the course, the institution, students, possible careers after the course…Remember to check these out on the day.

Look out anything you have been asked to take or feel would be useful.

On the day

Keep calm! Use your time to look around, talk to students and investigate the surroundings. Find out answers to all your questions – write them down.

At the interview have to hand any papers that you have been asked to bring, and your own checklist of questions and reminders, including your Record of Achievement if you have one. If possible, try not to be rushing for the first available train home. If your schedule does not include a tour of the area, make time yourself for detective work around the campus and the town.

Afterwards

Afterwards you should keep a record of everything you found out, and review how successful the day was. If you do not keep a record, it may be difficult to look back in a couple of months' time and remember, for example, whether this was the course which you thought was too theoretical, or whether that was the place where the halls of residence were four miles from the lecture theatres.

And what of your own performance on the day? Do not just forget it, however badly you think it went. If you go into the next interview and are asked the same question which caught you out last time, will you now know how to answer it?

Photograph: Mark Jarvis

Letts STUDY GUIDES
THE INDEPENDENT

Making Your Application

For the majority of Higher Education courses at universities and colleges, application is made through UCAS (Universities and Colleges Admissions Service). Your school, college or local careers service will be able to provide you with an application form, *UCAS Handbook* and instructions, and will be able to offer advice and help with completion of the form.

UCAS allows you to make up to six choices on your form. You should use prospectuses, course leaflets and other sources of reference (teachers, career advisers, videos, visits, current and former students, ECCTIS, and an atlas!) to help find out the details you need to make your choices of course and institution. Because of the limitation on the number of choices allowed, and the fact that many people apply before they have obtained the necessary academic qualifications for entry to higher education, a strategy is necessary to ensure that you do secure a place on a desirable course at a suitable institution.

Some Pointers

The UCAS application form you complete may be the first of many forms that you will have to fill in. Application forms are often your first contact with an organisation and on this evidence alone in some cases decisions are made about offering you an interview or a place. There are some general rules which apply to all application forms:
- check the closing date;
- allow plenty of time for the completion of the form - forms always take longer than you think and you need to give your referee time to add his/her statement;
- read the instructions carefully before you start;
- look at what each question actually asks;
- photocopy a blank form and practise well before tackling the one you will eventually submit;
- ask a friend, parent, teacher or careers adviser to review your draft, looking at content, spelling and presentation and viewing it as a selector might;
- write clearly;
- pay special attention to questions which ask you about yourself and interests, experience, etc;
- note the amount of space given to sections on personal statements or additional information as this is usually a guide to the importance that selectors attach to these items;
- keep a photocopy of the final version as it will provide the agenda for any subsequent interview.

UCAS deadlines

The normal deadline for applications to reach UCAS is 15 December 1997 (but see paragraph on methods of application for art and design), but if you are including Oxford or Cambridge among your six choices, their closing date for both the UCAS form and any additional information is 15 October 1997. Full details are included in the *UCAS Handbook* and in prospectuses

The earlier you apply for a course the better, especially if it is a popular one (but see section below on methods of application for art and design). Admissions tutors may receive only a handful of forms daily in October; by December several hundreds can arrive each day.

Interviews and decisions take place in the spring term, Christmas to Easter (if you have applied by 15 December). If your form arrives after 15 December, your chances of being considered will be severely restricted as sufficient offers may have been made to fill all the available places.

Methods of application for art and design

Students may apply for art and design courses through UCAS via one or both of two equal pathways. These are identified as Routes A and B and an institution's entry in the *UCAS Handbook* will indicate which courses are available through which route.

Applicants for art and design courses, like all UCAS applicants, have up to six choices. However, because of time constraints imposed by the sequential interview procedure, applicants choosing courses recruited through Route B are restricted to a maximum of four. Such applicants may use their remaining choices for any courses recruited through Route A.

In Route A, application forms should be submitted from September 1997 and by 15 December 1997 in order to ensure consideration. Copy application forms will be sent simultaneously to all Route A institutions listed on the form. Decisions on these applications will normally be due by the end of March 1998.

In Route B, application forms should be submitted between the beginning of January 1997 and 24 March 1998. Applicants through Route B may make a maximum of four choices and should indicate the order in which they wish to be interviewed. Copy application forms will be sent to institutions sequentially in order of interview preference. Interviews will take place from early April 1998.

Applicants who wish to apply for courses through both Route A and Route B should submit their Route A choices by 15 December. They are able to indicate, by ticking a box on the form, if they intend later to add choices for consideration through Route B. At the appropriate time UCAS will send them the necessary documentation to add choices and declare an interview preference.

Portfolios

Most art and design courses require applicants to submit a portfolio which, along with the interview, is crucial in an institution's decision to offer you a place. The central importance of a well-constructed portfolio cannot be overestimated since it is the main evidence a course tutor has of your creative ability and likely potential.

Clearing

UCAS operates a Clearing system which provides details of unfilled places to unplaced applicants. This comes into play during the summer and eligible applicants are automatically sent full details about Clearing arrangements and the publication of lists of UCAS course vacancies. You should plan to be at home from mid August as you may well have vital decisions and arrangements to make. A reappraisal of your options may be necessary and you cannot do that from far away places.

UCAS

APPLICATIONS FLOWCHARTS

*Standard UCAS
Applications and Route A
Art & Design Applications*

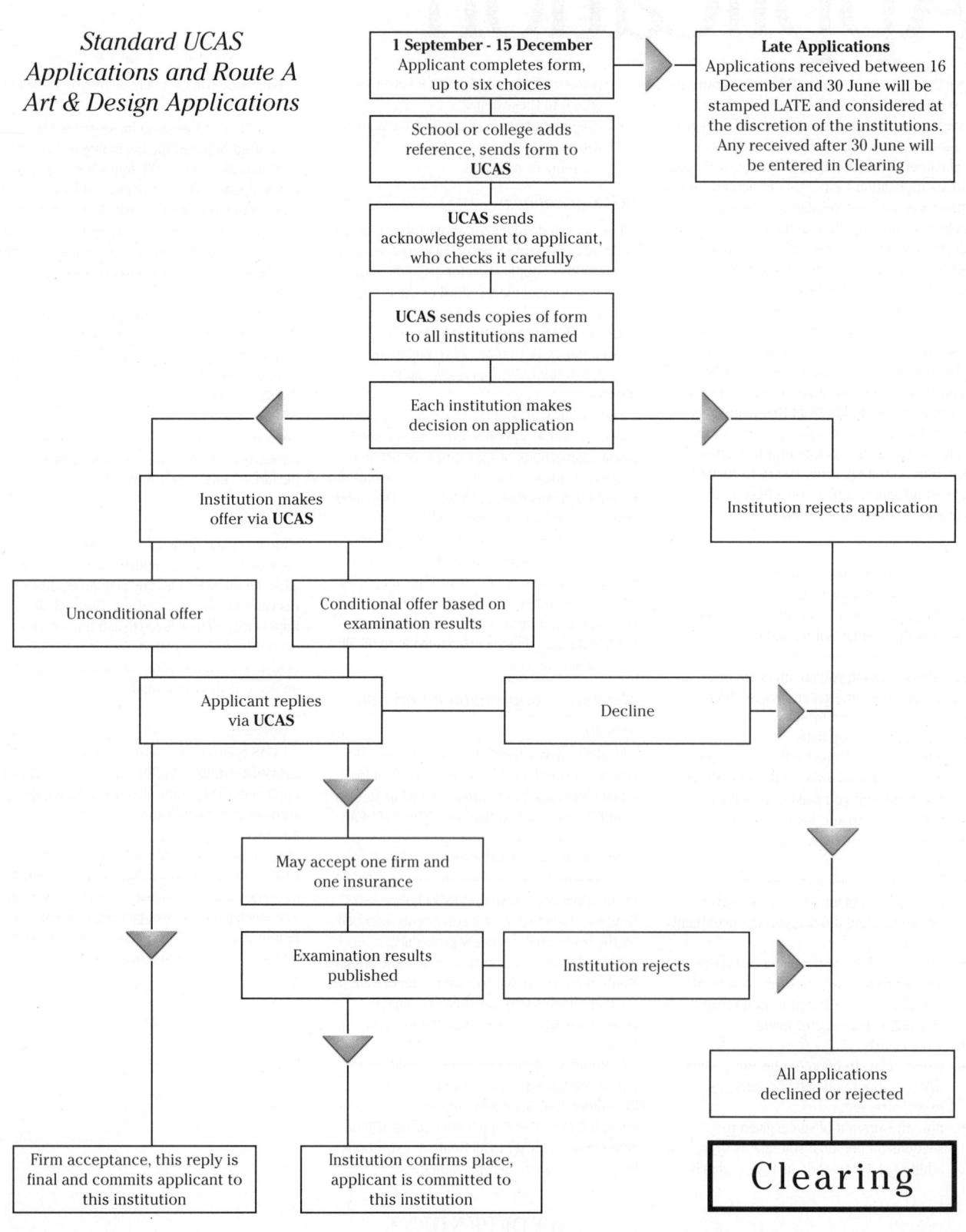

1 September - 15 December
Applicant completes form,
up to six choices

Late Applications
Applications received between 16
December and 30 June will be
stamped LATE and considered at
the discretion of the institutions.
Any received after 30 June will
be entered in Clearing

School or college adds
reference, sends form to
UCAS

UCAS sends
acknowledgement to applicant,
who checks it carefully

UCAS sends copies of form
to all institutions named

Each institution makes
decision on application

Institution makes
offer via **UCAS**

Institution rejects application

Unconditional offer

Conditional offer based on
examination results

Applicant replies
via **UCAS**

Decline

May accept one firm and
one insurance

Examination results
published

Institution rejects

All applications
declined or rejected

Firm acceptance, this reply is
final and commits applicant to
this institution

Institution confirms place,
applicant is committed to
this institution

Clearing

Applications for Admission to Courses in Art & Design

*Applications through **both** Route A and Route B*

A maximum of six choices of institution/course is available

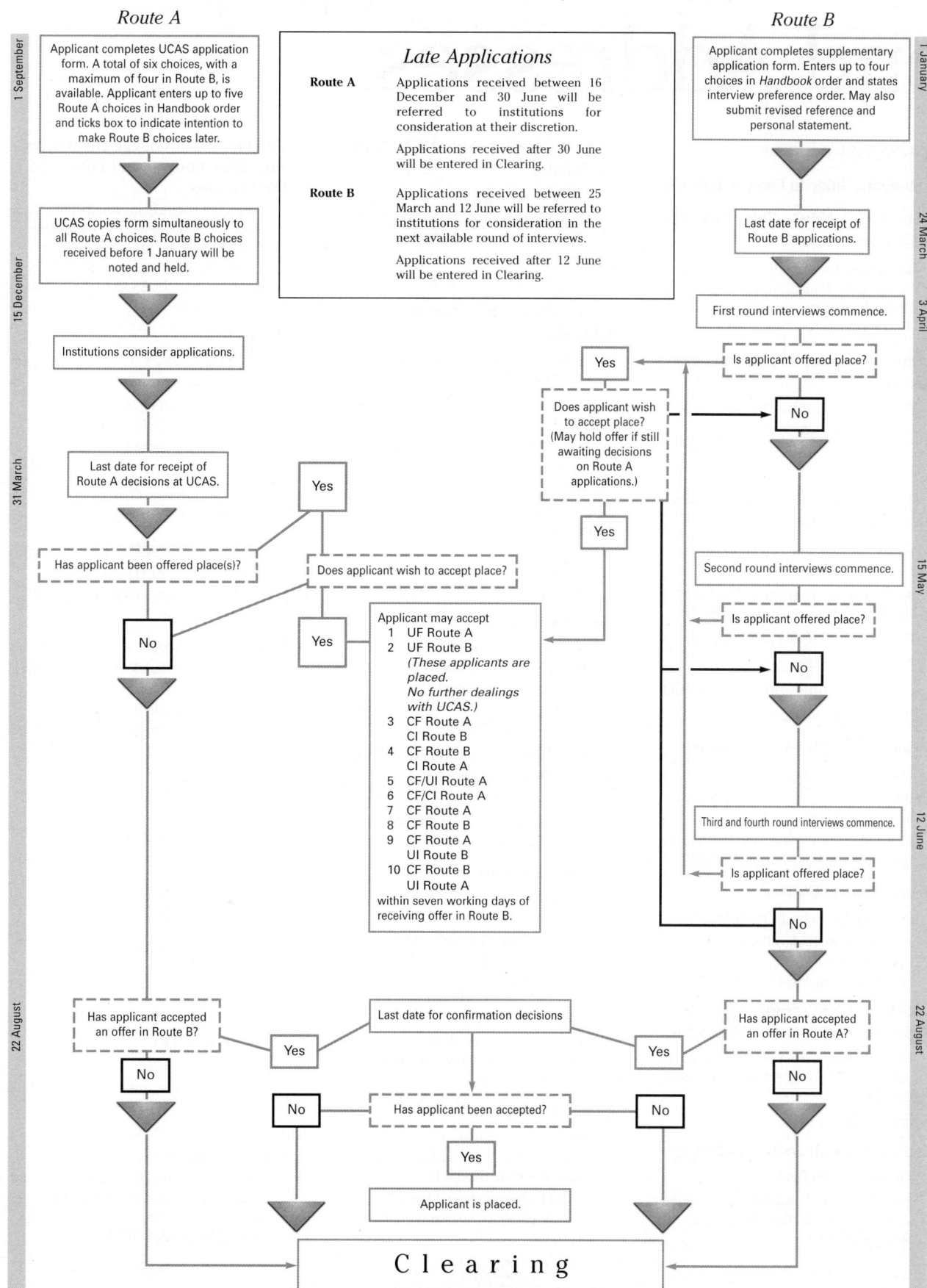

Some Useful Publications and Addresses

Choosing Courses

A Student's Guide to Entry to Law 1998

A Student's Guide to Entry to Media Studies 1998

Both published by and available from: UCAS, Fulton House, Jessop Avenue, Cheltenham, Gloucestershire GL50 3SH
Price £10.00.

A Student's Guide to Entry to Medicine

Published by and available from: UCAS, Fulton House, Jessop Avenue, Cheltenham, Gloucestershire GL50 3SH
Price £6.00.

A Guide to Art and Design Courses: On Course for 1998

Published by: Trotman and Co Ltd. in association with UCAS
Available from: Trotman and Co Ltd., 12 Hill Rise, Richmond, Surrey TW10 6UA
Price £9.99 (excluding p&p), special student price £7.95.

A Guide to Getting into Mathematics

Price £7.99 (excluding p&p)

A Guide to Getting into Teaching

Price £6.95 (excluding p&p)
Both published by: Trotman and Co Ltd. in association with UCAS
Available from: Trotman and Co Ltd., 12 Hill Rise, Richmond, Surrey TW10 6UA.

Degree Course Guides

Published by: Hobsons Publishing Plc
Available from: Biblios Publishers' Distribution Services Ltd., Star Road, Partridge Green, West Sussex RH13 8LD.

COSHEP/UCAS Entrance Guide to Higher Education in Scotland 1998

Copies available from: John Smith & Son (Glasgow), 57 St Vincent Street, Glasgow G2 5TB
Price £7.00.

Getting Into University and College

Author: Stephen Lamley
Published by and available from: Trotman and Co Ltd., 12 Hill Rise, Richmond, Surrey TW10 6UA.

How to Complete Your UCAS Form - 1998 Entry

Author: Tony Higgins
Published by and available from: Trotman and Co Ltd., 12 Hill Rise, Richmond, Surrey TW10 6UA
Price £6.95 plus £1.60 p&p.

A Parent's Guide to Higher Education

Published by: Trotman and Co Ltd. in association with UCAS
Available from: Trotman and Co Ltd., 12 Hill Rise, Richmond, Surrey TW10 6UA
Price £6.99 (excluding p&p). Summary version (8 pages) free of charge from UCAS.

The Potter Guide to Higher Education

Published annually and available from: Dalebank Books, Arden Lodge, Savile Park Road, Halifax HX1 2XR.

Sixth Form Choices

Author: John Handley
Published by and available from: Northcote House Publishers Ltd, Plymbridge House, Estover, Plymouth PL6 7PZ. Tel: 01752 695745.

The Sixthformers Guide to Visiting Universities and Colleges

Published annually and available from: ISCO Publications, 12A Princess Way, Camberley, Surrey GU15 3SP.

The Student Book

Published annually by: Pan Macmillan Publishers Ltd.
Available from: Trotman and Co Ltd., 12 Hill Rise, Richmond, Surrey TW10 6UA.

Survey of HND Courses

Author: Eric Whittington
Published by and available from: Trotman and Co Ltd., 12 Hill Rise, Richmond, Surrey TW10 6UA.

UCAS Handbook

Published annually by: UCAS, Fulton House, Jessop Avenue, Cheltenham, Gloucestershire GL50 3SH
Available (free of charge) from: UCAS and schools, careers offices and public libraries.

University and College Open Days, Pre-Taster Courses and Education Conventions

Published annually in association with Cambridge Occupational Analysts by: UCAS, Fulton House, Jessop Avenue, Cheltenham, Gloucestershire GL50 3SH
Available from: UCAS and schools and careers offices.

Which Degree?

Which University?

Both published annually by: Hobsons Publishing Plc
Available from: Biblios Publishers' Distribution Services Ltd., Star Road, Partridge Green, West Sussex RH13 8LD.

Studying in Europe

SOCRATES/ERASMUS: The UK Guide

Available from: ISCO Publications, 12a Princess Way, Camberley, Surrey GU15 3SP.

Studying in Europe

Authors: Anne Bariet and Olivier Rollot
Published by: Hobsons Publishing Plc
Available from: Biblios Publishers' Distribution Services Ltd., Star Road, Partridge Green, West Sussex RH13 8LD.

Deferred Entry

Gap Activity Projects

Published by Gap Activity Projects (GAP) Ltd., GAP House, 44 Queen's Road, Reading, Berkshire RG1 4BB.
Tel: 01734 594914.

Opportunities in the Gap Year

Published by and available from: ISCO Publications, 12a Princess Way, Camberley, Surrey GU15 3SP.

Taking a year Off

Author: Val Butcher
Published by and available from: Trotman and Co Ltd., 12 Hill Rise, Richmond, Surrey TW10 6UA.

Gap Year Guidebook

Published by and available from: Peridot Press, 2 Blenheim Crescent, London W11 1NN. Price: £8.95 plus 50p postage and packing. Tel: 0171 221 7404.

Sponsorship

Sponsorship for Students

Published annually by: Hobsons Publishing Plc.

Available from: Biblios Publishers' Distribution Services Ltd., Star Road, Partridge Green, West Sussex RH13 8LD.

Engineering Opportunities for Students and Graduates

Published annually by The Institution of Mechanical Engineers, and available (free of charge) from: Northgate Avenue, Bury St Edmunds, Suffolk IP32 6BN.

Student Finance

Students' Money Matters

Author: Gwenda Thomas

Published by and available from: Trotman and Co Ltd., 12 Hill Rise, Richmond, Surrey TW10 6UA

Price £7.95 plus £1.60 p&p.

Students' Grants and Loans: A Brief Guide

Published annually and available (free of charge) from: Department for Education and Employment, Publications Section, PO Box 6927, London E3 3NZ. Tel: 0171 510 0150.

Students' Grants in Scotland

Published annually and available (free of charge) from: The Student Awards Agency for Scotland (SAAS), Gyleview House, 3 Redheughs Rigg, South Gyle, Edinburgh EH12 9HH.

Awards and Loans to Students

Published annually and available (free of charge) from: Department of Education for N. Ireland, Balloo Road, Bangor, Co Down BT19 7PR.

The Student Loan Scheme

Published by and available (free of charge) from: Student Loans Company Ltd., 100 Bothwell Street, Glasgow G2 7JD.

Information for Students with Disabilities

Higher Education and Disability A Guide to Higher Education for People with Disabilities

Published annually by Hobsons Publishing and SKILL: National Bureau for Students with Disabilities. Circulated free of charge to all schools, colleges and careers services in the UK.

Available for sale from: SKILL, 336 Brixton Road, London SW9 7AA.
Tel: 0171 274 0565.

Financial Assistance for Students with Disabilities in Higher Education

Published annually by and available from: SKILL, 336 Brixton Road, London SW9 7AA.

SKILL Information Sheets

A range of free and priced leaflets. Available from SKILL.

Information for Mature Students

How to Win as a Mature Student

Published by : Kogan Page, 120 Pentonville Road, London N1 9JN. Tel: 0171 278 0433.

The Mature Students' Handbook

Authors: Iris Rosier and Lynn Earnshaw

Published by and available from: Trotman and Co Ltd., 12 Hill Rise, Richmond, Surrey TW10 6UA.

The Mature Student's Guide to Higher Education

Published by and available (free of charge) from: UCAS, Fulton House, Jessop Avenue, Cheltenham, Gloucestershire GL50 3SH.

Information for Overseas Students

Studying and Living in Britain 1997 – The British Council's Guide

Published by and available from: Northcote House Publishers Ltd., Plymbridge House, Estover Road, Plymouth PL6 7PZ.

British University and College Courses

Published by and available from: Trotman and Co Ltd., 12 Hill Rise, Richmond, Surrey TW10 6UA.

Awards for First Degree Study at Commonwealth Universities

Published by and available from: ACU, John Foster House, 36 Gordon Square, London WC1H 0PF.

Career Planning

Getting into...Series

Published by and available from: Trotman and Co Ltd., 12 Hill Rise, Richmond, Surrey TW10 6UA

Price £6.95 plus £1.60 for postage and handling

Includes the following titles:

Getting into Accountancy, Business Studies and Economics;

Getting into Art and Design;

Getting into The City;

Getting into Computing;

Getting into Dental School;

Getting into Engineering;

Getting into Languages;

Getting into Law;

Getting into the Media;

Getting into Medical School;

Getting into Nursing;

Getting into Psychology;

Getting into Teaching;

Getting into Veterinary Science.

Occupations

Published annually by: COIC

Available from: COIC, PO Box 348, Bristol BS99 7FE.

The Penguin Careers Guide: 10th Edition

Authors: Anna Alston and Anne Daniel

Published by: Penguin Books

What Do Graduates Do?

Published annually by: AGCAS in association with UCAS and CSU

Available from: CSU, 4th Floor, Armstrong House, Oxford Road, Manchester M1 7ED. Tel: 0161 236 9816. Price £5.95

UCAS Annual Report 1996 entry

A comprehensive statistical report published by and available from UCAS. Price £12.

UCAS Statistical Summary 1996 entry

Statistical data for applicants from the UK only. Published by and available from UCAS. Price £5.

Video

A Life of Knowledge

A six part guide to the world of Higher Education. Available from UCAS. Price £17.99.

AN OUTLINE
DESCRIPTION OF THE
UNIVERSITIES AND
COLLEGES FROM
WHICH TO CHOOSE

UNIVERSITIES

&

COLLEGES

1998

List of Institutions

Institution		Page

Letts STUDY GUIDES
THE INDEPENDENT

GET IN
WITH A GUIDE

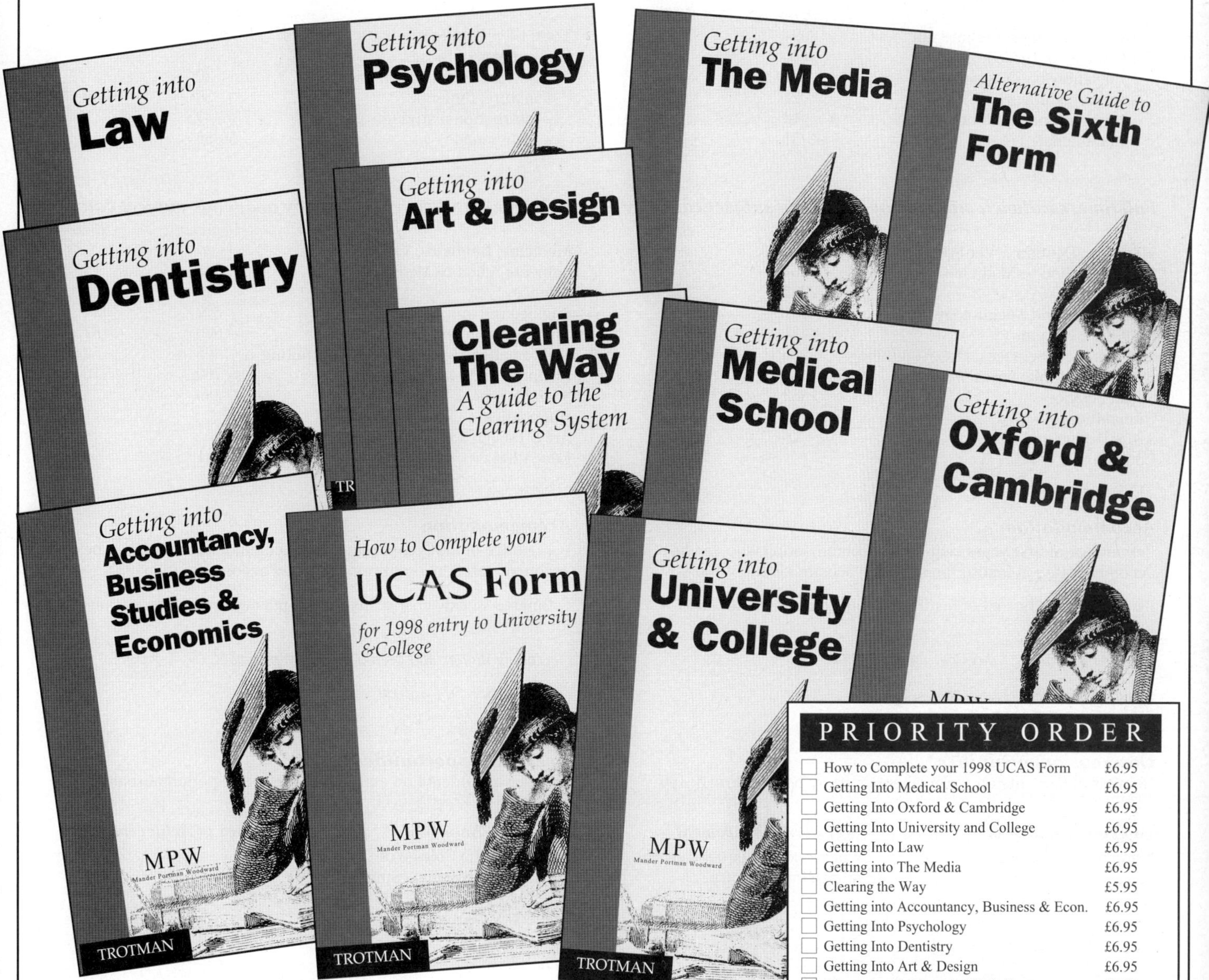

Getting into Law

Getting into Psychology

Getting into The Media

Alternative Guide to **The Sixth Form**

Getting into Dentistry

Getting into **Art & Design**

Clearing The Way *A guide to the Clearing System*

Getting into Medical School

Getting into **Oxford & Cambridge**

Getting into **Accountancy, Business Studies & Economics**

How to Complete your **UCAS Form** *for 1998 entry to University & College*

Getting into **University & College**

MPW *Mander Portman Woodward*

TROTMAN

Getting into higher education may be the toughest challenge you've yet faced.

MPW Guides can help.

Written by experts with a wealth of experience, *MPW Guides* are set out in straightforward language. They give clear, practical advice to help you win a place on the course of your choice. You'll find *MPW Guides* in all good bookshops.

To get your *Guides* fast, phone 0181-332 2132

How to Complete your **UCAS Form** *for 1998 entry to University & College* **Video** MPW *Mander Portman Woodward* TROTMAN

With more than twenty years experience of guiding students through the applications procedures for higher education, MPW (Mander Portman Woodward) has Colleges in London, Cambridge, Birmingham and Bristol. We cover a wide range of A-Level and GCSE subjects in courses lasting from ten weeks (retakes) to two years and we teach in small groups or individually. MPW offers a unique blend of expert tuition, close supervision, study skills and exam technique.

If you would like more information about MPW, telephone us on 0345-585597.

PRIORITY ORDER

☐	How to Complete your 1998 UCAS Form	£6.95
☐	Getting Into Medical School	£6.95
☐	Getting Into Oxford & Cambridge	£6.95
☐	Getting Into University and College	£6.95
☐	Getting Into Law	£6.95
☐	Getting into The Media	£6.95
☐	Clearing the Way	£5.95
☐	Getting into Accountancy, Business & Econ.	£6.95
☐	Getting Into Psychology	£6.95
☐	Getting Into Dentistry	£6.95
☐	Getting Into Art & Design	£6.95
☐	Alternative Guide to the Sixth Form	£5.95
☐	Video: How to Complete your UCAS Form	£29.38 inc vat

+Post and Packing: £1.60 for first item, 50p for each extra item.

Ring us and and quote your Access/Visa No.
0181-332 2132

Telephone 0171 835 1355 for more information about MPW

Trotman & Co Limited
12 Hill Rise, Richmond, Surrey TW10 6UA. (98)

MPW
GUIDES

The University of Aberdeen

Admissions Office, University Office, Regent Walk, Aberdeen, AB24 3FX

Tel: 01224 273504 Fax: 01224 272031
admoff@admin.abdn.ac.uk   http://www.abdn.ac.uk

A20

Datafile

1996-97 Student Numbers

Total number of all students   11094

	Degree	HND
Total FT/SW undergraduate numbers	8094	
Percentages of these		
– on sandwich programmes	1	
– mature students	21	
– international students	12	
– male/female	49/51	

Full-time/sandwich students by academic subject category

	Degree	HND
Medicine, Dentistry, Vet Science	824	
Subjects Allied to Medicine	301	
Science	2281	
Engineering and Technology	581	
Built Environment	231	
Mathematical Sciences, IT & Computing	285	
Business and Management	482	
Social Sciences	1432	
Humanities	1661	
Art & Design and Perf Arts	16	
Education		

Accommodation

Percentage of first years requiring accommodation who can be accommodated in institution-managed accommodation: 100%

Estimated weekly cost of institution-managed accommodation for 32 weeks:

(including 3 meals 7 days per week) £68.00

(no food) £40.00

(other…) £46.00

*Overseas opportunities**

Number of students on a placement or study period abroad: 100

Compacts/Networks
Summer School for Access.

Record of Achievement
Will request if required by the Admissions Selector.

Interviewing
Generally do not, although some for Medicine.

Campus locations
Old Aberdeen, Foresterhill (Medical School & Subjects Allied to Medicine).

Open Days
Open Door Visiting Policy. All welcome by appointment. Telephone 01224 272090, or e-mail schlia@admin.abdn.ac.uk.

*Excludes those on compulsory language course placements.

University of Abertay Dundee

Information & Recruitment Division, Bell Street, Dundee, DD1 1HG

Tel: 01382 308080 Fax: 01382 308877
l.balfour@abertay-dundee.ac.uk   http://www.tay.ac.uk/

A30

Datafile

1996-97 Student Numbers

Total number of all students   4141

	Degree	HND
Total FT/SW undergraduate numbers	3230	484
Percentages of these		
– on sandwich programmes	30	
– mature students	30	30
– international students	7	3
– male/female	50/50	50/50

Full-time/sandwich students by academic subject category

	Degree	HND
Medicine, Dentistry, Vet Science		
Subjects Allied to Medicine	315	15
Science	315	52
Engineering and Technology	300	181
Built Environment	660	67
Mathematical Sciences, IT & Computing	400	53
Business and Management	760	116
Social Sciences	480	
Humanities		
Art & Design and Perf Arts		
Education		

Accommodation

Percentage of first years requiring accommodation who can be accommodated in institution-managed accommodation: 95%

Estimated weekly cost of institution-managed accommodation for 36 weeks:

(including dinner and breakfast   days per week) £

(no food) £35.50 – £50.00

(other…) £

*Overseas opportunities**

Number of students on a placement or study period abroad: 60

Compacts/Networks
Links with Fife College of Further Education via Summer School for Access. Abertay Fife University Centre.

Record of Achievement

Interviewing
No interviews held but may invite applicants to informal visits.

Campus locations
Dundee city centre.

Open Days
Information Days held in February and March 1998. Open Days held on 22 & 23 September 1997.

*Excludes those on compulsory language course placements.

The University of Wales, Aberystwyth

Undergraduate Admissions Office, Old College, King Street,
Aberystwyth, Ceredigion, SY23 2AX

Tel: 01970 622021 Fax: 01970 627410
ait@aber.ac.uk http://www.aber.ac.uk

A40

Datafile

1996-97 Student Numbers

	Degree	HND
Total number of all students	6900	
Total FT/SW undergraduate numbers	5353	274
Percentages of these		
– on sandwich programmes	3	25
– mature students	18	25
– international students	11	3
– male/female	50/50	50/50

Full-time/sandwich students by academic subject category

	Degree	HND
Medicine, Dentistry, Vet Science		
Subjects Allied to Medicine		
Science	1788	274
Engineering and Technology		
Built Environment		
Mathematical Sciences, IT & Computing	342	
Business and Management	319	
Social Sciences	1191	
Humanities	1259	
Art & Design and Perf Arts	419	
Education	35	

Accommodation

Percentage of first years requiring accommodation who can be accommodated in institution-managed accommodation: 100%

Estimated weekly cost of institution-managed accommodation for 30-39 weeks:

(including dinner and breakfast 6-7 days per week) £50.63

(no food) £33.25

(other…) £

Overseas opportunities*

Number of students on a placement or study period abroad: 58

Compacts/Networks

Dinefwr, West Glam, Shropshire, Walsall, North East Worcestershire Partnership and Marches Consortium.

Record of Achievement

Used as additional evidence in marginal cases to decide whether to issue or confirm an offer/place.

Interviewing

Majority of offers made based on the UCAS form. Mature students interviewed due to qualifications.

Campus locations

Two Campuses, Penglius and Llanbrdarn, one mile apart and both nearly one mile from the town.

Open Days

1 July 1997 and 7 July 1998.

*Excludes those on compulsory language course placements.

Amersham & Wycombe College

Customer Services (Admissions), Stanley Hill, Amersham, Bucks, HP7 9HN

Tel: 01494 735500 Fax: 01494 735566

A55

Datafile

1996-97 Student Numbers

	Degree	HND
Total number of all students	6240	
Total FT/SW undergraduate numbers		192
Percentages of these		
– on sandwich programmes		
– mature students		20
– international students		1
– male/female		50/50

Full-time/sandwich students by academic subject category

	Degree	HND
Medicine, Dentistry, Vet Science		
Subjects Allied to Medicine		
Science		
Engineering and Technology		
Built Environment		
Mathematical Sciences, IT & Computing		
Business and Management		37
Social Sciences		
Humanities		
Art & Design and Perf Arts		155
Education		

Accommodation

There is no institution-managed accommodation. Students are advised to contact the institution for information about local accommodation options.

Overseas opportunities*

Number of students on a placement or study period abroad:

Compacts/Networks

Record of Achievement

RoAs requested at interview and students encouraged to maintain them throughout courses.

Interviewing

Art, Design & Performing Arts are interviewed and Travel & Tourism Management are discretionary.

Campus locations

Amersham and Chesham.

Open Days

Available throughout year. Contact Customer Services on 01494 735500.

*Excludes those on compulsory language course placements.

Anglia Polytechnic University

Senior Admissions Officer, Anglia Polytechnic University, East Road, Cambridge, CB1 1PT

Tel: 01223 363271 Fax: 01223 576156

degaalap@bridge.anglia.ac.uk

A60

Datafile

1996-97 Student Numbers

Total number of all students   13997

	Degree	HND
Total FT/SW undergraduate numbers	6464	544
Percentages of these		
– on sandwich programmes		1
– mature students	37	27
– international students	14	3
– male/female	41/59	70/30

Full-time/sandwich students by academic subject category

	Degree	HND
Medicine, Dentistry, Vet Science		
Subjects Allied to Medicine	460	
Science	649	4
Engineering and Technology	182	21
Built Environment	171	22
Mathematical Sciences, IT & Computing	484	186
Business and Management	859	235
Social Sciences	1385	
Humanities	1282	
Art & Design and Perf Arts	484	76
Education	508	

Accommodation

Percentage of first years requiring accommodation who can be accommodated in institution-managed accommodation: 30%

Estimated weekly cost of institution-managed accommodation for 39 weeks:

(including dinner and breakfast   days per week) £

(no food) £52.00

(other...) £

Overseas opportunities*

Number of students on a placement or study period abroad: 70

Compacts/Networks	Record of Achievement
Anglia Compact, Essex Consortium.	

Interviewing	Campus locations
Interviews held for Education, Nursing and Social Work provided other criteria are satisfied.	Chelmsford, Cambridge and Brentwood.

Open Days

18 January 1998, 22 March 1998 and 26 April 1998.

*Excludes those on compulsory language course placements.

Askham Bryan College

Registrar, Askham Bryan College, Askham Bryan, York, YO2 3PR

Tel: 01904 772277 Fax: 01904 772288

A70

Datafile

1996-97 Student Numbers

Total number of all students   590

	Degree	HND
Total FT/SW undergraduate numbers	59	167
Percentages of these		
– on sandwich programmes		33
– mature students	90	52
– international students	11	6
– male/female	50/50	60/40

Full-time/sandwich students by academic subject category

	Degree	HND
Medicine, Dentistry, Vet Science		
Subjects Allied to Medicine		
Science	38	117
Engineering and Technology		
Built Environment		
Mathematical Sciences, IT & Computing		
Business and Management	21	50
Social Sciences		
Humanities		
Art & Design and Perf Arts		
Education		

Accommodation

Percentage of first years requiring accommodation who can be accommodated in institution-managed accommodation: 60%

Estimated weekly cost of institution-managed accommodation for 39 weeks:

(including dinner and breakfast 5 days per week) £65.00

(no food) £40.00

(other...) £

Overseas opportunities*

Number of students on a placement or study period abroad:

Compacts/Networks	Record of Achievement

Interviewing	Campus locations
All prospective students are offered an information day visit.	One site at Askham Bryan College in York.

Open Days

By invitation during the Winter and Spring.

*Excludes those on compulsory language course placements.

Aston University

The Registry, Aston University, Aston Triangle, Birmingham, B4 7ET

Tel: 0121 359 6313 Fax: 0121 333 6350
prospectus@aston.ac.uk http://www.aston.ac.uk

A80

Datafile

1996-97 Student Numbers

	Degree	HND
Total number of all students 5200		
Total FT/SW undergraduate numbers	4062	
Percentages of these		
– on sandwich programmes	76	
– mature students	6	
– international students	3	
– male/female	52/48	

Full-time/sandwich students by academic subject category

	Degree	HND
Medicine, Dentistry, Vet Science		
Subjects Allied to Medicine	279	
Science	598	
Engineering and Technology	669	
Built Environment		
Mathematical Sciences, IT & Computing	327	
Business and Management	1163	
Social Sciences	536	
Humanities	490	
Art & Design and Perf Arts		
Education		

Accommodation

Percentage of first years requiring accommodation who can be accommodated in institution-managed accommodation: 100%

Estimated weekly cost of institution-managed accommodation for 38 weeks:

(including dinner and breakfast   days per week) £

(no food) £21.85 – £31.85

(other…) £

Overseas opportunities*
Number of students on a placement or study period abroad: 30

Compacts/Networks
Midlands Regional Compact. Foundation Programme with Matthew Boulton College of F & H Education.

Record of Achievement
May be requested if the applicant is invited for interview.

Interviewing
Policy varies with department. Students made an offer without interview will be invited to visit.

Campus locations
Aston Triangle, Birmingham.

Open Days
All subjects on 30 April 1997 and 29 September 1997. Contact Admissions Tutors for each subject.

*Excludes those on compulsory language course placements.

University of Wales, Bangor

Senior Assistant Registrar, University of Wales, Bangor, Gwynedd, LL57 2DG

Tel: 01248 382017 Fax: 01248 370451
k102@bangor.ac.uk

B06

Datafile

1996-97 Student Numbers

	Degree	HND
Total number of all students 7654		
Total FT/SW undergraduate numbers	5223	
Percentages of these		
– on sandwich programmes	1	
– mature students	33	
– international students	5	
– male/female	41/59	

Full-time/sandwich students by academic subject category

	Degree	HND
Medicine, Dentistry, Vet Science		
Subjects Allied to Medicine	208	
Science	1552	
Engineering and Technology	193	
Built Environment	34	
Mathematical Sciences, IT & Computing	84	
Business and Management	320	
Social Sciences	457	
Humanities	1134	
Art & Design and Perf Arts	126	
Education	552	

Accommodation

Percentage of first years requiring accommodation who can be accommodated in institution-managed accommodation: 100%

Estimated weekly cost of institution-managed accommodation for weeks:

(including dinner and breakfast 5 days per week) £54.57

(no food) £34.00 – £36.00

(other…) £43.00

Overseas opportunities*
Number of students on a placement or study period abroad:

Compacts/Networks
Compact arrangements with some local schools.

Record of Achievement
Admissions Tutors may, in some cases, request the Record of Achievement.

Interviewing
Some schools or departments interview candidates and others invite candidates to visit Bangor.

Campus locations
Bangor and Wrexham.

Open Days
To be held in Spring/Summer 1998. Contact School and Colleges Liaison Officer for information.

*Excludes those on compulsory language course placements.

38

Barking College

Admissions Officer, Barking College, Dagenham Road, Dagenham, RM7 0XU

Tel: 01708 766841 Fax: 01708 731067

B11

Datafile

1996-97 Student Numbers

Total number of all students 6000

	Degree	HND
Total FT/SW undergraduate numbers	8	34
Percentages of these		
– on sandwich programmes		
– mature students	25	20
– international students		
– male/female	0	6

Full-time/sandwich students by academic subject category

	Degree	HND
Medicine, Dentistry, Vet Science		
Subjects Allied to Medicine		
Science		
Engineering and Technology		
Built Environment		
Mathematical Sciences, IT & Computing		
Business and Management		
Social Sciences		
Humanities		
Art & Design and Perf Arts	8	34
Education		

Accommodation

There is no institution-managed accommodation. Students are advised to contact the institution for information about local accommodation options.

Overseas opportunities*

Number of students on a placement or study period abroad:

Compacts/Networks

Record of Achievement
Students can bring their Record of Achievement to support their application.

Interviewing
Students must bring their portfolio of work and other relevant work to support their application.

Campus locations
One site College: Rush Green Campus.

Open Days

Please contact College for confirmation of Open Days.

*Excludes those on compulsory language course placements.

Barnsley College

H E Administrative Officer, Client Services Team, Old Mill Lane Site, Barnsley College, Church Street, Barnsley, S70 2AX

Tel: 01226 730191 Fax: 01226 216166
clientservices@barnsley.ac.uk   http://www.barnsley.ac.uk

B13

Datafile

1996-97 Student Numbers

Total number of all students 17801

	Degree	HND
Total FT/SW undergraduate numbers	898	509
Percentages of these		
– on sandwich programmes		
– mature students	47	34
– international students	1	1
– male/female	53/47	57/43

Full-time/sandwich students by academic subject category

	Degree	HND
Medicine, Dentistry, Vet Science		
Subjects Allied to Medicine		
Science	11	
Engineering and Technology	16	
Built Environment		
Mathematical Sciences, IT & Computing		37
Business and Management	73	60
Social Sciences	99	
Humanities	347	145
Art & Design and Perf Arts	305	222
Education	47	45

Accommodation

Percentage of first years requiring accommodation who can be accommodated in institution-managed accommodation: 15%

Estimated weekly cost of institution-managed accommodation for 36 weeks:

(including dinner and breakfast   days per week) £

(no food) £40.00

(other…) £

Overseas opportunities*

Number of students on a placement or study period abroad: 41

Compacts/Networks
Local Compact in Barnsley and franchising with local universities for Science/Engineering.

Record of Achievement
RoAs are considered at interview. There is an opportunity for RoAs to be updated on all courses.

Interviewing
Interviews occur for Art, Design, Catering and Music. Interviews for other courses discretionary.

Campus locations
The College has five main sites all within five minutes walk of each other and the town centre.

Open Days

Open Days held in March, May and October. Contact Client Services Team for details.

*Excludes those on compulsory language course placements.

Basford Hall College

Enquiries & Admissions, Basford Hall College, Stockhill Lane, Nottingham, NG6 0NB

Tel: 0115 970 4541 Fax: 0115 942 2334
bits@basford.demon.co.uk www.demon.co.uk./basford/basford.html

B14

Datafile

1996-97 Student Numbers

Total number of all students   11000

	Degree	HND
Total FT/SW undergraduate numbers		40
Percentages of these		
– on sandwich programmes		
– mature students		45
– international students		
– male/female		87/13

Full-time/sandwich students by academic subject category

	Degree	HND
Medicine, Dentistry, Vet Science		
Subjects Allied to Medicine		
Science		
Engineering and Technology		
Built Environment		
Mathematical Sciences, IT & Computing		
Business and Management		
Social Sciences		
Humanities		
Art & Design and Perf Arts		40
Education		

Accommodation

There is no institution-managed accommodation. Students are advised to contact the institution for information about local accommodation options.

Overseas opportunities*

Number of students on a placement or study period abroad:

Compacts/Networks

HND Furniture Course is franchised through Buckinghamshire College of Higher Educaiton.

Record of Achievement

We continue to maintain RoAs and encourage students to bring them to interviews.

Interviewing

All applicants are interviewed and a portfolio is required.

Campus locations

Nottingham.

Open Days

By arrangement with HND Tutor.

*Excludes those on compulsory language course placements.

University of Bath

Admissions Office, University of Bath, Bath, BA2 7AY

Tel: 01225 826697 Fax: 01225 826366
d.l.driscoll@bath.ac.uk http://www.bath.ac.uk

B16

Datafile

1996-97 Student Numbers

Total number of all students   7835

	Degree	HND
Total FT/SW undergraduate numbers	4876	
Percentages of these		
– on sandwich programmes	66	
– mature students	10	
– international students	6	
– male/female	57/43	

Full-time/sandwich students by academic subject category

	Degree	HND
Medicine, Dentistry, Vet Science		
Subjects Allied to Medicine	175	
Science	1299	
Engineering and Technology	1095	
Built Environment	203	
Mathematical Sciences, IT & Computing	452	
Business and Management	657	
Social Sciences	557	
Humanities	420	
Art & Design and Perf Arts		
Education	18	

Accommodation

Percentage of first years requiring accommodation who can be accommodated in institution-managed accommodation: 100%

Estimated weekly cost of institution-managed accommodation for 39 weeks:

(including dinner and breakfast   days per week) £

(no food) £39.40

(other…) £47.21

Overseas opportunities*

Number of students on a placement or study period abroad: 481

Compacts/Networks

Foundation course for Science/Engineering at Strode College.

Record of Achievement

Interviewing

Most applicants offered non-selective interviews. Selective interviews for Pharmacy and Social Work.

Campus locations

A compact campus on one site, one mile from the centre of Bath which is very walkable.

Open Days

14 May 1997, 8 July 1997, 16 September 1997, 14 May 1998, 2 July 1998 and 16 September 1998.

*Excludes those on compulsory language course placements.

INDEPENDENT ON SUNDAY

Bath College of Higher Education

Registry, Bath College of H E, Newton Park, Bath, BA2 9BN

Tel: 01225 875875 Fax: 01225 875444

B20

Datafile

1996-97 Student Numbers

Total number of all students   3141

	Degree	HND
Total FT/SW undergraduate numbers	2077	
Percentages of these		
– on sandwich programmes		
– mature students	41	
– international students	4	
– male/female	27/73	

Full-time/sandwich students by academic subject category

	Degree	HND
Medicine, Dentistry, Vet Science		
Subjects Allied to Medicine	55	
Science	168	
Engineering and Technology		
Built Environment		
Mathematical Sciences, IT & Computing		
Business and Management	151	
Social Sciences	264	
Humanities	402	
Art & Design and Perf Arts	623	
Education	647	

Accommodation

Percentage of first years requiring accommodation who can be accommodated in institution-managed accommodation: 100%

Estimated weekly cost of institution-managed accommodation for 40 weeks:

(including dinner and breakfast   days per week) £

(no food) £40.00

(other…) £

Overseas opportunities*

Number of students on a placement or study period abroad: 45

Compacts/Networks

Six linked/local Access courses. First year of BSc Soc Sci course runs also at Strode College.

Record of Achievement

Useful only at the interview.

Interviewing

All suitable applicants for ITT and Art and Design courses are interviewed.

Campus locations

Newton Park is a rural campus four miles west of Bath. Sion Hill is one mile north of city centre.

Open Days

Invitation days for applicants on Modular Scheme courses. Open Week for Art & Design in February.

Excludes those on compulsory language course placements.

Bell College of Technology

Registry Admissions, Bell College of Technology, Almada Street, Hamilton, Lanarkshire, Scotland, ML3 0JB

Tel: 01698 283100 Fax: 01698 282131
registry@bell.ac.uk

B26

Datafile

1996-97 Student Numbers

Total number of all students   2268

	Degree	HND
Total FT/SW undergraduate numbers	456	931
Percentages of these		
– on sandwich programmes		
– mature students	15	15
– international students		
– male/female	70/30	52/48

Full-time/sandwich students by academic subject category

	Degree	HND
Medicine, Dentistry, Vet Science		
Subjects Allied to Medicine		
Science	121	77
Engineering and Technology	112	144
Built Environment	52	84
Mathematical Sciences, IT & Computing	65	57
Business and Management	106	404
Social Sciences		165
Humanities		
Art & Design and Perf Arts		
Education		

Accommodation

Percentage of first years requiring accommodation who can be accommodated in institution-managed accommodation: 10%

Estimated weekly cost of institution-managed accommodation for 39 weeks:

(including dinner and breakfast   days per week) £

(no food) £39.00

(other…) £

Overseas opportunities*

Number of students on a placement or study period abroad:

Compacts/Networks

Record of Achievement

Interviewing

Applicants may be requested to attend interview. All who receive offers will be invited to visit.

Campus locations

Open Days

Dates to be arranged. Contact Marketing Manager at a later date for details.

Excludes those on compulsory language course placements.

Letts STUDY GUIDES
THE INDEPENDENT

The University of Birmingham

Director of Admissions, The University of Birmingham, Edgbaston, Birmingham, B15 2TT

Tel: 0121 414 3697 Fax: 0121 414 3850
prospectus@birmingham.ac.uk

B32

Datafile

1996-97 Student Numbers

Total number of all students   18876

	Degree	HND
Total FT/SW undergraduate numbers	12671	
Percentages of these		
– on sandwich programmes	1	
– mature students	9	
– international students	8	
– male/female	52/48	

Full-time/sandwich students by academic subject category

	Degree	HND
Medicine, Dentistry, Vet Science	1252	
Subjects Allied to Medicine	545	
Science	2560	
Engineering and Technology	2009	
Built Environment	44	
Mathematical Sciences, IT & Computing	741	
Business and Management	770	
Social Sciences	1554	
Humanities	2691	
Art & Design and Perf Arts	289	
Education	216	

Accommodation

Percentage of first years requiring accommodation who can be accommodated in institution-managed accommodation: 100%

Estimated weekly cost of institution-managed accommodation for 30-40 weeks:

(including dinner and breakfast 6 days per week) £64.00 – £80.00

(no food) £34.00 – £50.00

(other…) £33.00

Overseas opportunities*

Number of students on a placement or study period abroad: 317

Compacts/Networks

Record of Achievement

RoAs welcome at interview but please do not send via post in case of loss.

Interviewing

Campus locations

Policy varies: interviews given for Medicine and other departments hold Open Days before offers.

Open Days

13 September 1997, 24 March 1998 and 25 March 1998.

*Excludes those on compulsory language course placements.

Birmingham College of Food, Tourism and Creative Studies

Admissions Office, Summer Row, Birmingham, B3 1JB

Tel: 0121 604 1040 Fax: 0121 200 1376
admissions@bcftcs.ac.uk http://www.bcftcs.ac.uk

B35

Datafile

1996-97 Student Numbers

Total number of all students

	Degree	HND
Total FT/SW undergraduate numbers	1087	1169
Percentages of these		
– on sandwich programmes	35	52
– mature students	23	25
– international students	19	17
– male/female	34/66	43/57

Full-time/sandwich students by academic subject category

	Degree	HND
Medicine, Dentistry, Vet Science		
Subjects Allied to Medicine		
Science		
Engineering and Technology		
Built Environment		
Mathematical Sciences, IT & Computing		
Business and Management	1087	1169
Social Sciences		
Humanities		
Art & Design and Perf Arts		
Education		

Accommodation

Percentage of first years requiring accommodation who can be accommodated in institution-managed accommodation: 65%

Estimated weekly cost of institution-managed accommodation for 39 weeks:

(including dinner and breakfast   days per week) £

(no food) £35.00 – £52.00

(other…)

Overseas opportunities*

Number of students on a placement or study period abroad: 123

Compacts/Networks

Arrangements exist with institutions nationally and internationally. Admissions Office has information.

Record of Achievement

RoAs will be taken into consideration if presented at interview.

Interviewing

Mature and non-standard applicants under consideration are normally interviewed.

Campus locations

The College is situated on a single site in central Birmingham.

Open Days

Pre-application Open Day on 13 September 1997. All applicants with an offer are invited to visit.

*Excludes those on compulsory language course placements.

Bishop Grosseteste College

College Registry, Bishop Grosseteste College, Newport, Lincoln, LN1 3DY

Tel: 01522 527347 Fax: 01522 530243

B38

Datafile

1996-97 Student Numbers

Total number of all students 809

	Degree	HND
Total FT/SW undergraduate numbers	790	
Percentages of these		
– on sandwich programmes		
– mature students	15	
– international students		
– male/female	14/86	

Full-time/sandwich students by academic subject category

	Degree	HND
Medicine, Dentistry, Vet Science		
Subjects Allied to Medicine		
Science		
Engineering and Technology		
Built Environment		
Mathematical Sciences, IT & Computing		
Business and Management		
Social Sciences		
Humanities	67	
Art & Design and Perf Arts	50	
Education	673	

Accommodation

Percentage of first years requiring accommodation who can be accommodated in institution-managed accommodation: 100%

Estimated weekly cost of institution-managed accommodation for 32-35 weeks:

(including 3 meals 5 days per week) £57.50

(no food) £

(other…) £

Overseas opportunities*

Number of students on a placement or study period abroad:

Compacts/Networks

Record of Achievement

RoAs can be brought to interview.

Interviewing

It is a DFEE requirement that all applications for ITT are interviewed.

Campus locations

B G C is a twenty-one acre, single site, residential campus in the uphill area of Lincoln.

Open Days

Family Visiting Days: 2 March and 19 October 1997.
Sixth Form Open Days: 19 June and 25 June 1997.

*Excludes those on compulsory language course placements.

Blackburn College

Student Services, Blackburn College, Feilden Street, Blackburn, Lancashire, BB2 1LH

Tel: 01254 55144 Fax: 01254 682700

B40

Datafile

1996-97 Student Numbers

Total number of all students

	Degree	HND
Total FT/SW undergraduate numbers		
Percentages of these		
– on sandwich programmes		
– mature students		
– international students		
– male/female		

Full-time/sandwich students by academic subject category

	Degree	HND
Medicine, Dentistry, Vet Science		
Subjects Allied to Medicine		
Science		
Engineering and Technology		
Built Environment		
Mathematical Sciences, IT & Computing		
Business and Management		
Social Sciences		
Humanities		
Art & Design and Perf Arts		
Education		

Accommodation

Percentage of first years requiring accommodation who can be accommodated in institution-managed accommodation: 10%

Estimated weekly cost of institution-managed accommodation for 36 weeks:

(including dinner and breakfast   days per week) £

(no food) £

(other…) £42.00

Overseas opportunities*

Number of students on a placement or study period abroad:

Compacts/Networks

Record of Achievement

We encourage all students to bring their RoA to interviews.

Interviewing

All students have the opportunity to attend interviews if required.

Campus locations

Town centre – close to rail and bus stations.

Open Days

Art & Design – 2, 3, 10, 11, 17, 18 February 1998, by appointment.
General – 12 March, 21 May 1998.

*Excludes those on compulsory language course placements.

Blackpool and the Fylde College

College Information Office, Ashfield Road, Bispham, Blackpool, Lancashire, FY2 0HB

Tel: 01253 352352 Fax: 01253 356127

B41

Datafile

1996-97 Student Numbers

Total number of all students   34000

	Degree	HND
Total FT/SW undergraduate numbers	505	605
Percentages of these		
– on sandwich programmes		
– mature students	48	41
– international students	1	1
– male/female	58/42	59/41

Full-time/sandwich students by academic subject category

	Degree	HND
Medicine, Dentistry, Vet Science		
Subjects Allied to Medicine		
Science		
Engineering and Technology		58
Built Environment		41
Mathematical Sciences, IT & Computing		
Business and Management	163	442
Social Sciences		
Humanities		
Art & Design and Perf Arts	342	64
Education		

Accommodation

There is no institution-managed accommodation. Students are advised to contact the institution for information about local accommodation options.

Overseas opportunities*

Number of students on a placement or study period abroad: 40

Compacts/Networks

Record of Achievement

Interviewing

At Admissions Tutor's discretion. Interviews held at Open Days for certain courses.

Campus locations

Five main compuses across the Fylde Coast.

Open Days

Open Days are held regularly. Please contact Sharon Potts in the Marketing Office for details.

Excludes those on compulsory language course placements.

Bolton Institute of Higher Education

Senior Assistant Registrar, Bolton Institute, Deane Road, Bolton, BL3 5AB

Tel: 01204 528851 Fax: 01204 399074
enquiries@bolton.ac.uk.

B44

Datafile

1996-97 Student Numbers

Total number of all students   7006

	Degree	HND
Total FT/SW undergraduate numbers	3098	626
Percentages of these		
– on sandwich programmes		
– mature students	47	19
– international students	3	7
– male/female	55/45	90/10

Full-time/sandwich students by academic subject category

	Degree	HND
Medicine, Dentistry, Vet Science		
Subjects Allied to Medicine	57	
Science	484	
Engineering and Technology	758	103
Built Environment	85	84
Mathematical Sciences, IT & Computing	122	120
Business and Management	565	253
Social Sciences	269	
Humanities	455	
Art & Design and Perf Arts	237	66
Education	63	

Accommodation

Percentage of first years requiring accommodation who can be accommodated in institution-managed accommodation: 99%

Estimated weekly cost of institution-managed accommodation for 40 weeks:

(including dinner and breakfast   days per week) £

(no food) £39.50

(other...) £

Overseas opportunities*

Number of students on a placement or study period abroad: 9

Compacts/Networks

Record of Achievement

Bring RoA if invited for interview.

Interviewing

Most applicants are not interviewed. Mature and non-standard applicants may attend interviews.

Campus locations

Bolton has three sites within walking distance of each other.

Open Days

Open Days arranged by individual Faculties. Please contact the Institute for details.

Excludes those on compulsory language course placements.

Bournemouth University

The Registry, Studland House, 12 Christchurch Road, Bournemouth, Dorset, BH1 3NA

Tel: 01202 524111 Fax: 01202 503869
postmaster@bournemouth.ac.uk http://www.bournemouth.ac.uk

B50

Datafile

1996-97 Student Numbers

Total number of all students   10865

	Degree	HND
Total FT/SW undergraduate numbers	6321	668
Percentages of these		
– on sandwich programmes	58	
– mature students	25	22
– international students	2	1
– male/female	57/43	55/45

Full-time/sandwich students by academic subject category

	Degree	HND
Medicine, Dentistry, Vet Science		
Subjects Allied to Medicine	273	
Science	837	99
Engineering and Technology	472	
Built Environment	51	
Mathematical Sciences, IT & Computing	956	180
Business and Management	2032	389
Social Sciences	357	
Humanities	514	
Art & Design and Perf Arts	829	
Education		

Accommodation

Percentage of first years requiring accommodation who can be accommodated in institution-managed accommodation: 100%

Estimated weekly cost of institution-managed accommodation for 40 weeks:

(including dinner and breakfast days per week) £

(no food) £47.50 – £50.00

(other...) £

Overseas opportunities*

Number of students on a placement or study period abroad:

Compacts/Networks

Record of Achievement

Interviewing

Some courses require applicants to attend an interview – see prospectus for details.

Campus locations

Talbot campus is the main campus situated in Poole. Landsdowne campus is in the town centre.

Open Days

Published annually – details in prospectus.

Excludes those on compulsory language course placements.

Bournemouth and Poole College of Art and Design

Admissions, Wallisdown, Poole, Dorset, BH12 5HH

Tel: 01202 537729 Fax: 01202 537729

B53

Datafile

1996-97 Student Numbers

Total number of all students   1450

	Degree	HND
Total FT/SW undergraduate numbers	179	421
Percentages of these		
– on sandwich programmes		
– mature students	12	37
– international students	3	3
– male/female	14/16	40/30

Full-time/sandwich students by academic subject category

	Degree	HND
Medicine, Dentistry, Vet Science		
Subjects Allied to Medicine		
Science		
Engineering and Technology		
Built Environment		
Mathematical Sciences, IT & Computing		
Business and Management		
Social Sciences		
Humanities		
Art & Design and Perf Arts	179	421
Education		

Accommodation

There is no institution-managed accommodation. Students are advised to contact the institution for information about local accommodation options.

Overseas opportunities*

Number of students on a placement or study period abroad: 20

Compacts/Networks

HELDS (Higher Education Links Dorset Students) Dorset Compacts.

Record of Achievement

Interviewing

Interviews for first choice candidates. Places offered at all choices subject to availability.

Campus locations

Wallisdown and Boscombe.

Open Days

Please contact the College for details on 01202 363224.

Excludes those on compulsory language course placements.

Letts STUDY GUIDES
THE INDEPENDENT

The University of Bradford

Schools Liaison Office, Richmond Road, Bradford, West Yorkshire, BD7 1DP

Tel: 01274 383081 Fax: 01274 385810
ug-admissions@bradford.ac.uk

B56

Datafile

1996-97 Student Numbers

Total number of all students   9512

	Degree	HND
Total FT/SW undergraduate numbers	6216	
Percentages of these		
– on sandwich programmes	45	
– mature students	12	
– international students	6	
– male/female	54/46	

Full-time/sandwich students by academic subject category

	Degree	HND
Medicine, Dentistry, Vet Science		
Subjects Allied to Medicine	665	
Science	1392	
Engineering and Technology	1436	
Built Environment		
Mathematical Sciences, IT & Computing	323	
Business and Management	765	
Social Sciences	870	
Humanities	765	
Art & Design and Perf Arts		
Education		

Accommodation

Percentage of first years requiring accommodation who can be accommodated in institution-managed accommodation: 100%

Estimated weekly cost of institution-managed accommodation for 30 weeks:

(including dinner and breakfast 7 days per week) £60.00

(no food) £37.00

(other…) £50.00

Overseas opportunities*

Number of students on a placement or study period abroad: 200

Compacts/Networks

The Going On Scheme links the University, 5 other local HEIs and 6 local schools for HE awareness.

Record of Achievement

Bring a summary, if invited to interview.

Interviewing

Depends on dept. Some interview all applicants (eg. Applied Social Studies), others do not interview.

Campus locations

Main campus, Management Centre and School of Health Studies.

Open Days

16 April 1997 and 10 September 1997.

*Excludes those on compulsory language course placements.

Bradford and Ilkley Community College

Admissions Officer, Great Horton Road, Bradford, West Yorkshire, BD7 1AY

Tel: 01274 753026 Fax: 01274 741060
admissions@bilk.ac.uk http;//wcb.bilk.ac.uk/bicchome.htm/

B60

Datafile

1996-97 Student Numbers

Total number of all students

	Degree	HND
Total FT/SW undergraduate numbers	2312	548
Percentages of these		
– on sandwich programmes		
– mature students	95	50
– international students	10	19
– male/female	36/64	50/50

Full-time/sandwich students by academic subject category

	Degree	HND
Medicine, Dentistry, Vet Science		
Subjects Allied to Medicine	779	
Science		
Engineering and Technology		56
Built Environment		18
Mathematical Sciences, IT & Computing		
Business and Management	608	332
Social Sciences		
Humanities		
Art & Design and Perf Arts	306	142
Education	619	

Accommodation

Percentage of first years requiring accommodation who can be accommodated in institution-managed accommodation: 75%

Estimated weekly cost of institution-managed accommodation for 38 weeks:

(including dinner and breakfast   days per week) £

(no food) £36.00

(other…) £46.00

Overseas opportunities*

Number of students on a placement or study period abroad: 5

Compacts/Networks

Record of Achievement

Interviewing

Policy varies with some departments interviewing selected applicants.

Campus locations

Bradford and Ilkley.

Open Days

Various dates. Contact Schools Liaison Officer on 01274 753189.

*Excludes those on compulsory language course placements.

Bretton Hall

Admissions, Bretton Hall, West Bretton, Nr. Wakefield, West Yorkshire, WF4 4LG

Tel: 01924 830261

B66

University of Brighton

Admissions Academic Registry, Mithras House, University of Brighton, Lewes Road, Brighton, East Sussex, BN2 4AT

Tel: 01273 600900 Fax: 01273 642825
admissions@bton.@.uk. http://www.bton.ac.uk.

B72

Datafile

1996-97 Student Numbers

Total number of all students   2380

	Degree	HND
Total FT/SW undergraduate numbers	1866	
Percentages of these		
– on sandwich programmes		
– mature students	27	
– international students	2	
– male/female	32/78	

Full-time/sandwich students by academic subject category

	Degree	HND
Medicine, Dentistry, Vet Science		
Subjects Allied to Medicine	19	
Science		
Engineering and Technology		
Built Environment		
Mathematical Sciences, IT & Computing		
Business and Management		
Social Sciences	87	
Humanities	244	
Art & Design and Perf Arts	1068	
Education	467	

Accommodation

Percentage of first years requiring accommodation who can be accommodated in institution-managed accommodation: 100%

Estimated weekly cost of institution-managed accommodation for 37 weeks:

(including dinner and breakfast   days per week) $65.00

(no food) $50.00

(other...) £

Overseas opportunities*

Number of students on a placement or study period abroad:

Compacts/Networks	Record of Achievement

Interviewing	Campus locations
All QTS applicants are interviewed and 90% of our remaining programmes are subject to interview.	

Open Days
15 June 1997.

*Excludes those on compulsory language course placements.

Datafile

1996-97 Student Numbers

Total number of all students   15000

	Degree	HND
Total FT/SW undergraduate numbers	7738	637
Percentages of these		
– on sandwich programmes	42	12
– mature students	38	20
– international students	12	6
– male/female	45/55	50/50

Full-time/sandwich students by academic subject category

	Degree	HND
Medicine, Dentistry, Vet Science		
Subjects Allied to Medicine	406	54
Science	1025	54
Engineering and Technology	641	93
Built Environment	412	68
Mathematical Sciences, IT & Computing	814	153
Business and Management	1505	232
Social Sciences	268	
Humanities	445	
Art & Design and Perf Arts	1059	37
Education	1163	

Accommodation

Percentage of first years requiring accommodation who can be accommodated in institution-managed accommodation: 76%

Estimated weekly cost of institution-managed accommodation for 35 weeks:

(including dinner and breakfast 7 days per week) $63.00

(no food) $42.00 – $53.00

(other...) £37.00 – £42.00

Overseas opportunities*

Number of students on a placement or study period abroad: 350

Compacts/Networks	Record of Achievement
	RoA may be required but most Admissions Tutors find the information in the UCAS form sufficient.

Interviewing	Campus locations
Applicants are interviewed for a significant number of courses.	Brighton/Eastbourne. Franchise Colleges: Brighton, Chichester, Hastings, Northbrook, Eastbourne and Plumpton.

Open Days
Students encouraged to attend departmental Open or Selection Days but we will always endeavour to arrange individual visits, if necessary.

*Excludes those on compulsory language course placements.

University of Bristol

Admissions Office, Senate House, Tyndall Avenue, Bristol, BS8 1TH

Tel: 0117 928 9000 Fax: 0117 925 1424
admissions@bristol.ac.uk www.bris.ac.uk

B78

Datafile

1996-97 Student Numbers

Total number of all students   11122

	Degree	HND
Total FT/SW undergraduate numbers	8726	
Percentages of these		
– on sandwich programmes		
– mature students	13	
– international students	9	
– male/female	51/49	

Full-time/sandwich students by academic subject category

	Degree	HND
Medicine, Dentistry, Vet Science	1372	
Subjects Allied to Medicine	293	
Science	1847	
Engineering and Technology	930	
Built Environment		
Mathematical Sciences, IT & Computing	475	
Business and Management	102	
Social Sciences	1552	
Humanities	1861	
Art & Design and Perf Arts	205	
Education	89	

Accommodation

Percentage of first years requiring accommodation who can be accommodated in institution-managed accommodation: 100%

Estimated weekly cost of institution-managed accommodation for 30 weeks:

(including dinner and breakfast 7 days per week) £54.00 – £76.00

(no food) £29.00 – £47.00

(other…) £24.00 – £36.00

Overseas opportunities*

Number of students on a placement or study period abroad: 200

Compacts/Networks

Record of Achievement

Interviewing

Varies among departments.

Campus locations

Teaching buildings on central site. Halls of Residence are one to three miles from University.

Open Days

University Preview Day:14 May 1997. Science and Engineering Open Day: 2 July 1997.

*Excludes those on compulsory language course placements.

University of the West of England, Bristol

Admissions and Student Recruitment, Frenchay Campus, Coldharbour Lane, Bristol, BS16 1QY

Tel: 0117 965 6261 Fax: 0117 976 3804
admissions@uwe.ac.uk.

B80

Datafile

1996-97 Student Numbers

Total number of all students   23412

	Degree	HND
Total FT/SW undergraduate numbers	11642	1121
Percentages of these		
– on sandwich programmes	32	15
– mature students	20	
– international students	2	2
– male/female	48/52	

Full-time/sandwich students by academic subject category

	Degree	HND
Medicine, Dentistry, Vet Science		
Subjects Allied to Medicine	680	
Science	1638	116
Engineering and Technology	734	242
Built Environment	1097	79
Mathematical Sciences, IT & Computing	1137	236
Business and Management	1455	365
Social Sciences	1727	
Humanities	1190	19
Art & Design and Perf Arts	917	64
Education	1067	

Accommodation

Percentage of first years requiring accommodation who can be accommodated in institution-managed accommodation: 85%

Estimated weekly cost of institution-managed accommodation for 46 weeks:

(including dinner and breakfast days per week) £

(no food) £39.00

(other…) £

Overseas opportunities*

Number of students on a placement or study period abroad:

Compacts/Networks

Special arrangements with schools and colleges in the South-West.

Record of Achievement

We recognise the value of RoAs and, if invited for interview, students should bring theirs.

Interviewing

Faculty of Art, Media & Design, Health, Social Care & Education interview. Others at Open Days.

Campus locations

An Associate Faculty in Glos., 5 campuses around Bristol and Centres in Bath, Gloucester & Swindon.

Open Days

Held during Autumn/Summer Terms for applicants with places. Other visits by arrangements.

*Excludes those on compulsory language course placements.

British College of Naturopathy and Osteopathy

Academic Registry, Life House, 3 Sumpter Close, 120/122 Finchley Road, London, NN3 5HR

Tel: 0171 435 6464 Fax: 0171 431 3630
bmg@bo.ac.uk.

B81

Datafile

1996-97 Student Numbers

Total number of all students   213

	Degree	HND
Total FT/SW undergraduate numbers	197	
Percentages of these		
– on sandwich programmes		
– mature students	50	
– international students	15	
– male/female	50	

Full-time/sandwich students by academic subject category

	Degree	HND
Medicine, Dentistry, Vet Science		
Subjects Allied to Medicine	197	
Science		
Engineering and Technology		
Built Environment		
Mathematical Sciences, IT & Computing		
Business and Management		
Social Sciences		
Humanities		
Art & Design and Perf Arts		
Education		

Accommodation

There is no institution-managed accommodation. Students are advised to contact the institution for information about local accommodation options.

*Overseas opportunities**

Number of students on a placement or study period abroad: 4

Compacts/Networks   *Record of Achievement*

Interviewing   *Campus locations*

All applicants are interviewed.   One.

Open Days

February and March.

*Excludes those on compulsory language course placements.

The British Institute in Paris (University of London)

Head of Department of French Studies, Department d'etudes Francaises, Institut Britannique de Paris, 11 rue de Constantine, 75340 Paris Cedex 07, France,

Tel: 1 44 11 73 83/4 Fax: 1 45 50 31 55

B82

Datafile

1996-97 Student Numbers

Total number of all students   2080

	Degree	HND
Total FT/SW undergraduate numbers	132	32
Percentages of these		
– on sandwich programmes		
– mature students	10	30
– international students	20	22
– male/female	13/87	30/70

Full-time/sandwich students by academic subject category

	Degree	HND
Medicine, Dentistry, Vet Science		
Subjects Allied to Medicine		
Science		
Engineering and Technology		
Built Environment		
Mathematical Sciences, IT & Computing		
Business and Management		
Social Sciences		
Humanities	132	32
Art & Design and Perf Arts		
Education		

Accommodation

There is no institution-managed accommodation. Students are advised to contact the institution for information about local accommodation options.

*Overseas opportunities**

Number of students on a placement or study period abroad:

Compacts/Networks   *Record of Achievement*

RoAs are taken into consideration as part of the admissions process.

Interviewing   *Campus locations*

All short-listed applicants are interviewed.

The British Institute in Paris is situated on the Esplanade des Invalides in the city centre.

Open Days

No Open Days. Applicants listed for interview can attend in London or Paris (two day student tour).

*Excludes those on compulsory language course placements.

Brunel University, West London

Undergraduate Admissions, Registry, Brunel University, Uxbridge, UB8 3PH

Tel: 01895 274000 Fax: 01895 232806
courses@brunel.ac.uk http://httpl.brunel.ac.uk.8080/

B84

Datafile

1996-97 Student Numbers

Total number of all students   12378

	Degree	HND
Total FT/SW undergraduate numbers	7491	286
Percentages of these		
– on sandwich programmes	46	
– mature students	32	30
– international students	3	2
– male/female	58/42	58/42

Full-time/sandwich students by academic subject category

	Degree	HND
Medicine, Dentistry, Vet Science		
Subjects Allied to Medicine	245	
Science	1336	
Engineering and Technology	1573	
Built Environment		
Mathematical Sciences, IT & Computing	927	163
Business and Management	1025	123
Social Sciences	1077	
Humanities	697	
Art & Design and Perf Arts	291	
Education	320	

Accommodation

Percentage of first years requiring accommodation who can be accommodated in institution-managed accommodation: 70%

Estimated weekly cost of institution-managed accommodation for 36 weeks:

(including dinner and breakfast days per week) £

(no food) £35.00 – £41.00

(other...) £47.00

Overseas opportunities*

Number of students on a placement or study period abroad: 235

Compacts/Networks	Record of Achievement
	Individual departments have own policies. Students should only present RoA if requested.

Interviewing	Campus locations
Individual departments have different policies.	Uxbridge, Twickenham, Osterley, Runnymede.

Open Days

Uxbridge - 21/5/97, 2/7/97, 26/9/97. Twic/Oster - 14/5/97, 1/7/97, 15/9/97. Runn - 24/9/97.

*Excludes those on compulsory language course placements.

The University of Buckingham

Admissions Office, University of Buckingham, Buckingham, MK18 1EG

Tel: 01280 814080 Fax: 01280 824081
admissions@buck.ac.uk http://www.buck.ac.uk

B90

Datafile

1996-97 Student Numbers

Total number of all students   884

	Degree	HND
Total FT/SW undergraduate numbers	709	
Percentages of these		
– on sandwich programmes		
– mature students	52	
– international students	65	
– male/female	56/44	

Full-time/sandwich students by academic subject category

	Degree	HND
Medicine, Dentistry, Vet Science		
Subjects Allied to Medicine		
Science	26	
Engineering and Technology		
Built Environment		
Mathematical Sciences, IT & Computing	22	
Business and Management	228	
Social Sciences	270	
Humanities	163	
Art & Design and Perf Arts		
Education		

Accommodation

Percentage of first years requiring accommodation who can be accommodated in institution-managed accommodation: 100%

Estimated weekly cost of institution-managed accommodation for 40 weeks:

(including dinner and breakfast days per week) £

(no food) £58.00

(other...) £

Overseas opportunities*

Number of students on a placement or study period abroad: 13

Compacts/Networks	Record of Achievement
	Admissions Tutors will examine applicants' RoAs if brought to interview.

Interviewing	Campus locations
The University invites all applicants resident in the UK to interview.	Buckingham has two sites ten minutes walk apart.

Open Days

Subject-specific interview/visit days are held throughout the term. Informal visits are possible.

*Excludes those on compulsory language course placements.

Buckinghamshire College of Higher Education

Admissions Office, Queen Alexandra Road, High Wycombe, Bucks, HP11 2JZ

Tel: 01494 522141 Fax: 01494 524392

B94

Datafile

1996-97 Student Numbers

Total number of all students   9800

	Degree	HND
Total FT/SW undergraduate numbers	4486	840
Percentages of these		
– on sandwich programmes	3	
– mature students	2	1
– international students	1	1
– male/female	45/55	17/83

Full-time/sandwich students by academic subject category

	Degree	HND
Medicine, Dentistry, Vet Science		
Subjects Allied to Medicine	586	
Science		
Engineering and Technology	359	115
Built Environment	29	31
Mathematical Sciences, IT & Computing	178	146
Business and Management	1774	416
Social Sciences	546	
Humanities	185	
Art & Design and Perf Arts	829	132
Education		

Accommodation

Percentage of first years requiring accommodation who can be accommodated in institution-managed accommodation: 95%

Estimated weekly cost of institution-managed accommodation for weeks:

(including 3 meals 7 days per week) £46.00 – £60.00

(no food) £46.00-£48.00

(other…) £50.00

Overseas opportunities*

Number of students on a placement or study period abroad: 85

Compacts/Networks

Contact institution.

Record of Achievement

Interviewing

By arrangement.

Campus locations

High Wycombe, Newland Park and Wellesbourne.

Open Days

Contact institution.

*Excludes those on compulsory language course placements.

Cambridge University

Intercollegiate Applications Office, Kellet Lodge, Tennis Court Road, Cambridge, CB2 1QJ

Tel: 01 223 333308 Fax: 01 223 366383
ucam-undergraduate-admissionselists.cam.ac.uk
http://www.cam.ac.uk/cambuniv/prospstudents.html

C05

Datafile

1996-97 Student Numbers

Total number of all students

	Degree	HND
Total FT/SW undergraduate numbers	10736	
Percentages of these		
– on sandwich programmes	1	
– mature students	4	
– international students	10	
– male/female	57/43	

Full-time/sandwich students by academic subject category

	Degree	HND
Medicine, Dentistry, Vet Science	1456	
Subjects Allied to Medicine	134	
Science	1609	
Engineering and Technology	1402	
Built Environment	194	
Mathematical Sciences, IT & Computing	1044	
Business and Management		
Social Sciences	1958	
Humanities	2759	
Art & Design and Perf Arts	178	
Education	2	

Accommodation

Percentage of first years requiring accommodation who can be accommodated in institution-managed accommodation: 95%

Estimated weekly cost of institution-managed accommodation for 24 weeks:

(including dinner and breakfast 7 days per week) £87.00

(no food) £

(other…) £

Overseas opportunities*

Number of students on a placement or study period abroad:

Compacts/Networks

Record of Achievement

RoAs may be requested to be brought to interview.

Interviewing

Most UK applicants are interviewed.

Campus locations

Cambridge.

Open Days

Details listed in Prospectus and circulated to schools and colleges in January and February.

*Excludes those on compulsory language course placements.

Cambridge Business College

Director of Studies, Cambridge Business College, 16 Brooklands Avenue, Cambridge, CB2 2BB

Tel: 01223 363159 Fax: 01223 323009
dennisp@bsg.ac.uk

C07

Datafile

1996-97 Student Numbers

Total number of all students   110

	Degree	HND
Total FT/SW undergraduate numbers	30	30
Percentages of these		
– on sandwich programmes	20	20
– mature students	10	10
– international students	60	60
– male/female	50/50	50/50

Full-time/sandwich students by academic subject category

	Degree	HND
Medicine, Dentistry, Vet Science		
Subjects Allied to Medicine		
Science		
Engineering and Technology		
Built Environment		
Mathematical Sciences, IT & Computing		
Business and Management	40	40
Social Sciences	30	30
Humanities		
Art & Design and Perf Arts		
Education		

Accommodation

Percentage of first years requiring accommodation who can be accommodated in institution-managed accommodation: 100%

Estimated weekly cost of institution-managed accommodation for 10 weeks:

(including dinner and breakfast 7 days per week) £70.00

(no food) £60.00

(other…) £

Overseas opportunities*

Number of students on a placement or study period abroad: 20

Compacts/Networks   Record of Achievement

Interviewing

All suitable applicants will be interviewed either in Cambridge or locally.

Campus locations

Cambridge - south side near botanical gardens.

Open Days

We are always open and welcome visits Monday to Friday in term time.

*Excludes those on compulsory language course placements.

Canterbury Christ Church College of Higher Education

Admissions Office, North Holmes Road, Canterbury, Kent, CT1 1QU

Tel: 01227 767700 Fax: 01227 470442
admissions@cant.ac.uk.

C10

Datafile

1996-97 Student Numbers

Total number of all students   8568

	Degree	HND
Total FT/SW undergraduate numbers	3173	38
Percentages of these		
– on sandwich programmes		
– mature students	37	43
– international students	1	
– male/female	65/35	84/16

Full-time/sandwich students by academic subject category

	Degree	HND
Medicine, Dentistry, Vet Science	262	
Subjects Allied to Medicine		
Science	315	
Engineering and Technology		
Built Environment		
Mathematical Sciences, IT & Computing	134	23
Business and Management	411	15
Social Sciences	326	
Humanities	522	
Art & Design and Perf Arts	348	
Education	855	

Accommodation

Percentage of first years requiring accommodation who can be accommodated in institution-managed accommodation: 67%

Estimated weekly cost of institution-managed accommodation for 32-42 weeks:

(including dinner and breakfast 7 days per week) £66.00

(no food) £46.50

(other…) £

Overseas opportunities*

Number of students on a placement or study period abroad:

Compacts/Networks   Record of Achievement

Interviewing

Every Wednesday during term time.

Campus locations

Main site in North Holmes Rd Mariowe Centre (city centre) and Art Department Research Centre in Northgate.

Open Days

Twice a year, usually November and June, by invitation only.

*Excludes those on compulsory language course placements.

University of Wales, Cardiff

Admissions Officer, University of Wales, Cardiff, PO Box 494, Cardiff, Wales, CF1 3YL

Tel: 01222 874404 Fax: 01222 874130 Prospectus Request: 01222 874899
prospectus@cf.ac.uk http://www.cf.ac.uk

C15

Datafile

1996-97 Student Numbers

Total number of all students   14262

	Degree	HND
Total FT/SW undergraduate numbers	11294	
Percentages of these		
– on sandwich programmes	12	
– mature students	16	
– international students	16	
– male/female	46/54	

Full-time/sandwich students by academic subject category

	Degree	HND
Medicine, Dentistry, Vet Science	445	
Subjects Allied to Medicine	374	
Science	2260	
Engineering and Technology	1187	
Built Environment	527	
Mathematical Sciences, IT & Computing	592	
Business and Management	1305	
Social Sciences	1329	
Humanities	2787	
Art & Design and Perf Arts	210	
Education	278	

Accommodation

Percentage of first years requiring accommodation who can be accommodated in institution-managed accommodation: 100%

Estimated weekly cost of institution-managed accommodation for 33 weeks:

(including dinner and breakfast   days per week) £51.00 – £59.00

(no food) £31.00 – £47.00

(other…) £

Overseas opportunities *

Number of students on a placement or study period abroad:

Compacts/Networks

Record of Achievement

Admissions Tutors will examine applicants' RoA if brought to an interview.

Interviewing

Most applicants considered are invited to a Departmental Visit Day (may include an interview).

Campus locations

Academic Depts, Halls of Residence, University Union and city centre all within close proximity.

Open Days

22 April 1997 and 28 April 1998.

*Excludes those on compulsory language course placements.

University of Wales Institute Cardiff

Admissions Unit, PO Box 377, Western Avenue, Cardiff, Wales, CF5 2SG

Tel: 01222 506012/13 Fax: 01222 506911
admissions@uwic.ac.uk http://www.uwic.ac.uk

C20

Datafile

1996-97 Student Numbers

Total number of all students   7348

	Degree	HND
Total FT/SW undergraduate numbers	4097	943
Percentages of these		
– on sandwich programmes	22	17
– mature students	30	26
– international students	5	5
– male/female	39/61	39/61

Full-time/sandwich students by academic subject category

	Degree	HND
Medicine, Dentistry, Vet Science		
Subjects Allied to Medicine	1046	12
Science	428	111
Engineering and Technology	63	105
Built Environment	44	50
Mathematical Sciences, IT & Computing	99	110
Business and Management	952	482
Social Sciences	93	
Humanities	54	
Art & Design and Perf Arts	644	73
Education	674	

Accommodation

Percentage of first years requiring accommodation who can be accommodated in institution-managed accommodation: 90%

Estimated weekly cost of institution-managed accommodation for 35-40 weeks:

(including dinner and breakfast 7 days per week) £65.00

(no food) £41.00

(other…) £45.00

Overseas opportunities *

Number of students on a placement or study period abroad: 44

Compacts/Networks

Compact arrangements with several local schools and FE Colleges.

Record of Achievement

Compact applicants to bring RoA if required to attend for interview.

Interviewing

Interview for Art, Education, Social Work, Speech and Language Therapy and Sports courses.

Campus locations

Colchester Avenue, Cyncoed, Howard Gardens and Llandaff.

Open Days

General Open Days second Wednesday of each month. Individual course Open Days are also held.

*Excludes those on compulsory language course placements.

Carmarthenshire College

Admissions Unit, Graig Campus, Sandy Road, Llanelli, Dyfed, SA15 4DW

Tel: 01554 759165 Fax: 01267 221515
postmaster@ccta.ac.uk www.ccta.ac.uk

C22

Datafile

1996-97 Student Numbers

Total number of all students

	Degree	HND
Total FT/SW undergraduate numbers	29	400
Percentages of these		
– on sandwich programmes		
– mature students	69	39
– international students		2
– male/female	67/33	52/48

Full-time/sandwich students by academic subject category

	Degree	HND
Medicine, Dentistry, Vet Science		
Subjects Allied to Medicine		
Science		
Engineering and Technology		
Built Environment		
Mathematical Sciences, IT & Computing		
Business and Management		
Social Sciences		
Humanities		
Art & Design and Perf Arts	29	400
Education		

Accommodation

Percentage of first years requiring accommodation who can be accommodated in institution-managed accommodation: 12%

Estimated weekly cost of institution-managed accommodation for 34 weeks:

(including dinner and breakfast   days per week) £

(no food) £50.00

(other...) £

Overseas opportunities*

Number of students on a placement or study period abroad:

Compacts/Networks

Record of Achievement

Interviewing

Students will be expected to attend an interview at Carmarthen with a Portfolio of work.

Campus locations

Jobs Well & Pibwrlwyd Carmarthen.

Open Days

24 January, 29 January, 7 February, 17 October, 22 October and 7 November 1997.

*Excludes those on compulsory language course placements.

University of Central England in Birmingham

Recruitment Unit, UCE, Perry Barr, Birmingham, B42 2SU

Tel: 0121 331 5595 Fax: 0121 331 6358

C25

Datafile

1996-97 Student Numbers

Total number of all students   24838

	Degree	HND
Total FT/SW undergraduate numbers	7664	903
Percentages of these		
– on sandwich programmes	11	1
– mature students	36	3
– international students	8	1
– male/female	44/56	75/25

Full-time/sandwich students by academic subject category

	Degree	HND
Medicine, Dentistry, Vet Science		
Subjects Allied to Medicine	781	
Science		58
Engineering and Technology	701	137
Built Environment	558	89
Mathematical Sciences, IT & Computing	668	216
Business and Management	1503	233
Social Sciences	1049	
Humanities	278	
Art & Design and Perf Arts	1601	170
Education	525	

Accommodation

Percentage of first years requiring accommodation who can be accommodated in institution-managed accommodation: 95%

Estimated weekly cost of institution-managed accommodation for 40 weeks:

(including dinner and breakfast   days per week) £

(no food) £42.00

(other...) £

Overseas opportunities*

Number of students on a placement or study period abroad:

Compacts/Networks

Faculty based agreements.

Record of Achievement

On an individual basis.

Interviewing

Interviews for Art & Design and Architecture/Landscape Arch (with portfolio), ITT, Social Work. Postal interview for Media.

Campus locations

Main campus – Perry Barr. Art and Design Birmingham city centre, Gosta Green. Education and Nursing Edgbaston.

Open Days

Faculties run their own Open Days either for the faculty or indiviual courses.

*Excludes those on compulsory language course placements.

University of Central Lancashire

Course Enquiries, University of Central Lancashire, Foster Building, Preston, PR1 2HE

Tel: 01772 892400 Fax: 01772 892935
http://www.uclan.ac.uk

C30

Datafile

1996-97 Student Numbers

Total number of all students — 18487

	Degree	HND
Total FT/SW undergraduate numbers	11675	1760
Percentages of these		
– on sandwich programmes	3	8
– mature students	50	43
– international students	2	1
– male/female	50/50	52/48

Full-time/sandwich students by academic subject category

	Degree	HND
Medicine, Dentistry, Vet Science		
Subjects Allied to Medicine	1672	252
Science	1923	289
Engineering and Technology	703	106
Built Environment	343	53
Mathematical Sciences, IT & Computing	1126	170
Business and Management	2130	321
Social Sciences	1309	197
Humanities	1517	228
Art & Design and Perf Arts	949	144
Education		

Accommodation

Percentage of first years requiring accommodation who can be accommodated in institution-managed accommodation: 100%

Estimated weekly cost of institution-managed accommodation for 38 weeks:

(including dinner and breakfast   days per week) £

(no food) £45.00 – £50.00

(other...) £

Overseas opportunities*

Number of students on a placement or study period abroad: 170

Compacts/Networks

Franchised course arrangements with FE Colleges and progression routes from many Access Courses.

Record of Achievement

RoAs valued and used during interviews. Summary copies can be forwarded in support of application.

Interviewing

Only mature and non-standard applicants are interviewed unless there is specific course needs.

Campus locations

Single site campus in Preston town centre which is also close to good road and rail links.

Open Days

22 May 1997. Organised campus tours are available throughout the year. Contact the University for details.

*Excludes those on compulsory language course placements.

The Central School of Speech and Drama

Admissions/Registry, Embassy Theatre, 64 Eton Avenue, London, NW3 3HY

Tel: 0171 7228183 Fax: 0171 7224132

C35

Datafile

1996-97 Student Numbers

Total number of all students — 691

	Degree	HND
Total FT/SW undergraduate numbers	463	
Percentages of these		
– on sandwich programmes		
– mature students	45	
– international students	14	
– male/female	45/55	

Full-time/sandwich students by academic subject category

	Degree	HND
Medicine, Dentistry, Vet Science		
Subjects Allied to Medicine	94	
Science		
Engineering and Technology		
Built Environment		
Mathematical Sciences, IT & Computing		
Business and Management		
Social Sciences		
Humanities		
Art & Design and Perf Arts	369	
Education		

Accommodation

There is no institution-managed accommodation. Students are advised to contact the institution for information about local accommodation options.

Overseas opportunities*

Number of students on a placement or study period abroad:

Compacts/Networks

Record of Achievement

Not normally part of Admissions procedure but RoAs can be requested occasionally.

Interviewing

Offers are made after attending an interview or audition. Art & Design requires a Portfolio.

Campus locations

Swiss Cottage, London, NW3. Camden, London, NW1.

Open Days

Visits can be made by contacting relevant Dept. Art & Design have Open Days between October and March.

*Excludes those on compulsory language course placements.

Cheltenham and Gloucester College of Higher Education

Admissions Office, The Park, Cheltenham, Glos, GL50 2QF

Tel: 01242 532824/6 Fax: 01242 256759
admissions@chelt.ac.uk

C50

Datafile

1996-97 Student Numbers

Total number of all students   8000

	Degree	HND
Total FT/SW undergraduate numbers	4822	720
Percentages of these		
– on sandwich programmes	22	20
– mature students	40	30
– international students	2	2
– male/female	40/60	40/60

Full-time/sandwich students by academic subject category

	Degree	HND
Medicine, Dentistry, Vet Science		
Subjects Allied to Medicine	97	
Science	820	170
Engineering and Technology		
Built Environment	227	
Mathematical Sciences, IT & Computing	449	150
Business and Management	1230	400
Social Sciences	245	
Humanities	501	
Art & Design and Perf Arts	712	
Education	541	

Accommodation

Percentage of first years requiring accommodation who can be accommodated in institution-managed accommodation: 56%

Estimated weekly cost of institution-managed accommodation for 35 weeks:

(including 2/3 meals 5/7 days per week) $60.00 – $72.00

(no food) $43.00 – $53.00

(other…) $

Overseas opportunities*

Number of students on a placement or study period abroad:

Compacts/Networks

Arrangements with colleges and schools in Gloucestershire, Evesham and Chippenham.

Record of Achievement

Viewed at interview.

Interviewing

For selective courses only, eg. BEd, BA Fine Art and BA Fashion.

Campus locations

The Park, Francis Close Hall and Pittville. All are situated in Cheltenham.

Open Days

19 April 1997, 28 June 1997, 15 October 1997, 25 October 1997 and 12 November 1997.

*Excludes those on compulsory language course placements.

University College Chester

Undergraduate Admissions Co-ordinator, University College Chester, Cheyney Road, Chester, CH1 4BJ

Tel: 01244 375444 Fax: 01244 373379

C55

Datafile

1996-97 Student Numbers

Total number of all students

	Degree	HND
Total FT/SW undergraduate numbers	2905	
Percentages of these		
– on sandwich programmes	19	
– mature students	30	
– international students	1	
– male/female	26/74	

Full-time/sandwich students by academic subject category

	Degree	HND
Medicine, Dentistry, Vet Science		
Subjects Allied to Medicine	729	
Science	268	
Engineering and Technology		
Built Environment		
Mathematical Sciences, IT & Computing	172	
Business and Management		
Social Sciences	166	
Humanities	350	
Art & Design and Perf Arts	169	
Education	1051	

Accommodation

Percentage of first years requiring accommodation who can be accommodated in institution-managed accommodation: 70%

Estimated weekly cost of institution-managed accommodation for 32 weeks:

(including dinner and breakfast 7 days per week) $59.50 – $64.40

(no food) $29.40 – $43.40

(other…) $

Overseas opportunities*

Number of students on a placement or study period abroad: 68

Compacts/Networks

Compacts with Birkenhead VI Form, Wirral Post- 16 Compact, Walbottle High School.

Record of Achievement

College supports the RoA HE Project. Applicants who are interviewed are asked to bring examples.

Interviewing

Applicants to Art programmes are interviewed. Half of Drama applicants participate in work-shop.

Campus locations

Reaseheath Agricultural College, Nantwich; Welsh College of Horticulture, Northop, Chester Campus.

Open Days

Not known at present.

*Excludes those on compulsory language course placements.

56

Chichester Institute of Higher Education

Admissions Office, College Lane, Chichester, W. Sussex, PO19 4PE

Tel: 01243 816000 Fax: 01243 816080
chihe@dial.pipex.com http://www.chihe.ac.uk

C58

Datafile

1996-97 Student Numbers

Total number of all students   3700

	Degree	HND
Total FT/SW undergraduate numbers	2350	
Percentages of these		
– on sandwich programmes		
– mature students	63	
– international students	5	
– male/female	30/70	

Full-time/sandwich students by academic subject category

	Degree	HND
Medicine, Dentistry, Vet Science		
Subjects Allied to Medicine	176	
Science	340	
Engineering and Technology		
Built Environment		
Mathematical Sciences, IT & Computing	20	
Business and Management		
Social Sciences	133	
Humanities	575	
Art & Design and Perf Arts	321	
Education	785	

Accommodation

Percentage of first years requiring accommodation who can be accommodated in institution-managed accommodation: 70%

Estimated weekly cost of institution-managed accommodation for 33 weeks:

(including dinner and breakfast 7 days per week) £55.00 – £70.00

(no food) £

(other…) £

Overseas opportunities*
Number of students on a placement or study period abroad: 10

Compacts/Networks
Founder Member of the Southern & Wessex Access Federation (SAFE & WAF). Links with Access Provs.

Record of Achievement
Records of Achievement are welcomed.

Interviewing
Interviews for Teacher Ed, Performance and mature students compulsory. Other courses discretionary.

Campus locations
Chichester (Bishop Otter Campus) and Bognor Regis (Bognor Regis Campus).

Open Days
17 October, 1997, 14 March & 27 May 1998. Health, Sports, Dance and Art by arrangement. Contact Marketing.

*Excludes those on compulsory language course placements.

City University

Undergraduate Admissions Office, City University, Northampton Square, London, EC1V 0HB

Tel: 0171 4778028 Fax: 0171 4778995
r.s.broom@city.ac.uk http://www.city.ac.uk

C60

Datafile

1996-97 Student Numbers

Total number of all students   10249

	Degree	HND
Total FT/SW undergraduate numbers	4844	
Percentages of these		
– on sandwich programmes	6	
– mature students	34	
– international students	22	
– male/female	51/49	

Full-time/sandwich students by academic subject category

	Degree	HND
Medicine, Dentistry, Vet Science		
Subjects Allied to Medicine	1428	
Science	202	
Engineering and Technology	712	
Built Environment		
Mathematical Sciences, IT & Computing	598	
Business and Management	849	
Social Sciences	783	
Humanities	103	
Art & Design and Perf Arts	73	
Education		

Accommodation

Percentage of first years requiring accommodation who can be accommodated in institution-managed accommodation: 65%

Estimated weekly cost of institution-managed accommodation for 30 weeks:

(including dinner and breakfast 7 days per week) £81.00

(no food) £69.71

(other…) £

Overseas opportunities*
Number of students on a placement or study period abroad: 24

Compacts/Networks
Kingsway Connect, City and Islington Connect, Hackney Compact.

Record of Achievement
Applicants are encouraged to bring RoAs to interview.

Interviewing
Interview procedures vary according to Department.

Campus locations
Northampton Square and the Barbican Centre in London.

Open Days
Departments contact applicants, direct, to advise on Open Days.

*Excludes those on compulsory language course placements.

 *Letts* STUDY GUIDES THE INDEPENDENT

City of Bristol College

Admissions Office, Marksbury Centre, Marksbury Road, Bedminster, Bristol, BS3 5JT

Tel: 0117 963 9033 Fax: 0117 963 6682

C63

Datafile

1996-97 Student Numbers

Total number of all students

	Degree	HND
Total FT/SW undergraduate numbers		
Percentages of these		
– on sandwich programmes		
– mature students		
– international students		
– male/female		

Full-time/sandwich students by academic subject category

	Degree	HND
Medicine, Dentistry, Vet Science		
Subjects Allied to Medicine		
Science		
Engineering and Technology		
Built Environment		
Mathematical Sciences, IT & Computing		
Business and Management		
Social Sciences		
Humanities		
Art & Design and Perf Arts		
Education		

Accommodation

There is no institution-managed accommodation. Students are advised to contact the institution for information about local accommodation options.

Overseas opportunities*

Number of students on a placement or study period abroad:

Compacts/Networks

Record of Achievement

Interviewing

Campus locations

Open Days

Excludes those on compulsory language course placements.

City College Manchester

Head of Admissions, City College Manchester, Arden Centre, Sale Road, Manchester, M23 0DD

Tel: 0161 9571790 Fax: 0161 9453854
admissions@manchester-city-coll.ac.uk
http://www.manchester-city-coll.ac.uk

C66

Datafile

1996-97 Student Numbers

Total number of all students

	Degree	HND
Total FT/SW undergraduate numbers	145	251
Percentages of these		
– on sandwich programmes		
– mature students	56	51
– international students		
– male/female	48/52	60/40

Full-time/sandwich students by academic subject category

	Degree	HND
Medicine, Dentistry, Vet Science		
Subjects Allied to Medicine		24
Science		
Engineering and Technology		45
Built Environment		
Mathematical Sciences, IT & Computing		3
Business and Management		68
Social Sciences		
Humanities		
Art & Design and Perf Arts	145	156
Education		

Accommodation

There is no institution-managed accommodation. Students are advised to contact the institution for information about local accommodation options.

Overseas opportunities*

Number of students on a placement or study period abroad:

Compacts/Networks

The College works closely with local schools by supporting curriculum development and transition.

Record of Achievement

Positively welcomes RoA. CCM has a programme of accreditation of the RoA process with NMU.

Interviewing

Interviews are arranged through the Admissions and Guidance Office.

Campus locations

Four main sites within Manchester city. Three in the south of the city and one in the north.

Open Days

29 October 1997.

Excludes those on compulsory language course placements.

City of Liverpool Community College

Admissions/Information Office, Hope St. Centre, Hope St., Liverpool, L1 9EB

Tel: 0151 252 3000 Fax: 0151 7072597

C67

Clarendon College

Admissions, Pelham Avenue, Mansfield Road, Nottingham, N65 1AL

Tel: 0115 960 7201 Fax: 0115 969 3315

C68

Datafile

1996-97 Student Numbers

		Degree	HND
Total number of all students	15659		
Total FT/SW undergraduate numbers		62	189
Percentages of these			
– on sandwich programmes			
– mature students		98	55
– international students			
– male/female		24/76	46/54

Full-time/sandwich students by academic subject category

	Degree	HND
Medicine, Dentistry, Vet Science		
Subjects Allied to Medicine	62	
Science		
Engineering and Technology		69
Built Environment		
Mathematical Sciences, IT & Computing		
Business and Management		49
Social Sciences		
Humanities		
Art & Design and Perf Arts		71
Education		

Accommodation

There is no institution-managed accommodation. Students are advised to contact the institution for information about local accommodation options.

*Overseas opportunities**

Number of students on a placement or study period abroad:

Compacts/Networks

Merseyside Training Partnership, COLCC/University of Ulster, Salford FE/HE Consortium & COLCC/JMU.

Record of Achievement

College policy being developed.

Interviewing

See prospectus.

Campus locations

Riversdale, Bankfield, Greenbank and Clarence.

Open Days

Contact Fran Parkinson, Marketing Manager, on 0151 2524655.

*Excludes those on compulsory language course placements.

Datafile

1996-97 Student Numbers

		Degree	HND
Total number of all students	17188		
Total FT/SW undergraduate numbers			104
Percentages of these			
– on sandwich programmes			
– mature students			26
– international students			2
– male/female			39/61

Full-time/sandwich students by academic subject category

	Degree	HND
Medicine, Dentistry, Vet Science		
Subjects Allied to Medicine		
Science		
Engineering and Technology		
Built Environment		
Mathematical Sciences, IT & Computing		
Business and Management		40
Social Sciences		
Humanities		
Art & Design and Perf Arts		64
Education		

Accommodation

There is no institution-managed accommodation. Students are advised to contact the institution for information about local accommodation options.

*Overseas opportunities**

Number of students on a placement or study period abroad:

Compacts/Networks

Magpie Consortium, Bigwood School, Elliott Durham, Glaisdale, Henry Mellish.

Record of Achievement

Taken into account.

Interviewing

All applicants are interviewed.

Campus locations

All close to city centre.

Open Days

One Open Day held in October, January and April.

*Excludes those on compulsory language course placements.

Cleveland College of Art and Design

Admissions Officer, Cleveland Col of Art & Design, Green Lane, Linthorpe, Middlesbrough, TS5 7RJ

Tel: 01642 829973 Fax: 01642 823467

C71

Datafile

1996-97 Student Numbers

Total number of all students 2000

	Degree	HND
Total FT/SW undergraduate numbers	248	190
Percentages of these		
– on sandwich programmes		
– mature students	47	39
– international students	1	3
– male/female	44/56	80/20

Full-time/sandwich students by academic subject category

	Degree	HND
Medicine, Dentistry, Vet Science		
Subjects Allied to Medicine		
Science		
Engineering and Technology		
Built Environment		
Mathematical Sciences, IT & Computing		
Business and Management		
Social Sciences		
Humanities		
Art & Design and Perf Arts	248	190
Education		

Accommodation

There is no institution-managed accommodation. Students are advised to contact the institution for information about local accommodation options.

Overseas opportunities*

Number of students on a placement or study period abroad:

Compacts/Networks

Record of Achievement

Interviewing

Students interviewed with their Portfolio of work.

Campus locations

Green Lane, Middlesbrough, Burlam Road, Middlesbrough, Church Square, Hartlepool.

Open Days

Normally held in February. Please contact College for details.

*Excludes those on compulsory language course placements.

Colchester Institute

Assistant Registrar/Admissions, Sheepen Road, Colchester, Essex, CO3 3LL

Tel: 01206 718000 Fax: 01206 763041

C75

Datafile

1996-97 Student Numbers

Total number of all students 8827

	Degree	HND
Total FT/SW undergraduate numbers	595	286
Percentages of these		
– on sandwich programmes	1	33
– mature students	36	21
– international students	2	2
– male/female	40/60	52/48

Full-time/sandwich students by academic subject category

	Degree	HND
Medicine, Dentistry, Vet Science		
Subjects Allied to Medicine		
Science		45
Engineering and Technology		
Built Environment		
Mathematical Sciences, IT & Computing		
Business and Management	98	191
Social Sciences		
Humanities	115	
Art & Design and Perf Arts	382	50
Education		

Accommodation

Percentage of first years requiring accommodation who can be accommodated in institution-managed accommodation:

Estimated weekly cost of institution-managed accommodation for 36 weeks:

(including dinner and breakfast   days per week) £

(no food) £40.00

(other…) £30.00

Overseas opportunities*

Number of students on a placement or study period abroad: 40

Compacts/Networks

Regional College of Anglia Polytechnic University and part of their Compact arrangement.

Record of Achievement

If invited for interview please bring Record of Achievement.

Interviewing

Interviews held at discretion of Admissions Tutors but for some courses an interview is vital.

Campus locations

Colchester and Clacton on Sea.

Open Days

Departments hold Open Days/Functions for prospective students. Contact appropriate Dept.

*Excludes those on compulsory language course placements.

Cordwainers College

Admissions, Cordwainers College, 182 Mare Street, London, E8 3RE

Tel: 0181 985 0273 Fax: 0181 985 9340

C77

Datafile

1996-97 Student Numbers

Total number of all students 352

	Degree	HND
Total FT/SW undergraduate numbers	52	123
Percentages of these		
– on sandwich programmes		
– mature students	20	43
– international students	11	52
– male/female	16/84	28/72

Full-time/sandwich students by academic subject category

	Degree	HND
Medicine, Dentistry, Vet Science		
Subjects Allied to Medicine		
Science		
Engineering and Technology		56
Built Environment		
Mathematical Sciences, IT & Computing		
Business and Management		
Social Sciences		
Humanities		
Art & Design and Perf Arts	52	67
Education		

Accommodation

Percentage of first years requiring accommodation who can be accommodated in institution-managed accommodation:

Estimated weekly cost of institution-managed accommodation for 42 weeks:

(including dinner and breakfast   days per week) £

(no food) £

(other...) £58.50

Overseas opportunities*

Number of students on a placement or study period abroad:

Compacts/Networks

Developing network with Sweden, Denmark and Finland in saddlery technology.

Record of Achievement

Interviewing

All suitable overseas applicants must send appropriate Portfolio by post prior to decision.

Campus locations

Single site.

Open Days

5 and 6 February 1997. Other days by appointment.

*Excludes those on compulsory language course placements.

Cornwall College with Duchy College

Student Services, Cornwall College, Pool, Redruth, Cornwall, TR15 3RD

Tel: 01209 712911 Fax: 01209 718802
enquiries@corncoll.ac.uk

C78

Datafile

1996-97 Student Numbers

Total number of all students 21500

	Degree	HND
Total FT/SW undergraduate numbers	150	240
Percentages of these		
– on sandwich programmes		
– mature students	59	46
– international students	2	
– male/female	61/39	41/59

Full-time/sandwich students by academic subject category

	Degree	HND
Medicine, Dentistry, Vet Science		
Subjects Allied to Medicine		
Science	75	94
Engineering and Technology	25	
Built Environment		
Mathematical Sciences, IT & Computing		
Business and Management		146
Social Sciences	50	
Humanities		
Art & Design and Perf Arts		
Education		

Accommodation

Percentage of first years requiring accommodation who can be accommodated in institution-managed accommodation: 30%

Estimated weekly cost of institution-managed accommodation for 39 weeks:

(including dinner and breakfast 7 days per week) £65.00

(no food) £40.00

(other...) £

Overseas opportunities*

Number of students on a placement or study period abroad:

Compacts/Networks

The College works with local schools and University of Plymouth.

Record of Achievement

The College operates RoA and encourages students to bring their RoA if they attend for interview.

Interviewing

All home applicants are invited for an interview but attendance is not compulsory.

Campus locations

Pool, Redruth, Falmouth, Stoke Climsland (Duchy College) courses are generally on a single site.

Open Days

Please telephone Student Services for details.

*Excludes those on compulsory language course placements.

Courtauld Institute of Art (University of London)

Secretary to the Registrar, Somerset House, Strand, London, WC2R 0RN

Tel: 0171 873 2645 Fax: 0171 873 2410

C80

Datafile

1996-97 Student Numbers

Total number of all students   402

	Degree	HND
Total FT/SW undergraduate numbers	115	
Percentages of these		
– on sandwich programmes		
– mature students	16	
– international students	2	
– male/female	26/74	

Full-time/sandwich students by academic subject category

	Degree	HND
Medicine, Dentistry, Vet Science		
Subjects Allied to Medicine		
Science		
Engineering and Technology		
Built Environment		
Mathematical Sciences, IT & Computing		
Business and Management		
Social Sciences		
Humanities	115	
Art & Design and Perf Arts		
Education		

Accommodation

There is no institution-managed accommodation. Students are advised to contact the institution for information about local accommodation options.

Overseas opportunities*

Number of students on a placement or study period abroad:

Compacts/Networks

Record of Achievement

Interviewing

Policy of normally interviewing applicants who are seriously considered for admission.

Campus locations

Open Days

Open Days will be held in mid-May and early October. Enquiries: 0171 873 2645.

Excludes those on compulsory language course placements.

Coventry University

Academic Registry, Coventry University, Priory Street, Coventry, CV1 5FB

Tel: 01203 631313 Fax: 01203 838793

C85

Datafile

1996-97 Student Numbers

Total number of all students   16775

	Degree	HND
Total FT/SW undergraduate numbers	9282	937
Percentages of these		
– on sandwich programmes	36	25
– mature students	40	24
– international students	9	6
– male/female	59/41	60/40

Full-time/sandwich students by academic subject category

	Degree	HND
Medicine, Dentistry, Vet Science		
Subjects Allied to Medicine	676	
Science	1551	115
Engineering and Technology	2527	240
Built Environment	221	17
Mathematical Sciences, IT & Computing	1134	48
Business and Management	1132	396
Social Sciences	1097	
Humanities	528	
Art & Design and Perf Arts	416	121
Education		

Accommodation

Percentage of first years requiring accommodation who can be accommodated in institution-managed accommodation: 80%

Estimated weekly cost of institution-managed accommodation for 40 weeks:

(including 2 meals 5 days per week) $64.50

(no food) $36.00 – $50.00

(other…) $30.00 – $35.00

Overseas opportunities*

Number of students on a placement or study period abroad:

Compacts/Networks

Compact agreements with schools in Warwickshire and the West Midlands. Franchised at FE Colleges.

Record of Achievement

If sent will be considered otherwise not required.

Interviewing

Art & Design, Maths, Computing, Nursing, Perf Arts and Social Work. Mature students are also interviewed.

Campus locations

City centre single site well served by motorway, air, rail and bus services.

Open Days

23 April 1997.

Excludes those on compulsory language course placements.

Cranfield University

Shrivenham: Undergraduate Admissions Office, Swindon, SN6 8LA

Tel: 01793 785400 Fax: 01793 783966 laxon@rmcs.cranfield.ac.uk

Silsoe: Student Recruitment Executive, Silsoe, Beds MK45 4DT

Tel: 01525 863318 Fax: 01525 863316
Silsoe: recruitment@silsoe.cranfield.ac.uk

C90

Datafile

1996-97 Student Numbers

Total number of all students   2965

	Degree	HND
Total FT/SW undergraduate numbers		
Percentages of these	637	113
– on sandwich programmes	152	85
– mature students	227	27
– international students	37	2
– male/female	76/24	72/28

Full-time/sandwich students by academic subject category

	Degree	HND
Medicine, Dentistry, Vet Science		
Subjects Allied to Medicine	97	
Science	74	85
Engineering and Technology	287	
Built Environment		
Mathematical Sciences, IT & Computing	125	
Business and Management	54	28
Social Sciences		
Humanities		
Art & Design and Perf Arts		
Education		

Accommodation

Percentage of first years requiring accommodation who can be accommodated in institution-managed accommodation: 100%

Estimated weekly cost of institution-managed accommodation for 30 weeks:

(including 2-3 meals 7 days per week) £53.50 – £80.00

(no food) £42.00 – £45.00

(other...) £

Overseas opportunities*

Number of students on a placement or study period abroad: 37

Compacts/Networks

Ryecotewood College and Bedford College.

Record of Achievement

Applicants are asked to bring RoA to interview.

Interviewing

All applicants are invited for interview.

Campus locations

Cranfield, Shrivenham and Silsoe.

Open Days

Shrivenham: May and October. Silsoe: February, May, July, September, October and November.

Excludes those on compulsory language course placements.

Croydon College

Admissions Registrar, Croydon College, Fairfield, Croydon, CR9 1DX

Tel: 0181 760 5892 Fax: 0181 760 5880

C92

Datafile

1996-97 Student Numbers

Total number of all students   12000

	Degree	HND
Total FT/SW undergraduate numbers	496	291
Percentages of these		
– on sandwich programmes		9
– mature students	58	49
– international students	1	
– male/female	44/56	43/57

Full-time/sandwich students by academic subject category

	Degree	HND
Medicine, Dentistry, Vet Science		
Subjects Allied to Medicine		
Science		
Engineering and Technology		18
Built Environment		
Mathematical Sciences, IT & Computing		
Business and Management	170	153
Social Sciences	90	
Humanities		
Art & Design and Perf Arts	236	120
Education		

Accommodation

There is no institution-managed accommodation. Students are advised to contact the institution for information about local accommodation options.

Overseas opportunities*

Number of students on a placement or study period abroad: 15

Compacts/Networks

None.

Record of Achievement

Applicants are asked to bring RoA to interview.

Interviewing

Most applicants will be asked to an interview. Art & Design applicants should bring a sample portfolio.

Campus locations

Located in centre of town, close to all facilities and with rail, bus and road access.

Open Days

11 March 1997, 7 October 1997 and September 1998. Details from College Marketing.

Excludes those on compulsory language course placements.

Cumbria College of Art and Design

Registrar, Brampton Road, Carlisle, Cumbria, CA3 9AY

Tel: 01228 25333 Fax: 01228 514491

C95

Datafile

1996-97 Student Numbers

Total number of all students   900

	Degree	HND
Total FT/SW undergraduate numbers	566	88
Percentages of these		
– on sandwich programmes		
– mature students	433	75
– international students		
– male/female	25/75	48/52

Full-time/sandwich students by academic subject category

	Degree	HND
Medicine, Dentistry, Vet Science		
Subjects Allied to Medicine		
Science		
Engineering and Technology		
Built Environment		
Mathematical Sciences, IT & Computing		
Business and Management	49	34
Social Sciences		
Humanities		
Art & Design and Perf Arts	517	54
Education		

Accommodation

Percentage of first years requiring accommodation who can be accommodated in institution-managed accommodation: 20%

Estimated weekly cost of institution-managed accommodation for weeks:

(including dinner and breakfast   days per week) £

(no food) £43.00 – £48.00

(other…) £

Overseas opportunities*

Number of students on a placement or study period abroad:

Compacts/Networks

Record of Achievement

Interviewing

All Art & Design applicants are interviewed.

Campus locations

Open Days

Open Days held in Spring & Autumn Terms. Other visits can be arranged on request.

*Excludes those on compulsory language course placements.

Dartington College of Arts

Registry, Totnes, Devon, TQ9 6EJ

Tel: 01803 861620 Fax: 01803 863569
registry@dartington.ac.uk http://www.dartington.ac.uk

D13

Datafile

1996-97 Student Numbers

Total number of all students   472

	Degree	HND
Total FT/SW undergraduate numbers	456	
Percentages of these		
– on sandwich programmes		
– mature students	41	
– international students	1	
– male/female	47/53	

Full-time/sandwich students by academic subject category

	Degree	HND
Medicine, Dentistry, Vet Science		
Subjects Allied to Medicine		
Science		
Engineering and Technology		
Built Environment		
Mathematical Sciences, IT & Computing		
Business and Management		
Social Sciences		
Humanities		
Art & Design and Perf Arts	456	
Education		

Accommodation

Percentage of first years requiring accommodation who can be accommodated in institution-managed accommodation: 95%

Estimated weekly cost of institution-managed accommodation for 33-34 weeks:

(including dinner and breakfast   days per week) £

(no food) £38.00 – £41.00

(other…) £

Overseas opportunities*

Number of students on a placement or study period abroad: 45

Compacts/Networks

For specific regional Performance Arts courses (Access/BTEC) interviews are guaranteed.

Record of Achievement

RoA used to establish applicants eligibility for interview. Final decision based on interviews.

Interviewing

Interviews held at Dartington. Successful applicants (via video/audio tape/questionnaire) may visit.

Campus locations

Situated on the Dartington Hall Estate near Totnes, within a few miles of Dartmoor and South Devon coast.

Open Days

Main Open Day in October. Informal/Group visits can be arranged. Contact Registry for details.

*Excludes those on compulsory language course placements.

De Montfort University

Admissions Division, The Gateway, Leicester, LE1 9BH

Tel: 0116 2551551 Fax: 0116 2577515

D26

Datafile

1996-97 Student Numbers

Total number of all students   28000

	Degree	HND
Total FT/SW undergraduate numbers	14149	1313
Percentages of these		
– on sandwich programmes	29	2
– mature students	38	30
– international students	3	1
– male/female	50/50	50/50

Full-time/sandwich students by academic subject category

	Degree	HND
Medicine, Dentistry, Vet Science		
Subjects Allied to Medicine	1277	
Science	1667	269
Engineering and Technology	1202	171
Built Environment	364	71
Mathematical Sciences, IT & Computing	1661	258
Business and Management	2029	433
Social Sciences	1706	40
Humanities	1323	
Art & Design and Perf Arts	1858	71
Education	1062	

Accommodation

Percentage of first years requiring accommodation who can be accommodated in institution-managed accommodation: 63%

Estimated weekly cost of institution-managed accommodation for 32 weeks:

(including 3 meals 7 days per week) £51.35

(no food) £37.70 – £47.20

(other...) £33.00 – £52.00

Overseas opportunities*

Number of students on a placement or study period abroad: 108

Compacts/Networks

Well-established PTP linking 100 schools and colleges. Schemes feature projects, visits etc.

Record of Achievement

Used extensively as criterion for off-setting reduced admissions offers as part of PTP scheme.

Interviewing

Mandatory for Nursing, Teaching and pilot AGNVQ applicants. Encouraged for mature, PTP, disabled.

Campus locations

Leicester City, Milton Keynes, Caythorpe Court, Riseholme, Holbeach, Lincoln City and Bedford.

Open Days

Open Days are arranged within each school. Please contact the School Office via above telephone number.

*Excludes those on compulsory language course placements.

University of Derby

Admissions Office, Kedleston Road, Derby, DE22 1GB

Tel: 01332 622289 Fax: 01332 294861
m.a.crowther@derby.ac.uk http://www.derby.ac.uk

D39

Datafile

1996-97 Student Numbers

Total number of all students   11941

	Degree	HND
Total FT/SW undergraduate numbers	7370	992
Percentages of these		
– on sandwich programmes	12	
– mature students	34	19
– international students	2	1
– male/female	43/57	68/32

Full-time/sandwich students by academic subject category

	Degree	HND
Medicine, Dentistry, Vet Science		
Subjects Allied to Medicine	674	
Science	1093	61
Engineering and Technology	258	112
Built Environment	69	22
Mathematical Sciences, IT & Computing	433	108
Business and Management	1479	689
Social Sciences	625	
Humanities	911	
Art & Design and Perf Arts	1195	
Education	633	

Accommodation

Percentage of first years requiring accommodation who can be accommodated in institution-managed accommodation: 90%

Estimated weekly cost of institution-managed accommodation for 35 weeks:

(including dinner and breakfast   days per week) £

(no food) £36.00 – £48.00

(other...) £

Overseas opportunities*

Number of students on a placement or study period abroad: 100

Compacts/Networks

Compact agreement with some local schools and colleges. Progression to some university programmes guaranteed.

Record of Achievement

Compact agreement requires Record of Achievement.

Interviewing

Interviews are required for some programmes.

Campus locations

Five sites within a three mile radius of Derby city centre.

Open Days

Academic Departments hold indiviual Open Days. Contact Admissions for further details.

*Excludes those on compulsory language course placements.

Dewsbury College

Admissions Office, Halifax Road, Dewsbury, West Yorkshire, WF13 2AS

Tel: 01924 465916 Fax: 01924 457047
dewsbury.ac.uk

D45

Datafile

1996-97 Student Numbers

Total number of all students   9000

	Degree	HND
Total FT/SW undergraduate numbers		280
Percentages of these		
– on sandwich programmes		
– mature students		10
– international students		1
– male/female		50/50

Full-time/sandwich students by academic subject category

	Degree	HND
Medicine, Dentistry, Vet Science		
Subjects Allied to Medicine		
Science		
Engineering and Technology		
Built Environment		
Mathematical Sciences, IT & Computing		
Business and Management		30
Social Sciences		30
Humanities		
Art & Design and Perf Arts		220
Education		

Accommodation

There is no institution-managed accommodation. Students are advised to contact the institution for information about local accommodation options.

Overseas opportunities*

Number of students on a placement or study period abroad:

Compacts/Networks

Record of Achievement
Students who bring RoAs to interview will have them inspected.

Interviewing
No applicant accepted without an interview.

Campus locations
Halifax Rd Campus - Dewsbury, Wheelwright Campus - Dewsbury and Cambridge St. Campus - Batley.

Open Days
Details on application to the Marketing Office.

Excludes those on compulsory language course placements.

Doncaster College

Academic Registry, Waterdale, Doncaster, DN1 3EX

Tel: 01302 553718 Fax: 01302 553559
www.don.ac.uk

D52

Datafile

1996-97 Student Numbers

Total number of all students   27000

	Degree	HND
Total FT/SW undergraduate numbers	469	245
Percentages of these		
– on sandwich programmes	11	3
– mature students	81	40
– international students		
– male/female	50/50	72/28

Full-time/sandwich students by academic subject category

	Degree	HND
Medicine, Dentistry, Vet Science		
Subjects Allied to Medicine		
Science		
Engineering and Technology	61	48
Built Environment		
Mathematical Sciences, IT & Computing	63	63
Business and Management	94	82
Social Sciences	168	
Humanities	83	
Art & Design and Perf Arts		52
Education		

Accommodation

Percentage of first years requiring accommodation who can be accommodated in institution-managed accommodation: 95%

Estimated weekly cost of institution-managed accommodation for 36 weeks:

(including dinner and breakfast   days per week) £

(no food) £42.00

(other…) £

Overseas opportunities*

Number of students on a placement or study period abroad:

Compacts/Networks

Record of Achievement
Applicants are invited to bring RoAs to interviews.

Interviewing
Policy varies - for most mature and all non standard applicants an interview is compulsory.

Campus locations
Waterdale, Church View and High Melton.

Open Days
Telephone 01302 553755 for details.

Excludes those on compulsory language course placements.

Dudley College of Technology

Admissions Office, Dudley College of Technology, The Broadway, Dudley, DY1 4AS

Tel: 01384 455433 Fax: 01384 454246
mark.ellerby@dudleycol.ac.uk

D58

Datafile

1996-97 Student Numbers

Total number of all students   25000

	Degree	HND
Total FT/SW undergraduate numbers		204
Percentages of these		
– on sandwich programmes		
– mature students		10
– international students		5
– male/female		59/41

Full-time/sandwich students by academic subject category

	Degree	HND
Medicine, Dentistry, Vet Science		
Subjects Allied to Medicine		
Science		
Engineering and Technology		
Built Environment		12
Mathematical Sciences, IT & Computing		12
Business and Management		110
Social Sciences		
Humanities		
Art & Design and Perf Arts		70
Education		

Accommodation

Percentage of first years requiring accommodation who can be accommodated in institution-managed accommodation: 100%

Estimated weekly cost of institution-managed accommodation for 30 weeks:

(including dinner and breakfast 7 days per week) £70.00

(no food) £50.00

(other...) £

Overseas opportunities*

Number of students on a placement or study period abroad: 12

Compacts/Networks

Compact with local universities, arrangements exist for students to progress to degree courses.

Record of Achievement

Candidates are encouraged to complete an RoA and bring to interview.

Interviewing

All applicants will be invited for interview.

Campus locations

Broadway site, Dudley. Mons Hill site - one mile from Broadway.

Open Days

Applicants are welcome to view the college at any time. Offers are not contingent on attendance at Open Days.

Excludes those on compulsory language course placements.

University of Dundee

University Admissions Office, The University of Dundee, Dundee, Scotland, DD1 4HN

Tel: 01382 344028 Fax: 01382 221554
g.g.black@dundee.ac.uk http://www.dundee.ac.uk

D65

Datafile

1996-97 Student Numbers

Total number of all students   8491

	Degree	HND
Total FT/SW undergraduate numbers	6124	
Percentages of these		
– on sandwich programmes		
– mature students	22	
– international students	4	
– male/female	49/51	

Full-time/sandwich students by academic subject category

	Degree	HND
Medicine, Dentistry, Vet Science	1005	
Subjects Allied to Medicine	172	
Science	899	
Engineering and Technology	445	
Built Environment	472	
Mathematical Sciences, IT & Computing	211	
Business and Management	472	
Social Sciences	1255	
Humanities	465	
Art & Design and Perf Arts	686	
Education	42	

Accommodation

Percentage of first years requiring accommodation who can be accommodated in institution-managed accommodation: 100%

Estimated weekly cost of institution-managed accommodation for 31-38 weeks:

(including 2-3 meals 7 days per week) £60.90

(no food) £32.41 – £48.09

(other...) £

Overseas opportunities*

Number of students on a placement or study period abroad: 200

Compacts/Networks

Arrangements exist with a number of local FE colleges to admit students to some courses.

Record of Achievement

Not a significant factor in the selection process.

Interviewing

Vocational courses (eg. Architecture, Dentistry) interview applicants. Other courses discretionary.

Campus locations

City centre. Medical and Nursing Schools in suburbs. School of Nursing in Kirkcaldy (30 miles from Dundee)

Open Days

18 June 1997, 17 June 1998. Art & Design Visit 5/6 November 1997 & Show 14-20 June 1997. Visits September/October.

Excludes those on compulsory language course placements.

The University of Durham

Undergraduate Admissions Office, Old Shire Hall, Old Elvet, Durham, DH1 3HP

Tel: 0191 374 2000 Fax: 0191 374 7250
http://www.dur.ac.uk

D86

Datafile

1996-97 Student Numbers

Total number of all students   11200

	Degree	HND
Total FT/SW undergraduate numbers	7600	
Percentages of these		
– on sandwich programmes		
– mature students	14	
– international students	4	
– male/female	50/50	

Full-time/sandwich students by academic subject category

	Degree	HND
Medicine, Dentistry, Vet Science		
Subjects Allied to Medicine	86	
Science	2131	
Engineering and Technology	338	
Built Environment		
Mathematical Sciences, IT & Computing	554	
Business and Management	42	
Social Sciences	1732	
Humanities	2191	
Art & Design and Perf Arts	123	
Education	389	

Accommodation

Percentage of first years requiring accommodation who can be accommodated in institution-managed accommodation: 95%

Estimated weekly cost of institution-managed accommodation for 28 weeks:

(including 3 meals 7 days per week) £70.00

(no food) £

(other…) £

Overseas opportunities*

Number of students on a placement or study period abroad:

Compacts/Networks

Record of Achievement
Varies.

Interviewing
Varies.

Campus locations
City of Durham - all Colleges and Departments except for our campus at Stockton-on-Tees.

Open Days

University-wide Open Days held for applicants who are made an offer without an interview.

*Excludes those on compulsory language course placements.

University of East Anglia

Admissions Office, The Registry, University of East Anglia, Norwich, Norfolk, NR4 7TJ

Tel: 01603 592216 Fax: 01603 458596
admissions@uea.ac.uk http://www.uea.ac.uk

E14

Datafile

1996-97 Student Numbers

Total number of all students   9591

	Degree	HND
Total FT/SW undergraduate numbers	5874	
Percentages of these		
– on sandwich programmes		
– mature students	34	
– international students	6	
– male/female	49/51	

Full-time/sandwich students by academic subject category

	Degree	HND
Medicine, Dentistry, Vet Science		
Subjects Allied to Medicine	657	
Science	1034	
Engineering and Technology	133	
Built Environment		
Mathematical Sciences, IT & Computing	436	
Business and Management	284	
Social Sciences	1372	
Humanities	1843	
Art & Design and Perf Arts	115	
Education		

Accommodation

Percentage of first years requiring accommodation who can be accommodated in institution-managed accommodation: 100%

Estimated weekly cost of institution-managed accommodation for 34-38 weeks:

(including dinner and breakfast days per week) £

(no food) £34.00 – £52.00

(other…) £

Overseas opportunities*

Number of students on a placement or study period abroad: 270

Compacts/Networks
We have a compact arrangement with four Essex Colleges.

Record of Achievement
May be brought to interviews or used to structure personal statements on the UCAS form.

Interviewing
Applications are examined on an indiviual basis. Interviews may be part of the selection process.

Campus locations
One campus in Norwich.

Open Days

1 May 1997, 10 July 1997 and 2 October 1997. Please telephone to book a place.

*Excludes those on compulsory language course placements.

University of East London

Admissions Unit, Longbridge, Road, Dagenham, Essex, RM8 2AS

Tel: 0181 849 3443 Fax: 0181 849 3438

E28

Datafile

1996-97 Student Numbers

	Degree	HND
Total number of all students 11700		
Total FT/SW undergraduate numbers	7820	420
Percentages of these		
– on sandwich programmes	5	
– mature students	61	61
– international students	15	15
– male/female	45/55	67/33

Full-time/sandwich students by academic subject category

	Degree	HND
Medicine, Dentistry, Vet Science		
Subjects Allied to Medicine	760	
Science	1260	79
Engineering and Technology	750	112
Built Environment	110	
Mathematical Sciences, IT & Computing	780	99
Business and Management	830	130
Social Sciences	2200	
Humanities	550	
Art & Design and Perf Arts	490	
Education	90	

Accommodation

Percentage of first years requiring accommodation who can be accommodated in institution-managed accommodation:

Estimated weekly cost of institution-managed accommodation for weeks:

(including dinner and breakfast   days per week) £

(no food) £52.50

(other…) £

Overseas opportunities*

Number of students on a placement or study period abroad:

Compacts/Networks
Within London/Essex. Generally progressionary rather than concessionary in nature.

Record of Achievement
RoAs will be considered.

Interviewing
Please consult the prospectus.

Campus locations
Barking and Stratford.

Open Days
February, March and June each year.

*Excludes those on compulsory language course placements.

East Surrey College (incorporating Reigate School of Art and Design)

Admissions Office, Reigate School of Art & Design, East Surrey College, 127 Blackborough Road, Reigate, Surrey, RH2 7DE

Tel: 01737 766137 Fax: 01737 768643

E32

Datafile

1996-97 Student Numbers

	Degree	HND
Total number of all students 275		
Total FT/SW undergraduate numbers		30
Percentages of these		
– on sandwich programmes		100
– mature students		84
– international students		
– male/female		41/59

Full-time/sandwich students by academic subject category

	Degree	HND
Medicine, Dentistry, Vet Science		
Subjects Allied to Medicine		
Science		
Engineering and Technology		
Built Environment		
Mathematical Sciences, IT & Computing		
Business and Management		
Social Sciences		
Humanities		
Art & Design and Perf Arts		30
Education		

Accommodation

There is no institution-managed accommodation. Students are advised to contact the institution for information about local accommodation options.

Overseas opportunities*

Number of students on a placement or study period abroad:

Compacts/Networks

Record of Achievement
Bring to interview if available, but not essential.

Interviewing
The policy is to interview all applicants who should bring a portfolio of work to the interview.

Campus locations
Reigate in Surrey.

Open Days
Open Days normally held in November and June. Applicants can arrange to visit at other times.

*Excludes those on compulsory language course placements.

Edge Hill University College

Admissions Unit, St Helens Road, Ormskirk, Lancs, L39 4QP

Tel: 01695 584312 Fax: 01695 579997
ibisona@admin.ehche.ac.uk

E42

Datafile

1996-97 Student Numbers

Total number of all students   6125

	Degree	HND
Total FT/SW undergraduate numbers	2943	450
Percentages of these		
– on sandwich programmes		
– mature students	30	65
– international students		
– male/female	30/70	15/85

Full-time/sandwich students by academic subject category

	Degree	HND
Medicine, Dentistry, Vet Science		
Subjects Allied to Medicine	20	450
Science	542	
Engineering and Technology		
Built Environment	123	
Mathematical Sciences, IT & Computing	24	
Business and Management	174	
Social Sciences	402	
Humanities	653	
Art & Design and Perf Arts	59	
Education	946	

Accommodation

Percentage of first years requiring accommodation who can be accommodated in institution-managed accommodation: 100%

Estimated weekly cost of institution-managed accommodation for 33 weeks:

(including dinner and breakfast 6 days per week) £56.00

(no food) £32.50

(other...) £41.44

Overseas opportunities*

Number of students on a placement or study period abroad:

Compacts/Networks	Record of Achievement
We have Compact arrangements with several local schools and colleges.	Bring to an interview if called.

Interviewing	Campus locations
Mandatory for QTS. Rarely used for other courses.	Ormskirk.

Open Days
7 May 1997 and 17 August 1997.

Excludes those on compulsory language course placements.

The University of Edinburgh

Schools Liaison Service, 57 George Square, Edinburgh, Scotland, EH8 9JU

Tel: 0131 6504360 Fax: 0131 6684565
slo@ed.ac.uk http://www.ed.ac.uk

E56

Datafile

1996-97 Student Numbers

Total number of all students   17562

	Degree	HND
Total FT/SW undergraduate numbers	12965	
Percentages of these		
– on sandwich programmes		
– mature students	10	
– international students	7	
– male/female	51/49	

Full-time/sandwich students by academic subject category

	Degree	HND
Medicine, Dentistry, Vet Science	1459	
Subjects Allied to Medicine	208	
Science	3197	
Engineering and Technology	1093	
Built Environment	202	
Mathematical Sciences, IT & Computing	709	
Business and Management	878	
Social Sciences	2026	
Humanities	3010	
Art & Design and Perf Arts	183	
Education		

Accommodation

Percentage of first years requiring accommodation who can be accommodated in institution-managed accommodation: 100%

Estimated weekly cost of institution-managed accommodation for 39 weeks:

(including dinner and breakfast 7 days per week) £72.00

(no food) £46.00

(other...) £46.00

Overseas opportunities*

Number of students on a placement or study period abroad: 350

Compacts/Networks	Record of Achievement
	RoA not used as part of admissions selection process.

Interviewing	Campus locations
Interviewing is rarely part of admissions process except in: Veterinary Medicine, Music & Divinity.	Edinburgh.

Open Days
17 June 1998. Open Day mid-October 1997 pre-UCAS Visit Day.

Excludes those on compulsory language course placements.

The University of Essex

Admissions Office, Wivenhoe Park, Colchester, Essex, CO4 3SQ

Tel: 01206 873666 Fax: 01206 873423
admit@essex.ac.uk   http://www.essex.ac.uk

E70

Datafile

1996-97 Student Numbers

Total number of all students   5673

	Degree	HND
Total FT/SW undergraduate numbers	4054	
Percentages of these		
– on sandwich programmes	1	
– mature students	27	
– international students	30	
– male/female	53/47	

Full-time/sandwich students by academic subject category

	Degree	HND
Medicine, Dentistry, Vet Science		
Subjects Allied to Medicine	5	
Science	642	
Engineering and Technology	208	
Built Environment		
Mathematical Sciences, IT & Computing	484	
Business and Management	284	
Social Sciences	1211	
Humanities	1213	
Art & Design and Perf Arts	7	
Education		

Accommodation

Percentage of first years requiring accommodation who can be accommodated in institution-managed accommodation: 100%

Estimated weekly cost of institution-managed accommodation for 39 weeks:

(including dinner and breakfast days per week) £

(no food) £34.00 – £53.00

(other…) £

Overseas opportunities*

Number of students on a placement or study period abroad: 123

Compacts/Networks

Compacts with some Colleges and Schools. Accreditation Consortium of South Anglia and franchise arrangements.

Record of Achievement

RoA considered during application process. Applicants should send RoA only if required.

Interviewing

One third of applicants interviewed. Special emphasis on mature and GNVQ applicants.

Campus locations

One site two miles outside town.

Open Days

Information about Open Days is available from the Student Recruitment Office on 01206 872002.

*Excludes those on compulsory language course placements.

European Business School, London

External Relations, Regent's College, Regent's Park, London, NW1 4NS

Tel: 0171 487 7507 Fax: 0171 487 7465
exrel@regents.ac.uk

E77

Datafile

1996-97 Student Numbers

Total number of all students   650

	Degree	HND
Total FT/SW undergraduate numbers	650	
Percentages of these		
– on sandwich programmes	100	
– mature students	15	
– international students	80	
– male/female	60/40	

Full-time/sandwich students by academic subject category

	Degree	HND
Medicine, Dentistry, Vet Science		
Subjects Allied to Medicine		
Science		
Engineering and Technology		
Built Environment		
Mathematical Sciences, IT & Computing		
Business and Management	650	
Social Sciences		
Humanities		
Art & Design and Perf Arts		
Education		

Accommodation

Percentage of first years requiring accommodation who can be accommodated in institution-managed accommodation:

Estimated weekly cost of institution-managed accommodation for weeks:

(including 3 meals 7 days per week) £165.00

(no food) £

(other…) £

Overseas opportunities*

Number of students on a placement or study period abroad: 100

Compacts/Networks

Record of Achievement

These should be produced for interviews.

Interviewing

All degree applicants must attend entrance tests and interviews.

Campus locations

One Campus - Regent's College.

Open Days

Held every month. Contact External Relations for list of dates and invitation details.

*Excludes those on compulsory language course placements.

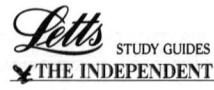

Letts STUDY GUIDES
THE INDEPENDENT

University of Exeter

Admissions Office, University of Exeter, Northcote House, The Queen's Drive, Exeter, EX4 4QJ

Tel: 01392 263032 Fax: 01392 263857
j.a.clissold@exeter.ac.uk http://info.ex.ac.uk/exeterhome.html

E84

Datafile

1996-97 Student Numbers

Total number of all students   10634

	Degree	HND
Total FT/SW undergraduate numbers	6602	59
Percentages of these		
– on sandwich programmes	2	
– mature students	13	40
– international students	5	2
– male/female	49/51	80/20

Full-time/sandwich students by academic subject category

	Degree	HND
Medicine, Dentistry, Vet Science		
Subjects Allied to Medicine	166	
Science	1003	23
Engineering and Technology	467	36
Built Environment		
Mathematical Sciences, IT & Computing	509	
Business and Management	172	
Social Sciences	1532	
Humanities	1792	
Art & Design and Perf Arts	202	
Education	759	

Accommodation

Percentage of first years requiring accommodation who can be accommodated in institution-managed accommodation:

Estimated weekly cost of institution-managed accommodation for 30-50 weeks:

(including 3 meals 7 days per week) £77.35

(no food) £40.95

(other...) £94.74

Overseas opportunities*

Number of students on a placement or study period abroad: 125

Compacts/Networks
None.

Record of Achievement
Considered together with other information.

Interviewing
Where applicable.

Campus locations
Streatham campus, St Lukes campus - Exeter, Camborne Sch of Mines - Pool, Redruth, Cornwall.

Open Days
26 June 1997, 3 July 1997. Contact: Mr J Pickering, Schools Liaison Officer.

*Excludes those on compulsory language course placements.

Falmouth College of Arts

Admissions Office, Falmouth College of Arts, Woodlane, Falmouth, Cornwall, TR11 4RA

Tel: 01326 211077 Fax: 01326 212261
joefalmouth.ac.uk

F33

Datafile

1996-97 Student Numbers

Total number of all students   1500

	Degree	HND
Total FT/SW undergraduate numbers	930	124
Percentages of these		
– on sandwich programmes		
– mature students		
– international students	82	
– male/female	46/54	

Full-time/sandwich students by academic subject category

	Degree	HND
Medicine, Dentistry, Vet Science		
Subjects Allied to Medicine		
Science		
Engineering and Technology		
Built Environment		
Mathematical Sciences, IT & Computing		
Business and Management		
Social Sciences		
Humanities		
Art & Design and Perf Arts	930	124
Education		

Accommodation

There is no institution-managed accommodation. Students are advised to contact the institution for information about local accommodation options.

Overseas opportunities*

Number of students on a placement or study period abroad:

Compacts/Networks

Record of Achievement

Interviewing
Studio programme students are interviewed with portfolio. Telephone and postal interviews used.

Campus locations
Falmouth.

Open Days
Telephone the Admissions Office for details.

*Excludes those on compulsory language course placements.

Farnborough College of Technology

Admissions Administrator, Boundary Road, Farnborough, Hants, GU14 6SB

Tel: 01252 391212 Fax: 01252 549682

F66

Datafile

1996-97 Student Numbers
Total number of all students

	Degree	HND
Total FT/SW undergraduate numbers	502	752
Percentages of these		
– on sandwich programmes		
– mature students		
– international students		
– male/female		

Full-time/sandwich students by academic subject category

	Degree	HND
Medicine, Dentistry, Vet Science		
Subjects Allied to Medicine		
Science	93	162
Engineering and Technology	179	236
Built Environment		
Mathematical Sciences, IT & Computing	33	66
Business and Management	197	268
Social Sciences		
Humanities		
Art & Design and Perf Arts		
Education		

Accommodation
Percentage of first years requiring accommodation who can be accommodated in institution-managed accommodation: 70%

Estimated weekly cost of institution-managed accommodation for weeks:

(including dinner and breakfast 6 days per week) £61.00

(no food) £35.00

(other...) £25.00

Overseas opportunities *
Number of students on a placement or study period abroad:

Compacts/Networks
Surrey Compact.

Record of Achievement

Interviewing

Campus locations

Open Days
20 June 1997, 22 June 1997 and October 1997.

*Excludes those on compulsory language course placements.

University of Glamorgan

Admissions, Pontypridd, Mid Glamorgan, CF37 1DL

Tel: 01443 482684 Fax: 01443 482014

G14

Datafile

1996-97 Student Numbers
Total number of all students   15179

	Degree	HND
Total FT/SW undergraduate numbers	7958	1688
Percentages of these		
– on sandwich programmes	6	1
– mature students	9	15
– international students	6	1
– male/female	58/42	73/27

Full-time/sandwich students by academic subject category

	Degree	HND
Medicine, Dentistry, Vet Science		
Subjects Allied to Medicine	452	
Science	643	248
Engineering and Technology	883	151
Built Environment	315	58
Mathematical Sciences, IT & Computing	605	251
Business and Management	901	647
Social Sciences	1330	165
Humanities	772	
Art & Design and Perf Arts	345	55
Education		

Accommodation
Percentage of first years requiring accommodation who can be accommodated in institution-managed accommodation: 46%

Estimated weekly cost of institution-managed accommodation for 37 weeks:

(including 1 meal 5 days per week) £54.00

(no food) £36.00 – £46.00

(other...) £65.00

Overseas opportunities *
Number of students on a placement or study period abroad:

Compacts/Networks
Compact arrangements with local schools & colleges. Contact the University for information.

Record of Achievement
Students are encouraged to continue with RoAs whilst at the University.

Interviewing
Applicants for Design courses are normally interviewed and asked to bring a portfolio.

Campus locations
Two sites - Law/Nursing/Midwifery one mile from main campus. Franchised colleges throughout Wales.

Open Days
1 July 1997, 10 October 1997 and 5 November 1997. All schools and Depts offer Open Days to applicants.

*Excludes those on compulsory language course placements.

Glamorgan Centre for Art and Design Technology

UCAS Coordinator, Glyntaff Road, Pontypridd, South Wales, CF37 4AT

Tel: 01443 486841 Fax: 01443 485783
p.hodges@pontypridd.ac.uk

G20

Datafile

1996-97 Student Numbers

Total number of all students   350

	Degree	HND
Total FT/SW undergraduate numbers		55
Percentages of these		
– on sandwich programmes		10
– mature students		
– international students		78/22
– male/female		

Full-time/sandwich students by academic subject category

	Degree	HND
Medicine, Dentistry, Vet Science		
Subjects Allied to Medicine		
Science		
Engineering and Technology		
Built Environment		
Mathematical Sciences, IT & Computing		
Business and Management		
Social Sciences		
Humanities		
Art & Design and Perf Arts		55
Education		

Accommodation

There is no institution-managed accommodation. Students are advised to contact the institution for information about local accommodation options.

Overseas opportunities*

Number of students on a placement or study period abroad:

Compacts/Networks

Record of Achievement

Interviewing
Art portfolio required.

Campus locations
Single site.

Open Days

Tuesdays and Wednesdays 10.30am/1.30pm, February/March.

Excludes those on compulsory language course placements.

University of Glasgow

Central Admissions Service, University of Glasgow, Glasgow, Scotland, G12 8QQ

Tel: 0141 3304275 Fax: 0141 3304413
Prospectus requests: 0141 330 4440
admissions@mis.gla.ac.uk http://www.gla.ac.uk/admissions/

G28

Datafile

1996-97 Student Numbers

Total number of all students   18100

	Degree	HND
Total FT/SW undergraduate numbers	14960	
Percentages of these		
– on sandwich programmes		
– mature students	5	
– international students	9	
– male/female	46/54	

Full-time/sandwich students by academic subject category

	Degree	HND
Medicine, Dentistry, Vet Science	1946	
Subjects Allied to Medicine	587	
Science	3146	
Engineering and Technology	1470	
Built Environment	230	
Mathematical Sciences, IT & Computing	648	
Business and Management	650	
Social Sciences	1756	
Humanities	2935	
Art & Design and Perf Arts	1280	
Education	101	

Accommodation

Percentage of first years requiring accommodation who can be accommodated in institution-managed accommodation: 100%

Estimated weekly cost of institution-managed accommodation for 30-37 weeks:

(including 2-3 meals 7 days per week) £63.00

(no food) £40.00

(other…) £

Overseas opportunities*

Number of students on a placement or study period abroad:

Compacts/Networks
Member of Glasgow Community Colleges Group. Agreement with Clydebank College.

Record of Achievement
Not normally requested.

Interviewing
Interviews are not part of procedure except for Medicine/Veterinary/Dentistry/Music/Architecture/Nursing.

Campus locations
The University is planning to establish a campus at Chrichton College, Dumfries. Subject to approval.

Open Days

24 September 1997. Faculty of Arts, Science & Soc Sciences hold Open Days in February and March 1998

Excludes those on compulsory language course placements.

Glasgow Caledonian University

Admissions Office, City Campus, 70 Cowcaddens Road, Glasgow, G4 0BA

Tel: 0141 331 3334 Fax: 0141 331 3449
d.black@gcal.ac.uk

G42

Datafile

1996-97 Student Numbers

Total number of all students   13262

	Degree	HND
Total FT/SW undergraduate numbers	9316	363
Percentages of these		
– on sandwich programmes	11	
– mature students	32	1
– international students	3	1
– male/female	42/58	38/62

Full-time/sandwich students by academic subject category

	Degree	HND
Medicine, Dentistry, Vet Science		
Subjects Allied to Medicine	2434	
Science	981	21
Engineering and Technology	840	33
Built Environment	609	
Mathematical Sciences, IT & Computing	426	
Business and Management	3194	254
Social Sciences	656	
Humanities	175	55
Art & Design and Perf Arts		
Education		

Accommodation

Percentage of first years requiring accommodation who can be accommodated in institution-managed accommodation: 80%

Estimated weekly cost of institution-managed accommodation for 37 weeks:

(including dinner and breakfast 5 days per week) £56.00

(no food) £43.00

(other...) £

Overseas opportunities*

Number of students on a placement or study period abroad: 200

Compacts/Networks	Record of Achievement
	Considered on an individual basis if appropriate.

Interviewing	Campus locations
Yes, when appropriate.	City Campus, Southbrave Campus and St James Campus are all in Glasgow.

Open Days
17 September 1997.

*Excludes those on compulsory language course placements.

Gloucestershire College of Arts and Technology

The Registry, Brunswick Road, Gloucester, Gloucestershire, GL1 1HU

Tel: 01452 426557 Fax: 01452 426531

G45

Datafile

1996-97 Student Numbers

Total number of all students   35000

	Degree	HND
Total FT/SW undergraduate numbers		250
Percentages of these		
– on sandwich programmes		
– mature students		25
– international students		10
– male/female		76/24

Full-time/sandwich students by academic subject category

	Degree	HND
Medicine, Dentistry, Vet Science		
Subjects Allied to Medicine		
Science		
Engineering and Technology		113
Built Environment		54
Mathematical Sciences, IT & Computing		
Business and Management		22
Social Sciences		41
Humanities		
Art & Design and Perf Arts		20
Education		

Accommodation

There is no institution-managed accommodation. Students are advised to contact the institution for information about local accommodation options.

Overseas opportunities*

Number of students on a placement or study period abroad:

Compacts/Networks	Record of Achievement
Partner of University of the West of England.	

Interviewing	Campus locations
	Park Campus in Cheltenham and Brunswick Campus in Gloucester.

Open Days
Termly - dates on request.

*Excludes those on compulsory language course placements.

Goldsmiths College (University of London)

Admissions Office, Goldsmiths College, University of London, New Cross, London, SE14 6NW

Tel: 0171 919 7282 Fax: 0171 919 7509
admissions@gold.ac.uk http://www.gold.ac.uk

G56

Datafile

1996-97 Student Numbers

Total number of all students   5500

	Degree	HND
Total FT/SW undergraduate numbers	3459	
Percentages of these		
– on sandwich programmes	4	
– mature students	47	
– international students	15	
– male/female	33/67	

Full-time/sandwich students by academic subject category

	Degree	HND
Medicine, Dentistry, Vet Science		
Subjects Allied to Medicine	60	
Science	311	
Engineering and Technology		
Built Environment		
Mathematical Sciences, IT & Computing	112	
Business and Management		
Social Sciences	700	
Humanities	936	
Art & Design and Perf Arts	936	
Education	390	

Accommodation

Percentage of first years requiring accommodation who can be accommodated in institution-managed accommodation: 100%

Estimated weekly cost of institution-managed accommodation for 38 weeks:

(including dinner and breakfast 5 days per week) £65.00

(no food) £46.00

(other…) £52.00

Overseas opportunities*
Number of students on a placement or study period abroad:

Compacts/Networks
Operate the Goldsmiths Lewisham Access Scheme (GLAS) encouraging applicants from the local area.

Record of Achievement
Applicants invited to interview are asked to bring their RoA.

Interviewing
Interviews for teacher training, Visual Arts, Design, Drama, Music & Mathematics.

Campus locations
One campus in New Cross (South East London) 15 minutes by train from Charing Cross.

Open Days
Open Days arranged by Departments. Contact them direct. Group visits to college can be arranged.

*Excludes those on compulsory language course placements.

University of Greenwich

Head of Admissions, Wellington Street, Woolwich, SE18 6PF

Tel: 0181 3318598 Fax: 0181 3319856
n.r.cumming@greenwich.ac.uk

G70

Datafile

1996-97 Student Numbers

Total number of all students   16297

	Degree	HND
Total FT/SW undergraduate numbers	8062	951
Percentages of these		
– on sandwich programmes	21	11
– mature students	60	49
– international students	5	2
– male/female	50/50	64/36

Full-time/sandwich students by academic subject category

	Degree	HND
Medicine, Dentistry, Vet Science		
Subjects Allied to Medicine	1224	89
Science	1597	50
Engineering and Technology	407	141
Built Environment	454	120
Mathematical Sciences, IT & Computing	729	237
Business and Management	1299	314
Social Sciences	898	
Humanities	575	
Art & Design and Perf Arts	4	
Education	875	

Accommodation

Percentage of first years requiring accommodation who can be accommodated in institution-managed accommodation: 100%

Estimated weekly cost of institution-managed accommodation for 40 weeks:

(including 1 meal 5 days per week) £59.00

(no food) £59.00

(other…) £45.00

Overseas opportunities*
Number of students on a placement or study period abroad:

Compacts/Networks
Partnership with 8 Associate Colleges and Compact arrangements with 25 Schools in Kent & S E London.

Record of Achievement
Should be available if called for interview.

Interviewing
Interviews required for Nursing, Midwifery and teacher-training. Mature and non standard entries require interview.

Campus locations
Chatham, Dartford (Kent) Eltham, Woolwich (S E London) and Roehampton (S W London).

Open Days
General Open Day 17 September 1997. Contact Enquiry Unit on 0800 005006 (44 3318590 internal).

*Excludes those on compulsory language course placements.

Gyosei International College

Admissions Office, London Road, Reading, Berkshire, RG1 5AQ

Tel: 01189 209357 Fax: 01189 310137

G96

Datafile

1996-97 Student Numbers

Total number of all students   350

	Degree	HND
Total FT/SW undergraduate numbers		
Percentages of these		
– on sandwich programmes		
– mature students		
– international students	80	
– male/female	60/40	

Full-time/sandwich students by academic subject category

	Degree	HND
Medicine, Dentistry, Vet Science		
Subjects Allied to Medicine		
Science		
Engineering and Technology		
Built Environment		
Mathematical Sciences, IT & Computing		
Business and Management	160	
Social Sciences	75	
Humanities	75	
Art & Design and Perf Arts		
Education		

Accommodation

Percentage of first years requiring accommodation who can be accommodated in institution-managed accommodation: 100%

Estimated weekly cost of institution-managed accommodation for 10 weeks:

(including 3 meals 7 days per week) £70.00 – £85.00

(no food) £50.00

(other…) £

Overseas opportunities*

Number of students on a placement or study period abroad: 15

Compacts/Networks

Not applicable.

Record of Achievement

We have a positive approach towards RoA.

Interviewing

Admissions Committee/College Representatives.

Campus locations

London Road campus, Reading, Berkshire RG1 5AQ.

Open Days

Personal visits welcome. Contact Admissions Office for further information.

*Excludes those on compulsory language course placements.

Halton College

Admissions Office, Kingsway, Widnes, Cheshire, WA8 7QQ

Tel: 0151 423 1391 Fax: 0151 420 2408
halton.college@cityscape.co.uk

H06

Datafile

1996-97 Student Numbers

Total number of all students

	Degree	HND
Total FT/SW undergraduate numbers		
Percentages of these		
– on sandwich programmes	100	
– mature students		10
– international students		
– male/female	70/30	50/50

Full-time/sandwich students by academic subject category

	Degree	HND
Medicine, Dentistry, Vet Science		
Subjects Allied to Medicine		
Science	10	69
Engineering and Technology		
Built Environment		
Mathematical Sciences, IT & Computing		
Business and Management		
Social Sciences		46
Humanities		
Art & Design and Perf Arts		
Education		

Accommodation

There is no institution-managed accommodation. Students are advised to contact the institution for information about local accommodation options.

Overseas opportunities*

Number of students on a placement or study period abroad:

Compacts/Networks

Birmingham TEC sector Compact available.

Record of Achievement

Required by all school leavers.

Interviewing

Most applicants accepted without interview. Evidence of portfolio of work is an advantage.

Campus locations

Aston Arts, Whitehead Road.

Open Days

12 February 1997. During Spring - to be decided.

*Excludes those on compulsory language course placements.

Letts STUDY GUIDES
THE INDEPENDENT

Handsworth College

Admissions, The Council House, Soho Road, Birmingham, B21 9DP

Tel: 0121 551 6031 Fax: 0121 523 4447

H09

Datafile

1996-97 Student Numbers

Total number of all students   20000

	Degree	HND
Total FT/SW undergraduate numbers	14	61
Percentages of these		
– on sandwich programmes		
– mature students	12	14
– international students		3
– male/female	55/45	30/70

Full-time/sandwich students by academic subject category

	Degree	HND
Medicine, Dentistry, Vet Science		
Subjects Allied to Medicine		
Science		
Engineering and Technology		
Built Environment		
Mathematical Sciences, IT & Computing		1
Business and Management		28
Social Sciences	13	
Humanities	1	
Art & Design and Perf Arts		32
Education		

Accommodation

There is no institution-managed accommodation. Students are advised to contact the institution for information about local accommodation options.

Overseas opportunities*

Number of students on a placement or study period abroad:

Compacts/Networks

Record of Achievement

Interviewing

Campus locations

Open Days

Excludes those on compulsory language course placements.

Harper Adams Agricultural College

Admissions Secretary, Harper Adams Agricultural College, Newport, Shropshire, TF10 8NB

Tel: 01952 815000 Fax: 01952 814783
gpodmore@haac.ac.uk http://www.haac.ac.uk

H12

Datafile

1996-97 Student Numbers

Total number of all students   1664

	Degree	HND
Total FT/SW undergraduate numbers	908	587
Percentages of these		
– on sandwich programmes	100	100
– mature students	19	16
– international students	4	8
– male/female	69/31	66/34

Full-time/sandwich students by academic subject category

	Degree	HND
Medicine, Dentistry, Vet Science		
Subjects Allied to Medicine		
Science	825	542
Engineering and Technology	83	45
Built Environment		
Mathematical Sciences, IT & Computing		
Business and Management		
Social Sciences		
Humanities		
Art & Design and Perf Arts		
Education		

Accommodation

Percentage of first years requiring accommodation who can be accommodated in institution-managed accommodation: 100%

Estimated weekly cost of institution-managed accommodation for 32 weeks:

(including 3 meals 5 days per week) £53.00 – £79.00

(no food) £

(other...) £

Overseas opportunities*

Number of students on a placement or study period abroad: 25

Compacts/Networks

Associate Colleges:
Reaseheath, (Nantwich, Cheshire) and Rodbaston (Penkridge, Staffordshire).

Record of Achievement

Interviewing

All applicants (not overseas) required to attend for interview/counselling held every Wednesday.

Campus locations

The entire College & associated 200 hectare mixed farm is two and a half miles west of Newport.

Open Days

Land-based industries 14 & 15 July 1997, 13 & 14 July 1998. Family Day 31 May 1997 & 6 June 1998.

Excludes those on compulsory language course placements.

Herefordshire College of Technology

MIS, Herefordshire College of Technology, Folly Lane, Hereford, Herefordshire, HR1 1LS

Tel: 01432 352235 Fax: 01432 353449

H16

Datafile

1996-97 Student Numbers

Total number of all students   16000

	Degree	HND
Total FT/SW undergraduate numbers	51	109
Percentages of these		
– on sandwich programmes		
– mature students	63	54
– international students		
– male/female	51/49	52/48

Full-time/sandwich students by academic subject category

	Degree	HND
Medicine, Dentistry, Vet Science		
Subjects Allied to Medicine		
Science		
Engineering and Technology		
Built Environment		
Mathematical Sciences, IT & Computing		
Business and Management	51	109
Social Sciences		
Humanities		
Art & Design and Perf Arts		
Education		

Accommodation

There is no institution-managed accommodation. Students are advised to contact the institution for information about local accommodation options.

Overseas opportunities*

Number of students on a placement or study period abroad:

Compacts/Networks

Agreement with PGL for outdoor pursuits, watersports programme and work experience.

Record of Achievement

Not essential but desirable.

Interviewing

No formal interviews - Open Day and small discussion groups held.

Campus locations

Single site situated half a mile from the city centre.

Open Days

Usually in March/April. Contact Institution.

*Excludes those on compulsory language course placements.

Herefordshire College of Art and Design

Administration Officer, Folly Lane, Hereford, HR1 1LT

Tel: 01432 273359 Fax: 01432 341099

H18

Datafile

1996-97 Student Numbers

Total number of all students   161

	Degree	HND
Total FT/SW undergraduate numbers	161	
Percentages of these		
– on sandwich programmes		
– mature students	40	
– international students	1	
– male/female	18/82	

Full-time/sandwich students by academic subject category

	Degree	HND
Medicine, Dentistry, Vet Science		
Subjects Allied to Medicine		
Science		
Engineering and Technology		
Built Environment		
Mathematical Sciences, IT & Computing		
Business and Management		
Social Sciences		
Humanities		
Art & Design and Perf Arts	161	
Education		

Accommodation

There is no institution-managed accommodation. Students are advised to contact the institution for information about local accommodation options.

Overseas opportunities*

Number of students on a placement or study period abroad:

Compacts/Networks

Record of Achievement

Taken into consideration when applying and at interview.

Interviewing

Applicants interviewed with portfolio of work, including contextual and/or theoretical studies.

Campus locations

Hereford (one site).

Open Days

Open Days are usually held in mid-February. Individuals can arrange to visit by appointment.

*Excludes those on compulsory language course placements.

Heriot-Watt University, Edinburgh

Admissions Office, Heriot-Watt University, Riccarton, Edinburgh,
Scotland, EH14 4AS

Tel: 0131 4513376 Fax: 0131 4513630
p.s.mclean@hw.ac.uk http://www.hw.ac.uk/

H24

Datafile

1996-97 Student Numbers

Total number of all students   5662

	Degree	HND
Total FT/SW undergraduate numbers	4426	
Percentages of these		
– on sandwich programmes	11	
– mature students	22	
– international students	13	
– male/female	67/33	

Full-time/sandwich students by academic subject category

	Degree	HND
Medicine, Dentistry, Vet Science		
Subjects Allied to Medicine		
Science	726	
Engineering and Technology	1085	
Built Environment	850	
Mathematical Sciences, IT & Computing	617	
Business and Management	654	
Social Sciences	244	
Humanities	250	
Art & Design and Perf Arts		
Education		

Accommodation

Percentage of first years requiring accommodation who can be accommodated in institution-managed accommodation: 100%

Estimated weekly cost of institution-managed accommodation for 32-38 weeks:

(including dinner and breakfast 7 days per week) £57.00

(no food) £36.00

(other...) £

Overseas opportunities*

Number of students on a placement or study period abroad: 101

Compacts/Networks

Record of Achievement
Not normally part of admissions procedure but requested occasionally.

Interviewing
Varies according to departments but most applicants invited to visit.

Campus locations
University campus at Riccarton on western outskirts of Edinburgh. College of Art is central.

Open Days

1 & 2 September 1997. Departments also hold Open Days. For further information contact 0131 4513450.

Excludes those on compulsory language course placements.

University of Hertfordshire

Hatfield Campus, College Lane, Hatfield, Herts, AL10 9AB

Tel: 01707 284800 Fax: 01707 284870
http://www.herts.ac.uk

H36

Datafile

1996-97 Student Numbers

Total number of all students   17000

	Degree	HND
Total FT/SW undergraduate numbers	10500	650
Percentages of these		
– on sandwich programmes	37	3
– mature students	40	22
– international students	8	1
– male/female	52/48	72/28

Full-time/sandwich students by academic subject category

	Degree	HND
Medicine, Dentistry, Vet Science		
Subjects Allied to Medicine	1500	
Science	1540	70
Engineering and Technology	2020	110
Built Environment	50	
Mathematical Sciences, IT & Computing	1230	340
Business and Management	1600	120
Social Sciences	1040	
Humanities	680	
Art & Design and Perf Arts	650	
Education	490	

Accommodation

Percentage of first years requiring accommodation who can be accommodated in institution-managed accommodation: 52%

Estimated weekly cost of institution-managed accommodation for 40 weeks:

(including dinner and breakfast   days per week) £

(no food) £47.00

(other...) £

Overseas opportunities*

Number of students on a placement or study period abroad:

Compacts/Networks
A number of University courses are taught at Associate Colleges.

Record of Achievement
Considered on an individual basis.

Interviewing
Policy varies according to department.

Campus locations
Hatfield, Hertford, Watford and St Albans.

Open Days

Departments offer Open Days to applicants.

Excludes those on compulsory language course placements.

Hertford Regional College

Admissions & Examinations, Hertford Regional College, Ware Centre, Scotts Road, Ware, Hertfordshire, SG12 9JF

Tel: 01920 465441 Fax: 01920 462772
sfb1@sfb1.demon.co.uk

H37

Datafile

1996-97 Student Numbers

	Degree	HND
Total number of all students 13341		
Total FT/SW undergraduate numbers	54	
Percentages of these		
– on sandwich programmes		
– mature students	10	
– international students		
– male/female	66/34	

Full-time/sandwich students by academic subject category

	Degree	HND
Medicine, Dentistry, Vet Science		
Subjects Allied to Medicine		
Science		
Engineering and Technology		
Built Environment		
Mathematical Sciences, IT & Computing		
Business and Management		
Social Sciences		
Humanities		
Art & Design and Perf Arts	54	
Education		

Accommodation

There is no institution-managed accommodation. Students are advised to contact the institution for information about local accommodation options.

Overseas opportunities*

Number of students on a placement or study period abroad:

Compacts/Networks

DipHE Programmes validated by Middlesex Univ and also an Assoc College of the Univ of Hertfordshire.

Record of Achievement

RoA welcomed and encouraged.

Interviewing

Suitable applicants are individually interviewed by staff and a student representative.

Campus locations

Ware in Hertfordshire.

Open Days

Visits any time by appointment - Open Week from 8-11 December 1997.

*Excludes those on compulsory language course placements.

Heythrop College (University of London)

Academic Registrar, Heythrop College, University of London, Kensington Square, London, W8 5HQ

Tel: 0171 795 6600 Fax: 0171 795 4200
a.clarkson@ic.ac.uk

H48

Datafile

1996-97 Student Numbers

	Degree	HND
Total number of all students 422		
Total FT/SW undergraduate numbers	129	
Percentages of these		
– on sandwich programmes		
– mature students	60	
– international students	15	
– male/female	65/35	

Full-time/sandwich students by academic subject category

	Degree	HND
Medicine, Dentistry, Vet Science		
Subjects Allied to Medicine		
Science		
Engineering and Technology		
Built Environment		
Mathematical Sciences, IT & Computing		
Business and Management		
Social Sciences		
Humanities	129	
Art & Design and Perf Arts		
Education		

Accommodation

Percentage of first years requiring accommodation who can be accommodated in institution-managed accommodation: 100%

Estimated weekly cost of institution-managed accommodation for 30 weeks:

(including dinner and breakfast 7 days per week) £75.00

(no food) £45.00

(other...) £

Overseas opportunities*

Number of students on a placement or study period abroad: 1

Compacts/Networks

Record of Achievement

Interviewing

All suitable applicants are interviewed and have an opportunity to meet students at the campus.

Campus locations

Kensington.

Open Days

Two general Open Days are held every November and February. Group visits welcome, by prior arrangement.

*Excludes those on compulsory language course placements.

Letts STUDY GUIDES
THE INDEPENDENT

Holborn College

Admissions Office, Holborn College, 200 Greyhound Road, London, W14 9RY

Tel: 0171 385 3377 Fax: 0171 381 3377
hlt@holborncollege.ac.uk http://www.holborncollege.ac.uk

H50

Datafile

1996-97 Student Numbers

Total number of all students   800

	Degree	HND
Total FT/SW undergraduate numbers	350	
Percentages of these		
– on sandwich programmes		
– mature students	65	
– international students	75	
– male/female	50/50	

Full-time/sandwich students by academic subject category

	Degree	HND
Medicine, Dentistry, Vet Science		
Subjects Allied to Medicine		
Science		
Engineering and Technology		
Built Environment		
Mathematical Sciences, IT & Computing		
Business and Management		
Social Sciences	350	
Humanities		
Art & Design and Perf Arts		
Education		

Accommodation

There is no institution-managed accommodation. Students are advised to contact the institution for information about local accommodation options.

Overseas opportunities*

Number of students on a placement or study period abroad:

Compacts/Networks

Record of Achievement

Interviewing

Mature applicants interviewed in certain circumstances.

Campus locations

Main campus on Greyhound Road, W14.

Open Days

Tuesday and Thursday afternoons from 2pm-4.30pm February to September. Other times by arrangement.

Excludes those on compulsory language course placements.

The University of Huddersfield

Admissions Office, The University of Huddersfield, Queensgate, Huddersfield, West Yorkshire, HD1 3DH

Tel: 01484 422288 Fax: 01484 516151
prospectus@hud.ac.uk http://www.hud.ac.uk

H60

Datafile

1996-97 Student Numbers

Total number of all students   14034

	Degree	HND
Total FT/SW undergraduate numbers	7363	3448
Percentages of these		
– on sandwich programmes	48	15
– mature students	29	25
– international students	1	1
– male/female	51/49	50/50

Full-time/sandwich students by academic subject category

	Degree	HND
Medicine, Dentistry, Vet Science		
Subjects Allied to Medicine	180	
Science	692	30
Engineering and Technology	552	60
Built Environment	236	44
Mathematical Sciences, IT & Computing	455	306
Business and Management	2147	387
Social Sciences	567	
Humanities	1300	
Art & Design and Perf Arts	1155	16
Education	167	

Accommodation

Percentage of first years requiring accommodation who can be accommodated in institution-managed accommodation: 80%

Estimated weekly cost of institution-managed accommodation for 36-41 weeks:

(including dinner and breakfast 5 days per week) £62

(no food) £44.00

(other...) £38.00

Overseas opportunities*

Number of students on a placement or study period abroad:

Compacts/Networks

Bradford Going On Project, Barnsley & Doncaster HE Access Project and East Lancashire ELPACT.

Record of Achievement

RoAs are not formally required but applicants invited for interviews may bring theirs along.

Interviewing

Many applicants attend selection interviews. Some courses hold informal Open Days for applicants.

Campus locations

Main Queensgate campus is in the town centre. Other facilities are located on nearby campuses.

Open Days

Main Open Day held in late April/early May. Contact School & College Liaison Office to arrange visit.

Excludes those on compulsory language course placements.

The University of Hull

Admissions Office, Cottingham Road, Hull, HU6 7RX

Tel: 01482 466200 Fax: 01482 442290
g.d.fourie@admin.hull.ac.uk http://www.hull.ac.uk

H72

Datafile

1996-97 Student Numbers

Total number of all students   7654

	Degree	HND
Total FT/SW undergraduate numbers	6491	
Percentages of these		
– on sandwich programmes		
– mature students	11	
– international students	7	
– male/female	50/50	

Full-time/sandwich students by academic subject category

	Degree	HND
Medicine, Dentistry, Vet Science		
Subjects Allied to Medicine	599	
Science	1318	
Engineering and Technology	491	
Built Environment		
Mathematical Sciences, IT & Computing	502	
Business and Management	764	
Social Sciences	1519	
Humanities	1930	
Art & Design and Perf Arts	205	
Education	256	

Accommodation

Percentage of first years requiring accommodation who can be accommodated in institution-managed accommodation: 100%

Estimated weekly cost of institution-managed accommodation for 31 weeks:

(including dinner and breakfast   days per week) £68.67

(no food) £39.69

(other...) £33.75

Overseas opportunities*

Number of students on a placement or study period abroad: 109

Compacts/Networks

Four Associated Colleges.

Record of Achievement

Bring to interview or visit day.

Interviewing

Mature applicants usually interviewed.

Campus locations

Two sites.

Open Days

One general Open Day in May. Visits arranged on request. Most applicants invited to visit.

Excludes those on compulsory language course placements.

Imperial College of Science, Technology and Medicine (University of London)

Assistant Registrar/Admissions, Registry, Imperial College of Science, Technology & Medicine, London, SW7 2AZ

Tel: 0171 594 8014 Fax: 0171 594 8004
admissions@ic.ac.uk http://www.ic.ac.uk

I50

Datafile

1996-97 Student Numbers

Total number of all students   8046

	Degree	HND
Total FT/SW undergraduate numbers	5225	
Percentages of these		
– on sandwich programmes	1	
– mature students	15	
– international students	22	
– male/female	71/29	

Full-time/sandwich students by academic subject category

	Degree	HND
Medicine, Dentistry, Vet Science	625	
Subjects Allied to Medicine		
Science	1682	
Engineering and Technology	2162	
Built Environment		
Mathematical Sciences, IT & Computing	751	
Business and Management	5	
Social Sciences		
Humanities		
Art & Design and Perf Arts		
Education		

Accommodation

Percentage of first years requiring accommodation who can be accommodated in institution-managed accommodation: 100%

Estimated weekly cost of institution-managed accommodation for 34-38 weeks:

(including dinner and breakfast   days per week) £57.31 – £74.81

(no food) £40.81 – £58.31

(other...) £

Overseas opportunities*

Number of students on a placement or study period abroad: 84

Compacts/Networks

None.

Record of Achievement

Interviewing

Selected applicants are invited for interview.

Campus locations

South Kensington in London.

Open Days

19 June 1997.

Excludes those on compulsory language course placements.

Jews' College (University of London)

Registrar, Albert Road, Hendon, London, NW4 2SJ

Tel: 0181 203 6427 Fax: 0181 203 6420
jewscoll@ulcc.clusi.ac.uk

J50

Datafile

1996-97 Student Numbers

Total number of all students 120

	Degree	HND
Total FT/SW undergraduate numbers	70	
Percentages of these		
– on sandwich programmes		
– mature students	6	
– international students		
– male/female	3/57	

Full-time/sandwich students by academic subject category

	Degree	HND
Medicine, Dentistry, Vet Science		
Subjects Allied to Medicine		
Science		
Engineering and Technology		
Built Environment		
Mathematical Sciences, IT & Computing		
Business and Management		
Social Sciences		
Humanities	70	
Art & Design and Perf Arts		
Education		

Accommodation

Percentage of first years requiring accommodation who can be accommodated in institution-managed accommodation: 30%

Estimated weekly cost of institution-managed accommodation for 30 weeks:

(including dinner and breakfast days per week) £

(no food) £50.00 – £55.00

(other…) £

Overseas opportunities*

Number of students on a placement or study period abroad:

Compacts/Networks

Record of Achievement

Interviewing

All potential students are interviewed.

Campus locations

Small campus in London.

Open Days

As per student request.

Excludes those on compulsory language course placements.

Keele University

Admissions & Recruitment Office, Keele University, Keele, Staffs, ST5 5BG

Tel: 01782 621111 Fax: 01782 632343
aaa06@admin.keele.ac.uk
http://www.keele.ac.uk/depts/aa/homepage.htm

K12

Datafile

1996-97 Student Numbers

Total number of all students 9609

	Degree	HND
Total FT/SW undergraduate numbers	4078	
Percentages of these		
– on sandwich programmes		
– mature students	20	
– international students	9	
– male/female	50/50	

Full-time/sandwich students by academic subject category

	Degree	HND
Medicine, Dentistry, Vet Science		
Subjects Allied to Medicine	244	
Science	625	
Engineering and Technology	25	
Built Environment		
Mathematical Sciences, IT & Computing	222	
Business and Management	372	
Social Sciences	1246	
Humanities	1140	
Art & Design and Perf Arts	81	
Education	123	

Accommodation

Percentage of first years requiring accommodation who can be accommodated in institution-managed accommodation: 100%

Estimated weekly cost of institution-managed accommodation for 37 weeks:

(including dinner and breakfast days per week) £

(no food) £30.00 – £46.00

(other…) £

Overseas opportunities*

Number of students on a placement or study period abroad: 160

Compacts/Networks

Compact Schools & Colleges:
Staffs, Dudley, Walsall, Salop & Wirral.

Record of Achievement

Interviewing

Mature applicants may be asked to interview. Not normally required of other applicants.

Campus locations

Keele, Staffs.

Open Days

Two Open Days in May and October, in addition to Visit Days for applicants throughout Spring Term.

Excludes those on compulsory language course placements.

The University of Kent at Canterbury

The Admissions Officer, The University, Canterbury, Kent, CT2 7NZ

Tel: 01227 827272 Fax: 01227 452196
admissions@ukc.ac.uk http://www.ukc.ac.uk

K24

Datafile

1996-97 Student Numbers

Total number of all students   10032

	Degree	HND
Total FT/SW undergraduate numbers	5807	
Percentages of these		
– on sandwich programmes	4	
– mature students	22	
– international students	21	
– male/female	50/50	

Full-time/sandwich students by academic subject category

	Degree	HND
Medicine, Dentistry, Vet Science		
Subjects Allied to Medicine	68	
Science	1002	
Engineering and Technology	408	
Built Environment	6	
Mathematical Sciences, IT & Computing	550	
Business and Management	902	
Social Sciences	1909	
Humanities	1741	
Art & Design and Perf Arts	322	
Education		

Accommodation

Percentage of first years requiring accommodation who can be accommodated in institution-managed accommodation: 100%

Estimated weekly cost of institution-managed accommodation for 30 weeks:

(including dinner and breakfast 7 days per week) £67.34

(no food) £44.00

(other...) £

Overseas opportunities *

Number of students on a placement or study period abroad: 236

Compacts/Networks

We have a number of Compacts with Schools and FE Colleges in Kent and Essex.

Record of Achievement

RoAs are not formally requested but students invited for interview may bring theirs along.

Interviewing

Generally, we do not interview students with standard qualifications or those living overseas.

Campus locations

Canterbury - one site.

Open Days

Annual Open Day on 27 June 1997. UCAS Visit Days from November-March. Contact Admissions Office.

*Excludes those on compulsory language course placements.

Kent Institute of Art and Design

Registry Office, Kent Institute of Art & Design, Oakwood Park, Maidstone, Kent, ME16 8AG

Tel: 01622 757286 Fax: 01622 692003
mfaupel@kiad.ac.uk http://kiad.ac.uk/kiad.htm

K36

Datafile

1996-97 Student Numbers

Total number of all students   2428

	Degree	HND
Total FT/SW undergraduate numbers	1136	409
Percentages of these		
– on sandwich programmes		
– mature students	50	40
– international students	16	7
– male/female	55/45	50/50

Full-time/sandwich students by academic subject category

	Degree	HND
Medicine, Dentistry, Vet Science		
Subjects Allied to Medicine		
Science		
Engineering and Technology		
Built Environment	142	
Mathematical Sciences, IT & Computing		
Business and Management		
Social Sciences		
Humanities		
Art & Design and Perf Arts	994	409
Education		

Accommodation

Percentage of first years requiring accommodation who can be accommodated in institution-managed accommodation: 60%

Estimated weekly cost of institution-managed accommodation for 43 weeks:

(including dinner and breakfast days per week) £

(no food) £40.00 – £45.00

(other...) £

Overseas opportunities *

Number of students on a placement or study period abroad: 140

Compacts/Networks

Compact arrangements exist between own FE and HE courses. Other compacts being developed.

Record of Achievement

RoAs are welcome at interviews.

Interviewing

All applicants interviewed where practicable, including most International students.

Campus locations

Canterbury, Maidstone and Rochester.

Open Days

Open Days take place in February and November. For confirmation please telephone.

*Excludes those on compulsory language course placements.

Kidderminster College

Student Admissions, Hoo Road, Kidderminster, Worcs, DY10 1LX

Tel: 01562 820811 Fax: 01562 748504
staff@kcfe.prestel.ac.uk.

K42

Datafile

1996-97 Student Numbers

Total number of all students   5500

	Degree	HND
Total FT/SW undergraduate numbers	127	83
Percentages of these		
– on sandwich programmes		
– mature students	56	25
– international students		
– male/female	8/92	53/47

Full-time/sandwich students by academic subject category

	Degree	HND
Medicine, Dentistry, Vet Science		
Subjects Allied to Medicine		
Science		
Engineering and Technology		
Built Environment		
Mathematical Sciences, IT & Computing		
Business and Management		24
Social Sciences		
Humanities		32
Art & Design and Perf Arts		27
Education		

Accommodation

There is no institution-managed accommodation. Students are advised to contact the institution for information about local accommodation options.

Overseas opportunities*

Number of students on a placement or study period abroad:

Compacts/Networks

Record of Achievement

Interviewing

Short-listed applicants are interviewed.

Campus locations

Kidderminster.

Open Days

Contact College for details.

*Excludes those on compulsory language course placements.

King Alfred's Winchester

Admissions Office, Winchester, Hampshire, SO22 4NR

Tel: 01962 841515 Fax: 01962 827406
admissions@wkac.ac.uk http://www.wkac.ac.uk

K48

Datafile

1996-97 Student Numbers

Total number of all students   5425

	Degree	HND
Total FT/SW undergraduate numbers	3161	
Percentages of these		
– on sandwich programmes		
– mature students	38	
– international students	1	
– male/female	28/72	

Full-time/sandwich students by academic subject category

	Degree	HND
Medicine, Dentistry, Vet Science		
Subjects Allied to Medicine	334	
Science	182	
Engineering and Technology		
Built Environment		
Mathematical Sciences, IT & Computing	40	
Business and Management	129	
Social Sciences	4	
Humanities	960	
Art & Design and Perf Arts	377	
Education	1305	

Accommodation

Percentage of first years requiring accommodation who can be accommodated in institution-managed accommodation: 100%

Estimated weekly cost of institution-managed accommodation for 30-40 weeks:

(including dinner and breakfast   days per week) £

(no food) £51.50 – £54.50

(other…) £67.00 – £70.00

Overseas opportunities*

Number of students on a placement or study period abroad: 27

Compacts/Networks

No formal arrangements yet but developing a close relationship with local schools and colleges.

Record of Achievement

Interviewing

Suitable applicants interviewed for ITT, Nursing and Midwifery, Learning Disabilities, Drama, Arts.

Campus locations

Winchester.

Open Days

June and October 1997, dates to be announced.

*Excludes those on compulsory language course placements.

King's College London (University of London)

UCAS Section Supervisor, Central Registry, Cornwall House, Waterloo Road, London, SE1 8WA

Tel: 0171 836 5454
ucas.enquires@kcl.ac.uk http://www.kcl.ac.uk

K60

Datafile

1996-97 Student Numbers

Total number of all students   12868

	Degree	HND
Total FT/SW undergraduate numbers	8531	
Percentages of these		
– on sandwich programmes		
– mature students	19	
– international students	10	
– male/female	42/58	

Full-time/sandwich students by academic subject category

	Degree	HND
Medicine, Dentistry, Vet Science	893	
Subjects Allied to Medicine	2237	
Science	1497	
Engineering and Technology	418	
Built Environment		
Mathematical Sciences, IT & Computing	535	
Business and Management	262	
Social Sciences	1000	
Humanities	1526	
Art & Design and Perf Arts	89	
Education	74	

Accommodation

Percentage of first years requiring accommodation who can be accommodated in institution-managed accommodation: 100%

Estimated weekly cost of institution-managed accommodation for 31-40 weeks:

(including 10-16 meals days per week) £76.30 – £109.20

(no food) £37.87 – £59.92

(other...) £70.00

Overseas opportunities*

Number of students on a placement or study period abroad: 199

Compacts/Networks

None.

Record of Achievement

Refer to Admissions Tutors (telephone number in prospectus).

Interviewing

Refer to Admissions Tutors (telephone number in prospectus).

Campus locations

The Strand in London, Kensington, King's Road in Chelsea and Waterloo.

Open Days

1 May 1997. Campus tours from May to October 1997.

*Excludes those on compulsory language course placements.

Kingston University

Admissions Office, River House, 53-57 High Street, Kingston-Upon-Thames, Surrey, KT1 1LQ

Tel: 0181 547 2000 Fax: 0181 547 7080
d.milner-walker@kingston.ac.uk http:/www.king.ac.uk

K84

Datafile

1996-97 Student Numbers

Total number of all students   13314

	Degree	HND
Total FT/SW undergraduate numbers	8490	675
Percentages of these		
– on sandwich programmes	18	2
– mature students	22	15
– international students	3	2
– male/female	51/49	71/29

Full-time/sandwich students by academic subject category

	Degree	HND
Medicine, Dentistry, Vet Science		
Subjects Allied to Medicine	368	
Science	1489	53
Engineering and Technology	1007	174
Built Environment	376	
Mathematical Sciences, IT & Computing	1123	107
Business and Management	799	272
Social Sciences	1282	
Humanities	738	
Art & Design and Perf Arts	749	69
Education	559	

Accommodation

Percentage of first years requiring accommodation who can be accommodated in institution-managed accommodation: 96%

Estimated weekly cost of institution-managed accommodation for 42 weeks:

(including dinner and breakfast days per week) £

(no food) £48.50 – £56.50

(other...) £

Overseas opportunities*

Number of students on a placement or study period abroad:

Compacts/Networks

A number of University courses are taught at Network colleges.

Record of Achievement

Considered on an individual basis.

Interviewing

Decided on an individual basis.

Campus locations

Penrhyn Road, Kingston Hill, Roehampton Vale and Knights Park.

Open Days

Date to be confirmed.

*Excludes those on compulsory language course placements.

The University of Wales, Lampeter

Admissions and Recruitment Office, University of Wales, College Street, Lampeter, Ceredigion, Wales, SA48 7ED

Tel: 01670 423530 Fax: 01670 423423
alexa@admin.lamp.ac.uk. http://www.lamp.ac.uk

L07

Datafile

1996-97 Student Numbers

Total number of all students　　　1496

	Degree	HND
Total FT/SW undergraduate numbers	1496	
Percentages of these		
– on sandwich programmes		
– mature students	26	
– international students	6	
– male/female	50/50	

Full-time/sandwich students by academic subject category

	Degree	HND
Medicine, Dentistry, Vet Science		
Subjects Allied to Medicine		
Science	94	
Engineering and Technology		
Built Environment		
Mathematical Sciences, IT & Computing	66	
Business and Management	19	
Social Sciences	98	
Humanities	1215	
Art & Design and Perf Arts		
Education		

Accommodation

Percentage of first years requiring accommodation who can be accommodated in institution-managed accommodation: 100%

Estimated weekly cost of institution-managed accommodation for 32-36 weeks:

(including dinner and breakfast　days per week) £

(no food) £37.00 – £65.00

(other…) £

Overseas opportunities*

Number of students on a placement or study period abroad: 45

Compacts/Networks

Record of Achievement
Acceptable.

Interviewing
All mature students interviewed. Many departments interview and some interview at Open Days.

Campus locations
University of Wales, Lampeter (one campus).

Open Days
16 June, 20 September 1997, 11 February, 4 March, 13 June 1998 and others for specific departments.

*Excludes those on compulsory language course placements.

Lancaster University

Undergraduate Admissions Office, External Relations, Lancaster University, Lancaster, LA1 4YW

Tel: 01524 65201 Fax: 01524 846243
ugadmissions@lancaster.ac.uk http://www.lancs.ac.uk

L14

Datafile

1996-97 Student Numbers

Total number of all students　　　10333

	Degree	HND
Total FT/SW undergraduate numbers	7630	
Percentages of these		
– on sandwich programmes	12	
– mature students	21	
– international students	7	
– male/female	48/52	

Full-time/sandwich students by academic subject category

	Degree	HND
Medicine, Dentistry, Vet Science		
Subjects Allied to Medicine	160	
Science	1480	
Engineering and Technology	240	
Built Environment		
Mathematical Sciences, IT & Computing	500	
Business and Management	650	
Social Sciences	1850	
Humanities	1950	
Art & Design and Perf Arts	250	
Education		

Accommodation

Percentage of first years requiring accommodation who can be accommodated in institution-managed accommodation: 100%

Estimated weekly cost of institution-managed accommodation for 31-38 weeks:

(including dinner and breakfast　days per week) £

(no food) £30.00 – £47.00

(other…) £

Overseas opportunities*

Number of students on a placement or study period abroad: 300

Compacts/Networks

Record of Achievement

Interviewing
Some Departments do interview as standard practice. Others only interview in special cases.

Campus locations
The University campus is based at Bailrigg on the outskirts of Lancaster.

Open Days
All applicants are invited to visit for Dept Open Days. Guardians/parents are welcome to attend.

*Excludes those on compulsory language course placements.

Lansdowne College

Head of Law, Lansdowne College, 40/44 Bark Road, London, W2 4AT

Tel: 0171 616 4410 Fax: 0171 616 4401

L20

Datafile

1996-97 Student Numbers

	Degree	HND
Total number of all students 400		
Total FT/SW undergraduate numbers	50	
Percentages of these		
– on sandwich programmes		
– mature students	27	
– international students	15	
– male/female	50/50	

Full-time/sandwich students by academic subject category

	Degree	HND
Medicine, Dentistry, Vet Science		
Subjects Allied to Medicine		
Science		
Engineering and Technology		
Built Environment		
Mathematical Sciences, IT & Computing		
Business and Management		
Social Sciences	50	
Humanities		
Art & Design and Perf Arts		
Education		

Accommodation

Percentage of first years requiring accommodation who can be accommodated in institution-managed accommodation: 10%

Estimated weekly cost of institution-managed accommodation for 27 weeks:

(including dinner and breakfast 7 days per week) $156.00

(no food) $119.00

(other...) $

Overseas opportunities *

Number of students on a placement or study period abroad:

Compacts/Networks	Record of Achievement
None.	Required at interview.

Interviewing	Campus locations
Applicants normally interviewed as interview plays a vital part in selection.	West London (Bayswater).

Open Days
By arrangement.

Excludes those on compulsory language course placements.

University of Leeds

Access & Information Office, University of Leeds, Leeds, LS2 9JT

Tel: 0113 233 2332 Fax: 0113 233 2334

L23

Datafile

1996-97 Student Numbers

	Degree	HND
Total number of all students 23607		
Total FT/SW undergraduate numbers	16099	
Percentages of these		
– on sandwich programmes	1	
– mature students	8	
– international students	7	
– male/female	52/48	

Full-time/sandwich students by academic subject category

	Degree	HND
Medicine, Dentistry, Vet Science	1391	
Subjects Allied to Medicine	1394	
Science	4158	
Engineering and Technology	2641	
Built Environment	58	
Mathematical Sciences, IT & Computing	1089	
Business and Management	813	
Social Sciences	2172	
Humanities	4378	
Art & Design and Perf Arts	292	
Education	674	

Accommodation

Percentage of first years requiring accommodation who can be accommodated in institution-managed accommodation: 100%

Estimated weekly cost of institution-managed accommodation for 30 weeks:

(including dinner and breakfast 6 days per week) $55.00 – $70.00

(no food) $30.00 – $50.00

(other...) $37.00

Overseas opportunities *

Number of students on a placement or study period abroad: 200

Compacts/Networks	Record of Achievement
	Sometimes requested when invited for interview.

Interviewing	Campus locations
Varies from one Department to another.	Academic Departments all on single campus site close to city centre.

Open Days
7 May 1997 and 2 July 1997. Individuals and parties wishing to visit contact 0113 2333996.

Excludes those on compulsory language course placements.

Leeds, Trinity and All Saints University College

Admissions, Brownberrie Lane, Horsforth, Leeds, LS18 5HD

Tel: 0113 283 7123 Fax: 0113 283 7200
http://www.tasc.ac.uk

L24

Datafile

1996-97 Student Numbers

Total number of all students   2100

	Degree	HND
Total FT/SW undergraduate numbers	1887	
Percentages of these		
– on sandwich programmes		
– mature students	18	
– international students	2	
– male/female	34/66	

Full-time/sandwich students by academic subject category

	Degree	HND
Medicine, Dentistry, Vet Science		
Subjects Allied to Medicine		
Science		
Engineering and Technology		
Built Environment		
Mathematical Sciences, IT & Computing		
Business and Management	487	
Social Sciences		
Humanities	771	
Art & Design and Perf Arts		
Education	739	

Accommodation

Percentage of first years requiring accommodation who can be accommodated in institution-managed accommodation: 100%

Estimated weekly cost of institution-managed accommodation for 33 weeks:

(including 3 meals 7 days per week) £58.18

(no food) £

(other...) £66.18

Overseas opportunities*

Number of students on a placement or study period abroad: 25

Compacts/Networks

Record of Achievement
RoA welcome, but not essential.

Interviewing
All applicants to the School of Education are interviewed. In other subject areas some are interviewed.

Campus locations
One location in Horsforth, Leeds.

Open Days
1 July 1997.

*Excludes those on compulsory language course placements.

Leeds Metropolitan University

Course Enquiries Office, Leeds Metropolitan University, Calverley Street, Leeds, LS1 3HE

Tel: 0113 283 3113 Fax: 0113 283 3114
course-enquiries@lmu.ac.uk http://www.lmu.ac.uk

L27

Datafile

1996-97 Student Numbers

Total number of all students   21000

	Degree	HND
Total FT/SW undergraduate numbers	9100	1100
Percentages of these		
– on sandwich programmes	28	21
– mature students	49	31
– international students	2	2
– male/female	50/50	67/33

Full-time/sandwich students by academic subject category

	Degree	HND
Medicine, Dentistry, Vet Science		
Subjects Allied to Medicine	1250	
Science	380	
Engineering and Technology	690	180
Built Environment	860	40
Mathematical Sciences, IT & Computing	1030	290
Business and Management	2360	590
Social Sciences	770	
Humanities	460	
Art & Design and Perf Arts	520	
Education	780	

Accommodation

Percentage of first years requiring accommodation who can be accommodated in institution-managed accommodation:

Estimated weekly cost of institution-managed accommodation for 41 weeks:

(including 9 meals days per week) £54.50

(no food) £47.00

(other...) £35.00

Overseas opportunities*

Number of students on a placement or study period abroad: 125

Compacts/Networks
LMU Progression Module, Leeds Family of Schools Project, West & North Yorkshire Access Network.

Record of Achievement
The University relies heavily on the UCAS form. RoAs should be brought to interview if up-to-date.

Interviewing
Most hold informal Open Days. Interview/portfolio inspection for Art & Design, Architecture courses.

Campus locations
Leeds city centre and Beckett Park (Headingley).

Open Days
Afternoon sessions in Spring Term for Art & Design. Details of Visitor Trail – contact Liaison Officer.

*Excludes those on compulsory language course placements.

Leeds College of Art and Design

Student Services, Jacob Kramer Building, Blenheim Walk, Leeds, LS2 9AQ

Tel: 0113 243 3848 Fax: 0113 244 5916

L28

Datafile

1996-97 Student Numbers

Total number of all students   3000

	Degree	HND
Total FT/SW undergraduate numbers	230	25
Percentages of these		
– on sandwich programmes		
– mature students	1	4
– international students	2	
– male/female	28/72	4/96

Full-time/sandwich students by academic subject category

	Degree	HND
Medicine, Dentistry, Vet Science		
Subjects Allied to Medicine		
Science		
Engineering and Technology		
Built Environment		
Mathematical Sciences, IT & Computing		
Business and Management		
Social Sciences		
Humanities		
Art & Design and Perf Arts	230	25
Education		

Accommodation

There is no institution-managed accommodation. Students are advised to contact the institution for information about local accommodation options.

Overseas opportunities*

Number of students on a placement or study period abroad: 15

Compacts/Networks

Record of Achievement
Not necessary.

Interviewing
Route A in January/February. Route B from April. See prospectus for details. Portfolio is crucial.

Campus locations
Jacob Kramer Building, Vernon Street and Rossington Street all in Leeds.

Open Days
Usually held during November and February. Other dates by arrangement with course leaders.

*Excludes those on compulsory language course placements.

Leeds College of Music

Admissions Tutor, 3 Quarry Hill, Leeds, L52 7PD

Tel: 0113 243 2491 Fax: 0113 243 8798

L30

Datafile

1996-97 Student Numbers

Total number of all students   600

	Degree	HND
Total FT/SW undergraduate numbers	220	
Percentages of these		
– on sandwich programmes		
– mature students	25	
– international students	5	
– male/female	83/17	

Full-time/sandwich students by academic subject category

	Degree	HND
Medicine, Dentistry, Vet Science		
Subjects Allied to Medicine		
Science		
Engineering and Technology		
Built Environment		
Mathematical Sciences, IT & Computing		
Business and Management		
Social Sciences		
Humanities		
Art & Design and Perf Arts	220	
Education		

Accommodation

There is no institution-managed accommodation. Students are advised to contact the institution for information about local accommodation options.

Overseas opportunities*

Number of students on a placement or study period abroad:

Compacts/Networks

Record of Achievement

Interviewing
By audition.

Campus locations
Single site. Links with USA and Northern Europe.

Open Days
Details on request from the External Relations Office.

*Excludes those on compulsory language course placements.

University of Leicester

Admissions Office, University of Leicester, Leicester, LE1 7RH

Tel: 0116 252 2295 Fax: 0116 252 2447
admissions@le.ac.uk http://www.le.ac.uk

L34

Datafile

1996-97 Student Numbers

Total number of all students   13040

	Degree	HND
Total FT/SW undergraduate numbers	6754	
Percentages of these		
– on sandwich programmes	2	
– mature students	16	
– international students	9	
– male/female	49/51	

Full-time/sandwich students by academic subject category

	Degree	HND
Medicine, Dentistry, Vet Science		
Subjects Allied to Medicine	785	
Science	12	
Engineering and Technology	1637	
Built Environment	387	
Mathematical Sciences, IT & Computing		
Business and Management	271	
Social Sciences		
Humanities	1971	
Art & Design and Perf Arts	1691	
Education		

Accommodation

Percentage of first years requiring accommodation who can be accommodated in institution-managed accommodation: 100%

Estimated weekly cost of institution-managed accommodation for 30 weeks:

(including dinner and breakfast 7 days per week) £64.00

(no food) £34.00

(other…) £34.79

Overseas opportunities*

Number of students on a placement or study period abroad: 100

Compacts/Networks

Member of the Leicestershire Progression Accord wth local schools and colleges.

Record of Achievement

Not formally requested. Applicants invited for interview may wish to bring their RoA.

Interviewing

Applicants invited to visit days. Some applicants are interviewed.

Campus locations

Leicester is a single site campus on the edge of the city adjacent to Victoria Park.

Open Days

24 September 1997, 20 May and 23 September 1998. Contact 0116 252 2674 for visits/clearing visits.

Excludes those on compulsory language course placements.

Leicester South Fields College

Central Admissions, Leicester South Fields College, Aylestone Road, Leicester, LE2 7LW

Tel: 0116 224 2000 Fax: 0116 224 2190

L36

Datafile

1996-97 Student Numbers

Total number of all students   8821

	Degree	HND
Total FT/SW undergraduate numbers		154
Percentages of these		
– on sandwich programmes		28
– mature students		56
– international students		27
– male/female		42/58

Full-time/sandwich students by academic subject category

	Degree	HND
Medicine, Dentistry, Vet Science		
Subjects Allied to Medicine		
Science		
Engineering and Technology		
Built Environment		
Mathematical Sciences, IT & Computing		4
Business and Management		41
Social Sciences		
Humanities		
Art & Design and Perf Arts		109
Education		

Accommodation

There is no institution-managed accommodation. Students are advised to contact the institution for information about local accommodation options.

Overseas opportunities*

Number of students on a placement or study period abroad:

Compacts/Networks

Record of Achievement

RoA welcomed and encouraged.

Interviewing

Selected applicants are interviewed.

Campus locations

Leicester.

Open Days

End of November and during February. Contact the College for specific dates and times.

Excludes those on compulsory language course placements.

INDEPENDENT
ON SUNDAY

University of Lincolnshire and Humberside

Central Admissions Unit, Cottingham Road, Kingston upon Hull, HU6 7RT

Tel: 01482 440550 Fax: 01482 463310
marketing@ac.humber.uk   http://www.humber.ac.uk

L39

Datafile

1996-97 Student Numbers

Total number of all students   13010

	Degree	HND
Total FT/SW undergraduate numbers	9097	1649
Percentages of these		
– on sandwich programmes		16
– mature students		57
– international students		8
– male/female	50/50	50/50

Full-time/sandwich students by academic subject category

	Degree	HND
Medicine, Dentistry, Vet Science		
Subjects Allied to Medicine	294	114
Science	475	173
Engineering and Technology	446	199
Built Environment	224	7
Mathematical Sciences, IT & Computing	189	224
Business and Management	2516	596
Social Sciences	1362	
Humanities	739	
Art & Design and Perf Arts	1511	130
Education		

Accommodation

Percentage of first years requiring accommodation who can be accommodated in institution-managed accommodation: 85%

Estimated weekly cost of institution-managed accommodation for 33 weeks:

(including 12 meals per week) £55.00 – £60.00

(no food) £36.00 – £44.00

(other…) £33.00 – £44.00

Overseas opportunities*

Number of students on a placement or study period abroad: 200

Compacts/Networks

Compacts with 6 schools & colleges and franchise arrangements with numerous colleges.

Record of Achievement

Interviewing

Lincoln campus - single awards only, Grimsby campus - all awards, Humberside campus - Arts.

Campus locations

Lincoln University campus and Lincoln University campus Great Grimsby. Humberside University campus, Kingston upon Hull.

Open Days

Contact Education Liaison Officer: 01482 440550 X3230.

*Excludes those on compulsory language course placements.

The University of Liverpool

Faculty Admissions, Sub-Deans, Liverpool, L69 3BX

Tel: 0151 794 2000 Fax: 0151 708 6502
http://www.liv.ac.uk/netscape.svga.liverpool.homepage.html

L41

Datafile

1996-97 Student Numbers

Total number of all students   10264

	Degree	HND
Total FT/SW undergraduate numbers	10264	
Percentages of these		
– on sandwich programmes		
– mature students	17	
– international students	9	
– male/female	51/49	

Full-time/sandwich students by academic subject category

	Degree	HND
Medicine, Dentistry, Vet Science	1577	
Subjects Allied to Medicine	800	
Science	2212	
Engineering and Technology	1027	
Built Environment	292	
Mathematical Sciences, IT & Computing	643	
Business and Management	253	
Social Sciences	1464	
Humanities	1897	
Art & Design and Perf Arts	99	
Education		

Accommodation

Percentage of first years requiring accommodation who can be accommodated in institution-managed accommodation: 100%

Estimated weekly cost of institution-managed accommodation for 31-39 weeks:

(including dinner and breakfast 7 days per week) £63.75

(no food) £41.00

(other…) £

Overseas opportunities*

Number of students on a placement or study period abroad: 140

Compacts/Networks

For details of Compact arrangements contact Dr I A Pickering, Head of Service, SCILAS.

Record of Achievement

Students to bring RoA with them if attending an interview or Open Day.

Interviewing

Faculty practice varies. Students normally invited to Open Day but some Faculties interview.

Campus locations

Liverpool.

Open Days

Open Day usually in May. See prospectus for details.

*Excludes those on compulsory language course placements.

Liverpool Hope University College

Admissions Office, Hope Park, Liverpool, L16 9JD

Tel: 0151 2913000 Fax: 0151 2913048

L46

Datafile

1996-97 Student Numbers

Total number of all students

	Degree	HND
Total FT/SW undergraduate numbers	3430	
Percentages of these		
– on sandwich programmes		
– mature students	35	
– international students	2	
– male/female	35/65	

Full-time/sandwich students by academic subject category

	Degree	HND
Medicine, Dentistry, Vet Science		
Subjects Allied to Medicine		
Science	1201	
Engineering and Technology		
Built Environment		
Mathematical Sciences, IT & Computing	508	
Business and Management		
Social Sciences	418	
Humanities	1498	
Art & Design and Perf Arts	519	
Education	1091	

Accommodation

Percentage of first years requiring accommodation who can be accommodated in institution-managed accommodation: 100%

Estimated weekly cost of institution-managed accommodation for 33 weeks:

(including dinner and breakfast 7 days per week) £55.00

(no food) £52.00

(other…) £

Overseas opportunities*

Number of students on a placement or study period abroad: 65

Compacts/Networks

Partnership agreement with 26 schools and colleges in North West. Recommended students have offers.

Record of Achievement

Interviewees are encouraged to bring their RoA to interview.

Interviewing

BA (Euro St), B Design, BEd and BSc (Health and Phys Rec St) only make offers through interviews.

Campus locations

Single site in Liverpool in a quiet residential area three miles from the city centre.

Open Days

Successful applicants are invited to a Visit Day. To arrange visits contact School Liaison Officer.

Excludes those on compulsory language course placements.

The Liverpool Institute for Performing Arts

Admissions Office, Liverpool Institute for Performing Arts, Mount Street, Liverpool, L1 9HF

Tel: 0151 330 3232 Fax: 0151 330 3131
admissions@lipa.ac.uk

L48

Datafile

1996-97 Student Numbers

Total number of all students   430

	Degree	HND
Total FT/SW undergraduate numbers	365	
Percentages of these		
– on sandwich programmes		
– mature students	42	
– international students	24	
– male/female	53/47	

Full-time/sandwich students by academic subject category

	Degree	HND
Medicine, Dentistry, Vet Science		
Subjects Allied to Medicine		
Science		
Engineering and Technology		
Built Environment		
Mathematical Sciences, IT & Computing		
Business and Management		
Social Sciences		
Humanities		
Art & Design and Perf Arts	365	
Education		

Accommodation

Percentage of first years requiring accommodation who can be accommodated in institution-managed accommodation: 90%

Estimated weekly cost of institution-managed accommodation for   weeks:

(including dinner and breakfast   days per week) £

(no food) £40.00

(other…) £

Overseas opportunities*

Number of students on a placement or study period abroad:

Compacts/Networks

Record of Achievement

Accepted as part of the criteria of assessment.

Interviewing

Offers made through audition/interview.

Campus locations

One site only - Mount Street.

Open Days

Not held at present.

Excludes those on compulsory language course placements.

Liverpool John Moores University

Recruitment Team, Roscoe Court, 4 Rodney Street, Liverpool, L1 2TZ

Tel: 0151 231 5090 Fax: 0151 231 3194

recruitment@livjm.ac.uk http://www.livjm.ac.uk

L51

Datafile

1996-97 Student Numbers

Total number of all students   19524

	Degree	HND
Total FT/SW undergraduate numbers	11491	552
Percentages of these		
– on sandwich programmes	18	22
– mature students	34	37
– international students	8	11
– male/female	50/50	80/20

Full-time/sandwich students by academic subject category

	Degree	HND
Medicine, Dentistry, Vet Science		
Subjects Allied to Medicine	840	
Science	2321	
Engineering and Technology	1050	233
Built Environment	654	67
Mathematical Sciences, IT & Computing	807	142
Business and Management	1400	110
Social Sciences	1137	
Humanities	1236	
Art & Design and Perf Arts	1030	
Education	1016	

Accommodation

Percentage of first years requiring accommodation who can be accommodated in institution-managed accommodation: 90%

Estimated weekly cost of institution-managed accommodation for 39 weeks:

(including dinner and breakfast   days per week) £

(no food) £31.00 – £50.00

(other…) £

Overseas opportunities*

Number of students on a placement or study period abroad: 80

Compacts/Networks   Record of Achievement

Compact arrangements with Merseyside schools and further links being forged all the time.

Interviewing   Campus locations

No policy of interviewing except for teaching, pharmacy, auditioned courses and mature students.

Over 20 teaching/learning buildings throughout the city. I M Marsh campus 4 miles from Aigburth.

Open Days

Individual departments have Open Days. All unconditional places are invited for a tour.

*Excludes those on compulsory language course placements.

London Guildhall University

Course Enquiries Unit, 133 Whitechapel High Street, London, E1 7QA

Tel: 0171 320 1616 Fax: 0171 320 1422

info@lgu.ac.uk http://www.lgu.ac.uk

L55

Datafile

1996-97 Student Numbers

Total number of all students   13900

	Degree	HND
Total FT/SW undergraduate numbers	6372	567
Percentages of these		
– on sandwich programmes	8	
– mature students	50	52
– international students	4	4
– male/female	47/53	55/45

Full-time/sandwich students by academic subject category

	Degree	HND
Medicine, Dentistry, Vet Science		
Subjects Allied to Medicine		
Science	463	
Engineering and Technology	391	172
Built Environment		
Mathematical Sciences, IT & Computing	584	69
Business and Management	1624	192
Social Sciences	1961	
Humanities	688	
Art & Design and Perf Arts	661	134
Education		

Accommodation

Percentage of first years requiring accommodation who can be accommodated in institution-managed accommodation: 55%

Estimated weekly cost of institution-managed accommodation for 40 weeks:

(including 1/2 meals 7 days per week) £68.00

(no food) £46.00 – £63.00

(other…) £

Overseas opportunities*

Number of students on a placement or study period abroad: 110

Compacts/Networks   Record of Achievement

Compact with Barking & Dagenham. Connect Scheme with Camden and Path Scheme with Tower Hamlets.

Interviewing   Campus locations

Most applicants to Art & Design courses are interviewed. Limited interviews on other courses.

7 teaching sites in London plus franchised courses at South Thames and Southwark Colleges.

Open Days

Post-application Open Days held in Spring and pre-application Open Day dates to be confirmed.

*Excludes those on compulsory language course placements.

The London Institute

Communications & Marketing Department, 65 Davies Street, London, W17 2DA

Tel: 0171 514 6000 Fax: 0171 514 6131

L65

London School of Economics and Political Science (University of London)

Undergraduate Admission Office, PO Box 13401, Houghton Street, London, WC2A 2AS

Tel: 0171 955 7124 Fax: 0171 831 1684
ug-admissions@ise.ac.uk

L72

Datafile

1996-97 Student Numbers

Total number of all students   15521

	Degree	HND
Total FT/SW undergraduate numbers	5302	1374
Percentages of these		
– on sandwich programmes	1	
– mature students	70	57
– international students	15	9
– male/female	36/64	26/74

Full-time/sandwich students by academic subject category

	Degree	HND
Medicine, Dentistry, Vet Science		
Subjects Allied to Medicine		
Science		113
Engineering and Technology	719	236
Built Environment		
Mathematical Sciences, IT & Computing		
Business and Management	261	576
Social Sciences		
Humanities	311	52
Art & Design and Perf Arts	4011	397
Education		

Accommodation

Percentage of first years requiring accommodation who can be accommodated in institution-managed accommodation:

Estimated weekly cost of institution-managed accommodation for 33-52 weeks:

(including dinner and breakfast 7 days per week) £69.20 – £89.09

(no food) £54.17 – £63.64

(other…) £

Overseas opportunities*

Number of students on a placement or study period abroad: 100

Compacts/Networks

Record of Achievement

Interviewing

Most applicants are interviewed (depending on course). Contact individual College for details.

Campus locations

The Institute comprises of five constituent Colleges and most have several sites in London.

Open Days

All Colleges hold Open Days/Exhibitions. Contact individual College administrators for details.

*Excludes those on compulsory language course placements.

Datafile

1996-97 Student Numbers

Total number of all students   6449

	Degree	HND
Total FT/SW undergraduate numbers	2707	
Percentages of these		
– on sandwich programmes		
– mature students	14	48
– international students	48	
– male/female	58/42	

Full-time/sandwich students by academic subject category

	Degree	HND
Medicine, Dentistry, Vet Science		
Subjects Allied to Medicine		
Science	32	
Engineering and Technology		
Built Environment		
Mathematical Sciences, IT & Computing	94	
Business and Management	577	
Social Sciences	1826	
Humanities	178	
Art & Design and Perf Arts		
Education		

Accommodation

Percentage of first years requiring accommodation who can be accommodated in institution-managed accommodation: 30%

Estimated weekly cost of institution-managed accommodation for 30-39 weeks:

(including dinner and breakfast 7 days per week) £89.00

(no food) £68.00

(other…) £

Overseas opportunities*

Number of students on a placement or study period abroad:

Compacts/Networks

Record of Achievement

Interviewing

Interviews for special cases and for some of the smaller courses.

Campus locations

Central London.

Open Days

7 May 1997 and 25 September 1997.

*Excludes those on compulsory language course placements.

Loughborough College of Art and Design

Admissions Officer, Loughborough, Leicestershire, LE11 3GE

Tel: 01509 261515 Fax: 01509 265515
v.dawson@lcad.ac.uk

L78

Datafile

1996-97 Student Numbers

Total number of all students   1018

	Degree	HND
Total FT/SW undergraduate numbers	624	87
Percentages of these		
– on sandwich programmes		
– mature students	33	18
– international students	1	1
– male/female	32/68	71/29

Full-time/sandwich students by academic subject category

	Degree	HND
Medicine, Dentistry, Vet Science		
Subjects Allied to Medicine		
Science		
Engineering and Technology		
Built Environment		
Mathematical Sciences, IT & Computing		
Business and Management		
Social Sciences		
Humanities		
Art & Design and Perf Arts	624	87
Education		

Accommodation

Percentage of first years requiring accommodation who can be accommodated in institution-managed accommodation: 100%

Estimated weekly cost of institution-managed accommodation for 32 weeks:

(including dinner and breakfast   days per week) £

(no food) £45.00

(other...) £

Overseas opportunities*

Number of students on a placement or study period abroad:10

Compacts/Networks

Record of Achievement

RoAs are considered during interview. Primary emphasis is placed on the applicant's portfolio.

Interviewing

First choice applicants guaranteed an interview. Interview procedure is selective in second choice.

Campus locations

Loughborough (two sites). All HE courses operate from Epinal Way Campus, one mile from town centre.

Open Days

Students are welcome in Spring Term and can visit during Jan/Feb to view exhibition of student work.

*Excludes those on compulsory language course placements.

Loughborough University

Undergraduate Admissions Office, Loughborough University, Ashby Road, Loughborough, Leics, LE11 3TU

Tel: 01509 263171 Fax: 01509 223905
h.e.jones@lboro.ac.uk

L79

Datafile

1996-97 Student Numbers

Total number of all students   10200

	Degree	HND
Total FT/SW undergraduate numbers	7580	
Percentages of these		
– on sandwich programmes	38	
– mature students	14	
– international students	12	
– male/female	67/33	

Full-time/sandwich students by academic subject category

	Degree	HND
Medicine, Dentistry, Vet Science		
Subjects Allied to Medicine	200	
Science	730	
Engineering and Technology	2410	
Built Environment	215	
Mathematical Sciences, IT & Computing	695	
Business and Management	1125	
Social Sciences	865	
Humanities	500	
Art & Design and Perf Arts	55	
Education	785	

Accommodation

Percentage of first years requiring accommodation who can be accommodated in institution-managed accommodation: 100%

Estimated weekly cost of institution-managed accommodation for 30 weeks:

(including 2-3 meals 7 days per week) £67.00

(no food) £38.00

(other...) £

Overseas opportunities*

Number of students on a placement or study period abroad: 60

Compacts/Networks

NE Midlands Access Partnership, Leic Progression Accord, SE Midlands Open Coll Network, Mid Compact.

Record of Achievement

Discretion of Admissions Tutors.

Interviewing

Discretion of Admissions Tutors.

Campus locations

Open Days

Wednesday 24 June 1998.

*Excludes those on compulsory language course placements.

Lowestoft College

Lowestoft College, St Peters Street, Lowestoft, Suffolk, NR32 2NB

Tel: 01502 583521 Fax: 01502 500031
info@lowestoft.ac.uk

L82

Datafile

1996-97 Student Numbers

Total number of all students   1200

	Degree	HND
Total FT/SW undergraduate numbers		
Percentages of these		
– on sandwich programmes		
– mature students		20
– international students		
– male/female		60/40

Full-time/sandwich students by academic subject category

	Degree	HND
Medicine, Dentistry, Vet Science		
Subjects Allied to Medicine		
Science		
Engineering and Technology		
Built Environment		
Mathematical Sciences, IT & Computing		
Business and Management		
Social Sciences		
Humanities		
Art & Design and Perf Arts		37
Education		

Accommodation

There is no institution-managed accommodation. Students are advised to contact the institution for information about local accommodation options.

Overseas opportunities*

Number of students on a placement or study period abroad:

Compacts/Networks
Anglia Polytechnic University Compact Scheme.

Record of Achievement
Yes.

Interviewing
All applicants seen with portfolio of work.

Campus locations

Open Days

Visits can be made by prior arrangement throughout the academic year.

Excludes those on compulsory language course placements.

LSU College of Higher Education

Registry, LSU College of HE, The Avenue, Southampton, Hampshire, SO17 1BG

Tel: 01703 225333 Fax: 01703 230944

L86

Datafile

1996-97 Student Numbers

Total number of all students   1891

	Degree	HND
Total FT/SW undergraduate numbers	1732	
Percentages of these		
– on sandwich programmes		
– mature students	35	
– international students	1	
– male/female	23/77	

Full-time/sandwich students by academic subject category

	Degree	HND
Medicine, Dentistry, Vet Science		
Subjects Allied to Medicine	80	
Science	161	
Engineering and Technology		
Built Environment		
Mathematical Sciences, IT & Computing	14	
Business and Management		
Social Sciences	199	
Humanities	598	
Art & Design and Perf Arts	42	
Education	797	

Accommodation

Percentage of first years requiring accommodation who can be accommodated in institution-managed accommodation: 100%

Estimated weekly cost of institution-managed accommodation for   weeks:

(including 3 meals 7 days per week) £65.00

(no food) £

(other…) £

Overseas opportunities*

Number of students on a placement or study period abroad:

Compacts/Networks

Record of Achievement

Interviewing
All Teacher Training and Podiatry applicants are interviewed.

Campus locations
All on one site.

Open Days

12 March 1997, 26 April 1997 and 12 November 1997. 11 March 1998 and a date in April/May 1998.

Excludes those on compulsory language course placements.

University of Luton

Admissions Manager, University of Luton, Park Square, Luton, Beds, LU1 3JU

Tel: 01582 489286 Fax: 01582 489323
pat.herber@luton.ac.uk.

L93

Datafile

1996-97 Student Numbers

Total number of all students   14000

	Degree	HND
Total FT/SW undergraduate numbers	7587	840
Percentages of these		
– on sandwich programmes	1	1
– mature students	55	32
– international students	12	7
– male/female	48/52	63/37

Full-time/sandwich students by academic subject category

	Degree	HND
Medicine, Dentistry, Vet Science	524	19
Subjects Allied to Medicine	781	246
Science	348	68
Engineering and Technology	314	30
Built Environment	386	135
Mathematical Sciences, IT & Computing	1504	132
Business and Management	1782	150
Social Sciences	829	
Humanities	681	52
Art & Design and Perf Arts	436	7
Education		

Accommodation

Percentage of first years requiring accommodation who can be accommodated in institution-managed accommodation: 100%

Estimated weekly cost of institution-managed accommodation for 40 weeks:

(including dinner and breakfast 7 days per week) $40.00 – $50.00

(no food) £

(other...) £

Overseas opportunities*

Number of students on a placement or study period abroad: 15

Compacts/Networks

A partnership is under development with local schools and colleges. Local Open College Network.

Record of Achievement

Evidence contained in RoAs will contribute to admissions decision.

Interviewing

Applicants are interviewed for specialist courses or where they have non-standard qualifications.

Campus locations

Open Days

17 September 1997, 16 November 1997, 5 February 1998, 5 March 1998, 15 March 1998 & 16 April 1998.

*Excludes those on compulsory language course placements.

Manchester College of Arts and Technology

City Centre Campus, Lower Hardman Street, Manchester M3 3ER

Tel: 0161 953 5995 Fax: 0161 953 2259

jim.whitham@mancat.ac.uk

M10

Datafile

1996-97 Student Numbers

Total number of all students   34000

	Degree	HND
Total FT/SW undergraduate numbers	60	19
Percentages of these		
– on sandwich programmes		
– mature students	49	9
– international students		1
– male/female	62/38	79/21

Full-time/sandwich students by academic subject category

	Degree	HND
Medicine, Dentistry, Vet Science		
Subjects Allied to Medicine		
Science		
Engineering and Technology		
Built Environment		19
Mathematical Sciences, IT & Computing		
Business and Management		
Social Sciences		
Humanities		
Art & Design and Perf Arts	60	
Education		

Accommodation

Percentage of first years requiring accommodation who can be accommodated in institution-managed accommodation:

Estimated weekly cost of institution-managed accommodation for 39 weeks:

(including dinner and breakfast   days per week) £

(no food)

(other...) £

Overseas opportunities*

Number of students on a placement or study period abroad:

Compacts/Networks

Record of Achievement

Interviewing

Campus locations

Central Manchester. Openshaw. Moston. Lever Street.

Open Days

*Excludes those on compulsory language course placements.

The University of Manchester

University Admissions Office, University of Manchester, Manchester, M13 9PL

Tel: 0161 275 2077 Fax: 0161 275 2047

http://www.man.ac.uk

M20

Datafile

1996-97 Student Numbers

Total number of all students   22507

	Degree	HND
Total FT/SW undergraduate numbers	14826	
Percentages of these		
– on sandwich programmes	1	
– mature students	8	
– international students	7	
– male/female	51/49	

Full-time/sandwich students by academic subject category

	Degree	HND
Medicine, Dentistry, Vet Science	1739	
Subjects Allied to Medicine	434	
Science	2845	
Engineering and Technology	1034	
Built Environment	458	
Mathematical Sciences, IT & Computing	1010	
Business and Management	1221	
Social Sciences	1354	
Humanities	3800	
Art & Design and Perf Arts	258	
Education	261	

Accommodation

Percentage of first years requiring accommodation who can be accommodated in institution-managed accommodation: 100%

Estimated weekly cost of institution-managed accommodation for 38 weeks:

(including 2/3 meals 6 days per week) £66.00

(no food) £35.00 – £57.00

(other…) £

Overseas opportunities *

Number of students on a placement or study period abroad: 655

Compacts/Networks

Links with local schools in Manchester and member of Greater Manchester Open College Foundation.

Record of Achievement

Students attending interviews/Open Days should bring RoAs to interview.

Interviewing

Each department has own policy but all applicants offered a place attend an interview or Open Day.

Campus locations

Manchester (one site), one mile from the city centre and close to main transport links.

Open Days

16 June 1997, 17 June 1997 and 8 September 1997.

Excludes those on compulsory language course placements.

The University of Manchester Institute of Science and Technology (UMIST)

Undergraduate Admissions Office, UMIST, P O Box 88, Manchester, M60 1QD

Tel: 0161 236 3311 Fax: 0161 228 7040

ug.prospectus@umist.ac.uk http://www.umist.ac.uk

M25

Datafile

1996-97 Student Numbers

Total number of all students   6490

	Degree	HND
Total FT/SW undergraduate numbers	4668	
Percentages of these		
– on sandwich programmes	5	
– mature students	17	
– international students	20	
– male/female	67/33	

Full-time/sandwich students by academic subject category

	Degree	HND
Medicine, Dentistry, Vet Science		
Subjects Allied to Medicine	183	
Science	720	
Engineering and Technology	2012	
Built Environment	237	
Mathematical Sciences, IT & Computing	706	
Business and Management	657	
Social Sciences		
Humanities	91	
Art & Design and Perf Arts	62	
Education		

Accommodation

Percentage of first years requiring accommodation who can be accommodated in institution-managed accommodation: 100%

Estimated weekly cost of institution-managed accommodation for 31-51 weeks:

(including dinner and breakfast 6-7 days per week) £65.00 – £70.00

(no food) £34.00 – £52.00

(other…) £

Overseas opportunities *

Number of students on a placement or study period abroad: 112

Compacts/Networks

Record of Achievement

RoA may be used to supplement the application.

Interviewing

All short-listed UK-based applicants invited to attend Open Day/informal interview.

Campus locations

City centre campus very close to main transport links in Manchester.

Open Days

9 October 1997, 20 May 1998 & 17 June 1998. Provisional 8 October 1998. Contact 0161 200 4023.

Excludes those on compulsory language course placements.

The Manchester Metropolitan University

Applications Section, Academic Division, All Saints, Manchester, M15 6BH

Tel: 0161 2471035 Fax: 0161 2476390

prospectus@mmu.ac.uk http://www.mmu.ac.uk

M40

Datafile

1996-97 Student Numbers

Total number of all students   30635

	Degree	HND
Total FT/SW undergraduate numbers	16328	1634
Percentages of these		
– on sandwich programmes	18	18
– mature students	30	18
– international students	5	4
– male/female	44/56	56/44

Full-time/sandwich students by academic subject category

	Degree	HND
Medicine, Dentistry, Vet Science		
Subjects Allied to Medicine	1027	
Science	1820	327
Engineering and Technology	1254	183
Built Environment	386	
Mathematical Sciences, IT & Computing	1105	272
Business and Management	2641	784
Social Sciences	2670	
Humanities	1876	
Art & Design and Perf Arts	1835	68
Education	1714	

Accommodation

Percentage of first years requiring accommodation who can be accommodated in institution-managed accommodation: 50%

Estimated weekly cost of institution-managed accommodation for 34 weeks:

(including 2/3 meals 7 days per week) £38.70 – £61.50

(no food) £35.00 – £40.30

(other…) £

Overseas opportunities*

Number of students on a placement or study period abroad:

Compacts/Networks
Member of Greater Manchester Open College Federation.

Record of Achievement
Admissions Tutors consider RoAs to aid final decision.

Interviewing
Applicants may be interviewed at the discretion of the department - refer to MMU prospectus.

Campus locations
Central Manchester (five sites), Crewe and Alsager.

Open Days

For details contact Marketing Office, Bellhouse Building, Lower Ormond St, Manchester, M15 6BX.

Excludes those on compulsory language course placements.

Matthew Boulton College of Further and Higher Education

College Admissions Unit, Sherlock Street, Birmingham, B5 7DB

Tel: 0121 4464545 Fax: 0121 4463105

M60

Datafile

1996-97 Student Numbers

Total number of all students

	Degree	HND
Total FT/SW undergraduate numbers	69	43
Percentages of these		
– on sandwich programmes		
– mature students	75	30
– international students		5
– male/female	20/80	70/30

Full-time/sandwich students by academic subject category

	Degree	HND
Medicine, Dentistry, Vet Science	69	
Subjects Allied to Medicine		
Science		
Engineering and Technology		
Built Environment		
Mathematical Sciences, IT & Computing		
Business and Management		43
Social Sciences		
Humanities		
Art & Design and Perf Arts		
Education		

Accommodation

There is no institution-managed accommodation. Students are advised to contact the institution for information about local accommodation options.

Overseas opportunities*

Number of students on a placement or study period abroad:

Compacts/Networks

Record of Achievement
The College is keen to see the RoA at applicant's interview.

Interviewing
Procedure differs depending on course.

Campus locations
Single site.

Open Days

Please contact the College Information Centre for details.

Excludes those on compulsory language course placements.

Letts STUDY GUIDES
THE INDEPENDENT

Mid-Cheshire College

Admissions Office, Hartford Campus, Chester Road, Northwich, Cheshire, CW8 1LJ

Tel: 01606 74444 Fax: 01606 75101

M77

Datafile

1996-97 Student Numbers

Total number of all students   6500

	Degree	HND
Total FT/SW undergraduate numbers		94
Percentages of these		
– on sandwich programmes		
– mature students		5
– international students		1
– male/female		42/58

Full-time/sandwich students by academic subject category

	Degree	HND
Medicine, Dentistry, Vet Science		
Subjects Allied to Medicine		
Science		
Engineering and Technology		
Built Environment		
Mathematical Sciences, IT & Computing		
Business and Management		
Social Sciences		
Humanities		
Art & Design and Perf Arts		94
Education		

Accommodation

There is no institution-managed accommodation. Students are advised to contact the institution for information about local accommodation options.

Overseas opportunities*

Number of students on a placement or study period abroad:

Compacts/Networks

Record of Achievement

Will take into consideration if available - emphasis on portfolio.

Interviewing

All applicants interviewed - portfolio of work and sketchbooks and evidence of written material.

Campus locations

Hartford campus, Northwich and London Road Studios, Northwich.

Open Days

Through December to March. Contact Student Services to arrange visit.

Excludes those on compulsory language course placements.

Middlesex University

Admissions Enquiries, Middlesex University, White Hart Lane, London, N17 8HR

Tel: 0181 362 5898 Fax: 0181 362 5649
admissions@mdx.ac.uk mdx.ac.uk/www/admissions/admit.htm

M80

Datafile

1996-97 Student Numbers

Total number of all students   23000

	Degree	HND
Total FT/SW undergraduate numbers	14227	329
Percentages of these		
– on sandwich programmes	20	2
– mature students	46	43
– international students	19	5
– male/female	43/57	66/34

Full-time/sandwich students by academic subject category

	Degree	HND
Medicine, Dentistry, Vet Science		
Subjects Allied to Medicine	520	19
Science	1127	
Engineering and Technology	560	72
Built Environment	17	7
Mathematical Sciences, IT & Computing	636	119
Business and Management	3323	1
Social Sciences	1748	
Humanities	1797	37
Art & Design and Perf Arts	1971	74
Education	364	

Accommodation

Percentage of first years requiring accommodation who can be accommodated in institution-managed accommodation: 70%

Estimated weekly cost of institution-managed accommodation for 39 weeks:

(including dinner and breakfast   days per week) £

(no food) £46.62 – £53.90

(other…) £

Overseas opportunities*

Number of students on a placement or study period abroad: 450

Compacts/Networks

Arrangements with selected schools & colleges. Progression Links with many Access Programmes.

Record of Achievement

Interviewing

A & D, Perf Arts, ITT, Nursing, Herbal Medicine & Soc Work require interview/audition. Others attend Open Days.

Campus locations

Bounds Green, Cat Hill, Enfield, Hendon, Tottenham, Trent Park, Ivy House, Bedford and 4 N. London hospitals.

Open Days

17 June 1997. Group visits can be arranged. Contact Education Liaison Office 0181 3625000.

Excludes those on compulsory language course placements.

Moray House Institute of Education

Registry, Moray House Institute of Education, Holyrood Road, Edinburgh, EH8 8AQ

Tel: 0131 556 8455 Fax: 0131 557 3458

M90

Datafile

1996-97 Student Numbers

	Degree	HND
Total number of all students	1960	
Total FT/SW undergraduate numbers	1450	
Percentages of these		
– on sandwich programmes		
– mature students	15	
– international students	4	
– male/female	30/70	

Full-time/sandwich students by academic subject category

	Degree	HND
Medicine, Dentistry, Vet Science		
Subjects Allied to Medicine		
Science		
Engineering and Technology		
Built Environment		
Mathematical Sciences, IT & Computing		
Business and Management		
Social Sciences		
Humanities		
Art & Design and Perf Arts		
Education	1450	

Accommodation

Percentage of first years requiring accommodation who can be accommodated in institution-managed accommodation: 100%

Estimated weekly cost of institution-managed accommodation for 36 weeks:

(including dinner and breakfast 7 days per week) £56.00

(no food) £

(other…) £

Overseas opportunities *

Number of students on a placement or study period abroad:

Compacts/Networks

Record of Achievement
RoA may be taken into account at interview.

Interviewing
All students to be offered places on professional training courses will normally be interviewed.

Campus locations
Holyrood Campus and Cramond Campus.

Open Days
Last Tuesday in November each year.

*Excludes those on compulsory language course placements.

Napier University

Information Office, 219 Colinton Road, Edinburgh, EH14 1DJ

Tel: 0131 455 4330 Fax: 0131 455 4666
info@napier.ac.uk http://www.napier.ac.uk

N07

Datafile

1996-97 Student Numbers

	Degree	HND
Total number of all students	11467	
Total FT/SW undergraduate numbers	6270	
Percentages of these		
– on sandwich programmes		
– mature students	38	
– international students	2	
– male/female	60/40	

Full-time/sandwich students by academic subject category

	Degree	HND
Medicine, Dentistry, Vet Science		
Subjects Allied to Medicine		
Science	755	
Engineering and Technology	990	
Built Environment	404	
Mathematical Sciences, IT & Computing	457	
Business and Management	2577	
Social Sciences	227	
Humanities		
Art & Design and Perf Arts	560	
Education		

Accommodation

Percentage of first years requiring accommodation who can be accommodated in institution-managed accommodation: 85%

Estimated weekly cost of institution-managed accommodation for 41 weeks:

(including dinner and breakfast   days per week) £

(no food) £48.50

(other…) £

Overseas opportunities *

Number of students on a placement or study period abroad:

Compacts/Networks

Record of Achievement

Interviewing
Policy varies according to department.

Campus locations
Nine locations in Edinburgh, plus Livingston and Melrose campuses.

Open Days
University Open Day 9 September 1998. Faculty/Department Open Days throughout year. Call for further information.

*Excludes those on compulsory language course placements.

Nene College of Higher Education

The Academic Registrar, Park Campus, Boughton Green Road, Northampton, NN2 7AL

Tel: 01604 735500 Fax: 01604 720636
admissions@nene.ac.uk http://www.nene.ac.uk

N14

Datafile

1996-97 Student Numbers

Total number of all students   9658

	Degree	HND
Total FT/SW undergraduate numbers	5808	915
Percentages of these		
– on sandwich programmes	9	3
– mature students	28	22
– international students	1	1
– male/female	37/63	68/32

Full-time/sandwich students by academic subject category

	Degree	HND
Medicine, Dentistry, Vet Science		
Subjects Allied to Medicine	324	
Science	997	53
Engineering and Technology	248	142
Built Environment	44	90
Mathematical Sciences, IT & Computing	316	132
Business and Management	925	369
Social Sciences	802	
Humanities	648	
Art & Design and Perf Arts	761	129
Education	743	

Accommodation

Percentage of first years requiring accommodation who can be accommodated in institution-managed accommodation: 70%

Estimated weekly cost of institution-managed accommodation for 40 weeks:

(including dinner and breakfast   days per week) £

(no food) $40.00 – $50.00

(other…) £

Overseas opportunities*

Number of students on a placement or study period abroad:

Compacts/Networks
Northampton Compact, Northamptonshire Local Students Partnership, National Recruitment Network.

Record of Achievement
Considered on an individual basis.

Interviewing
BA QTS & studio based Art courses will interview suitable applicants. Other courses will not normally interview.

Campus locations
Northampton.

Open Days
26 April 1997, 10 September 1997. April and September 1998.

*Excludes those on compulsory language course placements.

University of Newcastle Upon Tyne

Admissions Office, 10 Kensington Terrace, Newcastle upon Tyne, NE1 7RU

Tel: 0191 222 6138 Fax: 0191 222 6139
admissions-enquiries@ncl.ac.uk http://www.ncl.ac.uk

N21

Datafile

1996-97 Student Numbers

Total number of all students   11673

	Degree	HND
Total FT/SW undergraduate numbers	9689	
Percentages of these		
– on sandwich programmes	2	
– mature students	20	
– international students	6	
– male/female	54/46	

Full-time/sandwich students by academic subject category

	Degree	HND
Medicine, Dentistry, Vet Science	1178	
Subjects Allied to Medicine	219	
Science	2335	
Engineering and Technology	1315	
Built Environment	505	
Mathematical Sciences, IT & Computing	558	
Business and Management	456	
Social Sciences	1386	
Humanities	1467	
Art & Design and Perf Arts	270	
Education	1	

Accommodation

Percentage of first years requiring accommodation who can be accommodated in institution-managed accommodation:

Estimated weekly cost of institution-managed accommodation for 52 weeks:

(including dinner and breakfast 5 days per week) £55.20

(no food) £33.46

(other…) £

Overseas opportunities*

Number of students on a placement or study period abroad: 104

Compacts/Networks
None.

Record of Achievement
Candidates are welcome to bring RoA to interviews or Open Day.

Interviewing
Varies according to department.

Campus locations
Single city centre campus.

Open Days
Some departments organise instead of interviews. University also centrally organises Visit Days.

*Excludes those on compulsory language course placements.

Newcastle College

Admissions Officer, Rye Hill Campus, Scotswood Road, Newcastle upon Tyne, NE4 7SA

Tel: 0191 200 4110 Fax: 0191 272 4297
s.doughty@ncl.coll.ac.uk http://www.ncl-coll.ac.uk

N23

Datafile

1996-97 Student Numbers

Total number of all students   18000

	Degree	HND
Total FT/SW undergraduate numbers	15	1500
Percentages of these		
– on sandwich programmes		2
– mature students		30
– international students		3
– male/female	60/40	58/42

Full-time/sandwich students by academic subject category

	Degree	HND
Medicine, Dentistry, Vet Science		
Subjects Allied to Medicine		
Science		70
Engineering and Technology		30
Built Environment		
Mathematical Sciences, IT & Computing		100
Business and Management		400
Social Sciences		
Humanities		
Art & Design and Perf Arts	15	900
Education		

Accommodation

Percentage of first years requiring accommodation who can be accommodated in institution-managed accommodation: 20%

Estimated weekly cost of institution-managed accommodation for 43 weeks:

(including dinner and breakfast days per week) £

(no food) £48.00

(other...) £

Overseas opportunities *

Number of students on a placement or study period abroad:

Compacts/Networks

Record of Achievement
Students are welcome to bring their RoA to interview.

Interviewing
Route B applicants interviewed and portfolio inspected. Other applicants may be interviewed.

Campus locations
Rye Hill Campus, Sandyford Campus, John Marley Centre, Waterloo House.

Open Days
HE Advice Day – date to be confirmed. HE Advice Week (Art & Design) in February. Contact College for details.

*Excludes those on compulsory language course placements.

New College Durham

Admissions Officer, New College Durham, Framwellgate Moor, Durham, DH1 5ES

Tel: 0191 375 4210 Fax: 0191 375 4222
admissions@newdur.ac.uk

N28

Datafile

1996-97 Student Numbers

Total number of all students   9243

	Degree	HND
Total FT/SW undergraduate numbers	228	464
Percentages of these		
– on sandwich programmes		7
– mature students	57	19
– international students	12	10
– male/female	30/70	41/59

Full-time/sandwich students by academic subject category

	Degree	HND
Medicine, Dentistry, Vet Science		
Subjects Allied to Medicine	228	
Science		
Engineering and Technology		19
Built Environment		
Mathematical Sciences, IT & Computing		
Business and Management		445
Social Sciences		
Humanities		
Art & Design and Perf Arts		
Education		

Accommodation

Percentage of first years requiring accommodation who can be accommodated in institution-managed accommodation: 100%

Estimated weekly cost of institution-managed accommodation for 36 weeks:

(including dinner and breakfast days per week) £

(no food) £21.25 – £32.50

(other...) £

Overseas opportunities *

Number of students on a placement or study period abroad: 20

Compacts/Networks
Close links with local schools.

Record of Achievement
Applicants encouraged to bring RoA.

Interviewing
All suitable applicants offered chance to attend Open Days and talk to staff.

Campus locations
Neville's Cross one mile from Durham city centre.

Open Days
To be arranged. Check with Admissions Officer on 0191 375 4210.

*Excludes those on compulsory language course placements.

Newham College of Further Education

Secretary, School of Art, Design & Fashion, Newham College of FE,
East Ham Campus, High Street South, London, E6 4ER

Tel: 0181 257 4204 Fax: 0181 257 4308

N31

Datafile

1996-97 Student Numbers

Total number of all students 14000

	Degree	HND
Total FT/SW undergraduate numbers		121
Percentages of these		
– on sandwich programmes		
– mature students		20
– international students		4
– male/female		70/30

Full-time/sandwich students by academic subject category

	Degree	HND
Medicine, Dentistry, Vet Science		
Subjects Allied to Medicine		
Science		
Engineering and Technology		
Built Environment		
Mathematical Sciences, IT & Computing		
Business and Management		
Social Sciences		
Humanities		
Art & Design and Perf Arts		121
Education		

Accommodation

There is no institution-managed accommodation. Students are
advised to contact the institution for information about local
accommodation options.

Overseas opportunities*

Number of students on a placement or study period abroad:

Compacts/Networks

Record of Achievement

Interviewing

All suitable applicants
interviewed (with portfolio of
work if considered
appropriate).

Campus locations

East Ham. Stratford.

Open Days

Open Days held January to March but enquiries welcomed
throughout academic year.

*Excludes those on compulsory language course placements.

Newman College of Higher Education

Admissions Registry, Newman College of HE, Genners Lane, Bartley
Green, Birmingham, B32 3NT

Tel: 0121 476 1181 Fax: 0121 476 1196
registry@newman.ac.uk www.newman.ac.uk

N36

Datafile

1996-97 Student Numbers

Total number of all students 1275

	Degree	HND
Total FT/SW undergraduate numbers	1030	
Percentages of these		
– on sandwich programmes		
– mature students	32	
– international students	4	
– male/female	25/75	

Full-time/sandwich students by academic subject category

	Degree	HND
Medicine, Dentistry, Vet Science		
Subjects Allied to Medicine		
Science	93	
Engineering and Technology		
Built Environment		
Mathematical Sciences, IT & Computing	5	
Business and Management		
Social Sciences	15	
Humanities	164	
Art & Design and Perf Arts	15	
Education	757	

Accommodation

Percentage of first years requiring accommodation who can be
accommodated in institution-managed accommodation: 90%

Estimated weekly cost of institution-managed accommodation
for 33 weeks:

(including dinner and breakfast 7 days per week) £55.00

(no food) £

(other…) £

Overseas opportunities*

Number of students on a placement or study period abroad:

Compacts/Networks

Compact students are assured
an interview.

Record of Achievement

Helpful if brought to interview.

Interviewing

All ITT offers made after
interview. Majority of joint
honours places offered after
interview.

Campus locations

Single site.

Open Days

20 September 1997, 6 May 1998. Also during November 1997.
Open morning for Access students.

*Excludes those on compulsory language course placements.

University of Wales College, Newport

University Information Centre, UWCN, Caerleon Campus, PO Box 101, Newport, NP6 1YH

Tel: 01633 432432 Fax:: 01633 432154
uic@newport.ac.uk   http://www.newport.ac.uk

Datafile

1996-97 Student Numbers

Total number of all students   8000

	Degree	HND
Total FT/SW undergraduate numbers	2205	395
Percentages of these		
– on sandwich programmes		
– mature students	21	66
– international students	1	37
– male/female	47/53	49/51

Full-time/sandwich students by academic subject category

	Degree	HND
Medicine, Dentistry, Vet Science		
Subjects Allied to Medicine	129	
Science	76	
Engineering and Technology	34	79
Built Environment		
Mathematical Sciences, IT & Computing	124	148
Business and Management	205	166
Social Sciences		
Humanities	270	
Art & Design and Perf Arts	789	
Education	578	

Accommodation

Percentage of first years requiring accommodation who can be accommodated in institution-managed accommodation: 100%

Estimated weekly cost of institution-managed accommodation for 37 weeks:

(including dinner and breakfast   days per week) £

(no food) £44.00 – £50.00

(other...) £38.00 – £40.00

Overseas opportunities*

Number of students on a placement or study period abroad: 150

Compacts/Networks

Compacts with Gwent Tertiary College, Filton College & Loughborough College of Art & Design.

Record of Achievement

Accreditation of Prior Achievement (APA) system in place.

Interviewing

Interview for ITT courses and, often, Art & Design courses. Other courses depend on faculty policy.

Campus locations

Newport and Caerleon.

Open Days

There are normally six Visit Days per year. For details telephone Information Centre (01633 432432).

*Excludes those on compulsory language course placements.

The Norwich School of Art and Design

St George Street, Norwich NR3 1BB

Tel: 01603 610561 Fax: 01603 615728

Datafile

1996-97 Student Numbers

Total number of all students

	Degree	HND
Total FT/SW undergraduate numbers	554	86
Percentages of these		
– on sandwich programmes		
– mature students	63	41
– international students	2	
– male/female	41/59	48/52

Full-time/sandwich students by academic subject category

	Degree	HND
Medicine, Dentistry, Vet Science		
Subjects Allied to Medicine		
Science		
Engineering and Technology		
Built Environment		
Mathematical Sciences, IT & Computing		
Business and Management		
Social Sciences		
Humanities		
Art & Design and Perf Arts	554	86
Education		

Accommodation

Percentage of first years requiring accommodation who can be accommodated in institution-managed accommodation: 59%

Estimated weekly cost of institution-managed accommodation for 41 weeks:

(including dinner and breakfast   days per week) £

(no food) £40.00

(other...) £

Overseas opportunities*

Number of students on a placement or study period abroad: 28

Compacts/Networks

Record of Achievement

Interviewing

Contact the School.

Campus locations

Open Days

Contact the School.

*Excludes those on compulsory language course placements.

Letts STUDY GUIDES
THE INDEPENDENT

Northbrook College Sussex

Admissions Office, Littlehampton Road, Worthing, West Sussex, BN12 6NU

Tel: 01903 830057 Fax: 01903 265303
admissions@ubcol.ac.uk http://www.ubcol.ac.uk

N41

Datafile

1996-97 Student Numbers

Total number of all students   8000

	Degree	HND
Total FT/SW undergraduate numbers	110	424
Percentages of these		
– on sandwich programmes		
– mature students	25	20
– international students	7	7
– male/female	50/50	60/40

Full-time/sandwich students by academic subject category

	Degree	HND
Medicine, Dentistry, Vet Science		
Subjects Allied to Medicine		
Science		
Engineering and Technology		54
Built Environment		
Mathematical Sciences, IT & Computing		30
Business and Management		100
Social Sciences		
Humanities		
Art & Design and Perf Arts	110	240
Education		

Accommodation

There is no institution-managed accommodation. Students are advised to contact the institution for information about local accommodation options.

Overseas opportunities*

Number of students on a placement or study period abroad: 12

Compacts/Networks   Record of Achievement

Interviewing

All intending applicants are interviewed by course team member(s).

Campus locations

Worthing (three sites), Shoreham Airport.

Open Days

Please telephone for dates. No appointment necessary.

Excludes those on compulsory language course placements.

Nescot

Admissions Unit, Reigate Road, Ewell, Surrey, KT17 3DS

Tel: 0181 394 1731 Fax: 0181 394 3030
lclewlow@nescot.ac.uk

N49

Datafile

1996-97 Student Numbers

Total number of all students   5400

	Degree	HND
Total FT/SW undergraduate numbers	364	433
Percentages of these		
– on sandwich programmes	2	13
– mature students	52	23
– international students	1	8
– male/female	50/50	68/32

Full-time/sandwich students by academic subject category

	Degree	HND
Medicine, Dentistry, Vet Science		
Subjects Allied to Medicine	110	
Science	114	84
Engineering and Technology		
Built Environment	18	57
Mathematical Sciences, IT & Computing	58	73
Business and Management	64	108
Social Sciences		
Humanities		
Art & Design and Perf Arts		110
Education		

Accommodation

Percentage of first years requiring accommodation who can be accommodated in institution-managed accommodation: 2%

Estimated weekly cost of institution-managed accommodation for 50 weeks:

(including dinner and breakfast   days per week) £

(no food) £50.00

(other…) £

Overseas opportunities*

Number of students on a placement or study period abroad: 8

Compacts/Networks   Record of Achievement

Students applying through the Surrey HE Compact are guaranteed interviews.

Interviewing

Varies according to department.

Campus locations

Open Days

Telephone to arrange visits.

Excludes those on compulsory language course placements.

The North East Wales Institute of Higher Education

Admissions, NEWI, Plas Coch, Mold Road, Wrexham, LL11 2AW

Tel: 01978 290666 Fax: 01978 290008
k.mitchell@newi.ac.uk

Datafile

1996-97 Student Numbers

Total number of all students   4200

	Degree	HND
Total FT/SW undergraduate numbers	1721	538
Percentages of these		
– on sandwich programmes		
– mature students	20	25
– international students	5	5
– male/female	40/60	70/30

Full-time/sandwich students by academic subject category

	Degree	HND
Medicine, Dentistry, Vet Science		
Subjects Allied to Medicine	250	
Science	118	64
Engineering and Technology	123	109
Built Environment	115	59
Mathematical Sciences, IT & Computing	148	109
Business and Management	165	102
Social Sciences		
Humanities	184	
Art & Design and Perf Arts	230	95
Education	388	

Accommodation

Percentage of first years requiring accommodation who can be accommodated in institution-managed accommodation: 90%

Estimated weekly cost of institution-managed accommodation for weeks:

(including dinner and breakfast   days per week) £

(no food) £40.00 – £50.00

(other...) £

Overseas opportunities*

Number of students on a placement or study period abroad:

Compacts/Networks
Wirral Post 16 Compact Scheme.

Record of Achievement
Where available RoAs should be brought to interview.

Interviewing
All applicants, where practical, are interviewed or offered the opportunity to visit.

Campus locations
Wrexham.

Open Days
Visits can be arranged at most times by contacting Admissions.

Excludes those on compulsory language course placements.

North East Worcestershire College

Admissions, Peakman Street, Redditch, Worcs, B98 8DW

Tel: 01527 570020 Fax: 01527 572901

Datafile

1996-97 Student Numbers

Total number of all students   9624

	Degree	HND
Total FT/SW undergraduate numbers		
Percentages of these		255
– on sandwich programmes		
– mature students		45
– international students		3
– male/female		65/35

Full-time/sandwich students by academic subject category

	Degree	HND
Medicine, Dentistry, Vet Science		
Subjects Allied to Medicine		
Science		
Engineering and Technology		18
Built Environment		
Mathematical Sciences, IT & Computing		23
Business and Management		96
Social Sciences		11
Humanities		
Art & Design and Perf Arts		107
Education		

Accommodation

There is no institution-managed accommodation. Students are advised to contact the institution for information about local accommodation options.

Overseas opportunities*

Number of students on a placement or study period abroad:

Compacts/Networks

Record of Achievement
If applicants have RoAs they will be considered as part of the admissions process.

Interviewing

Campus locations
New college is based on two campuses in the heart of England close to Birmingham.

Open Days
Held in Autumn & Winter. Visits arranged at any time by appointment. Information Office 01527 572522/3.

Excludes those on compulsory language course placements.

Northern College

Assistant Secretary (Registry), Aberdeen Campus, Northern College, Hilton Place, Aberdeen, AB24 4FA

Tel: 01224 283500 Fax: 01224 283900

N60

Datafile

1996-97 Student Numbers

Total number of all students   1202

	Degree	HND
Total FT/SW undergraduate numbers	870	
Percentages of these		
– on sandwich programmes		
– mature students	19	
– international students		
– male/female	13/87	

Full-time/sandwich students by academic subject category

	Degree	HND
Medicine, Dentistry, Vet Science		
Subjects Allied to Medicine		
Science		
Engineering and Technology		
Built Environment		
Mathematical Sciences, IT & Computing		
Business and Management		
Social Sciences		
Humanities		
Art & Design and Perf Arts		
Education	870	

Accommodation

Percentage of first years requiring accommodation who can be accommodated in institution-managed accommodation: 100%

Estimated weekly cost of institution-managed accommodation for 37 weeks:

(including dinner and breakfast 5 days per week) £60.50

(no food) £42.00

(other...) £

Overseas opportunities*

Number of students on a placement or study period abroad:

Compacts/Networks

Record of Achievement

Interviewing

Selected applicants are interviewed before offers made.

Campus locations

Aberdeen and Dundee.

Open Days

To be announced.

*Excludes those on compulsory language course placements.

North Lincolnshire College

Registry, North Lincolnshire College, Monks Road, Lincoln, LN2 5HQ

Tel: 01522 510530 Fax: 01522 512930

N62

Datafile

1996-97 Student Numbers

Total number of all students   8750

	Degree	HND
Total FT/SW undergraduate numbers	236	179
Percentages of these		
– on sandwich programmes		
– mature students	53	24
– international students	1	
– male/female	64/36	67/33

Full-time/sandwich students by academic subject category

	Degree	HND
Medicine, Dentistry, Vet Science		
Subjects Allied to Medicine		
Science		
Engineering and Technology		12
Built Environment		
Mathematical Sciences, IT & Computing	29	26
Business and Management		40
Social Sciences	43	
Humanities		
Art & Design and Perf Arts		
Education	164	101

Accommodation

Percentage of first years requiring accommodation who can be accommodated in institution-managed accommodation: 100%

Estimated weekly cost of institution-managed accommodation for 38 weeks:

(including dinner and breakfast days per week) £

(no food) £42.50

(other...) £

Overseas opportunities*

Number of students on a placement or study period abroad:

Compacts/Networks

Member of NE Access Partnership (NEMAP), Access & Music Courses validated by Open College Networks.

Record of Achievement

RoA welcome at interview and its continuation is supported by College.

Interviewing

Interview arrangements vary according to programme.

Campus locations

Park Street Centre for DipSW. Monks Road site for all other HE programmes.

Open Days

Open Days for specific HE programmes are normally held during the Spring Term.

*Excludes those on compulsory language course placements.

University of North London

Admissions, 166-220 Holloway Road, London, N7 8DB

Tel: 0171 753 3355 Fax: 0171 753 3272
admissions@unl.ac.uk http://www.unl.ac.uk/

N63

Datafile

1996-97 Student Numbers

Total number of all students   13030

	Degree	HND
Total FT/SW undergraduate numbers	7398	765
Percentages of these		
– on sandwich programmes	15	15
– mature students	66	48
– international students	10	5
– male/female	44/56	56/44

Full-time/sandwich students by academic subject category

	Degree	HND
Medicine, Dentistry, Vet Science		
Subjects Allied to Medicine	540	
Science	903	36
Engineering and Technology	421	49
Built Environment	128	
Mathematical Sciences, IT & Computing	748	94
Business and Management	1954	586
Social Sciences	786	
Humanities	1471	
Art & Design and Perf Arts	373	
Education	74	

Accommodation

Percentage of first years requiring accommodation who can be accommodated in institution-managed accommodation: 8%

Estimated weekly cost of institution-managed accommodation for 38 weeks:

(including 1 meal 5 days per week) £64.00

(no food) £54.00

(other...) £

Overseas opportunities*

Number of students on a placement or study period abroad: 300

Compacts/Networks

Compact Partnerships with a number of schools and colleges, to enhance degree/diploma opportunities.

Record of Achievement

London Compact Scheme students requested to maintain RoA.

Interviewing

Practice varies according to subject.

Campus locations

Islington. Highbury.

Open Days

To be announced. Telephone 0171 753 3355 for information.

*Excludes those on compulsory language course placements.

University of Northumbria at Newcastle

Admissions, Student Administration Office, Ellison Building, Ellison Place, Newcastle upon Tyne, NE1 8ST

Tel: 0191 227 4064 Fax: 0191 227 3009
rg.admissions@unn.ac.uk http://www.unn.ac.uk

N77

Datafile

1996-97 Student Numbers

Total number of all students

	Degree	HND
Total FT/SW undergraduate numbers	10028	874
Percentages of these		
– on sandwich programmes	39	17
– mature students	51	31
– international students	7	2
– male/female	50/50	70/30

Full-time/sandwich students by academic subject category

	Degree	HND
Medicine, Dentistry, Vet Science		
Subjects Allied to Medicine	568	
Science	1196	34
Engineering and Technology	779	109
Built Environment	922	119
Mathematical Sciences, IT & Computing	943	205
Business and Management	2064	407
Social Sciences	1245	
Humanities	525	
Art & Design and Perf Arts	1301	
Education	485	

Accommodation

Percentage of first years requiring accommodation who can be accommodated in institution-managed accommodation: 90%

Estimated weekly cost of institution-managed accommodation for 32-46 weeks:

(including dinner and breakfast 7 days per week) £63.00

(no food) £39.00 – £41.00

(other...) £49.50

Overseas opportunities*

Number of students on a placement or study period abroad: 224

Compacts/Networks

Record of Achievement

Applicants may bring RoAs to interview.

Interviewing

Varies according to department. Applicants not invited to interview are invited to Open Days.

Campus locations

Newcastle City, Coach Lane (Newcastle suburb), Carlisle, Longhirst, Morpeth, Northumberland.

Open Days

7 May 1997. Campus tour second Wednesday of most months. Bookings and details 0191 227 4265.

*Excludes those on compulsory language course placements.

Northumberland College

Advice Centre, Northumberland College, College Road, Ashington, Northumberland, NE63 9RG

Tel: 01670 841200 Fax: 01670 841201

Datafile

1996-97 Student Numbers

Total number of all students

	Degree	HND
Total FT/SW undergraduate numbers		45
Percentages of these		
– on sandwich programmes		
– mature students		2
– international students		
– male/female		60/40

Full-time/sandwich students by academic subject category

	Degree	HND
Medicine, Dentistry, Vet Science		
Subjects Allied to Medicine		
Science		
Engineering and Technology		
Built Environment		
Mathematical Sciences, IT & Computing		
Business and Management		
Social Sciences		
Humanities		
Art & Design and Perf Arts		45
Education		

Accommodation

Percentage of first years requiring accommodation who can be accommodated in institution-managed accommodation: 100%

Estimated weekly cost of institution-managed accommodation for 35 weeks:

(including dinner and breakfast   days per week) £

(no food) £35.00

(other…) £

Overseas opportunities*

Number of students on a placement or study period abroad:

Compacts/Networks

Record of Achievement

Interviewing

Campus locations
Single site.

Open Days

Visits available during normal College working hours by prior arrangement.

*Excludes those on compulsory language course placements.

North Warwickshire and Hinckley College

Manager - Guidance Unit, Hinckley Road, Nuneaton, Warwickshire, CU11 6BH

Tel: 01203 349321 Fax: 01203 329056

Datafile

1996-97 Student Numbers

Total number of all students   20000

	Degree	HND
Total FT/SW undergraduate numbers	67	68
Percentages of these		
– on sandwich programmes		
– mature students	61	40
– international students		
– male/female	57/43	53/47

Full-time/sandwich students by academic subject category

	Degree	HND
Medicine, Dentistry, Vet Science		
Subjects Allied to Medicine		
Science		
Engineering and Technology	16	
Built Environment		
Mathematical Sciences, IT & Computing	27	
Business and Management		
Social Sciences	24	
Humanities		
Art & Design and Perf Arts		68
Education		

Accommodation

There is no institution-managed accommodation. Students are advised to contact the institution for information about local accommodation options.

Overseas opportunities*

Number of students on a placement or study period abroad:

Compacts/Networks
Associate College of Universities of Warwick and Coventry and Member of Central Access Network.

Record of Achievement
Requested at interview.

Interviewing
All applicants are interviewed.

Campus locations
Nuneaton and Hinckley.

Open Days

Visits by arrangement.

*Excludes those on compulsory language course placements.

Norwich City College

Registry, Ipswich Road, Norwich, Norfolk, NR2 2LJ

Tel: 01603 773136 Fax: 01603 773334

Datafile

1996-97 Student Numbers

Total number of all students   18194

	Degree	HND
Total FT/SW undergraduate numbers	448	530
Percentages of these		
– on sandwich programmes	19	35
– mature students	52	30
– international students	7	1
– male/female	37/63	63/37

Full-time/sandwich students by academic subject category

	Degree	HND
Medicine, Dentistry, Vet Science		
Subjects Allied to Medicine		
Science	69	
Engineering and Technology		93
Built Environment		
Mathematical Sciences, IT & Computing	49	123
Business and Management	206	305
Social Sciences		
Humanities	92	
Art & Design and Perf Arts		
Education		

Accommodation

Percentage of first years requiring accommodation who can be accommodated in institution-managed accommodation: 100%

Estimated weekly cost of institution-managed accommodation for 36 weeks:

(including dinner and breakfast   days per week) £

(no food) £36.25

(other...) £

Overseas opportunities*

Number of students on a placement or study period abroad: 18

Compacts/Networks

Partner in Anglia Polytechnic University Compact Scheme. Scheme students may get lower points offer.

Record of Achievement

If RoA available it will be considered as part of the admissions process.

Interviewing

We try to interview all applicants but may make offers before interview and visit to the College.

Campus locations

One site which is ten minutes walk away from Norwich city centre.

Open Days

14 November 1997 1pm-8pm and 15 November 1997 10am-1pm.

Excludes those on compulsory language course placements.

The University of Nottingham

Admissions & Schools Liaison Office, Registrars Department, The University of Nottingham, Trent Building, University Park, Nottingham, NG7 2RD

Tel: 0115 951 5756 Fax: 0115 951 5795
http://www.nottingham.ac.uk

Datafile

1996-97 Student Numbers

Total number of all students   21600

	Degree	HND
Total FT/SW undergraduate numbers	9800	
Percentages of these		
– on sandwich programmes		
– mature students	11	
– international students	9	
– male/female	55/45	

Full-time/sandwich students by academic subject category

	Degree	HND
Medicine, Dentistry, Vet Science	850	
Subjects Allied to Medicine	300	
Science	2460	
Engineering and Technology	1600	
Built Environment	380	
Mathematical Sciences, IT & Computing	660	
Business and Management	270	
Social Sciences	1430	
Humanities	1740	
Art & Design and Perf Arts	60	
Education	50	

Accommodation

Percentage of first years requiring accommodation who can be accommodated in institution-managed accommodation: 100%

Estimated weekly cost of institution-managed accommodation for 30-44 weeks:

(including dinner and breakfast 7 days per week) £69.60

(no food) £32.00

(other...) £

Overseas opportunities*

Number of students on a placement or study period abroad: 100

Compacts/Networks

Member of NE Midlands Access Partnership (NEMAP), Part of OCN, Member of TRAK 14-20 Compact.

Record of Achievement

Only to be submitted if requested.

Interviewing

Policy varies: some departments interview before offers eg. Medicine. Check prospectus for details.

Campus locations

University Park, Nottingham. Sutton Bonington Campus.

Open Days

Annual Open Day on 30 June 1997. Recommend booking in advance. 29 June 1998 (provisional).

Excludes those on compulsory language course placements.

The Nottingham Trent University

The Registry, The Nottingham Trent University, Burton Street, Nottingham, NG1 4BU

Tel: 0115 941 8418 Fax: 0115 948 6063

N91

Oxford University

Oxford College Admissions Office, University Offices, Wellington Square, Oxford, OX1 2JD

Tel: 01865 270207 Fax: 01865 270708
undergraduate.admissions@admin.ox.ac.uk

O33

Datafile

1996-97 Student Numbers

Total number of all students   23689

	Degree	HND
Total FT/SW undergraduate numbers	15518	2302
Percentages of these		
– on sandwich programmes	44	41
– mature students	18	17
– international students	3	2
– male/female	54/46	67/33

Full-time/sandwich students by academic subject category

	Degree	HND
Medicine, Dentistry, Vet Science		
Subjects Allied to Medicine	478	
Science	1606	610
Engineering and Technology	2145	594
Built Environment	1107	256
Mathematical Sciences, IT & Computing	1131	330
Business and Management	1696	512
Social Sciences	2162	
Humanities	1858	
Art & Design and Perf Arts	2249	
Education	1086	

Accommodation

Percentage of first years requiring accommodation who can be accommodated in institution-managed accommodation: 65%

Estimated weekly cost of institution-managed accommodation for 32 weeks:

(including dinner and breakfast 5 days per week) £65.00

(no food) £48.51

(other…) £35.42

Overseas opportunities*

Number of students on a placement or study period abroad: 200

Compacts/Networks

Individual arrangements with schools & colleges. Contact Access Coordinator 0115 9418418 ext 2340.

Record of Achievement

Applicants should bring RoA if invited to interview. May be used as a basis for discussion.

Interviewing

Each faculty has own policy regarding interviews. Most interview mature/non-standard applicants.

Campus locations

Main campus in city centre and 2 campuses 4 miles away at Clifton. Franchised colleges throughout country.

Open Days

Contact relevant faculty direct for details. Liaison Service arrange visits (0115 948 6540).

*Excludes those on compulsory language course placements.

Datafile

1996-97 Student Numbers

Total number of all students   15420

	Degree	HND
Total FT/SW undergraduate numbers	10989	
Percentages of these		
– on sandwich programmes		
– mature students	2	
– international students	12	
– male/female	59/41	

Full-time/sandwich students by academic subject category

	Degree	HND
Medicine, Dentistry, Vet Science	613	
Subjects Allied to Medicine	73	
Science	2271	
Engineering and Technology	633	
Built Environment		
Mathematical Sciences, IT & Computing	770	
Business and Management	93	
Social Sciences	1959	
Humanities	4346	
Art & Design and Perf Arts	231	
Education		

Accommodation

Percentage of first years requiring accommodation who can be accommodated in institution-managed accommodation: 100%

Estimated weekly cost of institution-managed accommodation for 25 weeks:

(including 3 meals 7 days per week) £71.00

(no food) £43.47

(other…) £

Overseas opportunities*

Number of students on a placement or study period abroad: 95

Compacts/Networks

No Compacts/Networks.

Record of Achievement

Applicants are invited to bring their RoA if called for interview.

Interviewing

The majority of our applicants are interviewed.

Campus locations

Oxford City.

Open Days

Many Colleges/Depts Open Days first half of year. Science 1 & 2 July 1997. Details in prospectus.

*Excludes those on compulsory language course placements.

Oxford Westminster College

Registry, Westminster College, Oxford, OX2 9AT

Tel: 01865 247644 Fax: 01865 251847

registry@ox-west.ac.uk http://www.ox-west.ac.uk

O50

Datafile

1996-97 Student Numbers

Total number of all students   2337

	Degree	HND
Total FT/SW undergraduate numbers	870	
Percentages of these		
– on sandwich programmes		
– mature students	31	
– international students	6	
– male/female	16/84	

Full-time/sandwich students by academic subject category

	Degree	HND
Medicine, Dentistry, Vet Science		
Subjects Allied to Medicine		
Science		
Engineering and Technology		
Built Environment		
Mathematical Sciences, IT & Computing		
Business and Management		
Social Sciences		
Humanities	272	
Art & Design and Perf Arts		
Education	598	

Accommodation

Percentage of first years requiring accommodation who can be accommodated in institution-managed accommodation: 95%

Estimated weekly cost of institution-managed accommodation for 33 weeks:

(including dinner and breakfast 5 days per week) £60.00 – £70.00

(no food) £

(other…) £

Overseas opportunities*

Number of students on a placement or study period abroad: 27

Compacts/Networks

Record of Achievement

RoA required for undergraduates.

Interviewing

On-going during year whilst courses are open.

Campus locations

College site.

Open Days

18 June 1997, 29 August 1997, 1 October 1997.

Excludes those on compulsory language course placements.

Oxford Brookes University

Admissions Office, Oxford Brooks University, Gipsy Lane Campus, Headington, Oxford, Oxon, OX3 0BP

Tel: 01865 483040 Fax: 01865 483983

O66

Datafile

1996-97 Student Numbers

Total number of all students   11598

	Degree	HND
Total FT/SW undergraduate numbers	6954	85
Percentages of these		
– on sandwich programmes	25	55
– mature students	34	35
– international students	15	16
– male/female	44/56	95/5

Full-time/sandwich students by academic subject category

	Degree	HND
Medicine, Dentistry, Vet Science		
Subjects Allied to Medicine	1110	
Science	896	
Engineering and Technology	468	56
Built Environment	650	29
Mathematical Sciences, IT & Computing	978	
Business and Management	1235	
Social Sciences	293	
Humanities	724	
Art & Design and Perf Arts	189	
Education	411	

Accommodation

Percentage of first years requiring accommodation who can be accommodated in institution-managed accommodation: 85%

Estimated weekly cost of institution-managed accommodation for 42 weeks:

(including 12 meals   days per week) £66.10

(no food) £44.10

(other…) £

Overseas opportunities*

Number of students on a placement or study period abroad: 200

Compacts/Networks

Record of Achievement

Interviewing

Campus locations

Open Days

Please contact School & College Liaison Officer (01865 484887).

Excludes those on compulsory language course placements.

Oxfordshire School of Art and Design

Administrator, Oxfordshire School of Art & Design, Broughton Road, Banbury, Oxon, OX16 9QA

Tel: 01295 257979 Fax: 01295 250381
mikecobb@oxfe.ac.uk http://161.73.64.249/banbury/default.htm

O80

Datafile

1996-97 Student Numbers

Total number of all students   7000

	Degree	HND
Total FT/SW undergraduate numbers	60	150
Percentages of these		
– on sandwich programmes		
– mature students		4
– international students	1	5
– male/female	46/54	42/58

Full-time/sandwich students by academic subject category

	Degree	HND
Medicine, Dentistry, Vet Science		
Subjects Allied to Medicine		
Science		
Engineering and Technology		
Built Environment		
Mathematical Sciences, IT & Computing		
Business and Management		20
Social Sciences		
Humanities		
Art & Design and Perf Arts	60	130
Education		

Accommodation

There is no institution-managed accommodation. Students are advised to contact the institution for information about local accommodation options.

Overseas opportunities*

Number of students on a placement or study period abroad: 20

Compacts/Networks

Compacts exist with many colleges in the region.

Record of Achievement

RoAs are used throughout the College and as part of the admissions process.

Interviewing

Interviews from March onwards, with discussions centred on portfolios or showreels.

Campus locations

One campus in the centre of Banbury.

Open Days

22 February 1998, 26 February 1998 and 22 June 1998.

*Excludes those on compulsory language course placements.

University of Paisley

Admissions Office, University of Paisley, Paisley, PA1 2BE

Tel: 0141 848 3859 Fax: 0141 848 3623
fras-apo@paisley.ac.uk

P20

Datafile

1996-97 Student Numbers

Total number of all students   8786

	Degree	HND
Total FT/SW undergraduate numbers	5659	17
Percentages of these		
– on sandwich programmes	22	
– mature students	20	41
– international students	6	
– male/female	50/50	71/29

Full-time/sandwich students by academic subject category

	Degree	HND
Medicine, Dentistry, Vet Science		
Subjects Allied to Medicine	994	
Science	56	
Engineering and Technology	765	17
Built Environment		
Mathematical Sciences, IT & Computing	267	
Business and Management	1361	
Social Sciences	46	
Humanities	1593	
Art & Design and Perf Arts		
Education	377	

Accommodation

Percentage of first years requiring accommodation who can be accommodated in institution-managed accommodation: 65%

Estimated weekly cost of institution-managed accommodation for 31 weeks:

(including dinner and breakfast   days per week) £56.46

(no food) £24.20 – £31.84

(other…) £

Overseas opportunities*

Number of students on a placement or study period abroad:

Compacts/Networks

Record of Achievement

May be taken into account but would not replace essential qualifications for entry.

Interviewing

A number of departments interview applicants or hold informal information sessions.

Campus locations

Paisley and Ayr.

Open Days

Paisley - September (date to be confirmed). Ayr - September (date to be confirmed).

*Excludes those on compulsory language course placements.

University of Plymouth

Admissions Officer, University Registry, University of Plymouth, Drake Circus, Plymouth, Devon, PL4 8AA

Tel: 01752 232135 Fax: 01752 232141
ctodd@plymouth.ac.uk http://www.plym.ac.uk

P60

Datafile

1996-97 Student Numbers

Total number of all students

	Degree	HND
Total FT/SW undergraduate numbers	11758	2102
Percentages of these		
– on sandwich programmes	23	10
– mature students	35	32
– international students	6	4
– male/female	53/47	61/39

Full-time/sandwich students by academic subject category

	Degree	HND
Medicine, Dentistry, Vet Science		
Subjects Allied to Medicine	692	32
Science	3210	404
Engineering and Technology	1503	284
Built Environment	337	49
Mathematical Sciences, IT & Computing	783	72
Business and Management	1792	812
Social Sciences	1137	
Humanities	447	
Art & Design and Perf Arts	1059	449
Education	798	

Accommodation

Percentage of first years requiring accommodation who can be accommodated in institution-managed accommodation: 33%

Estimated weekly cost of institution-managed accommodation for 42 weeks:

(including dinner and breakfast   days per week) £

(no food) £30.10 – £39.20

(other...) £

Overseas opportunities*

Number of students on a placement or study period abroad: 280

Compacts/Networks

Progression Accord with regional schools, FE/HE Network across SW Peninsula and Channel Islands.

Record of Achievement

Not normally requested.

Interviewing

Some applicants will be called for interview, but this varies from programme to programme.

Campus locations

Plymouth, Exeter, Exmouth and Seale-Hayne.

Open Days

University-wide Open Day in June for students, parents and advisors. For details 01752 233985.

Excludes those on compulsory language course placements.

Plymouth College of Art and Design

Admissions Officer, Tavistock Place, Plymouth, Devon, PL4 8AT

Tel: 01752 203434 Fax: 01752 203444

P65

Datafile

1996-97 Student Numbers

Total number of all students   1310

	Degree	HND
Total FT/SW undergraduate numbers	14	284
Percentages of these		
– on sandwich programmes		
– mature students	43	51
– international students	7	
– male/female	64/36	55/45

Full-time/sandwich students by academic subject category

	Degree	HND
Medicine, Dentistry, Vet Science		
Subjects Allied to Medicine		
Science		
Engineering and Technology		
Built Environment		
Mathematical Sciences, IT & Computing		
Business and Management		
Social Sciences		
Humanities		
Art & Design and Perf Arts	14	284
Education		

Accommodation

There is no institution-managed accommodation. Students are advised to contact the institution for information about local accommodation options.

Overseas opportunities*

Number of students on a placement or study period abroad: 10

Compacts/Networks

Record of Achievement

Please bring with portfolio.

Interviewing

Normally it is College policy to interview all first choice applicants.

Campus locations

Within the city centre of Plymouth.

Open Days

November 1997, February and March 1998. Contact the College for further details.

Excludes those on compulsory language course placements.

University of Portsmouth

Admissions Office, University of Portsmouth, University House, Winston Churchill Avenue, Portsmouth, PO1 2UP

Tel: 01705 876543 Fax: 01705 843082
admissions@reg.port.ac.uk http://www.port.ac.uk

P80

Datafile

1996-97 Student Numbers

Total number of all students   16650

	Degree	HND
Total FT/SW undergraduate numbers	1244	760
Percentages of these		
– on sandwich programmes	17	
– mature students	25	
– international students	7	3
– male/female	52/48	

Full-time/sandwich students by academic subject category

	Degree	HND
Medicine, Dentistry, Vet Science		
Subjects Allied to Medicine	1222	
Science	1878	24
Engineering and Technology	1459	182
Built Environment	618	
Mathematical Sciences, IT & Computing	1197	242
Business and Management	1568	234
Social Sciences	2232	
Humanities	1218	
Art & Design and Perf Arts	670	78
Education	432	

Accommodation

Percentage of first years requiring accommodation who can be accommodated in institution-managed accommodation: 50%

Estimated weekly cost of institution-managed accommodation for 39 weeks:

(including dinner and breakfast 7 days per week) £60.00 – £65.00

(no food) £38.00 – £43.00

(other…) £

Overseas opportunities*

Number of students on a placement or study period abroad: 156

Compacts/Networks

Colleges: Portsmouth, Havant, St Vincent, Itchen. Hampshire Open College Path Network, (Tower Hamlets).

Record of Achievement

Bring RoA if invited for interview.

Interviewing

Applicants for Art, Design & Media, English & Creative Studies and Radiography are interviewed.

Campus locations

Portsmouth (three sites), Basingstoke, Guildford and Chichester.

Open Days

Open Days every Wednesday afternoon in Term time. Information Day 7 May 1997. For details contact College.

*Excludes those on compulsory language course placements.

Queen Margaret College, Edinburgh

Admissions Officer, Queen Margaret College, Clerwood Terrace, Edinburgh, Scotland, EH12 8TS

Tel: 0131 317 3247 Fax: 0131 317 3248

Q25

Datafile

1996-97 Student Numbers

Total number of all students   3224

	Degree	HND
Total FT/SW undergraduate numbers	2375	
Percentages of these		
– on sandwich programmes		
– mature students	30	
– international students	9	
– male/female	20/80	

Full-time/sandwich students by academic subject category

	Degree	HND
Medicine, Dentistry, Vet Science		
Subjects Allied to Medicine	1164	
Science	97	
Engineering and Technology		
Built Environment		
Mathematical Sciences, IT & Computing		
Business and Management	678	
Social Sciences		
Humanities	272	
Art & Design and Perf Arts	164	
Education		

Accommodation

Percentage of first years requiring accommodation who can be accommodated in institution-managed accommodation: 70%

Estimated weekly cost of institution-managed accommodation for 38 weeks:

(including dinner and breakfast 5 days per week) £61.70

(no food) £37.79

(other…) £47.24

Overseas opportunities*

Number of students on a placement or study period abroad: 20

Compacts/Networks

Record of Achievement

Interviewing

Selection procedures vary according to course. Some courses, particularly Health Care, interview.

Campus locations

Corstorphine, Leith and the Gateway Theatre which are all in Edinburgh.

Open Days

The annual College Open Day is normally held in September.

*Excludes those on compulsory language course placements.

Queen Mary and Westfield College (University of London)

Admissions Office, Queen Mary & Westfield College, Mile End Road, London, E1 4NS

Tel: 0171 975 5511 Fax: 0171 975 5588
admissions@qmw.ac.uk http://www.qmw.ac.uk

Q50

Datafile

1996-97 Student Numbers
Total number of all students   7940

	Degree	HND
Total FT/SW undergraduate numbers	6390	
Percentages of these		
– on sandwich programmes		
– mature students	19	
– international students	17	
– male/female	56/44	

Full-time/sandwich students by academic subject category

	Degree	HND
Medicine, Dentistry, Vet Science	1410	
Subjects Allied to Medicine	110	
Science	1050	
Engineering and Technology	810	
Built Environment		
Mathematical Sciences, IT & Computing	600	
Business and Management	70	
Social Sciences	1100	
Humanities	1170	
Art & Design and Perf Arts	70	
Education		

Accommodation
Percentage of first years requiring accommodation who can be accommodated in institution-managed accommodation: 95%

Estimated weekly cost of institution-managed accommodation for 31-38 weeks:

(including dinner and breakfast   days per week) $69.99

(no food) $57.00

(other...) $55.00

Overseas opportunities*
Number of students on a placement or study period abroad: 75

Compacts/Networks
Essex & Havering VI Form College Consortium, Hackney Compact Scheme S (Tower Hamlets), Redbridge HE Compact.

Record of Achievement
Departments will request RoAs if required by admissions tutors.

Interviewing
Departmental policy varies. Mile End (Main campus); Medicine and Dentistry also taught at Whitechapel, Charterhouse Square.

Campus locations

Open Days
Campus Tours 0171 775 3064. Queen Mary participates in the University of London Open Day. Some Departments offer Open Days.

Excludes those on compulsory language course placements.

The Queen's University of Belfast

Admissions Officer, Admissions Office, Queen's University, Belfast, BT7 1NN

Tel: 01232 245133 Fax: 01232 247895
s.wisener@qub.ac.uk http://web.qub.ac.uk

Q75

Datafile

1996-97 Student Numbers
Total number of all students

	Degree	HND
Total FT/SW undergraduate numbers	9199	
Percentages of these		
– on sandwich programmes	3	
– mature students	12	
– international students	11	
– male/female	49/51	

Full-time/sandwich students by academic subject category

	Degree	HND
Medicine, Dentistry, Vet Science	904	
Subjects Allied to Medicine	194	
Science	1894	
Engineering and Technology	1182	
Built Environment	192	
Mathematical Sciences, IT & Computing	879	
Business and Management	530	
Social Sciences	1717	
Humanities	1645	
Art & Design and Perf Arts	62	
Education		

Accommodation
Percentage of first years requiring accommodation who can be accommodated in institution-managed accommodation: 88%

Estimated weekly cost of institution-managed accommodation for 32-38 weeks:

(including dinner and breakfast 7 days per week) $55.50

(no food) $50.41

(other...) $37.00

Overseas opportunities*
Number of students on a placement or study period abroad: 150

Compacts/Networks
No official Compacts.

Record of Achievement
Some selectors may ask to see applicants' RoA.

Interviewing
Occasionally applicants to certain courses may be called for interviews.

Campus locations
Belfast (one site).

Open Days
4 & 5 September 1997. Specific department Open Days for invited applicants December - March.

Excludes those on compulsory language course placements.

Letts STUDY GUIDES
THE INDEPENDENT

Ravensbourne College of Design and Communication

Assistant Registrar Admissions, Ravensbourne College of Design & Communication, Walden Road, Chislehurst, Kent, BR7 5SN

Tel: 0181 289 4907 Fax: 0181 325 8320

R06

Reading College and School of Art and Design

Information & Guidance, Crescent Road, Reading, Berks, RG1 5RQ

Tel: 0118 9675555 Fax: 0118 9675001

R10

Datafile

1996-97 Student Numbers

Total number of all students   730

	Degree	HND
Total FT/SW undergraduate numbers	450	130
Percentages of these		
– on sandwich programmes		
– mature students	22	13
– international students	4	1
– male/female	60/40	66/34

Full-time/sandwich students by academic subject category

	Degree	HND
Medicine, Dentistry, Vet Science		
Subjects Allied to Medicine		
Science		
Engineering and Technology	20	130
Built Environment		
Mathematical Sciences, IT & Computing		
Business and Management		
Social Sciences		
Humanities		
Art & Design and Perf Arts	430	
Education		

Accommodation

Percentage of first years requiring accommodation who can be accommodated in institution-managed accommodation: 50%

Estimated weekly cost of institution-managed accommodation for 15 weeks:

(including dinner and breakfast days per week) £

(no food) £53.00

(other...) £

Overseas opportunities*

Number of students on a placement or study period abroad: 6

Compacts/Networks

Record of Achievement

Will be taken into account together with evidence of motivation, ability and academic worth.

Interviewing

Practice varies among courses - a very high proportion are interviewed.

Campus locations

Single site in Chislehurst, Kent.

Open Days

All courses have Open Days which welcome potential applicants - details on request.

*Excludes those on compulsory language course placements.

Datafile

1996-97 Student Numbers

Total number of all students   10000

	Degree	HND
Total FT/SW undergraduate numbers	25	334
Percentages of these		
– on sandwich programmes		
– mature students	26	15
– international students		1
– male/female	63/37	59/41

Full-time/sandwich students by academic subject category

	Degree	HND
Medicine, Dentistry, Vet Science		
Subjects Allied to Medicine		
Science		
Engineering and Technology		33
Built Environment		
Mathematical Sciences, IT & Computing		40
Business and Management		70
Social Sciences		
Humanities		
Art & Design and Perf Arts	25	227
Education		

Accommodation

There is no institution-managed accommodation. Students are advised to contact the institution for information about local accommodation options.

Overseas opportunities*

Number of students on a placement or study period abroad:

Compacts/Networks

Compacts: Reading University, Oxford Brooks University, Lincolnshire & Humberside University.

Record of Achievement

The College values RoAs as indicators of past success and future potential.

Interviewing

Campus locations

Kings Road, Wokingham Road, Reading. Raymond Road, Maidenhead.

Open Days

Information Guidance Centres (all 3 campuses):
Mon-Thurs 0830-1900, Friday 0930-1630, (Kings Rd) Saturday 0930-1230.

*Excludes those on compulsory language course placements.

The University of Reading

Schools & Colleges Liaison Office, The University of Reading, PO Box 217, Reading, RG6 2AH

Tel: 0118 987 5123 Fax: 0118 931 4404
ug-prospectus@reading.ac.uk www.reading.ac.uk/UG

R12

Datafile

1996-97 Student Numbers

Total number of all students   13061

	Degree	HND
Total FT/SW undergraduate numbers	7701	
Percentages of these		
– on sandwich programmes		
– mature students	25	
– international students	15	
– male/female	45/55	

Full-time/sandwich students by academic subject category

	Degree	HND
Medicine, Dentistry, Vet Science		
Subjects Allied to Medicine	311	
Science	1770	
Engineering and Technology	410	
Built Environment	239	
Mathematical Sciences, IT & Computing	372	
Business and Management	467	
Social Sciences	1019	
Humanities	1577	
Art & Design and Perf Arts	375	
Education	635	

Accommodation

Percentage of first years requiring accommodation who can be accommodated in institution-managed accommodation: 97%

Estimated weekly cost of institution-managed accommodation for 30 weeks:

(including 19 meals per week) £73.00

(no food) £40.50

(other...) £

Overseas opportunities*

Number of students on a placement or study period abroad: 75

Compacts/Networks

A Compact exists with several schools in the surrounding area.

Record of Achievement

RoA may be requested from applicants.

Interviewing

Some departments use selection interviews but most decide from the application form.

Campus locations

Main Whiteknights campus (most subjects) and nearby the Faculty of Education & Community Studies.

Open Days

27 June 1997, 28 June 1997, 26 June 1998 and 27 June 1998.

*Excludes those on compulsory language course placements.

University College of Ripon and York St John

Admissions Registry, Lord Mayor's Walk, York, YO3 7EX

Tel: 01904 616850 Fax: 01904 616921
l.waghorn@ucrysj.ac.uk http://www/ucrysj.ac.uk

R24

Datafile

1996-97 Student Numbers

Total number of all students   3993

	Degree	HND
Total FT/SW undergraduate numbers	3094	
Percentages of these		
– on sandwich programmes		
– mature students	23	
– international students	5	
– male/female	34/66	

Full-time/sandwich students by academic subject category

	Degree	HND
Medicine, Dentistry, Vet Science		
Subjects Allied to Medicine	209	
Science	75	
Engineering and Technology		
Built Environment		
Mathematical Sciences, IT & Computing	44	
Business and Management	222	
Social Sciences	327	
Humanities	799	
Art & Design and Perf Arts	620	
Education	798	

Accommodation

Percentage of first years requiring accommodation who can be accommodated in institution-managed accommodation: 85%

Estimated weekly cost of institution-managed accommodation for 31 weeks:

(including 3 meals 7 days per week) £62.00 – £69.10

(no food) £39.00 – £41.00

(other...) £

Overseas opportunities*

Number of students on a placement or study period abroad: 90

Compacts/Networks

Thomas Danby College, Askham Bryan College, links with FE providers, in York, Selby, Harrogate.

Record of Achievement

Applicants may be asked to bring RoA to interview.

Interviewing

OT, ITT and mature students interviewed. Film, TV, Theatre, Art & Design are extensively interviewed.

Campus locations

York and Ripon.

Open Days

Please see prospectus. Usually two Wednesdays a month in December, February, March and May.

*Excludes those on compulsory language course placements.

The Robert Gordon University

The Admissions Office, The Robert Gordon University, Schoolhill, Aberdeen, Scotland, AB10 1FR

Tel: 01224 262105 Fax: 01224 262133
j.youngson@rgu.ac.uk

R36

Datafile

1996-97 Student Numbers

Total number of all students   6097

	Degree	HND
Total FT/SW undergraduate numbers	5173	434
Percentages of these		
– on sandwich programmes	24	
– mature students	20	20
– international students	5	1
– male/female	49/51	88/12

Full-time/sandwich students by academic subject category

	Degree	HND
Medicine, Dentistry, Vet Science		
Subjects Allied to Medicine	988	44
Science	357	86
Engineering and Technology	606	91
Built Environment	546	102
Mathematical Sciences, IT & Computing	372	76
Business and Management	1573	79
Social Sciences		
Humanities	288	
Art & Design and Perf Arts	438	
Education	5	

Accommodation

Percentage of first years requiring accommodation who can be accommodated in institution-managed accommodation: 100%

Estimated weekly cost of institution-managed accommodation for 34-36 weeks:

(including dinner and breakfast 7 days per week) £52.00 – £57.00

(no food) £42.50 – £58.00

(other...) £

Overseas opportunities*

Number of students on a placement or study period abroad:

Compacts/Networks

Record of Achievement

Interviewing

As most applicants attend Open/Selection Days, only a minority are interviewed.

Campus locations

Eight campuses throughout the city.

Open Days

3 October 1998. Open/Visit days are held for most courses from February to April for all applicants.

*Excludes those on compulsory language course placements.

Roehampton Institute London

Admissions Office, Roehampton Institute, Roehampton Lane, London, SW15 5PU

Tel: 0181 392 3000 Fax: 0181 392 3220
admissions@roehampton.ac.uk

R48

Datafile

1996-97 Student Numbers

Total number of all students   6500

	Degree	HND
Total FT/SW undergraduate numbers	4678	
Percentages of these		
– on sandwich programmes		
– mature students	35	
– international students	2	
– male/female	25/75	

Full-time/sandwich students by academic subject category

	Degree	HND
Medicine, Dentistry, Vet Science		
Subjects Allied to Medicine	106	
Science	630	
Engineering and Technology	101	
Built Environment		
Mathematical Sciences, IT & Computing	68	
Business and Management	324	
Social Sciences	549	
Humanities	945	
Art & Design and Perf Arts	632	
Education	1323	

Accommodation

Percentage of first years requiring accommodation who can be accommodated in institution-managed accommodation: 60%

Estimated weekly cost of institution-managed accommodation for 36 weeks:

(including 12 meals days per week) £70.00

(no food) £58.00

(other...) £63.00

Overseas opportunities*

Number of students on a placement or study period abroad: 80

Compacts/Networks

Surrey HE Compact, Surrey and South West London Access Agency.

Record of Achievement

Considered on an individual basis.

Interviewing

See individual subject entries in prospectus. All applicants for ITT, Art & Dance are interviewed.

Campus locations

Digby Stuart College, Froebel College, Southlands College and Whitelands College.

Open Days

All provisional: 21 May, 22 July, 8 & 25 Oct, 12 Nov 1997. 18 Feb, 18 March, 29 April, 20 May 1998.

*Excludes those on compulsory language course placements.

Rose Bruford College

Admissions Office, Rose Bruford College, Lamorbey Park, Burnt Oak Lane, Sidcup, Kent, DA15 9DF

Tel: 0181 300 3024 Fax: 0181 308 0542
admiss@bruford.ac.uk

R51

Datafile

1996-97 Student Numbers

Total number of all students   545

	Degree	HND
Total FT/SW undergraduate numbers	482	
Percentages of these		
– on sandwich programmes		
– mature students	38	
– international students	9	
– male/female	40/60	

Full-time/sandwich students by academic subject category

	Degree	HND
Medicine, Dentistry, Vet Science		
Subjects Allied to Medicine		
Science		
Engineering and Technology		
Built Environment		
Mathematical Sciences, IT & Computing		
Business and Management		
Social Sciences		
Humanities		
Art & Design and Perf Arts	482	
Education		

Accommodation

Percentage of first years requiring accommodation who can be accommodated in institution-managed accommodation: 30%

Estimated weekly cost of institution-managed accommodation for   weeks:

(including dinner and breakfast   days per week) £

(no food) £60.00

(other...) £

Overseas opportunities*

Number of students on a placement or study period abroad: 2

Compacts/Networks

Record of Achievement

Interviewing

The interview or audition is an important part of the selection process for most applicants.

Campus locations

Lamorbey Park Campus, Sidcup, Kent. Greenwich Campus, Deptford, London.

Open Days

Dates for Theatre Design Open Days available from the Admissions Office.

*Excludes those on compulsory language course placements.

Royal Agricultural College

Admissions Office, Royal Agricultural College, Cirencester, Gloucestershire, GL7 6JS

Tel: 01285 652531 Fax: 01285 650219
sbur@racregis.demon.co.uk.

R54

Datafile

1996-97 Student Numbers

Total number of all students   550

	Degree	HND
Total FT/SW undergraduate numbers	398	
Percentages of these		
– on sandwich programmes	50	
– mature students	10	
– international students	10	
– male/female	70/30	

Full-time/sandwich students by academic subject category

	Degree	HND
Medicine, Dentistry, Vet Science		
Subjects Allied to Medicine		
Science	150	
Engineering and Technology		
Built Environment		
Mathematical Sciences, IT & Computing		
Business and Management	248	
Social Sciences		
Humanities		
Art & Design and Perf Arts		
Education		

Accommodation

Percentage of first years requiring accommodation who can be accommodated in institution-managed accommodation: 100%

Estimated weekly cost of institution-managed accommodation for 30 weeks:

(including 3 meals 7 days per week) £98.00

(no food) £

(other...) £

Overseas opportunities*

Number of students on a placement or study period abroad:

Compacts/Networks

Record of Achievement

Not essential.

Interviewing

All applicants interviewed.

Campus locations

Open Days

More informal visits arranged.

*Excludes those on compulsory language course placements.

Royal Free Hospital School of Medicine (University of London)

Admissions Officer, The Registry, Royal Free Hospital School of Medicine, Rowland Hill Street, London, NW3 2PF

Tel: 0171 830 2686 Fax: 0171 435 4359

R60

Datafile

1996-97 Student Numbers
Total number of all students   582

	Degree	HND
Total FT/SW undergraduate numbers	582	
Percentages of these		
– on sandwich programmes		
– mature students	10	
– international students	6	
– male/female	48/52	

Full-time/sandwich students by academic subject category

	Degree	HND
Medicine, Dentistry, Vet Science		
Subjects Allied to Medicine	564	
Science	18	
Engineering and Technology		
Built Environment		
Mathematical Sciences, IT & Computing		
Business and Management		
Social Sciences		
Humanities		
Art & Design and Perf Arts		
Education		

Accommodation
Percentage of first years requiring accommodation who can be accommodated in institution-managed accommodation: 100%

Estimated weekly cost of institution-managed accommodation for 30 weeks:

(including dinner and breakfast 7 days per week) £80.00

(no food) £50.00

(other…) £

Overseas opportunities*
Number of students on a placement or study period abroad: 95

Compacts/Networks

Record of Achievement
RoA may be brought to interview.

Interviewing
Short-listed candidates are called for interview.

Campus locations
Hampstead.

Open Days
11 March 1997 and 15 April 1997.

*Excludes those on compulsory language course placements.

Royal Holloway, University of London

Schools & International Liaison Office, Royal Holloway, University of London, Egham, Surrey, TW20 0EX

Tel: 01784 443399 Fax: 01784 471381
liaison-office@rhbnc.ac.uk http://www.rhbnc.ac.uk

R72

Datafile

1996-97 Student Numbers
Total number of all students   5476

	Degree	HND
Total FT/SW undergraduate numbers	4391	
Percentages of these		
– on sandwich programmes		
– mature students	22	
– international students	15	
– male/female	46/54	

Full-time/sandwich students by academic subject category

	Degree	HND
Medicine, Dentistry, Vet Science		
Subjects Allied to Medicine	70	
Science	1113	
Engineering and Technology	50	
Built Environment		
Mathematical Sciences, IT & Computing	340	
Business and Management	510	
Social Sciences	383	
Humanities	1409	
Art & Design and Perf Arts	516	
Education		

Accommodation
Percentage of first years requiring accommodation who can be accommodated in institution-managed accommodation: 100%

Estimated weekly cost of institution-managed accommodation for 30-50 weeks:

(including dinner and breakfast   days per week) £

(no food) £

(other…) £45.00 – £65.00

Overseas opportunities*
Number of students on a placement or study period abroad: 180

Compacts/Networks
Special routes for certain applicants in Surrey (Tower Hamlets & Essex & Havering VI Form Consortium).

Record of Achievement
Not significant.

Interviewing
Most applicants will be invited for an interview (or in some departments for Open Days).

Campus locations
Egham, 20 miles (30 minutes by train) to the West of London, near Windsor Great Park and the River Thames.

Open Days
19/20 March & early October. Summer Campus Tours. Groups/visitors welcome. Contact School Liaison Office.

*Excludes those on compulsory language course placements.

INDEPENDENT ON SUNDAY

Royal Veterinary College (University of London)

Registry, The Royal Veterinary College, Royal College Street, London, NW1 0TU

Tel: 0171 468 5149 Fax: 0171 388 2342

R84

Datafile

1996-97 Student Numbers

Total number of all students   652

	Degree	HND
Total FT/SW undergraduate numbers	510	
Percentages of these		
– on sandwich programmes		
– mature students	18	
– international students	9	
– male/female	34/66	

Full-time/sandwich students by academic subject category

	Degree	HND
Medicine, Dentistry, Vet Science		
Subjects Allied to Medicine	499	
Science		
Engineering and Technology	11	
Built Environment		
Mathematical Sciences, IT & Computing		
Business and Management		
Social Sciences		
Humanities		
Art & Design and Perf Arts		
Education		

Accommodation

Percentage of first years requiring accommodation who can be accommodated in institution-managed accommodation: 80%

Estimated weekly cost of institution-managed accommodation for 30 weeks:

(including 2-3 meals 7 days per week) £70.00 – £90.00

(no food) £37.00 – £44.00

(other...) £

Overseas opportunities*

Number of students on a placement or study period abroad:

Compacts/Networks

Record of Achievement

Interviewing

Selected applicants are called for interview.

Campus locations

Camden Town, London NW1 and Hawkshead near Potters Bar, Herts.

Open Days

College Open Day for prospective applicants is held at Hawkshead campus in May.

*Excludes those on compulsory language course placements.

Rycotewood College

Admissions, Priest End, Thame, Oxon, OX9 2AF

Tel: 01844 212501 Fax: 01844 218809
enquiries-rycote@oxfe.ac.uk www.oxfe.ac.uk

R95

Datafile

1996-97 Student Numbers

Total number of all students   750

	Degree	HND
Total FT/SW undergraduate numbers		112
Percentages of these		
– on sandwich programmes		
– mature students		
– international students		
– male/female		

Full-time/sandwich students by academic subject category

	Degree	HND
Medicine, Dentistry, Vet Science		
Subjects Allied to Medicine		
Science		
Engineering and Technology		44
Built Environment		
Mathematical Sciences, IT & Computing		
Business and Management		
Social Sciences		
Humanities		
Art & Design and Perf Arts		68
Education		

Accommodation

Percentage of first years requiring accommodation who can be accommodated in institution-managed accommodation:

Estimated weekly cost of institution-managed accommodation for 36 weeks:

(including dinner and breakfast 5 days per week) £73.00

(no food) £

(other...) £

Overseas opportunities*

Number of students on a placement or study period abroad: 20

Compacts/Networks

Record of Achievement

Should be brought to interview.

Interviewing

All UK based applicants are invited for interview. Career advice interviews are offered.

Campus locations

Thame, Oxfordshire.

Open Days

Exhibition of work in June. Open Days throughout the year. Telephone 01844 212501 for details.

*Excludes those on compulsory language course placements.

Scottish Agricultural College

Academic Registry, Scottish Agricultural College, Auchincruive, Ayr, Scotland, KA6 5HW

Tel: 01292 525350 Fax: 01292 525349
etsu@au.sac.ac.uk http://www.sac.ac.uk

S01

Datafile

1996-97 Student Numbers

Total number of all students   1211

	Degree	HND
Total FT/SW undergraduate numbers	337	540
Percentages of these		
– on sandwich programmes	10	18
– mature students	30	35
– international students	7	2
– male/female	59/41	67/33

Full-time/sandwich students by academic subject category

	Degree	HND
Medicine, Dentistry, Vet Science		
Subjects Allied to Medicine		
Science	120	349
Engineering and Technology		20
Built Environment		
Mathematical Sciences, IT & Computing		
Business and Management	217	171
Social Sciences		
Humanities		
Art & Design and Perf Arts		
Education		

Accommodation

Percentage of first years requiring accommodation who can be accommodated in institution-managed accommodation: 40%

Estimated weekly cost of institution-managed accommodation for 32 weeks:

(including dinner and breakfast 7 days per week) £56.00

(no food) £30.00

(other…) £

Overseas opportunities*

Number of students on a placement or study period abroad: 7

Compacts/Networks

No formal arrangements but participation in Compact initiatives organised by Local Education Business Partnership.

Record of Achievement

RoAs are welcomed and are considered together with other evidence of qualifications/development.

Interviewing

All applicants visit College to discuss intended course. In most cases there is no formal interview.

Campus locations

Aberdeen, Ayr (Auchincruive), Edinburgh.

Open Days

Individual courses organise Open Days to which applicants are invited.

*Excludes those on compulsory language course placements.

The Scottish College of Textiles

Netherdale, Galashiels, Selkirkshire, Scotland, TD1 3HF

Tel: 0800 163200 Fax: 01896 758965
guntere@scot.hw.ac.uk http://www.hw.ac.uk/texwww

S02

Datafile

1996-97 Student Numbers

Total number of all students   709

	Degree	HND
Total FT/SW undergraduate numbers	541	110
Percentages of these		
– on sandwich programmes		
– mature students	19	14
– international students	1	1
– male/female	20/80	56/44

Full-time/sandwich students by academic subject category

	Degree	HND
Medicine, Dentistry, Vet Science		
Subjects Allied to Medicine		
Science	5	
Engineering and Technology	406	
Built Environment		
Mathematical Sciences, IT & Computing	24	33
Business and Management	106	77
Social Sciences		
Humanities		
Art & Design and Perf Arts		
Education		

Accommodation

Percentage of first years requiring accommodation who can be accommodated in institution-managed accommodation: 100%

Estimated weekly cost of institution-managed accommodation for 33 weeks:

(including dinner and breakfast 5 days per week) £55.00

(no food) £39.00

(other…) £

Overseas opportunities*

Number of students on a placement or study period abroad:

Compacts/Networks

Record of Achievement

Interviewing

All students for Textiles Design are interviewed with portfolio. Other courses may interview.

Campus locations

One campus.

Open Days

Open Days held in September, October and February each year. Contact College for details.

*Excludes those on compulsory language course placements.

The University of Salford

Undergraduate Admissions, Faraday House, Salford, Greater Manchester, M5 4WT

Tel: 0161 745 5641 Fax: 0161 745 3126

S03

Datafile

1996-97 Student Numbers

Total number of all students   15266

	Degree	HND
Total FT/SW undergraduate numbers	9033	1647
Percentages of these		
– on sandwich programmes	25	
– mature students	38	31
– international students	6	6
– male/female	41/59	39/61

Full-time/sandwich students by academic subject category

	Degree	HND
Medicine, Dentistry, Vet Science		
Subjects Allied to Medicine	749	
Science	1362	139
Engineering and Technology	1644	424
Built Environment	389	47
Mathematical Sciences, IT & Computing	884	
Business and Management	1166	611
Social Sciences	616	
Humanities	1144	194
Art & Design and Perf Arts	1079	232
Education		

Accommodation

Percentage of first years requiring accommodation who can be accommodated in institution-managed accommodation: 90%

Estimated weekly cost of institution-managed accommodation for 31 weeks:

(including 2-3 meals 7 days per week) £64.40

(no food) £34.65 – £49.00

(other...) £

Overseas opportunities*

Number of students on a placement or study period abroad: 35

Compacts/Networks

Progressive arrangements exist with a number of local and regional colleges and schools.

Record of Achievement

As per departments.

Interviewing

Departmental decision.

Campus locations

One site.

Open Days

As per departments plus Institution Open Day on 15 May 1997.

Excludes those on compulsory language course placements.

Salisbury College

Registrar, Southampton Road, Salisbury, Wilts, SP1 2LW

Tel: 01722 323711 Fax: 01722 326006

S07

Datafile

1996-97 Student Numbers

Total number of all students

	Degree	HND
Total FT/SW undergraduate numbers	39	238
Percentages of these		
– on sandwich programmes		
– mature students	26	57
– international students	1	
– male/female	50/50	57/43

Full-time/sandwich students by academic subject category

	Degree	HND
Medicine, Dentistry, Vet Science		
Subjects Allied to Medicine		
Science		
Engineering and Technology		
Built Environment		3
Mathematical Sciences, IT & Computing		
Business and Management		52
Social Sciences		
Humanities		
Art & Design and Perf Arts	39	186
Education		

Accommodation

There is no institution-managed accommodation. Students are advised to contact the institution for information about local accommodation options.

Overseas opportunities*

Number of students on a placement or study period abroad:

Compacts/Networks

None.

Record of Achievement

Taken into account as appropriate.

Interviewing

Portfolio and interview generally for Art & Design.

Campus locations

One site.

Open Days

Various, contact for details. Open Access for intending applicants by appointment.

Excludes those on compulsory language course placements.

Letts STUDY GUIDES
THE INDEPENDENT

Sandwell College

Central Enquiries, Wednesbury Campus, Woden Road South,
Wednesbury, West Midlands, WS10 0PE

Tel: 0800 622006 Fax: 0121 2536104

S08

Datafile

1996-97 Student Numbers

	Degree	HND
Total number of all students	20000	
Total FT/SW undergraduate numbers		230
Percentages of these		
– on sandwich programmes		
– mature students		30
– international students		1
– male/female		70/30

Full-time/sandwich students by academic subject category

	Degree	HND
Medicine, Dentistry, Vet Science		
Subjects Allied to Medicine		
Science		
Engineering and Technology		76
Built Environment		
Mathematical Sciences, IT & Computing		
Business and Management		111
Social Sciences		
Humanities		
Art & Design and Perf Arts		55
Education		

Accommodation

Percentage of first years requiring accommodation who can be accommodated in institution-managed accommodation: 80%

Estimated weekly cost of institution-managed accommodation for 36 weeks:

(including dinner and breakfast   days per week) £

(no food) £35.00

(other…) £

Overseas opportunities*

Number of students on a placement or study period abroad:

Compacts/Networks
University of Wolverhampton and University of Central England (Engineering programmes).

Record of Achievement
Taken into account when offers are made.

Interviewing
Applicants will be invited for interview in most cases.

Campus locations
Wednesbury - HND Business, West Bromwich - HND Design Photography & Smethwick - HND Engineering.

Open Days
Visits by arrangement. Please contact Central Enquiries.

*Excludes those on compulsory language course placements.

School of Oriental and African Studies (University of London)

Registry, SOAS, Thornhaugh Street, Russell Square, London, WC1H 0XG

Tel: 0171 6372388 Fax: 0171 4364211
registrar@soas.ac.uk http://www.soas.ac.uk

S09

Datafile

1996-97 Student Numbers

	Degree	HND
Total number of all students	2500	
Total FT/SW undergraduate numbers	1394	
Percentages of these		
– on sandwich programmes		
– mature students	44	
– international students	19	
– male/female	36/64	

Full-time/sandwich students by academic subject category

	Degree	HND
Medicine, Dentistry, Vet Science		
Subjects Allied to Medicine		
Science		
Engineering and Technology		
Built Environment		
Mathematical Sciences, IT & Computing		
Business and Management	6	
Social Sciences	639	
Humanities	740	
Art & Design and Perf Arts	9	
Education		

Accommodation

Percentage of first years requiring accommodation who can be accommodated in institution-managed accommodation: 75%

Estimated weekly cost of institution-managed accommodation for 38 weeks:

(including dinner and breakfast   days per week) £

(no food) £71.00

(other…) £

Overseas opportunities*

Number of students on a placement or study period abroad: 35

Compacts/Networks
None.

Record of Achievement
May be requested at the discretion of individual admissions tutors.

Interviewing
Many likely applicants are interviewed and those made offers are invited to an intro/info session.

Campus locations
Bloomsbury.

Open Days
School-wide Open Day in early September. In Terms 1 & 2 Information sessions every Wednesday.

*Excludes those on compulsory language course placements.

University College Scarborough

Head of External Relations &, Recruitment, Filey Road, Scarborough, North Yorkshire, YO11 3AZ

Tel: 01723 362392 Fax: 01723 370815
lizpa@ucscarb.ac.uk www.ucscarb.ac.uk

S10

Datafile

1996-97 Student Numbers

Total number of all students   1430

	Degree	HND
Total FT/SW undergraduate numbers	1430	
Percentages of these		
– on sandwich programmes		
– mature students	46	
– international students	1	
– male/female	40/60	

Full-time/sandwich students by academic subject category

	Degree	HND
Medicine, Dentistry, Vet Science		
Subjects Allied to Medicine		
Science	260	
Engineering and Technology		
Built Environment		
Mathematical Sciences, IT & Computing		
Business and Management	170	
Social Sciences	100	
Humanities	280	
Art & Design and Perf Arts	260	
Education	360	

Accommodation

Percentage of first years requiring accommodation who can be accommodated in institution-managed accommodation: 85%

Estimated weekly cost of institution-managed accommodation for 30 weeks:

(including 2-3 meals 7 days per week) £72.00

(no food) £52.00

(other…) £

Overseas opportunities*

Number of students on a placement or study period abroad: 2

Compacts/Networks

Record of Achievement
RoA is viewed positively and when presented, is taken into consideration in assessing ability.

Interviewing
Interview practice varies. All applicants invited to visit College. Teaching department interviews.

Campus locations
Single site a mile from the centre of Scarborough and three minutes walk from the coast.

Open Days
16 October 1997.

Excludes those on compulsory language course placements.

The School of Pharmacy (University of London)

Registry, The School of Pharmacy, University of London, 29/39 Brunswick Road, London, WC1N 1AX

Tel: 0171 7535800 Fax: 0171 7535829
registry@cua.ulsop.ac.uk http://194.66.95.129

S12

Datafile

1996-97 Student Numbers

Total number of all students   690

	Degree	HND
Total FT/SW undergraduate numbers	384	
Percentages of these		
– on sandwich programmes	16	
– mature students	13	
– international students	27	
– male/female	37/63	

Full-time/sandwich students by academic subject category

	Degree	HND
Medicine, Dentistry, Vet Science		
Subjects Allied to Medicine		
Science	384	
Engineering and Technology		
Built Environment		
Mathematical Sciences, IT & Computing		
Business and Management		
Social Sciences		
Humanities		
Art & Design and Perf Arts		
Education		

Accommodation

Percentage of first years requiring accommodation who can be accommodated in institution-managed accommodation: 95%

Estimated weekly cost of institution-managed accommodation for 30 weeks:

(including 2-3 meals 7 days per week) £80.00

(no food) £58.00

(other…) £

Overseas opportunities*

Number of students on a placement or study period abroad: 10

Compacts/Networks

Record of Achievement

Interviewing
Mature students with qualifications other than A levels are usually called to interview.

Campus locations
One location in Bloomsbury, London, near Russell Square, Kings Cross, St Pancras, Euston.

Open Days
March, May, November - write for exact details. Open Days in Feb/March for students with offers.

Excludes those on compulsory language course placements.

Letts STUDY GUIDES
THE INDEPENDENT

School of Slavonic and East European Studies (University of London)

Registry, School of Slavonic & East European Studies, Senate House, Malet Street, London, WC1E 7HU

Tel: 0171 637 4934 Fax: 0171 436 8916
c.morley@@ssees.ac.uk http://www.ssees.ac.uk

S15

Datafile

1996-97 Student Numbers

Total number of all students   550

	Degree	HND
Total FT/SW undergraduate numbers	330	
Percentages of these		
– on sandwich programmes		
– mature students	45	
– international students	10	
– male/female	50/50	

Full-time/sandwich students by academic subject category

	Degree	HND
Medicine, Dentistry, Vet Science		
Subjects Allied to Medicine		
Science		
Engineering and Technology		
Built Environment		
Mathematical Sciences, IT & Computing		
Business and Management		
Social Sciences		
Humanities	330	
Art & Design and Perf Arts		
Education		

Accommodation

Percentage of first years requiring accommodation who can be accommodated in institution-managed accommodation: 70%

Estimated weekly cost of institution-managed accommodation for 30 weeks:

(including dinner and breakfast 7 days per week) £83.00

(no food) £

(other...) £50.00

Overseas opportunities*

Number of students on a placement or study period abroad: 80

Compacts/Networks

Record of Achievement

Interviewing
At Admissions Tutors' discretion.

Campus locations
Bloomsbury.

Open Days
November, December, January. Visits by individual arrangement.

*Excludes those on compulsory language course placements.

The University of Sheffield

Undergraduate Admissions Office, 14 Favell Road, Sheffield, S3 7QX

Tel: 0114 222 4127 Fax: 0114 272 8014
ug.admissions@sheffield.ac.uk
http://www.sheffield.ac.uk/uni/admin/admit/

S18

Datafile

1996-97 Student Numbers

Total number of all students   21356

	Degree	HND
Total FT/SW undergraduate numbers	12913	
Percentages of these		
– on sandwich programmes		
– mature students	19	
– international students	8	
– male/female	51/49	

Full-time/sandwich students by academic subject category

	Degree	HND
Medicine, Dentistry, Vet Science	1183	
Subjects Allied to Medicine	1496	
Science	2529	
Engineering and Technology	1472	
Built Environment	509	
Mathematical Sciences, IT & Computing	736	
Business and Management	659	
Social Sciences	1848	
Humanities	2298	
Art & Design and Perf Arts	101	
Education	19	

Accommodation

Percentage of first years requiring accommodation who can be accommodated in institution-managed accommodation: 99%

Estimated weekly cost of institution-managed accommodation for 31-39 weeks:

(including 2-3 meals 5 days per week) £64.45

(no food) £32.85 – £42.00

(other...) £

Overseas opportunities*

Number of students on a placement or study period abroad: 117

Compacts/Networks
Compact arrangements with 10 local schools and colleges. Early outreach project with 22 schools.

Record of Achievement
RoAs are not normally considered as part of the admissions process.

Interviewing
Interview policy varies according to department.

Campus locations
Single site in one area of the city.

Open Days
7 May 1997, 24 June 1997 and 7 October 1997.

*Excludes those on compulsory language course placements.

Sheffield Hallam University

Admissions Office, Sheffield Hallam University, City Campus,
Pond Street, Sheffield S1 1WB

Tel: 0114 253 3490 (from 1st Jan 1998 0114 225 555)
Fax: 0114 253 4023 (from 1st Jan 1998 0114 225 4023)
c.arnold@shu.ac.uk   http://www.shu.ac.uk/

S21

Datafile

1996-97 Student Numbers

Total number of all students

	Degree	HND
Total FT/SW undergraduate numbers	11192	1982
Percentages of these		
– on sandwich programmes	50	34
– mature students	36	27
– international students	3	2
– male/female	56/44	70/30

Full-time/sandwich students by academic subject category

	Degree	HND
Medicine, Dentistry, Vet Science		
Subjects Allied to Medicine	652	
Science	816	213
Engineering and Technology	1429	377
Built Environment	994	184
Mathematical Sciences, IT & Computing	1155	361
Business and Management	2775	719
Social Sciences	783	75
Humanities	999	
Art & Design and Perf Arts	685	53
Education	256	

Accommodation

Percentage of first years requiring accommodation who can be accommodated in institution-managed accommodation: 30%

Estimated weekly cost of institution-managed accommodation for 33-46 weeks:

(including dinner and breakfast 5 days per week) £66.00

(no food) £42.00

(other...) £

Overseas opportunities*

Number of students on a placement or study period abroad:

Compacts/Networks

GNVQ Compacts, Associate College and franchise agreements exist. contact SHU for details.

Record of Achievement

The Institution welcomes and encourages Records of Achievement.

Interviewing

Most mature applicants are interviewed and for certain courses an interview is mandatory.

Campus locations

Sheffield (five sites).

Open Days

General Open Day in May. Specific course Open Days for applicants receiving an offer.

Excludes those on compulsory language course placements.

Sheffield College

Central Admissions, The Sheffield College, PO Box 730, Sheffield, S8 8YY

Tel: 0114 260 3007 Fax: 0114 260 2301

S22

Datafile

1996-97 Student Numbers

Total number of all students   27758

	Degree	HND
Total FT/SW undergraduate numbers	160	240
Percentages of these		
– on sandwich programmes		
– mature students	90	50
– international students	1	1
– male/female		

Full-time/sandwich students by academic subject category

	Degree	HND
Medicine, Dentistry, Vet Science		
Subjects Allied to Medicine		
Science	35	
Engineering and Technology	50	
Built Environment	20	
Mathematical Sciences, IT & Computing		
Business and Management		
Social Sciences	55	95
Humanities		28
Art & Design and Perf Arts		118
Education		

Accommodation

Percentage of first years requiring accommodation who can be accommodated in institution-managed accommodation:

Estimated weekly cost of institution-managed accommodation for 35 weeks:

(including dinner and breakfast   days per week) £

(no food) £45.00

(other...) £

Overseas opportunities*

Number of students on a placement or study period abroad:

Compacts/Networks

Compact with two Universities in Sheffield. Also College status with Sheffield Hallam University.

Record of Achievement

Interviewing

Campus locations

Sheffield.

Open Days

Please contact the College for details of individual areas. Campus visits by appointment.

Excludes those on compulsory language course placements.

Shrewsbury College of Arts and Technology

Registrar, Shrewsbury College of Arts & Technology, London Road, Shrewsbury, Shropshire, SY2 6PR

Tel: 01743 231544 Fax: 01743 241684

S23

Datafile

1996-97 Student Numbers

Total number of all students   9000

	Degree	HND
Total FT/SW undergraduate numbers	8	79
Percentages of these		
– on sandwich programmes		
– mature students	100	90
– international students	1	
– male/female	88/12	61/39

Full-time/sandwich students by academic subject category

	Degree	HND
Medicine, Dentistry, Vet Science		
Subjects Allied to Medicine		
Science		
Engineering and Technology		
Built Environment		
Mathematical Sciences, IT & Computing		
Business and Management		58
Social Sciences		
Humanities		
Art & Design and Perf Arts	8	21
Education		

Accommodation

There is no institution-managed accommodation. Students are advised to contact the institution for information about local accommodation options.

Overseas opportunities*

Number of students on a placement or study period abroad:

Compacts/Networks

Record of Achievement

Not considered.

Interviewing

Interview route B applicants. Offers to route A applicants if meet academic criteria.

Campus locations

Main campus - London Road. Radbrook, Bridgnorth.

Open Days

Telephone college to arrange visit.

Excludes those on compulsory language course placements.

University College of St Martin, Lancaster and Cumbria

Admissions Office, Bowerham Road, Lancaster, Lancashire, LA1 3JD

Lancaster: Tel: 01524 384444 Fax: 01524 384567
Ambleside: Tel: 015394 30211 Fax: 015394 30305
admissions@ucsm.ac.uk

S24

Datafile

1996-97 Student Numbers

Total number of all students   7100

	Degree	HND
Total FT/SW undergraduate numbers	3489	
Percentages of these		
– on sandwich programmes		
– mature students	30	
– international students	1	
– male/female	24/76	

Full-time/sandwich students by academic subject category

	Degree	HND
Medicine, Dentistry, Vet Science		
Subjects Allied to Medicine	865	
Science	255	
Engineering and Technology		
Built Environment		
Mathematical Sciences, IT & Computing	23	
Business and Management	31	
Social Sciences	244	
Humanities	343	
Art & Design and Perf Arts	188	
Education	1540	

Accommodation

Percentage of first years requiring accommodation who can be accommodated in institution-managed accommodation: 99%

Estimated weekly cost of institution-managed accommodation for 30 weeks:

(including 3 meals 7 dyas per week) £65.00

(no food) £43.00

(other…) £58.00

Overseas opportunities*

Number of students on a placement or study period abroad: 50

Compacts/Networks

Member of Open College of the North West.

Record of Achievement

Valuable but not essential in the selection process.

Interviewing

Suitably qualified applicants for professional courses are interviewed. Mature/special needs – seen individually.

Campus locations

Lancaster, Ambleside, Carlisle.

Open Days

9 July 1997, 3 September 1997, 14 September 1997, 5 October 1997 and 15 October 1997.

Excludes those on compulsory language course placements.

Solihull College

Advice Centre, Solihull College, Blossomfield Road, Solihull, B91 1SB

Tel: 0121 711 6025 Fax: 0121 711 2316
enquiries@staff.solihull.ac.uk http//:www.solihull.ac.uk

S26

Datafile

1996-97 Student Numbers

Total number of all students   2500

	Degree	HND
Total FT/SW undergraduate numbers	184	187
Percentages of these		
– on sandwich programmes		
– mature students	68	48
– international students	1	
– male/female	50/50	55/45

Full-time/sandwich students by academic subject category

	Degree	HND
Medicine, Dentistry, Vet Science		
Subjects Allied to Medicine		
Science	10	
Engineering and Technology	13	13
Built Environment		
Mathematical Sciences, IT & Computing		20
Business and Management	20	139
Social Sciences	25	
Humanities		
Art & Design and Perf Arts	100	15
Education	16	

Accommodation

There is no institution-managed accommodation. Students are advised to contact the institution for information about local accommodation options.

Overseas opportunities*

Number of students on a placement or study period abroad: 20

Compacts/Networks

Member of Central Access Network.

Record of Achievement

We request applicants to bring their RoA to interview.

Interviewing

All applicants are interviewed.

Campus locations

All campuses are within Solihull.

Open Days

14 June 1997. Visitors also welcome by appointment.

Excludes those on compulsory language course placements.

University of Southampton

Academic Registrar's, Department, Highfield, Southampton, SO17 1BJ

Tel: 01703 595000 Fax: 01703 593037
prospenq@soton.ac.uk http://www.soton.ac.uk

S27

Datafile

1996-97 Student Numbers

Total number of all students   14073

	Degree	HND
Total FT/SW undergraduate numbers	11040	
Percentages of these		
– on sandwich programmes		
– mature students	13	
– international students	7	
– male/female	53/47	

Full-time/sandwich students by academic subject category

	Degree	HND
Medicine, Dentistry, Vet Science	755	
Subjects Allied to Medicine	1164	
Science	1641	
Engineering and Technology	1275	
Built Environment		
Mathematical Sciences, IT & Computing	644	
Business and Management	268	
Social Sciences	1675	
Humanities	1562	
Art & Design and Perf Arts	894	
Education		

Accommodation

Percentage of first years requiring accommodation who can be accommodated in institution-managed accommodation: 100%

Estimated weekly cost of institution-managed accommodation for 39-50 weeks:

(including dinner and breakfast 5 days per week) $67.00 – $72.00

(no food) $34.00 – $40.00

(other...) $51.57 – $53.00

Overseas opportunities*

Number of students on a placement or study period abroad: 600

Compacts/Networks

Compact arrangement with Totton College.

Record of Achievement

The University encourages the compilation of RoAs.

Interviewing

Applicants invited to interview at departments' discretion. Mature applicants are interviewed.

Campus locations

Main campus, Highfield. Avenue campus. Southampton Oceanography Centre. Winchester School of Art.

Open Days

24 & 25 June 1997. Winchester School of Art on Tuesdays/Thursdays in February. Booking required.

Excludes those on compulsory language course placements.

Somerset College of Arts and Technology

Admissions & Student Services, Wellington Road, Taunton, Somerset, TA1 5AX

Tel: 01823 366366 Fax: 01823 355418

S28

Datafile

1996-97 Student Numbers

Total number of all students 13000

	Degree	HND
Total FT/SW undergraduate numbers	226	292
Percentages of these		
– on sandwich programmes		
– mature students		
– international students		
– male/female	41/59	40/60

Full-time/sandwich students by academic subject category

	Degree	HND
Medicine, Dentistry, Vet Science		
Subjects Allied to Medicine		
Science		
Engineering and Technology		59
Built Environment		20
Mathematical Sciences, IT & Computing		
Business and Management		34
Social Sciences	43	42
Humanities		11
Art & Design and Perf Arts	150	159
Education		

Accommodation

Percentage of first years requiring accommodation who can be accommodated in institution-managed accommodation: 75%

Estimated weekly cost of institution-managed accommodation for 39 weeks:

(including dinner and breakfast   days per week) £

(no food) £45.00

(other…) £

Overseas opportunities *

Number of students on a placement or study period abroad:

Compacts/Networks

Record of Achievement

Students are encouraged to bring RoA to interview and have the opportunity to update RoA at College.

Interviewing

Prospective students will normally be invited for interview.

Campus locations

Taunton, Somerset.

Open Days

Several Open Days are offered during the year. Contact the College or faculty for details.

*Excludes those on compulsory language course placements.

Southampton Institute

Marketing Service, East Park Terrace, Southampton, Hants, SO14 0YN

Tel: 01703 319039 Fax: 01703 334161
http://www.solent.ac.uk

S30

Datafile

1996-97 Student Numbers

Total number of all students 14898

	Degree	HND
Total FT/SW undergraduate numbers	7483	1899
Percentages of these		
– on sandwich programmes	11	9
– mature students	22	18
– international students	2	3
– male/female	58/42	67/33

Full-time/sandwich students by academic subject category

	Degree	HND
Medicine, Dentistry, Vet Science		
Subjects Allied to Medicine		
Science	300	
Engineering and Technology	783	243
Built Environment	376	41
Mathematical Sciences, IT & Computing	435	128
Business and Management	2592	910
Social Sciences	730	201
Humanities	875	
Art & Design and Perf Arts	1392	376
Education		

Accommodation

Percentage of first years requiring accommodation who can be accommodated in institution-managed accommodation: 95%

Estimated weekly cost of institution-managed accommodation for 38 weeks:

(including dinner and breakfast   days per week) £

(no food) £68.00

(other…) £64.00

Overseas opportunities *

Number of students on a placement or study period abroad: 21

Compacts/Networks

Hants Education Support Service, Eastleigh, Itchen, Totton, Southampton City, Fareham, IOW colleges.

Record of Achievement

Varies.

Interviewing

Design course applicants are invited for portfolio viewing from January.

Campus locations

Southampton, Warsash.

Open Days

Course Open Days held January - April. Details sent with offer letter. Institute Open Day in May.

*Excludes those on compulsory language course placements.

South Bank University

Admissions Office, G66, 103 Borough Road, London, SE1 0AA

Tel: 0171 815 8158 Fax: 0171 815 8273
enrol@sbu.ac.uk http://www.sbu.ac.uk

S33

Datafile

1996-97 Student Numbers

Total number of all students   18308

	Degree	HND
Total FT/SW undergraduate numbers	7961	998
Percentages of these		
– on sandwich programmes	47	46
– mature students	56	41
– international students	11	5
– male/female	55/45	67/33

Full-time/sandwich students by academic subject category

	Degree	HND
Medicine, Dentistry, Vet Science		
Subjects Allied to Medicine	358	
Science	743	19
Engineering and Technology	1373	235
Built Environment	788	85
Mathematical Sciences, IT & Computing	783	300
Business and Management	2183	359
Social Sciences	951	
Humanities	381	
Art & Design and Perf Arts		
Education	401	

Accommodation

Percentage of first years requiring accommodation who can be accommodated in institution-managed accommodation: 50%

Estimated weekly cost of institution-managed accommodation for 42 weeks:

(including dinner and breakfast   days per week) £

(no food) £66.00

(other...) £

Overseas opportunities*

Number of students on a placement or study period abroad:

Compacts/Networks

Compacts exist with schools, VI form colleges, Institutions. Education Liaison Officer visits schools.

Record of Achievement

To be submitted upon request.

Interviewing

Interviews: Teaching, Nursing, Radiography, Architecture, Engineering and foundation course.

Campus locations

Majority of sites located on Southwark Campus, close to London's Southbank.

Open Days

Applicants with a place invited to School Open Days. General University Open Day held in May/June.

*Excludes those on compulsory language course placements.

Sparsholt College Hampshire

College Registrar, Sparsholt College Hampshire, Sparsholt, Winchester, SO21 2NF

Tel: 01962 776441 Fax: 01962 776587
zspacin@hantsnet.hants.gov.uk

S34

Datafile

1996-97 Student Numbers

Total number of all students   4500

	Degree	HND
Total FT/SW undergraduate numbers	55	167
Percentages of these		
– on sandwich programmes	55	36
– mature students	16	37
– international students	2	
– male/female	100/0	60/40

Full-time/sandwich students by academic subject category

	Degree	HND
Medicine, Dentistry, Vet Science		
Subjects Allied to Medicine		
Science		42
Engineering and Technology		
Built Environment		
Mathematical Sciences, IT & Computing		
Business and Management		21
Social Sciences	1	
Humanities	55	104
Art & Design and Perf Arts		
Education		

Accommodation

Percentage of first years requiring accommodation who can be accommodated in institution-managed accommodation: 100%

Estimated weekly cost of institution-managed accommodation for 31 weeks:

(including 1-2 meals 7 days per week) £70.00 – £78.00

(no food) £40.00

(other...) £

Overseas opportunities*

Number of students on a placement or study period abroad:

Compacts/Networks

Record of Achievement

Interviewing

Viewing days throughout the year.

Campus locations

Single site campus.

Open Days

10 May 1998.

*Excludes those on compulsory language course placements.

Southport College

Admissions Office, Southport College, Mornington Road, Southport, PR9 0TT

Tel: 01704 500606 Fax: 01704 546240

S35

Datafile

1996-97 Student Numbers

Total number of all students

	Degree	HND
Total FT/SW undergraduate numbers	36	
Percentages of these		
– on sandwich programmes		
– mature students		
– international students		
– male/female		

Full-time/sandwich students by academic subject category

	Degree	HND
Medicine, Dentistry, Vet Science		
Subjects Allied to Medicine		
Science		
Engineering and Technology		
Built Environment		
Mathematical Sciences, IT & Computing		
Business and Management		
Social Sciences		
Humanities		
Art & Design and Perf Arts		
Education		

Accommodation

There is no institution-managed accommodation. Students are advised to contact the institution for information about local accommodation options.

Overseas opportunities*

Number of students on a placement or study period abroad:

Compacts/Networks

Record of Achievement

Interviewing

Campus locations

Open Days

Please contact College for details.

*Excludes those on compulsory language course placements.

University of St Andrews

Admissions Office, Old Union Building, North Street, St Andrews, Fife, KY16 9AJ

Tel: 01334 462150 Fax: 01334 463388
admissions@st.andrews.ac.uk.

S36

Datafile

1996-97 Student Numbers

Total number of all students   5653

	Degree	HND
Total FT/SW undergraduate numbers	4860	
Percentages of these		
– on sandwich programmes		
– mature students	141	
– international students	151	
– male/female	46/54	

Full-time/sandwich students by academic subject category

	Degree	HND
Medicine, Dentistry, Vet Science	344	
Subjects Allied to Medicine	112	
Science	1338	
Engineering and Technology		
Built Environment		
Mathematical Sciences, IT & Computing	232	
Business and Management	200	
Social Sciences	584	
Humanities	2050	
Art & Design and Perf Arts		
Education		

Accommodation

Percentage of first years requiring accommodation who can be accommodated in institution-managed accommodation: 100%

Estimated weekly cost of institution-managed accommodation for 30 weeks:

(including dinner and breakfast 7 days per week) £58.17

(no food) £28.14

(other…) £63.63

Overseas opportunities*

Number of students on a placement or study period abroad:

Compacts/Networks
None.

Record of Achievement
Accepted as an indication of performance, but not required.

Interviewing
Most applicants interviewed. Interviews in special cases eg: mature/disabled students.

Campus locations
St. Andrews is a small University with a single site integrated into the town of St. Andrews.

Open Days

Individual visits encouraged. Arranged by Visitor Centre on 01334 463324. Science Open Day in June.

*Excludes those on compulsory language course placements.

St Andrew's College, Glasgow

Organiser of Initial Teacher Education, St Andrew's College,
Duntocher Road, Bearsden, Glasgow, G61 4QA

Tel: 0141 943 3400 Fax: 0141 943 0106

S37

Datafile

1996-97 Student Numbers

Total number of all students   841

	Degree	HND
Total FT/SW undergraduate numbers	640	
Percentages of these		
– on sandwich programmes		
– mature students	16	
– international students	5	
– male/female	15/85	

Full-time/sandwich students by academic subject category

	Degree	HND
Medicine, Dentistry, Vet Science		
Subjects Allied to Medicine		
Science		
Engineering and Technology		
Built Environment		
Mathematical Sciences, IT & Computing		
Business and Management		
Social Sciences		
Humanities		
Art & Design and Perf Arts		
Education	640	

Accommodation

Percentage of first years requiring accommodation who can be
accommodated in institution-managed accommodation: 100%

Estimated weekly cost of institution-managed accommodation
for 36 weeks:

(including dinner and breakfast 7 days per week) £65.00

(no food) £

(other...) £

Overseas opportunities*

Number of students on a placement or study period abroad:

Compacts/Networks   Record of Achievement

Interviewing   Campus locations

Open Days
15 September 1997.

*Excludes those on compulsory language course placements.

Southwark College

Information Centre, Southwark College, Waterloo Centre, The Cut,
London, SE1 8LE

Tel: 0171 815 1600 Fax: 0171 261 1301
ucas@southwark.ac.uk www.southwark.ac.uk

S38

Datafile

1996-97 Student Numbers

Total number of all students   7000

	Degree	HND
Total FT/SW undergraduate numbers		93
Percentages of these		
– on sandwich programmes		
– mature students		14
– international students		2
– male/female		69/31

Full-time/sandwich students by academic subject category

	Degree	HND
Medicine, Dentistry, Vet Science		
Subjects Allied to Medicine		
Science		
Engineering and Technology		
Built Environment		
Mathematical Sciences, IT & Computing		11
Business and Management		
Social Sciences		
Humanities		
Art & Design and Perf Arts		88
Education		

Accommodation

There is no institution-managed accommodation. Students are
advised to contact the institution for information about local
accommodation options.

Overseas opportunities*

Number of students on a placement or study period abroad:

Compacts/Networks   Record of Achievement

RoAs are welcomed and form
part of the interview process.

Interviewing   Campus locations

Design applicants are   Surrey Docks Centre, London.
interviewed with portfolio.
Other courses are at the tutors'
discretion.

Open Days
Open Days schedule available from Information Centre. Visits
arranged through Course Leaders.

*Excludes those on compulsory language course placements.

Stafford College

Admissions Unit, Stafford College, Earl Street, Stafford, ST16 2QR

Tel: 01785 223800   Fax: 01785 259953

71134.2402@compuserve.com

S39

Datafile

1996-97 Student Numbers

Total number of all students   2500

	Degree	HND
Total FT/SW undergraduate numbers	200	260
Percentages of these		
– on sandwich programmes	40	40
– mature students	35	15
– international students	3	2
– male/female	40/60	50/50

Full-time/sandwich students by academic subject category

	Degree	HND
Medicine, Dentistry, Vet Science		
Subjects Allied to Medicine		
Science	20	
Engineering and Technology		
Built Environment		
Mathematical Sciences, IT & Computing	40	
Business and Management	140	160
Social Sciences		
Humanities		
Art & Design and Perf Arts		100
Education		

Accommodation

There is no institution-managed accommodation. Students are advised to contact the institution for information about local accommodation options.

Overseas opportunities*

Number of students on a placement or study period abroad:

Compacts/Networks

Record of Achievement
May be used to enhance qualifications offered.

Interviewing
All interviewed. Portfolio viewed for all Art & Design courses.

Campus locations
Stafford town.

Open Days

Details from Admissions Unit.

Excludes those on compulsory language course placements.

St George's Hospital Medical School (University of London)

Admissions Officer, St George's Hospital Medical School, Cranmer Terrace, London, SW17 0RE

Tel: 0181 725 5992 Fax: 0181 725 3426
w.evans@sghms.ac.uk.

S49

Datafile

1996-97 Student Numbers

Total number of all students   1020

	Degree	HND
Total FT/SW undergraduate numbers	894	
Percentages of these		
– on sandwich programmes		
– mature students	10	
– international students	7	
– male/female	60/40	

Full-time/sandwich students by academic subject category

	Degree	HND
Medicine, Dentistry, Vet Science		
Subjects Allied to Medicine	862	
Science		
Engineering and Technology		
Built Environment		
Mathematical Sciences, IT & Computing		
Business and Management		
Social Sciences		
Humanities		
Art & Design and Perf Arts		
Education		

Accommodation

Percentage of first years requiring accommodation who can be accommodated in institution-managed accommodation: 100%

Estimated weekly cost of institution-managed accommodation for 30 weeks:

(including dinner and breakfast   days per week) £

(no food) £42.00

(other…) £

Overseas opportunities*

Number of students on a placement or study period abroad: 150

Compacts/Networks

Record of Achievement
The RoA does not play any part in the selection process.

Interviewing
400-500 applicants interviewed. Those made an offer must first have attended for interview.

Campus locations
One campus only.

Open Days

Informal tours of School are held on the last Wednesday of every month, except July & December.

Excludes those on compulsory language course placements.

St Helens College

Student Services, St Helens College, Brook Street, St Helens, WA10 1PZ

Tel: 01744 623338

S51

Datafile

1996-97 Student Numbers

Total number of all students   15000

	Degree	HND
Total FT/SW undergraduate numbers	70	435
Percentages of these		
– on sandwich programmes		
– mature students		
– international students		
– male/female		

Full-time/sandwich students by academic subject category

	Degree	HND
Medicine, Dentistry, Vet Science		
Subjects Allied to Medicine		54
Science	15	
Engineering and Technology		33
Built Environment		9
Mathematical Sciences, IT & Computing		27
Business and Management	15	146
Social Sciences		
Humanities	40	15
Art & Design and Perf Arts		164
Education		

Accommodation

Percentage of first years requiring accommodation who can be accommodated in institution-managed accommodation: 25%

Estimated weekly cost of institution-managed accommodation for 36 weeks:

(including dinner and breakfast   days per week) £

(no food) £35.00

(other...) £

Overseas opportunities*

Number of students on a placement or study period abroad:

Compacts/Networks

An Associate College of Liverpool John Moores University. Member of Merseyside Open College Federation.

Record of Achievement

RoAs welcomed in support of application.

Interviewing

Most applicants are not required to attend for interview.

Campus locations

Town Centre, St Helens; Newton; Technology Centre, St Helens.

Open Days

Open Day in November 1997 and June 1998. Potential students encouraged to visit.

*Excludes those on compulsory language course placements.

St Loye's School of Occupational Therapy

Administrator, Millbrook House, Millbrook Lane, Topsham Road, Exeter, EX2 6ES

Tel: 01392 219774 Fax: 01392 435357
http://www.ex.ac.uk/affiliate/stloyes

S54

Datafile

1996-97 Student Numbers

Total number of all students   265

	Degree	HND
Total FT/SW undergraduate numbers	265	
Percentages of these		
– on sandwich programmes		
– mature students	48	
– international students	16	
– male/female	15/85	

Full-time/sandwich students by academic subject category

	Degree	HND
Medicine, Dentistry, Vet Science		
Subjects Allied to Medicine	265	
Science		
Engineering and Technology		
Built Environment		
Mathematical Sciences, IT & Computing		
Business and Management		
Social Sciences		
Humanities		
Art & Design and Perf Arts		
Education		

Accommodation

Percentage of first years requiring accommodation who can be accommodated in institution-managed accommodation: 50%

Estimated weekly cost of institution-managed accommodation for 36 weeks:

(including 1 meal 5 days per week) £50.00

(no food) £

(other...) £

Overseas opportunities*

Number of students on a placement or study period abroad:

Compacts/Networks

Record of Achievement

Interviewing

All applicants are interviewed.

Campus locations

Single site.

Open Days

Four Open Days held each year. Contact School for information.

*Excludes those on compulsory language course placements.

The University College of St Mark & St John

Admissions Officer, The University College of St Mark & St John, Derriford Road, Plymouth, Devon, PL6 8BH

Tel: 01752 636827 Fax: 01752 636849

S59

Datafile

1996-97 Student Numbers

	Degree	HND
Total number of all students	3140	
Total FT/SW undergraduate numbers	2247	
Percentages of these		
– on sandwich programmes		
– mature students	40	
– international students	6	
– male/female	31/69	

Full-time/sandwich students by academic subject category

	Degree	HND
Medicine, Dentistry, Vet Science		
Subjects Allied to Medicine	160	
Science	4	
Engineering and Technology		
Built Environment		
Mathematical Sciences, IT & Computing	72	
Business and Management	138	
Social Sciences	178	
Humanities	357	
Art & Design and Perf Arts	153	
Education	1435	

Accommodation

Percentage of first years requiring accommodation who can be accommodated in institution-managed accommodation: 100%

Estimated weekly cost of institution-managed accommodation for 40 weeks:

(including 3 meals 7 days per week) £54.00

(no food) £41.50

(other…) £

Overseas opportunities *

Number of students on a placement or study period abroad: 15

Compacts/Networks

The College is exploring more formal links with colleges/schools.

Record of Achievement

Students are encouraged to bring RoA to interview.

Interviewing

All ITT courses require an interview. Applicants with BA offers (not interviewed), invited to Open Days.

Campus locations

The College campus is five miles north of Plymouth city centre.

Open Days

Open Days provided for applicants offered places without interviews. General Open Days also held.

Excludes those on compulsory language course placements.

St Mary's University College

Admissions Office, St Mary's University College, Waldegrave Road, Twickenham, TW1 4SX

Tel: 0181 2404000 Fax: 0181 2404255

S64

Datafile

1996-97 Student Numbers

	Degree	HND
Total number of all students	2456	
Total FT/SW undergraduate numbers	2078	
Percentages of these		
– on sandwich programmes		
– mature students	17	
– international students	11	
– male/female	34/66	

Full-time/sandwich students by academic subject category

	Degree	HND
Medicine, Dentistry, Vet Science		
Subjects Allied to Medicine		
Science	427	
Engineering and Technology		
Built Environment		
Mathematical Sciences, IT & Computing	17	
Business and Management		
Social Sciences	105	
Humanities	686	
Art & Design and Perf Arts	148	
Education	695	

Accommodation

Percentage of first years requiring accommodation who can be accommodated in institution-managed accommodation: 85%

Estimated weekly cost of institution-managed accommodation for 31 weeks:

(including 1-2 meals 7 days per week) £65.00 – £85.00

(no food) £63.00

(other…) £

Overseas opportunities *

Number of students on a placement or study period abroad: 5

Compacts/Networks

Member of Surrey and South West London Access Agency and the Surrey University Compact Scheme.

Record of Achievement

Required for BA(QTS) applicants; RoA should be brought to interview.

Interviewing

Selected BA(QTS), Sport Rehabilitation, and Single Honours Degree applicants are interviewed.

Campus locations

Single site campus in Twickenham.

Open Days

Applicants are invited to an Open Day once an offer has been made.

Excludes those on compulsory language course placements.

Staffordshire University

Assistant Registrar, Admissions, Staffordshire University, College Road, Stoke on Trent, ST4 2DE

Tel: 01782 292752 Fax: 01782 745422

admissions@staffs.ac.uk http://www.staffs.ac.uk

S72

Datafile

1996-97 Student Numbers

Total number of all students   11609

	Degree	HND
Total FT/SW undergraduate numbers	10754	383
Percentages of these		
– on sandwich programmes	30	
– mature students	34	19
– international students	4	1
– male/female	57/43	63/37

Full-time/sandwich students by academic subject category

	Degree	HND
Medicine, Dentistry, Vet Science		
Subjects Allied to Medicine	610	
Science	1837	38
Engineering and Technology	545	
Built Environment	237	
Mathematical Sciences, IT & Computing	1576	142
Business and Management	1762	171
Social Sciences	1772	
Humanities	910	
Art & Design and Perf Arts	1452	32
Education		

Accommodation

Percentage of first years requiring accommodation who can be accommodated in institution-managed accommodation: 59%

Estimated weekly cost of institution-managed accommodation for 40 weeks:

(including dinner and breakfast   days per week) £

(no food) £27.00 – £50.00

(other...) £

Overseas opportunities*

Number of students on a placement or study period abroad: 148

Compacts/Networks
Midlands Regional Compact, Priority Application Scheme at Staffordshire, University & College Access Network.

Record of Achievement
At discretion of Admissions Tutors.

Interviewing
At discretion of Admissions Tutors.

Campus locations
Stoke, Stafford and at franchise centres.

Open Days
5 July 1997, 9 July 1997, 15 October 1997. Information from Student Recruitment: 01782 292709.

*Excludes those on compulsory language course placements.

The University of Stirling

Admissions Office, University of Stirling, Stirling, FK9 4LA

Tel: 01786 467044 Fax: 01786 466800

http://www.stir.ac.uk

S75

Datafile

1996-97 Student Numbers

Total number of all students   7500

	Degree	HND
Total FT/SW undergraduate numbers	4500	
Percentages of these		
– on sandwich programmes		
– mature students	25	
– international students	10	
– male/female	50/50	

Full-time/sandwich students by academic subject category

	Degree	HND
Medicine, Dentistry, Vet Science		
Subjects Allied to Medicine		
Science	990	
Engineering and Technology		
Built Environment		
Mathematical Sciences, IT & Computing	180	
Business and Management	945	
Social Sciences	675	
Humanities	1260	
Art & Design and Perf Arts		
Education	450	

Accommodation

Percentage of first years requiring accommodation who can be accommodated in institution-managed accommodation: 100%

Estimated weekly cost of institution-managed accommodation for 30 weeks:

(including dinner and breakfast   days per week) £

(no food) £40.00

(other...) £

Overseas opportunities*

Number of students on a placement or study period abroad: 150

Compacts/Networks
SWAP.

Record of Achievement
Not required.

Interviewing
Only in special cases.

Campus locations
Stirling.

Open Days
12 September 1997, 11 September 1998.

*Excludes those on compulsory language course placements.

Stockport College of Further & Higher Education

Academic Registry, Stockport College, Wellington Road South, Stockport, SK1 3UQ

Tel: 0161 9583416 Fax: 0161 9583305

S76

Datafile

1996-97 Student Numbers

Total number of all students   15000

	Degree	HND
Total FT/SW undergraduate numbers	116	735
Percentages of these		
– on sandwich programmes		
– mature students	50	30
– international students		5
– male/female	48/52	51/49

Full-time/sandwich students by academic subject category

	Degree	HND
Medicine, Dentistry, Vet Science		
Subjects Allied to Medicine	52	115
Science		29
Engineering and Technology		130
Built Environment		18
Mathematical Sciences, IT & Computing		
Business and Management		168
Social Sciences		
Humanities		
Art & Design and Perf Arts		275
Education	64	

Accommodation

There is no institution-managed accommodation. Students are advised to contact the institution for information about local accommodation options.

Overseas opportunities*

Number of students on a placement or study period abroad:

Compacts/Networks

Record of Achievement
Considered on an individual Basis.

Interviewing

Campus locations

Open Days

Students welcomed who want to visit the College. Contact Fiona Hobson on 0161 9583425 for details.

*Excludes those on compulsory language course placements.

The University of Strathclyde

Schools & Colleges Liaison, University of Strathclyde, Graham Hills Building, 40 George Street, Glasgow, G1 1QE

Tel: 0141 5524400 Fax: 0141 5527362
j.foulds@mis.strath.ac.uk http://www.strath.ac.uk

S78

Datafile

1996-97 Student Numbers

Total number of all students   14000

	Degree	HND
Total FT/SW undergraduate numbers	10400	
Percentages of these		
– on sandwich programmes		
– mature students	30	
– international students	10	
– male/female	50/50	

Full-time/sandwich students by academic subject category

	Degree	HND
Medicine, Dentistry, Vet Science		
Subjects Allied to Medicine	590	
Science	2041	
Engineering and Technology	2060	
Built Environment	500	
Mathematical Sciences, IT & Computing	855	
Business and Management	1621	
Social Sciences	1035	
Humanities	703	
Art & Design and Perf Arts		
Education	995	

Accommodation

Percentage of first years requiring accommodation who can be accommodated in institution-managed accommodation: 100%

Estimated weekly cost of institution-managed accommodation for 37 weeks:

(including 2-3 meals 7 days per week) £60.35

(no food) £43.15

(other…) £

Overseas opportunities*

Number of students on a placement or study period abroad:

Compacts/Networks

Record of Achievement

Interviewing
Education Faculty courses require interviews. Science/Engineering Faculty hold a few interviews.

Campus locations
Main campus in city centre and Faculty of Education in west end of Glasgow.

Open Days

8 September 1997 6pm-8pm. 9 September 1997 10am-4pm. Information about visits in prospectus.

*Excludes those on compulsory language course placements.

University College Suffolk

Registry (Admissions), Suffolk College, Ipswich, IP4 1LT

Tel: 01473 255885 Fax: 01473 230054

S81

Datafile

1996-97 Student Numbers

Total number of all students   31971

	Degree	HND
Total FT/SW undergraduate numbers	1367	610
Percentages of these		
– on sandwich programmes		
– mature students	57	31
– international students	2	1
– male/female	38/62	63/37

Full-time/sandwich students by academic subject category

	Degree	HND
Medicine, Dentistry, Vet Science		
Subjects Allied to Medicine	414	
Science	42	18
Engineering and Technology	13	42
Built Environment		21
Mathematical Sciences, IT & Computing	64	75
Business and Management	325	139
Social Sciences	23	32
Humanities	139	78
Art & Design and Perf Arts	364	208
Education	288	

Accommodation

There is no institution-managed accommodation. Students are advised to contact the institution for information about local accommodation options.

Overseas opportunities*

Number of students on a placement or study period abroad:

Compacts/Networks

Most degrees validated by UEA.

Record of Achievement

Interviewing

Interviews for Art & Design (portfolio), Performing Arts (audition), Social Work, Nursing & Radiography.

Campus locations

Ipswich but some Nursing and Midwifery in Great Yarmouth and Bury St Edmunds.

Open Days

Various Open Days throughout the year. Please contact Marketing on 01473 296520 for details.

Excludes those on compulsory language course placements.

University of Sunderland

Student Recruitment, Unit 4C, Technology Park, Chester Road, Sunderland, SR2 7PS

Tel: 0191 515 3000 Fax: 0191 515 3805
student-helpline@sunderland.ac.uk http://www.sunderland.ac.uk

S84

Datafile

1996-97 Student Numbers

Total number of all students   14405

	Degree	HND
Total FT/SW undergraduate numbers	9337	621
Percentages of these		
– on sandwich programmes	16	1
– mature students	35	29
– international students	10	6
– male/female	51/49	72/38

Full-time/sandwich students by academic subject category

	Degree	HND
Medicine, Dentistry, Vet Science		
Subjects Allied to Medicine	861	
Science	2099	53
Engineering and Technology	947	27
Built Environment	128	56
Mathematical Sciences, IT & Computing	832	160
Business and Management	1154	248
Social Sciences	679	
Humanities	1104	
Art & Design and Perf Arts	747	77
Education	786	

Accommodation

Percentage of first years requiring accommodation who can be accommodated in institution-managed accommodation: 98%

Estimated weekly cost of institution-managed accommodation for   weeks:

(including 1 meal 7 days per week) $54.00

(no food) $40.00

(other…) $30.00 – $40.00

Overseas opportunities*

Number of students on a placement or study period abroad: 27

Compacts/Networks

Progressive arrangements exist with a number of local and regional colleges and schools.

Record of Achievement

Interviewing

Interviews are a vital part of selection for Art & Design, Teaching, Social Work, Community Work.

Campus locations

Three sites around Sunderland.

Open Days

All schools hold regular Open Days. Details will be forwarded to prospective students who apply.

Excludes those on compulsory language course placements.

The University of Surrey

Undergraduate Admissions Office, The Registry, University of Surrey, Guildford, Surrey, GU2 5XH

Tel: 01483 259305 Fax: 01483 300803

S87

Datafile

1996-97 Student Numbers

Total number of all students   8515

	Degree	HND
Total FT/SW undergraduate numbers	5079	
Percentages of these		
– on sandwich programmes	81	
– mature students	24	
– international students	21	
– male/female	48/52	

Full-time/sandwich students by academic subject category

	Degree	HND
Medicine, Dentistry, Vet Science		
Subjects Allied to Medicine	934	
Science	954	
Engineering and Technology	1275	
Built Environment		
Mathematical Sciences, IT & Computing	298	
Business and Management	575	
Social Sciences	414	
Humanities	391	
Art & Design and Perf Arts	238	
Education		

Accommodation

Percentage of first years requiring accommodation who can be accommodated in institution-managed accommodation: 100%

Estimated weekly cost of institution-managed accommodation for 28-38 weeks:

(including dinner and breakfast   days per week) £

(no food) £33.95 – £45.50

(other...) £50.75 – £51.80

Overseas opportunities *

Number of students on a placement or study period abroad: 91

Compacts/Networks
Surrey HE Compact arrangements apply to many local schools and colleges.

Record of Achievement
Varies according to departments.

Interviewing
Varies according to departments.

Campus locations

Open Days

For details of Open Days contact Marketing on 01483 259192.

*Excludes those on compulsory language course placements.

Surrey Institute of Art and Design

Registry Service, Falkner Road, Farnham, Surrey, GU9 7DS

Tel: 01252 732286 Fax: 01252 718313
registry@surrart.ac.uk http://www.surrart.ac.uk

S88

Datafile

1996-97 Student Numbers

Total number of all students   3000

	Degree	HND
Total FT/SW undergraduate numbers	2290	
Percentages of these		
– on sandwich programmes		
– mature students	35	
– international students	5	
– male/female	55/45	

Full-time/sandwich students by academic subject category

	Degree	HND
Medicine, Dentistry, Vet Science		
Subjects Allied to Medicine		
Science		
Engineering and Technology		
Built Environment		
Mathematical Sciences, IT & Computing		
Business and Management		
Social Sciences		
Humanities	105	
Art & Design and Perf Arts	2185	
Education		

Accommodation

Percentage of first years requiring accommodation who can be accommodated in institution-managed accommodation: 75%

Estimated weekly cost of institution-managed accommodation for 35 weeks:

(including dinner and breakfast   days per week) £

(no food) £47.00

(other...) £

Overseas opportunities *

Number of students on a placement or study period abroad:

Compacts/Networks
We have a range of Compact arrangements with FE colleges.

Record of Achievement
Certificate and transcripts only, at present.

Interviewing
Many but not all applicants are interviewed.

Campus locations
Farnham and Epsom.

Open Days

Held October and February.

*Excludes those on compulsory language course placements.

University of Sussex

Admissions Officer, Undergraduate Admissions, Sussex House, University of Sussex, Brighton, Sussex, BN1 9RH

Tel: 01273 678416 Fax: 01273 678545
ug.admissions@sussex.ac.uk http://www.sussex.ac.uk

S90

Datafile

1996-97 Student Numbers

Total number of all students   8816

	Degree	HND
Total FT/SW undergraduate numbers	6627	22
Percentages of these		
– on sandwich programmes	1	
– mature students	32	69
– international students	20	5
– male/female	50/50	90/10

Full-time/sandwich students by academic subject category

	Degree	HND
Medicine, Dentistry, Vet Science		
Subjects Allied to Medicine	41	
Science	1540	
Engineering and Technology	604	22
Built Environment		
Mathematical Sciences, IT & Computing	539	
Business and Management		
Social Sciences	1812	
Humanities	1694	
Art & Design and Perf Arts	61	
Education	12	

Accommodation

Percentage of first years requiring accommodation who can be accommodated in institution-managed accommodation: 95%

Estimated weekly cost of institution-managed accommodation for 30-38 weeks:

(including dinner and breakfast days per week) £

(no food) £43.00 – £46.00

(other...) £

Overseas opportunities*

Number of students on a placement or study period abroad: 314

Compacts/Networks

Record of Achievement
Applicants are requested to bring the summary sheet to interview.

Interviewing
We call for visit or interview as many suitable applicants as possible. They can also visit the University.

Campus locations
Lewes Tertiary College, Croydon College, Crawley College, Chichester College of A, S & T.

Open Days
Please contact the Schools and Colleges Liaison Section on 01273 678416 for Open Day information.

*Excludes those on compulsory language course placements.

Sutton Coldfield College

Sutton Coldfield College, Design Centre, 90 Upper Holland Road, Sutton Coldfield, West Midlands, B72 1RD

Tel: 0121 362 1158 Fax: 0121 321 3180

S91

Datafile

1996-97 Student Numbers

Total number of all students

	Degree	HND
Total FT/SW undergraduate numbers	35	
Percentages of these		
– on sandwich programmes		
– mature students		
– international students		
– male/female		

Full-time/sandwich students by academic subject category

	Degree	HND
Medicine, Dentistry, Vet Science		
Subjects Allied to Medicine		
Science		
Engineering and Technology		
Built Environment		
Mathematical Sciences, IT & Computing		
Business and Management		
Social Sciences		
Humanities		
Art & Design and Perf Arts	35	
Education		

Accommodation

There is no institution-managed accommodation. Students are advised to contact the institution for information about local accommodation options.

Overseas opportunities*

Number of students on a placement or study period abroad:

Compacts/Networks

Record of Achievement
Not mandatory.

Interviewing
All first choice and most second and third choice applicants are interviewed.

Campus locations
College site in Sutton Coldfield and new Design Centre one mile away.

Open Days
We welcome applicants to visit and seek advice every Thursday afternoon by appointment.

*Excludes those on compulsory language course placements.

University of Wales Swansea

Undergraduate Admissions Office, The Registry, Singleton Park, Swansea, Wales, SA2 8PP

Tel: 01792 295111 Fax: 01792 295110
admissions@swan.ac.uk http://www.swan.ac.uk

S93

Datafile

1996-97 Student Numbers

Total number of all students   9548

	Degree	HND
Total FT/SW undergraduate numbers	6663	
Percentages of these		
– on sandwich programmes	1	
– mature students	19	
– international students	7	
– male/female	46/54	

Full-time/sandwich students by academic subject category

	Degree	HND
Medicine, Dentistry, Vet Science		
Subjects Allied to Medicine	593	
Science	1280	
Engineering and Technology	787	
Built Environment		
Mathematical Sciences, IT & Computing	306	
Business and Management	478	
Social Sciences	1398	
Humanities	1821	
Art & Design and Perf Arts		
Education		

Accommodation

Percentage of first years requiring accommodation who can be accommodated in institution-managed accommodation: 97%

Estimated weekly cost of institution-managed accommodation for 31-40 weeks:

(including dinner and breakfast 7 days per week) £64.45

(no food) £35.00

(other…) £48.35

Overseas opportunities *

Number of students on a placement or study period abroad: 72

Compacts/Networks

Compacts with East Dyfed, West Glam, Mid Glam St Julians School (Newport), NE Hereford & Worcester.

Record of Achievement

Send summary direct to Undergraduate Admissions Office and bring RoA to interview if requested.

Interviewing

Applicants not interviewed are invited to Open Days.

Campus locations

Swansea.

Open Days

Open Days are held in spring, summer and autumn. Contact Schools Liaison Office on 01792 295784.

Excludes those on compulsory language course placements.

Swansea Institute of Higher Education

The Registry, Swansea Institute of Higher Education, Townhill Road, Swansea, SA2 0UT

Tel: 01792 481000 Fax: 01792 481263
enquiry@sihe.ac.uk http://sihe.ac.uk

S96

Datafile

1996-97 Student Numbers

Total number of all students   4294

	Degree	HND
Total FT/SW undergraduate numbers	1909	865
Percentages of these		
– on sandwich programmes	10	4
– mature students	39	12
– international students	3	2
– male/female	49/51	66/34

Full-time/sandwich students by academic subject category

	Degree	HND
Medicine, Dentistry, Vet Science		
Subjects Allied to Medicine		
Science		
Engineering and Technology	249	129
Built Environment	28	55
Mathematical Sciences, IT & Computing	99	95
Business and Management	548	351
Social Sciences	158	
Humanities		
Art & Design and Perf Arts	186	235
Education	473	

Accommodation

Percentage of first years requiring accommodation who can be accommodated in institution-managed accommodation: 60%

Estimated weekly cost of institution-managed accommodation for   weeks:

(including dinner and breakfast   days per week) £

(no food) £37.00

(other…) £

Overseas opportunities *

Number of students on a placement or study period abroad:

Compacts/Networks

With local schools in S.W. Wales.

Record of Achievement

Bring RoA to interview if requested.

Interviewing

Campus locations

Townhill (Education, Humanities, A & D), Alexandra Road (A & D), Mount Pleasant- all others.

Open Days

Contact Faculty.

Excludes those on compulsory language course placements.

University of Wales College of Medicine

Undergraduate Admissions Officer, University of Wales College of Medicine, Heath Park, Cardiff, CF4 4XN

Tel: 01222 742027 Fax: 01222 742914

W10

Datafile

1996-97 Student Numbers

Total number of all students 27300

	Degree	HND
Total FT/SW undergraduate numbers	110	204
Percentages of these		
– on sandwich programmes		
– mature students	5	5
– international students	2	2
– male/female	55/45	50/50

Full-time/sandwich students by academic subject category

	Degree	HND
Medicine, Dentistry, Vet Science		
Subjects Allied to Medicine		
Science		
Engineering and Technology		25
Built Environment		
Mathematical Sciences, IT & Computing		18
Business and Management		80
Social Sciences		
Humanities		
Art & Design and Perf Arts	110	99
Education		

Accommodation

Percentage of first years requiring accommodation who can be accommodated in institution-managed accommodation: 60%

Estimated weekly cost of institution-managed accommodation for weeks:

(including dinner and breakfast days per week) £

(no food) £50.00

(other...) £

Overseas opportunities*

Number of students on a placement or study period abroad:

Compacts/Networks

Record of Achievement
Please bring your RoA.

Interviewing
Art & Design students are invited for interview and portfolio review.

Campus locations
Swindon.

Open Days
Please telephone for information.

Excludes those on compulsory language course placements.

University College Warrington

University College Registry, Padgate Campus, Crab Lane, Warrington, WA2 0DB

Tel: 01925 494494 Fax: 01925 816077
registry.he@warr.ac.uk http//www.warr.ac.uk/unicoll.html

W17

Datafile

1996-97 Student Numbers

Total number of all students 9834

	Degree	HND
Total FT/SW undergraduate numbers		84
Percentages of these		
– on sandwich programmes		
– mature students		92
– international students		
– male/female		51/49

Full-time/sandwich students by academic subject category

	Degree	HND
Medicine, Dentistry, Vet Science		
Subjects Allied to Medicine		
Science		
Engineering and Technology		
Built Environment		
Mathematical Sciences, IT & Computing		
Business and Management		44
Social Sciences		
Humanities		
Art & Design and Perf Arts		40
Education		

Accommodation

There is no institution-managed accommodation. Students are advised to contact the institution for information about local accommodation options.

Overseas opportunities*

Number of students on a placement or study period abroad:

Compacts/Networks

Record of Achievement

Interviewing
All applicants are normally interviewed.

Campus locations
All Higher Education courses are currently offered from the Ashton campus.

Open Days
14 March 1997, 17 June 1997.

Excludes those on compulsory language course placements.

The University of Warwick

Undergraduate Admissions Office, University of Warwick, Gibbet Hill Road, Coventry, CV4 7AL

Tel: 01203 523523 Fax: 01203 524649

ugadmissions@admin.warwick.ac.uk www.csv.warwick.ac.uk

W20

Datafile

1996-97 Student Numbers

Total number of all students   13000

	Degree	HND
Total FT/SW undergraduate numbers	6038	827
Percentages of these		
– on sandwich programmes	5	
– mature students	33	35
– international students	6	4
– male/female	55/45	72/48

Full-time/sandwich students by academic subject category

	Degree	HND
Medicine, Dentistry, Vet Science		
Subjects Allied to Medicine	260	
Science	780	28
Engineering and Technology	606	227
Built Environment	25	13
Mathematical Sciences, IT & Computing	773	248
Business and Management	1295	271
Social Sciences	1216	40
Humanities	649	
Art & Design and Perf Arts	434	
Education		

Accommodation

Percentage of first years requiring accommodation who can be accommodated in institution-managed accommodation: 80%

Estimated weekly cost of institution-managed accommodation for   weeks: £26.00 – £42.00

(including dinner and breakfast   days per week) £

(no food) £

(other…) £

Overseas opportunities *

Number of students on a placement or study period abroad:

Compacts/Networks

Record of Achievement

Interviewing

Campus locations

Open Days

Open Days take place at regular intervals on a School basis. Please contact the University for further details.

*Excludes those on compulsory language course placements.

Warwickshire College, Royal Leamington Spa & Moreton Morrell

Admissions Office, Warwick New Road, Leamington Spa, Warks, CV32 5JE

Tel: 01926 318000 Fax: 01926 318111

s.aslam@midwarks.demon.co.uk.

W25

Datafile

1996-97 Student Numbers

Total number of all students   27000

	Degree	HND
Total FT/SW undergraduate numbers	4564	1481
Percentages of these		
– on sandwich programmes	15	20
– mature students	55	33
– international students	29	15
– male/female	38/62	49/51

Full-time/sandwich students by academic subject category

	Degree	HND
Medicine, Dentistry, Vet Science		
Subjects Allied to Medicine	220	
Science	350	
Engineering and Technology	40	20
Built Environment		
Mathematical Sciences, IT & Computing	376	254
Business and Management	1509	1186
Social Sciences	880	
Humanities	563	
Art & Design and Perf Arts	626	21
Education		

Accommodation

There is no institution-managed accommodation. Students are advised to contact the institution for information about local accommodation options.

Overseas opportunities *

Number of students on a placement or study period abroad: 250

Compacts/Networks

West London Higher Education Compact, Windsor & Slough Compact. Open College Network.

Record of Achievement

TVU encourages applicants to refer to their RoA and welcomes the additional information provided.

Interviewing

We interview applicants claiming advanced standing, requesting accreditation of prior learning/experience.

Campus locations

Ealing and Slough.

Open Days

25 June, 30 July, 29 October, 26 November 1997. 20 May, 24 June, 29 July 1998. Tel: 0181 231 2742.

*Excludes those on compulsory language course placements.

Trinity College Carmarthen

The Registry, Trinity College Carmarthen, College Road,
Carmarthenshire, SA31 3EP

Tel: 01267 676767 Fax: 01267 676766

T80

Datafile

1996-97 Student Numbers

Total number of all students   1633

	Degree	HND
Total FT/SW undergraduate numbers	1377	
Percentages of these		
– on sandwich programmes		
– mature students	20	
– international students	2	
– male/female	40/60	

Full-time/sandwich students by academic subject category

	Degree	HND
Medicine, Dentistry, Vet Science		
Subjects Allied to Medicine		
Science	182	
Engineering and Technology		
Built Environment		
Mathematical Sciences, IT & Computing		
Business and Management		
Social Sciences		
Humanities	484	
Art & Design and Perf Arts	51	
Education	660	

Accommodation

Percentage of first years requiring accommodation who can be
accommodated in institution-managed accommodation:

Estimated weekly cost of institution-managed accommodation
for 39 weeks:

(including dinner and breakfast 5 days per week) £63.00

(no food) £49.50

(other…) £53.00

Overseas opportunities*

Number of students on a placement or study period abroad: 30

Compacts/Networks

Record of Achievement

All interviewees are invited to
bring their RoA.

Interviewing

Interviews essential for
Teacher Training. BA and BSc
applicants may be invited to
interviews.

Campus locations

Carmarthen - single site on the
outskirts of Carmarthen market
town, one mile from town
centre.

Open Days

Visits may be arranged at any convenient time. Please contact the
Registry Office for details.

*Excludes those on compulsory language course placements.

University of Ulster

Admissions Officer, University of Ulster, Cromore Road, Coleraine,
County Londonderry, BT52 1SA

Tel: 01265 44141 Fax: 01265 324908
ja.elliott@ulst.ac.uk http://www.ulst.ac.uk

U20

Datafile

1996-97 Student Numbers

Total number of all students   19340

	Degree	HND
Total FT/SW undergraduate numbers	10767	985
Percentages of these		
– on sandwich programmes	42	60
– mature students	25	7
– international students	19	9
– male/female	42/58	61/39

Full-time/sandwich students by academic subject category

	Degree	HND
Medicine, Dentistry, Vet Science		
Subjects Allied to Medicine	1563	
Science	1325	110
Engineering and Technology	880	240
Built Environment	637	31
Mathematical Sciences, IT & Computing	940	266
Business and Management	1920	318
Social Sciences	760	20
Humanities	1398	
Art & Design and Perf Arts	1030	
Education	314	

Accommodation

Percentage of first years requiring accommodation who can be
accommodated in institution-managed accommodation: 90%

Estimated weekly cost of institution-managed accommodation
for 32-37 weeks:

(including dinner and breakfast   days per week) £

(no food) £25.00 – £32.00

(other…) £

Overseas opportunities*

Number of students on a placement or study period abroad: 120

Compacts/Networks

Compacts with schools and
colleges offering first AGNVQ
in N Ireland. Validating Agency
for Access.

Record of Achievement

Will be considered as part of
overall application.

Interviewing

Where an interview forms part
of the selection procedure this
is identified in the prospectus.

Campus locations

Coleraine, Jordanstown,
Belfast, Magee.

Open Days

Magee: late March/early April, Belfast: early June, Coleraine: mid
June, Jordanstown: mid September.

*Excludes those on compulsory language course placements.

United Medical and Dental Schools of Guy's and St Thomas's (University of London)

Admissions Office, St Thomas's Hospital, Lambeth Palace Road, London, SE1 7EH

Tel: 0171 922 8013 Fax: 0171 928 0069

U60

Datafile

1996-97 Student Numbers

Total number of all students   2262

	Degree	HND
Total FT/SW undergraduate numbers	1625	

Percentages of these
- on sandwich programmes
- mature students   10
- international students   7
- male/female   51/49

Full-time/sandwich students by academic subject category

	Degree	HND
Medicine, Dentistry, Vet Science		
Subjects Allied to Medicine	136	
Science		
Engineering and Technology		
Built Environment		
Mathematical Sciences, IT & Computing		
Business and Management		
Social Sciences		
Humanities		
Art & Design and Perf Arts		
Education		

Accommodation

Percentage of first years requiring accommodation who can be accommodated in institution-managed accommodation: 100%

Estimated weekly cost of institution-managed accommodation for 31 weeks:

(including dinner and breakfast   days per week) £

(no food) £50.00

(other...) £

Overseas opportunities *

Number of students on a placement or study period abroad: 225

Compacts/Networks

Record of Achievement
Summary RoA may be brought to interview.

Interviewing
No places offered without interview.

Campus locations
Central London: Guy's at London Bridge, St Thomas's by Westminster Bridge.

Open Days

Contact Admissions Office for details. Advance booking essential.

*Excludes those on compulsory language course placements.

University College London (University of London)

The Registrar, University College London, Gower Street, London, WC1E 6BT

Tel: 0171 380 7365 Fax: 0171 380 7920
degree-info@ucl.ac.uk http://www.ucl.ac.uk

U80

Datafile

1996-97 Student Numbers

Total number of all students   14348

	Degree	HND
Total FT/SW undergraduate numbers	8856	

Percentages of these
- on sandwich programmes
- mature students   21
- international students   11
- male/female   50/50

Full-time/sandwich students by academic subject category

	Degree	HND
Medicine, Dentistry, Vet Science	1012	
Subjects Allied to Medicine	567	
Science	2009	
Engineering and Technology	904	
Built Environment	293	
Mathematical Sciences, IT & Computing	608	
Business and Management	29	
Social Sciences	1201	
Humanities	2090	
Art & Design and Perf Arts	143	
Education		

Accommodation

Percentage of first years requiring accommodation who can be accommodated in institution-managed accommodation: 100%

Estimated weekly cost of institution-managed accommodation for 30 weeks:

(including dinner and breakfast 7 days per week) £80.00

(no food) £39.00 – £57.00

(other...) £

Overseas opportunities *

Number of students on a placement or study period abroad: 73

Compacts/Networks
None.

Record of Achievement
Applicants may bring their summary RoA to interview.

Interviewing
Policy of normally interviewing applicants who are being seriously considered for admission.

Campus locations
Single compact site in centre of London.

Open Days

Open Days throughout the year. Contact Schools & Colleges Liaison Officer for information.

*Excludes those on compulsory language course placements.

Swindon College

Admissions Office, Swindon College, Regent Circus, Swindon, SN1 1PT

Tel: 01793 498308 Fax: 01793 641794

S98

Datafile

1996-97 Student Numbers

Total number of all students   2034

	Degree	HND
Total FT/SW undergraduate numbers	1237	
Percentages of these		
– on sandwich programmes		
– mature students	13	
– international students	7	
– male/female	35/65	

Full-time/sandwich students by academic subject category

	Degree	HND
Medicine, Dentistry, Vet Science	744	
Subjects Allied to Medicine	466	
Science	27	
Engineering and Technology		
Built Environment		
Mathematical Sciences, IT & Computing		
Business and Management		
Social Sciences		
Humanities		
Art & Design and Perf Arts		
Education		

Accommodation

Percentage of first years requiring accommodation who can be accommodated in institution-managed accommodation: 100%

Estimated weekly cost of institution-managed accommodation for 51 weeks:

(including dinner and breakfast   days per week) £

(no food) £30.50

(other...) £

Overseas opportunities *

Number of students on a placement or study period abroad: 225

Compacts/Networks

None.

Record of Achievement

Applicants invited to bring RoA to interviews.

Interviewing

No offers made without interview (except Physiotherapy, only mature applicants interviewed).

Campus locations

None.

Open Days

Medicine - monthly visits (invitation), Dentistry in March & July. Individual visits departmentally.

Excludes those on compulsory language course placements.

Tameside College

Student Services, Tameside College, Ashton Campus, Beaufort Road, Ashton-under-Lyne, Lancs, OL6 6NX

Tel: 0161 330 6911 Fax: 0161 343 2738
info@tamesidecollege.ac.uk

T10

Datafile

1996-97 Student Numbers

Total number of all students   1100

	Degree	HND
Total FT/SW undergraduate numbers	55	150
Percentages of these		
– on sandwich programmes		
– mature students	25	40
– international students	1	1
– male/female	50/50	53/47

Full-time/sandwich students by academic subject category

	Degree	HND
Medicine, Dentistry, Vet Science		
Subjects Allied to Medicine		45
Science		
Engineering and Technology		10
Built Environment		
Mathematical Sciences, IT & Computing		
Business and Management	355	37
Social Sciences		
Humanities	320	82
Art & Design and Perf Arts	35	21
Education		

Accommodation

Percentage of first years requiring accommodation who can be accommodated in institution-managed accommodation: 90%

Estimated weekly cost of institution-managed accommodation for 32 weeks:

(including dinner and breakfast   days per week) £

(no food) £24.00 – £32.00

(other...) £

Overseas opportunities *

Number of students on a placement or study period abroad: 80

Compacts/Networks

Member of Manchester Open College Federation. Networks with a range of local schools.

Record of Achievement

RoA may be requested if deemed necessary.

Interviewing

Applicants for certain specialist courses and those with non-standard applications.

Campus locations

All provision is located on one campus.

Open Days

During the autumn/winter terms. Please telephone the Registry for information on 01925 494494.

Excludes those on compulsory language course placements.

Letts STUDY GUIDES
THE INDEPENDENT

University of Teesside

Middlesbrough, Cleveland TS1 3BA

Tel: 01642 218121 Fax: 01642 384201
H.Cummins@tees.ac.uk

T20

Datafile

1996-97 Student Numbers

Total number of all students   15932

	Degree	HND
Total FT/SW undergraduate numbers	7716	
Percentages of these		
– on sandwich programmes		
– mature students	10	
– international students	9	
– male/female	52/48	

Full-time/sandwich students by academic subject category

	Degree	HND
Medicine, Dentistry, Vet Science		
Subjects Allied to Medicine		
Science	1059	
Engineering and Technology	900	
Built Environment		
Mathematical Sciences, IT & Computing	1031	
Business and Management	679	
Social Sciences	1668	
Humanities	1442	
Art & Design and Perf Arts	179	
Education	758	

Accommodation

Percentage of first years requiring accommodation who can be accommodated in institution-managed accommodation: 100%

Estimated weekly cost of institution-managed accommodation for 30 weeks:

(including dinner and breakfast 7 days per week) £59.40

(no food) £32.80 – £45.00

(other…) £

Overseas opportunities*

Number of students on a placement or study period abroad: 103

Compacts/Networks
None.

Record of Achievement
RoA may be considered as part of individual's application.

Interviewing
All ITT and mature applicants short-listed will be interviewed. Others may be interviewed.

Campus locations
Single site on the edge of Coventry.

Open Days

7 May, 24 September 1997. 29 April, 6 May 1998. Advance booking essential. Contact 01203 523648.

*Excludes those on compulsory language course placements.

Thames Valley University

Recruitment (Registry Services), Thames Valley University, St Mary's Road, Ealing, London, W5 5RF

Tel: 0181 579 5000 Fax: 0181 231 2900
christine.marchant@tvu.ac.uk http://www.tvu.uk

T40

Datafile

1996-97 Student Numbers

Total number of all students   18000

	Degree	HND
Total FT/SW undergraduate numbers		91
Percentages of these		
– on sandwich programmes		
– mature students		10
– international students		
– male/female		30/70

Full-time/sandwich students by academic subject category

	Degree	HND
Medicine, Dentistry, Vet Science		
Subjects Allied to Medicine		
Science		
Engineering and Technology		
Built Environment		
Mathematical Sciences, IT & Computing		
Business and Management		
Social Sciences		30
Humanities		
Art & Design and Perf Arts		61
Education		

Accommodation

Percentage of first years requiring accommodation who can be accommodated in institution-managed accommodation: 5%

Estimated weekly cost of institution-managed accommodation for 30 weeks:

(including 1 meal 7 days per week) £70.00

(no food) £52.00

(other…) £

Overseas opportunities*

Number of students on a placement or study period abroad:

Compacts/Networks
Compacts with Coventry University and DeMontfort University.

Record of Achievement
All applicants will be asked for their RoA.

Interviewing
All applicants are interviewed.

Campus locations
Royal Leamington Spa centre, Moreton Morrell centre.

Open Days

Art & Design courses have Open Day.

*Excludes those on compulsory language course placements.

Welsh College of Music and Drama

Administrative Assistant, Welsh College of Music & Drama, Cathays Park, Cardiff, CF1 3ER

Tel: 01222 342854 Fax: 01222 237639
joycet.@wcmd.ac.uk

W30

Datafile

1996-97 Student Numbers

	Degree	HND
Total number of all students 513		
Total FT/SW undergraduate numbers	266	50
Percentages of these		
– on sandwich programmes		
– mature students	38	11
– international students	4	
– male/female	29/71	78/22

Full-time/sandwich students by academic subject category

	Degree	HND
Medicine, Dentistry, Vet Science		
Subjects Allied to Medicine		
Science		
Engineering and Technology		
Built Environment		
Mathematical Sciences, IT & Computing		
Business and Management		
Social Sciences		
Humanities		
Art & Design and Perf Arts	266	50
Education		

Accommodation

There is no institution-managed accommodation. Students are advised to contact the institution for information about local accommodation options.

Overseas opportunities*

Number of students on a placement or study period abroad:

Compacts/Networks

Record of Achievement

Interviewing

Campus locations
Central Cardiff.

Open Days

Excludes those on compulsory language course placements.

West Herts College, Watford

UCAS Coordinator, West Herts College, Hempstead Road, Watford, Herts, WD1 3EZ

Tel: 01923 812565 Fax: 01923 812540

W40

Datafile

1996-97 Student Numbers

	Degree	HND
Total number of all students 28000		
Total FT/SW undergraduate numbers	250	800
Percentages of these		
– on sandwich programmes	10	
– mature students	25	15
– international students	15	10
– male/female	60/40	50/50

Full-time/sandwich students by academic subject category

	Degree	HND
Medicine, Dentistry, Vet Science		
Subjects Allied to Medicine		60
Science	25	
Engineering and Technology	35	40
Built Environment		
Mathematical Sciences, IT & Computing	20	20
Business and Management	30	430
Social Sciences		
Humanities	25	
Art & Design and Perf Arts	105	250
Education		

Accommodation

There is no institution-managed accommodation. Students are advised to contact the institution for information about local accommodation options.

Overseas opportunities*

Number of students on a placement or study period abroad:

Compacts/Networks
Associate College of the University of Hertfordshire.

Record of Achievement
Used at interview.

Interviewing
All applicants are invited for interview.

Campus locations
Watford, Hemel Hempstead.

Open Days
By individual programmes.

Excludes those on compulsory language course placements.

Westhill College of Higher Education

Wesley Park Road, Selly Oak, Birmingham, B29 6LL

Tel: 0121 415 2206 Fax: 0121 415 5399
v.haynes@westhill.ac.uk

W43

Datafile

1996-97 Student Numbers

Total number of all students   1257

	Degree	HND
Total FT/SW undergraduate numbers	898	
Percentages of these		
– on sandwich programmes		
– mature students	42	
– international students	1	
– male/female	20/80	

Full-time/sandwich students by academic subject category

	Degree	HND
Medicine, Dentistry, Vet Science		
Subjects Allied to Medicine	106	
Science		
Engineering and Technology		
Built Environment		
Mathematical Sciences, IT & Computing		
Business and Management		
Social Sciences		
Humanities	325	
Art & Design and Perf Arts	65	
Education	402	

Accommodation

Percentage of first years requiring accommodation who can be accommodated in institution-managed accommodation: 100%

Estimated weekly cost of institution-managed accommodation for 31 weeks:

(including 2-3 meals 5 days per week) £62.00

(no food) £

(other…) £

Overseas opportunities*

Number of students on a placement or study period abroad:

Compacts/Networks
Liaison with Open College Network of the West Midlands and member of Birmingham Compact.

Record of Achievement
The College will take into account any RoAs submitted.

Interviewing
Applicants who receive offers are invited to course Open Day.

Campus locations
One campus situated 4 miles south of Birmingham city centre.

Open Days
24 April 1997, 8 October 1997, 28 April 1998.

Excludes those on compulsory language course placements.

Weston College

Departmental Secretary, Weston College, Dept of Creative Arts & Design, Knightstone Road, Weston-super-Mare, Somerset, BS23 2AL

Tel: 01934 411411 Fax: 01934 411410

W47

Datafile

1996-97 Student Numbers

Total number of all students   5800

	Degree	HND
Total FT/SW undergraduate numbers	57	
Percentages of these		
– on sandwich programmes		
– mature students	22	
– international students		
– male/female	56/44	

Full-time/sandwich students by academic subject category

	Degree	HND
Medicine, Dentistry, Vet Science		
Subjects Allied to Medicine		
Science		
Engineering and Technology		
Built Environment		
Mathematical Sciences, IT & Computing		
Business and Management		
Social Sciences		
Humanities		
Art & Design and Perf Arts	57	
Education		

Accommodation

There is no institution-managed accommodation. Students are advised to contact the institution for information about local accommodation options.

Overseas opportunities*

Number of students on a placement or study period abroad:

Compacts/Networks
The programme is validated by the University of the West of England, Bristol.

Record of Achievement

Interviewing
All suitable applicants are invited to attend an interview with a portfolio of work.

Campus locations
Main Site (Knightstone) and the Westcliff Annexe.

Open Days
Throughout February or by appointment at any other time.

Excludes those on compulsory language course placements.

154

University of Westminster

Central Student Administration, University of Westminster, Metford House, 15-18 Clipstone Street, London, W1M 8JS

Tel: 0171 911 5000 Fax: 0171 911 5858

W50

Datafile

1996-97 Student Numbers

Total number of all students   18268

	Degree	HND
Total FT/SW undergraduate numbers	7857	604
Percentages of these		
– on sandwich programmes	15	
– mature students	43	38
– international students	7	71
– male/female	48/52	50/50

Full-time/sandwich students by academic subject category

	Degree	HND
Medicine, Dentistry, Vet Science		
Subjects Allied to Medicine	170	13
Science	632	22
Engineering and Technology	674	46
Built Environment	810	
Mathematical Sciences, IT & Computing	1046	306
Business and Management	1495	217
Social Sciences	1293	
Humanities	564	
Art & Design and Perf Arts	1173	
Education		

Accommodation

Percentage of first years requiring accommodation who can be accommodated in institution-managed accommodation:

Estimated weekly cost of institution-managed accommodation for weeks:

(including dinner and breakfast   days per week) £

(no food) £58.00

(other...) £

Overseas opportunities*

Number of students on a placement or study period abroad: 55

Compacts/Networks   Record of Achievement

Interviewing   Campus locations

Design & Architecture applicants may be interviewed. Others subject to academic profile.

Central London, Harrow.

Open Days

28 August 1997 (provisional). Many courses invite applicants offered a place to specific Open Days.

*Excludes those on compulsory language course placements.

Westminster College

Admissions, Westminster College, Vincent Square, London, SW1P 2PD

Tel: 0171 828 1222 Fax: 0171 931 0347

W52

Datafile

1996-97 Student Numbers

Total number of all students

	Degree	HND
Total FT/SW undergraduate numbers		320
Percentages of these		
– on sandwich programmes		
– mature students		100
– international students		30
– male/female		48/52

Full-time/sandwich students by academic subject category

	Degree	HND
Medicine, Dentistry, Vet Science		
Subjects Allied to Medicine		
Science		
Engineering and Technology		
Built Environment		
Mathematical Sciences, IT & Computing		
Business and Management		320
Social Sciences		
Humanities		
Art & Design and Perf Arts		
Education		

Accommodation

There is no institution-managed accommodation. Students are advised to contact the institution for information about local accommodation options.

Overseas opportunities*

Number of students on a placement or study period abroad: 70

Compacts/Networks   Record of Achievement

Nottingham Trent University (BA degree).

Interviewing   Campus locations

Mature applicants and those with non standard entry qualifications are normally interviewed.

Central London, Westminster.

Open Days

19 November 1997, 29 January 1998, 9 May 1998.

*Excludes those on compulsory language course placements.

West Thames College

Admissions Officer, West Thames College, London Road, Isleworth, Middlesex, TW7 4HS

Tel: 0181 568 0244 Fax: 0181 569 7787
enquiry@west-thames.ac.uk.

W65

Wigan and Leigh College

Marketing Manager, PO Box 53, Parsons Walk, Wigan, Lancashire, WN1 1RS

Tel: 01942 501528 Fax: 01942 501533

W67

West Thames College

Datafile

1996-97 Student Numbers

Total number of all students   5818

	Degree	HND
Total FT/SW undergraduate numbers		167
Percentages of these		
– on sandwich programmes		14
– mature students		49
– international students		10
– male/female		69/31

Full-time/sandwich students by academic subject category

	Degree	HND
Medicine, Dentistry, Vet Science		
Subjects Allied to Medicine		
Science		9
Engineering and Technology		14
Built Environment		
Mathematical Sciences, IT & Computing		
Business and Management		46
Social Sciences		
Humanities		
Art & Design and Perf Arts		98
Education		

Accommodation

There is no institution-managed accommodation. Students are advised to contact the institution for information about local accommodation options.

Overseas opportunities*

Number of students on a placement or study period abroad: 12

Compacts/Networks

Record of Achievement
RoA will be taken into consideration as part of the application process (where RoA is available).

Interviewing
All applicants interviewed before being offered a place (except overseas). Art & Design - portfolio required.

Campus locations
Single site campus in Isleworth.

Open Days
3-14 Feb 1997 - HND Art & Design, 12 Feb - International Trade. Contact College for details.

Excludes those on compulsory language course placements.

Wigan and Leigh College

Datafile

1996-97 Student Numbers

Total number of all students   15000

	Degree	HND
Total FT/SW undergraduate numbers	71	596
Percentages of these		
– on sandwich programmes		
– mature students	40	10
– international students		2
– male/female	60/40	60/40

Full-time/sandwich students by academic subject category

	Degree	HND
Medicine, Dentistry, Vet Science		
Subjects Allied to Medicine		18
Science		
Engineering and Technology		48
Built Environment		19
Mathematical Sciences, IT & Computing	20	53
Business and Management	42	235
Social Sciences		
Humanities	9	
Art & Design and Perf Arts		133
Education		90

Accommodation

Percentage of first years requiring accommodation who can be accommodated in institution-managed accommodation: 10%

Estimated weekly cost of institution-managed accommodation for   weeks:

(including dinner and breakfast   days per week) £

(no food) £

(other…) £45.00

Overseas opportunities*

Number of students on a placement or study period abroad: 30

Compacts/Networks

Record of Achievement
RoA encouraged and welcomed.

Interviewing
Applicants can be interviewed on request.

Campus locations
Wigan Campus, Leigh Campus, town centre locations.

Open Days
HE Convention 23 April 1997. Higher Performing Arts Events 16-18 June 1997. A & D 1-7 June 1997.

Excludes those on compulsory language course placements.

Wimbledon School of Art

Academic Registrar, Wimbledon College of Art, Merton Hall Road, London, SW19 3QA

Tel: 0181 540 0231 Fax: 0181 543 1750
art@wimbledon.ac.uk http://www.education.com.hk/wimbledon

W69

Datafile

1996-97 Student Numbers

Total number of all students   729

	Degree	HND
Total FT/SW undergraduate numbers	381	
Percentages of these		
– on sandwich programmes		
– mature students	73	
– international students	11	
– male/female	24/76	

Full-time/sandwich students by academic subject category

	Degree	HND
Medicine, Dentistry, Vet Science		
Subjects Allied to Medicine		
Science		
Engineering and Technology		
Built Environment		
Mathematical Sciences, IT & Computing		
Business and Management		
Social Sciences		
Humanities		
Art & Design and Perf Arts	381	
Education		

Accommodation

Percentage of first years requiring accommodation who can be accommodated in institution-managed accommodation: 8%

Estimated weekly cost of institution-managed accommodation for 52 weeks:

(including dinner and breakfast days per week) £

(no food) £55.00

(other...) £

Overseas opportunities *

Number of students on a placement or study period abroad: 10

Compacts/Networks

Record of Achievement

Interviewing

Route B application. All applicants interviewed.

Campus locations

Open Days

Thursday afternoons in Spring Term - contact School for more information.

Excludes those on compulsory language course placements.

Wirral Metropolitan College

Higher Education Coordinator, Carlett Park Campus, Eastham, Wirral, Merseyside, L62 0AY

Tel: 0151 551 7926 Fax: 0151 551 7701
gill.mullen@wmc.ac.uk.

W73

Datafile

1996-97 Student Numbers

Total number of all students   25000

	Degree	HND
Total FT/SW undergraduate numbers	240	210
Percentages of these		
– on sandwich programmes		
– mature students	84	37
– international students		
– male/female	32/68	62/38

Full-time/sandwich students by academic subject category

	Degree	HND
Medicine, Dentistry, Vet Science		
Subjects Allied to Medicine		
Science	74	6
Engineering and Technology		
Built Environment		18
Mathematical Sciences, IT & Computing		
Business and Management		173
Social Sciences		
Humanities	47	
Art & Design and Perf Arts	112	20
Education		

Accommodation

There is no institution-managed accommodation. Students are advised to contact the institution for information about local accommodation options.

Overseas opportunities *

Number of students on a placement or study period abroad:

Compacts/Networks

Wirral Post 16 Compact.

Record of Achievement

Available and encouraged.

Interviewing

All suitable applicants offered interview.

Campus locations

Birkenhead, Eastham, International Business and Management Centre in Birkenhead.

Open Days

Arranged through Compact.

Excludes those on compulsory language course placements.

University of Wolverhampton

Admissions and Records Unit, University of Wolverhampton,
Compton Road West, Wolverhampton, WV3 9DX

Tel: 01902 321000 Fax: 01902 323744
a.fitzpatrick@wlv.aC.UK http://www.wlv.ac.uk

W75

Datafile

1996-97 Student Numbers

Total number of all students   11013

	Degree	HND
Total FT/SW undergraduate numbers	10266	747
Percentages of these		
– on sandwich programmes	20	10
– mature students	16	15
– international students	3	1
– male/female	45/55	62/38

Full-time/sandwich students by academic subject category

	Degree	HND
Medicine, Dentistry, Vet Science		
Subjects Allied to Medicine	809	75
Science	1163	113
Engineering and Technology	325	11
Built Environment	174	36
Mathematical Sciences, IT & Computing	897	148
Business and Management	1705	310
Social Sciences	1342	
Humanities	1409	
Art & Design and Perf Arts	1423	54
Education	1019	

Accommodation

Percentage of first years requiring accommodation who can be accommodated in institution-managed accommodation: 80%

Estimated weekly cost of institution-managed accommodation for 38 weeks:

(including dinner and breakfast   days per week) £

(no food) £35.50

(other…) £41.10

Overseas opportunities*

Number of students on a placement or study period abroad:

Compacts/Networks

The University has over 100 compacts with schools and colleges locally and regionally.

Record of Achievement

A RoA can be used as part of entry qualifications particularly for Compact students.

Interviewing

Applicants for Art & Design, Teacher Training and Social Work are interviewed.

Campus locations

Wolverhampton, Telford, Dudley and Walsall.

Open Days

Many departmental Open Days. Please contact the University for information and visit arrangements.

*Excludes those on compulsory language course placements.

Worcester College of Higher Education

Henwick Grove, Worcester WR2 6AJ

Tel: 01905 855111 Fax: 01905 855132

W80

Datafile

1996-97 Student Numbers

Total number of all students

	Degree	HND
Total FT/SW undergraduate numbers	2800	128
Percentages of these		
– on sandwich programmes	3	
– mature students	37	15
– international students	1	
– male/female	35/65	68/32

Full-time/sandwich students by academic subject category

	Degree	HND
Medicine, Dentistry, Vet Science		
Subjects Allied to Medicine	465	
Science	482	47
Engineering and Technology		
Built Environment		
Mathematical Sciences, IT & Computing	83	
Business and Management	128	21
Social Sciences	535	
Humanities	367	
Art & Design and Perf Arts	111	60
Education	522	

Accommodation

Percentage of first years requiring accommodation who can be accommodated in institution-managed accommodation:

Estimated weekly cost of institution-managed accommodation for 35 weeks:

(including dinner and breakfast   days per week) £

(no food) £42.00

(other…) £

Overseas opportunities*

Number of students on a placement or study period abroad:

Compacts/Networks

Compacts with several West Midland Schools/Colleges.

Record of Achievement

Interviewing

Applicants for QTS, BSc Horticulture and some HNDs, are interviewed.

Campus locations

Worcester, Pershore (Horticulture), Kidderminster (HND Business and Media).

Open Days

Please contact Registry for dates.

*Excludes those on compulsory language course placements.

Worcester College of Technology

Registrar, Deansway, Worcester, WR1 2JF

Tel: 01905 725555 Fax: 01905 28906

W81

Datafile

1996-97 Student Numbers

Total number of all students 16000

	Degree	HND
Total FT/SW undergraduate numbers	12	250
Percentages of these		
– on sandwich programmes		
– mature students	40	20
– international students	8	5
– male/female	57/43	58/42

Full-time/sandwich students by academic subject category

	Degree	HND
Medicine, Dentistry, Vet Science		
Subjects Allied to Medicine		
Science		
Engineering and Technology	6	8
Built Environment		
Mathematical Sciences, IT & Computing		20
Business and Management		184
Social Sciences		
Humanities		
Art & Design and Perf Arts		37
Education		

Accommodation

There is no institution-managed accommodation. Students are advised to contact the institution for information about local accommodation options.

Overseas opportunities*

Number of students on a placement or study period abroad:

Compacts/Networks
None. Access students welcomed.

Record of Achievement
The College welcomes RoAs and will consider them as part of the admissions process.

Interviewing
All applicants will be interviewed.

Campus locations
Main campus in centre of Worcester, by River Severn. Easy access: Birmingham, Stratford, Wales.

Open Days

Visits to College can be arranged by contacting the Course Director for individual courses.

Excludes those on compulsory language course placements.

Writtle College

Registrar, Writtle College, Chelmsford, Essex, CM1 3RR

Tel: 01245 420705 Fax: 01245 420456
postmaster@writtle.ac.uk http://www.writtle.ac.uk

W85

Datafile

1996-97 Student Numbers

Total number of all students 1830

	Degree	HND
Total FT/SW undergraduate numbers	613	438
Percentages of these		
– on sandwich programmes		98
– mature students	25	19
– international students	11	18
– male/female	50/50	64/36

Full-time/sandwich students by academic subject category

	Degree	HND
Medicine, Dentistry, Vet Science		
Subjects Allied to Medicine		
Science	565	438
Engineering and Technology	48	
Built Environment		
Mathematical Sciences, IT & Computing		
Business and Management		
Social Sciences		
Humanities		
Art & Design and Perf Arts		
Education		

Accommodation

Percentage of first years requiring accommodation who can be accommodated in institution-managed accommodation: 90%

Estimated weekly cost of institution-managed accommodation for 39 weeks:

(including   meals   days per week) £66.00 – £76.00

(no food) £

(other…) £

Overseas opportunities*

Number of students on a placement or study period abroad: 27

Compacts/Networks
Offer interviews to Compact applicants.

Record of Achievement
Applicants attending interview sessions are encouraged to bring their RoA for dicussion.

Interviewing
Applicants are invited to view the College and have an informal interview with staff.

Campus locations
Three miles west of Chelmsford. London 40 minutes by train, Stansted Airport 25 minutes away by car.

Open Days

Open Houses on a Wednesday, once a month. Full details upon request. Open Day 1st Sunday in June.

Excludes those on compulsory language course placements.

Wye College (University of London)

Admissions Officer, Wye College, University of London, Wye, Ashford, Kent, TN25 5AH

Tel: 01233 812401 Fax: 01233 813320
registry@wye.ac.uk http://www.wye.ac.uk

W90

Datafile

1996-97 Student Numbers

Total number of all students   800

	Degree	HND
Total FT/SW undergraduate numbers	500	
Percentages of these		
– on sandwich programmes	25	
– mature students	26	
– international students	11	
– male/female	55/45	

Full-time/sandwich students by academic subject category

	Degree	HND
Medicine, Dentistry, Vet Science		
Subjects Allied to Medicine		
Science	390	
Engineering and Technology		
Built Environment		
Mathematical Sciences, IT & Computing		
Business and Management	110	
Social Sciences		
Humanities		
Art & Design and Perf Arts		
Education		

Accommodation

Percentage of first years requiring accommodation who can be accommodated in institution-managed accommodation: 100%

Estimated weekly cost of institution-managed accommodation for 10 weeks:

(including dinner and breakfast   days per week) £

(no food) £37.00

(other...) £80.00

Overseas opportunities*

Number of students on a placement or study period abroad: 6

Compacts/Networks

Record of Achievement

Interviewing

All suitable applicants are offered interview.

Campus locations

Single site campus.

Open Days

See prospectus.

Excludes those on compulsory language course placements.

The University of York

Undergraduate Admissions Office, University of York, Heslington, York, YO1 5DD

Tel: 01904 433533 Fax: 01904 433538
admissions@york.ac.uk http://www.york.ac.uk

Y50

Datafile

1996-97 Student Numbers

Total number of all students   6751

	Degree	HND
Total FT/SW undergraduate numbers	5085	
Percentages of these		
– on sandwich programmes	4	
– mature students	12	
– international students	10	
– male/female	50/50	

Full-time/sandwich students by academic subject category

	Degree	HND
Medicine, Dentistry, Vet Science		
Subjects Allied to Medicine		
Science	1237	
Engineering and Technology	317	
Built Environment		
Mathematical Sciences, IT & Computing	567	
Business and Management	55	
Social Sciences	1341	
Humanities	1330	
Art & Design and Perf Arts	127	
Education	111	

Accommodation

Percentage of first years requiring accommodation who can be accommodated in institution-managed accommodation: 100%

Estimated weekly cost of institution-managed accommodation for 28 weeks:

(including dinner and breakfast   days per week) £

(no food) £32.00

(other...) £

Overseas opportunities*

Number of students on a placement or study period abroad: 60

Compacts/Networks

Associate Institution: York College of H.E. Validate degrees of: University College Scarborough. Connect.

Record of Achievement

May be requested at admissions tutors' discretion.

Interviewing

Policy varies. Applicants receiving offers without interview are invited to attend departmental group visit.

Campus locations

Main campus: Heslington (1½ miles south of city centre). King's Manor campus York city centre.

Open Days

13 May 1998. For details contact Schools Liaison on 01904 433196.

Excludes those on compulsory language course placements.

160

York College of Further and Higher Education

Student Services, York College of Further and Higher Education, Tadcaster Road, York, YO2 1UA

Tel: 01904 770200 Fax: 01904 770499

Y70

Datafile

1996-97 Student Numbers

Total number of all students   8587

	Degree	HND
Total FT/SW undergraduate numbers	42	182
Percentages of these		
– on sandwich programmes		
– mature students	45	33
– international students	2	3
– male/female	64/36	56/44

Full-time/sandwich students by academic subject category

	Degree	HND
Medicine, Dentistry, Vet Science		
Subjects Allied to Medicine		
Science		
Engineering and Technology		7
Built Environment	16	
Mathematical Sciences, IT & Computing		
Business and Management	26	63
Social Sciences		
Humanities		
Art & Design and Perf Arts		112
Education		

Accommodation

There is no institution-managed accommodation. Students are advised to contact the institution for information about local accommodation options.

Overseas opportunities*

Number of students on a placement or study period abroad:

Compacts/Networks

Record of Achievement
Students with a RoA are asked to bring it to interview.

Interviewing
Please contact College for details.

Campus locations
York - single site.

Open Days

College Open Evenings in November. HND A & D Open Days in February. Contact College for details.

*Excludes those on compulsory language course placements.

Yorkshire Coast College of Further and Higher Education

Admissions Office, Lady Edith Drive, Scarborough, North Yorkshire, YO12 5RN

Tel: 01723 372105 Fax: 01723 501918
admissions@ycoastco.ac.uk
http://www.cdconnect.co.uk/ycc.html

Y80

Datafile

1996-97 Student Numbers

Total number of all students   5800

	Degree	HND
Total FT/SW undergraduate numbers		258
Percentages of these		
– on sandwich programmes		
– mature students		
– international students		
– male/female		50/50

Full-time/sandwich students by academic subject category

	Degree	HND
Medicine, Dentistry, Vet Science		
Subjects Allied to Medicine		
Science		
Engineering and Technology		
Built Environment		
Mathematical Sciences, IT & Computing		36
Business and Management		145
Social Sciences		12
Humanities		
Art & Design and Perf Arts		65
Education		

Accommodation

There is no institution-managed accommodation. Students are advised to contact the institution for information about local accommodation options.

Overseas opportunities*

Number of students on a placement or study period abroad:

Compacts/Networks
Member of Open College of the North West.

Record of Achievement
Students are encouraged to bring RoA to interview and to update it while at College.

Interviewing
All students will be invited to the College prior to the start of their course.

Campus locations
Scarborough (two sites).

Open Days

Open Days can be arranged via Central Admissions.

*Excludes those on compulsory language course placements.

Letts STUDY GUIDES
THE INDEPENDENT

WHY ARE YOU READING THIS ADVERTISEMENT?

Presumably because you want to be better educated, which is why you need to know that The Independent and Independent on Sunday are the newspapers for you.

- We publish listings of available higher education courses after the summer results come out

- We are the best title for graduate career opportunities

- We offer a students discount

and above all, we offer the paper for people with a mind of their own.

3

COURSE
TABLES

User Guide

The third section of the Guide contains the Course Tables. These provide you with detailed information relating to predicted entry requirements and historical admissions statistics.

Please note that predicted entry requirements are a guide only. By the time institutions receive your application, various factors may have affected course entry requirements and you may find that you are asked for higher grades than are stated in the Guide. Offers may also vary among individual applicants.

When consulting the Tables you will need to refer back to this introductory section in order to understand fully what is contained in the Tables, and how you can interpret the information within them. A brief summary of the abbreviations is also given inside the back cover and on the bookmark.

How to use the Course Tables

Identify the subjects which interest you. Look them up one at a time in the List of Tables which appears at the end of this text, or in the general index at the back of the book, to identify the appropriate Course Table(s).

Work down the Course Table and identify individual courses or groups of courses which you wish to investigate further. Read along each line: the various columns will be explained in the following pages.

Courses containing more than one subject

There are wide variations in the structure of the courses listed. Each Course Table covers courses which are predominantly in one broad subject area, for example Biology in Table 9.

Courses comprising two main subjects are included in the Tables for both subjects. You need to check prospectuses to discover the amount of time devoted to each subject during the course. Some multiple subject or combined programmes, coded with the letter 'Y' at the beginning, appear in the final Table (72) and in Subject Tables where that subject can be a significant part of your studies. Course descriptions for these programmes appear immediately after Table 72.

Letts STUDY GUIDES
THE INDEPENDENT

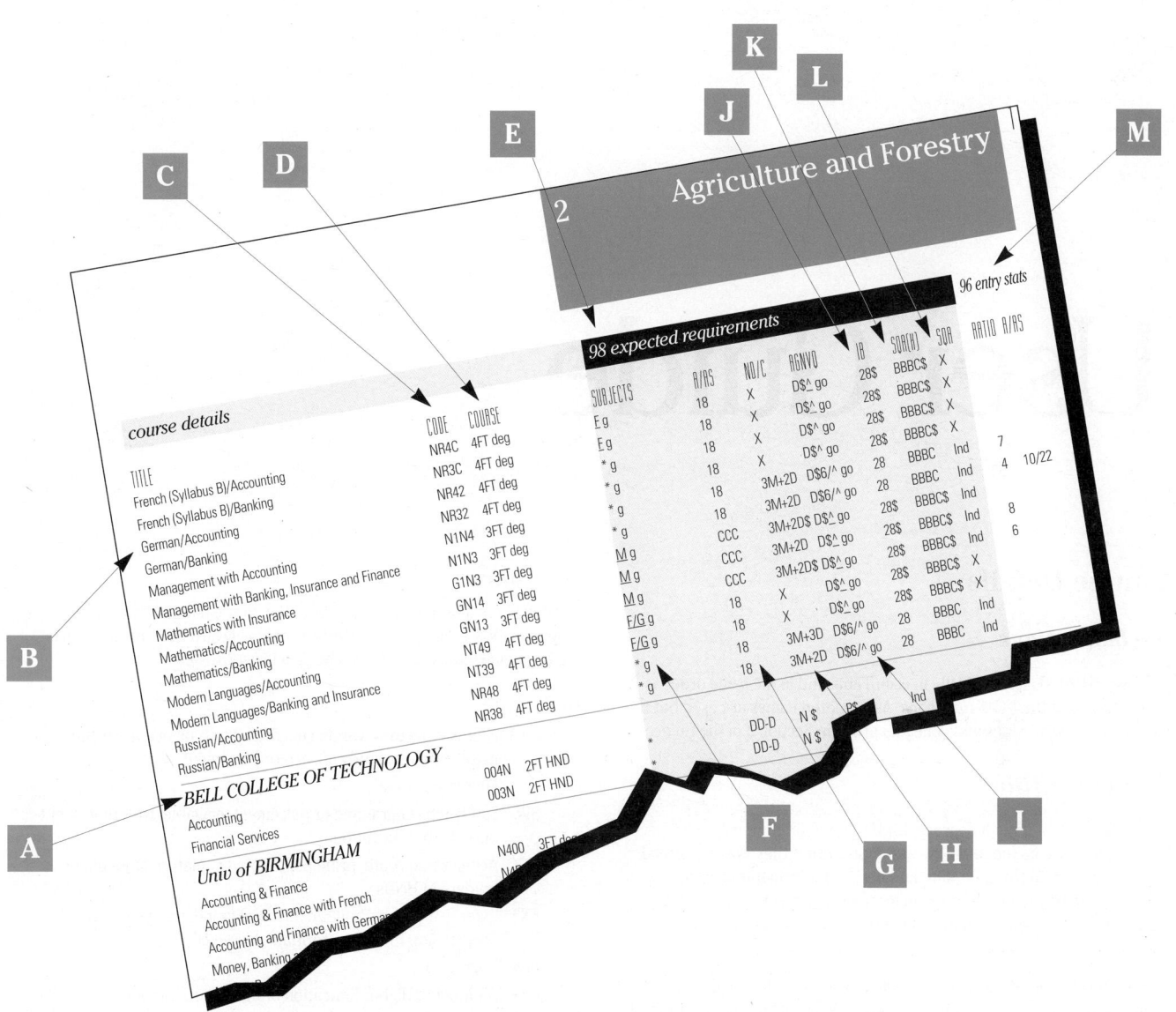

C **D** **E** **J** **K** **L** **M**

2 Agriculture and Forestry

98 expected requirements   96 entry stats

course details

CODE   COURSE

TITLE

SUBJECTS	R/RS	ND/C	AGNVQ	IB	SQA(C)	SQA	RATIO R/RS

French (Syllabus B)/Accounting	NR4C	4FT deg	
French (Syllabus B)/Banking	NR3C	4FT deg	
German/Accounting	NR42	4FT deg	
German/Banking	NR32	4FT deg	
Management with Accounting	N1N4	3FT deg	
Management with Banking, Insurance and Finance	N1N3	3FT deg	
Mathematics with Insurance	G1N3	3FT deg	
Mathematics/Accounting	GN14	3FT deg	
Mathematics/Banking	GN13	3FT deg	
Modern Languages/Accounting	NT49	4FT deg	
Modern Languages/Banking and Insurance	NT39	4FT deg	
Russian/Accounting	NR48	4FT deg	
Russian/Banking	NR38	4FT deg	

Requirements columns:

SUBJECTS	R/RS	ND/C	AGNVQ	IB	SQA(C)	SQA	RATIO R/RS
E g	18	X	D$⌃ go	28$	BBBC$	X	
E g	18	X	D$⌃ go	28$	BBBC$	X	
	18	X	D$^ go	28$	BBBC$	X	
	18	X	D$^ go	28$	BBBC$	X	7
* g	18	3M+2D	D$6/⌃ go	28	BBBC	Ind	4 10/22
* g	18	3M+2D	D$6/⌃ go	28	BBBC	Ind	
* g	18	3M+2D$	D$⌃ go	28$	BBBC$	Ind	8
M g	CCC	3M+2D	D$⌃ go	28$	BBBC$	Ind	6
M g	CCC	3M+2D$	D$⌃ go	28$	BBBC$	X	
M g	CCC	X	D$⌃ go	28$	BBBC$	X	
F/G g	18	X	D$⌃ go	28$	BBBC	Ind	
F/G g	18	3M+3D	D$6/⌃ go	28	BBBC	Ind	
* g	18	3M+2D	D$6/⌃ go	28			
* g							
*	DD-D	N $	Ps		Ind		
*	DD-D	N $					

BELL COLLEGE OF TECHNOLOGY   004N   2FT HND
003N   2FT HND

Accounting

Financial Services

Univ of BIRMINGHAM   N400   3FT deg

Accounting & Finance

Accounting & Finance with French

Accounting and Finance with German

Money, Banking

A **B** **F** **G** **H** **I**

Course Tables

The next few pages deal with the structure of the Course Tables. To help you to interpret the Tables, please refer to the above page sample, locate each area in turn and refer to the explanations overleaf.

User Guide

Course Details

A – Institutions

These are listed alphabetically in each Table and in the same order as they appear in the *UCAS Handbook*. Abbreviated names are used but the full titles of universities and colleges appear in Section 2 of the Guide.

B – Course Title

For each institution, all degrees, DipHE and HND courses are listed. All courses are included on the assumption that they have approval to run in 1998. More up-to-date and detailed information can be obtained from the institutions themselves. Prospectuses and the *UCAS Handbook* will indicate if a course was subject to approval at the time of going to press.

Combined Studies programmes which appear in Table 72 will also appear in Subject Tables with the overall title given first and the relevant subject area in *italics* underneath.

C – Course Code

The UCAS course code is included to help you cross-refer to the *UCAS Handbook* and to prospectuses.

Codes with E as the first or last letter are Art and Design courses recruited through Route B in UCAS - see article on Making your Application, page 23.

Codes can give you some indication of the type and structure of a course. Degrees in two subjects in equal combination will have two initial letters (eg CR12); degrees in two subjects in major/minor combination will have two letters separated by a number (eg C1R2).

▼ appears alongside the course code if the course offered may also be available at other sites.

D – Course

Details here aim to inform you about the nature and duration of the qualification(s) on offer and the type of final award. Key information is given below but remember to check in prospectuses.

Key:

eg 3 Number of years, varying according to type of course and involvement of study abroad or placement

FT Full-time course

SW Sandwich programme or placement available, with time spent outside the institution

ACC Accelerated route, principally aimed at mature students or holders of HNDs

EXT Extended course, built on an initial foundation year with progression to the appropriate degree/HND

deg Degree

Dip Diploma of Higher Education or Institution Diploma

HND Higher National Diploma

Expected Entry Requirements

E – 98 Expected requirements

These are shown for a number of qualifications and are for guidance only. Check with institutions and prospectuses before finalising your choice.

Note that these are *expected* requirements. Institutions may change them for a variety of reasons and may make higher or lower offers to individual applicants.

Where a column appears blank, you must check with institutions and their prospectuses for details. Requirements may be too complex to express in the space available here or there may be several possible routes of entry. New courses may not have had entry requirements set at the time of going to press. A blank column may also reflect that few applicants have previously sought entry from this route.

F – A/AS Subject patterns (Subj's)

This column indicates which A level or AS subjects are essential for entry to the course. The codes used for individual subjects are listed below.

Institutions will often accept two AS subjects in place of one A level. In some cases, eg Medicine, two AS subjects are required to substitute for a third A level.

If a subject is essential at A level, the subject code is underlined. Note that the number of subjects specified will frequently differ from the total number of A levels/AS required for entry since the latter may include a wide range of acceptable subjects.

These subject patterns should be used as an indication of what should be included by applicants offering other qualifications.

Institutions may specify GCSE (or equivalent) passes as general entry or course requirement. This is indicated by the symbol 'g'. Consult prospectuses for detailed information.

G – GCE A/AS (A/AS)

In this column offers may be expressed in terms of a points total or range of points or grades. Ranges are ABCDE. Points are calculated as follows:

A level

Grade A = 10 points, B = 8, C = 6, D = 4, E = 2

AS

Grade A = 5 points, B = 4, C = 3, D = 2 , E = 1

X signifies that A/AS alone are not sufficient for entry.

A range of grades or points may indicate the different offers likely to be made to applicants taking different numbers of subjects or the various options or streams available within a course. Check the prospectus for details.

Key to abbreviations used in subject patterns

+ **and** (eg M+C = mathematics and chemistry)

/ **or** (eg M/P = mathematics or physics)

_ **A level required, AS not acceptable** (underlined) eg M = mathematics A level required

() **select a given number from** (the subjects in the brackets) eg 2(M/P/C) = two from mathematics, physics, chemistry

A	Art	D	Dance	G	German
Ac	Accounting	Ds	Design and Technology	Gk	Greek
Ad	Art and Design	E	English (Language/Literature)	Gl	Geology
Ap	Approved subject from restricted list	Ec	Economics	Gy	Geography
Ar	Any Art or Design subject	Ee	English Language	H	History
B	Biology	El	English Literature	Ha	History of Art
Bu	Business Studies	En	Environmental Science	He	Home Economics
C	Chemistry	Es	Electronics	I	Italian
Cl	Classical Language	F	French	Ir	Irish
Cm	Communication Studies	Fa	Foundation Art course	L	1 Modern Foreign Language
Cs	Computing			2L	2 Modern Foreign Languages
				Ln	Latin
				Lw	Law

M	Mathematics	R	Russian	*	No specified subjects
Me	Media Studies	Re	Religious Studies	g	GCSE subjects, or equivalent, required other than those listed for A/AS
Mu	Music	S	1 Science		
P	Physics	2S	2 Sciences		
Pa	Performing Arts	So	Sociology	/*	Entry point varies according to qualifications held
Pe	Physical Education	Sp	Spanish		
Pf	Portfolio of work required	Ss	Sports Studies		
Ph	Any Physical Science	St	Statistics		
Pl	Polish	T	Theatre Studies		
Po	Politics	Tx	Textiles		
Ps	Psychology	W	Welsh		
Pt	Portuguese				
Py	Photography				

H – National Diploma/Certificate (ND/C)

Successful completion of the relevant National Certificate/Diploma is assumed. This alone may be sufficient for entry, or you may also be required to achieve a minimum performance in constituent units as indicated below. Offers usually relate to final year performance but contact the institution for advice.

The A/AS subject patterns may give some guidance to the suitability of your overall experience and BTEC qualification.

Key:

N	Completion of National Certificate or Diploma overall
M	Merit grades required: specified number given where appropriate
D	Distinction grades required: specified number given where appropriate
MO	Grades of merit in all units, or equivalent overall/average
DO	Distinctions required in all units
M+D	No standard offer: but some merit and distinction grades will be expected
HN	Completion of Higher National Certificate/Diploma
$	Specific units must be included
Ind	Considered on an individual basis – refer to institution
X	Not normally sufficient for entry

I – Advanced GNVQ (AGNVQ)

Although many institutions are now able to set entry requirements in terms of AGNVQ, you should check with the institution or prospectus for detailed information.

Key:

P	Pass in AGNVQ required
M	Merit in AGNVQ required
D	Distinction in AGNVQ required

The following may be used after P, M or D to indicate essential requirements as detailed:

one of the following abbreviations/symbols to show if AGNVQ must be in a specific subject, or one of several subjects, or any subject.

A	Art and Design
B	Business
C	Construction and the Built Environment
E	Engineering
G	Health and Social Care
H	Hospitality and Catering
I	Information Technology
J	Management Studies
K	Land and Environment
L	Leisure and Tourism
N	Manufacturing
Q	Performing Arts and Entertainment Industries
R	Retail and Distributive Services
S	Science
T	Media: Communication and Production
$	Specific AGNVQ subjects acceptable
*	No specified subject – any AGNVQ acceptable
+	NVQs or other additional qualification, eg Coaching Awards, Hygiene Certificate, required
eg 6	Number of additional units in AGNVQ required, eg 6. Underlined if one or more of these must be in a specific subject
^	A level, or possibly AS, must be held in addition to AGNVQ. Underlined if A/AS must be in a specific subject
gi	GCSE or intermediate GNVQ required
go	GCSE required
/	Indicates alternative
eg	MB6gi = Merit in AGNVQ in Business plus 6 additional units (one or more in specified subjects) plus either GCSE subjects or intermediate GNVQ

eg	PL6/^gi = Pass in AGNVQ in Leisure and Tourism plus either 6 additional units or A/AS (both to include specified subjects) plus either GCSE subjects or intermediate GNVQ
eg	D*^go = Distinction in any AGNVQ plus A/AS plus GCSE subjects
Ind	Considered on an individual basis – refer to institution
X	Not normally sufficient for entry

J – International Baccalaureate (IB)

Again, not every institution is able to set entry requirements in specific terms of IB, but if they can, this is given as follows:

Key:

eg 26	Points score with assumption that applicants will also pass the Diploma
D	Successful completion of Diploma
Ind	Considered on an individual basis – refer to institution
$	Specific subjects and/or grades must be included – A/AS subject pattern may give guidance
X	Not normally sufficient for entry

K – Scottish Highers (SQA(H))

Key:

ABCD	Number of Highers and bands required
CSYS	CSYS required in addition to Highers – refer to institution or prospectus
Ind	Considered on an individual basis – refer to institution
$	Specified subjects/grades must be included – A/AS subject pattern may give guidance
X	Not normally sufficient for entry

L – SQA National (SQA)

Not every institution receives sufficient applications from holders of SQA National Awards to enable them to define their requirements. Where they can, abbreviations used are:

Key:

eg20	Number of modules to be passed
N	Completion of National Certificate
HN	Completion of Higher National Certificate/Diploma required
Ind	Considered on an individual basis – refer to institution or prospectus
$	Specific units must be included – A/AS subject pattern may give guidance or refer to institution or prospectus
X	Not normally sufficient for entry

Entry statistics

M – 96 Entry statistics

Statistics of any kind cannot always be taken at face value. Some institutions choose not to display historical statistics for various very good reasons; the space available does not allow for any explanation and, by themselves, the figures might be unhelpful at best or misleading. It is also not always possible to calculate statistics for every course as developments in course structure and content can mean that many courses offered for 1998 have no obvious predecessor in 1996 on which comparisons can be based. Courses can vary in popularity from year to year and it would not be fair to applicants to give an impression from one year which will not necessarily be reflected in another.

The statistics shown are based upon UK applicants who applied for entry in 1996.

The figures that are given are presented as two statistics: the first (*Ratio*) indicates the number of applications compared to acceptances, calculated to a ratio of one; the second records the range of *A/AS* points scores held by those accepted on the course.

Remember that each student can make several applications through UCAS. Each of those applications is counted separately for these statistics but the student is only recorded once as an acceptance.

The **A/AS** points score is calculated on the points system described above in section G. It includes applicants' scores from examinations sat in the year of entry to HE and, for degree courses, only from those with at least 2 A/AS passes. The points scores do not include the many applicants accepted with other qualifications. The top and bottom 10% have also been removed to eliminate high or low aberrations. Please interpret these figures in the way that they are intended, ie as a guide and not a precise indicator of the recruitment pattern for that subject in an institution.

A Word about Course Codes

You will notice, when using this book, that each course is allocated a particular four-character code. This code is unique to that course at that institution. This is how UCAS and, indeed, the institution itself can identify exactly to which course you are applying. But how is the code made up? Does it in fact matter? Is it a random invention or does it have meaning?

Subjects of study are grouped together with other similar subjects and each group labelled with a letter of the alphabet. Biological Sciences, for example, are group C. Within each group are listed the various principal subjects which logically belong together. Each subject is identified by the group letter - in our example, C - followed by a single number. The Biological Sciences group are, therefore, Biology C1, Botany C2, Zoology C3, etc. All subjects are treated in the same way, eg Software Engineering is G7 (part of group G: Mathematical Sciences and Informatics); Accountancy is N4 (part of group N: Business and Administrative Studies).

The code given to a course is derived from codes given to the particular subjects taught within it. UCAS looks at the content of each course to determine the subjects, codes those subjects and, from there, allocates a code to the course. The title of the course is ignored from the point of view of the code eventually allocated to it. The course code has four characters to make the system flexible enough to cope with distinctions between related subjects and to allow for combinations of subjects within one course.

When a single subject is involved, the coding process is easy. Biology, subject code C1, has the course code C100. The zeros merely act as a 'filler' for the third and fourth characters. When two subjects are combined together in one course their two subject codes make up the course code. A major/minor combination of Biology with Software Engineering, where Biology is the major, would have the course code of C1G7. If Software Engineering is the major element the course code would be G7C1.

Often two subjects are combined as an equally-balanced combination, ie where the subjects are studied in the same proportion. Biology and Software Engineering could

therefore be coded as CG17 or GC71. The codes could not be CG71 or GC17 as that would be a combination of C7 (Biochemistry) and G1 (Mathematics).

By looking at the codes allocated to the various courses, therefore, you can often get a good idea of what subjects each course covers. You can also see the need to fill in your application form clearly and legibly. It would be a shame to do all that hard work and then have your chosen institution consider you for totally the wrong course.

List of Course Tables

| course details | | | 98 expected requirements | | | | | | | 96 entry stats | |

TITLE	CODE	COURSE	SUBJECTS	A/AS	NO/C	AGNVQ	IB	SQA(H)	SQA	RATIO	A/AS
Univ of ABERDEEN											
Accountancy	N400	3FT/4FT deg	* g	BBC	Ind	M$ go	30$	BBBB$	Ind	5	
Accountancy with French	N4R1	4FT deg	* g	BBC	Ind	M$ go	30$	BBBB$	Ind	13	
Accountancy with Gaelic	N4Q5	4FT deg	* g	BBC	Ind	M$ go	30$	BBBB$	Ind		
Accountancy with German	N4R2	4FT deg	* g	BBC	Ind	M$ go	30$	BBBB$	Ind		
Accountancy with Spanish	N4R4	4FT deg	* g	BBC	Ind	M$ go	30$	BBBB$	Ind		
Accountancy-Economics	NL41	4FT deg	* g	BBC	Ind	M$ go	30$	BBBB$	Ind	11	
Accountancy-Entrepreneurship	NN4C	4FT deg	* g	BBC	Ind	M$ go	30$	BBBB$	Ind		
Accountancy-French	NR41	4FT/5FT deg	* g	BBC	Ind	M$ go	30$	BBBB$	Ind	4	
Accountancy-Geography	NL48	4FT deg	* g	BBC	Ind	M$ go	30$	BBBB$	Ind	6	
Accountancy-German	NR42	4FT/5FT deg	* g	BBC	Ind	M$ go	30$	BBBB$	Ind		
Accountancy-Management Studies	NN14	4FT deg	* g	BBC	Ind	M$ go	30$	BBBB$	Ind	9	
Accountancy-Philosophy	NV47	4FT deg	* g	BBC	Ind	M$ go	30$	BBBB$	Ind		
Accountancy-Social Research	LN34	4FT deg	* g	BBC	Ind	M$ go	30$	BBBB$	Ind		
Accountancy-Sociology	NL43	4FT deg	* g	BBC	Ind	M$ go	30$	BBBB$	Ind		
Accountancy-Statistics	NG44	4FT deg	M g	BBC	Ind	M$ go	30$	BBBB$	Ind	7	
Chemistry with Accountancy	F1N4	4FT deg	C+2S/C+M+S g	CCD	Ind	MS go	24$	BBBC$	Ind		
Law (with options in Accountancy) (LLB)	M3N4	3FT/4FT deg	* g	BBB	Ind	X	34$	ABBBB$	Ind	4	
Univ of ABERTAY DUNDEE											
Accounting	N400	4FT deg	*	BC	Ind	Ind	Ind	BBBC	Ind		
Applied Chemistry with Management Accounting	F1N4	4FT/5SW deg	C	DD	Ind	Ind	Ind	BCC	Ind		
Financial Services	N300	2FT deg		X	HN	X	Ind	X	HN		
Taxation	N310	4FT deg		CC	Ind	Ind	Ind	BBCC	Ind		
Accounting	004N	2FT HND	*	C	Ind	Ind	Ind	BC	Ind		
Univ of Wales, ABERYSTWYTH											
Accounting and Finance	N400	3FT deg	* g	18	3M+3D	M6/^ g	29	BBBCC	Ind		
Accounting and Finance with Welsh	N4Q5	3FT deg	W g	18	3M+3D$ M^ g		29$	BBBCC$	Ind		
Accounting and Finance with a European Language	N4T9	4FT deg	L g	18	3M+3D$ M^ g		29$	BBBCC$	Ind		
Accounting and Finance/Economics	LN14	3FT deg	* g	18	3M+3D	M^ g	29	BBBCC	Ind		
Accounting and Finance/Law	MN34	3FT deg	* g	BBB	DO $	D g	32$	BBBCC$	Ind		
Accounting/Computer Science	GN54	3FT deg	* g	20	3M+2D	M6 g	30	BBBCC	Ind		
Accounting/Mathematics	GN14	3FT deg	M g	18	3M+3D$ M^ g		29$	BBBCC$	Ind		
Accounting/Statistics	GN44	3FT deg	M g	18	3M+3D$ M^ g		29$	BBBCC$	Ind		
Financial Management	N300	3FT deg	* g	18	3M+3D	M6/^ g	29	BBBCC	Ind		
Financial Mathematics	G1N3	3FT deg	M g	16	1M+5D$ M^ g		28$	BBBCC$	Ind		
Information Management, Accounting and Finance	GN5L	3FT deg	* g	18	1M+5D	M6 g	29	BBBCC	Ind		
ANGLIA Poly Univ											
Accounting	N400▼	3FT deg	*	14	6M	M	Dip	BBCC	N		
Business Administration (Financial Services)	N300▼	3FT deg	* g	14	6M	M go	Dip	BBCC	N		
Business Studies (Financial Services)	N301▼	3FT deg	* g	14	6M	M go	Dip	BBCC	Ind		
ASTON Univ											
Accounting for Management	N420	3FT/4SW deg	* g	BBB	3M+7D	DB6/^ go	31	AABBB	Ind	10	20/28
Business Computing & IT	NG45	3FT/4SW deg	* g	BBB	3M+7D	DB6/^ go	31	AABBB	Ind	11	20/26
Univ of Wales, BANGOR											
Accounting and Finance	N400	3FT deg	* g	18	3M+2D	D$6/^ go	28	BBBC	Ind	5	8/24
Banking,Insurance and Finance	N340	3FT deg	* g	18	3M+2D	D$6/^ go	28	BBBC	Ind	8	7/20
Banking/Accounting	NN34	3FT deg	* g	18	3M+2D	D$6/^ go	28	BBBC	Ind		
Economics/Accounting	LN14	3FT deg	* g	18	3M+2D	D$6/^ go	28	BBBC	Ind	13	
French (Syllabus A)/Accounting	NR41	4FT deg	F g	18	X	D$^ go	28$	BBBC$	X		
French (Syllabus A)/Banking	NR31	4FT deg	F g	18	X	D$^ go	28$	BBBC$	X		

Accountancy and Finance 1

	course details			98 expected requirements						96 entry stats
TITLE	CODE	COURSE	SUBJECTS	A/AS	NO/C	RGNVQ	IB	SQA(H)	SQA	RATIO A/AS
French (Syllabus B)/Accounting	NR4C	4FT deg	E g	18	X	D$^ go	28$	BBBC$	X	
French (Syllabus B)/Banking	NR3C	4FT deg	E g	18	X	D$^ go	28$	BBBC$	X	
German/Accounting	NR42	4FT deg	* g	18	X	D$^ go	28$	BBBC$	X	
German/Banking	NR32	4FT deg	* g	18	X	D$^ go	28$	BBBC$	X	
Management with Accounting	N1N4	3FT deg	* g	18	3M+2D	D$6/^ go	28	BBBC	Ind	7
Management with Banking, Insurance and Finance	N1N3	3FT deg	* g	18	3M+2D	D$6/^ go	28	BBBC	Ind	4 10/22
Mathematics with Insurance	G1N3	3FT deg	M g	CCC	3M+2D$	D$^ go	28$	BBBC$	Ind	
Mathematics/Accounting	GN14	3FT deg	M g	CCC	3M+2D	D$^ go	28$	BBBC$	Ind	8
Mathematics/Banking	GN13	3FT deg	M g	CCC	3M+2D$	D$^ go	28$	BBBC$	Ind	6
Modern Languages/Accounting	NT49	4FT deg	F/G g	18	X	D$^ go	28$	BBBC$	X	
Modern Languages/Banking and Insurance	NT39	4FT deg	F/G g	18	X	D$^ go	28$	BBBC$	X	
Russian/Accounting	NR48	4FT deg	* g	18	3M+3D	D$6/^ go	28	BBBC	Ind	
Russian/Banking	NR38	4FT deg	* g	18	3M+2D	D$6/^ go	28	BBBC	Ind	

BELL COLLEGE OF TECHNOLOGY

Accounting	004N	2FT HND	*	DD-D	N $	P$	Ind	CC	18$	
Financial Services	003N	2FT HND	*	DD-D	N $	P$	Ind	CC	12$	

Univ of BIRMINGHAM

Accounting & Finance	N400	3FT deg	*	BBC	Ind	D+^	32	ABBBB	Ind	10 20/28
Accounting & Finance with French	N4R1	4FT deg	F	BBC	Ind	D+^	32	ABBBB	Ind	7 20/28
Accounting and Finance with German	N4R2	4FT deg	G	BBC	Ind	D+^	32	ABBB	Ind	
Money, Banking and Finance	N300	3FT deg	*	BBB	Ind	D+^	33	ABBBB	Ind	8 22/28
Money, Banking and Finance with French	N3R1	4FT deg	F	BBB	Ind	D+^	33	ABBBB	Ind	6 26/26
Money, Banking and Finance with German	N3R2	4FT deg	G	BBB	Ind	D+^	33	ABBBB	Ind	3 24/30
Money, Banking and Finance with Italian	N3R3	4FT deg	L	BBB	Ind	D+^	33	ABBBB	Ind	
Money, Banking and Finance with Portuguese	N3R5	4FT deg	*	BBB	Ind	D+^	33	ABBBB	Ind	
Money, Banking and Finance with Spanish	N3R4	4FT deg	L	BBB	Ind	D+^	33	ABBBB	Ind	8

BLACKBURN COLL

Accounting and Finance	N420	3FT/4SW deg	* g	12-14	11M+3D	M$	Ind	Ind	Ind	

BLACKPOOL & FYLDE COLL

Business and Finance	31NN	2FT HND	*	4	3M	P$	Ind	Ind	Ind	

BOLTON INST

Accountancy	N400	3FT deg	* g	CD	M0	M	24	Ind	Ind	
Accountancy and Biology	CN14	3FT deg	* g	CD	M0	M*	24	BBCC	Ind	
Accountancy and Business Economics	LN14	3FT deg	* g	CD	M0	M*	24	BBCC	Ind	
Accountancy and Business Information Systems	NG45	3FT deg	* g	CD	M0	M*	24	BBCC	Ind	
Accountancy and Business Studies	NN14	3FT deg	* g	CD	M0	M*	24	BBCC	Ind	
Accountancy and Community Studies	LN54	3FT deg	* g	CD	M0	M*	24	BBCC	Ind	
Accountancy and Computing	GN54	3FT deg	* g	CD	M0	M*	24	BBCC	Ind	
Accountancy and Creative Writing	NW49	3FT deg	* g	CD	M0	M*	24	BBCC	Ind	
Accountancy and Environmental Studies	FN94	3FT deg	* g	CD	M0	M*	24	BBCC	Ind	
Accountancy and Film & TV Studies	NW45	3FT deg	* g	CD	M0	M*	24	BBCC	Ind	
Accountancy and French	NR41	3FT deg	F g	CD	Ind	Ind	24	BBCC	Ind	
Accountancy and Gender and Women's Studies	MN94	3FT deg	* g	CD	M0	M*	24	BBCC	Ind	
Accountancy and German	NR42	3FT deg	G g	CD	Ind	Ind	24	BBCC	Ind	
Accountancy and History	NVK1	3FT deg	* g	CD	M0	M*	24	BBCC	Ind	
Accountancy and Human Resource Management	NN1K	3FT deg	* g	CD	M0	M*	24	BBCC	Ind	
Accountancy and Law	NM43	3FT deg	* g	CD	M0	M*	24	BBCC	Ind	
Accountancy and Leisure Studies	NL4H	3FT deg	* g	CD	M0	M*	24	BBCC	Ind	
Accountancy and Literature	NQ42	3FT deg	* g	CD	M0	M*	24	BBCC	Ind	
Accountancy and Marketing	NN45	3FT deg	* g	CD	M0	M*	24	BBCC	Ind	

course details / 98 expected requirements / 96 entry stats

TITLE	CODE	COURSE	SUBJECTS	A/AS	NQ/C	AGNVQ	IB	SQA(H)	SQA	RATIO A/AS
Accountancy and Mathematics	GN14	3FT deg	M g	DD	Ind	Ind	24	BBCC	Ind	
Accountancy and Operations Management	NN24	3FT deg	* g	CD	MO	M*	24	BBCC	Ind	
Accountancy and Organisations, Mgt and Work	NN47	3FT deg	* g	CD	MO	M*	24	BBCC	Ind	
Accountancy and Peace and War Studies	NV41	3FT deg	* g	CD	MO	M*	24	BBCC	Ind	
Accountancy and Philosophy	NV47	3FT deg	* g	CD	MO	M*	24	BBCC	Ind	
Accountancy and Psychology	NL47	3FT deg	* g	12	MO	D*	24	BBCC	Ind	
Accountancy and Sociology	LN34	3FT deg	* g	CD	MO	M	24	Ind	Ind	
Accountancy and Statistics	GN44	3FT deg	* g	CD	MO	M	24	Ind	Ind	
Accountancy and Theatre Studies	NW44	3FT deg	Me/T g	CD	Ind	Ind	24	BBCC	Ind	
Accountancy and Tourism Studies	NP47	3FT deg	* g	CD	MO	M*	24	BBCC	Ind	
Accountancy and Urban and Cultural Studies	KN44	3FT deg	* g	CD	MO	M*	24	BBCC	Ind	
Art and Design History and Accountancy	NV44	3FT deg	* g	CD	MO	M*	24	BBCC	Ind	
Design and Accountancy	NW42	3FT deg	* g	CD	MO	M*	24	BBCC	Ind	
Visual Arts and Accountancy	NW41	3FT deg	* g	CD	MO	M*	24	BBCC	Ind	
BOURNEMOUTH Univ										
Accounting	N400	3FT deg	* g	16	MO+3D	Ind go	30	BBBB	Ind	4	8/20
Financial Services	N300	4SW deg	* g	12-14	MO+2D	M$ go	30	BBBB	Ind	1	6/16
Univ of BRIGHTON										
Accountancy with Law	NM43	3FT/4SW deg	* g	18	2M+4D	M$6/^/D$go Dip	BBBB	Ind	
Accounting and Finance	N420	3FT/4SW deg	* g	18	2M+4D	M$6/^/D$go Dip	BBBB	Ind	
Business Studies with Finance (4-year sandwich)	N1N3	4SW deg	* g	18	MO+5D	D$ go	28$	BBBB$	Ind	
International Finance and Capital Market Studies	N350	3FT/4SW deg	* g	18	2M+4D	M$6/^/D$go Dip	BBBB	Ind	
Univ of BRISTOL										
Economics and Accounting	LN14	3FT deg	M	BBC	Ind	D$^ | 32$	CSYS	Ind	12	22/28
Economics and Accounting with Law	LN1K	3FT deg	M	BBC	Ind	D$^ | 32$	CSYS	Ind	10	24/28
Economics and Accounting with Study in Cont Eur	NL41	4FT deg	M+L	BBC	Ind	D$^ | 32$	CSYS	Ind	4	24/30
Economics and Accounting with a Language	LN1L	3FT deg	M	BBC	Ind	D$^ | 32$	CSYS	Ind	8	28/30
BRISTOL, Univ of the W of England										
Accounting and Finance	N420	3FT/4SW deg	* g	16	MO+2D	M$6/^ go	24	BBCC	Ind	
Finance	N301	3FT/4SW deg	* g	16	MO+2D	M$6/^ go	24	BBCC	Ind	
Joint Honours Programme *Accounting and Economics*	Y401	3FT deg	M g	14-16	5M $	M$ go	24$	BCCC$	Ind	
Joint Honours Programme *Accounting and Statistics*	Y401	3FT deg	* g	14-16	5M	M$ go	24	BCCC	Ind	
Business Studies (Finance)	003N	2FT/3SW HND	* g	8	MO	M$ go	24	CCC	Ind	
BRUNEL Univ, West London										
Business Studies/Accounting	N1N4	3FT deg	Ec g	18	MO $	M go	26$	BCCC$	Ind	
Computer Studies/Accounting	G5N4	3FT deg	* g	16	MO $	M go	26$	BCCC$	Ind	
Economics and Business Finance	LNC3	3FT deg	* g	20	M+D	D^	28$	Ind	Ind	8	16/20
Economics and Business Finance (4 Yrs Thick SW)	LND3	4SW deg	* g	20	M+D	D^	28$	Ind	Ind	
Economics and Business Finance (4 Yrs Thin SW)	LN13	4SW deg	* g	20	M+D	D^	28$	Ind	Ind	5	16/26
Leisure Management/Accounting	N7N4	3FT deg	* g	18	MO $	M* go	26$	BCCC$	Ind	
Sport Sciences/Accounting	B6NK	3FT deg	* g	18	1M+3D	D	29	BBCC	Ind	
Univ of BUCKINGHAM										
Accounting and Finance with English Language St	N4Q3	2FT deg	* g	16	3M+2D	M	26	BCCC	Ind	
Accounting and Finance with French	N4R1	2FT deg	* g	16	3M+2D	M	26	BCCC	Ind	
Accounting and Finance with Spanish	N4R4	2FT deg	* g	16	3M+2D	M	26	BCCC	Ind	
Accounting and Financial Management	NN43	2FT deg	* g	16	3M+2D	M	26	BCCC	Ind	
Accounting with Economics	N4L1	2FT deg	* g	16	3M+2D	M	26	BCCC	Ind	
Financial Services	N300	2FT deg	* g	16	3M+2D	M	26	BCCC	Ind	

Accountancy and Finance 1

course details			98 expected requirements							96 entry stats	
TITLE	CODE	COURSE	SUBJECTS	A/AS	NO/C	AGNVQ	IB	SQA(H)	SQA	RATIO	A/AS
Information Systems with Accounting	G5N4	2FT deg	* g	12	3M+2D	M	24	CCCC	Ind		
Law with Accounting and Finance	M3N4	2FT deg	*	18	3M+2D	M	26	BCCC	Ind		
Law with Finance	M3N3	2FT deg	M* g	18	3M+2D	M	26	BCCC	Ind		
BUCKINGHAMSHIRE COLLEGE											
Business Administration with Finance	N1N3	3FT deg		8	MO	M	27	CCCC	Ind		
Business Studies with Finance	N1NH	4SW deg		8	MO+2D	M	27	CCCC	Ind		
Business Studies with Finance	31NN	2FT HND		4	3M	P	Ind	Ind	Ind		
CARDIFF Univ of Wales											
Accounting	N400	3FT deg	*	BBC-BBB	Ind	Ind	Ind	Ind	Ind	4	20/28
Accounting and Economics	LN14	3FT deg	*	BBC-BBB	Ind	Ind	Ind	Ind	Ind	5	20/26
Accounting and Management	NN14	3FT deg	*	BBC-BBB	Ind	Ind	Ind	Ind	Ind	6	20/28
Accounting with French	N4R1	4FT deg	F	BBC-BBB	Ind	Ind	Ind	Ind	Ind	7	
Accounting with German	N4R2	4FT deg	L g	BBC-BBB	Ind	Ind	Ind	Ind	Ind	5	
Accounting with Italian	N4R3	4FT deg	L g	BBC-BBB	Ind	Ind	Ind	Ind	Ind		
Accounting with Spanish	N4R4	4FT deg	Sp	BBC-BBB	Ind	Ind	Ind	Ind	Ind		
Banking and Finance	N300	3FT deg	*	BBC-BBB	Ind	Ind	Ind	Ind	Ind	9	20/26
Banking and Finance with French	N3R1	4FT deg	F	BBC-BBB	Ind	Ind	Ind	Ind	Ind	12	
Banking and Finance with German	N3R2	4FT deg	G	BBC-BBB	Ind	Ind	Ind	Ind	Ind	8	
Banking and Finance with Italian	N3R3	4FT deg	L	BBC-BBB	Ind	Ind	Ind	ABBBB	Ind		
Banking and Finance with Spanish	N3R4	4FT deg	Sp	BBC-BBB	Ind	Ind	Ind	Ind	Ind		
Univ of CENTRAL ENGLAND											
Accountancy	N400	3FT deg	* g	14	M+4D $	D6	24	CCCC	Ind	7	10/18
Business Administration with Accountancy	N1N4	3FT deg	* g	14	M+3D	D	22	CCCC	Ind	8	10/14
Business Administration with Finance	N1N3	3FT deg	* g	14	M+3D	D	22	CCCC	Ind	10	10/18
Business Economics and Finance	LN13	3FT deg	* g	14	M+3D	D	24	CCCC			
Economics with Accountancy	L1N4	3FT deg	* g	14	M+3D	D	24	CCCC	Ind	26	
Finance	N300	4SW deg	* g	14	M+3D	D6	24	CCCC			
Finance with Accountancy	N3N4	3FT deg	* g	14	M+3D	D6				7	10/20
Finance with Economics	N3L1	3FT deg	* g	14	M+3D	D6					
Finance with Law	N3M3	3FT deg	* g	14	M+3D	D6	24	CCCC			
Finance with Marketing	N3N5	3FT deg	* g	14	M+3D	D6					
Univ of CENTRAL LANCASHIRE											
Accounting	N400	3FT deg	* g	14	MO+2D	M$6/^	26	BBCC	Ind		
Accounting and Financial Studies	N420	3FT deg	* g	14	MO+2D	M$6/^	26	BBCC	Ind		
Accounting and Financial Studies (Year 2 entry)	N421	3FT deg									
Combined Honours Programme Accounting	Y400	3FT deg	* g	12	MO	M$6/^	26	BCCC	Ind		
Business with Finance	024N	2FT HND		8	MO	M$	24	CCC	Ind		
CHELTENHAM & GLOUCESTER COLL of HE											
Business Computer Systems and Financial Mgt	GNMH	3FT deg	*	8-12	MO	M	26	CCCC	Ind		
Business Computer Systems and Financial Ser Mgt	NG35	3FT deg	*	8-12	MO	M	24	CCCC	Ind		
Business Computer Systems with Financ Serv Mgt	G5NH	3FT deg	*	8	MO	M	24	CCCC	Ind		
Business Computer Systems with Financial Mgt	NGH5	3FT deg	*	8	MO	M	26	CCCC	Ind		
Business Info Technology and Financial Mgt	GNMJ	3FT deg	*	8-12	MO	M	26	CCCC	Ind		
Business Info Technology and Financial Serv Mgt	GN53	3FT deg	*	8-12	MO	M	24	CCCC	Ind		
Business Info Technology with Financial Mgt	NGJ5	3FT deg	*	8-12	MO	M	26	CCCC	Ind		
Business Info Technology with Financial Serv Mgt	G5N3	3FT deg	*	8-12	MO	M	24	CCCC	Ind		
Business Management and Financial Management	NND3	4SW deg	*	8-12	4M+3D	MB3	26	CCCC	Ind		
Business Management and Financial Services Mgt	NN13	4SW deg	*	12-16	4M+3D	MB3	26	CCCC	Ind		
Business Management with Financial Management	N1NJ	4SW deg	*	12	4M+3D	MB3	26	CCCC	Ind		

TITLE	CODE	COURSE	SUBJECTS	A/AS	ND/C	AGNVQ	IB	SQA(H)	SQA	RATIO A/AS
Business Management with Financial Services Mgt	N1N3	4SW deg	*	12-16	4M+3D	MB3	26	CCCC	Ind	
Catering Management and Financial Management	NN37	4SW deg	*	8-12	MO	MH3	26	CCCC	Ind	
Catering Management and Financial Services Mgt	NN7H	4SW deg	*	8-12	MO	MH3	26	CCCC	Ind	
Catering Management with Financial Management	N7NH	4SW deg	*	8	MO	MH3	26	CCCC	Ind	
Catering Management with Financial Services Mgt	N7NJ	4SW deg	*	8	MO	MH3	26	CCCC	Ind	
Computing and Financial Management	GNNH	3FT deg	*	8-12	MO	P3	26	CCCC	Ind	
Computing and Financial Services Management	GN5H	3FT deg	*	8-12	MO	P3	24	CCCC	Ind	
Computing with Financial Management	NG3M	3FT deg	*	8	MO	M	26	CCCC	Ind	
Computing with Financial Services Management	G5NJ	3FT deg	*	8-10	MO	M	24	CCCC	Ind	
Countryside Planning and Financial Management	DN23	3FT deg	*	8-12	MO	MK	26	CCCC	Ind	
Countryside Planning with Financial Management	D2N3	3FT deg	*	8-12	MO	MK	26	CCCC	Ind	
Environmental Policy and Financial Management	FNX3	3FT deg	*	8-10	MO	MK	26	CCCC	Ind	
Environmental Policy with Financial Management	F9NH	3FT deg	*	8-12	MO	M3	26	CCCC	Ind	
Financial Management and Financial Services Mgt	N303	4SW deg	*	10	5M+2D	MB3	26	CCCC	Ind	
Financial Management and Geology	NF36	3FT deg	S	8-12	5M+2D	M3	26	CCCC	Ind	
Financial Management and Hotel Management	NN73	4SW deg	*	8-12	5M+2D	M3	26	CCCC	Ind	
Financial Management and Human Resource Mgt	NNCH	4SW deg	*	10-14	5M+2D	MB3	26	CCCC	Ind	
Financial Management and Leisure Management	NN3R	4SW deg	*	10-16	5M+2D	M3L	26	CCCC	Ind	
Financial Management and Marketing Management	NN35	4SW deg	*	8-12	5M+2D	MB3	26	CCCC	Ind	
Financial Management and Multimedia	NGHM	3FT deg	*	8-12	5M+2D	M3	26	CCCC	Ind	
Financial Management and Natural Resource Mgt	FN93	3FT deg	*	8-10	MO	MK	26	CCCC	Ind	
Financial Management and Psychology	NL37	3FT deg	g	10-14	5M+2D	M3	26	CCCC	Ind	
Financial Management and Sociological Studies	NL33	3FT deg	*	10-14	5M+2D	M3	26	CCCC	Ind	
Financial Management and Sport and Exercise Sci	BN63	3FT deg	S	10-14	5M+2D	ML3	26	CCCC	Ind	
Financial Management and Tourism Management	NP37	4SW deg	*	10-16	5M+2D	ML3	26	CCCC	Ind	
Financial Management and Women's Studies	MN93	3FT deg	*	8-12	5M+2D	M3	26	CCCC	Ind	
Financial Management with Business Comp Systems	GN5J	4SW deg	*	8-12	MO	M3	26	CCCC	Ind	
Financial Management with Business Info Tech	GNM3	4SW deg	*	8-12	MO	M3	26	CCCC	Ind	
Financial Management with Business Management	N3ND	4SW deg	*	10	5M+2D	M3	26	CCCC	Ind	
Financial Management with Catering Management	N3NR	4SW deg	*	10	5M+2D	M3	26	CCCC	Ind	
Financial Management with Computing	GNN3	4SW deg	*	8-12	MO	M3	26	CCCC	Ind	
Financial Management with Countryside Planning	N3D2	4SW deg	*	10	5M+2D	M3	26	CCCC	Ind	
Financial Management with Environmental Policy	N3FX	4SW deg	*	10	5M+2D	M3	26	CCCC	Ind	
Financial Management with Financial Services Mgt	N301	4SW deg	*	10	5M+2D	M3	26	CCCC	Ind	
Financial Management with Geology	N3F6	4SW deg	*	8-10	MO	M3	26	CCCC	Ind	
Financial Management with Hotel Management	N3N7	4SW deg	*	10	5M+2D	M3	26	CCCC	Ind	
Financial Management with Human Resource Mgt	N3NC	4SW deg	*	10	5M+2D	M3	26	CCCC	Ind	
Financial Management with Leisure Management	NN3T	4SW deg	*	10-16	5M+2D	M3	26	CCCC	Ind	
Financial Management with Marketing Management	N3N5	4SW deg	*	10	5M+2D	M3	26	CCCC	Ind	
Financial Management with Multimedia	GNNJ	4SW deg	*	8-12	5M+2D	M3	26	CCCC	Ind	
Financial Management with Natural Resource Mgt	N3F9	4SW deg	*	10	5M+2D	M3	26	CCCC	Ind	
Financial Management with Psychology	N3L7	4SW deg	g	10-14	5M+2D	M3	26	CCCC	Ind	
Financial Management with Sociological Studies	N3L3	4SW deg	*	10-14	5M+2D	M3	26	CCCC	Ind	
Financial Management with Sport & Exercise Sci	N3B6	4SW deg	*	10-14	5M+2D	M3	26	CCCC	Ind	
Financial Management with Tourism Management	N3P7	4SW deg	*	10-14	5M+2D	M3	26	CCCC	Ind	
Financial Management with Women's Studies	N3M9	4SW deg	*	10	5M+2D	M3	26	CCCC	Ind	
Financial Services Mgt and Hotel Management	NN7J	4SW deg	*	10-12	5M+2D	M3	26	CCCC	Ind	
Financial Services Mgt and Human Resource Mgt	NNHC	4SW deg	*	10	5M+2D	M3	26	CCCC	Ind	
Financial Services Mgt and Leisure Management	NNRH	4SW deg	*	10-14	5M+2D	ML3	26	CCCC	Ind	
Financial Services Mgt and Marketing Management	NNH5	4SW deg	*	10	5M+2D	MB3	26	CCCC	Ind	
Financial Services Mgt and Multimedia	NG3N	3FT deg	*	8-12	5M+2D	M3	26	CCCC	Ind	
Financial Services Mgt and Psychology	LN73	3FT deg	g	10-14	5M+2D	M3	26	CCCC	Ind	

Accountancy and Finance 1

TITLE	CODE	COURSE	SUBJECTS	A/AS	NO/C	AGNVQ	IB	SQA(H)	SQA	RATIO A/AS
course details			**98 expected requirements**							**96 entry stats**
Financial Services Mgt and Sport & Exercise Sci	NB36	3FT deg	S	10-14	5M+2D	M3	26	CCCC	Ind	
Financial Services Mgt and Tourism Management	PN73	4SW deg	*	10-14	5M+2D	ML3	26	CCCC	Ind	
Financial Services Mgt with Business Comp Systs	N3GN	4SW deg	*	8-12	MO	M3	26	CCCC	Ind	
Financial Services Mgt with Business Info Tech	N3G5	4SW deg	*	8-12	MO	M3	26	CCCC	Ind	
Financial Services Mgt with Business Mgt	N3N1	4SW deg	*	10-12	4M+3D	M3	26	CCCC	Ind	
Financial Services Mgt with Catering Management	N3NT	4SW deg	*	8-12	5M+2D	M3	26	CCCC	Ind	
Financial Services Mgt with Computing	N3GM	4SW deg	*	8-12	MO	M3	26	CCCC	Ind	
Financial Services Mgt with Financial Management	N302	4SW deg	*	10	5M+2D	M3	26	CCCC	Ind	
Financial Services Mgt with Hotel Management	NNT3	4SW deg	*	10-12	5M+2D	M3	26	CCCC	Ind	
Financial Services Mgt with Human Resource Mgt	NN31	4SW deg	*	10	5M+2D	M3	26	CCCC	Ind	
Financial Services Mgt with Leisure Management	NNHT	4SW deg	*	10-14	5M+2D	M3	26	CCCC	Ind	
Financial Services Mgt with Marketing Management	N3NM	4SW deg	*	10	5M+2D	M3	26	CCCC	Ind	
Financial Services Mgt with Mod Lang (French)	N3R1	4SW deg	g	8-10	MO	M3	26	CCCC	Ind	
Financial Services Mgt with Multimedia	NGJN	4SW deg	*	8-12	5M+2D	M3	26	CCCC	Ind	
Financial Services Mgt with Psychology	N3LR	4SW deg	g	8-12	5M+2D	M3	26	CCCC	Ind	
Financial Services Mgt with Sport & Exercise Sci	N3BP	4SW deg	g	10-12	5M+2D	M3	26	CCCC	Ind	
Financial Services Mgt with Tourism Management	N3PR	4SW deg	*	10-14	5M+2D	M3	26	CCCC	Ind	
Geology with Financial Management	F6N3	3FT deg	*	8	MO	M3	26	CCCC	Ind	
Hotel Management with Financial Management	N7N3	4SW deg	*	12	5M+2D	MH3	26	CCCC	Ind	
Hotel Management with Financial Services Mgt	NNR3	4SW deg	*	12	5M+2D	MH3	26	CCCC	Ind	
Human Resource Mgt with Financial Management	N1NH	4SW deg	*	10	5M+2D	MB3	26	CCCC	Ind	
Human Resource Mgt with Financial Services Mgt	NNC3	3FT deg	*	10	5M+2D	MB3	26	CCCC	Ind	
Marketing Management with Financial Management	N5N3	4SW deg	*	12	5M+2D	MB3	26	CCCC	Ind	
Marketing Management with Financial Services Mgt	N5NH	4SW deg	*	12	5M+2D	MB3	26	CCCC	Ind	
Multimedia with Financial Management	NGHN	3FT deg	*	8-12	MO	MI3	26	CCCC	Ind	
Multimedia with Financial Services Management	NGJM	3FT deg	*	8-12	MO	MI3	26	CCCC	Ind	
Natural Resource Mgt with Financial Mgt	F9N3	3FT deg	*	8-12	MO	M3	26	CCCC	Ind	
Psychology with Financial Management	L7N3	3FT deg	g	12-16	5M+2D	M3^	26	CCCC	Ind	
Psychology with Financial Services Management	L7NH	3FT deg	g	12-16	5M+2D	M3^	26	CCCC	Ind	
Sociological Studies with Financial Management	L3N3	3FT deg	*	12	MO	MG3	26	CCCC	Ind	
Sport & Exercise Sciences with Financial Mgt	B6NH	3FT deg	S	12-16	MO	ML3	26	CCCC	Ind	
Sport & Exercise Sciences with Financial Ser Mgt	B6N3	3FT deg	S	12-16	4M+3D	ML3	26	CCCC	Ind	
Tourism Management with Financial Management	P7N3	4SW deg	*	12-16	5M+2D	ML3	26	CCCC	Ind	
Tourism Management with Financial Services Mgt	P7NH	4SW deg	*	12-16	5M+2D	ML3	26	CCCC	Ind	
Women's Studies with Financial Management	M9N3	3FT deg	*	8-12	MO	M3	26	CCCC	Ind	
Financial Management	003N	2FT HND	*	2	P	P	Ind	Ind	Ind	
Financial Services Management	053N	2FT HND	*	2	N	P	Ind	Ind	Ind	
CITY Univ										
Banking and International Finance	N302	3FT/4SW deg	* g	BBB	DO	D*^	30$	AAABB	Ind	11	18/28
Economics/Accountancy	LN14	3FT deg	* g	BBC	3M+4D	D*^	28$	BBBBB	Ind	16	18/24
Insurance and Investment	N330	3FT/4SW deg	* g	BBC	2M+5D	D	$	AAABB	Ind	2	17/24
Investment and Financial Risk Management	N350	3FT/4SW deg	* g	BBC	2M+5D	D	$	AAABB	Ind	
COVENTRY Univ										
Mathematical Studies & Accounting	GN94	3FT/4SW deg	M g	14-18	Ind	Ind	Ind	Ind	Ind	
Mathematical Studies & Finance	GN93	3FT/4SW deg	M g	14-18	Ind	Ind	Ind	Ind	Ind	
CROYDON COLL										
Business St (Accounting & Fin) (Yr 3 entry opt)	N1N4	3FT deg	*	6	MO $	M$/P$3	Ind	Ind		
Business Studies (Accounting and Finance)	34NN	2FT HND	*	E	N $	P$	Ind	Ind		

| course details | | | | 98 expected requirements | | | | | | 96 entry stats |

TITLE	CODE	COURSE	SUBJECTS	A/AS	ND/C	RGNVQ	IB	SQA(H)	SQA	RATIO A/AS
DE MONTFORT Univ										
Accounting and Finance	N420▼	3FT/4SW deg	* g	14	MO	D	X	BBBB	N	10/20
Business Economics/Accounting	LN14▼	3FT deg	* g	18	3M+3D	M	32	AABB	X	
Business/Accounting	NN14▼	3FT deg	* g	18	3M+3D	M	32	AABB	X	
Finance/Business	NN31▼	3FT deg	* g	18	3M+3D	M	32	AABB	X	
Finance/Business Economics	LN13▼	3FT deg	* g	18	3M+3D	M	32	AABB	X	
Human Resource Management/Accounting	NN64▼	3FT deg	* g	18	3M+3D	M	32	AABB	Ind	
Human Resource Management/Finance	NN63▼	3FT deg	* g	18	3M+3D	M	32	AABB	Ind	
Law/Accounting	MN34▼	3FT deg	* g	BBC	6D	M^	30$	BBBBB$	X	
Law/Finance	MN33▼	3FT deg	* g	BBC	6D	M^	30$	BBBBB$	X	
Management/Accounting	NN1K▼	3FT deg	* g	18	3M+3D	M	32	AABB	X	
Management/Finance	NN13▼	3FT deg	* g	18	3M+3D	M	32	AABB	X	
Marketing/Accounting	NN54▼	3FT deg	* g	18	3M+3D	M	32	AABB	X	
Marketing/Finance	NN35▼	3FT deg	* g	18	3M+3D	M	32	AABB	X	
Public Policy/Accounting	LN44▼	3FT deg	* g	18	3M+3D	M	32	AABB	X	
Public Policy/Finance	LN43▼	3FT deg	* g	18	3M+3D	M	32	AABB	X	
Combined Studies *Accounting*	Y400▼	3FT/4SW deg	*	12	2M+4D	M	30	BBB	Ind	
Univ of DERBY										
Accounting	N400	3FT deg	*	14	MO+2D	M$	28	BBCC	Ind	8	8/16
Management Accountancy	N410	3FT deg	*	14	MO+2D	D$	28	BBCC	Ind	
Credit Accumulation Modular Scheme *Accounting*	Y600	3FT deg	*	10	MO	M	Ind	CCCC	Ind	
Univ of DUNDEE										
Accountancy	N400	3FT/4FT deg	* g	CCC	MO+D	D$	29$	BBBBC$	HN$	4	12/20
Accountancy and Applied Computing	GN54	4FT deg	S g	14	5M $	M$	25$	BBBC$	N$	5
Accountancy and Chemistry	FN14	4FT deg	2S g	14	5M $	M$	25$	BBCC$	N$	
Accountancy and Mathematics	GN14	4FT deg	M g	14	5M $	M$^	25$	BBBC$	N$	9
Finance	N300	3FT/4FT deg	* g	CCC	MO+D	D$	29$	BBBC$	HN$	8	14/14
Univ of DURHAM										
Accounting and Economics	N420	3FT deg	* g	18	Ind	Ind	Ind	AAABB	Ind	
Univ of EAST ANGLIA										
Accountancy	N400	3FT deg	* g	BBB-BBC	MO+3D	D	30$	ABBBB	Ind	4	14/24
Accountancy with Business Management	N4N1	3FT deg								
Accountancy with Law	N4M3	3FT deg	* g	BBB-BBC	HN		30$	ABBBB	X	4	18/21
Business Finance and Economics	NL41	3FT deg	* g	BBC	3M+3D	D	30	BBBBB	Ind	10	20/22
Business Information Systems	GN54	3FT deg	*	BBB-BBC	MO+4D	D^	30$	BBBBB	Ind	5
Computerised Accountancy	NG45	3FT deg	M	BBB-BBC	MO+3D	D^	30$	ABBBB	Ind	6	22/26
Economics with Accountancy	L1N4	3FT deg	*	BCC	3M+3D		30	BBBBB	Ind	15
Univ of EAST LONDON										
Accounting & Finance and Economics	NL41	3FT deg	* g	14	MO	MB	Ind	Ind	Ind	4
Accounting & Finance and Law	NM43	3FT deg	* g	14	MO	D	Ind	Ind	Ind	7
Accounting & Finance and Maths, Stats & Comp	NG49	3FT deg	* g	14	MO	M$	Ind	Ind	Ind	
Accounting & Finance with Bus Information Systs	G5N4	3FT deg	* g	14	MO	M	Ind	Ind	Ind	
Accounting & Finance with Economics	N4L1	3FT deg	* g	14	M	D	Ind	Ind	Ind	
Accounting & Finance with European Studies	N4T2	3FT deg	* g	14	MO	M	Ind	Ind	Ind	
Accounting & Finance with Information Technology	N4G5	3FT deg	* g	14	MO	MB	Ind	Ind	Ind	
Accounting & Finance with Law	N4M3	3FT deg	* g	14	MO	MB	Ind	Ind	Ind	
Accounting & Finance with Maths, Stats & Comp	N4G9	3FT deg	* g	14	MO	MB	Ind	Ind	Ind	
Accounting and Finance	N420	3FT deg	* g	12	N	MB	Ind	Ind	Ind	10	10/18

Accountancy and Finance ▼   1

TITLE	CODE	COURSE	SUBJECTS	A/AS	NO/C	AGNVQ	IB	SQA(H)	SQA	RATIO A/AS
Accounting with Business Mathematics	N401	3FT deg	*g	14	N	MB	Ind	Ind	Ind	17
Business Info Systems/Accounting & Finance	NG47	3FT deg	*g	12	MO	MB	Ind	Ind	Ind	
Business Studies/Business Admin (Bus Finance)	N1N3	4FT deg	*g	14	MO	MB	Ind	Ind	Ind	
Economics with Accounting & Finance	L1N4	3FT deg	*g	12	MO	M	Ind	Ind	Ind	
Health Studies with Accounting & Finance	L4N4	3FT deg	*g	12	MO	M	Ind	Ind	Ind	
Information Technology with Accounting & Finance	G5NK	3FT deg	*g	12	MO	M	Ind	Ind	Ind	
Law with Accounting & Finance	M3N4	3FT deg	*g	14	MO	M				
Maths, Stats & Computing with Acc & Finance	G9N4	3FT deg	*g	12	MO	M	Ind	Ind	Ind	
Professional Accounting Studies	N400	3FT deg	*g	14	MO	MB	Ind	Ind	Ind	
Three-Subject Degree *Accounting and Finance*	Y600	3FT deg	*g	12	MO	M	Ind	Ind	Ind	

Univ of EDINBURGH

TITLE	CODE	COURSE	SUBJECTS	A/AS	NO/C	AGNVQ	IB	SQA(H)	SQA	RATIO A/AS
Business Studies and Accounting	NN14	4FT deg	g	BBB	Ind		34$	ABBB	Ind	7
Economics and Accounting	LN14	4FT deg	g	BBB	Ind		34$	ABBB	Ind	10
Law and Accountancy	MN34	4FT deg	g	ABB	X		32	AAABB	X	5

Univ of ESSEX

TITLE	CODE	COURSE	SUBJECTS	A/AS	NO/C	AGNVQ	IB	SQA(H)	SQA	RATIO A/AS
Accounting	N400	3FT deg	*g	20	MO+3D	D	28	BBBB	Ind	
Accounting and Economics	NL41	3FT deg	*g	20	MO+3D	D	28	BBBB	Ind	41
Accounting and Finance	N420	3FT deg	M	BCC	MO+3D$	Ind	28$	CSYS	Ind	
Accounting and Management	NN14	3FT deg	*g	20	MO+3D	D	28	BBBB	Ind	
Accounting and Sociology	NL43	3FT deg	*g	20	MO+3D	D	28	BBBB	Ind	
Mathematics and Finance	GN13	3FT deg	M	BBC	MO+4D	D^	30$	CSYS	Ind	11

Univ of EXETER

TITLE	CODE	COURSE	SUBJECTS	A/AS	NO/C	AGNVQ	IB	SQA(H)	SQA	RATIO A/AS
Accounting & Financial Studies	N420	3FT deg	*g	24	2M+3D	D$	36	Ind	Ind	8 20/28
Accounting & Financial Studies with European St	N421	4FT deg	L g	24	2M+3D	D$	36	Ind	Ind	6
Business and Accounting Studies	NN14	3FT deg	*g	24	2M+3D	D$	36	Ind	Ind	11 22/28
Business and Accounting Studies with European St	NN1K	4FT deg	L g	24	2M+3D	D$	36	Ind	Ind	14
Mathematics with Accounting	G1N4	3FT deg	M	22	MO	M/D$^	34$	Ind	Ind	

FARNBOROUGH COLL of Technology

TITLE	CODE	COURSE	SUBJECTS	A/AS	NO/C	AGNVQ	IB	SQA(H)	SQA	RATIO A/AS
Accounting	N400	3FT deg		10	Ind	M*	Ind	Ind	Ind	6 16/22

Univ of GLAMORGAN

TITLE	CODE	COURSE	SUBJECTS	A/AS	NO/C	AGNVQ	IB	SQA(H)	SQA	RATIO A/AS
Accounting & Finance and Biological Science	CN14	3FT deg	M/S g	12	Ind	M$	Ind	Ind	Ind	
Accounting & Finance and Mathematics	GN14	3FT deg	M g	12	Ind	M$	Ind	Ind	Ind	
Accounting and Computing	G5N4	3FT/4SW deg	*g	12	7M	M$	Ind	Ind	Ind	7 14/16
Accounting and Finance	N420	3FT/4SW deg	*g	14	MO+2D$	M$	Ind	Ind	Ind	4 8/16
Business Accounting	N410	3FT/4SW deg	*g	14	MO+2D	M$	Ind	Ind	Ind	
Financial Risk Management	N350	3FT deg								
International Accounting	N401	3FT deg	*g	14	MO+2D$	M$	Ind	Ind	Ind	
Law with Accounting and Finance	M3N4	3FT deg	*g	18	Ind	Ind	Ind	Ind	Ind	
Mathematics and Accounting & Finance	GN1K	3FT deg								
Mathematics with Accounting & Finance	G1NK	3FT deg								
Combined Studies (Honours) *Accounting & Finance*	Y400	3FT deg	*g	8-16	Ind	Ind	Ind	Ind	Ind	
Joint Honours *Accounting & Finance*	Y401	3FT deg	*g	8-16	Ind	Ind	Ind	Ind	Ind	
Major/Minor Honours *Accounting & Finance*	Y402	3FT deg	*g	8-16	Ind	Ind	Ind	Ind	Ind	
Business Administration (Accounting & Finance)	024N▼	2FT HND	*g	6	MO	P$	Ind	Ind	Ind	5 2/4

course details   **98 expected requirements**   *96 entry stats*

		course details		**98 expected requirements**							**96 entry stats**	
TITLE	CODE	COURSE	SUBJECTS	A/AS	NQ/C	RGNVQ	IB	SQA(H)	SQA	RATIO A/AS	

TITLE	CODE	COURSE	SUBJECTS	A/AS	NQ/C	RGNVQ	IB	SQA(H)	SQA	RATIO	A/AS
Univ of GLASGOW											
Accountancy	N400	4FT deg		BBB	HN		32	AAABB	X	6	16/20
Accountancy with Finance	N4N3	4FT deg		BBB	HN		32	AAABB	X		
Accountancy with International Accounting	N401	4FT deg		BBB	HN		32	AAABB	X		
Accountancy with Languages	N4T9	4FT deg		BBB	HN		32	AAABB	X		
Accountancy/Economics	LN1K	4FT deg		BBB	HN		32$	AAABB	X	16	
Business Economics/Accountancy	LNC4	4FT deg		BBC	N	M	30	BBBB	N		
Economics/Accountancy	LND4	4FT deg		BBC	8M	M	30	BBBB	Ind	3	
Financial and Legal Studies	MN34	4FT deg		BBB	HN		32	AAABB	X		
GLASGOW CALEDONIAN Univ											
Accountancy	N402	2FT Dip	E	CC	Ind		Ind	BBC$	Ind	4	
Accountancy	N400	3FT/4FT deg	E+M	BC	Ind		Ind	BBBC$	Ind	3	
Accountancy with Decision Sciences	N4N2	3FT/4FT deg	E+M	BC	Ind		Ind	BBBC$	Ind		
Accountancy with Economics	N4L1	3FT/4FT deg	E+M	BC	Ind		Ind	BBBC$	Ind		
Accountancy with Law	N4M3	3FT/4FT deg	E+M	BC	Ind		Ind	BBBC$	Ind		
Accountancy with Management	N4N1	3FT/4FT deg	E+M	BC	Ind		Ind	BBBC$	Ind		
Financial Mathematics	GN13	3FT deg	M	CD	Ind		Ind	BBC	Ind	2	
Financial Services	N300	3FT/4FT deg	E+L g	BC	Ind		Ind	BBBC$	Ind	3	
Risk Management	NN39	3FT/4FT deg	E+M+L	BC	Ind		Ind	BBBC$	Ind	3	
Univ of GREENWICH											
Accounting and Finance	N400	3FT deg	* g	14	MO+4D	M	24	CCC	Ind		
Applied Statistics with Accounting and Finance	G4N4	3FT/4SW deg	* g	CE	3M	Ind	Ind	CCC	Ind		
Economics with Banking	L1NH	3FT deg	* g	14	3M	Ind	Ind	Ind	Ind		
Finance and Financial Information Systems	N350	3FT deg	* g	16	MO+4D	M	24	CCC	Ind		
Financial Services	N310	3FT deg	* g	16	MO+4D	M	24	CCC	Ind		
HERIOT-WATT Univ											
Accountancy and Finance	NN34	4FT deg	* g	BCC	Ind	M$ go	Ind	ABBB	Ind		
Accountancy with French	N4R1	4FT deg	L g	BCC	Ind		Ind	ABBB$	Ind		
Accountancy with German	N4R2	4FT deg	L g	BCC	Ind		Ind	ABBB$	Ind		
Accountancy with Spanish	N4R4	4FT deg	L g	BCC	Ind		Ind	ABBB$	Ind		
Business and Finance	NN1H	4FT deg	*	CCC	HN	Ind	30	BBBB			
Economics and Accountancy	LN14	4FT deg	*	BCC	HN	M$ go	Ind	ABBB	Ind		
Economics and Finance	LN13	4FT deg	*	CCC	HN	M$ go	28	BBBB	HN		
International Business and Finance	NN13	4FT deg	L	CCC	Ind		Ind	BBBB	Ind		
Mathematics with Finance	G1N3	4FT deg	M	CDE		M$^					
Combined Studies *Accountancy and Finance*	Y300	4FT deg	*	CCC	Ind	M$ go	30	BBBB	Ind		
Univ of HERTFORDSHIRE											
Accounting	N400	3FT/4SW deg	* g	18	DO	DB	28$	BBBB	Ind	6	8/18
Accounting and Law	NM43	3FT/4SW deg	* g	18	DO	DB	28	BBBC	Ind		
Accounting and Management Information Systems	GN54	3FT/4SW deg	* g	18	DO	DB	28$	BBBB		7	10/20
Business Joint Honours	NN41	3FT/4SW deg	* g	18	DO	DB	28	BBBB		4	8/20
Financial Services	N300	3FT/4SW deg	* g	18	DO	DB	28	BBBB	Ind		
Univ of HUDDERSFIELD											
Accountancy	N401	2FT Dip	* g	12	3M+3D	M$ go	Ind	BBB	Ind		
Accountancy and Finance	N420	3FT deg	* g	12	3M+3D	M$ go	Ind	BBCC	Ind		
Accountancy with Environmental Studies	N4F9	3FT deg	* g	12	3M+3D	M$ go	Ind	BBCC	Ind		
Financial Management and Economics	LN13	3FT deg	* g	14	3M+3D	M$ go	Ind	BBCC	Ind		
Law and Accountancy	MN34	3FT deg	* g	16	3M+3D	M go	Ind	BBCC	Ind		
Management and Accountancy	NN14	3FT deg	* g	16	3M+3D	M$ go	Ind	BBCC	Ind		

Accountancy and Finance 1

			98 expected requirements							96 entry stats	
course details											
TITLE	CODE	COURSE	SUBJECTS	A/AS	NO/C	AGNVQ	IB	SQA(H)	SQA	RATIO A/AS	
Univ of HULL											
Accounting	N400	3FT deg	* g	BCC	MO+4D	D$^ go	28	BBCCC	Ind	5	16/26
Accounting (International)	N401	3FT deg	* g	20	DO	D$+	28	BBBCC	Ind		
Economics and Accounting	LN14	3FT deg	* g	BCC	MO	M*^ go	28$	BBCCC	Ind	5	12/26
KEELE Univ											
Finance and American Studies (4 Yrs)	QN43	4FT deg	*	BCC	Ind	Ind	28	BBBB	Ind		
Finance and Applied Social Studies	LN53	3FT deg	* g	BBB-BBC	Ind	Ind	30	CSYS	Ind		
Finance and Applied Social Studies (4 Yrs)	NL35	4FT deg	*	BBC	Ind	Ind	30	BBBB	Ind		
Finance and Astrophysics	FN53	3FT deg	P g	BCC	Ind	M$^	28$	CSYS	Ind		
Finance and Biochemistry	CN73	3FT deg	C g	BCC	Ind	M$^	28$	CSYS	Ind		
Finance and Biochemistry (4 Yrs)	CN7H	4FT deg	*	BCC	Ind	Ind	28	BBB	Ind		
Finance and Biological & Medicinal Chem (4 Yrs)	FN1H	4FT deg	*	BCC	Ind	Ind	28	BBBB	Ind		
Finance and Biological and Medicinal Chemistry	FN13	3FT deg	C g	BCC	Ind	M$^	28$	CSYS	Ind		
Finance and Biology	CN13	3FT deg	S g	BCC	Ind	M$^	28$	CSYS	Ind		
Finance and Biology (4 Yrs)	NC31	4FT deg	*	BCC	Ind	Ind	28	BBBB	Ind		
Finance and Business Administration	NN39	3FT deg	* g	BBC-BCC	Ind	Ind	30	CSYS	Ind		
Finance and Business Administration (4 Yrs)	NN3X	4FT deg	*	BCC	Ind	Ind	28	BBBB	Ind		
Finance and Chemistry	FNC3	3FT deg	C g	BCC	Ind	M$^	28$	CSYS	Ind		
Finance and Chemistry	NF31	4FT deg	*	BCC	Ind	Ind	28	BBBB	Ind		
Finance and Computer Science (4 Yrs)	NG35	4FT deg	* g	BCC	Ind	Ind	28	BBBB	Ind		
Finance and Criminology	MNH3	3FT deg	* g	BBB	Ind	Ind	32	CSYS	Ind		
Finance and Criminology (4 Yrs)	MNHH	4FT deg	*	BBB	Ind	Ind	32	BBBB	Ind		
Finance and Economics	LN13	3FT deg	* g	BCC	Ind	Ind	28	CSYS	Ind		
Finance and Economics (4 Yrs)	NL31	4FT deg	*	BCC	Ind	Ind	28	BBBB	Ind		
Finance and Educational Studies (4 Yrs)	XN93	4FT deg	* g	BCC	Ind	Ind	28	BBBB	Ind		
Finance and Electronic Music	NW3J	3FT deg	Mu g	BCC	Ind	D$^	28$	CSYS	Ind		
Finance and Electronic Music (4 Yrs)	WNJ3	4FT deg	*	BCC	Ind	Ind	28	BBBB	Ind		
Finance and English	NQ33	3FT deg	E	BBC	Ind	D$^	30$	CSYS	Ind		
Finance and English (4 Yrs)	QN33	4FT deg	*	BBC	Ind	Ind	30	BBBB	Ind		
Finance and Environmental Management	FNX3	3FT deg	* g	BCC	Ind	Ind	28	CSYS	Ind		
Finance and Environmental Management (4 Yrs)	NF3X	4FT deg	*	BCC	Ind	Ind	28	BBBB	Ind		
Finance and French	NR31	3FT deg	F	BBC-BCC	Ind	D$^	28$	CSYS	Ind		
Finance and Geology	FN63	3FT deg	S g	BCC	Ind	M$^	28$	CSYS	Ind		
Finance and History	NV31	3FT deg	* g	BBC-BCC	Ind	Ind	28	CSYS	Ind		
Finance and History (4 Yrs)	VN13	4FT deg	*	BBC-BCC	Ind	Ind	28	BBBB	SQA		
Finance and International History	NVHC	3FT deg	* g	BCC	Ind	Ind	28	CSYS	Ind		
Finance and Mathematics	GN13	3FT deg	M	BCC	Ind	M$^	28$	CSYS	Ind		
Finance and Music	NW33	3FT deg	Mu g	BCC	Ind	D$^	28$	CSYS	Ind		
Finance and Physics	FN33	3FT deg	P g	BCC	Ind	M$^	28	CSYS	Ind		
Finance and Psychology	CN83	3FT deg	* g	BBB	Ind	Ind	32	CSYS	Ind		
Finance and Russian	NR38	3FT deg	R g	BCC	Ind	D$^	28$	CSYS	Ind		
Finance and Russian Studies	NR3W	3FT deg	* g	BCC	Ind	D$	28	CSYS	Ind		
Finance and Statistics	GN43	3FT deg	M	BCC	Ind	M$^	28$	CSYS	Ind		
Finance and Visual Arts	NW31	3FT deg	*	BBC-BCC	Ind	Ind	28	CSYS	Ind		
French and Finance (4 Yrs)	RN13	4FT deg	*	BCC	Ind	Ind	28	BBB	Ind		
Geography and Finance	LN83	3FT deg	Gy g	BCC	Ind	D$^	28$	CSYS	Ind		
Geology and Finance (4 Yrs)	NF36	4FT deg	*	BCC	Ind	Ind	28	BBBB	Ind		
Human Resource Management and Finance	NN3Q	3FT deg	* g	BBC-BCC	Ind	D	28	CSYS	Ind		
Human Resource Management and Finance (4 Yrs)	NN63	4FT deg	*	BBC-BCC	Ind	Ind	28	BBBB	Ind		
International History and Finance (4 Yrs)	NV3D	4FT deg	*	BCC	Ind	Ind	28	BBBB	Ind		
International Politics and Finance	MNC3	3FT deg	* g	BCC	Ind	Ind	28	CSYS	Ind		
International Politics and Finance (4 Yrs)	NM3C	4FT deg	*	BCC	Ind	Ind	28	BBBB	Ind		

course details			98 expected requirements							96 entry stats	
TITLE	CODE	COURSE	SUBJECTS	A/AS	NO/C	AGNVQ	IB	SQA(H)	SQA	RATIO A/AS	
Latin and Finance (4 Yrs)	QN63	4FT deg	*	BCC	Ind	Ind	28	BBBB	Ind		
Law and Finance	MN33	3FT deg	* g	BBB	Ind	Ind	32	CSYS	Ind		
Management Science and Finance	NN13	3FT deg	* g	BCC	Ind	Ind	28	CSYS	Ind		
Management Science and Finance (4 Yrs)	NN31	4FT deg	*	BCC	Ind	Ind	28	BBBB	Ind		
Marketing and Finance	NN35	3FT deg	* g	BBC-BCC	Ind	Ind	28	CSYS	Ind		
Mathematics and Finance (4 Yrs)	NG31	4FT deg	*	BCC	Ind	Ind	28	BBBB	Ind		
Music and Finance (4 Yrs)	WN33	4FT deg	*	BBC-BCC	Ind	Ind	28	BBBB	Ind		
Philosophy and Finance (4 Yrs)	VN73	4FT deg	*	BBC-BCC	Ind	Ind	28	BBBB	Ind		
Politics and Finance	MN13	3FT deg	* g	BCC	Ind	Ind	28	CSYS	Ind		
Politics and Finance (4 Yrs)	NM31	4FT deg	*	BCC	Ind	Ind	28	BBBB	Ind		
Sociology & Social Anthropology & Finance(4 Yrs)	NL33	4FT deg	* g	BBC-BCC	Ind	Ind	28	BBBB	Ind		
Statistics and Finance (4 Yrs)	NG34	4FT deg	*	BCC	Ind	Ind	28	BBBB	Ind		
Univ of KENT											
Accounting & Finance	N400	3FT deg	* g	20	3M+3D	M$ go	28	BBBB	Ind	7	16/24
Accounting & Finance and Business Administration	NN41	3FT deg	* g	24	1M+5D	D$ go	32	AABB			
Accounting & Finance and Management Science	NN14	3FT deg	M	18	Ind	Ind	26$	BBBB$	Ind	7	16/24
Accounting & Finance with Computing	N4G5	3FT deg	* g	20	3M+4D	M$ go	28	BBBB	Ind	7	
Accounting & Finance with French Bus St (4 Yrs)	N4N1	4FT deg	F g	18	Ind	Ind	26$	BBBB$	Ind	7	
Accounting & Finance with German (4 Yrs)	N402	4FT deg	G g	18	Ind	Ind	26$	BBBB$	Ind		
Accounting and Finance	N420▼	3FT deg		20	6M	M	28	BBBB	Ind	1	6/14
Actuarial Science	N320	3FT deg	M	24	Ind	Ind	32	Ind	Ind	5	18/30
British and French Accounting & Finance (4 Yrs)	N403	4FT deg	F g	18	Ind	Ind	26$	BBBB$	Ind		
Computing and Accounting & Finance	GN54	3FT deg	* g	20	3M+3D	M$ go	28	BBBB	Ind		
Economics/Accounting and Finance	LN14	3FT deg	* g	20	3M+3D	M$ go	28	BBBB	Ind	4	14/20
Ind Relations & Human Resource Mgt (Accounting)	NN46	3FT deg	* g	20	3M+3D	M$ go	28	BBBB	Ind		
Mathematics and Accounting	GNC4	3FT/4SW deg	M	22	Ind	Ind	30$	ABBB$	Ind	7	20/26
Physics with Finance	F3N3	3FT deg	M+P	18	5M $	Ind	26$	BBBC$	Ind		
Politics & Government/Accounting and Finance	MN14	3FT deg	* g	BCC	3M+3D	M$ go	28	BBBB	Ind		
Social Anthropology/Accounting and Finance	LN64	3FT deg	* g	20	3M+3D	M$ go	28	BBBB	Ind		
Social Policy & Admin/Accounting and Finance	LN44	3FT deg	* g	20	3M+3D	M$ go	28	BBBB	Ind		
Sociology/Accounting and Finance	NL43	3FT deg	* g	20	3M+3D	M$ go	28	BBBB	Ind		
KINGSTON Univ											
Accounting and Finance	N420	3FT deg	*	CCC	3M+5D	Ind	Ind	Ind	Ind	9	10/22
Accounting and Law	MN34	3FT deg	*	CCC	3M+5D	Ind	Ind	CCCCC	Ind	5	14/20
Univ of Wales, LAMPETER											
Management Techniques and American Literature	NQ41	3FT deg			Ind	Ind	Ind	Ind	Ind		
LANCASTER Univ											
Accounting and Economics	NL41	3FT deg	* g	BBC	DO $		30	ABBBB	Ind		
Accounting and Finance	N400	3FT deg	* g	24	DO $		32	AABBB	Ind		
Accounting, Finance and Computer Science	NG45	3FT deg	M g	BBC	DO $		30$	ABBBB$	Ind		
Accounting, Finance and Mathematics	NG41	3FT deg	M g	BBC	DO $		30$	ABBBB$	Ind		
Finance	N300	3FT deg	* g	24	DO $		32	AABBB$	Ind		
Finance and Economics	NL31	3FT deg	* g	24	DO $		32	AABBB$	Ind		
French Studies and Accounting and Finance	NR41	4SW deg	M+F g	BBC	DO $		32$	AABBB$	Ind		
German Studies and Accounting and Finance	NR42	4SW deg	M+G/L g	BBC	DO $		32$	AABBB$	Ind		
Italian Studies and Accounting and Finance	NR43	4SW deg	M+I/L g	BBC	DO $		32$	AABBB$	Ind		
Spanish Studies and Accounting and Finance	NR44	4SW deg	M+Sp/L g	BBC	DO $		30$	AABBB$	Ind		
Univ of LEEDS											
Accounting and Finance	N420	3FT deg	g	BBB	Ind	Ind	32	CSYS	Ind	14	22/30
Accounting-Computer Science	GN54	3FT/4FT deg	M g	BBC	Ind	Ind	30$	CSYS	Ind	10	

Accountancy and Finance 1

course details			98 expected requirements							96 entry stats	
TITLE	CODE	COURSE	SUBJECTS	A/AS	NO/C	AGNVQ	IB	SQA(H)	SQA	RATIO	A/AS
Accounting-Information Systems	G5NK	3FT/4FT deg	g	BBC	Ind	Ind	30$	CSYS	Ind	11	
Mathematics with Finance	G1N3	3FT deg	M g	24	Ind	Ind	32$	CSYS	Ind		

LEEDS METROPOLITAN Univ

Accounting and Finance	N420	3FT/4SW deg	* g	CCD	4M+3D	DB/MB6/^ go	28	BBBCC	Ind	9	10/22

Univ of LINCOLNSHIRE and HUMBERSIDE

Accountancy	N400	3FT deg	* g	12	3M+1D	M	24	CCCC	Ind		
Accountancy and Administration	NN14	3FT deg	* g	12	3M+1D	M	24	CCCC	Ind		
Accountancy and Business	NN41	3FT deg	* g	12	3M+1D	M	24	CCCC	Ind		
Accountancy and Finance	N420	3FT deg	* g	12	3M+1D	M	24	CCCC	Ind		
Accountancy and French	NR41	3FT deg	F g	12	3M+1D	M	24	CCCC	Ind		
Accountancy and German	NR42	3FT deg	G g	12	3M+1D	M	24	CCCC	Ind		
Accountancy and Human Resource Management	NN64	3FT deg	* g	12	3M+1D	M	24	CCCC	Ind		
Accountancy and Information Systems	GN54	3FT deg	* g	12	3M+1D	M	24	CCCC	Ind		
Accountancy and Media Technology	NP44	3FT deg	* g	12	3M+1D	M	24	CCCC	Ind		
Accountancy and Modern Languages	NT49	3FT deg	L g	12	3M+1D	M	24	CCCC	Ind		
Accountancy and Spanish	NR44	3FT deg	Sp g	12	3M+1D	M	24	CCCC	Ind		
Administration and Finance	NN13	3FT deg	* g	12	3M+1D	M	24	CCCC	Ind		
Computing and Accountancy	GN5K	3FT deg	* g	12	3M+1D	M	24	CCCC	Ind		
Finance and Computing	NG35	3FT deg	* g	12	3M+1D	M	24	CCCC	Ind		
Finance and French	NR31	3FT deg	F g	12	3M+1D	M	24	CCCC	Ind		
Finance and German	NR32	3FT deg	G g	12	3M+1D	M	24	CCCC	Ind		
Finance and Human Resource Management	NN36	3FT deg	* g	12	3M+1D	M	24	CCCC	Ind		
Finance and Information Systems	GN53	3FT deg	* g	12	3M+1D	M	24	CCCC	Ind		
Finance and Marketing	NN35	3FT deg	* g	12	3M+1D	M	24	CCCC	Ind		
Finance and Media Technology	NP34	3FT deg	* g	12	3M+1D	M	24	CCCC	Ind		
Finance and Modern Languages	NT3X	3FT deg	L g	12	3M+1D	M	24	CCCC	Ind		
Finance and Spanish	NR34	3FT deg	Sp g	12	3M+1D	M	24	CCCC	Ind		
Management and Finance	NN1J ▼	3FT deg	* g								
Marketing and Accountancy	NN45	3FT deg	* g	12	3M+1D	M	24	CCCC	Ind		
European Technology and Finance	93JN	2FT HND	* g	4		P					
Finance and Technology	39NJ	2FT HND	* g	4		P					

Univ of LIVERPOOL

Accounting	N400	3FT deg	M/Ec	BCC	Ind	Ind	Ind	Ind	Ind	15	18/26
Accounting and Computer Science	GN54	3FT deg	M/Ec	CCC	Ind	Ind	Ind	Ind	Ind	16	18/20
Economics and Accounting	LNC4	3FT deg	M/Ec	BCC	Ind	Ind	Ind	Ind	Ind	24	

LIVERPOOL JOHN MOORES Univ

Accounting and Finance	N420	3FT deg		16	3M+4D	D/M^	Ind			12	12/22

LONDON GUILDHALL Univ

3D/Spatial Design and Accounting	NW4F	3FT deg	Pf g	DD	MO	M$ go	24	Ind	Ind		
3D/Spatial Design and Financial Services	NW3F	3FT deg	Pf g	DD	MO	M$ go	24	Ind	Ind		
3D/Spatial Design and Taxation	NWHF	3FT deg	Pf g	DD	MO	M$ go	24	Ind	Ind		
Accounting Studies	N401	3FT deg									
Accounting and Finance	N400	3FT deg	* g	CDD	DO	D$ go	24	Ind	Ind		
Business Economics and Accounting	LNC4	3FT deg	* g	DD	MO	M$ go	24	Ind	Ind		
Business Information Technology and Accounting	GN74	3FT deg	* g	DD	MO	M$ go	24	Ind	Ind		
Business and Accounting	NN14	3FT deg	* g	CD-DDD	MO+4D	M$ go	26	Ind	Ind		
Communications & Audio Vis Prod St & Accounting	NP44	3FT deg	* g	CC-CDD	MO+6D	D$ go	26	Ind	Ind		
Computing and Accounting	GN54	3FT deg	* g	DD	MO	M$ go	24	Ind	Ind		
Design Studies and Accounting	NW42	3FT deg	* g	CD-DDD	MO+2D	M$ go	24	Ind	Ind		
Development Studies and Accounting	MN94	3FT deg	* g	DD	MO	M$ go	24	Ind	Ind		

			98 expected requirements							96 entry stats

course details

TITLE	CODE	COURSE	SUBJECTS	A/AS	ND/C	AGNVQ	IB	SQA(H)	SQA	RATIO A/AS
Economics and Accounting	LN14	3FT deg	* g	DD	MO	M$ go	24	Ind	Ind	
English and Accounting	NQ43	3FT deg	* g	CD-DDD	MO+2D	M$ go	24	Ind	Ind	
European Studies and Accounting	NT42	3FT deg	* g	DD	MO	M$ go	24	Ind	Ind	
Financial Services	N302	1FT deg								
Financial Services	N301	3FT deg	* g	CDD	6M+4D	M$ go	24	Ind	Ind	
Financial Services & Business Information Techn	GN73	3FT deg	* g	DD	MO	M$ go	24	Ind	Ind	
Financial Services and Accounting	NN34	3FT deg	* g	DD	MO	M$ go	24	Ind	Ind	
Financial Services and Business	NN13	3FT deg	* g	CD-DDD	MO+2D	M$ go	26	Ind	Ind	
Financial Services and Business Economics	LNC3	3FT deg	* g	DD	MO	M$ go	24	Ind	Ind	
Financial Services and Computing	GN53	3FT deg	* g	DD	MO	M$ go	24	Ind	Ind	
Financial Services and Design Studies	NW32	3FT deg	* g	CD-DDD	MO+2D	M$ go	26	Ind	Ind	
Financial Services and Development Studies	MN93	3FT deg	* g	DD	MO	M$ go	24	Ind	Ind	
Financial Services and Economics	LN13	3FT deg	* g	DD	MO	M$ go	24	Ind	Ind	
Financial Services and English	NQ33	3FT deg	* g	CD-DDD	MO+2D	M$ go	26	Ind	Ind	
Financial Servs & Commun & Audio Visual Prod St	NP34	3FT deg	* g	CC-CDD	MO+4D	M$ go	26	Ind	Ind	
Financial Studies and European Studies	NT32	3FT deg	* g	DD	MO	M$ go	24	Ind	Ind	
Fine Art and Accounting	NW41	3FT deg	Pf g	CC-CDD	MO+2D	M$ go	26	Ind	Ind	
Fine Art and Financial Services	NW31	3FT deg	Pf g	CC-CDD	MO+2D	M$ go	26	Ind	Ind	
French and Accounting	NR41	4FT deg	* g	DD	MO	M$ go	24	Ind	Ind	
French and Financial Services	NR31	4FT deg	* g	DD	MO	M$ go	24	Ind	Ind	
German and Accounting	NR42	4FT deg	* g	DD	MO	M$ go	24	Ind	Ind	
German and Financial Services	NR32	4FT deg	* g	DD	MO	M$ go	24	Ind	Ind	
Insurance Studies	N341	1FT deg								
Insurance Studies	N340	3FT deg	* g	CDD	6M+4D	M$ go	24	Ind	Ind	
International Relations and Accounting	MNC4	3FT deg	* g	DD	MO	M$ go	24	Ind	Ind	
International Relations and Financial Services	MNC3	3FT deg	* g	DD	MO	M$ go	24	Ind	Ind	
Law and Accounting	MN34	3FT deg	* g	CC-CDD	MO+4D	M$ go	26	Ind	Ind	
Law and Financial Services	MN33	3FT deg	* g	CC-CDD	MO+2D	M$ go	26	Ind	Ind	
Marketing and Accounting	NN45	3FT deg	* g	CD-DDD	MO+2D	M$ go	26	Ind	Ind	
Marketing and Financial Services	NN35	3FT deg	* g	CD-DDD	MO+2D	M$ go	26	Ind	Ind	
Mathematics and Accounting	GN14	3FT deg	* g	DD	MO	M$ go	24	Ind	Ind	
Mathematics and Financial Services	GN13	3FT deg	* g	DD	MO	M$ go	24	Ind	Ind	
Modern History and Accounting	NV41	3FT deg	* g	DD	MO	M$ go	24	Ind	Ind	
Modern History and Financial Services	NV31	3FT deg	* g	DD	MO	M$ go	24	Ind	Ind	
Multimedia Systems and Accounting	GNM4	3FT deg	* g	DD	MO	M$ go	24	Ind	Ind	
Multimedia Systems and Financial Services	GNM3	3FT deg	* g	DD	MO	M$ go	24	Ind	Ind	
Politics and Accounting	MN14	3FT deg	* g	DD	MO	M$ go	24	Ind	Ind	
Politics and Financial Services	MN13	3FT deg	* g	DD	MO	M$ go	24	Ind	Ind	
Product Development & Manuf & Financial Services	JN43	3FT deg	* g	DD	MO	M$ go	24	Ind	Ind	
Product Development & Manufacture & Accounting	JN44	3FT deg	* g	DD	MO	M$ go	24	Ind	Ind	
Psychology and Accounting	CN84	3FT deg	* g	CD-DDD	MO+2D	M$ go	24	Ind	Ind	
Psychology and Financial Services	CN83	3FT deg	* g	CD-DDD	MO+2D	M$ go	26	Ind	Ind	
Social Policy & Management & Financial Services	LN43	3FT deg	* g	CD-DDD	MO	M$ go	24	Ind	Ind	
Social Policy & Management and Accounting	LN44	3FT deg	* g	CD-DDD	MO	M$ go	24	Ind	Ind	
Sociology and Accounting	LN34	3FT deg	* g	CD-DDD	MO	M$ go	24	Ind	Ind	
Sociology and Financial Services	LN33	3FT deg	* g	CD-DDD	MO	M$ go	24	Ind	Ind	
Spanish and Accounting	NR44	4FT deg	* g	DD	MO	M$ go	24	Ind	Ind	
Spanish and Financial Services	NR34	4FT deg	* g	DD	MO	M$ go	24	Ind	Ind	
Taxation & Communications & Audio Visual Prod St	NPH4	3FT deg	* g	CC-CDD	MO+3D	M$ go	26	Ind	Ind	
Taxation and Accounting	NN4H	3FT deg	* g	DD	MO	M$ go	24	Ind	Ind	
Taxation and Business	NN1H	3FT deg	* g	CD-DDD	MO	M$ go	24	Ind	Ind	
Taxation and Business Economics	LNCH	3FT deg	* g	DD	MO	M$ go	24	Ind	Ind	

Accountancy and Finance 1

course details			98 expected requirements							96 entry stats	
TITLE	CODE	COURSE	SUBJECTS	A/AS	NO/C	AGNVQ	IB	SQA(H)	SQA	RATIO	A/AS
Taxation and Business Information Technology	GN7H	3FT deg	* g	DD	M0	M$ go	24	Ind	Ind		
Taxation and Computing	GN5H	3FT deg	* g	DD	M0	M$ go	24	Ind	Ind		
Taxation and Design Studies	NWH2	3FT deg	* g	CD-DDD	M0+2D	M$ go	24	Ind	Ind		
Taxation and Development Studies	MN9H	3FT deg	* g	DD	M0	M$ go	24	Ind	Ind		
Taxation and Economics	LN1H	3FT deg	* g	DD	M0	M$ go	24	Ind	Ind		
Taxation and English	NQH3	3FT deg	* g	CD-DDD	M0+2D	M$ go	26	Ind	Ind		
Taxation and European Studies	NTH2	3FT deg	* g	DD	M0	M$ go	24	Ind	Ind		
Taxation and Financial Services	NN3H	3FT deg	* g	DD	M0	M$ go	24	Ind	Ind		
Taxation and Fine Art	NWH1	3FT deg	* g	CC-CDD	M0+2D	M$ go	24	Ind	Ind		
Taxation and French	NRH1	4FT deg	* g	DD	M0	M$ go	24	Ind	Ind		
Taxation and German	NRH2	4FT deg	* g	DD	M0	M$ go	24	Ind	Ind		
Taxation and International Relations	MNCH	3FT deg	* g	DD	M0	M$ go	24	Ind	Ind		
Taxation and Law	MN3H	3FT deg	* g	CC-CDD	M0+2D	M$ go	26	Ind	Ind		
Taxation and Marketing	NN5H	3FT deg	* g	CD-DDD	M0	M$ go	24	Ind	Ind		
Taxation and Mathematics	GN1H	3FT deg	* g	DD	M0	M$ go	24	Ind	Ind		
Taxation and Modern History	NVH1	3FT deg	* g	DD	M0	M$ go	24	Ind	Ind		
Taxation and Multimedia Systems	GNMH	3FT deg	* g	DD	M0	M$ go	24	Ind	Ind		
Taxation and Politics	MN1H	3FT deg	* g	DD	M0	M$ go	24	Ind	Ind		
Taxation and Product Development & Manufacture	JN4H	3FT deg	* g	DD	M0	M$ go	24	Ind	Ind		
Taxation and Psychology	CN8H	3FT deg	* g	CD-DDD	M0	M$ go	24	Ind	Ind		
Taxation and Social Policy & Management	LN4H	3FT deg	* g	CD-DDD	M0	M$ go	24	Ind	Ind		
Taxation and Sociology	LN3H	3FT deg	* g	CD-DDD	M0	M$ go	24	Ind	Ind		
Taxation and Spanish	NRH4	4FT deg	* g	DD	M0	M$ go	24	Ind	Ind		
Textile Furnishing Design and Accounting	NW4G	3FT deg	Pf g	DD	M0	M$ go	24	Ind	Ind		
Textile Furnishing Design and Financial Services	NW3G	3FT deg	Pf g	DD	M0	M$ go	24	Ind	Ind		
Textile Furnishing Design and Taxation	NWHG	3FT deg	Pf g	DD	M0	M$ go	24	Ind	Ind		
Modular Programme *Accounting Studies*	Y420▼	3FT deg	* g	EE	M0	P	24	Ind	Ind		
Modular Programme *Accounting Studies*	Y400	3FT deg	* g	CC-DD	M0	M$ go	24	Ind	Ind		
Modular Programme *Financial Services*	Y400	3FT deg	* g	CC-DD	M0	M$ go	24	Ind	Ind		
Modular Programme *Taxation*	Y400	3FT deg	* g	CC-DD	M0	M$ go	24	Ind	Ind		
Business and Finance	3N1N	2FT HND	* g	C-DE	M0	P$ go	24	Ind	Ind		

LSE: LONDON Sch of Economics (Univ of London)

TITLE	CODE	COURSE	SUBJECTS	A/AS	NO/C	AGNVQ	IB	SQA(H)	SQA	RATIO	A/AS
Accounting & Finance	NN34	3FT deg	g	ABB	Ind	X	$	Ind	Ind	15	26/30
Actuarial Science	N321	3FT deg	M	BBB-AAB	Ind	X	$	Ind	Ind		
Business Mathematics and Statistics *Actuarial Science*	Y240	3FT deg	M	BBB-AAB	Ind	X	$	Ind	Ind		

LOUGHBOROUGH Univ

TITLE	CODE	COURSE	SUBJECTS	A/AS	NO/C	AGNVQ	IB	SQA(H)	SQA	RATIO	A/AS
Accounting and Financial Management (4 Yr SW)	NN34	4SW deg	* g	BBC	4D	D*6/^ go	30	Ind	Ind	6	20/28
Banking and Finance (4 Yr SW)	N301	4SW deg	* g	BBC	4D	D*6/^ go	30	Ind	Ind	6	20/30
Business Economics and Finance	L1NK	3FT deg	* g	20	3D	D*6/^ go	30	Ind	Ind	5	18/24
Economics with Accounting	L1N4	3FT deg	* g	20	3D	D*6/^ go	30	Ind	Ind	4	16/28
Mathematics with Accountancy	G1N4	3FT deg	M	BCC			28$	Ind			
Mathematics with Accountancy (4 Yr SW)	G1NK	4SW deg	M	BCC			28$	Ind			

LUTON Univ

TITLE	CODE	COURSE	SUBJECTS	A/AS	NO/C	AGNVQ	IB	SQA(H)	SQA	RATIO	A/AS
Accounting	N420	3FT deg	g	12-16	M0/D0	M/D	32	BBBB	Ind	7	8/24
Accounting with Applied Statistics	N4G4	3FT deg	g	12-16	M0/D0	M/D	32	BBCC	Ind		
Accounting with Built Environment	N4NV	3FT deg	g	12-16	M0/D0	M/D	32	BBCC	Ind		
Accounting with Business	NNK1	3FT deg	g	12-16	M0/D0	M/D	32	BBCC	Ind		

course details

98 expected requirements

96 entry stats

TITLE	CODE	COURSE	SUBJECTS	A/AS	NO/C	AGNVQ	IB	SQA(H)	SQA	RATIO A/AS
Accounting with Business Systems	NNL1	3FT deg	g	12-16	MO/DO	M/D	32	BBCC	Ind	
Accounting with Contemporary History	N4VC	3FT deg	g	12-16	MO/DO	M/D	32	BBCC	Ind	
Accounting with Digital System Design	NHKQ	3FT deg	g	12-16	MO/DO	M/D	32	BBCC	Ind	
Accounting with Electronic Systems Design	N4H6	3FT deg		12-16	MO/DO	M/D	32	BBCC	Ind	
Accounting with French	N4RC	3FT deg	F g	12-16	MO/DO	M/D	32	BBCC	Ind	
Accounting with German	N4RF	3FT deg	G g	12-16	MO/DO	M/D	32	BBCC	Ind	
Accounting with Health Studies	N4BX	3FT deg		12-16	MO/DO	M/D	32	BBCC	Ind	
Accounting with Japanese	N4T4	3FT deg	L g	12-16	MO/DO	M/D	32	BBCC	Ind	
Accounting with Journalism	N4PP	3FT deg	g	12-16	MO/DO	M/D	32	BBCC	Ind	
Accounting with Management	NN41	3FT deg	g	12-16	MO/DO	M/D	32	BBCC	Ind	
Accounting with Mathematical Sciences	N4GC	3FT deg	g	12-16	MO/DO	M/D	32	BBCC	Ind	
Accounting with Mathematics	N4GD	3FT deg	g	12-16	MO/DO	M/D	32	BBCC	Ind	
Accounting with Media Practices	NPKK	3FT deg	g	12-16	MO/DO	M/D	32	BBCC	Ind	
Accounting with Media Production	NPLK	3FT deg	g	12-16	MO/DO	M/D	32	BBCC	Ind	
Accounting with Multimedia	NPLL	3FT deg	g	12-16	MO/DO	M/D	32	BBCC	Ind	
Accounting with Organisational Behaviour	N4LT	3FT deg	g	12-16	MO/DO	M/D	32	BBCC	Ind	
Accounting with Politics	N4MD	3FT deg	g	12-16	MO/DO	M/D	32	BBCC	Ind	
Accounting with Psychology	NL4T	3FT deg	g	12-16	MO/DO	M/D	32	BBCC	Ind	
Accounting with Public Policy & Management	NM4D	3FT deg	g	12-16	MO/DO	M/D	32	BBCC	Ind	
Accounting with Travel & Tourism	N4PR	3FT deg	g	12-16	MO/DO	M/D	32	BBCC	Ind	
Applied Statistics and Accounting	GN4K	3FT deg	g	12-16	MO/DO	M/D	32	BBCC	Ind	
Building Conservation and Accounting	KN24	3FT deg	g	12-16	MO/DO	M/D	32	BBCC	Ind	
Built Environment and Accounting	NNK8	3FT deg	g	12-16	MO/DO	M/D	32	BBCC	Ind	
Built Environment with Accounting	N8NK	3FT deg	g	12-16	MO/DO	M/D	32	BBCC	Ind	
Business Systems and Accounting	NNKC	3FT deg	g	12-16	MO/DO	M/D	32	BBCC	Ind	
Business Systems with Accounting	N1N4	3FT deg	g	12-16	MO/DO	M/D	32	BBCC	Ind	
Computer Applications and Accounting	GN64	3FT deg		12-16	MO/DO	M/D	32	BBCC	Ind	
Computer Science and Accounting	NGK5	3FT deg	g	12-16	MO/DO	M/D	32	BBCC	Ind	
Contemporary History and Accounting	NVK1	3FT deg	g	12-16	MO/DO	M/D	32	BBCC	Ind	
Digital Systems Design and Accounting	NHK6	3FT deg	g	12-16	MO/DO	M/D	32	BBCC	Ind	
Digital Systems Design with Accounting	H6NL	3FT deg	g	12-16	MO/DO	M/D	32	BBCC	Ind	
Electronic System Design and Accounting	NHKP	3FT deg	g	12-16	MO/DO	M/D	32	BBCC	Ind	
Electronic System Design with Accounting	HN6K	3FT deg	g	12-16	MO/DO	M/D	32	BBCC	Ind	
Environmental Science and Accounting	NFK9	3FT deg	g	12-16	MO/DO	M/D	32	BBCC	Ind	
Environmental Science with Accounting	F9NK	3FT deg	g	12-16	MO/DO	M/D	32	BBCC	Ind	
Environmental Studies with Accounting	F9NL	3FT deg		12-16	MO/DO	M/D	32	BBCC	Ind	
European Language Studies and Accounting	NTK2	3FT deg	L g	12-16	MO/DO	M/D	32	BBCC	Ind	
European Language Studies with Accounting	T2NK	4FT deg	L g	12-16	MO/DO	M/D	32	BBCC	Ind	
Health Science and Accounting	NBK9	3FT deg	g	12-16	MO/DO	M/D	32	BBCC	Ind	
Health Science with Accounting	B9NL	3FT deg	g	12-16	MO/DO	M/D	32	BBCC	Ind	
Health Studies and Accounting	NBKX	3FT deg	g	12-16	MO/DO	M/D	32	BBCC	Ind	
Housing Studies and Accounting	KN44	3FT deg	g	12-16	MO/DO	M/D	32	BBCC	Ind	
Journalism and Accounting	PN64	3FT deg		12-16	MO/DO	M/D	32	BBCC	Ind	
Law and Accounting	NMK3	3FT deg	g	12-16	MO/DO	M/D	32	BBCC	Ind	
Law with Accounting	M3N4	3FT deg	g	12-16	MO/DO	M/D	32	BBCC	Ind	
Linguistics and Accounting	NQK1	3FT deg	g	12-16	MO/DO	M/D	32	BBCC	Ind	
Linguistics with Accounting	Q1NK	3FT deg	g	12-16	MO/DO	M/D	32	BBCC	Ind	
Mapping Science and Accounting	NFK8	3FT deg	g	12-16	MO/DO	M/D	32	BBCC	Ind	
Mapping Science with Accounting	F8NL	3FT deg	g	12-16	MO/DO	M/D	32	BBCC	Ind	
Mathematical Sciences and Accounting	GN14	3FT deg	g	12-16	MO/DO	M/D	32	BBCC	Ind	
Mathematical Sciences with Accounting	G1N4	3FT deg	g	12-16	MO/DO	M/D	32	BBCC	Ind	
Mathematics and Accounting	NG41	3FT deg	g	12-16	MO/DO	M/D	32	BBCC	Ind	

Accountancy and Finance 1

course details			98 expected requirements							96 entry stats	
TITLE	CODE	COURSE	SUBJECTS	A/AS	NO/C	AGNVQ	IB	SQA(H)	SQA	RATIO A/AS	
Media Practices and Accounting	NPK4	3FT deg	g	12-16	MO/DO	M/D	32	BBCC	Ind		
Media Practices with Accounting	P4NL	3FT deg	g	12-16	MO/DO	M/D	32	BBCC	Ind		
Media Production and Accounting	NPKL	3FT deg	g	12-16	MO/DO	M/D	32	BBCC	Ind		
Media Production with Accounting	PN44	3FT deg	g	12-16	MO/DO	M/D	32	BBCC	Ind		
Modern History and Accounting	NVKC	3FT deg	g	12-16	MO/DO	M/D	32	BBCC	Ind		
Modern History with Accounting	V1N4	3FT deg	g	12-16	MO/DO	M/D	32	BBCC	Ind		
Organisational Behaviour and Accounting	NLK7	3FT deg	g	12-16	MO/DO	M/D	32	BBCC	Ind		
Physical Geography and Accounting	NFKV	3FT deg	g	12-16	MO/DO	M/D	32	BBCC	Ind		
Physical Geography with Accounting	FN84	3FT deg	g	12-16	MO/DO	M/D	32	BBCC	Ind		
Planning Studies and Accounting	KN4K	3FT deg	g	12-16	MO/DO	M/D	32	BBCC	Ind		
Politics and Accounting	NMK1	3FT deg	g	12-16	MO/DO	M/D	32	BBCC	Ind		
Politics with Accounting	M1NL	3FT deg	g	12-16	MO/DO	M/D	32	BBCC	Ind		
Property Studies and Accounting	KN2K	3FT deg	g	12-16	MO/DO	M/D	32	BBCC	Ind		
Psychology and Accounting	NLKR	3FT deg	g	12-16	MO/DO	M/D	32	BBCC	Ind		
Psychology with Accounting	L7NL	3FT deg	g	12-16	MO/DO	M/D	32	BBCC	Ind		
Public Policy & Management with Accounting	MN14	3FT deg	g	12-16	MO/DO	M/D	32	BBCC	Ind		
Public Policy and Management and Accounting	NMKC	3FT deg	g	12-16	MO/DO	M/D	32	BBCC	Ind		
Travel & Tourism with Accounting	P7NK	3FT deg	g	12-16	MO/DO	M/D	32	BBCC	Ind		
Travel and Tourism and Accounting	NPK7	3FT deg	g	12-16	MO/DO	M/D	32	BBCC	Ind		
Women's Studies and Accounting	MN94	3FT deg		12-16	MO/DO	M/D	32	BBCC	Ind		
Women's Studies with Accounting	M9N4	3FT deg		12-16	MO/DO	M/D	32	BBCC	Ind		
Univ of MANCHESTER											
Accounting and Finance	N420	3FT deg	g	BBC	M+6D	D^	32	ABBBB	Ind	10	20/28
Accounting and Law	MN34	4FT deg	g	ABB	Ind	D^	32$	CSYS	X	7	24/30
Accounting with Business Information Systems	N4G5	3FT deg	g	BBC	M+6D	D^	32	ABBBB	Ind	7	18/28
Finance	N300	3FT deg	M	BBB	X	D^	28$	CSYS	X	5	18/24
MANCHESTER METROPOLITAN Univ											
Accounting and Finance	N420	3FT deg	* g	16	MO+8D	D	26$	BBBCC	Ind		10/20
Accounting and Finance in Europe (French)	N4R1	4FT deg	F g	18	MO+8D	D^	26$	BBBBC	Ind		
Accounting and Finance in Europe (German)	N4R2	4FT deg	G g	18	MO+8D	D^	26$	BBBBC	Ind		
Accounting and Finance in Europe (Spanish)	N4R4	4FT deg	Sp g	18	MO+8D	D^	26$	BBBBC	Ind		
Financial Services	N300	3FT deg	* g	16	MO+8D	D	26$	BBBCC	Ind		10/20
MIDDLESEX Univ											
Accounting and Finance	N420▼	3FT deg	* g	16	MO+1D	D$ go	26	CCCC	Ind		
Management Accounting	N400▼	3FT deg	* g	16	MO+1D	D$ go	26	Ind	Ind		
Money Banking and Finance	N300▼	4SW deg	* g	12	5M	M$ go	26	Ind	Ind		
Joint Honours Degree *Accounting*	Y400	3FT deg	* g	16	MO+1D	D$ go	26	CCCC	Ind		
NAPIER Univ											
Accounting	N401	2FT Dip	*	CC	N	M	Ind	CCC	Ind	2	6/7
Accounting	N400	3FT/4FT deg	*	CDD	Ind	Ind	Ind	BBCC$	Ind	5	
Accounting and Information Management	NP42	3FT/4FT deg	*	CDE	Ind	Ind	Ind	BCCC$	Ind		
Business Economics and Financial Services	LN13	3FT deg									
Business Economics with Financial Services	L1N3	3FT deg									
Financial Services	N420	3SW/4SW deg	E g	CCD	Ind	Ind	Ind	BBCC	Ind	4	
Financial Services with Business Economics	N3L1	3FT deg									
Mathematics with Financial Studies	G1N3	4FT/5SW deg	M	CC	Ind	Ind	Ind	BBC	Ind		
NENE COLLEGE											
Accountancy and Finance	N420	3FT deg	* g	10	M+2D	M	Ind	CCC	Ind		8/18
Business Enterprise	NN13	3FT deg									

course details			98 expected requirements							96 entry stats	
TITLE	CODE	COURSE	SUBJECTS	A/AS	ND/C	RGNVQ	IB	SQA(H)	SQA	RATIO	A/AS
Univ of NEWCASTLE											
Accounting and Computing Science	NG45	3FT deg	M	20	4M+1D	Ind	30$	AAABB	Ind	8	18/23
Accounting and Financial Analysis	N400	3FT deg	* g	BB-BCC	5D		30	AAAAB	Ind	9	18/28
Accounting and Law	NM43	3FT deg	* g	BBB	5D		30	AAAAB	Ind	21	26/28
Accounting and Mathematics	NG41	3FT deg	M	20	4M+1D	Ind	30$	AAABB	Ind	10	20/24
Accounting and Statistics	NG44	3FT deg	M	20	4M+1D	Ind	30$	AAABB	Ind	11	
Economics and Accounting	LN14	3FT deg	* g	BB-BCC	5D		30	AAAAB	Ind	12	18/22
French with Accounting	R1N4	4FT deg	F+M/Ec	BBC			$	AABBB$			
German with Accounting	R2N4	4FT deg	G+M/Ec	20			$	ABBBB$			
Spanish with Accounting	R4N4	4FT deg	Sp+M/Ec	BCC			$	ABBBB$			
Combined Studies (BA) _Accounting_	Y400	3FT deg	M	ABC-BBB	5D	Ind	35$	AAAB	Ind		
Univ of Wales COLLEGE, NEWPORT											
Accounting Practice	N400	3FT deg		8-10	MO	D$	24	CCCC	Ind		
Accounting and Finance	NN34	3FT deg	*	8-10	MO	D$	24	CCCC	Ind		
Accounting and Legal Studies	MN34	3FT deg	*	8-10	MO	D$	24	CCCC	Ind		
Business and Accounting	NN14	3FT deg	*	8-10	MO	D$	24	CCCC	Ind		
Accounting and Finance	43NN	2FT HND	*	4	4M	M$	Ind	Ind	Ind		
NESCOT											
Management and Financial Services	NN13	4FT deg	*								
Management and Financial Services	NN31	3FT deg	*	DD	MO	M	Dip	Ind	N$		
NORTH EAST WALES INST of HE											
Business Studies with Accountancy	N1N4	3FT deg		6-12	3M	M$	Ind	CCC	N$		
Univ of NORTH LONDON											
Accounting and Finance	N420	3FT deg	* g	14	MO+4D$	Ind	Ind	CCCC$	Ind	17	6/18
Combined Honours _Accounting_	Y400	3FT deg	* g	14	MO+4D$	Ind	Ind	CCCC$	Ind		
Accounting and Business Management	41NN	2FT HND	* g	6	10M	Ind	Ind	CCC	Ind		
Univ of NORTHUMBRIA											
Accountancy	N400	3FT deg	* g	CCC	MO+4D	D4	26	BBBCC	Ind	6	16/22
Accounting	N401	2FT Dip	* g	10	MO	M	24	CCCC	Ind	3	10/14
Accounting and Finance (DipHE-1 year top up)	N420	1FT deg	X	X	X	X	X	X	X		
Financial Studies	N300	3FT deg	* g	CCC	MO+4D	D+4	24	BBBCC	Ind	3	13/18
Mathematics with Mathematical Finance	G1N3	3FT/4SW deg	M g	8-12	Ind	Ind	24$	BBC$	Ind		
Business and Accountancy	43NN	2FT HND	* g	DD	MO	M	24	CCC	Ind	8	8/16
NORWICH: City COLL											
Accounting and Finance	N420	3FT deg	* g	EE	Ind	Ind	Ind	Ind	Ind		
Accounting and Finance (HND top up)	N421	1FT deg		X	HN	X	X	X	X		
Univ of NOTTINGHAM											
Industrial Economics with Accounting	LN14	3FT deg	* g	BBB	Ind	D*6/^ go	32	AAABB	Ind	11	22/30
Industrial Economics with Insurance	L1N3	3FT deg	* g	BBB	Ind	D*6/^ go	32	AAABB	Ind	10	
NOTTINGHAM TRENT Univ											
Accounting	N400	1FT Dip	* g	8	MO	D	Ind	Ind	Ind		
Accounting and Finance	N421	3FT deg	* g	16	3D $		Ind	Ind	Ind	11	14/20
Accounting and Finance (4 year sandwich)	N420	4SW deg	* g	16	3D $		Ind	Ind	Ind	14	14/22
Financial Services	N300	4SW deg	* g	16	M+D $		Ind	Ind	Ind	5	14/24
Business and Finance	31NN▼	2FT/3SW HND	* g	CD	Ind	Ind	Ind	Ind	Ind		

Accountancy and Finance   1

course details			98 expected requirements							96 entry stats
TITLE	CODE	COURSE	SUBJECTS	A/AS	ND/C	RGNVQ	IB	SQA(H)	SQA	RATIO A/AS

OXFORD BROOKES Univ

TITLE	CODE	COURSE	SUBJECTS	A/AS	ND/C	RGNVQ	IB	SQA(H)	SQA	RATIO A/AS
Accounting and Finance	N420	3FT deg			Ind		Ind	Ind	Ind	
Anthropology/Accounting and Finance	LN64	3FT deg	* g	BCC	Ind	D*3/M*^	Ind	Ind	Ind	
Biological Chemistry/Accounting and Finance	CN74	3FT deg	S g	DD-BCC	Ind		Ind	Ind	Ind	
Biology/Accounting and Finance	CN14	3FT deg	S g	DD-BCC	Ind	MS/DS3	Ind	Ind	Ind	1
Business Admin and Mgt/Accounting and Finance	NN14	3FT deg	* g	BCC-BBC	Ind	MB4/DB3	Ind	Ind	Ind	6 16/24
Cartography/Accounting and Finance	FN84	3FT deg	* g	DDD-BCC	Ind	M*/D*3	Ind	Ind	Ind	
Cell Biology/Accounting and Finance	CNC4	3FT deg	* g	CC-BCC	Ind		Ind	Ind	Ind	
Combined Studies/Accounting and Finance	NY44	3FT deg		X		X	X	X		
Computer Systems/Accounting and Finance	GN64	3FT deg	* g	BC-BCC	Ind	M*/D*3	Ind	Ind	Ind	6
Computing Mathematics/Accounting and Finance	GN94	3FT deg	* g	CD-BCC	Ind	M*/D*3	Ind	Ind	Ind	
Computing/Accounting and Finance	GN54	3FT deg	* g	CDD-BCC	Ind	M*/D*3	Ind	Ind	Ind	5 12/17
Ecology/Accounting and Finance	CN94	3FT deg	* g	CD-BCC	Ind	MS/D*3	Ind	Ind	Ind	
Economics/Accounting and Finance	LN14	3FT deg	* g	BB-BCC	Ind	M*3/D*3	Ind	Ind	Ind	7 14/20
Educational Studies/Accounting and Finance	NX49	3FT deg	* g	CC-BCC	Ind	M*3/D*3	Ind	Ind	Ind	
Electronics/Accounting and Finance	HN64	3FT deg	S/M	CC-BCC	Ind	MS/D*3	Ind	Ind	Ind	
English Studies/Accounting and Finance	NQ43	3FT deg	* g	AB-BCC	Ind	M*^/D*3	Ind	Ind	Ind	
Environmental Chemistry/Accounting and Finance	NF41	3FT deg	* g		Ind		Ind	Ind	Ind	
Environmental Policy/Accounting and Finance	KN34	3FT deg								
Environmental Sciences/Accounting and Finance	FNX4	3FT deg	S g	CD-BCC	Ind	DS/D*3	Ind	Ind	Ind	
Exercise and Health/Accounting and Finance	NB46	3FT deg	S	DD-BCC	Ind	MS/D*3	Ind	Ind	Ind	
Fine Art/Accounting and Finance	NW41	3FT deg	Pf+A g	BC-BCC	Ind	MA^/D*3	Ind	Ind	Ind	
Food Science and Nutrition/Accounting & Finance	DN44	3FT deg	S g	DD-BCC	Ind	MS/D*3	Ind	Ind	Ind	
French Language and Contemp Studies/Acc and Fin	NR4C	4SW deg	F g	CDD-BCC	Ind	M^/D*3	Ind	Ind	Ind	
French Language and Literature/Accounting & Fin	NR41	4SW deg	F g	CDD-BCC	Ind	M^/D*3	Ind	Ind	Ind	
Geography and the Phys Env/Accounting & Finance	FNV4	3FT deg	* g	BB-BCC	Ind	M*/D*3	Ind	Ind	Ind	
Geography/Accounting and Finance	LN84	3FT deg	* g	BB-BCC	Ind	M*/D*3	Ind	Ind	Ind	
Geology/Accounting and Finance	FN64	3FT deg	S/M	DD-BCC	Ind	PS/D*3	Ind	Ind	Ind	
Geotechnics/Accounting and Finance	HN24	3FT deg	S/M/Ds/Es	DD-BCC	Ind	MS/D*3	Ind	Ind	Ind	
German Language and Contemp Stud/Acc & Finance	NR4F	4SW deg	G g	DDD-BCC	Ind	M^/D*3	Ind	Ind	Ind	3
German Language and Literature/Accounting & Fin	NR42	4SW deg	G g	DDD-BCC	Ind	M^/D*3	Ind	Ind	Ind	2
German Studies/Accounting and Finance	NR4G	4SW deg	G g	DDD-BCC	Ind	M^/D*3	Ind	Ind	Ind	
Health Care/Accounting and Finance (Post Exp)	BN74	3FT deg		X		X	X	X		
History of Art/Accounting and Finance	NV44	3FT deg	* g	BCC	Ind	M^/D*3	Ind	Ind	Ind	
History/Accounting and Finance	NV41	3FT deg	* g	BB-CCD	Ind	M^/D*3	Ind	Ind	Ind	6
Hospitality Management St/Accounting and Finance	NN47	3FT deg	* g	DDD-BCC	Ind	M*3/D*3	Ind	Ind	Ind	7
Human Biology/Accounting and Finance	BN14	3FT deg	* g	CC-BCC	Ind		Ind	Ind	Ind	
Information Systems/Accounting and Finance	GNM4	3FT deg	* g	CDD-BCC	Ind	M*/D*3	Ind	Ind	Ind	6
Intelligent Systems/Accounting and Finance	GN84	3FT deg	* g	CD-BCC	Ind	M*/D*3	Ind	Ind	Ind	
Law/Accounting and Finance	MN34	3FT deg	* g	BCC-BBB	Ind	D*3	Ind	Ind	Ind	17
Leisure Planning/Accounting and Finance	KNH4	3FT deg								
Marketing Management/Accounting and Finance	NN4N	3FT deg	* g	BCC	Ind	D*3	Ind	Ind	Ind	12
Mathematics/Accounting and Finance	GN14	3FT deg	M	DD-BCC	Ind	M^D*3	Ind	Ind	Ind	8 16/18
Music/Accounting and Finance	NW43	3FT deg	Mu g	DD-BCC	Ind	M/D*3	Ind	Ind	Ind	
Palliative Care/Accounting and Finance(Post Exp)	BNR4	3FT deg		X		X	X	X		
Planning Studies/Accounting and Finance	KN44	3FT deg	* g	DDD-BCC	Ind	M*/D*3	Ind	Ind	Ind	
Politics/Accounting and Finance	MN14	3FT deg	* g	AB-BCC	Ind	M^/D*3	Ind	Ind	Ind	4
Psychology/Accounting and Finance	CN84	3FT deg	* g	BCC-BBC	Ind	M^/D*3	Ind	Ind	Ind	
Publishing/Accounting and Finance	NP45	3FT deg	* g	BB-CCD	Ind	M$3/D*3	Ind	Ind	Ind	
Rehabilitation/Accounting and Finance (Post Exp)	BNT4	3FT deg		X		X	X	X		
Sociology/Accounting and Finance	LN34	3FT deg	* g	BCC	Ind	M*^/D*3	Ind	Ind	Ind	
Software Engineering/Accounting and Finance	GN74	3FT deg	* g	CDD-BCC	Ind	M*/D*3	Ind	Ind	Ind	

course details			98 expected requirements							96 entry stats
TITLE	CODE	COURSE	SUBJECTS	A/AS	ND/C	RGNVQ	IB	SQA(H)	SQA	RATIO A/AS
Statistics/Accounting and Finance	GN44	3FT deg	* g	DD-BCC	Ind	M*/D*3	Ind	Ind	Ind	5
Telecommunications/Accounting and Finance	HNP4	3FT deg								
Tourism/Accounting and Finance	NP47	3FT deg	* g	BCC-CCD	Ind	M*3/D*3	Ind	Ind	Ind	4
Transport Planning/Accounting and Finance	NN49	3FT deg	* g	BCC-DDD	Ind	M*/D*3	Ind	Ind	Ind	
Water Resources/Accounting and Finance	HNF4	3FT deg								

Univ of PAISLEY

Accounting	N400	3FT/4SW/5SW deg	E g	CCC	Ind	Ind	Ind	BCCC$	Ind	5
Business Information Technology & Accounting	GN74	4SW/5SW deg	* g	CC	Ind	Ind	Ind	BCCC$	Ind	
Mathematical Sciences with Finance	G1N3	3FT/4FT/5SW deg	M+S g	CCC-EE	Ind	Ind	Ind	BCC$	Ind	7
Physics with Finance	F3N3	3FT/4FT/5SW deg	M+P g	CCC-EE	Ind	Ind	Ind	BCC$	Ind	

Univ of PLYMOUTH

Accounting and Finance	N420	3FT deg	* g	CCD-CCC	MO	M18/M12^	Ind	BBCC$	Ind	8 12/18
Applied Economics with Accounting	L1N4	3FT deg	* g	CCD-CDD	MO	M$^	Ind	BCCC	Ind	

Univ of PORTSMOUTH

Accountancy Studies (For MARA Diploma Holders)	N420	2FT deg	Ac	X	X	X	X	X	X	
Accounting	N400	3FT/4SW deg	*	16	5M+1D	D$6/^ go	Dip	CCCCC	Ind	4 6/20
Accounting and Business Information Systems	NG45	3FT/4SW deg	*	16	5M+1D	D$6/^ go	Dip	CCCCC	Ind	4 6/16
Accounting and Economics	NL41	3FT deg	* g	16	4M+2D	D$6/^ go	Dip	CCCCC	Ind	
Accounting and Finance	NN34	3FT/4SW deg	* g	14	5M+1D	D$6/^ go	Dip	CCCCC	Ind	
Business and Finance (HND Top-up)	NN13	1FT deg	Bu	X	MO+2D	X	X	X	HN	
Financial Services	N300	4FT/4SW deg	* g	14	5M+1D	D$6/^ go	Dip	CCCCC	Ind	4 6/20
International Finance and Trade	N350	4SW deg	* g	14	5M+1D	D$6/^ go	Dip	CCCCC	Ind	3 8/20
Law and Accounting	MN34	3FT/4SW deg	*	18	MO+2D	D$6/^ go	Dip	BBBCC	Ind	

QUEEN'S Univ Belfast

Accounting	N400	3FT deg	* g	ABB	7D	D*^ go	34$	AAABB	Ind	7 24/30
Accounting with French	N4R1	4FT deg	F g	ABB	X	D*_^ go	34$	AAABB	X	4 24/30
Accounting with German	N4R2	4FT deg	G g	ABB	X	D*_^ go	34$	AAABB	X	
Accounting with Italian	N4R3	4FT deg	* g	ABB	7D	D*^ go	34$	AAABB	Ind	
Accounting with Spanish	N4R4	4FT deg	* g	ABB	7D	D*^ go	34$	AAABB	Ind	9
Finance	N300	4SW deg	* g	BBB	1M+6D	D*^ go	32$	AABBB	Ind	8 22/28
Finance with French	N3R1	4SW deg	F g	BBB	X	D*_^ go	32$	AABBB	X	8
Finance with German	N3R2	4SW deg	G g	BBB	X	D*_^ go	32$	AABBB	Ind	
Finance with Italian	N3R3	4SW deg	* g	BBB	1M+6D	D*^ go	32$	AABBB	Ind	
Finance with Spanish	N3R4	4SW deg	* g	BBB	1M+6D	D*^ go	32$	AABBB	Ind	
Information Management	P2N4	3FT deg	* g	BBC	2M+5D	D*6/^ go	30$	AABB	Ind	8 20/24
Law and Accounting	MN34	4FT deg	* g	AAB	7D	D*^ go	35$	AAABB	Ind	8 26/30

READING COLLEGE AND SCHOOL OF ART AND DESIGN

Business and Finance	31NN	2FT HND								

Univ of READING

Accounting and Economics	LN14	3FT deg	* g	BBC	Ind	D$6/^ go	31	BBBB	Ind	9 16/24
Chemistry with Accounting	F1N4	3FT deg	C g	18	4M+1D$	DS_^ go	29$	BBBC$	Ind	
Chemistry with Accounting with a year in Europe	F1NL	4FT deg	C g	18	4M+1D$	DS_^ go	29$	BBBC$	Ind	
International Securities, Investment and Banking	N302	3FT deg	* g	ABB	Ind	Ind	33	ABBBB	Ind	

ROBERT GORDON Univ

Accounting and Finance	N420	3FT/4FT deg	* g	CCC	Ind	Ind	Ind	BBBC$	Ind	4

SCOTTISH COLLEGE of TEXTILES

Accounting	004N	2FT HND	* g	D	Ind	Ind	Ind	CC	Ind	3

Accountancy and Finance 1

course details			98 expected requirements							96 entry stats	
TITLE	CODE	COURSE	SUBJECTS	A/AS	NQ/C	AGNVQ	IB	SQA(H)	SQA	RATIO	A/AS
Univ of SALFORD											
Accounting	N401	3FT Dip									
Finance and Accounting	NN34	3FT deg	g	BCC-CCC	DO	D^	Ind	Ind	Ind	6	14/24
Property Management and Investment	K4N3	3FT/4SW deg		BCC-CCC	4M+1D	M	Ind	Ind	Ind		
Business and Finance (Finance)	003N	2FT HND		DD	MO	M	24	CC	Ind	7	3/13
Univ of SHEFFIELD											
Accounting & Financial Management and Economics	NL41	3FT deg	* g	24	3M+3D	D^	32	AABB	Ind	11	22/28
Accounting & Financial Management and Info Mgt	NP42	3FT deg	* g	24	3M+3D	D6/^	32	AABB	Ind	20	
Accounting & Financial Management and Maths	NG4D	3FT deg	M g	24	3M+3D$	D^	32$	AABB$	Ind	7	20/28
Accounting and Financial Management	N420	3FT deg	* g	24	3M+3D	D^	32	AABB	Ind	11	20/28
Computer Science with Accounting	G5N4	3FT deg	M g	24	3M+3D$	D^	32$	AABB$	Ind	46	
SHEFFIELD HALLAM Univ											
Accounting and Business Information Technology	N350	3SW deg	g	16-18	MO+3D$	M	Ind	Ind	Ind		
Accounting and Management Control	N400	3FT/4SW deg	g	16-18	MO+3D$	M	Ind	Ind	Ind		
Financial Serv/Diplome/Matrise en Banque Assur	N301	3FT deg	F	18	3M+3D	M	Ind	Ind	Ind		
Financial Services	N300	3FT/4SW deg	* g	16-18	3M+3D	M	Ind	Ind	Ind		
International Financial and Legal Studies	MN33	4FT deg	F/G	14	3M+3D	M	Ind	Ind	Ind		
Combined Studies *Accountancy*	Y400	3FT deg	* g	14	2M	M	Ind	Ind	Ind		
Combined Studies *Financial Studies*	Y400	3FT deg	* g	14	2M	M	Ind	Ind	Ind		
Univ of SOUTHAMPTON											
Accounting and Finance	NN43	3FT deg	* g	24	Ind	D$^ go	32	AABBB	Ind	9	18/26
Accounting and French	NR41	4FT deg	F g	22	Ind	D$^ go	30$	ABBBB$	Ind		
Accounting and German	NR42	4FT deg	G g	22	Ind	D$^ go	30$	ABBBB$	Ind	8	
Accounting and Law	NM43	4FT deg	* g	24	Ind	D$^ go	32	AABBB	Ind	7	20/28
Accounting and Spanish	NR44	4FT deg	Sp g	22	Ind	D$^ go	30$	ABBBB$	Ind		
Accounting with Economics	NL41	3FT deg	* g	24	Ind	D$^ go	32	AABBB	Ind	7	18/24
Economics and Finance	L1NJ	3FT deg	* g	24	Ind	D$^ go	32	AABBB	Ind	6	
Economics with Actuarial Studies	L1N3	3FT deg	M	22	Ind	D$^ go	30$	ABBBB$	Ind	6	18/26
Management Sciences and Accounting	NNC4	3FT deg	* g	22	Ind	D$^ go	30	ABBBB	Ind		
Mathematics with Actuarial Studies	G1N3	3FT deg	M	BBC	Ind	Ind	30	ABBBB	Ind	6	14/30
Mathematics with Finance	G1NH	3FT deg	M	BBC	Ind	Ind	30	ABBBB	Ind	8	18/28
SOUTHAMPTON INST											
Accountancy	N400	3FT deg	*	10	MO	M$	Dip	CCCC	N	4	6/18
Accountancy and Law	NM43	3FT deg	*	10	MO	M$	Dip	CCCC	N	6	7/10
Financial Services	N300	3FT deg	*	10	MO	M$	Dip	CCCC	N		6/12
SOUTH BANK Univ											
Accounting and Finance	N420	3FT deg	M/Ac/Ec g	CC	DO	MB go	Ind	Ind	Ind		
Business Information Technology and Accounting	GN74	3FT deg	M g	12-16	4M+2D	M go	Ind	Ind	Ind		
Computing and Accounting	GN54	3FT deg	Ac/Ec/M g	12-16	4M+2D	M go	Ind	Ind	Ind		
Economics and Accounting	LN14	3FT deg	Bu/Ec g	12-16	4M+2D	M go	Ind	Ind	Ind		
English Studies and Accounting	NQ43	3FT deg	E+Ac/Ec g	14-18	X	M^ go	Ind	Ind	Ind		
European Studies and Accounting	NT42	3FT deg	Ac/Ec g	14-18	2M+4D	M go	Ind	Ind	Ind		
Food Policy and Accounting	DN44	3FT deg	S+Ac/Ec g	12-16	4M+2D	M go	Ind	Ind	Ind		
French and Accounting	NR41	3FT deg	F+Ac/Ec g	12-16	4M+2D	M go	Ind	Ind	Ind		
History and Accounting	NV41	3FT deg	H+Ac/Ec g	12-16	4M+2D	M^ go	Ind	Ind	Ind		
Housing and Accounting	KN4K	3FT deg	Ac/Ec g	14-18	2M+4D	M go	Ind	Ind	Ind		
Human Biology and Accounting	BN14	3FT deg	S g	12-16	4M+2D	M go	Ind	Ind	Ind		
Human Resource Management and Accounting	NN64	3FT deg	Ac/Ec g	14-18	2M+4D	M go	Ind	Ind	Ind		

| | | | 98 expected requirements | | | | | | | 96 entry stats |
| **course details** | | | | | | | | | | |
TITLE	CODE	COURSE	SUBJECTS	A/AS	ND/C	RGNVQ	IB	SQA(H)	SQA	RATIO A/AS
Law and Accounting	MN34	3FT deg	Ec/Ac g	14-18	2M+4D	D go	Ind	Ind	Ind	
Management and Accounting	NN41	3FT deg	Ac/Ec g	12-16	4M+2D	M go	Ind	Ind	Ind	
Marketing and Accounting	NN45	3FT deg	Ac/Ec g	14-18	2M+4D	M go	Ind	Ind	Ind	
Nutrition and Accounting	BN44	3FT deg	S+Ac/Ec g	12-16	4M+2D	M go	Ind	Ind	Ind	
Social Policy and Accounting	LN4K	3FT deg	Ac/Ec g	12-16	4M+2D	M go	Ind	Ind	Ind	
Sociology and Accounting	LN34	3FT deg	Ac/Ec g	12-16	4M+2D	M go	Ind	Ind	Ind	
Spanish - ab initio and Accounting	NR44	3FT deg	Ec/Ac g	12-16	4M+2D	M go	Ind	Ind	Ind	
Spanish and Accounting	NR4K	3FT deg	Sp+Ac/Ec g	14-18	2M+4D	M go	Ind	Ind	Ind	
Sports Science and Accounting	BN64	3FT deg	S+Ec/Ac g	12-16	4M+2D	M go	Ind	Ind	Ind	
Technology and Accounting	JN94	3FT deg	Ac/Ec g	12-16	4M+2D	M go	Ind	Ind	Ind	
Tourism and Accounting	NP47	3FT deg	L+Ac/Ec g	12-16	4M+2D	M go	Ind	Ind	Ind	
Urban Studies and Accounting	KN4L	3FT deg	Ec/Bu g	14-18	2M+4D	M go	Ind	Ind	Ind	
World Theatre and Accounting	NW44	3FT deg	Ac/Ec g	14-18	2M+4D	M go	Ind	Ind	Ind	

STAFFORDSHIRE Univ

Accounting	N400	3FT deg	g	CCD	MO+2D		27	CCC		
Accounting Information Technology	N4G5	3FT/4SW deg	g	12	Ind	D	27	CCC	Ind	3 7/18
Accounting and Business	N4N1	3FT deg	g	CCD	MO+2D	M$	24	BBC		
Applied Statistics/Accounting	GN44	3FT deg	g	12	Ind	M	27	CCC	Ind	
Business and Financial Economics	LN14	3FT deg	g	14	4M	M$	24	BBC	Ind	2 6/17
Financial Decision Making	N300	3FT deg	g	12	Ind	M	27	CCC	Ind	
International Finance and Business	NN13	4FT deg	g	CCD	MO+2D	M$	24	BBB		
Law/Accounting	MN34	3FT deg	g	16	MO+2D	M$	24	BBB	Ind	3 8/18

Univ of STIRLING

Accountancy	N400	4FT deg	g	BCC	HN	Ind	33	BBBB	HN	
Accountancy/Business Law	MN34	4FT deg	g	BCC	HN	Ind	33	BBBB	HN	
Accountancy/Business Studies	NN1K	4FT deg	g	BCC	HN	Ind	33	BBBB	HN	
Accountancy/Computing Science	GN54	4FT deg	g	BCC	HN	Ind	33	BBBB	HN	
Accountancy/Economics	LN14	4FT deg	g	BCC	HN	Ind	33	BBBB	HN	
Accountancy/French Language	NR4C	4FT deg	g	BCC	HN	Ind	33	BBBB	HN	
Accountancy/German Language	NR4F	4FT deg	g	BCC	HN	Ind	33	BBBB	HN	
Accountancy/Management Science	NN14	4FT deg	g	BCC	HN	Ind	33	BBBB	HN	
Accountancy/Marketing	NN45	4FT deg	g	BCC	HN	Ind	33	BBBB	HN	
Accountancy/Mathematics	GN14	4FT deg	M g	BCC	HN	Ind	33	BBBB	HN	
Accountancy/Spanish Language	NR4K	4FT deg	g	BCC	HN	Ind	33	BBBB	HN	
Accountancy/Sports Studies	NB46	4FT deg	g	BCC	HN	Ind	33	BBBB	HN	
Business Studies/Financial Studies	NN13	4FT deg	g	BBC	Ind	Ind	33	BBBB	HN	
Economics/Financial Studies	LN13	4FT deg	g	CCC	Ind	Ind	28	BBCC	HN	
Financial Studies	N310	4FT deg	g	BCC	Ind	Ind	31	BBBC	HN	
Financial Studies/Computing Science	NG35	4FT deg	g	CCC	Ind	Ind	28	BBCC	HN	
Financial Studies/French Language	N3R1	4FT deg	g	BCC	Ind	Ind	31	BBBC	HN	
Financial Studies/German Language	N3R2	4FT deg	g	BCC	Ind	Ind	31	BBBC	HN	
Financial Studies/Human Resources Management	NN3C	4FT deg	g	BCC	HN	Ind	31	BBBC	HN	
Financial Studies/Japanese	NT34	4FT deg	g	BCC	Ind	Ind	31	BBBC	HN	
Financial Studies/Management Science	NN31	4FT deg	g	BCC	Ind	Ind	31	BBBC	HN	
Financial Studies/Marketing	NN35	4FT deg	g	BBC	Ind	Ind	33	BBBB	HN	
Financial Studies/Mathematics	GN13	4FT deg	M g	CCC	Ind	Ind	28	BBCC	HN	
Financial Studies/Spanish Language	N3R4	4FT deg	g	BCC	Ind	Ind	31	BBBC	HN	
Financial Studies/Sports Studies	NB36	4FT deg	g	BCC	Ind	Ind	31	BBBC	HN	
Mathematics and its Applications with Fin St	G1N3	4FT deg	M g	CCC	Ind	Ind	28	BBCC	HN	

Accountancy and Finance 1

TITLE	CODE	COURSE	SUBJECTS	A/AS	NO/C	AGNVQ	IB	SQA(H)	SQA	RATIO A/AS
Univ of STRATHCLYDE										
Business with Accounting as a principal subject	N400	3FT/4FT deg	M g	BBC	Ind	Ind	32$	AAABB$	Ind	
Engineering with Business Mgt (Accounting)	H1N4	5FT deg	M+P g	BBB	HN		32$	AAAA$	HN	
Mathematics, Statistics and Accounting	GN44	4FT deg	M g	BBC	Ind		36$	AAABB$	Ind	
Mathematics, Statistics and Finance	GN43	4FT deg	M g	CD	HN		30$	BBBC$	Ind	
Mechanical Engineering with Financial Management	H3N3	5FT deg	M+P	BBB	HN		32$	AABBB$	HN	
Physics and Mathematical Finance	FN33	5FT deg	M+P	BBB	Ind	Ind		AABB$	Ind	
Technology and Business Studies with Accounting	HN14	3FT/4FT deg	M g	BBC	HN $		34$	AAABB$	HN$	
UNIVERSITY COLLEGE SUFFOLK										
Business Studies with Accounting	N1NK	3FT deg								
Business Studies with Financial Services	N1N3	3FT deg								
Business (Financial Services)	3CNN	2FT HND	*	E	N	P*	Ind	Ind	Ind	
Business and Finance	31NN	2FT HND	*	E	N	P*	Ind	Ind	Ind	
Univ of SUNDERLAND										
Accounting and Business	N400	3FT deg	* g	18	1M+4D$	D	26	BBBCC	N$	12 12/16
Accounting and Computing	NG45	3FT/4SW deg	* g	4-8	4M $	M*	24$	CCCC	N	5 8/16
Accounting and Economics	NL41	3FT deg	* g	18	2M+3D$	M*	24	CCCC	N	6/11
Accounting and Mathematics	NG41	3FT/4SW deg	M g	4-8	4M $	M*^	24	CCCC	N	6 6/12
Univ of Wales SWANSEA										
Actuarial Studies	G4N3	3FT deg	M	BBB	X	D$^ go	32$	AABBB$	X	
Actuarial Studies with a year abroad	G4NH	4FT deg	M	BBB	X	D$^ go	32$	AABBB$	X	
SWANSEA INST of HE										
Accounting	N400	3FT deg	g	10	MO+2D	M$ go	Ind	Ind	Ind	3 4/26
Univ of TEESSIDE										
Accounting & Finance	N420	3FT deg	* g	12	3M+3D	D	Ind	Ind	HN	4 6/20
Modular Degree Scheme	Y401	3FT deg								
Accounting and Finance										
Business and Financial Services	31NN▼	2FT HND								
THAMES VALLEY Univ										
Accountancy and Business Finance (Ealing)	N420▼	3FT deg	* g	10-12	MO	M	24	CCC		
Accounting with Business	N4N1	2FT/3FT Dip/deg		2-12	N/MO	P/M	24	CC		
Accounting with Economics	N4L1	3FT deg		8-12	MO	M	26	CCC		
Accounting with English Language Studies	N4Q1	3FT deg		8-12	MO	M	26	CCC		
Accounting with Finance	N4N3	3FT deg		8-12	MO	M	26	CCC		
Accounting with French	N4R1	3FT deg		8-12	MO	M	26	CCC		
Accounting with German	N4R2	3FT deg		8-12	MO	M	26	CCC		
Accounting with Information Systems	N4G5	3FT deg		8-12	MO	M	26	CCC		
Accounting with Law	N4M3	3FT deg		8-12	MO	M	26	CCC		
Accounting with Retail Management	N4NM	3FT deg		8-12	MO	M	26	CCC		
Accounting with Spanish	N4R4	3FT deg		8-12	MO	M	26	CCC		
Business Administration with Accounting	N1NK	3FT deg		8-12	MO	M	26	CCC		
Business Administration with Finance	N1NH	3FT deg		8-12	MO	M	26	CCC		
Business Economics with Accounting	L1NK	3FT deg		8-12	MO	M	26	CCC		
Business Economics with Finance	L1NH	3FT deg		8-12	MO	M	26	CCC		
Business Studies with Accounting (Dip)	N1N4	3FT/4SW deg		12	MO	M	26			
Business Studies with Finance (Dip)	N1N3	3FT/4SW deg		12	MO	M	26			
Economics with Accounting	L1N4	3FT deg		8-12	MO	M	26	CCC		
Economics with Finance	L1N3	3FT deg		8-12	MO	M	26	CCC		
Finance with Accounting	N3N4	3FT deg		8-12	MO	M	26	CCC		

TITLE	CODE	COURSE	SUBJECTS	A/AS	ND/C	AGNVQ	IB	SQA(H)	SQA	RATIO A/AS
Finance with Business	N3N1	3FT deg		8-12	MO	M	26	CCC		
Finance with Business Economics	N3LC	3FT deg		8-12	MO	M	26	CCC		
Finance with Economics	N3L1	3FT deg		8-12	MO	M	26	CCC		
Finance with English Language Studies	N3Q1	3FT deg		8-12	MO	M	26	CCC		
Finance with French	N3R1	3FT deg		8-12	MO	M	26	CCC		
Finance with German	N3R2	3FT deg		8-12	MO	M	26	CCC		
Finance with Information Management	N3P2	3FT deg		8-12	MO	M	26	CCC		
Finance with Information Systems	N3G5	3FT deg		8-12	MO	M	26	CCC		
Finance with Spanish	N3R4	3FT deg		8-12	MO	M	26	CCC		
Human Resource Management with Accounting	N6N4	3FT deg		8-12	MO	M	26	CCC		
Human Resource Management with Finance	N6N3	3FT deg		8-12	MO	M	26	CCC		
Information Management with Accounting	P2N4	3FT deg		8-12	MO	M	26	CCC		
Marketing with Accounting	N5N4	3FT deg		8-12	MO	M	26	CCC		
Marketing with Finance	N5N3	3FT deg		8-12	MO	M	26	CCC		

Univ of ULSTER

TITLE	CODE	COURSE	SUBJECTS	A/AS	ND/C	AGNVQ	IB	SQA(H)	SQA	RATIO A/AS
Accounting	N400▼	3FT deg	* g	BBC	MO+4D	D*6/^ gi	32	ABBB	Ind	11	20/28
Accounting	N401▼	2FT Dip	* g	CDD	Ind	D* gi	26	BCCC	Ind	10	12/18
Banking and Finance (Hons)	N300▼	3FT deg	* g	BBC	MO+4D	D*6/^ gi	32	ABBB	Ind	14	16/20

Univ of WARWICK

TITLE	CODE	COURSE	SUBJECTS	A/AS	ND/C	AGNVQ	IB	SQA(H)	SQA	RATIO A/AS
Accounting and Finance	NN34	3FT deg	g	ABB	DO $	D$6/^ | 32$	AAABB		13	24/30

WEST HERTS COLL

TITLE	CODE	COURSE	SUBJECTS	A/AS	ND/C	AGNVQ	IB	SQA(H)	SQA	RATIO A/AS
Business and Finance	31NN	2FT HND								3	

WIGAN and LEIGH COLL

TITLE	CODE	COURSE	SUBJECTS	A/AS	ND/C	AGNVQ	IB	SQA(H)	SQA	RATIO A/AS
Business and Legal Studies	31NN▼	2FT HND		DD	N	P					

Univ of WOLVERHAMPTON

TITLE	CODE	COURSE	SUBJECTS	A/AS	ND/C	AGNVQ	IB	SQA(H)	SQA	RATIO A/AS
Accounting (Specialist Route)	N400	3FT deg	g	14	4M	M	24	BBCC	Ind	30	16/20
Accounting and Finance	N420	4SW deg	g	16	4M	D	24	BBBB$	Ind	6	14/22
Combined Degrees *Accounting*	Y401	3FT deg	g	14	4M	M	24	BBBB	Ind		

				98 expected requirements						96 entry stats	

course details — **98 expected requirements** — *96 entry stats*

TITLE	CODE	COURSE	SUBJECTS	A/AS	ND/C	RGNVQ	IB	SQA(H)	SQA	RATIO	A/AS
Univ of ABERDEEN											
Agricultural Economics	D2LC	4FT deg	2S/S+M g	CDD	Ind	MS go	24$	BBBC$	Ind	11	
Agriculture	D200	4FT deg	2S/S+M g	CDD	Ind	MS go	24$	BBBC$	Ind	6	
Animal Science	D220	4FT deg	2S/S+M g	CDD	Ind	MS go	24$	BBBC$	Ind	3	
Animal Science	D222	4FT deg	3S/2S+M g	CCD	Ind	MS go	24$	BBBC$	Ind	10	
Arboriculture and Amenity Forestry	D310	4FT deg	2S/S+M g	CDD	Ind	MS go	24$	BBBC$	Ind	5	
Biological Sciences of Agriculture	CD12	4FT deg	3S/2S+M g	CCD	Ind	MS go	24$	BBBC$	Ind		
Countryside and Environmental Management	D2N8	4FT deg	3S/2S+M g	CCD	Ind	MS go	24$	BBBC$	Ind	15	
Countryside and Environmental Management	D2NV	4FT deg	* g	BBC	Ind	M$ go	30$	BBBB$	Ind	3	
Crop Science	D242	4FT deg	3S/2S+M g	CCD	Ind	MS go	24$	BBBC$	Ind	4	
Crop Science	D240	4FT deg	2S/S+M g	CDD	Ind	MS go	24$	BBBC$	Ind	4	
Crop and Soil Sciences	D962	4FT deg	3S/2S+M g	CCD	Ind	MS go	24$	BBBC$	Ind		
Ecology	D230	4FT deg	3S/2S+M g	CCD	Ind	MS go	24$	BBBC$	Ind	9	
Environmental Microbiology (Micr & Soil Science)	CD59	4FT deg	C+2S/C+S+M g	CCD	Ind	MS go	24$	BBBC$	Ind		
Environmental Microbiology with Indust Placement	DC95	5FT deg	C+2S/C+S+M g	CCD	Ind	MS go	24$	BBBC$	Ind		
Forest Management	D300	4FT deg	2S/S+M g	CDD	Ind	MS go	24$	BBBC$	Ind	5	
Geography with Soil Science	F8D9	4FT deg	3S/2S+M g	CCD	Ind	MS go	24$	BBBC$	Ind	2	
Plant and Soil Science	CDFX	4FT deg	3S/2S+M g	CCD	Ind	MS go	24$	BBBC$	Ind	3	
Soil Science	D960	4FT deg	3S/2S+M g	CCD	Ind	MS go	24$	BBBC$	Ind		
Univ of ABERTAY DUNDEE											
Forest Products Technology	CD93	4FT/5SW deg	B/C	DE	Ind	Ind	Ind	BCC	Ind		
Univ of Wales, ABERYSTWYTH											
Agricultural Science	D206	3FT deg	B/C g	12	MO $	MS g	26$	BCCCC$	Ind		
Agricultural and Food Marketing	D270	3FT deg	* g	12	MO	M g	26	BCCCC	Ind		
Agriculture	D201	4SW deg	B/C g	10	MO $	MS g	26$	BCCCC$	Ind		
Agriculture with Business Studies	D2N1	3FT deg	* g	12	MO	M g	26	BCCCC	Ind		
Countryside Management	D255	3FT deg	B/C g	12	MO $	MS g	26$	BCCCC$	Ind		
Equine Science	D224	3FT deg	B/C g	12	MO $	MS g	26$	BCCCC$	Ind		
Rural Resources Management	D253	3FT deg	* g	12	MO	M g	26	BCCCC	Ind		
Agriculture	102D	3SW HND	* g	2	N $	PS g	Dip$	DD$	N		
Countryside Management	552D	3SW HND	* g	2	N $	PS g	Dip$	DD$	N		
Equine Studies	422D	3SW HND	* g	2	N $	PS g	Dip$	DD$	N		
ANGLIA Poly Univ											
Animal Behaviour and Ecology and Conservation	CD12▼	3FT deg	S	10	3M	P	Dip	BCCC	N	2	6/20
Audiotechnology and Ecology and Conservation	HD6F▼	3FT deg	S	16	8M	D	Dip$	BBCCC	N		
Biology and Ecology and Conservation	DC21▼	3FT deg	B	10	3M	P	Dip$	BCCC	N	11	
Biomedical Science and Ecology and Conservation	DB29▼	3FT deg	B	10	3M	P go	Dip$	BCCC	N		
Business and Ecology and Conservation	DN21▼	3FT deg	* g	10	3M	P go	Dip	BCCC	Ind	2	
Chemistry and Ecology and Conservation	DF21▼	3FT deg	S	10	3M	P	Dip$	BCCC	N		
Communication Studies and Ecology & Conservation	DP23▼	3FT deg	Ap	14	6M	M+/^ go	Dip$	BBCC	Ind	2	
Computer Science and Ecology and Conservation	DG25▼	3FT deg	* g	10	3M	P go	Dip	BCCC	N		
Countryside Management	D255▼	3FT deg	* g	8	2M	P go	Dip	CCCC	Ind		
Countryside Management and Law	DM23▼	3FT deg	* g	8	2M	P go	Dip	CCCC	Ind		
Ecology & Conservation & Real Time Computer Syst	DG2M▼	3FT deg	* g	10	3M	P go	Dip	BCCC	N		
Ecology & Conservation and Ophthalmic Dispensing	BD52▼	3FT deg	* g	10	3M	P go	Dip	BCCC	N		
Ecology and Conservation & Instrumentation Elect	DH26▼	3FT deg	S g	10	2M	M go	Dip$	BCCC	N		
Ecology and Conservation & Maths or Stats/St.Mod	DG21▼	3FT deg	g	10	2M	M go	Dip	BCCC	N		
Ecology and Conservation and French	DR21▼	4FT deg	* g	12	4M	M+/^ go	Dip	BCCC	N		
Ecology and Conservation and Geography	DF28▼	3FT deg	Gy g	10	2M	M go	Dip$	BCCC	N	4	
Ecology and Conservation and Geology	DF26▼	3FT deg	* g	10	2M	M go	Dip	BCCC	N	2	
Ecology and Conservation and German	DR22▼	4FT deg	* g	12	4M $	M+/^	Dip	BCCC	N		

	course details		98 expected requirements							96 entry stats	
TITLE	CODE	COURSE	SUBJECTS	A/AS	ND/C	AGNVQ	IB	SQA(H)	SQA	RATIO	A/AS
Ecology and Conservation and Imaging Science	DW25▼	3FT deg	S g	10	2M	M go	Dip$	BCCC	N		
Ecology and Conservation and Italian	DR23▼	4FT deg	* g	12	4M	M+/^	Dip	BCCC	N		
Ecology and Conservation and Psychology	CD82▼	3FT deg	S g	16	3M	M go	Dip$	BBCCC	N		
Ecology and Conservation and Spanish	DR24▼	4FT deg	* g	12	4M	M+/^ go	Dip	BCCC	N		

ASKHAM BRYAN COLL

Agriculture	002D	3SW HND	*	2	MO	M$	Ind	CC	Ind	4	2/8
Horticulture	052D	3SW HND	*	2	MO	M$	Ind	CC	Ind	3	4/12

Univ of Wales, BANGOR

Agroforestry	DD32	4SW deg	2S g	CCD	3M $	MS6/^ go	26$	BBBC$	Ind	5	
Agroforestry	DD23	3FT deg	2S g	CCD	3M $	MS6/^ go	26$	BBBC$	Ind	9	
Applied Biology	D242	3FT deg	B+C g	CDD	3M $	DS^ go	26$	BBCC$	Ind	12	
Ecology	D230	3FT deg	B+S g	CCD	3M $	DS^ go	28$	BBCC$	Ind	6	
Forestry	D300	3FT deg	2S g	CCD	3M $	MS6/^ go	26$	BBBC	Ind	3	6/26
Forestry	D301	4SW deg	2S g	CCD	3M $	MS6/^ go	26$	BBCC	Ind	5	
Forestry and Forest Products	D322	3FT deg	2S g	CCD	3M $	MS6/^ go	26$	BBCC$	Ind	3	
Forestry and Forest Products	D323	4SW deg	2S g	CCD	3M $	MS6/^ go	26$	BBBC$	Ind	8	
Rural Resource Management	D254	4SW deg	2S g	CCD	3M $	MS6/^ go	26$	BBBC$	Ind	4	8/22
Rural Resource Management	D253	3FT deg	2S g	CCD	3M $	MS6/^ go	26$	BBBC$	Ind	4	8/18
World Agriculture	D200	3FT deg	2S g	CDD	3M $	MS6/^ go	26$	BBBC$	Ind	4	8/26
World Agriculture with Industrial Experience	D201	4FT deg	2S g	CDD	3M $	MS6/^ go	26$	BBBC$	Ind		
Zoology with Animal Ecology	C3D2	3FT deg	B+S g	BCC	4M $	DS^ go	28$	BBBC$	Ind	5	11/20
Agriculture	002D	2FT HND	B/C/S g	2-8	N $	P$	Ind	CC$	Ind		

Univ of BIRMINGHAM

Environmental Science and Policy	F9D2	3FT deg	*	BCC	Ind	Ind	30	Ind	Ind		

BOLTON INST

Conservation Biology	D230	3FT deg	S g	CD	MO	M*	24	BBCC	Ind		

BOURNEMOUTH Univ

Land-based Enterprise	D253	4SW deg	S/Gy/Ec g	12-14	MO	M$ go	Ind	CCC	Ind	1	8/14
Land-based Enterprise	352D	3FT HND	* g	2	MO	M$ go	Ind	Ind	Ind	1	4/8

Univ of BRIGHTON

Forestry Studies	003D▼	3FT/2ACC HND	* g	2-4	N	P	15	Ind	Ind		
Horse Studies	422D▼	3FT/2ACC HND	* g	2-4	N	P	15	Ind	Ind		

BRISTOL, Univ of the W of England

Animal Science	D220▼	3FT deg	B g	8	N $	MS go	24	CCC	N$		
Equine Science	D234▼	3FT/4SW deg	B g	12	4M $	MS go	24	BCC	Ind		
Land Use	D253▼	3FT deg	B g	8	3M $	MS go	24	CCC	N$		
Animal Science	022D▼	2FT HND	B g	4	N $	PS go	24	CC	N$		
Golf Course Management (Cannington College)	182D▼	3SW HND	* g	E	2M	P$ go	24	CD	N		
Horse Studies	432D▼	2FT/3SW HND	B g	6	2M $	PS go	24	CC	N$		
Horticulture (Cannington College)	052D▼	3SW HND	* g	E	2M	P$ go	24	CD	N		
Land Use	352D▼	2FT/3SW HND	B g	2	N$	PS go	24	C	N$		

BUCKINGHAMSHIRE COLLEGE

Global Forest Resources and Forest Products Tech	D315	3FT deg		8-10	MO	M	Ind	CCC	Ind		

Univ of CENTRAL ENGLAND

Horticulture	052D	2FT HND	*	E	N	P	Dip	Ind	Ind	3	
Land Administration	652D	2FT HND		2	P	P					2/5

				98 expected requirements						96 entry stats

TITLE	CODE	COURSE	SUBJECTS	A/AS	ND/C	AGNVQ	IB	SQA(H)	SQA	RATIO A/AS
Univ of CENTRAL LANCASHIRE										
Agriculture	D204▼	4SW deg								
Agriculture (HND top-up)	D200▼	1FT deg			HN $					
Arboriculture	D314▼	4SW deg								
Arboriculture (1 year top-up)	D311▼	1FT deg			HN					
Environmental Land Management	F9D2▼	4FT deg	S g	14	MO+3D	MS6/^	26$	BBCC	Ind	
Equine Science and Management	D224▼	4SW deg	S	DD	MO	M$	24$	CCC		
Equine Science and Management (1 year top-up)	D221▼	1FT deg			HN					
Horticulture	D253▼	4SW deg	S g	DD	MO	M$	24	BCC		
Horticulture (1 year top-up)	D251▼	1FT deg			HN					
International Forestry (year 3 top-up)	D301▼	1FT deg			HN					
Social and Community Forestry	D302▼	3FT/4SW deg	S g	DD	MO+3D	M$	24$	CCC	Ind	
Turf Science and Golf Course Management	D254▼	4SW deg	S g	DD	MO	M$	26$	BCCC	Ind	
Turf Science and Golf Course Management (top-up)	D255▼	1FT deg			HN					
Agriculture	002D▼	3SW HND	S	EE	N	P$	24	CCC	Ind	
Agriculture (Dairy Herd Management)	322D▼	2FT HND	S	EE	N	P$	24	CCC	Ind	
Agriculture (Intensive Crop Production)	042D▼	3SW HND								
Amenity Horticulture (Landscape Design and Mgt)	32KD▼	2FT HND	*	EE	N	P$	24	CCC	Ind	
Animal Management and Welfare	12ND▼	3SW HND	S g	EE	N $	P$	24$	CCC	Ind	
Animal Science	022D▼	2FT HND	* g	E	N	P		CC		
Arboriculture	013D▼	3SW HND	S	EE	N	P$	24	CCC	Ind	
Commercial Floral Design	752D▼	2FT HND	*	EE	N	P$	Dip	CCC	N	
Ecology and Conservation Management	82ND▼	3SW HND	*	EE	N	P$	24	CCC	N	
Environmental Land Management	2D9F▼	2FT HND	S	E	N	P$	24	CCC	N	
Equine Science and Management	422D▼	3SW HND	*	EE	N	P$	24	CCC	N	
Forestry	003D▼	2FT/3SW HND		E	N	P	24	CCC	N	
Game and Wildlife Management	8FND▼	2FT HND	*	E	N	P$	24$	CCC	Ind	
Horticulture	052D▼	3SW HND	*	EE	N	P$	Ind	CCC	Ind	
Land Based Industries	028D▼	3SW HND	*	EE	N	P$	Ind	CCC	Ind	
Turf Science and Golf Course Management	152D▼	3SW HND	*	E	N	P$	24	CCC	N	
CHELTENHAM & GLOUCESTER COLL of HE										
Business Management and Countryside Planning	DN2C	3FT deg	*	10-14	4M+3D	MB3	26	CCCC	Ind	
Business Management with Countryside Planning	N1D9	4SW deg	*	12	4M+3D	MB3	26	CCCC	Ind	
Countryside Planning	D255	3FT deg	*	10	MO	MK	24	CCCC	Ind	
Countryside Planning and English Studies	DQ23	3FT deg	E	10-14	4M+3D	MK	26	CCCC	Ind	
Countryside Planning and Environmental Policy	DF29	3FT deg	*	8-10	MO	MK	24	CCCC	Ind	
Countryside Planning and Financial Management	DN23	3FT deg	*	8-12	MO	MK	26	CCCC	Ind	
Countryside Planning and Geography	DL2V	3FT deg	*	10-12	MO	M3	24	CCCC	Ind	
Countryside Planning and Geology	DF26	3FT deg	S	8	MO	MK	26	CCCC	Ind	
Countryside Planning and Human Geography	DL28	3FT deg	*	8-12	5M+2D	MK	26	CCCC	Ind	
Countryside Planning and Human Resource Mgt	DN21	3FT deg	*	8-12	MO	MK	26	CCCC	Ind	
Countryside Planning and Information Technology	GD52	3FT deg	*	8-12	MO	M	24	CCCC	Ind	
Countryside Planning and Leisure Management	DN2R	3FT deg	*	8-14	5M+2D	M$	26	CCCC	Ind	
Countryside Planning and Marketing Management	DN25	3FT deg	*	8-12	MO	M$	26	CCCC	Ind	
Countryside Planning and Physical Geography	DF28	3FT deg	*	8-12	5M+2D	MK	26	CCCC	Ind	
Countryside Planning and Sport and Exercise Sci	DBF6	3FT deg	S	8-14	5M+2D	MK/DL	26	CCCC	Ind	
Countryside Planning and Tourism Management	DP27	3FT deg	*	8-14	4M+2D	M$	26	CCCC	Ind	
Countryside Planning with Business Management	D2NC	3FT deg	*	8-12	5M+2D	M$	26	CCCC	Ind	
Countryside Planning with English Studies	D2Q3	3FT deg	E	8-12	MO	MK	26	CCCC	Ind	
Countryside Planning with Environmental Policy	D2F9	3FT deg	*	8-12	MO	MK	26$	CCCC	Ind	
Countryside Planning with Financial Management	D2N3	3FT deg	*	8-12	MO	MK	26	CCCC	Ind	
Countryside Planning with Geography	D2LV	3FT deg	*	8	MO	M	24	CCCC	Ind	

course details			98 expected requirements							96 entry stats	
TITLE	CODE	COURSE	SUBJECTS	A/AS	ND/C	RGNVQ	IB	SQA(H)	SQA	RATIO	A/AS
Countryside Planning with Geology	D2F6	3FT deg	*	8	MO	MK	26	CCCC	Ind		
Countryside Planning with Human Geography	D2L8	3FT deg	*	8-12	MO	MK	26	CCCC	Ind		
Countryside Planning with Human Resource Mgt	D2N1	3FT deg	*	8-12	MO	MK	26	CCCC	Ind		
Countryside Planning with Information Technology	D2G5	3FT deg	*	8	MO	M	24	CCCC	Ind		
Countryside Planning with Leisure Management	D2N7	3FT deg	*	8-14	MO	MK	26$	CCCC	Ind		
Countryside Planning with Marketing Management	D2N5	3FT deg	*	8-12	MO	MK	26	CCCC	Ind		
Countryside Planning with Modern Langs (French)	D2R1	3FT deg	g	8-12	MO	MK	26	CCCC	Ind		
Countryside Planning with Physical Geography	D2F8	3FT deg	*	8-12	5M+2D	MK	26	CCCC	Ind		
Countryside Planning with Sport and Exercise Sci	D2B6	3FT deg	S	8-14	5M+2D	MK	26	CCCC	Ind		
Countryside Planning with Tourism Management	D2PT	3FT deg	*	8-14	MO	MK	26$	CCCC	Ind		
English Studies with Countryside Planning	Q3D2	3FT deg	E	12	4M+3D	M^	26	CCCC	Ind		
Environmental Policy with Countryside Planning	F9D2	3FT deg	*	8-10	MO	M3	26$	CCCC	Ind		
Financial Management with Countryside Planning	N3D2	4SW deg	*	10	5M+2D	M3	26	CCCC	Ind		
Geography with Countryside Planning	L8DF	3FT deg	*	8-12	MO	M3^	26	CCCC	Ind		
Geology with Countryside Planning	F6D2	3FT deg	*	8	MO	M3	26	CCCC	Ind		
Human Geography with Countryside Planning	L8D2	3FT deg	*	12	5M+2D	M3	26	CCCC	Ind		
Human Resource Mgt with Countryside Planning	N1D2	4SW deg	*	10	5M+2D	MB3	26	CCCC	Ind		
Information Technology with Countryside Planning	G7D2	3FT deg	*	8	MO	M	24	CCCC	Ind		
Leisure Management with Countryside Planning	N7D2	4SW deg	*	12-16	4M+3D	ML3	26	CCCC	Ind		
Marketing Management with Countryside Planning	N5D2	4SW deg	*	12	3M+2D	MB3	26	CCCC	Ind		
Physical Geography with Countryside Planning	F8D9	3FT deg	*	8-12	4M+3D	M3^	26	CCCC	Ind		
Sport & Exercise Sciences with Countryside Plan	B6DF	3FT deg	*	12-16	4M+3D	ML3	26	CCCC	Ind		
Tourism Management with Countryside Planning	P7D2	4SW deg	*	12-16	4M+3D	ML3	26	CCCC	Ind		

UNIVERSITY COLLEGE CHESTER

| Environmental Science (Rural Environmen Protect) | F9D2 | 4FT deg | * g | Ind | Ind | P | Ind | Ind | Ind | 1 | |

CORDWAINERS COLL

| Saddlery Technology | 29WD | 2FT HND | | | N | | Ind | Ind | Ind | | |

CORNWALL COLLEGE WITH DUCHY COLLEGE

| Equine Science | 422D | 2FT HND | * | C | 5M $ | P$ | Ind | Ind | Ind | | |
| Horse Studies | 322D | 2FT HND | * | C | 5M $ | P$ | Ind | Ind | Ind | | |

COVENTRY Univ

Equine Studies	DN21	4SW deg	* g	14	M+2D	MD	28	BBBC	Ind	5	12/22
Equine and Sport Sciences	BD62	3FT deg									
Recreation and the Countryside	N7D9	3FT/4SW deg	* g	12	Ind	M	Ind	Ind	Ind		
Horse Studies (Management and Technology)	12ND	3SW HND	* g	2	N	P	Ind	CC	Ind	3	2/16

CRANFIELD Univ

Agricultural Technology and Management	D9N1	4SW deg	S g	CDD	4M	M$6/^ go	27$	BBCC	Ind	5	
Agriculture	D200	4SW deg	S g	CDD	4M	M$6/^ go	27$	BBCC	Ind		
Agriculture	002D	3SW HND	*	E	N	P$	Ind	CC	Ind	6	4/ 8

DE MONTFORT Univ

Agriculture (Crop Production/Crop Protection)	D240▼	3FT deg	S g	CD	MO	M	Ind	BBBB	Ind		
Animal Science (Behavioural Studies)	D221▼	3FT deg	S g	CD	MO	M	Ind	BBBB	Ind	5	6/18
Equine Science	D220▼	3FT deg	S g	CD	MO	M	Ind	BBBB	Ind	8	12/22
Equine Sports Science	BD62▼	3FT deg	S g	CD	MO	M	Ind	BBBB	Ind		
Forestry	D300▼	3FT deg	S g	CD	MO	M	Ind	BBBB	Ind		
Landscape Ecology	D254▼	3FT deg	g	CD	MO	M	Ind	BBBB	Ind		
Rural Land Management	D252▼	3FT deg	* g	14	5M	M	26$	BBBB	Ind		
Agriculture (Crop Production/Crop Protection)	042D▼	2FT HND	S g	E	N	P	Ind	BB	Ind	2	
Animal Science(Equine Science/Behavioural Studs)	022D▼	2FT HND	S g	4	N	P	Ind	BB	Ind	2	2/16

			98 expected requirements							96 entry stats	
TITLE	CODE	COURSE	SUBJECTS	A/AS	ND/C	AGNVQ	IB	SQA(H)	SQA	RATIO	A/AS
Business Administration (Agricultural)	19ND▼	2FT HND	* g	E	N	P	Ind	CC	Ind	3	
Forestry	003D▼	2FT HND	S g	2	N	P	Ind	BB	Ind	3	
Horse Studies	122D▼	2FT HND	S g	4	N	P	Ind	BB	Ind	5	4/14
Landscape Ecology	052D▼	2FT HND	S g	2	N	P	Ind	BB	Ind	2	

Univ of DERBY

Conservation and Countryside Management	D255	3FT deg	*	10	N $	M$	26	CCCD	Ind		
Integrated Land Management	23DK▼	2FT HND		4	N $	P$	Dip$	CCD	Ind	5	
Organic Agriculture	002D▼	2FT HND		2	N $	PS	Dip	DD		1	

Univ of DUNDEE

Ecology	CD12	4FT deg	C+S/2S g	16	5M $	M$	25$	BBBC$	N$	31	

Univ of EAST ANGLIA

Conservation Management	D260	3FT deg	B/Gy/En	CD	Ind		Ind	Ind	Ind	15	
Conservation and Biodiversity	CD92	2FT Dip	B/Gy/En	DD	Ind		Ind	Ind	Ind	7	
Development Studies/Natural Resources	D268	3FT deg	* g	CCC	3M		Ind	Ind	Ind	4	
Environmental Landscape Management	D255	3FT deg									

Univ of EAST LONDON

Restoration Ecology (3 or 4 years- placement)	D235	3/4FT deg	* g	12	MO	M$	Ind	Ind	Ind	1	
Extended Science	Y108	4FT deg	* g	8-10	MO	M	Ind	Ind	Ind		
Restoration Ecology											

Univ of EDINBURGH

Agricultural Economics	DL21	4FT deg	S g	CCD	MO $		Dip$	BBBC$	N$	12	
Agricultural Science	D206	4FT deg	C+B/M/P g	CCD	MO $		Dip$	BBBC$	N$		
Agricultural Science (Animal Science)	D220	4FT deg	C+B/M/P g	CCD	MO $		Dip$	BBBC$	N$	5	14/22
Agricultural Science (Crop Science)	D240	4FT deg	C+B/M/P g	CCD	MO $		Dip$	BBBC$	N$		
Agricultural Science with Environmental Science	D8F9	4FT deg	C+B/M/P g	CCD	MO $		Dip$	BBBC$	N$	13	
Agriculture	D200	4FT deg	2(B/C/M/P) g	CCD	MO $		Dip$	BBBC$	N$	10	
Agriculture, Forestry and Rural Economy	DD23	4FT deg	2(B/C/M/P) g	CCD	MO $		Dip$	BBBC$	N$	4	14/18
Forestry	D300	4FT deg	2(B/C/M/P) g	CCC	MO $		Dip$	BBBB$	N$	10	16/22

Univ of ESSEX

Ecology and Conservation	D230	3FT deg	2S	18	MO	D	28	BBBC	Ind		
Ecology and Conservation (4 years inc found yr)	D238	4FT deg									

Univ of GLAMORGAN

Animal Science	322D▼	2FT HND	S g	D	N	P	Ind	Ind	Ind		
Animal Science	122D▼	2FT HND	S g	D	N $	P$	Ind	Ind	Ind	5	
Landscape Science	052D	2FT HND	g	D	N $	P$	Ind	Ind	Ind	6	

Univ of GLASGOW

Agricultural Botany	D820	4FT deg	2S	BBC-CCC	N	M	24$	BBBB$	N	3	
Agricultural Botany (with work placement)	D821	4FT deg	2S	BBC-CCC	N	M	24$	BBBB$	N		
Agricultural, Food and Environmental Chemistry	D860	4FT deg	C/M+S	BBC-CCC	N	M	24$	BBBB$	N	5	

Univ of GREENWICH

Environmental Conservation	D260	3FT/4SW deg	g	12	3M	Ind	Ind	BCC$	Ind		
Environmental Conservation (Extended)	D268	4FT/5SW deg	g	4		Ind	Ind	Ind	Ind		
Garden Design	D259▼	3FT/4SW deg	* g	14	5M	M	24	BBB			
Horticulture (Commercial)	D250▼	4SW deg	2S g	8	N		Dip	CCC			
Horticulture (Extended)	D258▼	5EXTSW deg	* g	4	Ind	Ind	Dip	CC	Ind		
Landscape Management (Land Use)	D2K3▼	4SW deg	* g	14	HN	M	24	BBB	HN		
Natural Resource Management (3FT/4SW)	FD82	3FT/4SW deg	* g	12	3M	Ind	Dip	CCC	Ind		
Natural Resource Management (Extended)	FD8F	4FT/5SW deg	g	4	Ind	Ind	Ind	Ind	Ind		

TITLE	CODE	COURSE	SUBJECTS	A/AS	ND/C	AGNVQ	IB	SQA(H)	SQA	RATIO	A/AS
Garden Design	252D▼	3SW HND	* g	6			Dip	BB			
Horticulture (Commercial)	152D▼	3SW HND	S g	2	N		Dip	CC			
Landscape Management (Land Use)	3K2D▼	2FT HND	* g	6			Dip	BB			

HARPER ADAMS Agric COLL

TITLE	CODE	COURSE	SUBJECTS	A/AS	ND/C	AGNVQ	IB	SQA(H)	SQA	RATIO	A/AS
Agri-Food Marketing with Business Studies	DN25	3FT/4SW deg	* g	8-12	MO	M$	Dip	CCCC	Ind	2	8/20
Agri-Food Production with Marketing and Mgt	D271	3FT/4SW deg	* g	8-12	MO	M$	Dip	CCCC	Ind		
Agriculture	D200	3FT/4SW deg	S g	8-12	MO	M$	Dip	CCCC	Ind	5	8/24
Agriculture with Agricultural Marketing	D270	3FT/4SW deg	S g	8-12	MO	M$	Dip	CCCC	Ind	6	14/18
Agriculture with Animal Science	D220	3FT/4SW deg	S g	8-12	MO	M$	Dip	CCCC	Ind	7	12/18
Agriculture with Crop Management	D240	3FT/4SW deg	S g	8-12	MO	M$	Dip	CCCC	Ind	7	
Agriculture with Land and Farm Management	D2N8	3FT/4SW deg	S g	8-12	MO	M$	Dip	CCCC	Ind	4	8/22
Agriculture with Rural Enterprise	D2N1	3FT/4SW deg	S g	8-12	MO	M$	Dip	CCCC			
Animal Health	D830	3FT/4SW deg	B g	8-12	MO	MS	26$	CCCC$	Ind		
International Agri-Food Production and Marketing	D201	4FT deg	S g	8-12	MO	M$	Dip	CCCC	Ind	6	
Negotiated Studies for the Land-based Industries	D900	3FT/4SW deg	* g	8-12	MO	M$	Dip	CCCC	Ind		
Rural Enterprise	DN21	3FT/4SW deg	* g	8-12	MO	M$	Dip	CCCC	Ind		
Rural Enterprise and Land Management	DN28	3FT/4SW deg	* g	14-16	MO	M$	Dip	BBCC	Ind	4	12/28
Agri-Food Marketing and Business Studies	072D	2FT/3SW HND	* g	2-8	N	P$	Ind	CC	N	2	4/10
Agriculture	002D▼	2FT/3SW HND	* g	2-8	N	P$	Ind	CC	N	3	2/10
Agriculture with Animal Production	622D	2FT/3SW HND	* g	2-8	N	P$	Ind	CC	N	4	2/6
Agriculture with Crop Production	042D	2FT/3SW HND	* g	2-8	N	P$	Ind	CC	N	13	
Agriculture with Land and Farm Management	8N2D	2FT/3SW HND	* g	2-8	N	P$	Ind	CC	N	3	2/10
Animal Care, Science and Business Management	022D▼	2FT HND	* g	2-8	N	P$	Ind	CC	N	5	4/9
Golf Course Management	152D▼	3SW HND	* g	2-8	N	P$	Ind	CC	N	2	2/10

Univ of HERTFORDSHIRE

TITLE	CODE	COURSE	SUBJECTS	A/AS	ND/C	AGNVQ	IB	SQA(H)	SQA	RATIO	A/AS
Landbased Technologies	109D▼	2FT/3SW HND	* g	6-20	N	P	24	CCC	Ind		

Univ of KENT

TITLE	CODE	COURSE	SUBJECTS	A/AS	ND/C	AGNVQ	IB	SQA(H)	SQA	RATIO	A/AS
Biodiversity Conservation and Environmental Mgt	CD92	3FT deg	S g	BCC	MO	Ind	28$	BBBB$	Ind		

Univ of LEEDS

TITLE	CODE	COURSE	SUBJECTS	A/AS	ND/C	AGNVQ	IB	SQA(H)	SQA	RATIO	A/AS
Animal Nutrition and Physiology	D224	3FT deg	B+M/C/P g	CDD	4M $	Ind	22$	BBCC	Ind	3	8/22
Animal Science	D220	3FT deg	B+M/C/P g	CDD	4M $	Ind	22$	BBCCC	Ind	5	8/22

Univ of LINCOLNSHIRE and HUMBERSIDE

TITLE	CODE	COURSE	SUBJECTS	A/AS	ND/C	AGNVQ	IB	SQA(H)	SQA	RATIO	A/AS
Countryside Management	D952▼	3FT deg	g	12	3M+1D	M	24	CCCC	Ind		
Equine Science Management	D220▼	3FT deg	* g	12	Ind	Ind	Ind	Ind	Ind		
Garden Design	D252▼	3FT deg	g								
Agriculture	002D▼	2FT HND	g	6	Ind	Ind	Ind	Ind	Ind		
Countryside Management	352D▼	2FT HND	g	6	MO	P	Ind	CC	Ind		
Equine Management	022D▼	2FT HND	* g	6	Ind	Ind	Ind	Ind	Ind		

LIVERPOOL JOHN MOORES Univ

TITLE	CODE	COURSE	SUBJECTS	A/AS	ND/C	AGNVQ	IB	SQA(H)	SQA	RATIO	A/AS
Countryside Management	D255	3FT deg	S g	8	3M	M	Ind	CCCC		6	8/10
Earth Science and Countryside Management	FD92	3FT deg	S g	8	3M	M	Ind	CCCC		6	8/12
Human Geography and Countryside Management	LD82	3FT deg	Gy+S g	12	5M+3D	PS^	28$	BBCC		9	

LSU COLL of HE

TITLE	CODE	COURSE	SUBJECTS	A/AS	ND/C	AGNVQ	IB	SQA(H)	SQA	RATIO	A/AS
European Studies with Ecology	T2D2	3FT deg									
Geography and Ecology	DL28	3FT deg									
Life Sciences and Ecology	DC29	3FT deg									
Politics and Ecology	DM21	3FT deg									
Politics with Ecology	M1D2	3FT deg	S	DD	Ind		Ind	Ind	Ind		
Sports Science and Ecology	DB26	3FT deg									

TITLE	CODE	COURSE	SUBJECTS	A/AS	ND/C	RGNVQ	IB	SQA(H)	SQA	RATIO	A/AS
MIDDLESEX Univ											
Garden Design	W2D2▼	3FT deg									
NENE COLLEGE											
Countryside Management	D255	1FT deg									
Equine Studies with Estates Studies	D2N8	1FT deg									
Animal Welfare	022D▼	2FT HND		E	P	P	24	CC	Ind		
Equine Studies with Estates Studies	8N2D	2FT HND		2	N	P		CC	Ind		
Univ of NEWCASTLE											
Agriculture	D200	3FT deg	B/C g	CCD	Ind	Ind	Ind	BBBB$	Ind	4	10/28
Agronomy	D244	3FT deg	B/C g	CCD	Ind	Ind	Ind	BBBB$	Ind	2	
Animal Production Science	D224	3FT deg	B/C g	CCD	Ind	Ind	Ind	BBBB$	Ind	2	
Countryside Management	D255	3FT deg	* g	CCC	MO		Ind	AABB	Ind	4	14/22
Domestic Animal Science	D220	3FT deg	2S g	CCD	Ind	Ind	Ind	AABB	Ind	4	14/20
Ecological Resource Management	F9D2	3FT deg	2(S/Ec/Gy/M) g	CCD	4M	M$^ go	26$	BBBB$	Ind		
Entomology and Pest Management	CD32	3FT deg	2S g	CCD	Ind	Ind	Ind	AABB	Ind		
Environmental Science and Agricultural Ecology	DF29	3FT deg	2S g	CCC	Ind	Ind	Ind	ABBB	Ind	3	10/22
Environmental and Ecological Engineering	HD2F	4FT deg	* g	CCC	3M $		26	BBCCC	Ind	10	
Environmental and Ecological Engineering	HD22	3FT deg	M+C/P	CCC	MO $		28$	CSYS$	Ind	14	
Farm Business Management	D202	3FT deg	B/C g	CCD	Ind	Ind	Ind	BBBB$	Ind	5	
Rural Economics and Environmental Management	DL21	3FT deg	* g	CCC	Ind	Ind	Ind	BBBB	Ind	3	
Rural Environmental Management	D234	3FT deg	* g	CCC	Ind	Ind	Ind	BBBB	Ind		
Rural Environmental Management and Marketing	DD24	3FT deg	* g	CCC	Ind	Ind	Ind	BBBB	Ind		
Rural Environmental and Business Management	DN21	3FT deg	* g	CCC	Ind	Ind	Ind	BBBB	Ind	5	16/16
Rural Resource Management	D253	3FT deg	B/C g	CCD	Ind	Ind	Ind	BBBB$	Ind	38	
NEW COLLEGE DURHAM											
Arboriculture - Urban Woodland Management	013D▼	2FT HND		2	N	Ind	Ind	Ind	Ind		
NESCOT											
Applied Animal Science	D220	3FT deg	S	EE	N	M	Dip	Ind	N$		
Applied Animal Science	D228	4FT deg	*								
Applied Ecology	D230	3FT deg	Ap	EE	N	M	Dip	Ind	N$		
Applied Ecology	D238	4FT deg	*								
Animal Science	022D	2FT HND	S	E	N	P	Dip	CC	N	2	
Nature Conservation for Leisure and Tourism	7N2D	2FT HND	*	E	N	P	Dip	Ind	N$		
Univ of NORTHUMBRIA											
Landscape Ecology	D250	3FT deg	Gy/S g	12	3M	M$	26	BBB$	Ind		
Univ of NOTTINGHAM											
Agricultural Biochemistry with European Studies	D8T2	4FT deg	2(M/S/Gy) g	CC-CDD	3M $	MS	24$	CSYS$	N$	1	
Agricultural Biochemistry (allows specialisation)	D850	3FT deg	2(M/S/Gy)	CC-CDD	3M $	MS	24$	CSYS$	N$	4	
Agriculture	D200	3FT deg	2(M/S/Gy)	CC-CDD	3M $	MS	24$	CSYS$	N$	9	12/22
Agriculture with European Studies	D2T2	4FT deg	2(M/S/Gy) g	CC-CDD	3M $	MS	24$	CSYS$	N$		
Agriculture with Technology	D206	4FT deg	2(M/S/Gy)	CC-CDD	3M $	MS	24$	CSYS$	N$	3	
Animal Science (allows specialisation)	D220	3FT deg	2(M/S/Gy)	CC-CDD	3M $	MS	24$	CSYS$	N$	8	12/22
Animal Science with European Studies (4 Yrs)	D2TF	4FT deg	2(M/S/Gy) g	CC-CDD	3M $	MS	24$	CSYS$	N$	7	
Applied Biology	D820	3FT deg	2(M/S/Gy) g	CC-CDD	3M $	MS	24$	CSYS$	N$	8	12/26
Applied Biology with European Studies	D8TF	4FT deg	2(M/S/Gy) g	CC-CDD	3M $	MS	24$	CSYS$	N$	5	
Biotechnology in Agriculture (allows specialis)	D8J8	3FT deg	2(M/S/Gy)	CC-CDD	3M $	MS	24$	CSYS$	N$	13	
Biotechnology in Agriculture with Euro Studies	D8TG	4FT deg	2(M/S/Gy) g	CC-CDD	3M $	MS	24$	CSYS$	N$		
Horticulture (allows specialisation)	D250	3FT deg	2(M/S/Gy)	CC-CDD	3M $	MS	24$	CSYS$	N$	5	
Horticulture with European Studies	D2TG	4FT deg	2(M/S/Gy) g	CC-CDD	3M $	MS	24$	CSYS$	N$		

course details — 98 expected requirements — 96 entry stats

| | | | 98 expected requirements | | | | | | | 96 entry stats |
| course details | | | | | | | | | | |

TITLE	CODE	COURSE	SUBJECTS	A/AS	ND/C	AGNVQ	IB	SQA(H)	SQA	RATIO A/AS
Horticulture with Technology	D256	4FT deg	2(M/S/Gy)	CC-CDD	3M $	MS	24$	CSYS$	N$	
Plant and Crop Science (allows specialisation)	D240	3FT deg	2(M/S/Gy)	CC-CDD	3M $	MS	24$	CSYS$	N$	3
Plant and Crop Science with European Studies	D2T9	4FT deg	2(M/S/Gy) g	CC-CDD	3M $	MS	24$	CSYS$	N$	

NOTTINGHAM TRENT Univ

TITLE	CODE	COURSE	SUBJECTS	A/AS	ND/C	AGNVQ	IB	SQA(H)	SQA	RATIO A/AS
Countryside Management	DN21▼	3FT deg	* g	16	5M	Ind	Ind	Ind	Ind	
Countryside Management (Extended)	DN2D▼	4EXTFT deg	* g		Ind	Ind	Ind	Ind	Ind	
Equine Studies	D239▼	4SW deg	S g	CD	Ind	Ind	Dip	C	$	5 8/22
Agriculture	002D▼	3SW HND	S g	EE	N	Ind	Dip	DD	N	5
Agriculture, Marketing Supply Management	072D▼	3SW HND	S g	EE	N	Ind	Dip	DD	N	
Animal Care	522D▼	2FT HND	S g	EE	N	Ind	Dip	DD	N	
Applied Equine Studies	932D▼	3SW HND	S g	EE	N	Ind	Dip	DD	N	4 2/14

Univ of PLYMOUTH

TITLE	CODE	COURSE	SUBJECTS	A/AS	ND/C	AGNVQ	IB	SQA(H)	SQA	RATIO A/AS
Agriculture	D200	3FT/4SW deg	2(S/Gy/Ec) g	10	3M	MS	Ind	CCC$	Ind	4 6/20
Agriculture and Countryside Management	D201	3FT/4SW deg	2(S/Gy/Ec) g	10	3M	M$	Ind	BBCC	Ind	5 8/18
Agriculture and the Environment	DF29	4SW deg	2(S/Gy/Ec) g	10	3M	M$	Ind	CCC	Ind	
Agriculture with Rural Estate Management	D2N8	4SW deg	2(S/Gy/Ec) g	12	3M	M$	Ind	CCC	Ind	1
Ecology	D230	3FT deg	B g	12-16	4M $	MS^	Ind	BBC	Ind	6 12/20
Ecology with Geography	D2F8	3FT deg	B g	16	4M $	MS^	Ind	BBC	Ind	4
Ecology with Geology	D2F6	3FT deg	B g	14-16	4M $	MS^	Ind	BBC	Ind	
Extended Eng (Land Based Inds) Found Yr (Bicton)	D208	1FT/4EXT deg	* g	2	Ind	Ind	Ind	Ind	Ind	1 6/6
Food Management	D203	4SW/3FT deg	He g	8	N $	M$	Ind	Ind	Ind	8
Food Production	D202	4SW/3FT deg	Ap g	8	3M	P$	Ind	Ind	Ind	3
Geography with Ecology	F8D2	3FT deg	Gy+B g	16-18	X	M$^	Ind	Ind	Ind	3 10/16
Geology with Ecology	F6D2	3FT deg	S+B g	12	4M	MS	Ind	Ind	Ind	2
Marine Biology and Ecology	CD12	3FT deg	B+S g	CCD	4M $	MS^	Ind	Ind	Ind	
Mathematics with Ecology	G1D2	3FT deg	M g	10-15	MO $	M$^	Ind	Ind	Ind	
Modern Languages with Ecology	T9D2	3FT/4SW deg	L g	C	Ind	Ind	Ind	Ind	Ind	
Rural Resource Management	D253	4SW deg	2(S/Gy/Ec) g	12	3M	M$	Ind	Ind	Ind	3 10/23
Statistics (Applied) with Ecology	G4D2	3FT deg	M/St g	10	MO $	M$	Ind	BBCC	Ind	
Extended Science (Foundation Year) *Agriculture*	Y108▼	1FT/4EXT deg	S	2	Ind	P$	Ind	Ind	Ind	
Agriculture	002D	2FT/3SW HND	* g	2	N	PS/PB	Ind	DD	Ind	2 2/14
Countryside Recreation Management (Bicton)	259D	2FT HND	* g	8	MO	Ind	Ind	Ind	Ind	3 4/12
Rural Resource Management	352D	2FT/3SW HND	S g	2	N $	P$	Ind	Ind	Ind	2 2/12

QUEEN'S Univ Belfast

TITLE	CODE	COURSE	SUBJECTS	A/AS	ND/C	AGNVQ	IB	SQA(H)	SQA	RATIO A/AS
Agricultural Science	D800	4FT deg	C+B/P/M g	CCC	X	Ind	28$	X	Ind	5 14/24
Agriculture	D200	3FT/4FT deg	C/B g	CDD	Ind	Ind	26$	BBCC	Ind	4 12/22
Plant Science	D825	3FT/4FT deg	C+B g	CCC	Ind	Ind	27$	BBBC	Ind	

Univ of READING

TITLE	CODE	COURSE	SUBJECTS	A/AS	ND/C	AGNVQ	IB	SQA(H)	SQA	RATIO A/AS
Agricultural Botany	D820	3FT deg	2S g	CDD	MO	MS6/^ gi	28$	BBCC	Ind	2
Agricultural Botany with International Studies	D8TX	4FT deg	2S g	CDD	MO	MS6/^ gi	28$	BBCC	Ind	2
Agricultural Botany with Studies in Europe	D8T2	4FT deg	2S g	CDD	MO	MS6/^ gi	28$	BBCC	Ind	
Agriculture	D200	3FT deg	S g	CDD	MO	MS6/^ gi	28$	BBCC	Ind	6 12/25
Animal Science	D220	3FT deg	B/C g	CDD	MO	MS6/^ gi	28$	BBCC	Ind	7 14/24
Crop Protection	D242	3FT deg	2S g	CCC	MO	MS6/^ gi	28$	BBBC	Ind	
Crop Protection with Studies in Europe	D2TX	4FT deg	2S g	CCC	MO	MS6/^ gi	28$	BBBC	Ind	
Crop Science	D240	3FT deg	2S g	CDD	MO	MS6/^ gi	28$	BBCC	Ind	3
Crop Science with International Studies	D2TY	4FT deg	2S g	CDD	MO	MS6/^ gi	28$	BBCC	Ind	
Crop Science with Studies in Europe	D2TF	4FT deg	2S g	CDD	MO	MS6/^ gi	28$	BBCC	Ind	
Habitat and Soil Management	D963	3FT deg	2S g	CCC	MO	MS6/^ gi	28$	BBBC	Ind	1
Horticulture	D251	4SW deg	B/C g	CDD	MO	MS6/^ gi	28$	BBCC	Ind	5
Horticulture	D250	3FT deg	B/C g	CDD	MO	MS6/^ gi	28$	BBCC	Ind	5

Agriculture and Forestry 2

	course details		98 expected requirements							96 entry stats	
TITLE	CODE	COURSE	SUBJECTS	A/AS	ND/C	AGNVQ	IB	SQA(H)	SQA	RATIO	A/AS
Horticulture with Studies in Europe	D2TG	4FT deg	B/C g	CDD	MO	MS6/^ gi	28$	BBCC	Ind	5	
Landscape Management	D255	4SW deg	B/En/Gy g	CCD	MO	M$6/^ gi	28$	BBCC	Ind	4	12/18
Landscape Management with Studies in Europe	D2T9	4FT deg	B/En/Gy g	CCD	MO	M$6/^ gi	28$	BBCC	Ind	7	
Rural Environmental Sciences	D230	3FT deg	2S g	CDD	MO	MS6/^ gi	28$	BBCC	Ind	1	10/13
Rural Resource Management	D253	3FT deg	S g	CDD	MO	MS6/^ gi	28$	BBCC	Ind	7	12/24

ROEHAMPTON INST

TITLE	CODE	COURSE	SUBJECTS	A/AS	ND/C	AGNVQ	IB	SQA(H)	SQA	RATIO	A/AS
Business Computing and Natural Resource Studies	DG27▼	3FT deg	g	12	4M	M	26	BCC	N		
Ecology & Conservation	CD92▼	3FT deg	g	12	3M	P$ go	24	CCC	N$		
Natural Resource St and English Lang & Linguist	DQ2H▼	3FT deg	g	CC	2M+2D	M$^ go	30	BBC	N$		
Natural Resource Studies	D268▼	3FT deg	g	DD	3M	P$ go	24	CCC	N$		
Natural Resource Studies & Drama & Theatre Studs	DW2L▼	3FT deg	E/T g	16	2M+2D	M$^ go	30	BBC	N$		
Natural Resource Studies & Environmental Studies	DF29▼	3FT deg	B/Gy	DD	4M $	P$ go	24	CCC	N$		
Natural Resource Studies and App Consumer Studs	DN29▼	3FT deg	g	12	3M	P$ go	24	CCC	N$		
Natural Resource Studies and Art for Community	DW21▼	3FT deg	g	DD	3M	P$ go	24	CCC	N$		
Natural Resource Studies and Biology	CD12▼	3FT deg	B g	12	3M	P$ go	24	CCC	N$		
Natural Resource Studies and Business Studies	DN21▼	3FT deg	g	DD	3D	M$ go	26	BCC	N$		
Natural Resource Studies and Dance Studies	DW24▼	3FT deg	g	CC	2M+2D	M$^ go	30	BBC	N$		
Natural Resource Studies and Education	DX29▼	3FT deg	g	DD	3M	P$ go	30	CCC	N$		
Natural Resource Studies and English Literature	DQ23▼	3FT deg	E g	CC	2M+2D	M^ go	30	BBC	N$		
Natural Resource Studies and French	DR21▼	4FT deg	F g	12	3M	P^ go	24	CCC	N$		
Natural Resource Studies and Geography	DL28▼	3FT deg	Gy g	DD	3M	P$ go	24	CCC	N$		
Natural Resource Studies and Health Studies	BD92▼	3FT deg	g	12	3M	P$ go	24	CCC	N$		
Natural Resource Studies and History	DV21▼	3FT deg	H g	DD	3M	P^ go	24	CCC	N$		
Natural Resource Studies and Music	DW23▼	3FT deg	Mu g	DD	3M	P^ go	24	CCC	N$		
Natural Resource Studs & Film & Television Studs	DP24▼	3FT deg	g	16	2M+2D	M$^ go	30	BBC	N$		
Natural Resource Studs and Human & Social Biol	CDC2▼	3FT deg	g	12	3M	P$ go	24	CCC	N$		
Psychology and Natural Resource Studies	DL27▼	3FT deg	g	CC	3D	M$ go	30	BBC	N$		
Social Policy & Admin & Natural Resource Studs	DL24▼	3FT deg	g	DD	3M	P$ go	24	CCC	N$		
Sociology and Natural Resource Studies	DL23▼	3FT deg	g	DD	3M	P$ go	24	CCC	N$		
Spanish and Natural Resource Studies	DR24▼	4FT deg	Sp g	12	3M	P$ go	24	CCC	N$		
Sport Studies and Natural Resource Studies	DB26▼	3FT deg	g	12	2M+2D	M$ go	28	BCC	N$		
Theology & Relig Studs & Natural Resource Studs	DV28▼	3FT deg	g	DD	3M	P$ go	24	CCC	N$		
Women's Studies and Natural Resource Studies	DM29▼	3FT deg	g	DD	3M	P$ go	24	CCC	N$		

ROYAL Agric COLL

TITLE	CODE	COURSE	SUBJECTS	A/AS	ND/C	AGNVQ	IB	SQA(H)	SQA	RATIO	A/AS
Agriculture	D800	3FT/4SW deg	2S g	12	MO		26$	CCC$	Ind		
Agriculture and Land Management	DN28	3FT/4SW deg	2S g	12	MO		26$	CCC$	Ind	8	10/22
Crop Production Ecology and Management	D240	3FT/4SW deg	2S g	12	MO		26$	CCC$	Ind		
Farm Mechanization and Management (post HND)	DH21	1FT deg	X	HN		X	X	X	8		
International Agricultural and Equine Bus Mgt	DN21	3FT/4SW deg	2S g	12	MO		26$	CCC$	Ind	4	8/26
International Agriculture, Land and Business Mgt	DN2C	3FT/4SW deg	2S g	12	MO		26$	CCC$	Ind	4	11/20

SCOTTISH Agric COLL

TITLE	CODE	COURSE	SUBJECTS	A/AS	ND/C	AGNVQ	IB	SQA(H)	SQA	RATIO	A/AS
Applied Plant and Animal Science	D220▼	3FT/4FT deg	B/C	CDD	Ind	MS	Ind	BBB$	Ind	2	
Food Production and Land Use	DN28▼	3FT/4FT deg	S	CC	Ind	M$	Ind	BCC$	Ind	1	
Food Production, Manufacturing & Marketing	DD24▼	3FT/4FT deg	S	CC	Ind	MS	Ind	BCC$	Ind	6	
Landscape Management and Design	D2K3▼	3FT/4FT deg	S/Gy	CD	Ind	M$	Ind	BCC$	Ind		
Rural Resource Management	D253▼	3FT/4FT deg	S	CD	Ind	M$	Ind	BCC$	Ind	4	
Rural Business Management _Farm Management_	Y400▼	3FT/4FT deg	S/M	CD	Ind	Ind	Ind	BBC$	Ind		
Agricultural Science	008D▼	2FT HND	B/C	D	N $	PS	Ind	CC$	Ind	5	
Agriculture	002D▼	2FT/3SW HND	S	D	N $	P$	Ind	CC$	N	2	
Biotechnology	.528D▼	2FT HND	B/C	D	N $	PS	Ind	CC$	Ind	2	
Countryside Recreation & Conservation Mgt	552D▼	2FT HND	*	D	N $	P$	Ind	CC	Ind	4	

	course details			98 expected requirements							96 entry stats
TITLE	CODE	COURSE	SUBJECTS	A/AS	ND/C	RGNVQ	IB	SQA(H)	SQA	RATIO A/AS
Horticulture	052D▼	2FT HND	S	D	N $	P$	Ind	CC$	N$	1
Horticulture with Plantsmanship	452D▼	2FT HND	S	D	N $	P$	Ind	CC$	Ind	2
Poultry Production and Management	222D▼	2FT HND	*	D	N $	P$	Ind	CC	N	1
Rural Business Management	652D▼	2FT HND	*	D	N $	P$	Ind	CC	Ind	
Rural Recreation and Tourism	27DP▼	2FT HND	*	D	N $	P$	Ind	CC	Ind	2
Rural Resource Management	352D▼	2FT HND	S	D	N $	P$	Ind	CC$	Ind	3
SHEFFIELD HALLAM Univ										
Countryside Recreation Management	DN27	3FT deg	*	14	8M+2D	M	Ind	Ind	Ind	
Combined Studies *Countryside Management*	Y400	3FT deg	*	14	2M	M	Ind	Ind	Ind	
SOUTH BANK Univ										
Conservation	D260	3FT/4SW deg	B/C g	CC	M	M	Ind	Ind	Ind	
Foundation Conservation	D261	4EXT deg					Ind	Ind	Ind	
SPARSHOLT COLLEGE Hampshire										
Aquaculture and Fishery Management	D280	3FT deg	S	DD	MO	M	Ind	Ind	Ind	
Agriculture-Production and Management	002D	2FT/3SW HND	*	EE	N	P	Ind	Ind	Ind	
Applied Biology (Animal Management/Equine Sci)	21DC	2FT HND	S	EE	N	P	Ind	Ind	Ind	
Fishery Studies/Fish Farming and Fishery Mgt	082D	2FT HND	S	D	MO	M	Ind	Ind	Ind	
Forestry (Lowland Management)	003D	2FT/3SW HND	*	EE	N	P	Ind	Ind	Ind	
Wildlife Management	032D	2FT HND	S	EE	MO	M	Ind	Ind	Ind	
Univ of ST ANDREWS										
Quantitative Ecology	D230	4FT deg	M g	BCC	X	Ind	28$	BBBC$	Ind	
Univ of STIRLING										
Conservation Management	D255	4FT deg	S g	CCC	Ind	Ind	31	BBBC	HN	
Univ of STRATHCLYDE										
Horticulture	D250	4FT deg	C+S g	CD	HN		24	BBB$	HN	
Horticulture with Horticultural Management	D2N9	4FT deg	C g	CD	HN		24	BBB$	HN	
Science Studies (Pass Degree) *Horticulture*	Y100	3FT deg	M+S	DD	Ind		Ind	CCC$	Ind	
UNIVERSITY COLLEGE SUFFOLK										
Animal Science and Welfare	122D	2FT HND	S	E	N $	P$	Ind	Ind	Ind	
Univ of SUNDERLAND										
Countryside Recreation and Leisure	DN27	3FT deg	* g	12	M6	M	Ind	CCCC	N	
Countryside Recreation and Leisure (Foundation)	DN2T	4EXT deg	*		Ind	Ind	Ind	Ind	Ind	
Univ of SUSSEX										
Ecology and Conservation	CD92	3FT deg	S g	BCC	MO $	MS6 go	$	Ind	Ind	
TRINITY COLL Carmarthen										
Rural Environment	DF29	3FT deg	S/Gy g	DD-CC	Ind		Ind	Ind	Ind	2 4/12
Univ of WOLVERHAMPTON										
Equine Studies	D224	3FT deg	g	DD	N	M	24	CCCC	Ind	
Plant & Crop Science	CD2F	3FT/4SW deg		DD	N	M	24	CCCC	Ind	
Applied Sciences *Plant and Crop Science*	Y100	3FT/4SW deg	B g	DD	N	M	24	CCCC	Ind	
Applied Sciences (4 Yrs) *Plant and Crop Science*	Y110▼	4FT deg	*							
Combined Degrees *Plant and Crop Science*	Y401	3FT/4SW deg	B g	DD	N	M	24	CCCC	Ind	
Equine Studies	422D	2FT HND	g	E	N	P	24	BBBB	Ind	

TITLE	CODE	COURSE	SUBJECTS	A/AS	NO/C	AGNVQ	IB	SQA(H)	SQA	RATIO A/AS	
WORCESTER COLL of HE											
Horticulture	D250▼	4FT deg	S	DD	Ind	M	Ind	Ind	Ind	2	12/24
Equine Studies	432D▼	2FT HND		E	N	Ind	Ind	Ind	Ind	10	
Horticulture (Crop Technology)	142D▼	2FT HND	S	E	N	Ind	Ind	Ind	Ind	1	
Horticulture (Garden Design and Management)	152D▼	2FT HND	S	E	N	Ind	Ind	Ind	Ind	2	4/16
WRITTLE COLL											
Agriculture	D201	3FT/4SW deg	Ap g	12	MO	M	Ind	Ind	Ind	11	12/14
Agriculture (Business Management)	D2N1	3FT/4SW deg	Ap g	12	MO	M	Ind	Ind	Ind		
Agriculture (Post HND)	D200	1FT deg	* g	X	HN	Ind				2	
Agriculture (Science)	D2Y1	3FT/4SW deg	Ap g	14	MO	M	Ind	Ind	Ind		
Animal Science	D221	3FT deg	Ap g	16	MO	M	Ind	Ind	Ind		
Equine Studies	D234	3FT deg	Ap g	16	MO	M	Ind	Ind	Ind	8	10/22
Horticultural Crop Production	D251	3FT/4SW deg	Ap g	10	MO	M	Ind	Ind	Ind	1	
Horticulture	D250	3FT/4SW deg	Ap g	10	MO	M	Ind	Ind	Ind	3	4/12
Horticulture (Business Management)	DN21	3FT/4SW deg	Ap g	10	MO	M	Ind	Ind	Ind		
Landscape and Amenity Management	D255	3FT/4SW deg	Ap g	10	MO	M	Ind	Ind	Ind		
Rural Environmental Management	D257	3FT deg	Ap g	12	MO	M	Ind	Ind	Ind		
Agriculture (Business Management)	1FND	2FT/3SW HND	Ap g	6	N	M	Ind	Ind	Ind		
Agriculture (Crops)	042D	2FT/3SW HND	Ap g	6	N	M	Ind	Ind	Ind	2	
Agriculture (Livestock)	022D	2FT/3SW HND	Ap g	6	N	M	Ind	Ind	Ind	8	
Agriculture (Mechanisation)	32HD	2FT/3SW HND	Ap g	6	N	M	Ind	Ind	Ind	3	
Equine Studies	432D	2FT/3SW HND	Ap g	6	N	M	Ind	Ind	Ind	4	2/14
Horticulture (Commercial Crop Production)	152D	2FT/3SW HND	Ap g	4	N	M	Ind	Ind	Ind	1	
Horticulture (Landscape and Amenity Management)	552D	2FT/3SW HND	Ap g	4	N	M	Ind	Ind	Ind	5	
Horticulture (Nursery)	452D	2FT/3SW HND	Ap g	4	N	M	Ind	Ind	Ind		
Horticulture (Retailing)	072D	2FT/3SW HND	Ap g	4	N	M	Ind	Ind	Ind	8	
Horticulture (Sports Turf and Golf Course Mgt)	652D	2FT/3SW HND	Ap g	4	N	M	Ind	Ind	Ind	6	
Rural Resource Management	352D	2FT/3SW HND	Ap g	6	N	M	Ind	Ind	Ind	5	
Science (Applied Biology for Animal Care)	122D	3FT HND	Ap g	6	N	M	Ind	Ind	Ind		
WYE COLL (Univ of London)											
Agricultural Business Management	D2N1	3FT deg	S+Ec	14	2M+1D$	Ind	25$	BBCCC$	Ind		
Agriculture	D200	3FT deg	B	14	2M+1D$	Ind	25$	BBCCC$	Ind		
Agriculture and the Environment	D206	3FT deg	B	14	2M+1D$	Ind	25$	BBCCC$	Ind		
Animal Agriculture	D222	3FT deg	B+C	14	2M+1D$	Ind	25$	BBCCC$	Ind		
Animal Sciences	D220	3FT deg	C+B	14	2M+1D$	Ind	25$	BBCCC$	Ind		
Countryside Management	D255	3FT deg	Gy+B/Ec	16	2M+1D$	Ind	25$	BBBCC$	Ind		
Equine Business Management	D2ND	4SW deg	Ec/M/B	16	2M+1D	Ind	25	BBCCC	Ind		
Equine Sciences (with foundation)	D224	4SW deg	C+B	18	2M+1D$	Ind	25$	BBBCC$	Ind		
Horticultural Business Management	D2NC	3FT/4SW deg	S+Ec	14	2M+1D$	Ind	25$	BBCCC$	Ind		
Horticulture	D250	3FT deg	B+C	14	2M+1D$	Ind	25$	BBCCC$	Ind		

course details			98 expected requirements							96 entry stats	
TITLE	CODE	COURSE	SUBJECTS	A/AS	ND/C	AGNVQ	IB	SQA(H)	SQA	RATIO	A/AS
Univ of Wales, ABERYSTWYTH											
American Studies	Q400	3FT deg	E/H g	18	1M+5D$	M^ g	29$	BBBCC$	Ind		
Art History/American Studies	QV44	3FT deg	E/H g	18	1M+5D$	MA^ g	29$	BBBCC$	Ind		
Art/American Studies	QW41	3FT deg	E/H+(A/Ad) g	18	1M+5D$	MA^ g	29$	BBBCC$	Ind		
Drama/American Studies	QW44	3FT deg	E/H g	20	1M+5D$	MQ6/^ g	30$	BBBBC$	Ind		
Education/American Studies	QX49	3FT deg	E/H g	18	1M+5D$	M^ g	29$	BBBCC$	Ind		
English/American Studies	QQ34	3FT deg	El	20	1M+5D$	M^ g	30$	BBBBC$	Ind		
Film and Television Studies/American Studies	QW45	3FT deg	E/H g	20	1M+5D$	MQ^ g	30$	BBBBC$	Ind		
French/American Studies	QR41	4FT deg	F+E/H g	18	1M+5D$	M^ g	29$	BBBCC$	Ind		
Geography/American Studies	LQ84	3FT deg	Gy+E/H g	20-22	3M+2D$	M^ g	31$	BBBBC$	Ind		
German/American Studies	QR42	4FT deg	E/H+G g	18	1M+5D$	M^ g	29$	BBBCC$	Ind		
History/American Studies	QV41	3FT deg	E/H g	18-20	1M+5D$	M^ g	30$	BBBCC$	Ind		
Information and Library Studies/American Studies	PQ24	3FT deg	E/H g	18	1M+5D$	M^ g	29$	BBBCC$	Ind		
International Politics and The Americas	MQ14	3FT deg	* g	20	1M+5D	M6 g	30	BBBCC	Ind		
Irish/American Studies	QQK5	4FT deg	E/H g	18	1M+5D$	M^ g	29$	BBBCC$	Ind		
Pure Mathematics/American Studies	GQ14	3FT deg	M+E/H g	18	1M+5D$	M^ g	29$	BBBCC$	Ind		
Spanish/American Studies	QR44	4FT deg	E/H+L g	18	1M+5D$	M^ g	29$	BBBCC$	Ind		
Welsh History/American Studies	QVK1	3FT deg	E/H g	18-20	1M+5D$	M^ g	30$	BBBCC$	Ind		
Welsh/American Studies	QQ45	3FT deg	E/H+W g	18	1M+5D$	M^ g	29$	BBBCC$	Ind		
Univ of BIRMINGHAM											
African Studies/American Studies	QT47	3FT deg	*	BBB	Ind	D*^	32	ABBB	Ind		
American Studies	Q400	4FT deg	*	ABB	Ind	D*^	34	ABBB	Ind	21	24/30
American Studies/English	QQ34	3FT deg	*	BBB	Ind	D*^	32	ABBB	Ind	12	24/30
American Studies/French Studies	QR41	4FT deg	F	BBB	Ind	D*_^	32$	ABBB	Ind		
American Studies/Geography	LQ84	3FT deg	Gy	BBB	Ind	D*_^	32$	ABBB	Ind	18	
American Studies/Hispanic Studies	QR44	4FT deg	*	BBB	Ind	D*^	32	ABBB	Ind	17	
American Studies/History	QV41	3FT deg	*	BBB	Ind	D*^	32	ABBB	Ind	8	22/26
American Studies/Media & Cultural Studies	PQ44	3FT deg	*	BBB	Ind	D*^	32	ABBB	Ind	44	
American Studies/Portuguese	QR45	4FT deg	*	BBB	Ind	D*^	32	ABBB	Ind		
BRUNEL Univ, West London											
American Studies	Q400	3FT deg	H/So/El g	16	MO $	M$ go	26$	BCCC$	Ind		
American Studies/Art	Q4W1	3FT deg	A g	14	MO $	M* go	22$	BCCC$	Ind		
Drama/American Studies	QW44	3FT deg	T g	BC	MO $	P go	22$	BCCC$	Ind		
English/American Studies	QQ34	3FT deg	E g	14	MO $	M* go	24$	BCCC$	Ind		
Film & TV Studies/American Studies	Q4W5	3FT deg	Ap g	20	MO $	M* go	28$	BBCC	Ind		
History/American Studies	QV41	3FT deg	H g	14	MO $	M* go	22$	BCCC$	Ind		
Music/American Studies	QW43	3FT deg	* g	14	MO $	M* go	26$	BCCC$	Ind		
CANTERBURY CHRIST CHURCH COLL of HE											
American Studies with Art	Q4W1	4FT deg	A g	CC	MO	M	24	Ind	Ind	1	
American Studies with Business Studies	Q4N1	4FT deg	* g	CC	MO	M	24	Ind	Ind	2	
American Studies with English	Q4Q3	4FT deg	E g	CC	MO	M	24	Ind	Ind	3	10/14
American Studies with French	Q4R1	4FT deg	F g	CC	MO	M	24	Ind	Ind		
American Studies with Geography	Q4L8	4FT deg	Gy g	CC	MO	M	24	Ind	Ind	4	
American Studies with History	Q4V1	4FT deg	H g	CC	MO	M	24	Ind	Ind	2	
American Studies with Information Technology	Q4G5	4FT deg	* g	CC	MO	M	24	Ind	Ind		
American Studies with Mathematics	Q4G1	4FT deg	M g	DD	Ind	Ind	24	Ind	Ind		
American Studies with Music	Q4W3	4FT deg	Mu g	CC	MO	M	24	Ind	Ind		
American Studies with Psychology	Q4L7	4FT deg	Ps g	CC	MO	M	24	Ind	Ind	9	
American Studies with Radio,Film & Television St	Q4W5	4FT deg	* g	CC	MO	M	24	Ind	Ind	34	
American Studies with Religious Studies	Q4V8	4FT deg	* g	CC	MO	M	24	Ind	Ind		
American Studies with Science	Q4Y1	4FT deg	S g	DD	Ind	Ind	24	Ind	Ind		

American Studies 3

course details			98 expected requirements							96 entry stats	
TITLE	CODE	COURSE	SUBJECTS	A/AS	ND/C	RGNVQ	IB	SQA(H)	SQA	RATIO	A/AS
American Studies with Social Science	Q4L3	4FT deg	* g	CC	MO	M	24	Ind	Ind	2	8/14
American Studies with Sport Science	Q4B6	4FT deg	* g	CC	MO	M	24	Ind	Ind		
American Studies with Statistics	Q4G4	4FT deg	M g	DD	Ind	Ind	24	Ind	Ind		
Art and American Studies	QW41	3FT deg	A g	CC	MO	M	24	Ind	Ind	2	
Art with American Studies	W1Q4	3FT deg	A g	CC	MO	M	24	Ind	Ind	4	
Business Studies and American Studies	QN41	3FT deg	* g	CC	MO	M	24	Ind	Ind	1	
Business Studies with American Studies	N1Q4	3FT deg	* g	CC	MO	M	24	Ind	Ind	1	10/14
English and American Studies	QQ43	3FT deg	E	CC	MO	M	24	Ind	Ind	1	6/16
English with American Studies	Q3Q4	3FT deg	E	CC	MO	M	24	Ind	Ind	3	6/16
French and American Studies	QR41	3FT deg	F g	CC	MO	M	24	Ind	Ind		
Geography and American Studies	QL48	3FT deg	Gy g	CC	MO	M	24	Ind	Ind	5	
Geography with American Studies	L8Q4	3FT deg	Gy g	CC	MO	M	24	Ind	Ind	11	
History and American Studies	QV41	3FT deg	H g	CC	MO	M	24	Ind	Ind		
History with American Studies	V1Q4	3FT deg	H g	CC	MO	M	24	Ind	Ind	2	
Information Technology and American Studies	GQ54	3FT deg	* g	CC	MO	M	24	Ind	Ind		
Information Technology with American Studies	G5Q4	3FT deg	* g	CC	MO	M	24	Ind	Ind		
Mathematics and American Studies	GQ14	3FT deg	M g	DD	Ind	Ind	24	Ind	Ind	1	
Mathematics with American Studies	G1Q4	3FT deg	M g	DD	Ind	Ind	24	Ind	Ind		
Music and American Studies	WQ34	3FT deg	Mu g	CC	MO	M	24	Ind	Ind	1	
Music with American Studies	W3Q4	3FT deg	Mu g	CC	MO	M	24	Ind	Ind	2	
Psychology and American Studies	LQ74	3FT deg	Ps g	CC	MO	M	24	Ind	Ind	5	
Psychology with American Studies	L7Q4	3FT deg	Ps g	CC	MO	M	24	Ind	Ind		
Radio, Film and Television Studs and American St	QW45	3FT deg	* g	CC	MO	M	24	Ind	Ind	13	
Radio,Film & Television Studies with American St	W5Q4	3FT deg	* g	CC	MO	M	24	Ind	Ind	7	10/20
Religious Studies and American Studies	QV48	3FT deg	* g	CC	MO	M	24	Ind	Ind		
Religious Studies with American Studies	V8Q4	3FT deg	* g	CC	MO	M	24	Ind	Ind		
Science and American Studies	QY41	3FT deg	S g	DD	Ind	Ind	24	Ind	Ind		
Social Science and American Studies	QL43	3FT deg	* g	CC	MO	M	24	Ind	Ind	1	
Social Science with American Studies	L3Q4	3FT deg	* g	CC	MO	M	24	Ind	Ind	5	
Sport Science and American Studies	BQ64	3FT deg	* g	CC	MO	M	24	Ind	Ind		
Sport Science with American Studies	B6Q4	3FT deg	* g	CC	MO	M	24	Ind	Ind		
Statistics and American Studies	GQ44	3FT deg	M g	DD	Ind	Ind	24	Ind	Ind		
Statistics with American Studies	G4Q4	3FT deg	M g	DD	Ind	Ind	24	Ind	Ind		
Univ of CENTRAL LANCASHIRE											
American Studies	Q400	3FT deg	E	18	Ind	D$^	30$	BBBB	Ind		
Combined Honours Programme American Studies	Y400	3FT deg	EI	14	X	D*^	28$	BBCC	Ind		
DE MONTFORT Univ											
Humanities Combined Honours American Studies	Y300▼	3FT deg	* g	BCD-CCD	MO	M$^	28$	ABBB	Ind		
Humanities Joint Honours American Studies	Y301▼	3FT deg	* g	CCD	MO	M$^	26$	ABBB	Ind		
Univ of DERBY											
American Studies	Q400	3FT deg	*	14	Ind	M$	28	BBCC	Ind		
Credit Accumulation Modular Scheme American Studies	Y600	3FT deg	*	12	MO	M	Ind	CCCC	Ind		
Univ of DUNDEE											
American Studies	Q400	4FT deg	* g	BCC	Ind	D$	29	BBBC	Ind	15	
American Studies and Business Economics & Mkt	Y600	4FT deg	* g	BCC	Ind	D$	29	BBBC	Ind		
American Studies and Economics	QL41	4FT deg	* g	BCC	Ind	D$	29	BBBC	Ind		
American Studies and English	QQ34	4FT deg	E g	BCC	Ind	D$^	29$	BBBC$	Ind	7	
American Studies and Environmental Science	FQ94	4FT deg	* g	BCC	Ind	D$	29	BBBC	Ind		

course details | 98 expected requirements | 96 entry stats

TITLE	CODE	COURSE	SUBJECTS	A/AS	NO/C	AGNVQ	IB	SQA(H)	SQA	RATIO A/AS
American Studies and Financial Economics	QL4C	4FT deg	* g	BCC	Ind	D$	29	BBBC	Ind	
American Studies and Geography	LQ84	4FT deg	* g	BCC	Ind	D$	29	BBBC	Ind	13
American Studies and Modern History	QV41	4FT deg	* g	BCC	Ind	D$	29	BBBC	Ind	6
American Studies and Philosophy	QV47	4FT deg	* g	BCC	Ind	D$	29	BBBC	Ind	
American Studies and Political Science	MQ14	4FT deg	* g	BCC	Ind	D$	29	BBBC	Ind	13
American Studies and Psychology	LQ74	4FT deg	* g	BCC	Ind	D$	29	BBBC	Ind	9
American and Contemporary European Studies	QT42	4FT deg	* g	BCC	Ind	D$	29	BBBC	Ind	12
Arts and Social Sciences *American Studies*	Y400	3FT deg	* g	BCC	Ind	D$	29	BBBC	Ind	

Univ of EAST ANGLIA

TITLE	CODE	COURSE	SUBJECTS	A/AS	NO/C	AGNVQ	IB	SQA(H)	SQA	RATIO A/AS
American Studies (4 Yrs)	Q400	4FT deg	E	BBB	X		28$	ABBBB	X	9 16/28
American and English Literature (4 Yrs)	QQ43	4FT deg	E	BBB	X		28$	ABBBB	X	9 20/30
English and American Literature	QQ34	3FT deg	E	ABB-BBB	X		30$	AABBB	X	6 22/30
Film and American Studies	QW45	4FT deg	E	ABB-BBB	X		30$	AABBB	X	19 22/30

Univ of EDINBURGH

TITLE	CODE	COURSE	SUBJECTS	A/AS	NO/C	AGNVQ	IB	SQA(H)	SQA	RATIO A/AS
American Studies	Q430	4FT deg	H/Po/Sp g	BBB	Ind	Ind	Dip$	BBBB$	Ind	
Social Science *Canadian Studies*	Y200	3FT deg	*	BBB	Ind		34	ABBB	Ind	

Univ of ESSEX

TITLE	CODE	COURSE	SUBJECTS	A/AS	NO/C	AGNVQ	IB	SQA(H)	SQA	RATIO A/AS
English and United States Literature	Q420	3FT deg	*	22	MO+3D	Ind	28	BBBB	Ind	5 18/20
United States Studies (4 Yrs)	Q408	4FT deg	*	20	MO+2D	Ind	28	BBBB	Ind	6 16/24

Univ of EXETER

TITLE	CODE	COURSE	SUBJECTS	A/AS	NO/C	AGNVQ	IB	SQA(H)	SQA	RATIO A/AS
American & Postcolonial Studies and Italian	QR4H	3FT deg	L g	BBB-BCC		D$	34			
American Studies	Q400	4FT deg	*	BBB-BCC	MO	D$	34	Ind	Ind	
English & American & Postcolonial St with Eur St	QQ34	4FT deg	E	BBB-BCC	MO	M/D$^	32$			
English and American & Postcolonial Studies	QQ43	3FT deg	E	BBB-BCC	MO	M/D$^	32$			
Music and American & Postcolonial Studies	QW4H	3FT deg	Mu	BCC	MO	M/D$^	32$			
Physics with North American Study	F3Q4	4FT deg	M+P	BC-CC	MO	M$^	28$			
Theoretical Physics with North American Study	F3QK	4FT deg	M+P	BC-CC	MO	M$^	28$			

Univ of GLAMORGAN

TITLE	CODE	COURSE	SUBJECTS	A/AS	NO/C	AGNVQ	IB	SQA(H)	SQA	RATIO A/AS
American Studies and English Studies	QQ43	3FT deg	* g	12	5M	M$	Ind	Ind	Ind	
American Studies and History	QV41	3FT deg	* g	12	5M	M$	Ind	Ind	Ind	
American Studies and Media Studies	QP44	3FT deg	Me/T/E g	14	5M	M$	Ind	Ind	Ind	
American Studies with English Studies	Q4Q3	3FT deg	E g	12	5M	M$	Ind	Ind	Ind	
American Studies with Media Studies	Q4P4	3FT deg	Me/T/E g	14	5M	M$	Ind	Ind	Ind	
English Studies with American Studies	Q3Q4	3FT deg	* g	12	Ind	Ind	Ind	Ind	Ind	
Government with American Studies	M1Q4	3FT deg	* g	12	Ind	Ind	Ind	Ind	Ind	
Humanities (American Studies)	Q400	3FT deg	* g	CC	5M	M$	24	CCCC	HN	23
Media Studies with American Studies	P4Q4	3FT deg	Me/T/E g	14	Ind	Ind	Ind	Ind	Ind	
Combined Studies (Honours) *American Studies*	Y400	3FT deg	* g	8-16	Ind	Ind	Ind	Ind	Ind	
Joint Honours *American Studies*	Y401	3FT deg	* g	8-16	Ind	Ind	Ind	Ind	Ind	
Major/Minor Honours *American Studies*	Y402	3FT deg	* g	8-16	Ind	Ind	Ind	Ind	Ind	

Univ of HULL

TITLE	CODE	COURSE	SUBJECTS	A/AS	NO/C	AGNVQ	IB	SQA(H)	SQA	RATIO A/AS
American Studies (4 Yrs)	Q401	4FT deg	E/H/T	BBC-BCC	Ind	Ind	28$	ABBCC	Ind	6 20/24
American Studies/Drama	QW44	3FT deg	E/T	BBB-BCC	Ind	D$^ go	30	AAABB	Ind	
American Studies/English	QQ43	3FT deg	E	BBB-BCC	Ind	M$^/6 gi	28$	ABBCC	Ind	15 18/28
American Studies/History	QV41	3FT deg	H	BBB-BCC	Ind	M*^ gi	28$	ABBCC	Ind	13 22/24
Gender Studies and American Studies	MQ94	3FT deg	*	BBB-BCC	Ind	M$6/^ go	26	BBCCC	Ind	

course details

KEELE Univ

TITLE	CODE	COURSE	SUBJECTS	A/AS	ND/C	AGNVQ	IB	SQA(H)	SQA	RATIO	A/AS
Ancient History and American Studies (4 Yrs)	QVK1	4FT deg	*	BCC	Ind	Ind	28	BBBB	Ind		
Applied Social Studies and American Studies	LQ54	3FT deg	*	BBC-BCC	Ind	Ind	30	CSYS	Ind		
Astrophysics and American Studies	FQ54	3FT deg	P g	BCC	Ind	D$^	28$	CSYS	Ind		
Astrophysics and American Studies	QF45	4FT deg	*	BCC	Ind	Ind	28	BBBB	Ind		
Biochemistry and American Studies	CQ74	3FT deg	C g	BCC	Ind	D$^	28$	CSYS	Ind		
Biochemistry and American Studies (4 Yrs)	QC47	4FT deg	*	BCC	Ind	Ind	28	BBBB	Ind		
Biology and American Studies	CQ14	3FT deg	S g	BCC	Ind	D$^	28$	CSYS	Ind		
Biology and American Studies (4 Yrs)	QC41	4FT deg	*	BCC	Ind	Ind	28	BBBB	Ind		
Business Administration and American St (4 Yrs)	QN49	4FT deg	*	BCC	Ind	Ind	28	BBBB	Ind		
Classical Studies and American Studies (4 Yrs)	QQ84	4FT deg	*	BCC	Ind	Ind	28	BBBB			
Criminology and American Studies	MQH4	3FT deg	*	BBB	Ind	Ind	32	CSYS	Ind	27	
Criminology and American Studies (4 Yrs)	QM4H	4FT deg	*	BBB	Ind	Ind	32	BBBB	Ind	7	
Economics and American Studies	LQ14	3FT deg	* g	BCC	Ind	Ind	28	CSYS	Ind		
Electronic Music and American Studies	QW4J	3FT deg	Mu	BCC	Ind	D$^	28$	CSYS	Ind		
Electronic Music and American Studies (4 Yrs)	WQJ4	4FT deg	*	BCC	Ind	Ind	28	BBBB	Ind		
English and American Studies	QQ34	3FT deg	E	BBC	Ind	D$^	30$	CSYS	Ind	9	20/30
English and American Studies (4 Yrs)	QQ43	4FT deg	*	BBC	Ind	Ind	30	BBBB	Ind	4	16/24
Environmental Management and American Studies	FQX4	3FT deg	* g	BCC	Ind	Ind	28	CSYS	Ind		
Finance and American Studies (4 Yrs)	QN43	4FT deg	*	BCC	Ind	Ind	28	BBBB	Ind		
French and American Studies	QR41	3FT deg	F	BBC-BCC	Ind	D$^	28$	CSYS	Ind	2	
French/Russian or Russ Studies and American St	QT4X	3FT deg	F+R	BBC	Ind	D$^	30$	CSYS			
Geography and American Studies	LQ84	3FT deg	Gy	BCC	Ind	D$^	28$	CSYS	Ind	6	16/20
Geography and American Studies (4 Yrs)	QL48	4FT deg	*	BCC	Ind	Ind	28	BBBB	Ind	9	
Geology and American Studies (4 Yrs)	QF46	4FT deg	* g	BCC	Ind	Ind	28	BBBB	Ind		
German and American Studies (4 Yrs)	RQ24	4FT deg	* g	BCC	Ind	Ind	28	BBBB	Ind		
History and American Studies	QV41	3FT deg	*	BBC	Ind	Ind	30	CSYS	Ind	6	18/28
History and American Studies (4 Yrs)	VQ14	4FT deg	*	BBC	Ind	Ind	30	BBBB	Ind		
Human Resource Management and American Studies	NQ64	3FT deg	*	BCC	Ind	Ind	28	CSYS	Ind		
Human Resource Management and American Studies	QN46	4FT deg	*	BCC	Ind	Ind	28	BBBB	Ind		
International History and American St (4 Yrs)	VQC4	4FT deg	*	BBC-BCC	Ind	Ind	28	BBBB	Ind	4	
International History and American Studies	QV4C	3FT deg	*	BBC-BCC	Ind	Ind	28	CSYS	Ind	4	20/22
International Politics and American Studies	MQC4	3FT deg	*	BCC	Ind	Ind	28	CSYS	Ind	5	
Latin and American Studies (4 Yrs)	QQ64	4FT deg	*	BCC	Ind	Ind	28	BBBB	Ind		
Law and American Studies	MQ34	3FT deg	*	BBB	Ind	Ind	32	CSYS	Ind	7	22/24
Law and American Studies	QM43	4FT deg	*	BBB	Ind	Ind	32	BBBB	Ind	9	
Marketing and American Studies	NQ54	3FT deg	*	BBC	Ind	Ind	30	CSYS	Ind	9	
Mathematics and American Studies (4 Yrs)	QG41	4FT deg	* g	BCC	Ind	Ind	28	BBBB	Ind		
Music and American Studies	QW43	3FT deg	Mu	BBC	Ind	D$^	30	CSYS	Ind		
Music and American Studies (4 Yrs)	WQ34	4FT deg	*	BBC	Ind	Ind	30	BBBB	Ind		
Philosophy and American Studies (4 Yrs)	VQ74	4FT deg	*	BCC	Ind	Ind	28	BBBB	Ind		
Physics and American Studies	FQ34	3FT deg	P g	BCC	Ind	D$^	28$	CSYS	Ind		
Physics and American Studies (4 Yrs)	QF43	4FT deg	*	BCC	Ind	Ind	28	BBBB	Ind		
Politics and American Studies	MQ14	3FT deg	*	BBC-BCC	Ind	Ind	30	CSYS	Ind	3	18/20
Politics and American Studies (4 Yrs)	QM41	4FT deg	*	BBC-BCC	Ind	Ind	30	BBBB	Ind	14	
Psychology and American Studies	CQ84	3FT deg	* g	BBB	Ind	Ind	32	CSYS	Ind	6	
Psychology and American Studies (4 Yrs)	QC48	4FT deg	*	BBB	Ind	Ind	32	ABBB	Ind	5	
Russian Studies and American Studies	QRK8	3FT deg	*	BCC	Ind	Ind	28	CSYS	Ind		
Russian Studies and American Studies (4 Yrs)	RQ8K	4FT deg	*	BCC	Ind	Ind	28	BBBB	Ind		
Russian and American Studies	QR48	3FT deg	R	BCC	Ind	D$^	28$	CSYS	Ind		
Russian and American Studies (4 Yrs)	RQ84	4FT deg	*	BCC	Ind	Ind	28	BBBB	Ind		
Sociology & Social Anthrop & American St (4 Yrs)	QL43	4FT deg	*	BBC-BCC	Ind	Ind	28	BBBB	Ind		

			98 expected requirements							96 entry stats
TITLE	CODE	COURSE	SUBJECTS	A/AS	NO/C	AGNVQ	IB	SQA(H)	SQA	RATIO A/AS
Statistics and American Studies (4 Yrs)	QG44	4FT deg	* g	BCC	Ind	Ind	28	BBBB	Ind	
Visual Arts and American Studies	QW41	3FT deg	*	BBC	Ind	D$^	30	CSYS	Ind	
Visual Arts and American Studies	WQ14	4FT deg	*	BBC	Ind	Ind	30	BBBB	Ind	1

Univ of KENT

American Studies (Art & Film)	Q4W5	4FT deg	*	26	6D	Ind	34	Ind	Ind	12
American Studies (History)	Q401	4FT deg	H	22	2M+4D	Ind	30	Ind	Ind	12 16/24
American Studies (Literature)	Q400	4FT deg	E	22	2M+4D	Ind	30	Ind	Ind	8 18/24

KING ALFRED'S WINCHESTER

American Studies	Q400	3FT deg	* g	14	6M	M	24	BCC	N	
Archaeology and American Studies	FQ44	3FT deg	* g	14	6M	M	24	BCC	N	
Business Studies and American Studies	NQ14	3FT deg	* g	14	6M	M	24	BCC	N	6
Contemporary Cultural Studies and American Studs	MQ94	3FT deg	* g	14	6M	M	24	BCC	N	3
Drama Studies and American Studies	QW44	3FT deg	* g	14	6M	M	24	BCC	N	2 8/16
English Studies and American Studies	QQ34	3FT deg	E	14	X	X	24$	BCC$	X	3 8/22
Geography and American Studies	LQ84	3FT deg	Gy g	14	X	X	24$	BCC$	X	4
History and American Studies	QV41	3FT deg	H g	14	X	X	24$	BCC$	X	8
Japanese Language and American Studies	QT44	3FT deg	L g	14	X	X	24$	BCC$	X	
Media & Film Studies and American Studies	PQ44	3FT deg	* g	14	6M	M	24	BCC	N	7 8/16
Philosophy and American Studies	QV47	3FT deg	* g	14	6M	M	24	BCC	N	3
Religious Studies and American Studies	QV48	3FT deg	* g	14	6M	M	24	BCC	N	

KING'S COLL LONDON (Univ of London)

United States and Latin-American Studies	Q450	4FT deg	E+H+L	BBC-BCC			$	Ind	Ind	4 20/28

Univ of Wales, LAMPETER

Ancient History and American Literature	QV41	3FT deg			Ind	Ind	Ind	Ind	Ind	
Anthropology and American Literature	LQ64	3FT deg			Ind	Ind	Ind	Ind	Ind	
Archaeology and American Literature	QV46	3FT deg			Ind	Ind	Ind	Ind	Ind	
Australian Studies and American Literature	LQ6K	3FT deg			Ind	Ind	Ind	Ind	Ind	
Church History and American Literature	QV4C	3FT deg			Ind	Ind	Ind	Ind	Ind	
Classical Studies and American Literature	QQ48	3FT deg			Ind	Ind	Ind	Ind	Ind	
Cultural Studies in Geography and American Lit	LQ84	3FT deg			Ind	Ind	Ind	Ind	Ind	
English Literature and American Literature	QQ34	3FT deg	E		Ind	Ind	Ind	Ind	Ind	
Geography and American Literature	LQ8K	3FT deg	Gy		Ind	Ind	Ind	Ind	Ind	
German Studies and American Literature	QR4F	3FT deg			Ind	Ind	Ind	Ind	Ind	
German and American Literature	QR42	3FT deg	G		Ind	Ind	Ind	Ind	Ind	
Greek and American Literature	QQ74	3FT deg	g		Ind	Ind	Ind	Ind	Ind	
History and American Literature	QV4D	3FT deg	H		Ind	Ind	Ind	Ind	Ind	
Informatics and American Literature	GQ54	3FT deg			Ind	Ind	Ind	Ind	Ind	
Islamic Studies and American Literature	QT4P	3FT deg			Ind	Ind	Ind	Ind	Ind	
Latin and American Literature	QQ64	3FT deg	Ln		Ind	Ind	Ind	Ind	Ind	
Medieval Studies and American Literature	VQ14	3FT deg			Ind	Ind	Ind	Ind	Ind	
Modern Historical Studies & American Literature	VQ1K	3FT deg	H		Ind	Ind	Ind	Ind	Ind	
Philosophical Studies and American Literature	QV47	3FT deg			Ind	Ind	Ind	Ind	Ind	
Religious Studies and American Literature	QV48	3FT deg			Ind	Ind	Ind	Ind	Ind	
Theology and American Literature	QV4V	3FT deg			Ind	Ind	Ind	Ind	Ind	
Victorian Studies and American Literature	QVK1	3FT deg			Ind	Ind	Ind	Ind	Ind	
Welsh Studies and American Literature	QQ5K	3FT deg			Ind	Ind	Ind	Ind	Ind	
Welsh and American Literature	QQ45	3FT deg			Ind	Ind	Ind	Ind	Ind	
Women's Studies and American Literature	MQ94	3FT deg			Ind	Ind	Ind	Ind	Ind	
Combined Honours American Literature	Y400	3FT deg		14-16	Ind	Ind	Ind	Ind	Ind	

course details			98 expected requirements							96 entry stats	
TITLE	CODE	COURSE	SUBJECTS	A/AS	NO/C	RGNVQ	IB	SQA(H)	SQA	RATIO	A/AS
LANCASTER Univ											
American Studies (second year in USA)	Q400	3FT deg	E/H	BBB-BBC	Ind		32	ABBBB	Ind		
American Studies and Women's Studies	QM49	3FT deg	E/H	BBC	Ind		32	ABBBB	Ind		
Univ of LEICESTER											
American Studies	Q400	3FT deg	*	BCC	Ind	D$^	30	ABBBB	Ind		18/22
American Studies with a year in USA	Q401	4FT deg	*	BCC	Ind	D$^	30	ABBBB	Ind		
Combined Arts American Studies	Y300	3FT deg	* g	BCC	DO	D$^	30$	BBBBB	X		
LIVERPOOL HOPE Univ COLL											
American Studies (Honours)	Q400	4FT deg	*	12	8M	M$	Ind	Ind	Ind	4	8/18
Drama & Theatre Studies/American Studies	QW44	3FT deg	g	12	8M	M$ go	Ind	Ind	Ind	5	
English/American Studies	QQ43	3FT deg	El	12	8M	P*^	Ind	Ind	Ind	7	8/24
Environmental Studies/American Studies	QF49	3FT deg	B/Gy/En	12	8M	ML /P*^	Ind	Ind	Ind		
European Studies/Americal Studies	QT42	3FT deg	*	12	8M	M$	Ind	Ind	Ind		
French/American Studies	QR41	3FT deg	F	12	8M	P$^	Ind	Ind	Ind	11	
Geography/American Studies	QF48	3FT deg	Gy	12	8M	P$^	Ind	Ind	Ind		
History/American Studies	QV41	3FT deg	H	12	8M	P$^	Ind	Ind	Ind	4	6/20
Human & Applied Biology/American Studies	QC41	3FT deg	B g	12	8M	MS /P$^	Ind	Ind	Ind	1	
Mathematics/American Studies	QG41	3FT deg	M	12	8M	P*^	Ind	Ind	Ind	4	
Music/American Studies	QW43	3FT deg	Mu	12	8M	P$^	Ind	Ind	Ind		
Psychology/American Studies	QC48	3FT deg	g	12	8M	M$ go	Ind	Ind	Ind	10	
Sociology/American Studies	QL43	3FT deg	*	12	8M	M$	Ind	Ind	Ind	13	
LIVERPOOL JOHN MOORES Univ											
History and American Studies	QV41	3FT deg		12-20	5M+3D	PT^	28$				
Lit, Life & Thought and American St (AS Jnt Awd)	QQ34	3FT deg	E	12-20	5M+3D	PT^	28$	BBBC		4	13/20
Univ of MANCHESTER											
American and Latin-American Studies	QR46	4FT deg	Sp	BBC			28$	ABBBB$		10	
English and American Literature	QQ34	3FT deg	E	ABB	Ind		32$	AABBB$		11	26/30
UMIST (Manchester)											
Civil Engineering with N American Studies (MEng)	H2Q4	4FT deg	M+P g	BBC	Ind	Ind	30$	CSYS	Ind		
International Mgt with American Bus St (4 Yrs)	N1Q4	4FT deg	* g	ABB	1M+6D	Ind	35	CSYS	Ind	10	26/30
MANCHESTER METROPOLITAN Univ											
Applied Social Studies/American Studies	LQ34	3FT deg	*	CC	M	D	28	CCCC	Ind		
Business Studies/American Studies	NQ14	3FT deg	*	CC	M	D	29	BBB	Ind		
Dance/American Studies	QW44	3FT deg	*	CC	M+D	D	28	CCCC	Ind		
Drama/American Studies	QW4K	3FT deg	*	CC	M+D	D	28	CCCC	Ind		
English/American Studies	QQ34	3FT deg	*	CC	M+D	D	28	CCCC	Ind		
Geography/American Studies	LQ84	3FT deg	*	CC	M+D	D	28	CCCC	Ind		
Health Studies/American Studies	BQ94	3FT deg	*	CC	M+D	D	28	CCCC	Ind		
History/American Studies	QV41	3FT deg	*	CC	M+D	D	28	CCCC	Ind		
Leisure Studies/American Studies	LQ44	3FT deg	*	CC	M+D	D	28	CCCC	Ind		
Music/American Studies	QW43	3FT deg	*	CC	M+D	D	28	CCCC	Ind		
Philosophy/American Studies	QV47	3FT deg	*	CC	M+D	D	28	CCCC	Ind		
Religious Studies/American Studies	QV48	3FT deg	*	CC	M+D	D	28	CCCC	Ind		
Sport/American Studies	BQ64	3FT deg	S	BC	M+D	DS	28	CCCC	Ind		
Visual Arts/American Studies	QW41	3FT deg	*	CC	M+D	D	28	CCCC	Ind		
Writing/American Studies	QW4L	3FT deg	*	CC	M+D	D	28	CCCC	Ind		
MIDDLESEX Univ											
American Studies	Q400▼	3FT deg	* g	12-16	5M	M$ go	28	Ind	Ind		

course details | 98 expected requirements | 96 entry stats

TITLE	CODE	COURSE	SUBJECTS	A/AS	ND/C	RGNVQ	IB	SQA(H)	SQA	RATIO	A/AS
Joint Honours Degree *American Studies*	Y400	4FT deg	* g	12-16	5M	Ind	28	BCCC	Ind		

NENE COLLEGE

TITLE	CODE	COURSE	SUBJECTS	A/AS	ND/C	RGNVQ	IB	SQA(H)	SQA	RATIO	A/AS
American St with Personal & Organisational Devel	Q4N6	3FT deg		DD	5M	M	24	CCC	Ind		
American Studies	Q400	3FT deg		CD	5M	M	24	CCC	Ind		6/20
American Studies with Architectural Studies	Q4V4	3FT deg		DD	5M	M	24	CCC	Ind		
American Studies with Art and Design	Q4W2	3FT deg		DD	5M	M	24	CCC	Ind		
American Studies with Business Administration	Q4N1	3FT deg	g	DD	5M	M	24	CCC	Ind		
American Studies with Drama	Q4W4	3FT deg		DD	5M	M	24	CCC	Ind		
American Studies with Education	Q4X9	3FT deg		DD	5M	M	24	CCC	Ind		
American Studies with English	Q4Q3	3FT deg		DD	5M	M	24	CCC	Ind		7/12
American Studies with European Union Studies	Q4T2	3FT deg		DD	5M	M	24	CCC	Ind		
American Studies with Geography	Q4F8	3FT deg		DD	5M	M	24	CCC	Ind		
American Studies with History	Q4V1	3FT deg		DD	5M	M	24	CCC	Ind		
American Studies with History of Art	Q4VK	3FT deg		DD	5M	M	24	CCC	Ind		
American Studies with Industrial Archaeology	Q4V6	3FT deg		DD	5M	M	24	CCC	Ind		
American Studies with Law	Q4M3	3FT deg		DD	5M	M	24	CCC	Ind		
American Studies with Media and Popular Culture	Q4P4	3FT deg		DD	5M	M	24	CCC	Ind		6/16
American Studies with Philosophy	Q4V7	3FT deg		DD	5M	M	24	CCC	Ind		
American Studies with Sociology	Q4L3	3FT deg		DD	5M	M	24	CCC	Ind		
American Studies with Sport Studies	Q4N7	3FT deg		DD	5M	M	24	CCC	Ind		
American Studies with Third World Development	Q4M9	3FT deg		DD	5M	M	24	CCC	Ind		
Art and Design with American Studies	W2Q4	3FT deg		DD	5M	M	24	CCC	Ind		
Business Administration with American Studies	N1Q4	3FT deg	g	10	M+1D	M	24	BCC	Ind		
Drama with American Studies	W4Q4	3FT deg		10	5M+1D	M	24	CCC	Ind		
Education with American Studies	X9Q4	3FT deg		DD	5M	M	24	CCC	Ind		
English with American Studies	Q3Q4	3FT deg		CC	4M+1D	M	24	CCC	Ind		10/18
French with American Studies	R1Q4	3FT deg	F	DD	5M	In	24	CCC	Ind		
Geography with American Studies	F8Q4	3FT deg	Gy	8	5M	M	24	CCC	Ind		
History with American Studies	V1Q4	3FT deg		CD	5M	M	24	CCC	Ind		
Industrial Archaeology with American Studies	V6Q4	3FT deg		10	5M	M	24	CCC	Ind		
Law with American Studies	M3Q4	3FT deg	g	10	3M+2D	M	24	CCC	Ind		
Sociology with American Studies	L3Q4	3FT deg		10	5M	M	24	CCC	Ind		
Sport Studies with American Studies	N7Q4	3FT deg	Ss/Pe	12	M+2D	M	24	BBB	Ind		

Univ of NOTTINGHAM

TITLE	CODE	COURSE	SUBJECTS	A/AS	ND/C	RGNVQ	IB	SQA(H)	SQA	RATIO	A/AS
American Studies	Q400	3FT deg	E/H/Po	BBB-BBC						19	22/30
American Studies and History	QV41	3FT deg	H	BBC						14	24/28
American Studies and Philosophy	QV47	3FT deg	E	BBC						9	
American and English Studies	QQ34	3FT deg	E	BBC						31	28/30

QUEEN'S Univ Belfast

TITLE	CODE	COURSE	SUBJECTS	A/AS	ND/C	RGNVQ	IB	SQA(H)	SQA	RATIO	A/AS
American Studies (Single only)	Q400	3FT deg	E g	BCC	X	D*^ go	29$	ABBB	X	16	

Univ of READING

TITLE	CODE	COURSE	SUBJECTS	A/AS	ND/C	RGNVQ	IB	SQA(H)	SQA	RATIO	A/AS
American Studies	Q400	3FT deg	*	BBC	Ind	DB^	31	BBBB	Ind	13	20/30

Univ College of RIPON & YORK ST JOHN

TITLE	CODE	COURSE	SUBJECTS	A/AS	ND/C	RGNVQ	IB	SQA(H)	SQA	RATIO	A/AS
American Studies (History)	QV41	3FT deg		CDD	M0+2D	M+^	30	BBBB		4	10/20
American Studies (Literature)	QQ42	3FT deg	E	CDD	M0	M*^	30	BBBB		6	8/20
English/American Studies	Q3Q4	3FT deg	E	16	Ind	M*^	30	BBBB			
History/American Studies	V1Q4	3FT deg	H	14	X	M*^	30	BBBB			

Univ of SHEFFIELD

TITLE	CODE	COURSE	SUBJECTS	A/AS	ND/C	RGNVQ	IB	SQA(H)	SQA	RATIO	A/AS
American Studies	Q400	4FT deg	H+El g	BBB	X	X	32$	ABBB$	Ind	14	24/28

American Studies 3

course details			98 expected requirements							96 entry stats	
TITLE	CODE	COURSE	SUBJECTS	A/AS	ND/C	AGNVQ	IB	SQA(H)	SQA	RATIO	A/AS
STAFFORDSHIRE Univ											
American Studies	Q400	3FT deg	g	CD	MO+2D	M	27	BBC			
Cultural Studies/American Studies	LQ64	3FT deg	g	CD	MO+2D	M	27	BBC	Ind	9	
Development Studies/American Studies	MQY4	3FT deg	g	12	MO+2D	M	27	BBC	Ind		
Film Studies/American Studies	WQ54	3FT deg	g	CD	MO+2D	M	27	BBC	Ind	3	4/18
French/American Studies	RQ14	3FT/4SW deg	F g	CD	MO+2D	M^	27	BBC	Ind		
Geography/American Studies	LQ84	3FT deg	g	CC	MO+2D	M	27	BBB	Ind	3	6/18
German/American Studies	RQ24	3FT/4SW deg	G g	CD	MO+2D	M^	27	BBC	Ind		
History of Art and Design/American Studies	VQ44	3FT deg	g	CD	MO+2D	M	27	BBC	Ind		
History/American Studies	VQ14	3FT deg	H g	CD	MO+2D	M	27	BBC	Ind	6	8/18
International Relations/American Studies	MQ1K	3FT deg	g	12	MO+2D	M	27	BBC	Ind	2	8/18
Law/American Studies	MQ34	3FT deg	g	CCC	HN	M^	27	BBBB	Ind	4	6/22
Legal Studies/American Studies	MQ3K	3FT deg	g	CCC	HN	M^	27	BBBB	Ind		
Literature/American Studies	QQ34	3FT deg	El g	12	MO+2D	M	27	BBC	Ind	4	6/16
Media Studies/American Studies	PQ44	3FT deg	g	CD	MO+2D	M	27	BBC	Ind	6	8/18
Philosophy/American Studies	VQ74	3FT deg	g	CD	MO+2D	M	27	BBC	Ind	4	
Politics/American Studies	MQC4	3FT deg	g	12	MO+2D	M	27	BBC	Ind	6	
Sociology/American Studies	LQ34	3FT deg	g	12	MO+2D	M	27	BBC	Ind	6	
Spanish/American Studies	RQ44	3FT/4SW deg	g	CD	MO+2D	M^	27	BBC	Ind	2	
Women's Studies/American Studies	MQ9K	3FT deg	g	12	MO+2D	M	27	BBC	Ind	1	
Univ of SUNDERLAND											
Biology with American Studies	C1Q4	3FT deg	B/C	8	3M	M	Ind	Ind	Ind		
English with American Studies	Q3Q4	3FT deg	El g	12	Ind	M	24$	BCCC$	Ind	5	8/16
French with American Studies	R1Q4	4FT deg	F g	10	Ind	M	24$	CCCC$	N$	3	
Geography with American Studies	L8Q4	3FT deg	Gy g	12	N $	M	24$	BCCC$	N$	5	
Geology with American Studies	F6Q4	3FT deg	*	8	3M	M	Ind	Ind	Ind		
History with American Studies	V1Q4	3FT deg	H g	12	Ind	M	24	BCCC	Ind	4	6/10
Media Studies with American Studies	P4Q4	3FT deg	* g	12	Ind	M	24	BCCC	Ind	15	
Philosophy with American Studies	V7Q4	3FT deg	*	8	3M	Ind	Ind	Ind	Ind		
Physiology with American Studies	B1Q4	3FT deg	*	8	3M	M	Ind	Ind	Ind		
Politics with American Studies	M1Q4	3FT deg	* g	12	3M	M	24	BCCC	N	4	
Psychology with American Studies	C8Q4	3FT deg	* g	14	MO	M	26$	BBCC$	N	3	8/22
Sociology with American Studies	L3Q4	3FT deg	* g	12	3M	M	24	BCCC	N	3	6/8
Univ of SUSSEX											
American Studies (History)	Q4V1	4FT deg	*	BBB	MO	M*6	$	Ind	Ind		
American Studies (Literature)	Q4Q3	4FT deg	*	BBB	MO	M*6	$	Ind	Ind		
American Studies (Social Studies)	Q4M9	4FT deg	*	BBB	MO	M*6	$	Ind	Ind		
Biology with North American Studies	C1Q4	4FT deg	2S g	BBC	MO $	MS6 go	$	Ind	Ind		
Chemical Physics with N. American Studs (MChem)	F3QL	4FT deg	C/P/Ph+M g	BCC	MO $	MS^ go	$	Ind	Ind		
Chemistry with North American Studies	F1Q4	4FT deg	C+S g	BCC	MO $	MS^ go	$	Ind	Ind		
Chemistry with North American Studies (MChem)	F1QL	4FT deg	C+S g	BCC	MO $	MS^ go	$	Ind	Ind		
Elec & Electronic Eng with N American St (MEng)	H5QK	4FT deg	M	BCC	MO $	MS^	$	Ind	Ind		
Electronic Engineering with N Amer St (MEng)	H6QK	4FT deg	M	BCC	MO $	MS^	$	Ind	Ind		
English Language in English and American Studies	Q3QK	3FT deg	*	BBB	MO	M*6	$	Ind	Ind		
English in English and American Studies	Q3Q4	3FT deg	*	BBB	MO	M*6	$	Ind	Ind		
Environmental Science with North American St	F9Q4	4FT deg	2(C/P/M) g	BCC	MO $	MS go	$	Ind	Ind		
History in English and American Studies	V1Q4	3FT deg	*	BBB	MO	M*6	$	Ind	Ind		
History of Art in English and American Studies	V4Q4	3FT deg	*	BBB	MO	M*6	$	Ind	Ind		
Intellectual History in English & American St	V1QK	3FT deg	*	BBB	MO	M*6	$	Ind	Ind		
International Relations in Eng and American St	M1QK	3FT deg	*	BBC	MO	M*6	$	Ind	Ind		
Law in English and American Studies	M3QK	3FT deg	*	BBB	MO	M*6	$	Ind	Ind		

			98 expected requirements							96 entry stats	

TITLE	CODE	COURSE	SUBJECTS	A/AS	ND/C	AGNVQ	IB	SQA(H)	SQA	RATIO A/AS	
Law with North American Studies	M3Q4	4FT deg	*	BBB	MO	M*6	$	Ind	Ind		
Mathematics & Stats with North Amer St (MMath)	G4QK	4FT deg	M	BCC	MO $	MS^	$	Ind	Ind		
Mathematics and Statistics with N Amer Studies	G4Q4	4FT deg	M	BCC	MO $	MS^	$	Ind	Ind		
Mathematics with North American Studies	G1Q4	4FT deg	M	BCC	MO $	MS^	$	Ind	Ind		
Mathematics with North American Studies (MMath)	G1QK	4FT deg	M	BCC	MO $	MS^	$	Ind	Ind		
Mechanical Eng with North American St (MEng)	H3Q4	4FT deg	M	BCC	MO $	MS^	$	Ind	Ind		
Music in English and American Studies	W3Q4	3FT deg	Mu	BBC	MO $	M*^	$	Ind	Ind		
Philosophy in English and American Studies	V7Q4	3FT deg	*	BBB	MO	M*6	$	Ind	Ind		
Physics with North American Studies	F3Q4	4FT deg	M+P	CCC	MO $	MS^	$	Ind	Ind		
Physics with North American Studies (MPhys)	F3QK	4FT deg	M+P	CCC	MO $	MS^	$	Ind	Ind		
Politics in English and American Studies	M1QL	3FT deg	*	BBC	MO	M*6	$	Ind	Ind		
Politics with North American Studies	M1Q4	4FT deg	*	BBC	MO	M*6	$	Ind	Ind		
Psychology with North American Studies	C8Q4	4FT deg	* g	BBB	MO $	M*6 go	$	Ind	Ind		
Twentieth Cent Music St in English & Amer St	W3QK	3FT deg	Mu	BBC	MO $	M*^	$	Ind	Ind		

Univ of Wales SWANSEA

TITLE	CODE	COURSE	SUBJECTS	A/AS	ND/C	AGNVQ	IB	SQA(H)	SQA	RATIO	A/AS
American Studies	Q400	4FT deg	E	BBC	X	X	30	ABBBB	Ind	3	16/24
American Studies and Anthropology	LQ64	3FT deg	*	BBC	Ind	Ind	30	ABBBB	Ind	4	
American Studies and Economic History	VQ34	3FT deg	*	BBC	Ind	Ind	30	ABBBB	Ind		
American Studies and Geography	LQ84	3FT deg	Gy	BBC	1M+5D$	Ind	30$	ABBBB$	Ind	12	
American Studies and Politics	MQ14	3FT deg	*	BBC	1M+5D	Ind	30	ABBBB	Ind	6	
American Studies and Social History	VQ3K	3FT deg	*	BBC	Ind	Ind	30	ABBBB	Ind	5	
American Studies and Sociology	LQ34	3FT deg	*	BBC	Ind	Ind	30	ABBBB	Ind	11	
English/American Studies	QQ34	3FT deg	E	BBB-BBC	X	X	30$	ABBBB$	X	3	18/28
French/American Studies	QR41	4FT deg									
German/American Studies	QR42	4FT deg									
History/American Studies	VQ14	3FT deg	*	BBC	Ind	Ind	30	ABBBB	Ind	3	16/24
Italian/American Studies	QR43	4FT deg									
Law and American Studies	MQ34	3FT deg	*	BBB	Ind	Ind	32	ABBBB	Ind		
Philosophy/American Studies	VQ74	3FT deg	*	BBC	1M+5D	Ind	30	ABBBB	Ind		
Russian/American Studies	QR48	4FT deg									
Spanish/American Studies	QR44	4FT deg									
Welsh/American Studies	QQ45	4FT deg									
Welsh/American Studies	QQ54	3FT deg	W	BCC	1M+5D$	X	28$	BBBBB$	X		

THAMES VALLEY Univ

TITLE	CODE	COURSE	SUBJECTS	A/AS	ND/C	AGNVQ	IB	SQA(H)	SQA	RATIO	A/AS
American Studies with English	Q4Q3	3FT deg		8-12	MO	M	26	CCC			
American Studies with English Language Studies	Q4Q1	3FT deg		8-12	MO	M	26	CCC			
American Studies with European Studies	Q4T2	3FT deg		8-12	MO	M	26	CCC			
American Studies with French	Q4R1	3FT deg		8-12	MO	M	26	CCC			
American Studies with German	Q4R2	3FT deg		8-12	MO	M	26	CCC			
American Studies with History	Q4V1	3FT deg		8-12	MO	M	26	CCC			
American Studies with International Studies	Q4MX	3FT deg		8-12	MO	M	26	CCC			
American Studies with Language and Communication	Q4PH	3FT deg		8-12	MO	M	26	CCC			
American Studies with Media Studies	Q4W9	3FT deg		8-12	MO	M	26	CCC			
American Studies with Music	Q4W3	3FT deg		8-12	MO	M	26	CCC			
American Studies with Politics & Int Relations	Q4M1	3FT deg		8-12	MO	M	26	CCC			
American Studies with Psychology	Q4C8	3FT deg		8-12	MO	M	26	CCC			
American Studies with Sociology	Q4L3	3FT deg		8-12	MO	M	26	CCC			
American Studies with Spanish	Q4R4	3FT deg		8-12	MO	M	26	CCC			
American Studies with Visual Cultures	Q4W1	3FT deg		8-12	MO	M	26	CCC			
American Studies with Women's Studies	Q4M9	3FT deg		8-12	MO	M	26	CCC			
English Lang and Communications with American St	Q1Q4	3FT deg		8-12	MO	M	24	CCC			

American Studies 3

course details			98 expected requirements							96 entry stats	
TITLE	CODE	COURSE	SUBJECTS	A/AS	ND/C	AGNVQ	IB	SQA(H)	SQA	RATIO	A/AS
English with American Studies	Q3Q4	3FT deg		8-12	MO	M	26	CCC			
European Studies with American Studies	T2Q4	3FT deg		8-12	MO	M	26	CCC			
History with American Studies	V1Q4	3FT deg		8-12	MO	M	26	CCC			
International Studies with American Studies	M9Q4	3FT deg		8-12	MO	M	26	CCC			
Politics and Int Relations with American Studies	M1Q4	3FT deg		8-12	MO	M	26	CCC			
Sociology with American Studies	L3Q4	3FT deg		8-12	MO	M	26	CCC			
Spanish with American Studies	R4Q4	3FT deg		8-12	MO	M	26	CCC			
Univ of ULSTER											
Modern Studies in the Humanities *American Studies*	Y321▼	3FT/4FT deg	*	CCC	MO+3D	D*6/^ gi	28	BBBC	Ind		
Univ of WARWICK											
Comparative American Studs (4 Yrs inc 1 yr abr)	Q404	4FT deg	H/E g	BBB	X	X	32$	AABBB$		7	22/28
English and American Literature	QQ34	3FT deg	E+H/L g	ABB-BBB	X	X	34$	AAABB$		9	24/30
Univ of WOLVERHAMPTON											
American Studies	Q400	3FT deg	*	12	4M	M	24	BBBB	Ind	1	
Combined Degrees *American Studies*	Y401	3FT/4SW deg	*	12	4M	M	24	BBBB	Ind		

course details			98 expected requirements							96 entry stats	
TITLE	CODE	COURSE	SUBJECTS	A/AS	ND/C	AGNVQ	IB	SQA(H)	SQA	RATIO	A/AS
Univ of ABERDEEN											
Biomedical Science (Physiology)	B9B1	4FT deg	C+2S/C+M+S g	BBC	Ind	MS go	34$	AABB$	Ind		
Genetics	C400	4FT deg	3S/2S+M g	CCD	Ind	MS go	24$	BBBC$	Ind	8	
Genetics (Immunology)	C450	4FT deg	3S/2S+M g	CCD	Ind	MS go	24$	BBBC$	Ind	5	
Genetics (Immunology) with Industrial Placement	C451	5FT deg	3S/2S+M g	CCD	Ind	MS go	24$	BBBC$	Ind		
Genetics with Industrial Placement	C401	5FT deg	3S/2S+M g	CCD	Ind	MS go	24$	BBBC$	Ind		
Microbiology-Genetics	CC54	4FT deg	3S/2S+M g	CCD	Ind	MS go	24$	BBBC$	Ind	7	
Microbiology-Genetics with Industrial Placement	CC45	5FT deg	3S/2S+M g	CCD	Ind	MS go	24$	BBBC$	Ind		
Molecular Biology (Biochemistry-Genetics)	CC74	4FT deg	3S/2S+M g	CCD	Ind	MS go	24$	BBBC$	Ind	3	
Molecular Biology with Industrial Placement	CC47	5FT deg	3S/2S+M g	CCD	Ind	MS go	24$	BBBC$	Ind		
Neuroscience	B170	4FT deg	3S/2S+M g	CCD	Ind	MS$/^	24$	BBBC$	Ind	11	
Physiology	B100	4FT deg	3S/2S+M g	CCD	Ind	MS go	24$	BBBC$	Ind	10	
Univ of ABERTAY DUNDEE											
Forensic Psychobiology	B160	4FT/5SW deg			Ind	Ind	Ind		Ind		
Univ of Wales, ABERYSTWYTH											
Genetics	C400	3FT deg	B/C g	16-18	3M $	MS6/^ g	29$	BBBCC$	Ind		
Genetics/Biochemistry	CC47	3FT deg	C g	16-18	3M $	MS^ g	29$	BBBCC$	Ind		
ANGLIA Poly Univ											
Biology and Forensic Science	BC11▼	3FT deg	g	10	3M	P go	Dip	BCCC			
Chemistry and Forensic Science	BF11▼	3FT deg	g	10	3M	P go	Dip	BCCC			
Computer Science and Forensic Science	BG15▼	3FT deg	g	12	4M	M go	Dip	BCCC			
Criminology and Forensic Science	BM13▼	3FT deg	g	12	4M	M go	Dip	BCCC	Ind		
Forensic Science and Law	MB31▼	3FT deg	g	14	6M	M go	Dip	BBCC	Ind		
Forensic Science and Psychology	BC18▼	3FT deg	g	16	8M	D go	Dip	BBCC			
BARNSLEY COLL											
Science Foundation *Anatomy and Cell Biology*	Y100	4EXT deg									
Science Foundation *Genetics*	Y100	4EXT deg									
Science Foundation *Physiology*	Y100	4EXT deg									
Univ of BATH											
Sport and Exercise Science	BC17	3FT deg	S	22	Ind	Ind	30$	Ind	Ind		
Sport and Exercise Science (4 Yr SW)	BC1R	4SW deg	S	22	Ind	Ind	30$	Ind	Ind		
Sport and Exercise Science (with year abroad)	BC1T	4FT deg	S	22	Ind	Ind	30$	Ind	Ind		
Univ of BIRMINGHAM											
Biological Sciences (Genetics)	C400	3FT deg	B+S/M/Gy/Gl/Ps g	BCC	Ind	Ind	30	Ind	Ind	9	18/26
Sport and Exercise Sciences	BC17	3FT deg	S g	BBB	Ind		32	Ind	Ind	16	22/30
BOLTON INST											
Human Biology	B150	3FT deg									
Univ of BRADFORD											
Cellular Pathology	B162	3FT deg	2S g	BB-CCD	3M $	MS4	Ind	Ind	Ind	5	14/16
Medical Engineering	H1BC	4SW deg	2S g	22	5M $	M$4/^	Ind	Ind	Ind		
Medical Engineering	H1B1	3FT deg	2S g	22	5M $	M$4/^	Ind	Ind	Ind		
Medical Engineering (Foundation Yr)	H1BD	4FT/5SW deg	* g	18			Ind	Ind	Ind		6/12
Medical Engineering (MEng)	HBCD	4FT/5SW deg					Ind	Ind	Ind		
Univ of BRIGHTON											
Pharmaceutical and Chemical Sciences	FB31	3FT/4SW deg	C g	12	MO $	MS go	Dip$	CCBB$	Ind		

course details			98 expected requirements							96 entry stats	
TITLE	CODE	COURSE	SUBJECTS	A/AS	ND/C	AGNVQ	IB	SQA(H)	SQA	RATIO	A/AS
Univ of BRISTOL											
Anatomical Science	B140	3FT deg	2S	BCC	Ind	D$^	28$	BBBBC	Ind	9	20/26
Cellular and Molecular Pathology	B162	3FT deg	C+2(B/M/P) g	BCC	Ind	D$^	28$	CSYS	Ind	4	18/30
Equine Science	D220	3FT deg	2S	ABB-BBB	Ind	D$^	32$	AABBB	Ind	12	22/28
Physiology	B100	3FT deg	2S g	BCC	Ind	D$^	28$	BBBBC	Ind	11	18/30
BRISTOL, Univ of the W of England											
Applied Physiology and Pharmacology	BB12	4SW deg	B+C g	12	4M $	MS go	24$	BCC$	Ind		
CAMBRIDGE Univ											
Natural Sciences Anatomy	Y160▼	3FT deg	2(S/M) g	AAA-AAB	Ind			Ind	CSYS	Ind	
Natural Sciences Genetics	Y160▼	3FT deg	2(S/M) g	AAA-AAB	Ind			Ind	CSYS	Ind	
Natural Sciences Neuroscience	Y160▼	3FT deg	2(S/M) g	AAA-AAB	Ind			Ind	CSYS	Ind	
Natural Sciences Pathology	Y160▼	3FT deg	2(S/M) g	AAA-AAB	Ind			Ind	CSYS	Ind	
Natural Sciences Physiology	Y160▼	3FT deg	2(S/M) g	AAA-AAB	Ind			Ind	CSYS	Ind	
CARDIFF Univ of Wales											
Anatomical Science	B141	3FT deg	C g	CCC						6	16/22
Biochemistry and Physiology	BC17	3FT deg	C+B/M/P g	CCC	MO $	MS6/^ go	26$	BBBC$	Ind	2	14/20
Genetics	C400	3FT deg	B+C/M/P g	BBB-BCC	MO $	Ind	30$	BBBB$	Ind	4	16/24
Genetics	C401	4SW deg	B+C/M/P g	BBB-BCC	MO $	Ind	30$	BBBB$	Ind	7	18/20
Neuroscience	B172	3FT deg	C+B g	BBC	3M+2D$	Ind	Ind	BBBB	Neuroscience	8	
Neuroscience	B173	4SW deg	C+B	BBC	3M+2D$	Ind	Ind	BBBB	Ind	2	18/26
Physiology	B100	3FT deg	C+B/M/P g	BCC	3M+2D$	MS^ go	26$	BBBC$	Ind	4	16/24
Physiology and Psychology	BC18	3FT deg	B/C+M/P g	BCC	MO+3D$	DS^ go	Ind	BBBB$	Ind	14	
Preliminary Year Anatomical Science	Y101	4FT deg	*		Ind		Ind	Ind	Ind		
Preliminary Year Genetics	Y101	4FT/5SW deg	* g		Ind	Ind	Ind	Ind	Ind		
Preliminary Year Neuroscience	Y101	4FT/5FT deg	*		Ind		Ind	Ind	Ind		
Preliminary Year Physiology	Y101	4FT deg	*	BCC	Ind	M^ go	Ind	Ind	Ind		
Univ of CENTRAL LANCASHIRE											
Neuroscience	B172	3FT deg	C+S	DD	3M $	M$6/^	24$	BCCC$	$		
Physiology/Pharmacology	BB12	3FT deg	C+S	DDD	MO $	MS6/^	26$	BBCC	$		
Combined Honours Programme Physiology/Pharmacology	Y400	3FT deg	C g	8	3M $	MS	24$	CCC	$		
Univ of DUNDEE											
Anatomical Sciences	B140	4FT deg	C+S/2S g	16	5M $	M$	25$	BBBC$	N$	5	14/18
Anatomical and Physiological Sciences	B120	4FT deg	C+S/2S g	16	5M $	M$	25$	BBBC$	N$	2	18/26
Biochemistry and Physiological Sciences	CB71	4FT deg	C+S/2S g	16	5M $	M$	25$	BBBC$	N$	10	
Chemistry and Physiological Sciences	FB11	4FT deg	C+S/2S g	16	5M $	M$	25$	BBBC$	N$		
Molecular Genetics	C420	4FT deg	C+S/2S g	16	5M $	M$	25$	BBBC$	N$	6	
Pharmacology and Physiological Sciences	BB21	4FT deg	C+S/2S g	16	5M $	M$	25$	BBBC$	N$	8	
Physiological Sciences	B100	4FT deg	C+S/2S g	16	5M $	M$	25$	BBBC$	N$	5	
Univ of EAST ANGLIA											
Zoology and Physiology	BC13	3FT deg	C+P/M/B	CCC	3D $		28$	BBBCC$	Ind	9	16/22

TITLE	CODE	COURSE	SUBJECTS	A/AS	NO/C	RGNVQ	IB	SQA(H)	SQA	RATIO A/AS

course details — *98 expected requirements* — *96 entry stats*

Univ of EAST LONDON

TITLE	CODE	COURSE	SUBJECTS	A/AS	NO/C	RGNVQ	IB	SQA(H)	SQA	RATIO A/AS
Archaeological Sciences and Biology	FB41	3FT deg	* g	12	MO	M				
Human Physiology	B100	3FT/4SW deg	* g	12	MO	MS	Ind	Ind	Ind	3
Psychology with Biology	L7B1	3FT deg	* g	12	MO	M				
Extended Science *Human Physiology*	Y108	4FT deg	* g	8-10	MO	M	Ind	Ind	Ind	

Univ of EDINBURGH

TITLE	CODE	COURSE	SUBJECTS	A/AS	NO/C	RGNVQ	IB	SQA(H)	SQA	RATIO A/AS
Anatomical Sciences	B140	4FT deg	C+2(B/M/P) g	BBC	MO $		Dip$	BBBB$	N$	15
Genetics	C400	4FT deg	C+2(B/M/P) g	BBC	MO $		Dip$	BBBB$	N$	9	24/28
Neuroscience	B172	4FT deg	C+2(B/M/P) g	BBC	MO $		Dip$	BBBB$	N$	8	20/24
Physiology	B100	4FT deg	C+2(B/M/P) g	BBC	MO $		Dip$	BBBB$	N$	7	20/28

Univ of GLASGOW

TITLE	CODE	COURSE	SUBJECTS	A/AS	NO/C	RGNVQ	IB	SQA(H)	SQA	RATIO A/AS
Anatomy	B140	4FT deg	C/M+S	BBC-CCC	N	M	24$	BBBB$	N	9
Anatomy (with work placement)	B141	4FT deg	C/M+S	BBC-CCC	N	M	24$	BBBB$	N	
Genetics	C400	4FT deg	C/M+S	BBC-CCC	N	M	24$	BBBB$	N	4
Genetics (with work placement)	C401	4FT deg	C/M+S	BBC-CCC	N	M	24$	BBBB$	N	
Molecular and Cellular Pathology	B166	4FT deg	C/M+S	BBC-CCC	N	M	24$	BBB	N	5
Neuroscience	B172	4FT deg	C/M+S	BBC-CCC	N	M	24$	BBBB$	N	7
Neuroscience (with work placement)	B173	4FT deg	C/M+S	BBC-CCC	N	M	24$	BBBB$	N	
Physiology	B100	4FT deg	C/M+S	BBC-CCC	N	M	24$	BBBB$	N	6
Physiology (with work placement)	B101	4FT deg	C/M+S	BBC-CCC	N	M	24$	BBBB$	N	
Physiology with Sports Science	B1B6	4FT deg	C/M+S	BBC-CCC	N	M	24$	BBBB$	N	
Physiology/Psychology	BC18	4FT deg	C/M+S	BBC-CCC	N	M	24$	BBBB$	N	5

Univ of GREENWICH

TITLE	CODE	COURSE	SUBJECTS	A/AS	NO/C	RGNVQ	IB	SQA(H)	SQA	RATIO A/AS
Applied Biology (Physiology)	B150	3FT/4SW deg	B+S g	10	3M	MS	Dip	BCC	Ind	
Exercise Physiology and Nutrition	BB14	3FT/4SW deg	B+C	12	3M	MS	Dip	BCC	Ind	
Health and Physiology	BB91	3FT deg	B g	12	N	X	22	Ind	Ind	
Health with Physiology	B9B1	3FT deg	S g	12	N	X	22	Ind	Ind	

Univ of HERTFORDSHIRE

TITLE	CODE	COURSE	SUBJECTS	A/AS	NO/C	RGNVQ	IB	SQA(H)	SQA	RATIO A/AS
Applied Geology/Human Biology	F6B1	3FT deg	S g	12	3M $	MS gi	24$	CCCC$	Ind	
Applied Statistics/Human Biology	G4B1	3FT deg	S g	12	3M $	MS gi	24$	CCCC$	Ind	
Astronomy/Human Biology	F5B1	3FT deg	M+S g	12	3M $	M$ gi	24$	CCCC$	Ind	
Chemistry/Human Biology	F1B1	3FT deg	C+S g	12	3M $	MS gi	24$	CCCC$	Ind	
Computing/Human Biology	G5B1	3FT deg	S g	12	3M $	MS gi	24$	CCCC$	Ind	1
Economics/Human Biology	L1B1	3FT deg	S g	12	3M $	MS gi	24$	CCCC$	Ind	
Electronic Music/Human Biology	W3B1	3FT deg	Mu+S	14	MO $	MS^ gi	26$	BCCC$	Ind	2
Electronics/Human Biology	H6B1	3FT deg	S g	12	3M $	MS gi	24$	CCCC$	Ind	
Environmental Science/Human Biology	F9B1	3FT deg	S g	14	MO $	MS gi	26$	BCCC$	Ind	8
European Studies/Human Biology	T2B1	3FT deg	S g	14	MO $	MS gi	26$	BCCC$	Ind	
Human Biology	B150	3FT deg	S g	16	3M $	MS gi	26	BCCC$	Ind	
Human Biology/Applied Geology	B1F6	3FT deg	S g	12	3M $	MS gi	24$	CCCC$	Ind	
Human Biology/Applied Statistics	B1G4	3FT deg	S g	12	3M $	MS gi	24$	CCCC$	Ind	1
Human Biology/Astronomy	B1F5	3FT deg	M g	12	3M $	MS gi	24$	CCCC$	Ind	
Human Biology/Chemistry	B1F1	3FT deg	S+C	12	3M $	MS gi	24$	CCCC$	Ind	10
Human Biology/Computing	B1G5	3FT deg	S g	12	3M $	MS gi	24$	CCCC$	Ind	2
Human Biology/Economics	B1L1	3FT deg	S g	12	3M $	MS gi	26$	CCCC$	Ind	
Human Biology/Electronic Music	B1W3	3FT deg	S+Mu g	14	MO $	MS^ gi	26$	BCCC$	Ind	
Human Biology/Electronics	B1H6	3FT deg	S g	12	3M $	MS gi	24$	CCCC$	Ind	
Human Biology/Environmental Science	B1F9	3FT deg	S g	14	MO $	MS gi	26$	BCCC$	Ind	2
Human Biology/European Studies	B1T2	3FT deg	S g	14	MO $	MS gi	26$	BCCC$	Ind	

TITLE	CODE	COURSE	SUBJECTS	A/AS	NO/C	AGNVQ	IB	SQA(H)	SQA	RATIO	A/AS
Human Biology/Law	B1M3	3FT deg	S g	20	4M+4D	DS gi	26$	BBBC$	Ind	6	
Human Biology/Manufacturing Systems	B1H7	3FT deg	S g	12	3M $	MS gi	24$	CCCC$	Ind	2	
Human Biology/Mathematics	B1G1	3FT deg	S+M g	12	3M $	MS^ gi	24$	CCCC$	Ind	2	
Human Biology/Operational Research	B1N2	3FT deg	S g	12	3M $	MS gi	24$	CCCC$	Ind	1	
Human Biology/Philosophy	B1V7	3FT deg	S g	14	MO $	MS gi	26$	BCCC$	Ind	1	
Human Biology/Psychology	B1C8	3FT deg	S g	20	4M+4D	DS gi	26$	BBBC$	Ind	8	
Law/Human Biology	M3B1	3FT deg	S g	20	4M+4D	D$ gi	26$	BBBC$	Ind	5	
Manufacturing Systems/Human Biology	H7B1	3FT deg	S g	12	3M $	MS gi	24$	CCCC$	Ind		
Mathematics/Human Biology	G1B1	3FT deg	M+S	12	3M $	MS^ gi	24$	CCCC$	Ind	3	
Operational Research/Human Biology	N2B1	3FT deg	S g	12	3M $	MS gi	24$	CCCC$	Ind		
Philosophy/Human Biology	V7B1	3FT deg	S g	14	MO $	MS gi	26$	BCCC$	Ind		
Physiology	C1B1	3FT/4SW deg	2S g	14-16	4M $	Ind	24	BCCC	Ind	11	
Physiology with a year in Europe	B101	4FT deg	2S g	14-16	4M $	Ind	24	BCCC	Ind		
Physiology with a year in North America	B102	4FT deg	2S g	14-16	4M $	Ind	24	BCCC	Ind		
Psychology/Human Biology	C8B1	3FT deg	S g	20	4M+4D	D$ gi	26$	BBBC$	Ind	7	16/20

KEELE Univ

TITLE	CODE	COURSE	SUBJECTS	A/AS	NO/C	AGNVQ	IB	SQA(H)	SQA	RATIO	A/AS
Neuroscience and Astrophysics	BF15	3FT deg	P+S	BCC-CCC Ind	M$^		26$	CSYS	Ind		
Neuroscience and Astrophysics (4 Yrs)	BF1M	4FT deg	*	BCC-CCC Ind	Ind		26$	BBBB	Ind		
Neuroscience and Biochemistry	BC17	3FT deg	C+S	BCC-CCC Ind	MS^		26$	CSYS	Ind	1	
Neuroscience and Biochemistry (4 Yrs)	BC1T	4FT deg	*	BCC-CCC Ind	Ind		26	BBBB	Ind		
Neuroscience and Biological & Medicinal Chem	BFCC	4FT deg	*	BCC-CCC Ind	Ind		26	BBBB	Ind		
Neuroscience and Biological and Medicinal Chem	BFCD	3FT deg	C+S	BCC-CCC Ind	MS^		26$	CSYS	Ind		
Neuroscience and Chemistry	BF11	3FT deg	C+S	BCC-CCC Ind	M$^		26$	CSYS	Ind		
Neuroscience and Chemistry (4 Yrs)	BF1C	4FT deg	*	BCC-CCC Ind	Ind		26	BBBB	Ind		
Neuroscience and Computer Science	BG15	3FT deg	2S	BCC-CCC Ind	MS^		26$	CSYS	Ind	1	
Neuroscience and Computer Science (4 Yrs)	BG1M	4FT deg	*	BCC-CCC Ind	Ind		26	BBBB	Ind		
Neuroscience and Geology	BF16	3FT deg	2S	BCC-CCC Ind	MS^		26$	CSYS	Ind		
Neuroscience and Geology (4 Yrs)	BF1P	4FT deg	*	BCC-CCC Ind	Ind		26	BBBB	Ind		
Neuroscience and Mathematics	BG11	3FT deg	S+M	BCC-CCC Ind	MS^		26$	CSYS	Ind		
Neuroscience and Mathematics (4 Yrs)	BG1C	4FT deg	*	BCC-CCC Ind	Ind		26	BBBB	Ind		
Neuroscience and Physics	BF1H	3FT deg	P+S	BCC-CCC Ind	M$^		26$	CSYS	Ind		
Neuroscience and Psychology	BC18	3FT deg	2S	BBB-BBC Ind	D$^		30$	CSYS	Ind	1	18/26
Neuroscience and Statistics	BG14	3FT deg	S+M	BCC-CCC Ind	M$^		26$	CSYS	Ind		
Physics and Neurosciences (4 Yrs)	BF13	4FT deg	*	BCC-CCC Ind	Ind		26	BBBB	Ind		
Psychology and Neurosciences (4 Yrs)	BC1V	4FT deg	*	BBB-BBC Ind	Ind		30	BBBB	Ind		
Statistics and Neurosciences (4 Yrs)	BG1K	4FT deg	*	BCC-CCC Ind	Ind		26	BBBB	Ind		

KING'S COLL LONDON (Univ of London)

TITLE	CODE	COURSE	SUBJECTS	A/AS	NO/C	AGNVQ	IB	SQA(H)	SQA	RATIO	A/AS
Biochemistry and Physiology	BC17	3FT/4SW deg	C+B/M/P	BCC	MO+3D	MS^	Ind	BCCC	Ind	3	18/20
Human Biology	B150	3FT deg	C+B	BCC			Ind	BCCC	Ind	3	12/24
Molecular Genetics	C400	3FT deg	C+M/B/P	BCC			Ind	BCCC	Ind	7	16/20
Physiology	B100	3FT/4SW deg	C+S	BCC	MO+3D	MS^	Ind	BCCC	Ind	4	14/28
Physiology and Pharmacology	BB12	3FT/4SW deg	C+S	BCC	MO+3D	MS^	Ind	BCCC	Ind	3	16/30

LANCASTER Univ

TITLE	CODE	COURSE	SUBJECTS	A/AS	NO/C	AGNVQ	IB	SQA(H)	SQA	RATIO	A/AS
Biochemistry with Animal Physiology	C7B1	3FT deg	C+B/M/P g	BCC	5M $		30$	BBBBC$	Ind		
Biochemistry with Genetics	C7C4	3FT deg	C+B/M/P g	BCC	5M $		30$	BBBBC$	Ind		

Univ of LEEDS

TITLE	CODE	COURSE	SUBJECTS	A/AS	NO/C	AGNVQ	IB	SQA(H)	SQA	RATIO	A/AS
Biochemistry-Genetics	CC47	3FT/4FT deg	C+B g	BCC	1M+5D$ Ind		28$	BBBBC	Ind	10	22/28
Biochemistry-Physiology	CB71	3FT/4FT deg	C+P/M/B g	BCC	1M+5D$ Ind		28$	BBBBC	Ind	5	
Genetics	C400	3FT deg	B+C g	CCC	1M+4D$ Ind		26$	BBBCC	Ind	6	18/28
Genetics-Microbiology	CC45	3FT/4FT deg	C+B g	BCC	1M+5D$ Ind		28$	BBBBC	Ind	22	

			98 expected requirements							96 entry stats	
course details											
TITLE	CODE	COURSE	SUBJECTS	A/AS	NO/C	AGNVQ	IB	SQA(H)	SQA	RATIO	A/AS
Human Biology	B150	3FT deg	2(B/C/M/P) g	CCC	1M+4D$	D$^ go	26$	BBBCC	Ind	10	20/28
Human Biology-Physiology	B151	3FT deg	C+M/P/B	BCC	Ind	Ind	Ind	Ind	Ind		
Human Genetics	C402	3FT deg	B+C g	CCC	1M+4D$	Ind	26$	BBBCC	Ind	3	16/30
Pharmacology-Physiology	BB12	3FT deg	C+M/P/B	BCC	1M+5D$	Ind	28$	BBBBC	Ind	6	20/22
Physiology	B100	3FT deg	C+S g	CCC	1M+4D$	Ind	26$	BBBCC	Ind	4	16/26
Sports Science and Physiology	BB16	3FT deg	B/C/M/P g	BBC	1M+5D$	Ind	30$	ABBBB	Ind		

LEEDS METROPOLITAN Univ

Human Biology	B150	3FT deg	B g	14	Ind	M$3/△ go	26$	BBBC$	Ind	5	10/18

Univ of LEICESTER

Biological Sciences (Animal Physiology)	B124	3FT deg	B+C g	18-20	DO $	D$4/△ gi	28$	BBBCC	Ind	8	16/22
Biological Sciences (Genetics)	C400	3FT deg	B+C g	20	DO $	D$4/△ gi	28$	BBBCC	Ind	5	16/28

Univ of LIVERPOOL

Anatomy and Human Biology	B140	3FT deg	B	CCC	MO $		31$	BBBCC$	Ind	9	18/24
Applied Genetics	C410	4FT deg	B+S g	18	MO $	DS^ g	31$	BBBCC$	Ind		
Genetics	C400	3FT deg	B+S g	18	MO $	DS^ go	31$	BBBCC$	Ind	8	16/26
Human Evolution	V6B1	3FT deg	2S	CCC	MO $	DS^ go	31	BBBCC	Ind	3	14/20
Physiology	B100	3FT deg	C+B	CCC	MO $	DS^ go	31$	BBBCC$	Ind	7	14/24
BSc Combined Honours *Genetics*	Y100	3FT deg	B	18	MO $	Ind	31$	BBBCC$	Ind		
BSc Combined Honours *Physiology*	Y100	3FT deg	C+B/P/M	CCC	MO $	DS^ g	31$	BBBCC$	Ind		

LOUGHBOROUGH Univ

Human Biology	B150	3FT deg	* g	18	3D	DS6/△ go	30	Ind	Ind	6	18/24
Human Biology (4 Yr SW)	B151	4SW deg	* g	18	3D	DS6/△ go	30	Ind	Ind	4	18/28

LUTON Univ

Biology with Human Biology	C1B1	3FT deg	g	12-16	MO/DO	M/D	32	BBCC	Ind		
Business Systems with Human Biology	N1BC	3FT deg	g	12-16	MO/DO	M/D	32	BBCC	Ind		
Business with Human Biology	N1B1	3FT deg	g	12-16	MO/DO	M/D	32	BBCC	Ind		
Environmental Science with Human Biology	F9B1	3FT deg	g	12-16	MO/DO	M/D	32	BBCC	Ind		
Environmental Studies with Human Biology	F9BC	3FT deg		12-16	MO/DO	M/D	32	BBCC	Ind		
European Language Studies with Human Biology	T2B1	4FT deg	L g	12-16	MO/DO	M/D	32	BBCC	Ind		
Geography with Human Biology	F8B1	3FT deg	g	12-16	MO/DO	M/D	32	BBCC	Ind		
Geology with Human Biology	F6B1	3FT deg	g	12-16	MO/DO	M/D	32	BBCC	Ind		
Health Science with Human Biology	B9B1	3FT deg	g	12-16	MO/DO	M/D	32	BBCC	Ind		
Health Studies with Human Biology	B9BC	3FT deg	g	12-16	MO/DO	M/D	32	BBCC	Ind		
Human Biology and Artificial Intelligence	GB81	3FT deg		12-16	MO/DO	M/D	32	BBCC	Ind		
Human Biology and Biology	BC11	3FT deg	g	12-16	MO/DO	M/D	32	BBCC	Ind		
Human Biology and Business	BN11	3FT deg	g	12-16	MO/DO	M/D	32	BBCC	Ind		
Human Biology and Business Systems	BN1C	3FT deg	g	12-16	MO/DO	M/D	32	BBCC	Ind		
Human Biology and Computer Science	BG15	3FT deg	g	12-16	MO/DO	M/D	32	BBCC	Ind		
Human Biology and Environmental Science	BF19	3FT deg	g	12-16	MO/DO	M/D	32	BBCC	Ind		
Human Biology and European Language Studies	BT12	3FT deg	L g	12-16	MO/DO	M/D	32	BBCC	Ind		
Human Biology and Geography	BF18	3FT deg	g	12-16	MO/DO	M/D	32	BBCC	Ind		
Human Biology and Geology	BF16	3FT deg	g	12-16	MO/DO	M/D	32	BBCC	Ind		
Human Biology and Health Science	BB19	3FT deg	g	12-16	MO/DO	M/D	32	BBCC	Ind		
Human Biology and Health Studies	BB1X	3FT deg	g	12-16	MO/DO	M/D	32	BBCC	Ind		
Law and Human Biology	BM13	3FT deg	g	12-16	MO/DO	M/D	32	PBCC	Ind		
Law with Human Biology	M3B1	3FT deg	g	12-16	MO/DO	M/D	32	BBCC	Ind		
Leisure Studies and Human Biology	BN17	3FT deg	g	12-16	MO/DO	M/D	32	BBCC	Ind		
Leisure Studies with Human Biology	N7B1	3FT deg	g	12-16	MO/DO	M/D	32	BBCC	Ind		

				98 expected requirements						96 entry stats

TITLE	CODE	COURSE	SUBJECTS	A/AS	NO/C	AGNVQ	IB	SQA(H)	SQA	RATIO A/AS
Mapping Science and Human Biology	BF1V	3FT deg	g	12-16	MO/DO	M/D	32	BBCC	Ind	
Mapping Science with Human Biology	F8BC	3FT deg	g	12-16	MO/DO	M/D	32	BBCC	Ind	
Marketing and Human Biology	BN15	3FT deg	g	12-16	MO/DO	M/D	32	BBCC	Ind	
Marketing with Human Biology	N5B1	3FT deg	g	12-16	MO/DO	M/D	32	BBCC	Ind	
Pharmacology and Human Biology	BB21	3FT deg								
Physical Geography and Human Biology	BF1W	3FT deg	g	12-16	MO/DO	M/D	32	BBCC	Ind	
Physical Geography with Human Biology	F8BD	3FT deg	g	12-16	MO/DO	M/D	32	BBCC	Ind	
Psychology and Human Biology	BL17	3FT deg	g	12-16	MO/DO	M/D	32	BBCC	Ind	
Psychology with Human Biology	L7B1	3FT deg	g	12-16	MO/DO	M/D	32	BBCC	Ind	
Public Policy & Management and Human Biology	BM1C	3FT deg	g	12-16	MO/DO	M/D	32	BBCC	Ind	
Public Policy & Management with Human Biology	M1B1	3FT deg	g	12-16	MO/DO	M/D	32	BBCC	Ind	
Regional Planning & Dev with Human Biology	K4B1	3FT deg	g	12-16	MO/DO	M/D	32	BBCC	Ind	
Regional Planning & Development & Human Biology	BK14	3FT deg	g	12-16	MO/DO	M/D	32	BBCC	Ind	
Travel & Tourism with Human Biology	P7B1	3FT deg	g	12-16	MO/DO	M/D	32	BBCC	Ind	
Travel and Tourism and Human Biology	BP17	3FT deg	g	12-16	MO/DO	M/D	32	BBCC	Ind	

Univ of MANCHESTER

TITLE	CODE	COURSE	SUBJECTS	A/AS	NO/C	AGNVQ	IB	SQA(H)	SQA	RATIO A/AS
Anatomical Sciences	B140	3FT deg	B g	BCC	2M+4D$	D^	28$	BBBCC$	Ind	13 20/30
Anatomical Sciences with Industrial Experience	B141	4SW deg	B g	BCC	2M+4D$	D^	28$	BBBBC$	Ind	6 20/24
Anatomical Sciences with a Modern Language	B144	4FT deg	B+L	BCC	2M+4D$	D^	28$	BBBBC$	Ind	
Genetics	C400	3FT deg	C	BBC	2M+4D$	D^	28$	BBBBC$	Ind	10 20/30
Genetics with Industrial Experience	C401	4SW deg	C	BBC	2M+4D$	D^	28$	BBBBC$	Ind	10 24/28
Genetics with a Modern Language	C402	4FT deg	C+L	BBC	2M+4D$	D^	28$	BBBBC$	Ind	5
Neuroscience	B172	3FT deg	B+C	BCC	2M+4D$	D^	28$	BBBBC	Ind	30
Neuroscience with Industrial Experience	B173	4SW deg	B+C	BCC	2M+4D$	D^	28$	BBBBC	Ind	17
Neuroscience with a Modern Language	B174	4FT deg	B+L+C	BCC	2M+4D$	D^	28$	BBBBC	Ind	12
Pharmacology and Physiology	BB12	3FT deg	C	BCC	2M+4D$	D^	28$	BBBBC	Ind	19
Pharmacology and Physiology with Ind Exp	BB1F	4SW deg	C	BCC	2M+4D$	D^	28$	BBBBC	Ind	
Physiology	B100	3FT deg	C	BCC	2M+4D$	D^	28$	BBBBC$	Ind	16 24/28
Physiology with Industrial Experience	B101	4SW deg	C	BCC	2M+4D$	D^	28$	BBBBC$	Ind	
Physiology with a Modern Language	B102	4FT deg	C+L	BCC	2M+4D$	D^	28$	BBBBC$	Ind	
Psychology and Neuroscience	BC18	3FT deg	B	BBC	1M+5D$	D^	30$	ABBBC$	Ind	21 20/28
Psychology and Neuroscience with Ind Exp	BC1V	4SW deg	B	BBC	1M+5D$	D^	30$	ABBBB	Ind	9 24/28

NENE COLLEGE

TITLE	CODE	COURSE	SUBJECTS	A/AS	NO/C	AGNVQ	IB	SQA(H)	SQA	RATIO A/AS
Earth Science with Human Biological Studies	F9B1	3FT deg		DD	5M	M	24	CCC	Ind	
Ecology with Human Biological Studies	C9B1	3FT deg		DD	5M	M	24	CCC	Ind	
Education with Human Biological Sciences	X9B1	3FT deg		DD	5M	M	24	CCC	Ind	
Human Biological St with Fossils and Evolution	B1F6▼	3FT deg	S	DE	5M	M	24	CCC	Ind	
Human Biological St with Industrial Archaeology	B1V6	3FT deg	S	DE	5M	M	24	CCC	Ind	
Human Biological St with Wastes Mgt & the Envir	B1FX	3FT deg	S	DE	5M	M	24	CCC	Ind	
Human Biological Studies with Chem & the Environ	B1F1	3FT deg	S	DE	5M	M	24	CCC	Ind	
Human Biological Studies with Earth Science	B1F9	3FT deg	S	DE	5M	M	24	CCC	Ind	
Human Biological Studies with Ecology	B1C9	3FT deg	S	DE	5M	M	24	CCC	Ind	
Human Biological Studies with Education	B1X9	3FT deg	S	DE	5M	M	24	CCC	Ind	
Human Biological Studies with Health Studies	B1L5▼	3FT deg	S	DE	5M	M	24	CCC	Ind	
Human Biological Studies with Philosophy	B1V7▼	3FT deg	S	DE	5M	M	24	CCC	Ind	
Human Biological Studies with Psychology	B1C8▼	3FT deg	S g	DE	5M	M	24	CCC	Ind	4/12
Human Biological Studies with Sociology	B1L3▼	3FT deg	S	DE	5M	M	24	CCC	Ind	6/ 8
Human Biological Studies with Sport Studies	B1N7▼	3FT deg	S	DE	5M	M	24	CCC	Ind	
Psychology with Human Biological Studies	C8B1▼	3FT deg	g	CC	5M+1D	M	24	CCC	Ind	12/16
Sociology with Human Biological Studies	L3B1▼	3FT deg		10	5M	M	24	CCC	Ind	
Sport Studies with Human Biological Studies	N7B1▼	3FT deg	Ss/Pe	12	M+2D	M	24	BBB	Ind	

course details | 98 expected requirements | 96 entry stats

TITLE	CODE	COURSE	SUBJECTS	A/AS	ND/C	AGNVQ	IB	SQA(H)	SQA	RATIO	A/AS
Univ of NEWCASTLE											
Genetics	C400	3FT deg	2S g	BCC	Ind		Ind	CSYS	X	5	18/26
Physiological Sciences	B100	3FT deg	C+S g	BCC	Ind	Ind	Ind	AABBB$	Ind	7	20/30
NESCOT											
Applied Human Physiology	B150	3FT deg	S	EE	N	M	Dip	Ind	N$	4	
Applied Human Physiology	B158	4FT deg	*								
Univ of NORTHUMBRIA											
Biomedical Sciences and Chemistry	BF11	3FT/4SW deg	B+C	12	5M+1D	MS gi	24$	CCCCC$	Ind	6	
NORWICH: City COLL											
Combined Science *Heredity*	Y100	3FT/4FT deg	2S	10	5M		Ind	Ind	Ind		
Combined Science *Human Physiology*	Y100	3FT/4FT deg	2S	10	5M		Ind	Ind	Ind		
Univ of NOTTINGHAM											
Biochemistry and Genetics	CC47	3FT deg	C+B/M g	AAB	Ind	Ind	Ind	Ind	Ind	10	28/30
Genetics	C400	3FT deg	B/C g	ABB	Ind	Ind	Ind	Ind	Ind	7	26/30
Human Genetics	C410	3FT deg	B/C g	ABB	Ind	Ind	Ind	Ind	Ind	7	26/30
Neuroscience	B172	3FT/4SW deg	B+C g	BBC	Ind	Ind	30$	Ind	Ind	8	22/30
NOTTINGHAM TRENT Univ											
Geography and Human Sciences	BL18	3FT deg	* g	12	Ind	Ind	Ind	Ind	Ind		10/20
Physiology and Pharmacology	BB12	4SW deg	S g	DDE	Ind	Ind	Dip	C	$	5	8/16
OXFORD Univ											
Physiological Sciences	B100	3FT deg	*	AAB	DO		36	AAAAA	Ind	2	28/30
Physiology with Philosophy	B1V7	3FT deg	*	AAB	DO		36	AAAAA	Ind		
Physiology with Psychology	B1C8	3FT deg	*	AAB	DO		36	AAAAA	Ind	2	28/30
Human Sciences *Genetics, Evolution*	Y400	3FT deg	*	AAB-ABB	DO		36	AAAAA	Ind		
Human Sciences *Human Biology, Animal Behaviour*	Y400	3FT deg	*	AAB-ABB	DO		36	AAAAA	Ind		
Psychology, Philosophy and Physiology *Physiology*	Y620	3FT deg	*	AAB	DO		36	AAAAA	Ind		
OXFORD BROOKES Univ											
Geography and the Phys Env/Human Biology	BF1V	3FT deg			Ind		Ind	Ind	Ind		
Human Biology	B150	2ACC/3FT deg	S g	DD	Ind	MS	Ind	Ind	Ind	3	6/16
Human Biology/Accounting and Finance	BN14	3FT deg	* g	CC-BCC	Ind		Ind	Ind	Ind		
Human Biology/Anthropology	BL16	3FT deg			Ind		Ind	Ind	Ind		
Human Biology/Biological Chemistry	BC17	3FT deg			Ind		Ind	Ind	Ind		
Human Biology/Biology	BC11	3FT deg			Ind		Ind	Ind	Ind		
Human Biology/Business Admin and Management	BN11	3FT deg			Ind		Ind	Ind	Ind		
Human Biology/Cartography	BF18	3FT deg			Ind		Ind	Ind	Ind		
Human Biology/Cell Biology	BC1C	3FT deg			Ind		Ind	Ind	Ind		
Human Biology/Combined Studies	BY14	3FT deg		X		X	X	X	Ind		
Human Biology/Computer Systems	BG16	3FT deg			Ind		Ind	Ind	Ind		
Human Biology/Computing	BG15	3FT deg			Ind		Ind	Ind	Ind		
Human Biology/Computing Mathematics	BG19	3FT deg			Ind		Ind	Ind	Ind		
Human Biology/Ecology	BC19	3FT deg			Ind		Ind	Ind	Ind		
Human Biology/Economics	BL11	3FT deg			Ind		Ind	Ind	Ind		
Human Biology/Educational Studies	BX19	3FT deg			Ind		Ind	Ind	Ind		
Human Biology/Electronics	BH16	3FT deg									
Human Biology/English Studies	BQ13	3FT deg									

Anatomy/Physiology/Genetics 4
Genetics

TITLE	CODE	COURSE	SUBJECTS	A/AS	ND/C	RGNVQ	IB	SQA(H)	SQA	RATIO A/AS
Human Biology/Environmental Chemistry	BF11	3FT deg								
Human Biology/Environmental Policy	BK13	3FT deg								
Human Biology/Environmental Sciences	BF1X	3FT deg								
Human Biology/Exercise and Health	BB16	3FT deg								
Human Biology/Fine Art	BW11	3FT deg								
Human Biology/Food Science and Nutrition	BD14	3FT deg								
Human Biology/French Language and Contemp Stds	BR1C	3FT deg								
Human Biology/French Language and Literature	BR11	3FT deg								
Human Biology/Geography	BL18	3FT deg								
Human Biology/Geology	BF16	3FT deg								
Human Biology/Geotechnics	BH12	3FT deg								
Human Biology/German Language and Contemp Stud	BR1F	3FT deg								
Human Biology/German Language and Literature	BR12	3FT deg								
Human Biology/German Studies	BR1G	3FT deg								
Human Biology/Health Care (Post Exp)	BB17	3FT deg	X		X		X	X		
Human Biology/History	BV11	3FT deg								
Human Biology/History of Art	BV14	3FT deg								
Human Biology/Hospitality Management Studies	BN17	3FT deg								
Information Systems/Human Biology	BG1M	3FT deg								
Intelligent Systems/Human Biology	BG18	3FT deg								
Law/Human Biology	BM13	3FT deg								
Leisure Planning/Human Biology	BK1H	3FT deg								
Marketing Management/Human Biology	BN1N	3FT deg								
Mathematics/Human Biology	BG11	3FT deg								
Music/Human Biology	BW13	3FT deg								
Palliative Care/Human Biology (Post Exp)	BB1R	3FT deg	X		X		X	X		
Planning Studies/Human Biology	BK14	3FT deg								
Politics/Human Biology	BM11	3FT deg								
Psychology/Human Biology	BC18	3FT deg								
Publishing/Human Biology	BP15	3FT deg								
Rehabilitation/Human Biology (Post Exp)	BB1T	3FT deg	X		X		X	X		
Sociology/Human Biology	BL13	3FT deg								
Software Engineering/Human Biology	BG17	3FT deg								
Statistics/Human Biology	BG14	3FT deg								
Telecommunications/Human Biology	BH1P	3FT deg								
Tourism/Human Biology	BP17	3FT deg								
Transport Planning/Human Biology	BN19	3FT deg								
Water Resources/Human Biology	BH1F	3FT deg								
Extended Science *Human Biology*	Y100	4FT deg	* g	EE	Ind	P*	Ind	Ind	Ind	
Univ of PORTSMOUTH										
Human Biology and Health Science	BB19	3FT deg	2S	14	3M $	MS6/^	Dip	BBB	Ind	
QUEEN MARY & WESTFIELD COLL (Univ of London)										
Genetics	C400	3FT deg	B+C/P/M	16	6M $	MS^/DS	26$	BBBCC		
Genetics/Microbiology	C4C5	3FT deg	B+C/P/M	16	6M $	MS^/DS	26$	BBBCC		
QUEEN'S Univ Belfast										
Anatomy	B140	3FT/4FT deg	B/C g	CCC	Ind	Ind	28$	BBBC	Ind	45
Genetics	C400	3FT/4FT deg	B+C g	CCC	Ind	Ind	28$	BBBC	Ind	8 18/24
Physiology	B100	3FT/4FT deg	B/C g	CCC	Ind	Ind	28$	BBBC	Ind	14 16/20
Univ of READING										
Pathobiology	B164	3FT deg	C g	18	4M+1D$	DS^ go	29$	BBBC$	Ind	8 13/22

course details			98 expected requirements							96 entry stats	
TITLE	CODE	COURSE	SUBJECTS	A/AS	ND/C	AGNVQ	IB	SQA(H)	SQA	RATIO	A/AS
Physiology and Biochemistry	BC17	3FT deg	B/C g	18	4M+1D$	DS^ go	29$	BBBC$	Ind	4	12/16
Psychology and Physiology	CB81	3FT deg	C g	BCC	3M+2D$	DS^ go	30$	BBBB$	Ind	22	

ROYAL HOLLOWAY, Univ of London

Biochemistry with Physiology	C7B1	3FT deg	B+C g	BCC	3M+2D	DS^	28$	BBBCC$		5	
Molecular Biology and Genetics	CC46	3FT deg	B+C g	BCC	3M+2D	DS^	28$	BBBCC$			
Zoology with Physiology	C3B1	3FT deg	B+C/S g	BCC	4M	DS^	28$	BBBCC$		4	14/20
Science Foundation Year *Physiology*	Y100	4FT deg	*		Ind	Ind	Ind	Ind			

Univ of SALFORD

Physiology with Biochemistry	BC17	3FT/4SW deg	g	BCC-CCD	4M	MS	Ind	Ind	Ind		7/13

Univ of SHEFFIELD

Anatomy and Cell Biology	B120	3FT deg	C+S g	20	5M+1D$	DS6/^	29$	BBBB$	Ind	7	20/26
Biochemistry and Genetics	CC74	3FT deg	C+S g	BCC	4M+2D$	DS^	29$	BBBB$	Ind	7	20/28
Biochemistry and Physiology	CB71	3FT/4EXT deg	C+S g	BCC	4M+2D	DS6/^	30$	BBBB$	Ind	5	
Biomedical Science Foundation Year (4 Yrs)	B101	4FT deg	g	20	4M+2D	DS6/^	30	BBBB	Ind		
Genetics	C400	3FT deg	C+S g	BCD	6M $	DS^	28$	BBBC$	Ind	14	20/24
Genetics and Microbiology	CC45	3FT deg	C+S g	BCD	6M $	DS^	28$	BBBC$	Ind	7	20/22
Neuroscience	B172	3FT deg	C/B+S g	20	4M+2D$	DS6/^	30$	BBBB$	Neuro	13	18/28
Physiology	B100	3FT deg	C+S g	20	4M+2D	DS6/^	30$	BBBB$	Ind	20	18/26
Physiology and Pharmacology	BB12	3FT/4EXT deg	S+C g	20	4M+2D	DS6/^	30$	BBBB$	Ind	6	18/28
Zoology and Genetics	CC34	3FT/4EXT deg	C+S g	BCD	6M $	D^	28$	BBBC$	Ind	37	

Univ of SOUTHAMPTON

Biochemistry with Physiology	C7B1	3FT deg	C+B/P/M/Gy g	BCC	$	M^	$	Ind	Ind	5	
Physiology	B100	3FT deg	C+B/P/M/Gy g	BCC	$	M^	$	Ind	Ind	5	14/28
Physiology and Biochemistry	BC17	3FT deg	C+B/P/M g	BCC	$	M^	$	Ind	Ind	2	18/24
Physiology and Pharmacology	BB12	3FT/4SW deg	C+B/P/M g	BCC	$	M^	$	Ind	Ind	5	18/22
Physiology with Biochemistry	B1C7	3FT deg	C+B/P/M/Gy g	BCC	$	M^	$	Ind	Ind		
Physiology with Nutrition	B1B4	3FT deg	C+B/P/M/Gy g	BCC	$	M^	$	Ind	Ind	14	
Physiology with Pharmacology	B1B2	3FT/4SW deg	C+B/P/M/Gy g	BCC	$	M^	$	Ind	Ind	4	
Physiology with Psychology	B1C8	3FT deg	C+B/P/M/Gy g	BCC	$	M^	$	Ind	Ind	6	
Psychology with Physiology	C8B1	3FT deg	B g	22	Ind	D$^ go	30$	ABBBB$	Ind	29	

SOUTH BANK Univ

Foundation Human Biology	B151	4EXT deg					Ind	Ind	Ind		
Human Biology	B150	3FT/4SW deg	S g	CC	MO	M go	Ind	Ind	Ind		
Human Biology and Accounting	BN14	3FT deg	S g	12-16	4M+2D	M go	Ind	Ind	Ind		
Human Biology and Computing	BG15	3FT deg	S+M g	12-16	4M+2D	M go	Ind	Ind	Ind		
Human Biology and English Studies	BQ13	3FT deg	E+S g	14-18	X	M^ go	Ind	Ind	Ind		
Human Biology and Environmental Policy	FB91	3FT deg	S g	12-16	4M+2D	M go	Ind	Ind	Ind		
Human Biology and European Studies	BT12	3FT deg	S g	14-18	2M+4D	M go	Ind	Ind	Ind		
Human Biology and Health Studies	BL14	3FT deg	S g	12-16	4M+2D	M go	Ind	Ind	Ind		
Human Biology and Housing	BK1K	3FT deg	S g	14-18	2M+4D	M go	Ind	Ind	Ind		
Human Geography and Human Biology	BL18	3FT deg	S/Gy g	12-16	4M+2D	M go	Ind	Ind	Ind		
Human Resource Management and Human Biology	BN16	3FT deg	S g	14-18	2M+4D	M go	Ind	Ind	Ind		
Law and Human Biology	BM13	3FT deg	S g	14-18	2M+4D	M go	Ind	Ind	Ind		
Management and Human Biology	BN11	3FT deg	S g	12-16	4M+2D	M go	Ind	Ind	Ind		
Marketing and Human Biology	BN15	3FT deg	S g	14-18	2M+4D	M go	Ind	Ind	Ind		
Media Studies and Human Biology	BP14	3FT deg	S+E g	14-18	2M+4D	M go	Ind	Ind	Ind		
Politics and Human Biology	BM11	3FT deg	S g	12-16	4M+2D	M go	Ind	Ind	Ind		
Product Design and Human Biology	BH17	3FT deg	S+Ad/A g	12-16	4M+2D	M go	Ind	Ind	Ind		
Psychology and Human Biology	BC18	3FT deg	S g	14-18	2M+4D	M go	Ind	Ind	Ind		

				98 expected requirements							96 entry stats

TITLE	CODE	COURSE	SUBJECTS	A/AS	ND/C	RGNVQ	IB	SQA(H)	SQA	RATIO A/AS	
Technology and Human Biology	BJ19	3FT deg	S g	12-16	4M+2D	M go	Ind	Ind	Ind		
Tourism and Human Biology	BP17	3FT deg	S+L g	12-16	4M+2D	M go	Ind	Ind	Ind		
Urban Studies and Human Biology	BK1L	3FT deg	S g	14-18	2M+4D	M go	Ind	Ind	Ind		
World Theatre and Human Biology	BW14	3FT deg	S g	14-18	2M+4D	M go	Ind	Ind	Ind		

Univ of ST ANDREWS

Experimental Pathology	B166	3FT/4FT deg	B/C/Gy/M/P g	BCC	Ind	Ind	28	BBBC$	Ind	6	
Genetics	C400	3FT/4FT deg	C g	BCC	Ind	Ind	28	BBBC$	Ind	8	
Neuroscience	B172	3FT/4FT deg	B/C/Gy/M/P g	BCC	Ind	Ind	28$	BBBC	Ind	16	
Physiology	B100	3FT/4FT deg	B/C/Gy/M/P g	BCC	Ind	Ind	28	BBBC$	Ind	16	
General Degree of BSc *Experimental Pathology*	Y100	3FT deg	B/C/Gy/M/P g	BCC	Ind	Ind	28	BBBC$	Ind		
General Degree of BSc *Genetics*	Y100	3FT deg	C g	BCC	Ind	Ind	28	BBBC$	Ind		
General Degree of BSc *Neuroscience*	Y100	3FT deg	B/C/Gy/M/P g	BCC	Ind	Ind	28$	BBBC$	Ind		
General Degree of BSc *Physiology*	Y100	3FT deg	B/C/Gy/M/P g	BCC	Ind	Ind	28	BBBC$	Ind		

STAFFORDSHIRE Univ

Biochemistry and Physiology	BC17	3FT deg	B g	12	4M	M^	24	BCC	Ind	2	8/18
Extended Biochemistry and Physiology (4 yr)	CB7D	4EXT deg	g	4	1M	P	24	CCC	Ind		
Foundation Biochemistry and Physiology	CB7C▼	4EXT deg	*	4	N	P	24	CCC	Ind		
Human Biology	B159	4EXT deg	g	4	1M	P	24	CCC			
Human Biology	B150	3FT deg	g								
Physiology/Computing	BG15	3FT deg									
Physiology/Electronics	BH16	3FT deg									
Physiology/Molecular Biology	BC16	3FT deg	B g	12	4M	M	24	BCC			
Psychology/Physiology	BL17	3FT deg									
Sport Sciences and Applied Statistics	BG14	3FT deg	S	14	Ind	D	Ind	BBCC	Ind		

Univ of STRATHCLYDE

Science Studies (Pass Degree) *Physiology*	Y100	3FT deg	M+S	DD	Ind		Ind	CCC$	Ind		

UNIVERSITY COLLEGE SUFFOLK

Applied Biological Science with Human Science	C1B1	3FT deg	S	EE	N $	PS	Ind	Ind	Ind		
Art & Design with Human Science	W2B1	3FT deg	S+Pf	EE	N $	P$	Ind	Ind	Ind		
Art & Design with Human Science	E2B1	3FT deg	S+Pf	EE	N $	P$	Ind	Ind	Ind		
Behavioural Studies with Human Science	L7B1	3FT deg	S	DD	N $	P$	Ind	Ind	Ind		
Business Studies with Human Science	N1B1	3FT deg	S	EE	N $	P$	Ind	Ind	Ind		
Early Childhood Studies with Human Science	X9B1	3FT deg	S	DD	N $	P$	Ind	Ind	Ind		
Environmental Studies with Human Science	F9B1	3FT deg	S	EE	N $	P$	Ind	Ind	Ind		
Information Technology with Human Science	G5B1	3FT deg	S	EE	N $	P$	Ind	Ind	Ind		
Media Studies with Human Science	P4B1	3FT deg	S	CE	N $	P$	Ind	Ind	Ind		
Product Design & Manufacture with Human Science	H7B1	3FT deg	S	EE	N $	P$	Ind	Ind	Ind		

Univ of SUNDERLAND

Biology and Physiology	CB11▼	3FT deg	B/C g	8	N $	M	24$	CCCC$	N$	2	
Biology with Physiology	C1B1	3FT deg	B/C	8	3M	M	Ind	Ind	Ind		
Business Studies and Physiology	NB11	3FT/4SW deg	*	8	3M	M	Ind	Ind	Ind		
Business Studies with Physiology	N1B1	3FT/4SW deg	*	8	3M	M	Ind	Ind	Ind		
Chemistry and Physiology	FB11▼	3FT deg	C/B g	8	N $	M	24$	CCCC$	N$		
Chemistry with Physiology	F1B1	3FT deg	C	8	3M	M	Ind	Ind	Ind		
Computer Studies and Physiology	GB51	3FT deg	B/C g	8	N	M	24$	CCCC$	N		
Computer Studies with Physiology	G5B1	3FT/4SW deg	*	8	3M	M	Ind	Ind	Ind		

course details | 98 expected requirements | 96 entry stats

TITLE	CODE	COURSE	SUBJECTS	A/AS	NVQ/C	AGNVQ	IB	SQA(H)	SQA	RATIO A/AS
English and Physiology	QB31	3FT deg	*	10	4M	M	Ind	Ind	Ind	
English with Physiology	Q3B1	3FT deg	*	10	4M	M	Ind	Ind	Ind	
French and Physiology	RB11	4FT deg	B/C+F g	8	N $	M	24$	CCCC$	N$	
Geography and Physiology	LB81	3FT deg	*	8	3M	M	Ind	Ind		
Geography with Physiology	L8B1	3FT deg	*	8	3M	M	Ind	Ind	Ind	
Geology and Physiology	FB61	3FT deg	*	8	3M	M	Ind	Ind		
Geology with Physiology	F6B1	3FT deg	*	8	3M	M	Ind	Ind	Ind	
History and Physiology	VB11	3FT deg	*	10	4M	M	Ind	Ind		
History of Art and Design and Physiology	VB41	3FT deg	*	8	3M	M	Ind	Ind		
History with Physiology	V1B1	3FT deg	*	10	4M	M	Ind	Ind	Ind	
Mathematics and Physiology	GB11	3FT deg	M	8	3M	M	Ind	Ind		
Mathematics with Physiology	G1B1	3FT deg	M	8	3M	M	Ind	Ind	Ind	
Media Studies and Physiology	PB41	3FT deg	*	24	Ind	Ind	Ind	Ind		
Media Studies with Physiology	P4B1	3FT deg	*	24	Ind	Ind	Ind	Ind	Ind	
Neurosciences and Biocomputing	BG15	3FT/4SW deg	C+S	8	N $	PS	24$	CCCC$	N$	
Pharmacology and Physiology	BB12	3FT/4SW deg	2S	8	N$	PS	24$	CCCC$	N$	
Philosophy and Physiology	VB71	3FT deg	*	8	3M	Ind	Ind			
Philosophy with Physiology	V7B1	3FT deg	*	8	3M	M	Ind	Ind	Ind	
Physiology	B110▼	3FT/4SW deg	S/M/Gy/Ss/Ps g	10	3M $	Ind	24$	CCCC$	N$	1 6/22
Physiology (Foundation)	B118▼	4EXT/5EXTSW deg	*							1
Physiology and Biocomputing	BG1M	3FT/4SW deg	C+S	8	N $	PS	24$	CCCC$	N$	
Physiology and Biomedical Science	BB19	3FT/4SW deg	2S	8	N $	PS	24$	CCCC$	N$	
Physiology and Business Studies	BN11	3FT/4SW deg	C+S	8	N $	PS	24$	CCCC$	N$	
Physiology and Politics	BM11	3FT deg	*	8	3M	M	Ind	Ind		
Physiology and Psychology	BC18	3FT deg	B/C g	12	3M $	M	26$	BCCC$	N$	9
Physiology and Religious Studies	BV18	3FT deg	*	8	3M	M	Ind	Ind		
Physiology and Sociology	BL13	3FT deg	*	10	4M	M	Ind	Ind		
Physiology and Spanish	BR14	4SW deg	*	8	3M	M	Ind	Ind		
Physiology with American Studies	B1Q4	3FT deg	*	8	3M	M	Ind	Ind	Ind	
Physiology with Biology	B1C1	3FT deg	*	8	3M	M	Ind	Ind	Ind	
Physiology with Business Studies	B1N1	3FT deg	*	8	3M	M	Ind	Ind	Ind	
Physiology with Chemistry	B1F1	3FT deg	*	8	3M	M	Ind	Ind	Ind	
Physiology with Comparative Literature	B1Q2	3FT deg	*	8	3M	M	Ind	Ind	Ind	
Physiology with Computer Studies	B1G5	3FT deg	*	8	3M	M	Ind	Ind	Ind	
Physiology with Economics	B1L1	3FT deg	*	8	3M	M	Ind	Ind	Ind	
Physiology with French	B1R1	3FT deg	*	8	3M	M	Ind	Ind	Ind	
Physiology with Gender Studies	B1M9	3FT deg	*	8	3M	M	Ind	Ind	Ind	
Physiology with Geography	B1L8	3FT deg	*	8	3M	M	Ind	Ind	Ind	
Physiology with German	B1R2	3FT deg	*	8	3M	M	Ind	Ind	Ind	
Physiology with History	B1V1	3FT deg	*	10	4M	M	Ind	Ind	Ind	
Physiology with History of Art and Design	B1V4	3FT deg	*	8	3M	M	Ind	Ind	Ind	
Physiology with Mathematics	B1G1	3FT deg	*	8	3M	M	Ind	Ind	Ind	
Physiology with Media Studies	B1P4	3FT deg	*	24	Ind	Ind	Ind	Ind	Ind	
Physiology with Philosophy	B1V7	3FT deg	*	8	3M	M	Ind	Ind	Ind	
Physiology with Politics	B1M1	3FT deg	*	8	3M	M	Ind	Ind	Ind	
Physiology with Psychology	B1C8	3FT deg	*	10	4M	M^	Ind	Ind	Ind	
Physiology with Religious Studies	B1V8	3FT deg	*	8	3M	M	Ind	Ind	Ind	
Physiology with Sociology	B1L3	3FT deg	*	10	4M	M	Ind	Ind	Ind	
Physiology with Spanish	B1R4	3FT deg	*	8	3M	M	Ind	Ind	Ind	
Politics with Physiology	M1B1	3FT deg	*	8	3M	M	Ind	Ind	Ind	
Psychology with Physiology	C8B1	3FT deg	*	10	4M	M^	Ind	Ind	Ind	
Religious Studies with Physiology	V8B1	3FT deg	*	8	3M	M	Ind	Ind	Ind	

course details			98 expected requirements							96 entry stats
TITLE	CODE	COURSE	SUBJECTS	A/AS	ND/C	AGNVQ	IB	SQA(H)	SQA	RATIO A/AS
Univ of SUSSEX										
Molecular Genetics in Biotechnology	C4JV	4SW deg	2S g	BCD	MO $	MS6 go	$	Ind	Ind	
Molecular Genetics in Biotechnology	C4J8	3FT deg	2S g	BCD	MO $	MS6 go	$	Ind	Ind	
Molecular Genetics in Biotechnology with French	C4R1	4FT deg	2S g	BCD	MO $	MS6 go	$	Ind	Ind	
Molecular Genetics in Biotechnology with German	C4R2	4FT deg	2S g	BCD	MO $	MS6 go	$	Ind	Ind	
Molecular Genetics in Biotechnology with Spanish	C4R4	4FT deg	2S g	BCD	MO $	MS6 go	$	Ind	Ind	
Neuroscience	B172	3FT deg	2S g	BCC	MO $	MS6 go	$	Ind	Ind	
Univ of Wales SWANSEA										
Genetics	C400	3FT deg	B	BCC-CCC	2M+3D$	DS^	28$	BBBC$	Ind	8 14/16
UNIVERSITY COLL LONDON (Univ of London)										
Anatomy and Developmental Biology	B143	3FT deg	C+S g	BBC-BBB	3M+MO$	Ind	32$	Ind	Ind	8 18/26
Genetics	C400	3FT deg	C+B/M/P g	BCC-BBB	3M+2D$	Ind	32$	Ind	Ind	8 20/30
Human Genetics	C402	3FT deg	C+B/M/P g	BCC-BBB	3M+2D$	Ind	32$	Ind	Ind	10
Microbiology and Genetics	CC54	3FT deg	C+B/M/P g	BCC-BBB	3M+2D$	Ind	32$	Ind	Ind	24
Neuroscience	B172	3FT deg	2S g	BBC	MO+2D$	Ind	32$	Ind	Ind	8 22/28
Physiology	B100	3FT deg	C+B/M/P g	BCC	MO+2D$	Ind	32$	Ind	Ind	4 18/26
Physiology and Pharmacology	BB12	3FT deg	C+B/M/P g	BCC	MO+2D$	Ind	32$	Ind	Ind	3 16/26
Univ of WESTMINSTER										
Physiology	B100	3FT deg	B/C	DD	3M		Ind	Ind	Ind	4 6/16
Univ of WOLVERHAMPTON										
Genetics & Molecular Biology	C4C6	3FT/4SW deg	B g	DD	N	M	24	CCCC	Ind	
Applied Sciences *Genetics and Molecular Biology*	Y110	4FT deg	*							
Applied Sciences *Genetics and Molecular Biology*	Y100	3FT/4SW deg	B g	DD	N	M	24	CCCC	Ind	
Applied Sciences *Human Physiology*	Y100	3FT/4SW deg	B g	DD	N	M	24	CCCC	Ind	
Applied Sciences (4 Yr) *Human Physiology*	Y110	4FT deg	*							
Combined Degrees *Genetics and Molecular Biology*	Y401	3FT/4SW deg	B g	DD	N	M	24	CCCC	Ind	
Combined Degrees *Human Physiology*	Y401	3FT/4SW deg	B g	DD	N	M	24	CCCC	Ind	
Physiology & Pharmacology	21BB	2FT HND	S g	D	N	M	24	CCCC	Ind	5 2/6
Univ of YORK										
Genetics	C404	4SW deg	B+C g	BCC	5M $	MS6/^	28$	BBBB$	N$	
Genetics	C400	3FT deg	B+C g	BCC	5M $	MS6/^	28$	BBBB$	N$	18/24

course details			98 expected requirements							96 entry stats	
TITLE	CODE	COURSE	SUBJECTS	A/AS	NO/C	RGNVQ	IB	SQA(H)	SQA	RATIO	A/AS
Univ of Wales, BANGOR											
History with Archaeology	V1V6	3FT deg	H g	18	Ind	D*^ go	28$	BBBC$	Ind	5	10/22
Welsh History with Archaeology	V1VQ	3FT deg	H g	CCD	Ind	D*^ go	28$	BBCC$	Ind	3	14/22
Univ of BIRMINGHAM											
African Studies/Ancient History & Archaeology	TV76	3FT deg	*	BBB	Ind	D*^	32	ABBB	Ind		
Ancient Hist & Archaeology/E Mediterranean Hist	VV1Q	3FT deg	* g	BBB	Ind	D*^	32	ABBB	Ind		
Ancient Hist & Archaeology/Modern Greek Studies	TV26	4FT deg	* g	BBB	Ind	D*^	32	ABBB	Ind		
Ancient History & Arch/Artificial Intelligence	GV86	3FT deg	* g	BBB	Ind	D*^	32	ABBB	Ind		
Ancient History & Archaeology/Computer Studies	GV56	3FT deg	* g	BBB	Ind	D*^	32	ABBB	Ind	1	
Ancient History & Archaeology/English	QV36	3FT deg	*	BBB	Ind	D*^	32	ABBB	Ind	11	
Ancient History & Archaeology/French Studies	RV16	4FT deg	F	BBB	Ind	D*^	32$	ABBB	Ind		
Ancient History & Archaeology/Geography	LV86	3FT deg	Gy	BBB	Ind	D*^	32$	ABBB	Ind	11	
Ancient History & Archaeology/German Studies	RV26	4FT deg	G	BBB	Ind	D*^	32$	ABBB	Ind		
Ancient History & Archaeology/Hispanic Studies	RV46	4FT deg	*	BBB	Ind	D*^	32	ABBB	Ind		
Ancient History & Archaeology/History	VV16	3FT deg	*	BBB	Ind	D*^	32	ABBB	Ind	32	
Ancient History & Archaeology/History of Art	VV46	3FT deg	*	BBB	Ind	D*^	32	ABBB	Ind		
Ancient History & Archaeology/Italian	RV36	4FT deg	*	BBB	Ind	D*^	32	ABBB	Ind		
Ancient History & Archaeology/Latin	QV66	3FT deg	Ln	BBB	Ind	D*^	32$	ABBB	Ind		
Ancient History & Archaeology/Mathematics	GV16	3FT deg	M	ABB-ABC	Ind	D*^	32$	ABBB	Ind	3	
Ancient History & Archaeology/Philosophy	VV67	3FT deg	*	BBB	Ind	D*^	32	ABBB	Ind		
Ancient History & Archaeology/Portuguese	RV56	4FT deg	*	BBB	Ind	D*^	32	ABBB	Ind		
Ancient History & Archaeology/Russian	RV86	4FT deg	*	BBB	Ind	D*^	32	ABBB	Ind		
Ancient History & Archaeology/Sport & Recr Studs	VB66	3FT deg	*	BBB	Ind	D*^	32	ABBB	Ind		
Ancient History & Archaeology/Theology	VV68	3FT deg	*	BBB	Ind	D*^	32	ABBB	Ind	8	
Ancient History and Archaeology	VVC6	3FT deg	* g	BBC	Ind	D*^	32	ABBB	Ind	6	18/28
Archaeology	V600	3FT deg	* g	BBC	Ind	D*^	32	ABBB	Ind	18	18/24
Classics and Classical Archaeology	QV86	3FT deg	*	BBC-BCC	Ind	D*^	32	ABBB	Ind	6	24/28
BOURNEMOUTH Univ											
Archaeology	F400	3FT deg	2(H/Gy/G/M/C)g	14-16	MO	Ind go	Ind	CCCCC	Ind	4	7/16
Conservation Science Foundation Programme	FF49▼	4EXT deg	* g	12	MO	Ind go	Ind	CCCCC	Ind	1	4/12
Practical Archaeology	004F▼	2FT HND	H/Gy/M/S g	C-DD	N	Ind go	Ind	CC	Ind	3	2/14
Univ of BRADFORD											
Archaeological Chemistry	FF14	3FT deg	C g	BCC	3M+1D	DS^	Ind	Ind	Ind		
Archaeological Chemistry	FF41	4SW deg	C g	BCC	2M+1D	DS^	Ind	Ind	Ind		
Archaeological Sciences	F401	4SW deg	S g	BCC	3M+1D	DS^	Ind	Ind	Ind		
Archaeological Sciences	F400	3FT deg	S g	BCC	3M+1D	DS^	Ind	Ind	Ind		
Archaeology	V603	4SW deg	* g	BCC	3M+1D	DS^	Ind	Ind	Ind	1	6/18
Archaeology	V600	3FT deg	* g	BCC	3M+1D	DS^	Ind	Ind	Ind	4	10/16
Bioarchaeology	F4C9	3FT deg	B g	BCC	3M+1D	DS^	Ind	Ind	Ind		
Bioarchaeology	F4CX	4SW deg	B g	BCC	3M+1D	DS^	Ind	Ind	Ind		
Univ of BRISTOL											
Ancient Mediterranean Studies	V640	3FT deg	H/Cl g	BBC	Ind	D$^	28$	BBBBB	Ind	14	
Archaeology	V600	3FT deg	g	BBC	Ind	D$^	28$	BBBBB	Ind	13	12/28
Archaeology and Geology	VF66	3FT deg	S	BBC	Ind	D$^	28$	BBBBB	Ind	44	
CAMBRIDGE Univ											
Archaeology and Anthropology	LV66▼	3FT deg	* g	AAB	Ind		Ind	CSYS	Ind	2	28/30
CARDIFF Univ of Wales											
Archaeological Conservation	F480	3FT deg	C	BCC	3M+2D		Ind	AABB	Ind		
Archaeology	F402	3FT deg	*	BCC	3M+2D	M^	Ind	ABBB	Ind		

Archaeology 5

TITLE	CODE	COURSE	SUBJECTS	A/AS	NQ/C	AGNVQ	IB	SQA(H)	SQA	RATIO	A/AS
Archaeology	V600	3FT deg	*	BCC	3M+2D	M^	Ind	ABBB	Ind	4	16/24
Archaeology and Ancient History	VVC6	3FT deg	*	BCC	Ind		Ind	AAABB	X	6	18/26
Archaeology and Medieval History	VV1P	3FT deg	H	BBC-BCC	X		Ind	AABBB	X	9	
Cultural Criticism/Archaeology	MV96	3FT deg	E	ABC	X		Ind	AAABB	X		
Education/Archaeology	XV96	3FT deg		BCC	Ind		Ind	AABB	X		
English Literature/Archaeology	QV36	3FT deg	E	ABB	X		Ind	AAAA	X		
French/Archaeology	RV16	4FT deg	E	BBC	Ind		Ind	AABB	Ind		
German/Archaeology	RV26	4FT deg	G	BCC	Ind		Ind	AABB	X		
History of Ideas/Archaeology	VVD6	3FT deg	*	BBC	Ind		Ind	AABB	X	1	
History/Archaeology	VV16	3FT deg	H	BBC-BCC	X		Ind	AABBB	X	5	
Italian/Archaeology	RV36	4FT deg	L	BCC	Ind		Ind	Ind	Ind		
Philosophy/Archaeology	VV76	3FT deg	*	BBC	Ind		Ind	AABB	X		
Religious Studies/Archaeology	VV86	3FT deg	*	BCC	Ind		Ind	AABB	X		
Social Philosophy and Applied Ethics/Archaeology	VV6R	3FT deg	*	BBC	Ind		Ind	AABB	X		
Sociology/Archaeology	LV36	3FT deg	*	BCC	3M+2D		Ind	Ind	X		
Welsh History/Archaeology	VV6C	3FT deg	H	BBC-BCC	X		Ind	AABBB	X		
Welsh/Archaeology	QV56	3FT deg	W	BCC	X		Ind	X	X		

Univ of DURHAM

TITLE	CODE	COURSE	SUBJECTS	A/AS	NQ/C	AGNVQ	IB	SQA(H)	SQA	RATIO	A/AS
Ancient History and Archaeology	VF14	3FT deg	*	BCC	MO	Ind	28	AAABB	Ind	8	22/26
Anthropology and Archaeology	LF64	3FT deg	*	BBC	MO	Ind	28	AAABB	Ind	10	20/28
Archaeology	F400	3FT deg	*	BCC	MO	Ind	28	AAABB	Ind	4	18/28
Archaeology	F402	3FT deg	*	BCD	MO	Ind	26	ABBBB	Ind	7	20/30
Archaeology and History	FV41	3FT deg	*	BBC	MO	Ind	30	AAABB	Ind	12	
Natural Sciences *Archaeology*	Y160	3FT deg	2S	ABB	Ind	X	33	CSYS	X		
Social Sciences Combined *Archaeology*	Y220	3FT deg	*	ABC	MO	Ind	32	AAABB	Ind		

Univ of EAST ANGLIA

TITLE	CODE	COURSE	SUBJECTS	A/AS	NQ/C	AGNVQ	IB	SQA(H)	SQA	RATIO	A/AS
History,English,with Landscape Archaeology Minor	V1V6	3FT deg	H	ABC-BCC	X		30	BBBBB	X	4	18/26
Anthropology, Archaeology and Art History *Archaeology*	Y400	3FT deg	*	BBC	Ind		Ind	BBBBB	Ind		

Univ of EAST LONDON

TITLE	CODE	COURSE	SUBJECTS	A/AS	NQ/C	AGNVQ	IB	SQA(H)	SQA	RATIO	A/AS
Anthropology and Archaeological Sciences	FL46	3FT deg	* g	12	MO	M	Ind	Ind	Ind	2	8/14
Anthropology with Archaeological Sciences	L6F4	3FT deg	* g	12	MO	M	Ind	Ind	Ind		
Archaeological Sciences & Information Technology	FG45	3FT deg	* g	12	MO	M$	Ind	Ind	Ind		
Archaeological Sciences and Biology	FB41	3FT deg	* g	12	MO	M					
Archaeological Sciences and Economics	FL41	3FT deg	* g	12	MO	MB	Ind	Ind	Ind		
Archaeological Sciences and Educ & Community St	FX49	3FT deg	* g	12	MO	M	Ind	Ind	Ind		
Archaeological Sciences and Environmental Sci	FF4X	3FT deg	* g	12	MO	M					
Archaeological Sciences and French	FR41	3FT deg	* g	12	MO	M^	Ind	Ind	Ind		
Archaeological Sciences and German	VR62	3FT deg	* g	12	MO	M	Ind	Ind	Ind		
Archaeological Sciences and Health Studies	FL4K	3FT deg	* g	12	MO	M					
Archaeological Sciences and History	FV4C	3FT deg	* g	12	MO	M					
Archaeological Sciences and Maths, Stats & Comp	FG49	3FT deg	* g	12	MO	M$	Ind	Ind	Ind		
Archaeological Sciences and Sociology	FL43	3FT deg	* g	12	MO	M$	Ind	Ind	Ind		
Archaeological Sciences and Spanish	FR44	3FT deg	* g	12	MO	M^	Ind	Ind	Ind		
Biology and Archaeological Sciences	CF14	3FT deg	* g	12	MO	M	Ind	Ind	Ind		
Biology with Archaeological Sciences	C1F4	3FT deg	* g	12	MO	M	Ind	Ind	Ind		
Economics with Archaeological Sciences	L1F4	3FT deg	* g	12	MO	M	Ind				
Education & Community Studies w. Archaeology Sci	X9F4	3FT deg	* g	12	MO	M					
Environmental Sciences with Archaeological Sci	F9F4	3FT deg	* g	12	MO	M					
European Studies with Archaeological Sciences	T2F4	3FT deg	* g	12	MO	M	Ind	Ind			

TITLE	CODE	COURSE	SUBJECTS	A/AS	ND/C	AGNVQ	IB	SQA(H)	SQA	RATIO A/AS
Health Studies with Archaeological Sciences	BF9K	3FT deg	* g	12	MO	M				
History with Archaeological Sciences	V1F4	3FT deg	* g	12	MO	M				
Information Technology with Archaeological Sci	G5F4	3FT deg	* g	12	MO	M	Ind	Ind	Ind	
Maths, Stats & Computing with Archaeological Sci	G9F4	3FT deg	* g	12	MO	M	Ind	Ind	Ind	
Psychology with Archaeological Sciences	L7F4	3FT deg	* g	12	MO	M				
Sociology with Archaeological Sciences	L3F4	3FT deg	* g	12	MO	M	Ind	Ind	Ind	
Three-Subject Degree *Archaeological Sciences*	Y600	3FT deg	* g	12	MO	M	Ind	Ind	Ind	

Univ of EDINBURGH

TITLE	CODE	COURSE	SUBJECTS	A/AS	ND/C	AGNVQ	IB	SQA(H)	SQA	RATIO A/AS
Ancient Civilisations of the Med and Middle East	VV61	4FT deg	g	BBB	Ind	Ind	Dip$	BBBB	Ind	
Ancient History and Classical Archaeology	VV16	4FT deg	g	BBB	Ind	Ind	Dip$	BBBB	Ind	
Archaeology	V600	4FT deg	*	BBB	Ind		34$	ABBB	Ind	7
Archaeology and Scottish Ethnology	VV69	4FT deg	g	BBB	Ind	Ind	34	ABBB	Ind	
Archaeology and Social Anthropology	VL66	4FT deg	*	AAB	Ind		38$	ABBB	Ind	8
Celtic and Archaeology	QV56	4FT deg	L g	BBB	Ind	Ind	Dip$	BBBB$	Ind	
Classical Archaeology and Greek or Latin	QV86	4FT deg	g	BBB	Ind	Ind	Dip$	BBBB	Ind	
Environmental Archaeology	V680	4FT deg	2(Gy/Gl/S/M) g	CCC	MO $		Dip$	BBBB$	N$	6
Geography and Archaeology	LV86	4FT deg	*	ABB	Ind		36$	AABB	Ind	12
Social Science *Archaeology*	Y200	3FT deg	*	BBB	Ind		34$	ABBB	Ind	

Univ of EXETER

TITLE	CODE	COURSE	SUBJECTS	A/AS	ND/C	AGNVQ	IB	SQA(H)	SQA	RATIO A/AS
Ancient History and Archaeology	VVC6	3FT deg	*	BCC	MO	M/D$	30	Ind	Ind	14 18/22
Archaeology	V600	3FT deg	*	BBC-BCC	MO	M/D$	32	Ind	Ind	11 12/24
Archaeology with European Study	V601	4FT deg	L	BBC-BCC	MO	MD$	32$	Ind	Ind	9
History and Archaeology	VV16	3FT deg	*	BBC-BCC	MO	M$	32	Ind	Ind	8 16/24
History and Archaeology with European Study	VV1P	4FT deg	L	BBC-BCC	MO	M/D$	32	Ind	Ind	

Univ of GLASGOW

TITLE	CODE	COURSE	SUBJECTS	A/AS	ND/C	AGNVQ	IB	SQA(H)	SQA	RATIO A/AS
Anthropology/Archaeology	LV66	4FT deg		BBC	N	M	30	BBBB	Ind	
Archaeology	V602	4FT deg	2S	BBC-CCC	N	M	24$	BBBB$	N	5
Archaeology	V600	4FT deg		BBC	HN	M	30	BBBB	Ind	9
Archaeology/Celtic	QV56	4FT deg		BBC	HN	M	30	BBBB	Ind	
Archaeology/Classical Hebrew	VV86	4FT deg		BBC	HN	M	30	BBBB	Ind	
Archaeology/Computing Science	GV56	4FT deg	2S	BBC-CCC	N	M	24$	BBBB$	N	5
Archaeology/Czech	TV16	5FT deg		BBC	HN	M	30	BBBB	Ind	
Archaeology/Economic and Social History	VV36	4FT deg		BBC	HN	M	30	BBBB	Ind	
Archaeology/Economics	LV16	4FT deg		BBC	HN	M	30	BBBB	Ind	
Archaeology/English	QV36	4FT deg		BBC	HN	M	30	BBBB	Ind	4
Archaeology/Film and Television Studies	VW65	4FT deg		BBB	HN	D	32	AABB	Ind	
Archaeology/Geography	FV86	4FT deg	2S	BBC-CCC	N	M	24$	BBBB$	N	
Archaeology/Geography	LV86	4FT deg		BBC	HN	M	30	BBBB	Ind	7
Archaeology/Geology	FV66	4FT deg	2S	BBC-CCC	N	M	24$	BBBB$	N	8
Archaeology/German	RV26	5FT deg		BBC	HN	M	30	BBBB	Ind	
Archaeology/Greek	QV76	4FT deg		BBC	HN	M	30	BBBB	Ind	
Archaeology/Hispanic Studies	RV46	5FT deg		BBC	HN	M	30	BBBB	Ind	2
Archaeology/History	VV16	4FT deg		BBC	HN	M	30	BBBB	Ind	6
Archaeology/History of Art	VV46	4FT deg		BBC	HN	M	30	BBBB	Ind	16
Archaeology/Italian	RV36	5FT deg		BBC	HN	M	30	BBBB	Ind	
Archaeology/Latin	QV66	4FT deg		BBC	HN	M	30	BBBB	Ind	
Archaeology/Mathematics	GV16	4FT deg		BBC	HN	M	30	BBBB	Ind	
Archaeology/Music	VW63	4FT deg		BBC	HN	M	30	BBBB	Ind	
Archaeology/Philosophy	VV67	4FT deg		BBC	HN	M	30	BBBB	Ind	4

Archaeology 5

course details			98 expected requirements							96 entry stats
TITLE	CODE	COURSE	SUBJECTS	R/AS	NO/C	AGNVQ	IB	SQA(H)	SQA	RATIO R/AS
Archaeology/Politics	MV16	4FT deg		BBC	HN	M	30	BBBB	Ind	
Archaeology/Psychology	CV86	4FT deg		BBC	HN	M	30	BBBB	Ind	9
Archaeology/Russian	RV86	5FT deg		BBC	HN	M	30	BBBB	Ind	
Archaeology/Scottish History	VVCP	4FT deg		BBC	HN	M	30	BBBB	Ind	
Archaeology/Sociology	LV36	4FT deg		BBC	HN	M	30	BBBB	Ind	
Archaeology/Theatre Studies	VW64	4FT deg		BBC	HN	M	30	BBBB	Ind	
Business Economics/Archaeology	LVC6	4FT deg		BBC	N	M	30	BBBB	N	
Celtic Civilisation/Archaeology	QV5P	4FT deg		BBC	HN	M	30	BBBB	Ind	
Classical Civilisation/Archaeology	QV86	4FT deg		BBC	HN	M	30	BBBB	Ind	24
Economic and Social History/Archaeology	VV63	4FT deg		BBC	HN	M	30	BBBB	Ind	
Economics/Archaeology	VL61	4FT deg		BBC	HN	M	30	BBBB	Ind	
Geography/Archaeology	VL68	4FT deg		BBC	8M	M	30	BBBB	Ind	
Islamic Studies/Archaeology	TV66	4FT deg		BBC	N	M	30	BBBB	Ind	
Management Studies/Archaeology	NVC6	4FT deg		BBC	HN	M	30	BBBB	Ind	
Management Studies/Archaeology	NV16	4FT deg		BBC	8M	M	30	BBBB	Ind	
Philosophy/Archaeology	VV76	4FT deg		BBC	8M	M	30	BBBB	Ind	
Politics/Archaeology	VM61	4FT deg		BBC	8M	M	30	BBBB	Ind	
Psychology/Archaeology	VC68	4FT deg		BBC	8M	M	30	BBBB	Ind	4
Sociology/Archaeology	VL63	4FT deg		BBC	8M	M	30	BBBB	Ind	
Theology & Religious Studies/Archaeology	VV6V	4FT deg		BBC	HN	M	30	BBBB	Ind	

KING ALFRED'S WINCHESTER

Archaeology	F400	3FT deg	H g	14	X	X	24$	BCC$	X	
Archaeology and American Studies	FQ44	3FT deg	* g	14	6M	M	24	BCC	N	
Business Studies and Archaeology	FN41	3FT deg	* g	14	6M	M	24	BCC	N	
Computing and Archaeology	FG45	3FT deg	* g	14	6M	M	24	BCC	N	
Education Studies and Archaeology	FX49	3FT deg	* g	14	6M	M	24	BCC	N	
Geography and Archaeology	FL48	3FT deg	Gv g	14	X	X	24$	BCC$	X	
History and Archaeology	FV4C	3FT deg	H g	14	X	X	24$	BCC$	X	
Music (World) and Archaeology	FW43	3FT deg	* g	14	6M	M	24	BCC	N	
Religious Studies and Archaeology	FV48	3FT deg	* g	14	6M	M	24	BCC	N	
Social Biology and Archaeology	CF14	3FT deg	B g	14	6M $	M	24$	BCC$	N$	
Visual Studies and Archaeology	FW42	3FT deg	A/Ad g	14	6M $	M	24$	BCC$	X	

KING'S COLL LONDON (Univ of London)

Classical Archaeology	V614	3FT deg		BCC						10

KINGSTON Univ

Nutrition	F400	3FT deg								

Univ of Wales, LAMPETER

Ancient History and Archaeology	VVC6	3FT deg		16	Ind	Ind	Ind	Ind	Ind	
Archaeology	V600	3FT deg	*	16	Ind	Ind	Ind	Ind	Ind	
Archaeology and American Literature	QV46	3FT deg			Ind	Ind	Ind	Ind	Ind	
Archaeology and Ancient History	VV1Q	3FT deg	*	16	Ind	Ind	Ind	Ind	Ind	
Archaeology and Anthropology	LV66	3FT deg	*	16	Ind	Ind	Ind	Ind	Ind	
Archaeology and Anthropology	LV6P	3FT deg	*	16-18	Ind	Ind	Ind	Ind	Ind	
Australian Studies and Archaeology	LV6Q	3FT deg			Ind	Ind	Ind	Ind	Ind	
Church History and Archaeology	VV1P	3FT deg	*	16	Ind	Ind	Ind	Ind	Ind	
Classical Studies and Archaeology	QV86	3FT deg	*	16	Ind	Ind	Ind	Ind	Ind	
Cultural Studies in Geography and Archaeology	LVVP	3FT deg	*	16	Ind	Ind	Ind	Ind	Ind	
English Literature and Archaeology	QV36	3FT deg	E	16-18	Ind	Ind	Ind	Ind	Ind	
Environment and Archaeology	FV96	3FT deg	* g	18	Ind	Ind	Ind	Ind	Ind	
French and Archaeology	RV16	4FT deg	F	16	Ind	Ind	Ind	Ind	Ind	

course details			98 expected requirements							96 entry stats	
TITLE	CODE	COURSE	SUBJECTS	A/AS	NO/C	RGNVQ	IB	SQA(H)	SQA	RATIO	A/AS
Geography and Archaeology	LV86	3FT deg	Gy	16	Ind	Ind	Ind	Ind	Ind		
German Studies and Archaeology	RVF6	4FT deg	*	16-18	Ind	Ind	Ind	Ind	Ind		
German and Archaeology	RV26	4FT deg	G	16	Ind	Ind	Ind	Ind	Ind		
Greek and Archaeology	QV76	3FT deg	* g	16	Ind	Ind	Ind	Ind	Ind		
History and Archaeology	VV16	3FT deg	H	16	Ind	Ind	Ind	Ind	Ind		
Informatics and Archaeology	GV56	3FT deg	*	14-16	Ind	Ind	Ind	Ind	Ind		
Islamic Studies and Archaeology	TV66	3FT deg	*	16	Ind	Ind	Ind	Ind	Ind		
Latin and Archaeology	QV66	3FT deg	* g	16	Ind	Ind	Ind	Ind	Ind		
Management Techniques and Archaeology	NV1P	3FT deg	*	18	Ind	Ind	Ind	Ind	Ind		
Medieval Studies and Archaeology	VV61	3FT deg	*	16	Ind	Ind	Ind	Ind	Ind		
Modern Historical Studies and Archaeology	VVCP	3FT deg			Ind	Ind	Ind	Ind	Ind		
Philosophical Studies and Archaeology	VV67	3FT deg	*	16	Ind	Ind	Ind	Ind	Ind		
Religious Studies and Archaeology	VVP8	3FT deg	*	16	Ind	Ind	Ind	Ind	Ind		
Theology and Archaeology	VV68	3FT deg	*	18	Ind	Ind	Ind	Ind	Ind		
Victorian Studies and Archaeology	VVD6	3FT deg	*	18	Ind	Ind	Ind	Ind	Ind		
Welsh Studies and Archaeology	QVN6	3FT deg	*	16	Ind	Ind	Ind	Ind	Ind		
Welsh and Archaeology	QVM6	3FT/4FT deg	W	18	Ind	Ind	Ind	Ind	Ind		
Women's Studies and Archaeology	MV96	3FT deg	*	18	Ind	Ind	Ind	Ind	Ind		
Combined Honours *Archaeology*	Y400	3FT deg	*	14-16	Ind	Ind	Ind	Ind	Ind		

Univ of LEICESTER

TITLE	CODE	COURSE	SUBJECTS	A/AS	NO/C	RGNVQ	IB	SQA(H)	SQA	RATIO	A/AS
Ancient History and Archaeology	VV61	3FT deg	*	BCC	MO	D$^	30	BBBBB	Ind		20/26
Archaeology	V600	3FT deg	*	20	MO	D$^	28	BBBBB	Ind		14/22
Archaeology	F400	3FT deg	*	20	MO	D$^	28	BBBBB	Ind		
Archaeology and Sociology	LV36	3FT deg	*	18-20	MO	D$^	28	BBBBB	Ind		8/18
Geography and Archaeology	FF48	3FT deg	Gy g	BCD	5D $	D$^	28$	BBBBB$	Ind		16/24
History and Archaeology	VV16	3FT deg	H g	20	MO	D$^	28	BBBBB$	Ind		18/30
Combined Arts *Archaeology*	Y300	3FT deg	* g	BCC	DO	D$^	30$	BBBBB	Ind		
Combined Science *Archaeology*	Y100	3FT deg	* g	CCC	MO	D$^	28$	BBBCC$	Ind		

Univ of LIVERPOOL

TITLE	CODE	COURSE	SUBJECTS	A/AS	NO/C	RGNVQ	IB	SQA(H)	SQA	RATIO	A/AS
Ancient History and Archaeology	VV16	3FT deg	*	BCC	Ind	Ind	30	BBBB	Ind	6	14/28
Archaeology (Arts)	V600	3FT deg	*	CCC	MO		30	BBBB	Ind	6	16/26
Archaeology (Science)	V602	3FT deg	S	CCC	MO $		30$	BBBCC$	Ind	4	16/20
Geography and Archaeology	LV86	3FT deg	Gy g	BCC	MO $	Ind	Ind	Ind	Ind	6	20/24
Human Evolution	V6B1	3FT deg	2S	CCC	MO $	DS^ go	31	BBBCC	Ind	3	14/20
Oriental Studies: Egyptology	V630	3FT deg	*	BCC	MO		30	BBBB	Ind	10	18/22
Arts Combined *Archaeology*	Y401	3FT deg	*	BBC-BBB	Ind	Ind	30$	ABBB	Ind		
Arts Combined *Egyptology*	Y401	3FT deg	*	BBC-BBB	Ind	Ind	30$	ABBB	Ind		
BA Combined Honours *Archaeology*	Y200	3FT deg	*	BBB	Ind	Ind	Ind	Ind			
BA Combined Honours *Egyptology*	Y200	3FT deg	* g	BBB	Ind	Ind	Ind	Ind	Ind		
BSc Combined Honours *Archaeology*	Y100	3FT deg	2S	18	MO $	Ind	30$	BBBCC$	Ind		

Univ of MANCHESTER

TITLE	CODE	COURSE	SUBJECTS	A/AS	NO/C	RGNVQ	IB	SQA(H)	SQA	RATIO	A/AS
Ancient History and Archaeology	VV16	3FT deg		BCD-BCC						9	14/22
Archaeology	V600	4FT deg		BCC				BBBBC			
Art and Archaeology of the Ancient World	VW61	3FT deg		BBC	5M		28	BBBCC		8	18/20
Geography and Archaeology	LV86	3FT deg	Gy	BBC-BBB	MO	D^	30	ABBBB	X	7	14/26

Archaeology 5

			98 expected requirements							96 entry stats

TITLE	CODE	COURSE	SUBJECTS	A/AS	ND/C	AGNVQ	IB	SQA(H)	SQA	RATIO A/AS
Greek and Archaeology	QV76	3FT deg	Gk	BBC	X	X	30	BBBBB	X	
Latin and Archaeology	QV66	3FT deg	Ln	BBC	X	X	30$	BBBBB	X	

NENE COLLEGE

TITLE	CODE	COURSE	SUBJECTS	A/AS	ND/C	AGNVQ	IB	SQA(H)	SQA	RATIO A/AS
American Studies with Industrial Archaeology	Q4V6	3FT deg		DD	5M	M	24	CCC	Ind	
Art and Design with Industrial Archaeology	W2V6	3FT deg		DD	5M	M	24	CCC	Ind	
Earth Science with Industrial Archaeology	F9V6	3FT deg		DD	5M	M	24	CCC	Ind	
Economics with Industrial Archaeology	L1V6	3FT deg	g	6	5M	M	24	CCC	Ind	
Energy Management with Industrial Archaeology	J9V6	3FT deg	g	EE	3M	P	24	CCC	Ind	
English with Industrial Archaeology	Q3V6	3FT deg		CC	4M+1D	M	24	CCC	Ind	
French with Industrial Archaeology	R1V6	3FT deg	F	DD	5M	Ind	24	CCC	Ind	
Geography with Industrial Archaeology	F8V6	3FT deg	Gy	8	5M	M	24	CCC	Ind	
History with Industrial Archaeology	V1V6	3FT deg		CD	5M	M	24	CCC	Ind	
Human Biological St with Industrial Archaeology	B1V6	3FT deg	S	DE	5M	M	24	CCC	Ind	
Ind Archaeology with Chemistry & the Environment	V6F1	3FT deg		10	5M	M	24	CCC	Ind	
Ind Archaeology with Fossils and Evolution	V6F6	3FT deg		10	5M	M	24	CCC	Ind	
Ind Archaeology with Wastes Mgt & the Environ	V6FX	3FT deg		10	5M	M	24	CCC	Ind	
Industrial Archaeology with American Studies	V6Q4	3FT deg		10	5M	M	24	CCC	Ind	
Industrial Archaeology with Architectural St	V6V4	3FT deg		10	5M	M	24	CCC	Ind	
Industrial Archaeology with Art and Design	V6W2	3FT deg		10	5M	M	24	CCC	Ind	
Industrial Archaeology with Earth Science	V6F9	3FT deg		10	5M	M	24	CCC	Ind	
Industrial Archaeology with Energy Management	V6J9	3FT deg	g	10	5M	M	24	CCC	Ind	
Industrial Archaeology with French	V6R1	3FT deg	F	10	5M	M	24	CCC	Ind	
Industrial Archaeology with Geography	V6F8	3FT deg		10	5M	M	24	CCC	Ind	
Industrial Archaeology with History	V6V1	3FT deg		10	5M	M	24	CCC	Ind	
Industrial Archaeology with Ind & Enterprise	V6H1	3FT deg	g	10	5M	M	24	CCC	Ind	
Industrial Archaeology with Management Science	V6G4	3FT deg	g	10	5M	M	24	CCC	Ind	
Industrial Archaeology with Property Management	V6N8	3FT deg		10	5M	M	24	CCC	Ind	
Industry & Enterprise with Ind Archaeology	H1V6	3FT deg	g	EE	3M	P	24	CCC	Ind	
Law with Industrial Archaeology	M3V6	3FT deg	g	10	3M+2D	M	24	CCC	Ind	
Management Science with Industrial Archaeology	G4V6	3FT deg	g	DD	5M	M	24	CCC	Ind	

Univ of NEWCASTLE

TITLE	CODE	COURSE	SUBJECTS	A/AS	ND/C	AGNVQ	IB	SQA(H)	SQA	RATIO A/AS
Ancient History and Archaeology	VV16	3FT deg	*	BCC-BBC	DO		Ind	Ind	Ind	8 18/28
Archaeology	V600	3FT deg	*	BCC-CCC	MO	X	Ind	Ind	Ind	12 16/24
Combined Studies (BA) *Archaeology*	Y400	3FT deg	*	ABC-CCC	5D	Ind	35$	AAAB	Ind	

Univ of Wales COLLEGE, NEWPORT

TITLE	CODE	COURSE	SUBJECTS	A/AS	ND/C	AGNVQ	IB	SQA(H)	SQA	RATIO A/AS
English and Archaeology	QV36	3FT deg		10	M+D	D$	Ind	Ind	Ind	
Environmental Studies and Archaeology	FV96	3FT deg		10	M+D	D$	Ind	Ind	Ind	
European Studies and Archaeology	VT62	3FT deg		10	M+D	D$	Ind	Ind	Ind	
Geography and Archaeology	LV86	3FT deg		10	M+D	D$	Ind	Ind	Ind	
History and Archaeology	VV16	3FT deg		10	M+D	D$	Ind	Ind	Ind	
Information Technology and Archaeology	GV56	3FT deg		10	M+D	D$	Ind	Ind	Ind	
Sports Studies and Archaeology	BV66	3FT deg		10	M+D	D$	Ind	Ind	Ind	

Univ of NOTTINGHAM

TITLE	CODE	COURSE	SUBJECTS	A/AS	ND/C	AGNVQ	IB	SQA(H)	SQA	RATIO A/AS
Ancient History and Archaeology	VVC6	3FT deg		BCC						28 22/28
Archaeology	V600	3FT deg		BCC						13 16/26
Archaeology and Classical Civilisation	QVV6	3FT deg		BCC						15
Archaeology and English Language	QV36	3FT deg	E	BBC						5
Archaeology and Geography	LV86	3FT deg	Gy	BBC						14 24/28
Archaeology and History	VV16	3FT deg	H	BBC						26
Archaeology and Latin	QV66	3FT deg	Ln	BBC						

			98 expected requirements							96 entry stats	
course details											
TITLE	CODE	COURSE	SUBJECTS	A/AS	ND/C	RGNVQ	IB	SQA(H)	SQA	RATIO	A/AS
OXFORD Univ											
Archaeology and Anthropology	LV66	3FT deg	*	AAB-ABB	DO		36	AAAAA	Ind	3	22/30
QUEEN'S Univ Belfast											
Archaeology	V602	3FT deg	* g	BCC	3M+4D	D*6/^ go	29$	ABBB	Ind	11	22/28
Archaeology - Palaeoecology and Geography	VF68	3FT/4FT deg	Gv g	CCC	X	Ind	28$	BBBC	X	7	16/22
Archaeology-Palaeoecology	V600	3FT/4FT deg	* g	CCC	Ind	D*6/^ go	28$	ABBB	Ind	7	16/18
Archaeology/Ancient History	VVC6	3FT deg	* g	BCC	3M+4D	D*6/^ go	29$	ABBB	Ind	13	
Biblical Studies/Archaeology	VV68	3FT deg	* g	BCC	3M+4D	D*6/^ go	29$	ABBB	Ind		
Byzantine Studies/Archaeology	VQ68	3FT/4FT deg	* g	BCC	3M+4D	D*6/^ go	29$	ABBB	Ind	2	
Celtic/Archaeology	VQ65	3FT/4FT deg	* g	BCC	3M+4D	D*6/^ go	29$	ABBB	Ind	20	
English/Archaeology	VQ63	3FT deg	E g	BCC	X	D*_^ go	29$	ABBB	X	6	
Greek/Archaeology	VQ67	3FT/4FT deg	* g	BCC	3M+4D	D*6/^ go	29$	ABBB	Ind		
History & Philosophy of Science/Archaeology	VV65	3FT deg	* g	BCC	3M+4D	D*6/^ go	29$	ABBB	Ind		
Modern History/Archaeology	VV61	3FT deg	* g	BCC	3M+4D	D*6/^ go	29$	ABBB	Ind	7	
Social Anthropology/Archaeology	VL66	3FT deg	* g	BCC	3M+4D	D*6/^ go	29$	ABBB	Ind	10	
Univ of READING											
Ancient History and Archaeology	VV61	3FT deg	*	BCC	Ind	D*6/^	30	BBBB	Ind	9	14/18
Archaeology	V600	3FT deg	*	BCC	Ind	D*6/^	30	BBBB	Ind	9	14/26
Archaeology and History	VV16	3FT deg	*	BCC	Ind	D*6/^	30	BBBB	Ind	7	16/30
Archaeology and History of Art	VV64	3FT deg	*	BBC	Ind	D$6/^	31	BBBB	Ind	13	
Archaeology and Italian	VR63	4FT deg	* g	BCC	Ind	D$6/^ go	30	BBBB	Ind	2	
Chemistry with Archaeology	F1V6	3FT deg	C g	18	4M+1D$	DS^ go	29$	BBBC$	Ind	3	14/17
Chemistry with Archaeology with a year in Europe	F1VP	4FT deg	C g	18	4M+1D$	DS^ go	29$	BBBC$	Ind		
Latin and Archaeology	QV66	3FT deg	* g	BCC	Ind	D*6/^ go	30	BBBB	Ind	2	
ROYAL HOLLOWAY, Univ of London											
Archaeology and Ancient History	VV16	3FT deg	*	BBC			30				
Archaeology and History	VV61	3FT deg	g	BBB-BBC			30				
Archaeology and History with a year in Europe	VV6C	4FT deg	L g	BBB-BBC			30$				
SOAS:Sch of Oriental & African St (U of London)											
History of Art/Archaeology (Asia,Africa)	V620	3FT deg		20	Ind		30	BBBCC	Ind	2	14/22
History of Art/Archaeology and African Studies	VT67	3FT deg		20	Ind		30	BBBCC	Ind		
History of Art/Archaeology and Amharic	TV76	4FT deg		20	Ind		30	BBBCC	Ind		
History of Art/Archaeology and Arabic	TV66	4FT deg		22	Ind		31	BBBBC	Ind	5	
History of Art/Archaeology and Bengali	TV56	3FT deg		20	Ind		30	BBBCC	Ind		
History of Art/Archaeology and Burmese	TVM6	4FT deg		20	Ind		30	BBBCC	Ind		
History of Art/Archaeology and Chinese	TV36	4FT deg		24	Ind		32	BBBBB	Ind	7	
History of Art/Archaeology and Geography	LV86	3FT deg		20	Ind		30	BBBCC	Ind		
History of Art/Archaeology and Georgian	TV96	3FT deg		22	Ind		31	BBBBC	Ind		
History of Art/Archaeology and Gujarati	TV5P	3FT deg		20	Ind		30	BBBCC	Ind		
History of Art/Archaeology and Hausa	TVR6	4FT deg		20	Ind		30	BBBCC	Ind		
History of Art/Archaeology and Hebrew	QV96	4FT deg		22	Ind		31	BBBBC	Ind		
History of Art/Archaeology and Hindi	TVMP	3FT/4FT deg		20	Ind		30	BBBCC	Ind		
History of Art/Archaeology and History	VV16	3FT deg		20	Ind		30	BBBCC	Ind	6	
Indonesian and History of Art/Archaeology	TVMQ	3FT/4FT deg		20	Ind		30	BBBCC	Ind	1	
Japanese and History of Art/Archaeology	TV46	4FT deg		24	Ind		32	BBBBB	Ind		
Korean and History of Art/Archaeology	TVNP	4FT deg		16	Ind		28	BBCCC	Ind		
Linguistics and History of Art/Archaeology	QV36	3FT deg									
Music and History of Art/Archaeology	VWP3	3FT deg		20	Ind		30	BBBCC	Ind	1	
Nepali and History of Art/Archaeology	TV5Q	3FT deg		20	Ind		30	BBBCC	Ind		
Persian and History of Art/Archaeology	TVQ6	3FT deg		22	Ind		31	BBBBC	Ind		

Archaeology 5

			98 expected requirements							96 entry stats

TITLE	CODE	COURSE	SUBJECTS	A/AS	ND/C	AGNVQ	IB	SQA(H)	SQA	RATIO A/AS
Sanskrit and History of Art/Archaeology	QVX6	3FT deg		20	Ind		30	BBBCC	Ind	
Sinhalese and History of Art/Archaeology	TVN6	3FT deg		20	Ind		30	BBBCC	Ind	
Social Anthropology and History of Art/Archaeolo	LV66	3FT deg		22	Ind		31	BBBBC	Ind	12
South Asian Studies and History of Art/Archaeol	VTP5	3FT deg								
Study of Religions and History of Art/Archaeolog	VV68	3FT deg		20	Ind		30	BBBCC	Ind	4
Swahili and History of Art/Archaeology	TVT6	4FT deg		20	Ind		30	BBBCC	Ind	
Tamil and History of Art/Archaeology	TVNQ	3FT deg		20	Ind		30	BBBCC	Ind	
Thai and History of Art/Archaeology	VT65	3FT/4FT deg		20	Ind		30	BBBCC	Ind	
Turkish and History of Art/Archaeology	TVP6	4FT deg		22	Ind		31	BBBBC	Ind	
Urdu and History of Art/Archaeology	VT6M	3FT deg		20	Ind		30	BBBCC	Ind	
Vietnamese and History of Art/Archaeology	VT6N	4FT deg		20	Ind		30	BBBCC	Ind	

Univ of SHEFFIELD

TITLE	CODE	COURSE	SUBJECTS	A/AS	ND/C	AGNVQ	IB	SQA(H)	SQA	RATIO A/AS
Archaeological Science	F410	3FT deg	* g	BBC	4M+2D	D6/^	30	ABBB	Ind	
Archaeological Science and Geography	FF48	3FT deg	Gy g	BBC	4M+2D	D6/^	30$	ABBB$	Ind	
Archaeological Science and Geology	FF46	3FT deg	* g	BCC	5M+1D	D6/^	29	BBBB	Ind	
Archaeology and Prehistory	F400	3FT deg	* g	BBB-BBC	6M	D^	31	ABBB	Ind	
Archaeology and Prehistory and Medieval History	FV41	3FT deg	H g	BBB	4M+2D$	D^	32$	AABB$	Ind	
Landscape Design and Archaeology (Grad Dip Opt)	KF34	3FT/4FT deg	2S g	CCC	6M	D^	28$	BBBC$	Ind	

Univ of SOUTHAMPTON

TITLE	CODE	COURSE	SUBJECTS	A/AS	ND/C	AGNVQ	IB	SQA(H)	SQA	RATIO A/AS
Archaeology	V600	3FT deg	*	BCD-CCC	Ind	Ind	26	Ind	Ind	6 13/24
Archaeology and Geography	VL68	3FT deg	Gy	BCC	Ind	Ind	26	Ind	Ind	10 16/28
Archaeology and History	VV61	3FT deg	H	BCC	Ind	Ind	26	Ind	Ind	11 18/24
Archaeology and Iberian Studies	VR64	4FT deg	Sp/Pt	BCD-CCC	Ind	Ind	26	Ind	Ind	5

Univ of ST ANDREWS

TITLE	CODE	COURSE	SUBJECTS	A/AS	ND/C	AGNVQ	IB	SQA(H)	SQA	RATIO A/AS
Ancient History and Archaeology	VV16	3FT deg	* g	BBB	X	Ind	30$	BBBB	Ind	
Mediaeval History and Archaeology	VV1P	4FT deg	* g	BBB	X	Ind	30$	BBBB	Ind	

TRINITY COLL Carmarthen

TITLE	CODE	COURSE	SUBJECTS	A/AS	ND/C	AGNVQ	IB	SQA(H)	SQA	RATIO A/AS
Archaeology	V600	3FT deg	* g	DD-CC	Ind		Ind	Ind	Ind	4 6/16
English/Archaeology	QV36	3FT deg	E g	DD-CC	Ind		Ind	Ind	Ind	
Heritage Conservation (Archaeology)	VW62	3FT deg	* g	DD-CC	Ind		Ind	Ind	Ind	3
History/Archaeology	VV16	3FT deg	H g	DD-CC	Ind		Ind	Ind	Ind	8
Religious Studies/Archaeology	VV68	3FT deg	g	DD-CC	Ind		Ind	Ind	Ind	4
Theatre Studies/Archaeology	VW64	3FT deg	g	DD-CC	Ind		Ind	Ind	Ind	2
Welsh Studies/Archaeology	QV56	3FT deg	g	DD-CC	Ind		Ind	Ind	Ind	
Humanities Archaeology	Y320	3FT deg	* g	DD-CC	Ind		Ind	Ind	Ind	

UNIVERSITY COLL LONDON (Univ of London)

TITLE	CODE	COURSE	SUBJECTS	A/AS	ND/C	AGNVQ	IB	SQA(H)	SQA	RATIO A/AS
Archaeological Conservation	F480	3FT deg	C g	BCC-BBC	3M	Ind	30$	BBBCC	Ind	7
Archaeology (Egyptian)	F432	3FT deg	* g	BBC-BBB	3M	Ind	30	BBBCC	Ind	7 12/20
Archaeology (Greek and Roman)	F445	3FT deg	g	BCC-BBC	3M	Ind	30	BBBCC	Ind	10
Archaeology (Medieval)	F426	3FT deg	* g	BCC-BBC	3M	Ind	30	BBBCC	Ind	5 20/22
Archaeology (Medieval) and History of Art	VV64	3FT deg	g	BBC	3M	Ind	30$	BBBCC	Ind	
Archaeology (Western Asia)	F420	3FT deg	* g	BCC-BBC	3M	Ind	30	BBBCC	Ind	5
Archaeology BA (General)	F400	3FT deg	* g	BCC-BBC	3M	Ind	30	BBBCC	Ind	4 20/28
Archaeology BSc (General)	F402	3FT deg	* g	BCC-BBC	3M	Ind	30	BBBCC	Ind	5 18/24
Archaeology, Classics and Classical Art	VQ68	4FT deg	g	BCC-BBB	3M	Ind	30$	BBBCC	Ind	5 24/26

Univ of WARWICK

TITLE	CODE	COURSE	SUBJECTS	A/AS	ND/C	AGNVQ	IB	SQA(H)	SQA	RATIO A/AS
Ancient History and Classical Archaeology	VV16	3FT deg	* g	BCC	X	X	30	BBBBC		13 20/28

TITLE	CODE	COURSE	SUBJECTS	A/AS	ND/C	AGNVQ	IB	SQA(H)	SQA	RATIO A/AS
Univ of YORK										
Archaeology	V600	3FT deg	*	BBC	M+D	D$^	30	BBBC	Ind	18/28
Archaeology	V602	3FT deg	*	BBC	M+D	D$^	30	BBBC	Ind	
Archaeology/Education	V6X9	3FT deg	*	BBC	M+D	D$^	30	BBBC	Ind	
Archaeology/History (Equal)	VV16	3FT deg	H	24	Ind	D$_^	32$	BBBB$	Ind	

course details — *98 expected requirements* — *96 entry stats*

Architecture 6

			98 expected requirements							96 entry stats	
TITLE	CODE	COURSE	SUBJECTS	A/AS	ND/C	RGNVQ	IB	SQA(H)	SQA	RATIO	A/AS
Univ of BATH											
Architectural Studies	K100	4SW deg	M	24	Ind	D^	30	AAABB	Ind	9	20/28
Univ of BRIGHTON											
Architectural Design	K100	3FT deg	* g	18	4M+2D	M6/^ go	26	BBBB	Ind		
Building Studies	K200	3FT/4SW deg	* g	12	5M $	MC go	Dip	BBCC	Ind		
Interior Architecture	E260	3FT deg	Fa+Pf g		MO $	M$ go	Ind	Ind	Ind		
Interior Architecture	W260	3FT deg	Fa+Pf g		MO $	M$ go	Ind	Ind	Ind		
Building Studies (Architectural Technology)	632K▼	2FT/3SW HND	* g	E	3M $	P$ go	Ind	Ind	Ind		
BRISTOL, Univ of the W of England											
Architecture and Planning	KK14	4FT deg	* g	16-18	4M+2D	M*3/^ go	24	BBCC	Ind		
CAMBRIDGE Univ											
Architecture	K100▼	3FT deg	* g	AAA-AAB	Ind		Ind	CSYS	Ind	6	28/30
CARDIFF Univ of Wales											
Architectural Studies	K100	5SW deg	*	22	Ind	Ind	Ind	Ind		4	20/28
Univ of CENTRAL ENGLAND											
Architecture	K100	3FT deg	*	8	2M		24	BBCC	Ind	9	10/22
DE MONTFORT Univ											
Architecture	K100▼	3FT deg	* g	16	4M+2D	M$ go	30	BBBB	Ind	5	12/20
Architecture & Urban Studies	KK14▼	3FT deg	* g	16	4M+2D	M$ go	30	BBBB	Ind	5	
Univ of DERBY											
Architectural Technology and Innovation	K101	3FT deg		10	4M	M$	26	CCCD	Ind	2	6/10
Credit Accumulation Modular Scheme Architectural Design	Y600	3FT deg	*	8	MO	M	Ind	CCCC	Ind		
Univ of DUNDEE											
Architecture (BSc/BArch)	K100	5FT deg	* g	BCC	6M $	D$	30$	BBBC	HN$	6	14/26
Univ of EAST LONDON											
Architecture	K100	3FT deg	* g	12	N	D$	Ind	Ind	Ind	12	
Univ of EDINBURGH											
Architectural Design	K100	4FT deg	g	ABB	Ind		36$	AABB	Ind	11	
Architectural Studies	K101	4FT deg	g	ABB	Ind		36$	AABB		13	
Structural Engineering with Architecture	H2K1	4FT deg	M+P	ABB				BBBBB			
Structural Engineering with Architecture (MEng)	H2KC	4FT deg	M+P	ABB				BBBBB			
Social Science Architectural History	Y200	3FT deg	*	BBB	Ind		34$	ABBB	Ind		
Univ of GLAMORGAN											
Architectural and Building Conservation	KK21	2FT deg			Ind	M$	Ind	Ind	Ind		
Architectural and Building Conservation	12KK▼	2FT HND	g	4-6	N $	P$	Ind	Ind	Ind	1	
Univ of GLASGOW											
Architecture (BArch Ordinary/Honours)	K100	4FT deg	g	BCC	5M		30	BBBC	Ind	8	16/28
Civil Eng with Architecture (MEng or BEng)	H2K1	4FT/5FT deg	M+P	CCD	4M $	M$	24$	BBBB$	N$		
Univ of GREENWICH											
Architecture	K100	3FT deg	* g	14	3M-5M	M	24	BBB	Ind		
HERIOT-WATT Univ											
Architecture	K100▼	4FT deg	* g	BCC	HN	M$ go	30	BBBB	HN		
Housing Studies	K110▼	4FT deg	*	BCC	Ind	M$ go	28	BBBB	Ind		

TITLE	CODE	COURSE	SUBJECTS	A/AS	NO/C	RGNVQ	IB	SQA(H)	SQA	RATIO	A/AS
Univ of HUDDERSFIELD											
Architectural Computer Aided Technology	GK51	3FT deg	* g	12	5M	M$4/^ go	Ind	Ind	Ind		
Architecture/Architecture (International)	K100	6SW deg	Pf g	14	5M	M$ go	Ind	Ind	Ind		
Architectural Studies	001K	2FT HND	* g	6	3M	P$ go	Ind	Ind	Ind		
KENT INST of A & D											
Architecture	K100▼	3FT deg	H g	16	N	P go	32	ABC	Ind	12	8/20
Interior Architecture	W2K9▼	3FT deg	Fa	12	N	P+	24	ABC	Ind	20	
Interior Architecture	E2K9▼	3FT deg	Fa	12	N	P+	24	ABC	Ind		
KINGSTON Univ											
Architecture	K100	3FT deg	*	20	5M	Ind^	28	BBBCC	Ind	7	14/26
Univ of LEEDS											
Architectural Engineering (4 Yrs)	H2KC	4FT deg	M g	CCC	3M+2D$	Ind	26$	BBBCC	Ind	5	12/26
Civil Engineering with Architecture	H2K1	3FT/4FT deg	M g	CCC	3M+2D$	Ind	26$	BBBCC	Ind	6	14/22
LEEDS METROPOLITAN Univ											
Architecture	K100	3FT deg	Pf g	16-20	7M	D$ go	Dip	BBBBC	Ind	4	8/20
Univ of LINCOLNSHIRE and HUMBERSIDE											
Architecture	K100	3FT deg	Pf g	12	3M+1D	M	24	CCCC	Ind		
Univ of LIVERPOOL											
Architecture	K100	3FT deg	* g	BBB	Ind	Ind	30	BBBBB	Ind	9	16/26
LIVERPOOL JOHN MOORES Univ											
Architectural Studies	K100	3FT deg	Pf	CCC	3M+2D	D$				7	10/20
LUTON Univ											
Architecture	K100	3FT deg	g	12-16	MO/DO	M/D	32	BBCC	Ind	11	10/16
Business and Property Studies	NK2D	3FT deg		12-16	MO/DO	M/D	32	BBCC	Ind		
Univ of MANCHESTER											
Architecture	K100	3FT deg		BBB				AABBB		14	20/28
Structural Eng with Arch (Int Eur Prog) (MEng)	H2KC	4FT deg		18	4M+2D$		30$	Ind	Ind	5	26/30
Structural Engineering with Arch (Japanese)	HK21	4SW deg									
Structural Engineering with Architecture	H2K1	4FT deg		18	4M+2D$		30$	Ind	Ind	9	16/18
Structural Engineering with Architecture (4 Yrs)	H2KD	4FT deg								3	
MANCHESTER METROPOLITAN Univ											
Architecture	K100	3FT deg	Pf	BCC	5M		Dip	BBCC	HN		14/26
MIDDLESEX Univ											
Architecture	K100▼	3FT deg									
Univ of NEWCASTLE											
Architectural Studies	K100	3FT deg	* g	24	MD	M* go	30	AAAB	Ind	5	18/30
Combined Studies (BA) *History of Architecture*	Y400	3FT deg	*	ABC-BBB	5D	Ind	35$	AAAB	Ind		
NORTH EAST WALES INST of HE											
Architectural Design	K100	3FT deg		6-12	3M	M$	Ind	CCC	N$		
Building (Architecture)	11HK	2FT HND		2-6	2M	P$	Ind	CC	N$		
Univ of NORTH LONDON											
Architecture	K100	3FT deg	Pf	CC	3M	M	Ind	Ind	Ind	17	10/16
Univ of NORTHUMBRIA											
Architectural Design and Management	KK12	3FT deg	* g	16	4M+2D	D gi	26	BBCCC	Ind		

Architecture 6

TITLE	CODE	COURSE	SUBJECTS	A/AS	NO/C	RGNVQ	IB	SQA(H)	SQA	RATIO A/AS
Architectural Environmental Design	K236	4FT deg	M g	12	6M	MC2/^	24	BCCCC$			
Architectural and Urban Conservation	KK14	3FT deg	* g	14	5M+1D	M gi	24	BCCC	Ind		
Univ of NOTTINGHAM										
Architectural Studies	K102	3FT deg	* g	BBB	M+D	D*^ go	32	CSYS	Ind	31
Architecture	K100	3FT deg	* g	BBB	M+D	D*^ go	32	CSYS	Ind	16 26/30
NOTTINGHAM TRENT Univ										
Architectural Technology	K101	4SW deg	M+S	14	6M	M+1	Ind	Ind	Ind	
OXFORD BROOKES Univ										
Architecture	K100	3FT deg	Pf g	16	4M	M$3	Ind	Ind	Ind	6 10/24
Univ of PAISLEY										
Structural Eng with Architectural Studies (MEng)	H2KD	5SW deg	M g	CCC	Ind	Ind	Ind	ABBC$	Ind	
Structural Engineering with Architectural Studs	H2K1	4SW deg	M g	CDD	Ind	Ind	Ind	BBBC$	Ind	9
Univ of PLYMOUTH										
Architecture	K100	3FT deg	* g	18	4M+1D$	D$	Ind	Ind	Ind	6 10/24
Univ of PORTSMOUTH										
Architecture	K100	3FT deg	*	CCC	5M+1D	D*6/^	28	BBBB	Ind	4 10/22
QUEEN'S Univ Belfast										
Architecture	K100	3FT deg	* g	BCC	Ind	Ind	29$	ABBB	Ind	6 18/28
ROBERT GORDON Univ										
Architecture	K100	4FT/5SW deg	E+Pf g	CCD	N	Ind	Ind	BBCC$	Ind	6
Architecture with Languages	K1T2	5SW deg	E+F/G+M/S+Pf	CCD	N	Ind	Ind	BBCC$	Ind	4
Interior Architecture	K1W2	4FT/5SW deg	E+Pf g	CCD	N	Ind	Ind	BBCC$	Ind	6
Univ of SHEFFIELD										
Architecture (post grad dip option)	K100	3FT/5FT/6FT deg	Pf g	BBB	3M+3D	D^	32	AABB	Ind	10 24/28
Civil Engineering with Architecture	H2K1	3FT/4FT deg	M+S+Pf g	BCC	5M+1D$	M$^	28$	BBBB$	Ind	10 18/24
Structural Engineering and Architecture	HK21	4FT deg	M+S+Pf g	BBB	X	D^	32$	AABB$	Ind	4 20/30
SHEFFIELD HALLAM Univ										
Architectural Technology	K230	4SW deg	*	16	6M	M$2	Ind	BBBCC	Ind	
Combined Studies Architectural Technology	Y400	3FT deg	M	14	2M	M	Ind	Ind	Ind	
SOUTHAMPTON INST										
Interior Architecture	K1W2	3FT deg	Ad/Ha/Ds	10-12	MO	M$	Dip	CCCC	N	
Interior Architecture (with Foundation Year)	K1WF▼	4FT deg	*	2-4	N	P$	Dip	CCCC	N	
SOUTH BANK Univ										
Architecture	K100	3FT deg	Pf/M+E+A g	CC	4M	M go	Ind	Ind	Ind	
Foundation Architecture	K108	4EXT deg					Ind	Ind	Ind	
Urban Studies and Technology	KJ94	3FT deg	* g	14-18	2M+4D	M go	Ind	Ind	Ind	
Univ of STRATHCLYDE										
Architectural Studies	K100	4FT deg	M/P	BBC	HN		Ind	BBBBC$	HN	
Architectural Studies with European Studies	K1T2	4FT deg	M/P+L	BBC	HN		Ind	BBBBC$	HN	
UNIVERSITY COLL LONDON (Univ of London)										
Architecture	K100	3FT deg	* g	BBC	3M	Ind	30	BBBCC	Ind	10 20/30
Univ of WESTMINSTER										
Architecture	K100	3FT deg	*	BC-CC	3M			BBB		15 12/24

course details | 98 expected requirements | 96 entry stats

	course details			98 expected requirements							96 entry stats
TITLE	CODE	COURSE	SUBJECTS	A/AS	NO/C	AGNVQ	IB	SQA(H)	SQA	RATIO A/AS

Univ of Wales, ABERYSTWYTH

TITLE	CODE	COURSE	SUBJECTS	A/AS	NO/C	AGNVQ	IB	SQA(H)	SQA	RATIO A/AS
Art	W150	3FT deg	A/Ad g	18	1M+5D$	MA6 g	29$	BBBCC$	Ind	
Art	E150	3FT deg	A/Ad g	18	1M+5D$	MA6 g	29$	BBBCC$	Ind	
Art History with Art	V4W1	3FT deg	A/Ad g	18	1M+5D$	MA6 g	29$	BBBCC$	Ind	
Art History/Art	VW41	3FT deg	A/Ad	18	1M+5D$	MA6 g	29$	BBBCC$	Ind	
Art with Art History	W1V4	3FT deg	A/Ad g	18	1M+5D$	MA6 g	29$	BBBCC$	Ind	
Art/American Studies	QW41	3FT deg	E/H+(A/Ad) g	18	1M+5D$	MA^ g	29$	BBBCC$	Ind	
Drama/Art	WW14	3FT deg	A/Ad g	20	1M+5D$	MQ/A^ g	30$	BBBBC$	Ind	
Education/Art	WX19	3FT deg	A/Ad g	18	1M+5D$	MA6 g	29$	BBBCC$	Ind	
English/Art	QW31	3FT deg	El+A/Ad	20	1M+5D$	MA^ g	30$	BBBBC$	Ind	
Film and Television Studies/Art	WW15	3FT deg	A/Ad g	20	1M+5D$	MA/Q^ g	30$	BBBBC$	Ind	
French/Art	RW11	4FT deg	F+A/Ad g	18	1M+5D$	MA^ g	29$	BBBCC$	Ind	
Geography/Art	LW81	3FT deg	Gy+A/Ad g	20-22	3M+2D$	MA^ g	31$	BBBBC$	Ind	
History/Art	VW11	3FT deg	A/Ad g	18-20	1M+5D$	MA^ g	30$	BBBCC$	Ind	
Information and Library Studies/Art	PW21	3FT deg	A/Ad g	18	1M+5D$	MA6 g	29$	BBBCC$	Ind	
Irish/Art	QWM1	4FT deg	A/Ad g	18	1M+5D$	MA6 g	29$	BBBCC$	Ind	
Italian/Art	RW31	4FT deg	A/Ad+L g	18	1M+5D$	MA^ g	29$	BBBCC$	Ind	
Pure Mathematics/Art	GW11	3FT deg	M+A/Ad g	18	1M+5D$	MA^ g	29$	BBBCC$	Ind	
Spanish/Art	RW41	4FT deg	A/Ad+L g	18	1M+5D$	MA^ g	29$	BBBCC$	Ind	
Welsh History/Art	VWC1	3FT deg	A/Ad g	18-20	1M+5D$	MA^ g	30$	BBBCC$	Ind	
Welsh/Art	QW51	3FT deg	W+A/Ad g	18	1M+5D$	MA^ g	29$	BBBCC$	Ind	

AMERSHAM & WYCOMBE COLL

TITLE	CODE	COURSE	SUBJECTS	A/AS	NO/C	AGNVQ	IB	SQA(H)	SQA	RATIO A/AS
Graphic Design	012E	2FT HND	Fa+Pf		N	P $	Ind	Ind	Ind	
Textile Design	022E	2FT HND	Fa+Pf		N	P $	Ind	Ind	Ind	

ANGLIA Poly Univ

TITLE	CODE	COURSE	SUBJECTS	A/AS	NO/C	AGNVQ	IB	SQA(H)	SQA	RATIO A/AS
Art History and Graphic Arts	WV24▼	3FT deg	A	16	6M	M+/^	Dip$	BBCC	Ind	4
Art History and Studio Art	WV94▼	3FT deg	A	14	6M	M+/^	Dip$	BBCC	Ind	2 10/20
Art History and Studio Art	EV94▼	3FT deg	A	14	6M	M+/^	Dip$	BBCC	Ind	
Business and Graphic Arts	NW12▼	3FT deg	A g	14	6M	M+/^ go	Dip$	BBBC	Ind	
Communication Studies and Graphic Arts	PW32▼	3FT deg	Ap	14	6M	M+/^	Dip$	BBCC	Ind	4 12/20
English and Graphic Arts	QW32▼	3FT deg	A+E	14	6M	M+/^	Dip$	BBCC	Ind	11
European Philosophy & Literature & Graphic Arts	VW72▼	3FT deg	A	14	6M	M+/^	Dip$	BBCC	Ind	
French and Graphic Arts	RW12▼	4FT deg	A g	14	6M	M+/^ go	Dip$	BBCC	Ind	
Geography and Graphic Arts	LW82▼	3FT deg	A+Gy	14	6M	M	Dip$	BBCC	Ind	
German and Graphic Arts	RW22▼	4FT deg	A g	14	6M	M+/^ go	Dip$	BBCCC	Ind	
Graphic Arts	E210▼	3FT deg	A+Pf g	14	6M	M	Dip$	BBCC	Ind	
Graphic Arts	W210▼	3FT deg	A+Pf g	14	6M	M	Dip$	BBCC	Ind	15
Graphic Arts and History	VW12▼	3FT deg	A	14	6M	M+/^	Dip$	BBCC	Ind	
Graphic Arts and Imaging Science	WW25▼	3FT deg	A+S	12	4M	M	Dip$	BCCC	Ind	
Graphic Arts and Italian	RW32▼	4FT deg	A g	14	6M	M+/^ go	Dip$	BBCC	Ind	
Graphic Arts and Law	MW32▼	3FT deg	A	14	6M	M	Dip$	BBCC	Ind	
Graphic Arts and Maths or Stats/Stat Modelling	GW12▼	3FT deg	A g	14	6M	M go	Dip$	BBCC	Ind	3
Graphic Arts and Music	WW32▼	3FT deg	Mu+A	14	6M	M+/^	Dip$	BBCC	Ind	
Graphic Arts and Real Time Computer Systems	WG25▼	3FT deg	A g	14	6M	M+/^ go	Dip$	BBCC	Ind	
Graphic Arts and Sociology	LW32▼	3FT deg	A	14	6M	M+/^	Dip$	BBCC	Ind	2
Graphic Arts and Spanish	RW42▼	4FT deg	A g	14	6M	M+/^ go	Dip$	BBCC	Ind	1
Graphic Arts and Women's Studies	WM29▼	3FT deg	A	14	6M	M+/^	Dip$	BBCC	Ind	
Illustration	W215▼	3FT deg	Fa g	16	8M	D go	Dip$	BBCCC	Ind	28
Illustration	E215▼	3FT deg	Fa g	16	8M	D go	Dip$	BBCCC	Ind	
Design (Graphic Design)	112W▼	2FT HND	A/Fa+Pf	8	2M	P	Dip	CCCC	Ind	
Design (Studio Crafts)	002W▼	2FT HND	A/Fa+Pf	8	2M	P	Dip	CCCC	Ind	
Informational Illustration	512W▼	2FT HND	A/Fa+Pf	8	2M	P	Dip	CCCC	Ind	

			98 expected requirements							96 entry stats
course details										
TITLE	CODE	COURSE	SUBJECTS	A/AS	NO/C	AGNVQ	IB	SQA(H)	SQA	RATIO A/AS
BARKING COLL										
Product Design (Extended)	E778	1EXT deg	M/P+Pf g	A	N	P				
Modelmaking	092E	2FT HND	Pf g	A	N	P				
Modelmaking	092W	2FT deg								
BARNSLEY COLL										
Combined Studies *Design*	E401	3FT deg	Pf g	EE	4M	M*	Ind	Ind	Ind	
Combined Studies *Design*	Y401	3FT deg	Pf g	EE	4M	M*	Ind	Ind	Ind	
Combined Studies *Fine Art*	Y401	3FT deg	Pf g	EE	4M	M*	Ind	Ind	Ind	
Combined Studies *Fine Art*	E401	3FT deg	Pf g	EE	4M	M*	Ind	Ind	Ind	
Design (Crafts) Multi-Disciplinary Option	62WE	2FT HND	Pf g	E	2M	P*	Ind	Ind	Ind	
Design (Crafts) Multi-Disciplinary Option	62WW	2FT HND	Pf g	E	2M	P*	Ind	Ind	Ind	
Design (Crafts) Textile Option	022E	2FT HND	Pf g	E	2M	P*	Ind	Ind	Ind	
Design (Crafts) Textile Option	022W	2FT HND	Pf g	E	2M	P*	Ind	Ind	Ind	
Design (Crafts) Three Dimensional Option	062W	2FT HND	Pf g	E	2M	P*	Ind	Ind	Ind	
Design (Crafts) Three Dimensional Option	062E	2FT HND	Pf g	E	2M	P*	Ind	Ind	Ind	
Graphic Design	012E	2FT HND	Pf g	E	2M	P*	Ind	Ind	Ind	
Graphic Design	012W	2FT HND	Pf g	E	2M	P*	Ind	Ind	Ind	
Industrial Design	032W	2FT HND	Pf g	E	2M	P*	Ind	Ind	Ind	
Industrial Design	032E	2FT HND	Pf g	E	2M	P*	Ind	Ind	Ind	
BASFORD HALL COLL										
Furniture Studies	024E	2FT HND	A/Ad/Ar/Ds/Ha	D-E	N	P	Ind	Ind	Ind	
BATH COLL of HE										
Creative Arts	W900	3FT deg	2(A/E/Mu/T)/Fa		N		Ind	$	$	9 10/20
Fine Art (Painting)	E101	3FT deg	Fa+Pf		N		Ind	X	X	
Fine Art (Painting)	W101	3FT deg	Fa+Pf		N		Ind	X	X	
Fine Art (Sculpture)	W102	3FT deg	Fa+Pf		N		Ind	X	X	
Fine Art (Sculpture)	E102	3FT deg	Fa+Pf		N		Ind	X	X	
Graphic Design	E200	3FT deg	Fa+Pf		N		Ind	X	X	
Graphic Design	W200	3FT deg	Fa+Pf		N		Ind	X	X	
Three Dimensional Design: Ceramics	W260	3FT deg	*		N		Ind	$	$	
Three Dimensional Design: Ceramics	E260	3FT deg	Fa+Pf		N		Ind	X	X	
Modular Programme (DipHE) *Art*	Y460	2FT Dip	A		N		Ind	$	$	
Modular Programme (DipHE) *Design & Technology*	Y460	2FT Dip	*		N		Ind	$	$	
Modular Programme (DipHE) *Textile Design Studies*	Y460	2FT Dip	A/Tx		N		Ind	$	$	
BLACKBURN COLL										
Graphic Design	E210	3FT deg	Fa+Pf g	2-4	N $	PA		Ind	Ind	
Graphic Design	W210	3FT deg	Fa+Pf g	2-4	N $	PA		Ind	Ind	
Visual Arts and Culture (Fine Art)	W150	3FT deg	Fa+Pf g	2-4	N $	PA		Ind	Ind	
Visual Arts and Culture (Fine Art)	E150	3FT deg	Fa+Pf g	2-4	N $	PA		Ind	Ind	
Textile Design	022W	2FT HND	Fa+Pf g	2-4	N $	PA		Ind	Ind	
Textile Design	022E	2FT HND	Fa+Pf g	2-4	N $	PA		Ind	Ind	
BLACKPOOL & FYLDE COLL										
Design (Graphic Design)	W210	3FT deg	*	10	4M		Ind	Ind	Ind	
Design (Graphic Design)	E210	3FT deg	*	10	4M		Ind	Ind	Ind	

			98 expected requirements							96 entry stats

course details

TITLE	CODE	COURSE	SUBJECTS	A/AS	ND/C	AGNVQ	IB	SQA(H)	SQA	RATIO A/AS
Design (Scientific & Natural History Illustrat)	E216	3FT deg	*	10	4M		Ind	Ind	Ind	
Design (Scientific & Natural History Illustrat)	W216	3FT deg	*	10	4M		Ind	Ind	Ind	
Design (Technical and Information Illustration)	W217	3FT deg	*	10	4M		Ind	Ind	Ind	
Design (Technical and Information Illustration)	E217	3FT deg	*	10	4M		Ind	Ind	Ind	
Design (Publications)	62PE	2FT HND	*	10	4M		Ind	Ind	Ind	
Design (Publications)	62PW	2FT HND	*	10	4M		Ind	Ind	Ind	

BOLTON INST

TITLE	CODE	COURSE	SUBJECTS	A/AS	ND/C	AGNVQ	IB	SQA(H)	SQA	RATIO A/AS
Accountancy and Creative Writing	NW49	3FT deg	* g	CD	MO	M*	24	BBCC	Ind	
Art & Design History and Creative Writing	VW49	3FT deg	* g	CD	MO	M*	24	BBCC	Ind	
Art & Design History and Design	EV24	3FT deg	* g	CD	MO	M*	24	BBCC	Ind	
Art & Design History and Visual Arts	EW41	3FT deg	* g	CD	MO	M*	24	BBCC	Ind	
Art and Design	EW12	3FT deg	* g	CD	MO	M*	24	BBCC	Ind	
Biology and Creative Writing	WC91	3FT deg	* g	CD	MO	M*	24	BBCC	Ind	
Business Economics and Creative Writing	LW19	3FT deg	* g	CD	MO	M*	24	BBCC	Ind	
Business Info Systems and Creative Writing	WG95	3FT deg	* g	CD	MO	M*	24	BBCC	Ind	
Business Studies and Creative Writing	NW1X	3FT deg	* g	CD	MO	M*	24	BBCC	Ind	
Business Studies and Creative Writing	WW2X	3FT deg	* g	CD	MO	M*	24	BBCC	Ind	
Community Studies and Creative Writing	LW5X	3FT deg	* g	CD	MO	M*	24	BBCC	Ind	
Computer Aided Product Design	HW72	3FT deg	M/S/Ad/Ds	10	3M	M$	Ind	Ind	Ind	
Computer Aided Product Design	HW7F	4FT deg	M/S/Ad/Ds	4	N	P$	Ind	Ind	Ind	
Computing and Creative Writing	GW5X	3FT deg	* g	CD	MO	M*	24	BBCC	Ind	
Creative Writing and Environmental Studies	FW9X	3FT deg	* g	CD	MO	M*	24	BBCC	Ind	
Creative Writing and European Cultural Studies	WT92	3FT deg	* g	CD	MO	M*	24	BBCC	Ind	
Creative Writing and Film and TV Studies	WW95	3FT deg	Me/T g	CD	Ind	Ind	24	BBCC	Ind	
Creative Writing and Gender and Women's Studies	WM99	3FT deg	* g	CD	MO	M*	24	BBCC	Ind	
Creative Writing and History	VW1X	3FT deg	* g	CD	MO	M*	24	BBCC	Ind	
Creative Writing and Human Resource Management	NW1Y	3FT deg	* g	CD	MO	M*	24	BBCC	Ind	
Creative Writing and Law	MW3X	3FT deg	* g	CD	MO	M*	24	BBCC	Ind	
Creative Writing and Leisure Studies	LWH9	3FT deg	* g	CD	MO	M*	24	BBCC	Ind	
Creative Writing and Literature	WQ92	3FT deg	* g	CD	MO	M*	24	BBCC	Ind	
Creative Writing and Marketing	NW5X	3FT deg	* g	CD	MO	M*	24	BBCC	Ind	
Creative Writing and Mathematics	GW5Y	3FT deg	* g	CD	MO	M*	24	BBCC	Ind	
Creative Writing and Operations Management	NW29	3FT deg	* g	CD	MO	M*	24	BBCC	Ind	
Creative Writing and Peace and War Studies	WV9C	3FT deg	* g	CD	MO	M*	24	BBCC	Ind	
Creative Writing and Philosophy	WV97	3FT deg	* g	CD	MO	M*	24	BBCC	Ind	
Creative Writing and Psychology	LW7X	3FT deg	* g	12	MO	D*	24	BBCC	Ind	
Creative Writing and Sociology	LW3X	3FT deg	* g	CD	MO	M	24	Ind	Ind	
Creative Writing and Theatre Studies	WW94	3FT deg	Me/T g	CD	Ind	Ind	24	BBCC	Ind	
Creative Writing and Tourism Studies	PW7X	3FT deg	* g	CD	MO	M*	24	BBCC	Ind	
Creative Writing and Urban and Cultural Studies	WL93	3FT deg	* g	CD	MO	M*	24	BBCC	Ind	
Design	E200	3FT deg	* g	CD	MO		24	BBCC	Ind	
Design and Accountancy	NW42	3FT deg	* g	CD	MO	M*	24	BBCC	Ind	
Design and Architectural Technology	KW22	3FT deg	* g	10	MO	M*	Ind	Ind	Ind	
Design and Biology	CW12	3FT deg	* g	CD	MO	M*	24	BBCC	Ind	
Design and Business Economics	LW12	3FT deg	* g	CD	MO	M*	24	BBCC	Ind	
Design and Business Information Systems	GW52	3FT deg	* g	CD	MO	M*	24	BBCC	Ind	
Design and Business Studies	WN21	3FT deg	* g	CD	MO	M*	24	BBCC	Ind	
Design and Community Studies	LW52	3FT deg	* g	CD	MO	M*	24	BBCC	Ind	
Design and Computing	GW5F	3FT deg	* g	CD	MO	M*	24	BBCC	Ind	
Design and Creative Writing	WW29	3FT deg	* g	CD	MO	M*	24	BBCC	Ind	
Design and Environmental Studies	FW92	3FT deg	* g	CD	MO	M*	24	BBCC	Ind	
Design and European Cultural Studies	TW22	3FT deg	* g	CD	MO	M*	24	BBCC	Ind	

course details | **98 expected requirements** | *96 entry stats*

TITLE	CODE	COURSE	SUBJECTS	A/AS	NO/C	AGNVQ	IB	SQA(H)	SQA	RATIO A/AS
Design and Film & TV Studies	WW25	3FT deg	Me/T g	CD	Ind	Ind	24	BBCC	Ind	
Design and French	RW12	3FT deg	F g	CD	Ind	Ind	24	BBCC	Ind	
Design and Gender & Women's Studies	MW92	3FT deg	* g	CD	MO	M*	24	BBCC	Ind	
Design and German	RW22	3FT deg	G g	CD	Ind	Ind	24	BBCC	Ind	
Design and History	VW12	3FT deg	* g	CD	MO	M*	24	BBCC	Ind	
Design and Human Resource Management	NW12	3FT deg	* g	CD	MO	M*	24	BBCC	Ind	
Design and Law	MW32	3FT deg	* g	CD	MO	M*	24	BBCC	Ind	
Design and Leisure Studies	LWH2	3FT deg	* g	CD	MO	M*	24	BBCC	Ind	
Design and Literature	QW22	3FT deg	* g	CD	MO	M*	24	BBCC	Ind	
Design and Marketing	NW52	3FT deg	* g	CD	MO	M*	24	BBCC	Ind	
Design and Mathematics	GW12	3FT deg	* g	CD	MO	M*	24	BBCC	Ind	
Design and Operations Management	NW22	3FT deg	* g	CD	MO	M*	24	BBCC	Ind	
Design and Organisations, Management & Work	NW72	3FT deg	* g	CD	MO	M*	24	BBCC	Ind	
Design and Peace & War Studies	VWC2	3FT deg	* g	CD	MO	M*	24	BBCC	Ind	
Design and Philosophy	VW72	3FT deg	* g	CD	MO	M*	24	BBCC	Ind	
Design and Psychology	LW72	3FT deg	* g	12	MO	D*	24	BBCC	Ind	
Design and Simulation/Virtual Environment	GW72	3FT deg	* g	10	MO	M*	Ind	Ind	Ind	
Design and Theatre Studies	WW24	3FT deg	Me/T g	CD	Ind	Ind	24	BBCC	Ind	
Design and Tourism Studies	PW72	3FT deg	* g	CD	MO	M*	24	BBCC	Ind	
Design and Urban & Cultural Studies	LW32	3FT deg	* g	CD	MO	M*	24	BBCC	Ind	
Gender & Women's Studies and Sociology	LW3Y	3FT deg	* g	CD	MO	M	24	Ind	Ind	
Simulation and Virtual Environment	H7W2	3FT deg	M/S	10	3M	M$	Ind	Ind	Ind	
Simulation and Virtual Environment (4 yrs)	H7WF	4FT deg	M/S	4	N	P$	Ind	Ind	Ind	
Textiles (Technology and Design)	JW42	3FT deg	* g	10	3M	M*	Ind	Ind	Ind	
Textiles (Technology and Design)	JW4F	4FT deg	* g	4	N	P*	Ind	Ind	Ind	
Visual Arts	E150	3FT deg	g	CD	MO	M*	24	BBCC	Ind	
Visual Arts and Accountancy	NW41	3FT deg	* g	CD	MO	M*	24	BBCC	Ind	
Visual Arts and Biology	CW11	3FT deg	* g	CD	MO	M*	24	BBCC	Ind	
Visual Arts and Business Economics	LW11	3FT deg	* g	CD	MO	M*	24	BBCC	Ind	
Visual Arts and Business Information Systems	GW51	3FT deg	* g	CD	MO	M*	24	BBCC	Ind	
Visual Arts and Business Studies	NW1C	3FT deg	* g	CD	MO	M*	24	BBCC	Ind	
Visual Arts and Community Studies	LW51	3FT deg	* g	CD	MO	M*	24	BBCC	Ind	
Visual Arts and Computing	GW5C	3FT deg	* g	CD	MO	M*	24	BBCC	Ind	
Visual Arts and Creative Writing	QW31	3FT deg	g	CD	MO	M*	24	BBCC	Ind	
Visual Arts and Design	EW21	3FT deg	g	CD	MO	M*	24	BBCC	Ind	
Visual Arts and Environmental Studies	FW91	3FT deg	* g	CD	MO	M*	24	BBCC	Ind	
Visual Arts and European Cultural Studies	TW21	3FT deg	* g	CD	MO	M*	24	BBCC	Ind	
Visual Arts and Film and TV Studies	WW51	3FT deg	Me/T g	CD	Ind	Ind	24	BBCC	Ind	
Visual Arts and French	WR11	3FT deg	F g	CD	Ind	Ind	24	BBCC	Ind	
Visual Arts and Gender & Women's Studies	MW91	3FT deg	* g	CD	MO	M*	24	BBCC	Ind	
Visual Arts and Gender & Women's Studies	MW9X	3FT deg	* g	CD	MO	M*	24	BBCC	Ind	
Visual Arts and German	WR12	3FT deg	G g	CD	Ind	Ind	24	BBCC	Ind	
Visual Arts and History	VW11	3FT deg	* g	CD	MO	M*	24	BBCC	Ind	
Visual Arts and Law	MW31	3FT deg	* g	CD	MO	M*	24	BBCC	Ind	
Visual Arts and Leisure Studies	LW31	3FT deg	* g	CD	MO	M*	24	BBCC	Ind	
Visual Arts and Literature	QW21	3FT deg	* g	10	MO	M*	24	BBCC	Ind	
Visual Arts and Marketing	NW51	3FT deg	* g	CD	MO	M*	24	BBCC	Ind	
Visual Arts and Mathematics	GW11	3FT deg	* g	DD	MO	M*	24	BBCC	Ind	
Visual Arts and Operations Management	NW21	3FT deg	* g	CD	MO	M*	24	BBCC	Ind	
Visual Arts and Organisations, Management & Work	NW71	3FT deg	* g	CD	MO	M*	24	BBCC	Ind	
Visual Arts and Peace & War Studies	VWC1	3FT deg	* g	CD	MO	M*	24	BBCC	Ind	
Visual Arts and Philosophy	VW71	3FT deg	* g	10	MO	M*	24	BBCC	Ind	

| | | | 98 expected requirements | | | | | | | 96 entry stats | |

TITLE	CODE	COURSE	SUBJECTS	A/AS	ND/C	AGNVQ	IB	SQA(H)	SQA	RATIO A/AS	
Visual Arts and Product Design	WH17	3FT deg	* g	10	MO	M*	Ind	Ind	Ind		
Visual Arts and Psychology	LW71	3FT deg	* g	12	MO	D*	24	BBCC	Ind		
Visual Arts and Theatre Studies	WW41	3FT deg	* g	10	MO	M*	24	BBCC	Ind		
Visual Arts and Tourism Studies	PW71	3FT deg	* g	CD	MO	M*	24	BBCC	Ind		
Visual Arts and Urban & Cultural Studies	KW41	3FT deg	* g	CD	MO	M*	24	BBCC	Ind		
Design and Technology	92JW	2FT HND	M/S/Ad/Ds	4	N	P$	Ind	Ind	Ind		

BOURNEMOUTH Univ

TITLE	CODE	COURSE	SUBJECTS	A/AS	ND/C	AGNVQ	IB	SQA(H)	SQA	RATIO	A/AS
Computer Visualisation and Animation	W270	3FT deg	A/M g	18-22	MO+4D	D$ go	Ind	ABBBB	Ind	11	16/28
Creative Advertising	W215	3FT deg	* g	BBC	MO+5D	D$^ go	30	ABBBB	Ind	21	16/22
Creative Advertising	E215	3FT deg	* g	BBC	MO+5D	D$^ go	30	ABBBB	Ind		
Interior Design	E260	4SW deg	A/Ad/Ds g	12-16	MO $	M$ go	Ind	CCCC	Ind		
Interior Design	W260	4SW deg	A/Ad/Ds g	12-16	MO $	M$ go	Ind	CCCC	Ind	4	8/18
Product Design	W230	4SW deg	2(Ar/M/P) g	CC-CCE	MO	M$ go	Ind	CCCC	Ind	7	8/18
Product Design	E230	4SW deg	2(Ar/M/P) g	CC-CCE	MO	M$ go	Ind	CCCC	Ind		
Product Design Visualisation	E231	4SW deg	2(Ar/M/P) g	BC-CCC	MO	M$ go	Ind	CCCC	Ind		
Product Design Visualisation	W231	4SW deg	2(Ar/M/P) g	BC-CCC	MO	M$ go	Ind	CCCC	Ind	4	6/19

BOURNEMOUTH and POOLE COLLEGE of A & D

TITLE	CODE	COURSE	SUBJECTS	A/AS	ND/C	AGNVQ	IB	SQA(H)	SQA	RATIO A/AS	
Costume Design for the Stage and Screen	E490	3FT deg	Pf	E	N $	P	Ind	Ind	N$		
Fine Art	E100	3FT deg	Pf	EE	N $	P	Ind	Ind	N$		
Graphic Design	E210	3FT deg	Pf	EE	N $	P	Ind	Ind	N$		
Integrated Three Dimensional Design	E260	3FT deg	Pf	EE	N $	P	Ind	Ind	N$		
Arts and Event Administration	11WE	2FT HND		E	N $	P	Ind	Ind	N$		
Arts and Event Administration	11WN	2FT HND		E	N $	P	Ind	Ind	N$		
Design (Animation)	072E	2FT HND	Pf	E	N $	P	Ind	Ind	N$		
Design (Design Modelmaking)	092E	2FT HND	Pf	E	N $	P	Ind	Ind	N$		
Design (Editorial/Nat History/Tech Illustration)	512E	2FT HND	Pf	E	N $	P	Ind	Ind	N$		
Design (Fashion/Fashion Marketing)	022E	2FT HND	Pf	E	N $	P	Ind	Ind	N$		
Design (Photography)	082E	2FT HND	Pf	E	N $	P	Ind	Ind	N$		

BRADFORD & ILKLEY Comm COLL

TITLE	CODE	COURSE	SUBJECTS	A/AS	ND/C	AGNVQ	IB	SQA(H)	SQA	RATIO A/AS	
Art and Design	WW12	3FT deg	A/Pf	C	N	Ind	$	Ind	Ind		
Art and Design	EW12	3FT deg	A/Pf	C	N	Ind	$	Ind	Ind		
Communication Design (Level 3 only)	E213	3FT deg	A/Pf		HN	X		Ind	Ind		
Communication Design (Level 3 only)	W213	3FT deg	A/Pf		HN	X		Ind	Ind		
Design Crafts & Manufacture	E230	3FT deg	A/Pf	C	N	Ind		Ind	Ind		
Design Crafts & Manufacture	W230	3FT deg	A/Pf	C	N	Ind		Ind	Ind		
European Textile Design	W220	3FT deg	A/Pf	C	N	Ind	$	Ind	Ind		
European Textile Design	E220	3FT deg	A/Pf	C	N	Ind	$	Ind	Ind		
Design (Communications)	012E	2FT HND	A/Pf	C	N	Ind	$	Ind	Ind		
Design (Communications)	012W	2FT HND	A/Pf	C	N	Ind	$	Ind	Ind		

BRETTON HALL

TITLE	CODE	COURSE	SUBJECTS	A/AS	ND/C	AGNVQ	IB	SQA(H)	SQA	RATIO	A/AS
Arts and Education (Art)	XW92	3FT deg	A	CC	MO		Ind	CCC	Ind	3	8/20
Fashion	W220	3FT deg	Pf	CD-CC	Ind		Ind	CCC	Ind		
Fashion	E220	3FT deg	Pf	CD-CC	Ind		Ind	CCC	Ind		
Fine Art (Ceramics)	W190	3FT deg	Pf	CD-CC	Ind		Ind	CCC	Ind		
Fine Art (Ceramics)	E190	3FT deg	Pf	CC	MO		Ind	CCC	Ind		
Fine Art (Painting and Printmaking)	E170	3FT deg	Pf	CC	MO		Ind	CCC	Ind		
Fine Art (Painting and Printmaking)	W170	3FT deg	Pf	CD-CC	Ind		Ind	CCC	Ind		
Fine Art (Sculpture)	W130	3FT deg	Pf	CD-CC	Ind		Ind	CCC	Ind		
Fine Art (Sculpture)	E130	3FT deg	Pf	CD-CC	MO		Ind	CCC	Ind		
Graphic Design	E210	3FT deg	Pf	CC	MO		Ind	CCC	Ind		

			98 expected requirements							96 entry stats
TITLE	CODE	COURSE	SUBJECTS	A/AS	ND/C	AGNVQ	IB	SQA(H)	SQA	RATIO A/AS
Graphic Design	W210	3FT deg	Pf	CC	MO		Ind	CCC	Ind	
Textile and Surface Pattern Design	W225	3FT deg	Pf	CD-CC	MO		Ind	CCC	Ind	
Textile and Surface Pattern Design	E225	3FT deg	Pf	CD-CC	MO		Ind	CCC	Ind	

Univ of BRIGHTON

TITLE	CODE	COURSE	SUBJECTS	A/AS	ND/C	AGNVQ	IB	SQA(H)	SQA	RATIO A/AS
Art and Design (Craft)	006W▼	2FT HND								
Art and Design (Craft)	006E▼	2FT HND								
Art and Design (Fine Art)	001W▼	2FT HND								
Art and Design (Fine Art)	001E▼	2FT HND								
Critical Fine Art Practice	E100	3FT deg	Fa+Pf g	X	N $	Ind$ go	Ind$	Ind$	Ind$	
Critical Fine Art Practice	W100	3FT deg	Fa+Pf g	X	N $	Ind$ go	Ind$	Ind$	Ind$	
Dance with Visual Practice	E4W1	3FT deg	Fa+Pf g		N $	Ind$ go	Ind$	Ind$	Ind$	
Dance with Visual Practice	W4W1	3FT deg	Fa+Pf g		N $	Ind$ go	Ind$	Ind$	Ind$	
Fashion Design with Business St(4-year sandwich)	E2ND	4SW deg	Fa+Pf g		N $	Ind$ go	Ind$	Ind$	Ind$	
Fashion Design with Business St(4-year sandwich)	W2ND	4SW deg	Fa+Pf g		N $	Ind$ go	Ind$	Ind$	Ind$	
Fashion Textiles Des with Bus St (4-yr sandwich)	W2NC	4SW deg	Fa+Pf g		N $	Ind$ go	Ind$	Ind$	Ind$	
Fashion Textiles Des with Bus St (4-yr sandwich)	E2NC	4SW deg	Fa+Pf g		N $	Ind$ go	Ind$	Ind$	Ind$	
Fine Art Painting	E120	3FT deg	Fa+Pf g		N $	Ind$ go	Ind$	Ind$	Ind$	
Fine Art Painting	W120	3FT deg	Fa+Pf g		N $	Ind$ go	Ind$	Ind$	Ind$	
Fine Art Printmaking	W140	3FT deg	Fa+Pf g		N $	Ind$ go	Ind$	Ind$	Ind$	
Fine Art Printmaking	E140	3FT deg	Fa+Pf g		N $	Ind$ go	Ind$	Ind$	Ind$	
Fine Art Sculpture	E130	3FT deg	Fa+Pf g		N $	Ind$ go	Ind$	Ind$	Ind$	
Fine Art Scuplture	W130	3FT deg	Fa+Pf g		N $	Ind$ go	Ind$	Ind$	Ind$	
Graphic Design	W210	3FT deg	Fa+Pf g		N $	Ind$ go	Ind$	Ind$	Ind$	
Graphic Design	E210	3FT deg	Fa+Pf g		N $	Ind$ go	Ind$	Ind$	Ind$	
Illustration	E215	3FT deg	Fa+Pf g		N $	Ind$ go	Ind$	Ind$	Ind$	
Illustration	W215	3FT deg	Fa+Pf g		N $	Ind$ go	Ind$	Ind$	Ind$	
Music with Visual Practice	E3W1	3FT deg	Fa+Pf g		N $	Ind$ go	Ind$	Ind$	Ind$	
Music with Visual Practice	W3W1	3FT deg	Fa+Pf g		N $	Ind$ go	Ind$	Ind$	Ind$	
Product Design (4 year sandwich)	W231	4SW deg	Pf+M+P/S g	18	5M $	ME/M$^	25$	BBBC$	Ind	
Product Design (4 year sandwich)	E231	4SW deg	M+P/g+Pf	18	5M $	ME/M$^	25$	BBBC$	Ind	
Theatre with Visual Practice	E4WC	3FT deg	Fa+Pf g		N $	Ind$ go	Ind$	Ind$	Ind$	
Theatre with Visual Practice	W4WC	3FT deg	Fa+Pf g		N $	Ind$ go	Ind$	Ind$	Ind$	
Three Dimensional Crafts	E610	3FT deg	Fa+Pf g		N $	Ind$ go	Ind$	Ind$	Ind$	
Three Dimensional Crafts	W610	3FT deg	Fa+Pf g		N $	Ind$ go	Ind$	Ind$	Ind$	
Three Dimensional Design for Production	W230	3FT deg	Fa+Pf g		N $	Ind$ go	Ind$	Ind$	Ind$	
Three Dimensional Design for Production	E230	3FT deg	Fa+Pf g		N $	Ind$ go	Ind$	Ind$	Ind$	
2D/3D Design and Communication	002E▼	2FT HND	Fa/Ad/Ar		N $	Ind$	Ind$	Ind$	Ind$	
2D/3D Design and Communication	002W▼	2FT HND	Fa/Ad/Ar		N $	Ind$	Ind$	Ind$	Ind$	
Art and Design (Craft)	006E	2FT HND	Fa		N	A				
Art and Design (Crafts)	006W	2FT HND								
Art and Design (Fine Art)	001E	2FT HND	Fa		N	A				
Art and Design (Fine Art)	001W	2FT HND								

BRISTOL, Univ of the W of England

TITLE	CODE	COURSE	SUBJECTS	A/AS	ND/C	AGNVQ	IB	SQA(H)	SQA	RATIO A/AS
Ceramics	E233	3FT deg	Fa+Pf g		N $	PA go	Dip$	Ind	N$	
Fashion/Texile Design	E226	3FT deg	Fa+Pf g		N $	PA go	Dip$	Ind	N$	
Fine Art	E100	3FT deg	Fa+Pf g		N $	PA go	Dip$	Ind	N$	
Fine Art in Context	E190	3FT deg	Fa+Pf g		N $	PA go	Dip$	Ind	N$	
Graphic Design	E211	3FT deg	Fa+Pf g		N $	P$ go	Dip$	Ind	N$	
Illustration	E214	3FT deg	Fa+Pf g		N $	P$ go	Dip$	Ind	N$	
Time-Based Media	E253	3FT deg	Fa+Pf g		N $	P$ go	Dip$	Ind	N$	
Community Arts (Bath College)	199W▼	2FT HND	* g	E	N	P* gi	24	Ind	N	

TITLE	CODE	COURSE	SUBJECTS	A/AS	ND/C	AGNVQ	IB	SQA(H)	SQA	RATIO A/AS	
BRUNEL Univ, West London											
American Studies/Art	Q4W1	3FT deg	A g	14	MO $	M* go	22$	BCCC$	Ind		
Drama/Art	W4W1	3FT deg	T+A g	BC	MO $	P go	22$	BCCC$	Ind		
English/Art	Q3W1	3FT deg	E+A g	14	MO $	M* go	24$	BCCC$	Ind		
History/Art	V1W1	3FT deg	H+A g	14	MO $	M* go	22$	BCCC$	Ind		
Industrial Design and Technology	HW72	3FT deg	Ds	CCC	4M $	Ind	26	CCCCC$	Ind		
Industrial Design and Technology (Thick SW)	HW7F	4SW deg	Ds	CCC	4M $	Ind	26	CCCCC$	Ind		
Music/Art	W3W1	3FT deg	A g	14	MO $	M* go	26$	BCCC$	Ind		
BUCKINGHAMSHIRE COLLEGE											
Business Information Tech with Image Processing	G7W2	3FT deg		8-10	MO	M	Ind	CCC	Ind		
Ceramics with Glass	WJ23	3FT deg									
Ceramics with Glass	EJ23	3FT deg		CC	1D		Ind	Ind	Ind		
Computer Aided Design (Conversion to degree)	HW72	1FT/2FT deg			HN				HN		
Computer Engineering with Image Processing	G5W2	3FT deg		8-10	MO	M	Ind	CCC	Ind		
Computing with Image Processing	G5WF	3FT deg		8-10	MO	M	Ind	CCC	Ind		
Design Technology	W240	3FT deg		8-10	MO	M	Ind	CCC	Ind		
Design Technology with Management	W2N1	3FT deg									
Design Technology with Marketing	W2N5	3FT deg									
Designed Metalwork & Jewellery	W2W6	3FT deg									
Designed Metalwork & Jewellery	E2W6	3FT deg		CC	1D		Ind	Ind	Ind		
Furniture & Related Product Design	EJ24	3FT deg		CC	1D		Ind	Ind	Ind		
Furniture & Related Product Design	WJ24	3 deg									
Furniture Design & Craftsmanship	EW26	3FT deg		CD	1D		Ind	Ind	Ind		
Furniture Design & Craftsmanship	WW26	3FT deg		8-12	Ind		Ind	Ind	Ind	6	10/14
Furniture Restoration & Craftsmanship	W610	3FT deg		8-12	Ind		Ind	Ind	Ind		
Furniture Restoration & Craftsmanship	E610	3FT deg		8-12	Ind		Ind	Ind	Ind		
Graphic Design & Advertising	E2P3	3FT deg		CC	1D		Ind	Ind	Ind		
Graphic Design & Advertising	W2P3	3FT deg									
Interior Design	W260	3FT deg									
Interior Design	E260	3FT deg		10	2D	M	27	CCCC	Ind		
Product Design	H7W2	3FT deg		8-10	MO	M	Ind	CCC	Ind		
Textile Design & Surface Decoration	E220	3FT deg		CC	1D		Ind	Ind	Ind		
Textile Design & Surface Decoration	W220	3FT deg									
Three Dimensional Multi-Disciplinary Design	W200	3FT deg									
Three Dimensional Multi-Disciplinary Design	E200	3FT deg		CC	1D		Ind	Ind	Ind		
Building Design	22WK	2FT HND		4	N	P	Ind	CC	Ind		
Design (Furniture)	016E	2FT HND		4-8	Ind	M	Ind	Ind	Ind		
Design (Furniture)	016W	2FT HND		4-8	Ind	M	Ind	Ind	Ind	3	
Furniture Studies	42JE	2FT HND									
Furniture Studies	42JW	2FT HND									
CANTERBURY CHRIST CHURCH COLL of HE											
American Studies with Art	Q4W1	4FT deg	A g	CC	MO	M	24	Ind	Ind	1	
Art	W100	3FT deg	A g	CC	MO	M	24	Ind	Ind	12	
Art and American Studies	QW41	3FT deg	A g	CC	MO	M	24	Ind	Ind	2	
Art and Social Science	LW31	3FT deg	A g	CC	MO	M	24	Ind	Ind	4	
Art with American Studies	W1Q4	3FT deg	A g	CC	MO	M	24	Ind	Ind	4	
Art with Business Studies	W1N1	3FT deg	A g	CC	MO	M	24	Ind	Ind	14	
Art with Early Childhood Studies	W1X9	3FT deg	A g	CC	MO	M	24	Ind	Ind		
Art with English	W1Q3	3FT deg	E+A	CC	MO	M	24	Ind	Ind	4	12/16
Art with French	W1R1	3FT deg	A+F g	CC	MO	M	24	Ind	Ind		
Art with Geography	W1L8	3FT deg	A+Gy g	CC	MO	M	24	Ind	Ind	4	
Art with History	W1V1	3FT deg	A+H g	CC	MO	M	24	Ind	Ind	11	
Art with Information Technology	W1G5	3FT deg	A g	CC	MO	M	24	Ind	Ind	10	

course details   **98 expected requirements**   *96 entry stats*

course details			98 expected requirements							96 entry stats	
TITLE	CODE	COURSE	SUBJECTS	A/AS	ND/C	AGNVQ	IB	SQA(H)	SQA	RATIO A/AS	
Art with Marketing	W1N5	3FT deg	A g	CC	MO	M	24	Ind	Ind	5	
Art with Mathematics	W1G1	3FT deg	A+M g	DD	Ind	Ind	24	Ind	Ind		
Art with Media Studies	W1P4	3FT deg	A g	CC	MO	M	24	Ind	Ind		
Art with Music	W1W3	3FT deg	A+Mu g	CC	MO	M	24	Ind	Ind		
Art with Psychology	W1L7	3FT deg	A+Ps g	CC	MO	M	24	Ind	Ind	31	
Art with Radio, Film & Television Studies	W1W5	3FT deg	A g	CC	MO	M	24	Ind	Ind	45	
Art with Religious Studies	W1V8	3FT deg	A g	CC	MO	M	24	Ind	Ind	3	
Art with Science	W1Y1	3FT deg	A+S g	DD	Ind	Ind	24	Ind	Ind		
Art with Social Science	W1L3	3FT deg	A g	CC	MO	M	24	Ind	Ind	2	
Art with Sport Science	W1B6	3FT deg	A g	CC	MO	M	24	Ind	Ind		
Art with Statistics	W1G4	3FT deg	A+M g	DD	Ind	Ind	24	Ind	Ind		
Art with Tourism Studies	W1P7	3FT deg	A g	CC	MO	M	24	Ind	Ind	3	
Business Studies and Art	WN11	3FT deg	A g	CC	MO	M	24	Ind	Ind	7	
Business Studies with Art	N1W1	3FT deg	A g	CC	MO	M	24	Ind	Ind	12	
Early Childhood Studies and Art	XW91	3FT deg	A g	CC	MO	M	24	Ind	Ind	1	
Early Childhood Studies with Art	X9W1	3FT deg	A g	CC	MO	M	24	Ind	Ind	4	
English and Art	WQ13	3FT deg	E+A	CC	MO	M	24	Ind	Ind	16	
English with Art	Q3W1	3FT deg	E+A	CC	MO	M	24	Ind	Ind	4	10/20
French and Art	RW11	3FT deg	F+A g	CC	MO	M	24	Ind	Ind		
Geography and Art	LW81	3FT deg	Gy+A g	CC	MO	M	24	Ind	Ind	3	
Geography with Art	L8W1	3FT deg	Gy+A g	CC	MO	M	24	Ind	Ind	10	
History and Art	VW11	3FT deg	A+H g	CC	MO	M	24	Ind	Ind	2	
History with Art	V1W1	3FT deg	A+H g	CC	MO	M	24	Ind	Ind		
Information Technology and Art	WG15	3FT deg	A g	CC	MO	M	24	Ind	Ind		
Information Technology with Art	G5W1	3FT deg	A g	CC	MO	M	24	Ind	Ind		
Marketing and Art	NW51	3FT deg	A g	CC	MO	M	24	Ind	Ind	2	
Marketing with Art	N5W1	3FT deg	A g	CC	MO	M	24	Ind	Ind	7	
Mathematics and Art	WG11	3FT deg	A+M g	DD	Ind	Ind	24	Ind	Ind	4	
Mathematics with Art	G1W1	3FT deg	M+A g	DD	Ind	Ind	24	Ind	Ind		
Media Studies and Art	PW41	3FT deg	A g	CC	MO	M	24	Ind	Ind		
Media Studies with Art	P4W1	3FT deg	A g	CC	MO	M	24	Ind	Ind		
Music and Art	WW13	3FT deg	A+Mu g	CC	MO	M	24	Ind	Ind	2	
Music with Art	W3W1	3FT deg	Mu+A g	CC	MO	M	24	Ind	Ind		
Psychology and Art	LW71	3FT deg	Ps+A g	CC	MO	M	24	Ind	Ind		
Psychology with Art	L7W1	3FT deg	Ps+A g	CC	MO	M	24	Ind	Ind	10	
Radio, Film and Television Studies and Art	WW51	3FT deg	A g	CC	MO	M	24	Ind	Ind	19	
Radio, Film and Television Studies with Art	W5W1	3FT deg	A g	CC	MO	M	24	Ind	Ind	9	
Religious Studies and Art	VW81	3FT deg	A g	CC	MO	M	24	Ind	Ind	3	
Religious Studies with Art	V8W1	3FT deg	A g	CC	MO	M	24	Ind	Ind		
Religious Studies with Early Childhood Studies	V8W9	3FT deg	* g	CC	MO	M	24	Ind	Ind		
Science and Art	YW11	3FT deg	A+S g	DD	Ind	Ind	24	Ind	Ind		
Science with Art	Y1W1	3FT deg	A+S g	DD	Ind	Ind	24	Ind	Ind		
Social Science with Art	L3W1	3FT deg	A g	CC	MO	M	24	Ind	Ind	2	
Sport Science and Art	WB16	3FT deg	A g	CC	MO	M	24	Ind	Ind		
Sport Science with Art	B6W1	3FT deg	A g	CC	MO	M	24	Ind	Ind		
Statistics and Art	GW41	3FT deg	M+A g	DD	Ind	Ind	24	Ind	Ind		
Statistics with Art	G4W1	3FT deg	M+A g	DD	Ind	Ind	24	Ind	Ind		
Tourism Studies and Art	PW71	3FT deg	A g	CC	MO	M	24	Ind	Ind		
Tourism Studies with Art	P7W1	3FT deg	A g	CC	MO	M	24	Ind	Ind	5	

Univ of Wales INST, CARDIFF

Architectural Design and Technology	E236	3FT deg	Ad/Ds g	EE	N	PA go	Ind	CCCC	Ind		
Art and Aesthetics	EX19	3FT deg	Fa g	EE	N	MA go					
Art and Aesthetics	WX19	3FT deg	Fa g	EE	N	MA go	Ind	Ind	Ind		

course details			98 expected requirements							96 entry stats
TITLE	CODE	COURSE	SUBJECTS	A/AS	ND/C	AGNVQ	IB	SQA(H)	SQA	RATIO A/AS
Ceramics	E232	3FT deg	Fa+Pf g	4	N	Ind	Ind	Ind	Ind	
Ceramics	W232	3FT deg	Fa+Pf g	4	N	Ind	Ind	Ind	Ind	
Design Engineering	HW12	3FT deg		EE	N	P$	Ind	CCCC	Ind	
Design Engineering	EW12	3FT deg		EE	N	P$	Ind	CCCC	Ind	
Fine Art	E100	3FT deg	Fa+Pf g	EE	N	Ind	Ind	Ind	Ind	
Fine Art	W100	3FT deg	Fa+Pf g	EE	N	Ind	Ind	Ind	Ind	
Graphic Communication	W211	3FT deg	Ad g		HN					
Graphic Communication	E211	3FT deg	Ad g		HN					
Industrial Design	E230	3FT deg	Fa g	4	N	Ind	Ind	Ind	Ind	
Industrial Design	W230	3FT deg	Fa g	4	N	Ind	Ind	Ind	Ind	
Interior Architecture	W260	3FT deg	Fa g	4	N	Ind	Ind	Ind	Ind	
Interior Architecture	E260	3FT deg	Fa g	4	N	Ind	Ind	Ind	Ind	
Architectural Design and Technology	632E	2FT HND	* g	12	3M	M$ go	Ind	CC	Ind	
Design (Graphic Communication)	112W	2 HND	A/Ad g	E	N	P go	Ind	CC	Ind	
Design (Graphic Communication)	112E	2FT HND	A/Ad g	E	N	P go	Ind	CC	Ind	
Design (Textile/Surface Pattern Design)	022W	2FT HND	A/Ad/Tx g	E	N	P go	Ind	CC	Ind	
Design (Textile/Surface Pattern Design)	022E	2FT HND	A/Ad/Tx g	E	N	P go	Ind	CC	Ind	

CARMARTHENSHIRE COLLEGE

Art and Design (Top-up)	EW12	1FT deg								
Art and Design (Top-up)	WW12	1FT deg		X	X	X	X	X	X	
Fashion/Textiles/Surface Decoration	522W	2FT HND		X	Ind	Ind	Ind	X	Ind	
Fashion/Textiles/Surface Decoration	522E	2FT HND		X	Ind	Ind	Ind	X	Ind	
Fine Art	001W	2FT HND		X	Ind	Ind	Ind	X	Ind	
Fine Art	001E	2FT HND		X	Ind	Ind	Ind	X	Ind	
Graphics/Illustration/Wildlife	612E	2FT HND		X	Ind	Ind	Ind	X	Ind	
Graphics/Illustration/Wildlife	612W	2FT HND		X	Ind	Ind	Ind	X	Ind	
Three-Dimensional Design	062E	2FT HND		X	Ind	Ind	Ind	X	Ind	
Three-Dimensional Design	062W	2FT HND		X	Ind	Ind	Ind	X	Ind	

Univ of CENTRAL ENGLAND

Art & Design by Negotiated Study	E150	3FT deg	Fa/Pf	18	MO	M$	28	BBBB	Ind	
Art & Design by Negotiated Study	W150	3FT deg	Fa/Pf	18	MO	M$	28	BBBB	Ind	61
Art and Design	WW12▼	2FT Dip	Fa/Pf	18	MO	M$	28	BBBB	Ind	
Art and Design	EW12▼	2FT Dip	Fa/Pf	18	MO	M$	28	BBBB	Ind	
Design, Media & Management	E290	3FT deg	* g	18	MO	M$	28	BBBB	Ind	
Design, Media and Management	W290	3FT deg	* g	18	MO	M$	28	BBBB	Ind	9 12/20
Fashion Design	E220	3FT deg	Fa/Pf	18	MO	M$	28	BBBB	Ind	
Fashion Design	W220	3FT deg	Fa/Pf	18	MO	M$	28	BBBB	Ind	
Fine Art	E101	3FT deg	Fa/Pf	18	MO	M$	28	BBBB	Ind	
Fine Art	W101	3FT deg	Fa/Pf	18	MO	M$	28	BBBB	Ind	15 14/28
Jewellery and Silversmithing	WW26	3FT deg	Fa/Pf	18	MO	M$	28	BBBB	Ind	7
Jewellery and Silversmithing	EW26	3FT deg	Fa/Pf	18	MO	M$	28	BBBB	Ind	
Textile Design	W221	3FT deg	Fa/Pf	18	MO	M$	28	BBBB	Ind	
Textile Design	E221	3FT deg	Fa/Pf	18	MO	M$	28	BBBB	Ind	
Three-Dimensional Design (Ceramics with Glass)	EJ23	3FT deg	Fa/Pf	18	MO	M$	28	BBBB	Ind	
Three-Dimensional Design (Ceramics with Glass)	WJ23	3FT deg	Fa/Pf	18	MO	M$	28	BBBB	Ind	12
Three-Dimensional Design (Furniture Design)	W236	3FT deg	Fa/Pf	18	MO	M$	28	BBBB	Ind	15
Three-Dimensional Design (Furniture Design)	E236	3FT deg	Fa/Pf	18	MO	M$	28	BBBB	Ind	
Three-Dimensional Design (Industrial Design)	E231	3FT deg	Fa/Pf	18	MO	M$	28	BBBB	Ind	
Three-Dimensional Design (Industrial Design)	W231	3FT deg	Fa/Pf	18	MO	M$	28	BBBB	Ind	6 13/16
Three-Dimensional Design (Interior Design)	W260	3FT deg	Fa/Pf	18	MO	M$	28	BBBB	Ind	15
Three-Dimensional Design (Interior Design)	E260	3FT deg	Fa/Pf	18	MO	M$	28	BBBB	Ind	
Visual Communication	EW32	3FT deg	Fa/Pf	18	MO	M$	28	BBBB	Ind	

TITLE	CODE	COURSE	SUBJECTS	A/AS	NO/C	RGNVQ	IB	SQA(H)	SQA	RATIO A/AS
Visual Communication	PW32	3FT deg	Fa/Pf	18	MO	M$	28	BBBB	Ind	20
Visual Communication (Graphic Design)	W210	3FT deg	Fa/Pf	18	MO	M$	28	BBBB	Ind	63 12/20
Visual Communication (Graphic Design)	E210	3FT deg	Fa/Pf	18	MO	M$	28	BBBB	Ind	
Visual Communication (Illustration)	E215	3FT deg	Fa/Pf	18	MO	M$	28	BBBB	Ind	
Visual Communication (Illustration)	W215	3FT deg	Fa/Pf	18	MO	M$	28	BBBB	Ind	24 14/20
Visual Communication (Information Media)	WP23	3FT deg	Fa/Pf	18	MO	M$	28	BBBB	Ind	
Visual Communication (Information Media)	EP23	3FT deg	Fa/Pf	18	MO	M$	28	BBBB	Ind	
Visual Communication (Time-Based Media)	EH26	3FT deg	FA/Pf	18	MO	M$	28	BBBB	Ind	
Visual Communication (Time-Based Media)	WH26	3FT deg	Fa/Pf	18	MO	M$	28	BBBB	Ind	
Design (Gemmology)	066W	2FT HND	Fa/Pf	8	N	P	24	CCC	Ind	
Design (Gemmology)	066E	2FT HND	Fa/Pf	8	N	P	24	CCC	Ind	
Design (Horology)	016E	2FT HND	Fa/Pf	8	N	P	24	CCC	Ind	
Design (Horology)	016W	2FT HND	Fa/Pf	8	N	P	24	CCC	Ind	
Design (Jewellery and Silversmithing)	62WW	2FT HND	Fa/Pf	8	N	P	24	CCC	Ind	
Design (Jewellery and Silversmithing)	62WE	2FT HND	Fa/Pf	8	N	P	24	CCC	Ind	

Univ of CENTRAL LANCASHIRE

TITLE	CODE	COURSE	SUBJECTS	A/AS	NO/C	RGNVQ	IB	SQA(H)	SQA	RATIO A/AS
Art & Design (Year 0)	EW12	4FT deg	*							
Creative Advertising	E211	3FT deg	Pf							
Fashion	EJ24	4SW deg	Pf							
Fashion Promotion	EJ2K	4SW deg	Pf							
Fine Art	E100	3FT deg	Pf							
Furniture	E261	3FT deg	Pf							
Graphic Design	E210	3FT/4SW deg	Pf							
Illustration	E215	3FT deg	Pf							
Industrial Design	W231	3FT deg	1(Ad/Ds)	18	MO	D$6/^	28	BBBB	Ind	
Jewellery	E262	3FT deg	Pf							
Surface Pattern	E263	3FT deg	Pf							
Tableware	E264	3FT deg	Pf							
Combined Honours Programme Design Studies	Y400	3FT deg	*	10	MO $	M$6/^	24	BCCC	Ind	
Furniture Design	24WJ▼	2FT HND	Ar	E	N $	P$	Ind	CC$	Ind	

CENTRAL SCHOOL of Speech & Drama

TITLE	CODE	COURSE	SUBJECTS	A/AS	NO/C	RGNVQ	IB	SQA(H)	SQA	RATIO A/AS
Theatre Practice:Des/Pupp/Crafts/StageMan/TecArt	WW24	3FT deg	Pf g	CC	Ind	Ind$^	Ind	CC	Ind	
Theatre Practice:Des/Pupp/Crafts/StageMan/TecArt	EW24	3FT deg	Pf g	CC	Ind	Ind$^	Ind	CC	Ind	

CHELTENHAM & GLOUCESTER COLL of HE

TITLE	CODE	COURSE	SUBJECTS	A/AS	NO/C	RGNVQ	IB	SQA(H)	SQA	RATIO A/AS
Business Management and Fashion	WN21	3FT deg	*	10-14	4M+3D	MB3	26	CCCC	Ind	
Business Management with Fashion	N1W2	4SW deg	*	12	4M+3D	MB3	26	CCCC	Ind	
English Studies and Fashion	WQ23	3FT deg	E	12	4M+3D	M^	26	CCCC	Ind	
English Studies and Visual Arts	QW31	3FT deg	E+A	10-14	4M+3D	MA3	26	CCCC	Ind	
English Studies with Fashion	Q3W2	3FT deg	E	12	4M+3D	M^	26	CCCC	Ind	
English Studies with Visual Arts	Q3W1	3FT deg	E	10-14	4M+3D	MA3	26	CCCC	Ind	
Fashion Design Technology	W225	3FT deg	*	8-12	MO	MA3	26	CCCC	Ind	
Fashion Design Technology	E225	3FT deg	*	8-12	MO	MA3	26	CCCC	Ind	
Fashion and Marketing Management	WN25	3FT deg	*	10-14	MO	MB3	26	CCCC	Ind	
Fashion and Media Communications	WP24	3FT deg	*	10-14	MO	MT3	26	CCCC	Ind	
Fashion and Visual Arts	WW21	3FT deg	A	8-12	5M+2D	MA3	26	CCCC	Ind	
Fashion and Women's Studies	WM29	3FT deg	*	10-14	MO	M3	26	CCCC	Ind	
Fashion with Business Management	W2N1	3FT deg	*	10-14	MO	M3	26	CCCC	Ind	
Fashion with Combined Arts	W2Y3	3FT deg	*	10-14	MO	M3	26	CCCC	Ind	
Fashion with English Studies	W2Q3	3FT deg	*	10-14	MO	M^	26	CCCC	Ind	
Fashion with Marketing Management	W2N5	3FT deg	*	10-14	MO	M3	26	CCCC	Ind	

course details   98 expected requirements   96 entry stats

TITLE	CODE	COURSE	SUBJECTS	A/AS	ND/C	AGNVQ	IB	SQA(H)	SQA	RATIO A/AS
Fashion with Media Communications	W2P4	3FT deg	*	10-14	MO	MT3	26	CCCC	Ind	
Fashion with Visual Arts	W2W1	3FT deg	*	8-12	5M+2D	MA3	26	CCCC	Ind	
Fashion with Women's Studies	W2M9	3FT deg	*	10-14	MO	M3	26	CCCC	Ind	
Fine Art (Painting)	E110	3FT deg	Fa+A/Ad		MO	Ind	X	X	Ind	
Fine Art (Painting)	W110	3FT deg	Fa+A/Ad		MO	Ind	X	X	Ind	
Fine Art (Printmaking)	W140	3FT deg	Fa+A/Ad		MO	Ind	X	X	Ind	
Fine Art (Printmaking)	E140	3FT deg	Fa+A/Ad		MO	Ind	X	X	Ind	
Fine Art (Sculpture)	E130	3FT deg	Fa+A/Ad		MO	Ind	X	X	Ind	
Fine Art (Sculpture)	W130	3FT deg	Fa+A/Ad		MO	Ind	X	X	Ind	
Geography and Visual Arts	LW81	3FT deg	A	10-14	5M+2D	MA3	26	CCCC	Ind	
Geography with Visual Arts	L8W1	3FT deg	*	10-14	5M+2D	MA3	26	CCCC	Ind	
History and Visual Arts	VW11	3FT deg	A	10-14	5M+2D	MA3	26	CCCC	Ind	
History with Visual Arts	V1W1	3FT deg	*	10-14	5M+2D	MA3	26	CCCC	Ind	
Human Geography and Visual Arts	LW8C	3FT deg	*	10	MO	MA3	26	CCCC	Ind	
Human Geography with Visual Arts	L8WC	3FT deg	*	10	MO	M3	26	CCCC	Ind	
Marketing Management with Fashion	N5W2	4SW deg	*	12	5M+2D	MB3	26	CCCC	Ind	
Media Communication with Fashion	P4W2	3FT deg	*	12	5M+2D	MT3	26	CCCC	Ind	
Media Communications and Visual Arts	PW41	3FT deg	*	12	5M+2D	MA3	26	CCCC	Ind	
Media Communications with Visual Arts	P4W1	3FT deg	*	12	5M+2D	M3	26	CCCC	Ind	
Multimedia and Visual Arts	GW51	3FT deg	*	10-14	5M+2D	MA3	26	CCCC	Ind	
Multimedia with Visual Arts	G5WC	4SW deg	*	10-14	5M+2D	MA3	26	CCCC	Ind	
Multimedia with Visual Arts	G5W1	3FT deg	*	10-14	5M+2D	MA3	26	CCCC	Ind	
Performance Arts and Visual Arts	WW41	3FT deg	A	10-14	5M+2D	MA3	26	CCCC	Ind	
Performance Arts with Visual Arts	W4W1	3FT deg	*	10-14	5M+2D	MA3	26	CCCC	Ind	
Professional Media (Graphics)	E210	3FT deg	Fa	12	5M+2D	Ind	Ind	Ind	Ind	
Professional Media (Graphics)	W210	3FT deg	Fa	12	5M+2D	Ind	Ind	Ind	Ind	
Professional Media (Graphics,Photography,Video)	E270	3FT deg	A/Ad/Fa	12	5M+2D	Ind	Ind	Ind	Ind	
Professional Media (Graphics,Photography,Video)	W270	3FT deg	A/Ad/Fa	12	5M+2D	Ind	Ind	Ind	Ind	
Professional Media (Video)	E280	3FT deg	Fa	12	5M+2D	Ind	Ind	Ind	Ind	
Professional Media (Video)	W280	3FT deg	Fa	12	5M+2D	Ind	Ind	Ind	Ind	
Psychology with Visual Arts	L7W1	3FT deg	* g	12-16	4M+3D	M3	26	CCCC	Ind	
Religious Studies and Visual Arts	VW81	3FT deg	A	8-12	5M+2D	MA3	26	CCCC	Ind	
Religious Studies with Visual Arts	V8W1	3FT deg	*	8-12	5M+2D	MA3	26	CCCC	Ind	
Sport & Exercise Sciences and Visual Arts	BW61	3FT deg	A	12-16	4M+3D	MA3	26	CCCC	Ind	
Sport and Exercise Sciences with Visual Arts	B6W1	3FT deg	*	14	4M+3D	MA3	26	CCCC	Ind	
Visual Arts and Women's Studies	WM19	3FT deg	A	8-12	5M+2D	MA3	26	CCCC	Ind	
Visual Arts with Combined Arts	W1Y3	3FT deg	A	10-14	5M+2D	MA3	26	CCCC	Ind	
Visual Arts with English Studies	W1Q3	3FT deg	A	10-14	5M+2D	MA3	26	CCCC	Ind	
Visual Arts with Fashion	W1W2	3FT deg	A	8-12	5M+2D	MA3	26	CCCC	Ind	
Visual Arts with Geography	W1L8	3FT deg	A	10-14	5M+2D	MA3	26	CCCC	Ind	
Visual Arts with History	W1V1	3FT deg	A	10-14	5M+2D	MA3	26	CCCC	Ind	
Visual Arts with Human Geography	W1LV	3FT deg	A	10-14	5M+2D	MA3	26	CCCC	Ind	
Visual Arts with Media Communications	W1P4	3FT deg	A	10-14	5M+2D	MA3	26	CCCC	Ind	
Visual Arts with Modern Languages (French)	W1T9	3FT deg	A g	10-14	5M+2D	MA3	26	CCCC	Ind	
Visual Arts with Multimedia	W1G5	3FT deg	A	10-14	5M+2D	MA3	26	CCCC	Ind	
Visual Arts with Performance Arts	W1W4	3FT deg	A	10-14	5M+2D	MA3	26	CCCC	Ind	
Visual Arts with Psychology	W1L7	3FT deg	A	10-14	5M+2D	MA3	26	CCCC	Ind	
Visual Arts with Religious Studies	W1V8	3FT deg	A	10-14	5M+2D	MA3	26	CCCC	Ind	
Visual Arts with Sport & Exercise Sciences	W1B6	3FT deg	A	10-14	5M+2D	MA3	26	CCCC	Ind	
Visual Arts with Women's Studies	W1M9	3FT deg	A	10-12	5M+2D	MA3	26	CCCC	Ind	
Women's Studies with Fashion	M9W2	3SW deg	*	8-12	MO	M3	26	CCCC	Ind	
Women's Studies with Visual Arts	M9W1	3FT deg	*	10-12	5M+2D	M3	26	CCCC	Ind	

			98 expected requirements							96 entry stats	

TITLE	CODE	COURSE	SUBJECTS	A/AS	ND/C	AGNVQ	IB	SQA(H)	SQA	RATIO	A/AS
UNIVERSITY COLLEGE CHESTER											
Art and Biology	WC91	3FT deg	B	12	M	P^	Ind	CCCC	$	3	
Art and Computer Science/IT	WG95	3FT deg	g	12	M	P^	Ind	CCCC	$		
Art and Drama and Theatre Studies	WW94	3FT deg	*	CC	M	P^	Ind	CCCC	$	11	
Art and English Literature	WQ93	3FT deg	E	CC	M	P^	Ind	CCCC	$	13	
Art and Geography	WF98	3FT deg	Gy/Gl	CC	M	P^	Ind	CCCC	$		
Art and History	WV91	3FT deg	H/Ec/So	CC	M	P^	Ind	CCCC	$		
Art and Mathematics	WG91	3FT deg	M	12	M	P^	Ind	CCCC	$	4	
Art and Physical Education/Sports Science	WB96	3FT deg	*	12	M	P^	Ind	CCCC	$		
Art and Psychology	WL97	3FT deg	g	12	M	P^	Ind	CCCC	$	10	14/20
Art and Theology and Religious Studies	WV98	3FT deg	*	12	M	P^	Ind	CCCC	$	5	
Art with Biology	W9C1	3FT deg	B	12	MO	P^	Ind	CCCC	$		
Art with Computer Science/IT	W9G5	3FT deg	g	12	MO	P^	Ind	CCCC	$	4	
Art with Drama and Theatre Studies	W9W4	3FT deg	*	CC	M	P^	Ind	CCCC	$		
Art with English Literature	W9Q3	3FT deg	E	CC	M	P^	Ind	CCCC	$	6	18/20
Art with French	W9R1	3FT deg	g	12	M	P^	Ind	CCCC	$		
Art with Geography	W9F8	3FT deg	Gy/Gl	CC	M	P^	Ind	CCCC	$		
Art with German	W9R2	3FT deg	g	12	M	P^	Ind	CCCC	$		
Art with History	W9V1	3FT deg	H/Ec/So	CC	M	P^	Ind	CCCC	$	8	
Art with Mathematics	W9G1	3FT deg	M	12	M	P^	Ind	CCCC	$		
Art with Physical Education/Sports Science	W9B6	3FT deg	*	12	M	P^	Ind	CCCC	$		
Art with Psychology	W9L7	3FT deg	g	12	M	P^	Ind	CCCC	$	6	
Art with Theology and Religious Studies	W9V8	3FT deg	*	12	M	P^	Ind	CCCC	$		
Biology with Art	C1W9	3FT deg	B	12	M	P^	Ind	CCCC	$		
Computer Science/IT with Art	G5W9	3FT deg	g	12	M	M	Ind	CCCC	$		
Drama and Theatre Studies with Art	W4W9	3FT deg	*	CC	M	M	Ind	CCCC	$	14	
English with Art	Q3W9	3FT deg	E	CC	M	P^	Ind	CCCC	$	12	
Geography with Art	F8W9	3FT deg	Gy/Gl	CC	M	P^	Ind	CCCC	$	6	
History with Art	V1W9	3FT deg	H/Ec/So	CC	M	M	Ind	CCCC	$		
Mathematics with Art	G1W9	3FT deg	M	12	M	P^	Ind	CCCC	$	1	
Physical Education/Sports Science with Art	B6W9	3FT deg	*	CC	M	P^	Ind	CCCC	$		
Psychology with Art	L7W9	3FT deg	g	12	M	M	Ind	CCCC	$	32	
Theology and Religious Studies with Art	V8W9	3FT deg	*	12	M	M	Ind	CCCC	$	4	
CHICHESTER INSTITUTE OF HIGHER EDUCATION											
Art	W100	3FT deg	A+Pf	12	Ind	M^+	Ind	Ind	Ind		
Art and Dance	WW14	3FT deg	A+Pf	12	Ind	M$+^	Ind	Ind	Ind	3	
Art and English	WQ13	3FT deg	E+A+Pf	12	Ind	M$+^	Ind	Ind	Ind	7	14/22
Art and English Language Teaching (EFL)	WQ11	3FT deg	A+Pf	12	Ind	M^+	Ind	Ind	Ind		
Art and Geography	WL18	3FT deg	Gy+A+Pf	12	Ind	M$+^	Ind	Ind	Ind	6	
Art and History	WV11	3FT deg	H+A+Pf	12	Ind	M$+^	Ind	Ind	Ind		
Art and Mathematics	GW11	3FT deg	M+A+Pf	12	Ind	M$+^	Ind	Ind	Ind		
Art and Media Studies	PW41	3FT deg	A+Pf	12	Ind	M$+^	Ind	Ind	Ind	11	
Art and Music	WW13	3FT deg	A+Mu+Pf	12	Ind	M$+^	Ind	Ind	Ind	5	
Art and Study of Religions	WV18	3FT deg	A+Pf	12	Ind	M$+^	Ind	Ind	Ind	6	
Art and Theology	WV1V	3FT deg	A+Pf	12	Ind	M^+	Ind	Ind	Ind		
Art with Dance	W1W4	3FT deg	A+Pf	12	Ind	M$+^	Ind	Ind	Ind		
Art with Dance	E1W4	3FT deg	A+Pf	12	Ind	M$+^	Ind	Ind	Ind		
Art with Education Studies (Opt. QTS) (P)	W1X9	3FT/4FT deg	A+Pf g	12	Ind	M$+^ go	Ind	Ind	Ind	6	6/18
Art with English	E1Q3	3FT deg	A+Pf	12	Ind	M$+^	Ind	Ind	Ind		
Art with English	W1Q3	3FT deg	A+Pf	12	Ind	M$+^	Ind	Ind	Ind		
Art with English Language Teaching (EFL)	W1Q1	3FT deg	A+Pf	12	Ind	M$+^	Ind	Ind	Ind		
Art with English Language Teaching (EFL)	E1Q1	3FT deg	A+Pf	12	Ind	M$+^	Ind	Ind	Ind		

course details			**98 expected requirements**							*96 entry stats*	
TITLE	CODE	COURSE	SUBJECTS	A/AS	ND/C	AGNVQ	IB	SQA(H)	SQA	RATIO	A/AS
Art with Geography	W1L8	3FT deg	A+Pf	12	Ind	M$+^	Ind	Ind	Ind		
Art with Geography	E1L8	3FT deg	A+Pf	12	Ind	M$+^	Ind	Ind	Ind		
Art with History	E1V1	3FT deg	A+Pf	12	Ind	M$+^	Ind	Ind	Ind		
Art with History	W1V1	3FT deg	A+Pf	12	Ind	M$+^	Ind	Ind	Ind		
Art with Mathematics	W1G1	3FT deg	A+Pf g	12	Ind	M$+^	Ind	Ind	Ind		
Art with Mathematics	E1G1	3FT deg	A+Pf g	12	Ind	M$+^	Ind	Ind	Ind		
Art with Music	E1W3	3FT deg	A+Pf	12	Ind	M$+^	Ind	Ind	Ind		
Art with Music	W1W3	3FT deg	A+Pf	12	Ind	M$+^	Ind	Ind	Ind		
Art with Related Arts	W1W9	3FT deg	A+Pf	12	Ind	M$+^	Ind	Ind	Ind		
Art with Related Arts	E1W9	3FT deg	A+Pf	12	Ind	M$+^	Ind	Ind	Ind		
Art with Study of Religions	E1V8	3FT deg	A+Pf g	12	Ind	M$+^	Ind	Ind	Ind		
Art with Study of Religions	W1V8	3FT deg	A+Pf	12	Ind	M$+^	Ind	Ind	Ind		
Art with Theology	W1VV	3FT deg	A+Pf	12	Ind	M$	Ind	Ind	Ind		
Dance with Art	W4W1	3FT deg	Pf	12	Ind	M$+	Ind	Ind	Ind		
Dance with Related Arts	W4W9	3FT deg	Pf	12	Ind	M$+	Ind	Ind	Ind	10	12/16
English with Art	Q3W1	3FT deg	E	12	Ind	M^	Ind	Ind	Ind	13	
English with Related Arts	Q3W9	3FT deg	E	12	Ind	M^	Ind	Ind	Ind	3	
Geography with Art	L8W1	3FT deg	Gy	12	Ind	M$	Ind	Ind	Ind		
Geography with Related Arts	L8W9	3FT deg	Gy	12	Ind	M$	Ind	Ind	Ind		
History with Art	V1W1	3FT deg	H	12	Ind	M$	Ind	Ind	Ind		
History with Related Arts	V1W9	3FT deg	H	12	Ind	M$	Ind	Ind	Ind		
Media Studies with Art	P4W1	3FT deg		12							
Media Studies with Related Arts	P4W9	3FT deg		12							
Music with Art	W3W1	3FT deg	Mu	12	Ind	M$+	Ind	Ind	Ind	3	
Music with Related Arts	W3W9	3FT deg	Mu	12	Ind	M$+	Ind	Ind	Ind	5	
Related Arts and Art	WW19	3FT deg	A+Pf	12	Ind	M$+	Ind	Ind	Ind		
Related Arts and Art	EW19	3FT deg	A+Pf	12	Ind	M$+	Ind	Ind	Ind		
Related Arts and Dance	WW49	3FT deg	Pf	12	Ind	M$+	Ind	Ind	Ind		6/18
Related Arts and English	QW39	3FT deg	E	12	Ind	M+^	Ind	Ind	Ind	1	8/14
Related Arts and Geography	WL98	3FT deg	Gy	12	Ind	M$+	Ind	Ind	Ind		
Related Arts and History	WV91	3FT deg	H	12	Ind	M$+	Ind	Ind	Ind		
Related Arts and Media Studies	WP94	3FT deg	Pf	12	Ind	M$+	Ind	Ind	Ind		
Related Arts and Music	WW39	3FT deg	Mu	12	Ind	M$+	Ind	Ind	Ind		6/ 8
Related Arts and Study of Religions	WV98	3FT deg	*	12	Ind	M$	Ind	Ind	Ind		
Related Arts and Theology	WV9V	3FT deg	Pf	12	Ind	M$	Ind	Ind	Ind		
Study of Religions with Art	V8W1	3FT deg	*	12	Ind	M$	Ind	Ind	Ind	2	
Study of Religions with Related Arts	V8W9	3FT deg	*	12	Ind	M$	Ind	Ind	Ind		
Theology with Art	V8WC	3FT deg	Pf	12	Ind	M$	Ind	Ind	Ind		
Theology with Related Arts	V8WX	3FT deg	*	12	Ind	M$	Ind	Ind	Ind		
Women's Studies and Related Arts	MW99	3FT deg	*	12	Ind	M$	Ind	Ind	Ind		

CITY OF BRISTOL COLLEGE

Design (Computer Graphics)	072W	2FT HND									
Design (Computer Graphics)	072E	2FT HND									
Design (Visual Communications)	012E	2FT HND									
Design (Visual Communications)	012W	2FT HND									

CITY COLLEGE Manchester

Arts Work in the Community	099W	2FT HND		EE	N $	PA					
Arts Work in the Community	099E	2FT HND		EE	N $	PA					
Design Crafts (Metal, Ceramics and Textiles)	26WE	2FT HND	Pf								
Design Crafts (Metal, Ceramics and Textiles)	26WW	2FT HND	Pf								
Graphic Design	012W	2FT HND	Pf								
Graphic Design	012E	2FT HND	Pf								

course details				98 expected requirements						96 entry stats	
TITLE	CODE	COURSE	SUBJECTS	A/AS	NO/C	AGNVQ	IB	SQA(H)	SQA	RATIO	A/AS
CITY of LIVERPOOL Comm COLL											
Clothing Technology	24WJ	2FT HND									
Clothing Technology	24WE	2FT HND									
Fine and Applied Arts	071E	2FT HND									
Fine and Applied Arts	071W	2FT HND									
Theatre Costume Interpretation	084E	2FT HND									
CLEVELAND COLLEGE of A & D											
Design Crafts for the Entertainment Industries	E460	3FT deg	Fa/Pf		N	P	Ind	Ind	N		
Fine Art	E100	3FT deg	Fa/Pf		N	P	Ind	Ind	N		
International Textiles and Surface Pattern	E220	3FT deg	Fa/Pf		N	P	Ind	Ind	N		
Design (Typography and Graphic Communication)	002E	2FT HND	Fa/Pf		N	P	Ind	Ind	N		
Graphic Design	012E	2FT HND	Fa/Pf		N	P	Ind	Ind	N		
COLCHESTER INST											
Art and Design (Multidisciplinary)	E200	3FT deg	Pf	EE	Ind	MA	Ind	Ind	Ind		
Art and Design (Multidisciplinary)	W200	3FT deg	Pf	EE	Ind	MA	Ind	Ind	Ind		
Art and Design (Multidisciplinary)	002W	2FT HND	Pf	EE	N $	PA	Ind	Ind	Ind		
Art and Design (Multidisciplinary)	002E	2FT HND	Pf	EE	N $	PA	Ind	Ind	Ind		
CORDWAINERS COLL											
Design, Marketing & Prod Dev (Footwear & Access)	JW42	3FT deg			N	PA	Dip	Ind	Ind		
Design, Marketing & Prod Dev (Footwear & Access)	EW42	3FT deg			N	PA	Dip	Ind	Ind		
Design (Footwear and Accessories)	24WE	2FT HND			N		Ind	Ind	Ind		
Design (Footwear and Accessories)	24WJ	2FT HND			N		Ind	Ind	Ind		
Saddlery Technology	29WD	2FT HND			N		Ind	Ind	Ind		
COVENTRY Univ											
Art and Craft Studies	WW26	3FT deg	Pf+Fa g	X	Ind	Ind	Ind	Ind	Ind		
Art and Craft Studies	EW26	3FT deg	Pf+Fa g	X	Ind	Ind	Ind	Ind	Ind		
Arts Practice and Cultural Policy	E990	1FT deg		X	HN	X	X	X	X		
Arts Practice and Cultural Policy	W990	1FT deg		X	HN	X	X	X	X		
Consumer Product Design (MDes)	W230	3FT/4SW deg	Pf g	X	Ind	Ind	Ind	Ind	Ind		
Consumer Product Design (MDes)	E230	3FT/4SW deg	Pf g	X	Ind	Ind	Ind	Ind	Ind		
Fine Art	E100	3FT deg	Pf+Fa g	X	Ind	Ind	X	X	X		
Fine Art	W100	3FT deg	Pf+Fa g	X	Ind	Ind	X	X	X		
Graphic Design	W210	3FT deg	Pf+Fa g	X	Ind	Ind	Ind	Ind	Ind		
Graphic Design	E210	3FT deg	Pf+Fa g	X	Ind	Ind	Ind	Ind	Ind		
Transport Design (MDes)	EH27	3FT/4SW deg	Pf g	X	Ind	Ind	Ind	Ind	Ind		
Transport Design (MDes)	WH27	3FT/4SW deg	Pf g	X	Ind	Ind	Ind	Ind	Ind		
CROYDON COLL											
Design (Theatre Studies)	WW42	3FT deg	Fa+Pf		N $	PA2/Q2					
Design (Theatre Studies)	EW42	3FT deg	Fa+Pf		N $	PA2/Q2					
Fashion with Business (yr 3 entry option)	E4N1	3FT deg	Fa+Pf		N $	PA2					
Fashion with Business (yr 3 entry option)	J4N1	3FT deg	Fa+Pf		N $	PA2					
Fine Art (Printmaking & Book Arts)	JW56	3FT deg	Fa+Pf		N $	PA2					
Fine Art (Printmaking and Book Arts)	EW56	3FT deg	Fa+Pf		N $	PA2					
Graphic Design (Yr 3 entry option)	E210	3FT deg	Fa+Pf		N $	PA2					
Graphic Design (yr 3 entry option)	W210	3FT deg	Fa+Pf		N $	PA2					
Photomedia	WW25	3FT deg	Fa+Pf		N $	PA2					
Photomedia	EW25	3FT deg	Fa+Pf		N $	PA2					
CUMBRIA COLL of A & D											
Creative Arts	W900	3FT deg		CC	N	M	Ind	BB	Ind	3	6/22
Creative Arts	E900	3FT deg		CC	N	M			Ind		

course details | 98 expected requirements | 96 entry stats

TITLE	CODE	COURSE	SUBJECTS	A/AS	NO/C	AGNVQ	IB	SQA(H)	SQA	RATIO	A/AS
Design Crafts	E610	3FT deg			N	M	Dip		Ind		
Design Crafts	W610	3FT deg			N	M	Dip		Ind	3	
Fine Art	W100	3FT deg			N	M	Dip		Ind	1	
Fine Art	E100	3FT deg			N	M	Dip		Ind		
Graphic Design	E210	3FT deg			N	M	Dip		Ind		
Graphic Design	W210	3FT deg			N	M	Dip		Ind		
Visual Arts and Culture	W150	3FT deg		CC	N	M	Ind	BB	Ind	1	
Visual Arts and Culture	E150	3FT deg		CC	N	M	Dip	BB	Ind		
Design Crafts	016E	2FT HND			N	M	Dip		Ind		
Design Crafts	016W	2FT HND			N	M	Dip		Ind		
Graphic Design	012W	2FT HND			N	M	Dip		Ind		
Graphic Design	012E	2FT HND			N	M	Dip		Ind		

DARTINGTON COLL of Arts

TITLE	CODE	COURSE	SUBJECTS	A/AS	NO/C	AGNVQ	IB	SQA(H)	SQA	RATIO	A/AS
Visual Performance	W430	3FT deg	A/Fa/Pf	BE	10M	Ind	26$	CCC$	Ind	4	
Visual Performance	E430	3FT deg	A/Fa/Pf	BE	10M	Ind	26$	CCC$	Ind		
Visual Performance with Arts Management	E4NC	3FT deg	A/Fa/Pf	BE	10M	Ind	26$	CCC$	Ind		
Visual Performance with Arts Management	W4NC	3FT deg	A/Fa/Pf	BE	10M	Ind	26$	CCC$	Ind	4	

DE MONTFORT Univ

TITLE	CODE	COURSE	SUBJECTS	A/AS	NO/C	AGNVQ	IB	SQA(H)	SQA	RATIO	A/AS
Arts Management	W9N1▼	3FT deg	*g	CCD	MO	M^	28$	ABBB	Ind	3	14/22
Conservation and Restoration	W160▼	3FT deg	S g	16	MO	Ind$	$	CSYS$	Ind	4	6/18
Conservation and Restoration	E160▼	3FT deg	S g	16	MO	Ind$	$	CSYS$	Ind		
Design Management	E290▼	3FT deg	A/Ds g	14	6M	M	26$	BBB	N$		
Design Management	W290▼	3FT deg	A/Ds g	14	6M	M	26$	BBB	N$	3	10/18
Fashion and Associated Studies	W221▼	3FT deg	Ad g	10	MO	P					
Fashion and Associated Studies	E221▼	2FT Dip	Ad g	10	MO	P	Dip	BBCC	Ind		
Fashion and Textile Design	E220▼	3FT deg	Fa g	14	6M	M	26$	BBBB			
Fashion and Textile Design	W220▼	3FT deg	Fa g	14	6M	M	Dip	BBBB	Ind	5	10/22
Fine Art	E100▼	3FT deg	Fa g		MO		Dip	BBBB	Ind		
Fine Art	E101▼	3FT deg	Fa g	10	N	P	Ind	X	Ind		
Fine Art	W100▼	3FT deg	Fa								
Fine Art	W101▼	3FT deg	Fa	10	N	P	Ind	X	Ind		
Fine Art and Visual	EW19▼	3FT deg	Fa g	12-18	MO	D	Dip	BBCC	Ind		
Fine Art and Visual Culture	WW19▼	3FT deg	Fa g	12-18	MO	D	Dip	BBCC	Ind		
Graphic Design and Illustration	E210▼	3FT deg	Fa g	14	6M	D	Dip	BBBB	Ind		
Graphic Design and Illustration	W210▼	3FT deg	Fa g	14	6M	D	Dip	BBBB	Ind	35	22/26
Historic and Contemporary Decorative Crafts	E610▼	2FT Dip	Ad g	12-18	MO	D	Dip	BBCC	Ind		
Historic and Contemporary Decorative Crafts	W610▼	3FT deg	Ad g	12-18	MO	D	Dip	BBCC	Ind		
Industrial Design	W230▼	3FT deg	Fa g	14	3M+3D	D	26	BBBB	Ind		
Industrial Design	E230▼	3FT deg	Fa g	14	3M+3D	D	26	BBBB	Ind		
Multi-Media Design	E280▼	3FT deg	Fa g	18	4M+4D	D	32$	AABB	Ind		
Multi-Media Design	W280▼	3FT deg	Fa g	18	4M+4D	D	32$	AABB	Ind	5	8/24
The Study of Visual Culture	W901▼	3FT deg	Ha g	12-18	MO	P	Dip	BBCC	Ind		
The Study of Visual Culture	E901▼	3FT deg	Ha g	12-18	MO	P	Dip	BBCC	Ind		
Three-Dimensional Design	E260▼	3FT deg	Fa/2(A/M/S/L) g	14-16	MO	D	26$	BBBB	Ind		
Three-Dimensional Design	W260▼	3FT deg	Fa/2(A/M/S/L) g	14-16	MO	D	26$	BBBB	Ind	6	4/22
Valuation and Auctioneering: Chattels & Fine Art	EN18▼	3FT deg		14	5M	M	26$	BBBB	Ind		
Valuation and Auctioneering: Chattels & Fine Art	WN18▼	3FT deg		14	5M	M	26$	BBBB	Ind		
Humanities Combined Honours *Fine Art*	Y300▼	3FT deg	A/Fa g	CCD	MO	MA^	26$	ABBB	Ind		
Humanities Joint Honours *Fine Art*	Y301▼	3FT deg	A/Fa g	CCD	MO	X	26$	ABBB	Ind		
Floristry	036W▼	2FT HND	*g	2	N	P	Ind	BB	Ind		

TITLE	CODE	COURSE	SUBJECTS	A/AS	ND/C	AGNVQ	IB	SQA(H)	SQA	RATIO A/AS
Univ of DERBY										
Applied Arts	E201	3FT deg		X	Ind	Ind	X	X	Ind	
Applied Arts	W201	4FT deg	*	18	Ind	Ind	30	BBBBC	Ind	11
Biological Imaging	CW12	4FT deg	B	CC	MO $	M^	26$	CCCC$	Ind	3 6/28
Biological Imaging	EW12	3FT deg	B+A	CDD	MO $	M^	28$	BBCC$	Ind	
Ecodesign	HW72	3FT deg		12-14	8M	D	28	BBCC		
Ecodesign	EW72	3FT deg		12-14	8M	D	28	BBCC		
Fashion Studies	E221	4SW deg	A/Fa+Pf		Ind	Ind	$	$	Ind	
Fine Art	E100	3FT deg		X	Ind	Ind	X	X	Ind	
Fine Art	W100	4EXT deg	*	18	Ind	Ind	30	BBBBC	Ind	23
Graphic Design	W211	4EXT deg	*	18	Ind	Ind	30	BBBBC	Ind	114
Graphic Design	E211	3FT deg		X	Ind	Ind	X	X	Ind	
Photography and Time-based Media	E280	3FT deg		X	Ind	Ind	X	X	Ind	
Photography and Time-based Media	W280	4EXT deg	Ph	18	Ind	Ind$	Ind	Ind	Ind	
Textile Design	W220	4EXT deg	Tx	18	Ind	Ind	X	X	Ind	133
Textile Design	E220	3FT deg	A/Fa+Pf		Ind	Ind	$	$	Ind	
Credit Accumulation Modular Scheme *Fine Art*	Y600	3FT deg	A+Pf/Fa		Ind	MA	Ind	Ind	Ind	
Credit Accumulation Modular Scheme *Visual Communications*	Y600	3FT deg	Pf+Fa		Ind	MA	Ind	Ind	Ind	
DEWSBURY COLL										
Photography	W550	3FT deg								
Photography	E550	3FT deg								
Design (Communications) Graphic Option	012W	2FT HND	Fa+Pf	X	N	PA				
Design (Communications) Graphic Option	012E	2FT HND	Fa+Pf	X	N	PA				
Design (Communications) Media Production Option	034E	2FT HND	Fa+Pf	X	N	PA				
Design (Communications) Media Production Option	034P	2FT HND	Fa+Pf	X	N	PA				
Design (Fashion/Surface Pattern) Surf Patt Opt	522W	2FT HND	Fa+Pf	X	N	PA				
Design (Fashion/Surface Pattern) Surf Patt Opt	522E	2FT HND	Fa+Pf	X	N	PA				
Design (Spatial Design) Interior and Exhibition	062E	2FT HND	Fa+Pf	X	N	PA				
Design (Spatial Design) Interior and Exhibition	062W	2FT HND	Fa+Pf	X	N	PA				
DONCASTER COLL										
Design (Advertising)	32PE	2FT HND								
DUDLEY COLLEGE of Technology										
Art and Design (Electronic Graphics)	112E	2FT HND	* g	2	Ind	Ind				
Design (Three Dimensional Design)	062E	2FT HND	* g	2	Ind	Ind				
Design Glass (including Ceramics)	332E	2FT HND	* g	2	Ind	Ind				
Univ of DUNDEE										
Animation & Electronic Media	E270	3FT deg	Fa+Pf	X	Ind	Ind	X	X	Ind	
Ceramics	E232	3FT deg	Fa+Pf	X	Ind	Ind	X	X	Ind	
Constructed Textiles	E220	3FT deg	Fa+Pf	X	Ind	Ind	X	X	Ind	
Drawing and Painting	E115	3FT deg	Fa+Pf	X	Ind	Ind	X	X	Ind	
Graphic Design	E210	3FT deg	Fa+Pf	X	Ind	Ind	X	X	Ind	
Illustration and Print Making	E215	3FT deg	Fa+Pf	X	Ind	Ind	X	X	Ind	
Interior and Environmental Design	E265	4FT deg	Pf	BB-EE	Ind	Ind	Ind	CCC$	Ind	
Jewellery and Metalwork	E660	3FT deg	Fa+Pf	X	Ind	Ind	X	X	Ind	
Printed Textiles	E225	3FT deg	Fa+Pf	X	Ind	Ind	X	X	Ind	
Printmaking	E140	3FT deg	Fa+Pf	X	Ind	Ind	X	X	Ind	
Sculpture	E130	3FT deg	Fa+Pf	X	Ind	Ind	X	X	Ind	
Time Based Art	E560	3FT deg	Fa+Pf	X	Ind	Ind	X	X	Ind	

course details

98 expected requirements

96 entry stats

			98 expected requirements							96 entry stats	
TITLE	**CODE**	**COURSE**	**SUBJECTS**	**A/AS**	**NO/C**	**AGNVQ**	**IB**	**SQA(H)**	**SQA**	**RATIO**	**A/AS**
Univ of EAST ANGLIA											
English Literature with Creative Writing Minor	Q3W9	3FT deg	E	ABB-BBB	X		30$	AABBB	X	50	22/24
Univ of EAST LONDON											
Art and Design	W211	3FT deg	* g	12	MO	M	Ind	Ind	Ind		
Art and Design	E211	3FT deg	* g	12	MO	MA	Ind	Ind	Ind		
Business Studies and Design-Visual Communication	NW12	3FT deg	* g	12	N	MA	Ind	Ind	Ind		
Business Studies with Design - Textile Design	N1W2	3FT deg	* g	14	MO	MB					
Business Studies with Design-Visual Commun	N1WF	3FT deg	* g	14	MO	MB					
Communication Studies and Design-Visual Commun	PW32	3FT deg	* g	12	MO	MA	Ind	Ind	Ind		
Communication Studies with Design-Visual Commun	P3WF	3FT deg	* g	12	MO	M	Ind	Ind			
Design	E200	3FT deg	*	12	N	MA	Ind	Ind	Ind		
Design	W200	3FT deg	*	12	N	MA	Ind	Ind	Ind	30	
Design - Visual Communic & Hist of Art Des &Film	VW42	3FT deg	* g	12	MO	M$	Ind	Ind	Ind		
Design - Visual Communic w. Hist of Art Des&Film	W2V4	3FT deg	* g	12	MO	M	Ind	Ind	Ind		
Design - Visual Communication and French	RW12	3FT deg	* g	12	MO	M^	Ind	Ind	Ind		
Design - Visual Communication and German	RW22	3FT deg	* g	12	MO	M^	Ind	Ind	Ind		
Design - Visual Communication and IT	GW52	3FT deg	* g	12	MO	M$	Ind	Ind	Ind		
Design - Visual Communication and Spanish	RW42	3FT deg	* g	12	MO	M^	Ind	Ind	Ind		
Design - Visual Communication with Business St	W2N1	3FT deg	* g	12	MO	M	Ind	Ind	Ind		
Design - Visual Communication with Comm Studies	W2P3	3FT deg	* g	12	MO	M	Ind	Ind	Ind		
Design - Visual Communication with Fash Des&Mktg	W2J4	3FT deg	* g	12	MO	M	Ind	Ind	Ind		
Design - Visual Communication with French	W2R1	3FT deg	* g	12	MO	M	Ind	Ind	Ind		
Design - Visual Communication with German	W2R2	3FT deg	* g	12	MO	M	Ind	Ind	Ind		
Design - Visual Communication with Italian	W2R3	3FT deg	* g	12	MO	M	Ind	Ind	Ind		
Design - Visual Communication with Spanish	W2R4	3FT deg	* g	12	MO	M	Ind	Ind	Ind		
Fashion Design	E220	3FT deg	* g	12	4M	MA	Ind	Ind	Ind		
Fashion Design with Marketing	E2N5	4SW deg	* g	12	MO	MA	Ind	Ind	Ind		
Fashion Design with Marketing	E2NM	3FT deg	* g	12	4M	MA	Ind	Ind	Ind		
Fine Art	E100	3FT deg	* g	12	MO	MA	Ind	Ind	Ind		
French with Design - Visual Communication	R1W2	3FT deg	* g	12	MO	M	Ind				
German with Design - Visual Communication	R2W2	3FT deg	* g	12	MO	M	Ind				
Graphic Design and Communication	E210	3FT deg	*	12	MO	M	Ind	Ind	Ind		
Graphic Design and Communication	W210	3FT deg	*	12	MO		Ind	Ind	Ind		
History of Art Design & Film w.Design-Vis Commun	V4W2	3FT deg	* g	12	MO	M	Ind	Ind			
Information Technology with Design - Visual Comm	G5W2	3FT deg	* g	12	MO	M	Ind	Ind	Ind		
Printed Textile Design and Surface Decoration	W221	3FT deg	* g	12	MO	MA	Ind				
Printed Textile Design and Surface Decoration	E221	3FT deg	* g	12	MO	MA	Ind				
Spanish with Design - Visual Communication	R4W2	3FT deg	* g	12	MO	M	Ind				
Three-Subject Degree *Design-Textiles*	Y600	3FT deg	* g	12	MO	M	Ind	Ind	Ind		
Three-Subject Degree *Design-Visual Communication*	Y600	3FT deg	* g	12	MO	M	Ind	Ind	Ind		
EAST SURREY COLL											
Fine Art and Design (Modular)	21WE	2FT HND	*	X	N	Ind	Ind	Ind	Ind		
Lettering: Architect Heraldic, Calligraphic	26WE	2FT HND	*	X	N	PA	Ind	Ind	N		
EDGE HILL Univ COLLEGE											
Art & Design and Communication Studies	PW32	3FT deg	A	CC	3M+3D	MA / P*^	Dip	BBCC	Ind	2	10/14
Art & Design and Drama	WW24	3FT deg	A	CC	3M+3D	MA / P*^	Dip	BBCC	Ind		
Art & Design and English	QW32	3FT deg	A+E	CC	X	X	Dip	BBCC$	X	2	7/18
Univ of EDINBURGH											
Fine Art	W150	5FT deg	Pf g	BBB	Ind	Ind	Dip$	BBBB$	Ind		

			98 expected requirements							96 entry stats	
TITLE	**CODE**	**COURSE**	**SUBJECTS**	**A/AS**	**ND/C**	**AGNVQ**	**IB**	**SQA(H)**	**SQA**	**RATIO**	**A/AS**
Univ of EXETER											
Arts in Society	WW49	3FT deg	*	CC-DD	MO	M$	28	Ind	Ind		
English and Fine Art	QW31	3FT deg	E+Pf	BBB-BCC	MO	M/D$^	32$	Ind	Ind	9	18/30
French and Fine Art	RW11	4FT deg	F+Pf	22-24	MO	M/D$^	34$	Ind	Ind	7	26/30
Italian and Fine Art	RW31	4FT deg	L+Pf g	20-22	MO	M$	32$	Ind	Ind	5	
FALMOUTH COLLEGE of Arts											
Fine Art	W100	3FT deg									
Fine Art	E100	3FT deg	Fa g		N		24	CC	N		
Graphic Communication (Corporate Design)	E213	3FT deg	Fa g	CC	N		24	CC	N		
Graphic Communication (Corporate Design)	W213	3FT deg	A/Ad g	CC	N		24	CC	N	16	
Graphic Communication (Graphic Design)	W214	3FT deg	Fa g	CC	N		24	CC	N	29	10/14
Graphic Communication (Graphic Design)	E214	3FT deg	Fa g	CC	N		24	CC	N		
Graphic Communication (Information Design)	E212	3FT deg	A/Ad g	CC	N		24	CC	N		
Graphic Communication (Information Design)	W212	3FT deg	A/Ad g	CC	N		24	CC	N	12	
Illustration	E215	3FT deg	Fa		N				N		
Illustration	W215	3FT deg								34	18/25
Studio Ceramics	W232	3FT deg									
Studio Ceramics	E232	3FT deg	Fa	CC	N		24	CC	N		
FARNBOROUGH COLL of Technology											
Design Technology (Multi Media Video & Animation)	52GW	2FT HND		8	Ind	M*	Ind	Ind	Ind	6	
Leisure Studies (Entertainment and Event Mgt)	17WN	2FT HND	g	6	Ind	P*	Ind	Ind	Ind	12	
Univ of GLAMORGAN											
Art Practice	W990	3FT deg			Ind	Ind	Ind	Ind	Ind		
Art Practice	E990	3FT deg			Ind	Ind	Ind	Ind	Ind		
Built Heritage	W250	3FT deg			Ind	Ind	Ind	Ind	Ind		
Design and Technology	E240	3FT deg			Ind	Ind	Ind	Ind	Ind		
Design and Technology	W240	3FT deg			Ind	Ind	Ind	Ind	Ind		
English Studies and Visual Arts	QW31	3FT deg	A g	12	Ind	Ind	Ind	Ind	Ind		
Geography and Visual Arts	LW81	3FT deg	A g	12	Ind	Ind	Ind	Ind	Ind		
Graphic Design and Production	W210	3FT deg			Ind	Ind	Ind	Ind	Ind		
Graphic Design and Production	E210	3FT deg			Ind	Ind	Ind	Ind	Ind		
Mathematics with Art	G1W1	3FT deg	M/A g	12	Ind	Ind	Ind	Ind	Ind		
Media Studies and Visual Arts	PW41	3FT deg	Me/T/E g	14	Ind	Ind	Ind	Ind	Ind		
Product Design	E230	3FT deg	A/Ad/Ds g	CC	Ind	Ind	Ind	Ind	Ind		
Product Design	H3W2	3FT deg	A/Ad/Ds g	CC	MO $	M$	Ind	Ind	Ind	9	10/11
Product Design	W2H3	3FT deg	A/Ad/Ds g	CC	MO $	M$	Ind	Ind	Ind	15	
Psychology and Visual Arts	LW71	3FT deg	A g	CC	Ind	Ind	Ind	Ind	Ind		
Psychology with Visual Arts	L7W1	3FT deg	A g	CC	5M	M	Ind	Ind	Ind		
Sports Equipment Design	E2HH	3FT deg									
Textile Design and Garment Manufacture	E225	3FT deg			Ind	Ind	Ind	Ind	Ind		
Textile Design and Garment Manufacture	W225	3FT deg			Ind	Ind	Ind	Ind	Ind		
Theatre and Media Drama and Visual Arts	WW14	3FT deg	T/E/Me+A g	14	Ind	Ind	Ind	Ind	Ind		
Visual Arts with Art History	W1V4	3FT deg	A g	12	5M	M	Ind	Ind	Ind		
Combined Studies (Honours) *Art (Visual Arts)*	Y400	3FT deg	A g	8-16	Ind	Ind	Ind	Ind	Ind		
Combined Studies (Honours) *Design*	Y400	3FT deg	* g	8-16	Ind	Ind	Ind	Ind	Ind		
Joint Honours *Art (Visual Arts)*	Y401	3FT deg	A g	8-16	Ind	Ind	Ind	Ind	Ind		
Major/Minor Honours *Art (Visual Arts)*	Y402	3FT deg	A g	8-16	Ind	Ind	Ind	Ind	Ind		

course details			98 expected requirements							96 entry stats	

TITLE	CODE	COURSE	SUBJECTS	A/AS	NO/C	RGNVQ	IB	SQA(H)	SQA	RATIO A/AS	
Major/Minor Honours *Design*	Y402	3FT deg	* g	8-16	Ind	Ind	Ind	Ind	Ind		
Graphic Design and Print Technology	52JW▼	2FT HND			Ind	Ind	Ind	Ind	Ind		
Graphic Design and Production	012W	2FT HND			Ind	Ind	Ind	Ind	Ind		
Graphic Design and Production	012E	2FT HND			Ind	Ind	Ind	Ind	Ind		
Industrial Design	132E	2FT HND									
Industrial Design - (Pembrokeshire)	032W▼	2FT HND	g	4-6	N	P$	Ind	Ind	Ind	3	
Product Design	3H2E	2FT HND	A/Ad/Ds g		Ind	Ind	Ind	Ind	Ind		
Textile Design and Garment Manufacture	522W	2FT HND			Ind	Ind	Ind	Ind	Ind		
Textile Design and Garment Manufacture	522E	2FT HND			Ind	Ind	Ind	Ind	Ind		

GLAMORGAN CENTRE FOR ART AND DESIGN TECHNOLOGY

Art and Design (Animation)	072E	2FT HND	Fa+Pf		Ind	PA	Ind	Ind	Ind		

Univ of GLASGOW

Design: Product Design Eng (MEng or BEng)	H3W2	4FT/5FT deg	M	CDD	MO	Ind	24$	BBBB$	N$	5	

GLASGOW CALEDONIAN Univ

Applied Graphics Technology	GW52	2FT deg		X	Ind		Ind	X	HN		
Interior Design	W260	2FT deg		X	Ind		Ind	X	HN		
Medical Illustration	BW92	3FT/4FT deg		X	Ind		Ind	X	HN		

GLOUCESTERSHIRE COLLEGE of Arts and Technology

Visual Communication and Graphic Design	012E	2FT HND	* g	E	MO $	P			Ind		

GOLDSMITHS COLL (Univ of London)

Anthropology and Communication Studies	LW69	3FT deg		BBC	DO	D	Dip	BBBCC	N		12/24
Art (Studio Practice) and History of Art	VW41	3FT deg	Fa+Pf	BC	MO	M	Dip	BCCCC	N	12	20/30
Art(Studio Prac)& Hist of Art-For O'seas Student	WV14	4EXT deg	Pf							5	
Communication Studies and Sociology	LW39	3FT deg		BBC	DO	D	Dip	ABBBB	N	7	16/28
Design Studies (4 Yrs)	E200	4FT deg	Pf	CC	MO	M	Dip	BCCCC	N		
Eco-Design (4 Yrs)	E201	4FT deg	Pf	CC	MO	M	Dip	BCCCC	N		
Fine Art (4 Yrs Ext) (For Overseas Students)	W105	4EXT deg	Pf							34	
Fine Art (Studio Pract with Contemp Crit Theory)	E100	3FT deg	Fa+Pf	CC	MO	M	Dip	BCCCC	N		
Media and Communications	W901	3FT deg	*	BBB	DO	D	Dip	AABBB	N		
Textiles	E220	3FT deg	Fa+Pf	CC	MO	M	Dip	BCCCC	N		
Textiles (4 Yrs Ext Degree)-For O'seas Students	W221	4FT deg	F								

Univ of GREENWICH

Arts Management	W9N1	3FT deg	* g	16	MO+4D	M	24	CCC	Ind		
Arts Management/Language	WT99	3FT deg	* g	16	MO+4D	M	24	CCC	Ind		
Design Studies	W200	3FT/4SW deg	* g	16	5M	M	24	CCC	Ind		
Technology and Design	JW92	3FT/4SW deg	* g	12	4M	M	24	BCC	Ind		

HANDSWORTH COLL

Clothing	2W4E	2FT HND	*	E		M					

HEREFORDSHIRE COLLEGE of A & D

Design Crafts (Mixed Media)	WW29	3FT deg	Fa/Pf g	4	N	P$6	Ind	Ind	N		
Design Crafts (Mixed Media)	EW29	3FT deg	Fa/Pf g	4	N	P$6	Ind	Ind	N		
Illustration	E215	3FT deg	Fa/Pf g	4	N	P$6	Ind	Ind	N		
Illustration	W215	3FT deg	Fa/Pf g	4	N	P$6	Ind	Ind	N		
Art & Design (Illustration)	62WW	2FT HND	Fa/Pf g	2	N	P$6	Ind	Ind	N		
Art & Design (Illustration)	62WE	2FT HND	Fa/Pf g	2	N	P$6	Ind	Ind	N		

Univ of HERTFORDSHIRE

Applied Arts Practice	WW12	3FT deg	Fa g	X	X	Ind	Ind	Ind	Ind		

			98 expected requirements							**96 entry stats**

course details

TITLE	CODE	COURSE	SUBJECTS	A/AS	ND/C	AGNVQ	IB	SQA(H)	SQA	RATIO A/AS
Applied Arts Practice	EW12	3FT deg	Fa g	X	X	Ind	Ind	Ind	Ind	
Art in the Public Domain	E990	3FT deg	* g	X	X	Ind	Ind	Ind	Ind	
Art in the Public Domain	W990	3FT deg	* g	X	X	Ind	Ind	Ind	Ind	
Fine Art	W100	3FT deg	Fa g	X	X	Ind	Ind	Ind	Ind	
Fine Art	E100	3FT deg	Fa g	X	X	Ind	Ind	Ind	Ind	
Histories of Art and Visual Culture	EV14	3FT deg	Fa/Ap g	10	X	Ind	Ind	Ind	Ind	
Histories of Art and Visual Culture	WV14	3FT deg	Fa/Ap g	10	X	Ind	Ind	Ind	Ind	
Model Design	W290	3FT deg	Fa g	X	X	Ind	Ind	Ind	Ind	
Model Design	E290	3FT deg	Fa g	X	X	Ind	Ind·	Ind	Ind	
Two Dimensional Design	E210	3FT deg	Fa g	X	X	Ind	Ind	Ind	Ind	
Two Dimensional Design	W210	3FT deg	Fa g	X	X	Ind	Ind	Ind	Ind	
Design and Creative Arts	42WE▼	2FT HND								

HERTFORD REGIONAL COLL

TITLE	CODE	COURSE	SUBJECTS	A/AS	ND/C	AGNVQ	IB	SQA(H)	SQA	RATIO A/AS
3D Design - Furniture, Interior, Industrial	W260	2FT Dip								
3D Design - Furniture, Interior, Industrial	E260	2FT Dip								
Visual Communication Design - Graphic Design	E210	2FT Dip								
Visual Communication Design - Graphic Design	W210	2FT Dip								

Univ of HUDDERSFIELD

TITLE	CODE	COURSE	SUBJECTS	A/AS	ND/C	AGNVQ	IB	SQA(H)	SQA	RATIO A/AS
Design, Culture and Marketing	WN25	3FT/4SW deg	Pf+A/Ad/Fa g	10-12	N	Ind	Ind	Ind	Ind	
Design, Culture and Marketing	EN25	3FT/4SW deg	Pf+A/Ad/Fa g	10-12	N	Ind	Ind	Ind	Ind	
Fashion with Manufacture,Marketing and Promotion	E2N5	3FT/4SW deg	Pf+A/Ad/Fa g	10-12	N	Ind	Ind	Ind	Ind	
Fashion with Manufacture,Marketing and Promotion	W2N5	3FT/4SW deg	Pf+A/Ad/Fa g	10-12	N	Ind	Ind	Ind	Ind	
Fine Art (Drawing and Painting) with Marketing	EN15	3FT/4SW deg	Pf+A/Ad/Fa g	10-12	N	Ind	Ind	Ind	Ind	
Fine Art (Drawing and Painting) with Marketing	WN15	3FT/4SW deg	Pf+A/Ad/Fa g	10-12	N	Ind	Ind	Ind	Ind	
Industrial Design	E230	3FT/4SW deg	Pf+Ar g	14	N	M$ gi	Ind	Ind	Ind	
Industrial Design	W230	3FT/4SW deg	Pf+Ar g	14	N	M$ gi	Ind	Ind	Ind	
Interior Design	W260	3FT/4SW deg	Pf+A/Ad/Fa g	10-12	N	Ind	Ind	Ind	Ind	
Interior Design	E260	3FT/4SW deg	Pf+A/Ad/Fa g	10-12	N	Ind	Ind	Ind	Ind	
Product Design	HW72	4SW deg	Pf+Ar g	14	N	M$ gi	Ind	Ind	Ind	
Product Design	EW72	4SW deg	Pf+Ar g	14	N	M$ gi	Ind	Ind	Ind	
Surface Pattern	W225	3FT/4SW deg	Pf+A/Ad/Fa g	10-12	N	Ind	Ind	Ind	Ind	
Surface Pattern	E225	3FT/4SW deg	Pf+A/Ad/Fa g	10-12	N	Ind	Ind	Ind	Ind	
Textile Design	EJ24	2FT Dip	Pf+A/Ad/Fa g	6-8	Ind	Ind	Ind	Ind	Ind	
Textile Design	JW42	3FT/4SW deg	Pf+A/Ad/Fa g	8-12	Ind	Ind	Ind	Ind	Ind	
Textile Design	WJ24	2FT Dip	Pf+A/Ad/Fa g	6-8	Ind	Ind	Ind	Ind	Ind	
Textile Design	EW42	3FT/4SW deg	Pf+A/Ad/Fa g	8-12	Ind	Ind	Ind	Ind	Ind	
Transport Design	EW92	3FT/4SW deg	Pf+A/Ad/Fa g	10-12	N	Ind	Ind	Ind	Ind	
Transport Design	NW92	3FT/4SW deg	Pf+A/Ad/Fa g	10-12	N	Ind	Ind	Ind	Ind	
Product Design	27WE	3SW HND	Pf+Ar g	8	N	P$ gi	Ind	Ind	Ind	
Product Design	27WH	3SW HND	Pf+Ar g	8	N	P$ gi	Ind	Ind	Ind	

KEELE Univ

TITLE	CODE	COURSE	SUBJECTS	A/AS	ND/C	AGNVQ	IB	SQA(H)	SQA	RATIO A/AS
Finance and Visual Arts	NW31	3FT deg	*	BBC-BCC	Ind	Ind	28	CSYS	Ind	
Visual Arts and American Studies	WQ14	4FT deg	*	BBC	Ind	Ind	30	BBBB	Ind	1
Visual Arts and American Studies	QW41	3FT deg	*	BBC	Ind	D$^	30	CSYS	Ind	
Visual Arts and Ancient History	VWD1	3FT deg	*	BBC	Ind	D$^	30	CSYS	Ind	
Visual Arts and Applied Social Studies (4 Yrs)	WL15	4FT deg	*	BBC-BCC	Ind	Ind	28	BBBB	Ind	
Visual Arts and Biochemistry	CW71	3FT deg	C	BCC	Ind	D$^	28$	CSYS	Ind	
Visual Arts and Biochemistry (4 Yrs)	WC17	4FT deg	*	BCC	Ind	Ind	28	BBBB	Ind	
Visual Arts and Biological and Med Chem (4 Yrs)	WF1C	4FT deg	* g	BCC	Ind	Ind	28	BBBB	Ind	
Visual Arts and Biology (4 Yrs)	WC11	4FT deg	* g	BCC	Ind	Ind	28	BBBB	Ind	
Visual Arts and Business Administration (4 Yrs)	WN19	4FT deg	*	BBC-BCC	Ind	Ind	28	BBBB	Ind	

| | | | 98 expected requirements | | | | | | | 96 entry stats |
| course details | | | | | | | | | | |

TITLE	CODE	COURSE	SUBJECTS	A/AS	ND/C	AGNVQ	IB	SQA(H)	SQA	RATIO A/AS
Visual Arts and Chemistry	FW11	3FT deg	C	BCC	Ind	D$^	28$	CSYS	Ind	
Visual Arts and Chemistry (4 Yrs)	WF11	4FT deg	*	BCC	Ind	Ind	28	BBBB	Ind	
Visual Arts and Classical Studies	QW81	3FT deg	*	BCC	Ind	D$^	28	CSYS	Ind	
Visual Arts and Computer Science	GW51	3FT deg	*	BCC	Ind	D$^	28	CSYS	Ind	2
Visual Arts and Computer Science (4 Yrs)	WG15	4FT deg	*	BCC	Ind	Ind	28	BBBB	Ind	
Visual Arts and Criminology (4 Yrs)	WM1H	4FT deg	*	BBB	Ind	Ind	32	BBBB	Ind	
Visual Arts and Economics (4 Yrs)	WL11	4FT deg	*	BCC	Ind	Ind	28	BBBB	Ind	
Visual Arts and Educational Studies	XW91	4FT deg	*	BCC	Ind	Ind	28	BBBB	Ind	
Visual Arts and Electronic Music	WW1J	3FT deg	Mu	BCC	Ind	D$^	28	CSYS	Ind	
Visual Arts and Electronic Music (4 Yrs)	WWJ1	4FT deg	*	BCC	Ind	Ind	28	BBBB	Ind	
Visual Arts and English	QW31	3FT deg	E	BBC	Ind	D$^	30$	CSYS	Ind	13
Visual Arts and English (4 Yrs)	WQ13	4FT deg	*	BBC	Ind	Ind	30	BBBB	Ind	15
Visual Arts and Environmental Management (4 Yrs)	WF1X	4FT deg	* g	BCC	Ind	Ind	28	BBBB	Ind	
Visual Arts and French	RW11	3FT deg	F	BCC	Ind	D$^	28$	CSYS	Ind	
Visual Arts and French (4 Yrs)	WR11	4FT deg	*	BCC	Ind	Ind	28	BBBB	Ind	
Visual Arts and Geology	FW61	3FT deg	S	BCC	Ind	D$^	28$	CSYS	Ind	
Visual Arts and Geology (4 Yrs)	WF16	4FT deg	*	BCC	Ind	Ind	28	BBBB	Ind	
Visual Arts and German	RW21	3FT deg	G	BCC	Ind	D$^	28$	CSYS	Ind	
Visual Arts and History (4 Yrs)	VW11	4FT deg	*	BBC-BCC	Ind	Ind	28	BBBB	Ind	
Visual Arts and Human Resource Management	NW61	3FT deg	*	BBC-BCC	Ind	D$^	28	CSYS	Ind	
Visual Arts and Human Resource Management	WN16	4FT deg	*	BBC-BCC	Ind	Ind	28	BBBB	Ind	
Visual Arts and International History	VWC1	3FT deg	*	BCC	Ind	D$^	28	CSYS	Ind	
Visual Arts and International History (4 Yrs)	WV1C	4FT deg	*	BCC	Ind	Ind	28	BBBB	Ind	
Visual Arts and International Politics (4 Yrs)	WM1C	4FT deg	*	BCC	Ind	Ind	28	BBBB	Ind	
Visual Arts and Marketing	NW51	3FT deg	*	BBC	Ind	D$^	30	CSYS	Ind	
Visual Arts and Mathematics	WG11	4FT deg	*	BCC	Ind	Ind	28	BBBB	Ind	
Visual Arts and Mathematics	GW11	3FT deg	M	BCC	Ind	D$^	28$	CSYS	Ind	
Visual Arts and Music	WW31	3FT deg	Mu	BCC	Ind	D$^	28$	BBBB	Ind	
Visual Arts and Music (4 Yrs)	WW13	4FT deg	*	BCC	Ind	Ind	28	BBBB	Ind	
Visual Arts and Philosophy	VW71	3FT deg	*	BCC	Ind	D$^	28	CSYS	Ind	5
Visual Arts and Philosophy (4 Yrs)	WV17	4FT deg	*	BBC-BCC	Ind	Ind	28	BBBB	Ind	
Visual Arts and Physics	FW31	3FT deg	P	BCC	Ind	D$^	28$	CSYS	Ind	
Visual Arts and Politics	MW11	3FT deg	*	BCC	Ind	D$^	28	CSYS	Ind	
Visual Arts and Politics	WM11	4FT deg	*	BCC	Ind	Ind	28	BBBB	Ind	
Visual Arts and Psychology	CW81	3FT deg	* g	BBB	Ind	D$^	32	CSYS	Ind	10
Visual Arts and Russian	RW81	3FT deg	R	BCC	Ind	D$^	28$	CSYS	Ind	
Visual Arts and Russian Studies	RWV1	3FT deg	*	BCC	Ind	D$^	28	D$^	Ind	
Visual Arts and Sociology & Social Anthropology	WL13	4FT deg	*	BBC	Ind	Ind	30	BBBB	Ind	
Visual Arts and Sociology & Social Anthropology	LW31	3FT deg	*	BBC-BCC	Ind	D$^	28	CSYS	Ind	
Visual Arts and Statistics	GW41	3FT deg	M	BCC	Ind	D$^	28$	CSYS	Ind	
Visual Arts and Statistics	WG14	4FT deg	*	BCC	Ind	Ind	28	BBBB	Ind	

KENT INST of A & D

Ceramics	E253▼	3FT deg	Fa	12	N	P+	24	ABC	Ind	
Ceramics	E232▼	2FT dip	Fa		N	P+				
Ceramics	W232▼	2FT dip	Fa		N	P+				
Ceramics	W253▼	3FT deg	Fa	12	N	P+	24	ABC	Ind	
European Fashion	E221▼	4FT deg	Fa		N	P+				
European Fashion	W221▼	4FT deg	Fa		N	P+				
Fashion Design	W220▼	3FT deg	Fa		N	P+				1
Fashion Design	E220▼	3FT deg	Fa		N	P+				
Fashion Technology	W225▼	3FT deg	Fa		N					32
Fashion Technology	E225▼	3FT deg	Fa		N					

Art and Design 7

TITLE	CODE	COURSE	SUBJECTS	A/AS	ND/C	AGNVQ	IB	SQA(H)	SQA	RATIO A/AS
Fine Art	W100▼	3FT deg	Fa		N	P+	24		Ind	
Fine Art	E100▼	3FT deg	Fa		N	P+	24		Ind	
Interior Architecture	W2K9▼	3FT deg	Fa	12	N	P+	24	ABC	Ind	20
Interior Architecture	E2K9▼	3FT deg	Fa	12	N	P+	24	ABC		
Interior Design	E260▼	3FT deg	Fa		N	P+				
Interior Design	W260▼	3FT deg	Fa		N	P+				
Modelmaking	E2W6▼	3FT deg	Fa		N	P+	24	ABC	Ind	
Modelmaking	W2W6▼	3FT deg	Fa		N	P+	24	ABC	Ind	8
Product Design	W235▼	3FT deg	Fa		N	P+				
Product Design	E235▼	3FT deg	Fa		N	P+				
Silversmithing, Goldsmithing and Jewellery Desig	W660▼	3FT deg	Fa		N	P+			Ind	2
Silversmithing, Goldsmithing and Jewellery Desig	E660▼	3FT deg	Fa		N	P+			Ind	
Visual Communication: Combined Studies	E200▼	3FT deg	Fa		N	P+				
Visual Communication: Combined Studies	W200▼	3FT deg	Fa		N	P+				4
Visual Communication: Graphic Design	W211▼	3FT deg	Fa		N	P+				10
Visual Communication: Graphic Design	E211▼	3FT deg	Fa		N	P+				
Visual Communication: Illustration	E215▼	3FT deg	Fa		N	P+				
Visual Communication: Illustration	W215▼	3FT deg	Fa		N	P+				4
Visual Communication: Time Based Media	W265▼	3FT deg	Fa		N	P+				4
Visual Communication: Time Based Media	E265▼	3FT deg	Fa		N	P+				
Fashion Design and Technology	022W▼	2FT HND	Fa		N	P+	24		Ind	2
Fashion Design and Technology	022E▼	2FT HND	Fa		N	P+	24		Ind	
Graphic Design and Illustration	012E▼	2FT HND	Fa		N	P+				
Graphic Design and Illustration	012W▼	2FT HND	Fa		N	P+				4
Interior Design	062W▼	2FT HND	Fa		N					1
Interior Design	062E▼	2FT HND	Fa		N					
Modelmaking	092E▼	2FT HND	Fa		N	P+				
Modelmaking	092W▼	2FT HND	Fa		N	P+				2
Silversmithing, Goldsmithing and Jewellery Desig	066W▼	2FT HND	Fa		N	P+			Ind	1
Silversmithing, Goldsmithing and Jewellery Desig	066E▼	2FT HND	Fa		N	P+			Ind	

KIDDERMINSTER COLL

TITLE	CODE	COURSE	SUBJECTS	A/AS	ND/C	AGNVQ	IB	SQA(H)	SQA	RATIO A/AS
Design for Floorcoverings and Interior Textiles	E220	3FT deg	Pf+Fa/A	BC	N $		Ind	Ind	Ind	
Design for Floorcoverings and Interior Textiles	W220	3FT deg	Pf+Fa/A	BC	N $		Ind	Ind	Ind	

KING ALFRED'S WINCHESTER

TITLE	CODE	COURSE	SUBJECTS	A/AS	ND/C	AGNVQ	IB	SQA(H)	SQA	RATIO A/AS
Design and Technology	W240	3FT deg	A/Ad+Ds/Ad g	14	6M $	M	24$	BCC$	N$	1	10/18
Visual Studies and Archaeology	FW42	3FT deg	A/Ad g	14	6M $	M	24$	BCC$	X	
Visual Studies and Contemporary Culture Studies	MW92	3FT deg								
Visual Studies and Drama Studies	WW24	3FT deg								
Visual Studies and Education Studies	WX29	3FT deg								2
Visual Studies and English Studies	QW32	3FT deg	A/Ad+E	14	X	X	24$	BCC$	X	7
Visual Studies and History	VW12	3FT deg	A/Ad/H g	14	6M $	M	24$	BCC$	X	
Visual Studies and Media & Film Studies	PW42	3FT deg	A/Ad g	14	6M $	M	24$	BCC$	N$	9	12/20
Visual Studies and Philosophy	VW72	3FT deg								6
Visual Studies and Psychology	LW72	3FT deg	A/Ad g	14	6M $	M	24$	BCC$	N$	4	14/24

KINGSTON Univ

TITLE	CODE	COURSE	SUBJECTS	A/AS	ND/C	AGNVQ	IB	SQA(H)	SQA	RATIO A/AS
Fashion	E225	3FT deg	Fa+Pf		N	Ind	Ind	Ind	Ind	
Fine Art	E100	3FT deg	Fa+Pf		N	Ind	Ind	Ind	Ind	
Fine Art	W100	3FT deg	Fa+Pf		N	Ind	Ind	Ind	Ind	
Graphic Design	E210	3FT deg	Fa+Pf		N	Ind	Ind	Ind	Ind	
Illustration	E215	3FT deg	Fa+Pf		N	Ind	Ind	Ind	Ind	
Interior Design	E260	3FT deg	Fa+Pf		N	Ind	Ind	Ind	Ind	

			98 expected requirements							96 entry stats
course details										
TITLE	CODE	COURSE	SUBJECTS	A/AS	ND/C	RGNVQ	IB	SQA(H)	SQA	RATIO A/AS
Product & Furniture Design	E235	3FT deg	Fa+Pf		N	Ind	Ind	Ind	Ind	
Graphic Design	012E▼	2FT HND	Fa+Pf		N	Ind	Ind	Ind	Ind	

LANCASTER Univ

TITLE	CODE	COURSE	SUBJECTS	A/AS	ND/C	RGNVQ	IB	SQA(H)	SQA	RATIO A/AS
Art History and English	WQ13	3FT deg	E g	BBC	Ind $		32$	ABBBB$	Ind	
Art History and History	WV11	3FT deg	H	BBC-BCC	Ind $		30$	BBBBB$	Ind	
Art History and Religious Studies	WV18	3FT deg	*	BCC-BCD	MO		30	BBBBB	Ind	
Art: History and Culture: the twentieth century	W100	3FT deg	*	BCC	Ind		30	BBBBB	Ind	
Art: History and Culture: the twentieth century	E100	3FT deg	*	BCC	Ind		30	BBBBB	Ind	
Art: Practice and Theory	E150	3FT deg	Pf+A/Fa	BCC	Ind $		Ind$	BBBBB$	Ind	
Art: Practice and Theory	W150	3FT deg	Pf+A/Fa	BCC	Ind $		Ind$	BBBBB$	Ind	
Creative Arts	W900	3FT deg	Pf/T/A/Mu	BCC	M+D $		Ind$	BBBBB$	Ind	
French Studies and Art History	WR11	4SW deg	F	BCC	MO $		30$	BBBBB$	Ind	
German Studies and Art History	WR12	4SW deg	G/L	BCC	MO $		30$	BBBBB$	Ind	
Italian Studies and Art History	WR13	4SW deg	I/L	BCC	MO $		30$	BBBBB$	Ind	
Spanish Studies and Art History	WR14	4SW deg	Sp/L	BCC	MO $		30$	BBBBB$	Ind	
Culture, Media and Communication *Visual Representation*	Y400	3FT deg	*	BBB-BCC	M+D		30	ABBBB	Ind	

Univ of LEEDS

TITLE	CODE	COURSE	SUBJECTS	A/AS	ND/C	RGNVQ	IB	SQA(H)	SQA	RATIO A/AS
Fine Art	W150	4FT deg	* g	BBC	Ind	Ind	30	CSYS	Ind	29 20/28
Textile Design	WJ24	3FT deg	A g	BCC	Ind	Ind	28$	BBBBC	Ind	7 14/26

LEEDS METROPOLITAN Univ

TITLE	CODE	COURSE	SUBJECTS	A/AS	ND/C	RGNVQ	IB	SQA(H)	SQA	RATIO A/AS
Fine Art	E100	3FT deg	Fa+Pf g	X	N$	PA go	Ind	Ind	Ind	
Fine Art	W100	3FT deg								
Graphic Arts and Design (Graphic Arts)	W215	3FT deg								
Graphic Arts and Design (Graphic Arts)	E215	3FT deg	Fa+Pf g	X	N$	PA go	Ind	Ind	Ind	
Graphic Arts and Design (Graphic Design)	E210	3FT deg	Fa+Pf g	X	N$	PA go	Ind	Ind	Ind	
Graphic Arts and Design (Graphic Design)	W210	3FT deg								
Interior Design	W260	3FT deg								
Interior Design	E260	3FT deg	Fa+Pf g	X	N$	PA go	Ind	Ind	Ind	
Three Dimensional Design (Furniture)	E236	3FT deg	Fa+Pf g	X	N$	PA go	Ind	Ind	Ind	
Three Dimensional Design (Furniture)	W236	3FT deg								
Three Dimensional Design (Product)	W230	3FT deg								
Three Dimensional Design (Product)	E230	3FT deg	Fa+Pf g	X	N$	PA go	Ind	Ind	Ind	

LEEDS COLLEGE of A & D

TITLE	CODE	COURSE	SUBJECTS	A/AS	ND/C	RGNVQ	IB	SQA(H)	SQA	RATIO A/AS
Clothing/Fashion	E221	3FT deg								
Clothing/Fashion	W221	3FT deg								
Interior Design	W260	3FT deg	Fa/Pf g		Ind	Ind	Ind	Ind	Ind	
Interior Design	E260	3FT deg								
Printed Textiles and Surface Pattern Design	E222	3FT deg								
Printed Textiles and Surface Pattern Design	W222	3FT deg								
Visual Communications	W210	3FT deg	Fa/Pf g		Ind	Ind	Ind	Ind	Ind	
Visual Communications	E210	3FT deg								

LEICESTER SOUTH FIELDS COLL

TITLE	CODE	COURSE	SUBJECTS	A/AS	ND/C	RGNVQ	IB	SQA(H)	SQA	RATIO A/AS
Design (Surface Pattern)	522E	2FT HND	Fa g	4	N	P$	Dip	CSYS	N	

Univ of LINCOLNSHIRE and HUMBERSIDE

TITLE	CODE	COURSE	SUBJECTS	A/AS	ND/C	RGNVQ	IB	SQA(H)	SQA	RATIO A/AS
Animation	W270	3FT deg	g							
Animation	E270	3FT deg	g							
Fashion Promotion	N5W2▼	2FT HND	g		Ind	Ind	Ind	Ind	Ind	
Fine Art	E100	3FT deg	Pf g							
Fine Art	W100	3FT deg	Pf g							

			98 expected requirements							96 entry stats	

TITLE	CODE	COURSE	SUBJECTS	A/AS	ND/C	AGNVQ	IB	SQA(H)	SQA	RATIO A/AS	
Graphic Design	W211	3FT deg	Pf g								
Graphic Design	E211	3FT deg	Pf g								
Illustration	W215	3FT deg	g								
Illustration	E215	3FT deg	g								
Interactive Design	E275	3FT deg	g								
Interactive Design	W275	3FT deg	g								
Interior Design	E260	3FT deg	Pf g	10	4M	M	24	CCC			
Interior Design	W260	3FT deg	Pf g	10	4M	M	24	CCC			
Museum and Exhibition Design	PW12	3FT deg	* g	10	4M	M	24	CCC	Ind		
Museum and Exhibition Design	EW12	3FT deg	* g	10	4M	M	24	CCC	Ind		
Interior Design	062E▼	2FT HND	* g								
Interior Design	062W▼	2FT HND	* g								

LIVERPOOL HOPE Univ COLL

TITLE	CODE	COURSE	SUBJECTS	A/AS	ND/C	AGNVQ	IB	SQA(H)	SQA	RATIO A/AS	
Design	E200	3FT deg	A/Fa		Ind	MA	Ind	Ind	Ind		
Drama & Theatre Studies/Art	WW94	3FT deg	A/Fa g	12	8M	MA /P*^ go	Ind	Ind	Ind	9	
English/Art	WQ93	3FT deg	El+A/Fa	12	8M	PA^	Ind	Ind	Ind	7	12/20
Environmental Studies/Art	WF99	3FT deg	B/Gy/En+A/Fa	12	8M	PA^	Ind	Ind	Ind	3	
European Studies/Art	WT92	3FT deg	A/Fa	12	8M	MA /P*^	Ind	Ind	Ind		
French/Art	WR91	3FT deg	A/Fa+F	12	8M	PA^	Ind	Ind	Ind	4	
Geography/Art	WF98	3FT deg	A/Fa+Gy	12	8M	P$^	Ind	Ind	Ind	9	
History/Art	WV91	3FT deg	H+A/Fa	12	8M	PA^	Ind	Ind	Ind	8	
Human & Applied Biology/Art	WC91	3FT deg	B+A/Fa g	12	8M	P$^	Ind	Ind	Ind	4	
Mathematics/Art	WG91	3FT deg	A/Fa+M	12	8M	PA^	Ind	Ind	Ind		
Music/Art	WW93	3FT deg	A/Fa+Mu	12	8M	PQ^	Ind	Ind	Ind	2	
Psychology/Art	WC98	3FT deg	A/Fa g	12	8M	MA /P*^ go	Ind	Ind	Ind	6	10/22
Sociology/Art	WL93	3FT deg	A/Fa	12	8M	MA /P*^	Ind	Ind	Ind	12	

LIVERPOOL JOHN MOORES Univ

TITLE	CODE	COURSE	SUBJECTS	A/AS	ND/C	AGNVQ	IB	SQA(H)	SQA	RATIO A/AS	
Fashion and Textiles	E220	3FT deg	Pf+Fa	X			X	X	X		
Fine Art	E100	3FT deg	Pf+Fa	X			X	X	X		
Graphic Design	E210	3FT deg	Pf+Fa	X			X	X	X		
Lit,Life & Thought & Imaginative Writing IW JntA	WQ93	3FT deg	E/H+Pf	12-20	5M+3D	PT^	28$	BBBC		8	14/24
Screen Studs and Imaginative Writing (IW jt awd)	WW59	3FT deg	E	BB	5M+3D	D^	28$			22	
Theatre Studies and Imaginative Writing	WW94	3FT deg	E+T	BB	7D	X	28$	BBCC		7	12/20
Visual Studies and Art History Studies	VW41	3FT deg	Pf	12	5M+2D	M$	28$	CCCC			
Visual Studies and Product Design	WH17	3FT deg	Pf/Fa	CC	5M+3D	D$/M$6^	28$	CCCC		1	8/14

LONDON GUILDHALL Univ

TITLE	CODE	COURSE	SUBJECTS	A/AS	ND/C	AGNVQ	IB	SQA(H)	SQA	RATIO A/AS	
3D/Spatial Des & Communs & Audio Visual Prod St	PW4F	3FT deg	Pf g	CC-CDD	MO+4D	M$ go	26	Ind	Ind		
3D/Spatial Design & Product Development & Manuf	JW4F	3FT deg	Pf g	CD-DDD	MO+3D	M$ go	24	Ind	Ind		
3D/Spatial Design and Accounting	NW4F	3FT deg	Pf g	DD	MO	M$ go	24	Ind	Ind		
3D/Spatial Design and Business	NW1F	3FT deg	Pf g	CD-DDD	MO+4D	M$ go	26	Ind	Ind		
3D/Spatial Design and Business Economics	LWCF	3FT deg	Pf g	DD	MO	M$ go	24	Ind	Ind		
3D/Spatial Design and Business Information Techn	GW7F	3FT deg	Pf g	DD	MO	M$ go	24	Ind	Ind		
3D/Spatial Design and Computing	GW5F	3FT deg	Pf g	DD	MO	M$ go	24	Ind	Ind		
3D/Spatial Design and Design Studies	WW2F	3FT deg	Pf g	CD-DDD	MO+3D	M$ go	24	Ind	Ind		
3D/Spatial Design and Development Studies	MW9F	3FT deg	Pf g	DD	MO	M$ go	24	Ind	Ind		
3D/Spatial Design and Economics	LW1F	3FT deg	Pf g	DD	MO	M$ go	24	Ind	Ind		
3D/Spatial Design and English	QW3F	3FT deg	Pf g	CD-DDD	MO+4D	M$ go	26	Ind	Ind		
3D/Spatial Design and European Studies	TW2F	3FT deg	Pf g	DD	MO	M$ go	24	Ind	Ind		
3D/Spatial Design and Financial Services	NW3F	3FT deg	Pf g	DD	MO	M$ go	24	Ind	Ind		
3D/Spatial Design and Fine Art	WW1F	3FT deg	Pf g	CC-CDD	MO+5D	D$ go	26	Ind	Ind		
3D/Spatial Design and French	RW1F	4FT deg	Pf g	DD	MO	M$ go	24	Ind	Ind		

course details			**98 expected requirements**						*96 entry stats*	
TITLE	CODE	COURSE	SUBJECTS	A/AS	NO/C	AGNVQ	IB	SQA(H)	SQA	RATIO A/AS
3D/Spatial Design and German	RW2F	4FT deg	Pf g	DD	MO	M$ go	24	Ind	Ind	
3D/Spatial Design and International Relations	MWCF	3FT deg	Pf g	DD	MO	M$ go	24	Ind	Ind	
3D/Spatial Design and Law	MW3F	3FT deg	Pf g	CC-CDD	MO+5D	D$ go	26	Ind	Ind	
3D/Spatial Design and Marketing	NW5F	3FT deg	Pf g	CD-DDD	MO+3D	M$ go	24	Ind	Ind	
3D/Spatial Design and Mathematics	GW1F	3FT deg	Pf g	DD	MO	M$ go	24	Ind	Ind	
3D/Spatial Design and Modern History	VW1F	3FT deg	Pf g	DD	MO	M$ go	24	Ind	Ind	
3D/Spatial Design and Multimedia Systems	GWMF	3FT deg	Pf g	DD	MO	M$ go	24	Ind	Ind	
3D/Spatial Design and Politics	MW1F	3FT deg	Pf g	DD	MO	M$ go	24	Ind	Ind	
3D/Spatial Design and Psychology	CW8F	3FT deg	Pf g	CC-CDD	MO+5D	D$ go	26	Ind	Ind	
3D/Spatial Design and Social Policy & Management	LW4F	3FT deg	Pf g	DD	MO	M$ go	24	Ind	Ind	
3D/Spatial Design and Sociology	LW3F	3FT deg	Pf g	DD	MO	M$ go	24	Ind	Ind	
3D/Spatial Design and Spanish	RW4F	4FT deg	Pf g	DD	MO	M$ go	24	Ind	Ind	
3D/Spatial Design and Taxation	NWHF	3FT deg	Pf g	DD	MO	M$ go	24	Ind	Ind	
3D/Spatial Design and Textile Furnishing Design	WWFG	3FT deg	Pf g	DD	MO	M$ go	24	Ind	Ind	
Design St and Communications & Audio Vis Prod St	PW42	3FT deg	* g	CC	MO+4D	D$ go	26	Ind	Ind	
Design Studies	W204	3FT deg	* g	CD	Ind		Dip	BCC	Ind	
Design Studies	E204	3FT deg	* g	CD	Ind		Dip	BCC	Ind	
Design Studies & Business Information Technology	GW72	3FT deg	* g	CD-DDD	MO+2D	M$ go	24	Ind	Ind	
Design Studies and Accounting	NW42	3FT deg	* g	CD-DDD	MO+2D	M$ go	24	Ind	Ind	
Design Studies and Business	NW12	3FT deg	* g	CC-CDD	MO+4D	M$ go	26	Ind	Ind	
Design Studies and Business Economics	LWC2	3FT deg	* g	CD-DDD	MO+2D	M$ go	24	Ind	Ind	
Design Studies and Computing	GW52	3FT deg	* g	CD-DDD	MO+2D	M$ go	24	Ind	Ind	
Development Studies and Design Studies	MW92	3FT deg	* g	CD-DDD	MO+2D	M$ go	24	Ind	Ind	
Economics and Design Studies	LW12	3FT deg	* g	CD-DDD	MO+2D	M$ go	24	Ind	Ind	
English and Design Studies	QW32	3FT deg	* g	CC-CDD	MO+4D	M$ go	26	Ind	Ind	
European Studies and Design Studies	TW22	3FT deg	* g	CD-DDD	MO+2D	M$ go	26	Ind	Ind	
Financial Services and Design Studies	NW32	3FT deg	* g	CD-DDD	MO+2D	M$ go	26	Ind	Ind	
Fine Art	W100	3FT deg	Fa/Pf g		Ind	Ind	Ind	Ind	Ind	
Fine Art	E100	3FT deg	Fa+Pf g		Ind	Ind	Ind	Ind	Ind	
Fine Art & Communications & Audio Visual Prod St	PW41	3FT deg	Pf g	BC-CCC	MO+6D	D$ go	28	Ind	Ind	
Fine Art and Accounting	NW41	3FT deg	Pf g	CC-CDD	MO+2D	M$ go	26	Ind	Ind	
Fine Art and Business	NW11	3FT deg	Pf g	CC-CDD	MO+4D	D$ go	26	Ind	Ind	
Fine Art and Business Economics	LWC1	3FT deg	Pf g	CC-CDD	MO+2D	M$ go	26	Ind	Ind	
Fine Art and Business Information Technology	GW71	3FT deg	Pf g	CC-CDD	MO+2D	M$ go	26	Ind	Ind	
Fine Art and Computing	GW51	3FT deg	Pf g	CC-CDD	MO+2D	M$ go	26	Ind	Ind	
Fine Art and Design Studies	WW12	3FT deg	Pf g	CC-CDD	MO+4D	M$ go	26	Ind	Ind	
Fine Art and Development Studies	MW91	3FT deg	Pf g	CC-CDD	MO+2D	M$ go	26	Ind	Ind	
Fine Art and Economics	LW11	3FT deg	Pf g	CC-CDD	MO+2D	M$ go	26	Ind	Ind	
Fine Art and English	QW31	3FT deg	Pf g	CC-CDD	MO+4D	M$ go	26	Ind	Ind	
Fine Art and European Studies	TW21	3FT deg	Pf g	CC-CDD	MO+2D	M$ go	26	Ind	Ind	
Fine Art and Financial Services	NW31	3FT deg	Pf g	CC-CDD	MO+2D	M$ go	26	Ind	Ind	
French and Design Studies	RW12	4FT deg	* g	CD-DDD	MO+2D	M$ go	26	Ind	Ind	
French and Fine Art	RW11	4FT deg	* g	CC-CDD	MO+2D	M$ go	26	Ind	Ind	
Furniture Design and Technology	EW4F	3FT deg	Fa+Pf g		3M		X	Ind	Ind	
German and Design Studies	RW22	4FT deg	* g	CD-DDD	MO+2D	M$ go	26	Ind	Ind	
German and Fine Art	RW21	4FT deg	* g	CC-CDD	MO+2D	M$ go	26	Ind	Ind	
Interior Design and Technology	EW42	3FT deg	Fa+Pf g		3M	Ind	X	Ind	Ind	
International Relations and Design Studies	MWC2	3FT deg	* g	CD-DDD	MO+2D	M$ go	26	Ind	Ind	
International Relations and Fine Art	MWC1	3FT deg	* g	CC-CDD	MO+2D	M$ go	26	Ind	Ind	
Law and Design Studies	MW32	3FT deg	* g	CC-CDD	MO+4D	M$ go	26	Ind	Ind	
Law and Fine Art	MW31	3FT deg	* g	BC-CCC	MO+6D	D$ go	28	Ind	Ind	
Marketing and Design Studies	NW52	3FT deg	* g	CC-CDD	MO+4D	M$ go	26	Ind	Ind	

	course details			**98 expected requirements**						*96 entry stats*
TITLE	CODE	COURSE	SUBJECTS	A/AS	NO/C	AGNVQ	IB	SQA(H)	SQA	RATIO A/AS
Marketing and Fine Art	NW51	3FT deg	* g	CC-CDD	MO+4D	M$ go	26	Ind	Ind	
Mathematics and Design Studies	GW12	3FT deg	* g	CD-DDD	MO	M$ go	24	Ind	Ind	
Mathematics and Fine Art	GW11	3FT deg	* g	CC-CDD	MO+2D	M$ go	26	Ind	Ind	
Modern History and Design Studies	VW12	3FT deg	* g	CD-DDD	MO+2D	M$ go	24	Ind	Ind	
Modern History and Fine Art	VW11	3FT deg	* g	CC-CDD	MO+2D	M$ go	26	Ind	Ind	
Multimedia Systems and Design Studies	GWM2	3FT deg	* g	CD-DDD	MO	M$ go	24	Ind	Ind	
Multimedia Systems and Fine Art	GWM1	3FT deg	* g	CC-CDD	MO+2D	M$ go	26	Ind	Ind	
Politics and Design Studies	MW12	3FT deg	* g	CD-DDD	MO+2D	M$ go	24	Ind	Ind	
Politics and Fine Art	MW11	3FT deg	* g	CC-CDD	MO+2D	M$ go	26	Ind	Ind	
Product Development & Manufacture & Design Studs	JW42	3FT deg	* g	CD-DDD	MO	M$ go	24	Ind	Ind	
Product Development & Manufacture and Fine Art	JW41	3FT deg	* g	CD-DDD	MO+2D	M$ go	26	Ind	Ind	
Psychology and Design Studies	CW82	3FT deg	* g	CC-CDD	MO+3D	M$ go	26	Ind	Ind	
Psychology and Fine Art	CW81	3FT deg	* g	CC	MO+4D	M$ go	26	Ind	Ind	
Silversmithing, Jewellery and Allied Crafts	W240	3FT deg	Fa/Pf g		Ind	Ind	Ind	Ind	Ind	
Silversmithing, Jewellery and Allied Crafts	E240	3FT deg	Fa/Pf g		Ind	Ind	Ind	Ind	Ind	
Social Policy & Management and Design Studies	LW42	3FT deg	* g	CD-DDD	MO	M$ go	24	Ind	Ind	
Social Policy & Management and Fine Art	LW41	3FT deg	* g	CC-CDD	MO+2D	M$ go	26	Ind	Ind	
Sociology and Design Studies	LW32	3FT deg	* g	CC-CDD	MO+2D	M$ go	26	Ind	Ind	
Sociology and Fine Art	LW31	3FT deg	* g	CC	MO+4D	M$ go	26	Ind	Ind	
Spanish and Design Studies	RW42	4FT deg	* g	CD-DDD	MO+2D	M$ go	26	Ind	Ind	
Spanish and Fine Art	RW41	4FT deg	* g	CC-CDD	MO+2D	M$ go	24	Ind	Ind	
Taxation and Design Studies	NWH2	3FT deg	* g	CD-DDD	MO+2D	M$ go	24	Ind	Ind	
Taxation and Fine Art	NWH1	3FT deg	* g	CC-CDD	MO+2D	M$ go	24	Ind	Ind	
Textile Furnish Des & Commun & Audio Vis Prod St	PW4G	3FT deg	Pf g	CC-CDD	MO	M$ go	24	Ind	Ind	
Textile Furnishing Des & International Relations	MWCG	3FT deg	Pf g	DD	MO	M$ go	24	Ind	Ind	
Textile Furnishing Design & Social Policy & Mgt	LW4G	3FT deg	Pf g	DD	MO	M$ go	24	Ind	Ind	
Textile Furnishing Design and Accounting	NW4G	3FT deg	Pf g	DD	MO	M$ go	24	Ind	Ind	
Textile Furnishing Design and Business	NW1G	3FT deg	Pf g	CD-DDD	MO	M$ go	24	Ind	Ind	
Textile Furnishing Design and Business Economics	LWCG	3FT deg	Pf g	DD	MO	M$ go	24	Ind	Ind	
Textile Furnishing Design and Business IT	GW7G	3FT deg	Pf g	DD	MO	M$ go	24	Ind	Ind	
Textile Furnishing Design and Computing	GW5G	3FT deg	Pf g	DD	MO	M$ go	24	Ind	Ind	
Textile Furnishing Design and Design Studies	WW2G	3FT deg	Pf g	CD-DDD	MO	M$ go	24	Ind	Ind	
Textile Furnishing Design and Development Studs	MW9G	3FT deg	Pf g	DD	MO	M$ go	24	Ind	Ind	
Textile Furnishing Design and Economics	LW1G	3FT deg	Pf g	DD	MO	M$ go	24	Ind	Ind	
Textile Furnishing Design and English	QW3G	3FT deg	Pf g	CD-DDD	MO+2D	M$ go	24	Ind	Ind	
Textile Furnishing Design and European Studies	TW2G	3FT deg	Pf g	DD	MO	M$ go	24	Ind	Ind	
Textile Furnishing Design and Financial Services	NW3G	3FT deg	Pf g	DD	MO	M$ go	24	Ind	Ind	
Textile Furnishing Design and Fine Art	WW1G	3FT deg	Pf g	CC-CDD	MO+4D	M$ go	26	Ind	Ind	
Textile Furnishing Design and French	RW1G	4FT deg	Pf g	DD	MO	M$ go	24	Ind	Ind	
Textile Furnishing Design and German	RW2G	4FT deg	Pf g	DD	MO	M$ go	24	Ind	Ind	
Textile Furnishing Design and Law	MW3G	3FT deg	Pf g	CC-CDD	MO	M$ go	24	Ind	Ind	
Textile Furnishing Design and Manufacture	E420	3FT deg	Fa+Pf g		3M		X	Ind	Ind	
Textile Furnishing Design and Marketing	NW5G	3FT deg	Pf g	CD-DDD	MO	M$ go	24	Ind	Ind	
Textile Furnishing Design and Mathematics	GW1G	3FT deg	Pf g	DD	MO	M$ go	24	Ind	Ind	
Textile Furnishing Design and Modern History	VW1G	3FT deg	Pf g	DD	MO	M$ go	24	Ind	Ind	
Textile Furnishing Design and Multimedia Systems	GWMG	3FT deg	Pf g	DD	MO	M$ go	24	Ind	Ind	
Textile Furnishing Design and Politics	MW1G	3FT deg	Pf g	DD	MO	M$ go	24	Ind	Ind	
Textile Furnishing Design and Psychology	CW8G	3FT deg	Pf g	CD-DDD	MO+2D	M$ go	24	Ind	Ind	
Textile Furnishing Design and Sociology	LW3G	3FT deg	Pf g	CD-DDD	MO+2D	M$ go	24	Ind	Ind	
Textile Furnishing Design and Spanish	RW4G	4FT deg	Pf g	DD	MO	M$ go	24	Ind	Ind	
Textile Furnishing Design and Taxation	NWHG	3FT deg	Pf g	DD	MO	M$ go	24	Ind	Ind	
Modular Programme *3D/Spatial Design*	Y400	3FT deg	* g	CC-DD	MO	M$ go	24	Ind	Ind	

course details			98 expected requirements							96 entry stats	
TITLE	CODE	COURSE	SUBJECTS	A/AS	NO/C	AGNVQ	IB	SQA(H)	SQA	RATIO	A/AS
Modular Programme *Design Studies*	Y400	3FT deg	* g	CC-DDD	MO	M$ go	24	Ind	Ind		
Modular Programme *Fine Art*	Y400	3FT deg	* g	BB-CC	MO+4D	D/M$ go	26	Ind	Ind		
Modular Programme *Textile Furnishing Design*	Y400	3FT deg	* g	CC-DD	MO	M$ go	24	Ind	Ind		
Design (Interior Design)	062E	2FT HND	Pf g		N		Dip	Ind	Ind		
Design (Silversmithing,Jewellery & Allied Craft)	042E	2FT HND	Pf g		N		$	Ind	Ind		
Furniture (Design and Realisation)	024E	2FT HND	Pf g	D	Ind	Ind	Dip	Ind	Ind		
Furniture (Design and Realisation)	024J	2FT HND	Pf g	D	Ind	Ind	Dip	Ind	Ind		

LONDON INST

Ceramic Design	E233	3FT deg									
Design-(Design and Public Art)	E200	3FT deg									
Design-(Design and Puglic Art)	W200	3FT deg									
Design-(Interior Design)	W260	3FT deg									
Design-(Interior Design)	E260	3FT deg									
Design-(Textile Design)	E221	3FT deg									
Design-(Textile Design)	W221	3FT deg									
Environment and Industry Related-Art and Design	E240	3FT deg									
Fashion	E220	3FT deg									
Fashion Management	WN21	3FT deg								8	12/18
Film and Video	W280	3FT deg								32	12/26
Fine Art (Combined Media)	W103	3 deg									
Fine Art (Painting)	W104	3FT deg									
Fine Art (Sculpture)	W105	3FT deg									
Fine Art: (Combined Media)	E103	3FT deg									
Fine Art: (Critical Fine Art Practice)	E110	3FT deg									
Fine Art: (Film & Video)	E113	3FT deg									
Fine Art: (Painting)	E111	3FT deg									
Fine Art: (Painting)	E104	3FT deg									
Fine Art: (Printmaking and Photomedia)	E114	3FT deg									
Fine Art: (Sculpture)	E112	3FT deg									
Fine Art: (Sculpture)	E105	3FT deg									
Graphic Design	W210	3FT deg									
Graphic Design	E211	3FT deg									
Graphic Design	E210	3FT deg									
Graphic and Media Design	E212	3FT deg									
Jewellery Design	E660	3FT deg									
Print Media (Book Arts and Crafts)	WW26	3FT deg									
Print Media (Book Arts and Crafts)	EW26	3FT deg									
Print Media (Surface Design)	EW2P	3FT deg									
Print Media (Surface Design)	WW2P	3FT deg									
Product Design	E230	3FT deg									
Retail Design Management	EW52	3FT deg									
Retail Design Management	NW5F	3FT deg									
Textile Design	E225	3FT deg									
Visual Arts: Ceramics	W151	3FT deg									
Visual Arts: Ceramics	E151	3FT deg									
Visual Arts: Drawing	W152	3FT deg									
Visual Arts: Drawing	E152	3FT deg									
Visual Arts: Painting	E153	3FT deg									
Visual Arts: Painting	W153	3FT deg									
Visual Arts: Sculpture	W154	3FT deg									

Art and Design 7

course details			98 expected requirements							96 entry stats	
TITLE	CODE	COURSE	SUBJECTS	A/AS	ND/C	RGNVQ	IB	SQA(H)	SQA	RATIO	A/AS
Visual Arts: Sculpture	E154	3FT deg									
Visual Arts: Silversmithing and Metalwork	E155	3FT deg									
Visual Arts: Silversmithing and Metalwork	W155	3FT deg									
Visual Merchandising	NW52	3FT deg									
Retail Design	25WE	2FT HND									
Typographic Design	012E	2FT HND									
LOUGHBOROUGH COLLEGE of A & D											
Fine Art (Painting)	E120	3FT deg	Fa g		N	PA<u>3</u>/^ gi	Ind	CCCC	N		
Fine Art (Printmaking)	E140	3FT deg	Fa g		N	PA<u>3</u>/^ gi	Ind	CCCC	N		
Fine Art (Sculpture)	E130	3FT deg	Fa g		N	PA<u>3</u>/^ gi	Ind	CCCC	N		
Graphic Communication	E210	3FT deg	Fa g		N	PA<u>3</u>/^ gi	Ind	CCCC	N		
Illustration	E215	3FT deg	Fa g		N	PA<u>3</u>/^ gi	Ind	CCCC	N		
Textile Design (Printed Textiles)	E221	3FT deg	Fa g		N	PA<u>3</u>/^ gi	Ind	CCCC	N		
Textile Design (Multi-Media Textiles)	E220	3FT deg	Fa g		N	PA<u>3</u>/^ gi	Ind	CCCC	N		
Textile Design (Woven Textiles)	E222	3FT deg	Fa g		N	PA<u>3</u>/^ gi	Ind	CCCC	N		
Three Dimensional Design (Ceramics)	E232	3FT deg	Fa g		N	PA<u>3</u>/^ gi	Ind	CCCC	N		
Three Dimensional Design (Furniture)	E235	3FT deg	Fa g		N	PA<u>3</u>/^ gi	Ind	CCCC	N		
Three Dimensional Design (Silversmithing & Jewel)	E660	3FT deg	Fa g		N	PA<u>3</u>/^ gi	Ind	CCCC	N		
LOWESTOFT COLL											
Design (Informational Illustration)	512E	2FT HND	Fa+Pf	8	N	PA	Ind	Ind	Ind		
Design (Studio Crafts)	62WE	2FT HND	Fa+Pf	8	N	PA	Ind	Ind	Ind		
Graphic Design	012E	2FT HND	Fa+Pf	8	N	PA	Ind	Ind	Ind		
LSU COLL of HE											
Art (Combined)	W100	3FT deg									
Art and English	EQ13	3FT deg									
Art and History	EV11	3FT deg									
Art and Psychology	EL17	3FT deg									
Art with English	E1Q3	3FT deg	<u>A+E</u>	CD	Ind		Ind	Ind	Ind		
Art with English	W1Q3	3FT deg	<u>A+E</u>	CD	Ind		Ind	Ind	Ind	5	8/18
Art with History	W1V1	3FT deg	<u>A+H</u>	CD	Ind		Ind	Ind	Ind		
Art with History	E1V1	3FT deg	<u>A+H</u>	CD	Ind		Ind	Ind	Ind		
Art with Psychology	W1L7	3FT deg	<u>A</u>	DD	Ind		Ind	Ind	Ind	5	10/20
Art with Psychology	E1L7	3FT deg	<u>A</u>	DD	Ind		Ind	Ind	Ind		
English and Art	WQ13	3FT deg									
English with Art	Q3W1	3FT deg									
History and Art	WV11	3FT deg									
History with Art	V1W1	3FT deg									
Psychology and Art	WL17	3FT deg									
LUTON Univ											
Biology with Animation	C1WF	3FT deg	g	12-16	MO/DO	M/D	32	BBCC	Ind		
Business Systems with Animation	N1WG	3FT deg	g	12-16	MO/DO	M/D	32	BBCC	Ind		
Business with Animation	N1WF	3FT deg	g	12-16	MO/DO	M/D	32	BBCC	Ind		
Contemp British & Euro History with Animation	V1WF	3FT deg	g	12-16	MO/DO	M/D	32	BBCC	Ind		
Creative Design	W200	3FT deg		12-16	MO/DO	M/D	32	BBCC	Ind		
Creative Design & Comp Visualisation & Animation	GWN2	3FT deg		12-16	MO/DO	M/D	32	BBCC	Ind		
Creative Design and Building Conservation	KW22	3FT deg		12-16	MO/DO	M/D	32	BBCC	Ind		
Creative Design and Business	WN21	3FT deg		12-16	MO/DO	M/D	32	BBCC	Ind		
Design	W208	1FT deg		Ind	Ind	Ind	Ind	Ind		
Design and Manufacturing	HW72	3FT deg	g	12-16	MO/DO	M/D	32	BBCC	Ind	17	
Digital Systems Design with Animation	H6WG	3FT deg	g	12-16	MO/DO	M/D	32	BBCC	Ind		

course details — 98 expected requirements — 96 entry stats

TITLE	CODE	COURSE	SUBJECTS	A/AS	NO/C	AGNVQ	IB	SQA(H)	SQA	RATIO A/AS
Electronic System Design with Animation	H6W2	3FT deg	g	12-16	MO/DO	M/D	32	BBCC	Ind	
Environmental Science with Animation	F9WF	3FT deg	g	12-16	MO/DO	M/D	32	BBCC	Ind	
European Language Studies with Animation	T2WF	4FT deg	L g	12-16	MO/DO	M/D	32	BBCC	Ind	
Geology with Animation	F6WF	3FT deg	g	12-16	MO/DO	M/D	32	BBCC	Ind	
Graphic Design	W211	3FT deg	A+Pf g	12-16	MO/DO	M/D	32	BBCC	Ind	15 6/20
Graphic Design	E211	3FT deg	A+Pf g	12-16	MO/DO	M/D	32	BBCC	Ind	
History of Design & Architecture & Creative Des	WV24	3FT deg		12-16	MO/DO	M/D	32	BBCC	Ind	
Human Centred Computing and Creative Design	GWM2	3FT deg		12-16	MO/DO	M/D	32	BBCC	Ind	
Industrial Design	E230	4SW deg	Pf g	12-16	MO/DO	M/D	32	BBCC	Ind	
Industrial Design	W230	4SW deg	Pf g	12-16	MO/DO	M/D	32	BBCC	Ind	24
Integrated Engineering with Animation	H1WF	3FT deg	g	12-16	MO/DO	M/D	32	BBCC	Ind	
Interior Design	W235	3FT deg	A+Pf g	12-16	MO/DO	M/D	32	BBCC	Ind	113
Interior Design	E235	3FT deg	A+Pf g	12-16	MO/DO	M/D	32	BBCC	Ind	
Journalism and Creative Design	PW62	3FT deg		12-16	MO/DO	M/D	32	BBCC	Ind	
Leisure Studies with Animation	N7WF	3FT deg	g	12-16	MO/DO	M/D	32	BBCC	Ind	
Linguistics with Animation	Q1WF	3FT deg	g	12-16	MO/DO	M/D	32	BBCC	Ind	
Mapping Science with Animation	F8WF	3FT deg	g	12-16	MO/DO	M/D	32	BBCC	Ind	
Marketing and Creative Design	WN25	3FT deg		12-16	MO/DO	M/D	32	BBCC	Ind	
Marketing with Animation	N5WF	3FT deg	g	12-16	MO/DO	M/D	32	BBCC	Ind	
Media Performance with Animation	W4WF	3FT deg	Pf g	12-16	MO/DO	M/D	32	BBCC	Ind	
Media Performance with Design	W4W2	3FT deg		12-16	MO/DO	M/D	32	BBCC	Ind	
Media Practices with Animation	P4WF	3FT deg	g	12-16	MO/DO	M/D	32	BBCC	Ind	
Media Production with Animation	PW42	3FT deg								
Media Production with Design	P4WG	3FT deg								
Media Production with Photography	P4W9	3FT deg	g	12-16	MO/DO	M/D	32	BBCC	Ind	
Modern English Studies with Animation	Q3WF	3FT deg	g	12-16	MO/DO	M/D	32	BBCC	Ind	
New Media Technology with Animation	P4W2	3FT deg	g	12-16	MO/DO	M/D	32	BBCC	Ind	
Physical Geography with Animation	F8WG	3FT deg	g	12-16	MO/DO	M/D	32	BBCC	Ind	
Product Design	W231	3FT deg	A g	12-16	MO/DO	M/D	32	BBCC	Ind	11
Product Design	E231	3FT deg	A g	12-16	MO/DO	M/D	32	BBCC	Ind	
Psychology with Animation	L7WG	3FT deg	g	12-16	MO/DO	M/D	32	BBCC	Ind	
Social Studies with Animation	L3WF	3FT deg	g	12-16	MO/DO	M/D	32	BBCC	Ind	
Stage & Screen Technology and Creative Design	WP24	3FT deg		12-16	MO/DO	M/D	32	BBCC	Ind	
Graphic Design	112E	2FT HND	Fa+Pf g	4-8	N/MO	P/M	26	CCDD	Ind	
Graphic Design	112W	2FT HND	Fa+Pf g	4-8	N/MO	P/M	26	CCDD	Ind	23
Interior Design	062W	2FT HND	Pf g	4-8	N/MO	P/M	26	CCDD	Ind	

MANCHESTER COLLEGE OF ARTS AND TECHNOLOGY

TITLE	CODE	COURSE	SUBJECTS	A/AS	NO/C	AGNVQ	IB	SQA(H)	SQA	RATIO A/AS
Furniture Design and Making	EJ24	3FT deg								
Furniture Design and Making	WJ24	3FT deg								
Furniture Restoration and Conservation	WW26	3FT deg								
Furniture Restoration and Conservation	EW26	3FT deg								

UMIST (Manchester)

TITLE	CODE	COURSE	SUBJECTS	A/AS	NO/C	AGNVQ	IB	SQA(H)	SQA	RATIO A/AS
Textile Design and Design Management	J4W2	3FT deg	* g	18	5M	Ind	28	BBBCC	Ind	4 12/24
Textile Design and Design Management with Ind	J4WG	3FT deg	* g	18	5M	Ind	28	BBBCC	Ind	

MANCHESTER METROPOLITAN Univ

TITLE	CODE	COURSE	SUBJECTS	A/AS	NO/C	AGNVQ	IB	SQA(H)	SQA	RATIO A/AS
Crafts	E600	3FT deg	Fa g		Ind		Ind	Ind	Ind	
Crafts	W600	3FT deg	Fa g		Ind		Ind	Ind	Ind	
Creative Arts	W430	3FT deg	* g	DD	3M	D	28	CCC	Ind	6/22
Design & Technology/Business Studies	NW12	3FT deg	*	CD	M+D	D	28	CCCC	Ind	
Design and Art Direction	W200	3FT deg	Pf+Fa							
Design and Art Direction	E200	3FT deg	Pf+Fa							

Art and Design

course details			**98 expected requirements**							**96 entry stats**
TITLE	CODE	COURSE	SUBJECTS	A/AS	ND/C	AGNVQ	IB	SQA(H)	SQA	RATIO A/AS
Drama/Dance	WW2K	3FT deg	*	DD	M+D	DQ	28	CCCC	Ind	
Embroidery	E620	3FT deg	Fa+Pf g	4	N		Ind	CCCC	N	
Embroidery	W620	3FT deg	Fa+Pf g	4	N		Ind	CCCC	N	
English/Design & Technology	QW3F	3FT deg	*	CD	M+D	D	28	CCCC	Ind	
Fashion	J471	3FT deg	Fa+Pf g	4	N		Ind	CCCC	N	
Fashion	E471	3FT deg	Fa+Pf g	4	N		Ind	CCCC	N	
Fashion Design with Technology	JW42	4SW deg	Fa/A+Pf g	12	Ind	M	Ind	Ind	Ind	10/20
Fashion Design with Technology	EW4F	4SW deg	Fa/A+Pf g	12	Ind	M	Ind	Ind	Ind	
Fine Art	E100	3FT deg	Fa g	4	Ind		Ind	Ind	Ind	
Fine Art	W100	3FT deg	Fa g	4	Ind		Ind	Ind	Ind	
Geography/Design & Technology	LW82	3FT deg	*	CC	M+D	D	28	CCCC	Ind	
History/Design & Technology	VW12	3FT deg	*	CC	M+D	D	28	CCCC	Ind	
Illustration with Animation	W217	3FT deg	* Pf	CC	Ind		Ind	Ind	Ind	
Illustration with Animation	E217	3FT deg	* Pf	CC	Ind		Ind	Ind	Ind	
Interactive Arts	W920	3FT deg	Fa+Pf g	6	Ind		Ind	Ind	Ind	
Interactive Arts	E920	3FT deg	Fa+Pf g	6	Ind		Ind	Ind	Ind	
Interactive and Broadcast Media	PW42	3FT deg	Fa+Pf	CC	Ind		Ind	Ind	Ind	
Interactive and Broadcast Media	EW42	3FT deg	Fa+Pf	CC	Ind		Ind	Ind	Ind	
Interior Design	W260	3FT deg	Pf/Ar	12-14	Ind	Ind	Ind	Ind	Ind	
Interior Design	E260	3FT deg	Pf/Fa/Ar	6	Ind	Ind	Ind	Ind	Ind	
Leisure Studies/Design & Technology	LW42	3FT deg	*	CC	M+D	D	28	CCCC	Ind	
Sport/Design & Technology	BW62	3FT deg	S	BC	M+D	DS	28	CCCC	Ind	
Textiles	E410	3FT deg	Fa+Pf g	4	N		Ind	CCCC	N	
Textiles	J410	3FT deg	Fa+Pf g	4	N		Ind	CCCC	N	
Three Dimensional Design	W230	3FT deg	Pf/Ar/Ds	12-14	Ind	Ind	Ind	Ind	Ind	
Three Dimensional Design	E230	3FT deg	Pf/Fa/Ar/D$	6	Ind	Ind	Ind	Ind	Ind	
Visual Arts/American Studies	QW41	3FT deg	*	CC	M+D	D	28	CCCC	Ind	
Visual Arts/Applied Social Studies	LW31	3FT deg	*	CC	M+D	D	28	CCCC	Ind	
Visual Arts/Cultural Studies	LWH1	3FT deg	*	CC	M+D	D	28	CCCC	Ind	
Visual Arts/Dance	WW14	3FT deg	*	DD	M+D	DQ/A	28	CCCC	Ind	
Visual Arts/Design & Technology	WW12	3FT deg	*	DD	M+D	DQ/A	28	CCCC	Ind	
Visual Arts/Drama	WW1K	3FT deg	*	DD	M+D	DQ/A	28	CCCC	Ind	
Visual Arts/English	QW31	3FT deg	*	CC	M+D	D	28	CCCC	Ind	
Visual Arts/Geography	LW81	3FT deg	*	CC	M+D	D	28	CCCC	Ind	
Visual Arts/Health Studies	BW91	3FT deg	*	CC	M+D	D	28	CCCC	Ind	
Visual Arts/History	VW11	3FT deg	*	CC	M+D	D	28	CCCC	Ind	
Visual Arts/Leisure Studies	LW41	3FT deg	*	CC	M+D	D	28	CCCC	Ind	
Visual Arts/Music	WW13	3FT deg	*	DD	M+D	DQ/A	28	CCCC	Ind	
Visual Arts/Philosophy	VW71	3FT deg	*	CC	M+D	D	28	CCCC	Ind	
Visual Arts/Religious Studies	VW81	3FT deg	*	CC	M+D	D	28	CCCC	Ind	
Visual Arts/Sport	BW61	3FT deg	*	CC	M+D	D	28	CCCC	Ind	
Writing/Visual Arts	WW1L	3FT deg	*	DD	M+D	DQ/A	28	CCCC	Ind	
Design (Fashion with Technology)	24WE	2FT HND	Pf g	4	Ind	P	Ind	Ind	Ind	
Design (Fashion with Technology)	24WJ	2FT HND	Pf g	4	Ind	P	Ind	Ind	Ind	4/20

MID-CHESHIRE COLLEGE

Art and Design (3D Craft and Design)	062E	2FT HND	Pf+Fa/Ar	A-E	N	PA	Ind	Ind	Ind	
Art and Design (Fine Art)	001E	2FT HND	Pf+Fa/Ar	A-E	N	PA	Ind	Ind	Ind	
Art and Design (Graphic Communication)	012E	2FT HND	Pf+Fa/Ar	A-E	N	PA	Ind	Ind	Ind	
Art and Design (Photography)	055E	2FT HND	Pf+Fa/Ar	A-E	N	PA	Ind	Ind	Ind	
Art and Design (Textile Design)	522E	2FT HND	Pf+Fa/Ar	A-E	N	PA	Ind	Ind	Ind	

| | | | 98 expected requirements | | | | | | | 96 entry stats |

TITLE	CODE	COURSE	SUBJECTS	A/AS	ND/C	AGNVQ	IB	SQA(H)	SQA	RATIO A/AS

MIDDLESEX Univ

TITLE	CODE	COURSE	SUBJECTS	A/AS	ND/C	AGNVQ	IB	SQA(H)	SQA	RATIO A/AS
Art Practice in the Community	W990▼	3FT deg	Fa/Fp				Ind	Ind	Ind	
Ceramics Design	E233▼	3FT deg	Fa/Pf		N	X	X	X	X	
Constructed Textiles	E221▼	3FT deg	Fa/Pf		N	X	X	X	X	
Design and Technology	W240▼	3FT deg	Ds g	DD	5M	X	Ind	Ind	Ind	
Fashion	E220▼	3FT deg	Fa/Pf		N	X	X	X	X	
Fine Art	E100▼	3FT deg	Fa/Pf		N	X	Ind	Ind	Ind	
Furniture Design	E262▼	3FT deg	Fa/Pf		N	X	X	X	X	
Garden Design	W299▼	3FT deg	Fa/Pf	EE	N	X	Ind	Ind	Ind	
Garden Design	W2D2▼	3FT deg								
Garden Design	E299▼	3FT deg	Fa/Pf	EE	N	X	X	X	X	
Interior Design	E261▼	3FT deg	Fa/Pf		N	X	X	X	X	
Jewellery Design	E660▼	3FT deg	Fa/Pf		N	X	X	X	X	
Metals Design	E238▼	3FT deg	Fa/Pf		N	X	X	X	X	
Printed Textiles & Decoration	EW26▼	3FT deg	Fa/Pf		N	X	X	X	X	
Product Design	E230▼	3FT deg	Fa/Pf g	10	3M	M$ go	X	X	X	
Product Design	W230▼	3FT deg	Fa/Pf g	10	3M	M$ go	X	X	X	
Three Dimensional Design	E260▼	3FT deg	Fa/Pf		N	X	X	X	X	
Visual Communication Design	E210▼	3FT deg	Fa/Pf		N	X	X	X	X	
Joint Honours Degree *Arts Practice in the Community*	Y400	3FT deg	Fa/Pf	12-16	N	Ind	Ind	Ind	Ind	
Joint Honours Degree *Education Design Technology*	Y400	3FT deg	Ds g	12-16	5M	X	24	Ind	Ind	
Fashion	022E▼	2FT HND	Fa/Pf	2	N	PA	Ind	Ind	Ind	
Fine Art	001E▼	2FT HND	Fa/Pf	2	N	PA	Ind	Ind	Ind	
Graphic Design	012E▼	2FT HND	Fa/Pf	2	N	PA	Ind	Ind	Ind	
Public Art Project Management	11NE▼	2FT HND								
Three-Dimensional Design	062E▼	2FT HND	Fa/Pf	2	N	PA	Ind	Ind	Ind	

NAPIER Univ

TITLE	CODE	COURSE	SUBJECTS	A/AS	ND/C	AGNVQ	IB	SQA(H)	SQA	RATIO A/AS
Graphic Communications Management	W210	3FT/4FT deg	*	CC	Ind	Ind	Ind	BBC	Ind	3 10/13
Interior Design	W260	3FT/4FT deg	Pf	CC	Ind	Ind	Ind	BBCC	Ind	
Interior Design	E260	3FT/4FT deg	Pf	CC	Ind	Ind	Ind	BBCC	Ind	

NENE COLLEGE

TITLE	CODE	COURSE	SUBJECTS	A/AS	ND/C	AGNVQ	IB	SQA(H)	SQA	RATIO A/AS
American Studies with Art and Design	Q4W2	3FT deg		DD	5M	M	24	CCC	Ind	
Art and Design with American Studies	W2Q4	3FT deg		DD	5M	M	24	CCC	Ind	
Art and Design with Architectural Studies	W2V4	3FT deg		DD	5M	M	24	CCC	Ind	
Art and Design with Business Administration	W2N1	3FT deg	g	DD	5M	M	24	CCC	Ind	
Art and Design with Drama	W2W4	3FT deg		DD	5M	M	24	CCC	Ind	8/14
Art and Design with Education	W2X9	3FT deg		DD	5M	M	24	CCC	Ind	6/12
Art and Design with English	W2Q3	3FT deg		DD	5M	M	24	CCC	Ind	6/20
Art and Design with French	W2R1	3FT deg	F	DD	5M	M	24	CCC	Ind	
Art and Design with Geography	W2F8	3FT deg		DD	5M	M	24	CCC	Ind	
Art and Design with History	W2V1	3FT deg		DD	5M	M	24	CCC	Ind	
Art and Design with History of Art	W2VK	3FT deg		DD	5M	M	24	CCC	Ind	
Art and Design with Industrial Archaeology	W2V6	3FT deg		DD	5M	M	24	CCC	Ind	
Art and Design with Industry and Enterprise	W2H1	3FT deg	g	DD	5M	M	24	CCC	Ind	
Art and Design with Law	W2M3	3FT deg	g	DD	5M	M	24	CCC	Ind	
Art and Design with Marketing Communications	W2N5	3FT deg		DD	5M	M	24	CCC	Ind	
Art and Design with Media and Popular Culture	W2P4	3FT deg		DD	5M	M	24	CCC	Ind	8/22
Art and Design with Music	W2W3	3FT deg	Mu	DD	5M	M	24	CCC	Ind	
Art and Design with Philosophy	W2V7	3FT deg		DD	5M	M	24	CCC	Ind	
Art and Design with Psychology	W2C8	3FT deg	g	DD	5M	M	24	CCC	Ind	8/20

			98 expected requirements							*96 entry stats*
TITLE	**CODE**	**COURSE**	**SUBJECTS**	**A/AS**	**NO/C**	**AGNVQ**	**IB**	**SQA(H)**	**SQA**	**RATIO A/AS**
Art and Design with Sociology	W2L3	3FT deg		DD	5M	M	24	CCC	Ind	
Art and Design with Sport Studies	W2N7	3FT deg		DD	5M	M	24	CCC	Ind	
Business Administration with Art and Design	N1W2	3FT deg	g	10	M+1D	M	24	BCC	Ind	
Drama with Art and Design	W4W2	3FT deg		10	5M+1D	M	24	CCC	Ind	
Education with Art and Design	X9W2	3FT deg		DD	5M	M	24	CCC	Ind	
English with Art and Design	Q3W2	3FT deg		CC	4M+1D	M	24	CCC	Ind	
Fashion and Textiles	W220	3FT deg		EE	D	M	24	CCC	Ind	
Fashion and Textiles	E220	3FT deg		EE	D	M	24	CCC	Ind	
French with Art and Design	R1W2	3FT deg	F	DD	5M	Ind	24	CCC	Ind	
Graphic Communications	W212	3FT deg		4	N	D	24	CCC	Ind	
Graphic Communications	E212	3FT deg		4	N	D	24	CCC	Ind	
History with Art and Design	V1W2	3FT deg		CD	5M	M	24	CCC	Ind	
Industrial Archaeology with Art and Design	V6W2	3FT deg		10	5M	M	24	CCC	Ind	
Industry and Enterprise with Art and Design	H1W2	3FT deg	g	EE	3M	P	24	CCC	Ind	
Information Systems with Art and Design	G5W2	3FT deg		6	5M	M	24	CCC	Ind	
Mathematics with Art and Design	G1W2	3FT deg	M	DD	Ind	Ind	24	CCC	Ind	
Music with Art and Design	W3W2	3FT deg	Mu	DD	5M	M	24	CCC	Ind	
Product Design (Route A)	HW72	3FT deg	g	4	3M	P	24	CCC	Ind	
Product Design (Route B)	EW72	3FT deg								
Psychology with Art and Design	C8W2	3FT deg	g	CC	5M+1D	M	24	CCC	Ind	
Sociology with Art and Design	L3W2	3FT deg		10	5M	M	24	CCC	Ind	
Sport Studies with Art and Design	N7W2	3FT deg	Ss/Pe	12	M+2D	M	24	BBB	Ind	
Visual Arts	E150	3FT deg	A/Ad/Ds	12	N	D	24	CCC	Ind	
Visual Arts	W150	3FT deg	A/Ad/Ds	12	N	D	24	CCC	Ind	
Design (Fashion)	522W	2FT HND		2	N	M	Ind	CC	Ind	8/12
Design (Fashion)	522E	2FT HND		2	N	M		CC	Ind	
Design (Graphic Design)	112E	2FT HND		2	N	M	24	CCC	Ind	
Design (Graphic Design)	112W	2FT HND		2	N	M	24	CCC	Ind	
Product Design (Route A)	27WH	2FT HND	g	2	N	P		CC	Ind	
Product Design (Route B)	27WE	2FT HND								

Univ of NEWCASTLE

Fine Art	W150	4FT deg	Pf	EE	N		24	CCCCC	HN	15 14/28
Fine Art	E150	4FT deg								

NEWCASTLE COLL

Design (Advertising)	112W▼	2FT HND
Design (Advertising)	112E▼	2FT HND
Design (Fashion Design)	022E▼	2FT HND
Design (Fashion Design)	022W▼	2FT HND
Design (Graphic Design)	012W▼	2FT HND
Design (Graphic Design)	012E▼	2FT HND
Design (Interior Design)	162E▼	2FT HND
Design (Interior Design)	162W▼	2FT HND
Design (Newspaper Design and Infographics)	212W▼	2FT HND
Design (Newspaper Design and Infographics)	212E▼	2FT HND
Design (Photography)	055E▼	2FT HND
Design (Photography)	055W▼	2FT HND
Design (Three Dimensional Studies)	062W▼	2FT HND
Design (Three Dimensional Studies)	062E▼	2FT HND
Design (Time Based Media)	034E▼	2FT HND
Design (Time-based Media)	034W▼	2FT HND

			98 expected requirements							96 entry stats
course details										
TITLE	CODE	COURSE	SUBJECTS	A/AS	ND/C	AGNVQ	IB	SQA(H)	SQA	RATIO A/AS
NEWHAM COLLEGE of F E										
Design (Graphic Design)	012E	2FT HND	* g		Ind	Ind	Ind	Ind	Ind	
Univ of Wales COLLEGE, NEWPORT										
Animation	E270	3FT deg								
Animation	W270	3FT deg	Pf	6	M+D	P$	Ind	Ind	Ind	
Design Futures	W240	3FT deg	Pf	6	M+D	P$	Ind	Ind	Ind	
Design Futures	E240	3FT deg								
Fashion and Textiles	W220	3FT deg								
Fashion and Textiles	E220	3FT deg								
Graphics	E210	3FT deg								
Graphics	W210	3FT deg	Pf	6	M+D	P$	Ind	Ind	Ind	
Interactive Arts	W920	3FT deg	Pf	6	M+D	P$	$	$	$	
Interactive Arts	E920	3FT deg								
Media and Visual Culture	E150	3FT deg								
Media and Visual Culture	W150	3FT deg	Pf	6	M+D	P$	Ind	Ind	Ind	
Multimedia	WG25	3FT deg	Pf	6	M+D	P$	Ind	Ind	Ind	
Multimedia	EG25	3FT deg								
Electronic Computer Aided Design	2W1H	2FT HND	*	2	N	P$	Ind	Ind	Ind	
NORWICH School of A & D										
Cultural Studies	EV94	3FT deg	*	4	Ind		Ind	Ind	Ind	
Cultural Studies	WV94	3FT deg	*	4	Ind		Ind	Ind	Ind	8/22
Fine Art	E100	3FT deg	Fa/Pf g	4	N		Ind	Ind	Ind	
Graphic Design	E210	3FT deg	Fa/Pf g	4	N	Ind	Ind	Ind	Ind	
Textiles	E220	3FT deg	Fa/Pf g	4	N		Ind	Ind	Ind	
Visual Studies	E150	3FT deg	Fa/Pf g	4	N		Ind	Ind	Ind	
Design (Graphic Design)	012E	2FT HND	Fa/Pf g	4	N	Ind	Ind	Ind	Ind	
NORTHBROOK COLLEGE Sussex										
Fine Art: Painting	E100	3FT deg	Fa	2	N					
Fine Art: Painting	W100	3FT deg	Fa	2	N					
Marketing and Design Management	N5W2	3FT deg		10	4M	M				
Menswear Design	E221	3FT deg	Fa	2	N	D	Ind	Ind	Ind	
Surface Pattern with Textiles	E220	3FT deg	Fa/Ar		N	P	Ind	Ind	Ind	
Design (Textiles)	022E	2FT HND	Fa/Ar		N	P	Ind	Ind	Ind	
Fashion Design Promotion with Computer Aided-Des	1H4J	2FT HND	Fa		N	Ind	Dip	SQA	Ind	
Graphic Design and Illustration	012E	2FT HND	Fa		N		Ind	Ind	Ind	
Three Dimensional Design	062E	2FT HND	Fa/Ar		N	P	Ind	Ind	Ind	
NESCOT										
Building Technology and Design	KW22	2FT/3SW deg	*	EE	N	M	Dip	Ind	N$	
Building Technology and Design	KW2F	4FT deg	*							
Imaging Technology	WW25	3FT deg	Py	EE	MO	M	Dip	Ind	N$	
Imaging Technology	WW2M	4FT deg	*							
NORTH EAST WALES INST of HE										
Animation	W270	3FT deg	Pf		Ind	Ind	Ind	Ind	Ind	
Animation	E270	3FT deg	Pf		Ind	Ind	Ind	Ind	Ind	
Animation/Electronic and Digital Design	WH25	3FT deg	Pf		Ind	Ind	Ind	Ind	Ind	
Animation/Electronic and Digital Design	EH25	3FT deg	Pf		Ind	Ind	Ind	Ind	Ind	
Animation/Illustration	E216	3FT deg	Pf		Ind	Ind	Ind	Ind	Ind	
Animation/Illustration	W216	3FT deg	Pf		Ind	Ind	Ind	Ind	Ind	
Ceramics	E232	3FT deg	Pf		Ind	Ind	Ind	Ind	Ind	
Ceramics	W232	3FT deg	Pf		Ind	Ind	Ind	Ind	Ind	

			SUBJECTS	A/AS	ND/C	AGNVQ	IB	SQA(H)	SQA	RATIO A/AS
TITLE	**CODE**	**COURSE**								
Ceramics/Glass	EJ23	3 deg	Pf		Ind	Ind	Ind	Ind	Ind	
Ceramics/Glass	WJ23	3FT deg	Pf		Ind	Ind	Ind	Ind	Ind	
Ceramics/Jewellery Metalwork	WJ63	3 deg	Pf		Ind	Ind	Ind	Ind	Ind	
Ceramics/Jewellery Metalwork	EJ63	3FT deg	Pf		Ind	Ind	Ind	Ind	Ind	
Ceramics/Small Business Practice	EJ13	3 deg	Pf		Ind	Ind	Ind	Ind	Ind	
Ceramics/Small Business Practice	WJ13	3FT deg	Pf		Ind	Ind	Ind	Ind	Ind	
Design (Small Business Practice)	W2N1	3FT deg	Pf							
Design (Small Business Practice)	E2N1	3FT deg	Pf							
Electronic and Digital Design	E2H5	3FT deg	Pf							
Electronic and Digital Design	W2H5	3FT deg	Pf							
Glass	W234	3FT deg	Pf		Ind	Ind	Ind	Ind	Ind	
Glass	E234	3FT deg	Pf		Ind	Ind	Ind	Ind	Ind	
Glass/Jewellery Metalwork	EJ6H	3FT deg	Pf		Ind	Ind	Ind	Ind	Ind	
Glass/Jewellery Metalwork	WJ6H	3FT deg	Pf		Ind	Ind	Ind	Ind	Ind	
Glass/Small Business Practice	WJ1H	3FT deg	Pf		Ind	Ind	Ind	Ind	Ind	
Glass/Small Business Practice	EJ1H	3FT deg	Pf		Ind	Ind	Ind	Ind	Ind	
Graphic Design/Electronic and Digital Design	WH2M	3FT deg	Pf		Ind	Ind	Ind	Ind	Ind	
Graphic Design/Electronic and Digital Design	EH2M	3FT deg	Pf		Ind	Ind	Ind	Ind	Ind	
Graphics	E210	3FT deg	Pf		Ind	Ind	Ind	Ind	Ind	
Graphics	W210	3FT deg	Pf		Ind	Ind	Ind	Ind	Ind	
Illustration	W215	3FT deg	Pf		Ind	Ind	Ind	Ind	Ind	
Illustration	E215	3FT deg	Pf		Ind	Ind	Ind	Ind	Ind	
Illustration/Glass	WJ2H	3FT deg	Pf		Ind	Ind	Ind	Ind	Ind	
Illustration/Glass	EJ2H	3FT deg	Pf		Ind	Ind	Ind	Ind	Ind	
Jewellery Metalwork/Small Business Practice	WN61	3FT deg	Pf		Ind	Ind	Ind	Ind	Ind	
Jewellery Metalwork/Small Business Practice	EN61	3FT deg	Pf		Ind	Ind	Ind	Ind	Ind	
Jewellery/Metalwork	E660	3FT deg	Pf		Ind	Ind	Ind	Ind	Ind	
Jewellery/Metalwork	W660	3FT deg	Pf		Ind	Ind	Ind	Ind	Ind	
Graphic Design	012W	2FT HND	Pf		Ind	Ind	Ind	Ind	Ind	
Graphic Design	012E	2FT HND	Pf		Ind	Ind	Ind	Ind	Ind	
Illustration	512E	2FT HND	Pf		Ind	Ind	Ind	Ind	Ind	
Illustration	512W	2FT HND	Pf		Ind	Ind	Ind	Ind	Ind	

NORTH EAST WORCESTERSHIRE COLL

			SUBJECTS	A/AS	ND/C	AGNVQ	IB	SQA(H)	SQA	RATIO A/AS
Design (Ceramics)	332E	2FT HND	Pf+Fa/2(Ar/Ha/L)	4	N	MA				
Design (Communications)	012E	2FT HND	Pf+Fa/2(Ar/Ha/L)	4	N	MA				
Design (Theatre Studies)	064E	2FT HND	Pf+Fa/2(Ar/Ha/L)	4	N	MA				
Media (Design-Electronic Media)	42PE	2FT HND	Pf		N	Ind	Ind	Ind	Ind	

Univ of NORTH LONDON

			SUBJECTS	A/AS	ND/C	AGNVQ	IB	SQA(H)	SQA	RATIO A/AS
Interior Design	W260	3FT/4FT deg	A g		X	Ind	Ind	Ind	Ind	
Interior Design	E260	3FT/4FT deg	A g		X	Ind	Ind	Ind	Ind	

Univ of NORTHUMBRIA

			SUBJECTS	A/AS	ND/C	AGNVQ	IB	SQA(H)	SQA	RATIO A/AS
Art History and Fine Art	E101	3	Fa	18	MO+4D		26	BBBCC	Ind	
Art History and Information Studies	W151	3FT deg	E/H/A	18	MO+4D		26	BBBCC	Ind	4 12/16
Design and Design History	W201	3FT deg	H+A/E+Pf/Fa	18	MO+4D		26	Ind	Ind	3 8/14
Design for Industry	E230	4SW deg	Fa+Pf g		N	N	X	X	X	
Fashion	E220	4SW deg	Fa+Pf g		N	M	X	X	X	
Fashion Marketing	E221	4SW deg	Fa+Pf g		N$		X	X	X	
Fine Art	E100	3FT deg	Fa+Pf g	X	X		X	X	X	
Graphic Design	E210	3FT deg	Fa+Pf g		N		X	X	X	
History of Modern Art, Design and Film	WW25	3FT deg	E/H	16-20	MO+4D		26	CCCCC	Ind	3 14/22
Multi Media Design	WP25	3FT deg			N	Ind	Ind	Ind	X	

TITLE	CODE	COURSE	SUBJECTS	A/AS	ND/C	AGNVQ	IB	SQA(H)	SQA	RATIO A/AS
Multimedia Design	EP25	3FT deg			N	Ind	Ind	Ind	X	
Three Dimensional Design	E260	3FT deg	Fa+Pf g		N$	M	X	X	X	
Transportation Design	EJ29	3FT deg	Fa g	4	N$			Ind		
Transportation Design	WJ29	3FT deg	Fa g	4	N $			Ind		

NORTH WARWICKSHIRE and HINCKLEY COLL

TITLE	CODE	COURSE	SUBJECTS	A/AS	ND/C	AGNVQ	IB	SQA(H)	SQA	RATIO A/AS
Art and Design	W151▼	2FT Dip	Fa+Pf		N	Ind	Ind	Ind	N	
Art and Design	E151▼	2FT Dip	Fa+Pf		N	Ind	Ind	Ind	N	
Ceramics with Glass	32JE▼	2FT HND	Fa+Pf		N	Ind	Ind	Ind	N	
Ceramics with Glass	32JW▼	2FT HND	Fa+Pf		N	Ind	Ind	Ind	N	
Fashion and Textiles	074J▼	2FT HND	Fa+Pf		N	Ind	Ind	Ind	N	
Fashion and Textiles	074E▼	2FT HND	Fa+Pf		N	Ind	Ind	Ind	N	
Visual Communication	23WE▼	2FT HND	Fa+Pf		N	Ind	Ind	Ind	N	
Visual Communication	23WP▼	2FT HND	Fa+Pf		N	Ind	Ind	Ind	N	

NOTTINGHAM TRENT Univ

TITLE	CODE	COURSE	SUBJECTS	A/AS	ND/C	AGNVQ	IB	SQA(H)	SQA	RATIO A/AS
Clothing Studies with Textiles	JW42	4SW deg	Fa g	12	Ind	Ind	Ind	Ind	Ind	4 12/24
Decorative Arts	E170	3FT deg	Fa/Ad g		Ind	Ind	Ind	Ind	Ind	
Design Studies	W200	3FT deg	* g	14	Ind	Ind	Ind	Ind	Ind	8 14/26
Fashion Design	E220	3FT deg	Fa g		Ind	Ind	Ind	Ind	Ind	
Fine Art	E100	3FT deg	Fa g		Ind	Ind	Ind	Ind	Ind	
Furniture and Product Design	E230	4SW deg	Fa/Ds/A g		Ind	Ind	Ind	Ind	Ind	
Graphic Design	E210	3FT deg	Fa/A g		Ind	Ind	Ind	Ind	Ind	
Interior Architecture & Design	E260	4SW deg	Fa g	18	Ind	Ind	Ind	Ind	Ind	
Knitwear Design	E222	4SW deg	Fa g		Ind	Ind	Ind	Ind	Ind	
Television Production Design	E280	3FT deg	Fa+A g		Ind	Ind	Ind	Ind	Ind	
Textile Design	E221	3FT deg	Fa g	14	Ind	Ind	Ind	Ind	Ind	
Fashion Technology	022E▼	2FT HND	g	4-6	Ind	Ind	Ind	Ind	Ind	

OXFORD Univ

TITLE	CODE	COURSE	SUBJECTS	A/AS	ND/C	AGNVQ	IB	SQA(H)	SQA	RATIO A/AS
Fine Art	W100	3FT deg	*	ABB-BBB	DO		34	AAABB	Ind	7 24/30

OXFORD BROOKES Univ

TITLE	CODE	COURSE	SUBJECTS	A/AS	ND/C	AGNVQ	IB	SQA(H)	SQA	RATIO A/AS
Fine Art	E100	3FT deg	Pf+A	BC	Ind	MA^	Ind	Ind	Ind	
Fine Art/Accounting and Finance	NW41	3FT deg	Pf+A g	BC-BCC	Ind	MA^/D*3	Ind	Ind	Ind	
Fine Art/Anthropology	LW61	3FT deg	Pf+A	BC-BCC	Ind	MA^	Ind	Ind	Ind	
Fine Art/Biological Chemistry	CW71	3FT deg								
Fine Art/Biology	CW11	3FT deg	Pf+A+S g	DD-BC	Ind	MA^/MS	Ind	Ind	Ind	
Fine Art/Business Administration and Management	NW11	3FT deg	Pf+A g	BC-BBC	Ind	MA^/MB4	Ind	Ind	Ind	
Fine Art/Cartography	FW81	3FT deg	Pf+A g	BC-DDD	Ind	MA^	Ind	Ind	Ind	
Fine Art/Cell Biology	CWC1	3FT deg								
Fine Art/Combined Studies	WY14	3FT deg		X		X	X	X		
Fine Art/Computer Systems	GW61	3FT deg	Pf+A g	CDD-BC	Ind	MA^	Ind	Ind	Ind	
Fine Art/Computing	GW51	3FT deg	Pf+A g	CDD-BC	Ind	MA^	Ind	Ind	Ind	
Fine Art/Computing Mathematics	GW91	3FT deg	Pf+A g	CD-BC	Ind	MA^	Ind	Ind	Ind	
Fine Art/Ecology	CW91	3FT deg	Pf+A g	BC-DDD	Ind	MA^/MS	Ind	Ind	Ind	
Fine Art/Economics	LW11	3FT deg	Pf+A g	CCD-BB	Ind	MA^/M*3	Ind	Ind	Ind	
Fine Art/Educational Studies	WX19	3FT deg	Pf+A	BC-DDD	Ind	MA^/M*3	Ind	Ind	Ind	
Fine Art/Electronics	HW61	3FT deg	S/M+Pf+A	CC-BC	Ind	M$/MA^	Ind	Ind	Ind	
Fine Art/English Studies	QW31	3FT deg	Pf+A	BC-AB	Ind	MA^	Ind	Ind	Ind	
Fine Art/Environmental Chemistry	WF11	3FT deg								
Fine Art/Environmental Policy	KW31	3FT deg								
Fine Art/Environmental Sciences	FWX1	3FT deg	Pf+A+S g	CD-BC	Ind	MA^/DS	Ind	Ind	Ind	
Fine Art/Exercise and Health	WB16	3FT deg	Pf+A+S	DD-BC	Ind	MA^/MS	Ind	Ind	Ind	

course details			98 expected requirements							96 entry stats

TITLE	CODE	COURSE	SUBJECTS	A/AS	ND/C	AGNVQ	IB	SQA(H)	SQA	RATIO A/AS
Food Science and Nutrition/Fine Art	DW41	3FT deg	Pf+A+S g	DD-BC	Ind	MS/MA^	Ind	Ind	Ind	
French Language and Contemp Studies/Fine Art	RWC1	4SW deg	F+Pf+A	BC-DDD	Ind	MA^	Ind	Ind	Ind	
French Language and Literature/Fine Art	RW11	4SW deg	F+Pf+A	BC-DDD	Ind	MA^	Ind	Ind	Ind	6
Geography and the Phys Env/Fine Art	FWV1	3FT deg								
Geography/Fine Art	LW81	3FT deg	Pf+A g	BC-BB	Ind	MA^	Ind	Ind	Ind	
Geology/Fine Art	FW61	3FT deg	S/M+Pf+A g	DD-BC	Ind	PS/MA^	Ind	Ind	Ind	
Geotechnics/Fine Art	HW21	3FT deg	Pf+S/M+A/Ds/Es	BC-DD	Ind	M$^	Ind	Ind	Ind	
German Language and Contemp Stud/Fine Art	RWF1	4SW deg	G+Pf+A	BC-DDD	Ind	MA^	Ind	Ind	Ind	
German Language and Literature/Fine Art	RW21	4SW deg	G+Pf+A	BC-DDD	Ind	MA^	Ind	Ind	Ind	
German Studies/Fine Art	WR1G	4SW deg			Ind		Ind	Ind	Ind	
Health Care/Fine Art (Post Exp)	BW71	3FT deg		X		X	X	X		
History of Art/Fine Art	VW41	3FT deg	Pf+A	BC-BCC	Ind	MA^	Ind	Ind	Ind	9 18/24
History/Fine Art	VW11	3FT deg	Pf+A	BC-BB	Ind	MA^	Ind	Ind	Ind	
Hospitality Management Studies/Fine Art	NW71	3FT deg	Pf+A	BC-DDD	Ind	MA^/M*3	Ind	Ind	Ind	
Human Biology/Fine Art	BW11	3FT deg								
Information Systems/Fine Art	GWM1	3FT deg	A+Pf g	CDD-BC	Ind	MA^	Ind	Ind	Ind	
Intelligent Systems/Fine Art	GW81	3FT deg	Pf+A g	CC-BC	Ind	MA^	Ind	Ind	Ind	
Law/Fine Art	MW31	3FT deg	Pf+A	BC-BBB	Ind	MA^/D*3	Ind	Ind	Ind	
Leisure Planning/Fine Art	KWH1	3FT deg								
Marketing Management/Fine Art	NWN1	3FT deg	Pf+A g	BC-BCC	Ind	MA^/D*3	Ind	Ind	Ind	
Mathematics/Fine Art	GW11	3FT deg	M+Pf+A	DD-BC	Ind	MA^	Ind	Ind	Ind	
Music/Fine Art	WW13	3FT deg	Mu+Pf+A	DD-BC	Ind	MA^	Ind	Ind	Ind	11
Palliative Care/Fine Art (Post Exp)	BWR1	3FT deg		X		X	X	X		
Planning Studies/Fine Art	KW41	3FT deg	Pf+A g	DDD-BC	Ind	MA^	Ind	Ind	Ind	
Politics/Fine Art	MW11	3FT deg	Pf+A	BC-AB	Ind	MA^	Ind	Ind	Ind	
Psychology/Fine Art	CW81	3FT deg	A+Pf g	BC-BBC	Ind	MA^	Ind	Ind	Ind	13
Publishing/Fine Art	PW51	3FT deg	Pf+A g	BC-BB	Ind	MA^/M$3	Ind	Ind	Ind	
Rehabilitation/Fine Art (Post Exp)	BWT1	3FT deg		X		X	X	X		
Sociology/Fine Art	LW31	3FT deg	Pf+A g	BC-BCC	Ind	MA^	Ind	Ind	Ind	
Software Engineering/Fine Art	GW71	3FT deg	Pf+A g	CDD-BC	Ind	MA^	Ind	Ind	Ind	
Statistics/Fine Art	GW41	3FT deg	Pf+A g	DD-BC	Ind	MA^	Ind	Ind	Ind	
Telecommunications/Fine Art	HWP1	3FT deg								
Tourism/Fine Art	PW71	3FT deg	Pf+A g	BC-CCD	Ind	MA^/M*3	Ind	Ind	Ind	
Transport Planning/Fine Art	NW91	3FT deg	Pf+A g	CC-BC	Ind	MA^	Ind	Ind	Ind	
Water Resources/Fine Art	HWF1	3FT deg								

OXFORDSHIRE SCHOOL of A & D

TITLE	CODE	COURSE	SUBJECTS	A/AS	ND/C	AGNVQ	IB	SQA(H)	SQA	RATIO A/AS
Fine Art	W100	3FT deg	Fa+Pf		N	MA gi	Ind	Ind	Ind	
Fine Art	E100	3FT deg	Fa+Pf		N	MA gi	Ind	Ind	Ind	
Fine Art and History of Art and Design	VW41	3FT deg	Fa+Pf	8	N	MA6 gi	Ind	Ind	Ind	
Fine Art and History of Art and Design	EW41	3FT deg	Fa+Pf	8	N	MA6 gi	Ind	Ind	Ind	
Graphic Design/Illustration	E215	2FT deg		X	HN			X		
Design Crafts	016W	2FT HND			N	MA gi	Ind	Ind	Ind	
Design Crafts	016E	2FT HND			N	MA gi	Ind	Ind	Ind	
Graphic Design	012W	2FT HND			N	MA gi	Ind	Ind	Ind	
Graphic Design	012E	2FT HND			N	MA gi	Ind	Ind	Ind	

Univ of PLYMOUTH

TITLE	CODE	COURSE	SUBJECTS	A/AS	ND/C	AGNVQ	IB	SQA(H)	SQA	RATIO A/AS
Art History with Heritage and Landscape	V4WF	3FT deg	Ap g	CCD	MO+3D	D$^	Ind	Ind	Ind	4
Art History with Media Arts	V4WG	3FT deg	Ap g	CCD	MO+3D	D$^	Ind	Ind	Ind	15
Art History with Visual Arts	V4W2	3FT deg	Ap g	CCD	MO+3D	D$^	Ind	Ind	Ind	5
Cult Interpret & Pract with Heritage & Landscape	Y3W2	3FT deg	Ap g	CCD	MO+3D	D$^	Ind	Ind	Ind	
Cult Interpretation & Practice with Media Arts	Y3WF	3FT deg	Ap g	CCD	MO+3D	D$^	Ind	Ind	Ind	

				98 expected requirements						96 entry stats	
course details											
TITLE	CODE	COURSE	SUBJECTS	A/AS	NO/C	AGNVQ	IB	SQA(H)	SQA	RATIO	A/AS
Cultural Interpret and Practice with Visual Arts	Y3WG	3FT deg	Ap g	CCD	MO+3D	D$^	Ind	Ind	Ind		
Design and Italian	WR23	3FT deg	Fa+Ap g	Ind	MO	MA go	Ind	Ind	Ind		
Design and Italian	ER23	3FT deg	Fa+Ap g	Ind	MO	MA go	Ind	Ind	Ind		
Design: Illustration	E215	3FT deg	Fa+Ap g	Ind	MO	MA^	Ind	Ind	Ind		
Design: Illustration	W215	3FT deg	Fa+Ap g	Ind	MO	MA^	Ind	Ind	Ind		
Design: Photography	W280	3FT deg	Fa+Ap g	Ind	MO	MA^	Ind	Ind	Ind		
Design: Photography	E280	3FT deg	Fa+Ap g	Ind	MO	MA^	Ind	Ind	Ind		
Design: Typography	E210	3FT deg	Fa+Ap g	Ind	MO	M$^	Ind	Ind	Ind		
Design: Typography	W210	3FT deg	Fa+Ap g	Ind	MO	M$^	Ind	Ind	Ind		
Designer Maker	W231	3FT deg	Fa+Ap g	Ind	Ind	MA^	Ind	Ind	Ind		
Designer Maker	E231	3FT deg	Fa+Ap g	Ind	Ind	MA^	Ind	Ind	Ind		
Designer for Industry	E230	3FT deg	Fa+Ap g	Ind	Ind	MA^	Ind	Ind	Ind		
Designer for Industry	W230	3FT deg	Fa+Ap g	Ind	Ind	MA^	Ind	Ind	Ind		
English with Heritage and Landscape	Q3WG	3FT deg	Ap g	BBC	MO+3D	D$^	Ind	Ind	Ind	2	
English with Media Arts	Q3WF	3FT deg	Ap g	BBC	MO+3D	D$^	Ind	Ind	Ind	9	12/26
English with Visual Arts	Q3W2	3FT deg	Ap g	BBC	MO+3D	D$^	Ind	Ind	Ind	2	12/18
Fine Art	W100	3FT deg	Fa+Ap g	Ind	MA	MA^	Ind	Ind	Ind		
Fine Art	E100	3FT deg	Fa+Ap g	Ind	MA	MA^	Ind	Ind	Ind		
Fine Art Contextual Practice	E101	3FT deg	Fa+Ap g	Ind	MA	MA^	Ind	Ind	Ind		
Fine Art Contextual Practice	W101	3FT deg	Fa+Ap g	Ind	MA	MA^	Ind	Ind	Ind		
Heritage & Landscape w. Cult Interpret & Pract	W2Y3	3FT deg	Ap g	CCD	MO+3D	D$^	Ind	Ind	Ind		
Heritage and Landscape	W250	3FT deg	Ap g	CCD	MO+3D	D$^	Ind	Ind	Ind	6	
Heritage and Landscape with Art History	W2VL	3FT deg	Ap g	CCD	MO+3D	D$^	Ind	Ind	Ind	3	
Heritage and Landscape with Education Studies	W2XX	3FT deg	Ap g	CCD	MO+3D	DS^	Ind	Ind	Ind		
Heritage and Landscape with English	W2QJ	3FT deg	Ap g	CCD	MO+3D	D$^	Ind	Ind	Ind		
Heritage and Landscape with History	W2VD	3FT deg	Ap g	CCD	MO+3D	D$^	Ind	Ind	Ind	16	
Heritage and Landscape with Media Arts	W207	3FT deg	Ap g	CCD	MO+3D	D$^	Ind	Ind	Ind		
Heritage and Landscape with Music	W2WH	3FT deg	Ap g	CCD	MO+3D	D$^	Ind	Ind	Ind		
Heritage and Landscape with Theatre & Perfor St	W2WL	3FT deg	Ap g	CCD	MO+3D	D$^	Ind	Ind	Ind	2	
Heritage and Landscape with Visual Arts	W206	3FT deg	Ap g	CCD	MO+3D	D$^	Ind	Ind	Ind	3	
History with Heritage and Landscape	V1WG	3FT deg	Ap g	CCD	MO+3D	D$^	Ind	Ind	Ind	11	
History with Media Arts	V1WF	3FT deg	Ap g	CCD	MO+3D	D$^	Ind	Ind	Ind	4	
History with Visual Arts	V1W2	3FT deg	Ap g	CCD	MO+3D	D$^	Ind	Ind	Ind		
Media Arts with Art History	W2VK	3FT deg	Ap g	CCD	MO+3D	D$^	Ind	Ind	Ind	7	
Media Arts with Cult Interpretation and Practice	W2YH	3FT deg	Ap g	CCD	MO+3D	D$^	Ind	Ind	Ind		
Media Arts with Education Studies	W2XY	3FT deg	Ap g	CCD	MO+3D	D$^	Ind	Ind	Ind	5	
Media Arts with English	W2QH	3FT deg	Ap g	CCD	MO+3D	D$^	Ind	Ind	Ind	5	12/22
Media Arts with Heritage and Landscape	W205	3FT deg	Ap g	CCD	MO+3D	D$^	Ind	Ind	Ind	3	
Media Arts with History	W2V1	3FT deg	Ap g	CCD	MO+3D	D$^	Ind	Ind	Ind	3	
Media Arts with Music	W2W3	3FT deg	Ap g	CCD	MO+3D	D$^	Ind	Ind	Ind		
Media Arts with Theatre & Performance Studies	W2WK	3FT deg	Ap g	CCD	MO+3D	D$^	Ind	Ind	Ind	12	14/20
Media Arts with Visual Arts	W204	3FT deg	Ap g	CCD	MO+3D	D$^	Ind	Ind	Ind	5	12/24
MediaLab Arts	GW59	4SW deg	Ap g	16	Ind	D$	Ind	Ind	Ind	5	14/24
Theatre & Perfor St with Heritage & Landscape	W4WF	3FT deg	Ap g	CCD	MO+3D	D$^	Ind	Ind	Ind	2	
Theatre & Performance St with Visual Arts	W4W2	3FT deg	Ap g	CCD	MO+3D	D$^	Ind	Ind	Ind	8	16/22
Theatre and Performance St with Media Arts	W4WG	3FT deg	Ap g	CCD	MO+3D	D$^	Ind	Ind	Ind	6	14/20
Three Dimensional Design	W260	3FT deg	Fa+Ap g	Ind	M $	D$^	Ind	Ind	Ind		
Three Dimensional Design	E260	3FT deg	Fa+Ap g	Ind	M $	D$^	Ind	Ind	Ind		
Visual Arts with Art History	W2V4	3FT deg	Ap g	CCD	MO+3D	D$^	Ind	Ind	Ind		
Visual Arts with Cult Interpretation & Practice	W2YJ	3FT deg	Ap g	CCD	MO+3D	D$^	Ind	Ind	Ind		
Visual Arts with Education Studies	W2X9	3FT deg	Ap g	CCD	MO+3D	D$^	Ind	Ind	Ind	2	
Visual Arts with English	W2Q3	3FT deg	Ap g	CCD	MO+3D	D$^	Ind	Ind	Ind	3	

Art and Design 7

	course details			98 expected requirements						96 entry stats	
TITLE	CODE	COURSE	SUBJECTS	A/AS	ND/C	AGNVQ	IB	SQA(H)	SQA	RATIO	A/AS
Visual Arts with Heritage and Landscape	W208	3FT deg	Ap g	CCD	MO+3D	D$^	Ind	Ind	Ind	4	
Visual Arts with History	W2VC	3FT deg	Ap g	CCD	MO+3D	D$^	Ind	Ind	Ind		
Visual Arts with Media Arts	W203	3FT deg	Ap g	CCD	MO+3D	D$^	Ind	Ind	Ind	8	14/20
Visual Arts with Music	W2WJ	3FT deg	Ap g	CCD	MO+3D	D$^	Ind	Ind	Ind		
Visual Arts with Theatre and Performance Studies	W2W4	3FT deg	Ap g	CCD	MO+3D	D$^	Ind	Ind	Ind	5	12/16
Interior Design (South Devon College)	062W	2FT HND	* g	4	Ind	P	Ind	Ind	Ind		

PLYMOUTH COLLEGE of A & D

Ceramics, Glass and Metals	W233	1FT deg		X	HN	X	X	X			
Ceramics, Glass and Metals	E233	1FT deg		X	HN	X	X	X			
Ceramics with Glass	332W	2FT HND	Fa/Ad		N	P	Ind	Ind	Ind		
Ceramics with Glass	332E	2FT HND	Fa/Ad		N	P	Ind	Ind	Ind		
Design Metals	056E	2FT HND	Fa/Ad		N	P	Ind	Ind	Ind		
Design Metals	056W	2FT HND	Fa/Ad		N	P	Ind	Ind	Ind		
Graphic Design	012W	2FT HND	Fa/Ad		N	P	Ind	Ind	Ind		
Graphic Design	012E	2FT HND	Fa/Ad		N	P	Ind	Ind	Ind		

Univ of PORTSMOUTH

Art and Creative Studies	WW19	3FT deg	A/Fa+Pf	18	N	Ind	Dip	Ind	Ind		
Art and Creative Studies	EW19	3FT deg	A/Fa+Pf		N	Ind	Dip	Ind	Ind		
Art and English	EQ13	3FT deg	E+Fa/Pf		N	Ind	Dip	Ind	Ind		
Art and English	WQ13	3FT deg	E+Fa/Pf	18	N	Ind	Dip	Ind	Ind		
Art, Design and Media	E900	3FT deg	Fa/Pf		N	Ind	Dip	Ind	Ind		
Art, Design and Media	W900	3FT deg	A/Fa/Pf	18	N	Ind	Dip	Ind	Ind	9	8/22
English and Creative Studies	QW39	3FT deg	E+Pf	BCC	X	D$6/^	Ind	AABBB	Ind	6	12/24
Textiles for Fashion	E220▼	3FT deg	Pf		N $	P$			N$		
Textiles for Fashion	W220▼	3FT deg	Pf		N $	P$			N$		
Computer Animation	072W	2FT HND	Pf	Ind	Ind	Ind	Ind	Ind	Ind		
Computer Animation	072E	2FT HND	Pf	Ind	Ind	Ind	Ind	Ind	Ind		
Restoration and Decorative Studies	071E	2FT HND	Fa/Pf	X	MO $	M$	X	X	Ind		
Restoration and Decorative Studies	071W	2FT HND	Fa/Pf	X	MO $	M$	X	X	Ind		
Textiles for Fashion	022W▼	2FT HND	Pf		N $	P$	Dip	Ind	Ind		
Textiles for Fashion	022E▼	2FT HND	Pf		N $	P$	Dip	Ind	Ind		
Visual Communications	012E▼	2FT HND	Pf		N	P*	Dip	Ind	Ind		
Visual Communications	012W▼	2FT HND	Pf		N	P*	Dip	Ind	Ind		

RAVENSBOURNE COLLEGE of Design and Communication

Broadcast Design	E2H6	3FT deg	M/P	E	N	PT	Ind	Ind	Ind		
Design	E200	3FT deg	Ad	E	N	P	Ind	Ind	Ind		
Fashion (Fashion/Textiles)	E220	3FT deg	Ad	E	N	PA^	Ind	Ind	Ind		
Furniture and Related Product Design	E231	3FT deg	Ad	E	N	PA	Ind	Ind	Ind		
Interaction Design	E291	3FT deg	Ad	E	N	PA	Ind	Ind	Ind		
Interior Design	E260	3FT deg	Ad	E	N	PA	Ind	Ind	Ind		
Product Design	E230	3FT deg	Ad	E	N	PA	Ind	Ind	Ind		
Visual Communication Design	E210	3FT deg	Ad	E	N	PA	Ind	Ind	Ind		

READING COLLEGE AND SCHOOL OF ART AND DESIGN

Design (Fashion)	W220	2FT/3FT HND/deg			N	PA	$	$	N		
Design (Fashion)	E220	2FT/3FT HND/deg			N	PA	$	$	N		
Design (Three Dimensional Studies)	E261	3FT deg									
Design (Three Dimensional Studies)	W261	3FT deg									
Fine Art	E100	3FT deg									
Fine Art	W100	3FT deg									
Graphic Design	E210	2FT/3FT HND/deg			N	PA	$	$	N		

TITLE	CODE	COURSE	SUBJECTS	A/AS	ND/C	AGNVQ	IB	SQA(H)	SQA	RATIO	A/AS
Graphic Design	W210	2FT/3FT HND/deg			N	PA	$	$	N		
Interdisciplinary Design	W200	1FT deg			HN						
Interdisciplinary Design	E200	1FT deg			HN						
Product Design	032E	2FT HND			N	P$	$	$	N		
Product Design	032W	2FT HND			N	P$	$	$	N		

Univ of READING

TITLE	CODE	COURSE	SUBJECTS	A/AS	ND/C	AGNVQ	IB	SQA(H)	SQA	RATIO	A/AS
Art	E150	4FT deg	*	BB-EE	Ind	MA^	Ind	Ind	Ind		
Art	W150	4FT deg	*	BB-EE	Ind	MA^	Ind	Ind	Ind	11	10/28
Art and History of Art	VW41	4FT deg	*	BBC	Ind	DA^	31	BBBB	Ind	20	
Art and History of Art	EV14	4FT deg	*	BBC	Ind	DA^	31	BBBB	Ind		
Art and Philosophy	EV17	4FT deg	*	BCC	Ind	DA^	30	BBBB	Ind		
Art and Philosophy	VW71	4FT deg	*	BCC	Ind	DA^	30	BBBB	Ind		
Art and Psychology	EC18	4FT deg	* g	BCC	Ind	DA^ go	30	BBBB	Ind		
Art and Psychology	CW81	4FT deg	* g	BCC	Ind	DA^ go	30	BBBB	Ind	18	18/26
Typography and Graphic Communication	W210	4FT deg	*	20	Ind	DA6/^	30	BBBB	Ind	5	12/28
Typography and Graphic Communication	E210	4FT deg	*	20	Ind	DA6/^	30	BBBB	Ind		

Univ College of RIPON & YORK ST JOHN

TITLE	CODE	COURSE	SUBJECTS	A/AS	ND/C	AGNVQ	IB	SQA(H)	SQA	RATIO	A/AS
Applied Social Sciences/Design & Technology	L3W2	3FT deg		CC	M	MA	27	BBBC			
Art & Design	WW12	3FT deg	A+Pf	BC-CDD	MO	MA6/^	27	BBBB			
Art and Design	EW12	3FT deg	A+Pf	BC-CDD	MO	MA6/^	27	BBBB			
Art/Design and Technology	E1W2	3FT deg	A+Pf	BC-CDD	MO+2D	MA6/^	27	BBBB			
Art/Design and Technology	W1W2	3FT deg	A+Pf	BC-CDD	M	MA6/^	27	BBBB		4	
Art/English	W1Q3	3FT deg	A+E+Pf	BC-CCD	Ind	MA^	27	BBBB		3	10/24
Art/English	E1Q3	3FT deg	A+E+Pf	BC-CCD	Ind	MA^	27	BBBB			
Art/History	E1V1	3FT deg	A+H+Pf	BC-CCD	Ind	MA^	27	BBBB			
Art/History	W1V1	3FT deg	A+H+Pf	BC-CCD	Ind	MA^	27	BBBB		11	
Design & Technology/Education	W2X9	3FT deg	Pf g	CD	M	MA	27	BBBC			
Design & Technology/Education	WX29	3FT deg	Pf g	CD	M	MA	27	BBBC			
Design and Technology/Applied Social Sciences	W2L3	3FT deg	Pf	CD	M	MA	27	BBBC			
Design and Technology/Applied Social Sciences	E2L3	3FT deg	Pf	CD	MO	MA	27	BBBC			
Design and Technology/Art	E2W1	3FT deg	A+Pf	CD	MO	MA / M*^	27	BBBC			
Design and Technology/Art	W2W1	3FT deg	A+Pf	CD	MO	MA / M*^	27	BBBC		2	8/18
Design and Technology/Management Studies	W2N1	3FT deg	Pf g	CD	MO	MA	27	BBBC		3	6/20
Design and Technology/Management Studies	E2N1	3FT deg	Pf g	CD	MO	MA	27	BBBC			
English/Art	Q3W1	3FT deg	E+A+Pf	16	Ind	Ind	30	BBBB		5	
History/Art	V1W1	3FT deg	A+H+Pf	14	X	MA^	30	BBBB		3	

ROBERT GORDON Univ

TITLE	CODE	COURSE	SUBJECTS	A/AS	ND/C	AGNVQ	IB	SQA(H)	SQA	RATIO	A/AS
Design for Industry	W230	4FT deg	E g	DD	Ind	Ind	Ind	BBC$	Ind	6	
Interior Architecture	K1W2	4FT/5SW deg	E+Pf g	CCD	N	Ind	Ind	BBCC$	Ind	6	

ROEHAMPTON INST

TITLE	CODE	COURSE	SUBJECTS	A/AS	ND/C	AGNVQ	IB	SQA(H)	SQA	RATIO	A/AS
Applied Consumer Studies and Art for Community	WN19▼	3FT deg	g	12	4M	P$ go	26	BCC	N	2	
Art For Community	W150▼	3FT deg	*	DD	3M	P$	24	CCC	N	2	8/18
Biology and Art for Community	WC11▼	3FT deg	B	12	4M $	P$ go	26	CCC	N$		
Business Studies and Art for Community	NW11▼	3FT deg	g	DD	3D	M$ go	26	BCC	N$		
Calligraphy & Bookbinding	PW52▼	3FT deg	g	DD	4M	P$	26	BCC	N	2	
Dance Studies and Art for Community	WW14▼	3FT deg	*	CC	2M+2D	M$	30	BBC	Ind	4	
Drama & Theatre Studies and Art for Community	WW1L▼	3FT deg	T/E	16	3D	M$^	30	BBC	Ind	4	
Education and Art for Community	WX19▼	3FT deg	*	DD	3M	P$	24	CCC	N	1	6/20
English Lang & Linguistics and Art for Community	WQ1H▼	3FT deg	E/L	CC	2M+2D$	M$^	30	BBC	Ind	2	
English Literature and Art for Community	WQ13▼	3FT deg	E	CC	2M+2D$	M^	28	BBC	Ind	4	

course details

TITLE	CODE	COURSE	SUBJECTS	A/AS	ND/C	AGNVQ	IB	SQA(H)	SQA	RATIO A/AS
Environmental Studies and Art for Community	WF19▼	3FT deg	B/Gy	DD	4M $	P$ go	26	BCC	N$	3
French and Art for Community	WR11▼	4FT deg	F	12	4M $	P^	26	BCC	N$	
Geography and Art for Community	WL18▼	3FT deg	Gy	DD	4M $	P$ go	26	BCC	N$	5
Health Studies and Art for Community	BW91▼	3FT deg	g	12	3M	P$	24	CCC	N$	
History and Art for Community	WV11▼	3FT deg	H	DD	4M $	P^	26	BCC	N$	2
Human & Social Biology and Art for Community	WC1C▼	3FT deg	B	12	3M $	P$	24	CCC	N$	
Music and Art for Community	WW13▼	3FT deg	Mu	DD	4M $	P^	26	BCC	N$	4
Natural Resource Studies and Art for Community	DW21▼	3FT deg	g	DD	3M	P$ go	24	CCC	N$	
Psychology and Art for Community	WL17▼	3FT deg	g	CC	3D	M$ go	30	BBC	Ind	6
Social Policy & Admin and Art for Community	WL14▼	3FT deg	g	DD	3M	P$ go	24	CCC	N	3
Sociology and Art for Community	WL13▼	3FT deg	g	DD	3M	P$ go	24	CCC	N	1
Sport Studies and Art for Commmunity	BW61▼	3FT deg	S g	12	3D	MS go	30	BBC	N$	
Theology & Religious Studs and Art for Community	WV18▼	3FT deg	*	DD	3M	P$	24	CCC	N	1
Women's Studies and Art for Community	WM19▼	3FT deg	*	DD	3M	P$	24	CCC	N	

ROSE BRUFORD COLL

Lighting Design	W4W2	3FT deg	*							7	9/22
Scenic Construction and Stage Properties	W4W6	3FT deg	*							5	
Theatre Design	W460	3FT deg	*								
Theatre Design	E460	3FT deg									

RYCOTEWOOD COLL

Design (Furniture Restoration/Conservation)	016E	2FT HND			N	P	Ind	ABC	N	
Design (Furniture Restoration/Conservation)	016W	2FT HND			N	P	Ind	ABC	N	
Design (Furniture)	632W	2FT HND	Fa/Ar	CC	N	P	Ind	ABC	N	
Design (Furniture)	632E	2FT HND	Fa/Ar	CC	N	P	Ind	ABC	N	
Design (Modelmaking)	092E	2FT HND	Fa/Ar	CC	N	P	Ind	ABC	N	
Design (Modelmaking)	092W	2FT HND	Fa/Ar	CC	N	P	Ind	ABC	N	

SCOTTISH COLLEGE of TEXTILES

Textile Design	W220	4FT deg	A g	CC	Ind	MA	Dip	BBC	HN	3	10/22

Univ of SALFORD

Design Studies	W200	3FT deg	* g	4	3M	P	Ind	CCCC	Ind	9	8/20
Design Studies	E200	3FT deg	Ad	4	3M	P	Ind	CCCC	Ind		
Fashion Design (Design Practice)	E225	3FT deg	Ad	4	3M	M	Ind	CCCC	Ind		
Fashion Design (Design Practice)	E226	3FT Dip		6-14	3M	M					
Fashion Design (Design Practice)	W226	2FT Dip		6-14	3M	M	Ind	Ind	Ind		
Fashion Design (Design Practice)	W225	3FT deg		4	3M	M	Ind	CCCC	Ind	20	
Graphic Design (Design Practice)	W210	3FT deg	Ad	4	3M	M	Ind	CCCC	Ind	141	
Graphic Design (Design Practice)	W212	2FT Dip	Ad	6-14	3M	M	Ind	CC	Ind		
Graphic Design (Design Practice)	E210	3FT deg	Ad	4	3M	M	Ind	CCCC	Ind		
Graphic Design (Design Practice)	E212	3FT Dip		6-14	3M	M	Ind	CC	Ind		
Product Design and Development	E230	3FT deg	g	4	3M	M	Ind	CCCC	Ind		
Product Design and Development	W230	3FT deg	g	4	3M	M	Ind	CCCC	Ind	10	6/22
Spatial Design (Design Practice)	E236	3FT Dip		6-14	3M	M					
Spatial Design (Design Practice)	W236	2FT Dip	Ad	6-14	3M	M	Ind	CC	Ind		
Spatial Design (Design Practice)	W235	3FT deg	Ad	4	3M	M	Ind	CCCC	Ind	16	
Spatial Design (Design Practice)	E235	3FT deg	Ad	4	3M	M	Ind	Ind	Ind		
Visual Arts and Culture	E100	3FT deg	Ad	4	3M	M	Ind	CCCC	Ind		
Visual Arts and Culture	W100	3FT deg		4	3M	M	Ind	CCCC	Ind	9	20/22
Fashion Design	522W	2FT HND	* g	2	2M	M	Ind	CCC		9	
Fashion Design	522E	2FT HND	* g	2	2M	M					
Graphic Design	012E	2FT HND	*	2	N	P					
Graphic Design	012W	2FT HND	*	2	N	P	24	CC	Ind	27	

course details			98 expected requirements							96 entry stats	
TITLE	CODE	COURSE	SUBJECTS	A/AS	ND/C	AGNVQ	IB	SQA(H)	SQA	RATIO	A/AS
SALISBURY COLL											
Design (Graphic Design)	012E	2FT HND	Pf		N	Ind	Ind	Ind	Ind		
Design (Graphic Design)	012W	2FT HND	Pf		N	Ind	Ind	Ind	Ind		
Univ College SCARBOROUGH											
Fine Art	E100	3FT deg	A g	CD	Ind	M	28$	Ind	Ind		
Fine Art	W100	3FT deg	A g	CD	Ind	M	28$	Ind	Ind		
Visual Art with Arts	E1Y3	3FT deg	A g	CD	Ind	M	28$	Ind	Ind		
Visual Art with Arts	W1Y3	3FT deg	A g	CD	Ind	M	28$	Ind	Ind		
Visual Art with Social Sciences	W1Y2	3FT deg	A g	CD	Ind	M	28$	Ind	Ind		
Visual Art with Social Sciences	E1Y2	3FT deg	A g	CD	Ind	M	28$	Ind	Ind		
SHEFFIELD HALLAM Univ											
Fine Art (Combined and Media Arts)	E100	3FT deg									
Fine Art (Painting and Printmaking)	E120	3FT deg									
Fine Art (Sculpture)	E130	3FT deg									
Industrial Design (Product)	E230	3FT deg	A/Ds/M/P	CC	3M	PA3/^	Ind	Ind	Ind		
Industrial Design (Product)	W230	3FT deg	A/Ds/M/P/	CC	3M	PA3/^	Ind	Ind	Ind		
Industrial Design (With Applied Technologies)	W240	3FT deg	A/Ds/P/M	CC	3M	PA3/^	Ind	Ind	Ind		
Industrial Design (with Applied Technologies)	E240	3FT deg	A/Ds/M/P	CC	3M	PA3/^	Ind	Ind	Ind		
Metalwork and Jewellery	E660	3FT deg	Ar/E	EE	N	PA	Ind	Ind	Ind		
Packaging Design	E210	3FT deg	Ar	CC	3M	PA3/^	Ind	Ind	Ind		
Packaging Design	W210	3FT deg	Ar	CC	3M	PA3/^	Ind	Ind	Ind		
Combined Studies Art	Y400	3FT deg	*	18	2M	M	Ind	Ind	Ind		
Combined Studies Design	Y400	3FT deg	*	18	2M	M	Ind	Ind	Ind		
Combined Studies Technology (Design Technology)	Y400	3FT deg	*	18	2M	M	Ind	Ind	Ind		
SHEFFIELD COLL											
Design (Communications)	012E	2FT HND	* g	X	Ind	DA	Ind	Ind	Ind		
SHREWSBURY COLLEGE OF ARTS & TECHNOLOGY											
Furniture Design	EJ24	3FT deg	Fa+Pf		N $	Ind			N$		
Art and Design (Textiles)	022E	2FT HND									
Design (Furniture)	42JE	2FT HND	Fa+Pf		N $	Ind			N$		
Design (Graphics)	002E	2FT HND									
Design (Interior Design)	062E	2FT HND									
Univ College of St MARTIN, LANCASTER AND CUMBRIA											
Applied Community Studies/Art and Design	LW51	3FT deg	A	CD-DDE	3M+2D$	MA	28$	BCCC$	Ind	2	
Art and Design	W100	3FT deg	A	CC-CDE	3M+2D$	MA	28$	BBCC$	Ind	5	10/16
Art and Design	E100	3FT deg	A	CC-CDE	3M+2D$	MA	28$	BBCC$	Ind		
Art and Design/Applied Community Studies	WL1M	3FT deg	A	CC-CDE	3M+2D$	MA	28$	BBCC$	Ind	1	
Art and Design/Drama	WW14	3FT deg	A	CC-CDE	3M+2D$	MA	28$	BBCC$	Ind	4	
Art and Design/English	WQ1H	3FT deg	A+E	CC-CDE	3M+2D$	MA^	28$	BBCC$	Ind	10	
Art and Design/Geography	WL1V	3FT deg	A+Gy	CC-CDE	3M+2D$	MA^	28$	BBCC$	Ind	2	
Art and Design/Health Administration	WL1K	3FT deg	A	CC-CDE	3M+2D$	MA	28$	BBCC$	Ind		
Art and Design/Health Studies	WB19	3FT deg	A	CC-CDE	3M+2D	MA	28$	BBCC$	Ind	2	
Art and Design/History	WV1C	3FT deg	A+H	CC-CDE	3M+2D$	MA	28$	BBCC$	Ind		
Art and Design/Mathematics	WG11	3FT deg	A+M	CC-CDE	3M+2D$	MA^	28$	BBCC$	Ind		
Art and Design/Religious Studies	WV18	3FT deg	A	CC-CDE	3M+2D$	MA	28$	BBCC$	Ind		
Art and Design/Science,Technology and Society	WY11	3FT deg	A g	CC-CDE	3M+2D	MA	28$	BBCC$	Ind		
English/Art and Design	QW3C	3FT deg	E+A	BC-BDE	X	MA^	28$	BBBC$	Ind	12	

course details			98 expected requirements							96 entry stats	
TITLE	CODE	COURSE	SUBJECTS	A/AS	ND/C	AGNVQ	IB	SQA(H)	SQA	RATIO	A/AS
Geography/Art and Design	LW8C	3FT deg	Gy+A	CD-DDE	X	X	28$	BCCC$	Ind		
Health Studies/Art and Design	BW91	3FT deg	A	CD-DDE	3M+2D$	MA	28$	BCCC$	Ind		
History/Art and Design	VW1C	3FT deg	H+A	CD-DDE	X	X	28$	BCCC$	Ind		
Mathematics/Art and Design	GW1C	3FT deg	A+M	DD-DEE	X	X	28$	BCCC$	Ind		
Religious Studies/Art and Design	VW8C	3FT deg	A	CD-DDE	X	M^	28$	BCCC	Ind	3	
Science, Technology and Society/Art and Design	WYC1	3FT deg	A g	CD-DDE	X	M^	28$	BCCC$	Ind		

SOLIHULL COLL

Fine Art	E100	3FT deg	Fa+Pf		N	PA	Ind	Ind	Ind		
Fine Art	W100	3FT deg	Fa+Pf		N	PA	Ind	Ind	Ind		
Graphics	W210	3FT deg	Fa+Pf g		N	PA go	Ind	Ind	Ind		
Graphics	E210	3FT deg	Fa+Pf g		N	PA go	Ind	Ind	Ind		
Fashion/Knitwear	24WE	2FT HND	Fa+Pf		N	PA	Ind	Ind	Ind		
Fashion/Knitwear	24WJ	2FT HND	Fa+Pf		N	PA	Ind	Ind	Ind		

Univ of SOUTHAMPTON

Fashion	WW2P▼	4FT deg									
Fashion	EW26▼	3FT deg									
Fashion	WW26▼	3FT deg									
Fine Art	W150▼	3FT deg									
Fine Art	E150▼	3FT deg									
Fine Art	W154▼	4FT deg									
Textile Art	W204▼	4FT deg									
Textile Art	W202▼	3FT deg									
Textile Art	E202▼	3FT deg									
Textiles/Fashion	E221▼	3FT deg									
Textiles/Fashion	W221▼	3FT deg									
Textiles/Fashion	W224▼	4FT deg									

SOMERSET COLLEGE of Arts and Technology

BA(Hons) Design (Packaging) (HND Top-up)	EW52	1ACC deg		X	HN	X	X	X	HN		
Design (Fashion)	W220	3FT deg	Fa+Pf			Ind	Ind	Ind	Ind		
Design (Fashion)	E220	3FT deg	Fa+Pf		Ind	Ind	Ind	Ind	Ind		
Design (Fashion/Textiles)	E221	3FT deg	Fa+Pf			Ind	Ind	Ind	Ind		
Design (Fashion/Textiles)	W221	3FT deg	Fa+Pf			Ind	Ind	Ind	Ind		
Design (Packaging)	JW52	1ACC deg		X	HN	X	X	X	HN		
Design (Surface Pattern)	W226	3FT deg	Fa+Pf			Ind	Ind	Ind	Ind		
Design (Surface Pattern)	E226	3FT deg	Fa+Pf			Ind	Ind	Ind	Ind		
Design (Textiles and Surface Pattern)	W225	3FT deg	Fa+Pf			Ind	Ind	Ind	Ind		
Design (Textiles and Surface Pattern)	E225	3FT deg	Fa+Pf			Ind	Ind	Ind	Ind		
Design (Textiles)	W227	3FT deg	Fa+Pf			Ind	Ind	Ind	Ind		
Design (Textiles)	E227	3FT deg	Fa+Pf			Ind	Ind	Ind	Ind		
Design (Graphic Design)	012W	2FT HND	Fa+Pf			Ind	Ind	Ind	Ind		
Design (Graphic Design)	012E	2FT HND	Fa+Pf			Ind	Ind	Ind	Ind		
Design (Product Design and Manufacture)	045E	2FT HND	Ad/Ds/Fa+Pf			Ind	Ind	Ind	Ind		

SOUTHAMPTON INST

Fashion	W225	3FT deg	Pf	12-14	MO	M$	Dip	CCCC	N	6	10/20
Fashion	E225	3FT deg	Pf	12-14	MO	M$	Dip	CCCC	N		
Fashion (with Foundation Year)	E228▼	4FT deg	Pf	4	N	P$	Dip	CCCC	N		
Fashion (with Foundation Year)	W228▼	4FT deg	Pf	4	N	P$	Dip	CCCC	N	10	
Fine Art	W100	3FT deg	Pf	18	MO	M$	Dip	BBBC	N	9	10/24
Fine Art	E100	3FT deg	Pf	18	MO	M$	Dip	BBBC	N		
Fine Art (with Foundation Year)	E108▼	4FT deg	Pf	6	MO	P$	Dip	CCCC	N		

course details			98 expected requirements							96 entry stats	
TITLE	CODE	COURSE	SUBJECTS	A/AS	NO/C	AGNVQ	IB	SQA(H)	SQA	RATIO	A/AS
Fine Art (with Foundation Year)	W108▼	4FT deg	Pf	6	MO	P$	Dip	CCCC	N	5	12/18
Graphic Design	W211	3FT deg	Pf	18	MO	M$	Dip	BBBBC	N	6	8/22
Graphic Design	E211	3FT deg	Pf	18	MO	M$	Dip	BBBBC	N		
Graphic Design (with Foundation Year)	E218▼	4FT deg	Pf	4	N	P$	Dip	CCCC	N		
Graphic Design (with Foundation Year)	W218▼	4FT deg	Pf	4	N	P$	Dip	CCCC	N	13	14/26
Interior Architecture	K1W2	3FT deg	Ad/Ha/Ds	10-12	MO	M$	Dip	CCCC	N		
Interior Architecture (with Foundation Year)	K1WF▼	4FT deg	*	2-4	N	P$	Dip	CCCC	N		
International Design	W215	3FT deg	Pf	18	MO	M$	Dip	BBBBC	N		
International Design	E215	3FT deg	Pf	18	MO	M$	Dip	BBBBC	N		
Marketing Design	N5W2	3FT deg	*	10	MO	M$	Dip	CCCC	N	2	8/18
Product Design with Marketing	W2N5	3FT deg	Pf	12	MO	M$	Dip	CCCC	N	8	8/22
Product Design with Marketing	E2N5	3FT deg	Pf	12	MO	M$	Dip	CCCC	N		
Product Design with Marketing (with Foundation)	E2NM▼	4FT deg	Pf	4	N	P$	Dip	CCCC	N		
Product Design with Marketing (with Foundation)	W2NM▼	4FT deg	Pf	4	N	P$	Dip	CCCC	N		
Design (Communications)	012W	2FT HND	*	8	MO	M	15$	CCCC	$		
Design (Communications)	012E	2FT HND	*	8	MO	M	15$	CCCC	$		
Design (Graphic Design)	112E	2FT HND	*	4-8	MO	P$	Dip	CCCC	N		
Design (Graphic Design)	112W	2FT HND	*	4-8	MO	P$	Dip	CCCC	N	4	2/12

SOUTH BANK Univ

Arts Management	WN11	3FT/4SW deg	* g	CC	MO	M$	Ind	Ind	Ind		
Media Special Effects	HW62	3FT deg	2(Ar/Fa/Me/T) g	CC-CD	MO	M$ go	Ind	Ind	Ind		

SOUTHPORT COLL

Fine Art	E100	3FT deg	Fa+Pf		N $				N$		

SOUTHWARK COLL

Combined Crafts Design	006E	2FT HND	Fa+Pf		N	PA2 gi	Ind	Ind	Ind		
Combined Crafts Design	006W	2FT HND	Fa+Pf		N	PA2 gi	Ind	Ind	Ind		
Graphic Design	012W	2FT HND	Fa+Pf		N	PA2 gi	Ind	Ind	Ind		
Graphic Design	012E	2FT HND	Fa+Pf		N	PA2 gi	Ind	Ind	Ind		
Textile Design	022W	2FT HND	Fa+Pf		N	PA2 gi	Ind	Ind	Ind		
Textile Design	022E	2FT HND	Fa+Pf		N	PA2 gi	Ind	Ind	Ind		

STAFFORD COLL

Design (Figurative Sculpture)	031W	2FT HND	Ad/Fa/Pf			MA go	X				
Design (Figurative Sculpture)	031E	2FT HND	Ad/Fa/Pf			MA go	X				
Design (Typography)	012E	2FT HND	Ad/Fa/Pf			MA go	X				
Design (Typography)	012W	2FT HND	Ad/Fa/Pf			MA go	X				

ST HELENS COLL

Building Studies (Design)	22WK	2FT HND	*	2	N	PC	Ind	Ind	Ind		
Design (3D Craft)	62WE	2FT HND	Pf	2	N	M*	Ind	Ind	Ind		
Design (3D Craft)	62WW	2FT HND	Pf	2	N	M*	Ind	Ind	Ind		
Design (Computer-Aided Art and Design)	082W	2FT HND	Pf	2	N	M*	Ind	Ind	Ind		
Design (Computer-Aided Art and Design)	082E	2FT HND	Pf	2	N	M*	Ind	Ind	Ind		
Design (Graphic Design)	012W	2FT HND	Pf	2	N	M*	Ind	Ind	Ind		
Design (Graphic Design)	012E	2FT HND	Pf	2	N	M*	Ind	Ind	Ind		
Design (Illustration)	512E	2FT HND	Pf	2	N	M*	Ind	Ind	Ind		
Design (Illustration)	512W	2FT HND	Pf	2	N	M*	Ind	Ind	Ind		

THE UNIVERSITY COLLEGE OF ST MARK AND ST JOHN

Art & Design/Community Studies	W1L5	3FT deg		4	MO	M	Dip	CCCC	Ind		
Art & Design/History	W1V1	3FT deg		4	MO	M	Dip	CCCC	Ind		
Art & Design/Leisure & Tourism Studies	W1P7	3FT deg		4	MO	M	Dip	CCCC	Ind		

course details			98 expected requirements							96 entry stats	
TITLE	CODE	COURSE	SUBJECTS	A/AS	NO/C	AGNVQ	IB	SQA(H)	SQA	RATIO	A/AS
Art & Design/Public Relations	W1P3	3FT deg		4	MO	M	Dip	CCCC	Ind		
Art and Design/Media Studies	W1P4	3FT deg		4	MO	M	Dip	CCCC	Ind		
Art and Design/Theology and Philosophy	W1V8	3FT deg		4	MO	M	Dip	CCCC	Ind		
Community Studies/Art & Design	L5W1	3FT deg		4	MO	M	Dip	CCCC	Ind		
History/Art & Design	V1W1	3FT deg	H	12	MO	M	Dip	Ind	Ind		
Leisure & Tourism Studies/Art & Design	P7W1	3FT deg		8	MO	M	Ind	Ind	Ind		
Media Studies/Art and Design	P4W1	3FT deg		16	MO	M	Ind	Ind	Ind		
Public Relations/Art & Design	P3W1	3FT deg		16	MO	M	Ind	Ind	Ind		
Theology & Philosophy/Art & Design	V8W1	3FT deg	Re	4	MO	M	Dip	CCCC	Ind		

STAFFORDSHIRE Univ

Design (Level Zero)	E208	1FT deg	Pf	EE	Ind	M					
Design (Level Zero)	W208	1FT deg	Pf g	EE	Ind	M$	Ind	Ind	Ind		
Design (Semester Zero)	W218	1FT deg	Pf g	E	Ind	Ind	Ind	Ind	Ind		
Design (Semester Zero)	E218	1FT deg									
Design Management	W290	3FT deg	Pf	DD	3M	MA	Ind	Ind	Ind	1	8/12
Design: Ceramic Arts	W233	3FT deg	Pf	EE	3M	MA	Ind	Ind	Ind		
Design: Ceramic Arts	E233	3FT deg	Pf	EE	3M	MA	Ind	Ind	Ind		
Design: Ceramics	E232	3FT deg	Pf	EE	3M	MA	Ind	Ind	Ind		
Design: Ceramics	W232	3FT deg	Pf	EE	3M	MA	Ind	Ind	Ind		
Design: Crafts	W600	3FT deg	Pf	EE	3M	MA	Ind	Ind	Ind	25	
Design: Crafts	E600	3FT deg	Pf	EE	3M	MA	Ind	Ind	Ind		
Design: Electronic Graphics	E211	3FT deg	Pf	EE	3M	MA	Ind	Ind	Ind		
Design: Electronic Graphics	W211	3FT deg	Pf	EE	3M	MA	Ind	Ind	Ind	19	
Design: Glass	W234	3FT deg	Pf	EE	3M	MA	Ind	Ind	Ind	6	
Design: Glass	E234	3FT deg	Pf	EE	3M	MA	Ind	Ind	Ind		
Design: Graphics	E210	3FT deg	Pf	EE	3M	MA	Ind	Ind	Ind		
Design: Graphics	W210	3FT deg	Pf	EE	3M	MA	Ind	Ind	Ind	9	6/22
Design: Multimedia Graphics	W212	3FT deg	Pf	EE	3M	MA	Ind	Ind	Ind	14	
Design: Multimedia Graphics	E212	3FT deg	Pf	EE	3M	MA	Ind	Ind	Ind		
Design: Product Design	E230	3FT deg	Pf	EE	3M	MA	Ind	Ind	Ind		
Design: Product Design	W230	3FT deg	Pf	EE	3M	MA	Ind	Ind	Ind	21	8/13
Design: Surface Pattern	W202	3FT deg	Pf	EE	3M	MA	Ind	Ind	Ind	37	
Design: Surface Pattern	E202	3FT deg	Pf		Ind	MA	Ind	Ind	Ind		
Fine Art	E100	3FT deg	Pf		Ind	Ind	Ind	Ind	Ind		
Fine Art	W100	3FT deg	Pf		Ind	Ind	Ind	Ind	Ind	7	
Fine Art (Level Zero)	E101	3FT deg	Pf								
Fine Art (Level Zero)	W101	3FT deg	Pf		Ind	Ind	Ind	Ind	Ind		
Graphics, Imaging and Visualisation	GW52	3FT deg	g	12	Ind	M	27	CCC			
Graphics, Imaging and Visualisation	GW5F	3FT deg									
Product Design Technology	E231	3FT deg	Ds+Pf	12	3M	MA	Ind	Ind	Ind		
Product Design Technology	W231	3FT deg	Pf	EE	3M	MA	Ind	Ind	Ind		
Design: Ceramics	232E	2FT HND	Pf		Ind	PA	Ind	Ind	Ind		
Design: Ceramics	232W	2FT HND	Pf		Ind	PA	Ind	Ind	Ind	3	

STOCKPORT COLL of F and HE

Design (Advertising)	082E	2FT HND	Pf		N	P	Ind				
Design (Graphic Design)	012E	2FT HND	Pf		N	P	Ind				
Design (Illustration and Visual Studies)	512E	2FT HND	Pf		N	P	Ind				
Design (Lettering/Typography)	112E	2FT HND	Pf		N	P	Ind				
Design (Multi Media Textiles)	022E	2FT HND	Pf		N	P	Ind				
Design (Surface Pattern/Printed Textiles)	122E	2FT HND	Pf		N	P	Ind				

course details			98 expected requirements							96 entry stats
TITLE	CODE	COURSE	SUBJECTS	A/AS	ND/C	AGNVQ	IB	SQA(H)	SQA	RATIO A/AS
Univ of STRATHCLYDE										
Community Arts	WX99	3FT/4FT deg	g	CC	Ind		Ind	BBC$	HN	
UNIVERSITY COLLEGE SUFFOLK										
Applied Biological Science with Art & Design	C1W2	3FT deg	S+Pf	EE	N $	PS	Ind	Ind	Ind	
Art & Design	W200	3FT deg	Pf	EE	N $	P$	Ind	Ind	Ind	
Art & Design	E200	3FT deg	Pf	EE	N $	P$	Ind	Ind	Ind	
Art & Design and Applied Biological Science	EC21	3FT deg	Pf	EE	N $	P$	Ind	Ind	Ind	
Art & Design and Applied Biological Science	WC21	3FT deg	Pf	EE	N $	P$	Ind	Ind	Ind	
Art & Design and Behavioural Studies	EW7F	3FT deg	Pf	EE	N $	P$	Ind	Ind	Ind	
Art & Design and Behavioural Studies	LW72	3FT deg	Pf	EE	N $	P$	Ind	Ind	Ind	
Art & Design and Business Studies	EN21	3FT deg	Pf	EE	N $	P$	Ind	Ind	Ind	
Art & Design and Business Studies	WN21	3FT deg	Pf	EE	N $	P$	Ind	Ind	Ind	
Art & Design and Cultural Studies	WY23	3FT deg	Pf	EC	N $	P$	Ind	Ind	Ind	
Art & Design and Cultural Studies	EY23	3FT deg	Pf	EC	N $	P$	Ind	Ind	Ind	
Art & Design and Early Childhood Studies	EW92	3FT deg	Pf	DE	N $	P$	Ind	Ind	Ind	
Art & Design and Early Childhood Studies	XW92	3FT deg	Pf	DE	N $	P$	Ind	Ind	Ind	
Art & Design and Environmental Studies	FW9F	3FT deg	Pf	EE	N $	P$	Ind	Ind	Ind	
Art & Design and Environmental Studies	EW9F	3FT deg	Pf	EE	N $	P$	Ind	Ind	Ind	
Art & Design and Information Technology	EW52	3FT deg	Pf	EE	N $	P$	Ind	Ind	Ind	
Art & Design and Information Technology	GW52	3FT deg	Pf	EE	N $	P$	Ind	Ind	Ind	
Art & Design and Literary Studies	WQ22	3FT deg	E+Pf	EC	N $	P$	Ind	Ind	Ind	
Art & Design and Literary Studies	EQ22	3FT deg	E+Pf	EC	N $	P$	Ind	Ind	Ind	
Art & Design and Management	EW12	3FT deg	Pf	EE	N $	P$	Ind	Ind	Ind	
Art & Design and Management	NW12	3FT deg	Pf	EE	N $	P$	Ind	Ind	Ind	
Art & Design and Media Studies	EW42	3FT deg	Pf	CE	N $	P$	Ind	Ind	Ind	
Art & Design and Media Studies	PW42	3FT deg	Pf	CE	N $	P$	Ind	Ind	Ind	
Art & Design and Product Design and Manufacture	HW72	3FT deg	Pf	EE	N $	P$	Ind	Ind	Ind	
Art & Design and Product Design and Manufacture	EW72	3FT deg	Pf	EE	N $	P$	Ind	Ind	Ind	
Art & Design with Behavioural Studies	E2L3	3FT deg	Pf	EE	N $	P$	Ind	Ind	Ind	
Art & Design with Behavioural Studies	W2L3	3FT deg	Pf	EE	N $	P$	Ind	Ind	Ind	
Art & Design with Business Studies	W2ND	3FT deg	Pf	EE	N $	P$	Ind	Ind	Ind	
Art & Design with Business Studies	E2ND	3FT deg	Pf	EE	N $	P$	Ind	Ind	Ind	
Art & Design with Cultural Studies	E2Y3	3FT deg	Pf	EE	N $	P$	Ind	Ind	Ind	
Art & Design with Cultural Studies	W2Y3	3FT deg	Pf	EE	N $	P$	Ind	Ind	Ind	
Art & Design with Early Childhood Studies	W2XX	3FT deg	Pf	EE	N $	P$	Ind	Ind	Ind	
Art & Design with Early Childhood Studies	E2XX	3FT deg	Pf	EE	N $	P$	Ind	Ind	Ind	
Art & Design with Education Studies	E2X9	3FT deg	Pf	EE	N $	P$	Ind	BBC$	HN	
Art & Design with Education Studies	W2X9	3FT deg	Pf	EE	N $	P$	Ind	Ind	Ind	
Art & Design with Human Science	W2B1	3FT deg	S+Pf	EE	N $	P$	Ind	Ind	Ind	
Art & Design with Human Science	E2B1	3FT deg	S+Pf	EE	N $	P$	Ind	Ind	Ind	
Art & Design with Information Technology	E2G5	3FT deg	Pf	EE	N $	P$	Ind	Ind	Ind	
Art & Design with Information Technology	W2G5	3FT deg	Pf	EE	N $	P$	Ind	Ind	Ind	
Art & Design with Literary Studies	W2Q2	3FT deg	Pf	EE	N $	P$	Ind	Ind	Ind	
Art & Design with Literary Studies	E2Q2	3FT deg	Pf	EE	N $	P$	Ind	Ind	Ind	
Art & Design with Management	E2NC	3FT deg	Pf	EE	N $	P$	Ind	Ind	Ind	
Art & Design with Management	W2NC	3FT deg	Pf	EE	N $	P$	Ind	Ind	Ind	
Art & Design with Media Studies	W2P4	3FT deg	Pf	EE	N $	P$	Ind	Ind	Ind	
Art & Design with Media Studies	E2P4	3FT deg	Pf	EE	N $	P$	Ind	Ind	Ind	
Art & Design with Social Policy	E2L4	3FT deg	Pf	EE	N $	P$	Ind	Ind	Ind	
Art & Design with Social Policy	W2L4	3FT deg	Pf	EE	N $	P$	Ind	Ind	Ind	
Behavioural Studies with Art & Design	L7W2	3FT deg	Pf	DD	N $	P$	Ind	Ind	Ind	
Business Studies with Art & Design	N1W2	3FT deg	Pf	EE	N $	P$	Ind	Ind	Ind	

course details			98 expected requirements							96 entry stats
TITLE	CODE	COURSE	SUBJECTS	A/AS	ND/C	AGNVQ	IB	SQA(H)	SQA	RATIO A/AS
Design Studies	E210	1FT deg								
Design Studies	W210	1FT deg								
Early Childhood Studies with Art & Design	X9W2	3FT deg	Pf	DD	N $	P$	Ind	Ind	Ind	
Environmental Studies with Art & Design	F9W2	3FT deg	S/Gy	EE	N $	P$	Ind	Ind	Ind	
Information Technology with Art & Design	G5W2	3FT deg	Pf	EE	N $	P$	Ind	Ind	Ind	
Media Studies with Art & Design	P4W2	3FT deg	Pf	CE	N $	P$	Ind	Ind	Ind	
Design (Spatial)	062W	2FT HND	Pf	E	N $	P$	Ind	Ind	Ind	
Design (Spatial)	062E	2FT HND	Pf	E	N $	P$	Ind	Ind	Ind	
Graphic Design Communication	012E	2FT HND	Pf	E	N $	P$	Ind	Ind	Ind	
Graphic Design Communication	012W	2FT HND	Pf	E	N $	P$	Ind	Ind	Ind	
Model Making and Visual Effects	572W	2FT HND	Pf	E	N $	P$	Ind	Ind	Ind	
Model Making and Visual Effects	572E	2FT HND	Pf	E	N $	P$	Ind	Ind	Ind	

Univ of SUNDERLAND

TITLE	CODE	COURSE	SUBJECTS	A/AS	ND/C	AGNVQ	IB	SQA(H)	SQA	RATIO A/AS
3D Design (Glass, Architectural Glass, Ceramics)	W265	3FT deg	* g	CC	N $		24$	CCCCC	N$	
3D Design (Glass, Architectural Glass, Ceramics)	E265	3FT deg	* g	CC	N $		24$	CCCCC	N$	
Arts and Design	E900	3FT deg	Pf g		Ind		X		Ind	
Arts and Design	W900	3FT deg	Pf g		Ind		X		Ind	4 6/20
Electronic Media Design	W270	3FT deg	Pf g		Ind	Ind	X	Ind	Ind	
Electronic Media Design	E270	3FT deg	Pf g		Ind	Ind	X	Ind	Ind	
Fine Art	E100	5EXT deg	Pf g			*	Ind	Ind		
Illustration and Design	W215	3FT deg	Pf g		Ind	Ind	X	Ind	Ind	
Illustration and Design	E215	3FT deg	Pf g		Ind	Ind	X	Ind	Ind	
Information Design	E212	3FT deg	Pf g		HN		X		X	
Modelmaking	W260	3FT deg	Pf g		Ind	Ind	X	Ind	Ind	
Modelmaking	E260	3FT deg	Pf g		Ind	Ind	X	Ind	Ind	
Product Design	HW72	3FT deg	*	10	3M	M	24	CCC	N	
Technology Design	W240	3FT/4SW deg	*	12	3M	P	24	CCC	N	
Themed Leisure Management and Design	N7W2	3FT deg	* g	18	1M+4D	D	26	BBBCC	N$	
Information Design	212E	2FT HND	Pf g		X	MA gi	X		X	

SURREY INST of A & D

TITLE	CODE	COURSE	SUBJECTS	A/AS	ND/C	AGNVQ	IB	SQA(H)	SQA	RATIO A/AS
Animation	E270	3FT deg	Fa		N					
Animation	W270	3FT deg	Fa		N					10 12/26
Design Management	W290	3FT deg	Fa	12-16	N					5 10/20
Design Management	E290	3FT deg	Fa	12-16	N					
Fashion	E2J4▼	3FT deg	Fa		N					
Fashion	W2J4▼	3FT deg	Fa		N					12 14/18
Fashion Promotion and Illustration	W211▼	3FT deg	Fa		N					6 10/24
Fashion Promotion and Illustration	E211▼	3FT deg	Fa		N					
Fine Art	E100	3FT deg	Fa		N					
Fine Art	W100	3FT deg	Fa		N					24
Graphic Design	W210▼	3FT deg	Fa		N					16 12/20
Graphic Design	E210▼	3FT deg	Fa		N					
Interior Design	E260	3FT deg	Fa		N					
Interior Design	W260	3FT deg	Fa		N					14
Packaging Design	W2J5	3FT deg	Fa		N					4
Packaging Design	E2J5	3FT deg	Fa		N					
Textiles	E220	3FT deg	Fa		N					
Textiles	W220	3FT deg	Fa		N					7 10/24
Three-Dimensional Design (Ceramics)	W231	3FT deg	Fa		N					6
Three-Dimensional Design (Ceramics)	E231	3FT deg	Fa		N					
Three-Dimensional Design (Glass)	E232	3FT deg	Fa		N					

| | | | 98 expected requirements | | | | | | | 96 entry stats | |

TITLE	CODE	COURSE	SUBJECTS	A/AS	NO/C	AGNVQ	IB	SQA(H)	SQA	RATIO	A/AS
Three-Dimensional Design (Glass)	W232	3FT deg	Fa		N					8	
Three-Dimensional Design (Metals)	W233	3FT deg	Fa		N					24	
Three-Dimensional Design (Metals)	E233	3FT deg	Fa		N						
Visual Communication	E212	3FT deg	Fa		N						
Visual Communication	W212	3FT deg	Fa		N						

SUTTON COLDFIELD COLL

TITLE	CODE	COURSE	SUBJECTS	A/AS	NO/C	AGNVQ	IB	SQA(H)	SQA	RATIO	A/AS
Fashion and Textiles Design (Surface Pattern)	E220	3FT deg	Fa+Pf	DE	N	Ind	Ind	Ind	Ind		

SWANSEA INST of HE

TITLE	CODE	COURSE	SUBJECTS	A/AS	NO/C	AGNVQ	IB	SQA(H)	SQA	RATIO	A/AS
Architectural Stained Glass	E232	2FT/3FT deg		12	M	M	Ind	Ind	Ind		
Architectural Stained Glass	W232	2FT/3FT deg		12	M	M	Ind	Ind	Ind		
Ceramics	W233	2FT/3FT deg		12	M	M	Ind	Ind	Ind		
Ceramics	E233	2FT/3FT deg		12	M	M	Ind	Ind	Ind		
Design in the Environment	E250	3FT deg									
Design in the Environment	W250	3FT deg									
Fine Art (Interdisciplinary)	W100	3FT deg									
Fine Art (Interdisciplinary)	E100	3FT deg									
General Illustration	E215	2FT/3FT deg		12	M	M	Ind	Ind	Ind		
General Illustration	W215	2FT/3FT deg		12	M	M	Ind	Ind	Ind	6	8/24
Graphic Design	E212	2FT/3FT deg		12	M	M	Ind	Ind	Ind		
Graphic Design	W212	2FT/3FT deg		12	M	M	Ind	Ind	Ind		
Media (A V & Electromed, Video & Mov Image)	E280	3FT deg		12	M	M	Ind	Ind	Ind		
Media (A V & Electromed, Video & Mov Image)	W280	3FT deg		12	M	M	Ind	Ind	Ind		
Painting and Drawing	W151	3FT deg		12	M	M	Ind	Ind	Ind	7	
Painting and Drawing	E151	3FT deg		12	M	M	Ind	Ind	Ind		
Photography in the Arts	E281	2FT/3FT deg		12	M	M	Ind	Ind	Ind		
Photography in the Arts	W281	2FT/3FT deg		12	M	M	Ind	Ind	Ind		
Technical Graphics	E210	2FT/3FT deg		12	M	M	Ind	Ind	Ind		
Technical Graphics	W210	2FT/3FT deg		12	M	M	Ind	Ind	Ind	12	
Virtual Reality	WG2M	3FT deg									
Virtual Reality	WG2N▼	3FT deg									
Virtual Reality	EG2N▼	3FT deg									
Virtual Reality	EG2M	3FT deg									
Design Technology	21WH	2FT HND		E	N		Ind	Ind	N	2	
Design Technology	21WE	2FT HND		E	N		Ind	Ind	N		

SWINDON COLL

TITLE	CODE	COURSE	SUBJECTS	A/AS	NO/C	AGNVQ	IB	SQA(H)	SQA	RATIO	A/AS
Design (5 Options)	W200	3FT deg	Fa/Pf	X	MO	MA	Ind	Ind	Ind		
Design (5 Options)	E200	3FT deg	Fa/Pf	X	MO	MA	Ind	Ind	Ind		
Graphic Design	012E	2FT HND	Fa/Pf	X	N	M$	Ind	Ind	Ind		
Graphic Design	012W	2FT HND	Fa/Pf	X	N	M$	Ind	Ind	Ind		
Illustration	521W	2FT HND	Fa/Pf	X	N	M$	Ind	Ind	Ind		
Illustration	521E	2FT HND	Fa/Pf	X	N	M$	Ind	Ind	Ind		
Packaging Design	25WE	2FT HND	Fa/Pf	8-12	N	M$	Ind	Ind	Ind		
Packaging Design	25WJ	2FT HND	Fa/Pf	8-12	N	M$	Ind	Ind	Ind		

TAMESIDE COLLEGE

TITLE	CODE	COURSE	SUBJECTS	A/AS	NO/C	AGNVQ	IB	SQA(H)	SQA	RATIO	A/AS
Design Crafts	002E	2FT HND		2	N	PA					
Fashion Design and Technology	022E	2FT HND		2	N	PA					
Fine Art Comtemporary Media	001E	2FT HND		2	N	PA					
Graphic Design	012E	2FT HND		2	N	PA					

Art and Design 7

TITLE	CODE	COURSE	98 expected requirements							96 entry stats	
			SUBJECTS	A/AS	NO/C	AGNVQ	IB	SQA(H)	SQA	RATIO	A/AS
Univ of TEESSIDE											
Creative Visualisation	WG25	4SW deg	* g	8-12	Ind	M	Ind	CCCC	Ind	1	10/20
Design Marketing	E2N5	3FT deg	Pf g		N	M$	Ind	CCC	N		
Design Marketing	W2N5	3FT deg	Pf g		N	M$	Ind	CCC	N	6	8/20
Design with a Modern Language	W2T9	3FT deg	Pf g		N	M$	Ind	CCC	Ind		
Design with a Modern Language	E2T9	3FT deg	Pf g		N	M$	Ind	CCC	Ind		
Graphic Design	W210	3FT deg	Pf+Ad/Ds g		N	M$	Ind	CCC	N	15	8/24
Graphic Design	E210	3FT deg	Pf+Ad/Ds g		N	M$	Ind	CCC	N		
Industrial Design	E230	3FT deg	Pf+Ad/Ds g		N	M$	Ind	Ind	Ind		
Industrial Design	W230	3FT deg	Pf+Ad/Ds g		N	M$	Ind	Ind	Ind	6	12/18
Information Society	GW52	4SW deg	* g	8-12	Ind	M	Ind	CCCC	Ind		
Interior Architecture and Design	W235	3FT deg	Pf g		N	M$	Ind	Ind	Ind	11	16/18
Interior Architecture and Design	E235	3FT deg	Pf g		N	M$	Ind	Ind	Ind		
Visualisation	G5W2	4SW deg	* g	8-12	Ind	M	Ind	CCCC	Ind	2	10/22
Visualisation	2W5G	2FT HND	* g	4	Ind	P	Ind	CC	Ind		
THAMES VALLEY Univ											
American Studies with Media Studies	Q4W9	3FT deg		8-12	MO	M	26	CCC			
American Studies with Visual Cultures	Q4W1	3FT deg		8-12	MO	M	26	CCC			
Digital Arts with Advertising	W9P3	3FT deg		8-12	MO	M		CCC			
Digital Arts with Business	W9N1	3FT deg		8-12	MO	M		CCC			
Digital Arts with Information Management	W9P2▼	3FT deg		8-12	MO	M		CCC			
Digital Arts with Information Systems	W9G5	3FT deg		8-12	MO	M		CCC			
Digital Arts with Media Studies	W932	3FT deg		8-12	MO	M		CCC			
Digital Arts with Multi-Media Computing	W9GM	3FT deg		8-12	MO	M		CCC			
Digital Arts with Photography	W9W5	3FT deg		8-12	MO	M		CCC			
Digital Arts with Radio Broadcasting	W9H6	3FT deg		8-12	MO	M		CCC			
Digital Arts with Sound and Music Recording	W9W3	3FT deg		8-12	MO	M		CCC			
Digital Arts with Video Production	W9W4	3FT deg		8-12	MO	M		CCC			
Digital Arts with Visual Cultures	W9W1	3FT deg		8-12	MO	M		CCC			
English Languages & Communications with Media St	Q1W9	3FT deg		8-12	MO	M	26	CCC			
English with Media Studies	Q3W9	3FT deg		8-12	MO	M	26	CCC			
English with Visual Cultures	Q3W1	3FT deg		8-12	MO	M	26	CCC			
Food and Drink Consumer Studies with Media St	D4W9	3FT deg		8-12	MO	M	26	CCC			
French with Media Studies	R1W9	3FT deg		8-12	MO	M	26	CCC			
German with Media Studies	R2W9	3FT deg		8-12	MO	M	26	CCC			
History with Visual Cultures	V1W1	3FT deg		8-12	MO	M	26	CCC			
Information Management with Digital Arts	P2W9	3FT deg		8-12	MO	M	26	CCC			
Information Management with Media Studies	P2WX	3FT deg		8-12	MO	M	26	CCC			
Marketing with Media Studies	N5W9	3FT deg		8-12	MO	M	26	CCC			
Media Arts	W930	3FT dip									
Media Arts with Advertising	W9PH	3FT deg		8-12	MO	M	26	CCC			
Media Arts with Business	W9NC	3FT deg		8-12	MO	M	26	CCC			
Media Arts with Digital Arts	W931	3FT deg		8-12	MO	M	26	CCC			
Media Arts with English	W9Q3	3FT deg		8-12	MO	M	26	CCC			
Media Arts with English Language Studies	W9Q1	3FT deg		8-12	MO	M	26	CCC			
Media Arts with French	W9R1	3FT deg		8-12	MO	M	26	CCC			
Media Arts with German	W9R2	3FT deg		8-12	MO	M	26	CCC			
Media Arts with Marketing	W9N5	3FT deg		8-12	MO	M	26	CCC			
Media Arts with Multi-Media Computing	W9GN	3FT deg		8-12	MO	M	26	CCC			
Media Arts with Music	W9WH	3FT deg		8-12	MO	M	26	CCC			
Media Arts with Photography	W9WM	3FT deg		8-12	MO	M	26	CCC			
Media Arts with Radio Broadcasting	W9HP	3FT deg		8-12	MO	M	26	CCC			

course details				98 expected requirements						96 entry stats
TITLE	CODE	COURSE	SUBJECTS	A/AS	NO/C	RGNVQ	IB	SQA(H)	SQA	RATIO A/AS
Media Arts with Sociology	W9L3	3FT deg								
Media Arts with Sound and Music Recording	W9WJ	3FT deg								
Media Arts with Sound and Music Recording	W9WY	3FT deg		8-12	MO	M	26	CCC		
Media Arts with Spanish	W9R4	3FT deg		8-12	MO	M	26	CCC		
Media Arts with Video Production	W9WK	3FT deg		8-12	MO	M	26	CCC		
Media Arts with Visual Cultures	W9WC	3FT deg		8-12	MO	M	26	CCC		
Media Arts with Women's Studies	W9M9	3FT deg		8-12	MO	M	26	CCC		
Multi-Media Computing with Digital Arts	G5W9	3FT deg		8-12	MO	M	26	CCC		
Multi-Media Computing with Media Studies	G5WX	3FT deg		8-12	MO	M	26	CCC		
Multi-Media Computing with Visual Cultures	G5W1	3FT deg		8-12	MO	M	26	CCC		
Psychology with Media Studies	C8W9	3FT deg		8-12	MO	M	26	CCC		
Sociology with Media Studies	L3W9	3FT deg		8-12	MO	M	26	CCC		
Sociology with Visual Cultures	L3W1	3FT deg		8-12	MO	M	26	CCC		
Spanish with Media Studie	R4W9	3FT deg		8-12	MO	M	26	CCC		
Spanish with Visual Cultures	R4W1	3FT deg		8-12	MO	M	26	CCC		
Tourism with Media Studies	P7W9	3FT deg		8-12	MO	M	26	CCC		

TRINITY COLL Carmarthen

TITLE	CODE	COURSE	SUBJECTS	A/AS	NO/C	RGNVQ	IB	SQA(H)	SQA	RATIO A/AS
Heritage Conservation (Archaeology)	VW62	3FT deg	* g	DD-CC	Ind		Ind	Ind	Ind	3

Univ of ULSTER

TITLE	CODE	COURSE	SUBJECTS	A/AS	NO/C	RGNVQ	IB	SQA(H)	SQA	RATIO A/AS
Combined Studies in Art and Design	EW1F▼	2FT/SW/Dip								
Combined Studies in Art and Design	EW12▼	3FT/4SW deg	Pf			Ind				
Design	E200▼	3FT/4SW deg	Pf			Ind				
Design	E201▼	2FT/SW/Dip								
Fine and Applied Arts	EW22▼	2FT/SW/Dip								
Fine and Applied Arts	EW21▼	3FT/4SW deg	Pf			Ind				
Technology and Design	HW12▼	2FT/3FT/4SW Dip/deg	S/Cs/M	CCD	MO+2D	Ind	27	BBCC	Ind	7 14/22
Textiles and Fashion Design	E220▼	3FT/4SW deg	Pf			Ind				
Textiles and Fashion Design	E221▼	2FT/SW/Dip								
Visual Communication	E211▼	2FT/SW/DIP								
Visual Communication	E210▼	3FT/4SW deg	Pf			Ind				

UNIVERSITY COLL LONDON (Univ of London)

TITLE	CODE	COURSE	SUBJECTS	A/AS	NO/C	RGNVQ	IB	SQA(H)	SQA	RATIO A/AS
Fine Art (4 Yrs)	W150	4FT deg	Pf g	EE	3M	MA go	Dip	BCCCC	Ind	32 16/30
Italian and Design (4 Yrs)	RW32	4FT deg	g	BCC	3M	MA^ go	30$	BBBCC$	Ind	4 18/26

Univ Col WARRINGTON

TITLE	CODE	COURSE	SUBJECTS	A/AS	NO/C	RGNVQ	IB	SQA(H)	SQA	RATIO A/AS
Graphic Design	002E	2FT HND	*	12	Ind	Ind$	Ind	Ind	Ind	
Graphic Design	002W	2FT HND	*	12	Ind	Ind$	Ind	Ind	Ind	

WARWICKSHIRE COLLEGE, ROYAL LEAMINGTON SPA

TITLE	CODE	COURSE	SUBJECTS	A/AS	NO/C	RGNVQ	IB	SQA(H)	SQA	RATIO A/AS
Design (Heritage Display)	052E	2FT HND								
Design (Visual Communication)	23WE	2FT HND								

WEST HERTS COLL

TITLE	CODE	COURSE	SUBJECTS	A/AS	NO/C	RGNVQ	IB	SQA(H)	SQA	RATIO A/AS
Graphic Design	012E	2FT HND	Pf	2	N					
Typographic Design	112E	2FT HND		2	N					

WESTHILL COLL

TITLE	CODE	COURSE	SUBJECTS	A/AS	NO/C	RGNVQ	IB	SQA(H)	SQA	RATIO A/AS
Humanities - English Lit, English Language & Art	Q3W1	3FT deg	* g	CC	4M+2D	M^	Ind	Ind	Ind	
Humanities - Visual Arts	W150	3FT deg	* g	CC	4M+2D	M^	Ind	Ind	Ind	
Humanities - Creative Arts	Y4W9	3FT deg	* g	CC	4M+2D	M^	Ind	Ind	Ind	

Art and Design

	course details			98 expected requirements						96 entry stats
TITLE	CODE	COURSE	SUBJECTS	A/AS	NO/C	RGNVQ	IB	SQA(H)	SQA	RATIO A/AS
WESTON COLL										
Integrating Art and Design	EW12	2FT Dip	Fa+Pf		N $	P$			N$	
Integrating Art and Design	WW12	2FT Dip	Fa/Pf		N $	P$			N$	
Univ of WESTMINSTER										
Contemporary Media Practice	W900▼	3FT deg	*	12	3M	D	Ind	Ind	Ind	16 8/24
Design Futures	W200▼	3FT deg	*	14	MO		Ind	Ind	Ind	11
Fashion	E220▼	3FT deg								
Graphic Information Design	E210▼	3FT deg								
Graphic Information Design	W210▼	3FT deg								
Illustration	E215▼	3FT deg								
Mixed-Media Art	WP24▼	3FT deg	*	14-16	4M+3D	D	28	BBB		14
Workshop Ceramics	E610▼	3FT deg								
Workshop Ceramics	W610▼	3FT deg								
WEST THAMES COLL										
Graphic Design and Advertising	23WE	2FT HND	Ar/Fa/E/Ha/Pf		N	M$	Ind	Ind	Ind	
Industrial Design	032E	2FT HND	Ar/Fa/E/Ha/Pf		N	M$	Ind	Ind	Ind	
WIGAN and LEIGH COLL										
Fashion Design	24WE▼	2FT HND	Ad		N	P$		Ind	Ind	
Graphic Communication Design	012E▼	2FT HND	Ad		N	P$		Ind	Ind	
Textiles and Surface Pattern Design	522E▼	2FT HND	Ad		N	P$		Ind	Ind	
Three Dimensional Craft Design	62WE▼	2FT HND	Ad		N	P$		Ind	Ind	
WIMBLEDON School of Art										
Fine Art (Painting)	E120	3FT deg	Fa+Pf							
Fine Art (Sculpture)	E130	3FT deg	Fa+Pf							
Theatre Design	E2W4	3FT deg	Fa+Pf							
Theatre Design (Costume Design)	E220	3FT deg	Fa+Pf							
Theatre Design (Costume Interpretation)	E221	3FT deg	Fa+Pf							
Theatre Design (Technical Arts Design)	E2WK	3FT deg	Fa+Pf							
Theatre Design (Technical Arts Interpretation)	E2WL	3FT deg	Fa+Pf							
WIRRAL METROPOLITAN COLLEGE										
Fine Art	W100	3FT deg			Ind	Ind	Ind	Ind	Ind	
Design (Multi-option)	002W	2FT HND			Ind	Ind	Ind	Ind	Ind	
Univ of WOLVERHAMPTON										
Animation (Route A)	E271	3FT deg	A/Ad/Ds+Pf	12	4M	M	24	BBBB	Ind	
Animation (Route B)	W271	3FT deg	A/Ad/Ds+Pf	12	4M	M	24	BBBB	Ind	
Art for Society	E101	3FT deg	A/Ad/Ds	14	4M	M	24	BBBB	Ind	
Art for Society	W101	3FT deg	A/Ad/Ds	14	4M	M	24	BBBB	Ind	3
Ceramics	WJ23	3FT deg	A/Ad/Ds+Pf	12	4M	M	24	BBBB	Ind	3
Ceramics	EJ23	3FT deg	A/Ad/Ds+Pf	12	4M	M	24	BBBB	Ind	
Computer Aided Product Design	EW7F	3FT/4SW deg	g	8	2M		Ind	Ind	Ind	
Computer Aided Product Design	HW7F	3FT/4SW deg	g	8	2M		Ind	Ind	Ind	
Computer Aided Product Design	HW72	3FT/4SW deg	g	8	2M		Ind	Ind	Ind	3 6/17
Design & Technology	EJ29	3FT deg	A/Ds+Pf	8	N	M	24	CCCC	Ind	
Design Studies	E200	3FT deg	*	12	4M	M	24	BBBB	Ind	
Design Studies	W200	3FT deg	*	12	4M	M	24	BBBB	Ind	11
Design and Technology	WJ29	3FT deg	A/Ds+Pf	8	N	M	24	CCCC	Ind	7 8/15
Furniture Design	WJ24	3FT deg	A/Ad/Ds+Pf	12	4M	M	24	BBBB	Ind	
Furniture Design	EJ24	3FT deg	A/Ad/Ds+Pf	12	4M	M	24	BBBB	Ind	__ __
Glass	E223	3FT deg	A/Ad/Ds+Pf	12	4M	M	24	BBBB	Ind	

course details | 98 expected requirements | 96 entry stats

TITLE	CODE	COURSE	SUBJECTS	A/AS	ND/C	AGNVQ	IB	SQA(H)	SQA	RATIO	A/AS
Glass	W223	3FT deg	A/Ad/Ds+Pf	12	4M	M	24	BBBB	Ind		
Graphic Communication	W210	3FT deg	A/Ad/Ds+Pf	12	4M	M	24	BBBB	Ind	17	14/18
Graphic Communication	E210	3FT deg	A/Ad/Ds+Pf	12	4M	M	24	BBBB	Ind		
Illustration	E215	3FT deg	A/Ad/Ds+Pf	12	4M	M	24	BBBB	Ind		
Illustration	W215	3FT deg	A/Ad/Ds+Pf	12	4M	M	24	BBBB	Ind	23	10/15
Interactive Multimedia Communication	W270	4SW deg		18	4D	D	28	BBBB	Ind		
Interactive Multimedia Communications	E270	4SW deg		18	4D	D	28	BBBB	Ind		
Painting	E120	3FT deg	A/Ad/Ds+Pf	12	4M	M	24	BBBB	Ind		
Painting	W120	3FT deg	A/Ad/Ds+Pf	12	4M	M	24	BBBB	Ind		
Printmaking	W221	3FT deg	A/Ad/Ds+Pf	12	4M	M	24	BBBB	Ind	5	
Printmaking	E221	3FT deg	A/Ad/Ds+Pf	12	4M	M	24	BBBB	Ind		
Sculpture	E130	3FT deg	A/Ad/Ds+Pf	12	4M	M	24	BBBB	Ind		
Sculpture	W130	3FT deg	A/Ad/Ds+Pf	12	4M	M	24	BBBB	Ind		
Woods, Metals & Plastics	E260	3FT deg	A/Ad/Ds+Pf	12	4M	M	24	BBBB	Ind		
Woods, Metals and Plastics	W260	3FT deg	A/Ad/Ds+Pf	12	4M	M	24	BBBB	Ind		
Applied Sciences *Computer Aided Design*	Y100	3FT/4SW deg	S g	DD	N	M	24	CCCC	Ind		
Applied Sciences (4 Yrs) *Computer Aided Design*	Y110▼	4FT deg	*								
Combined Degrees *Animation*	Y401	3FT deg	A/Ad/Ds+Pf	12	4M	M	24	BBBB	Ind		
Combined Degrees *Animation*	E401	3FT deg	A/Ad/Ds+Pf	12	4M	M	24	BBBB	Ind		
Combined Degrees *Art For Society*	E401	3FT deg	A/Ad/Ds	14	4M	M	24	BBBB	Ind		
Combined Degrees *Art For Society*	Y401	3FT deg	A/Ad/Ds	14	4M	M	24	BBBB	Ind		
Combined Degrees *Ceramics*	Y401	3FT deg	A/Ad/Ds	12	4M	M	24	BBBB	Ind		
Combined Degrees *Ceramics*	E401	3FT deg	A/Ad/Ds	12	4M	M	24	BBBB	Ind		
Combined Degrees *Computer Aided Design*	Y401	3FT/4SW deg	g	DD	N	M	24	CCCC	Ind		
Combined Degrees *Design Studies*	Y401	3FT deg	*	12	4M	M	24	BBBB	Ind		
Combined Degrees *Design Studies*	E401	3FT deg	*	12	4M	M	24	BBBB	Ind		
Combined Degrees *Design and Technology*	Y401	3FT deg		8	N	M	24	CCCC	SQA		
Combined Degrees *Design for Floor Covering & Interior Textiles*	Y401	3FT/4SW deg	A/Ad/Ds	12	4M	M	24	BBBB	Ind		
Combined Degrees *Design for Floor Covering & Interior Textiles*	E401	3FT/4SW deg	A/Ad/Ds	12	4M	M	24	BBBB	Ind		
Combined Degrees *Electronic Media*	E401	3FT/4SW deg	A/Ad/Ds	12	4M	M	24	BBBB	Ind		
Combined Degrees *Electronic Media*	Y401	3FT/4SW deg	A/Ad/Ds	12	4M	M	24	BBBB	Ind		
Combined Degrees *Furniture Design*	Y401	3FT deg	A/Ad/Ds+Pf	12	4M	M	24	BBBB	Ind		
Combined Degrees *Furniture Design*	E401	3FT deg	A/Ad/Ds+Pf	12	4M	M	24	BBBB	Ind		
Combined Degrees *Glass*	E401	3FT deg	A/Ad/Ds	12	4M	M	24	BBBB	Ind		
Combined Degrees *Glass*	Y401	3FT deg	A/Ad/Ds	12	4M	M	24	BBBB	Ind		
Combined Degrees *Graphic Communication*	Y401	3FT deg	A/Ad/Ds+Pf	12	4M	M	24	BBBB	Ind		

	course details			98 expected requirements							96 entry stats
TITLE	CODE	COURSE	SUBJECTS	A/AS	NO/C	AGNVQ	IB	SQA(H)	SQA	RATIO A/AS
Combined Degrees *Graphic Communication*	E401	3FT deg	A/Ad/Ds+Pf	12	4M	M	24	BBBB	Ind	
Combined Degrees *Illustration*	E401	3FT deg	A/Ad/Ds+Pf	12	4M	M	24	BBBB	Ind	
Combined Degrees *Illustration*	Y401	3FT deg	A/Ad/Ds+Pf	12	4M	M	24	BBBB	Ind	
Combined Degrees *Painting*	Y401	3FT deg	A/Ad/Ds+Pf	12	4M	M	24	BBBB	Ind	
Combined Degrees *Painting*	E401	3FT deg	A/Ad/Ds+Pf	12	4M	M	24	BBBB	Ind	
Combined Degrees *Photography*	E401	3FT deg	A/Ad/Ds+Pf	12	4M	M	24	BBBB	Ind	
Combined Degrees *Photography*	Y401	3FT deg	A/Ad/Ds+Pf	12	4M	M	24	BBBB	Ind	
Combined Degrees *Printmaking*	Y401	3FT deg	A/Ad/Ds+Pf	12	4M	M	24	BBBB	Ind	
Combined Degrees *Printmaking*	E401	3FT deg	A/Ad/Ds+Pf	12	4M	M	24	BBBB	Ind	
Combined Degrees *Sculpture*	E401	3FT deg	A/Ad/Ds+Pf	12	4M	M	24	BBBB	Ind	
Combined Degrees *Sculpture*	Y401	3FT deg	A/Ad/Ds+Pf	12	4M	M	24	BBBB	Ind	
Combined Degrees *Woods, Metals and Plastics*	Y401	3FT deg	A/Ad/Ds+Pf	12	4M	M	24	BBBB	Ind	
Combined Degrees *Woods, Metals and Plastics*	E401	3FT deg	A/Ad/Ds+Pf	12	4M	M	24	BBBB	Ind	
Design	42PE	2FT HND	A/Ds+Pf	E	N	P	24	CCCC	Ind	
Design	42PW	2FT HND	A/Ds+Pf	E	N	P	24	CCCC	Ind	9
Design (Figurative Sculpture and Modelling)	031W	2FT HND	A/Ds+Pf	E	N	P	24	CCCC	Ind	
Design (Figurative Sculpture and Modelling)	031E	2FT HND	A/Ds+Pf	E	N	P	24	CCCC	Ind	
Design (Furniture)	42JE	2FT HND	A/Ds+Pf	E	N	P	24	CCCC	Ind	
Design (Furniture)	42JW▼	2FT HND	A/Ds+Pf	E	N	P	24	CCCC	Ind	
Design (Typography)	012W	2FT HND	A/Ds+Pf	E	N	P	24	CCCC	Ind	
Design (Typography)	012E	2FT HND	A/Ds+Pf	E	N	P	24	CCCC	Ind	

WORCESTER COLL of HE

Biological Science/Art and Design	WC91	3FT deg	S+A	DD	Ind	Ind	Ind	Ind	Ind	
Business Management/Art and Design	WN91	3FT deg	A	DD	Ind	M	Ind	Ind	Ind	
Drama/Art and Design	WW94	3FT deg	A	DD	Ind	M	Ind	Ind	Ind	6
Education Studies/Art & Design	WX99	3FT deg	A	DD	Ind	M	Ind	Ind	Ind	2
English and Literary Studies/Art and Design	WQ93	3 deg	A	CC	Ind	M	Ind	Ind	Ind	
Geography/Art & Design	WL98	3FT deg	A	DD	Ind	M	Ind	Ind	Ind	7
Health Studies/Art & Design	WB99	3FT deg	A g	DD	Ind	M	Ind	Ind	Ind	2
History/Art & Design	WV91	3FT deg	A	DD	Ind	M	Ind	Ind	Ind	4
Information Technology/Art & Design	WG95	3FT deg	A	DD	Ind	M	Ind	Ind	Ind	8
Psychology/Art & Design	WL97	3FT deg	A g	CC	Ind	M	Ind	Ind	Ind	5 10/18
Sociology/Art & Design	WL93	3FT deg	A	DD	Ind	M	Ind	Ind	Ind	2
Women's Studies/Art and Design	WM99	3FT deg	A	DD	Ind	M	Ind	Ind	Ind	
Design	002W▼	2FT HND	A	E	N	PA	Ind	Ind	Ind	

WORCESTER COLLEGE of Technology

Design (Communications Electronic Graphics)	012E	2FT HND	*	2	N	M				

YORK COLLEGE of F and HE

Design (Fashion)	022W	2FT HND	*	X	Ind	PA	Ind	Ind	Ind	
Design (Fashion)	022E	2FT HND	*	X	Ind	PA	Ind	Ind	Ind	
Design (Graphic Design)	012E	2FT HND	*	X	Ind	PA	Ind	Ind	Ind	

course details			98 expected requirements							96 entry stats
TITLE	CODE	COURSE	SUBJECTS	A/AS	NQ/C	AGNVQ	IB	SQA(H)	SQA	RATIO A/AS
Design (Graphic Design)	012W	2FT HND	*	X	Ind	PA	Ind	Ind	Ind	
Design Crafts (Clay, Metal, Stone and Wood)	26WW	2FT HND	*	X	Ind	PA	Ind	Ind	Ind	
Design Crafts (Clay, Metal, Stone and Wood)	26WE	2FT HND	*	X	Ind	PA	Ind	Ind	Ind	

YORKSHIRE COAST COLLEGE of F and HE

Fashion/Costume	022E	2FT HND	Fa+Pf		N	M	Ind	Ind	Ind	
Graphic Design	012E	2FT HND	Fa+Pf		N	M	Ind	Ind	Ind	

Biochemistry/Biophysics/ Biotechnology 8

course details			98 expected requirements							96 entry stats	
TITLE	CODE	COURSE	SUBJECTS	A/AS	ND/C	AGNVQ	IB	SQA(H)	SQA	RATIO	A/AS
Univ of ABERDEEN											
Biochemistry	C700	4FT deg	3S/2S+M g	CCD	Ind	MS go	24$	BBBC$	Ind	7	
Biochemistry (Immunology)	C7C9	4FT deg	3S/2S+M g	CCD	Ind	MS go	24$	BBBC$	Ind	6	
Biochemistry (Immunology) with Indust Placement	C7CX	5FT deg	3S/2S+M g	CCD	Ind	MS go	24$	BBBC$	Ind		
Biochemistry (Parasitology)	C7C3	4FT deg	3S/2S+M g	CCD	Ind	MS go	24$	BBBC$	Ind		
Biochemistry with Industrial Placement	C701	5FT deg	3S/2S+M g	CCD	Ind	MS go	24$	BBBC$	Ind		
Biochemistry-Microbiology	CC75	4FT deg	C+2S/C+S+M g	CCD	Ind	MS go	24$	BBBC$	Ind	9	
Biochemistry-Microbiology with Indust Placement	CC57	5FT deg	C+2S/C+S+M g	CCD	Ind	MS go	24$	BBBC$	Ind		
Biomedical Science (Molecular Biology)	B9C6	4FT deg	C+2S/C+M+S g	BBC	Ind	MS go	34$	AABB$	Ind		
Biotechnology (Applied Molecular Biology)	J800	4FT deg	3S/2S+M g	CCD	Ind	MS go	24$	BBBC$	Ind	7	
Molecular Biology (Biochemistry-Genetics)	CC74	4FT deg	3S/2S+M g	CCD	Ind	MS go	24$	BBBC$	Ind	3	
Molecular Biology with Industrial Placement	CC47	5FT deg	3S/2S+M g	CCD	Ind	MS go	24$	BBBC$	Ind		
Univ of ABERTAY DUNDEE											
Biological Chemistry	C740	4FT/5SW deg		DE	Ind	Ind	Ind	BCC	Ind		
Univ of Wales, ABERYSTWYTH											
Biochemistry	C700	3FT deg	C g	16-18	3M $	MS6/^ g	29$	BBBCC$	Ind		
Genetics/Biochemistry	CC47	3FT deg	C g	16-18	3M $	MS^ g	29$	BBBCC$	Ind		
Microbiology and Biochemistry	CC57	3FT deg	B/C g	16-18	3M $	MS6/^ g	29$	BBBCC$	Ind		
Information and Library St/an approved Sci Sub Biochemistry	PY21	3FT deg	B+C g	16-18	3M $	MS6/^ g	29$	BBBCC$	Ind		
ANGLIA Poly Univ											
Cell and Molecular Biology	C620▼	3FT deg	B g	10	3M	P go	Dip	BCCC	N	8	
Univ of Wales, BANGOR											
Biochemistry	C700	3FT deg	C+S g	CCD	3M $	DS^ go	26$	BBCC$	Ind	4	12/22
Biochemistry and Chemistry	CF71	3FT deg	C+S g	CDD	3M $	MS3 go	26$	BCCC$	Ind	4	
Biology with Biochemistry	C1C7	3FT deg	B+C g	CCD	3M $	DS^ go	26$	BBCC$	Ind	5	
Biomolecular Sciences	C650	3FT deg	S g	CDD	3M $	DS^ go	26$	BBCC$	Ind	3	
Marine Biology and Biochemistry	CC17	3FT deg	B+C+S g	CCC	4M $	DS^ go	28$	BBBC$	Ind	15	
BARNSLEY COLL											
Science Foundation Animal and Plant Biology	Y100	4EXT deg									
Science Foundation Biochemistry	Y100	4EXT deg									
Science Foundation Biotechnology	Y100	4EXT deg									
Univ of BATH											
Biochemistry	C702	3FT deg									
Biochemistry (MBioc)	C700	4FT deg	C+B	20	Ind	Ind	30		Ind	4	22/30
Sport and Exercise Science	BC17	3FT deg	S	22	Ind	Ind	30$	Ind	Ind		
Sport and Exercise Science (4 Yr SW)	BC1R	4SW deg	S	22	Ind	Ind	30$	Ind	Ind		
Sport and Exercise Science (with year abroad)	BC1T	4FT deg	S	22	Ind	Ind	30$	Ind	Ind		
Univ of BIRMINGHAM											
Biochemistry	C700	3FT deg	C+B/P/M g	BCC	Ind	Ind	30	Ind	Ind	6	18/28
Biochemistry with Biotechnology	C7J8	3FT deg	C+B/P/M g	BCC	Ind	Ind	30	Ind	Ind	4	24/28
Biochemistry with Molecular and Cell Biology	C7C6	3FT deg	C+B/P/M g	BCC	Ind	Ind	30	Ind	Ind	7	22/30
Biochemistry, Medical	C720	3FT deg	C+B/P/M g	BCC	Ind	Ind	30	Ind	Ind	3	18/28
Biological Sciences (Biotechnology)	J800	3FT deg	B+S/M/Gy/Gl/Ps g	BCC	Ind	Ind	30	Ind	Ind	11	
Mathematics and Sports Science	GC17	3FT deg	M+B/C/P	ABB-ABC	Ind	Ind	30	Ind	Ind	12	24/30
Psychology and Sports Science	CC87	3FT deg	S g	BBB	Ind	Ind	33	Ind	Ind	17	22/28
Sport and Exercise Sciences	BC17	3FT deg	S g	BBB	Ind		32	Ind	Ind	16	22/30

			98 expected requirements							96 entry stats	

course details | | | | | | | | | | *96 entry stats* |

TITLE	CODE	COURSE	SUBJECTS	A/AS	ND/C	AGNVQ	IB	SQA(H)	SQA	RATIO	A/AS
Univ of BRADFORD											
Biochemistry	C760	3FT deg	2S g	BB-CCD	3M $	MS4	Ind	Ind	$	10	12/14
Univ of BRISTOL											
Biochemistry	C700	3FT deg	C+S g	BBC	Ind	D$^	32$	CSYS	HN	9	22/30
Biochemistry with Medical Biochemistry	C720	3FT deg	C+S g	BBC	Ind	D$^	32$	CSYS	HN	23	26/28
Biochemistry with Molecular Biology and Biotechn	C7C6	3FT deg	C+S g	BBC	Ind	D$^	32$	CSYS	HN	12	24/30
BRISTOL, Univ of the W of England											
Applied Biochemistry and Molecular Biology	CC76	4SW deg	B+C g	12	4M $	MS go	24$	BCC$	Ind		
Biotechnology	J800	4SW deg	B+C g	12	4M $	MS go	24$	BCC$	Ind		
BRUNEL Univ, West London											
Applied Biochemistry	C711	3FT deg	C+B/M/P g	CCC-CCD	MO+4D$	MS2/^	26$	CSYS	Ind	30	
Applied Biochemistry (4 Yrs Thick SW)	C712	4SW deg	C+B/M/P g	CCC-CCD	MO+4D$	MS2/^	26$	CSYS	Ind	8	
Applied Biochemistry (4 Yrs Thin SW)	C710	4SW deg	C+B/M/P g	CCC-CCD	MO+4D$	MS2/^	26$	CSYS	Ind	6	10/12
Medical Biochemistry	C721	3FT deg	C+B/M/P g	CCC	MO+4D$	MS2/^	26$	CSYS	Ind	7	12/16
Medical Biochemistry (4 Yrs Thick SW)	C722	4SW deg	C+B/M/P g	CCC	MO+4D$	MS2/^	26$	CSYS	Ind	5	
Medical Biochemistry (4 Yrs Thin SW)	C720	4SW deg	C+B/M/P g	CCC	MO+4D$	MS2/^	26$	CSYS	Ind	3	8/18
CAMBRIDGE Univ											
Natural Sciences *Biochemistry*	Y160▼	3FT deg	2(S/M)	AAA-AAB	Ind		Ind	CSYS	Ind		
Natural Sciences *Biochemistry and Molecular Biology*	Y160▼	3FT deg	2(S/M)	AAA-AAB	Ind		Ind	CSYS	Ind		
Natural Sciences *Molecular Cell Biology*	Y160▼	3FT deg	2(S/M)	AAA-AAB	Ind		Ind	CSYS	Ind		
CARDIFF Univ of Wales											
Biochemistry	C701	4SW deg	C+B/M/P g	BCC	MO $	MS6/^ go	28$	BBBB$	Ind	6	20/28
Biochemistry	C700	3FT deg	C+B/M/P g	BCC	MO $	MS6/^ go	28$	BBBB$	Ind	7	18/26
Biochemistry and Chemistry	CF71	3FT deg	C+B/M/P g	CCC	MO $	MS6/^ go	26$	BBBB$	Ind	3	14/30
Biochemistry and Physiology	BC17	3FT deg	C+B/M/P g	CCC	MO $	MS6/^ go	26$	BBBC$	Ind	2	14/20
Biochemistry with Medical Biochemistry	C720	3FT deg	C+B/M/P g	BCC	MO $	MS6/^ go	28$	BBBB$	Ind	5	18/26
Biochemistry with Molecular Biology	C7C6	3FT deg	C+B/M/P g	BCC	4M $	MS6/^ go	28$	BBBC$	Ind	7	
Biotechnology	J801	4SW deg	B+C/M/P g	BBB-BCC	MO $	Ind	30$	BBBB$	Ind	3	16/30
Biotechnology	J800	3FT deg	B+C/M/P g	BBB-BCC	MO $	Ind	30$	BBBB$	Ind	7	
Medical Molecular Biology	C624	3FT deg	C+B/M/P g	BCC	MO $	MS6/^ go	28$	BBBB$	Ind	6	
Preliminary Year *Biochemistry*	Y101	4FT/5SW deg	* g		Ind	M*6 go	Ind	Ind	Ind		
Preliminary Year *Biotechnology*	Y101	4FT/5SW deg	* g		Ind	Ind	Ind	Ind	Ind		
Univ of CENTRAL LANCASHIRE											
Applied Biochemistry	C710	3FT deg	C+S	DDD	MO $	MS6/^	26$	BCCC	$		
Biological Chemistry	C740	3FT/4SW deg	S+C	DD	MO $	MS6/^	24$	CCC	$		
Cell and Molecular Biology	C620	3FT deg	S+C	DDD	MO $	MS6/^	26$	BCCC	Ind		
Combined Honours Programme *Biochemistry*	Y400	3FT deg	B+C g	8	3M $	MS	24$	CCC	$		
COVENTRY Univ											
Applied Chemistry with Biochemistry	F1CR	4FT/5SW deg			Ind	Ind	Ind	Ind	Ind		
Applied Chemistry with Biochemistry	F1C7	3FT/4SW deg	C	DD	3M	MS	Ind	Ind	Ind	11	
Biochemistry	C700	3FT/4SW deg	C+B g	10	3M $	Ind	Ind	CCC$	HN$	3	6/14
Biochemistry	C709	4FT/5SW deg			Ind	Ind	Ind	Ind	Ind		
Biochemistry with Study in Europe	C7T9	4FT/5SW deg			Ind	Ind	Ind	Ind	Ind		
Biochemistry with Study in Europe	C7T2	4FT deg	C+B g	10	3M $	Ind	Ind	CCC$	HN$	5	

Biochemistry/Biophysics/ Biotechnology 8

			98 expected requirements							96 entry stats	
TITLE	CODE	COURSE	SUBJECTS	A/AS	ND/C	AGNVQ	IB	SQA(H)	SQA	RATIO	A/AS
Biochemistry	007C	2FT HND	C/B	2	N	Ind	Ind	DDDD$	N	9	
Biochemistry	807C	3FT HND			Ind	Ind	Ind	Ind	Ind		
Biological Sciences (Foundation)	856C	3FT HND			Ind	Ind	Ind	Ind	Ind		

DE MONTFORT Univ

TITLE	CODE	COURSE	SUBJECTS	A/AS	ND/C	AGNVQ	IB	SQA(H)	SQA	RATIO	A/AS
Biomedical Science	B940▼	3FT/4SW deg	B+C g	12-16	6M $	MS6 gi	28$	BBBB$	X	9	11/20
Biomedical Sciences with Business (Extended)	B9NC▼	4FT/5SW deg	* g	2	N	P	Dip	Ind	X		
Biomedical Sciences with Business Studies	B9N1▼	3FT/4SW deg	B g	12-14	Ind	MS	$	BBB	X	2	4/16
Chemistry and Biomedical Sciences	FB19▼	3FT/4SW	B+C	10	4M $	M	24$	BBB	$		6/12
Medical Statistics and Biophysics	CG64▼	3FT deg	P g		Ind	Ind	Ind	Ind	Ind		

Univ of DUNDEE

TITLE	CODE	COURSE	SUBJECTS	A/AS	ND/C	AGNVQ	IB	SQA(H)	SQA	RATIO	A/AS
Biochemistry	C700	4FT deg	C+S/2S g	16	5M $	M$	25$	BBBC$	N$	5	16/24
Biochemistry and Pharmacology	BC27	4FT deg	C+S/2S g	16	5M $	M$	25$	BBBC$	N$	5	
Biochemistry and Physiological Sciences	CB71	4FT deg	C+S/2S g	16	5M $	M$	25$	BBBC$	N$	10	
Biological Chemistry	CF7C	4FT deg	C+S/2S g	16	5M $	M$	25$	BBBC$	N$	5	
Chemistry and Biochemistry	FC17	4FT deg	C+S/2S g	16	5M $	M$	25$	BBBC$	N$	9	
Molecular Biology	C620	4FT deg	C+S/2S g	16	5M $	M$	25$	BBBC$	N$	5	

Univ of DURHAM

TITLE	CODE	COURSE	SUBJECTS	A/AS	ND/C	AGNVQ	IB	SQA(H)	SQA	RATIO	A/AS
Molecular Biology and Biochemistry	CC67	3FT deg	C+2(M/P/B)	BCC-CCC	3M+2D$	Ind	28	AAABB	Ind	9	22/30
Molecular Biology and Biochemistry	CC6R	4SW deg	C+2(M/P/B)	BCC-CCC	3M+2D$	Ind	28	AAABB	Ind	2	

Univ of EAST ANGLIA

TITLE	CODE	COURSE	SUBJECTS	A/AS	ND/C	AGNVQ	IB	SQA(H)	SQA	RATIO	A/AS
Biochemistry	C700	3FT deg	C+M/P+B	BCD	3D $		28$	BBBCC$	Ind	7	14/24
Biochemistry with Biology	C7C1	3FT deg	C+P/M/B	CCC	3D $		28$	BBBCC$	Ind	8	
Biochemistry with a Year in Europe (4 Yrs)	C701	4FT deg	C+M/P+B	CCB	3D $		29$	BBBCC$	Ind	4	
Biochemistry with a Year in N America (4 Yrs)	C702	4FT deg	C+M/P+B	ABB-BBB	5D $		32$	AAABB$	Ind	15	
Molecular Biology and Genetics	C630	3FT deg	C+P/M/B	CCC	3D $		28$	BBBCC$	Ind	4	12/20

Univ of EAST LONDON

TITLE	CODE	COURSE	SUBJECTS	A/AS	ND/C	AGNVQ	IB	SQA(H)	SQA	RATIO	A/AS
Biochemistry	C700	3FT/4SW deg	* g	12	MO	MS	Ind	Ind	Ind	22	
Biotechnology	J800	4SW deg	* g	12	MO		Ind	Ind	Ind	8	
French with Biology	R1C6	3FT deg	* g	12	MO	M	Ind				
Medical Biochemistry	C720	4SW deg	* g	12	N		Ind	Ind	Ind	13	
Medical Biotechnology	J820	4SW deg	* g	12	MO		Ind	Ind	Ind	4	
Extended Science _Biochemistry_	Y108	4FT deg	* g	8-10	MO	M	Ind	Ind	Ind		
Extended Science _Biotechnology_	Y108	4FT deg	* g	8-10	MO	M	Ind	Ind	Ind		
Extended Science _Medical Biochemistry_	Y108	4FT deg	* g	8-10	MO	M	Ind	Ind	Ind		
Extended Science _Medical Biotechnology_	Y108	4FT deg	* g	8-10	MO	M	Ind	Ind	Ind		

Univ of EDINBURGH

TITLE	CODE	COURSE	SUBJECTS	A/AS	ND/C	AGNVQ	IB	SQA(H)	SQA	RATIO	A/AS
Biochemistry	C700	4FT deg	C+2(B/M/P) g	BBC	MO $		Dip$	BBBB$	N$	7	20/30
Molecular Biology	C620	4FT deg	C+2(B/M/P) g	BBC	MO $		Dip$	BBBB$	N$	3	18/26

Univ of ESSEX

TITLE	CODE	COURSE	SUBJECTS	A/AS	ND/C	AGNVQ	IB	SQA(H)	SQA	RATIO	A/AS
Biochemistry	C700	3FT deg	C+S/M g	18	MO	D	28	BBBB$	Ind	3	12/16
Biochemistry (4 years)	C701	4FT deg	C+S/M g	18	MO	D	28	BBBB$	Ind		
Biochemistry and Molecular Medicine	C720	3FT deg	C+S/M g	16	MO	D	28	BBBB$	Ind		
Biochemistry and Molecular Medicine (4 years)	C721	4SW deg	C+S/M g	16	MO	D	28	BBBB$	Ind	5	
Biochemistry and Psychology	CC78	3FT deg	C+S/M g	20	MO $	D	28$	BBBC	Ind	1	14/18
Sports Science with Biochemistry	B6C7	3FT deg	C+S	18	MO	D	28$	BBBC	Ind		

course details			98 expected requirements							96 entry stats	
TITLE	CODE	COURSE	SUBJECTS	A/AS	NO/C	AGNVQ	IB	SQA(H)	SQA	RATIO	A/AS
Univ of EXETER											
Biological and Medicinal Chemistry	CF71	3FT deg	C+B g	CCC	4M	M$^	30$	Ind	Ind	6	8/30
Univ of GLAMORGAN											
Biotechnology	J800	3FT/4SW deg	B/C/P g	DD	5M $	M$	Ind	Ind	Ind	6	6/ 8
Univ of GLASGOW											
Biochemistry	C700	4FT deg	C/M+S	BBC-CCC N	M		24$	BBBB$	N	5	
Biochemistry (with work placement)	C701	5FT deg	C/M+S	BBC-CCC N	M		24$	BBBB$	N	6	
Environmental Biogeochemistry	CF76	4FT deg	C/M+S	BBC-CCC N	M		24$	BBBB$	N	7	
Medical Biochemistry	C720	4FT deg	C/M+S	BBC-CCC N	M		24$	BBBB$	N	6	
Medical Biochemistry (with work placement)	C721	5FT deg	C/M+S	BBC-CCC N	M		24$	BBBB$	N	6	
Molecular Biology	C620	4FT deg	C/M+S	BBC-CCC N	M		24$	BBBB$	N	5	
Molecular Biology (with work placement)	C621	4FT deg	C/M+S	BBC-CCC N	M		24$	BBBB$	N		
Univ of GREENWICH											
Applied Biology (Biotechnology)	J800	3FT/4SW deg	B+C g	10	3M	MS	Dip	BCC	Ind		
Biochemistry	C700	3FT/4SW deg	B+C g	10	3M	MS	Dip	BCC	Ind		
Biochemistry with European Study	C701	3FT/4SW deg	B+C g	10	3M	MS	Dip	BCC	Ind		
HALTON COLL											
Science (Biomolecular Sciences)	007C	2FT HND	B/C	2	N	P	Ind	Ind	N		
HERIOT-WATT Univ											
Biochemistry	C700	4FT deg	C	DDD	MO	M$ go	28	BBB$	Ind		
Chemistry with Biochemistry	F1C7	4FT deg	C+S	DDD	$	M$ go	28	BBCC	$		
Chemistry with Biochemistry (MChem)	F1CR	5FT deg	C+S	DDD	$	M$ go	28	BBCC	$		
Univ of HERTFORDSHIRE											
Biochemistry	C1C7	3FT/4SW deg	2S g	14-16	4M $	Ind	24	BCCCC	Ind	9	
Biochemistry with a year in North America	C702	4FT deg	2S g	14-16	4M $	Ind	24	BCCC	Ind		
Biochmemistry with a year in Europe	C701	4FT deg	2S g	14-16	4M $	Ind	24	BCCC	Ind		
Biological Chemistry	C740	3FT/4SW deg	C	8-12	4M $	Ind	Ind	Ind	Ind	3	
Biological Chemistry (Extended)	C748▼	4FT deg	* g	2	Ind	Ind	Ind	Ind	Ind		
Biotechnology	C1J8	3FT/4SW deg	2S g	14-16	4M $	Ind	24	BCCCC	Ind	12	
Biotechnology with a year in Europe	J801	3FT deg									
Biotechnology with a year in North America	J802	3FT deg									
Molecular Biology	C1C6	3FT/4SW deg	2S g	14-16	4M $	Ind	24	BCCC	Ind	14	
Molecular Biology with a year in Europe	C621	4FT deg	2S g	14-16	4M $	Ind	24	BCCC	Ind		
Molecular Biology with a year in North America	C622	4FT deg	2S g	14-16	4M $	Ind	24	BCCC	Ind		
Applied Biology (Biochemistry)	7C1C	2FT/3SW HND	B+C g	4-6	N	Ind	Ind	Ind	N	4	
Applied Biology (Microbiology)	6C1C	2FT HND	B+C g	4-6	N	Ind	Ind	Ind	N	8	
Univ of HUDDERSFIELD											
Biochemistry	C700	3FT/4SW deg	C g	10-18	3M $	MS go	Ind	Ind	Ind		
Biology (Molecular and Cellular)	C621	3FT/4SW deg	S g	10-18	3M $	MS go	Ind	Ind	Ind		
Chemistry with Biochemistry	F1C7	3FT/4SW deg	C g	10	3M $	MS gi	Ind	BCC	Ind		
Chemistry with Biotechnology	F1J8	3FT/4SW deg	C g	10	3M $	MS gi	Ind	BCC	Ind		
Science (Extended) Biochemistry	Y108	4FT/5SW deg	* g	EE	N	P$ gi	Ind	Ind	Ind		
Science (Extended) Biology (Molecular and Cellular)	Y108	4FT/5SW deg	* g	EE	N	P$ gi	Ind	Ind	Ind		
IMPERIAL COLL (Univ of London)											
Biochemistry	C700	3FT deg	C+M/P/B	BCC	DO		30$	Ind	Ind	5	22/30
Biochemistry with Management	C7N1	3FT deg	C+M/P/B	BCC	DO		30$	Ind	Ind	5	
Biochemistry with Mgt and a Year in Ind/Research	C7ND	4FT deg	C+M/P/B	BCC	DO		30$	Ind	Ind	5	22/30

Biochemistry/Biophysics/ Biotechnology 8

			98 expected requirements							96 entry stats	
TITLE	CODE	COURSE	SUBJECTS	A/AS	NO/C	AGNVQ	IB	SQA(H)	SQA	RATIO	A/AS
Biochemistry with a Year in Europe (4 Yrs)	C702	4FT deg	C+M/P/B g	BBC	DO		30$	Ind	Ind	8	28/30
Biochemistry with a Year in Industry/Research	C701	4FT deg	C+M/P/B	BBC	DO		30$	Ind	Ind	7	22/28
Biotechnology	J800	3FT deg	C+M/P/B	BCC	DO		30$	Ind	Ind		
Biotechnology with a Year in Europe (4 Yrs)	J801	4FT deg	C+M/P/B g	BBC	DO		30$	Ind	Ind	5	
Biotechnology with a Year in Industry/Research	J802	4FT deg	C+M/P/B	BBC	DO		30$	Ind	Ind	6	
Chemistry and Biochemistry	FC17	4FT deg	C+M/P g	BBC	HN		32	CSYS		3	22/30
Chemistry and Biochemistry with a Yr in Industry	CF71	5SW deg	C+M/P g	BBC	HN		32	CSYS		14	
Chemistry and Biotechnology	FJ18	4FT deg	C+M/P g	BBC	HN		32	CSYS			
Chemistry and Biotechnology with a Yr in Ind	JF81	5SW deg	C+M/P g	BBC	HN		32	CSYS			

KEELE Univ

Biochemistry	C700	3FT deg	C g	BCC-CCC	Ind	M$^	26$	CSYS	Ind		
Biochemistry and American Studies	CQ74	3FT deg	C g	BCC	Ind	D$^	28$	CSYS	Ind		
Biochemistry and American Studies (4 Yrs)	QC47	4FT deg	*	BCC	Ind	Ind	28	BBBB	Ind		
Biochemistry and Ancient History	CV7D	3FT deg	C g	BCC	Ind	D$^	28$	CSYS	Ind		
Biochemistry and Ancient History (4 Yrs)	VCD7	4FT deg	*	BCC	Ind	Ind	28	BBBB	Ind		
Biochemistry and Applied Social Studies	CL75	3FT deg	C g	BCC	Ind	D$^	28$	CSYS	Ind		
Biochemistry and Applied Social Studies (4 Yrs)	LC57	4FT deg	*	BCC	Ind	Ind	28	BBBB	Ind		
Biochemistry and Astrophysics	CF75	3FT deg	P+C g	BCC-CCC	Ind	M$^	26$	CSYS	Ind		
Biochemistry and Astrophysics (4 Yrs)	FC57	4FT deg	*	BCC-CCC	Ind	Ind	26	BBBB	Ind		
Biological & Med Chem and Biochemistry (4 Yrs)	FCC7	4FT deg	*	BCC-CCC	Ind	Ind	26	BBBB	Ind		
Biological & Medicinal Chem and Biochemistry	CF7C	3FT deg	C g	BCC-CCC	Ind	M$^	26$	CSYS	Ind		
Biology and Biochemistry	CC17	3FT deg	C g	BCC-CCC	Ind	M$^	26$	CSYS	Ind		
Biology and Biochemistry (4 Yrs)	CC71	4FT deg	*	BCC-CCC	Ind	Ind	26$	BBBB	Ind		
Biology and Biochemistry (MSci)	CC7C	4FT deg	C	BCC-CCC	Ind	M$^	26$	CSYS	Ind		
Business Administration and Biochemistry	CN79	3FT deg	C g	BCC	Ind	D$^	28$	CSYS	Ind		
Business Administration and Biochemistry (4 Yrs)	NC97	4FT deg	*	BCC	Ind	Ind	28	BBBB	Ind		
Chemistry and Biochemistry	CF71	3FT deg	C g	BCC-CCC	Ind	M$^	26$	CSYS	Ind		
Chemistry and Biochemistry (4 Yrs)	FC17	4FT deg	*	BCC-CCC	Ind	Ind	26	BBBB	Ind		
Chemistry and Biochemistry (MSci)	FC1R	4FT deg	C	BCC-CCC	Ind	M$^	26$	CSYS	Ind		
Classical Studies and Biochemistry	CQ78	3FT deg	C g	BCC	Ind	D$^	28$	CSYS	Ind		
Classical Studies and Biochemistry (4 Yrs)	QC87	4FT deg	*	BCC	Ind	Ind	28	BBBB	Ind		
Computer Science and Biochemistry	CG75	3FT deg	C g	BCC-CCC	Ind	M$^	26$	CSYS	Ind		
Computer Science and Biochemistry (4 Yrs)	GC57	4FT deg	*	BCC-CCC	Ind	Ind	26	BBBB	Ind		
Economics and Biochemistry	CL71	3FT deg	C g	BCC	Ind	D$^	28$	CSYS	Ind		
Economics and Biochemistry (4 Yrs)	LC17	4FT deg	*	BCC	Ind	Ind	28	BBBB	Ind		
Educational Studies and Biochemistry	CX79	3FT deg	C g	BCC	Ind	D$^	28$	CSYS	Ind		
Educational Studies and Biochemistry (4 Yrs)	XC97	4FT deg	*	BCC	Ind	Ind	28	BBBB	Ind		
Electronic Music and Biochemistry	CW7J	3FT deg	Mu+C g	BCC	Ind	D$^	28$	CSYS	Ind		
Electronic Music and Biochemistry (4 Yrs)	WCJ7	4FT deg	*	BCC	Ind	Ind	28	BBBB	Ind		
Environmental Management & Biochemistry (4 Yrs)	FCX7	4FT deg	* g	BCC	Ind	Ind	28	BBBB	Ind		
Environmental Management and Biochemistry	CF7X	3FT deg	C g	BCC	Ind	D$^	28$	BBBB	Ind		
Finance and Biochemistry	CN73	3FT deg	C g	BCC	Ind	M$^	28$	CSYS	Ind		
Finance and Biochemistry (4 Yrs)	CN7H	4FT deg	*	BCC	Ind	Ind	28	BBB	Ind		
French and Biochemistry	CR71	3FT deg	C+F g	BCC	Ind	D$^	28$	CSYS	Ind		
French and Biochemistry (4 Yrs)	RC17	4FT deg	*	BCC	Ind	Ind	28	BBBB	Ind		
French/German and Biochemistry	CT79	3FT deg	F+G+C g	BBC	Ind	D$^	30$	CSYS	Ind		
French/German and Biochemistry (4 Yrs)	TC97	4FT deg	G	BBC	Ind	Ind	30$	BBBB	Ind		
French/Russian or Russian St and Biochem (4 Yrs)	TCX7	4FT deg	*	BCC	Ind	Ind	28	BBBB	Ind		
French/Russian or Russian Studs and Biochemistry	CT7X	3FT deg	F+R+C g	BBC-BCC	Ind	D$^	28$	CSYS	Ind		
Geography and Biochemistry	CL78	3FT deg	Gy+C g	BCC	Ind	D$^	28$	CSYS	Ind		
Geography and Biochemistry (4 Yrs)	LC87	4FT deg	*	BCC	Ind	Ind	28	BBBB	Ind		
German and Biochemistry	CR72	3FT deg	C+G g	BCC	Ind	D$^	28$	CSYS	Ind		

| | | | 98 expected requirements | | | | | | | 96 entry stats | |
| course details | | | | | | | | | | | |
TITLE	CODE	COURSE	SUBJECTS	A/AS	NQ/C	AGNVQ	IB	SQA(H)	SQA	RATIO	A/AS
German and Biochemistry (4 Yrs)	RC27	4FT deg	G	BCC	Ind	Ind	28$	BBBB	Ind		
German/Russian or Russian St and Biochem (4 Yrs)	TCY7	4FT deg	G	BCC	Ind	Ind	28$	BBBB	Ind		
German/Russian or Russian St and Biochemistry	CT7Y	3FT deg	G+R+C g	BBC-BCC	Ind	D$^	28$	CSYS	Ind		
History and Biochemistry	CV71	3FT deg	C g	BCC	Ind	D$^	28$	CSYS	Ind		
History and Biochemistry (4 Yrs)	VC17	4FT deg	*	BCC	Ind	Ind	28	BBBB	Ind		
International Politics and Biochemistry	CM7C	3FT deg	C	BCC	Ind	D$^	28$	CSYS	Ind		
International Politics and Biochemistry (4 Yrs)	MCC7	4FT deg	*	BCC	Ind	Ind	28	BBBB	Ind		
Latin and Biochemistry	CQ76	3FT deg	C+Ln g	BCC	Ind	D$^	28$	CSYS	Ind		
Latin and Biochemistry (4 Yrs)	QC67	4FT deg	*	BCC	Ind	Ind	28	BBBB	Ind		
Law and Biochemistry	CM73	3FT deg	C g	BBB	Ind	D$^	32$	CSYS	Ind		
Law and Biochemistry (4 Yrs)	MC37	4FT deg	*	BBB	Ind	Ind	32	BBBB	Ind		
Management Science and Biochemistry	CN71	3FT deg	C g	BCC	Ind	D$^	28$	CSYS	Ind		
Management Science and Biochemistry (4 Yrs)	NC17	4FT deg	*	BCC	Ind	Ind	28	BBBB	Ind		
Marketing and Biochemistry	CN75	3FT deg	C g	BCC	Ind	D$^	28$	CSYS	Ind		
Music and Biochemistry	CW73	3FT deg	Mu+C g	BCC	Ind	D$^	28$	CSYS	Ind		
Music and Biochemistry (4 Yrs)	WC37	4FT deg	*	BCC	Ind	Ind	28	BBBB	Ind		
Neuroscience and Biochemistry	BC17	3FT deg	C+S	BCC-CCC	Ind	MS^	26$	CSYS	Ind		
Neuroscience and Biochemistry (4 Yrs)	BC1T	4FT deg	*	BCC-CCC	Ind	Ind	26	BBBB	Ind		
Philosophy and Biochemistry	CV77	3FT deg	C g	BCC	Ind	D$^	28$	CSYS	Ind		
Philosophy and Biochemistry (4 Yrs)	VC77	4FT deg	*	BCC	Ind	Ind	28	BBBB	Ind		
Physics and Biochemistry	CF73	3FT deg	P+C g	BCC-CCC	Ind	M$^	26$	CSYS	Ind		
Physics and Biochemistry (4 Yrs)	FC37	4FT deg	*	BCC-CCC	Ind	Ind	26	BBBB	Ind		
Physics and Biochemistry (MSci)	FC3R	4FT deg	P+C	BCC-CCC	Ind	M$^	26$	CSYS	Ind		
Psychology and Biochemistry	CC87	3FT deg	C g	BBB-BCC	Ind	D$^	28$	CSYS	Ind		
Psychology and Biochemistry (4 yrs)	CC78	4FT deg	*	BBB-BCC	Ind	Ind	32	ABBB	Ind		
Russian Studies and Biochemistry	CRR8	3FT deg	C g	BCC	Ind	D$^	28$	CSYS	Ind		
Russian Studies and Biochemistry (4 Yrs)	RC8R	4FT deg	*	BCC	Ind	Ind	28	BBBB	Ind		
Russian and Biochemistry	CR78	3FT deg	C+R g	BCC	Ind	D$^	28$	CSYS	Ind		
Russian and Biochemistry (4 Yrs)	RC87	4FT deg	*	BCC	Ind	Ind	28	BBBB	Ind		
Sociol & Soc Anthrop and Biochemistry (4 Yrs)	LC37	4FT deg	*	BCC	Ind	Ind	28	BBBB	Ind		
Sociology & Social Anthroplogy and Biochemistry	CL73	3FT deg	C g	BCC	Ind	D$^	28$	CSYS	Ind		
Visual Arts and Biochemistry	CW71	3FT deg	C	BCC	Ind	D$^	28$	CSYS	Ind		
Visual Arts and Biochemistry (4 Yrs)	WC17	4FT deg	*	BCC	Ind	Ind	28	BBBB	Ind		

Univ of KENT

TITLE	CODE	COURSE	SUBJECTS	A/AS	NQ/C	AGNVQ	IB	SQA(H)	SQA	RATIO	A/AS
Biochemistry	C700	3FT deg	C g	BCC	MO $	Ind	28$	BBBB$	Ind	5	10/18
Biochemistry	C702	4SW deg	C g	BCC	MO $	Ind	28$	BBBB$	Ind	4	10/26
Biochemistry with Biotechnology	C780	3FT deg	C g	BCC	MO $	Ind	28$	BBBB$	Ind	12	
Biochemistry with Cell and Molecular Biology	C736	3FT deg	C g	BCC	MO $	Ind	28$	BBBB$	Ind	3	
Biochemistry with Medical Biosciences	C720	3FT deg	C g	BCC	MO $	Ind	28$	BBBB$	Ind	17	
Biochemistry with Neuroscience	C730	3FT deg	C g	BCC	MO $	Ind	28$	BBBB$	Ind	6	
Biochemistry with a year in Europe	C701	4FT deg	C g	BCC	MO $	Ind	28$	BBBB$	Ind	13	
Molecular & Cellular Biology with a Yr in Europe	C623	4FT deg	C g	BCC	MO $	Ind	28$	BBBB$	Ind	1	
Molecular and Cellular Biology	C621	4SW deg	C g	BCC	MO $	Ind	28$	BBBB$	Ind	2	
Molecular and Cellular Biology	C620	3FT deg	C g	BCC	MO $	Ind	28$	BBBB$	Ind	6	

KING'S COLL LONDON (Univ of London)

TITLE	CODE	COURSE	SUBJECTS	A/AS	NQ/C	AGNVQ	IB	SQA(H)	SQA	RATIO	A/AS
Biochemistry	C700	3FT deg	C+B/M/P	BBC	5M	M	Ind	BCCCC	Ind	5	16/26
Biochemistry and Immunology	CC79	3FT deg	C+B/M/P	BCC	5M	M	Ind	BCCCC	Ind	3	18/22
Biochemistry and Microbiology	CC57	3FT deg	C+S	BCC	5M	M	Ind	BCCCC	Ind	7	
Biochemistry and Pharmacology	BC27	3FT deg	C+B/M/P	BBC	5M	M	Ind	BCCCC	Ind	5	18/24
Biochemistry and Physiology	BC17	3FT/4SW deg	C+B/M/P	BCC	MO+3D	MS^	Ind	BCCCC	Ind	3	18/20
Biochemistry with a European Language	C7T9	4SW deg	C+S+L	BBC	Ind	Ind	Ind	BCCCC	Ind	4	18/22

Biochemistry/Biophysics/ Biotechnology 8

			98 expected requirements							**96 entry stats**	
course details											
TITLE	CODE	COURSE	SUBJECTS	A/AS	NO/C	RGNVQ	IB	SQA(H)	SQA	RATIO	A/AS
Biomolecular Sciences	C650	3FT deg	C+M/B/P	BCC			Ind	BCCCC	Ind	10	22/24
Biotechnology	J800	3FT deg	C+S	BCC	5M	M	Ind	BCCCC	Ind	4	16/22
Chemistry with Biochemistry	F1C7	3FT/4SW deg	C+S	18	4M $	Ind	28$	BBCCC	Ind	22	
Chemistry with Biochemistry	F1CR	4FT deg	C+S	18	4M $	Ind	28$	BBCCC	Ind		
Medical Biochemistry	C720	3FT deg	C+M/B/P	BBC	5M	M	Ind	BCCCC	Ind	5	16/24
Molecular Biology	C620	3FT deg	C+S	BCC			Ind	BCCCC	Ind	9	
Molecular Biology and Immunology	CC69	3FT deg	C+S	BCC	5M	M	Ind	BCCCC	Ind	3	14/20
Molecular Biophysics	C610	3FT deg	C+M/P	BCC			Ind	BCCCC	Ind	3	
KINGSTON Univ											
Biochemistry	C700	3FT deg	B+C g	10	N	Ind	Ind	CCC	Ind	3	4/15
Biochemistry	C708▼	4EXT deg	*		Ind		Ind	Ind	Ind	1	
LANCASTER Univ											
Biochemistry	C700	3FT deg	C+B/M/P g	BCC	5M $		30$	BBBCC$	Ind		
Biochemistry (inc a year in the USA or Canada)	C702	3FT deg	C+B/M/P g	BBC	5M $		30$	BBBBB$	Ind		
Biochemistry with Animal Physiology	C7B1	3FT deg	C+B/M/P g	BCC	5M $		30$	BBBBC$	Ind		
Biochemistry with Genetics	C7C4	3FT deg	C+B/M/P g	BCC	5M $		30$	BBBBC$	Ind		
Biochemistry with Microbiology	C7C5	3FT deg	C+B/M/P g	BCC	5M $		30$	BBBBC$	Ind		
Univ of LEEDS											
Biochemistry	C700	3FT/4FT deg	C+S g	BCC	1M+5D$ DS^ go		28$	BBBBC	Ind	7	18/30
Biochemistry with Cell Biology	C7CQ	3FT/4FT deg	C+S g	BCC	1M+5D$ DS^ go		28$	BBBBC	Ind		
Biochemistry with Medical Biochemistry	C720	3FT/4FT deg	C+S g	BCC	1M+5D$ DS^ go		28$	BBBBC	Ind	5	20/26
Biochemistry with Molecular Biology	C7C6	3FT/4FT deg	C+S g	BCC	1M+5D$ DS^ go		28$	BBBBC	Ind	4	18/30
Biochemistry with Plant Biochemistry	C730	3FT/4FT deg	C+S g	BCC	1M+5D$ DS^ go		28$	BBBBC	Ind		
Biochemistry-Chemistry	CF71	3FT/4FT deg	C+M/P g	BCC	1M+5D$ Ind		28$	BBBBC	Ind	11	
Biochemistry-Food Science	CD74	3FT/4FT deg	C+M/P/B g	CCC	1M+5D$ Ind		28$	BBBBC	Ind		
Biochemistry-Genetics	CC47	3FT/4FT deg	C+B g	BCC	1M+5D$ Ind		28$	BBBBC	Ind	10	22/28
Biochemistry-Microbiology	CC57	3FT/4FT deg	C+B g	BCC	1M+5D$ Ind		28$	BBBBC	Ind	8	
Biochemistry-Molecular Plant Biology	CC27	3FT/4FT deg	C+B g	BCC	1M+5D$ Ind		28$	BBBBC	Ind		
Biochemistry-Pharmacology	CB72	3FT/4FT deg	C+P/M/B g	BCC	1M+5D$ Ind		28$	BBBBC	Ind	7	
Biochemistry-Physiology	CB71	3FT/4FT deg	C+P/M/B g	BCC	1M+5D$ Ind		28$	BBBBC	Ind	5	
Biochemistry-Zoology	CC37	3FT/4FT deg	C+B g	BCC	1M+5D$ Ind		28$	BBBBC	Ind	5	
Biotechnology	J800	3FT/4FT deg	C+S g	BCC	1M+5D$ DS^ go		28$	BBBBC	Ind	7	16/26
Univ of LEICESTER											
Biological Chemistry	CF71	3FT deg	C g	18	5M	M/DS^ gi	28$	BBBCC$	Ind		10/20
Biological Chemistry (MChem)	CF7C	4FT deg	C g	CCC	5M	DS^ gi	28$	BBBCC$	Ind		
Biological Chemistry (Sandwich)	CFRD	3FT deg	C g	18-20	5M $	DS^ gi	28$	BBCCC$	Ind		
Biological Chemistry (USA)	CFR1	3FT deg	C g	22-24	Ind	DS^ gi	30$	ABBBC$	Ind		
Biological Sciences (Biochemistry)	C700	3FT/4SW deg	B+C g	20	DO $	D$4/^ gi	28$	BBBBC$	Ind		18/20
Biological Sciences (Molecular Biology)	C620	3FT deg	B+C g	18-20	DO $	D$4/^ gi	28$	BBBCC$	Ind		
Medical Biochemistry	C720	3FT/4SW deg	C+B g	BCC	Ind	DS^ gi	30$	ABBBC$	Ind		16/28
Univ of LIVERPOOL											
Biochemistry	C701	4FT deg	C+S g	20	MO $	DS^ go	31$	BBBCC$	Ind	10	18/30
Biochemistry	C700	3FT deg	C+S g	20	MO $	DS^ go	31$	BBBCC$	Ind	4	16/26
Biomolecular Sciences (2+2)	C650	4FT deg	C+S g	4	MO $	Ind	24$	CCCDD$	Ind	1	8/14
Cell Biology and Biochemistry	CC17	4FT deg	C+B g	18	MO $	DS^ go	31$	BBBCC$	Ind		
Cell Biology and Biochemistry	CC1R	3FT deg	C+B g	18	MO $	DS^ go	31$	BBBCC$	Ind	2	
Microbial Biotechnology	C5J8	3FT deg	B+S g	18	MO $	DS^ go	31$	BBBCC$	Ind	5	
Molecular Biology	C620	3FT deg	C+S g	18	MO $	DS^ go	31$	BBBCC$	Ind		
Molecular Biology	C621	4FT deg	C+S g	18	MO $	Ind	31$	BBBCC$	Ind	8	
BSc Combined Honours Biochemistry	Y100	3FT deg	C	20	MO $	Ind	31$	BBBCC$	Ind		

course details			98 expected requirements							96 entry stats	
TITLE	CODE	COURSE	SUBJECTS	A/AS	ND/C	RGNVQ	IB	SQA(H)	SQA	RATIO	A/AS
LIVERPOOL JOHN MOORES Univ											
App Biochemistry & App Microbiology (Foundation)	CC7M	4FT/5SW deg									
Applied Biochemistry	C710	3FT/4SW deg		8	3M	M				6	8/16
Applied Biochemistry & Applied Microbiology	CC75	3FT/4SW deg		8	3M	M				6	10/14
Applied Biochemistry (Foundation)	C718	4FT/5SW deg									
Biophysics	C600	3FT/4SW deg	2S g	DD	3M	M				7	
Biophysics (Foundation)	C608	4FT/5SW deg									
Biotechnology	J800	3FT/4SW deg	C	8	3M	M				17	
Biotechnology (Foundation)	J808	4FT/5SW deg									
Biotechnology Management	J801	3FT deg		10	3M	M					
Biotechnology Management (Extended)	J809	3FT deg									
Molecular Biology	C620	3FT/4SW deg	2S	CD	3M	M				2	
Molecular Biology (Foundation)	C628	3FT deg									
LUTON Univ											
Biochemistry with Business	C7N1	3FT deg	g	12-16	MO/DO	M/D	32	BBCC	Ind		
Biochemistry with Business Systems	C7NC	3FT deg	g	12-16	MO/DO	M/D	32	BBCC	Ind		
Biochemistry with Environmental Sciences	C7F9	3FT deg	g	12-16	MO/DO	M/D	32	BBCC	Ind		
Biochemistry with French	C7R1	3FT deg	F g	12-16	MO/DO	M/D	32	BBCC	Ind		
Biochemistry with Geography	C7F8	3FT deg	g	12-16	MO/DO	M/D	32	BBCC	Ind		
Biochemistry with Geology	C7F6	3FT deg	g	12-16	MO/DO	M/D	32	BBCC	Ind		
Biochemistry with Health Science	C7B9	3FT deg	g	12-16	MO/DO	M/D	32	BBCC	Ind		
Biochemistry with Leisure Studies	C7N7	3FT deg	g	12-16	MO/DO	M/D	32	BBCC	Ind		
Biochemistry with Marketing	C7N5	3FT deg	g	12-16	MO/DO	M/D	32	BBCC	Ind		
Biochemistry with Physical Geography	C7FV	3FT deg	g	12-16	MO/DO	M/D	32	BBCC	Ind		
Biochemistry with Psychology	C7L7	3FT deg	g	12-16	MO/DO	M/D	32	BBCC	Ind		
Biochemistry with Public Policy and Management	C7M1	3FT deg	g	12-16	MO/DO	M/D	32	BBCC	Ind		
Biochemistry with Regional Planning and Dev	C7K4	3FT deg	g	12-16	MO/DO	M/D	32	BBCC	Ind		
Biochemistry with Travel & Tourism	C7P7	3FT deg	g	12-16	MO/DO	M/D	32	BBCC	Ind		
Biology with Biotechnology	C1J8	3FT deg	g	12-16	MO/DO	M/D	32	BBCC	Ind		
Biotechnology with Business	J8N1	3FT deg	g	12-16	MO/DO	M/D	32	BBCC	Ind		
Biotechnology with Business Systems	J8NC	3FT deg	g	12-16	MO/DO	M/D	32	BBCC	Ind		
Biotechnology with Environmental Science	J8F9	3FT deg	g	12-16	MO/DO	M/D	32	BBCC	Ind		
Biotechnology with French	J8R1	3FT deg	F g	12-16	MO/DO	M/D	32	BBCC	Ind		
Biotechnology with Geography	J8F8	3FT deg	g	12-16	MO/DO	M/D	32	BBCC	Ind		
Biotechnology with Geology	J8F6	3FT deg	g	12-16	MO/DO	M/D	32	BBCC	Ind		
Biotechnology with Health Science	J8B9	3FT deg	g	12-16	MO/DO	M/D	32	BBCC	Ind		
Biotechnology with Leisure Studies	J8N7	3FT deg	g	12-16	MO/DO	M/D	32	BBCC	Ind		
Biotechnology with Marketing	J8N5	3FT deg	g	12-16	MO/DO	M/D	32	BBCC	Ind		
Biotechnology with Pharmacology	J8B2	3FT deg	g	12-16	MO/DO	M/D	32	BBCC	Ind		
Biotechnology with Physical Geography	J8FV	3FT deg	g	12-16	MO/DO	M/D	32	BBCC	Ind		
Biotechnology with Psychology	J8L7	3FT deg	g	12-16	MO/DO	M/D	32	BBCC	Ind		
Biotechnology with Public Policy & Management	J8M1	3FT deg	g	12-16	MO/DO	M/D	32	BBCC	Ind		
Biotechnology with Regional Planning & Dev	J8K4	3FT deg	g	12-16	MO/DO	M/D	32	BBCC	Ind		
Biotechnology with Travel & Tourism	J8P7	3FT deg	g	12-16	MO/DO	M/D	32	BBCC	Ind		
Business Systems and Biochemistry	CN7C	3FT deg	g	12-16	MO/DO	M/D	32	BBCC	Ind		
Business Systems and Biotechnology	JN8C	3FT deg	g	12-16	MO/DO	M/D	32	BBCC	Ind		
Business Systems with Biochemistry	N1CR	3FT deg	g	12-16	MO/DO	M/D	32	BBCC	Ind		
Business Systems with Biotechnology	N1JV	3FT deg	g	12-16	MO/DO	M/D	32	BBCC	Ind		
Business and Biochemistry	CN71	3FT deg	g	12-16	MO/DO	M/D	32	BBCC	Ind		
Business and Biotechnology	JN81	3FT deg	g	12-16	MO/DO	M/D	32	BBCC	Ind		
Business with Biochemistry	N1C7	3FT deg	g	12-16	MO/DO	M/D	32	BBCC	Ind		
Business with Biotechnology	N1J8	3FT deg	g	12-16	MO/DO	M/D	32	BBCC	Ind		
Computer Science and Biochemistry	CG75	3FT deg	g	12-16	MO/DO	M/D	32	BBCC	Ind		

Biochemistry/Biophysics/ Biotechnology   8

course details			98 expected requirements							96 entry stats
TITLE	CODE	COURSE	SUBJECTS	A/AS	ND/C	RGNVQ	IB	SQA(H)	SQA	RATIO A/AS
Computer Science and Biotechnology	GJ58	3FT deg	g	12-16	MO/DO	M/D	32	BBCC	Ind	
Environmental Science and Biochemistry	CF79	3FT deg	g	12-16	MO/DO	M/D	32	BBCC	Ind	
Environmental Science and Biotechnology	FJ98	3FT deg	g	12-16	MO/DO	M/D	32	BBCC	Ind	
Environmental Science with Biochemistry	F9C7	3FT deg	g	12-16	MO/DO	M/D	32	BBCC	Ind	
Environmental Science with Biotechnology	F9J8	3FT deg	g	12-16	MO/DO	M/D	32	BBCC	Ind	
Environmental Studies with Biochemistry	F9CR	3FT deg		12-16	MO/DO	M/D	32	BBCC	Ind	
Environmental Studies with Biotechnology	F9JV	3FT deg		12-16	MO/DO	M/D	32	BBCC	Ind	
European Language Studies and Biochemistry	CT72	3FT deg	L g	12-16	MO/DO	M/D	32	BBCC	Ind	
European Language Studies and Biotechnology	JT82	3FT deg	L g	12-16	MO/DO	M/D	32	BBCC	Ind	
European Language Studies with Biochemistry	T2C7	3FT deg	L g	12-16	MO/DO	M/D	32	BBCC	Ind	
European Language Studies with Biotechnology	T2J8	3FT deg	L g	12-16	MO/DO	M/D	32	BBCC	Ind	
Geography and Biochemistry	CF78	3FT deg	g	12-16	MO/DO	M/D	32	BBCC	Ind	
Geography and Biotechnology	FJ88	3FT deg	g	12-16	MO/DO	M/D	32	BBCC	Ind	
Geography with Biochemistry	F8C7	3FT deg	g	12-16	MO/DO	M/D	32	BBCC	Ind	
Geography with Biotechnology	F8J8	3FT deg	g	12-16	MO/DO	M/D	32	BBCC	Ind	
Geology and Biochemistry	CF76	3FT deg	g	12-16	MO/DO	M/D	32	BBCC	Ind	
Geology with Biochemistry	F6C7	3FT deg	g	12-16	MO/DO	M/D	32	BBCC	Ind	
Geology with Biotechnology	F6J8	3FT deg	g	12-16	MO/DO	M/D	32	BBCC	Ind	
Health Science and Biochemistry	BC97	3FT deg	g	12-16	MO/DO	M/D	32	BBCC	Ind	
Health Science and Biotechnology	BJ98	3FT deg	g	12-16	MO/DO	M/D	32	BBCC	Ind	
Health Science with Biochemistry	B9C7	3FT deg	g	12-16	MO/DO	M/D	32	BBCC	Ind	
Health Science with Biotechnology	B9J8	3FT deg	g	12-16	MO/DO	M/D	32	BBCC	Ind	
Health Studies and Biochemistry	BCX7	3FT deg	g	12-16	MO/DO	M/D	32	BBCC	Ind	
Health Studies and Biotechnology	BJX8	3FT deg	g	12-16	MO/DO	M/D	32	BBCC	Ind	
Health Studies with Biochemistry	B9CR	3FT deg	g	12-16	MO/DO	M/D	32	BBCC	Ind	
Health Studies with Biotechnology	B9JV	3FT deg	g	12-16	MO/DO	M/D	32	BBCC	Ind	
Leisure Studies and Biochemistry	CN77	3FT deg	g	12-16	MO/DO	M/D	32	BBCC	Ind	
Leisure Studies and Biotechnology	JN87	3FT deg	g	12-16	MO/DO	M/D	32	BBCC	Ind	
Leisure Studies with Biochemistry	N7C7	3FT deg	g	12-16	MO/DO	M/D	32	BBCC	Ind	
Leisure Studies with Biotechnology	N7J8	3FT deg	g	12-16	MO/DO	M/D	32	BBCC	Ind	
Marketing and Biochemistry	CN75	3FT deg	g	12-16	MO/DO	M/D	32	BBCC	Ind	
Marketing and Biotechnology	JN85	3FT deg	g	12-16	MO/DO	M/D	32	BBCC	Ind	
Marketing with Biochemistry	N5C7	3FT deg	g	12-16	MO/DO	M/D	32	BBCC	Ind	
Marketing with Biotechnology	N5J8	3FT deg	g	12-16	MO/DO	M/D	32	BBCC	Ind	
Pharmacology and Biotechnology	BJ28	3FT deg	g	12-16	MO/DO	M/D	32	BBCC	Ind	
Physical Geography and Biochemistry	CF7V	3FT deg	g	12-16	MO/DO	M/D	32	BBCC	Ind	
Physical Geography and Biotechnology	FJX8	3FT deg	g	12-16	MO/DO	M/D	32	BBCC	Ind	
Physical Geography with Biochemistry	F8CR	3FT deg	g	12-16	MO/DO	M/D	32	BBCC	Ind	
Physical Geography with Biotechnology	F8JV	3FT deg	g	12-16	MO/DO	M/D	32	BBCC	Ind	
Psychology and Biochemistry	CL77	3FT deg	g	12-16	MO/DO	M/D	32	BBCC	Ind	
Psychology with Biochemistry	L7C7	3FT deg	g	12-16	MO/DO	M/D	32	BBCC	Ind	
Public Policy & Management with Biochemistry	M1C7	3FT deg	g	12-16	MO/DO	M/D	32	BBCC	Ind	
Public Policy & Management with Biotechnology	M1J8	3FT deg	g	12-16	MO/DO	M/D	32	BBCC	Ind	
Public Policy and Management and Biochemistry	CM7C	3FT deg	g	12-16	MO/DO	M/D	32	BBCC	Ind	
Public Policy and Management and Biotechnology	JM8C	3FT deg	g	12-16	MO/DO	M/D	32	BBCC	Ind	
Regional Planning & Develop with Biochemistry	K4C7	3FT deg	g	12-16	MO/DO	M/D	32	BBCC	Ind	
Regional Planning & Develop with Biotechnology	K4J8	3FT deg	g	12-16	MO/DO	M/D	32	BBCC	Ind	
Regional Planning and Develop and Biotechnology	JK84	3FT deg	g	12-16	MO/DO	M/D	32	BBCC	Ind	
Regional Planning and Development & Biochemistry	CK74	3FT deg	g	12-16	MO/DO	M/D	32	BBCC	Ind	
Travel & Tourism with Biochemistry	P7C7	3FT deg	g	12-16	MO/DO	M/D	32	BBCC	Ind	
Travel & Tourism with Biotechnology	P7J8	3FT deg	g	12-16	MO/DO	M/D	32	BBCC	Ind	
Travel and Tourism and Biochemistry	CP77	3FT deg	g	12-16	MO/DO	M/D	32	BBCC	Ind	
Travel and Tourism and Biotechnology	JP87	3FT deg	g	12-16	MO/DO	M/D	32	BBCC	Ind	

course details			98 expected requirements							96 entry stats	
TITLE	CODE	COURSE	SUBJECTS	A/AS	NO/C	AGNVQ	IB	SQA(H)	SQA	RATIO	A/AS
Univ of MANCHESTER											
Biochemistry	C700	3FT deg	C g	BBC	2M+4D$	D^	28$	BBBBC$	Ind	9	20/28
Biochemistry with Biotechnology with Ind Exp	C7J8	4SW deg	C g	BBC	2M+4D$	D^	28$	BBBBC$	Ind	9	
Biochemistry with Industrial Experience	C701	4SW deg	C g	BBC	2M+4D$	D^	28$	BBBBC$	Ind	5	20/28
Biochemistry with a Modern Language	C705	4FT deg	C+L g	BBC	2M+4D$	D^	28$	BBBBC$	Ind	4	20/30
Microbiology with Biotechnology	C5J8	4SW deg	B+C	BCD	3M+3D$	D^	26$	BBBBC$	Ind	17	
Molecular Biology	C620	3FT deg	C	BCC	2M+4D$	D^	28$	BBBBC	Ind	3	22/30
Molecular Biology with Industrial Experience	C621	4SW deg	C	BCC	2M+4D$	D^	28$	BBBBC	Ind	3	22/30
Molecular Biology with a Modern Language	C622	4FT deg	C+L	BCC	2M+4D$	D^	28$	BBBBC	Ind		
UMIST (Manchester)											
Biochemistry	C700	3FT/4SW deg	C+2S g	18-20	4M $	Ind	30$	CSYS	N$	4	12/30
Biochemistry (with Applied Molecular Biology)	C7C6	3FT/4SW deg	C+2S g	18-20	4M $	Ind	30$	CSYS	N$	5	20/30
Biochemistry (with Biotechnology)	C7J8	3FT/4SW deg	C+2S g	18-20	4M $	Ind	30$	CSYS	N$	5	22/30
Biochemistry (with Clinical Biochemistry)	C722	3FT/4SW deg	C+2S g	18-20	4M $	Ind	30$	CSYS	N$	4	16/24
Biochemistry with German	C7R2	4FT deg	C+2S g	18-20	4M $	Ind	30$	CSYS	N$	4	
Chemical Engineering and Biotechnology (MEng)	HJ88	4FT deg	M+C g	BBC	MO+3D$	Ind	30$	CSYS$	Ind	6	20/30
NAPIER Univ											
Applied Microbiology & Biotechnology (comm Yr 1)	CJ58	4FT/5SW deg	B/C	DD	Ind	Ind	Ind	BBC	Ind		
Univ of NEWCASTLE											
Biochemistry	C700	3FT deg	C+S g	BCC	Ind		Ind	CSYS	X	6	16/26
Molecular Biology	C620	3FT deg	C+S g	BCC	Ind		Ind	CSYS	X	11	
NESCOT											
Biochemistry	C700	3FT deg	S	EE	N	M	Dip	Ind	N$	6	
Biochemistry	C708	4FT deg	*							2	
Biotechnology	J801	3FT deg	S	EE	N	M	Dip	Ind	N$		
Biotechnology	J808	4FT deg	*								
NORTH EAST WALES INST of HE											
Biotechnology	J800	3FT deg		4-8	3M	M$	Ind	CCC	N$		
Biochemistry	007C	2FT HND		2-4	N	P$	Ind	CC	N$		
Univ of NORTH LONDON											
Biochemistry	C700	3FT/4SW/4EXT deg	B+C	CC	3M $	MS	$	Ind	Ind	12	6/ 8
Combined Honours *Biochemistry*	Y100	3FT/4SW/4EXT deg	B+C	CC	3M $	MS	$	Ind	Ind		
Univ of NORTHUMBRIA											
Chemistry with Biochemistry	F1C7	3FT/4SW deg	C+S/M g	10	3M	MS gi	24$	CCCC$	Ind	6	
NORWICH: City COLL											
Combined Science *Biochemistry*	Y100	3FT/4FT deg	2S	10	5M		Ind	Ind	Ind		
Combined Science *Molecular Biology*	Y100	3FT/4FT deg	2S	10	5M		Ind	Ind	Ind		
Univ of NOTTINGHAM											
Biochemistry & Biological Chemistry (MSci)	C701	4FT deg	C+2(B/P/M) g	BBC-BCC	Ind	Ind	Ind	Ind	Ind	7	24/30
Biochemistry & Biomedical Physics	CC76	3FT deg	C+P+M g	BBC	Ind	Ind	Ind	Ind	Ind	7	
Biochemistry and Biological Chemistry	C700	3FT deg	C+2(B/P/M) g	BBC-BCC	Ind	Ind	Ind	Ind	Ind	41	24/30
Biochemistry and Biomedical Physics (MSci)	CCR6	4FT deg	C+P+M g	BBC	Ind	Ind	Ind	Ind	Ind	8	
Biochemistry and Genetics	CC47	3FT deg	C+B/M g	AAB	Ind	Ind	Ind	Ind	Ind	10	28/30
Biotechnology in Agriculture (allows specialis)	D8J8	3FT deg	2(M/S/Gy)	CC-CDD	3M $	MS	24$	CSYS$	N$	13	
Nutritional Biochemistry (allows specialisation)	C770	3FT deg	2(M/S/Gy)	CC-CDD	3M $	MS	24$	CSYS$	N$	14	
Nutritional Biochemistry with European Studies	C7T2	4FT deg	2(M/S/Gy) g	CC-CDD	3M $	MS	24$	CSYS$	N$		

Biochemistry/Biophysics/ Biotechnology   8

course details			*98 expected requirements*							*96 entry stats*
TITLE	CODE	COURSE	SUBJECTS	A/AS	ND/C	AGNVQ	IB	SQA(H)	SQA	RATIO A/AS
NOTTINGHAM TRENT Univ										
Biochemistry and Microbiology	CC57	4SW deg	S g	DDE	Ind	Ind	Dip	C	$	8 6/10
OXFORD Univ										
Molecular and Cellular Biochemistry	C700	4FT deg	C+M+S/C+2S	AAB	DO		36	AAAAA	Ind	2 28/30
OXFORD BROOKES Univ										
Biological Chemistry/Accounting and Finance	CN74	3FT deg	S g	DD-BCC	Ind		Ind	Ind	Ind	
Biological Chemistry/Anthropology	CL76	3FT deg	S g	DD-BCC	Ind		Ind	Ind	Ind	
Biological Chemistry/Biology	CC71	3FT deg					Ind	Ind	Ind	
Business Administration and Mgt/Biological Chem	CN71	3FT deg			Ind		Ind	Ind	Ind	
Cartography/Biological Chemistry	CF78	3FT deg								
Cell Biology/Biological Chemistry	CCC7	3FT deg								
Combined Studies/Biological Chemistry	CY74	3FT deg		X		X	X	X		
Computer Systems/Biological Chemistry	CG76	3FT deg								
Computing Mathematics/Biological Chemistry	CG79	3FT deg								
Computing/Biological Chemistry	CG75	3FT deg								
Ecology/Biological Chemistry	CC79	3FT deg								
Economics/Biological Chemistry	CL71	3FT deg								
Educational Studies/Biological Chemistry	CX79	3FT deg								
Electronics/Biological Chemistry	CH76	3FT deg								
English Studies/Biological Chemistry	CQ73	3FT deg								
Environmental Chemistry/Biological Chemistry	CF71	3FT deg								
Environmental Policy/Biological Chemistry	CK73	3FT deg								
Environmental Sciences/Biological Chemistry	CF79	3FT deg								
Exercise and Health/Biological Chemistry	CB76	3FT deg								
Fine Art/Biological Chemistry	CW71	3FT deg								
Food Science and Nutrition/Biological Chemistry	CD74	3FT deg								
French Language and Contemp Studies/Bio Chem	CR7C	3FT deg								
French Language and Literature/Biological Chem	CR71	3FT deg								
Geography and the Phys Env/Biological Chemistry	FCV7	3FT deg								
Geography/Biological Chemistry	CL78	3FT deg								
Geology/Biological Chemistry	CF76	3FT deg								
Geotechnics/Biological Chemistry	CH72	3FT deg								
German Language and Contemp Stud/Biological Chem	CR7F	3FT deg								
German Language and Literature/Biological Chem	CR72	3FT deg								
German Studies/Biological Chemistry	CR7G	3FT deg								
Health Care/Biological Chemistry (Post Exp)	BC77	3FT deg		X		X	X	X		
History of Art/Biological Chemistry	CV74	3FT deg								
History/Biological Chemistry	CV71	3FT deg								
Hospitality Management Studies/Biological Chem	CN77	3FT deg								
Human Biology/Biological Chemistry	BC17	3FT deg			Ind		Ind	Ind	Ind	
Information Systems/Biological Chemistry	CG7M	3FT deg								
Intelligent Systems/Biological Chemistry	CG78	3FT deg								
Law/Biological Chemistry	CM73	3FT deg								
Leisure Planning/Biological Chemistry	CK7H	3FT deg								
Marketing Management/Biological Chemistry	CN7N	3FT deg								
Mathematics/Biological Chemistry	CG71	3FT deg								
Music/Biological Chemistry	CW73	3FT deg								
Palliative Care/Biological Chemistry (Post Exp)	BCR7	3FT deg		X		X	X	X		
Planning Studies/Biological Chemistry	CK74	3FT deg								
Politics/Biological Chemistry	CM71	3FT deg								
Psychology/Biological Chemistry	CC78	3FT deg								

			98 expected requirements							96 entry stats	
TITLE	CODE	COURSE	SUBJECTS	A/AS	NO/C	RGNVQ	IB	SQA(H)	SQA	RATIO	A/AS
Publishing/Biological Chemistry	CP75	3FT deg									
Rehabilitation/Biological Chemistry (Post Exp)	BCT7	3FT deg	X		X	X	X				
Retail Management/Biological Chemistry	CN75	3FT deg									
Sociology/Biological Chemistry	CL73	3FT deg									
Software Engineering/Biological Chemistry	CG77	3FT deg									
Statistics/Biological Chemistry	CG74	3FT deg									
Telecommunications/Biological Chemistry	CH7P	3FT deg									
Tourism/Biological Chemistry	CP77	3FT deg									
Transport Planning/Biological Chemistry	CN79	3FT deg									
Water Resources/Biological Chemistry	CH7F	3FT deg									

Univ of PAISLEY

Applied Biochemistry	C710	3FT/4FT/5SW deg	B/C g	CCC-EE	Ind	Ind	Ind	BCC$	Ind	6	
Biochemistry and Microbiology	CC75	4FT/5SW deg	* g	CCC-EE	Ind	Ind	Ind	BCC$	Ind		
Biotechnology	J800	4FT/5SW deg	* g	CCC-EE	Ind	Ind	Ind	BCC$	Ind	6	
Immunology and Biochemistry	CC79	3FT deg	* g	CCC-EE	Ind	Ind	Ind	BCC$	Ind		

Univ of PORTSMOUTH

Biochemistry	C700	3FT deg	2S	10	3M $	M$6/^	Dip	BBB	Ind		8/14
Biomolecular Science	C650	3FT deg	2S	10	3M $	M$6/^	Dip	BBB	Ind		
Biotechnology	J800	3FT deg	2S	10	3M $	M$6/^	Dip	BBB	Ind		
Molecular Biology	C621	3FT deg	C+S	10	3M	M$	Dip	BBB	Ind	4	6/8
Molecular Biology	C628▼	4EXT deg	*	Ind	Ind	Ind	Ind	Ind	Ind	2	

QUEEN MARY & WESTFIELD COLL (Univ of London)

Biochemistry	C700	3FT deg	C+B/P/M	16	6M $	MS^/DS	26$	BBBCC			
Biochemistry/Microbiology	C7C5	3FT deg	C+B/P/M	16	6M $	MS^/DS	26$	BBBCC			
Chemistry with Biochemistry	F1C7	3FT deg	C+B/P/M	CCC	5M $	DS	26$	BBBCC			
Molecular Biology	C620	3FT deg	B+C/P/M	16	6M $	DS	26$	BBBCC			

QUEEN'S Univ Belfast

Biochemistry	C700	3FT/4FT deg	C+B/M/P g	CCC	Ind	Ind	28$	BBBC	Ind	8	16/26
Molecular Biology	C620	3FT/4FT deg	C+B g	CCC	Ind	Ind	28$	BBBC	Ind	11	

Univ of READING

Biochemistry	C700	3FT deg	C g	18	4M+1D$	DS^ go	29$	BBBC$	Ind	16	16/20
Biotechnology	J800	4SW deg	2S g	CDD	MO	MS6/^ gi	28$	BBCC	Ind	5	14/22
Molecular Biology	C620	3FT deg	B+C g	18	4M+1D$	DS^ go	29$	BBBC$	Ind	6	
Physiology and Biochemistry	BC17	3FT deg	B/C g	18	4M+1D$	DS^ go	29$	BBBC$	Ind	4	12/16

ROBERT GORDON Univ

Biosciences with Biomedical Sciences	C9B9	3FT/4FT deg	B/C g	EE	N	Ind	Ind	CCC$	Ind		

ROYAL HOLLOWAY, Univ of London

Biochemistry	C700	3FT deg	C+B/M/P g	BCC	3M+2D	DS^	28$	BBBCC$		6	14/18
Biochemistry (Biotechnology)	CJ78	3FT/4SW deg	C+B/M/P g	BCC	3M+2D	DS^	28$	BBBCC$		6	
Biochemistry (Medical)	C720	3FT deg	C+B g	BCC	3M+2D	DS^	28$	BBBCC$		3	14/22
Biochemistry for Management	C7NC	3FT deg	C+B/M/P g	BCC	3M+2D	DS^	28$	BBBCC$		12	
Biochemistry with German	C7R2	3FT/4FT deg	C+G+B/M/P g	BCC	3M+2D	DS^	28$	BBBCC$			
Biochemistry with Physiology	C7B1	3FT deg	B+C g	BCC	3M+2D	DS^	28$	BBBCC$		5	
Biochemistry with Psychology	C7C8	3FT deg	C+B/M/P g	BCC	3M+2D	DS^	28$	BBBCC$			
Molecular Biology and Genetics	CC46	3FT deg	B+C g	BCC	3M+2D	DS^	28$	BBBCC$			
Foundation Programme *Biochemistry*	Y408	4FT deg									
Science Foundation Year *Biochemistry*	Y100	4FT deg	*		Ind	Ind	Ind	Ind			

Biochemistry/Biophysics/Biotechnology 8

TITLE	CODE	COURSE	SUBJECTS	A/AS	ND/C	AGNVQ	IB	SQA(H)	SQA	RATIO	A/AS
Univ of SALFORD											
Biochemical Sciences (3/4Yrs)	C700	3FT/4SW deg	g	BBC-CCD	4M	MS	Ind	Ind	Ind	4	10/20
Biochemical Sciences with studies in USA	C702	3FT deg	3S g	BBC-CCD	3M+2D	D	Ind	Ind	Ind	9	
Biochemistry & Geography (3 or 4 Yrs)	CF78	3FT/4SW deg	B/C+Gy	BBC-CCD	3M	M	Ind	Ind	Ind		
Biochemistry and Chemistry (3 or 4 Yrs)	FC17	3FT/4SW deg	C	BCC-CCD	3M	M	Ind	Ind	Ind	5	
Biochemistry and Economics (3 or 4 Yrs)	LC17	3FT/4SW deg	C	BCC-CCD	3M	M	Ind	Ind	Ind	1	
Biochemistry and Physics (3 or 4 Yrs)	FC37	3FT/4SW deg	C+P	BCC-CCD	3M	M	Ind	Ind	Ind	1	
Chemistry with Biochemistry	F1C7	4FT deg	C+S/M	BC	N	P					
Physiology with Biochemistry	BC17	3FT/4SW deg	g	BCC-CCD	4M	MS	Ind	Ind	Ind		7/13
Univ of SHEFFIELD											
Biochemistry	C700	3FT deg	C+S g	BCC	4M+2D$	DS^	29$	BBBB$	Ind	10	22/30
Biochemistry and Biotechnology	CJ78	3FT deg	C+S g	18	6M $	DS^	28$	BBBC$	Ind	14	
Biochemistry and Genetics	CC74	3FT deg	C+S g	BCC	4M+2D$	DS^	29$	BBBB$	Ind	7	20/28
Biochemistry and Microbiology	CC75	3FT deg	C+S g	BCC	5M+1D$	DS^	29$	BBBB$	Ind	15	
Biochemistry and Physiology	CB71	3FT/4EXT deg	C+S g	BCC	4M+2D	DS6/^	30$	BBBB$	Ind	5	
Biological Chemistry	C741	3FT deg	C+S g	24	3M+3D$	D^	32$	AABB$			
Biological Chemistry (MChem)	C740	4FT deg	C+S g	24	3M+3D$	D^	32$	AABB$			
Biotechnology and Microbiology	JC85	3FT/4EXT deg	C+S g	18	6M $	DS^	28$	BBBC$	Ind	11	
Chemical Engineering with Biotechnology(3/4 Yrs)	H8J8	3FT/4FT deg	M+C g	BBC-BCC	5M+1D$	X	30$	CSYS	Ind	7	
Medical Biochemistry	C720	3FT deg	C+S g	BCC	4M+2D$	D^	29$	BBBB$	Ind	11	22/30
Molecular Biology	C620	3FT deg	C+S g	BCD	6M	DS^	28$	BBBC$	Ind	12	
SHEFFIELD HALLAM Univ											
Biomedical Sciences	B940	4SW deg	B+S	10	3M	M$	Ind	Ind	Ind		
Mathematics with Biomedical Sciences	G1B9	3FT/4SW deg	M/St/B	EE	3M	P	Ind	Ind	Ind		
Combined Studies *Biomedical Sciences*	Y400	3FT deg	S	8-10	2M	M	Ind	Ind	Ind		
Biomedical Sciences	049B	2FT HND	B	D	N $	P$	Ind	Ind	Ind		
Univ of SOUTHAMPTON											
Biochemistry	C700	3FT/4SW deg	C+B/P/M/Gy g	BCC	$	M^	$	Ind	Ind	8	18/26
Biochemistry and Chemistry (4 Yrs)	CF71	4FT deg	C+B/P/M/Gy g	BCC	$	M^	$	Ind	Ind		
Biochemistry and Pharmacology	CB72	3FT/4SW deg	C+B/P/M/Gy g	BCC	$	M^	$	Ind	Ind	6	
Biochemistry and Physiology with Foundation Year	CB7F	4FT deg									
Biochemistry with Chemistry	C7F1	3FT/4SW deg	C+B/P/M/Gy g	BCC	$	M^	$	Ind	Ind	9	
Biochemistry with Nutrition	C7B4	3FT deg	C+B/P/M/Gy g	BCC	$	M^	$	Ind	Ind	2	
Biochemistry with Pharmacology	C7B2	3FT/4SW deg	C+B/P/M/Gy g	BCC	$	M^	$	Ind	Ind	5	
Biochemistry with Physiology	C7B1	3FT deg	C+B/P/M/Gy g	BCC	$	M^	$	Ind	Ind	5	
Chemistry and Biochemistry (4 Yrs)	FC17	4FT deg	C+S g	BBC	Ind	Ind	30$	CSYS	Ind	3	22/30
Chemistry with Biochemistry	F1C7	3FT deg	C+S g	18	Ind	Ind	28$	CSYS	Ind	5	
Physiology and Biochemistry	BC17	3FT deg	C+B/P/M g	BCC	$	M^	$	Ind	Ind	2	18/24
Physiology with Biochemistry	B1C7	3FT deg	C+B/P/M/Gy g	BCC	$	M^	$	Ind	Ind		
SOUTH BANK Univ											
Biochemistry	C700	3FT/4SW deg	B/C/P g	BC	MO	M go	Ind	Ind	Ind		
Biotechnology	J800	3FT/4SW deg	B/C/P g	BC	MO	M go	Ind	Ind	Ind		
Univ of ST ANDREWS											
Biochemistry	C700	3FT/4FT deg	C g	CCC	Ind	Ind	28	BBCC	Ind	5	
Biochemistry with Biotechnology	C7J8	3FT/4FT deg	C g	CCC	Ind	Ind	28	BBCC	Ind	8	
Biochemistry with Microbiology	C7C5	3FT/4FT deg	C g	CCC	Ind	Ind	28	BBCC	Ind	7	
Chemistry-Biochemistry	CF71	3FT/4FT deg	C g	CCC	Ind	Ind	28$	BBCC$	Ind	6	
General Degree of BSc *Biochemistry*	Y100	3FT deg	C g	CCC	Ind	Ind	28	BBCC	Ind		

			98 expected requirements							96 entry stats	

course details / 98 expected requirements / 96 entry stats

TITLE	CODE	COURSE	SUBJECTS	A/AS	NO/C	RGNVQ	IB	SQA(H)	SQA	RATIO	A/AS
STAFFORDSHIRE Univ											
Biochemistry and Microbiology	CC75	3FT deg	B	12	4M	M^	24	BCC	Ind	9	8/10
Biochemistry and Molecular Biology	CC6R	4EXT deg	g	4	1M	P	24	CCC			
Biochemistry and Molecular Biology	CC67	3FT deg									
Biochemistry and Physiology	BC17	3FT deg	B g	12	4M	M^	24	BCC	Ind	2	8/18
Chemistry/Biochemistry	FC17	3FT deg	S	8	3M	M	24	BCC	Ind		
Computing/Biochemistry	CG75	3FT deg									
Extended Biochemistry and Microbiology (4 yr)	CC5T	4EXT deg	g	4	1M	P	24	CCC	Ind	1	
Extended Biochemistry and Physiology (4 yr)	CB7D	4EXT deg	g	4	1M	P	24	CCC	Ind		
Foundation Biochemistry and Chemistry	CF7C▼	4EXT deg	*	4	N	P	24	CCC	Ind		
Foundation Biochemistry and Microbiology	CC5R▼	4EXT deg	*	4	N	P	24	CCC	Ind		
Foundation Biochemistry and Physiology	CB7C▼	4EXT deg	*	4	N	P	24	CCC	Ind		
Physics/Biochemistry	CF73	3FT deg									
Physiology/Molecular Biology	BC16	3FT deg	B g	12	4M	M	24	BCC			
Univ of STIRLING											
Biochemistry	C700	4FT deg	C g	CCD	Ind	Ind	28	BBCC	HN		
Molecular and Cell Biology	CC16	4FT deg	S g	CCD	Ind	Ind	28	BBCC	HN		
STOCKPORT COLL of F and HE											
Biochemistry	C700	4FT deg	B+C/M	EE	N	PS	Dip	BBCC	N		
Univ of STRATHCLYDE											
Biochemistry and Biotechnology	CJ78	4FT deg	C+B+M/P g	CCC	HN		Ind	BBC$	HN		
Biochemistry and Food Science	CD74	4FT deg	C+B+M/P g	CCC	HN		Ind	BBC$	HN		
Biochemistry and Immunology	CC79	4FT deg	C+B+M/P g	CCC	Ind		Ind	BBC$	Ind		
Biochemistry and Microbiology	CC75	4FT deg	C+B/M+P g	CCC	HN		Ind	BBC$	HN		
Biochemistry and Molecular Biology	CC76	4FT deg	C+B+M/P g	CCC	HN		Ind	BBC$	HN		
Biochemistry and Pharmacology	CB72	4FT deg	C+B+M/P g	CCC	HN		Ind	BBC$	HN		
Chemical Engineering with Process Biotechnology	H8J8	4FT deg	C+M+P	CCD			Ind	BBBB$			
Science Studies (Pass Degree) *Biochemistry*	Y100	3FT deg	M+S	DD	Ind		Ind	CCC$	Ind		
Univ of SUNDERLAND											
Cellular and Molecular Biology	C620	3FT/4SW deg	B+C g	10	N $	PS	24$	CCCC$	N$		
Univ of SURREY											
Biochemistry	C700	3FT/4SW deg	C+M/P/B g	BCC-CCC	3M+3D$		30$	AABBB$	X	5	6/28
Biochemistry with a Foundation Year	C705	4FT/5SW deg	*	CCC	5M $	D	30$	ABBBB	Ind	10	
Biochemistry, Medical	C720	3FT/4SW deg	C+M/P/B g	BCC-CCC	3M+3D$		30$	AABBB$	X	4	12/22
Biochemistry, Toxicology	C706	3FT/4SW deg	C+M/P/B g	BCC-CCC	3M+3D$		30$	AABBB$	X	3	10/22
Molecular Biology	C620	3FT/4SW deg	C+M/P/B g	BCC-CCC	3M+3D$		30$	AABBB$	X	5	8/16
Univ of SUSSEX											
Biochemistry	C700	3FT deg	C+S g	BCD	MO $	MS6 go	$	Ind	Ind		
Biochemistry	C706	4SW deg	C+S g	BCD	MO $	MS6 go	$	Ind	Ind		
Biochemistry with European Studies (French)	C7R1	4FT deg	C+S g	BCC	MO $	MS6 go	$	Ind	Ind		
Biochemistry with European Studies (German)	C7R2	4FT deg	C+S g	BCC	MO $	MS6 go	$	Ind	Ind		
Biochemistry with European Studies (Spanish)	C7R4	4FT deg	C+S g	BCC	MO $	MS6 go	$	Ind	Ind		
Biochemistry with Management Studies	C7N1	3FT deg	C+S g	BCD	MO $	MS6 go	$	Ind	Ind		
Biochemistry with Neurobiology	C7C1	3FT deg	C+S g	BCD	MO $	MS6 go	$	Ind	Ind		
Biomolecular Science	C704	3FT deg	C+S g	BCD	MO $	MS6 go	$	Ind	Ind		
Molecular Genetics in Biotechnology	C4J8	3FT deg	2S g	BCD	MO $	MS6 go	$	Ind	Ind		
Molecular Genetics in Biotechnology	C4JV	4SW deg	2S g	BCD	MO $	MS6 go	$	Ind	Ind		

Biochemistry/Biophysics/ Biotechnology 8

	course details			98 expected requirements							96 entry stats	
TITLE	CODE	COURSE	SUBJECTS	A/AS	NO/C	AGNVQ	IB	SQA(H)	SQA	RATIO	A/AS
Univ of Wales SWANSEA											
Biochemistry	C700	3FT deg	C	BCC-CCC	2M+3D$	DS^	28$	BBBCC$	Ind	3	10/20
Biochemistry (with Italian)	C7R3	4FT deg	C	BCC-CCC	2M+3D$	X	28$	BBBCC$	Ind		
Biochemistry with a yr in Industry	C701	4FT deg	C	BCC-CCC	2M+3D$	DS^	28$	BBBCC$	Ind		
Univ of TEESSIDE											
Process Biotechnology	J801	3FT/4SW deg	S/M	8	3M		Ind	CCC	3M	2	4/18
Biotechnology	008J	2FT HND	S	4	N	P	Ind	CC	N	2	2/4
Univ of ULSTER											
Applied Biochemical Sciences (4 Yr SW inc DIS)	C710▼	4SW deg	C/B	CCC	MO+3D	DS6/^ gi	28	BBBC	Ind	6	14/24
UNIVERSITY COLL LONDON (Univ of London)											
Biochemistry	C700	3FT deg	C+S/M g	BCC-BBB	MO+2D$	Ind	32$	Ind	Ind	8	18/26
Biotechnology	J800	3FT deg	C+B/M/P g	BCC-BBB	MO+2D$	Ind	32$	Ind	Ind	8	24/28
Molecular Biology	C620	3FT deg	C+S/M g	BCC-BBB	MO+2D$	Ind	32$	Ind	Ind	4	
Univ of WARWICK											
Biochemistry	C700	3FT deg	C/S+B g	20-22	DO $	DS^	28$	BBBBB$		8	16/30
Univ of WESTMINSTER											
Biochemistry & Microbiology	CC75	3FT deg	B/C	CC-CD	3M	M			Ind	6	4/10
Biotechnology	J800	3FT deg	C	CC-CD	3M	M			Ind	6	
Univ of WOLVERHAMPTON											
Applied Chemistry with Biochemical Science	F1C7	3FT/4SW deg	C g	DD	N	M	24	CCCC	Ind		
Biochemistry	C700	3FT/4SW deg	C/B g	DD	N	M	24	CCCC	Ind	4	8/14
Biochemistry with Food Science	C7D4	3FT/4SW deg	C/B g	DD	N	M	24	CCCC	Ind		
Biochemistry with Molecular Biology	C7C6	3FT/4SW deg	C/B g	DD	N	M	24	CCCC	Ind		
Biochemistry with Pharmacology	C7B2	3FT/4SW deg	C g	DD	N	M	24	CCCC	Ind		
Biotechnology	J800	3FT/4SW deg		DD	N	M	24	CCCC	Ind		
Cell & Molecular Biology	C620	3FT/4SW deg		DD	N	M	24	CCCC	Ind		
Genetics & Molecular Biology	C4C6	3FT/4SW deg	B g	DD	N	M	24	CCCC	Ind		
Applied Sciences *Biochemistry*	Y100	3FT/4SW deg	S g	DD	N	M	24	CCCC$	Ind		
Applied Sciences *Biotechnology*	Y100	3FT/4SW deg	B g	DD	N	M	24	CCCC$	Ind		
Applied Sciences *Genetics and Molecular Biology*	Y100	3FT/4SW deg	B g	DD	N	M	24	CCCC	Ind		
Applied Sciences *Genetics and Molecular Biology*	Y110	4FT deg	*								
Applied Sciences (4 Yrs) *Biochemistry*	Y110▼	4FT deg	*								
Applied Sciences (4 Yrs) *Biotechnology*	Y110▼	4FT deg	*								
Combined Degrees *Biochemistry*	Y401	3FT/4SW deg	B/C g	DD	N	M	24	CCCC	HN		
Combined Degrees *Biotechnology*	Y401	3FT/4SW deg	B g	DD	N	M	24	CCCC	Ind		
Combined Degrees *Genetics and Molecular Biology*	Y401	3FT/4SW deg	B g	DD	N	M	24	CCCC	Ind		
Biochemistry	007C	2FT HND	C/B g	D	N	M	24	CCCC	Ind	1	
Biotechnology and Microbiology	008J	2FT HND	B g	D	N	M	24	CCCC	Ind	2	
WRITTLE COLL											
Engineering (Biological Processes)	J800	3FT deg	Ap g	14	MO	M	Ind	Ind	Ind		

course details			98 expected requirements							96 entry stats
TITLE	CODE	COURSE	SUBJECTS	A/AS	ND/C	AGNVQ	IB	SQA(H)	SQA	RATIO A/AS
WYE COLL (Univ of London)										
Biochemistry	C700	3FT deg	C+B	14	2M+1D$ Ind		25$	BBCCC$ Ind		
Univ of YORK										
Biochemistry	C700	3FT deg	C+B/M/P g	BCC	5M $	MS6/^	28$	BBBB$	N$	16/28
Biochemistry (4 Yr SW)	C705	4SW deg	C+B/M/P g	BCC	5M $	MS6/^	28$	BBBB$	N$	18/28
Biochemistry with a year in Europe	C701	4SW deg	C+B/M/P g	BCC	5M $	MS6/^	28$	BBBB$	N$	

			98 expected requirements							96 entry stats	
TITLE	CODE	COURSE	SUBJECTS	A/AS	NO/C	AGNVQ	IB	SQA(H)	SQA	RATIO	A/AS
Univ of ABERDEEN											
Biochemistry (Immunology)	C7C9	4FT deg	3S/2S+M g	CCD	Ind	MS go	24$	BBBC$	Ind	6	
Biochemistry (Immunology) with Indust Placement	C7CX	5FT deg	3S/2S+M g	CCD	Ind	MS go	24$	BBBC$	Ind		
Biological Sciences of Agriculture	CD12	4FT deg	3S/2S+M g	CCD	Ind	MS go	24$	BBBC$	Ind		
Biology	C100	4FT deg	3S/2S+M g	CCD	Ind	MS go	24$	BBBB$	Ind	6	
Biology (Ecology)	C162	4FT deg	3S/2S+M g	CCD	Ind	MS go	24$	BBBC$	Ind		
Biology (Environmental Science)	C160	4FT deg	3S/2S+M g	CCD	Ind	MS go	24$	BBBB$	Ind	7	
Univ of ABERTAY DUNDEE											
Biology & Chemistry	CF11	4FT/5SW deg	C	CD	Ind	Ind	Ind	BBC	Ind		
Biology & Computing	CG15	4FT/5SW deg	g	CD	Ind	Ind	Ind	BBC	Ind		
Biotechnology	C930	4FT deg	B/C	DE	Ind	Ind	Ind	BCC	Ind		
Environmental Biotechnology	C9F9	4FT deg	B/C	DE	Ind	Ind	Ind	BCC	Ind		
Forest Products Technology	CD93	4FT/5SW deg	B/C	DE	Ind	Ind	Ind	BCC	Ind		
Management & Biology	CN11	4FT/5SW deg	g	CD	Ind	Ind	Ind	BBC	Ind		
Medical Biotechnology	C9B9	4FT deg	B/C	DE	Ind	Ind	Ind	BCC	Ind		
Microbial Biotechnology	C9C5	4FT deg	B/C	DE	Ind	Ind	Ind	BCC	Ind		
Plant & Animal Cell Biotechnology	C9C2	4FT deg	B/C	DE	Ind	Ind	Ind	BCC	Ind		
Psychology with Biology	CC81	4FT/5SW deg	E	CD	Ind	Ind	Ind	BBC	Ind		
Biological Sciences	021C	2FT HND	B/C	D	Ind	Ind	Ind	BC	Ind		
Univ of Wales, ABERYSTWYTH											
Biology	C100	3FT deg	B/C g	16-18	3M $	MS6/^ g	29$	BBBCC$	Ind		
Environmental Biology	C160	3FT deg	B/C g	16-18	3M $	MS6/^ g	29$	BBBCC$	Ind		
Life Sciences (4 yrs)	C980	4FT deg	* g		N $	PS g	Dip				
Marine and Freshwater Biology	C174	3FT deg	B/C g	16-18	3M $	MS6/^ g	29$	BBBCC$	Ind		
Information and Library St/an approved Sci Sub *Biology*	PY21	3FT deg	B/C g	16-18	3M $	MS6/^ g	29$	BBBCC$	Ind		
ANGLIA Poly Univ											
Animal Behaviour and Biology	C156▼	3FT deg	B	10	3M	P	Dip	BCCC	N	5	9/16
Animal Behaviour and Biomedical Science	BC91▼	3FT deg	B	10	3M	P	Dip	BCCC	N	5	
Animal Behaviour and Chemistry	CF1C▼	3FT deg	S	10	3M	P	Dip	BCCC	N		
Animal Behaviour and Ecology and Conservation	CD12▼	3FT deg	S	10	3M	P	Dip	BCCC	N	2	6/20
Animal Behaviour and French	CR1C▼	4FT deg	g	12	4M	P go	Dip	BCCC	N		
Animal Behaviour and Geography	CF1V▼	3FT deg	Gy g	10	3M	P go	Dip	BCCC	N	5	
Animal Behaviour and Geology	CF1P▼	3FT deg		10	3M	P	Dip	BCCC	N	1	
Animal Behaviour and German	CR1F▼	4FT deg	g	12	4M	P go	Dip	BCCC	N		
Animal Behaviour and Imaging Science	CW15▼	3FT deg	S	10	3M	P	Dip	BCCC			
Animal Behaviour and Italian	CR1H▼	4FT deg	g	12	4M	P go	Dip	BCCC	N		
Animal Behaviour and Maths or Stats/Stat Mod.	CG1C▼	3FT deg	g	10	3M	P go	Dip	BCCC	N		
Animal Behaviour and Psychology	CC1V▼	3FT deg	S g	16	8M	M go	Dip	BBCCC	N	5	
Animal Behaviour and Spanish	CR1K▼	4FT deg	g	12	4M	P go	Dip	BCCC	N		
Audiotechnology and Biology	HC6C▼	3FT deg	B	16	8M	D	Dip$	BBCCC			
Biological Sciences	C120▼	3FT deg	B	10	3M	P	Dip$	BCCC	N	4	6/20
Biology and Biomedical Science	CB19▼	3FT deg	B	10	3M	P	Dip$	BCCC	N	3	
Biology and Chemistry	CF11▼	3FT deg	B	10	3M	P	Dip$	BCCC	N	4	
Biology and Computer Science	CG15▼	3FT deg	B	10	3M	P	Dip$	BCCC	N		
Biology and Ecology and Conservation	DC21▼	3FT deg	B	10	3M	P	Dip$	BCCC	N	11	
Biology and Food Science	CD14▼	3FT deg	g	10	3M	P go	Dip	BCCC			
Biology and Forensic Science	BC11▼	3FT deg	g	10	3M	P go	Dip	BCCC			
Biology and French	CR11▼	4FT deg	B g	12	4M	P+/^	Dip$	BCCC	N		
Biology and Geography	CF18▼	3FT deg	B+Gy	10	3M	P	Dip$	BCCC	N	13	
Biology and Geology	CF16▼	3FT deg	B	10	3M	P	Dip$	BCCC	N	4	

course details			98 expected requirements							96 entry stats	
TITLE	CODE	COURSE	SUBJECTS	A/AS	NO/C	RGNVQ	IB	SQA(H)	SQA	RATIO	A/AS
Biology and German	CR12▼	4FT deg	B g	12	4M	P+/^ go	Dip$	BCCC	N		
Biology and Imaging Science	CW1M▼	3FT deg	B	10	3M	P	Dip$	BCCC	N		
Biology and Instrumentation Electronics	CH16▼	3FT deg	B	10	3M	P	Dip$	BCCC	N		
Biology and Italian	CR13▼	4FT deg	B g	12	4M	P+/^ go	Dip$	BCCC	N		
Biology and Maths or Stats/Statistical Mod.	CG11▼	3FT deg	B g	10	3M	P go	Dip$	BCCC	N		
Biology and Ophthalmic Dispensing	BC51▼	3FT deg	B	10	3M	P go	Dip$	BCCC	N	2	
Biology and Psychology	CC18▼	3FT deg	B	16	8M	D go	Dip$	BBCCC	N	10	
Biology and Spanish	CR14▼	4FT deg	B g	12	4M	M+/^ go	Dip$	BCCC	N		
Biomedical Science and Ophthalmic Dispensing	BC59▼	3FT deg	B	10	3M	P go	Dip$	BCCC	N	3	
Environmental Biology	C160▼	3FT deg	B	10	3M	P gi	Dip$	BCCC	N	17	

ASTON Univ

TITLE	CODE	COURSE	SUBJECTS	A/AS	NO/C	RGNVQ	IB	SQA(H)	SQA	RATIO	A/AS
Applied and Human Biology	C112	3FT/4SW deg	B g	20	5M+5D$	D$6/^ go	31$	BBBBB$	Ind	4	14/24
Applied and Human Biology (Year Zero)	C118	4FT/5SW deg									
Business Administration/Biology	CN11	3FT/4SW deg	B g	20	5M+5D$	D$^ go	30$	BBBBB$	Ind	3	16/26
Business Administration/Biology (Year Zero)	CN1C	4FT/5SW deg									
Chemistry/Biology	CF11	3FT/4SW deg	B+C g	18	X	X	29$	BBBBC$	Ind	6	
Chemistry/Biology (Year Zero)	CF1D	4FT/5SW deg									
Computer Science/Biology	CG15	3FT/4SW deg	B g	18	5M+5D$	D$6/^ go	29$	BBBBC$	Ind	4	
Computer Science/Biology (Year Zero)	CG1M	4FT/5SW deg									
Electronics/Biology	HC61	3FT/4SW deg	B+M/P g	18	X	X	29$	BBBBC$	Ind		
Environmental Science & Technology/Biology	CF19	3FT/4SW deg	B g	18	5M+5D$	D$6/^ go	29$	BBBBC$	Ind		
Environmental Science/Biology (Year Zero)	CF9X	4FT/5SW deg									
Ergonomics/Biology	CJ1X	3FT/4SW deg	B g	20		D$^ go	30$	BBBBB$	Ind		
European Studies/Biology	CT12	3FT/4SW deg	B g	18	X	D$^ go	29	BBBBC	Ind		
European Studies/Biology (Year Zero)	CT1F	4FT/5SW deg									
Health & Safety Management/Biology	CJ19	3FT/4SW deg	B g	18	5M+5D$	D$^ go	29$	BBBBC$	Ind	2	
Health & Safety Management/Biology (Year Zero)	CJ9X	4FT/5SW deg									
Human Psychology/Biology	CL17	3FT/4SW deg	B g	20	3M+7D$	D$^ go	30$	BBBBB$	Ind	4	20/26
Human Psychology/Biology (Year Zero)	CL1R	4FT/5SW deg									
Mathematics/Biology	CG11	3FT/4SW deg	B+M g	20	X	X	31$	ABBBB$	Ind	9	
Medicinal Chemistry/Biology	CF1C	3FT/4SW deg	C+B g	20	3M+7D$	X	31$	ABBBB$	Ind		
Product Design (Engineering)/Biology	CH17	3FT/4SW deg	B g	18	5M+5D$	D$^ go	29	BBBBC$	Ind		
Social Studies/Biology	CL14	3FT/4SW deg	B g	18	5M+5D$	D$^ go	29$	BBBBC$	Ind	2	
Social Studies/Biology (Year Zero)	CL1K	4FT/5SW deg									

Univ of Wales, BANGOR

TITLE	CODE	COURSE	SUBJECTS	A/AS	NO/C	RGNVQ	IB	SQA(H)	SQA	RATIO	A/AS
Biology	C100	3FT deg	B+S g	CDD	3M $	DS^ go	28$	BBCC$	Ind	4	10/22
Biology with Biochemistry	C1C7	3FT deg	B+C g	CCD	3M $	DS^ go	26$	BBCC$	Ind	5	
Biology with European Dimension	C1T2	4FT deg	B+F+S g	CDD	X	DS^ go	28$	BBCC$	X		
Environmental Biology	C160	3FT deg	2S g	CCD	5M $	DS^ go	28$	BBBC$	Ind	6	10/14
Marine Biology	C170	3FT deg	B+2S g	BCC	5M $	DS^ go	30$	BBBB$	Ind	12	18/28
Marine Biology and Biochemistry	CC17	3FT deg	B+C+S g	CCC	4M $	DS^ go	28$	BBBC$	Ind	15	
Marine Biology and Oceanography	CF17	3FT deg	B+2S g	CCD	4M $	DS^ go	28$	BBBC$	Ind	4	12/20
Marine Biology and Zoology	CC13	3FT deg	B+2S g	CCC	4M $	DS^ go	28$	BBBC$	Ind	27	

BARNSLEY COLL

TITLE	CODE	COURSE	SUBJECTS	A/AS	NO/C	RGNVQ	IB	SQA(H)	SQA	RATIO	A/AS
Science Foundation *Biological Sciences*	Y100	4EXT deg									

Univ of BATH

TITLE	CODE	COURSE	SUBJECTS	A/AS	NO/C	RGNVQ	IB	SQA(H)	SQA	RATIO	A/AS
Applied Biology	C111	4SW deg	B+S	20	Ind	DS^	28$	Ind	Ind	5	18/30
Biology	C100	3FT deg	B+S	20	Ind	DS^	28$	Ind	Ind	7	16/28
Molecular and Cellular Biology	C140	3FT deg	B+C	20	Ind	Ind	28$	Ind	Ind	3	14/26
Molecular and Cellular Biology	C141	4SW deg	B+C	20	Ind	Ind	28$	Ind	Ind	3	16/28

course details			98 expected requirements							96 entry stats	
TITLE	CODE	COURSE	SUBJECTS	A/AS	ND/C	AGNVQ	IB	SQA(H)	SQA	RATIO	A/AS
Natural Sciences *Biology*	Y160	3FT deg	S/M+S/M	20	Ind	DS	30	Ind	Ind		
Natural Sciences *Biology*	Y161	4SW deg	S/M+S/M	20	Ind	DS	30	Ind	Ind		

BATH COLL of HE

Environmental Biology	C160	3FT deg	S		Ind		Ind	$	$	5	4/20
Combined Awards *Environmental Biology*	Y400	3FT deg	S		N		Ind	$	$		
Modular Programme (DipHE) *Environmental Biology*	Y460	2FT Dip	S		N		Ind	$	$		

BELL COLLEGE OF TECHNOLOGY

Applied Biological Sciences	C910	3FT deg	2(B/C/Gy/M/P)	DD	Ind	Ind	Ind	CCC$	Ind		
Applied Biological Sciences	019C	2FT HND	S	D	Ind	Ind	Ind	CC$	Ind		

Univ of BIRMINGHAM

Biological Sci with Study in Continental Europe	C101	4FT deg	B+S/M/Gy/Gl/Ps g	BCC	Ind	Ind	30	Ind	Ind	3	20/30
Biological Sciences	C100	3FT deg	B+S/M/Gy/Gl/Ps g	BCC	Ind	Ind	30	Ind	Ind	6	16/28
Biological Sciences (Environmental Biology)	C160	3FT deg	B+S/M/Gy/Gl/Ps g	BCC	Ind	Ind	30	Ind	Ind	13	
Geology with Biology	F6C1	3FT deg	B+S g	BBC-CCC	Ind	Ind	30	Ind	Ind		

BOLTON INST

Accountancy and Biology	CN14	3FT deg	* g	CD	MO	M*	24	BBCC	Ind		
Art and Design History and Biology	VC41	3FT deg	* g	CD	MO	M*	24	BBCC	Ind		
Biology	C100	3FT deg	* g	CD	MO	M*	24	BBCC	Ind		
Biology and Business Economics	CL11	3FT deg	* g	CD	MO	M*					
Biology and Business Information Systems	GC51	3FT deg	* g	CD	MO	M*	24	BBCC	Ind		
Biology and Business Studies	CN11	3FT deg	* g	CD	MO	M*	24	BBCC	Ind		
Biology and Community Studies	LC51	3FT deg	* g	CD	MO	M*	24	BBCC	Ind		
Biology and Computing	CG15	3FT deg	* g	CD	MO	M*	24	BBCC	Ind		
Biology and Creative Writing	WC91	3FT deg	* g	CD	MO	M*	24	BBCC	Ind		
Biology and Environmental Studies	CF19	3FT deg	* g	CD	MO	M*	24	BBCC	Ind		
Biology and European Cultural Studies	TC21	3FT deg	* g	CD	MO	M*	24	BBCC	Ind		
Biology and Film & TV Studies	CW15	3FT deg	Me/T g	CD	Ind	Ind	24	BBCC	Ind		
Biology and French	CR11	3FT deg	F g	CD	Ind	Ind	24	BBCC	Ind		
Biology and Gender & Women's Studies	MC91	3FT deg	* g	CD	MO	M*	24	BBCC	Ind		
Biology and German	CR12	3FT deg	G g	CD	Ind	Ind	24	BBCC	Ind		
Biology and History	CV11	3FT deg	* g	CD	MO	M*	24	BBCC	Ind		
Biology and Human Resource Management	CN1C	3FT deg	* g	CD	MO	M*	24	BBCC	Ind		
Biology and Law	CM13	3FT deg	* g	CD	MO	M*	24	BBCC	Ind		
Biology and Leisure Studies	CL1H	3FT deg	* g	CD	MO	M*	24	BBCC	Ind		
Biology and Literature	CQ12	3FT deg	* g	CD	MO	M*	24	BBCC	Ind		
Biology and Marketing	CN15	3FT deg	* g	CD	MO	M*	24	BBCC	Ind		
Biology and Mathematics	CG11	3FT deg	M g	DD	Ind	Ind	24	BBCC	Ind		
Biology and Operations Management	CN12	3FT deg	* g	CD	MO	M*	24	BBCC	Ind		
Biology and Organisations, Management & Work	CN17	3FT deg	* g	CD	MO	M*	24	BBCC	Ind		
Biology and Peace and War Studies	CV1C	3FT deg	* g	CD	MO	M*	24	BBCC	Ind		
Biology and Philosophy	CV17	3FT deg	* g	CD	MO	M*	24	BBCC	Ind		
Biology and Psychology	CL17	3FT deg	* g	12	MO	D*	24	BBCC	Ind		
Biology and Statistics	CG14	3FT deg	* g	CD	MO	M	24	Ind	Ind		
Biology and Theatre Studies	WC41	3FT deg	Me/T g	CD	Ind	Ind	24	BBCC	Ind		
Biology and Tourism Studies	CP17	3FT deg	* g	CD	MO	M*	24	BBCC	Ind		
Biology and Urban and Cultural Studies	CK14	3FT deg	* g	CD	MO	M*	24	BBCC	Ind		
Design and Biology	CW12	3FT deg	* g	CD	MO	M*	24	BBCC	Ind		

course details — 98 expected requirements — 96 entry stats

TITLE	CODE	COURSE	SUBJECTS	A/AS	NO/C	RGNVQ	IB	SQA(H)	SQA	RATIO	A/AS
Human Resource Management and Mathematics	NC11	3FT deg	M g	DD	Ind	Ind	24	BBCC	Ind		
Visual Arts and Biology	CW11	3FT deg	* g	CD	MO	M*	24	BBCC	Ind		
Univ of BRADFORD											
Applied Ecology	C910	3FT deg	B+S g	BB-CCC	3M $	MS4/^					
Applied Ecology (4 Years)	C911	4SW deg	B+S g	BB-CCC	3M $	MS4/^					
Bioarchaeology	F4C9	3FT deg	B g	BCC	3M+1D	DS^	Ind	Ind	Ind		
Bioarchaeology	F4CX	4SW deg	B g	BCC	3M+1D	DS^	Ind	Ind	Ind		
BRADFORD & ILKLEY Comm COLL											
Applied Sciences *Biology*	001Y	2FT HND	S g	2	N $	P		Ind	Ind		
Univ of BRIGHTON											
Biological Sciences	C120	3FT/4SW deg	Ap g	12	Ind	M$ go	Dip$	BBCC$	Ind		
Biology and Chemistry	CF11	3FT/4SW deg	B/C g	12	MO $	M$	Dip$	BBCC$	Ind		
Biology and Computing	CG15	3FT/4SW deg	S g	12	MO $	M$	Dip$	BBCC$	Ind		
Biology and Energy Studies	CJ19	3FT/4SW deg	S g	12	MO $	M$	Dip$	BBCC$	Ind		
Biology and Geography	CF18	3FT/4SW deg	S g	12	MO $	M$	Dip$	BBCC$	Ind		
Biology and Mathematics	CG11	3FT/4SW deg	M g	12	MO $	M$	Dip$	BBCC$	Ind		
Applied Biology	011C▼	2FT HND	S g	E	N $	P$ go	24$	Ind	Ind		
Wine Studies	589C▼	2FT HND	S g	2-4	N	P	15	Ind	Ind		
Univ of BRISTOL											
Biology	C100	3FT deg	B+S g	BBC	Ind	D$^	32$	CSYS	Ind	10	22/30
Biology and Geography	CF18	3FT deg	B+Gy g	BBC	Ind	D$^	32$	CSYS	Ind	7	22/30
Geology and Biology	FC61	3FT deg	B+S g	BBC	Ind	D$^	32$	CSYS	Ind	16	
BRISTOL, Univ of the W of England											
Applied Biological Sciences	C110	4SW deg	B+C g	12	4M $	MS go	24$	BCC$	Ind		
Biology and Chemistry	CF11	3FT/4SW deg	B+C g	8	3M $	PS go	24$	CCC$	Ind		
Biology and Environmental Science	CF19	3FT/4SW deg	B+C g	8	3M $	PS go	24$	CCC$	Ind		
Biology and Information Technology in Science	CG15	3FT/4SW deg	B+C g	8	3M $	PS go	24$	CCC$	Ind		
Biology and Psychology	CC18	3FT/4SW deg	B+C g	8	3M $	PS go	24$	CCC$	Ind		
Biomedical Sciences	C980	4SW deg	B+C g	12	4M $	MS go	24$	BCC$	Ind		
Biomedical Sciences and Chemistry	BF91	3FT/4SW deg	B+C g	8	3M $	PS go	24$	CCC$	Ind		
Business Studies with Combined Science	C9N1	3FT/4SW deg	S/M g	12	4M $	MS go	24$	BCC$	Ind		
Environmental Biology	C160	4SW deg	B+S g	10	3M $	MS go	24$	BC$	Ind		
Joint Honours Programme *Education and Science*	Y401	3FT deg	S g	14-16	5M $	M$ go	24$	BCCC$	Ind		
Joint Honours Programme *Law and Science*	Y401	3FT deg	S g	14-16	5M $	M$ go	24$	BCCC$	Ind		
Science Foundation Year *Applied Biological Sciences*	Y120	5EXTSW deg	M/S g	E	N $	PS go	24$	Ind	N$		
Science Foundation Year *Biomedical Sciences*	Y120	5EXTSW deg	M/S g	E	N $	PS go	24$	Ind	N$		
Science (Applied Biology)	011C▼	2FT HND	B g	2	N $	PS go	24$	CD$	Ind		
BRUNEL Univ, West London											
Applied Biology	C111	3FT deg	B+C g	16-18	MO+4D$	MS2/^	26$	CSYS	Ind	6	
Applied Biology (4 Yrs Thick SW)	C112	4SW deg	B+C g	16-18	MO+4D$	MS2/^	26$	CSYS	Ind	11	
Applied Biology (4 Yrs Thin SW)	C110	4SW deg	B+C g	16-18	MO+4D$	MS2/^	26$	CSYS	Ind	4	12/18
Medical Biology	C130	3FT deg	B+C g	16-18	MO+4D$	MS2/^	26$	CSYS	Ind	5	8/18
Medical Biology (4 Yrs Thick SW)	C132	4SW deg	B+C g	16-18	MO+4D$	MS2/^	26$	CSYS	Ind	6	
Medical Biology (4 Yrs Thin SW)	C131	4SW deg	B+C g	16-18	MO+4D$	MS2/^	26$	CSYS	Ind	4	12/16

course details			98 expected requirements							96 entry stats	
TITLE	CODE	COURSE	SUBJECTS	A/AS	ND/C	AGNVQ	IB	SQA(H)	SQA	RATIO	A/AS
CAMBRIDGE Univ											
Biological Sciences with Education Studies (BA)	C1X9▼	3FT deg	* g	AAB	Ind		Ind	CSYS	Ind		
Natural Sciences *Animal Biology*	Y160▼	3FT deg	2(S/M) g	AAA-AAB	Ind		Ind	CSYS	Ind		
Natural Sciences *Biology of Cells*	Y160▼	3FT deg	2(S/M) g	AAA-AAB	Ind		Ind	CSYS	Ind		
Natural Sciences *Biology of Organisms*	Y160▼	3FT deg	2(S/M) g	AAA-AAB	Ind		Ind	CSYS	Ind		
Natural Sciences *Quantitative Biology*	Y160▼	3FT deg	2(S/M) g	AAA-AAB	Ind		Ind	CSYS	Ind		
CANTERBURY CHRIST CHURCH COLL of HE											
Environmental Biology	C160	3FT deg	S g	DD	Ind	Ind	24	Ind	Ind		
CARDIFF Univ of Wales											
Applied Biology	C111	4SW deg	B+C/M/P g	BBB-BCC	MO $	Ind	30$	BBBB$	Ind	6	18/28
Applied Biology	C110	3FT deg	B+C/M/P g	BBB-BCC	MO $	Ind	30$	BBBB$	Ind	8	
Biology	C101	4SW deg	B+C/M/P g	BBB-BCC	MO $	Ind	30$	BBBB$	Ind	3	16/24
Biology	C100	3FT deg	B+C/M/P g	BBB-BCC	MO $	Ind	30$	BBBB$	Ind	4	18/28
Ecology and Environmental Management	C900	3FT deg	B+C/M/P g	BBB-BCC	MO $	Ind	30$	BBBB$	Ind	13	
Ecology and Environmental Management	C901	4SW deg	B+C/M/P g	BBB-BCC	MO $	Ind	30$	BBBB$	Ind	17	
Preliminary Year *Applied Biology*	Y101	4FT/5SW deg	* g		Ind	Ind	Ind	Ind	Ind		
Preliminary Year *Biology*	Y101	4FT/5SW deg	* g		Ind	Ind	Ind	Ind	Ind		
Preliminary Year *Ecology and Environmental Management*	Y101	4FT/5SW deg	* g		Ind	Ind	Ind	Ind	Ind		
Univ of Wales INST, CARDIFF											
Applied Biology	011C	2FT/3SW HND	B/C g	E	N	PS go	Ind	CC	Ind	4	2/6
Univ of CENTRAL LANCASHIRE											
Applied Biology	C110	3FT deg	C+S	DDD	MO $	MS6/^	26$	BCCC	$		
Applied Biology	011C	2FT HND	C	DD	N $	MS	24$	CCC	$		
UNIVERSITY COLLEGE CHESTER											
Applied Biology	C110	2FT Dip	g	4	Ind	Ind	Dip	CC	$	2	5/6
Applied Biology	C111	3FT deg	B g	10	M	P	Ind	CCC	$		
Art and Biology	WC91	3FT deg	B	12	M	P^	Ind	CCCC	$	3	
Art with Biology	W9C1	3FT deg	B	12	MO	P^	Ind	CCCC	$		
Biology and Computer Studies/IT	CG15	3FT deg	B g	10	M	P^	Ind	CCCC	$		
Biology and Drama and Theatre Studies	CW14	3FT deg	B	12	M	P^	Ind	CCCC	$		
Biology and English Literature	CQ13	3FT deg	B+E	CC	M	P^	Ind	CCCC	$		
Biology and Geography	CF18	3FT deg	B+Gy/Gl	CD	M	P^	Ind	CCCC	$	10	
Biology and History	CV11	3FT deg	B+H/Ec/So	12	M	P^	Ind	CCCC	$		
Biology and Physical Education/Sports Science	CB16	3FT deg	B	10	M	P^	Ind	CCCC	$		
Biology and Psychology	CL17	3FT deg	B g	10	M	P^	Ind	CCCC	$	4	8/13
Biology and Theology and Religious Studies	CV18	3FT deg	B	12	M	P^	Ind	CCCC	$	1	
Biology with Art	C1W9	3FT deg	B	12	M	P^	Ind	CCCC	$		
Biology with Computer Science/IT	C1G5	3FT deg	B g	10	M	P^	Ind	CCCC	$	2	
Biology with Drama and Theatre Studies	C1W4	3FT deg	B	12	M	P^	Ind	CCCC	$		
Biology with English Literature	C1Q3	3FT deg	B+E	CC	M	P^	Ind	CCCC	$		
Biology with French	C1R1	3FT deg	B g	12	M	P^	Ind	CCCC	$	2	
Biology with Geography	C1F8	3FT deg	B+Gy/Gl	CD	M	P^	Ind	CCCC	$		
Biology with German	C1R2	3FT deg	B g	12	M	P^	Ind	CCCC	$		
Biology with History	C1V1	3FT deg	B+H/Ec/So	12	M	P^	Ind	CCCC	$		

course details			98 expected requirements							96 entry stats	
TITLE	CODE	COURSE	SUBJECTS	A/AS	ND/C	AGNVQ	IB	SQA(H)	SQA	RATIO	A/AS
Biology with Mathematics	C1G1	3FT deg	B+M	10	M	P^	Ind	CCCC	$		
Biology with Physical Education/Sports Science	C1B6	3FT deg	B	10	M	P^	Ind	CCCC	$		
Biology with Psychology	C1L7	3FT deg	B g	10	M	P^	Ind	CCCC	$		
Biology with Social Science	C1L3	3FT deg	B g	10	M	P^	Ind	CCCC	$		
Biology with Theology and Religious Studies	C1V8	3FT deg	B	12	M	P^	Ind	CCCC	$		
Biosciences with a European Language (French)	C9R1	3FT deg	B g	12	MO	P^	Ind	CCCC	$		
Biosciences with a European Language (German)	C9R2	3FT deg	B g	12	MO	P^	Ind	CCCC	$		
Computer Science/IT with Biology	G5C1	3FT deg	B g	10	M	P^	Ind	CCCC	$	2	
Drama and Theatre Studies with Biology	W4C1	3FT deg	B	12	M	P^	Ind	CCCC	$		
English with Biology	Q3C1	3FT deg	E+B	12	M	P^	Ind	CCCC	$		
Geography with Biology	F8C1	3FT deg	Gy/Gl+B	CD	M	P^	Ind	CCCC	$	6	
History with Biology	V1C1	3FT deg	H/Ec/So+B	12	M	P^	Ind	CCCC	$		
Mathematics and Biology	GC11	3FT deg	B+M	10	M	P^	Ind	CCCC	$	6	
Mathematics with Biology	G1C1	3FT deg	M+B	10	M	P^	Ind	CCCC	$		
PE/Sports Science with Biology	B6C1	3FT deg	B	10	M	P^	Ind	CCCC	$		
Psychology with Biology	L7C1	3FT deg	B g	10	M	P^	Ind	CCCC	$	7	
Theology and Religious Studies with Biology	V8C1	3FT deg	B	12	M	P^	Ind	CCCC	$		
Combined Subjects (4 Yrs) Franchised *Plant & Animal Biology*	Y400	4FT deg	*		Ind	Ind	Ind	$	$		

COVENTRY Univ

Applied Ecology	C911	3FT deg									
Biological Sciences	C119	4FT/5SW deg			Ind	Ind	Ind	Ind	Ind		
Biological Sciences (BSc/MSc)	C110	3FT/4SW deg	B g	10	3M $	Ind	Ind	CCC$	HN$	5	4/14
Biological Sciences and Business	CN11	3FT deg									
Biological Sciences and Economics	CL1C	4FT/5SW deg			Ind	Ind	Ind	Ind	Ind		
Biological Sciences and Geography	CF1V	4FT/5SW deg			Ind	Ind	Ind	Ind	Ind		
Biological Sciences with Study in Europe	C1T9	4FT/5SW deg			Ind	Ind	Ind	Ind	Ind		
Biological Sciences with Study in Europe	C1T2	4FT deg	B g	10	3M $	Ind	Ind	CCC$	HN$		
Bioscience Communications	C9G5	3FT/4SW deg									
Chemistry and Biological Sciences	F1CC	4FT/5SW deg			Ind	Ind	Ind	Ind	Ind		
Chemistry and Biological Sciences	FC11	3FT/4SW deg	B+C g	CD	3M	MS	Ind	Ind	Ind	6	
Computing and Biological Sciences	GC51	3FT/4SW deg	B g	10	3M $		Ind	CCC$	Ind	10	
Computing and Biological Sciences	GC5C	4FT/5SW deg			Ind	Ind	Ind	Ind	Ind		
Economics and Biological Sciences	CL11	3FT/4SW deg	B g	10	3M $	Ind	Ind	CCC$	Ind	4	
Geography and Biological Sciences	CL18	3FT/4SW deg									
Mathematics and Biological Sciences	CG11	3FT/4SW deg	M+B/C	12-18	3M $	Ind	Ind	Ind	Ind		
Psychology and Biological Sciences	CC18	3FT/4SW deg	* g	CC	3M+3D	M^ go	Ind	BBB	Ind	1	9/12
Statistics and Biological Sciences	GC41	3FT/4SW deg	M/St+B/C g	12-16	3M $	M	Ind	Ind	Ind	4	
Statistics and Biological Sciences	GC4C	4FT/5SW deg		2	N $	P	Ind	Ind	Ind		
Biological Sciences	011C▼	2FT HND	B	2	N	P	Ind	Ind	Ind		

DE MONTFORT Univ

Biology, Appl (Biotechn, Envir Biol, Toxicology)	C110▼	3FT deg	B/C/P g	8-10	MO $	MS	28$	BBCCC$	N$	7	6/14
Combined Sciences *Biology*	Y100▼	2FT Dip	B/C g	4-6	N	P	Dip	BCC	Ind		
Combined Sciences *Biology*	Y108▼	3FT deg	g	2	N	P	Dip	CC	Ind		
Combined Studies *Biology*	Y400▼	3FT/4SW deg	B g	10	MO	M	30	BBB	Ind		
Biology, Applied	011C▼	2FT HND	B/C/P g	2-4	N $	PS	24$	ABCD$	N$	3	2/6

Univ of DERBY

Biological Imaging	CW12	4FT deg	B	CC	MO $	M^	26$	CCCC$	Ind	3	6/28
Biology	C100	3FT deg	B	10	N $	MS	26$	CCCD$	Ind	7	8/18

Biology 9

			98 expected requirements							96 entry stats	
TITLE	CODE	COURSE	SUBJECTS	A/AS	ND/C	AGNVQ	IB	SQA(H)	SQA	RATIO	A/AS
Biology	C101	4FT deg	B	10	N $	MS	26$	CCCD$	Ind		
Biology and Chemistry	CF11	3FT deg	S	10	N $	MS	26$	CCCD$	Ind	12	
Biology and Environmental Studies	CF19	3FT deg	S	10	N $	MS	26$	CCCD$	Ind	44	
Biology and Geography	CF18	3FT deg	S	10	N $	PS^	26$	CCCD$	Ind	9	
Biology and Geology	CF16	3FT deg	S	10	N $	MS	26$	CCCD$	Ind	8	
Biology and Heritage Conservation	CF1C	3FT deg	S	10	N $	MS	26$	CCCD$	Ind		
Environmental Monitoring & Management and Biolog	FC91	3FT deg	S	10	N $	MS	26$	CCCD$	Ind		
Human Sciences	C900	3FT deg	*	10	N $	M$	26	CCCD	Ind		
Credit Accumulation Modular Scheme Biology	Y600	3FT deg	S	8	MO $	M$	Ind	CCCC$	Ind		
Applied Biology	011C▼	2FT HND	S	2	N $	PS	Dip	DD			

Univ of DUNDEE

Biology	C100	4FT deg	C+S/2S g	16	5M $	M$	25$	BBBC$	N$	8	14/18
Ecology	CD12	4FT deg	C+S/2S g	16	5M $	M$	25$	BBBC$	N$	31	

Univ of DURHAM

Biology	C100	3FT deg	B+C	BCC-CCC	3M+2D$	Ind	28	AAABB	Ind	7	20/30
Cell Biology	C140	3FT deg	B+C	BCC-CCC	3M+2D$	Ind	28	AAABB	Ind	12	
Ecology	C910	3FT deg	B+C	BCC-CCC	3M+2D$	Ind	28	AAABB	Ind	26	
Natural Sciences Biology	Y160	3FT deg	B+S	ABB	Ind	X	33$	CSYS$	X		

Univ of EAST ANGLIA

Biochemistry with Biology	C7C1	3FT deg	C+P/M/B	CCC	3D $		28$	BBBCC$	Ind	8	
Biological Sciences with Deferred Specialisation	C100	3FT deg	C+P/M/B	CCC	3D $		28$	BBBCC$	Ind	6	12/28
Biological Sciences with a Year in Eur(4 Yrs)	C101	4FT deg	C+P/M/B	BCC	3D $		29$	BBBCC$	Ind	8	15/24
Biological Sciences with a Yr in N America(4Yr)	C102	4FT deg	C+P/M/B	ABB-BBB	5D $		32$	AAABB$	Ind	10	24/28
Cell Biology	C140	3FT deg	C+P/M/B	CCC	3D $		28$	BBBCC$	Ind	12	
Conservation and Biodiversity	CD92	2FT Dip	B/Gy/En	DD	Ind		Ind	Ind	Ind	7	
Ecology	C900	3FT deg	B g	BBC	3D $		30$	AAABB$	Ind	4	18/26
Ecology with Biology	C9C1	3FT deg	C+P/M/B	CCC	3D $		28$	BBBCC$	Ind	5	
Ecology, Single Subject, w Year in N America(4Yr)	C902	4FT deg	B g	ABB	3D $		32	AAABB	Ind	5	24/28
Ecology, Single subj, with a year in Europe (4Yrs)	C903	4FT deg	B g	BBB	3D $		30	AABBB	Ind	5	

Univ of EAST LONDON

Anthropology and Biology	LC61	3FT deg	* g	12	MO	M	Ind	Ind	Ind		
Anthropology with Biology	L6C1	3FT deg	* g	12	MO	M	Ind	Ind	Ind		
Applied Biology	C110	4SW deg	* g	12	MO	M	Ind	Ind	Ind	7	8/14
Biocomputing	CG1M	3FT/4SW deg	* g	12	MO	MS	Ind	Ind	Ind	10	
Biology and Archaeological Sciences	CF14	3FT deg	* g	12	MO	M	Ind	Ind	Ind		
Biology and Business Studies	CN1D	3FT deg	* g	16	MO	M	Ind	Ind	Ind		
Biology and Education & Community Studies	CX19	3FT deg	* g	12	MO	M	Ind	Ind	Ind	4	
Biology and Environmental Sciences	CF19	3FT deg	* g	12	MO	M	Ind	Ind	Ind		
Biology and French	CR11	3FT deg	* g	12	MO	M^	Ind	Ind	Ind		
Biology and German	CR12	3FT deg	* g	12	MO	M^	Ind	Ind	Ind		
Biology and Health Studies	BC91	3FT deg	* g	12	MO	M$	Ind	Ind	Ind		
Biology and Information Technology	CG15	3FT deg	* g	12	MO	M$	Ind	Ind	Ind		
Biology and Maths, Stats & Computing	CG19	3FT deg	* g	12	MO	M$	Ind	Ind	Ind		
Biology and Psychosocial Studies	CL17	3FT deg	* g	12	MO	M$	Ind	Ind	Ind		
Biology and Spanish	CR14	3FT deg	* g	12	MO	M^	Ind	Ind	Ind		
Biology with Anthropology	C1L6	3FT deg	* g	12	MO	M	Ind	Ind	Ind		
Biology with Archaeological Sciences	C1F4	3FT deg	* g	12	MO	M	Ind	Ind	Ind		
Biology with Business Studies	C1N1	3FT deg	* g	12	MO	M	Ind	Ind	Ind		
Biology with Education & Community Studies	C1X9	3FT deg	* g	12	MO	M	Ind	Ind	Ind		
Biology with Health Studies	C1B9	3FT deg	* g	12	MO	M	Ind	Ind	Ind		

course details			98 expected requirements							96 entry stats	
TITLE	CODE	COURSE	SUBJECTS	A/AS	ND/C	AGNVQ	IB	SQA(H)	SQA	RATIO	A/AS
Biology with Information Technology	C1G5	3FT deg	* g	12	MO	M	Ind	Ind	Ind		
Biology with Maths, Stats & Computing	C1G9	3FT deg	* g	12	MO	M	Ind	Ind	Ind		
Biology with Psychology	CC18	3FT deg	* g	12	MO	D^	Ind	Ind	Ind		
Biology with Psychosocial Studies	C1L7	3FT deg	* g	12	MO	M	Ind	Ind	Ind		
Business Studies with Biology	N1C1	3FT deg	* g	14	MO	MB					
Education & Community Studies with Biology	X9C1	3FT deg	* g	12	MO	M					
Environmental Sciences with Biology	F9C1	3FT deg	* g	12	MO	M	Ind	Ind			
German with Biology	R2C1	3FT deg	* g	12	MO	M					
Health Studies with Biology	B9C1	3FT deg	* g	12	MO	M	Ind	Ind	Ind		
Human Biology	C198	3FT/4SW deg	* g	12	MO	PS	Ind	Ind	Ind	6	
Immunology	C920	4SW deg	* g	12	MO	MS	Ind	Ind	Ind	6	
Infectious Diseases	C921	4SW deg	* g	12	N	MS	Ind	Ind	Ind	3	
Information Technology with Biology	G5C1	3FT deg	* g	12	MO	M	Ind	Ind	Ind		
Maths, Stats & Computing with Biology	G9C1	3FT deg	* g	12	MO	M	Ind	Ind	Ind		
Psychosocial Studies with Biology	L7C1	3FT deg	* g	12	MO	M	Ind	Ind	Ind		
Spanish with Biology	R4C1	3FT deg	* g	12	MO	M	Ind				
Wildlife Conservation	C901	3FT/4SW deg	* g	12	MO	PS	Ind	Ind	Ind	4	10/14
Extended Science *Applied Biology*	Y108	4FT deg	* g	8-10	MO	M	Ind	Ind	Ind		
Extended Science *Human Biology*	Y108	4FT deg	* g	8-10	MO	M	Ind	Ind	Ind		
Extended Science *Immunology*	Y108	4FT deg	* g	8-10	MO	M	Ind	Ind	Ind		
Extended Science *Infectious Diseases*	Y108	4FT deg	* g	8-10	MO	M	Ind	Ind	Ind		
Three-Subject Degree *Biology*	Y600	3FT deg	* g	12	MO	M	Ind	Ind	Ind		
EDGE HILL Univ COLLEGE											
Biology and Geography	CL18	3FT deg	S+Gy g	DD	X	PS^ go	Dip	BBCC$	Ind		
Biology and Mathematics	CG11	3FT deg	S g	DD	3M+3D	PS^ go	Dip	BBCC$	Ind		
Biology and Sports Studies	BC61	3FT deg	S g	CD	3M+3D	PS^ go	Dip	BBCC$	Ind		
Conservation Biology	C161	3FT deg	2(B/C) g	CD	3M+3D	MS / P*^	Dip	BBCC	Ind		
Field Biology and Habitat Management	C162	3FT deg	B/C/(B+C) g	CD	3M+3D	MS / P*^	Dip	BBCC$	Ind	2	6/12
Univ of EDINBURGH											
Biological Sciences	C100	4FT deg	C+2(B/M/P) g	BBC	MO $		Dip$	BBBB$	N$	5	18/30
Biological Sciences (Integrated Honours)	C120	4FT deg	C+2(B/M/P) g	BBC	MO $		Dip$	BBBB$	N$	4	20/28
Developmental Biology	C150	4FT deg	C+2(B/M/P) g	BBC	MO $		Dip$	BBBB$	N$	3	
Ecological Science	C900	4FT deg	2(B/C/M/P) g	CCC	MO $		Dip$	BBBB$	N$	5	20/24
Ecological Science with Environmental Science	C9F9	4FT deg	2(B/C/M/P) g	CCC	MO $		Dip$	BBBB$	N$	4	18/26
Immunology	C920	4FT deg	C+2(B/M/P) g	BBC	MO $		Dip$	BBBB$	N$	14	
Univ of ESSEX											
Biological Sciences	C100	3FT deg	2S	18	MO	D	28	BBBC	Ind	2	8/18
Biosciences (4 years inc Foundation year)	C102	4FT deg	* g	4	N	M	Dip	BBCC	Ind		
Cell and Molecular Biology	C140	3FT deg	2S	18	MO	D	28	BBBB	Ind	10	
Ecology and Environmental Biology	C160	3FT deg	2S	18	MO	D	28	BBBB	Ind	4	10/18
Ecology and Environmental Biology (4 years)	C161	4FT deg	* g	4	N	M	Dip	BBCC	Ind	1	
Marine and Freshwater Biology	C175	4FT deg	* g	4	N	M	Dip	BBCC	Ind		
Marine and Freshwater Biology	C174	3FT deg	2S	18	MO	D	28	BBBB	Ind		
Sports Science with Biology	B6C1	3FT deg	2S	18	MO	D	28	BBBC	Ind		
Univ of EXETER											
Biological Sciences	C100	3FT deg	B+S/B+2S g	CCC	4M	M$^	32$	Ind	Ind	5	12/26
Biology and Geography	CF18	3FT deg	Gy+B g	22	4M	M$^	34$	Ind	Ind	6	12/26

Biology   9

TITLE	CODE	COURSE	SUBJECTS	A/AS	ND/C	AGNVQ	IB	SQA(H)	SQA	RATIO	A/AS
Univ of GLAMORGAN											
Accounting & Finance and Biological Science	CN14	3FT deg	M/S g	12	Ind	M$	Ind	Ind	Ind		
Biological Sci and Environmental Pollution Sci	CF19▼	3FT/4SW deg	M/S g	DD	5M $	M$	Ind	Ind	Ind	3	6/20
Biological Science and Minerals Surveying Sci	CJ11	3FT/4SW deg	M/S g	DD	5M $	M$	Ind	Ind	Ind		
Biological Science and Sociology	CL13	3FT deg	M/S g	12	Ind	Ind	Ind	Ind	Ind		
Biological Science and Sports Science	BC61	3FT deg	M/S g	DD	5M $	M$	Ind	Ind	Ind		
Biological Science with Chemical Science	C1F1	3FT/4SW deg	M/S g	DD	5M $	M$	Ind	Ind	Ind		
Biological Science with Environmental Pollution	C1F9	3FT/4SW deg	M/S g	DD	5M $	M$	Ind	Ind	Ind	3	
Biological Science with Geological Science	C1F6	3FT/4FT deg	M/S g	DD	5M $	M$	Ind	Ind	Ind		
Biological Science with Minerals Surveying Sci	C1J1	3FT/4SW deg	M/S g	DD	5M $	M$	Ind	Ind	Ind		
Biological Science with Sports Science	C1B6	3FT deg	M/S g	DD	5M $	M$	Ind	Ind	Ind		
Biology	C100	3FT/4SW deg	P/B/C g	DD	5M $	M$	Ind	Ind	Ind	7	4/10
Chemical Science and Biological Science	FC11	3FT/4SW deg	M/S g	DD	5M $	M$	Ind	Ind	Ind	2	
Chemical Science with Biological Science	F1C1	3FT/4SW deg	M/S g	DD	5M $	M$	Ind	Ind	Ind	4	
Environmental Pollution Sci with Biological Sci	F9C1	3FT/4SW deg	M/S g	DD	5M $	M$	Ind	Ind	Ind		
Forensic Measurement with Biology	CF11	3FT deg	M/S g	DD	5M $	M$	Ind	Ind	Ind		
Geological Science and Biological Science	FC61	3FT/4SW deg	M/S g	DD	5M $	M$	Ind	Ind	Ind		
Geological Science with Biological Science	F6C1	3FT/4SW deg	M/S g	DD	5M $	M$	Ind	Ind	Ind		
Minerals Surveying with Biological Science	J1C1	3FT/4SW deg	M/S g	DD	5M $	M$	Ind	Ind	Ind		
Sports Science with Biological Science	B6C1	3FT deg	M/S g	DD	5M $	M$	Ind	Ind	Ind		
Combined Studies (Honours) *Biological Science*	Y400	3FT deg	M/S g	8-16	Ind	Ind	Ind	Ind	Ind		
Joint Honours *Biological Science*	Y401	3FT deg	M/S g	8-16	Ind	Ind	Ind	Ind	Ind		
Major/Minor Honours *Biological Science*	Y402	3FT deg	M/S g	8-16	Ind	Ind	Ind	Ind	Ind		
Marine Wildlife Conservation	119C▼	2FT HND									
Univ of GLASGOW											
Aquatic Bioscience	C174	4FT deg	C/M+S	BBC-CCC	N	M	24$	BBBB$	N	6	
Aquatic Bioscience (with work placement)	C175	4FT deg	C/M+S	BBC-CCC	N	M	24$	BBBB$	N		
Biotechnology	C110	4FT deg	C/M+S	BBC-CCC	N	M	24$	BBBB$	N		
Cell Biology	C140	4FT deg	C/M+S	BBC-CCC	N	M	24$	BBBB$	N	8	
Cell Biology (with work placement)	C142	4FT deg	C/M+S	BBC-CCC	N	M	24$	BBBB$	N		
Immunology	C920	4FT deg	C/M+S	BBC-CCC	N	M	24$	BBBB$	N	5	
GLASGOW CALEDONIAN Univ											
Applied Biosciences	C120	3FT/4FT deg	C+B/M/E	DDD	Ind		Ind	BCCC$	Ind	7	
Applied Biosciences	C121	2FT Dip	C+B/M/E	EE	Ind		Ind	CCC$	Ind	5	
Univ of GREENWICH											
Applied Biology	C110▼	3FT/4SW deg	B+C g	10	3M	MS	Dip	BCC	Ind		
Applied Biology (Ecology)	C910	3FT/4SW deg	B+S g	10	3M	MS	Dip	BCC	Ind		
Applied Biology and Law	CM13	3FT deg	B+C g	12	M+D	M	Dip	Ind	Ind		
Applied Biology with European Study	C111	3FT/4SW deg	B+C g	10	3M	MS	Dip	BCC	Ind		
Applied Biology with French	C1R1	3FT/4SW deg	B+C g	10	3M	MS	Dip	CCC	Ind		
Applied Biology with German	C1R2	3FT/4SW deg	B+C g	10	3M	MS	Dip	CCC	Ind		
Applied Biology with Law	C1M3	3FT deg	B+C g	12	M+D	M	Dip	Ind	Ind		
Applied Biology with Spanish	C1R4	3FT/4SW deg	B+C g	10	3M	MS	Dip	CCC	Ind		
Environmental Biology	C160	3FT/4SW deg	B g	10	3M	MS	Dip	CCC	Ind		
Environmental Biology with European Study	C161	3FT/4SW deg	B g	10	3M	MS	Dip	CCC	Ind		
Human Ecology	C911	3FT/4SW deg	B/Gy/C/M/Ec g	8	MO	M$ go	Ind	BCC$	Ind		
Science and Society	C900	3FT deg	S	10	3M	$	Dip	Ind	Ind		
Applied Biology	001C▼	2FT HND	2S g	4	N $	MS	Ind	Ind	Ind		

| | | | 98 expected requirements | | | | | | | 96 entry stats | |
| course details | | | | | | | | | | | |
TITLE	CODE	COURSE	SUBJECTS	A/AS	ND/C	RGNVQ	IB	SQA(H)	SQA	RATIO	A/AS
HALTON COLL											
Science (Biological Sciences)	001C	2FT HND	B/C	2	N	P	Ind	Ind	N	3	
HERIOT-WATT Univ											
Applied Marine Biology	C170	4FT deg	C	DDD	MO	M$ go	28	BBB$	Ind		
Applied Psychology with Biology	L7C1	4FT deg	*	CCC	HN	M$ go	30	BBBC	Ind		
Biological Sciences	C120	4FT deg	C	DDD	MO	M$ go	28	BBB$	Ind		
Brewing and Distilling	C980	4FT deg	C	DDD	MO	M$ go	28	BBB$	Ind		
Chem Eng with Brewing and Distilling Tech (MEng)	H8C9	5FT deg	C+M	CCD		M$ go	30	BBBB	$		
Combined Studies *Biological Science*	Y100	4FT deg	C	DDE	Ind	M$ go	26	BCCC	Ind		
Univ of HERTFORDSHIRE											
Applied Biology	C110	3FT/4SW deg	2S g	14-16	4M $	Ind	24	BCCCC	Ind	4	8/18
Applied Biology (Extended)	C118▼	4FT/5SW deg	* g	2	Ind	Ind	Ind	Ind	Ind		4/6
Applied Biology with a year in Europe	C111	4FT deg	2S g	14-16	4M $	Ind	24	BCCC	Ind	3	
Applied Biology with a year in North America	C112	4FT deg	2S g	14-16	4M $	Ind	24	BCCC	Ind	10	
Applied Biology with deferred ch. of specialism	C113	4FT/4SW deg	2S g	14-16	4M $	Ind	24	BCCC	Ind	14	
Biochemistry	C1C7	3FT/4SW deg	2S g	14-16	4M $	Ind	24	BCCCC	Ind	9	
Biotechnology	C1J8	3FT/4SW deg	2S g	14-16	4M $	Ind	24	BCCCC	Ind	12	
Ecology and Agric Biol with a year in Europe	C911	4FT deg	* g	14-18	4M	Ind	24	BBCCC	Ind		
Ecology and Agric Biol with a year in N.America	C912	4FT deg	* g	14-18	4M	Ind	24	BBCCC	Ind		
Ecology and Agricultural Biology	C910	3FT/4SW deg	* g	14-18	4M	Ind	24	BBCCC	Ind		
Microbiology	C1C5	3FT/4SW deg	2S g	14-16	4M $	Ind	24	BCCCC	Ind	9	
Molecular Biology	C1C6	3FT/4SW deg	2S g	14-16	4M $	Ind	24	BCCC	Ind	14	
Pharmacology	C1B2	3FT/4SW deg	2S g	14-16	4M $	Ind	24	BCCC	Ind	7	10/14
Physiology	C1B1	3FT/4SW deg	2S g	14-16	4M $	Ind	24	BCCC	Ind	11	
Combined Modular Scheme *Human Biology*	Y100	3FT deg	S g	12	3M $	MS gi	24$	CCCC$	Ind		
Combined Modular Scheme *Human Biology (Extended)*	Y108▼	4EXT deg	* g	4	N $	Ind	Dip$	DDDD$	Ind		
Applied Biology	011C	2FT HND	B+C g	4-6	N	Ind	Ind	Ind	N	3	4/6
Applied Biology (Biochemistry)	7C1C	2FT/3SW HND	B+C g	4-6	N	Ind	Ind	Ind	N	4	
Applied Biology (Microbiology)	6C1C	2FT HND	B+C g	4-6	N	Ind	Ind	Ind	N	8	
Applied Biology (Pharmacology)	2B1C	2FT HND	B+C g	4-6	N	Ind	Ind	Ind	N	5	
Univ of HULL											
Aquatic Biology	C174	3FT deg	2S	BCC-CCD	MO $	M$^ gi	26$	BBCCC	Ind	6	10/22
Aquatic Biology (with a year in industry)	C175	4FT deg	2S	BCC-CCD	MO $	M$^ gi	28$	BBCCC	Ind		
Biology	C100	3FT deg	2S	BCC-CCD	MO $	M$^ gi	26$	BBCCC	Ind	5	12/24
Biology (Yr 1 Franchised)	C101	4FT deg	*	CD	Ind	P$ gi	24	Ind	Ind	2	4/10
Environmental Biology	C160	3FT deg	2S	BCC-CCD	MO $	M$^ gi	26$	BBCCC	Ind	4	12/28
Environmental Biology and Geography	CF18	3FT deg	Gy+S	BCC	MO $	M$^ gi	26	BBCCC	Ind	9	16/26
Marine Biology	C170	3FT deg	2S	BCC-CCD	MO $	M$^ gi	28$	BBCCC	Ind		
Molecular Biology and Biotechnology	C140	3FT deg	C+S	BCC-CCD	MO $	M$^ gi	26$	BBCCC	Ind	4	
Physical Education and Sports Science with Biol	B6C1	3FT deg	B	18-20	MO $	M$^/6	28$	BBBCC	Ind		
IMPERIAL COLL (Univ of London)											
Applied Biology (4Yr SW)	C110	4SW deg	B+C/M/P	BBB	Ind	X	32$	Ind	Ind	12	24/30
Biology	C100	3FT deg	B+C/M/P	BCC	MO+2D	Ind	30$	Ind	Ind	6	20/28
Biology with Management	C1N1	3FT deg	B+C/M/P	BCC	MO+2D	Ind	30$	Ind	Ind	21	
Biology with Microbiology	C1C5	3FT deg	B+C/M/P	BCC	MO+2D	Ind	30$	Ind	Ind	7	
Biology with a Year in Europe (4 Yrs)	C102	4SW deg	B+C/M/P g	BBC	MO+2D	Ind	30$	Ind	Ind	4	22/28
Ecology	C900	3FT deg	B+C/M/P	BCC	MO+2D	Ind	30$	Ind	Ind	7	

course details | 98 expected requirements | 96 entry stats

TITLE	CODE	COURSE	SUBJECTS	A/AS	NO/C	AGNVQ	IB	SQA(H)	SQA	RATIO A/AS
KEELE Univ										
Biological and Medicinal Chemistry and Biology	CF1C	3FT deg	C g	BCC-CCC	Ind	M$^	26$	CSYS	Ind	2
Biology	C100	3FT deg	S g	BCC-CCC	Ind	M$^	26$	CSYS	Ind	61
Biology and American Studies	CQ14	3FT deg	S g	BCC	Ind	D$^	28$	CSYS	Ind	
Biology and American Studies (4 Yrs)	QC41	4FT deg	*	BCC	Ind	Ind	28	BBBB	Ind	
Biology and Ancient History	CV1D	3FT deg	S g	BCC	Ind	D$^	28$	CSYS	Ind	
Biology and Ancient History (4 Yrs)	VCD1	4FT deg	*	BCC	Ind	Ind	28	BBBB	Ind	1
Biology and Applied Social Studies	CL15	3FT deg	S g	BCC	Ind	D$^	28$	CSYS	Ind	2
Biology and Applied Social Studies (4 Yrs)	LC51	4FT deg	*	BCC	Ind	Ind	28	BBBB		
Biology and Astrophysics	CF15	3FT deg	P g	BCC-CCC	Ind	M$^	26$	CSYS	Ind	
Biology and Astrophysics (4 Yrs)	FC51	4FT deg	*	BCC-CCC	Ind	Ind	26	BBBB	Ind	
Biology and Biochemistry	CC17	3FT deg	C g	BCC-CCC	Ind	M$^	26$	CSYS	Ind	3
Biology and Biochemistry (4 Yrs)	CC71	4FT deg	*	BCC-CCC	Ind	Ind	26$	BBBB	Ind	5
Biology and Biochemistry (MSci)	CC7C	4FT deg	C	BCC-CCC	Ind	M$^	26$	CSYS	Ind	
Biology and Biological & Medicinal Chem (4 Yrs)	FCC1	4FT deg	*	BCC-CCC	Ind	Ind	26	BBBB	Ind	
Biology and Chemistry (MSci)	FC1C	4FT deg	C	BCC-CCC	Ind	M$^	26$	CSYS	Ind	
Biology and Mathematics (MSci)	CG1C	4FT deg	S+M	BCC-CCC	Ind	M$^	26$	CSYS	Ind	
Biomedical Sciences	C931	4FT deg	*	BCC-CCC	Ind	Ind	26	BBBB	Ind	20
Biomedical Sciences	C930	3FT deg	C	BCC-CCC	Ind	M$^ | 26$	CSYS	Ind	6	14/24
Chemistry and Biology	CF11	3FT deg	C g	BCC-CCC	Ind	M$^	26$	CSYS	Ind	4
Chemistry and Biology (4 Yrs)	FC11	4FT deg	*	BCC-CCC	Ind	Ind	26	BBBB	Ind	
Classical Studies and Biology	CQ18	3FT deg	S g	BCC	Ind	D$^	28$	CSYS	Ind	
Classical Studies and Biology (4 Yrs)	QC81	4FT deg	*	BCC	Ind	Ind	28	BBBB	Ind	
Computer Science and Biology	CG15	3FT deg	S g	BCC-CCC	Ind	M$^	26$	CSYS	Ind	
Computer Science and Biology (4 Yrs)	GC51	4FT deg	*	BCC-CCC	Ind	Ind	26	BBBB	Ind	
Criminology and Biology (4 Yrs)	MCH1	4FT deg	*	BBB-BCC	Ind	Ind	28	BBBB	Ind	
Economics and Biology (4 Yrs)	LC11	4FT deg	* g	BCC	Ind	Ind	28	BBBB	Ind	
Educational Studies and Biology	CX19	3FT deg	S g	BCC	Ind	D$^	28$	CSYS	Ind	
Educational Studies and Biology (4 Yrs)	XC91	4FT deg	*	BCC	Ind	Ind	28	BBBB	Ind	8
Electronic Music and Biology	CW1J	3FT deg	Mu+S g	BCC	Ind	D$^	28$	CSYS	Ind	
English and Biology	CQ13	3FT deg	S+E g	BCC	Ind	D$^	28$	CSYS	Ind	8
English and Biology (4 Yrs)	QC31	4FT deg	*	BCC	Ind	Ind	28	BBBB	Ind	8
Environmental Management and Biology	CF1X	3FT deg	S g	BCC	Ind	D$^ | 28$	CSYS	Ind	4	18/22
Environmental Management and Biology (4 Yrs)	FCX1	4FT deg	*	BCC	Ind	Ind	28	BBBB	Ind	3
Finance and Biology	CN13	3FT deg	S g	BCC	Ind	M$^	28$	CSYS	Ind	
Finance and Biology (4 Yrs)	NC31	4FT deg	*	BCC	Ind	Ind	28	BBBB	Ind	
French and Biology	CR11	3FT deg	S+F g	BCC	Ind	D$^	28$	CSYS	Ind	3
French and Biology (4 Yrs)	RC11	4FT deg	*	BCC	Ind	Ind	28	BBBB	Ind	
French/German and Biology	CT19	3FT deg	F+G+S g	BBC	Ind	D$^	30$	CSYS	Ind	
French/German and Biology (4 Yrs)	TC91	4FT deg	g	BBC	Ind	Ind	30	BBBB	Ind	
French/Russian or Russian St and Biology (4 Yrs)	TCX1	4FT deg	*	BCC	Ind	Ind	28	BBBB	Ind	
French/Russian or Russian Studies and Biology	CT1X	3FT deg	F+R+S g	BBC-BCC	Ind	D$^	28$	CSYS	Ind	
Geography and Biology	CL18	3FT deg	S+Gy g	BCC	Ind	D$^	28$	CSYS	Ind	11
Geography and Biology (4 Yrs)	LC81	4FT deg	*	BCC	Ind	Ind	28	BBBB	Ind	
Geology and Biology	CF16	3FT deg	S g	BCC-CCC	Ind	M$^	26$	CSYS	Ind	
Geology and Biology (4 Yrs)	FC61	4FT deg	*	BCC-CCC	Ind	Ind	26	BBBB	Ind	1
German and Biology	CR12	3FT deg	S+G g	BCC	Ind	D$^	28$	CSYS	Ind	
German and Biology (4 Yrs)	RC21	4FT deg	G	BCC	Ind	Ind	28$	BBBB	Ind	
German/Russian or Russian St and Biology (4 Yrs)	TCY1	4FT deg	g	BBC	Ind	Ind	30	BBBB	Ind	
German/Russian or Russian Studies and Biology	CT1Y	3FT deg	G+R+S g	BBC-BCC	Ind	D$^	28$	CSYS	Ind	
Human Resource Management and Biology	NC61	4FT deg	*	BCC	Ind	Ind	28	BBBB	Ind	
Human Resource Management and Biology	CN16	3FT deg	S g	BCC	Ind	D$^	28$	CSYS	Ind	

course details | 98 expected requirements | 96 entry stats

TITLE	CODE	COURSE	SUBJECTS	A/AS	NO/C	AGNVQ	IB	SQA(H)	SQA	RATIO A/AS
International History and Biology	CV1C	3FT deg	S g	BCC	Ind	D$^	28$	CSYS	Ind	
International History and Biology (4 Yrs)	VCC1	4FT deg	*	BCC	Ind	Ind	28	BBBB	Ind	2
International Politics and Biology	CM1C	3FT deg	S g	BCC	Ind	D$^	28$	CSYS	Ind	
International Politics and Biology (4 Yrs)	MCC1	4FT deg	*	BCC	Ind	Ind	28	BBBB	Ind	
Latin and Biology	CQ16	3FT deg	S+Ln g	BCC	Ind	D$^	28$	CSYS	Ind	
Law and Biology	CM13	3FT deg	S g	BBB	Ind	D$^	32$	CSYS	Ind	
Law and Biology (4 Yrs)	MC31	4FT deg	*	BBB	Ind	Ind	32	BBBB	Ind	
Management Science and Biology	CN11	3FT deg	S g	BCC	Ind	D$^	28$	CSYS	Ind	12
Marketing and Biology	CN15	3FT deg	S g	BCC	Ind	D$^	28$	CSYS	Ind	
Mathematics and Biology	CG11	3FT deg	S+M g	BCC-CCC	Ind	M$^	26$	CSYS	Ind	
Mathematics and Biology (4 Yrs)	GC11	4FT deg	*	BCC-CCC	Ind	Ind	26	BBBB	Ind	
Music and Biology	CW13	3FT deg	Mu+S g	BCC	Ind	D$^	28$	CSYS	Ind	3
Philosophy and Biology	CV17	3FT deg	S g	BCC	Ind	D$^	28$	CSYS	Ind	
Physics and Biology	CF13	3FT deg	P g	BCC-CCC	Ind	M$^	26$	CSYS	Ind	2
Physics and Biology (4 Yrs)	FC31	4FT deg	*	BCC-CCC	Ind	Ind	26	BBBB	Ind	
Physics and Biology (MSci)	FC3C	4FT deg	P	BCC-CCC	Ind	M$^	26$	CSYS	Ind	
Politics and Biology (4 Yrs)	MC11	4FT deg	* g	BCC	Ind	Ind	28	BBBB	Ind	
Psychology and Biology	CC81	3FT deg	S g	BBB-BCC	Ind	D$^	28$	CSYS	Ind	7
Psychology and Biology (4 Yrs)	CC18	4FT deg	*	BBB	Ind	Ind	32	ABBB	Ind	
Russian Studies and Biology	CRC8	3FT deg	S g	BCC	Ind	D$^	28$	CSYS	Ind	
Russian Studies and Biology (4 Yrs)	RC8C	4FT deg	*	BCC	Ind	Ind	28	BBBB	Ind	
Russian and Biology	CR18	3FT deg	S+R g	BCC	Ind	D$^	28$	CSYS	Ind	
Russian and Biology (4 Yrs)	RC81	4FT deg	*	BCC	Ind	Ind	28	BBBB	Ind	
Sociology & Social Anthropology and Biology	CL13	3FT deg	S g	BCC	Ind	D$^	28$	CSYS	Ind	5
Statistics and Biology	CG14	3FT deg	S+M g	BCC-CCC	Ind	M$^	26$	CSYS	Ind	
Statistics and Biology (4 Yrs)	GC41	4FT deg	*	BCC-CCC	Ind	Ind	26	BBBB	Ind	
Visual Arts and Biology (4 Yrs)	WC11	4FT deg	* g	BCC	Ind	Ind	28	BBBB	Ind	

Univ of KENT

TITLE	CODE	COURSE	SUBJECTS	A/AS	NO/C	AGNVQ	IB	SQA(H)	SQA	RATIO A/AS
Biodiversity Conservation and Environmental Mgt	CD92	3FT deg	S g	BCC	MO	Ind	28$	BBBB$	Ind	
Biological Chemistry	F1C1	3FT deg	C g	16	MO $	Ind	24$	BBCC$	Ind	6
Biological Chemistry with Studies Abroad	F1CC	4FT deg	C g	16	MO $	Ind	24$	BBCC$	Ind	
Biological Chemistry with Studies Abroad (MChem)	F1CD	4FT deg	C g	16	MO $	Ind	24$	BBCC$	Ind	
Biological Sciences	C100	3FT/4SW deg	C g	BCC	MO $	Ind	28$	BBBB$	Ind	5 10/24
Biology with a foundation year (4 Yrs)	C101	4FT deg	* g		N	Ind	Dip	Ind	Ind	1 6/14

KING ALFRED'S WINCHESTER

TITLE	CODE	COURSE	SUBJECTS	A/AS	NO/C	AGNVQ	IB	SQA(H)	SQA	RATIO A/AS
Social Biology and Archaeology	CF14	3FT deg	B g	14	6M $	M	24$	BCC$	N$	
Social Biology and Business Studies	CN11	3FT deg	B g	14	6M $	M	24$	BCC$	N$	5
Social Biology and Computing	CG15	3FT deg	B g	14	6M $	M	24$	BCC$	N$	
Social Biology and Education Studies	CX19	3FT deg	B g	14	4M $	M	24$	CCC$	N$	
Social Biology and Geography	CL18	3FT deg	B+Gy g	14	X	X	24$	BCC$	N$	7
Social Biology and Media & Film Studies	CP14	3FT deg	B g	14	6M $	M	24$	BCC$	N$	
Social Biology and Psychology	CL17	3FT deg	B g	14	6M $	M	24$	BCC$	N$	5
Sports Studies and Social Biology	CL1H	3FT deg	B g	14	6M $	M	24$	BCC$	N$	

KING'S COLL LONDON (Univ of London)

TITLE	CODE	COURSE	SUBJECTS	A/AS	NO/C	AGNVQ	IB	SQA(H)	SQA	RATIO A/AS
Biochemistry and Immunology	CC79	3FT deg	C+B/M/P	BCC	5M	M	Ind	BCCCC	Ind	3 18/22
Biological Sciences	C120	3FT deg	B+S g	BCC	Ind	Ind	Ind	BBCCC	Ind	6 14/24
Biological Sciences with a European Language	C1T9	3FT deg	B+S+L g	BCC	Ind	Ind	Ind	BBCCC	Ind	8
Biomedical Science	BC99	3FT deg	C+S	BCC	MO+3D$	Ind	30	BBCCC	Ind	5 16/26
Cell Biology	C140	3FT deg	C+S	BCC			Ind	BCCCC	Ind	
Chemistry with Bioscience (4 Yrs) (MSci)	F1C1	4FT deg	C+S	18	4M $	Ind	28$	BBCCC	Ind	
Human Environmental Science	C1F9	3FT/4SW deg	B+C	BCC	Ind	Ind	Ind	BBCCC	Ind	11

Biology 9

TITLE	CODE	COURSE	SUBJECTS	A/AS	ND/C	AGNVQ	IB	SQA(H)	SQA	RATIO	A/AS
Immunology	C920	3FT deg	S+C	BCC	5M	M	Ind	BCCCC	Ind	4	18/20
Molecular Biology and Immunology	CC69	3FT deg	C+S	BCC	5M	M	Ind	BCCCC	Ind	3	14/20

KINGSTON Univ

TITLE	CODE	COURSE	SUBJECTS	A/AS	ND/C	AGNVQ	IB	SQA(H)	SQA	RATIO	A/AS
Applied Biology	C111	3FT deg	B/C g	10	N	Ind	Ind	CCC	Ind	4	4/16
Applied Biology	C118▼	4EXT deg	*		Ind		Ind	Ind	Ind	1	
Applied Biology & Chemistry	CF11	3FT deg	B/C g	8	3M $	Ind	Ind	CCC	Ind	14	
Applied Biology & Geography	CF18	3FT deg	Gy+B/C g	12	Ind	Ind	Ind	BCCC	Ind	4	
Applied Biology & Physics	CF13	3FT deg	2(P/B/C) g	10	3M $	Ind	Ind	CCC	Ind		
Applied Biology and French	CR11	4FT deg	2(B/C/F) g	10	Ind	Ind	Ind	CCC	Ind	5	

LANCASTER Univ

TITLE	CODE	COURSE	SUBJECTS	A/AS	ND/C	AGNVQ	IB	SQA(H)	SQA	RATIO	A/AS
Biochemistry with Biomedicine	BC79	3FT deg									
Biological Sciences	C100	3FT deg	2(M/P/C/B) g	CCC	MO $		28$	BBBCC$	Ind		
Biological Sciences (inc a yr in USA or Canada)	C102	3FT deg	2(M/P/C/B) g	BBC	MO $		30$	BBBBC$	Ind		
Biological Sciences with Biomedicine	C1B9	3FT deg	2(M/P/C/B) g	CCC	MO $		28$	BBBCC$	Ind		
Ecology	C900	3FT deg	2(B/C/M/P/Gy) g	BCC	MO $		30$	BBBBB$	Ind		
Ecology (inc a year in USA or Canada)	C902	3FT deg	2(B/C/M/P/Gy) g	BBB	MO $		32$	AABBB$	Ind		
Combined Science *Biological Sciences*	Y158	3FT deg	2(S/M) g	CCD	MO $		28$	BBBB$	Ind		
Combined Science (inc a year in USA or Canada) *Biological Sciences*	Y155	3FT deg	2(S/M) g	BBB	Ind $		30$	ABBBB$	Ind		

Univ of LEEDS

TITLE	CODE	COURSE	SUBJECTS	A/AS	ND/C	AGNVQ	IB	SQA(H)	SQA	RATIO	A/AS
Applied Biology	C110	3FT/4FT deg	B+M/C/P g	BBC	1M+5D$	Ind	30	BBBBC	Ind	7	18/26
Applied Biology-Chemistry	CFC1	3FT/4FT deg	C+B+P/M g	BCC	1M+5D$	Ind	28	BBBBC	Ind	12	
Applied Biology-Management Studies	C1NC	3FT/4FT deg	B+C/M/P/Ec g	BCC	1M+5D$	Ind	28	BBBBC	Ind	5	
Biology	C100	3FT deg	B g	BCC	1M+5D$	Ind	28$	BBBBC	Ind	8	18/26
Biology-History and Philosophy of Science	CV15	3FT/4FT deg	B g	BCC	1M+5D$	Ind	28$	BBBBC	Ind	4	20/26
Biology-Mathematics	CG11	3FT/4FT deg	B+M g	BCC	1M+5D$	Ind	28$	BBBBC	Ind	11	
Biology-Statistics	CG14	3FT/4FT deg	B+M g	BCC	1M+5D$	Ind	28$	BBBBC	Ind	3	
Ecology	C900	3FT deg	B g	BCC	1M+5D$	Ind	28$	BBBBC	Ind	9	16/24
Microbiology with Immunology	C5C9	3FT deg	2S g	BBC	3M+2D$	Ind	30$	ABBBC	Ind		

Univ of LEICESTER

TITLE	CODE	COURSE	SUBJECTS	A/AS	ND/C	AGNVQ	IB	SQA(H)	SQA	RATIO	A/AS
Biological Sciences	C100	3FT deg	B+C g	18-20	DO $	D$4/^ gi	28$	BBBCC$	Ind		14/28
Biological Sciences (Cell Biology)	C140	3FT deg	B+C g	18-20	DO $	D$4/^ gi	28$	BBBCC$	Ind		
Biological Sciences (Environmental Biology)	C900	3FT deg	B+C g	18-20	DO $	D$4/^ gi	28$	BBBCC$	Ind		16/20
BSc with integrated foundation *Biology*	Y101	4EXT deg	* g		N	*			Ind		
Combined Science *Biological Sciences*	Y100	3FT deg	B/C g	CCC	MO	D$^	28$	BBBCC$	Ind		

Univ of LIVERPOOL

TITLE	CODE	COURSE	SUBJECTS	A/AS	ND/C	AGNVQ	IB	SQA(H)	SQA	RATIO	A/AS
Applied Biology	C110	4FT deg	B+S g	18	MO $	DS^ go	31$	BBBCC$	Ind	15	18/24
Applied Cell Science	C141	4FT deg	C+B g	18	MO $	DS^ go	31$	BBBCC$	Ind		
Biological and Medical Sciences (Options)	C130	3FT deg	2S g	18	MO $	DS^ go	31$	BBBCC$	Ind	2	14/26
Biology (Options)	C100	3FT deg	B+S g	18	MO $	DS^ go	31$	BBBCC$	Ind	12	16/28
Cell Biology	C140	3FT deg	B+C g	18	MO $	DS^ go	31$	BBBCC$	Ind	14	
Cell Biology and Biochemistry	CC1R	3FT deg	C+B g	18	MO $	DS^ go	31$	BBBCC$	Ind	2	
Cell Biology and Biochemistry	CC17	4FT deg	C+B g	18	MO $	DS^ go	31$	BBBCC$	Ind		
Environmental Biology	C160	3FT deg	B+S g	18	MO $	DS^ go	31$	BBBCC$	Ind	16	18/28
Geography and Biology	CF18	3FT deg	B g	22	MO $	Ind	31$	BBBCC$	Ind	6	20/30
Life Sciences (2+2)	C980	4FT deg	* g	EE	N $	Ind	Ind	CCDDD$	Ind	2	10/16
Life Sciences with a European Language	C1T2	4FT deg	B+S g	18	MO $	Ind	31$	BBBCC$	Ind	3	14/24
Marine Biology	C170	3FT deg	B+S g	18	MO $	Ind	31$	BBBCC$	Ind	12	17/26

	course details			98 expected requirements						96 entry stats
TITLE	CODE	COURSE	SUBJECTS	A/AS	ND/C	AGNVQ	IB	SQA(H)	SQA	RATIO A/AS
Arts Combined	Y401	3FT deg	B	BBC-BBB	Ind	Ind	30$	ABBB$	Ind	
Biology										
BA Combined Honours	Y200	3FT deg	g	BBB	Ind	Ind	Ind	Ind	Ind	
Biology										

LIVERPOOL HOPE Univ COLL

TITLE	CODE	COURSE	SUBJECTS	A/AS	ND/C	AGNVQ	IB	SQA(H)	SQA	RATIO A/AS
Human & Applied Biology and Music	CW13	3FT deg								
Human & Applied Biology/American Studies	QC41	3FT deg	B g	12	8M	MS /P$^	Ind	Ind	Ind	1
Human & Applied Biology/Art	WC91	3FT deg	B+A/Fa g	12	8M	P$^	Ind	Ind	Ind	4
Human & Applied Biology/Drama & Theatre Studies	CW14	3FT deg	B g	12	8M	MS /P*^ go	Ind	Ind	Ind	4
Human & Applied Biology/Environmental Studies	CF19	3FT deg	En/B g	10	6M	MS /P*^ go	Ind	Ind	Ind	
Human & Applied Biology/French	RC11	3FT deg	B+F g	12	8M	P$^	Ind	Ind	Ind	
Human & Applied Biology/Geography	CF18	3FT deg	B+Gy g	10	6M	MS /P*^ go	Ind	Ind	Ind	
Human & Applied Biology/History	CV11	3FT deg	H+B g	12	8M	PS^ go	Ind	Ind	Ind	5
Information Technology/Human & Applied Biology	CG15	3FT deg	B g	10	6M	M$ /M*^ go	Ind	Ind	Ind	
Psychology/Human & Applied Biology	CC18	3FT deg	B g	10	6M	MS /P*^ go	Ind	Ind	Ind	11 12/14
Sociology/Human & Applied Biology	CL13	3FT deg	B g	12	8M	M$ go	Ind	Ind	Ind	
Sport, Recreation & P.E./Human & Applied Biology	CB16	3FT deg	B g	10	6M	M$ /P*^ go	Ind	Ind	Ind	
Theology & Religious St/Human & Applied Biology	CV18	3FT deg	B g	12	8M	M$ /M*^ go	Ind	Ind	Ind	2

LIVERPOOL JOHN MOORES Univ

TITLE	CODE	COURSE	SUBJECTS	A/AS	ND/C	AGNVQ	IB	SQA(H)	SQA	RATIO A/AS
Applied Biology	C110▼	3FT/4SW deg	B	8	3M	M				5 6/20
Applied Biology (Foundation)	C118	4FT/5SW deg								
Applied Ecology	C910	3FT/4SW deg	B	8	3M	M				5 8/16
Applied Ecology (Foundation)	C918	4FT/5SW deg								7
Biological and Chemical Sciences (Foundation)	CF1C	4FT/5SW deg								
Psychology and Biology	CC18	3FT deg		10-12	5M	M go				

LSU COLL of HE

TITLE	CODE	COURSE
Life Sciences and Ecology	DC29	3FT deg
Life Sciences and Geography	CL98	3FT deg
Psychology and Life Sciences	CL97	3FT deg
Sports Science and Life Sciences	CB96	3FT deg

LUTON Univ

TITLE	CODE	COURSE	SUBJECTS	A/AS	ND/C	AGNVQ	IB	SQA(H)	SQA	RATIO A/AS
Biology	C100	3FT deg	g	12-16	MO/DO	M/D	32	BBCC	Ind	9 4/8
Biology and Applied Statistics	CG14	3FT deg	g	12-16	MO/DO	M/D	32	BBCC	Ind	
Biology with Animation	C1WF	3FT deg	g	12-16	MO/DO	M/D	32	BBCC	Ind	
Biology with Applied Statistics	C1G4	3FT deg	g	12-16	MO/DO	M/D	32	BBCC	Ind	
Biology with Biotechnology	C1J8	3FT deg	g	12-16	MO/DO	M/D	32	BBCC	Ind	
Biology with Business	C1N1	3FT deg	g	12-16	MO/DO	M/D	32	BBCC	Ind	1
Biology with Business Systems	C1NC	3FT deg	g	12-16	MO/DO	M/D	32	BBCC	Ind	
Biology with Contemporary History	C1V1	3FT deg	g	12-16	MO/DO	M/D	32	BBCC	Ind	
Biology with Digital System Design	C1HP	3FT deg	g	12-16	MO/DO	M/D	32	BBCC	Ind	
Biology with Environmental Science	C1F9	3FT deg	g	12-16	MO/DO	M/D	32	BBCC	Ind	1
Biology with French	C1R1	3FT deg	F g	12-16	MO/DO	M/D	32	BBCC	Ind	
Biology with Geographical Information Systems	C161	3FT deg	g	12-16	MO/DO	M/D	32	BBCC	Ind	
Biology with Geography	CFDV	3FT deg	g	12-16	MO/DO	M/D	32	BBCC	Ind	
Biology with Health Science	C1B9	3FT deg	g	12-16	MO/DO	M/D	32	BBCC	Ind	
Biology with Health Studies	C1BX	3FT deg		12-16	MO/DO	M/D	32	BBCC	Ind	
Biology with Human Biology	C1B1	3FT deg	g	12-16	MO/DO	M/D	32	BBCC	Ind	
Biology with Japanese	C1T4	3FT deg	L g	12-16	MO/DO	M/D	32	BBCC	Ind	
Biology with Journalism	C1P6	3FT deg	g	12-16	MO/DO	M/D	32	BBCC	Ind	
Biology with Leisure Studies	C1N7	3FT deg	g	12-16	MO/DO	M/D	32	BBCC	Ind	
Biology with Management	CN1D	3FT deg	g	12-16	MO/DO	M/D	32	BBCC	Ind	

Biology 9

TITLE	CODE	COURSE	SUBJECTS	A/AS	NO/C	AGNVQ	IB	SQA(H)	SQA	RATIO A/AS
Biology with Mapping Science	C1F8	3FT deg	g	12-16	MO/DO	M/D	32	BBCC	Ind	
Biology with Marketing	C1N5	3FT deg	g	12-16	MO/DO	M/D	32	BBCC	Ind	
Biology with Mathematical Sciences	C1GC	3FT deg	g	12-16	MO/DO	M/D	32	BBCC	Ind	
Biology with Mathematics	C1GD	3FT deg	g	12-16	MO/DO	M/D	32	BBCC	Ind	
Biology with Media Production	C1PL	3FT deg	g	12-16	MO/DO	M/D	32	BBCC	Ind	
Biology with Multimedia	C1PK	3FT deg	g	12-16	MO/DO	M/D	32	BBCC	Ind	
Biology with Organisational Behaviour	C1L7	3FT deg	g	12-16	MO/DO	M/D	32	BBCC	Ind	
Biology with Physical Geography	C1FV	3FT deg	g	12-16	MO/DO	M/D	32	BBCC	Ind	
Biology with Politics	C1M1	3FT deg	g	12-16	MO/DO	M/D	32	BBCC	Ind	
Biology with Pollution Studies	CFC9	3FT deg	g	12-16	MO/DO	M/D	32	BBCC	Ind	
Biology with Psychology	C1LR	3FT deg	g	12-16	MO/DO	M/D	32	BBCC	Ind	
Biology with Publishing	C1P5	3FT deg	g	12-16	MO/DO	M/D	32	BBCC	Ind	
Biology with Video Production	C1W5	3FT deg	g	12-16	MO/DO	M/D	32	BBCC	Ind	
Business Systems and Biology	CN1C	3FT deg	g	12-16	MO/DO	M/D	32	BBCC	Ind	
Business Systems with Biology	N1CC	3FT deg	g	12-16	MO/DO	M/D	32	BBCC	Ind	
Business and Biology	CN11	3FT deg	g	12-16	MO/DO	M/D	32	BBCC	Ind	
Business with Biology	N1C1	3FT deg	g	12-16	MO/DO	M/D	32	BBCC	Ind	
Computer Applications and Biology	GC61	3FT deg		12-16	MO/DO	M/D	32	BBCC	Ind	
Computer Science and Biology	CG15	3FT deg	g	12-16	MO/DO	M/D	32	BBCC	Ind	
Ecology (Eco Tech) and Leisure Studies	CN97	3FT deg	g	12-16	MO/DO	M/D	32	BBCC	Ind	
Ecology (Eco Tech) with Environmental Science	C9F9	3FT deg	g	12-16	MO/DO	M/D	32	BBCC	Ind	
Ecology (Eco Tech) with Geographical Info System	C901	3FT deg	g	12-16	MO/DO	M/D	32	BBCC	Ind	
Ecology (Eco Tech) with Geography	C9F8	3FT deg	g	12-16	MO/DO	M/D	32	BBCC	Ind	
Ecology (Eco Tech) with Geology	C9F6	3FT deg	g	12-16	MO/DO	M/D	32	BBCC	Ind	
Ecology (Eco Tech) with Leisure Studies	C9N7	3FT deg	g	12-16	MO/DO	M/D	32	BBCC	Ind	
Ecology (Eco Tech) with Mapping Science	C9FV	3FT deg	g	12-16	MO/DO	M/D	32	BBCC	Ind	
Ecology (Eco Tech) with Organis Behaviour	C9L7	3FT deg	g	12-16	MO/DO	M/D	32	BBCC	Ind	
Ecology (Eco Tech) with Physical Geography	C9FW	3FT deg	g	12-16	MO/DO	M/D	32	BBCC	Ind	
Ecology (Eco Tech) with Politics	C9M1	3FT deg	g	12-16	MO/DO	M/D	32	BBCC	Ind	
Ecology (Eco Tech) with Public Policy & Mgt	C9MC	3FT deg	g	12-16	MO/DO	M/D	32	BBCC	Ind	
Ecology (Eco Tech) with Regional Planning & Dev	C9K4	3FT deg	g	12-16	MO/DO	M/D	32	BBCC	Ind	
Ecology (Eco Tech) with Travel & Tourism	C9P7	3FT deg	g	12-16	MO/DO	M/D	32	BBCC	Ind	
Ecology (Ecological Tech) and Mapping Science	CF9W	3FT deg	g	12-16	MO/DO	M/D	32	BBCC	Ind	
Environmental Sci with Ecology & Biodiversity	F9C9	3FT deg	g	12-16	MO/DO	M/D	32	BBCC	Ind	
Environmental Science and Biology	CF19	3FT deg	g	12-16	MO/DO	M/D	32	BBCC	Ind	5
Environmental Science and Ecology & Biodiversity	CF99	3FT deg	g	12-16	MO/DO	M/D	32	BBCC	Ind	
Environmental Science with Biology	F9C1	3FT deg	g	12-16	MO/DO	M/D	32	BBCC	Ind	3
Environmental Studies with Biology	F9CX	3FT deg		12-16	MO/DO	M/D	32	BBCC	Ind	
Environmental Studs with Ecology & Biodiversity	F9CY	3FT deg		12-16	MO/DO	M/D	32	BBCC	Ind	
European Language Studies and Biology	CT12	3FT deg	L g	12-16	MO/DO	M/D	32	BBCC	Ind	
European Language Studies with Biology	T2C1	4FT deg	L g	12-16	MO/DO	M/D	32	BBCC	Ind	
Geography and Biology	FC81	3FT deg	g	12-16	MO/DO	M/D	32	BBCC	Ind	
Geography and Ecology & Biodiversity	CF98	3FT deg	g	12-16	MO/DO	M/D	32	BBCC	Ind	
Geography with Biology	F8CD	3FT deg	g	12-16	MO/DO	M/D	32	BBCC	Ind	
Geography with Ecology & Biodiversity	F8C9	3FT deg	g	12-16	MO/DO	M/D	32	BBCC	Ind	
Geology and Ecology & Biodiversity	CF96	3FT deg	g	12-16	MO/DO	M/D	32	BBCC	Ind	
Geology with Ecology & Biodiversity	F6C9	3FT deg	g	12-16	MO/DO	M/D	32	BBCC	Ind	
Health Science and Biology	CB19	3FT deg	g	12-16	MO/DO	M/D	32	BBCC	Ind	
Health Science with Biology	B9C1	3FT deg	g	12-16	MO/DO	M/D	32	BBCC	Ind	4
Health Studies and Biology	CB1X	3FT deg	g	12-16	MO/DO	M/D	32	BBCC	Ind	
Health Studies and Ecology and Biodiversity	BC99	3FT deg	g	12-16	MO/DO	M/D	32	BBCC	Ind	
Health Studies with Ecology & Biodiversity	B9C9	3FT deg	g	12-16	MO/DO	M/D	32	BBCC	Ind	
Human Biology and Biology	BC11	3FT deg	g	12-16	MO/DO	M/D	32	BBCC	Ind	

			98 expected requirements							96 entry stats	

course details   **98 expected requirements**   *96 entry stats*

TITLE	CODE	COURSE	SUBJECTS	A/AS	NO/C	AGNVQ	IB	SQA(H)	SQA	RATIO	A/AS
Law and Biology	CM13	3FT deg	g	12-16	MO/DO	M/D	32	BBCC	Ind		
Law with Biology	M3C1	3FT deg	g	12-16	MO/DO	M/D	32	BBCC	Ind		
Leisure Studies and Biology	CN17	3FT deg	g	12-16	MO/DO	M/D	32	BBCC	Ind		
Leisure Studies and Ecology & Biodiversity	CF97	3FT deg		12-16	MO/DO	M/D	32	BBCC	Ind		
Leisure Studies with Biology	N7C1	3FT deg	g	12-16	MO/DO	M/D	32	BBCC	Ind		
Leisure Studies with Ecology & Biodiversity	N7C9	3FT deg	g	12-16	MO/DO	M/D	32	BBCC	Ind		
Linguistics and Biology	CQ11	3FT deg	g	12-16	MO/DO	M/D	32	BBCC	Ind		
Linguistics with Biology	Q1C1	3FT deg	g	12-16	MO/DO	M/D	32	BBCC	Ind		
Mapping Science and Biology	CF18	3FT deg	g	12-16	MO/DO	M/D	32	BBCC	Ind		
Mapping Science and Ecology & Biodiversity	CN9W	3FT deg	g	12-16	MO/DO	M/D	32	BBCC	Ind		
Mapping Science with Biology	F8C1	3FT deg	g	12-16	MO/DO	M/D	32	BBCC	Ind		
Mapping Science with Ecology & Biodiversity	F8CY	3FT deg	g	12-16	MO/DO	M/D	32	BBCC	Ind		
Marketing and Biology	CN15	3FT deg	g	12-16	MO/DO	M/D	32	BBCC	Ind		
Marketing with Biology	N5C1	3FT deg	g	12-16	MO/DO	M/D	32	BBCC	Ind		
Mathematical Sciences and Biology	CG11	3FT deg	g	12-16	MO/DO	M/D	32	BBCC	Ind		
Mathematical Sciences with Biology	G1C1	3FT deg	g	12-16	MO/DO	M/D	32	BBCC	Ind		
Mathematics and Biology	GC11	3FT deg	g	12-16	MO/DO	M/D	32	BBCC	Ind		
Media Practices and Biology	CP14	3FT deg	g	12-16	MO/DO	M/D	32	BBCC	Ind		
Media Practices with Biology	P4C1	3FT deg	g	12-16	MO/DO	M/D	32	BBCC	Ind		
Media Production and Biology	CP1L	3FT deg	g	12-16	MO/DO	M/D	32	BBCC	Ind		
Media Production with Biology	P4CC	3FT deg	g	12-16	MO/DO	M/D	32	BBCC	Ind		
Modern History and Biology	CV1C	3FT deg	g	12-16	MO/DO	M/D	32	BBCC	Ind		
Modern History with Biology	V1CC	3FT deg	g	12-16	MO/DO	M/D	32	BBCC	Ind		
Organisational Behaviour and Biology	CL17	3FT deg	g	12-16	MO/DO	M/D	32	BBCC	Ind		
Organisational Behaviour and Ecol & Biodiversity	CL97	3FT deg	g	12-16	MO/DO	M/D	32	BBCC	Ind		
Pharmacology and Biology	BC21	3FT deg		12-16	MO/DO	M/D	32	BBCC	Ind		
Physical Geography and Biology	CF1V	3FT deg	g	12-16	MO/DO	M/D	32	BBCC	Ind		
Physical Geography and Ecology & Biodiversity	CF9V	3FT deg	g	12-16	MO/DO	M/D	32	BBCC	Ind		
Physical Geography with Biology	F8CC	3FT deg	g	12-16	MO/DO	M/D	32	BBCC	Ind		
Physical Geography with Ecology & Biodiversity	F8CX	3FT deg		12-16	MO/DO	M/D	32	BBCC	Ind		
Politics and Biology	CM11	3FT deg	g	12-16	MO/DO	M/D	32	BBCC	Ind		
Politics and Ecology & Biodiversity	CM91	3FT deg	g	12-16	MO/DO	M/D	32	BBCC	Ind		
Politics with Biology	M1C1	3FT deg	g	12-16	MO/DO	M/D	32	BBCC	Ind		
Politics with Ecology & Biodiversity	M1C9	3FT deg	g	12-16	MO/DO	M/D	32	BBCC	Ind		
Psychology and Biology	CL1R	3FT deg	g	12-16	MO/DO	M/D	32	BBCC	Ind	9	
Psychology with Biology	L7CC	3FT deg	g	12-16	MO/DO	M/D	32	BBCC	Ind	10	
Public Policy & Mgt with Ecology & Biodiversity	M1CX	3FT deg	g	12-16	MO/DO	M/D	32	BBCC	Ind		
Public Policy and Management and Biology	CM1C	3FT deg	g	12-16	MO/DO	M/D	32	BBCC	Ind		
Public Policy and Management with Biology	M1CC	3FT deg	g	12-16	MO/DO	M/D	32	BBCC	Ind		
Public Policy and Mgt and Ecology & Biodiversity	CM9C	3FT deg	g	12-16	MO/DO	M/D	32	BBCC	Ind		
Regional Plan and Dev and Ecology & Biodiversity	CK94	3FT deg	g	12-16	MO/DO	M/D	32	BBCC	Ind		
Regional Planning & Dev with Eco & Biodiversity	K4C9	3FT deg	g	12-16	MO/DO	M/D	32	BBCC	Ind		
Travel & Tourism with Ecology (Ecological Tech)	P7C9	3FT deg	g	12-16	MO/DO	M/D	32	BBCC	Ind		
Travel and Tourism and Biology	CP17	3FT deg	g	12-16	MO/DO	M/D	32	BBCC	Ind		
Travel and Tourism and Ecology & Biodiversity	CP97	3FT deg	g	12-16	MO/DO	M/D	32	BBCC	Ind		
Travel and Tourism with Biology	P7C1	3FT deg	g	12-16	MO/DO	M/D	32	BBCC	Ind		
Women's Studies and Biology	MC91	3FT deg		12-16	MO/DO	M/D	32	BBCC	Ind		
Women's Studies with Biology	M9C1	3FT deg		12-16	MO/DO	M/D	32	BBCC	Ind		
Applied Biology	011C	2FT HND	g	4-8	N-MO	P/M	26	CCDD	Ind	3	2/8

Univ of MANCHESTER

TITLE	CODE	COURSE	SUBJECTS	A/AS	NO/C	AGNVQ	IB	SQA(H)	SQA	RATIO	A/AS
Biology	C100	3FT deg	B+C g	BCC	2M+4D$	D^	28$	BBBBC$	Ind	9	20/30
Biology and Geology	CF16	3FT deg	B g	BCD	3M+3D$	D^	26$	BBBCC$	Ind	9	18/22

Biology 9

course details			98 expected requirements							96 entry stats	
TITLE	CODE	COURSE	SUBJECTS	A/AS	ND/C	AGNVQ	IB	SQA(H)	SQA	RATIO	A/AS
Biology with Industrial Experience	C101	4SW deg	B+C g	BCC	2M+4D$	D^	28$	BBBBC$	Ind	5	20/30
Biology with a Modern Language	C106	4FT deg	B+C+L g	BCC	2M+4D$	D^	28$	BBBBC$	Ind	8	20/26
Cell Biology	C140	3FT deg	B+C	CCC	3M+3D$	D^	26$	BBBCC$	Ind	29	
Cell Biology with Industrial Experience	C141	4SW deg	B+C	CCC	3M+3D$	D^	26$	BBBCC$	Ind	5	
Cell Biology with a Modern Language	C142	4FT deg	B+C+L	CCC	3M+3D$	D^	26$	BBBCC$	Ind		
Environmental Biology	C160	3FT deg	B+C	BCD	3M+3D$	D^	26$	BBBCC$	Ind	8	20/30
Environmental Biology with Industrial Experience	C161	4SW deg	B+C	BCD	3M+3D$	D^	26$	BBBCC$	Ind	9	
Environmental Biology with a Mod Lang	C163	4FT deg	B+C+L	BCD	3M+3D$	D^	26$	BBBCC$	Ind	10	
Life Sciences	C102	3FT deg	B+C	BCC	2M+4D$	D^	28$	BBBBC$	Ind	5	22/30
Life Sciences with Industrial Experience	C105	4SW deg	B+C	BCC	2M+4D$	D^	28$	BBBBC$	Ind	3	22/30
Life Sciences with a Modern Language	C103	4FT deg	B+C+L	BCC	2M+4D$	D^	28$	BBBBC$	Ind	4	

MANCHESTER METROPOLITAN Univ

TITLE	CODE	COURSE	SUBJECTS	A/AS	ND/C	AGNVQ	IB	SQA(H)	SQA	RATIO	A/AS
Biological Sciences (3 Yr route)	C120	3FT deg	B+S g	12	5M	M	Dip$	BBB$	Ind		
Biological Sciences (4 year route)	C129	4FT deg	* g	8	X	M	Dip	BBB	Ind		
Biology	C100	3FT deg	* g	12-18	MO	M$	28	BBCCC	Ind		
Biology/Applicable Mathematics	CG11	3FT deg	M g	12	5M $	M$	27$	BCCCC$	Ind		
Business Mathematics/Biology	CG1C	3FT deg	M/P/Ec g	12	5M $	M$	27$	BCCCC$	Ind		
Chemistry/Biology	CF11	3FT deg	C g	12	N $	M$	24$	CCCC$	Ind		
Electronics/Biology	CH1P	3FT deg	* g	12	5M	M$	27	BCCCC	Ind		
Environmental Studies/Biology	CF19	3FT deg	* g	14		M$					
Geography/Biology	CL18	3FT deg	Gy g	14	MO $	M$	28$	BBCCC$	Ind		
Life Science/Business Studies	CN11	3FT deg	*	CC	M+D	D	28	CCCC	Ind		
Life Science/English	CQ13	3FT deg	*	CC	M+D	D	28	CCCC	Ind		
Life Science/Environmental Science	CF1X	3FT deg	* g	DD	M+D	D	28	CCCC	Ind		
Life Science/Geography	CL1V	3FT deg	* g	DD	M+D	D	28	CCCC	Ind		
Life Science/Health Studies	BC91	3FT deg	*	CC	M+D	D	28	CCCC	Ind		
Life Science/Leisure Studies	CL14	3FT deg	* g	DD	M+D	D	28	CCCC	Ind		
Materials Science/Biology	CF12	3FT deg	M/P/C g	12	4M $	M$	26$	CCCCC$	Ind		
Psychology/Biology	CL17	3FT deg	* g	18	MO	D$	28	BBCCC	Ind		12/20
Social Studies of Technology/Biology	CL13	3FT deg	* g	12	5M	M$	27	BCCCC	Ind		
Sport/Life Science	BC61	3FT deg	S	BC	M+D	DS	28	CCCC	Ind		
Combined Studies (Foundation) Biology	Y108▼	4FT deg	M/P	E	2M $	P$	$	$	Ind		
Applied Biological Sciences	011C	2FT HND	B/C g	CD-E	N	P	X	BB$	Ind		2/7

MIDDLESEX Univ

TITLE	CODE	COURSE	SUBJECTS	A/AS	ND/C	AGNVQ	IB	SQA(H)	SQA	RATIO	A/AS
Joint Honours Degree Biological Sciences	Y400	3FT deg	* g	10	5M	M$ go	24	CCCC	Ind		

NAPIER Univ

TITLE	CODE	COURSE	SUBJECTS	A/AS	ND/C	AGNVQ	IB	SQA(H)	SQA	RATIO	A/AS
Biological Sciences (common 1st year)	C120	4FT/5SW deg	B/C	DD	Ind	Ind	Ind	BBC	Ind		
Environmental Biology (common 1st year)	C160	4FT/5SW deg	B/C	DD	Ind	Ind	Ind	BBC	Ind		
Applied Biological Sciences	021C	2FT HND	C/B	DE	Ind	Ind	Ind	CCC	Ind		

NENE COLLEGE

TITLE	CODE	COURSE	SUBJECTS	A/AS	ND/C	AGNVQ	IB	SQA(H)	SQA	RATIO	A/AS
Earth Science with Ecology	F9C9	3FT deg		DD	5M	M	24	CCC	Ind		
Ecology with Chemistry and the Environment	C9F1	3FT deg		DD	5M	M	24	CCC	Ind		
Ecology with Earth Science	C9F9	3FT deg		DD	5M	M	24	CCC	Ind		
Ecology with Energy Management	C9J9	3FT deg		DD	5M	M	24	CCC	Ind		
Ecology with Fossils and Evolution	C9F6	3FT deg		DD	5M	M	24	CCC	Ind		
Ecology with Geography	C9F8	3FT deg		DD	5M	M	24	CCC	Ind		
Ecology with Human Biological Studies	C9B1	3FT deg		DD	5M	M	24	CCC	Ind		
Ecology with Industry and Enterprise	C9H1	3FT deg	g	DD	5M	M	24	CCC	Ind		
Ecology with Management Science	C9G4	3FT deg	g	DD	5M	M	24	CCC	Ind		

course details — 98 expected requirements — 96 entry stats

TITLE	CODE	COURSE	SUBJECTS	A/AS	ND/C	AGNVQ	IB	SQA(H)	SQA	RATIO A/AS
Ecology with Wastes Management & the Environment	C9FX	3FT deg		DD	5M	M	24	CCC	Ind	
Economics with Ecology	L1C9	3FT deg	g	6	5M	M	24	CCC	Ind	
Energy Management with Ecology	J9C9	3FT deg	g	EE	3M	P	24	CCC	Ind	
Geography with Ecology	F8C9	3FT deg	Gy	8	5M	M	24	CCC	Ind	
Human Biological Studies with Ecology	B1C9	3FT deg	S	DE	5M	M	24	CCC	Ind	
Information Systems with Ecology	G5C9	3FT deg		6	5M	M	24	CCC	Ind	
Law with Ecology	M3C9	3FT deg	g	10	3M+2D	M	24	CCC	Ind	
Mathematics with Ecology	G1C9	3FT deg	M	DD	Ind	Ind	24	CCC	Ind	

Univ of NEWCASTLE

TITLE	CODE	COURSE	SUBJECTS	A/AS	ND/C	AGNVQ	IB	SQA(H)	SQA	RATIO	A/AS
Applied Biology	C110	3FT/4SW deg	2S g	CCC	Ind	Ind	Ind	BBBB$	Ind	6	12/22
Biological Sciences	C100	3FT deg	B+C	CC-BCC	Ind	Ind	26$	ABBB	Ind	6	18/28
Biology of Plants and Animals	C180	3FT deg	B+C	CCD	Ind	Ind	Ind	Ind	Ind	3	10/18
Environmental Biology	C160	3FT deg	B+2S	CCC	Ind	Ind	Ind	AABB$	Ind	6	12/28
Marine Biology	C170	3FT deg	B+C	BBC-BCC	HN	Ind	30$	AABB	Ind	9	18/28
Combined Studies (BSc) *Biological Sciences*	Y100	3FT deg	B+S	20	4M+1D	Ind	28$	AAABB	Ind		

NEWMAN COLLEGE OF HIGHER EDUCATION

TITLE	CODE	COURSE	SUBJECTS	A/AS	ND/C	AGNVQ	IB	SQA(H)	SQA
Biological Science and Geography	CF18	3FT deg	*	CC	3M	M*	Dip	CCC	Ind
Biological Science and History	CV11	3FT deg	*	CC	3M	M*	Dip	CCC	Ind
Biological Science and Social & Applied Psychol.	CL17	3FT deg	*	CC	3M	M*	Dip	CCC	Ind
Biological Science and Theology	CV18	3FT deg	*	CC	3M	M*	Dip	CCC	Ind
English and Biological Science	CQ13	3FT deg	*	CC	3M	M*	Dip	CCC	Ind
Expressive English and Biological Science	CW14	3FT deg	*	CC	3M	M*	Dip	CCC	Ind
Information Technology and Biological Science	CG15	3FT deg	*	CC	3M	M*	Dip	CCC	Ind
PE & Sports Studies and Biological Science	CX19	3FT deg	*	CC	3M	M*	Dip	CCC	Ind

NESCOT

TITLE	CODE	COURSE	SUBJECTS	A/AS	ND/C	AGNVQ	IB	SQA(H)	SQA	RATIO
Applied Biology	C118	4FT deg	*							3
Applied Biology	C110	3FT deg	S	EE	N	M	Dip	Ind	N$	11
Biological Imaging	CJ1M	3FT deg	*	EE	N	M	Dip	Ind	N$	
Biological Sciences	C121	2FT Dip	S	EE	N	M	Dip	Ind	N$	
Immunology	C928	4FT deg	*							1
Immunology	C920	3FT deg	S	EE	N	M	Dip	Ind	N$	9
Applied Biology	011C	2FT HND	S	D	N	P	Dip	Ind	N$	18

NORTH EAST WALES INST of HE

TITLE	CODE	COURSE	SUBJECTS	A/AS	ND/C	AGNVQ	IB	SQA(H)	SQA
Biology	C100	3FT deg		4-8	3M	M$	Ind	CCC	N$
Biology and Media Practice	CP14	3FT deg		4-8	3M	M$	Ind	CCC	N$
Environmental Biology	C910	3FT deg		4-8	4M	M$	Ind	CCC	N$
Applied Biology	011C	2FT HND		2-4	2M	P$	Ind	CC	N$

Univ of NORTH LONDON

TITLE	CODE	COURSE	SUBJECTS	A/AS	ND/C	AGNVQ	IB	SQA(H)	SQA	RATIO	A/AS
Biological Science and Education Studies	CX19	3FT/4SW/4EXT deg	B	12	Ind	Ind	Ind	Ind	Ind		
Biological Science and French	CR11	4FT deg	B	CD	Ind	Ind	Ind	Ind	Ind		
Biological Science and German	CR12	4FT deg	B	CC	Ind	Ind	Ind	Ind	Ind		
Biological Science and Philosophy	CV17	3FT/4SW/4EXT deg	B	CD	Ind	Ind	Ind	Ind	Ind		
Biological Sciences	C120	3FT/4SW/4EXT deg	B	CC	3M $	MS	$	Ind	Ind	8	8/20
Biology/Chemistry/Food Science Foundation	CF11▼	4FT/5SW deg			Ind	Ind	Ind	INd	Ind	1	
Ecology	CF99	3FT/4SW/4EXT deg	B/2S	CC	3M $	MS	$	Ind	Ind	4	
Environmental Management and Ecological Science	CF9X	3FT/4SW/4EXT deg	B/2S	CC	3M $	MS	Ind	Ind	Ind		
Sports and Biological Sciences	CB16	3FT/4SW/4EXT deg	B/(Ss+S)	12	4M $	MS	$	Ind	Ind		
Combined Honours *Biological Sciences*	Y100	3FT/4SW/4EXT deg	B	CC	3M $	MS	$	Ind	Ind		
Biology	011C	2FT HND	B/C	E	N $	PS	$	Ind	Ind	5	

Biology 9

TITLE	CODE	COURSE	SUBJECTS	A/AS	NO/C	RGNVQ	IB	SQA(H)	SQA	RATIO	A/AS
Univ of NORTHUMBRIA											
Applied Biology	C100	3FT deg	B g	10	3M	MS gi	24$	CCC$	Ind		
Applied Statistics and Life Sciences	GC49	3FT deg	B+M/S g	12	Ind	Ind	24$	CCCC$	Ind		
NORWICH: City COLL											
Environmental Biology	C160	3FT/4FT deg	2S	10	5M	P$ go	Ind	Ind	Ind	4	
Human Life Sciences	C980	3FT/4FT deg	2S	12	5M	P$ go	Ind	Ind	Ind	4	
Human Life Sciences and Psychology	CL97	3FT/4FT deg	2S	10	5M	P$ go	Ind	Ind	Ind		
Human Life Sciences with Psychology	C9L7	3FT/4FT deg	2S	10	5M	P$ go	Ind	Ind	Ind		
Psychology with Human Life Sciences	L7C9	3FT deg	S	12	5M	P	Ind	Ind	Ind		
Combined Science *Ecology*	Y100	3FT/4FT deg	2S	10	5M		Ind	Ind	Ind		
Combined Science *Population Biology*	Y100	3FT/4FT deg	2S	10	5M		Ind	Ind	Ind		
Univ of NOTTINGHAM											
Biology	C100	3FT deg	2S/B+C g	ABB-BBB	Ind	Ind	Ind	Ind	Ind	11	26/30
Environmental Biology	C160	3FT deg	2(M/S/Gy)	CC-CDD	3M $	MS	24$	CSYS$	N$	8	12/24
Environmental Biology with European Studies	C1T2	4FT deg	2(M/S/Gy) g	CC-CDD	3M $	MS	24$	CSYS$	N$	6	
Environmental Life Science	C162	3FT deg	B+C/M/P g	BBB	Ind	Ind	Ind	Ind	Ind	16	26/28
Molecular Cell Biology	C140	3FT deg	C+B+M/P/Gy/L	BBC	Ind	Ind	Ind	Ind	Ind	7	26/30
NOTTINGHAM TRENT Univ											
Applied Biology	C110	4SW deg	S g	DDE	Ind	Ind	Dip	C	$	6	6/16
Applied Biology (Extended)	C118▼	4EXT/5EXTSW deg	* g		Ind	Ind	Ind	Ind	Ind	3	
Biology and Chemistry	CF11	3FT deg	B+C g	10	Ind	Ind	Dip	C	Ind	10	
Biology and Computing	CG15	3FT deg	B g	10	Ind	Ind	Dip	C	Ind	7	7/12
Biology and Mathematics	CG11	3FT deg	B+M	10	Ind	Ind	Dip	C	Ind	3	8/10
Biology and Physics	CF13	3FT deg	B+M/P g	10	Ind	Ind	Dip	C	Ind	4	
Environmental Conservation & Mgt & Biology	FC91	3FT deg	B g	10	Ind	Ind	Dip	C	Ind	10	10/20
Information Technology for Sciences and Biology	GC51	3FT deg	B g	10	Ind	Ind	Dip	C	Ind	2	
Sport & Exercise Science and Biology	BC61	3FT deg	B g	18	Ind	Ind	Dip	B	Ind		
Science (Applied Biology)	011C▼	2FT/3SW HND	S g	EE	N		Dip	DD	$	2	2/8
OXFORD Univ											
Biological Sciences	C100	3FT deg	B+C/M/P	AAB-ABB	DO		36	AAAAA	Ind	2	26/30
OXFORD BROOKES Univ											
Biological Chemistry/Biology	CC71	3FT deg					Ind	Ind	Ind		
Biology	C100	3FT deg									
Biology/Accounting and Finance	CN14	3FT deg	S g	DD-BCC	Ind	MS/DS3	Ind	Ind	Ind	1	
Biology/Anthropology	CL16	3FT deg	S g	DD-BCC	Ind	MS^	Ind	Ind	Ind	2	14/20
Business Administration and Management/Biology	CN11	3FT deg	S g	DD-BCC	Ind	MS/MB4	Ind	Ind	Ind	7	
Cartography/Biology	CF18	3FT deg	S g	DD-DDD	Ind	MS	Ind	Ind	Ind		
Cell Biology/Accounting and Finance	CNC4	3FT deg	* g	CC-BCC	Ind		Ind	Ind	Ind		
Cell Biology/Anthropology	CLC6	3FT deg									
Cell Biology/Biological Chemistry	CCC7	3FT deg									
Cell Biology/Biology	C142	3FT deg									
Cell Biology/Business Administration and Mgt	CNC1	3FT deg									
Cell Biology/Cartography	CFC8	3FT deg									
Cell and Molecular Biology	C140	3FT deg	S g	DD	Ind	PS^	Ind	Ind	Ind	5	6/14
Combined Studies/Biology	CY14	3FT deg		X		X	X	X			
Combined Studies/Cell Biology	CYC4	3FT deg		X		X	X	X			
Computer Systems/Biology	CG16	3FT deg	S g	DD-CDD	Ind	MS	Ind	Ind	Ind		
Computer Systems/Cell Biology	CGC6	3FT deg									

course details			**98 expected requirements**							**96 entry stats**	
TITLE	CODE	COURSE	SUBJECTS	A/AS	ND/C	AGNVQ	IB	SQA(H)	SQA	RATIO A/AS	
Computing Mathematics/Cell Biology	CGC9	3FT deg									
Computing/Biology	CG15	2ACC/3FT deg	S g	DD-BC	Ind	MS	Ind	Ind	Ind	6	
Computing/Cell Biology	CGC5	3FT deg									
Ecology/Accounting and Finance	CN94	3FT deg	* g	CD-BCC	Ind	MS/D*3	Ind	Ind	Ind		
Ecology/Anthropology	CL96	3FT deg	* g	CD-BCC	Ind	MS/M*^	Ind	Ind	Ind	2	
Ecology/Biological Chemistry	CC79	3FT deg									
Ecology/Biology	CC19	2ACC/3FT deg	S g	DD-CD	Ind	MS	Ind	Ind	Ind	7	
Ecology/Business Administration and Management	CN91	3FT deg	* g	CD-BBC	Ind	MS/MB4	Ind	Ind	Ind		
Ecology/Cartography	FC89	3FT deg	* g	DD-DDD	Ind	MS	Ind	Ind	Ind		
Ecology/Cell Biology	CCC9	3FT deg									
Ecology/Combined Studies	CY94	3FT deg		X		X	X	X			
Ecology/Computer Systems	CG96	3FT deg	* g	CD-BC	Ind	MS	Ind	Ind	Ind		
Ecology/Computing	CG95	3FT deg	* g	CD-BC	Ind	MS	Ind	Ind	Ind		
Ecology/Economics	CL91	3FT deg	* g	CD-BB	Ind	MS/M*3	Ind	Ind	Ind		
Economics/Biology	CL11	3FT deg	S g	DD-BB	Ind	MS/M*3	Ind	Ind	Ind	46	
Economics/Cell Biology	CLC1	3FT deg									
Educational Studies/Biology	CX19	3FT deg	S g	DD-CC	Ind	MS/M*3	Ind	Ind	Ind		
Educational Studies/Cell Biology	CXC9	3FT deg									
Educational Studies/Ecology	CX99	3FT deg	* g	CD-CC	Ind	MS/M*3	Ind	Ind	Ind		
Electronics/Cell Biology	CHC6	3FT deg									
English Studies/Biology	CQ13	3FT deg	S g	DD-AB	Ind	M*^/MS	Ind	Ind	Ind		
English Studies/Cell Biology	CQC3	3FT deg									
English Studies/Ecology	CQ93	3FT deg	* g	CD-AB	Ind	MS/M*^	Ind	Ind	Ind	10	
Environmental Biology	C160	3FT deg	S g	CD	Ind	MS	Ind	Ind	Ind	6	8/18
Environmental Chemistry/Biology	FC11	3FT deg									
Environmental Chemistry/Cell Biology	CFC1	3FT deg									
Environmental Chemistry/Ecology	CF91	3FT deg									
Environmental Policy/Biology	CK13	3FT deg									
Environmental Policy/Cell Biology	CKC3	3FT deg									
Environmental Policy/Ecology	CK93	3FT deg									
Environmental Sciences/Biology	CF1X	3FT deg	S g	DD-CD	Ind	MS/DS	Ind	Ind	Ind		
Environmental Sciences/Cell Biology	CFCX	3FT deg									
Environmental Sciences/Ecology	CF9X	3FT deg	S g	CD	Ind	MS/DS	Ind	Ind	Ind	10	
Exercise and Health/Biology	CB16	3FT deg	S g	DD	Ind	MS	Ind	Ind	Ind		
Exercise and Health/Cell Biology	BC6C	3FT deg									
Exercise and Health/Ecology	CB96	3FT deg	S g	DD-CD	Ind	MS	Ind	Ind	Ind		
Fine Art/Biology	CW11	3FT deg	Pf+A+S g	DD-BC	Ind	MA^/MS	Ind	Ind	Ind		
Fine Art/Cell Biology	CWC1	3FT deg									
Fine Art/Ecology	CW91	3FT deg	Pf+A g	BC-DDD	Ind	MA^/MS	Ind	Ind	Ind		
Food Science and Nutrition/Biology	CD14	3FT deg	S g	DD	Ind	MS	Ind	Ind	Ind	6	
Food Science and Nutrition/Cell Biology	CDC4	3FT deg									
Food Science and Nutrition/Ecology	DC49	3FT deg	S g	DD-CD	Ind	MS	Ind	Ind	Ind		
French Language and Contemp Studies/Biology	CR1C	4SW deg	F+S g	DD-CC	Ind	MS^	Ind	Ind	Ind		
French Language and Contemp Studies/Cell Biology	CRCC	3FT deg									
French Language and Contemp Studies/Ecology	CR9C	4SW deg	F g	CD-CC	Ind	MS^	Ind	Ind	Ind		
French Language and Literature/Cell Biology	CRC1	3FT deg									
Geography and the Phys Env/Biology	CF1V	3FT deg									
Geography and the Phys Env/Cell Biology	CFCV	3FT deg									
Geography and the Phys Env/Ecology	CF9V	3FT deg									
Geography/Biology	CL18	3FT deg	S g	DD-CDD	Ind	MS	Ind	Ind	Ind	10	
Geography/Cell Biology	CLC8	3FT deg									
Geography/Ecology	CL98	3FT deg	* g	CD-BB	Ind	MS	Ind	Ind	Ind		

			98 expected requirements							96 entry stats
course details										
TITLE	CODE	COURSE	SUBJECTS	A/AS	ND/C	AGNVQ	IB	SQA(H)	SQA	RATIO A/AS
Geology/Biology	CF16	3FT deg	S/M g	DD	Ind	PS/MS	Ind	Ind	Ind	7
Geology/Cell Biology	CFC6	3FT deg								
Geology/Ecology	FC69	3FT deg	S/M g	DD-CD	Ind	PS/MS	Ind	Ind	Ind	
Geotechnics/Biology	CH12	3FT deg	S/M/Ds/Es g	DD-DDD	Ind	M$	Ind	Ind	Ind	
Geotechnics/Cell Biology	CHC2	3FT deg								
Geotechnics/Ecology	CH92	3FT deg	S/M/Ds/Es g	DD-CC	Ind	M$	Ind	Ind	Ind	
German Language and Contemp Stud/Biology	CR1F	4SW deg	G+S g	DD-DDD	Ind	MS^	Ind	Ind	Ind	1
German Language and Contemp Stud/Cell Biology	CRCF	3FT deg								
German Language and Contemp Stud/Ecology	CR9F	4SW deg	G g	CD-DDD	Ind	MS^	Ind	Ind	Ind	
German Language and Literature/Biology	CR12	4SW deg	G+S g	DD-DDD	Ind	MS^	Ind	Ind	Ind	
German Language and Literature/Cell Biology	CRC2	3FT deg								
German Language and Literature/Ecology	CR92	4SW deg	G g	CD-DDD	Ind	MS^	Ind	Ind	Ind	
German Studies/Biology	CR1G	4SW deg			Ind		Ind	Ind	Ind	
German Studies/Cell Biology	CRCG	3FT deg								
German Studies/Ecology	CR9G	4SW deg			Ind		Ind	Ind	Ind	
Health Care/Biology (Post Exp)	BC71	3FT deg		X		X	X	X		
Health Care/Cell Biology (Post Exp)	BC7C	3FT deg		X		X	X	X		
Health Care/Ecology (Post Exp)	BC79	3FT deg		X		X	X	X		
History of Art/Cell Biology	CVC4	3FT deg								
History/Biology	CV11	3FT deg	S g	DD-BB	Ind	MS/M^	Ind	Ind	Ind	2
History/Cell Biology	CVC1	3FT deg								
History/Ecology	CV91	3FT deg	* g	CD-BB	Ind	MS/M^	Ind	Ind	Ind	
Hospitality Management Studies/Biology	CN17	3FT deg	S/M g	DD-CC	Ind	MS/M*3	Ind	Ind	Ind	
Hospitality Management Studies/Cell Biology	CNC7	3FT deg								
Hospitality Management Studies/Ecology	CN97	3FT deg	* g	DD-DDD	Ind	MS/M*3	Ind	Ind	Ind	
Human Biology/Biology	BC11	3FT deg			Ind		Ind	Ind	Ind	
Human Biology/Cell Biology	BC1C	3FT deg			Ind		Ind	Ind	Ind	
Human Biology/Ecology	BC19	3FT deg			Ind		Ind	Ind	Ind	
Information Systems/Biology	CG1M	3FT deg	S g	DD-BC	Ind	MS	Ind	Ind	Ind	1
Information Systems/Cell Biology	CGCM	3FT deg								
Information Systems/Ecology	CG9M	3FT deg	* g	CD-BC	Ind	MS	Ind	Ind	Ind	
Intelligent Systems/Biology	CG18	3FT deg	S g	DD-CD	Ind	MS	Ind	Ind	Ind	
Intelligent Systems/Cell Biology	CGC8	3FT deg								
Intelligent Systems/Ecology	CG98	3FT deg	* g	CD	Ind	MS	Ind	Ind	Ind	
Law/Cell Biology	CMC3	3FT deg								
Leisure Planning/Biology	CK1H	3FT deg								
Leisure Planning/Cell Biology	CKCH	3FT deg								
Leisure Planning/Ecology	CK9H	3FT deg								
Marketing Management/Biology	CN1N	3FT deg	S g	DD-BCC	Ind	MS/D*3	Ind	Ind	Ind	7
Marketing Management/Cell Biology	CNCN	3FT deg								
Marketing Management/Ecology	CN9N	3FT deg	* g	CD-BCC	Ind	MS/D*3	Ind	Ind	Ind	3
Mathematics/Biology	CG11	2ACC/3FT deg	M g	DD-DDE	Ind	MS^	Ind	Ind	Ind	
Mathematics/Cell Biology	CGC1	3FT deg								
Mathematics/Ecology	CG91	3FT deg	M g	DD-CD	Ind	MS/M^	Ind	Ind	Ind	
Music/Biology	CW13	3FT deg	Mu+S g	DD	Ind	MS	Ind	Ind	Ind	1
Music/Cell Biology	CWC3	3FT deg								
Music/Ecology	CW93	3FT deg	Mu+S g	DD-CD	Ind	MS	Ind	Ind	Ind	
Palliative Care/Biology (Post Exp)	BCR1	3FT deg		X		X	X	X		
Palliative Care/Cell Biology (Post Exp)	BCRC	3FT deg		X		X	X	X		
Palliative Care/Ecology (Post Exp)	BCR9	3FT deg		X		X	X	X		
Planning Studies/Biology	CK14	3FT deg	S g	CC-DD	Ind	MS	Ind	Ind	Ind	
Planning Studies/Cell Biology	CKC4	3FT deg								

TITLE	CODE	COURSE	SUBJECTS	A/AS	ND/C	AGNVQ	IB	SQA(H)	SQA	RATIO A/AS
Planning Studies/Ecology	CK94	3FT deg	* g	CD-CC	Ind	MS	Ind	Ind	Ind	
Politics/Cell Biology	CMC1	3FT deg								
Psychology/Biology	CC18	3FT deg	S g	DD-BBC	Ind	MS/M*^	Ind	Ind	Ind	14 16/18
Psychology/Cell Biology	CCC8	3FT deg								
Psychology/Ecology	CC89	3FT deg	* g	CD-BBC	Ind	MS/M*^	Ind	Ind	Ind	
Publishing/Biology	CP15	3FT deg	S g	DD-BB	Ind	MS/M$3	Ind	Ind	Ind	
Publishing/Cell Biology	CPC5	3FT deg								
Publishing/Ecology	CP95	3FT deg	* g	CD-BB	Ind	MS/M$3	Ind	Ind	Ind	
Rehabilitation/Biology (Post Exp)	BCT1	3FT deg	X		X		X	X		
Rehabilitation/Cell Biology (Post Exp)	BCTC	3FT deg	X		X		X	X		
Rehabilitation/Ecology (Post Exp)	BCT9	3FT deg	X		X		X	X		
Retail Management/Biology	CN15	3FT deg	S/M g	DD-CCD	Ind		Ind	Ind	Ind	
Retail Management/Ecology	CN95	3FT deg	* g	CD-CCD	Ind		Ind	Ind	Ind	
Sociology/Biology	CL13	3FT deg	S/M g	DD-BCC	Ind	MS/M*^	Ind	Ind	Ind	
Sociology/Cell Biology	CLC3	3FT deg								
Sociology/Ecology	CL93	3FT deg	* g	CD-BCC	Ind	MS/M*^	Ind	Ind	Ind	
Software Engineering/Biology	CG17	3FT deg	S g	DD-BC	Ind	MS	Ind	Ind	Ind	
Software Engineering/Cell Biology	CGC7	3FT deg								
Software Engineering/Ecology	CG97	3FT deg	S g	CD-BC	Ind	MS	Ind	Ind	Ind	
Statistics/Biology	CG14	2ACC/3FT deg	S/M g	DD	Ind	MS	Ind	Ind	Ind	4
Statistics/Cell Biology	CGC4	3FT deg								
Statistics/Ecology	CG94	3FT deg	S g	DD-CD	Ind	MS	Ind	Ind	Ind	
Telecommunications/Biology	CH1P	3FT deg								
Telecommunications/Cell Biology	CHCP	3FT deg								
Telecommunications/Ecology	CH9P	3FT deg								
Tourism/Biology	CP17	3FT deg	S g	DD-BC	Ind	MS/M*3	Ind	Ind	Ind	
Tourism/Cell Biology	CPC7	3FT deg								
Tourism/Ecology	CP97	3FT deg	* g	CD-BC	Ind	MS/M*3	Ind	Ind	Ind	
Transport Planning/Cell Biology	CNC9	3FT deg								
Water Resources/Biology	CH1F	3FT deg								
Water Resources/Cell Biology	CHCF	3FT deg								
Water Resources/Ecology	CH9F	3FT deg								
Extended Science *Biology*	Y100	4FT deg	* g	EE	Ind	P*	Ind	Ind	Ind	
Extended Science *Cell and Molecular Biology*	Y100	4FT deg	* g	EE	Ind	P*	Ind	Ind	Ind	
Extended Science *Environmental Biology*	Y100	4FT deg	* g	EE	Ind	P*	Ind	Ind	Ind	

Univ of PAISLEY

TITLE	CODE	COURSE	SUBJECTS	A/AS	ND/C	AGNVQ	IB	SQA(H)	SQA	RATIO A/AS
Biology	C100	3FT/4FT/5SW deg	* g	CCC-EE	Ind	Ind	Ind	BCC$	Ind	3
Biology with European Language	C1T2	3FT/4FT/5SW deg	* g	CCC-EE	Ind	Ind	Ind	BCC$	Ind	2
Biology with Management	C1N1	3FT/4FT/5SW deg	* g	CCC-EE	Ind	Ind	Ind	BCC$	Ind	6
Environmental Biology	C160	4FT/5SW deg	* g	CCC-EE	Ind	Ind	Ind	BCC$	Ind	3
Immunology and Biochemistry	CC79	3FT deg	* g	CCC-EE	Ind	Ind	Ind	BCC$	Ind	
Immunology and Microbiology	CC59	3FT/4FT deg	* g	CCC-EE	Ind	Ind	Ind	BCC$	Ind	
Psychology and Biology	CC81	3FT/4FT deg	* g	CC	Ind	Ind	Ind	BCCC$	Ind	

Univ of PLYMOUTH

TITLE	CODE	COURSE	SUBJECTS	A/AS	ND/C	AGNVQ	IB	SQA(H)	SQA	RATIO A/AS
Biological Sciences	C100	3FT deg	Ap g	10-14	4M	MS	Ind	BBC	Ind	4 8/20
Biomedical Sciences	C130	3FT deg	B g	10-14	Ind	Ind	Ind	BBBB	Ind	
Biotechnology with Business	C9N1	3FT/4SW deg	B+Bu g	16	4M	MS^	Ind	BBBB	Ind	
Biotechnology with Chemistry	C9F1	3FT/4SW deg	B+C g	10-14	4M	MS^	Ind	BBBB	Ind	
Biotechnology with Computing	C9G5	3FT/4SW deg	B g	12-14	4M	MS^	Ind	BBBB	Ind	

| | | | 98 expected requirements | | | | | | | 96 entry stats | |
| course details | | | | | | | | | | | |

TITLE	CODE	COURSE	SUBJECTS	A/AS	ND/C	AGNVQ	IB	SQA(H)	SQA	RATIO	A/AS
Biotechnology with French	C9R1	3FT/4SW deg	B+F g	12-14	4M	MS^	Ind	BBBB	Ind		
Biotechnology with Mathematics	C9G1	3FT/4SW deg	B g	12-14	4M	MS^	Ind	BBBB	Ind	2	
Cell Biology and Immunology with Chemistry	C1F1	3FT/4SW deg	B+C g	12-14	4M	MS^	Ind	BBBB	Ind	4	
Cell Biology and Immunology with Computing	C1G5	3FT/4SW deg	B g	10-14	4M	MS^	Ind	BBBB	Ind	1	
Cell Biology and Immunology with French	C1R1	3FT/4SW deg	B+F g	12-14	4M	MS^	Ind	BBBB	Ind		
Cell Biology and Immunology with Statistics	C1G4	3FT/4SW deg	B g	10-14	4M	MS^	Ind	BBBB	Ind		
Chemistry with Human Biology	F1C9	3FT deg	C+B g	CC	3M	MS^	Ind	CCCC	Ind		
Human Biology with Chemistry	C9FC	3FT/4SW deg	B+C g	12-14	4M $	MS^	Ind	BBBB	Ind	8	
Human Biology with Computing	C9GN	3FT/4SW deg	B g	10-14	4M $	MS^	Ind	BBBB	Ind	3	
Human Biology with French	C9RC	3FT/4SW deg	B+F g	BCC	4M $	M$^	Ind	BBBB	Ind		
Human Biology with Psychology	C9C8	3FT/4SW deg	B g	14-18	4M $	Ind	Ind	BBBB	Ind	9	16/16
Human Biology with Statistics	C9GL	3FT/4SW deg	B g	10-14	4M $	M$^	Ind	BBBB	Ind	2	
Marine Biology	C170	3FT deg	B+C g	CCC-BCC	4M $	MS^	Ind	BBBB	Ind	18	16/26
Marine Biology and Ecology	CD12	3FT deg	B+S g	CCD	4M $	MS^	Ind	Ind	Ind		
Marine Biology with Chemistry	C1FD	3FT deg	B+C g	CCC	4M $	MS^	Ind	BBBB	Ind	8	
Marine Biology with Microbiology	C1C5	3FT deg	B+C g	CCC	4M $	MS^	Ind	BBBB	Ind	21	
Marine Biology with Ocean Science	C1F7	3FT deg	B+C g	CCC	4M $	MS^	Ind	BBBB	Ind	50	
Mathematics with Human Biology	G1C9	3FT deg	M g	10-15	MO $	M$^	Ind	BBCC	Ind		
Modern Languages with Human Biology	T9C9	3FT/4SW deg	L g	C	Ind	Ind	Ind	Ind	Ind		
Ocean Science with Marine Biology	F7CC	3FT deg	S g	CCC	5M $	M$	Ind	CCCC	Ind	17	
Psychology with Human Biology	C8C9	3FT/4SW deg	B g	BBC	MO+3D	M12^	Ind	BBBC$	Ind	7	16/26
Sociology with Human Biology	L3C9	3FT deg	B g	BBC	2M+3D$	M$^	Ind	BBBC$	Ind	6	
Statistics (App) with Human Biology	G4C9	3FT deg	M/St g	10	MO $	M$^	Ind	BBCC	Ind	1	
Extended Science (Foundation year) Biology	Y108▼	1FT/4EXT deg	S	2	Ind	P$	Ind	Ind	Ind		

Univ of PORTSMOUTH

TITLE	CODE	COURSE	SUBJECTS	A/AS	ND/C	AGNVQ	IB	SQA(H)	SQA	RATIO	A/AS
Biology	C100	3FT deg	2S	8	3M $	M$6/^	Dip	BBB	Ind	3	4/18
Cell Biology	C140	3FT deg	2S	10	3M $	M$6/^	Dip	BBB	Ind		
Ecological Chemical Monitoring (Extended)	CF9X	4FT deg	*	Ind	Ind	Ind	Ind	Ind	Ind		
Ecological and Chemical Monitoring	CF99	3FT deg	C+S	8	N $	M$6/^	Dip	Ind	Ind		
Environmental Biology	C160	3FT deg	2S	10	3M $	M$6/^	Dip	BBB	Ind		
Extended Biology Degree Scheme	C108	4FT deg	*	4	Ind	P*	Ind	Ind	Ind	1	4/13
Marine Biology	C170	3FT deg	2S	12	3M $	M$6/^	Dip	BBB	Ind		6/16

QUEEN MARY & WESTFIELD COLL (Univ of London)

TITLE	CODE	COURSE	SUBJECTS	A/AS	ND/C	AGNVQ	IB	SQA(H)	SQA	RATIO	A/AS
Biological Chemistry	F1C1	3FT deg	C+B/P/M	CCC	5M $	DS	26$	BBBCC			
Biology	C100	3FT deg	B+C/P/M	16	6M $	MS^/DS	26$	BBBCC			
Biology and Chemistry	CF11	3FT deg	B+C	CCC	6M $	DS	26$	BBBCC			
Biology with Business Studies	C1N1	3FT deg	B+C/P/M/Ec/Bu	16	6M $	MS^/DS	26$	BBBCC			
Ecology	C910	3FT deg	B+C/P/M	16	6M $	MS^/DS	26$	BBBCC			
Marine & Freshwater Biology	C172	3FT deg	B+C/P/M	16C	6M $	MS^/DS	26$	BBBCC			

QUEEN'S Univ Belfast

TITLE	CODE	COURSE	SUBJECTS	A/AS	ND/C	AGNVQ	IB	SQA(H)	SQA	RATIO	A/AS
Biological Sciences	C100	3FT/4FT deg	B+C g	CCC	Ind	Ind	28$	BBBC	Ind	6	16/24
Environmental Biology	C160	3FT/4FT deg	B+C g	CCC	Ind	Ind	28$	BBBC	Ind	11	18/22
Marine Biology	C170	3FT/4FT deg	B+C g	CCC	Ind	Ind	28$	BBBC	Ind		

Univ of READING

TITLE	CODE	COURSE	SUBJECTS	A/AS	ND/C	AGNVQ	IB	SQA(H)	SQA	RATIO	A/AS
Biological Sciences	C100	3FT deg	B g	18	4M+1D$	DS^ go	29$	BBBC$	Ind	10	14/24
Environmental Biology	C160	3FT deg	B g	18	4M+1D$	DS^ go	29$	BBBC$	Ind	8	12/22
Environmental Biosciences	C165	3FT deg	S g	18	4M+1D$	DS^ go	29$	BBBC$	Ind		

Univ College of RIPON & YORK ST JOHN

TITLE	CODE	COURSE	SUBJECTS	A/AS	ND/C	AGNVQ	IB	SQA(H)	SQA	RATIO	A/AS
Life Science and Health Studies	C9B9	3FT deg	g	DD	M	M	27	BBCC		3	6/12

	course details		98 expected requirements							96 entry stats
TITLE	CODE	COURSE	SUBJECTS	A/AS	ND/C	AGNVQ	IB	SQA(H)	SQA	RATIO A/AS
ROBERT GORDON Univ										
Applied Biosciences and Chemistry	CF91	3FT/4FT deg	B/C g	EE	N	Ind	Ind	CCC$	Ind	3
Biosciences with Biomedical Sciences	C9B9	3FT/4FT deg	B/C g	EE	N	Ind	Ind	CCC$	Ind	
Applied Science (Applied Biological Sciences)	019C	2FT HND	B/C g	E	N	Ind	Ind	CC$	Ind	4
Applied Science (Applied Biosciences and Chem)	91CC	2FT HND	S g	E	N	Ind	Ind	CC$	Ind	
ROEHAMPTON INST										
Biological Sciences	C120▼	3FT deg	B	12	3M	P$ go	24	CCC	N$	11
Biology and Applied Consumer Studies	CN19▼	3FT deg	B g	12	4M $	P$ go	26	CCC	N$	
Biology and Art for Community	WC11▼	3FT deg	B	12	4M $	P$ go	26	CCC	N$	
Business Computing and Biology	CG17▼	3FT deg	B g	12	3D	M$ go	26	BCC	N$	
Business Studies and Biology	CN11▼	3FT deg	B g	12	3D $	M$ go	26	BCC	N$	6
Dance Studies and Biology	CW14▼	3FT deg	B	CC	2M+2D$	M$ go	30	BBC	Ind	2
Drama & Theatre Studies and Biology	CW1L▼	3FT deg	B+T/E	16	3D $	M$^ go	30	BBB	Ind	
Ecology & Conservation	CD92▼	3FT deg	g	12	3M	P$ go	24	CCC	N$	
Education and Biology	CX19▼	3FT deg	B	12	3M $	P$ go	24	CCC	N$	2
English Language & Linguistics and Biology	CQ1H▼	3FT deg	E/L+B	CC	2M+2D$	M$^ go	30	BBC	N$	
English Literature and Biology	CQ13▼	3FT deg	E+B	CC	2M+2D$	M^ go	28	BBC	N$	
Environmental Studies and Biology	CF19▼	3FT deg	B g	12	4M $	P$ go	26	BCC	N$	
Film & Television Studies & Human & Social Biol	CPC4▼	3FT deg	B	16	2M+2D$	M$^	30	BBC	N$	
Film & Television Studies and Biology	CP14▼	3FT deg	B g	16	2M+2D$	M$^	30	BBC	N$	
French and Biology	CR11▼	4FT deg	F+B	12	4M $	P^ go	26	BCC	N$	
Geography and Biology	CL18▼	3FT deg	B+Gy	12	4M $	P$ go	26	BCC	N$	3
Health Studies and Biology	BC91▼	3FT deg	B	12	4M $	P$ go	26	BCC	N$	4
History and Biology	CV11▼	3FT deg	B+H	12	4M $	P^ go	26	CCC	N$	
Human & Social Biol and English Lang & Linguist	QCHC▼	3FT deg	B+E/L	CC	2M+2D$	M$	30	BBC	Ind	
Human & Social Biol and Environmental Studies	FC9C▼	3FT deg	B g	12	4M $	P$ go	26	BCC	N$	
Human & Social Biology and Applied Consumer St	CNC9▼	3FT deg	B g	12	4M $	P$ go	26	BCC	N$	2
Human & Social Biology and Art for Community	WC1C▼	3FT deg	B	12	3M $	P$	24	CCC	N$	
Human & Social Biology and Business Computing	GC7C▼	3FT deg	g	12	3D	M$ go	26	BCC	N$	
Human & Social Biology and Business Studies	NC1C▼	3FT deg	B g	12	3D $	M$ go	26	BCC	N$	2
Human & Social Biology and Dance Studies	WC4C▼	3FT deg	B	CC	2M+2D	M$^	30	BBC	Ind	
Human & Social Biology and Drama & Theatre Studs	CWCL▼	3FT deg	E/T+B	16	2M+2D	M$^	30	BBC	N$	
Human & Social Biology and Education	XC9C▼	3FT deg	B	12	3M	P$	24	CCC	N	2
Human & Social Biology and English Literature	QC3C▼	3FT deg	B+E	CC	2M+2D$	M^	28	BBC	Ind	
Human & Social Biology and French	CRC1▼	4FT deg	F+B	12	4M $	P^	26	BCC	N$	
Human & Social Biology and Geography	LC8C▼	3FT deg	B+Gy	12	4M $	P$ go	26	BCC	N$	
Human & Social Biology and Health Studies	CBC9▼	3FT deg	B	12	4M	P$ go	26	BCC	N$	1
Human & Social Biology and History	VC1C▼	3FT deg	B+H	12	4M $	P^	24	CCC	N$	
Music and Biology	CW13▼	3FT deg	B+Mu	12	4M $	P^ go	26	BCC	N$	
Music and Human & Social Biology	CWC3▼	3FT deg	B+Mu	12	4M $	P^ go	26	BCC	N$	
Natural Resource Studies and Biology	CD12▼	3FT deg	B g	12	3M	P$ go	24	CCC	N$	
Natural Resource Studs and Human & Social Biol	CDC2▼	3FT deg	g	12	3M	P$ go	24	CCC	N$	
Psychology and Biology	CL17▼	3FT deg	B g	CC	3D $	M$ go	30	BBB	N$	10
Psychology and Human & Social Biology	LC7C▼	3FT deg	B g	CC	3D	M$ go	30	BBB	Ind	3
Social Policy & Admin and Human & Social Biology	LC4C▼	3FT deg	B g	12	3M	P$	24	CCC	N$	
Social Policy & Administration and Biology	CL14▼	3FT deg	B	12	4M $	P$ go	26	BCC	N$	
Sociology and Biology	CL13▼	3FT deg	B g	12	4M $	P$ go	26	BCC	N$	
Sociology and Human & Social Biology	CLC3▼	3FT deg	B g	12	3M	P$ go	24	CCC	N$	3
Spanish and Biology	CR14▼	4FT deg	Sp+B	12	2M+2D$	P$ go	28	BBC	N$	
Spanish and Human & Social Biology	CRC4▼	4FT deg	Sp+B	12	2M+2D$	P$ go	28	BBC	N$	
Sport Studies and Biology	CB16▼	3FT deg	B g	12	3D $	MS go	30	BBB	N$	
Sport Studies and Human & Social Biology	CBC6▼	3FT deg	B g	12	3D $	MS go	30	BBB	N$	

			98 expected requirements							96 entry stats	
course details											
TITLE	CODE	COURSE	SUBJECTS	A/AS	ND/C	AGNVQ	IB	SQA(H)	SQA	RATIO	A/AS
Theology & Religious St and Human & Social Biol	CVC8▼	3FT deg	B	DD	3M	P$ go	24	CCC	N$		
Theology & Religious Studies and Biology	CV18▼	3FT deg	B	12	4M $	P$ go	26	BCC	N$		
Women's Studies and Biology	CM19▼	3FT deg	B	12	3M $	P$ go	24	CCC	N$		
Women's Studies and Human & Social Biology	CM1X▼	3FT deg	B	12	3M	P$ go	24	CCC	N$		

ROYAL HOLLOWAY, Univ of London

TITLE	CODE	COURSE	SUBJECTS	A/AS	ND/C	AGNVQ	IB	SQA(H)	SQA	RATIO	A/AS
Biology	C100	3FT deg	B+C/S g	BCC	4M	DS^	28$	BBBCC$		5	12/24
Biology and Geography	CF18	3FT deg	B+Gy+C/S g	BCC	Ind	DS^	28$	BBBBC$		8	
Biology for Management	C1NC	3FT deg	B+C/S g	BCC	4M	DS^	28$	BBBCC$		9	
Biology with Environmental Studies	C1F9	3FT deg	B+C/S g	BCC	4M	DS^	28$	BBBCC$		6	
Environmental Biology	C160	3FT deg	B+C/S g	BCC	4M	DS^	28$	BBBCC$		5	
Geology and Biology	FC61	3FT deg	B+C/S g	BBC-CCC	Ind	D^	28$	BBBCC$		8	
Foundation Programme Biology	Y408	4FT deg									
Science Foundation Year Biology	Y100	4FT deg	*		Ind	Ind	Ind	Ind			
Science Foundation Year Molecular Cell Biology	Y100	4FT deg	*		Ind	Ind	Ind	Ind			

SCOTTISH Agric COLL

TITLE	CODE	COURSE	SUBJECTS	A/AS	ND/C	AGNVQ	IB	SQA(H)	SQA	RATIO	A/AS
Aquaculture	C172▼	3FT/4FT deg	S	CD	Ind	M$	Ind	BBC$	Ind	2	

Univ of SALFORD

TITLE	CODE	COURSE	SUBJECTS	A/AS	ND/C	AGNVQ	IB	SQA(H)	SQA	RATIO	A/AS
Biological Sciences (3/4 Yrs)	C100	3FT/4SW deg	g	BBC-CCD	4M	M	Ind	Ind	Ind	4	12/20
Biological Sciences with studies in USA	C102	3FT deg	g	BBC-CCD	3M+2D	D	Ind	Ind	Ind	12	18/22
Biology and Chemistry (3 or 4 yr SW)	FC11	3FT/4SW deg	B+C g	BCC-CCD	3M	M	Ind	Ind	Ind	5	
Biology and Geography (3 or 4 yr SW)	CF18	3FT/4SW deg	B/C+Gy g	BCC-CCD	3M	M	Ind	Ind	Ind	4	
Biology and Information Technology	GC51	3FT/4SW deg		BCC-CCD	3M	M	Ind	Ind	Ind		
Economics and Physiology	LC19	3FT/4SW deg		BCC-CCD	3M	M	Ind	Ind	Ind		
Environmental Biological Science	C160	3FT/4SW deg	g	BBC-CCD	4M	M	Ind	Ind	Ind		
Geography and Physiology	FC89	3FT/4SW deg		BCC-CCD	3M	M	Ind	Ind	Ind		
Physiology and Information Technology	CG95	3FT/4SW deg		BCC-CCD	3M	M	Ind	Ind	Ind		
Physiology and Physics (3 or 4 yr SW)	CF93	3FT/4SW deg	P+B/C	BCC-CCD	3M	M	Ind	Ind	Ind		

Univ College SCARBOROUGH

TITLE	CODE	COURSE	SUBJECTS	A/AS	ND/C	AGNVQ	IB	SQA(H)	SQA	RATIO	A/AS
Coastal Marine Biology	CD12	3FT deg	B g	DD	Ind	P	27$	Ind	Ind		

Univ of SHEFFIELD

TITLE	CODE	COURSE	SUBJECTS	A/AS	ND/C	AGNVQ	IB	SQA(H)	SQA	RATIO	A/AS
Animal and Plant Biology	C180	3FT deg	2S g	20	5M+1D$	DS6/^	29$	BBBB$	Ind	6	22/30
Animal and Plant Sciences Foundation Year (4 Yr)	C102	4FT deg	g	20	5M+1D	DS6/^	29	BBBB	Ind		
Biological Sciences	C120	3FT deg	B+S g	20	5M+1D$	DS6/^	29$	BBBB$	Ind	7	20/28
Biological Sciences (including a Foundation Yr)	C101	4FT deg	g	20	5M+1D	DS6/^	29	BBBB	Ind		
Biological Sciences and Philosophy	CV17	3FT deg	B+S g	24	3M+3D$	DS6/^	32$	AABB$	Ind	7	
Ecology	C910	3FT deg	2S g	20	6M $	DS6/^	30$	BBBB$	Ind	10	20/30
Ecology and Geography	CF98	3FT/4EXT deg	Gy g	BBC	4M+2D$	DS^	30$	AABB$	Ind	9	
Landscape Design and Ecology (Grad Dip Opt)	KC39	3FT/4FT deg	B+S g	CCC	6M $	D^	28$	BBBC$	Landsc		
Molecular Biology and Biotechnology Found Yr	C103	4FT deg	g	BCD	6M	DS^	28	BBBC	Ind		

SHEFFIELD HALLAM Univ

TITLE	CODE	COURSE	SUBJECTS	A/AS	ND/C	AGNVQ	IB	SQA(H)	SQA	RATIO	A/AS
Applied Biological Sciences (1 Year)	C120	1FT deg		X	HN	X	X	X	X		

Univ of SOUTHAMPTON

TITLE	CODE	COURSE	SUBJECTS	A/AS	ND/C	AGNVQ	IB	SQA(H)	SQA	RATIO	A/AS
Biology	C100	3FT deg	B g	BCC	5M+1D$	Ind^	28$	BBBBC	Ind	8	18/28
Biology with Chemistry	C1F1	3FT deg	B+C g	BCC	5M+1D$	Ind^	28$	BBBBC	Ind	3	20/24
Biology with Computer Science	C1G5	3FT deg	B+M g	BCC	5M+1D$	Ind^	28$	BBBBC	Ind	18	
Biology with Foundation Year	C108	4FT deg									
Biology with Oceanography	C1F7	3FT deg	B+M/C g	BCC	5M+1D$	Ind^	28$	BBBBC	Ind	4	16/28

TITLE	CODE	COURSE	SUBJECTS	A/AS	ND/C	AGNVQ	IB	SQA(H)	SQA	RATIO	A/AS
course details			**98 expected requirements**							**96 entry stats**	
Geology with Biology	F6C1	3FT deg	B+S g	18-20	Ind	Ind	28$	BBBBC	Ind	3	12/24
Molecular Cell Biology	C140	3FT deg	C+B/P/M/Gy g	BCC	$	M^	$	Ind	Ind	5	14/24
Oceanography with Marine Biology	F7CC	3FT deg	B+S/M g	BBB-BCC	Ind	Ind	30$	ABBBB	Ind	14	20/28
Physiology and Biochemistry with Nutrition	C901	3FT deg	C+B/P/M/Gy g	BCC	$	M^	$	Ind	Ind	4	

SOUTH BANK Univ

TITLE	CODE	COURSE	SUBJECTS	A/AS	ND/C	AGNVQ	IB	SQA(H)	SQA	RATIO	A/AS
Applied Biology	C110	3FT/4SW deg	S/M g	DD	MO	P go	Ind	Ind	Ind		
Foundation Applied Biology	C118	4EXT deg					Ind	Ind	Ind		
Applied Biology	011C	2FT HND	S/2S g	E	N	P go	Ind	Ind	Ind		

SPARSHOLT COLLEGE Hampshire

TITLE	CODE	COURSE	SUBJECTS	A/AS	ND/C	AGNVQ	IB	SQA(H)	SQA	RATIO	A/AS
Applied Biology (Animal Management/Equine Sci)	21DC	2FT HND	S	EE	N	P	Ind	Ind	Ind		

Univ of ST ANDREWS

TITLE	CODE	COURSE	SUBJECTS	A/AS	ND/C	AGNVQ	IB	SQA(H)	SQA	RATIO	A/AS
Behavioural Biology	C155	3FT/4FT deg	B/C/Gy/M/P	BBC	Ind	Ind	28$	BBBB$	Ind	15	
Biology	C100	3FT/4FT deg	B/C/Gy/M/P g	BBC	Ind	Ind	28$	BBBB$	Ind	7	18/28
Biology with French (Science)	C1R1	4FT deg	B/C/Gy/M/P g	BBC	Ind	Ind	28$	BBBB$	Ind	3	
Biology with French (with Integ Year Abroad)	C1RC	4FT/5FT deg	B/C/Gy/M/P g	BBC	Ind	Ind	28$	BBBB$	Ind	7	
Biology with German (Science)	C1R2	4FT deg	B/C/Gy/M/P g	BBC	Ind	Ind	28$	BBBB$	Ind	1	
Biology with German (with Integrated Yr Abroad)	C1RF	4FT/5FT deg	B/C/Gy/M/P g	BBC	X	Ind	28$	BBBB$	Ind	3	
Cell and Molecular Biology	C140	3FT/4FT deg	B/C/Gy/M/P g	CCC	Ind	Ind	28$	BBBC$	Ind	13	
Environmental Biology	C160	3FT/4FT deg	B/C/Gy/M/P g	BBC	Ind	Ind	28$	BBBB$	Ind	39	
Environmental Biology-Geography	FC81	3FT/4FT deg	B/C/Gy/M/P g	BBB	Ind	Ind	30$	BBBB$	Ind	13	
Environmental Biology-Geology	CF16	3FT/4FT deg	B/C/Gy/M/P g	CCC	Ind	Ind	28$	BBBC$	Ind	6	
Environmental Biology-Marine	C176	3FT/4FT deg	B/C/Gy/M/P g	ABB	Ind	Ind	30$	ABBB$	Ind	11	24/30
Environmental Biology-Plant	CC12	3FT/4FT deg	B/C/Gy/M/P g	BBC	Ind	Ind	28$	BBBB$	Ind		
General Degree of BSc *Behavioural Biology*	Y100	3FT deg	B/C/Gy/M/P g	CCC	Ind	Ind	28$	BBBC$	Ind		
General Degree of BSc *Biology*	Y100	3FT deg	B/C/Gy/M/P g	CCC	Ind	Ind	28$	BBBC$	Ind		
General Degree of BSc *Cell and Molecular Biology*	Y100	3FT deg	B/C/Gy/M/P g	CCC	Ind	Ind	28$	BBBC$	Ind		
General Degree of BSc *Environmental Biology*	Y100	3FT deg	B/C/Gy/M/P g	CCC	Ind	Ind	28$	BBBC$	Ind		
General Degree of BSc *Marine and Environmental Biology*	Y100	3FT deg	B/C/Gy/M/P g	CCC	Ind	Ind	28$	BBBC$	Ind		

ST HELENS COLL

TITLE	CODE	COURSE	SUBJECTS	A/AS	ND/C	AGNVQ	IB	SQA(H)	SQA	RATIO	A/AS
Brewing Technology	089C	2FT HND	B/C/P	2	N	P$	Ind	Ind	Ind		

ST MARY'S Univ COLL

TITLE	CODE	COURSE	SUBJECTS	A/AS	ND/C	AGNVQ	IB	SQA(H)	SQA	RATIO	A/AS
Classical Studies and Biology	CQ18	3FT deg	B/C	4-8	Ind	Ind	Ind	BBBB$	Ind		
Education Studies and Biology	CX1X	3FT deg	B/C	4-8	Ind	Ind	Ind	BBBBB$	Ind		
English and Biology	QC31	3FT deg	E+B/C	8-12	X	X	Ind	BBBBB$	X		
Environmental Investigation Studies and Biology	CF18	3FT deg	B/C	4-8	Ind	Ind	Ind	BBBB	Ind		
Environmental Studies and Biology	CF1X	3FT deg	B/C	4-8	Ind	Ind	Ind	BBBB	Ind		
Gender Studies and Biology	CM19	3FT deg	B/C	4-8	Ind	Ind	Ind	BBBBB$	Ind		
Geography and Biology	FC81	3FT deg	Gy+B/C	4-8	Ind	Ind	Ind	BBBBB$	Ind		
Heritage Management and Biology	CN19	3FT deg	B/C	4-8	Ind	Ind	Ind	BBBBB$	Ind		
Irish Studies and Biology	CQ15	3FT deg	B/C	4-8	Ind	Ind	Ind	BBBBB$	Ind		
Management Studies and Biology	CN11	3FT deg	B/C g	4-8	Ind	Ind	Ind	BBBBB$	Ind		
Media Arts and Biology	CP14	3FT deg	B/C	4-8	Ind	Ind	Ind	BBBB	Ind		
Sociology and Biology	CL13	3FT deg	B/C	4-8	Ind	Ind	Ind	BBBBB$	Ind		
Sport Rehabilitation and Biology	BC91	3FT deg	B g	12-14	X	X	Ind	BBBBB$	X		
Sport Science and Biology	CB16	3FT deg	B/C g	8-12	Ind	Ind	Ind	BBBBB$	Ind		
Theology and Religious Studies and Biology	VC81	3FT deg	B/C	4-8	Ind	Ind	Ind	BBBBB$	Ind		

Biology 9

| | | | 98 expected requirements | | | | | | | 96 entry stats | |

TITLE	CODE	COURSE	SUBJECTS	A/AS	ND/C	AGNVQ	IB	SQA(H)	SQA	RATIO	A/AS
STAFFORDSHIRE Univ											
Applied Biology	C110	3FT deg	B	12	4M	M^	24	BCC	Ind	4	6/16
Applied Ecology	C910	3FT deg									
Applied Ecology	C919	4EXT deg	g	4	1M	P	24	CCC		2	
Biology/Applied Statistics	CG14	3FT deg	S	8	3M	M^	24	BCC	Ind	2	
Chemistry/Biology	CF11	3FT deg	S g	8	3M	M	24	BCC	Ind		
Computing/Biology	CG15	3FT deg	S	8	3M	M	24	BCC	Ind	8	
Ecology/Computing	CG95	3FT deg									
Electronics/Biology	CH16	3FT deg	S	8	3M	M	24	BCC	Ind		
Environmental Biology	C160	3FT deg	B	12	4M	M	24	BCC	Ind	6	8/16
Environmental Science and Biology	CF19	3FT deg	S g	8	3M	M	24	BCC	Ind	5	
Extended Applied Biology (4 yr)	C119	4EXT deg	g	4	1M	P	24	CCC	Ind	1	
Extended Environmental Biology (4 yr)	C169	4EXT deg	g	4	1M	P	24	CCC	Ind		
Foundation Applied Biology	C118▼	4EXT deg	*	4	N	P	24	CCC	Ind	4	
Foundation Biology and Chemistry	CF1C▼	4EXT deg	*	4	N	P	24	CCC	Ind		
Foundation Biology and Computing	CG1M▼	4EXT deg	*	4	N	P	24	CCC	Ind	6	
Foundation Biology and Electronics	CH1P▼	4EXT deg	*	4	N	P	24	CCC	Ind		
Foundation Biology and Geology	CF1P	4EXT deg	*	4	N	P	24	CCC			
Foundation Biology and Physics	CF1H▼	4EXT deg	*	4	N	P	24	CCC			
Foundation Environmental Biology	C168▼	4EXT deg	*	4	N	P	24	CCC	Ind		
Geography/Biology	CL18	3FT deg	S/Gy	8	3M	M	24	BCC	Ind	9	
Geography/Ecology	CL98	3FT deg									
Geology/Biology	CF16	3FT deg	S/Gy g	8	3M	M	24	BCC	Ind		
Geology/Ecology	CF96	3FT deg									
Physics/Biology	CF13	3FT deg	S g	8	3M	M	24	BCC	Ind		
Psychology/Biology	CL17	3FT deg	g	18	3M+3D	D/M^	27	BBB	Ind	12	14/18
Sport Sciences and Biology	BC61	3FT deg	S	14	Ind	D	Ind	BBCC	Ind		
Applied Biology	011C	2FT HND	B/C	2	N	P	24	CCC	Ind	7	
Univ of STIRLING											
Aquaculture	C172	4FT deg	S g	CCD	Ind	Ind	28	BBCC	HN		
Biology	C100	4FT deg	S g	CCD	Ind	Ind	28	BBCC	HN		
Biology/Computing Science	CG15	4FT deg	S g	CCD	Ind	Ind	28	BBCC	HN		
Biology/Management Science	CN11	4FT deg	S g	CCD	Ind	Ind	28	BBCC	HN		
Biology/Mathematics	CG11	4FT deg	S+M	CCC	Ind	Ind	28	BBCC	HN		
Biology/Psychology	CC18	4FT deg	S g	CCD	Ind	Ind	28	BBCC	HN		
Ecology	C900	4FT deg	S g	CCD	Ind	Ind	28	BBCC	HN		
Environmental Biology	C160	4FT deg	S g	CCD	Ind	Ind	28	BBCC	HN		
Environmental Science/Biology	CF19	4FT deg	S g	CCC	Ind	Ind	31	BBBC	HN		
Marine Biology	C170	4FT deg	S g	CCD	Ind	Ind	28	BBCC	HN		
Mathematics and its Applications with Biology	G1C1	4FT deg	M+S g	CCC	Ind	Ind	28	BBCC	HN		
Molecular and Cell Biology	CC16	4FT deg	S g	CCD	Ind	Ind	28	BBCC	HN		
STOCKPORT COLL of F and HE											
Biology	C100	4FT deg	B+M/C	EE	N	PS	Dip	BBCC	N		
Univ of STRATHCLYDE											
Biochemistry and Immunology	CC79	4FT deg	C+B+M/P g	CCC	Ind		Ind	BBC$	Ind		
Biological Sciences	C120	3FT deg	C+B+M/P g	CCC	HN		Ind	BBC$	HN		
Bioscience with Modelling	C910	4FT deg	C+B+M/P g	CCC	HN		Ind	BBC$	HN		
Environmental Health	CH92	4FT deg	M+C+P/B	CCC	HN		36$	BBBB$	HN		
Immunology and Microbiology	CC59	4FT deg	C+B+M/P g	CCC	Ind		Ind	BBC$	Ind		
Immunology and Pharmacology	CB92	4FT deg	C+B+M/P g	CCC	Ind		Ind	BBC$	Ind		
Mathematical Biology	GC11	4FT deg	M+C g	CD	Ind		30$	BBCC$	Ind		

course details			98 expected requirements							96 entry stats	
TITLE	CODE	COURSE	SUBJECTS	A/AS	ND/C	RGNVQ	IB	SQA(H)	SQA	RATIO A/AS	
Science Studies (Pass Degree)	Y100	3FT deg	M+S	DD	Ind		Ind	CCC$	Ind		
Biology											
UNIVERSITY COLLEGE SUFFOLK											
Applied Biological Sci and Early Childhood Studs	CX19	3FT deg	S	ED	N $	PS	Ind	Ind	Ind		
Applied Biological Sci with Early Childhood St	C1X9	3FT deg	S	EE	N $	PS	Ind	Ind	Ind		
Applied Biological Science and Environmental St	CF19	3FT deg	S	EE	N $	PS	Ind	Ind	Ind		
Applied Biological Science and Information Techn	CG15	3FT deg	S	EE	N $	PS	Ind	Ind	Ind		
Applied Biological Science with Art & Design	C1W2	3FT deg	S+Pf	EE	N $	PS	Ind	Ind	Ind		
Applied Biological Science with Behavioural St	C1L3	3FT deg	S	EE	N $	PS	Ind	Ind	Ind		
Applied Biological Science with Business Studies	C1N1	3FT deg	S	EE	N $	PS	Ind	Ind	Ind		
Applied Biological Science with Cultural Studies	C1Y3	3FT deg	S	EE	N $	PS	Ind	Ind	Ind		
Applied Biological Science with Education Studs	C1XX	3FT deg	S	EE	N $	PS	Ind	Ind	Ind		
Applied Biological Science with Environmental St	C1F9	3FT deg	S	EE	N $	PS	Ind	Ind	Ind		
Applied Biological Science with Human Science	C1B1	3FT deg	S	EE	N $	PS	Ind	Ind	Ind		
Applied Biological Science with Information Tech	C1G5	3FT deg	S	EE	N $	PS	Ind	Ind	Ind		
Applied Biological Science with Literary Studies	C1Q2	3FT deg	S	EE	N $	PS	Ind	Ind	Ind		
Applied Biological Science with Management	C1NC	3FT deg	S	EE	N $	PS	Ind	Ind	Ind		
Applied Biological Science with Media Studies	C1P4	3FT deg	S	EE	N $	PS	Ind	Ind	Ind		
Applied Biological Science with Social Policy	C1L4	3FT deg	S	EE	N $	PS	Ind	Ind	Ind		
Art & Design and Applied Biological Science	EC21	3FT deg	Pf	EE	N $	P$	Ind	Ind	Ind		
Art & Design and Applied Biological Science	WC21	3FT deg	Pf	EE	N $	P$	Ind	Ind	Ind		
Behavioural Studies with Applied Biological Sci	L7C1	3FT deg	S	DD	N $	P$	Ind	Ind	Ind		
Business Studies and Applied Biological Science	CN11	3FT deg	S	EE	N $	P$	Ind	Ind	Ind		
Business Studies with Applied Biological Science	N1C9	3FT deg	S	EE	N $	P$	Ind	Ind	Ind		
Cultural Studies and Applied Biological Science	YC31	3FT deg	S	CE	N $	P$	Ind	Ind	Ind		
Early Childhood Studies with Applied Biol Sci	X9CC	3FT deg	S	DD	N $	P$	Ind	Ind	Ind		
Environmental Studies with Applied Biol Science	F9C1	3FT deg	S/Gy	EE	N $	P$	Ind	Ind	Ind		
Information Technology with Appl Biological Sci	G5C1	3FT deg	S	EE	N $	P$	Ind	Ind	Ind		
Literary Studies and Applied Biological Science	QC21	3FT deg	E/S	CE	N $	P$	Ind	Ind	Ind		
Media Studies and Applied Biological Science	CP14	3FT deg	S	CE	N $	P$	Ind	Ind	Ind		
Media Studies with Applied Biological Science	P4C1	3FT deg	*	CE	N $	P$	Ind	Ind	Ind		
Product Design & Manuf with Applied Biol Science	H7C1	3FT deg	*	EE	N $	P$	Ind	Ind	Ind		
Product Design & Manufacture & Applied Biol Sci	HC71	3FT deg	S	EE	N $	P$	Ind	Ind	Ind		
Univ of SUNDERLAND											
Biocomputing	CG1M	3FT deg	* g	4-8	4M	M*	24	CCCC	N		
Biological Science	C110▼	3FT/4SW deg	B+C g	10	N $	PS	24$	CCCC$	N$	5	5/16
Biological Science (Foundation)	C118▼	4EXT/5EXTSW deg	*							2	
Biology and Chemistry	CF11▼	3FT deg	C+B g	8	N $		24$	CCCC$	N$	4	
Biology and Computer Studies	CG15	3FT deg	B/C g	8	N $	M	24$	CCCC$	N$	3	
Biology and Economics	CL11	3FT deg	B/C	8	3M	M	Ind	Ind	Ind		
Biology and English	CQ13	3FT deg	B/C	10	4M	M	Ind	Ind	Ind		
Biology and French	CR11▼	4FT deg	B/C+F g	8	N $	M	24$	CCCC$	N$		
Biology and Geography	CL18▼	3FT deg	B+Gy/Gl g	10	N $	M	24$	CCCC$	N$	5	
Biology and Geology	CF16	3FT deg	B/C+Gy/Gl g	8	N $	M	24$	CCCC$	N$	2	
Biology and German	CR12▼	4FT deg	B/C+G g	8	N $	M	24$	CCCC$	N$		
Biology and History	CV11	3FT deg	B/C	10	4M	M	Ind	Ind	Ind		
Biology and History of Art and Design	CV14	3FT deg	B/C	8	3M	M	Ind	Ind	Ind		
Biology and Mathematics	CG11	3FT deg	B/C+M g	8	N $	M	24$	CCCC$	N$		
Biology and Media Studies	CP14	3FT deg	B/C	24	Ind	Ind	Ind	Ind	Ind		
Biology and Physiology	CB11▼	3FT deg	B/C g	8	N $	M	24$	CCCC$	N$	2	
Biology and Psychology	CC18	3FT deg	g	`12	MO	M	24$	BCCC$	N	5	10/16
Biology and Religious Studies	CV18	3FT deg	B/C	8	3M	M	Ind	Ind	Ind		

Biology 9

	course details			98 expected requirements							96 entry stats
TITLE	CODE	COURSE	SUBJECTS	A/AS	ND/C	RGNVQ	IB	SQA(H)	SQA	RATIO A/AS	
Biology and Sociology	CL13	3FT deg	B/C	10	4M	M	Ind	Ind	Ind		
Biology with American Studies	C1Q4	3FT deg	B/C	8	3M	M	Ind	Ind	Ind		
Biology with Chemistry	C1F1	3FT deg	B/C	8	3M	M	Ind	Ind	Ind		
Biology with Comparative Literature	C1Q2	3FT deg	B/C	8	3M	M	Ind	Ind	Ind		
Biology with Economics	C1L1	3FT deg	B/C	8	3M	M	Ind	Ind	Ind		
Biology with English	C1Q3	3FT deg	B/C	10	4M	M	Ind	Ind	Ind		
Biology with European Studies	C1T2	3FT deg	B/C	8	3M	M	Ind	Ind	Ind		
Biology with French	C1R1	3FT deg	B/C	8	3M	M	Ind	Ind	Ind		
Biology with Geography	C1L8	3FT deg	B/C	8	3M	M	Ind	Ind	Ind		
Biology with Geology	C1F6	3FT deg	B/C	8	3M	M	Ind	Ind	Ind		
Biology with German	C1R2	3FT deg	B/C	8	3M	M	Ind	Ind	Ind		
Biology with History	C1V1	3FT deg	B/C	10	4M	M	Ind	Ind	Ind		
Biology with History of Art and Design	C1V4	3FT deg	B/C	8	3M	M	Ind	Ind	Ind		
Biology with Mathematics	C1G1	3FT deg	B/C	8	3M	M	Ind	Ind	Ind		
Biology with Media Studies	C1P4	3FT deg	B/C	24	6M	X	Ind	Ind	Ind		
Biology with Physiology	C1B1	3FT deg	B/C	8	3M	M	Ind	Ind	Ind		
Biology with Psychology	C1C8	3FT deg	B/C	10	4M	M^	Ind	Ind	Ind		
Biology with Religious Studies	C1V8	3FT deg	B/C	8	3M	M	Ind	Ind	Ind		
Biology with Sociology	C1L3	3FT deg	B/C	10	4M	M	Ind	Ind	Ind		
Economics with Biology	L1C1	3FT deg	*	8	3M	M	Ind	Ind	Ind		
English with Biology	Q3C1	3FT deg	B/C	10	4M	M	Ind	Ind	Ind		
Environmental Biology	C160▼	3FT/4SW deg	B/C g	8	3M $	M$	24$	CCCC$	N$	4	6/10
Environmental Biology (Foundation)	C168▼	4EXT deg	*		Ind	Ind	Ind	Ind	Ind	1	
French with Biology	R1C1	3FT deg	F+B/C	8	3M	M	Ind	Ind	Ind		
Geography with Biology	L8C1	3FT deg	*	8	3M	M	Ind	Ind	Ind		
Geology with Biology	F6C1	3FT deg	*	8	3M	M	Ind	Ind	Ind		
German with Biology	R2C1	4SW deg	G	8	3M	M	Ind	Ind	Ind		
History with Biology	V1C1	3FT deg	*	10	4M	M	Ind	Ind	Ind		
Mathematics with Biology	G1C1	3FT deg	M	8	3M	M	Ind	Ind	Ind		
Media Studies with Biology	P4C1	3FT deg	*	24	Ind	Ind	Ind	Ind	Ind		
Physiology with Biology	B1C1	3FT deg	*	8	3M	M	Ind	Ind	Ind		
Psychology with Biology	C8C1	3FT deg	*	10	4M	M^	Ind	Ind	Ind		
Religious Studies with Biology	V8C1	3FT deg	*	3M	M	Ind	Ind	Ind	Ind		
Sociology with Biology	L3C1	3FT deg	*	10	4M	M	Ind	Ind	Ind		
Applied Biology	011C	2FT/3SW HND	B/C g	2	Ind	PS	24$	CC$	X	2	2/6

Univ of SUSSEX

Biochemistry with Neurobiology	C7C1	3FT deg	C+S g	BCD	MO $	MS6 go	$	Ind	Ind		
Biological Sciences	C120▼	4FT deg									
Biology	C100	3FT deg	2S g	BCC	MO $	MS6 go	$	Ind	Ind		
Biology with European Studies (French)	C1R1	4FT deg	2S g	BCC	MO $	MS6 go	$	Ind	Ind		
Biology with European Studies (German)	C1R2	4FT deg	2S g	BCC	MO $	MS6 go	$	Ind	Ind		
Biology with European Studies (Spanish)	C1R4	4FT deg	2S g	BCC	MO $	MS6 go	$	Ind	Ind		
Biology with Management Studies	C1N1	3FT deg	2S g	BCC	MO $	MS6 go	$	Ind	Ind		
Biology with North American Studies	C1Q4	4FT deg	2S g	BBC	MO $	MS6 go	$	Ind	Ind		
Ecology and Conservation	CD92	3FT deg	S g	BCC	MO $	MS6 go	$	Ind	Ind		

Univ of Wales SWANSEA

Biological Sciences	C102	3FT deg	B	BCC-CCC	2M+3D$	DS^	28$	BBBCC$	Ind	7	14/26
Biological Sciences	C101	4FT deg	*		Ind	DS go	Ind	Ind	Ind	1	
Biological Sciences (with French)	C1R1	4FT deg	B+F	BCC	X	X	28$	ABBCC$	Ind	5	
Biological Sciences (with German)	C1R2	4FT deg	B+G	BCC	X	X	28$	ABBCC$	Ind	12	
Biological Sciences (with Italian)	C1R3	4FT deg	B	BCC	X	X	28$	ABBCC$	Ind	5	
Biological Sciences (with Spanish)	C1R4	4FT deg	B+Sp	BCC	X	X	28$	ABBCC$	Ind	3	

TITLE	CODE	COURSE	SUBJECTS	A/AS	ND/C	AGNVQ	IB	SQA(H)	SQA	RATIO	A/AS
Biological Sciences and Geography	CL18	3FT deg	B+Gy	BBC-BCC	1M+5D$	Ind	28$	BBBBB$	Ind	6	16/24
Biological Sciences and Psychology	CC18	3FT deg	B g	BBC	1M+5D$	Ind	30$	ABBBB$	Ind	7	18/26
Biological Sciences with deferred choice of spec	C100	3FT deg	B	BCC-CCC	2M+3D$	DS^	28$	BBBCC$	Ind	13	14/26
Biology	C104	3FT deg	B+C	CCC	2M+3D$	DS^	28$	BBBCC$	Ind	6	14/20
Environmental Biology	C160	3FT deg	B	BCC-CCC	2M+3D$	DS^	28$	BBBCC$	Ind	6	12/24
Marine Biology	C170	3FT deg	B	BCC	1M+5D$	X	28$	ABBCC$	Ind	8	14/26

THAMES VALLEY Univ

TITLE	CODE	COURSE	SUBJECTS	A/AS	ND/C	AGNVQ	IB	SQA(H)	SQA	RATIO	A/AS
Food and Drink Consumer St with Culinary Arts	D4C9	3FT deg		8-12	MO	M	26	CCC			
Hospitality Management with Culinary Arts	N7C9	3FT deg		8-12	MO	M	26	CCC			
Leisure Management with Culinary Arts	N7CX	3FT deg		8-12	MO	M	26	CCC			

Univ of ULSTER

TITLE	CODE	COURSE	SUBJECTS	A/AS	ND/C	AGNVQ	IB	SQA(H)	SQA	RATIO	A/AS
Biological Sciences (3 Yrs)	C102▼	3FT deg	B	CDD	MO+1D	M*6/^ gi	26	BCCC	Ind	107	
Biological Sciences Hons (4 Yr SW inc DIS)	C100▼	4SW deg	B g	CCD	MO+2D	DS6/^ gi	27	BBCC	Ind	9	14/20
Biotechnology (4 Yr SW inc DIS)	C930▼	4SW deg	B g	CCD	MO+2D	DS6/^ gi	27	BBCC	Ind	14	20/20
Science with Management (4 Yr SW inc Dip)	C9N1▼	4SW deg	B/C g	CCD	MO+2D	DS6/^ gi	27	BBCC	Ind	9	14/20
Science (Applied Biology)	001C▼	2FT HND	B+C g		Ind	MS gi	Ind	Ind	Ind	7	7/14
Science (Chemistry with Biology)	1C1F▼	2FT HND	C g		Ind	MS gi	Ind	Ind	Ind	6	4/12

UNIVERSITY COLL LONDON (Univ of London)

TITLE	CODE	COURSE	SUBJECTS	A/AS	ND/C	AGNVQ	IB	SQA(H)	SQA	RATIO	A/AS
Biology	C100	3FT deg	C+B/M/P g	BCC-BBB	3M+2D$	Ind	32$	Ind	Ind	7	20/30
Cell Biology	C140	3FT deg	C+B/M/P g	CCC-BBC	MO+2D$	Ind	32$	Ind	Ind	2	20/24
Ecology	C910	3FT deg	C+B/M/P g	BCC-BBB	3M+2D$	Ind	32$	Ind	Ind	11	
Immunology	C920	3FT deg	C+2(B/M/P) g	BBC	MO+2D$	Ind	32$	Ind	Ind	4	22/28

Univ of WARWICK

TITLE	CODE	COURSE	SUBJECTS	A/AS	ND/C	AGNVQ	IB	SQA(H)	SQA	RATIO	A/AS
Biological Sciences	C100	3FT deg	C/S+B g	20	DO $	DS^	28$	BBBBC$		9	16/28

Univ of WESTMINSTER

TITLE	CODE	COURSE	SUBJECTS	A/AS	ND/C	AGNVQ	IB	SQA(H)	SQA	RATIO	A/AS
Applied Biology	C110	3FT deg	B/C	CC-CD	3M	M			Ind		
Applied Ecology	C910	3FT deg		CC-CD	3M	M			Ind		
Biological Sciences	C120	3FT deg	B/C	CC-CD	3M	M			Ind	5	4/14
Biological Sciences (4 years with foundation)	C128	4EXT deg	B/C	DD	3M					2	
Applied Biology	011C	2FT HND	B/C	D	2M					11	

WIRRAL METROPOLITAN COLLEGE

TITLE	CODE	COURSE	SUBJECTS	A/AS	ND/C	AGNVQ	IB	SQA(H)	SQA	RATIO	A/AS
Life Sciences	C980	4FT deg			Ind	Ind	Ind	Ind	Ind		

Univ of WOLVERHAMPTON

TITLE	CODE	COURSE	SUBJECTS	A/AS	ND/C	AGNVQ	IB	SQA(H)	SQA	RATIO	A/AS
Biological Sciences	C120	3FT/4SW deg	B g	DD	N	M	24	CCCC	Ind	3	4/20
Ecology	C910	3FT/4SW deg		DD	N	M	24	CCCC	Ind		
Applied Sciences *Biology*	Y100	3FT/4SW deg	B g	DD	N	M	24	CCCC$	Ind		
Applied Sciences *Ecology*	Y100	3FT/4SW deg		DD	N	M	24	CCCC	Ind		
Applied Sciences *Human Biology*	Y100	3FT/4SW deg	S g	DD	N	M	24	CCCC	Ind		
Applied Sciences (4 Yrs) *Biology*	Y110	4FT deg	*								
Applied Sciences (4 Yrs) *Ecology*	Y110	4FT deg	*								
Applied Sciences (4 Yrs) *Human Biology*	Y110▼	4FT deg	*								
Combined Degrees *Biology*	Y401	3FT/4SW deg	B g	DD	N	M	24	CCCC	Ind		
Combined Degrees *Ecology*	Y401	3FT/4SW deg		DD	N	M	24	CCCC	Ind		

Biology 9

	course details			98 expected requirements							96 entry stats
TITLE	CODE	COURSE	SUBJECTS	A/AS	NO/C	AGNVQ	IB	SQA(H)	SQA	RATIO A/AS
Combined Degrees *Human Biology*	Y401	3FT/4SW deg	S g	DD	N	M	24	CCCC	Ind	
Applied Biology	011C	2FT HND	B g	D	N	M	24	CCCC$	Ind	6

WORCESTER COLL of HE

TITLE	CODE	COURSE	SUBJECTS	A/AS	NO/C	AGNVQ	IB	SQA(H)	SQA	RATIO A/AS
Biological Science	C120	3FT deg	S	EE	N	P	Ind	Ind	Ind	3
Biological Science/Art and Design	WC91	3FT deg	S+A	DD	Ind	Ind	Ind	Ind	Ind	
Business Management/Biological Science	CN11	3FT deg	S	DD	Ind	M	Ind	Ind	Ind	
Drama/Biological Science	CW14	3FT deg	S	DD	Ind	M	Ind	Ind	Ind	3
Economy and Society/Biological Science	CL11	3FT deg	S	DD	Ind	M	Ind	Ind	Ind	
Education Studies/Biological Science	CX19	3FT deg	S	DD	Ind	M	Ind	Ind	Ind	10
Environmental Science/Biological Science	CF19	3FT deg	S	EE	N	P	Ind	Ind	Ind	1
Geography/Biological Science	CL18	3FT deg	S	EE	N	P	Ind	Ind	Ind	
Health Studies/Biological Science	CB19	3FT deg	S g	DD	Ind	M	Ind	Ind	Ind	1
History/Biological Science	CV11	3FT deg	S	DD	Ind	M	Ind	Ind	Ind	
Information Technology/Biological Science	CG15	3FT deg	S	DD	Ind	M	Ind	Ind	Ind	
Psychology/Biological Science	CL17	3FT deg	S g	CC	Ind	M	Ind	Ind	Ind	4
Sociology/Biological Science	CL13	3FT deg	S	DD	Ind	M	Ind	Ind	Ind	
Sports Studies/Biological Science	CB16	3FT deg	S	CC	Ind	M	Ind	Ind	Ind	
Urban Studies/Biological Science	CL1V	3FT deg	S	DE	Ind	Ind	Ind	Ind	Ind	

WYE COLL (Univ of London)

TITLE	CODE	COURSE	SUBJECTS	A/AS	NO/C	AGNVQ	IB	SQA(H)	SQA	RATIO A/AS
Biology	C100	3FT deg	C+B	14	2M+1D$	Ind	25$	BBCCC$	Ind	
Environmental Biology	C160	3FT deg	B/C	14	2M+1D$	Ind	25$	BBCCC$	Ind	

Univ of YORK

TITLE	CODE	COURSE	SUBJECTS	A/AS	NO/C	AGNVQ	IB	SQA(H)	SQA	RATIO A/AS
Animal Physiology	C184	4SW deg	B+C g	BCC	5M $	MS6/^	28$	BBBB$	N$	
Animal Physiology	C182	3FT deg	B+C g	BCC	5M $	MS6/^	28$	BBBB$	N$	
Applied and Environmental Biology	C160	3FT deg	B+C g	BCC	5M $	MS6/^	28$	BBBB$	N$	
Applied and Environmental Biology	C164	4SW deg	B+C g	BCC	5M $	MS6/^	28$	BBBB$	N$	
Biology	C100	3FT deg	B+C g	BCC	5M $	MS6/^	28$	BBBB$	N$	18/28
Biology (4 Yr SW)	C107	4SW deg	B+C g	BCC	5M $	MS6/^	28$	BBBB$	N$	18/26
Biology (with a year in Europe) (4 Yrs)	C101	4SW deg	B+C g	BCC	5M $	MS6/^	28$	BBBB$	N$	
Biology/Education	C1X9	3FT deg	B+C g	BCC	5M $	MS6/^	28$	BBBB$	N$	
Ecology, Conservation and Environment	C910	3FT deg	B+C g	BCC	5M $	MS6/^	28$	BBBB$	N$	
Ecology, Conservation and Environment (4 Yr SW)	C914	4SW deg	B+C g	BCC	5M $	MS6/^	28$	BBBB$	N$	
Environmental Biology and Env Management	CC91	3FT deg	B+S/M/Ec g	BBC	Ind	DS^	28$	BBBB$	Ind	20/30
Environmental Economics and Env Management	CL91	3FT deg	M/S g	BBC	Ind	DS^	28$	BBBB$	Ind	16/30
Mathematics/Biostatistics	G1CX	3FT deg	M	22	HN$	D$^	30$	CSYS$	HN$	
Molecular Cell Biology	C144	4SW deg	B+C g	BCC	5M $	MS6/^	28$	BBBB$	N$	
Molecular Cell Biology	C140	3FT deg	B+C g	BCC	5M $	MS6/^	28$	BBBB$	N$	

course details			98 expected requirements							96 entry stats
TITLE	CODE	COURSE	SUBJECTS	A/AS	NO/C	RGNVQ	IB	SQA(H)	SQA	RATIO A/AS
Univ of ABERDEEN										
Geography with Plant Science	F8C2	4FT deg	3S/2S+M g	CCD	Ind	MS go	24$	BBBC$	Ind	
Plant Science	C200	4FT deg	3S/2S+M g	CCD	Ind	MS go	24$	BBBC$	Ind	8
Plant Science (Cell and Molecular)	C250	4FT deg	3S/2S+M g	CCD	Ind	MS go	24$	BBBC$	Ind	
Plant Science (Plant Ecology)	C260	4FT deg	3S/2S+M g	CCD	Ind	MS go	24$	BBBC$	Ind	3
Plant and Soil Science	CDFX	4FT deg	3S/2S+M g	CCD	Ind	MS go	24$	BBBC$	Ind	3
Univ of ABERTAY DUNDEE										
Plant & Animal Cell Biotechnology	C9C2	4FT deg	B/C	DE	Ind	Ind	Ind	BCC	Ind	
Univ of Wales, ABERYSTWYTH										
Botany	C200	3FT deg	B/C g	16-18	3M $	MS6/^ g	29$	BBBCC$	Ind	
Information and Library St/an approved Sci Sub *Botany*	PY21	3FT deg	B/C g	16-18	3M $	MS6/^ g	29$	BBBCC$	Ind	
Univ of Wales, BANGOR										
Botany with Marine Botany	C208	3FT deg	B g	CD	3M $	D$^ go	26$	BBBC$	Ind	3
Plant Biology	C200	3FT deg	B g	CDD	3M $	D$^ go	26$	BBBC$	Ind	3
BARNSLEY COLL										
Science Foundation *Molecular Biology*	Y100	4EXT deg								
Science Foundation *Plant Sciences*	Y100	4EXT deg								
Univ of BIRMINGHAM										
Biological Sciences (Plant Biology)	C260	3FT deg	B+S/M/Gy/Gl/Ps g	BCC	Ind	Ind	30	Ind	Ind	
Univ of BRISTOL										
Botany	C200	3FT deg	B+S g	BBC	Ind	D$^	32$	CSYS	Ind	24
BRISTOL, Univ of the W of England										
Applied Plant Biology	C210	4SW deg	B+C g	12	4M $	MS go	24$	BCC$	Ind	
CAMBRIDGE Univ										
Natural Sciences *Plant Sciences*	Y160▼	3FT deg	2(S/M) g	AAA-AAB	Ind		Ind	CSYS	Ind	
Univ of DUNDEE										
Botany	C200	4FT deg	C+S/2S g	16	5M $	M$	25$	BBBC$	N$	
Univ of DURHAM										
Plant Sciences	C200	3FT deg	B+C	BCC-CCC	3M+2D$	Ind	28	AAABB	Ind	
Univ of EAST ANGLIA										
Plant Biology	C260	3FT deg	C+P/M/B	CCC	3D $		28$	BBBCC$	Ind	
Univ of EDINBURGH										
Plant Science	C200	4FT deg	C+2(B/M/P) g	BBC	MO $		Dip$	BBBB$	N$	11
Univ of GLASGOW										
Botany	C200	4FT deg	C/M+S	BBC-CCC	N	M	24$	BBBB$	N	5
Botany (with work placement)	C201	4FT deg	C/M+S	BBC-CCC	N	M	24$	BBBB$	N	
IMPERIAL COLL (Univ of London)										
Plant Science	C200	3FT deg	B+C/M/P	BCC	MO+2D	Ind	30$	Ind	Ind	7
Univ of LEEDS										
Biochemistry-Molecular Plant Biology	CC27	3FT/4FT deg	C+B g	BCC	1M+5D$	Ind	28$	BBBBC	Ind	
Molecular Plant Biology	C250	3FT/4FT deg	B+C g	BCC	1M+4D$	Ind	28$	BBBBC	Ind	

Botany 10

course details			**98 expected requirements**							**96 entry stats**
TITLE	CODE	COURSE	SUBJECTS	A/AS	NO/C	RGNVQ	IB	SQA(H)	SQA	RATIO A/AS
Univ of LEICESTER										
Biological Sciences (Plant Science)	C200	3FT deg	B+C g	18-20	DO $	D$4/^ gi	28$	BBBCC$	Ind	
Univ of LIVERPOOL										
Plant Science	C200	3FT deg	B+S g	18	MO $	DS^ go	31$	BBBCC$	Ind	
BSc Combined Honours *Plant Science*	Y100	3FT deg	B	18	MO $	Ind	31$	BBBCC$	Ind	
LIVERPOOL JOHN MOORES Univ										
Applied Plant Science	C210	3FT/4SW deg		8	3M	M				
Applied Plant Science (Foundation)	C218	4FT/5SW deg								
LUTON Univ										
Business Systems with Plant Biology	N1CF	3FT deg	g	12-16	MO/DO	M/D	32	BBCC	Ind	
Business with Plant Biology	N1C2	3FT deg	g	12-16	MO/DO	M/D	32	BBCC	Ind	
Environmental Science with Plant Biology	F9C2	3FT deg	g	12-16	MO/DO	M/D	32	BBCC	Ind	
Environmental Studies with Plant Biology	F9CF	3FT deg		12-16	MO/DO	M/D	32	BBCC	Ind	
European Language Studies with Plant Biology	T2C2	4FT deg	L g	12-16	MO/DO	M/D	32	BBCC	Ind	
Geography with Plant Biology	F8C2	3FT deg	g	12-16	MO/DO	M/D	32	BBCC	Ind	
Geology with Plant Biology	F6C2	3FT deg	g	12-16	MO/DO	M/D	32	BBCC	Ind	
Health Science with Plant Biology	B9C2	3FT deg	g	12-16	MO/DO	M/D	32	BBCC	Ind	
Health Studies with Plant Biology	B9CF	3FT deg		12-16	MO/DO	M/D	32	BBCC	Ind	
Leisure Studies with Plant Biology	N7C2	3FT deg	g	12-16	MO/DO	M/D	32	BBCC	Ind	
Marketing with Plant Biology	N5C2	3FT deg	g	12-16	MO/DO	M/D	32	BBCC	Ind	
Physical Geography with Plant Biology	F8CF	3FT deg	g	12-16	MO/DO	M/D	32	BBCC	Ind	
Plant Biology and Business	CN21	3FT deg	g	12-16	MO/DO	M/D	32	BBCC	Ind	
Plant Biology and Business Systems	CN2C	3FT deg	g	12-16	MO/DO	M/D	32	BBCC	Ind	
Plant Biology and Computer Science	CG25	3FT deg	g	12-16	MO/DO	M/D	32	BBCC	Ind	
Plant Biology and Environmental Science	CF29	3FT deg	g	12-16	MO/DO	M/D	32	BBCC	Ind	
Plant Biology and European Language Studies	CT22	3FT deg	L g	12-16	MO/DO	M/D	32	BBCC	Ind	
Plant Biology and Geography	CF28	3FT deg	Gy	12-16	MO/DO	M/D	32	BBCC	Ind	
Plant Biology and Geology	CF26	3FT deg	g	12-16	MO/DO	M/D	32	BBCC	Ind	
Plant Biology and Health Science	BC92	3FT deg	g	12-16	MO/DO	M/D	32	BBCC	Ind	
Plant Biology and Health Studies	BCX2	3FT deg	g	12-16	MO/DO	M/D	32	BBCC	Ind	
Plant Biology and Leisure Studies	CN27	3FT deg	g	12-16	MO/DO	M/D	32	BBCC	Ind	
Plant Biology and Marketing	CN25	3FT deg	g	12-16	MO/DO	M/D	32	BBCC	Ind	
Plant Biology and Physical Geography	CF2V	3FT deg	g	12-16	MO/DO	M/D	32	BBCC	Ind	
Plant Biology with Business	C2N1	3FT deg	g	12-16	MO/DO	M/D	32	BBCC	Ind	
Plant Biology with Business Systems	C2NC	3FT deg	g	12-16	MO/DO	M/D	32	BBCC	Ind	
Plant Biology with Environmental Science	C2F9	3FT deg	g	12-16	MO/DO	M/D	32	BBCC	Ind	
Plant Biology with French	C2R1	3FT deg	F g	12-16	MO/DO	M/D	32	BBCC	Ind	
Plant Biology with Geography	C2F8	3FT deg	g	12-16	MO/DO	DS^	32	BBCC	Ind	
Plant Biology with Geology	C2F6	3FT deg	g	12-16	MO/DO	M/D	32	BBCC	Ind	
Plant Biology with Health Science	C2B9	3FT deg	g	12-16	MO/DO	M/D	32	BBCC	Ind	
Plant Biology with Health Studies	C2BX	3FT deg		12-16	MO/DO	M/D	32	BBCC	Ind	
Plant Biology with Leisure Studies	C2N7	3FT deg	g	12-16	MO/DO	M/D	32	BBCC	Ind	
Plant Biology with Marketing	C2N5	3FT deg	g	12-16	MO/DO	M/D	32	BBCC	Ind	
Plant Biology with Physical Geography	C2FV	3FT deg	g	12-16	MO/DO	M/D	32	BBCC	Ind	
Plant Biology with Psychology	C2L7	3FT deg	g	12-16	MO/DO	M/D	32	BBCC	Ind	
Plant Biology with Public Policy & Management	C2M1	3FT deg	g	12-16	MO/DO	M/D	32	BBCC	Ind	
Plant Biology with Regional Planning and Dev	C2K4	3FT deg	g	12-16	MO/DO	M/D	32	BBCC	Ind	
Plant Biology with Travel & Tourism	C2P7	3FT deg	g	12-16	MO/DO	M/D	32	BBCC	Ind	
Psychology and Plant Biology	CL27	3FT deg	g	12-16	MO/DO	M/D	32	BBCC	Ind	
Psychology with Plant Biology	L7C2	3FT deg	g	12-16	MO/DO	M/D	32	BBCC	Ind	

course details   98 expected requirements   96 entry stats

TITLE	CODE	COURSE	SUBJECTS	A/AS	ND/C	AGNVQ	IB	SQA(H)	SQA	RATIO A/AS
Public Policy & Management with Plant Biology	M1C2	3FT deg	g	12-16	MO/DO	M/D	32	BBCC	Ind	
Public Policy and Management and Plant Biology	CM21	3FT deg	g	12-16	MO/DO	M/D	32	BBCC	Ind	
Regional Planning & Develop with Plant Biology	K4C2	3FT deg	g	12-16	MO/DO	M/D	32	BBCC	Ind	
Regional Planning & Development & Plant Biology	CK24	3FT deg	g	12-16	MO/DO	M/D	32	BBCC	Ind	
Travel & Tourism with Plant Biology	P7C2	3FT deg	g	12-16	MO/DO	M/D	32	BBCC	Ind	
Travel and Tourism and Plant Biology	CP27	3FT deg	g	12-16	MO/DO	M/D	32	BBCC	Ind	

Univ of MANCHESTER

Plant Science	C200	3FT deg	B+C	BCD	3M+3D$	D^	26$	BBBCC$	Ind	5
Plant Science with Industrial Experience	C210	4SW deg	B+C	BCD	3M+3D$	D^	26$	BBBCC$	Ind	
Plant Science with a Modern Language	C201	4FT deg	B+C+L	BCD	3M+3D$	D^	26$	BBBCC$	Ind	

Univ of NEWCASTLE

Plant Science	C260	3FT deg	2S g	CCC-CCD	Ind	Ind	26$	ABBB$	Ind	2

Univ of NOTTINGHAM

Plant Life Science	C2C5	3FT deg	B+C/M g	BCC	Ind	Ind	Ind	Ind	Ind	14

NOTTINGHAM TRENT Univ

Plant and Environmental Biology	CF29	4SW deg	S g	DDE	Ind	Ind	Dip	C	$	2

Univ of PLYMOUTH

Plant Sciences	C200	3FT/4SW deg	B g	10-14	4M $	MS	Ind	BBC	Ind	2 6/16

QUEEN'S Univ Belfast

Plant Science	C260	3FT/4FT deg	C+B g	CCC	Ind	Ind	28$	BBBC	Ind	

Univ of READING

Botany	C200	3FT deg	B g	16	5M $	DS^ go	28$	BBBC$	Ind	4 19/28
Botany and Zoology	CC23	3FT deg	B g	16	5M $	DS^ go	28$	BBBC$	Ind	5 12/18
Environmental Plant Science	C254	3FT deg	2S g	16	5M$	DS^ go	28$	BBBC$	Ind	3

ROYAL HOLLOWAY, Univ of London

Botany (Plant Biology)	C200	3FT deg	B+C/S g	BCC	4M	DS^	28$	BBBCC$		11
Science Foundation Year *Botany*	Y100	4FT deg	*		Ind	Ind	Ind	Ind		

Univ of SHEFFIELD

Plant Sciences	C200	3FT deg	2S g	20	6M $	DS6/^	30$	BBBB$	Ind	12

Univ of SOUTHAMPTON

Plant Science	C200	3FT deg	B g	BCC	5M+1D$	Ind^	28$	BBBBC	Ind	

Univ of ST ANDREWS

Environmental Biology-Plant	CC12	3FT/4FT deg	B/C/Gy/M/P g	BBC	Ind	Ind	28$	BBBB$	Ind	

Univ of WOLVERHAMPTON

Plant & Crop Science	CD2F	3FT/4SW deg		DD	N	M	24	CCCC	Ind	

WYE COLL (Univ of London)

Plant Sciences	C200	3FT deg	C+B	14	2M+1D$	Ind	25$	BBCCC$	Ind	

course details			98 expected requirements							96 entry stats
TITLE	CODE	COURSE	SUBJECTS	A/AS	ND/C	AGNVQ	IB	SQA(H)	SQA	RATIO A/AS
Univ of ABERTAY DUNDEE										
Building Engineering & Management	K250	4FT/5SW deg	g	DD	Ind	Ind	Ind	BCC	Ind	
Building Surveying	K260	4FT/5SW deg	g	DD	Ind	Ind	Ind	BCC	Ind	
Quantity Surveying	K280	4FT/5SW deg	g	DD	Ind	Ind	Ind	BCC	Ind	
Building Maintenance Management	402K	2FT HND	g	D	Ind	Ind	Ind	BC	Ind	
Building Services Engineering	042K	2FT HND	g	D	Ind	Ind	Ind	BC	Ind	
Construction Management	052K	2FT HND	g	D	Ind	Ind	Ind	BC	Ind	
Quantity Surveying	082K	2FT HND	g	D	Ind	Ind	Ind	BC	Ind	
ANGLIA Poly Univ										
Architectural Design	K236▼	3FT deg	*	8	2M	P	Ind	CCCC	Ind	4
Architectural Design Technology	632K▼	2FT HND	* g	10	3M	P go	Ind	BCCC	Ind	
Building Economics and Design	K281▼	3FT deg	* g	10	3M	P go	Dip	BCCC	N	1
Building Surveying	K260▼	3FT deg	* g	10	3M	P go	Dip	BCCC	N	
Business Studies and Construction Management	NK12▼	3FT deg	g	10	3M	P go	Dip	BCCC	Ind	
Construction Engineering	K200▼	3FT deg	* g	8	N	M go	Dip	CCCC		
Construction Management	K250▼	3FT/4FT deg	* g	10	3M	P go	Dip	BCCC	Ind	4
Construction Management and Multimedia	KG25▼	3FT deg	* g	10	3M	P go	Dip	BCCC	Ind	
Construction Mgt and Business Information Systs	GKN2▼	3FT deg	* g	10	3M	P go	Dip	BCCC	Ind	
Energy Management	K246▼	3FT deg	* g	10	3M	P go	Dip	BCCC	Ind	
Energy and Environmental Conservation	K247▼	3FT deg	* g	10	3M	P go	Dip	BCCC	Ind	
Facilities Management	K241▼	3FT deg	* g	10	3M	P go	Ind	BCCC	Ind	
Facilities Management and Law	KM23▼	3FT deg	g	10	3M	P go	Dip	BCCC	Ind	
Quantity Surveying	K280▼	3FT deg	g	8	2M	P gi	Dip	CCCC	Ind	
Architectural Design Technology	632K▼	2FT HND	* g	10	3M	P go	Ind	BCCC	Ind	
Building Economics and Design	182K▼	2FT HND		4	N	P		CCC	N	
Building Management	002K▼	3SW HND	* g	4	N	P go	Dip	CCC	N	2
Energy and Environmental Studies	542K▼	2FT HND	* g	10	3M	P go	Dip	BCCC	Ind	
BELL COLLEGE OF TECHNOLOGY										
Architectural Technology	K236	3FT deg	* g	CD	Ind	Ind	Ind	BBC$	Ind	
Construction Engineering and Management	K250	3FT deg	* g	CD	Ind	Ind	Ind	BBC$	Ind	
Facilities Management	K240	3FT deg	* g	CD	Ind	Ind	Ind	BBC$	Ind	
Architectural Technology	632K	2FT HND	* g	D	N $	PC	Ind	CC$	Ind	
Building Inspection and Supervision	152K	2FT HND	* g	D	N $	PC	Ind	CC$	Ind	
Building Maintenance Management	252K	2FT HND	* g	D	N $	PC	Ind	CC$	Ind	
Building Services	142K	2FT HND	* g	D	N $	PC	Ind	CC$	Ind	
Construction Management	052K	2FT HND	* g	D	N $	PC	Ind	CC$	Ind	
Quantity Surveying	082K	2FT HND	* g	D	N $	PC	Ind	CC$	Ind	
BLACKBURN COLL										
Building Studies	002K	2FT HND		2		P				
BLACKPOOL & FYLDE COLL										
Building Studies	002K	2FT HND	*	2	N	P*	Ind	Ind	Ind	
BOLTON INST										
Architectural Tech & Occupational Hlth & Safety	KN26	3FT deg	* g	10	3M	M*	Ind	Ind	Ind	
Architectural Tech & Simulation/Virtual Environ	KG27	3FT deg	* g	10	3M	M*	Ind	Ind	Ind	
Architectural Technology	K237	3FT deg	* g	4	N	P*	Ind	Ind	Ind	
Architectural Technology	K235	3FT deg	* g	10	3M	M*	Ind	Ind	Ind	
Architectural Technology	K236	4FT deg	* g	4	N	P*	Ind	Ind	Ind	
Architectural Technology and French	KR21	3FT deg	F g	10	3M	Ind	Ind	Ind	Ind	
Architectural Technology and German	KR22	3FT deg	G g	10	3M	Ind	Ind	Ind	Ind	

| | | | 98 expected requirements | | | | | | 96 entry stats |
| course details | | | | | | | | | |

TITLE	CODE	COURSE	SUBJECTS	R/AS	NO/C	AGNVQ	IB	SQA(H)	SQA	RATIO A/AS
Architectural Technology and Law	KM23	3FT deg	* g	10	3M	M*	Ind	Ind	Ind	
Building Surveying	K263	3FT deg	* g	4	N	P*	Ind	Ind	Ind	
Building Surveying	K264	4FT deg	* g	4	N	P*	Ind	Ind	Ind	
Building Surveying	K260	3FT/4SW deg	* g	10	3M	M*	Ind	Ind	Ind	
Building Surveying & Occupational Hlth & Safety	KNF6	3FT deg	* g	10	3M	M*	Ind	Ind	Ind	
Building Surveying & Simulation/Virtual Environ	KGF7	3FT deg	* g	10	3M	M*	Ind	Ind	Ind	
Building Surveying and Environmental Studies	KFF9	3FT deg	* g	10	3M	M*	Ind	Ind	Ind	
Building Surveying and French	KRF1	3FT deg	F g	10	3M	Ind	Ind	Ind	Ind	
Building Surveying and German	KRF2	3FT deg	G g	10	3M	Ind	Ind	Ind	Ind	
Building Surveying and Law	KMF3	3FT deg	* g	10	3M	M*	Ind	Ind	Ind	
Civil Engineering and Construction	HK22	3FT deg	M/S g	10	3M	M$	Ind	Ind	Ind	
Civil Engineering and Quantity Surveying	HK2F	3FT deg	M/S g	10	3M	M$	Ind	Ind	Ind	
Construction	K203	3FT deg	* g	4	N	P*	Ind	Ind	Ind	
Construction Management	K254	4FT deg	* g	4	N	P*	Ind	Ind	Ind	
Construction Management	K250	3FT/4SW deg	* g	10	3M	M*	Ind	Ind	Ind	
Construction and Environmental Studies	KFG9	3FT deg	* g	10	3M	M*	Ind	Ind	Ind	
Construction and Environmental Technology	KKG3	3FT deg	S g	10	3M	M$	Ind	Ind	Ind	
Construction and French	KRG1	3FT deg	F g	10	3M	Ind	Ind	Ind	Ind	
Construction and German	KRG2	3FT deg	G g	10	3M	Ind	Ind	Ind	Ind	
Construction and Law	KMG3	3FT deg	* g	10	3M	M*	Ind	Ind	Ind	
Construction and Occupational Health & Safety	KNG6	3FT deg	* g	10	3M	M*	Ind	Ind	Ind	
Construction and Simulation/Virtual Environment	KGG7	3FT deg	* g	10	3M	M*	Ind	Ind	Ind	
Design and Architectural Technology	KW22	3FT deg	* g	10	MO	M*	Ind	Ind	Ind	
Environmental Studies and Quantity Surveying	FK9F	3FT deg								
Environmental Technology and Quantity Surveying	KK3F	3FT deg	S g	10	3M	M$	Ind	Ind	Ind	
French and Quantity Surveying	RK1F	3FT deg	F g	10	3M	Ind	Ind	Ind	Ind	
German and Quantity Surveying	RK2F	3FT deg	G g	10	3M	Ind	Ind	Ind	Ind	
Law and Quantity Surveying	MK3F	3FT deg	* g	10	3M	Ind	Ind	Ind	Ind	
Occupational Health & Safety & Quantity Surv	NK6F	3FT deg	* g	10	3M	M*	Ind	Ind	Ind	
Quantity Surveying	K283	3FT deg	* g	4	N	P*	Ind	Ind	Ind	
Quantity Surveying	K284	4FT deg	* g	4	N	P*	Ind	Ind	Ind	
Quantity Surveying	K280	3FT/4SW deg	* g	10	3M	M*	Ind	Ind	Ind	
Building Studies	002K	2FT/3SW HND	* g	4	N	P	Ind	Ind	Ind	
Construction Studies	052K	3FT deg								

BRADFORD & ILKLEY Comm COLL

TITLE	CODE	COURSE	SUBJECTS	R/AS	NO/C	AGNVQ	IB	SQA(H)	SQA	RATIO A/AS
Building Studies (2 Yrs)	002K	2FT HND	g	2	N$	P		Ind	Ind	

Univ of BRIGHTON

TITLE	CODE	COURSE	SUBJECTS	R/AS	NO/C	AGNVQ	IB	SQA(H)	SQA	RATIO A/AS
Architectural Structures (MEng)	HK22	3FT/4SW/4FT/5SW de	M g	18	2M+3D$	MC2/^ gi	26$	BBBB$	Ind	
Building Studies	K200	3FT/4SW deg	* g	12	5M $	MC go	Dip	BBCC	Ind	
Building Surveying	K260	3FT/4SW deg	* g	12	6M	M$	Dip	BBCC	Ind	
Construction Management	K250	3FT/4SW deg	*	12	MO	M	Dip	CCCC	Ind	
Project Management for Construction	K251	3FT/4SW deg	*	12	MO	M	Dip	CCCC	Ind	
Building Services Engineering	042K▼	2FT HND	* g	E	N	P	Ind	Ind	Ind	
Building Studies (Architectural Technology)	632K▼	2FT/3SW HND	* g	E	3M $	P$ go	Ind	Ind	Ind	
Building Studies (Building Technology & Manageme	052K▼	2FT/3SW HND	* g	E	3M $	P$ go	Ind	Ind	Ind	
Building Studies (Quantity Surveying)	082K▼	2FT/3SW HND	* g	E	3M $	P$ go	Ind	Ind	Ind	

BRISTOL, Univ of the W of England

TITLE	CODE	COURSE	SUBJECTS	R/AS	NO/C	AGNVQ	IB	SQA(H)	SQA	RATIO A/AS
Building Engineering and Management	K200	3FT/4SW deg	M/P g	10-12	5M $	P*3/^ go	24$	BC$	Ind	
Building Production Engineering	H7K2	3FT/4SW deg	M/P g	10-12	5M $	P*3/^ go	24$	BC$	Ind	
Building Surveying	K260	3FT deg	* g	14-16	5M+1D$	M*2/^ go	24	BCCC	Ind	

 INDEPENDENT ON SUNDAY

			98 expected requirements							96 entry stats	
TITLE	CODE	COURSE	SUBJECTS	A/AS	NO/C	AGNVQ	IB	SQA(H)	SQA	RATIO	A/AS
Built Environment Studies	K2K3	3FT deg	* g	8-10	4M	P*2/^ go	24	CCC	Ind		
Built Environment Studies	K2KH	4EXT deg	* g	2-4	2M	P* go	24	CC	Ind		
Construction Management	K251	1FT/2FT deg	g	X	HN $	X	X	X	Ind		
Construction Management	K252	3FT/4SW deg	M/P g	12-14	MO $	M$1/^ go	24$	BCC$	Ind		
Quantity Surveying	K280	3FT/4SW deg	* g	12-14	6M	M*1/^ go	24	BCC	Ind		
Building Studies	002K	2FT/3SW HND	* g	2-4	2M $	P* go	24	CD	Ind		

BRUNEL Univ, West London

Mech Eng with Bld Serv (4/5 Yrs Thick SW) (MEng)	H3K2	4SW/5SW deg	M+P	BCC	4M+1D$ DE^		28$	BBBBB$	Ind	6	
Mech Eng with Build Serv (4/5 Yrs Thin SW)(MEng)	H3KF	4SW/5SW deg	M+P	BCC	4M+1D$ DE^		28$	BBBBB$	Ind		
Mech Engineering with Building Services (MEng)	H3KG	3FT/4FT deg	M+P	BCC	4M+1D$ DE^		28$	BBBBB$	Ind		

BUCKINGHAMSHIRE COLLEGE

Architectural Technology	K236	3FT deg		8-10	MO	M	Ind	CCCC	Ind		
Building Design	K200	3FT deg		6-10	5M	M	Ind	CCC	Ind		
Building Design with Facilities Management	K201	3FT deg		6-10	5M	M	Ind	CCC	Ind		
Building Management	K253	3FT deg		8-10	MO	M	Ind	CCC	Ind		
Building Management (Conversion to degree)	K254	2FT deg			HN				HN		
Building Processes (1 yr conversion to Degree)	K251	1FT deg		HN					HN	1	
Building Design	22WK	2FT HND		4	N	P	Ind	CC	Ind		
Building Management	052K	2FT HND		4	N	P	Ind	CC	Ind		

Univ of Wales INST, CARDIFF

Architectural Design and Technology	K236	3FT deg	Ad/Ds g	EE	N	PA go	Ind	CCCC	Ind		
Architectural Design and Technology	632K	2FT HND	* g	2	3M	M$ go	Ind	CC	Ind		

Univ of CENTRAL ENGLAND

Building Management	K250	3FT deg		8	2M	M	24	CCCC	Ind		
Building Management (Facilities Management)	K243	3FT deg		8	2M	M	24	CCCC	Ind		
Building Management (IT)	K252	3FT deg		8	2M	M	24	CCCC	Ind		
Building Management (Project Management)	K251	3FT deg		8	2M	M	24	CCCC	Ind		
Building Services Engineering	K240	3FT deg	*	8	2M	M	24	CCCC	Ind		
Building Services Engineering (Facilities Mgt)	K241	3FT deg	*	8	2M	M	24	CCCC	Ind		
Building Services Engineering (IT in Property)	K242	3FT deg	*	8	2M	M	24	CCCC	Ind		
Building Surveying	K260	3FT deg	*	8	2M	P	24	CCCC	Ind	13	10/12
Quantity Surveying	K280	3FT/4SW deg	*	8	2M	M	24	CCCC	Ind	9	10/14
Building Studies	012K▼	2FT HND	*	2	N	P	Dip	CCCC	Ind	3	
Building Studies	002K	2FT HND	*	2	N	P	Dip	CCCC	Ind	3	2/4

Univ of CENTRAL LANCASHIRE

Architectural Technology	K236	3FT deg	*	8	PO+4M	M	26	CCC			
Building Management (Year Zero)	K251▼	4FT deg	* g								
Building Services Engineering	K240	3FT/4SW deg	M	12	5M	D$	26	BCCC	Ind		
Building Surveying	K260	3FT/4SW deg	*	12	MO	M*	26	BCCC	Ind		
Construction Project Management	K201	3FT/4SW deg	*	8	4M	M*	24	CCC	Ind		
Fire Safety	K256	1FT deg			HN $						
Fire Safety	K255	3FT deg	* g	8	MO	M*	24	CCC	Ind		
Quantity Surveying	K280	3FT/4SW deg	*	8	4M	M*	24	CCC	Ind		
Building Studies	002K	2FT/3SW HND	*	E	N	P	Ind	CC	Ind		

COVENTRY Univ

Architectural Design Technology	K236	3FT/4SW deg	* g	14	5M	MC	Ind	Ind	Ind		
Architectural Design Technology with European St	K237	3FT/4SW deg	* g	14	5M	MC	Ind	Ind	Ind		
Building Structures Engineering	KH22	3FT/4SW deg	M+S g	18	5M $	MC	Ind	Ind	Ind	13	
Building Structures Engineering (Extended)	KHF2	4FT/5SW deg	* g	12	3M	M	Ind	Ind	Ind	2	

course details			98 expected requirements							96 entry stats	
TITLE	CODE	COURSE	SUBJECTS	A/AS	NO/C	RGNVQ	IB	SQA(H)	SQA	RATIO	A/AS
Building Surveying	K260	3FT/4SW deg	* g	14	5M	MC	Ind	Ind	Ind	12	8/14
Building Surveying with European Studies	K2TG	3FT/4SW deg	* g	14	5M	MC	Ind	Ind	Ind		
Built Environment Studies	HK22	3FT/4SW deg	* g	10	4M	MC	Ind	Ind	Ind		
Construction Management	K200	3FT/4SW deg	* g	14	5M	MC	Ind	Ind	Ind	6	
Construction Management with European Studies	K2T2	4FT deg	* g	14	5M	MC	Ind	Ind	Ind		
Building	002K	2FT/3SW HND	* g	4	2M $	PC	Ind	Ind	Ind	3	2/4
DE MONTFORT Univ											
Building Surveying	K260▼	3FT deg	* g	10-14	4M+1D	D	Dip	BBBB	Ind	5	6/22
Construction Technology and Management	K214▼	4SW deg	* g	10	6M	M	24	BBB	Ind	7	
Building Studies	002K▼	3SW HND	* g	E	N	P	Dip	BB	Ind	5	
Univ of DERBY											
Construction Management	K252	3FT deg	*	10	4M	M$	26	CCCD	Ind	8	
Building Studies	002K	2FT HND	*	2-4	N	P	Dip	CCD	Ind	16	
DONCASTER COLL											
Building Services Engineering	042K	2FT HND		E	N		Ind	Ind	Ind		
DUDLEY COLLEGE of Technology											
Building Services Engineering	042K	2FT HND	* g	2	Ind	Ind					
Building Studies	002K	2FT HND	* g	2	Ind	Ind					
Univ of DUNDEE											
Civil Engineering and Building	HK22	4FT deg	M g	12	5M $	Ind	Ind	BBCC$	N$	6	
Univ of EDINBURGH											
Civil Engineering and Construction Mgt (BEng)	HK22	4FT deg	M+P	CCC	MO $		Dip$	BBBB$	N$		
Civil Engineering and Construction Mgt (MEng)	HK2F	5FT deg	M+P	BCC	MO $		Dip$	BBBB	N$		
Univ of GLAMORGAN											
Architectural Technology	K236	3FT deg			Ind	M$	Ind	Ind	Ind		
Architectural and Building Conservation	KK21	2FT deg			Ind	M$	Ind	Ind	Ind		
Building Surveying	K260	4SW deg	* g	10	5M $	M$	Ind	Ind	Ind	4	10/14
Construction Health and Safety	K2N6	3FT deg			Ind	Ind	Ind	Ind	Ind		
Construction Management	K250	3FT deg	g	10-12	Ind	Ind	Ind	Ind	Ind		
Construction Management Foundation Year	K208	3FT deg	* g	E	Ind	Ind	Ind	Ind	Ind		
Quantity Surveying	K280	4SW deg	* g	10	5M	M$	Ind	Ind	Ind	6	
Surveying	K261	4SW deg	* g	10	Ind	Ind	Ind	Ind	Ind		
Combined Studies (Honours) *Building Economics*	Y400	3FT deg	* g	8-16	Ind	Ind	Ind	Ind	Ind		
Combined Studies (Honours) *Building Management*	Y400	3FT deg	* g	8-16	Ind	Ind	Ind	Ind	Ind		
Joint Honours *Building Economics*	Y401	3FT deg	* g	8-16	Ind	Ind	Ind	Ind	Ind		
Joint Honours *Building Management*	Y401	3FT deg	* g	8-16	Ind	Ind	Ind	Ind	Ind		
Major/Minor Honours *Building Management*	Y402	3FT deg	* g	8-16	Ind	Ind	Ind	Ind	Ind		
Architectural and Building Conservation	12KK▼	2FT HND	g	4-6	N $	P$	Ind	Ind	Ind	1	
Building Studies	002K▼	2FT/3SW HND	* g	2	N	P$	Ind	Ind	Ind	6	
Construction Management	052K	2FT HND			Ind	Ind	Ind	Ind	Ind		
Quantity Surveying	082K	2FT HND	* g	D	Ind	Ind	Ind	Ind	Ind		
GLASGOW CALEDONIAN Univ											
Architectural Technology	K236	2FT deg		X	Ind		Ind	X	HN	5	
Building Control	K200	2FT deg		X	Ind		Ind	X	HN	4	
Building Services Engineering	K240	3FT deg	M+S+E	DE	Ind		Ind	CCC$	Ind	2	

| | | | 98 expected requirements | | | | | | | 96 entry stats | |
| course details | | | | | | | | | | | |
TITLE	CODE	COURSE	SUBJECTS	A/AS	ND/C	AGNVQ	IB	SQA(H)	SQA	RATIO	A/AS
Building Services Engineering	K241	4SW deg	M+E+S g	DDE	Ind		Ind	BCCC$	Ind		
Building Surveying	K260	4SW deg	M+E+S g	CCE	Ind		Ind	BCCC$	Ind	2	
Construction Management	K251	4SW deg	M g	CD-DD	Ind		Ind	BBC$	Ind		
Quantity Surveying	K280	4SW deg	E+M	DD	Ind		Ind	BCCC$	Ind	4	
GLOUCESTERSHIRE COLLEGE of Arts and Technology											
Building Studies	002K	2FT HND	* g	E	N $	P*			Ind		
Univ of GREENWICH											
Building Surveying	K260	3FT/4SW deg	* g	16	5M	M	24	CCC	Ind		
Building Surveying with Conservation Studies	K261	3FT/4SW deg	* g	16	5M	M	24	CCC	Ind		
Building Surveying with Information Technology	K2GM	3FT/4SW deg	* g	16	5M	M	24	CCC	Ind		
Design and Construction Management	K252	3FT/4SW deg	* g	16	5M	M	24	CCC	Ind		
Design and Construction Management with I.T.	K2GN	3FT/4SW deg	* g	16	5M	M	24	CCC	Ind		
Estate Management with Conservation Studies	N8K2	3FT/4SW deg	* g	16	5M	M	24	CCC	Ind		
Facilities Management	K240	3FT/4SW deg	* g	16	5M	M	24	CCC	Ind		
Property Management	K241	3FT/4SW deg	* g	16	5M	M	24	CCC	Ind		
Quantity Surveying	K280	3FT/4SW deg	* g	16	5M	Ind	24	CCC	Ind		
Quantity Surveying with Information Technology	K2G5	3FT/4SW deg	* g	16	5M	Ind	24	CCC	Ind		
Building Studies	002K▼	2FT HND	* g	4	N $	P	Dip	Ind	Ind		
HERIOT-WATT Univ											
Building Economics and Quantity Surveying	K270	4FT deg	*	CCD	MO	M$ go	34	BBCC	Ind		
Building Surveying	K260	4FT deg	*	CCD	MO	M$ go	34	BBCC	Ind		
Construction Management	K200	4FT deg	*	CCD	MO	M$ go	34	BBCC	Ind		
Environmental Services Engineering	K241	4FT deg	*	CCD	MO	M$ go	34	BBCC	Ind		
Environmental Services Engineering (MEng)	K242	5FT deg	M	BCC		M$ go	30	AAABB	Ind		
Estate Management	K2N8	4FT deg	*	CCD	MO	M$ go	34	BBCC	Ind		
Combined Studies / Building	Y100	4FT deg	*	DDE	Ind	M$ go	26	BCCC	Ind		
Univ of HERTFORDSHIRE											
Building Services Engineering	K240	3FT/4SW deg	M+P/S	14	3M $	Ind	$	Ind	Ind	3	
Building Services Engineering	K241	4FT/5SW deg	M+2S	22	5M		Ind	Ind	Ind		
Building Services Engineering (Extended)	K248▼	4FT/5SW deg	*	2	N	Ind	$	Ind	Ind		
Building Studies	002K▼	2FT/3SW HND	*	2-4	N	P	Ind	Ind	Ind	11	
Univ of HUDDERSFIELD											
Architectural Technology	K236	3FT deg	* g	8-10	5M	M$ go	Ind	Ind	Ind		
Building Conservation	K290	3FT deg	* g	10-16	5M	MC4/^ go	Ind	BBB	Ind		
KINGSTON Univ											
Building Surveying	K260	4SW deg	*	12	N	M$	24	Ind	Ind	5	10/14
Construction Economics	K250	4SW deg	*	12	N	M$	24	Ind	Ind	3	
Property Studies	K2N8	4SW deg	*	12	N	M$	24	Ind	Ind	3	
Quantity Surveying	K280	4SW deg	*	12	N	M$	24	Ind	Ind	7	
LEEDS METROPOLITAN Univ											
Architectural Technology	K236	3FT deg	* g	14-16	M+D	M$ go	Ind	BBBC	Ind		
Building Surveying	K260	3FT/4SW deg	* g	16-18	6M	D*/M*4/^ go	26	BBBCC	Ind	6	10/22
Construction Management	K250	3FT/4SW deg	* g	10	3M $	M$ go	Dip	BBCC	Ind	4	10/14
Project Management	KN2X	1FT deg									
Project Management (Construction)	KN29	3FT/4SW deg	* g	EE	N	P$ go	Dip	CCC	Ind	4	
Quantity Surveying	K280	4SW deg	* g	14-16	5M	D*/M*3/^ go	24	BBBC	Ind	5	10/20
Building Studies	002K▼	2FT HND	* g	D	N	PC go	22	BC	Ind	4	2/14

course details			98 expected requirements							96 entry stats	
TITLE	CODE	COURSE	SUBJECTS	A/AS	NO/C	AGNVQ	IB	SQA(H)	SQA	RATIO A/AS	

Univ of LINCOLNSHIRE and HUMBERSIDE

Architectural Technology	K236	3FT deg	Pf g	12	3M+1D	M	24	CCCC	Ind		

Univ of LIVERPOOL

Building Management and Technology	K200	3FT deg	* g	18	Ind	Ind	Ind	Ind	Ind	3	
Building Management and Technology	K201	4SW deg	* g	18	Ind	Ind	Ind	Ind	Ind	5	18/20

LIVERPOOL JOHN MOORES Univ

Building Surveying	K260	4SW deg		16	4M+4D	DC				8	8/20
Construction Management	K250	3FT/4SW deg		DD	3M+2D	DC				3	4/12
Quantity Surveying	K280	3FT/4SW deg		16	5M	D$/MC				7	6/20
Urban Estate Management	K281	3FT deg		14	5M	D$/M$6				7	8/20
Building Technology	002K	2FT/3SW HND		D	3M	PC				5	3/8

LOUGHBOROUGH Univ

Building Services Engineering	K241	4SW deg	M g	20	3M+2D	DC6/^ go	28$	Ind	Ind	1	
Building Services Engineering	K240	3FT deg	M g	20	3M+2D	DC6/^ go	28$	Ind	Ind	5	
Building Services Engineering	K242	5SW deg	M g	22	3M+2D	DC6/^ go	28$	Ind	Ind		
Building Services Engineering	K243	4FT deg	M g	22	3M+2D	DC6/^ go	28$	Ind	Ind		
Civil and Building Engineering (4 Yr MEng)	H2K2	4FT deg	M g	22	3M+2D	DE6/^ go	28$	Ind	Ind		
Civil and Building Engineering (5 Yr SW MEng)	H2KF	5SW deg	M g	22	3M+2D	DE6/^ go	28$	Ind	Ind	6	
Commercial Mgt and Quantity Surveying (4 Yr SW)	HK22	4SW deg	* g	22	3M+2D	D*6/^ go	28	Ind	Ind	4	12/26
Construction Engineering Management (4 Yr SW)	K291	4SW deg	* g	20	3M+2D	DC6/^ go	28	Ind	Ind	3	14/24

LUTON Univ

Building Conservation	K290	3FT deg		12-16	MO/DO	M/D	32	BBCC	Ind		
Building Conservation and Accounting	KN24	3FT deg	g	12-16	MO/DO	M/D	32	BBCC	Ind		
Building Conservation and British Studies	VK92	3FT deg		12-16	MO/DO	M/D	32	BBCC	Ind		
Building Surveying	K260	3FT deg	g	12-16	MO/DO	M/D	32	BBCC	Ind	8	
Built Environment and Building Conservation	KN28	3FT deg		12-16	MO/DO	M/D	32	BBCC	Ind		
Business and Building Conservation	KN21	3FT deg	g	12-16	MO/DO	M/D	32	BBCC	Ind		
Computer Applications and Building Conservation	KG26	3FT deg		12-16	MO/DO	M/D	32	BBCC	Ind		
Construction Management	K250	3FT/4SW deg	g	12-16	MO/DO	M/D	32	BBCC	Ind	15	
Creative Design and Building Conservation	KW22	3FT deg		12-16	MO/DO	M/D	32	BBCC	Ind		
Environmental Science and Building Conservation	KF29	3FT deg		12-16	MO/DO	M/D	32	BBCC	Ind		
History of Des & Architecture & Building Conserv	KV24	3FT deg		12-16	MO/DO	M/D	32	BBCC	Ind		
Housing Studies and Building Conservation	KK42	3FT deg	g	12-16	MO/DO	M/D	32	BBCC	SQA		
Journalism and Building Conservation	PK62	3FT deg		12-16	MO/DO	M/D	32	BBCC	Ind		
Law and Building Conservation	KM23	3FT deg	g	12-16	MO/DO	M/D	32	BBCC	Ind		
Mapping Science and Building Conservation	KF2W	3FT deg		12-16	MO/DO	M/D	32	BBCC	Ind		
Marketing and Building Conservation	KN25	3FT deg		12-16	MO/DO	M/D	32	BBCC	Ind		
Mathematical Sciences and Building Conservation	KG2C	3FT deg		12-16	MO/DO	M/D	32	BBCC	Ind		
Mathematics and Building Conservation	KG21	3FT deg		12-16	MO/DO	M/D	32	BBCC	Ind		
Physical Geography and Building Conservation	KG2V	3FT deg		12-16	MO/DO	M/D	32	BBCC	Ind		
Planning Studies and Building Conservation	KK4F	3FT deg	g	12-16	MO/DO	M/D	32	BBCC	Ind		
Property Studies and Accounting	KN2K	3FT deg	g	12-16	MO/DO	M/D	32	BBCC	Ind		
Property Studies and Building Conservation	K201	3FT deg	g	12-16	MO/DO	M/D	32	BBCC	Ind		
Property Studies and Business	KN2C	3FT deg	g	12-16	MO/DO	M/D	32	BBCC	Ind		
Property Studies and Housing Studies	KK2K	3FT deg	g	12-16	MO/DO	M/D	32	BBCC	Ind		
Property Studies and Law	KM2H	3FT deg	g	12-16	MO/DO	M/D	32	BBCC	Ind		
Property Studies and Planning Studies	KK4G	3FT deg	g	12-16	MO/DO	M/D	32	BBCC	Ind		
Public Policy & Mgt and Building Conservation	KM21	3FT deg	g	12-16	MO/DO	M/D	32	BBCC	Ind		
Public Policy and Management and Property Studs	KM2C	3FT deg	g	12-16	MO/DO	M/D	32	BBCC	Ind		
Regional Plan & Dev and Building Conservation	KK24	3FT deg	g	12-16	MO/DO	M/D	32	BBCC	Ind		

TITLE	CODE	COURSE	SUBJECTS	A/AS	ND/C	AGNVQ	IB	SQA(H)	SQA	RATIO A/AS
course details			**98 expected requirements**							**96 entry stats**
Regional Planning & Development and Property St	KK2L	3FT deg	g	12-16	MO/DO	M/D	32	BBCC	Ind	
Sociology with Built Environment	L3K2	3FT deg		12-16	MO/DO	M/D	32	BBCC	Ind	
Architectural Technology	632K	2FT HND	g	4-8	N/MO	P/M	26	CCDD	Ind	
Building Management	052K	2FT HND	g	4-8	N/MO	P/M	26	CCDD	Ind	
Building Surveying	062K	2FT HND	g	4-8	N/MO	P/M	26	CCDD	Ind	
Fire Studies	652K	2FT HND	g	4-8	N/MO	P/M	26	CCDD	Ind	
Quantity Surveying	082K	2FT HND	g	4-8	N/MO	P/M	26	CCDD	Ind	
UMIST (Manchester)										
Building Services Engineering	K240	3FT deg	P g	18	2M+2D$	M$6/^ go	30$	ABBB$	Ind	5
Commercial Management & Quantity Survey (4 Yrs)	K285	4SW deg	* g	20	2M+2D$	M$6/^ go | 30$	ABBB$	Ind	3	14/24
Construction Management	K258	3FT deg	* g	18	2M+2D$	M$6/^ go | 30$	ABBB$	Ind	8	14/18
NAPIER Univ										
Architectural Technology	K236	3FT/4FT deg	*	CCC	MO	M$	Ind	BBCC	Ind	4
Building Engineering and Management	K250	3FT/4FT deg	*	CCC	MO	M$	Ind	BBCC	Ind	4
Building Surveying	K260	3FT/4FT deg	*	CCC	MO	M$	Ind	BBCC	Ind	5
Quantity Surveying	K280	3FT/4FT deg	*	CCC	MO	M$	Ind	BBCC	Ind	10
NENE COLLEGE										
Architectural Technology	K210	3FT deg		EE	4M	P	24	CCC	Ind	
Quantity Surveying	K280	4SW deg		10	6M	M	24	CCC	Ind	
Architectural Technology	012K	2FT HND		E	N	P	24	CCC	Ind	6/10
Construction Management	052K▼	2FT HND		E	N	P		CC	Ind	
Quantity Surveying	082K	2FT HND		E	N	P		CC	Ind	
NESCOT										
Building Technology and Design	KW22	2FT/3SW deg	*	EE	N	M	Dip	Ind	N$	
Building Technology and Design	KW2F	4FT deg	*							
Facilities Management	K240	3FT deg	*	EE	N	M	Dip	Ind	N$	
Facilities Management	K248	4FT deg	*							
Building Studies	002K▼	2FT/3SW HND	*	E	N	P	Dip	Ind	N$	9
Facilities Management	142K	2FT/3SW HND	*	E	N	P	Dip	Ind	N$	
NORTH EAST WALES INST of HE										
Construction Management	KN21	3FT deg		6-12	3M	M$	Ind	CCC	N$	
Estate Management with Conservation & the Envir	N835	3FT deg		6-10	3M	M$	Ind	CCC	N$	
Estate Management with Development and Planning	N831	3FT deg		6-10	3M	M$	Ind	CCC	N$	
Estate Management with Residential Property Mgt	N820	3FT deg		6-10	3M	M$	Ind	CCC	N$	
Estate Management with Valuations and Surveying	N810	3FT deg		6-10	3M	M$	Ind	CCC	N$	
Heritage Management	KN99	3FT deg		4-10	3M	M$	Ind	CCC	N$	
Quantity Surveying with Project Management	K281	3FT deg		10	3M	M$	Ind	CCC	N$	
Building (Architecture)	11HK	2FT HND		2-6	2M	P$	Ind	CC	N$	
Building (Management)	052K	2FT HND		2-4	N	P$	Ind	CC	N$	
Building (Quantity Surveying)	082K	2FT HND		2-4	2M	P$	Ind	CC	N$	
Univ of NORTH LONDON										
Facilities Management	K240	3FT/4SW deg	* g	12-14	MO+4D$	Ind	Ind	Ind	Ind	
Univ of NORTHUMBRIA										
Architectural Design and Management	KK12	3FT deg	* g	16	4M+2D	D gi	26	BBCCC	Ind	
Building Design Management	K252	3FT/4SW deg	* g	14	5M	M gi	24	CCCCC	Ind	
Building Project Management	K253	3FT/4SW deg	* g	14	5M	M gi	24	CCCCC	Ind	
Building Surveying	K260	4SW deg	* g	14	5M+1D	M gi	24	BCCC	Ind	5	8/24
Construction Management	K251	3FT/4SW deg	* g	14	5M	M gi	24	CCCCC	Ind	
Planning and Development Surveying	KK24	3FT/4SW deg	* g	14	5M+1D	M gi	24	BCCC	Ind	2	6/14

course details			98 expected requirements							96 entry stats	
TITLE	CODE	COURSE	SUBJECTS	A/AS	ND/C	AGNVQ	IB	SQA(H)	SQA	RATIO	R/AS
Quantity Surveying	K280	4SW deg	* g	14	5M	M gi	24	BCCC	Ind	4	8/16
Building Design	002K	2FT HND	* g	6	3M	P gi	24	CCC	Ind	4	2/ 6
Building Production	012K	2FT HND	* g	6	3M	P gi	24	CCC	Ind		
Building Surveying	062K	2FT HND	* g	6	3M	P gi	24	CCC			
Quantity Surveying	082K	2FT HND	* g	6	3M	P gi	24	CCC	Ind		
Univ of NOTTINGHAM											
Building Environment Engineering	H3K2	3FT deg	P+M	CCD-CDD	Ind	Ind	28$	Ind	Ind	3	16/24
NOTTINGHAM TRENT Univ											
Building	K201	4SW deg	* g	14	7M $	Ind	Ind	CCC	Ind		
Building Surveying	K260	3FT/4SW deg	* g	16	6M	Ind	Ind	CCC	Ind	6	8/14
Construction Management	K200	4SW deg	* g	14	7M $		Ind	CCC	Ind	5	6/16
Construction Management (Extended)	K258▼	5EXTSW deg	* g		Ind	Ind	Ind	Ind	Ind	2	
Facilities Management	K240	3FT/4SW deg	* g	16	3M	M$	Ind	Ind	Ind		
Property and Surveying	K265	3FT/4SW deg	* g	16	3M	M$	Ind	Ind	Ind		
Quantity Surveying	K280	4SW deg	* g	16	5M		Ind	CCC	Ind	5	8/22
Quantity Surveying (Extended)	K288▼	5EXTSW deg	* g		Ind	Ind	Ind	Ind	Ind	5	
Rural Land and Property Management	KN28▼	3FT deg	* g	16	5M	Ind	Ind	Ind	Ind		
Architectural Technology	632K	3SW HND	* g	6	2M	Ind	Ind	Ind	Ind		
Building Engineering Services Quantity Surveying	062K	3SW HND	* g	6	3M	Ind	Ind	Ind	Ind		
Building Studies	002K	3SW HND	* g	6	3M $	Ind	Ind	Ind	Ind	7	2/12
Quantity Surveying	082K	3SW HND	* g	6	3M		Ind	Ind	Ind	1	2/ 6
OXFORD BROOKES Univ											
Building	K200	4SW deg	* g	CC-DDD	Ind	M*	Ind	Ind	Ind	2	6/10
Building Studies	002K	3FT HND	* g	E	Ind		Ind	Ind	Ind	5	
Univ of PAISLEY											
Construction Management	K250	4SW deg	M g	CD	Ind	Ind	Ind	BBC$	Ind	3	
Construction and Environmental Management	FK92	4SW	M g	CD	Ind	Ind	Ind	BBC$	Ind		
Univ of PLYMOUTH											
Building Surv and the Environ Stage 1 deg module	K266	3FT/4SW deg	Ap g	10	4M	M$^	Ind	BCCC	Ind		
Building Surveying and the Environment	K265	3FT/4SW deg	Ap g	10	4M	M$^	Ind	BCCC	Ind		
Construction Management and the Environment	K255	3FT/4SW deg	Ap g	10	Ind	M$_^	Ind	BCCC	Ind		
Quantity Surveying and the Environment	K285	3FT/4SW deg	Ap g	10	4M	M$^	Ind	BCCC	Ind		
European Building Design & Management (S Devon)	1GNK	2FT/3SW HND	* g	2	N	P$	Ind	Ind	Ind		
European Building Design & Mgt (Somerset)	1FNK	2FT/3SW HND	* g	2	N	P$	Ind	Ind	Ind		
Univ of PORTSMOUTH											
Quantity Surveying	K280	3FT deg	*	12	5M	M$6/^	Dip	BBCC	Ind	4	6/16
Building Studies	002K▼	2FT HND	*	4	N	P	Dip	Ind	Ind		
QUEEN'S Univ Belfast											
Architectural Engineering	K236	3FT/4FT deg	M+S g	BCC	Ind	Ind	29$	BBBC	Ind	17	16/24
READING COLLEGE AND SCHOOL OF ART AND DESIGN											
Building Studies	002K	2FT HND									
Univ of READING											
Building Construction and Management	K254	3FT deg	* g	20	6M+2D	D$6/^ gi	30	BBBB	Ind	15	
Building Services Eng Design & Management	K240	3FT deg	* g	20	6M+2D	D$6/^ gi	30	BBBB	Ind	3	
Building Surveying	K260	3FT deg	* g	20	6M+2D	D$6/^ gi	30	BBBB	Ind	4	
Construction Management Engineering & Surveying	K285	3FT deg	* g	20	6M+2D	D$6/^ gi	30	BBBB	Ind	3	
Quantity Surveying	K280	3FT deg	* g	20	6M+2D	D$6/^ gi	30	BBBB	Ind	13	

	course details			98 expected requirements								96 entry stats

TITLE	CODE	COURSE	SUBJECTS	A/AS	NO/C	AGNVQ	IB	SQA(H)	SQA	RATIO A/AS	
ROBERT GORDON Univ											
Architectural Technology	K236	3FT/4FT deg	E g	CCD	N	Ind	Ind	BBCC$	Ind	3	
Building Surveying	K260	3FT/4SW/4FT/5SW de	E g	CCC	Ind	Ind	Ind	BCC$	Ind	6	
Construction Management	K250	3FT/4FT deg	E g	CCC	N	Ind	Ind	BCC$	Ind	5	
Quantity Surveying	K280	3FT/4SW/4FT/5SW de	E g	CCC	Ind	Ind	Ind	BCC$	Ind	4	
Architectural Technology	632K	2FT HND	E g	DE	N	Ind	Ind	CCC$	Ind	5	
Building Surveying	062K	2FT HND	E g	DE	N	Ind	Ind	CCC$	Ind	4	
Construction Management	992K	2FT HND	E g	DE	N	Ind	Ind	CCC$	Ind	4	
Quantity Surveying	082K	2FT HND	E g	DE	N	Ind	Ind	CCC$	Ind	9	
Univ of SALFORD											
Building	K200	3FT deg	* g	16	3M	M	30	Ind	Ind		
Building Surveying (3yr or 4yr S/W)	K260	3FT/4SW deg	* g	BCC-CCC	4M+1D	M	Ind	Ind	Ind	5	10/24
Construction	K201	3FT deg	* g	16	3M	M	30	Ind	Ind		
Construction Management	KN21	4FT deg									
Construction Management (4 Yrs)	K2N1	4SW deg	* g	BBC	3M+2D	M	Ind	Ind	Ind	6	14/22
Quantity Surveying (3/4 Yrs)	K280	3FT/4SW deg	* g	BCC-CCC	4M+1D	M	Ind	Ind	Ind	9	14/18
Building Studies	002K	2FT HND		4	N	P	24	CC	Ind	15	
SHEFFIELD HALLAM Univ											
Building Surveying	K260	4SW deg	*	16	6M	M$2	Ind	BBBCC	Ind		
Construction Management	K250	4SW deg	*	16	6M	M$2	Ind	BBBCC	Ind		
Construction and the Built Environ (Foundation)	K258▼	4EXT/5EXTSW									
Quantity Surveying	K280	4SW deg	*	16	6M	M$2	Ind	Ind	Ind		
Combined Studies *Architectural Technology*	Y400	3FT deg	M	14	2M	M	Ind	Ind	Ind		
Combined Studies *Construction*	Y400	3FT deg	*	14	2M	M	Ind	Ind	Ind		
Combined Studies *Surveying*	Y400	3FT deg	*	14	2M	M	Ind	Ind	Ind		
Building Studies	002K▼	2FT HND	* g	E	N	P$	Ind	Ind	Ind		
SOUTHAMPTON INST											
Architectural Technology	K236	3FT deg	S	10-12	MO	M$	Dip	CCCC	N		
Architectural Technology (with Foundation)	K238▼	4FT deg	*	2-4	N	P$	Dip	CCCC	N		
Building Studies	K200	3FT deg	*	8	MO	M$	Dip	CCCC	N		
Building Studies (with Foundation)	K201	4FT deg	*	2-4	N	P$	Dip	CCCC	N		
Construction	K252	3FT deg	*	4-8	MO	M$	Dip	CCCC	N	2	6/8
Construction (with Foundation Year)	K258▼	4FTdeg	*	2-4	N	P$	Dip	CCCC	N	12	
Building Studies	002K▼	2FT HND	*	2-6	N	P$	Dip	CCCC	N	3	4/6
SOUTH BANK Univ											
Architectural Engineering	K236	3FT deg	* g	14-18	2M+4D	M go	Ind	Ind	Ind		
Architectural Technology	K235	3FT deg	* g	14-18	2M+4D	M go	Ind	Ind	Ind		
Building Services Engineering	K240	3FT deg	M/P/C/Cs/Ds g	DD	MO	M$ go	Ind	Ind	Ind		
Building Services Engineering	K245	1/1/2FT deg			HN		Ind	Ind	Ind		
Building Surveying	K260	3FT/4SW deg	* g	CC	3M	M go	Ind	Ind	Ind		
Construction Studies	K252	3FT/4SW deg	* g	CC	3M $	M go	Ind	Ind	Ind		
Construction Studies	K251	1FT deg			HN		Ind	Ind	Ind		
Foundation Building Surveying	K268	4EXT deg					Ind	Ind	Ind		
Foundation Construction Management	K258	4EXT deg					Ind	Ind	Ind		
Foundation Quantity Surveying	K288	4EXT deg					Ind	Ind	Ind		
Quantity Surveying	K280	3FT/4SW deg	g	CC	3M	M go	Ind	Ind	Ind		
Building Services Engineering	042K	2FT HND	M/P/C/Cs/Ds g	E	N	P go	Ind	Ind	Ind		
Construction Studies	002K	2FT/3SW HND	M+S g	E	N	P go	Ind	Ind	Ind		

course details			98 expected requirements							96 entry stats	
TITLE	CODE	COURSE	SUBJECTS	A/AS	ND/C	AGNVQ	IB	SQA(H)	SQA	RATIO	A/AS
ST HELENS COLL											
Building Studies (Design)	22WK	2FT HND	*	2	N	PC	Ind	Ind	Ind		
Building Studies (Production)	002K	2FT HND	*	2	N	PC	Ind	Ind	Ind		
STAFFORDSHIRE Univ											
Building Surveying	K260	3FT deg	g	12	4M	M$	24	BBC	Ind	5	6/12
Facilities Management	K240	3FT deg	g	12	4M	M$	24	BBC	Ind		
Property and Construction	K200	3FT deg	g	12	4M	M$	24	BBC	Ind	3	
Property with Business Studies	K2N1	3FT deg	g	12	4M	M$	24	BBC	Ind		6/ 8
Property with French	K2R1	3FT deg	g	12	4M	M$	24	BBC	Ind		
Property with Geography	K2F8	3FT deg	g	12	4M	M$	24	BBC	Ind		
Property with German	K2R2	3FT deg	g	12	4M	M$	24	BBC	Ind		
Property with Spanish	K2R4	3FT deg	g	12	4M	M$	24	BBC	Ind		
Quantity Surveying	K280	3FT deg	g	12	4M	M$	24	BBC	Ind	4	8/12
STOCKPORT COLL of F and HE											
Building Studies	002K	2FT/3SW HND	* g	2	N	PC	Ind	Ind	Ind		
Univ of STRATHCLYDE											
Building Design Engineering	K210	4FT deg	M+P	BCC	HN		30$	BBBB$	HN		
Building Design Engineering	K212	5FT deg	M+P	BBB	Ind		32$	AAAB$	Ind		
UNIVERSITY COLLEGE SUFFOLK											
Building Studies	002K	2FT HND	*	E	N $	P$	Ind	Ind	Ind		
SWANSEA INST of HE											
Project and Construction Management	K250	3FT deg		EE	HN	P	Ind	Ind	HN	3	
Building Studies	002K	2FT HND		E	N	P	Ind	Ind	N	2	
Univ of TEESSIDE											
Construction Management	K250	3FT deg	M+S	8	3M		Ind	CCC	Ind		
Modular Degree Scheme *Construction Management*	Y401	3FT deg									
Science and Technology Combined Honours Scheme *Construction Management*	Y108	3FT deg									
Building Studies	002K	2FT HND	S/M	4	N	P	Ind	Ind	Ind	7	
Univ of ULSTER											
Architectural Technology & Mgt(4 Yr SW inc DIS)	K235▼	4SW deg	M/Ph/A g	BCC	MO+4D	Ind	30	BBBB	Ind	16	16/24
Building Engineering and Mgt (4 Yr SW inc DIS)	K250▼	4SW deg	M/S	CCD	MO+2D	Ind	27	BBCC	Ind	14	16/18
Building Production Engineering	K210▼	3FT deg	M+Ph	CDD	MO+1D	Ind	26	BCCC	Ind	5	14/16
Surveying with Specialisms (4 Yr SW inc DIS)	K260▼	4SW deg		BCC	MO+4D	Ind	30	BBBB			
UNIVERSITY COLL LONDON (Univ of London)											
Construction Management	K250	3FT deg	* g	DDD	3M	Ind	26	BCCCC	Ind	3	10/20
Univ of WESTMINSTER											
Architectural Engineering	K236	3FT deg	M/P	CC	3M					3	12/18
Building Engineering	K240	3FT deg	*	12	3M				Ind		
Building Engineering (with foundation)	K248	4EXT deg		E	N		Ind		Ind		
Building Surveying	K260	3FT deg	*	CC	3M		Ind		Ind	6	
Building Surveying (with foundation)	K268	4EXT deg	*	D	N		Ind		Ind	3	
Construction Management (Sandwich)	K250	4SW deg	*	DE	3M		Ind	Ind	Ind	3	
Construction Management (with foundation)	K258	5SW deg	*	D	N		Ind	Ind	Ind	5	
Facilities Management	K241	3FT deg									
Facilities Management with foundation	K249	3FT deg									
Quantity Surveying	K280	3FT deg	*	CC	4M	M	Ind	BBB		4	
Quantity Surveying (with foundation)	K288	4EXT deg	*	D	N	P	Ind	Ind		4	

Building and Surveying 11

course details			98 expected requirements							96 entry stats
TITLE	CODE	COURSE	SUBJECTS	A/AS	ND/C	AGNVQ	IB	SQA(H)	SQA	RATIO A/AS
WIGAN and LEIGH COLL										
Building Studies (Information Technology)	25KG▼	2FT HND		DE	N	P$	Dip		N	
Building Studies (Management)	052K▼	2FT HND		DE	N	P$	Dip		N	
Building Studies (Quantity Surveying)	082K▼	2FT HND		DE	N	P$	Dip		N	
Building Studies (Services)	042K▼	2FT HND		DE	N	P$	Dip	N		
WIRRAL METROPOLITAN COLLEGE										
Building Studies	002K	2FT HND			Ind	Ind	Ind	Ind	Ind	
Univ of WOLVERHAMPTON										
Building Management	K250	3FT/4SW deg	* g	DD	N	M	24	CCCC	Ind	7
Building Surveying	K260	3FT/4SW deg	* g	DD	N	M	24	CCCC	Ind	9
Computer Aided Design & Construction	H1K2	3FT/4SW deg	* g	DD	N	M	24	CCCC	Ind	4
Quantity Surveying	K280	3FT/4SW deg	* g	DD	N	M	24	CCCC	Ind	9
Applied Sciences *Construction Studies*	Y100	3FT/4SW deg	S g	DD	N	M	24	CCCC	Ind	
Applied Sciences (4 Yrs) *Construction Studies*	Y110▼	4FT deg	*							
Combined Degrees *Construction Studies*	Y401	3FT/4SW deg	g	DD	N	M	24	CCCC	Ind	
Building Studies	002K	2FT HND	* g	D	N	M	24	CCCC	Ind	4 4/7

course details   98 expected requirements   96 entry stats

TITLE	CODE	COURSE	SUBJECTS	A/AS	ND/C	AGNVQ	IB	SQA(H)	SQA	RATIO A/AS
Univ of ABERDEEN										
Accountancy-Entrepreneurship	NN4C	4FT deg	* g	BBC	Ind	M$ go	30$	BBBB$	Ind	
Accountancy-Management Studies	NN14	4FT deg	* g	BBC	Ind	M$ go	30$	BBBB$	Ind	9
Agricultural Economics-Management Studies	LN11	4FT deg	* g	BBC	Ind	M$ go	30$	BBBB$	Ind	
Celtic-Management Studies	QN51	4FT deg	* g	BBC	Ind	M$ go	30$	BBBB$	Ind	
Chemistry with Management Studies	F1N1	4FT deg	C+2S/C+M+S g	CCD	Ind	MS go	24$	BBBC$	Ind	
Computing Science-Management Studies	GN5C	3FT/4FT deg	M+S g	CCD	Ind	MS go	24$	BBBC$	Ind	6
Computing-Entrepreneurship	NGC5	4FT deg	* g	BBC	Ind	M$ go	30 $	BBBB$	Ind	
Countryside and Environmental Management	D2N8	4FT deg	3S/2S+M g	CCD	Ind	MS go	24$	BBBC$	Ind	15
Countryside and Environmental Management	D2NV	4FT deg	* g	BBC	Ind	M$ go	30$	BBBB2$	Ind	3
Economic History-Management Studies	NV13	4FT deg	* g	BBC	Ind	M$ go	30$	BBBB$	Ind	2
Economics-Entrepreneurship	NLC1	4FT deg	* g	BBC	Ind	M$ go	30$	BBBB$	Ind	
Economics-Management Studies	LN1C	4FT deg	* g	BBC	Ind	M$ go	30$	BBBB$	Ind	5
English-Entrepreneurship	QN3C	4FT deg	* g	BBC	Ind	M$ go	30$	BBBB$	Ind	
English-Management Studies	QN31	4FT deg	* g	BBC	Ind	M$ go	30$	BBBB$	Ind	3
Entrepreneurship	N122	4FT deg	* g	BBC	Ind	M$ go	30$	BBBB$	Ind	
Entrepreneurship-Geography	LN8C	4FT deg	* g	BBC	Ind	M$ go	30$	BBBB$	Ind	
Entrepreneurship-Hispanic Studies	NRC4	4FT deg	* g	BBC	Ind	M$ go	30$	BBBB$	Ind	
Entrepreneurship-Hispanic Studies (4 Yrs)	NRCK	4FT deg	* g	BBC	Ind	M$ go	30$	BBBB$	Ind	
Entrepreneurship-History	NVC1	4FT deg	* g	BBC	Ind	M$ go	30$	BBBB$	Ind	
Entrepreneurship-Mathematics	GN1C	4FT deg	* g	BBC	Ind	M$ go	30$	BBBB$	Ind	
Entrepreneurship-Social Research	NLC3	4FT deg	* g	BBC	Ind	M$ go	30$	BBBB$	Ind	
Entrepreneurship-Sociology	LNHC	4FT deg	* g	BBC	Ind	M$ go	30$	BBBB$	Ind	
European Management Studies	N1T2	4FT deg	L g	BBC	Ind	M$^ go	30$	BBBB$	Ind	7
French-Entrepreneurship	RN1C	5FT deg	* g	BBC	Ind	M$ go	30$	BBBB$	Ind	
French-Entrepreneurship (4 Yrs)	NRC1	4FT deg	* g	BBC	Ind	M$ go	30$	BBBB$	Ind	
French-Management Studies	RN11	4FT/5FT deg	* g	BBC	Ind	M$ go	30$	BBBB$	Ind	13
French-Management Studies (4 Yrs)	NR11	4FT deg	* g	BBC	Ind	M$ go	30$	BBBB$	Ind	
Geography-Management Studies	LN81	4FT deg	* g	BBC	Ind	M$ go	30$	BBBB$	Ind	11
German-Management Studies	RN21	4FT/5FT deg	* g	BBC	Ind	M$ go	30$	BBBB$	Ind	7
German-Management Studies (4 Yrs)	NR12	4FT deg	* g	BBC	Ind	M$ go	30$	BBBB$	Ind	
Hispanic Studies-Management Studies	RN41	4FT/5FT deg	* g	BBC	Ind	M$ go	30$	BBBB$	Ind	2
Hispanic Studies-Management Studies (4 Yrs)	NR14	4FT deg	* g	BBC	Ind	M$ go	30$	BBBB$	Ind	
History-Management Studies	NV11	4FT deg	* g	BBC	Ind	M$ go	30$	BBBB$	Ind	13
Information Systems-Management Studies	GN51	4FT deg	M g	BBC	Ind	M$ go	30$	BBBB$	Ind	8
International Relations-Management Studies	MN1C	4FT deg	* g	BBC	Ind	M$ go	30$	BBBB$	Ind	6
Law (with options in Management Studies) (LLB)	M3N1	3FT/4FT deg	* g	BBB	Ind	X	34$	ABBBB$	Ind	3
Management Studies	N100	4FT deg	* g	BBC	Ind	M$ go	30$	BBBB$	Ind	6
Mathematics-Management Studies	GN11	4FT deg	M g	BBC	Ind	M$ go	30$	BBBB$	Ind	
Philosophy-Management Studies	VN71	4FT deg	* g	BBC	Ind	M$ go	30$	BBBB$	Ind	
Politics-Management Studies	MN11	4FT deg	* g	BBC	Ind	M$ go	30$	BBBB$	Ind	5
Social Research-Management Studies	LN3C	4FT deg	* g	BBC	Ind	M$ go	30$	BBBB$	Ind	6
Sociology-Management Studies	LN31	4FT deg	* g	BBC	Ind	M$ go	30$	BBBB$	Ind	4
Statistics-Management Studies	GN41	4FT deg	M g	BBC	Ind	M$ go	30$	BBBB$	Ind	
Univ of ABERTAY DUNDEE										
Applied Chemistry with Business Management	F1NC	4FT/5SW deg	C	DD	Ind	Ind	Ind	BCC	Ind	
Business Administration	N100	2FT deg		X	HN	Ind	Ind	X	HN	
Business Engineering	HN11	4FT/5SW deg	M+P/C/Ds	CD	Ind	Ind	Ind	BBCC	Ind	
Business Engineering with French, German or Span	HN1C	4FT deg								
Business Studies	N120	4SW deg	*	DDD	Ind	Ind	Ind	BBCC	Ind	
Commerce	N130	4FT deg	E	DD	Ind	Ind	Ind	BBC	Ind	
Engineering Management	HN1D	4FT deg								

Business and Management

12

				98 expected requirements							96 entry stats

course details

TITLE	CODE	COURSE	SUBJECTS	A/AS	ND/C	AGNVQ	IB	SQA(H)	SQA	RATIO A/AS
European Business Management with Languages	N140	4FT deg	E+F/G/Sp	DD	Ind	Ind	Ind	BCC	Ind	
Management & Biology	CN11	4FT/5SW deg	g	CD	Ind	Ind	Ind	BBC	Ind	
Management & Chemistry	FN11	4FT/5SW deg	C	CD	Ind	Ind	Ind	BBC	Ind	
Management & Computing	GN51	4FT/5SW deg	*	CD	Ind	Ind	Ind	BBC	Ind	
Management & Mathematics	GN11	4FT/5SW deg	M	CD	Ind	Ind	Ind	BBC	Ind	
Marketing, Management & Consumer Electronics	N5H6	4FT/5SW deg	*	DD	Ind	Ind	Ind	BCC	Ind	
Marketing, Management & Consumer Electronics	H6N5	4FT/5SW deg	*	DD	Ind	Ind	Ind	BCC	Ind	
Mathematics with Business Methods	G1N1	4FT/5SW deg	M	CD	Ind	Ind	Ind	BBC	Ind	
Quality Systems	NN19	3FT deg								
Retail & Distribution Management	N550	4FT/5SW deg	*	DDD	Ind	Ind	Ind	BBCC	Ind	

Univ of Wales, ABERYSTWYTH

Agriculture with Business Studies	D2N1	3FT deg	* g	12	MO	M g	26	BCCCC	Ind	
Business Economics	L112	3FT deg	* g	18	3M+3D	M^ g	29	BBBCC	Ind	
Business Studies	N122	3FT deg	* g	18	3M+3D	M6 g	29	BBBCC	Ind	
Business Studies with a Modern Language	N1T9	4FT deg	L g	18	3M+3D$	M^ g	29$	BBBCC$	Ind	
Business Studies/Welsh	NQ15	3FT deg	W g	18	3M+3D$	M^ g	29$	BBBCC$	Ind	
Business/Law	MN31	3FT deg	* g	BBB	DO $	D g	32$	BBBCC$	Ind	
Economics and Marketing	LN15	3FT deg	* g	18	3M+3D	M^ g	29	BBBCC	Ind	
Modern Languages with Business Studies	T9N1	4FT deg	L g	18	1M+5D$	M^ g	29$	BBBCC$	Ind	
Physics with Business Studies	F3N1	3FT deg	P+M g	14	3M $	MS^ g	27$	BBCCC$	Ind	

ANGLIA Poly Univ

Art History and Business	NV14▼ 3FT deg		*	14	6M	M*	Dip	BBCC	Ind	5
Audiotechnology and Business	HN6C▼ 3FT deg		S	16	8M	D	Dip$	BBCCC	N	4
Business	N100▼ 3FT deg		* g	10	3M	P go	Dip	BCCC	N	4/ 8
Business Administration	N124▼ 3FT deg		* g	14	6M	M go	Dip	BBCC	N	5 8/22
Business Administration (Corporate Admin)	N151▼ 3FT deg		* g	14	6M	M go	Dip	BBCC	N	
Business Administration (Human Resource Mgt)	N130▼ 3FT deg		* g	14	6M	M go	Dip	BBCC	N	
Business Administration (Marketing Management)	N500▼ 3FT deg		* g	14	6M	M go	Dip	BBCC	N	
Business Studies	N120▼ 4SW deg		* g	14	6M	M^ go	Dip	BBCC	Ind	5 8/20
Business Studies (Corporate Administration)	N152▼ 3FT deg		* g	14	6M	M go	Dip	BBCC	Ind	
Business Studies (Human Resource Management)	N131▼ 3FT deg		* g	14	6M	M go	Dip	BBCC	Ind	
Business Studies (Marketing Management)	N501▼ 3FT deg		* g	14	6M	M go	Dip	BBCC	Ind	
Business Studies and Business Information Systs	GN51▼ 3FT deg		* g	14	6M	M go	Dip	BBCC	Ind	3
Business Studies and Construction Management	NK12▼ 3FT deg		g	10	3M	P go	Dip	BCCC	Ind	
Business Studies and Leisure Planning & Develop	NL1H▼ 3FT deg		* g	14	6M	M go	Dip	BBCC	Ind	
Business Studies and Multimedia	HN61▼ 3FT deg		* g	14	6M	M go	Dip	BBCC	Ind	
Business Studies and Product Design	NHC7▼ 3FT deg		* g	14	6M	M go	Dip	BBCC	Ind	14
Business and Chemistry	NF11▼ 3FT deg		S g	10	3M	P go	Dip$	BCCC	Ind	2
Business and Communication Studies	PN31▼ 3FT deg		Ap	14	6M	M+/^ go	Dip$	BBCC	Ind	8
Business and Computer Science	NG15▼ 3FT deg		* g	10	3M	P go	Dip	BCCC	Ind	6
Business and Ecology and Conservation	DN21▼ 3FT deg		* g	10	3M	P go	Dip	BCCC	Ind	2
Business and English	NQ13▼ 3FT deg		E g	12	4M	M+/^ go	Dip$	BCCC	Ind	5 11/16
Business and English Language Studies	NQ11▼ 3FT deg		g	10	3M	P go	Dip	BCCC		
Business and European Philosophy and Literature	NV17▼ 3FT deg		* g	12	4M	M+/^ go	Dip	BCCC	Ind	
Business and Food Science	DN41▼ 3FT deg									
Business and French	NR11▼ 4FT deg		* g	12	4M	M+/^ go	Dip	BCCC	Ind	10
Business and Geography	NL18▼ 3FT deg		Gy g	12	4M	M+/^ go	Dip$	BCCC	Ind	5 10/18
Business and German	NR12▼ 4FT deg		* g	12	4M	M+/^ go	Dip	BCCC	Ind	4
Business and Graphic Arts	NW12▼ 3FT deg		A g	14	6M	M+/^ go	Dip$	BBBC	Ind	
Business and History	NV11▼ 3FT deg		* g	12	4M	M+/^ go	Dip	BCCC	Ind	19
Business and Instrumentation Electronics	NH16▼ 3FT deg		S g	10	3M	P go	Dip$	BCCC	Ind	
Business and Italian	NR13▼ 4FT deg		* g	12	4M	M go	Dip	BCCC	Ind	2

course details | 98 expected requirements | 96 entry stats

TITLE	CODE	COURSE	SUBJECTS	A/AS	ND/C	AGNVQ	IB	SQA(H)	SQA	RATIO	A/AS
Business and Law	NM13▼	3FT deg	* g	14	6M	M go	Dip	BBCC	Ind	11	14/18
Business and Maths or Stats/Statistical Mod.	NG11▼	3FT deg	* g	10	3M	P go	Dip	BCCC	Ind	3	
Business and Music	NW13▼	3FT deg	Mu g	12	4M	M+/^ go	Dip$	BCCC	Ind	2	14/14
Business and Ophthalmic Dispensing	BN51▼	3FT deg	* g	10	3M	P go	Dip	BCCC	Ind	6	
Business and Politics	NM11▼	3FT deg	* g	14	6M	M go	Dip	BBCC	Ind	5	
Business and Psychology	CN81▼	3FT deg	* g	16	8M	D go	Dip	BBCCC	Ind	7	
Business and Real Time Computer Systems	NG1M▼	3FT deg	* g	10	3M	P go	Dip	BCCC	Ind		
Business and Social Policy	NL14▼	3FT deg	* g	12	4M	M go	Dip	BCCC	Ind	2	
Business and Sociology	NL13▼	3FT deg	* g	12	4M	M go	Dip	BCCC	Ind	8	12/16
Business and Spanish	NR14▼	4FT deg	* g	12	4M	M+/^ go	Dip	BCCC	Ind	4	
Business and Women's Studies	NM19▼	3FT deg	* g	10	3M	P go	Dip	BCCC	Ind	1	
Estate Management	N800▼	3FT deg	*	8	2M	P	Dip	CCCC	Ind		
European Business (French Programme)	N122▼	4FT deg	F g	10	3M	P go	Dip	BCCC	Ind	6	6/18
European Business (German Programme)	N1R2▼	4FT deg	G g	10	3M	P go	Dip	BCCC	Ind	3	10/10
Law and Property Management	NMV3▼	3FT deg									
Optical Management	BN5C▼	3FT deg	* g	10	3M	P go	Dip	BCCC			
Business Studies	001N▼	2FT HND	* g	12	4M	P go	Dip	BCCC	N		
Business Studies	021N▼	2FT HND	* g	14	6M	M go	Dip	BBCC	Ind	6	7/20

ASKHAM BRYAN COLL

Business Management	N120	1FT deg		X	HN+8M	X	X	X	X	6	
Land Management and Technology	N800	1FT deg		X	HN+8M	X	X	X	X	2	
Business	051N	3SW HND	* g	2	MO	M$	Ind	CC	Ind	3	

ASTON Univ

Business Administration/Biology	CN11	3FT/4SW deg	B g	20	5M+5D	D$^ go	30$	BBBBB$	Ind	3	16/26
Business Administration/Biology (Year Zero)	CN1C	4FT/5SW deg									
Business Administration/Computer Sci (Year Zero)	GN5C	4FT/5SW deg									
Chemistry/Business Administration	FN11	3FT/4SW deg	C g	20	3M+7D$	D$^ go	30$	BBBBB$	Ind	10	
Chemistry/Business Administration (Year Zero)	FN1D	4FT/5SW deg									
Computer Science/Business Administration	GN51	3FT/4SW deg	* g	20	3M+7D	D$6/^ go	30	BBBBB	Ind	5	18/28
Electronic Engineering with Management Studies	H6ND	4SW deg	M+Ph g	20	5M+5D	D$6/^ go	30$	BBBBB$	Ind		
Electronic Engineering with Management Studies	H6N1	3FT deg	M+Ph g	20	5M+5D	D$6/^ go	30$	BBBBB$	Ind		
Electronic Systems Engineering with Mgt Studies	H6NC	4FT deg	M+Ph g	24	1M+9D	D$6/^ go	33$	AABBB	Ind		
Electronics/Business Administration	HN61	3FT/4SW deg	M/P g	20	5M+5D	D$6/^ go	30$	BBBBB$	Ind	5	
Engineering Management/Business Administration	HNR1	3FT/4SW deg	S g	20	5M+5D	D$6/^ go	30$	BBBBB$	Ind		
Environmental Sci & Tech/Business Admin (Yr Z)	FN9C	4FT/5SW deg									
Environmental Sci & Technology/Business Admin	FN91	3FT/4SW deg	S g	20	5M+5D$	D$^ go	30$	BBBBB$	Ind		
Ergonomics/Business Administration	JNX1	3FT/4SW deg	* g	20	5M+5D	D$6/^ go	30	BBBBB	Ind		
European Studies/Business Administration	NT12	3FT/4SW deg	* g	20	5M+5D	D6/^ go	30	BBBBB	Ind		
French/Business Administration	NR11	4SW deg	F g	20	X	D$^ go	30$	BBBBB$	Ind	4	16/24
German/Business Administration	NR12	4SW deg	G g	20	X	D$^ go	30$	BBBBB$	Ind	3	18/24
Human Psychology/Business Admin (Year Zero)	NL17	4FT/5SW deg									
Human Psychology/Business Administration	LN71	3FT/4SW deg	* g	22	3M+7D	D$6/^ go	31	ABBBB	Ind	6	20/28
International Business and French	NRC1	4SW deg	F g	BBB	3M+7D	D$^ go	31$	AABBB$	Ind	6	20/30
International Business and German	NRD2	4SW deg	G g	BBB	3M+7D	D$^ go	31$	AABBB$	Ind	6	20/30
International Business, French and German	NT1F	4SW deg	F+G g	BBB	3M+7D	D$^ go	31$	AABBB$	Ind		
Logistics	J9NX	3FT deg	* g	18	8M+2D	D$6/^ go	29	BBBBC	Ind	2	14/20
Logistics	J9N9	4SW deg	* g	18	8M+2D	D$6/^ go	29	BBBBC	Ind	2	13/20
Managerial and Administrative Studies	N128	4SW deg	* g	BBB	3M+7D	DB6/^ go	31	AABBB	Ind	5	20/28
Marketing	N500	4SW deg	* g	BBB	3M+7D	DB6/^ go	31	AABBB	Ind	10	20/28
Mathematics/Business Administration	GN11	3FT/4SW deg	M g	20	X	D$^ go	31$	ABBBB$	Ind	12	
Medicinal Chemistry/Business Administration	FN1C	3FT/4SW deg	C g	20	3M+7D$	D$^ go	31$	ABBBB$	Ind		
Operations Management	N220	3FT/4SW deg	* g	BBB	3M+7D	DB6/^ go	31	AABBB	Ind		

| course details | | | 98 expected requirements | | | | | | | 96 entry stats | |

TITLE	CODE	COURSE	SUBJECTS	A/AS	ND/C	AGNVQ	IB	SQA(H)	SQA	RATIO	A/AS
Organisation Studies	N130	3FT/4SW deg	* g	BBB	3M+7D	DB6/^ go	31	AABBB	Ind	7	
Product Design (Engineering)/Business Admin	HN71	3FT/4SW deg	S g	20	5M+5D$	D$^ go	30$	BBBBB			
Psychology & Management (Year Zero)	LN7D	4FT/5SW deg									
Psychology and Management	LN7C	3FT/4SW deg	* g	BBC	3M+7D	D$6/^ go	32	ABBBB	Ind	7	18/26
Public Policy & Management/Business Admin	MN1C	3FT/4SW deg	* g	20	3M+7D	D$6/^ go	30	BBBBB	Ind	3	18/22
Social Studies/Business Administration	LN41	3FT/4SW deg	* g	20	3M+7D	D$6/^ go	30	BBBBB	Ind	3	16/24
Transport Management	N920	3FT deg	* g	18	8M+2D	D$6/^ go	29	BBBBC	Ind	4	16/18
Transport Management	N921	4SW deg	* g	18	8M+2D	D$6/^ go	29	BBBBC	Ind	5	16/22

Univ of Wales, BANGOR

Business and Social Administration	L4N1	3FT deg	* g	12	4M	M$ go	Ind	Ind	Ind		
Computer Systems with Business Studies	H6N1	3FT deg	* g	CC	3M	M$6/^ go	26	BBCC	Ind	5	8/16
French Syllabus (B) and Management	NR1C	4FT deg	F g	18	X	D$^ go	28$	BBBC$	X		
Management and Chemistry	NF11	3FT deg	C g	CDD	3M $	MS3 go	26$	BBCC$	Ind		
Management and French Syllabus (A)	NR11	4FT deg	F g	18	X	D$^ go	28$	BBBC$	X		
Management and German	NR12	4FT deg	* g	18	X	D$^ go	28	BBBC	X		
Management and Mathematics	NG11	3FT deg	M g	18	5M $	D$^ go	28$	BBBC$	Ind		
Management with Accounting	N1N4	3FT deg	* g	18	3M+2D	D$6/^ go	28	BBBC	Ind	7	
Management with Banking, Insurance and Finance	N1N3	3FT deg	* g	18	3M+2D	D$6/^ go	28	BBBC	Ind	4	10/22
Management with Economics	N1L1	3FT deg	* g	18	3M+2D	D$6/^ go	28	BBBC	Ind	3	10/16
Management/Welsh	NQ15	3FT deg	W g	18	X	D*^ go	Ind	X	X		

BARNSLEY COLL

Business and Management Studies	N100	3FT deg	*	EE	4M	M*	Ind	Ind	Ind		
Business	021N	2FT HND	* g	E	2M	P*	Ind	Ind	Ind		

Univ of BATH

Business Administration	N122	4SW deg	*	BBB	Ind	D^	30	Ind	Ind	7	20/28
Chemistry with Management (with year abroad)	F1NC	4FT deg	C g	18	Ind	D^	28	Ind	Ind		
International Mgt and Modern Lang-French (4 Yr)	NR11	4SW deg	F	BBB	Ind	Ind	30	Ind	Ind	7	24/30
International Mgt and Modern Lang-German (4 Yr)	NR12	4SW deg	G	BBB	Ind	Ind	30	Ind	Ind	5	22/30
Sociology with Industrial Relations (4 Yr SW)	L3N6	4SW deg	*	22	1M+5D$	Ind	30	ABBBB	Ind	7	

BATH COLL of HE

Combined Awards *Business Studies*	Y400	3FT deg		N			Ind	$	$		
Modular Programme (DipHE) *Business Studies*	Y460	2FT Dip		N			Ind	$	$		

BELL COLLEGE OF TECHNOLOGY

Manufacturing Engineering and Management	HN71	3FT deg	* g	DD	Ind	Ind	Ind	CCC$	Ind		
Premises Management	N800	3FT deg	* g	CD	Ind	Ind	Ind	BBC$	Ind		
Quality Management with Business Studies	N9N1	4FT deg	E/Ee g	BBB-CC	Ind	Ind	Ind	BBB$	Ind		
Retail Business Management	N111	2FT Dip	Ap g	DDEE-DE	Ind	Ind	Ind	CCC$	18$		
Administration and Information Management	12NP	2FT HND	Ap g	DD-D	N $	P$	Ind	CC$	N$		
Business Administration	051N	2FT HND	Ap g	DD-D	N $	P$	Ind	CC$	N$		
Business Administration with Travel and Tourism	7P1N	2FT HND	Ap g	DD-D	N $	P$	Ind	CC$	12$		
Logistics Management	099N	2FT HND	* g	D	N	P$	Ind	CC$	Ind		
Manufacturing Engineering and Management	17NH	2FT HND	* g	D	N $	P$	Ind	CC$	Ind		
Quality Management	039N	2FT HND	* g	DD-D	N $	P$	Ind	CC$	Ind		
Retail Management	011N	2FT HND	Ap g	DD-D	N $	P$	Ind	CC$	N$		
Small Business Management	221N	2FT HND	Ap g	DD-D	N $	P$	Ind	CC$	18$		

Univ of BIRMINGHAM

BCom (Business Administration) Honours	N100	3FT deg	*	BBB	Ind	D+^	32	ABBBB	Ind	9	24/30
BCom (Business Administration) with French	NR11	4FT deg	F	BBB	Ind	D+^	32	ABBBB	Ind	8	24/30

course details | 98 expected requirements | 96 entry stats

TITLE	CODE	COURSE	SUBJECTS	A/AS	ND/C	AGNVQ	IB	SQA(H)	SQA	RATIO	A/AS
BCom (Business Administration) with German	NR12	4FT deg	G	BBC	Ind	D+^	32	ABBBB	Ind	5	24/30
BCom (Business Administration) with Italian	NR13	4FT deg	L	BBC	Ind	D+^	32	ABBBB	Ind	16	
BCom (Business Administration) with Japanese	NT14	4FT deg	L	BBC	Ind	D+^	32	ABBBB	Ind		
BCom (Business Administration) with Portuguese	NR15	4FT deg	L	BBC	Ind	D+^	32	ABBBB	Ind		
BCom (Business Administration) with Spanish	NR14	4FT deg	L	BBC	Ind	D+^	32	ABBBB	Ind	10	22/28
BCom (Russian Studies)	NR98	3FT/4FT deg	R/*	BBC	Ind	D+^	32	ABBBB	Ind		
Business Studies/French Studies	RN11	4FT deg	F g	BBB	Ind	D*^	32$	ABBB	Ind	16	24/28
Business Studies/German Studies	RN21	4FT deg	G g	BBB	Ind	D*^	32$	ABBB	Ind	14	
Business Studies/Hispanic Studies	RN41	4FT deg	* g	BBB	Ind	D*^	32	ABBB	Ind	5	24/28
Business Studies/Italian	RN31	4FT deg	* g	BBB	Ind	D*^	32	ABBB	Ind	22	
Business Studies/Portuguese	RN51	4FT deg	* g	BBB	Ind	D*^	32	ABBB	Ind	6	
Chemical Engineering with Management (c)	H8N1	4FT deg	M+C	BBC	4M+1D$	Ind	32$	Ind	Ind	2	14/30
Chemistry with Business Studies	F1N1	3FT deg	C+M	BBB	Ind	Ind	34	Ind	Ind	6	14/26
Computer Science/Software Engineering w. Bus St	G5N1	3FT deg	S g	BBB	Ind	Ind	30	Ind	Ind	8	16/24
Law and Business Studies	MN31	3FT deg	g	AAB	DO	D$^ go	34$	CSYS	Ind	27	28/30
Manufacturing Eng & Business St with Found Year	H7N1	4FT/5FT deg	* g	BBC	6M+D$	M*^ go	30$	BBBC$	Ind	3	14/22
Manufacturing Engineering and Business Studies	HN71	3FT/4FT deg	M g	BBC	6M+1D$	D$^ go	32$	CSYS	Ind		
Manufacturing Engineering and Commerce	H7NC	4FT deg	M	BBC	6M+1D$	D$^ go	32$	CSYS	Ind	2	18/28
Mechanical Engineering & Bus St with Found Yr	H3N1	4FT/5FT deg	* g	BBC	6M+1D$	M*^ go	30$	BBBC$	Ind	9	
Mechanical Engineering and Business Studies	HN31	3FT/4FT deg	M+P	BBC	6M+1D$	D$^ go	32$	CSYS	Ind		
Physics with Business Studies	F3N1	3FT/4FT deg	P+M	BBC	Ind	Ind	30	Ind	Ind		
Mechanical Engineering, Manuf and Management Management	Y600	4FT deg	M+P	BBB	X	X	33$	CSYS	X		

BIRMINGHAM COLL of Food, Tourism & Creative St

Food and Consumer Management	DN49	3FT deg	* g	10	MO	M$ gi	Ind	Ind	Ind	4	4/22
Food and Retail Management	DN45	3FT/4SW deg	* g	10	MO	M$ gi	Ind	Ind	Ind		
Tourism Business Management	PN71	3FT deg	* g	12	MO	M$ gi	Ind	Ind	Ind	5	6/16
Food and Consumer Management (Home Economics)	94ND	2FT HND	*	4	3M	P$	Ind	Ind	Ind	2	6/8

BLACKBURN COLL

Business Administration (HND Top-up)	N122	1FT deg		X	HN						
Business Studies	N120	3FT deg									
Management	N100	3FT deg		12	M	M					
Business	001N	2FT HND									
Business and Finance	091N	2FT HND		2	N	P					
Business and Markteting	51NN	2FT HND									
Business and Personnel	61NN	2FT HND									

BLACKPOOL & FYLDE COLL

Business Studies (Service Industries)	N120	2FT deg			HN		X	X	Ind		
Business and Finance	31NN	2FT HND	*	4	3M	P$	Ind	Ind	Ind		
Business and Marketing	51NN	2FT HND	*	4	3M	P$	Ind	Ind	Ind		
Business and Personnel	61NN	2FT HND	*	4	3M	P$	Ind	Ind	Ind		
Performing Arts	1N4W	2FT HND	E/T	2	N		Ind	Ind	Ind		

BOLTON INST

Accountancy and Business Studies	NN14	3FT deg	* g	CD	MO	M*	24	BBCC	Ind		
Accountancy and Human Resource Management	NN1K	3FT deg	* g	CD	MO	M*	24	BBCC	Ind		
Accountancy and Marketing	NN45	3FT deg	* g	CD	MO	M*	24	BBCC	Ind		
Accountancy and Operations Management	NN24	3FT deg	* g	CD	MO	M*	24	BBCC	Ind		
Architectural Tech & Occupational Hlth & Safety	KN26	3FT deg	* g	10	3M	M*	Ind	Ind	Ind		
Art & Design History and Business Studies	VN41	3FT deg	* g	CD	MO	M*	24	BBCC	Ind		
Art and Design History and Human Resource Mgt	NV14	3FT deg	* g	CD	MO	M*	24	BBCC	Ind		
Art and Design History and Marketing	NV54	3FT deg	* g	CD	MO	M*	24	BBCC	Ind		

| | | | 98 expected requirements | | | | | | 96 entry stats |

course details

TITLE	CODE	COURSE	SUBJECTS	A/AS	ND/C	AGNVQ	IB	SQA(H)	SQA	RATIO A/AS
Art and Design History and Operations Management	NV24	3FT deg	* g	CD	MO	M*	24	BBCC	Ind	
Biology and Business Studies	CN11	3FT deg	* g	CD	MO	M*	24	BBCC	Ind	
Biology and Human Resource Management	CN1C	3FT deg	* g	CD	MO	M*	24	BBCC	Ind	
Biology and Marketing	CN15	3FT deg	* g	CD	MO	M*	24	BBCC	Ind	
Biology and Operations Management	CN12	3FT deg	* g	CD	MO	M*	24	BBCC	Ind	
Building Surveying & Occupational Hlth & Safety	KNF6	3FT deg	* g	10	3M	M*	Ind	Ind	Ind	
Business Administration	N150	1FT deg	* g		HN	Ind	Ind	Ind	Ind	
Business Economics and Business Studies	LN11	3FT deg	* g	CD	MO	M*	24	BBCC	Ind	
Business Economics and Human Resource Management	NL11	3FT deg	* g	CD	MO	M*	24	BBCC	Ind	
Business Economics and Marketing	LN15	3FT deg	* g	CD	MO	M*	24	BBCC	Ind	
Business Economics and Operations Management	LN12	3FT deg	* g	CD	MO	M*	24	BBCC	Ind	
Business Info Systems and Human Resource Mgt	GN5C	3FT deg	* g	CD	MO	M*	24	BBCC	Ind	
Business Information Systems and Marketing	GN55	3FT deg	* g	CD	MO	M*	24	BBCC	Ind	
Business Information Systems and Operations Mgt	GN52	3FT deg	* g	CD	MO	M*	24	BBCC	Ind	
Business Studies	N100	3FT deg	* g	CD	MO	M*	24	BBCC	Ind	
Business Studies and Civil Engineering	HN21	3FT deg	M g	10	3M	M$	Ind	Ind	Ind	
Business Studies and Community Studies	LN5C	3FT deg	* g	CD	MO	M*	24	BBCC	Ind	
Business Studies and Computing	GN51	3FT deg	* g	CD	MO	M*	24	BBCC	Ind	
Business Studies and Creative Writing	NW1X	3FT deg	* g	CD	MO	M*	24	BBCC	Ind	
Business Studies and Environmental Studies	FN91	3FT deg	* g	CD	MO	M*	24	BBCC	Ind	
Business Studies and European Cultural Studies	TN21	3FT deg	* g	CD	MO	M*	24	BBCC	Ind	
Business Studies and Film & TV Studies	NW1M	3FT deg	Me/T g	CD	Ind	Ind	24	BBCC	Ind	
Business Studies and French	NR11	3FT deg	F g	CD	Ind	Ind	24	BBCC	Ind	
Business Studies and Gender & Women's Studies	MN9C	3FT deg	* g	CD	MO	M*	24	BBCC	Ind	
Business Studies and German	NR12	3FT deg	G g	CD	Ind	Ind	24	BBCC	Ind	
Business Studies and History	NV11	3FT deg	* g	CD	MO	M*	24	BBCC	Ind	
Business Studies and Human Resource Management	NN1C	3FT deg	* g	CD	MO	M*	24	BBCC	Ind	
Business Studies and Law	NM13	3FT deg	* g	CD	MO	M g	24	BBCC	Ind	
Business Studies and Leisure Studies	NL1H	3FT deg	* g	CD	MO	M*	24	BBCC	Ind	
Business Studies and Literature	NQ12	3FT deg	* g	CD	MO	M*	24	BBCC	Ind	
Business Studies and Marketing	NN15	3FT deg	* g	CD	MO	M*	24	BBCC	Ind	
Business Studies and Mathematics	GN11	3FT deg	M g	DD	Ind	Ind	24	BBCC	Ind	
Business Studies and Operations Management	NN12	3FT deg	* g	CD	MO	M*	24	BBCC	Ind	
Business Studies and Organisations, Mgt & Work	NNC7	3FT deg	* g	CD	MO	M*	24	BBCC	Ind	
Business Studies and Peace and War Studies	NM19	3FT deg	* g	CD	MO	M*	24	BBCC	Ind	
Business Studies and Philosophy	NV17	3FT deg	* g	CD	MO	M*	24	BBCC	Ind	
Business Studies and Psychology	LN71	3FT deg	* g	12	MO	D*	24	BBCC	Ind	
Business Studies and Sociology	LN3C	3FT deg	* g	CD	MO	M	24	Ind	Ind	
Business Studies and Statistics	GN41	3FT deg	* g	CD	MO	M	24	Ind	Ind	
Business Studies and Theatre Studies	WN41	3FT deg	Me/T g	CD	Ind	Ind	24	BBCC	Ind	
Business Studies and Tourism Studies	NP17	3FT deg	* g	CD	MO	M*	24	BBCC	Ind	
Business Studies and Urban and Cultural Studies	KN41	3FT deg	* g	CD	MO	M*	24	BBCC	Ind	
Civil Engineering and Occupational Hlth & Safety	HN26	3FT deg	M/S g	10	3M	M$	Ind	Ind	Ind	
Community Studies and Human Resource Management	LN51	3FT deg	* g	CD	MO	M*	24	BBCC	Ind	
Community Studies and Marketing	LN55	3FT deg	* g	CD	MO	M*	24	BBCC	Ind	
Community Studies and Operations Management	LN52	3FT deg	* g	CD	MO	M*	24	BBCC	Ind	
Computing Studies and Human Resource Management	GN5D	3FT deg	* g	CD	MO	M*	24	BBCC	Ind	
Computing and Marketing	GN5M	3FT deg	* g	CD	MO	M*	24	BBCC	Ind	
Computing and Operations Management	GN5F	3FT deg	* g	CD	MO	M*	24	BBCC	Ind	
Construction and Occupational Health & Safety	KNG6	3FT deg	* g	10	3M	M*	Ind	Ind	Ind	
Creative Writing and Human Resource Management	NW1Y	3FT deg	* g	CD	MO	M*	24	BBCC	Ind	
Creative Writing and Marketing	NW5X	3FT deg	* g	CD	MO	M*	24	BBCC	Ind	

course details | .98 expected requirements | .96 entry stats

TITLE	CODE	COURSE	SUBJECTS	A/AS	ND/C	AGNVQ	IB	SQA(H)	SQA	RATIO A/AS
Creative Writing and Operations Management	NW29	3FT deg	* g	CD	MO	M*	24	BBCC	Ind	
Design and Business Studies	WN21	3FT deg	* g	CD	MO	M*	24	BBCC	Ind	
Design and Human Resource Management	NW12	3FT deg	* g	CD	MO	M*	24	BBCC	Ind	
Design and Marketing	NW52	3FT deg	* g	CD	MO	M*	24	BBCC	Ind	
Design and Operations Management	NW22	3FT deg	* g	CD	MO	M*	24	BBCC	Ind	
Electronics and Occupational Health & Safety	HNP6	3FT deg	M/S	10	3M	M$	Ind	Ind	Ind	
Electronics and Technology Management	HNP9	3FT deg	M/S/Bu	10	3M	M$	Ind	Ind	Ind	
Environmental St & Occupational Health & Safety	FN96	3FT deg	* g	10	MO	M*	Ind	Ind	Ind	
Environmental Studies and Human Resource Mgt	FN9C	3FT deg	* g	CD	MO	M*	24	BBCC	Ind	
Environmental Studies and Marketing	FN95	3FT deg	* g	CD	MO	M*	24	BBCC	Ind	
Environmental Studies and Operations Management	FN92	3FT deg	* g	CD	MO	M*	24	BBCC	Ind	
Environmental Tech & Occupational Hlth & Safety	KN36	3FT deg	S g	10	3M	M$	Ind	Ind	Ind	
European Cultural Studies and Human Resource Mgt	NT12	3FT deg	* g	CD	MO	M*	24	BBCC	Ind	
European Cultural Studies and Marketing	NT52	3FT deg	* g	CD	MO	M*	24	BBCC	Ind	
European Cultural Studies and Operations Mgt	NT22	3FT deg	* g	CD	MO	M*	24	BBCC	Ind	
Film and TV Studies and Human Resource Mgt	NW15	3FT deg	Me/T g	CD	Ind	Ind	24	BBCC	Ind	
Film and TV Studies and Marketing	NW55	3FT deg	Me/T g	CD	Ind	Ind	24	BBCC	Ind	
Film and TV Studies and Operations Management	NW25	3FT deg	Me/T g	CD	Ind	Ind	24	BBCC	Ind	
French and Human Resource Management	NR1C	3FT deg	F g	CD	Ind	Ind	24	BBCC	Ind	
French and Marketing	NR51	3FT deg	F g	CD	Ind	Ind	24	BBCC	Ind	
French and Occupational Health & Safety	RN16	3FT deg	F g	10	Ind	Ind	Ind	Ind	Ind	
French and Operations Management	NR21	3FT deg	F g	CD	Ind	Ind	24	BBCC	Ind	
French and Technology Management	RN19	3FT deg	F g	10	3M	Ind	Ind	Ind	Ind	
Gender and Women's Studies and Marketing	MN95	3FT deg	* g	CD	MO	M*	24	BBCC	Ind	
Gender and Women's Studies and Operations Mgt	MN92	3FT deg	* g	CD	MO	M*	24	BBCC	Ind	
Gender and Women's Studs and Human Resource Mgt	MN91	3FT deg	* g	CD	MO	M*	24	BBCC	Ind	
German and Human Resource Management	NR1F	3FT deg	G g	CD	Ind	Ind	24	BBCC	Ind	
German and Marketing	NR52	3FT deg	G g	CD	Ind	Ind	24	BBCC	Ind	
German and Occupational Health & Safety	RN26	3FT deg	G g	10	Ind	Ind	Ind	Ind	Ind	
German and Operations Management	NR22	3FT deg	G g	CD	Ind	Ind	Ind	Ind	Ind	
German and Technology Management	RN29	3FT deg	G g	10	3M	Ind	Ind	Ind	Ind	
History and Human Resource Management	NV1C	3FT deg	* g	CD	MO	M*	24	BBCC	Ind	
History and Marketing	NV51	3FT deg	* g	CD	MO	M*	24	BBCC	Ind	
History and Operations Management	NV21	3FT deg	* g	CD	MO	M*	24	BBCC	Ind	
History and Organisations, Management & Work	NVD7	3FT deg	* g	CD	MO	M*	24	BBCC	Ind	
Human Resource Management	N130	3FT deg	* g	CD	MO	M*	24	BBCC	Ind	
Human Resource Management and Law	MN31	3FT deg	* g	CD	MO	M*	24	BBCC	Ind	
Human Resource Management and Leisure Studies	LNH1	3FT deg	* g	CD	MO	M*	24	BBCC	Ind	
Human Resource Management and Literature	NQ1F	3FT deg	* g	CD	MO	M*	24	BBCC	Ind	
Human Resource Management and Marketing	NN1M	3FT deg	* g	CD	MO	M*	24	BBCC	Ind	
Human Resource Management and Mathematics	NG11	3FT deg	M g	CD	Ind	Ind	24	BBCC	Ind	
Human Resource Management and Mathematics	NC11	3FT deg	M g	DD	Ind	Ind	24	BBCC	Ind	
Human Resource Management and Operations Mgt	NN21	3FT deg	* g	CD	Ind	Ind	24	BBCC	Ind	
Human Resource Management and Peace and War St	NV1D	3FT deg	* g	CD	MO	M*	24	BBCC	Ind	
Human Resource Management and Philosophy	NV1R	3FT deg	* g	CD	MO	M*	24	BBCC	Ind	
Human Resource Management and Psychology	LN7C	3FT deg	* g	12	MO	D*	24	BBCC	Ind	
Human Resource Management and Sociology	LN3D	3FT deg	* g	CD	MO	M	24	Ind	Ind	
Human Resource Management and Statistics	GN4C	3FT deg	* g	CD	MO	M	24	Ind	Ind	
Human Resource Management and Technology Mgt	NNC9	3FT deg	* g	10	MO	Ind	Ind	Ind	Ind	
Human Resource Management and Theatre Studies	NW14	3FT deg	Me/T g	CD	Ind	Ind	24	BBCC	Ind	
Human Resource Management and Tourism Studies	NP1R	3FT deg	* g	CD	MO	M*	24	BBCC	Ind	
Human Resource Mgt & Occupational Hlth & Safety	NNC6	3FT deg	* g	10	MO	Ind	Ind	Ind	Ind	

Business and Management 12

TITLE	CODE	COURSE	SUBJECTS	A/AS	NO/C	AGNVQ	IB	SQA(H)	SQA	RATIO A/AS
Human Resource Mgt & Organisations, Mgt & Work	NN71	3FT deg	* g	CD	MO	M*	24	BBCC	Ind	
Human Resource Mgt and Urban and Cultural Studs	LN31	3FT deg	* g	CD	MO	M*	24	BBCC	Ind	
International Business (French)	N1R1	3FT deg	* g	CD	MO	M*	24	BBCC	Ind	
International Business (German)	N1R2	3FT deg	* g	CD	MO	M*	24	BBCC	Ind	
International Business (Spanish)	N1R4	3FT deg	* g	CD	MO	M*	24	BBCC	Ind	
Law and Marketing	MN35	3FT deg	* g	CD	MO	M*	24	BBCC	Ind	
Law and Operations Management	MN32	3FT deg	* g	CD	MO	M*	24	BBCC	Ind	
Leisure Studies and Marketing	LNH5	3FT deg	* g	CD	MO	M*	24	BBCC	Ind	
Leisure Studies and Operations Management	LN32	3FT deg	* g	CD	MO	M*	24	BBCC	Ind	
Literature and Marketing	NQ52	3FT deg	* g	CD	MO	M*	24	BBCC	Ind	
Literature and Operations Management	NQ22	3FT deg	* g	CD	MO	M*	24	BBCC	Ind	
Man Systs Design & Occupational Health & Safety	HN76	3FT deg	M/S g	10	3M	M$	Ind	Ind	Ind	
Manufacturing Systems Design and Technology Mgt	HNR9	4FT deg	M/S/Bu g	4	N	P$	Ind	Ind	Ind	
Manufacturing Systems Design and Technology Mgt	HN79	3FT deg								
Marketing	N500	3FT deg	* g	CD	MO	M*	24	BBCC	Ind	
Marketing and Mathematics	GN15	3FT deg	M g	CD	Ind	Ind	24	BBCC	Ind	
Marketing and Motor Vehicle Studies	NH5J	3FT deg	M/S g	10	3M	M$	Ind	Ind	Ind	
Marketing and Operations Management	NN52	3FT deg	* g	CD	MO	M*	24	BBCC	Ind	
Marketing and Organisations, Management & Work	NN75	3FT deg	* g	CD	MO	M*	24	BBCC	Ind	
Marketing and Peace & War Studies	NV5C	3FT deg	* g	CD	MO	M*	24	BBCC	Ind	
Marketing and Philosophy	VN75	3FT deg	* g	CD	MO	M	24	BBCC	Ind	
Marketing and Sociology	LN3M	3FT deg	* g	CD	MO	M	24	Ind	Ind	
Marketing and Statistics	GN45	3FT deg	* g	CD	MO	M	24	Ind	Ind	
Marketing and Tourism Studies	NP5R	3FT deg	* g	CD	MO	M*	24	BBCC	Ind	
Marketing and Urban & Cultural Studies	LN35	3FT deg	* g	CD	MO	M*	24	BBCC	Ind	
Mathematics and Operations Management	GN12	3FT deg	M g	CD	Ind	Ind	24	BBCC	Ind	
Motor Vehicle St & Occupational Health & Safety	HNJ6	3FT deg								
Motor Vehicle Studies and Technology Management	HNJ9	3FT deg	M/S/Bu g	10	3M	M$	Ind	Ind	Ind	
Occupational Health & Safety & Quantity Surv	NK6F	3FT deg	* g	10	3M	M*	Ind	Ind	Ind	
Occupational Health & Safety and Technology Mgt	NN69	3FT deg	* g	10	3M	M*	Ind	Ind	Ind	
Operations Management & Sociology	LN3G	3FT deg	* g	CD	MO	M	24	Ind	Ind	
Operations Management and Peace and War Studies	NV2C	3FT deg	* g	CD	MO	M*	24	BBCC	Ind	
Operations Management and Philosophy	NV27	3FT deg	* g	CD	MO	M*	24	BBCC	Ind	
Operations Management and Psychology	LN72	3FT deg	* g	12	MO	D*	24	BBCC	Ind	
Operations Management and Theatre Studies	NW24	3FT deg	Me/T g	CD	Ind	Ind	24	BBCC	Ind	
Operations Management and Tourism Studies	NP27	3FT deg	* g	CD	Ind	Ind	24	BBCC	Ind	
Operations Management and Urban and Cultural St	LN3F	3FT deg	* g	CD	Ind	Ind	24	BBCC	Ind	
Operations Mgt & Organisations, Mgt & Work	NN27	3FT deg	* g	CD	Ind	Ind	24	BBCC	Ind	
Product Design and Technology Management	HNTX	4FT deg	M/S/Ad/Ds/Bu	4	N	P$	Ind	Ind	Ind	
Product Design and Technology Management	HNT9	3FT deg	M/S/As/Ds/Bu	10	3M	M$	Ind	Ind	Ind	
Simulation/Virtual Environ and Technology Mgt	GN79	3FT deg	M/S/Bu	10	3M	M$	Ind	Ind	Ind	
Simulation/Virtual Environment and Technol Mgt	GN7X	4FT deg	M/S/Bu	4	N	P$	Ind	Ind	Ind	
Textiles (Technology and Management)	JN41	3FT deg	* g	10	3M	M*	Ind	Ind	Ind	
Textiles (Technology and Management)	JN4C	4FT deg	* g	4	N	P*	Ind	Ind	Ind	
Textiles (Technology and Marketing)	JN4M	4FT deg	* g	4	N	P*	Ind	Ind	Ind	
Textiles (Technology and Marketing)	JN45	3FT deg	* g	10	3M	M*	Ind	Ind	Ind	
Theatre Studies and Marketing	NW54	3FT deg	* g	CD	MO	M*	24	BBCC	Ind	
Visual Arts and Business Studies	NW1C	3FT deg	* g	CD	MO	M*	24	BBCC	Ind	
Visual Arts and Marketing	NW51	3FT deg	* g	CD	MO	M*	24	BBCC	Ind	
Visual Arts and Operations Management	NW21	3FT deg	* g	CD	MO	M*	24	BBCC	Ind	
Business Studies	001N	2FT HND	* g	E	3M	P	Dip	Ind	N	

TITLE	CODE	COURSE	SUBJECTS	A/AS	ND/C	AGNVQ	IB	SQA(H)	SQA	RATIO	A/AS
BOURNEMOUTH Univ											
Advertising Management	N510	3FT deg	* g	BB-BCC	MO+4D	D$^ go	30	ABBBB	Ind	12	18/26
Business Administration	N121	1FT deg									
Business Studies	N120	4SW deg	* g	14-16	MO+4D	D$ go	Ind	BBBB	Ind	11	13/22
Business Studies with Languages	N1T9	4SW deg									10/18
International Marketing Management	N501	4SW deg	F/Sp/G/I g	16-18	MO+3D$	D$ go	26	BBBB	Ind	9	13/23
Leisure Marketing	N580	3FT deg	* g	14-18	DO	D$ go	Ind	BBBBB	Ind		
Retail Management	N110	4SW deg	* g	16-22	MO+4D	D$ go	30	BBB	Ind	6	12/20
Business	021N▼	2FT HND	* g	2	3M	P$ go	Ind	CCC	Ind	7	2/12
Tourism and Business	71PN▼	2FT HND	* g	4	4M	P$ go	Ind	CCC	Ind	9	4/10
BOURNEMOUTH and POOLE COLLEGE of A & D											
Arts and Event Administration	11WN	2FT HND		E	N $	P	Ind	Ind	N$		
Univ of BRADFORD											
Business and Management Studies	N121	4SW deg	* g	22	DO	DB^	Ind	Ind	Ind	5	16/28
Business and Management Studies	N120	3FT deg	* g	22	DO	DB^	Ind	Ind	Ind	7	12/24
Chemistry with Business & Management St (MChem)	F1ND	4FT deg	C+S g	BBC			Ind	Ind	Ind		
Chemistry with Business & Management Studies	F1NC	4SW deg	C+S g	BCD	3M+5D$	DS^	Ind	Ind	Ind	16	
Chemistry with Business & Management Studies	F1N1	3FT deg	C+S g	BCD	3M+5D$	DS^	Ind	Ind	Ind		
Computing with Management	G5N1	3FT deg	* g	22	3M+2D	D$4/^	Ind	Ind	Ind	6	
Computing with Management	G5NC	4SW deg	* g	22	3M+2D	D$4/^	Ind	Ind	Ind	5	12/20
International Management and French	N1R1	4SW deg	F g	22	DO $	D$^	Ind	Ind	Ind	5	16/28
International Management and German	N1R2	4SW deg	G g	22	DO $	D$^	Ind	Ind	Ind	5	14/24
International Management and Spanish	N1R4	4SW deg	Sp g	22	DO $	D$^	Ind	Ind	Ind	11	
Manufacturing Management and Technology	NJ19	4SW deg	* g	BB-CCC	3M $	M$4/^	Ind	Ind	Ind		
Manufacturing Management and Technology	NJ1X	3FT deg	* g	BB-CCC	3M $	M$4/^	Ind	Ind	Ind		
Pharmaceutical Management	B2N1	3FT deg	S g	CCD	5M $	MS4/^	Ind	Ind	Ind	2	12/18
Technology and Management	JN91	4SW deg	* g	BB-CCC	3M $	M$4/^	Ind	Ind	Ind	1	4/16
Technology and Management (3 Years)	JN9C	3FT deg	* g	BB-CCC	3M $	M$4/^	Ind	Ind	Ind	2	
BRADFORD & ILKLEY Comm COLL											
Business Administration	N150	3FT deg	g	6	DO	M	Ind	Ind	HN		
Law and European Business	MN31	3FT deg		6	DO	M+	Ind	Ind	Ind		
Management and Organizations	N100	3FT deg		8	MO	M	Ind	Ind	HN		
Office Systems Management	N1G7	3FT deg	g	8	MO	M	Ind	Ind			
Ophthalmic Dispensing with Management	B5N1	3FT deg			Ind	P					
Organization Studies	N153	3FT deg	*	8	MO	M	Ind	Ind	HN		
Business (general)	001N	2FT HND	g	2	MO	P	Ind	Ind	N		
Business and Finance (2 Yrs)	021N	2FT HND	*	2	MO	P	Ind	Ind	N		
Business and Marketing	51NN	2FT HND	*	2	MO	P	Ind	Ind	N		
Business and Personnel	031N	2FT HND	*	2	MO	P	Ind	Ind	N		
Univ of BRIGHTON											
Business Administration (HND top-up)	N122	1/2FT deg	g	X	MO $	X	X	X	X		
Business Studies	N120	4SW deg	* g	18	MO+5D	D$ go	28$	BBBB$	Ind		
Business Studies with Finance (4-year sandwich)	N1N3	4SW deg	* g	18	MO+5D	D$ go	28$	BBBB$	Ind		
Business Studies with Law	N1M3	3FT/4SW deg	* g	18	MO+5D	D$ go	28$	BBBB$	Ind		
Business Studies with Marketing(4-year sandwich)	N1N5	4SW deg	* g	18	MO+5D	D$ go	28$	BBBB$	Ind		
Computing and Operational Research	GN52	3FT/4SW deg	M g	12	MO $	M$	Dip$	BBCC$	Ind		
Energy Science with Management	J9N1	3FT/4SW deg	M/S/P g	12	5M $	MS/M^	Dip$	BBBC$	Ind		
European Business with Technology	N1J9	4SW deg	* g	14	5M	M6/^$ go	Dip$	Ind	Ind		
Fashion Design with Business St(4-year sandwich)	E2ND	4SW deg	Fa+Pf g		N $	Ind$ go	Ind$	Ind$	Ind$		
Fashion Design with Business St(4-year sandwich)	W2ND	4SW deg	Fa+Pf g		N $	Ind$ go	Ind$	Ind$	Ind$		

Business and Management 12

course details | 98 expected requirements | 96 entry stats

TITLE	CODE	COURSE	SUBJECTS	A/AS	ND/C	AGNVQ	IB	SQA(H)	SQA	RATIO A/AS
Fashion Textiles Des with Bus St (4-yr sandwich)	W2NC	4SW deg	Fa+Pf g		N $	Ind$ go	Ind$	Ind$	Ind$	
Fashion Textiles Des with Bus St (4-yr sandwich)	E2NC	4SW deg	Fa+Pf g		N $	Ind$ go	Ind$	Ind$	Ind$	
Food Retail Management	N550	3FT/4SW deg	* g	12	MO	M go	Dip	BBCC	Ind	
International Business	N140	4SW deg	L g	16	MO+5D	M$^ go	26$	BBBB$	Ind	
Language Studies with Business	T9N1	3FT/4SW deg	F/G g	14	2M+3D$ Ind		Dip$	BBCC$	Ind	
Mathematics and Operational Research	GN12	3FT/4SW deg	M g	12	MO $	M$	Dip$	BBCC$	Ind	
Mathematics for Management	G1N1	3FT/4SW deg	M g	12	Ind	Ind	Dip$	BBCC$	Ind	
Physics with Management	F3N1	3FT/4SW deg	M/P/S g	12	5M $	MS/M^	Dip$	BBBC$	Ind	
Statistics for Management	G4N1	3FT/4SW deg	M g	12	Ind	Ind	Dip$	BBCC$	Ind	
Tourism Management	PN71	3FT/4SW deg	* g	12	MO	M go	Dip	BBCC	Tourism	
Travel Management	P701	3FT/4SW deg	* g	12	MO	M go	Dip	BBCC	Tourism	
Business and Finance	021N	2FT HND	* g	DD	MO+2D$	M$ go	24$	CCCC$	Ind	
Business and Marketing	51NN	2FT HND	* g	DD	MO+2D$	M$ go	24$	CCCC$	Ind	
Business and Personnel	61NN	2FT HND	* g	DD	MO+2D$	M$ go	24$	CCCC$	Ind	
Mathematical Studies (Business Applications)	1N1G	2FT HND	M g	4	Ind	Ind	24$	CC$	Ind	

BRISTOL, Univ of the W of England

TITLE	CODE	COURSE	SUBJECTS	A/AS	ND/C	AGNVQ	IB	SQA(H)	SQA	RATIO A/AS
Business Administration	N100	3FT deg	* g	16	MO+2D	M$6/^ go	24	BBCC	Ind	
Business Studies	N120	4SW deg	* g	16	MO+2D	M$6/^ go	24	BBCC	Ind	
Business Studies with Combined Science	C9N1	3FT/4SW deg	S/M g	12	4M $	MS go	24$	BCC$	Ind	
Business Studies with Tourism	N121	1FT deg	* g	X	HN $	X	X	X	Ind	
EFL and Business Systems	QN31	3FT deg	g	14-22	5M	M*^ go	24$	BCCC$	Ind	
EFL, French and Business Systems	TN91	3FT deg	g	14-22	5M	M*^ go	24$	BCCC$	Ind	
EFL, German and Business Systems	TN9C	3FT deg	g	14-22	5M	M*^ go	24$	BCCC$	Ind	
EFL, Spanish and Business Systems	TN9D	3FT deg	g	14-22	5M	M*^ go	24$	BCCC$	Ind	
European Business Studies with Tourism	N1PR	4FT deg	* g	16	MO+2D	M$6/^ go	24	BBCC	Ind	
French and Business Systems	RN11	3FT deg	F g	14-22	5M	M*^ go	24$	BCCC$	Ind	
French, German and Business Systems	TNX1	3FT deg	F/G g	14-22	5M	M*^ go	24$	BCCC$	Ind	
French, Spanish and Business Systems	TNXC	3FT deg	F/Sp g	14-22	5M	M*^ go	24$	BCCC$	Ind	
German and Business Systems	RN21	3FT deg	G g	14-22	5M	M*^ go	24$	BCCC$	Ind	
German, Spanish and Business Systems	TNXD	3FT deg	G/Sp g	14-22	5M	M*^ go	24$	BCCC$	Ind	
International Business Studies	N140	4FT deg	* g	16	MO+2D	M$6/^ go	24	BBCC	Ind	
Marketing	N500	3FT/4SW deg	* g	16	MO+2D	M$6/^ go	24	BBCC	Ind	
Spanish and Business Systems	RN41	3FT deg		14-22	5M	M*^ go	24$	BCCC$	Ind	
Joint Honours Programme *Marketing and Languages*	Y401	4FT deg	L g	14-16	5M $	M$ go	24$	BCCC$	Ind	
Joint Honours Programme *Marketing and Statistics*	Y401	3FT deg	M g	14-16	5M $	M$ go	24$	BCCC$	Ind	
Science Foundation Year *Business Studies with Combined Science*	Y120	4EXT/5EXTSW deg	M/S g	E	N $	PS go	24$	Ind	N$	
Business Administration	051N	2FT/3SW HND	* g	8	MO	M$ go	24	CCC	Ind	
Business Studies (Marketing)	005N▼	2FT/3SW HND	* g	8	MO	M$ go	24	CCC	Ind	

BRUNEL Univ, West London

TITLE	CODE	COURSE	SUBJECTS	A/AS	ND/C	AGNVQ	IB	SQA(H)	SQA	RATIO A/AS
Business Studies/Accounting	N1N4	3FT deg	Ec g	18	MO $	M go	26$	BCCC$	Ind	
Chemistry with Management	F1NC	3FT deg	C g	CCD	3M $	MS2/^	26$	BBCCC$	Ind	25
Chemistry with Management (4 Yrs Thick SW)	F1ND	4SW deg	C g	CCD	3M $	MS2/^	26$	BBCCC$	Ind	10
Chemistry with Management (4 Yrs Thin SW)	F1N1	4SW deg	C g	CCD	3M $	MS2/^	26$	BBCCC$	Ind	2
Chemistry with Management (MChem)	FN1D	4SW deg	C g	BBB	6D $	DS4/^	32$	AABBB$	Ind	
Computer Studies/Business Studies	N1G5	3FT deg	Ec g	18	MO $	M go	26$	BCCC$	Ind	5
Economics and Management	LNC1	3FT deg	* g	20	M+D	D^	28$	Ind	Ind	11
Economics and Management (4 Yrs Thick SW)	LND1	4SW deg	* g	20	M+D	D^	28$	Ind	Ind	
Economics and Management (4 Yrs Thin SW)	LN11	4SW deg	* g	20	M+D	D^	28$	Ind	Ind	5 16/26
Health Service Administration	LN41	3FT deg	B	12-20	Ind	MG	Ind	Ind	Ind	

course details			98 expected requirements							96 entry stats	
TITLE	CODE	COURSE	SUBJECTS	A/AS	ND/C	RGNVQ	IB	SQA(H)	SQA	RATIO	A/AS
Management Studies	N103	3FT deg	*	20-24	5D	D^	28	Ind	Ind	7	14/22
Management Studies (4 Yrs Thick SW)	N102	4SW deg	*	20-24	5D	D^	28	Ind	Ind	6	16/24
Management Studies (4 Yrs Thin SW)	N101	4SW deg	*	20-24	5D	D^	28	Ind	Ind	6	15/26
Management Studies and Law	NM13	3FT deg	*	20-24	5D	D^	28	Ind	Ind	11	20/24
Management Studies and Law (4 Yrs Thick SW)	NM1J	4SW deg	*	20-24	5D	D^	28	Ind	Ind		
Management Studies and Law (4 Yrs Thin SW)	NM1H	4SW deg	*	20-24	5D	D^	28	Ind	Ind	10	
Manu Eng w. Mgt & Bus Stud(MEng) (4Yrs Thick SW)	H7NC	4SW/5SW deg	M	CCC	4M+1D$	DE^	28$	AABBB$	Ind	4	
Manuf Eng with Mgt & Bus St(MEng)(4 Yrs Thin SW)	H7N1	4SW/5SW deg	M	CCC	4M+1D$	DE^	28$	AABBB$	Ind	1	6/15
Manufacturing Eng with Mgt and Bus Studs (MEng)	H7ND	3FT/4FT deg	M	CCC	4M+1D$	DE^	28$	AABBB$	Ind	4	
Materials Engineering with Management (3/4 Yrs)	J5ND	3FT/4FT deg	2(M/P/C/Ds)	CCC-DDD	3M $	ME/S^	26$	CCCCC$	Ind	2	
Materials Engineering with Management (4/5 Yrs)	J5NC	4SW/5SW deg	2(M/P/C/Ds)	CC-DD	3M $	ME/S^	26$	CCCC$	Ind		
Materials Engineering with Management (4/5 Yrs)	J5N1	4SW/5SW deg	2(M/P/C/Ds)	CCC-DDD	3M $	ME/S^	26$	CCCCC$	Ind		
Materials Engineering with Mgt (4/5 Yr Thick SW)	J521	4SW/5SW deg	2(M/P/C/Ds)	CCC-DDD	3M $	ME/S^	26$	CCCCC$	Ind		
Mathematical & Management Studs (4 Yrs Thick SW)	GN1D	4SW deg	M	BBC-BCC	3M+2D$	P^	29$	BBBC$	Ind	7	
Mathematical and Management St (4 Yrs Thin SW)	GN11	4SW deg	M	BBC-BCC	3M+2D$	P^	29$	BBBC$	Ind	2	16/18
Mathematical and Management Studies	GN1C	3FT deg	M	BBC-BCC	3M+2D$	P^	29$	BBBC$	Ind	23	
Mathematics & Statistics with Mgt(4 Yrs Thin SW)	G1N1	4SW deg	M	BBC-BCC	3M+2D$	P^	29$	BBBC$	Ind	2	12/20
Mathematics & Statistics with Mgt(4Yrs Thick SW)	G1ND	4SW deg	M	BBC-BCC	3M+2D$	P^	29$	BBBC$	Ind	9	
Mathematics and Statistics with Management	G1NC	3FT deg	M	BBC-BCC	3M+2D$	P^	29$	BBBC$	Ind	5	14/18
Physics with Management Studies	F3N1	3FT deg	P+M	CC	3M $	Ind^	26$	CCCCC$	Ind	3	
Physics with Management Studies (4 Yrs Thick SW)	F3ND	4SW deg	P+M	CC	3M $	Ind^	26$	CCCCC$	Ind	2	
Physics with Management Studies (4 Yrs Thin SW)	F3NC	4SW deg	P+M	CC	3M $	Ind^	26$	CCCCC$	Ind		
Sport Sciences/Business Studies	B6NC	3FT deg	Ec g	18	1M+3D	D	29	BBCC	Ind		
Business and Finance	421N	2FT HND	* g	8	MO	M	24	CCCC	Ind		

Univ of BUCKINGHAM

Business Studies	N120	2FT deg	* g	14	3M+2D	M	26	BCCC	Ind	15	
Business Studies with Information Systems	N1G5	2FT deg	* g	14	3M+2D	M	26	BCCC	Ind		
Business Studies with Tourism	N1P7	2FT deg	* g	14	3M+2D	M	26	BCCC	Ind	16	
Information Systems with Business Studies	G5N1	2FT deg	* g	12	5M	M	24	CCCC	Ind		
Information Systems with Operations Management	G5N2	2FT deg	* g	12	5M	M	24	BCCC	Ind		
Law with Business Studies	M3N1	2FT deg	M* g	18	3M+2D	M	26	BCCC	Ind		
Marketing with French	N5R1	2FT deg	*	16	3M+2D	M	26	BCCC	Ind		
Marketing with Spanish	N5R4	2FT deg	*	16	3M+2D	M	26	BCCC	Ind		
Psychology with Business Studies	C8N1	2FT deg	* g	14	5M	M	26	BCCC	Ind		

BUCKINGHAMSHIRE COLLEGE

Business Administration	N122	3FT deg		8	MO+2D	M	27	CCCC	Ind	3	4/13
Business Administration (Conversion to degree)	N120	1FT deg			HN					5	
Business Administration and Human Resources Mgt	NN16	3FT deg		8	MO	M	27	CCCC	Ind		
Business Administration and Languages	NT1F	3FT deg		8	MO	M	27	CCCC	Ind		
Business Administration and Law	MN31	3FT deg		8	MO	M	27	CCCC	Ind		
Business Administration and Marketing	NN15	3FT deg		8	MO	M	27	CCCC	Ind		
Business Administration with Economics	N1L1	3FT deg		8	MO	M	27	CCCC	Ind		
Business Administration with European Studies	N1T2	3FT deg		8	2D	M	27	CCCC	Ind		
Business Administration with Finance	N1N3	3FT deg		8	MO	M	27	CCCC	Ind		
Business Administration with French	N1R1	3FT deg	F g	8	MO	M	27	CCCC	Ind	6	
Business Administration with German	N1R2	3FT deg	G g	8	MO	M	27	CCCC	Ind	14	
Business Administration with Human Resources Mgt	N130	3FT deg		8	MO+2D	M	27	CCCC	Ind		
Business Administration with Italian	N1R3	3FT deg	I g	8	MO+2D	M	27	CCCC	Ind	4	
Business Administration with Law	N1M3	3FT deg		8	MO+2D	M	27	CCCC	Ind		
Business Administration with Leisure Management	N1L7	3FT deg									
Business Administration with Logistics	N1N9	3FT deg		8	MO+2D	M	27	CCCC	Ind		

Business and Management 12

			98 expected requirements							96 entry stats	
TITLE	CODE	COURSE	SUBJECTS	A/AS	ND/C	AGNVQ	IB	SQA(H)	SQA	RATIO	A/AS
Business Administration with Marketing	N1N5	3FT deg		8	MO+2D	M	27	CCCC	Ind		
Business Administration with Spanish	N1R4	3FT deg	Sp g	8	MO+2D	M	27	CCCC	Ind	3	
Business Administration with Tourism	N1P7	3FT deg									
Business Information Technology with Management	G7N1	3FT deg									
Business Information Technology with Marketing	G7N5	3FT deg		8-10	MO	M	Ind	CCC	Ind		
Business Studies	N100	4SW deg		8	MO+2D	M	27	CCCC	Ind	6	6/20
Business Studies and Human Resources Management	NN1P	4SW deg		8	MO	M	27	CCCC	Ind		
Business Studies and Languages	NT1G	4SW deg	L g	8	MO	M	27	CCCC	Ind		
Business Studies and Law	MN3C	4SW deg			MO	M	27	CCCC	Ind		
Business Studies with Economics	N1LC	3FT deg		8	MO	M	27	CCCC	Ind		
Business Studies with European Studies	N1TF	4SW deg		8	M)+2D	M	27	CCCC	Ind		
Business Studies with Finance	N1NH	4SW deg		8	MO+2D	M	27	CCCC	Ind		
Business Studies with French	N1RD	4SW deg	F g	8	MO+2D	M	27	CCCC	Ind		
Business Studies with German	N1RG	4SW deg	G g	8	MO	M	27	CCCC	Ind		
Business Studies with Human Resources Management	N131	4SW deg		8	MO	M	27	CCCC	Ind		
Business Studies with Italian	N1RJ	4SW deg	I g	8	MO	M	27	CCCC	Ind		
Business Studies with Law	N1MH	4SW deg		8	MO	M	27	CCCC	Ind		
Business Studies with Leisure Management	N1NR	3FT deg									
Business Studies with Logistics	N1NX	4SW deg		8	MO	M	27	CCCC	Ind		
Business Studies with Marketing	N1NM	4SW deg		8	MO	M	27	CCCC	Ind		
Business Studies with Spanish	N1RL	4SW deg	Sp g	8	MO	M	27	CCCC	Ind		
Business Studies with Tourism	N1PR	3FT deg									
Computer Aided Design with Management	H1N1	3FT deg		8-10	MO	M	Ind	CCC	Ind		
Computer Aided Design with Marketing	H1N5	3FT deg		8-10	MO	M	Ind	CCC	Ind		
Computer Engineering with Management	G5N1	3FT deg		8-10	MO	M	Ind	CCC	Ind		
Computer Engineering with Marketing	G5N5	3FT deg		8-10	MO	M	Ind	CCC	Ind		
Computing with Management	G5NC	3FT deg		8-10	MO	M	Ind	CCC	Ind		
Computing with Marketing	G5NM	3FT deg		8-10	MO	M	Ind	CCC	Ind		
Design Technology with Management	W2N1	3FT deg									
Design Technology with Marketing	W2N5	3FT deg									
European Business Studies (French)	NR11	4SW deg	F g	8	MO	M	27	CCCC	Ind		
European Business Studies (German)	NR12	4SW deg	G g	8	MO	M	27	CCCC	Ind		
European Business Studies (Italian)	NR13	4SW deg	I g	8	MO	M	27	CCCC	Ind		
European Business Studies (Spanish)	NR14	4SW deg	Sp g	8	MO	M	27	CCCC	Ind		
Forest Products Technology with Management	J5N1	3FT deg		8-10	MO	M	Ind	CCC	Ind		
Forest Products Technology with Marketing	J5N5	3FT deg		8-10	MO	M	Ind	CCC	Ind		
Human Resources Management	N600	3FT deg		8	MO	M	27	CCCC	Ind		
Human Resources Management and Languages	NT62	3FT deg		8	MO	M	27	CCCC	Ind		
Human Resources Management and Law	MN36	3FT deg		8	MO	M	27	CCCC	Ind		
Human Resources Management and Marketing	NN65	3FT deg		8	MO	M	27	CCCC	Ind		
Human Resources Management with Economics	N6L1	3FT deg		8	MO	M	27	CCCC	Ind		
Human Resources Management with European Studies	N6T2	3FT deg		8	MO	M	27	CCCC	Ind		
Human Resources Management with French	N6R1	3FT deg		8	MO	M	27	CCCC	Ind		
Human Resources Management with German	N6R2	3FT deg		8	MO	M	27	CCCC	Ind		
Human Resources Management with Italian	N6R3	3FT deg		8	MO	M	27	CCCC	Ind		
Human Resources Management with Law	N6M3	3FT deg		8	MO	M	27	CCCC	Ind		
Human Resources Management with Spanish	N6R4	3FT deg		8	MO	M	27	CCCC	Ind		
International Business & Marketing Logistics	NN1M	3FT deg									
International Business Studies (French)	N1RC	4SW deg	L	8	MO	M	27	CCCC	Ind		
International Business Studies (German)	N1RF	4SW deg	L	8	MO	M	27	CCCC	Ind		
International Business Studies (Italian)	N1RH	4SW deg	L	8	MO	M	27	CCCC	Ind		
International Business Studies (Spanish)	N1RK	4SW deg	L	8	MO	M	27	CCCC	Ind		

course details				**98 expected requirements**						*96 entry stats*
TITLE	CODE	COURSE	SUBJECTS	A/AS	NO/C	AGNVQ	IB	SQA(H)	SQA	RATIO A/AS
International Marketing	N500	3FT deg		8	MO	M	27	CCCC	Ind	
International Marketing with French	N5R1	3FT deg	F g	8	MO	M	27	CCCC	Ind	
International Marketing with German	N5R2	3FT deg	G g	8	MO	M	27	CCCC	Ind	
International Marketing with Italian	N5R3	3FT deg	I g	8	MO	M	27	CCCC	Ind	
International Marketing with Spanish	N5R4	3FT deg	Sp g	8	MO	M	27	CCCC	Ind	
Leisure Management with Marketing	N7N5	3FT deg		8-10	1D	M	27	CCCC	Ind	
Marketing and Languages	NT52	3FT deg		8	MO	M	27	CCCC	Ind	
Marketing and Law	MN35	3FT deg		8	MO	M	27	CCCC	Ind	
Music Industry Management	W3N1	3FT deg		8-10	1D	M	27	CCCC	Ind	3 8/20
Product Design with Management	H7ND	3FT deg		8-10	MO	M	Ind	CCC	Ind	
Product Design with Marketing	H7N5	3FT deg		8-10	MO	M	Ind	CCC	Ind	
Tourism with Marketing	P7N5	3FT deg		8-10	1D	M	27	CCCC	Ind	
Business Studies	421N	2FT HND		4-6	4M	P	Ind	CCC	Ind	3 2/5
Business Studies with Finance	31NN	2FT HND		4	3M	P	Ind	Ind	Ind	
Business Studies with French	11RN	2FT HND		4	3M	P	Ind	Ind	Ind	
Business Studies with German	21RN	2FT HND		4	3M	P	Ind	Ind	Ind	
Business Studies with Human Resources Management	61NN	2FT HND		4	3M	P	Ind	Ind	Ind	
Business Studies with Italian	31RN	2FT HND		4	3M	P	Ind	Ind	Ind	
Business Studies with Marketing	51NN	2FT HND		4	3M	P	Ind	Ind	Ind	
Business Studies with Russian	81RN	2FT HND		4	3M	P	Ind	Ind	Ind	
Business Studies with Spanish	41RN	2FT HND		4	3M	P	Ind	Ind	Ind	

CANTERBURY CHRIST CHURCH COLL of HE

American Studies with Business Studies	Q4N1	4FT deg	* g	CC	MO	M	24	Ind	Ind	2
Art with Business Studies	W1N1	3FT deg	A g	CC	MO	M	24	Ind	Ind	14
Art with Marketing	W1N5	3FT deg	A g	CC	MO	M	24	Ind	Ind	5
Business Information Technology	GN51	2FT Dip	* g	CC	MO	M	24	Ind	Ind	1
Business Studies and American Studies	QN41	3FT deg	* g	CC	MO	M	24	Ind	Ind	1
Business Studies and Art	WN11	3FT deg	A g	CC	MO	M	24	Ind	Ind	7
Business Studies and Social Science	NL13	3FT deg	* g	CC	MO	M	24	Ind	Ind	4
Business Studies with American Studies	N1Q4	3FT deg	* g	CC	MO	M	24	Ind	Ind	1 10/14
Business Studies with Art	N1W1	3FT deg	A g	CC	MO	M	24	Ind	Ind	12
Business Studies with Early Childhood Studies	N1X9	3FT deg	* g	CC	MO	M	24	Ind	Ind	
Business Studies with English	N1Q3	3FT deg	E	CC	MO	M	24	Ind	Ind	10
Business Studies with French	N1R1	3FT deg	F g	CC	MO	M	24	Ind	Ind	
Business Studies with Geography	N1L8	3FT deg	Gy g	CC	MO	M	24	Ind	Ind	4 18/20
Business Studies with History	N1V1	3FT deg	H g	CC	MO	M	24	Ind	Ind	6
Business Studies with Information Technology	N1G5	3FT deg	* g	CC	MO	M	24	Ind	Ind	4 6/16
Business Studies with Marketing	N1N5	3FT deg	* g	CC	MO	M	24	Ind	Ind	4 6/20
Business Studies with Mathematics	N1G1	3FT deg	M g	DD	Ind	Ind	24	Ind	Ind	5
Business Studies with Media Studies	N1P4	3FT deg	* g	CC	MO	M	24	Ind	Ind	
Business Studies with Music	N1W3	3FT deg	Mu g	CC	MO	M	24	Ind	Ind	3
Business Studies with Psychology	N1L7	3FT deg	Ps g	CC	MO	M	24	Ind	Ind	27
Business Studies with Radio,Film & Television St	N1W5	3FT deg	* g	CC	MO	M	24	Ind	Ind	
Business Studies with Religious Studies	N1V8	3FT deg	* g	CC	MO	M	24	Ind	Ind	
Business Studies with Science	N1Y1	3FT deg	S g	DD	Ind	Ind	24	Ind	Ind	
Business Studies with Social Science	N1L3	3FT deg	* g	CC	MO	M	24	Ind	Ind	3
Business Studies with Sport Science	N1B6	3FT deg	* g	CC	MO	M	24	Ind	Ind	
Business Studies with Statistics	N1G4	3FT deg	M g	DD	Ind	Ind	24	Ind	Ind	
Business Studies with Tourism Studies	N1P7	3FT deg	* g	CC	MO	M	24	Ind	Ind	4 8/14
Early Childhood Studies and Business Studies	XN91	3FT deg	* g	CC	MO	M	24	Ind	Ind	
Early Childhood Studies with Business Studies	X9N1	3FT deg	* g	CC	MO	M	24	Ind	Ind	5
English and Business Studies	QN31	3FT deg	E	CC	MO	M	24	Ind	Ind	2

Business and Management 12

course details

TITLE	CODE	COURSE	SUBJECTS	A/AS	ND/C	AGNVQ	IB	SQA(H)	SQA	RATIO A/AS
English with Business Studies	Q3N1	3FT deg	E	CC	MO	M	24	Ind	Ind	5
English with Marketing	Q3N5	3FT deg	E	CC	MO	M	24	Ind	Ind	4
French and Business Studies	NR11	3FT deg	F g	CC	MO	M	24	Ind	Ind	
Geography and Business Studies	NL18	3FT deg	Gy g	CC	MO	M	24	Ind	Ind	
Geography with Business Studies	L8N1	3FT deg	Gy g	CC	MO	M	24	Ind	Ind	5 12/20
Geography with Marketing	L8N5	3FT deg	Gy g	CC	MO	M	24	Ind	Ind	
History and Business Studies	VN11	3FT deg	H g	CC	MO	M	24	Ind	Ind	4
History with Business Studies	V1N1	3FT deg	H g	CC	MO	M	24	Ind	Ind	12
History with Marketing	V1N5	3FT deg	H g	CC	MO	M	24	Ind	Ind	
Information Technology and Business Studies	NG15	3FT deg	* g	CC	MO	M	24	Ind	Ind	7
Information Technology with Business Studies	G5N1	3FT deg	* g	CC	MO	M	24	Ind	Ind	3
Information Technology with Marketing	G5N5	3FT deg	* g	CC	MO	M	24	Ind	Ind	
Marketing and Art	NW51	3FT deg	A g	CC	MO	M	24	Ind	Ind	2
Marketing and Business Studies	NN15	3FT deg	* g	CC	MO	M	24	Ind	Ind	4
Marketing and English	NQ53	3FT deg	E g	CC	MO	M	24	Ind	Ind	2
Marketing and French	NR51	3FT deg	F g	CC	MO	M	24	Ind	Ind	
Marketing and Geography	LN85	3FT deg	Gy g	CC	MO	M	24	Ind	Ind	
Marketing and History	NV51	3FT deg	H g	CC	MO	M	24	Ind	Ind	
Marketing and Information Technology	GN55	3FT deg	* g	CC	MO	M	24	Ind	Ind	
Marketing and Social Science	NL53	3FT deg	* g	CC	MO	M	24	Ind	Ind	1
Marketing with Art	N5W1	3FT deg	A g	CC	MO	M	24	Ind	Ind	7
Marketing with Business Studies	N5N1	3FT deg	* g	CC	MO	M	24	Ind	Ind	3
Marketing with English	N5Q3	3FT deg	E g	CC	MO	M	24	Ind	Ind	
Marketing with French	N5R1	3FT deg	F g	CC	MO	M	24	Ind	Ind	
Marketing with Geography	N5L8	3FT deg	Gy g	CC	MO	M	24	Ind	Ind	4
Marketing with History	N5V1	3FT deg	H g	CC	MO	M	24	Ind	Ind	
Marketing with Information Technology	N5G5	3FT deg	* g	CC	MO	M	24	Ind	Ind	3
Marketing with Mathematics	N5G1	3FT deg	M g	DD	Ind	Ind	24	Ind	Ind	
Marketing with Music	N5W3	3FT deg	Mu g	CC	MO	M	24	Ind	Ind	
Marketing with Psychology	N5L7	3FT deg	Ps g	CC	MO	M	24	Ind	Ind	
Marketing with Radio, Film and Television Studs	N5W5	3FT deg	* g	CC	MO	M	24	Ind	Ind	
Marketing with Religious Studies	N5V8	3FT deg	* g	CC	MO	M	24	Ind	Ind	
Marketing with Science	N5Y1	3FT deg	S g	DD	Ind	Ind	24	Ind	Ind	
Marketing with Social Science	N5L3	3FT deg	* g	CC	MO	M	24	Ind	Ind	6/18
Marketing with Sport Science	N5B6	3FT deg	* g	CC	MO	M	24	Ind	Ind	
Marketing with Statistics	N5G4	3FT deg	M g	DD	Ind	Ind	24	Ind	Ind	
Mathematics and Business Studies	NG11	3FT deg	M g	DD	Ind	Ind	24	Ind	Ind	
Mathematics and Marketing	NG51	3FT deg	M g	DD	Ind	Ind	24	Ind	Ind	
Mathematics with Business Studies	G1N1	3FT deg	M g	DD	Ind	Ind	24	Ind	Ind	4
Mathematics with Marketing	G1N5	3FT deg	M g	DD	Ind	Ind	24	Ind	Ind	
Media Studies and Business Studies	PN41	3FT deg	* g	CC	MO	M	24	Ind	Ind	
Media Studies with Business Studies	P4N1	3FT deg	* g	CC	MO	M	24	Ind	Ind	
Music and Business Studies	WN31	3FT deg	Mu g	CC	MO	M	24	Ind	Ind	2
Music and Marketing	NW53	3FT deg	Mu g	CC	MO	M	24	Ind	Ind	
Music with Business Studies	W3N1	3FT deg	Mu g	CC	MO	M	24	Ind	Ind	6
Music with Marketing	W3N5	3FT deg	Mu g	CC	MO	M	24	Ind	Ind	3
Psychology and Business Studies	NL17	3FT deg	Ps g	CC	MO	M	24	Ind	Ind	
Psychology and Marketing	NL57	3FT deg	Ps g	CC	MO	M	24	Ind	Ind	
Psychology with Business Studies	L7N1	3FT deg	Ps g	CC	MO	M	24	Ind	Ind	11
Psychology with Marketing	L7N5	3FT deg	Ps g	CC	MO	M	24	Ind	Ind	
Radio, Film and Television St and Business St	NW15	3FT deg	* g	CC	MO	M	24	Ind	Ind	6
Radio, Film & Television Studies with Business St	W5N1	3FT deg	* g	CC	MO	M	24	Ind	Ind	24

TITLE	CODE	COURSE	SUBJECTS	A/AS	ND/C	AGNVQ	IB	SQA(H)	SQA	RATIO	A/AS
Radio,Film & Television Studies with Marketing	W5N5	3FT deg	* g	CC	MO	M	24	Ind	Ind	5	10/18
Radio,Film and Television Studies and Marketing	WN55	3FT deg	* g	CC	MO	M	24	Ind	Ind	25	
Religious Studies and Business Studies	VN81	3FT deg	* g	CC	MO	M	24	Ind	Ind		
Religious Studies and Marketing	VN85	3FT deg	* g	CC	MO	M	24	Ind	Ind		
Religious Studies with Business Studies	V8N1	3FT deg	* g	CC	MO	M	24	Ind	Ind		
Religious Studies with Marketing	V8N5	3FT deg	* g	CC	MO	M	24	Ind	Ind		
Science and Business Studies	YN11	3FT deg	S g	DD	Ind	Ind	24	Ind	Ind		
Science and Marketing	NY51	3FT deg	S g	DD	Ind	Ind	24	Ind	Ind		
Science with Business Studies	Y1N1	3FT deg	S g	DD	Ind	Ind	24	Ind	Ind	1	
Social Science with Business Studies	L3N1	3FT deg	* g	CC	MO	M	24	Ind	Ind	7	
Social Science with Marketing	L3N5	3FT deg	* g	CC	MO	M	24	Ind	Ind		
Sport Science and Business Studies	NB16	3FT deg	* g	CC	MO	M	24	Ind	Ind		
Sport Science and Marketing	BN65	3FT deg	* g	CC	MO	M	24	Ind	Ind		
Sport Science with Business Studies	B6N1	3FT deg	* g	CC	MO	M	24	Ind	Ind		
Sport Science with Marketing	B6N5	3FT deg	* g	CC	MO	M	24	Ind	Ind		
Statistics and Business Studies	GN41	3FT deg	M g	DD	Ind	Ind	24	Ind	Ind		
Statistics and Marketing	GN45	3FT deg	M g	DD	Ind	Ind	24	Ind	Ind		
Statistics with Business Studies	G4N1	3FT deg	M g	DD	Ind	Ind	24	Ind	Ind		
Statistics with Marketing	G4N5	3FT deg	M g	DD	Ind	Ind	24	Ind	Ind		
Tourism Studies and Business Studies	PN71	3FT deg	* g	CC	MO	M	24	Ind	Ind	2	6/10
Tourism Studies with Business Studies	P7N1	3FT deg	* g	CC	MO	M	24	Ind	Ind	2	

CARDIFF Univ of Wales

TITLE	CODE	COURSE	SUBJECTS	A/AS	ND/C	AGNVQ	IB	SQA(H)	SQA	RATIO	A/AS
Accounting and Management	NN14	3FT deg	*	BBC-BBB	Ind	Ind	Ind	Ind	Ind	6	20/28
Business Administration	N122	3FT deg	*	BBC-BBB	Ind	Ind	Ind	Ind	Ind	4	20/26
Business Administration with French	N1R1	4FT deg	F g	BBC-BBB	Ind	Ind	Ind	Ind	Ind	11	20/26
Business Administration with German	N1R2	4FT deg	L g	BBC-BBB	Ind	Ind	Ind	Ind	Ind	9	
Business Administration with Italian	N1R3	4FT deg	L g	BBC-BBB	Ind	Ind	Ind	Ind	Ind	6	
Business Administration with Spanish	N1R4	4FT deg	Sp g	BBC-BBB	Ind	Ind	Ind	Ind	Ind	10	
Business Studies with Japanese	NT14	4FT deg	*	BBC-BBB	Ind	Ind	Ind	Ind	Ind	6	20/26
Economics and Management Studies	LN11	3FT deg	*	BBC-BBB	Ind	Ind	Ind	Ind	Ind	4	18/28
International Transport	N920	3FT deg		BCC-CCC	2M+2D		Ind			2	10/24
International Transport	N921	4SW deg		BCC-CCC	2M+2D		Ind			2	12/24
Maritime Studies	N925	4SW deg		BCC-CCC	2M+2D		Ind			6	
Maritime Studies	N924	3FT deg		BCC-CCC	2M+2D		Ind			12	
Sociology and Industrial Relations	LN36	3FT deg	*	BBC-BBB	7M+7D		Ind	AABBB	Ind	7	

Univ of Wales INST, CARDIFF

TITLE	CODE	COURSE	SUBJECTS	A/AS	ND/C	AGNVQ	IB	SQA(H)	SQA	RATIO	A/AS
Business Management (post HND)	N150	1FT deg	g		HN					6	
Business Studies	N120	3FT deg	* g	12	4M+2D		Ind	CCCC	Ind	11	10/18
Consumer Protection	N984	3FT deg									
European Business Management	N140	3FT deg	L g	10	MO	M*△ go	Ind	CCCC	Ind	3	4/14
Manufacturing Systems and Manufacturing Mgt	H7N1	4FT deg	* g	4	N	M$ gi	Ind	CCCC	Ind	8	
Business and Finance: Administration	051N	2FT HND	* g	6	MO	MB go	Ind	CC	Ind	8	2/12

Univ of CENTRAL ENGLAND

TITLE	CODE	COURSE	SUBJECTS	A/AS	ND/C	AGNVQ	IB	SQA(H)	SQA	RATIO	A/AS
Business Admin with Business Information Syts	N150	3FT deg	* g	14	M+3D	D	22	CCCC	Ind	10	10/14
Business Administration	N121	3FT deg	* g	14	M+3D	D	24	CCCC	Ind		
Business Administration with Accountancy	N1N4	3FT deg	* g	14	M+3D	D	22	CCCC	Ind	8	10/14
Business Administration with Enterprise	N125	3FT deg	* g	14	M+3D	D	22	CCCC			
Business Administration with Finance	N1N3	3FT deg	* g	14	M+3D	D	22	CCCC	Ind	10	10/18
Business Administration with French	N1R1	3FT deg	* g	14	M+3D	D	22	CCCC			
Business Administration with German	N1R2	3FT deg	* g	14	M+3D	D	22	CCCC			
Business Administration with Human Resource Mgt	N130	3FT deg	* g	14	M+3D	D	22	CCCC	Ind	10	10/16

| | | | 98 expected requirements | | | | | | | 96 entry stats | |
| course details | | | | | | | | | | | |
TITLE	CODE	COURSE	SUBJECTS	A/AS	ND/C	GNVQ	IB	SQA(H)	SQA	RATIO	A/AS
Business Administration with Law	N1M3	3FT deg	* g	14	M+3D	D	24	CCCCC	Ind	9	12/18
Business Administration with Marketing	N1N5	3FT deg	* g	14	M+3D	D	22	CCCC	Ind	9	10/20
Business Administration with Spanish	N1R4	3FT deg	Sp g	14	M+3D	D	22	CCCC			
Business Studies	N120	4SW deg	* g	CCD	M+3D	M	24	CCCCC	Ind	9	12/19
Business Studies for Property	NK14	3FT deg		8	2M	M					4/8
Economics with Management	L1N1	3FT deg	* g	14	M+3D	D	24	CCCC	Ind	7	12/20
Economics with Marketing	L1N5	3FT deg	* g	14	M+3D	D	24	CCCC	Ind		
Engineering Systems & Management (MEng)	HN11	4FT/5SW deg	M g	12	3M $	ME1	24	CCC	Ind		
Engineering with Business Studies	H1N1	3FT/4SW deg	* g	12	3M	M* go	24	CCC	Ind	4	
Engineering with Business Studies Found Year	H1ND▼	4FT/5SW deg	*	2	N	P*	Ind	CC	Ind		
Estate Management	N800	3FT deg	*	8	2M	M	24	CCCC	Ind	7	6/14
European Business and Languages	NT12	3FT deg	* g	14	M+3D	M	22	CCCC	Ind	21	12/14
Finance with Marketing	N3N5	3FT deg	* g	14	M+3D	D6					
Management of Manufacturing Systems	H7N1	3FT/4SW deg	M g	12	3M $	ME1	24$	CCC$	Ind		
Management of Manufacturing Systems Found Year	H7NC▼	4FT/5SW deg	* g	2	N	P*	Ind	CC	Ind		
Manufacturing Technology & Mgt Foundation Year	HN7C▼	4FT/5SW deg	*	2	N	P*	Ind	CC	Ind	1	
Manufacturing Technology and Management	HN71	3FT/4SW deg	* g	12	3M	M* go	24	CCC	Ind	20	
Marketing	N500	3FT deg	g	16	M+3D	M	24	CCCCC		6	10/20
Marketing with French	N5R1	3FT deg	* g	16	M+3D	M	24	CCCCC			
Marketing with German	N5R2	3FT deg	* g	16	M+3D	M	24	CCCCC			
Marketing with Spanish	N5R4	3FT deg	* g	16	M+3D	M	24	CCCCC			
Technology with Business	J9N1	3FT/4SW deg	* g	12	3M	M* go	24	CCC	Ind		
Business & Finance (South Birmingham College)	021N▼	2FT HND	*	4	3M	P	22	CCCC	Ind	4	2/4
Business and Finance	421N	2FT HND	* g	8	M+2D	M	24	CCCC	Ind	6	6/10

Univ of CENTRAL LANCASHIRE

TITLE	CODE	COURSE	SUBJECTS	A/AS	ND/C	GNVQ	IB	SQA(H)	SQA	RATIO	A/AS
Business Computing	GN51	3FT deg	*	12	MO	D*6/^	26	BCCC	Ind		
Business Enterprise (Year 3 Entry)	N121	1FT deg			HN $						
Business Information Technology	G5N1	4SW deg	* g	12	MO+2D	M$	26	BCCC	Ind		
Business Studies	N120	4SW deg	* g	16	MO+6D	M$6/^	28	BBBC	Ind		
Chemistry and International Business	FN11	3FT deg	* g	DD	MO	MS6/^	24$	CCC	$		
International Business	NT19	3FT deg	* g	14	MO+2D	M$6/^	26	BBCC	Ind		
Languages for International Business	T9N1	4SW deg	L	14	Ind	M$^	26$	BBCC$	Ind		
Management	N100	3FT deg	* g	16	MO+3D	M$6/^	28	BBBC	Ind		
Marketing	N500	3FT deg	* g	16	MO+3D	M$6/^	28	BBBC	Ind		
Organisation St(Yr 2 Entry or via Combined Hons)	N153	2FT deg			HN						
Combined Honours Programme. *Business*	Y400	3FT deg	* g	16	MO+3D	D$6/^	28	BBBC	Ind		
Combined Honours Programme *Business Information Systems*	Y400	3FT deg	* g	12	MO	M$6/^	26	BCCC	Ind		
Combined Honours Programme *Management*	Y400	3FT deg	* g	16	MO+3D	D$6/^	28	BBCC	Ind		
Combined Honours Programme *Marketing*	Y400	3FT deg	*	16	MO+3D	D$6/^	28	BBBC	Ind		
Combined Honours Programme *Public Relations*	Y400	3FT deg	*	16	MO+3D	D$6/^	28	BBBC	Ind		
Animal Management and Welfare	12ND▼	3SW HND	S g	EE	N $	P$	24$	CCC	Ind		
Business Studies	421N	2FT HND	* g	8	MO	M$	24	CCC	Ind		
Business with Information Management	15NG	2FT HND	* g	8	MO	M$	24	CCC	Ind		
Business with Languages	9T1N	2FT HND	* g	8	MO	M$	24	CCC	Ind		
Business with Marketing	5N1N	2FT HND	* g	8	MO	M$	24	CCC	Ind		
Business with Personnel	6N1N	2FT HND	* g	8	MO	M$	24	CCC	Ind		
Business with Tourism and Leisure	7P1N	2FT HND	* g	8	MO	M$	24	CCC	Ind		
Ecology and Conservation Management	82ND▼	3SW HND	*	EE	N	P$	24	CCC	N		

TITLE	CODE	COURSE	SUBJECTS	A/AS	NO/C	RGNVQ	IB	SQA(H)	SQA	RATIO A/AS
		course details		*98 expected requirements*						*96 entry stats*
Environmental Business Studies	921N▼	2FT HND	*	8	N	P$	24	CCC	Ind	6
Game and Wildlife Management	8FND▼	2FT HND	*	E	N	P$	24$	CCC	Ind	
Land Based Industries	081N▼	3SW HND								

CHELTENHAM & GLOUCESTER COLL of HE

TITLE	CODE	COURSE	SUBJECTS	A/AS	NO/C	RGNVQ	IB	SQA(H)	SQA
Business Computer Systems & Business Inform Tech	GNNC	3FT deg	*	8	MO	M	24	CCCC	Ind
Business Computer Systems and Business Mgt	NG15	3FT deg	*	12	5M+2D	MB3	24	CCCC	Ind
Business Computer Systems and Computing	GN5C	3FT deg	*	8	MO	M	24	CCCC	Ind
Business Computer Systems and Human Resource Mgt	GNND	3FT deg	*	8-12	MO	M	26	CCCC	Ind
Business Computer Systems and Marketing Mgt	GNN5	3FT deg	*	8-12	MO	M	26	CCCC	Ind
Business Computer Systems with Business Mgt	G5ND	3FT deg	*	8-12	MO	MB3	24	CCCC	Ind
Business Computer Systems with Computing	N1GM	3FT deg	*	8	MO	M	24	CCCC	Ind
Business Computer Systems with Human Res Mgt	GNMC	3FT deg	*	8-12	MO	M	26	CCCC	Ind
Business Computer Systems with Marketing Mgt	NG55	3FT deg	*	8-12	MO	M	26	CCCC	Ind
Business Info Technology and Business Mgt	GN51	3FT deg	*	12	MO	MB3	24	CCCC	Ind
Business Info Technology and Human Resource Mgt	NGC5	3FT deg	*	8-12	MO	M	26	CCCC	Ind
Business Info Technology and Marketing Mgt	GN5M	3FT deg	*	8-12	MO	M	26	CCCC	Ind
Business Info Technology with Business Mgt	G5N1	3FT deg	*	8-12	MO	M	24	CCCC	Ind
Business Info Technology with Human Resource Mgt	GNMD	3FT deg	*	8-12	MO	M	26	CCCC	Ind
Business Info Technology with Marketing Mgt	GN55	3FT deg	*	8-12	MO	M	26	CCCC	Ind
Business Management and Catering Management	NN17	4SW deg	*	12	5M+2D	MB3	26	CCCC	Ind
Business Management and Computing	NG1M	3FT deg	*	12	5M+2D	MB3	26	CCCC	Ind
Business Management and Countryside Planning	DN2C	3FT deg	*	10-14	4M+3D	MB3	26	CCCC	Ind
Business Management and Environmental Policy	FN91	3FT deg	*	10-14	4M+3D	MB3	26	CCCC	Ind
Business Management and Fashion	WN21	3FT deg	*	10-14	4M+3D	MB3	26	CCCC	Ind
Business Management and Financial Management	NND3	4SW deg	*	8-12	4M+3D	MB3	26	CCCC	Ind
Business Management and Financial Services Mgt	NN13	4SW deg	*	12-16	4M+3D	MB3	26	CCCC	Ind
Business Management and Geography	LN8D	3FT deg	*	12	MO	MB3	26	CCCC	Ind
Business Management and Geology	NF16	3FT deg	g	8-12	5M+2D	MB3	26	CCCC	Ind
Business Management and History	NV11	3FT deg	H	12-16	4M+3D	MB3	26	CCCC	Ind
Business Management and Hotel Management	NN1R	4SW deg	*	12-16	4M+3D	MB3	26	CCCC	Ind
Business Management and Human Geography	NL18	3FT deg	*	12-16	4M+3D	MB3	26	CCCC	Ind
Business Management and Human Resource Mgt	N132	4SW deg	*	12	4M+3D	MB3	26	CCCC	Ind
Business Management and Leisure Management	NNR1	4SW deg	*	12-16	4M+3D	MB3	26	CCCC	Ind
Business Management and Marketing Management	NNC5	4SW deg	*	12	4M+3D	MB3	26	CCCC	Ind
Business Management and Multimedia	NG1N	3FT deg	*	12	4M+3D	MB3	26	CCCC	Ind
Business Management and Natural Resource Mgt	NF19	3FT deg	*	12	4M+3D	MB3	26	CCCC	Ind
Business Management and Physical Geography	NF18	3FT deg	*	12	4M+3D	MB3	26$	CCCC	Ind
Business Management and Psychology	NL17	3FT deg	g	12-16	4M+3D	MB3	26	CCCC	Ind
Business Management and Sociological Studies	NL13	3FT deg	*	12-16	4M+3D	MB3	26	CCCC	Ind
Business Management and Sport & Exercise Sci	NB16	3FT deg	S	12-16	4M+3D	MB3	26	CCCC	Ind
Business Management and Tourism Management	NN1T	4SW deg	*	12-16	4M+3D	MB3	26	CCCC	Ind
Business Management and Women's Studies	NM19	3FT deg	*	12	5M+2D	MB3	26	CCCC	Ind
Business Management with Business Comp Systems	N1GN	4SW deg	*	12	5M+2D	MB3	26	CCCC	Ind
Business Management with Business Info Tech	N1G5	4SW deg	*	12	5M+2D	MB3	26	CCCC	Ind
Business Management with Catering Management	N1N7	4SW deg	*	12	4M+3D	MB3	26	CCCC	Ind
Business Management with Computing	N125	4SW deg	*	12	4M+3D	MB3	26	CCCC	Ind
Business Management with Countryside Planning	N1D9	4SW deg	*	12	4M+3D	MB3	26	CCCC	Ind
Business Management with Environmental Policy	N1F9	4SW deg	*	12	4M+3D	MB3	26	CCCC	Ind
Business Management with Fashion	N1W2	4SW deg	*	12	4M+3D	MB3	26	CCCC	Ind
Business Management with Financial Management	N1NJ	4SW deg	*	12	4M+3D	MB3	26	CCCC	Ind
Business Management with Financial Services Mgt	N1N3	4SW deg	*	12-16	4M+3D	MB3	26	CCCC	Ind
Business Management with Geography	N1LW	4SW deg	*	12	MO	MB3	24	CCCC	Ind

Business and Management 12

TITLE	CODE	COURSE	SUBJECTS	A/AS	NO/C	AGNVQ	IB	SQA(H)	SQA	RATIO A/AS
Business Management with Geology	N1F6	4SW deg	*	12	4M+3D	MB3	26	CCCC	Ind	
Business Management with History	N1V1	4SW deg	*	12	4M+3D	MB3	26	CCCC	Ind	
Business Management with Hotel Management	N1NR	4SW deg	*	12-16	4M+3D	MB3	26	CCCC	Ind	
Business Management with Human Geography	N1LV	4SW deg	*	12	4M+3D	MB3	26	CCCC	Ind	
Business Management with Human Resource Mgt	N100	4SW deg	*	12	4M+3D	MB3	26	CCCC	Ind	
Business Management with Leisure Management	N1NT	4SW deg	*	12-16	4M+3D	MB3	26	CCCC	Ind	
Business Management with Marketing Management	N1NM	4SW deg	*	12	4M+3D	MB3	26	CCCC	Ind	
Business Management with Modern Lang (French)	N1R1	4SW deg	g	12-16	4M+3D	MB3	26	CCCC	Ind	
Business Management with Multimedia	NGCN	4SW deg	*	12	4M+3D	MB3	26	CCCC	Ind	
Business Management with Natural Resource Mgt	N1FX	4SW deg	*	12	4M+3D	MB3	26	CCCC	Ind	
Business Management with Physical Geography	N1FV	4SW deg	*	12	4M+3D	MB3	26	CCCC	Ind	
Business Management with Psychology	N1L7	4SW deg	g	12-16	4M+3D	MB3	26	CCCC	Ind	
Business Management with Sociological Studies	N1L3	4SW deg	*	12-16	4M+3D	MB3	26	CCCC	Ind	
Business Management with Sport and Exercise Sci	N1B6	4SW deg	S	12-16	4M+3D	MB3	26	CCCC	Ind	
Business Management with Tourism Management	N1PT	4SW deg	*	12-16	4M+3D	MB3	26	CCCC	Ind	
Business Management with Women's Studies	N1M9	4SW deg	*	12	4M+3D	MB3	26	CCCC	Ind	
Business and Finance	N124	2FT Dip	*	6	6M	P	Ind	Ind	Ind	
Catering Management and Human Resource Mgt	NN7D	4SW deg	*	8-12	MO	MH3	26	CCCC	Ind	
Catering Management and Marketing Management	NN57	4SW deg	*	8-12	MO	MH3	26	CCCC	Ind	
Catering Management with Business Management	N7N1	4SW deg	*	8-12	5M+2D	MH3	24	CCCC	Ind	
Catering Management with Human Resource Mgt	N7NC	4SW deg	*	8	MO	MH3	26	CCCC	Ind	
Catering Management with Marketing Management	N7N5	4SW deg	*	8	MO	MH3	26	CCCC	Ind	
Computing and Human Resource Management	NGD5	3FT deg	*	8-12	MO	M	26	CCCC	Ind	
Computing and Marketing Management	GN5N	3FT deg	*	8-12	MO	M	26	CCCC	Ind	
Computing with Business Computer Systems	G5NC	3FT deg	*	8	MO	P3	24	CCCC	Ind	
Computing with Human Resource Management	GNN1	3FT deg	*	8	MO	M	26	CCCC	Ind	
Computing with Marketing Management	GNM5	3FT deg	*	8	MO	M	26	CCCC	Ind	
Countryside Planning and Human Resource Mgt	DN21	3FT deg	*	8-12	MO	MK	26	CCCC	Ind	
Countryside Planning and Marketing Management	DN25	3FT deg	*	8-12	MO	M$	26	CCCC	Ind	
Countryside Planning with Business Management	D2NC	3FT deg	*	8-12	5M+2D	M$	26	CCCC	Ind	
Countryside Planning with Human Resource Mgt	D2N1	3FT deg	*	8-12	MO	MK	26	CCCC	Ind	
Countryside Planning with Marketing Management	D2N5	3FT deg	*	8-12	MO	MK	26	CCCC	Ind	
Environmental Policy and Human Resource Mgt	FNY1	3FT deg	*	8-12	MO	M3	26	CCCC	Ind	
Environmental Policy and Marketing Management	FNX5	3FT deg	*	8-12	MO	M3	26	CCCC	Ind	
Environmental Policy with Business Management	F9N1	3FT deg	*	8-12	5M+2D	M3	26	CCCC	Ind	
Environmental Policy with Human Resource Mgt	FN9C	3FT deg	*	8-12	MO	M3	26	CCCC	Ind	
Environmental Policy with Marketing Management	F9NM	3FT deg	*	8-12	MO	M3	26	CCCC	Ind	
Fashion and Marketing Management	WN25	3FT deg	*	10-14	MO	MB3	26	CCCC	Ind	
Fashion with Business Management	W2N1	3FT deg	*	10-14	MO	M3	26	CCCC	Ind	
Fashion with Marketing Management	W2N5	3FT deg	*	10-14	MO	M3	26	CCCC	Ind	
Financial Management and Human Resource Mgt	NNCH	4SW deg	*	10-14	5M+2D	MB3	26	CCCC	Ind	
Financial Management and Marketing Management	NN35	4SW deg	*	8-12	5M+2D	MB3	26	CCCC	Ind	
Financial Management with Business Management	N3ND	4SW deg	*	10	5M+2D	M3	26	CCCC	Ind	
Financial Management with Human Resource Mgt	N3NC	4SW deg	*	10	5M+2D	M3	26	CCCC	Ind	
Financial Management with Marketing Management	N3N5	4SW deg	*	10	5M+2D	M3	26	CCCC	Ind	
Financial Services Mgt and Human Resource Mgt	NNHC	4SW deg	*	10	5M+2D	M3	26	CCCC	Ind	
Financial Services Mgt and Marketing Management	NNH5	4SW deg	*	10	5M+2D	MB3	26	CCCC	Ind	
Financial Services Mgt with Business Mgt	N3N1	4SW deg	*	10-12	4M+3D	M3	26	CCCC	Ind	
Financial Services Mgt with Human Resource Mgt	NN31	4SW deg	*	10	5M+2D	M3	26	CCCC	Ind	
Financial Services Mgt with Marketing Management	N3NM	4SW deg	*	10	5M+2D	M3	26	CCCC	Ind	
Geography and Human Resource Management	LN8C	3FT deg	*	12	MO	MB3	26	CCCC	Ind	
Geography and Marketing Management	LN8M	3FT deg	*	12	MO	MB3	26	CCCC	Ind	

course details			98 expected requirements							96 entry stats
TITLE	CODE	COURSE	SUBJECTS	A/AS	ND/C	RGNVQ	IB	SQA(H)	SQA	RATIO A/AS
Geography with Business Management	L8ND	3FT deg	*	12	MO	M3^	26	CCCC	Ind	
Geography with Human Resource Management	LNVC	3FT deg	*	12	MO	MB3	26	CCCC	Ind	
Geography with Marketing Management	L8NM	3FT deg	*	12	MO	MB3	26	CCCC	Ind	
Geology and Human Resource Management	FN61	3FT deg	*	8-12	5M+2D	MB3	26	CCCC	Ind	
Geology and Marketing Management	FN65	3FT deg	*	8-12	5M+2D	MB3	26	CCCC	Ind	
Geology with Business Management	F6N1	3FT deg	*	8-12	5M+2D	M3	26	CCCC	Ind	
Geology with Human Resource Management	F6NC	3FT deg	*	8	MO	M3	26	CCCC	Ind	
Geology with Marketing Management	F6N5	3FT deg	*	8	MO	M3	26	CCCC	Ind	
History with Business Management	V1N1	3FT deg	H	12	5M+2D	M3^	26	CCCC	Ind	
Hotel Management and Human Resource Management	NN71	4SW deg	*	12	5M+2D	MH3	26	CCCC	Ind	
Hotel Management and Marketing Management	NN75	4SW deg	*	12	5M+2D	M$3	26	CCCC	Ind	
Hotel Management with Business Management	NNRC	4SW deg	*	12	4M+3D	MH3	26	CCCC	Ind	
Hotel Management with Human Resource Management	N7ND	4SW deg	*	12	5M+2D	MH3	26	CCCC	Ind	
Hotel Management with Marketing Management	N7NM	4SW deg	*	12	5M+2D	MH3	26	CCCC	Ind	
Human Geography and Human Resource Management	LN81	3FT deg	*	12	5M+2D	MB3	26	CCCC	Ind	
Human Geography and Marketing Management	LN85	3FT deg	*	12	5M+2D	MB3	26	CCCC	Ind	
Human Geography with Business Management	L8NC	3FT deg	*	12	5M+2D	M3	26	CCCC	Ind	
Human Geography with Human Resource Management	L8N1	3FT deg	*	12	5M+2D	M3	26	CCCC	Ind	
Human Geography with Marketing Management	L8N5	3FT deg	Gy	12	5M+2D	M3	26	CCCC	Ind	
Human Resource Management and Leisure Mgt	NNCR	4SW deg	*	12-16	5M+2D	MB3	26	CCCC	Ind	
Human Resource Management and Marketing Mgt	NN15	4SW deg	*	12	5M+2D	MB3	26	CCCC	Ind	
Human Resource Management and Physical Geography	FN81	3FT deg	*	8-12	5M+2D	MB3	26	CCCC	Ind	
Human Resource Management and Psychology	NLC7	3FT deg	g	12-16	5M+2D	MB3	26	CCCC	Ind	
Human Resource Management and Sociological Studs	NLC3	3FT deg	*	12	5M+2D	MB3	26	CCCC	Ind	
Human Resource Management and Sport & Exer Sci	BN61	3FT deg	S	12	5M+2D	M$3	26	CCCC	Ind	
Human Resource Management and Tourism Management	NP17	4SW deg	*	12-16	5M+2D	M$3	26	CCCC	Ind	
Human Resource Management and Women's Studies	MN91	3FT deg	*	8-12	MO	MB3	26	CCCC	Ind	
Human Resource Mgt and Natural Resource Mgt	FNX1	3FT deg	*	8-12	MO	M3	26	CCCC	Ind	
Human Resource Mgt with Business Computer Systs	GN5D	4SW deg	*	8-12	MO	MB3	26	CCCC	Ind	
Human Resource Mgt with Business Info Technology	GNM1	4SW deg	*	8-12	MO	MB3	26	CCCC	Ind	
Human Resource Mgt with Business Management	N131	4SW deg	*	12	5M+2D	MB3	26	CCCC	Ind	
Human Resource Mgt with Catering Management	NN7C	4SW deg	*	8-12	MO	MB3	26	CCCC	Ind	
Human Resource Mgt with Computing	NGCM	4SW deg	*	8-12	MO	MB3	26	CCCC	Ind	
Human Resource Mgt with Countryside Planning	N1D2	4SW deg	*	10	5M+2D	MB3	26	CCCC	Ind	
Human Resource Mgt with Environmental Policy	NF1X	4SW deg	*	10	5M+2D	MB3	26	CCCC	Ind	
Human Resource Mgt with Financial Management	N1NH	4SW deg	*	10	5M+2D	MB3	26	CCCC	Ind	
Human Resource Mgt with Financial Services Mgt	NNC3	3FT deg	*	10	5M+2D	MB3	26	CCCC	Ind	
Human Resource Mgt with Geography	NLCV	4SW deg	*	12	MO	MB3	26	CCCC	Ind	
Human Resource Mgt with Geology	N1FP	4SW deg	*	8-12	MO	MB3	26	CCCC	Ind	
Human Resource Mgt with Hotel Management	NNC7	4SW deg	*	10	5M+2D	MB3	26	CCCC	Ind	
Human Resource Mgt with Human Geography	N1L8	3FT deg	*	10	5M+2D	MB3	26	CCCC	Ind	
Human Resource Mgt with Leisure Management	NNRD	4SW deg	*	12-16	5M+2D	MB3	26	CCCC	Ind	
Human Resource Mgt with Marketing Management	N1N5	4SW deg	*	10	5M+2D	MB3	26	CCCC	Ind	
Human Resource Mgt with Modern Languages(French)	N1RD	4SW deg	g	10	5M+2D	MB3	26	CCCC	Ind	
Human Resource Mgt with Multimedia	NGDM	4SW deg	*	12	5M+2D	MB3	26	CCCC	Ind	
Human Resource Mgt with Natural Resource Mgt	N1FY	4SW deg	*	10	5M+2D	MB3	26	CCCC	Ind	
Human Resource Mgt with Physical Geography	N1F8	4SW deg	*	10-14	5M+2D	MB3	26	CCCC	Ind	
Human Resource Mgt with Psychology	N1LR	4SW deg	g	12	5M+2D	MB3	26	CCCC	Ind	
Human Resource Mgt with Sociological Studies	N1LH	4SW deg	*	12	5M+2D	MB3	26	CCCC	Ind	
Human Resource Mgt with Sport and Exercise Sci	NBC6	4SW deg	*	12	5M+2D	MB3	26	CCCC	Ind	
Human Resource Mgt with Tourism Management	N1P7	4SW deg	*	12-16	5M+2D	MB3	26	CCCC	Ind	
Human Resource Mgt with Women's Studies	N1MX	4SW deg	*	10	5M+2D	MB3	26	CCCC	Ind	

Business and Management 12

TITLE	CODE	COURSE	SUBJECTS	A/AS	NC/C	AGNVQ	IB	SQA(H)	SQA	RATIO A/AS
Leisure Management and Marketing Management	NN5R	4SW deg	*	12-16	5M+2D	M$3	26	CCCC	Ind	
Leisure Management with Marketing Management	N7NN	4SW deg	*	12-16	5M+2D	ML3	26	CCCC	Ind	
Marketing Management and Multimedia	NGM5	3FT deg	*	12	5M+2D	MB3	26	CCCC	Ind	
Marketing Management and Natural Resource Mgt	FN95	3FT deg	*	8-12	M0	M3	26	CCCC	Ind	
Marketing Management and Physical Geography	FN85	3FT deg	*	12	5M+2D	MB3	26	CCCC	Ind	
Marketing Management and Psychology	NL57	3FT deg	g	12	5M+2D	MB3	26	CCCC	Ind	
Marketing Management and Sociological Studies	NL53	3FT deg	*	12	5M+2D	MB3	26	CCCC	Ind	
Marketing Management and Sport and Exercise Sci	BN65	3FT deg	S	12-16	5M+2D	M$3	26	CCCC	Ind	
Marketing Management and Tourism Management	NP57	4SW deg	*	12-16	5M+2D	M$3	26	CCCC	Ind	
Marketing Management and Women's Studies	MN95	3FT deg	*	8-12	M0	MB3	26	CCCC	Ind	
Marketing Management with Business Computer Syst	N5G5	4SW deg	*	8-12	M0	MB3	26	CCCC	Ind	
Marketing Management with Business Info Tech	N5GM	4SW deg	*	8-12	M0	MB3	26	CCCC	Ind	
Marketing Management with Business Management	N5NC	4SW deg	*	12	5M+2D	MB3	26	CCCC	Ind	
Marketing Management with Catering Management	N5N7	4SW deg	*	12	5M+2D	MB3	26	CCCC	Ind	
Marketing Management with Computing	N5GN	4SW deg	*	8-12	M0	MB3	26	CCCC	Ind	
Marketing Management with Countryside Planning	N5D2	4SW deg	*	12	3M+2D	MB3	26	CCCC	Ind	
Marketing Management with Environmental Policy	N5FX	4SW deg	*	12	5M+2D	MB3	26	CCCC	Ind	
Marketing Management with Fashion	N5W2	4SW deg	*	12	5M+2D	MB3	26	CCCC	Ind	
Marketing Management with Financial Management	N5N3	4SW deg	*	12	5M+2D	MB3	26	CCCC	Ind	
Marketing Management with Financial Services Mgt	N5NH	4SW deg	*	12	5M+2D	MB3	26	CCCC	Ind	
Marketing Management with Geography	N5LV	4SW deg	*	12	M0	MB3	26	CCCC	Ind	
Marketing Management with Geology	N5F6	4SW deg	*	8-12	M0	MB3	26	CCCC	Ind	
Marketing Management with Hotel Management	N5NR	4SW deg	*	12	5M+2D	MB3	26	CCCC	Ind	
Marketing Management with Human Geography	N5L8	4SW deg	*	12	5M+2D	MB3	26	CCCC	Ind	
Marketing Management with Human Resource Mgt	N5N1	4SW deg	*	12	5M+2D	MB3	26	CCCC	Ind	
Marketing Management with Leisure Management	N5NT	4SW deg	*	12-16	5M+2D	MB3	26	CCCC	Ind	
Marketing Management with Modern Langs (French)	N5R1	4SW deg	g	12	5M+2D	MB3	26	CCCC	Ind	
Marketing Management with Multimedia	NGN5	4SW deg	*	12	5M+2D	MB3	26	CCCC	Ind	
Marketing Management with Natural Resource Mgt	N5F9	4SW deg	*	12	5M+2D	MB3	26	CCCC	Ind	
Marketing Management with Physical Geography	N5F8	4SW deg	*	12	5M+2D	MB3	26	CCCC	Ind	
Marketing Management with Psychology	N5L7	4SW deg	g	12	5M+2D	MB3	26	CCCC	Ind	
Marketing Management with Sociological Studies	N5L3	4SW deg	*	12	5M+2D	MB3	26	CCCC	Ind	
Marketing Management with Sport and Exercise Sci	N5B6	4SW deg	S	12	5M+2D	MB3	26	CCCC	Ind	
Marketing Management with Tourism Management	N5P7	4SW deg	*	12-16	5M+2D	MB3	26	CCCC	Ind	
Marketing Management with Women's Studies	N5M9	4SW deg	*	8-12	M0	MB3	26	CCCC	Ind	
Multimedia with Business Management	NGDN	3FT deg	*	12	5M+2D	MI3	26	CCCC	Ind	
Multimedia with Marketing Management	NGMM	3FT deg	*	8-12	M0	MI3	26	CCCC	Ind	
Natural Resource Mgt with Business Mgt	F9NC	3FT deg	*	8-12	5M+2D	M3	26	CCCC	Ind	
Natural Resource Mgt with Human Resource Mgt	F9ND	3FT deg	*	8-12	M0	M3	26	CCCC	Ind	
Natural Resource Mgt with Marketing Mgt	F9N5	3FT deg	*	8-12	M0	M3	26	CCCC	Ind	
Physical Geography with Business Management	F8NC	3FT deg	*	8-12	M0	M3^	26	CCCC	Ind	
Physical Geography with Human Resource Mgt	F8N1	3FT deg	*	8-12	5M+2D	M3^	26	CCCC	Ind	
Physical Geography with Marketing Management	F8N5	3FT deg	.*	8-12	M0	M3^	26	CCCC	Ind	
Psychology with Business Management	L7N1	3FT deg	g	12-16	4M+3D	M3^	26	CCCC	Ind	
Psychology with Human Resource Management	L7NC	3FT deg	g	12-16	5M+2D	M3^	26	CCCC	Ind	
Psychology with Marketing Management	L7N5	3FT deg	g	12-16	5M+2D	M3^	26	CCCC	Ind	
Sociological Studies with Business Management	L3N1	3FT deg	*	12	4M+3D	MG3	26	CCCC	Ind	
Sociological Studies with Human Resource Mgt	L3NC	3FT deg	*	12	M0	MG3	26	CCCC	Ind	
Sociological Studies with Marketing Management	L3N5	3FT deg	*	12	M0	MG3	26	CCCC	Ind	
Sport & Exercise Sciences with Business Mgt	B6N1	3FT deg	S	12-16	4M+3D	ML3	26	CCCC	Ind	
Sport & Exercise Sciences with Human Res Mgt	B6NC	3FT deg	S	12-16	M0	ML3	26	CCCC	Ind	
Sport & Exercise Sciences with Marketing Mgt	B6NM	3FT deg	S	12-16	M0	ML3	26	CCCC	Ind	

TITLE	CODE	COURSE	SUBJECTS	A/AS	ND/C	AGNVQ	IB	SQA(H)	SQA	RATIO A/AS
course details			*98 expected requirements*							*96 entry stats*
Tourism Management with Business Management	P7N1	4SW deg	*	12-16	4M+3D	ML3	26	CCCC	Ind	
Tourism Management with Human Resource Mgt	P7NC	4SW deg	*	12-16	5M+2D	ML3	26	CCCC	Ind	
Tourism Management with Marketing Management	P7N5	4SW deg	*	12-16	5M+2D	ML3	26	CCCC	Ind	
Women's Studies with Business Management	M9N1	3FT deg	*	12	M0	M3	26	CCCC	Ind	
Women's Studies with Human Resource Management	M9NC	3FT deg	*	8-12	M0	M3	26	CCCC	Ind	
Women's Studies with Marketing Management	M9N5	3FT deg	*	8-12	M0	M3	26	CCCC	Ind	
Business Management	001N	2FT HND		4	P	P	Ind	Ind	Ind	
Human Resources Management	031N	2FT HND	*	2	N	P	Ind	Ind	Ind	
Marketing Management	055N	2FT HND	*	4	N	P	Ind	Ind	Ind	

UNIVERSITY COLLEGE CHESTER

TITLE	CODE	COURSE	SUBJECTS	A/AS	ND/C	AGNVQ	IB	SQA(H)	SQA	RATIO A/AS
Business Information Systems	GN51	3FT deg	g	10	M0	P	Ind	CCCC	$	

CHICHESTER INSTITUTE OF HIGHER EDUCATION

TITLE	CODE	COURSE	SUBJECTS	A/AS	ND/C	AGNVQ	IB	SQA(H)	SQA	RATIO A/AS
Recreation Studies	NB19	3FT deg	*	12	Ind	M$	Ind	Ind	Ind	

CITY Univ

TITLE	CODE	COURSE	SUBJECTS	A/AS	ND/C	AGNVQ	IB	SQA(H)	SQA	RATIO A/AS
Business Studies (with optional language)	N120	3FT/4SW deg	* g	24	D0	DB6/^	31$	AAABB	Ind	15 20/26
Design and Management in Engineering	HN71	3FT deg	*	18	3M+2D	D$^	27	BBBBB	HN	
Management and Systems	N100	3FT/4SW deg	* g	BBC	3M+4D	DB	26	AAABB	N$	6 15/24
Property Valuation and Finance	N800	3FT/4SW deg	* g	BBC	3M+2D	D	$	BBBBC	Ind	5 18/20
Statistical Sci with Management St (Foundation)	G4ND	4EXT deg	M		Ind		Ind	Ind	Ind	4
Statistical Science with Management Studies	G4N1	3FT deg	M	BCC	Ind		Ind	ABBBB	Ind	6
Statistical Science with Mgt St (with Study Abrd)	G4NC	4SW deg	M	BCC	Ind		Ind	ABBBB	Ind	1

CITY COLLEGE Manchester

TITLE	CODE	COURSE	SUBJECTS	A/AS	ND/C	AGNVQ	IB	SQA(H)	SQA	RATIO A/AS
Business Management	001N	2FT HND		EE	N	PB				

CITY of LIVERPOOL Comm COLL

TITLE	CODE	COURSE	SUBJECTS	A/AS	ND/C	AGNVQ	IB	SQA(H)	SQA	RATIO A/AS
Business and Finance	021N	2FT HND								

COLCHESTER INST

TITLE	CODE	COURSE	SUBJECTS	A/AS	ND/C	AGNVQ	IB	SQA(H)	SQA	RATIO A/AS
Business Studies	021N	2FT HND	* g	E	N	P$	Ind	Ind	Ind	5 4/14

CORNWALL COLLEGE WITH DUCHY COLLEGE

TITLE	CODE	COURSE	SUBJECTS	A/AS	ND/C	AGNVQ	IB	SQA(H)	SQA	RATIO A/AS
Business Administration	N122	1FT deg								
Business and Finance	N190	2FT HND		4	5M	M$	24	CCC	Ind	

COVENTRY Univ

TITLE	CODE	COURSE	SUBJECTS	A/AS	ND/C	AGNVQ	IB	SQA(H)	SQA	RATIO A/AS
American and European Business	N145	3FT deg	* g	14	M0	M	24	Ind	Ind	
Applied Chemistry with Management Studies	F1N1	3FT/4SW deg	C	DD	3M	MS	Ind	Ind	Ind	7
Applied Chemistry with Management Studies	F1NC	4FT/5SW deg			Ind	Ind	Ind	Ind	Ind	
Biological Sciences and Business	CN11	3FT deg								
Business Administration	N150	3FT deg	* g	14	M0	M	24	Ind	Ind	92
Business Decision Methods	NG14	4FT/5SW deg	*	2	N	P	Ind	Ind	Ind	3
Business Decision Methods	GN41	3FT/4SW deg	*	12-16	Ind		Ind	Ind	Ind	16
Business Enterprise	N122	4FT deg	* g	8	M	M	Ind	CCC	Ind	
Business Information Technology	GNM1	4FT/5SW deg	*	2	N	P	Ind	Ind	Ind	1
Business Information Technology	GN51	3FT deg	* g	12	M0	Ind	Ind	CCCC	Ind	7 8/16
Business Studies	N120	4SW deg	* g	16	M+3D	M	Dip	CCC	Ind	13 10/20
Business Studies with French	N1RC	4SW deg	E g	16	M+3D	M	Dip	CCC	Ind	25 16/24
Business Studies with German	N1R2	4SW deg	* g	16	M+3D	M	Dip	CCC	Ind	9 12/18
Business Studies with Italian	N1R3	4SW deg	* g	16	M+3D	M	Dip	CCC	Ind	
Business Studies with Portuguese	N1R5	4SW deg	* g	16	M+3D	M	Dip	CCC	Ind	
Business Studies with Russian	N1R8	4SW deg	* g	16	M+3D	M	Dip	CCC	Ind	
Business Studies with Spanish	N1R4	4SW deg	* g	16	M+3D	M	Dip	CCC	Ind	13

374

TITLE	CODE	COURSE	SUBJECTS	A/AS	ND/C	AGNVQ	IB	SQA(H)	SQA	RATIO	A/AS
Business and Technology	HN11▼	3FT deg	*	8	3M	M+	24	CCCC	Ind	2	4/13
Equine Studies	DN21	4SW deg	*g	14	M+2D	MD	28	BBBC	Ind	5	12/22
European Business and Technology	HN1C▼	4FT deg	*g	8	3M	M+	24	CCCC	Ind	2	10/12
Extended Business Information Technology	GN5C	4FT deg	*	2	N		Dip	Ind	Ind		
International Disaster Engineering & Management	JN91	3FT/4SW deg	*g	14	5M	MC	Ind	Ind	Ind	2	6/22
International Disaster Engineering & Management	JN9C	4FT deg	*g	10	3M	P	Ind	Ind	Ind		
Manufacturing Management and Business	H7N1	3FT/4SW/4FT/5SW deg	*	12-18	3M $	M+	24$	BBCC$	Ind	3	
Manufacturing Management and Business	HN7D	3FT deg									
Materials Technology with Management	J5NC	3FT deg	*g	12	Ind	Ind	Ind	Ind	Ind		
Materials Technology with Management	J5N1	3FT deg	*g	12	Ind	Ind	Ind	Ind	Ind		
Statistics and Operational Research	GN4F	4FT/5SW deg	*	2	N	P	Ind	Ind	Ind		
Statistics and Operational Research	GN42	3FT deg	M/St g	12-16	Ind	M	Ind	Ind	Ind	20	
Business	421N▼	2FT HND	*	8	M+	M	Dip	CCC	Ind	5	2/10
Business Information Technology	15NG▼	2FT HND		4	4M	P	Ind	Ind	Ind	4	2/4
Horse Studies (Management and Technology)	12ND	3SW HND	*g	2	N	P	Ind	CC	Ind	3	2/16

CRANFIELD Univ

TITLE	CODE	COURSE	SUBJECTS	A/AS	ND/C	AGNVQ	IB	SQA(H)	SQA	RATIO	A/AS
Agricultural Technology and Management	D9N1	4SW deg	S g	CDD	4M	M$6/^ go	27$	BBCC	Ind	5	
Business Information Systems	N1G5	3FT deg	*g	CC-CCC	3M	M$ go	Ind	CSYS		1	
Business Management and the Environment	N1F9	4SW deg	g	CDD	4M	M$6/^ go	27	BBCC	Ind	19	
Business Management for the Food & Related Inds	N100	4SW deg	g	CDD	4M	M$6/^ go	27	BBCC	Ind		
Command & Control, Communications & Info Systems	GN51	3FT deg	*g	CC-CCC	3M	M$ go	Ind	CSYS	Ind	2	
Environment Management	F9N8	4SW deg	S g	CDD	4M	M$6/^ go	27$	BBCC	Ind	6	14/18
Information Systems Management	GN5C	3FT deg	*g	CC-CCC	3M	M$ go	Ind	CSYS	Ind	3	
Management and Logistics	NN19	3FT deg	*g	CC-CCC	3M	M$ go	Ind	CSYS	Ind	1	
Marketing and Food Management	N5D4	4SW deg	S g	CDD	4M	M$6/^ go	27$	BBCC	Ind	8	
Business and Finance	001N	2FT HND	*	E	N	P$	Ind	CC	Ind	6	2/4
Rural Environment Management	8N9F	3SW HND	*	E	N	P$	Ind	CC	Ind	4	4/8

CROYDON COLL

TITLE	CODE	COURSE	SUBJECTS	A/AS	ND/C	AGNVQ	IB	SQA(H)	SQA	RATIO	A/AS
Business St (Accounting & Fin) (Yr 3 entry opt)	N1N4	3FT deg	*	6	MO $	M$/P$3	Ind	Ind			
Business St (Business & Law) (yr 3 entry opt)	NM13	3FT deg	*	6	MO $	M$/P$3	Ind	Ind			
Business Studies (European St) (Yr 3 entry opt)	N150	3FT deg	*	6	MO $	M$/P$3	Ind	Ind			
Business Studies (Hum Res Mgt) (Yr 3 entry opt)	N130	3FT deg	*	6	MO $	M$/P$3	Ind	Ind			
Business Studies (Marketing) (Yr 3 entry option)	N500	3FT deg	*	6	MO $	M$/P$3	Ind	Ind			
Business Studies (Yr 3 entry option)	N100	3FT deg	*	6	MO $	M$/P$3	Ind	Ind			
Fashion with Business (yr 3 entry option)	E4N1	3FT deg	Fa+Pf		N $	PA2					
Fashion with Business (yr 3 entry option)	J4N1	3FT deg	Fa+Pf		N $	PA2					
Hospitality and Business Management (yr 3 entry)	NN17	3FT deg	*	6	MO $	P$2	Ind	Ind			
Business Studies	001N	2FT HND	*	E	N $	P$	Ind	Ind			
Business Studies (Business and Law)	31MN	2FT HND	*	E	N $	P$	Ind	Ind			
Business Studies (European Studies)	051N	2FT HND	*	E	N $	P$	Ind	Ind			
Business Studies (Human Resources Mgt)	031N	2FT HND	*	E	N $	P$	Ind	Ind			
Business Studies (Marketing)	005N	2FT HND	*	E	N $	P$	Ind	Ind			

CUMBRIA COLL of A & D

TITLE	CODE	COURSE	SUBJECTS	A/AS	ND/C	AGNVQ	IB	SQA(H)	SQA	RATIO	A/AS
Heritage Management	P7N9	3FT deg	*	EE	N	M	Ind	BB	Ind	3	
Tourism and Heritage Management	79PN	2FT HND	*	E	N	M	Ind	B	Ind	2	2/4

DARTINGTON COLL of Arts

TITLE	CODE	COURSE	SUBJECTS	A/AS	ND/C	AGNVQ	IB	SQA(H)	SQA	RATIO	A/AS
Music with Arts Management	W3N1	3FT deg	Mu	CD	10M	Ind	26$	CCCC$	Ind	5	
Performance Writing with Arts Management	W4ND	3FT deg		BC	10M	Ind	26$	BBCC	Ind	2	
Theatre with Arts Management	W4N1	3FT deg		BB	10M	Ind	26$	BBCC	Ind	17	
Visual Performance with Arts Management	W4NC	3FT deg	A/Fa/Pf	BE	10M	Ind	26$	CCC$	Ind	4	
Visual Performance with Arts Management	E4NC	3FT deg	A/Fa/Pf	BE	10M	Ind	26$	CCC$	Ind		

course details   98 expected requirements   96 entry stats

TITLE	CODE	COURSE	SUBJECTS	A/AS	ND/C	AGNVQ	IB	SQA(H)	SQA	RATIO	A/AS
DE MONTFORT Univ											
Arts Management	W9N1 ▼ 3FT deg		* g	CCD	MO	M^	28$	ABBB	Ind	3	14/22
Biomedical Sciences with Business (Extended)	B9NC ▼ 4FT/5SW deg		* g	2	N	P	Dip	Ind	X		
Biomedical Sciences with Business Studies	B9N1 ▼ 3FT/4SW deg		B g	12-14	Ind	MS	$	BBB	X	2	4/16
Business (BS)	N100 ▼ 3FT deg			12	10M+2D	M	Ind	BCCC	Ind	10	6/12
Business Administration	N122 ▼ 3FT deg		* g	16	3M+3D		32	ABBB		5	8/16
Business Economics/Business	LN11 ▼ 3FT deg		* g	18	3M+3D	M	32	AABB	X		
Business Studies	N121 ▼ 4SW deg		* g	18	3M+3D		32	AABB	X	15	8/18
Business Studies	N120 ▼ 4SW deg		* g	18	3M+3D	M	32	AABB	X	7	11/22
Business/Accounting	NN14 ▼ 3FT deg		* g	18	3M+3D	M	32	AABB	X		
Chemistry with Business Studies	F1N1 ▼ 3FT/4SW deg		*	12	3M $	M	24$	BBB	$	8	
Chemistry with Business Studies (Extended)	F1ND ▼ 4FT/5SW deg		*	2	N	P	24	CC	$	3	
Finance/Business	NN31 ▼ 3FT deg		* g	18	3M+3D	M	32	AABB	X		
Human Resource Management	N130 ▼ 3FT deg		* g	18	3M+3D	M	32	AABB	Ind		
Human Resource Management/Accounting	NN64 ▼ 3FT deg		* g	18	3M+3D	M	32	AABB	Ind		
Human Resource Management/Business	NN61 ▼ 3FT deg		* g	18	3M+3D	M	32	AABB	Ind		
Human Resource Management/Business Economics	LN16 ▼ 3FT deg		* g	18	3M+3D	M	32	AABB	Ind		
Human Resource Management/Finance	NN63 ▼ 3FT deg		* g	18	3M+3D	M	32	AABB	Ind		
Industrial and Business Systems	N1H7 ▼ 4SW deg		* g	14	4M	M	26	BBBB	Ind	3	
Information Systems with Management	G5N1 ▼ 3FT/4SW deg		* g	12-18	2M+2D	D	30	BBBC$	Ind		
Land Management	N801 ▼ 3FT deg		* g	14	5M	Ind	Dip	BBBB	Ind	4	
Land Management	N800 ▼ 3FT deg		* g	14	5M	M	26$	BBBB	Ind	7	8/14
Law and Human Resource Management	M3N1 ▼ 3FT deg		* g	BBC	6D	M^	30	BBBBB	X		
Law and Marketing	M3N5 ▼ 3FT deg		* g	BBC	6D	M^	30	BBBBB	X		
Law/Business	MN31 ▼ 3FT deg		* g	BBC	6D	M^	30$	BBBBB$	X		
Management Science	G9N1 ▼ 4SW deg		* g	12	3M+1D	M$ go	Ind	Ind	Ind	1	4/16
Management/Accounting	NN1K ▼ 3FT deg		* g	18	3M+3D	M	32	AABB	X		
Management/Business	N124 ▼ 3FT deg		* g	18	3M+3D	M	32	AABB	X		
Management/Business Economics	LN1C ▼ 3FT deg		* g	18	3M+3D	M	32	AABB	X		
Management/Finance	NN13 ▼ 3FT deg		* g	18	3M+3D	M	32	AABB	X		
Management/Human Resource Management	NN16 ▼ 3FT deg		* g	18	3M+3D	M	32	AABB	X		
Management/Law	MN3C ▼ 3FT deg		* g	18	3M+3D	M	32	AABB	X		
Marketing	N500 ▼ 3FT deg		* g	18	3M+3D	M	32	AABB	X		
Marketing/Accounting	NN54 ▼ 3FT deg		* g	18	3M+3D	M	32	AABB	X		
Marketing/Business	NN51 ▼ 3FT deg		* g	18	3M+3D	M	32	AABB	X		
Marketing/Business Economics	LN51 ▼ 3FT deg		* g	18	3M+3D	M	32	AABB	X		
Marketing/Finance	NN35 ▼ 3FT deg		* g	18	3M+3D	M	32	AABB	X		
Marketing/Human Resource Management	NN65 ▼ 3FT deg		* g	18	3M+3D	M	32	AABB	X		
Marketing/Management	NN15 ▼ 3FT deg		* g	18	3M+3D	M	32	AABB	X		
Physics with Business Studies	F3N1 ▼ 3FT/4SW deg		*	12	Ind	M	24$	BBB	$	8	
Property and Business	NN18 ▼ 3FT deg		* g	14	5M	Ind	Dip	BBBB	Ind	1	
Public Policy/Business	LN41 ▼ 3FT deg		* g	18	3M+3D	M	32	AABB	X		
Public Policy/Human Resource Management	LN46 ▼ 3FT deg		* g	18	3M+3D	M	32	AABB	X		
Public Policy/Management	LN4C ▼ 3FT deg		* g	18	3M+3D	M	32	AABB	X		
Public Policy/Marketing	LN45 ▼ 3FT deg		* g	18	3M+3D	M	32	AABB	X		
Valuation and Auctioneering: Chattels & Fine Art	WN18 ▼ 3FT deg			14	5M	M	26$	BBBB	Ind		
Valuation and Auctioneering: Chattels & Fine Art	EN18 ▼ 3FT deg			14	5M	M	26$	BBBB	Ind		
Combined Studies *Human Resource Management*	Y400 ▼ 3FT/4SW deg		* g	14	2M+4D	D	30	BBB	Ind		
Combined Studies *Management Science*	Y400 ▼ 3FT/4SW deg		* g	10	MO	M	30	BBB	Ind		
Combined Studies *Marketing*	Y400 ▼ 3FT/4SW deg		* g	12	2M+4D	M	30	BBB	Ind		

Business and Management 12

course details			98 expected requirements							96 entry stats	
TITLE	CODE	COURSE	SUBJECTS	A/AS	NO/C	AGNVQ	IB	SQA(H)	SQA	RATIO	A/AS
Humanities Combined Honours *Arts Management*	Y300▼	3FT deg	* g	CCD	MO	M$^	26$	ABBB	Ind		
Humanities Joint Honours *Arts Management*	Y301▼	3FT deg	* g	CCD	MO	M$^	30$	ABBB	Ind		
Business Administration (Agricultural)	19ND▼	2FT HND	* g	E	N	P	Ind	CC	Ind	3	
Business and Finance	321N▼	2FT HND	* g	8	3M+2D	M	24	CCCC	$	13	4/16
Business and Finance	421N▼	2FT HND	* g	8	3M+2D	M	24	CCCC	$	7	4/12
Land Administration	008N▼	2FT HND	* g	6	N	P	Dip	BB	Ind	2	2/6
Management Science	1N9G▼	2FT HND	* g	4	2M	P$ go	Ind	Ind	Ind	3	1/5

Univ of DERBY

TITLE	CODE	COURSE	SUBJECTS	A/AS	NO/C	AGNVQ	IB	SQA(H)	SQA	RATIO	A/AS
Business Administration	N122	3FT deg	*	14	MO+2D	D$	28	BBCC	Ind	12	10/18
Business Decision Analysis	G730	4SW deg	M	8	3M $	M$	Dip$	CCCD$	Ind		9/10
Business Studies	N120	4SW deg	*	14	MO+2D	D$	28	BBCC	Ind	10	12/20
Enterprise Management	N123	3FT deg		14	MO+2D	D$	28	BBCC	Ind		
European Management	N140	3FT deg	g	14	MO+2D	D$	28	BBCC	Ind		
Human Resource Management	N130	3FT deg	*	14	MO+2D	D$	28	BBCC	Ind	5	10/20
International Business	N141	4SW deg	F/G/Sp	14	MO+2D$	D$^	28$	BBCC$	Ind	13	10/16
Management	N100	3FT deg		14	MO+2D	D$	28	BBCC	Ind		
Marketing	N500	3FT deg	*	14	MO+2D	D$	28	BBCC	Ind	9	12/22
Retail Management	N110	3FT deg		14	MO+2D	D$	28	BBCC	Ind		
Tech Mgt, Innovation and Business Psychology	J9NC	3FT deg	*	10	4M	M$	26	CCCD	Ind		
Tech Mgt, Innovation and Human Resource Mgt	J9N1	3FT deg	*	10	4M	M$	26	CCCD	Ind		
Technology Management, Innovation and Marketing	J9N5	3FT deg	*	10	4M	M$	26	CCCD	Ind		
Credit Accumulation Modular Scheme *Business Administration*	Y600	3FT deg	*	12	MO	M	Ind	CCCC	Ind		
Credit Accumulation Modular Scheme *Human Resource Management*	Y600	3FT deg	*	12	MO	M	Ind	CCCC	Ind		
Credit Accumulation Modular Scheme *Management*	Y600	3FT deg	*	12	MO	M	Ind	CCCC	Ind		
Credit Accumulation Modular Scheme *Marketing*	Y600	3FT deg	*	12	MO	M	Ind	CCCC	Ind		
Business Management (Pathways)	021N▼	2FT HND	*	4	MO	M$	Dip	CCD	Ind	2	2/8
Civil Engineering (Management)	12NH	2FT HND	*	4	N	P	Dip	CCD	Ind	4	4/6
European Business	041N	2FT HND	g	4	MO	M$	Dip$	CCD$	Ind	1	2/10

DEWSBURY COLL

TITLE	CODE	COURSE	SUBJECTS	A/AS	NO/C	AGNVQ	IB	SQA(H)	SQA	RATIO	A/AS
Business	001N	2FT HND	g	E	N	P$					

DONCASTER COLL

TITLE	CODE	COURSE	SUBJECTS	A/AS	NO/C	AGNVQ	IB	SQA(H)	SQA	RATIO	A/AS
Business Administration	N150	3FT deg		12	3M	M	Ind	Ind	Ind	15	
Business Administration (HND Conversion)	N151	2FT deg			HN						
Business Studies	N100	4SW deg		12	3M	M	Ind	Ind	Ind	7	
Business Studies (HND Conversion)	N108	2FT deg			HN					4	
Business and Marketing	NN15	4SW deg		12		M	Ind	Ind	Ind		
Business and Marketing (HND Conversion)	NN1M	2FT deg			HN						
Business and Personnel	NN16	4SW deg		12		M	Ind	Ind	Ind		
Business and Personnel (HND Conversion)	NN1P	2FT deg			HN						
Integrated Business Technology (1 Year top-up)	GN51	1FT deg			HN		Ind	Ind	HN		
Business Studies	001N	1FT HND								4	
Business and Finance	021N	2FT HND		EE	N		Ind	Ind	Ind	8	
Business and Marketing	51NN	1FT HND								9	
Business and Personnel	61NN	1FT HND								6	

course details			98 expected requirements							96 entry stats
TITLE	CODE	COURSE	SUBJECTS	A/AS	NO/C	RGNVQ	IB	SQA(H)	SQA	RATIO A/AS
DUDLEY COLLEGE of Technology										
Business	001N	2FT HND	* g	2	Ind	Ind				
Business and Finance	091N	2FT HND	* g	2	Ind	Ind				
Business and Marketing	51NN	2FT HND	* g	2	Ind	Ind				
Business and Personnel	61NN	2FT HND	* g	2	Ind	Ind				
Univ of DUNDEE										
Business Economics and Marketing	LN15	4FT deg	* g	BCC	Ind	D$	29	BBBC	Ind	2
Civil Engineering and Management	HN21	4FT deg	M g	12	5M $	Ind	Ind	BBCC$	N$	
Electronic Engineering with Management	H6N1	3FT/4FT deg	M+P/Ds g	12	5M $	M$^	26$	BBCC$	N$	12
Electronic Engineering with Management (MEng)	H6NC	4FT/5FT deg	M+P/Ds g	12	5M $	M$^	26$	BBCC$	N$	
Manufacturing Engineering and Management	HN71	3FT/4FT deg	M+P/Ds g	8	5M $	M$^	26$	BBCC$	N$	14
Arts and Social Sciences Business Economics and Marketing	Y400	3FT deg	* g	BCC	Ind	D$	29	BBBC	Ind	
Univ of DURHAM										
Chinese and Management Studies	TN31	4FT deg	*	BBC	Ind	Ind	31	AABBB	Ind	12
Japanese and Management Studies	TN41	4FT deg	*	BBC	Ind	Ind	31	AABBB	Ind	8 22/30
Social Sciences Combined Management Studies	Y220	3FT deg	*	ABC	MO	Ind	32	AAABB	Ind	
Univ of EAST ANGLIA										
Accountancy with Business Management	N4N1	3FT deg								
Business Management	N100	3FT deg	* g	BBC	MO+3D	D	30$	ABBBB	Ind	6 16/26
Chemistry with Business St and 1yr in Eur (4yr)	F1NC	4FT deg	C+B/M/P	BCC	MO+3D$	Ind	28$	ABBB$	Ind	
Chemistry with Business Studies	F1N1	3FT deg	C+B/M/P	CCC	MO+1D$	Ind	27$	BBBB$	Ind	6
Electronics with Business	H6N1	3FT deg	M+S	CCD	4M $	M^	28$	BBBC	N$	
Euro Bus Studs w Hons Lang-1 from Fr,Ger,Danish	T9N1	4FT deg	F/G	BBC	X		30	AAABB	X	4 18/28
Honours Language with Management Studies	T2N1	4FT deg	L	BBC	X		30	AAABB	X	6 20/24
Mathematics with Management Studies	G1N1	3FT deg	M	BCC	Ind		32$	BBBC$	X	6 12/20
Univ of EAST LONDON										
Biology and Business Studies	CN1D	3FT deg	* g	16	MO	M	Ind	Ind	Ind	
Biology with Business Studies	C1N1	3FT deg	* g	12	MO	M	Ind	Ind	Ind	
Business St with Computing & Business Info Systs	N1G5	3FT deg	* g	14	MO	MB				
Business Studies and Cultural Studies	LNP1	3FT deg	* g	14	MO	M				
Business Studies and Design-Visual Communication	NW12	3FT deg	* g	12	N	MA	Ind	Ind	Ind	
Business Studies and Economics	LN11	3FT deg	* g	12	N	MB	Ind	Ind	Ind	14
Business Studies and Education & Community St	NX19	3FT deg	* g	12	MO	M	Ind	Ind	Ind	
Business Studies and French	NR11	3FT deg	* g	12	MO	M^	Ind	Ind	Ind	
Business Studies and German	NR12	3FT deg	* g	12	MO	M^	Ind	Ind	Ind	
Business Studies and Health Studies	BN91	3FT deg	* g	16	MO	M	Ind	Ind	Ind	
Business Studies and Hist of Art Design & Film	NV14	3FT deg	* g	12	MO	M$	Ind	Ind	Ind	
Business Studies and Information Technology	NG15	3FT deg	* g	12	MO	M				
Business Studies and Maths, Stats & Computing	GN91	3FT deg	* g	12	MO	M$	Ind	Ind	Ind	
Business Studies and Spanish	RN41	3FT deg	* g	12	MO	M^	Ind	Ind	Ind	7
Business Studies and Women's Studies	NM1X	3FT deg	* g	14	MO	MB				
Business Studies with Biology	N1C1	3FT deg	* g	14	MO	MB				
Business Studies with Cultural Studies	N1L6	3FT deg	* g	14	MO	MB				
Business Studies with Design - Textile Design	N1W2	3FT deg	* g	14	MO	MB				
Business Studies with Design-Visual Commun	N1WF	3FT deg	* g	14	MO	MB				
Business Studies with Economics	N1L1	3FT deg	* g	14	MO	MB				
Business Studies with Education & Community St	N1X9	3FT deg	* g	14	MO	MB				
Business Studies with Fashion Design & Marketing	N1J4	3FT deg	* g	14	MO	MB				
Business Studies with French	N1R1	3FT deg	* g	14	MO	MB				

Business and Management 12

course details			**98 expected requirements**							*96 entry stats*
TITLE	CODE	COURSE	SUBJECTS	A/AS	ND/C	AGNVQ	IB	SQA(H)	SQA	RATIO A/AS
Business Studies with German	N1R2	3FT deg	* g	14	MO	MB				
Business Studies with Health Studies	N1B9	3FT deg	* g	14	MO	MB				
Business Studies with Hist of Art Design & Film	N1V4	3FT deg	* g	14	MO	MB				
Business Studies with Information Technology	N1GM	3FT deg	* g	14	MO	MB				
Business Studies with Italian	N1R3	3FT deg	* g	14	MO	MB				
Business Studies with Maths Stats & Computing	N1G9	3FT deg	* g	14	MO	MB				
Business Studies with Sociology	N1L3	3FT deg	* g	14	MO	MB				
Business Studies with Spanish	N1R4	3FT deg	* g	14	MO	MB				
Business Studies with Women's Studies	N1M9	3FT deg	* g	14	MO	MB				
Business Studies/Bus Admin (Human Resource Mgt)	N1N6	4FT deg	* g	14	MO	MB				
Business Studies/Business Admin (Bus Finance)	N1N3	4FT deg	* g	14	MO	MB	Ind	Ind	Ind	
Business Studies/Business Admin (Marketing)	N1N5	4FT deg	* g	14	MO	MB				
Business Studies/Business Administration	N120	4SW deg	* g	12-16	DO	DB	Ind	Ind	Ind	19 10/18
Computing & Information Systems with Bus St	G5N1	3FT deg	* g	14	MO	M	Ind	Ind	Ind	
Cultural Studies and Business Studies	LN61	3FT deg	* g	14	MO	M				
Cultural Studies with Business Studies	L6N1	3FT deg	* g	14	MO	M	Ind	Ind	Ind	
Design - Textile Design with Business Studies	J4N1	3FT deg	* g	12	MO	M	Ind	Ind	Ind	
Design - Visual Communication with Business St	W2N1	3FT deg	* g	12	MO	M	Ind	Ind	Ind	
Economics with Business Studies	L1N1	3FT deg	* g	12	MO	M	Ind			
Education & Community Studies with Business St	X9N1	3FT deg	* g	12	MO	M				
European Studies with Business Studies	T2N1	3FT deg	* g	12	MO	M	Ind	Ind		
Fashion Design with Marketing	E2NM	3FT deg	* g	12	4M	MA	Ind	Ind	Ind	
Fashion Design with Marketing	E2N5	4SW deg	* g	12	MO	MA	Ind	Ind	Ind	
French with Business Studies	R1N1	3FT deg	* g	12	MO	M	Ind			
German with Business Studies	R2N1	3FT deg	* g	12	MO	M				
Health Services Management	B9N1	3FT deg	* g	12	MO	MG	Ind	Ind	Ind	3
Health Studies with Business Studies	B9NC	3FT deg	* g	12	MO	M	Ind	Ind	Ind	
History of Art Design & Film with Business St	V4N1	3FT deg	* g	12	MO	M	Ind	Ind	Ind	
Industrial Studies	N611	3FT/4SW deg	* g	14	MO	MN	Ind	Ind		
Information Technology with Business Studies	G5NC	3FT deg	* g	12	MO	M	Ind	Ind	Ind	
International Business/International Bus. Admin	N146	4FT/SW deg	* g	12	MO	M	Ind	Ind	Ind	
Law with Business Studies	M3N1	3FT deg	* g	14	MO	M				
Maths, Stats & Computing with Business Studies	G9N1	3FT deg	* g	12	MO	M	Ind	Ind	Ind	
Politics with Business Studies	M1N1	3FT deg	* g	12	MO	M	Ind			
Politics/Business Studies	MN11	3FT deg	* g	12	MO	M	Ind			
Social Policy Research with Business Studies	L4N1	3FT deg	* g	12	MO	M	Ind	Ind		
Sociology with Business Studies	L3N1	3FT deg	* g	12	MO	M	Ind	Ind	Ind	
Spanish with Business Studies	R4N1	3FT deg	* g	12	MO	M	Ind			
Technology Management	JN91	4FT deg	* g	14	MO	M				
Third World & Development Studies with Bus Stds	M9N1	3FT deg								
Women's Studies with Business Studies	M9NC	3FT deg	* g	12	MO	M	Ind			
Three-Subject Degree	Y600	3FT deg	* g	12	MO	M	Ind	Ind	Ind	
Business Studies										
Business and Computing	51GN	2FT HND	* g	12	MO	M				
Business and Finance	421N	2FT HND	* g	12	MO	M	Ind	Ind	Ind	9 4/8
EDGE HILL Univ COLLEGE										
Business and Management Studies	N126	3FT deg	* g	CC	3D $	M* / P*^	Dip	BBCC	Ind	3 6/16
Organization and Management Studies	N130	3FT deg	* g	CC	3M+3D	M* / P*^ go	Dip	BBCC$	Ind	
Univ of EDINBURGH										
Arabic and Business Studies	TN61	4FT deg	g	BBB	Ind	Ind	Dip$	BBBB	Ind	
BCom (with or without Honours)	N120	3FT/4FT deg	g	BBB	Ind		34$	ABBB	Ind	6

course details

TITLE	CODE	COURSE	SUBJECTS	A/AS	ND/C	RGNVQ	IB	SQA(H)	SQA	RATIO A/AS
Business Studies and Accounting	NN14	4FT deg	g	BBB	Ind		34$	ABBB	Ind	7
Business Studies and Economics	NL11	4FT deg	g	BBB	Ind		34$	ABBB	Ind	9
Business Studies and French	NR11	4FT deg	F g	BBB	Ind		34$	ABBB	Ind	7
Business Studies and Geography	NL18	4FT deg	M	ABB			36	AABB		
Business Studies and German	NR12	4FT deg	L g	BBB	Ind		34$	ABBB$	Ind	10
Business Studies and Law	NM13	4FT deg	g	ABB	Ind		36$	AABB	Ind	16
Business Studies and Mathematics	NG11	4FT deg	M	BBB	Ind		34$	ABBB	Ind	10
Business Studies and Spanish	NR14	4FT deg	L g	BBB	Ind		34$	ABBB$	Ind	10
Business Studies and Statistics	NG14	4FT deg	M	BBB	Ind		34	ABBB	Ind	
Computer Science and Management Science	GN51	4FT deg	M	CCC	MO $		Dip$	BBBB$	N$	8	22/24
French and Business Studies	RN11	4FT deg	F g	BBB	Ind	Ind	Dip$	BBBB$	Ind	
German and Business Studies	RN21	4FT deg	L g	BBB	Ind	Ind	Dip$	BBBB$	Ind	
International Business (MA Hons)	N145	4FT deg	g	AAB	Ind		38$	AABB	Ind	
Italian and Business Studies	RN31	4FT deg	L g	BBB	Ind		Dip$	BBBB$	Ind	
Law and Business Studies	MN31	4FT deg	g	ABB	X		32	AAABB	X	9
Mathematics and Business Studies	GN11	4FT deg	M	BBC	MO $		Dip$	ABBC$	N$	5	20/30
Mechanical Eng with Management Techniques (BEng)	H3N1	4FT deg	M+P	CCC	MO $		Dip$	BBBB$	N$	8	18/26
Mechanical Engineering with Mgt Techniques	H3NC	5FT deg	M+P	CCC	MO $		Dip$	BBBB$	N$	
Psychology and Business Studies	LN71	4FT deg	g	AAB	Ind		38	AABB	Ind	9
Russian Studies and Business Studies	RN81	4FT deg	L g	BBB	Ind	Ind	Dip$	BBBB$	Ind	
Spanish and Business Studies	RN41	4FT deg	L g	BBB	Ind	Ind	Dip$	BBBB$	Ind	
Statistics and Business Studies	GN41	4FT deg	M	BBB	MO $		Dip$	ABBB	N$	
Social Science *Business Studies*	Y200	3FT deg	* g	BBB	Ind		34$	ABBB	Ind	

Univ of ESSEX

TITLE	CODE	COURSE	SUBJECTS	A/AS	ND/C	RGNVQ	IB	SQA(H)	SQA	RATIO A/AS
Accounting and Management	NN14	3FT deg	* g	20	MO+3D	D	28	BBBB	Ind	
Mathematics and Operational Research	GN12	3FT deg	M	18	MO $	D^	28$	CSYS	Ind	8

EUROPEAN Business School

TITLE	CODE	COURSE	SUBJECTS	A/AS	ND/C	RGNVQ	IB	SQA(H)	SQA	RATIO A/AS
Euro Bus Admin with French + one beginner lang	N1RC	4SW deg	L	12	Ind		Ind	Ind	Ind	
Euro Bus Admin with German + one beginner lang	N1RF	4SW deg	L	12	Ind		Ind	Ind	Ind	
Euro Bus Admin with Italian + one beginner lang	N1RH	4SW deg	L	12	Ind		Ind	Ind	Ind	
Euro Bus Admin with Russian + one beginner lang	N1RV	4SW deg	L	12	Ind		Ind	Ind	Ind	
Euro Bus Admin with Spanish + one beginner lang	N1RK	4SW deg	L	12	Ind		Ind	Ind	Ind	
European Business Administration (Test+Int)	N1T2	4SW deg	L	12	Ind		Ind	Ind	Ind	5
International Bus St: French + one beginner lang	NR11	4FT deg								
International Bus St: German + one beginner lang	NR12	4FT deg								
International Bus St: Italian +one beginner lang	NR13	4FT deg								
International Bus St: Japan + one beginner lang	NT14	4FT deg								
International Bus St: Russian +one beginner lang	NR18	4FT deg								
International Bus St: Spanish +one beginner lang	NR14	4FT deg								
International Bus Studs with French (Test+Int)	N1R1	4SW deg		12	Ind		Ind	Ind	Ind	
International Bus Studs with German (Test+Int)	N1R2	4SW deg		12	Ind		Ind	Ind	Ind	
International Bus Studs with Italian (Test+Int)	N1R3	4SW deg		12	Ind		Ind	Ind	Ind	
International Bus Studs with Japanese (Test+Int)	N1T4	4SW deg		12	Ind		Ind	Ind	Ind	
International Bus Studs with Russian (Test+Int)	N1R8	4SW deg		12	Ind		Ind	Ind	Ind	
International Bus Studs with Spanish (Test+Int)	N1R4	4SW deg		12	Ind		Ind	Ind	Ind	
International Business & Mgt Studies with French	N1RD	4SW deg		12	Ind		Ind	Ind	Ind	
International Business & Mgt Studies with German	N1RG	4SW deg		12	Ind		Ind	Ind	Ind	
International Business & Mgt Studs with Italian	N1RJ	4SW deg		12	Ind		Ind	Ind	Ind	
International Business & Mgt Studs with Japanese	N1TL	4SW deg		12	Ind		Ind	Ind	Ind	
International Business & Mgt Studs with Russian	N1RW	4SW deg		12	Ind		Ind	Ind	Ind	
International Business & Mgt Studs with Spanish	N1RL	4SW deg		12	Ind		Ind	Ind	Ind	

TITLE	CODE	COURSE	SUBJECTS	A/AS	ND/C	AGNVQ	IB	SQA(H)	SQA	RATIO	A/AS
			98 expected requirements							*96 entry stats*	
International Business Studies (2 languages)	N1TX	4FT deg									
International Business Studies (Test+Int)	N1T9	4SW deg	*	12	Ind		Ind	Ind	Ind	12	
International Business and Management Studies	N145	4SW deg		12	Ind		Ind	Ind	Ind		
International Management Studies (Test+Int)	N160	3/4SW deg		12	Ind		Ind	Ind	Ind		

Univ of EXETER

TITLE	CODE	COURSE	SUBJECTS	A/AS	ND/C	AGNVQ	IB	SQA(H)	SQA	RATIO	A/AS
Business and Accounting Studies	NN14	3FT deg	* g	24	2M+3D	D$	36	Ind	Ind	11	22/28
Business and Accounting Studies with European St	NN1K	4FT deg	L g	24	2M+3D	D$	36	Ind	Ind	14	
Business and Management Studies	N100	3FT deg	g	24	2M+3D	D$	36				
Business and Management Studies with European St	N101	4FT deg	L g	24	2M+3D	D$	36				
Computer Science with Management Science	G5N2	3FT deg	M	20	M0+2D	M$^	32$	Ind	Ind	16	
Management Science with Information Technology	GN52	3FT deg	M/St	BBC	M0+2D	M/D$^	34$	Ind	Ind	5	14/22
Management Science with Media Computing	N2GM	3FT deg	M/St	BBC	M0+2D	M/D$^	34$	Ind	Ind	9	
Mathematical Statistics and Operational Research	GN42	3FT deg	M/St	22	M0	M/D$^	34$	Ind	Ind	3	13/28
Mathematical Stats & Op Research with Euro Studs	GN4F	4FT deg	M/St g	22	M0	M/D$^	34$	Ind	Ind	5	
Media Computing with Management Science	G5NF	3FT deg	M/St	20	M0+2D	M$^	32$	Ind	Ind		

FARNBOROUGH COLL of Technology

TITLE	CODE	COURSE	SUBJECTS	A/AS	ND/C	AGNVQ	IB	SQA(H)	SQA	RATIO	A/AS
Business Administration	N122	3FT deg		10	Ind	M*	Ind	Ind	Ind	4	6/16
Environmental Management and Business	F9N1	3FT deg		DE	4M	P* go	Ind	Ind	Ind		
Marketing	N501	3FT deg		10	Ind	M*	Ind	Ind	Ind	6	
Antiques and Collection Management	1N4J	2FT HND		6	Ind	P*	Ind	Ind	Ind	2	2/4
Business Studies (European Business)	041N	2FT HND		4	N	P*	Ind	Ind	Ind	6	
Business and Finance	091N	2FT HND		4	N	P*	Ind	Ind	Ind		
Business and Marketing	51NN	2FT HND		4	N	P*	Ind	Ind	Ind		
Business and Personnel	61NN	2FT HND		4	N	P*	Ind	Ind	Ind		

Univ of GLAMORGAN

TITLE	CODE	COURSE	SUBJECTS	A/AS	ND/C	AGNVQ	IB	SQA(H)	SQA	RATIO	A/AS
American Business Studies	N160	4SW deg	* g	14	M0+3D	M$	Ind	Ind	Ind		
Business Information Management	N100	4SW deg	* g	14	M0+3D	M$	Ind	Ind	Ind	9	
Business Studies	N120	4SW deg	* g	14	M0+3D	M$	Ind	Ind	Ind	3	8/16
Business Studies and Economics	NL11	3FT deg	* g	14	M0+3D	M$	Ind	Ind	Ind		
Computing and Business	GN51	3FT deg	* g	CC	7M	M$	Ind	Ind	Ind		
Computing with Business	G5N1	3FT/4SW deg	* g	CC	7M	M$	Ind	Ind	Ind	8	8/12
Construction Health and Safety	K2N6	3FT deg			Ind	Ind	Ind	Ind	Ind		
Electronics with European Business Studies	H6N1	3FT/4SW deg	M+S/Cs g	8	3M $	M$	Ind	Ind	Ind		
Enterprise and Small Business	N122	4SW deg	* g	14	M0+3D	M$	Ind	Ind	Ind	3	
Estate Management Surveying	N800	4SW deg	* g	10	Ind	Ind	Ind	Ind	Ind	7	8/14
European and International Business Admin	N140	4SW deg	* g	14	M0+3D	M$	Ind	Ind	Ind	8	
Government with American Business	M1NC	3FT deg	* g	12-14	M0+3D	M	Ind	Ind	Ind		
Government with European & International Bus	M1ND	3FT deg	* g	12-14	M0+3D$	M$	Ind	Ind	Ind		
Human Resource Management	N620	4SW deg	* g	14	M0+3D	M$	Ind	Ind	Ind	4	8/14
Law and Business Studies	MN31	3FT deg	* g	18	M0+3D	D$	Ind	Ind	Ind		
Law with Business Studies	M3N1	3FT deg	* g	18	Ind	Ind	Ind	Ind	Ind		
Marketing	N500	4SW deg	* g	14	M0+3D	M$	Ind	Ind	Ind	5	8/16
Marketing with Languages	N5T9	4SW deg	* g	14	M0+3D	M$	Ind	Ind	Ind	3	
Mathematics and Business Studies	GN1C	3FT deg									
Mathematics with Business Studies	G1N1	3FT deg	M g	14	Ind	Ind	Ind	Ind	Ind		
Purchasing and Supply Chain Management	N550	4SW deg	* g	14	M0+3D	M$	Ind	Ind	Ind	12	
Retail Management (4 year Sandwich)	N110	4SW deg	* g	14	M0+3D	M$	Ind	Ind	Ind		
Statistics and Business Studies	GN41	3FT deg	M g	14	Ind	Ind	Ind	Ind	Ind		
Technology & Business Studies	H8N1	3FT deg	g	DD	N $	M$	Ind	Ind	Ind		6/10
Combined Studies (Honours) Business Studies	Y400	3FT deg	* g	8-16	Ind	Ind	Ind	Ind	Ind		

course details | 98 expected requirements | 96 entry stats

TITLE	CODE	COURSE	SUBJECTS	A/AS	ND/C	AGNVQ	IB	SQA(H)	SQA	RATIO A/AS	
Combined Studies (Honours) *Marketing*	Y400	3FT deg	* g	8-16	Ind	Ind	Ind	Ind	Ind		
Combined Studies (Honours) *Real Estate Management*	Y400	3FT deg	* g	8-16	Ind	Ind	Ind	Ind	Ind		
Joint Honours *Business Studies*	Y401	3FT deg	* g	8-16	Ind	Ind	Ind	Ind	Ind		
Joint Honours *Marketing*	Y401	3FT deg	* g	8-16	Ind	Ind	Ind	Ind	Ind		
Joint Honours *Real Estate Management*	Y401	3FT deg	* g	8-16	Ind	Ind	Ind	Ind	Ind		
Major/Minor Honours *Business Studies*	Y402	3FT deg	* g	8-16	Ind	Ind	Ind	Ind	Ind		
Major/Minor Honours *Marketing*	Y402	3FT deg	* g	8-16	Ind	Ind	Ind	Ind	Ind		
Business Admin (Hum Res Mgt)	031N	2FT HND	* g	6	MO	P$	Ind	Ind	Ind		
Business Administration	051N▼	2FT HND	* g	6	MO	P$	Ind	Ind	Ind	3	2/12
Business Administration (European Business)	141N	2FT HND	* g	6	MO	P$	Ind	Ind	Ind	3	
Business Administration (Executive Secretarial)	071N	2FT HND	* g	6	MO	P$	Ind	Ind	Ind	31	
Business Administration (Marketing)	005N	2FT HND	* g	6	MO	P$	Ind	Ind	Ind	4	2/4
Business Administration (Public Sector)	501N	2FT HND	* g	6	MO	P$	Ind	Ind	Ind	24	
Business Information Technology	1N5G▼	2FT HND	* g	D	N	P$	Ind	Ind	Ind	3	2/6
Land Administration	008N	2FT HND			Ind	Ind	Ind	Ind	Ind		
Manufacturing and Business Studies	17NH	2FT HND	M/P/S g	D	N $	P$	Ind	Ind	Ind		

Univ of GLASGOW

TITLE	CODE	COURSE	SUBJECTS	A/AS	ND/C	AGNVQ	IB	SQA(H)	SQA	RATIO A/AS	
Business Economics and Business History	LN1C	4FT deg		BBC	N	M	30	BBBB	N		
Computing Science/Management Studies	NG15	4FT deg	M+S	BBC-CCC	N	M	24$	BBBB$	N	7	
Economic and Social History/Management Studies	NV13	4FT deg		BBC	8M	M	30	BBBB	Ind		
Geography/Management Studies	LN81	4FT deg		BBC	8M	M	30	BBBB	Ind	9	
Management Studies	N100	4FT deg		BBC	8M	M	30	BBBB	Ind	16	20/24
Management Studies with Celtic	N1Q5	4FT deg		BBC	8M	M	30	BBBB	Ind		
Management Studies with Czech	N1T1	4FT deg		BBC	8M	M	30	BBBB	Ind		
Management Studies with French	N1R1	4FT deg		BBC	8M	M	30	BBBB	Ind		
Management Studies with German	N1R2	4FT deg		BBC	8M	M	30	BBBB	Ind	12	
Management Studies with Italian	N1R3	4FT deg		BBC	8M	M	30	BBBB	Ind		
Management Studies with Polish	N1TC	4FT deg		BBC	8M	M	30	BBBB	Ind		
Management Studies with Russian	N1R8	3FT deg		BBC	8M	M	30	BBBB	Ind	5	
Management Studies/Archaeology	NV16	4FT deg		BBC	8M	M	30	BBBB			
Management Studies/Archaeology	NVC6	4FT deg		BBC	HN	M	30	BBBB	Ind		
Management Studies/Celtic	NQ15	4FT deg		BBC	HN	M	30	BBBB	Ind		
Management Studies/Classical Civilisation	NQ1V	4FT deg		BBC	8M	M	30	BBBB	Ind		
Management Studies/Classical Civilisation	NQ18	4FT deg		BBC	HN	M	30	BBBB		2	
Management Studies/Computing	NGC5	4FT deg		BBC	HN	M	30	BBBB	Ind	26	
Management Studies/Computing Science	GN51	4FT deg		BBC	8M	M	30	BBBB	Ind	18	
Management Studies/Czech	NT11	5FT deg		BBC	HN	M	30	BBBB	Ind		
Management Studies/Economics	LN11	4FT deg		BBC	8M	M	30	BBBB	Ind	5	
Management Studies/English	NQ1H	4FT deg		BBC	HN	M	30	BBBB	Ind	9	
Management Studies/French	NRC1	5FT deg		BBC	HN	M	30	BBBB	Ind	15	
Management Studies/German	NR12	5FT deg		BBC	HN	M	30	BBBB	Ind	7	
Management Studies/Greek	NQ17	4FT deg		BBC	HN	M	30	BBBB	Ind		
Management Studies/Hispanic Studies	NR14	5FT deg		BBC	HN	M	30	BBBB	Ind	7	
Management Studies/History	NV11	4FT deg		BBC	8M	M	30	BBBB	Ind	6	
Management Studies/History	NVC1	4FT deg		BBC	HN	M	30	MABBB	Ind	10	
Management Studies/History of Art	NV14	4FT deg		BBC	HN	M	30	BBBB	Ind		
Management Studies/Italian	NR13	5FT deg		BBC	HN	M	30	BBBB	Ind		

Business and Management 12

course details			98 expected requirements							96 entry stats	
TITLE	CODE	COURSE	SUBJECTS	A/AS	ND/C	AGNVQ	IB	SQA(H)	SQA	RATIO A/AS	
Management Studies/Latin	NQ16	4FT deg		BBC	HN	M	30	BBBB	Ind		
Management Studies/Mathematics	GN1C	4FT deg		BBC	8M	M	30	BBBB	Ind	11	
Management Studies/Mathematics	GNC1	4FT deg		BBC	HN	M	30	BBBB	Ind	11	
Management Studies/Philosophy	NV17	4FT deg		BBC	8M	M	30	BBBB	Ind	3	
Management Studies/Philosophy	NVC7	4FT deg		BBC	HN	M	30	BBBB	Ind		
Management Studies/Physics	FN31	4FT deg		BBC	HN	M	30	BBBB	Ind		
Management Studies/Polish	NT1C	5FT deg		BBC	HN	M	30	BBBB	Ind		
Management Studies/Politics	MN11	4FT deg		BBC	8M	M	30	BBBB	Ind	6	
Management Studies/Psychology	CN81	4FT deg		BBC	8M	M	30	BBBB	Ind	10	
Management Studies/Psychology	CN8C	4FT deg		BBC	HN	M	30	BBBB	Ind	14	
Management Studies/Russian	NR18	5FT deg		BBC	HN	M	30	BBBB	Ind		
Management Studies/Scottish History	NVCC	4FT deg		BBC	8M	M	30	BBBB	Ind	4	
Management Studies/Scottish History	NV1C	4FT deg		BBC	HN	M	30	BBBB	Ind	4	
Management Studies/Scottish Literature	NQ12	4FT deg		BBC	HN	M	30	BBBB	Ind		
Management Studies/Social and Urban Policy	LN41	4FT deg		BBC	8M	M	30	BBBB	Ind		
Management Studies/Sociology	LN31	4FT deg		BBC	8M	M	30	BBBB	Ind	6	
Management Studies/Statistics	GN41	4FT deg		BBC	8M	M	30	BBBB	Ind	8	
Management Studies/Theology & Religious Studies	NV18	4FT deg		BBC	HN	M	30	BBBB	Ind		
Mathematics/Management Studies	NG11	4FT deg	M+S	BBC-CCC	N	M	24$	BBBB$	N	11	

GLASGOW CALEDONIAN Univ

TITLE	CODE	COURSE	SUBJECTS	A/AS	ND/C	AGNVQ	IB	SQA(H)	SQA	RATIO A/AS	
Accountancy with Decision Sciences	N4N2	3FT/4FT deg	E+M	BC	Ind		Ind	BBBC$	Ind		
Accountancy with Management	N4N1	3FT/4FT deg	E+M	BC	Ind		Ind	BBBC$	Ind		
Business	N123	3FT/4FT deg	E+M g	BC	Ind		Ind	BBBC$	Ind	2	
Business Studies	N120	4SW/5SW deg	M+E	BCC	Ind		Ind	BBBC$	Ind	7	12/16
Business Studies	N121	2FT Dip	E	BD-CCD	Ind		Ind	BBC$	Ind	5	
Business and Information Management	N1G5	3FT/4SW deg	E g	CC	Ind		Ind	BBB$	Ind	2	
Business and Languages	N140	3FT/4FT deg	E+L g	BC	Ind		Ind	BBCC$	Ind	4	
Business and Manufacturing Systems Eng (BEng)	HN71	4FT deg	M	CD	Ind		Ind	BBC$	Ind		
Consumer & Management St (Fashion with Business)	JN49	3SW/4SW deg	E g	CD	Ind		Ind	BBC$	Ind	5	
Consumer & Management St (Food Product Develop)	DN49	3SW/4SW deg	E g	CD	Ind		Ind	BBC$	Ind	3	
Consumer and Management Studies (General)	N980	3FT/4SW deg	E	CD	Ind		Ind	BBC$	Ind	6	
Consumer and Management Studies (Home Economics)	NN97	3FT/4FT deg	E g	CD	Ind		Ind	BBC$	Ind	3	
Consumer and Trading Standards	N984	3FT/4FT deg	g	CD	Ind		Ind	BBC$	Ind	3	
European Business Studies	N141	4FT deg	L+E g	BCC	Ind		Ind	BBBC$	Ind	5	
Information Management Systems	NP14	4FT deg	M+E+Cs	CC-DDD	Ind		Ind	BCCC	Ind	1	
Information and Business Administration	N1GM	3FT deg	E	DD	Ind		Ind	BCCC$	Ind		
Information and Business Administration	N170	2FT Dip	E g	DE	Ind		Ind	CCC$	Ind	4	
International Travel with Information Systems	GN59	4SW deg	E+M g	CCC	Ind		Ind	BBCC$	Ind	6	
Law with Administrative Studies	M3N1	3FT/4FT deg	E+M	BC-CC	Ind		Ind	BBBC$	Ind	3	
Management Science	N100	3FT deg	E+M	CD				BBC$	Ind	7	
Marketing and Communication	NP53	3FT/4SW deg	E+L	CC	Ind		Ind	BBC$	Ind	8	12/24
Mathematics for Business Analysis	G1NC	4FT/5SW deg	M+E	CD	Ind		Ind	BBC$	Ind	4	
Media Technology Management	PN41	2FT deg		X	Ind		Ind	X	Ind		
Property Management and Development/Property St	N830	3FT/4FT deg	E+M	CC	Ind		Ind	BCCC$	Ind	4	
Public Administration and Management	MN11	3FT/4FT deg	E+Po	CC	Ind		Ind	BBB$	Ind	3	
Retail Management	N553	3FT/4SW deg	E+M	CC	Ind		Ind	BBCC$	Ind	7	
Risk Management	NN39	3FT/4FT deg	E+M+L	BC	Ind		Ind	BBBC$	Ind	3	

GLOUCESTERSHIRE COLLEGE of Arts and Technology

TITLE	CODE	COURSE	SUBJECTS	A/AS	ND/C	AGNVQ	IB	SQA(H)	SQA	RATIO A/AS	
Business and Finance	091N	2FT HND	* g	CC	MO $	P*			Ind		

TITLE	CODE	COURSE	SUBJECTS	A/AS	ND/C	AGNVQ	IB	SQA(H)	SQA	RATIO A/AS
Univ of GREENWICH										
Applied Chemistry and Business Management	FN11	3FT/4SW deg	C g	8	3M	MS	Dip	CCC	Ind	
Applied Chemistry with Business Management	F1N1	3FT/4SW deg	C g	8	3M	MS	Dip	CCC	Ind	
Applied Statistics with Business Management	G4N1	3FT/4SW deg	* g	CE	3M	Ind	Ind	CCC$	Ind	
Arts Management	W9N1	3FT deg	* g	16	MO+4D	M	24	CCC	Ind	
Arts Management/Language	WT99	3FT deg	* g	16	MO+4D	M	24	CCC	Ind	
Business Administration	N122	3FT deg	* g	16	MO+4D	M	24	CCC	Ind	
Business Administration (HND Top Up)	N123	1FT deg								
Business Administration/Language	NT1X	3FT deg	* g	16	MO+4D	M	24	CCC	Ind	
Business Studies	N120	4SW deg	* g	16	MO+4D	M	24	CCC	Ind	
Business Studies/Language	NT1Y	4FT deg	* g	16	MO+4D	M	24	CCC	Ind	
Business Systems Modelling	G9N1	3FT/4SW deg	* g	CE	3M	Ind	Ind	CCC$	Ind	
Business: Central/Eastern Europe	N140	3FT deg	* g	16	MO+4D	M	24	CCC	Ind	
Civil Engineering with Project Management	H2N1	3FT/4SW deg	M+S g	16	6M	M$2	24	Ind	Ind	
Engineering and Business Management	HN11	3FT/4SW deg	* g	8	4M $	M	Dip	CCCC$	Ind	
Engineering and Business Management	HN1D	4EXT deg	* g	4	Ind	Ind	Ind	Ind	Ind	
Estate Management	N800	3FT/4SW deg	* g	16	5M	M	24	CCC	Ind	
Estate Management with Conservation Studies	N8K2	3FT/4SW deg	* g	16	5M	M	24	CCC	Ind	
Estate Management with Information Technology	N8G5	3FT/4SW deg	* g	16	5M	M	24	CCC	Ind	
Health and Management	BN91	3FT deg	* g	12	N	M$	22	Ind	Ind	
Health with Management	B9N1	3FT deg	* g	12	N	M$	22	Ind	Ind	
Heritage Management	N801	3FT deg	* g	16	MO+4D	M	24	CCC	Ind	
Heritage Management/Language	NT99	3FT deg	* g	16	MO+4D	M	24	CCC	Ind	
Information Systems with Business Management	GN51	3FT/4SW deg	* g	8-10	8M	M$ go	Ind	CCC	Ind	
International Business	N145	4SW deg	* g	16	MO+4D	M	24	CCC	Ind	
International Business/Language	NT12	4SW deg	* g	16	MO+4D	M	24	CCC	Ind	
International Marketing	N502	4SW deg	* g	16	MO+4D	M	24	CCC	Ind	
International Marketing/Language	NT52	4SW deg	* g	16	MO+4D	M	24	CCC	Ind	
Leisure Property Development	N803	3FT/4SW deg	* g	16	5M	M	24	CCC	Ind	
Management Science	GN11	3FT/4SW deg	M g	CE	3M $	Ind	Ind	CCC$	Ind	
Management and Industrial Sciences	N105	3FT deg	* g	12	1M+1D	Ind	24	CCC	Ind	
Marketing	N501	3FT/4SW deg	* g	16	MO+4D	M	24	CCC	Ind	
Marketing Communications	NN15	3FT deg	* g	16	MO+4D	M	24	CCC	Ind	
Marketing Communications/Language	NT5X	3FT deg	* g	16	MO+4D	M	24	CCC	Ind	
Marketing/Language	TN95	3FT/4SW deg	* g	16	MO+4D	M	24	CCC	Ind	
Motor Vehicle Engineering with Management (BEng)	H3N1	3FT deg	* g	6	2/3M	P	Ind	Ind	Ind	
Operations Management	N220	3FT/4SW deg	* g	16	MO+4D	M	24	CCC	Ind	
Operations Management/Language	NT29	3FT/4SW deg	* g	16	MO+4D	M	24	CCC	Ind	
Personnel Management	N611	3FT/4SW deg	* g	16	MO+4D	M	24	CCC	Ind	
Personnel Management/Language	NT69	3FT/4SW deg	* g	16	MO+4D	M	24	CCC	Ind	
Property Valuations	N810	3FT/4SW deg	* g	16	5M	M	24	CCC	Ind	
Tourism Management	P7N1	3FT deg	* g	16	MO+4D	M	24	CCC	Ind	
Business Studies	421N▼	2FT HND	* g	6	MO	P		CC	Ind	
GYOSEI International COLL										
Business Studies	N100	3FT/4FT deg	*		BCC	Ind	Ind	Ind	Ind	
Business with Culture Studies	N1L3	3FT/4FT deg	*		BCC	Ind	Ind	Ind	Ind	
Business with Language Studies	N1T9	3FT/4FT deg	*		BCC	Ind	Ind	Ind	Ind	
HALTON COLL										
Business	021N	2FT HND	*	4	MO	P	Ind	Ind	Ind	5
Engineering with Management Studies	1N1H	2FT HND	M/P	2	N	P	Ind	Ind	N	

Business and Management 12

	course details		98 expected requirements							96 entry stats	
TITLE	CODE	COURSE	SUBJECTS	A/AS	ND/C	AGNVQ	IB	SQA(H)	SQA	RATIO	A/AS

HARPER ADAMS Agric COLL

TITLE	CODE	COURSE	SUBJECTS	A/AS	ND/C	AGNVQ	IB	SQA(H)	SQA	RATIO	A/AS
Agri-Food Marketing with Business Studies	DN25	3FT/4SW deg	* g	8-12	MO	M$	Dip	CCCC	Ind	2	8/20
Agricultural Engineering with Marketing and Mgt	H3N1	3FT/4SW deg	M/S g	8-12	MO $	M$	Dip	CCCC$	Ind	4	
Agriculture with Land and Farm Management	D2N8	3FT/4SW deg	S g	8-12	MO	M$	Dip	CCCC	Ind	4	8/22
Agriculture with Rural Enterprise	D2N1	3FT/4SW deg	S g	8-12	MO	M$	Dip	CCCC	Ind		
Rural Enterprise	DN21	3FT/4SW deg	* g	8-12	MO	M$	Dip	CCCC	Ind		
Rural Enterprise and Land Management	DN28	3FT/4SW deg	* g	14-16	MO	M$	Dip	BBCC	Ind	4	12/28
Agriculture with Land and Farm Management	8N2D	2FT/3SW HND	* g	2-8	N	P$	Ind	CC	N	3	2/10

HEREFORDSHIRE COLLEGE of Technology

TITLE	CODE	COURSE	SUBJECTS	A/AS	ND/C	AGNVQ	IB	SQA(H)	SQA	RATIO	A/AS
Business Studies	021N	2FT HND	*	2	Ind	M	Ind	CC	N	3	2/10

HERIOT-WATT Univ

TITLE	CODE	COURSE	SUBJECTS	A/AS	ND/C	AGNVQ	IB	SQA(H)	SQA	RATIO	A/AS
Business and Economics	LN11	4FT deg	* g	CCC	MO	M$ go	30	BBBB	Ind		
Business and Finance	NN1H	4FT deg	*	CCC	HN	Ind	30	BBBB			
Estate Management	K2N8	4FT deg	*	CCD	MO	M$ go	34	BBCC	Ind		
Industrial and Business Studies	HN71	4FT deg	M	CDD	HN	M$ go	28	BBB	HN		
International Business and Finance	NN13	4FT deg	L	CCC	Ind		Ind	BBBB	Ind		
International Business and Langs:French/German	NT19	4FT deg	L	BBC	Ind	Ind	Ind	AABB	Ind		
International Business and Langs:French/Russian	NTC9	4FT deg	L	BBC	Ind	Ind	Ind	AABB	Ind		
International Business and Langs:French/Spanish	NTD9	4FT deg	L	BBC	Ind	Ind	Ind	AABB	Ind		
International Business and Langs:German/Russian	NTCX	4FT deg	L	BBC	Ind	Ind	Ind	AABB	Ind		
International Business and Langs:German/Spanish	NT1X	4FT deg	L	BBC	Ind	Ind	Ind	AABB	Ind		
International Business and Langs:Spanish/Russian	NT1Y	4FT deg	L	BBC	Ind	Ind	Ind	AABB	Ind		
International Management	N145	4FT deg	*	CCC		M$ go	30	BBBB	Ind		
Management	N124	4FT deg	* g	CCC	MO	M$^ go	30	BBBB	Ind		
Management with Business Law	N1M3	4FT deg	*	CCC		M$ go	30	BBBB	Ind		
Management with Human Resource Management	N1N6	4FT deg	*	CCC		M$ go	30	BBBB	Ind		
Management with Marketing	N1N5	4FT deg	*	CCC		M$ go	30	BBBB	Ind		
Management with Operations Management	N1N2	4FT deg	*	CCC		M$ go	30	BBBB	Ind		
Combined Studies *Business Organisation*	Y300	4FT deg	*	CCC	Ind	M$ go	30	BBBB	Ind		

Univ of HERTFORDSHIRE

TITLE	CODE	COURSE	SUBJECTS	A/AS	ND/C	AGNVQ	IB	SQA(H)	SQA	RATIO	A/AS
Applied Geology/Business	F6N1	3FT deg	* g	18	4M+4D	M$ gi	26$	BBBC	Ind		
Applied Geology/Operational Research	F6N2	3FT deg	S g	12	3M $	M$ gi	24$	CCCC$	Ind		
Applied Physics/Operational Research	F3N2	3FT deg	M+P	12	3M $	M$ gi	24$	CCCC$	Ind		
Applied Statistics/Business	G4N1	3FT deg	*	18	4M+4D	M$6 gi	26	BBBC	Ind		
Applied Statistics/Operational Research	G4N2	3FT deg	*	12	3M	M$ gi	24	CCCC	Ind	6	
Astronomy/Business	F5N1	3FT deg	M g	16	6M+2D	M$6 gi	26$	BBCC$	Ind		
Astronomy/Operational Research	F5N2	3FT deg	M g	12	3M $	M$ gi	24$	CCCC$	Ind		
Business Administration	N121	3FT deg	* g	18	4M+4D	M$6 gi	26	BBBC	Ind		
Business Decision Sciences	GN42	3FT/4SW deg	g	12	MO	Ind $	24$	Ind		1	4/14
Business Joint Honours	NN41	3FT/4SW deg	* g	18	DO	DB	28	BBBB		4	8/20
Business Studies	N120	4SW deg	* g	18	DO	DB	28	BBBB		11	12/20
Business/Applied Geology	N1F6	3FT deg	* g	18	4M+4D	M$6 gi	26$	BBBC$	Ind		
Business/Applied Statistics	N1G4	3FT deg	*	18	4M+4D	M$6 gi	26	BBBC	Ind		
Business/Astronomy	N1F5	3FT deg	M g	16	6M+2D	M$6 gi	26$	BBCC$	Ind		
Business/Chemistry	N1F1	3FT deg	C g	18	4M+4D	M$6 gi	26$	BBBC$	Ind	3	
Business/Computing	N1G5	3FT deg	*	18	4M+4D	M$6 gi	26	BBBC	Ind	5	14/20
Business/Economics	N1L1	3FT deg	*	18	4M+4D	M$6 gi	26	BBBC	Ind	11	
Business/Electronic Music	N1W3	3FT deg	Mu	18	4M+4D	M$^ gi	26$	BBBC	Ind		
Business/Electronics	N1H6	3FT deg	* g	18	4M+4D	M$6 gi	26$	BBBC$	Ind		
Business/Environmental Science	N1F9	3FT deg	*	18	4M+4D	M$6 gi	26	BBBC	Ind	13	

course details

98 expected requirements

96 entry stats

TITLE	CODE	COURSE	SUBJECTS	A/AS	ND/C	AGNVQ	IB	SQA(H)	SQA	RATIO	A/AS
Business/European Studies	N1T2	3FT deg	*	18	4M+4D	M$6 gi	26	BBBC	Ind	3	
Business/Law	N1M3	3FT deg	*	20	4M+4D	D$ gi	26	BBBC	Ind	7	14/20
Business/Manufacturing Systems	N1H7	3FT deg	*	18	4M+4D	M$6 gi	26	BBBC	Ind		
Business/Mathematics	N1G1	3FT deg	M	18	4M+4D	M$^ gi	26$	BBBC$	Ind	7	
Business/Operational Research	N1N2	3FT deg	*	18	4M+4D	M$6 gi	26	BBBC	Ind		
Business/Psychology	N1C8	3FT deg	*	20	4M+4D	D$ gi	26	BBBC	Ind	10	18/20
Chemistry/Business	F1N1	3FT deg	C g	18	4M+4D	MS^ gi	26$	BBBC$	Ind		
Chemistry/Operational Research	F1N2	3FT deg	C g	12	3M $	MS gi	24$	CCCC$	Ind		
Computing/Business	G5N1	3FT deg	*	18	4M+4D	M$6 gi	26	BBBC	Ind	13	
Economics/Business	L1N1	3FT deg	*	18	4M+4D	M$6 gi	26	BBBC	Ind	11	
Electronic Music/Business	W3N1	3FT deg	Mu	18	4M+4D	M$^ gi	26$	BBBC$	Ind	2	
Electronic Music/Operational Research	W3N2	3FT deg	Mu	14	MO $	M$^ gi	26$	BCCC$	Ind		
Electronics/Business	H6N1	3FT deg	* g	18	4M+4D	M$6 gi	26$	BBBC$	Ind		
Electronics/Operational Research	H6N2	3FT deg	* g	12	3M $	M$ gi	24$	CCCC$	Ind		
Engineering Management	HN11	3FT/4SW deg	*	14	3M $	Ind	$	Ind	Ind	1	4/14
Engineering Management (Extended)	HN1C▼	4FT/5SW deg	*	2	N	Ind	Dip$	Ind	Ind	7	
Environmental Science/Business	F9NC	3FT deg	*	18	4M+4D	M$^ gi	26	BBBC	Ind		
European Studies/Business	T2N1	3FT deg	*	18	4M+4D	M$6 gi	26	BBBC	Ind	10	
European Studies/Operational Research	T2N2	3FT deg	*	14	MO	M$ gi	26	BCCC	Ind		
Human Biology/Operational Research	B1N2	3FT deg	S g	12	3M $	MS gi	24$	CCCC$	Ind	1	
Innovation and Enterprise Technology (extended)	HN7C	4FT deg									
International Business Studies	N145	4SW deg	F/G/S g	18	DO $	DB	28$	BBBB$	Ind		
Law/Business	M3N1	3FT deg	*	20	4M+4D	D$ gi	26	BBBC	Ind	19	
Law/Operational Research	M3N2	3FT deg	*	20	4M+4D	D$ gi	26	BBBC	Ind		
Linguistic Science/Operational Research	Q1N2	3FT deg	*	14	MO $	M$ gi	26	BCCC	Ind		
Manufacturing Systems/Business	H7N1	3FT deg	*	18	4M+4D	M$6 gi	26	BBBC	Ind		
Manufacturing Systems/Operational Research	H7N2	3FT deg	*	12	3M	M$ gi	24	CCCC	Ind		
Mathematics for Business Analysis	G1NF	3FT deg									
Mathematics/Business	G1N1	3FT deg	M	18	4M+4D	M$^ gi	26$	BBBC$	Ind	6	
Mathematics/Operational Research	G1N2	3FT deg	M	12	3M $	M$^ gi	24$	CCCC$	Ind		
Operational Research	N200	3FT deg	*	12	3M $	M$ gi	24$	CCCC$	Ind		
Operational Research/Applied Geology	N2F6	3FT deg	* g	12	3M $	M$ gi	24$	CCCC$	Ind		
Operational Research/Applied Physics	N2F3	3FT deg	M+P	12	3M $	M$ gi	24$	CCCC$	Ind		
Operational Research/Applied Statistics	N2G4	3FT deg	*	12	3M	M$ gi	24	CCCC	Ind	1	
Operational Research/Astronomy	N2F5	3FT deg	M g	12	3M $	M$ gi	24$	CCCC$	Ind		
Operational Research/Business	N2N1	3FT deg	*	18	4M+4D	M$6 gi	26	BBBC	Ind		
Operational Research/Chemistry	N2F1	3FT deg	C g	12	3M $	MS gi	24$	CCCC$	Ind		
Operational Research/Electronic Music	N2W3	3FT deg	Mu	14	MO $	M$^ gi	26$	BCCC	Ind		
Operational Research/Electronics	N2H6	3FT deg	* g	12	3M $	M$ gi	24$	CCCC$	Ind		
Operational Research/European Studies	N2T2	3FT deg	*	14	MO	M$ gi	26	BCCC	Ind		
Operational Research/Human Biology	N2B1	3FT deg	S g	12	3M $	MS gi	24$	CCCC$	Ind		
Operational Research/Law	N2M3	3FT deg	*	20	4M+4D	D$ gi	26	BBBC	Ind		
Operational Research/Linguistic Science	N2Q1	3FT deg	*	14	MO $	M$ gi	26	BCCC	Ind		
Operational Research/Manufacturing Systems	N2H7	3FT deg	*	12	3M	M$ gi	24	CCCC	Ind		
Operational Research/Mathematics	N2G1	3FT deg	M	12	3M $	M$^ gi	24$	CCCC$	Ind		
Operational Research/Philosophy	N2V7	3FT deg	*	14	MO	M$ gi	26	BCCC	Ind		
Operational Research/Psychology	N2C8	3FT deg	*	20	4M+4D	D$ gi	26	BBBC	Ind		
Philosophy/Operational Research	V7N2	3FT deg	*	14	MO	M$ gi	26	BCCC	Ind		
Psychology/Business	C8N1	3FT deg	*	20	4M+4D	D$ gi	26	BBBC	Ind	14	
Psychology/Operational Research	C8N2	3FT deg	*	20	4M+4D	D$ gi	26	BBBC	Ind	6	
Combined Modular Scheme Business	Y100	3FT deg	*	18	4M+4D	M$6 gi	26	BBBC	Ind		

Business and Management 12

TITLE	CODE	COURSE	SUBJECTS	A/AS	ND/C	RGNVQ	IB	SQA(H)	SQA	RATIO A/AS
98 expected requirements ... **96 entry stats**										
Combined Modular Scheme *Operational Research*	Y100	3FT deg	*	12	3M	M$ gi	24	CCCC	Ind	
Combined Modular Scheme *Operational Research (Extended)*	Y109▼	4EXT deg	*	4	N	P$ gi	Dip	DDDD	Ind	
Business	021N▼	2FT HND	*	2	N	Ind	24	Ind	Ind	4 2/12
Business	121N▼	2FT HND	* g	2	MO	Ind	24	CCCD	Ind	
Business with Finance	091N▼	2FT HND	* g	2	MO	Ind	24	CCCD	Ind	
Business with Leisure and Tourism	71PN▼	2FT HND	* g	2	MO	Ind	24	CCCD	Ind	
Business with Marketing	51NN▼	2FT HND	* g	2	MO	Ind	24	CCCD	Ind	
Business with Personnel	61NN▼	2FT HND	* g	2	MO	Ind	24	CCCD	Ind	

Univ of HUDDERSFIELD

TITLE	CODE	COURSE	SUBJECTS	A/AS	ND/C	RGNVQ	IB	SQA(H)	SQA	RATIO A/AS
Business Administration	N122	1FT deg	X	X	MO	X	X	X	HNMO	
Business Studies	N120	3FT/4SW deg	* g	16	MO+4D	M$ go	26	BBCC	Ind	
Business Studies with Environmental Management	N1F9	3FT/4SW deg	* g	16	MO+4D	M$ go	26	BBCC	Ind	
Business Studies with a Modern Language	N1T9	3FT/4SW deg	Ap g	16	MO+4D	M$ go	26	BBCC	Ind	
Chemistry with Business	F1N1	3FT/4SW deg	C g	10	3M $	MS gi	Ind	BCC	Ind	
Computing and Business Analysis	GN51	4SW deg	* g	14-16	MO	M go	Ind	BBB	Ind	
Design, Culture and Marketing	EN25	3FT/4SW deg	Pf+A/Ad/Fa g	10-12	N	Ind	Ind	Ind	Ind	
Design, Culture and Marketing	WN25	3FT/4SW deg	Pf+A/Ad/Fa g	10-12	N	Ind	Ind	Ind	Ind	
Environmental Sustainability	F9N1	3FT deg	* g	14-16	Ind	Ind	Ind	Ind	Ind	
European Logistics Management	N921	3FT/4SW deg	L g	14-18	Ind	Ind	Ind	BBB	Ind	
Fashion with Manufacture, Marketing and Promotion	E2N5	3FT/4SW deg	Pf+A/Ad/Fa g	10-12	N	Ind	Ind	Ind	Ind	
Fashion with Manufacture, Marketing and Promotion	W2N5	3FT/4SW deg	Pf+A/Ad/Fa g	10-12	N	Ind	Ind	Ind	Ind	
Fine Art (Drawing and Painting) with Marketing	WN15	3FT/4SW deg	Pf+A/Ad/Fa g	10-12	N	Ind	Ind	Ind	Ind	
Fine Art (Drawing and Painting) with Marketing	EN15	3FT/4SW deg	Pf+A/Ad/Fa g	10-12	N	Ind	Ind	Ind	Ind	
Food Supply Chain Management	DN49	3FT/4SW deg	* g	14-18	Ind	Ind	Ind	BBB	Ind	
International Business with Modern Languages	N1TX	4FT/4SW deg	Ap g	16	MO+4D	M$ go	26	BBCC	Ind	
Logistics and Supply Chain Management	N9H7	3FT/4SW deg	* g	14-18	Ind	Ind	Ind	BBB	Ind	
Management Sciences	N100	4SW deg	* g	18-20	MO	M go	Ind	BBB	Ind	
Management and Accountancy	NN14	3FT deg	* g	16	3M+3D	M$ go	Ind	BBCC	Ind	
Manufacturing and Operations Management	HN71	4SW deg	* g	14	4M	M go	Ind	Ind	Ind	
Marketing	N500	4SW deg	* g	14	MO	M go	28	BBB	Ind	
Marketing and Innovation	N501	4SW deg	* g	14	MO+4D	M$ go	28	BBB	Ind	
Marketing with a Modern Language	N5T9	4SW deg	* g	14	MO	M go	28	BBB	Ind	
Marketing, Retailing and Distribution	N555	4SW deg	* g	14	MO+4D	M$ go	28	BBB	Ind	
Product Development	H3N9	3FT/4SW deg	* g	14	4M	M	Ind	Ind	Ind	
Technology with Business Studies	J9N1	4SW deg	S g	12	4M	M$ go	Ind	Ind	Ind	
Textile Management and Marketing	NN15	3FT/4SW deg	* g	10-12	Ind	Ind	Ind	Ind	Ind	
Transport Design	EW92	3FT/4SW deg	Pf+A/Ad/Fa g	10-12	N	Ind	Ind	Ind	Ind	
Transport Design	NW92	3FT/4SW deg	Pf+A/Ad/Fa g	10-12	N	Ind	Ind	Ind	Ind	
Transport and Logistics Management	N920	4SW deg	* g	14-18	Ind	Ind	Ind	BBB	Ind	
Business and Finance	421N	2FT HND	* g	6	MO	P	Ind	CCC	Ind	
Decision Sciences	25NG	3SW HND	* g	4	N	P go	Ind	CCC	Ind	

Univ of HULL

TITLE	CODE	COURSE	SUBJECTS	A/AS	ND/C	RGNVQ	IB	SQA(H)	SQA	RATIO A/AS
Business Studies	N120	3FT deg	* g	BBB	DO	D*^ go	28$	BBBCC	Ind	11 18/26
Business Studies/Dutch	NT12	4FT deg	* g	BBC-BCC	Ind	D*_ go	26$	BCCCC	Ind	4
Business Studies/French	NR11	4FT deg	F g	BBC-BCC	Ind $	D*_ go	26$	BBCCC	Ind	11 18/24
Business Studies/German	NR12	4FT deg	G g	BBC-BCC	Ind $	D*_ go	26$	BBCCC	Ind	6 16/26
Business Studies/Italian	NR13	4FT deg	L g	BBC-BCC	Ind $	D*_ go	26$	BBCCC	Ind	5 20/22
Business Studies/Scandinavian Studies	NR17	4FT deg	* g	BBC-BCC	Ind	D*_ go	26$	BCCCC	Ind	
Business Studies/Spanish	NR14	4FT deg	L g	BBC-BCC	Ind $	D*_ go	26$	BBCCC	Ind	4 18/24
Computer Systems Eng with Bus Studies (MEng)	G6N1	4FT deg	S+M g	BCC	M+D $	ME^ gi	26$	BBBCC	Ind	

course details | 98 expected requirements | 96 entry stats

TITLE	CODE	COURSE	SUBJECTS	A/AS	ND/C	AGNVQ	IB	SQA(H)	SQA	RATIO	A/AS
Computer and Management Sciences	GN51	3FT deg	M	BCC-CCC	MO+D $	M$^ go	26$	BBBCC	Ind	17	
Economics and Management Sciences	LN11	3FT deg	M	BBC-BCC	MO $	M*^ go	26$	Ind	Ind	5	
Information Management	N1G5	3FT deg	M g	BBC-BCC	M+4D	M*6/^ go	28$	BBCCC	Ind	3	14/20
Management	N100	3FT deg	* g	BBC-BCC	M+4D	M*6/^ go	26$	BBCCC	Ind	13	18/24
Management (International) (4 Yrs)	N140	4FT deg	* g	BBC-BCC	M+4D	M*6/^ go	28$	BBCCC	Ind	5	18/24
Management Sciences	NN12	3FT deg	M g	BBC-BCC	MO $	M*^ go	28$	Ind	Ind	5	18/22
Management Sciences (International) (4 Yrs)	N141	4FT deg	M g	BBC-BCC	MO $	M*^ go	28$	Ind	Ind	4	22/24
Management/Sociological Systems	LN31	3FT deg	* g	BBC	MO+3D	D$^/6 go	28$	BBBBC	Ind		
Mathematics and Management Sciences	NG11	3FT deg	M	BBC-BCD	MO $	M$^ go	28$	Ind	Ind	7	16/20
Physical Education and Sports Science with Mgt	B6N1	3FT deg	*	18-20	3M	M$6 gi	25$	BBBCC	Ind		
Politics with Management	M1N1	3FT deg	* g	BBC-BCC	MO $	M*6/^ go	28$	BBCCC	Ind		

IMPERIAL COLL (Univ of London)

TITLE	CODE	COURSE	SUBJECTS	A/AS	ND/C	AGNVQ	IB	SQA(H)	SQA	RATIO	A/AS
Biochemistry with Management	C7N1	3FT deg	C+M/P/B	BCC	DO		30$	Ind	Ind	5	
Biochemistry with Mgt and a Year in Ind/Research	C7ND	4FT deg	C+M/P/B	BCC	DO		30$	Ind	Ind	5	22/30
Biology with Management	C1N1	3FT deg	B+C/M/P	BCC	MO+2D	Ind	30$	Ind	Ind	21	
Chemistry with Management	F1N1	3FT deg	C+M/P	BBC	HN		32	CSYS		25	
Chemistry with Management	F1ND	4FT deg	C+M/P	BBC	HN		32	CSYS		5	
Chemistry with Management and a Yr in Industry	F1NC	4SW deg	C+M/P	BBC	HN		32	CSYS		19	
Electrical & Electronic Eng with Mgt (MEng)	H5NC	4FT deg	M+P g	AAB-BBB	HN/DO$ X		$	CSYS$	HN$	4	26/30
Materials with Management	J5N1	3FT deg	M+P/C	18	HN		$	BBBB	$	5	
Materials with Management and a Year Abroad	J5NC	4FT deg	M+P/C g	18	HN		$	BBBB	$		
Mathematics with Management	G1N1	3FT deg	M	BBC-ACC	Ind	X	Ind	Ind	Ind	10	24/30

KEELE Univ

TITLE	CODE	COURSE	SUBJECTS	A/AS	ND/C	AGNVQ	IB	SQA(H)	SQA	RATIO	A/AS
Biol & Medicinal Chemistry and Business Admin	FNC9	3FT deg	C g	BCC	Ind	D$^	28$	CSYS	Ind		
Biol and Med Chem and Human Resource Management	FNC6	3FT deg	C g	BCC	Ind	D$^	28$	CSYS	Ind		
Business Admin and Applied Social Studs (4 Yrs)	NL95	4FT deg	*	BBC	Ind	Ind	30	BBBB	Ind		
Business Admin and Biological & Med Chem (4 Yrs)	NF9C	4FT deg	*	BCC	Ind	Ind	28	BBBB	Ind		
Business Administration and American St (4 Yrs)	QN49	4FT deg	*	BCC	Ind	Ind	28	BBBB	Ind		
Business Administration and Ancient Hist (4 Yrs)	VND9	4FT deg	*	BCC	Ind	Ind	28	BBBB	Ind		
Business Administration and Ancient History	NV9D	3FT deg	*	BCC	Ind	Ind	28	CSYS	Ind	6	
Business Administration and Applied Social Studs	LN59	3FT deg	*	BBC	Ind	Ind	30	CSYS	Ind	5	
Business Administration and Astrophysics	FN59	3FT deg	P g	BCC	Ind	D$^	28$	CSYS	Ind		
Business Administration and Astrophysics (4 Yrs)	NF95	4FT deg	*	BCC	Ind	Ind	28	BBBB	Ind		
Business Administration and Biochemistry	CN79	3FT deg	C g	BCC	Ind	D$^	28$	CSYS	Ind		
Business Administration and Biochemistry (4 Yrs)	NC97	4FT deg	*	BCC	Ind	Ind	28	BBBB	Ind		
Chemistry and Business Administration	FN19	3FT deg	C g	BCC	Ind	D$^	28$	CSYS	Ind	13	
Chemistry and Business Administration (4 Yrs)	NF91	4FT deg	*	BCC	Ind	Ind	28	BBBB	Ind		
Classical Studies and Business Admin (4 Yrs)	QN89	4FT deg	*	BCC	Ind	Ind	28	BBBB	Ind		
Computer Science and Business Admin (4 Yrs)	NG95	4FT deg	*	BCC	Ind	Ind	28	BBBB	Ind		
Criminology and Business Administration (4 Yrs)	NM9H	4FT deg	*	BBB-BCC	Ind	Ind	28	BBBB	Ind		
Economics and Business Administration (4 Yrs)	NL91	4FT deg	* g	BCC	Ind	Ind	28	BBBB	Ind		
Educational Studies and Business Admin (4 Yrs)	XN99	4FT deg	*	BBC-BCC	Ind	Ind	28	BBBB	Ind		
Educational Studies and Business Administration	NX99	3FT deg	*	BCC	Ind	Ind	28	CSYS	Ind	4	
English and Business Administration (4 Yrs)	QN39	4FT deg	*	BBC	Ind	Ind	30	BBBB	Ind		
Environmental Management and Business Admin	FNX9	3FT deg	* g	BCC	Ind	Ind	28	CSYS	Ind	16	
Environmental Mgt and Business Admin (4 Yrs)	NF9X	4FT deg	*	BCC	Ind	Ind	28	BBBB	Ind	15	
Finance and Business Administration	NN39	3FT deg	* g	BBC-BCC	Ind	Ind	30	CSYS	Ind		
Finance and Business Administration (4 Yrs)	NN3X	4FT deg	*	BCC	Ind	Ind	28	BBBB	Ind		
French and Business Administration	NR91	3FT deg	F	BBC-BCC	Ind	D$^	28$	CSYS	Ind	4	16/24
French and Business Administration (4 Yrs)	RN19	4FT deg	*	BBC-BCC	Ind	Ind	28	BBBB	Ind	63	
French/German and Business Admin (4 Yrs)	TN99	4FT deg	g	BBC	Ind	Ind	30	BBBB	Ind		

Business and Management 12

TITLE	CODE	COURSE	SUBJECTS	A/AS	ND/C	AGNVQ	IB	SQA(H)	SQA	RATIO A/AS
French/German and Business Administration	NT99	3FT deg	F+G	BBC	Ind	D$^	30$	CSYS	Ind	2
French/Russian or Russian St and Bus Admin(4Yrs)	TNX9	4FT deg	*	BBC	Ind	Ind	30	BBBB	Ind	
French/Russian or Russian Studies and Bus Admin	NT9X	3FT deg	F+R	BBC	Ind	D$^	30$	CSYS	Ind	
Geography and Business Administration (4 Yrs)	NF98	4FT deg	* g	BCC	Ind	Ind	28	BBBB	Ind	
Geology and Business Administration	FN69	3FT deg	S g	BCC	Ind	D$^	28$	CSYS	Ind	
Geology and Business Administration (4 Yrs)	NF96	4FT deg	*	BCC	Ind	Ind	28	BBBB	Ind	
German and Business Administration	NR92	3FT deg	G	BBC-BCC	Ind	D$^	28$	CSYS	Ind	6
German and Business Administration (4 Yrs)	RN29	4FT deg	G	BBC-BCC	Ind	Ind	28$	BBBB	Ind	15
German/Russian or Russ St and Bus Admin (4 Yrs)	TNY9	4FT deg	g	BCC	Ind	Ind	30	BBBB	Ind	
German/Russian or Russian St and Business Admin	NT9Y	3FT deg	G+R	BBC	Ind	D$^	30$	CSYS	Ind	
Hum Res M and French/Russian or Russian St(4Yrs)	TNX6	4FT deg	*	BBC-BCC	Ind	D$^	28	BBBB	Ind	
Hum Res Mgt and German/Russ or Russ St (4 Yrs)	TNY6	4FT deg	G	BCC	Ind	Ind	28$	BBBB	Ind	
Human Res Mgt and French/Russian or Russian St	NT6X	3FT deg	F+R	BBC-BCC	Ind	D$^	28$	CSYS	Ind	
Human Res Mgt and German/Russian or Russian St	NT6Y	3FT deg	G+R	BBC-BCC	Ind	D$^	28$	CSYS	Ind	
Human Resource Management and American Studies	NQ64	3FT deg	*	BCC	Ind	Ind	28	CSYS	Ind	
Human Resource Management and American Studies	QN46	4FT deg	*	BCC	Ind	Ind	28	BBBB	Ind	
Human Resource Management and Ancient History	NV6D	3FT deg	*	BCC	Ind	Ind	28	CSYS	Ind	2
Human Resource Management and Applied Social St	LN56	3FT deg	*	BBC	Ind	Ind	30	CSYS	Ind	4
Human Resource Management and Astrophysics	FN56	3FT deg	P g	BCC	Ind	D$^	28$	CSYS	Ind	
Human Resource Management and Biology	NC61	4FT deg	*	BCC	Ind	Ind	28	BBBB	Ind	
Human Resource Management and Biology	CN16	3FT deg	S g	BCC	Ind	D$^	28$	CSYS	Ind	
Human Resource Management and Business Admin	NN69	3FT deg	*	BBC	Ind	Ind	30	CSYS	Ind	8 20/28
Human Resource Management and Chemistry	FN16	3FT deg	C g	BCC	Ind	D$^	28$	CSYS	Ind	
Human Resource Management and Chemistry (4 Yrs)	NF61	4FT deg	*	BCC	Ind	Ind	28	BBBB	Ind	
Human Resource Management and Classical Studies	QN86	4FT deg	*	BCC	Ind	Ind	28	BBBB	Ind	
Human Resource Management and Classical Studies	NQ68	3FT deg	*	BCC	Ind	Ind	28	CSYS	Ind	
Human Resource Management and Computer Science	GN56	3FT deg	* g	BCC	Ind	Ind	28	CSYS	Ind	
Human Resource Management and Economics	LN16	3FT deg	* g	BCC	Ind	Ind	28	CSYS	Ind	6
Human Resource Management and Economics (4 Yrs)	NL61	4FT deg	*	BCC	Ind	Ind	28	BBBB	Ind	
Human Resource Management and Educational Studs	NX69	3FT deg	*	BCC	Ind	Ind	28	CSYS	Ind	
Human Resource Management and Electronic Music	NW6J	3FT deg	Mu	BCC	Ind	D$^	28$	CSYS	Ind	
Human Resource Management and Env Mgt (4 Yrs)	NF6X	4FT deg	*	BCC	Ind	Ind	28	BBBB	Ind	
Human Resource Management and Environmental Mgt	FNX6	3FT deg	* g	BCC	Ind	Ind	28	CSYS	Ind	5
Human Resource Management and Finance	NN3Q	3FT deg	* g	BBC-BCC	Ind	D	28	CSYS	Ind	
Human Resource Management and Finance (4 Yrs)	NN63	4FT deg	*	BBC-BCC	Ind	Ind	28	BBBB	Ind	
Human Resource Management and French	NR61	3FT deg	F	BCC	Ind	D$^	28$	CSYS	Ind	2
Human Resource Management and French (4 Yrs)	RN16	4FT deg	*	BCC	Ind	Ind	28	BBBB	Ind	
Human Resource Management and French/German	NT69	3FT deg	F+G	BBC	Ind	D$^	30$	CSYS	Ind	
Human Resource Management and Geography	LN86	3FT deg	Gy	BCC	Ind	D$^	28$	CSYS	Ind	
Human Resource Management and Geography (4 Yrs)	NL68	4FT deg	*	BCC	Ind	Ind	28	BBBB	Ind	
Human Resource Management and German	NR62	3FT deg	G	BCC	Ind	D$^	28$	CSYS	Ind	
Human Resource Management and German (4 Yrs)	RN26	4FT deg	G	BCC	Ind	Ind	28$	BBBB	Ind	2
Human Resource Management and History	VN16	4FT deg	*	BBC-BCC	Ind	Ind	28	BBBB	Ind	
Human Resource Management and History	NV61	3FT deg	*	BBC-BCC	Ind	Ind	28	CSYS	Ind	
Human Resource Management and Philosophy	NV67	3FT deg	*	BCC	Ind	Ind	28	CSYS	Ind	
Human Resource Management and Philosophy	VN76	4FT deg	*	BBC-BCC	Ind	Ind	28	BBBB	Ind	
Human Resource Mgt and Ancient History (4 Yrs)	VND6	4FT deg	*	BCC	Ind	Ind	28	BBBB	Ind	
Human Resource Mgt and App Social St (4 Yrs)	NL65	4FT deg	*	BBC	Ind	Ind	30	BBBB	Ind	3
Human Resource Mgt and Astrophysics (4 Yrs)	NF65	4FT deg	*	BCC	Ind	Ind	28	BBBB	Ind	
Human Resource Mgt and Biol Med Chem (4 Yrs)	NF6C	4FT deg	*	BCC	Ind	Ind	28	BBBB	Ind	
Human Resource Mgt and Business Admin (4 Yrs)	NN96	4FT deg	*	BBC	Ind	Ind	30	BBBB	Ind	14
Human Resource Mgt and Computer Science (4 Yrs)	NG65	4FT deg	*	BCC	Ind	Ind	28	BBBB	Ind	1

course details | 98 expected requirements | 96 entry stats

TITLE	CODE	COURSE	SUBJECTS	A/AS	NO/C	AGNVQ	IB	SQA(H)	SQA	RATIO	A/AS
Human Resource Mgt and Educational Studs (4 Yrs)	XN96	4FT deg	*	BCC	Ind	Ind	28	BBBB	Ind		
Human Resource Mgt and Electronic Music (4 Yrs)	WNJ1	4FT deg	*	BCC	Ind	Ind	28	BBBB	Ind		
Human Resource Mgt and French/German (4 Yrs)	TN96	4FT deg	G	BCC	Ind	Ind	28$	BBBB	Ind		
International History and Business Admin (4 Yrs)	VNC9	4FT deg	*	BCC	Ind	Ind	28	BBBB	Ind		
International Politics and Business Admin(4 Yrs)	NM9C	4FT deg	*	BCC	Ind	Ind	28	BBBB	Ind		
International Politics and Human Resource Mgt	MNC6	3FT deg	*	BCC	Ind	Ind	28	CSYS	Ind		
International Politics and Human Resource Mgt	NM6C	4FT deg	*	BBC-BCC	Ind	Ind	28	BBBB	Ind	3	
Latin and Human Resource Management (4 Yrs)	QN66	4FT deg	*	BCC	Ind	Ind	28	BBBB	Ind		
Law and Business Administration	MN39	3FT deg	*	BBB	Ind	Ind	32	CSYS	Ind	8	22/26
Law and Business Administration (4 Yrs)	NM93	4FT deg	*	BBB	Ind	Ind	32	BBBB	Ind	8	
Law and Human Resource Management	MN36	3FT deg	*	BBB	Ind	Ind	32	CSYS	Ind	5	
Law and Human Resource Management (4 Yrs)	NM63	4FT deg	*	BBB	Ind	Ind	32	BBBB	Ind		
Management Sci & German/Russian or Russ (4 Yrs)	TNY1	4FT deg	*	BBC	Ind	Ind	30	BBBB	Ind		
Management Science and Astrophysics	FN51	3FT deg	P g	BCC	Ind	D$^	28$	CSYS	Ind		
Management Science and Astrophysics (4 Yrs)	NF15	4FT deg	*	BCC	Ind	Ind	28	BBBB	Ind		
Management Science and Biochemistry	CN71	3FT deg	C g	BCC	Ind	D$^	28$	CSYS	Ind		
Management Science and Biochemistry (4 Yrs)	NC17	4FT deg	*	BCC	Ind	Ind	28	BBBB	Ind		
Management Science and Biology	CN11	3FT deg	S g	BCC	Ind	D$^	28$	CSYS	Ind	12	
Management Science and Computer Science	GN51	3FT deg	* g	BCC	Ind	Ind	28	CSYS	Ind	4	14/16
Management Science and Computer Science (4 Yrs)	NG15	4FT deg	*	BCC	Ind	Ind	28	BBBB	Ind	5	
Management Science and Economics	LN11	3FT deg	* g	BCC	Ind	D$	28	CSYS	Ind		
Management Science and Economics (4 Yrs)	NL11	4FT deg	*	BCC	Ind	Ind	28	BBBB	Ind		
Management Science and Finance	NN13	3FT deg	* g	BCC	Ind	Ind	28	CSYS	Ind		
Management Science and Finance (4 Yrs)	NN31	4FT deg	*	BCC	Ind	Ind	28	BBBB	Ind		
Management Science and French (4 Yrs)	RN11	4FT deg	* g	BCC	Ind	Ind	28	BBBB	Ind		
Management Science and French/German (4 Yrs)	TN91	4FT deg	* g	BBC	Ind	Ind	30	BBBB	Ind		
Management Science and German	NR12	3FT deg	G g	BCC	Ind	D$^	28$	CSYS	Ind	5	
Management Science and German (4 Yrs)	RN21	4FT deg	* g	BCC	Ind	Ind	28	BBBB	Ind	10	
Management Science and Human Resource Mgt(4 Yrs)	NN61	4FT deg	* g	BCC	Ind	Ind	28	BBBB	Ind		
Management Science and Law	MN31	3FT deg	* g	BBB	Ind	Ind	32	CSYS	Ind		
Marketing and American Studies	NQ54	3FT deg	*	BBC	Ind	Ind	30	CSYS	Ind	9	
Marketing and Ancient History	NV5D	3FT deg	*	BCC	Ind	Ind	28	CSYS	Ind		
Marketing and Astrophysics	FN55	3FT deg	P g	BCC	Ind	D$^	28$	CSYS	Ind		
Marketing and Biochemistry	CN75	3FT deg	C g	BCC	Ind	D$^	28$	CSYS	Ind		
Marketing and Biology	CN15	3FT deg	S g	BCC	Ind	D$^	28$	CSYS	Ind		
Marketing and Classical Studies	NQ58	3FT deg	*	BCC	Ind	Ind	28	CSYS	Ind		
Marketing and Computer Science	GN55	3FT deg	* g	BCC	Ind	Ind	28	CSYS	Ind		
Marketing and Criminology	MNH5	3FT deg	*	BBB	Ind	Ind	32	CSYS	Ind		
Marketing and Economics	LN15	3FT deg	* g	BCC	Ind	Ind	28	CSYS	Ind	14	
Marketing and Educational Studies	NX59	3FT deg	*	BCC	Ind	Ind	28	CSYS	Ind		
Marketing and Electronic Music	NW5J	3FT deg	Mu	BCC	Ind	D$^	28	CSYS	Ind		
Marketing and English	NQ53	3FT deg	E	BBC	Ind	D$^	30$	CSYS	Ind	16	
Marketing and Environmental Management	FNX5	3FT deg	* g	BCC	Ind	Ind	28	CSYS	Ind		
Marketing and Finance	NN35	3FT deg	* g	BBC-BCC	Ind	Ind	28	CSYS	Ind		
Marketing and Geography	LN85	3FT deg	Gy	BCC	Ind	D$^	28$	CSYS	Ind	8	21/26
Marketing and Geology	FN65	3FT deg	S g	BCC	Ind	D$^	28$	CSYS	Ind		
Marketing and German	NR52	3FT deg	G	BCC	Ind	D$^	28$	CSYS	Ind	6	
Marketing and German/Russian or Russian Studies	NT5Y	3FT deg	G+R	BBC	Ind	D$^	30$	CSYS	Ind		
Marketing and History	NV51	3FT deg	*	BBC	Ind	Ind	30	CSYS	Ind	9	
Marketing and Human Resource Management	NN56	3FT deg	*	BBC	Ind	Ind	30	CSYS	Ind	22	
Marketing and International History	NV5C	3FT deg	*	BCC	Ind	Ind	28	CSYS	Ind	6	
Marketing and Latin	NQ56	3FT deg	Ln	BCC	Ind	D$^	28$	CSYS	Ind		

Business and Management 12

course details

98 expected requirements

96 entry stats

TITLE	CODE	COURSE	SUBJECTS	A/AS	ND/C	AGNVQ	IB	SQA(H)	SQA	RATIO A/AS
Marketing and Law	MN35	3FT deg	*	BBB	Ind	Ind	32	CSYS	Ind	30
Mathematics and Business Administration (4 Yrs)	NG91	4FT deg	*	BCC	Ind	Ind	28	BBBB	Ind	
Mathematics and Management Science	GN11	3FT deg	M g	BCC	Ind	D$^	28$	CSYS	Ind	6
Mathematics and Management Science (4 Yrs)	NG11	4FT deg	*	BCC	Ind	Ind	28	BBBB	Ind	
Mathematics and Marketing	GN15	3FT deg	M	BCC	Ind	D$^	28$	CSYS	Ind	
Mgt Science and German/Russian or Russian Studs	NT1Y	3FT deg	G+R g	BCC	Ind	D$^	28$	CSYS	Ind	
Music and Human Resource Management (4 Yrs)	WN36	4FT deg	*	BCC	Ind	Ind	28	BBBB	Ind	
Music and Marketing	NW53	3FT deg	Mu	BCC	Ind	D$^	28$	CSYS	Ind	
Physics and Business Administration	FN39	3FT deg	P g	BCC	Ind	D$^	28$	CSYS	Ind	
Physics and Business Administration (4 Yrs)	NF93	4FT deg	*	BCC	Ind	Ind	28	BBBB	Ind	
Physics and Human Resource Management	FN36	3FT deg	P	BCC	Ind	D$^	28$	CSYS	Ind	
Physics and Human Resource Management (4 Yrs)	NF63	4FT deg	*	BCC	Ind	Ind	28	BBBB	Ind	
Physics and Management Science	FN31	3FT deg	P g	BCC	Ind	D$^	28$	CSYS	Ind	1
Physics and Management Science (4 Yrs)	NF13	4FT deg	*	BCC	Ind	Ind	28	BBBB	Ind	
Physics and Marketing	FN35	3FT deg	P	BCC	Ind	D$^	28$	CSYS	Ind	
Politics and Business Administration	MN19	3FT deg	*	BCC	Ind	Ind	28	CSYS	Ind	18
Politics and Business Administration (4 Yrs)	NM91	4FT deg	*	BCC	Ind	Ind	28	BBBB	Ind	4
Politics and Marketing	MN15	3FT deg	*	BCC	Ind	Ind	28	CSYS	Ind	
Psychology and Business Administration (4 Yrs)	NC98	4FT deg	*	BBB	Ind	Ind	32	ABBB	Ind	
Psychology and Human Resource Management	CN86	3FT deg	* g	BBB	Ind	Ind	32	CSYS	Ind	20
Psychology and Human Resource Management (4 Yrs)	NC68	4FT deg	*	BBB	Ind	Ind	32	ABBB	Ind	
Russian Studies & Business Administration(4 Yrs)	RNV9	4FT deg	*	BCC	Ind	Ind	28	BBBB	Ind	
Russian Studies and Business Administration	NR9V	3FT deg	*	BCC	Ind	Ind	28	CSYS	Ind	
Russian Studies and Human Resource Management	NR6V	3FT deg	*	BCC	Ind	Ind	28	CSYS	Ind	
Russian Studies and Human Resource Mgt (4 Yrs)	RNV6	4FT deg	*	BCC	Ind	Ind	28	BBBB	Ind	
Russian Studies and Management Science	NR1V	3FT deg	* g	BCC	Ind	Ind	28	CSYS	Ind	
Russian Studies and Management Science (4 Yrs)	RN8C	4FT deg	*	BCC	Ind	Ind	28	BBBB	Ind	
Russian Studies and Marketing	NR5V	3FT deg	*	BCC	Ind	Ind	28	CSYS	Ind	
Russian and Business Administration	NR98	3FT deg	R	BCC	Ind	D$^	28$	CSYS	Ind	3
Russian and Business Administration (4 Yrs)	RN89	4FT deg	*	BCC	Ind	Ind	28	BBBB	Ind	
Russian and Human Resource Management	NR68	3FT deg	R	BCC	Ind	D$^	28$	CSYS	Ind	
Russian and Human Resource Management (4 Yrs)	RN86	4FT deg	*	BCC	Ind	Ind	28	BBBB	Ind	
Russian and Management Science	NR18	3FT deg	R g	BCC	Ind	D$^	28$	CSYS	Ind	
Russian and Management Science (4 Yrs)	RN81	4FT deg	*	BCC	Ind	Ind	28	BBBB	Ind	
Russian and Marketing	NR58	3FT deg	R	BCC	Ind	D$^	28$	CSYS	Ind	
Sociol & Soc Anthrop and Human Resource Mgt(4Yr)	NLP3	4FT deg	*	BCC	Ind	Ind	28	BBBB	Ind	1
Sociol & Social Anthrop and Human Resource Mgt	LN3P	3FT deg	*	BCC	Ind	Ind	28	CSYS	Ind	4
Sociol & Social Anthropology and Business Admin	LN39	3FT deg	*	BCC	Ind	Ind	28	CSYS	Ind	6 18/28
Sociology & Social Anthropology and Marketing	LN35	3FT deg	*	BCC	Ind	Ind	28	CSYS	Ind	9
Statistics and Business Administration (4 Yrs)	NG94	4FT deg	* g	BCC	Ind	Ind	28	BBBB	Ind	
Statistics and Management Science	GN41	3FT deg	M g	BCC	Ind	D$^	28$	CSYS	Ind	13
Statistics and Management Science (4 Yrs)	NG14	4FT deg	*	BCC	Ind	Ind	28	BBBB	Ind	
Statistics and Marketing	GN45	3FT deg	M	BCC	Ind	D$^	28$	CSYS	Ind	
Visual Arts and Business Administration (4 Yrs)	WN19	4FT deg	*	BBC-BCC	Ind	Ind	28	BBBB	Ind	
Visual Arts and Human Resource Management	NW61	3FT deg	*	BBC-BCC	Ind	D$^	28	CSYS	Ind	
Visual Arts and Human Resource Management	WN16	4FT deg	*	BBC-BCC	Ind	Ind	28	BBBB	Ind	
Visual Arts and Marketing	NW51	3FT deg	*	BBC	Ind	D$^	30	CSYS	Ind	

Univ of KENT

TITLE	CODE	COURSE	SUBJECTS	A/AS	ND/C	AGNVQ	IB	SQA(H)	SQA	RATIO A/AS
Accounting & Finance and Business Administration	NN41	3FT deg	* g	24	1M+5D	D$ go	32	AABB		
Accounting & Finance and Management Science	NN14	3FT deg	M	18	Ind	Ind	26$	BBBB$	Ind	7 16/24
Accounting & Finance with French Bus St (4 Yrs)	N4N1	4FT deg	F g	18	Ind	Ind	26$	BBBB$	Ind	7
Business Administration	N122	3FT deg	* g	24	1M+5D	D$ go	32$	AABB	Ind	14/22

course details   98 expected requirements   96 entry stats

TITLE	CODE	COURSE	SUBJECTS	A/AS	ND/C	AGNVQ	IB	SQA(H)	SQA	RATIO A/AS	
Business Administration & Politics & Government	MN11	3FT deg	* g	24	1M+5D	D$ go	32	AABB	Ind		
Business Administration (Euro Management)(4 Yrs)	N123	4FT deg	F/G/Sp	22	Ind	Ind	30$	ABBB$	Ind		
Business Administration and Economics	LN11	3FT deg	* g	24	1M+5D	D$ go	32	AABB	Ind		
Business Mathematics	G1N1	3FT/4SW deg	M	20	Ind	Ind	28$	BBBB$	Ind	12	
Business Studies (4 Yrs)	N120▼	4FT deg		16	Ind	Ind	Ind	Ind	Ind	3	
Chemistry and Business Administration	FN11	3FT deg	C g	20	3M+2D$	Ind	28$	BBBB$	Ind		
Chemistry with Business Studies	FN1D	3FT deg	C g	16	MO $	Ind	24$	BBCC$	Ind		
Chemistry with Business Studs with Studs Abroad	FNCC	4FT deg	C g	16	MO $	Ind	24$	BBCC$	Ind		
Chemistry with Management Science	F1N1	3FT deg	C g	16	MO $	Ind	24$	BBCC$	Ind	17	
Chemistry with Mgt Sci with Studs Abroad (MChem)	F1ND	4FT deg	C g	16	MO $	Ind	24$	BBCC$	Ind		
Chemistry with Mgt Science with Studies Abroad	F1NC	4FT deg	C g	16	MO $	Ind	24$	BBCC$	Ind		
Computer Sci and Business Admin with a yr in Ind	GN5C	4FT deg									
Computer Science and Business Administration	GN51	3FT deg	* g	20	Ind	Ind	28	BBBB	Ind		
Computer Science with Management Science	G5N1	3FT deg	M	BCC	Ind	Ind	28$	BBBB$	Ind	6	10/23
Computer Science with Mgt Sci & a yr in Industry	G5NC	4FT deg	M	BCC	Ind	Ind	28$	BBBB$	Ind		
European Management Sci & Business Admin (4 Yrs)	N151	4FT deg	M	20	1M+5D	Ind	28$	Ind	Ind		
European Management Science (France)	N140	4FT deg	M+F	20	1M+5D	Ind	28$	Ind	Ind	2	14/22
European Management Science (Germany)	N142	4FT deg	M+G	20	1M+5D	Ind	28$	Ind	Ind	6	
European Management Science (Italy) (4 Yrs)	N143	4FT deg	M+L	20	1M+5D	Ind	28$	Ind	Ind		
European Management Science (Spain) (4 Yrs)	N144	4FT deg	M+L	20	1M+5D	Ind	28$	Ind	Ind	2	
European Management Science with Computing	N1GM	4FT deg	M+L	20	1M+5D	Ind	28$	Ind	Ind		
Ind Relations & Human Res Mgt (Soc Pol & Admin)	NL64	3FT deg	* g	20	3M+3D	M$ go	28	BBBB	Ind	5	
Ind Relations & Human Resource Mgt	N610	3FT deg	* g	CCC	4M+2D	M$ go	26	BBBB	Ind	3	12/26
Ind Relations & Human Resource Mgt (Accounting)	NN46	3FT deg	* g	20	3M+3D	M$ go	28	BBBB	Ind		
Ind Relations & Human Resource Mgt (Economics)	LN16	3FT deg	* g	20	3M+3D	M$ go	28	BBBB	Ind	3	
Ind Relations & Human Resource Mgt (Pol & Gov)	MN16	3FT deg	* g	BCC	3M+3D	M$ go	28	BBBB	Ind	4	
Ind Relations & Human Resource Mgt (Soc Psychol)	LN76	3FT deg	* g	26	6D	D$ go	33	AAAB	Ind		
Ind Relations & Human Resource Mgt (Sociology)	LN36	3FT deg	* g	20	3M+3D	M$ go	28	BBBB	Ind	9	
Industrial Relations & Human Resource Mgt (Law)	MN36	3FT deg	* g	26	6D	D$ go	33	AAAB	Ind	7	
Management Science	N100	3FT/4SW deg	M	20	1M+5D	Ind	28$	Ind	Ind	5	14/24
Management Science and Business Administration	N150	3FT deg	M	20	1M+5D	Ind	28$	Ind	Ind		
Management Science and Computing	NG15	3FT/4SW deg	M	20	1M+5D	Ind	28$	Ind	Ind	5	
Management Science with Computing	N1G5	3FT/4SW deg	M	20	1M+5D	Ind	28$	Ind	Ind	1	14/20
Mathematics and Management Science	GN11	3FT/4SW deg	M	20	Ind	Ind	28$	BBBB$	Ind	13	
Mathematics with Management Science	G1NC	3FT/4SW deg	M	20	Ind	Ind	28$	BBBB$	Ind		
Physics and Business Adminstration	FN31	3FT deg	M+P	20	3M+2D$	Ind	28$	BBBB$	Ind		
Physics with Business Studies	F3ND	3FT deg	M+P	18	5M $	Ind	26$	BBBC$	Ind		
Physics with Management Science	F3N1	3FT deg	M+P	18	5M $	Ind	26$	BBBC$	Ind		
Social Policy and Public Management	LN41	3FT deg	* g	18	4M+2D	M$ go	26	BBBB	Ind		

KING ALFRED'S WINCHESTER

Business Administration	N150	1FT deg	g	X	HN	X	X	X	HN	2	
Business Communications	PN31	3FT deg	* g	14	6M $	M	24$	CCC$	N$		
Business Studies and American Studies	NQ14	3FT deg	* g	14	6M	M	24	BCC	N	6	
Business Studies and Archaeology	FN41	3FT deg	* g	14	6M	M	24	BCC	N		
Business and Environmental Management	FN91	3FT deg	* g	14	6M	M	24	BCC	N	2	
Computing and Business Studies	GN51	3FT deg	* g	14	6M	M	24	BCC	N	2	7/18
Design & Technology and Business Studies	JN91	3FT deg	Ds/Ad g	14	6M	M	24$	BCC$	N$		
Drama Studies and Business Studies	NW14	3FT deg	* g	14	6M	M	24	BCC	N	2	12/16
Japanese Language and Business Culture	T4N1	3FT deg	L g	14	X	X	24$	BCC$	X		
Japanese Language and Business Studies	NT14	3FT deg	L g	14	X	X	24$	BCC$	X	3	
Media & Film Studies and Business Studies	NP14	3FT deg	* g	14	6M	M	24	BCC	N	5	10/12
Philosophy and Business Studies	NV17	3FT deg	* g	14	6M	M	24	BCC	N	1	

Business and Management 12

| | | | 98 expected requirements | | | | | | | 96 entry stats | |
| course details | | | | | | | | | | | |
TITLE	CODE	COURSE	SUBJECTS	A/AS	NQ/C	AGNVQ	IB	SQA(H)	SQA	RATIO	A/AS
Psychology and Business Studies	LN71	3FT deg	* g	14	6M	M	24	BCC	N	8	
Social Biology and Business Studies	CN11	3FT deg	B g	14	6M $	M	24$	BCC$	N$	5	
Sports Studies and Business Studies	NL1H	3FT deg	* g	14	6M	M	24	BCC	N		

KING'S COLL LONDON (Univ of London)

TITLE	CODE	COURSE	SUBJECTS	A/AS	NQ/C	AGNVQ	IB	SQA(H)	SQA	RATIO	A/AS
Business Management	N100	3FT deg	*	ABB	5M+5D	D$	30	ABBBB	Ind	37	24/30
Chemistry and Management	FN11	3FT deg	C+S	20	5M $	Ind	28$	BBBCC	X		
Chemistry with Management	F1N1	3FT deg	C+S	18	4M $	Ind	28$	BBCCC	Ind	4	16/18
Chemistry with Management with a year abroad	F1ND	4SW deg	C+S	18	5M $	Ind	28$	BBCCC	Ind	4	
Chemistry with Management with a yr in Industry	F1NC	4SW deg	C+S	18	5M $	Ind	28$	BBCCC	Ind	5	18/24
Computer Science with Management	G5N1	3FT/4SW deg	M	20	X	X	30$	ABBBB$	X	7	16/24
French with Management	R1N1	4FT deg	F	BBC						7	20/26
Manufacturing Systems Engineering with Mgt	H7N1	3FT deg	M+P	BCC	MO+1D		28	BBCCC$	Ind	6	18/18
Manufacturing Systems and Management	HN71	3FT deg	M+P	BCC	MO+1D		28	BBCCC$	Ind	5	
Mathematics and Management	GN11	3FT deg	M	20	X		28$	AABBB$	X	4	16/28
Pharmacology with Management	B2N1	4SW deg	C+B/M/P	ABB	X	X	Ind	AAABB	X	14	
Physics with Management	F3N1	3FT deg	M+P	18	2M+1D		28$	AABBB	Ind	13	

KINGSTON Univ

TITLE	CODE	COURSE	SUBJECTS	A/AS	NQ/C	AGNVQ	IB	SQA(H)	SQA	RATIO	A/AS
Applied Geology with Business Management	F6NC▼	4EXT deg			Ind		Ind	Ind	Ind		
Applied Geology with Business Management	F6ND	4FT deg									
Applied Geology with Business Management	F6N1	3FT deg		10-12	Ind	Ind	Ind	Ind	Ind		
Business Administration (1 year HND top-up)	N122	1FT deg									
Business Economics	L1N1	3FT deg	* g	16	MO	Ind^	Ind	BBCCC	HN	5	8/16
Business Studies	N120	4SW deg	*	BCC-CCC	3M+5D	Ind	30$	BBCC	Ind	20	14/22
Business Studies (European Programme)	N1T9	4SW deg	L	CCC	3M+5D	Ind	30$	BBCC	Ind	12	14/22
Chemistry with Business Management	F1N1	3FT deg	C g	8	3M	M	Ind	CCC	Ind	12	
Chemistry with Business Management	F1NC▼	4EXT/5EXTSW deg	*		Ind		Ind	Ind	Ind	1	
Chemistry with Business Management	F1ND	4SW deg	C g	8	3M	M	Ind	CCC	Ind	4	
Mathematics with Business Management	G1NC	4SW deg	M g	10	Ind	Ind	Ind	Ind	Ind	2	6/14
Mathematics with Business Management	G1ND▼	4EXT deg			Ind		Ind	Ind	Ind	3	
Mathematics with Business Management	G1N1	3FT deg	M g	10	Ind	Ind	Ind	Ind	Ind	10	
Physics with Business Management	F3NC▼	4EXT/5EXTSW deg	*		Ind		Ind	Ind	Ind		
Physics with Business Management	F3ND	4SW deg	P/M	12	2M $	Ind	Ind	CCC	Ind		
Physics with Business Management	F3N1	3FT deg	P/M	12	2M $	Ind	Ind	CCC	Ind	7	
Property Studies	K2N8	4SW deg	*	12	N	M$	24	Ind	Ind	3	
Statistics with Business Management	G4N1	3FT deg	M g	10	Ind	Ind	Ind	Ind	Ind	4	
Statistics with Business Management	G4NC	4SW deg	M g	10	Ind	Ind	Ind	Ind	Ind	2	6/10
Statistics with Business Management	G4ND▼	4EXT deg			Ind	Ind	Ind	Ind	Ind	4	
Urban Estate Management	N800	4SW deg	*	12	N	M$	24	Ind	Ind	3	6/18
Business and Finance	421N▼	2FT HND	*	DD-EE	Ind	Ind	Ind	Ind	Ind	6	2/10

Univ of Wales, LAMPETER

TITLE	CODE	COURSE	SUBJECTS	A/AS	NQ/C	AGNVQ	IB	SQA(H)	SQA	RATIO	A/AS
Management Techniques and Ancient History	NV11	3FT deg	*	16	Ind	Ind	Ind	Ind	Ind		
Management Techniques and Anthropology	NL16	3FT deg	*	16	Ind	Ind	Ind	Ind	Ind		
Management Techniques and Archaeology	NV1P	3FT deg	*	18	Ind	Ind	Ind	Ind	Ind		
Management Techniques and Australian Studies	LN61	3FT deg			Ind	Ind	Ind	Ind	Ind		
Management Techniques and Church History	NV1C	3FT deg	*	16	Ind	Ind	Ind	Ind	Ind		
Management Techniques and Classical Studies	NQ18	3FT deg	*	16	Ind	Ind	Ind	Ind	Ind		
Management Techniques and Cultural St in Geog	LN1V	3FT deg	*	16	Ind	Ind	Ind	Ind	Ind		
Management Techniques and English Literature	NQ13	3FT deg	E	18	Ind	Ind	Ind	Ind	Ind		
Management Techniques and French	NR11	3FT deg	F	16	Ind	Ind	Ind	Ind	Ind		
Management Techniques and Geography	LN81	3FT deg	Gy	16	Ind	Ind	Ind	Ind	Ind		
Management Techniques and German	NR12	3FT deg	G	16	Ind	Ind	Ind	Ind	Ind		

course details			98 expected requirements							96 entry stats

TITLE	CODE	COURSE	SUBJECTS	A/AS	NO/C	AGNVQ	IB	SQA(H)	SQA	RATIO A/AS
Management Techniques and German Studies	NR1F	3FT deg	*	16	Ind	Ind	Ind	Ind	Ind	
Management Techniques and Greek	NQ17	3FT deg	* g	16	Ind	Ind	Ind	Ind	Ind	
Management Techniques and History	NVCC	3FT deg	H	16	Ind	Ind	Ind	Ind	Ind	
Management Techniques and Informatics	GN51	3FT deg	*	16	Ind	Ind	Ind	Ind	Ind	
Management Techniques and Islamic Studies	NT16	3FT deg	*	16	Ind	Ind	Ind	Ind	Ind	
Management Techniques and Latin	NQ16	3FT deg	* g	16	Ind	Ind	Ind	Ind	Ind	
Medieval Studies and Management Techniques	NV1D	3FT deg	*	16	Ind	Ind	Ind	Ind	Ind	
Modern Historical Studies and Mgt Techniques	VN11	3FT deg			Ind	Ind	Ind	Ind	Ind	
Philosophical Studies and Management Techniques	NV17	3FT deg	*	16	Ind	Ind	Ind	Ind	Ind	
Religious Studies and Management Techniques	NV18	3FT deg	*	14	Ind	Ind	Ind	Ind	Ind	
Theology and Management Techniques	NV1V	3FT deg	*	14	Ind	Ind	Ind	Ind	Ind	
Tourism and Heritage Management	PN79	3FT deg		16-18	Ind	Ind	Ind	Ind	Ind	
Victorian Studies and Management Techniques	NVC1	3FT deg	*	14	Ind	Ind	Ind	Ind	Ind	
Welsh Studies and Management Techniques	NQ1M	3FT deg	*	14	Ind	Ind	Ind	Ind	Ind	
Welsh and Management Techniques	NQ15	3FT deg	W	14	Ind	Ind	Ind	Ind	Ind	
Women's Studies and Management Techniques	MN91	3FT deg	*	14	Ind	Ind	Ind	Ind	Ind	
Combined Honours *Management Techniques*	Y400	3FT deg	*	14-16	Ind	Ind	Ind	Ind	Ind	

LANCASTER Univ

Advertising and Marketing	N501	3FT deg	* g	ABB	MO+5D		34	AAABB	Ind	
Advertising and the Econ of Competitive Strategy	LN1N	4SW deg	* g	BBB	MO+3D		30	ABBBB	Ind	
Advertising, Economics and Marketing	LN1M	3FT deg	* g	BBB	MO+3D		30	ABBBB	Ind	
Business Studies	N102	3FT deg	* g	BBC	MO+4D		30	AABBB	Ind	
Business Studies (inc a year in USA or Canada)	N103	3FT deg	* g	AAB	MO+4D		35	AAAAA	Ind	
Computer Modelling for Business	NG25	3FT deg	M/S g	BCC	MO $		30$	BBBBB$	Ind	
Economics and Management Science	NL21	3FT deg	M	BBC	Ind $		30$	ABBBB$	Ind	
Educational Studies and Organisation Studies	XN91	3FT deg	*	BCC	MO		30	BBBBB	Ind	
Electronic Engineering with Management Sci(MEng)	H6NC	4FT/5SW deg	M+P/Cs/Es/Ds g	20	MO+2D		30$	AABBB$	Ind	
Electronic Engineering with Management Science	H6N1	3FT/4SW deg	M+P/Cs/Es/Ds g	20	MO+1D		30$	BBBBB$	Ind	
European Management (French)	N1R1	4FT/5SW deg	F g	ABB	MO+5D		32$	AABBB$	Ind	
European Management (German)	N1R2	4FT/5SW deg	G/L g	ABB	MO+5D		32$	AABBB$	Ind	
European Management (Italian)	N1R3	4FT/5SW deg	I/L g	ABB	MO+5D		32$	AABBB$	Ind	
European Management (Spanish)	N1R4	4FT/5SW deg	Sp/* g	ABB	MO+5D		32$	AABBB$	Ind	
French Studies and Marketing	RN15	4SW deg	F g	BBC	MO+4D		32$	ABBBB$	Ind	
German Studies and Marketing	RN25	4SW deg	G/L g	BBC	MO+4D		32$	ABBBB$	Ind	
International Business (Economics)	N140	3FT deg	* g	BBC	MO+4D		32	ABBBB	Ind	
International Business(Econ) (inc yr in USA/Can)	N145	3FT deg	* g	AAB	MO+4D		32	ABBBB	Ind	
Italian Studies and Marketing	RN35	4SW deg	I/L g	BBC	MO+4D		32$	ABBBB$	Ind	
Management (inc a year in USA or Canada)	N101	4SW deg	* g	AAB	MO+5D		35	AAAAA	Ind	
Management (incl a year's work placement)	N100	4SW deg	* g	ABB	MO+5D		33	AAAAB	Ind	
Management Science	N200	3FT deg	M/S	BBC	MO $		30$	ABBBB$	Ind	
Management Science (inc a year in USA or Canada)	N201	3FT deg	M/S	AAB	MO $		30$	ABBBB$	Ind	
Marketing	N500	3FT deg	* g	BBB-BBC	MO+4D		32$	ABBBB$	Ind	
Marketing/USA-Canada	N502	3FT deg	* g	AAB	MO+4D		34$	AAABB$	Ind	
Mathematics and Operational Research	NG21	3FT deg	M	22	MO $		30$	ABBBB$	Ind	
Mechanical Engineering with Management Sci(MEng)	H3ND	4FT/5SW deg	M+P/Cs/Es/Ds g	20	MO+2D		30$	BBBBB$	Ind	
Mechanical Engineering with Management Science	H3N1	3FT/4SW deg	M+P/Cs/Es/Ds g	20	MO+1D		30$	BBBBB$	Ind	
Operations Management	N220	3FT deg	* g	BCC	Ind		30	BBBBB	Ind	
Operations Mgt (inc a year in USA or Canada)	N221	3FT deg	* g	AAB	Ind		30	BBBBB	Ind	
Organisation Studies	N126	3FT deg	*	BCC	MO+2D		30	BBBBB	Ind	
Organisation Studies and Human Resource Mgt	N130	3FT deg	*	BCC	MO+2D		30	BBBBB	Ind	
Organisation Studies and Psychology	CN81	3FT deg	* g	BBC	DO		32	ABBBB	Ind	

Business and Management

			98 expected requirements							96 entry stats	
course details											
TITLE	CODE	COURSE	SUBJECTS	A/AS	NO/C	AGNVQ	IB	SQA(H)	SQA	RATIO	A/AS
Organisation Studies with Industrial Relations	N1N6	3FT deg	*	BCC	MO+2D		30	BBBBB	Ind		
Organisation Studs (inc a year in USA or Canada)	N127	3FT deg	*	AAB	MO+2D		30	BBBBB	Ind		
Organisational Studies and Sociology	NL13	3FT deg	*	BCC	MO+2D		30	BBBBB	Ind		
Spanish Studies and Marketing	RN45	4SW deg	Sp/L g	BBC	MO+4D		32$	ABBBB$	Ind		
Culture, Media and Communication *Marketing*	Y400	3FT deg	*	BBB-BBC	M+D $		30	ABBBB	Ind		
Economics & Mathematics & Operational Research *Operational Research*	Y642	3FT deg	M	BCC	MO $		30$	BBBBB$	Ind		

Univ of LEEDS

TITLE	CODE	COURSE	SUBJECTS	A/AS	NO/C	AGNVQ	IB	SQA(H)	SQA	RATIO	A/AS
Applied Biology-Management Studies	C1NC	3FT/4FT deg	B+C/M/P/Ec g	BCC	1M+5D$	Ind	28	BBBBC	Ind	5	
Arabic-Management Studies	TN61	4FT deg	Cl/L g	BBC	Ind	Ind	30$	CSYS	Ind		
Chemistry-Management Studies	FN11	3FT/4FT deg	C+M/P g	BCC	1M+5D$	Ind	28$	BBBBC	Ind	6	20/28
Chinese-Management Studies	TN31	4FT deg	L g	BBC	Ind	Ind	30$	CSYS	Ind	10	
Computer Science-Management Studies	GN51	3FT/4FT deg	M g	BBC	1M+5D$	Ind	28$	BBBBC	Ind	14	20/26
Economics and Industrial Studies (3 Yrs)	LN16	3FT deg	g	BBC	Ind	Ind	30$	CSYS	Ind	7	22/28
Economics-Management Studies	LN11	3FT deg	g	BBB	Ind	Ind	32$	CSYS	Ind	10	24/30
French-Management Studies	RN11	4FT deg	F g	BBB	Ind	Ind	32$	CSYS	Ind	14	24/30
Gender Studies - Industrial Studies	MN96	3FT deg	* g	BCC	Ind	Ind	28$	CSYS			
Geography-Management Studies	FN81	3FT/4FT deg	Gy+C/B/M/P g	BBB	Ind	Ind	32$	CSYS	Ind	4	24/26
Geography-Management Studies	LN81	3FT deg	Gy g	ABB	Ind	Ind	33$	CSYS	Ind	14	26/30
German-Management Studies	RN21	4FT deg	G g	BBC	Ind	Ind	30$	CSYS	Ind	9	22/30
Information Systems-Management Studies	G5NC	3FT/4FT deg	g	BBC	1M+5D$	Ind	30$	ABBBB	Ind	13	18/24
Italian-Management Studies	RN31	4FT deg	I g	BBC	Ind	Ind	30$	CSYS	Ind	15	
Italian-Management Studies B	RNH1	4FT deg	L g	BBC	Ind	Ind	30$	CSYS	Ind		
Japanese-Management Studies	TN41	4FT deg	L g	BBB	Ind	Ind	32$	CSYS	Ind	10	26/30
Management Studies	N100	3FT deg	g	BBB	Ind	D$^ go	32$	CSYS	Ind	16	22/28
Management Studies-Mathematics	GN11	3FT/4FT deg	M g	BBC	1M+5D$	Ind	30$	CSYS	Ind	6	20/28
Management Studies-Pharmacology	BN21	3FT deg	2(B/C/M/P) g	BCC	2M+5D	Ind	28$	BBBBC	Ind	3	20/24
Management Studies-Philosophy	VN71	3FT deg	g	BBC	Ind	Ind	30	CSYS	Ind	15	
Management Studies-Portuguese	RN51	4FT deg	L g	BBC	Ind	Ind	30$	CSYS	Ind	8	
Management Studies-Psychology	NC18	3FT deg	g	ABB	Ind	Ind	33	CSYS	Ind	12	26/30
Management Studies-Russian	RN81	4FT deg	R g	BBC	Ind	Ind	30$	CSYS	Ind		
Management Studies-Russian B	RNV1	4FT deg	L g	BBC	Ind	Ind	30$	CSYS	Ind		
Management Studies-Spanish	RN41	4FT deg	Sp g	BBC	Ind	Ind	30$	CSYS	Ind	11	22/30
Management Studies-Statistics	GN41	3FT/4FT deg	M g	BBC	1M+5D$	Ind	30$	CSYS	Ind	25	
Mgt with Mechanical & Manufacturing Engineering	H3N1	3FT/4FT deg	M g	BBC	1M+5D$	D$^ go	30$	CSYS	Ind	10	16/28
Textile Management	J4N1	3FT deg	* g	CCC	Ind	Ind	26$	BBBCC	Ind	3	10/22

LEEDS, TRINITY & ALL SAINTS Univ COLL

TITLE	CODE	COURSE	SUBJECTS	A/AS	NO/C	AGNVQ	IB	SQA(H)	SQA	RATIO	A/AS
French-Management	RN11	4FT deg	F g	BCC-CCD	Ind	X	24$	BBCCC	Ind	6	8/17
Geography-Management	LN81	3FT deg	Gy g	CCD-CD	MO	X	24$	BBCCC	Ind	11	10/16
History-Management	VN11	3FT deg	H g	BCC-BC	Ind	X	24	BBBCC	Ind	3	6/20
Management	N100	3FT deg	* g	BCC-CCD	MO	Ind	24	BBCCC	Ind	7	6/20
Mathematics-Management	GN11	3FT deg	M g	CCC-DE	Ind	X	24	BBCCC	Ind	5	10/14
Media-Management	PN41	3FT deg	* g	BCC-CC	MO	$	24	BBCCC	Ind	11	8/24
Psychology-Management	LN71	3FT deg	* g	BCC-BD	MO	X	24	BBCCC	Ind	7	8/20
Sociology-Management	LN31	3FT deg	* g	BCC-CCD	MO	X	24	BBCCC	Ind	3	10/20
Spanish-Management	RN41	4FT deg	Sp g	BCC-CCD	Ind	X	24$	BBCCC	Ind	8	
Sport, Health and Leisure-Management	BN61	3FT deg	* g	BBB-CCC	MO+3D	Ind	26	AABBB	Ind		

LEEDS METROPOLITAN Univ

TITLE	CODE	COURSE	SUBJECTS	A/AS	NO/C	AGNVQ	IB	SQA(H)	SQA	RATIO	A/AS
Business Studies	N120	4SW deg	* g	CCD	2M+5D	DB/MB^ go	28	BBBB	Ind	21	16/24
Events Management	P3N5	3FT/4SW deg	* g	12	MO	M$ go	26	BBCC	Ind		10/16

course details — 98 expected requirements — 96 entry stats

TITLE	CODE	COURSE	SUBJECTS	A/AS	NO/C	AGNVQ	IB	SQA(H)	SQA	RATIO	A/AS
Occupational Health and Safety .	BN96	3FT deg	Ph g	12	1M+3D	MS/DG^ go	28$	CCCCC$	Ind	3	8/20
Project Management	KN2X	1FT deg									
Project Management (Construction)	KN29	3FT/4SW deg	* g	EE	N	P$ go	Dip	CCC	Ind	4	
Retailing	N110	3FT/4SW deg	* g	12	MO	M$ go	26	BBCC	Ind		
Service Sector Management	N111	1FT deg									
Business	421N	2FT/3SW HND	* g	DE	4M+2D	MB go	22	BCC	Ind	18	4/12

Univ of LINCOLNSHIRE and HUMBERSIDE

TITLE	CODE	COURSE	SUBJECTS	A/AS	NO/C	AGNVQ	IB	SQA(H)	SQA	RATIO	A/AS
Accountancy and Administration	NN14	3FT deg	* g	12	3M+1D	M	24	CCCC	Ind		
Accountancy and Business	NN41	3FT deg	* g	12	3M+1D	M	24	CCCC	Ind		
Accountancy and Human Resource Management	NN64	3FT deg	* g	12	3M+1D	M	24	CCCC	Ind		
Administration and Computing	GN5C	3FT deg	* g	12	3M+1D	M	24	CCCC	Ind		
Administration and Finance	NN13	3FT deg	* g	12	3M+1D	M	24	CCCC	Ind		
Administration and French	NR1D	3FT deg	F g	12	3M+1D	M	24	CCCC	Ind		
Administration and German	NR1G	3FT deg	G g	12	3M+1D	M	24	CCCC	Ind		
Administration and Human Resource Management	NN16	3FT deg	* g	12	3M+1D	M	24	CCCC	Ind		
Administration and Information Systems	GNND	3FT deg	* g	12	3M+1D	M	24	CCCC	Ind		
Administration and Media Technology	NP1K	3FT deg	* g	12	3M+1D	M	24	CCCC	Ind		
Administration and Modern Languages	NT1Y	3FT deg	L g	12	3M+1D	M	24	CCCC	Ind		
Administration and Spanish	NR1K	3FT deg	Sp g	12	3M+1D	M	24	CCCC	Ind		
Administrative Management	N170	3FT deg	* g	12	3M+1D	M	24	CCCC	Ind		
Applied Social Science and Business	LN3C	3FT deg	* g	12	3M+1D	M	24	CCCC	Ind		
Business Studies	N120▼	4SW deg	* g	14	2M+2D	M	24	BCCC	Ind		
Business and Finance	N190	3FT deg	* g	12	3M+1D	M	24	CCCC	Ind		
Business and French	RN11	3FT deg	F g	12	3M+1D	M	24	CCCC	Ind		
Business and German	RN21	3FT deg	G g	12	3M+1D	M	24	CCCC	Ind		
Business and Human Resource Management	NN1P	3FT deg	* g	12	3M+1D	M	24	CCCC	Ind		
Business and Marketing	NN1M	3FT deg	* g	12	3M+1D		24	CCCC	Ind		
Business and Media Technology	NP1L	3FT deg	* g	12	3M+1D		24	CCCC	Ind		
Business and Modern Languages	NT19	3FT deg	L g	12	3M+1D		24	CCCC	Ind		
Business and Social Work	NL15	3FT deg	* g	14	2M+2D		24	BCCC	Ind		
Business and Spanish	RN41	3FT deg	Sp g	12	3M+1D		24	CCCC	Ind		
Communications and Management	NP13▼	3FT deg	* g	16	1M+3D	D	24	BBCCC	Ind		
Computing and Business	NG1M	3FT deg	* g	12	3M+1D	M	24	CCCC	Ind		
Computing and Human Resource Management	GN56	3FT deg	* g	12	3M+1D	M	24	CCCC	Ind		
Computing and Marketing	GN5M	3FT deg	* g	12	3M+1D	M	24	CCCC	Ind		
Criminology and Management	MNH1▼	3FT deg	* g	16	1M+3D	D	24	BBCCC	Ind		
Economics and Management	LN1D▼	3FT deg	* g	16	1M+3D	D	24	BBCCC	Ind		
Environmental Studies and Management	FN91	3FT deg	M/P/C/B/He g	8	3M	P	Ind	CCC$	Ind		
European Business Studies	N145	4SW deg	L g	14	2M+2D	M	24	BCCC$	Ind		
European Marketing	N146	4SW deg	L g	12	3M+1D	M	24	CCCC$	Ind		
Fashion Promotion	N5W2▼	2FT HND	g		Ind	Ind	Ind	Ind	Ind		
Finance and Human Resource Management	NN36	3FT deg	* g	12	3M+1D	M	24	CCCC	Ind		
Finance and Marketing	NN35	3FT deg	* g	12	3M+1D	M	24	CCCC	Ind		
Food Science and Management	DN41	3FT deg	M/P/C/B/He g	8	3M		Ind	CCC$	Ind		
Food Technology and Management	DN4C	3FT deg	M/P/C/B/He g	8	3M	P	Ind	CCC$	Ind		
French and Human Resource Management	NR61	3FT deg	F g	12	3M+1D	M	24	CCCC	Ind		
German and Human Resource Management	NR62	3FT deg	G g	12	3M+1D	M	24	CCCC	Ind		
Health Studies and Management	LN41▼	3FT deg	* g	16	1M+3D	D	24	BBCCC	Ind		
Human Resource Management	N600	3FT deg	* g	12	3M+1D	M	24	CCCC	Ind		
Human Resource Management and Information Systs	GN5P	3FT deg	* g	12	3M+1D	M	24	CCCC	Ind		
Human Resource Management and Marketing	NN65	3FT deg	* g	12	3M+1D	M	24	CCCC	Ind		
Human Resource Management and Modern Languages	NT62	3FT deg	L g	12	3M+1D	M	24	CCCC	Ind		

Business and Management 12

TITLE	CODE	COURSE	SUBJECTS	A/AS	NO/C	AGNVQ	IB	SQA(H)	SQA	RATIO A/AS
Human Resource Management and Spanish	NR64	3FT deg	Sp g	12	3M+1D	M	24	CCCC	Ind	
Human Resource Management and Technology	JN96	3FT deg	* g	12	3M+1D	M	24	CCCC	Ind	
Information Systems and Marketing	GN55	3FT deg	* g	12	3M+1D	M	24	CCCC	Ind	
International Business Studies	N1T9	4FT deg	* g	16	1M+3D	D	24	BBCCC	Ind	
International Relations and Management	MN11▼	3FT deg	* g	16	1M+3D	D	24	BBCCC	Ind	
Journalism and Management	NP16▼	3FT deg	* g	18	1M+4D	D	26	BBBCC	Ind	
Law and Management	MN3D▼	3FT deg	* g	16	1M+3D	D	24	BBCCC	Ind	
Management	N100▼	3FT deg	* g	16	1M+3D	D	24	BBCCC	Ind	
Management and Finance	NN1J▼	3FT deg	* g							
Management and Information Systems	NG1N▼	3FT deg	* g							
Management and Marketing	NN1N▼	3FT deg	* g							
Management and Media	NP14▼	3FT deg	* g	18	1M+4D	D	26	BBBCC	Ind	
Management and Politics	MN1C▼	3FT deg	* g	16	1M+3D	D	24	BBCCC	Ind	
Management and Psychology	CN81▼	3FT deg	* g	18	1M+4D	D	26	BBBCC	Ind	
Management and Social Policy	LN4C▼	3FT deg	* g	14	2M+2D	M	24	BCCC	Ind	
Management and Tourism	NP1R▼	3FT deg	* g	14	2M+2D	M	24	BCCC	Ind	
Marketing	N500	3FT deg	* g	14	2M+2D	M	24	BCCC	Ind	
Marketing and Accountancy	NN45	3FT deg	* g	12	3M+1D	M	24	CCCC	Ind	
Marketing and Administration	NN51	3FT deg	* g	12	3M+1D	M	24	CCCC	Ind	
Marketing and French	NR51	3FT deg	F g	12	3M+1D	M	24	CCCC	Ind	
Marketing and German	NR52	3FT deg	G g	12	3M+1D	M	24	CCCC	Ind	
Marketing and Media Technology	NP54	3FT deg	* g	12	3M+1D	M	24	CCCC	Ind	
Marketing and Modern Languages	NT5X	3FT deg	L g	12	3M+1D	M	24	CCCC	Ind	
Marketing and Spanish	NR54	3FT deg	Sp g	12	3M+1D	M	24	CCCC	Ind	
Marketing and Tourism Operations	NP5R▼	3FT deg	g	8		M				
Nutrition and Management	BN41	3FT deg	M/P/C/B/He g	8	3M		Ind	CC$	Ind	
Social Work and Administration	LN5C	3FT deg	g	14	Ind	Ind	Ind	BCCC	Ind	
Business	021N▼	2FT HND	* g	4		P	24	C	Ind	
Business and Information Systems	15NG	2FT HND	* g	4	2M	P	24	C	Ind	
European Technology and Business	19NJ	2FT HND	* g	4		P				
European Technology and Marketing	95JN	2FT HND	* g	4		P				
Marketing and Technology	59NJ	2FT HND	* g							

Univ of LIVERPOOL

TITLE	CODE	COURSE	SUBJECTS	A/AS	NO/C	AGNVQ	IB	SQA(H)	SQA	RATIO A/AS
Business Economics	LN11	3FT deg	M/Ec	BCC	Ind	Ind	Ind	Ind	Ind	13 20/28
Geophysics with Business Studies	F6N1	3FT deg	M+P g	18	MO $	DS^ go	31$	BBBCC$	Ind	
Integrated Eng with Industrial Management (BEng)	H1ND	4EXT deg	*	18	3M $		30$	BBBCC	Ind	4
Integrated Eng with Industrial Management (BEng)	H1N1	3FT deg	M+P	20	4M+1D$		30$	BBBBB	Ind	4
Integrated Eng with Industrial Management (MEng)	H1NC	4SW deg	M+P	20	4M+1D$		30$	BBBBB	Ind	4
Manufacturing Engineering and Management (BEng)	H7N1	3FT deg	M+P	20	4M+1D$		30$	BBBBB	Ind	7
Materials Science and Management Studies	F2N1	3FT deg	M+P/C	18	4M+1D$		30$	BBBBB	Ind	
Mathematics with Management	G1N1	3FT deg	M g	20	MO $	DS^ go	31$	BBBCC$	Ind	5 14/28
Mechanical Engineering with Management (BEng)	H3N1	3FT deg	M+P	20	4M+1D$		30$	BBBBB	Ind	
Mechanical Engineering with Management (MEng)	H3NC	4FT deg	M+P	20	4M+1D$		30$	BBBBB	Ind	6
BSc Combined Honours Management	Y100	3FT deg	2S	18	MO $	Ind	31$	BBBCC$	Ind	

LIVERPOOL JOHN MOORES Univ

TITLE	CODE	COURSE	SUBJECTS	A/AS	NO/C	AGNVQ	IB	SQA(H)	SQA	RATIO A/AS
Business Administration	N122	3FT deg		16	3M+4D	D/M^				12 14/22
Business Decision Analysis	N2G5	3FT deg		16	3M+4D	D/M^				4 11/16
Business Studies	N120▼	3FT/4SW deg	* g	16	3M+4D	D/M^				18 16/24
Consumer Studies	N980	3FT deg		CC	5M	M				6 6/16
Economics and Business	LN11	3FT deg		14-16	5M+3D	D/M^		BCCC		
Food and Nutrition and Business	DN41	3FT deg		14-16	5M+3D	D/M^	28$	BCCC		

course details

98 expected requirements

96 entry stats

TITLE	CODE	COURSE	SUBJECTS	A/AS	NQ/C	AGNVQ	IB	SQA(H)	SQA	RATIO A/AS
International Business Studies with French	N1R1	4SW deg	F	16	3M+4D					15 12/24
International Business Studies with German	N1R2	4SW deg		16	3M+4D					11 14/18
International Business Studies with Italian	N1R3	4SW deg		16	3M+4D					5 10/14
International Business Studies with Japanese	N1T4	4SW deg		16	3M+4D		Ind			40
International Business Studies with Russian	N1R8	4SW deg		16	3M+4D					
International Business Studies with Spanish	N1R4	4SW deg	*	16	3M+4D					6 12/20
Law and Business	MN3D	3FT deg		CCC	MO+5D	D^	28$	BBBC		11 16/24
Maritime Business and Management	N910	3FT/4SW deg		10	3M	M				2
Maritime and Intermodal Transport	N921	3FT/4SW deg		10	3M	M				6
Media and Cultural St & Marketing (Mkt Jnt Awd)	NP54	3FT deg		14-18	5M+3D	X	28$	BBBC		6 14/26
Product Design and Business	NH17	3FT deg	Ar+Pf	14-16	5M+3D	D/M^	28$	BCCC		
Public Service Management	N105	3FT deg		14	5M+3D	D/M^				3 12/16
Technology Management	HN71	3FT/4SW deg	* g	10	4M	M				2 6/18
Technology Management (Extended)	HN7C▼	4EXT/5EXTSW deg	* g	6	3M					4
Transport	N920	3FT deg		10	3M	D				
Business and Finance	421N	2FT HND	* g	10	MO		Ind			13 8/14

LONDON GUILDHALL Univ

TITLE	CODE	COURSE	SUBJECTS	A/AS	NQ/C	AGNVQ	IB	SQA(H)	SQA	RATIO A/AS
3D/Spatial Design and Business	NW1F	3FT deg	Pf g	CD-DDD	MO+4D	M$ go	26	Ind	Ind	
3D/Spatial Design and Marketing	NW5F	3FT deg	Pf g	CD-DDD	MO+3D	M$ go	24	Ind	Ind	
Business Administration	N122	3FT deg	* g	CC-CDD	DO $	M$ go	26	Ind	Ind	
Business Economics and Business	LNC1	3FT deg	* g	CD-DDD	MO+4D	M$ go	26	Ind	Ind	
Business Information Technology and Business	GN71	3FT deg	* g	CD-DDD	MO+4D	M$ go	26	Ind	Ind	
Business Studies	N120	4SW deg	* g	CC	DO	M$ go	26	Ind	Ind	
Business and Accounting	NN14	3FT deg	* g	CD-DDD	MO+4D	M$ go	26	Ind	Ind	
Communications & Audio Vis Prod St & Business	NP14	3FT deg	* g	CC-CDD	MO+6D	D$ go	26	Ind	Ind	
Computing and Business	GN51	3FT deg	* g	CD-DDD	MO+4D	M$ go	24	Ind	Ind	
Design Studies and Business	NW12	3FT deg	* g	CC-CDD	MO+4D	M$ go	26	Ind	Ind	
Development Studies and Business	MN91	3FT deg	* g	CD-DDD	MO+2D	M$ go	24	Ind	Ind	
Economics and Business	LN11	3FT deg	* g	CD-DDD	MO+2D	M$ go	24	Ind	Ind	
English and Business	NQ13	3FT deg	* g	CC-CDD	MO+4D	M$ go	26	Ind	Ind	
European Business Studies	N1T9	4FT deg	* g	CC-CDD	DO		26	Ind	Ind	
European Studies and Business	NT12	3FT deg	* g	CC-CCD	MO+4D	M$ go	26	Ind	Ind	
Financial Services and Business	NN13	3FT deg	* g	CD-DDD	MO+2D	M$ go	26	Ind	Ind	
Fine Art and Business	NW11	3FT deg	Pf g	CC-CDD	MO+4D	D$ go	26	Ind	Ind	
French and Business	NR11	4FT deg	* g	CD-DDD	MO+2D	M$ go	26	Ind	Ind	
German and Business	NR12	4FT deg	* g	CD-DDD	MO+2D	M$ go	24	Ind	Ind	
International Relations and Business	MNC1	3FT deg	* g	CD-DDD	MO+2D	M$ go	26	Ind	Ind	
Law and Business	MN31	3FT deg	* g	CC-CDD	MO+4D	M$ go	26	Ind	Ind	
Marketing and Accounting	NN45	3FT deg	* g	CD-DDD	MO+2D	M$ go	26	Ind	Ind	
Marketing and Business Economics	LNC5	3FT deg	* g	CD-DDD	MO+2D	M$ go	26	Ind	Ind	
Marketing and Business Information Technology	GN75	3FT deg	* g	CD-DDD	MO+2D	M$ go	26	Ind	Ind	
Marketing and Communications & Audio Vis Prod St	NP54	3FT deg	* g	CC-CDD	MO+4D	D$ go	26	Ind	Ind	
Marketing and Computing	GN55	3FT deg	* g	CD-DDD	MO+2D	M$ go	26	Ind	Ind	
Marketing and Design Studies	NW52	3FT deg	* g	CC-CDD	MO+4D	M$ go	26	Ind	Ind	
Marketing and Development Studies	MN95	3FT deg	* g	CD-DDD	MO+2D	M$ go	26	Ind	Ind	
Marketing and Economics	LN15	3FT deg	* g	CD-DDD	MO+2D	M$ go	26	Ind	Ind	
Marketing and English	NQ53	3FT deg	* g	CC-CDD	MO+4D	D$ go	26	Ind	Ind	
Marketing and European Studies	NT52	3FT deg	* g	CD-DDD	MO+2D	M$ go	26	Ind	Ind	
Marketing and Financial Services	NN35	3FT deg	* g	CD-DDD	MO+2D	M$ go	26	Ind	Ind	
Marketing and Fine Art	NW51	3FT deg	* g	CC-CDD	MO+4D	M$ go	26	Ind	Ind	
Marketing and French	NR51	4FT deg	* g	CD-DDD	MO+2D	M$ go	26	Ind	Ind	
Marketing and German	NR52	4FT deg	* g	CD-DDD	MO+2D	M$ go	26	Ind	Ind	

Business and Management 12

course details | 98 expected requirements | 96 entry stats

TITLE	CODE	COURSE	SUBJECTS	A/AS	NO/C	AGNVQ	IB	SQA(H)	SQA	RATIO A/AS
Marketing and International Relations	MNC5	3FT deg	* g	CD-DDD	MO+2D	M$ go	26	Ind	Ind	
Marketing and Law	MN35	3FT deg	* g	CC-CDD	MO+4D	M$ go	26	Ind	Ind	
Mathematics and Business	GN11	3FT deg	* g	CD-DDD	MO+2D	M$ go	24	Ind	Ind	
Mathematics and Marketing	GN15	3FT deg	* g	CD-DDD	MO+2D	M$ go	26	Ind	Ind	
Mathematics with Business Applications	G1N1	3FT deg	M g	DE-EE	MO	P$ go	24	Ind	Ind	
Modern History and Business	NV11	3FT deg	* g	CD-DDD	MO+2D	M$ go	26	Ind	Ind	
Modern History and Marketing	NV51	3FT deg	* g	CD-DDD	MO+2D	M$ go	24	Ind	Ind	
Multimedia Systems and Business	GNM1	3FT deg	* g	CD-DDD	MO+2D	M$ go	26	Ind	Ind	
Multimedia Systems and Marketing	GNM5	3FT deg	* g	CD-DDD	MO+2D	M$ go	26	Ind	Ind	
Politics and Business	MN11	3FT deg	* g	CD-DDD	MO+2D	M$ go	24	Ind	Ind	
Politics and Marketing	MN15	3FT deg	* g	CD-DDD	MO+2D	M$ go	24	Ind	Ind	
Product Development & Manufacture and Business	JN41	3FT deg	* g	CD-DDD	MO+2D	M$ go	24	Ind	Ind	
Product Development & Manufacture and Marketing	JN45	3FT deg	* g	CD-DDD	MO+2D	M$ go	24	Ind	Ind	
Psychology and Business	CN81	3FT deg	* g	CC-CDD	MO+4D	M$ go	26	Ind	Ind	
Psychology and Marketing	CN85	3FT deg	* g	CC-CDD	MO+2D	M$ go	26	Ind	Ind	
Social Policy & Management and Business	LN41	3FT deg	* g	CD-DDD	MO	M$ go	24	Ind	Ind	
Social Policy & Management and Marketing	LN45	3FT deg	* g	CD-DDD	MO	M$ go	24	Ind	Ind	
Sociology and Business	LN31	3FT deg	* g	CC-CDD	MO+2D	M$ go	26	Ind	Ind	
Sociology and Marketing	LN35	3FT deg	* g	CC-CDD	MO+2D	M$ go	26	Ind	Ind	
Spanish and Business	NR14	4FT deg	* g	CD-DDD	MO+2D	M$ go	24	Ind	Ind	
Spanish and Marketing	NR54	4FT deg	* g	CD-DDD	MO+2D	M$ go	26	Ind	Ind	
Taxation and Business	NN1H	3FT deg	* g	CD-DDD	MO	M$ go	24	Ind	Ind	
Taxation and Marketing	NN5H	3FT deg	* g	CD-DDD	MO	M$ go	24	Ind	Ind	
Textile Furnishing Design and Business	NW1G	3FT deg	Pf g	CD-DDD	MO	M$ go	24	Ind	Ind	
Textile Furnishing Design and Marketing	NW5G	3FT deg	Pf g	CD-DDD	MO	M$ go	24	Ind	Ind	
Modular Programme *Business*	Y400	3FT deg	* g	CC-DDD	MO+2D	M$ go	24	Ind	Ind	
Modular Programme *Business Information Technology*	Y420▼	3FT deg	* g	EE	MO	P	24	Ind	Ind	
Modular Programme *Business Information Technology*	Y400	3FT deg	* g	CC-DD	MO	M$ go	24	Ind	Ind	
Modular Programme *Marketing*	Y400	3FT deg	* g	CC-DDD	MO+2D	M$ go	24	Ind	Ind	
Business	001N	2FT HND	* g	C-DE	MO	P$ go	24	Ind	Ind	
Business and Finance	3N1N	2FT HND	* g	C-DE	MO	P$ go	24	Ind	Ind	
Business and Marketing	5N1N	2FT HND	* g	C-DE	MO	P$ go	24	Ind	Ind	
Business and Personnel	6N1N	2FT HND	* g	C-DE	MO	P$ go	24	Ind	Ind	
European Business	041N	2FT HND	* g	C-DE	MO	P$ go	24	Ind	Ind	

LONDON INST

TITLE	CODE	COURSE								RATIO A/AS
Business Communication	NP13	3FT deg								3	6/20
Fashion Management	WN21	3FT deg								8	12/18
Marketing and Advertising	NP53	3FT deg								34	10/20
Retail Design Management	EW52	3FT deg									
Retail Design Management	NW5F	3FT deg									
Retail Logistics	N550	3FT deg									
Retail Management	N553	3FT deg								11	6/22
Visual Merchandising	NW52	3FT deg									
Business	021N	2FT HND								5	2/6
Marketing and Advertising	35PN	2FT HND								26	
Retail Design	25WE	2FT HND									
Retail Management	355N	2FT HND								7	2/12

		course details		98 expected requirements							96 entry stats	
TITLE	CODE	COURSE	SUBJECTS	A/AS	NQ/C	AGNVQ	IB	SQA(H)	SQA	RATIO	A/AS

LSE: LONDON Sch of Economics (Univ of London)

TITLE	CODE	COURSE	SUBJECTS	A/AS	NQ/C	AGNVQ	IB	SQA(H)	SQA	RATIO	A/AS
Industrial Relations & Human Resource Management	NN16	3FT deg	g	ABB	Ind	X	$	Ind	Ind	14	26/28
Management	N103	3FT deg	g	ABB	Ind	X	$	Ind	Ind		
Management Sciences	N101	3FT deg	M	BBB	Ind	X	$	Ind	Ind		
Business Mathematics and Statistics *Business Methods*	Y240	3FT deg	M	BBB-AAB	Ind	X	$	Ind	Ind		

LOUGHBOROUGH Univ

TITLE	CODE	COURSE	SUBJECTS	A/AS	NQ/C	AGNVQ	IB	SQA(H)	SQA	RATIO	A/AS
Computing and Management	GN5D	3FT deg	*	20	3D	DI6/^ go	28	Ind	Ind	4	16/22
Computing and Management (4 Yr SW)	GN51	4SW deg	*	20	3D	DI6/^ go	28	Ind	Ind	4	16/28
European Business (4 Yr SW)	N140	4SW deg	F/G g	BBC			28$	Ind		7	20/28
Information and Management	PN21	3FT deg	* g	22	2M+3D	D*6/^ go	28	Ind	Ind		
Information and Management (4 Yr SW)	PN2C	4SW deg	* g	22	2M+3D	D*6/^ go	28	Ind	Ind		
Management Sciences (4 Yr SW)	N101	4SW deg	* g	BBC	4D	D*6/^ go	30	Ind	Ind	4	20/28
Materials with Business Studies	J5N1	3FT deg	M	20	5M	DE6/^ go	28$	Ind	Ind	2	14/16
Materials with Business Studies (4 Yr SW)	J5NC	4SW deg	M	20	5M	DE6/^ go	28$	Ind	Ind	4	
Mathematics with Management	G1N1	3FT deg	M	BCC			28$	Ind			
Mathematics with Management (4 Yr SW)	G1NC	4SW deg	M	BCC			28$	Ind			
Physics with Management	F3N1	3FT deg	M+P	BCC	3M+2D	DS6/^ go	28$	Ind	Ind		
Physics with Management (4 Yr SW)	F3NC	4SW deg	M+P	BCC	3M+2D	DS6/^ go	28$	Ind	Ind		
Physics with Management and a year in Europe	F3ND	4SW deg	M+P	BCC	3M+2D	DS6/^ go	28$	Ind	Ind		
Retail Management (4 Yr SW)	N110	4SW deg	* g	BBC	4D	D*6/^ go	30	Ind	Ind	6	20/28
Retail Management (Automotive) (4 Yr SW)	N111	4SW deg	* g	BBC	4D	D*6/^ go	30	Ind	Ind		
Transport Management and Planning	N920	3FT deg	*	20	2D	D*6/^ go	28	Ind	Ind	5	
Transport Management and Planning (4 Yr SW)	N921	4SW deg	*	20	2D	D*6/^ go	28	Ind	Ind	4	20/28

LUTON Univ

TITLE	CODE	COURSE	SUBJECTS	A/AS	NQ/C	AGNVQ	IB	SQA(H)	SQA	RATIO	A/AS
Accounting with Built Environment	N4NV	3FT deg	g	12-16	MO/DO	M/D	32	BBCC	Ind		
Accounting with Business	NNK1	3FT deg	g	12-16	MO/DO	M/D	32	BBCC	Ind		
Accounting with Business Systems	NNL1	3FT deg	g	12-16	MO/DO	M/D	32	BBCC	Ind		
Accounting with Management	NN41	3FT deg	g	12-16	MO/DO	M/D	32	BBCC	Ind		
Biochemistry with Business	C7N1	3FT deg	g	12-16	MO/DO	M/D	32	BBCC	Ind		
Biochemistry with Business Systems	C7NC	3FT deg	g	12-16	MO/DO	M/D	32	BBCC	Ind		
Biochemistry with Marketing	C7N5	3FT deg	g	12-16	MO/DO	M/D	32	BBCC	Ind		
Biology with Business	C1N1	3FT deg	g	12-16	MO/DO	M/D	32	BBCC	Ind	1	
Biology with Business Systems	C1NC	3FT deg	g	12-16	MO/DO	M/D	32	BBCC	Ind		
Biology with Management	CN1D	3FT deg	g	12-16	MO/DO	M/D	32	BBCC	Ind		
Biology with Marketing	C1N5	3FT deg	g	12-16	MO/DO	M/D	32	BBCC	Ind		
Biotechnology with Business	J8N1	3FT deg	g	12-16	MO/DO	M/D	32	BBCC	Ind		
Biotechnology with Business Systems	J8NC	3FT deg	g	12-16	MO/DO	M/D	32	BBCC	Ind		
Biotechnology with Marketing	J8N5	3FT deg	g	12-16	MO/DO	M/D	32	BBCC	Ind		
Broadcasting & Media Technology with Business	H6N1	3FT deg		12-16	MO/DO	M/D	32	BBCC	Ind		
Built Environment	N801	3FT deg		12-16	MO/DO	M/D	32	BBCC	Ind		
Built Environment	N808	1FT deg		Ind	Ind		Ind	Ind	Ind		
Built Environment and Accounting	NNK8	3FT deg	g	12-16	MO/DO	M/D	32	BBCC	Ind		
Built Environment and Applied Statistics	GN48	3FT deg	g	12-16	MO/DO	M/D	32	BBCC	Ind		
Built Environment and British Studies	VN98	3FT deg		12-16	MO/DO	M/D	32	BBCC	Ind		
Built Environment and Building Conservation	KN28	3FT deg		12-16	MO/DO	M/D	32	BBCC	Ind		
Built Environment w Lang & Stylistics in English	N8QG	3FT deg	g	12-16	MO/DO	M/D	32	BBCC	Ind		
Built Environment with Accounting	N8NK	3FT deg	g	12-16	MO/DO	M/D	32	BBCC	Ind		
Built Environment with Applied Statistics	N8G4	3FT deg	g	12-16	MO/DO	M/D	32	BBCC	Ind		
Built Environment with British Studies	N8V9	3FT deg		12-16	MO/DO	M/D	32	BBCC	Ind		
Built Environment with Business	N8N1	3FT deg	g	12-16	MO/DO	M/D	32	BBCC	Ind		

course details

TITLE	CODE	COURSE	SUBJECTS	A/AS	ND/C	AGNVQ	IB	SQA(H)	SQA	RATIO A/AS	
Built Environment with Business Systems	N8NC	3FT deg	g	12-16	MO/DO	M/D	32	BBCC	Ind		
Built Environment with Chinese	N8T3	3FT deg		12-16	MO/DO	M/D	32	BBCC	Ind		
Built Environment with Contemporary History	N8V1	3FT deg	g	12-16	MO/DO	M/D	32	BBCC	Ind		
Built Environment with Environmental Science	N8F9	3FT deg	g	12-16	MO/DO	M/D	32	BBCC	Ind		
Built Environment with Geographical Info Systems	N811	3FT deg	g	12-16	MO/DO	M/D	32	BBCC	Ind		
Built Environment with Geography	NF8W	3FT deg	g	12-16	MO/DO	M/D	32	BBCC	Ind		
Built Environment with Geology	N8F6	3FT deg	g	12-16	MO/DO	M/D	32	BBCC	Ind		
Built Environment with Health Studies	N8BX	3FT deg		12-16	MO/DO	M/D	32	BBCC	Ind		
Built Environment with Journalism	N8P6	3FT deg	g	12-16	MO/DO	M/D	32	BBCC	Ind		
Built Environment with Leisure Studies	N8N7	3FT deg	g	12-16	MO/DO	M/D	32	BBCC	Ind		
Built Environment with Management	N8ND	3FT deg	g	12-16	MO/DO	M/D	32	BBCC	Ind		
Built Environment with Mapping Science	N8F8	3FT deg	g	12-16	MO/DO	M/D	32	BBCC	Ind		
Built Environment with Marketing	N8N5	3FT deg	g	12-16	MO/DO	M/D	32	BBCC	Ind		
Built Environment with Mathematical Sciences	N8G1	3FT deg	g	12-16	MO/DO	M/D	32	BBCC	Ind		
Built Environment with Mathematics	N8GC	3FT deg	g	12-16	MO/DO	M/D	32	BBCC	Ind		
Built Environment with Media Production	N8PL	3FT deg	g	12-16	MO/DO	M/D	32	BBCC	Ind		
Built Environment with Organisational Behaviour	N8L7	3FT deg	g	12-16	MO/DO	M/D	32	BBCC	Ind		
Built Environment with Physical Geography	N8FV	3FT deg	g	12-16	MO/DO	M/D	32	BBCC	Ind		
Built Environment with Politics	N8M1	3FT deg	g	12-16	MO/DO	M/D	32	BBCC	Ind		
Built Environment with Public Policy and Mgt	N8MC	3FT deg	g	12-16	MO/DO	M/D	32	BBCC	Ind		
Built Environment with Regional Planning and Dev	N8K4	3FT deg	g	12-16	MO/DO	M/D	32	BBCC	Ind		
Built Environment with Social Studies	N8L3	3FT deg	g	12-16	MO/DO	M/D	32	BBCC	Ind		
Business	N123	1FT deg	*	Ind	Ind		Ind	Ind	Ind		
Business Administration	N122	3FT deg	g	12-16	MO/DO	M/D	32	BBCC	Ind	8	6/18
Business Decision Management	GN51	3FT deg	g	12-16	MO/DO	M/D	32	BBCC	Ind		
Business Studies (Options)	N120	4SW deg	g	12-16	MO/DO	M/D	32	BBCC	Ind	9	6/20
Business Systems and Accounting	NNKC	3FT deg	g	12-16	MO/DO	M/D	32	BBCC	Ind		
Business Systems and Applied Statistics	GN4C	3FT deg	g	12-16	MO/DO	M/D	32	BBCC	Ind		
Business Systems and Artificial Intelligence	GN8C	3FT deg		12-16	MO/DO	M/D	32	BBCC	Ind		
Business Systems and Biochemistry	CN7C	3FT deg	g	12-16	MO/DO	M/D	32	BBCC	Ind		
Business Systems and Biology	CN1C	3FT deg	g	12-16	MO/DO	M/D	32	BBCC	Ind		
Business Systems and Biotechnology	JN8C	3FT deg	g	12-16	MO/DO	M/D	32	BBCC	Ind		
Business Systems and Built Environment	NN8C	3FT deg	g	12-16	MO/DO	M/D	32	BBCC	Ind		
Business Systems w Lang & Stylistics in English	N101	3FT deg	g	12-16	MO/DO	M/D	32	BBCC	Ind		
Business Systems with Accounting	N1N4	3FT deg	g	12-16	MO/DO	M/D	32	BBCC	Ind		
Business Systems with Animation	N1WG	3FT deg	g	12-16	MO/DO	M/D	32	BBCC	Ind		
Business Systems with Applied Statistics	N1GK	3FT deg	g	12-16	MO/DO	M/D	32	BBCC	Ind		
Business Systems with Biochemistry	N1CR	3FT deg	g	12-16	MO/DO	M/D	32	BBCC	Ind		
Business Systems with Biology	N1CC	3FT deg	g	12-16	MO/DO	M/D	32	BBCC	Ind		
Business Systems with Biotechnology	N1JV	3FT deg	g	12-16	MO/DO	M/D	32	BBCC	Ind		
Business Systems with Built Environment	N1NV	3FT deg	g	12-16	MO/DO	M/D	32	BBCC	Ind		
Business Systems with Communication Systs Design	N1HQ	3FT deg		12-16	MO/DO	M/D	32	BBCC	Ind		
Business Systems with Comparative Literature	N1QF	3FT deg	g	12-16	MO/DO	M/D	32	BBCC	Ind		
Business Systems with Digital Systems Design	N103	3FT deg	g	12-16	MO/DO	M/D	32	BBCC	Ind		
Business Systems with Electronic Systems Design	N126	3FT deg		12-16	MO/DO	M/D	32	BBCC	Ind		
Business Systems with French	N1RC	3FT deg	F g	12-16	MO/DO	M/D	32	BBCC	Ind		
Business Systems with Geographical Info Systems	N104	3FT deg	g	12-16	MO/DO	M/D	32	BBCC	Ind		
Business Systems with Geography	N1F8	3FT deg	g	12-16	MO/DO	M/D	32	BBCC	Ind		
Business Systems with Geology	N1FP	3FT deg	g	12-16	MO/DO	M/D	32	BBCC	Ind		
Business Systems with German	N1RF	3FT deg	G g	12-16	MO/DO	M/D	32	BBCC	Ind		
Business Systems with Health Science	N1B9	3FT deg	g	12-16	MO/DO	M/D	32	BBCC	Ind		
Business Systems with Human Biology	N1BC	3FT deg	g	12-16	MO/DO	M/D	32	BBCC	Ind		

course details			98 expected requirements							96 entry stats

TITLE	CODE	COURSE	SUBJECTS	A/AS	ND/C	AGNVQ	IB	SQA(H)	SQA	RATIO A/AS
Business Systems with Italian	N1RH	3FT deg	I g	12-16	MO/DO	M/D	32	BBCC	Ind	
Business Systems with Journalism	N1PP	3FT deg	g	12-16	MO/DO	M/D	32	BBCC	Ind	
Business Systems with Leisure Studies	N1N7	3FT deg	g	12-16	MO/DO	M/D	32	BBCC	Ind	
Business Systems with Management	N1ND	3FT deg		12-16	MO/DO	M/D	32	BBCC	Ind	
Business Systems with Mapping Science	N106	3FT deg	g	12-16	MO/DO	M/D	32	BBCC	Ind	
Business Systems with Marketing	N1N5	3FT deg	g	12-16	MO/DO	M/D	32	BBCC	Ind	16
Business Systems with Mathematical Sciences	N1GD	3FT deg	g	12-16	MO/DO	M/D	32	BBCC	Ind	
Business Systems with Mathematics	NG1D	3FT deg	g	12-16	MO/DO	M/D	32	BBCC	Ind	
Business Systems with Media Practices	N1P4	3FT deg	g	12-16	MO/DO	M/D	32	BBCC	Ind	
Business Systems with Media Production	N1PK	3FT deg	g	12-16	MO/DO	M/D	32	BBCC	Ind	
Business Systems with Modern English Studies	N1QH	3FT deg	g	12-16	MO/DO	M/D	32	BBCC	Ind	
Business Systems with Multimedia	N108	3FT deg	g	12-16	MO/DO	M/D	32	BBCC	Ind	
Business Systems with Organisational Behaviour	N1L7	3FT deg	g	12-16	MO/DO	M/D	32	BBCC	Ind	
Business Systems with Plant Biology	N1CF	3FT deg	g	12-16	MO/DO	M/D	32	BBCC	Ind	
Business Systems with Politics	N1MD	3FT deg	g	12-16	MO/DO	M/D	32	BBCC	Ind	
Business Systems with Psychology	N1LT	3FT deg	g	12-16	MO/DO	M/D	32	BBCC	Ind	
Business Systems with Public Policy and Mgt	N109	3FT deg	g	12-16	MO/DO	M/D	32	BBCC	Ind	
Business Systems with Regional Planning and Dev	N1KK	3FT deg	g	12-16	MO/DO	M/D	32	BBCC	Ind	
Business Systems with Social Studies	N1LH	3FT deg	g	12-16	MO/DO	M/D	32	BBCC	Ind	
Business Systems with Spanish	N1RK	3FT deg	Sp g	12-16	MO/DO	M/D	32	BBCC	Ind	
Business Systems with Travel and Tourism	N1P7	3FT deg	g	12-16	MO/DO	M/D	32	BBCC	Ind	
Business and Applied Statistics	GN41	3FT deg	g	12-16	MO/DO	M/D	32	BBCC	Ind	
Business and Artificial Intelligence	GN81	3FT deg		12-16	MO/DO	M/D	32	BBCC	Ind	
Business and Biochemistry	CN71	3FT deg	g	12-16	MO/DO	M/D	32	BBCC	Ind	
Business and Biology	CN11	3FT deg	g	12-16	MO/DO	M/D	32	BBCC	Ind	
Business and Biotechnology	JN81	3FT deg	g	12-16	MO/DO	M/D	32	BBCC	Ind	
Business and Building Conservation	KN21	3FT deg	g	12-16	MO/DO	M/D	32	BBCC	Ind	
Business and Built Environment	NN81	3FT deg	g	12-16	MO/DO	M/D	32	BBCC	Ind	
Business and Property Studies	NK2D	3FT deg		12-16	MO/DO	M/D	32	BBCC	Ind	
Business with Animation	N1WF	3FT deg	g	12-16	MO/DO	M/D	32	BBCC	Ind	
Business with Applied Statistics	N1G4	3FT deg	g	12-16	MO/DO	M/D	32	BBCC	Ind	
Business with Biochemistry	N1C7	3FT deg	g	12-16	MO/DO	M/D	32	BBCC	Ind	
Business with Biology	N1C1	3FT deg	g	12-16	MO/DO	M/D	32	BBCC	Ind	
Business with Biotechnology	N1J8	3FT deg	g	12-16	MO/DO	M/D	32	BBCC	Ind	
Business with Built Environment	N1N8	3FT deg	g	12-16	MO/DO	M/D	32	BBCC	Ind	
Business with Contemporary History	N1V1	3FT deg	g	12-16	MO/DO	M/D	32	BBCC	Ind	1
Business with Digital Systems Design	N1HP	3FT deg	g	12-16	MO/DO	M/D	32	BBCC	Ind	
Business with Electronic Systems Design	N1H6	3FT deg		12-16	MO/DO	M/D	32	BBCC	Ind	
Business with Environmental Science	N1F9	3FT deg	g	12-16	MO/DO	M/D	32	BBCC	Ind	
Business with French	N1R1	3FT deg	F g	12-16	MO/DO	M/D	32	BBCC	Ind	
Business with Geography	N1FW	3FT deg	g	12-16	MO/DO	M/D	32	BBCC	Ind	
Business with Geology	N1F6	3FT deg	g	12-16	MO/DO	M/D	32	BBCC	Ind	
Business with German	N1R2	3FT deg	G g	12-16	MO/DO	M/D	32	BBCC	Ind	
Business with Health Studies	N1BX	3FT deg		12-16	MO/DO	M/D	32	BBCC	Ind	
Business with Human Biology	N1B1	3FT deg	g	12-16	MO/DO	M/D	32	BBCC	Ind	
Business with Italian	N1R3	3FT deg	I g	12-16	MO/DO	M/D	32	BBCC	Ind	
Business with Japanese	N1T4	3FT deg	L g	12-16	MO/DO	M/D	32	BBCC	Ind	
Business with Journalism	N1P6	3FT deg	g	12-16	MO/DO	M/D	32	BBCC	Ind	
Business with Language & Stylistics in English	N1QG	3FT deg	g	12-16	MO/DO	M/D	32	BBCC	Ind	
Business with Linguistics	N1Q1	3FT deg	g	12-16	MO/DO	M/D	32	BBCC	Ind	
Business with Literary Studies in English	N1Q2	3FT deg	g	12-16	MO/DO	M/D	32	BBCC	Ind	
Business with Mathematical Sciences	N1GC	3FT deg	g	12-16	MO/DO	M/D	32	BBCC	Ind	

Business and Management 12

course details   98 expected requirements   96 entry stats

TITLE	CODE	COURSE	SUBJECTS	A/AS	NO/C	AGNVQ	IB	SQA(H)	SQA	RATIO A/AS
Business with Mathematics	NGCD	3FT deg	g	12-16	MO/DO	M/D	32	BBCC	Ind	
Business with Media Production	N1PL	3FT deg	g	12-16	MO/DO	M/D	32	BBCC	Ind	
Business with Modern English Studies	N1Q3	3FT deg	g	12-16	MO/DO	M/D	32	BBCC	Ind	
Business with Multimedia	N110	3FT deg	g	12-16	MO/DO	M/D	32	BBCC	Ind	
Business with Physical Geography	N1FV	3FT deg	g	12-16	MO/DO	M/D	32	BBCC	Ind	
Business with Plant Biology	N1C2	3FT deg	g	12-16	MO/DO	M/D	32	BBCC	Ind	
Business with Politics	N1M1	3FT deg	g	12-16	MO/DO	M/D	32	BBCC	Ind	3
Business with Pollution Studies	NF1Y	3FT deg	g	12-16	MO/DO	M/D	32	BBCC	Ind	
Business with Psychology	N1LR	3FT deg	g	12-16	MO/DO	M/D	32	BBCC	Ind	
Business with Public Policy and Management	N1MC	3FT deg	g	12-16	MO/DO	M/D	32	BBCC	Ind	
Business with Regional Planning and Development	N1K4	3FT deg	g	12-16	MO/DO	M/D	32	BBCC	Ind	
Business with Social Studies	N1L3	3FT deg	g	12-16	MO/DO	M/D	32	BBCC	Ind	3
Business with Spanish	N1R4	3FT deg	Sp g	12-16	MO/DO	M/D	32	BBCC	Ind	
Business with Video Production	N1W5	3FT deg	g	12-16	MO/DO	M/D	32	BBCC	Ind	
Communication System Design and Business Systems	GN61	3FT deg	g	12-16	MO/DO	M/D	32	BBCC	Ind	
Communication System Design with Business Systs	G6N1	3FT deg	g	12-16	MO/DO	M/D	32	BBCC	Ind	
Communication System Design with Management	G6NC	3FT deg	g	12-16	MO/DO	M/D	32	BBCC	Ind	
Communication System Design with Marketing	G6N5	3FT deg	g	12-16	MO/DO	M/D	32	BBCC	Ind	
Computer Applications and Built Environment	GN68	3FT deg		12-16	MO/DO	M/D	32	BBCC	Ind	
Computer Applications and Business	GN6D	3FT deg		12-16	MO/DO	M/D	32	BBCC	Ind	
Computer Science and Built Environment	NG85	3FT deg	g	12-16	MO/DO	M/D	32	BBCC	Ind	
Computer Science and Business	NG15	3FT deg	g	12-16	MO/DO	M/D	32	BBCC	Ind	10
Computer Science and Business Systems	NGC5	3FT deg	g	12-16	MO/DO	M/D	32	BBCC	Ind	5
Contemp British & Euro History with Business	V1N1	3FT deg	g	12-16	MO/DO	M/D	32	BBCC	Ind	
Contemp British & Euro History with Management	V1ND	3FT deg	g	12-16	MO/DO	M/D	32	BBCC	Ind	
Contemp British & Euro History with Marketing	V1N5	3FT deg	g	12-16	MO/DO	M/D	32	BBCC	Ind	
Contemporary History and Business	NV11	3FT deg	g	12-16	MO/DO	M/D	32	BBCC	Ind	2
Creative Design and Business	WN21	3FT deg		12-16	MO/DO	M/D	32	BBCC	Ind	
Design Marketing	N510	3FT deg		12-16	MO/DO	M/D	32	BBCC	Ind	
Digital Systems Design and Business	NH1P	3FT deg	g	12-16	MO/DO	M/D	32	BBCC	Ind	
Digital Systems Design and Business Systems	NHCP	3FT deg	g	12-16	MO/DO	M/D	32	BBCC	Ind	
Digital Systems Design with Management	HN6D	3FT deg	g	12-16	MO/DO	M/D	32	BBCC	Ind	
Digital Systems Design with Marketing	H6NM	3FT deg	g	12-16	MO/DO	M/D	32	BBCC	Ind	
Electronic System Design and Business	HN61	3FT deg	g	12-16	MO/DO	M/D	32	BBCC	Ind	
Electronic System Design and Business Systems	HN6C	3FT deg	g	12-16	MO/DO	M/D	32	BBCC	Ind	
Electronic System Design with Business	HN6P	3FT deg	g	12-16	MO/DO	M/D	32	BBCC	Ind	
Electronic System Design with Business Systems	HNP1	3FT deg	g	12-16	MO/DO	M/D	32	BBCC	Ind	
Electronic System Design with Management	HNQ1	3FT deg	g	12-16	MO/DO	M/D	32	BBCC	Ind	
Electronic System Design with Marketing	HN6M	3FT deg	g	12-16	MO/DO	M/D	32	BBCC	Ind	
Environmental Science and Built Environment	NF89	3FT deg	g	12-16	MO/DO	M/D	32	BBCC	Ind	
Environmental Science and Business	NF19	3FT deg	g	12-16	MO/DO	M/D	32	BBCC	Ind	
Environmental Science with Built Environment	F9N8	3FT deg	g	12-16	MO/DO	M/D	32	BBCC	Ind	
Environmental Science with Business	F9N1	3FT deg	g	12-16	MO/DO	M/D	32	BBCC	Ind	
Environmental Science with Management	FN9D	3FT deg	g	12-16	MO/DO	M/D	32	BBCC	Ind	
Environmental Science with Marketing	F9N5	3FT deg	g	12-16	MO/DO	M/D	32	BBCC	Ind	
Environmental Studies with Built Environment	F9NV	3FT deg		12-16	MO/DO	M/D	32	BBCC	Ind	
Environmental Studies with Business	F9NC	3FT deg		12-16	MO/DO	M/D	32	BBCC	Ind	
Environmental Studies with Management	F9NY	3FT deg		12-16	MO/DO	M/D	32	BBCC	Ind	
Environmental Studies with Marketing	F9NM	3FT deg		12-16	MO/DO	M/D	32	BBCC	Ind	
Estate Management	N800	3FT deg	g	12-16	MO/DO	M/D	32	BBCC	Ind	12
European Language Studies and Business	NT12	3FT deg	L g	12-16	MO/DO	M/D	32	BBCC	Ind	
European Language Studies and Business Systems	NTC2	3FT deg	L g	12-16	MO/DO	M/D	32	BBCC	Ind	

course details

98 expected requirements

96 entry stats

TITLE	CODE	COURSE	SUBJECTS	A/AS	NQ/C	AGNVQ	IB	SQA(H)	SQA	RATIO A/AS
European Language Studies with Business	T2N1	4FT deg	L g	12-16	MO/DO	M/D	32	BBCC	Ind	
European Language Studies with Business Systems	T2NC	4FT deg	L g	12-16	MO/DO	M/D	32	BBCC	Ind	
European Language Studies with Management	T2ND	4FT deg	L g	12-16	MO/DO	M/D	32	BBCC	Ind	
European Language Studies with Marketing	T2N5	4FT deg	L g	12-16	MO/DO	M/D	32	BBCC	Ind	
Geography and Built Environment	FN88	3FT deg	g	12-16	MO/DO	M/D	32	BBCC	Ind	
Geography and Business Systems	FN81	3FT deg	g	12-16	MO/DO	M/D	32	BBCC	Ind	
Geography with Built Environment	F8NW	3FT deg	g	12-16	MO/DO	M/D	32	BBCC	Ind	
Geography with Business Systems	FN8D	3FT deg	g	12-16	MO/DO	M/D	32	BBCC	Ind	
Geology and Built Environment	NF86	3FT deg	g	12-16	MO/DO	M/D	32	BBCC	Ind	
Geology and Business	NF16	3FT deg	g	12-16	MO/DO	M/D	32	BBCC	Ind	
Geology and Business Systems	NFC6	3FT deg	g	12-16	MO/DO	M/D	32	BBCC	Ind	
Geology with Built Environment	F6N8	3FT deg	g	12-16	MO/DO	M/D	32	BBCC	Ind	
Geology with Business	F6N1	3FT deg	g	12-16	MO/DO	M/D	32	BBCC	Ind	
Geology with Business Systems	F6NC	3FT deg	g	12-16	MO/DO	M/D	32	BBCC	Ind	
Geology with Management	FN61	3FT deg	g	12-16	MO/DO	M/D	32	BBCC	Ind	
Geology with Marketing	F6N5	3FT deg	g	12-16	MO/DO	M/D	32	BBCC	Ind	
Health Science and Business Systems	NBC9	3FT deg	g	12-16	MO/DO	M/D	32	BBCC	Ind	
Health Science with Business Systems	B9NC	3FT deg	g	12-16	MO/DO	M/D	32	BBCC	Ind	
Health Studies and Built Environment	NB8X	3FT deg	g	12-16	MO/DO	M/D	32	BBCC	Ind	
Health Studies and Business	NB1X	3FT deg	g	12-16	MO/DO	M/D	32	BBCC	Ind	3
Health Studies with Management	B9ND	3FT deg	g	12-16	MO/DO	M/D	32	BBCC	Ind	
Health Studies with Marketing	B9N5	3FT deg	g	12-16	MO/DO	M/D	32	BBCC	Ind	
History of Design and Architecture and Built Env	VN48	3FT deg		12-16	MO/DO	M/D	32	BBCC	Ind	
Housing Studies and Business	NK1K	3FT deg	g	12-16	MO/DO	M/D	32	BBCC	Ind	
Human Biology and Business	BN11	3FT deg	g	12-16	MO/DO	M/D	32	BBCC	Ind	
Human Biology and Business Systems	BN1C	3FT deg	g	12-16	MO/DO	M/D	32	BBCC	Ind	
Human Resource Management	N130	3FT deg		12-16	MO/DO	M/D	32	BBCC	Ind	
Integrated Engineering with Business	H1N1	3FT deg	g	12-16	MO/DO	M/D	32	BBCC	Ind	
Integrated Engineering with Business Systems	H1NC	3FT deg	g	12-16	MO/DO	M/D	32	BBCC	Ind	
Integrated Engineering with Marketing	H1N5	3FT deg	g	12-16	MO/DO	M/D	32	BBCC	Ind	
International Marketing	N501	4SW deg	L g	12-16	MO/DO	M/D	32	BBCC	Ind	3
Journalism and Business	PN61	3FT deg		12-16	MO/DO	M/D	32	BBCC	Ind	
Journalism and Business Systems	PN6C	3FT deg		12-16	MO/DO	M/D	32	BBCC	Ind	
Language & Stylistics in Engl and Business Syst	NQCG	3FT deg	g	12-16	MO/C	M/D	32	BBCC	Ind	
Language & Stylistics in English & Built Environ	NQ8G	3FT deg	g	12-16	MO/C	M/D	32	BBCC	Ind	
Language & Stylistics in English and Business	NQ1G	3FT deg	g	12-16	MO/DO	M/D	32	BBCC	Ind	
Law and Business	NM13	3FT deg	g	12-16	MO/DO	M/D	32	BBCC	Ind	25
Law and Business Systems	NMC3	3FT deg	g	12-16	MO/DO	M/D	32	BBCC	Ind	
Law with Business	MN31	3FT deg	g	12-16	MO/DO	M/D	32	BBCC	Ind	
Law with Business Systems	M3NC	3FT deg	g	12-16	MO/DO	M/D	32	BBCC	Ind	
Law with Management	M3ND	3FT deg	g	12-16	MO/DO	M/D	32	BBCC	Ind	
Law with Marketing	M3N5	3FT deg	g	12-16	MO/DO	M/D	32	BBCC	Ind	
Leisure Studies with Marketing	N7N5	3FT deg	g	12-16	MO/DO	M/D	32	BBCC	Ind	
Linguistics and Business	NQ11	3FT deg	g	12-16	MO/DO	M/D	32	BBCC	Ind	
Linguistics with Business	Q1N1	3FT deg	g	12-16	MO/DO	M/D	32	BBCC	Ind	
Linguistics with Marketing	Q1N5	3FT deg	g	12-16	MO/DO	M/D	32	BBCC	Ind	
Literary Studies in English and Business	NQ12	3FT deg	g	12-16	MO/DO	M/D	32	BBCC	Ind	
Literary Studies in English with Business	Q2N1	3FT deg		12-16	MO/DO	M/D	32	BBCC	Ind	
Literary Studies in English with Marketing	Q2N5	3FT deg		12-16	MO/DO	M/D	32	BBCC	Ind	
Management Science	N124	3FT deg	g	12-16	MO/DO	M/D	32	BBCC	Ind	
Mapping Science and Built Environment	NF88	3FT deg	g	12-16	MO/DO	M/D	32	BBCC	Ind	
Mapping Science and Business Systems	NFC8	3FT deg	g	12-16	MO/DO	M/D	32	BBCC	Ind	

Business and Management 12

TITLE	CODE	COURSE	SUBJECTS	A/AS	NO/C	AGNVQ	IB	SQA(H)	SQA	RATIO	A/AS
Mapping Science and Ecology & Biodiversity	CN9W	3FT deg	g	12-16	MO/DO	M/D	32	BBCC	Ind		
Mapping Science with Built Environment	F8N8	3FT deg	g	12-16	MO/DO	M/D	32	BBCC	Ind		
Mapping Science with Business Systems	F8NC	3FT deg	g	12-16	MO/DO	M/D	32	BBCC	Ind		
Marketing	N500	3FT deg	g	12-16	MO/DO	M/D	32	BBCC	Ind	8	8/16
Marketing and Applied Statistics	GN45	3FT deg	g	12-16	MO/DO	M/D	32	BBCC	Ind		
Marketing and Biochemistry	CN75	3FT deg	g	12-16	MO/DO	M/D	32	BBCC	Ind		
Marketing and Biology	CN15	3FT deg	g	12-16	MO/DO	M/D	32	BBCC	Ind		
Marketing and Biotechnology	JN85	3FT deg	g	12-16	MO/DO	M/D	32	BBCC	Ind		
Marketing and Building Conservation	KN25	3FT deg		12-16	MO/DO	M/D	32	BBCC	Ind		
Marketing and Built Environment	NN85	3FT deg	g	12-16	MO/DO	M/D	32	BBCC	Ind		
Marketing and Communication System Design	GN65	3FT deg	g	12-16	MO/DO	M/D	32	BBCC	Ind		
Marketing and Computer Applications	GN6M	3FT deg		12-16	MO/DO	M/D	32	BBCC	Ind		
Marketing and Computer Science	GN55	3FT deg	g	12-16	MO/DO	M/D	32	BBCC	Ind		
Marketing and Computer Visualisation & Animation	GNN5	3FT deg		12-16	MO/DO	M/D	32	BBCC	Ind		
Marketing and Contemporary History	VN15	3FT deg	g	12-16	MO/DO	M/D	32	BBCC	Ind		
Marketing and Creative Design	WN25	3FT deg		12-16	MO/DO	M/D	32	BBCC	Ind		
Marketing and Digital Systems Design	HNP5	3FT deg	g	12-16	MO/DO	M/D	32	BBCC	Ind		
Marketing and Electronic System Design	HNP6	3FT deg	g	12-16	MO/DO	M/D	32	BBCC	Ind		
Marketing and Environmental Science	FN95	3FT deg	g	12-16	MO/DO	M/D	32	BBCC	Ind		
Marketing and European Language Studies	TN25	3FT deg	L g	12-16	MO/DO	M/D	32	BBCC	Ind	3	
Marketing and Geology	FN65	3FT deg	g	12-16	MO/DO	M/D	32	BBCC	Ind	1	
Marketing and Health Studies	BNX5	3FT deg	g	12-16	MO/DO	M/D	32	BBCC	Ind		
Marketing and Human Biology	BN15	3FT deg	g	12-16	MO/DO	M/D	32	BBCC	Ind		
Marketing and Human Centred Computing	GNM5	3FT deg		12-16	MO/DO	M/D	32	BBCC	Ind		
Marketing and Journalism	PN65	3FT deg		12-16	MO/DO	M/D	32	BBCC	Ind		
Marketing and Language & Stylistics in English	QNG5	3FT deg	g	12-16	MO/DO	M/D	32	BBCC	Ind		
Marketing and Law	MN35	3FT deg	g	12-16	MO/DO	M/D	32	BBCC	Ind	6	
Marketing and Leisure Studies	NN57	3FT deg	g	12-16	MO/DO	M/D	32	BBCC	Ind		
Marketing and Linguistics	QN15	3FT deg	g	12-16	MO/DO	M/D	32	BBCC	Ind		
Marketing and Literary Studies in English	QN25	3FT deg	g	12-16	MO/DO	M/D	32	BBCC	Ind		
Marketing with Animation	N5WF	3FT deg	g	12-16	MO/DO	M/D	32	BBCC	Ind		
Marketing with Applied Statistics	N5G4	3FT deg	g	12-16	MO/DO	M/D	32	BBCC	Ind		
Marketing with Biochemistry	N5C7	3FT deg	g	12-16	MO/DO	M/D	32	BBCC	Ind		
Marketing with Biology	N5C1	3FT deg	g	12-16	MO/DO	M/D	32	BBCC	Ind		
Marketing with Biotechnology	N5J8	3FT deg	g	12-16	MO/DO	M/D	32	BBCC	Ind		
Marketing with Built Environment	N5N8	3FT deg	g	12-16	MO/DO	M/D	32	BBCC	Ind		
Marketing with Communication System Design	N5H6	3FT deg		12-16	MO/DO	M/D	32	BBCC	Ind		
Marketing with Contemporary History	N5V1	3FT deg	g	12-16	MO/DO	M/D	32	BBCC	Ind		
Marketing with Digital Systems Design	N5HP	3FT deg	g	12-16	MO/DO	M/D	32	BBCC	Ind		
Marketing with Electronic Systems Design	N5HQ	3FT deg		12-16	MO/DO	M/D	32	BBCC	Ind		
Marketing with Environmental Science	N5F9	3FT deg	g	12-16	MO/DO	M/D	32	BBCC	Ind		
Marketing with French	N5R1	3FT deg	F g	12-16	MO/DO	M/D	32	BBCC	Ind		
Marketing with Geographical Information Systems	N5F8	3FT deg	g	12-16	MO/DO	M/D	32	BBCC	Ind		
Marketing with Geology	N5F6	3FT deg	g	12-16	MO/DO	M/D	32	BBCC	Ind		
Marketing with German	N5R2	3FT deg	G g	12-16	MO/DO	M/D	32	BBCC	Ind		
Marketing with Health Studies	N5BX	3FT deg		12-16	MO/DO	M/D	32	BBCC	Ind		
Marketing with Human Biology	N5B1	3FT deg	g	12-16	MO/DO	M/D	32	BBCC	Ind		
Marketing with Italian	N5R3	3FT deg	I g	12-16	MO/DO	M/D	32	BBCC	Ind		
Marketing with Japanese	N5T4	3FT deg	g	12-16	MO/DO	M/D	32	BBCC	Ind		
Marketing with Journalism	N5P6	3FT deg	g	12-16	MO/DO	M/D	32	BBCC	Ind		
Marketing with Land Reclamation	N5K3	3FT deg	g	12-16	MO/DO	M/D	32	BBCC	Ind		
Marketing with Language & Stylistics in English	N5QG	3FT deg	L g	12-16	MO/DO	M/D	32	BBCC	Ind		

| | | | | 98 expected requirements | | | | | | 96 entry stats |

TITLE	CODE	COURSE	SUBJECTS	A/AS	NO/C	AGNVQ	IB	SQA(H)	SQA	RATIO A/AS
Marketing with Leisure Studies	N5N7	3FT deg	g	12-16	MO/DO	M/D	32	BBCC	Ind	
Marketing with Linguistics	N5Q1	3FT deg	g	12-16	MO/DO	M/D	32	BBCC	Ind	
Marketing with Literary Studies in English	N5Q2	3FT deg	g	12-16	MO/DO	M/D	32	BBCC	Ind	
Marketing with Mathematics	NG5C	3FT deg	g	12-16	MO/DO	M/D	32	BBCC	Ind	
Marketing with Media Production	N5PL	3FT deg	g	12-16	MO/DO	M/D	32	BBCC	Ind	16
Marketing with Modern English Studies	N5Q3	3FT deg	g	12-16	MO/DO	M/D	32	BBCC	Ind	
Marketing with Multimedia	N5PK	3FT deg	g	12-16	MO/DO	M/D	32	BBCC	Ind	
Marketing with Plant Biology	N5C2	3FT deg	g	12-16	MO/DO	M/D	32	BBCC	Ind	
Marketing with Politics	N5M1	3FT deg	g	12-16	MO/DO	M/D	32	BBCC	Ind	
Marketing with Psychology	N5LR	3FT deg	g	12-16	MO/DO	M/D	32	BBCC	Ind	3
Marketing with Public Policy and Management	N5MC	3FT deg	g	12-16	MO/DO	M/D	32	BBCC	Ind	
Marketing with Regional Planning and Development	N5K4	3FT deg	g	12-16	MO/DO	M/D	32	BBCC	Ind	
Marketing with Social Studies	N5L3	3FT deg	g	12-16	MO/DO	M/D	32	BBCC	Ind	
Marketing with Spanish	N5R4	3FT deg	Sp g	12-16	MO/DO	M/D	32	BBCC	Ind	
Marketing with Travel and Tourism	N5P7	3FT deg	g	12-16	MO/DO	M/D	32	BBCC	Ind	
Mathematical Sciences and Built Environment	GN18	3FT deg	g	12-16	MO/DO	M/D	32	BBCC	Ind	
Mathematical Sciences and Business	GN11	3FT deg	g	12-16	MO/DO	M/D	32	BBCC	Ind	
Mathematical Sciences and Business Systems	GN1C	3FT deg	g	12-16	MO/DO	M/D	32	BBCC	Ind	
Mathematical Sciences and Marketing	GN15	3FT deg	g	12-16	MO/DO	M/D	32	BBCC	Ind	
Mathematical Sciences with Built Environment	G1N8	3FT deg	g	12-16	MO/DO	M/D	32	BBCC	Ind	
Mathematical Sciences with Business	G1N1	3FT deg	g	12-16	MO/DO	M/D	32	BBCC	Ind	
Mathematical Sciences with Business Systems	G1NC	3FT deg	g	12-16	MO/DO	M/D	32	BBCC	Ind	
Mathematical Sciences with Management	G1ND	3FT deg	g	12-16	MO/DO	M/D	32	BBCC	Ind	
Mathematical Sciences with Marketing	G1N5	3FT deg	g	12-16	MO/DO	M/D	32	BBCC	Ind	
Mathematics and Built Environment	NG81	3FT deg	g	12-16	MO/DO	M/D	32	BBCC	Ind	
Mathematics and Business	NG11	3FT deg	g	12-16	MO/DO	M/D	32	BBCC	Ind	
Mathematics and Business Systems	NGC1	3FT deg	g	12-16	MO/DO	M/D	32	BBCC	Ind	
Mathematics and Marketing	NG51	3FT deg	g	12-16	MO/DO	M/D	32	BBCC	Ind	
Media Performance with Performance Management	W4N9	3FT deg		12-16	MO/DO	M/D	32	BBCC	Ind	
Media Practices with Performance Management	P4N9	3FT deg		12-16	MO/DO	M/D	32	BBCC	Ind	
Media Production and Business	NP1L	3FT deg	g	12-16	MO/DO	M/D	32	BBCC	Ind	
Media Production and Business Systems	NPCL	3FT deg	g	12-16	MO/DO	M/D	32	BBCC	Ind	
Media Production and Marketing	NP5L	3FT deg	g	12-16	MO/DO	M/D	32	BBCC	Ind	
Media Production with Business	P4N1	3FT deg	g	12-16	MO/DO	M/D	32	BBCC	Ind	7
Media Production with Marketing	P4N5	3FT deg	g	12-16	MO/DO	M/D	32	BBCC	Ind	
Media Production with Performance Management	P4NX	3FT deg								
Modern English Studies and Business	NQ13	3FT deg	g	12-16	MO/DO	M/D	32	BBCC	Ind	7
Modern English Studies and Business Systems	NQC3	3FT deg	g	12-16	MO/DO	M/D	32	BBCC	Ind	
Modern English Studies and Marketing	NQ53	3FT deg	g	12-16	MO/DO	M/D	32	BBCC	Ind	
Modern English Studies with Business	Q3N1	3FT deg	g	12-16	MO/DO	M/D	32	BBCC	Ind	1
Modern English Studies with Business Systems	Q3NC	3FT deg	g	12-16	MO/DO	M/D	32	BBCC	Ind	
Modern English Studies with Management	Q3ND	3FT deg	g	12-16	MO/DO	M/D	32	BBCC	Ind	
Modern English Studies with Marketing	Q3N5	3FT deg	g	12-16	MO/DO	M/D	32	BBCC	Ind	
Modern History and Business	NV1C	3FT deg	g	12-16	MO/DO	M/D	32	BBCC	Ind	
Modern History and Business Systems	NVCC	3FT deg	g	12-16	MO/DO	M/D	32	BBCC	Ind	
Modern History and Marketing	NV5C	3FT deg	g	12-16	MO/DO	M/D	32	BBCC	Ind	
Modern History with Business Systems	V1NC	3FT deg	g	12-16	MO/DO	M/D	32	BBCC	Ind	
Modern History with Marketing	V1NM	3FT deg	g	12-16	MO/DO	M/D	32	BBCC	Ind	
Organisational Behaviour and Built Environment	NL87	3FT deg	g	12-16	MO/DO	M/D	32	BBCC	Ind	
Organisational Behaviour and Business Systems	NLC7	3FT deg	g	12-16	MO/DO	M/D	32	BBCC	Ind	2
Physical Geography and Built Environment	NF8V	3FT deg	g	12-16	MO/DO	M/D	32	BBCC	Ind	
Physical Geography and Business	NF1V	3FT deg	g	12-16	MO/DO	M/D	32	BBCC	Ind	

Business and Management 12

course details			98 expected requirements							96 entry stats
TITLE	CODE	COURSE	SUBJECTS	A/AS	NO/C	AGNVQ	IB	SQA(H)	SQA	RATIO A/AS
Physical Geography and Marketing	NF5V	3FT deg	g	12-16	MO/DO	M/D	32	BBCC	Ind	
Physical Geography with Built Environment	F8NV	3FT deg	g	12-16	MO/DO	M/D	32	BBCC	Ind	
Physical Geography with Business	F8N1	3FT deg	g	12-16	MO/DO	M/D	32	BBCC	Ind	
Physical Geography with Marketing	F8N5	3FT deg	g	12-16	MO/DO	M/D	32	BBCC	Ind	
Planning Studies and Built Environment	KN48	3FT deg	g	12-16	MO/DO	M/D	32	BBCC	Ind	
Planning Studies and Business	KN41	3FT deg	g	12-16	MO/DO	M/D	32	BBCC	Ind	
Planning Studies and Business Systems	KN4D	3FT deg	g	12-16	MO/DO	M/D	32	BBCC	Ind	
Plant Biology and Business	CN21	3FT deg	g	12-16	MO/DO	M/D	32	BBCC	Ind	
Plant Biology and Business Systems	CN2C	3FT deg	g	12-16	MO/DO	M/D	32	BBCC	Ind	
Plant Biology and Marketing	CN25	3FT deg	g	12-16	MO/DO	M/D	32	BBCC	Ind	
Plant Biology with Business	C2N1	3FT deg	g	12-16	MO/DO	M/D	32	BBCC	Ind	
Plant Biology with Business Systems	C2NC	3FT deg	g	12-16	MO/DO	M/D	32	BBCC	Ind	
Plant Biology with Marketing	C2N5	3FT deg	g	12-16	MO/DO	M/D	32	BBCC	Ind	
Politics and Built Environment	NM81	3FT deg	g	12-16	MO/DO	M/D	32	BBCC	Ind	
Politics and Business	NM11	3FT deg	g	12-16	MO/DO	M/D	32	BBCC	Ind	12
Politics and Business Systems	NMC1	3FT deg	g	12-16	MO/DO	M/D	32	BBCC	Ind	
Politics and Marketing	NM51	3FT deg	g	12-16	MO/DO	M/D	32	BBCC	Ind	
Politics with Built Environment	M1N8	3FT deg	g	12-16	MO/DO	M/D	32	BBCC	Ind	
Politics with Business	M1N1	3FT deg	g	12-16	MO/DO	M/D	32	BBCC	Ind	
Politics with Business Systems	M1NC	3FT deg	g	12-16	MO/DO	M/D	32	BBCC	Ind	
Politics with Management	MN1D	3FT deg	g	12-16	MO/DO	M/D	32	BBCC	Ind	
Politics with Marketing	M1N5	3FT deg	g	12-16	MO/DO	M/D	32	BBCC	Ind	
Property Studies and Business	KN2C	3FT deg	g	12-16	MO/DO	M/D	32	BBCC	Ind	
Psychology and Business	NL1R	3FT deg	g	12-16	MO/DO	M/D	32	BBCC	Ind	52
Psychology and Business Systems	NLCR	3FT deg	g	12-16	MO/DO	M/D	32	BBCC	Ind	
Psychology and Marketing	NL5R	3FT deg	g	12-16	MO/DO	M/D	32	BBCC	Ind	13
Psychology with Business Systems	L7N1	3FT deg	g	12-16	MO/DO	M/D	32	BBCC	Ind	
Psychology with Management	LN71	3FT deg	g	12-16	MO/DO	M/D	32	BBCC	Ind	
Psychology with Marketing	L7N5	3FT deg	g	12-16	MO/DO	M/D	32	BBCC	Ind	9
Public Policy & Management and Business Systems	NMCC	3FT deg	g	12-16	MO/DO	M/D	32	BBCC	Ind	
Public Policy & Management with Built Environ	M1NV	3FT deg	g	12-16	MO/DO	M/D	32	BBCC	Ind	
Public Policy and Management and Built Environ	NM8C	3FT deg	g	12-16	MO/DO	M/D	32	BBCC	Ind	
Public Policy and Management and Business	NM1C	3FT deg	g	12-16	MO/DO	M/D	32	BBCC	Ind	2
Public Policy and Management and Marketing	NM5C	3FT deg	g	12-16	MO/DO	M/D	32	BBCC	Ind	
Public Policy and Management with Marketing	M1NM	3FT deg	g	12-16	MO/DO	M/D	32	BBCC	Ind	
Regional Planning & Development & Built Environ	NK84	3FT deg	g	12-16	MO/DO	M/D	32	BBCC	Ind	
Regional Planning & Development & Business Systs	NKC4	3FT deg	g	12-16	MO/DO	M/D	32	BBCC	Ind	
Regional Planning & Development with Management	KN4C	3FT deg	g	12-16	MO/DO	M/D	32	BBCC	Ind	
Regional Planning and Dev with Business Systems	K4NC	3FT deg	g	12-16	MO/DO	M/D	32	BBCC	Ind	
Regional Planning and Development and Business	NK14	3FT deg	g	12-16	MO/DO	M/D	32	BBCC	Ind	
Regional Planning and Development and Marketing	NK54	3FT deg	g	12-16	MO/DO	M/D	32	BBCC	Ind	
Regional Planning and Development with Built Env	K4N8	3FT deg	g	12-16	MO/DO	M/D	32	BBCC	Ind	
Regional Planning and Development with Business	K4N1	3FT deg	g	12-16	MO/DO	M/D	32	BBCC	Ind	
Regional Planning and Development with Marketing	K4N5	3FT deg	g	12-16	MO/DO	M/D	32	BBCC	Ind	
Social Policy and Built Environment	LN48	3FT deg		12-16	MO/DO	M/D	32	BBCC	Ind	
Social Policy and Business	LN41	3FT deg		12-16	MO/DO	M/D	32	BBCC	Ind	
Social Policy with Built Environment	L4N8	3FT deg		12-16	MO/DO	M/D	32	BBCC	Ind	
Social Policy with Business	L4N1	3FT deg		12-16	MO/DO	M/D	32	BBCC	Ind	
Social Studies and Business	NL13	3FT deg	g	12-16	MO/DO	M/D	32	BBCC	Ind	
Social Studies and Business Systems	NLC3	3FT deg	g	12-16	MO/DO	M/D	32	BBCC	Ind	
Social Studies and Marketing	NL53	3FT deg	g	12-16	MO/DO	M/D	32	BBCC	Ind	
Social Studies with Business	L3N1	3FT deg	g	12-16	MO/DO	M/D	32	BBCC	Ind	

		course details				*98 expected requirements*				*96 entry stats*
TITLE	CODE	COURSE	SUBJECTS	A/AS	NO/C	AGNVQ	IB	SQA(H)	SQA	RATIO A/AS
Social Studies with Business Systems	L3NC	3FT deg	g	12-16	MO/DO	M/D	32	BBCC	Ind	
Social Studies with Marketing	L3N5	3FT deg	g	12-16	MO/DO	M/D	32	BBCC	Ind	
Sociology and Built Environment	LNH8	3FT deg		12-16	MO/DO	M/D	32	BBCC	Ind	
Sociology and Business	LNH1	3FT deg		12-16	MO/DO	M/D	32	BBCC	Ind	
Sociology and Marketing	LNH5	3FT deg		12-16	MO/DO	M/D	32	BBCC	Ind	
Sociology with Business	L3NX	3FT deg		12-16	MO/DO	M/D	32	BBCC	Ind	
Sociology with Marketing	L3NM	3FT deg		12-16	MO/DO	M/D	32	BBCC	Ind	
Software Engineering and Business Systems	GN7C	3FT deg		12-16	MO/DO	M/D	32	BBCC	Ind	
Stage & Screen Technology and Business	PNK1	3FT deg		12-16	MO/DO	M/D	32	BBCC	Ind	
Stage & Screen Technology and Marketing	PNK5	3FT deg		12-16	MO/DO	M/D	32	BBCC	Ind	
Travel & Tourism with Management	P7N1	3FT deg	g	12-16	MO/DO	M/D	32	BBCC	Ind	
Travel and Tourism and Marketing	NP57	3FT deg	g	12-16	MO/DO	M/D	32	BBCC	Ind	5
Travel and Tourism with Marketing	P7N5	3FT deg	g	12-16	MO/DO	M/D	32	BBCC	Ind	
Women's Studies and Built Environment	MN98	3FT deg		12-16	MO/DO	M/D	32	BBCC	Ind	
Women's Studies and Business Systems	MN9C	3FT deg		12-16	MO/DO	M/D	32	BBCC	Ind	
Women's Studies with Built Environment	M9N8	3FT deg		12-16	MO/DO	M/D	32	BBCC	Ind	
Women's Studies with Business Systems	M9NC	3FT deg		12-16	MO/DO	M/D	32	BBCC	Ind	
Business Studies	421N	2FT HND	g	4-8	N/MO	P/M	26	CCDD	Ind	7 2/6
Business and Property Studies	18NN	2FT HND	g	12-16	MO/DO	M/D	32	BBCC	Ind	

Univ of MANCHESTER

Computer Science with Business and Management	G5N1	3FT deg	S/M g	BBC	Ind	D$^	28$	BBBBB$	X	13 16/28
Engineering with Business	H1N1	3FT deg	M+P	18	Ind		30	AAAAA	Ind	10
Engineering with Business	H1NC	4FT deg	M+P	18	Ind		30	AAAAA	Ind	5
Engineering, Business and Management	HN11	3FT deg	M+P	18	Ind		30	AAAAA	Ind	14
Materials Science with Business & Mgt (MMatSci)	J5N9	4FT deg	2(M/P/C) g	CCC	4M+1D	DS	28$	CSYS	Ind	
Mathematics with Business and Management	G1N1	3FT deg	M	22-24	Ind		30$	CSYS	Ind	6 21/30
Physics with Business and Management (BSc/MPhys)	F3N1	3FT/4FT deg	M+P	BCC-BBC	4M+2D$	D^	30$	CSYS	Ind	4 20/20

UMIST (Manchester)

Civil Engineering and Environmental Mgt (MEng)	H2N8	4FT deg	M+P g	BCC	3M+3D$	Ind	30$	CSYS	Ind	2 18/22
Clothing Engineering and Management (4 Yrs)	J4N9	4SW deg	M/P/C g	18	5M	Ind	25	BBBCC	Ind	
Engineering Manufacture and Management (MEng)	H7N1	4FT deg	M+P g	BBB	DO $	Ind	32$	CSYS$	Ind	8 22/30
International Management with French	N1R1	4FT deg	F g	ABB	X	Ind	35$	CSYS$	Ind	4 20/30
International Management with German	N1R2	4FT deg	G g	BBC	X	Ind	30$	CSYS$	Ind	3 18/30
International Mgt with American Bus St (4 Yrs)	N1Q4	4FT deg	* g	ABB	1M+6D	Ind	35	CSYS	Ind	10 26/30
Management	N101	3FT deg	* g	BBB	3M+4D	D$^ go	32	CSYS	Ind	
Management & Marketing of Textiles with Ind Exp	J4NM	4SW deg	* g	BCC	4M+1D	M$6/^ go	30	BBBCC	Ind	
Management & Mkting of Textiles with a Mod Lang	J4N5	4FT deg	* g	BCC	X	Ind	Ind	BBBCC	Ind	5
Management (Decision Science)	N1N2	3FT deg	* g	BBB	3M+4D	D$^ go	32	CSYS	Ind	
Management (Employment and Organisation)	N1N6	3FT deg	* g	BBB	3M+4D	D$^ go	32	CSYS	Ind	
Management (Human Resources)	N130	3FT deg	* g	BBB	3M+4D	D$^ go	32	CSYS	Ind	
Management (International Business Economics)	N146	3FT deg	* g	BBB	3M+4D	D$^ go	32	CSYS	Ind	
Management (International Studies)	N145	3FT deg	* g	BBB	3M+4D	D$^ go	32	CSYS	Ind	
Management (Marketing)	N1N5	3FT deg	* g	BBB	3M+4D	D$^ go	32	CSYS	Ind	
Management (Operations and Technology)	N125	3FT deg	* g	BBB	3M+4D	D$^ go	32	CSYS	Ind	
Management and Chemical Sciences	NF11	3FT deg	C g	18	3M+1D	MS6/^ go	30	CSYS	Ind	3 14/18
Management and Information Technology	GN51	3FT deg								
Management and Marketing of Textiles	J4N1	3FT deg	* g	BCC	4M+1D	D$6/^ go	30	BBBCC	Ind	2 10/22
Materials Science with Business and Mgt (4 Yrs)	J5N9	4FT deg	2(M/P/C) g	CCC	4M+1D$	Ind	28$	CSYS	Ind	
Mathematics and Management Sciences	GN11	3FT deg	M g	BBC	Ind	M*^ go	30$	CSYS	Ind	4 16/26
Paper Science with Management	J5N1	3FT deg	M/P/C g	CCD	3M	DS^	27$	BBBC$	Ind	6
Textile Technology and Management	J4NC	3FT deg	M/P/C g	18	5M $	Ind	25	BBBCC	Ind	13
Textile Technology and Mgt with Industrial Exp	J4ND	4SW deg	M/P/C	18	5M $	Ind	25	BBBCC	Ind	

Business and Management 12

TITLE	CODE	COURSE	SUBJECTS	A/AS	NO/C	AGNVQ	IB	SQA(H)	SQA	RATIO A/AS
MANCHESTER METROPOLITAN Univ										
Business	N120	4SW deg	* g	20	M+D	D* go	24	BBBB	Ind	14/22
Business Administration	N122	3FT deg	*	CC	2M+3D	D	Ind	BBB	Ind	9/18
Business Administration	N100	1FT deg			HN $					
Business Administration (HND top-up)	N123	1FT deg								
Business Studies/American Studies	NQ14	3FT deg	*	CC	M	D	29	BBB	Ind	
Business Studies/Applied Social Studies	LN31	3FT deg	*	CC	M	D	28	BBB	Ind	
Business in Europe-French Route	N1R1	4FT deg	F g	BBC	Ind	DB	24$	Ind	Ind	14/24
Business in Europe-German Route	N1R2	4FT deg	G g	BBC	Ind	DB	24$	Ind	Ind	14/18
Business in Europe-Italian Route	N1R3	4FT deg	* g	BBC	Ind	DB	24$	Ind	Ind	14/20
Business in Europe-Spanish Route	N1R4	4FT deg	* g	BBC	Ind	DB	24$	Ind	Ind	10/22
Business with Leisure (HND top-up)	N1NR	1FT deg								10/16
Business with Sport (HND top-up)	NN1R	1FT deg								
Consumer Product Marketing and Technology	N510	3FT deg	* g	12	Ind	M	24	CCCC	Ind	
Consumer Protection	N984	3FT deg	* g	12	Ind	M	24	CCCC	Ind	10/20
Cultural Studies/Business Studies	LNH1	3FT deg	*	CC	M+D	D	28	CCCC	Ind	
Dance/Business Studies	NW14	3FT deg	*	CC	M+D	D	28	CCCC	Ind	
Design & Technology/Business Studies	NW12	3FT deg	*	CD	M+D	D	28	CCCC	Ind	
Drama/Business Studies	NW1K	3FT deg	*	CC	M+D	D	28	CCCC	Ind	
Electronic Eng with Management with Study in Eur	H6NC	4SW deg	M+P	10	MO $	ME2	24$	CCC$	Ind	
Electronic Engineering with Management	H6N1	3FT/4SW deg	M+P	10	MO $	ME2	24$	CCC$	Ind	
English/Business Studies	NQ13	3FT deg	*	CC	M+D	D	28	CCCC	Ind	
Environmental Science/Business Studies	FN91	3FT deg	*	CC	M+D	D	28	CCCC	Ind	
Food Manufacturing Management	D4N1	4SW deg	S g	8-10	Ind	M	24	CCCC	Ind	6/12
Food Manufacturing Management (Foundation)	D4NC	5SW deg	M/P	E	2M $	P$	$	$	Ind	
Geography/Business Studies	LN81	3FT deg	*	CC	M+D	D	28	CCCC	Ind	
Health Studies/Business Studies	BN91	3FT deg	*	CC	M+D	D	28	CCCC	Ind	
History/Business Studies	NV11	3FT deg	*	CC	M+D	D	28	CCCC	Ind	
International Business	N145	4FT deg	* g	BBC	Ind	DB	24	Ind	Ind	
Leisure Studies/Business Studies	LN41	3FT deg	*	CC	M+D	D	28	CCCC	Ind	
Life Science/Business Studies	CN11	3FT deg	*	CC	M+D	D	28	CCCC	Ind	
Manufacturing Management	HN71	3FT deg	* g	DDD	3M	M$	24$	BB$	Ind	10/16
Manufacturing Management (Foundation)	HN7C▼	4FT deg	M/P	E	2M $	P$	$	$	Ind	
Music/Business Studies	NW13	3FT deg	*	CC	M+D	D	28	CCCC	Ind	
Philosophy/Business Studies	NV17	3FT deg	*	CC	M+D	D	28	CCCC	Ind	
Religious Studies/Business Studies	NV18	3FT deg	*	CC	M+D	D	28	CCCC	Ind	
Retail Marketing	N550	4SW deg	* g	18	Ind	D	Ind	BBBB	Ind	10/24
Sport/Business Studies	BN61	3FT deg	S	BC	M+D	DS	28	CCCC	Ind	
Writing/Business Studies	NW1L	3FT deg	*	CC	M+D	D	28	CCCC	Ind	
Business	421N	2FT HND	* g	10	MO	M* go	Ind	CCCC	Ind	6/12
Business Administration	321N	2FT HND	* g	10	MO	M	Ind	CCCC	Ind	2/8
Business with Leisure	71NN	2FT HND	* g	4	M+D	M	24	C	Ind	2/8
Business with Sport	17NN	2FT HND	* g	4	3M	M	24	C	Ind	2/8
MATTHEW BOULTON COLL of F & HE										
Business	021N	2FT HND	*	4	MO		Dip		N	
MIDDLESEX Univ										
Business Administration	N122▼	3FT deg	* g	16	MO+1D	D$ go	26	Ind	Ind	8 9/20
Business Studies	N120▼	4SW deg	* g	16	MO+1D	D$ go	26	Ind	Ind	8 8/19
Electronic Engineering and Management	H6N1▼	3FT/4SW deg	S g	10	3M	M$ go	24	Ind	Ind	23
Electronics and Business	HN61▼	3FT deg	S g	10	3M	M$ go	24	Ind	Ind	
Environment and Business Management	FNY1▼	3FT deg	* g	12-16	5M	M$ go	26	Ind	Ind	5

course details | 98 expected requirements | 96 entry stats

TITLE	CODE	COURSE	SUBJECTS	A/AS	ND/C	AGNVQ	IB	SQA(H)	SQA	RATIO A/AS
Environmental Management and Policy	FNX1▼	3FT deg	* g	12-16	5M	M$ go	26	Ind	Ind	8
Housing Studies	KN48▼	3FT deg	* g	12	5M	M$ go	24	Ind	Ind	
Human Resource Management	N130▼	3FT deg	* g	16	MO+1D	D$ go	26	Ind	Ind	4	8/14
Industrial and Business Systems	J9N1▼	3FT/4SW deg	S g	10	3M	M$ go	24	CCCC	Ind	32
International Management	N140▼	3FT deg	* g	16	MO+1D	D$ go	26	Ind	Ind	
Manufacturing Engineering and Management	HN71▼	3FT/4SW deg	S g	10	3M	M$ go	24	Ind	Ind	7
Manufacturing Management	H7N1▼	3FT deg	S g	10	3M	M$ go	24	Ind	Ind	
Marketing	N500▼	3FT deg	* g	16	MO+1D	D$ go	26	Ind	Ind	2
Mathematics for Business	G1N1▼	4SW deg	M g	8	MO	M$^ go	24	CCCC	Ind	4
Occupational Health and Safety Management	N610▼	1FT deg	X	X	X	X	X	X	X	
Water Science and Management	FN9C▼	3FT deg	* g	12-16	5M	M$ go	28	BBCC	Ind	5
Joint Honours Degree Business Information Systems	Y400	3FT deg	* g	12-16	5M	M$ go	24	CCCC	Ind	
Joint Honours Degree Business Policy	Y400	3FT deg	* g	16	MO	M$ go	26	CCCC	Ind	
Joint Honours Degree Business Studies	Y400	3FT deg	* g	16	MO+1D	M$ go	26	BCCCC	Ind	
Joint Honours Degree Human Resource Management	Y400	3FT deg	* g	12-16	MO+1D	M$ go	26	CCCC	Ind	
Joint Honours Degree Management	Y400	3FT deg	* g	14-16	MO+1D	D$ go	26	CCCC	Ind	
Joint Honours Degree Marketing	Y400	3FT deg	* g	16	MO+1D	D$ go	26	CCCC	Ind	
Electronic Systems with Business Studies	16NH▼	2FT HND	S g	E	N	P$ go	24	Ind	Ind	3
Housing Studies	84NK▼	2FT HND	* g	E	N	P$ go				
Public Art Project Management	11NE▼	2FT HND								

NAPIER Univ

Business Administration	N120	3FT/4FT deg	*	BC-CDD	M+D	DB	Ind	BBCC$	Ind	16
Business Information Management	N122	3FT/4FT deg	*	CD-CEE	Ind	Ind	Ind	BCCC$	Ind	5
Business Studies	N100	4SW/5SW deg	*	BC-CDD	M+D	DB	Ind	BBCC$	Ind	7	10/14
Business Studies and Languages	NT12	4SW/5SW deg	*	CDD	Ind	Ind	Ind	BBCC	Ind	
Commerce	N150	3SW/4SW deg	*	CDE-CC	Ind	Ind	Ind	BBCC$	Ind	3	8/12
Engineering with Management	H1N1	3FT/4SW deg	M	CD	Ind	Ind	Ind	BBB$	Ind	6
Estate Management	N800	3FT/4FT deg	*	CCC	MO	M$	Ind	BBCC	Ind	5
Hospitality and Marketing	NN57	3FT/4FT deg	*	CCD	Ind	Ind	Ind	BBCC	Ind	
Languages and Export Management	NT59	3FT/4FT deg	F/G	CDE	Ind	Ind	Ind	BBCC$	Ind	3	8/14
Languages and Marketing	NT5X	3FT/4FT deg	*	CCD	Ind	Ind	Ind	BBCC	Ind	
Management and Technology	HN11	3FT/4FT deg	*	DD	Ind	Ind	Ind	BBC	Ind	2
Marketing Management	NN15	3FT/4FT deg	*	DDD	Ind	Ind	Ind	BBCC	Ind	5	8/16
Marketing and Tourism	NP57	3FT/4FT deg	*	CCD	Ind	Ind	Ind	BBCC	Ind	
Science with Management Studies	Y1N1	4FT/5SW deg	2(M/P/C/B)	DD	Ind	Ind	Ind	BCC	Ind	
Social and Management Sciences	LN31	3FT/4FT deg	g	CD	Ind	Ind	Ind	BCCC	Ind	3	10/12
Transport Studies	NJ99	3FT/4FT deg		CC	Ind	Ind	Ind	BBCC	Ind	
Transport Studies with Information Management	N9P2	3FT/4FT deg		CC	Ind	Ind	Ind	BBCC	Ind	
Business Administration	221N	2FT HND	*	EE-D	Ind	Ind	Ind	CC	Ind	4	3/ 6

NENE COLLEGE

American St with Personal & Organisational Devel	Q4N6	3FT deg		DD	5M	M	24	CCC	Ind	
American Studies with Business Administration	Q4N1	3FT deg	g	DD	5M	M	24	CCC	Ind	
Art and Design with Business Administration	W2N1	3FT deg	g	DD	5M	M	24	CCC	Ind	
Art and Design with Marketing Communications	W2N5	3FT deg	g	DD	5M	M	24	CCC	Ind	
Bus Admin with Personal & Organisational Develop	N1N6	3FT deg	g	10	M+1D	M	24	BCC	Ind	
Business Admin with Industry and Enterprise	N1H1	3FT deg	g	10	M+1D	M	24	BCC	Ind	
Business Admin with Marketing Communications	N1N5	3FT deg	g	10	M+1D	M	24	BCC	Ind	9/16

course details			98 expected requirements							96 entry stats

TITLE	CODE	COURSE	SUBJECTS	A/AS	ND/C	AGNVQ	IB	SQA(H)	SQA	RATIO A/AS
Business Admin with Media and Popular Culture	N1P4	3FT deg	g	10	M+1D	M	24	BCC	Ind	
Business Admin with Third World Development	N1M9	3FT deg	g	10	M+1D	M	24	BCC	Ind	
Business Admin with Wastes Mgt & the Environment	N1FX	3FT deg	g	10	M+1D	M	24	BCC	Ind	
Business Administration and Management (Top-up)	N150	1FT deg								
Business Administration with American Studies	N1Q4	3FT deg	g	10	M+1D	M	24	BCC	Ind	
Business Administration with Architectural St	N1V4	3FT deg	g	10	M+1D	M	24	BCC	Ind	
Business Administration with Art and Design	N1W2	3FT deg	g	10	M+1D	M	24	BCC	Ind	
Business Administration with Economics	N1L1	3FT deg	g	10	M+1D	M	24	BCC	Ind	6/14
Business Administration with Energy Management	N1J9	3FT deg	g	10	M+1D	M	24	BCC	Ind	
Business Administration with English	N1Q3	3FT deg	g	10	M+1D	M	24	BCC	Ind	
Business Administration with European Union St	N1T2	3FT deg	g	10	M+1D	M	24	BCC	Ind	
Business Administration with Geography	N1F8	3FT deg	g	10	M+1D	M	24	CCC	Ind	
Business Administration with Health Studies	N1L5	3FT deg	g	10	M+1D	M	24	BCC	Ind	
Business Administration with History	N1V1	3FT deg	g	10	M+1D	M	24	BCC	Ind	
Business Administration with Information Systems	N1G5	3FT deg	g	10	M+1D	M	24	BCC	Ind	8/12
Business Administration with Law	N1M3	3FT deg	g	10	M+1D	M	24	BCC	Ind	10/15
Business Administration with Management Science	N1G4	3FT deg	g	10	M+1D	M	24	BCC	Ind	
Business Administration with Mathematics	N1G1	3FT deg	M	10	M+1D	M	24	BCC	Ind	
Business Administration with Politics	N1M1	3FT deg	g	10	M+1D	M	24	BCC	Ind	
Business Administration with Property Management	N1N8	3FT deg	g	10	M+1D	M	24	BCC	Ind	
Business Administration with Psychology	N1C8	3FT deg	g	10	M+1D	M	24	BCC	Ind	6/14
Business Enterprise	NN13	3FT deg								
Business Studies	N120	4SW deg	g	12	M+1D	M	24	CCC	Ind	8/20
Drama with Marketing Communications	W4N5	3FT deg		10	5M+1D	M	24	CCC	Ind	
Drama with Personal and Organisational Develop	W4N6	3FT deg		10	5M+1D	M	24	CCC	Ind	
Earth Science with Business Administration	F9N1	3FT deg	g	DD	5M	M	24	CCC	Ind	
Earth Science with Personal & Organisational Dev	F9N6	3FT deg		DD	5M	M				
Economics with Business Administration	L1N1	3FT deg	g	6	5M	M	24	CCC	Ind	
Economics with Personal and Organisational Devel	L1N6	3FT deg	g	6	5M	M	24	CCC	Ind	
Education with Personal and Organisational Devel	X9N6	3FT deg		DD	5M	M	24	CCC	Ind	
Energy Management with Business Administration	J9N1	3FT deg	g	EE	3M	P	24	CCC	Ind	
Energy Management with Property Management	J9N8	3FT deg	g	EE	3M	P	24	CCC	Ind	
English with Business Administration	Q3N1	3FT deg	g	CC	4M+1D	M	24	CCC	Ind	
English with Marketing Communications	Q3N5▼	3FT deg		CC	4M+1D	M	24	CCC	Ind	
English with Personal and Organisational Develop	Q3N6▼	3FT deg		CC	4M+1D	M	24	CCC	Ind	
Equine Studies with Estates Studies	D2N8	1FT deg								
European Business (French)	NR11	4SW deg	F g	8	M+D	M	24	CCC	Ind	
European Business (German)	NR12	4SW deg	G g	8	M+D	M	24	CCC	Ind	
European Business (Italian)	NR13	4SW deg	I g	8	M+D	M	24	CCC	Ind	
European Business (Spanish)	NR14	4SW deg	Sp g	8	M+D	M	24	CCC	Ind	
French with Marketing Communications	R1N5	3FT deg		DD	5M	Ind	24	CCC	Ind	
Geography with Business Administration	F8N1	3FT deg	Gy g	8	5M	M	24	CCC	Ind	8/24
Geography with Marketing Communications	F8N5	3FT deg	Gy	8	5M	M	24	CCC	Ind	
Geography with Personal and Organisational Devel	F8N6	3FT deg	Gy	8	5M	M	24	CCC	Ind	
Geography with Property Management	F8N8	3FT deg	Gy	8	5M	M	24	CCC	Ind	
History with Business Administration	V1N1	3FT deg	g	CD	5M	M	24	CCC	Ind	
History with Marketing Communications	V1N5▼	3FT deg		CD	5M	M	24	CCC	Ind	
Ind & Enterprise with Marketing Communication	H1N5	3FT deg	g	EE	3M	P	24	CCC	Ind	
Ind & Enterprise/Personal & Organisational Devel	H1N6	3FT deg	g	EE	3M	P	24	CCC	Ind	
Industrial Archaeology with Property Management	V6N8	3FT deg		10	5M	M	24	CCC	Ind	
Industry & Enterprise with Business Admin	H1N1	3FT deg	g	EE	3M	P	24	CCC	Ind	4/7
Industry and Enterprise with Property Management	H1N8	3FT deg	g	EE	3M	P	24	CCC	Ind	

course details | 98 expected requirements | 96 entry stats

TITLE	CODE	COURSE	SUBJECTS	A/AS	ND/C	AGNVQ	IB	SQA(H)	SQA	RATIO A/AS
Info Systs with Personal & Organisational Devel	G5N6	3FT deg		6	5M	M	24	CCC	Ind	
Information Systems with Business Administration	G5N1	3FT deg	g	6	5M	M	24	CCC	Ind	
Law with Business Administration	M3N1	3FT deg	g	10	3M+2D	M	24	CCC	Ind	6/20
Law with Marketing Communications	M3N5	3FT deg	g	10	3M+2D	M	24	CCC	Ind	
Law with Personal and Organisational Development	M3N6	3FT deg	g	10	3M+2D	M	24	CCC	Ind	
Law with Property Management	M3N8	3FT deg	g	10	3M+2D	M	24	CCC	Ind	
Management Science with Business Administration	G4N1	3FT deg	g	DD	5M	M	24	CCC	Ind	
Management Science with Marketing Communications	G4N5	3FT deg	g	DD	5M	M	24	CCC	Ind	
Management Science with Property Management	G4N8	3FT deg	g	DD	5M	M	24	CCC	Ind	
Mathematics with Business Administration	G1N1	3FT deg	M	DD	Ind	Ind	24	CCC	Ind	
Mathematics with Marketing Communications	G1N5	3FT deg	M	DD	Ind	Ind	24	CCC	Ind	
Mgt Sci with Personal & Organisational Develop	G4N6	3FT deg	g	EE	5M	M	24	CCC	Ind	
Music with Business Administration	W3N1	3FT deg	Mu g	DD	5M	M	24	CCC	Ind	
Music with Personal & Organisational Development	W3N6	3FT deg	Mu	DD	5M	M	24	CCC	Ind	
Politics with Business Administration	M1N1	3FT deg	g	DD	5M	M	24	CCC	Ind	
Politics with Personal Organisational Develop	M1N6	3FT deg		CD	5M	M	24	CCC	Ind	
Psychology with Business Administration	C8N1	3FT deg	g	CC	5M+1D	M	24	CCC	Ind	
Psychology with Personal & Organisational Devel	C8N6▼	3FT deg	g	CC	5M+D	M	24	CCC	Ind	
Sociology with Marketing Communications	L3N5▼	3FT deg		10	5M	M	24	CCC	Ind	
Sociology with Personal & Organisational Develop	L3N6▼	3FT deg		10	5M	M	24	CCC	Ind	
Sociology with Property Management	L3N8	3FT deg		10	5M	M	24	CCC	Ind	
Sport St with Personal & Organisational Develop	N7N6▼	3FT deg	SS/Pe	12	M+2D	M	24		Ind	
Sport Studies with Property Management	N7N8	3FT deg	Ss/Pe	12	M+2D	M	24	BBB	Ind	
Business and Finance	421N▼	2FT HND	g	6	4M	P	24	CC	Ind	2/9
Countryside Management	98FN	2FT HND		E	P	P	24	CC	Ind	
Equine Studies with Estates Studies	8N2D	2FT HND		2	N	P		CC	Ind	

Univ of NEWCASTLE

TITLE	CODE	COURSE	SUBJECTS	A/AS	ND/C	AGNVQ	IB	SQA(H)	SQA	RATIO A/AS
Agri-Business Economics and Management	NL11	3FT deg	* g	CCC	Ind	Ind	Ind	BBBB	Ind	3	14/23
Agri-Business Management	N180	4FT deg	* g	CCC	Ind	Ind	Ind	BBBB	Ind	5	10/20
Agri-Business Management and Marketing	DN41	3FT deg	* g	CCC	Ind	Ind	Ind	BBBB	Ind	3	12/24
Business Management	N100	3FT deg	* g	24	Ind	Ind	32	AAAAB	Ind	15	22/28
Economics and Business Management	LN11	3FT/4SW deg	* g	BBB	Ind	Ind	Ind	AABBB	Ind	18	24/30
European Business Management	N140	4FT deg	* g	24	Ind	Ind	32	AAAAB	Ind	14	22/28
International Business Management	N141	4FT deg	L g	24	Ind	Ind	32$	AAAAB$	Ind	14	24/30
Rural Environmental and Business Management	DN21	3FT deg	* g	CCC	Ind	Ind	Ind	BBBB	Ind	5	16/16

NEWCASTLE COLL

TITLE	CODE	COURSE
Beauty Therapy Management	018W▼	2FT HND
Business	001N▼	2FT HND
Business (Management of Caring)	091N▼	2FT HND
Leisure Studies	053L▼	2FT HND

NEW COLLEGE DURHAM

TITLE	CODE	COURSE	SUBJECTS	A/AS	ND/C	AGNVQ	IB	SQA(H)	SQA
Management and Administration	N100	1FT deg							
Business	021N	2FT/3SW HND	g	2	N	Ind	Ind	Ind	Ind
Business and Finance	421N	2FT HND	g	2	N	Ind	Ind	Ind	Ind
Business and Personnel	031N	2FT HND	g	2	N	Ind	Ind	Ind	Ind

Univ of Wales COLLEGE, NEWPORT

TITLE	CODE	COURSE	SUBJECTS	A/AS	ND/C	AGNVQ	IB	SQA(H)	SQA
Business Administration	N150	3FT deg	*	8-10	MO	D$	24	CCCC	Ind
Business Information Technology	GN71	3FT deg	*	8-10	3M	D$	Ind	Ind	Ind
Business Studies	N128	3FT/4FT HND/deg							
Business and Accounting	NN14	3FT deg	*	8-10	MO	D$	24	CCCC	Ind

			98 expected requirements							96 entry stats

TITLE	CODE	COURSE	SUBJECTS	A/AS	ND/C	RGNVQ	IB	SQA(H)	SQA	RATIO A/AS
Business and Legal Studies	MN31	3FT deg	*	8-10	MO	D$	24	CCCC	Ind	
Social Welfare and Organisations	LN41	3FT deg		8	MO	M				
Business Administration	421N	2FT HND	*	4	4M	M$	Ind	Ind	Ind	
Business Information Technology	17NG	2FT HND		2	N	P$	Ind	Ind	Ind	
European Business Studies	041N	2FT HND	*	4	4M	M$	Ind	Ind	Ind	
NORTHBROOK COLLEGE Sussex										
Information Systems and Business Management	GN51	3FT deg								
Marketing and Design Management	N5W2	3FT deg		10	4M	M				
Business Studies	021N	2FT HND	*	6-8	3M	Ind	Dip	Ind	Ind	
Business Studies with Languages	2T1N	2FT HND	*	6-8	3M	Ind	Dip	Ind	Ind	
Business and Marketing	51NN	2FT HND	*	6-8	3M	Ind	Dip	Ind	Ind	
Business and Travel and Tourism Management	71PN	2FT HND	*	6-8	3M	Ind	Dip	Ind	Ind	
International Business Management	541N	2FT HND	*	6-8	3M	Ind	Dip	Ind	Ind	
NESCOT										
Business Studies	N120	3FT deg	*	DD	MO	M*	Dip	Ind	N	7
Business Studies	N128	4FT deg	*							14
Management and Financial Services	NN13	4FT deg	*							
Management and Financial Services	NN31	3FT deg	*	DD	MO	M	Dip	Ind	N$	
Business	021N	2FT HND	*	D	6M	M	Dip	Ind	N$	5 3/10
NORTH EAST WALES INST of HE										
Aeronautical & Mechanical Eng with Business Stds	H4N1	3FT deg		4-8	3M	M$	Ind	CCC	N$	
Business Studies	N100	3FT deg		6-12	3M	M$	Ind	CCC	N$	5/18
Business Studies with Accountancy	N1N4	3FT deg		6-12	3M	M$	Ind	CCC	N$	
Business Studies with Human Resource Management	N1N6	3FT deg		6-12	3M	M$	Ind	CCC	N$	
Business Studies with Marketing	N1N5	3FT deg		6-12	3M	M$	Ind	CCC	N$	
Business and Media Studies	NP14	3FT deg		6-12	3M	M$		CCC	N$	
Construction Management	KN21	3FT deg		6-12	3M	M$	Ind	CCC	N$	
Design (Small Business Practice)	W2N1	3FT deg	Pf							
Design (Small Business Practice)	E2N1	3FT deg	Pf							
Electrical and Electronic Eng with Bus Studies	H6N1	3FT deg		4-8	3M	M$	Ind	CCC	N$	
Glass/Small Business Practice	WJ1H	3FT deg	Pf		Ind	Ind	Ind	Ind	Ind	
Heritage Management	KN99	3FT deg		4-10	3M	M$	Ind	CCC	N$	
Jewellery Metalwork/Small Business Practice	EN61	3FT deg	Pf		Ind	Ind	Ind	Ind	Ind	
Jewellery Metalwork/Small Business Practice	WN61	3FT deg	Pf		Ind	Ind	Ind	Ind	Ind	
Manufacturing Systems Engineering with Bus St	H7ND	3FT deg		4-8	3M	M$	Ind	CCC	N$	
Business	021N	2FT HND		2-6	N	P$	Ind	CC	N$	4/ 8
Business Information Technology	1N5G	2FT HND		2-4	2M	P$	Ind	CC	N$	
Manufacturing Management	1N7H	2FT HND		2-4	2M	P$	Ind	CC	N$	
NORTH EAST WORCESTERSHIRE COLL										
Business	021N	2FT HND								
NORTH LINCOLNSHIRE COLLEGE										
Business Administration	051N	2FT HND	* g	DD	MO $	M$	Ind	Ind	Ind	
Univ of NORTH LONDON										
Business Administration	N150	3FT deg	* g	14	MO+4D	Ind	Ind	CCCC	Ind	
Business Economics and Consumer Studies	LN15	3FT/4SW deg	* g	CC	Ind	D* go	Ind	Ind	Ind	10
Business Economics and Finance	N124	3FT deg	* g	14	MO+4D	Ind	Ind	CCCC	Ind	14 8/19
Business Information Systems	G5N1	3FT/4SW/4EXT deg	M/P/Cs/St/Es	CC	4M $	M* go	$	Ind	Ind	12
Business Studies	N120	4SW deg	* g	14	MO+4D	Ind	Ind	CCCC	Ind	16 8/18
Business and Applied Psychology	NL17	3FT deg	* g	CC	MO+4D	D	Ind	CCCCC	Ind	

course details

TITLE	CODE	COURSE	SUBJECTS	A/AS	ND/C	AGNVQ	IB	SQA(H)	SQA	RATIO A/AS
Business and Communications Engineering	HN61	3FT/4SW/4EXT deg	M+P/Es/Cs/Ds	12	MO+4D	DE go	Ind	Ind	Ind	
Business and Computing	GN51	3FT/4SW/4EXT deg	M/Cs/P/Es/St	12	MO+4D	D* go	Ind	Ind	Ind	
Business and Law	MN31	3FT deg	* g	CC	Ind	Ind	Ind	Ind	Ind	
Business and Philosophy	NV17	3FT deg	* g	12	MO+4D	D	Ind	Ind	Ind	
Business and Politics	NM11	3FT deg	* g	CC	MO+4D	D	Ind	CCCCC	Ind	
Business and Polymer Engineering	JN41	3FT/4SW/4EXT deg	M/Ph	CD	MO+4D	DE	Ind	Ind	Ind	
Business and Sociology	LN31	3FT deg	*	CC	Ind	Ind	Ind	Ind	Ind	
Chemistry and Business	FN11	3FT/4SW/4EXT deg	C g	12-14	MO+4D	DS	Ind	Ind	Ind	
Comm & Cultural Studies & Business	LNP1	3FT deg	Me/Cm/E/So g	CC	Ind	Ind	Ind	Ind	Ind	
Communication & Cultural Studies & Arts Mgt	LN61	3FT deg	Cm/Me/E/So g	CC	MO	M	Ind	Ind	Ind	8
Computer Electronics and Business	HNP1	3FT/4SW/4EXT deg	M+P/Es/Cs/Ds	12	MO+4D	DE go	Ind	Ind	Ind	
Decision Systems and Business	N240	3FT deg	M/Ph/Ec/Cs g	12	3M $	M	Ind	Ind	Ind	
Education Studies and Business	NX19	3FT deg	* G	12	MO+4D	D	Ind	Ind	Ind	
Electronics and International Business	HN6C	3FT/4SW/4EXT deg	M+P/Es/Cs/Ds	12	MO+4D	DE go	Ind	Ind	Ind	
European Studies and International Business	NT12	3FT deg	* g	12	MO+4D	D	Ind	Ind	Ind	
Film Studies and Arts Management	NWC5	3FT deg	* g	BC	MO+4D	D	Ind	Ind	Ind	
Food & Consumer Studies	DN49	3FT/4SW/4EXT deg	He/M/Ec/Ph	CC	4M $	M$	24	Ind	Ind	6
Human Resource Studies and Consumer Studies	NN15	3FT/4SW deg	* g	CC	MO+4D	DS	Ind	Ind	Ind	13
Human Resource Studies and Public Administration	NL14	3FT deg	* g	CC	MO+4D	M	Ind	Ind	Ind	4
Human Resource Studies and Women's Studies	NM19	3FT deg	* g	CC	MO+4D	D	Ind	Ind	Ind	
Information Technology and Business	GN5C	3FT/4SW/4EXT deg	M/Cs/P/Es/St g	12	MO+4D	Ind	Ind	Ind	Ind	
International Business	N140	4SW deg	* g	14	MO+4D	Ind	Ind	CCCC	Ind	9 8/20
International Business and French	NR11	4FT deg	* g	CC	MO+4D	D	Ind	Ind	Ind	14
International Business and German	NR12	4FT deg	* g	CC	MO+4D	D	Ind	Ind	Ind	15
International Business and Politics	NMC1	3FT deg	* g	CC	MO+4D	D	Ind	Ind	Ind	
International Business and Polymers	NJ1K	3FT deg	M/Ph	CC	MO+4D	D$	Ind	Ind	Ind	
International Business and Spanish	NR14	4FT deg	* g	CC	MO+4D	D	Ind	Ind	Ind	7
Marketing and Communication & Cultural Studies	LN65	3FT deg	Cm/Me/E/So g	CC	Ind	Ind	Ind	Ind	Ind	
Marketing and French	NR51	4FT deg	* g	CC	MO+4D	D	Ind	Ind	Ind	
Marketing and Social Research	LN35	3FT deg	* g	CC	MO+4D	D	Ind	Ind	Ind	
Marketing and Spanish & Latin American Studies	NR54	4FT deg	* g	CC	MO+4D	D	Ind	Ind	Ind	
Mathematical Sciences and Business	GN11	3FT/4SW/4EXT deg	* g	10-12	MO+4D	Ind	Ind	Ind	Ind	
Mathematics and Business	GN1C	3FT/4SW/4EXT deg	M g	12	X	Ind	Ind	Ind	Ind	
Psychology (Applied) and Human Resource Studies	LN71	3FT deg	* g	CC	Ind	Ind	Ind	Ind	Ind	
Purchasing and Logistics	NN59	1FT Dip	*	X	X	X	X	X	X	
Retail Management and Geography	NL18	3FT deg	* g	12-14	MO+4D	D	Ind	Ind	Ind	
Sociology and Marketing	LN3M	3FT deg	* g	CC	Ind	Ind	Ind	Ind	Ind	
Statistics and Business	GN41	3FT/4SW/4EXT deg	* g	12	4M-2D$	Ind	Ind	Ind	Ind	
Theatre Studies and Arts Management	NWC4	3FT deg	* g	CC	MO+4D	D	Ind	Ind	Ind	
Combined Honours *Business*	Y400	3FT deg	* g	14	MO+4D	Ind	Ind	CCCC	Ind	
Combined Honours *Business Economics*	Y400	3FT deg	* g	14	MO+4D	Ind	Ind	CCCC	Ind	
Combined Honours *Business Operations Management*	Y400	3FT/4SW deg	* g	14	MO+4D	Ind	Ind	CCCC	Ind	
Combined Honours *Consumer Studies*	Y100	3FT/4SW/4EXT deg	*	CC	4M	M*	$	Ind	Ind	
Combined Honours *International Business*	Y400	3FT deg	* g	14	MO+4D	Ind	Ind	CCCC	Ind	
Combined Honours *Law in Business*	Y400	3FT deg	* g	14	MO+4D	Ind	Ind	CCCC	Ind	
Combined Honours *Marketing*	Y400	3FT deg	* g	14	MO+4D	Ind	Ind	CCCC	Ind	
Combined Honours *Retail Management*	Y400	3FT deg	* g	14	MO+4D	Ind	Ind	CCCC	Ind	

TITLE	CODE	COURSE	SUBJECTS	A/AS	NO/C	AGNVQ	IB	SQA(H)	SQA	RATIO A/AS
Accounting and Business Management	41NN	2FT HND	* g	6	10M	Ind	Ind	CCC	Ind	
Business Management	021N▼	2FT HND	* g	6	10M	Ind	Ind	CCC	Ind	10 2/6
Hospitality and Business Management	17NN	2FT HND	* g	4	8M	Ind	Ind	CCC	Ind	
Human Resource and Business Management	031N	2FT HND	* g	6	10M	Ind	Ind	CCC	Ind	
Marketing and Business Management	5CNN	2FT HND	* g	6	10M	Ind	Ind	CCC	Ind	
Operations and Business Management	21NN	2FT HND	* g	6	10M	Ind	Ind	Ind	Ind	

Univ of NORTHUMBRIA

TITLE	CODE	COURSE	SUBJECTS	A/AS	NO/C	AGNVQ	IB	SQA(H)	SQA	RATIO A/AS
Business Administration	N150▼	3FT deg	g	12	MO+2D	D	24	BCCCC	Ind	3
Business Studies	N120▼	4SW deg	* g	CCC	MO+4D	D+4	26	BBBCC	Ind	7 12/26
Business Systems and Information Technology	GN15	3FT deg	* g	12	MO+2D	D	26	BCCCC	Ind	
Computing for Business	G5N1	4SW deg	* g	12	4M	M gi	24	CCCC	Ind	5 10/20
Engineering with Business Studies	H1ND	3FT/4SW deg	* g	12	3M	M gi	24	CCCC	Ind	5
Human Resource Management	N130	4SW deg	* g	CCC	MO+4D	D4	26	BBBCC	Ind	7 16/24
International Business Administration	N140	3FT deg	* g	CCC	MO+4D	D4	26	BBBCC	Ind	20
International Business Studies	N1T9	4SW deg	* g	CCC	MO+4D	D4	26	BBBCC	Ind	4 14/26
International Business and Technology	H1N1	4FT deg	* g	12	MO	M gi	24	CCCC	Ind	2 10/16
International Business and Technology	H1NC	5EXT deg	*-g	2-4	Ind	Ind	Ind	Ind	Ind	2
Logistics (top up course)	N901	3FT deg	X	X	HN	X	X	X	HN	1
Marketing	N550	4SW deg	* g	CCC	MO+4D	D4	Ind	BBBCC	Ind	10 14/24
Mathematics with Business Administration	G1N1	3FT/4SW deg	M g	8-12	Ind	Ind	24$	BBC$	Ind	2 10/20
Mathematics with Business Administration (Ext)	G1NC	4EXT/5EXTSW deg	* g	2-4	Ind	Ind	Ind	Ind	Ind	
Secretarial and Business Administration	N172	3FT deg	* g	12	MO+2D	D	24	BCCCC	Ind	4 10/20
Combined Honours *Business Administration*	Y400▼	3FT deg	g	12-20	MO+3D	DB	26	BBCCC	Ind	
Business Administration	015N	2FT HND	* g	DD	MO	M	24	CCC	Ind	8/14
Business and Marketing Management	005N	2FT HND	* g	DD	MO	M	24	CCC	Ind	11 8/16
Business and Personnel/Resource Management	031N	2FT HND	* g	DD	MO	M	24	CCC	Ind	7 6/13

NORWICH: City COLL

TITLE	CODE	COURSE	SUBJECTS	A/AS	NO/C	AGNVQ	IB	SQA(H)	SQA	RATIO A/AS
Business Administration	N121	3FT deg	* g	EE	Ind	Ind	Ind	Ind	Ind	
Business Administration (HND top up)	N122	1FT deg		X	HN	X	X	X	X	
Human Resource Management	N130	3FT deg	* g	EE	Ind	P	Ind	Ind	Ind	
Human Resource Management (HND top up)	N131	1FT deg		X	HN	X	X	X	X	
Marketing	N500	3FT deg	* g	EE	Ind	P	Ind	Ind	Ind	
Marketing (HND top up)	N501	1FT deg		X	HN	X	X	X	X	
Business	001N	2FT HND	* g	E	N	P go	Ind	Ind	Ind	
Business and Finance	021N	2FT HND	* g	E	N	P* go	Ind	CC	Ind	2 2/15
Business and Marketing	51NN	2FT HND	* g	E	N	P* go	Ind	Ind	Ind	
Business and Personnel	61NN	2FT HND	* g	E	N	P* go	Ind	Ind	Ind	

Univ of NOTTINGHAM

TITLE	CODE	COURSE	SUBJECTS	A/AS	NO/C	AGNVQ	IB	SQA(H)	SQA	RATIO A/AS
Chemistry and Management Studies	FN11	3FT deg	C+P/M g	BBC-BBB	Ind	Ind	28$	CSYS	Ind	8 26/30
Computer Science and Management Studies	GN51	3FT deg	M	BBB	Ind		Ind	Ind	Ind	14 26/30
Industrial Economics	L1N1	3FT deg	* g	BBB	Ind	D*6/^ go	32	AAABB	Ind	5 24/30
Management Studies	N100	3FT deg	* g	BBB	Ind	D*6/^ go	32	AAABB	Ind	74 26/30
Management Studies with East European Studies	N1T1	3FT deg	g	BBB	Ind	D*6/△ go	32	AAABB	Ind	24/24
Management Studies with French	N1R1	4FT deg	E g	BBB	Ind	D*△ go	32$	AAABB$	Ind	26 24/30
Management Studies with German	N1R2	4FT deg	G g	BBB	Ind	D*△ go	32$	AAABB$	Ind	24 24/28
Management Studies with Portuguese	N1R5	4FT deg	L g	BBB	Ind	D*6/^ go	32	AAABB	Ind	4
Management Studies with Spanish	N1R4	4FT deg	S g	BBB	Ind	D*△ go	32$	AAABB$	Ind	13 26/28
Mathematics and Management Studies	GN11	3FT deg	M	AAB-ABB	Ind	Ind	Ind	Ind	Ind	10 28/30

course details			98 expected requirements							96 entry stats	
TITLE	CODE	COURSE	SUBJECTS	A/AS	ND/C	AGNVQ	IB	SQA(H)	SQA	RATIO	A/AS
NOTTINGHAM TRENT Univ											
Business Administration	N122	3FT deg	* g	18	M+D $	Ind	Ind	Ind	Ind	56	16/26
Business Administration & Environmental Studies	NF19▼	3FT deg	* g	12	Ind	M$ go	Ind	Ind	Ind	3	8/14
Business Administration & Urban Studies	NK14▼	3FT deg	* g	12	Ind	M$ go	Ind	Ind	Ind	3	8/14
Business Studies	N120	4SW deg	* g	18	M+D $		Ind	Ind	Ind	36	16/24
Business and Quality Management	N126	4SW deg	* g	16	M+D $		Ind	Ind	Ind	9	14/24
Civil Engineering with Management	H2N1	3FT/4SW deg	M+P	14	4M+D	D/MC6	Ind	Ind	Ind		
Countryside Management	DN21▼	3FT deg	* g	16	5M	Ind	Ind	Ind	Ind		
Countryside Management (Extended)	DN2D▼	4EXTFT deg	* g		Ind	Ind	Ind	Ind	Ind		
Economics and Industrial Management	LN16	3FT deg	* g	12	Ind	M$ go	Ind	Ind	Ind	2	9/14
Estate Surveying	N810	3FT/4SW deg	* g	16	5M		Ind	CCC	Ind	3	8/18
European Business with French	N1R1	4SW deg	F g	18	M+D $		24$	Ind	Ind	11	14/24
European Business with German	N1R2	4SW deg	G g	16	M+D $		24$	Ind	Ind	10	14/26
European Business with Spanish	N1R4	4SW deg	Sp g	16	M+D $		24$	Ind	Ind	24	20/23
Health and Safety Management (Extended)	N619▼	4EXT/5EXTSW deg	* g		Ind	Ind	Ind	Ind	Ind	4	
Industrial Management	N611	3FT/4SW deg	* g	10-14	3M $	Ind	Ind	DD$	$	2	10/18
Industrial Management (Extended)	N618▼	4EXT/5EXTSW deg	* g		Ind	Ind	Ind	Ind	Ind		
Industrial Management and Psychology	CN86	3FT deg	* g	12	Ind	Ind	Ind	Ind	Ind		10/14
Occupational Health and Safety Management	N610	3FT/4SW deg	S g	12	N		24$	Ind	N	1	6/20
Property Development	N831	3FT/4SW deg	* g	16	5M	Ind	Ind	Ind	Ind		
Residential Development	N830	4SW deg	* g	14	6M $		Ind	CCC	Ind		
Rural Land and Property Management	KN28▼	3FT deg	* g	16	5M	Ind	Ind	Ind	Ind		
Urban and Rural Open Space Management	N801▼	3FT/4SW deg	* g	14	Ind	Ind	Ind	Ind	Ind		
Urban and Rural Open Space Management (Extended)	N808▼	4EXT/5EXTSW deg	* g		Ind	Ind	Ind	Ind	Ind		
Working with Technology	GN51	3FT deg	* g	8	3M	M	Ind	CCCC	N	2	6/14
Business Administration	051N▼	2FT HND	* g	CD	M+D	M$	Ind	Ind	Ind	7	2/16
Business Studies	421N	2FT/3SW HND	* g	CD	M+D	M$	Ind	Ind	Ind	27	10/17
Business and Finance	31NN▼	2FT/3SW HND	* g	CD	Ind	Ind	Ind	Ind	Ind		
Estate Surveying	018N	2FT HND	* g	4-6	3M		Ind	Ind	Ind	3	2/ 6
Rural Land Management	208N▼	3SW HND	S g	E	N	Ind	Dip	D	N	4	10/12
OXFORD Univ											
Economics and Management	LN11	3FT deg	*		AAB	DO		36	AAAAA	Ind	7	28/30
Engineering, Economics and Management Management	Y630	4FT deg	M+P		AAB	DO		36	AAAAA	Ind		
Materials, Economics and Management Management	Y634	4FT deg	2S		AAB-ABB	DO		36	AAAAA	Ind		
OXFORD BROOKES Univ											
Business Admin and Mgt/Accounting and Finance	NN14	3FT deg	* g	BCC-BBC	Ind	MB4/DB3	Ind	Ind	Ind	6	16/24
Business Administration and Management/Biology	CN11	3FT deg	S g	DD-BCC	Ind	MS/MB4	Ind	Ind	Ind	7	
Business Administration and Mgt/Anthropology	LN61	3FT deg	* g	BCC-BBC	Ind	MB4/^4	Ind	Ind	Ind		
Business Administration and Mgt/Biological Chem	CN71	3FT deg			Ind		Ind	Ind	Ind		
Business and Management	N122	3FT/4SW deg	* g	CCC-BCD	Ind	MB4	Ind	Ind	Ind	6	10/20
Business and Retail Management	NN51	3FT deg			Ind		Ind	Ind	Ind		
Cartography/Business Administration & Management	FN81	3FT deg	* g	CC-BBC	Ind	MB/MB4	Ind	Ind	Ind		
Cell Biology/Business Administration and Mgt	CNC1	3FT deg									
Combined Studies/Business Administration and Mgt	NY14	3FT deg		X		X	X	X			
Computer Systems/Business Admin and Management	GN61	3FT deg	* g	BC-BBC	Ind	MB/MB4	Ind	Ind	Ind	12	
Computing Mathematics/Business Admin & Mgt	GN91	3FT deg	* g	CD-BBC	Ind	M*/MB4	Ind	Ind	Ind		
Computing/Business Administration & Management	GN51	3FT deg	* g	CDD-BBC	Ind	M*/MB4	Ind	Ind	Ind	11	
Ecology/Business Administration and Management	CN91	3FT deg	* g	CD-BBC	Ind	MS/MB4	Ind	Ind	Ind		
Economics/Business Administration & Management	LN11	3FT deg	* g	BB-BBC	Ind	MB3	Ind	Ind	Ind	9	
Educational Studies/Business Admin & Management	NX19	3FT deg	* g	CC-BBC	Ind	M*3/MB4	Ind	Ind	Ind		

	course details			*98 expected requirements*							*96 entry stats*
TITLE	CODE	COURSE	SUBJECTS	A/AS	ND/C	AGNVQ	IB	SQA(H)	SQA	RATIO	A/AS
Electronics/Business Administration & Management	HN61	3FT deg	S/M	CC-BBC	Ind	M$/MB4	Ind	Ind	Ind		
English Studies/Business Administration & Mgt	NQ13	3FT deg	* g	AB-BCC	Ind	M*^/MB4	Ind	Ind	Ind	15	
Environmental Chemistry/Bus Admin & Management	NF11	3FT deg									
Environmental Policy/Business Admin & Mgt	KN31	3FT deg									
Environmental Sciences/Business Admin & Mgt	FNX1	3FT deg	S g	CD-BBC	Ind	MB4/DS	Ind	Ind	Ind	6	
Estate Management	N800	3FT deg	* g	16	Ind	D	Ind	Ind	Ind	3	11/22
European Business Studies	N140	4SW deg	F/G g	18	Ind	MN4	Ind	Ind	Ind	11	8/22
Exercise and Health/Business Admin & Management	NB16	3FT deg	S	DD-BBC	Ind	MS/MB4	Ind	Ind	Ind		
Fine Art/Business Administration and Management	NW11	3FT deg	Pf+A g	BC-BBC	Ind	MA^/MB4	Ind	Ind	Ind		
Food Science and Nutrition/Bus Admin & Mgt	DN41	3FT deg	S g	DD-BBC	Ind	MS/MB4	Ind	Ind	Ind	8	
French Language & Literature/Business Adm & Mgt	NR11	4SW deg	F g	CDD-BBC	Ind	M^/MB4	Ind	Ind	Ind	13	
French Language and Contemp St/Bus Adm & Mgt	NR1C	4SW deg	F g	CDD-BBC	Ind	MB^/4	Ind	Ind	Ind	10	
Geography and the Phys Env/Business Admin & Mgt	FNV1	3FT deg									
Geography and the Phys Env/Marketing Management	FNVN	3FT deg									
Geography/Business Administration & Management	LN81	3FT deg	* g	CCD-BBC	Ind	M*/MB4	Ind	Ind	Ind	40	
Geology/Business Administration and Management	FN61	3FT deg	S/M	DD-BBC	Ind	PS/MB4	Ind	Ind	Ind		
Geotechnics/Business Administration & Management	HN21	3FT deg	S/M/Ds/Es	DD-BBC	Ind	M$/MB4	Ind	Ind	Ind		
German Language and Contemp Stud/Bus Admin & Mgt	NR1F	4SW deg	G g	DDD-BBC	Ind	M^/MB4	Ind	Ind	Ind		
German Language and Lit/Business Admin and Mgt	NR12	4SW deg	G g	DDD-BBC	Ind	M^/MB4	Ind	Ind	Ind		
German Studies/Business Administration and Mgt	RNG1	4SW deg			Ind		Ind	Ind	Ind		
Health Care/Business Admin & Mgt (Post Exp)	BN71	3FT deg		X		X	X	X			
History of Art/Business Administration & Mgt	NV14	3FT deg	* g	BCC-BBC	Ind	M^/MB4	Ind	Ind	Ind	8	
History/Business Administration & Management	NV11	3FT deg	* g	BB-BBC	Ind	M^/MB4	Ind	Ind	Ind	15	
Hospitality Mgt Studs/Business Admin and Mgt	NN17	3FT deg	* g	DDD-BBC	Ind	M*3/MB4	Ind	Ind	Ind	8	
Human Biology/Business Admin and Management	BN11	3FT deg			Ind		Ind	Ind	Ind		
Information Systems/Business Admin & Management	GNM1	3FT deg	* g	CDD-BBC	Ind	MB/MB4	Ind	Ind	Ind	5	
Information Systems/Retail Management	GNM5	3FT deg			Ind		Ind	Ind	Ind	4	
Intelligent Systems/Business Admin & Management	GN81	3FT deg	* g	CD-BBC	Ind	M*/MB4	Ind	Ind	Ind		
International Business Management	N145	3FT deg									
Lang for Bus:Italian-Ab Initio/Spanish-Post GCSE	TN91	4FT deg									
Langs for Bus:Italian-Ab Initio/English-Post A	NQCJ	4FT deg									
Langs for Bus:Italian-Ab Initio/French-Post A	TNGC	4FT deg									
Langs for Bus:Italian-Ab Initio/French-Post GCSE	NT1Q	4FT deg									
Langs for Bus:Italian-Ab Initio/German-Ab Initio	NRD2	4FT deg									
Langs for Bus:Italian-Ab Initio/German-Post A	TNGD	4FT deg									
Langs for Bus:Italian-Ab Initio/German-Post GCSE	T2N1	4FT deg									
Langs for Bus:Italian-Ab Initio/Japanese-Ab Init	NTC4	4FT deg									
Langs for Bus:Italian-Ab Initio/Spanish-Ab Init	NRCK	4FT deg									
Langs for Bus:Italian-Ab Initio/Spanish-Post A	TNYD	4FT deg									
Langs for Business:English/Japanese-Ab Initio	NT14	4FT deg	E	BC-CDD	Ind	M*^	Ind	Ind	Ind		
Languages for Bus:Italian/Japanese-Ab Initio	NTCK	4FT deg	I	BC-CDD	Ind	M*^	Ind	Ind	Ind		
Languages for Business:English/French-Post A	NTCF	4FT deg	E+F	BC-CDD	Ind	M*^	Ind	Ind	Ind		
Languages for Business:English/French-Post GCSE	NT12	4FT deg	E g	BC-CDD	Ind	M*^	Ind	Ind	Ind	1	
Languages for Business:English/German-Ab Initio	NR1G	4FT deg	E	BC-CDD	Ind	M*^	Ind	Ind	Ind	1	
Languages for Business:English/German-Post A	TNF1	4FT deg	E+G	BC-CDD	Ind	M*^	Ind	Ind	Ind		
Languages for Business:English/German-Post GCSE	NTDG	4FT deg	E g	BC-CDD	Ind	M*^	Ind	Ind	Ind		
Languages for Business:English/Italian Ab Initio	NR13	4FT deg	E	BC-CDD	Ind	M*^	Ind	Ind	Ind		
Languages for Business:English/Italian-Post A	NTCX	4FT deg	E+I	BC-CDD	Ind	M*^	Ind	Ind	Ind		
Languages for Business:English/Italian-Post GCSE	NT19	4FT deg	E g	BC-CDD	Ind	M*^	Ind	Ind	Ind		
Languages for Business:English/Spanish-Ab Initio	NR14	4FT deg	E	BC-CDD	Ind	M*^	Ind	Ind	Ind		
Languages for Business:English/Spanish-Post A	TNX1	4FT deg	E+Sp	BC-CDD	Ind	M*^	Ind	Ind	Ind	1	
Languages for Business:English/Spanish-Post GCSE	NTDY	4FT deg	E g	BC-CDD	Ind	M*^	Ind	Ind	Ind		

course details
98 expected requirements
96 entry stats

TITLE	CODE	COURSE	SUBJECTS	A/AS	NO/C	RGNVQ	IB	SQA(H)	SQA	RATIO A/AS
Languages for Business:French/English-Post A	NQCH	4FT deg	F+E	BC-CDD	Ind	M*^	Ind	Ind	Ind	
Languages for Business:French/German-Ab Initio	NRCF	4FT deg	F	BC-CDD	Ind	M*^	Ind	Ind	Ind	
Languages for Business:French/German-Post A	TNFC	4FT deg	F+G	BC-CDD	Ind	M*^	Ind	Ind	Ind	6
Languages for Business:French/German-Post GCSE	TN21	4FT deg	F g	BC-CDD	Ind	M*^	Ind	Ind	Ind	3
Languages for Business:French/Italian-Ab Initio	NR1H	4FT deg	F	BC-CDD	Ind	M*^	Ind	Ind	Ind	5 14/22
Languages for Business:French/Italian-Post A	NTCY	4FT deg	F+I	BC-CDD	Ind	M*^	Ind	Ind	Ind	2
Languages for Business:French/Italian-Post GCSE	NT1X	4FT deg	F g	BC-CDD	Ind	M*^	Ind	Ind	Ind	4
Languages for Business:French/Japanese-Ab Initio	NT1K	4FT deg	F	BC-CDD	Ind	M*^	Ind	Ind	Ind	12
Languages for Business:French/Spanish-Ab Initio	NR1K	4FT deg	F	BC-CDD	Ind	M*^	Ind	Ind	Ind	8
Languages for Business:French/Spanish-Post A	TNXC	4FT deg	F+Sp	BC-CDD	Ind	M*^	Ind	Ind	Ind	4 18/22
Languages for Business:French/Spanish-Post GCSE	TNYC	4FT deg	F g	BC-CDD	Ind	M*^	Ind	Ind	Ind	5
Languages for Business:German/English-Post A	NQ1H	4FT deg	G+E	BC-CDD	Ind	M*^	Ind	Ind	Ind	
Languages for Business:German/French-Post A	NTCG	4FT deg	G+F	BC-CDD	Ind	M*^	Ind	Ind	Ind	5
Languages for Business:German/French-Post GCSE	NT1F	4FT deg	G g	BC-CDD	Ind	M*^	Ind	Ind	Ind	
Languages for Business:German/Italian-Ab Initio	NR1J	4FT deg	G	BC-CDD	Ind	M*^	Ind	Ind	Ind	2
Languages for Business:German/Italian-Post A	NTD9	4FT deg	G+I	BC-CDD	Ind	M*^	Ind	Ind	Ind	
Languages for Business:German/Italian-Post GCSE	NT1Y	4FT deg	G g	BC-CDD	Ind	M*^	Ind	Ind	Ind	
Languages for Business:German/Japanese-Ab Initio	NT1L	4FT deg	G	BC-CDD	Ind	M*^	Ind	Ind	Ind	2
Languages for Business:German/Spanish-Ab Initio	NR1L	4FT deg	G	BC-CDD	Ind	M*^	Ind	Ind	Ind	2
Languages for Business:German/Spanish-Post A	TNXD	4FT deg	G+Sp	BC-CDD	Ind	M*^	Ind	Ind	Ind	
Languages for Business:German/Spanish-Post GCSE	TN9C	4FT deg	G g	BC-CDD	Ind	M*^	Ind	Ind	Ind	
Languages for Business:Italian/English-Post A	NQ1J	4FT deg	I+E	BC-CDD	Ind	M*^	Ind	Ind	Ind	
Languages for Business:Italian/French-Post A	NTD2	4FT deg	I+F	BC-CDD	Ind	M*^	Ind	Ind	Ind	
Languages for Business:Italian/French-Post GCSE	NT1G	4FT deg	I	BC-CDD	Ind	M*^	Ind	Ind	Ind	
Languages for Business:Italian/German-Ab Initio	NRCG	4FT deg	I	BC-CDD	Ind	M*^	Ind	Ind	Ind	6
Languages for Business:Italian/German-Post A	TNFD	4FT deg	I+G	BC-CDD	Ind	M*^	Ind	Ind	Ind	
Languages for Business:Italian/German-Post GCSE	TN2C	4FT deg	I g	BC-CDD	Ind	M*^	Ind	Ind	Ind	
Languages for Business:Italian/Spanish-Ab Initio	NRC4	4FT deg	I	BC-CDD	Ind	M*^	Ind	Ind	Ind	2
Languages for Business:Italian/Spanish-Post A	TNY1	4FT deg	I+Sp	BC-CDD	Ind	M*^	Ind	Ind	Ind	
Languages for Business:Italian/Spanish-Post GCSE	TN9D	4FT deg	I g	BC-CDD	Ind	M*^	Ind	Ind	Ind	
Languages for Business:Span/Japanese-Ab Initio	NTCL	4FT deg	Sp	BC-CDD	Ind	M*^	Ind	Ind	Ind	
Languages for Business:Spanish/English-Post A	NQC3	4FT deg	Sp+E	CDD-BC	Ind	M*^	Ind	Ind	Ind	
Languages for Business:Spanish/French-Post A	NTDF	4FT deg	Sp+F	BC-CDD	Ind	M*^	Ind	Ind	Ind	5
Languages for Business:Spanish/French-Post GCSE	NTC2	4FT deg	Sp g	BC-CDD	Ind	M*^	Ind	Ind	Ind	8
Languages for Business:Spanish/German-Ab Initio	NRC2	4FT deg	Sp	BC-CDD	Ind	M*^	Ind	Ind	Ind	
Languages for Business:Spanish/German-Post A	TNG1	4FT deg	Sp+G	BC-CDD	Ind	M*^	Ind	Ind	Ind	
Languages for Business:Spanish/German-Post GCSE	TN2D	4FT deg	Sp g	BC-CDD	Ind	M*^	Ind	Ind	Ind	
Languages for Business:Spanish/Italian-Ab Initio	NRC3	4FT deg	Sp	BC-CDD	Ind	M*^	Ind	Ind	Ind	5
Languages for Business:Spanish/Italian-Post A	NTDX	4FT deg	Sp+I	BC-CDD	Ind	M*^	Ind	Ind	Ind	
Languages for Business:Spanish/Italian-Post GCSE	NTC9	4FT deg	Sp g	BC-CDD	Ind	M*^	Ind	Ind	Ind	
Law/Business Administration & Management	MN31	3FT deg	* g	BBC-BBB	Ind	MB4/D*3	Ind	Ind	Ind	14
Leisure Planning/Business Administration and Mgt	KNH1	3FT deg								
Marketing Management	N500	3FT deg								
Marketing Management/Accounting and Finance	NN4N	3FT deg	* g	BCC	Ind	D*3	Ind	Ind	Ind	12
Marketing Management/Anthropology	LN6N	3FT deg	* g	BCC	Ind	M*^/D*3	Ind	Ind	Ind	
Marketing Management/Biological Chemistry	CN7N	3FT deg								
Marketing Management/Biology	CN1N	3FT deg	S g	DD-BCC	Ind	MS/D*3	Ind	Ind	Ind	7
Marketing Management/Business Admin & Management	NN1N	3FT deg	* g	BCC-BBC	Ind	MB4/D*3	Ind	Ind	Ind	68
Marketing Management/Cartography	FN8N	3FT deg	* g	DDD-BCC	Ind	M*/D*3	Ind	Ind	Ind	
Marketing Management/Cell Biology	CNCN	3FT deg								
Marketing Management/Combined Studies	NYN4	3FT deg		X		X	X	X		
Marketing Management/Computer Systems	GN6N	3FT deg	* g	CDD-BCC	Ind	M*/D*3	Ind	Ind	Ind	

			98 expected requirements							96 entry stats

TITLE	CODE	COURSE	SUBJECTS	A/AS	NO/C	AGNVQ	IB	SQA(H)	SQA	RATIO A/AS
Marketing Management/Computing	GN5N	3FT deg	* g	CDD-BCC	Ind	M*/D*3	Ind	Ind	Ind	3
Marketing Management/Computing Mathematics	GN9N	3FT deg	* g	CD-BCC	Ind	M*/D*3	Ind	Ind	Ind	
Marketing Management/Ecology	CN9N	3FT deg	* g	CD-BCC	Ind	MS/D*3	Ind	Ind	Ind	3
Marketing Management/Economics	LN1N	3FT deg	* g	CCD-BCC	Ind	M*3/D*3	Ind	Ind	Ind	11
Marketing Management/Educational Studies	NXN9	3FT deg	* g	CC-BCC	Ind	M*3/D*3	Ind	Ind	Ind	
Marketing Management/Electronics	HN6N	3FT deg	S/M g	CC-BCC	Ind	M$/D*3	Ind	Ind	Ind	
Marketing Management/English Studies	NQN3	3FT deg	* g	AB-BCC	Ind	M*^/D*3	Ind	Ind	Ind	
Marketing Management/Environmental Chemistry	FN1N	3FT deg								
Marketing Management/Environmental Policy	KN3N	3FT deg								
Marketing Management/Environmental Sciences	FNXN	3FT deg	S g	CD-BCC	Ind	DS/DS3	Ind	Ind	Ind	3
Marketing Management/Exercise and Health	NBN6	3FT deg	S g	DD-BCC	Ind	MS/D*3	Ind	Ind	Ind	
Marketing Management/Fine Art	NWN1	3FT deg	Pf+A g	BC-BCC	Ind	MA^/D*3	Ind	Ind	Ind	
Marketing Management/Food Science and Nutrition	DN4N	3FT deg	S g	DD-BCC	Ind	MS/D*3	Ind	Ind	Ind	
Marketing Management/French Lang and Contemp St	NRNC	4SW deg	F g	CC-BCC	Ind	M^/D*3	Ind	Ind	Ind	11
Marketing Management/French Language and Lit	NRN1	4SW deg	F g	CC-BCC	Ind	M^/D*3	Ind	Ind	Ind	
Marketing Management/Geography	LN8N	3FT deg	* g	BB-CCD	Ind	M*/D*3	Ind	Ind	Ind	25
Marketing Management/Geology	FN6N	3FT deg	S/M g	DD-BCC	Ind	PS/D*3	Ind	Ind	Ind	2
Marketing Management/Geotechnics	HN2N	3FT deg	S/M/Ds/Es g	DD-BCC	Ind	M$/D*3	Ind	Ind	Ind	
Marketing Management/German Lang & Contemp Stud	NRNF	4SW deg	G g	DDD-BCC	Ind	M^/D*3	Ind	Ind	Ind	
Marketing Management/German Language and Lit	NRN2	4SW deg	G g	DDD-BCC	Ind	M^/D*3	Ind	Ind	Ind	
Marketing Management/German Studies	NRNG	4SW deg	G g	DDD-BCC	Ind	M^/D*3				
Marketing Management/Health Care (Post Exp)	BN7N	3FT deg	X			X	X	X		
Marketing Management/History	NVN1	3FT deg	* g	BB-BCC	Ind	M^/D*B	Ind	Ind	Ind	3
Marketing Management/History of Art	NVN4	3FT deg	* g	BB-BCC	Ind	M^/D*3	Ind	Ind	Ind	2 14/20
Marketing Management/Hospitality Management St	NN7N	3FT deg	* g	DDD-BCC	Ind	M*3/D*3	Ind	Ind	Ind	4
Marketing Management/Human Biology	BN1N	3FT deg								
Marketing Management/Information Systems	GNMN	3FT deg	* g	CDD-BCC	Ind	M*/D*3	Ind	Ind	Ind	1
Marketing Management/Intelligent Systems	GN8N	3FT deg	* g	CD-BCC	Ind	M*/D*3	Ind	Ind	Ind	6
Marketing Management/Law	MN3N	3FT deg	* g	BCC-BBB	Ind	D*3	Ind	Ind	Ind	13
Marketing Management/Leisure Planning and Mgt	KNHN	3FT deg								
Mathematics/Business Administration & Management	GN11	3FT deg	M	DD-BBC	Ind	MB4/M^	Ind	Ind	Ind	13
Mathematics/Marketing Management	GN1N	3FT deg	M g	DD-BCC	Ind	M^/D*3	Ind	Ind	Ind	8
Music/Business Administration & Management	NW13	3FT deg	Mu g	DD-BBC	Ind	M/MB4	Ind	Ind	Ind	16
Music/Marketing Management	NWN3	3FT deg	Mu g	DD-BCC	Ind	M/D*3	Ind	Ind	Ind	
Palliative Care/Business Admin and Mgt(Post Exp)	BNR1	3FT deg		X		X	X	X		
Palliative Care/Marketing Management (Post Exp)	BNRN	3FT deg		X		X	X	X		
Planning Studies/Business Administration & Mgt	KN41	3FT deg	* g	DDD-BBC	Ind	M*/MB4	Ind	Ind	Ind	5
Planning Studies/Marketing Management	KN4N	3FT deg	* g	DDD-BCC	Ind	M*/D*3	Ind	Ind	Ind	
Politics/Business Administration and Management	MN11	3FT deg	* g	AB-CCC	Ind	M^/MB3	Ind	Ind	Ind	
Politics/Marketing Management	NMN1	3FT deg	* g	CCC-AB	Ind	M^/D*3	Ind	Ind	Ind	6
Psychology/Business Administration & Management	CN81	3FT deg	* g	BBC-BBC	Ind	M^/MB4	Ind	Ind	Ind	79
Psychology/Marketing Management	CN8N	3FT deg	* g	BCC-BBC	Ind	M^/D*3	Ind	Ind	Ind	74
Publishing/Business Administration & Management	NP15	3FT deg	* g	BB-CCD	Ind	MB4/M$3	Ind	Ind	Ind	2
Publishing/Marketing Management	NPN5	3FT deg	* g	BB-CCD	Ind	M$3/D*3	Ind	Ind	Ind	17
Rehabilitation/Business Admin and Mgt (Post Exp)	BNT1	3FT deg	X			X	X	X		
Rehabilitation/Marketing Management (Post Exp)	BNTN	3FT deg	X			X	X	X		
Retail Management/Biological Chemistry	CN75	3FT deg								
Retail Management/Biology	CN15	3FT deg	S/M g	DD-CCD	Ind		Ind	Ind	Ind	
Retail Management/Computer Systems	GN65	3FT deg			Ind		Ind	Ind	Ind	
Retail Management/Computing	GN55	3FT deg	* g	CDD-CCD	Ind		Ind	Ind	Ind	1
Retail Management/Computing Mathematics	GN95	3FT deg	* g	CD-CCD	Ind		Ind	Ind	Ind	
Retail Management/Ecology	CN95	3FT deg	* g	CD-CCD	Ind		Ind	Ind	Ind	

 *Letts* STUDY GUIDES
THE INDEPENDENT

TITLE	CODE	COURSE	SUBJECTS	A/AS	ND/C	AGNVQ	IB	SQA(H)	SQA	RATIO A/AS
course details				*98 expected requirements*						*96 entry stats*
Retail Management/Electronics	HN65	3FT deg	S/M g	CD-CCD	Ind		Ind	Ind	Ind	
Retail Management/Environmental Chemistry	FN15	3FT deg								
Retail Management/Environmental Policy	KN35	3FT deg								
Retail Management/Environmental Sciences	FNX5	3FT deg	S/M g	CD-CCD	Ind		Ind	Ind	Ind	
Retail Management/Exercise & Health	NB56	3FT deg	S/M g	DD-CCD	Ind		Ind	Ind	Ind	
Retail Management/Food Science and Nutrition	DN45	3FT deg	S/M g	DD-CCD	Ind		Ind	Ind	Ind	
Retail Management/Geology	FN65	3FT deg	S/M g	DD-CCD	Ind		Ind	Ind	Ind	
Retail Management/Geotechnics	HN25	3FT deg	S/M g	DD-CCD	Ind		Ind	Ind	Ind	
Retail Management/Intelligent Systems	GN85	3FT deg	* g	CD-CCD	Ind		Ind	Ind	Ind	1
Retail Management/Mathematics	GN15	3FT deg	M g	DD-CCD	Ind		Ind	Ind	Ind	
Retail Management/Music	NW53	3FT deg	Mu g	DD-CCD	Ind		Ind	Ind	Ind	
Retail Management/Planning Studies	KN45	3FT deg	* g	DD-CCD	Ind		Ind	Ind	Ind	3
Sociology/Business Administration & Management	LN31	3FT deg	* g	BCC-BBC	Ind	M*^/MB4	Ind	Ind	Ind	17
Sociology/Marketing Management	LN3N	3FT deg	* g	BCC	Ind	M*^/D*3	Ind	Ind	Ind	22
Sociology/Retail Management	LN35	3FT deg	* g	CCD-BCC	Ind		Ind	Ind	Ind	
Software Engineering/Business Admin and Mgt	GN71	3FT deg	* g	CDD-BBC	Ind	M*/MB4	Ind	Ind	Ind	
Software Engineering/Marketing Management	GN7N	3FT deg	* g	CDD-BCC	Ind	M*/D*3	Ind	Ind	Ind	
Software Engineering/Retail Management	GN75	3FT deg			Ind		Ind	Ind	Ind	
Statistics/Business Administration & Management	GN41	3FT deg	* g	DD-BBC	Ind	M*/MB4	Ind	Ind	Ind	14
Statistics/Marketing Management	GN4N	3FT deg	* g	DD-BCC	Ind	M*/D*3	Ind	Ind	Ind	3
Technology Management	JN91	3FT/4SW deg	* g	DDD	Ind	M$	Ind	Ind	Ind	2 6/22
Telecommunications/Business Administration & Mgt	NH1P	3FT deg								
Telecommunications/Marketing Management	HNPN	3FT deg								
Tourism/Business Administration & Management	NP17	3FT deg	* g	CCD-BBC	Ind	M*3/MB4	Ind	Ind	Ind	87
Tourism/Marketing Management	PN7N	3FT deg	* g	CCD-BCC	Ind	M*3/D*3	Ind	Ind	Ind	81
Transport Planning/Accounting and Finance	NN49	3FT deg	* g	BCC-DDD	Ind	M*/D*3	Ind	Ind	Ind	
Transport Planning/Anthropology	LN69	3FT deg	* g	BCC-DDD	Ind	M*^	Ind	Ind	Ind	
Transport Planning/Biological Chemistry	CN79	3FT deg								
Transport Planning/Business Administration & Mgt	NN19	3FT deg	* g	BBC-DDD	Ind	M*/MB4	Ind	Ind	Ind	7
Transport Planning/Cartography	FN89	3FT deg	* g	CC-DDD	Ind	M*	Ind	Ind	Ind	2
Transport Planning/Cell Biology	CNC9	3FT deg								
Transport Planning/Combined Studies	NY94	3FT deg		X		X	X	X		
Transport Planning/Computer Systems	GN69	3FT deg	* g	CDD-BC	Ind	M*	Ind	Ind	Ind	
Transport Planning/Computing	GN59	3FT deg	* g	BC-DDD	Ind	M*	Ind	Ind	Ind	
Transport Planning/Computing Mathematics	GN99	3FT deg	* g	CD-CC	Ind	M*	Ind	Ind	Ind	
Transport Planning/Economics	LN19	3FT deg	* g	BB-DDD	Ind	M*/M*3	Ind	Ind	Ind	1
Transport Planning/Educational Studies	NX99	3FT deg	* g	CC-DDD	Ind	M*/M*3	Ind	Ind	Ind	
Transport Planning/English Studies	NQ93	3FT deg	* g	AB-DDD	Ind	M*^	Ind	Ind	Ind	
Transport Planning/Environmental Chemistry	NF91	3FT deg								
Transport Planning/Environmental Policy	KN39	3FT deg								
Transport Planning/Environmental Sciences	FNX9	3FT deg	S g	CD-CC	Ind	M*/DS	Ind	Ind	Ind	
Transport Planning/Exercise and Health	NB96	3FT deg	S g	DD-CC	Ind	MS	Ind	Ind	Ind	
Transport Planning/Fine Art	NW91	3FT deg	Pf+A g	CC-BC	Ind	MA^	Ind	Ind	Ind	
Transport Planning/Food Science and Nutrition	DN49	3FT deg	S g	DD-CC	Ind	MS	Ind	Ind	Ind	
Transport Planning/French Language & Contemp St	NR9C	4SW deg	F g	CC-CDD	Ind	M*^	Ind	Ind	Ind	
Transport Planning/French Language & Literature	NR91	4SW deg	F g	CC-CDD	Ind	M*^	Ind	Ind	Ind	
Transport Planning/Geography	LN89	3FT deg	* g	BB-DDD	Ind	M*	Ind	Ind	Ind	7
Transport Planning/Geology	FN69	3FT deg	S/M g	DD-CC	Ind	PS/M*	Ind	Ind	Ind	
Transport Planning/Geotechnics	HN29	3FT deg	S/M/Ds/Es	CC-DD	Ind	M$	Ind	Ind	Ind	
Transport Planning/German Language & Contemp St	NR9F	4SW deg	G	CD-CC	Ind	M*^	Ind	Ind	Ind	
Transport Planning/German Language & Literature	NR92	4SW deg	G	CD-CC	Ind	M*^	Ind	Ind	Ind	
Transport Planning/German Studies	NR9G	4SW deg	G	CD-CC	Ind	M*^	Ind	Ind	Ind	

				98 expected requirements						96 entry stats
TITLE	**CODE**	**COURSE**	**SUBJECTS**	**A/AS**	**ND/C**	**AGNVQ**	**IB**	**SQA(H)**	**SQA**	**RATIO A/AS**
Transport Planning/Health Care (Post Exp)	BN79	3FT deg	X		X	X	X			
Transport Planning/History	NV91	3FT deg	* g	BB-DDD	Ind	M*^	Ind	Ind	Ind	1
Transport Planning/Hospitality Management Studs	NN79	3FT deg	* g	CC-DDD	Ind	M*/M*3	Ind	Ind	Ind	
Transport Planning/Human Biology	BN19	3FT deg								
Transport Planning/Information Systems	GNM9	3FT deg	* g	CC-BC	Ind	M*	Ind	Ind	Ind	
Transport Planning/Intelligent Systems	GN89	3FT deg	* g	CD-CC	Ind	M*	Ind	Ind	Ind	
Transport Planning/Leisure Planning & Management	KNH9	3FT deg								
Transport Planning/Marketing Management	NNN9	3FT deg	* g	BCC-DDD	Ind	M*/D*3	Ind	Ind	Ind	
Transport Planning/Mathematics	GN19	3FT deg	M	DD-CC	Ind	M*_^	Ind	Ind	Ind	
Transport Planning/Music	NW93	3FT deg	Mu	DD-CC	Ind	M*	Ind	Ind	Ind	
Transport Planning/Palliative Care (Post Exp)	BNR9	3FT deg	X		X	X	X			
Transport Planning/Physical Geography	FNV9	3FT deg								
Transport Planning/Planning Studies	KN49	3FT deg	* g	DD-DDD	Ind	M*	Ind	Ind	Ind	
Transport Planning/Psychology	CN89	3FT deg	* g	BBC-DDD	Ind	M*^	Ind	Ind	Ind	
Transport Planning/Publishing	NP95	3FT deg	* g	BB-DDD	Ind	M*/M$3	Ind	Ind	Ind	
Transport Planning/Rehabilitation	BNT9	3FT deg	X		X	X	X			
Transport Planning/Retail Management	NN59	3FT deg	* g	CCD-DDD	Ind		Ind	Ind	Ind	
Transport Planning/Sociology	LN39	3FT deg	* g	BCC-DDD	Ind	M*^	Ind	Ind	Ind	
Transport Planning/Software Engineering	GN79	3FT deg	* g	DDD-BC	Ind	M*	Ind	Ind	Ind	
Transport Planning/Statistics	GN49	3FT deg	* g	DD-CC	Ind	M*	Ind	Ind	Ind	
Transport Planning/Telecommunications	HNP9	3FT deg								
Transport Planning/Tourism	PN79	3FT deg	* g	BB-DDD	Ind	M*/M*3	Ind	Ind	Ind	5
Water Resources/Business Administration and Mgt	HNF1	3FT deg								
Water Resources/Marketing Management	HNFN	3FT deg								
Water Resources/Transport Planning	HNF9	3FT deg								

Univ of PAISLEY

Biology with Management	C1N1	3FT/4FT/5SW deg	* g	CCC-EE	Ind	Ind	Ind	BCC$	Ind	6
Business Administration (1 Year)	N151▼	1FT/2FT deg	X	X	HN	X	X	X	HN	2
Business Analysis	N240	3FT/4FT deg	* g	CCD	Ind	Ind	Ind	BCC	Ind	
Business Economics	LN11	3FT/4FT/4SW deg	* g	CCD	Ind	Ind	Ind	BCC	Ind	5
Business Information Technology & Marketing	GN75	4SW/5SW deg	* g	CC	Ind	Ind	Ind	BCCC	Ind	
Business and Management	N100	3FT/4FT/5SW deg	* g	BC-CCD	Ind	Ind	Ind	BBBC	Ind	4
Chemistry with Management	F1N1	3FT/4FT/5SW deg	* g	CCC-EE	Ind	Ind	Ind	BCC$	Ind	5
Land Economics	N820	4SW/5SW deg	* g	CC	Ind	Ind	Ind	BBB$	Ind	
Manufacturing Systems with Management	H7N1	4SW/5SW deg	M g	DD	Ind	Ind	Ind	BCC$	Ind	3
Manufacturing Systems with Management	H7NC	2FT Dip	M g	DD	Ind	Ind	Ind	CCC$	Ind	
Manufacturing Systems with Management (MEng)	H7ND	5SW deg	M g	CCC	Ind	Ind	Ind	BBC$	Ind	
Marketing	N500	3FT/4SW/5SW deg	* g	CC	Ind	Ind	Ind	BCCC	Ind	4	6/12
Mathematical Sciences with Management	G1N1	3FT/4FT/5SW deg	M+S g	CCC-EE	Ind	Ind	Ind	BCC$	Ind	
Physics with Management	F3N1	3FT/4FT/5SW deg	M+P g	CCC-EE	Ind	Ind	Ind	BCC$	Ind	10
Technology and Management	JN91	3FT/4SW/5SW deg	* g	DD	Ind	Ind	Ind	BCC	Ind	5

Univ of PLYMOUTH

Agriculture with Rural Estate Management	D2N8	4SW deg	2(S/Gy/Ec) g	12	3M	M$	Ind	CCC	Ind	1
Applied Economics with Business	L1NC	3FT deg	* g	CCD-CDD	MO	M$^	Ind	BCCC	Ind	4	10/18
Applied Economics with Transport	L1N9	3FT deg	* g	CCD-CDD	MO	M$^	Ind	BCCC	Ind	
Biotechnology with Business	C9N1	3FT/4SW deg	B+Bu g	16	4M	MS^	Ind	BBBB	Ind	
Business Administration	N150	3FT deg	* g	CCC-DDD	MO	M12^	Ind	CCCCC	Ind	
Business Economics with Transport	L1NX	3FT deg	* g	CDD-CCD	MO	M$^	Ind	BCCC	Ind	
Business Studies	N120	4SW deg	* g	CCC-CCD	MO	M12^	Ind	BBCC$	Ind	9	14/22
Business Studies Stage one degree modules	N121	4SW deg	* g	CCC-CCD	MO	M12^	Ind	BBCC$	Ind	
Business of Perfumery	N550	4SW deg	* g	CCC-CCD	MO	M12^	Ind	BBCC$	Ind	4

course details | 98 expected requirements | 96 entry stats

TITLE	CODE	COURSE	SUBJECTS	A/AS	NO/C	AGNVQ	IB	SQA(H)	SQA	RATIO A/AS
Chemistry with Business	F1N1	3FT deg	C+Bu g	CCD	3M	MS^	Ind	CCCC	Ind	
Design Technology and Business	H7N1	3FT/4SW deg	Ap g	10-11	5M $	M$	Ind	Ind	Ind	2 6/18
Electronics and Business Management	HN6C	3FT deg	Ap g	6	2M	ME^	Ind	Ind	Ind	
European Economics with Business	L1ND	3FT deg	* g	CDD-CCD	MO	M$^	Ind	BCCC	Ind	
European Economics with Transport	L1NY	3FT deg	* g	CDD-CCD	MO	M$^	Ind	BCCC	Ind	
Fisheries Studies with Maritime Business	J6N1	3FT deg	Ap g	14	5M $	M$	Ind	Ind	Ind	
Geography with Transport	F8N9	3FT deg	Gy g	16-18	X	M$^	Ind	Ind	Ind	28
Geology with Business	F6N1	3FT deg	S+Bu g	CCD	4M	MS	Ind	Ind	Ind	
Hydrography with Fisheries Science	F8NX	3FT deg	2(M/P/C/Ap) g	14	5M $	M$	Ind	Ind	Ind	
Hydrography with Maritime Business	F8N1	3FT deg	2(M/P/C/Ap) g	14	5M $	M$	Ind	Ind	Ind	
International Business	N140	4FT/4SW deg	F/G/I/Sp g	CCD-CCC	MO	M12^	Ind	BBCC	Ind	6 14/24
International Business with French	N1R1	4SW deg	F g	CCD-CCC	MO	M12^	Ind	BBCC	Ind	10 16/22
International Business with German	N1R2	4SW deg	G g	CCD-CCC	MO	M12^	Ind	BBCC	Ind	15 12/20
International Business with Italian	N1R3	4SW deg	I g	CCD-CCC	MO	M12^	Ind	BBCC	Ind	
International Business with Modern Languages	N1TX	4FT/4SW deg	L g	CCD-CCC	MO	M12^	Ind	BBCC	Ind	
International Business with Spanish	N1R4	4FT/4SW deg	Sp g	CCD-CCC	MO	M12^	Ind	BBCC	Ind	12 14/22
Law with Business	M3N1	3FT deg	Ap g	BCC-BBC	DO	D12^	Ind	BBBB$	Ind	20 16/22
Law with Transport	M3N9	3FT deg	Ap g	BCC-BBC	DO	D12^	Ind	BBBB$	Ind	
Marine Navigation with Fisheries Business Studs	J9N9	3FT deg	2(M/P/C) g	14	5M $	M$	Ind	CCCC	Ind	
Marine Navigation with Fisheries Science	J9NX	3FT deg	2(M/P/C) g	14	5M $	M$	Ind	CCCC	Ind	
Marine Navigation with Maritime Business	J9NY	3FT deg	2(M/P/C) g	14	5M $	M$	Ind	CCCC	Ind	1
Marine Technology with Fisheries Business Studs	J6NY	3FT deg	2(M/P/C) g	14	5M $	M$	Ind	CCCC	Ind	
Marine Technology with Maritime Business	J6NC	3FT deg	2(M/P/C) g	14	5M $	M$	Ind	CCCC	Ind	
Maritime Business	N100	3FT deg	* g	18	5M	M$	Ind	CCCC	Ind	5
Maritime Business with Astronomy	N1F5	3FT deg	* g	18	5M	M$	Ind	CCCC	Ind	
Maritime Business with Fisheries Business Studs	N1NX	3FT deg	* g	18	5M	M$	Ind	CCCC	Ind	
Maritime Business with Fisheries Science	N1NY	3FT deg	M/P/C g	18	5M	M$	Ind	CCCC	Ind	1
Maritime Business with Fisheries Technology	N1J6	3FT deg	* g	18	5M	M$	Ind	CCCC	Ind	
Maritime Business with Hydrography	N1F8	3FT deg	* g	18	5M	M$	Ind	CCCC	Ind	
Maritime Business with Marine Navigation	N1J9	3FT deg	* g	18	5M	M$	Ind	CCCC	Ind	8
Maritime Business with Maritime History	N1V1	3FT deg	* g	18	5M	M$	Ind	CCCC	Ind	5
Maritime Business with Maritime Law	N1M3	3FT deg	* g	18	5M	M$	Ind	CCCC	Ind	4
Maritime Business with Ocean Science	N1F7	3FT deg	* g	18	5M	M$	Ind	CCCC	Ind	
Maritime Business with Transport	N1N9	3FT deg	* g	18	5M	M$	Ind	CCCC	Ind	9
Maritime Business with Underwater Studies	N1FX	3FT deg	M/P/C g	18	5M	M$	Ind	CCCC	Ind	
Marketing	N500	4SW deg	* g	CCD-CCC	MO	M12^	Ind	BBCC$	Ind	10 14/20
Modern Languages with Business	T9N1	3FT/4SW deg	L g	C	Ind	Ind	Ind	Ind	Ind	
Ocean Science with Maritime Business	F7N1	3FT deg	S g	14-16	5M $	M$	Ind	CCCC	Ind	
Personnel Management	N160	4SW deg	Ap g	CCD-CCC	MO	M12^	Ind	BBCC$	Ind	10 12/22
Political Economy with Business	LN1C	3FT deg	Ap g	CDD-CCD	MO $	M$^	Ind	BCCC	Ind	
Political Economy with Transport	LN1X	3FT deg	Ap g	CDD-CCD	MO $	M$^	Ind	BCCC	Ind	
Politics with Transport	M1N9	3FT deg	* g	14	4M	M$	Ind	BBBC$	Ind	
Rural Estate Management	N800	4SW deg	2(S/Gy/Ec) g	12	3M $	M$	Ind	Ind	Ind	4 6/20
Statistics (App) with Management Science	G4N1	3FT deg	M/St g	10	MO $	M$	Ind	BBCC	Ind	2 10/16
Statistics (Applied) and Business	GN41	3FT deg	M/St g	10-15	MO $	M$	Ind	BBCC	Ind	
Statistics (Applied) with Business	G4NC	3FT deg	M/St g	10	MO $	M$	Ind	BBCC	Ind	
Statistics(App) and Mgt Sci with Transport	G4N9	3FT deg	M/St g	10	MO $	M$	Ind	BBCC	Ind	
Statistics(App) with Transport	G4NX	3FT deg	M/St g	10	MO $	M$	Ind	BBCC	Ind	
Transport	N920	3FT deg	* g	14	5M	M$	Ind	CCCC	Ind	6 10/16
Transport with Applied Economics	N9L1	3FT deg	Ec g	CCD	5M	M$	Ind	CCCC	Ind	
Transport with Geography	N9FW	3FT deg	Gy g	16	5M	M$	Ind	Ind	Ind	8
Transport with Maritime Law	N9MH	3FT deg	* g	14	5M	M$	Ind	CCCC	Ind	5

Business and Management 12

TITLE	CODE	COURSE	SUBJECTS	A/AS	NO/C	AGNVQ	IB	SQA(H)	SQA	RATIO A/AS
Underwater Studies with Maritime Business	F9NC	3FT deg	Ap g	14-16	5M $	M$	Ind	CCCC	Ind	
Extended Science (Foundation Year) *Rural Estate Management*	Y108▼	1FT/4EXT deg	S	2	Ind	P$	Ind	Ind	Ind	
Business & Finance(Travel & Tour opt) (S Devon)	121N	2FT HND	* g	4	MO	M*	Ind	Ind	Ind	3 4/13
Business and Finance (Retailing) (Plymouth CFE)	055N	2FT HND	*	2	MO	MB	Ind	Ind	Ind	2 2/6
Business and Finance (Somerset)	221N	2FT HND	*	6	MO	MB	Ind	Ind	Ind	3 4/18
Electronic Business Management (Somerset)	16NH	2FT HND	*	4	N $	P$	Ind	Ind	Ind	3
Electronics and Business Management	1PNH	2FT HND	Ap g	4	N $	PE^	Ind	Ind	Ind	
European Building Design & Management (S Devon)	1GNK	2FT/3SW HND	* g	2	N	P$	Ind	Ind	Ind	
European Building Design & Mgt (Somerset)	1FNK	2FT/3SW HND	* g	2	N	P$	Ind	Ind	Ind	

Univ of PORTSMOUTH

TITLE	CODE	COURSE	SUBJECTS	A/AS	NO/C	AGNVQ	IB	SQA(H)	SQA	RATIO A/AS
Business Administration	N122	3FT deg	* g	18	MO+2D	D$6/^ go	Dip	BBBBC	Ind	
Business Studies	N120	4SW deg	* g	18	MO+2D	D$6/^ go	Dip	BBBBC	Ind	7 12/20
Business and Finance (HND Top-up)	NN13	1FT deg	Bu	X	MO+2D	X	X	X	HN	
Business and Marketing (HND Top-up)	NN15	1FT deg	Bu	X	MO+2D	X	X	X	HN	
Business and Personnel (HND Top-up)	NN16	1FT deg	Bu	X	MO+2D	X	X	X	HN	
Economic and Business Policy	LN11	3FT deg	* g	16	4M+2D	D$6/^ go	Dip	CCCCC	Ind	7/12
Engineering Management	HN11	3FT deg	2(M/P/C/Cs/Es)	16	4M $	M$6/^	26	BBBB	N$	
Engineering with Business Management (BEng/MEng)	H1NC	3FT/4SW deg	2(M/P/C/Es/Cs)	16	4M $	M$6/^	26$	BBBB	N$	1 8/13
European Business	N140	4SW deg	F/G/Sp	18	X	D$^	Dip	CCCCC	Ind	4 12/22
Extended Business Degree Scheme	N128	4EXT/5EXTSW deg	*		Ind	Ind	Ind	Ind	Ind	3
International Business Studies	N145	4FT deg	* g	18	MO+2D	D$6/^ go	Dip	BCCCC	Ind	
Land Management	N800	3FT deg	*	14	6M	M*6/^	Dip	BBCC	Ind	5 4/16
Languages and International Trade	TN21	4FT deg	L	12	5M	M*6/^	25	BCCC	Ind	5 4/14
Law and Business	MN31	3FT deg	*	18	MO+2D	D$6/^ go	Dip	BBBCC	Ind	
Leisure Resource Management	NN78	3FT deg	*	14	6M	M*6/^	Dip	BBCC	Ind	
Property Development	N830	3FT deg	*							
Technology Management	N126	3FT/4SW deg	*	16	MO	D$6/^	26	BBBB	Ind	1 6/16
Business	001N▼	2FT HND	*	8	MO+1D	M*6/^	Dip	CCCC	Ind	

QUEEN MARGARET COLL

TITLE	CODE	COURSE	SUBJECTS	A/AS	NO/C	AGNVQ	IB	SQA(H)	SQA	RATIO A/AS
Applied Consumer Studies	N980	3FT/4FT deg	* g	DD	M+D	P* go	Dip	BCC	N	3 4/18
Applied Food Science with Marketing	D4N5	3FT/4FT deg	* g	EE	M+D	P$ go	Dip	CCC	N	3
Retail Business	N550	3FT/4FT deg	* g	DD	M+D	P* go	Dip	BCC	N	3 4/10
Combined Studies *Business Organisation*	Y600	3FT/4FT deg	*	BC	M+D	M/D$^ go	Ind	BBBC	Ind	
Combined Studies *Consumer Studies*	Y600	3FT/4FT deg	*	BC	M+D	M/D$^ go	Ind	BBBC	Ind	
Combined Studies *Marketing*	Y600	3FT/4FT deg	*	BC	M+D	M/D$^ go	Ind	BBBC	Ind	

QUEEN MARY & WESTFIELD COLL (Univ of London)

TITLE	CODE	COURSE	SUBJECTS	A/AS	NO/C	AGNVQ	IB	SQA(H)	SQA	RATIO A/AS
Biology with Business Studies	C1N1	3FT deg	B+C/P/M/Ec/Bu	16	6M $	MS^/DS	26$	BBBCC		
Chemistry with Business Studies	F1N1	3FT deg	C+B/P/M	CCC	5M $	DS	26$	BBBCC		
Computer Science with Business Studies	G5N1	3FT deg	g	BCC	3M+2D	D^	28$			
Engineering with Business Studies	H1N1	3FT deg	M	CDD-BCC	5M $	M$^	24$	BBBCC		
French with Business Studies	R1N1	4FT deg	F	18		M^	30$			
German with Business Studies	R2N1	4FT deg	G g	18		M^	30$			
Hispanic Studies with Business Studies	R4N1	4FT deg	g	18		M^				
Mathematics with Business Studies	G1N1	3FT deg	M			M$^				
Physics with Business Studies	F3N1	3FT deg	M+P	24		MS^				
Russian with Business Studies	R8N1	4FT deg	g	18		M^				

TITLE	CODE	COURSE	SUBJECTS	A/AS	ND/C	AGNVQ	IB	SQA(H)	SQA	RATIO A/AS
QUEEN'S Univ Belfast										
Computer Science with Bus Admin (inc prof exp)	GNMD	4SW deg								
Computer Science with Bus Admin (inc prof exp)	GNMC	4SW deg								
Computer Science with Business Administration	G5NC	3FT deg								
Computer Science with Business Administration	G5ND	3FT deg								
Management	N100	3FT deg	* g	BBB	2M+5D	D*^ go	32$	AABBB	Ind	6 22/26
Management with Business Economics	N1L1	3FT deg	* g	BBB	2M+5D	D*^ go	32$	AABBB	Ind	8
Management with Computer Science	N1G5	3FT deg	M/Cs g	BBB	X	D*^ go	32$	X	Ind	
Management with Economic and Social History	N1V3	3FT deg	* g	BBB	2M+5D	D*^ go	32$	AABBB	Ind	
Management with Economics	N1LC	3FT deg	* g	BBB	2M+5D	D*^ go	32$	AABBB	Ind	
Management with European Area Studies	N1T2	3FT deg	L/* g	BBB	2M+5D	D*^ go	32$	AABBB	Ind	
Management with French	N1R1	3FT deg	E g	BBB	X	D*^ go	32$	AABBB	X	5 22/28
Management with German	N1R2	3FT deg	G g	BBB	X	D*^ go	32$	AABBB	X	1
Management with Italian	N1R3	3FT deg	* g	BBB	2M+5D	D*^ go	32$	AABBB	Ind	
Management with Social Policy	N1L4	3FT deg	* g	BBB	2M+5D	D*^ go	32$	AABBB	Ind	
Management with Sociology	N1L3	3FT deg	* g	BBB	2M+5D	D*^ go	32$	AABBB	Ind	
Management with Spanish	N1R4	3FT deg	* g	BBB	2M+5D	D*^ go	32$	AABBB	Ind	2
Statistics and Operational Research	GN42	3FT/4FT deg	M g	CCC	Ind	D*^ go	28$	BBBC	Ind	12
READING COLLEGE AND SCHOOL OF ART AND DESIGN										
Business	021N	2FT HND								
Business and Finance	31NN	2FT HND								
Business and Marketing	51NN	2FT HND								
Business and Personnel	61NN	2FT deg								
Univ of READING										
Business Economics and Organisational Studies	LN11	3FT deg	* g	BCC	Ind	D$6/^ go	30	BBBB	Ind	12 18/26
French and Management Studies	NR11	4FT deg	E g	BBC	Ind	DB^ go	31$	BBBB$	Ind	8 14/26
German and Management Studies	NR12	4FT deg	* g	BBC	Ind	DB^ go	31	BBBB	Ind	28
International Management & Bus Admin with French	N1R1	4FT deg	F g	BBB	Ind	DB^ go	32$	ABBB$	Ind	
International Management & Bus Admin with German	N1R2	4FT deg	* g	BBB	Ind	DB^ go	32	ABBB	Ind	
International Management & Bus Admin with Ital	N1R3	4FT deg	* g	BBB	Ind	DB^ go	32	ABBB	Ind	
International Management with Japanese	N1T4	4FT deg	* g	BBB	Ind	DB^ go	32	ABBB	Ind	
Italian and Management Studies	NR13	4FT deg	* g	BCC	Ind	DB^ go	30	BBBB	Ind	9
Land Management	N800	3FT deg	* g	22	6M+2D	D$6/^ gi	30	BBBB	Ind	3
Management and Business Administration	N120	3FT deg	* g	BBB	Ind	DB^ go	32	ABBB	Ind	14 18/26
Univ College of RIPON & YORK ST JOHN										
Design and Technology/Management Studies	W2N1	3FT deg	Pf g	CD	MO	MA	27	BBBC		3 6/20
Design and Technology/Management Studies	E2N1	3FT deg	Pf g	CD	MO	MA	27	BBBC		
Environmental Science/Management Studies	F9N1	3FT deg	g	DD	M	M*	27	BBCC		2 8/20
Geography/Management Studies	L8N1	3FT deg	Gy g	CCD	X	M*^ g	30	BBBB		5 10/22
Physical Education/Management Studies	B6N1	3FT deg	g	BB-CCC	MO+3D	D$6/^ g	30	ABBB		
ROBERT GORDON Univ										
Applied Science and Management	FN91	3FT/4FT deg	S g	EE	N	Ind	Ind	BCC	Ind	
Business Administration	N122	3FT/4FT deg	E g	CCC	Ind	Ind	Ind	BBCC$	Ind	7
Business Computing	NG15	3FT/4FT deg	* g	DD	N	Ind	Ind	CCC$	Ind	3
Business Studies	N100	4SW/5SW deg	E g	CCC	Ind	Ind	Ind	BBCC$	Ind	4
Consumer Product Management	N980	3FT/4FT deg	* g	EE	N	Ind	Ind	CCC$	Ind	2
European Business Admin with Languages	N1T9	4FT deg	E+F/G g	CCC	Ind	Ind	Ind	BBBC$	Ind	4
Food Science with Management	D4N1	3FT/4FT deg	S g	DE	N	Ind	Ind	BCC$	Ind	27
Technology and Business	JN91	3FT/4FT deg	S g	EE	N	Ind	Ind	BCC$	Ind	1

Business and Management 12

TITLE	CODE	COURSE	SUBJECTS	A/AS	ND/C	AGNVQ	IB	SQA(H)	SQA	RATIO A/AS
ROEHAMPTON INST										
Applied Consumer Studies and Art for Community	WN19▼3FT deg		g	12	4M	P$ go	26	BCC	N	
Biology and Applied Consumer Studies	CN19▼3FT deg		B g	12	4M $	P$ go	26	CCC	N$	
Business Computing and Applied Consumer Studies	GN79▼3FT deg		g	12	3D	M$ go	26	BCC	N$	
Business Studies	N120▼3FT deg		g	DD	3D	MB^ go	26	BCC	N$	5 6/14
Business Studies and Applied Consumer Studies	NN19▼3FT deg		g	12	3D	M$ go	26	BCC	N$	14
Business Studies and Art for Community	NW11▼3FT deg		g	DD	3D	M$ go	26	BCC	N$	
Business Studies and Biology	CN11▼3FT deg		B g	12	3D $	M$ go	26	BCC	N$	6
Business Studies and Business Computing	GN71▼3FT deg		g	12	3D	M$ go	26	BCC	N$	
Dance Studies and Applied Consumer Studies	NW94▼3FT deg		g	CC	2M+2D$	M$ go	30	BBC	N$	
Dance Studies and Business Studies	NW14▼3FT deg		g	CC	3D	M$ go	30	BBC	Ind	12
Drama & Theatre Studies and Business Studies	NW1L▼3FT deg		T/E g	16	3D	M$^ go	30	BBC	Ind	19
Drama & Theatre Studs and Applied Consumer Studs	NWX4▼3FT deg		E/T g	16	2M+2D$	M$^ go	30	BBC	N$	
Education and Applied Consumer Studies	NX99▼3FT deg		g	12	4M	P$ go	26	BCC	N$	
Education and Business Studies	NX19▼3FT deg		g	DD	3D	M$ go	26	BCC	N	3
English Language & Linguist and App Consumer St	QN39▼3FT deg		E/L g	CC	2M+2D$	M$^	30	BBC	N$	
English Language & Linguist and Business Studies	QN31▼3FT deg		E/L g	CC	3D $	M$^ go	30	BBC	N$	
English Literature and Applied Consumer Studies	NQ93▼3FT deg		E g	CC	2M+2D$	M^ go	28	BBC	N$	
English Literature and Business Studies	NQ13▼3FT deg		E g	CC	3D $	M^ go	28	BBC	N$	4 12/16
Environmental Studies and Applied Consumer Studs	FN99▼3FT deg		B/Gy g	12	4M $	P$ go	26	BCC	N$	
Environmental Studies and Business Studies	NF19▼3FT deg		B/Gy g	DD	3D $	M$ go	26	BCC	N$	3
Film & Television Studies and Business Studies	NP14▼3FT deg		g	16	3D	M$^ go	30	BBC	N$	15
Film & Television Studs & Applied Consumer Studs	NP94▼3FT deg		g	16	2M+2D$	M$^ go	30	BBC	N$	
French and Applied Consumer Studies	NR91▼4FT deg		F g	12	4M $	P^ go	26	BCC	N$	
French and Business Studies	NR11▼4FT deg		F g	12	3D $	M^ go	26	BCC	N$	6
Geography and Applied Consumer Studies	NL98▼3FT deg		Gy g	12	4M $	P$ go	26	BCC	N$	
Geography and Business Studies	NL18▼3FT deg		Gy g	DD	3D $	M$ go	26	BCC	N$	5
Health Studies and Applied Consumer Studies	NB99▼3FT deg		B g	12	4M $	P$ go	26	BCC	N$	
Health Studies and Business Studies	BN91▼3FT deg		B g	12	3D	M$ go	26	BCC	Ind	8
History and Applied Consumer Studies	NV91▼3FT deg		H g	12	4M $	P^ go	26	BCC	N$	
History and Business Studies	NV11▼3FT deg		H g	DD	3D $	M^ go	26	BCC	N$	5
Human & Social Biology and Applied Consumer St	CNC9▼3FT deg		B g	12	4M $	P$ go	26	BCC	N$	2
Human & Social Biology and Business Studies	NC1C▼3FT deg		B g	12	3D $	M$ go	26	BCC	N$	2
Marketing French and Spanish	NT59▼4FT deg		F g	12	2M+2D$	P^	26	BCC	N$	7 6/10
Music and Applied Consumer Studies	NW93▼3FT deg		Mu g	12	4M $	P^	26	BCC	N$	
Music and Business Studies	NW13▼3FT deg		Mu g	DD	3D $	M^ go	26	BCC	N$	17
Natural Resource Studies and App Consumer Studs	DN29▼3FT deg		g	12	3M	P$ go	24	CCC	N$	
Natural Resource Studies and Business Studies	DN21▼3FT deg		g	DD	3D	M$ go	26	BCC	N$	
Psychology and Applied Consumer Studies	LN79▼3FT deg		g	CC	3D	M$ go	30	BBC	N$	
Psychology and Business Studies	NL17▼3FT deg		g	CC	3D	M$ go	30	BBC	N$	14
Retail & Product Management	N550▼3FT deg		g	12	3M	P$ go	24	CCC	N	2 4/12
Social Policy & Admin & Applied Consumer Studs	LN49▼3FT deg		g	12	4M	P$ go	26	BCC	N	2
Social Policy & Admin and Business Studies	NL14▼3FT deg		g	DD	3D	M$ go	26	BCC	N$	4
Sociology and Applied Consumer Studies	LN39▼3FT deg		g	12	4M	P$ go	26	BCC	N	
Sociology and Business Studies	NL13▼3FT deg		g	DD	3D	M$ go	26	BCC	N$	3 8/12
Spanish and Applied Consumer Studies	NR94▼4FT deg		Sp g	12	2M+2D$	P$ go	28	BBC	N$	1
Spanish and Business Studies	NR14▼4FT deg		Sp g	12	3D	M$ go	28	BBC	N$	3
Sport Studies and Applied Consumer Studies	NB96▼3FT deg		S g	12	3D	MS go	30	BBC	N$	
Sport Studies and Business Studies	NB16▼3FT deg		S g	12	3D	MS go	30	BBC	Ind	
Theology & Religious Studies and App Consumer St	NV98▼3FT deg		g	12	4M	P$ go	26	BCC	N	
Theology & Religious Studies and Business Studs	NV18▼3FT deg		g	DD	3D	M$ go	26	BCC	N$	2
Women's Studies and Applied Consumer Studies	NM99▼3FT deg		g	12	4M	P$ go	26	BCC	N	
Women's Studies and Business Studies	NM19▼3FT deg		g	DD	3D	M$ go	26	BCC	N$	

course details			98 expected requirements							96 entry stats	
TITLE	CODE	COURSE	SUBJECTS	A/AS	NO/C	RGNVQ	IB	SQA(H)	SQA	RATIO	A/AS
ROYAL Agric COLL											
Agriculture and Land Management	DN28	3FT/4SW deg	2S g	12	MO		26$	CCC$	Ind	8	10/22
International Agribusiness Management	N180	3FT/4SW deg	2S g	12	MO		26$	CCC$	Ind	2	7/20
International Agricultural and Equine Bus Mgt	DN21	3FT/4SW deg	2S g	12	MO		26$	CCC$	Ind	4	8/26
International Agriculture, Land and Business Mgt	DN2C	3FT/4SW deg	2S g	12	MO		26$	CCC$	Ind	4	11/20
Rural Estate Management	N800	3FT deg	* g	4	5M		Dip	CCC	Ind	3	4/18
Rural Land Management	N802	3FT deg	* g	12	MO		26$	CCCC	Ind	3	10/22
ROYAL HOLLOWAY, Univ of London											
Biochemistry for Management	C7NC	3FT deg	C+B/M/P g	BCC	3M+2D	DS^	28$	BBBCC$		12	
Biology for Management	C1NC	3FT deg	B+C/S g	BCC	4M	DS^	28$	BBBCC$		9	
Computer Science with Management Studies	G5N1	3FT/4SW deg	M	BCC-BBC	MO+3D	D^	30$	Ind		5	12/24
Economics and Management Studies	LN11	3FT deg	*	BBB	Ind		32	Ind		12	18/26
Economics with Management Studies	L1N1	3FT deg	*	BBB	Ind		32	Ind		3	
Electronics with Management Studies	H6N1	3FT deg	M+P/S	BCC-BBC	MO+2D	D^	30	Ind		6	
French and Management Studies	RN11	4FT deg	F	BBC-ABC	Ind		30$	Ind		6	18/24
French with Management Studies	R1N1	4FT deg	F	BBC-ABC			28$	Ind		1	14/16
German and Management Studies	RN21	4FT deg	G	BBC	Ind		30$	BBBBC$		11	
German with Management Studies	R2N1	4FT deg	G	BCC			28$	BBBBC$			
Italian and Management Studies	RN31	4FT deg	L/Ln	BBC	Ind		30	Ind		12	
Italian with Management Studies	R3N1	4FT deg	L/Ln	BBC			30	BBCCC$		3	
Management Studies	N100	3FT deg	*	BBC-BBB	2M+3D	D^	30	Ind		6	18/28
Management Studies and Spanish	NR14	4FT deg	Sp	BBB-BBC	Ind	D^	Ind	Ind			
Management Studies with Economics	N1L1	3FT deg	*	BBC-BBB	2M+3D	D^	30	Ind			
Management Studies with French	N1R1	3FT deg	F	BBB	2M+3D	D^	30	Ind		7	
Management Studies with German	N1R2	3FT deg	G	BBC-BBB	2M+3D	D^	30	Ind		5	
Management Studies with Italian	N1R3	3FT deg	L/Ln	BBC-BBB	2M+3D	D^	30	Ind			
Management Studies with Japanese Studies	N1T4	3FT deg	L g	BBC-BBB	2M+3D	D^	30	Ind			
Management Studies with Mathematics	N1G1	3FT deg	M	BBC-BBB	2M+3D	D^	30	Ind			
Management Studies with Social Policy	N1L4	3FT deg	*	BBC-BBB	2M+3D	D^	30	Ind		6	
Management Studies with Spanish	N1R4	3FT deg	L	BBC-BBB	2M+3D	D^	30	Ind		8	
Management and Information Systems	NG15	3FT deg	M	BBC-BBB	Ind	D^	30$	Ind			
Mathematics and Management Studies	GN11	3FT deg	M	BCC-BBC	Ind	D^	Ind	Ind		17	
Mathematics with Management Studies	G1N1	3FT deg	M	BCC-BBC	Ind	D^	Ind	Ind		1	16/22
Mathematics with Operational Research	G1N2	3FT deg	M	BCC-BBC	Ind	D^	Ind	Ind			
Music with Management Studies	W3N1	3FT deg	Mu	BCC-BBC			Ind	ABBCC$		4	
Physics for Management	F3NC	3FT deg	M+P	BCC-BBC	5M	DS^	30$	BBBCC$		5	
Social Policy with Management Studies	L4N1	3FT deg	*	BCC-BCC	Ind	D^	Ind	Ind			
Sociology with Management Studies	L3N1	3FT deg	*	BCC-BBC	Ind	D^	Ind	Ind		6	
Foundation Programme *Management*	Y408	4FT deg									
RYCOTEWOOD COLL											
Business and Management	091N	2FT HND	Bu/E/Ac	10	N	P	Ind	ABC	N		
SCOTTISH Agric COLL											
Environmental Protection and Management	KN38▼	3FT/4FT deg	2S g	CDD	Ind	M$	Ind	BBCC$	Ind	3	
Food Production and Land Use	DN28▼	3FT/4FT deg	S	CC	Ind	M$	Ind	BCC$	Ind	1	
Rural Business Management *Agricultural Business Management*	Y400▼	3FT/4FT deg	S/M	CD	Ind	Ind	Ind	BBC$	Ind		
Rural Business Management *Rural Enterprise and Development*	Y400▼	3FT/4FT deg	S/M	CD	Ind	Ind	Ind	BBC$	Ind		
Environmental Protection and Management	83NK▼	2FT HND	S	D	N $	P$	Ind	CC$	Ind	1	

Business and Management 12

			98 expected requirements							96 entry stats	
course details											
TITLE	CODE	COURSE	SUBJECTS	A/AS	NO/C	AGNVQ	IB	SQA(H)	SQA	RATIO	A/AS
SCOTTISH COLLEGE of TEXTILES											
Administration	N120	4FT deg	*	CC	N	M$	Dip	BBC	HN	2	
Quality Management	NN12	4FT deg	* g	CC	Ind	M$	Dip	BBC	HN	5	
Textiles and Fashion Design Management	J4NM	4FT deg	* g	CC	Ind	M$	Dip	BBC	HN	5	
Textiles with Marketing	J4N5	4FT deg	* g	CC	Ind	M$	Dip	BBC	HN	8	
Business Studies	021N	2FT HND	*	D	Ind	Ind	Ind	CC	Ind	2	
Univ of SALFORD											
Business Operation & Contr (inc Maths & Mgt Sci)	G4N1	3FT/4SW deg	M	BCC	X	X	Ind	Ind	Ind	2	12/28
Business Operation & Control with St in N Amer	G4NC	3FT/4SW deg	M	BBB	X	X	Ind	Ind	Ind	5	
Business Studies	N120	3FT/4SW deg	* g	BCC-CCC	D	D^	Ind	Ind	Ind	8	14/22
Chemistry with Business Studies (3/4 Yrs)	F1N1	3FT/4SW deg	C+S/M	BC	N	P	30$	Ind	Ind	14	
Computers Management & Electronics (3 or 4 Yrs)	H6N1	3FT/4SW deg		CCC	Ind	Ind	Ind	Ind	Ind	2	
Computers, Management and Electronics	H6NC	4FT deg									
Construction Management	KN21	4FT deg									
Construction Management (4 Yrs)	K2N1	4SW deg	* g	BBC	3M+2D	M	Ind	Ind	Ind	6	14/22
Environmental Technology and Management	K3N1	3FT/4SW deg	S g	EEE	Ind	M	Ind	Ind	Ind		
European Business Studies (3/4 yrs)	N145	3FT/4SW deg		18-22	DO	D	Ind	Ind	Ind		
Information Technology	G5N1▼	3FT deg	g	CCC	DO	D^	Ind	Ind	Ind	3	12/22
Manufacturing Management	H7NC	4FT deg									
Manufacturing Management (NEWI) (4 Yrs)	H7N1	3FT/4SW deg	M/S	18	3M+1D$	M	Ind	Ind	Ind	11	
Manufacturing Management with European Studies	H7ND	4SW deg									
Modern Languages and Marketing Studies (4 Yrs)	NT59	4SW deg	L g	ABC-BBC	X	X	Ind	Ind	X	3	18/28
Business and Finance (Languages in Business)	041N	2FT HND	L	4	5M	M	24	CC	Ind	6	2/6
Business and Finance (Marketing)	005N	2FT HND		DD	MO	M	24	CC	Ind	5	2/12
Business and Finance (Personnel)	016N	2FT HND		DD	MO	M	24	CC	Ind	10	4/10
Food Industry Management	1N4D	2FT HND	* g	2	3M	P	24	CC	Ind	7	
SANDWELL COLL											
Business	001N	2FT HND	*	E	N	P$	Ind	Ind	Ind		
Business Marketing	51NN	2FT HND	*	E	N	P$	Ind	Ind	Ind		
Business and Finance	091N	2FT HND	*	E	N	P$	Ind	Ind	Ind		
Business and Personnel	61NN	2FT HND	*	E	N	P$	Ind	Ind	Ind		
SOAS:Sch of Oriental & African St (U of London)											
Management and Amharic	NT17	4FT deg	g	20	Ind		30	BBBCC	Ind		
Management and Arabic	NT16	4FT deg	g	22	Ind		31	BBBBC	Ind	16	
Management and Bengali	NT15	3FT deg	g	20	Ind		30	BBBCC	Ind		
Management and Burmese	NT1M	4FT deg		20	Ind		30	BBBCC	Ind		
Management and Chinese	NT13	4FT deg	g	24	Ind		32	BBBBB	Ind	23	
Management and Gujarati	NTC5	3FT deg	g	20	Ind		30	BBBCC	Ind		
Management and Hausa	NT1R	4FT deg	g	20	Ind		30	BBBCC	Ind		
Management and Hebrew	NQ19	4FT deg	g	22	Ind		31	BBBBC	Ind		
Management and Hindi	NT1N	3FT/4FT deg	g	20	Ind		30	BBBCC	Ind		
Management and Indonesian	NTCM	3FT/4FT deg	g	20	Ind		30	BBBCC	Ind		
Management and Japanese	NT14	4FT deg	g	24	Ind		32	BBBBB	Ind	15	
Management and Korean	NTCN	4FT deg	g	16	Ind		28	BBCCC	Ind		
Nepali and Management	NTD5	3FT deg	g	20	Ind		30	BBBCC	Ind		
Persian and Management	NT1Q	3FT deg	g	22	Ind		31	BBBBC	Ind		
Sanskrit and Management	NQ1X	3FT deg	g	20	Ind		30	BBBCC	Ind		
Sinhalese and Management	NTDM	3FT deg	g	20	Ind		30	BBBCC	Ind		
South Asian Studies and Management	TNM1	3FT deg									
Swahili and Management	NT1T	4FT deg	g	20	Ind		30	BBBCC	Ind		
Tamil and Management	NTDN	3FT deg	g	20	Ind		30	BBBCC	Ind		

course details   98 expected requirements   96 entry stats

TITLE	CODE	COURSE	SUBJECTS	A/AS	ND/C	AGNVQ	IB	SQA(H)	SQA	RATIO A/AS
Thai and Management	TN51	3FT/4FT deg	g	20	Ind		30	BBBCC	Ind	
Turkish and Management	NT1P	4FT deg	g	22	Ind		31	BBBBC	Ind	
Urdu and Management	TN5C	3FT deg	g	20	Ind		30	BBBCC	Ind	3
Vietnamese and Management	TN5D	4FT deg	g	20	Ind		30	BBBCC	Ind	

Univ College SCARBOROUGH

TITLE	CODE	COURSE	SUBJECTS	A/AS	ND/C	AGNVQ	IB	SQA(H)	SQA	RATIO A/AS
Business and Management	N122	3FT deg	* g	DD	Ind	P	27$	Ind	Ind	
Management with Arts	N1Y3	3FT deg	* g	DD	Ind	P	27$	Ind	Ind	
Management with Sciences	N1Y1	3FT deg	* g	DD	Ind	P	27$	Ind	Ind	
Management with Social Sciences	N1Y2	3FT deg	* g	DD	Ind	P	27$	Ind	Ind	
Marketing with Arts	N5Y3	3FT deg	* g	DD	Ind	P	27$	Ind	Ind	
Marketing with Sciences	N5Y1	3FT deg	* g	DD	Ind	P	27$	Ind	Ind	
Marketing with Social Sciences	N5Y2	3FT deg	* g	DD	Ind	P	27$	Ind	Ind	

Univ of SHEFFIELD

TITLE	CODE	COURSE	SUBJECTS	A/AS	ND/C	AGNVQ	IB	SQA(H)	SQA	RATIO A/AS
Business Studies	N120	3FT deg	* g	26	2M+4D	D^	33	AAAB	Ind	14 24/30
Business Studies and Economics	NL11	3FT deg	* g	26	2M+4D	D^	33	AAAB	Ind	11 24/30
Business Studies and Information Management	NP12	3FT deg	* g	24	3M+3D	D^	32	AABB	Ind	14 22/26
Business Studies and Japanese Studies	NT14	4FT deg	* g	BBC	4M+2D	D^	30	ABBB	Ind	9 20/28
Chinese Studies and Business Studies	TN31	4FT deg	* g	BBC	4M+2D	D^	30	ABBB	Ind	9
French and Business Studies	RN11	4FT deg	F g	BBC	X	D^	30$	ABBB$	Ind	9 22/28
German and Business Studies	RN21	4FT deg	G g	BBC	X	D^	30$	ABBB$	German	24
Hispanic Studies and Business Studies	RN41	4FT deg	Sp g	BBC	X	D^	30$	ABBB$	Ind	13 22/26
Korean Studies and Business Studies	TN51	4FT deg	* g	BBC	4M+2D	D^	30	ABBB		
Management and Mathematics	NG11	3FT deg	M g	24	3M+3D$	D^	32$	AABB$	Ind	13 22/24
Russian and Business Studies	RN81	4FT deg	L g	BBC	X	D^	30$	ABBB$	Ind	

SHEFFIELD HALLAM Univ

TITLE	CODE	COURSE	SUBJECTS	A/AS	ND/C	AGNVQ	IB	SQA(H)	SQA	RATIO A/AS
Business Property Management	N801	3FT/4SW deg	*	12-16	5M	M	Ind	Ind	Ind	
Business Studies (1Yr top-up)	N122	1FT deg		X	HN	X	X	X	X	
Business Studies (Full-Time)	N120	3FT deg	g	18	M+D	M4/^	Ind	Ind	Ind	
Business Studies (Sandwich)	N121	4SW deg	g	18	M+D	M4/^	Ind	Ind	Ind	
Business and Technology	NJ19	4SW deg	* g	EE	3M	P	Ind	CCCC	Ind	
Computing & Management Science (Foundation Year)	GN5D▼	5EXT deg								
Computing Mathematics with Business Studies	GN11	4SW deg	M/St	12	5M	M	Ind	Ind	Ind	
Computing and Management Sciences	GN51	4SW deg	*	12	5M	M	Ind	Ind	Ind	
Engineering with Business Studies	H1N1	3FT/4SW deg	M/P/C/Ph	8	3M $	M$	Ind	Ind	Ind	
Engineering with Business Studies (Extended)	H1NC▼	4EXTFT/5EXTSW deg								
Food Marketing Management	DN45	3FT/4SW deg	g	10	10M	M	Ind	Ind	Ind	
International Business with Language (French)	N1R1	4SW deg	F	16	X	M4/^	Ind	Ind	Ind	
International Business with Language (German)	N1R2	4SW deg	G	16	X	M4/^	Ind	Ind	Ind	
International Business with Language (Italian)	N1R3	4SW deg	g	16	M+D	M gi	Ind	Ind	Ind	
International Business with Language (Spanish)	N1R4	4SW deg	g	16	M+D	M gi	Ind	Ind	Ind	
Property Development	N830	3FT/4SW deg	*	12-16	5M	M	Ind	Ind	Ind	
Public Policy and Management (Sandwich)	NM11	4SW deg	g	14	M+D	M4/^	Ind	Ind	Ind	
Residential Development and Agency	N831	3FT/4SW deg	*	12-16	5M	M	Ind	Ind	Ind	
Urban Land Economics	N800	3FT/4SW deg	*	12-16	5M	M	Ind	Ind	Ind	
Urban Land Valuation (1 Year top-up)	N810	1FT deg		X	HN	X	X	X	X	
Combined Studies *Business Information Systems*	Y400	3FT deg	M	14	2M	M	Ind	Ind	Ind	
Combined Studies *Business Studies*	Y400	3FT deg	* g	14	2M	M	Ind	Ind	Ind	
Combined Studies *Business and Technology*	Y400	3FT deg	S	8-10	2M	M	Ind	Ind	Ind	
Combined Studies *Environmental Management*	Y400	3FT deg	*	14	2M	M	Ind	Ind	Ind	

Business and Management 12

TITLE	CODE	COURSE	SUBJECTS	A/AS	NO/C	AGNVQ	IB	SQA(H)	SQA	RATIO	A/AS
course details			**98 expected requirements**							**96 entry stats**	
Combined Studies *Food Marketing*	Y400	3FT deg	*	14	2M	M	Ind	Ind	Ind		
Combined Studies *Housing Management*	Y400	3FT deg	*	16	2M	M	Ind	Ind	Ind		
Combined Studies *Industrial Studies*	Y400	3FT deg	S	8-10	2M	M	Ind	Ind	Ind		
Combined Studies *Property Development and Management*	Y400	3FT deg	*	16	2M	M	Ind	Ind	Ind		
Business Decision Methods	037G	2FT/3SW HND	M/St	E	M $	P	Ind	Ind	Ind		
Business Property Management	038N	2FT HND	*	4	1M	P	Ind	Ind	Ind		
Business Studies	421N▼	2FT HND	*	8	MO	M2/^	Ind	Ind	Ind		
Business and Technology	91JN	2FT HND	*	2	N	P	Ind	Ind	Ind		
Estate Agency	018N	2FT HND	*	4	1M	P	Ind	Ind	Ind		

SHREWSBURY COLLEGE OF ARTS & TECHNOLOGY

TITLE	CODE	COURSE	SUBJECTS	A/AS	NO/C	AGNVQ	IB	SQA(H)	SQA	RATIO	A/AS
Business and Finance	421N	2FT HND		2		P	Ind	Ind	Ind		

Univ College of St MARTIN, LANCASTER AND CUMBRIA

TITLE	CODE	COURSE	SUBJECTS	A/AS	NO/C	AGNVQ	IB	SQA(H)	SQA	RATIO	A/AS
Applied Community Studies/Business Mgt Studies	LN51	3FT deg	*	CD-DDE	3M+2D	M	28	BCCC			
Business Management Studies/Applied Community St	NL1M	3FT deg	*	CD-CEE	3M+2D	M*	28	BCCC			
Business Management Studies/Drama	NW14	3FT deg	*	CD-CEE	3M+2D	M*	28	BCCC			
Business Management Studies/English	NQ13	3FT deg	E	CD-CEE	3M+2D	M	28$	BCCC$			
Business Management Studies/Geography	NL18	3FT deg	Gy	CD-DDE	X	M^	28$	BCCC$			
Business Management Studies/Health Admin	NL14	3FT deg	*	CD-CEE	3M+2D	M	28	BCCC			
Business Management Studies/Health Studies	NB19	3FT deg	*	CD-CEE	3M+2D	M*	28	BCCC			
Business Management Studies/History	NV11	3FT deg	H	CD-CEE	X	M^	28$	BCCC$			
Business Management Studies/Mathematics	NG11	3FT deg	M	CD-CEE	3M+2D	M^	28$	BCCC$			
Business Management Studies/Religious Studies	NV18	3FT deg	*	CD-CEE	3M+2D	M	28	BCCC			
Business Management Studies/Sci, Technol & Soc	NY11	3FT deg	g	CD-CEE	3M+2D	M	28	BCCC			
Business Studies	N100	3FT deg	*	CD-CEE	3M+2D	M	28	BCCC			
English/Business Management Studies	QN31	3FT deg	E	BC-BDE	X	P^	28$	BBBC$			
Geography/Business Management Studies	LN81	3FT deg	Gy	CD-DDE	X	P^	28$	BCCC$			
Health Studies/Business Management Studies	BN91	3FT deg	*	CD-DDE	3M+2D	M*	28	BCCC			
History/Business Management Studies	VN11	3FT deg	H	CD-DDE	3M+2D	P^	28$	BCCC$			
Mathematics/Business Management Studies	GN11	3FT deg	M	DD-DEE	X	P^	28$	BCCC$			
Religious Studies/Business Management Studies	VN81	3FT deg	*	CD-DDE	3M+2D	M	28	BCCC			
Science, Technology and Society/Business Mgt St	YN11	3FT deg	g	CD-DDE	3M+2D	M*	28	BCCC			

SOLIHULL COLL

TITLE	CODE	COURSE	SUBJECTS	A/AS	NO/C	AGNVQ	IB	SQA(H)	SQA	RATIO	A/AS
Business	021N	2FT HND	*	E	N	P	Dip	Ind	Ind		
Retail Management	055N	2FT HND	*	E	N	P	Dip	Ind	Ind		

Univ of SOUTHAMPTON

TITLE	CODE	COURSE	SUBJECTS	A/AS	NO/C	AGNVQ	IB	SQA(H)	SQA	RATIO	A/AS
Management Sciences	N100	3FT deg	* g	22	Ind	D$^ go	30	ABBBB	Ind	10	20/26
Management Sciences and Accounting	NNC4	3FT deg	* g	22	Ind	D$^ go	30	ABBBB	Ind		
Management Sciences and French	NRC1	4FT deg	F g	22	Ind	D$^ go	30$	ABBBB$	Ind	7	18/26
Management Sciences and German	NRC2	4FT deg	G g	22	Ind	D$^ go	30$	ABBBB$	Ind	4	20/20
Management Sciences and Spanish	NRC4	4FT deg	Sp g	22	Ind	D$^ go	30$	ABBBB$	Ind	11	
Mathematics with Operational Research	G1N2	3FT deg	M	BBC	Ind	Ind	30	ABBBB	Ind	12	

SOUTHAMPTON INST

TITLE	CODE	COURSE	SUBJECTS	A/AS	NO/C	AGNVQ	IB	SQA(H)	SQA	RATIO	A/AS
Business Administration	N122	3FT deg	*	10	MO	M$	Dip	CCCC	N	4	6/18
Business Administration (HND top-up)	N123	1/2FT deg		X	HN $	X	X	X	HN$		
Business Studies	N120	4SW deg	*	12	MO	M$	Dip	CCCC	N	5	10/19
Business Technology Management	J9N1	3FT deg	*	4	MO	M$	Dip	CCCC	N	2	6/12
Business Technology Management (with Foundation)	J9NC▼	4FT deg	*	2-4	N	M$	Dip	CCCC	N	1	

course details | 98 expected requirements | 96 entry stats

TITLE	CODE	COURSE	SUBJECTS	A/AS	NO/C	RGNVQ	IB	SQA(H)	SQA	RATIO	A/AS
Business and Law	NM13	3FT deg	*	10	MO	M$	Dip	CCCC	N	3	8/14
Engineering with Business	H1N1	3FT deg	M/P	4-10	MO	M$	Dip	CCCC	N	5	
Engineering with Business (with Foundation)	H1NC▼	4FT deg	*	2-4	N	P$	Dip	CCCC	N	2	
Fine Art Valuation Studies	N813	3FT deg	*	6-14	MO	M$	Dip	CCCC	N		
Fine Arts Valuation	N812	3FT deg	*	6-14	MO	M$	Dip	CCCC	N	1	6/20
Human Resource Management	N131	3FT deg	*	10	MO	M$	Dip	CCCC	N	3	8/18
International Business	N141	3FT deg	*	10	MO	M$	Dip	CCCC	N	4	8/14
International Transport Management	N925	3FT deg	*	10-12	MO	M$	Dip	CCCC	N		
Marketing	N500	3FT deg	*	12	MO	M$	Dip	CCCC	N	6	10/18
Marketing Design	N5W2	3FT deg	*	10	MO	M$	Dip	CCCC	N	2	8/18
Product Design with Marketing	W2N5	3FT deg	Pf	12	MO	M$	Dip	CCCC	N	8	8/22
Product Design with Marketing	E2N5	3FT deg	Pf	12	MO	M$	Dip	CCCC	N		
Product Design with Marketing (with Foundation)	E2NM▼	4FT deg	Pf	4	N	P$	Dip	CCCC	N		
Product Design with Marketing (with Foundation)	W2NM▼	4FT deg	Pf	4	N	P$	Dip	CCCC	N		
Real Estate Valuation	N810	3FT deg	*	6	MO	M$	Dip	CCCC	N	3	6/20
Real Estate Valuation (with Foundation Year)	N818▼	4FT deg	*	2-4	N	P$	Dip	CCCC	N	11	
Retail Management	N110	3FT deg	*	10	MO	M$	Dip	CCCC	N		
Sports Studies with Business	NN17	3FT deg	*	12	MO	M*4 gi	Dip	CCCC	N		8/16
Business	001N	2FT HND	*	6	MO	P$	Dip	CCCC	N	2	4/ 6
Business and Finance	421N▼	2FT HND	*	6	MO	P$	Dip	CCCC	N	3	2/12
Business and Marketing	51NN	2FT HND	*	6	MO	P$	Dip	CCCC	N	2	4/ 8
Business and Personnel	031N	2FT HND	*	6	MO	P$	Dip	CCCC	N	4	4/ 6

SOUTH BANK Univ

TITLE	CODE	COURSE	SUBJECTS	A/AS	NO/C	RGNVQ	IB	SQA(H)	SQA	RATIO	A/AS
Arts Management	WN11	3FT/4SW deg	* g	CC	MO	M$	Ind	Ind	Ind		
Business Administration	N150	3FT deg	* g	CC	3D	D go	Ind	Ind	Ind		
Business School Common Foundation Programme	N128	4EXT deg					Ind	Ind	Ind		
Business Studies	N120	4SW deg	* g	BC	3D	D go	Ind	Ind	Ind		
Business Studies with Languages	N1T9	4SW deg	* g	CC	3D	M go	Ind	Ind	Ind		
Electronic Engineering Management	H6N1	3FT deg	M+S g	CC	5M	M go	Ind	Ind	Ind		
Electronic Engineering Management (top-up)	HN61	1/2FT deg			HN						
Estate Management	N800	3FT/4SW deg	* g	CB	4M	M go	Ind	Ind	Ind		
Food and Consumer Studies	DN49	3FT/4SW deg	S/2S g	DD	4M	MS go	Ind	Ind	Ind		
Foundation Estate Management	N808	4EXT deg					Ind	Ind	Ind		
Foundation Occupational & Environmental Hygiene	BN9Q	4EXT deg					Ind	Ind	Ind		
Foundation Occupational Health and Safety	BNXQ	3FT deg					Ind	Ind	Ind		
Human Resource Management & Environmental Policy	FN96	3FT deg	* g	14-18	2M+4D	M go	Ind	Ind	Ind		
Human Resource Management and Accounting	NN64	3FT deg	Ac/Ec g	14-18	2M+4D	M go	Ind	Ind	Ind		
Human Resource Management and Business Info Tech	GN76	3FT deg	M g	14-18	2M+4D	M go	Ind	Ind	Ind		
Human Resource Management and Computing	GN56	3FT deg	M g	14-18	2M+4D	M go	Ind	Ind	Ind		
Human Resource Management and Economics	LN16	3FT deg	Ec/Bu g	14-18	2M+4D	M go	Ind	Ind	Ind		
Human Resource Management and English Studies	QN36	3FT deg	E g	14-18	X	M^ go	Ind	Ind	Ind		
Human Resource Management and European Studies	NT62	3FT deg	* g	14-18	2M+4D	M go	Ind	Ind	Ind		
Human Resource Management and Food Policy	DN46	3FT deg	S g	14-18	2M+4D	M go	Ind	Ind	Ind		
Human Resource Management and French	NR61	3FT deg	F g	14-18	2M+4D	M go	Ind	Ind	Ind		
Human Resource Management and German	NR62	3FT deg	G g	14-18	2M+4D	M^ go	Ind	Ind	Ind		
Human Resource Management and German - ab initio	NR6F	3FT deg	* g	14-18	2M+4D	M go	Ind	Ind	Ind		
Human Resource Management and Health Studies	NL64	3FT deg	S g	14-18	2M+4D	M go	Ind	Ind	Ind		
Human Resource Management and History	NV61	3FT deg	H g	14-18	2M+4D	M go	Ind	Ind	Ind		
Human Resource Management and Housing	KN46	3FT deg	* g	14-18	2M+4D	M go	Ind	Ind	Ind		
Human Resource Management and Human Biology	BN16	3FT deg	S g	14-18	2M+4D	M go	Ind	Ind	Ind		
Human Resource Management and Human Geography	LN86	3FT deg	Gy	14-18	2M+4D	M go	Ind	Ind	Ind		
Law and Human Resource Management	MN36	3FT deg	* g	14-18	2M+4D	M go	Ind	Ind	Ind		

Business and Management 12

TITLE	CODE	COURSE	SUBJECTS	A/AS	NO/C	RGNVQ	IB	SQA(H)	SQA	RATIO A/AS
Management and Accounting	NN41	3FT deg	Ac/Ec g	12-16	4M+2D	M go	Ind	Ind	Ind	
Management and Business Information Technology	GN71	3FT deg	M g	12-16	4M+2D	M go	Ind	Ind	Ind	
Management and Economics	LN11	3FT deg	Bu/Ec g	12-16	4M+2D	M go	Ind	Ind	Ind	
Management and Environmental Policy	FN91	3FT deg	* g	14-18	2M+4D	M go	Ind	Ind	Ind	
Management and European Studies	NT12	3FT deg	* g	14-18	2M+4D	M go	Ind	Ind	Ind	
Management and Food Policy	DN41	3FT deg	S g	12-16	4M+2D	M go	Ind	Ind	Ind	
Management and French	NR11	3FT deg	F g	12-16	4M+2D	M go	Ind	Ind	Ind	
Management and German	NR1F	3FT deg	G g	14-18	2M+4D	M go	Ind	Ind	Ind	
Management and German - ab initio	NR12	3FT deg	g	12-16	4M+2D	M go	Ind	Ind	Ind	
Management and Health Studies	LN41	3FT deg	S g	12-16	4M+2D	M go	Ind	Ind	Ind	
Management and History	NV11	3FT deg	H g	12-16	4M+2D	M^ go	Ind	Ind	Ind	
Management and Housing	KN4C	3FT deg	* g	14-18	2M+4D	M go	Ind	Ind	Ind	
Management and Human Biology	BN11	3FT deg	S g	12-16	4M+2D	M go	Ind	Ind	Ind	
Management and Human Geography	LN81	3FT deg	Gy g	12-16	4M+2D	M go	Ind	Ind	Ind	
Management and Law	MN31	3FT deg	* g	14-18	2M+4D	D go	Ind	Ind	Ind	
Marketing and Accounting	NN45	3FT deg	Ac/Ec g	14-18	2M+4D	M go	Ind	Ind	Ind	
Marketing and Business Information Technology	GN75	3FT deg	M g	12-16	2M+4D	M go	Ind	Ind	Ind	
Marketing and Computing	GN55	3FT deg	M g	14-18	2M+4D	M go	Ind	Ind	Ind	
Marketing and Economics	LN15	3FT deg	Ec/Bu g	12-16	2M+4D	M go	Ind	Ind	Ind	
Marketing and English Studies	QN35	3FT deg	E g	14-18	X	M^ go	Ind	Ind	Ind	
Marketing and Environmental Policy	FN95	3FT deg	* g	14-18	2M+4D	M go	Ind	Ind	Ind	
Marketing and European Studies	NT52	3FT deg	* g	14-18	2M+4D	M go	Ind	Ind	Ind	
Marketing and Food Policy	DN45	3FT deg	S g	14-18	2M+4D	M go	Ind	Ind	Ind	
Marketing and French	NR51	3FT deg	F g	12-16	2M+4D	M^ go	Ind	Ind	Ind	
Marketing and German	NR52	3FT deg	G g	12-16	2M+4D	M^ go	Ind	Ind	Ind	
Marketing and German - ab initio	NR5F	3FT deg	* g	14-18	2M+4D	M go	Ind	Ind	Ind	
Marketing and Health Studies	LN45	3FT deg	S g	14-18	2M+4D	M go	Ind	Ind	Ind	
Marketing and History	NV51	3FT deg	H g	14-18	2M+4D	M^ go	Ind	Ind	Ind	
Marketing and Housing	KN45	3FT deg	* g	14-18	2M+4D	M go	Ind	Ind	Ind	
Marketing and Human Biology	BN15	3FT deg	S g	14-18	2M+4D	M go	Ind	Ind	Ind	
Marketing and Human Geography	LN85	3FT deg	Gy g	14-18	2M+4D	M go	Ind	Ind	Ind	
Marketing and Human Resource Management	NN56	3FT deg	* g	12-16	2M+4D	M go	Ind	Ind	Ind	
Marketing and Law	MN35	3FT deg	* g	14-18	2M+4D	D go	Ind	Ind	Ind	
Marketing and Management	NN51	3FT deg	* g	12-16	2M+4D	M go	Ind	Ind	Ind	
Media Studies and Human Resource Management	NP64	3FT deg	E g	14-18	2M+4D	D go	Ind	Ind	Ind	
Media Studies and Management	NP14	3FT deg	E g	14-18	2M+4D	D go	Ind	Ind	Ind	
Media Studies and Marketing	NP54	3FT deg	E g	14-18	2M+4D	D go	Ind	Ind	Ind	
Modern Languages and International Business	TN91	4SW deg	F/G/Sp g	CC	DO $	M go	Ind	Ind	Ind	
Modern Languages and International Studies	TN21	4SW deg	F/G/Sp g	CC	DO	M go	Ind	Ind	Ind	
Nutrition and Human Resource Management	BN46	3FT deg	S g	14-18	2M+4D	M go	Ind	Ind	Ind	
Nutrition and Management	BN41	3FT deg	S g	12-16	4M+2D	M go	Ind	Ind	Ind	
Nutrition and Marketing	BN45	3FT deg	S g	14-18	2M+4D	M go	Ind	Ind	Ind	
Occupational Health and Safety	BNY6	3FT deg	2S g	DD	N	M go	Ind	Ind	Ind	
Occupational and Environmental Hygiene	BNX6	3FT/4SW deg	2S g	DD	N	M go	Ind	Ind	Ind	
Planning and Human Resource Management	KN4Q	3FT deg	* g	14-18	2M+4D	M go	Ind	Ind	Ind	
Planning and Management	KN41	3FT deg	* g	14-18	2M+4D	M go	Ind	Ind	Ind	
Planning and Marketing	KN4M	3FT deg	* g	14-18	2M+4D	M go	Ind	Ind	Ind	
Politics and Human Resource Management	MN1P	3FT deg	* g	14-18	2M+4D	M go	Ind	Ind	Ind	
Politics and Management	MN11	3FT deg	g	12-16	4M+2D	M go	Ind	Ind	Ind	
Politics and Marketing	MN15	3FT deg	* g	14-18	2M+4D	M go	Ind	Ind	Ind	
Product Design and Human Resource Management	HN76	3FT deg	Ad g	14-18	2M+4D	M go	Ind	Ind	Ind	
Product Design and Management	HN71	3FT deg	Ad g	12-16	4M+2D	M go	Ind	Ind	Ind	

course details

TITLE	CODE	COURSE	SUBJECTS	A/AS	ND/C	AGNVQ	IB	SQA(H)	SQA	RATIO A/AS
Product Design and Marketing	HN75	3FT deg	Ad g	14-18	2M+4D	M go	Ind	Ind	Ind	
Psychology and Human Resource Management	CN86	3FT deg	S g	14-18	2M+4D	M go	Ind	Ind	Ind	
Psychology and Management	CN81	3FT deg	S g	14-18	2M+4D	M go	Ind	Ind	Ind	
Psychology and Marketing	CN85	3FT deg	S g	14-18	2M+4D	M go	Ind	Ind	Ind	
Social Policy and Human Resource Management	LN46	3FT deg	* g	14-18	2M+4D	M go	Ind	Ind	Ind	
Social Policy and Management	LN4C	3FT deg	* g	12-16	4M+2D	M go	Ind	Ind	Ind	
Social Policy and Marketing	LN4M	3FT deg	* g	14-18	4M+2D	M go	Ind	Ind	Ind	
Sociology and Human Resource Management	LN36	3FT deg	* g	14-18	2M+4D	M go	Ind	Ind	Ind	
Sociology and Management	LN31	3FT deg	* g	12-16	4M+2D	M go	Ind	Ind	Ind	
Sociology and Marketing	LN35	3FT deg	* g	14-18	2M+4D	M go	Ind	Ind	Ind	
Spanish - ab initio and Human Resource Mgt	NR6K	3FT deg	* g	14-18	2M+4D	M go	Ind	Ind	Ind	
Spanish - ab initio and Management	NR14	3FT deg	* g	12-16	4M+2D	M go	Ind	Ind	Ind	
Spanish - ab initio and Marketing	NP5K	3FT deg	* g	14-18	2M+4D	M go	Ind	Ind	Ind	
Spanish and Human Resource Management	NR64	3FT deg	Sp g	14-18	2M+4D	M^ go	Ind	Ind	Ind	
Spanish and Management	NR1K	3FT deg	Sp g	14-18	2M+4D	M^ go	Ind	Ind	Ind	
Spanish and Marketing	NR54	3FT deg	Sp g	14-18	2M+4D	M^ go	Ind	Ind	Ind	
Sports Science and Human Resource Management	BN66	3FT deg	S g	14-18	2M+4D	M go	Ind	Ind	Ind	
Sports Science and Management	BN61	3FT deg	S g	12-16	4M+2D	M go	Ind	Ind	Ind	
Sports Science and Marketing	BN65	3FT deg	S g	14-18	2M+4D	M go	Ind	Ind	Ind	
Technology and Human Resource Management	JN96	3FT deg	* g	14-18	2M+4D	M go	Ind	Ind	Ind	
Technology and Management	JN91	3FT deg	* g	12-16	4M+2D	M go	Ind	Ind	Ind	
Technology and Marketing	NJ59	3FT deg	* g	14-18	2M+4D	M go	Ind	Ind	Ind	
Tourism and Human Resource Management	NP67	3FT deg	L g	14-18	2M+4D	M^ go	Ind	Ind	Ind	
Tourism and Marketing	NP57	3FT deg	L g	14-18	2M+4D	M^ go	Ind	Ind	Ind	
Urban Studies and Human Resource Management	KN4P	3FT deg	* g	14-18	2M+4D	M go	Ind	Ind	Ind	
Urban Studies and Management	KN4D	3FT deg	* g	14-18	2M+4D	M go	Ind	Ind	Ind	
Urban Studies and Marketing	KN4N	3FT deg	* g	14-18	2M+4D	M go	Ind	Ind	Ind	
World Theatre and Human Resource Management	NW64	3FT deg	* g	14-18	2M+4D	M go	Ind	Ind	Ind	
World Theatre and Management	NW14	3FT deg	* g	14-18	2M+4D	M go	Ind	Ind	Ind	
World Theatre and Marketing	NW54	3FT deg	* g	14-18	2M+4D	M go	Ind	Ind	Ind	
Business Studies	421N	2FT HND	* g	C	MO	M go	Ind	Ind	Ind	
Land Management	108N	2FT HND	* g	D	2M	P go	Ind	Ind	Ind	

SPARSHOLT COLLEGE Hampshire

TITLE	CODE	COURSE	SUBJECTS	A/AS	ND/C	AGNVQ	IB	SQA(H)	SQA	RATIO A/AS
Business and Finance (Agricult/Equine Business)	421N	2FT HND	*	DD	N	P	Ind	Ind	Ind	3

Univ of ST ANDREWS

TITLE	CODE	COURSE	SUBJECTS	A/AS	ND/C	AGNVQ	IB	SQA(H)	SQA	RATIO A/AS
Management (Arts)	N100	4FT deg	* g	BBB	X	Ind	30	BBBB	Ind	8 26/26
Management (Science)	N101	4FT deg	g	BBB	X	Ind	28$	BBBB	Ind	
Management Sciences (Science)	N104	4FT deg	M g	BBB	Ind	Ind	28$	BBBB$	Ind	
Management Sciences-Chemistry	FN11	4FT deg	C+M	CCC	Ind	Ind	28$	BBBC$	Ind	11
Management Sciences-Computer Science	GN51	4FT deg	M g	CCC	Ind	Ind	28$	BBBC$	Ind	28
Management Sciences-Economics	LN11	4FT deg	M g	BBC	Ind	Ind	28$	BBBB$	Ind	
Management Sciences-Geography (Science)	FN81	4FT deg	M g	BBB	Ind	Ind	30$	BBBB$	Ind	14
Management Sciences-Geology	FN61	4FT deg	M g	CCC	Ind	Ind	28$	BBBC$	Ind	
Management-Arabic	NT1P	4FT deg	* g	BBB	X	Ind	30$	BBBB	Ind	
Management-Chemistry	FN1C	4FT deg	C g	BCC	Ind	Ind	28$	BBBC$	Ind	
Management-Classics	NQ18	4FT deg		BBB	Ind	Ind	30$	BBBB$	Ind	
Management-Computer Science	GN5C	4FT deg	M g	CCC	X	Ind	28$	BBBC$	Ind	
Management-Economics (Arts)	NL11	4FT deg	* g	BBB	X	Ind	30$	BBBB	Ind	7 24/28
Management-Economics (Science)	LN1C	4FT deg	* g	BBB	X	Ind	28$	BBBB$	Ind	
Management-French	NR11	4FT deg	F g	BBB	X	Ind	30	BBBB$	Ind	
Management-French with Year Abroad	NR1C	4FT/5FT deg	F g	BBB	X	Ind	30	BBBB$	Ind	8

Business and Management 12

course details			98 expected requirements							96 entry stats
TITLE	CODE	COURSE	SUBJECTS	A/AS	NQ/C	AGNVQ	IB	SQA(H)	SQA	RATIO A/AS
Management-Geography (Arts)	NL18	4FT deg	* g	BBB	X	Ind	30$	BBBB	Ind	7
Management-Geography (Science)	FN8C	4FT deg	* g	BBB	X	Ind	30$	BBBB$	Ind	
Management-Geology	FN6C	4FT deg	* g	CCC	X	Ind	28$	BBBC$	Ind	
Management-German	NR12	4FT deg	* g	BBB	X	Ind	30$	BBBB	Ind	
Management-German with Year Abroad	NR1F	4FT/5FT deg	* g	BBB	X	Ind	30$	BBBB	Ind	8
Management-International Relations (Arts)	MN11	4FT deg	* g	AAB	X	Ind	36$	AAAB	Ind	7
Management-Italian	NR13	4FT deg	* g	BBB	X	Ind	34$	BBBB	Ind	
Management-Italian with Year Abroad	NR1H	4FT/5FT deg	* g	BBB	X	Ind	30$	BBBB	Ind	
Mathematics-Management Sciences	GN11	4FT deg	M g	BBB	Ind	Ind	28$	BBBB$	Ind	6
Modern History-Management	NV11	4FT deg	* g	BBB	X	Ind	30$	BBBB	Ind	
Modern Languages with Management	T9NC	4FT deg	* g	BBB	X	Ind	30$	BBBB	Ind	
Modern Languages with Mgt (Integ Year Abroad)	T9N1	4FT/5FT deg	* g	BBB	X	Ind	30$	BBBB	Ind	5
Philosophy-Management	VN71	4FT deg	* g	BBB	X	Ind	30$	BBBB	Ind	4
Psychology-Management (Arts)	LN71	4FT deg	* g	ABB	X	Ind	32$	BBBBB	Ind	7
Russian with Year Abroad-Management	NRC8	4FT/5FT deg	* g	BBB	X	Ind	30$	BBBB	Ind	
Russian-Management	NR18	4FT deg	* g	BBB	X	Ind	30$	BBBB	Ind	
Spanish with Year Abroad-Management	NRC4	4FT/5FT deg	* g	BBB	X	Ind	30	BBBB	Ind	11
Spanish-Management	NR14	4FT deg	* g	BBB	X	Ind	32$	BBBB	Ind	
Statistics-Management Sciences	GN41	4FT deg	M g	BBB	Ind	Ind	28$	BBBB$	Ind	6
General Degree of BSc Management Sciences (Science)	Y100	3FT deg	M g	CCC	Ind	Ind	28$	BBBC$	Ind	
General Degree of MA Management (Arts)	Y450	3FT deg	* g	BBB	X	Ind	30$	BBBB	Ind	

ST HELENS COLL

Business	001N	2FT HND	*		2	N	P*	Dip	Ind	Ind
Business and Finance	091N	2FT HND	*		2	N	P*	Dip	Ind	Ind
Business and Marketing	51NN	2FT HND	*		2	N	P*	Dip	Ind	Ind
Business and Personnel	61NN	2FT HND	*		2	N	P*	Dip	Ind	Ind

ST MARY'S Univ COLL

Heritage Management and Biology	CN19	3FT deg	B/C	4-8	Ind	Ind	Ind	BBBB$	Ind	
Heritage Management and Classical Studies	NQ98	3FT deg	*	4-8	Ind	Ind	Ind	BBBB	Ind	
Heritage Management and Drama	NW94	3FT deg	*	8-12	Ind	Ind	Ind	BBBB	Ind	
Heritage Management and Education Studies	NX9X	3FT deg	*	4-8	Ind	Ind	Ind	BBBB	Ind	
Heritage Management and English	NQ93	3FT deg	E	8-12	X	X	Ind	BBBB$	X	
Heritage Management and Environ Investigation St	FN99	3FT deg	S/2S	4-8	Ind	Ind	Ind	BBBB$	Ind	
Heritage Management and Environmental Studies	FNX9	3FT deg	*	4-8	Ind	Ind	Ind	BBBB	Ind	
Heritage Management and Gender Studies	MN99	3FT deg	*	4-8	Ind	Ind	Ind	BBBB	Ind	
History and Heritage Management	NV91	3FT deg	H	4-8	Ind	Ind	Ind	BBBB$	Ind	
Integrated Scientific Studies and Heritage Mgt	NY91	3FT deg	S/2S	4-8	Ind	Ind	Ind	BBBB$	Ind	
Irish Studies and Heritage Management	NQ95	3FT deg	*	4-8	Ind	Ind	Ind	BBBB	Ind	
Management Studies and Biology	CN11	3FT deg	B/C g	4-8	Ind	Ind	Ind	BBBB$	Ind	
Management Studies and Drama	NW14	3FT deg	* g	8-12	Ind	Ind	Ind	BBBB	Ind	
Management Studies and English	NQ13	3FT deg	E g	8-12	X	X	Ind	BBBB$	X	
Management Studies and Environ Investigation St	FN91	3FT deg	S/2S g	4-8	Ind	Ind	Ind	BBBB$	Ind	
Management Studies and Environmental Studies	FNX1	3FT deg	* g	4-8	Ind	Ind	Ind	BBBB	Ind	
Management Studies and Gender Studies	MN91	3FT deg	* g	4-8	Ind	Ind	Ind	BBBB	Ind	
Management Studies and Geography	FN81	3FT deg	Gy g	4-8	Ind	Ind	Ind	BBBB$	Ind	
Management Studies and History	NV11	3FT deg	H g	4-8	Ind	Ind	Ind	BBBB$	Ind	
ManGement Studies and Integrated Scientific St	NY11	3FT deg	S/2S g	4-8	Ind	Ind	Ind	BBBB$	Ind	
Management Studies and Irish Studies	NQ15	3FT deg	* g	4-8	Ind	Ind	Ind	BBBB	Ind	
Management Studies and Media Arts	NP14	3FT deg	* g	8-12	Ind	Ind	Ind	BBBB	Ind	
Mathematics and Heritage Management	GN19	3FT deg	M	4-8	X	X	Ind	BBBB$	X	

course details | 98 expected requirements | 96 entry stats

TITLE	CODE	COURSE	SUBJECTS	A/AS	ND/C	AGNVQ	IB	SQA(H)	SQA	RATIO A/AS
Mathematics and Management Studies	GN11	3FT deg	M	4-8	X	X	Ind	BBBB$	X	
Sociology and Heritage Management	LN39	3FT deg	*	4-8	Ind	Ind	Ind	BBBB	Ind	
Sport Rehabilitation and Management Studies	BN91	3FT deg	B g	12-14	X	X	Ind	BBBB$	X	
Sport Science and Heritage Management	BN69	3FT deg	S g	8-12	Ind	Ind	Ind	BBBB$	Ind	
Theology and Religious Studies and Management St	NV18	3FT deg	* g	4-8	Ind	Ind	Ind	BBBB	Ind	

STAFFORDSHIRE Univ

TITLE	CODE	COURSE	SUBJECTS	A/AS	ND/C	AGNVQ	IB	SQA(H)	SQA	RATIO A/AS
Accounting and Business	N4N1	3FT deg	g	CCD	MO+2D	M$	24	BBC		
Business Administration	N150	3FT deg	g	12	MO	M	24	BCC	Ind	6/18
Business Enterprise	N110	3FT deg	g	10	MO	M	24	BCC	Ind	1 4/10
Business Studies	N120	3FT/4SW deg	g	CCD	MO+2D	M$	24	BBB	Ind	5 10/20
Business Studies with Operations Management	N1N2	3FT/4SW deg	g	CCD	MO+2D	M$	24	BBB	Ind	5
Business Studies with Tourism	N1P7	3FT/4SW deg	g	CCD	MO+2D	M$	24	BBB	Ind	6 8/22
Business Studies/Applied Statistics	NG14	3FT deg	g	16	Ind	M	24	BBC	Ind	
Business and Quality Management	N122	3FT deg	g	10	MO	M	24	BCC		2
Chemistry/Business Studies	FN11	3FT deg	S g	12	4M	M	24	BCC	Ind	
Electronics/Business Studies	HN61	3FT deg	S g	12	4M	M	24	BCC	Ind	
Enterprise and Business Computing	N111	3FT deg	g	10	MO	M	24	BCC	Ind	1
Enterprise and Entrepreneurship	N121	3FT deg	*	10	MO	M	24	BCC	Ind	3
Environmental Transportation Studies	N921	3FT deg	g	8	3M	M$				
Environmental Transportation Studies	FN99	4EXT deg	g	EE	P $	P$	Ind	Ind	Ind	
Extended Manufacturing Engineering with Business	H7ND	5EXT/6EXTSW deg	*	4	N	P$	24	CCC	Ind	
Foundation Enterprise,Innovation & Communication	NP1H▼	3FT/4FT deg	g							
Foundation Technology Management	GN51▼	5EXTSW deg		Ind	Ind	Ind	Ind	Ind	Ind	3
French/Business Studies	RN11	3FT/4SW deg	F g	CCD	MO+2D	M$^	26	BBB	Ind	7 8/14
Geography/Business Studies	LN81	3FT deg	g	16	4M+2D	M	28	AAB	Ind	5 12/20
German/Business Studies	RN21	3FT/4SW deg	G g	CCD	MO+2D	M$^	26	BBB	Ind	
Human Resource Management	N130	3FT/4SW deg	g	CCD	MO+2D	M$	24	BBB	Ind	6 10/22
Industrial Marketing	N510	3FT deg	g	8	3M	M$	24	BCC	Ind	
Industrial Marketing	N519	4EXT deg	g	EE	P $	P$	Ind	Ind	Ind	
Information Systems/Business Studies	GN5C	3FT deg	g	16	Ind	M	24	BBB	Ind	3
International Business Communications	N140	3FT deg	g	10	MO	M	24	BCC	Ind	2
International Business Management	N145	3FT/4SW deg	g	CCD	MO+2D	M$	24	BBB	Ind	
International Finance and Business	NN13	4FT deg	g	CCD	MO+2D	M$	24	BBB		
Law/Business Studies	MN31	3FT deg	g	18	HN	M^	26	BBBB	Ind	6 10/24
Legal Studies/Business Studies	MN3C	3FT deg	g	18	HN	M^	26	BBBB	Ind	9
Manufacturing Engineering with Business	H7NC	3FT deg		10	3M	M$				
Marketing	N500	3FT/4SW deg	g	CCD	MO+2D	D	24	BBB	Ind	7 10/20
Physics/Business Studies	FN31	3FT deg	S g	12	4M	M	24	BCC	Ind	
Politics/Business Studies	MNC1	3FT deg	g	16	MO+2D	M$	24	BBB	Ind	6
Property with Business Studies	K2N1	3FT deg	g	12	4M	M$	24	BBC	Ind	6/ 8
Sociology/Business Studies	LN31	3FT deg	g	CCD	MO+2D	M$	24	BBB	Ind	4 12/12
Spanish/Business Studies	RN41	3FT/4SW deg	g	CCD	MO+2D	M$^	26	BBB	Ind	
Technology Management	GNM1	4SW deg	g	12	Ind	M	Ind	CCC	Ind	22
Transportation Studies/Management Informatics	N929	4EXT deg	g	EE	P $	P$	Ind	Ind	Ind	
Transportation Studies/Management/Informatics	N920	3FT deg	g	8	3M	M$				
Valuation Surveying	N810	3FT deg	g	12	4M	M$	24	BBC	Ind	7
Business	421N▼	2FT HND	g	2	4M	M	24	BCC	Ind	4 2/6
Manufacturing Engineering with Business	1N7H▼	2FT HND	M/P	2	N	P$	24	CCC	Ind	

Univ of STIRLING

TITLE	CODE	COURSE	SUBJECTS	A/AS	ND/C	AGNVQ	IB	SQA(H)	SQA	RATIO A/AS
Accountancy/Business Studies	NN1K	4FT deg	g	BCC	HN	Ind	33	BBBB	HN	
Accountancy/Management Science	NN14	4FT deg	g	BCC	HN	Ind	33	BBBB	HN	

Business and Management 12

course details			98 expected requirements							96 entry stats
TITLE	CODE	COURSE	SUBJECTS	A/AS	NO/C	RGNVQ	IB	SQA(H)	SQA	RATIO A/AS
Accountancy/Marketing	NN45	4FT deg	g	BCC	HN	Ind	33	BBBB	HN	
Biology/Management Science	CN11	4FT deg	S g	CCD	Ind	Ind	28	BBCC	HN	
Business Studies	N120	4FT deg	g	BBC	Ind	Ind	33	BBBB	HN	
Business Studies/Business Law	MN31	4FT deg	g	BCC	Ind	Ind	33	BBBB	HN	
Business Studies/Computing Science	NG15	4FT deg	g	CCC	Ind	Ind	28	BBCC	HN	
Business Studies/Economics	LN1D	4FT deg	g	BBB	Ind	Ind	33	BBBB	HN	
Business Studies/English Studies	NQ13	4FT deg	g	BBC	HN	Ind	33	BBBB	HN	
Business Studies/Film & Media Studies	NP14	4FT deg	g	BBC	Ind	Ind	35	ABBB	HN	
Business Studies/Financial Studies	NN13	4FT deg	g	BBC	Ind	Ind	33	BBBB	HN	
Business Studies/French Language	NRCC	4FT deg	g	CCC	Ind	Ind	31	BBBC	HN	
Business Studies/German Language	NRCF	4FT deg	g	CCC	Ind	Ind	31	BBBC	HN	
Business Studies/Japanese	N1T4	4FT deg	g	BCC	Ind	Ind	31	BBBC	HN	
Business Studies/Mathematics	GN11	4FT deg	M g	CCC	Ind	Ind	28	BBCC	HN	
Business Studies/Politics	MN11	4FT deg	g	BBC	Ind	Ind	33	BBBB	HN	
Business Studies/Psychology	CN81	4FT deg	g	BBC	Ind	Ind	33	BBBB	HN	
Business Studies/Social Policy	NL14	4FT deg	g	BBC	Ind	Ind	33	BBBB	HN	
Business Studies/Sociology	NL13	4FT deg	g	BBC	Ind	Ind	33	BBBB	HN	
Business Studies/Spanish Language	NRCK	4FT deg	g	CCC	Ind	Ind	31	BBBC	HN	
Business Studies/Sports Studies	NB16	4FT deg	g	BBC	Ind	Ind	33	BBBB	HN	
Business and Management	N100	4FT deg	g	BBC	Ind	Ind	33	BBBB	HN	
Computing Science/Management Science	GN51	4FT deg	g	CCC	Ind	Ind	28	BBCC	HN	
Computing Science/Marketing	GN55	4FT deg	g	CCC	Ind	Ind	28	BBCC	HN	
Economics/Marketing	NL51	4FT deg	g	CCC	Ind	Ind	28	BBCC	HN	
Environmental Science/Management Science	FN91	4FT deg	S g	CCC	Ind	Ind	31	BBBC	HN	
Film & Media Studies/Marketing	PN45	4FT deg	g	BBC	Ind	Ind	35	ABBB	HN	
Financial Studies/Human Resources Management	NN3C	4FT deg	g	BCC	HN	Ind	31	BBBC	HN	
Financial Studies/Management Science	NN31	4FT deg	g	BCC	Ind	Ind	31	BBBC	HN	
Financial Studies/Marketing	NN35	4FT deg	g	BBC	Ind	Ind	33	BBBB	HN	
French/Human Resources Management	NR1D	4FT deg	g	CCC	Ind	Ind	31	BBBC	HN	
German/Human Resources Management	NR1G	4FT deg	g	CCC	Ind	Ind	31	BBBC	HN	
Human Resources Management	N130	4FT deg	g	BBC	Ind	Ind	33	BBBB	HN	
Human Resources Management/Business Law	MN36	4FT deg	g	BCC	Ind	Ind	33	BBBB	HN	
Human Resources Management/Economics	NL11	4FT deg	g	CCC	Ind	Ind	28	BBCC	HN	
Human Resources Management/Marketing	NN15	4FT deg	g	BBC	Ind	Ind	33	BBBB	HN	
Human Resources Management/Politics	MN1C	4FT deg	g	BBC	Ind	Ind	33	BBBB	HN	
Human Resources Management/Psychology	NL17	4FT deg	g	BBC	Ind	Ind	33	BBBB	HN	
Human Resources Management/Social Policy	NL1K	4FT deg	g	BBC	Ind	Ind	33	BBBB	HN	
Human Resources Management/Sociology	NL1H	4FT deg	g	BBC	Ind	Ind	33	BBBB	HN	
Human Resources Management/Sports Studies	NBC6	4FT deg	g	BBC	Ind	Ind	33	BBBB	HN	
Japanese/Human Resources Management	NT1K	4FT deg	g	BCC	Ind	Ind	31	BBBC	HN	
Management Science	N106	4FT deg	g	BCC	Ind	Ind	31	BBBC	HN	
Management Science/Business Law	NM13	4FT deg	g	BCC	Ind	Ind	33	BBBB	HN	
Management Science/French Language	NR1C	4FT deg	g	CCC	Ind	Ind	31	BBBC	HN	
Management Science/German Language	NR1F	4FT deg	g	CCC	Ind	Ind	31	BBBC	HN	
Management Science/Japanese	NT14	4FT deg	g	BCC	Ind	Ind	31	BBBC	HN	
Management Science/Marketing	N1N5	4FT deg	g	BBC	Ind	Ind	33	BBBB	HN	
Management Science/Mathematics	GN12	4FT deg	M g	CCC	Ind	Ind	28	BBCC	HN	
Management Science/Psychology	CNV1	4FT deg	g	BBC	Ind	Ind	33	BBBB	HN	
Management Science/Spanish Language	NR1K	4FT deg	g	CCC	Ind	Ind	31	BBBC	HN	
Management Science/Sports Studies	NBD6	4FT deg	g	BCC	Ind	Ind	31	BBBC	HN	
Marketing	N500	4FT deg	g	BBC	Ind	Ind	33	BBBB	HN	
Marketing/Business Law	MN35	4FT deg	g	BCC	Ind	Ind	33	BBBB	HN	

	course details			98 expected requirements						96 entry stats
TITLE	CODE	COURSE	SUBJECTS	A/AS	ND/C	AGNVQ	IB	SQA(H)	SQA	RATIO A/AS
Marketing/French Language	N5R1	4FT deg	g	CCC	Ind	Ind	31	BBBC	HN	
Marketing/German Language	N5R2	4FT deg	g	CCC	Ind	Ind	31	BBBC	HN	
Marketing/Japanese	N5T4	4FT deg	g	BCC	Ind	Ind	31	BBBC	HN	
Marketing/Psychology	CN85	4FT deg	g	BBC	Ind	Ind	33	BBBB	HN	
Marketing/Social Policy	LN45	4FT deg	g	BBC	Ind	Ind	33	BBBB	HN	
Marketing/Sociology	LN35	4FT deg	g	BBC	Ind	Ind	33	BBBB	HN	
Marketing/Spanish Language	N5R4	4FT deg	g	CCC	Ind	Ind	31	BBBC	HN	
Marketing/Sports Studies	NB56	4FT deg	g	BBC	Ind	Ind	33	BBBB	HN	
Mathematics and its Applications with Mgt Sci	G1N1	4FT deg	M g	CCC	Ind	Ind	28	BBCC	HN	
Modern Languages/Business Studies	NT19	4FT deg	L g	CCC	Ind	Ind	31	BBBC	HN	
Modern Languages/Marketing	TN95	4FT deg	L g	CCC	Ind	Ind	31	BBBC	HN	
Social Policy/Management Science	LN41	4FT deg	g	BCC	Ind	Ind	31	BBBC	HN	
Sociology/Management Science	LN31	4FT deg	g	BCC	Ind	Ind	31	BBBC	HN	
Spanish Language/Human Resources Management	NR14	4FT deg	g	CCC	Ind	Ind	31	BBBC	HN	

STOCKPORT COLL of F and HE

Business	421N	2FT HND	* g	2	Ind	PB/M*	Ind	Ind	Ind	
Business and Finance	091N	2FT HND	* g	2	Ind	PB/M*	Ind	Ind	Ind	
Business and Marketing	51NN	2FT HND	g	2	Ind	PB/M*	Ind	Ind	Ind	
Business and Personnel	61NN	2FT HND	g	2	Ind	PB/M*	Ind	Ind	Ind	
Customer Services and Sales	055N	2FT HND	g	2	Ind	PB/M*	Ind	Ind	Ind	

Univ of STRATHCLYDE

Business	N150	3FT/4FT deg	g	BBC	Ind		32$	ABBBC$	Ind	
Business and Software Development	GN59	4FT deg	M	CCC	HN		Ind	BBBB$	HN	
Electrical and Mech Engineering with Business St	H3N1	5FT deg	M+P+E	BBC	Ind	Ind	36$	AABBC$	Ind	
Eng with Business Mgt & Euro St(Int Euro Option)	H1ND	5FT deg	M+P g	BBB	HN		32$	AAAA$	HN	
Eng with Business Mgt & Euro St(Int Euro Option)	H1NC	5FT deg	M+P g	BBB	HN		32$	AAAA$	HN	
Eng with Business Mgt & Euro St(Int Euro Option)	H1N1	5FT deg	M+P g	CCC	HN		30$	BBBB$	HN	
Horticulture with Horticultural Management	D2N9	4FT deg	C g	CD	HN		24	BBB$	HN	
International Business and Modern Languages	NT19	5FT deg	L g	BBC	Ind		32$	ABBBB$	Ind	
Manufacturing Engineering and Management	HN71	4FT deg	M+P g	BCC	HN	Ind	34$	BBBBC$	HN	
Manufacturing Sciences and Engineering/Dip Mgt	H1NX	5SW deg	M+P	BCC			35$	AABBC$		
Mathematics, Statistics and Management Science	GN11	4FT deg	M g	CD	Ind		30$	BBCC$	Ind	
Technology and Business Studies	HN19	3FT/4FT deg	M g	CCC	HN $		24$	BBBB$	HN$	

UNIVERSITY COLLEGE SUFFOLK

Applied Biological Science with Business Studies	C1N1	3FT deg	S	EE	N $	PS	Ind	Ind	Ind	
Applied Biological Science with Management	C1NC	3FT deg	S	EE	N $	PS	Ind	Ind	Ind	
Art & Design and Business Studies	EN21	3FT deg	Pf	EE	N $	P$	Ind	Ind	Ind	
Art & Design and Business Studies	WN21	3FT deg	Pf	EE	N $	P$	Ind	Ind	Ind	
Art & Design and Management	EW12	3FT deg	Pf	EE	N $	P$	Ind	Ind	Ind	
Art & Design and Management	NW12	3FT deg	Pf	EE	N $	P$	Ind	Ind	Ind	
Art & Design with Business Studies	W2ND	3FT deg	Pf	EE	N $	P$	Ind	Ind	Ind	
Art & Design with Business Studies	E2ND	3FT deg	Pf	EE	N $	P$	Ind	Ind	Ind	
Art & Design with Management	E2NC	3FT deg	Pf	EE	N $	P$	Ind	Ind	Ind	
Art & Design with Management	W2NC	3FT deg	Pf	EE	N $	P$	Ind	Ind	Ind	
Behavioural Studies and Business Studies	LN7C	3FT deg	*	DE	N $	P$	Ind	Ind	Ind	
Behavioural Studies and Management	LN71	3FT deg	*	DE	N $	P$	Ind	Ind	Ind	
Behavioural Studies with Business Studies	L7N1	3FT deg	*	DD	N $	P$	Ind	Ind	Ind	
Behavioural Studies with Management	L7NC	3FT deg	*	DD	N $	P$	Ind	Ind	Ind	
Business Studies	N120	3FT deg	*	EE	N $	P*	Ind	Ind	Ind	
Business Studies and Applied Biological Science	CN11	3FT deg	S	EE	N $	P$	Ind	Ind	Ind	
Business Studies and Cultural Studies	NY13	3FT deg	*	CE	N $	P$	Ind	Ind	Ind	

Business and Management

			course details				*98 expected requirements*					*96 entry stats*

TITLE	CODE	COURSE	SUBJECTS	A/AS	NO/C	AGNVQ	IB	SQA(H)	SQA	RATIO A/AS
Business Studies and Early Childhood Studies	NX19	3FT deg	*	DE	N $	P$	Ind	Ind	Ind	
Business Studies and Environmental Studies	FN91	3FT deg	S	EE	N $	P$	Ind	Ind	Ind	
Business Studies and Literary Studies	NQ12	3FT deg	E	EC	N $	P$	Ind	Ind	Ind	
Business Studies and Management	N121	3FT deg	*	EE	N $	P$	Ind	Ind	Ind	
Business Studies with Accounting	N1NK	3FT deg								
Business Studies with Applied Biological Science	N1C9	3FT deg	S	EE	N $	P$	Ind	Ind	Ind	
Business Studies with Art & Design	N1W2	3FT deg	Pf	EE	N $	P$	Ind	Ind	Ind	
Business Studies with Behavioural Studies	N1L3	3FT deg	*	EE	N $	P$	Ind	Ind	Ind	
Business Studies with Cultural Studies	N1Y3	3FT deg	*	EE	N $	P$	Ind	Ind	Ind	
Business Studies with Early Childhood Studies	N1XX	3FT deg	*	EE	N $	P$	Ind	Ind	Ind	
Business Studies with Economics	N1LC	3FT deg								
Business Studies with Education Studies	N1X9	3FT deg	*	EE	N $	P$	Ind	Ind	Ind	
Business Studies with Environmental Studies	N1F9	3FT deg	*	EE	N $	P$	Ind	Ind	Ind	
Business Studies with Financial Services	N1N3	3FT deg								
Business Studies with Human Science	N1B1	3FT deg	S	EE	N $	P$	Ind	Ind	Ind	
Business Studies with Information Technology	N1G5	3FT deg	*	EE	N $	P$	Ind	Ind	Ind	
Business Studies with Leisure Studies	N1LH	3FT deg	*	EE	N $	P$	Ind	Ind	Ind	
Business Studies with Literary Studies	N1Q2	3FT deg	*	EE	N $	P$	Ind	Ind	Ind	
Business Studies with Management	N100	3FT deg	*	EE	N $	P$	Ind	Ind	Ind	
Business Studies with Marketing	N1N5	3FT deg								
Business Studies with Media Studies	N1P4	3FT deg		EE	N $	P$	Ind	Ind	Ind	
Business Studies with Personnel	N1N6	3FT deg								
Business Studies with Small Business	N122	3FT deg								
Business Studies with Social Policy	N1L4	3FT deg	*	EE	N $	P$	Ind	Ind	Ind	
Business Studies with Tourism Studies	N1P7	3FT deg	*	EE	N $	P$	Ind	Ind	Ind	
Cultural Studies and Management	YN31	3FT deg	*	CE	N $	P$	Ind	Ind	Ind	
Early Childhood Studies and Management	XN91	3FT deg	*	DE	N $	P$	Ind	Ind	Ind	
Early Childhood Studies with Business Studies	X9N1	3FT deg	*	DD	N $	P$	Ind	Ind	Ind	
Early Childhood Studies with Management	X9NC	3FT deg	*	DD	N $	P$	Ind	Ind	Ind	
Environmental Studies and Management	FN9C	3FT deg	S/Gy	EE	N $	P$	Ind	Ind	Ind	
Environmental Studies with Business Studies	F9N1	3FT deg	S/Gy	EE	N $	P$	Ind	Ind	Ind	
Environmental Studies with Management	F9NC	3FT deg	S/Gy	EE	N $	P$	Ind	Ind	Ind	
Information Technology and Business Studies	GN51	3FT deg	*	EE	N	P*	Ind	Ind	Ind	
Information Technology and Management	GN5C	3FT deg	*	EE	N $	P$	Ind	Ind	Ind	
Information Technology with Management	G5N1	3FT deg	*	EE	N $	P$	Ind	Ind	Ind	
Literary Studies and Management	QN2C	3FT deg	E	CE	N $	P$	Ind	Ind	Ind	
Media Studies and Business Studies	PN41	3FT deg	*	CE	N $	P$	Ind	Ind	Ind	
Media Studies and Management	PN4C	3FT deg	*	CE	N $	P$	Ind	Ind	Ind	
Media Studies with Business Studies	P4NC	3FT deg	*	CE	N $	P$	Ind	Ind	Ind	
Product Design & Manufacture and Business Studs	HN71	3FT deg	*	EE	N $	P$	Ind	Ind	Ind	
Product Design & Manufacture and Management	HN7C	3FT deg	*	EE	N $	P$	Ind	Ind	Ind	
Product Design & Manufacture with Art & Design	H7N2	3FT deg	Pf	EE	N $	P$	Ind	Ind	Ind	
Product Design & Manufacture with Business Studs	H7N1	3FT deg	*	EE	N $	P$	Ind	Ind	Ind	
Product Design & Manufacture with Management	H7NC	3FT deg	*	EE	N $	P$	Ind	Ind	Ind	
Business	001N	2FT HND	*	E	N	P*	Ind	Ind	Ind	
Business (European Environment)	21TN	2FT HND	*	E	N	P*	Ind	Ind	Ind	
Business (Financial Services)	3CNN	2FT HND	*	E	N	P*	Ind	Ind	Ind	
Business (Law)	31MN	2FT HND	*	E	N	P*	Ind	Ind	Ind	
Business (Tourism)	71PN	2FT HND	*	E	N	P*	Ind	Ind	Ind	
Business and Finance	31NN	2FT HND	*	E	N	P*	Ind	Ind	Ind	
Business and Marketing	51NN	2FT HND	*	E	N	P*	Ind	Ind	Ind	
Business and Personnel	61NN	2FT HND	*	E	N	P*	Ind	Ind	Ind	

course details | 98 expected requirements | 96 entry stats

TITLE	CODE	COURSE	SUBJECTS	A/AS	ND/C	AGNVQ	IB	SQA(H)	SQA	RATIO A/AS
Univ of SUNDERLAND										
Business Admin (Relevant vocational exp reqd)	N127	2FT deg		X	N $	X	X	X	X	47
Business Administration	N122	3FT deg	* g	18	1M+4D	D	26	BBBCC	N$	4
Business Administration	N128	1FT deg	*	X	X	X	X	X	X	
Business Studies	N120	4SW deg	* g	18	1M+4D$	D	26	BBBCC	N$	5 11/24
Business Studies and Computer Studies	NG15	3FT deg	* g	10	N	M	24	CCCC	N	3 6/ 8
Business Studies and Economics	NL11	3FT/4SW deg	*	8	3M	M	Ind	Ind	Ind	
Business Studies and English	NQ13	3FT/4SW deg	*	10	4M	M	Ind	Ind	Ind	
Business Studies and French	NR11	4FT deg	F g	10	N $	M	24$	CCCC$	N$	5
Business Studies and Geography	NL18	3FT deg	Gy/Gl g	12	3M $	M	24$	BCCC$	N$	6
Business Studies and Geology	NF16	3FT deg	Gy/Gl/S g	10	N $	M	24$	CCCC$	N$	
Business Studies and German	NR12	4FT deg	G g	10	N $	M	24$	CCCC$	N$	11
Business Studies and History	NV11	3FT/4SW deg	*	10	4M	M	Ind	Ind	Ind	
Business Studies and History of Art and Design	NV14	3FT/4SW deg	*	8	3M	M	Ind	Ind	Ind	
Business Studies and Mathematics	NG11	3FT/4SW deg	M	8	3M	M	Ind	Ind	Ind	
Business Studies and Physiology	NB11	3FT/4SW deg	*	8	3M	M	Ind	Ind	Ind	
Business Studies and Psychology	NC18	3FT deg	g	14	MO	M	26$	BBCC$	N	8 8/12
Business Studies and Religious Studies	NV18	3FT/4SW deg	*	8	3M	M	Ind	Ind	Ind	
Business Studies with Chemistry	N1F1	3FT/4SW deg	*	8	3M	M	Ind	Ind	Ind	
Business Studies with Economics	N1L1	3FT/4SW deg	*	8	3M	M	Ind	Ind	Ind	
Business Studies with English	N1Q3	3FT/4SW deg	*	10	4M	M	Ind	Ind	Ind	
Business Studies with French	N1R1	3FT/4SW deg	*	8	3M	M	Ind	Ind	Ind	
Business Studies with Geography	N1L8	3FT/4SW deg	*	8	3M	M	Ind	Ind	Ind	
Business Studies with Geology	N1F6	3FT/4SW deg	*	8	3M	M	Ind	Ind	Ind	
Business Studies with German	N1R2	3FT/4SW deg	*	8	3M	M	Ind	Ind	Ind	
Business Studies with History	N1V1	3FT/4SW deg	*	10	4M	M	Ind	Ind	Ind	
Business Studies with History of Art and Design	N1V4	3FT/4SW deg	*	8	3M	M	Ind	Ind	Ind	
Business Studies with Mathematics	N1G1	3FT/4SW deg	*	8	3M	M	Ind	Ind	Ind	
Business Studies with Media Studies	N1P4	3FT/4SW deg	*	24	Ind	Ind	Ind	Ind	Ind	
Business Studies with Physiology	N1B1	3FT/4SW deg	*	8	3M	M	Ind	Ind	Ind	
Business Studies with Psychology	N1C8	3FT/4SW deg	*	10	4M	M^	Ind	Ind	Ind	
Business Studies with Religious Studies	N1V8	3FT/4SW deg	*	8	3M	M	Ind	Ind	Ind	
Business Studies with Sociology	N1L3	3FT/4SW deg	*	10	4M	M	Ind	Ind	Ind	
Business and Corporate Values	N103	3FT deg	* g	18	1M+4D	D	26	BBBCC	N$	4
Business and Human Resource Management	N130	3FT deg	* g		1M+4D	D	26	BBBCC	N$	5
Business and Legal Studies	MN31	3FT deg	* g	18	1M+4D	D	26	BBBCC	N	6 10/16
Business and Management Studies	N101	3FT deg	* g	18	1M+4D	D	26	BBBCC	N	5 12/24
Business and Marketing	NN15	3FT deg	* g	18	1M+4D	D	26	BBBCC	N	5 14/18
Chemistry and Business Studies	FN11	3FT/4SW deg	C+S	8	N $	PS	24$	CCCC$	N$	
Chemistry with Business Studies	F1N1	3FT deg	C	8	3M	M	Ind	Ind	Ind	
Economics with Business Studies	L1N1	3FT deg	*	8	3M	M	Ind	Ind	Ind	
English with Business Studies	Q3N1	3FT/4SW deg	*	10	4M	M	Ind	Ind	Ind	
French with Business Studies	R1N1	4FT deg	F	8	3M	M	Ind	Ind	Ind	
Geography with Business Studies	L8N1	3FT deg	*	8	3M	M	Ind	Ind	Ind	
Geology with Business Studies	F6N1	3FT deg	*	8	3M	M	Ind	Ind	Ind	
German with Business Studies	R2N1	4SW deg	G	8	3M	M	Ind	Ind	Ind	
History with Business Studies	V1N1	3FT deg	*	10	4M	M	Ind	Ind	Ind	
International Business	N143	3FT deg	* g	18	1M+4D$	D	26	BBBCC	N$	3
International Business with French	N1RC	3FT deg	* g	18	1M+4D$	D	26	BBBCC	N$	
International Business with German	N1RF	3FT deg	* g	18	1M+4D$	D	26	BBBCC	N$	
International Business with Japanese	N1T4	3FT deg	* g	18	1M+4D$	D	26	BBBCC	N$	
International Business with Spanish	N1RK	3FT deg	* g	18	1M+4D$	D	26	BBBCC	N$	

Business and Management 12

TITLE	CODE	COURSE	SUBJECTS	A/AS	NQ/C	AGNVQ	IB	SQA(H)	SQA	RATIO	A/AS
International Business/Diplom Betriebswirt	N142	4SW deg	G g	18	1M+4D$	D	26	BBBCC	N$		
International Business/Licences-Maitrises	N141	4SW deg	E g	18	1M+4D$	D	26	BBBCC	N$	13	
Manufacturing Operations Management	H7N1 ▼	3FT/4SW deg	* g	10	3M $	M	24	CCC	N $	2	
Manufacturing Operations Management (Foundation)	H7NC ▼	4EXT/5EXTSW deg	*	2	N	P	24	CC	N		
Mathematics with Business Studies	G1N1	3FT deg	M	8	3M	M	Ind	Ind	Ind		
Media Studies with Business Studies	P4N1	3FT deg	*	24	Ind	Ind	Ind	Ind	Ind		
Pharmacology and Business Studies	BN21	3FT/4SW deg	C+S	8	N $	PS	24$	CCCC$	N$		
Physiology and Business Studies	BN11	3FT/4SW deg	C+S	8	N $	PS	24$	CCCC$	N$		
Physiology with Business Studies	B1N1	3FT deg	*	8	3M	M	Ind	Ind	Ind		
Product Design (Foundation)	HN7D	4FT deg	*								
Product Design Management	HN71 ▼	3FT deg	* g	10	3M $	M	24	CCC	N	3	6/12
Product Design Management (Foundation)	HN7C ▼	4EXT deg	*	2	N	P	24	CC	N		
Psychology with Business Studies	C8N1	3FT deg	*	10	4M	M^	Ind	Ind	Ind		
Religious Studies with Business Studies	V8N1	3FT deg	*	8	3M	M	Ind	Ind	Ind		
Sociology with Business Studies	L3N1	3FT deg	*	10	4M	M	Ind	Ind	Ind		
Technology Management	JN91 ▼	3FT/4SW deg	* g	10	N	M	24	CCCC	N	3	
Business and Finance	021N	2FT HND	* g	10	5M	M	24	CCCC	N$	4	4/10

Univ of SURREY

Mathematics with Business Studies	G1NC	4SW deg	M	18-20	Ind	Ind	Ind	CSYS	Ind	5	18/20
Mathematics with Business Studies	G1N1	3FT deg	M	18-20	Ind	Ind	Ind	CSYS	Ind	6	14/20
Physics with Management Studies	F3N1	3FT/4SW deg	M+P	BBB-CC	M $	MS^	$	Ind	Ind	7	
Retail Management	N110	4SW deg	* g	BCC-CCC	MO+3D	Ind	30$	BBBB	Ind	5	14/22

Univ of SUSSEX

Biochemistry with Management Studies	C7N1	3FT deg	C+S g	BCD	MO $	MS6 go	$	Ind	Ind		
Biology with Management Studies	C1N1	3FT deg	2S g	BCC	MO $	MS6 go	$	Ind	Ind		
Chemistry with Management Studies	F1N1	3FT deg	C+S g	CCC	MO $	MS go	$	Ind	Ind		
Chemistry with Management Studies (MChem)	F1NC	4FT deg	C+S g	CCC	MO $	MS go	$	Ind	Ind		
Electronic Engineering with Business Management	H6N1	3FT deg	M	BCC	MO $	MS^	$	Ind	Ind		
Environmental Science with Management Studies	F9N1	3FT deg	2(C/P/M) g	CCC	MO $	MS go	$	Ind	Ind		
Mathematics & Stats with Management St (MMath)	G4NC	4FT deg	M	BCC	MO $	MS^	$	Ind	Ind		
Mathematics and Stats with Management Studs	G4N1	3FT deg	M	BCC	MO $	MS^	$	Ind	Ind		
Mathematics with Management Studies	G1N1	3FT deg	M	BCC	MO $	MS^	$	Ind	Ind		
Mathematics with Management Studies (MMath)	G1ND	4FT deg	M	BCC	MO $	MS^	$	Ind	Ind		
Mechanical Engineering with Business Management	H3N1	3FT deg	M	BCC	MO $	MS^	$	Ind	Ind		
Physics with Management Studies	F3N1	3FT deg	M+P	CCC	MO $	MS^	$	Ind	Ind		
Physics with Management Studies (MPhys)	F3NC	4FT deg	M+P	CCC	MO $	MS^	$	Ind	Ind		

Univ of Wales SWANSEA

American Business Studies (4 Yrs)	N166	4FT deg	* g	ABC-BBB	6D	D$^ go	32	AABBB	Ind	3	18/26
American Management Science	N165	4FT deg	M	ABC-BBB	X	D$^ go	32$	AABBB$	X	2	16/28
Business Management and Economics	NL11	3FT deg	* g	22-24	1M+5D$	D$^ go	30$	ABBBB$	Ind	8	18/22
Business Studies	N120	3FT deg	* g	ABC-BBB	6D	D$^ go	32	AABBB	Ind	14	14/26
Business Studies with a year abroad	N121	4FT deg	* g	ABC-BBB	6D	D$^ go	32	AABBB	Ind	10	16/24
Catalan/Spanish (with Business Studies)	R4NC	4FT deg	Sp g	BBC	1M+5D$	Ind	30$	ABBBB$	Ind		
Chemistry with Business Management	FN11	3FT deg	C	BCD-CCC	3M+2D$	MS^/DS	26$	BBBCC$	Ind		
Chemistry with Business Mgt (with a year abroad)	FN1C	4FT deg	C	BBC-BCC	2M+3D$	DS^	30$	ABBBB$	Ind		
Chemistry with Business Mgt (with a year in Ind)	FN1D	4FT deg	C	BCD-CCC	3M+2D$	MS^/DS	26$	BBBCC$	Ind		
Euro Bus St with deferred choice of a Mod Lang	N1TX	4FT deg	L g	ABC-BBB	Ind	D$^ go	32$	AABBB$	Ind		
Euro Mgt Sci with deferred choice of a Mod Lang	N1TY	4FT deg	L+M	ABC-BBB	X	D$^ go	32$	AABBB$	Ind	2	
European Business Studies (France)	N1R1	4FT deg	F g	ABC-BBB	Ind	D$^ go	32$	AABBB$	Ind	3	18/26
European Business Studies (Germany)	N1R2	4FT deg	G g	ABC-BBB	Ind	D$^ go	32$	AABBB$	Ind	3	
European Business Studies (Italy)	N1R3	4FT deg	I g	ABC-BBB	Ind	D$^ go	32$	AABBB$	Ind	2	

course details			98 expected requirements							96 entry stats	
TITLE	CODE	COURSE	SUBJECTS	A/AS	NO/C	AGNVQ	IB	SQA(H)	SQA	RATIO	A/AS
European Business Studies (Spain)	N1R4	4FT deg	Sp g	ABC-BBB	Ind	D$^ go	32$	AABBB$	Ind	2	
European Management Science (France)	N1RC	4FT deg	F+M	ABC-BBB	X	X	32$	AABBB$	Ind	2	12/26
European Management Science (Germany)	N1RF	4FT deg	G+M	ABC-BBB	X	X	32$	AABBB$	Ind	3	
European Management Science (Italy)	N1RH	4FT deg	I+M	ABC-BBB	X	D$^ go	32$	AABBB$	Ind		
European Management Science (Spain)	N1RK	4FT deg	Sp+M	ABC-BBB	X	D$^ go	32$	AABBB$	Ind	1	14/18
European Master in Business Sciences (MSc)	N140	4FT deg	* g	ABB-BBB	X	D$^ go	32	AABBB	X		
French (with Business Studies)	R1N1	4FT deg	F g	BBC	1M+5D$	Ind	30$	ABBBB$	Ind	5	18/24
German (with Business Studies)	R2N1	4FT deg	G g	BBC	1M+5D$	Ind	30$	ABBBB$	Ind	4	16/20
Italian (with Business Studies)	R3N1	4FT deg	I/L g	BBC	1M+5D$	Ind	30$	ABBBB$	Ind	6	
Law and Business Studies	MN31	3FT deg	* g	BBB	6D	Ind	32	AABBB	Ind	6	16/24
Management Sci and Statistics with a year abroad	GN4C	4FT deg	M	BBC	X	D$^ go	32$	AABBB$	Ind	1	
Management Science	N108	3FT deg	M	ABC-BBB	X	D$^ go	32$	AABBB$	Ind	5	16/26
Management Science (with Mathematics)	G1N1	3FT deg	M	BBC	X	D$^ go	32$	AABBB$	Ind	8	
Management Science (with a year abroad)	N109	4FT deg	M	ABC-BBB	X	D$^ go	32$	AABBB$	Ind	4	16/24
Management Science and Statistics	GN41	3FT deg	M	BBC	X	D$^ go	32$	AABBB$	Ind	5	
Management Science with Maths (with a yr abroad)	G1NC	4FT deg	M	BBC	X	D$^ go	32$	AABBB$	Ind		
Operational Research	N200	3FT deg	M	BBB	X	D$^ go	32$	AABBB$	Ind		
Russian (with Business Studies)	R8N1	4FT deg	L/* g	BBC-BCD	1M+5D$	Ind	26$	BBBBC$	Ind	2	
Spanish (with Business Studies)	R4N1	4FT deg	L/* g	BBC	1M+5D$	Ind	30$	ABBBB$	Ind	4	12/22
Welsh (with Business Studies)	Q5N1	3FT/4FT deg	W	CCC-CCD	1M+4D$	X	Ind	Ind	Ind	3	
SWANSEA INST of HE											
Business Administration	N150	3FT deg	g	10	MO+2D	M$ go	Ind	Ind	Ind	22	
Business Studies	N120	4SW deg	g	10	MO+2D	M$ go	Ind	Ind	Ind	3	6/16
European Business Studies	N140	4SW deg	L g	10	MO+3D	M$ go	Ind	Ind	Ind		
Logistics Management	N930	3FT deg	*	10		M	Ind	Ind	Ind		
Management of Innovation	HN11	3FT deg	g	10	MO+2D	M go	Ind	Ind	Ind		
Marketing	N500	3FT deg	g	10	MO+2D	M$ go	Ind	Ind	Ind		
Personnel	N610	3FT deg	g	10	MO+2D	M$ go	Ind	Ind	Ind		
Transport Management	N921	3FT deg	*	10	6M	M	Ind	Ind	Ind	3	
Business	021N	2FT HND	g	4	3M	P$ go	Ind	Ind	Ind	3	2/7
Business & Finance	421N	2FT HND	g	4	3M	P$ go	Ind	Ind	Ind	5	4/8
Business and Marketing	011N	2FT HND	g	4	3M	P$ go	Ind	Ind	Ind	4	2/6
Business and Personnel	031N	2FT HND	g	4	3M	P$ go	Ind	Ind	Ind	5	2/8
Business and Retail Management	111N	2FT HND	g	4	3M	PS go	Ind	Ind	Ind		
European Business	9T1N	2FT HND	L g	4	Ind	Ind	Ind	Ind	Ind	2	
Management of Innovation	11HN	2FT HND	g	E	MO	P go	Ind	Ind	Ind		
Transport Management	229N	2FT HND	*	E	N	P$	Ind	Ind	Ind	3	
SWINDON COLL											
Business	021N	2FT HND	* g	4	3M	P	Ind	Ind	N		
Business and Finance	091N	2FT HND	* g	4	3M	P	Ind	Ind	N		
Business and Marketing	51NN	2FT HND	* g	4	3M	P	Ind	Ind	N		
Business and Personnel	61NN	2FT HND	* g	4	3M	P	Ind	Ind	N		
TAMESIDE COLLEGE											
Business	021N	2FT HND		2	N	P					
Business and Finance	091N	2FT HND		2	N	P					
Business and Marketing	15NN	2FT HND		2	N	P					
Business and Personnel	16NN	2FT HND		2	N	P					
Univ of TEESSIDE											
Applied Statistics for Business	GN41	3FT/4SW deg	* g	8-12	Ind	M	Ind	CCCC	Ind	2	8/22
Business Administration (HND top-up)	N150	1FT deg		X	MO			X		4	

Business and Management 12

course details | 98 expected requirements | 96 entry stats

TITLE	CODE	COURSE	SUBJECTS	A/AS	NO/C	AGNVQ	IB	SQA(H)	SQA	RATIO A/AS
Business Administration-Hospitality (HND top-up)	N123	1FT deg		X	MO			X		
Business Administration-Leisure (HND top-up)	N125	1FT deg		X	MO			X		
Business Informatics (HND top-up)	NG14	1FT deg		X	HN	M		X		5
Business Management (Generic)	N101	3FT deg	* g	12	3M+3D	D	Ind	Ind	Ind	
Business Studies (with major/minor pathways)	N120	4SW deg	* g	12	3M+3D	D	Ind	Ind	Ind	4 6/18
Design Marketing	W2N5	3FT deg	Pf g		N	M$	Ind	CCC	N	6 8/20
Design Marketing	E2N5	3FT deg	Pf g		N	M$	Ind	CCC	N	
Human Resource Management	N130	3FT deg	* g	12	3M+3D	D	Ind	Ind	Ind	3 6/20
International Business Studies	N145	3FT deg	* g	12	3M+3D	D	Ind	Ind	Ind	
Marketing	N500	3FT deg	* g	12	3M+3D	D	Ind	Ind	Ind	5 6/18
Organisational Behaviour	N154	3FT/4SW deg	* g	12	3M+3D	D	Ind	Ind	Ind	
Statistics and Operational Research	GN42	3FT/4SW deg	M	8-12	Ind	M	Ind	CCCC	Ind	
Modular Degree Scheme *Business Studies*	Y401	3FT deg								
Modular Degree Scheme *Human Resource Management*	Y401	3FT deg								
Modular Degree Scheme *Marketing*	Y401	3FT deg								
Applied Statistics for Business	4G1N	2FT HND	* g	4	N	P	Ind	CC	Ind	
Business and Administration	051N▼	2FT HND								
Business and Countryside Tourism	17NP▼	2FT HND								
Business and European St (incorp Kaufmann Awd)	12NT▼	2FT HND								
Business and European Studies	21TN▼	2FT HND								
Business and Finance	091N▼	2FT HND								
Business and Financial Services	31NN▼	2FT HND								
Business and Human Resource Management	031N▼	2FT HND								
Business and Marketing	51NN▼	2FT HND								
Business and Travel and Tourism	71PN▼	2FT HND								

THAMES VALLEY Univ

TITLE	CODE	COURSE	SUBJECTS	A/AS	NO/C	AGNVQ	IB	SQA(H)	SQA	RATIO A/AS
Accounting with Business	N4N1	2FT/3FT Dip/deg		2-12	N/MO	P/M	24	CC		
Accounting with Retail Management	N4NM	3FT deg		8-12	MO	M	26	CCC		
Business Administration	N122	3FT deg	* g	8-12	MO	M	26	CCC		
Business Administration with Accounting	N1NK	3FT deg		8-12	MO	M	26	CCC		
Business Administration with Advertising	N1PH	3FT deg		8-12	MO	M	26	CCC		
Business Administration with Economics	N1LC	3FT deg		8-12	MO	M	26	CCC		
Business Administration with English Language St	N1QC	3FT deg		8-12	MO	M	26	CCC		
Business Administration with Finance	N1NH	3FT deg		8-12	MO	M	26	CCC		
Business Administration with French	N1RC	3FT deg		8-12	MO	M	26	CCC		
Business Administration with German	N1RF	3FT deg		8-12	MO	M	26	CCC		
Business Administration with Health Studies	N1LK	3FT deg		8-12	MO	M	26	CCC		
Business Administration with Human Resource Mgt	N1NP	3FT deg		8-12	MO	M	26	CCC		
Business Administration with Information Mgt	N1PF	3FT deg		8-12	MO	M	26	CCC		
Business Administration with Information Systems	N1GM	3FT deg		8-12	MO	M	26	CCC		
Business Administration with Marketing	N1NM	3FT deg		8-12	MO	M	26	CCC		
Business Administration with Spanish	N1RK	3FT deg		8-12	MO	M	26	CCC		
Business Economics with Business	L1NC	3FT deg		8-12	MO	M	26	CCC		
Business Economics with Marketing	L1NM	3FT deg		8-12	MO	M	26	CCC		
Business Studies (Dip)	N120	3FT/4SW deg	* g	8-12	MO	M	26	CCC		
Business Studies with Accounting (Dip)	N1N4	3FT/4SW deg		12	MO	M	26			
Business Studies with Advertising (Dip)	N1P3	3FT/4SW deg		12	MO	M	26			
Business Studies with Business Economics (Dip)	N1LD	3FT/4SW deg		12	MO	M	26			
Business Studies with Economics (Dip)	N1L1	3FT/4SW deg		12	MO	M	26			
Business Studies with English Language St (Dip)	N1Q1	3FT/4SW deg		12	MO	M	26			

course details | 98 expected requirements | 96 entry stats

TITLE	CODE	COURSE	SUBJECTS	A/AS	ND/C	AGNVQ	IB	SQA(H)	SQA	RATIO A/AS
Business Studies with Finance (Dip)	N1N3	3FT/4SW deg		12	MO	M	26			
Business Studies with French (Dip)	N1R1▼	3FT/4SW deg	* g	10-12	MO+2D	M	26	CCC		
Business Studies with German (Dip)	N1R2▼	3FT/4SW deg	* g	10-12	MO+2D	M	26	CCC		
Business Studies with Human Resource Mgt (Dip)	N1N6	3FT/4SW deg		8-12	MO	M	26	CCC		
Business Studies with Information Mgt (Dip)	N1P2	3FT/4SW deg		8-12	MO	M	26	CCC		
Business Studies with Information Systems (Dip)	N1G5	3FT/4SW deg		8-12	MO	M	26	CCC		
Business Studies with Law (Dip)	N1M3	3FT/4SW deg		8-12	MO	M	26	CCC		
Business Studies with Marketing (Dip)	N1N5	3FT/4SW deg		8-12	MO	M	26	CCC		
Business Studies with Politics & Int Rels (Dip)	N1M1	3FT/4SW deg		8-12	MO	M	26	CCC		
Business Studies with Retail Management	N1NN	3FT/4SW deg		8-12	MO	M	26	CCC		
Business Studies with Spanish	N1R4▼	3FT/4SW deg	* g	10-12	MO+2D	M	26	CCC		
Digital Arts with Business	W9N1	3FT deg		8-12	MO	M		CCC		
Economics with Business	L1N1	3FT deg		8-12	MO	M	26	CCC		
Economics with Marketing	L1N5	3FT deg		8-12	MO	M	26	CCC		
English Lang and Communications with Business	Q1N1	3FT deg		8-12	MO	M	24	CCC		
Environmental Policy and Mgt with Business	F9N1	3FT deg		8-12	MO	M	26	CCC		
Environmental Policy and Mgt with Marketing	F9N5	3FT deg		8-12	MO	M	26	CCC		
European Studies with Business	T2N1	3FT deg		8-12	MO	M	26	CCC		
Finance with Business	N3N1	3FT deg		8-12	MO	M	26	CCC		
Food and Drink Consumer St with Food Servs Mgt	D4N9	3FT deg		8-12	MO	M	26	CCC		
Food and Drink Consumer Studies with Business	D4N1	3FT deg		8-12	MO	M	26	CCC		
Food and Drink Consumer Studies with Marketing	D4N5	3FT deg		8-12	MO	M	26	CCC		
Food and Drink Consumer Studies with Retail Mgt	D4NM	3FT deg		8-12	MO	M	26	CCC		
French with Business	R1N1	3FT deg		8-12	MO	M	26	CCC		
German with Business	R2N1	3FT deg		8-12	MO	M	26	CCC		
Health Studies with Business	L4N1	3FT deg		8-12	MO	M	26	CCC		
History with Business	V1N1	3FT deg		8-12	MO	M	26	CCC		
Hospitality Management with Business	N7N1	2FT/3FT Dip/deg		2-12	N/MO	P/M	24	CC		
Hospitality Management with Food Services Mgt	N7N9	3FT deg		8-12	MO	M	26	CCC		
Hospitality Management with Human Resource Mgt	N7N6	3FT deg		8-12	MO	M	26	CCC		
Hospitality Management with Marketing	N7N5	3FT deg		8-12	MO	M	26	CCC		
Hospitality Management with Retail Management	N7NM	3FT deg		8-12	MO	M	26	CCC		
Human Resource Management with Accounting	N6N4	3FT deg		8-12	MO	M	26	CCC		
Human Resource Management with Business	N6N1	3FT deg		8-12	MO	M	26	CCC		
Human Resource Management with Community Law	N6MH	3FT deg		8-12	MO	M	26	CCC		
Human Resource Management with Economics	N6L1	3FT deg		8-12	MO	M	26	CCC		
Human Resource Management with Finance	N6N3	3FT deg		8-12	MO	M	26	CCC		
Human Resource Management with French	N6R1	3FT deg		8-12	MO	M	26	CCC		
Human Resource Management with German	N6R2	3FT deg		8-12	MO	M	26	CCC		
Human Resource Management with Marketing	N6N5	3FT deg		8-12	MO	M	26	CCC		
Human Resource Management with Psychology	N6C8	3FT deg		8-12	MO	M	26	CCC		
Human Resource Management with Spanish	N6R4	3FT deg		8-12	MO	M	26	CCC		
Human Resource Mgt with Business Economics	N6LC	3FT deg		8-12	MO	M	26	CCC		
Human Resource Mgt with English Language Studies	N6Q1	3FT deg		8-12	MO	M	26	CCC		
Information Management with Business	P2N1	3FT deg		8-12	MO	M	26	CCC		
Information Management with Retail Management	P2NM	3FT deg		8-12	MO	M	26	CCC		
International Studies with Business	M9N1	3FT deg		8-12	MO	M	26	CCC		
International Studies with Marketing	M9N5	3FT deg		8-12	MO	M	26	CCC		
Law with Business	M3N1	3FT deg		8-12	MO	M	26	CCC		
Leisure Management with Business	N7NC	3FT deg		8-12	MO	M	26	CCC		
Leisure Management with Food Services Management	N7NX	3FT deg		8-12	MO	M	26	CCC		
Leisure Management with Human Resource Mgt	N7NP	3FT deg		8-12	MO	M	26	CCC		

Business and Management 12

			98 expected requirements							96 entry stats
TITLE	CODE	COURSE	SUBJECTS	A/AS	NO/C	AGNVQ	IB	SQA(H)	SQA	RATIO A/AS
Leisure Management with Marketing	N7NN	3FT deg		8-12	MO	M	26	CCC		
Marketing with Accounting	N5N4	3FT deg		8-12	MO	M	26	CCC		
Marketing with Advertising	N5P3	3FT deg		8-12	MO	M	26	CCC		
Marketing with Business	N5N1	3FT deg		8-12	MO	M	26	CCC		
Marketing with English Language Studies	N5Q1	3FT deg		8-12	MO	M	26	CCC		
Marketing with Finance	N5N3	3FT deg		8-12	MO	M	26	CCC		
Marketing with French	N5R1	3FT deg		8-12	MO	M	26	CCC		
Marketing with German	N5R2	3FT deg		8-12	MO	M	26	CCC		
Marketing with Media Studies	N5W9	3FT deg		8-12	MO	M	26	CCC		
Marketing with Multi-Media Computing	N5G5	3FT deg		8-12	MO	M	26	CCC		
Marketing with Psychology	N5C8	3FT deg		8-12	MO	M	26	CCC		
Marketing with Retail Management	N5NM	3FT deg		8-12	MO	M	26	CCC		
Marketing with Spanish	N5R4	3FT deg		8-12	MO	M	26	CCC		
Media Arts with Business	W9NC	3FT deg		8-12	MO	M	26	CCC		
Media Arts with Marketing	W9N5	3FT deg		8-12	MO	M	26	CCC		
Multi-Media Computing with Business	G5N1	3FT deg		8-12	MO	M	26	CCC		
Multi-Media Computing with Marketing	G5N5	3FT deg		8-12	MO	M	26	CCC		
Politics & International Relations with Business	M1N1	3FT deg		8-12	MO	M	26	CCC		
Psychology with Business	C8N1	3FT deg		8-12	MO	M	26	CCC		
Psychology with Human Resource Management	C8N6	3FT deg		8-12	MO	M	26	CCC		
Psychology with Marketing	C8N5	3FT deg		8-12	MO	M	26	CCC		
Recreation Management with Business	N7ND	3FT deg		8-12	MO	M	26	CCC		
Sociology with Business	L3N1	3FT deg		8-12	MO	M	26	CCC		
Sociology with Marketing	L3N5	3FT deg		8-12	MO	M	26	CCC		
Spanish with Business	R4N1	3FT deg		8-12	MO	M	26	CCC		
Tourism with Business	P7N1	3FT deg		8-12	MO	M	26	CCC		
Tourism with Food Services Management	P7N9	3FT deg		8-12	MO	M	26	CCC		
Tourism with Hotel Management	P7ND	3FT deg		8-12	MO	M	26	CCC		
Tourism with Human Resource Management	P7N6	3FT deg		8-12	MO	M	26	CCC		
Tourism with Marketing	P7N5	3FT deg		8-12	MO	M	26	CCC		
Tourism with Retail Management	P7NM	3FT deg		8-12	MO	M	26	CCC		
Business Studies	021N▼	2FT/3SW HND	* g	4	N	P	24	CC		
Hospitality and Tourism	7P1N▼	3SW HND	*	4	MO	P	24	CC		
Multi-Media Computing	1N4P	2FT HND	* g	2-4	N	P	24	CC		

Univ of ULSTER

TITLE	CODE	COURSE	SUBJECTS	A/AS	NO/C	AGNVQ	IB	SQA(H)	SQA	RATIO A/AS
Business St with Specialisms (4 Yr SW inc DIS)	N125▼	4SW deg	* g	BCC	MO+4D	D*6/^ gi	30	BBBB	Ind	14 16/22
Business Studies (4 Yr SW inc DIS)	N120▼	4SW deg	* g	BBC	MO+4D	D*6/^ gi	32	ABBB	Ind	21 22/28
Business Studies with Japanese (4 Yr inc DAS)	N1T4▼	4SW deg	* g	CCC	MO+3D	D*6/^ gi	28	BBBC	Ind	9 16/20
Business with Computing (3 Yr/4 Yr SW inc DIS)	N1G5▼	3FT/4SW deg	* g	BCC	MO+4D	D*6/^ gi	29	BBBB	Ind	16 16/28
Computing with Enterprise Studies	G5N1▼	4SW deg	* g	BCC	MO+4D	D*6/^ gi	30	BBBB	Ind	
Computing with Marketing	G5N5▼	4SW deg	* g	BCC	MO+4D	D*6/^ gi	30	BBBB	Ind	
Consumer Studies (3 Yr/4 Yr SW inc DIS)	N980▼	3FT/4SW deg	* g	CCC	MO+3D	D*6/^ gi	28	BBBC	Ind	18 18/24
Engineering with Business (4 Yr SW inc DIS)	H1N1▼	4SW deg	S/M	CCC	MO+3D	Ind	28	BBBB	Ind	
European Business Studies (4 Yr Options)	N140▼	4SW deg	L g	BCC	MO+4D	D6/^ gi	30	BBBB	Ind	9 16/26
International Business Communication	NT19▼	4SW deg	L g	CCC	MO+3D	D^ gi	28	BBBC	Ind	9 14/20
Psychology with Organisational Science	C8N2▼	3FT deg	g	CCC	MO+3D	D*6/^ gi	28	BBBC	Ind	6 10/20
Retail Distribution Management	NN59▼	3FT deg	* g	BCC	MO+4D	D*6/^ gi	30	BBBB	Ind	16 16/20
Science with Management (4 Yr SW inc Dip)	C9N1▼	4SW deg	B/C g	CCD	MO+2D	DS6/^ gi	27	BBCC	Ind	9 14/20
Business & Related St (3 Yr SW inc CIS or CAS)	521N▼	3SW HND	* g	CDD	Ind	D* gi	26	BCCC	Ind	18 12/18

			98 expected requirements							96 entry stats	
course details											
TITLE	CODE	COURSE	SUBJECTS	A/AS	NO/C	RGNVQ	IB	SQA(H)	SQA	RATIO	A/AS
UNIVERSITY COLL LONDON (Univ of London)											
Chemistry with Management Studies	F1N1	3FT deg	C+M/P/B g	CCC-BBB	MO $	Ind	28$	BCCCC$	N$	31	
Chemistry with Management Studies (MSci)	F1NC	4FT deg	C+M/P/B g	CCC-BBB	MO $	Ind	28$	BCCCC$	N$		20/24
Dutch with Management Studies (4 Yrs)	T2N1	4FT deg	g	BCC-BBC	3M	D$^ go	26$	BBBCC	Ind	2	
Electronic Engineering with Management Studies	H6N1	3FT deg	M+P g	ABB-AAB	DO $	X	30$	BBBCC$	Ind	6	
Engineering with Business Finance	H130	3FT deg	M g	BBC-ABB	Ind	Ind	32$	BBBBC$	Ind	5	22/28
Italian and Business Studies (4 Yrs)	RN31	4FT deg	g	BCC-BBC	3M	M$^ go	30	BBBCC$	Ind	6	16/26
Mathematics with Management Studies	G1N1	3FT deg	M g	ABC-ABB	MO $	Ind	30$	AAABB$	N$	9	24/28
Mathematics with Management Studies (MSci)	G1NC	4FT deg	M g	ABC-ABB	MO $	Ind	30$	AAABB$	N$	4	
Scandinavian Studies with Management St (4 Yrs)	R7N1	4FT deg	* g	CC	3M	X	26$	BBCCC	Ind	2	12/14
Statistics and Operational Research with Mgt St	G4N1	3FT deg	M g	BCC	MO $	Ind	30$	BCCCC$	N$	7	22/24
Statistics,Computing,Operational Res & Economics *Operational Research*	Y624	3FT deg	M g	BCC	MO $	Ind	30$	BBCCC$	N$		
Statistics,Operational Res & a European Language *Operational Research*	Y625	3FT deg	M g	BCC	MO $	Ind	30$	BBCCC$	N$		
Univ Col WARRINGTON											
Leisure Studies with Business Management and IT	NN71	3FT deg	* g	10-12	Ind	Ind	Ind	Ind	Ind		
Media St with Bus Mgt & IT (Multi-Media Journal)	NP1K	3FT deg	* g	16	Ind	Ind	Ind	Ind	Ind	3	8/16
Media St with Bus Mgt and IT (Music Record Prod)	NP1L	3FT deg	* g	16	Ind	Ind	Ind	Ind	Ind		
Media Studs with Bus Mgt & IT (Radio Production)	NPD4	3FT deg	* g	16	Ind	Ind	Ind	Ind	Ind	4	10/24
Media Studs with Bus Mgt & IT (Television Prod)	NPC4	3FT deg	* g	16	Ind	Ind	Ind	Ind	Ind	4	9/22
Performing Arts with Business Management and IT	NW14	3FT deg	* g	12-14	Ind	Ind	Ind	Ind	Ind	3	4/20
Sports Studies with Business Management and IT	BN61	3FT deg	* g	12-14	Ind	Ind	Ind	Ind	Ind		
Business	001N	2FT HND	* g	6	Ind	Ind	Ind	Ind	Ind	2	
Univ of WARWICK											
Applied Mathematics and Business Studies	G1N1	3FT deg	M g	AAA-AAB	X	X	36$	CSYS$			
Chemistry and Business Studies	FN11	3FT deg	C+S/M g	BCC	M+D $	DS^	28$	BBBBB$		11	16/18
Chemistry with Management	F1N1	3FT deg	C+S/M g	BBB	M+D $	DS^	30$	AABBB$			
Computer Science and Business Studies	GN51	3FT deg	* g	ABB	Ind	D$^	33	AAABB		9	24/30
Computer and Management Sciences	GN5C	3FT deg	M g	ABB	Ind	D$^	33$	AAABB$		11	26/28
Engineering and Business Studies	H1N1	3FT deg	M+S g	CCC	5M+1D$	D$^	28$	BBBBC$		4	16/24
German & Business Studies (4 Yrs inc yr abroad)	RN21	4FT deg	G g	BBB	X	X	32$	ABBBB$		6	22/30
International Business (4 Yrs inc yr abroad)	N140	4FT deg	F/G/I g	AAB-ABB	X	Ind	36$	AAAAB$		12	26/30
Law and Business Studies (3/4 years)	MN31	3FT/4FT deg	* g	ABB-BBB	Ind	Ind	34	AAABB			
Management Sciences	N100	3FT deg	g	ABB	DO $	D$6/^	32	AAABB		9	24/30
Mathematics and Business Studies	G1NC	3FT deg	M g	AAA-AAB	X	X	36$	CSYS$		11	26/30
Physics and Business Studies	FN31	3FT deg	P+M g	BBC	3M+2D$	DS^	30$	ABBBB$		5	
Maths-Operational Research-Statistics-Economics *Operational Research*	Y602	3FT deg	M g	ABC	X	X	32$	AABBB$			
WEST HERTS COLL											
Advertising & Marketing Communications	N510	1FT deg									
Business Administration (1 Year Top-Up to HND)	N122	1FT deg		X	HN		X	X		11	
Business Administration (Care Management)	N150	3FT deg									
Media Production Management	EP14	3FT deg	*	4	N						
Advertising & Marketing Communications	025N	2FT HND									
Business (Options)	421N	2FT HND	*	2						1	2/6
Business and Finance	31NN	2FT HND								3	
Business and Marketing	51NN	2FT HND								3	4/10
Business and Personnel	031N	2FT HND								5	

Business and Management 12

course details | 98 expected requirements | 96 entry stats

TITLE	CODE	COURSE	SUBJECTS	A/AS	NO/C	AGNVQ	IB	SQA(H)	SQA	RATIO	A/AS
Univ of WESTMINSTER											
Business Administration	N121▼	3FT deg	*	12	MO+3D	D	26		Ind	13	10/18
Business Information Management and Finance	NG15	4SW deg	*	CC	MO+2D		28	BBBB	Ind		
Business Studies	N120	4SW deg	*	14	MO+3D	D	26	BBB	Ind	14	13/24
Business Studies (Services)	N900	3FT deg	*	14	MO+3D	D	26	BBB	Ind	7	14/20
Business Studies (Services-Finance)	N902	3FT deg	*	14-16	MO+3D	D	26	BBB	Ind		
Business Studies (Services-Retail)	N901	3FT deg	*	14-16	MO+3D	D	26	BBB	Ind		
Business Studies (Services-Travel)	N903	3FT deg	*	14-16	MO+3D	D	26	BBB	Ind		
Economics for Business	LN11	3FT deg	*	BC	MO+3D	D	26	BBB	Ind	7	11/18
Environmental Science and Business Management	FN91	3FT deg	B	CD	3M	M	26$		Ind	5	6/12
European Management	N140▼	4FT deg	*	BC	MO+3D	D	26	BBB			
Industrial Systems & Business Mgt (Sandwich)	HN71	4SW deg	*	12	6M	M	26	BBC		1	10/16
Industrial Systems & Business Mgt (with found)	HN11	5EXT deg	*	D-E	N	P				10	
International Business	N1T9	4FT deg	*	BC	MO+3D	D	26	BBB		11	12/18
Managing Business Information	NG17	3FT deg		CC	MO+2D	D	26	BBB			
Statistics and Operational Research	GN42	3FT deg	M	CD		M	Ind	Ind	Ind		
Urban Property	N830	3FT deg	*	12-14	3M	M	Ind	BBB			
Urban Property (with foundation)	N835	4FT deg				P					
WESTMINSTER COLLEGE											
Business	001N	2FT HND		8	Ind	Ind	24	Ind	Ind		
Business & Finance	091N	2FT HND		8	Ind	Ind	24	Ind	Ind		
Business & Marketing	51NN	2FT HND		8	Ind	Ind	24	Ind	Ind		
Business & Personnel	61NN	2FT HND		8	Ind	Ind	24	Ind	Ind		
WEST THAMES COLL											
Business and Finance (International Trade)	091N	2FT HND	Bu								
WIGAN and LEIGH COLL											
Business Studies	N100▼	4FT deg									
Business	001N▼	2FT HND		DD	N	P					
Business and Finance	091N▼	2FT HND		DD	N	P					
Business and Legal Studies	31NN▼	2FT HND		DD	N	P					
Business and Marketing	51NN▼	2FT HND		DD	N	P					
Business and Personnel	61NN▼	2FT HND		DD	N	P					
Business with Hospitality, Leisure and Tourism	71NN▼	2FT HND		6	N	Ind	Dip		N		
WIRRAL METROPOLITAN COLLEGE											
Business	021N	2FT HND			Ind	Ind	Ind	Ind	Ind		
Univ of WOLVERHAMPTON											
Business (Specialist Route)	N120	3FT deg	g	14	4M	M	24	BBBB	Ind	19	
Business Economics	L1N1	3FT deg		14	4M	M	24	BBBB	Ind	6	6/14
Business Information Systems	GN51	3FT/4SW deg	*	12	4M	M	24	BBBB	Ind	3	6/13
Business Studies	N121	4SW deg	g	16	4M	D	24	BBBB$	Ind	7	10/20
Civil Engineering Management	H2NC	3FT/4SW deg	*g	DD	N	M	24	CCCC	Ind	37	
European Business Administration	N141	4SW deg	g	16	4M	D	24	BBBB	Ind	2	10/22
European Civil Engineering Management	H2N1	3FT/4SW deg	*g	DD	N	M	24	CCCC	Ind	7	
Human Resource Management (Specialist Route)	N130	3FT deg	g	14	4M	M	24	BBBB	Ind	17	14/20
Marketing (Specialist Route)	N501	3FT deg	g	14	4M	M	24	BBBB	Ind	70	
Mathematical Business Analysis	GN12	4SW deg	M	12	4M	M	24	BBBB	Ind	2	8/18
Applied Sciences *Business*	Y100	3FT/4SW deg	g	14	4M	M	24	BBBB	Ind		
Applied Sciences *Decision Sciences*	Y100	3FT/4SW deg	S g	DD	N	M	24	CCCC	Ind		

| | | | *98 expected requirements* | | | | | | | *96 entry stats* |

TITLE	CODE	COURSE	SUBJECTS	A/AS	ND/C	AGNVQ	IB	SQA(H)	SQA	RATIO A/AS
Applied Sciences (4 Yrs) *Decision Sciences*	Y110▼	4FT deg	*							
Combined Degrees *Business*	Y401	3FT deg	g	14	4M	M	24	BBBB	Ind	
Combined Degrees *Business Information Management*	Y401	3FT deg	g	14	4M	M	24	BBBB	Ind	
Combined Degrees *Human Resource Management*	Y401	3FT deg	g	14	4M	M	24	BBBB	Ind	
Combined Degrees *Marketing*	Y401	3FT deg	g	14	4M	M	24	BBBB	Ind	
Combined Degrees *Quality Management*	Y401	3FT deg		10	4M	M	24	BBBB	Ind	
Business & Finance	421N▼	2FT HND	g	12	4M	M	24	BBBB	Ind	4 2/11

WORCESTER COLL of HE

TITLE	CODE	COURSE	SUBJECTS	A/AS	ND/C	AGNVQ	IB	SQA(H)	SQA	RATIO A/AS
Business Management/Art and Design	WN91	3FT deg	A	DD	Ind	M	Ind	Ind	Ind	
Business Management/Biological Science	CN11	3FT deg	S	DD	Ind	M	Ind	Ind	Ind	
Drama/Business Management	NW14	3FT deg		DD	Ind	M	Ind	Ind	Ind	7
Economy and Society/Business Management	NL11	3FT deg		DD	Ind	M	Ind	Ind	Ind	2
Education Studies/Business Management	NX19	3FT deg		DD	Ind	M	Ind	Ind	Ind	2
Environmental Science/Business Management	NF19	3FT deg		DD	Ind	M	Ind	Ind	Ind	3
Geography/Business Management	NL18	3FT deg		DD	Ind	M	Ind	Ind	Ind	12
Health Studies/Business Management	NB19	3FT deg	g	DD	Ind	M	Ind	Ind	Ind	3
History/Business Management	NV11	3FT deg		DD	Ind	M	Ind	Ind	Ind	11
Information Technology/Business Management	NG15	3FT deg		DD	Ind	M	Ind	Ind	Ind	2 7/16
Psychology/Business Management	NL17	3FT deg	g	CC	Ind	M	Ind	Ind	Ind	12
Sociology/Business Management	NL13	3FT deg		DD	Ind	M	Ind	Ind	Ind	25
Sports Studies/Business Management	NB16	3FT deg		CC	Ind	M	Ind	Ind	Ind	
Urban Studies/Business Management	NL1V	3FT deg		DD	Ind	M	Ind	Ind	Ind	3
Women's Studies/Business Management	NM19	3FT deg		DD	Ind	M	Ind	Ind	Ind	
Business Studies	021N▼	2FT HND		E	N	Ind	Ind	Ind	Ind	16

WORCESTER COLLEGE of Technology

TITLE	CODE	COURSE	SUBJECTS	A/AS	ND/C	AGNVQ	IB	SQA(H)	SQA	RATIO A/AS
Business	001N	2FT HND	*	2	N	P				

WRITTLE COLL

TITLE	CODE	COURSE	SUBJECTS	A/AS	ND/C	AGNVQ	IB	SQA(H)	SQA	RATIO A/AS
Agricultural Engineering with Business Mgt	H3N1	3FT/4SW deg	* g	12	MO	M+	Ind	Ind	Ind	3
Agriculture (Business Management)	D2N1	3FT/4SW deg	Ap g	12	MO	M	Ind	Ind	Ind	
Business Management	N100	3FT deg	Ap g	12	MO	M	Ind	Ind	Ind	
Horticulture (Business Management)	DN21	3FT/4SW deg	Ap g	10	MO	M	Ind	Ind	Ind	
Land Management and Technology	N805	3FT deg	Ap g	12	MO	M	Ind	Ind	Ind	
Agriculture (Business Management)	1FND	2FT/3SW HND	Ap g	6	N	M	Ind	Ind	Ind	
Land Management and Technology	508N	2FT/3SW HND	Ap g	6	N	M	Ind	Ind	Ind	

WYE COLL (Univ of London)

TITLE	CODE	COURSE	SUBJECTS	A/AS	ND/C	AGNVQ	IB	SQA(H)	SQA	RATIO A/AS
Agricultural Business Management	D2N1	3FT deg	S+Ec	14	2M+1D$	Ind	25$	BBCCC$	Ind	
Business Studies	N120	4SW deg	Ec	14	2M+1D$	Ind	25$	BBCCC$	Ind	
Business and the Environment	N1F9	4FT deg								
Equine Business Management	D2ND	4SW deg	Ec/M/B	16	2M+1D	Ind	25	BBCCC	Ind	
Horticultural Business Management	D2NC	3FT/4SW deg	S+Ec	14	2M+1D$	Ind	25$	BBCCC$	Ind	
International Business	N140	4FT deg								

Business and Management 12

course details			98 expected requirements							96 entry stats
TITLE	CODE	COURSE	SUBJECTS	A/AS	ND/C	AGNVQ	IB	SQA(H)	SQA	RATIO A/AS
Univ of YORK										
Electronic Engineering with Business Management	H6NC	4SW deg	M+S	BBB	MO+3D$	D$^	30$	CSYS$	Ind	
Electronic Engineering with Business Management	H6N1	3FT deg	M+S	BBB	MO+3D$	D$^	30$	CSYS$	Ind	
Electronic Engineering with Business Management	H6ND	4FT deg	M+S	BBB	MO+3D$	D$^	30$	CSYS$	Ind	
Information Technology, Business Mgt & Language	G5N1	3FT deg	* g	24	HN	D$^ go	32	BBBB	Ind	24/26
Information Technology, Business Mgt & Language	G5NC	4SW deg	* g	24	HN	D$^ go	32	BBBB	Ind	22/30
Physics with Business Management	F3N1	3FT/4FT deg	M+P	BCC	Ind	DS^	28$	CSYS$	Ind	
Physics with Business Management (Europe)	F3NC	4FT deg	M+P g	BCC	Ind	DS^	28$	CSYS$	Ind	
YORK COLLEGE of F and HE										
Business	021N	2FT HND	*	2	MO	M	Ind	Ind	Ind	
YORKSHIRE COAST COLLEGE of F and HE										
Business Studies	021N	2FT HND	*	2	N	P	Ind	Ind	Ind	

TITLE	CODE	COURSE	SUBJECTS	A/AS	ND/C	RGNVQ	IB	SQA(H)	SQA	RATIO A/AS
course details			**98 expected requirements**							**96 entry stats**
Univ of ABERDEEN										
Chemistry	F100	4FT deg	C+2S/C+M+S g	CCD	Ind	MS go	24$	BBBC$	Ind	7
Chemistry (MChem)	F105	4FT deg	C+2S g	CCD	Ind	MS go	24$	BBBC$	Ind	
Chemistry with Accountancy	F1N4	4FT deg	C+2S/C+M+S g	CCD	Ind	MS go	24$	BBBC$	Ind	
Chemistry with Biomedical Sciences	F1B9	4FT deg	C+2S/C+M+S g	CCD	Ind	MS go	24$	BBBC$	Ind	
Chemistry with Environmental Chemistry	F140	4FT deg	C+2S/C+M+S g	CCD	Ind	MS go	24$	BBBC$	Ind	8
Chemistry with French	F1R1	4FT deg	C+2S/C+M+S g	CCD	Ind	MS go	24$	BBBC$	Ind	7
Chemistry with German	F1R2	4FT deg	C+2S/C+M+S g	CCD	Ind	MS go	24$	BBBC$	Ind	3
Chemistry with Management Studies	F1N1	4FT deg	C+2S/C+M+S g	CCD	Ind	MS go	24$	BBBC$	Ind	
Chemistry with New Materials Technology	F1J5	4FT deg	C+2S/C+S+M g	CCD	Ind	MS go	24$	BBBC$	Ind	5
Chemistry with Physics	F1F3	4FT deg	C+2S/C+S+M g	CCD	Ind	MS go	24$	BBBC$	Ind	
Chemistry with Spanish	F1R4	4FT deg	C+2S/C+M+S g	CCD	Ind	MS go	24$	BBBC$	Ind	
Chemistry with a year in Canada	F102	4FT deg	C+2S/C+M+S g	CCD	Ind	MS go	24$	BBBC$	Ind	
Chemistry with a year in Japan	F106	5FT deg	C+2S/C+M+S g	CCD	Ind	MS go	24$	BBBC$	Ind	
Physics with Chemistry	F3F1	4FT deg	M+2S g	CCD	Ind	MS go	24$	BBBC$	Ind	
Univ of ABERTAY DUNDEE										
Applied Chemistry	F110	4FT/5SW deg	C	DD	Ind	Ind	Ind	BCC	Ind	
Applied Chemistry with Business Management	F1NC	4FT/5SW deg	C	DD	Ind	Ind	Ind	BCC	Ind	
Applied Chemistry with Economics	F1L1	4FT/5SW deg	C	DD	Ind	Ind	Ind	BCC	Ind	
Applied Chemistry with Environmental Chemistry	F140	4FT/5SW deg	C	DD	Ind	Ind	Ind	BCC	Ind	
Applied Chemistry with Management Accounting	F1N4	4FT/5SW deg	C	DD	Ind	Ind	Ind	BCC	Ind	
Applied Chemistry with Materials Chemistry	F111	4FT/5SW deg	C	DD	Ind	Ind	Ind	BCC	Ind	
Applied Chemistry with Pharmaceutical Chemistry	F126	4FT/5SW deg	C	DD	Ind	Ind	Ind	BCC	Ind	
Applied Chemistry with a European Language	F1T2	4FT/5SW deg	C	DD	Ind	Ind	Ind	BCC	Ind	
Applied Pharmaceutical Science	F127	4FT/5SW deg			Ind	Ind	Ind		Ind	
Biology & Chemistry	CF11	4FT/5SW deg	<u>C</u>	CD	Ind	Ind	Ind	BBC	Ind	
Chemistry & Computing	FG15	4FT/5SW deg	<u>C</u>	CD	Ind	Ind	Ind	BBC	Ind	
Chemistry & Mathematics	FG11	4FT/5SW deg	<u>C+M</u>	CD	Ind	Ind	Ind	BBC	Ind	
Management & Chemistry	FN11	4FT/5SW deg	<u>C</u>	CD	Ind	Ind	Ind	BBC	Ind	
Applied Chemistry	011F	2FT HND	C	D	Ind	Ind	Ind	BC	Ind	
ANGLIA Poly Univ										
Animal Behaviour and Chemistry	CF1C▼	3FT deg	<u>S</u>	10	3M	P	Dip	BCCC	N	
Audiotechnology and Chemistry	HF6C▼	3FT deg	<u>S</u>	16	8M	D	Dip$	BBCCC	N	
Biology and Chemistry	CF11▼	3FT deg	<u>B</u>	10	3M	P	Dip$	BCCC	N	4
Biomedical Science and Chemistry	BF91▼	3FT deg	<u>B</u>	10	3M	P go	Dip$	BCCC	N	4
Business and Chemistry	NF11▼	3FT deg	<u>S</u> g	10	3M	P go	Dip$	BCCC	Ind	2
Chemistry	F100▼	3FT deg	<u>S</u> g	8	2M	P go	Dip$	CCCC	N	7
Chemistry and Computer Science	FG15▼	3FT deg	<u>S</u>	10	3M	P go	Dip$	BCCC	N	
Chemistry and Ecology and Conservation	DF21▼	3FT deg	<u>S</u>	10	3M	P	Dip$	BCCC	N	
Chemistry and Food Science	DF41▼	3FT deg								
Chemistry and Forensic Science	BF11▼	3FT deg	g	10	3M	P go	Dip	BCCC		
Chemistry and French	FR11▼	4FT deg	<u>S</u> g	12	4M	M go	Dip$	BCCC	Ind	
Chemistry and Geography	FF18▼	3FT deg	<u>S+Gy</u> g	12	4M	M go	Dip$	BCCC	N	
Chemistry and Geology	FF16▼	3FT deg	<u>S</u> g	10	3M	P go	Dip$	CCCC	N	
Chemistry and German	FR12▼	4FT deg	<u>S</u> g	12	4M $	M go	Dip$	BCCC	Ind	
Chemistry and Imaging Science	FW15▼	3FT deg	<u>S</u> g	10	3M	P go	Dip$	BCCC	N	
Chemistry and Instrumentation Electronics	FH16▼	3FT deg	<u>S</u> g	8	2M	P go	Dip$	CCCC	N	
Chemistry and Italian	FR13▼	4FT deg	<u>S</u> g	12	4M	M go	Dip$	BCCC	Ind	
Chemistry and Maths or Stats/Stat Modelling	FG11▼	3FT deg	<u>S</u> g	8	2M	P go	Dip$	CCCC	N	3
Chemistry and Ophthalmic Dispensing	BF51▼	3FT deg	<u>S</u> g	10	3M	P	Dip$	BCCC	N	
Chemistry and Psychology	CF81▼	3FT deg	<u>S</u> g	16	8M	M go	Dip$	BBCCC	N	

TITLE	CODE	COURSE	SUBJECTS	A/AS	ND/C	AGNVQ	IB	SQA(H)	SQA	RATIO	A/AS
Chemistry and Spanish	FR14▼	4FT deg	S g	12	4M	M go	Dip$	BCCC	Ind		
Chemistry in Society	F101▼	3FT deg	S g	8	2M	P	Dip$	CCCC	Ind		
Medicinal Chemistry	F120▼	3FT deg	S	8	2M	P	Dip$	CCCC	N	4	

ASTON Univ

TITLE	CODE	COURSE	SUBJECTS	A/AS	ND/C	AGNVQ	IB	SQA(H)	SQA	RATIO	A/AS
Applied Chemistry	F110	4SW deg	C g	18	7M+3D$	D$6/△ go	30$	BBBBC$	Ind	2	12/22
Applied Chemistry (Year Zero)	F118	3FT/5SW deg									
Chemical Engineering and App Chem (MEng)	FH18	4FT/5SW deg	C+M g	26	10D $	D$6/△ go	34$	AAABB$	Ind	3	20/30
Chemistry	F100	3FT deg	C g	18	7M+3D$	D$6/△ go	30$	BBBBC$	Ind	8	14/24
Chemistry (Year Zero)	F108	4FT deg									
Chemistry/Biology	CF11	3FT/4SW deg	B+C g	18	X	X	29$	BBBBC$	Ind	6	
Chemistry/Biology (Year Zero)	CF1D	4FT/5SW deg									
Chemistry/Business Administration	FN11	3FT/4SW deg	C g	20	3M+7D$	D$△ go	30$	BBBBB$	Ind	10	
Chemistry/Business Administration (Year Zero)	FN1D	4FT/5SW deg									
Electronics/Chemistry	HF61	3FT/4SW deg	C+M/P g	18	X	X	29$	BBBBC$	Ind		
Engineering Management/Chemistry	FH1R	3FT/4SW deg	C g	18	X	D$△ go	29$	BBBBC$	Ind		
Environmental Science & Technology/Chemistry	FF19	3FT/4SW deg	C g	18	5M+5D$	D$6/△ go	29$	BBBBC$	Ind		
Environmental Science/Chemistry (Year Zero)	FF1Y	4FT/5SW deg									
Ergonomics/Chemistry	FJ1X	3FT/4SW deg	C g	20		D$△ go	30$	BBBBB$	Ind		
European Studies/Chemistry	FT12	3FT/4SW deg	C g	18	X	D$△ go	29	BBBBC	Ind		
European Studies/Chemistry (Year Zero)	FT1F	4FT/5SWdeg									
French/Chemistry	FR11	4SW deg	C+F g	20	X	X	30$	BBBBB$	Ind		
German/Chemistry	FR12	4SW deg	C+G g	18	X	X	29$	BBBBC$	Ind	6	
German/Chemistry (Year Zero)	FR1F	5SW deg									
Health & Safety Management/Chemistry	FJ19	3FT/4SW deg	C g	18	5M+5D$	D$△ go	29$	BBBBC$	Ind	2	
Health & Safety Mgt/Chemistry (Year Zero)	JF91	4FT/5SW deg									
Human Psychology/Chemistry	FL17	3FT/4SW deg	C g	20	3M+7D$	D$△ go	30$	BBBBB$	Ind	14	
Human Psychology/Chemistry (Year Zero)	FL1R	4FT/5SW deg									
Mathematics/Chemistry	FG11	3FT/4SW deg	C+M g	20	X	X	31$	ABBBB$	Ind	7	
Medicinal Chemistry/Biology	CF1C	3FT/4SW deg	C+B g	20	3M+7D$	X	31$	ABBBB$	Ind		
Medicinal Chemistry/Business Administration	FN1C	3FT/4SW deg	C g	20	3M+7D$	D$△ go	31$	ABBBB$	Ind		
Medicinal Chemistry/Chemistry	F120	3FT/4SW deg	C g	20	3M+7D$	D$△ go	31$	ABBBB$	Ind		
Medicinal Chemistry/Computer Science	FG15	3FT/4SW deg	C g	20	3M+7D$	D$△ go	31$	ABBBB$	Ind		
Medicinal Chemistry/Engineering Management	FH1T	3FT/4SW deg	C g	20	3M+7D$	D$△ go	30	BBBBB$	Ind		
Medicinal Chemistry/French	FR1C	4SW deg	C+F g	20	3M+7D$	X	30$	BBBBB$	Ind		
Medicinal Chemistry/German	FRC2	4SW deg	C+G g	20	3M+7D$	X	30$	BBBBB$	Ind		
Medicinal Chemistry/Health & Safety Management	FJ1Y	3FT/4SW deg	C g	20	3M+7D$	D$△ go	30$	BBBBB$	Ind		
Pharmaceutical Sciences	F126	3FT/4SW deg	C g	22	3M+7D$	X	32$	ABBBB$	Ind		
Product Design (Engineering)/Medicinal Chemistry	FH17	3FT/4SW deg	C g	20	5M+5D$	D$△ go	30$	BBBBB			
Public Policy & Management/Chemistry	MF11	3FT/4SW deg	C g	20	3M+7D$	D$△ go	30$	BBBBB$	Ind		
Public Policy & Management/Chemistry (Year Zero)	MF1D	4FT/5SW deg									
Public Policy & Management/Medicinal Chem (YrZ)	FM11	4FT/5SW deg									
Public Policy & Management/Medicinal Chemistry	MF1C	3FT/4SW deg	C g	20	5M+5D$	D$△ go	30$	BBBBB$	Ind		
Social Studies/Medicinal Chemistry	LF41	3FT/4SW deg	C g	20	5M+5D$	D$△ go	30$	BBBBB$	Ind		
Social Studies/Medicinal Chemistry (Year Zero)	LF4C	4FT/5SW deg									

Univ of Wales, BANGOR

TITLE	CODE	COURSE	SUBJECTS	A/AS	ND/C	AGNVQ	IB	SQA(H)	SQA	RATIO	A/AS
Biochemistry and Chemistry	CF71	3FT deg	C+S g	CDD	3M $	MS3 go	26$	BCCC$	Ind	4	
Chemistry	F100	3FT deg	C g	14	3M $	MS3 go	26$	BBCC$	Ind	4	6/14
Chemistry and Physical Education	FB16	3FT deg	C g	14	3M $	MS3 go	26$	BBCC$	Ind		
Chemistry and Sports Science	BF61	3FT deg	C g	14	3M $	MS3 go	26$	BBCC$	Ind		
Chemistry with European Experience	F102	4SW deg	C g	14	3M $	MS3 go	26$	BBCC$	Ind		
Chemistry with Industrial Experience	F103	4SW deg	C g	14	3M $	MS3 go	26$	BBCC$	Ind	4	10/18

course details			98 expected requirements							96 entry stats	
TITLE	CODE	COURSE	SUBJECTS	A/AS	NO/C	AGNVQ	IB	SQA(H)	SQA	RATIO	A/AS
Environmental Chemistry	F141	3FT deg	C g	14	3M $	MS3 go	26$	BBCC$	Ind	6	8/12
Instrumental Methods for Science Laboratories	F180	2FT dip	* g								
MChem	F104	4FT deg	C g	20-24	3M+2D$	DS^ go	30$	BBBB$	Ind		
Management and Chemistry	NF11	3FT deg	C g	CDD	3M $	MS3 go	26$	BBCC$	Ind		
Marine Chemistry	F140	3FT deg	C g	14	3M $	MS3 go	26$	BCCC$	Ind	4	6/14

BARNSLEY COLL

Science Foundation *Chemistry*	Y100	4EXT deg									

Univ of BATH

Chemistry	F100	3FT deg	C g	18	Ind	D^	28$	Ind	Ind	8	12/30
Chemistry	F101	4SW deg	C g	18	Ind	D^	28$	Ind	Ind	6	16/28
Chemistry (4 years full time with study abroad)	F105	4FT deg	C g	18	Ind	D^	28$	Ind	Ind	32	
Chemistry (MChem)	F103	4FT deg	C g	18	Ind	D^	28$	Ind	Ind	10	18/30
Chemistry (MChem) (4 Yr SW)	F104	4SW deg	C g	18	Ind	D^	28$	Ind	Ind	10	
Chemistry (with study abroad)	F107	4FT deg	C g	18	Ind	D^	28$	Ind	Ind	8	
Chemistry with Management (3 Yrs)	F146	3FT deg	C g	18	Ind	D^	28$	Ind	Ind	5	18/24
Chemistry with Management (4 Yr SW)	F145	4SW deg	C g	18	Ind	D^	28$	Ind	Ind	5	12/20
Chemistry with Management (with year abroad)	F1NC	4FT deg	C g	18	Ind	D^	28	Ind	Ind		
Natural Sciences *Chemistry*	Y160	3FT deg	S/M+S/M	20	Ind	DS	30	Ind	Ind		
Natural Sciences *Chemistry*	Y161	4SW deg	S/M+S/M	20	Ind	DS	30	Ind	Ind		

BELL COLLEGE OF TECHNOLOGY

Chemistry with Instrumental Analysis	F180	3FT deg	C+S	DD-DE	Ind	Ind	Ind	CCC$	Ind		
Chemistry with Instrumental Analysis	081F	2FT HND	C/S	D	Ind	Ind	Ind	CC	Ind		

Univ of BIRMINGHAM

Chemistry	F100	3FT deg	C+M	BBB	Ind	Ind	34	Ind	Ind	9	16/30
Chemistry (MNatSc)	F101	4FT deg	C+M g	AAB	Ind	Ind	34	Ind	Ind	5	28/30
Chemistry with Analytical Science	F180	3FT deg	C+M	BBB	Ind	Ind	34	Ind	Ind	7	16/30
Chemistry with Bioorganic Chemistry	F130	3FT deg	C+M	BBB	Ind	Ind	34	Ind	Ind	4	18/28
Chemistry with Business Studies	F1N1	3FT deg	C+M	BBB	Ind	Ind	34	Ind	Ind	6	14/26
Chemistry with Environmental Chemistry	F140	3FT deg	C+M	BBB	Ind	Ind	34	Ind	Ind	6	17/26
Chemistry with French	F1R1	3FT deg	C+M	BBB	Ind	Ind	34	Ind	Ind	6	
Chemistry with Polymer Science	F170	3FT deg	C+M	BBB	Ind	Ind	34	Ind	Ind	17	
Chemistry with Study in Continental Europe	F102	4FT deg	C+M g	BBB	Ind	Ind	34	Ind	Ind	8	

Univ of BRADFORD

Archaeological Chemistry	FF41	4SW deg	C g	BCC	2M+1D	DS^	Ind	Ind	Ind		
Archaeological Chemistry	FF14	3FT deg	C g	BCC	3M+1D	DS^	Ind	Ind	Ind		
Chemistry	F100	3FT deg	C+S g	BC-CDD	3M+3D$	DS^	Ind	Ind	Ind	23	
Chemistry	F101	4SW deg	C+S g	BC-CDD	3M+3D$	DS^	Ind	Ind	Ind	6	
Chemistry (MChem)	F102	4FT deg	C+S g	BCC			Ind	Ind	Ind		
Chemistry with Business & Management St (MChem)	F1ND	4FT deg	C+S g	BBC			Ind	Ind	Ind		
Chemistry with Business & Management Studies	F1NC	4SW deg	C+S g	BCD	3M+5D$	DS^	Ind	Ind	Ind	16	
Chemistry with Business & Management Studies	F1N1	3FT deg	C+S g	BCD	3M+5D$	DS^	Ind	Ind	Ind		
Chemistry with Pharmaceutical & Foren Sc (MChem)	F1BG	4FT deg	C+S g	BBB			Ind	Ind	Ind		
Chemistry with Pharmaceutical & Forensic Science	F1BF	4SW deg	C+S g	BCC	3M+5D$	DS^	Ind	Ind	Ind		
Chemistry with Pharmaceutical & Forensic Science	F1B2	3FT deg	C+S g	BCC	3M+5D$	DS^	Ind	Ind	Ind	5	12/26

BRADFORD & ILKLEY Comm COLL

Applied Sciences *Chemistry*	001Y	2FT HND	S g	2	N $	P		Ind	Ind		

TITLE	CODE	COURSE	SUBJECTS	A/AS	ND/C	AGNVQ	IB	SQA(H)	SQA	RATIO A/AS
course details			**98 expected requirements**							**96 entry stats**
Univ of BRIGHTON										
Biology and Chemistry	CF11	3FT/4SW deg	B/C g	12	MO $	M$	Dip$	BBCC$	Ind	
Chemistry and Computing	FG15	3FT/4SW deg	S g	12	MO $	M$	Dip$	BBCC$	Ind	
Chemistry and Energy Studies	FJ19	3FT/4SW deg	S g	12	MO $	M$	Dip$	BBCC$	Ind	
Chemistry and Physics	FF13	3FT/4SW deg	C/P g	12	MO $	M$	Dip$	BBCC$	Ind	
Chemistry and Statistics	FG14	3FT/4SW deg	C/St g	12	MO $	M$	Dip$	BBCC$	Ind	
Univ of BRISTOL										
Chemistry	F100	3FT deg	C g	CCC	Ind	D$^	26$		Ind	9 20/30
Chemistry (MSci)	F103	4FT deg	C g	CCC	Ind	D$^	26$	BBBCC	Ind	10 18/28
Chemistry and Law	FM13	4FT deg	C g	ABB	Ind	D$^	33$	AAABB	Ind	4 24/30
Chemistry with Environmental Science	F140	3FT deg	C g	CCC	Ind	D$^	26$	BBBCC	Ind	7 18/26
Chemistry with Environmental Science (MSci)	F143	4FT deg	C g	CCC	Ind	D$^	26$	BBBCC	Ind	
Chemistry with Study in Continental Europe	F101	4FT deg	C g	CCC	Ind	D$^	26$	BBBCC	Ind	11 26/30
Chemistry with a Preliminary Yr	F108	4FT deg	g		Ind	D$^			Ind	
BRISTOL, Univ of the W of England										
Applied Chemical Sciences	F110	3FT/4SW deg	C/P g	6	N $	PS go	24$	CC$	N$	
Biology and Chemistry	CF11	3FT/4SW deg	B+C g	8	3M $	PS go	24$	CCC$	Ind	
Biomedical Sciences and Chemistry	BF91	3FT/4SW deg	B+C g	8	3M $	PS go	24$	CCC$	Ind	
Chemistry and Environmental Science	FF19	3FT/4SW deg	C g	6	N $	PS go	24$	CC$	N$	
Chemistry and Information Technology in Science	FG15	3FT/4SW deg	C g	6	N $	PS go	24$	CC$	N$	
Chemistry and Psychology	FC18	3FT/4SW deg	C g	6	N $	PS go	24$	CC$	N$	
Environmental Chemistry	F140	3FT/4SW deg	C/P g	6	N $	PS go	24$	CC$	N$	
Science Foundation Year *Applied Chemical Sciences*	Y120	4EXT/5EXTSW deg	M/S g	E	N $	PS go	24$	Ind	N$	
Science Foundation Year *Environmental Chemistry (Foundation)*	Y120	4EXT/5EXTSW deg	M/S g	E	N $	PS go	24$	Ind	N$	
BRUNEL Univ, West London										
Applied Chemistry (4 Yrs Thick SW)	F111	4SW deg	C g	CCD	3M $	MS2/^	26$	BBCCC$	Ind	5
Applied Chemistry (4 Yrs Thin SW)	F110	4SW deg	C g	CCD	3M $	MS2/^	26$	BBCCC$	Ind	6
Chemistry	F100	3FT deg	C g	CCD	3M $	MS2/^	26$	BBCCC$	Ind	7 8/20
Chemistry (MChem)	F101	4SW deg	C g	BBB	6D $	DS4/^	32$	AABBB$	Ind	
Chemistry with Management	F1NC	3FT deg	C g	CCD	3M $	MS2/^	26$	BBCCC$	Ind	25
Chemistry with Management (4 Yrs Thick SW)	F1ND	4SW deg	C g	CCD	3M $	MS2/^	26$	BBCCC$	Ind	10
Chemistry with Management (4 Yrs Thin SW)	F1N1	4SW deg	C g	CCD	3M $	MS2/^	26$	BBCCC$	Ind	2
Chemistry with Management (MChem)	FN1D	4SW deg	C g	BBB	6D $	DS4/^	32$	AABBB$	Ind	
Chemistry with a Foundation Year	F102	4FT deg	*							
Medicinal and Environmental Chem (4 Yrs Thin SW)	F120	4SW deg	C g	CCD	3M $	MS2/^	26$	BBCCC$	Ind	2
Medicinal and Environmental Chem(4 Yrs Thick SW)	F121	4SW deg	C g	CCD	3M $	MS2/^	26$	BBCCC$	Ind	3
Medicinal and Environmental Chemistry	F122	3FT deg	C g	CCD	3M $	MS2/^	26$	BBCCC$	Ind	10
Medicinal and Environmental Chemistry (MChem)	F123	4SW deg	C g	BBB	6D $	DS4/^	32$	AABBB$	Ind	
CAMBRIDGE Univ										
Natural Sciences *Chemistry*	Y160▼	3FT/4FT deg	2(S/M) g	AAA-AAB	Ind		Ind	CSYS	Ind	
CARDIFF Univ of Wales										
Biochemistry and Chemistry	CF71	3FT deg	C+B/M/P g	CCC	MO $	MS6/^ go	26$	BBBB$	Ind	3 14/30
Chemistry	F100	3FT deg	C+S/M g	16-18	4M $	DS6	Ind	BBBB	Ind	3 12/26
Chemistry	F103	4FT deg	C+S/M g	18	Ind	Ind	Ind	Ind	Ind	
Chemistry and Physics	FF13	3FT deg	P+C+M g	CCC	Ind		Ind	Ind	Ind	8
Chemistry with Industrial Experience	F101	4SW deg	C+S/M g	16-18	4M $	DS6	Ind	BBBB	Ind	4 12/26
Preliminary Year *Chemistry*	Y121	4FT/5SW deg	*		Ind	Ind	Ind	Ind	Ind	

| course details | | | 98 expected requirements | | | | | | | 96 entry stats |

TITLE	CODE	COURSE	SUBJECTS	A/AS	NO/C	AGNVQ	IB	SQA(H)	SQA	RATIO A/AS
Univ of CENTRAL LANCASHIRE										
Applied Chemistry	F110	3FT/4SW deg	C+S	DD	MO $	MS6/^	24$	CCC	$	
Chemistry	F100	3FT/4SW deg	S+C	DD	MO $	MS6/^	24$	CCC	$	
Chemistry (MChem)	F101	4FT deg	C+S	12	MO $	MS6/^	26$	BCCC	Ind	
Chemistry and International Business	FN11	3FT deg	* g	DD	MO	MS6/^	24$	CCC	$	
Combined Honours Programme Chemistry	Y400	3FT deg	C g	8	3M $	PS	26$	BCCC	$	
Chemistry	001F	2FT/3SW HND	C	E	N $	PS	24$	CCC	$	
COVENTRY Univ										
Applied Chemistry	F110	3FT/4SW deg	C	DD	3M	MS	Ind	Ind	Ind	8
Applied Chemistry	F119	4FT/5SW deg			Ind	Ind	Ind	Ind	Ind	
Applied Chemistry with Biochemistry	F1C7	3FT/4SW deg	C	DD	3M	MS	Ind	Ind	Ind	11
Applied Chemistry with Biochemistry	F1CR	4FT/5SW deg			Ind	Ind	Ind	Ind	Ind	
Applied Chemistry with Management Studies	F1NC	4FT/5SW deg			Ind	Ind	Ind	Ind	Ind	
Applied Chemistry with Management Studies	F1N1	3FT/4SW deg	C	DD	3M	MS	Ind	Ind	Ind	7
Applied Chemistry with Polymer Science	F1J4	3FT/4SW deg	C	DD	3M	MS	Ind	Ind	Ind	7
Applied Chemistry with Polymer Science	F1J5	4FT/5SW deg			Ind	Ind	Ind	Ind	Ind	
Chemistry and Biological Sciences	FC11	3FT/4SW deg	B+C g	CD	3M	MS	Ind	Ind	Ind	6
Chemistry and Biological Sciences	F1CC	4FT/5SW deg			Ind	Ind	Ind	Ind	Ind	
Chemistry and Computing	FG1N	4FT/5SW deg			Ind	Ind	Ind	Ind	Ind	
Chemistry and Geography	FL1W	4FT/5SW deg			Ind	Ind	Ind	Ind	Ind	
Chemistry and Materials Technology	JF51	4FT/5SW deg			Ind	Ind	Ind	Ind	Ind	
Chemistry and Mathematics	FG1D	4FT/5SW deg			Ind	Ind	Ind	Ind	Ind	
Chemistry and Statistics	FG1L	4FT/5SW deg			Ind	Ind	Ind	Ind	Ind	
Computing and Chemistry	FG15	3FT/4SW deg	C	DD	3M	MS	Ind	Ind	Ind	19
Environmental Chemistry	F140	3FT/4SW deg	C	CD	3M	MS	Ind	Ind	Ind	12
Environmental Chemistry	F149	4FT/5SW deg			Ind	Ind	Ind	Ind	Ind	
Geography and Chemistry	FL18	3FT/4SW deg	C+Gy	10	3M	MS	Ind	Ind	Ind	4
Materials Technology and Chemistry	FJ15	3FT/4SW deg	C+P/M	CC	Ind	Ind	Ind	Ind	Ind	
Mathematics and Chemistry	FG11	3FT/4SW deg	C+M	DD	Ind	Ind	Ind	Ind	Ind	10
Pharmaceutical Chemistry	F129	4FT/5SW deg			Ind	Ind	Ind	Ind	Ind	
Pharmaceutical Chemistry	F126	3FT/4SW deg	C+B	CD	3M	MS	Ind	Ind	Ind	4	6/18
Statistics and Chemistry	FG14	3FT/4SW deg	C	CD	3M	MS	Ind	Ind	Ind	
Applied Chemistry	811F	3FT HND			Ind	Ind	Ind	Ind	Ind	
Applied Chemistry	011F	2FT HND	C	D	P	PS	Ind	DDDD$	N	4
Pharmaceutical Chemistry	621F	2FT HND	C	E	P	PS	Ind	Ind	Ind	9
DE MONTFORT Univ										
Chemistry	F100▼	3FT deg	C	12	3M $		24$	BBB		
Chemistry	F101▼	3FT deg	C	12	3M $		24$	BBB		
Chemistry Options	F102▼	3FT deg	C	12	3M $		24$	BBB		
Chemistry and Biomedical Sciences	FB19▼	3FT/4SW	B+C	10	4M $	M	24$	BBB	$	6/12
Chemistry with Business Studies	F1N1▼	3FT/4SW deg	*	12	3M $	M	24$	BBB	$	8
Chemistry with Business Studies (Extended)	F1ND▼	4FT/5SW deg	*	2	N	P	24	CC	$	3
Chemistry, Applied	F110▼	3FT/4SW deg	C g	8	3M $	M	24$	BBB	$	4	4/14
Chemistry, Applied (Extended)	F118▼	4FT/5SW deg	C	2	N	P	24	CC	$	1
Combined Sciences Chemistry	Y108▼	3FT deg	g	2	N	P	Dip	CC	Ind	
Combined Sciences Chemistry	Y100▼	2FT Dip	g	4-6	N	P	Dip	BCC	Ind	
Combined Studies Chemistry	Y400▼	3FT/4SW deg	* g	10	MO	M	30	BBB	Ind	
Chemistry	001F▼	2FT HND	C	2	N	P	24$	CCC	$	2	2/8
Pharmaceutical Chemistry	621F▼	2FT HND	C g	2	N	P	24	CCC		

Chemistry 13

			98 expected requirements							96 entry stats
TITLE	CODE	COURSE	SUBJECTS	A/AS	NO/C	AGNVQ	IB	SQA(H)	SQA	RATIO A/AS
Univ of DERBY										
Biology and Chemistry	CF11	3FT deg	S	10	N $	MS	26$	CCCD$	Ind	12
Biology and Heritage Conservation	CF1C	3FT deg	S	10	N $	MS	26$	CCCD$	Ind	
Chemistry and Environmental Monitoring & Mgt	FF1X	3FT deg	S	10	N $	MS	26$	CCCD$	Ind	
Chemistry and Environmental Studies	FF19	3FT deg	S	10	N $	MS	26$	CCCD$	Ind	
Chemistry and Geology	FF16	3FT deg	S	10	N $	MS	26$	CCCD$	Ind	
Chemistry and Heritage Conservation	F140	3FT deg	S	10	N $	MS	26$	CCCD$	Ind	
Environmental Monitoring & Mgt and Heritage Con	FF9C	3FT deg	S	10	N $	MS	26$	CCCD$	Ind	
Environmental Studies and Heritage Conservation	FF91	3FT deg	S	10	N $	MS	26$	CCCD$	Ind	
Geography and Heritage Conservation	FF81	3FT deg	Gy	10	N $	MS	26$	CCCD$	Ind	
Credit Accumulation Modular Scheme *Heritage Conservation*	Y600	3FT deg	*	8	MO	M	Ind	CCCC	Ind	
Univ of DUNDEE										
Accountancy and Chemistry	FN14	4FT deg	2S g	14	5M $	M$	25$	BBCC$	N$	
Biological Chemistry	CF7C	4FT deg	C+S/2S g	16	5M $	M$	25$	BBBC$	N$	5
Chemistry	F100	4FT deg	2S g	14	5M $	M$	25$	BBCC$	N$	10
Chemistry	F101	3FT deg	2S g	10	5M $	M$	25$	BCC$	N$	7
Chemistry and Applied Computing	FG15	4FT deg	2S g	14	5M $	M$	25$	BBBC$	N$	7
Chemistry and Biochemistry	FC17	4FT deg	C+S/2S g	16	5M $	M$	25$	BBBC$	N$	9
Chemistry and Business Economics and Marketing	LF11	4FT deg	2S g	14	5M $	M$	25$	BBCC$	N$	
Chemistry and Economics	FL11	4FT deg	2S g	14	5M $	M$	25$	BBCC$	N$	
Chemistry and Environmental Science	FF19	4FT deg	C+S/2S g	14	5M $	M$	25$	BBCC$	N$	13
Chemistry and Mathematics	FG11	4FT deg	M+S g	14	5M $	M$^	25$	BBCC$	N$	
Chemistry and Microbiology	CF51	4FT deg	C+S/2S g	16	5M $	M$	25$	BBBC$	N$	1
Chemistry and Pharmacology	FB12	4FT deg	C+S/2S g	16	5M $	M$	25$	BBBC$	N$	24
Chemistry and Physics	FF13	4FT deg	M+S g	10	5M $	M$^	25$	BBCC$	N$	4
Chemistry and Physiological Sciences	FB11	4FT deg	C+S/2S g	16	5M $	M$	25$	BBBC$	N$	
Chemistry and Statistics	FG14	4FT deg	M+S g	14	5M $	M$^	25$	BBCC$	N$	
Medicinal Chemistry	F120	4FT deg	C+S/2S g	16	5M $	M$	25$	BBBC$	N$	4
Univ of DURHAM										
Chemistry	F100	3FT deg	C+M/P	18-20	5M $	Ind	28$	AAABB	Ind	8 22/30
Chemistry (4 Yrs)	F104	4FT deg	C+M/P	18-20	5M $	Ind	28$	AAABB	Ind	4 22/30
Natural Sciences *Chemistry*	Y160	3FT deg	C+S	ABB	Ind	X	33$	CSYS$	X	
Univ of EAST ANGLIA										
Biological & Medicinal Chem with 1yr in Eur(4yr)	F126	4FT deg	C+B/M/P g	BCC	MO+3D$	Ind	28$	ABBB$	Ind	4
Biological and Medicinal Chemistry	F125	3FT deg	C+B/M/P	CCC	MO+1D$	Ind	27$	BBBB$	Ind	3 10/20
Chemical Physics	FF31	3FT deg	C+P+M	BCC	MO+3D$	Ind	28$	ABBB$	Ind	9
Chemistry	F100	3FT deg	C+P+M/P	CCC	MO+1D$	Ind	27$	BBBB$	Ind	5 6/20
Chemistry & Mathematics with 1yr in Europe(4Yrs)	FG1C	4FT deg	M+C g	BCC	MO+3D$	Ind	28$	ABBB$	Ind	2
Chemistry (MChem)	F101	4FT deg	C+M/P	BCC	MO+3D$	Ind	28$	ABBB$	Ind	7
Chemistry and Mathematics	FG11	3FT deg	M+C	BCC	MO+3D$	Ind	28$	ABBB$	Ind	18
Chemistry w Adv Materials & 1 yr in N.Amer (3yr)	F167	3FT deg	C+M/P	BBB	DO $	Ind	31$	AAABB$	Ind	4
Chemistry w Adv Materials and 1yr in Eur (4yr)	F165	4FT deg	C+M/P g	BCC	MO+3D	Ind	28$	ABBB$	Ind	
Chemistry w Analytical Sci with 1yr in Eur(4yr)	F182	4FT deg	C+B/M/P g	BCC	MO+3D$	Ind	28$	ABBB$	Ind	
Chemistry with Advanced Materials	F166	3FT deg	C+M/P	CCC	MO+1D$	Ind	27$	BBBB$	Ind	4
Chemistry with Analytical Science	F181	3FT deg	C+B/M/P	CCC	MO+1D$	Ind	27	BBBB$	Ind	11
Chemistry with Business St and 1yr in Eur (4yr)	F1NC	4FT deg	C+B/M/P	BCC	MO+3D$	Ind	28$	ABBB$	Ind	
Chemistry with Business Studies	F1N1	3FT deg	C+B/M/P	CCC	MO+1D$	Ind	27$	BBBB$	Ind	6
Chemistry with Mathematics	F1G1	3FT deg	C+M	CCC	MO+1D$		27$	BBBB$	Ind	
Chemistry with Mathematics and 1yr in Eur(4 Yrs)	F1GC	4FT deg	C+M g	BCC	MO+3D$		28$	ABBB$	Ind	

			98 expected requirements							96 entry stats	
TITLE	**CODE**	**COURSE**	**SUBJECTS**	**A/AS**	**NO/C**	**AGNVQ**	**IB**	**SQA(H)**	**SQA**	**RATIO**	**A/AS**
Chemistry with a year in Europe (4 Yrs)	F106	4FT deg	C+B/M/P g	BCC	MO+3D$ Ind		28	ABBB$	Ind	13	
Chemistry with a year in North America (3 Yrs)	F102	3FT deg	C+M/P	BBB	DO $	Ind	31$	AAABB$ Ind		4	24/30
Environmental Chemistry	FF19	3FT deg	C+M/P	CCC	MO+1D$ Ind		27$	BBBB$	Ind	5	8/26
Environmental Chemistry with 1yr in Europe(4yrs)	FF1X	4FT deg	C+M/P g	BCC	MO+3D$ Ind		28$	ABBB$	Ind	1	

Univ of EDINBURGH

Chemistry	F100	4FT deg	C+M+P/B g	CCD	MO $		Dip$	BBBC$	N$	7	14/30
Chemistry (MChem)	F104	5FT deg	C+M+P/B g	CCD	MO $		Dip$	BBBC$		5	26/28
Chemistry with Industrial Experience	F102	5FT deg	C+M+P/B g	CCD	MO $		Dip$	BBBC	N$		
Chemistry with Industrial Experience	F101	5SW deg	C+M+P/B g	CCD	MO $		Dip$	BBBC$	N$	6	16/26
Chemistry with a Year in Europe	F1T9	4FT deg	C+M+L	CCD	MO $		Dip$	BBBC$	N$	9	
Chemistry with a year in Europe	F1TX	5FT deg	C+M+L	CCD	MO $		Dip$	BBBC	N$		
Environmental Chemistry	F140	4FT deg	C+B/GI/M/P g	CCD	MO $		Dip$	BBBC$	N$	5	20/26
Environmental Chemistry (MChem)	F144	5FT deg	C+B/M/P g	CCD	MO $		Dip$	BBBBC$ N$		9	
Environmental Chemistry with Indust Experience	F143	5FT deg	C+B/GI/M/P g	CCD	MO $		Dip$	BBBC$	N$		
Environmental Chemistry with Industrial Exp	F142	5SW deg	C+B/GI/M/P g	CCD	MO $		Dip$	BBBC$	N$	4	
Environmental Chemistry with a Year in Europe	F141	4FT deg	L+C+B/GI/M/P g	CCD	MO $		Dip$	BBBC	N$	6	
Environmental Chemistry with a year in Europe	F145	5FT deg	L+C+B/GI/M/P g	CCD	MO $		Dip$	BBBC	N$		

Univ of EXETER

Biological and Medicinal Chemistry	CF71	3FT deg	C+B g	CCC	4M	M$^	30$	Ind	Ind	6	8/30
Chemistry	F100	3FT deg	C/S g	CCC	MO	M$^	30$	Ind	Ind	9	10/30
Chemistry (MChem)	F103	4FT deg	C/S g	CCC	MO	M$^	30$	Ind	Ind	9	16/26
Chemistry and Law	FM13	3FT deg	C/S g	BCC	DO	M/D$^	32$	Ind	Ind	6	14/18
Chemistry with European Study	F104	4FT deg	C/S g	CCC	MO	M$^	30$	Ind	Ind	1	
Chemistry with Industrial Experience	F162	4FT deg	C/S g	CCC	MO	M$^	30$	Ind	Ind		

Univ of GLAMORGAN

Biological Science with Chemical Science	C1F1	3FT/4SW deg	M/S g	DD	5M $	M$	Ind	Ind	Ind		
Chemical Sci with Environmental Pollution Sci	F1F9	3FT/4SW deg	M/S g	DD	5M $	M$	Ind	Ind	Ind	2	
Chemical Science and Biological Science	FC11	3FT/4SW deg	M/S g	DD	5M $	M$	Ind	Ind	Ind	2	
Chemical Science and Environmental Pollution Sci	FF19	3FT/4SW deg	M/S g	DD	5M $	M$	Ind	Ind	Ind		
Chemical Science and Geological Science	FF16	3FT/4SW deg	M/S g	DD	5M $	M$	Ind	Ind	Ind		
Chemical Science and Minerals Surveying Science	FJ11	3FT/4SW deg	M/S g	DD	5M $	M$	Ind	Ind	Ind		
Chemical Science and Sports Science	BF61	3FT deg	M/S g	DD	5M $	M$	Ind	Ind	Ind		
Chemical Science with Biological Science	F1C1	3FT/4SW deg	M/S g	DD	5M $	M$	Ind	Ind	Ind	4	
Chemical Science with Geological Science	F1F6	3FT/4SW deg	M/S g	DD	5M $	M$	Ind	Ind	Ind	2	
Chemical Science with Minerals Surveying Science	F1J1	3FT/4SW deg	M/S g	DD	5M $	M$	Ind	Ind	Ind		
Chemical Science with Sports Science	F1B6	3FT deg	M/S g	DD	5M $	M$	Ind	Ind	Ind		
Chemistry	F100	3FT/4SW deg	M/S g	DD	5M $	M$	Ind	Ind	Ind	14	
Environmental Pollution Sci with Chemical Sci	F9F1	3FT/4SW deg	M/S g	DD	5M $	M$	Ind	Ind	Ind		
Forensic Measurement	F125	3FT deg	M/S g	DD	5M $	M$	Ind	Ind	Ind		
Forensic Measurement with Biology	CF11	3FT deg	M/S g	DD	5M $	M$	Ind	Ind	Ind		
Forensic Measurement with Criminal Justice	FM13	3FT deg	M/S+Lw/Ps/So g	14	Ind	Ind	Ind	Ind	Ind		
Geological Science with Chemical Science	F6F1	3FT/4SW deg	M/S g	DD	5M $	M$	Ind	Ind	Ind		
Minerals Surveying with Chemical Science	J1F1	3FT/4SW deg	M/S g	DD	5M $	M$	Ind	Ind	Ind		
Sports Science with Chemical Science	B6F1	3FT deg	M/S g	DD	5M $	M$	Ind	Ind	Ind		
Combined Studies (Honours) *Chemical Science*	Y400	3FT deg	M/S g	8-16	Ind	Ind	Ind	Ind	Ind		
Combined Studies (Honours) *Forensic Measurement*	Y400	3FT deg	M/S g	8-16	Ind	Ind	Ind	Ind	Ind		
Joint Honours *Chemical Science*	Y401	3FT deg	M/S g	8-16	Ind	Ind	Ind	Ind	Ind		
Joint Honours *Forensic Measurement*	Y401	3FT deg	* g	8-16	Ind	Ind	Ind	Ind	Ind		

TITLE	CODE	COURSE	SUBJECTS	A/AS	NO/C	RGNVQ	IB	SQA(H)	SQA	RATIO A/AS
Major/Minor Honours *Chemical Science*	Y402	3FT deg	M/S g	8-16	Ind	Ind	Ind	Ind	Ind	
Major/Minor Honours *Forensic Measurement (Major only)*	Y402	3FT deg	M/S g	8-16	Ind	Ind	Ind	Ind	Ind	
Science (Chemistry)	001F	2FT HND	C g	E	N $	P$	Ind	Ind	Ind	7

Univ of GLASGOW

Chemistry	F100	4FT deg	C/M+S	BBC-CCC	N	M	24$	BBBB$	N	8
Chemistry with Medicinal Chemistry	F103	4FT deg	C/M+S	BBC-CCC	N	M	24$	BBBB$	N	14
Chemistry/Geology	FF16	4FT deg	C/M+S	BBC-CCC	N	M	24$	BBBB$	N	6
Environmental Chemistry	F140	4FT deg	C/M+S	BBC-CCC	N	M	24$	BBBB$	N	7
Environmental Chemistry/Geography	FF18	4FT deg	C/M+S	BBC-CCC	N	M	24$	BBBB$	N	

GLASGOW CALEDONIAN Univ

| Chemistry with Info Tech and Instrumentation | F1G5 | 3FT/4FT deg | M+S | DD-DE | Ind | | Ind | CCC$ | Ind | 3 |

Univ of GREENWICH

Applied Chemistry	F110	3FT/4SW deg	C+S g	8	3M	MS	Dip	CCC	Ind	
Applied Chemistry (MChem)	F113	4FT deg	C+M	18	3D	Ind	Dip	ABB	Ind	
Applied Chemistry and Business Management	FN11	3FT/4SW deg	C g	8	3M	MS	Dip	CCC	Ind	
Applied Chemistry and Law	FM13	3FT deg	B+C g	12	M+D	M	Dip	Ind	Ind	
Applied Chemistry with Business Management	F1N1	3FT/4SW deg	C g	8	3M	MS	Dip	CCC	Ind	
Applied Chemistry with European St (MChem)	F114	3FT deg	C+M	18	3D	Ind	Dip	ABB	Ind	
Applied Chemistry with European Study	F111	3FT/4SW deg	C+S g	8	3M	MS	Dip	CCC	Ind	
Applied Chemistry with French	F1R1	3FT/4SW deg	C+S g	8	3M	MS	Dip	CCC	Ind	
Applied Chemistry with German	F1R2	3FT/4SW deg	C+S g	8	3M	MS	Dip	CCC	Ind	
Applied Chemistry with Law	F1M3	3FT deg	B+C g	12	M+D	M	Dip	Ind	Ind	
Applied Chemistry with Spanish	F1R4	3FT/4SW deg	C+S g	8	3M	MS	Dip	CCC	Ind	
Environmental Chemistry	F140	3FT/4SW deg	C+S g	8	3M	MS	Dip	CCC	Ind	
Environmental Chemistry with European Study	F141	3FT/4SW deg	C g	10	3M	MS	Dip	CCC	Ind	
Medicinal Chemistry	F120	3FT/4SW deg	C	8	3M	MS	Dip	CCC	Ind	
Medicinal Chemistry with European Study	F121	3FT deg	C	8	3M	MS	Dip	CCC	Ind	
Science (Chemistry)	001F	2FT HND	C g	2	N	MS	Dip	CC	Ind	

HALTON COLL

| Chemistry | F100 | 3SW deg | C | 2 | N | P | Ind | Ind | N | 2 |
| Science (Chemical Sciences) | 001F | 2FT HND | C | 2 | N | P | Ind | Ind | N | 2 |

HERIOT-WATT Univ

Chem with Polymers & Electronic Materials(MChem)	F115	5FT deg	C+S	DDD	$	M$ go	28	BBCC	$	
Chemical Engineering with Pharmaceutical Chemist	H8F1	5FT deg	C+M	CCD		M$ go	30	BBBB	$	
Chemistry	F100	3FT/4FT deg	C+S	DDD	$	Ind	28	BBCC	$	
Chemistry (MChem)	F101	4FT deg	C+S	DDD	$	M$ go	28	BBCC	$	
Chemistry with Biochemistry	F1C7	4FT deg	C+S	DDD	$	M$ go	28	BBCC	$	
Chemistry with Biochemistry (MChem)	F1CR	5FT deg	C+S	DDD	$	M$ go	28	BBCC	$	
Chemistry with Computer Science	F1G5	4FT deg	C+S	DDD	$	M$ go	28	BBCC	$	
Chemistry with Computer Science (MChem)	F1GM	5FT deg	C+S	DDD	$	M$ go	28	BBCC	$	
Chemistry with Environmental Economics	F1L1	4FT deg	C+S	DDD	$	M$ go	28	BBCC	$	
Chemistry with Environmental Economics (MChem)	F1LC	6FT deg	C+S	DDD	$	M$ go	28	BBCC	$	
Chemistry with French	F1R1	4FT deg	C+S+L	CCD	$	M$ go	28	BBB	$	
Chemistry with German	F1R2	4FT deg	C+S+L	CCD	$	M$ go	28	BBB	$	
Chemistry with Industrial Experience (MChem)	F102	5SW deg	C+S	DDD	$	M$ go	28	BBCC	$	
Chemistry with Pharmaceutical Chemistry	F125	4FT deg	C+S	DDD	$	M$ go	28	BBCC	$	
Chemistry with Pharmaceutical Chemistry (MChem)	F126	5FT deg	C+S	DDD	$	M$ go	28	BBCC	$	
Chemistry with Polymers and Electronic Materials	F114	4FT deg	C+S	DDD	$	MS go	28	BBCC	$	

			98 expected requirements							**96 entry stats**
course details										
TITLE	CODE	COURSE	SUBJECTS	A/AS	NO/C	RGNVQ	IB	SQA(H)	SQA	RATIO A/AS
Chemistry with Spanish	F1R4	4FT deg	C+S+L	CCD	$	MS^ go	28	BBB	$	
Chemistry with a European Language (MChem)	F1T2	5FT deg	C+S+L	CCD	$	Ind	28	BBB	Ind	
Colour Chemistry	F110	4FT deg	C+S	DDD	$	M$ go	28	BBCC	$	
Colour Chemistry (MChem)	F176	5FT deg	C+S	DDD	$	M$ go	28	BBCC	Ind	
Combined Studies *Chemistry*	Y100	4FT deg	C	DDE	Ind	M$ go	26	BCCC	Ind	

Univ of HERTFORDSHIRE

TITLE	CODE	COURSE	SUBJECTS	A/AS	NO/C	RGNVQ	IB	SQA(H)	SQA	RATIO A/AS
Applied Geology/Chemistry	F6F1	3FT deg	C g	12	3M $	MS gi	24$	CCCC$	Ind	
Applied Physics/Chemistry	F3F1	3FT deg	M+P+C	12	3M $	M$ gi	24$	CCCC$	Ind	2
Biological Chem with deferred ch. of specialism	F133	4FT/4SW deg	C	8-12	4M $	Ind	Ind	Ind	Ind	2
Biological Chemistry	C740	3FT/4SW deg	C	8-12	4M $	Ind	Ind	Ind	Ind	3
Biological Chemistry (Extended)	C748▼	4FT deg	* g	2	Ind	Ind	Ind	Ind	Ind	
Biological Chemistry with a year in Europe	F131	4FT deg	C	8-12	4M $	Ind	Ind	Ind	Ind	
Biological Chemistry with a yr in North America	F132	4FT deg	C	8-12	4M $	Ind	Ind	Ind	Ind	6
Business/Chemistry	N1F1	3FT deg	C g	18	4M+4D	M$6 gi	26$	BBBC$	Ind	3
Chemistry	F110	3FT/4SW deg	C	8-12	4M	Ind	Ind	Ind	Ind	5 8/24
Chemistry (Extended)	F118▼	4EXT/5EXTSW deg	* g	2	Ind	Ind	Ind	Ind	Ind	
Chemistry (MChem)	F100	4FT deg	C	8-12	4M $	Ind	Ind	Ind	Ind	9
Chemistry with Analytical Chemistry	F180	3FT/4SW deg	C	8-12	4M $	Ind	Ind	Ind	Ind	5
Chemistry with Medicinal Chemistry	F120	3FT/4SW deg	C	8-12	4M $	Ind	Ind	Ind	Ind	13
Chemistry with a year in Europe	F101	4FT deg	C	8-12	4M $	Ind	Ind	Ind	Ind	
Chemistry with a year in North America	F102	4FT deg	C	8-12	4M $	Ind	Ind	Ind	Ind	9
Chemistry with deferred choice of specialism	F103	4FT/4SW deg	C	8-12	4M $	Ind	Ind	Ind	Ind	
Chemistry/Applied Geology	F1F6	3FT deg	C g	12	3M $	MS gi	24$	CCCC$	Ind	
Chemistry/Applied Physics	F1F3	3FT deg	C+M+P	12	3M $	MS gi	24$	CCCC$	Ind	
Chemistry/Business	F1N1	3FT deg	C g	18	4M+4D	MS^ gi	26$	BBBC$	Ind	
Chemistry/Computing	F1G5	3FT deg	C g	12	3M $	MS gi	24$	CCCC$	Ind	
Chemistry/Economics	F1L1	3FT deg	C g	12	3M $	MS gi	24$	CCCC$	Ind	
Chemistry/Electronic Music	F1W3	3FT deg	C+Mu g	14	MO $	MS^ gi	26$	BCCC$	Ind	
Chemistry/Environmental Science	F1F9	3FT deg	C g	14	MO $	MS gi	26$	BCCC$	Ind	1
Chemistry/Human Biology	F1B1	3FT deg	C+S g	12	3M $	MS gi	24$	CCCC$	Ind	
Chemistry/Law	F1M3	3FT deg	C g	20	4M+4D	DS gi	26$	BBBC$	Ind	4
Chemistry/Linguistic Science	F1Q1	3FT deg	C g	12	MO $	MS gi	26$	BCCC$	Ind	
Chemistry/Manufacturing Systems	F1H7	3FT deg	C g	12	3M $	MS gi	24$	CCCC$	Ind	
Chemistry/Mathematics	F1G1	3FT deg	C+M g	12	3M $	MS^ gi	24$	CCCC$	Ind	
Chemistry/Operational Research	F1N2	3FT deg	C g	12	3M $	MS gi	24$	CCCC$	Ind	
Computing/Chemistry	G5F1	3FT deg	C g	12	3M $	MS gi	24$	CCCC$	Ind	
Economics/Chemistry	L1F1	3FT deg	C g	12	3M $	MS gi	24$	CCCC$	Ind	
Electronic Music/Chemistry	W3F1	3FT deg	Mu+C g	14	MO $	MS^ gi	26$	BCCC$	Ind	
Environmental Chem with Deferred Choice of spec	F143	4FT/4SW deg	S	8-12	4M	Ind	Ind	Ind	Ind	
Environmental Chemistry	F140	3FT/4SW deg	S	8-12	4M	Ind	Ind	Ind	Ind	11
Environmental Chemistry (Extended)	F148▼	4EXT/5EXTSW deg	* g	2	Ind	Ind	Ind	Ind	Ind	
Environmental Chemistry with a year in Europe	F141	4FT deg	S	8-12	4M	Ind	Ind	Ind	Ind	
Environmental Chemistry with a year in N America	F142	4FT deg	S	8-12	4M	Ind	Ind	Ind	Ind	
Environmental Science/Chemistry	F9F1	3FT deg	C g	14	MO $	MS gi	26$	BCCC$	Ind	
Human Biology/Chemistry	B1F1	3FT deg	S+C	12	3M $	MS gi	24$	CCCC$	Ind	10
Law/Chemistry	M3F1	3FT deg	C g	20	4M+4D	D$ gi	26$	BBBC$	Ind	
Linguistic Science/Chemistry	Q1F1	3FT deg	C g	12	MO $	MS gi	26$	BCCC$	Ind	
Manufacturing Systems/Chemistry	H7F1	3FT deg	C g	12	3M $	MS gi	24$	CCCC$	Ind	
Mathematics/Chemistry	G1F1	3FT deg	M+C g	12	3M $	MS^ gi	24$	CCCC$	Ind	
Operational Research/Chemistry	N2F1	3FT deg	C g	12	3M $	MS gi	24$	CCCC$	Ind	
Combined Modular Scheme *Chemistry*	Y100	3FT deg	C g	12	3M $	MS gi	24$	CCCC$	Ind	

Chemistry 13

TITLE	CODE	COURSE	SUBJECTS	A/AS	ND/C	AGNVQ	IB	SQA(H)	SQA	RATIO A/AS
			98 expected requirements							**96 entry stats**
Combined Modular Scheme	Y108▼	4EXT deg	* g	4	N $	Ind	Dip$	DDDD$	Ind	
Chemistry (Extended)										
Chemistry	001F	2FT HND	C	2-4	N $	Ind	Ind	Ind	Ind	3

Univ of HUDDERSFIELD

TITLE	CODE	COURSE	SUBJECTS	A/AS	ND/C	AGNVQ	IB	SQA(H)	SQA	RATIO A/AS
Chemistry	F100	3FT/4SW deg	C g	10	3M $	MS gi	Ind	BCC	Ind	
Chemistry (MChem)	F101	5SW deg	C g	10	3M $	MS gi	Ind	Ind	Ind	
Chemistry with Analytical Chemistry	F180	3FT/4SW deg	C g	10	3M $	MS gi	Ind	BCC	Ind	
Chemistry with Biochemistry	F1C7	3FT/4SW deg	C g	10	3M $	MS gi	Ind	BCC	Ind	
Chemistry with Biotechnology	F1J8	3FT/4SW deg	C g	10	3M $	MS gi	Ind	BCC	Ind	
Chemistry with Business	F1N1	3FT/4SW deg	C g	10	3M $	MS gi	Ind	BCC	Ind	
Chemistry with Chemical Engineering	F1H8	3FT/4SW deg	C g	10	3M $	MS gi	Ind	BCC	Ind	
Chemistry with Environmental Science	F1F9	3FT/4SW deg	C g	10	3M $	MS gi	Ind	BCC	Ind	
Chemistry with Food Science	F1D4	3FT/4SW deg	C g	10	3M $	MS gi	Ind	BCC	Ind	
Chemistry with Medicinal Chemistry	F120	3FT/4SW deg	C g	10	3M $	MS gi	Ind	BCC	Ind	
Science (Extended)	Y108	4FT/5SW deg	* g	EE	N	P$ gi	Ind	Ind	Ind	
Chemistry (all pathways)										
Chemistry	001F	3SW HND	C g	2	N	PS gi	Ind	CC	N	

Univ of HULL

TITLE	CODE	COURSE	SUBJECTS	A/AS	ND/C	AGNVQ	IB	SQA(H)	SQA	RATIO A/AS
Chemistry	F100	3FT deg	C	CCD	MO $	M$^ gi	26$	BCCCC	Ind	4 6/22
Chemistry	F101	4FT deg	*	DD	N	P$ gi	24	BCCCC	Ind	1
Chemistry (MChem)	F102	4FT deg	C	BCC	MO+3D$	M$^ gi	26$	BBCCC	Ind	10
Chemistry with 21st Century Materials	F166	3FT deg	C	CCD	MO $	M$^ gi	26$	BCCCC	Ind	24
Chemistry with 21st Century Materials (MChem)	F167	4FT deg	C	BCC	MO+3D$	M$^ gi	26$	BBBCC		
Chemistry with Analyt Chem and Toxicol (MChem)	F186	4FT deg	C	BCC	MO+3D$	M$^ gi	26$	BBBCC		
Chemistry with Analyt Chem and Toxicology(Indus)	F185	4FT deg	C	CCD	MO $	M$^ gi	26$	BCCCC	Ind	3 8/24
Chemistry with Analytical Chem & Toxicol (MChem)	F187	4FT deg	C	18	MO $	M$^/6	26$	BBBCC	Ind	
Chemistry with Analytical Chem and Toxicology	F184	3FT deg	C	CCD	MO $	M$^ gi	26$	BCCCC	Ind	6
Chemistry with Drug Design and Toxicol (MChem)	F131	4FT deg	C	BCC	MO+3D$	M$^ gi	26$	BBBCC		
Chemistry with Environmental Toxicology	F1F9	3FT deg	C g	CCD	MO $	M$^ gi	26$	BCCCC	Ind	
Chemistry with Environmental Toxicology (MChem)	F1FX	4FT deg	C	BCC	MO+3D$	M$^ gi	26$	BBBCC		
Chemistry with French	F1R1	4FT deg	C g	CCD	MO $	M$^ go	26$	BCCCC	Ind	
Chemistry with French (MChem)	F1RC	4FT deg	C g	BCC	MO+3D$	M$^ gi	26$	BBBCC		
Chemistry with German	F1R2	4FT deg	C g	CCD	MO $	M$^ go	26$	BCCCC	Ind	8
Chemistry with German (MChem)	F1RF	4FT deg	C g	BCC	MO+3D$	M$^ gi	26$	BBBCC		
Chemistry with Quality Management	F1H8	3FT deg	C	CCD	MO $	M$^ gi	26$	BCCCC	Ind	13
Chemistry with Quality Management (MChem)	F1HV	4FT deg	C	BCC	MO+3D$	M$^ gi	26$	BBBCC		
Chemistry with Sports Science	F1B6	3FT deg								
Chemistry, Drug Design and Toxicology	F130	3FT deg	C	CCD	MO $	M$^ gi	26$	BCCCC	Ind	5 6/24
Physical Education and Sports Science with Chem	B6F1	3FT deg	C	18-20	MO $	M$6	26$	BBBCC		

IMPERIAL COLL (Univ of London)

TITLE	CODE	COURSE	SUBJECTS	A/AS	ND/C	AGNVQ	IB	SQA(H)	SQA	RATIO A/AS
Chemistry (MSci)	F103	4FT deg	C+M/P	BBC	HN		32	CSYS		5 24/30
Chemistry and Biochemistry	FC17	4FT deg	C+M/P g	BBC	HN		32	CSYS		3 22/30
Chemistry and Biochemistry with a Yr in Industry	CF71	5SW deg	C+M/P g	BBC	HN		32	CSYS		14
Chemistry and Biotechnology	FJ18	4FT deg	C+M/P g	BBC	HN		32	CSYS		
Chemistry and Biotechnology with a Yr in Ind	JF81	5SW deg	C+M/P g	BBC	HN		32	CSYS		
Chemistry with Management	F1ND	4FT deg	C+M/P	BBC	HN		32	CSYS		5
Chemistry with Management	F1N1	3FT deg	C+M/P	BBC	HN		32	CSYS		25
Chemistry with Management and a Yr in Industry	F1NC	4SW deg	C+M/P	BBC	HN		32	CSYS		19
Chemistry with Med Chem & a Yr in Ind (MSci)	F125	5SW deg	C+M/P g	BBC	HN		32	CSYS		5 28/30
Chemistry with Medicinal Chemistry (MSci)	F124	4FT deg	C+M/P g	BBC	HN		32	CSYS		13
Chemistry with a Year in Europe (MSci)	F104	4FT deg	C+M/P g	BBC	HN		32	CSYS		4 24/30
Chemistry with a Year in Industry (MSci)	F105	5SW deg	C+M/P	BBC	HN		32	CSYS		5 28/30

course details			98 expected requirements							96 entry stats
TITLE	CODE	COURSE	SUBJECTS	A/AS	ND/C	RGNVQ	IB	SQA(H)	SQA	RATIO A/AS
KEELE Univ										
Biol & Med Chem and German/Russian or Russian St	FTCY	3FT deg	G+R+P/C g	BBC-BCC	Ind	D$^	28$	CSYS	Ind	
Biol & Medicinal Chem and Astrophysics (4 Yrs)	FFC5	4FT deg	*	BCC-CCC	Ind	Ind	26	BBBB	Ind	
Biol & Medicinal Chemistry and Business Admin	FNC9	3FT deg	C g	BCC	Ind	D$^	28$	CSYS	Ind	
Biol and Med Chem and Human Resource Management	FNC6	3FT deg	C g	BCC	Ind *	D$^	28$	CSYS	Ind	
Biol and Medicinal Chem and Computer Science	FGC5	3FT deg	C g	BCC-CCC	Ind	M$^	26$	CSYS	Ind	
Biological & Med Chem and Ancient Hist (4 Yrs)	VFDC	4FT deg	*	BCC	Ind	Ind	28	BBBB	Ind	
Biological & Med Chem and Biochemistry (4 Yrs)	FCC7	4FT deg	*	BCC-CCC	Ind	Ind	26	BBBB	Ind	
Biological & Medicinal Chem and Biochemistry	CF7C	3FT deg	C g	BCC-CCC	Ind	M$^	26$	CSYS	Ind	17
Biological & Medicinal Chem and Electronic Music	FWCJ	3FT deg	Mu+C	BCC	Ind	D$^	28$	CSYS	Ind	
Biological & Medicinal Chem and Environment Mgt	FFCX	3FT deg	C g	BCC	Ind	D$^	28$	CSYS	Ind	
Biological and Med Chem and Ancient History	FVCD	3FT deg	C g	BCC	Ind	D$^	28$	CSYS	Ind	
Biological and Medicinal Chem and Int History	FVCC	3FT deg	C g	BCC	Ind	D$^	28$	CSYS	Ind	
Biological and Medicinal Chem and Mathematics	FGC1	3FT deg	M+C g	BCC-CCC	Ind	M$^	26$	CSYS	Ind	1
Biological and Medicinal Chemistry and Astrophys	FF5C	3FT deg	P+C g	BCC-CCC	Ind	M$^	26$	CSYS	Ind	
Biological and Medicinal Chemistry and Biology	CF1C	3FT deg	C g	BCC-CCC	Ind	M$^	26$	CSYS	Ind	2
Biological and Medicinal Chemistry and Economics	FLC1	3FT deg	C g	BCC	Ind	D$^	28$	CSYS	Ind	
Biological and Medicinal Chemistry and Educ St	FXC9	3FT deg	C g	BCC	Ind	D$^	28$	CSYS	Ind	
Biological and Medicinal Chemistry and English	FQC3	3FT deg	C+E g	BBC-BCC	Ind	D$^	28$	CSYS	Ind	
Biological and Medicinal Chemistry and Geography	FLC8	3FT deg	C+Gy g	BCC	Ind	D$^	28$	CSYS	Ind	
Biological and Medicinal Chemistry and Geology	FF6C	3FT deg	C g	BCC-CCC	Ind	M$^	26$	CSYS	Ind	
Biological and Medicinal Chemistry and German	FRC2	3FT deg	G+C g	BCC	Ind	D$^	28$	CSYS	Ind	
Biological and Medicinal Chemistry and History	FVC1	3FT deg	C g	BCC	Ind	D$^	28$	CSYS	Ind	
Biological and Medicinal Chemistry and Latin	FQC6	3FT deg	Ln+C g	BCC	Ind	D$^	28$	CSYS	Ind	
Biological and Medicinal Chemistry and Law	FMC3	3FT deg	C g	BBB-BCC	Ind	D$^	30$	CSYS	Ind	3
Biology and Biological & Medicinal Chem (4 Yrs)	FCC1	4FT deg	*	BCC-CCC	Ind	Ind	26	BBBB	Ind	
Biology and Chemistry (MSci)	FC1C	4FT deg	C	BCC-CCC	Ind	M$^	26$	CSYS	Ind	
Business Admin and Biological & Med Chem (4 Yrs)	NF9C	4FT deg	*	BCC	Ind	Ind	28	BBBB	Ind	
Chemistry	F100	3FT deg	C g	BCC-CCC	Ind	M$^	26$	CSYS	Ind	12
Chemistry and Ancient History	FV1D	3FT deg	C g	BCC	Ind	D$^	28$	CSYS	Ind	
Chemistry and Ancient History (4 Yrs)	VFD1	4FT deg	*	BCC	Ind	Ind	28	BBBB	Ind	
Chemistry and Astrophysics	FF15	3FT deg	P+C g	BCC-CCC	Ind	M$^	26$	CSYS	Ind	
Chemistry and Astrophysics (4 Yrs)	FF51	4FT deg	*	BCC-CCC	Ind	Ind	26$	BBBB	Ind	
Chemistry and Astrophysics (MSci)	FF5D	4FT deg	C+P	BCC-CCC	Ind	M$^	26$	CSYS	Ind	
Chemistry and Biochemistry	CF71	3FT deg	C g	BCC-CCC	Ind	M$^	26$	CSYS	Ind	3
Chemistry and Biochemistry (4 Yrs)	FC17	4FT deg	*	BCC-CCC	Ind	Ind	26	BBBB	Ind	3
Chemistry and Biochemistry (MSci)	FC1R	4FT deg	C	BCC-CCC	Ind	M$^	26$	CSYS	Ind	
Chemistry and Biology	CF11	3FT deg	C g	BCC-CCC	Ind	M$^	26$	CSYS	Ind	4
Chemistry and Biology (4 Yrs)	FC11	4FT deg	*	BCC-CCC	Ind	Ind	26	BBBB	Ind	
Chemistry and Business Administration	FN19	3FT deg	C g	BCC	Ind	D$^	28$	CSYS	Ind	13
Chemistry and Business Administration (4 Yrs)	NF91	4FT deg	*	BCC	Ind	Ind	28	BBBB	Ind	
Classical St and Biological and Med Chem (4 Yrs)	QF8C	4FT deg	*	BCC	Ind	Ind	28	BBBB	Ind	
Classical Studies and Chemistry	FQ18	3FT deg	C g	BCC	Ind	D$^	28$	CSYS	Ind	
Classical Studies and Chemistry (4 Yrs)	QF81	4FT deg	*	BCC	Ind	Ind	28	BBBB	Ind	
Classical Studs and Biological & Medicinal Chem	FQC8	3FT deg	C g	BCC	Ind	D$^	28$	CSYS	Ind	
Computer Science and Astrophysics (MSci)	GFMC	4FT deg	*	BCC-CCC	Ind	Ind	28	BBBB	Ind	
Computer Science and Chemistry	FG15	3FT deg	C g	BCC-CCC	Ind	M$^	26$	CSYS	Ind	9
Computer Science and Chemistry (MSci)	GF5D	4FT deg	C	BCC-CCC	Ind	M$^	26$	CSYS	Ind	
Criminology and Biological & Med Chem (4 yrs)	MFHC	4FT deg	*	BBB-BCC	Ind	Ind	28	BBB		
Criminology and Chemistry (4 Yrs)	MFH1	4FT deg	*	BBB-BCC	Ind	Ind	28	BBBB	Ind	
Economics and Chemistry	FL11	3FT deg	C g	BCC	Ind	D$^	28$	CSYS	Ind	
Educational Studies and Chemistry	FX19	3FT deg	C g	BCC	Ind	D$^	28$	CSYS	Ind	

Chemistry 13

	course details			98 expected requirements							96 entry stats
TITLE	CODE	COURSE	SUBJECTS	A/AS	ND/C	AGNVQ	IB	SQA(H)	SQA	RATIO A/AS
Electronic Music and Biol and Med Chem (4 Yrs)	WFJC	4FT deg	*	BCC	Ind	Ind	28	BBBB	Ind	
Electronic Music and Chemistry	FW1J	3FT deg	Mu+C g	BCC	Ind	D$^	28$	CSYS	Ind	
Electronic Music and Chemistry (4 Yrs)	WFJ1	4FT deg	*	BCC	Ind	Ind	28	BBBB	Ind	
English and Biological & Medicinal Chem (4 Yrs)	QF3C	4FT deg	*	BCC	Ind	Ind	28	BBBB	Ind	
English and Chemistry	FQ13	3FT deg	C+E g	BCC	Ind	D$^	28$	CSYS	Ind	1
English and Chemistry (4 Yrs)	QF31	4FT deg	*	BCC	Ind	Ind	28	BBBB	Ind	
Environmental Management and Chemistry	FFX1	3FT deg	C g	BCC	Ind	D$^	28$	CSYS	Ind	
Finance and Biological & Medicinal Chem (4 Yrs)	FN1H	4FT deg	*	BCC	Ind	Ind	28	BBBB	Ind	
Finance and Biological and Medicinal Chemistry	FN13	3FT deg	C g	BCC	Ind	M$^	28$	CSYS	Ind	
Finance and Chemistry	NF31	4FT deg	*	BCC	Ind	Ind	28	BBBB	Ind	
Finance and Chemistry	FNC3	3FT deg	C g	BCC	Ind	M$^	28$	CSYS	Ind	
French/Russian or Russian Studies and Chemistry	FT1X	3FT deg	F+R+C g	BBC-BCC	Ind	D$^	28$	CSYS	Ind	
Geography and Biological and Med Chem (4 Yrs)	LF8C	4FT deg	*	BCC	Ind	Ind	28	BBBB	Ind	
Geography and Chemistry	FL18	3FT deg	Gy+C g	BCC	Ind	D$^	28$	CSYS	Ind	2
Geography and Chemistry (4 Yrs)	LF81	4FT deg	*	BCC	Ind	Ind	28	BBBB	Ind	
Geology and Biological & Medicinal Chem (4 Yrs)	FFC6	4FT deg	*	BCC-CCC	Ind	Ind	26	BBBB	Ind	
Geology and Chemistry	FF16	3FT deg	C g	BCC-CCC	Ind	M$^	26$	CSYS	Ind	
Geology and Chemistry (4 Yrs)	FF61	4FT deg	*	BCC-CCC	Ind	Ind	26	BBBB	Ind	
Geology and Chemistry (MSci)	FF6D	4FT deg	C	BCC-CCC	Ind	M$^	26$	CSYS	Ind	
German and Biological and Medicine Chem (4 Yrs)	RF2C	4FT deg	* g	BCC	Ind	Ind	28	BBBB	Ind	
German and Chemistry	FR12	3FT deg	C+G g	BCC	Ind	D$^	28$	CSYS	Ind	2
German and Chemistry (4 Yrs)	RF21	4FT deg	G	BCC	Ind	Ind	28$	BBBB	Ind	
German/Russian or Russian St & Bio Med Chemistry	TFYC	4FT deg	G g	BCC	Ind	D$^	28$	BBBB	Ind	
German/Russian or Russian St and Chem (4 Yrs)	TFY1	4FT deg	G	BCC	Ind	Ind	28$	BBBB	Ind	
German/Russian or Russian Studies and Chemistry	FT1Y	3FT deg	G+R+C g	BBC-BCC	Ind	D$^	28$	CSYS	Ind	
History and Biological and Med Chemistry (4 Yrs)	VF1C	4FT deg	*	BCC	Ind	Ind	28	BBBB	Ind	
History and Chemistry	FV11	3FT deg	C g	BCC	Ind	D$^	28$	CSYS	Ind	4
History and Chemistry (4 Yrs)	VF11	4FT deg	*	BCC	Ind	Ind	28	BBBB	Ind	
Human Resource Management and Chemistry	FN16	3FT deg	C g	BCC	Ind	D$^	28$	CSYS	Ind	
Human Resource Management and Chemistry (4 Yrs)	NF61	4FT deg	*	BCC	Ind	Ind	28	BBBB	Ind	
Human Resource Mgt and Biol Med Chem (4 Yrs)	NF6C	4FT deg	*	BCC	Ind	Ind	28	BBBB	Ind	
Int History and Biological and Med Chem (4 Yrs)	VFCC	4FT deg	*	BCC	Ind	Ind	28	BBBB	Ind	
International History and Chemistry	FV1C	3FT deg	C g	BCC	Ind	D$^	28$	CSYS	Ind	
International History and Chemistry (4 Yrs)	VFC1	4FT deg	*	BCC	Ind	Ind	28	BBBB	Ind	
Latin and Biological and Medicinal Chem (4 Yrs)	QF6C	4FT deg	*	BCC	Ind	Ind	28	BBBB	Ind	
Latin and Chemistry	FQ16	3FT deg	Ln+C g	BCC	Ind	D$^	28$	CSYS	Ind	
Latin and Chemistry (4 Yrs)	QF61	4FT deg	*	BCC	Ind	Ind	28	BBBB	Ind	
Law and Biological and Medicinal Chem (4 Yrs)	MF3C	4FT deg	*	BBB	Ind	Ind	32	ABBB	Ind	
Law and Chemistry	FM13	3FT deg	C g	BBB-BBC	Ind	D$^	30$	CSYS	Ind	4
Law and Chemistry (4 Yrs)	MF31	4FT deg	*	BBB	Ind	Ind	32	BBBB	Ind	
Mathematics and Chemistry	FG11	3FT deg	M+C g	BCC-CCC	Ind	M$^	26$	CSYS	Ind	6
Mathematics and Chemistry (4 Yrs)	GF11	4FT deg	*	BCC-CCC	Ind	Ind	26	BBBB	Ind	4
Mathematics and Chemistry (MSci)	GFC1	4FT deg	M+C	BCC-CCC	Ind	M$^	26$	CSYS	Ind	
Maths and Biological & Medicinal Chem (4 Yrs)	GF1C	4FT deg	*	BCC-CCC	Ind	Ind	26	BBBB	Ind	
Music and Biological & Medicinal Chemistry	FWC3	3FT deg	Mu/C g	BCC	Ind	D$^	28$	CSYS	Ind	
Music and Biological and Medicinal Chem (4 Yrs)	WF3C	4FT deg	*	BCC	Ind	Ind	28	BBBB	Ind	
Music and Chemistry	FW13	3FT deg	Mu+C g	BCC	Ind	D$^	28$	CSYS	Ind	
Music and Chemistry (4 Yrs)	WF31	4FT deg	*	BCC	Ind	Ind	28	BBBB	Ind	
Neuroscience and Biological & Medicinal Chem	BFCC	4FT deg	*	BCC-CCC	Ind	Ind	26	BBBB	Ind	
Neuroscience and Biological and Medicinal Chem	BFCD	3FT deg	C+S	BCC-CCC	Ind	M$^	26$	CSYS	Ind	
Neuroscience and Chemistry	BF11	3FT deg	C+S	BCC-CCC	Ind	M$^	26$	CSYS	Ind	
Neuroscience and Chemistry (4 Yrs)	BF1C	4FT deg	*	BCC-CCC	Ind	Ind	26	BBBB	Ind	

course details | 98 expected requirements | 96 entry stats

TITLE	CODE	COURSE	SUBJECTS	A/AS	ND/C	AGNVQ	IB	SQA(H)	SQA	RATIO A/AS
Philosophy and Biological & Medicinal Chemistry	VF7C	4FT deg	*	BCC	Ind	Ind	28	BBBB	Ind	
Philosophy and Biological and Medicinal Chem	FVC7	3FT deg	C	BCC	Ind	D$^	28$	CSYS	Ind	
Philosophy and Chemistry	FV17	3FT deg	C	BCC	Ind	D$^	28$	CSYS	Ind	
Philosophy and Chemistry (4 Yrs)	VF71	4FT deg	*	BCC	Ind	Ind	28	BBBB	Ind	
Physics and Biological & Medicinal Chem (4 Yrs)	FFC3	4FT deg	*	BCC-CCC	Ind	Ind	26$	BBBB	Ind	
Physics and Biological and Medicinal Chemistry	FFCH	3FT deg	P+C g	BCC-CCC	Ind	M$^	26$	CSYS	Ind	
Physics and Chemistry	FF13	3FT deg	P+C g	BCC-CCC	Ind	M$^	26$	CSYS	Ind	5
Physics and Chemistry (4 Yrs)	FF31	4FT deg	*	BCC-CCC	Ind	Ind	26	BBBB	Ind	
Physics and Chemistry (MSci)	FF3C	4FT deg	P+C g	BCC-CCC	Ind	M$^	26$	CSYS	Ind	
Politics and Biological & Medicinal Chem (4 Yrs)	MF1C	4FT deg	*	BCC	Ind	Ind	28	BBBB	Ind	
Politics and Biological and Medicinal Chemistry	FMC1	3FT deg	C g	BCC	Ind	D$^	28$	CSYS	Ind	
Politics and Chemistry	FM11	3FT deg	C g	BCC	Ind	D$^	28$	CSYS	Ind	
Politics and Chemistry (4 Yrs)	MF11	4FT deg	*	BCC	Ind	Ind	28	BBBB	Ind	
Psychology and Biological & Medicinal Chemistry	FCC8	4FT deg	*	BBB-BCC	Ind	Ind	28	ABBB	Ind	
Psychology and Chemistry (4 Yrs)	FC18	4FT deg	*	BBB-BCC	Ind	Ind	28	BBBB	Ind	
Russian Studies and Biolgical & Med Chem (4 Yrs)	RFVC	4FT deg	*	BCC	Ind	Ind	28	BBBB	Ind	
Russian Studies and Chemistry	FRC8	3FT deg	C g	BCC	Ind	D$^	28$	CSYS	Ind	
Russian Studies and Chemistry (4 Yrs)	RF8C	4FT deg	*	BCC	Ind	Ind	28	BBBB	Ind	
Russian Studs and Biological and Medicinal Chem	FRCV	3FT deg	C g	BCC	Ind	D$^	28$	CSYS	Ind	
Russian and Biological and Medicinal Chem(4 Yrs)	RFWC	4FT deg	*	BCC	Ind	Ind	28	BBBB	Ind	
Russian and Biological and Medicinal Chemistry	FRCW	3FT deg	R/C g	BCC	Ind	D$^	28$	CSYS	Ind	
Russian and Chemistry	FR18	3FT deg	C+R g	BCC	Ind	D$^	28$	CSYS	Ind	
Russian and Chemistry (4 Yrs)	RF81	4FT deg	*	BCC	Ind	Ind	28	BBBB	Ind	
Sociol & Soc Anthrop and Biological & Med Chem	LF3C	4FT deg	*	BCC	Ind	Ind	28	BBBB	Ind	
Sociol & Soc Anthrop and Biological & Med Chem	FLC3	3FT deg	C g	BCC	Ind	D$^	28$	CSYS	Ind	
Sociol & Soc Anthropology and Chemistry (4 Yrs)	LF31	4FT deg	*	BCC	Ind	Ind	28	BBBB	Ind	
Sociology & Social Anthropology and Chemistry	FL13	3FT deg	C g	BCC	Ind	D$^	28$	CSYS	Ind	
Statistics and Biological & Medicinal Chem(4Yrs)	GF4C	4FT deg	*	BCC-CCC	Ind	Ind	26	BBBB	Ind	
Statistics and Biological and Medicinal Chem	FGC4	3FT deg	M/C g	BCC-CCC	Ind	M$^	26$	CSYS	Ind	
Statistics and Chemistry	FG14	3FT deg	M+C g	BCC-CCC	Ind	M$^	26$	CSYS	Ind	
Statistics and Chemistry (4 Yrs)	GF41	4FT deg	*	BCC-CCC	Ind	Ind	26	BBBB	Ind	
Visual Arts and Biological and Med Chem (4 Yrs)	WF1C	4FT deg	* g	BCC	Ind	Ind	28	BBBB	Ind	
Visual Arts and Chemistry	FW11	3FT deg	C	BCC	Ind	D$^	28$	CSYS	Ind	
Visual Arts and Chemistry (4 Yrs)	WF11	4FT deg	*	BCC	Ind	Ind	28	BBBB	Ind	

Univ of KENT

TITLE	CODE	COURSE	SUBJECTS	A/AS	ND/C	AGNVQ	IB	SQA(H)	SQA	RATIO A/AS
Biological Chemistry	F1C1	3FT deg	C g	16	MO $	Ind	24$	BBCC$	Ind	6
Biological Chemistry with Studies Abroad	F1CC	4FT deg	C g	16	MO $	Ind	24$	BBCC$	Ind	
Biological Chemistry with Studies Abroad (MChem)	F1CD	4FT deg	C g	16	MO $	Ind	24$	BBCC$	Ind	
Chemistry	F100	3FT deg	C g	16	MO $	Ind	24$	BBCC$	Ind	11 8/12
Chemistry (MChem)	F103	4FT deg	C g	16	MO $	Ind	24$	BBCC$	Ind	
Chemistry and Business Administration	FN11	3FT deg	C g	20	3M+2D$	Ind	28$	BBBB$	Ind	
Chemistry with Business Studies	FN1D	3FT deg	C g	16	MO $	Ind	24$	BBCC$	Ind	
Chemistry with Business Studs with Studs Abroad	FNCC	4FT deg	C g	16	MO $	Ind	24$	BBCC$	Ind	
Chemistry with Env Sci with Studies Abroad	F1FX	4FT deg	C g	16	MO $	Ind	24$	BBCC$	Ind	
Chemistry with Environ Sci with St Abrd (MChem)	F1FY	4FT deg	C g	16	MO $	Ind	24$	BBCC$	Ind	
Chemistry with Environmental Science	F1F9	3FT deg	C g	16	MO $	Ind	24$	BBCC$	Ind	14
Chemistry with Management Science	F1N1	3FT deg	C g	16	MO $	Ind	24$	BBCC$	Ind	17
Chemistry with Mgt Sci with Studs Abroad (MChem)	F1ND	4FT deg	C g	16	MO $	Ind	24$	BBCC$	Ind	
Chemistry with Mgt Science with Studies Abroad	F1NC	4FT deg	C g	16	MO $	Ind	24$	BBCC$	Ind	
Chemistry with Studies Abroad	F101	4FT deg	C g	16	MO $	Ind	24$	BBCC$	Ind	9
Chemistry with Studies Abroad (MChem)	F102	4FT deg	C g	16	MO $	Ind	24$	BBCC$	Ind	
Chemistry with a foundation year (4 Yrs)	F105	4FT deg	* g		N	Ind	Dip	Ind	Ind	1

TITLE	CODE	COURSE	SUBJECTS	A/AS	ND/C	AGNVQ	IB	SQA(H)	SQA	RATIO	A/AS
			98 expected requirements							*96 entry stats*	
Pharmaceutical Chemistry	F127	3FT deg	C g	16	MO $	Ind	24$	BBCC$	Ind	5	
Pharmaceutical Chemistry with St Abroad (MChem)	F129	4FT deg	C g	16	MO $	Ind	24$	BBCC$	Ind		
Pharmaceutical Chemistry with Studies Abroad	F128	4FT deg	C g	16	MO $	Ind	24$	BBCC$	Ind		

KING'S COLL LONDON (Univ of London)

TITLE	CODE	COURSE	SUBJECTS	A/AS	ND/C	AGNVQ	IB	SQA(H)	SQA	RATIO	A/AS
Biological Chemistry	F131	4FT deg	C+S	18	4M $	Ind	28$	BBCCC	Ind		
Biological Chemistry	F130	3FT/4SW deg	C+S	18	4M $	Ind	28$	BBCCC	Ind	3	
Chemical Sciences	F105	3FT deg	C	14	3M $	Ind	28$	BBCCC	Ind		12/18
Chemistry	F100	3FT deg	C+S	18	4M $	Ind	28$	BBCCC	Ind	9	10/20
Chemistry (MSci)	F103	4FT deg	C+S	18	4M $	Ind	28$	BBCCC	Ind		18/24
Chemistry and Analytical Chemistry	F181	4FT deg	C+M	18	4M $	Ind	28$	BBBCC	Ind		
Chemistry and Management	FN11	3FT deg	C+S	20	5M $	Ind	28$	BBBCC	X		
Chemistry and Mathematics	FG11	3FT deg	C+M	BCC	X	Ind	28$	BBBCC	X	21	
Chemistry and Mathematics (4 years) (MSci)	FG1C	4FT deg	C+M	BCC	X	Ind	28$	BBBCC	X	1	
Chemistry and Philosophy	FV17	3FT deg	C+S	BBB	X	Ind	28$	BBBBB	X		
Chemistry and Physics	FF13	3FT deg	C+P+M	CCC	3M+1D$	Ind	28$	BBBCC	Ind	11	
Chemistry and Physics (4 years) (MSci)	FF1H	4FT deg	C+P+M	CCC	3M+1D$	Ind	28$	BBBCC	Ind		
Chemistry with Analytical Chemistry	F180	3FT/4SW deg	C+M	18	4M $	Ind	28$	BBCCC	Ind	5	
Chemistry with Biochemistry	F1C7	3FT/4SW deg	C+S	18	4M $	Ind	28$	BBCCC	Ind	22	
Chemistry with Biochemistry	F1CR	4FT deg	C+S	18	4M $	Ind	28$	BBCCC	Ind		
Chemistry with Bioscience (4 Yrs) (MSci)	F1C1	4FT deg	C+S	18	4M $	Ind	28$	BBCCC	Ind		
Chemistry with Computer Science	F1GM	4FT deg	C+M	18	4M $	Ind	28$	BBCCC	Ind		
Chemistry with Computer Science	F1G5	3FT/4SW deg	C+M	18	4M $	Ind	28$	BBCCC	Ind	9	
Chemistry with Management	F1N1	3FT deg	C+S	18	4M $	Ind	28$	BBCCC	Ind	4	16/18
Chemistry with Management with a year abroad	F1ND	4SW deg	C+S	18	5M $	Ind	28$	BBCCC	Ind	4	
Chemistry with Management with a yr in Industry	F1NC	4SW deg	C+S	18	5M $	Ind	28$	BBCCC	Ind	5	18/24
Chemistry with Philosophy of Science	F1V5	3FT deg	C+S	18	4M $	Ind	28$	BBCCC	Ind	6	
Chemistry with a year abroad (4 Yrs)	F101	4SW deg	C+S	18	5M $	Ind	28$	BBBCC	Ind	5	
Chemistry with a year in Industry (4 Yrs)	F115	4SW deg	C+S	18	5M $	Ind	28$	BBBCC	Ind	5	16/22
Theoretical and Computational Chemistry	F152	3FT/4SW deg	C+M	18	4M $			28$	BBCCC	Ind	
Theoretical and Computational Chemistry	F151	4FT deg									

KINGSTON Univ

TITLE	CODE	COURSE	SUBJECTS	A/AS	ND/C	AGNVQ	IB	SQA(H)	SQA	RATIO	A/AS
Applied Biology & Chemistry	CF11	3FT deg	B/C g	8	3M $	Ind	Ind	CCC	Ind	14	
Applied Chemistry	F111	4SW deg	C g	8	3M $	M	Ind	CCC	Ind	3	
Applied Chemistry	F118▼	4EXT/5EXTSW deg	*		Ind		Ind	Ind	Ind	1	
Applied Chemistry	F110	3FT deg	C g	8	3M $	M	Ind	CCC	Ind	4	
Chemistry	F108▼	4EXT/5EXTSW deg	*		Ind		Ind	Ind	Ind		
Chemistry (MChem)	F105	4FT deg									
Chemistry (MChem)	F104	4FT deg									
Chemistry and French	FR11	4FT deg	C/F g	8	Ind	Ind	Ind	CCC	Ind		
Chemistry with Business Management	F1ND	4SW deg	C g	8	3M	M	Ind	CCC	Ind	4	
Chemistry with Business Management	F1NC▼	4EXT/5EXTSW deg	*		Ind		Ind	Ind	Ind	1	
Chemistry with Business Management	F1N1	3FT deg	C g	8	3M	M	Ind	CCC	Ind	12	
Chemistry/GRSC	F101	4SW deg	C g	8	3M $	M	Ind	CCC	Ind	5	
Chemistry/GRSC	F100	3FT deg	C g	8	3M $	M	Ind	Ind	Ind	5	
Computing & Chemistry	FG15	3FT deg	C g	8	3M $	Ind	Ind	CCC	Ind	5	
Medicinal Chemistry	F128▼	4EXT/5EXTSW deg	*		Ind	Ind	Ind	Ind	Ind	3	
Medicinal Chemistry	F120	3FT deg	C g	8	3M $	M	Ind	CCC	Ind	3	
Medicinal Chemistry	F121	4SW deg	C	8	3M $	M+	Ind	CCC	Ind	10	
Physics and Chemistry	FF31	3FT deg	P/C g	8	3M $	Ind	Ind	CCC	Ind	3	
Chemistry	001F	2FT HND	C	2	$	PS	Ind	Ind	Ind	2	2/8

			98 expected requirements							96 entry stats	
course details											
TITLE	CODE	COURSE	SUBJECTS	A/AS	NQ/C	AGNVQ	IB	SQA(H)	SQA	RATIO A/AS	

LANCASTER Univ

TITLE	CODE	COURSE	SUBJECTS	A/AS	NQ/C	AGNVQ	IB	SQA(H)	SQA	RATIO	A/AS
Chem w. Polymer Sci(inc yr in USA/Canada)(MChem)	F175	4FT deg	C g	BCD	M+D $		32$	AABBB$	Ind		
Chemistry	F100	3FT deg	C g	CCD	MO $		28$	BBBB$	Ind		
Chemistry (MChem)	F105	4FT deg	C g	CCD	MO $		28$	BBBB$	Ind		
Chemistry (MChem)(inc a year in the USA/Canada)	F103	4FT deg	C g	BCD	M/D $		32$	AABBB$	Ind		
Chemistry (inc a year in USA or Canada)	F102	3FT deg	C g	BCD	M/D $		32$	AABBB$	Ind		
Chemistry with French Studies (4 years)	F1R1	4SW deg	C+F g	18	MO $		28$	BBBB$	Ind		
Chemistry with German Studies (4 years)	F1R2	4SW deg	C+G/L g	18	MO $		28$	BBBB$	Ind		
Chemistry with Italian Studies (4 years)	F1R3	4SW deg	C+I/L g	18	MO $		28$	BBBB$	Ind		
Chemistry with Polymer Science (MChem)	F173	4FT deg	C g	CCD	MO $		28$	BBBB$	Ind		
Chemistry with Spanish Studies (4 years)	F1R4	4SW deg	C+Sp/L g	18	MO $		28$	BBBB$	Ind		
Environmental Chemistry	F140	3FT deg	C+B/M/P g	CCD	MO $		28$	BBCC$	Ind		
Environmental Chemistry (MChem)	F142	4FT deg	C+B/M/P g	CCD	MO $		28$	BBCC$	Ind		
Environmental Chemistry (inc a yr in USA/Canada)	F143	4FT deg	C+B/M/P g	BBC	DO $		32$	ABBB$	Ind		
Environmental Chemistry (inc a yr in USA/Canada)	F141	3FT deg	C+B/M/P g	BBC	DO $		32$	ABBB$	Ind		
Combined Science *Chemistry*	Y158	3FT deg	C g	CCD	MO $		28$	BBBB$	Ind		
Combined Science (inc a year in USA or Canada) *Chemistry*	Y155	3FT deg	C g	BBB	Ind $		32$	ABBBB$	Ind		

Univ of LEEDS

TITLE	CODE	COURSE	SUBJECTS	A/AS	NQ/C	AGNVQ	IB	SQA(H)	SQA	RATIO	A/AS
Applied Biology-Chemistry	CFC1	3FT/4FT deg	C+B+P/M g	BCC	1M+5D$	Ind	28	BBBBC	Ind	12	
Biochemistry-Chemistry	CF71	3FT/4FT deg	C+M/P g	BCC	1M+5D$	Ind	28$	BBBBC	Ind	11	
Chemistry	F100	3FT/4FT deg	C+M/P g	CCC	1M+4D$	Ind	26$	BBBCC	Ind	8	16/30
Chemistry with Analytical Chemistry	F180	3FT/4FT deg	C+M/P g	CCC	1M+4D$	Ind	26$	BBBCC	Ind	7	12/24
Chemistry-Computer Science	FG15	3FT/4FT deg	C+M g	BCC	1M+5D$	Ind	28$	BBBBC	Ind	6	
Chemistry-French	FR11	4FT deg	C+F+M/P	BBC	Ind	Ind	30$	CSYS	Ind		
Chemistry-German	FR12	4FT deg	C+G+M/P	BBC	Ind	Ind	30$	CSYS	Ind		
Chemistry-History and Philosophy of Science	FV15	3FT/4FT deg	C+M/P g	BCC	Ind	Ind	28$	BBBBC	Ind	3	
Chemistry-Management Studies	FN11	3FT/4FT deg	C+M/P g	BCC	1M+5D$	Ind	28$	BBBBC	Ind	6	20/28
Chemistry-Mathematics	FG11	3FT/4FT deg	C+M g	BBC	1M+5D$	Ind	30$	ABBBC	Ind	13	
Chemistry-Pharmacology	BF21	3FT/4FT deg	C+B/M/P g	BCC	2M+5D$	Ind	28$	BBBBC	Ind	19	
Chemistry-Philosophy	FV17	3FT/4FT deg	C+M/P g	BCC	1M+5D$	Ind	28$	BBBBC	Ind		
Chemistry-Physics	FF13	3FT/4FT deg	C+M+P g	BCC	1M+5D$	Ind	28$	BBBBC	Ind	21	
Colour Chemistry	F176	3FT deg	C+M/P/B g	CCD	1M+3D$ DS6/^ go		24$	BBCCC	Ind	1	6/26
Colour and Polymer Chemistry	F174	3FT deg	C+M/P/B g	CCD	1M+3D$ DS6/^ go		24$	BBCCC	Ind	3	10/16
Medicinal Chemistry	F120	3FT/4FT deg	C+M/P g	CCC	1M+4D$	Ind	26$	BBBCC	SQA	3	14/30
Molecular Science and Technology	FF31	3FT/4FT deg	C+P+M g	CCC	Ind	Ind	26$	BBBCC	Ind		

Univ of LEICESTER

TITLE	CODE	COURSE	SUBJECTS	A/AS	NQ/C	AGNVQ	IB	SQA(H)	SQA	RATIO	A/AS
Biological Chemistry	CF71	3FT deg	C g	18	5M	M/DS^ gi	28$	BBBCC$	Ind		10/20
Biological Chemistry (MChem)	CF7C	4FT deg	C g	CCC	5M	DS^ gi	28$	BBBCC$	Ind		
Biological Chemistry (Sandwich)	CFRD	3FT deg	C g	18-20	5M $	DS^ gi	28$	BBCCC$	Ind		
Biological Chemistry (USA)	CFR1	3FT deg	C g	22-24	Ind	DS^ gi	30$	ABBB$	Ind		
Chemistry	F100	3FT deg	C g	18	5M $	DS^	28$	BBBCC$	Ind		12/26
Chemistry (2+2)	F103	4EXT deg	C g	E	N	Ind	24$	Ind	Ind		
Chemistry (Europe)	F1T9	4FT deg	C g	20	5M $	DS^ gi	30$	ABBBC	Ind		
Chemistry (Europe) (MChem)	F108	4FT deg	C g	20	5M $	DS^	30$	ABBBC	Ind		
Chemistry (MChem)	F105	4FT deg	C g	18	5M $	DS^	28$	BBBCC$	Ind		16/24
Chemistry (Sandwich)	F101	4SW deg	C g	20	5M $	DS^	30$	ABBBC	Ind		16/24
Chemistry (Sandwich) (MChem)	F106	4/5SW deg	C g	20	5M $	DS^	30$	ABBBC	Ind		
Chemistry (USA)	F102	3FT deg	C+M+P g	24	Ind	DS^	32$	ABBBB	Ind		18/28
Chemistry (USA) (MChem)	F107	4FT deg	C+M+P g	24	Ind	DS^	32$	ABBBB	Ind		20/24
BSc with integrated foundation *Chemistry*	Y101	4EXT deg	* g		N	*			Ind		

Chemistry 13

			98 expected requirements							96 entry stats	
course details											
TITLE	CODE	COURSE	SUBJECTS	A/AS	ND/C	RGNVQ	IB	SQA(H)	SQA	RATIO	A/AS
Combined Science *Chemistry*	Y100	3FT deg	C g	CCC	MO $	DS^	28$	BBBCC$	Ind		

Univ of LIVERPOOL

TITLE	CODE	COURSE	SUBJECTS	A/AS	ND/C	RGNVQ	IB	SQA(H)	SQA	RATIO	A/AS
Chemical Sciences (2+2)	F106	4FT deg	S g	EE	N	Ind	24$	CCCDD$	Ind	1	6/8
Chemistry	F100	3FT deg	C+S g	14	MO $	DS^ go	31$	BBBCC$	Ind	4	12/22
Chemistry (MChem)	F102	4FT deg	C+S g	20	MO $	DS^ go	31$	BBBCC$		7	22/26
Chemistry with Industrial Chemistry	F160	4FT deg	C+S g	14	MO $	Ind	31$	BBBCC$	Ind	6	10/22
Chemistry with Industrial Chemistry (MChem)	F161	4FT deg	C+S g	20	MO $	Ind	31$	BBBCC$			
Chemistry with Materials Science	FF12	3FT deg	C+S g	14	MO $	DS^ go	31$	BBBCC$	Ind	15	
Chemistry with Oceanography	F1F7	3FT deg	C+S g	14	MO $	DS^ go	31$	BBBCC$	Ind	6	16/24
Chemistry with Pharmacology	F1B2	3FT deg	C+S g	20	MO $	Ind	31$	BBBCC$	Ind	6	12/26
Chemistry with Pharmacology (MChem)	F1BF	4FT deg	C+S g	20	MO $	Ind	31$	BBBCC$	Ind	5	
Chemistry with a European Language	F1TF	4FT deg	C+S g	14	MO $	Ind	31$	BBBCC$	Ind	12	
Chemistry with a European Language (MChem)	F1T2	4FT deg	C+S g	20	MO $	Ind	31$	BBBCC$	Ind	8	
Oceanography with Chemistry	F7F1	3FT deg	C+S g	16	MO $	DS^ go	31$	BBBCC$	Ind	15	
BSc Combined Honours *Chemistry*	Y100	3FT deg	C+S	20	MO $	Ind	30$	BBBCC$			

LIVERPOOL JOHN MOORES Univ

TITLE	CODE	COURSE	SUBJECTS	A/AS	ND/C	RGNVQ	IB	SQA(H)	SQA	RATIO	A/AS
Applied Chemistry	F110	3FT/4SW deg	C	8	3M	M				7	7/14
Applied Chemistry with Environmental Chemistry	F111	3FT deg	C	8	3M	M					
Applied Chemistry with Industrial Chemistry	F112	3FT deg	C	8	3M	M				24	
Biological and Chemical Sciences (Foundation)	CF1C	4FT/5SW deg									
Chemistry (MChem)	F100	4FT deg	C g	10	3M	M					6/14
Pharmaceutical and Chemical Science	F125	3FT deg	C	CCC	DO	D^					12/20

LOUGHBOROUGH Univ

TITLE	CODE	COURSE	SUBJECTS	A/AS	ND/C	RGNVQ	IB	SQA(H)	SQA	RATIO	A/AS
Chemistry	F100	3FT deg	C	18	3M+2D	DS6/^ go	28$	Ind	Ind	9	16/22
Chemistry (4 Yr MChem)	F102	4FT deg	C	18	3M+2D	DS6/^ go	28$	Ind	Ind		
Chemistry (4 Yr SW)	F101	4SW deg	C	18	3M+2D	DS6/^ go	28$	Ind	Ind	18	
Chemistry (5 Yr MChem)	F103	5SW deg	C	18	3M+2D	DS6/^ go	28$	Ind	Ind		
Chemistry and Physical Education and Sports Sci	FB16	3FT deg	C	20	3M+2D		30$	Ind	Ind		
Chemistry with Analytical Chemistry	F180	3FT deg	C	16	3M+2D	DS6/^ go	28$	Ind	Ind	6	
Chemistry with Analytical Chemistry (4 Yr SW)	F181	4SW deg	C	16	3M+2D	DS6/^ go	28$	Ind	Ind	10	
Chemistry with Analytical Chemistry (MChem)	F183	5SW deg	C	18	3M+2D	DS6/^ go	28$	Ind	Ind		
Chemistry with Analytical Chemistry (MChem)	F182	4FT deg	C	18	3M+2D	DS6/^ go	28$	Ind	Ind		
Chemistry with Polymer Chemistry & Tech (MChem)	F172	4FT deg	C	18	3M+2D	DS6/^ go	28$	Ind	Ind		
Chemistry with Polymer Chemistry & Tech (MChem)	F173	5SW deg	C	18	3M+2D	DS6/^ go	28$	Ind	Ind		
Chemistry with Polymer Chemistry/Tech (4 Yr SW)	F171	4SW deg	C	16	3M+2D	DS6/^ go	28$	Ind	Ind		
Chemistry with Polymer Chemistry/Technology	F170	3FT deg	C	16	3M+2D	DS6/^ go	28$	Ind	Ind	7	
Chemistry with a European Language	F1T2	4SW deg	C	16	3M+2D	DS6/^ go	28$	Ind	Ind		
Chemistry with a European Language (MChem)	F1TF	5SW deg	C	16	3M+2D	DS6/^ go	28$	Ind	Ind		
Medicinal and Pharmaceutical Chemistry	F126	3FT deg	C	16	3M+2D	DS6/^ go	28$	Ind	Ind	6	10/26
Medicinal and Pharmaceutical Chemistry (4 Yr SW)	F127	4SW deg	C	16	3M+2D	DS6/^ go	28$	Ind	Ind	2	10/22
Medicinal and Pharmaceutical Chemistry (MChem)	F129	5SW deg	C	18	3M+2D	DS6/^ go	28$	Ind	Ind		
Medicinal and Pharmaceutical Chemistry (MChem)	F128	4FT deg	C	18	3M+2D	DS6/^ go	28$	Ind	Ind		

Univ of MANCHESTER

TITLE	CODE	COURSE	SUBJECTS	A/AS	ND/C	RGNVQ	IB	SQA(H)	SQA	RATIO	A/AS
Chemistry	F100	3FT/4FT deg	C	CCC	3M+2D$		25$	CSYS	Ind	4	10/26
Chemistry and Physics	FF13	3FT deg	C+P+M	CCC	4M+2D$		30$	CSYS	Ind	5	
Chemistry with Industrial Experience	F101	4SW deg	C	CCC	3M+2D$		25$	CSYS	Ind	5	14/28
Chemistry with Medicinal Chemistry	F1B3	3FT deg	C+B	BCC	3M+2D$		30$	CSYS	Ind	3	12/22
Chemistry with Patent Law	F1M3	4SW deg	C	ABB	X		35$	CSYS	X	5	
Chemistry with Polymer Science	F170	3FT/4SW deg	C	CCC	3M+2D$		25$	CSYS	Ind	11	
Chemistry with Studies in Europe	F102	4FT deg	C+F/G/I/S	CCC	X		30$	CSYS	X	8	20/28

	course details			**98 expected requirements**							**96 entry stats**	
TITLE		CODE	COURSE	SUBJECTS	A/AS	NO/C	RGNVQ	IB	SQA(H)	SQA	RATIO	A/AS

UMIST (Manchester)

TITLE	CODE	COURSE	SUBJECTS	A/AS	NO/C	RGNVQ	IB	SQA(H)	SQA	RATIO	A/AS
Analytical Chemistry	F180	3FT deg	C g	18	3M+1D	MS6/^ go	30	CSYS	Ind	8	
Analytical Chemistry (MChem)	F181	4FT deg	C g	18	3M+1D	MS6/^ go	30	CSYS	Ind		
Chemical Physics	F112	3FT deg	C g	18	3M+1D	MS6/^ go	30	CSYS	Ind		
Chemical Physics (MChem)	F113	4FT deg	C g	18	3M+1D	MS6/^ go	30	CSYS	Ind		
Chemistry	F100	3FT deg	C g	18	3M+1D	MS6/^ go	30	CSYS	Ind	8	10/24
Chemistry (MChem)	F105	4FT deg	C g	18	3M+1D	MS6/^ go	30	CSYS	Ind		18/24
Chemistry and Polymer Science and Tech (MChem)	FJ14	4FT deg	C g	18	3M+1D	MS6/^ go	30	CSYS	Ind	2	20/24
Chemistry with French (MChem)	F1RC	4FT deg	C g	18	3M+1D	MS6/^ go	30	CSYS	Ind	7	
Chemistry with German (MChem)	F1RF	4FT deg	C g	18	3M+1D	MS6/^ go	30	CSYS	Ind	19	
Chemistry with Industrial Placement (MChem)	F103	4SW deg	C g	18	3M+1D	MS6/^ go	30	CSYS	Ind		12/26
Chemistry with Polymer Science	F1J4	3FT deg	C g	18	3M+1D	MS6/^ go	30	CSYS	Ind	4	
Chemistry with Spanish (MChem)	F1RL	4FT deg	C g	18	3M+1D	MS6/^ go	30	CSYS	Ind	8	
Computer-Aided Chemistry (MChem)	F104	4FT deg	C g	18	3M+1D	M$6/^ go	30	CSYS	Ind	2	
Computer-aided Chemistry	F102	3FT deg	C g	18	3M+1D	M$6/^ go	30	CSYS	Ind	25	
Environmental Chemistry	F140	3FT deg	C g	18	3M+1D	MS6/^ go	30	CSYS	Ind	14	
Environmental Chemistry (MChem)	F141	4FT deg	C g	18	3M+1D	MS6/^ go	30	CSYS	Ind		
Industrial Chemistry	F160	3FT deg	C g	18	3M+1D	MS6/^ go	30	CSYS	Ind	6	
Industrial Chemistry (MChem)	F161	4FT deg	C g	18	3M+1D	MS6/^ go	30	CSYS	Ind		
Management and Chemical Sciences	NF11	3FT deg	C g	18	3M+1D	MS6/^ go	30	CSYS	Ind	3	14/18
Medicinal Chemistry	F126	3FT deg	C g	18	3M+1D	MS6/^ go	30	CSYS	Ind	6	16/22
Medicinal Chemistry (MChem)	F127	4FT deg	C g	18	3M+1D	MS6/^ go	30	CSYS	Ind	2	

MANCHESTER METROPOLITAN Univ

TITLE	CODE	COURSE	SUBJECTS	A/AS	NO/C	RGNVQ	IB	SQA(H)	SQA	RATIO	A/AS
Chemical Science	F101	4FT deg	C g	4	3M	PS	Dip	CC$	N$		10/10
Chemistry (MChem)	F100	3FT deg	C g	8-10	5M $	MS	26$	BCCC$	N$		4/10
Chemistry with Study in Europe	F102	4FT deg	C g	10	5M $	MS	26$	BCCC$	N$		
Chemistry with Study in Industry (MChem)	F110	4SW deg	C g	10	5M	MS	26$	BCCC$	N$		4/10
Chemistry/Applicable Mathematics	FG11	3FT deg	M+C g	12	4M $	M$	26$	CCCCC$	Ind		
Chemistry/Applied Physics	FF13	3FT deg	C+P/M g	12	4M $	M$	26$	CCCCC$	Ind		
Chemistry/Biology	CF11	3FT deg	C g	12	N $	M$	24$	CCCC$	Ind		
Computer Technology/Chemistry	GFM1	3FT deg	C g	12	5M $	M$	27$	BCCC$	Ind		
Computing Science/Chemistry	FG15	3FT deg	C g	12	5M $	M$	27$	BCCC$	Ind		
Economics/Chemistry	FL11	3FT deg	C g	14	MO $	M$	28$	BBCC$	Ind		
Electronics/Chemistry	FH1P	3FT deg	C g	12	5M $	M$	27$	BCCC$	Ind		
Environmental Studies/Chemistry	FF19	3FT deg	C g	14	MO $	M$	28$	BBCC$	Ind		
European Studies/Chemistry	FT12	3FT deg	C g	14	MO $	M$	28$	BBCC$	Ind		
Languages/Chemistry	FT19	3FT deg	C g	14	MO $	M$	28$	BBCC$	Ind		
Materials Science/Chemistry	FF12	3FT deg	C g	12	N $	M$	24$	CCCC$	Ind		
Physics Studies/Chemistry	FF31	3FT deg	C+P/M g	12	4M $	M$	26$	CCCCC$	Ind		
Polymer Science/Chemistry	FJ14	3FT deg	C g	12	N $	M$	24$	CCCC$	Ind		
Psychology/Chemistry	FL17	3FT deg	C g	18	MO $	D$	28$	BBCC$	Ind		
Scientific Instrumentation/Chemistry	FH16	3FT deg	C+P/M g	12	4M $	M$	26$	CCCCC$	Ind		
Social Studies of Technology/Chemistry	FL13	3FT deg	C g	12	5M $	M$	27$	BCCCC$	Ind		
Combined Studies (Foundation) Chemistry	Y108▼	4FT deg	M/P	E	2M $	P$	$	$	Ind		
Chemistry	001F	2FT HND	C g	2	1M $	PS	Dip	CC$	N$		2/6

NAPIER Univ

TITLE	CODE	COURSE	SUBJECTS	A/AS	NO/C	RGNVQ	IB	SQA(H)	SQA	RATIO	A/AS
Applied Chemistry	F110	4FT/5SW deg	2(M/P/C/B)	DD	Ind	Ind	Ind	BCC	Ind		
Chemistry	001F	2FT HND	C/M/P	D	Ind	Ind	Ind	CC	Ind		

TITLE	CODE	COURSE	SUBJECTS	A/AS	ND/C	AGNVQ	IB	SQA(H)	SQA	RATIO A/AS
NENE COLLEGE										
Earth Science with Chemistry and the Environment	F9F1	3FT deg		DD	5M	M	24	CCC	Ind	
Ecology with Chemistry and the Environment	C9F1	3FT deg		DD	5M	M	24	CCC	Ind	
Human Biological Studies with Chem & the Environ	B1F1	3FT deg	S	DE	5M	M	24	CCC	Ind	
Ind Archaeology with Chemistry & the Environment	V6F1	3FT deg		10	5M	M	24	CCC	Ind	
Mathematics with Chemistry and the Environment	G1F1	3FT deg	M	DD	Ind	Ind	24	CCC	Ind	
Sport Studies with Chemistry and the Environment	N7F1	3FT deg	Ss/Pe	12	M+2D	M	24	BBB	Ind	
Univ of NEWCASTLE										
Chemistry	F100	3FT deg	C g	BCD-CCC	Ind		Ind	BBBB$	Ind	9	12/26
Chemistry (MChem)	F103	4FT deg	C g	BCD-CCC	Ind		Ind	BBBB$	Ind	7
Chemistry (with Foundation Year)	F101	4FT deg	* g	16	Ind		Ind	BBBB		2	8/14
Chemistry (with industrial training)	F102	4SW deg	C g	BCD-CCC	Ind		Ind	BBBB$	Ind	6	14/26
Chemistry and Mathematics	FG11	3FT deg	C+M	18	4M	Ind	28$	AABBB	Ind	8
Chemistry and Physics	FF13	3FT deg	C+P+M	18	4M	Ind	28$	AABBB	Ind	
Chemistry and Statistics	FG14	3FT deg	C+M	18	4M	Ind	28$	AABBB	Ind	
Chemistry with Applied Chemistry	F111	4SW deg	C g	BCD-CCC	Ind		Ind	BBBB$	Ind	8
Chemistry with Applied Chemistry (MChem)	F113	4FT deg	C g	BCD-CCC	Ind		Ind	BBBB$	Ind	4
Chemistry with European Studies (French)	F1TF	4FT deg	C g	BCC	Ind		Ind	ABBB$	Ind	
Chemistry with European Studies (German)	F1TG	4FT deg	C g	BCC	Ind		Ind	ABBB$	Ind	
Chemistry with European Studies (Spanish)	F1T2	4FT deg	C g	BCC	Ind		Ind	ABBB$	Ind	
Chemistry with Medicinal Chemistry	F126	3FT deg	C g	BCD-CCC	Ind		Ind	BBBB$	Ind	4	16/26
Chemistry with Medicinal Chemistry (MChem)	F123	4FT deg	C g	BCD-CCC	Ind		Ind	BBBB$	Ind	5
Chemistry with Medicinal Chemistry (w. Ind. Tr.)	F122	4SW deg	C g	BCD-CCC	Ind		Ind	BBBB$	Ind	7	14/22
Chemistry with study in North America (3 years)	F104	3FT deg	C+M	BCC	Ind		Ind	ABBB$	Ind	
Chemistry with study in North America (MChem)	F105	4FT deg	C+M	BCC	Ind		Ind	ABBB$	Ind	
Combined Studies (BSc) *Chemistry*	Y100	3FT deg	C+S	18	4M	Ind	28$	AABBB	Ind	
NORTH EAST WALES INST of HE										
Environmental Chemistry	F140	3FT deg		4-8	3M	M$	Ind	CCC	N$	
Univ of NORTH LONDON										
Biological Chemistry	F130	3FT/4SW/4EXT deg	C+B	12	3M $	MS	24$	Ind	Ind	18
Biology/Chemistry/Food Science Foundation	CF11▼	4FT/5SW deg			Ind	Ind	Ind	INd	Ind	1
Chemistry	F100	3FT/4SW/4EXT deg	C	12	3M $	MS	24$	Ind	Ind	5
Chemistry Foundation	F108	4FT/5SW deg			Ind	Ind	Ind	Ind	Ind	1
Chemistry and Business	FN11	3FT/4SW/4EXT deg	C g	12-14	MO+4D	DS	Ind	Ind	Ind	
Chemistry and Education Studies	FX19	3FT/4SW/4EXT deg	C	CD	Ind	Ind	Ind	Ind	Ind	
Chemistry and French	FR11	4FT deg	C	CD	Ind	Ind	Ind	Ind	Ind	
Chemistry and German	FR12	4FT deg	C	CC	Ind	Ind	Ind	Ind	Ind	
Chemistry and Information Technology	F1G5	3FT/4SW/4EXT deg	C	12	3M $	MS	24$	Ind	Ind	7
Chemistry and Philosophy	FV17	3FT/4SW/4EXT deg	C	12	Ind	Ind	Ind	Ind	Ind	
Chemistry by Research	F180	3FT/4SW deg	C	16	X	X	Ind	Ind	X	
Pharmaceutical Science	F126	3FT/4SW/4EXT deg	B+C	CC	3M $	MS	Ind	Ind	Ind	6/ 8
Combined Honours *Chemistry*	Y100	3FT/4SW/4EXT deg	C	12	3M $	MS	24$	Ind	Ind	
Chemistry	001F	2FT/3SW HND	C	E	N $	PS	$	Ind	Ind	10
Univ of NORTHUMBRIA										
Applied Chemistry	F110	3FT/4SW deg	C+S/M g	10	3M	MS gi	24$	CCC$	Ind	9	6/16
Applied Chemistry	F118	5EXT deg	* g	2-4	N	P	Ind	Ind	Ind	
Biomedical Sciences and Chemistry	BF11	3FT/4SW deg	B+C	12	5M+1D	MS gi	24$	CCCCC$	Ind	6
Chemical and Life Sciences	F111	2FT Dip	B g	4	N	PS gi	24$	CCC$	Ind	1
Chemistry	F101	4FT deg	C+S/M g	10	3M	MS gi	24$	CCCC$	Ind	

course details			98 expected requirements							96 entry stats
TITLE	CODE	COURSE	SUBJECTS	A/AS	ND/C	AGNVQ	IB	SQA(H)	SQA	RATIO A/AS
Chemistry with Analytical Chemistry	F180	3FT/4SW deg	C+S/M g	10	3M	MS gi	24$	CCCC$	Ind	23
Chemistry with Biochemistry	F1C7	3FT/4SW deg	C+S/M g	10	3M	MS gi	24$	CCCC$	Ind	6
Chemistry with Biomedical Sciences	F1B9	3FT/4SW deg	C+S/M g	10	3M	MS gi	24$	CCCC$	Ind	3
Chemistry with Chemical Engineering	F1H8	3FT/4SW deg	C+S/M g	10	3M	MS gi	24$	CCCC$	Ind	10
Chemistry with Environmental Chemistry	F1F9	3FT/4SW deg	C+S/M g	10	3M	MS gi	24$	CCCC$	Ind	
Chemistry with Food Science	F170	3FT/4SW deg	C+S/M g	10	3M	MS gi	24$	CCCC$	Ind	

Univ of NOTTINGHAM

TITLE	CODE	COURSE	SUBJECTS	A/AS	ND/C	AGNVQ	IB	SQA(H)	SQA	RATIO A/AS
Chemistry	F100	3FT deg	C+P/M g	BCD	Ind	Ind	28$	CSYS	Ind	17 20/30
Chemistry (MSci)(4 Yrs)	F101	4FT deg	C+P/M g	BCD	Ind	Ind	28$	CSYS	Ind	5 20/30
Chemistry and Management Studies	FN11	3FT deg	C+P/M g	BBC-BBB	Ind	Ind	28$	CSYS	Ind	8 26/30
Chemistry and Molecular Physics	FF31	3FT deg	C+P+M	BBB-BBC	Ind	Ind	32$	Ind	Ind	
Chemistry and Molecular Physics (MSci)(4 Yrs)	FFH1	4FT deg	C+P+M	BBB-BBC	Ind	Ind	32$	Ind	Ind	5 24/30
Chemistry of Materials	FJ15	3FT deg	C+P/M g	CCD	HN		28$	CSYS	HN	7 14/20
Chemistry of Materials (MSci) (4 Yrs)	FJC5	4FT deg	C+P/M g	CCD	HN		28$	CSYS	HN	

NOTTINGHAM TRENT Univ

TITLE	CODE	COURSE	SUBJECTS	A/AS	ND/C	AGNVQ	IB	SQA(H)	SQA	RATIO A/AS
Applied Chemistry	F110	4SW deg	C g	14	3M	MS go	Ind	B	Ind	8 6/12
Biology and Chemistry	CF11	3FT deg	B+C g	10	Ind	Ind	Dip	C	Ind	10
Chemistry & Environmental Systems & Monitoring	FF19	3FT deg	C g	DD	Ind	Ind	Dip	C	Ind	4
Chemistry (2+2)	F109	4FT deg	C g	E	Ind	PS go	Ind	D	Ind	
Chemistry (Extended)	F108▼	4EXT/5EXTSW deg	* g		Ind	Ind	Ind	Ind	Ind	
Chemistry (Full-Time)	F100	3FT deg	C g	14	3M	MS go	Ind	B	Ind	22
Chemistry (MChem)	F103	4FT deg	C g	14	3M	MS go	Ind	B	Ind	6/18
Chemistry and Computing	FG15	3FT deg	C g	10	Ind	Ind	Dip	C	Ind	11
Chemistry and Mathematics	FG11	3FT deg	C+M	10	Ind	Ind	Dip	C	Ind	
Chemistry and Physics	FF13	3FT deg	C+M/P g	10	Ind	Ind	Dip	C	Ind	
Chemistry in Europe	F101	4SW deg	C g	16	5M	DS go	Ind	BB	Ind	
Chemistry in Europe (MChem)	F104	4FT deg	C g	16	5M	DS go	Ind	BB	Ind	1
Chemistry with Study in the USA	F102	3FT deg	C g	20	5M	DS go	Ind	ABB	Ind	32
Chemistry with Study in the USA (MChem)	F105	4FT deg	C g	20	5M	DS go	Ind	ABB	Ind	2 16/26
Environmental Conservation & Management and Chem	FF91	3FT deg	C g	10	Ind	Ind	Dip	C	Ind	5
Information Technology for Sciences & Chemistry	GF51	3FT deg	C g	10	Ind	Ind	Dip	C	Ind	4
Medicinal Chemistry	F120	3FT deg	C g	16	5M	DS go	Ind	BB	Ind	
Medicinal Chemistry (MChem)	F121	4FT deg	C g	16	5M	DS go	Ind	BB	Ind	
Sport & Exercise Science and Chemistry	BF61	3FT deg	C+B/Pe/Ss g	16	Ind	Ind	Dip	B	Ind	
Science (Chemistry)	001F	2FT/3SW HND	C g	E	N	PS go	Ind	D	Ind	3

OXFORD Univ

TITLE	CODE	COURSE	SUBJECTS	A/AS	ND/C	AGNVQ	IB	SQA(H)	SQA	RATIO A/AS
Chemistry	F100	4FT deg	C+B/M/P	AAB	DO		36	AAAAA	Ind	2 28/30

OXFORD BROOKES Univ

TITLE	CODE	COURSE	SUBJECTS	A/AS	ND/C	AGNVQ	IB	SQA(H)	SQA	RATIO A/AS
Environmental Chemistry/Accounting and Finance	NF41	3FT deg	* g		Ind		Ind	Ind	Ind	
Environmental Chemistry/Anthropology	LF71	3FT deg								
Environmental Chemistry/Biological Chemistry	CF71	3FT deg								
Environmental Chemistry/Biology	FC11	3FT deg								
Environmental Chemistry/Bus Admin & Management	NF11	3FT deg								
Environmental Chemistry/Cartography	FF81	3FT deg								
Environmental Chemistry/Cell Biology	CFC1	3FT deg								
Environmental Chemistry/Combined Studies	FY14	3FT deg		X		X	X	X		
Environmental Chemistry/Computer Systems	GF61	3FT deg								
Environmental Chemistry/Computing	GF51	3FT deg								
Environmental Chemistry/Computing Mathematics	GF91	3FT deg								
Environmental Chemistry/Ecology	CF91	3FT deg								

course details

98 expected requirements

96 entry stats

TITLE	CODE	COURSE	SUBJECTS	A/AS	ND/C	AGNVQ	IB	SQA(H)	SQA	RATIO A/AS
Environmental Chemistry/Economics	FL11	3FT deg								
Environmental Chemistry/Educational Studies	XF91	3FT deg								
Environmental Chemistry/Electronics	HF61	3FT deg								
Environmental Chemistry/English Studies	QF31	3FT deg								
Environmental Policy/Environmental Chemistry	FK13	3FT deg								
Environmental Sciences/Environmental Chemistry	FF19	3FT deg								
Exercise and Health/Environmental Chemistry	BF61	3FT deg								
Fine Art/Environmental Chemistry	WF11	3FT deg								
Food Science and Nutrition/Environmental Chem	FD14	3FT deg								
French Language and Contemp Studies/Environ Chem	RF1C	3FT deg								
French Language and Literature/Environ Chemistry	RF11	3FT deg								
Geography and the Phys Env/Environmental Chem	FF1V	3FT deg								
Geography/Environmental Chemistry	FF8C	3FT deg								
Geology/Environmental Chemistry	FF61	3FT deg								
Geotechnics/Environmental Chemistry	HF21	3FT deg								
German Language and Contemp Stud/Environ Chem	RF2C	3FT deg								
German Language and Literature/Environmental Che	RF21	3FT deg								
German Studies/Environmental Chemistry	RF2D	3FT deg								
Health Care/Environmental Chemistry (Post Exp)	BF71	3FT deg	X		X	X	X			
History of Art/Environmental Chemistry	VF41	3FT deg								
History/Environmental Chemistry	VF11	3FT deg								
Hospitality Management Stds/Environmental Chem	NF71	3FT deg								
Human Biology/Environmental Chemistry	BF11	3FT deg								
Information Systems/Environmental Chemistry	GF5C	3FT deg								
Intelligent Systems/Environmental Chemistry	GF81	3FT deg								
Law/Environmental Chemistry	MF31	3FT deg								
Leisure Planning/Environmental Chemistry	FK1H	3FT deg								
Marketing Management/Environmental Chemistry	FN1N	3FT deg								
Mathematics/Environmental Chemistry	GF11	3FT deg								
Music/Environmental Chemistry	WF31	3FT deg								
Palliative Care/Environmental Chem (Post Exp)	BFR1	3FT deg	X		X	X	X			
Planning Studies/Environmental Chemistry	FK14	3FT deg								
Politics/Environmental Chemistry	MF11	3FT deg								
Psychology/Environmental Chemistry	FC18	3FT deg								
Publishing/Environmental Chemistry	FP15	3FT deg								
Rehabilitation/Environmental Chemistry(Post Exp)	BFT1	3FT deg	X		X	X	X			
Retail Management/Environmental Chemistry	FN15	3FT deg								
Sociology/Environmental Chemistry	LF31	3FT deg								
Software Engineering/Environmental Chemistry	GF71	3FT deg								
Statistics/Environmental Chemistry	GF41	3FT deg								
Telecommunications/Environmental Chemistry	FH1P	3FT deg								
Tourism/Environmental Chemistry	PF71	3FT deg								
Transport Planning/Environmental Chemistry	NF91	3FT deg								
Water Resources/Environmental Chemistry	FH1F	3FT deg								

Univ of PAISLEY

Chemistry	F100	3FT/4FT/5SW deg	* g	CCC-EE	Ind	Ind	Ind	BCC$	Ind	7
Chemistry with Management	F1N1	3FT/4FT/5SW deg	* g	CCC-EE	Ind	Ind	Ind	BCC$	Ind	5
Industrial Chemistry	F160	5SW deg	M+S g	CCC-EE	Ind	Ind	Ind	BCC$	Ind	3
Medicinal Chemistry	F120	3								
Psychology and Chemistry	CF81	3FT/4FT deg	* g	CC	Ind	Ind	Ind	BCCC$	Ind	

course details			98 expected requirements							96 entry stats
TITLE	CODE	COURSE	SUBJECTS	A/AS	NO/C	RGNVQ	IB	SQA(H)	SQA	RATIO A/AS
Univ of PLYMOUTH										
Biotechnology with Chemistry	C9F1	3FT/4SW deg	B+C g	10-14	4M	MS^	Ind	BBBB	Ind	
Cell Biology and Immunology with Chemistry	C1F1	3FT/4SW deg	B+C g	12-14	4M	MS^	Ind	BBBB	Ind	4
Chemistry (Analytical) (MChem Option)	F180	3FT/4FT deg	C g	CC	3M	MS^	Ind	CCCC	Ind	13
Chemistry (Applied) (MChem Option)	F110	3FT/4FT deg	C g	CC	3M	MS^	Ind	CCCC	Ind	22
Chemistry (Environmental) (MChem Option)	F140	3FT/4FT deg	C g	CC	3M	MS^	Ind	CCCC	Ind	7
Chemistry with Astronomy	F1F5	3FT deg	C g	CC	3M	MS^	Ind	CCCC	Ind	5
Chemistry with Business	F1N1	3FT deg	C+Bu g	CCD	3M	MS^	Ind	CCCC	Ind	
Chemistry with Computing	F1G5	3FT deg	C g	CC	3M	MS^	Ind	CCCC	Ind	4
Chemistry with French	F1R1	3FT deg	C+F g	CC	3M	MS^	Ind	CCCC	Ind	
Chemistry with Geology	F1F6	3FT deg	C g	CC	3M	MS^	Ind	CCCC	Ind	
Chemistry with German	F1R2	3FT deg	C+G g	CC	3M	MS^	Ind	CCCC	Ind	
Chemistry with Human Biology	F1C9	3FT deg	C+B g	CC	3M	MS^	Ind	CCCC	Ind	
Chemistry with Italian	F1R3	3FT deg	C g	CC	3M	MS^	Ind	CCCC	Ind	
Chemistry with Languages	F1T9	3FT deg	C+L g	CC	3M	MS^	Ind	CCCC	Ind	
Chemistry with Mathematics	F1G1	3FT deg	C+M g	CC	3M	MS^	Ind	CCCC	Ind	5
Chemistry with Microbiology	F1C5	3FT deg	C+B g	CC	3M	MS^	Ind	CCCC	Ind	2
Chemistry with Ocean Science	F1F7	3FT deg	C g	CC	3M	MS^	Ind	CCCC	Ind	
Chemistry with Resources, Manufac & the Environ	F1F9	3FT deg	C g	CC	3M	MS^	Ind	CCCC	Ind	
Chemistry with Spanish	F1R4	3FT deg	C+Sp g	CC	3M	MS^	Ind	CCCC	Ind	
Chemistry with Statistics	F1G4	3FT deg	C g	CC	3M	MS^	Ind	CCCC	Ind	
Geology with Chemistry	F6F1	3FT deg	S+C g	12	4M	MS	Ind	CCC	Ind	
Human Biology with Chemistry	C9FC	3FT/4SW deg	B+C g	12-14	4M $	MS^	Ind	BBBB	Ind	8
Marine Biology with Chemistry	C1FD	3FT deg	B+C g	CCC	4M $	MS^	Ind	BBBB	Ind	8
Mathematics with Chemistry	G1F1	3FT deg	M g	10-15	MO $	MS$^	Ind	Ind	Ind	
Microbiology with Chemistry	C5F1	3FT/4SW deg	B+C g	12-16	4M $	MS	Ind	BBBB	Ind	3
Ocean Science with Chemistry	F7F1	3FT deg	S g	14-16	5M $	M$	Ind	BBBB	Ind	
Statistics (App) with Chemistry	G4F1	3FT deg	M/St g	10	MO $	M$	Ind	BBCC	Ind	
Extended Science (Foundation year) Chemistry	Y108▼	1FT/4EXT deg	S	2	Ind	P$	Ind	Ind	Ind	
Univ of PORTSMOUTH										
Applied Chemistry	F110	4SW deg	C+S	8	N $	M$6/^	Dip	Ind	Ind	4 6/18
Applied Chemistry	F118▼	4FT deg	*		Ind	P*	Ind	Ind	Ind	1
Chemistry and Computing	FG15	3FT deg	C	10	N $	MS6/^	Dip	Ind	Ind	
Chemistry and Computing	FG1M▼	4FT deg	*		Ind	Ind	Ind	Ind	Ind	Ind
Chemistry and Geographical Science	FF1V▼	4FT deg	*	Ind	Ind	Ind	Ind	Ind	Ind	
Chemistry and Geographical Science	FF18	3FT deg	C+Gy	14	4M	MS6/^	26	BBBB	Ind	
Chemistry and Geology	FF16	3FT deg	C	10	3M	MS6/^	26	BBBB	Ind	
Chemistry and Geology	FF1P▼	4FT deg	*		Ind	Ind	Ind	Ind	Ind	
Chemistry and Mathematics	FG1C▼	4FT deg	*		Ind	Ind	Ind	Ind	Ind	
Chemistry and Mathematics	FG11	3FT deg	C+M	10	1M $	MS6/^	Dip	BCCC	Ind	9
Chemistry and Physics	FF13	3FT deg	C+P	10	N $	MS6/^	Dip	Ind	Ind	
Chemistry and Physics	FF1J▼	4FT deg	*		Ind	Ind	Ind	Ind	Ind	
Chemistry and Statistics	FG1K▼	4FT deg	*		Ind	Ind	Ind	Ind	Ind	
Chemistry and Statistics	FG14	3FT deg	C+M	10	N $	MS6/^	Dip	Ind	Ind	
Pharmaceutical and Medicinal Chemistry	F128	4FT deg	*		Ind	Ind	Ind	Ind	Ind	
Pharmaceutical and Medicinal Chemistry	F126	3FT deg	C+S	12	3M $	M$6/^	Dip	BBB	Ind	6/16
QUEEN MARY & WESTFIELD COLL (Univ of London)										
Biological Chemistry	F1C1	3FT deg	C+B/P/M	CCC	5M $	DS	26$	BBBCC		
Biology and Chemistry	CF11	3FT deg	B+C	CCC	6M $	DS	26$	BBBCC		
Chemistry	F100	3FT deg	C+B/P/M	CCC	5M $	DS	26$	BBBCC		

TITLE	CODE	COURSE	SUBJECTS	A/AS	NO/C	AGNVQ	IB	SQA(H)	SQA	RATIO	A/AS
course details			_98 expected requirements_							_96 entry stats_	
Chemistry (MSci)	F101	4FT deg	C+B/P/M	CCC	6M $	DS	26$	BBBCC			
Chemistry and German	FR1F	4FT deg	C+G	BCC	5M $	DS^	26$	BBBCC			
Chemistry and Mathematics	FG11	3FT deg	C+M	CCC	6M $	DS^	26$	BBBCC			
Chemistry and Physics	FF13	3FT deg	C+P	CCC	5M $	DS	26$	BBBCC			
Chemistry with Biochemistry	F1C7	3FT deg	C+B/P/M	CCC	5M $	DS	26$	BBBCC			
Chemistry with Business Studies	F1N1	3FT deg	C+B/P/M	CCC	5M $	DS	26$	BBBCC			
Environmental Chemistry	F140	3FT deg	C+B/P/M	18	MO	DS	26$				
Pharmaceutical Chemistry	F126	3FT deg	C+B/P/M.	CCC	6M $	DS	26$	BBBCC			
Science and Engineering (4 yrs with Foundation) Chemistry	Y157	4EXT deg		E	N	P					

QUEEN'S Univ Belfast

TITLE	CODE	COURSE	SUBJECTS	A/AS	NO/C	AGNVQ	IB	SQA(H)	SQA	RATIO	A/AS
Chemistry	F100	3FT/4FT deg	C g	CCC	Ind	Ind	28$	BBBC	Ind	4	16/28
Chemistry and Computer Science	FG15	3FT/4FT deg	C+M/Cs g	CCC	Ind	Ind	28$	BBBC	Ind	5	
Chemistry with Extended Studies in Europe	F102	4FT deg	C g	CCC	X	Ind	28$	X	Ind		
Environmental Chemistry	F140	3FT/4FT deg	C g	CCC	Ind	Ind	28$	BBBC	Ind	8	
Environmental Chemistry with Ext St in Europe	F142	4FT deg	C g	CCC	X	Ind	28$	X	Ind	3	

Univ of READING

TITLE	CODE	COURSE	SUBJECTS	A/AS	NO/C	AGNVQ	IB	SQA(H)	SQA	RATIO	A/AS
Chemistry	F100	3FT deg	C g	18	4M+1D$	DS^ go	29$	BBBC$	Ind	6	10/18
Chemistry (MChem)	F103	4FT deg	C g	18	4M+1D$	DS^ go	29$	BBBC$	Ind	6	14/24
Chemistry with Accounting	F1N4	3FT deg	C g	18	4M+1D$	DS^ go	29$	BBBC$	Ind		
Chemistry with Accounting with a year in Europe	F1NL	4FT deg	C g	18	4M+1D$	DS^ go	29$	BBBC$	Ind		
Chemistry with Archaeology	F1V6	3FT deg	C g	18	4M+1D$	DS^ go	29$	BBBC$	Ind	3	14/17
Chemistry with Archaeology with a year in Europe	F1VP	4FT deg	C g	18	4M+1D$	DS^ go	29$	BBBC$	Ind		
Chemistry with Computer Sci with a year in Eur	F1GM	4FT deg	C g	18	4M+1D$	DS^ go	29$	BBBC$	Ind	3	
Chemistry with Computer Science	F1G5	3FT deg	C g	18	4M+1D$	DS^ go	29$	BBBC$	Ind	8	
Chemistry with Economics	F1L1	3FT deg	C g	18	4M+1D$	DS^ go	29$	BBBC$	Ind	2	14/16
Chemistry with Economics with a year in Europe	F1LC	4FT deg	C g	18	4M+1D$	DS^ go	29$	BBBC$	Ind		
Chemistry with Food Science	F1D4	3FT deg	C g	18	4M+1D$	DS^ go	29$	BBBC$	Ind		
Chemistry with a year in Europe (MChem)	F104	4FT deg	C g	18	4M+1D$	DS^ go	29$	BBBC$	Ind		
Chemistry with a year in Industry (MChem)	F105	4FT deg	C g	18	4M+1D$	DS^ go	29$	BBBC$	Ind		
Environmental Chemistry	F140	3FT deg	C g	18	4M+1D$	DS^ go	29$	BBBC$	Ind	6	
Environmental Chemistry with a year in Europe	F142	4FT deg	C g	18	4M+1D$	DS^ go	29$	BBBC$	Ind	11	
Environmental Geochemistry	F141	3FT deg	C g	18	4M+1D$	DS^ go	29$	BBBC$	Ind	3	12/20

ROBERT GORDON Univ

TITLE	CODE	COURSE	SUBJECTS	A/AS	NO/C	AGNVQ	IB	SQA(H)	SQA	RATIO	A/AS
Applied Biosciences and Chemistry	CF91	3FT/4FT deg	B/C g	EE	N	Ind	Ind	CCC$	Ind	3	
Applied Chemistry	F110	3FT/4FT deg	C+S g	EE	N	Ind	Ind	CCC$	Ind	5	
Applied Science (Analytical with Environ Sci)	9F1F	2FT HND	S g	E	N	Ind	Ind	CC$	Ind		
Applied Science (Applied Chemistry)	011F	2FT HND	S g	E	N	Ind	Ind	CC$	Ind	6	

Univ of SALFORD

TITLE	CODE	COURSE	SUBJECTS	A/AS	NO/C	AGNVQ	IB	SQA(H)	SQA	RATIO	A/AS
Applied Chemistry (4 Yrs)	F110	4SW deg	C+S/M	BC	N	P	30$	Ind	Ind	7	
Biochemistry and Chemistry (3 or 4 Yrs)	FC17	3FT/4SW deg	C	BCC-CCD	3M	M	Ind	Ind	Ind	5	
Biology and Chemistry (3 or 4 yr SW)	FC11	3FT/4SW deg	B+C g	BCC-CCD	3M	M	Ind	Ind	Ind	5	
Chemical Analysis	F112	3FT deg	C	8	Ind	Ind	28	CC	Ind		
Chemical Sciences (4 Yrs)	F106	4FT deg	C	8	Ind	Ind	Ind	Ind	Ind	1	4/6
Chemistry	F100	3FT deg	C+M/S	BC	N	P	30$	Ind	Ind	5	6/14
Chemistry and Economics (3 or 4 Yrs)	FL11	3FT/4SW deg	C	BCC-CCD	3M	M	Ind	Ind	Ind	1	
Chemistry and Information Technology	FG15	3FT/4SW deg		BCC-CCD	3M	M	Ind	Ind	Ind		
Chemistry and Physics (3 or 4 Yrs)	FF13	3FT/4SW deg	C+P	BCC-CCD	3M	M	Ind	Ind	Ind		
Chemistry with Additional St in Europe (4 Yrs)	F101	4SW deg	C+S/M	BC	N	P	30$	Ind	Ind	3	
Chemistry with Analytical Chemistry (MChem)	F180	3FT/4SW deg	C+S/M	BC	N	P	30$	Ind	Ind	13	
Chemistry with Biochemistry	F1C7	4FT deg	C+S/M	BC	N	P					

course details			98 expected requirements							96 entry stats	
TITLE	CODE	COURSE	SUBJECTS	A/AS	NQ/C	AGNVQ	IB	SQR(H)	SQR	RATIO	A/AS
Chemistry with Business Studies (3/4 Yrs)	F1N1	3FT/4SW deg	C+S/M	BC	N	P	30$	Ind	Ind	14	
Chemistry with Industrial Experience (4 Yrs)	F105	4SW deg	C+S/M	BC	Ind	P	30$	Ind	Ind	10	
Chemistry with Medicinal Chemistry (3/4 Yrs)	F120	3FT/4SW deg	C+S	16-18	Ind	D	30$	Ind	Ind		
Chemistry with a Foundation Year	F107	4FT deg			Ind	P	Ind	Ind	Ind	1	
Chemistry with studies in North America	F102	3FT deg	C+M/S	BC	N	P	30$	Ind	Ind		
Environmental Chemistry	F140	3FT deg	C+S	16-18	Ind	M	30$	Ind	Ind	10	
Analytical Chemistry	081F	2FT HND	C	2-4	N	M	Ind	CC	Ind	14	

Univ of SHEFFIELD

TITLE	CODE	COURSE	SUBJECTS	A/AS	NQ/C	AGNVQ	IB	SQR(H)	SQR	RATIO	A/AS
Chemistry	F100	3FT deg	C g	20	5M+1D$	DS^	29$	BBBB$	Ind	8	16/26
Chemistry	F105	4FT deg	C g	20	5M+1D$	DS^	29$	BBBB$	Ind	4	18/30
Chemistry Foundation Year (4 or 5 Yrs)	F101	4FT/5FT deg	g	20	5M+1D	D^	29	BBBB	Ind		
Chemistry and Astronomy	FF15	3FT deg	C+M g	BBB	3M+3D$	X	32$	AABB$	Ind	10	
Chemistry and Materials Science	FJ15	3FT/4EXT deg	C+M/P g	BCC	5M+1D$	DS^	29$	BBBB$	Ind	5	
Chemistry and Mathematics	FG1D	3FT/4EXT deg	C+M g	BBC	5M+1D$	DS^	29$	ABBC$	Ind	6	26/30
Chemistry with Study in Australia	F108	4FT deg	C g	26	2M+4D$	DS^	33$	AABB$			
Chemistry with Study in Europe	F107	4FT deg	C+L g	BBB	3M+3D$	DS^	32$	AABB$	Ind	4	22/30
Chemistry with Study in Industry	F106	4FT deg	C g	22	4M+2D$	DS^	30$	ABBB$	Ind	5	22/30
Chemistry with Study in the USA	F109	4FT deg	C g	26	2M+4D$	DS^	33$	AABB$			

SHEFFIELD HALLAM Univ

TITLE	CODE	COURSE	SUBJECTS	A/AS	NQ/C	AGNVQ	IB	SQR(H)	SQR	RATIO	A/AS
Applied Chemistry	F110	4SW deg	C	10	3M	MS	Ind	Ind	Ind		
Biomedical Chemistry	F103	4SW deg	B+C	10	3M	M$	Ind	Ind	Ind		
Environmental Chemistry	F140	4SW deg	C	10	3M	MS	Ind	Ind	Ind		
Pharmaceutical Chemistry	F126	4SW deg									
Combined Studies Chemistry	Y400	3FT deg	C	8-10	2M	M	Ind	Ind	Ind		
Chemistry	001F	2FT HND	C	E	N	PS	Ind	Ind	Ind		

Univ of SOUTHAMPTON

TITLE	CODE	COURSE	SUBJECTS	A/AS	NQ/C	AGNVQ	IB	SQR(H)	SQR	RATIO	A/AS
Biochemistry and Chemistry (4 Yrs)	CF71	4FT deg	C+B/P/M/Gy g	BCC	$	M^	$	Ind	Ind		
Biochemistry with Chemistry	C7F1	3FT/4SW deg	C+B/P/M/Gy g	BCC	$	M^	$	Ind	Ind	9	
Biology with Chemistry	C1F1	3FT deg	B+C g	BCC	5M+1D$	Ind^	28$	BBBBC	Ind	3	20/24
Chemistry	F100	3FT deg	C+S g	18	Ind	Ind	28$	CSYS	Ind	7	18/26
Chemistry (inc professional training) (MChem)	F101	4FT deg	C+S g	22	Ind	Ind	30$	CSYS	Ind	6	22/30
Chemistry and Biochemistry (4 Yrs)	FC17	4FT deg	C+S g	BBC	Ind	Ind	30$	CSYS	Ind	3	22/30
Chemistry and Mathematics (4 Yrs)	FG11	4FT deg	C+M g	BBC	Ind	Ind	30$	CSYS	Ind	3	20/30
Chemistry with Biochemistry	F1C7	3FT deg	C+S g	18	Ind	Ind	28$	CSYS	Ind	5	
Chemistry with Computer Science	F1G5	3FT deg	C+M	18	Ind	Ind	28$	CSYS	Ind	4	16/30
Chemistry with Environmental Sciences	F1F9	3FT deg	C+S g	18	Ind	Ind	28$	CSYS	Ind	12	
Chemistry with Geology	F1F6	3FT deg	C+S g	18	Ind	Ind	28$	CSYS	Ind	4	
Chemistry with Mathematics	F1G1	3FT deg	C+M	18	Ind	Ind	28$	CSYS	Ind	4	
Chemistry with Medicinal Chemistry	F120	3FT deg	C+S g	18	Ind	Ind	28$	CSYS	Ind	15	
Chemistry with Oceanography	F1F7	3FT deg	C+S g	18	Ind	Ind	28$	CSYS	Ind	3	18/24
Chemistry with Pharmacology	F1B2	3FT deg	C+S g	18	Ind	Ind	28$	CSYS	Ind	13	
Chemistry with Physics	F1F3	3FT deg	C+P+M	CCC	Ind	Ind	28$	CSYS	Ind		
Geology with Chemistry	F6F1	3FT deg	C+S g	18-20	Ind	Ind	28$	BBBBC$	Ind	2	
Marine Environmental Chemistry	F7F1	3FT deg	C+S/M g	BCC	Ind	Ind	30$	BBBBC	Ind	11	
Mathematics with Chemistry	G1F1	3FT deg	M+C	BBC	Ind	Ind	30	ABBBB	Ind	8	
Physics with Chemistry	F3F1	3FT deg	M+P+C g	BCE	Ind	Ind	28$	AAABB	Ind		

Univ of ST ANDREWS

TITLE	CODE	COURSE	SUBJECTS	A/AS	NQ/C	AGNVQ	IB	SQR(H)	SQR	RATIO	A/AS
Chemistry	F100	3FT/4FT deg	C g	CCC	Ind	Ind	28$	BBBC$	Ind	4	16/30
Chemistry and Advanced Chemistry	F101	3FT/4FT deg	C g	CCC	Ind	Ind	28$	BBBC$	Ind		
Chemistry with Applied Chemistry	F110	3FT/4FT deg	C g	CCC	Ind	Ind	28$	BBBC$	Ind		

Chemistry 13

course details   98 expected requirements   96 entry stats

TITLE	CODE	COURSE	SUBJECTS	A/AS	ND/C	AGNVQ	IB	SQA(H)	SQA	RATIO A/AS
Chemistry with Biological Chemistry	F130	3FT/4FT deg	C g	CCC	Ind	Ind	28$	BBBC$	Ind	
Chemistry with Catalysis	F160	3FT/4FT deg	C g	CCC	Ind	Ind	28$	BBBC$	Ind	
Chemistry with French	F1R1	4FT deg	C g	CCC	Ind	Ind	28$	BBBC$	Ind	
Chemistry with French (with Integ Year Abroad)	F1RC	4FT/5FT deg	C g	CCC	Ind	Ind	28$	BBBC$	Ind	
Chemistry with German	F1R2	4FT deg	C g	CCC	Ind	Ind	28$	BBBC	Ind	
Chemistry with German (with Integ Year Abroad)	F1RF	4FT/5FT deg	C g	CCC	Ind	Ind	28$	BBBC$	Ind	
Chemistry with Industrial Placement	F111	4FT/5FT deg	C g	CCC	Ind	Ind	28$	BBBC$	Ind	
Chemistry with Materials Chemistry	F112	3FT/4FT deg	C g	CCC	Ind	Ind	28$	BBBC$	Ind	
Chemistry with Pharmacology	F1B2	3FT/4FT deg	C g	CCC	Ind	Ind	28$	BBBC$	Ind	21
Chemistry-Biochemistry	CF71	3FT/4FT deg	C g	CCC	Ind	Ind	28$	BBCC$	Ind	6
Computer Science-Chemistry	FG15	3FT/4FT deg	M+C	CCC	Ind	Ind	28$	BBCC$	Ind	7
Management Sciences-Chemistry	FN11	4FT deg	C+M	CCC	Ind	Ind	28$	BBBC$	Ind	11
Management-Chemistry	FN1C	4FT deg	C g	BCC	Ind	Ind	28$	BBBC$	Ind	
Mathematics-Chemistry	FG11	3FT/4FT deg	C+M	CCC	Ind	Ind	28$	BBCC$	Ind	5
Physics-Chemistry	FF13	3FT/4FT deg	C+P+M	CCC	Ind	Ind	28$	BBCC$	Ind	10
General Degree of BSc Chemistry	Y100	3FT deg	C g	CCC	Ind	Ind	28$	BBBC$	Ind	

STAFFORDSHIRE Univ

TITLE	CODE	COURSE	SUBJECTS	A/AS	ND/C	AGNVQ	IB	SQA(H)	SQA	RATIO A/AS
Applied and Analytical Chemistry	F110	3FT deg	C g	8	4M	M^	24	BCC	Ind	7
Applied and Analytical Chemistry (MChem)	F180	3FT deg								
Chemical Sciences	F102	3FT deg	C g	8	4M	M	24	BCC	Ind	
Chemistry	F100	3FT deg	C g	10	4M	M	24	BCC	Ind	8
Chemistry (MChem)	F101	4FT deg	C g	12	4M	M	24	BCC	Ind	
Chemistry/Applied Statistics	FG14	3FT deg	S	8	3M	M	24	BCC	Ind	
Chemistry/Biochemistry	FC17	3FT deg	S	8	3M	M	24	BCC	Ind	
Chemistry/Biology	CF11	3FT deg	S g	8	3M	M	24	BCC	Ind	
Chemistry/Business Studies	FN11	3FT deg	S g	12	4M	M	24	BCC	Ind	
Chemistry/Ceramic Science	FJ13	3FT deg	S g	8	3M	M	24	BCC	Ind	
Computing/Chemistry	FG15	3FT deg	S	8	3M	M	24	BCC	Ind	
Electronics/Chemistry	FH16	3FT deg	S	8	3M	M	24	BCC	Ind	
Environmental Chemistry	F148	3FT deg	C	10	4M	M	24	BCC	Ind	18
Environmental Science and Chemistry	FF19	3FT deg	S	8	3M	M	24	BCC	Ind	4
Extended Applied and Analytical Chemistry (4 yr)	F119	4EXT deg	g	4	N	M	24	CCC	Ind	2
Extended Chemistry (4 yr)	F109	4EXT deg	g	4	1M	M	24	CCC	Ind	2
Extended Environmental Chemistry (4 yr)	F147	4EXT deg	g	4	N	M	24	CCC	Ind	1
Foundation Applied and Analytical Chemistry	F118▼	4EXT deg	*	4	N	P	24	CCC	Ind	
Foundation Biochemistry and Chemistry	CF7C▼	4EXT deg	*	4	N	P	24	CCC	Ind	
Foundation Biology and Chemistry	CF1C▼	4EXT deg	*	4	N	P	24	CCC	Ind	
Foundation Chemistry	F108▼	4EXT deg	*	4	N	P	24	BCC	Ind	
Foundation Chemistry and Computing	FG1M▼	4EXT deg	*	4	N	P	24	CCC	Ind	
Foundation Chemistry and Electronics	FH1P▼	4EXT deg	*	4	N	P	24	CCC	Ind	
Foundation Chemistry and Geology	FF1P	4EXT deg	*	4	N	P	24	CCC		
Foundation Chemistry and Physics	FF1H▼	4EXT deg	*	4	N	P	24	CCC	Ind	
Foundation Environmental Chemistry	F149▼	4EXT deg	*	4	N	P	24	BCC	Ind	
Geography/Chemistry	FL18	3FT deg	S g	8	3M	M	24	BCC	Ind	
Geology/Chemistry	FF16	3FT deg	S	8	3M	M	24	BCC	Ind	
Physics/Chemistry	FF13	3FT deg	P+C	8	3M	M	24	BCC	Ind	
Sport Sciences and Chemistry	BF61	3FT deg	S	14	Ind	D	Ind	BBCC	Ind	
Chemistry	001F	2FT HND	C	2	N	P	24	CCC	Ind	2

Univ of STIRLING

TITLE	CODE	COURSE	SUBJECTS	A/AS	ND/C	AGNVQ	IB	SQA(H)	SQA	RATIO A/AS
Chemistry (General Degree only)	F100	3/4FT deg	C g	CCD	Ind	Ind	28	BBCC	HN	
Environmental Analysis	FF19	4FT deg	S g	CCC	HN	Ind	31	BBBC	HN	

				98 expected requirements						96 entry stats	
course details											
TITLE	CODE	COURSE	SUBJECTS	A/AS	ND/C	RGNVQ	IB	SQA(H)	SQA	RATIO	A/AS
STOCKPORT COLL of F and HE											
Chemistry	F100	4FT deg	C+M/B/P	EE	N	PS	Dip	BBCC	N		
Univ of STRATHCLYDE											
Applied Chemistry	F110	4FT deg	C+M+S	CCC	HN		28$	BBBB$	HN		
Chemistry	F100	4FT deg	C+M+P	CCC	HN		28$	BBBB$	HN		
Chemistry (MSci)	F103	5FT deg	C+M+P	ABB	HN		34$	AABB$	HN		
Forensic and Analytical Chemistry	F1B9	4FT deg	C+M+P	ABB	HN		30$	AABB$	HN		26/30
Science Studies (Pass Degree) *Chemistry*	Y100	3FT deg	M+S	DD	Ind		Ind	CCC$	Ind		
Univ of SUNDERLAND											
Biology and Chemistry	CF11▼	3FT deg	C+B g	8	N $		24$	CCCC$	N$	4	
Biology with Chemistry	C1F1	3FT deg	B/C	8	3M	M	Ind	Ind	Ind		
Business Studies with Chemistry	N1F1	3FT/4SW deg	*	8	3M	M	Ind	Ind	Ind		
Chemical and Pharmaceutical Science	FB13▼	3FT/4SW deg	C g	12	MO $	MS	24$	CCCCC$	N$	3	8/17
Chemical and Pharmaceutical Science (Foundation)	FBC3▼	4EXT/5EXTSW deg	*							3	
Chemistry and Business Studies	FN11	3FT/4SW deg	C+S	8	N $	PS	24$	CCCC$	N$		
Chemistry and Computer Studies	FG15	3FT deg	C g	8	N $	M	24$	CCCC$	N$		
Chemistry and Economics	FL11	3FT deg	C g	8	N $	M	24$	CCCC$	N$		
Chemistry and English	FQ13	3FT deg	C	10	4M	M	Ind	Ind	Ind		
Chemistry and Geography	FL18	3FT deg	C	8	3M	M	Ind	Ind	Ind		
Chemistry and Geology	FF16	3FT deg	C+Gy/Gl g	8	N $	M	24$	CCCC$	N$		
Chemistry and German	FR12▼	4FT deg	G+C g	8	N $	M	24$	CCCC$	N$	1	
Chemistry and History of Art and Design	FV14	3FT deg	C	8	3M	M	Ind	Ind	Ind		
Chemistry and Information Systems	FG1M	3FT/4SW deg	C+S	8	N $	PS	24$	CCCC$	N$		
Chemistry and Mathematics	FG11	3FT deg	M+C g	8	N $	M	24$	CCCC$	N$		
Chemistry and Philosophy	FV17	3FT deg	C	8	3M	M	Ind	Ind	Ind		
Chemistry and Physiology	FB11▼	3FT deg	C/B g	8	N $	M	24$	CCCC$	N$		
Chemistry and Politics	FM11	3FT deg	C	8	3M	M	Ind	Ind	Ind		
Chemistry and Psychology	FC18	3FT deg	C	10	4M	M	Ind	Ind	Ind		
Chemistry and Religious Studies	FV18	3FT deg	C	8	3M	M	Ind	Ind	Ind		
Chemistry and Sociology	FL13	3FT deg	C	10	4M	M	Ind	Ind	Ind		
Chemistry and Spanish	FR14	4FT deg	C	8	3M	M	Ind	Ind	Ind		
Chemistry with Business Studies	F1N1	3FT deg	C	8	3M	M	Ind	Ind	Ind		
Chemistry with Computer Studies	F1G5	3FT deg	C	8	3M	M	Ind	Ind	Ind		
Chemistry with Economics	F1L1	3FT deg	C	8	3M	M	Ind	Ind	Ind		
Chemistry with English	F1Q3	3FT deg	C	10	4M	M	Ind	Ind	Ind		
Chemistry with Geography	F1L8	3FT deg	C	8	3M	M	Dip	Ind	Ind		
Chemistry with Geology	F1F6	3FT deg	C	8	3M	M	Ind	Ind	Ind		
Chemistry with German	F1R2	3FT deg	C	8	3M	M	Ind	Ind	Ind		
Chemistry with History of Art and Design	F1V4	3FT deg	C	8	3M	M	Ind	Ind	Ind		
Chemistry with Mathematics	F1G1	3FT deg	C	8	3M	M	Ind	Ind	Ind		
Chemistry with Philosophy	F1V7	3FT deg	C	8	3M	M	Ind	Ind	Ind		
Chemistry with Physiology	F1B1	3FT deg	C	8	3M	M	Ind	Ind	Ind		
Chemistry with Politics	F1M1	3FT deg	C	8	3M	M	Ind	Ind	Ind		
Chemistry with Psychology	F1C8	3FT deg	C	10	4M	M^	Ind	Ind	Ind		
Chemistry with Religious Studies	F1V8	3FT deg	C	8	3M	M	Ind	Ind	Ind		
Chemistry with Sociology	F1L3	3FT deg	C	10	4M	M	Ind	Ind	Ind		
Chemistry with Spanish	F1R4	3FT deg	C	8	3M	M	Ind	Ind	Ind		
Computer Studies with Chemistry	G5F1	3FT/4SW deg	*	8	3M	M	Ind	Ind	Ind		
Economics with Chemistry	L1F1	3FT deg	*	8	3M	M	Ind	Ind	Ind		
English with Chemistry	Q3F1	3FT deg	C	10	4M	M	Ind	Ind	Ind		

Chemistry 13

TITLE	CODE	COURSE	SUBJECTS	A/AS	NO/C	AGNVQ	IB	SQA(H)	SQA	RATIO A/AS
French with Chemistry	R1F1	4FT deg								
Geography with Chemistry	L8F1	3FT deg	*	8	3M	M	Ind	Ind	Ind	
Geology with Chemistry	F6F1	3FT deg	*	8	3M	M	Ind	Ind	Ind	
German with Chemistry	R2F1	4SW deg	G	8	3M	M	Ind	Ind	Ind	
Mathematics with Chemistry	G1F1	3FT deg	M	8	3M	M	Ind	Ind	Ind	
Philosophy with Chemistry	V7F1	3FT deg	*	8	3M	Ind	Ind	Ind	Ind	
Physiology with Chemistry	B1F1	3FT deg	*	8	3M	M	Ind	Ind	Ind	
Politics with Chemistry	M1F1	3FT deg	*	8	3M	M	Ind	Ind	Ind	
Psychology with Chemistry	C8F1	3FT deg	*	10	4M	M^	Ind	Ind	Ind	
Religious Studies with Chemistry	V8F1	3FT deg	*	8	3M	M	Ind	Ind	Ind	
Sociology with Chemistry	L3F1	3FT deg	*	10	4M	M	Ind	Ind	Ind	

Univ of SURREY

TITLE	CODE	COURSE	SUBJECTS	A/AS	NO/C	AGNVQ	IB	SQA(H)	SQA	RATIO A/AS
Analytical and Environmental Chemistry	F189	4SW deg	C+M+S g	20	Ind		Ind	Ind	Ind	
Analytical and Environmental Chemistry	F188	3FT deg	C+M+S g	20	Ind		Ind	Ind	Ind	
Chemistry	F100	3FT deg	C+M+S g	18	4M+1D$		24$	Ind	Ind	11
Chemistry	F103	4SW deg	C+M+S	18	4M+1D$		Ind	Ind	Ind	2 10/14
Chemistry (MChem)	F110	4SW deg	C+2S g	20	Ind		Ind	Ind	Ind	
Chemistry (with Initial Teacher Training)	F107	4SW deg	C+M+S g	20	Ind		Ind	Ind	Ind	
Chemistry for Europe (France)	F101	4SW deg	C+M+S g	20	4M+1D$		Ind	Ind	Ind	2
Chemistry for Europe (Germany)	F104	4SW deg	C+M+S g	20	4M+1D$		Ind	Ind	Ind	1
Chemistry with Management Studies	F106	4SW deg	C+M+S g	20	4M+1D$		Ind	Ind	Ind	3 14/22
Chemistry with a Foundation Year	F105	4FT/5SW deg	C g	18	4M+1D$		Ind	Ind	Ind	6/10
Computer-Aided Chemistry	F102	4SW deg	C+M+S g	22	4M+1D$		Ind	Ind	Ind	3 15/26
Computer-Aided Chemistry (MChem)	F152	4SW deg	C+2S g	22	Ind		Ind	Ind	Ind	

Univ of SUSSEX

TITLE	CODE	COURSE	SUBJECTS	A/AS	NO/C	AGNVQ	IB	SQA(H)	SQA	RATIO A/AS
Chemistry	F100	3FT deg	C+S g	CCC	MO $	MS go	$	Ind	Ind	
Chemistry	F104	4SW deg	C+S g	CCC	MO $	MS go	$	Ind	Ind	
Chemistry (MChem)	F103	4FT deg	C+S g	CCC	MO $	MS go	$	Ind	Ind	
Chemistry with European Studies (French)	F1R1	4FT deg	C+S g	CCC	MO $	MS go	$	Ind	Ind	
Chemistry with European Studies (French) (MChem)	F1RD	4FT deg	C+S g	CCC	MO $	MS go	$	Ind	Ind	
Chemistry with European Studies (German)	F1R2	4FT deg	C+S g	CCC	MO $	MS go	$	Ind	Ind	
Chemistry with European Studies (German) (MChem)	F1RG	4FT deg	C+S g	CCC	MO $	MS go	$	Ind	Ind	
Chemistry with European Studies (Spanish)	F1R4	4FT deg	C+S g	CCC	MO $	MS go	$	Ind	Ind	
Chemistry with European Studs (Spanish) (MChem)	F1RL	4FT deg	C+S g	CCC	MO $	MS go	$	Ind	Ind	
Chemistry with Management Studies	F1N1	3FT deg	C+S g	CCC	MO $	MS go	$	Ind	Ind	
Chemistry with Management Studies (MChem)	F1NC	4FT deg	C+S g	CCC	MO $	MS go	$	Ind	Ind	
Chemistry with North American Studies	F1Q4	4FT deg	C+S g	BCC	MO $	MS^ go	$	Ind	Ind	
Chemistry with North American Studies (MChem)	F1QL	4FT deg	C+S g	BCC	MO $	MS^ go	$	Ind	Ind	
Chemistry with Polymer Science	F1J4	3FT deg	C+S g	CCC	MO $	MS go	$	Ind	Ind	
Chemistry with Polymer Science (MChem)	F1JK	4FT deg	C+S g	CCC	MO $	MS go	$	Ind	Ind	
Medicinal Chemistry	F120	3FT deg	C+S g	CCC	MO $	MS go	$	Ind	Ind	
Medicinal Chemistry (MChem)	F121	4FT deg	C+S g	CCC	MO $	MS go	$	Ind	Ind	
Molecular Sciences	F102▼	4FT deg	*							
Molecular Sciences	F101▼	4FT deg	*							
Polymer Science	F1JL	4SW deg	C+S g	CCC	MO $	MS go	$	Ind	Ind	

Univ of Wales SWANSEA

TITLE	CODE	COURSE	SUBJECTS	A/AS	NO/C	AGNVQ	IB	SQA(H)	SQA	RATIO A/AS
Biomol and Biomed Chem with a year abroad	F194	4FT deg	C+B	BBC-BCC	2M+3D$	DS^	30$	ABBBB$	Ind	2
Biomol and Biomed Chem with a year in Industry	F193	4FT deg	C+B	BCD-CCC	3M+2D$	MS^/DS	26$	BBBCC$	Ind	
Biomolecular and Biomedical Chemistry	F192	3FT deg	C+B	BCD-CCC	3M+2D$	MS^/DS	26$	BBBCC$	Ind	2
Chem and Analytical Sci with a yr in Ind (4 Yrs)	F181	4FT deg	C	BCD-CCC	3M+2D$	MS^/DS	26$	BBBCC$	Ind	5
Chem and Analytical Science with a year abroad	F182	4FT deg	C	BBC-BCC	2M+3D$	DS^	30$	ABBCC$	Ind	3

	course details			**98 expected requirements**							**96 entry stats**	
TITLE	CODE	COURSE	SUBJECTS	A/AS	ND/C	RGNVQ	IB	SQA(H)	SQA	RATIO A/AS	
Chem with Computer Sci with a year in Industry	F1GM	4FT deg	C	BCD-CCC	3M+2D$	MS^/DS	26$	BBBCC$	Ind		
Chem with Env Chem with a year in Industry	F1FC	4FT deg	C	BCD-CCC	3M+2D$	MS^/DS	26$	BBBCC$	Ind		
Chemical and Analytical Science	F180	3FT deg	C	BCD-CCC	3M+2D$	MS^/DS	28$	BBBBB$	Ind	3	
Chemistry	F100	3FT deg	C	BCD-CCC	3M+2D$	MS^/DS	28$	BBBBB$	Ind	8	12/16
Chemistry (Integrated Course)	F107	4FT deg	*	CD	M+D	MS	Dip	Ind	Ind	2	
Chemistry (MChem)	F103	4FT deg	C	BCD	3M+2D$	MS^/DS	28$	BBBBB$	Ind	8	
Chemistry with Business Management	FN11	3FT deg	C	BCD-CCC	3M+2D$	MS^/DS	26$	BBBCC$	Ind		
Chemistry with Business Mgt (with a year abroad)	FN1C	4FT deg	C	BBC-BCC	2M+3D$	DS^	30$	ABBBB$	Ind		
Chemistry with Business Mgt (with a year in Ind)	FN1D	4FT deg	C	BCD-CCC	3M+2D$	MS^/DS	26$	BBBCC$	Ind		
Chemistry with Computer Sci with a year abroad	F1GN	4FT deg	C	BBC-BCC	2M+3D$	DS^	30$	ABBBB$	Ind		
Chemistry with Computer Science	F1G5	3FT deg	C	BCD-CCC	3M+2D$	MS^/DS	26$	BBBCC$	Ind	5	
Chemistry with Environ Chem with a yr abroad	F144	4FT deg	C	BBC-BCC	2M+3D$	DS^	30$	ABBBB$	Ind	5	
Chemistry with Environmental Chemistry	F161	3FT deg	C	BCD-CCC	3M+2D$	MS^/DS	26$	BBBCC$	Ind	2	
Chemistry with Law	F111	3FT deg	C	BCD-CCC	3M+2D$	MS^/DS	26$	BBBCC$	Ind		
Chemistry with Law with a year abroad	F1MH	4FT deg	C	BBC-BCC	2M+3D$	DS^	30$	ABBBB$	Ind	4	
Chemistry with Law with a year in Industry	F1MJ	4FT deg	C	BCD-CCC	3M+2D$	MS^/DS	26$	BBBCC$	Ind	5	
Chemistry with a year abroad	F102	4FT deg	C	BBC-BCC	2M+3D$	DS^	30$	ABBBB$	Ind	11	
Chemistry with a year in Industry	F101	4FT deg	C	BCD-CCC	3M+2D$	MS^/DS	26$	BBBCC$	Ind	22	
Chemistry with a yr abroad (MChem)	F104	4FT deg	C	BBC-BCC	1M+4D$	DS^	32$	AABBB$	Ind		
Chemistry with a yr in industry (MChem)	F105	4FT deg	C	BCD	3M+2D$	MS^/DS	28$	BBBBB$	Ind		

Univ of TEESSIDE

TITLE	CODE	COURSE	SUBJECTS	A/AS	ND/C	RGNVQ	IB	SQA(H)	SQA	RATIO A/AS	
Chemical Technology	F161	3FT deg	B/C/M/P	6-8	2M	M	Ind	CCC	Ind		
Chemistry	F100	3FT/4SW deg	C+S	8	3M		Ind	CCC	3M	4	8/16
Chemistry and Medicinal Science	F120	3FT deg	C+S	8	3M		Ind	CCC	3M		
Modular Degree Scheme _Chemical Technology_	Y401	3FT deg									
Modular Degree Scheme _Chemistry_	Y401	3FT deg									
Science and Technology Combined Honours Scheme _Chemical Technology_	Y108	3FT deg									
Science and Technology Combined Honours Scheme _Chemistry_	Y108	3FT deg									
Chemistry	001F	2FT HND	C	C	N		Ind	CC	N	10	

Univ of ULSTER

TITLE	CODE	COURSE	SUBJECTS	A/AS	ND/C	RGNVQ	IB	SQA(H)	SQA	RATIO A/AS	
Science (Chemistry with Biology)	1C1F▼	2FT HND	C g		Ind	MS gi	Ind	Ind	Ind	6	4/12

UNIVERSITY COLL LONDON (Univ of London)

TITLE	CODE	COURSE	SUBJECTS	A/AS	ND/C	RGNVQ	IB	SQA(H)	SQA	RATIO A/AS	
Chemical Physics	F112	3FT deg	C+M+P g	BCC-BBB	MO $	Ind	30$	BBCCC$	N$		
Chemical Physics (MSci)	F113	4FT deg	C+M+P g	BCC-BBB	MO $	Ind	30$	BBCCC$	N$	4	
Chemistry	F100	3FT deg	C+M/P/B g	CCC-BBB	MO $	Ind	28$	BCCCC$	N$	29	
Chemistry (MSci)	F101	4FT deg	C+M/P/B g	CCC-BBB	MO D	Ind	28$	BCCCC$	N$	3	16/28
Chemistry with Management Studies	F1N1	3FT deg	C+M/P/B g	CCC-BBB	MO $	Ind	28$	BCCCC$	N$	31	
Chemistry with Management Studies (MSci)	F1NC	4FT deg	C+M/P/B g	CCC-BBB	MO $	Ind	28$	BCCCC$	N$		20/24
Chemistry with Materials Science	F1F2	3FT deg	C+M+P g	BCC-BBB	MO $	Ind	30$	BBCCC$	N$		
Chemistry with Materials Science (MSci)	F1FF	4FT deg	C+M+P g	BCC-BBB	MO $	Ind	30$	BBCCC$	N$	2	
Chemistry with Mathematics	F1G1	3FT deg	C+M g	BCC-BBB	MO $	Ind	30$	BBCCC$	N$		
Chemistry with Mathematics (MSci)	F1GC	4FT deg	C+M g	BCC-BBB	MO $	Ind	30$	BBCCC$	N$	2	
Chemistry with a European Language	F1T2	3FT deg	C+M/P/B g	CCC-BBB	MO $	Ind	28$	BCCCC$	N$		
Chemistry with a European Language (MSci)	F1TF	4FT deg	C+M/P/B g	CCC-BBB	MO $	Ind	28$	BCCCC$	N$	3	14/26
Medicinal Chemistry	F126	3FT deg	C+B/M/P g	CCC-BBB	MO $	Ind	28$	BCCCC$	N$		
Medicinal Chemistry (MSci)	F121	4FT deg	C+B/M/P g	CCC-BBB	MO $	Ind	28$	BCCCC$	N$	2	14/30
Physical Sciences _Chemistry_	Y100	3FT deg	S g	CCC-BCC	$	Ind	28$	BCCCC$	N$		

		course details		98 expected requirements						96 entry stats	
TITLE	CODE	COURSE	SUBJECTS	A/AS	ND/C	AGNVQ	IB	SQA(H)	SQA	RATIO	A/AS
Univ of WARWICK											
Chemistry	F100	3FT deg	C+S/M g	BCC	M+D $	DS^	28$	BBBBB$		6	12/26
Chemistry (MChem)	F105	4FT deg	C+S/M g	BCC	M+D $	DS^	28$	BBBBB$		7	18/30
Chemistry and Business Studies	FN11	3FT deg	C+S/M g	BCC	M+D $	DS^	28$	BBBBB$		11	16/18
Chemistry with Industrial Environ Chem (MChem)	F145	4FT deg	C+S/M g	BCC	M+D $	DS^	28$	BBBBB$			
Chemistry with Industrial Environ Chemistry	F140	3FT deg	C+S/M g	BCC	M+D $	DS^	28$	BBBBB$		6	20/28
Chemistry with Management	F1N1	3FT deg	C+S/M g	BBB	M+D $	DS^	30$	AABBB$			
Chemistry with Medicinal Chemistry	F121	3FT deg	C+S/M g	BCC	M+D $	DS^	28$	BBBBB$		8	12/24
Chemistry with Medicinal Chemistry (MChem)	F125	4FT deg	C+S/M g	BCC	M+D $	DS$	28$	BBBBB$		4	14/22
Chemistry with Psychology	F1C8	3FT deg	C+S/M g	BCC	M+D $	DS^	28$	BBBBB$		5	16/20
Univ of WOLVERHAMPTON											
Applied Chemistry	F110	3FT/4SW deg	g	DD	N	M	24	CCCC$	Ind	9	
Applied Chemistry with Analytical Science	F180	3FT/4SW deg	C g	DD	N	M	24	CCCC	Ind		
Applied Chemistry with Biochemical Science	F1C7	3FT/4SW deg	C g	DD	N	M	24	CCCC	Ind		
Applied Chemistry with Polymer Science	F1J4	3FT/4SW deg	C g	DD	N	M	24	CCCC	Ind		
Medicinal Chemistry	F120	3FT/4SW deg	C g	DD	N	M	24	CCCC	Ind		
Applied Sciences *Chemistry*	Y100	3FT/4SW deg	C g	DD	N	M	24	CCCC	Ind		
Applied Sciences (4 Yrs) *Chemistry*	Y110▼	4FT deg	*								
Combined Degrees *Chemistry*	Y401	3FT/4SW deg	C g	DD	N	M	24	CCCC	Ind		
Applied Chemistry	011F	2FT HND	C g	D	N	M	24	CCCC$	Ind	3	
Univ of YORK											
Chemistry	F100	3FT deg	C+M/P/B	CCC	Ind $	DS6/^	27$	CSYS$	Ind$		14/28
Chemistry	F102	4FT deg	C+M/P/B	CCC	Ind $	DS6/^	27$	CSYS$	Ind$		16/30
Chemistry with a year in Europe	F101	4FT deg	C+M/P/B g	CCC	Ind $	DS6/^	27$	CSYS$	Ind$		20/30
Chemistry, Life Systems & Pharmaceuticals (Euro)	F123	4FT deg	C+M/P/B g	CCC	Ind $	DS6/^	27$	CSYS$	Ind$		22/28
Chemistry, Life Systems and Pharmaceuticals	F124	4FT deg	C+M/P/B	CCC	Ind $	DS6/^	27$	CSYS$	Ind$		16/26
Chemistry, Life Systems and Pharmaceuticals	F122	3FT deg	C+M/P/B	CCC	Ind $	DS6/^	27$	CSYS$	Ind$		20/24
Chemistry, Management and Industry	F162	3FT deg	C+M/P/B	CCC	Ind $	DS6/^	27$	CSYS$	Ind$		
Chemistry, Management and Industry	F164	4FT deg	C+M/P/B	CCC	Ind $	DS6/^	27$	CSYS$	Ind$		26/28
Chemistry, Management and Industry (Europe)	F163	4FT deg	C+M/P/B g	CCC	Ind $	DS6/^	27$	CSYS$	Ind$		
Chemistry, Resources and Environment (Europe)	F143	4FT deg	C+M/P/B g	CCC	Ind $	DS6/^	27$	CSYS$	Ind$		
Chemistry, Resources and the Environment	F144	4FT deg	C+M/P/B	CCC	Ind $	DS6/^	27$	CSYS$	Ind$		
Chemistry, Resources and the Environment	F142	3FT deg	C+M/P/B	CCC	Ind $	DS6/^	27$	CSYS$	Ind$		

course details			98 expected requirements							96 entry stats
TITLE	CODE	COURSE	SUBJECTS	A/AS	ND/C	AGNVQ	IB	SQA(H)	SQA	RATIO A/AS
Univ of ABERDEEN										
Cultural History with Film Studies	V9W5	4FT deg	* g	BBC	Ind	M$ go	30$	BBBB$	Ind	
English with Film Studies	Q3W5	4FT deg	* g	BBC	Ind	M$ go	30$	BBBB$	Ind	5
French with Film Studies	R1W5	4FT/5FT deg	* g	BBC	Ind	M$ go	30$	BBBB$	Ind	17
French with Film Studies (4 Yrs)	R1WM	4FT deg	* g	BBC	Ind	M$ go	30$	BBBB$	Ind	
German with Film Studies	R2W5	4FT/5FT deg	* g	BBC	Ind	M$ go	30$	BBBB$	Ind	2
German with Film Studies (4 Yrs)	R2WM	4FT deg	* g	BBC	Ind	M$ go	30$	BBBB$	Ind	
Hispanic Studies with Film Studies	R4W5	4FT/5FT deg	* g	BBC	Ind	M$ go	30$	BBBB$	Ind	3
Hispanic Studies with Film Studies (4 Yrs)	R4WM	4FT deg	* g	BBC	Ind	M$ go	30$	BBBB$	Ind	
History of Art with Film Studies	V4W5	4FT deg	* g	BBC	Ind	M$ go	30$	BBBB$	Ind	5
History with Film Studies	V1W5	4FT deg	* g	BBC	Ind	M$ go	30$	BBBB$	Ind	18
Philosophy with Film Studies	V7W5	4FT deg	* g	BBC	Ind	M$ go	30$	BBBB$	Ind	4
Religious Studies with Film Studies	V8W5	4FT deg	* g	BBC	Ind	M$ go	30$	BBBB$	Ind	
Univ of Wales, ABERYSTWYTH										
Film and Television Studies	W520	3FT deg	* g	20	1M+5D	MQ6 g	30	BBBBC	Ind	
Film and Television Studies/American Studies	QW45	3FT deg	E/H g	20	1M+5D$	MQ^ g	30$	BBBBC$	Ind	
Film and Television Studies/Art	WW15	3FT deg	A/Ad g	20	1M+5D$	MA/Q^ g	30$	BBBBC$	Ind	
Film and Television Studies/Art History	VW45	3FT deg	* g	20	1M+5D	MA/Q^ g	30	BBBBC	Ind	
Film and Television Studies/Drama	WW54	3FT deg	* g	20	1M+5D	M6 g	30	BBBBC	Ind	
Film and Television Studies/Education	WX59	3FT deg	* g	20	1M+5D	MQ6 g	30	BBBBC	Ind	
Film and Television Studies/English	QW35	3FT deg	El	20	1M+5D$	MQ^ g	30$	BBBBC$	Ind	
French/Film and Television Studies	RW15	4FT deg	F g	20	1M+5D$	MQ^ g	30$	BBBBC$	Ind	
Geography/Film and Television Studies	LW85	3FT deg	Gy g	20-22	1M+5D$	MQ^ g	30$	BBBBC$	Ind	
German/Film and Television Studies	RW25	4FT deg	G g	20	1M+5D$	MQ^ g	30$	BBBBC$	Ind	
Information and Library Studies/Film & TV St	PW25	3FT deg	* g	20	1M+5D	MQ6 g	30	BBBBC	Ind	
Irish/Film and Television Studies	QW55	3FT deg	* g	20	1M+5D$	MQ6 g	30$	BBBBC$	Ind	
Italian/Film and Television Studies	RW35	4FT deg	L g	20	1M+5D$	MQ^ g	30$	BBBBC$	Ind	
Pure Mathematics/Film and Television Studies	GW15	3FT deg	M g	20	1M+5D$	MQ^ g	30$	BBBBC$	Ind	
Spanish/Film and Television Studies	RW45	4FT deg	L g	20	1M+5D$	MQ^ g	30$	BBBBC$		
Welsh History/Film and Television Studies	VW1M	3FT deg	* g	20	1M+5D	MQ6 g	30	BBBBC	Ind	
Welsh/Film and Television Studies	QW5M	3FT deg	W g	20	1M+5D$	MQ^ g	30$	BBBBC$	Ind	
ANGLIA Poly Univ										
Animal Behaviour and Imaging Science	CW15▼	3FT deg	S	10	3M	P	Dip	BCCC	N	
Audiotechnology and Imaging Science	HW65▼	3FT deg	S	16	8M	D	Dip$	BBCCC	N	
Biology and Imaging Science	CW1M▼	3FT deg	B	10	3M	P	Dip$	BCCC	N	
Biomedical Science and Imaging Science	BW95▼	3FT deg	B g	10	3M	P go	Dip$	BCCC	N	
Chemistry and Imaging Science	FW15▼	3FT deg	S g	10	3M	P go	Dip$	BCCC	N	
Computer Science and Imaging Science	GW5M▼	3FT deg	S g	10	3M	P go	Dip$	BCCC	N	
Ecology and Conservation and Imaging Science	DW25▼	3FT deg	S g	10	2M	M go	Dip$	BCCC	N	
Geography and Imaging Science	FW85▼	3FT deg	S+Gy g	12	4M	M go	Dip$	BCCC	N	
Graphic Arts and Imaging Science	WW25▼	3FT deg	A+S	12	4M	M	Dip$	BCCC	Ind	
Imaging Science and Instrumentation Electronics	HW6M▼	3FT deg	S	10	3M	P	Dip	BCCC	N	
Imaging Science and Maths or Stats/Stat Mod.	GWC5▼	3FT deg	S g	10	3M	P	Dip	BCCC	N	
Imaging Science and Ophthalmic Dispensing	BW55▼	3FT deg	S	10	3M	P	Dip	BCCC	N	
Imaging Science and Psychology	CW85▼	3FT deg	S g	16	8M	D go	Dip$	BBCCC	Ind	
Imaging Science and Real Time Computer Systems	GW55▼	3FT deg	S g	10	3M	P go	Dip$	BCCC	N	
Univ of Wales, BANGOR										
English with Film Studies	Q3W5	3FT deg	E/El g	CCC	X	D*^ go	28$	BBBC$	X	

course details			98 expected requirements							96 entry stats
TITLE	CODE	COURSE	SUBJECTS	A/AS	NO/C	AGNVQ	IB	SQA(H)	SQA	RATIO A/AS
BATH COLL of HE										
Combined Awards	Y400	3FT deg	*		N		Ind	$	$	
Creative Studies in English (Film)										
Modular Programme (DipHE)	Y460	2FT Dip	*		N		Ind	$	$	
Creative Studies in English (Film)										
BLACKPOOL & FYLDE COLL										
Design (Photography)	W550	3FT deg	*	10	4M		Ind	Ind	Ind	
Design (Photography)	E550	3FT deg	*	10	4M		Ind	Ind	Ind	
BOLTON INST										
Accountancy and Film & TV Studies	NW45	3FT deg	* g	CD	MO	M*	24	BBCC	Ind	
Art & Design History and Film & TV Studies	WV54	3FT deg	Me/T g	CD	Ind	Ind	24	BBCC	Ind	
Art and Design History and Film and TV Studies	VW45	3FT deg	Me/T g	CD	MO	Ind	24	BBCC	Ind	
Biology and Film & TV Studies	CW15	3FT deg	Me/T g	CD	Ind	Ind	24	BBCC	Ind	
Business Economics and Film and TV Studies	LW15	3FT deg	Me/T g	CD	Ind	Ind	24	BBCC	Ind	
Business Info Systems and Film & TV Studies	GW55	3FT deg	Me/T g	CD	Ind	Ind	24	BBCC	Ind	
Business Studies and Film & TV Studies	NW1M	3FT deg	Me/T g	CD	Ind	Ind	24	BBCC	Ind	
Community Studies and Film & TV Studies	LW55	3FT deg	Me/T g	CD	Ind	Ind	24	BBCC	Ind	
Computing and Film & TV Studies	GW5M	3FT deg	Me/T g	CD	Ind	Ind	24	BBCC	Ind	
Creative Writing and Film and TV Studies	WW95	3FT deg	Me/T g	CD	Ind	Ind	24	BBCC	Ind	
Design and Film & TV Studies	WW25	3FT deg	Me/T g	CD	Ind	Ind	24	BBCC	Ind	
Environmental Studies and Film & TV Studies	FW95	3FT deg	Me/T g	CD	Ind	Ind	24	BBCC	Ind	
European Cultural Studies and Film & TV Studies	TW25	3FT deg	Me/T g	CD	Ind	Ind	24	BBCC	Ind	
Film & TV Studies and German	RW25	3FT deg	Me/T+G g	CD	Ind	Ind	24	BBCC	Ind	
Film & TV Studies and Mathematics	GW15	3FT deg	M g	CD	MO	M*	24	BBCC	Ind	
Film & TV Studies and Psychology	LW75	3FT deg	Me/T g	12	Ind	Ind	24	BBCC	Ind	
Film & TV Studies and Theatre Studies	WW54	3FT deg	Me/T g	CD	Ind	Ind	24	BBCC	Ind	
Film & TV Studies and Tourism Studies	PW75	3FT deg	Me/T g	CD	Ind	Ind	24	BBCC	Ind	
Film & TV Studies and Urban & Cultural Studies	WL53	3FT deg	Me/T g	CD	Ind	Ind	24	BBCC	Ind	
Film and TV St and Organisations, Mgt & Work	NW75	3FT deg	Me/T g	CD	Ind	Ind	24	BBCC	Ind	
Film and TV Studies and French	RW15	3FT deg	Me/T+F g	CD	Ind	Ind	24	BBCC	Ind	
Film and TV Studies and History	WV51	3FT deg	Me/T g	CD	Ind	Ind	24	BBCC	Ind	
Film and TV Studies and Human Resource Mgt	NW15	3FT deg	Me/T g	CD	Ind	Ind	24	BBCC	Ind	
Film and TV Studies and Law	MW35	3FT deg	Me/T g	CD	Ind	Ind	24	BBCC	Ind	
Film and TV Studies and Literature	WQ52	3FT deg	Me/T g	CD	Ind	Ind	24	BBCC	Ind	
Film and TV Studies and Marketing	NW55	3FT deg	Me/T g	CD	Ind	Ind	24	BBCC	Ind	
Film and TV Studies and Operations Management	NW25	3FT deg	Me/T g	CD	Ind	Ind	24	BBCC	Ind	
Film and TV Studies and Peace and War Studies	WV5C	3FT deg	Me/T g	CD	Ind	Ind	24	BBCC	Ind	
Film and TV Studies and Philosophy	WV57	3FT deg	Me/T g	CD	Ind	Ind	24	BBCC	Ind	
Film and TV Studies and Sociology	LW35	3FT deg	Me/T g	CD	MO	M	24	Ind	Ind	
Gender and Women's Studies and Film and TV Studs	MW95	3FT deg	Me/T g	CD	Ind	Ind	24	BBCC	Ind	
Leisure Studies and Film & TV Studies	LWH5	3FT deg	Me/T g	CD	Ind	Ind	24	BBCC	Ind	
Visual Arts and Film and TV Studies	WW51	3FT deg	Me/T g	CD	Ind	Ind	24	BBCC	Ind	
BOURNEMOUTH Univ										
Scriptwriting for Film and Television	W520	3FT deg	* g	18-22	MO+4D	D$ go	Ind	ABBBB	Ind	9 8/26
Television and Video Production	W521	3FT deg								16/26
BOURNEMOUTH and POOLE COLLEGE of A & D										
Design (Film and Television Production)	025E	2FT HND	Pf	E	N$	P	Ind	Ind	N$	
BRADFORD & ILKLEY Comm COLL										
Electronic Imaging and Media Communication	PW45	2FT HND								
Design (Photography)	055E	2FT HND	A/Pf	C	N	Ind	$	Ind	Ind	
Design (Photography)	055W	2FT HND	A/Pf	C	N	Ind	$	Ind	Ind	

TITLE	CODE	COURSE	SUBJECTS	A/AS	ND/C	AGNVQ	IB	SQA(H)	SQA	RATIO A/AS
course details			*98 expected requirements*							*96 entry stats*
Univ of BRIGHTON										
Editorial Photography	W555	3FT deg	Fa+Pf g	X	N $	Ind$ go	Ind$	Ind$	Ind$	
Editorial Photography	E555	3FT deg	Fa+Pf g	X	N $	Ind$ go	Ind$	Ind$	Ind$	
BRISTOL, Univ of the W of England										
Art and Visual Culture	E500	3FT deg	Fa+Pf g		N $	PA go	Dip$	Ind	N$	
BRUNEL Univ, West London										
Film & TV Studies/American Studies	Q4W5	3FT deg	Ap g	20	MO $	M* go	28$	BBCC	Ind	
Film & TV Studies/Drama	W4W5	3FT deg	Ap+T g	20	MO $	M* go	28$	BBCC$	Ind	
Film & TV Studies/English	Q3W5	3FT deg	Ap+E g	20	MO $	M* go	28$	BBCC$	Ind	
Film and Television Studies	W520	3FT deg	Me/Cm/E g	20	MO $	M$ go	28$	BBCC$	Ind	
History/Film & TV Studies	V1W5	3FT deg	H+Ap g	20	MO $	M* go	28$	BBCC$	Ind	
Music/Film & TV Studies	W3W5	3FT deg	Ap g	20	MO $	M* go	28$	BBCC$	Ind	
BUCKINGHAMSHIRE COLLEGE										
Film and English Studies	QW25	3FT deg		12	2D	M	27	CCCC	Ind	
Film and Media	PW45	3FT deg		12	2D	M	27	CCCC	Ind	3 10/18
Film and Visual Arts	VW45	3FT deg		12	2D	M	27	CCCC	Ind	
Film with Media & Video Production	W5P4	3FT deg		12	2D	M	27	CCCC	Ind	
Media with Film & Video Production	P4W5	3FT deg		12	2D	M	27	CCCC	Ind	
CANTERBURY CHRIST CHURCH COLL of HE										
American Studies with Radio,Film & Television St	Q4W5	4FT deg	* g	CC	MO	M	24	Ind	Ind	34
Art with Radio, Film & Television Studies	W1W5	3FT deg	A g	CC	MO	M	24	Ind	Ind	45
Business Studies with Radio,Film & Television St	N1W5	3FT deg	* g	CC	MO	M	24	Ind	Ind	
Early Childhood Studies with Radio, Film & TV St	X9W5	3FT deg	* g	CC	MO	M	24	Ind	Ind	
English with Radio, Film and Television Studies	Q3W5	3FT deg	E	CC	MO	M	24	Ind	Ind	20 12/20
Geography with Radio, Film & Television Studies	L8W5	3FT deg	Gy g	CC	MO	M	24	Ind	Ind	11
History with Radio, Film And Television Studies	V1W5	3FT deg	H g	CC	MO	M	24	Ind	Ind	
Marketing with Radio, Film and Television Studs	N5W5	3FT deg	* g	CC	MO	M	24	Ind	Ind	
Mathematics with Radio, Film & Television Studs	G1W5	3FT deg	M g	DD	Ind	Ind	24	Ind	Ind	
Media Studies with Radio, Film & Television St	P4W5	3FT deg	* g	CC	MO	M	24	Ind	Ind	
Music with Radio, Film and Television Studies	W3W5	3FT deg	Mu g	CC	MO	M	24	Ind	Ind	
Radio, Film & TV Studs with Early Childhood St	W5X9	3FT deg	* g	CC	MO	M	24	Ind	Ind	
Radio, Film & Television Studies and Media Studs	PW45	3FT deg	* g	CC	MO	M	24	Ind	Ind	
Radio, Film & Television Studies with English	W5Q3	3FT deg	E g	CC	MO	M	24	Ind	Ind	14 15/16
Radio, Film & Television Studies with French	W5R1	3FT deg	F g	CC	MO	M	24	Ind	Ind	
Radio, Film & Television Studies with Geography	W5L8	3FT deg	Gy g	CC	MO	M	24	Ind	Ind	
Radio, Film & Television Studies with Media St	W5P4	3FT deg	* g	CC	MO	M	24	Ind	Ind	
Radio, Film & Television Studies with Science	W5Y1	3FT deg	S g	CC	MO	M	24	Ind	Ind	
Radio, Film & Television Studies with Statistics	W5G4	3FT deg	M g	CC	MO	M	24	Ind	Ind	
Radio, Film & Television Studies with Tourism St	W5P7	3FT deg	* g	CC	MO	M	24	Ind	Ind	32
Radio, Film & Television Studs with Religious St	W5V8	3FT deg	* g	CC	MO	M	24	Ind	Ind	5
Radio, Film and TV Studs and Early Childhood St	XW95	3FT deg	* g	CC	MO	M	24	Ind	Ind	
Radio, Film and Television St and Business St	NW15	3FT deg	* g	CC	MO	M	24	Ind	Ind	6
Radio, Film and Television St and Social Science	WL53	3FT deg	* g	CC	MO	M	24	Ind	Ind	2
Radio, Film and Television Studies and Art	WW51	3FT deg	A g	CC	MO	M	24	Ind	Ind	19
Radio, Film and Television Studies and English	QW35	3FT deg	E g	CC	MO	M	24	Ind	Ind	24
Radio, Film and Television Studies and Geography	WL58	3FT deg	Gy g	CC	MO	M	24	Ind	Ind	
Radio, Film and Television Studies and History	VW15	3FT deg	H g	CC	MO	M	24	Ind	Ind	
Radio, Film and Television Studies and Music	WW53	3FT deg	Mu g	CC	MO	M	24	Ind	Ind	19
Radio, Film and Television Studies with Art	W5W1	3FT deg	A g	CC	MO	M	24	Ind	Ind	9
Radio, Film and Television Studies with Music	W5W3	3FT deg	Mu g	CC	MO	M	24	Ind	Ind	

			98 expected requirements							96 entry stats	

course details

TITLE	CODE	COURSE	SUBJECTS	A/AS	NO/C	RGNVQ	IB	SQA(H)	SQA	RATIO	A/AS
Radio, Film and Television Studs and American St	QW45	3FT deg	* g	CC	MO	M	24	Ind	Ind	13	
Radio, Film and Television Studs and Mathematics	GW15	3FT deg	M g	DD	Ind	Ind	24	Ind	Ind		
Radio, Film and Television Studs with Social St	W5L3	3FT deg	* g	CC	MO	M	24	Ind	Ind	3	
Radio,Film & Television Studies with American St	W5Q4	3FT deg	* g	CC	MO	M	24	Ind	Ind	7	10/20
Radio,Film & Television Studies with Business St	W5N1	3FT deg	* g	CC	MO	M	24	Ind	Ind	24	
Radio,Film & Television Studies with History	W5V1	3FT deg	H g	CC	MO	M	24	Ind	Ind		
Radio,Film & Television Studies with Marketing	W5N5	3FT deg	* g	CC	MO	M	24	Ind	Ind	5	10/18
Radio,Film & Television Studies with Mathematics	W5G1	3FT deg	M g	CC	MO	M	24	Ind	Ind		
Radio,Film and Television Studies and Marketing	WN55	3FT deg	* g	CC	MO	M	24	Ind	Ind	25	
Religious Studies and Radio, Film and TV Studies	WV58	3FT deg	* g	CC	MO	M	24	Ind	Ind		
Religious Studs with Radio, Film and TV Studies	V8W5	3FT deg	* g	CC	MO	M	24	Ind	Ind		
Science and Radio, Film and Television Studies	WY51	3FT deg	S g	DD	Ind	Ind	24	Ind	Ind		
Science with Radio, Film & Television Studies	Y1W5	3FT deg	S g	DD	Ind	Ind	24	Ind	Ind		
Social Science with Radio Film and Television St	L3W5	3FT deg	* g	CC	MO	M	24	Ind	Ind		
Statistics and Radio, Film and Television Studs	GW45	3FT deg	M g	DD	Ind	Ind	24	Ind	Ind		
Statistics with Radio, Film & Television Studies	G4W5	3FT deg	M g	DD	Ind	Ind	24	Ind	Ind		
Tourism Studies and Radio, Film and TV Studies	PW75	3FT deg	* g	CC	MO	M	24	Ind	Ind	20	
Tourism Studies with Radio, Film & Television St	P7W5	3FT deg	* g	CC	MO	M	24	Ind	Ind		
CARMARTHENSHIRE COLLEGE											
Photography/Media/Multi-Media	555W	2FT HND		X	Ind	Ind	Ind	X	Ind		
Photography/Media/Multi-Media	555E	2FT HND		X	Ind	Ind	Ind	X	Ind		
Univ of CENTRAL ENGLAND											
Visual Communication (Photography)	E550	3FT deg	Fa/Pf	18	MO	M$	28	BBBB	Ind		
Visual Communication (Photography)	W550	3FT deg	Fa/Pf	18	MO	M$	28	BBBB	Ind	27	
Univ of CENTRAL LANCASHIRE											
Film and Media Studies	PW45	3FT deg	*	16	MO+5D	D$6/^	28	BBBB$	Ind		
Combined Honours Programme Media Technology	Y400	3FT deg	* g	14	MO	M$6/^	26	BBCC	Ind		
CHELTENHAM & GLOUCESTER COLL of HE											
Professional Media (Photography)	E550	3FT deg	Fa	12	5M+2D	Ind	Ind	Ind	Ind		
Professional Media (Photography)	W550	3FT deg	Fa	12	5M+2D	Ind	Ind	Ind	Ind		
CLEVELAND COLLEGE of A & D											
Photography	E550	3FT deg	Fa/Pf		N	P	Ind	Ind	N		
Film and Television Production	53WE	2FT HND	Fa/Pf		N	P	Ind	Ind	N		
CROYDON COLL											
Photomedia	EW25	3FT deg	Fa+Pf		N $	PA2					
Photomedia	WW25	3FT deg	Fa+Pf		N $	PA2					
CUMBRIA COLL of A & D											
Media (Creative Digital Technology)	055E	2FT HND		C	N	M	$	B	Ind		
Univ of DERBY											
Film and Television Studies	W520	3FT deg	*	CC	3M+3D	M^	26	CCCC	Ind	14	11/20
Credit Accumulation Modular Scheme Film and Television Studies	Y600	3FT deg	*	14	MO	M	28	BBCC	Ind		
Credit Accumulation Modular Scheme Photography	Y600	3FT deg	Pf		Ind	MA	Ind	Ind	Ind		
Univ of EAST ANGLIA											
Film and American Studies	QW45	4FT deg	E	ABB-BBB	X		30$	AABBB	X	19	22/30
Film and English Studies	QW35	3FT deg	E	BBB-BBC	X		30$	ABBBB	X	18	24/30

course details			98 expected requirements							96 entry stats
TITLE	CODE	COURSE	SUBJECTS	A/AS	ND/C	AGNVQ	IB	SQA(H)	SQA	RATIO A/AS
FALMOUTH COLLEGE of Arts										
Photographic Communication	E550	3FT deg	Fa	CC	N		24	CC	N	
Photographic Communication	W550	3FT deg								33
Univ of GLAMORGAN										
Humanities (Visual Arts)	W503	3FT deg	* g	CC	5M	M$	24	CCCC	HN	1
Univ of GLASGOW										
Archaeology/Film and Television Studies	VW65	4FT deg		BBB	HN	D	32	AABB	Ind	
Celtic/Film and Television Studies	QW55	4FT deg		BBB	HN	D	32	AABB	Ind	4
Classical Hebrew/Film and Television Studies	VW85	4FT deg		BBB	HN	D	32	AABB	Ind	
Czech/Film and Television Studies	WT51	5FT deg		BBB	HN	D	32	AABB	HN	
English/Film and Television Studies	QW35	4FT deg		BBB	HN	D	32	AABB	Ind	6 26/28
Film and Television St/Social and Urban Policy	LW45	4FT deg		BBB	HN	D	32	AABB	HN	
Film and Television St/Theology & Religious St	VWV5	4FT deg		BBB	HN	D	32	AABB	HN	1
Film and Television Studies/Classical Hebrew	QW95	4FT deg		BBB	HN	D	32	AABB	HN	
Film and Television Studies/French	RW15	5FT deg		BBB	HN	D	32	AABB	HN	7
Film and Television Studies/Geography	LW85	4FT deg		BBB	HN	D	32	AABB	HN	
Film and Television Studies/German	RW25	5FT deg		BBB	HN	D	32	AABB	HN	5
Film and Television Studies/Greek	QW75	4FT deg		BBB	HN	D	32	AABB	HN	
Film and Television Studies/Hispanic Studies	RW45	5FT deg		BBB	HN	D	32	AABB	HN	6
Film and Television Studies/History	VW15	4FT deg		BBB	HN	D	32	AABB	HN	13
Film and Television Studies/History of Art	VW45	4FT deg		BBB	HN	D	32	AABB	HN	47
Film and Television Studies/Italian	RW35	5FT deg		BBB	HN	D	32	AABB	HN	15
Film and Television Studies/Latin	QW65	4FT deg		BBB	HN	D	32	AABB	HN	
Film and Television Studies/Mathematics	GW15	4FT deg		BBB	HN	D	32	AABB	HN	4
Film and Television Studies/Music	WW35	4FT deg		BBB	HN	D	32	AABB	HN	14
Film and Television Studies/Philosophy	VW75	4FT deg		BBB	HN	D	32	AABB	HN	9
Film and Television Studies/Physics	FW35	4FT deg		BBB	HN	D	32	AABB	HN	
Film and Television Studies/Polish	TW15	5FT deg		BBB	HN	D	32	AABB	HN	
Film and Television Studies/Politics	MW15	4FT deg		BBB	HN	D	32	AABB	HN	12
Film and Television Studies/Russian	RW85	5FT deg		BBB	HN	D	32	AABB	HN	
Film and Television Studies/Scottish History	VWC5	4FT deg		BBB	HN	D	32	AABB	HN	7
Film and Television Studies/Scottish Literature	QW25	4FT deg		BBB	HN	D	32	AABB	HN	16
Film and Television Studies/Sociology	LW35	4FT deg		BBB	HN	D	32	AABB	HN	9
Theatre Studies/Film and Television Studies	WW45	4FT deg		BBB	HN	D	32	AABB	HN	11 24/28
Univ of HUDDERSFIELD										
Creative Imaging	EW52	3FT/4SW deg	Pf+<u>A/Ad</u>/Fa g	12-14	MO	M4/<u>^</u> go	Ind	Ind	Ind	
Creative Imaging	GW52	3FT/4SW deg	Pf+<u>A/Ad</u>/Fa g	12-14	MO	M4/<u>^</u> go	Ind	Ind	Ind	
Univ of KENT										
American Studies (Art & Film)	Q4W5	4FT deg	*	26	6D	Ind	34	Ind	Ind	12
European Arts (Film Studies)	W511	3FT deg		26	6D	Ind	34	Ind	Ind	
Film Studies	W510	3FT deg	*	26	6D	Ind	34	Ind	Ind	
Film Studies/Classical Studies	QW85	3FT deg	*	22	2M+4D	Ind	30	Ind	Ind	
Film Studies/Comparative Literary Studies	WQ52	3FT deg	*	22	2M+4D	Ind	30	Ind	Ind	
Film Studies/Computing	WG55	3FT deg	*	22	2M+4D	Ind	30	Ind	Ind	
Film Studies/Drama	WWK5	3FT deg	*	24	1M+5D	Ind	32	Ind	Ind	9 22/26
Film Studies/English	QW35	3FT deg	E	24	1M+5D	Ind	32	Ind	Ind	8 22/28
Film Studies/English (Post-Colonial Literatures)	WQ5J	3FT deg	E	24	1M+5D	Ind	32	Ind	Ind	
Film Studies/English Language	WQ53	3FT deg	E	22	2M+4D	Ind	30	Ind	Ind	41
Film Studies/European Studies	TW25	4FT deg	L	22	2M+4D	Ind	30	Ind	Ind	
French/Film Studies	RW15	4FT deg	F	22	2M+4D	Ind	30	Ind	Ind	21

			98 expected requirements							96 entry stats
course details										
TITLE	CODE	COURSE	SUBJECTS	A/AS	ND/C	AGNVQ	IB	SQA(H)	SQA	RATIO A/AS
German/Film Studies	RW25	4FT deg	G	22	2M+4D	Ind	30	Ind	Ind	
History and Theory of Art/Film Studies	VW45	3FT deg	*	22	2M+4D	Ind	30	Ind	Ind	
History/Film Studies	VW15	3FT deg	*	24	1M+5D	Ind	32	Ind	Ind	8
Italian/Film Studies	RW35	4FT deg	*	22	2M+4D	Ind	30	Ind	Ind	
Linguistics/Film Studies	WQ51	3FT deg	*	22	2M+4D	Ind	30	Ind	Ind	
Philosophy/Film Studies	VW75	3FT deg	*	22	2M+4D	Ind	30	Ind	Ind	4 20/22
Spanish/Film Studies	WR54	4FT deg	*	22	2M+4D	Ind	30	Ind	Ind	
Theology/Film Studies	VW85	3FT deg	*	22	2M+4D	Ind	30	Ind	Ind	
KENT INST of A & D										
Editorial and Advertising Photography	W552▼	3FT deg	Fa		N	P+				21
Editorial and Advertising Photography	E552▼	3FT deg	Fa		N	P+				
Visual Communication: Photography	E550▼	3FT deg	Fa		N	P+				
Visual Communication: Photography	W550▼	3FT deg	Fa		N	P+				10
KING ALFRED'S WINCHESTER										
Drama, Theatre and Television Studies	W4W5	3FT deg	* g	20-24	MO $	D	24	BBB	X	13 14/24
Media and Film Studies	P4W5	3FT deg	* g	14	6M	M	24	BCC	N	
LEICESTER SOUTH FIELDS COLL										
Photography	055E	2FT HND	Fa g	4	N	P$	Dip	CSYS	N	
LIVERPOOL JOHN MOORES Univ										
Screen Studies and Media and Cultural Studies	PW45	3FT deg	E	BB-BCC	5M+3D	X	28$	BBBC		7 20/28
Screen Studs and Imaginative Writing (IW jt awd)	WW59	3FT deg	E	BB	5M+3D	D^	28$			22
Theatre Studies & Screen Studies (SS Jnt Awd)	WW54	3FT deg	T+E	BB	7D	X	28$	BBCC		19
LONDON GUILDHALL Univ										
Communications and Audio Visual Production Studs	PW45	3FT deg	* g	BC-CCD	MO+2D		24	Ind	Ind	
Modular Programme *Communications and Audio Visual Production Studs*	Y400	3FT deg	* g	BB-CC	MO+4D	D/M$ go	26	Ind	Ind	
LONDON INST										
Photography	W550	3FT deg								20 8/24
Fashion Styling and Photography	58WE	2FT HND								
LUTON Univ										
Biology with Video Production	C1W5	3FT deg	g	12-16	MO/DO	M/D	32	BBCC	Ind	
Business with Video Production	N1W5	3FT deg	g	12-16	MO/DO	M/D	32	BBCC	Ind	
Contemp Br & Euro History with Video Production	V1W5	3FT deg	g	12-16	MO/DO	M/D	32	BBCC	Ind	
Contemp British & Euro History with Film Studies	V1WM	3FT deg	g	12-16	MO/DO	M/D	32	BBCC	Ind	
Contemp British & Euro History with TV Studies	V1WN	3FT deg	g	12-16	MO/DO	M/D	32	BBCC	Ind	
Digital Systems Design with Photography	H6WN	3FT deg	g	12-16	MO/DO	M/D	32	BBCC	Ind	
Digital Systems Design with TV Studies	HW6N	3FT deg	g	12-16	MO/DO	M/D	32	BBCC	Ind	
Digital Systems Design with Video Production	H6WM	3FT deg	g	12-16	MO/DO	M/D	32	BBCC	Ind	
Electronic System Design with Photography	HW65	3FT deg	g	12-16	MO/DO	M/D	32	BBCC	Ind	
Electronic System Design with TV Studies	HWP5	3FT deg	g	12-16	MO/DO	M/D	32	BBCC	Ind	
Electronic System Design with Video Production	HW6M	3FT deg	g	12-16	MO/DO	M/D	32	BBCC	Ind	
Environmental Science with Photography	F9W5	3FT deg	g	12-16	MO/DO	M/D	32	BBCC	Ind	
Environmental Studies with Photography	F9WM	3FT deg	g	12-16	MO/DO	M/D	32	BBCC	Ind	
European Language Studies with Film Studies	T2WM	4FT deg	L g	12-16	MO/DO	M/D	32	BBCC	Ind	
European Language Studies with Photography	T2WN	4FT deg	L g	12-16	MO/DO	M/D	32	BBCC	Ind	
European Language Studies with Video Production	T2W5	4FT deg	L g	12-16	MO/DO	M/D	32	BBCC	Ind	
Integrated Engineering with Video Production	H1W5	3FT deg	g	12-16	MO/DO	M/D	32	BBCC	Ind	
Law with TV Studies	M3W5	3FT deg	g	12-16	MO/DO	M/D	32	BBCC	Ind	
Leisure Studies with Photography	N7W5	3FT deg	g	12-16	MO/DO	M/D	32	BBCC	Ind	

course details | 98 expected requirements | 96 entry stats

TITLE	CODE	COURSE	SUBJECTS	A/AS	NO/C	AGNVQ	IB	SQA(H)	SQA	RATIO A/AS
Leisure Studies with TV Studies	N7WM	3FT deg	g	12-16	MO/DO	M/D	32	BBCC	Ind	
Linguistics with TV Studies	Q1W5	3FT deg	g	12-16	MO/DO	M/D	32	BBCC	Ind$	
Literary Studies in English with Film Studies	Q2W5	3FT deg		12-16	MO/DO	M/D	32	BBCC	Ind	
Literary Studies in English with TV Studies	Q2WM	3FT deg		12-16	MO/DO	M/D	32	BBCC	Ind	
Media Performance with Photography	W4WN	3FT deg		12-16	MO/DO	M/D	32	BBCC	Ind	
Media Performance with Radio	WW4M	3FT deg		12-16	MO/DO	M/D	32	BBCC	Ind	
Media Performance with TV Studies	WW45	3		12-16	MO/DO	M/D	32	BBCC	Ind	
Media Performance with Video Production	W4W5	3FT deg	Pf g	12-16	MO/DO	M/D	32	BBCC	Ind	
Media Performancewith Film Studies	W4WM	3FT deg		12-16	MO/DO	M/D	32	BBCC	Ind	
Media Practices with Film Studies	WP54	3FT deg		12-16	MO/DO	M/D	32	BBCC	Ind	
Media Practices with Photography	WP5K	3FT deg		12-16	MO/DO	M/D	32	BBCC	Ind	
Media Practices with Radio	WP5L	3FT deg		12-16	MO/DO	M/D	32	BBCC	Ind	
Media Practices with TV Studies	PW4M	3FT deg		12-16	MO/DO	M/D	32	BBCC	Ind	
Media Practices with Video Production	P4W5	3FT deg	g	12-16	MO/DO	M/D	32	BBCC	Ind	
Media Production with Film Studies	P4WM	3FT deg	g	12-16	MO/DO	M/D	32	BBCC	Ind	
Media Production with Radio	WPM4	3FT deg								
Media Production with TV Studies	PW45	3FT deg	g	12-16	MO/DO	M/D	32	BBCC	Ind	
Media Production with Video Production	PW4N	3FT deg								
Media Technology with Photography	P4WN	3FT deg		12-16	MO/DO	M/D	32	BBCC	Ind	
Modern English Studies with Film Studies	Q3W5	3FT deg	g	12-16	MO/DO	M/D	32	BBCC	Ind	
Modern English Studies with Photography	Q3WM	3FT deg	g	12-16	MO/DO	M/D	32	BBCC	Ind	
Modern English Studies with TV Studies	Q3WN	3FT deg	g	12-16	MO/DO	M/D	32	BBCC	Ind	
Physical Geography with Video Production	F8WM	3FT deg	g	12-16	MO/DO	M/D	32	BBCC	Ind	
Politics with Film Studies	M1W5	3FT deg	g	12-16	MO/DO	M/D	32	BBCC	Ind	
Politics with TV Studies	M1WM	3FT deg	g	12-16	MO/DO	M/D	32	BBCC	Ind	
Psychology with Film Studies	L7W5	3FT deg		12-16	MO/DO	M/D	32	BBCC	Ind	
Psychology with Photography	L7WN	3FT deg	g	12-16	MO/DO	M/D	32	BBCC	Ind	
Psychology with TV Studies	LW75	3FT deg		12-16	MO/DO	M/D	32	BBCC	Ind	
Psychology with Video Production	L7WM	3FT deg	g	12-16	MO/DO	M/D	32	BBCC	Ind	
Regional Planning & Development with Photography	K4W5	3FT deg	g	12-16	MO/DO	M/D	32	BBCC	Ind	
Social Studies with Film Studies	L3WM	3FT deg	g	12-16	MO/DO	M/D	32	BBCC	Ind	
Social Studies with TV Studies	L3WN	3FT deg	g	12-16	MO/DO	M/D	32	BBCC	Ind	
Social Studies with Video Production	L3W5	3FT deg	g	12-16	MO/DO	M/D	32	BBCC	Ind	
Travel & Tourism with Photography	P7WM	3FT deg	g	12-16	MO/DO	M/D	32	BBCC	Ind	
Travel and Tourism with Video Production	P7W5	3FT deg	g	12-16	MO/DO	M/D	32	BBCC	Ind	

Univ of MANCHESTER

TITLE	CODE	COURSE	SUBJECTS	A/AS	NO/C	AGNVQ	IB	SQA(H)	SQA	RATIO A/AS
Drama and Screen Studies	WW45	3FT deg	El	BBC	4M+6D		32	AAABB	HN$	

MANCHESTER METROPOLITAN Univ

TITLE	CODE	COURSE	SUBJECTS	A/AS	NO/C	AGNVQ	IB	SQA(H)	SQA	RATIO A/AS
History of Film, Photography and Graphic Media	VW45	3FT deg	*	18	N	Ind	Ind	Ind	Ind	6/22
Photography	JW55	3FT deg	Pf	CC	Ind		Ind	Ind	Ind	8/22
Photography	EW55	3FT deg	Pf	CC	Ind		Ind	Ind	Ind	

MIDDLESEX Univ

TITLE	CODE	COURSE	SUBJECTS	A/AS	NO/C	AGNVQ	IB	SQA(H)	SQA	RATIO A/AS
Joint Honours Degree Film Studies	Y400	3FT deg	* g	12-16	MO	Ind	28	Ind	Ind	

NAPIER Univ

TITLE	CODE	COURSE	SUBJECTS	A/AS	NO/C	AGNVQ	IB	SQA(H)	SQA	RATIO A/AS
Photography, Film and Television	W500	3FT/4FT deg	Pf	CD	Ind	Ind	Ind	BCCC	Ind	20 12/22
Photography, Film and Television	E500	3FT/4FT deg	Pf	CD	Ind	Ind	Ind	BCCC	Ind	

Univ of NEWCASTLE

TITLE	CODE	COURSE	SUBJECTS	A/AS	NO/C	AGNVQ	IB	SQA(H)	SQA	RATIO A/AS
Combined Studies (BA) Film Studies	Y400	3FT deg	*	ABC-BBB	5D	Ind	35$	AAAB	Ind	

Cinematics – Film, TV, Photography — 14

course details			98 expected requirements							96 entry stats
TITLE	CODE	COURSE	SUBJECTS	A/AS	ND/C	AGNVQ	IB	SQA(H)	SQA	RATIO A/AS
Univ of Wales COLLEGE, NEWPORT										
Documentary Photography	W550	3FT deg	Pf	6	M+D	P$	Ind	Ind	Ind	
Documentary Photography	E550	3FT deg								
Film And Video	W520	3FT deg	Pf	6	M+D	P$	Ind	Ind	Ind	
Film and Video	E520	3FT deg								
Photographic Art	E551	3FT deg								
Photographic Art	W551	3FT deg	Pf	6	M+D	P$	Ind	Ind	Ind	
NORTHBROOK COLLEGE Sussex										
Photography, Media and Society	W5L3	3FT deg	Fa/Me/Py/Ar	2	N		Ind	Ind	Ind	
Photography, Media and Society	E5L3	3FT deg	Fa/Me/Py/Ar	2	N		Ind	Ind	Ind	
Design (Audio Visual)	035E	2FT HND	Fa/Me/Py/Ar		N		Ind	Ind	Ind	
NESCOT										
Imaging Technology	WW25	3FT deg	Py	EE	MO	M	Dip	Ind	N$	
Imaging Technology	WW2M	4FT deg	*							
Design (Photomedia)	055W	2FT HND	Py	C	MO	P	Dip	Ind	N$	5
NORTH EAST WALES INST of HE										
Film and Television Design	025W	2FT HND	Pf		Ind	Ind	Ind	Ind	Ind	
Film and Television Design	025E	2FT HND	Pf		Ind	Ind	Ind	Ind	Ind	
Univ of NORTH LONDON										
Communication & Cultural Studies and Film Studs	LW65	3FT deg	E/So/Me/Cm	BC	Ind	M	Ind	Ind	Ind	6	10/20
Film Studies and Arts Management	NWC5	3FT deg	* g	BC	MO+4D	D	Ind	Ind	Ind	
Combined Honours *Film Studies*	Y300	3FT/4FT deg	E/So	BC	Ind	Ind	Ind	Ind	Ind	
Univ of NORTHUMBRIA										
Contemporary Photographic Practice	E550	3FT deg	Fa+Pf g		X		X	X	X	
English and Film Studies	QW35	3FT deg	E	BBC	MO+4D		26	BBBCC	Ind	14	18/24
History of Modern Art, Design and Film	WW25	3FT deg	E/H	16-20	MO+4D		26	CCCCC	Ind	3	14/22
Media Production	E510	3FT deg	Fa/Pf g		N$		X	X	X	
NORTHUMBERLAND COLLEGE										
Design (Communications) Television Operations	54WW	2FT HND	2(Ad/M/E)	BE-BBC	N	P	Ind	Ind	Ind	
Design (Communications) Television Operations	54WE	2FT HND	2(Ad/M/E)	BE-BBC	N	P	Ind	Ind	Ind	
NOTTINGHAM TRENT Univ										
Photography	E550	3FT deg	Fa g	12	Ind	Ind	Ind	Ind	Ind	
Photography in Europe	E551	3FT deg	Fa g	12	Ind	Ind	Ind	Ind	Ind	
Photography and Imaging	065W▼	2FT HND	* g		Ind	Ind	Ind	Ind	Ind	
PLYMOUTH COLLEGE of A & D										
Photomedia	W555	1FT deg		X	HN	X	X	X		
Photomedia	E555	1FT deg		X	HN	X	X	X		
READING COLLEGE AND SCHOOL OF ART AND DESIGN										
Design (Photography)	E550	2FT/3FT HND/deg			N	PA	$	$	N	
Design (Photography)	W550	2FT/3FT HND/deg			N	PA	$	$	N	
Photography and Digital Imaging	W560	3FT deg								
Photography and Digital Imaging	E560	3FT deg								
Univ of READING										
Italian with Film Studies	R3W5	4FT deg	* g	BCC	Ind	D$6/^ go	30	BBBB	Ind	8

TITLE	CODE	COURSE	SUBJECTS	A/AS	NQ/C	AGNVQ	IB	SQA(H)	SQA	RATIO A/AS
SALISBURY COLL										
Professional Communications (Photo or TV & Film)	E500	1FT deg	Pf	X	HN	X	X	X	Ind	
Professional Communications (Photo or TV & Film)	W500	1FT deg	Pf	X	HN	X	X	X	Ind	
Design (Photography or Television & Film)	005W	2FT HND	Pf		N	Ind	Ind	Ind	Ind	
Design (Photography or Television & Film)	005E	2FT HND	Pf		N	Ind	Ind	Ind	Ind	
SANDWELL COLL										
Design (Photography)	055E	2FT HND	* g	A-E	N	Ind	Dip	ABC	Ind	
Design (Photography)	055W	2FT HND	* g	A-E	N	Ind	Dip	ABC	Ind	
SHEFFIELD HALLAM Univ										
Film Studies	W510	3FT deg	*	BB-BCC	3M+2D	P^	Ind	Ind	Ind	
Film and Literature	QW25	3FT deg	*	BB-BCC	3M+2D	P^	Ind	Ind	Ind	
Combined Studies _Film Studies_	Y400	3FT deg	*	18	2M	M	Ind	Ind	Ind	
Univ of SOUTHAMPTON										
English and Film	QW35	3FT deg	E							
French and Film	RW15	4FT deg	F	BBC		Ind		Ind	Ind	
German and Film	RW25	4FT deg	G	BBC						
Spanish and Film	RW45	4FT deg	Sp	BBC						
SOUTHAMPTON INST										
Film Studies	W510	3FT deg	*	18	MO	M$	Dip$	BBBBC	N$	11 12/26
Photography	W551	3FT deg	Pf	18	MO	M$	Dip	BBBBC	N	
Photography	E551	3FT deg	Pf	18	MO	M$	Dip	BBBBC	N	
SOUTH BANK Univ										
World Theatre and Human Geography	LW85	3FT deg	Gy g	14-18	2M+4D	M go	Ind	Ind	Ind	
ST HELENS COLL										
Design (Photography)	055W	2FT HND	Pf	2	N	M*	Ind	Ind	Ind	
Design (Photography)	055E	2FT HND	Pf	2	N	M*	Ind	Ind	Ind	
Design (Television and Video)	035W	2FT HND	*	2	N	M*	Ind	Ind	Ind	
Design (Television and Video)	035E	2FT HND	*	2	N	M*	Ind	Ind	Ind	
STAFFORDSHIRE Univ										
Design: Photography	E550	3FT deg	Pf	EE	3M	MA	Ind	Ind	Ind	
Design: Photography	W550	3FT deg	Pf	EE	3M	MA	Ind	Ind	Ind	39
Film Studies	W510	3FT deg	g	CD	MO+2D	M	27	BBC		
Film Studies/American Studies	WQ54	3FT deg	g	CD	MO+2D	M	27	BBC	Ind	3 4/18
Film Studies/Cultural Studies	LW65	3FT deg	g	CD	MO+2D	M	27	BBC	Ind	2 12/18
Film Studies/Development Studies	MWY5	3FT deg	g	12	MO+2D	M	27	BBC	Ind	
Film Studies/European Culture	LWP5	3FT deg	g	CD	MO+2D	M	27	BBC	Ind	
Film, Television and Radio	W520	3FT deg	g	BC	MO+2D	M	Ind	BBB	Ind	6 6/22
German/Film Studies	RW25	3FT/4SW deg	G g	CD	MO+2D	M^	27	BBC	Ind	
History/Film Studies	VW15	3FT deg	H g	CD	MO+2D	M	27	BBC	Ind	9
Information Systems/Film Studies	GW55	3FT deg	g	12	Ind	M	Ind	BBB	Ind	4
International Relations/Film Studies	MWC5	3FT deg	g	12	MO+2D	M	27	BBC	Ind	2
Literature/Film Studies	QW35	3FT deg	EL g	CD	MO+2D	M	27	BBC	Ind	4 6/18
Media Studies/Film Studies	PW45	3FT deg	g	CD	MO+2D		27	BBC		
Philosophy/Film Studies	VW75	3FT deg	g	CD	MO+2D	M	27	BBC	Ind	4
Politics/Film Studies	MWCM	3FT deg	g	12	MO+2D	M	27	BBC	Ind	
Psychology/Film Studies	LW75	3FT deg	g	18	3M+3D	Ind	27	BBB	Ind	23
Spanish/Film Studies	RW45	3FT/4SW deg	g	CD	MO+2D	M^	27	BBC	Ind	
Women's Studies/Film Studies	MW95	3FT deg	g	12	MO+2D	M	27	BBC	Ind	

INDEPENDENT ON SUNDAY

course details			98 expected requirements							96 entry stats
TITLE	CODE	COURSE	SUBJECTS	A/AS	ND/C	AGNVQ	IB	SQA(H)	SQA	RATIO A/AS
STOCKPORT COLL of F and HE										
Documentary Photography	E550	3FT deg	Pf		N	P	Ind			
Design (Photography and Contemporary Imaging)	065E	2FT HND	Pf		N	P	Ind			
Univ of SUNDERLAND										
Photography, Video and Digital Imaging	W551	3FT deg	Pf g	CC	3M	Ind	24	CCCCC	N	33
Photography, Video and Digital Imaging	E551	3FT deg	Pf g	CC	3M	Ind	24	CCCCC	N	
SURREY INST of A & D										
Film and Video	E500	3FT deg	Fa		N					
Film and Video	W500	3FT deg	Fa		N					20 8/28
Photography	W550	3FT deg	Fa		N					17 12/20
Photography	E550	3FT deg	Fa		N					
SWANSEA INST of HE										
Photojournalism	E5P6	3FT deg		12		M	Ind	Ind	Ind	
Photojournalism	W5P6	3FT deg		12		M	Ind	Ind	Ind	85
TAMESIDE COLLEGE										
Photography	055E	2FT HND		2	N	PA				
THAMES VALLEY Univ										
Digital Arts with Photography	W9W5	3FT deg		8-12	MO	M		CCC		
Media Arts with Photography	W9WM	3FT deg		8-12	MO	M	26	CCC		
Multi-Media Computing with Photography	G5W5	3FT deg		8-12	MO	M	26	CCC		
Univ of WARWICK										
Film and Literature	QW25	3FT deg	El/L g	AAB	X	X	36$	AAAAB$		10 24/30
French with Film Studies (4 Yrs inc yr abroad)	R1W5	4FT deg	F g	BCC	X	X	30$	ABBBB$		9 22/28
Italian with Film Studies (4 Yrs inc yr abroad)	R3W5	4FT deg	E/L g	BBC	X	X	29$	ABBCC$		13
WEST HERTS COLL										
Imagemaking and Design	E560	3FT deg	Pf	4	N					
Univ of WESTMINSTER										
Film, Video and Photo Arts (Photo & Multimedia)	W550▼	3FT deg	*	CC	5M+2D	D	Ind	BBB		21 16/24
Film, Video and Photographic Arts (Film)	W520▼	3FT deg	*	CC	5M+2D	D	Ind	BBB		56 14/30
Photographic and Electronic Imaging Sciences	WJ55▼	3FT deg	P/C/M	DE	N	M	Ind	Ind	Ind	4 8/20
Univ of WOLVERHAMPTON										
Photography	W550	3FT deg	A/Ad/Ds+Pf	12	4M	M	24	BBBB	Ind	35
Photography	E550	3FT deg	A/Ad/Ds+Pf	12	4M	M	24	BBBB	Ind	
Combined Degrees *Film Studies*	Y401	3FT deg		12	4M	M	24	BBBB	Ind	
Combined Degrees *Photography*	E401	3FT deg	A/Ad/Ds+Pf	12	4M	M	24	BBBB	Ind	
Combined Degrees *Photography*	Y401	3FT deg	A/Ad/Ds+Pf	12	4M	M	24	BBBB	Ind	

	course details			98 expected requirements							96 entry stats
TITLE	CODE	COURSE	SUBJECTS	A/AS	ND/C	RGNVQ	IB	SQA(H)	SQA	RATIO A/AS

Univ of ABERDEEN

TITLE	CODE	COURSE	SUBJECTS	A/AS	ND/C	RGNVQ	IB	SQA(H)	SQA	RATIO A/AS
Computing	G502	4FT deg	M g	BBC	Ind	M$ go	30$	BBBB$	Ind	6
Computing Science	G500	4FT deg	M+2S g	CCD	Ind	MS go	24$	BBBC$	Ind	5
Computing Science (Artificial Intelligence)	G5G8	4FT deg	M+2S g	CCD	Ind	MS go	24$	BBBC$	Ind	12
Computing Science (Business Computing)	G520	4FT deg	M+2S g	CCD	Ind	MS go	24$	BBBC$	Ind	9
Computing Science with French	G5R1	4FT deg	M+2S g	CCD	Ind	MS go	24$	BBBC$	Ind	2
Computing Science with German	G5R2	4FT deg	M+2S g	CCD	Ind	MS go	24$	BBBC$	Ind	3
Computing Science with Spanish	G5R4	4FT deg	M+2S g	CCD	Ind	MS go	24$	BBBC$	Ind	
Computing Science-Engineering	GH56	4FT deg	M+2S g	CCD	Ind	MS go	24$	BBBC$	Ind	14
Computing Science-Management Studies	GN5C	3FT/4FT deg	M+S g	CCD	Ind	MS go	24$	BBBC$	Ind	6
Computing Science-Mathematics	GGMC	4FT deg	M+2S g	CCD	Ind	MS go	24$	BBBC$	Ind	6
Computing Science-Psychology	GC58	4FT deg	M+2S g	CCD	Ind	MS go	24$	BBBC$	Ind	6
Computing Science-Statistics	GG54	4FT deg	M+2S g	CCD	Ind	MS go	24$	BBBC$	Ind	
Computing-Entrepreneurship	NGC5	4FT deg	* g	BBC	Ind	M$ go	30 $	BBBB$	Ind	
Computing-Mathematics	GG51	4FT deg	M g	BBC	Ind	M$ go	30$	BBBB$	Ind	5
Computing-Statistics	GG4M	4FT deg	M g	BBC	Ind	M$ go	30$	BBBB$	Ind	
Electronic & Software Engineering	H6G7	4FT deg	M+P/Ds g	CC	Ind	M$ go	26$	BBBCC$	Ind	14
Informatics	G522	4FT deg	M g	BBC	Ind	M$ go	30$	BBBB$	Ind	
Information Systems-Management Studies	GN51	4FT deg	M g	BBC	Ind	M$ go	30$	BBBB$	Ind	8

Univ of ABERTAY DUNDEE

TITLE	CODE	COURSE	SUBJECTS	A/AS	ND/C	RGNVQ	IB	SQA(H)	SQA	RATIO A/AS
Biology & Computing	CG15	4FT/5SW deg	g	CD	Ind	Ind	Ind	BBC	Ind	
Business Computing	G561	4FT/5SW deg	*	CD	Ind	Ind	Ind	BBC	Ind	
Chemistry & Computing	FG15	4FT/5SW deg	C	CD	Ind	Ind	Ind	BBC	Ind	
Computing	G500	4FT/5SW deg	*	CD	Ind	Ind	Ind	BBC	Ind	
Computing & Mathematics	GG51	4FT/5SW deg	M	CD	Ind	Ind	Ind	BBC	Ind	
Information & Communication Technology	G600	4FT/5SW deg	M	CD	Ind	Ind	Ind	BBC	Ind	
Management & Computing	GN51	4FT/5SW deg	*	CD	Ind	Ind	Ind	BBC	Ind	
Mathematical Sciences	G1G5	4FT/5SW deg	M	CD	Ind	Ind	Ind	BBC	Ind	
Computing: Software Development	005G	2FT HND	*	D	Ind	Ind	Ind	CC	Ind	

Univ of Wales, ABERYSTWYTH

TITLE	CODE	COURSE	SUBJECTS	A/AS	ND/C	RGNVQ	IB	SQA(H)	SQA	RATIO A/AS
Accounting/Computer Science	GN54	3FT deg	* g	20	3M+2D	M6 g	30	BBBCC	Ind	
Computer Science	G500	3FT deg	* g	20	3M+2D	M6 g	30	BBBCC	Ind	
Computer Science with French	G5R1	4FT deg	F g	20	1M+5D$	M^ g	30$	BBBBC$	Ind	
Computer Science with German	G5R2	4FT deg	G g	20	1M+5D$	M^ g	30$	BBBBC$	Ind	
Computer Science with Italian	G5R3	4FT deg	L g	20	1M+5D$	M^ g	30$	BBBBC$	Ind	
Computer Science with Spanish	G5R4	4FT deg	L g	20	1M+5D$	M^ g	30$	BBBBC$	Ind	
Computer Science/Geography	FG85	3FT deg	Gy g	20	3M+2D$	M^ g	30$	BBBCC$	Ind	
Computer Science/Mathematics	GG15	3FT deg	M g	20	3M+2D$	M^ g	30$	BBBCC$	Ind	
Computer Science/Physics	FG35	3FT deg	P+M g	20	X	MS6/^ g	30$	BBBCC$	Ind	
Computer Science/Statistics	GG45	3FT deg	M g	20	3M+2D$	M^ g	30$	BBBCC$	Ind	
Information Management, Accounting and Finance	GN5L	3FT deg	* g	18	1M+5D	M6 g	29	BBBCC	Ind	
Software Eng (inc integ ind & prof tr) (MEng)	G701	5SW deg	* g	22	3M+2D	D6 g	31	BBBBC	Ind	
Software Eng (inc integ ind & prof training)	G700	4SW deg	* g	20	3M+2D	M6 g	30	BBBCC	Ind	
Information and Library St/an approved Sci Sub *Computer Science*	PY21	3FT deg	* g	20	3M+2D	M6 g	30	BBBCC	Ind	

ANGLIA Poly Univ

TITLE	CODE	COURSE	SUBJECTS	A/AS	ND/C	RGNVQ	IB	SQA(H)	SQA	RATIO A/AS
Audiotechnology and Computer Science	HGPM▼	3FT deg	S	16	8M	D	Dip$	BBCCC	N	19
Audiotechnology and Real Time Computer Systems	HG6M▼	3FT deg	S	16	8M	D	Dip$	BCCCC	N	6
Biology and Computer Science	CG15▼	3FT deg	B	10	3M	P	Dip$	BCCC	N	
Biomedical Science and Computer Science	BG95▼	3FT deg	B	10	3M	P go	Dip$	BCCC	N	
Business Information Systems	G520▼	3FT deg	* g	8	3M	P go	Dip	CCCC	N	1 8/14

Computer Sciences and Engineering 15

TITLE	CODE	COURSE	SUBJECTS	A/AS	ND/C	AGNVQ	IB	SQA(H)	SQA	RATIO	A/AS
Business Studies and Business Information Systs	GN51▼	3FT deg	* g	14	6M	M go	Dip	BBCC	Ind	3	
Business and Computer Science	NG15▼	3FT deg	* g	10	3M	P go	Dip	BCCC	Ind	6	
Business and Real Time Computer Systems	NG1M▼	3FT deg	* g	10	3M	P go	Dip	BCCC	Ind		
Chemistry and Computer Science	FG15▼	3FT deg	S	10	3M	P go	Dip$	BCCC	N		
Communication Studies & Real Time Computer Systs	PG35▼	3FT deg	Ap g	14	6M	M+/^ go	Dip$	BBCC	Ind		
Communication Studies and Computer Science	GP53▼	3FT deg	Ap g	14	6M	M+/^ go	Dip$	BBCC	Ind		
Computer Science	G500▼	3FT deg	* g	10	3M	P go	Dip	BCCC	N	4	6/8
Computer Science and Ecology and Conservation	DG25▼	3FT deg	* g	10	3M	P go	Dip	BCCC	N		
Computer Science and Forensic Science	BG15▼	3FT deg	g	12	4M	M go	Dip	BCCC			
Computer Science and French	GR51▼	4FT deg	* g	12	4M	M go	Dip	BCCC	Ind	4	
Computer Science and Geology	GF56▼	3FT deg	* g	10	2M	P go	Dip	BCCC	N	4	
Computer Science and German	GR52▼	4FT deg	* g	12	4M	M go	Dip	BCCC	N		
Computer Science and Imaging Science	GW5M▼	3FT deg	S g	10	3M	P go	Dip$	BCCC	N		
Computer Science and Instrumentation Electronics	GH56▼	3FT deg	* g	10	3M	P go	Dip	BCCC	N	5	
Computer Science and Italian	GR53▼	4FT deg	* g	12	4M	M go	Dip	BCCC	N	1	
Computer Science and Maths or Stats/Stat Mod.	GG51▼	3FT deg	* g	10	3M	P go	Dip	BCCC	N	4	
Computer Science and Ophthalmic Dispensing	BG55▼	3FT deg	* g	10	3M	P go	Dip	BCCC	N		
Computer Science and Psychology	CG85▼	3FT deg	S g	16	8M	D go	Dip$	BBCC	N	3	
Computer Science and Spanish	GR54▼	4FT deg	* g	12	4M	M go	Dip	BCCC	N		
Construction Management and Multimedia	KG25▼	3FT deg									
Construction Mgt and Business Information Systs	GKN2▼	3FT deg	* g	10	3M	P go	Dip	BCCC	Ind		
Ecology & Conservation & Real Time Computer Syst	DG2M▼	3FT deg	* g	10	3M	P go	Dip	BCCC	N		
Graphic Arts and Real Time Computer Systems	WG25▼	3FT deg	A g	14	6M	M+/^ go	Dip$	BBCC	Ind		
Imaging Science and Real Time Computer Systems	GW55▼	3FT deg	S g	10	3M	P go	Dip$	BCCC	N		
Information Systems	G521▼	2FT deg	S g	10	3M	P go	Dip	BCCC			
Information Systems Development	G522▼	3FT deg	S g	10	3M	P go	Dip$	BCCC	N	2	
Information Systems and Multimedia	G524▼	3FT deg	* g	8	3M	P go	Dip	CCCC	N		
Information Systems and Product Design	GH57▼	3FT deg	S g	10	3M	P go	Ind$	BCCC	Ind		
Instrumentation Elects & Real Time Comp Systems	HG65▼	3FT deg	S g	10	3M	P go	Dip$	BCCC	N	2	
Maths or Stats/Stat Mod.& Real Time Comp.Systems	GG15▼	3FT deg	* g	10	3M	P go	Dip	BCCC	N		
Multimedia Development	G611▼	3FT deg	* g	10	3M	P go	Dip	BCCC			
Multimedia Systems	G610▼	3FT deg	* g	10	3M	P go	Dip	BCCC	Ind	2	10/16
Multimedia and Leisure Planning and Development	GL53▼	3FT deg	g	8	N	Ind go	Dip	CCCC	Ind		
Psychology and Real Time Computer Systems	CG8M▼	3FT deg	S g	16	8M	D	Dip$	BBCCC	N		
Software Engineering	G701▼	3FT deg	S g	10	3M	P gi	Dip	BCCC	Ind	5	
Business Information Technology	065G▼	2FT HND	* g	4	N	P go	Dip	CCC	N	1	2/4
Computing	105G▼	2FT HND	* g	10	3M	P go	Dip	BCCC	Ind	2	2/8

ASTON Univ

TITLE	CODE	COURSE	SUBJECTS	A/AS	ND/C	AGNVQ	IB	SQA(H)	SQA	RATIO	A/AS
Business Administration/Computer Sci (Year Zero)	GN5C	4FT/5SW deg									
Business Computing & IT	NG45	3FT/4SW deg	* g	BBB	3M+7D	DB6/^ go	31	AABBB	Ind	11	20/26
Computer Science/Biology	CG15	3FT/4SW deg	B g	18	5M+5D$	D$6/^ go	29$	BBBBC$	Ind	4	
Computer Science/Biology (Year Zero)	CG1M	4FT/5SW deg									
Computer Science/Business Administration	GN51	3FT/4SW deg	* g	20	3M+7D	D$6/^ go	30	BBBBB	Ind	5	18/28
Computing Science	G500	3FT/4SW deg	* g	20	5M+5D	D$6/^ go	30	BBBBC	Ind	9	16/24
Computing Science with European St (MEng)	G5T2	4FT deg	* g	22	3M+7D	D$6/^ go	32	ABBBB	Ind		
Electronic Engineering and Computer Science	GH56	3FT/4SW deg	M+Ph/Cs/Es g	20	5M+5D$	D$6/^ go	30$	BBBBB$	Ind	4	12/28
Electronics/Computer Science	HG65	3FT/4SW deg	M/P g	18	5M+5D$	D$6/^ go	29$	BBBBC$	Ind	9	
Engineering Management/Computer Science	GH57	3FT/4SW deg	S	18	5M+5D$	D$^ go	29$	BBBBC$	Ind		
Environmental Sci & Tech/Computer Sci (Yr Zero)	GF5X	4FT/5SW deg									
Environmental Science & Technology/Computer Sci	GF59	3FT/4SW deg	S g	18	5M+5D$	D$6/^ go	29$	BBBBC$	Ind		
Ergonomics/Computer Science	GJ5X	3FT/4SW deg	* g	20	5M+5D	D$6/^ go	30	BBBBB	Ind		
European Studies/Computer Science	GT52	3FT/4SW deg	* g	18	5M+5D	D$6/^ go	29	BBBBC	Ind		

course details			98 expected requirements							96 entry stats	
TITLE	CODE	COURSE	SUBJECTS	A/AS	ND/C	AGNVQ	IB	SQA(H)	SQA	RATIO	A/AS
European Studies/Computer Science (Year Zero)	GT5F	4FT/5SW deg									
French/Computer Science	GR51	4SW deg	F g	20	X	D$6/△ go	30$	BBBBB$	Ind	7	
German/Computer Science	GR52	4SW deg	G g	18	X	D$6/△ go	29$	BBBBC$	Ind	2	
German/Computer Science (Year Zero)	GR5F	5SW deg									
Health & Safety Management/Computer Science	GJ59	3FT/4SW deg	* g	18	5M+5D	D$6/^ go	29	BBBBC	Ind		
Health & Safety Mgt/Computer Science (Year Zero)	GJ5Y	4FT/5SW deg									
Human Psychology/Computer Science	LG75	3FT/4SW deg	* g	20	3M+7D	D$6/^ go	30	BBBBB	Ind	14	
Human Psychology/Computer Science (Year Zero)	LG7M	4FT/5SW deg									
Information Technology for Business	G560	3FT/4SW deg	* g	20	5M+5D	D$6/^ go	30	BBBBC	Ind	6	16/20
Mathematics/Computer Science	GG15	3FT/4SW deg	M g	20	X	D$^ go	31$	ABBBB$	Ind	7	14/22
Medicinal Chemistry/Computer Science	FG15	3FT/4SW deg	C g	20	3M+7D$	D$^ go	31$	ABBBB$	Ind		
Public Policy & Management/Computer Science	GM5C	4FT/5SW deg									
Public Policy & Management/Computer Science	GM51	3FT/4SW deg	* g	20	5M+5D	D$6/^ go	30	BBBBB	Ind		

Univ of Wales, BANGOR

| Information Technology and Applied Statistics | GG54 | 2FT dip | * g | | | | | | | | |

BARNSLEY COLL

| Science Foundation *Computer Science* | Y100 | 4EXT deg | | | | | | | | | |
| Computing | 005G | 2FT HND | Ap | E | 2M | Pl/B | Ind | Ind | Ind | | |

BASFORD HALL COLL

| Multimedia Computing | G535 | 2FT deg | | | | D | Ind | Ind | Ind | | |
| Business Information Systems | 025G | 2FT HND | | D-E | | M | Ind | Ind | Ind | | |

Univ of BATH

Computer Information Systems (3 Yrs)	G520	3FT deg	M	22	Ind	Ind	30	Ind	Ind	11	18/20
Computer Information Systems (4 Yr SW)	G521	4SW deg	M	22	Ind	Ind	30	Ind	Ind	12	18/22
Computer Science	G501	4SW deg	M	22	Ind	Ind	30	AABBC$	Ind		
Computer Science	G500	3FT deg	M	22	Ind	Ind	30	AABBC$	Ind		
Computer Software Theory	G700	3FT deg	M	22	Ind	Ind	30$	AABBC$	Ind	14	24/30
Computer Software Theory (4 Yr SW)	G701	4SW deg	M	22	Ind	Ind	30$	AABBC$	Ind	30	
Mathematics and Computing	G5GC	3FT deg	M	22	Ind	Ind	30$	AABBC$	Ind	8	22/26
Mathematics and Computing	G5G1	4SW deg	M	22	Ind	Ind	30$	AABBC$	Ind	3	20/28
Networks & Information Eng for the Euro Market	GGNQ	5SW deg	M	22	Ind	Ind	30$	AABBC$	Ind		
Networks & Information Eng for the Euro Market	GGMP	4FT deg	M	22	Ind	Ind	30$	AABBC$	Ind		
Networks & Information Engineering (3 Yrs)	GG56	3FT deg	M	22	Ind	Ind	30$	AABBC$	Ind		
Networks & Information Engineering (4 Yr SW)	GG5P	4SW deg	M	22	Ind	Ind	30$	AABBC$	Ind		
Networks & Information Engineering (4 Yrs)	GG6M	4FT deg	M	22	Ind	Ind	30$	AABBC$	Ind		
Networks & Information Engineering (5 Yr SW)	GG6N	5SW deg	M	22	Ind	Ind	30$	AABBC$	Ind		

BELL COLLEGE OF TECHNOLOGY

Applied Computing	G610	3FT deg	M+E	DD	Ind	Ind	Ind	CCC$	22$		
Applicable Mathematics with Computing	5G1G	2FT HND	M	D-E	Ind	Ind	Ind	CC$	18$		
Business Information Systems	027G	2FT HND	Ap g	DD-D	N $	P$	Ind	CC$	18$		
Computer Technology and Instrumentation	006G	2FT HND	S	D	Ind	Ind	Ind	CC	18		
Computing (Software Development)	007G	2FT HND	M/E/Cs	EE	Ind	Ind	Ind	CC$	18$		
Computing (Support)	105G	2FT HND	M/E/Cs	EE	Ind	Ind	Ind	CC$	18$		

Univ OF BIRMINGHAM

Ancient History & Arch/Artificial Intelligence	GV86	3FT deg	* g	BBB	Ind	D*^	32	ABBB	Ind		
Ancient History & Archaeology/Computer Studies	GV56	3FT deg	* g	BBB	Ind	D*^	32	ABBB	Ind	1	
Artificial Intelligence and Computer Science	GG58	3FT deg	S g	BBB	Ind	Ind	30	Ind	Ind	11	18/26
Artificial Intelligence/East Medit History	GVV1	3FT deg	* g	BBB	Ind	D*^	32	ABBB	Ind		
Artificial Intelligence/English	GQ83	3FT deg	* g	BBB	Ind	D*^	32	ABBB	Ind	4	

Computer Sciences and Engineering 15

			98 expected requirements							96 entry stats

course details — *98 expected requirements* — *96 entry stats*

TITLE	CODE	COURSE	SUBJECTS	A/AS	NO/C	AGNVQ	IB	SQA(H)	SQA	RATIO A/AS
Artificial Intelligence/French Studies	GR81	4FT deg	F g	BBB	Ind	D*^	32$	ABBB	Ind	
Artificial Intelligence/German Studies	GR82	4FT deg	G g	BBB	Ind	D*^	32$	ABBB	Ind	1
Artificial Intelligence/Hispanic Studies	GR84	4FT deg	* g	BBB	Ind	D*^	32	ABBB	Ind	
Artificial Intelligence/Italian	GR83	4FT deg	* g	BBB	Ind	D*^	32	ABBB	Ind	
Artificial Intelligence/Latin	GQ86	3FT deg	Ln g	BBB	Ind	D*^	32$	ABBB	Ind	
Artificial Intelligence/Modern Greek Studies	GT82	4FT deg	* g	BBB	Ind	D*^	32	ABBB	Ind	
Artificial Intelligence/Music	GW83	3FT deg	Mu g	AAB-ABB	Ind	D*^	32$	ABBB	Ind	1
Artificial Intelligence/Philosophy	GV87	3FT deg	* g	BBB	Ind	D*^	32	ABBB	Ind	
Artificial Intelligence/Portuguese	GR85	4FT deg	* g	BBB	Ind	D*^	32	ABBB	Ind	
Artificial Intelligence/Russian	GR88	4FT deg	* g	BBB	Ind	D*^	32	ABBB	Ind	
Artificial Intelligence/Theology	GV88	3FT deg	* g	BBB	Ind	D*^	32	ABBB	Ind	
Computer Science/Software Engineering	GG57	3FT deg	S g	BBB	Ind	Ind	30	Ind	Ind	8 16/30
Computer Science/Software Engineering w. Bus St	G5N1	3FT deg	S g	BBB	Ind	Ind	30	Ind	Ind	8 16/24
Computer Studies/East Mediterranean History	GVM1	3FT deg	* g	BBB	Ind	D*^	32	ABBB	Ind	
Computer Studies/English	GQ53	3FT deg	* g	BBB	Ind	D*^	32	ABBB	Ind	23
Computer Studies/French Studies	GR51	4FT deg	F g	BBB	Ind	D*^	32$	ABBB	Ind	
Computer Studies/German Studies	GR52	4FT deg	G g	BBB	Ind	D*^	32$	ABBB	Ind	
Computer Studies/Hispanic Studies	GR54	4FT deg	* g	BBB	Ind	D*^	32	ABBB	Ind	
Computer Studies/Italian	GR53	4FT deg	* g	BBB	Ind	D*^	32	ABBB	Ind	
Computer Studies/Latin	GQ56	3FT deg	Ln g	BBB	Ind	D*^	32$	ABBB	Ind	
Computer Studies/Modern Greek Studies	GT52	4FT deg	* g	BBB	Ind	D*^	32	ABBB	Ind	
Computer Studies/Music	GW53	3FT deg	Mu g	AAB-ABB	Ind	D*^	32$	ABBB	Ind	7
Computer Studies/Philosophy	GV57	3FT deg	* g	BBB	Ind	D*^	32	ABBB	Ind	
Computer Studies/Portuguese	GR55	4FT deg	* g	BBB	Ind	D*^	32	ABBB	Ind	
Computer Studies/Russian	GR58	4FT deg	* g	BBB	Ind	D*^	32	ABBB	Ind	
Computer Studies/Theology	GV58	3FT deg	* g	BBB	Ind	D*^	32	ABBB	Ind	
Electronic and Software Engineering (e)	GH76	3FT/4FT deg	M+P	BBB-BCC	2M+4D$	Ind	32$	Ind	Ind	5 10/28
Mathematics and Artificial Intelligence	GG18	3FT deg	M	ABC	Ind	Ind	30	Ind	Ind	17
Mathematics and Computer Science	GG15	3FT deg	M	ACC	Ind	Ind	30	Ind	Ind	10 20/28
Psychology and Artificial Intelligence	CG85	3FT deg	* g	BBB	Ind	Ind	33	Ind	Ind	19 24/28

BLACKBURN COLL

Computing (HND Top-Up)	G500	1FT deg		X	HN $			X		
Computing	005G	2FT HND				P				

BOLTON INST

Accountancy and Business Information Systems	NG45	3FT deg	* g	CD	MO	M*	24	BBCC	Ind	
Accountancy and Computing	GN54	3FT deg	* g	CD	MO	M*	24	BBCC	Ind	
Architectural Tech & Simulation/Virtual Environ	KG27	3FT deg	* g	10	3M	M*	Ind	Ind	Ind	
Art & Design History and Business Info Systems	GV54	3FT deg	* g	CD	MO	M*	24	BBCC	Ind	
Art & Design History and Computing	VG45	3FT deg	* g	CD	MO	M*	24	BBCC	Ind	
Biology and Business Information Systems	GC51	3FT deg	* g	CD	MO	M*	24	BBCC	Ind	
Biology and Computing	CG15	3FT deg	* g	CD	MO	M*	24	BBCC	Ind	
Building Surveying & Simulation/Virtual Environ	KGF7	3FT deg	* g	10	3M	M*	Ind	Ind	Ind	
Business Economics and Business Information Syst	GL51	3FT deg	* g	CD	MO	M*	24	BBCC	Ind	
Business Economics and Computing	GL5C	3FT deg	* g	CD	MO	M*	24	BBCC	Ind	
Business Info Systems and Creative Writing	WG95	3FT deg	* g	CD	MO	M*	24	BBCC	Ind	
Business Info Systems and Environmental Studies	GF59	3FT deg	* g	CD	MO	M*	24	BBCC	Ind	
Business Info Systems and European Cultural St	GT52	3FT deg	* g	CD	MO	M*	24	BBCC	Ind	
Business Info Systems and Film & TV Studies	GW55	3FT deg	Me/T g	CD	Ind	Ind	24	BBCC	Ind	
Business Info Systems and Gender & Women's Studs	GM59	3FT deg	* g	CD	MO	M*	24	BBCC	Ind	
Business Info Systems and History	GVM1	3FT deg	* g	CD	MO	M*	24	BBCC	Ind	
Business Info Systems and Human Resource Mgt	GN5C	3FT deg	* g	CD	MO	M*	24	BBCC	Ind	

| course details | | | 98 expected requirements | | | | | | | 96 entry stats |

TITLE	CODE	COURSE	SUBJECTS	A/AS	ND/C	AGNVQ	IB	SQA(H)	SQA	RATIO A/AS
Business Info Systems and Literature	GQ5F	3FT deg	* g	CD	MO	M*	24	BBCC	Ind	
Business Info Systems and Mathematics	GG51	3FT deg	M g	DD	Ind	Ind	24	BBCC	Ind	
Business Info Systems and Peace & War Studies	GVMC	3FT deg	* g	CD	MO	M*	24	BBCC	Ind	
Business Info Systems and Urban & Cultural St	GL5J	3FT deg	* g	CD	MO	M*	24	BBCC	Ind	
Business Info Systs & Organisations, Mgt & Work	GN57	3FT deg	* g	CD	MO	M*	24	BBCC	Ind	
Business Information Systems	G520	3FT deg	* g	CD	10-12M	M*	24	BBCC	Ind	
Business Information Systems and Community Studs	GL75	3FT deg	* g	CD	MO	M*	24	BBCC	Ind	
Business Information Systems and French	GR5C	3FT deg	F g	CD	Ind	Ind	24	BBCC	Ind	
Business Information Systems and German	GR5F	3FT deg	G g	CD	Ind	Ind	24	BBCC	Ind	
Business Information Systems and Law	GM5H	3FT deg	* g	CD	MO	M*	24	BBCC	Ind	
Business Information Systems and Leisure Studies	GLMH	3FT deg	* g	CD	MO	M*	24	BBCC	Ind	
Business Information Systems and Marketing	GN55	3FT deg	* g	CD	MO	M*	24	BBCC	Ind	
Business Information Systems and Operations Mgt	GN52	3FT deg	* g	CD	MO	M*	24	BBCC	Ind	
Business Information Systems and Philosophy	GV5R	3FT deg	* g	CD	MO	M*	24	BBCC	Ind	
Business Information Systems and Psychology	GL5R	3FT deg	* g	12	MO	D*	24	BBCC	Ind	
Business Information Systems and Sociology	LG35	3FT deg	* g	CD	MO	M	24	Ind	Ind	
Business Information Systems and Statistics	GG54	3FT deg	* g	CD	MO	M	24	Ind	Ind	
Business Information Systems and Textiles	GJ54	3FT deg	* g	CD	MO	M*	24	BBCC	Ind	
Business Information Systems and Theatre Studies	GW54	3FT deg	Me/T g	CD	Ind	Ind	24	BBCC	Ind	
Business Information Systems and Tourism Studies	GP5R	3FT deg	* g	CD	MO	M*	24	BBCC	Ind	
Business Studies and Computing	GN51	3FT deg	* g	CD	MO	M*	24	BBCC	Ind	
Civil Engineering and Simulation/Virtual Environ	HG27	3FT deg	M/S g	10	3M	M$	Ind	Ind	Ind	
Community Studies and Computing	LG55	3FT deg	* g	CD	MO	M*	24	BBCC	Ind	
Computing	G500	3FT deg	* g	CD	MO	M*	24	BBCC	Ind	
Computing Studies and Human Resource Management	GN5D	3FT deg	* g	CD	MO	M*	24	BBCC	Ind	
Computing and Creative Writing	GW5X	3FT deg	* g	CD	MO	M*	24	BBCC	Ind	
Computing and Electronics	GH5P	3FT deg	M/S g	10	3M	M$	Ind	Ind	Ind	
Computing and Environmental Studies	FG95	3FT deg	* g	CD	MO	M*	24	BBCC	Ind	
Computing and European Cultural Studies	GLM3	3FT deg	* g	CD	MO	M*	24	BBCC	Ind	
Computing and Film & TV Studies	GW5M	3FT deg	Me/T g	CD	Ind	Ind	24	BBCC	Ind	
Computing and French	GR51	3FT deg	F g	CD	Ind	Ind	24	BBCC	Ind	
Computing and Gender & Women's Studies	LG65	3FT deg	* g	CD	MO	M*	24	BBCC	Ind	
Computing and German	GR52	3FT deg	G g	CD	Ind	Ind	24	BBCC	Ind	
Computing and History	GV5C	3FT deg	* g	CD	MO	M*	24	BBCC	Ind	
Computing and Human Resource Management	GN5T	3FT deg	* g	CD	MO	M*	24	BBCC	Ind	
Computing and Law	GM53	3FT deg	* g	CD	MO	M*	24	BBCC	Ind	
Computing and Leisure Studies	GL5H	3FT deg	* g	CD	MO	M*	24	BBCC	Ind	
Computing and Literature	GQ52	3FT deg	* g	CD	MO	M*	24	BBCC	Ind	
Computing and Manufacturing Systems	GH57	3FT deg	* g	10	3M	M$	Ind	Ind	Ind	
Computing and Marketing	GN5M	3FT deg	* g	CD	MO	M*	24	BBCC	Ind	
Computing and Mathematics	GG15	3FT deg	M g	DD	Ind	Ind	24	BBCC	Ind	
Computing and Motor Vehicle Studies	GH5J	3FT deg	M/S g	10	3M	M$	Ind	Ind	Ind	
Computing and Operations Management	GN5F	3FT deg	* g	CD	MO	M*	24	BBCC	Ind	
Computing and Organisations, Management & Work	GN5R	3FT deg	* g	CD	MO	M*	24	BBCC	Ind	
Computing and Peace & War Studies	GV5D	3FT deg	* g	CD	MO	M*	24	BBCC	Ind	
Computing and Philosophy	GV57	3FT deg	* g	CD	MO	M*	24	BBCC	Ind	
Computing and Psychology	GL57	3FT deg	* g	12	MO	D*	24	BBCC	Ind	
Computing and Simulation/Virtual Environment	GG57	3FT deg								
Computing and Sociology	LG3M	3FT deg	* g	CD	MO	M	24	Ind	Ind	
Computing and Statistics	GG5K	3FT deg	* g	CD	MO	M	24	Ind	Ind	
Computing and Theatre Studies	WG45	3FT deg	Me/T g	CD	Ind	Ind	24	BBCC	Ind	
Computing and Tourism Studies	GP57	3FT deg	* g	CD	MO	M*	24	BBCC	Ind	

| | | | 98 expected requirements | | | | | | | 96 entry stats | |
| | | | | | | | | | | | |

TITLE	CODE	COURSE	SUBJECTS	A/AS	NO/C	AGNVQ	IB	SQA(H)	SQA	RATIO	A/AS
Computing and Urban and Cultural Studies	GL53	3FT deg	* g	CD	MO	M*	24	BBCC	Ind		
Construction and Simulation/Virtual Environment	KGG7	3FT deg	* g	10	3M	M*	Ind	Ind	Ind		
Creative Writing and Mathematics	GW5Y	3FT deg	* g	CD	MO	M*	24	BBCC	Ind		
Design and Business Information Systems	GW52	3FT deg	* g	CD	MO	M*	24	BBCC	Ind		
Design and Computing	GW5F	3FT deg	* g	CD	MO	M*	24	BBCC	Ind		
Design and Simulation/Virtual Environment	GW72	3FT deg	* g	10	MO	M*	Ind	Ind	Ind		
Electronic and Computer Engineering	GH6Q	4FT deg	M/S	4	N	P$	Ind	Ind	Ind		
Electronic and Computer Engineering	GH66	3FT deg	M+S	12	4M	M$	Ind	Ind	Ind		
Electronic and Computer Engineering (MEng)	HG6Q	4FT deg	M+S	18	3M+1D	M3$	Ind	Ind	Ind		
Electronics and Computer Engineering (Found)	GH6P	4FT/5FT deg		Ind	Ind	Ind	Ind	Ind			
Electronics and Leisure Computing Technology	HG67	4FT deg	* g	4	N	P*	Ind	Ind	Ind		
Electronics and Simulation/Virtual Environment	HGP7	3FT deg	M/S	10	3M	M$	Ind	Ind	Ind		
French and Simulation/Virtual Environment	RG17	3FT deg	F g	10	3M	Ind	Ind	Ind	Ind		
German and Simulation/Virtual Environment	RG27	3FT deg	G g	10	3M	Ind	Ind	Ind	Ind		
Leisure Computing Technology	G710	3FT deg	* g	10	3M	M*	Ind	Ind	Ind		
Man Systs Design & Simulation/Virtual Environ	HG77	3FT deg	M/S g	10	3M	M$	Ind	Ind	Ind		
Man Systs Design & Simulation/Virtual Environ	HGRT	4FT deg	M/S g	4	N	P$	Ind	Ind	Ind		
Motor Vehicle St and Simulation/Virtual Environ	HGJ7	3FT deg									
Product Des/Simulation & Virtual Environ (Found)	HG7R	4FT/5FT deg		Ind	Ind	Ind	Ind	Ind			
Product Design and Simulation/Virtual Environ	HGTT	4FT deg	M/S/Ad/Ds	4	N	P$	Ind	Ind	Ind		
Product Design and Simulation/Virtual Environ	HGT7	3FT deg	M/S/Ad/Ds	10	3M	M$	Ind	Ind	Ind		
Simulation/Virtual Environ and Technology Mgt	GN79	3FT deg	M/S/Bu	10	3M	M$	Ind	Ind	Ind		
Simulation/Virtual Environment and Technol Mgt	GN7X	4FT deg	M/S/Bu	4	N	P$	Ind	Ind	Ind		
Simulation/Virtual Environment and Textiles	GJ74	3FT deg	M/S	10	3M	M$	Ind	Ind	Ind		
Simulation/Virtual Environment and Transport St	GJ79	3FT deg	M/S	10	3M	M$	Ind	Ind	Ind		
Visual Arts and Business Information Systems	GW51	3FT deg	* g	CD	MO	M*	24	BBCC	Ind		
Visual Arts and Computing	GW5C	3FT deg	* g	CD	MO	M*	24	BBCC	Ind		
Business Information Technology	065G	2FT HND	* g	2	N	P	Dip	Ind	N		
Computing	105G	2FT HND	* g	E	N	P	Dip	Ind	N		

BOURNEMOUTH Univ

TITLE	CODE	COURSE	SUBJECTS	A/AS	NO/C	AGNVQ	IB	SQA(H)	SQA	RATIO	A/AS
Business Decision Computing	G522	4SW deg									
Business Information Systems (HND top-up)	G521	1FT deg									
Business Information Technology	G560	3FT deg	* g	10-12	MO $	M$ go	Ind	Ind	Ind	3	8/18
Computing	G710	4SW deg									
Information Systems Management	G520	4SW deg	* g	12	MO	M$ go	28	BBBB	Ind	2	9/18
Software Engineering Management	G700	4SW deg	* g	10	MO	M$ go	Ind	CCCC	Ind	2	8/20
Business Information Technology	265G▼	2FT HND	* g	6	3M	P$ go	Ind	Ind	Ind	3	2/12

Univ of BRADFORD

TITLE	CODE	COURSE	SUBJECTS	A/AS	NO/C	AGNVQ	IB	SQA(H)	SQA	RATIO	A/AS
Computer Science	G501	4SW deg	* g	18	3M+1D	D$4/^	Ind	Ind	Ind	6	6/18
Computer Science	G500	3FT deg	* g	18	3M+1D	D$4/^	Ind	Ind	Ind	5	10/14
Computing and Information Systems	G520	3FT deg	* g	18	3M+1D	D$4/^	Ind	Ind	Ind	10	
Computing and Information Systems	G521	4SW deg	* g	18	3M+1D	D$4/^	Ind	Ind	Ind	14	
Computing with Management	G5N1	3FT deg	* g	22	3M+2D	D$4/^	Ind	Ind	Ind	6	
Computing with Management	G5NC	4SW deg	* g	22	3M+2D	D$4/^	Ind	Ind	Ind	5	12/20
Health Informatics	G580	3FT deg	* g	18	3M+1D	D$4/^	Ind	Ind	Ind		
Health Informatics	G581	4SW deg	* g	18	3M+1D	D$4/^	Ind	Ind	Ind		
Multimedia Computing	G540	3FT deg	* g	18	3M+1D	D$4/^	Ind	Ind	Ind		
Multimedia Computing	G541	4SW deg	* g	18	3M+1D	D$4/^	Ind	Ind	Ind		
Networks Information Management	G531	4SW deg	* g	18	3M+1D	D$4/^	Ind	Ind	Ind		
Networks Information Management	G530	3FT deg	* g	18	3M+1D	D$4/^	Ind	Ind	Ind		
Software Engineering (MEng)	G700	4SW deg	* g	22	3M+2D	DS4/^	Ind	Ind	Ind	6	8/20

course details			98 expected requirements							96 entry stats	
TITLE	CODE	COURSE	SUBJECTS	A/AS	ND/C	RGNVQ	IB	SQA(H)	SQA	RATIO	A/AS
BRADFORD & ILKLEY Comm COLL											
Office Systems Management	N1G7	3FT deg	g	8	MO	M	Ind	Ind			
Software Engineering	007G	2FT HND	* g	2	N $	P		Ind	Ind		
Univ of BRIGHTON											
Biology and Computing	CG15	3FT/4SW deg	S g	12	MO $	M$	Dip$	BBCC$	Ind		
Chemistry and Computing	FG15	3FT/4SW deg	S g	12	MO $	M$	Dip$	BBCC$	Ind		
Computer Science (4-year sandwich)	G501	4SW deg	S g	16	DO	D$	Dip$	BBBC$	Ind		
Computer Studies	G500	3FT/4SW deg	* g	16	DO	D	Dip	BBBC	Ind		
Computing and Geography	GF58	3FT/4SW deg	S g	12	MO $	M$	Dip$	BBCC$	Ind		
Computing and Information Systs(4-year sandwich)	G560	4SW deg	* g	16	DO	D	Dip	BBBC	Ind		
Computing and Mathematics	GG51	3FT/4SW deg	M g	12	MO $	M$	Dip$	BBCC$	Ind		
Computing and Operational Research	GN52	3FT/4SW deg	M g	12	MO $	M$	Dip$	BBCC$	Ind		
Computing and Physics	GF53	3FT/4SW deg	S g	12	MO $	M$	Dip$	BBCC$	Ind		
Computing and Statistics	GG54	3FT/4SW deg	S g	12	MO $	M$	Dip$	BBCC$	Ind		
Electronic & Computer Engineering(Dip/BEng/MEng)	HG66	3FT/4SW 4FT/5SW deg	M+P/S/Ds	18	5M $	M$^	25$	BBCC$	Ind		
Software Engineering	G700	4SW deg	S g	16	DO $	D$	Dip$	BBBC$	Ind		
Computing (Information Systems)	025G▼	2FT HND	* g	4	MO	M	24	CC	Ind		
Computing (Real Time Systems)	005G▼	2FT HND	* g	4	MO	M	24	CC	Ind		
Computing (Software Engineering)	007G▼	2FT HND	* g	4	MO	M	24	CC	Ind		
Univ of BRISTOL											
Computer Science	G500	3FT deg	M	BBB-ABC	HN $	D$^	32$	CSYS	HN$	12	20/30
Computer Science (MEng)	G503	4FT deg	M	BBB-ABC	HN $	D$^	32$	CSYS	HN$	6	18/30
Computer Science and French	RG15	4FT deg	F g	BBC	Ind	D$^	30$	CSYS	Ind	13	
Computer Science and German	RG25	4FT deg	G g	BBB	Ind	D$^	30$	CSYS			
Computer Science and Italian	RG35	4FT deg	* g	BBC	Ind	D$^	30$	CSYS	Ind		
Computer Science and Russian	RG85	4FT deg	* g	BBC-BBD	Ind	D$^	30$	CSYS	Ind	2	
Computer Science and Spanish	RG45	4FT deg	* g	BBB-BBC	Ind	D$^	30$	CSYS	Ind		
Computer Science with Mathematics	G5G1	3FT deg	M	ABB	HN $	D$^	32$	CSYS	HN$	12	20/24
Computer Science with St in Cont Europe (MEng)	G501	4FT deg	M g	BBB-ABC	HN $	D$^	32$	CSYS	HN$	4	
BRISTOL, Univ of the W of England											
Biology and Information Technology in Science	CG15	3FT/4SW deg	B+C g	8	3M $	PS go	24$	CCC$	Ind		
Business Decision Analysis	G520	3FT/4SW deg	* g	14	3M $	M$ go	24$	BCCC$	Ind		
Business Information Systems	G562	4SW deg	* g	14	MO$	M$ go	24	BCCC	Ind		
Chemistry and Information Technology in Science	FG15	3FT/4SW deg	C g	6	N $	PS go	24$	CC$	N$		
Computer Science	G500	4SW deg	Cs/M/S g	14	MO	M$^ go	24	BCCC	N$		
Computing	G501	4SW deg	* g	14	MO	M$ go	24	BCCC	Ind		
Computing and Information Systems	GG65	4SW deg	* g	14	MO	M$ go	24	BCCC	Ind		
Computing for Real Time Systems	GG67	4SW deg	M/Cs/S g	14	MO $	M$ go	24$	BCCC$	N$		
Computing for Real Time Systems (Foundation)	GG6R▼	4EXT/5EXTSW deg	S g	2	N $	P$ go	24	CD	Ind		
EFL and Information Systems	QG35	3FT deg	g	14-22	5M	M*^ go	24$	BCCC$	Ind		
Environmental Sci and Information Tech in Sci	FG95	3FT/4SW deg	S g	6	N $	PS go	24$	CC$	Ind		
French and Information Systems	RG15	3FT deg	F g	14-22	5M	M*^ go	24$	BCCC$	Ind		
German and Information Systems	RG25	3FT deg	G g	14-22	5M	M*^ go	24$	BCCC$	Ind		
Information Systems and Social Science	G5L3	3FT deg	* g	14-16	5M-6M	M* go	24	BCCC	Ind		
Information Systems, EFL and French	G5Q3	3FT deg	g	14-22	5M	M*^ go	24$	BCCC$	Ind		
Information Systems, EFL and German	G5QH	3FT deg	g	14-22	5M	M*^ go	24$	BCCC$	Ind		
Information Systems, EFL and Spanish	G5QJ	3FT deg	g	14-22	5M	M*^ go	24$	BCCC$	Ind		
Information Systems, French and German	G5T9	3FT deg	F/G g	14-22	5M	M*^ go	24$	BCCC$	Ind		
Information Systems, French and Spanish	G5TX	3FT deg	F/Sp g	14-22	5M	M*^ go	24$	BCCC$	Ind		
Information Systems, German and Spanish	G5TY	3FT deg	G/Sp g	14-22	5M	M*^ go	24$	BCCC$	Ind		
Mathematics and Computing	GG15	3FT/4SW deg	M g	14	MO $	M$^ go	24$	BCCC$	N$		

Computer Sciences and Engineering · 15

TITLE	CODE	COURSE	SUBJECTS	A/AS	ND/C	RGNVQ	IB	SQA(H)	SQA	RATIO A/AS
Psychology and Information Technology in Science	CG85	3FT/4SW deg	S g	6	N $	PS go	24$	CC$	Ind	
Software Engineering	G700	4SW deg	Cs/M/S g	14	MO	M* go	24$	BCCC$	N$	
Spanish and Information Systems	RG45	3FT deg	Sp g	14-22	5M	M*^ go	24$	BCCC$	Ind	
Statistics and Computing	G4GM	3FT/4SW deg	M/St g	14	3M $	M*^ go	24$	BCCC$	N$	
Statistics and Information Systems	GG45	3FT/4SW deg	M/St g	14	MO	M*^ go	24$	BCCC$	N$	
Systems Analysis	G710	4SW deg	* g	14	MO	M* go	24	BCCC	Ind	
Business Decision Analysis	025G	2FT HND	* g	6	3M $	P$ go	24$	CC$	Ind	
Computing	105G	2FT HND	* g	6	3M	P$ go	24	CC	N$	
Computing Studies (Bridgwater College)	005G▼	2FT HND	* g	4	2M	P*6/^ go	24	CC	N$	
Information Systems	125G	2FT HND	* g	6	3M	P$ go	24	CC	Ind	
BRUNEL Univ, West London										
Computer Science	G502	3FT deg	S/M g	BBB-BCC	MO+3D$	D$4/^ go	30	BBBCC$	Ind	7 12/26
Computer Science (4 Yrs Thick SW)	G507	4SW deg	S/M g	BBB-BCC	MO+3D$	D$4/^ go	30	BBBCC$	Ind	7 18/24
Computer Science (4 Yrs Thin SW)	G500	4SW deg	S/M g	BBB-BCC	MO+3D$	D$4/^ go	30	BBBCC$	Ind	5 12/22
Computer Studies/Accounting	G5N4	3FT deg	* g	16	MO $	M go	26$	BCCC$	Ind	
Computer Studies/Business Studies	N1G5	3FT deg	Ec g	18	MO $	M go	26$	BCCC$	Ind	5
Computing in Business	G523	3FT deg	* g	BBB-BCC	MO+3D$	D$4/^ go	30	BBBCC	Ind	11
Computing in Business (4 Yrs Thick SW)	G524	4SW deg	* g	BBB-BCC	MO+3D$	D$4/^ go	30	BBBCC	Ind	7 14/18
Computing in Business (4 Yrs Thin SW)	G522	4SW deg	* g	BBB-BCC	MO+3D$	D$4/^ go	30	BBBCC	Ind	7
Health Information Science	L4G5	3FT deg	B	12-20	Ind	MG	Ind	Ind	Ind	
Leisure Management/Computer Studies	N7G5	3FT deg	* g	18	MO $	M* go	26$	BCCC$	Ind	
Mathematics with Computer Sci (4 Yrs Thick SW)	G1GN	4SW deg	M	BBC-BCC	3M+2D$	P^	29$	BBBC$	Ind	11
Mathematics with Computer Sci (4 Yrs Thin SW)	G1G5	4SW deg	M	BBC-BCC	3M+2D$	P^	29$	BBBC$	Ind	6
Mathematics with Computer Science	G1GM	3FT deg	M	BBC-BCC	3M+2D$	P^	29$	BBBC$	Ind	9
Physics with Computer Science	F3GM	3FT deg	P+M	CC	3M $	Ind^	26$	CCCCC	Ind	12
Physics with Computer Science (4 Yrs Thick SW)	F3GN	4SW deg	P+M	CC	3M $	Ind^	26$	CCCCC	Ind	3
Physics with Computer Science (4 Yrs Thin SW)	F3G5	4SW deg	P+M	CC	3M $	Ind^	26$	CCCCC$	Ind	3
Sport Sciences/Computer Studies	B6GM	3FT deg	* g	18	1M+3D	D	29	BBCC	Ind	
Business Information Technology	265G	2FT HND	Bu/Cs g	6	MO $	MB go	26$	CCCC	Ind	6
Computing (Information Systems for Business)	105G	2FT HND	* g	6	MO $	P go	20$	BCCC$	Ind	
Computing (Multi-Media Production)	45PG	2FT HND	* g	6	MO $	P go	24$	BCCC$	Ind	
Univ of BUCKINGHAM										
Business Studies with Information Systems	N1G5	2FT deg	* g	14	3M+2D	M	26	BCCC		
Information Systems	G500	2FT deg	* g	12	5M	M	24	CCCC	Ind	
Information Systems with Accounting	G5N4	2FT deg	* g	12	3M+2D	M	24	CCCC	Ind	
Information Systems with Business Studies	G5N1	2FT deg	* g	12	5M	M	24	CCCC	Ind	
Information Systems with Economics	G5L1	2FT deg	* g	12	5M	M	24	CCCC	Ind	
Information Systems with Operations Management	G5N2	2FT deg	* g	12	5M	M	24	BCCC	Ind	
Psychology with Information Systems	C8G5	2FT deg	* g	14	5M	M	24	CCCC	Ind	
BUCKINGHAMSHIRE COLLEGE										
Business Information Tech with Image Processing	G7W2	3FT deg		8-10	MO	M	Ind	CCC	Ind	
Business Information Technology	G720	3FT deg		8-10	MO	M	Ind	CCC	Ind	
Business Information Technology (Conv to Deg)	G721	1FT/2FT deg			HN					
Business Information Technology with Management	G7N1	3FT deg								
Business Information Technology with Marketing	G7N5	3FT deg		8-10	MO	M	Ind	CCC	Ind	
Business Information Technology with Multimedia	G7P4	3FT deg		8-10	MO	M	Ind	CCC	Ind	
Computer Engineering	G501	3FT deg		8-10	MO	M	Ind	CCC	Ind	2
Computer Engineering (Conv to Degree)	G502	1FT/2FT deg			HN					
Computer Engineering with Image Processing	G5W2	3FT deg		8-10	MO	M	Ind	CCC	Ind	
Computer Engineering with Management	G5N1	3FT deg		8-10	MO	M	Ind	CCC	Ind	
Computer Engineering with Marketing	G5N5	3FT deg		8-10	MO	M	Ind	CCC	Ind	

| | | | 98 expected requirements | | | | | | | 96 entry stats |

TITLE	CODE	COURSE	SUBJECTS	A/AS	ND/C	RGNVQ	IB	SQA(H)	SQA	RATIO A/AS
Computer Engineering with Multimedia	G6P4	3FT deg		8-10	MO	M	Ind	CCC	Ind	
Computing	G500	3FT deg		8-10	MO	M	Ind	CCC	Ind	
Computing (Conversion to degree)	G503	1FT/2FT deg			HN				HN	
Computing with Image Processing	G5WF	3FT deg		8-10	MO	M	Ind	CCC	Ind	
Computing with Management	G5NC	3FT deg		8-10	MO	M	Ind	CCC	Ind	
Computing with Marketing	G5NM	3FT deg		8-10	MO	M	Ind	CCC	Ind	
Computing with Multimedia	G5P4	3FT deg		8-10	MO	M	Ind	CCC	Ind	
Business Information Technology	027G	2FT HND		4	N	P	Ind	CC	Ind	
Computing	105G	2FT HND		4	N	P	Ind	CC	Ind	6

CAMBRIDGE Univ

TITLE	CODE	COURSE	SUBJECTS	A/AS	ND/C	RGNVQ	IB	SQA(H)	SQA	RATIO A/AS
Computer Science	G500▼	3FT deg	M g	AAA-AAB Ind			Ind	CSYS	Ind	4 28/30

CANTERBURY CHRIST CHURCH COLL of HE

TITLE	CODE	COURSE	SUBJECTS	A/AS	ND/C	RGNVQ	IB	SQA(H)	SQA	RATIO A/AS
American Studies with Information Technology	Q4G5	4FT deg	* g	CC	MO	M	24	Ind	Ind	
Art with Information Technology	W1G5	3FT deg	A g	CC	MO	M	24	Ind	Ind	10
Business Information Technology	GN51	2FT Dip	* g	CC	MO	M	24	Ind	Ind	1
Business Information Technology	G520	3FT deg	* g	CC	MO	M	24	Ind	Ind	3
Business Studies with Information Technology	N1G5	3FT deg	* g	CC	MO	M	24	Ind	Ind	4 6/16
Early Childhood Studies with Info Technology	X9G5	3FT deg	* g	CC	MO	M	24	Ind	Ind	1
English with Information Technology	Q3G5	3FT deg	E g	CC	MO	M	24	Ind	Ind	5
Geography with Information Technology	L8G5	3FT deg	Gy g	CC	MO	M	24	Ind	Ind	14
History with Information Technology	V1G5	3FT deg	H g	CC	MO	M	24	Ind	Ind	2
Information Technology and American Studies	GQ54	3FT deg	* g	CC	MO	M	24	Ind	Ind	
Information Technology and Art	WG15	3FT deg	A g	CC	MO	M	24	Ind	Ind	
Information Technology and Business Studies	NG15	3FT deg	* g	CC	MO	M	24	Ind	Ind	7
Information Technology and Early Childhood Studs	XG95	3FT deg	* g	CC	MO	M	24	Ind	Ind	
Information Technology and English	QG35	3FT deg	E g	CC	MO	M	24	Ind	Ind	
Information Technology and French	GR51	3FT deg	F g	CC	MO	M	24	Ind	Ind	
Information Technology and Geography	GL58	3FT deg	Gy g	CC	MO	M	24	Ind	Ind	2
Information Technology and History	VG15	3FT deg	H g	CC	MO	M	24	Ind	Ind	
Information Technology and Social Science	GL53	3FT deg	* g	CC	MO	M	24	Ind	Ind	
Information Technology with American Studies	G5Q4	3FT deg	* g	CC	MO	M	24	Ind	Ind	
Information Technology with Art	G5W1	3FT deg	A g	CC	MO	M	24	Ind	Ind	
Information Technology with Business Studies	G5N1	3FT deg	* g	CC	MO	M	24	Ind	Ind	3
Information Technology with Early Childhood St	G5X9	3FT deg	* g	CC	MO	M	24	Ind	Ind	
Information Technology with English	G5Q3	3FT deg	E g	CC	MO	M	24	Ind	Ind	
Information Technology with French	G5R1	3FT deg	F g	CC	MO	M	24	Ind	Ind	
Information Technology with Geography	G5L8	3FT deg	Gy g	CC	MO	M	24	Ind	Ind	
Information Technology with History	G5V1	3FT deg	H g	CC	MO	M	24	Ind	Ind	
Information Technology with Marketing	G5N5	3FT deg	* g	CC	MO	M	24	Ind	Ind	
Information Technology with Mathematics	G5G1	3FT deg	M g	DD	Ind	Ind	24	Ind	Ind	2
Information Technology with Media Studies	G5P4	3FT deg	* g	CC	MO	M	24	Ind	Ind	
Information Technology with Music	G5W3	3FT deg	Mu g	CC	MO	M	24	Ind	Ind	
Information Technology with Religious Studies	G5V8	3FT deg	* g	CC	MO	M	24	Ind	Ind	
Information Technology with Science	G5Y1	3FT deg	S g	DD	Ind	Ind	24	Ind	Ind	
Information Technology with Social Science	G5L3	3FT deg	* g	CC	MO	M	24	Ind	Ind	
Information Technology with Statistics	G5G4	3FT deg	M g	DD	Ind	Ind	24	Ind	Ind	
Information Technology with Tourism Studies	G5P7	3FT deg	* g	CC	MO	M	24	Ind	Ind	2
Marketing and Information Technology	GN55	3FT deg	* g	CC	MO	M	24	Ind	Ind	
Marketing with Information Technology	N5G5	3FT deg	* g	CC	MO	M	24	Ind	Ind	3
Mathematics and Information Technology	GG15	3FT deg	M g	DD	Ind	Ind	24	Ind	Ind	1
Mathematics with Information Technology	G1G5	3FT deg	M g	DD	Ind	Ind	24	Ind	Ind	11

	course details			98 expected requirements						96 entry stats	
TITLE	CODE	COURSE	SUBJECTS	A/AS	NO/C	AGNVQ	IB	SQA(H)	SQA	RATIO	A/AS
Media Studies and Information Technology	GP54	3FT deg	* g	CC	MO	M	24	Ind	Ind		
Media Studies with Information Technology	P4G5	3FT deg	* g	CC	MO	M	24	Ind	Ind		
Music and Information Technology	WG35	3FT deg	Mu g	CC	MO	M	24	Ind	Ind		
Music with Information Technology	W3G5	3FT deg	Mu g	CC	MO	M	24	Ind	Ind		
Religious Studies and Information Technology	GV58	3FT deg	* g	CC	MO	M	24	Ind	Ind		
Religious Studies with Information Technology	V8G5	3FT deg	* g	CC	MO	M	24	Ind	Ind		
Science and Information Technology	GY51	3FT deg	S g	DD	Ind	Ind	24	Ind	Ind		
Science with Information Technology	Y1G5	3FT deg	S g	DD	Ind	Ind	24	Ind	Ind	6	
Social Science with Information Technology	L3G5	3FT deg	* g	CC	MO	M	24	Ind	Ind	1	
Statistics and Information Technology	GG45	3FT deg	M g	DD	Ind	Ind	24	Ind	Ind		
Statistics with Information Technology	G4G5	3FT deg	M g	DD	Ind	Ind	24	Ind	Ind		
Tourism Studies and Information Technology	GP57	3FT deg	* g	CC	MO	M	24	Ind	Ind	1	
Tourism Studies with Information Technology	P7G5	3FT deg	* g	CC	MO	M	24	Ind	Ind		
Software Engineering	007G	2FT HND	* g	D	Ind	Ind	24	Ind	Ind	2	

CARDIFF Univ of Wales

Computer Science	G500	3FT deg	*	20-22	MO+2D	Ind	Ind	AABBB		4	12/26
Computer Systems	GH56	3FT deg	M	18-20	MO+2D		Ind	AABBB		39	
Computer Systems	HG66	3FT deg	M	18-24	5M $		28$	BBBC	Ind	5	14/16
Computing and Physics	FG35	3FT deg	P+M	CCC	Ind		Ind	Ind	Ind	5	
Pure Mathematics/Computing	GG15	3FT deg	M	BCC	3M+2D$	Ind	Ind	AABB	Ind	17	

Univ of Wales INST, CARDIFF

Business Information Systems	G561	3FT deg	* g	10	MO	MI go	Ind	CCCC	Ind	3	6/13
Business Information	027G	2FT HND	* g	2	3M	M$ gi	Ind	CC	Ind		
Computing	105G	2FT HND	* g	2	3M	M$ gi	Ind	CC	Ind	3	2/ 6

Univ of CENTRAL ENGLAND

Business Information Studies	G523	3FT deg	* g	12	MO	M	24	Ind		2	6/10
Business Information Technology	G720	3FT deg	* g	12	MO		Ind	Ind	Ind		
Business Systems Eng with French Found Yr	G5RC▼ 4FT/5SW deg		*	2	N	P*	Ind	CC	Ind		
Business Systems Eng with German Found Yr	G5RF▼ 4FT/5SW deg		*	2	N	P*	Ind	CC	Ind	2	
Business Systems Engineering	G522	3FT/4SW deg	* g	12	3M	M* go	24	CCC	Ind	2	
Business Systems Engineering Foundation Year	G528▼ 4FT/5SW deg		*	2	N	P*	Ind	CC	Ind		
Business Systems Engineering with French	G5R1	3FT/4SW deg	* g	12	3M	M* go	24	CCC	Ind	1	
Business Systems Engineering with German	G5R2	3FT/4SW deg	* g	12	3M	M* go	24	CCC	Ind		
Computing	G500	3FT deg	* g	12	MO		Ind	Ind	Ind	7	10/18
Industrial Information Technology	G560	3FT/4SW deg	* g	12	3M	M* go	24	CCC	Ind	1	
Industrial Information Technology Foundation Yr	G568▼ 4FT/5SW deg		*	2	N	P*	Ind	CC	Ind	1	
Information Systems	G520	3FT deg	Mu g	12	MO		Ind	Ind	Ind	6	
Software Design for Engineering Systems	G701	3FT/4SW deg	M g	12	3M $	ME1	24$	CCC$	Ind		
Software Design for Engineering Systems Found Yr	G709▼ 4FT/5SW deg		* g	2	N	P*	Ind	CC	Ind	2	
Software Engineering	G700	3FT deg	* g	12	MO		Ind	Ind	Ind	14	
Software Engineering Foundation Year	G708▼ 4EXT deg		*	2	N		Ind	Ind	Ind	3	
Business Information Technology	027G▼ 2FT HND		* g	4	N		Ind	Ind	Ind		
Computer Studies	205G▼ 2FT HND		* g	4	N		Ind	Ind	Ind		
Computing	005G▼ 2FT HND		* g	4	N		Ind	Ind	Ind	3	
Engineering - Software Development	007G	2FT/3SW HND	M/P	2	$	PE1	24	CC$	Ind		
Industrial Information Technology	065G	2FT/3SW HND	*	2	N	P*	24	CC	Ind		
Software Engineering	107G	2FT HND	* g	4	N		Ind	Ind	Ind		

Univ of CENTRAL LANCASHIRE

Business Computing	GN51	3FT deg	*	12	MO	D*6/^	26	BCCC	Ind		
Business Information Technology	G5N1	4SW deg	* g	12	MO+2D	M$	26	BCCC	Ind		

			98 expected requirements							96 entry stats	
course details											
TITLE	CODE	COURSE	SUBJECTS	A/AS	NO/C	AGNVQ	IB	SQA(H)	SQA	RATIO	A/AS
Computing	G500	3FT/4SW deg	* g	12	MO	D*6/^	26	BCCC	Ind	8	12/14
Software Engineering	G700	3FT/4SW deg	* g	12	MO	D$6	26	BCCC	Ind	5	8/20
Combined Honours Programme _Computing_	Y400	3FT deg	* g	14	MO	M$6/^	26	BCCC	Ind		
Business Information Technology	265G	2FT HND	*	6	3M	M*	24	CC	Ind	3	3/ 7
Business with Information Management	15NG	2FT HND	* g	8	MO	M$	24	CCC	Ind		
Computing	205G	2FT HND	* g	4	2M	M*	Ind	CC	Ind	2	2/ 8
Software Engineering	007G	2FT HND	Cs	4	2M	M$	Ind	CC	Ind	9	

CHELTENHAM & GLOUCESTER COLL of HE

Business Computer Systems & Business Inform Tech	GNNC	3FT deg	*	8	MO	M	24	CCCC	Ind		
Business Computer Systems and Business Mgt	NG15	3FT deg	*	12	5M+2D	MB3	24	CCCC	Ind		
Business Computer Systems and Computing	GN5C	3FT deg	*	8	MO	M	24	CCCC	Ind		
Business Computer Systems and Environmental Pol	GF59	3FT deg	*	8-12	MO	M	24	CCCC	Ind		
Business Computer Systems and Financial Mgt	GNMH	3FT deg	*	8-12	MO	M	26	CCCC	Ind		
Business Computer Systems and Financial Ser Mgt	NG35	3FT deg	*	8-12	MO	M	24	CCCC	Ind		
Business Computer Systems and Geography	GL5V	3FT deg	*	12	MO	M	24	CCCC	Ind		
Business Computer Systems and Geology	GF5P	3FT deg	S	8	MO	M	26	CCCC	Ind		
Business Computer Systems and Hotel Management	GN5R	3FT deg	*	8-12	MO	M	24	CCCC	Ind		
Business Computer Systems and Human Resource Mgt	GNND	3FT deg	*	8-12	MO	M	26	CCCC	Ind		
Business Computer Systems and Leisure Mgt	GN57	3FT deg	*	8-12	5M+2D	ML3	24	CCCC	Ind		
Business Computer Systems and Marketing Mgt	GNN5	3FT deg	*	8-12	MO	MB3	26	CCCC	Ind		
Business Computer Systems and Media Communicat	GP54	3FT deg	*	8-12	MO	M	24	CCCC	Ind		
Business Computer Systems and Multimedia	G520	3FT deg	*	8	MO	M	24	CCCC	Ind		
Business Computer Systems and Physical Geography	FG8M	3FT deg	*	8-12	MO	M	26	CCCC	Ind		
Business Computer Systems and Religious Studies	VG85	3FT deg	*	8	MO	M	24	CCCC	Ind		
Business Computer Systems and Women's Studies	GM5X	3FT deg	*	8-12	MO	M	24	CCCC	Ind		
Business Computer Systems with Busin Info Tech	G525	3FT deg	*	8	MO	M	24	CCCC	Ind		
Business Computer Systems with Business Mgt	G5ND	3FT deg	*	8-12	MO	MB3	24	CCCC	Ind		
Business Computer Systems with Computing	N1GM	3FT deg	*	8	MO	M	24	CCCC	Ind		
Business Computer Systems with Env Policy	G5F9	3FT deg	*	8	MO	M	24	CCCC	Ind		
Business Computer Systems with Financ Serv Mgt	G5NH	3FT deg	*	8	MO	M	24	CCCC	Ind		
Business Computer Systems with Financial Mgt	NGH5	3FT deg	*	8	MO	M	26	CCCC	Ind		
Business Computer Systems with Geography	G5LW	3FT deg	*	8	MO	M	24	CCCC	Ind		
Business Computer Systems with Geology	G5FQ	3FT deg	*	8	MO	M	26	CCCC	Ind		
Business Computer Systems with Hotel Management	G5NR	3FT deg	*	8-12	MO	M	24	CCCC	Ind		
Business Computer Systems with Human Res Mgt	GNMC	3FT deg	*	8-12	MO	M	26	CCCC	Ind		
Business Computer Systems with Leisure Mgt	G5N7	3FT deg	*	8-12	MO	M	24	CCCC	Ind		
Business Computer Systems with Marketing Mgt	NG55	3FT deg	*	8-12	MO	M	26	CCCC	Ind		
Business Computer Systems with Media Communic	G5P4	3FT deg	*	8-12	MO	M	24	CCCC	Ind		
Business Computer Systems with Modern Languages	G5T9	3FT deg	g	8-12	MO	M	24	CCCC	Ind		
Business Computer Systems with Multimedia	G521	3FT deg	*	8	MO	M	26	CCCC	Ind		
Business Computer Systems with Religious Studies	G5V8	3FT deg	*	8	MO	M	24	CCCC	Ind		
Business Computer Systems with Women's Studies	G5MX	3FT deg	*	8-12	MO	M	24	CCCC	Ind		
Business Computer Systs with Physical Geography	G5FW	3FT deg	*	8	MO	M	26	CCCC	Ind		
Business Info Technology and Business Mgt	GN51	3FT deg	*	12	MO	MB3	24	CCCC	Ind		
Business Info Technology and Catering Management	NG75	3FT deg	*	8	MO	M	24	CCCC	Ind		
Business Info Technology and Financial Mgt	GNMJ	3FT deg	*	8-12	MO	M	26	CCCC	Ind		
Business Info Technology and Financial Serv Mgt	GN53	3FT deg	*	8-12	MO	M	24	CCCC	Ind		
Business Info Technology and Hotel Management	GNM7	3FT deg	*	10-14	MO	M	24	CCCC	Ind		
Business Info Technology and Human Resource Mgt	NGC5	3FT deg	*	8-12	MO	M	26	CCCC	Ind		
Business Info Technology and Leisure Mgt	NGR5	3FT/4SW deg	*	10-14	5M+2D	ML3	24	CCCC	Ind		
Business Info Technology and Marketing Mgt	GN5M	3FT deg	*	8-12	MO	M	26	CCCC	Ind		

Computer Sciences and Engineering 15

TITLE	CODE	COURSE	SUBJECTS	A/AS	NO/C	RGNVQ	IB	SQA(H)	SQA	RATIO A/AS
Business Info Technology and Tourism Mgt	GP57	3FT/4SW deg	*	8-12	5M+2D	ML3	24	CCCC	Ind	
Business Info Technology with Bus Comp Systems	G523	3FT deg	*	8	M0	M	24	CCCC	Ind	
Business Info Technology with Business Mgt	G5N1	3FT deg	*	8-12	M0	M	24	CCCC	Ind	
Business Info Technology with Catering Mgt	G5NT	3FT deg	*	8-12	M0	M	24	CCCC	Ind	
Business Info Technology with Financial Mgt	NGJ5	3FT deg	*	8-12	M0	M	26	CCCC	Ind	
Business Info Technology with Financial Serv Mgt	G5N3	3FT deg	*	8-12	M0	M	24	CCCC	Ind	
Business Info Technology with Hotel Mgt	G501	3FT deg	*	8-12	M0	M	24	CCCC	Ind	
Business Info Technology with Human Resource Mgt	GNMD	3FT deg	*	8-12	M0	M	26	CCCC	Ind	
Business Info Technology with Leisure Management	GNNR	3FT/4SW deg	*	8-12	M0	M	24	CCCC	Ind	
Business Info Technology with Marketing Mgt	GN55	3FT deg	*	8-12	M0	M	26	CCCC	Ind	
Business Info Technology with Tourism Management	G5P7	3FT/4SW deg	*	8-12	M0	M	24	CCCC	Ind	
Business Management and Computing	NG1M	3FT deg	*	12	5M+2D	MB3	26	CCCC	Ind	
Business Management and Multimedia	NG1N	3FT deg	*	12	4M+3D	MB3	26	CCCC	Ind	
Business Management with Business Comp Systems	N1GN	4SW deg	*	12	5M+2D	MB3	26	CCCC	Ind	
Business Management with Business Info Tech	N1G5	4SW deg	*	12	5M+2D	MB3	26	CCCC	Ind	
Business Management with Multimedia	NGCN	4SW deg	*	12	4M+3D	MB3	26	CCCC	Ind	
Catering Management and Computing	GNNT	3FT deg	*	8	M0	MH3	24	CCCC	Ind	
Catering Management with Computing	NGTN	4SW deg	*	8	M0	MH3	24	CCCC	Ind	
Computing and Environmental Policy	GF5X	3FT deg	*	8-12	M0	P3	24	CCCC	Ind	
Computing and Financial Management	GNNH	3FT deg	*	8-12	M0	P3	26	CCCC	Ind	
Computing and Financial Services Management	GN5H	3FT deg	*	8-12	M0	P3	24	CCCC	Ind	
Computing and Geography	GL5W	3FT deg	*	8-12	M0	M	24	CCCC	Ind	
Computing and Geology	GF56	3FT deg	S	8	M0	P3	24	CCCC	Ind	
Computing and Hotel Management	GN5T	3FT deg	*	8-12	M0	M	24	CCCC	Ind	
Computing and Human Geography	LG85	3FT deg	*	8-12	M0	M	26	CCCC	Ind	
Computing and Human Resource Management	NGD5	3FT deg	*	8-12	M0	M	26	CCCC	Ind	
Computing and Information Technology	G527	3FT deg	*	8	M0	M	24	CCCC	Ind	
Computing and Marketing Management	GN5N	3FT deg	*	8-12	M0	M	26	CCCC	Ind	
Computing and Media Communications	GP5L	3FT deg	*	8-12	5M+2D	M	24	CCCC	Ind	
Computing and Multimedia	G561	3FT deg	*	8-12	M0	M	26	CCCC	Ind	
Computing and Physical Geography	GF58	3FT deg	*	8-12	M0	M	26	CCCC	Ind	
Computing and Tourism Management	GPM7	3FT deg	*	8-12	5M+2D	ML3	24	CCCC	Ind	
Computing and Women's Studies	GM5Y	3FT deg	*	8-12	M0	M	24	CCCC	Ind	
Computing with Business Computer Systems	G5NC	3FT deg	*	8	M0	P3	24	CCCC	Ind	
Computing with Business Management	G502	3FT deg	*	8	M0	MB3	24	CCCC	Ind	
Computing with Catering Management	NGTM	3FT deg	*	8	M0	M	24	CCCC	Ind	
Computing with Environmental Policy	G503	3FT deg	*	8-10	M0	M	24	CCCC	Ind	
Computing with Financial Management	NG3M	3FT deg	*	8	M0	M	26	CCCC	Ind	
Computing with Financial Services Management	G5NJ	3FT deg	*	8-10	M0	M	24	CCCC	Ind	
Computing with Geography	GLMV	3FT deg	*	8	M0	M3	24	CCCC	Ind	
Computing with Geology	G5FP	3FT deg	*	8	M0	P3	24	CCCC	Ind	
Computing with Hotel Management	G504	3FT deg	*	8-12	M0	M	24	CCCC	Ind	
Computing with Human Geography	G5LV	3FT deg	*	8	M0	M	26	CCCC	Ind	
Computing with Human Resource Management	GNN1	3FT deg	*	8	M0	M	26	CCCC	Ind	
Computing with Information Technology	G526	3FT deg	*	8	M0	M	24	CCCC	Ind	
Computing with Marketing Management	GNM5	3FT deg	*	8	M0	M	26	CCCC	Ind	
Computing with Media Communications	G5PL	3FT deg	*	8-12	M0	M	24	CCCC	Ind	
Computing with Modern Languages (French)	G5RD	3FT deg	g	8	M0	M	24	CCCC	Ind	
Computing with Multimedia	G505	3FT deg	*	8	M0	M	26	CCCC	Ind	
Computing with Physical Geography	G5FV	3FT deg	*	8	M0	M	26	CCCC	Ind	
Computing with Tourism Management	G5PR	3FT deg	*	8-12	M0	M	24	CCCC	Ind	
Computing with Women's Studies	G5MY	3FT deg	*	8-12	M0	M	24	CCCC	Ind	

course details

98 expected requirements

96 entry stats

TITLE	CODE	COURSE	SUBJECTS	A/AS	ND/C	AGNVQ	IB	SQA(H)	SQA	RATIO A/AS
Countryside Planning and Information Technology	GD52	3FT deg	*	8-12	MO	M	24	CCCC	Ind	
Countryside Planning with Information Technology	D2G5	3FT deg	*	8	MO	M	24	CCCC	Ind	
English Studies and Multimedia	QG35	3FT deg	E	12	4M+3D	M^	26	CCCC	Ind	
English Studies with Multimedia	Q3G5	3FT deg	E	12	4M+3D	M^	26	CCCC	Ind	
Environmental Policy and Information Technology	FG95	3FT deg	*	8-12	MO	M3	24	CCCC	Ind	
Environmental Policy with Business Computer Syst	F9GM	3FT deg	*	8-12	MO	M3	26	CCCC	Ind	
Environmental Policy with Computing	F9G5	3FT/4SW deg	*	8-12	MO	M3	26	CCCC	Ind	
Environmental Policy with Information Technology	F9GN	3FT/4SW deg	*	8-12	MO	M3	26	CCCC	Ind	
Financial Management and Multimedia	NGHM	3FT deg	*	8-12	5M+2D	M3	26	CCCC	Ind	
Financial Management with Business Comp Systems	GN5J	4SW deg	*	8-12	MO	M3	26	CCCC	Ind	
Financial Management with Business Info Tech	GNM3	4SW deg	*	8-12	MO	M3	26	CCCC	Ind	
Financial Management with Computing	GNN3	4SW deg	*	8-12	MO	M3	26	CCCC	Ind	
Financial Management with Multimedia	GNNJ	4SW deg	*	8-12	5M+2D	M3	26	CCCC	Ind	
Financial Services Mgt and Multimedia	NG3N	3FT deg	*	8-12	5M+2D	M3	26	CCCC	Ind	
Financial Services Mgt with Business Comp Systs	N3GN	4SW deg	*	8-12	MO	M3	26	CCCC	Ind	
Financial Services Mgt with Business Info Tech	N3G5	4SW deg	*	8-12	MO	M3	26	CCCC	Ind	
Financial Services Mgt with Computing	N3GM	4SW deg	*	8-12	MO	M3	26	CCCC	Ind	
Financial Services Mgt with Multimedia	NGJN	4SW deg	*	8-12	5M+2D	M3	26	CCCC	Ind	
Geography and Information Technology	GLM8	3FT deg	*	12	MO	M	24	CCCC	Ind	
Geography with Business Computer Systems	L8GN	3FT deg	*	12	MO	M3^	26	CCCC	Ind	
Geography with Computing	LGVM	3FT deg	*	8-12	MO	M3^	26	CCCC	Ind	
Geography with Information Technology	LGWM	3FT deg	*	8-12	MO	M	24	CCCC	Ind	
Geology and Information Technology	FG65	3FT deg	S	8	MO	M3	26	CCCC	Ind	
Geology and Multimedia	FG6M	3FT deg	*	8-12	MO	M3^	24	CCCC	Ind	
Geology with Business Computer Systems	F6GN	3FT deg	S	8	MO	M3	26	CCCC	Ind	
Geology with Computing	F6GM	3FT deg	S	8	MO	M3	26	CCCC	Ind	
Geology with Information Technology	F6G5	3FT deg	S	8	MO	M3	26	CCCC	Ind	
Geology with Multimedia	FGPM	3FT deg	*	8-12	MO	M3^	24	CCCC	Ind	
Hotel Management with Business Computer Systems	N7GM	4SW deg	*	12	5M+2D	MH3	26	CCCC	Ind	
Hotel Management with Business Info Technology	N7GN	4SW deg	*	12	5M+2D	MH3	26	CCCC	Ind	
Hotel Management with Computing	N7G5	4SW deg	*	8-12	5M+2D	MH3	26	CCCC	Ind	
Human Geography and Information Technology	GL58	3FT/4SW deg	*	8-12	MO	M3	24	CCCC	Ind	
Human Geography and Multimedia	GLN8	3FT deg	*	10-14	5M+2D	M3	26	CCCC	Ind	
Human Geography with Computing	L8GM	3FT deg	*	8-12	MO	M3	26	CCCC	Ind	
Human Geography with Information Technology	L8G5	3FT deg	*	12	4M+3D	M3	26	CCCC	Ind	
Human Geography with Multimedia	LG8M	3FT deg	*	10-14	5M+2D	M3	26	CCCC	Ind	
Human Resource Management and Multimedia	G567	3FT deg	*	8-12	5M+2D	MB3	26	CCCC	Ind	
Human Resource Mgt with Business Computer Systs	GN5D	4SW deg	*	8-12	MO	MB3	26	CCCC	Ind	
Human Resource Mgt with Business Info Technology	GNM1	4SW deg	*	8-12	MO	MB3	26	CCCC	Ind	
Human Resource Mgt with Computing	NGCM	4SW deg	*	8-12	MO	MB3	26	CCCC	Ind	
Human Resource Mgt with Multimedia	NGDM	4SW deg	*	12	5M+2D	MB3	26	CCCC	Ind	
Information Technology and Media Communications	GP5K	3FT deg	*	8-12	5M+2D	MT3	24	CCCC	Ind	
Information Technology and Multimedia	G560	3FT deg	*	8-12	MO	M3	26	CCCC	Ind	
Information Technology and Natural Resource Mgt	GF5Y	3FT deg	*	8	MO	M3	26	CCCC	Ind	
Information Technology and Physical Geography	FG85	3FT/4SW deg	*	8-12	MO	M3	24	CCCC	Ind	
Information Technology and Religious Studies	GV58	3FT/4SW deg	*	8	MO	M3	24	CCCC	Ind	
Information Technology and Women's Studies	GM59	3FT/4SW deg	*	8	MO	M	24	CCCC	Ind	
Information Technology with Computing	G524	3FT/4SW deg	*	8	MO	M3	24	CCCC	Ind	
Information Technology with Countryside Planning	G7D2	3FT deg	*	8	MO	M	24	CCCC	Ind	
Information Technology with Environmental Policy	G5FY	3FT deg	*	8-12	MO	M3	24	CCCC	Ind	
Information Technology with Geography	GLMW	3FT deg	*	8-12	MO	M3	24	CCCC	Ind	
Information Technology with Geology	G5F6	3FT/4SW deg	*	8	MO	M3	24	CCCC	Ind	

Computer Sciences and Engineering   15

	course details			98 expected requirements							96 entry stats
TITLE	CODE	COURSE	SUBJECTS	A/AS	NO/C	RGNVQ	IB	SQA(H)	SQA	RATIO A/AS
Information Technology with Human Geography	G5L8	3FT deg	*	8-12	MO	M3	24	CCCC	Ind	
Information Technology with Media Communications	G5PK	3FT deg	*	8-12	MO	M3	24	CCCC	Ind	
Information Technology with Modern Lang (French)	G5RC	3FT deg	F g	8	MO	M3	26	CCCC	Ind	
Information Technology with Multimedia	G562	3FT deg	*	8	MO	M3	26	CCCC	Ind	
Information Technology with Natural Resource Mgt	G5FX	3FT deg	*	8	MO	M3	26	CCCC	Ind	
Information Technology with Physical Geography	G5F8	3FT deg	*	8-12	MO	M3	24	CCCC	Ind	
Information Technology with Religious Studies	G5VV	3FT deg	*	8	MO	M3	24	CCCC	Ind	
Information Technology with Women's Studies	G5M9	3FT deg	*	8-12	MO	M3	24	CCCC	Ind	
Leisure Management and Multimedia	NGT5	3FT deg	*	12-16	5M+2D	ML3	26	CCCC	Ind	
Marketing Management and Multimedia	NGM5	3FT deg	*	12	5M+2D	MB3	26	CCCC	Ind	
Marketing Management with Business Computer Syst	N5G5	4SW deg	*	8-12	MO	MB3	26	CCCC	Ind	
Marketing Management with Business Info Tech	N5GM	4SW deg	*	8-12	MO	MB3	26	CCCC	Ind	
Marketing Management with Computing	N5GN	4SW deg	*	8-12	MO	MB3	26	CCCC	Ind	
Marketing Management with Multimedia	NGN5	4SW deg	*	12	5M+2D	MB3	26	CCCC	Ind	
Media Communications and Multimedia	PG45	3FT deg	*	12	5M+2D	MP3	26	CCCC	Ind	
Media Communications with Business Computer Syst	P4GM	3FT deg	*	12	5M+2D	MP3	26	CCCC	Ind	
Media Communications with Computing	P4GN	3FT deg	*	12	5M+2D	MP3	26	CCCC	Ind	
Media Communications with Information Tech	P4G5	3FT deg	*	12	5M+2D	MP3	26	CCCC	Ind	
Media Communications with Multimedia	PGK5	3FT deg	*	12	5M+2D	MP3	26	CCCC	Ind	
Multimedia Computing	G540	3FT deg	*	8-12	MO	M3	24	CCCC	Ind	
Multimedia Management	G542	3FT deg	*	8-12	MO	M3	24	CCCC	Ind	
Multimedia Marketing	G543	3FT deg	*	8-12	MO	M3	24	CCCC	Ind	
Multimedia Systems Design	G545	3FT deg	*	8-12	MO	M3	24	CCCC	Ind	
Multimedia and Physical Geography	GF5V	3FT deg	*	8-12	5M+2D	M3	26	CCCC	Ind	
Multimedia and Psychology	GL57	3FT deg	g	12	5M+2D	MI3	26	CCCC	Ind	
Multimedia and Sociological Studies	GL53	3FT deg	*	12	5M+2D	MI3	26	CCCC	Ind	
Multimedia and Tourism Management	GPN7	3FT deg	*	12-16	5M+2D	MI3	26	CCCC	Ind	
Multimedia and Visual Arts	GW51	3FT deg	*	10-14	5M+2D	MA3	26	CCCC	Ind	
Multimedia and Women's Studies	GMM9	3FT deg	*	8-12	MO	MI3	26	CCCC	Ind	
Multimedia with Business Computer Systems	G528	3FT deg	*	8-12	MO	MI3	26	CCCC	Ind	
Multimedia with Business Computer Systems	G569	4SW deg	*	8-12	MO	MI3	24	CCCC	Ind	
Multimedia with Business Management	G568	4SW deg	*	8-12	MO	MI3	24	CCCC	Ind	
Multimedia with Business Management	NGDN	3FT deg	*	12	5M+2D	MI3	26	CCCC	Ind	
Multimedia with Combined Arts	G5Y3	3FT deg	*	8-12	MO	MI3	24	CCCC	Ind	
Multimedia with Combined Arts	G5YH	4SW deg	*	8-12	MO	MI3	26	CCCC	Ind	
Multimedia with Computing	G573	4SW deg	*	8-12	MO	MI3	26	CCCC	Ind	
Multimedia with Computing	G564	3FT deg	*	8-12	MO	MI3	26	CCCC	Ind	
Multimedia with English Studies	G5Q3	3FT deg	E	8-12	MO	MI3	26	CCCC	Ind	
Multimedia with English Studies	G5QH	4SW deg	*	8-12	MO	MI3	24	CCCC	Ind	
Multimedia with Financial Management	G565	4SW deg	*	8-12	MO	MI3	24	CCCC	Ind	
Multimedia with Financial Management	NGHN	3FT deg	*	8-12	MO	MI3	26	CCCC	Ind	
Multimedia with Financial Services Management	NGJM	3FT deg	*	8-12	MO	MI3	26	CCCC	Ind	
Multimedia with Financial Services Management	G570	4SW deg	*	8-12	MO	MI3	24	CCCC	Ind	
Multimedia with Geology	GFMQ	4SW deg	*	8-12	MO	MI3	24	CCCC	Ind	
Multimedia with Geology	GFMP	3FT deg	*	8-12	MO	MI3	24	CCCC	Ind	
Multimedia with Human Geography	GLNV	3FT deg	*	8-12	MO	MI3				
Multimedia with Human Geography	GLNW	4SW deg	*	8-12	MO	MI3				
Multimedia with Human Resource Management	G571	4SW deg	*	8-12	MO	MI3	24	CCCC	Ind	
Multimedia with Human Resource Management	G566	3FT deg	*	8-12	MO	MI3	26	CCCC	Ind	
Multimedia with Information Technology	G563	3FT deg	*	8-12	MO	MI3	26	CCCC	Ind	
Multimedia with Information Technology	G572	4SW deg	*	8-12	MO	MI3	24	CCCC	Ind	
Multimedia with Leisure Management	GNMR	4SW deg	*	8-12	MO	MI3	24	CCCC	Ind	

Letts STUDY GUIDES
THE INDEPENDENT

			98 expected requirements							96 entry stats

TITLE	CODE	COURSE	SUBJECTS	A/AS	NO/C	AGNVQ	IB	SQA(H)	SQA	RATIO A/AS
Multimedia with Leisure Management	GNN7	3FT deg	*	12	5M+2D	MI3	26	CCCC	Ind	
Multimedia with Marketing Management	NGMM	3FT deg	*	8-12	MO	MI3	26	CCCC	Ind	
Multimedia with Marketing Management	GNMT	4SW deg	*	8-12	MO	MI3	24	CCCC	Ind	
Multimedia with Media Communications	GPMK	4SW deg	*	8-12	MO	MI3	24	CCCC	Ind	
Multimedia with Media Communications	PGL5	3FT deg	*	12	5M+2D	MI3	26	CCCC	Ind	
Multimedia with Modern Languages (French)	G5R1	3FT deg	g	8-12	MO	MI3	26	CCCC	Ind	
Multimedia with Modern Languages (French)	GRMC	4SW deg	F g	8-12	MO	MI3	24	CCCC	Ind	
Multimedia with Physical Geography	GF5W	3FT deg	*	8-12	MO	MI3	24	CCCC	Ind	
Multimedia with Physical Geography	GFM8	4SW deg	*	8-12	MO	MI3	24	CCCC	Ind	
Multimedia with Psychology	G5LR	4SW deg	M g	8-12	MO	MI3	24	CCCC	Ind	
Multimedia with Psychology	G5L7	3FT deg	g	8-12	MO	MI3	26	CCCC	Ind	
Multimedia with Sociological Studies	G5L3	3FT deg	*	8-12	MO	MI3	26	CCCC	Ind	
Multimedia with Sociological Studies	G5LH	4SW deg	*	8-12	MO	MI3	24	CCCC	Ind	
Multimedia with Tourism Management	GPMR	4SW deg	*	8-12	MO	MI3	24	CCCC	Ind	
Multimedia with Tourism Management	G5PT	3FT deg	*	12	5M+2D	MI3	26	CCCC	Ind	
Multimedia with Visual Arts	G5WC	4SW deg	*	10-14	5M+2D	MA3	26	CCCC	Ind	
Multimedia with Visual Arts	G5W1	3FT deg	*	10-14	5M+2D	MA3	26	CCCC	Ind	
Multimedia with Women's Studies	GMMY	4SW deg	*	8-12	MO	MI3	24	CCCC	Ind	
Multimedia with Women's Studies	GMMX	3FT deg	*	8-12	MO	MI3	26	CCCC	Ind	
Natural Resource Mgt with Info Technology	GFM9	3FT deg	*	8	MO	M3	26	CCCC	Ind	
Physical Geography with Business Computer Systs	F8GN	3FT deg	*	8-12	MO	M3^	26	CCCC	Ind	
Physical Geography with Computing	F8GM	3FT deg	*	8-12	MO	M3^	26	CCCC	Ind	
Physical Geography with Information Technology	F8G5	3FT deg	*	10	MO	M3^	26	CCCC	Ind	
Physical Geography with Multimedia	FG8N	3FT deg	*	8-12	MO	M3^	26	CCCC	Ind	
Psychology with Information Technology	L7G5	3FT deg	g	12-16	MO	M3^	26	CCCC	Ind	
Psychology with Multimedia	GLM7	3FT deg	g	12	5M+2D	M3^	26	CCCC	Ind	
Religious Studies with Business Computer Systems	V8GM	3FT deg	*	8	MO	M3^	26	CCCC	Ind	
Religious Studies with Information Technology	V8G5	3FT/4SW deg	*	8	MO	M3^	26	CCCC	Ind	
Sociological Studies with Multimedia	GLM3	3FT deg	*	12	MO	MG3	26	CCCC	Ind	
Tourism Management with Business Info Technology	P7G5	4SW deg	*	12	4M+3D	ML3	26	CCCC	Ind	
Tourism Management with Computing	P7GM	4SW deg	*	12	4M+3D	ML3	26	CCCC	Ind	
Tourism Management with Multimedia	GP5R	4SW deg	*	12	MO	ML3	26	CCCC	Ind	
Visual Arts with Multimedia	W1G5	3FT deg	A	10-14	5M+2D	MA3	26	CCCC	Ind	
Women's Studies with Business Computer Systems	M9GM	3FT deg	*	8-12	MO	M3	26	CCCC	Ind	
Women's Studies with Computing	M9GN	3FT deg	*	8-12	MO	M3	26	CCCC	Ind	
Women's Studies with Information Technology	M9G5	3FT deg	*	8-12	MO	M3	26	CCCC	Ind	
Women's Studies with Multimedia	GMN9	3FT deg	*	8	MO	M3	26	CCCC	Ind	
Business Information Technology	265G	3SW HND	*	4	4M	P	Ind	Ind	Ind	
Business Information Technology	165G	2FT HND	*	4	4M	P	Ind	Ind	Ind	
Computing	005G	2FT HND	*	2	2M	P	Ind	Ind	Ind	
Computing	105G	3SW HND	*	2	2M	P	Ind	Ind	Ind	
Information Systems	325G	3SW HND	*	2	N	P	Ind	Ind	Ind	
Information Systems	025G	2FT HND	*	2	N	P	Ind	Ind	Ind	
Multimedia Computing	045G	2FT HND	*	4	N	P	Ind	Ind	Ind	
Multimedia Computing	445G	3SW HND	*	4	N	P	Ind	Ind	Ind	
Multimedia Information Technology	365G	3SW HND	*	4	N	P	Ind	Ind	Ind	
Multimedia Information Technology	065G	2FT HND	*	4	N	P	Ind	Ind	Ind	
Multimedia Management	245G	3SW HND	*	4	N	P	Ind	Ind	Ind	
Multimedia Management	645G	2FT HND	*	4	N	P	Ind	Ind	Ind	
Multimedia Marketing	745G	3SW HND	*	4	N	P	Ind	Ind	Ind	
Multimedia Marketing	345G	2FT HND	*	4	N	P	Ind	Ind	Ind	
Multimedia Systems Design	145G	2FT HND	*	4	N	P	Ind	Ind	Ind	
Multimedia Systems Design	545G	3SW HND	*	4	N	P	Ind	Ind	Ind	

Computer Sciences and Engineering 15

| | | | 98 expected requirements | | | | | | | 96 entry stats |
| course details | | | | | | | | | | |

TITLE	CODE	COURSE	SUBJECTS	A/AS	NQ/C	AGNVQ	IB	SQA(H)	SQA	RATIO A/AS
UNIVERSITY COLLEGE CHESTER										
Art and Computer Science/IT	WG95	3FT deg	g	12	M	P^	Ind	CCCC	$	
Art with Computer Science/IT	W9G5	3FT deg	g	12	MO	P^	Ind	CCCC	$	4
Biology and Computer Studies/IT	CG15	3FT deg	B g	10	M	P^	Ind	CCCC	$	
Biology with Computer Science/IT	C1G5	3FT deg	B g	10	M	P^	Ind	CCCC	$	2
Business Information Systems	GN51	3FT deg	g	10	MO	P	Ind	CCCC	$	
Computer Science/IT & Drama and Theatre Studies	GW54	3FT deg	g	12	M	M	Ind	CCCC	$	5
Computer Science/IT & Theology and Religious St	GV58	3FT deg	g	12	M	M	Ind	CCCC	$	
Computer Science/IT and English Literature	GQ53	3FT deg	E g	12	M	P^	Ind	CCCC	$	3
Computer Science/IT and History	GV51	3FT deg	H/Ec/So g	12	M	M	Ind	CCCC	$	8
Computer Science/IT with Art	G5W9	3FT deg	g	12	M	M	Ind	CCCC	$	
Computer Science/IT with Biology	G5C1	3FT deg	B g	10	M	P^	Ind	CCCC	$	2
Computer Science/IT with Drama & Theatre Studies	G5W4	3FT deg	g	12	M	P^	Ind	CCCC		
Computer Science/IT with English Literature	G5Q3	3FT deg	E g	12	M	P^	Ind	CCCC	$	5
Computer Science/IT with French	G5R1	3FT deg	g	12	M	M	Ind	CCCC	$	6
Computer Science/IT with Geography	G5F8	3FT deg	Gy/Gl g	CD	M	P^	Ind	CCCC	$	
Computer Science/IT with German	G5R2	3FT deg	g	12	M	M	Ind	CCCC	$	3
Computer Science/IT with History	G5V1	3FT deg	H/Ec/So g	12	M	M	Ind	CCCC	$	2
Computer Science/IT with Mathematics	G5G1	3FT deg	M	10	M	P^	Ind	CCCC	$	4
Computer Science/IT with PE/Sports Science	G5B6	3FT deg	g	10	M	P^	Ind	CCCC	$	
Computer Science/IT with Psychology	G5L7	3FT deg	g	10	M	M	Ind	CCCC	$	7
Computer Science/IT with Social Science	G5L3	3FT deg	g	10	M	M	Ind	CCCC	$	
Computer Science/IT with Theology and Rel St	G5V8	3FT deg	g	12	M	P^	· Ind	CCCC	$	
Computer Studies/IT and Geography	GF58	3FT deg	Gy/Gl g	CD	3M	P^	Ind	CCCC	$	15
Computer Studies/IT and Mathematics	GG51	3FT deg	M	10	M	P^	Ind	CCCC	$	7
Computer Studies/IT and PE/Sports Science	GB56	3FT deg	g	10	M	P^	Ind	CCCC	$	
Computer Studies/IT and Psychology	GL57	3FT deg	g	10	M	M	Ind	CCCC	$	7
Drama and Theatre Studies with Computer Sc/IT	W4G5	3FT deg	g	12	M	M	Ind	CCCC	$	5
English with Computer Science/IT	Q3G5	3FT deg	E g	12	M	P^	Ind	CCCC	$	5
Geography and Geomatics	F8GM	3FT deg	Gy/Gl	10	M	P	Ind	CCCC	$	
Geography with Computer Science/IT	F8G5	3FT deg	Gy/Gl g	12	M	P^	Ind	CCCC	$	3
History with Computer Science/IT	V1G5	3FT deg	H/Ec/So g	12	M	M	Ind	CCCC	$	7
Mathematics with Computer Science/IT	G1G5	3FT deg	M	10	M	P^	Ind	CCCC	$	7
PE/Sports Science with Computer Science/IT	B6G5	3FT deg	g	10	M	P^	Ind	CCCC	$	
Psychology with Computer Science/IT	L7G5	3FT deg	g	10	M	M	Ind	CCCC	$	4 10/18
Theology and Religious St with Computer Sci/IT	V8G5	3FT deg	g	12	M	M	Ind	CCCC	$	
CITY Univ										
Business Computing Systems	G522	4SW deg	* g	BBC-BCC	5M	D$	Ind	Ind	Ind	4 12/22
Business Computing Systems (Foundation)	G710	4EXT deg	*		Ind		Ind	Ind	Ind	
Computer Systems Engineering	G600	3FT deg	M+P/Cs	CCD	3M+2D$	D$^	27$	ABBBB$	HN$	7 10
Computer Systems Engineering	G601	4SW deg	M+P/Cs	CCD	3M+2D$	D$^	27$	ABBBB$	HN$	
Computer Systems Engineering (Foundation)	G608	4EXT deg	M+P	EE	Ind $	M$	20$	ABB$	N$	6
Computing	G500	3FT/4SW deg	M/P/Cs/S g	20-22	2M+3D	D*^	28$	ABBBB	Ind	7 12/20
Computing (Dist Infor Systems & Comms) (BEng)	G520	3FT/4SW deg	M/P/Cs/S g	20-22	2M+3D	D*^	28$	ABBBB	Ind	
Computing (Foundation)	G505	5EXT deg	M/P/Cs/S g	8	Ind	M	Ind	Ind	Ind	
Economics/Computing	LG15	3FT deg	* g	BCC	3M+4D	D*^	28$	BBBBC	Ind	21
Mathematical Sci with Computer Sci (Foundation)	G1GM	4EXT Deg	*		Ind	Ind	Ind	Ind	Ind	
Mathematical Science with Computer Science	G1G5	3FT/4SW deg	M	BCD-CDD	Ind	D*^	26$	Ind	Ind	25
Media Communication Systems (BEng)	G610	4SW deg	*	BCC	3M+3D	D*^	28$	BBBBB	Ind	
Media Communication Systems (BEng)	G618	3FT deg	*	BCC	3M+3D	D*^	28$	BBBBB	Ind	
Software Engineering (BEng)	G700	4SW deg	M/P/Cs/S g	20-22	2M+3D	D*^	28$	ABBBB	Ind	7 14/26
Software Engineering (Foundation)	G708	5EXT deg	M/P/Cs/S g	8	Ind	M	Ind	Ind	Ind	19

TITLE	CODE	COURSE	SUBJECTS	A/AS	ND/C	AGNVQ	IB	SQA(H)	SQA	RATIO A/AS
CITY COLLEGE Manchester										
Business Information Technology	027G	2FT HND								
COVENTRY Univ										
Bioscience Communications	C9G5	3FT/4SW deg								
Business Information Technology	GN51	3FT deg	* g	12	MO	Ind	Ind	CCCC	Ind	7 8/16
Business Information Technology	GNM1	4FT/5SW deg	*	2	N	P	Ind	Ind	Ind	1
Business Information Technology (2+2 Scheme)	G561	4FT deg		4	4M		Ind	Ind	Ind	
Chemistry and Computing	FG1N	4FT/5SW deg			Ind	Ind	Ind	Ind	Ind	
Computer Hardware and Software Engineering	GG76	4FT/5SW deg	M+S	12-18	5M		24$	BBCC$	Ind	19
Computer Science	G500	3FT/4SW deg	* g	14	MO	M	Ind	CCCC	Ind	8 8/18
Computer Science	G501	4FT/5SW deg								
Computer Systems	G502	3FT/4SW deg	* g	14	MO		Ind	CCCC	Ind	
Computer Systems	G509	4FT/5SW deg								
Computer and Control Systems	GH66	4FT/5SW deg								
Computing	G504	3FT/4SW deg		14	MO		Ind	Ind	Ind	
Computing (2+2 Scheme)	G503	4FT deg	* g	4	4M		Ind	Ind	Ind	
Computing and Biological Sciences	GC5C	4FT/5SW deg			Ind	Ind	Ind	Ind	Ind	
Computing and Biological Sciences	GC51	3FT/4SW deg	B g	10	3M $		Ind	CCC$	Ind	10
Computing and Chemistry	FG15	3FT/4SW deg	C	DD	3M	MS	Ind	Ind	Ind	19
Computing with European Studies	G5T2	4FT deg	L g	12	Ind	M	Ind	CCCC	Ind	8
Computing with European Studies	GT59	5FT deg								
Economics and Computing	GL51	3FT/4SW deg	*	12	MO	M	Ind	Ind	Ind	6
Extended Business Information Technology	GN5C	4FT deg	*	2	N		Dip	Ind	Ind	
Geographical Information Systems	G562	3FT deg	* g	12	4M	M	Ind	Ind	Ind	8
Geography and Computing	LG85	3FT/4SW deg	* g	12	MO	M	Ind	Ind	Ind	4 8/14
Information Systems	G560	3FT/4SW deg	* g	12	1M	M	Ind	CCCC	Ind	11 10/14
Information Systems Management	G520	4FT/5SW deg								
Mathematics and Computing	GG15	3FT/4SW deg	M/Cs	12-16	3M $		Ind	Ind	Ind	13
Psychology and Computing	CG85	3FT/4SW deg	* g	CC	3M+3D	M go	Ind	BBB	Ind	5
Software Engineering	G700	3FT/4SW deg	* g	14	MO	M	Ind	CCCC	Ind	10 10/18
Statistics and Computing	GG45	3FT/4SW deg	M/Cs/St g	12-16	3M $	M	Ind	Ind	Ind	
Business Information Technology	15NG▼	2FT HND		4	4M	P	Ind	Ind	Ind	4 2/4
Computer Engineering	006G	3FT HND								
Computing	105G▼	2FT HND	* g	4	4M		Ind	Ind	Ind	5
Computing	805G	3FT HND								
Mathematics and Computing	51GG	2FT HND	M	2	N $	P	Ind	Ind	Ind	
Statistics and Computing	54GG	2FT HND	M/St/Cs	2	N $	P	Ind	Ind	Ind	
CRANFIELD Univ										
Business Information Systems	N1G5	3FT deg	* g	CC-CCC	3M	M$ go	Ind	CSYS		1
Command & Control, Communications & Info Systems	GN51	3FT deg	* g	CC-CCC	3M	M$ go	Ind	CSYS	Ind	2
Information Systems Management	GN5C	3FT deg	* g	CC-CCC	3M	M$ go	Ind	CSYS	Ind	3
Information Technology	G610	3FT/4SW deg	M g	BC-BCC	4M $		Ind	Ind	Ind	
Software Engineering	G700	3FT/4SW deg	* g	BC-CCC	4M	D$	Ind	Ind	Ind	7
DE MONTFORT Univ										
Business Information Systems	G521▼	4SW deg	* g	16	2M+2D	M	30	BBBC$	Ind	3 8/12
Computer Science	G500▼	4SW deg	* g	12-18	2M+2D	M	30	BBBC$	Ind	4 8/18
Computer and Information Systems	G520▼	3FT/4SW deg	* g	12-18	2M+2D	D	30	BBBC$	Ind	
Computing	G503▼	3/4FT deg	* g	8-14	4M $	P	28	BBCC$	Ind	
Computing	G501▼	3/4FT deg	* g	8-14	4M $	P	28	BBCC$	Ind	2 4/16
Information Systems with Management	G5N1▼	3FT/4SW deg	* g	12-18	2M+2D	D	30	BBBC$	Ind	
Information Technology	G560▼	4SW deg	*	8-16	4M	Ind	30	BBBB	Ind	9

TITLE	CODE	COURSE	SUBJECTS	A/AS	ND/C	AGNVQ	IB	SQA(H)	SQA	RATIO	A/AS
Mathematics with Computing	G1G5▼	4SW deg	M	12	3M+1D	M$ go	Ind	Ind	Ind	7	
Medical and Health Statistics	GG54▼	3FT/4SW deg	*	10-14	MO	M	Ind	Ind	Ind		6/14
Multi-Media Computing	G535▼	4SW deg	*	12-18	Ind	Ind	Ind	Ind	Ind		10/15
Software Engineering	G700▼	4SW deg	g	16	2M+2D	Ind	28	BBBB	Ind	6	8/19
Combined Sciences Computing	Y108▼	3FT deg	g	2	N	P	Dip	CC	Ind		
Combined Studies Computing	Y400▼	3FT/4SW deg	* g	12	2M+4D	M	30	BBB	Ind		
Combined Studies Computing-Enhanced Route	Y400▼	3FT/4SW deg	* g	12	2M+4D	M	30	BBB	Ind		
Humanities Combined Honours Business Information Systems	Y300▼	3FT deg	* g	CCD	MO	M$^	26$	ABBB	Ind		
Computing	105G▼	2FT HND	* g	4-6	3M $	P	26	CCCC$	Ind	3	2/24
Computing	305G▼	2FT HND	* g	4-6	3M $	P	26	CCCC$	Ind	4	2/ 6

Univ of DERBY

TITLE	CODE	COURSE	SUBJECTS	A/AS	ND/C	AGNVQ	IB	SQA(H)	SQA	RATIO	A/AS
Applicable Mathematics and Computing	GG15	4SW deg	M	8	3M $	M^	Dip$	CCCD$	Ind	13	
Artificial Intelligence	G801	4SW deg	*	10-12	3M $	M$	26$	CCCC	Ind		
Business Information Systems	G720	3FT deg		10-12	3M	M$	26$	CCCC	Ind		
Computer Studies	G501	4SW deg	*	10-12	3M	M$	26$	CCCC	Ind	7	6/14
Computer Studies (Artificial Intelligence)	G800	4SW deg	*	10-12	3M	M$	26$	CCCC	Ind		
Computer Studies (Networks & Communications)	G506	4SW deg	*	10-12	3M	M$	26$	CCCC	Ind		
Computer Studies (Software Engineering)	G5G7	4SW deg	*	10-12	3M	M$	26$	CCCC	Ind		
Computer Studies (Visualisation)	G700	4SW deg	*	10-12	3M	M$	26$	CCCC	Ind		
Creative Computing	G540	3FT deg		10-12	3M	M$	26$	CCCC	Ind		
Health Care Information Management	G580	3FT deg	*	12	4M+1D	M$	25	CCCD	Ind	7	
Information Systems	G520	4SW deg	*	10-12	3M	M$	26$	CCCC	Ind	9	
Information Systems (Artificial Intelligence)	G5G8	3FT deg	*	10-12	3M	M$	26$	CCCC	Ind		
Information Systems (Networks & Communications)	G5G6	3FT deg		10-12	3M	M$	26$	CCCC	Ind		
Information Systems (Visualisation)	G5GT	3FT deg		10-12	3M	M$	26$	CCCC	Ind		
Mathematical & Computer Studies	GG51	3FT deg	M	8	3M $	M^	Dip$	CCCD$	Ind		
Visualisation	G701	3FT deg									
Credit Accumulation Modular Scheme Computer Studies	Y600	3FT deg	*	8	MO	M	Ind	CCCC	Ind		
Credit Accumulation Modular Scheme Information Systems	Y600	3FT deg	*	8	MO	M	Ind	CCCC	Ind		
Computer Studies	105G	2FT HND	*	4	N	P	Dip	CCC	Ind	3	2/ 8

DONCASTER COLL

TITLE	CODE	COURSE	SUBJECTS	A/AS	ND/C	AGNVQ	IB	SQA(H)	SQA	RATIO	A/AS
Informatics	G510	2FT Dip		EE	N	P	Ind	Ind	Ind		
Integrated Business Technology (1 Year top-up)	GN51	1FT deg			HN		Ind	Ind	HN		
Business Information Technology	025G	2FT HND		EE	N	P	Ind	Ind	Ind	5	
Computer Studies/Software Engineering	005G	2FT HND		EE	N	P	Ind	Ind	Ind	4	

DUDLEY COLLEGE of Technology

TITLE	CODE	COURSE	SUBJECTS	A/AS	ND/C	AGNVQ	IB	SQA(H)	SQA	RATIO	A/AS
Business Information Technology	007G	2FT HND	* g	2	Ind	Ind					
Computer Studies	005G	2FT HND	* g	2	Ind	Ind					

Univ of DUNDEE

TITLE	CODE	COURSE	SUBJECTS	A/AS	ND/C	AGNVQ	IB	SQA(H)	SQA	RATIO	A/AS
Accountancy and Applied Computing	GN54	4FT deg	S g	14	5M $	M$	25$	BBBC$	N$	5	
Applied Computing	G510	4FT deg	S g	14	5M $	M$	25$	BBBC$	N$	5	
Applied Computing	G511	3FT deg	S g	10	5M $	M$	25$	BBCC$	N$	11	
Applied Computing and Digital Microelectronics	GHM6	4FT deg	M+S g	14	5M $	M$^	25$	BBBC$	N$	5	
Applied Computing and Economics	GL51	4FT deg	S g	14	5M $	M$	25$	BBBC$	N$	5	
Applied Computing and Financial Economics	GL5C	4FT deg	S g	14	5M $	M$	25$	BBBC$	N$		
Chemistry and Applied Computing	FG15	4FT deg	2S g	14	5M $	M$	25$	BBBC$	N$	7	

TITLE	CODE	COURSE	SUBJECTS	A/AS	ND/C	AGNVQ	IB	SQA(H)	SQA	RATIO A/AS	
Computing and Cognitive Science	CG85	4FT deg	S g	14	5M $	M$	25$	BBBC$	N$		
Electronic Eng and Microcomputer Systems (BEng)	HG66	3FT/4FT deg	M+P/Ds g	12	5M $	M$^	26$	BBCC$	N$		
Electronic Eng and Microcomputer Systems (MEng)	GH66	4FT/5FT deg	M+P/Ds g	12	5M $	M$^	26$	BBCC$	N$		
Mathematics and Applied Computing	GG15	4FT deg	M g	14	5M $	M$^	25$	BBBB$	N$	7	
Mathematics and Applied Computing	GG51	3FT deg	M g	10	5M $	M$^	25$	BBCC$	N$	6	
Physics and Applied Computing	FG35	4FT deg	M+S g	14	5M $	M$^	25$	BBBC$	N$	8	
Psychology and Applied Computing	LG75	4FT deg	S g	14	5M $	M$	25$	BBBC$	N$	3	

Univ of DURHAM

TITLE	CODE	COURSE	SUBJECTS	A/AS	ND/C	AGNVQ	IB	SQA(H)	SQA	RATIO A/AS	
Artificial Intelligence	G800	3FT deg	2S	20	Ind	Ind	30$	AABBB$	Ind	8	20/28
Computer Science	G500	3FT deg	2S	20	Ind	Ind	30$	AABBB$	Ind	7	22/30
Computer Science (European Studies)	G501	3FT deg	2S	20	Ind	Ind	30$	AABBB$	Ind		
Computer Science and Mathematics	GG51	3FT deg	M+S	24	X	X	32$	CSYS$	X	10	26/30
Information Systems Management	G520	3FT deg	2S	20	Ind	Ind	30$	AABBB$	Ind		
Software Engineering	G700	3FT deg	2S	20	Ind	Ind	30$	AABBB$	Ind	8	20/28
Natural Sciences *Computing*	Y160	3FT deg	2S	ABB	Ind	X	33$	CSYS$	X		

Univ of EAST ANGLIA

TITLE	CODE	COURSE	SUBJECTS	A/AS	ND/C	AGNVQ	IB	SQA(H)	SQA	RATIO A/AS	
Business Information Systems	GN54	3FT deg	*	BBB-BBC	MO+4D	D^	30$	BBBBB	Ind	5	
Computer Systems Eng with a Yr in N Amer (3 Yrs)	G601	3FT deg	M+S	BBB-BBC	5D $	D^	30$	ABBBB	HN	22	
Computer Systems Engineering	G600	3FT deg	M+S	CCC	4M $	M^	28$	BBBC	N$	11	
Computerised Accountancy	NG45	3FT deg	M	BBB-BBC	MO+3D	D^	30$	ABBBB	Ind	6	22/26
Computing Science	G500	3FT deg	* g	BBC-BCC	MO+3D	D+^	28$	BBBB	HN	5	12/28
Computing Science with a Year in N America(3 Yr)	G502	3FT deg	M	BBB-BBC	Ind	X	30$	BBBBB	HN	7	18/24
Computing and Mathematics	GG51	3FT deg	M	BC-CCC	Ind		32$	BBBC$	X	6	
Computing, Applied	G510	3FT deg	*	BBC-BCC	MO+3D	D^	28$	BBBB	Ind	2	14/28
Computing, Applied (2nd year in North America)	G511	3FT deg	*	BBB	Ind	X	30$	BBBBB	HN	15	
Mathematics with Computing	G1G5	3FT deg	M	BCC	Ind		32$	BBBC$	X	3	12/20

Univ of EAST LONDON

TITLE	CODE	COURSE	SUBJECTS	A/AS	ND/C	AGNVQ	IB	SQA(H)	SQA	RATIO A/AS	
Accounting & Finance with Bus Information Systs	G5N4	3FT deg	* g	14	MO	M	Ind	Ind	Ind		
Accounting & Finance with Information Technology	N4G5	3FT deg	* g	14	MO	MB	Ind	Ind	Ind		
Archaeological Sciences & Information Technology	FG45	3FT deg	* g	12	MO	M$	Ind	Ind	Ind		
Biocomputing	CG1M	3FT/4SW deg	* g	12	MO	MS	Ind	Ind	Ind	10	
Biology and Information Technology	CG15	3FT deg	* g	12	MO	M$	Ind	Ind	Ind		
Biology with Information Technology	C1G5	3FT deg	* g	12	MO	M	Ind	Ind	Ind		
Business Info Systems/Accounting & Finance	NG47	3FT deg	* g	12	MO	MB	Ind	Ind	Ind		
Business St with Computing & Business Info Systs	N1G5	3FT deg	* g	14	MO	MB					
Business Studies and Information Technology	NG15	3FT deg	* g	12	MO	M					
Business Studies with Information Technology	N1GM	3FT deg	* g	14	MO	MB					
Communication Studies and Information Technology	GP53	3FT deg	* g	12	MO	M$	Ind	Ind	Ind	1	
Communication Studies with Information Technol	P3G5	3FT deg	* g	12	MO	M	Ind	Ind			
Computer and Control Engineering	GH66	3FT/4SW deg	* g	12	3M	ME	Ind	Ind	Ind	44	
Computing & Business Info Systems and French	GR5C	3FT deg	* g	12	MO	M					
Computing & Business Info Systems and German	GR5F	3FT deg	* g	12	MO	M					
Computing & Business Info Systems and Spanish	GR5K	3FT deg	* g	12	MO	M					
Computing & Information Systems with Bus St	G5N1	3FT deg	* g	14	MO	M	Ind		Ind		
Computing and Business Information	G520	3FT/4SW deg	* g	12	N	M	Ind	Ind	Ind	4	
Cultural Studies and Information Technology	GL5P	3FT deg	* g	14	MO	M					
Cultural Studies with Information Technology	L6G5	3FT deg	* g	14	MO	M	Ind	Ind			
Design - Textile Design with Information Technol	J4G5	3FT deg	* g	12	MO	M	Ind	Ind	Ind		
Design - Visual Communication and IT	GW52	3FT deg	* g	12	MO	M$	Ind	Ind	Ind		
Distributed Information Systems	G521	4SW deg	* g	12	MO	M	Ind	Ind	Ind		

Computer Sciences and Engineering 15

	course details		98 expected requirements							96 entry stats
TITLE	CODE	COURSE	SUBJECTS	A/AS	NO/C	AGNVQ	IB	SQA(H)	SQA	RATIO A/AS
Education & Community Studies & Information Tech	GX59	3FT deg	* g	12	MO	M$	Ind	Ind	Ind	1
Education & Community Studies with IT	X9G5	3FT deg	* g	12	MO	M				
Environmental Sciences and Information Technol	GF59	3FT deg	* g	12	MO	M$	Ind	Ind	Ind	4
Environmental Sciences with Information Technol	F9G5	3FT deg	* g	12	MO	M	Ind	Ind	Ind	
European Studies with Information Technology	T2G5	3FT deg	* g	12	MO	M	Ind	Ind		
French and Information Technology	GR51	3FT deg	* g	12	MO	M$	Ind	Ind	Ind	1
French with Computing & Business Info Systems	R1G5	3FT deg	* g	12	MO	M	Ind			
French with Information Technology	R1GN	3FT deg	* g	12	MO	M	Ind			
French with Maths, Stats & Computing	R1GM	3FT deg	* g	12	MO	M				
German and Information Technology	GR52	3FT deg	* g	12	MO	M$	Ind	Ind	Ind	2
German with Computing & Business Info Systems	R2G5	3FT deg	* g	12	MO	M				
German with Information Technology	R2GM	3FT deg	* g	12	MO	M	Ind			
German/Business Information Systems	GR72	3FT deg	* g	12	MO	M^	Ind			
Health Studies and Information Technology	BG95	3FT deg	* g	12	MO	M	Ind	Ind	Ind	
Health Studies with Information Technology	B9G5	3FT deg	* g	12	MO	M	Ind	Ind	Ind	
History and Information Technology	GV51	3FT deg	* g	12	MO	M$	Ind	Ind	Ind	
History of Art Design & Film and IT	GV54	3FT deg	* g	12	MO	M$	Ind	Ind	Ind	
History of Art Design & Film with IT	V4G5	3FT deg	* g	12	MO	M	Ind	Ind		
History with Information Technology	V1G5	3FT deg	* g	12	MO	M	Ind	Ind		
Information Systems	G522	4SW deg	* g	12	MO	M	Ind	Ind	Ind	
Information Technology & Social Policy Research	GL54	3FT deg	* g	12	MO	M	Ind	Ind	Ind	
Information Technology & Third World & Devel St	GM5Y	3FT deg	* g	12	MO	M	Ind	Ind	Ind	3
Information Technology and Law	GM53	3FT deg	* g	12	MO	D	Ind	Ind	Ind	4
Information Technology and Linguistics	GQ51	3FT deg	* g	12	MO	X	Ind	Ind	Ind	
Information Technology and Maths, Stats & Comput	GG59	3FT deg	* g	12	MO	M	Ind	Ind	Ind	
Information Technology and Politics	MG15	3FT deg	* g	12	MO	M	Ind	Ind	Ind	
Information Technology and Social Sciences	GL5H	3FT deg	* g	12	MO	MB	Ind	Ind	Ind	3
Information Technology and Spanish	GR54	3FT deg	* g	12	MO	M^	Ind	Ind	Ind	1
Information Technology and Women's Studies	GM59	3FT deg	* g	12	MO	M	Ind	Ind	Ind	
Information Technology w. Hist of Art Des & Film	G5V4	3FT deg	* g	12	MO	M	Ind	Ind	Ind	
Information Technology with Accounting & Finance	G5NK	3FT deg	* g	12	MO	M	Ind	Ind	Ind	
Information Technology with Anthropology	G5L6	3FT deg	* g	12	MO	M	Ind	Ind	Ind	
Information Technology with Archaeological Sci	G5F4	3FT deg	* g	12	MO	M	Ind	Ind	Ind	
Information Technology with Biology	G5C1	3FT deg	* g	12	MO	M	Ind	Ind	Ind	
Information Technology with Business Studies	G5NC	3FT deg	* g	12	MO	M	Ind	Ind	Ind	
Information Technology with Communication St	G5P3	3FT deg	* g	12	MO	M	Ind	Ind	Ind	
Information Technology with Cultural Studies	GL5Q	3FT deg	* g	12	MO	M	Ind	Ind	Ind	
Information Technology with Design - Textile Des	G5J4	3FT deg	* g	12	MO	M	Ind	Ind	Ind	
Information Technology with Design - Visual Comm	G5W2	3FT deg	* g	12	MO	M	Ind	Ind	Ind	
Information Technology with Economics	G5L1	3FT deg	* g	12	MO	M	Ind	Ind	Ind	
Information Technology with Educ & Community St	G5X9	3FT deg	* g	12	MO	M	Ind	Ind	Ind	
Information Technology with Environmental Sci	G5F9	3FT deg	* g	12	MO	M	Ind	Ind	Ind	
Information Technology with European Studies	G5T2	3FT deg	* g	12	MO	M	Ind	Ind	Ind	
Information Technology with French	G5R1	3FT deg	* g	12	MO	M	Ind	Ind	Ind	
Information Technology with German	G5R2	3FT deg	* g	12	MO	M	Ind	Ind	Ind	
Information Technology with Health Studies	G5B9	3FT deg	* g	12	MO	M	Ind	Ind	Ind	
Information Technology with History	G5V1	3FT deg	* g	12	MO	M	Ind	Ind	Ind	
Information Technology with Italian	G5R3	3FT deg	* g	12	MO	M	Ind	Ind	Ind	
Information Technology with Law	G5M3	3FT deg	* g	12	MO	M	Ind	Ind	Ind	
Information Technology with Linguistics	G5Q1	3FT deg	* g	12	MO	M	Ind	Ind	Ind	
Information Technology with Maths Stats & Comput	G5G9	3FT deg	* g	12	MO	M	Ind	Ind	Ind	
Information Technology with Media Studies	G5P4	3FT deg	* g	12	MO	M	Ind	Ind	Ind	

			98 expected requirements							96 entry stats	

course details   **98 expected requirements**   *96 entry stats*

TITLE	CODE	COURSE	SUBJECTS	A/AS	ND/C	AGNVQ	IB	SQA(H)	SQA	RATIO	A/AS
Information Technology with Politics	G5M1	3FT deg	* g	12	MO	M	Ind	Ind	Ind		
Information Technology with Psychosocial Studies	G5L7	3FT deg	* g	12	MO	M	Ind	Ind	Ind		
Information Technology with Social Pol Research	G5L4	3FT deg	* g	12	MO	M	Ind	Ind	Ind		
Information Technology with Social Sciences	G5L3	3FT deg	* g	12	MO	M	Ind	Ind	Ind		
Information Technology with Spanish	G5R4	3FT deg	* g	12	MO	M	Ind	Ind	Ind		
Information Technology with Third World & Dev St	G5M9	3FT deg	* g	12	MO	M	Ind	Ind	Ind		
Information Technology with Women's Studies	G5MX	3FT deg	* g	12	MO	M	Ind	Ind	Ind		
Linguistics with Information Technology	Q1G5	3FT deg	* g	12	MO	M					
Mathematics & Computing	GG15	3/4FT deg	* g	12	MO	M$	Ind	Ind	Ind	9	
Maths, Stats & Computing with IT	G9G5	3FT deg	* g	12	MO	M	Ind	Ind	Ind		
Media Studies with Information Technology	P4G5	3FT deg	* g	14	MO	M					
Politics with Information Technology	M1G5	3FT deg	* g	12	MO	M	Ind				
Psychosocial Studies with Information Technology	L7G5	3FT deg	* g	12	MO	M	Ind	Ind	Ind		
Social Policy Research with IT	L4G5	3FT deg	* g	12	MO	M	Ind	Ind	Ind		
Social Sciences with Information Technology	L3G5	3FT deg	* g	12	MO	M	Ind	Ind	Ind		
Software Engineering	G700	3FT deg	* g	14	MO	M$	Ind	Ind	Ind	9	
Spanish with Computing & Business Info Systems	R4G5	3FT deg	* g	12	MO	M	Ind				
Spanish with Information Technology	R4GM	3FT deg	* g	12	MO	M	Ind				
Third World & Development Studies with IT	M9G5	3FT deg	* g	12	MO	M	Ind	Ind			
Women's Studies with Information Technology	M9GM	3FT deg	* g	12	MO	M	Ind				
Three-Subject Degree *Information Technology*	Y600	3FT deg	* g	12	MO	M	Ind	Ind	Ind		
Business and Computing	51GN	2FT HND	* g	12	MO	M					
Computing	105G	2FT HND	* g	12	MO	PI	Ind	Ind	Ind	5	6/8

EDGE HILL Univ COLLEGE

TITLE	CODE	COURSE	SUBJECTS	A/AS	ND/C	AGNVQ	IB	SQA(H)	SQA	RATIO	A/AS
Environmental Management and Information Systems	FG95	3FT deg	2(B/C/En/P) g	DD	3M+3D	MS / P*	Dip	BBCC	Ind		
Geography and Information Systems	GL58	3FT deg	Gv g	CD	X	P*^	Dip	BBCC$	Ind	6	
Information Systems and Communication Studies	GP53	3FT deg	* g	CC	3M+3D	M* / P*^	Dip	BBCC	Ind	5	6/20
Information Systems and Mathematics	GG15	3FT deg	* g	CD	3M+3D	M* / P*^	Dip	BBCC	Ind	2	
Sports Studies and Information Systems	BG65	3FT deg	* g	CC	3M+3D	M* / P*^	Dip	BBCC	Ind		

Univ of EDINBURGH

TITLE	CODE	COURSE	SUBJECTS	A/AS	ND/C	AGNVQ	IB	SQA(H)	SQA	RATIO	A/AS
Artificial Intelligence and Computer Science	GG58	4FT deg	M	CCC	MO $		Dip$	BBBB$	N$	3	18/30
Artificial Intelligence and Mathematics	GG18	4FT deg	M	BCC	MO $		Dip$	ABBC$	N$	4	22/30
Artificial Intelligence and Psychology	GL87	4FT deg	2S g	BBC	MO $		Dip$	BBBB$	N$		
Artificial Intelligence and Software Engineering	GG78	4FT deg	M	CCC	MO $		Dip$	BBBB$			
Computer Science	G500	4FT deg	M	CCC	MO $		Dip$	BBBB$	N$	5	18/30
Computer Science (BEng)	G501	4FT deg	M	CCC	MO $		Dip$	BBBB	N$	8	
Computer Science and Electronics (BEng)	GH56	4FT deg	M+P	CCC	MO $		Dip$	BBBB$	N$	7	
Computer Science and Management Science	GN51	4FT deg	M	CCC	MO $		Dip$	BBBB$	N$	8	22/24
Computer Science and Mathematics	GG15	4FT deg	M	BCC	MO $		Dip$	ABBC$	N$	9	
Computer Science and Physics	GF53	4FT deg	M+P	CCC	MO $		Dip$	BBBB$	N$		
Electronics and Computer Science (BEng)	HG65	4FT deg	M+P	CCC	MO $		Dip$	BBBB$	N$	5	
Linguistics and Artificial Intelligence	QG18	4FT deg	g	BBB	Ind	Ind	Dip$	BBBB	Ind		
Software Engineering (BEng)	G700	4FT deg	M	CCC	MO $		Dip$	BBBB$	N$	9	

Univ of ESSEX

TITLE	CODE	COURSE	SUBJECTS	A/AS	ND/C	AGNVQ	IB	SQA(H)	SQA	RATIO	A/AS
Cognitive Science	C8G5	3FT deg	* g	22	MO+2D	D	28	BBBB	Ind		
Computer Science	G500	3FT deg	* g	20	MO+2D	D	28	BBBB	Ind	4	8/24
Computer Science (Artificial Intelligence)	G800	3FT deg	* g	20	MO+2D	D	28	BBBB	Ind	6	10/20
Computer Science (Software Engineering)	G700	3FT deg	* g	20	MO+2D	D	28	BBBB	Ind	5	8/28
Computer Science (Systems Architecture)	G600	3FT deg	* g	20	MO+2D	D	28	BBBB	Ind	20	
Computer Science with French (4 Yrs)	G5R1	4FT deg	E g	20	MO+2D	Ind	28$	CSYS	Ind		

TITLE	CODE	COURSE	SUBJECTS	A/AS	ND/C	AGNVQ	IB	SQA(H)	SQA	RATIO	A/AS
Computer Science with German (4 Yrs)	G5R2	4FT deg	* g	20	MO+2D	Ind	28	BBBB	Ind	12	
Computer Science with Russian (4 Yrs)	G5R8	4FT deg	R g	20	MO+2D	Ind	28$	CSYS	Ind		
Computer Science with Spanish (4 Yrs)	G5R4	4FT deg	* g	20	MO+2D	Ind	28	BBBB	Ind		
Computers & Networks	H6G7	3FT/4FT deg	(P+M)/*	14-18	MO $	D	28	BBCC	Ind	6	
Information Systems & Networks (MEng)	HG6P	4FT deg	M+Cs/Es/P	BCC	MO $	Ind	28$	CSYS	Ind		
Mathematics and Computing	GG15	3FT deg	M	18	MO $	D^	28$	CSYS	Ind	25	
Philosophy and Artificial Intelligence	GV87	3FT deg	*	24	MO+2D	Ind	28	BBBB	Ind		

Univ of EXETER

TITLE	CODE	COURSE	SUBJECTS	A/AS	ND/C	AGNVQ	IB	SQA(H)	SQA	RATIO	A/AS
Cognitive Science	CGV5	3FT deg	M g	20	MO	M$^	32$	Ind	Ind	3	18/22
Computer Science	G500	3FT deg	* g	20	MO+2D	M$	32	Ind	Ind	13	18/30
Computer Science with European Study	G5T2	4FT deg	* g	20	MO+2D	M$	32	Ind	Ind	5	
Computer Science with Management Science	G5N2	3FT deg	M	20	MO+2D	M$^	32$	Ind	Ind	16	
Computer Science with Mathematics	G5G1	3FT deg	M	20	MO+2D	M$^	32$	Ind	Ind	13	
Computer Science with Statistics	G5G4	3FT deg	M/St	20	MO+2D	M$^	32$	Ind	Ind	5	
Management Science with Information Technology	GN52	3FT deg	M/St	BBC	MO+2D	M/D$^	34$	Ind	Ind	5	14/22
Management Science with Media Computing	N2GM	3FT deg	M/St	BBC	MO+2D	M/D$^	34$	Ind	Ind	9	
Mathematics with Computer Science	G1G5	3FT deg	M	22	MO	M/D$^	34$	Ind	Ind	14	
Mathematics with Media Computing	G1GM	3FT deg	M	22	MO	M/D$^	34$	Ind	Ind	2	
Media Computing	G502	3FT deg		20	MO+2D	M$	32	Ind	Ind	13	
Media Computing with European Study	G5TF	4FT deg	g	20	MO+2D	M$	32	Ind	Ind	2	
Media Computing with Management Science	G5NF	3FT deg	M/St	20	MO+2D	M$^	32$	Ind	Ind		
Media Computing with Mathematics	G5GC	3FT deg	M	20	MO+2D	M$^	32$	Ind	Ind		
Media Computing with Statistics	G5GK	3FT deg	M/St	20	MO+2D	M$^	32$	Ind	Ind		
Statistical Science with Information Technology	GGK5	3FT deg	M/St	22	MO+2D	M/D$^	34$	Ind	Ind	4	
Statistics with Media Computing	G4GM	3FT deg	M/St	22	MO+2D	M/D$^	34$	Ind	Ind	4	

FARNBOROUGH COLL of Technology

TITLE	CODE	COURSE	SUBJECTS	A/AS	ND/C	AGNVQ	IB	SQA(H)	SQA	RATIO	A/AS
Computing	G500	3FT deg		EE	Ind	P*	Ind	Ind	Ind	3	6/16
Business Information Technology	265G	2FT HND		E	N	P*	Ind	Ind	Ind	4	
Computing	005G	2FT HND		E	N	P*	Ind	Ind	Ind	6	
Design Technology (Multi Media Video & Animation)	52GW	2FT HND		8	Ind	M*	Ind	Ind	Ind	6	
Electronic and Computer Systems Engineering	66HG	2FT HND		E	N	P*	Ind	Ind	Ind	3	
Software Engineering	007G	2FT HND		E	N	P*	Ind	Ind	Ind	3	

Univ of GLAMORGAN

TITLE	CODE	COURSE	SUBJECTS	A/AS	ND/C	AGNVQ	IB	SQA(H)	SQA	RATIO	A/AS
Accounting and Computing	G5N4	3FT/4SW deg	* g	12	7M	M$	Ind	Ind	Ind	7	14/16
Business Information Technology	G721▼	3FT deg									
Computer Studies	G501	3FT/4SW deg	* g	12	7M	M$	Ind	Ind	Ind	5	8/17
Computer Studies (Foundation Year)	G508▼	4EXT deg	* g	E	Ind	Ind	Ind	Ind	Ind	1	
Computer Studies with Foreign Lang & Business	G5T9	3FT/4SW deg	* g	12	7M	M$	Ind	Ind	Ind	16	
Computing and Business	GN51	3FT deg	* g	CC	7M	M$	Ind	Ind	Ind		
Computing with Business	G5N1	3FT/4SW deg	* g	CC	7M	M$	Ind	Ind	Ind	8	8/12
Information Systems	G521	4SW deg	* g	CC	5M	M$	Ind	Ind	Ind	10	
Information Technology	G560	3FT/4SW deg	* g	CD	3M $	M$	Ind	BB	N$	3	
Information Technology	G561	3FT deg									
Information Technology with European Business St	G564	3FT deg	* g	CD	3M $	M$	Ind	Ind	Ind		
Multimedia Computing	G540	3FT deg	* g	12	Ind	M$	Ind	Ind	Ind		
Software Engineering	G700	3FT/4SW deg	* g	12	7M	M$	Ind	Ind	Ind	7	10/14
Combined Studies (Honours) *Computer Studies*	Y400	3FT deg	* g	8-16	Ind	Ind	Ind	Ind	Ind		
Combined Studies (Honours) *Information Systems*	Y400	3FT deg	* g	8-16	Ind	Ind	Ind	Ind	Ind		
Combined Studies (Honours) *Information Technology*	Y400	3FT deg	* g	8-16	Ind	Ind	Ind	Ind	Ind		

TITLE	CODE	COURSE	SUBJECTS	A/AS	NO/C	RGNVQ	IB	SQA(H)	SQA	RATIO	A/AS
Combined Studies (Honours) *Software Engineering*	Y400	3FT deg	*g	8-16	Ind	Ind	Ind	Ind	Ind		
Joint Honours *Computer Studies*	Y401	3FT deg	*g	8-16	Ind	Ind	Ind	Ind	Ind		
Joint Honours *Information Systems*	Y401	3FT deg	*g	8-16	Ind	Ind	Ind	Ind	Ind		
Major/Minor Honours *Computer Studies*	Y402	3FT deg	*g	8-16	Ind	Ind	Ind	Ind	Ind		
Major/Minor Honours *Information Systems*	Y402	3FT deg	*g	8-16	Ind	Ind	Ind	Ind	Ind		
Major/Minor Honours *Information Technology*	Y402	3FT deg	*g	8-16	Ind	Ind	Ind	Ind	Ind		
Major/Minor Honours *Software Engineering*	Y402	3FT deg	*g	8-16	Ind	Ind	Ind	Ind	Ind		
Business Information Technology	1N5G▼	2FT HND	*g	D	N	P$	Ind	Ind	Ind	3	2/6
Computing	105G▼	2FT HND	*g	D	3M	P$	Ind	Ind	Ind	2	2/12
Information Technology	065G	2FT HND	*g	D	N	P$	Ind	Ind	Ind		
Multimedia	53GP	2FT HND	*g	D	Ind	P$	Ind	Ind	Ind		
Software Engineering	007G	2FT HND	*g	D	Ind	P$	Ind	Ind	Ind	4	

Univ of GLASGOW

TITLE	CODE	COURSE	SUBJECTS	A/AS	NO/C	RGNVQ	IB	SQA(H)	SQA	RATIO	A/AS
Anthropology/Computing Science	LG65	4FT deg		BBC	N	M	30	BBBB	Ind	5	
Archaeology/Computing Science	GV56	4FT deg	2S	BBC-CCC	N	M	24$	BBBB$	N	5	
Business Economics/Computing Science	LGC5	4FT deg		BBC	N	M	30	BBBB	N		
Celtic Civilisation/Computing Science	GQ5M	4FT deg		BBC	HN	M	30	BBBB	Ind		
Celtic/Computing	GQ55	4FT deg		BBC	HN	M	30	BBBB	Ind	1	
Classical Civilisation/Computing Science	GQ58	4FT deg		BBC	HN	M	30	BBBB	Ind		
Computing Science	G500	4FT deg	M+S	BBC-CCC	N	M	24$	BBBB$	N	5	16/24
Computing Science/Geography	FG85	4FT deg	M+S	BBC-CCC	N	M	24$	BBBB$	N	7	
Computing Science/Geology	FG65	4FT deg	M+S	BBC-CCC	N	M	24$	BBBB$	N		
Computing Science/Management Studies	NG15	4FT deg	M+S	BBC-CCC	N	M	24$	BBBB$	N	7	
Computing Science/Psychology	CG85	4FT deg	M+S	BBC-CCC	N	M	24$	BBBB$	N	3	
Computing Science/Statistics	GG45	4FT deg	M+S	BBC-CCC	N	M	24$	BBBB$	N	8	
Computing/Classical Hebrew	GQ59	4FT deg		BBC	HN	M	30	BBBB	Ind		
Computing/Czech	GT51	5FT deg		BBC	HN	M	30	BBBB	Ind		
Computing/Economic History	GV53	4FT deg		BBC	HN	M	30	BBBB	Ind		
Computing/Economics	GL5C	4FT deg		BBC	HN	M	30	BBBB	Ind	2	
Computing/French	GR51	5FT deg		BBC	HN	M	30	BBBB	Ind	17	
Computing/Greek	GQ57	4FT deg		BBC	HN	M	30	BBBB	Ind		
Computing/History	GV51	4FT deg		BBC	HN	M	30	BBBB	Ind	7	
Computing/History of Art	GV54	4FT deg		BBC	HN	M	30	BBBB	Ind		
Computing/Latin	GQ56	4FT deg		BBC	HN	M	30	BBBB	Ind		
Computing/Music	GW53	4FT deg		BBC	HN	M	30	BBBB	Ind	3	
Computing/Philosophy	GV57	4FT deg		BBC	HN	M	30	BBBB	Ind		
Computing/Politics	GM51	4FT deg		BBC	HN	M	30	BBBB	Ind	4	
Computing/Psychology	GC58	4FT deg		BBC	HN	M	30	BBBB	Ind	12	
Computing/Russian	GR58	5FT deg		BBC	HN	M	30	BBBB	Ind		
Computing/Scottish History	GV5C	4FT deg		BBC	HN	M	30	BBBB	Ind		
Computing/Scottish Literature	GQ52	4FT deg		BBC	HN	M	30	BBBB	Ind		
Computing/Social and Urban Policy	GL5K	4FT deg		BBC	8M	M	30	BBBB	Ind		
Computing/Sociology	GL53	4FT deg		BBC	HN	M	30	BBBB	Ind		
Computing/Theatre Studies	GW54	4FT deg		BBC	HN	M	30	BBBB	Ind		
Economic and Social History/Computing Science	VG35	4FT deg		BBC	8M	M	30	BBBB	Ind		
Economics/Computing Science	GLN1	4FT deg		BBC	8N	M	30	BBBB	Ind		
Electronic and Software Engineering	GH76	4FT deg	M+S	BBC-CCC	N	M	24$	BBBB$	N	11	

TITLE	CODE	COURSE	SUBJECTS	A/AS	ND/C	AGNVQ	IB	SQA(H)	SQA	RATIO A/AS
Electronic and Software Engineering	GH7P	4FT deg	M+P	CCD	MO	ME	24$	BBBBC$	N$	9
Geography/Computing Science	LG85	4FT deg		BBC	8M	M	30	BBBB	Ind	10
Management Studies/Computing	NGC5	4FT deg		BBC	HN	M	30	BBBB	Ind	26
Management Studies/Computing Science	GN51	4FT deg		BBC	8M	M	30	BBBB	Ind	18
Mathematics/Computing Science	GG15	4FT deg	M+S	BBC-CCC	N	M	24$	BBBB$	N	7
Microcomputer Systems Engineering	GH66	4FT deg	M+P	CCD	MO	ME	24$	BBBBC$	N$	9
Philosophy/Computing Science	GVM7	4FT deg		BBC	8M	M	30	BBBB	Ind	
Politics/Computing Science	MG15	4FT deg		BBC	8M	M	30	BBBB	Ind	
Psychology/Computing Science	CG8M	4FT deg		BBC	8M	M	30	BBBB	Ind	8
Social and Urban Policy/Computing Science	GL54	4FT deg		BBC	8M	M	30	BBBB	Ind	
Sociology/Computing Science	LG35	4FT deg		BBC	8M	M	30	BBBB	Ind	
Software Engineering	G530	4FT deg	M+S	BBC-CCC	N	M	24$	BBBB$	N	7

GLASGOW CALEDONIAN Univ

TITLE	CODE	COURSE	SUBJECTS	A/AS	ND/C	AGNVQ	IB	SQA(H)	SQA	RATIO A/AS
Applied Graphics Technology	GW52	2FT deg		X	Ind		Ind	X	HN	
Business and Information Management	N1G5	3FT/4SW deg	E g	CC	Ind		Ind	BBB$	Ind	2
Chemistry with Info Tech and Instrumentation	F1G5	3FT/4FT deg	M+S	DD-DE	Ind		Ind	CCC$	Ind	3
Computer Studies	G500	3FT/5SW deg	M+E+L	CC-CDD	Ind		Ind	BBCC$	Ind	4
Information Technology Studies	GG57	2FT deg		X				X		
Information and Business Administration	N1GM	3FT deg	E	DD	Ind		Ind	BCCC$	Ind	
International Travel with Information Systems	GN59	4SW deg	E+M g	CCC	Ind		Ind	BBCC$	Ind	6

GOLDSMITHS COLL (Univ of London)

TITLE	CODE	COURSE	SUBJECTS	A/AS	ND/C	AGNVQ	IB	SQA(H)	SQA	RATIO A/AS
Computer Science and Statistics	GG54	3FT deg	M	DD	MO	M	Dip	BBBBC	N	
Computing and Information Systems	G520	3FT deg		CCC	MO	M	Dip	BBBBC	N	
Mathematics & Computer Sci with Wk Exp (4 Yrs)	GG1M	4FT deg	M	DD	MO	M	Dip	BCCC	N	
Mathematics and Computer Science	GG15	3FT deg	M	DD	MO	M	Dip	BCCC	N	4 14/16
Mathematics with Computer Sci with Wk Ex (4 Yrs)	G1GM	4FT deg	M	DD	MO	M	Dip	BCCC	N	9
Mathematics with Computer Science	G1G5	3FT deg	M	DD	MO	M	Dip	BCCC	N	8
Psychology with Computer Science	C8G5	3FT deg		BBC	MO	M	Dip	ABBBB	N	9
Statistics, Computer Science & Applicable Maths	GG45	3FT deg	M	DD	MO	M	Dip	BCCC	N	3

Univ of GREENWICH

TITLE	CODE	COURSE	SUBJECTS	A/AS	ND/C	AGNVQ	IB	SQA(H)	SQA	RATIO A/AS
Applied Statistics with Computing	G4G5	3FT/4SW deg	* g	CE	3M	Ind	Ind	CCC$	Ind	
Building Surveying with Information Technology	K2GM	3FT/4SW deg	* g	16	5M	M	24	CCC	Ind	
Computer Networking	G720	3FT/4SW deg	S/Cs/M g	14	4M	M$ g	24	CCCC	Ind	
Computer Systems with Software Engineering	G6G7	3FT/4SW deg	S/Cs/M g	14	4M	M$ g	24	CCCC	Ind	
Computing	G504	3FT deg	* g	8-10	8M	M$ go	Ind	CCC		
Computing Major/Minor	G506	3FT/4SW deg	* g	8-10	8M	M$ go	Ind	CCC	Ind	
Computing Science	G500	3FT/4SW deg	* g	8-10	8M	M$ go	Ind	CCC	Ind	
Design and Construction Management with I.T.	K2GN	3FT/4SW deg	* g	16	5M	M	24	CCC	Ind	
Estate Management with Information Technology	N8G5	3FT/4SW deg	* g	16	5M	M	24	CCC	Ind	
Geographical Information Systems	FG85	3FT/4SW deg	* g	12	3M	Ind	Dip	CCC	Ind	
Geographical Information Systems (Extended)	FG8M	4FT/5SW deg	g	4		Ind	Ind	Ind	Ind	
Information Systems	G561	3FT/4SW deg	* g	8-10	4M	P$ go	Ind	CCC	Ind	
Information Systems with Business Management	GN51	3FT/4SW deg	* g	8-10	8M	M$ go	Ind	CCC	Ind	
Mathematics with Computing	GG15	3FT/4SW deg	M g	CE	3M $	Ind	Ind	CCC$	Ind	
Multi Media Technology	G503▼	3FT deg	* g	8-12	8M	M$ go	Ind	CCC	Ind	
Quantity Surveying with Information Technology	K2G5	3FT/4SW deg	* g	16	5M	Ind	24	CCC	Ind	
Remote Sensing	GF58	3FT/4SW deg	* g	12	3M	Ind	Dip	CCC	Ind	
Remote Sensing (Extended)	GF5V	4FT/5SW deg	g	4	N	Ind	Ind	Ind	Ind	
Business Information Systems	017G▼	2FT HND	* g	2	2M	P$ go	Ind	C	Ind	
Computer Systems Engineering	006G▼	3FT HND	* g	2	2M	P$ go	Ind	C	Ind	
Computing	005G▼	2FT HND	* g	2	2M	P$ go	Ind	C	Ind	

| | | | 98 expected requirements | | | | | | | 96 entry stats | |
TITLE	CODE	COURSE	SUBJECTS	A/AS	ND/C	RGNVQ	IB	SQA(H)	SQA	RATIO	A/AS
HERIOT-WATT Univ											
Applied Psychology and Computer Science	GL57	4FT deg	M	CCC	HN	M$ go	30	BBBC$	Ind		
Chemistry with Computer Science	F1G5	4FT deg	C+S	DDD	$	M$ go	28	BBCC	$		
Chemistry with Computer Science (MChem)	F1GM	5FT deg	C+S	DDD	$	M$ go	28	BBCC	$		
Computer Science	G500	4FT deg	* g	CDD	N	M$ go	28	BBBC	N		
Computer Science (Automated Systems)	G700	4FT deg	* g	CDD	N	M$ go	28	BBBC	N		
Computer Science (Human Computer Interaction)	G570	4FT deg	* g	CDD	N	M$ go	28	BBBC	N		
Computer Science (Information Systems)	G520	4FT deg	* g	CDD	N	M$ go	28	BBBC	N		
Computer Science (Knowledge-Based Systems)	G560	4FT deg	* g	CDD	N	M$ go	28	BBBC	N		
Computing and Electronics	GH56	4FT deg	M+P	CDD	MO	M$ go	28	BBBC	Ind		
Information Systems Engineering	HG66	4FT deg	M+P	CDD	MO	M$^ go	28	BBBC	Ind		
Mathematics with Computer Science	G1G5	4FT deg	M	CDE	HN	M$^	28	BBB	HN		
Combined Studies 　　Computer Science	Y100	4FT deg	*	DDE	Ind	M$ go	26	BCCC	Ind		
Univ of HERTFORDSHIRE											
Accounting and Management Information Systems	GN54	3FT/4SW deg	* g	18	DO	DB	28$	BBBB		7	10/20
Applied Geology/Computing	F6G5	3FT deg	* g	12	3M $	M$ gi	24$	CCCC$	Ind	4	
Applied Physics/Computing	F3G5	3FT deg	M+P	12	3M $	M$ gi	24$	CCCC$	Ind	7	
Applied Statistics/Computing	G4G5	3FT deg	*	12	3M	M$ gi	24	CCCC	Ind	1	
Astronomy/Computing	F5G5	3FT deg	M g	12	3M $	M$ gi	24$	CCCC$	Ind	3	
Business Information Systems	G710	3FT/4SW deg	* g	18	DO	DB/I	28$	BBBB			
Business/Computing	N1G5	3FT deg	*	18	4M+4D	M$6 gi	26	BBBC	Ind	5	14/20
Chemistry/Computing	F1G5	3FT deg	C g	12	3M $	MS gi	24$	CCCC$	Ind		
Computer Science (1 year full-time)	G503	1FT deg	* g							2	
Computer Science (4 year sandwich)	G500	4SW deg	* g	14	MO	M$^ gi	28	Ind	Ind	2	7/18
Computer Science in Europe	G5T2	4SW deg	* g	18	MO	M$^ gi	30	Ind	Ind	7	
Computing Mathematics	GG15	3FT/4SW deg	M g	12	MO+D	M$^ gi	26	Ind	Ind	6	
Computing/Applied Geology	G5F6	3FT deg	* g	12	3M $	M$ gi	24$	CCCC$	Ind	6	
Computing/Applied Physics	G5F3	3FT deg	M+P	12	3M $	M$ gi	24$	CCCC$	Ind		
Computing/Applied Statistics	G5G4	3FT deg	* g	12	3M	M$ gi	24	CCCC	Ind		
Computing/Astronomy	G5F5	3FT deg	M g	12	3M $	M$ gi	24$	CCCC$	Ind		
Computing/Business	G5N1	3FT deg	*	18	4M+4D	M$6 gi	26	BBBC	Ind	13	
Computing/Chemistry	G5F1	3FT deg	C g	12	3M $	MS gi	24$	CCCC$	Ind		
Computing/Electronic Music	G5W3	3FT deg	Mu	14	MO $	M$^ gi	26$	BCCC$	Ind	8	
Computing/Electronics	G5H6	3FT deg	* g	12	3M $	M$ gi	24$	CCCC$	Ind	2	
Computing/European Studies	G5TF	3FT deg	*	14	MO	M$ gi	26	BCCC	Ind	2	
Computing/Human Biology	G5B1	3FT deg	S g	12	3M $	MS gi	24$	CCCC$	Ind	1	
Computing/Law	G5M3	3FT deg	*	20	4M+4D	D$ gi	26	BBBC	Ind		
Computing/Linguistic Science	G5Q1	3FT deg	*	14	MO	M$ gi	26	BCCC	Ind		
Computing/Manufacturing Systems	G5H7	3FT deg	*	12	3M	M$ gi	24	CCCC	Ind	2	
Computing/Mathematics	G5G1	3FT deg	M	12	3M $	M$^ gi	24$	CCCC$	Ind	13	
Computing/Philosophy	G5V7	3FT deg	*	14	MO	M$ gi	26	BCCC	Ind	2	
Computing/Psychology	G5C8	3FT deg	*	20	4M+4D	D$ gi	26	BBBC	Ind		
Electronic Music/Computing	W3G5	3FT deg	Mu	14	MO $	M$^ gi	26$	BCCC$	Ind	3	
Electronics/Computing	H6G5	3FT deg	* g	12	3M $	M$ gi	24$	CCCC$	Ind	6	
European Studies/Computing	T2G5	3FT deg	*	14	MO	M$ gi	26	BCCC	Ind		
Human Biology/Computing	B1G5	3FT deg	S g	12	3M $	MS gi	24$	CCCC$	Ind	2	
Informatics (1 year top-up from HND)	G504	1FT deg	*	X	MO $		Ind	Ind	Ind		
Information Systems	G520	4SW deg	* g	14	MO	M$^ gi	28	Ind	Ind	4	
Intelligent Systems	G800	3FT deg									
Law/Computing	M3G5	3FT deg	*	20	4M+4D	D$ gi	26	BBBC	Ind	7	
Linguistic Science/Computing	Q1G5	3FT deg	*	14	MO	M$ gi	26	BCCC	Ind		

Computer Sciences and Engineering 15

TITLE	CODE	COURSE	SUBJECTS	A/AS	ND/C	AGNVQ	IB	SQR(H)	SQR	RATIO	A/AS
Manufacturing Systems/Computing	H7G5	3FT deg	*	12	3M	M$ gi	24	CCCC	Ind		
Mathematics/Computing	G1G5	3FT deg	M	12	3M $	M$^ gi	24$	CCCC$	Ind	17	
Multimedia Systems	G5P4	3FT deg									
Philosophy/Computing	V7G5	3FT deg	*	14	MO	M$ gi	26	BCCC	Ind	4	
Psychology/Computing	C8G5	3FT deg	*	20	4M+4D	D$ gi	26	BBBC	Ind	19	
Software Engineering	G5G7	4SW deg	* g	14	MO	M$^ gi	28	Ind	Ind	5	10/16
Software Systems for the Arts and Media	G701	3FT deg	* g	10	MO	M*	Ind	Ind	Ind	2	6/22
Combined Modular Scheme Computing	Y100	3FT deg	*	12	3M	M$ gi	24	CCCC	Ind		
Combined Modular Scheme Computing (Extended)	Y109▼	4EXT deg	*	4	N	P$ gi	Dip	DDDD	Ind		
Business Decision Analysis	017G	2FT HND	g	4	N	M$	24$	CCCC	Ind	1	2/5
Business Information Technology	265G▼	2FT HND	* g	4	3M	P	24	Ind	Ind	3	
Computing	105G	2FT/3SW HND	* g	4	2M	P*	Ind	Ind	Ind	2	2/8
Computing (Business Systems)	205G	2FT HND	* g	4	2M	P*	Ind	Ind	Ind	8	
Computing (Computer Systems)	025G	2FT HND	* g	4	2M	P*	Ind	Ind	Ind	4	
Computing (Information Technology)	165G	2FT HND	* g	4	2M	P*	Ind	Ind	Ind		
Computing (Multimedia Systems)	065G	2FT HND	* g	4	2M	P*	Ind	Ind	Ind	4	
Computing (Software Engineering)	007G	2FT/3SW HND	* g	4	2M	P*	Ind	Ind	Ind		

Univ of HUDDERSFIELD

TITLE	CODE	COURSE	SUBJECTS	A/AS	ND/C	AGNVQ	IB	SQR(H)	SQR	RATIO	A/AS
Architectural Computer Aided Technology	GK51	3FT deg	* g	12	5M	M$4/^ go	Ind	Ind	Ind		
Combined Studies in Computing	G501	3FT/4SW deg	* g	18-20	MO	M go	Ind	BBB	Ind		
Computing (Software Development)	G700	4SW deg	* g	18-20	MO	M go	Ind	BBB	Ind		
Computing Science	G500	3FT deg	* g	14-16	MO	M go	Ind	BBB	Ind		
Computing and Business Analysis	GN51	4SW deg	* g	14-16	MO	M go	Ind	BBB	Ind		
Computing and Mathematics	GG51	3FT/4SW deg	M g	18-20	MO+1D$	M^ go	Ind	BBB	Ind		
Computing and Psychology	GL57	3FT deg	* g	14-16	MO	M go	Ind	BBB	Ind		
Computing and Statistics	GG54	3FT deg	* g	14-16	MO	M go	Ind	BBB	Ind		
Computing in Business	G523	4SW deg	* g	18-20	MO	M go	Ind	BBB	Ind		
Computing with a Modern European Language	GT52	4SW deg	* g	14-16	MO	M go	Ind	BBB	Ind		
Creative Imaging	EW52	3FT/4SW deg	Pf+A/Ad/Fa g	12-14	MO	M4/^ go	Ind	Ind	Ind		
Creative Imaging	GW52	3FT/4SW deg	Pf+A/Ad/Fa g	12-14	MO	M4/^ go	Ind	Ind	Ind		
Electronic Engineering and Computer Systems	GH56	4SW deg	M+S	12	4M $	M$ go	Ind	BBC	Ind		
Electronic Engineering and Computer Systems(Ext)	GH5P	5SW deg	* g	DD	N	P go	Dip	CCC	Ind		
Electronic Engineering and Computer Systs (MEng)	GHM6	5SW deg	M+S	CCC	3D $	M$3/^ go	Ind	Ind	Ind		
European Software Engineering	G7T2	1FT/2FT deg	g	X	HN	X	X	X	HN		
Interactive Media	G5P4	4SW deg	* g	18-20	MO	M go	Ind	BBB	Ind		
Scientific Computing	GG15	4SW deg	M g	18-20	MO+1D$	M^ go	Ind	BBB	Ind		
Software Engineering (MEng)	G701	5SW deg	* g	20-22	MO+2D	D go	Ind	Ind	Ind		
Virtual Reality Systems	GG57	3FT/4SW deg	S g	16-20	2D	M$ go	Ind	Ind	Ind		
Business Information Technology	265G	3SW HND	* g	4	N	P go	Ind	CCC	Ind		
Computing	105G	3SW HND	* g	4	N	P go	Ind	CCC	Ind		
Decision Sciences	25NG	3SW HND	* g	4	N	P go	Ind	CCC	Ind		
Multimedia	4P5G	3SW HND	* g	4	N	P go	Ind	CCC	Ind		
Software Engineering	007G	3SW HND	* g	4	N	P go	Ind	CCC	Ind		

Univ of HULL

TITLE	CODE	COURSE	SUBJECTS	A/AS	ND/C	AGNVQ	IB	SQR(H)	SQR	RATIO	A/AS
Computer Graphics and Mathematical Modelling	GG5D	4FT deg	* g	10	N	P	24	CCCCD	Ind		
Computer Graphics and Mathematical Modelling	GG5C	3FT deg	S+M	18	MO	M$+	26$	BBBCC	Ind		
Computer Science	G500	3FT deg	M	18	MO $	M$^ go	26$	BBCCC	Ind	9	12/22
Computer Science (Yr 1 franchised)	G501	4FT deg	*	CD	N	P$ gi	24	BCCCC	Ind	3	5/12
Computer Science with Info Eng (Yr 1 franchised)	G568	4FT deg	*	CD	N	M$^ go	24	BCCCC	Ind	9	
Computer Science with Information Engineering	G560	3FT deg	g	18	MO	M$^ go	26$	BBCCC	Ind	2	14/24

			98 expected requirements							96 entry stats	
TITLE	**CODE**	**COURSE**	**SUBJECTS**	**A/AS**	**NO/C**	**RGNVQ**	**IB**	**SQA(H)**	**SQA**	**RATIO**	**A/AS**
Computer Systems Eng with Bus Studies (MEng)	G6N1	4FT deg	S+M g	BCC	M+D $	ME^ gi	26$	BBBCC	Ind		
Computer Systems Engineering	G600	3FT deg	S+M	18	Ind	ME^ gi	26$	BBCCC	Ind	7	15/18
Computer Systems Engineering (4 Yrs)	G601	4FT deg	*	CD	N	P$ gi	24	BCCCC	Ind	3	
Computer and Management Sciences	GN51	3FT deg	M	BCC-CCC	M0+D $	M$^ go	26$	BBBCC	Ind	17	
Information Management	N1G5	3FT deg	M g	BBC-BCC	M+4D	M*6/^ go	28$	BBCCC	Ind	3	14/20
Software Engineering	G701	4FT deg	*	CD	N	P$^ gi	24	BCCCC	Ind	4	
Software Engineering	G700	3FT deg	M	18	MO $	M$^ go	26$	BBCCC	Ind	11	
Software Engineering with Industrial Experience	G702	4FT deg	M	18	MO $	M$^ gi	26$	BBCCC	Ind		
Software Engineering with Study Abroad	G703	4FT deg	M g	18	MO $	M$^ gi	26$	BBCCC	Ind		

IMPERIAL COLL (Univ of London)

Computing	G500	3FT deg	M	BBB	Ind		$	Ind	Ind	14	24/30
Computing (Artificial Intelligence) (4 years)	G800	4FT deg	M	BBB	Ind		$	Ind	Ind	15	26/30
Computing (Computational Management) (4 years)	G520	4FT deg	M	BBB	Ind		$	Ind	Ind	14	26/28
Computing (MEng)	G501	4FT deg	M	BBB	Ind		$	Ind	Ind	8	26/30
Computing (Mathematical Foundations) (4 years)	G550	4FT deg	M	BBB	Ind		$	Ind			
Computing (Software Engineering) (MEng)	G700	4FT deg	M	BBB	Ind		$	Ind	Ind	13	26/30
Computing(European Prog of Study) (MEng)	G502	4FT deg	M g	BBB	Ind		$	Ind	Ind	9	
Information Systems Engineering	HG65	3FT deg	M+P	BBB	HN/DO	X	$	CSYS$	HN$	12	
Information Systems Engineering (MEng)	GH56	4FT deg	M+P	BBB	HN/DO	X	$	CSYS$	HN$	4	26/30
Mathematics and Computer Science	GG15	3FT deg	M	BBC-ACC	Ind	X	Ind	Ind	Ind	11	26/30
Mathematics and Computer Science (MSci)	GG51	4FT deg	M	AAB	Ind	X	Ind	Ind	Ind	3	24/30

KEELE Univ

Biol and Medicinal Chem and Computer Science	FGC5	3FT deg	C g	BCC-CCC	Ind	M$^	26$	CSYS	Ind		
Computer Science	G500	3FT deg	*	BCC-CCC	Ind	M$^	26	CSYS	Ind	54	
Computer Science and Ancient History (4 Yrs)	VGD5	4FT deg	*	BCC	Ind	Ind	28	BBBB	Ind		
Computer Science and Applied Social Studies	GL55	3FT deg	*	BCC	Ind	D$^	28	CSYS	Ind		
Computer Science and Astrophysics	FG55	3FT deg	P g	BCC-CCC	Ind	M$^	26$	CSYS	Ind	13	
Computer Science and Astrophysics (4 Yrs)	GF55	4FT deg	*	BCC-CCC	Ind	Ind	26	BBBB	Ind	2	
Computer Science and Astrophysics (MSci)	GFMC	4FT deg	*	BCC-CCC	Ind	Ind	28	BBBB	Ind		
Computer Science and Biochemistry	CG75	3FT deg	C g	BCC-CCC	Ind	M$^	26$	CSYS	Ind		
Computer Science and Biochemistry (4 Yrs)	GC57	4FT deg	*	BCC-CCC	Ind	Ind	26	BBBB	Ind		
Computer Science and Biology	CG15	3FT deg	S g	BCC-CCC	Ind	M$^	26$	CSYS	Ind		
Computer Science and Biology (4 Yrs)	GC51	4FT deg	*	BCC-CCC	Ind	Ind	26	BBBB	Ind		
Computer Science and Business Admin (4 Yrs)	NG95	4FT deg	*	BCC	Ind	Ind	28	BBBB	Ind		
Computer Science and Chemistry	FG15	3FT deg	C g	BCC-CCC	Ind	M$^	26$	CSYS	Ind	9	
Computer Science and Chemistry (MSci)	GF5D	4FT deg	C	BCC-CCC	Ind	M$^	26$	CSYS	Ind		
Computer Science and Classical Studies (4 Yrs)	QG85	4FT deg	*	BCC	Ind	Ind	28	BBBB	Ind		
Computer Science and Mathematics (MSci)	GG5C	4FT deg	M	BCC-CCC	Ind	M$^	26$	CSYS	Ind		
Criminology and Computer Science	GM5H	3FT deg	* g	BBB-BCC	Ind	D$^	28	CSYS	Ind		
Criminology and Computer Science (4 Yrs)	MGH5	4FT deg	*	BBB	Ind	Ind	32	ABBB	Ind	2	
Economics and Computer Science	GL51	3FT deg	* g	BCC	Ind	Ind	28	CSYS	Ind	3	
Electronic Music and Computer Science	GW5J	3FT deg	Mu	BCC	Ind	D$^	28$	CSYS	Ind	6	
Electronic Music and Computer Science (4 Yrs)	WGJ5	4FT deg	*	BCC	Ind	Ind	28	BBBB	Ind	5	
English and Computer Science	GQ53	3FT deg	E	BCC	Ind	D$^	28$	CSYS	Ind	13	
English and Computer Science (4 Yrs)	QG35	4FT deg	*	BCC	Ind	Ind	28	BBBB	Ind		
Environmental Management and Computer Science	FGX5	3FT deg	* g	BCC	Ind	Ind	28	CSYS	Ind		
Finance and Computer Science (4 Yrs)	NG35	4FT deg	* g	BCC	Ind	Ind	28	BBBB	Ind		
French and Computer Science	GR51	3FT deg	F g	BCC	Ind	D$^	28$	CSYS	Ind		
French/Russian or Russian Studs and Comp Science	GT5X	3FT deg	F+R	BBC-BCC	Ind	D$^	28$	CSYS	Ind		
Geography and Computer Science	GL58	3FT deg	Gy g	BCC	Ind	D$^	28$	CSYS	Ind	4	15/18
Geography and Computer Science (4 Yrs)	LG85	4FT deg	*	BCC	Ind	Ind	28	BBBB	Ind		

Computer Sciences and Engineering   15

course details

TITLE	CODE	COURSE	SUBJECTS	A/AS	ND/C	AGNVQ	IB	SQA(H)	SQA	RATIO A/AS
Geology and Computer Science	FG65	3FT deg	S g	BCC-CCC	Ind	M$^	26$	CSYS	Ind	
Geology and Computer Science (4 Yrs)	GF56	4FT deg	*	BCC-CCC	Ind	Ind	26	BBBB	Ind	
Geology and Computer Science (MSci)	GF5P	4FT deg	S	BCC-CCC	Ind	M$^	26$	CSYS	Ind	
German and Computer Science (4 Yrs)	RG25	4FT deg	* g	BCC	Ind	Ind	28	BBBB	Ind	
History and Computer Science	GV51	3FT deg	* g	BCC	Ind	Ind	28	CSYS	Ind	
History and Computer Science (4 Yrs)	VG15	4FT deg	*	BCC	Ind	Ind	28	BBBB	Ind	
Human Resource Management and Computer Science	GN56	3FT deg	* g	BCC	Ind	Ind	28	CSYS	Ind	
Human Resource Mgt and Computer Science (4 Yrs)	NG65	4FT deg	*	BCC	Ind	Ind	28	BBBB	Ind	1
International History and Computer Sci (4 Yrs)	VGC5	4FT deg	*	BCC	Ind	Ind	28	BBBB	Ind	
International History and Computer Science	GV5C	3FT deg	* g	BCC	Ind	Ind	28	CSYS	Ind	
International Politics and Computer Science	GM5C	3FT deg	* g	BCC	Ind	Ind	28	CSYS	Ind	
Latin and Computer Science (4 Yrs)	QG65	4FT deg	* g	BCC	Ind	Ind	28	BBBB	Ind	
Law and Computer Science	GM53	3FT deg	*	BBB-BBC	Ind	Ind	30	CSYS	Ind	14
Law and Computer Science (4 Yrs)	MG35	4FT deg	*	BBB	Ind	Ind	32	BBBB	Ind	
Management Science and Computer Science	GN51	3FT deg	* g	BCC	Ind	Ind	28	CSYS	Ind	4 14/16
Management Science and Computer Science (4 Yrs)	NG15	4FT deg	*	BCC	Ind	Ind	28	BBBB	Ind	5
Marketing and Computer Science	GN55	3FT deg	* g	BCC	Ind	Ind	28	CSYS	Ind	
Mathematics and Computer Science	GG15	3FT deg	M	BCC-CCC	Ind	M$^	26$	CSYS	Ind	3 16/24
Mathematics and Computer Science (4 Yrs)	GG51	4FT deg	*	BCC-CCC	Ind	Ind	26	BBBB	Ind	
Music and Computer Science	GW53	3FT deg	Mu g	BCC	Ind	D$^	28$	CSYS	Ind	9
Music and Computer Science (4 Yrs)	WG35	4FT deg	*	BCC	Ind	Ind	28	BBBB	Ind	
Neuroscience and Computer Science	BG15	3FT deg	2S	BCC-CCC	Ind	MS^	26$	CSYS	Ind	1
Neuroscience and Computer Science (4 Yrs)	BG1M	4FT deg	*	BCC-CCC	Ind	Ind	26	BBBB	Ind	
Philosophy and Computer Science (4 Yrs)	VG75	4FT deg	* g	BCC	Ind	Ind	28	BBBB	Ind	
Physics and Computer Science	FG35	3FT deg	P g	BCC-CCC	Ind	M$^	26$	CSYS	Ind	4
Physics and Computer Science (4 Yrs)	GF53	4FT deg	*	BCC-CCC	Ind	Ind	26	BBBB	Ind	2
Physics and Computer Science (MSci)	GF5H	4FT deg	P g	BCC-CCC	Ind	M$^	26$	CSYS	Ind	
Politics and Computer Science	GM51	3FT deg	* g	BCC	Ind	D$^	28	CSYS	Ind	
Politics and Computer Science (4 Yrs)	MG15	4FT deg	*	BCC	Ind	Ind	28	BBBB	Ind	
Psychology and Computer Science	CG85	3FT deg	* g	BBB	Ind	Ind	32	CSYS	Ind	
Psychology and Computer Science (4 Yrs)	GC58	4FT deg	*	BBB	Ind	Ind	32	ABBB	Ind	6
Russian Studies and Computer Science	GRM8	3FT deg	* g	BCC	Ind	Ind	28	CSYS	Ind	
Russian Studies and Computer Science (4 Yrs)	RG8M	4FT deg	*	BCC	Ind	Ind	28	BBBB	Ind	
Russian and Computer Science	GR58	3FT deg	R	BCC	Ind	D$^	28$	CSYS	Ind	
Russian and Computer Science (4 Yrs)	RG85	4FT deg	*	BCC	Ind	Ind	28	BBBB	Ind	
Sociology & Soc Anthrop & Computer Sci (4 Yrs)	LG35	4FT deg	* g	BCC	Ind	Ind	28	BBBB	Ind	
Statistics and Computer Science	GG45	3FT deg	M	BCC-CCC	Ind	M$^	26$	CSYS	Ind	3
Statistics and Computer Science (4 Yrs)	GG54	4FT deg	*	BCC-CCC	Ind	Ind	26	BBBB	Ind	
Visual Arts and Computer Science	GW51	3FT deg	*	BCC	Ind	D$^	28	CSYS	Ind	2
Visual Arts and Computer Science (4 Yrs)	WG15	4FT deg	*	BCC	Ind	Ind	28	BBBB	Ind	

Univ of KENT

TITLE	CODE	COURSE	SUBJECTS	A/AS	ND/C	AGNVQ	IB	SQA(H)	SQA	RATIO A/AS
Accounting & Finance with Computing	N4G5	3FT deg	* g	20	3M+4D	M$ go	28	BBBB	Ind	7
Computer Sci and Business Admin with a yr in Ind	GN5C	4FT deg								
Computer Science	G500	3FT deg	* g	BCC	Ind	Ind	28	BBBBB	Ind	5 10/24
Computer Science (MEng)	G502	4FT deg	* g	BCC	Ind	Ind	28	BBBB	Ind	
Computer Science and Business Administration	GN51	3FT deg	* g	20	Ind	Ind	28	BBBB	Ind	
Computer Science with Management Science	G5N1	3FT deg	M	BCC	Ind	Ind	28$	BBBB$	Ind	6 10/23
Computer Science with Mgt Sci & a yr in Industry	G5NC	4FT deg	M	BCC	Ind	Ind	28$	BBBB$	Ind	
Computer Science with a year in Industry	G504	4FT deg	* g	BCC	Ind	Ind	28	BBBB	Ind	
Computing and Accounting & Finance	GN54	3FT deg	* g	20	3M+3D	M$ go	28	BBBB	Ind	
Computing and Economics	GLM1	3FT deg	* g	20	3M+3D	M$ go	28	BBBB	Ind	
Computing and Social Psychology	GL57	3FT deg	* g	26	6D	D$ go	33	AAAB	Ind	

course details			98 expected requirements							96 entry stats	
TITLE	CODE	COURSE	SUBJECTS	A/AS	ND/C	AGNVQ	IB	SQA(H)	SQA	RATIO	A/AS
Computing and Social Psychology	CG85	3FT deg	* g	26	6D+5D	D$ go	33	AAAB	Ind		
Computing and Social Statistics	GG54	3FT deg	M	20	Ind	Ind	28$	BBBB$	Ind		
Computing/Classical Studies	QG85	3FT deg	*	20	3M+3D	Ind	28	Ind	Ind		
Computing/Comparative Literary Studies	QG25	3FT deg	*	20	3M+3D	Ind	28	Ind	Ind		
Drama/Computing	WG45	3FT deg	*	22	2M+4D	Ind	30	Ind	Ind		
Economics with Computing	L1G5	3FT deg	* g	20	3M+3D	M$ go	28	BBBB	Ind	18	
English (Post-Colonial Literatures)/Computing	GQ5J	3FT deg	E	22	2M+4D	Ind	30$	Ind	Ind		
English Language/Computing	GQ53	3FT deg	E	20	3M+3D	Ind	28	Ind	Ind	4	
English/Computing	QG35	3FT deg	E	22	2M+4D	Ind	30	Ind	Ind		
European Computer Science	G501	4FT deg	M g	BCC	Ind	Ind	28$	BBBB$	Ind	17	
European Management Science with Computing	N1GM	4FT deg	M+L	20	1M+5D	Ind	28$	Ind	Ind		
European Studies/Computing	TG25	4FT deg	L	20	3M+3D	Ind	28	Ind	Ind	3	
Film Studies/Computing	WG55	3FT deg	*	22	2M+4D	Ind	30	Ind	Ind		
French/Computing	RG15	4FT deg	F	20	3M+3D	Ind	28	Ind	Ind	5	
German/Computing	RG25	4FT deg	G	20	3M+3D	Ind	28	Ind	Ind		
History and Theory of Art/Computing	VG45	3FT deg	*	20	3M+3D	Ind	28	Ind	Ind	1	
History/Computing	VG15	3FT deg	*	22	2M+4D	Ind	30	Ind	Ind	7	
Italian/Computing	RG35	4FT deg	*	20	3M+3D	Ind	28	Ind	Ind	1	
Linguistics/Computing	QG15	3FT deg	*	20	3M+3D	Ind	28	Ind	Ind		
Management Science and Computing	NG15	3FT/4SW deg	M	20	1M+5D	Ind	28$	Ind	Ind	5	
Management Science with Computing	N1G5	3FT/4SW deg	M	20	1M+5D	Ind	28$	Ind	Ind	1	14/20
Mathematics & Computer Science with a Yr in Ind	GG1M	4SW deg	M	20	Ind	Ind	28$	BBBB$	Ind		
Mathematics and Computer Science	GG15	3FT deg	M	20	Ind	Ind	28$	BBBB$	Ind	7	12/24
Philosophy/Computing	VG75	3FT deg	*	20	3M+3D	Ind	28	Ind	Ind	3	
Social Policy and Administration with Computing	L4G5	3FT deg	* g	20	3M+3D	M$ go	28	BBBB	Ind	3	
Social Psychology with Computing	C8G5	3FT deg	* g	BBB	1M+5D	D$ go	32	AABB	Ind		
Software Engineering	G700▼	3FT deg	* g	Ind	Ind	Ind	Ind	Ind	Ind		12/20
Spanish/Computing	GR54	4FT deg	*	20	3M+3D	Ind	28	Ind	Ind		
Statistics and Computer Science (3/4 Yrs)	GG45	3FT/4FT deg	M	20	Ind	Ind	28$	Ind	Ind		
Theology/Computing	VG85	3FT deg	*	20	3M+3D	Ind	28	Ind	Ind		

KING ALFRED'S WINCHESTER

Computing (Human Centred)	G500	3FT deg	* g	14	6M	M	24	BCC	N		
Computing and Archaeology	FG45	3FT deg	* g	14	6M	M	24	BCC	N		
Computing and Business Studies	GN51	3FT deg	* g	14	6M	M	24	BCC	N	2	7/18
Design & Technology and Computing	GJ59	3FT deg	Ds/Ad g	14	6M $	M	24$	BCC$	N$	1	
Geography and Computing	GL58	3FT deg	Gy g	14	X	X	24$	BCC$	X	5	
History and Computing	GV51	3FT deg	H g	14	X	X	24$	BCC$	X	2	
Music (World) and Computing	GW53	3FT deg	* g	14	6M	M	24	BCC	N	1	
Psychology and Computing	GL57	3FT deg	* g	14	6M	M	24	BCC	N	1	
Social Biology and Computing	CG15	3FT deg	B g	14	6M $	M	24$	BCC$	N$		
Sports Studies and Computing	GL5H	3FT deg	* g	14	6M	M	24	BCC	N		

KING'S COLL LONDON (Univ of London)

Chemistry with Computer Science	F1GM	4FT deg	C+M	18	4M $	Ind	28$	BBCCC	Ind		
Chemistry with Computer Science	F1G5	3FT/4SW deg	C+M	18	4M $	Ind	28$	BBCCC	Ind	9	
Computer Science	G500	3FT/4SW deg	M	20	X	X	30$	ABBBB$	X	8	16/26
Computer Science and Digital Electronics	GH56	3FT deg	M	20	X	X	30$	ABBBB$	X	9	
Computer Science with Management	G5N1	3FT/4SW deg	M	20	X	X	30$	ABBBB$	X	7	16/24
Computer Science with a year abroad	G501	3FT deg	M	20	X		30$	ABBBB$			
Computer Science with a year in Industry	G505	4FT deg	M	20	X		30$	ABBBB$			
Computer Syst and Electronics with a yr Industry	GH6Q	5FT deg	M	20	X		30$	ABBBB$			
Computer Systems & Electronics with 1 Yr abroad	GH6P	4FT deg	M+P	BBC	MO+3D		28	BBBCC$	Ind	10	

| | | | 98 expected requirements | | | | | | | 96 entry stats | |
| course details | | | | | | | | | | | |
TITLE	CODE	COURSE	SUBJECTS	A/AS	NO/C	AGNVQ	IB	SQA(H)	SQA	RATIO	A/AS
Computer Systems and Electronics	GH66	3FT deg	M+P	BBC	MO+3D		28	BBBCC$	Ind	7	18/30
Computer Systems and Electronics	GHP6	4FT deg									
French with Applied Computing	R1G5	4FT deg	F	BCC						4	
Geography with Applied Computing	L8G5	3FT deg	Gy	BCC						6	
German with Applied Computing	R2G5	4FT deg	G	BCC							
Hispanic Studies with Applied Computing	R4G5	4FT deg	Sp	BBC							
Mathematics and Computer Science	GG15	3FT deg	M	20	X		28	ABBBB$	X	4	12/24
Mathematics and Computer Science (Management)	GG1N	3FT deg	M	20	X		28	ABBBB$	X	4	16/26
Modern Greek with Applied Computing	T2G5	4FT deg	*	BCC							
Music with Applied Computing	W3G5	3FT deg	Mu	BBC						17	
Physics with Computer Science	F3G5	3FT deg	M+P	18	2M+1D		28$	AABBB	Ind	5	
Portuguese with Applied Computing	R5G5	3FT deg	E+H/L	BCC							
War Studies with Applied Computing	M9G5	3FT deg	*	BBC							

KINGSTON Univ

TITLE	CODE	COURSE	SUBJECTS	A/AS	NO/C	AGNVQ	IB	SQA(H)	SQA	RATIO	A/AS
Business Information Technology	G562	4SW deg	*	CCD	4M+4D	Ind	30$	Ind	Ind	8	10/20
Computer Information Systems Design	G561	4SW deg	* g	12-18	5D $	M*3	Ind	Ind	Ind	3	6/15
Computer Science	G500	4SW deg	*	10	5M $	M$3/^	24	Ind	Ind	6	6/18
Computing & Chemistry	FG15	3FT deg	C g	8	3M $	Ind	Ind	CCC	Ind	5	
Computing & Mathematics	GG15	3FT deg	M	10	3M $	Ind	Ind	CCC	Ind	5	12/16
Computing & Physics	FG35	3FT deg	P/M g	10	3M $	Ind	Ind	CCC	Ind		
Computing & Statistics	GG54	3FT deg	* g	10	3M $	Ind	Ind	CCC	Ind	3	
Computing Systems	G521	4SW deg	M	10	5M $	ME3/^	Ind	Ind	Ind	3	
Computing Systems	G520	3FT deg	M	10	5M $	ME3/^	Ind	Ind	Ind	1	
Electronic Engineering with Computing	H6GM▼	4FT/5SW deg	*	4-6	Ind		Ind	Ind	Ind	2	
Electronic Engineering with Computing(BEng/MEng)	H6G5	4SW/5SW deg	M+S/Cs/Ec/Es/Ds	8	5M $	ME3	Ind	Ind	Ind	4	
Electronic Engineering with Computing(BEng/MEng)	H6GN	3FT/4FT deg	M+S/Cs/Ec/Es/Ds	8	5M $	ME3	Ind	Ind	Ind	3	6/10
Geographical Information Systems	LG85▼	4EXT deg	*		Ind		Ind	Ind	Ind		
Geographical Information Systems	GL58	3FT deg	Gy	12	$	Ind	Ind	BCCC	Ind	2	6/20
Geography & Computing	FG85	3FT deg	Gy g	12	$	Ind	Ind	BCCC	Ind	7	
Geology & Computing	FG65	3FT deg	S	10	3M $	Ind	Ind	CCC	Ind	3	
Software Engineering	G700	4SW deg	*	10	5M $	Ind	24	Ind	Ind	5	7/26
Computer Applications	005G▼	2FT HND	*	4	$	P	Ind	Ind	Ind	7	5/14
Geographical Information Systems	85LG	2FT HND	Gy	8	$	Ind	Ind	CC	Ind	2	

Univ of Wales, LAMPETER

TITLE	CODE	COURSE	SUBJECTS	A/AS	NO/C	AGNVQ	IB	SQA(H)	SQA	RATIO	A/AS
Informatics and American Literature	GQ54	3FT deg			Ind	Ind	Ind	Ind	Ind		
Informatics and Ancient History	GV5C	3FT deg	*	14-16	Ind	Ind	Ind	Ind	Ind		
Informatics and Anthropology	GL56	3FT deg	*	14-16	Ind	Ind	Ind	Ind	Ind		
Informatics and Archaeology	GV56	3FT deg	*	14-16	Ind	Ind	Ind	Ind	Ind		
Informatics and Australian Studies	GL5P	3FT deg			Ind	Ind	Ind	Ind	Ind		
Informatics and Church History	GV51	3FT deg	*	14	Ind	Ind	Ind	Ind	Ind		
Informatics and Classical Studies	GQ58	3FT deg	*	16	Ind	Ind	Ind	Ind	Ind		
Informatics and Cultural Studies in Geography	GL5V	3FT deg		16	Ind	Ind	Ind	Ind	Ind		
Informatics and English Literature	GQ53	3FT deg	E	18	Ind	Ind	Ind	Ind	Ind		
Informatics and French	GR51	4FT deg	F	14-16	Ind	Ind	Ind	Ind	Ind		
Informatics and Geography	GL58	3FT deg	Gy	16	Ind	Ind	Ind	Ind	Ind		
Informatics and German	GR52	4FT deg	G	14-16	Ind	Ind	Ind	Ind	Ind		
Informatics and German Studies	GR5F	4FT deg	*	14-16	Ind	Ind	Ind	Ind	Ind		
Informatics and Greek	GQ57	3FT deg	* g	14-16	Ind	Ind	Ind	Ind	Ind		
Informatics and History	GV5D	3FT deg	H	14-16	Ind	Ind	Ind	Ind	Ind		
Information Management Informatics	GP52	2FTDip/3FTdeg	*	14	Ind	Ind	Ind	Ind	Ind		
Islamic Studies and Informatics	GT56	3FT deg	*	14	Ind	Ind	Ind	Ind	Ind		

			98 expected requirements							96 entry stats
course details										
TITLE	CODE	COURSE	SUBJECTS	A/AS	NQ/C	RGNVQ	IB	SQA(H)	SQA	RATIO A/AS
Latin and Informatics	GQ56	3FT deg	*g	16	Ind	Ind	Ind	Ind	Ind	
Management Techniques and Informatics	GN51	3FT deg	*	16	Ind	Ind	Ind	Ind	Ind	
Medieval Studies and Informatics	VG1M	3FT deg	*	16	Ind	Ind	Ind	Ind	Ind	
Modern Historical Studies and Informatics	VG1N	3FT deg			Ind	Ind	Ind	Ind	Ind	
Philosophical Studies and Informatics	GV57▼	3FT deg	*	16	Ind	Ind	Ind	Ind	Ind	
Religious Studies and Informatics	GV58	3FT deg	*	14	Ind	Ind	Ind	Ind	Ind	
Theology and Informatics	GV5V	3FT deg	*	14	Ind	Ind	Ind	Ind	Ind	
Victorian Studies and Informatics	VG15	3FT deg	*	14	Ind	Ind	Ind	Ind	Ind	
Welsh Studies and Informatics	GQ5N	3FT deg	*	14	Ind	Ind	Ind	Ind	Ind	
Welsh and Informatics	GQ55	3FT/4FT deg	W	14	Ind	Ind	Ind	Ind	Ind	
Women's Studies and Informatics	GM59	3FT deg	*	14	Ind	Ind	Ind	Ind	Ind	
Combined Honours *Informatics*	Y400	3FT deg	*	14-16	Ind	Ind	Ind	Ind	Ind	

LANCASTER Univ

TITLE	CODE	COURSE	SUBJECTS	A/AS	NQ/C	RGNVQ	IB	SQA(H)	SQA	RATIO A/AS
Accounting, Finance and Computer Science	NG45	3FT deg	M g	BBC	DO $		30$	ABBBB$	Ind	
Computer Modelling for Business	NG25	3FT deg	M/S g	BCC	MO $		30$	BBBBB$	Ind	
Computer Science	G500	3FT deg	*g	BCC	M+D $		30	BBBBB	Ind	
Computer Science and Linguistics	GQ51	3FT deg	*g	BBC	Ind		30	ABBBB	Ind	
Computer Science and Mathematics	GG15	3FT deg	M g	20	Ind $		30$	BBBBB$	Ind	
Computer Science and Music	GW53	3FT deg	Mu g	BCC	Ind $		30$	ABBBB$	Ind	
Computer Science with Multimedia Systems	G5P4	3FT deg	*g	BCC	M+D $		30	BBBBB	Ind	
Computer Science with Software Engineering	G5G7	3FT deg	*g	BCC	Ind		30	BBBBB	Ind	
Computer Systems Engineering (BEng)	GH66	3FT/4SW deg	M+P/Cs/Ds/Es g	20	MO+1D		30$	BBBBB$	Ind	
Computer Systems Engineering (MEng)	GH6P	4FT/5SW deg	M+P/Cs/Ds/Es g	20	MO+2D		30$	BBBBB$	Ind	
French Studies and Computing	GR51	4FT deg	F g	BCC	Ind $		30$	BBBBB$	Ind	
German Studies and Computing	GR52	4FT deg	G/L g	BCC	Ind $		30$	BBBBB$	Ind	
Italian Studies and Computing	GR53	4FT deg	I/L g	BCC	Ind $		30$	BBBBB$	Ind	
Spanish Studies and Computing	GR54	4FT deg	Sp/L	BCC	Ind $		30$	BBBBB$	Ind	
Combined Science *Computer Science*	Y158	3FT deg	*g	CCD	MO		28	BBBB	Ind	
Combined Science (inc a year in USA or Canada) *Computer Science*	Y155	3FT deg	*g	BBB	Ind		32	ABBBB	Ind	

Univ of LEEDS

TITLE	CODE	COURSE	SUBJECTS	A/AS	NQ/C	RGNVQ	IB	SQA(H)	SQA	RATIO A/AS
Accounting-Computer Science	GN54	3FT/4FT deg	M g	BBC	Ind	Ind	30$	CSYS	Ind	10
Accounting-Information Systems	G5NK	3FT/4FT deg	g	BBC	Ind	Ind	30$	CSYS	Ind	11
Artificial Intelligence-Mathematics	GG18	3FT/4FT deg	M g	BBC	1M+5D$	Ind	30$	ABBBC	Ind	12
Artificial Intelligence-Philosophy	GV87	3FT deg	M g	BBC	Ind	Ind	Ind	Ind	Ind	
Artificial Intelligence-Physics	FG38	3FT deg	M+P g	BCC	1M+5D$	Ind	28$	BBBBC	Ind	11
Chemistry-Computer Science	FG15	3FT/4FT deg	C+M g	BCC	1M+5D$	Ind	28$	BBBBC	Ind	6
Cognitive Science	CG8N	3FT deg	g	BBC	1M+5D$	Ind	30$	ABBBB	Ind	5	20/24
Computer Science	G500	3FT/4FT deg	M g	BBC	Ind	Ind	30$	ABBBB	Ind	8	16/26
Computer Science-Economics	GL51	3FT deg	M g	BBC	Ind	Ind	Ind	Ind	Ind	
Computer Science-French	GR51	4FT deg	F+M g	BBC		Ind	30$	ABBBB	Ind	
Computer Science-German	GR52	4FT deg	G+M g	BBC		Ind	30$	ABBBB	Ind	
Computer Science-Management Studies	GN51	3FT/4FT deg	M g	BBC	1M+5D$	Ind	28$	BBBBC	Ind	14	20/26
Computer Science-Mathematics	GG15	3FT/4FT deg	M g	BBC	1M+5D$	Ind	30$	ABBBC	Ind	10	20/24
Computer Science-Music	GW53	3FT/4FT deg	M+Mu g	BBC	1M+5D$	Ind	30$	ABBBB	Ind	12	
Computer Science-Philosophy	GV57	3FT deg	M g	BBC	Ind	Ind	Ind	Ind	Ind	
Computer Science-Physics	FG35	3FT/4FT deg	M+P g	BCC	1M+5D$	Ind	28$	BBBBC	Ind	
Computer Science-Statistics	GG45	3FT/4FT deg	M g	BCC	1M+5D$	Ind	28$	BBBBC	Ind	4
Electronic and Computer Engineering	H6G6	3FT/4FT deg	M+P g	BBC	1M+5D$	Ind	30$	ABBBC	Ind	10	18/24
Information Systems	G520	3FT/4FT deg	g	BBC	1M+5D$	Ind	30$	ABBBB	Ind	3	16/24

Computer Sciences and Engineering   15

TITLE	CODE	COURSE	SUBJECTS	A/AS	ND/C	AGNVQ	IB	SQA(H)	SQA	RATIO	A/AS
Information Systems-Management Studies	G5NC	3FT/4FT deg	g	BBC	1M+5D$	Ind	30$	ABBBB	Ind	13	18/24
Linguistics-Computing	QG15	3FT deg	L g	BBC	Ind	Ind	30$	ABBBB	Ind	6	
Philosophy-Computing	VG75	3FT deg	g	BBC	Ind	Ind	30$	ABBBB	Ind	5	

LEEDS, TRINITY & ALL SAINTS Univ COLL

TITLE	CODE	COURSE	SUBJECTS	A/AS	ND/C	AGNVQ	IB	SQA(H)	SQA	RATIO	A/AS
Media Information Technology-Information Culture	GP54	3FT deg	* g	BBB-CCC	MO	Ind	26	AABBB	Ind		

LEEDS METROPOLITAN Univ

TITLE	CODE	COURSE	SUBJECTS	A/AS	ND/C	AGNVQ	IB	SQA(H)	SQA	RATIO	A/AS
Business Computing	G710	3FT deg									6/10
Business Decision Analysis	G730	3FT/4SW deg	* g	12	M+D	M$ go	26	BBCC	Ind		10/14
Business Information Management	GP52	3FT/4SW deg	*/L g	12	Ind	D$^/D$ go	26	BBCC	Ind		
Business Information Systems	G520	3FT/4SW deg	* g	12	3M+2D	D$ go	26	BBCC	Ind	3	8/16
Business Information Technology	G562	1FT deg	*/L g	12	Ind	D$^/D$ go	26	BBCC	Ind	2	8/18
Computing	G501	3FT/4SW deg	* g	12	3M+1D	DI go	26	BBC	Ind	4	8/16
Information Systems	G521	3FT deg									
Business Computing	017G	2FT HND									2/6
Business Information Technology	265G	2FT/3SW HND	* g	6	5M	M$ go	20	BCC	Ind	3	2/8
Computing	105G	2FT/3SW HND	* g	6-8	4M $	MI go	20	BCC	Ind	5	2/6

Univ of LEICESTER

TITLE	CODE	COURSE	SUBJECTS	A/AS	ND/C	AGNVQ	IB	SQA(H)	SQA	RATIO	A/AS
Computer Science	G500	3FT deg	M g	20	Ind	D$^	28$	BBBBC$	Ind		12/20
Elec & Software Eng with Ind in Europe (MEng)	HG6R	5SW deg	M+P g	18	5M$	M$6^	30$	ABBBB$	Ind		
Electronic & Software Eng with Ind in Europe	HGQR	4FT deg	M+P g	18	5M$	M$6^	28$	BBBBC$	Ind		
Electronic & Software Engineering with Industry	HG6T	4FT deg	M$6^	18	5M$	M$6^	28$	BBBBC$	Ind		
Electronic and Software Eng with Industry (MEng)	HGQ7	5SW deg	M+P g	18	5M $	M$6^	28$	ABBBB$	Ind		
Electronic and Software Engineering	HG67	3FT deg	M+P g	18	5M $	M$6^	28$	BBBBC$	Ind		12/20
Electronic and Software Engineering (MEng)	HGP7	4FT deg	M+P g	18	5M $	M$6^	28$	ABBBB$	Ind		
Mathematics and Computer Science	GG15	3FT deg	M g	20	Ind	D$^	28$	BBBBC$	Ind		12/24
Mathematics and Computer Science (Europe)	GG1M	4FT deg	M g	20	Ind	D$^	28$	BBBBC$	Ind		
BSc with integrated foundation Computer Science	Y101	4EXT deg	* g		N	*			Ind		
Combined Arts Computer Science	Y300	3FT deg	* g	BCC	DO	D$^	30$	Ind	X		
Combined Science Computer Science	Y100	3FT deg	* g	CCC	MO $	D$^	28$	BBBCC$	Ind		

Univ of LINCOLNSHIRE and HUMBERSIDE

TITLE	CODE	COURSE	SUBJECTS	A/AS	ND/C	AGNVQ	IB	SQA(H)	SQA	RATIO	A/AS
Accountancy and Information Systems	GN54	3FT deg	* g	12	3M+1D	M	24	CCCC	Ind		
Administration and Computing	GN5C	3FT deg	* g	12	3M+1D	M	24	CCCC	Ind		
Administration and Information Systems	GNND	3FT deg	* g	12	3M+1D	M	24	CCCC	Ind		
Business Information Systems	G720	3FT deg	* g	12	3M+1D	M	24	CCCC	Ind		
Computing	G500	3FT deg	* g	12	3M+1D	M	24	CCCC	Ind		
Computing (Games, Simulation and Visual Reality)	G501	3FT deg									
Computing (Internet Technologies)	G502	3FT deg									
Computing (Multimedia and Systems Development)	G503	3FT deg									
Computing (Network Systems Support & Management)	G504	3FT deg									
Computing and Accountancy	GN5K	3FT deg	* g	12	3M+1D	M	24	CCCC	Ind		
Computing and Business	NG1M	3FT deg	* g	12	3M+1D	M	24	CCCC	Ind		
Computing and French	GR5C	3FT deg	F g	12	3M+1D	M	24	CCCC	Ind		
Computing and German	GR5F	3FT deg	G g	12	3M+1D	M	24	CCCC	Ind		
Computing and Human Resource Management	GN56	3FT deg	* g	12	3M+1D	M	24	CCCC	Ind		
Computing and Information Systems	G523	3FT deg	* g	12	3M+1D	M	24	CCCC	Ind		
Computing and Marketing	GN5M	3FT deg	* g	12	3M+1D	M	24	CCCC	Ind		
Computing and Media Technology	GP54	3FT deg	* g	12	3M+1D	M	24	CCCC	Ind		
Computing and Modern Languages	GT5X	3FT deg	L g	12	3M+1D	M	24	CCCC	Ind		

course details | 98 expected requirements | 96 entry stats

TITLE	CODE	COURSE	SUBJECTS	A/AS	ND/C	RGNVQ	IB	SQA(H)	SQA	RATIO A/AS
Computing and Spanish	G5RK	3FT deg								
Computing and Technology	GJ59	3FT deg	* g	12	3M+1D	M	24	CCCC	Ind	
Finance and Computing	NG35	3FT deg	* g	12	3M+1D	M	24	CCCC	Ind	
Finance and Information Systems	GN53	3FT deg	* g	12	3M+1D	M	24	CCCC	Ind	
Human Resource Management and Information Systs	GN5P	3FT deg	* g	12	3M+1D	M	24	CCCC	Ind	
Information Systems and French	GR51	3FT deg	F g	12	3M+1D	M	24	CCCC	Ind	
Information Systems and German	GR52	3FT deg	G g	12	3M+1D	M	24	CCCC	Ind	
Information Systems and Marketing	GN55	3FT deg	* g	12	3M+1D	M	24	CCCC	Ind	
Information Systems and Media Technology	GP5K	3FT deg	* g	12	3M+1D	M	24	CCCC	Ind	
Information Systems and Modern Languages	GT5Y	3FT deg	L g	12	3M+1D	M	24	CCCC	Ind	
Information Systems and Spanish	GR54	3FT deg	Sp g	12	3M+1D	M	24	CCCC	Ind	
Management and Information Systems	NG1N▼	3FT deg	* g							
Business Information Technology	165G▼	2FT HND	g	4	2M	P	24	C	Ind	
Business and Information Systems	15NG	2FT HND	* g	4	2M	P	24	C	Ind	
Business and Technology	065G	2FT HND								
Computing	105G▼	2FT HND	g	4	2M	P	24	C	Ind	
Information Systems	025G▼	2FT HND	g	4		P				

Univ of LIVERPOOL

TITLE	CODE	COURSE	SUBJECTS	A/AS	ND/C	RGNVQ	IB	SQA(H)	SQA	RATIO A/AS
Accounting and Computer Science	GN54	3FT deg	M/Ec	CCC	Ind	Ind	Ind	Ind	Ind	16 18/20
Business Economics and Computer Science	LG15	3FT deg	M/Ec	CCC	Ind	Ind	Ind	Ind	Ind	9 18/24
Computer Information Systems	G520	3FT deg	* g	18	MO $	DS^ go	31$	BBBCC$	Ind	3 12/22
Computer Information Systems	G521	4FT deg	* g	10	MO $	Ind	24$	CCCDD$	Ind	5/ 9
Computer Information Systems	G523	3FT deg	* g	18	MO $	Ind	31$	BBBCC$	Ind	
Computer Science	G500	3FT deg	M g	18	MO $	DS^ go	31$	BBBCC$	Ind	7 11/22
Computer Science with a European Language	G5T2	4FT deg	M g	18	MO $	Ind	31$	BBBCC$	Ind	5
Computer and Microelectronic Systems	GH66	3FT deg	M+P/Cs	22	3M+2D		30$	BBBBB	Ind	8
Economics and Computer Science	GL51	3FT deg	M/Ec	CCC	Ind	Ind	Ind	Ind	Ind	32
Mathematics and Computer Science	GG15	3FT deg	M g	20	MO $	D$^ go	31$	BBBCC$	Ind	7 16/30
Physics and Computer Science	FG35	3FT deg	M+P g	12	MO $	DS^ go	31$	BBBCC$	Ind	6
Arts Combined *Computer Science*	Y401	3FT deg	* g	BBC-BBB	Ind	Ind	30$	ABBB	Ind	
BA Combined Honours *Computer Science*	Y200	3FT deg	g	BBB	Ind	Ind	Ind	Ind	Ind	
BSc Combined Honours *Computer Information Systems*	Y100	3FT deg	* g	18	MO $	DS^ go	31$	BBBCC$	Ind	
BSc Combined Honours *Computer Science*	Y100	3FT deg	M g	18	MO $	Ind	31$	BBBCC$	Ind	

LIVERPOOL HOPE Univ COLL

TITLE	CODE	COURSE	SUBJECTS	A/AS	ND/C	RGNVQ	IB	SQA(H)	SQA	RATIO A/AS
Information Technology/Drama & Theatre Studies	GW54	3FT deg	g	12	8M	M* go	Ind	Ind	Ind	9
Information Technology/English	GQ53	3FT deg	El	12	8M	P*^	Ind	Ind	Ind	4
Information Technology/Environmental Studies	GF59	3FT deg	B/Gy/En g	10	6M	M$ go	Ind	Ind	Ind	3
Information Technology/European Studies	TG25	3FT deg	*	12	8M	M*	Ind	Ind	Ind	
Information Technology/French	GR51	3FT deg	F	12	8M	P*^	Ind	Ind	Ind	2
Information Technology/Geography	GF58	3FT deg	Gy g	10	6M	M$ go	Ind	Ind	Ind	
Information Technology/History	GV51	3FT deg	H	12	8M	P*^	Ind	Ind	Ind	4
Information Technology/Human & Applied Biology	CG15	3FT deg	B g	10	6M	M$ /M*^ go	Ind	Ind	Ind	
Mathematics/Information Technology	GG51	3FT deg	M	10	6M	P*^	Ind	Ind	Ind	5
Music/Information Technology	GW53	3FT deg	Mu	12	8M	MQ /P*^	Ind	Ind	Ind	2
Psychology/Information Technology	GC58	3FT deg	g	10	6M	M* go	Ind	Ind	Ind	4 8/18
Sociology/Information Technology	GL53	3FT deg	*	12	8M	M*	Ind	Ind	Ind	4

Computer Sciences and Engineering   15

TITLE	CODE	COURSE	SUBJECTS	A/AS	NO/C	AGNVQ	IB	SQA(H)	SQA	RATIO A/AS
course details			**98 expected requirements**							**96 entry stats**
LIVERPOOL JOHN MOORES Univ										
Applied Computer Technology	G610	3FT/4SW deg		12	5M	M				7 10/12
Applied Computer Technology (Foundation)	G618	4FT/5SW deg								10
Business Decision Analysis	N2G5	3FT deg		16	3M+4D	D/M^				4 11/16
Business Information Systems	G522	4SW deg	* g	16	3M+4D	D/M^				5 10/22
Computer Studies	G501▼	4SW deg	* g	14	MO+1D	D$				6 8/20
Software Engineering	G700	4SW deg	* g	14	MO+1D	D$				6 6/24
Computing	105G	2FT HND	* g	4	1M	M$				5 2/8
Electronics and Computers	6MHG	3EXT HND								
Engineering (Electronics and Computers)	65HG	2FT/3SW HND								5
LONDON GUILDHALL Univ										
3D/Spatial Design and Business Information Techn	GW7F	3FT deg	Pf g	DD	MO	M$ go	24	Ind	Ind	
3D/Spatial Design and Computing	GW5F	3FT deg	Pf g	DD	MO	M$ go	24	Ind	Ind	
3D/Spatial Design and Multimedia Systems	GWMF	3FT deg	Pf g	DD	MO	M$ go	24	Ind	Ind	
Business Information Technology & Bus Economics	GL7C	3FT deg	* g	DD	MO	M$ go	24	Ind	Ind	
Business Information Technology and Accounting	GN74	3FT deg	* g	DD	MO	M$ go	24	Ind	Ind	
Business Information Technology and Business	GN71	3FT deg	* g	CD-DDD	MO+4D	M$ go	26	Ind	Ind	
Communications & Audio Vis Prod St & Business IT	GP74	3FT deg	* g	CC-CDD	MO+6D	D$ go	26	Ind	Ind	
Computing & Communications & Audio Vis Prod St	GP54	3FT deg	* g	CC-CDD	MO+6D	D$ go	26	Ind	Ind	
Computing and Accounting	GN54	3FT deg	* g	DD	MO	M$ go	24	Ind	Ind	
Computing and Business	GN51	3FT deg	* g	CD-DDD	MO+4D	M$ go	24	Ind	Ind	
Computing and Business Economics	GL5C	3FT deg	* g	DD	MO	M$ go	24	Ind	Ind	
Computing and Business Information Technology	GG57	3FT deg	* g	DD	MO	M$ go	24	Ind	Ind	
Computing and Information Systems	G520	3FT deg	* g	CD	MO $	M$ go	$	Ind	Ind	
Computing with Human Factors	G5C8	3FT deg	* g	CD	MO $	M$ go	$	Ind	Ind	
Design Studies & Business Information Technology	GW72	3FT deg	* g	CD-DDD	MO+2D	M$ go	24	Ind	Ind	
Design Studies and Computing	GW52	3FT deg	* g	CD-DDD	MO+2D	M$ go	24	Ind	Ind	
Development St & Business Information Technology	GM79	3FT deg	* g	DD	MO	M$ go	24	Ind	Ind	
Development Studies and Computing	GM59	3FT deg	* g	DD	MO	M$ go	24	Ind	Ind	
Economics and Business Information Technology	GL71	3FT deg	* g	DD	MO	M$ go	24	Ind	Ind	
Economics and Computing	GL51	3FT deg	* g	DD	MO	M$ go	24	Ind	Ind	
English and Business Information Technology	GQ73	3FT deg	* g	CD-DDD	MO+2D	M$ go	24	Ind	Ind	
English and Computing	GQ53	3FT deg	* g	CD-DDD	MO+2D	M$ go	24	Ind	Ind	
European St & Business Information Technology	GT72	3FT deg	* g	DD	MO	M$ go	24	Ind	Ind	
European Studies and Computing	GT52	3FT deg	* g	DD	MO	M$ go	24	Ind	Ind	
Financial Services & Business Information Techn	GN73	3FT deg	* g	DD	MO	M$ go	24	Ind	Ind	
Financial Services and Computing	GN53	3FT deg	* g	DD	MO	M$ go	24	Ind	Ind	
Fine Art and Business Information Technology	GW71	3FT deg	Pf g	CC-CDD	MO+2D	M$ go	26	Ind	Ind	
Fine Art and Computing	GW51	3FT deg	Pf g	CC-CDD	MO+2D	M$ go	26	Ind	Ind	
French and Business Information Technology	GR71	4FT deg	* g	DD	MO	M$ go	24	Ind	Ind	
French and Computing	GR51	4FT deg	* g	DD	MO	M$ go	24	Ind	Ind	
German and Business Information Technology	GR72	4FT deg	* g	DD	MO	M$ go	24	Ind	Ind	
German and Computing	GR52	4FT deg	* g	DD	MO	M$ go	24	Ind	Ind	
International Relations and Business IT	GM7C	3FT deg	* g	DD	MO	M$ go	24	Ind	Ind	
International Relations and Computing	GM5C	3FT deg	* g	DD	MO	M$ go	24	Ind	Ind	
Law and Business Information Technology	GM73	3FT deg	* g	CC-CDD	MO+2D	M$ go	26	Ind	Ind	
Law and Computing	GM53	3FT deg	* g	CC-CDD	MO+2D	M$ go	26	Ind	Ind	
Marketing and Business Information Technology	GN75	3FT deg	* g	CD-DDD	MO+2D	M$ go	26	Ind	Ind	
Marketing and Computing	GN55	3FT deg	* g	CD-DDD	MO+2D	M$ go	26	Ind	Ind	
Mathematics and Business Information Technology	GG17	3FT deg	* g	DD	MO	M$ go	24	Ind	Ind	
Mathematics and Computing	GG15	3FT deg	* g	DD	MO	M$ go	24	Ind	Ind	
Modern History & Business Information Technology	GV71	3FT deg	* g	DD	MO	M$ go	24	Ind	Ind	

			98 expected requirements						96 entry stats	

course details   98 expected requirements   96 entry stats

TITLE	CODE	COURSE	SUBJECTS	A/AS	ND/C	AGNVQ	IB	SQA(H)	SQA	RATIO A/AS
Modern History and Computing	GV51	3FT deg	* g	DD	MO	M$ go	24	Ind	Ind	
Multimedia Systems	G5W5	3FT deg	* g	CD	MO	M$ go	$	Ind	Ind	
Multimedia Systems & Business Information Techn	GG7M	3FT deg	* g	DD	MO	M$ go	24	Ind	Ind	
Multimedia Systems and Accounting	GNM4	3FT deg	* g	DD	MO	M$ go	24	Ind	Ind	
Multimedia Systems and Business	GNM1	3FT deg	* g	CD-DDD	MO+2D	M$ go	26	Ind	Ind	
Multimedia Systems and Business Economics	GLMC	3FT deg	* g	DD	MO	M$ go	24	Ind	Ind	
Multimedia Systems and Computing	GG5M	3FT deg	* g	DD	MO	M$ go	24	Ind	Ind	
Multimedia Systems and Design Studies	GWM2	3FT deg	* g	CD-DDD	MO	M$ go	24	Ind	Ind	
Multimedia Systems and Development Studies	GMM9	3FT deg	* g	DD	MO	M$ go	24	Ind	Ind	
Multimedia Systems and Economics	GLM1	3FT deg	* g	DD	MO	M$ go	24	Ind	Ind	
Multimedia Systems and English	GQM3	3FT deg	* g	CD-DDD	MO+2D	M$ go	26	Ind	Ind	
Multimedia Systems and European Studies	GTM2	3FT deg	* g	DD	MO	M$ go	24	Ind	Ind	
Multimedia Systems and Financial Services	GNM3	3FT deg	* g	DD	MO	M$ go	24	Ind	Ind	
Multimedia Systems and Fine Art	GWM1	3FT deg	* g	CC-CDD	MO+2D	M$ go	26	Ind	Ind	
Multimedia Systems and French	GRM1	4FT deg	* g	DD	MO	M$ go	24	Ind	Ind	
Multimedia Systems and German	GRM2	4FT deg	* g	DD	MO	M$ go	24	Ind	Ind	
Multimedia Systems and International Relations	GMMC	3FT deg	* g	DD	MO	M$ go	24	Ind	Ind	
Multimedia Systems and Law	GMM3	3FT deg	* g	CC-CDD	MO+2D	M$ go	26	Ind	Ind	
Multimedia Systems and Marketing	GNM5	3FT deg	* g	CD-DDD	MO+2D	M$ go	26	Ind	Ind	
Multimedia Systems and Mathematics	GG1M	3FT deg	* g	DD	MO	M$ go	24	Ind	Ind	
Multimedia Systems and Modern History	GVM1	3FT deg	* g	DD	MO	M$ go	24	Ind	Ind	
Multimedia Systs and Communs & Audio Vis Prod St	GPM4	3FT deg	* g	CC-CDD	MO+2D	M$ go	26	Ind	Ind	
Politics and Business Information Technology	GM71	3FT deg	* g	DD	MO	M$ go	24	Ind	Ind	
Politics and Computing	GM51	3FT deg	* g	DD	MO	M$ go	24	Ind	Ind	
Politics and Multimedia Systems	GMM1	3FT deg	* g	DD	MO	M$ go	24	Ind	Ind	
Product Development & Manuf and Multimedia Systs	GJM4	3FT deg	* g	DD	MO	M$ go	24	Ind	Ind	
Product Development & Manufacture & Business IT	GJ74	3FT deg	* g	DD	MO	M$ go	24	Ind	Ind	
Product Development & Manufacture and Computing	GJ54	3FT deg	* g	DD	MO	M$ go	24	Ind	Ind	
Psychology and Business Information Technology	CG87	3FT deg	* g	CD-DDD	MO+2D	M$ go	26	Ind	Ind	
Psychology and Computing	CG85	3FT deg	* g	CD-DDD	MO+2D	M$ go	26	Ind	Ind	
Psychology and Multimedia Systems	CG8M	3FT deg	* g	CD-DDD	MO+2D	M$ go	26	Ind	Ind	
Social Policy & Management and Business IT	GL74	3FT deg	* g	CD-DDD	MO	M$ go	24	Ind	Ind	
Social Policy & Management and Computing	GL54	3FT deg	* g	CD-DDD	MO	M$ go	24	Ind	Ind	
Social Policy & Management and Multimedia Systs	GLM4	3FT deg	* g	CD-DDD	MO	M$ go	24	Ind	Ind	
Sociology and Business Information Technology	GL73	3FT deg	* g	CD-DDD	MO	M$ go	24	Ind	Ind	
Sociology and Computing	GL53	3FT deg	* g	CD-DDD	MO	M$ go	24	Ind	Ind	
Sociology and Multimedia Systems	GLM3	3FT deg	* g	CD-DDD	MO	M$ go	24	Ind	Ind	
Spanish and Business Information Technology	GR74	4FT deg	* g	DD	MO	M$ go	24	Ind	Ind	
Spanish and Computing	GR54	4FT deg	* g	DD	MO	M$ go	24	Ind	Ind	
Spanish and Multimedia Systems	GRM4	4FT deg	* g	DD	MO	M$ go	24	Ind	Ind	
Taxation and Business Information Technology	GN7H	3FT deg	* g	DD	MO	M$ go	24	Ind	Ind	
Taxation and Computing	GN5H	3FT deg	* g	DD	MO	M$ go	24	Ind	Ind	
Taxation and Multimedia Systems	GNMH	3FT deg	* g	DD	MO	M$ go	24	Ind	Ind	
Textile Furnishing Design and Business IT	GW7G	3FT deg	Pf g	DD	MO	M$ go	24	Ind	Ind	
Textile Furnishing Design and Computing	GW5G	3FT deg	Pf g	DD	MO	M$ go	24	Ind	Ind	
Textile Furnishing Design and Multimedia Systems	GWMG	3FT deg	Pf g	DD	MO	M$ go	24	Ind	Ind	
Modular Programme *Business Information Technology*	Y400	3FT deg	* g	CC-DD	MO	M$ go	24	Ind	Ind	
Modular Programme *Business Information Technology*	Y420▼	3FT deg	* g	EE	MO	P	24	Ind	Ind	
Modular Programme *Computing*	Y420▼	3FT deg	* g	EE	MO	P	24	Ind	Ind	
Modular Programme *Computing*	Y400	3FT deg	* g	CC-DD	MO	M$ go	24	Ind	Ind	

TITLE	CODE	COURSE	SUBJECTS	A/AS	ND/C	RGNVQ	IB	SQA(H)	SQA	RATIO A/AS
course details			*98 expected requirements*							*96 entry stats*
Modular Programme	Y400	3FT deg	* g	CC-DD	MO	M$ go	24	Ind	Ind	
Multimedia Systems										
Computing	105G	2FT HND	* g	C-DD	2M		24	Ind	Ind	

LOUGHBOROUGH Univ

TITLE	CODE	COURSE	SUBJECTS	A/AS	ND/C	RGNVQ	IB	SQA(H)	SQA	RATIO A/AS
Computer Science	G500	3FT deg	M/P	20	3D	DI6/^ go	28	Ind	Ind	7 16/24
Computer Science (4 Yr MComp)	G502	4FT deg	M/P	22	3D	DI6/^ go	28	Ind	Ind	
Computer Science (4 Yr SW)	G501	4SW deg	M/P	20	3D	DI6/^ go	28	Ind	Ind	3 14/26
Computer Science (5 Yr SW MComp)	G503	5SW deg	M/P	22	3D	DI6/^ go	28	Ind	Ind	
Computing and Management	GN5D	3FT deg	*	20	3D	DI6/^ go	28	Ind	Ind	4 16/22
Computing and Management (4 Yr SW)	GN51	4SW deg	*	20	3D	DI6/^ go	28	Ind	Ind	4 16/28
Computing with a Modern Language (4 Yr SW)	G5T2	4SW deg	F/G	20		DI6/^ go	28	Ind		4
Information and Computing	G562	3FT deg	* g	20	2M+3D	D*6/^ go	28	Ind	Ind	6
Information and Computing (4 Yr SW)	G563	4SW deg	* g	20	2M+3D	D*6/^ go	28	Ind	Ind	4 14/16
Mathematics and Computing	GG15	3FT deg	M	BCC			28$	Ind		4 14/24
Mathematics and Computing (4 Yr SW)	GG51	4SW deg	M	BCC			28$	Ind		3 14/26
Physics with Computing	F3G5	3FT deg	M+P	BCC	3M+2D	DS6/^ go	28$	Ind	Ind	
Physics with Computing (4 Yr SW)	F3GM	4SW deg	M+P	BCC	3M+2D	DS6/^ go	28$	Ind	Ind	
Physics with Computing and a year in Europe	F3GN	4FT deg	M+P	BCC	3M+2D	DS6/^ go	28$	Ind	Ind	
Politics with Computing	M1G5	3FT deg	* g	20	2M+3D	D*6/^ go	28	Ind	Ind	

LUTON Univ

TITLE	CODE	COURSE	SUBJECTS	A/AS	ND/C	RGNVQ	IB	SQA(H)	SQA	RATIO A/AS
Artificial Intelligence	G800	3FT deg		12-16	MO/DO	M/D	32	BBCC	Ind	
Broadcasting & Media Tech with Computer Syst Des	H6G6	3FT deg		12-16	MO/DO	M/D	32	BBCC	Ind	
Business Decision Management	GN51	3FT deg	g	12-16	MO/DO	M/D	32	BBCC	Ind	
Business Systems and Artificial Intelligence	GN8C	3FT deg		12-16	MO/DO	M/D	32	BBCC	Ind	
Business and Artificial Intelligence	GN81	3FT deg		12-16	MO/DO	M/D	32	BBCC	Ind	
Communication Syst Des & Artificial Intelligence	GH8Q	3FT deg		12-16	MO/DO	M/D	32	BBCC	Ind	
Communication System Design	G610	3FT deg	g	12-16	MO/DO	M/D	32	BBCC	Ind	
Communication System Design and Business Systems	GN61	3FT deg	g	12-16	MO/DO	M/D	32	BBCC	Ind	
Communication System Design with Business Systs	G6N1	3FT deg	g	12-16	MO/DO	M/D	32	BBCC	Ind	
Communication System Design with Management	G6NC	3FT deg	g	12-16	MO/DO	M/D	32	BBCC	Ind	
Communication System Design with Marketing	G6N5	3FT deg	g	12-16	MO/DO	M/D	32	BBCC	Ind	
Computer Applications	G611	3FT deg		12-16	MO/DO	M/D	32	BBCC	Ind	
Computer Applications & Artificial Intelligence	GG86	3FT deg		12-16	MO/DO	M/D	32	BBCC	Ind	
Computer Applications and Accounting	GN64	3FT deg		12-16	MO/DO	M/D	32	BBCC	Ind	
Computer Applications and Biology	GC61	3FT deg		12-16	MO/DO	M/D	32	BBCC	Ind	
Computer Applications and Building Conservation	KG26	3FT deg		12-16	MO/DO	M/D	32	BBCC	Ind	
Computer Applications and Built Environment	GN68	3FT deg		12-16	MO/DO	M/D	32	BBCC	Ind	
Computer Applications and Business	GN6D	3FT deg		12-16	MO/DO	M/D	32	BBCC	Ind	
Computer Applications and Communication Syst Des	GH6Q	3FT deg		12-16	MO/DO	M/D	32	BBCC	Ind	
Computer Science	G500	3FT deg	g	12-16	MO/DO	M/D	32	BBCC	Ind	13
Computer Science and Accounting	NGK5	3FT deg	g	12-16	MO/DO	M/D	32	BBCC	Ind	
Computer Science and Applied Statistics	GG45	3FT deg	g	12-16	MO/DO	M/D	32	BBCC	Ind	
Computer Science and Artificial Intelligence	GG85	3FT deg		12-16	MO/DO	M/D	32	BBCC	Ind	
Computer Science and Biochemistry	CG75	3FT deg	g	12-16	MO/DO	M/D	32	BBCC	Ind	
Computer Science and Biology	CG15	3FT deg	g	12-16	MO/DO	M/D	32	BBCC	Ind	
Computer Science and Biotechnology	GJ58	3FT deg	g	12-16	MO/DO	M/D	32	BBCC	Ind	
Computer Science and Built Environment	NG85	3FT deg	g	12-16	MO/DO	M/D	32	BBCC	Ind	
Computer Science and Business	NG15	3FT deg	g	12-16	MO/DO	M/D	32	BBCC	Ind	10
Computer Science and Business Systems	NGC5	3FT deg	g	12-16	MO/DO	M/D	32	BBCC	Ind	5
Computer Science and Communication System Design	GG65	3FT deg	g	12-16	MO/DO	M/D	32	BBCC	Ind	
Computer Science and Computer Applications	GGP5	3FT deg	g	12-16	MO/DO	M/D	32	BBCC	Ind	
Computer System Engineering	G601	3FT deg	g	12-16	MO/DO	M/D	32	BBCC	Ind	8

course details

TITLE	CODE	COURSE	SUBJECTS	A/AS	NO/C	RGNVQ	IB	SQA(H)	SQA	RATIO A/AS
Computer Visual & Animation & Artificial Intell	GG8N	3FT deg		12-16	MO/DO	M/D	32	BBCC	Ind	
Computer Visualisation & Animation & Comp Apps	GG6N	3FT deg		12-16	MO/DO	M/D	32	BBCC	Ind	
Computer Visualisation & Animation and Comp Sci	GG5N	3FT deg		12-16	MO/DO	M/D	32	BBCC	Ind	
Computer Visualisation and Animation	G540	3FT deg		12-16	MO/DO	M/D	32	BBCC	Ind	
Contemporary History and Computer Science	GV51	3FT deg	g	12-16	MO/DO	M/D	32	BBCC	Ind	2
Creative Design & Comp Visualisation & Animation	GWN2	3FT deg		12-16	MO/DO	M/D	32	BBCC	Ind	
Digital Systems Design & Artificial Intelligence	GH8P	3FT deg		12-16	MO/DO	M/D	32	BBCC	Ind	
Digital Systems Design and Computer Applications	GH6P	3FT deg		12-16	MO/DO	M/D	32	BBCC	Ind	
Digital Systems Design and Computer Science	GH5P	3FT deg	g	12-16	MO/DO	M/D	32	BBCC	Ind	2
Electronic Sys Design with Digital System Design	GHM6	3FT deg	g	12-16	MO/DO	M/D	32	BBCC	Ind	
Electronic Syst Design & Artificial Intelligence	GH86	3FT deg		12-16	MO/DO	M/D	32	BBCC	Ind	
Electronic System Design and Computer Applic	GH66	3FT deg		12-16	MO/DO	M/D	32	BBCC	Ind	
Electronic System Design and Computer Science	HG65	3FT deg	g	12-16	MO/DO	M/D	32	BBCC	Ind	
Electronic System Design and Digital Systems Des	GH5Q	3FT deg	g	12-16	MO/DO	M/D	32	BBCC	Ind	
Environmental Science & Artificial Intelligence	GF89	3FT deg		12-16	MO/DO	M/D	32	BBCC	Ind	
Environmental Science and Computer Science	GF59	3FT deg	g	12-16	MO/DO	M/D	32	BBCC	Ind	
European Language Studies and Computer Science	GT52	3FT deg	L g	12-16	MO/DO	M/D	32	BBCC	Ind	
Foundation Computing	G509	1FT deg	*		Ind	Ind	Ind	Ind	Ind	1
Geography and Artificial Intelligence	GF88	3FT deg		12-16	MO/DO	M/D	32	BBCC	Ind	
Geography and Computer Science	FG85	3FT deg	g	12-16	MO/DO	M/D	32	BBCC	Ind	
Geology and Computer Science	GF56	3FT deg	g	12-16	MO/DO	M/D	32	BBCC	Ind	
Health Science and Artificial Intelligence	GB89	3FT deg		12-16	MO/DO	M/D	32	BBCC	Ind	
Health Studies and Artificial Intelligence	GB8X	3FT deg		12-16	MO/DO	M/D	32	BBCC	Ind	
Health Studies and Computer Science	GB5X	3FT deg	g	12-16	MO/DO	M/D	32	BBCC	Ind	
History of Des & Arch & Artificial Intelligence	VG48	3FT deg		12-16	MO/DO	M/D	32	BBCC	Ind	
Human Biology and Artificial Intelligence	GB81	3FT deg		12-16	MO/DO	M/D	32	BBCC	Ind	
Human Biology and Computer Science	BG15	3FT deg	g	12-16	MO/DO	M/D	32	BBCC	Ind	
Human Centred Comp & Computer Visual & Animation	GGNM	3FT deg		12-16	MO/DO	M/D	32	BBCC	Ind	
Human Centred Computing	G530	3FT deg		12-16	MO/DO	M/D	32	BBCC	Ind	
Human Centred Computing & Computer Applications	GG6M	3FT deg		12-16	MO/DO	M/D	32	BBCC	Ind	
Human Centred Computing and Computer Science	GG5M	3FT deg		12-16	MO/DO	M/D	32	BBCC	Ind	
Human Centred Computing and Creative Design	GWM2	3FT deg		12-16	MO/DO	M/D	32	BBCC	Ind	
Information Systems	G522	3FT deg	g	12-16	MO/DO	M/D	32	BBCC	Ind	7
Information Systems Development	G520	3FT deg		12-16	MO/DO	M/D	32	BBCC	Ind	
Information Systems Networking	G521	3FT deg		12-16	MO/DO	M/D	32	BBCC	Ind	
Journalism and Computer Applications	PG66	3FT deg		12-16	MO/DO	M/D	32	BBCC	Ind	
Language & Stylistics in English & Computer Sci	GQ5G	3FT deg	g	12-16	MO/DO	M/D	32	BBCC	Ind	
Law and Computer Science	GM53	3FT deg	g	12-16	MO/DO	M/D	32	BBCC	Ind	9
Linguistics and Artificial Intelligence	GQ81	3FT deg		12-16	MO/DO	M/D	32	BBCC	Ind	
Linguistics and Computer Science	GQ51	3FT deg	g	12-16	MO/DO	M/D	32	BBCC	Ind	
Literary Studies in English and Computer Science	GQ52	3FT deg	g	12-16	MO/DO	M/D	32	BBCC	Ind	
Mapping Science and Artificial Intelligence	GF8W	3FT deg		12-16	MO/DO	M/D	32	BBCC	Ind	
Mapping Science and Computer Applications	GF6W	3FT deg		12-16	MO/DO	M/D	32	BBCC	Ind	
Mapping Science and Computer Science	GF58	3FT deg	g	12-16	MO/DO	M/D	32	BBCC	Ind	
Marketing and Communication System Design	GN65	3FT deg	g	12-16	MO/DO	M/D	32	BBCC	Ind	
Marketing and Computer Applications	GN6M	3FT deg		12-16	MO/DO	M/D	32	BBCC	Ind	
Marketing and Computer Science	GN55	3FT deg	g	12-16	MO/DO	M/D	32	BBCC	Ind	
Marketing and Computer Visualisation & Animation	GNN5	3FT deg		12-16	MO/DO	M/D	32	BBCC	Ind	
Marketing and Human Centred Computing	GNM5	3FT deg		12-16	COMMO	M/D	32	BBCC	Ind	
Mathematical Sciences & Artificial Intelligence	GG8C	3FT deg		12-16	MO/DO	M/D	32	BBCC	Ind	
Mathematical Sciences and Computer Applications	GG6C	3FT deg		12-16	MO/DO	M/D	32	BBCC	Ind	
Mathematical Sciences and Computer Science	GG15	3FT deg	g	12-16	MO/DO	M/D	32	BBCC	Ind	

Computer Sciences and Engineering   15

TITLE	CODE	COURSE	SUBJECTS	A/AS	ND/C	RGNVQ	IB	SQA(H)	SQA	RATIO A/AS	
Mathematics and Artificial Intelligence	GG81	3FT deg		12-16	MO/DO	M/D	32	BBCC	Ind		
Mathematics and Computer Science	GG51	3FT deg	g	12-16	MO/DO	M/D	32	BBCC	Ind		
Media Practices and Artificial Intelligence	GP84	3FT deg		12-16	MO/DO	M/D	32	BBCC	Ind		
Media Practices and Computer Science	GP54	3FT deg	g	12-16	MO/DO	M/D	32	BBCC	Ind		
Media Prod & Computer Visualisation & Animation	GPNL	3FT deg		12-16	MO/DO	M/D	32	BBCC	Ind		
Media Production and Artificial Intelligence	GP8L	3FT deg		12-16	MO/DO	M/D	32	BBCC	Ind		
Media Production and Computer Applications	GP6L	3FT deg		12-16	MO/DO	M/D	32	BBCC	Ind		
Media Production and Human Centred Computing	GPML	3FT deg		12-16	MO/DO	M/D	32	BBCC	Ind		
Media Tech & Computer Visualisation & Animation	GPNK	3FT deg		12-16	MO/DO	M/D	32	BBCC	Ind		
Media Technology and Computer Science	GP5K	3FT deg	g	12-16	MO/DO	M/D	32	BBCC	Ind		
Media Technology and Human Centred Computing	GPMK	3FT deg		12-16	MO/DO	M/D	32	BBCC	Ind		
Modern English Studies and Computer Science	GQ53	3FT deg	g	12-16	MO/DO	M/D	32	BBCC	Ind		
Organisational Behaviour and Computer Science	GL57	3FT deg	g	12-16	MO/DO	M/D	32	BBCC	Ind		
Physical Geography and Building Conservation	KG2V	3FT deg		12-16	MO/DO	M/D	32	BBCC	Ind		
Physical Geography and Computer Science	GF5V	3FT deg	g	12-16	MO/DO	M/D	32	BBCC	Ind		
Plant Biology and Computer Science	CG25	3FT deg	g	12-16	MO/DO	M/D	32	BBCC	Ind		
Psychology and Artificial Intelligence	GL87	3FT deg		12-16	MO/DO	M/D	32	BBCC	Ind		
Psychology and Computer Science	GL5R	3FT deg	g	12-16	MO/DO	M/D	32	BBCC	Ind	12	
Regional Planning & Development & Computer Sci	GK54	3FT deg	g	12-16	MO/DO	M/D	32	BBCC	Ind		
Social Studies and Computer Science	GL53	3FT deg	g	12-16	MO/DO	M/D	32	BBCC	Ind		
Software Eng & Comp Visualisation & Animation	GG7N	3FT deg		12-16	MO/DO	M/D	32	BBCC	Ind		
Software Engineering	G700	3FT deg		12-16	MO/DO	M/D	32	BBCC	Ind		
Software Engineering and Artificial Intelligence	GG78	3FT deg		12-16	MO/DO	M/D	32	BBCC	Ind		
Software Engineering and Business Systems	GN7C	3FT deg		12-16	MO/DO	M/D	32	BBCC	Ind		
Software Engineering and Communication Syst Des	GH7Q	3FT deg		12-16	MO/DO	M/D	32	BBCC	Ind		
Software Engineering and Computer Applications	GG67	3FT deg		12-16	MO/DO	M/D	32	BBCC	Ind		
Software Engineering and Computer Science	GG57	3FT deg		12-16	MO/DO	M/D	32	BBCC	Ind		
Software Engineering and Digitial Systems Design	GH7P	3FT deg		12-16	MO/DO	M/D	32	BBCC	Ind		
Software Engineering and European Language Studs	GT72	3FT deg		12-16	MO/DO	M/D	32	BBCC	Ind		
Software Engineering and Human Centred Computing	GG7M	3FT deg		12-16	MO/DO	M/D	32	BBCC	Ind		
Software Engineering and Mathematical Sciences	GG7C	3FT deg		12-16	MO/DO	M/D	32	BBCC	Ind		
Software Engineering and Mathematics	GG71	3FT deg		12-16	MO/DO	M/D	32	BBCC	Ind		
Stage & Screen Technol & Comp Visual & Animation	GPN4	3FT deg		12-16	MO/DO	M/D	32	BBCC	Ind		
Stage & Screen Technology and Human Centred Comp	GPM4	3FT deg		12-16	MO/DO	M/D	32	BBCC	Ind		
Travel and Tourism and Computer Science	GP57	3FT deg	g	12-16	MO/DO	M/D	32	BBCC	Ind		
Travel and Tourism with Computer Science	P7G5	3FT deg	g	12-16	MO/DO	M/D	32	BBCC	Ind		
Business Information Technology	265G	2FT HND	g	4-8	N/MO	P/M	26	CCDD	Ind	4	2/4
Computing	105G	2FT HND	g	4-8	N/MO	P/M	26	CCDD	Ind	7	2/8
Geographical Information Systems	58GF	2FT HND	g	4-8	N/MO	P/M	26	CCDD	Ind		

Univ of MANCHESTER

TITLE	CODE	COURSE	SUBJECTS	A/AS	ND/C	RGNVQ	IB	SQA(H)	SQA	RATIO A/AS	
Accounting with Business Information Systems	N4G5	3FT deg	g	BBC	M+6D	D^	32	ABBBB	Ind	7	18/28
Artificial Intelligence	G800	3FT deg	S/M g	BBC	Ind	DS^	28$	BBBBB$	X	12	20/24
Artificial Intelligence with Industrial Exp	G801	4FT deg	S/M g	BBC	Ind	DS^	28$	BBBBB$			
Computer Engineering	G600	3FT deg	S/M g	BBC	Ind	DS^	28$	BBBBB$	X	14	22/22
Computer Engineering with Industrial Exp	G601	4SW deg	S/M g	BBC	Ind	DS^	28$	BBBBB$	X	29	
Computer Science	G500	3FT deg	S/M g	BBC	Ind	DS^	28$	BBBBB$	X	7	18/30
Computer Science (MEng)	G501	4FT deg	S/M g	ABB	X	X	30$	AAABB$	X	5	22/30
Computer Science and Mathematics	GG15	3FT deg	M	BBC	X	D$^	30$	CSYS$	X	10	18/30
Computer Science with Business and Management	G5N1	3FT deg	S/M g	BBC	Ind	D$^	28$	BBBBB$	X	13	16/28
Computer Science with Industrial Experience	G505	4SW deg	M/S g	BBC	Ind	D$^	28$	BBBBB$	X	6	22/30
Computer Science with a Modern Language	G5T9	4FT deg	M+L	BBC	X	X	28$	BBBBB$	X	7	
Computing and Information Syst with Ind Exp	G507	4SW deg	S/M g	BBC	Ind	DS^	28$	BBBBB$	X	15	22/28

TITLE	CODE	COURSE	SUBJECTS	A/AS	NO/C	RGNVQ	IB	SQA(H)	SQA	RATIO A/AS
Computing and Information Systems	G506	3FT deg	S/M g	BBC	Ind	DS^	28$	BBBBB$	X	25
Software Engineering	G700	3FT deg								
Software Engineering with Industrial Experience	G701	3FT deg								

UMIST (Manchester)

TITLE	CODE	COURSE	SUBJECTS	A/AS	NO/C	RGNVQ	IB	SQA(H)	SQA	RATIO A/AS
Artificial Intelligence	G800	3FT deg	g	20	MO+3D	Ind	28	BBBBB	Ind	
Computation	G510	3FT deg	g	18	3M+2D	M$ go	28	AABBB	Ind	3 14/24
Computational Linguistics	G5Q1	3FT deg	* g	20	MO+3D	Ind	28	BBBBB	Ind	
Computational Linguistics (MLang Eng)	G5QC	4FT deg	* g	20	MO+3D	Ind	28	BBBBB	Ind	
Computer Systems Engineering	GH66	3FT deg	M+P g	BBC	Ind	DE^	30$	AABBB$	Ind	
Computer Systems Engineering (MEng)	GH6P	4FT deg	M+P g	BBC	Ind	DE^	30$	AABBB$	Ind	
Information Systems Engineering	G560	3FT deg	M g	18	3M+2D	Ind	28	AABBB	Ind	39
Management and Information Technology	GN51	3FT deg								
Microelectronic Systems Engineering	HG66	3FT deg	M+P g	BBC	Ind	DE^	32$	AABBB$	Ind	6
Microelectronic Systems Engineering (MEng)	HG6P	4FT deg	M+P g	BBC	Ind	DE^	32$	AABBB$	Ind	4
Software Engineering	G700	3FT deg	M+P g	BBC	Ind	DE^	30$	AABBB$	Ind	13 16/26
Software Engineering (MEng)	G701	4FT deg	M+P g	BBC	Ind	DE^	30$	AABBB$	Ind	7 18/30

MANCHESTER METROPOLITAN Univ

TITLE	CODE	COURSE	SUBJECTS	A/AS	NO/C	RGNVQ	IB	SQA(H)	SQA	RATIO A/AS
Business Informatics (HND top-up)	G720	1FT deg	* g		HN					
Business Information Technology	G562	4SW deg	* g	16	DO	D	Ind	CCCCC	Ind	12/20
Computer & Electronic Eng with Study in Eur	GH6P	4SW deg	M+P	10	MO $	ME2	24$	CCC$	Ind	
Computer Technology/Applicable Mathematics	GGM1	3FT deg	M g	12	5M $	M$	27	BCCCC$	Ind	
Computer Technology/Applied Physics	FG3M	3FT deg	M+P g	12	5M $	M$	27$	BCCCC$	Ind	
Computer Technology/Business Mathematics	GGMC	3FT deg	M/P/Ec g	12	5M $	M$	27$	BCCCC$	Ind	
Computer Technology/Chemistry	GFM1	3FT deg	C g	12	5M $	M$	27$	BCCCC$	Ind	
Computer and Electronic Engineering	GH66	3FT/4SW deg	M+P	10	MO $	ME2	24$	CCC$	Ind	
Computing	G500	4SW deg	* g	12	MO+2D	D$/M$4/^ go	24$	BBCCC	N$	10/20
Computing (Foundation)	G508▼	5SW deg	M/P	E	2M $	P$	$	$	Ind	
Computing Science/Applicable Mathematics	GG15	3FT deg	M g	16	1M+3D$	M$	28$	BBBC$	Ind	
Computing Science/Applied Physics	FG35	3FT deg	M+P g	12	5M $	M$	27$	BCCCC$	Ind	
Computing Science/Business Mathematics	GGC5	3FT deg	M/P/Ec g	16	1M+3D$	M$	28$	BBBCC$	Ind	
Computing Science/Chemistry	FG15	3FT deg	C g	12	5M $	M$	27$	BCCCC$	Ind	
Economics/Computer Technology	GLM1	3FT deg	* g	16	1M+3D	M$	28	BBBCC	Ind	
Economics/Computing Science	GL51	3FT deg	* g	16	1M+3D	M$	28	BBBCC	Ind	
Electronics/Computer Technology	GHMP	3FT deg	* g	12	5M	M$	27	BCCCC	Ind	
Electronics/Computing Science	GH5P	3FT deg	* g	12	5M	M$	27	BCCCC	Ind	
Environmental Studies/Computer Technology	FG9M	3FT deg	* g	16	1M+3D	M$	M$	BBBCC	Ind	
Environmental Studies/Computing Science	FG95	3FT deg	* g	16	1M+3D	M$	28	BBBCC	Ind	
European Studies/Computer Technology	GTM2	3FT deg	* g	16	1M+3D	M$	28	BBBCC	Ind	
European Studies/Computing Science	GT52	3FT deg	* g	16	1M+3D	M$	28	BBBCC	Ind	
Geography/Computer Technology	GLM8	3FT deg	* g	14	MO	M$	28	BBCCC	Ind	
Geography/Computing Science	GL58	3FT deg	* g	18	2M+4D	M$	29	BBBBC	Ind	
Information Systems	G521▼	4SW deg	* g	12	MO+2D	D$/M$4/^ go	24$	BBCCC	N$	14/16
Information Systems (Foundation)	G528▼	5SW deg	M/P	E	2M $	P$	$	$	Ind	
Information Technology	G560	4SW deg	* g	10	3M $		24$	CCC$	Ind	6/14
Information Technology (Foundation)	G568▼	5SW deg	M/P	E	2M $	P$	$	$	Ind	
Information Technology in Society	G563	3FT deg	* g	CC	Ind	Ind	Ind	Ind	Ind	8/14
Manufacturing/Computer Technology	GHM7	3FT deg	* g	12	5M	M$	27	BCCCC	Ind	
Manufacturing/Computing Science	GH57	3FT deg	* g	12	5M	M$	27	BCCCC	Ind	
Materials Science/Computer Technology	FG2M	3FT deg	M/P/C g	12	5M $	M$	27$	BCCCC$	Ind	
Materials Science/Computing Science	FG25	3FT deg	M/P/C g	12	5M $	M$	27$	BCCCC$	Ind	
Physics Studies/Computer Technology	FGHM	3FT deg	P/M g	12	5M $	M$	27$	BCCCC$	Ind	

course details — *98 expected requirements* — *96 entry stats*

			98 expected requirements							96 entry stats	

TITLE	CODE	COURSE	SUBJECTS	A/AS	NO/C	AGNVQ	IB	SQA(H)	SQA	RATIO A/AS	
Physics Studies/Computing Science	FGH5	3FT deg	P/M g	12	5M $	M$	27$	BCCCC$	Ind		
Psychology/Computer Technology	GLM7	3FT deg	* g	18	1M+3D	D$	28	BBBCC	Ind		
Psychology/Computing Science	GL57	3FT deg	* g	18	2M+4D	D$	29	BBBBC	Ind		
Social Studies of Technology/Computer Technology	GLM3	3FT deg	* g	12	5M	M$	27	BCCCC	Ind		
Social Studies of Technology/Computing Science	GL53	3FT deg	* g	16	1M+3D	M$	28	BBBCC	Ind		
Software Engineering	G700	4SW deg	* g	12	MO+2D	D$/M$4/^ go	24$	BBCCC	N$	10/24	
Software Engineering (Foundation)	G708▼	5SW deg	M/P	E	2M $	P$	$	$	Ind		
Combined Studies (Foundation) Computer Technology	Y108	4FT deg	M/P	E	2M $	P$	$	$	Ind		
Combined Studies (Foundation) Computing Science	Y108▼	4FT deg	M/P	E	2M $	P$	$	$	Ind		
Business Information Technology	265G	2FT HND	* g	6	MO	M	Ind	Ind	Ind	4/10	
Computing	105G	2FT HND	* g	6	3M	M$ go	Dip	CCC	N$	4/12	
Software Engineering	007G	2FT HND	* g	6	3M	M$	Dip	CCC	N$	6/ 8	

MIDDLESEX Univ

Applied Computing	G523▼	3FT deg	* g	12	5M	M$ go	26	CCCC	Ind		
Computer Systems	G500▼	3FT deg	S g	10	3M	M$ go	24	Ind	Ind		
Computing Foundation	G508▼	4EXT deg	* g	E	N	P* go	Ind	CC	Ind		
Geographical Information Technology	LG85▼	3FT deg	Gy g	12	5M	M$ go	24	Ind	Ind		
Intelligent Computer Systems	G801▼	3FT deg	* g	10	3M	M$ go	24	CCCC	Ind		
Joint Honours Degree Applied Computing	Y400	3FT deg	* g	12-16	5M	M$ go	26	CCCC	Ind		
Joint Honours Degree Cognitive Science	Y400	3FT/4SW deg	* g	12-16	5M	M$ go	28	Ind	Ind		
Joint Honours Degree Computer Systems	Y400	3FT deg	M+P g	12	3M	M$ go	24	CCCC	Ind		
Joint Honours Degree Information Technology	Y400	3FT deg	* g	12-16	5M	M$ go	24	CCCC	Ind		
Multidisciplinary Degree Electronic Communications	Y400	3FT deg	M+P g	10	3M	M$ go	24	CCCC	Ind		
Computing	105G▼	2FT HND	* g	4	N	M* go	Ind	CC	Ind		
Networking and Computer Systems	65GG▼	2FT HND	* g	E	N	P$ go	24	Ind	Ind		

MORAY HOUSE Institute of Education

Computer Science and Education	GX57	3FT/4FT deg	g	DD	Ind	Ind		CCC$	Ind		

NAPIER Univ

Applied Physics with Computing	F3G5	4FT deg	2(M/P/C/B)	DD	Ind	Ind	Ind	BCC	Ind		
Computing	G500	4SW/5SW deg	*	DD	Ind	Ind	Ind	BCC	Ind	3	8/14
Computing and Electronic Systems	GH5P	3FT/4FT deg						BBC			
Electronic and Computer Engineering	GH56	4SW deg	*	DD	Ind	Ind	Ind	BBC	Ind	7	
Information Systems	G520	4SW/5SW deg	*	DD	Ind	Ind	Ind	BCC	Ind	8	
Mathematics with Computing	G1G5	4FT/5SW deg	M	CC	Ind	Ind	Ind	BBC	Ind		
Software Engineering	G700	3FT/4FT deg	*	CD	Ind	Ind	Ind	BBB	Ind	4	6/18
Computing	005G	2FT HND	*	D	Ind	Ind	Ind	CC	Ind	2	2/ 4
Software Engineering	007G	2FT HND	*	D	Ind	Ind	Ind	CC	Ind	2	

NENE COLLEGE

Business Administration with Information Systems	N1G5	3FT deg	g	10	M+1D	M	24	BCC	Ind	8/12	
Business Information Systems	G521	3FT deg		6	5M	M	24	CCC	Ind	6/16	
Computer Communications	G560	3FT deg	g	EE	4M	M	24	CCC	Ind		
Computing	G500	3FT deg		6	5M	M	24	CCC	Ind	4/20	
Drama with Information Systems	W4G5	3FT deg		10	5M+1D	M	24	CCC	Ind		
Education with Information Systems	X9G5	3FT deg		DD	5M	M	24	CCC	Ind		
Energy Management with Information Systems	J9G5	3FT deg	g	EE	3M	P	24	CCC	Ind		

course details

TITLE	CODE	COURSE	SUBJECTS	A/AS	NO/C	AGNVQ	IB	SQA(H)	SQA	RATIO A/AS
French with Information Systems	R1G5	3FT deg	F	DD	5M	Ind	24	CCC	Ind	
Geography with Information Systems	F8G5	3FT deg	Gy	8	5M	M	24	CCC	Ind	
Industry and Enterprise with Information Systems	H1G5	3FT deg	g	EE	3M	P	24	CCC	Ind	
Info Systs with Personal & Organisational Devel	G5N6	3FT deg		6	5M	M	24	CCC	Ind	
Information Systems with Architectural Studies	G5V4	3FT deg		6	5M	M	24	CCC	Ind	
Information Systems with Art and Design	G5W2	3FT deg		6	5M	M	24	CCC	Ind	
Information Systems with Business Administration	G5N1	3FT deg	g	6	5M	M	24	CCC	Ind	
Information Systems with Ecology	G5C9	3FT deg		6	5M	M	24	CCC	Ind	
Information Systems with Education	G5X9	3FT deg		6	5M	M	24	CCC	Ind	
Information Systems with Energy Management	G5J9	3FT deg	g	6	5M	M	24	CCC	Ind	
Information Systems with English	G5Q3	3FT deg		6	5M	M	24	CCC	Ind	
Information Systems with European Union Studies	G5T2	3FT deg		6	5M	M	24	CCC	Ind	
Information Systems with French	G5R1	3FT deg	F	6	5M	M	24	CCC	Ind	
Information Systems with Geography	G5F8	3FT deg		6	5M	M	24	CCC	Ind	
Information Systems with History	G5V1	3FT deg		6	5M	M	24	CCC	Ind	
Information Systems with Industry and Enterprise	G5H1	3FT deg	g	6	5M	M	24	CCC	Ind	
Information Systems with Law	G5M3	3FT deg	g	6	5M	M	24	CCC	Ind	4/ 9
Information Systems with Management Science	G5G4	3FT deg	g	6	5M	M	24	CCC	Ind	
Information Systems with Mathematics	G5G1	3FT deg	M	6	5M	M	24	CCC	Ind	
Information Systems with Media & Popular Culture	G5P4	3FT deg		6	5M	M	24	CCC	Ind	
Information Systems with Philosophy	G5V7	3FT deg		6	5M	M	24	CCC	Ind	
Information Systems with Sociology	G5L3	3FT deg		6	5M	M	24	CCC	Ind	
Information Systems with Sport Studies	G5N7	3FT deg		6	5M	M	24	CCC	Ind	
Law with Information Systems	M3G5	3FT deg	g	10	3M+2D	M	24	CCC	Ind	
Management Science with Information Systems	G4G5	3FT deg	g	DD	5M	M	24	CCC	Ind	
Mathematics with Information Systems	G1G5	3FT deg	M	DD	Ind	Ind	24	CCC	Ind	
Sociology with Information Systems	L3G5	3FT deg		10	5M	M	24	CCC	Ind	
Sport Studies with Information Systems	N7G5	3FT deg	Ss/Pe	12	M+2D	M	24	BBB		
Business Information Technology	265G▼	2FT HND	g	2	3M	P		CC	Ind	2/ 6
Computer Systems	005G	2FT HND		2	2M	P		CC	Ind	
Computing	105G	2FT HND	g	2	3M	P		CC	Ind	2/10

Univ of NEWCASTLE

TITLE	CODE	COURSE	SUBJECTS	A/AS	NO/C	AGNVQ	IB	SQA(H)	SQA	RATIO A/AS
Accounting and Computing Science	NG45	3FT deg	M	20	4M+1D	Ind	30$	AAABB	Ind	8 18/23
Computer Systems Engineering	G601	4FT deg		Ind	Ind	Ind	Ind	Ind	Ind	
Computer Systems Engineering	G600	3FT deg	M+P	BCC	Ind	Ind	Ind	CSYS$	Ind	
Computing Science	G500	3FT deg	* g	18	Ind	Ind	Ind	ABBB	Ind	4 10/22
Computing Science	G501	4FT deg	* g	Ind	Ind	Ind	Ind	Ind	Ind	55
Computing Science and Economics	GL51	3FT deg	M	20	4M+1D	Ind	28$	AAABB	Ind	
Computing Science and Mathematics	GG15	3FT deg	M	18-20	Ind		28$	AAAB$	Ind	5 16/22
Computing Science and Physics	FG35	3FT deg	M+P	18	4M	Ind	28$	AABBB	Ind	
Computing Science and Psychology	CG85	3FT deg	M	24	Ind	Ind	30$	AAABB	Ind	
Computing Science and Statistics	GG45	3FT deg	M	18-20	Ind		28$	AAAB$	Ind	3
Computing Science and Surveying and Mapping Sci	GH5F	3FT deg	M	18	4M	Ind	28$	AABBB	Ind	5
Microelectronics and Software Engineering	HG67	4FT deg	* g	CCC	3M $	Ind	$	BCCCC$	$	7
Microelectronics and Software Engineering	GH76	3FT deg	M+P	BCC	6M $	Ind	$	CSYS$	$	12
Microelectronics and Software Engineering (MEng)	GHR6	5FT deg	* g	CCC	3M $	Ind	$	BCCCC$	$	
Microelectronics and Software Engineering (MEng)	GH7Q	4FT deg	M+P	BBC	5M+1D$	Ind	$	CSYS$	$	10
Software Engineering	G700	3FT deg	* g	18	Ind		Ind	ABBB	Ind	10 14/20
Combined Studies (BA) *Computing Science*	Y400	3FT deg	M g	ABC-BBB	5D	Ind	35$	AAAB	Ind	
Combined Studies (BSc) *Computing Science*	Y100	3FT deg	M+S	18	4M	Ind	28$	AABBB	Ind	

Computer Sciences and Engineering 15

TITLE	CODE	COURSE	SUBJECTS	A/AS	ND/C	AGNVQ	IB	SQA(H)	SQA	RATIO A/AS
course details			**98 expected requirements**							**96 entry stats**
NEWCASTLE COLL										
Computing (Business Information Technology)	027G▼	2FT HND								
Computing (Business Systems)	017G▼	2FT HND								
Software Engineering	007G▼	2FT HND								
NEWMAN COLLEGE OF HIGHER EDUCATION										
Geography and Information Technology	FG85	3FT deg	*	CC	3M	M*	Dip	CCC	Ind	
Information Technology and Biological Science	CG15	3FT deg	*	CC	3M	M*	Dip	CCC	Ind	
Information Technology and Expressive English	GW54	3FT deg	*	CC	3M	M*	Dip	CCC	Ind	
Information Technology and History	GV51	3FT deg	*	CC	3M	M*	Dip	CCC	Ind	
Information Technology and PE & Sports Studies	GX59	3FT deg	*	CC	3M	M*	Dip	CCC	Ind	
Univ of Wales COLLEGE, NEWPORT										
Business Information Technology	GN71	3FT deg	*	8-10	3M	D$	Ind	Ind	Ind	
Computing	G501	3FT deg		8-10	N	D$	Ind	Ind	Ind	
Information Technology	G508	3FT/4FT HND/deg								
Information Technology and Archaeology	GV56	3FT deg		10	M+D	D$	Ind	Ind	Ind	
Information Technology and English	GQ53	3FT deg		10	M+D	D$	Ind	Ind	Ind	
Information Technology and Environmental Studies	FG95	3FT deg		10	M+D	D$	Ind	Ind	Ind	
Information Technology and European Studies	GT52	3FT deg		10	M+D	D$	Ind	Ind	Ind	
Information Technology and Geography	GL58	3FT deg		10	M+D	D$	Ind	Ind	Ind	
Information Technology and History	GV51	3FT deg		10	M+D	D$	Ind	Ind	Ind	
Multimedia	EG25	3FT deg								
Multimedia	WG25	3FT deg	Pf	6	M+D	P$	Ind	Ind	Ind	
Sports Studies and Information Technology	BG65	3FT deg		10	M+D	D$	Ind	Ind	Ind	
Business Information Technology	17NG	2FT HND		2	N	P$	Ind	Ind	Ind	
Computing - Information Technology	105G	2FT HND	*	2	N	P$	Ind	Ind	Ind	
Industrial Information Technology	065G	2FT HND		2	N	P$	Ind	Ind	Ind	
NORTHBROOK COLLEGE Sussex										
Computing (Networking Technologies)	GG56	3FT deg								
Information Systems and Business Management	GN51	3FT deg								
Computing (Information Technology Management)	027G	2FT HND			N		Ind	Ind	Ind	
NESCOT										
Business Information Technology	G562	1FT deg	*		HN					
Computer Studies	G508	5SW deg	*							3
Computer Studies	G500	4SW deg	*	DD	MO	M	Dip	Ind	N$	9
Business Information Technology	265G	2FT HND	*	D	MO	M	Dip	Ind	N$	2
Computer Automation and Networking	027G	2FT HND	S	D	N	P	Dip	Ind	N$	2
Computing	105G	2FT HND	*	D	MO	P	Dip	Ind	N$	2
NORTH EAST WALES INST of HE										
Business Information Systems Management	G525	3FT deg		4-8	4M	M$	Ind	CCC	N$	
Computer Studies	G500	3FT deg		6-10	3M	M$	Ind	CCC	N$	
Multimedia Computing	G564	3FT deg		6-10	3M	M$	Ind	CCC	N$	
Business Information Technology	1N5G	2FT HND		2-4	2M	P$	Ind	CC	N$	
Computing	005G	2FT HND		2-4	2M	P$	Ind	CC	N$	
Multimedia Computing	465G	2FT HND		2-6	N	P$	Ind	CC	N$	
NORTH EAST WORCESTERSHIRE COLL										
Computing	005G	2FT HND								
NORTH LINCOLNSHIRE COLLEGE										
Electronics, Software and Systems Engineering	67HG	2FT HND	M/P g	2	$	P$	Ind	Ind	Ind	

			98 expected requirements							96 entry stats	
TITLE	CODE	COURSE	SUBJECTS	A/AS	ND/C	AGNVQ	IB	SQA(H)	SQA	RATIO	A/AS
Univ of NORTH LONDON											
Business Decision Analysis	G710	3FT/4SW/4EXT deg	* g	CC	4M $	M* go	$	Ind	Ind	2	
Business Information Systems	G5N1	3FT/4SW/4EXT deg	M/P/Cs/St/Es	CC	4M $	M* go	$	Ind	Ind	12	
Business and Computing	GN51	3FT/4SW/4EXT deg	M/Cs/P/Es/St	12	MO+4D	D* go	Ind	Ind	Ind		
Chemistry and Information Technology	F1G5	3FT/4SW/4EXT deg	C	12	3M $	MS	24$	Ind	Ind	7	
Computer Science & Discrete Maths	GG5C	3FT/4SW/4EXT deg	M/Cs/P/Es/St	CC	4M $	M* go	$	Ind	Ind	5	
Computer Science (4 Yrs)	G500	4SW/5EXT deg	M/Cs/P/Es/St	CC	4M $	M* go	$	Ind	Ind	9	6/14
Computing	G501	3FT/4SW/4EXT deg	M/Cs/P/Es/St	CC	4M $	M* go	$	Ind	Ind	13	6/20
Computing/Mathematics Foundation	GGN1▼	4FT/5SW deg			Ind	Ind	Ind	Ind	Ind	1	
French and Information Technology	GR51	4FT deg	M/Cs/P/Es/St	CD	Ind	Ind	Ind	Ind	Ind		
Information Technology and Business	GN5C	3FT/4SW/4EXT deg	M/Cs/P/Es/St g	12	MO+4D	Ind	Ind	Ind	Ind		
Mathematics and Computing	GG5D	3FT/4SW/4EXT deg	M	CC	X	M*^	$	Ind	Ind	40	
Multimedia Technology	G540	3FT/4SW/4EXT deg	* g	CC	3M $	M$ go	$	Ind	Ind		
Statistics and Computing	GGL5	3FT/4SW/4EXT deg	M/Cs/P/Es/St	CC	4M $	M* go	$	Ind	Ind	4	
Combined Honours Computer Electronics	Y100	3FT/4SW/4EXT deg	M+Es/Cs/Ds/P	CC	3M $	ME go	$	Ind	Ind		
Combined Honours Computing	Y100	3FT/4SW deg	M/Cs/P/Es/St	CC	4M $	MI go	$	Ind	Ind		
Combined Honours Information Systems	Y100	3FT/4SW/4EXT deg	M/Cs/P/Es/St	CC	3M $	M* go	$	Ind	Ind		
Combined Honours Information Technology	Y100	3FT/4SW/4EXT deg	M/Cs/P/Es/St	CC	3M $	M* go	$	Ind	Ind		
Computing	005G	2FT HND	M/Cs/P/Es/St g	D	2M $	P$ go	$	Ind	Ind		
Univ of NORTHUMBRIA											
Applied Statistics and Scientific Computing	GG45	3FT deg	M/S g	12	3M	Ind	24	CCCC	Ind		
Business Information Systems	G562	4SW deg	* g	CCD	MO+3D	D	24	BBCCC	Ind	3	12/18
Business Information Technology (1 year top-up)	G563	1FT deg	X	X	HN	X	X	X	HN	2	
Computing	G508	5EXT deg	* g	2-4	N	P gi	Ind	Ind	Ind	1	
Computing Studies	G502	4SW deg	* g	12	4M	M gi	24	CCCC	Ind	6	10/22
Computing Technology	G620	4SW deg	* g	12	4M	M gi	24	CCCC	Ind		
Computing for Business	G5N1	4SW deg	* g	12	4M	M gi	24	CCCC	Ind	5	10/20
Computing for Europe	G504	3FT/4SW deg	* g	12	4M	M gi	24	CCCC	Ind		
Computing for Industry	G501	4SW deg	* g	12	4M	M gi	24	CCCC	Ind	5	10/12
Computing with Cognitive Psychology	G5C8	4SW deg	* g	14	5M	M gi	24	BBBC	Ind		
Computing with Multi Media Design	GP54	4SW deg	* g	14	3M	M gi	24	BBBC	Ind		
Information and Communication Management	G560	3FT deg		12	3M+1D	M	24	CCCC	Ind	2	6/14
Mathematics and Scientific Computing	GG15	3FT deg	M g	8-12	Ind	Ind	24$	BBC$	Ind		
Psychology with Computing	C8G5	3FT deg	g	CCC	1M+4D	M^	26	BBBCC	Ind		
Scientific Computing	G510	3FT deg	M g	8-12	Ind	Ind	24$	BBC$			
Business Information Technology	265G	2FT HND	* g	DD	MO	M	24	CCC	Ind	4	6/10
Computing Studies	105G▼	3SW HND	* g	4-6	2M	P gi	24	CCC	Ind	4	4/9
Computing Technology	026G	3SW HND	* g	4-6	2M	P gi	24	CCC	Ind		
Computing for Business	305G	3SW HND	* g	4-6	2M	P gi	24	CCC	Ind	4	4/6
NORWICH: City COLL											
Business Information Systems (HND top up)	G562	1FT deg		X	HN	X	X	X	X	3	
Business Information Technology	265G	2FT HND	*	E	N	M* go	Ind	CC	Ind	3	
Computing	005G	2FT HND	*	E	N	M* go	Ind	CC	Ind	2	6/10
Univ of NOTTINGHAM											
Computer Sci, Artificial Intelligence & Psych	CG85	3FT deg	M	BBB-BBC	Ind		Ind	Ind	Ind	10	22/30
Computer Science	G500	3FT deg	M	BBB-BCC	Ind		Ind	Ind	Ind	11	18/30
Computer Science and Management Studies	GN51	3FT deg	M	BBB	Ind		Ind	Ind	Ind	14	26/30
Computer Systems Engineering	G600	3FT deg	M+P	BBB-BCC	Ind		Ind	Ind	Ind	19	18/26
Mathematics and Computer Science	GG51	3FT deg	M	AAB-ABB	Ind	Ind	Ind	Ind	Ind	9	26/30

course details			*98 expected requirements*							*96 entry stats*	
TITLE	CODE	COURSE	SUBJECTS	A/AS	ND/C	AGNVQ	IB	SQA(H)	SQA	RATIO	A/AS
NOTTINGHAM TRENT Univ											
Biology and Computing	CG15	3FT deg	B g	10	Ind	Ind	Dip	C	Ind	7	7/12
Business Information Systems	G522	4SW deg	* g	16	M+D $		Ind	Ind	Ind	9	12/24
Chemistry and Computing	FG15	3FT deg	C g	10	Ind	Ind	Dip	C	Ind	11	
Computer Studies	G501▼	3FT/4SW deg	* g	14	4M		Ind	Ind	Ind	5	10/22
Computer Studies (Extended)	G507▼	4EXT/5EXTSW deg	* g		Ind	Ind	Ind	Ind	Ind	1	
Computing Systems	G600	3FT/4SW deg	* g	14	4M $		Ind	CCC	$	6	10/18
Computing Systems (Extended)	G508▼	4EXT/5EXTSW deg	* g		Ind	Ind	Ind	Ind	Ind	1	
Computing and Environmental Systs and Monitoring	FGX5	3FT deg	S g	10	Ind	Ind	Dip	C	Ind	9	
Computing and Physics	FG35	3FT deg	M/P	10	Ind	Ind	Dip	C	Ind	4	10/14
Electronics and Computing	GH56	3FT/4SW deg	* g	18	4M $		Ind	BBB$	$	6	8/20
Electronics and Computing (Extended)	GH5P▼	4EXT/5EXTSW deg	* g		Ind	Ind	Ind	$	Ind	2	
Engineering Systems and Computing	GH51	3FT/4SW deg	* g	18	3M $	Ind	Ind	Ind	Ind		
Environmental Conservation & Mgt & Computing	FG95	3FT deg	S g	10	Ind	Ind	Dip	C	Ind	12	
Environmental Systs & Monitoring & IT for Sci's	FGXM	3FT deg	S g	10	Ind	Ind	Dip	C	Ind	5	
Information Technology for Sciences & Chemistry	GF51	3FT deg	C g	10	Ind	Ind	Dip	C	Ind	4	
Information Technology for Sciences & Maths	GG51	3FT deg	M g	10	Ind	Ind	Dip	C	Ind		
Information Technology for Sciences and Biology	GC51	3FT deg	B g	10	Ind	Ind	Dip	C	Ind	2	
Information Technology for Sciences and Physics	GF53	3FT deg	M/P g	10	Ind	Ind	Dip	C	Ind		
Information Technology for Scis & Env Cons & Mgt	GF59	3FT deg	S g	10	Ind	Ind	Dip	C	Ind		
Mathematical Methods for Information Tech (Ext)	G1GM▼	5EXTSW deg	* g		Ind	Ind	Ind	Ind	Ind	1	
Mathematical Methods for Information Technology	G1G5	4SW deg	M g	DD	Ind	Ind	Dip	C	$	3	6/16
Mathematics and Computing	GG15	3FT deg	M g	10	Ind	Ind	Dip	C	Ind	6	6/14
Sport & Exercise Science & IT for Science	BG6M	3FT deg	B+Pe/Ss g	16	Ind	Ind	Dip	B	Ind		
Sport & Exercise Science and Computing	BG65	3FT deg	B+Pe/Ss g	16	Ind	Ind	Dip	B	Ind		
Working with Technology	GN51	3FT deg	* g	8	3M	M	Ind	CCCC	N	2	6/14
Computer Studies	105G▼	2FT/3SW HND	* g	6	2M		Ind	Ind	Ind	4	2/10
Electronics and Computing	65HG▼	2FT HND	* g	4	4M $	Ind	Ind	CC$	$	4	
OXFORD Univ											
Computation	G500	3FT deg	M	AAB	DO		36	AAAAA	Ind	3	26/30
Engineering and Computing Science (4 Yrs)	GH51	4FT deg	M+P	AAB	DO		36	AAAAA	Ind	5	28/30
Mathematics and Computation	GG15	3FT deg	M	AAB	DO		36	AAAAA	Ind	2	28/30
OXFORD BROOKES Univ											
Computer Systems	G600	4SW deg	* g	CD-DDD	Ind	M*	Ind	Ind	Ind	10	
Computer Systems/Accounting and Finance	GN64	3FT deg	* g	BC-BCC	Ind	M*/D*3	Ind	Ind	Ind	6	
Computer Systems/Anthropology	GL66	3FT deg	* g	BC-BCC	Ind	M*^	Ind	Ind	Ind		
Computer Systems/Biological Chemistry	CG76	3FT deg									
Computer Systems/Biology	CG16	3FT deg	S g	DD-CDD	Ind	MS	Ind	Ind	Ind		
Computer Systems/Business Admin and Management	GN61	3FT deg	* g	BC-BBC	Ind	MB/MB4	Ind	Ind	Ind	12	
Computer Systems/Cartography	FG86	3FT deg	* g	DDD-BC	Ind	M*	Ind	Ind	Ind		
Computer Systems/Cell Biology	CGC6	3FT deg									
Computer Systems/Combined Studies	GY64	3FT deg		X		X	X	X			
Computing	G501	4SW deg	* g	CDD-BC	Ind	M*	Ind	Ind	Ind	4	8/16
Computing Mathematics/Computer Systems	GG69	3FT deg	* g	CD-BC	Ind	M*	Ind	Ind	Ind	3	
Computing Mathematics/Computing	GG59	3FT deg	* g	CD-CDD	Ind	M*	Ind	Ind	Ind		
Computing Science	G500	4SW deg	* g	DDD-CD	Ind	M*	Ind	Ind	Ind	6	9/22
Computing/Accounting and Finance	GN54	3FT deg	* g	CDD-BCC	Ind	M*/D*3	Ind	Ind	Ind	5	12/17
Computing/Anthropology	GL56	3FT deg	* g	CDD-BCC	Ind	M*^	Ind	Ind	Ind		
Computing/Biological Chemistry	CG75	3FT deg									
Computing/Biology	CG15	2ACC/3FT deg	S g	DD-BC	Ind	MS	Ind	Ind	Ind	6	
Computing/Business Administration & Management	GN51	3FT deg	* g	CDD-BBC	Ind	M*/MB4	Ind	Ind	Ind	11	

course details | .98 expected requirements | 96 entry stats

TITLE	CODE	COURSE	SUBJECTS	A/AS	ND/C	AGNVQ	IB	SQA(H)	SQA	RATIO A/AS
Computing/Cartography	FG85	3FT deg	* g	DDD-BC	Ind	M*	Ind	Ind	Ind	2
Computing/Cell Biology	CGC5	3FT deg								
Computing/Combined Studies	GY54	3FT deg		X		X	X	X		
Computing/Computer Systems	GG65	3FT deg	* g	CDD-BC	Ind	M*	Ind	Ind	Ind	3
Ecology/Computer Systems	CG96	3FT deg	* g	CD-BC	Ind	MS	Ind	Ind	Ind	
Ecology/Computing	CG95	3FT deg	* g	CD-BC	Ind	MS	Ind	Ind	Ind	
Economics/Computer Systems	GL61	3FT deg	* g	CDD-BB	Ind	M*/M*3	Ind	Ind	Ind	
Economics/Computing	GL51	3FT deg	* g	CDD-BB	Ind	M*/M*3	Ind	Ind	Ind	5
Educational Studies/Computer Systems	GX69	3FT deg	* g	DDD-BC	Ind	M*/M*3	Ind	Ind	Ind	
Educational Studies/Computing	GX59	3FT deg	* g	CC-CDD	Ind	M*/M*3	Ind	Ind	Ind	
Electronics/Computer Systems	GH66	3FT deg	S/M	CC-BC	Ind	M$	Ind	Ind	Ind	4
Electronics/Computing	GH56	2ACC/3FT deg	S/M	CDD-BB	Ind	M$	Ind	Ind	Ind	5
English Studies/Computer Systems	GQ63	3FT deg	* g	CDD-AB	Ind	M*^	Ind	Ind	Ind	1
English Studies/Computing	GQ53	3FT deg	* g	CDD-AB	Ind	M*^	Ind	Ind	Ind	8
Environmental Chemistry/Computer Systems	GF61	3FT deg								
Environmental Chemistry/Computing	GF51	3FT deg								
Environmental Policy/Computer Systems	KG36	3FT deg								
Environmental Policy/Computing	KG35	3FT deg								
Environmental Sciences/Computer Systems	FGX6	3FT deg	S g	CD-BC	Ind	M*/DS	Ind	Ind	Ind	
Environmental Sciences/Computing	FGX5	3FT deg	S g	CD-CDD	Ind	M*/DS	Ind	Ind	Ind	
Exercise and Health/Computer Systems	GB66	3FT deg	S g	DD-BC	Ind	MS	Ind	Ind	Ind	
Exercise and Health/Computing	GB56	3FT deg	S g	DD-BC	Ind	MS	Ind	Ind	Ind	
Fine Art/Computer Systems	GW61	3FT deg	Pf+A g	CDD-BC	Ind	MA^	Ind	Ind	Ind	
Fine Art/Computing	GW51	3FT deg	Pf+A g	CDD-BC	Ind	MA^	Ind	Ind	Ind	
Food Science and Nutrition/Computer Systems	DG46	3FT deg	S g	DD-BC	Ind	MS	Ind	Ind	Ind	
Food Science and Nutrition/Computing	DG45	3FT deg	S g	DD-BC	Ind	MS	Ind	Ind	Ind	
French Language and Contemp Studies/Comp Systs	GR6C	3FT deg	F g	CDD-BC	Ind	M*_^	Ind	Ind	Ind	
French Language and Contemp Studies/Computing	GR5C	4SW deg	F g	BC-CDD	Ind	M*_^	Ind	Ind	Ind	
French Language and Literature/Computer Systems	GR61	3FT deg	F g	CDD-BC	Ind	M*_^	Ind	Ind	Ind	
French Language and Literature/Computing	GR51	4SW deg	F g	BC-CDD	Ind	M*_^	Ind	Ind	Ind	
Geography and the Phys Env/Computer Systems	FGV6	3FT deg								
Geography and the Phys Env/Computing	FGV5	3FT deg								
Geography and the Phys Env/Informatiion Systems	FGVM	3FT deg								
Geography and the Phys Env/Intelligent Systems	FGV8	3FT deg								
Geography/Computer Systems	GL68	3FT deg	* g	CDD-BB	Ind	M*	Ind	Ind	Ind	
Geography/Computing	GL58	3FT deg	* g	CDD-BB	Ind	M*	Ind	Ind	Ind	
Geology/Computer Systems	FG66	3FT deg	* g	DD-BC	Ind	PS/MS	Ind	Ind	Ind	
Geology/Computing	FG65	3FT deg	S/M g	DD-BC	Ind	PS/MS	Ind	Ind	Ind	
Geotechnics/Computer Systems	GH62	3FT deg	S/M/Ds/Es	DD-BC	Ind	M$	Ind	Ind	Ind	
Geotechnics/Computing	GH52	3FT deg	S/M/Ds/Es g	CC-DD	Ind	M$	Ind	Ind	Ind	1
German Language and Contemp Stud/Computer System	GR6F	3FT deg	G g	DDD-BC	Ind	M*_^	Ind	Ind	Ind	
German Language and Contemp Stud/Computing	GR5F	4SW deg	G g	DDD-BC	Ind	M*_^	Ind	Ind	Ind	
German Language and Literature/Computer Systems	GR62	4FT deg	G g	DDD-BC	Ind	M*_^	Ind	Ind	Ind	
German Language and Literature/Computing	GR52	4SW deg	G g	DDD-BC	Ind	M*_^	Ind	Ind	Ind	
German Studies/Computer Systems	GR6G	4SW deg			Ind		Ind	Ind	Ind	
German Studies/Computing	GR5G	4SW deg			Ind		Ind	Ind	Ind	
Health Care/Computer Systems (Post Exp)	BG76	3FT deg		X		X	X	X		
Health Care/Computing (Post Exp)	BG75	3FT deg		X		X	X	X		
History of Art/Computer Systems	GV64	3FT deg	* g	CDD-BCC	Ind	M*^	Ind	Ind	Ind	
History of Art/Computing	GV54	3FT deg	* g	CDD-BCC	Ind	M*^	Ind	Ind	Ind	
History/Computer Systems	GV61	3FT deg	* g	CDD-BB	Ind	M*^	Ind	Ind	Ind	
History/Computing	GV51	3FT deg	* g	CDD-BB	Ind	M*^	Ind	Ind	Ind	2

Computer Sciences and Engineering 15

course details				*98 expected requirements*						*96 entry stats*
TITLE	CODE	COURSE	SUBJECTS	A/AS	ND/C	AGNVQ	IB	SQA(H)	SQA	RATIO A/AS
Hospitality Management Studies/Computer Systems	GN67	3FT deg	* g	DDD-BC	Ind	M*/M*3	Ind	Ind	Ind	
Hospitality Management Studies/Computing	GN57	3FT deg	* g	DDD-BC	Ind	M*/M*3	Ind	Ind	Ind	
Human Biology/Computer Systems	BG16	3FT deg			Ind		Ind	Ind	Ind	
Human Biology/Computing	BG15	3FT deg			Ind		Ind	Ind	Ind	
Information Systems	G520	4SW deg	g	DDD-CD	Ind	M*	Ind	Ind	Ind	6
Information Systems/Accounting and Finance	GNM4	3FT deg	* g	CDD-BCC	Ind	M*/D*3	Ind	Ind	Ind	6
Information Systems/Anthropology	GLM6	3FT deg	* g	CDD-BCC	Ind	M*^	Ind	Ind	Ind	1
Information Systems/Biological Chemistry	CG7M	3FT deg								
Information Systems/Biology	CG1M	3FT deg	S g	DD-BC	Ind	MS	Ind	Ind	Ind	1
Information Systems/Business Admin & Management	GNM1	3FT deg	* g	CDD-BBC	Ind	MB/MB4	Ind	Ind	Ind	5
Information Systems/Cartography	FG8M	3FT deg	* g	DDD-BC	Ind	M*	Ind	Ind	Ind	1
Information Systems/Cell Biology	CGCM	3FT deg								
Information Systems/Combined Studies	GYM4	3FT deg		X		X	X	X		
Information Systems/Computer Systems	GG6M	3FT deg	* g	CDD-BC	Ind	M*	Ind	Ind	Ind	3
Information Systems/Computing	G510	3FT deg	* g	CDD-BC	Ind	M*	Ind	Ind	Ind	5
Information Systems/Computing Mathematics	GGM9	3FT deg	* g	CD-BC	Ind	M*	Ind	Ind	Ind	
Information Systems/Ecology	CG9M	3FT deg	* g	CD-BC	Ind	MS	Ind	Ind	Ind	
Information Systems/Economics	GLM1	3FT deg	* g	CDD-BB	Ind	M*/M*3	Ind	Ind	Ind	
Information Systems/Educational Studies	GXM9	3FT deg	* g	CDD-BB	Ind	M*/M*3	Ind	Ind	Ind	
Information Systems/Electronics	GHM6	3FT deg	S/M	CC-BC	Ind	M$	Ind	Ind	Ind	
Information Systems/English Studies	GQM3	3FT deg	* g	CDD-BCC	Ind	M*^	Ind	Ind	Ind	
Information Systems/Environmental Chemistry	GF5C	3FT deg								
Information Systems/Environmental Policy	KG3M	3FT deg								
Information Systems/Environmental Sciences	FGXM	3FT deg	S g	CD-BC	Ind	M*/DS	Ind	Ind	Ind	
Information Systems/Exercise and Health	GBM6	3FT deg	S g	DD-BC	Ind	MS	Ind	Ind	Ind	
Information Systems/Fine Art	GWM1	3FT deg	A+Pf g	CDD-BC	Ind	MA^	Ind	Ind	Ind	
Information Systems/Food Science and Nutrition	DG4M	3FT deg	S g	DD-BC	Ind	MS	Ind	Ind	Ind	
Information Systems/French Lang & Contemp Studs	GRMC	3FT deg	F g	CC-BC	Ind	M*^	Ind	Ind	Ind	3
Information Systems/French Language & Literature	GRM1	3FT deg	F g	CC-BC	Ind	M*^	Ind	Ind	Ind	2
Information Systems/Geography	GLM8	3FT deg	* g	BC-BB	Ind	M*	Ind	Ind	Ind	
Information Systems/Geology	FG6N	3FT deg	M/S g	DD-BC	Ind	PS/M*	Ind	Ind	Ind	
Information Systems/Geotechnics	GHN2	3FT deg	S/M/Ds/Es g	DD-BC	Ind	M$	Ind	Ind	Ind	
Information Systems/German Lang and Contemp Stud	GRNF	3FT deg	G g	CD-BC	Ind	M*^	Ind	Ind	Ind	
Information Systems/German Language & Literature	GRN2	3FT deg	G g	CD-BC	Ind	M*^	Ind	Ind	Ind	
Information Systems/German Studies	GRMG	4SW deg	G g	CD-BC	Ind	M*^	Ind	Ind	Ind	
Information Systems/Health Care (Post Exp)	BG7M	3FT deg		X		X	X	X		
Information Systems/History	GVN1	3FT deg	* g	BC-BB	Ind	M*	Ind	Ind	Ind	
Information Systems/History of Art	GVN4	3FT deg	* g	CDD-BCC	Ind	M^	Ind	Ind	Ind	
Information Systems/Hospitality Management Studs	GNM7	3FT deg	* g	CC-BC	Ind	M*/M*3	Ind	Ind	Ind	
Information Systems/Human Biology	BG1M	3FT deg								
Information Systems/Retail Management	GNM5	3FT deg			Ind		Ind	Ind	Ind	4
Intelligent Systems	G800	4SW deg	* g	CDD-BC	Ind	M*	Ind	Ind	Ind	7
Intelligent Systems/Accounting and Finance	GN84	3FT deg	* g	CD-BCC	Ind	M*/D*3	Ind	Ind	Ind	
Intelligent Systems/Anthropology	GL86	3FT deg	* g	CD-BCC	Ind	M*/D*3	Ind	Ind	Ind	
Intelligent Systems/Biological Chemistry	CG78	3FT deg								
Intelligent Systems/Biology	CG18	3FT deg	S g	DD-CD	Ind	MS	Ind	Ind	Ind	
Intelligent Systems/Business Admin & Management	GN81	3FT deg	* g	CD-BBC	Ind	M*/MB4	Ind	Ind	Ind	
Intelligent Systems/Cartography	FG88	3FT deg	* g	CC-DDD	Ind	M*	Ind	Ind	Ind	
Intelligent Systems/Cell Biology	CGC8	3FT deg								
Intelligent Systems/Combined Studies	GY84	3FT deg		X		X	X	X		
Intelligent Systems/Computer Systems	GG68	3FT deg		CDD-BC	Ind	M*	Ind	Ind	Ind	
Intelligent Systems/Computing	GG58	3FT deg	* g	BC-CDD	Ind	M*	Ind	Ind	Ind	

course details

98 expected requirements

96 entry stats

TITLE	CODE	COURSE	SUBJECTS	A/AS	NO/C	RGNVQ	IB	SQA(H)	SQA	RATIO A/AS
Intelligent Systems/Computing Mathematics	GG89	3FT deg	* g	CD	Ind	M*	Ind	Ind	Ind	
Intelligent Systems/Ecology	CG98	3FT deg	* g	CD	Ind	MS	Ind	Ind	Ind	
Intelligent Systems/Economics	GL81	3FT deg	* g	CD-BB	Ind	M*/M*3	Ind	Ind	Ind	
Intelligent Systems/Educational Studies	GX89	3FT deg	* g	CD-CC	Ind	M*/M*3	Ind	Ind	Ind	
Intelligent Systems/Electronics	GH86	3FT deg	S/M	CD-CC	Ind	M$	Ind	Ind	Ind	
Intelligent Systems/English Studies	GQ83	3FT deg	* g	CD-AB	Ind	M*^	Ind	Ind	Ind	
Intelligent Systems/Environmental Chemistry	GF81	3FT deg								
Intelligent Systems/Environmental Policy	KG38	3FT deg								
Intelligent Systems/Environmental Sciences	FGX8	3FT deg	S g	CD	Ind	M*/DS	Ind	Ind	Ind	
Intelligent Systems/Exercise and Health	GB86	3FT deg	S g	DD-CD	Ind	MS	Ind	Ind	Ind	
Intelligent Systems/Fine Art	GW81	3FT deg	Pf+A g	CC-BC	Ind	MA^	Ind	Ind	Ind	
Intelligent Systems/Food Science and Nutrition	DG48	3FT deg	S g	DD-CD	Ind	MS	Ind	Ind	Ind	
Intelligent Systems/French Lang & Contemp Studs	GR8C	4SW deg	F g	CD-CC	Ind	M*^	Ind	Ind	Ind	
Intelligent Systems/French Lang and Literature	GR81	4SW deg	F g	CD-CC	Ind	M*^	Ind	Ind	Ind	
Intelligent Systems/Geography	GL88	3FT deg	* g	CD-BB	Ind	M*	Ind	Ind	Ind	
Intelligent Systems/Geology	FG68	3FT deg	S/M	DD-CD	Ind	M*/PS	Ind	Ind	Ind	
Intelligent Systems/Geotechnics	GH82	3FT deg	S/M/Ds/Es	CC-DD	Ind	M$	Ind	Ind	Ind	
Intelligent Systems/German Lang & Contemp Stud	GR8F	4SW deg	G g	CD-DDD	Ind	M*^	Ind	Ind	Ind	
Intelligent Systems/German Lang and Literature	GR82	4SW deg	G g	CD-DDD	Ind	M*^	Ind	Ind	Ind	
Intelligent Systems/German Studies	GR8G	4SW deg		CD-DDD	Ind	M*^	Ind	Ind	Ind	
Intelligent Systems/Health Care (Post Exp)	BG78	3FT deg	X			X	X	X	X	
Intelligent Systems/History	GV81	3FT deg	* g	BB-CD	Ind	M^	Ind	Ind	Ind	
Intelligent Systems/History of Art	GV84	3FT deg	* g	BCC-CD	Ind	M^	Ind	Ind	Ind	
Intelligent Systems/Hospitality Management Studs	GN87	3FT deg	* g	CC-DDD	Ind	M*/M*3	Ind	Ind	Ind	
Intelligent Systems/Human Biology	BG18	3FT deg								
Intelligent Systems/Information Systems	GGM8	3FT deg		CDD-BC	Ind	M*	Ind	Ind	Ind	
Law/Computer Systems	GM63	3FT deg	* g	CDD-BBB	Ind	M*/D*3	Ind	Ind	Ind	
Law/Computing	GM53	3FT deg	* g	CDD-BBB	Ind	M*/D*3	Ind	Ind	Ind	3
Law/Information Systems	GMM3	3FT deg	* g	CDD-BBB	Ind	M*/D*3	Ind	Ind	Ind	1
Law/Intelligent Systems	GM83	3FT deg	* g	CD-BBB	Ind	M*/D*3	Ind	Ind	Ind	
Leisure Planning/Computer Systems	KGH6	3FT deg								
Leisure Planning/Computing	KGH5	3FT deg								
Leisure Planning/Information Systems	KGHM	3FT deg								
Leisure Planning/Intelligent Systems	KGH8	3FT deg								
Marketing Management/Computer Systems	GN6N	3FT deg	* g	CDD-BCC	Ind	M*/D*3	Ind	Ind	Ind	
Marketing Management/Computing	GN5N	3FT deg	* g	CDD-BCC	Ind	M*/D*3	Ind	Ind	Ind	3
Marketing Management/Information Systems	GNMN	3FT deg	* g	CDD-BCC	Ind	M*/D*3	Ind	Ind	Ind	1
Marketing Management/Intelligent Systems	GN8N	3FT deg	* g	CD-BCC	Ind	M*/D*3	Ind	Ind	Ind	6
Mathematics/Computer Systems	GG61	3FT deg	M g	DD-BC	Ind	M*^	Ind	Ind	Ind	
Mathematics/Computing	GG15	2ACC/3FT deg	M	DD-BC	Ind	M*^	Ind	Ind	Ind	11
Mathematics/Information Systems	GGM1	3FT deg	M	DD-BC	Ind	M*^	Ind	Ind	Ind	
Mathematics/Intelligent Systems	GG18	3FT deg	M	DD-BC	Ind	M*^	Ind	Ind	Ind	5
Music/Computer Systems	GW63	3FT deg	Mu g	DD-BC	Ind	M*	Ind	Ind	Ind	
Music/Computing	GW53	3FT deg	Mu g	DD-BC	Ind	M*	Ind	Ind	Ind	
Music/Information Systems	GWM3	3FT deg	Mu g	DD-BC	Ind	M*	Ind	Ind	Ind	
Music/Intelligent Systems	GW83	3FT deg	Mu g	DD-CD	Ind	M*	Ind	Ind	Ind	
Palliative Care/Computer Systems (Post Exp)	BGR6	3FT deg		X		X	X	X	X	
Palliative Care/Computing (Post Exp)	BGR5	3FT deg		X		X	X	X	X	
Palliative Care/Information Systems (Post Exp)	BGRM	3FT deg		X		X	X	X	X	
Palliative Care/Intelligent Systems (Post Exp)	BGR8	3FT deg		X		X	X	X	X	
Planning Studies/Computer Systems	GK64	3FT deg	* g	DDD-BC	Ind	M*	Ind	Ind	Ind	
Planning Studies/Computing	GK54	3FT deg	* g	DDD-BC	Ind	M*	Ind	Ind	Ind	

Computer Sciences and Engineering 15

TITLE	CODE	COURSE	SUBJECTS	A/AS	NO/C	AGNVQ	IB	SQA(H)	SQA	RATIO A/AS
Planning Studies/Information Systems	GKM4	3FT deg	* g	DDD-BC	Ind	M*	Ind	Ind	Ind	
Planning Studies/Intelligent Systems	GK84	3FT deg	* g	DDD-BC	Ind	M*	Ind	Ind	Ind	
Politics/Computer Systems	GM61	3FT deg	* g	BC-AB	Ind	M*^	Ind	Ind	Ind	
Politics/Computing	GM51	3FT deg	* g	CDD-AB	Ind	M*^	Ind	Ind	Ind	2
Politics/Information Systems	GMM1	3FT deg	* g	CDD-AB	Ind	M*^	Ind	Ind	Ind	
Politics/Intelligent Systems	MG18	3FR deg	* g	CD-AB	Ind	M*^	Ind	Ind	Ind	
Psychology/Computer Systems	CG86	3FT deg	* g	CDD-BBC	Ind	M*^	Ind	Ind	Ind	
Psychology/Computing	CG85	3FT deg	* g	CDD-BBC	Ind	M*^	Ind	Ind	Ind	16
Psychology/Information Systems	CG8M	3FT deg		CD-BBC	Ind	M*^	Ind	Ind	Ind	
Psychology/Intelligent Systems	CG88	3FT deg	* g	CD-BBC	Ind	M*^	Ind	Ind	Ind	
Publishing/Computer Systems	GP65	3FT deg	* g	CDD-CCC	Ind	M*/M$3	Ind	Ind	Ind	
Publishing/Computing	GP55	3FT deg	* g	CDD-BB	Ind	M*/M$3	Ind	Ind	Ind	2
Publishing/Information Systems	GPM5	3FT deg	* g	CDD-BB	Ind	M*/M$3	Ind	Ind	Ind	
Publishing/Intelligent Systems	GP85	3FT deg	* g	CDD-BB	Ind	M*/M$3	Ind	Ind	Ind	
Rehabilitation/Computer Systems (Post Exp)	BGT6	3FT deg		X		X	X	X		
Rehabilitation/Computing (Post Exp)	BGT5	3FT deg		X		X	X	X		
Rehabilitation/Information Systems	BGTM	3FT deg		X		X	X	X		
Rehabilitation/Intelligent Systems (Post Exp)	BGT8	3FT deg		X		X	X	X		
Retail Management/Computer Systems	GN65	3FT deg			Ind		Ind	Ind	Ind	
Retail Management/Computing	GN55	3FT deg	* g	CDD-CCD	Ind		Ind	Ind	Ind	1
Retail Management/Intelligent Systems	GN85	3FT deg	* g	CD-CCD	Ind		Ind	Ind	Ind	1
Sociology/Computer Systems	GL63	3FT deg	* g	CDD-BCC	Ind	M*^	Ind	Ind	Ind	
Sociology/Information Systems	GLM3	3FT deg		CDD-BCC	Ind	M*^	Ind	Ind	Ind	
Sociology/Intelligent Systems	GL83	3FT deg	* g	CDD-BCC	Ind	M*^	Ind	Ind	Ind	2
Software Engineering	G700	4SW deg	* g	DDD-CD	Ind	M*	Ind	Ind	Ind	8
Software Engineering/Accounting and Finance	GN74	3FT deg	* g	CDD-BCC	Ind	M*/D*3	Ind	Ind	Ind	
Software Engineering/Anthropology	GL76	3FT deg	* g	CDD-BCC	Ind	M*^	Ind	Ind	Ind	
Software Engineering/Biological Chemistry	CG77	3FT deg								
Software Engineering/Biology	CG17	3FT deg	S g	DD-BC	Ind	MS	Ind	Ind	Ind	
Software Engineering/Business Admin and Mgt	GN71	3FT deg	* g	CDD-BBC	Ind	M*/MB4	Ind	Ind	Ind	
Software Engineering/Cartography	FG87	3FT deg	* g	DDD-CDD	Ind	M*	Ind	Ind	Ind	
Software Engineering/Cell Biology	CGC7	3FT deg								
Software Engineering/Combined Studies	GY74	3FT deg		X		X	X	X		
Software Engineering/Computer Systems	GG67	3FT deg	* g	CDD-BC	Ind	M*	Ind	Ind	Ind	5
Software Engineering/Computing	GG75	3FT deg	* g	CDD-BC	Ind	M*	Ind	Ind	Ind	3
Software Engineering/Computing Mathematics	GG79	3FT deg	* g	CD-BC	Ind	M*	Ind	Ind	Ind	
Software Engineering/Ecology	CG97	3FT deg	S g	CD-BC	Ind	MS	Ind	Ind	Ind	
Software Engineering/Economics	GL71	3FT deg	* g	CDD-BB	Ind	M*/M*3	Ind	Ind	Ind	
Software Engineering/Educational Studies	GX79	3FT deg	* g	CC-BC	Ind	M*/M*3	Ind	Ind	Ind	
Software Engineering/Electronics	GH76	3FT deg	S/M	CC-BC	Ind	M$	Ind	Ind	Ind	
Software Engineering/English Studies	GQ73	3FT deg	* g	CD-AB	Ind	M*^	Ind	Ind	Ind	
Software Engineering/Environmental Chemistry	GF71	3FT deg								
Software Engineering/Environmental Policy	KG37	3FT deg								
Software Engineering/Environmental Sciences	FGX7	3FT deg	S g	CD-BC	Ind	M*/DS	Ind	Ind	Ind	
Software Engineering/Exercise and Health	GB76	3FT deg	S g	DD-BC	Ind	MS	Ind	Ind	Ind	
Software Engineering/Fine Art	GW71	3FT deg	Pf+A g	CDD-BC	Ind	MA^	Ind	Ind	Ind	
Software Engineering/Food Science and Nutrition	DG47	3FT deg	S g	DD-BC	Ind	MS	Ind	Ind	Ind	
Software Engineering/French Lang & Literature	GR71	4FT deg	F g	CDD-BC	Ind	M*^	Ind	Ind	Ind	
Software Engineering/French Lang and Contemp St	GR7C	4FT deg	F g	CDD-BC	Ind	M*^	Ind	Ind	Ind	
Software Engineering/Geography	GL78	3FT deg	* g	CDD-BB	Ind	M*	Ind	Ind	Ind	
Software Engineering/Geology	FG67	3FT deg	M/S g	DD-BC	Ind	PS/M*	Ind	Ind	Ind	
Software Engineering/Geotechnics	GH72	3FT deg	S/M/Ds/Es g	DD-BC	Ind	M$	Ind	Ind	Ind	

course details   *98 expected requirements*   *96 entry stats*

course details | 98 expected requirements | 96 entry stats

TITLE	CODE	COURSE	SUBJECTS	A/AS	ND/C	AGNVQ	IB	SQA(H)	SQA	RATIO A/AS
Software Engineering/German Lang & Literature	GR72	4FT deg	G g	CDD-BC	Ind	M*-^	Ind	Ind	Ind	
Software Engineering/German Lang and Contemp St	GR7F	4FT deg	G g	CDD-BC	Ind	M*-^	Ind	Ind	Ind	
Software Engineering/German Studies	GR7G	4SW deg	G g	CDD-BC	Ind	M*-^	Ind	Ind	Ind	
Software Engineering/Health Care (Post Exp)	BG77	3FT deg		X		X	X	X		
Software Engineering/History	GV71	3FT deg	* g	CDD-BB	Ind	M*-^	Ind	Ind	Ind	
Software Engineering/History of Art	GV74	3FT deg	* g	CDD-BCC	Ind	M*-^	Ind	Ind	Ind	
Software Engineering/Hospitality Management Stds	GN77	3FT deg	* g	BB-BC	Ind	M*/M*3	Ind	Ind	Ind	
Software Engineering/Human Biology	BG17	3FT deg								
Software Engineering/Information Systems	GGM7	3FT deg	* g	CDD-BC	Ind	M*	Ind	Ind	Ind	
Software Engineering/Intelligent Systems	GG78	3FT deg	* g	CDD-BC	Ind	M*	Ind	Ind	Ind	
Software Engineering/Law	GM73	3FT deg	* g	CDD-BBB	Ind	M*/D*3	Ind	Ind	Ind	
Software Engineering/Leisure Planning & Mgt	KGH7	3FT deg								
Software Engineering/Marketing Management	GN7N	3FT deg	* g	CDD-BCC	Ind	M*/D*3	Ind	Ind	Ind	
Software Engineering/Mathematics	GG71	3FT deg	M g	DD-BC	Ind	M*-^	Ind	Ind	Ind	
Software Engineering/Music	GW73	3FT deg	Mu g	DD-BC	Ind	M*	Ind	Ind	Ind	
Software Engineering/Palliative Care (Post Exp)	BGR7	3FT deg		X		X	X	X		
Software Engineering/Physical Geography	FGV7	3FT deg								
Software Engineering/Planning Studies	GK74	3FT deg	* g	CD-CC	Ind	M*	Ind	Ind	Ind	
Software Engineering/Politics	GM71	3FT deg	* g	CD-AB	Ind	M*-^	Ind	Ind	Ind	
Software Engineering/Psychology	CG87	3FT deg	* g	CC-BC	Ind	M*-^	Ind	Ind	Ind	
Software Engineering/Publishing	GP75	3FT deg	* g	CDD-CCC	Ind	M*/M$3	Ind	Ind	Ind	
Software Engineering/Rehabilitation (Post Exp)	BGT7	3FT deg		X		X	X	X		
Software Engineering/Retail Management	GN75	3FT deg			Ind		Ind	Ind	Ind	
Software Engineering/Sociology	GL73	3FT deg	* g	CDD-BCC	Ind	M*-^	Ind	Ind	Ind	
Statistics/Computer Systems	GG64	3FT deg	* g	DD-BC	Ind	M*	Ind	Ind	Ind	
Statistics/Computing	GG45	2ACC/3FT deg	* g	DD-BC	Ind	M*	Ind	Ind	Ind	4
Statistics/Information Systems	GGM4	3FT deg	* g	DD-BC	Ind	M*	Ind	Ind	Ind	
Statistics/Intelligent Systems	GG48	3FT deg	* g	DD-CD	Ind	M*	Ind	Ind	Ind	
Statistics/Software Engineering	GG74	3FT deg	* g	DD-BC	Ind	M*	Ind	Ind	Ind	
Telecommunications/Computer Systems	GH6P	3FT deg								
Telecommunications/Computing	GH5P	3FT deg								
Telecommunications/Information Systems	GHMP	3FT deg								
Telecommunications/Intelligent Systems	GH8P	3FT deg								
Telecommunications/Software Engineering	GH7P	3FT deg								
Tourism/Computer Systems	GP67	3FT deg	* g	CDD-BC	Ind	M*/M*3	Ind	Ind	Ind	
Tourism/Computing	GP57	3FT deg	* g	CDD-BC	Ind	M*/M*3	Ind	Ind	Ind	2
Tourism/Information Systems	GPM7	3FT deg	* g	CDD-BC	Ind	M*/M*3	Ind	Ind	Ind	6
Tourism/Intelligent Systems	GP87	3FT deg	* g	CD-BC	Ind	M*/M*3	Ind	Ind	Ind	
Tourism/Software Engineering	GP77	3FT deg	* g	CDD-BC	Ind	M*/M*3	Ind	Ind	Ind	
Transport Planning/Computer Systems	GN69	3FT deg	* g	CDD-BC	Ind	M*	Ind	Ind	Ind	
Transport Planning/Computing	GN59	3FT deg	* g	BC-DDD	Ind	M*	Ind	Ind	Ind	
Transport Planning/Information Systems	GNM9	3FT deg	* g	CC-BC	Ind	M*	Ind	Ind	Ind	
Transport Planning/Intelligent Systems	GN89	3FT deg	* g	CD-CC	Ind	M*	Ind	Ind	Ind	
Transport Planning/Software Engineering	GN79	3FT deg	* g	DDD-BC	Ind	M*	Ind	Ind	Ind	
Water Resources/Computer Systems	GH6F	3FT deg								
Water Resources/Computing	GH5F	3FT deg								
Water Resources/Information Systems	HGFM	3FT deg								
Water Resources/Intelligent Systems	GH8F	3FT deg								
Water Resources/Software Engineering	GH7F	3FT deg								

Univ of PAISLEY

TITLE	CODE	COURSE	SUBJECTS	A/AS	ND/C	AGNVQ	IB	SQA(H)	SQA	RATIO A/AS
Applicable Mathematics with Computing	GG15	3FT/4FT/5SW deg	M+S g	CCC-EE	Ind	Ind	Ind	BCC$	Ind	14
Business Info Technology and Euro Languages	GT72	4SW/5SW deg	* g	CC	Ind	Ind	Ind	BBCC$	Ind	

Computer Sciences and Engineering   15

TITLE	CODE	COURSE	SUBJECTS	A/AS	NO/C	AGNVQ	IB	SQA(H)	SQA	RATIO	A/AS
			98 expected requirements							**96 entry stats**	
Business Information Technology	G720	4SW/5SW deg	* g	CC	Ind	Ind	Ind	BBC$	Ind		
Business Information Technology & Accounting	GN74	4SW/5SW deg	* g	CC	Ind	Ind	Ind	BCCC$	Ind		
Business Information Technology & Marketing	GN75	4SW/5SW deg	* g	CC	Ind	Ind	Ind	BCCC	Ind		
Computer Engineering	GH66	3FT/4FT/5SW deg	M+P g	DD	Ind	Ind	Ind	BBC$	Ind	12	
Computing Science	G500	3FT/4SW/5SW deg	M g	CC	Ind	Ind	Ind	BCCC$	Ind	5	
Computing Science (MEng)	G501	5FT/6SW deg	M g	CCC	Ind	Ind	Ind	BBBB$	Ind		
Computing Science, Stats & Operational Research	GG54	3FT/4SW/5SW deg	M g	CC	Ind	Ind	Ind	BCCC$	Ind		
Information Systems	G520	3FT/4SW/5SW deg	M g	CC	Ind	Ind	Ind	BCCC$	Ind	4	
Physics with Scientific Computing	F3G5	3FT/4FT/5SW deg	M+P g	CCC-EE	Ind	Ind	Ind	BCC$	Ind	3	
Software Engineering	G700	3FT/4SW/5SW deg	M g	CC	Ind	Ind	Ind	BCCC$	Ind	4	
Software Engineering (MEng)	G701	5FT/6SW deg	M g	CCC	Ind	Ind	Ind	BBBB$	Ind		

Univ of PLYMOUTH

TITLE	CODE	COURSE	SUBJECTS	A/AS	NO/C	AGNVQ	IB	SQA(H)	SQA	RATIO	A/AS
Applied Economics with Computing	L1G5	3FT deg	* g	CCD-CDD	MO	M$^	Ind	BCCC	Ind		
Biotechnology with Computing	C9G5	3FT/4SW deg	B g	12-14	4M	MS^	Ind	BBBB	Ind		
Business Economics with Computing	L1GM	3FT deg	* g	CDD-CCD	MO	M$^	Ind	BCCC	Ind		
Business Information Management Systems	G561	4SW deg	* g	CDD-CCD	MO	M12^	Ind	Ind	Ind	5	10/18
Cell Biology and Immunology with Computing	C1G5	3FT/4SW deg	B g	10-14	4M	MS^	Ind	BBBB	Ind	1	
Chemistry with Computing	F1G5	3FT deg	C g	CC	3M	MS^	Ind	CCCC	Ind	4	
Computer Engineering (MEng Option)	G563	3FT/4FT deg	Ap g	12	5M $	ME+	Ind	Ind	Ind		
Computer Systems and Networks	G600	4SW deg	Ap g	16	D+M $	D$^	Ind	BBBB	Ind	4	8/16
Computing	G500	3FT deg	Ap g	12	N $	M$	Ind	BBCC	Ind	7	4/16
Computing and Informatics	G501	4SW deg	Ap g	16	M+D $	D$^	Ind	BBBC	Ind		
European Economics with Computing	L1GN	3FT deg	* g	CDD-CCD	MO	M$^	Ind	BCCC	Ind		
Geography with Computing	F8G5	3FT deg	Gy g	16-18	X	M$^	Ind	ABBB	Ind	12	14/16
Geology with Computing	F6G5	3FT deg	S g	12	4M	MS	Ind	CCC	Ind	4	
Human Biology with Computing	C9GN	3FT/4SW deg	B g	10-14	4M $	MS^	Ind	BBBB	Ind	3	
Law with Computing	M3G5	3FT deg	Ap g	BCC-BBC	DO	D12^	Ind	BBBB$	Ind		
Mathematics with Computing	G1G5	3FT deg	M g	10-15	MO $	M$^	Ind	Ind	Ind	10	
MediaLab Arts	GW59	4SW deg	Ap g	16	Ind	D$	Ind	Ind	Ind	5	14/24
Microbiology with Computing	C5G5	3FT/4SW deg	B g	10-14	4M $	MS	Ind	BBBB	Ind		
Modern Languages with Computing	T9G5	3FT/4SW deg	L g	C	Ind	Ind	Ind	Ind	Ind		
Multimedia, Electronics and Music	G610	3FT deg	Ap g	6	2M	ME^	Ind	Ind	Ind		
Ocean Science with Computing	F7G5	3FT deg	S g	14-16	5M $	M$	Ind	CCCC	Ind	5	
Personal Computer Technology	G560	3FT deg	Ap g	6	2M	ME	Ind	Ind	Ind		
Political Economy with Computing	LG1N	3FT deg	Ap g	CDD-CCD	MO $	M$^	Ind	BCCC	Ind		
Politics with Computing	M1G5	3FT deg	* g	14	Ind	M$	Ind	BBBC$	Ind		
Psychology with Computing	C8G5	3FT/4SW deg	Ap g	BBC	MO+3D	M12^	Ind	BBBC$	Ind		
Sociology with Computing	L3G5	3FT deg	* g	14	Ind	M$	Ind	BBBC$	Ind	8	
Statistics(App) and Mgt Sci with Computing	G4GM	3FT deg	M/St g	10	MO $	M$	Ind	BBCC	Ind	3	
Statistics(App) with Computing	G4G5	3FT deg	M/St g	10	MO $	M$	Ind	BBCC	Ind	2	
Business Information Technology (Exeter College)	006G	2FT HND	* g	2-4	N	M$	Ind	Ind	Ind	2	2/4
Computing	105G	2FT HND	Ap g	8	M $	D$	Ind	CCCC	Ind	7	4/8
Multimedia, Electronics and Music	016G	2FT HND	Ap g	4	N $	PE^	Ind	Ind	Ind		
Personal Computer Technology	065G	2FT HND	Ap g	4	N $	PE^	Ind	Ind	Ind		

Univ of PORTSMOUTH

TITLE	CODE	COURSE	SUBJECTS	A/AS	NO/C	AGNVQ	IB	SQA(H)	SQA	RATIO	A/AS
Accounting and Business Information Systems	NG45	3FT/4SW deg	*	16	5M+1D	D$6/^ go	Dip	CCCCC	Ind	4	6/16
Business Information Systems	G521	4SW deg	*	16	6M	D* go	28	BBBB	Ind	4	4/20
Business Information Technology	G562	4SW deg	*	16	6M	D* go	28	BBBB	Ind	5	9/24
Chemistry and Computing	FG15	3FT deg	C	10	N $	MS6/^	Dip	Ind	Ind		
Chemistry and Computing	FG1M	▼4FT deg	*	Ind	Ind	Ind	Ind	Ind	Ind		
Computer Engineering	G601	3FT/4SW deg	2(M/P/Cs/Es)	14	4M $	M$6/^	26$	BBBC	N$		

course details | 98 expected requirements | 96 entry stats

TITLE	CODE	COURSE	SUBJECTS	A/AS	ND/C	RGNVQ	IB	SQA(H)	SQA	RATIO	A/AS
Computer Engineering (MEng)	G603	4FT/5SW deg	2(M/P/Cs/Es)	16	4M $	M$6/^	28	BBBB	N$		
Computer Science	G500	4SW deg	*	16	6M	D* go	28	BBBB	Ind	5	8/20
Computer Systs Engineering BSc (1 Year Top Up)	G602	1FT deg	Cs/Es	X	HN	X	X	X	HN		
Computing	GG57	3FT/4SW deg	*	16	6M	M* go	28	CCCC	Ind	3	
Computing and Geographical Science	FG8M▼	4FT deg	*	Ind	Ind	Ind	Ind	Ind	Ind		
Computing and Mathematics	GG1M▼	4FT deg	*	Ind	Ind	Ind	Ind	Ind	Ind		
Computing and Mathematics	GG15	3FT deg	M	8	1M $	M*6/^	Dip	BCCC	Ind	7	
Computing and Statistics	GG45	3FT deg	M	8	1M $	M*6/^	Dip	BCCC	Ind	8	
Computing and Statistics	GG4M▼	4FT deg	*	Ind	Ind	Ind	Ind	Ind	Ind		
Decision Analysis and Information Technology	G520	3FT deg	* g	14	4M	P*	Dip	BCCC	Ind	1	6/14
Electronic & Computer Engineering (MEng)	GH6P	4FT/5SW deg	2(M/P/Cs/Es)	16	4M $	M$6/^	28$	BBBB	N$		
Electronic and Computer Engin (Ext Route Avail)	GH66	3FT/4SW deg	2(M/P/Cs/Es)	14	4M $	M$6/^	26$	BBBC	N$	5	6/16
Geographical Science and Computing	FG85	3FT deg	Gy	16	3M	M$6/^	26	BBBB	Ind	5	
Information Technology and Society	GL53	4SW deg	*	14	6M	M* go	28	CCCC	Ind	2	6/16
Physical Electronics and Computing	FG35	3FT deg	P+M	8	N $	MS6/^	Dip		Ind		
Computer Systems Engineering	106G	2FT/3SW HND	M/P/Es/Cs	4	1M $	P$	Dip	CC	Ind		
Computing	105G▼	2FT HND	*	6	3M	M* go	Dip	CCC	Ind	2	2/10
Software Engineering	007G	2FT HND	*	6	3M	M$ go	Dip	CCC	Ind	5	2/ 9

QUEEN MARY & WESTFIELD COLL (Univ of London)

TITLE	CODE	COURSE	SUBJECTS	A/AS	ND/C	RGNVQ	IB	SQA(H)	SQA	RATIO	A/AS
Computer Science	G500	3FT deg		BCC	3M+2D	D^	28$				
Computer Science and Mathematics	GG15	3FT deg	M	BCC	3M+2D	D^	28$				
Computer Science with Business Studies	G5N1	3FT deg	g	BCC	3M+2D	D^	28$				
Computer Systems and Digital Electronics	G521	3FT deg	M+P/Es	BCC	3M+2D	D^	28$				
French, Linguistics and Computer Science	GR51	4FT deg	F	BBC-BCD	3D $	D^	28$				
German, Linguistics and Computer Science	GR52	4FT deg	G	BBC-BCD	3D $	D^	28$				
Hispanic Studs, Linguistics and Computer Science	GR5K	4FT deg	L	BBC-BCD	3D $	D^	28$				
Mathematics and Computing	GG51	3FT deg	M			M$^					
Physics and Computer Science	FG35	3FT deg	M+P	24	3M+2D	MS^	28$				
Physics with Computing	F3G5	3FT deg	M+P	24		MS^					
Russian, Linguistics and Computer Science	GR58	4FT deg	L	BBC-BCD	3D $	D^	28$				

QUEEN'S Univ Belfast

TITLE	CODE	COURSE	SUBJECTS	A/AS	ND/C	RGNVQ	IB	SQA(H)	SQA	RATIO	A/AS
Chemistry and Computer Science	FG15	3FT/4FT deg	C+M/Cs g	CCC	Ind	Ind	28$	BBBC	Ind	5	
Computer Sci & Stats and Operational Research	GG54	3FT/4FT deg	M g	CCC	Ind	D*^ go	28$	BBBC	Ind	3	
Computer Science (inc professional experiece)	G500	4SW deg	Cs/M g	CCC	Ind	D*^ go	28$	BBBC	Ind	5	16/30
Computer Science (inc professional experience)	G503	4SW/5SW deg	M+P g	BCC	Ind	Ind	29$	BBBC	Ind	13	
Computer Science (inc professional experience)	G506	4SW deg									
Computer Science Extended Course	G505	4SW/5SW deg									
Computer Science and Mathematics	GG51	3FT/4FT deg	M g	CCC	Ind	D*^ go	28$	BBBC	Ind	5	18/24
Computer Science and Physics	GF53	3FT/4FT deg	P+M g	CCC	Ind	Ind	28$	BBBC	Ind	14	
Computer Science with Bus Admin (inc prof exp)	GNMD	4SW deg									
Computer Science with Bus Admin (inc prof exp)	GNMC	4SW deg									
Computer Science with Business Administration	G5ND	3FT deg									
Computer Science with Business Administration	G5NC	3FT deg									
Electronic and Software Eng (inc prof exp)	HG67	4SW deg	M+P g	BCC	Ind	Ind	29$	BBBC	Ind	13	18/26
Management with Computer Science	N1G5	3FT deg	M/Cs g	BBB	X	D*^ go	32$	X	Ind		
Music/Computer Science	GW53	3FT deg	M/Cs g	BCC	X	D*^ go	29$	X	Ind	6	
Philosophy/Computer Science	GV57	3FT deg	M/Cs g	BCC	X	D*^ go	29$	X	Ind		

RAVENSBOURNE COLLEGE of Design and Communication

TITLE	CODE	COURSE	SUBJECTS	A/AS	ND/C	RGNVQ	IB	SQA(H)	SQA	RATIO	A/AS
Communications and Techology	G720	2FT deg	M/P/Cs/Es	E	N	PT	Ind	Ind	Ind		

Computer Sciences and Engineering   15

			98 expected requirements							96 entry stats	
TITLE	**CODE**	**COURSE**	**SUBJECTS**	**A/AS**	**ND/C**	**AGNVQ**	**IB**	**SQA(H)**	**SQA**	**RATIO A/AS**	
READING COLLEGE AND SCHOOL OF ART AND DESIGN											
Computing	005G	2FT deg									
Univ of READING											
Analytical Computer Science	G5G1	3FT deg	M g	20	3M+2D$	D$^	30$	BBBB$	Ind		
Applied Analytical Computer Science	G5GC	4SW deg	M g	20	3M+2D$	D$^	30$	BBBB$	Ind		
Applied Computer Science	G501	4SW deg	* g	20	3M+2D	D$^ go	30	BBBB	Ind		
Applied Computer Science and Cybernetics	GH5P	4SW deg	* g	20	3M+2D$	D$^ go	30$	BBBB	Ind		
Chemistry with Computer Sci with a year in Eur	F1GM	4FT deg	C g	18	4M+1D$	DS^ go	29$	BBBC$	Ind	3	
Chemistry with Computer Science	F1G5	3FT deg	C g	18	4M+1D$	DS^ go	29$	BBBC$	Ind	8	
Computational Mathematics	G1G5	3FT deg	M g	BCC	3M+2D$	D$^	30$	BBBB$	Ind		
Computer Science	G500	3FT deg	* g	20	3M+2D	D$^ go	30	BBBB	Ind	10	14/24
Computer Science and Cybernetics	GH56	3FT deg	* g	20	3M+2D$	D$^ go	30$	BBBB$	Ind	8	14/28
Computer Science with Philosophy	G5V7	3FT deg	* g	20	3M+2D	D$^ go	30	BBBB	Ind		
Intelligent Systems	GC88	3FT deg	B/C/M/P g	20	3M+2D$	D$^ go	30$	BBBB$	Ind	23	
Physics with Computer Science	F3G5	3FT deg	M+P	CCC	5M $	DS^	29$	BBBC$	Ind		
ROBERT GORDON Univ											
Business Computing	NG15	3FT/4FT deg	* g	DD	N	Ind	Ind	CCC$	Ind	3	
Computer Science	G500	4SW/5SW deg	M g	EE	N	Ind	Ind	CCC$	Ind	7	
Computing	G501	3FT/4FT deg	*	EE	N	Ind	Ind	CCC$	Ind	3	
Electronic and Computer Engineering	GH66	3FT/4FT deg	M+S	EE	N	Ind	Ind	BCC$	Ind	6	
Mathematics and Computing	G1G5	3FT/4FT deg	M g	DE	N	Ind	Ind	BCC$	Ind	6	
Computing	005G	2FT HND	*	EE	N	Ind	Ind	BC$	Ind	3	
ROEHAMPTON INST											
Business Computing	G710▼	3FT deg	g	12	2M+2D	M$ go	26	BCC	N$		
Business Computing and Applied Consumer Studies	GN79▼	3FT deg	g	12	3D	M$ go	26	BCC	N$		
Business Computing and Biology	CG17▼	3FT deg	B g	12	3D	M$ go	26	BCC	N$		
Business Computing and Natural Resource Studies	DG27▼	3FT deg	g	12	4M	M	26	BCC	N		
Business Studies and Business Computing	GN71▼	3FT deg	g	12	3D	M$ go	26	BCC	N$		
Dance Studies and Business Computing	GW74▼	3FT deg	g	CC	2M+2D	M$^ go	30	BBC	N$		
Drama & Theatre Studies and Business Computing	GW7L▼	3FT deg	E/T g	16	2M+2D	M$^ go	30	BBC	N$		
Education and Business Computing	GX79▼	3FT deg	g	12	3D	M$ go	26	BCC	N$		
English Lang & Linguist and Business Computing	GQ7H▼	3FT deg	g	CC	2M+2D	M$^ go	30	BBC	N$		
English Literature and Business Computing	GQ73▼	3FT deg	E g	CC	2M+2D	M^ go	30	BBC	N$		
Environmental Studies and Business Computing	GF79▼	3FT deg	g	12	3D	M$ go	26	BCC	N$		
Film & Television Studies and Business Computing	GP74▼	3FT deg	g	16	2M+2D	M$^ go	30	BBC	N$		
French and Business Computing	GR71▼	4FT deg	F g	12	3D	M^ go	26	BCC	N$		
Geography and Business Computing	GL78▼	3FT deg	Ge g	12	3D	M$ go	26	BCC	N$		
Health Studies and Business Computing	GB79▼	3FT deg	g	12	3D	M$ go	26	BCC	N$		
History and Business Computing	GV71▼	3FT deg	H g	12	3D	M^ go	26	BCC	N$		
Human & Social Biology and Business Computing	GC7C▼	3FT deg	g	12	3D	M$ go	26	BCC	N$		
Music and Business Computing	GW73▼	3FT deg	Mu g	12	3D	M^ go	26	BCC	N$		
Psychology and Business Computing	GL77▼	3FT deg	g	CC	3D	M^ go	30	BBC	N$		
Social Policy & Admin and Business Computing	GL74▼	3FT deg	g	12	3D	M$ go	26	BCC	N$		
Sociology and Business Computing	GL73▼	3FT deg	g	12	3D	M$ go	26	BCC	N$		
Spanish and Business Computing	GR74▼	3FT deg	Sp g	12	3D	M^ go	26	BCC	N$		
Sport Studies and Business Computing	GB76▼	3FT deg	S g	12	2M+2D	M$ go	28	BCC	N$		
Theology & Religious Studies and Business Comp	GV78▼	3FT deg	g	12	3D	M$ go	26	BCC	N$		
Women's Studies and Business Computing	GM79▼	3FT deg	g	12	3D	M$ go	26	BCC	N$		

			98 expected requirements							96 entry stats	
TITLE	CODE	COURSE	SUBJECTS	A/AS	ND/C	AGNVQ	IB	SQA(H)	SQA	RATIO	A/AS
ROYAL HOLLOWAY, Univ of London											
Cognitive Science	CG85	3FT deg	M	BBC	Ind	D^	30$	Ind			
Computer Science	G500	3FT/4SW deg	M	BCC-BBC	MO+3D	D^	30$	Ind		8	16/30
Computer Science and Discrete Mathematics	GG5C	3FT/4SW deg	M	BCC-BBC	MO+3D	D^	Ind	Ind			
Computer Science and Electronics	GH56	3FT/4SW deg	M+P/S	BCC-BBC	MO+2D	D^	30$	Ind			
Computer Science and Mathematics	GG51	3FT/4SW deg	M	BCC-BBC	MO+3D	D^	Ind	Ind		5	15/24
Computer Science and Physics	GF53	3FT/4SW deg	M+P	BCC-BBC	Ind	D^	30$	BBBCC$			
Computer Science with French	G5R1	3FT/4SW deg	M+F	BCC-BBC	MO+3D	D^	30$	Ind			
Computer Science with Management Studies	G5N1	3FT/4SW deg	M	BCC-BBC	MO+3D	D^	30$	Ind		5	12/24
Geology and Computing	FG65	3FT deg	M+S	BCC	Ind	D^	Ind	Ind		5	
Management and Information Systems	NG15	3FT deg	M	BBC-BBB	Ind	D^	30$	Ind			
Foundation Programme *Computer Science*	Y408	4FT deg									
Science Foundation Year *Computer Science*	Y100	4FT deg	*		Ind	Ind	Ind	Ind			
SCOTTISH COLLEGE of TEXTILES											
Computing for Industry	GH57	4FT deg	* g	CC	Ind	M$	Dip	BBC	HN	1	
Computing	005G	2FT HND	*	D	N	Ind	Ind	CC	Ind	2	
Univ of SALFORD											
Appl Comput & Math Modelling with Prelim Yr(4yr)	G518	4FT deg		Ind	Ind	Ind	Ind	Ind			
Applied Computing and Mathematical Modelling	G510	3FT/4FT deg	M	16	Ind	Ind	Ind	Ind	Ind		
Biology and Information Technology	GC51	3FT/4SW deg		BCC-CCD	3M	M	Ind	Ind	Ind		
Business Information Systems (3/4 Yrs)	G520	3FT/4SW deg	* g	18	MO+6D	M	Ind	Ind	Ind	7	10/20
Chemistry and Information Technology	FG15	3FT/4SW deg		BCC-CCD	3M	M	Ind	Ind	Ind		
Computer Science & Applied Mathematics (3/4 yr)	GG51	3FT/4SW deg	M	16	X	X	Ind	Ind	Ind		
Computer Science (3 or 4 Yrs)	G500	3FT/4SW deg	M	18	MO+6D	Ind	Ind	Ind	Ind	10	10/20
Computer Science and Inf Systs (3 or 4 Yrs)	G506	3FT/4SW deg	M	18	MO+6D	M	Ind	Ind	Ind	10	10/20
Computer Science and Information Systems	G505	4FT deg									
Computer Science and O R and Applied Statistics	GG54	3FT/4SW deg	M	16	X	X					
Economics and Information Technology	LG15	3FT/4SW deg		BCC-CCD	3M	M	Ind	Ind	Ind		
Geography and Information Technology	GF58	3FT/4SW deg		BCC-CCD	3M	M	Ind	Ind	Ind		
Info Tech with English for Professional Purposes	G5Q3	3FT deg		18	DO	M^/D	Ind	Ind	Ind		
Info Technology with Language Training in French	G5R1	3FT deg	g	CCC	DO	D^	Ind	Ind	Ind	3	
Info Technology with Language Training in German	G5R2	3FT deg	g	CCC	DO	D^	Ind	Ind	Ind		
Info Technology with Studies in Japan (4 Yrs)	G5T4	4SW deg	* g	20	DO	M/D^	Ind	Ind	Ind	10	
Information Technology	G5N1▼	3FT deg	g	CCC	DO	D^	Ind	Ind	Ind	3	12/22
Modelling of Physical and Financial Systems	G511	3FT deg									
Physics and Information Technology	FG35	3FT/4SW deg		BCC-CDD	3M	M	Ind	Ind	Ind		
Physiology and Information Technology	CG95	3FT/4SW deg		BCC-CCD	3M	M	Ind	Ind	Ind		
Software Development	G701	3FT deg	Cs	4	MO	P	Ind	CC	Ind	9	10/16
Software	107G	2FT HND	Cs	4	MO	P	Ind	CC	Ind	15	
SANDWELL COLL											
Animation and Graphics	67HG	2FT HND	A/Ad/Cs/Ds/M	DD-EE	N	P$	Ind	Ind	Ind		
Software Engineering	007G	2FT HND	Cs/Ds/M/P	DD-EE	N	P	Ind	Ind	Ind		
Univ of SHEFFIELD											
Artificial Intelligence and Computer Science	GG85	3FT deg	M g	BBC	4M+2D$	D^	30$	ABBB$			
Computer Science	G500	3FT deg	M g	BBC	4M+2D$	D^	30$	ABBB$	Ind	10	18/26
Computer Science Foundation Year (4 Yrs)	G501	4FT deg	g	BBC	4M+2D	D^	30	ABBB	Ind		
Computer Science and French	GR51	4FT deg	F+M g	BBC	4M+2D$	D^	30$	ABBB$	Ind	4	
Computer Science and German	GR52	4FT deg	G+M g	BBC	4M+2D$	D^	30$	ABBB$	Ind		
Computer Science and Mathematics	GG51	3FT/4EXT deg	M g	24	3M+3D$	D^	32$	AABB$	Ind	9	20/28

course details

			98 expected requirements							96 entry stats	
TITLE	CODE	COURSE	SUBJECTS	A/AS	ND/C	AGNVQ	IB	SQA(H)	SQA	RATIO	A/AS
Computer Science and Russian	GR58	4FT deg	L+M g	BBC	4M+2D$	D^	30$	ABBB$	Ind		
Computer Science and Spanish	GR54	4FT deg	M+L g	BBC	4M+2D$	D^	30$	ABBB$	Ind		
Computer Science with Accounting	G5N4	3FT deg	M g	24	3M+3D$	D^	32$	AABB$	Ind	46	
Computer Systems Engineering (3/4 Yrs)	G600	3FT/4FT deg	M g	BBB-BCC	3M+3D$	D^	31$	AABB	Ind	7	16/22
Software Engineering (3/4 Yrs)	G700	3FT/4FT deg	M g	BBC	3M+1D$	D^	30$	ABBB$	Ind	7	18/30
Software Engineering (including Foundation Year)	G701	4FT/5FT deg	* g	BBB-BCC	3M+D	D^	30	ABBB			
Software Engineering and Law (MEng)	GM73	4FT deg	M g	ABB	2M+4D$	X	33$	AAAB$			

SHEFFIELD HALLAM Univ

Applied Computing (1 year)	G610	1FT deg		X	HN	X	X	X	X		
Business Information Systems	G521	4SW deg	*	12	6M	M	Ind	Ind	Ind		
Computer and Information Engineering	G601	3FT/4SW deg	M+S	8	3M $	M$	Ind	Ind	Ind		
Computer and Information Engineering (Extended)	G608▼	4EXT/5EXTSW deg									
Computer and Network Engineering	GG67	3FT/4SW deg	M/S	8	3M $	M$	Ind	Ind	Ind		
Computer and Network Engineering (Extended)	GG6R▼	4EXT/5EXTSW deg									
Computing & Management Science (Foundation Year)	GN5D▼	5EXT deg									
Computing (Networks and Communication)	G600	4SW deg	*	12	6M	M	Ind	Ind	Ind		
Computing (Software Engineering)	G700	4SW deg	*	12	6M	M	Ind	Ind	Ind		
Computing and Management Sciences	GN51	4SW deg	*	12	5M	M	Ind	Ind	Ind		
Electronic Systems and Information Engineering	GH56	3FT/4SW deg	M+S	8	3M $	M$	Ind	Ind	Ind		
Electronic Systems and Information Engineering	GH5P▼	4EXT/5EXTSW deg									
Electronic and Computer Engineering	HG66	3FT/4SW deg	M+S	8	3M $	M$	Ind	Ind	Ind		
Electronic and Computer Engineering (Extended)	HG6P▼	4EXT/5EXTSW deg									
Electronics and Information Tech (1 Year top-up)	GG65	1FT deg		X	HN $	X	X	X	X		
European Computing	G7R1	4SW deg	g	12	6M	M	Ind	Ind	Ind		
Combined Studies *Business Information Systems*	Y400	3FT deg	M	14	2M	M	Ind	Ind	Ind		
Combined Studies *Business and Technology*	Y400	3FT deg	S	8-10	2M	M	Ind	Ind	Ind		
Combined Studies *Computing*	Y400	3FT deg	*	14	2M	M	Ind	Ind	Ind		
Combined Studies *Computing Mathematics*	Y400	3FT deg	M	14	2M	M	Ind	Ind	Ind		
Combined Studies *Systems Modelling*	Y400	3FT deg	M	14	2M	M	Ind	Ind	Ind		
Business Information Technology	165G▼	3SW HND	*	6	2M	P	Ind	Ind	Ind		
Computer Networks	206G	2FT/3SW HND	*	6	2M	P	Ind	Ind	Ind		
Computing	105G▼	2FT/3SW HND	*	6	2M	P	Ind	Ind	Ind		
Electronic and Information Engineering	265G▼	2FT/3SW HND	Cs/Es/M/P/Ph	E	N $	P$	Ind	Ind	Ind		
Software Engineering	007G	3SW HND	*	6	2M	P	Ind	Ind	Ind		

SHREWSBURY COLLEGE OF ARTS & TECHNOLOGY

Business Information Technology	265G	2FT HND		2		P	Ind	Ind	Ind		

Univ College of St MARTIN, LANCASTER AND CUMBRIA

Imaging Sciences/Applied Imaging	HJ65	2FT deg	g	E	N	PS	28	CCCC		1	

SOLIHULL COLL

Computing	005G	2FT HND	*	E	N	P	Dip	Ind	Ind		

Univ of SOUTHAMPTON

Biology with Computer Science	C1G5	3FT deg	B+M g	BCC	5M+1D$	Ind^	28$	BBBBC	Ind	18	
Chemistry with Computer Science	F1G5	3FT deg	C+M	18	Ind	Ind	28$	CSYS	Ind	4	16/30
Computer Sci with Image and Multimedia Systems	G5GP	3FT deg	M	22	Ind $	D^	30$	CSYS	Ind	10	20/30
Computer Science	G500	3FT deg	M	22	Ind $	D^	30$	CSYS	Ind	8	18/28
Computer Science and Modern Languages (4 Yrs)	GT59	4FT deg	M+L	22	Ind $	D^	30$	CSYS	Ind	9	

course details			98 expected requirements							96 entry stats	
TITLE	CODE	COURSE	SUBJECTS	A/AS	ND/C	AGNVQ	IB	SQA(H)	SQA	RATIO	A/AS
Computer Science with Artificial Intelligence	G5G8	3FT deg	M	22	Ind $	D^	30$	CSYS	Ind	10	20/30
Computer Science with Distributed Systs & Netwks	G5G6	3FT deg	M	22	Ind $	D^	30$	CSYS	Ind	5	
Computer Science with Parallel Computation	G5GQ	3FT deg	M	22	Ind $	D^	30$	CSYS	Ind		
Computer Science with Systems Integration	G520	3FT deg	M	22	Ind $	D^	30$	CSYS	Ind	29	
Geology with Computer Science	F6G5	3FT deg	M+S g	18-20	Ind	Ind	28$	BBBBC$	Ind		
Mathematics with Computer Science	G1G5	3FT deg	M	BBC	Ind	Ind	30	ABBBB	Ind	7	16/26
Physics with Computer Science	F3G5	3FT deg	M+P	BC	Ind	Ind	28$	AAABB	Ind	5	18/24
Software Engineering (MEng)	G700	4FT deg	M	24	Ind $	D^	32$	CSYS	Ind		
SOUTHAMPTON INST											
Business Information Technology	G562	4SW deg	*	8-10	MO	M$	Dip	CCCC	N	3	6/16
Business Information Technology(with Foundation)	G568▼	5SW deg	*	2-4	N	P$	Dip	CCCC	N	2	
Computer Studies	G501	3FT deg	*	8-10	MO	M$	Dip	CCCC	N	4	6/18
Computer Studies (with Foundation Year)	G502▼	4FT deg	*	2-4	N	P$	Dip	CCCC	N	2	
Business Information Technology	065G▼	2FT HND	* g	2	N	P$	Dip	CCCC	N		
Computing	105G	2FT HND	*	2	N	P$	Dip	CCCC	N	2	1/4
SOUTH BANK Univ											
Business Information Technology	G720	3FT/4SW deg	Cs/Bu/M g	CC	5M	M go	Ind	Ind	Ind		
Business Information Technology	G725	1/2FT deg			HN		Ind	Ind	Ind		
Business Information Technology and Accounting	GN74	3FT deg	M g	12-16	4M+2D	M go	Ind	Ind	Ind		
Computing Studies	G505	1/2FT deg			HN		Ind	Ind	Ind		
Computing Studies	G501	3FT/4SW deg	2S g	CD	5M $	M go	Ind	Ind	Ind		
Computing and Accounting	GN54	3FT deg	Ac/Ec/M g	12-16	4M+2D	M go	Ind	Ind	Ind		
Economics and Computing	GL51	3FT deg	M+Ec/Bu g	12-16	4M+2D	M go	Ind	Ind	Ind		
English Studies and Business Info Technology	GQ73	3FT deg	M+E g	14-18	X	M^ go	Ind	Ind	Ind		
Environmental Policy & Business Info Technology	FG97	3FT deg	M g	12-16	4M+2D	M go	Ind	Ind	Ind		
Environmental Policy and Computing	FG95	3FT deg	M g	12-16	4M+2D	M go	Ind	Ind	Ind		
European Studies and Business Information Tech	GT72	3FT deg	M g	14-18	2M+4D	M go	Ind	Ind	Ind		
European Studies and Computing	GT52	3FT deg	M g	14-18	2M+4D	M go	Ind	Ind	Ind		
Food Policy and Computing	DG45	3FT deg	S+M g	12-16	4M+2D	M go	Ind	Ind	Ind		
Foundation Computing Studies	G508	4EXT deg					Ind	Ind	Ind		
French and Business Information Technology	GR71	3FT deg	M+F g	12-16	4M+2D	M go	Ind	Ind	Ind		
French and Computing	GR51	3FT deg	M+F g	12-16	4M+2D	M go	Ind	Ind	Ind		
German - ab initio and Business Information Tech	GR72	3FT deg	M g	12-16	4M+2D	M go	Ind	Ind	Ind		
German - ab initio and Computing	GR52	3FT deg	M g	12-16	4M+2D	M go	Ind	Ind	Ind		
German and Business Information Technology	GR7F	3FT deg	M+G g	14-18	2M+4D	M go	Ind	Ind	Ind		
German and Computing	GR5F	3FT deg	M+G g	14-18	2M+4D	M go	Ind	Ind	Ind		
Health Informatics	GL5L	3FT deg	M g	CC	4M+2D	M go	Ind	Ind	Ind		
Health Studies & Business Information Technology	GL74	3FT deg	M+S g	12-16	4M+2D	M go	Ind	Ind	Ind		
Health Studies and Computing	GL54	3FT deg	M+S g	12-16	4M+2D	M go	Ind	Ind	Ind		
Housing and Business Information Technology	GK7L	3FT deg	M g	14-18	2M+4D	M go	Ind	Ind	Ind		
Housing and Computing	GK5L	3FT deg	M g	14-18	2M+4D	M go	Ind	Ind	Ind		
Human Biology and Computing	BG15	3FT deg	S+M g	12-16	4M+2D	M go	Ind	Ind	Ind		
Human Geography and Business Info Technology	GL78	3FT deg	M+Gy g	12-16	4M+2D	M go	Ind	Ind	Ind		
Human Geography and Computing	GL58	3FT deg	M+Gy g	12-16	4M+2D	M go	Ind	Ind	Ind		
Human Resource Management and Business Info Tech	GN76	3FT deg	M g	14-18	2M+4D	M go	Ind	Ind	Ind		
Human Resource Management and Computing	GN56	3FT deg	M g	14-18	2M+4D	M go	Ind	Ind	Ind		
Law and Business Information Technology	GM73	3FT deg	M g	14-18	2M+4D	D go	Ind	Ind	Ind		
Law and Computing	GM53	3FT deg	M g	14-18	2M+4D	D go	Ind	Ind	Ind		
Management and Business Information Technology	GN71	3FT deg	M g	12-16	4M+2D	M go	Ind	Ind	Ind		
Marketing and Business Information Technology	GN75	3FT deg	M g	12-16	2M+4D	M go	Ind	Ind	Ind		
Marketing and Computing	GN55	3FT deg	M g	14-18	2M+4D	M go	Ind	Ind	Ind		
Media Studies & Business Information Technology	GP74	3FT deg	M+E g	14-18	4M+2D	D go	Ind	Ind	Ind		

Computer Sciences and Engineering 15

TITLE	CODE	COURSE	SUBJECTS	A/AS	NO/C	AGNVQ	IB	SQA(H)	SQA	RATIO A/AS
Media Studies and Computing	GP54	3FT deg	M+E g	14-18	2M+4D	D go	Ind	Ind	Ind	
Multi-Media Engineering	GH76	3FT/4SW deg	M g	CC	5M	M go	Ind	Ind	Ind	
Nutrition and Computing	BG45	3FT deg	S+M g	12-16	4M+2D	M go	Ind	Ind	Ind	
Planning and Computing	GK54	3FT deg	M g	14-18	2M+4D	M go	Ind	Ind	Ind	
Politics and Business Information Technology	GM71	3FT deg	M g	12-16	4M+2D	M go	Ind	Ind	Ind	
Product Design & Business Information Technology	GH77	3FT deg	M+Ad g	12-16	4M+2D	M go	Ind	Ind	Ind	
Product Design and Computing	GH57	3FT deg	M+Ad g	12-16	4M+2D	M go	Ind	Ind	Ind	
Psychology and Business Information Technology	CG87	3FT deg	S g	14-18	2M+4D	M go	Ind	Ind	Ind	
Psychology and Computing	CG85	3FT deg	S+M g	14-18	4M+2D	M go	Ind	Ind	Ind	
Software Engineering for Real Time Systems	HG67	3FT deg	M+S	CD	M+D	M go	Ind	Ind	Ind	
Spanish - ab initio and Business Information Tec	GR74	3FT deg	M g	12-16	4M+2D	M go	Ind	Ind	Ind	
Spanish - ab initio and Computing	GR54	3FT deg	M g	12-16	4M+2D	M go	Ind	Ind	Ind	
Spanish and Business Information Technology	GR7K	3FT deg	Sp+M g	14-18	2M+4D	M go	Ind	Ind	Ind	
Spanish and Computing	GR5K	3FT deg	Sp+M g	14-18	2M+4D	M go	Ind	Ind	Ind	
Sports Science and Computing	BG65	3FT deg	S+M g	12-16	4M+2D	M go	Ind	Ind	Ind	
Technology and Computing	GJ59	3FT deg	M g	12-16	4M+2D	M go	Ind	Ind	Ind	
Tourism and Business Information Technology	GP77	3FT deg	M+L g	12-16	4M+2D	M go	Ind	Ind	Ind	
Urban Studies and Business Information Tech	GK7K	3FT deg	M g	14-18	2M+4D	M go	Ind	Ind	Ind	
Urban Studies and Computing	GK5K	3FT deg	M g	14-18	2M+4D	M go	Ind	Ind	Ind	
World Theatre and Business Information Tech	GW74	3FT deg	M g	14-18	2M+4D	M go	Ind	Ind	Ind	
World Theatre and Computing	GW54	3FT deg	M g	14-18	2M+4D	M go	Ind	Ind	Ind	
Business Information Technology	027G	2FT HND	S g	E	Ind	P go	Ind	Ind	Ind	
Computing Studies	105G	2FT HND	S g	E	3M	P go	Ind	Ind	Ind	

Univ of ST ANDREWS

TITLE	CODE	COURSE	SUBJECTS	A/AS	NO/C	AGNVQ	IB	SQA(H)	SQA	RATIO A/AS
Computer Science (BSc/MSci)	G500	3FT/4FT deg	M g	CCC	Ind	Ind	28$	BBCC$	Ind	9
Computer Science and Mathematics (BSc/MSci)	GG15	3FT/4FT deg	M g	CCC	Ind	Ind	28$	BBBC$	Ind	5
Computer Science-Chemistry	FG15	3FT/4FT deg	M+C	CCC	Ind	Ind	28$	BBCC$	Ind	7
Geology-Computer Science	FG65	3FT/4FT deg	M g	CCC	Ind	Ind	28$	BBCC$	Ind	
Logic and Philosophy of Science-Computer Science	GV5R	3FT/4FT deg	M g	BBB	Ind	Ind	28$	BBCC$	Ind	
Management Sciences-Computer Science	GN51	4FT deg	M g	CCC	Ind	Ind	28$	BBBC$	Ind	28
Management-Computer Science	GN5C	4FT deg	M g	CCC	X	Ind	28$	BBBC$	Ind	
Physics-Computer Science	GF53	4FT deg	M+P	CCC	Ind	Ind	28$	BBCC$	Ind	4
Statistics-Computer Science	GG45	3FT/4FT deg	M g	BCC	Ind	Ind	28$	BBBC$	Ind	
General Degree of BSc *Computer Science*	Y100	3FT deg	M g	CCC	Ind	Ind	28$	BBCC$	Ind	

ST HELENS COLL

TITLE	CODE	COURSE	SUBJECTS	A/AS	NO/C	AGNVQ	IB	SQA(H)	SQA	RATIO A/AS
Computer Games Production	016G	2FT HND	M/P/Es/Cs	2-6	N	P$	Ind	Ind	Ind	
Computing	005G	2FT HND	*	2	3M	M*	Ind	Ind	Ind	
Software Engineering	007G	2FT HND	M/P/Es/Cs	2-6	N	P$	Ind	Ind	Ind	

THE UNIVERSITY COLLEGE OF ST MARK AND ST JOHN

TITLE	CODE	COURSE	SUBJECTS	A/AS	NO/C	AGNVQ	IB	SQA(H)	SQA	RATIO A/AS
English (Literary Studies)/Information Techno	Q3G5	3FT deg	El	12-16	Ind	M	Ind	Ind	Ind	
English Language Studies/Information Technology	Q1G5	3FT deg		12	MO	M	Ind	Ind	Ind	
Geography/Information Technology	L8G5	3FT deg	Gy	8-10	MO	M	Ind	Ind	Ind	
Info Technology/English Language Studies	G5Q1	3FT deg		4	MO	M	Dip	CCCC	Ind	
Information Technology/English (Literary St)	G5Q3	3FT deg		4	MO	M	Dip	CCCC	Ind	
Information Technology/Geography	G5L8	3FT deg		4	MO	M	Dip	CCCC	Ind	
Information Technology/Media Studies	G5P4	3FT deg		4	MO	M	Dip	CCCC	Ind	
Information Technology/Public Relations	G5P3	3FT deg		4	MO	M	Dip	CCCC	Ind	
Information Technology/Sports Science	G5B6	3FT deg		4	MO	M	Dip	CCCC	Ind	
Media Studies/Information Technology	P4G5	3FT deg		16	MO	M	Ind	Ind	Ind	
Public Relations/Information Technology	P3GN	3FT deg		16	MO	M	Ind	Ind	Ind	
Sports Science/Information Technology	B6G5	3FT deg		8	MO	M	Ind	Ind	Ind	

course details | 98 expected requirements | 96 entry stats

TITLE	CODE	COURSE	SUBJECTS	A/AS	NVQ/C	AGNVQ	IB	SQA(H)	SQA	RATIO A/AS
STAFFORDSHIRE Univ										
Accounting Information Technology	N4G5	3FT/4SW deg	g	12	Ind	D	27	CCC	Ind	3 7/18
Business Communications & Technology	G725	3FT deg	g	12	Ind	M	27	CCC	Ind	
Business Computing	G711	3FT deg	g	12	Ind	M	27	CCC		
Business Decision Analysis	G710	4SW deg	M g	10	Ind	Ind	Ind	Ind	Ind	5
Business Information Technology	G562	4SW deg	* g	12	Ind	M	27	CCC	Ind	4 6/18
Computer & Electronics for Information Technol	HG65	4EXT deg	g	EE	P $	P$	Ind	Ind	Ind	
Computer Science	G501	4SW deg	g	12	Ind	M	27	CCC	Ind	4 4/18
Computer Science (MEng)	G502	5SW deg	g	12	Ind	M	27	CCC	Ind	4
Computer Systems	G600	3FT deg	g	12	Ind	M	27	CCC		
Computer Systems	G601	3FT deg								
Computing Science	G500	4SW deg	g	12	Ind	M	27	CCC	Ind	4 6/16
Computing and Applicable Mathematics	GG15	4SW deg	g	12	Ind	M	27	CCC	Ind	5
Computing and Electronics for Info Technology	GH5Q	3FT deg	g	8	3M $	M$	24	BCC	Ind	
Computing/Applied Statistics	GG54	3FT deg	g	10	Ind	Ind	Ind	Ind	Ind	4
Computing/Biochemistry	CG75	3FT deg								
Computing/Biology	CG15	3FT deg	S	8	3M	M	24	BCC	Ind	8
Computing/Ceramic Science	JG35	3FT deg	g	8	3M	M$	24	BCC	Ind	
Computing/Chemistry	FG15	3FT deg	S	8	3M	M	24	BCC	Ind	
Development Studies/Computing	GMMY	3FT deg	g	12	3M	M	Ind	BBB	Ind	
Distributed Interactive Systems	G611	3FT deg	g	12	Ind	M	27	CCC		
Distributed Interactive Systems	G610	3FT deg	g	12	Ind	M	27	CCC		
Ecology/Computing	CG95	3FT deg								
Electronics/Computing	GH56	3FT deg	S g	8	3M	M	24	BCC	Ind	5
Foundation Biology and Computing	CG1M▼	4EXT deg	*	4	N	P	24	CCC	Ind	6
Foundation Business Decision Analysis	G718▼	5EXTSW deg			Ind	Ind	Ind	Ind		
Foundation Business Information Technology	G561▼	5EXTSW deg	*	4	N	P	24	CCC	Ind	1
Foundation Chemistry and Computing	FG1M▼	4EXT deg	*	4	N	P	24	CCC	Ind	
Foundation Computer Science	G508▼	5EXTSW deg			Ind	Ind	Ind	Ind	Ind	
Foundation Computer Science	G507▼	5EXTSW deg			Ind	Ind	Ind	Ind	Ind	2
Foundation Computing Science	G509▼	5EXTSW deg			Ind	Ind	Ind	Ind	Ind	
Foundation Computing and Applicable Mathematics	GG1M▼	4EXT/5SW deg			Ind	Ind	Ind	Ind	Ind	
Foundation Electronics and Computing	HG6M▼	4EXT deg	*	4	N	P	24	CCC	Ind	
Foundation Geology and Computing	FG6M	4EXT deg	*	4	N	P	24	CCC		
Foundation Information Systems	G569▼	5EXTSW deg			Ind	Ind	Ind	Ind	Ind	
Foundation Information Systems	G528▼	5EXTSW deg			Ind	Ind	Ind	Ind	Ind	
Foundation Interactive Systems Design	GP5K▼	4EXT/5EXTSW deg	g	4	N	P	24	CCC	Ind	
Foundation Physics and Computing	FG3N▼	4EXT deg	*	4	N	P	24	CCC	Ind	
Foundation Software Engineering	G709▼	5EXTSW deg			Ind	Ind	Ind	Ind	Ind	2
Foundation Software Engineering	G708▼	5EXTSW deg			Ind	Ind	Ind	Ind	Ind	1
Foundation Technology Management	GN51▼	5EXTSW deg			Ind	Ind	Ind	Ind	Ind	3
Geography/Computing	GL58	3FT deg	*	8	3M	M	24	BBB	Ind	5
Geology/Computing	GF56	3FT deg	S	8	3M	M	24	BCC	Ind	26
Graphics, Imaging and Visualisation	GW52	3FT deg	g	12	Ind	M	27	CCC		
Graphics, Imaging and Visualisation	GW5F	3FT deg								
Information Systems	G521	4SW deg	g	12	Ind	M	27	BCC	Ind	7
Information Systems (MEng)	G520	5SW deg	g	12	Ind	M	27	CCC	Ind	12
Information Systems/Applied Statistics	GG45	3FT deg	g	10	Ind	Ind	Ind	Ind	Ind	1
Information Systems/Business Studies	GN5C	3FT deg	g	16	Ind	M	24	BBB	Ind	3
Information Systems/Computing	G529	3FT deg	g	12	Ind	M	27	CCC	Ind	
Information Systems/Cultural Studies	GL56	3FT deg	g	12	Ind	M	27	BBC	Ind	
Information Systems/Development Studies	GM5Y	3FT deg	g	12	3M	M	Ind	BBB	Ind	

			98 expected requirements							**96 entry stats**	
course details											
TITLE	CODE	COURSE	SUBJECTS	A/AS	ND/C	AGNVQ	IB	SQA(H)	SQA	RATIO	A/AS
Information Systems/Environmental Studies	GF59	3FT deg	g	12	Ind	M	24	BBC	Ind	1	
Information Systems/Film Studies	GW55	3FT deg	g	12	Ind	M	Ind	BBB	Ind	4	
Information Systems/French	GR51	3FT/4SW deg	F g	12	4M+2D	M^	26	BCC	Ind	2	
Information Systems/Geography	GL5V	3FT deg	g	CC	4M+1D	M	24	BBB	Ind	2	
Information Systems/German	GR52	3FT/4SW deg	G g	12	4M+2D	M^	26	BCC	Ind	2	
Information Systems/History	GV51	3FT deg	H g	12	Ind	M	27	BBB	Ind		
Information Systems/History of Art and Design	GV54	3FT deg	g	12	Ind	M	27	BBB	Ind		
Information Technology Strategy	G527	3FT deg									
Information Technology Strategy	G526	3FT deg	g	12	Ind	M	27	CCC			
Intelligent Systems	G800	3FT deg	g	12	Ind	M	27	CCC			
Intelligent Systems	G801	3FT deg									
Interactive Systems Design	GP54	4SW deg	g	12	Ind	M	Ind	CCC	Ind	4	8/12
International Relations/Information Systems	MG1M	3FT deg	g	12	3M	M	24	BCC	Ind		
Law/Information Systems	MG35	3FT deg	g	14	3D	M^	26	BBBB	Ind	6	
Legal Studies/Computing	GM53	3FT deg	g	18	HN	M^	Ind	BBB	Ind		
Legal Studies/Information Systems	MG3M	3FT deg	g	14	3D	M^	26	BBBB	Ind		
Literature/Information Systems	QG35	3FT deg	El g	12	MO+2D	M	27	BBC	Ind	2	
Media Studies/Information Systems	PG45	3FT deg	g	12	MO+2D	M	27	BBC	Ind	4	
Microbiology/Computing	CG55	3FT deg									
Microelectronics and Computer Engineering (MEng)	GH66	4FT/5SW deg	M+P	10	3M	M$	24	BCC	Ind	3	6/13
Multimedia Systems	G541	3FT deg	g	12	Ind	M	27	CCC			
Multimedia Systems	G540	3FT deg	g	12	Ind	M	27	CCC			
Philosophy/Information Systems	VG75	3FT deg	g	12	MO+2D	M	27	BBC	Ind		
Physics/Computing	FG35	3FT deg	S	8	3M	M	24	BCC	Ind		
Physiology/Computing	BG15	3FT deg									
Politics/Information Systems	MGC5	3FT deg	g	12	3M	M	24	BCC	Ind	1	
Psychology/Computing	LG75	3FT deg	g	18	3M+3D	Ind	27	BBB	Ind		
Sociology/Computing	LG35	3FT deg	g	12	3M	M	24	BBB	Ind		
Sociology/Information Systems	LG3M	3FT deg	g	12	3M	M	24	BBB	Ind	4	
Software Engineering	G700	4SW deg	g	12	Ind	M	27	CCC	Ind	4	6/18
Software Engineering (MEng)	G701	5SW deg	g	12	Ind	M	27	CCC	Ind	4	
Spanish/Information Systems	RG45	3FT/4SW deg		12	Ind	M^	27	BCC	Ind		
Sport Sciences and Information Systems	BG65	3FT deg	S	14	Ind	D	Ind	BBCC	Ind		
Technology Management	GNM1	4SW deg	g	12	Ind	M	Ind	CCC	Ind	22	
Women's Studies/Computing	GM51	3FT deg	g	12	Ind	M	Ind	BBB	Ind		
Women's Studies/Information Systems	MG95	3FT deg	g	12	3M	M	24	BCC	Ind		
Business Information Systems	225G	2FT HND	g	4	P	P	Ind	Ind	Ind		
Business Information Technology	265G▼	2FT HND	g	D	N	P	24	CCC	Ind	4	4/10
Computer Science	005G	2FT HND	g	4	N	P	Ind	Ind	Ind		
Computing	105G▼	2FT HND	g	D	N	P	24	CCC	Ind	4	2/10
Electronic Engineering	66HG	2FT HND	M/P g	2	N	P$	24	CCC	Ind		
Extended Electronic Engineering	6PHG	3EXT HND	g	2	N	P$	24	CCC	Ind		
Information Systems	125G	2FT HND	g	4	N	P	Ind	Ind	Ind		
Software Engineering	007G▼	2FT HND	g	D	N	P	24	CCC	Ind	4	2/6

Univ of STIRLING

Accountancy/Computing Science	GN54	4FT deg	g	BCC	HN	Ind	33	BBBB	HN		
Biology/Computing Science	CG15	4FT deg	S g	CCD	Ind	Ind	28	BBCC	HN		
Business Computing	G710	4FT deg	g	CCC	Ind	Ind	28	BBCC	HN		
Business Studies/Computing Science	NG15	4FT deg	g	CCC	Ind	Ind	28	BBCC	HN		
Computing Science	G500	4FT deg	g	CCC	Ind	Ind	28	BBCC	HN		
Computing Science/Economics	GL51	4FT deg	g	CCC	Ind	Ind	28	BBCC	HN		
Computing Science/Film & Media Studies	GW55	4FT deg	g	BBC	HN	Ind	35	ABBB	HN		

			98 expected requirements							96 entry stats

TITLE	CODE	COURSE	SUBJECTS	A/AS	ND/C	AGNVQ	IB	SQA(H)	SQA	RATIO A/AS
Computing Science/French Language	GR51	4FT deg	g	CCC	Ind	Ind	28	BBCC	HN	
Computing Science/German Language	GR52	4FT deg	g	CCC	Ind	Ind	28	BBCC	HN	
Computing Science/Japanese	GT54	4FT deg	g	CCC	Ind	Ind	28	BBCC	HN	
Computing Science/Management Science	GN51	4FT deg	g	CCC	Ind	Ind	28	BBCC	HN	
Computing Science/Marketing	GN55	4FT deg	g	CCC	Ind	Ind	28	BBCC	HN	
Computing Science/Mathematics	G5G1	4FT deg	M g	CCC	Ind	Ind	28	BBCC	HN	
Computing Science/Philosophy	GV57	4FT deg	g	CCC	Ind	Ind	28	BBCC	HN	
Computing Science/Psychology	CG85	4FT deg	g	CCC	Ind	Ind	28	BBCC	HN	
Computing Science/Sociology	GL53	4FT deg	g	CCC	Ind	Ind	28	BBCC	HN	
Computing Science/Spanish Language	GR54	4FT deg	g	CCC	Ind	Ind	28	BBCC	HN	
Environmental Science/Computing Science	FG95	4FT deg	S g	CCC	Ind	Ind	31	BBBC	HN	
Financial Studies/Computing Science	NG35	4FT deg	g	CCC	Ind	Ind	28	BBCC	HN	
Mathematics & its Applications with Comp Science	G1G5	4FT deg	M g	CCC	Ind	Ind	28	BBCC	HN	
Software Engineering	G700	4FT deg	g	CCC	Ind	Ind	28	BBCC	HN	

Univ of STRATHCLYDE

TITLE	CODE	COURSE	SUBJECTS	A/AS	ND/C	AGNVQ	IB	SQA(H)	SQA	RATIO A/AS
Business and Software Development	GN59	4FT deg	M	CCC	HN		Ind	BBBB$	HN	
Computer Science	G500	4FT deg	M	CCC	HN		Ind	BBBC$	HN	
Computer Science with Law	G5M3	4FT deg	M+E	CCC	HN		Ind	AABB$	HN	
Computer Science with Modern Languages	G5T9	4FT deg	E+M+L	CCC	HN		Ind	BBBBB$	HN	
Computer and Electronic Systems (BEng)	GH56	4FT deg	M+P	CCD	HN		Ind	ABBB$	HN	
Mathematics and Computer Science	GG15	4FT deg	M g	CD	Ind		30$	BBBC$	Ind	
Science Studies (Pass Degree) *Computer Science*	Y100	3FT deg	M+S	DD	Ind		Ind	CCC$	Ind	

UNIVERSITY COLLEGE SUFFOLK

TITLE	CODE	COURSE	SUBJECTS	A/AS	ND/C	AGNVQ	IB	SQA(H)	SQA	RATIO A/AS
Applied Biological Science and Information Techn	CG15	3FT deg	S	EE	N $	PS	Ind	Ind	Ind	
Applied Biological Science with Information Tech	C1G5	3FT deg	S	EE	N $	PS	Ind	Ind	Ind	
Art & Design and Information Technology	GW52	3FT deg	Pf	EE	N $	P$	Ind	Ind	Ind	
Art & Design and Information Technology	EW52	3FT deg	Pf	EE	N $	P$	Ind	Ind	Ind	
Art & Design with Information Technology	E2G5	3FT deg	Pf	EE	N $	P$	Ind	Ind	Ind	
Art & Design with Information Technology	W2G5	3FT deg	Pf	EE	N $	P$	Ind	Ind	Ind	
Behavioural Studies and Information Technology	GL57	3FT deg	*	DE	N $	P$	Ind	Ind	Ind	
Behavioural Studies with Information Technology	L7G5	3FT deg	*	DD	N $	P$	Ind	Ind	Ind	
Business Information Technology	G561	3FT deg	*	EE	N $	P*	Ind	Ind	Ind	
Business Studies with Information Technology	N1G5	3FT deg	*	EE	N $	P$	Ind	Ind	Ind	
Cultural Studies and Information Technology	YG35	3FT deg	*	CE	N $	P$	Ind	Ind	Ind	
Early Childhood Studies and Information Techn	XG95	3FT deg	*	DE	N $	P$	Ind	Ind	Ind	
Early Childhood Studies with Information Techn	X9GM	3FT deg	*	DD	N $	P$	Ind	Ind	Ind	
Environmental Studies and Information Technology	FG95	3FT deg	S/Gy	EE	N $	P$	Ind	Ind	Ind	
Environmental Studies with Information Technol	F9GM	3FT deg	S	EE	N $	P$	Ind	Ind	Ind	
Information Technology and Business Studies	GN51	3FT deg	*	EE	N	P*	Ind	Ind	Ind	
Information Technology and Management	GN5C	3FT deg	*	EE	N $	P$	Ind	Ind	Ind	
Information Technology with Appl Biological Sci	G5C1	3FT deg	S	EE	N $	P$	Ind	Ind	Ind	
Information Technology with Art & Design	G5W2	3FT deg	Pf	EE	N $	P$	Ind	Ind	Ind	
Information Technology with Behavioural Studies	G5L3	3FT deg	*	EE	N $	P$	Ind	Ind	Ind	
Information Technology with Early Childhood St	G5XX	3FT deg	*	EE	N $	P$	Ind	Ind	Ind	
Information Technology with Education Studies	G5X9	3FT deg	*	EE	N $	P$	Ind	Ind	Ind	
Information Technology with Environmental Studs	G5F9	3FT deg	S/Gy	EE	N $	P$	Ind	Ind	Ind	
Information Technology with Human Science	G5B1	3FT deg	S	EE	N $	P$	Ind	Ind	Ind	
Information Technology with Management	G5N1	3FT deg	*	EE	N $	P$	Ind	Ind	Ind	
Information Technology with Media Studies	G5P4	3FT deg	*	EE	N $	P$	Ind	Ind	Ind	
Information Technology with Social Policy	G5L4	3FT deg	*	EE	N $	P$	Ind	Ind	Ind	
Literary Studies and Information Technology	QG25	3FT deg	E	CE	N $	P$	Ind	Ind	Ind	

TITLE	CODE	COURSE	SUBJECTS	A/AS	ND/C	AGNVQ	IB	SQA(H)	SQA	RATIO	A/AS
course details			**98 expected requirements**							**96 entry stats**	
Media Studies and Information Technology	P4G5	3FT deg	*	CE	N $	P$	Ind	Ind	Ind		
Media Studies with Information Technology	P4GM	3FT deg	*	CE	N $	P$	Ind	Ind	Ind		
Product Design & Manufact with Information Techn	H7G5	3FT deg	*	EE	N $	P$	Ind	Ind	Ind		
Product Design & Manufacture & Information Techn	HG75	3FT deg	*	EE	N $	P$	Ind	Ind	Ind		
Software Engineering	G700	3FT deg	*	EE	N $	P$	Ind	Ind	Ind		
Business Information Technology	165G	2FT HND	*	E	N	P*	Ind	Ind	Ind		
Software Engineering	007G	2FT HND	*	E	N $	P$	Ind	Ind	Ind		
Univ of SUNDERLAND											
Accounting and Computing	NG45	3FT/4SW deg	* g	4-8	4M $	M*	24$	CCCC	N	5	8/16
Biocomputing	CG1M	3FT deg	* g	4-8	4M	M*	24	CCCC	N		
Biology and Computer Studies	CG15	3FT deg	B/C g	8	N $	M	24$	CCCC$	N$	3	
Business Computing	G523	3FT/4SW deg	* g	4-8	4M	M*	24	CCCC	N	2	4/16
Business Computing (Foundation)	G528▼	4EXT/5EXTSW deg	*							1	
Business Computing with French	G5R1	4SW deg	* g	4-8	4M	M* go	24	CCCC	N	5	
Business Computing with German	G5R2	4SW deg	* g	4-8	4M	M*	24	CCCC	N		
Business Computing with Spanish	G5R4	4SW deg	* g	4-8	4M	M*	24	CCCC	N	2	
Business Studies and Computer Studies	NG15	3FT deg	* g	10	N	M	24	CCCC	N	3	6/ 8
Chemistry and Computer Studies	FG15	3FT deg	C g	8	N $	M	24$	CCCC$	N$		
Chemistry and Information Systems	FG1M	3FT/4SW deg	C+S	8	N $	PS	24$	CCCC$	N$		
Chemistry with Computer Studies	F1G5	3FT deg	C	8	3M	M	Ind	Ind	Ind		
Computer Studies and Economics	GL51	3FT deg	* g	8	N	M	24	CCCC	N	3	
Computer Studies and English	GQ53	3FT deg	El g	10	Ind	M	24$	CCCC$	Ind	4	
Computer Studies and French	GR51	4FT deg	F g	8	N $	M	24$	CCCC$	N$		
Computer Studies and Geography	GL58	3FT deg	Gy/Gl g	10	N $	M	24$	CCCC$	N$	5	
Computer Studies and Geology	GF56	3FT deg	Gy/Gl g	8	N $	M	24	CCCC$	N$		
Computer Studies and German	GR52	4FT deg	G g	8	N $	M	24$	CCCC$	N$		
Computer Studies and History	GV51	3FT deg	H g	10	Ind	M	24$	CCCC	Ind	2	
Computer Studies and History of Art and Design	GV54	3FT/4SW deg	*	8	3M	M	Ind	Ind	Ind		
Computer Studies and Mathematics	GG51	3FT deg	M g	8	N $	M	24$	CCCC$	N$		
Computer Studies and Media Studies	GP54	3FT/4SW deg	*	24	Ind	Ind	Ind	Ind	Ind		
Computer Studies and Physiology	GB51	3FT deg	B/C g	8	N	M	24$	CCCC$	N		
Computer Studies and Psychology	GC58	3FT deg	* g	12	MO	M	24$	BCCC$	N	3	
Computer Studies and Religious Studies	GV58	3FT deg	* g	10	N	M	24	CCCC	N		
Computer Studies and Sociology	GL53	3FT deg	* g	10	N	M	24	CCCC	N		
Computer Studies and Spanish	GR54	3FT/4SW deg	*	8	3M	M	Ind	Ind	Ind		
Computer Studies with Chemistry	G5F1	3FT/4SW deg	*	8	3M	M	Ind	Ind	Ind		
Computer Studies with Economics	G5L1	3FT/4SW deg	*	8	3M	M	Ind	Ind	Ind		
Computer Studies with English	G5Q3	3FT/4SW deg	*	10	4M	M	Ind	Ind	Ind		
Computer Studies with Geography	G5L8	3FT/4SW deg	*	8	3M	M	Ind	Ind	Ind		
Computer Studies with Geology	G5F6	3FT/4SW deg	*	8	3M	M	Ind	Ind	Ind		
Computer Studies with History	G5V1	3FT/4SW deg	*	10	4M	M	Ind	Ind	Ind		
Computer Studies with History of Art and Design	G5V4	3FT/4SW deg	*	8	3M	M	Ind	Ind	Ind		
Computer Studies with Mathematics	G5G1	3FT/4SW deg	*	8	3M	M	Ind	Ind	Ind		
Computer Studies with Media Studies	G5P4	3FT deg	*	24	Ind	Ind	Ind	Ind	Ind		
Computer Studies with Physiology	G5B1	3FT/4SW deg	*	8	3M	M	Ind	Ind	Ind		
Computer Studies with Psychology	G5C8	3FT/4SW deg	*	10	4M	M^	Ind	Ind	Ind		
Computer Studies with Religious Studies	G5V8	3FT/4SW deg	*	8	3M	M	Ind	Ind	Ind		
Computer Studies with Sociology	G5L3	3FT/4SW deg	*	10	4M	M	Ind	Ind	Ind		
Computing	G500	3FT/4SW deg	* g	12	2M+2D	D*	24	BBCC	N	3	6/18
Economics with Computer Studies	L1G5	3FT deg	*	8	3M	M	Ind	Ind	Ind		
English with Computer Studies	Q3G5	3FT deg	*	10	4M	M	Ind	Ind	Ind		
French with Computer Studies	R1G5	4FT deg	F	8	3M	M	Ind	Ind	Ind		

course details   *98 expected requirements*   *96 entry stats*

TITLE	CODE	COURSE	SUBJECTS	A/AS	ND/C	ADVQ	IB	SQA(H)	SQA	RATIO A/AS
Geography with Computer Studies	L8G5	3FT deg	*	8	3M	M	Ind	Ind	Ind	
Geology with Computer Studies	F6G5	3FT deg	*	8	3M	M	Ind	Ind	Ind	
German with Computer Studies	R2G5	4SW deg	G	8	3M	M	Ind	Ind	Ind	
Global Information Systems	G520	4SW deg	* g	4-8	4M	M*	24	CCCC	N	3
History with Computer Studies	V1G5	3FT deg	*	10	4M	M	Ind	Ind	Ind	
Information Technology	G560▼	3FT/4SW deg	* g	10	N	M	24	CCCC	N	3
Interactive Media	G700	3FT deg	* g	4-8	4M	M*	24	CCCC	N	2
Mathematics with Computer Studies	G1G5	3FT deg	M	8	3M	M	Ind	Ind	Ind	
Media Studies with Computer Studies	P4G5	3FT deg	*	24	Ind	Ind	Ind	Ind	Ind	
Neurosciences and Biocomputing	BG15	3FT/4SW deg	C+S	8	N $	PS	24$	CCCC$	N$	
Pharmacology and Biocomputing	BG25	3FT/4SW deg	C+S	8	N $	PS	24$	CCCC$	N$	
Physiology and Biocomputing	BG1M	3FT/4SW deg	C+S	8	N $	PS	24$	CCCC$	N$	
Physiology with Computer Studies	B1G5	3FT deg	*	8	3M	M	Ind	Ind	Ind	
Psychology with Computer Studies	C8G5	3FT deg	*	10	4M	M^	Ind	Ind	Ind	
Religious Studies with Computer Studies	V8G5	3FT deg	*	8	3M	M	Ind	Ind	Ind	
Sociology with Computer Studies	L3G5	3FT deg	*	10	4M	M	Ind	Ind	Ind	
Business Information Technology	065G	2FT/3SW HND	* g	2-6	N	P*	Dip	CC	N	2 2/4
Business Information Technology for Returners	165G	2FT HND	*	4	N	P*	Dip	CC	N	1
Computing	105G	2FT/3SW HND	* g	2-6	N		Dip	CC	N	2 2/8
Computing for Returners	005G	2FT/3SW HND	*	4	N	P*	Dip	CC	N	2

Univ of SURREY

Computer Modelling for Physical Sciences	F3G5	3FT/4SW deg	M+P	BBB-CC	M $	MS^	$	Ind	Ind	
Computing & Information Technology	G560	3FT deg	* g	BBC-BCC	Ind	D$^ go	Ind	Ind	Ind	13
Computing & Information Technology	G561	4SW deg	* g	BBC/BCC	Ind	D$^ go	Ind	Ind	Ind	6 10/28
Computing & Mathematical Sciences	G510	3FT deg	M	18-20	Ind	Ind	Ind	CSYS	Ind	
Computing & Mathematical Sciences	G511	4SW deg	M	18-20	Ind	Ind	Ind	CSYS	Ind	
Mathematics and Computing Science	GG15	4SW deg	M	18-20	Ind	Ind	Ind	CSYS	Ind	5 14/20
Mathematics and Computing Science	GG1M	3FT deg	M	18-20	Ind	Ind	Ind	CSYS	Ind	9

Univ of SUSSEX

Artificial Intelligence in Cognitive & Comp Sci	G800	3FT deg	* g	BBC	MO	M*6 go	$	Ind	Ind	
Artificial Intelligence in European Studies	G8T2	4FT deg	* g	BBC	MO	M*6	$	Ind	Ind	
Computer Science	G500	3FT deg	M	BBC	MO $	M*^	$	Ind	Ind	
Computer Science and Artificial Intelligence	G575	3FT deg	g	BBC	MO $	M*6 go	$	Ind	Ind	
Computer Science with European Studies (French)	G5R1	4FT deg	M g	BBC	MO $	M*^ go	$	Ind	Ind	
Computer Science with European Studies (German)	G5R2	4FT deg	M g	BBC	MO $	M*^ go	$	Ind	Ind	
Computer Science with European Studies (Russian)	G5R8	4FT deg	M g	BBC	MO $	M*^ go	$	Ind	Ind	
Computer Science with European Studies (Spanish)	G5R4	4FT deg	M g	BBC	MO $	M*^ go	$	Ind	Ind	
Computer Science with European Studs (Italian)	G5R3	4FT deg	M g	BBC	MO $	M*^ go	$	Ind	Ind	
Computing Sciences	G502▼	4FT deg	*							
Economics with Comp and Quantitative Method	L1G5	3FT deg	* g	BBB	MO $	M*6 go	$	Ind	Ind	
Electronic Engineering and Computer Science	H6G5	3FT deg	M	BCC	MO $	MS^	$	Ind	Ind	
Linguistics in Cognitive and Computing Sciences	Q1G5	3FT deg	*	BBC	MO	M*6	$	Ind	Ind	
Mathematics and Artificial Intelligence	GG51	3FT deg	M	BCC	MO $	MS^	$	Ind	Ind	
Mathematics and Computer Science	GG15	3FT deg	M	BCC	MO $	MS^	$	Ind	Ind	
Mathematics and Stats with Computer Sc(MMat)	G4GM	4FT deg	M	BCC	MO $	MS^	$	Ind	Ind	
Mathematics and Stats with Computer Science	G4G5	3FT deg	M	BCC	MO $	MS^	$	Ind	Ind	
Mathematics with Computer Science	G1G5	3FT deg	M	BCC	MO $	MS^	$	Ind	Ind	
Mathematics with Computer Science (MMath)	G1GM	4FT deg	M	BCC	CMO $	MS^	$	Ind	Ind	
Philosophy in Cognitive and Computing Studies	V7G5	3FT deg	*	BBB	MO	M*6	$	Ind	Ind	
Psychology	C8GM	3FT deg	* g	BBB	MO $	M*6 go	$	Ind	Ind	

Computer Sciences and Engineering 15

TITLE	CODE	COURSE	SUBJECTS	A/AS	ND/C	RGNVQ	IB	SQA(H)	SQA	RATIO A/AS
Univ of Wales SWANSEA										
Chem with Computer Sci with a year in Industry	F1GM	4FT deg	C	BCD-CCC	3M+2D$	MS^/DS	26$	BBBCC$	Ind	
Chemistry with Computer Sci with a year abroad	F1GN	4FT deg	C	BBC-BCC	2M+3D$	DS^	30$	ABBBB$	Ind	
Chemistry with Computer Science	F1G5	3FT deg	C	BCD-CCC	3M+2D$	MS^/DS	26$	BBBCC$	Ind	5
Computer Science	G500	3FT deg	*	BBC-BCC	5D	Ind	30	ABBBB	Ind	5 16/26
Computer Science	G501	4FT deg	*	12	Ind	Ind	Ind	Ind	Ind	14
Computer Science (with French)	G5R1	4FT deg	F	BBC	4D $	Ind	28$	BBBBB$	Ind	4
Computer Science (with German)	G5R2	4FT deg	G	BBC	4D $	Ind	28$	BBBBB$	Ind	
Computer Science (with Italian)	G5R3	4FT deg	L	BBC	4D	Ind	28	BBBBB	Ind	
Computer Science (with Russian)	G5R8	4FT deg	L	BBD-BCC	4D	Ind	28	BBBBB	Ind	
Computer Science (with Spanish)	G5R4	4FT deg	L	BBC	4D	Ind	28	BBBBB	Ind	
Computer Science (with Welsh)	G5Q5	4FT deg	*	BCC	4D	Ind	28	BBBBC	Ind	
Computer Science and Psychology	CG85	3FT deg	* g	BBC-BCC	1M+5D	Ind	30	BBBBB	Ind	4
Computer Science and Topographic Science	GF58	3FT deg	M+Gy	BCC	4D $	Ind	28$	BBBBC$	Ind	4
Computer Science with Electronics	G5H6	3FT deg	M	BCC-BCC	5D $	Ind	30$	ABBBB$	Ind	7
Computing (MEng)	G503	4FT deg	M	BBC	5D $	D$	30$	ABBBB	Ind	8
Computing Mathematics	G5G1	3FT deg	M	BBC-BCC	5D $	Ind	30$	ABBBB$	Ind	20
Electronics with Comp Sci(Eur.Austral.N.Am o In)	H6GN	5FT deg	M+P g	BCC	1M+5D$	Ind	28$	BBBBB$	Ind	
Electronics with Comp Sci(Eur.Austral.N.Am.o In)	HG6M	4FT deg	M+P g	BCC	1M+5D$	Ind	28$	BBBBB$	Ind	
Electronics with Computing Science	H6G5	3FT deg	M+P g	BCC	1M+5D$	Ind	28$	BBBBB$	Ind	3
Electronics with Computing Science (MEng)	H6GM	4FT deg	M+P g	BCC	1M+5D$	Ind	28$	BBBBB$	Ind	
French (with Computer Studies)	R1G5	4FT deg	F	BBC	1M+5D$	Ind	28$	BBBBB$	Ind	2
German (with Computer Studies)	R2G5	4FT deg	G	BBC	1M+5D$	Ind	30$	ABBBB$	Ind	
Italian (with Computer Studies)	R3G5	4FT deg	L	BBC	1M+5D$	Ind	30$	ABBBB$	Ind	
Russian (with Computer Studies)	R8G5	4FT deg	L/*	BBC-BCD	1M+5D$	Ind	26$	BBBBC$	Ind	
Spanish (with Computer Studies)	R4G5	4FT deg	L/*	BBC	1M+5D$	Ind	30$	ABBBB$	Ind	
Welsh (with Computer Studies)	Q5G5	3FT/4FT deg	W	CCC-CCD	1M+4D$	X	Ind	Ind	Ind	
SWANSEA INST of HE										
Business Information Technology	G710	3FT deg	*	EE	2M	M	Ind	Ind	Ind	2
Computer Systems Engineering	G600	3FT deg	2S	EE	3M		Ind	Ind	Ind	5
Computer Systems Engineering (Foundation)	G608	4EXT deg								
Computing and Information Systems	G520	3FT deg	*	EE	2M	M	Ind	Ind	Ind	3 4/14
Multi Media	PG45	3FT deg		DD	N			Ind	N	4 8/18
Multi Media	EG45	3FT deg		DD	N			Ind	N	
Multi Media (Foundation)	EG4M▼	4EXT deg								
Multi Media (Foundation)	PG4M▼	4EXT deg								2
Software Engineering	G700	3FT deg	*	EE	2M	M	Ind	Ind	Ind	1
Virtual Reality	WG2N▼	3FT deg								
Virtual Reality	EG2M	3FT deg								
Virtual Reality	EG2N▼	3FT deg								
Virtual Reality	WG2M	3FT deg								
Business Information Technology	265G	2FT HND		E	N	P	Ind	Ind	N	3
Computing	105G	2FT/3SW HND		E	N	P	Ind	Ind	N	4
SWINDON COLL										
Computer Systems Engineering	006G	2FT HND	Cs/Ds/Es/L/M/P g	2	N	PE/I/S	Ind	Ind	N	
TAMESIDE COLLEGE										
Computing	005G	2FT HND		2	N	P				

course details			98 expected requirements							96 entry stats	
TITLE	CODE	COURSE	SUBJECTS	A/AS	ND/C	AGNVQ	IB	SQA(H)	SQA	RATIO	A/AS
Univ of TEESSIDE											
Business Computing	G710	4SW deg	* g	8-12	Ind	M	Ind	CCCC	Ind	5	6/14
Computer Aided Product Design Engineering	H7G5	3FT deg	M+S	8	3M		Ind	CCC	Ind		
Computer Science	G500	4SW deg	* g	8-12	Ind	M	Ind	CCCC	Ind	4	6/16
Computing and Mathematics	GG15	3FT/4SW deg	M	8-12	Ind	M	Ind	CCCC	Ind	4	6/10
Computing and Statistics	GG54	3FT/4SW deg	* g	8-12	Ind	M	Ind	CCCC	Ind	7	
Creative Visualisation	WG25	4SW deg	* g	8-12	Ind	M	Ind	CCCC	Ind	1	10/20
Informatics	G501	4SW deg				M					
Information Sciences	G520	3FT/4SW deg	* g	8-12	Ind	M	Ind	CCCC	Ind		
Information Society	GW52	4SW deg	* g	8-12	Ind	M	Ind	CCCC	Ind		
Information Technology	G560	4SW deg	* g	8-12	Ind	M	Ind	CCCC	Ind	5	7/13
International Business Information Technology	G562	4SW deg	* g	8-12	Ind	M	Ind	CCCC	Ind	19	
Multimedia	G540	3FT deg	* g	8-12	Ind	M	Ind	CCCC	Ind		
Social Science and Information Technology	GL53	3FT deg	* g	14	Ind	Ind	Ind	BCCCC	Ind		
Software Engineering	G700	4SW deg	* g	8-12	Ind	M	Ind	CCCC	Ind	4	8/18
Visualisation	G5W2	4SW deg	* g	8-12	Ind	M	Ind	CCCC	Ind	2	10/22
Modular Degree Scheme *Computer Aided Product Design Engineering*	Y401	3FT deg									
Modular Degree Scheme *Computing*	Y401	3FT deg									
Modular Degree Scheme *Information Technology*	Y401	3FT deg									
Modular Degree Scheme *Visualisation*	Y401	3FT deg									
Science and Technology Combined Honours Scheme *Computer Aided Product Design Engineering*	Y108	3FT deg									
Business Information Technology	265G	2FT HND	*	4	N	P	Ind	Ind	Ind	3	2/6
Computing	005G ▼	2FT HND	* g	4	N	P	Ind	CC	Ind	2	2/10
Multimedia	045G	2FT HND	* g	4	N	P	Ind	CC	Ind		
Software Engineering	007G	2FT HND	* g	4	N	P	Ind	CC	Ind	2	
Visualisation	2W5G	2FT HND	* g	4	Ind	P	Ind	CC	Ind		
THAMES VALLEY Univ											
Accounting with Information Systems	N4G5	3FT deg		8-12	MO	M	26	CCC			
Business Administration with Information Systems	N1GM	3FT deg		8-12	MO	M	26	CCC			
Business Computing	G710	2FT Dip		2-4	N	P	24	CC			
Business Economics with Information Systems	L1GM	3FT deg		8-12	MO	M	26	CCC			
Business Studies with Information Systems (Dip)	N1G5	3FT/4SW deg		8-12	MO	M	26	CCC			
Computing	G501	2FT Dip		2-4	N	P	24	CC			
Digital Arts with Information Systems	W9G5	3FT deg		8-12	MO	M		CCC			
Digital Arts with Multi-Media Computing	W9GM	3FT deg		8-12	MO	M		CCC			
Economics with Information Systems	L1G5	3FT deg		8-12	MO	M	26	CCC			
Finance with Information Systems	N3G5	3FT deg		8-12	MO	M	26	CCC			
Information Management with Information Systems	P2G5	3FT deg		8-12	MO	M	26	CCC			
Information Mgt with Multi-Media Computing	P2GM	3FT deg		8-12	MO	M	26	CCC			
Marketing with Multi-Media Computing	N5G5	3FT deg		8-12	MO	M	26	CCC			
Media Arts with Multi-Media Computing	W9GN	3FT deg		8-12	MO	M	26	CCC			
Multi-Media Comp with Sound and Music Recording	G5WH	3FT deg		8-12	MO	M	26	CCC			
Multi-Media Computing with Advertising	G5P3	3FT deg		8-12	MO	M	26	CCC			
Multi-Media Computing with Business	G5N1	3FT deg		8-12	MO	M	26	CCC			
Multi-Media Computing with Digital Arts	G5W9	3FT deg		8-12	MO	M	26	CCC			
Multi-Media Computing with English	G5Q3	3FT deg		8-12	MO	M	26	CCC			
Multi-Media Computing with English Language St	G5Q1	3FT deg		8-12	MO	M	26	CCC			
Multi-Media Computing with Information Mgt	G5P2	3FT deg		8-12	MO	M	26	CCC			
Multi-Media Computing with Information Systems	G5GM	3FT deg		8-12	MO	M	26	CCC			

course details				98 expected requirements						96 entry stats
TITLE	CODE	COURSE	SUBJECTS	A/AS	NQ/C	RGNVQ	IB	SQA(H)	SQA	RATIO A/AS
Multi-Media Computing with Lang & Communication	G5PH	3FT deg		8-12	MO	M	26	CCC		
Multi-Media Computing with Marketing	G5N5	3FT deg		8-12	MO	M	26	CCC		
Multi-Media Computing with Media Studies	G5WX	3FT deg		8-12	MO	M	26	CCC		
Multi-Media Computing with Photography	G5W5	3FT deg		8-12	MO	M	26	CCC		
Multi-Media Computing with Radio Broadcasting	G5H6	3FT deg		8-12	MO	M	26	CCC		
Multi-Media Computing with Sociology	G5L3	3FT deg		8-12	MO	M	26	CCC		
Multi-Media Computing with Video Production	G5W4	3FT deg		8-12	MO	M	26	CCC		
Multi-Media Computing with Visual Cultures	G5W1	3FT deg		8-12	MO	M	26	CCC		
Tourism with Information Systems	P7G5	3FT deg		8-12	MO	M	26	CCC		
Business Computing	017G	2FT HND		2-4	N	P	24	CC		
Business Information Technology	265G▼	2FT HND	* g	EE	2M	M	24	CC		

TRINITY COLL Carmarthen

Information Systems and Technologies	G520	3FT deg	* g	DD-CC	Ind		Ind	Ind	Ind	1

Univ of ULSTER

Business with Computing (3 Yr/4 Yr SW inc DIS)	N1G5▼	3FT/4SW deg	* g	BCC	MO+4D	D*6/^ gi	29	BBBB	Ind	16 16/28
Computing & Linguistics (4 Yr SW inc DIS or DAS)	GQ51▼	4SW deg	* g	BCC	MO+4D	D*6/^ gi	30	BBBB	Ind	4 14/16
Computing Science	G502▼	4SW deg	* g	CDD	MO+1D	M*6/^ gi	26	BCCC	Ind	9 12/16
Computing Science (Hons) (4 Yr SW inc DIS)	G500▼	4SW deg	* g	BCC	MO+4D	D*6/^ gi	30	BBBB	Ind	7 14/24
Computing with Enterprise Studies	G5N1▼	4SW deg	* g	BCC	MO+4D	D*6/^ gi	30	BBBB	Ind	
Computing with Marketing	G5N5▼	4SW deg	* g	BCC	MO+4D	D*6/^ gi	30	BBBB	Ind	
Electronics & Computing (Hons) (4 Yr SW inc DIS)	GH76▼	4SW deg	S	CCC	MO+3D	Ind	28	BBBC	Ind	10
Electronics and Computing (4 Yr SW inc DIS)	HG67▼	4SW deg	S	CDD	MO+1D	Ind	26	BCCC	Ind	7
Interactive Multimedia Systems Design	G532▼	2FT/3FT/4SW Dip/de	g	BCC-CD	MO+4D	DI6/^ gi	22	BBBB	Ind	
Software Engineering (4/5 Yr SW inc DIS)	G700▼	4SW/5SW deg	* g	BCC	MO+4D	D*6/^ gi	29	BBBB	Ind	12 16/28
Computing	105G▼	2FT HND	* g	CD	Ind	D* gi	22	CCD	Ind	11 8/12
Computing includes CIS	005G▼	3SW HND	* g	CD	Ind	D* gi	22	CCD	Ind	15 10/14

UNIVERSITY COLL LONDON (Univ of London)

Computer Science	G500	3FT deg	M g	BBB	MO $	Ind	32$	ABBBB$	Ind	13 22/30
Computer Science (MSci)	G501	4FT deg	M g	BBB	MO $	Ind	32$	ABBBB$	Ind	
Computer Science with Cognitive Science	G5C8	3FT deg	M g	BBB	MO $	Ind	32$	ABBBB$	Ind	8
Computer Science with Cognitive Science (MSci)	G5CV	4FT deg	M g	BBB	MO $	Ind	32$	ABBBB$	Ind	
Computer Science with Electronic Eng (MSci)	G5HP	4FT deg	M g	BBB	MO $	Ind	32$	ABBBB$	Ind	
Computer Science with Electronic Engineering	G5H6	3FT deg	M g	BBB	MO $	Ind	32$	ABBBB$	Ind	6 22/26
Electronic Eng with Comp Sci for Eur (MEng)	H6GM	4FT deg	M+P g	ABB-AAB	DO $	X	30$	BBBCC$	Ind	7
Electronic Engineering with Computer Science	H6G5	3FT deg	M+P g	ABB-AAB	DO $	X	30$	BBBCC$	Ind	16 28/30
Information Management	P2G5	3FT deg	g	BBC	MO $	Ind	30$	BBCCC$	N$	6 20/26
Mathematics and Computer Science	GG15	3FT deg	M g	ABC-ABB	MO $	Ind	30$	AAABB$	N$	12 24/26
Mathematics and Computer Science (MSci)	GG1M	4FT deg	M g	ABC-ABB	MO $	Ind	30$	AAABB$	N$	4 24/30
Physical Sciences Computer Science	Y100	3FT deg	S g	CCC-BCC	$	Ind	28$	BCCCC$	N$	
Statistics,Computing,Operational Res & Economics Computing	Y624	3FT deg	M g	BCC	MO $	Ind	30$	BBCCC$	N$	

Univ of WARWICK

Applied Mathematics with Computing	G1G5	3FT deg	M g	AAA-AAB	X	X	36$	CSYS$		4
Computer Science	G500	3FT deg	M g	ABB	Ind	D$^	33$	AAABB$		11 24/30
Computer Science and Business Studies	GN51	3FT deg	* g	ABB	Ind	D$^	33	AAABB		9 24/30
Computer Systems Engineering	GH66	3FT deg	M g	BBB	Ind	DS^	32$	AABBB$		6 22/30
Computer Systems Engineering	GH6P	4FT deg	M g	BBB	Ind	DS^	32$	AABBB$		
Computer and Management Sciences	GN5C	3FT deg	M g	ABB	Ind	D$^	33$	AAABB$		11 26/28
Mathematics with Computing	G1GN	3FT deg	M g	AAA-AAB	X	X	36$	CSYS$		6 26/30
Philosophy with Computer Science	V7G5	3FT deg	M g	BBB	X	X	32$	AABBB$		6
Physics with Computing	F3G5	3FT deg	P+M g	BBC	3M+2D$	DS^	30$	ABBBB$		7 20/28

TITLE	CODE	COURSE	SUBJECTS	A/AS	ND/C	AGNVQ	IB	SQA(H)	SQA	RATIO	A/AS
WEST HERTS COLL											
Business Information Technology	065G	2FT HND	*	2	N					2	
Univ of WESTMINSTER											
Artificial Intelligence	G800	3FT deg	*	CC	3M	M			Ind	6	6/13
Business Information Management and Finance	NG15	4SW deg	*	CC	MO+2D		28	BBBB	Ind		
Business Information Technology	G710	4SW deg	*	CC	MO+2D	D	26	BBB	Ind	7	10/20
Computational Mathematics	GG15	3FT deg	M	CD	N	M	Ind	Ind	Ind	6	4/10
Computer Communications and Networks	PG35	3FT deg	M/P/Cs	CC	3M	M	Ind	Ind	Ind		
Computer Systems Technology	G600	3FT deg	M/P	CC	N	M	Ind	Ind	Ind	7	8/12
Computing	G500	3FT deg	*	12	3M	M	Ind	Ind	Ind	6	4/15
Computing (with foundation)	G501	4FT deg	*	E	N						
Information Systems Engineering	G520	3FT deg	*	12	3M					3	4/12
Managing Business Information	NG17	3FT deg		CC	MO+2D	D	26	BBB			
Multimedia Computing	GP54▼	3FT deg		BC	4M	M	Ind	Ind	Ind	1	
Operational Research and Information Systems	GG45	3FT deg	M	CD		M	Ind	Ind	Ind		
Software Engineering	G700	3FT deg	*	12	3M	M	Ind	Ind	Ind	7	6/16
Computing (Artificial Intelligence)	008G▼	2FT HND								5	
Computing (Information Systems)	025G▼	2FT HND	*							3	2/10
Mathematical Studies (Business Support Systems)	017G▼	2FT HND	M	C	2M						
Software Engineering	007G▼	2FT HND	*	C	2M	M				6	
WIGAN and LEIGH COLL											
Information Technology	G560▼	3FT deg									
Building Studies (Information Technology)	25KG▼	2FT HND		DE	N	P$	Dip		N		
Business Information Technology	027G▼	2FT HND		DD	N	P					
Computing	005G▼	2FT HND		DD	N	P					
Software Engineering	007G▼	2FT HND		DD	N	P					
Univ of WOLVERHAMPTON											
Business Information Systems	GN51	3FT/4SW deg	*	12	4M	M	24	BBBB	Ind	3	6/13
Computing	G500	4SW deg	* g	DD	N	M	24	CCCC	Ind	4	6/16
Applied Sciences *Computing*	Y100	3FT/4SW deg	S g	DD	N	M	24	CCCC	Ind		
Applied Sciences (4 Yrs) *Computing*	Y110▼	4FT deg	*								
Combined Degrees *Computing*	Y401	3FT/4SW deg	g	DD	N	M	24	CCCC	Ind		
Computing	105G	2FT HND	* g	D	N	M	24	CCCC	Ind	3	2/9
WORCESTER COLL of HE											
Information Technology/Art & Design	WG95	3FT deg	A	DD	Ind	M	Ind	Ind	Ind	8	
Information Technology/Biological Science	CG15	3FT deg	S	DD	Ind	M	Ind	Ind	Ind		
Information Technology/Business Management	NG15	3FT deg		DD	Ind	M	Ind	Ind	Ind	2	7/16
Information Technology/Drama	WG45	3FT deg		DD	Ind	M	Ind	Ind	Ind		
Information Technology/Economy and Society	LG15	3FT deg		DD	Ind	M	Ind	Ind	Ind		
Information Technology/Education Studies	XG95	3FT deg		DD	Ind	M	Ind	Ind	Ind		
Information Technology/English & Literary St	QG35	3FT deg		CC	Ind	M	Ind	Ind	Ind	5	
Information Technology/Environmental Science	FG95	3FT deg		DD	Ind	M	Ind	Ind	Ind		
Information Technology/Geography	LG85	3FT deg		DD	Ind	M	Ind	Ind	Ind		
Information Technology/Health Studies	BG95	3FT deg	g	DD	Ind	M	Ind	Ind	Ind		
Information Technology/History	VG15	3FT deg		DD	Ind	M	Ind	Ind	Ind		
Psychology/Information Technology	GL57	3FT deg	g	CC	Ind	M	Ind	Ind	Ind	5	
Sociology/Information Technology	GL53	3FT deg		DD	Ind	M	Ind	Ind	Ind		
Sports Studies/Information Technology	GB56	3FT deg		CC	Ind	M	Ind	Ind	Ind		

Computer Sciences and Engineering   15

course details			98 expected requirements							96 entry stats
TITLE	CODE	COURSE	SUBJECTS	A/AS	NO/C	AGNVQ	IB	SQA(H)	SQA	RATIO A/AS
Urban Studies/Information Technology	GL5V	3FT deg	DD	Ind	M	Ind	Ind	Ind	
Women's Studies/Information Technology	MG95	3FT deg	DD	Ind	M	Ind	Ind	Ind	
WORCESTER COLLEGE of Technology									
Computing and Information Systems	025G	2FT HND	2	N					
Univ of YORK									
Computer Science	G500	3FT deg	M+Ph/B	24	HN $	D$^	32$	CSYS$	Ind$	22/30
Computer Science	G501	4SW deg	M+Ph/B	24	HN $	D$^	32$	CSYS$	Ind$	24/30
Computer Science/Mathematics (Equal)	GG5C	4SW deg	M	24	HN $	D$^	32$	CSYS$	HN$	
Computer Science/Mathematics (Equal)	GG51	3FT deg	M	24	HN $	D$^	32$	CSYS$	HN$	22/30
Computer Systems and Software Engineering	GG67	4FT deg	M+Ph/B	24	HN $	D$^	32$	CSYS$	Ind$	24/30
Information Technology, Business Mgt & Language	G5NC	4SW deg	* g	24	HN	D$^ go	32	BBBB	Ind	22/30
Information Technology, Business Mgt & Language	G5N1	3FT deg	* g	24	HN	D$^ go	32	BBBB	Ind	24/26
Mathematics/Computer Science (Equal) (MMath)	GG15	4FT deg	M	24	HN $	D$^	32$	CSYS$	HN$	

course details			98 expected requirements							96 entry stats	
TITLE	CODE	COURSE	SUBJECTS	A/AS	ND/C	AGNVQ	IB	SQA(H)	SQA	RATIO	A/AS
Univ of BIRMINGHAM											
Dentistry (BDS)	A200	5FT deg	C+S g	ABB	MO+4D		36$	AAAAB	Ind	20	22/30
Univ of BRISTOL											
Dentistry - First BDS (pre-dental) Entry	A204	6FT deg	* g	ABB	Ind	D$^	32$	AAAAB	Ind	12	
Dentistry - Second BDS Entry	A206	5FT deg	C+S g	ABB	Ind	X	32$	AAAAB	Ind	10	24/30
Univ of DUNDEE											
Dentistry (BDS)	A200	5FT deg	C+2(B/M/P) g	ABB	X	X	Ind	AAABB$	X	14	22/28
Dentistry BDS (Pre-dental year)	A204	6FT deg	* g	BBB	X	X	Ind	BBBBB$	X	2	
Univ of GLASGOW											
Dentistry (BDS)	A200	5FT deg	C+B/P/M	ABB	X		34$	AAAAB	X	6	24/30
KING'S COLL LONDON (Univ of London)											
Dentistry	A205	5FT deg	C+(2(M/S)/M/S+Ap	BBB	X	X	$	AABBB$	X	20	20/30
Foundation Course in Natural Sciences/Dentistry	A203	6FT deg	*	BBB	X	X	$	AABBB	X		
Univ of LEEDS											
Dentistry	A200	5FT deg	C g	BBB	Ind	Ind	32$	CSYS	Ind	24	22/30
Univ of LIVERPOOL											
Dentistry (BDS)	A200	5FT deg	C+S g	AAB-ABB	DO $		32$	AAABB	Ind	15	24/30
Univ of MANCHESTER											
Dentistry (BDS first-year entry)	A206	5FT deg	C/M/P/B/S g	ABB	4M+5D$	X	32$	ABBB$	Ind	11	22/28
Dentistry (BDS pre-dental year entry)	A204	6FT deg	g	ABB	Ind	D^	X	AAAA$	Ind		
Univ of NEWCASTLE											
Dentistry (First-Year Entry)	A206	5FT deg	B/C	ABB	Ind		X	AABBB	X	11	24/30
Dentistry (Pre-Dental)	A204	6FT deg	* g	ABB	X		X	X	X		
QUEEN MARY & WESTFIELD COLL (Univ of London)											
Dentistry	A200▼	5FT deg	C+S/2S g	BBB-BBC	X	X	32	X	X		
QUEEN'S Univ Belfast											
Dentistry	A200	5FT deg	C+2(P/M/B) g	AAB	X	X	35$	AAABB	X	5	26/30
Univ of SHEFFIELD											
Dentistry (First-Year Entry)	A204	6FT deg	* g	ABB	7M+4D	D^	33	AAABB	Ind	104	
Dentistry (Second-Year Entry)	A206	5FT deg	C+S g	ABB	7M+4D$	DS^	33$	AAABB$	Ind	19	24/30
UMDS of Guy's & St Thomas's (Univ of London)											
Dentistry	A200	5FT deg	C+S/M g	BBB	X	X	34$	CSYS$	X	9	22/30
Univ of WALES COLL of MEDICINE											
BDS (First-year entry) (Foundation Course)	A204	6FT deg	* g	ABB	MO+5D$	DS^ go	30	ABBBB$	Ind	29	
BDS (Second-year entry)	A206	5FT deg	C+B/P g	ABB	HN+5D$	X	30$	CSYS$	Ind	10	22/28

TITLE	CODE	COURSE	SUBJECTS	A/AS	ND/C	RGNVQ	IB	SQA(H)	SQA	RATIO A/AS

Univ of Wales, ABERYSTWYTH

TITLE	CODE	COURSE	SUBJECTS	A/AS	ND/C	RGNVQ	IB	SQA(H)	SQA	RATIO A/AS
Drama	W400	3FT deg	* g	20	1M+5D	MQ6 g	30	BBBBC	Ind	
Drama/American Studies	QW44	3FT deg	E/H g	20	1M+5D$	MQ6/^ g	30$	BBBBC$	Ind	
Drama/Art	WW14	3FT deg	A/Ad g	20	1M+5D$	MQ/A^ g	30$	BBBBC$	Ind	
Drama/Art History	VW44	3FT deg	* g	20	1M+5D	MQ/A6	30	BBBBC	Ind	
Education/Drama	WX49	3FT deg	* g	20	1M+5D	MQ6 g	30	BBBBC	Ind	
English/Drama	QW34	3FT deg	El	20	1M+5D$	MQ^ g	30$	BBBBC$	Ind	
Film and Television Studies/Drama	WW54	3FT deg	* g	20	1M+5D	M6 g	30	BBBBC	Ind	
French/Drama	RW14	4FT deg	F g	20	1M+5D$	MQ^ g	30$	BBBBC$	Ind	
Geography/Drama	LW84	3FT deg	Gy g	20-22	1M+5D$	MQ^ g	31$	BBBBC$	Ind	
German/Drama	RW24	4FT deg	G g	20	1M+5D$	MQ^ g	30$	BBBBC$	Ind	
Information and Library Studies/Drama	PW24	3FT deg	* g	20	1M+5D	MQ6 g	30	BBBBC	Ind	
Irish/Drama	QWM4	4FT deg	* g	20	1M+5D$	MQ6 g	30$	BBBBC$	Ind	
Italian/Drama	RW34	4FT deg	L g	20	1M+5D$	MQ^ g	30$	BBBBC$	Ind	
Pure Mathematics/Drama	GW14	3FT deg	M g	20	1M+5D$	MQ^ g	30$	BBBBC$	Ind	
Spanish/Drama	RW44	4FT deg	L g	20	1M+5D$	MQ^ g	30$	BBBBC$	Ind	
Welsh History/Drama	VWC4	3FT deg	* g	20	1M+5D	MQ^ g	30	BBBBC	Ind	
Welsh/Drama	QW54	3FT deg	W g	20	1M+5D$	MQ^ g	30$	BBBBC$	Ind	

AMERSHAM & WYCOMBE COLL

| Performing Arts (Music/Theatre) | 034W | 2FT HND | Pf | | N | P $ | Ind | Ind | Ind | |

Univ of Wales, BANGOR

| English with Creative Writing | Q3W4 | 3FT deg | E/El g | CCC | X | D*^ go | 28$ | BBBC$ | X | |
| Welsh Literature and Literature of the Media | Q5W4 | 3FT/4FT deg | W g | CCD | Ind | D*^ go | Ind | X | X | 3 14/26 |

BARNSLEY COLL

| Combined Studies
Performing Arts | Y400 | 3FT deg | * g | DD | 4M | M* | Ind | Ind | Ind | |

BATH COLL of HE

| Combined Awards
Creative Studies in English (Drama) | Y400 | 3FT deg | * | | N | | Ind | $ | $ | |
| Modular Programme (DipHE)
Creative Studies in English (Drama) | Y460 | 2FT Dip | * | | N | | Ind | $ | $ | |

Univ of BIRMINGHAM

Dance and Theatre Arts	W450	3FT deg	*	BCC	Ind	D*^	30	ABBB	Ind	10 16/24
Dance/East Mediterranean History	WV41	3FT deg	* g	BBB	Ind	D*^	32	ABBB	Ind	
Dance/English	WQ43	3FT deg	*	BBB	Ind	D*^	32	ABBB	Ind	35
Dance/French Studies	WR41	4FT deg	F	BBB	Ind	D*^	32$	ABBB	Ind	3
Dance/German Studies	WR42	4FT deg	G	BBB	Ind	D*^	32$	ABBB	Ind	
Dance/Hispanic Studies	WR44	4FT deg	*	BBB	Ind	D*^	32	ABBB	Ind	
Dance/History	WV4C	3FT deg	*	BBB	Ind	D*^	32	ABBB	Ind	
Dance/History of Art	WV44	3FT deg	*	BBB	Ind	D*^	32	ABBB	Ind	5
Dance/Italian	WR43	4FT deg	*	BBB	Ind	D*^	32	ABBB	Ind	
Dance/Latin	WQ46	3FT deg	Ln	BBB	Ind	D*^	32$	ABBB	Ind	
Dance/Media & Cultural Studies	WP44	3FT deg	*	BBB	Ind	D*^	32	ABBB	Ind	
Dance/Modern Greek Studies	WT42	4FT deg	* g	BBB	Ind	D*^	32	ABBB	Ind	
Dance/Music	WW43	3FT deg	Mu	AAB-ABB	Ind	D*^	32$	ABBB	Ind	14
Dance/Portuguese	WR45	4FT deg	*	BBB	Ind	D*^	32	ABBB	Ind	
Dance/Russian	WR48	4FT deg	*	BBB	Ind	D*^	32	ABBB	Ind	
Dance/Sport & Recreation Studies	WB4P	3FT deg	*	BBB	Ind	D*^	32	ABBB	Ind	
Drama and Theatre Arts	W420	3FT deg	*	BBB	Ind	D*^	32	ABBB	Ind	23 22/30
Drama/Classical Literature and Civilisation	QW84	3FT deg	*	BBB	Ind	D*^	32	ABBB	Ind	

										96 entry stats
course details			*98 expected requirements*							*96 entry stats*
TITLE	CODE	COURSE	SUBJECTS	A/AS	ND/C	AGNVQ	IB	SQA(H)	SQA	RATIO A/AS
Drama/East Mediterranean History	VWD4	3FT deg	* g	BBB	Ind	D*^	32	ABBB	Ind	
Drama/English	QW34	3FT deg	*	BBB	Ind	D*^	32	ABBB	Ind	38 26/30
Drama/French Studies	RW14	4FT deg	F	BBB	Ind	D*^	32$	ABBB	Ind	17
Drama/German Studies	RW24	4FT deg	G	BBB	Ind	D*^	32$	ABBB	Ind	
Drama/Hispanic Studies	RW44	4FT deg	*	BBB	Ind	D*^	32	ABBB	Ind	11
Drama/History	VW14	3FT deg	*	BBB	Ind	D*^	32	ABBB	Ind	
Drama/History of Art	VW44	3FT deg	*	BBB	Ind	D*^	32	ABBB	Ind	
Drama/Italian	RW34	4FT deg	*	BBB	Ind	D*^	32	ABBB	Ind	3
Drama/Latin	QW64	3FT deg	Ln	BBB	Ind	D*^	32$	ABBB	Ind	
Drama/Media & Cultural Studies	PW44	3FT deg	*	BBB	Ind	D*^	32	ABBB	Ind	103
Drama/Modern Greek Studies	TW24	4FT deg	* g	BBB	Ind	D*^	32	ABBB	Ind	
Drama/Music	WW34	3FT deg	Mu	AAB-ABB	Ind	D*^	32$	ABBB	Ind	
Drama/Portuguese	RW54	4FT deg	*	BBB	Ind	D*^	32	ABBB	Ind	
Drama/Russian	RW84	4FT deg	*	BBB	Ind	D*^	32	ABBB	Ind	
Drama/Sport & Recreation Studies	WB46	3FT deg	*	BBB	Ind	D*^	32	ABBB	Ind	

BISHOP GROSSETESTE COLL

Arts in the Community (Drama) (3 Yrs)	W400	3FT deg	*	CD	9M	M*^ go	Ind	Ind	Ind	

BLACKPOOL & FYLDE COLL

Performing Arts	1N4W	2FT HND	E/T	2	N		Ind	Ind	Ind	

BOLTON INST

Accountancy and Theatre Studies	NW44	3FT deg	Me/T g	CD	Ind	Ind	24	BBCC	Ind	
Art & Design History and Visual Arts	EW41	3FT deg	* g	CD	MO	M*	24	BBCC	Ind	
Art and Design History and Theatre Studies	VW44	3FT deg	Me/T g	CD	Ind	Ind	24	BBCC	Ind	
Biology and Theatre Studies	WC41	3FT deg	Me/T g	CD	Ind	Ind	24	BBCC	Ind	
Business Economics and Theatre Studies	LW14	3FT deg	Me/T g	CD	MO	M*	24	BBCC	Ind	
Business Information Systems and Theatre Studies	GW54	3FT deg	Me/T g	CD	Ind	Ind	24	BBCC	Ind	
Business Studies and Theatre Studies	WN41	3FT deg	Me/T g	CD	Ind	Ind	24	BBCC	Ind	
Community Studies and Theatre Studies	LW54	3FT deg	Me/T g	CD	Ind	Ind	24	BBCC	Ind	
Computing and Theatre Studies	WG45	3FT deg	Me/T g	CD	Ind	Ind	24	BBCC	Ind	
Creative Writing and Organisations, Mgt & Work	NW74	3FT deg	* g	CD	MO	M*	24	BBCC	Ind	
Creative Writing and Theatre Studies	WW94	3FT deg	Me/T g	CD	Ind	Ind	24	BBCC	Ind	
Design and Theatre Studies	WW24	3FT deg	Me/T g	CD	Ind	Ind	24	BBCC	Ind	
Environmental Studies and Theatre Studies	FW94	3FT deg	Me/T g	CD	Ind	Ind	24	BBCC	Ind	
European Cultural Studies and Theatre Studies	TW24	3FT deg	Me/T g	CD	Ind	Ind	24	BBCC	Ind	
Film & TV Studies and Theatre Studies	WW54	3FT deg	Me/T g	CD	Ind	Ind	24	BBCC	Ind	
French and Theatre Studies	RW14	3FT deg	F+Me/T g	CD	Ind	Ind	24	BBCC	Ind	
Gender & Women's Studies and Theatre Studies	WM49	3FT deg	Me/T g	CD	Ind	Ind	24	BBCC	Ind	
German and Theatre Studies	RW24	3FT deg	G+Me/T g	CD	Ind	Ind	24	BBCC	Ind	
History and Theatre Studies	WV41	3FT deg	Me/T g	CD	Ind	Ind	24	BBCC	Ind	
Human Resource Management and Theatre Studies	NW14	3FT deg	Me/T g	CD	Ind	Ind	24	BBCC	Ind	
Law and Theatre Studies	MW34	3FT deg	Me/T g	CD	Ind	Ind	24	BBCC	Ind	
Leisure Studies and Theatre Studies	WL4H	3FT deg	Me/T g	CD	Ind	Ind	24	BBCC	Ind	
Literature and Theatre Studies	WQ42	3FT deg	Me/T g	CD	Ind	Ind	24	BBCC	Ind	
Mathematics and Theatre Studies	WG41	3FT deg	M+Me/T g	CD	Ind	Ind	24	BBCC	Ind	
Operations Management and Theatre Studies	NW24	3FT deg	Me/T g	CD	Ind	Ind	24	BBCC	Ind	
Peace & War Studies and Theatre Studies	WV4C	3FT deg	Me/T g	CD	Ind	Ind	24	BBCC	Ind	
Philosophy and Theatre Studies	WV47	3FT deg	Me/T g	CD	Ind	Ind	24	BBCC	Ind	
Textiles and Theatre Studies	JW44	3FT deg	Me/T g	10	Ind	Ind	Ind	Ind	Ind	
Theatre Studies and Marketing	NW54	3FT deg	* g	CD	MO	M*	24	BBCC	Ind	
Theatre Studies and Psychology	WL47	3FT deg	Me/T g	12	Ind	Ind	24	BBCC	Ind	
Theatre Studies and Tourism Studies	PW74	3FT deg	Me/T g	CD	Ind	Ind	24	BBCC	Ind	

course details			98 expected requirements							96 entry stats	
TITLE	CODE	COURSE	SUBJECTS	A/AS	NO/C	AGNVQ	IB	SQA(H)	SQA	RATIO	A/AS
Theatre Studies and Urban & Cultural Studies	WL43	3FT deg	Me/T g	CD	Ind	Ind	24	BBCC	Ind		
Visual Arts and Theatre Studies	WW41	3FT deg	* g	10	MO	M*	24	BBCC	Ind		
BRETTON HALL											
Arts and Education (Drama)	XW94	3FT deg	T	CC	MO		Ind	CCC	Ind	3	10/20
Dance	W450	3FT deg	D	CC	MO $		Ind	CCC	Ind	9	10/26
English-Drama	Q3W4	3FT deg	E	CC-BB	MO $		Ind	CCC	Ind	7	8/26
Performance Management	W421	3FT deg	T	BB	MO $		Ind	BBB	Ind	8	8/20
Performing Arts (Drama/English)	W4Q3	3FT deg	T	BB	MO $		Ind	BBB	Ind	4	
Theatre (Acting)	W410	3FT deg	T	BB	MO $		Ind	BBB	Ind	21	14/28
Theatre (Acting: Devised Performance)	W423	3FT deg	T	BB	MO $		Ind	BBB	Ind	2	12/26
Theatre (Broadcast Acting)	W411	3FT deg	T	BB	MO $		Ind	BBB	Ind	11	12/22
Theatre (Design and Technology)	W460	3FT deg	T	BB	MO $		Ind	BBB	Ind	6	8/22
Univ of BRIGHTON											
Dance with Visual Practice	W4W1	3FT deg	Fa+Pf g		N $	Ind$ go	Ind$	Ind$	Ind$		
Dance with Visual Practice	E4W1	3FT deg	Fa+Pf g		N $	Ind$ go	Ind$	Ind$	Ind$		
Theatre with Visual Practice	E4WC	3FT deg	Fa+Pf g		N $	Ind$ go	Ind$	Ind$	Ind$		
Theatre with Visual Practice	W4WC	3FT deg	Fa+Pf g		N $	Ind$ go	Ind$	Ind$	Ind$		
Univ of BRISTOL											
Drama	W400	3FT deg	*	BCC	Ind	D$^	28$	BBBBB	Ind	35	22/30
Drama and English	WQ43	3FT deg	El g	BB	Ind	D$^	30$	AABBB	Ind	50	26/30
Drama and French	WR41	4FT deg	F	BC	Ind	D$^	28$	BBBBB	Ind	12	28/30
Drama and German	WR42	4FT deg	G	BC	Ind	D$^	28$	BBBBB	Ind		
Drama and Italian	WR43	4FT deg		BC	Ind	D$^	28$	BBBBB	Ind		
Drama and Spanish	WR44	4FT deg		BC	Ind	D$^	28$	BBBBB	Ind		
BRISTOL, Univ of the W of England											
Drama and Cultural & Media Studies	WL46	3FT deg	Ap g	BBC	3M+3D	M$^ go	30	ABBB	Ind		
Drama and English	WQ43	3FT deg	Ap g	BBC	3M+3D	M$^ go	30	ABBB	Ind		
Drama and History	WV41	3FT deg	Ap g	BCC	4M+2D	M$^ go	28	BBBB	Ind		
BRUNEL Univ, West London											
Drama/American Studies	QW44	3FT deg	T g	BC	MO $	P go	22$	BCCC$	Ind		
Drama/Art	W4W1	3FT deg	T+A g	BC	MO $	P go	22$	BCCC$	Ind		
English/Drama	QW34	3FT deg	E+T g	CB	MO $	M* go	24$	BCCC$	Ind		
Film & TV Studies/Drama	W4W5	3FT deg	Ap+T g	20	MO $	M* go	28$	BBCC$	Ind		
History/Drama	VW14	3FT deg	T+H g	BC	MO $	M* go	26$	BBCC$	Ind		
Modern Drama Studies	W400	3FT deg	T g	14	MO	M$ go	26$	BCCC$	Ind		
Music/Drama	WW34	3FT deg	T g	BC	MO $	M* go	22$	BCCC$	Ind		
CARMARTHENSHIRE COLLEGE											
Performing Arts	134W	2FT HND		X	Ind	Ind	Ind	X	Ind		
Performing Arts	134E	2FT HND		X	Ind	Ind	Ind	X	Ind		
Univ of CENTRAL ENGLAND											
Three-Dimensional Design (Theatre Design)	E460	3FT deg	Fa/Pf	18	MO	M$	28	BBBB	Ind		
Three-Dimensional Design (Theatre Design)	W460	3FT deg	Fa/Pf	18	MO	M$	28	BBBB	Ind		
Univ of CENTRAL LANCASHIRE											
Acting	W410▼	3FT deg	*								
Performing Arts	W430	3FT deg	*								

17   Drama, Dance and Performance Arts

			98 expected requirements							96 entry stats	
course details											
TITLE	CODE	COURSE	SUBJECTS	A/AS	ND/C	AGNVQ	IB	SQA(H)	SQA	RATIO A/AS	

CENTRAL SCHOOL of Speech & Drama

TITLE	CODE	COURSE	SUBJECTS	A/AS	ND/C	AGNVQ	IB	SQA(H)	SQA	RATIO A/AS	
Drama and Education	XW94	3FT deg	g	BCC	Ind	Ind	30	BBBBC	Ind		
Theatre Practice:Des/Pupp/Crafts/StageMan/TecArt	WW24	3FT deg	Pf g	CC	Ind	Ind$^	Ind	CC	Ind		
Theatre Practice:Des/Pupp/Crafts/StageMan/TecArt	EW24	3FT deg	Pf g	CC	Ind	Ind$^	Ind	CC	Ind		

CHELTENHAM & GLOUCESTER COLL of HE

TITLE	CODE	COURSE	SUBJECTS	A/AS	ND/C	AGNVQ	IB	SQA(H)	SQA	RATIO A/AS	
English Studies and Performance Arts	QW34	3FT deg	E	10-14	4M+3D	M3	26	CCCC	Ind		
English Studies with Performance Arts	Q3W4	3FT deg	E	10-14	4M+3D	M3	26	CCCC	Ind		
Media Communications and Performance Arts	PW44	3FT deg	*	12	5M+2D	M3	26	CCCC	Ind		
Media Communications with Performance Arts	P4W4	3FT deg	*	12	5M+2D	M3	26	CCCC	Ind		
Performance Arts and Religious Studies	WV48	3FT deg	*	8-12	5M+2D	M3	26	CCCC	Ind		
Performance Arts and Sport & Exercise Sciences	WB46	3FT deg	*	12-16	4M+3D	M3	26	CCCC	Ind		
Performance Arts and Visual Arts	WW41	3FT deg	A	10-14	5M+2D	MA3	26	CCCC	Ind		
Performance Arts and Women's Studies	WM49	3FT deg	*	8-12	5M+2D	M3	26	CCCC	Ind		
Performance Arts with Combined Arts	W4Y3	3FT deg	*	10-14	5M+2D	M3	26	CCCC	Ind		
Performance Arts with English Studies	W4Q3	3FT deg	*	10-14	5M+2D	M3	26	CCCC	Ind		
Performance Arts with Media Communications	W4P4	3FT deg	*	10-14	5M+2D	M3	26	CCCC	Ind		
Performance Arts with Religious Studies	W4V8	3FT deg	*	10-14	5M+2D	M3	26	CCCC	Ind		
Performance Arts with Sport & Exercise Sciences	W4B6	3FT deg	*	10-14	5M+2D	M3	26	CCCC	Ind		
Performance Arts with Visual Arts	W4W1	3FT deg	*	10-14	5M+2D	MA3	26	CCCC	Ind		
Performance Arts with Women's Studies	W4M9	3FT deg	*	8-12	5M+2D	M3	26	CCCC	Ind		
Religious Studies with Performance Arts	V8W4	3FT deg	*	8-12	5M+2D	M3	26	CCCC	Ind		
Sport & Exercise Sciences with Performance Arts	B6W4	3FT deg	*	14	4M+3D	M3	26	CCCC	Ind		
Visual Arts with Performance Arts	W1W4	3FT deg	A	10-14	5M+2D	MA3	26	CCCC	Ind		
Women's Studies with Performance Arts	M9W4	3FT deg	*	10-12	5M+2D	M3	26	CCCC	Ind		

UNIVERSITY COLLEGE CHESTER

TITLE	CODE	COURSE	SUBJECTS	A/AS	ND/C	AGNVQ	IB	SQA(H)	SQA	RATIO A/AS	
Art and Drama and Theatre Studies	WW94	3FT deg	*	CC	M	P^	Ind	CCCC	$	11	
Art with Drama and Theatre Studies	W9W4	3FT deg	*	CC	M	P^	Ind	CCCC	$		
Biology and Drama and Theatre Studies	CW14	3FT deg	B	12	M	P^	Ind	CCCC	$		
Biology with Drama and Theatre Studies	C1W4	3FT deg	B	12	M	P^	Ind	CCCC	$		
Computer Science/IT & Drama and Theatre Studies	GW54	3FT deg	g	12	M	M	Ind	CCCC	$	5	
Computer Science/IT with Drama & Theatre Studies	G5W4	3FT deg	g	12	M	P^	Ind	CCCC	$		
Drama & Theatre Studies & Theology & Rel St	WV48	3FT deg	*	12	M	M	Ind	CCCC	$	5	
Drama and Theatre St with Theology and Rel St	W4V8	3FT deg	*	12	M	M	Ind	CCCC	$	13	
Drama and Theatre Studies and English Lit	WQ43	3FT deg	E	12	M	P^	Ind	CCCC	$	16	16/26
Drama and Theatre Studies and Geography	WF48	3FT deg	Gy/Gl	CC	M	P^	Ind	CCCC	$		
Drama and Theatre Studies and History	WV41	3FT deg	H	CC	M	P^	Ind	CCCC	$		
Drama and Theatre Studies and Mathematics	WG41	3FT deg	M	12	M	P^	Ind	CCCC	$	2	
Drama and Theatre Studies and PE/Sports Science	WB46	3FT deg	*	CC	M	P^	Ind	CCCC			
Drama and Theatre Studies and Psychology	WL47	3FT deg	g	12	M	P	Ind	CCCC	$	24	
Drama and Theatre Studies with Art	W4W9	3FT deg	*	CC	M	M	Ind	CCCC	$	14	
Drama and Theatre Studies with Biology	W4C1	3FT deg	B	12	M	P^	Ind	CCCC	$		
Drama and Theatre Studies with Computer Sc/IT	W4G5	3FT deg	g	12	M	M	Ind	CCCC	$	5	
Drama and Theatre Studies with English	W4Q3	3FT deg	E	CC	M	P^	Ind	CCCC	$	23	14/16
Drama and Theatre Studies with Geography	W4F8	3FT deg	Gy/Gl	CC	M	P^	Ind	CCCC	$		
Drama and Theatre Studies with History	W4V1	3FT deg	H/Ec/So	CC	M	P^	Ind	CCCC	$		
Drama and Theatre Studies with Mathematics	W4G1	3FT deg	M	12	M	P^	Ind	CCCC	$		
Drama and Theatre Studies with PE/Sports Science	W4B6	3FT deg	*	12	M	P^	Ind	CCCC	$		
Drama and Theatre Studies with Psychology	W4L7	3FT deg	g	12	M	M	Ind	CCCC	$	21	
Drama with French	W4R1	3FT deg	g	12	M	M	Ind	CCCC	$	9	
Drama with German	W4R2	3FT deg	g	12	M	M	Ind	CCCC	$	3	
English with Drama and Theatre Studies	Q3W4	3FT deg	E	CC	M	P^	Ind	CCCC	$	31	

			98 expected requirements							96 entry stats	

course details

TITLE	CODE	COURSE	SUBJECTS	A/AS	ND/C	AGNVQ	IB	SQA(H)	SQA	RATIO	A/AS
Geography with Drama and Theatre Studies	F8W4	3FT deg	Gy/Gl	CC	M	P^	Ind	CCCC	$		
History with Drama and Theatre Studies	V1W4	3FT deg	H/Ec/So	CC	M	M	Ind	CCCC	$	7	
Mathematics with Drama and Theatre Studies	G1W4	3FT deg	M	12	M	P^	Ind	CCCC	$	2	
PE/Sports Science with Drama and Theatre Studies	B6W4	3FT deg	*	12	M	P^	Ind	CCCC	$		
Psychology with Drama and Theatre Studies	L7W4	3FT deg	g	12	M	P^	Ind	CCCC	$	10	
Theology and Rel St with Drama and Theatre Studs	V8W4	3FT deg	*	12	M	M	Ind	CCCC	$		

CHICHESTER INSTITUTE OF HIGHER EDUCATION

Art and Dance	WW14	3FT deg	A+Pf	12	Ind	M$+^	Ind	Ind	Ind	3	
Art with Dance	E1W4	3FT deg	A+Pf	12	Ind	M$+^	Ind	Ind	Ind		
Art with Dance	W1W4	3FT deg	A+Pf	12	Ind	M$+^	Ind	Ind	Ind		
Dance	W400	3FT deg	Pf	12	Ind	M$+	Ind	Ind	Ind		
Dance and English Language Teaching (EFL)	WQ41	3FT deg	Pf	12	Ind	M$+	Ind	Ind	Ind		
Dance and Geography	LW84	3FT deg	Gy+Pf	12	Ind	M$+	Ind	Ind	Ind		
Dance and History	VW14	3FT deg	H+Pf	12	Ind	M$+	Ind	Ind	Ind		
Dance and Mathematics	GW14	3FT deg	M+Pf	12	Ind	M$+^	Ind	Ind	Ind		
Dance and Media Studies	PW44	3FT deg	Pf	12	Ind	M$+	Ind	Ind	Ind	14	
Dance and Study of Religions	VW84	3FT deg	Pf	12	Ind	M$+	Ind	Ind	Ind		
Dance and Theology	WV48	3FT deg	Pf	12	Ind	M$+	Ind	Ind	Ind		
Dance with Art	W4W1	3FT deg	Pf	12	Ind	M$+	Ind	Ind	Ind		
Dance with Education Studies (Opt. QTS) (P)	W4X9	3FT/4FT deg	Pf g	12	Ind	M$+ go	Ind	Ind	Ind	9	8/20
Dance with English Language Teaching (EFL)	W4Q1	3FT deg	Pf g	12	Ind	M$+	Ind	Ind	Ind		
Dance with Environmental Science	W4F9	3FT deg	Pf g	12	Ind	M$+	Ind	Ind	Ind		
Dance with Geography	W4L8	3FT deg	Pf	12	Ind	M$+	Ind	Ind	Ind		
Dance with History	W4V1	3FT deg	Pf	12	Ind	M$+	Ind	Ind	Ind		
Dance with Mathematics	W4G1	3FT deg	Pf g	12	Ind	M$+	Ind	Ind	Ind	2	
Dance with Media Studies	W4P4	3FT deg	Pf	12	Ind	M$+	Ind	Ind	Ind		
Dance with Music	W4W3	3FT deg	Pf	12	Ind	M$+	Ind	Ind	Ind		
Dance with Related Arts	W4W9	3FT deg	Pf	12	Ind	M$+	Ind	Ind	Ind	10	12/16
Dance with Study of Religions	W4V8	3FT deg	Pf	12	Ind	M$+	Ind	Ind	Ind		
Dance with Theology	W4VV	3FT deg	Pf	12	Ind	M$	Ind	Ind	Ind		
Geography with Dance	L8W4	3FT deg	Gy	12	Ind	M$	Ind	Ind	Ind		
History with Dance	V1W4	3FT deg	H	12	Ind	M$	Ind	Ind	Ind	2	
Mathematics with Dance	G1W4	3FT deg	M	12	Ind	M^	Ind	Ind	Ind		
Media Studies with Dance	P4W4	3FT deg		12							
Music with Dance	W3W4	3FT deg	Mu	12	Ind	M$+	Ind	Ind	Ind	3	
Related Arts and Dance	WW49	3FT deg	Pf	12	Ind	M$+	Ind	Ind	Ind		6/18
Study of Religions with Dance	V8W4	3FT deg	*	12	Ind	M$	Ind	Ind	Ind		
Theology with Dance	V8WK	3FT deg	Pf	12	Ind	M$	Ind	Ind	Ind		

CITY COLLEGE Manchester

Acting Studies	W410	4FT deg									
Technical Theatre Arts	W460	3FT deg									
Technical Theatre Arts	E460	3FT deg									

CITY of LIVERPOOL Comm COLL

Community Dance	054E	2FT HND									
Community Dance	054W	2FT HND									
Community Theatre	024W	2FT HND									
Community Theatre	024E	2FT HND									
Theatre Costume Interpretation	084E	2FT HND									
Theatre Costume Interpretation	084W	2FT HND									

TITLE	CODE	COURSE	SUBJECTS	A/AS	NO/C	RGNVQ	IB	SQA(H)	SQA	RATIO A/AS
COVENTRY Univ										
Dance and Professional Practice	W450	3FT deg	D/Pa g	12-20	MO+3D	Ind	Ind	Ind	Ind	
Theatre and Professional Practice	W420	3FT deg	T/Pa g	12-20	MO+4D$	Ind	Ind	Ind	Ind	
Theatre Practice	234W▼	2FT HND	* g	4-20	4M+3D$	Ind				10 4/14
CROYDON COLL										
Design (Theatre Studies)	WW42	3FT deg	Fa+Pf		N $	PA2/Q2				
Design (Theatre Studies)	EW42	3FT deg	Fa+Pf		N $	PA2/Q2				
Design (Theatre Studies)	024E	3SW HND	Fa+Pf		N $	PA/Q				
Design (Theatre Studies)	024W	3SW HND	Fa+Pf		N $	PA/Q				
DARTINGTON COLL of Arts										
Performance Writing	W433	3FT deg		BC	10M	Ind	26$	BBCC	Ind	3 10/18
Performance Writing with Arts Management	W4ND	3FT deg		BC	10M	Ind	26$	BBCC	Ind	2
Theatre	W420	3FT deg		BB	10M	Ind	26$	BBCC	Ind	7 8/26
Theatre with Arts Management	W4N1	3FT deg		BB	10M	Ind	26$	BBCC	Ind	17
DE MONTFORT Univ										
Contemporary Dance	W450▼	3FT deg	g	18	D	D^	28$	BBBB	Ind	13 8/20
Contemporary Theatre	W451▼	3FT deg	g	20	D $	D^	28$	BBBB	Ind	20 10/26
Dance and Drama in Contemporary Culture	W455▼	3FT deg	g	12	7M+5D	M	Ind	BBCCC	Ind	3 6/18
Performing Arts	W430▼	3FT deg	g	10-18	MO	Ind	28$	BBBB	Ind	1 14/20
Textiles Design and Production	E461▼	4SW deg	g	12	6M $	M	24$	BBB	N	
Humanities Combined Honours *Performing Arts*	Y300▼	3FT deg	* g	CCD	MO	M$^	26$	ABBB	Ind	
Humanities Joint Honours *Performing Arts*	Y301▼	3FT deg	* g	CCD	MO	M$^	28$	ABBB	Ind	
Clothing	074E▼	2FT HND	Fa g	6	N $	P	Dip	BB	$	
Performing Arts	234W▼	2FT HND		4	5M+1D	D	Ind	CCC	Ind	4 2/12
Univ of DERBY										
Performing and Media Arts	W430	3FT deg	*	12	MO	M	26	BCCC	Ind	6 10/24
Credit Accumulation Modular Scheme *Dance*	Y600	3FT deg	*	12	MO	M	Ind	CCCC	Ind	
Credit Accumulation Modular Scheme *Theatre Studies*	Y600	3FT deg	*	14	MO+1D	M$	28	BBCC	Ind	
DUDLEY COLLEGE of Technology										
Media	004E	2FT HND	* g	2	Ind	Ind				
Performing Arts	034E	2FT HND	* g	2	Ind	Ind				
Univ of DURHAM										
Performing Arts	W430	3FT deg	*	18	Ind	Ind	Dip	BBBB	Ind	
Univ of EAST ANGLIA										
Drama	W400	3FT deg	E	BBB-BBC	X		30	Ind	X	14 20/28
English Literature and Drama	WQ43	3FT deg	E	ABB-BBB	X		30$	AABBB	X	27 28/30
Univ of EAST LONDON										
Acting	W400	3FT deg	* g	12	MO	M	Ind	Ind	Ind	2 8/22
EDGE HILL Univ COLLEGE										
Art & Design and Drama	WW24	3FT deg	A	CC	3M+3D	MA / P*^	Dip	BBCC	Ind	
Communication Studies and Drama	PW34	3FT deg	*	CC	3M+3D	M* / P*^	Dip	BBCC	Ind	4 8/16
Drama	W400	3FT deg	*	CC	3M+3D	M* / P*^	Dip	BBCC	Ind	
Drama and Applied Social Sciences	LW34	3FT deg	*	CC	3M+3D	M* / P*^	Dip	BBCC	Ind	
Drama and English	QW34	3FT deg	E	CC	X	P*^	Dip	BBCC$	X	7 8/20

Drama, Dance and Performance Arts　　17

TITLE	CODE	COURSE	SUBJECTS	A/AS	ND/C	RGNVQ	IB	SQA(H)	SQA	RATIO	A/AS
Univ of EXETER											
Arts in Society	WW49	3FT deg	*	CC-DD	MO	M$	28	Ind	Ind		
Drama	W400	3FT deg	*	BBC	MO+3D	M/D$	34	Ind	Ind	15	16/30
English and Drama	QW34	3FT deg	E	BBB-BCC	MO+3D	M/D$^	32$	Ind	Ind	27	24/28
German and Drama	RW24	4FT deg	G	BBB-BCC	MO+3D	M/D$^	32$	Ind	Ind		
Spanish and Drama (Beginners Spanish available)	RW44	4FT deg	Sp	BBC	MO+3D	M/D$^	34$	Ind	Ind	18	
Univ of GLAMORGAN											
English Studies and Theatre & Media Drama	QW34	3FT deg	Me/T/E g	14	Ind	Ind	Ind	Ind	Ind		
English Studies with Theatre and Media Drama	Q3W4	3FT deg	Me/T/E g	14	Ind	Ind	Ind	Ind	Ind		
Humanities (Theatre and Media Drama)	W401	3FT deg	* g	CC	5M	M$	24	CCCC	HN	1	6/16
Media Studies and Theatre & Media Drama	PW44	3FT deg	Me/T/E g	14	Ind	Ind	Ind	Ind	Ind		
Media Studies with Theatre and Media Drama	P4W4	3FT deg	Me/T/E g	14	Ind	Ind	Ind	Ind	Ind		
Psychology and Theatre & Media Drama	LW74	3FT deg	T/E g	14	Ind	Ind	Ind	Ind	Ind		
Theatre and Media Drama	W403	3FT deg	E/T g	CB	5M	M$	26	BCC	HN	5	14/26
Theatre and Media Drama and Visual Arts	WW14	3FT deg	T/E/Me+A g	14	Ind	Ind	Ind	Ind	Ind		
Theatre and Media Drama with Media Studies	W4P4	3FT deg	T/E/Me g	14	Ind	Ind	Ind	Ind	Ind		
Combined Studies (Honours) 　　Theatre & Media Drama	Y400	3FT deg	Me/T/E g	8-16	Ind	Ind	Ind	Ind	Ind		
Joint Honours 　　Theatre & Media Drama	Y401	3FT deg	Me/T/E g	8-16	Ind	Ind	Ind	Ind	Ind		
Major/Minor Honours 　　Theatre & Media Drama	Y402	3FT deg	Me/T/E g	8-16	Ind	Ind	Ind	Ind	Ind		
Univ of GLASGOW											
Archaeology/Theatre Studies	VW64	4FT deg		BBC	HN	M	30	BBBB	Ind		
Classical Hebrew/Theatre Studies	VWW4	4FT deg		BBC	HN	M	30	BBBB	Ind		
Computing/Theatre Studies	GW54	4FT deg		BBC	HN	M	30	BBBB	Ind		
Czech/Theatre Studies	TW14	5FT deg		BBC	HN	M	30	BBBB	Ind		
Islamic Studies/Theatre Studies	TW64	4FT deg		BBC	N	M	30	BBBB	Ind		
Social and Urban Policy/Theatre Studies	LW44	4FT deg		BBC	HN	M	30	BBBB	Ind		
Theatre Studies/Classical Hebrew	QW94	4FT deg		BBC	HN	M	30	BBBB	Ind		
Theatre Studies/Economic History	VW34	4FT deg		BBC	HN	M	30	BBBB	Ind		
Theatre Studies/Economics	LW14	4FT deg		BBC	HN	M	30	BBBB	Ind		
Theatre Studies/English	QW34	4FT deg		BBC	HN	M	30	BBBB	Ind	6	22/28
Theatre Studies/Film and Television Studies	WW45	4FT deg		BBB	HN	D	32	AABB	HN	11	24/28
Theatre Studies/French	RW14	5FT deg		BBC	HN	M	30	BBBB	Ind	3	
Theatre Studies/Geography	LW84	4FT deg		BBC	HN	M	30	BBBB	Ind		
Theatre Studies/German	RW24	5FT deg		BBC	HN	M	30	BBBB	Ind		
Theatre Studies/Greek	QW74	4FT deg		BBC	HN	M	30	BBBB	Ind		
Theatre Studies/Hispanic Studies	RW44	5FT deg		BBC	HN	M	30	BBBB	Ind		
Theatre Studies/History	VW14	4FT deg		BBC	HN	M	30	BBBB	Ind	3	
Theatre Studies/History of Art	VW44	4FT deg		BBC	HN	M	30	BBBB	Ind	6	
Theatre Studies/Italian	RW34	5FT deg		BBC	HN	M	30	BBBB	Ind		
Theatre Studies/Latin	QW64	4FT deg		BBC	HN	M	30	BBBB	Ind	1	
Theatre Studies/Mathematics	GWC4	4FT deg		BBC	HN	M	30	BBBB	Ind		
Theatre Studies/Music	WW34	4FT deg		BBC	HN	M	30	BBBB	Ind	12	
Theatre Studies/Philosophy	VW74	4FT deg		BBC	HN	M	30	BBBB	Ind	7	
Theatre Studies/Polish	TWC4	5FT deg		BBC	HN	M	30	BBBB	Ind		
Theatre Studies/Politics	MW14	4FT deg		BBC	HN	M	30	BBBB	Ind	7	
Theatre Studies/Psychology	CW84	4FT deg		BBC	HN	M	30	BBBB	Ind	9	
Theatre Studies/Russian	RW84	5FT deg		BBC	HN	M	30	BBBB	Ind		
Theatre Studies/Scottish History	VWC4	4FT deg		BBC	HN	M	30	BBBB	Ind		
Theatre Studies/Scottish Literature	QW24	4FT deg		BBC	HN	M	30	BBBB	Ind	5	

TITLE	CODE	COURSE	SUBJECTS	A/AS	ND/C	AGNVQ	IB	SQA(H)	SQA	RATIO	A/AS
Theatre Studies/Sociology	LW34	4FT deg		BBC	HN	M	30	BBBB	Ind	5	
Theology & Religious Studies/Theatre Studies	VWV4	4FT deg		BBC	HN	M	30	BBBB	Ind		

GLOUCESTERSHIRE COLLEGE of Arts and Technology

TITLE	CODE	COURSE	SUBJECTS	A/AS	ND/C	AGNVQ	IB	SQA(H)	SQA	RATIO	A/AS
Performing Arts	034W	2FT HND	* g	E	N	P			Ind		

GOLDSMITHS COLL (Univ of London)

TITLE	CODE	COURSE	SUBJECTS	A/AS	ND/C	AGNVQ	IB	SQA(H)	SQA	RATIO	A/AS
Drama and Theatre Arts	W420	3FT deg		BBC	DO	D	Dip	ABBBB	N	27	18/30
English and Theatre Arts	QW34	3FT deg	E	BBC	MO	M	Dip	ABBBB	N	8	14/30

Univ of HERTFORDSHIRE

TITLE	CODE	COURSE	SUBJECTS	A/AS	ND/C	AGNVQ	IB	SQA(H)	SQA	RATIO	A/AS
Performing Arts (Recruits from 234W)	W430▼	3FT deg	*	X	Ind	Ind	X	X	X	4	6/20
Design and Creative Arts	42WE▼	2FT HND									
Performing Arts	234W▼	2FT HND	*		Ind	Ind	Ind	Ind	Ind	9	4/16

Univ of HUDDERSFIELD

TITLE	CODE	COURSE	SUBJECTS	A/AS	ND/C	AGNVQ	IB	SQA(H)	SQA	RATIO	A/AS
Music with Theatre Studies (Practical Quals Req)	W3W4	3FT deg	Mu	CC	Ind	Ind	Ind	BBC	Ind		
Theatre Studies	W420	3FT deg	*	CCC	3M+4D	M$^	Ind	BBBC	Ind		
Theatre Studies and Media	WP44	3FT deg	*	CCC	3M+4D	M$^	Ind	BBBC	Ind		
Theatre Studies with Music	W4W3	3FT deg	Mu	CCC	3M+4D	Ind	Ind	BBBC	Ind		

Univ of HULL

TITLE	CODE	COURSE	SUBJECTS	A/AS	ND/C	AGNVQ	IB	SQA(H)	SQA	RATIO	A/AS
American Studies/Drama	QW44	3FT deg	E/T	BBB-BCC	Ind	D$^ go	30	AAABB	Ind		
Drama	W400	3FT deg	*	BBB-BCC	3M+4D	D$^ go	28	BBBCC	Ind	9	16/28
Drama/English	QW34	3FT deg	E	BBB-BCC	Ind	D$^ go	30	AAABB	Ind	19	24/30
Drama/French	RW14	4FT deg	F	BBB-BCC	Ind	D$_^ go	28$	ABBCC	Ind	27	
Drama/German	RW24	4FT deg	G	BBB-BCC	Ind	D$_^ go	28$	ABBCC	Ind		
Drama/Italian	RW34	4FT deg	L	BBB-BCC	Ind	D$_^ go	28$	ABBCC	Ind		
Drama/Music (Practical Standards Req)	WW34	3FT deg	Mu	BBB-BCC	Ind	D$_^ go	28$	BBCCC	Ind	10	
Drama/Theology	VW84	3FT deg		BBB-BCC	Ind	D$^ go	28	BBBCC	Ind		

Univ of KENT

TITLE	CODE	COURSE	SUBJECTS	A/AS	ND/C	AGNVQ	IB	SQA(H)	SQA	RATIO	A/AS
Drama and Theatre Studies	W421	4FT deg	*	24	1M+5D	Ind	32	Ind	Ind	8	20/26
Drama/Classical Studies	QW84	3FT deg	*	22	2M+4D	Ind	30	Ind	Ind		
Drama/Comparative Literary Studies	QWF4	3FT deg	*	22	2M+4D	Ind	30	Ind	Ind	3	
Drama/Computing	WG45	3FT deg	*	22	2M+4D	Ind	30	Ind	Ind		
English (Post-Colonial Literatures)/Drama	WQ4J	3FT deg	E	24	1M+5D	Ind	32$	Ind	Ind		
English Language/Drama	WQ43	3FT deg	E	22	2M+4D	Ind	30	Ind	Ind	4	22/24
English/Drama	QW34	3FT deg	E	24	1M+5D	Ind	32	Ind	Ind	10	18/28
European Studies/Drama	TW24	4FT deg	L	22	2M+4D	Ind	30	Ind	Ind	3	
Film Studies/Drama	WWK5	3FT deg	*	24	1M+5D	Ind	32	Ind	Ind	9	22/26
French/Drama	RW14	4FT deg	F	22	2M+4D	Ind	30	Ind	Ind	20	
German/Drama	RW24	4FT deg	G	22	2M+4D	Ind	30	Ind	Ind		
History and Theory of Art/Drama	VW44	3FT deg	*	22	2M+4D	Ind	30	Ind	Ind	9	
History/Drama	VW14	3FT deg	*	22	2M+4D	Ind	30	Ind	Ind	10	
Italian/Drama	RW34	4FT deg	*	22	2M+4D	Ind	30	Ind	Ind	8	
Linguistics/Drama	WQ41	3FT deg	*	22	2M+4D	Ind	30	Ind	Ind		
Philosophy/Drama	VW74	3FT deg	*	22	2M+4D	Ind	30	Ind	Ind		
Spanish/Drama	WR44	4FT deg	*	22	2M+4D	Ind	30	Ind	Ind		
Theology/Drama	VW84	3FT deg	*	22	2M+4D	Ind	30	Ind	Ind	2	

KIDDERMINSTER COLL

TITLE	CODE	COURSE	SUBJECTS	A/AS	ND/C	AGNVQ	IB	SQA(H)	SQA	RATIO	A/AS
Performing Arts (Theatre and Education)	94XW	2FT HND	T	BC	Ind		Ind	Ind	Ind	4	
Performing Arts (Theatre and Education)	94XE	2FT HND	T	BC	Ind		Ind	Ind	Ind		

TITLE	CODE	COURSE	SUBJECTS	A/AS	NO/C	RGNVQ	IB	SQA(H)	SQA	RATIO A/AS
course details			**98 expected requirements**							**96 entry stats**
KING ALFRED'S WINCHESTER										
Dance Studies and Contemporary Cultural Studies	MW9K	3FT deg	* g	14	6M	M	24	BCC	N	4
Drama Studies and American Studies	QW44	3FT deg	* g	14	6M	M	24	BCC	N	2 8/16
Drama Studies and Business Studies	NW14	3FT deg	* g	14	6M	M	24	BCC	N	2 12/16
Drama Studies and Contemporary Cultural Studies	MW94	3FT deg	* g	14	6M	M	24	BCC	N	3
Drama Studies and Dance Studies	W430	3FT deg	* g	14	6M	M	24	BCC	N	3 10/20
Drama, Theatre and Television Studies	W4W5	3FT deg	* g	20-24	MO $	D	24	BBB	X	13 14/24
Education Studies and Dance Studies	WXK9	3FT deg	* g	14	6M	M	24	BCC	N	15
Education Studies and Drama Studies	WX49	3FT deg	* g	14	6M	M	24	BCC	N	4
English Studies and Drama Studies	QW34	3FT deg	E	14	X	X	24$	BCC$	X	3 8/24
Geography and Drama Studies	LW84	3FT deg	Gy g	14	X	X	24$	BCC$	X	6
History and Drama Studies	VW14	3FT deg	H g	14	X	X	24$	BCC$	X	20
Media & Film Studies and Dance Studies	PW4K	3FT deg	* g	14	6M	M	24	BCC	N	9
Media & Film Studies and Drama Studies	PW44	3FT deg	* g	14	6M	M	24	BCC	N	5 10/18
Music (World) and Dance Studies	WW3K	3FT deg	* g	14	6M	M	24	BCC	N	2
Music (World) and Drama Studies	WW34	3FT deg	* g	14	6M	M	24	BCC	N	2
Performing Arts	W431	3FT deg	* g	14	6M	M	24	BCC	N	
Psychology and Dance Studies	LW7K	3FT deg	* g	14	6M	M	24	BCC	N	7
Psychology and Drama Studies	LW74	3FT deg	* g	14	6M	M	24	BCC	N	3 8/20
Sports Studies and Dance Studies	WLKH	3FT deg	* g	14	6M	M	24	BCC	N	
Visual Studies and Drama Studies	WW24	3FT deg								
LANCASTER Univ										
French Studies and Theatre Studies	WR41	4SW deg	F	BCC	MO $		30$	BBBBB$	Ind	
German Studies and Theatre Studies	WR42	4SW deg	G/L	BCC	MO $		30$	BBBBB$	Ind	
Independent Studies and Theatre Studies	YW44	3FT deg	*	BBC	Ind		Ind	Ind	Ind	
Italian Studies and Theatre Studies	WR43	4SW deg	I/L	BCC	MO $		30$	BBBBB$	Ind	
Spanish Studies and Theatre Studies	WR44	4SW deg	Sp/L	BCC	MO $		30$	BBBBB$	Ind	
Theatre Studies	W420	3FT deg	*	BBC	Ind		32	ABBBB	Ind	
Theatre Studies and Educational Studies	WX49	3FT deg	*	BBC	Ind		32	BBBBB	Ind	
Theatre Studies and English	WQ43	3FT deg	E g	BBC	Ind $		32$	BBBBB$	Ind	
Theatre Studies and Religious Studies	WV48	3FT deg	*	BBC-BCC	Ind		30	BBBBB	Ind	
Univ of LEEDS										
English Literature and Theatre Studies	QW34	3FT/4FT deg	E g	ABB	Ind	X	33$	CSYS	Ind	8 22/30
Univ of LINCOLNSHIRE and HUMBERSIDE										
Media Production	024E▼	2FT HND	g	6	2M	M	Ind	CCC	Ind	
LIVERPOOL HOPE Univ COLL										
Drama & Theatre Studies/American Studies	QW44	3FT deg	g	12	8M	M$ go	Ind	Ind	Ind	5
Drama & Theatre Studies/Art	WW94	3FT deg	A/Fa g	12	8M	MA /P*△ go	Ind	Ind	Ind	9
English/Drama & Theatre Studies	WQ43	3FT deg	El g	12	8M	P*△	Ind	Ind	Ind	7 12/20
European Studies/Drama & Theatre Studies	WT42	3FT deg	g	12	8M	M* go	Ind	Ind	Ind	
Geography/Drama & Theatre Studies	WF48	3FT deg	Gy g	12	8M	M$ go	Ind	Ind	Ind	3
History/Drama & Theatre Studies	WV41	3FT deg	H g	12	8M	P*△ go	Ind	Ind	Ind	16
Human & Applied Biology/Drama & Theatre Studies	CW14	3FT deg	B g	12	8M	MS /P*△ go	Ind	Ind	Ind	4
Information Technology/Drama & Theatre Studies	GW54	3FT deg	g	12	8M	M* go	Ind	Ind	Ind	9
Mathematics/Drama & Theatre Studies	WG41	3FT deg	M g	12	8M	P*△ go	Ind	Ind	Ind	
Music/Drama & Theatre Studies	WW43	3FT deg	Mu g	12	8M	MQ /P*△ go	Ind	Ind	Ind	3 10/20
Psychology/Drama & Theatre Studies	WC48	3FT deg	g	12	8M	M* go	Ind	Ind	Ind	13
Sport, Recreation & P.E./Drama & Theatre Studies	WB46	3FT deg	g	12	8M	M* go	Ind	Ind	Ind	
Theology & Religious Studies/Drama & Theatre St	WV48	3FT deg	g	12	8M	M* go	Ind	Ind	Ind	8

TITLE	CODE	COURSE	SUBJECTS	A/AS	ND/C	RGNVQ	IB	SQA(H)	SQA	RATIO A/AS
course details			**98 expected requirements**							**96 entry stats**
THE LIVERPOOL INSTITUTE FOR PERORMING ARTS										
Performing Arts	W431	3FT deg			Ind	Ind	Ind	Ind	Ind	
LIVERPOOL JOHN MOORES Univ										
Dance and Community Sport/Dance	WN47	3FT deg		12	5D	M	28$	CCCC		
Dance and Drama	W450	3FT deg	T	18	7D	X	28$	BBCC		
Drama	W400	3FT deg	T	18	7D	X	28$	BBCC		40	18/26
Theatre St & Lit, Life & Thought (Th St Jnt Awd)	QW34	3FT deg	E+T	BB	7D	X	28$	BBBC		8	12/20
Theatre St and Media & Cultural St(Th St Jt Awd)	PW44	3FT deg	T	BB	7D	X	28$	BBBC		9	14/20
Theatre Studies & Screen Studies (SS Jnt Awd)	WW54	3FT deg	T+E	BB	7D	X	28$	BBCC		19	
Theatre Studies and Imaginative Writing	WW94	3FT deg	E+T	BB	7D	X	28$	BBCC		7	12/20
LONDON INST										
Costume and Make up for the Performing Arts	E495	3FT deg								
Design Technology for the Fashion Industry	E470	3FT deg								
History of Art & Design	E400	3FT deg								
Theatre Design	E460	3FT deg								
LOUGHBOROUGH COLLEGE of A & D										
History of Art and Design with Studio Practice	E480	3FT deg								
LOUGHBOROUGH Univ										
Drama	W400	3FT deg	*	22	4D		30	Ind		14	18/26
Drama with English	W4Q3	3FT deg	*	22			30	Ind		5	20/28
LUTON Univ										
Media Performance	W430	3FT deg	Pf g	12-16	MO/DO	M/D	32	BBCC	Ind	4	6/18
Media Performance with Animation	W4WF	3FT deg	Pf g	12-16	MO/DO	M/D	32	BBCC	Ind	
Media Performance with Design	W4W2	3FT deg		12-16	MO/DO	M/D	32	BBCC	Ind	
Media Performance with Journalism	W4P6	3FT deg	Pf g	12-16	MO/DO	M/D	32	BBCC	Ind	
Media Performance with Performance Management	W4N9	3FT deg		12-16	MO/DO	M/D	32	BBCC	Ind	
Media Performance with Photography	W4WN	3FT deg		12-16	MO/DO	M/D	32	BBCC	Ind	
Media Performance with Radio	WW4M	3FT deg		12-16	MO/DO	M/D	32	BBCC	Ind	
Media Performance with Scriptwriting	W4PP	3FT deg		12-16	MO/DO	M/D	32	BBCC	Ind	
Media Performance with TV Studies	WW45	3		12-16	MO/DO	M/D	32	BBCC	Ind	
Media Performance with Video Production	W4W5	3FT deg	Pf g	12-16	MO/DO	M/D	32	BBCC	Ind	
Media Performancewith Film Studies	W4WM	3FT deg		12-16	MO/DO	M/D	32	BBCC	Ind	
Univ of MANCHESTER										
Drama	W400	3FT deg	El	BBC	4M+6D		32	AAABB	HN$	18	22/30
Drama and Screen Studies	WW45	3FT deg	El	BBC	4M+6D		32	AAABB	HN$	
Drama with English	W4Q3	4FT deg	E	BBB	4M+6D		32	AAABB	HN$	33	26/30
English and Drama	WQ43	4FT deg	E	BBB	4M+6D		32	AAABB	HN$	25	26/30
Music and Drama	WW34	3FT deg	Mu+E	BBC-BBB			30$	BBBBB		17	
MANCHESTER METROPOLITAN Univ										
Dance/American Studies	QW44	3FT deg	*	CC	M+D	D	28	CCCC	Ind	
Dance/Applied Social Studies	LW34	3FT deg	*	CC	M+D	D	28	CCCC	Ind	
Dance/Business Studies	NW14	3FT deg	*	CC	M+D	D	28	CCCC	Ind	
Dance/Cultural Studies	LWH4	3FT deg	*	CC	M+D	D	28	CCCC	Ind	
Drama/American Studies	QW4K	3FT deg	*	CC	M+D	D	28	CCCC	Ind	
Drama/Applied Social Studies	LW3K	3FT deg	*	CC	M+D	D	28	CCCC	Ind	
Drama/Business Studies	NW1K	3FT deg	*	CC	M+D	D	28	CCCC	Ind	
Drama/Cultural Studies	LWHK	3FT deg	*	CC	M+D	D	28	CCCC	Ind	
Drama/Dance	WW2K	3FT deg	*	DD	M+D	DQ	28	CCCC	Ind	
English/Dance	QW3K	3FT deg	*	CC	M+D	D	28	CCCC	Ind	

Drama, Dance and Performance Arts 17

course details			98 expected requirements							96 entry stats	
TITLE	CODE	COURSE	SUBJECTS	A/AS	ND/C	AGNVQ	IB	SQA(H)	SQA	RATIO	A/AS
English/Drama	QWH4	3FT deg	*	CC	M+D	D	28	CCCC	Ind		
Geography/Drama	LW8K	3FT deg	*	CC	M+D	D	28	CCCC	Ind		
Health Studies/Dance	BW94	3FT deg	*	CC	M+D	D	28	CCCC	Ind		
Health Studies/Drama	BW9K	3FT deg	*	CC	M+D	D	28	CCCC	Ind		
History/Dance	VW14	3FT deg	*	CC	M+D	D	28	CCCC	Ind		
History/Drama	VW1K	3FT deg	*	CC	M+D	D	28	CCCC	Ind		
Leisure Studies/Dance	LW44	3FT deg	*	CC	M+D	D	28	CCCC	Ind		
Leisure Studies/Drama	LW4K	3FT deg	*	CC	M+D	D	28	CCCC	Ind		
Music/Dance	WW34	3FT deg	*	DD	M+D	D	28	CCCC	Ind		
Music/Drama	WW3K	3FT deg	*	DD	M+D	D	28	CCCC	Ind		
Philosophy/Dance	VW74	3FT deg	*	CC	M+D	D	28	CCCC	Ind		
Philosophy/Drama	VW7K	3FT deg	*	CC	M+D	D	28	CCCC	Ind		
Religious Studies/Dance	VW84	3FT deg	*	CC	M+D	D	28	CCCC	Ind		
Religious Studies/Drama	VW8K	3FT deg	*	CC	M+D	D	28	CCCC	Ind		
Sport/Dance	BW64	3FT deg	S	BC	M+D	DS	28	CCCC	Ind		
Sport/Drama	BW6K	3FT deg	S	BC	M+D	DS	28	CCCC	Ind		
Theatre Arts (Acting)	W411	3FT deg	*	CC	Ind		Ind	Ind	Ind		10/30
Visual Arts/Dance	WW14	3FT deg	*	DD	M+D	DQ/A	28	CCCC	Ind		
Visual Arts/Drama	WW1K	3FT deg	*	DD	M+D	DQ/A	28	CCCC	Ind		
Writing/American Studies	QW4L	3FT deg	*	CC	M+D	D	28	CCCC	Ind		
Writing/Applied Social Studies	LW3L	3FT deg	*	CC	M+D	D	28	CCCC	Ind		
Writing/Business Studies	NW1L	3FT deg	*	CC	M+D	D	28	CCCC	Ind		
Writing/Cultural Studies	LWHL	3FT deg	*	CC	M+D	D	28	CCCC	Ind		
Writing/Dance	WW4L	3FT deg	*	DD	M+D	DQ/A	28	CCCC	Ind		
Writing/Drama	WWLK	3FT deg	*	DD	M+D	DQ/A	28	CCCC	Ind		
Writing/English	QW3L	3FT deg	*	CC	M+D	D	28	CCCC	Ind		
Writing/Geography	LW8L	3FT deg	*	CC	M+D	D	28	CCCC	Ind		
Writing/Health Studies	BW9L	3FT deg	*	CC	M+D	D	28	CCCC	Ind		
Writing/History	VW1L	3FT deg	*	CC	M+D	D	28	CCCC	Ind		
Writing/Leisure Studies	LW4L	3FT deg	*	CC	M+D	D	28	CCCC	Ind		
Writing/Music	WW3L	3FT deg	*	DD	M+D	DQ/A	28	CCCC	Ind		
Writing/Philosophy	VW7L	3FT deg	*	CC	M+D	D	28	CCCC	Ind		
Writing/Religious Studies	VW8L	3FT deg	*	CC	M+D	D	28	CCCC	Ind		
Writing/Sport	BW6L	3FT deg	*	CC	M+D	D	28	CCCC	Ind		
Writing/Visual Arts	WW1L	3FT deg	*	DD	M+D	DQ/A	28	CCCC	Ind		
MIDDLESEX Univ											
Acting	W411▼	3FT deg	*	Ind	Ind	Ind	Ind	Ind	Ind		
Acting	W410▼	3FT deg	* g	16	5M	Ind	Ind	Ind	Ind		
Dance	W455▼	3FT deg	D g	12-16	5M	MQ go	Ind	Ind	Ind		
Dance Performance	W450▼	3FT deg	D g	12-16	5M	MQ go	Ind	Ind	Ind		
Drama & Theatre Studies	W400▼	3FT deg	T/E g	12-16	5M	X	Ind	Ind	Ind		
Performing Arts - Dance	W430▼	3FT deg	D	12-16	3M+2D	MQ go	Ind	Ind	Ind		
Performing Arts - Drama	W431▼	3FT deg	T/E	12-16	3M+2D	MQ go	Ind	Ind	Ind		
Performing Arts - Music	WW34▼	3FT deg	Mu	12-16	3M+2D	MQ go	Ind	Ind	Ind		
Technical Theatre Arts	W443▼	3FT deg	T	12-16	5M	Ind	Ind	Ind	Ind		
Theatre Dance	W4W3▼	3FT deg	D		Ind	Ind	Ind	Ind	Ind		
Joint Honours Degree *Dance*	Y400	3FT deg	D g	12-16	5M	X	Ind	Ind	Ind		
Joint Honours Degree *Drama & Theatre Arts*	Y400	3FT deg	T/E g	12-16	5M	X	Ind	Ind	Ind		
Media Studies	004E▼	2FT HND									

course details | 98 expected requirements | 96 entry stats

TITLE	CODE	COURSE	SUBJECTS	A/AS	NO/C	AGNVQ	IB	SQA(H)	SQA	RATIO	R/AS
NENE COLLEGE											
American Studies with Drama	Q4W4	3FT deg		DD	5M	M	24	CCC	Ind		
Art and Design with Drama	W2W4	3FT deg		DD	5M	M	24	CCC	Ind		8/14
Drama with American Studies	W4Q4	3FT deg		10	5M+1D	M	24	CCC	Ind		
Drama with Art and Design	W4W2	3FT deg		10	5M+1D	M	24	CCC	Ind		
Drama with English	W4Q3	3FT deg		10	5M+1D	M	24	CCC	Ind		6/14
Drama with French	W4R1	3FT deg	F	10	5M+1D	M	24	CCC	Ind		
Drama with Geography	W4F8	3FT deg		10	5M+1D	M	24	CCC	Ind		
Drama with History	W4V1	3FT deg		10	5M+1D	M	24	CCC	Ind		
Drama with Information Systems	W4G5	3FT deg		10	5M+1D	M	24	CCC	Ind		
Drama with Law	W4M3	3FT deg									
Drama with Marketing Communications	W4N5	3FT deg		10	5M+1D	M	24	CCC	Ind		
Drama with Media and Popular Culture	W4P4	3FT deg		10	5M+1D	M	24	CCC	Ind		6/22
Drama with Music	W4W3	3FT deg	Mu	10	5M+1D	M	24	CCC	Ind		
Drama with Personal and Organisational Develop	W4N6	3FT deg		10	5M+1D	M	24	CCC	Ind		
Drama with Politics	W4M1	3FT deg		10	5M+1D	M	24	CCC	Ind		
Drama with Psychology	W4C8	3FT deg	g	10	5M+1D	M	24	CCC	Ind		6/16
English with Drama	Q3W4	3FT deg		CC	4M+1D	M	24	CCC	Ind		12/16
French with Drama	R1W4	3FT deg	F	DD	5M	Ind	24	CCC	Ind		
History with Drama	V1W4	3FT deg		CD	5M	M	24	CCC	Ind		
Music with Drama	W3W4	3FT deg	Mu	DD	5M	M	24	CCC	Ind		6/16
Performance Studies	W432	3FT deg		10	5M+1D	M	24	CCC	Ind		7/16
Psychology with Drama	C8W4	3FT deg	g	CC	5M+1D	M	24	CCC	Ind		
NEWCASTLE COLL											
Music Theatre	033W▼	2FT HND									
Performing Arts (Dance)	054W▼	2FT HND									
Performing Arts (Drama)	004W▼	2FT HND									
Performing Arts (Theatre and Media Production)	044W▼	2FT HND									
NEWMAN COLLEGE OF HIGHER EDUCATION											
Expressive English & Physical Ed. & Sports Stds.	WX4X	3FT deg	*	CC	3M	M*	Dip	CCC	Ind		
Expressive English & Social & Applied Psychology	LW74	3FT deg	*	CC	3M	M*	Dip	CCC	Ind		
Expressive English and Biological Science	CW14	3FT deg	*	CC	3M	M*	Dip	CCC	Ind		
Expressive English and Geography	FW84	3FT deg	*	CC	3M	M*	Dip	CCC	Ind		
History and Expressive English	WV41	3FT deg	*	CC	3M	M*	Dip	CCC	Ind		
Information Technology and Expressive English	GW54	3FT deg	*	CC	3M	M*	Dip	CCC	Ind		
Theology and Expressive English	VW84	3FT deg	*	CC	3M	M*	Dip	CCC	Ind		
NORTHBROOK COLLEGE Sussex											
Design (Theatre Studies)	064E	2FT HND	Fa		N	P$	Ind	Ind	Ind		
Performing Arts - Community Performance	034E	2FT HND	*		N	Ind	Ind	Ind	Ind		
Performing Arts - Stage Management	074E	2FT HND		2	N	Ind	Ind	Ind	Ind		
NESCOT											
Performing Arts	034W	2FT HND	T/Pa	D	6M	M	Dip	Ind	N$	6	4/7
Univ of NORTH LONDON											
Communication & Cultural Studies & Theatre Studs	LW64	3FT deg	Me/Cm/E/So	CC	MO	M	Ind	Ind	Ind	9	
Performing Arts	W430	3FT deg	D/T	CC	Ind	Ind	Ind	Ind	Ind		8/16
Theatre Studies and Arts Management	NWC4	3FT deg	*g	CC	MO+4D	D	Ind	Ind	Ind		
Combined Honours *Theatre Studies*	Y300	3FT deg	T/E	CC	Ind	Ind	Ind	Ind	Ind		

TITLE	CODE	COURSE	SUBJECTS	A/AS	ND/C	AGNVQ	IB	SQA(H)	SQA	RATIO	A/AS
Univ of NORTHUMBRIA											
Drama	W400	3FT deg		BC	MO+1D		24	BCC	Ind	13	8/18
NORTHUMBERLAND COLLEGE											
Design (Communications) Television Operations	54WW	2FT HND	2(Ad/M/E)	BE-BBC	N	P	Ind	Ind	Ind		
Design (Communications) Television Operations	54WE	2FT HND	2(Ad/M/E)	BE-BBC	N	P	Ind	Ind	Ind		
NOTTINGHAM TRENT Univ											
Contemporary Arts	W431	3FT deg	D/Mu/E/T g	12	Ind	Ind	Ind	Ind	Ind	7	10/20
Theatre Design	E460	3FT deg	Fa/A g		Ind	Ind	Ind	Ind	Ind		
Univ of PLYMOUTH											
Art History with Theatre & Performance Studies	V4W4	3FT deg	Ap g	CCD	MO+3D	D$^	Ind	Ind	Ind	6	
Cult Interpret & Practice with Theatre Perf St	Y3W4	3FT deg	Ap g	CCD	MO+3D	D$^	Ind	Ind	Ind		
English with Theatre and Performance Studies	Q3W4	3FT deg	Ap g	BBC	MO+3D	D$^	Ind	Ind	Ind	8	14/22
Heritage and Landscape with Theatre & Perfor St	W2WL	3FT deg	Ap g	CCD	MO+3D	D$^	Ind	Ind	Ind	2	
History with Theatre and Performance Studies	V1W4	3FT deg	Ap g	CCD	MO+3D	D$^	Ind	Ind	Ind		
Media Arts with Theatre & Performance Studies	W2WK	3FT deg	Ap g	CCD	MO+3D	D$^	Ind	Ind	Ind	12	14/20
Theatre & Perf St with Cult Interpret & Practice	W4Y3	3FT deg	Ap g	CCD	MO+3D	D$^	Ind	Ind	Ind		
Theatre & Perfor St with Heritage & Landscape	W4WF	3FT deg	Ap g	CCD	MO+3D	D$^	Ind	Ind	Ind	2	
Theatre & Performance St with Visual Arts	W4W2	3FT deg	Ap g	CCD	MO+3D	D$^	Ind	Ind	Ind	8	16/22
Theatre & Performance Studs with Art History	W4V4	3FT deg	Ap g	CCD	MO+3D	D$^	Ind	Ind	Ind	6	
Theatre and Performance St with Education St	W4X9	3FT deg	Ap g	CCD	MO+3D	D$^	Ind	Ind	Ind	4	
Theatre and Performance St with English	W4Q3	3FT deg	Ap g	CCD	MO+3D	D$^	Ind	Ind	Ind	7	10/24
Theatre and Performance St with Media Arts	W4WG	3FT deg	Ap g	CCD	MO+3D	D$^	Ind	Ind	Ind	6	14/20
Theatre and Performance Studies with History	W4V1	3FT deg	Ap g	CCD	MO+3D	D$^	Ind	Ind	Ind	3	
Theatre and Performance Studies with Music	WW4H	3FT deg	Ap g	CCD	MO+3D	D$^	Ind	Ind	Ind		
Visual Arts with Theatre and Performance Studies	W2W4	3FT deg	Ap g	CCD	MO+3D	D$^	Ind	Ind	Ind	5	12/16
Dance in the Community	054W	3FT HND	Ap g	5	MO	M$	Ind	Ind	Ind		
Drama in the Community (S Devon)	034W	2FT HND	Ap g	5	MO	M	Ind	Ind	Ind	3	2/9
QUEEN MARGARET COLL											
Acting	W410	3FT/4FT deg	*								
Drama Studies	W401	3FT/4FT deg	*	BCC	M+D	D$^ go	Ind	ABCCC	Ind	5	
Stage Management and Theatre Production	W470	3FT/4FT deg	*	DD	M+D	P$ go	Dip	BCC	N		
Combined Studies Theatre Studies	Y600	3FT/4FT deg	*	BC	M+D	M/D$^ go	Ind	BBBC	Ind		
QUEEN MARY & WESTFIELD COLL (Univ of London)											
English and Drama	QW34	3FT deg	E	22		M	30$				
French and Drama	WR41	4FT deg	F	20		M^	30$				
German and Drama	WR42	4FT deg	G	20		M^	30$				
Hispanic Studies and Drama	WRK4	4FT deg	L	20		M^	30$				
Russian and Drama (European Studies)	WR48	4FT deg	L	20		M^	30$				
Univ of READING											
English Literature and Film & Drama	QW34	3FT deg	El	BBC	Ind	D*^	31$	BBBB$	Ind	20	22/30
Film & Drama	W480	3FT deg	*	BBC	Ind	D*^	31	BBBB	Ind		
Film & Drama and Italian	RW34	4FT deg	* g	BBC	Ind	D*^ go	31	BBBB	Ind		
German and Film & Drama	RW24	4FT deg	* g	BBC	Ind	D$^	31	BBBB	Ind	5	
Theatre Arts Education and Deaf St (1999 entry)	W420	3FT deg		EE	MO	M	24	CCCC	Ind		
Univ College of RIPON & YORK ST JOHN											
Dance: Performance and Communication Arts	PW3K	3FT deg		CC	M	M$	27	BBBC			
Drama: Performance and Communication Arts	PW34	3FT deg		CC	M	M$	27	BBBC			
Film, TV, Literature & Theatre Studies	WQ42	3FT deg		AB-BBC	MO+3D	D$6/^	30	ABBBB		6	16/28

			98 expected requirements							96 entry stats	
course details											
TITLE	CODE	COURSE	SUBJECTS	A/AS	NO/C	AGNVQ	IB	SQA(H)	SQA	RATIO	A/AS
ROEHAMPTON INST											
Dance Studies	W450▼	3FT deg	*	CC	2M+2D	M$	30	BBC	N$	12	12/24
Dance Studies and Applied Consumer Studies	NW94▼	3FT deg	g	CC	2M+2D$	M$ go	30	BBC	N$		
Dance Studies and Art for Community	WW14▼	3FT deg	*	CC	2M+2D	M$	30	BBC	Ind	4	
Dance Studies and Biology	CW14▼	3FT deg	B	CC	2M+2D$	M$ go	30	BBC	Ind	2	
Dance Studies and Business Computing	GW74▼	3FT deg	g	CC	2M+2D	M$^ go	30	BBC	N$		
Dance Studies and Business Studies	NW14▼	3FT deg	g	CC	3D	M$ go	30	BBC	Ind	12	
Drama & Theatre Studies	W420▼	3FT deg	E/T	16	2M+2D$	M$^	30	BBC	N$	11	16/24
Drama & Theatre Studies and Art for Community	WW1L▼	3FT deg	T/E	16	3D	M$^	30	BBC	Ind	4	
Drama & Theatre Studies and Biology	CW1L▼	3FT deg	B+T/E	16	3D $	M$^ go	30	BBB	Ind		
Drama & Theatre Studies and Business Computing	GW7L▼	3FT deg	E/T g	16	2M+2D	M$^ go	30	BBC	N$		
Drama & Theatre Studies and Business Studies	NW1L▼	3FT deg	T/E g	16	3D	M$^ go	30	BBC	Ind	19	
Drama & Theatre Studies and Dance Studies	W430▼	3FT deg	T/E	16	3D	M$^	30	BBC	Ind	6	
Drama & Theatre Studs and Applied Consumer Studs	NWX4▼	3FT deg	E/T g	16	2M+2D$	M$^ go	30	BBC	N$		
Education and Dance Studies	WX49▼	3FT deg	*	CC	2M+2D	M$^	30	BBC	Ind	5	
Education and Drama & Theatre Studies	WXL9▼	3FT deg	T/E	16	3D	M$^	30	BBC	Ind	5	
English Language & Linguist/Drama & Theatre St	WQLH▼	3FT deg	E/L+E/T	16	3D $	M$^	30	BBC	Ind	6	
English Language & Linguistics/Dance Studies	WQ4H▼	3FT deg	E/L	CC	2M+2D$	M$^	30	BBC	Ind	3	
English Literature and Dance Studies	WQ43▼	3FT deg	E	CC	2M+2D$	M^	30	BBC	Ind	7	16/18
English Literature and Drama & Theatre Studies	WQL3▼	3FT deg	E	16	3D $	M^	30	BBC	Ind	7	16/22
Environmental Studies and Dance Studies	WF49▼	3FT deg	B/Gy	CC	2M+2D$	M$^ go	30	BBC	Ind		
Environmental Studies and Drama & Theatre St	WFL9▼	3FT deg	B/Gy+T/E	16	3D $	M$^ go	30	BBC	Ind		
Film & Television Studies and Dance Studies	PW44▼	3FT deg	*	16	2M+2D$	M$^	30	BBC	N$	14	
Film & Television Studies and Drama & Theatre St	PW4K▼	3FT deg	E/T	16	2M+2D$	M$^	30	BBC	N$	10	16/20
French and Dance Studies	WR41▼	4FT deg	F	CC	2M+2D$	M^	30	BBC	Ind		
French and Drama & Theatre Studies	WRL1▼	4FT deg	F+E/T	16	3D $	M^	30	BBC	Ind	6	
Geography and Dance Studies	WL48▼	3FT deg	Gy	CC	2M+2D$	M$^ go	30	BBC	Ind		
Geography and Drama & Theatre Studies	LW84▼	3FT deg	Gy+T/E	16	3D $	M$^ go	30	BBC	Ind		
Health Studies and Dance Studies	BW94▼	3FT deg	B	CC	2M+2D$	M$^ go	30	BBC	N$		
Health Studies and Drama & Theatre Studies	BW9L▼	3FT deg	B+E/T	16	2M+2D$	M$^ go	30	BBC	N$		
History and Dance Studies	WV41▼	3FT deg	H	CC	2M+2D$	M^	30	BBC	Ind		
History and Drama & Theatre Studies	WVL1▼	3FT deg	H+E/T	16	3D $	M^	30	BBC	Ind		
Human & Social Biology and Dance Studies	WC4C▼	3FT deg	B	CC	2M+2D	M$^	30	BBC	Ind		
Human & Social Biology and Drama & Theatre Studs	CWCL▼	3FT deg	E/T+B	16	2M+2D	M$^	30	BBC	N$		
Music and Dance Studies	WW43▼	3FT deg	Mu	CC	2M+2D$	M^	30	BBC	Ind	14	
Music and Drama & Theatre Studies	WWL3▼	3FT deg	Mu+T/E	16	3D $	M^	30	BBC	Ind	28	
Natural Resource Studies & Drama & Theatre Studs	DW2L▼	3FT deg	E/T g	16	2M+2D	M$^ go	30	BBC	N$		
Natural Resource Studies and Dance Studies	DW24▼	3FT deg	g	CC	2M+2D	M$^ go	30	BBC	N$		
Psychology and Dance Studies	WL47▼	3FT deg	g	CC	3D	M$^ go	30	BBC	Ind	9	
Psychology and Drama & Theatre Studies	WLL7▼	3FT deg	T/E g	16	3D	MS^ go	30	BBC	Ind	7	
Social Policy & Admin and Drama & Theatre Studs	LW4L▼	3FT deg	E/T	16	2M+2D$	M$^	30	BBC	N$	3	
Social Policy & Administration and Dance Studies	WL44▼	3FT deg	g	CC	2M+2D	M$^	30	BBC	Ind		
Sociology and Dance Studies	WL43▼	3FT deg	g	CC	2M+2D	M$^ go	30	BBC	Ind		
Sociology and Drama & Theatre Studies	WLL3▼	3FT deg	E/T g	16	3D	M$^ go	30	BBC	Ind	4	
Spanish and Dance Studies	RW44▼	4FT deg	Sp	CC	2M+2D$	M$^	30	BBC	N$	2	
Spanish and Drama & Theatre Studies	RW4L▼	4FT deg	Sp+E/T	16	2M+2D$	M$^	30	BBC	N$	3	
Sport Studies and Dance Studies	WB46▼	3FT deg	S g	CC	3D	M$^ go	30	BBC	Ind		
Sport Studies and Drama & Theatre Studies	BW6L▼	3FT deg	E/T g	16	2M+2D$	M$^ go	30	BBC	Ind		
Theology & Religious St/Drama & Theatre Studies	WVL8▼	3FT deg	E/T	16	3D	M$^	30	BBC	Ind	4	
Theology & Religious Studies and Dance Studies	WV48▼	3FT deg	*	CC	3D	M$^	30	BBC	Ind		
Women's Studies and Dance Studies	MW9K▼	3FT deg	*	CC	2M+2D	M$^	30	BBC	N$		
Women's Studies and Drama & Theatre Studies	WM49▼	3FT deg	T/E	16	3D	M$^	30	BBC	Ind		

TITLE	CODE	COURSE	SUBJECTS	A/AS	ND/C	AGNVQ	IB	SQA(H)	SQA	RATIO	A/AS
ROSE BRUFORD COLL											
Acting	W410	3FT deg	*								
Actor Musician	W4W3	3FT deg	*							10	16/23
Costume Production	W490	3FT deg	*								
Costume Production	E490	3FT deg	*								
Directing	W440	3FT deg	*								
Lighting Design	W4W2	3FT deg	*							7	9/22
Scenic Construction and Stage Properties	W4W6	3FT deg	*							5	
Stage Management	W470	3FT deg	*								
ROYAL HOLLOWAY, Univ of London											
Classical Studies and Drama	QW84	3FT deg	E/T g	BBC-BCC	Ind		30	Ind		7	
Drama and Music	WW43	3FT deg	Mu+E/T g	BBC	Ind		30$	CSYS		17	
Drama and Theatre Studies	W420	3FT deg	E/T g	BBC	Ind		30$	CSYS		11	18/28
English Language and Drama	QW3K	3FT deg	E g	ABC	Ind		30$	Ind			
English and Drama	QW34	3FT deg	E g	ABC	Ind		30$	Ind		14	22/30
French and Drama	RW14	4FT deg	F+E/T g	ABC-BBC	Ind		30$	Ind		6	18/26
Media Arts	W425	3FT deg	g	BBC	Ind	D^	Ind	Ind		10	20/28
Foundation Programme *Drama & Theatre Studies*	Y408	4FT deg									
Univ of SALFORD											
Media Technology	HW64	3FT deg	M/P	18	4M	D3	28	CCCCC	Ind	19	10/24
Media and Performance	W400	3FT deg		CC	4D	M/D$	28	BBBB	Ind	16	12/26
Media, Language and Business	WQ41	3FT deg	L g	18-24	6M	M/D^	28	BBBB	Ind	7	14/22
Performing Arts (3 or 4 Yrs)	W430	3FT/4FT deg		CC-D	4M	P	24	CCC	Ind		
Television and Radio	W431	3FT deg		BBC	6D	M	28	BBBB	Ind	18	16/24
Media Performance	004W	2FT HND		D	4M	P$/M	24	CCC	Ind	10	6/14
Media Production	014W	2FT HND		CD	M+D	P	24	CCC	Ind	24	6/10
Physical Theatre and Dance	054W	2FT HND	D	6-8	MO	M	24	CCC	Ind	4	6/12
Univ College SCARBOROUGH											
Dance	W450	3FT deg	* g	DD	Ind	P	27$	Ind	Ind		
Dance with Arts	W4YH	3FT deg	* g	DD	Ind	P	27$	Ind	Ind		
Dance with Social Sciences	W4YF	3FT deg	* g	DD	Ind	P	27$	Ind	Ind		
Theatre Studies	W420	3FT deg	T/E g	DD	Ind	P	27$	Ind	Ind		
Theatre Studies with Arts	W4Y3	3FT deg	T/E g	DD	Ind	P	27$	Ind	Ind		
Theatre Studies with Social Sciences	W4Y2	3FT deg	T/E g	DD	Ind	P	27$	Ind	Ind		
Univ College of St MARTIN, LANCASTER AND CUMBRIA											
Applied Community Studies/Drama	LW54	3FT deg	*	CD-DDE	3M+2D	M*	28$	BCCC	Ind	8	
Art and Design/Drama	WW14	3FT deg	A	CC-CDE	3M+2D$	MA	28$	BBCC$	Ind	4	
Business Management Studies/Drama	NW14	3FT deg	*	CD-CEE	3M+2D	M*	28	BCCC			
English/Drama	QW34	3FT deg	E	BC-BDE	X	P^	28$	BBBC$	Ind	5	12/24
Health Studies/Drama	BW94	3FT deg	*	CD-DDE	3M+2D	M*	28	BCCC	Ind	1	
History/Drama	VW14	3FT deg	H	CD-DDE	X	P^	28$	BCCC$	Ind		
Mathematics/Drama	GW14	3FT deg	M	DD-DEE	X	P^	28$	BCCC$	Ind		
Performing Arts (Drama, Dance or Music)	WW43	3FT deg	*	CC-CDE	3M+2D$	MQ	28$	BBCC		7	6/22
Science, Technology and Society/Drama	WY41	3FT deg	g	CD-DDE	3M+2D	M*	28	BCCC	Ind		
Social Ethics/Drama	VW74	3FT deg	*	CD-DDE	3M+2D	M*	28	BCCC	Ind	5	
SOUTHAMPTON INST											
Media with Cultural Studies	P400	3FT deg	*	18	M	M$	Dip	BBBBC	N	4	12/24

course details

98 expected requirements

96 entry stats

TITLE	CODE	COURSE	SUBJECTS	A/AS	ND/C	RGNVQ	IB	SQA(H)	SQA	RATIO A/AS
SOUTH BANK Univ										
Tourism and World Theatre	PW74	3FT deg	* g	14-18	2M+4D	M go	Ind	Ind	Ind	
Urban Studies and World Theatre	WK44	3FT deg	* g	14-18	2M+4D	M go	Ind	Ind	Ind	
World Theatre and Accounting	NW44	3FT deg	Ac/Ec g	14-18	2M+4D	M go	Ind	Ind	Ind	
World Theatre and Business Information Tech	GW74	3FT deg	M g	14-18	2M+4D	M go	Ind	Ind	Ind	
World Theatre and Computing	GW54	3FT deg	M g	14-18	2M+4D	M go	Ind	Ind	Ind	
World Theatre and Economics	LW14	3FT deg	Ec/Bu g	14-18	2M+4D	M go	Ind	Ind	Ind	
World Theatre and English Studies	QW34	3FT deg	E g	14-18	X	M^ go	Ind	Ind	Ind	
World Theatre and Environmental Policy	FW94	3FT deg	* g	14-18	2M+4D	M go	Ind	Ind	Ind	
World Theatre and European Studies	TW24	3FT deg	* g	14-18	2M+4D	M go	Ind	Ind	Ind	
World Theatre and Food Policy	DW44	3FT deg	S g	14-18	2M+4D	M go	Ind	Ind	Ind	
World Theatre and French	RW14	3FT deg	F g	14-18	2M+4D	M go	Ind	Ind	Ind	
World Theatre and German	RW24	3FT deg	G g	14-18	2M+4D	M go	Ind	Ind	Ind	
World Theatre and German - ab initio	RW2K	3FT deg	* g	14-18	2M+4D	M go	Ind	Ind	Ind	
World Theatre and Health Studies	LW44	3FT deg	S g	14-18	2M+4D	M go	Ind	Ind	Ind	
World Theatre and History	WV41	3FT deg	H g	14-18	2M+4D	M go	Ind	Ind	Ind	
World Theatre and Housing	KW44	3FT deg	* g	14-18	2M+4D	M go	Ind	Ind	Ind	
World Theatre and Human Biology	BW14	3FT deg	S g	14-18	2M+4D	M go	Ind	Ind	Ind	
World Theatre and Human Resource Management	NW64	3FT deg	* g	14-18	2M+4D	M go	Ind	Ind	Ind	
World Theatre and Law	MW34	3FT deg	* g	14-18	2M+4D	D go	Ind	Ind	Ind	
World Theatre and Management	NW14	3FT deg	* g	14-18	2M+4D	M go	Ind	Ind	Ind	
World Theatre and Marketing	NW54	3FT deg	* g	14-18	2M+4D	M go	Ind	Ind	Ind	
World Theatre and Media Studies	PW44	3FT deg	E g	14-18	2M+4D	D go	Ind	Ind	Ind	
World Theatre and Nutrition	BW44	3FT deg	S g	14-18	2M+4D	M go	Ind	Ind	Ind	
World Theatre and Planning	KW4L	3FT deg	* g	14-18	2M+4D	M go	Ind	Ind	Ind	
World Theatre and Politics	MW14	3FT deg	* g	14-18	2M+4D	M go	Ind	Ind	Ind	
World Theatre and Product Design	HW74	3FT deg	Ad g	14-18	2M+4D	M go	Ind	Ind	Ind	
World Theatre and Psychology	CW84	3FT deg	S g	14-18	2M+4D	M go	Ind	Ind	Ind	
World Theatre and Social Policy	LW4K	3FT deg	* g	14-18	2M+4D	M go	Ind	Ind	Ind	
World Theatre and Sociology	LW34	3FT deg	* g	14-18	2M+4D	M go	Ind	Ind	Ind	
World Theatre and Spanish	RW44	3FT deg	S g	14-18	2M+4D	M^ go	Ind	Ind	Ind	
World Theatre and Spanish - ab initio	RW4K	3FT deg	* g	14-18	2M+4D	M go	Ind	Ind	Ind	
World Theatre and Sports Science	BW64	3FT deg	S g	14-18	2M+4D	M go	Ind	Ind	Ind	
World Theatre and Technology	JW94	3FT deg	* g	14-18	2M+4D	M go	Ind	Ind	Ind	
ST MARY'S Univ COLL										
Drama	W400	3FT deg	*	12-14	Ind	Ind	Ind	BBBB	Ind	
Drama and Classical Studies	WQ48	3FT deg	*	8-12	Ind	Ind	Ind	BBBB	Ind	
Education Studies and Drama	WX4X	3FT deg	*	8-12	Ind	Ind	Ind	BBBB	Ind	
English and Drama	QW34	3FT deg	E	12-14	X	X	Ind	BBBB$	X	
Environmental Investigation Studies and Drama	FW94	3FT deg	S/2S	8-12	Ind	Ind	Ind	BBBB	Ind	
Environmental Studies and Drama	FWX4	3FT deg	*	8-12	Ind	Ind	Ind	BBBB	Ind	
Gender Studies and Drama	MW94	3FT deg	*	8-12	Ind	Ind	Ind	BBBB	Ind	
Geography and Drama	FW84	3FT deg	Gy	8-12	Ind	Ind	Ind	BBBB$	Ind	
Heritage Management and Drama	NW94	3FT deg	*	8-12	Ind	Ind	Ind	BBBB	Ind	
Integrated Scientific Studies and Drama	WY41	3FT deg	S/2S	8-12	Ind	Ind	Ind	BBBB$	Ind	
Irish Studies and Drama	QW54	3FT deg	*	8-12	Ind	Ind	Ind	BBBB	Ind	
Management Studies and Drama	NW14	3FT deg	* g	8-12	Ind	Ind	Ind	BBBB	Ind	
Media Arts and Drama	PW44	3FT deg	*	8-12	Ind	Ind	Ind	BBBB	Ind	
Sociology and Drama	WLL3	3FT deg	*	8-12	Ind	Ind	Ind	BBBB	Ind	
Sport Rehabilitation and Drama	BW94	3FT deg	B g	12-14	X	X	Ind	BBBB$	X	
Sport Science and Drama	WBL6	3FT deg	S g	12-14	Ind	Ind	Ind	BBBB$	Ind	
Theology and Religious Studies and Drama	VW84	3FT deg	*	8-12	Ind	Ind	Ind	BBBB	Ind	

course details			98 expected requirements							96 entry stats	
TITLE	CODE	COURSE	SUBJECTS	A/AS	ND/C	AGNVQ	IB	SQA(H)	SQA	RATIO	A/AS
STAFFORDSHIRE Univ											
Design: Media Production	E430	3FT deg	Pf		Ind	Ind	Ind	Ind	Ind		
UNIVERSITY COLLEGE SUFFOLK											
Performing Arts (Level 3 only)	W430	1FT deg	Pf	X	X	X	Ind	Ind	Ind		
Performing Arts (Production)	234W	2FT HND	Pf	E	N $	P$	Ind	Ind	Ind		
Univ of SURREY											
Dance and Culture	W452	3FT deg	D	BB-BBC	6D		30	ABBB	Ind	6	14/26
Dance and Culture	W453	4SW deg	D	BB-BBC	6D		30	ABBB	Ind	7	16/24
Univ of SUSSEX											
European Drama in European Studies	W4T2	4FT deg	* g	BCC	MO $	M*6 go	$	Ind	Ind		
SWANSEA INST of HE											
Joint Honours *English and Drama and Media*	Y300	3FT deg	8	N					N		
TAMESIDE COLLEGE											
Drama in the Community	004W	2FT HND	2	N	P						
THAMES VALLEY Univ											
Digital Arts with Video Production	W9W4	3FT deg		8-12	MO	M		CCC			
Media Arts with Video Production	W9WK	3FT deg		8-12	MO	M	26	CCC			
Multi-Media Computing with Video Production	G5W4	3FT deg		8-12	MO	M	26	CCC			
TRINITY COLL Carmarthen											
Astudiaethau Theatr/Astudiaethau Crefydd	WV48	3FT deg	T+Re g								
Cymraeg/Astudiaethau Theatr	WQ45	3FT deg	W+T g	DD-CC	Ind		Ind	Ind	Ind		
Hanes/Astudiaethau Theatr	WV41	3FT deg	H+T g	DD-CC	Ind		Ind	Ind	Ind		
Saesneg/Astudiaethau Theatr	WQ43	3FT deg	E+T g	DD-CC	Ind		Ind	Ind	Ind		
Theatr, Cerdd a'r Cyfryngau	W444	3FT deg	g	DD-CC	Ind		Ind	Ind	Ind	2	9/20
Theatre Studies	W420	3FT deg	T g	DD-CC	Ind		Ind	Ind	Ind	1	8/16
Theatre Studies/Archaeology	VW64	3FT deg	g	DD-CC	Ind		Ind	Ind	Ind	2	
Theatre Studies/English	QW34	3FT deg	T+E g	DD-CC	Ind		Ind	Ind	Ind	3	
Theatre Studies/History	VW14	3FT deg	T+H g	DD-CC	Ind		Ind	Ind	Ind		
Theatre Studies/Religious Studies	VW84	3FT deg	g	DD-CC	Ind		Ind	Ind	Ind		
Welsh Studies/Theatre Studies	QW54	3FT deg	g	DD-CC	Ind		Ind	Ind	Ind		
Dyniaethau *Saesneg*	Y321	3FT deg	E g	DD-CC	Ind		Ind	Ind	Ind		
Humanities *Theatre Studies*	Y320	3FT deg	T g	DD-CC	Ind		Ind	Ind	Ind		
Univ of ULSTER											
Theatre Studies	W420▼	3FT deg	*	CCC	MO+3D	D*6/^ gi	28	BBBC	Ind	6	16/24
Humanities Combined *Theatre Studies*	Y320▼	3FT/4SW deg	*	CCC	MO+3D	D*6/<u>^</u> gi	28	BBBC	Ind		
Univ Col WARRINGTON											
Performing Arts with Business Management and IT	NW14	3FT deg	* g	12-14	Ind	Ind	Ind	Ind	Ind	3	4/20
Univ of WARWICK											
English and Theatre Studies	QW34	3FT deg	E+H/L g	ABB	X	X	34	AAABB		14	24/30
Italian with Theatre Studies (4 Yrs inc yr abrd)	R3W4	4FT deg	E/L g	BCC	X	X	29$	ABBCC$			
Theatre and Performance Studies	W420	3FT deg	E/T/H g	BBB	X	X	32	AABBB$		11	22/30

			98 expected requirements							96 entry stats	
course details											
TITLE	CODE	COURSE	SUBJECTS	A/AS	ND/C	AGNVQ	IB	SQA(H)	SQA	RATIO A/AS	
WELSH COLL of Music and Drama											
Theatre Studies (Acting)	W410	3FT deg	* g	4-16	N	Ind	Dip	Ind	Ind		
Theatre Studies (Design)	W460	3FT deg	* g	4-16	N	P	Dip	Ind	Ind		
Theatre Studies (Design)	E460	3FT deg	* g	4-16	N	P	Dip	Ind	Ind		
Theatre Studies (Stage Management)	W470	3FT deg	* g	4-16	N	P	Dip	Ind	Ind		
WESTHILL COLL											
Humanities - Creative Arts _Dance_	Y4W9	3FT deg	* g	CC	4M+2D	M^	Ind	Ind	Ind		
Humanities - Creative Arts _Drama_	Y4W9	3FT deg	* g	CC	4M+2D	M^	Ind	Ind	Ind		
Univ of WOLVERHAMPTON											
Combined Degrees _Animation_	E401	3FT deg	A/Ad/Ds+Pf	12	4M	M	24	BBBB	Ind		
Combined Degrees _Dance_	Y401	3FT deg		10	4M	M	24	BBBB	Ind		
Combined Degrees _Theatre Studies_	Y401	3FT/4SW deg		12	4M	M	24	BBBB	Ind		
WORCESTER COLL of HE											
Drama/Art and Design	WW94	3FT deg	A	DD	Ind	M	Ind	Ind	Ind	6	
Drama/Biological Science	CW14	3FT deg	S	DD	Ind	M	Ind	Ind	Ind	3	
Drama/Business Management	NW14	3FT deg		DD	Ind	M	Ind	Ind	Ind	7	
Economy and Society/Drama	WL41	3FT deg		DD	Ind	M	Ind	Ind	Ind		
English and Literary Studies/Drama	WQ43	3FT deg		CC	Ind	M	Ind	Ind	Ind	5	12/24
Environmental Science/Drama	WF49	3FT deg		DD	Ind	M	Ind	Ind	Ind		
History/Drama	WV41	3FT deg		DD	Ind	M	Ind	Ind	Ind	3	
Information Technology/Drama	WG45	3FT deg		DD	Ind	M	Ind	Ind	Ind		
Psychology/Drama	WL47	3FT deg	g	CC	Ind	M	Ind	Ind	Ind	7	
Sociology/Drama	WL43	3FT deg		DD	Ind	M	Ind	Ind	Ind	4	
Urban Studies/Drama	WL4V	3FT deg		DD	Ind	M	Ind	Ind	Ind		
Women's Studies/Drama	WM49	3FT deg		DD	Ind	M	Ind	Ind	Ind		

Economics 18

Univ of ABERDEEN

TITLE	CODE	COURSE	SUBJECTS	A/AS	NO/C	AGNVQ	IB	SQA(H)	SQA	RATIO A/AS
Accountancy-Economics	NL41	4FT deg	* g	BBC	Ind	M$ go	30$	BBBB$	Ind	11
Agricultural Economics	D2LC	4FT deg	2S/S+M g	CDD	Ind	MS go	24$	BBBC$	Ind	11
Agricultural Economics-Management Studies	LN11	4FT deg	* g	BBC	Ind	M$ go	30$	BBBB$	Ind	
Celtic-Economics	QL51	4FT deg	* g	BBC	Ind	M$ go	30$	BBBB$	Ind	
Economic Science	L100	4FT deg	* g	BBC	Ind	M$ go	30$	BBBB$	Ind	4
Economics-Agricultural Economics	L134	4FT deg	* g	BBC	Ind	M$ go	30$	BBBB$	Ind	
Economics-Economic History	LV13	4FT deg	* g	BBC	Ind	M$ go	30$	BBBB$	Ind	
Economics-English	LQ13	4FT deg	* g	BBC	Ind	M$ go	30$	BBBB$	Ind	
Economics-Entrepreneurship	NLC1	4FT deg	* g	BBC	Ind	M$ go	30$	BBBB$	Ind	
Economics-French	LR11	4FT/5FT deg	* g	BBC	Ind	M$ go	30$	BBBB$	Ind	3
Economics-French (4 Yrs)	RL11	4FT deg	* g	BBC	Ind	M$ go	30$	BBBB$	Ind	
Economics-Geography	LL18	4FT deg	* g	BBC	Ind	M$ go	30$	BBBB$	Ind	
Economics-German	LR12	4FT/5FT deg	* g	BBC	Ind	M$ go	30$	BBBB$	Ind	
Economics-German (4 Yrs)	RL21	4FT deg	* g	BBC	Ind	M$ go	30$	BBBB$	Ind	
Economics-Hispanic Studies	LR14	5FT deg	* g	BBC	Ind	M$ go	30$	BBBB$	Ind	
Economics-Hispanic Studies (4Yrs)	RL41	4FT deg	* g	BBC	Ind	M$ go	30$	BBBB$	Ind	
Economics-International Relations	LM1C	4FT deg	* g	BBC	Ind	M$ go	30$	BBBB$	Ind	12
Economics-Management Studies	LN1C	4FT deg	* g	BBC	Ind	M$ go	30$	BBBB$	Ind	5
Economics-Mathematics	LG11	4FT deg	M g	BBC	Ind	M$ go	30$	BBBB$	Ind	
Economics-Philosophy	LV17	4FT deg	* g	BBC	Ind	M$ go	30$	BBBB$	Ind	6
Economics-Politics	LM11	4FT deg	* g	BBC	Ind	M$ go	30$	BBBB$	Ind	7
Economics-Sociology	LL13	4FT deg	* g	BBC	Ind	M$ go	30$	BBBB$	Ind	
Economics-Statistics	LG14	4FT deg	M g	BBC	Ind	M$ go	30$	BBBB$	Ind	
Law (with Options in Economics) (LLB)	M3L1	3FT/4FT deg	* g	BBB	Ind	X	34$	ABBBB$	Ind	5

Univ of ABERTAY DUNDEE

TITLE	CODE	COURSE	SUBJECTS	A/AS	NO/C	AGNVQ	IB	SQA(H)	SQA	RATIO A/AS
Applied Chemistry with Economics	F1L1	4FT/5SW deg	C	DD	Ind	Ind	Ind	BCC	Ind	
Economics	L100	4FT deg	*	CD	Ind	Ind	Ind	BBB	Ind	
Economics (with European Study)	L110	4FT deg	*	CD	Ind	Ind	Ind	BBB	Ind	
European Economy and Society	L170	4FT deg		CD	Ind	Ind	Ind	BBB	Ind	

Univ of Wales, ABERYSTWYTH

TITLE	CODE	COURSE	SUBJECTS	A/AS	NO/C	AGNVQ	IB	SQA(H)	SQA	RATIO A/AS
Accounting and Finance/Economics	LN14	3FT deg	* g	18	3M+3D	M^ g	29	BBBCC	Ind	
Economics	L100	3FT deg	* g	18	3M+3D	M^ g	29	BBBCC	Ind	
Economics (Major)	L178	3FT deg	* g	18	3M+3D	M^ g	29	BBBCC	Ind	
Economics and Marketing	LN15	3FT deg	* g	18	3M+3D	M^ g	29	BBBCC	Ind	
The Economics of Agriculture, Food & Rural Env	L130	3FT deg	* g	12	MO	M g	26	BCCCC	Ind	

ANGLIA Poly Univ

TITLE	CODE	COURSE	SUBJECTS	A/AS	NO/C	AGNVQ	IB	SQA(H)	SQA	RATIO A/AS
Business Economics	L100▼	3FT deg	* g	10	6M	P go	Dip	BCCC	N	2	6/15
Communication Studies and Economics	PL31▼	3FT deg	Ap g	14	6M	M+/^ go	Dip$	BBCC	Ind	4
Economics and English	LQ13▼	3FT deg	E g	12	4M	M+/^ go	Dip$	BCCC	Ind	
Economics and English Language Studies	LQ11▼	3FT deg	* g	12		go	Dip$	BCCC	Ind	
Economics and French	LR11▼	4FT deg	* g	12	4M	M+/^ go	Dip	BCCC	Ind	
Economics and Geography	LL18▼	3FT deg	Gy g	12	4M	M+/^ go	Dip	BCCC	Ind	11
Economics and German	LR12▼	4FT deg	* g	12	4M	M+/^ go	Dip	BCCC	Ind	
Economics and History	LV11▼	3FT deg	Ap g	12	4M	M+/^ go	Dip	BCCC	Ind	4
Economics and Italian	LR13▼	4FT deg	* g	12	4M	M+/^ go	Dip	BCCC	Ind	
Economics and Law	LM13▼	3FT deg	* g	14	6M	M go	Dip	BBCC	Ind	12
Economics and Maths or Statistics/Stat Modelling	LG11▼	3FT deg	* g	10	3M	P go	Dip	BCCC	Ind	
Economics and Music	LW13▼	3FT deg	Mu g	12	4M	M+/^	Dip$	BCCC	Ind	
Economics and Politics	LM11▼	3FT deg	* g	14	6M	M+/^	Dip$	BBCC	Ind	22
Economics and Social Policy	LL14▼	3FT deg	* g	12	4M	M go	Dip	BCCC	Ind	

course details | 98 expected requirements | 96 entry stats

TITLE	CODE	COURSE	SUBJECTS	A/AS	ND/C	RGNVQ	IB	SQA(H)	SQA	RATIO A/AS
Economics and Sociology	LL13▼	3FT deg	* g	12	4M	M go	Dip	BCCC	Ind	
Economics and Spanish	LR14▼	4FT deg	* g	12	4M	M go	Dip	BCCC	Ind	
Economics and Women's Studies	LM19▼	3FT deg	* g	12	4M	M go	Dip	BCCC	Ind	
European Business (French Programme)	L112▼	4FT deg	g	10	3M	P go	Dip	BCCC	Ind	
European Business (German Programme)	L113▼	4FT deg	g	10	3M	P go	Dip	BCCC	Ind	2
European Business (Spanish Programme)	L114▼	4FT deg	Sp g	10	3M	P go	Dip	BCCC	Ind	5

Univ of Wales, BANGOR

TITLE	CODE	COURSE	SUBJECTS	A/AS	ND/C	RGNVQ	IB	SQA(H)	SQA	RATIO A/AS
Economics	L100	3FT deg	* g	18	3M+2D	D$6/^ go	28	BBBC	Ind	4	10/24
Economics/Accounting	LN14	3FT deg	* g	18	3M+2D	D$6/^ go	28	BBBC	Ind	13
French (Syllabus A)/Economics	LR11	4FT deg	F g	18	X	D$^ go	28$	BBBC$	X
French (Syllabus B)/Economics	LR1C	4FT deg	F g	18	X	D$^ go	28$	BBBC$	X
German/Economics	LR12	4FT deg	* g	18	X	D$^ go	28$	BBBC$	X
History/Economics	LV11	3FT deg	H g	18	Ind	D*^ go	28$	BBBC$	Ind
Management with Economics	N1L1	3FT deg	* g	18	3M+2D	D$6/^ go	28	BBBC	Ind	3	10/16
Mathematics/Economics	GL11	3FT deg	M g	18	3M+2D$	D$^ go	28$	BBBC$	Ind	3
Modern Languages/Economics	LT19	4FT deg	F/G g	18	X	D$^ go	28$	BBBC$	X
Russian/Economics	LR18	4FT deg	* g	18	3M+2D	D$6/^ go	28	BBBC	Ind
Social Policy/Economics	LL14	3FT deg	* g	18	3M+2D	D$6/^ go	28	BBBC	Ind
Sociology/Economics	LL13	3FT deg	* g	18	3M+2D	D$6/^ go	28	BBBC	Ind	3

Univ of BATH

TITLE	CODE	COURSE	SUBJECTS	A/AS	ND/C	RGNVQ	IB	SQA(H)	SQA	RATIO A/AS
Economics	L100	3FT deg	g	22	Ind	D^	30	AABBB	Ind	10	20/28
Economics	L101	4SW deg	g	22	Ind	D^	30	AABBB	Ind	5	20/28
Economics and Politics	LM11	3FT deg	g	22	Ind	D^	30	Ind	Ind	9	20/26
Economics and Politics	LMC1	4SW deg	g	22	Ind	D^	30	Ind	Ind	5	22/28
Politics with Economics (3 Yrs)	M1L1	3FT deg	g	22	Ind	D^	30	Ind	Ind	7	22/26
Politics with Economics (4 Yr SW)	M1LC	4SW deg	g	22	Ind	D^	30	Ind	Ind	3	22/30

Univ of BIRMINGHAM

TITLE	CODE	COURSE	SUBJECTS	A/AS	ND/C	RGNVQ	IB	SQA(H)	SQA	RATIO A/AS
Economics	L100	3FT deg	*	BBB	Ind	D+^	32	ABBBB	Ind	8	24/30
Economics and Modern Economic History	LV13	3FT deg	*	BBC	Ind	D+^	32	ABBBB	Ind	7	24/28
Economics and Political Science	LM11	3FT deg	*	BBB	Ind	D+^	32	ABBBB	Ind	8	24/28
Economics and Statistics	GL41	3FT deg	M	BBC	Ind	D+^	32	ABBBB	Ind	17
Economics with French	L1R1	4FT deg	F	BBB	Ind	D+^	32	ABBBB	Ind	7	22/28
Economics with German	L1R2	4FT deg	G	BBC	Ind	D+^	32	ABBBB	Ind	7
Economics with Italian	L1R3	4FT deg	*	BBC	Ind	D+^	32	ABBBB	Ind
Economics with Portuguese	L1R5	4FT deg	*	BBC	Ind	D+^	32	ABBBB	Ind
Economics with Spanish	L1R4	4FT deg	*	BBC	Ind	D+^	32	ABBBB	Ind	4
Geography and Economics	LL81	3FT deg	Gy	BBB	Ind	D+^	32	ABBBB	Ind	15
International Studies with Economics	ML11	3FT deg	*	BBB	Ind	D+^	32	ABBBB	Ind	20
Mathematical Economics	L140	3FT deg	M	BBC	Ind	D+^	32	ABBBB	Ind	10	26/30
Planning and Economics	KL41	3FT deg	*	BBC	Ind	D+^	32	ABBBB	Ind	5
Russian and East European Studies and Economics	RL81	3FT/4FT deg	R/*	BBC	Ind	D+^		ABBBB	Ind

BOLTON INST

TITLE	CODE	COURSE	SUBJECTS	A/AS	ND/C	RGNVQ	IB	SQA(H)	SQA	RATIO A/AS
Accountancy and Business Economics	LN14	3FT deg	* g	CD	MO	M*	24	BBCC	Ind
Art and Design History and Business Economics	LV14	3FT deg	* g	CD	MO	M*	24	BBCC	Ind
Biology and Business Economics	CL11	3FT deg	* g	CD	MO	M*
Business Economics & Organisations, Mgt and Work	LN17	3FT deg	* g	CD	MO	M*	24	BBCC	Ind
Business Economics and Business Information Syst	GL51	3FT deg	* g	CD	MO	M*	24	BBCC	Ind
Business Economics and Business Studies	LN11	3FT deg	* g	CD	MO	M*	24	BBCC	Ind
Business Economics and Community Studies	LL15	3FT deg	* g	CD	MO	M*	24	BBCC	Ind
Business Economics and Computing	GL5C	3FT deg	* g	CD	MO	M*	24	BBCC	Ind

Economics 18

course details | 98 expected requirements | 96 entry stats

TITLE	CODE	COURSE	SUBJECTS	A/AS	ND/C	AGNVQ	IB	SQA(H)	SQA	RATIO A/AS
Business Economics and Creative Writing	LW19	3FT deg	* g	CD	MO	M*	24	BBCC	Ind	
Business Economics and Environmental Studies	FL91	3FT deg	* g	CD	MO	M*	24	BBCC	Ind	
Business Economics and European Cultural Studies	LT12	3FT deg	* g	CD	MO	M*	24	BBCC	Ind	
Business Economics and Film and TV Studies	LW15	3FT deg	Me/T g	CD	Ind	Ind	24	BBCC	Ind	
Business Economics and French	LR11	3FT deg	F g	CD	Ind	Ind	24	BBCC	Ind	
Business Economics and Gender and Women's Studs	LM19	3FT deg	* g	CD	MO	M*	24	BBCC	Ind	
Business Economics and German	LR12	3FT deg	G g	CD	Ind	Ind	24	BBCC	Ind	
Business Economics and History	LV11	3FT deg	* g	CD	MO	M*	24	BBCC	Ind	
Business Economics and Human Resource Management	NL11	3FT deg	* g	CD	MO	M*	24	BBCC	Ind	
Business Economics and Law	LM13	3FT deg	* g	CD	MO	M*	24	BBCC	Ind	
Business Economics and Leisure Studies	LL13	3FT deg	* g	CD	MO	M*	24	BBCC	Ind	
Business Economics and Literature	LQ12	3FT deg	* g	CD	MO	M*	24	BBCC	Ind	
Business Economics and Marketing	LN15	3FT deg	* g	CD	MO	M*	24	BBCC	Ind	
Business Economics and Mathematics	LG11	3FT deg	M g	DD	Ind	Ind	24	BBCC	Ind	
Business Economics and Operations Management	LN12	3FT deg	* g	CD	MO	M*	24	BBCC	Ind	
Business Economics and Peace and War Studies	LV1C	3FT deg	* g	CD	MO	M*	24	BBCC	Ind	
Business Economics and Philosophy	LV17	3FT deg	* g	CD	MO	M*	24	BBCC	Ind	
Business Economics and Psychology	LL17	3FT deg	* g	12	MO	D*	24	BBCC	Ind	
Business Economics and Sociology	LL1J	3FT deg	* g	CD	MO	M	24	Ind	Ind	
Business Economics and Theatre Studies	LW14	3FT deg	Me/T g	CD	MO	M*	24	BBCC	Ind	
Business Economics and Tourism Studies	LP17	3FT deg	* g	CD	MO	M*	24	BBCC	Ind	
Business Economics and Urban and Cultural Studs	LL1H	3FT deg	* g	CD	MO	M*	24	BBCC	Ind	
Design and Business Economics	LW12	3FT deg	* g	CD	MO	M*	24	BBCC	Ind	
Visual Arts and Business Economics	LW11	3FT deg	* g	CD	MO	M*	24	BBCC	Ind	

Univ of BRADFORD

TITLE	CODE	COURSE	SUBJECTS	A/AS	ND/C	AGNVQ	IB	SQA(H)	SQA	RATIO A/AS
Economics	L100	3FT deg	*	BB-CCC	Ind	M*4	Ind	Ind	Ind	2 6/16
Economics/History	LV11	3FT deg	*	BB-CCC	Ind	M*4	Ind	Ind	Ind	
Economics/Politics	LM11	3FT deg	*	BB-CCC	Ind	M*4	Ind	Ind	Ind	
Economics/Sociology	LL13	3FT deg	*	BB-CCC	Ind	M*4	Ind	Ind	Ind	

Univ of BRISTOL

TITLE	CODE	COURSE	SUBJECTS	A/AS	ND/C	AGNVQ	IB	SQA(H)	SQA	RATIO A/AS
Economics	L100	3FT deg	M	ABC	Ind	D$^	32$	CSYS	Ind	14 28/30
Economics and Accounting	LN14	3FT deg	M	BBC	Ind	D$^	32$	CSYS	Ind	12 22/28
Economics and Accounting with Law	LN1K	3FT deg	M	BBC	Ind	D$^	32$	CSYS	Ind	10 24/28
Economics and Accounting with Study in Cont Eur	NL41	4FT deg	M+L	BBC	Ind	D$^	32$	CSYS	Ind	4 24/30
Economics and Accounting with a Language	LN1L	3FT deg	M	BBC	Ind	D$^	32$	CSYS	Ind	8 28/30
Economics and Economic History	LV13	3FT deg	* g	BBC	Ind	D$^	32$	CSYS	Ind	5 22/30
Economics and Mathematics	LG11	3FT deg	M	ABC	Ind	D$^	32$	CSYS	Ind	7 24/30
Economics and Politics	LM11	3FT deg	* g	ABC	Ind	D$^	32$	CSYS	Ind	11 26/30
Economics and Sociology	LL13	3FT deg	* g	ABC	Ind	D$^	32$	CSYS	Ind	12
Economics with Statistics	L140	3FT deg	M	ABC	Ind	D$^	32$	CSYS	Ind	5 24/28
Economics with Statistics with Study in Cont Eur	L141	4FT deg	M+L	ABC	Ind	D$^	32$	CSYS	Ind	10
Economics with Study in Continental Europe	L101	4FT deg	M+L	ABC	Ind	D$^	32$	CSYS	Ind	11 30/30
Philosophy and Economics	VL71	3FT deg	* g	ABC	Ind	D$^	32$	CSYS	Ind	9 26/30

BRISTOL, Univ of the W of England

TITLE	CODE	COURSE	SUBJECTS	A/AS	ND/C	AGNVQ	IB	SQA(H)	SQA	RATIO A/AS
Economics	L100▼	3FT deg	* g	14-16	5M-6M	M* go	24	BCCC	Ind	
Joint Honours Programme *Accounting and Economics*	Y401	3FT deg	M g	14-16	5M $	M$ go	24$	BCCC$	Ind	
Joint Honours Programme *Economics and Mathematics*	Y401	3FT deg	M g	14-16	5M $	M$ go	24$	BCCC$	Ind	

course details			98 expected requirements							96 entry stats	
TITLE	CODE	COURSE	SUBJECTS	A/AS	NO/C	AGNVQ	IB	SQA(H)	SQA	RATIO	A/AS
BRUNEL Univ, West London											
Business Economics	L113	3FT deg	* g	20	M+D	M^	28$	Ind	Ind	19	
Business Economics (4 Yrs Thick SW)	L111	4SW deg	* g	20	M+D	M^	28$	Ind	Ind		
Business Economics (4 Yrs Thin SW)	L112	4SW deg	* g	20	M+D	M^	28$	Ind	Ind	6	16/28
Economics	L101	3FT deg	* g	20	M+D	M^	28$	Ind	Ind	7	16/22
Economics (4 Yrs Thick SW)	L106	4SW deg	* g	20	M+D	M^	28$	Ind	Ind		
Economics (4 Yrs Thin SW)	L100	4SW deg	* g	20	M+D	M^	28$	Ind	Ind	5	14/24
Economics and Business Finance	LNC3	3FT deg	* g	20	M+D	D^	28$	Ind	Ind	8	16/20
Economics and Business Finance (4 Yrs Thick SW)	LND3	4SW deg	* g	20	M+D	D^	28$	Ind	Ind		
Economics and Business Finance (4 Yrs Thin SW)	LN13	4SW deg	* g	20	M+D	D^	28$	Ind	Ind	5	16/26
Economics and Law	LMC3	3FT deg	* g	22-24	M+D	D^	30$	Ind	Ind	13	
Economics and Law (4 Yrs Thick SW)	LMD3	4SW deg	* g	22-24	M+D	D^	30$	Ind	Ind		
Economics and Law (4 Yrs Thin SW)	LM13	4SW deg	* g	22-24	M+D	D^	30$	Ind	Ind	11	
Economics and Management	LNC1	3FT deg	* g	20	M+D	D^	28$	Ind	Ind	11	
Economics and Management (4 Yrs Thick SW)	LND1	4SW deg	* g	20	M+D	D^	28$	Ind	Ind		
Economics and Management (4 Yrs Thin SW)	LN11	4SW deg	* g	20	M+D	D^	28$	Ind	Ind	5	16/26
Politics and Economics	LMCD	3FT deg	* g	BCC	5M	D^	28$	BBBCC	Ind	6	
Politics and Economics (4 Yrs Thick SW)	LM11	4SW deg	* g	BCC	5M	D^	28$	BBBCC	Ind		
Politics and Economics (4 Yrs Thin SW)	LM1C	4SW deg	* g	BCC	5M	D^	28$	BBBCC	Ind	6	
Univ of BUCKINGHAM											
Accounting with Economics	N4L1	2FT deg	* g	16	3M+2D	M	26	BCCC	Ind		
Business Economics	L112	2FT deg	M/Ec	14	3M+2D	M	26	BCCC	Ind		
Economics	L100	2FT deg	M/Ec	14	3M+2D	M	26	BCCC	Ind		
Economics with English Language Studies (EFL)	L1Q3	2FT deg	M g	14	3M+2D	M	26	BCCC	Ind		
Economics with French	L1R1	2FT deg	F/M g	14	3M+2D	M	26	BCCC	Ind		
Economics with Politics	L1M1	2FT deg	M g	14	3M+2D	M	26	BCCC	Ind		
Economics with Spanish	L1R4	2FT deg	Sp g	14	3M+2D	M	26	BCCC	Ind		
Information Systems with Economics	G5L1	2FT deg	* g	12	5M	M	24	CCCC	Ind		
Politics with Economics	M1L1	2FT deg	* g	14	3M+2D	M	26	BCCC	Ind		
Politics, Economics and Law *Economics*	Y618	2FT deg	* g	12	3M+2D	M	26	BCCC	Ind		
BUCKINGHAMSHIRE COLLEGE											
Business Administration with Economics	N1L1	3FT deg		8	MO	M	27	CCCC	Ind		
Business Studies with Economics	N1LC	3FT deg		8	MO	M	27	CCCC	Ind		
Human Resources Management with Economics	N6L1	3FT deg		8	MO	M	27	CCCC	Ind		
CAMBRIDGE Univ											
Economics	L100▼	3FT deg	* g	AAA-AAB	Ind		Ind	CSYS	Ind	3	28/30
Land Economy	KL41▼	3FT deg	* g	AAB	Ind		Ind	CSYS	Ind	2	26/30
CARDIFF Univ of Wales											
Accounting and Economics	LN14	3FT deg	*	BBC-BBB	Ind	Ind	Ind	Ind	Ind	5	20/26
Business Economics	L112	3FT deg	*	BBC-BBB	Ind	Ind	Ind	Ind	Ind	4	20/30
Business Economics with French	L1RC	4FT deg	F	BBC-BBB	Ind	Ind	Ind	Ind	Ind	20	
Business Economics with German	L1RF	4FT deg	G	BBC-BBB	Ind	Ind	Ind	Ind	Ind		
Business Economics with Italian	L1RH	4FT deg	L	BBC-BBB	Ind	Ind	Ind	Ind	Ind		
Business Economics with Spanish	L1RK	4FT deg	Sp	BBC-BBB	Ind	Ind	Ind	Ind	Ind	4	
Economics	L100	3FT deg	*	BBC-BBB	Ind	Ind	Ind	Ind	Ind	3	16/28
Economics and Management Studies	LN11	3FT deg	*	BBC-BBB	Ind	Ind	Ind	Ind	Ind	4	18/28
Economics with French	L1R1	4FT deg	F	BBC-BBB	Ind	Ind	Ind	Ind	Ind	8	
Economics with German	L1R2	4FT deg	G	BBC-BBB	Ind	Ind	Ind	Ind	Ind		
Economics with Italian	L1R3	4FT deg	L	BBC-BBB	Ind	Ind	Ind	Ind	Ind		

Economics 18

course details				**98 expected requirements**					**96 entry stats**	
TITLE	CODE	COURSE	SUBJECTS	A/AS	ND/C	AGNVQ	IB	SQA(H)	SQA	RATIO A/AS
Economics with Spanish	L1R4	4FT deg	Sp	BBC-BBB	Ind	Ind	Ind	Ind	Ind	
Education/Economics	XL91	3FT deg	*	BBC-BBB	Ind	Ind	Ind	Ind	Ind	
French/Economics	RL11	4FT deg	F	BBC-BBB	X		Ind	ABBBB	Ind	
German/Economics	RL21	4FT deg	G	BBC-BBB	X		Ind	AABB	X	
History of Ideas/Economics	VLD1	3FT deg	*	BBC-BBB	7M+7D		Ind	AAAB	Ind	
History/Economics	VL11	3FT deg	H	BBC-BBB	X		Ind	AAABB	X	6
Italian/Economics	RL31	4FT deg	L	BBC-BBB	X		Ind	AAAAB	X	
Philosophy/Economics	VL71	3FT deg	*	BBC-BBB	7M+7D		Ind	AAAB	Ind	9
Politics and Economics	LM11	3FT deg	*	BBC-BBB	7M+7D		Ind	AAAB	Ind	11
Portuguese/Economics	LR15	4FT deg	L	BBC-BBB	X		Ind	AAAB	X	
Social Philosophy and Applied Ethics/Economics	VLR1	3FT deg	*	BBC-BBB	7M+7D		Ind	AAAB	Ind	
Sociology and Economics	LL13	3FT deg	*	BBC-BBB	7M+7D		Ind	AAAB	Ind	9
Spanish/Economics	LR14	4FT deg	L	BBC-BBB	X		Ind	AAAB	X	
Welsh History/Economics	VLCC	3FT deg	H	BBC-BBB	X		Ind	AAABB	X	
Welsh/Economics	QL51	3FT deg	W	BBC-BBB	X		Ind	ABBBB	X	

Univ of CENTRAL ENGLAND

Business Economics	L112	3FT deg	* g	14	M+3D	D	24	CCCC		
Business Economics and Finance	LN13	3FT deg	* g	14	M+3D	D	24	CCCC		
Economics	L100	3FT deg	* g	14	M+3D	D	24	CCCC	Ind	4 8/16
Economics with Accountancy	L1N4	3FT deg	* g	14	M+3D	D	24	CCCC	Ind	26
Economics with Law	L1M3	3FT deg	* g	14	M+3D	D	24	CCCC	Ind	4 8/14
Economics with Management	L1N1	3FT deg	* g	14	M+3D	D	24	CCCC	Ind	7 12/20
Economics with Marketing	L1N5	3FT deg	* g	14	M+3D	D	24	CCCC	Ind	
Finance with Economics	N3L1	3FT deg	* g	14	M+3D	D6				

Univ of CENTRAL LANCASHIRE

Combined Honours Programme *Economics*	Y400	3FT deg	* g	12	MO+2D	M$6/^	26	BBCC	Ind	

CITY Univ

Economics	L100	3FT deg	* g	BCC	3M+4D	D*^	28$	BBBBC	Ind	12 18/24
Economics/Accountancy	LN14	3FT deg	* g	BBB	3M+4D	D*^	28$	BBBBB	Ind	16 18/24
Economics/Computing	LG15	3FT deg	* g	BCC	3M+4D	D*^	28$	BBBBC	Ind	21
Economics/Philosophy	LV17	3FT deg	* g	BCC	3M+4D	D*^	28$	BBBBC	Ind	12
Economics/Psychology	LL17	3FT deg	* g	BCC	3M+4D	D*^	28$	BBBBC	Ind	9
Economics/Sociology	LL13	3FT deg	* g	BCC	3M+4D	D*^	28$	BBBBC	Ind	7
Journalism/Economics	LP16	3FT/4SW deg	* g	BBC-CCC	Ind	D*^	Ind	Ind	Ind	18
Mathematical Science with Finance and Economics	G1L1	3FT/4SW deg	M	BBC-BCD	Ind	D*^	28$	Ind	Ind	4 12/16
Philosophy/Economics	LVC7	3FT deg	* g	BCC	3M+4D	D*^	28$	BBBBC	Ind	
Psychology/Economics	CL81	3FT deg	* g	BCC	3M+4D	D*^	28$	BBBBC	Ind	
Sociology/Economics	LLC3	3FT deg	* g	BCC	3M+4D	D*^	28$	BBBBC	Ind	4

COVENTRY Univ

American and European Economics	L105	3FT deg	* g	12-16	D	D	24	BCCCC	Ind	
Biological Sciences and Economics	CL1C	4FT/5SW deg			Ind	Ind	Ind	Ind	Ind	
Business Economics	L112	3FT deg	* g	12-16	M+2D	D	Ind	CCC	Ind	4 8/20
Economics	L100	3FT deg	* g	12-16	M+2D	D	Ind	CCC	Ind	4 6/22
Economics and Biological Sciences	CL11	3FT/4SW deg	B g	10	3M $	Ind	Ind	CCC$	Ind	4
Economics and Computing	GL51	3FT/4SW deg	*	12	MO	M	Ind	Ind	Ind	6
Economics and Law	LM13	3FT deg	* g	12-16	M+2D	M	Ind	CCC	Ind	
Financial Economics	L160	3FT deg	* g	12-16	2D	DD	Ind	CCC	Ind	6 6/16
French and Economics	LR11	4FT deg	F g	12	M+D	M	Ind	Ind	Ind	12
Geography and Economics	LL18	3FT/4SW deg	Ec/Gy g	12	Ind	M	Ind	Ind	Ind	10
German and Economics	LR12	4FT deg	G g	12	M+D	M	Ind	Ind	Ind	

			98 expected requirements							96 entry stats

TITLE	CODE	COURSE	SUBJECTS	A/AS	NO/C	AGNVQ	IB	SQA(H)	SQA	RATIO A/AS
International Economics	L115	3FT deg	* g	12-16	M+2D	M	Ind	CCC	Ind	
Mathematics and Economics	GL11	3FT/4SW deg	M/E g	14-18	3M $	M	M	Ind	Ind	7
Mathematics and Economics	GL1C	4FT/5SW deg	*	2	N	P	Ind	Ind	Ind	
Planning and Economics	LK14	3FT deg	* g	12-16	M+2D	M	Ind	CCC	Ind	
Statistics and Economics	LG14	3FT/4SW deg	M/E g	12-16	3M $	M	Ind	Ind	Ind	18

DE MONTFORT Univ

TITLE	CODE	COURSE	SUBJECTS	A/AS	NO/C	AGNVQ	IB	SQA(H)	SQA	RATIO A/AS
Business Economics/Accounting	LN14▼	3FT deg	* g	18	3M+3D	M	32	AABB	X	
Business Economics/Business	LN11▼	3FT deg	* g	18	3M+3D	M	32	AABB	X	
Economics	L100▼	3FT deg	* g	16	D	D	32	BBB	Ind	91
Economics and Management Science	L1G9▼	4SW deg	* g	12	3M+1D	M$ go	Ind	Ind	Ind	
Economics and Politics (Modular Scheme)	LM11▼	3FT deg	*	16	DO	D	Ind	Ind	Ind	
Economics and Psychology (Modular Scheme)	LL17▼	3FT deg	*	16	DO	D	Ind	Ind	Ind	
Economics and Sociology (Modular Scheme)	LL13▼	3FT deg	*	16	DO	D	Ind	Ind	Ind	
Finance/Business Economics	LN13▼	3FT deg	* g	18	3M+3D	M	32	AABB	X	
Human Resource Management/Business Economics	LN16▼	3FT deg	* g	18	3M+3D	M	32	AABB	Ind	
Law/Business Economics	LM13▼	3FT deg	* g	BBC	6D	M^	30$	BBBBB$	X	
Management Science and Economics	GL91▼	4SW deg	* g	12	3M+1D	M$ go	Ind	Ind	Ind	
Management/Business Economics	LN1C▼	3FT deg	* g	18	3M+3D	M	32	AABB	X	
Public Policy/Business Economics	LL41▼	3FT deg	* g	18	3M+3D	M	32	AABB	X	

Univ of DERBY

TITLE	CODE	COURSE	SUBJECTS	A/AS	NO/C	AGNVQ	IB	SQA(H)	SQA	RATIO A/AS
Financial Economics	L160	3FT deg	*	14	MO+2D	D$	28	BBCC	Ind	
Industrial Economics	L113	3FT deg	*	14	MO+2D	D$	28	BBCC	Ind	
Credit Accumulation Modular Scheme *Economics*	Y600	3FT deg	*	10	MO	M	Ind	CCCC	Ind	

Univ of DUNDEE

TITLE	CODE	COURSE	SUBJECTS	A/AS	NO/C	AGNVQ	IB	SQA(H)	SQA	RATIO A/AS
American Studies and Business Economics & Mkt	Y600	4FT deg	* g	BCC	Ind	D$	29	BBBC	Ind	
American Studies and Economics	QL41	4FT deg	* g	BCC	Ind	D$	29	BBBC	Ind	
American Studies and Financial Economics	QL4C	4FT deg	* g	BCC	Ind	D$	29	BBBC	Ind	
Applied Computing and Economics	GL51	4FT deg	S g	14	5M $	M$	25$	BBBC$	N$	5
Applied Computing and Financial Economics	GL5C	4FT deg	S g	14	5M $	M$	25$	BBBC$	N$	
Business Econ, Marketing and Operational Res	GL4D	4FT deg	M g	14	5M $	M$^	25$	BBBC$	N$	
Business Economics & Marketing & Contemp Euro St	Y601	4FT deg	* g	BCC	Ind	D$	29	BBBC	Ind	1
Business Economics & Marketing & Modern History	Y605	4FT deg	* g	BCC	Ind	D$	29	BBBC	Ind	
Business Economics and Marketing	LN15	4FT deg	* g	BCC	Ind	D$	29	BBBC	Ind	2
Business Economics and Marketing & Political Sci	Y607	4FT deg	* g	BCC	Ind	D$	29	BBBC	Ind	
Business Economics and Marketing and Environ Sci	Y602	4FT deg	* g	BCC	Ind	D$	29	BBBC	Ind	
Business Economics and Marketing and Geography	Y603	4FT deg	* g	BCC	Ind	D$	29	BBBC	Ind	1
Business Economics and Marketing and Mathematics	Y604	4FT deg	M g	BCC	Ind	D$^	29	BBBC	Ind	
Business Economics and Marketing and Philosophy	Y606	4FT deg	* g	BCC	Ind	D$	29	BBBC	Ind	
Business Economics and Marketing and Psychology	Y608	4FT deg	* g	BCC	Ind	D$	29	BBBC	Ind	
Chemistry and Business Economics and Marketing	LF11	4FT deg	2S g	14	5M $	M$	25$	BBCC$	N$	
Chemistry and Economics	FL11	4FT deg	2S g	14	5M $	M$	25$	BBCC$	N$	
Contemporary European St and Financial Economics	LTC2	4FT deg	* g	BCC	Ind	D$	29	BBBC	Ind	
Contemporary European Studies and Economics	LT12	4FT deg	* g	BCC	Ind	D$	29	BBBC	Ind	
Economics	L100	4FT deg	* g	CCC	Ind	D$	29	BBCC	Ind	4 18/18
Economics	L101	4FT deg	M g	14	5M $	M$^	25$	ABB$	N$	
Economics and Environmental Science	FL91	4FT deg	* g	BCC	Ind	D$	29	BBBC	Ind	
Economics and Geography	LL18	4FT deg	* g	BCC	Ind	D$	29	BBBC	Ind	10
Economics and Mathematics	LG11	4FT deg	M g	BCC	Ind	D$^	29$	BBBC$	Ind	
Economics and Modern History	LV11	4FT deg	* g	BCC	Ind	D$	29	BBBC	Ind	
Economics and Philosophy	LV17	4FT deg	* g	BCC	Ind	D$	29	BBBC	Ind	

Economics 18

			98 expected requirements							96 entry stats

course details

TITLE	CODE	COURSE	SUBJECTS	A/AS	ND/C	AGNVQ	IB	SQA(H)	SQA	RATIO A/AS
Economics and Political Science	LM11	4FT deg	* g	BCC	Ind	D$	29	BBBC	Ind	
Economics and Psychology	LL17	4FT deg	* g	BCC	Ind	D$	29	BBBC	Ind	5
Environmental Science and Financial Economics	FLX1	4FT deg	* g	BCC	Ind	D$	29	BBBC	Ind	
Financial Economics	L150	4FT deg	* g	CCC	Ind	D$	29	BBCC	Ind	15
Financial Economics	L160	4FT deg	M g	14	5M $	M$^	25$	ABB$	N$	
Financial Economics and Geography	LLC8	4FT deg	* g	BCC	Ind	D$	29	BBBC	Ind	
Financial Economics and Mathematics	GLC1	4FT deg	M g	BCC	Ind	D$^	29$	BBBC$	Ind	
Financial Economics and Modern History	LVC1	4FT deg	* g	BCC	Ind	D$	29	BBBC	Ind	
Financial Economics and Philosophy	LVC7	4FT deg	* g	BCC	Ind	D$	29	BBBC	HN	
Financial Economics and Political Science	LMC1	4FT deg	* g	BCC	Ind	D$	29	BBBC	Ind	
Financial Economics and Psychology	LLC7	4FT deg	* g	BCC	Ind	D$	29	BBBC	Ind	
Mathematics and Economics	GL11	4FT deg	M g	14	5M $	M$^	25$	BBBC$	N$	2
Mathematics and Financial Economics	GL1C	4FT deg	M g	14	5M $	M$^	25$	BBBC$	N$	
Statistics and Economics	GL41	4FT deg	M g	14	5M $	M$^	25$	BBBC$	N$	
Statistics and Financial Economics	GL4C	4FT deg	M g	14	5M $	M$^	25$	BBBC$	N$	
Arts and Social Sciences *Economics*	Y400	3FT deg	* g	BCC	Ind	D$	29	BBBC	Ind	
Arts and Social Sciences *Financial Economics*	Y400	3FT deg	* g	BCC	Ind	D$	29	BBBC	Ind	

Univ of DURHAM

TITLE	CODE	COURSE	SUBJECTS	A/AS	ND/C	AGNVQ	IB	SQA(H)	SQA	RATIO A/AS
Arabic with Economics	T6L1	4FT deg	* g	BBB	Ind	Ind	28	Ind	Ind	5	
Business Economics	L112	3FT deg	* g	ABC	Ind	X	32$	AAABB	Ind	9	24/30
Economics	L100	3FT deg	* g	ABC	Ind	X	32$	AAABB	Ind	8	24/30
Economics and History	LV11	3FT deg	* g	ABC	Ind	X	32$	AAABB	Ind	9	26/28
Economics and Law	LM13	3FT deg	* g	ABB	DO	X	32$	AAABB	HN	13	
Economics and Politics	LM11	3FT deg	* g	ABC	Ind	X	32$	AAABB	Ind	10	26/30
Economics and Sociology	LL13	3FT deg	* g	ABC	Ind	X	32$	AAABB	Ind		
Economics with French	L1R1	4FT deg	F g	ABC	Ind	X	32$	AAABB	Ind	10	28/28
Economics with Mathematics	L1G1	3FT deg	M	ABC	Ind	X	32$	Ind	Ind		
Environment and Development	L1F9▼	3FT deg	S	DD	Ind	Ind	Dip	CCCCC	Ind	2	6/16
Law with Economics	M3L1	3FT deg	* g	AAB	DO	X	32	AAABB	HN	16	
Mathematics and Economics	GL11	3FT deg	M	ABC	Ind	X	32$	AAABB$	Ind	9	26/30
Social Sciences Combined *Economics*	Y220	3FT deg	* g	ABC	Ind	Ind	32$	AAABB	Ind		

Univ of EAST ANGLIA

TITLE	CODE	COURSE	SUBJECTS	A/AS	ND/C	AGNVQ	IB	SQA(H)	SQA	RATIO A/AS
Business Finance and Economics	NL41	3FT deg	* g	BBC	3M+3D	D	30	BBBBB	Ind	10	20/22
Economics	L100	3FT deg	*	BBC	3M+3D		30	BBBBB	Ind	4	16/26
Economics and Economic and Social History	LV13	3FT deg	*	BBC	3M+3D		30	BBBBB	Ind	18	
Economics and Philosophy	LV17	3FT deg	*	BBC	3M+3D		30	BBBBB	Ind	8	
Economics with Accountancy	L1N4	3FT deg	*	BCC	3M+3D		30	BBBBB	Ind	15	
Economics with a Modern European Language	L1T2	4FT deg	L/*	BBC	3M+3D		30	BBBBB	Ind	4	
Mathematics with Economics	G1L1	3FT deg	M	BCC	Ind		32$	BBBC$	X	8	
Politics and Economics	LM11	3FT deg	*	BBC	3M+3D		30	BBBBB	Ind	5	20/28
Sociology and Economics	LL31	3FT deg	*	BBC	3M+3D		30	BBBBB	Ind	9	
Economic and Social Studies (4 years) *Economics*	Y200	4FT deg	*						Ind		

Univ of EAST LONDON

TITLE	CODE	COURSE	SUBJECTS	A/AS	ND/C	AGNVQ	IB	SQA(H)	SQA	RATIO A/AS
Accounting & Finance and Economics	NL41	3FT deg	* g	14	MO	MB	Ind	Ind	Ind	4
Accounting & Finance with Economics	N4L1	3FT deg	* g	14	M	D	Ind	Ind	Ind	
Applied Economics	L100	3FT deg	* g	12	MO	MB	Ind	Ind	Ind	10
Archaeological Sciences and Economics	FL41	3FT deg	* g	12	MO	MB	Ind	Ind	Ind	
Business Economics	L112	3FT deg	* g	12	MO		Ind	Ind	Ind	4

TITLE	CODE	COURSE	SUBJECTS	A/AS	NO/C	AGNVQ	IB	SQA(H)	SQA	RATIO A/AS
course details			**98 expected requirements**							**96 entry stats**
Business Studies and Economics	LN11	3FT deg	* g	12	N	MB	Ind	Ind	Ind	14
Business Studies with Economics	N1L1	3FT deg	* g	14	MO	MB				
Development Economics	L118	3FT deg	* g	12	MO	M	Ind	Ind	Ind	
Economics	L110	3FT deg	* g	12	MO	MB	Ind	Ind	Ind	4
Economics and Environmental Sciences	LF19	3FT deg	* g	12	MO	M				
Economics and French	LR11	3FT deg	* g	12	MO	M^	Ind	Ind	Ind	2
Economics and German	LR12	3FT deg	* g	12	MO	M^	Ind	Ind	Ind	
Economics and History	LV11	3FT deg	* g	12	MO	M	Ind	Ind	Ind	
Economics and Law	LM13	3FT deg	* g	12	MO	D	Ind	Ind	Ind	5
Economics and Maths, Stats & Computing	GL91	3FT deg	* g	12	MO	M$	Ind	Ind	Ind	
Economics and Politics	LM11	3FT deg	* g	12	MO	M	Ind	Ind	Ind	6
Economics and Psychosocial Studies	LL17	3FT deg	* g	12	MO	M$	Ind	Ind	Ind	
Economics and Social Policy Research	LL1K	3FT deg	* g	12	MO					
Economics and Social Sciences	LL1H	3FT deg	* g	12	MO	MB	Ind	Ind	Ind	
Economics and Spanish	LR14	3FT deg	* g	12	MO	M^	Ind	Ind	Ind	
Economics and Third World & Development Studies	LM1Y	3FT deg	* g	12	MO	M	Ind	Ind	Ind	
Economics with Accounting & Finance	L1N4	3FT deg	* g	12	MO	M	Ind	Ind	Ind	
Economics with Archaeological Sciences	L1F4	3FT deg	* g	12	MO	M	Ind			
Economics with Business Studies	L1N1	3FT deg	* g	12	MO	M	Ind			
Economics with Environmental Sciences	L1F9	3FT deg	* g	12	MO	M	Ind			
Economics with European Studies	L1T2	3FT deg	* g	12	MO	M	Ind			
Economics with French	L1R1	3FT deg	* g	12	MO	M	Ind			
Economics with German	L1R2	3FT deg	* g	12	MO	M	Ind			
Economics with History	L1V1	3FT deg	* g	12	MO	M	Ind			
Economics with Italian	L1R3	3FT deg	* g	12	MO	M	Ind			
Economics with Law	L1M3	3FT deg	* g	12	MO	M	Ind			
Economics with Maths, Stats & Computing	L1G9	3FT deg	* g	12	MO	M	Ind			
Economics with Politics	L1M1	3FT deg	* g	12	MO	M	Ind			
Economics with Psychosocial Studies	L1L7	3FT deg	* g	12	MO	M	Ind			
Economics with Social Policy Research	L1L4	3FT deg	* g	12	MO	M	Ind			
Economics with Social Sciences	L1Y2	3FT deg	* g	12	MO	M	Ind			
Economics with Spanish	L1R4	3FT deg	* g	12	MO	M	Ind			
Economics with Third World & Development Studies	L1M9	3FT deg	* g	12	MO	M	Ind			
Environmental Sciences with Economics	F9L1	3FT deg	* g	12	MO	M	Ind	Ind	Ind	
European Economics	L170	4SW deg	* g	12	MO	M	Ind	Ind	Ind	
European Studies with Economics	T2L1	3FT deg	* g	12	MO	M	Ind	Ind		
French with Economics	R1L1	3FT deg	* g	12	MO	M	Ind			
German with Economics	R2L1	3FT deg	* g	12	MO	M	Ind			
History with Economics	V1L1	3FT deg	* g	12	MO	M	Ind	Ind		
Information Technology with Economics	G5L1	3FT deg	* g	12	MO	M	Ind	Ind	Ind	
Maths, Stats & Computing with Economics	G9L1	3FT deg	* g	12	MO	M	Ind	Ind	Ind	
Politics with Economics	M1L1	3FT deg	* g	12	MO	M	Ind			
Psychosocial Studies with Economics	L7L1	3FT deg	* g	12	MO	M	Ind	Ind	Ind	
Social Policy Research with Economics	L4L1	3FT deg	* g	12	MO	M	Ind	Ind	Ind	
Social Sciences with Economics	L3L1	3FT deg	* g	12	MO	M	Ind	Ind	Ind	
Spanish with Economics	R4L1	3FT deg	* g	12	MO	M	Ind			
Third World & Development Studies with Economics	M9L1	3FT deg	* g	12	MO	M	Ind	Ind		
Three-Subject Degree *Economics*	Y600	3FT deg	* g	12	MO	M	Ind	Ind	Ind	

Univ of EDINBURGH

TITLE	CODE	COURSE	SUBJECTS	A/AS	NO/C	AGNVQ	IB	SQA(H)	SQA	RATIO A/AS
Agricultural Economics	DL21	4FT deg	S g	CCD	MO $		Dip$	BBBC$	N$	12
Arabic and Economics	TL61	4FT deg	g	BBB	Ind	Ind	Dip$	BBBB	Ind	

Economics 18

				98 expected requirements							96 entry stats	
TITLE	CODE	COURSE	SUBJECTS	A/AS	ND/C	RGNVQ	IB	SQA(H)	SQA	RATIO	A/AS
Business Studies and Economics	NL11	4FT deg	g	BBB	Ind		34$	ABBB	Ind	9	
Economics	L100	4FT deg	g	BBB	Ind		34$	ABBB	Ind	5	
Economics and Accounting	LN14	4FT deg	g	BBB	Ind		34$	ABBB	Ind	10	
Economics and Economic History	LV13	4FT deg	g	BBB	Ind		34$	ABBB	Ind	11	
Economics and Law	LM13	4FT deg	g	ABB	Ind		36$	AABB	Ind	33	
Economics and Mathematics	LG11	4FT deg	M	BBB	Ind		34$	ABBB	Ind	29	
Economics and Politics	LM11	4FT deg	g	ABB	Ind		36$	AABB	Ind	7	
Economics and Sociology	LL13	4FT deg	g	BBB	Ind		34$	ABBB	Ind	4	
Economics and Statistics	LG14	4FT deg	M	BBB	Ind		34$	ABBB	Ind	6	
Economics with Environmental Studies	L1F9	4FT deg		BBB			34	ABBB			
Geography and Economics	LL81	4FT deg	*	ABB	Ind		36$	AABB	Ind	31	
Law and Economics	ML31	4FT deg	g	ABB	X		32	AAABB	X	7	
Philosophy and Economics	VL71	4FT deg	g	BBB	Ind	Ind	Dip$	BBBB	Ind		
Social Policy and Economics	LL41	4FT deg	*	BBB	Ind		34$	ABBB	Ind		
Social Science	Y200	3FT deg	* g	BBB	Ind		34$	ABBB	Ind		
Economics											

Univ of ESSEX

TITLE	CODE	COURSE	SUBJECTS	A/AS	ND/C	RGNVQ	IB	SQA(H)	SQA	RATIO	A/AS
Accounting and Economics	NL41	3FT deg	* g	20	MO+3D	D	28	BBBB	Ind	41	
Economics	L100	3FT deg	g	22	MO+2D	D	28	BBBB	Ind	5	12/22
Economics (European Exchange)	L105	4FT deg	*	22	MO	D	28	BBBC	Ind		
Economics and Politics	LM11	3FT deg	* g	22	MO+2D	D	28	BBBB	Ind	16	
History and Economics	LV11	3FT deg	* g	20	MO+2D	Ind	28	BBBB	Ind	15	
International Economics and Trade Policy	L115	3FT deg	g	20	MO+2D	Ind	28	BBBB	Ind	11	
Mathematics with Economics	G1L1	3FT deg	M	CCC	MO $	Ind	28$	CSYS	Ind		
Mathematics, Operational Research and Economics	G4L1	3FT deg	M	18	MO $	D^	28	CSYS	Ind	14	
Statistics and Economics	GL41	3FT deg	M	CCC	MO $	Ind	28$	CSYS	Ind		

Univ of EXETER

TITLE	CODE	COURSE	SUBJECTS	A/AS	ND/C	RGNVQ	IB	SQA(H)	SQA	RATIO	A/AS
Business Economics	L112	3FT deg	* g	ABC	2M+3D	D$	36	Ind	Ind	7	18/28
Business Economics with European Study	L115	4FT deg	L g	ABC	2M+3D	D$	36	Ind	Ind	7	26/28
Economic & Political Development	LMD1	3FT deg	* g	BBB-CCC	2M+3D	M/D$	30	Ind	Ind	4	18/28
Economic & Political Development with Euro Study	LMDC	4FT deg	g	BBB-CCC	2M+3D	M/D$	30	Ind	Ind	3	
Economics	L100	3FT deg	* g	ABC	2M+3D	D$	36	Ind	Ind	6	20/28
Economics and Geography	LL18	3FT deg	Gv g	BBB	2M+3D	D$^	36$	Ind	Ind	6	20/26
Economics and Geography with European Study	LLC8	4FT deg	L+Gv g	BBB	2M+3D	D$^	36$	Ind	Ind	8	
Economics and Politics	LM11	3FT deg	* g	ABC	2M+3D	D$	36	Ind	Ind	5	16/28
Economics and Politics with European Study	LM1C	4FT deg	L g	ABC	2M+3D	D$	36	Ind	Ind	8	
Economics and Statistics	L142	3FT deg	M/St	BCC	2M+3D	M$^	32$	Ind	Ind	5	14/26
Economics and Statistics with European Study	L141	4FT deg	M/St+L	BCC	2M+3D	M$^	32$	Ind	Ind		
Economics of Agric, Food and Nat Res (Euro St)	L131	4FT deg	L g	BCC	2M+3D	M$	32	Ind	Ind		
Economics of Agriculture, Food & Nat Resources	L137	3FT deg	* g	BCC	2M+3D	M$	32	Ind	Ind	6	
Economics with European Study	L101	4FT deg	L g	ABC	2M+3D	D$	36	Ind	Ind	3	20/30
Managerial Statistics	L143	3FT deg	M/St	BCC	2M+3D	M/D$^	32$	Ind	Ind	6	
Managerial Statistics with European Study	L144	4FT deg	L+M/St	BCC	2M+3D	M/D$^	32$	Ind	Ind	2	
Mathematics with Economics	G1L1	3FT deg	M	22	2M+3D	M/D$^	34$	Ind	Ind	7	16/30

Univ of GLAMORGAN

TITLE	CODE	COURSE	SUBJECTS	A/AS	ND/C	RGNVQ	IB	SQA(H)	SQA	RATIO	A/AS
Business Studies and Economics	NL11	3FT deg	* g	14	MO+3D	M$	Ind	Ind	Ind		
Economics and Politics	LM1D	3FT deg									
Economics and Public Policy	LM1C	3FT deg									
Government and Economics	ML11	3FT deg	* g	12	MO+1D	M	Ind	Ind	Ind		
Combined Studies	Y400	3FT deg	* g	8-16	Ind	Ind	Ind	Ind	Ind		
Managerial Economics											

course details			98 expected requirements							96 entry stats
TITLE	CODE	COURSE	SUBJECTS	A/AS	ND/C	AGNVQ	IB	SQA(H)	SQA	RATIO A/AS
Combined Studies (Honours) *Business/Economics*	Y400	3FT deg	* g	8-16	Ind	Ind	Ind	Ind	Ind	
Major/Minor Honours *Managerial Economics*	Y402	3FT deg	* g	8-16	Ind	Ind	Ind	Ind	Ind	

Univ of GLASGOW

course details			98 expected requirements							96 entry stats
Accountancy/Economics	LN1K	4FT deg		BBB	HN		32$	AAABB	X	16
Agricultural Economics	L132	4FT deg		BCC	5M		28	BBBB	X	4
Agricultural Economics	L130	4FT deg	2S	BBC-CCC	N	M	24$	BBBB$	N	
Archaeology/Economics	LV16	4FT deg		BBC	HN	M	30	BBBB	Ind	
Business Economics and Business History	LN1C	4FT deg		BBC	N	M	30	BBBB	N	
Business Economics with Celtic	L1QM	4FT deg		BBC	N	M	30	BBBB	N	
Business Economics with Czech	L1TD	4FT deg		BBC	N	M	30	BBBB	N	
Business Economics with French	L1RC	4FT deg		BBC	N	M	30	BBBB	N	
Business Economics with German	L1RF	4FT deg		BBC	N	M	30	BBBB	N	
Business Economics with Hispanic Studies	L1RK	4FT deg		BBC	N	M	30	BBBB	N	
Business Economics with Italian	L1RH	4FT deg		BBC	N	M	30	BBBB	N	
Business Economics with Polish	L101	4FT deg		BBC	N	M	30	BBBB	N	
Business Economics with Russian	L1RV	4FT deg		BBC	N	M	30	BBBB	N	
Business Economics/Accountancy	LNC4	4FT deg		BBC	N	M	30	BBBB	N	
Business Economics/Archaeology	LVC6	4FT deg		BBC	N	M	30	BBBB	N	
Business Economics/Computing Science	LGC5	4FT deg		BBC	N	M	30	BBBB	N	
Business Economics/History	LVC1	4FT deg		BBC	N	M	30	BBBB	N	
Business Economics/Mathematics	LGC1	4FT deg		BBC	N	M	30	BBBB	N	
Business Economics/Politics	LMC1	4FT deg		BBC	N	M	30	BBBB	N	
Business Economics/Psychology	LCC8	4FT deg		BBC	N	M	30	BBBB	N	
Business Economics/Scottish History	LVCD	4FT deg		BBC	N	M	30	BBBB	N	
Business Economics/Social and Urban Policy	LLC4	4FT deg		BBC	N	M	30	BBBB	N	
Business Economics/Sociology	LLC3	4FT deg		BBC	N	M	30	BBBB	N	
Business Economics/Statistics	LGC4	4FT deg		BBC	N	M	30	BBBB	N	
Celtic/Economics	LQ15	4FT deg		BBC	8M	M	30	BBBB	Ind	
Classical Hebrew/Economics	LVCW	4FT deg		BBC	HN	M	30	BBBB	Ind	
Computing/Economics	GL5C	4FT deg		BBC	HN	M	30	BBBB	Ind	2
Czech/Economics	LTC1	5FT deg		BBC	HN	M	30	BBBB	Ind	
Economic and Social History/Economics	LV1H	4FT deg		BBC	8M	M	30	BBBB	Ind	3
Economics	L114	4FT deg		BBC	8M	M	30	BBBB	Ind	8
Economics	L116	4FT deg		BBC	HN	M	30	BBBB	Ind	14
Economics with Business Economics	L111	4FT deg		BBC	N	M	30	BBBB	N	
Economics with Celtic	L1Q5	4FT deg		BBC	8M	M	30	BBBB	Ind	
Economics with Czech	L1T1	4FT deg		BBC	8M	M	30	BBBB	Ind	
Economics with French	L1R1	4FT deg		BBC	8M	M	30	BBBB	Ind	
Economics with German	L1R2	4FT deg		BBC	8M	M	30	BBBB	Ind	
Economics with Hispanic Studies	L1R4	4FT deg		BBC	8M	M	30	BBBB	Ind	
Economics with Italian	L1R3	4FT deg		BBC	8M	M	30	BBBB	Ind	
Economics with Polish	L1TC	4FT deg		BBC	8M	M	30	BBBB	Ind	
Economics with Russian	L1R8	4FT deg		BBC	8M	M	30	BBBB	Ind	
Economics/Accountancy	LND4	4FT deg		BBC	8M	M	30	BBBB	Ind	3
Economics/Archaeology	VL61	4FT deg		BBC	HN	M	30	BBBB	Ind	
Economics/Computing Science	GLN1	4FT deg		BBC	8N	M	30	BBBB	Ind	
Economics/History	LV11	4FT deg		BBC	8M	M	30	BBBB	Ind	
Economics/Mathematics	GL11	4FT deg		BBC	8M	M	30	BBBB	Ind	
Economics/Politics	LM11	4FT deg		BBC	8M	M	30	BBBB	Ind	4
Economics/Psychology	LC18	4FT deg		BBC	HN	M	30	BBBB	Ind	6

course details			98 expected requirements							96 entry stats	
TITLE	CODE	COURSE	SUBJECTS	A/AS	ND/C	AGNVQ	IB	SQA(H)	SQA	RATIO A/AS	
Economics/Psychology	CL81	4FT deg		BBC	8M	M	30	BBBB	Ind	4	
Economics/Russian	LRD8	5FT deg		BBC	HN	M	30	BBBB	Ind		
Economics/Scottish History	LV1C	4FT deg		BBC	HN	M	30	BBBB	Ind		
Economics/Scottish History	LVCC	4FT deg		BBC	8M	M	30	BBBB	Ind		
Economics/Scottish Literature	LQ12	4FT deg		BBC	HN	M	30	BBBB	Ind		
Economics/Social and Urban Policy	LL14	4FT deg		BBC	8M	M	30	BBBB	Ind		
Economics/Sociology	LLD3	4FT deg		BBC	8M	M	30	BBBB	Ind	3	
Economics/Statistics	LG14	4FT deg		BBC	HN	M	30	BBBB	Ind	3	
Economics/Statistics	L148	4FT deg		BBC	8M	M	30	BBBB	Ind		
English/Economics	LQC3	4FT deg		BBC	HN	M	30	BBBB	Ind		
French/Economics	LR11	5FT deg		BBC	HN	M	30	BBBB	Ind	4	
Geography/Economics	LL18	4FT deg		BBC	8M	M	30	BBBB	Ind	13	
German/Economics	LRC2	5FT deg		BBC	HN	M	30	BBBB	Ind		
Greek/Economics	LQ17	4FT deg		BBC	HN	M	30	BBBB	Ind		
Hispanic Studies/Economics	LRC4	5FT deg		BBC	HN	M	30	BBBB	Ind		
History of Art/Economics	LV14	4FT deg		BBC	HN	M	30	BBBB	Ind		
History/Economics	LV1D	4FT deg		BBC	HN	M	30	BBBB	Ind	5	
Islamic Studies/Economics	TL61	4FT deg		BBC	N	M	30	BBBB	Ind		
Latin/Economics	LQ16	4FT deg		BBC	HN	M	30	BBBB	Ind		
Management Studies/Economics	LN11	4FT deg		BBC	8M	M	30	BBBB	Ind	5	
Mathematics/Economics	GL1C	4FT deg		BBC	HN	M	30	BBBB	Ind		
Music/Economics	LWC3	4FT deg		BBC	HN	M	30	BBBB	Ind		
Philosophy/Economics	LV1R	4FT deg		BBC	HN	M	30	BBBB	Ind		
Philosophy/Economics	LVD7	4FT deg		BBC	8M	M	30	BBBB	Ind	2	
Polish/Economics	LT11	5FT deg		BBC	HN	M	30	BBBB	Ind		
Theatre Studies/Economics	LW14	4FT deg		BBC	HN	M	30	BBBB	Ind		
Theology & Religious Studies/Economics	LV1V	4FT deg		BBC	HN	M	30	BBBB	Ind		

GLASGOW CALEDONIAN Univ

Accountancy with Economics	N4L1	3FT/4FT deg	E+M	BC	Ind		Ind	BBBC$	Ind		
Business Economics	L112	3FT/4FT deg	M+E	CDD	Ind		Ind	BBCC$	Ind	6	

GOLDSMITHS COLL (Univ of London)

Economics, Politics and Public Policy	LM11	3FT deg		BCD	MO	M	Dip	BCCCC	N	4	4/20
Politics with Economics	M1L1	3FT deg		BCD	MO	M	Dip	BBBBC	N	2	8/22
Social Policy with Economics	L4L1	3FT deg		BCD	MO	M	Dip	BBBBC	N		

Univ of GREENWICH

Economics	L114	3FT deg	* g	14	3M	Ind	Ind	Ind	Ind		
Economics and Psychology	LL17	3FT deg	* g	16	3M	Ind	Ind	ABC	Ind		
Economics with Banking	L1NH	3FT deg	* g	14	3M	Ind	Ind	Ind	Ind		
Economics with Economic Development	L115	3FT deg	* g	14	3M	Ind	Ind	Ind	Ind		
Economics with European Economics	L170	3FT deg	* g	14	3M	Ind	Ind	Ind	Ind		
Economics with Psychology	L1L7	3FT deg	* g	16	3M	Ind	Ind	ABC	Ind		
Economics with Sociology	L1L3	3FT deg	* g	14	3M	Ind	25	ABC	Ind		
Sociology & Economics	LL31	3FT deg	* g	14	3M	Ind	Ind	Ind	Ind		
Sociology with Economics	L3L1	3FT deg	* g	14	3M	Ind	Ind	Ind	Ind		

HERIOT-WATT Univ

Business and Economics	LN11	4FT deg	* g	CCC	MO	M$ go	30	BBBB	Ind		
Chemistry with Environmental Economics	F1L1	4FT deg	C+S	DDD	$	M$ go	28	BBCC	$		
Chemistry with Environmental Economics (MChem)	F1LC	6FT deg	C+S	DDD	$	M$ go	28	BBCC	$		
Economics	L100	4FT deg	*	CCC	HN	M$ go	28	BBBC	HN		
Economics and Accountancy	LN14	4FT deg	*	BCC	HN	M$ go	Ind	ABBB	Ind		

course details | 98 expected requirements | 96 entry stats

TITLE	CODE	COURSE	SUBJECTS	A/AS	ND/C	AGNVQ	IB	SQA(H)	SQA	RATIO A/AS
Economics and European Studies	LT12	4FT deg	L	BCC		M$ go	30	BBBB	Ind	
Economics and Finance	LN13	4FT deg	*	CCC	HN	M$ go	28	BBBB	HN	
Economics and Languages: French/German	LT19	4FT deg	L	BBC	Ind	Ind	Ind	AABB	Ind	
Economics and Languages: French/Russian	LTCX	4FT deg	L	BBC	Ind	Ind	Ind	AABB	Ind	
Economics and Languages: French/Spanish	LTDX	4FT deg	L	BBC	Ind	Ind	Ind	AABB	Ind	
Economics and Languages: German/Russian	LTDY	4FT deg	L	BBC	Ind	Ind	Ind	AABB	Ind	
Economics and Languages: German/Spanish	LT1X	4FT deg	L	BBC	Ind	Ind	Ind	AABB	Ind	
Economics and Languages: Spanish/Russian	LTCY	4FT deg	L	BBC	Ind	Ind	Ind	AABB	Ind	
Mathematics with Economics	G1L1	4FT deg	M	CDE	HN	M$^	28	BBB	HN	
Combined Studies *Economics*	Y300	4FT deg	*	CCC	Ind	M$ go	30	BBBB	Ind	

Univ of HERTFORDSHIRE

TITLE	CODE	COURSE	SUBJECTS	A/AS	ND/C	AGNVQ	IB	SQA(H)	SQA	RATIO A/AS
Applied Geology/Economics	F6L1	3FT deg	* g	12	3M	M$ gi	24$	CCCC$	Ind	
Applied Physics/Economics	F3L1	3FT deg	M+P	12	3M $	M$ gi	24$	CCCC$	Ind	
Applied Statistics/Economics	G4L1	3FT deg	*	12	3M	M$ gi	24	CCCC	Ind	
Astronomy/Economics	F5L1	3FT deg	M g	12	3M $	M$ gi	24$	CCCC$	Ind	
Business Economics	L112	3FT/4SW deg	* g	16	D0	D $	26	BBBC	Ind	
Business/Economics	N1L1	3FT deg	*	18	4M+4D	M$6 gi	26	BBBC	Ind	11
Chemistry/Economics	F1L1	3FT deg	C g	12	3M $	MS gi	24$	CCCC$	Ind	
Economics	L101	3FT/4SW deg	* g	16	D0	D $	26	BBBC	Ind	2 6/14
Economics	L102	3FT deg	* g	12	3M $	M$ gi	24	CCCC$	Ind	
Economics with options	L3L1	3FT deg	* g	14	M+D	Ind	26	BBCC	Ind	
Economics/Applied Geology	L1F6	3FT deg	* g	12	3M $	M$ gi	24$	CCCC$	Ind	
Economics/Applied Physics	L1F3	3FT deg	M+P	12	3M $	M$ gi	24$	CCCC$	Ind	
Economics/Applied Statistics	L1G4	3FT deg	*	12	3M $	M$ gi	24	CCCC	Ind	3
Economics/Astronomy	L1F5	3FT deg	M g	12	3M $	M$ gi	24$	CCCC$	Ind	
Economics/Business	L1N1	3FT deg	*	18	4M+4D	M$6 gi	26	BBBC	Ind	11
Economics/Chemistry	L1F1	3FT deg	C g	12	3M $	MS gi	24$	CCCC$	Ind	
Economics/Electronic Music	L1W3	3FT deg	Mu	14	MO $	M$^ gi	26$	BCCC$	Ind	
Economics/Electronics	L1H6	3FT deg	* g	12	3M $	M$ gi	24$	CCCC$	Ind	2
Economics/European Studies	L1T2	3FT deg	*	14	MO	M$ gi	26	BCCC	Ind	2
Economics/Human Biology	L1B1	3FT deg	S g	12	3M $	MS gi	24$	CCCC$	Ind	
Economics/Law	L1M3	3FT deg	*	20	4M+4D	D$ gi	26	BBBC	Ind	9
Economics/Linguistic Science	L1Q1	3FT deg	*	14	MO $	M$ gi	26	BCCC	Ind	
Economics/Manufacturing Systems	L1H7	3FT deg	*	12	3M	M$ gi	24	CCCC	Ind	1
Economics/Mathematics	L1G1	3FT deg	M	12	3M $	M$^ gi	24$	CCCC$	Ind	
Economics/Psychology	L1C8	3FT deg	*	20	4M+4D	D$ gi	26	BBBC	Ind	
Electronic Music/Economics	W3L1	3FT deg	Mu	14	MO $	M$^ gi	26$	BCCC$	Ind	
Electronics/Economics	H6L1	3FT deg	* g	12	3M $	M$ gi	24$	CCCC$	Ind	
European Studies/Economics	T2L1	3FT deg	*	14	MO	M$ gi	26	BCCC	Ind	1
Human Biology/Economics	B1L1	3FT deg	S g	12	3M $	MS gi	26$	CCCC$	Ind	
International Economics	L170	3FT/4SW deg	* g	16	D0	D $	26	BBBC	Ind	
Law/Economics	M3L1	3FT deg	*	20	4M+4D	D$ gi	26	BBBC	Ind	16
Linguistic Science/Economics	Q1L1	3FT deg	*	14	MO $	M$ gi	26	BCCC	Ind	
Manufacturing Systems/Economics	H7L1	3FT deg	*	12	3M	M$ gi	24	CCCC	Ind	1
Mathematics/Economics	G1L1	3FT deg	M	12	3M $	M$^ gi	24$	CCCC$	Ind	12
Politics/Economics	M1L1	3FT deg	* g	14	M+D	Ind	26	BBCC		
Psychology/Economics	C8L1	3FT deg	*	20	4M+4D	D$ gi	26	BBBC	Ind	5
Social Policy/Economics	L4L1	3FT deg	* g	14	M+D	Ind	26	BBCC	Ind	
Sociology/Economics	L3LC	3FT deg	* g	14	M+D	Ind	26	BBCC	Ind	
Combined Modular Scheme *Economics*	Y100	3FT deg	*	12	3M	M$ gi	24	CCCC	Ind	

Economics 18

			98 expected requirements							96 entry stats

course details / 98 expected requirements / 96 entry stats

TITLE	CODE	COURSE	SUBJECTS	A/AS	NO/C	AGNVQ	IB	SQA(H)	SQA	RATIO A/AS
Univ of HUDDERSFIELD										
Economics	L100	3FT/4SW deg	* g	14	3M+3D	M$ go	26	BBCC	Ind	
Financial Management and Economics	LN13	3FT deg	* g	14	3M+3D	M$ go	Ind	BBCC	Ind	
Politics and Economics	ML11	3FT deg	*	14	MO+3D	M6/^	Ind	BBBC	Ind	
Univ of HULL										
Economics	L100	3FT deg	* g	BCC	M+D	M*^ go	28	BBBCC	Ind	5	16/24
Economics and Accounting	LN14	3FT deg	* g	BCC	MO	M*^ go	28$	BBCCC	Ind	5	12/26
Economics and Business Economics	L112	3FT deg	* g	BCC	M+D	M*^ go	28	BBBCC	Ind	8	18/24
Economics and Economic History	VL31	3FT deg	* g	BBC-BCC	MO	M*^ go	26$	BBCCC	Ind	3	
Economics and Management Sciences	LN11	3FT deg	M	BBC-BCC	MO $	M*^ go	26$	Ind	Ind	5	
Economics/Geography	LL18	3FT deg	Gy g	BCC	Ind	M*^ go	28$	BBCCC	Ind	11	22/24
International and Financial Economics	L171	3FT deg	* g	BCC	M+D	M*^ go	28	BBBCC	Ind	9	
Mathematics and Economics	GL11	3FT deg	M	BCC-BCD	MO $	M$^ go | 26$	BBCCC	Ind	12	
Statistics and Economics	GL41	3FT deg	M	18-20	MO $	M$^ gi	26$	BBCCC	Ind	
Politics, Philosophy, Economics *Economics*	Y616	3FT deg	*	BBB	MO+2D	Ind	28	BBBCC	Ind	
KEELE Univ										
Biological and Medicinal Chemistry and Economics	FLC1	3FT deg	C g	BCC	Ind	D$^	28$	CSYS	Ind	
Economics and American Studies	LQ14	3FT deg	* g	BCC	Ind	Ind	28	CSYS	Ind	
Economics and Ancient History	LV1D	3FT deg	* g	BCC	Ind	Ind	28	CSYS	Ind	3
Economics and Ancient History (4 Yrs)	VLD1	4FT deg	*	BCC	Ind	Ind	28	BBBB	Ind	
Economics and Applied Social Studies	LL15	3FT deg	* g	BCC	Ind	Ind	28	CSYS	Ind	
Economics and Astrophysics	FL51	3FT deg	P g	BCC	Ind	D$^	28$	CSYS	Ind	2
Economics and Astrophysics (4 Yrs)	LF15	4FT deg	*	BCC	Ind	Ind	28	BBBB	Ind	
Economics and Biochemistry	CL71	3FT deg	C g	BCC	Ind	D$^	28$	CSYS	Ind	
Economics and Biochemistry (4 Yrs)	LC17	4FT deg	*	BCC	Ind	Ind	28	BBBB	Ind	
Economics and Biology (4 Yrs)	LC11	4FT deg	* g	BCC	Ind	Ind	28	BBBB	Ind	
Economics and Business Administration (4 Yrs)	NL91	4FT deg	* g	BCC	Ind	Ind	28	BBBB	Ind	
Economics and Chemistry	FL11	3FT deg	C g	BCC	Ind	D$^	28$	CSYS	Ind	
Economics and Classical Studies	LQ18	3FT deg	* g	BCC	Ind	Ind	28	CSYS	Ind	
Economics and Classical Studies (4 Yrs)	QL81	4FT deg	*	BCC	Ind	Ind	28	BBBB	Ind	
Economics and Computer Science	GL51	3FT deg	* g	BCC	Ind	Ind	28	CSYS	Ind	3
Economics and Criminology	LM1H	3FT deg	* g	BBB	Ind	Ind	32	CSYS	Ind	6
Economics and Criminology (4 Yrs)	MLH1	4FT deg	*	BBB	Ind	Ind	32	ABBB	Ind	
Educational Studies and Economics	LX19	3FT deg	* g	BCC	Ind	Ind	28	CSYS	Ind	
Electronic Music and Economics	LW1J	3FT deg	Mu g	BCC	Ind	D$^	28$	CSYS	Ind	
Electronic Music and Economics (4 Yrs)	WLJ1	4FT deg	*	BCC	Ind	Ind	28	BBBB	Ind	
English and Economics	LQ13	3FT deg	E g	BBC	Ind	D$^	30$	CSYS	Ind	3
English and Economics (4 Yrs)	QL31	4FT deg	*	BBC	Ind	Ind	30	BBBB	Ind	
Environmental Management and Economics	FLX1	3FT deg	* g	BCC	Ind	Ind	28	BBBB	Ind	
Finance and Economics	LN13	3FT deg	* g	BCC	Ind	Ind	28	CSYS	Ind	
Finance and Economics (4 Yrs)	NL31	4FT deg	*	BCC	Ind	Ind	28	BBBB	Ind	
French and Economics	LR11	3FT deg	F g	BCC	Ind	D$^	28$	CSYS	Ind	
French/German and Economics	LT19	3FT deg	F+G g	BBC	Ind	D$^	30$	CSYS	Ind	
French/Russian or Russian Studies and Economics	LT1X	3FT deg	F+R g	BBC-BCC	Ind	D$^	28$	CSYS	Ind	
Geography and Economics	LL18	3FT deg	Gy g	BCC	Ind	D$^ | 28$	CSYS	Ind	9	16/16
Geography and Economics (4 Yrs)	LL81	4FT deg	*	BCC	Ind	Ind	28	BBBB	Ind	10
Geology and Economics	FL61	3FT deg	S g	BCC	Ind	D$^	28$	CSYS	Ind	
Geology and Economics (4 Yrs)	LF16	4FT deg	*	BCC	Ind	Ind	28	BBBB	Ind	
German and Economics	LR12	3FT deg	G g	BCC	Ind	D$^	28$	CSYS	Ind	
German and Economics (4 Yrs)	RL21	4FT deg	G	BCC	Ind	Ind	28$	BBBB	Ind	

course details   98 expected requirements   96 entry stats

TITLE	CODE	COURSE	SUBJECTS	A/AS	ND/C	AGNVQ	IB	SQA(H)	SQA	RATIO	A/AS
German/Russian or Russian St and Econ (4 Yrs)	TLY1	4FT deg	G	BCC	Ind	Ind	28$	BBBB	Ind		
German/Russian or Russian Studies and Economics	LT1Y	3FT deg	G+R g	BBC-BCC	Ind	D$^	28$	CSYS	Ind		
History and Economics (4 Yrs)	VL11	4FT deg	* g	BCC	Ind	Ind	28	BBBB	Ind		
Human Resource Management and Economics	LN16	3FT deg	* g	BCC	Ind	Ind	28	CSYS	Ind	6	
Human Resource Management and Economics (4 Yrs)	NL61	4FT deg	*	BCC	Ind	Ind	28	BBBB	Ind		
International History and Economics	LV1C	3FT deg	* g	BCC	Ind	Ind	28	CSYS	Ind	2	18/18
International History and Economics (4 Yrs)	VLC1	4FT deg	*	BCC	Ind	Ind	28	BBBB	Ind		
International Politics and Economics	LM1C	3FT deg	* g	BCC	Ind	Ind	28	CSYS	Ind	3	
Latin and Economics	LQ16	3FT deg	Ln g	BCC	Ind	D$^	28$	CSYS	Ind		
Latin and Economics (4 Yrs)	QL61	4FT deg	*	BCC	Ind	Ind	28	BBBB	Ind		
Law and Economics	LM13	3FT deg	* g	BBB	Ind	Ind	32	CSYS	Ind	4	20/28
Law and Economics (4 Yrs)	ML31	4FT deg	*	BBB	Ind	Ind	32	BBBB	Ind		
Management Science and Economics	LN11	3FT deg	* g	BCC	Ind	D$	28	CSYS	Ind		
Management Science and Economics (4 Yrs)	NL11	4FT deg	*	BCC	Ind	Ind	28	BBBB	Ind		
Marketing and Economics	LN15	3FT deg	* g	BCC	Ind	Ind	28	CSYS	Ind	14	
Mathematics and Economics	GL11	3FT deg	M g	BCC	Ind	D$^	28$	CSYS	Ind	4	14/20
Mathematics and Economics (4 Yrs)	LG11	4FT deg	*	BCC	Ind	Ind	28	BBBB	Ind		
Music and Economics	LW13	3FT deg	Mu g	BCC	Ind	D$^	28$	CSYS	Ind		
Music and Economics (4 Yrs)	WL31	4FT deg	*	BCC	Ind	Ind	28	BBBB	Ind		
Philosophy and Economics	LV17	3FT deg	* g	BCC	Ind	Ind	28	CSYS	Ind	4	
Philosophy and Economics (4 Yrs)	VL71	4FT deg	*	BCC	Ind	Ind	28	BBBB	Ind		
Physics and Economics	FL31	3FT deg	P g	BCC	Ind	D$^	28$	CSYS	Ind	2	
Physics and Economics (4 Yrs)	LF13	4FT deg	*	BCC	Ind	Ind	28	BBBB	Ind		
Politics and Economics	LM11	3FT deg	* g	BCC	Ind	D$^	28	CSYS	Ind	4	17/22
Politics and Economics (4 Yrs)	ML11	4FT deg	*	BCC	Ind	Ind	28	BBBB	Ind		
Psychology and Economics	CL81	3FT deg	* g	BBB	Ind	Ind	32	CSYS	Ind		
Psychology and Economics (4 Yrs)	LC18	4FT deg	*	BBB	Ind	Ind	32	ABBB	Ind		
Russian Studies and Economics	LRC8	3FT deg	* g	BCC	Ind	Ind	28	CSYS	Ind		
Russian Studies and Economics (4 Yrs)	RL8C	4FT deg	*	BCC	Ind	Ind	28	BBBB	Ind		
Russian and Economics	LR18	3FT deg	R g	BCC	Ind	D$^	28$	CSYS	Ind		
Russian and Economics (4 Yrs)	RL81	4FT deg	*	BCC	Ind	Ind	28	BBBB	Ind		
Sociol & Soc Anthropology and Economics (4 Yrs)	LL31	4FT deg	*	BCC	Ind	Ind	28	BBBB	Ind		
Sociology & Social Anthropology and Economics	LL13	3FT deg	* g	BCC	Ind	Ind	28	CSYS	Ind	2	
Statistics and Economics	GL41	3FT deg	M g	BCC	Ind	D$^	28$	CSYS	Ind	8	
Statistics and Economics (4 Yrs)	LG14	4FT deg	*	BCC	Ind	Ind	28	BBBB	Ind		
Visual Arts and Economics (4 Yrs)	WL11	4FT deg	*	BCC	Ind	Ind	28	BBBB	Ind		

Univ of KENT

TITLE	CODE	COURSE	SUBJECTS	A/AS	ND/C	AGNVQ	IB	SQA(H)	SQA	RATIO	A/AS
Business Administration and Economics	LN11	3FT deg	* g	24	1M+5D	D$ go	32	AABB	Ind		
Computing and Economics	GLM1	3FT deg	* g	20	3M+3D	M$ go	28	BBBB	Ind		
Economics	L100	3FT deg	* g	20	3M+3D	M$ go	28	BBBB	Ind	8	16/26
Economics and Physics	LF13	3FT deg	M+P	18	Ind	Ind	26$	BBBB$	Ind		
Economics with Computing	L1G5	3FT deg	* g	20	3M+3D	M$ go	28	BBBB	Ind	18	
Economics with Econometrics	L141	3FT deg	M	18	Ind	Ind	26$	BBBB$	Ind	4	
Economics with a Language	L168	3FT deg	F/G g	18	Ind	Ind	26$	BBBB$	Ind	13	
Economics/Accounting and Finance	LN14	3FT deg	* g	20	3M+3D	M$ go	28	BBBB	Ind	4	14/20
European Economics (4 Yrs)	L171	4FT deg	* g	20	3M+3D	M$ go	28$	BBBB	Ind	5	
European Economics (French) (4 Yrs)	L176	4FT deg	F g	18	Ind	Ind	26$	BBBB$	Ind	5	
European Economics (German) (4 Yrs)	L174	4FT deg	G g	18	Ind	Ind	26$	BBBB$	Ind	4	
European Economics (Spanish) (4 Yrs)	L177	4FT deg	Sp g	18	Ind	Ind	26$	BBBB$	Ind	8	
European Studies (Economics) (4 Yrs)	LTC2	4FT deg	L g	20	Ind	Ind	28$	BBBB$	Ind	5	
Ind Relations & Human Resource Mgt (Economics)	LN16	3FT deg	* g	20	3M+3D	M$ go	28	BBBB	Ind	3	
Law/Economics	LM13	3FT deg	* g	26	6D	D$ go	33	AAAB	Ind	25	

| course details | | | 98 expected requirements | | | | | | | 96 entry stats | |

TITLE	CODE	COURSE	SUBJECTS	A/AS	ND/C	AGNVQ	IB	SQA(H)	SQA	RATIO	A/AS
Mathematics and Economics	GLC1	3FT/4SW deg	M	20	Ind	Ind	28$	BBBB$	Ind	4	18/26
Politics & Government/Economics	LM11	3FT deg	* g	BCC	3M+3D	M$ go	28	BBBB	Ind	16	
Social Anthropology/Economics	LL16	3FT deg	* g	20	3M+3D	M$ go	28	BBBB	Ind		
Social Policy & Administration/Economics	LL14	3FT deg	* g	20	3M+3D	M$ go	28	BBBB	Ind		
Sociology/Economics	LL13	3FT deg	* g	20	3M+3D	M$ go	28	BBBB	Ind	3	
Statistics and Economics	GL41	3FT/4SW deg	M	20	Ind	Ind	28$	BBBB$	Ind		
Urban Studies (Economics)	KL41	3FT deg	* g	20	3M+3D	M$ go	28	BBBB	Ind	3	

KINGSTON Univ

TITLE	CODE	COURSE	SUBJECTS	A/AS	ND/C	AGNVQ	IB	SQA(H)	SQA	RATIO	A/AS
Business Economics	L1N1	3FT deg	* g	16	MO	Ind^	Ind	BBCCC	HN	5	8/16
Economics	L100	3FT deg	* g	16	MO	Ind^	Ind	BBCCC	HN	4	8/16
English Language/Economics	LQ13	3FT deg	E g	14-16	MO	Ind^	Ind	BBCCC	HN		
Financial Economics	L160	3FT deg	* g	16	MO	Ind^	Ind	BBCCC	HN	8	
French/Economics	RL11	4FT deg	F g	14	MO	Ind^	Ind	BCCCC	HN	1	
Geography & Economics	FL81	3FT deg	Gy	12	N	Ind	Ind	BCCC	Ind	5	6/18
Geology & Economics	FL61	3FT deg	S	10	N	Ind	Ind	CCC	Ind		
German/Economics	RL21	4FT deg	G g	14	MO	Ind^	Ind	BCCCC	HN	4	
History of Ideas/Economics	VL71	3FT deg	* g	16	MO	Ind^	Ind	BBCCC	HN	3	
History/Economics	VL11	3FT deg	H g	16	MO	Ind^	Ind	BBCCC	HN	2	
Mathematics & Economics	GL11	3FT deg	M g	10	N	Ind	Ind	CCC	Ind	6	
Politics/Economics	ML11	3FT deg	* g	14	MO	Ind^	Ind	BCCCC	HN	2	6/17
Social and Economic History/Economics	LV13	3FT deg	* g	14	MO	Ind^	Ind	BCCCC	HN	8	
Sociology/Economics	LL31	3FT deg	* g	14	MO	Ind^	Ind	BCCCC	HN	8	
Spanish/Economics	RL41	4FT deg	Sp g	14	MO	Ind^	Ind	BCCCC	HN	2	
Statistics & Economics	GL41	3FT deg	M g	10	N	Ind	Ind	CCC	Ind	4	

Univ of Wales, LAMPETER

TITLE	CODE	COURSE	SUBJECTS	A/AS	ND/C	AGNVQ	IB	SQA(H)	SQA	RATIO	A/AS
Management Techniques and Cultural St in Geog	LN1V	3FT deg	*	16	Ind	Ind	Ind	Ind	Ind		

LANCASTER Univ

TITLE	CODE	COURSE	SUBJECTS	A/AS	ND/C	AGNVQ	IB	SQA(H)	SQA	RATIO	A/AS
Accounting and Economics	NL41	3FT deg	* g	BBC	DO $		30	ABBBB	Ind		
Advertising and the Econ of Competitive Strategy	LN1N	4SW deg	* g	BBB	MO+3D		30	ABBBB	Ind		
Advertising, Economics and Marketing	LN1M	3FT deg	* g	BBB	MO+3D		30	ABBBB	Ind		
Economics	L100	3FT deg	* g	BBC	MO+4D		32	ABBBB	Ind		
Economics (inc a year in USA or Canada)	L101	3FT deg	* g	AAB	MO+4D		32	ABBBB	Ind		
Economics and Geography	LL81	3FT deg	Gy g	BBC	Ind $		32$	ABBBB$	Ind		
Economics and International Relations	LM1C	3FT deg	* g	BBC	MO+4D		32	ABBBB	Ind		
Economics and Management Science	NL21	3FT deg	M	BBC	Ind $		30$	ABBBB$	Ind		
Economics and Mathematics	GL11	3FT deg	M	BCC	Ind $		30$	BBBBB$	Ind		
Economics and Modern History	VL11	3FT deg	H g	BBC	MO+4D		32$	ABBBB$	Ind		
Economics and Philosophy	LV17	3FT deg	* g	BBC-BCC	Ind		32	ABBBB	Ind		
Economics and Politics	ML11	3FT deg	* g	BBC	MO+4D		32	ABBBB	Ind		
Economics and Sociology	LL31	3FT deg	* g	22	MO+4D		32	ABBBB	Ind		
Finance and Economics	NL31	3FT deg	* g	24	DO $		32	AABBB$	Ind		
French Studies and Economics	RL11	4SW deg	F g	BBC	Ind		32$	ABBBB$	Ind		
German Studies and Economics	RL21	4SW deg	G/L g	BBC	Ind $		32$	ABBBB$	Ind		
Italian Studies and Economics	RL31	4SW deg	I/L g	BBC	MO+4D		32$	ABBBB$	Ind		
Spanish Studies and Economics	RL41	4SW deg	Sp/L g	BBC	MO+4D		32$	ABBBB$	Ind		
Economics & Mathematics & Operational Research Economics	Y642	3FT deg	M	BCC	DO $		30$	BBBBB$	Ind		
Philosophy and Politics and Economics Economics	Y616	3FT deg	* g	BBC	Ind		32	ABBBB	Ind		

course details			98 expected requirements							96 entry stats
TITLE	CODE	COURSE	SUBJECTS	A/AS	ND/C	AGNVQ	IB	SQA(H)	SQA	RATIO A/AS
Univ of LEEDS										
Chinese-Economics	LT13	4FT deg	L g	BBC	Ind	Ind	30$	CSYS	Ind	4
Computer Science-Economics	GL51	3FT deg	M g	BBC	Ind	Ind	Ind	Ind	Ind	
Economic Studies	L100	3FT deg	g	BBC	Ind	Ind	30	CSYS	Ind	8　22/30
Economics and Industrial Studies (3 Yrs)	LN16	3FT deg	g	BBC	Ind	Ind	30$	CSYS	Ind	7　22/28
Economics and Italian B	LR1H	4FT deg	L g	BBC						
Economics-Economic and Social History	LV13	3FT deg	g	BCC	Ind	Ind	28	CSYS	Ind	5　20/26
Economics-French	RL11	4FT deg	F g	BBC	Ind	Ind	30$	CSYS	Ind	13
Economics-Geography	LL18	3FT deg	Gy g	BBC	Ind	Ind	30$	CSYS	Ind	9　24/30
Economics-German	RL21	4FT deg	G g	BBC	Ind	Ind	30$	CSYS	Ind	8
Economics-History	VL11	3FT deg	g	BBC	Ind	Ind	30	CSYS	Ind	12　26/30
Economics-History with North American Studies	VL1C	4FT deg	g	BBC	Ind	Ind	30	CSYS	Ind	6
Economics-Italian	LR13	4FT deg	I g	BBC	Ind	Ind	Ind	Ind	Ind	
Economics-Japanese Studies	TL41	4FT deg	L g	BBB	Ind	Ind	32$	CSYS	Ind	
Economics-Management Studies	LN11	3FT deg	g	BBB	Ind	Ind	32$	CSYS	Ind	10　24/30
Economics-Mathematics	GL11	3FT/4FT deg	M g	BBC	1M+5D$	Ind	30$	ABBBB	Ind	10　22/28
Economics-Philosophy	VL71	3FT deg	g	BBC	Ind	Ind	30	CSYS	Ind	8　24/26
Economics-Politics	LM11	3FT deg	g	BBB	Ind	Ind	32	CSYS	Ind	11　24/28
Economics-Politics with North American Studies	LM1C	4FT deg	g	BBB	Ind	Ind	32	CSYS	Ind	5　22/28
Economics-Russian	RL81	4FT deg	R g	BBC	Ind	Ind	30$	CSYS	Ind	
Economics-Russian B	RLV1	4FT deg	L g	BBC	Ind	Ind	30$	CSYS	Ind	
Economics-Social Policy	LL14	3FT deg	g	BBC	Ind	Ind	30	CSYS	Ind	15
Economics-Sociology	LL13	3FT deg	g	BBB	Ind	Ind	32	CSYS	Ind	12
Economics-Spanish	RL41	4FT deg	Sp g	BBC	Ind	Ind	30$	CSYS	Ind	9
Economics-Statistics	GL41	3FT/4FT deg	M g	BBB	Ind	Ind	32$	CSYS	Ind	7
LEEDS METROPOLITAN Univ										
Economics and Public Policy	L100	3FT/4SW deg	* g	14	3M+3D	MB3/^ go	26	BBBC	Ind	3　10/20
Univ of LEICESTER										
BA/BSc with integ foundation (overseas students)	L101	4EXT deg	* g		N	*			Ind	
Business Economics	L113	3FT deg	M g	22	1M+5D	D$^	30$	CSYS$	Ind	16/20
Business Economics	L112	3FT deg	* g	BCC	1M+5D	D$^	30	ABBBB	Ind	16/24
Economics	L102	3FT deg	M g	BCC	1M+5D	D$^	30$	CSYS$	X	18/28
Economics	L100	3FT deg	* g	BCC	1M+5D	D$^	30	ABBBB	Ind	14/26
Economics and Economic History	LV13	3FT deg	* g	BCC	MO	D$^	28	BBBBC	Ind	14/16
Economics and Law	LM13	3FT deg	* g	BBB	6D	D$^	32	AABBB	Ind	20/26
Combined Arts 　Economics	Y300	3FT deg	* g	BCC	DO	D$^	30$	Ind	X	
Combined Science 　Economics	Y100	3FT deg	g	CCC	MO	D$^	28$	BBBCC$	Ind	
Univ of LINCOLNSHIRE and HUMBERSIDE										
Communications and Economics	LP13▼	3FT deg	* g	16	1M+3D	D	24	BBCCC	Ind	
Criminology and Economics	LM1H▼	3FT deg	* g	16	1M+3D	D	24	BBCCC	Ind	
Economics	L100▼	3FT deg	* g	16	1M+3D	D	24	BBCCC	Ind	
Economics and Health Studies	LL1K▼	3FT deg	* g	16	1M+3D	D	24	BBCCC	Ind	
Economics and International Relations	LM11▼	3FT deg	* g	16	1M+3D	D	24	BBCCC	Ind	
Economics and Journalism	LP16▼	3FT deg	* g	18	1M+4D	D	26	BBBCC	Ind	
Economics and Law	LM13▼	3FT deg	* g	16	1M+3D	D	24	BBCCC	Ind	
Economics and Management	LN1D▼	3FT deg	* g	16	1M+3D	D	24	BBCCC	Ind	
Economics and Media	LP14▼	3FT deg	* g	18	1M+4D	D	26	BBBCC	Ind	
Economics and Politics	LM1C▼	3FT deg	* g	16	1M+3D	D	24	BBCCC	Ind	
Economics and Psychology	CL81▼	3FT deg	* g	18	1M+4D	D	26	BBBCC	Ind	

			98 expected requirements							96 entry stats	
course details											
TITLE	CODE	COURSE	SUBJECTS	A/AS	NO/C	AGNVQ	IB	SQA(H)	SQA	RATIO	A/AS
Economics and Social Policy	LL14▼	3FT deg	* g	16	1M+3D	D	24	BBCCC	Ind		
Economics and Tourism	LP17▼	3FT deg	* g	16	1M+3D	D	24	BBCCC	Ind		
Univ of LIVERPOOL											
Business Economics	LN11	3FT deg	M/Ec	BCC	Ind	Ind	Ind	Ind	Ind	13	20/28
Business Economics and Computer Science	LG15	3FT deg	M/Ec	CCC	Ind	Ind	Ind	Ind	Ind	9	18/24
Economics	L100	3FT deg	M/Ec	BCC	Ind	Ind	Ind	Ind	Ind	16	18/30
Economics and Accounting	LNC4	3FT deg	M/Ec	BCC	Ind	Ind	Ind	Ind	Ind	24	
Economics and Computer Science	GL51	3FT deg	M/Ec	CCC	Ind	Ind	Ind	Ind	Ind	32	
Economics and Economic History	LV13	3FT deg	* g	BCC	Ind	Ind	Ind	Ind	Ind	8	
Economics and Mathematics	GL11	3FT deg	M	BCC	Ind	Ind	Ind	Ind	Ind	7	20/26
Financial Economics	L160	3FT deg	M/Ec	BCC	Ind	Ind	Ind	Ind	Ind	13	20/26
Arts Combined *Economics*	Y401	3FT deg	* g	BBC-BBB	Ind	Ind	30$	ABBB	Ind		
BA Combined Honours *Economics and Accounting*	Y200	3FT deg	g	BBB	Ind	Ind	Ind	Ind	Ind		
LIVERPOOL JOHN MOORES Univ											
Economics and Business	LN11	3FT deg		14-16	5M+3D	D/M^		BCCC			
Global Economy	L110	3FT deg									
History and Economics	LV11	3FT deg		12-14	5M+2D	PB	28$	CCCC		4	6/18
Human Geography and Economics	LL18	3FT deg	Gy	12	5M+3D	PB	28$	BBCC		5	14/18
Politics and Economics	LM11	3FT deg		12-14	5M+2D	PB^	28$	CCCC		6	12/18
LONDON GUILDHALL Univ											
3D/Spatial Design and Business Economics	LWCF	3FT deg	Pf g	DD	MO	M$ go	24	Ind	Ind		
3D/Spatial Design and Economics	LW1F	3FT deg	Pf g	DD	MO	M$ go	24	Ind	Ind		
Business Economics	L112	3FT deg	* g	CC	MO	M$ go	24	Ind	Ind		
Business Economics and Accounting	LNC4	3FT deg	* g	DD	MO	M$ go	24	Ind	Ind		
Business Economics and Business	LNC1	3FT deg	* g	CD-DDD	MO+4D	M$ go	26	Ind	Ind		
Business Information Technology & Bus Economics	GL7C	3FT deg	* g	DD	MO	M$ go	24	Ind	Ind		
Communications & Audio Visual Prod St & Bus Econ	LPC4	3FT deg	* g	CC-CDD	MO+6D	D$ go	26	Ind	Ind		
Computing and Business Economics	GL5C	3FT deg	* g	DD	MO	M$ go	24	Ind	Ind		
Design Studies and Business Economics	LWC2	3FT deg	* g	CD-DDD	MO+2D	M$ go	24	Ind	Ind		
Development Studies and Business Economics	LMC9	3FT deg	* g	DD	MO	M$ go	24	Ind	Ind		
Economic Studies	L101	3FT deg									
Economics	L100	3FT deg	* g	CC	MO	M$ go	24	Ind	Ind		
Economics & Communications & Audio Vis Prod St	LP14	3FT deg	* g	CC-CDD	MO+4D	M$ go	26	Ind	Ind		
Economics and Accounting	LN14	3FT deg	* g	DD	MO	M$ go	24	Ind	Ind		
Economics and Business	LN11	3FT deg	* g	CD-DDD	MO+2D	M$ go	24	Ind	Ind		
Economics and Business Information Technology	GL71	3FT deg	* g	DD	MO	M$ go	24	Ind	Ind		
Economics and Computing	GL51	3FT deg	* g	DD	MO	M$ go	24	Ind	Ind		
Economics and Design Studies	LW12	3FT deg	* g	CD-DDD	MO+2D	M$ go	24	Ind	Ind		
Economics and Development Studies	LM19	3FT deg	* g	DD	MO	M$ go	24	Ind	Ind		
English and Business Economics	LQC3	3FT deg	* g	CD-DDD	MO+2D	M$ go	24	Ind	Ind		
English and Economics	LQ13	3FT deg	* g	CD-DDD	MO+2D	M$ go	24	Ind	Ind		
European Studies and Business Economics	LTC2	3FT deg	* g	DD	MO	M$ go	24	Ind	Ind		
European Studies and Economics	LT12	3FT deg	* g	DD	MO	M$ go	24	Ind	Ind		
Financial Economics	L160	3FT deg	* g	CC	MO	M$ go	24	Ind	Ind		
Financial Services and Business Economics	LNC3	3FT deg	* g	DD	MO	M$ go	24	Ind	Ind		
Financial Services and Economics	LN13	3FT deg	* g	DD	MO	M$ go	24	Ind	Ind		
Fine Art and Business Economics	LWC1	3FT deg	Pf g	CC-CDD	MO+2D	M$ go	26	Ind	Ind		
Fine Art and Economics	LW11	3FT deg	Pf g	CC-CDD	MO+2D	M$ go	26	Ind	Ind		
French and Business Economics	LRC1	4FT deg	* g	DD	MO	M$ go	24	Ind	Ind		

course details			98 expected requirements							96 entry stats	
TITLE	CODE	COURSE	SUBJECTS	A/AS	NO/C	AGNVQ	IB	SQA(H)	SQA	RATIO	A/AS
French and Economics	LR11	4FT deg	* g	DD	MO	M$ go	24	Ind	Ind		
German and Business Economics	LRC2	4FT deg	* g	DD	MO	M$ go	24	Ind	Ind		
German and Economics	LR12	4FT deg	* g	DD	MO	M$ go	24	Ind	Ind		
International Relations and Business Economics	LMCC	3FT deg	* g	DD	MO	M$ go	24	Ind	Ind		
International Relations and Economics	LM1C	3FT deg	* g	DD	MO	M$ go	24	Ind	Ind		
Law and Business Economics	LMC3	3FT deg	* g	CC-CDD	MO+2D	M$ go	26	Ind	Ind		
Law and Economics	LM13	3FT deg	* g	CC-CDD	MO+2D	M$ go	26	Ind	Ind		
Legal and Economic St/Licence D'Administration	M3L1	3FT deg	F g	CCD	MO	X	24	Ind	Ind		
Marketing and Business Economics	LNC5	3FT deg	* g	CD-DDD	MO+2D	M$ go	26	Ind	Ind		
Marketing and Economics	LN15	3FT deg	* g	CD-DDD	MO+2D	M$ go	26	Ind	Ind		
Mathematics and Business Economics	GL1C	3FT deg	* g	DD	MO	M$ go	24	Ind	Ind		
Mathematics and Economics	GL11	3FT deg	* g	DD	MO	M$ go	24	Ind	Ind		
Modern History and Business Economics	LVC1	3FT deg	* g	DD	MO	M$ go	24	Ind	Ind		
Modern History and Economics	LV11	3FT deg	* g	DD	MO	M$ go	24	Ind	Ind		
Multimedia Systems and Business Economics	GLMC	3FT deg	* g	DD	MO	M$ go	24	Ind	Ind		
Multimedia Systems and Economics	GLM1	3FT deg	* g	DD	MO	M$ go	24	Ind	Ind		
Politics and Business Economics	LMC1	3FT deg	* g	DD	MO	M$ go	24	Ind	Ind		
Politics and Economics	LM11	3FT deg	* g	DD	MO	M$ go	24	Ind	Ind		
Product Development & Manufacture & Bus Econ	JL4C	3FT deg	* g	DD	MO	M$ go	24	Ind	Ind		
Product Development & Manufacture and Economics	JL41	3FT deg	* g	DD	MO	M$ go	24	Ind	Ind		
Psychology and Business Economics	CL8C	3FT deg	* g	CD-DDD	MO+2D	M$ go	26	Ind	Ind		
Psychology and Economics	CL81	3FT deg	* g	CD-DDD	MO+2D	M$ go	26	Ind	Ind		
Social Policy & Management & Business Economics	LL4C	3FT deg	* g	CD-DDD	MO	M$ go	24	Ind	Ind		
Social Policy & Management and Economics	LL14	3FT deg	* g	CD-DDD	MO	M$ go	24	Ind	Ind		
Sociology and Business Economics	LL3C	3FT deg	* g	CD-DDD	MO	M$ go	24	Ind	Ind		
Sociology and Economics	LL13	3FT deg	* g	CD-DDD	MO	M$ go	24	Ind	Ind		
Spanish and Business Economics	LRC4	4FT deg	* g	DD	MO	M$ go	24	Ind	Ind		
Spanish and Economics	LR14	4FT deg	* g	DD	MO	M$ go	24	Ind	Ind		
Taxation and Business Economics	LNCH	3FT deg	* g	DD	MO	M$ go	24	Ind	Ind		
Taxation and Economics	LN1H	3FT deg	* g	DD	MO	M$ go	24	Ind	Ind		
Textile Furnishing Design and Business Economics	LWCG	3FT deg	Pf g	DD	MO	M$ go	24	Ind	Ind		
Textile Furnishing Design and Economics	LW1G	3FT deg	Pf g	DD	MO	M$ go	24	Ind	Ind		
Modular Programme _Business Economics_	Y400	3FT deg	* g	CC-DD	MO	M$ go	24	Ind	Ind		
Modular Programme _Economics_	Y400	3FT deg	* g	CC-DD	MO	M$ go	24	Ind	Ind		
Modular Programme _Economics_	Y420▼	3FT deg	* g	EE	MO	P	24	Ind	Ind		

LSE: LONDON Sch of Economics (Univ of London)

Econometrics & Mathematical Economics	L140	3FT deg	<u>M</u>	ABB	Ind	X	$	Ind	Ind	5	26/30
Economic History and Economics	VL31	3FT deg	g	ABB	Ind	X	$	Ind	Ind	6	24/28
Economic History with Economics	V3L1	3FT deg	g	ABB	Ind	X	$	Ind	Ind	12	
Economic History with Population Studies	V3LC	3FT deg	g	ABB	Ind	X	$	Ind	Ind	8	
Economics	L101	3FT deg	g	AAB-ABB		X				10	26/30
Economics with Economic History	L1V3	3FT deg	g	AAB-ABB	Ind	X	$	Ind	Ind	8	28/30
Environmental Policy with Economics	F9L1	3FT deg	g	BBB	Ind	X	$	Ind	Ind		
Geography with Economics	L8L1	3FT deg	g	BBB	Ind	X	$	Ind	Ind	6	22/30
Government and Economics	LM11	3FT deg	g	ABB	Ind	X	$	Ind	Ind	46	28/30
Mathematics and Economics	GL11	3FT deg	<u>M</u>	ABB	Ind	X	$	Ind	Ind	6	28/30
Philosophy and Economics	LV17	3FT deg	g	ABB	Ind	X	$	Ind	Ind	12	24/30
Population Studies	L187	3FT deg	g	BBB	Ind	X	$	Ind	Ind		
Social Policy and Population Studies	LL41	3FT deg	g	BBB	Ind	X	$	Ind	Ind		

Economics 18

			98 expected requirements							96 entry stats	
TITLE	CODE	COURSE	SUBJECTS	A/AS	NO/C	RGNVQ	IB	SQA(H)	SQA	RATIO	A/AS
LOUGHBOROUGH Univ											
Business Economics and Finance	L1NK	3FT deg	* g	20	3D	D*<u>6</u>/^ go	30	Ind	Ind	5	18/24
Economics	L100	3FT deg	* g	20	3D	D*<u>6</u>/^ go	30	Ind	Ind	5	16/26
Economics with Accounting	L1N4	3FT deg	* g	20	3D	D*<u>6</u>/^ go	30	Ind	Ind	4	16/28
Economics with French	L1R1	3FT deg	<u>F</u> g	20				30$	Ind	13	
Economics with Geography	L1F8	3FT deg	<u>Gy</u>	20		D*<u>6</u>/^ go		30$	Ind	5	18/20
Economics with German	L1R2	3FT deg	<u>G</u> g	20				30$	Ind		
Economics with Politics	L1M1	3FT deg	* g	20	3D	D*<u>6</u>/^ go	30	Ind	Ind	9	18/18
Economics with Social Policy	L1L4	3FT deg	* g	20	3D	D*<u>6</u>/^ go	30	Ind	Ind	4	
Economics with Sociology	L1L3	3FT deg	* g	20	3D	D*<u>6</u>/^ go	30	Ind	Ind	6	
Economics with Spanish	L1R4	3FT deg	<u>Sp</u> g	20				30$	Ind		
Geography with Economics	LL18	3FT deg	<u>Gy</u>	BCC				30$	Ind	8	20/28
International Economics	L115	3FT deg	* g	20	3D	D*<u>6</u>/^ go	30	Ind	Ind	3	18/26
Mathematics with Economics	G1L1	3FT deg	<u>M</u>	BCC				28$	Ind	6	16/24
Mathematics with Economics (4 Yr SW)	G1LC	4SW deg	<u>M</u>	BCC				28$	Ind	4	
Politics with Economics	M1L1	3FT deg	* g	20	2M+3D	D*<u>6</u>/^ go	28	Ind	Ind		12/20
Univ of MANCHESTER											
Econometrics and Social Statistics	L146	3FT deg	* g	BBC	M+6D	D^	32	AABBB	Ind		
Economic History and Economics	LV13	3FT deg		BBC-BBB	Ind		30	CSYS$	Ind	7	22/26
Economics	L100	3FT deg	* g	BBC	M+6D	D^	32	AABBB	Ind	6	20/28
Economics	L102	3FT deg	M+Ec	BBC	X		Ind	AABB$	X	5	20/30
MANCHESTER METROPOLITAN Univ											
Economics	L100	3FT deg	* g	14	MO	Ind	24	Ind	Ind		8/18
Economics	L101	3FT deg	<u>M</u> g	14	MO	Ind	24	Ind	Ind		
Economics with French/Maitrise d'Econometrie	L103	4FT deg	<u>M+F</u> g	14	MO	Ind	24	Ind	Ind		
Economics with French/Maitrise de Sci Economique	L102	4FT deg	<u>F</u> g	14	MO	Ind	24	Ind	Ind		
Economics/Applicable Mathematics	GL11	3FT deg	M g	16	1M+3D$	M$	28$	BBBCC$	Ind		
Economics/Business Mathematics	GLC1	3FT deg	<u>M/P/Ec</u> g	16	1M+3D$	M$	28$	BBBCC$	Ind		
Economics/Chemistry	FL11	3FT deg	C g	14	MO $	M$	28$	BBCCC$	Ind		
Economics/Computer Technology	GLM1	3FT deg	* g	16	1M+3D	M$	28	BBBCC	Ind		
Economics/Computing Science	GL51	3FT deg	* g	16	1M+3D	M$	28	BBBCC	Ind		
Electronics/Economics	HLP1	3FT deg	* g	16	1M+3D	M$	28	BBBCC	Ind		
Environmental Studies/Economics	FL91	3FT deg	* g	18	2M+4D	M$	29	BBBBC	Ind		
European Studies/Economics	LT12	3FT deg	* g	18	2M+4D	M$	29	BBBBC	Ind		
Financial Econ with French/Maitrise en Banq Assc	L148	4FT deg	<u>F</u> g	14	MO	Ind	24	Ind	Ind		
Geography/Economics	LL18	3FT deg	* g	CCC	2M+4D	M$	29	BBBBC	Ind		14/18
Int Econ Studs with Sp/Licen en Ciencias Econom	L149	4FT deg	<u>L</u> g	14	MO	Ind	24	Ind	Ind		
Languages/Economics	LT19	3FT deg	* g	18	2M+4D	M$	29	BBBBC	Ind		
Manufacturing/Economics	HL71	3FT deg	* g	16	1M+3D	M$	28	BBBCC	Ind		
Materials Science/Economics	FL21	3FT deg	M/P/C g	16	1M+3D$	M$	28$	BBBCC$	Ind		
Polymer Science/Economics	JL41	3FT deg	C g	16	1M+3D$	M$	28$	BBBCC$	Ind		
Psychology/Economics	LL17	3FT deg	* g	CCC	2M+4D	D$	29	BBBBC	Ind		
Humanities/Social Studies Economics	Y400	3FT deg	* g	CDD	Ind	Ind	Ind	BBB	Ind		
MIDDLESEX Univ											
Business Economics	L110▼	3FT/4SW deg	* g	14	MO+1D	M$ go	26	Ind	Ind		
Economics	L100▼	3FT deg	* g	14	5M	M$ go	28	Ind	Ind		
Joint Honours Degree Business Economics	Y400	3FT deg	* g	16	3D	M$ go	28	Ind	Ind		
Joint Honours Degree Economics	Y400	3FT deg	* g	14	5M	M$ go	28	Ind	Ind		

TITLE	CODE	COURSE	SUBJECTS	A/AS	ND/C	AGNVQ	IB	SQA(H)	SQA	RATIO A/AS
NAPIER Univ										
Business Economics	L112	3FT deg								
Business Economics and Financial Services	LN13	3FT deg								
Business Economics with Financial Services	L1N3	3FT deg								
Financial Services with Business Economics	N3L1	3FT deg								
NENE COLLEGE										
Business Administration with Economics	N1L1	3FT deg	g	10	M+1D	M	24	BCC	Ind	6/14
Economics with Architectural Studies	L1V4	3FT deg	g	6	5M	M	24	CCC	Ind	
Economics with Business Administration	L1N1	3FT deg	g	6	5M	M	24	CCC	Ind	
Economics with Ecology	L1C9	3FT deg	g	6	5M	M	24	CCC	Ind	
Economics with Education	L1X9	3FT deg	g	6	5M	M	24	CCC	Ind	
Economics with Energy Management	L1J9	3FT deg	g	6	5M	M	24	CCC	Ind	
Economics with European Union Studies	L1T2	3FT deg	g	6	5M	M	24	CCC	Ind	
Economics with French	L1R1	3FT deg	F g	6	5M	M	24	CCC	Ind	
Economics with Geography	L1F8	3FT deg	g	6	5M	M	24	CCC	Ind	
Economics with Industrial Archaeology	L1V6	3FT deg	g	6	5M	M	24	CCC	Ind	
Economics with Industry and Enterprise	L1H1	3FT deg	g	6	5M	M	24	CCC	Ind	
Economics with Law	L1M3	3FT deg	g	6	5M	M	24	CCC	Ind	
Economics with Management Science	L1G4	3FT deg	g	6	5M	M	24	CCC	Ind	
Economics with Mathematics	L1G1	3FT deg	M	6	5M	M	24	CCC	Ind	
Economics with Media and Popular Culture	L1P4	3FT deg	g	6	5M	M	24	CCC	Ind	
Economics with Personal and Organisational Devel	L1N6	3FT deg	g	6	5M	M	24	CCC	Ind	
Economics with Philosophy	L1V7	3FT deg	g	6	5M	M	24	CCC	Ind	
Economics with Sociology	L1L3	3FT deg	g	6	5M	M	24	CCC	Ind	
Economics with Sport Studies	L1N7	3FT deg	g	6	5M	M	24	CCC	Ind	
Economics with Third World Development	L1M9	3FT deg	g	6	5M	M	24	CCC	Ind	
Economics with Wastes Management and the Environ	L1FX	3FT deg	g	6	5M	M	24	CCC	Ind	
Education with Economics	X9L1	3FT deg	g	DD	5M	M	24	CCC	Ind	
Energy Management with Economics	J9L1	3FT deg	g	EE	3M	P	24	CCC	Ind	
French with Economics	R1L1	3FT deg	F g	DD	5M	Ind	24	CCC	Ind	
Geography with Economics	F8L1	3FT deg	Gy g	8	5M	M	24	CCC	Ind	
History with Economics	V1L1	3FT deg	g	CD	5M	M	24	CCC	Ind	
Industry and Enterprise with Economics	H1L1	3FT deg	g	EE	3M	P	24	CCC	Ind	
Law with Economics	M3L1	3FT deg	g	10	3M+2D	M	24	CCC	Ind	
Management Science with Economics	G4L1	3FT deg	g	DD	5M	M	24	CCC	Ind	
Mathematics with Economics	G1L1	3FT deg	M	DD	Ind	Ind	24	CCC	Ind	
Sociology with Economics	L3L1	3FT deg	g	10	5M	M	24	CCC	Ind	
Sport Studies with Economics	N7L1	3FT deg	Ss/Pe g	12	M+2D	M	24	BBB	Ind	
Univ of NEWCASTLE										
Agri-Business Economics and Management	NL11	3FT deg	* g	CCC	Ind	Ind	Ind	BBBB	Ind	3 14/23
Computing Science and Economics	GL51	3FT deg	M	20	4M+1D	Ind	28$	AAABB	Ind	
Economics	L100	3FT deg	* g	BBC	Ind	Ind	30	AABB	Ind	8 18/26
Economics and Accounting	LN14	3FT deg	* g	BB-BCC	5D		30	AAAAB	Ind	12 18/22
Economics and Business Management	LN11	3FT/4SW deg	* g	BBB	Ind	Ind	Ind	AABBB	Ind	18 24/30
Economics and Geography	LL18	3FT deg	Gy g	BBB-BBC	Ind		32	AABBB	Ind	14
Economics and Mathematics	GL11	3FT deg	M	20	4M+1D	Ind	28$	AAABB	Ind	5 22/28
Economics and Social Policy	LL14	3FT deg	* g	BCC	Ind		30	ABBB	HN	5 20/28
Economics and Statistics	GL41	3FT deg	M	20	4M+1D	Ind	28$	AAABB	Ind	4
Financial and Business Economics	L161	3FT deg	* g	BBB	Ind	Ind	30	AABBB	Ind	26
Food Marketing and Rural Economics	DL41	3FT deg	* g	CCC	Ind	Ind	Ind	BBBB	Ind	
Politics and Economics	ML11	3FT deg	* g	BBB-BBC	Ind		Ind	AABB	Ind	9 22/28

TITLE	CODE	COURSE	SUBJECTS	A/AS	ND/C	RGNVQ	IB	SQA(H)	SQA	RATIO A/AS
Rural Economics and Environmental Management	DL21	3FT deg	* g	CCC	Ind	Ind	Ind	BBBB	Ind	3	
Rural and Environmental Economics	L120	3FT deg	* g	CCC	Ind	Ind	Ind	BBBB	Ind	3	
Combined Studies (BA)	Y400	3FT deg	M	ABC-BBB	5D	Ind	35$	AAAB	Ind		
Economics										

Univ of NORTH LONDON

TITLE	CODE	COURSE	SUBJECTS	A/AS	ND/C	RGNVQ	IB	SQA(H)	SQA	RATIO A/AS
Business Economics and Consumer Studies	LN15	3FT/4SW deg	* g	CC	Ind	D* go	Ind	Ind	Ind	10
Economics and History	LV11	3FT deg	H g	CC	Ind	Ind	Ind	Ind	Ind	
Economics and Sociology	LL13	3FT deg	* g	CC	MO+4D	Ind	Ind	Ind	Ind	
Philosophy and Economics	LV17	3FT deg	* g	12	Ind	Ind	Ind	Ind	Ind	
Politics and Economics	LM1C	3FT deg	* g	CC	Ind	Ind	Ind	Ind	Ind	
Combined Honours	Y400	3FT/4SW deg	* g	14	MO+4D	Ind	Ind	CCCC	Ind	
Economics										

Univ of NORTHUMBRIA

TITLE	CODE	COURSE	SUBJECTS	A/AS	ND/C	RGNVQ	IB	SQA(H)	SQA	RATIO A/AS
Economics	L100	3FT deg	Ec g	12	N	Ind	24	CCCC	N	5	10/18
Economics	L111	2FT Dip	Ec g	8	3M	Ind	24	CCCC	N	1	
French and Economics	LR11	3FT deg	F	CC	2M+2D	M^	24	BBCCC	Ind	
German and Economics	LR12	3FT deg		CG	2M+2D	M^	24	BBCCC	Ind	
Politics and Economics	LM11	3FT deg	g	14	Ind		24	BCCC	Ind	4	9/16
Russian and Economics	LR18	3FT deg		CC	2M+2D	M^	24	BBCCC	Ind	
Spanish and Economics	LR14	3FT deg		CC	2M+2D	M^	24	BBCCC	Ind	

Univ of NOTTINGHAM

TITLE	CODE	COURSE	SUBJECTS	A/AS	ND/C	RGNVQ	IB	SQA(H)	SQA	RATIO A/AS
Economics	L100	3FT deg	* g	AAB-ABB	X		32	Ind	X	11	26/30
Economics and Agricultural Economics	L134	3FT deg	* g	AAB-ABB	X		32	Ind	X	4	
Economics and Econometrics	L140	3FT deg	M	AAB-ABB	X		32$	Ind	X	7	28/30
Economics and Philosophy	LV17	3FT deg	* g	AAB-ABB	X		32	Ind	X	14	28/30
Economics with European Union Studies	L1T2	3FT deg	* g	AAB-ABB	X		32	Ind	X	9	26/30
Economics with French	L1R1	4FT deg	F g	AAB-ABB	X		32$	Ind	X	10	26/30
Economics with German	L1R2	4FT deg	G g	AAB-ABB	X		32$	Ind	X	3	26/30
Economics with Hispanic Studies	L1R4	4FT deg	L g	AAB-ABB	X		32$	Ind	X	11	
Economics with Russian	L1R8	4FT deg	L g	AAB-ABB	X		32$	Ind	X	8	
Industrial Economics	L1N1	3FT deg	* g	BBB	Ind	D*6/^ go	32	AAABB	Ind	5	24/30
Industrial Economics with Accounting	LN14	3FT deg	* g	BBB	Ind	D*6/^ go	32	AAABB	Ind	11	22/30
Industrial Economics with Insurance	L1N3	3FT deg	* g	BBB	Ind	D*6/^ go	32	AAABB	Ind	10	
Mathematics and Economics	GL11	3FT deg	M	AAB-ABB	Ind	Ind	Ind	Ind	Ind	13	28/30

NOTTINGHAM TRENT Univ

TITLE	CODE	COURSE	SUBJECTS	A/AS	ND/C	RGNVQ	IB	SQA(H)	SQA	RATIO A/AS
Business Economics	L112	3FT deg	* g	BB-CCC	1M+4D		Ind	BBBC	Ind	4	10/20
Economic Studies	L102	3FT deg	* g	14	Ind	Ind	Ind	BBBC	Ind	
Economics	L100	3FT deg	* g	BB-CCC	1M+4D	Ind	Ind	BBBC	Ind	4	10/20
Economics and Geography	LL18	3FT deg	* g	12	Ind	Ind	Ind	Ind	Ind		10/14
Economics and Industrial Management	LN16	3FT deg	* g	12	Ind	M$ go	Ind	Ind	Ind	2	9/14
European Economics in the Netherlands	L1T2	4FT deg	* g	14-16	1M+3D	Ind	Ind	BBCC	Ind	8	
European Economics with French	L1R1	4FT deg	F g	14-16	1M+3D	Ind	Ind	BBCC	Ind	5	12/18
European Economics with German	L1R2	4FT deg	G g	14-16	1M+3D	Ind	Ind	BBCC	Ind	6	
European Economics with Italian	L1R3	4FT deg	I g	14-16	1M+3D	Ind	Ind	BBCC	Ind	
European Economics with Spanish	L1R4	4FT deg	Sp g	14-16	1M+3D	Ind	Ind	BBCC	Ind	2	10/16
Mathematics & Statistics and Economics	GL11	3FT deg	M/Ec	12	Ind	M go	Ind	Ind	Ind	

OXFORD Univ

TITLE	CODE	COURSE	SUBJECTS	A/AS	ND/C	RGNVQ	IB	SQA(H)	SQA	RATIO A/AS
Economics and Management	LN11	3FT deg	*	AAB	DO		36	AAAAA	Ind	7	28/30
Modern History and Economics	LV11	3FT deg	H	AAB-ABB	DO		36	AAAAA	Ind	3	26/30
Engineering, Economics and Management	Y630	4FT deg	M+P	AAB	DO		36	AAAAA	Ind	
Economics										

| | | | 98 expected requirements | | | | | | | 96 entry stats | |
| course details | | | | | | | | | | | |
TITLE	CODE	COURSE	SUBJECTS	A/AS	ND/C	AGNVQ	IB	SQA(H)	SQA	RATIO	A/AS
Materials, Economics and Management *Economics*	Y634	4FT deg	2S	AAB-ABB	DO		36	AAAAA	Ind		
Philosophy, Politics and Economics *Economics*	Y616	3FT deg	*	AAB	DO		36	AAAAA	Ind		

OXFORD BROOKES Univ

TITLE	CODE	COURSE	SUBJECTS	A/AS	ND/C	AGNVQ	IB	SQA(H)	SQA	RATIO	A/AS
Business Economics	L112	3FT deg			Ind		Ind	Ind	Ind		
Ecology/Economics	CL91	3FT deg	* g	CD-BB	Ind	MS/M*3	Ind	Ind	Ind		
Economics/Accounting and Finance	LN14	3FT deg	* g	BB-BCC	Ind	M*3/D*3	Ind	Ind	Ind	7	14/20
Economics/Anthropology	LL16	3FT deg	* g	BB-CCD	Ind	M*^/3	Ind	Ind	Ind		
Economics/Biological Chemistry	CL71	3FT deg									
Economics/Biology	CL11	3FT deg	S g	DD-BB	Ind	MS/M*3	Ind	Ind	Ind	46	
Economics/Business Administration & Management	LN11	3FT deg	* g	BB-BBC	Ind	MB3	Ind	Ind	Ind	9	
Economics/Cartography	FL81	3FT deg	* g	DDD-BB	Ind	M*/M*3	Ind	Ind	Ind		
Economics/Cell Biology	CLC1	3FT deg									
Economics/Combined Studies	LY14	3FT deg		X		X	X	X			
Economics/Computer Systems	GL61	3FT deg	* g	CDD-BB	Ind	M*/M*3	Ind	Ind	Ind		
Economics/Computing	GL51	3FT deg	* g	CDD-BB	Ind	M*/M*3	Ind	Ind	Ind	5	
Economics/Computing Mathematics	GL91	3FT deg	* g	CD-BB	Ind	M*/M*3	Ind	Ind	Ind	5	
Educational Studies/Economics	LX19	3FT deg	* g	CC-BB	Ind	M*3	Ind	Ind	Ind		
Electronics/Economics	HL61	3FT deg	S/M	CC-BB	Ind	MS/M*3	Ind	Ind	Ind		
English Studies/Economics	LQ13	3FT deg	* g	CCD-AB	Ind	M*^M*3	Ind	Ind	Ind		
Environmental Chemistry/Economics	FL11	3FT deg									
Environmental Policy/Economics	KL31	3FT deg									
Environmental Sciences/Economics	FLX1	3FT deg	S g	CD-BB	Ind	M*3/DS	Ind	Ind	Ind	1	
Exercise and Health/Economics	LB16	3FT deg	S g	DD-BB	Ind	MS/M*3	Ind	Ind	Ind		
Fine Art/Economics	LW11	3FT deg	Pf+A g	CCD-BB	Ind	MA^/M*3	Ind	Ind	Ind		
Food Science and Nutrition/Economics	DL41	3FT deg	S g	DD-BB	Ind	MS/M*3	Ind	Ind	Ind		
French Language and Contemp Studies/Economics	LR1C	4SW deg	F g	CDD-BB	Ind	M^/M*3	Ind	Ind	Ind	2	
French Language and Literature/Economics	LR11	4SW deg	F g	CDD-BB	Ind	M^/M*3	Ind	Ind	Ind		
Geography and the Phys Env/Economics	FLV1	3FT deg									
Geography/Economics	LL18	3FT deg	* g	BB-CCD	Ind	M*/M*3	Ind	Ind	Ind	37	
Geology/Economics	FL61	3FT deg	S/M	DD-BB	Ind	PS/MS3	Ind	Ind	Ind		
Geotechnics/Economics	HL21	3FT deg	S/M/Ds/Es	DD-BB	Ind	MS/M*3	Ind	Ind	Ind		
German Language and Contemp Stud/Economics	LR1F	4SW deg	G g	DDD-BB	Ind	M^/M*3	Ind	Ind	Ind		
German Language and Literature/Economics	LR12	4SW deg	G g	DDD-BB	Ind	M^/M*3	Ind	Ind	Ind		
German Studies/Economics	LR1G	4SW deg			Ind		Ind	Ind	Ind		
Health Care/Economics (Post Exp)	BL71	3FT deg		X		X	X	X			
History of Art/Economics	LV14	3FT deg	* g	BB-CCD	Ind	M*^/3	Ind	Ind	Ind		
History/Economics	LV11	3FT deg	* g	BB-CCD	Ind	M^/M*3	Ind	Ind	Ind	9	
Hospitality Management Studies/Economics	LN17	3FT deg	* g	DDD-BB	Ind	M*3	Ind	Ind	Ind	2	
Human Biology/Economics	BL11	3FT deg			Ind		Ind	Ind	Ind		
Information Systems/Economics	GLM1	3FT deg	* g	CDD-BB	Ind	M*/M*3	Ind	Ind	Ind		
Intelligent Systems/Economics	GL81	3FT deg	* g	CD-BB	Ind	M*/M*3	Ind	Ind	Ind		
Law/Economics	LM13	3FT deg	* g	CCD-BBB	Ind	M*3/D*3	Ind	Ind	Ind	5	14/16
Leisure Planning/Economics	KLH1	3FT deg									
Marketing Management/Economics	LN1N	3FT deg	* g	CCD-BCC	Ind	M*3/D*3	Ind	Ind	Ind	11	
Mathematics/Economics	GL11	3FT deg	M	DD-BB	Ind	M*3/M^	Ind	Ind	Ind	11	
Music/Economics	LW13	3FT deg	Mu g	DD-BB	Ind	M/M*3	Ind	Ind	Ind	2	
Palliative Care/Economics (Post Exp)	BLR1	3FT deg		X		X	X	X			
Politics/Economics	LM11	3FT deg	* g	CCD-AB	Ind	M^/M*3	Ind	Ind	Ind	9	10/20
Psychology/Economics	CL81	3FT deg	* g	CCD-BBC	Ind	M^/M*3	Ind	Ind	Ind	6	
Publishing/Economics	LP15	3FT deg	* g	BB-CCD	Ind	M$3	Ind	Ind	Ind	1	

Economics 18

TITLE	CODE	COURSE	SUBJECTS	A/AS	NQ/C	AGNVQ	IB	SQA(H)	SQA	RATIO A/AS
98 expected requirements										*96 entry stats*
Rehabilitation/Economics (Post Exp)	BLT1	3FT deg		X		X	X	X		
Sociology/Economics	LL13	3FT deg	* g	BB-CCD	Ind	M*^/M*3	Ind	Ind	Ind	
Software Engineering/Economics	GL71	3FT deg	* g	CDD-BB	Ind	M*/M*3	Ind	Ind	Ind	
Statistics/Economics	GL41	3FT deg	* g	DD-BB	Ind	M*/M*3	Ind	Ind	Ind	3
Telecommunications/Economics	LH1P	3FT deg								
Tourism/Economics	LP17	3FT deg	* g	BB-CCD	Ind	M*3	Ind	Ind	Ind	5
Transport Planning/Economics	LN19	3FT deg	* g	BB-DDD	Ind	M*/M*3	Ind	Ind	Ind	1
Water Resources/Economics	HLF1	3FT deg								

Univ of PAISLEY

TITLE	CODE	COURSE	SUBJECTS	A/AS	NQ/C	AGNVQ	IB	SQA(H)	SQA	RATIO A/AS
Applied Economics	L110	5SW deg	* g	CCD	Ind	Ind	Ind	BCC	Ind	
Business Economics	LN11	3FT/4FT/4SW deg	* g	CCD	Ind	Ind	Ind	BCC	Ind	5

Univ of PLYMOUTH

TITLE	CODE	COURSE	SUBJECTS	A/AS	NQ/C	AGNVQ	IB	SQA(H)	SQA	RATIO A/AS
Applied Economics	L100	3FT deg	* g	CCD-CDD	MO	M$^	Ind	BCCC	Ind	34
Applied Economics with Accounting	L1N4	3FT deg	* g	CCD-CDD	MO	M$^	Ind	BCCC	Ind	
Applied Economics with Business	L1NC	3FT deg	* g	CCD-CDD	MO	M$^	Ind	BCCC	Ind	4 10/18
Applied Economics with Computing	L1G5	3FT deg	* g	CCD-CDD	MO	M$^	Ind	BCCC	Ind	
Applied Economics with French	L1R1	3FT deg	F g	CCD-CDD	MO	M$^	Ind	BCCC	Ind	
Applied Economics with Geography	L1F8	3FT deg	* g	CCD	MO	M$^	Ind	BCCC	Ind	7
Applied Economics with German	L1R2	3FT deg	G g	CCD-CDD	MO	M$^	Ind	BCCC	Ind	
Applied Economics with International Relations	LMCC	3FT deg	* g	CDD-CCD	MO	M$^	Ind	BCCC	Ind	
Applied Economics with Italian	L1R3	3FT deg	* g	CDD-CCD	MO	M$^	Ind	BCCC	Ind	
Applied Economics with Languages	L1T9	3FT deg	L g	CCD-CDD	MO	M$^	Ind	BCCC	Ind	5
Applied Economics with Law	L1M3	3FT deg	* g	BCC-BBC	MO	M$^	Ind	BBBB	Ind	12
Applied Economics with Maritime Law	LM1J	3FT deg	* g	CDD-CCD	MO	M$^	Ind	BCCC	Ind	
Applied Economics with Politics	L1M1	3FT deg	* g	CCD-CDD	MO	M$^	Ind	BCCC	Ind	12
Applied Economics with Psychology	L1C8	3FT deg	* g	BBC	MO	M$^	Ind	Ind	Ind	
Applied Economics with Res, Manuf & the Environ	L1F9	3FT deg	* g	CCD-CDD	MO	M$^	Ind	BCCC	Ind	
Applied Economics with Social Policy	L1L4	3FT deg	Ap g	CCD-CDD	MO	M$^	Ind	BCCC	Ind	7
Applied Economics with Sociology	L1L3	3FT deg	Ap g	CCD-CDD	MO	M$^	Ind	BCCC	Ind	
Applied Economics with Spanish	L1R4	3FT deg	Sp g	CCD-CDD	MO	M$^	Ind	BCCC	Ind	
Applied Economics with Statistics	L1G4	3FT deg	* g	CCD-CDD	MO	M$^	Ind	BCCC	Ind	14
Applied Economics with Transport	L1N9	3FT deg	* g	CCD-CDD	MO	M$^	Ind	BCCC	Ind	
Business Econ with Resources Manu and the Env	L1FX	3FT deg	* g	CDD-CCD	MO	M$^	Ind	BCCC	Ind	
Business Economics	L112	3FT deg	* g	CDD-CCD	MO	M$^	Ind	BCCC	Ind	
Business Economics with Computing	L1GM	3FT deg	* g	CDD-CCD	MO	M$^	Ind	BCCC	Ind	
Business Economics with French	L1RC	3FT deg	F g	CDD-CCD	MO	M$^	Ind	BCCC	Ind	
Business Economics with Geography	L1FV	3FT deg	* g	CCD	MO	M$^	Ind	BCCC	Ind	
Business Economics with German	L1RF	3FT deg	G g	CDD-CCD	MO	M$^	Ind	BCCC	Ind	
Business Economics with Italian	L1RH	3FT deg	* g	CDD-CCD	MO	M$^	Ind	BCCC	Ind	
Business Economics with Languages	L1TX	3FT deg	L g	CDD-CCD	MO	M$^	Ind	BCCC	Ind	
Business Economics with Law	L1MH	3FT deg	* g	BCC-BBC	MO	M$^	Ind	BBBB	Ind	
Business Economics with Maritime Law	MLH1	3FT deg	* g	CDD-CCD	MO	M$^	Ind	BCCC	Ind	
Business Economics with Politics	L1MC	3FT deg	* g	CDD-CCD	MO	M$^	Ind	BCCC	Ind	
Business Economics with Psychology	L1CV	3FT deg	* g	BBC	MO	M$^	Ind	Ind	Ind	
Business Economics with Social Policy	L1LK	3FT deg	Ap g	CDD-CCD	MO	M$^	Ind	BCCC	Ind	
Business Economics with Sociology	L1LH	3FT deg	Ap g	CDD-CCD	MO	M$^	Ind	BCCC	Ind	
Business Economics with Spanish	L1RK	3FT deg	Sp g	CDD-CCD	MO	M$^	Ind	BCCC	Ind	
Business Economics with Statistics	L1GK	3FT deg	* g	CDD-CCD	MO	M$^	Ind	BCCC	Ind	
Business Economics with Transport	L1NX	3FT deg	* g	CDD-CCD	MO	M$^	Ind	BCCC	Ind	
European Economics with Business	L1ND	3FT deg	* g	CDD-CCD	MO	M$^	Ind	BCCC	Ind	
European Economics with Computing	L1GN	3FT deg	* g	CDD-CCD	MO	M$^	Ind	BCCC	Ind	

TITLE	CODE	COURSE	SUBJECTS	A/AS	NO/C	AGNVQ	IB	SQA(H)	SQA	RATIO A/AS
European Economics with French	L1RD	3FT deg	E g	CDD-CCD	MO	M$^	Ind	BCCC	Ind	
European Economics with Geography	L1FW	3FT deg	* g	CDD-CCD	MO	M$^	Ind	BCCC	Ind	
European Economics with German	L1RG	3FT deg	G g	CDD-CCD	MO	M$^	Ind	BCCC	Ind	
European Economics with Italian	L1RJ	3FT deg	* g	CDD-CCD	MO	M$^	Ind	BCCC	Ind	
European Economics with Languages	L1TY	3FT deg	L g	CDD-CCD	MO	M$^	Ind	BCCC	Ind	
European Economics with Law	L1MJ	3FT deg	* g	BCC-BBC	MO	M$^	Ind	BBBB	Ind	
European Economics with Maritime Law	MLHC	3FT deg	* g	CDD-CCD	MO	M$^	Ind	BCCC	Ind	
European Economics with Politics	L1MD	3FT deg	* g	CDD-CCD	MO	M$^	Ind	BCCC	Ind	
European Economics with Psychology	L1CW	3FT deg	* g	BBC	MO	M$^	Ind	Ind	Ind	
European Economics with Resources,Manu & the Env	L1FY	3FT deg	* g	CDD-CCD	MO	M$^	Ind	BCCC	Ind	
European Economics with Social Policy	L1LL	3FT deg	Ap g	CDD-CCD	MO	M$^	Ind	BCCC	Ind	
European Economics with Sociology	L1LJ	3FT deg	Ap g	CDD-CCD	MO	M$^	Ind	BCCC	Ind	
European Economics with Spanish	L1RL	3FT deg	Sp g	CDD-CCD	MO	M$^	Ind	BCCC	Ind	
European Economics with Statistics	L1GL	3FT deg	* g	CDD-CCD	MO	M$^	Ind	BCCC	Ind	
European Economics with Transport	L1NY	3FT deg	* g	CDD-CCD	MO	M$^	Ind	BCCC	Ind	
Geography with Applied Economics	F8L1	3FT deg	Gy g	16-18	X	M$^	Ind	ABBB	Ind	16
Law with Applied Economics	M3L1	3FT deg	Ap g	BCC-BBC	DO	D12^	Ind	BBBB$	Ind	
Modern Languages with Applied Economics	T9L1	3FT/4SW deg	L g	C	Ind	Ind	Ind	Ind	Ind	
Political Economy with Business	LN1C	3FT deg	Ap g	CDD-CCD	MO $	M$^	Ind	BCCC	Ind	
Political Economy with Computing	LG1N	3FT deg	Ap g	CDD-CCD	MO $	M$^	Ind	BCCC	Ind	
Political Economy with French	LR1C	3FT deg	E g	CDD-CCD	MO $	M$^	Ind	BCCC	Ind	
Political Economy with Geography	LF1V	3FT deg	Ap g	CDD-CCD	MO $	M$^	Ind	BCCC	Ind	
Political Economy with German	LR1F	3FT deg	G g	CDD-CCD	MO $	M$^	Ind	BCCC	Ind	
Political Economy with Italian	LR1H	3FT deg	Ap g	CDD-CCD	MO $	M$^	Ind	BCCC	Ind	
Political Economy with Languages	LT1X	3FT deg	L g	CDD-CCD	MO $	M$^	Ind	BCCC	Ind	
Political Economy with Law	LM1H	3FT deg	Ap g	BCC-BBC	MO $	M$^	Ind	BBBB	Ind	
Political Economy with Maritime Law	MLHD	3FT deg	Ap g	CDD-CCD	MO $	M$^	Ind	BCCC	Ind	
Political Economy with Politics	LM1D	3FT deg	Ap g	CDD-CCD	MO $	M$^	Ind	BCCC	Ind	
Political Economy with Psychology	LC1V	3FT deg	Ap g	BBC	MO $	M$^	Ind	Ind	Ind	
Political Economy with Resources, Manu & the Env	LF1X	3FT deg	Ap g	CDD-CCD	MO $	M$^	Ind	BCCC	Ind	
Political Economy with Social Policy	LL1K	3FT deg	Ap g	CDD-CCD	MO $	M$^	Ind	BCCC	Ind	
Political Economy with Sociology	LL1H	3FT deg	Ap g	CDD-CCD	MO $	M$^	Ind	BCCC	Ind	
Political Economy with Spanish	LR1K	3FT deg	Sp g	CDD-CCD	MO $	M$^	Ind	BCCC	Ind	
Political Economy with Statistics	LG1K	3FT deg	Ap g	CDD-CCD	MO $	M$^	Ind	BCCC	Ind	
Political Economy with Transport	LN1X	3FT deg	Ap g	CDD-CCD	MO $	M$^	Ind	BCCC	Ind	
Politics with Applied Economics	M1L1	3FT deg	* g	14	Ind	M$	Ind	BBBC$	Ind	
Psychology with Applied Economics	C8L1	3FT/4SW deg	Ap g	BBC	MO+3D	M12^	Ind	BBBC$	Ind	8
Social Policy with Applied Economics	L4L1	3FT deg	* g	14	3M	M$	Ind	BBBC$	Ind	2
Sociology with Applied Economics	L3L1	3FT deg	* g	14	3M	M$	Ind	BBBC$	Ind	
Statistics (App) & Mgt Sci with App Economics	G4LC	3FT deg	M/St g	10-15	MO $	M$	Ind	BBCC	Ind	
Statistics (App) with Applied Economics	G4L1	3FT deg	M/St g	10	MO $	M$	Ind	BBCC	Ind	
Transport with Applied Economics	N9L1	3FT deg	Ec g	CCD	5M	M$	Ind	CCCC	Ind	

Univ of PORTSMOUTH

TITLE	CODE	COURSE	SUBJECTS	A/AS	NO/C	AGNVQ	IB	SQA(H)	SQA	RATIO A/AS
Accounting and Economics	NL41	3FT deg	* g	16	4M+2D	D$6/^ go	Dip	CCCCC	Ind	
Business Economics	L112	3FT deg	*	16	4M+2D	D$6/^ go	Dip	CCCCC	Ind	6/14
Economic and Business Policy	LN11	3FT deg	* g	16	4M+2D	D$6/^ go	Dip	CCCCC	Ind	7/12
Economics	L100	3FT deg	* g	16	4M+2D	D$6/^ go	Dip	CCCCC	Ind	4 8/16
Economics and Economic History	LV13	3FT deg	* g	16	4M+2D	D$6/^ go	Dip	CCCCC	Ind	1
Economics and Geography	LL18	3FT deg	*	14	4M+2D	D$6/^	Dip	CCCCC	Ind	4 10/22
Economics and Media Studies	LP14	3FT deg	*	16	4M+2D	D$6/^	Dip	CCCCC	Ind	
Law and Economics	ML31	3FT deg	*	18	MO+2D	D$6/^ go	Dip	BBBCC	Ind	

Economics 18

course details			98 expected requirements							96 entry stats	
TITLE	CODE	COURSE	SUBJECTS	A/AS	ND/C	AGNVQ	IB	SQA(H)	SQA	RATIO	A/AS
QUEEN MARY & WESTFIELD COLL (Univ of London)											
Business Economics	L112	3FT deg	M	BCC	3D	M^	30$	ABBBB			
Economics	L100	3FT deg	g	BCC		M	30$	BBBBB			
Economics and History	LV11	3FT deg	H g	BCC		M^	30$	BBBBB			
Economics and Politics	LM11	3FT deg	g	BBC		M	30$	BBBBB			
Economics/Statistics and Mathematics	LG1C	3FT deg	M g	BCC	5M	M$^	30$	BBBBB			
French and Economics	LR11	4FT deg	F g	20		M^	30$	BBBBB			
Geography and Economics	LL81	3FT deg	Gv g	BCC		M$^	30$	BBBBB			
German and Economics	LR1F	4FT deg	G	18		M^	30$	BBBBB			
Hispanic Studies and Economics	LR1K	4FT deg	L g	BCC		M^	30$	BBBBB			
Law and Economics	LM13	3FT deg	g	ABB	DO	D^	32$	AABBB			
Mathematics and Business Economics	GL11	3FT deg	M	BCC		M$^	30$	BBBBB			
Physics and Economics	FL31	3FT deg	M+P	24		MS^	30$	BBBBB			
Russian and Economics	LR1V	4FT deg	L g	BCC		M^	30$	BBBBB			
Statistics, Mathematics and Business Economics	GL41	3FT deg	M	BCC		M$^	30$	BBBBB			
QUEEN'S Univ Belfast											
Agricultural Economics and Management	L130	3FT deg	* g	CCC	3M+4D	D*6/^ go	28$	BBBB	Ind	5	14/22
Agriculture Economics and Mgt with ext St in Eur	L132	4FT deg	* g	CCC	3M+4D	D*6/^ go	28$	BBBB	Ind	1	
Economics	L100	3FT deg	* g	BBC	2M+5D	D*6/^ go	30$	AABB	Ind	5	20/26
Economics with French	L1R1	3FT deg									
Economics with German	L1R2	3FT deg									
Economics with Italian	L1R3	3FT deg									
Economics/Economic & Social History	LV13	3FT deg									
English/Economics	LQ13	3FT deg									
European Area Studies/Economics	LT1F	3FT deg									
French/Economics (4 years)	LR11	3FT deg									
German/Economics (4 years)	LR12	3FT deg									
Italian/Economics (4 years)	LR13	3FT deg									
Management with Business Economics	N1L1	3FT deg	* g	BBB	2M+5D	D*^ go	32$	AABBB	Ind	8	
Management with Economics	N1LC	3FT deg	* g	BBB	2M+5D	D*^ go	32$	AABBB	Ind		
Modern History/Economics	LV11	3FT deg									
Politics/Economics	LM11	3FT deg									
Scholastic Philosophy/Economics	LV1R	3FT deg									
Univ of READING											
Accounting and Economics	LN14	3FT deg	* g	BBC	Ind	D$6/^ go	31	BBBB	Ind	9	16/24
Agricultural Economics	L130	3FT deg	*	CDD	MO	M*6/^ gi	28	BBCC	Ind	4	12/24
Business Economics	L112	3FT deg	* g	BBC	Ind	D$6/^ go	31	BBBB	Ind	12	16/24
Business Economics and Organisational Studies	LN11	3FT deg	* g	BCC	Ind	D$6/^ go	30	BBBB	Ind	12	18/26
Chemistry with Economics	F1L1	3FT deg	C g	18	4M+1D$	DS^ go	29$	BBBC$	Ind	2	14/16
Chemistry with Economics with a year in Europe	F1LC	4FT deg	C g	18	4M+1D$	DS^ go	29$	BBBC$	Ind		
Economics	L100	3FT deg	* g	BBC	Ind	D$6/^ go	31	BBBB	Ind	10	18/30
Economics and Econometrics	L140	3FT deg	M g	BCC	Ind	D$6/^ go	30$	BBBB$	Ind		
Economics and Sociology	LL13	3FT deg	* g	BCC	Ind	D$^ go	30	BBBB	Ind	13	
French and Economics	LR11	4FT deg	F g	BBC	Ind	D$^ go	31$	BBBB$	Ind	9	
Geography and Economics (Regional Science)	LL18	3FT deg	* g	BBC	5M+3D	D$6/^ gi	31	BBBB	Ind	7	20/26
German and Economics	LR12	4FT deg	* g	BCC	Ind	D$^ go	30	BBBB	Ind		
History and Economics	LV11	3FT deg	* g	BBC	Ind	D$6/^ go	31	BBBB	Ind	5	
International Relations and Economics	ML11	3FT deg	* g	BBC	Ind	D$6/^ go	31	BBBB	Ind	12	
Italian and Economics	LR13	4FT deg	* g	BCC	Ind	D$6/^ go	30	BBBB	Ind	2	
Mathematics and Economics	GL11	3FT deg	M	BCC	3M+2D$	D$^	30$	BBBB$	Ind	11	
Politics and Economics	LM11	3FT deg	* g	BBC	Ind	D$6/^ go	31	BBBB	Ind	10	18/20

			98 expected requirements							96 entry stats	

course details   **98 expected requirements**   *96 entry stats*

TITLE	CODE	COURSE	SUBJECTS	A/AS	ND/C	AGNVQ	IB	SQA(H)	SQA	RATIO	A/AS
ROYAL HOLLOWAY, Univ of London											
Economics	L101	3FT deg	*	BBB	Ind		32	Ind		5	14/26
Economics and Management Studies	LN11	3FT deg	*	BBB	Ind		32	Ind		12	18/26
Economics and Mathematics	LG11	3FT deg	M	BBC-BBB	Ind		Ind	Ind			
Economics and Public Administration	LM11	3FT deg	*	BCC-BBB	Ind		Ind	Ind			
Economics and Social Policy	LL14	3FT deg	*	BCC-BBB	Ind		Ind	Ind		9	
Economics with French	L1R1	3FT deg	F	BBB	Ind		32	Ind			
Economics with German	L1R2	3FT deg	G	BBC-BBB	Ind		32	Ind			
Economics with Italian	L1R3	3FT deg	L/Ln	BBC-BBB	Ind		32	Ind			
Economics with Japanese Studies	L1T4	3FT deg	L g	BBB-BBC	Ind		32	Ind		6	
Economics with Management Studies	L1N1	3FT deg	*	BBB	Ind		32	Ind		3	
Economics with Mathematics	L1G1	3FT deg	M	BBC-BBB	Ind		32$	Ind		6	
Economics with Music	L1W3	3FT deg	Mu	BBC-BBB	Ind		32	Ind			
Economics with Political Studies	L1M1	3FT deg	*	BBC-BBB	Ind		32	Ind		7	
Economics with Social Policy	L1L4	3FT deg	*	BBC-BBB	Ind		32	Ind			
Economics with Sociology	L1L3	3FT deg	*	BBC-BBB	Ind		32	Ind			
Economics with Spanish	L1R4	3FT deg	L	BBC-BBB	Ind		32	Ind			
Financial and Business Economics	L160	3FT deg	*	BBB	Ind		32	Ind			
French with Economics	R1L1	4FT deg	F	BBC-ABC			28$	Ind			
German with Economics	R2L1	4FT deg	G	BCC			28$	BBBBC$			
Italian with Economics	R3L1	4FT deg	L/Ln	BBC			30	BBCCC$			
Management Studies with Economics	N1L1	3FT deg	*	BBC-BBB	2M+3D	D^	30	Ind			
Mathematics with Economics	G1L1	3FT deg	M	BCC	Ind	D^	Ind	Ind			
Mathematics with Economics and Management	G1LC	3FT deg	M	BCC-BBC	Ind	D^	Ind	Ind		20	
Social Policy with Economics	L4L1	3FT deg	*	BCC-BBC	Ind	D^	Ind	Ind			
Sociology and Economics	LL13	3FT deg	*	BCC-BBB	Ind	D^	Ind	Ind			
Sociology with Economics	L3L1	3FT deg	*	BCC-BBC	Ind	D^	Ind	Ind		1	
Foundation Programme *Economics*	Y408	4FT deg									
Univ of SALFORD											
Biochemistry and Economics (3 or 4 Yrs)	LC17	3FT/4SW deg	C	BCC-CCD	3M	M	Ind	Ind	Ind	1	
Business Economics	L112	3FT deg	* g	BCC	Ind	D	Ind	Ind	Ind	6	12/24
Business Economics with Gambling Studies	L101	3FT deg	* g	CCC	Ind	M	Ind	Ind	Ind		
Chemistry and Economics (3 or 4 Yrs)	FL11	3FT/4SW deg	C	BCC-CCD	3M	M	Ind	Ind	Ind	1	
Economics	L100	3FT deg	* g	BCC	Ind	D	Ind	Ind	Ind	3	10/22
Economics & Geography (3 or 4 Yrs)	LF18	3FT/4SW deg	Gy	BCC-CCD	3M	M	Ind	Ind	Ind	2	14/18
Economics and Information Technology	LG15	3FT/4SW deg		BCC-CCD	3M	M	Ind	Ind	Ind		
Economics and Physiology	LC19	3FT/4SW deg		BCC-CCD	3M	M	Ind	Ind	Ind		
Political Economy	L114	3FT deg	* g	CCC	Ind	D	Ind	Ind	Ind	4	
SOAS:Sch of Oriental & African St (U of London)											
Development Economics	L118	3FT deg	g	20	Ind		30	BBBCC	Ind	12	
Economics	L100	3FT deg	g	22	Ind		31	BBBBC	Ind	15	
Economics and African Studies	TL71	3FT deg	g	22	Ind		31	BBBBC	Ind		
Economics and Amharic	LT17	4FT deg	g	22	Ind		31	BBBBC	Ind		
Economics and Arabic	LT16	4FT deg	g	22	Ind		31	BBBBC	Ind	2	
Economics and Bengali	LT15	3FT deg	g	22	Ind		31	BBBBC	Ind		
Economics and Burmese	LT1M	4FT deg	g	22	Ind		31	BBBBC	Ind		
Economics and Chinese	LT13	4FT deg	g	24	Ind		32	BBBBB	Ind	11	
Economics and Development Studies	ML91	3FT deg	g	22	Ind		31	BBBBC	Ind	5	
Geography and Economics	LL18	3FT deg	g	22	Ind		31	BBBBC	Ind	14	
Georgian and Economics	LT19	3FT deg	g	22	Ind		31	BBBBC	Ind		

Economics 18

TITLE	CODE	COURSE	SUBJECTS	A/AS	NO/C	RGNVQ	IB	SQA(H)	SQA	RATIO A/AS
course details			98 expected requirements							96 entry stats
Gujarati and Economics	LT1N	3FT deg	g	22	Ind		31	BBBBC	Ind	
Hausa and Economics	LT1R	4FT deg	g	22	Ind		31	BBBBC	Ind	
Hebrew and Economics	LQ19	4FT deg	g	22	Ind		31	BBBBC	Ind	
Hindi and Economics	LTC5	3FT/4FT deg	g	22	Ind		31	BBBBC	Ind	2
History and Economics	LV11	3FT deg	g	22	Ind		31	BBBBC	Ind	8
Indonesian and Economics	LTCM	3FT/4FT deg	g	22	Ind		31	BBBBC	Ind	
Japanese and Economics	LT14	4FT deg	g	24	Ind		32	BBBBB	Ind	14
Korean and Economics	LTCN	4FT deg	g	22	Ind		31	BBBBC	Ind	
Law and Economics	LM13	3FT deg	g	24	Ind		32	BBBBB	Ind	8
Linguistics and Economics	LQ13	3FT deg								
Nepali and Economics	LTD5	3FT deg	g	22	Ind		31	BBBBC	Ind	
Persian and Economics	LT1Q	3FT deg	g	22	Ind		31	BBBBC	Ind	
Politics and Economics	LM11	3FT deg	g	22	Ind		31	BBBBC	Ind	3 18/26
Sanskrit and Economics	LQ1X	3FT deg	g	22	Ind		31	BBBBC	Ind	
Sinhalese and Economics	LTDM	3FT deg	g	22	Ind		31	BBBBC	Ind	
Social Anthropology and Economics	LL16	3FT deg	g	22	Ind		31	BBBBC	Ind	
South Asian Studies and Economics	TLM1	3FT deg								
Study of Religions and Economics	LV18	3FT deg	g	20	Ind		30	BBBCC	Ind	3
Swahili and Economics	LT1T	4FT deg	g	22	Ind		31	BBBBC	Ind	
Tamil and Economics	LTDN	3FT deg	g	22	Ind		31	BBBBC	Ind	
Thai and Economics	TL51	3FT/4FT deg	g	22	Ind		31	BBBBC	Ind	
Turkish and Economics	LT1P	4FT deg	g	22	Ind		31	BBBBC	Ind	
Urdu and Economics	TL5C	3FT deg	g	22	Ind		31	BBBBC	Ind	
Vietnamese and Economics	TL5D	4FT deg	g	22	Ind		31	BBBBC	Ind	

SSEES:Sch of Slavonic & E European St(U of London)

TITLE	CODE	COURSE	SUBJECTS	A/AS	NO/C	RGNVQ	IB	SQA(H)	SQA	RATIO A/AS
Economics with East European Studies	L1T1	3FT deg		BCC		Ind	28	BBBBB		

Univ of SHEFFIELD

TITLE	CODE	COURSE	SUBJECTS	A/AS	NO/C	RGNVQ	IB	SQA(H)	SQA	RATIO A/AS
Accounting & Financial Management and Economics	NL41	3FT deg	* g	24	3M+3D	D^	32	AABB	Ind	11 22/28
Business Studies and Economics	NL11	3FT deg	* g	26	2M+4D	D^	33	AAAB	Ind	11 24/30
Economics	L100	3FT deg	* g	22	4M+2D	D^	30	ABBB	Ind	10 22/30
Economics and Geography	LL18	3FT deg	Gy g	BBB	3M+3D$	D^	32$	AABB$	Ind	15 26/28
Economics and Japanese Studies	LT14	3FT deg	* g	BBC	4M+2D	D^	30	ABBB	Ind	6
Economics and Mathematics	LG1D	3FT deg	M g	24	3M+3D$	D^	32$	AABB$	Ind	4 20/30
Economics and Philosophy	LV17	3FT deg	* g	BBB	3M+3D	D^	32	AABB	Ind	9
Economics and Politics	LM11	3FT deg	* g	BBB	3M+3D	D^	32	AABB	Ind	11 24/30
Economics and Social Policy	LL14	3FT deg	* g	BBC	4D	D^	30	ABBB	Ind	18
Economics and Sociology	LL13	3FT deg	* g	BBC	4D	D^	30	ABBB	Ind	19
Economics and Statistics	LG14	3FT deg	M g	24	3M+3D$	D^	32$	AABB$	Ind	19
Economics with Econometrics	L140	3FT deg	M g	22	4M+2D$	D^	30$	ABBB$	Ind	9
French and Economics	RL11	4FT deg	F g	BBC	X	D^	30$	ABBB$	Ind	22
German and Economics	RL21	4FT deg	G g	BBC	X	D^	30$	ABBB$	Ind	8
Hispanic Studies and Economics	RL41	4FT deg	Sp g	BBC	X	D^	30$	ABBB$	Ind	
Korean Studies and Economics	TL51	4FT deg	* g	BBC	4M+2D	D^	30	ABBB	Ind	
Russian and Economics	RL81	4FT deg	L g	BBC	X	D^	30	ABBB	Ind	2
Economics with Mathematics and Statistics	Y620	3FT deg	M g	22	4M+2D$	D^	30$	ABBB$	Ind	
Economics										

Univ of SOUTHAMPTON

TITLE	CODE	COURSE	SUBJECTS	A/AS	NO/C	RGNVQ	IB	SQA(H)	SQA	RATIO A/AS
Accounting with Economics	NL41	3FT deg	* g	24	Ind	D$^ go	32	AABBB	Ind	7 18/24
Economics	L100	3FT deg	* g	24	Ind	D$^ go	32	AABBB	Ind	5 18/28
Economics and Econometrics	L140	3FT deg	M	24	Ind	D$^ go	32$	AABBB$	Ind	4 26/30
Economics and Economic History	LV13	3FT deg	* g	24	Ind	D$^ go	32	AABBB	Ind	

course details   98 expected requirements   *96 entry stats*

TITLE	CODE	COURSE	SUBJECTS	A/AS	ND/C	RGNVQ	IB	SQA(H)	SQA	RATIO	A/AS
Economics and Finance	L1NJ	3FT deg	*g	24	Ind	D$^ go	32	AABBB	Ind	6	
Economics and French	LR11	4FT deg	F g	24	Ind	D$^ go	32$	AABBB$	Ind	6	20/28
Economics and German	LR12	4FT deg	G g	24	Ind	D$^ go	32$	AABBB$	Ind	13	
Economics and Management Sciences	L112	3FT deg	*g	24	Ind	D$^ go	32	AABBB	Ind	10	20/28
Economics and Mathematics	LG11	3FT deg	M	24	Ind	D$^ go	32$	AABBB$	Ind	29	
Economics and Philosophy	VL71	3FT deg	*g	BCC	Ind	D$^ go	26	Ind	Ind		
Economics and Politics	LM11	3FT deg	*g	22	Ind	D$^ go	30	ABBBB	Ind	8	18/26
Economics with Actuarial Studies	L1N3	3FT deg	M	22	Ind	D$^ go	30$	ABBBB$	Ind	6	18/26
Mathematics with Economics	G1L1	3FT deg	M	BBC	Ind	Ind	30	ABBBB	Ind	7	20/30
Population Studies	L184	3FT deg	*g	20	Ind	D$^ go	28	BBBBC	Ind	2	14/24

SOUTH BANK Univ

TITLE	CODE	COURSE	SUBJECTS	A/AS	ND/C	RGNVQ	IB	SQA(H)	SQA	RATIO	A/AS
Economics and Accounting	LN14	3FT deg	Bu/Ec g	12-16	4M+2D	M go	Ind	Ind	Ind		
Economics and Computing	GL51	3FT deg	M+Ec/Bu g	12-16	4M+2D	M go	Ind	Ind	Ind		
English Studies and Economics	LQ13	3FT deg	Ec/Bu+E g	14-18	X	M^ go	Ind	Ind	Ind		
Environmental Policy and Economics	FL91	3FT deg	Ec/Bu g	12-16	4M+2D	M go	Ind	Ind	Ind		
European Studies and Economics	LT1F	3FT deg	Ec/Bu g	14-18	2M+4D	M go	Ind	Ind	Ind		
French and Economics	LR11	3FT deg	Ec/Bu+F g	12-16	4M+2D	M go	Ind	Ind	Ind		
German - ab initio and Economics	LR12	3FT deg	Ec/Bu g	12-16	4M+2D	M go	Ind	Ind	Ind		
German and Economics	LR1F	3FT deg	G g	14-18	2M+4D	M go	Ind	Ind	Ind		
Health Studies and Economics	LL14	3FT deg	Ec/Bu g	12-16	4M+2D	M go	Ind	Ind	Ind		
Housing and Economics	KL4C	3FT deg	Ec/Bu g	14-18	2M+4D	M go	Ind	Ind	Ind		
Human Geography and Economics	LL18	3FT deg	Ec/Bu+Gy g	12-16	4M+2D	M go	Ind	Ind	Ind		
Human Resource Management and Economics	LN16	3FT deg	Ec/Bu g	14-18	2M+4D	M go	Ind	Ind	Ind		
Law and Economics	LM13	3FT deg	Ec/Bu g	14-18	2M+4D	D go	Ind	Ind	Ind		
Management and Economics	LN11	3FT deg	Bu/Ec g	12-16	4M+2D	M go	Ind	Ind	Ind		
Marketing and Economics	LN15	3FT deg	Ec/Bu g	12-16	2M+4D	M go	Ind	Ind	Ind		
Media Studies and Economics	LP14	3FT deg	Ec/Bu+E g	14-18	2M+4D	D go	Ind	Ind	Ind		
Politics and Economics	LM11	3FT deg	Bu/Ec g	14-18	2M+4D	M go	Ind	Ind	Ind		
Product Design and Economics	HL71	3FT deg	Ad+Ec/Bu g	12-16	4M+2D	M go	Ind	Ind	Ind		
Psychology and Economics	CL81	3FT deg	Bu/Ec+S g	14-18	4M+2D	M go	Ind	Ind	Ind		
Social Policy and Health Studies	LL41	3FT deg	S g	12-16	4M+2D	M go	Ind	Ind	Ind		
Spanish - ab initio and Economics	LR14	3FT deg	Ec/Bu g	12-16	4M+2D	M go	Ind	Ind	Ind		
Spanish and Economics	LR1K	3FT deg	Sp+Ec/Bu g	14-18	2M+4D	M go	Ind	Ind	Ind		
Technology and Economics	JL91	3FT deg	Ec/Bu g	12-16	4M+2D	M go	Ind	Ind	Ind		
Tourism and Economics	LP17	3FT deg	Ec/Bu+L g	12-16	4M+2D	M go	Ind	Ind	Ind		
Urban Studies and Economics	LK14	3FT deg	Ec/Bu g	14-18	2M+4D	M go	Ind	Ind	Ind		
World Theatre and Economics	LW14	3FT deg	Ec/Bu g	14-18	2M+4D	M go	Ind	Ind	Ind		

Univ of ST ANDREWS

TITLE	CODE	COURSE	SUBJECTS	A/AS	ND/C	RGNVQ	IB	SQA(H)	SQA	RATIO	A/AS
Economics (Arts)	L100	4FT deg	*g	BBC	X	Ind	30$	BBBB	Ind	4	24/30
Economics (Science)	L102	4FT deg	B/C/M/B/Gy g	BCC	Ind	Ind	28$	BBBC$	Ind	5	
Economics with French	L1R1	4FT deg	M+F g	BCC	Ind	Ind	28$	BBBC$	Ind		
Economics with French (with Integ Year Abroad)	L1RC	4FT deg	M+F g	BCC	Ind	Ind	28$	BBBC$	Ind		
Economics-Ancient History	LV1D	4FT deg	*g	BBB	X	Ind	30$	BBBB	Ind		
Economics-Arabic	LT16	4FT deg	*g	BBB	X	Ind	30$	BBBB	Ind		
Economics-Biblical Studies	LV18	4FT deg	*g	BBB	X	Ind	30$	BBBB	Ind		
English-Economics	LQ13	4FT deg	*g	BBB	X	Ind	30$	BBBB	Ind		
French with Year Abroad-Economics	LRC1	4FT/5FT deg	F g	BBB	X	Ind	30$	BBBB	Ind		
French-Economics	LR11	4FT deg	F g	BBB	X	Ind	30$	BBBB$	Ind	3	
Geography-Economics	LL18	4FT deg	*g	BBB	X	Ind	30$	BBBB	Ind	15	
German with Year Abroad-Economics	LRC2	4FT/5FT deg	*g	BBB	X	Ind	30$	BBBB	Ind	3	
German-Economics	LR12	4FT deg	*g	BBB	X	Ind	30$	BBBB	Ind		

Economics 18

course details			98 expected requirements							96 entry stats	
TITLE	CODE	COURSE	SUBJECTS	A/AS	ND/C	RGNVQ	IB	SQA(H)	SQA	RATIO	A/AS
International Relations-Economics	LM11	4FT deg	* g	AAB	X	Ind	36$	AAAB	Ind	17	
Italian with Year Abroad-Economics	LR1H	4FT/5FT deg	* g	BBB	X	Ind	30$	BBBB	Ind		
Management Sciences-Economics	LN11	4FT deg	M g	BBC	Ind	Ind	28$	BBBB$	Ind		
Management-Economics (Arts)	NL11	4FT deg	* g	BBB	X	Ind	30$	BBBB	Ind	7	24/28
Management-Economics (Science)	LN1C	4FT deg	* g	BBB	X	Ind	28$	BBBB$	Ind		
Mathematics-Economics (Arts)	GL11	4FT deg	M g	BBB	X	Ind	30$	BBBB$	Ind	4	
Mathematics-Economics (Science)	GLC1	3FT/4FT deg	M g	BCC	Ind	Ind	28$	BBBC$	Ind	4	
Mediaeval History-Economics	LVC1	4FT deg	* g	BBB	X	Ind	30$	BBBB	Ind		
Modern History-Economics	LV11	4FT deg	* g	BBB	X	Ind	30$	BBBB	Ind	5	
Modern Languages with Economics	T9LC	4FT deg	* g	BBB	X	Ind	30$	BBBB	Ind		
Modern Languages with Economics (Int Yr Abroad)	T9L1	4FT/5FT deg	* g	BBB	X	Ind	30$	BBBB	Ind		
Philosophy-Economics	LV17	4FT deg	* g	BBB	X	Ind	30$	BBBB	Ind	12	
Psychology-Economics (Arts)	LL71	4FT deg	* g	ABB	X	Ind	32$	BBBBB	Ind	4	
Psychology-Economics (Science)	CLV1	4FT deg	* g	ABB	X	Ind	32$	BBBBB	Ind		
Russian with Year Abroad-Economics	LRC8	4FT/5FT deg	* g	BBB	X	Ind	30$	BBBB	Ind		
Russian-Economics	LR18	4FT deg	* g	BBB	X	Ind	30$	BBBB	Ind		
Social Anthropology-Economics	LL16	4FT deg	* g	BBB	X	Ind	32$	BBBB	Ind	2	
Spanish with Year Abroad-Economics	LRC4	4FT/5FT deg	* g	BBB	X	Ind	30$	BBBB	Ind		
Spanish-Economics	LR14	4FT deg	* g	BBB	X	Ind	32$	BBBB	Ind		
Statistics-Economics (Arts)	GLK1	4FT deg	M g	BBB	X	Ind	30$	BBBB$	Ind		
Statistics-Economics (Science)	GL41	4FT deg	M g	BCC	Ind	Ind	28$	BBBC$	Ind	6	
European Integration Studies Economics	Y602	4FT deg	* g	BBB	X	Ind	30$	BBBB	Ind		
General Degree of BSc Economics (Science)	Y100	3FT deg	B/C/Gy/M/P g	CCC	Ind	Ind	28$	BBBC$	Ind		
General Degree of MA Economics	Y450	3FT deg	* g	BBB	X	Ind	30$	BBBB	Ind		

STAFFORDSHIRE Univ

Business and Financial Economics	LN14	3FT deg	g	14	4M	M$	24	BBC	Ind	2	6/17
Economic Studies	L101	3FT deg	g	12	4M	M$		BBC			
Economic Studies/Development Studies	LM19	3FT deg	g	12	4M	M	24	BBC			
Economics	L100	3FT deg	g	12	4M	M$	Ind	BBC	Ind	7	6/14
Environmental Studies/Economic Studies	FL91	3FT deg									
European Economics	LT12	3FT deg	g	12	4M	M$	24	BBC	Ind	2	
Geography/Economic Studies	LL1V	3FT deg									
History/Economic Studies	LV1C	3FT deg	H g	12	MO+2D	M	27	BBC			
International Relations/Economic Studies	LM11	3FT deg									
Legal Studies/Economic Studies	LMCH	3FT deg									
Leisure Economics	L1N7	3FT deg	g	12	4M	M$		BBC			
Philisophy/Economic Studies	LVC7	3FT deg	g	12	MO+2D	M	27	BBC			
Politics/Economic Studies	LM1D	3FT deg	g	12	4M	M	24	BBC			
Sociology/Economic Studies	LL13	3FT deg									

Univ of STIRLING

Accountancy/Economics	LN14	4FT deg	g	BCC	HN	Ind	33	BBBB	HN		
Business Studies/Economics	LN1D	4FT deg	g	BBC	Ind	Ind	33	BBBB	HN		
Computing Science/Economics	GL51	4FT deg	g	CCC	Ind	Ind	28	BBCC	HN		
Ecological Economics	L120	4FT deg	S g	CCC	Ind	Ind	28	BBCC	HN		
Economic Policy	L108	4FT deg	g	CCC	Ind	Ind	28	BBCC	HN		
Economics	L100	4FT deg	g	CCC	Ind	Ind	28	BBCC	HN		
Economics/Business Law	L1M3	4FT deg	g	CCC	Ind	Ind	28	BBCC	HN		
Economics/Environmental Science	FL91	4FT deg	S g	CCC	Ind	Ind	31	BBBC	HN		
Economics/Financial Studies	LN13	4FT deg	g	CCC	Ind	Ind	28	BBCC	HN		

course details			98 expected requirements							96 entry stats
TITLE	CODE	COURSE	SUBJECTS	A/AS	ND/C	AGNVQ	IB	SQA(H)	SQA	RATIO A/AS
Economics/French Language	LR1C	4FT deg	g	CCC	Ind	Ind	31	BBBC	HN	
Economics/German Language	LR1F	4FT deg	g	CCC	Ind	Ind	31	BBBC	HN	
Economics/History	LV11	4FT deg	g	BCC	Ind	Ind	31	BBBC	HN	
Economics/Japanese	LT14	4FT deg	g	BCC	Ind	Ind	31	BBBC	HN	
Economics/Marketing	NL51	4FT deg	g	CCC	Ind	Ind	28	BBCC	HN	
Economics/Mathematics	GL11	4FT deg	M g	CCC	Ind	Ind	28	BBCC	HN	
Economics/Philosophy	LV17	4FT deg	g	CCC	Ind	Ind	28	BBCC	HN	
Economics/Politics	LM11	4FT deg	g	CCC	Ind	Ind	28	BBCC	HN	
Economics/Sociology	LL13	4FT deg	g	BCC	Ind	Ind	31	BBBC	HN	
Economics/Spanish Language	LR1K	4FT deg	g	CCC	Ind	Ind	31	BBBC	HN	
Economics/Sports Studies	LB16	4FT deg	g	CCC	Ind	Ind	28	BBCC	HN	
Human Resources Management/Economics	NL11	4FT deg	g	CCC	Ind	Ind	28	BBCC	HN	
Mathematics and its Applications with Economics	G1L1	4FT deg	M g	CCC	Ind	Ind	28	BBCC	HN	
Technological Economics	L188	4FT deg	g	BCC	Ind	Ind	31	BBBC	HN	
Politics, Philosophy and Economics	Y616	4FT deg	g	BCC	Ind	Ind	31	BBBC	HN	

Economics

Univ of STRATHCLYDE

Mathematics, Statistics and Economics	G1L1	4FT deg	M g	CD	Ind		30$	BBCC$	Ind	

UNIVERSITY COLLEGE SUFFOLK

Business Studies with Economics	N1LC	3FT deg								

Univ of SUNDERLAND

Accounting and Economics	NL41	3FT deg	* g	18	2M+3D$ M*		24	CCCC	N	6/11
Biology and Economics	CL11	3FT deg	B/C	8	3M	M	Ind	Ind	Ind	
Biology with Economics	C1L1	3FT deg	B/C	8	3M	M	Ind	Ind	Ind	
Business Economics	L112	3FT deg	* g	16	N $	M	26	BBCC	N$	1 6/14
Business Studies and Economics	NL11	3FT/4SW deg	*	8	3M	M	Ind	Ind	Ind	
Business Studies with Economics	N1L1	3FT/4SW deg	*	8	3M	M	Ind	Ind	Ind	
Chemistry and Economics	FL11	3FT deg	C g	8	N $	M	24$	CCCC$	N$	
Chemistry with Economics	F1L1	3FT deg	C	8	3M	M	Ind	Ind	Ind	
Computer Studies and Economics	GL51	3FT deg	* g	8	N	M	24	CCCC	N	3
Computer Studies with Economics	G5L1	3FT/4SW deg	*	8	3M	M	Ind	Ind	Ind	
Economics	L100	3FT deg	* g	14	2M+2D$ M		26	BBCCC	N$	4 5/18
Economics and English	LQ13	3FT deg	*	10	4M	M	Ind	Ind	Ind	
Economics and French	LR11	4FT deg	F g	8	N $	M	24$	CCCC$	N$	
Economics and Geography	LL18	3FT deg	Gy/Gl g	10	N $	M	24$	CCCC$	N$	6
Economics and Geology	LF16	3FT deg	Gy/Gl g	8	N $	M	24	CCCC$	N$	
Economics and History	LV11	3FT deg	H g	10	Ind	M	24$	CCCC	Ind	
Economics and Mathematics	LG11	3FT deg	M g	8	N $	M	24$	CCCC$	N$	
Economics and Media Studies	LP14	3FT deg	*	24	Ind	Ind	Ind	Ind	Ind	
Economics and Philosophy	LV17	3FT deg	* g	10	Ind	M	24	CCCC	Ind	2
Economics and Politics	LM11	3FT deg	* g	10	N	M	24	CCCC	N	
Economics and Psychology	LC18	3FT deg	* g	10	N	M	24$	CCCC$	N	
Economics and Religious Studies	LV18	3FT deg	*	8	3M	M	Ind	Ind	Ind	
Economics and Spanish	LR14	4FT deg	*	8	3M	M	Ind	Ind	Ind	
Economics with Biology	L1C1	3FT deg	*	8	3M	M	Ind	Ind	Ind	
Economics with Business Studies	L1N1	3FT deg	*	8	3M	M	Ind	Ind	Ind	
Economics with Chemistry	L1F1	3FT deg	*	8	3M	M	Ind	Ind	Ind	
Economics with Computer Studies	L1G5	3FT deg	*	8	3M	M	Ind	Ind	Ind	
Economics with English	L1Q3	3FT deg	*	10	4M	M	Ind	Ind	Ind	
Economics with French	L1R1	3FT deg	*	8	3M	M	Ind	Ind	Ind	
Economics with Geography	L1L8	3FT deg	*	8	3M	M	Ind	Ind	Ind	

Economics 18

			98 expected requirements							**96 entry stats**	
course details										*96 entry stats*	
TITLE	CODE	COURSE	SUBJECTS	A/AS	ND/C	AGNVQ	IB	SQA(H)	SQA	RATIO	A/AS
Economics with Geology	L1F6	3FT deg	*	8	3M	M	Ind	Ind	Ind		
Economics with History	L1V1	3FT deg	*	10	4M	M	Ind	Ind	Ind		
Economics with Mathematics	L1G1	3FT deg	*	8	3M	M	Ind	Ind	Ind		
Economics with Media Studies	L1P4	3FT deg	*	24	Ind	Ind	Ind	Ind	Ind		
Economics with Philosophy	L1V7	3FT deg	*	8	3M	M	Ind	Ind	Ind		
Economics with Politics	L1M1	3FT deg	*	8	3M	M	Ind	Ind	Ind		
Economics with Psychology	L1C8	3FT deg	*	10	4M	M^	Ind	Ind	Ind		
Economics with Religious Studies	L1V8	3FT deg	*	8	3M	M	Ind	Ind	Ind		
Economics with Sociology	L1L3	3FT deg	*	8	3M	M	Ind	Ind	Ind		
Economics with Spanish	L1R4	3FT deg	*	8	3M	M	Ind	Ind	Ind		
English with Economics	Q3L1	3FT deg	*	10	4M	M	Ind	Ind	Ind		
French with Economics	R1L1	4FT deg	F	8	3M	M	Ind	Ind	Ind		
Geography with Economics	L8L1	3FT deg	*	8	3M	M	Ind	Ind	Ind		
Geology with Economics	F6L1	3FT deg	*	8	3M	M	Ind	Ind	Ind		
History with Economics	V1L1	3FT deg	*	10	4M	M	Ind	Ind	Ind		
Mathematics with Economics	G1L1	3FT deg	M	8	3M	M	Ind	Ind	Ind		
Media Studies with Economics	P4L1	3FT deg	*	24	Ind	Ind	Ind	Ind	Ind		
Philosophy with Economics	V7L1	3FT deg	*	8	3M	Ind	Ind	Ind	Ind		
Physiology with Economics	B1L1	3FT deg	*	8	3M	M	Ind	Ind	Ind		
Politics with Economics	M1L1	3FT deg	*	8	3M	M	Ind	Ind	Ind		
Psychology with Economics	C8L1	3FT deg	*	10	4M	M^	Ind	Ind	Ind		
Religious Studies with Economics	V8L1	3FT deg	*	8	3M	M	Ind	Ind	Ind		

Univ of SURREY

Business Economics with Computing	L112	3FT/4SW deg	M+E g	BBB	Ind	M$^ go	32$	BBBB	Ind	5	18/26
Economics	L100	3FT/4SW deg	M+E g	BBB	Ind	M$^ go	32$	BBBB	Ind	6	16/22
Economics and Sociology	LLCH	3FT/4SW deg	M+E g	BCC	Ind	M$^ go	32$	BBBB	Ind	2	12/22
French and Economics with International Business	RL11	4SW deg	F g	22	3M+3D$		30$	ABBCC	Ind	4	14/22
German and Economics with International Business	RL21	4SW deg	G g	22	3M+3D$		30$	ABBCC	Ind	2	16/28
Russian and Economics w International Business	RL81	4SW deg	* g	18	3M+3D$		30	ABBCC	Ind	2	10/12

Univ of SUSSEX

Economics in African & Asian Studies	L1T5	3FT deg	* g	BBB	MO $	M*6 go	$	Ind	Ind		
Economics in European Studies	L1T2	4FT deg	* g	BBB	MO $	M*6 go	$	Ind	Ind		
Economics in Social Sciences	L1M9	3FT deg	* g	BBB	MO $	M*6 go	$	Ind	Ind		
Economics with Comp and Quantitative Method	L1G5	3FT deg	* g	BBB	MO $	M*6 go	$	Ind	Ind		
Economics with Development Studies	L1MY	3FT deg	* g	BBB	MO $	M*6 go	$	Ind	Ind		
Economics with Economic History	L1V3	3FT deg	* g	BBB	MO $	M*6 go	$	Ind	Ind		
Economics with French/Maitrise Internationale	L1RC	4FT deg	F+Ec/M	BBC	MO $	M*6 go	$	Ind	Ind		
Economics with Mathematics	L1G1	3FT deg	M/St	BBB	MO $	M*^ go	$	Ind	Ind		
Mathematics and Economics	GL11	3FT deg	M	BCC	MO $	MS^	$	Ind	Ind		
Mathematics and Statistics with Economics	G4L1	3FT deg	M	BCC	MO $	MS^	$	Ind	Ind		
Mathematics and Stats with Economics (MMath)	G4LC	4FT deg	M	BCC	MO $	MS^	$	Ind	Ind		
Mathematics with Economics	G1L1	3FT deg	M	BCC	MO $	MS^	$	Ind	Ind		
Mathematics with Economics (MMath)	G1LC	4FT deg	M	BCC	MO $	MS^	$	Ind	Ind		

Univ of Wales SWANSEA

Applied Economics	L110	3FT deg	M+Ec	24	Ind	Ind	32$	AABBB$	Ind		
Business Economics	L112	3FT deg	* g	22-24	1M+5D$	Ind	30$	ABBBB$	Ind	3	14/28
Business Economics	L113	3FT deg	* g	20-24	1M+5D	Ind	30$	BBBBB$	Ind	1	14/26
Business Management and Economics	NL11	3FT deg	* g	22-24	1M+5D$ D$^ go		30$	ABBBB$	Ind	8	18/22
Business, Economics and Law	LM13	3FT deg	* g	BBB	1M+5D$	Ind	30$	BBBBB$	Ind		
Development Studies and Economics	LM19	3FT deg	* g	BB-BBC	Ind	Ind	30	ABBBB	Ind		
Economic History and Economics	LV13	3FT deg	* g	BBC	Ind	Ind	30	ABBBB	Ind	2	

			SUBJECTS	A/AS	NO/C	AGNVQ	IB	SQA(H)	SQA	RATIO	A/AS
TITLE	**CODE**	**COURSE**									
Economics	L102	3FT deg	* g	20-24	1M+5D	Ind	30	ABBBB	Ind	2	12/22
Economics	L100	3FT deg	* g	20-24	1M+5D	Ind	30	ABBBB	Ind	3	10/22
Economics	L104	3FT deg	* g	20-24	1M+5D	Ind	30	ABBBB	Ind	2	10/22
Economics and Geography	LL81	3FT deg	Gy g	BBC	1M+5D$	Ind	30$	ABBBB$	Ind		
Economics and Geography	LLC8	3FT deg	Gy g	BBC	1M+5D$	Ind	30$	ABBBB$	Ind	2	16/24
Economics and Mathematics	GLD1	3FT deg	M g	BBC-BCC	Ind	Ind	28$	BBBBC$	Ind	4	
Economics and Politics	LM11	3FT deg	* g	BBC	1M+5D	Ind	30	ABBBB	Ind	2	14/22
Economics and Psychology	LL17	3FT deg	* g	BBB-BBC	1M+5D	Ind	30	ABBBB	Ind	8	
Economics and Social Policy	LL41	3FT deg	* g	BBC-BCC	1M+5D	Ind	28	BBBBB	Ind		
Economics and Statistics	L140	3FT deg	M g	BBC	Ind	Ind	30$	ABBBB$	Ind		
Financial Economics	L160	3FT deg	* g	22-24	1M+5D$	Ind	30$	BBBBB$	Ind		
French/Economics	LR11	4FT deg	F g	BBC	1M+5D$	Ind	30$	ABBBB$	Ind	9	
Geography/Economics	LL18	3FT deg	Gy g	BBC	1M+5D$	Ind	30$	ABBBB$	Ind	2	14/18
German/Economics	LR12	4FT deg									
History/Economics	LV11	3FT deg	* g	BBB-BBC	Ind	Ind	30	ABBBB	Ind	4	
Italian/Economics	LR13	4FT deg									
Law and Economics	ML31	3FT deg	* g	BBB-BBC	1M+5D	Ind	30$	ABBBB$	Ind	3	14/26
Russian Studies/Economics	LRC8	3FT deg	* g	BBB-BBC	1M+5D	Ind	30$	ABBBB$	Ind		
Russian/Economics	LR18	4FT deg									
Spanish/Economics	LR14	4FT deg	L/* g	BBC	1M+5D$	Ind	30$	ABBBB$	Ind	4	
Joint Hons with defer choice of specialisation (inc Economics)	Y220	3FT deg	* g	20-22	1M+5D	Ind	28	BBBBB	Ind		

Univ of TEESSIDE

Economics	L100	3FT deg	*	14-16	Ind		Ind	Ind	Ind		
Modular Degree Scheme *Economics*	Y401	3FT deg									

THAMES VALLEY Univ

Accounting with Economics	N4L1	3FT deg		8-12	M0	M	26	CCC			
Business Administration with Economics	N1LC	3FT deg		8-12	M0	M	26	CCC			
Business Economics with Accounting	L1NK	3FT deg		8-12	M0	M	26	CCC			
Business Economics with Business	L1NC	3FT deg		8-12	M0	M	26	CCC			
Business Economics with English Language Studies	L1QC	3FT deg		8-12	M0	M	26	CCC			
Business Economics with Finance	L1NH	3FT deg		8-12	M0	M	26	CCC			
Business Economics with French	L1RC	3FT deg		8-12	M0	M	26	CCC			
Business Economics with German	L1RF	3FT deg		8-12	M0	M	26	CCC			
Business Economics with Information Systems	L1GM	3FT deg		8-12	M0	M	26	CCC			
Business Economics with Law	L1MH	3FT deg		8-12	M0	M	26	CCC			
Business Economics with Marketing	L1NM	3FT deg		8-12	M0	M	26	CCC			
Business Economics with Spanish	L1RK	3FT deg		8-12	M0	M	26				
Business Studies with Business Economics (Dip)	N1LD	3FT/4SW deg		12	M0	M	26				
Business Studies with Economics (Dip)	N1L1	3FT/4SW deg		12	M0	M	26				
Economics with Accounting	L1N4	3FT deg		8-12	M0	M	26	CCC			
Economics with Business	L1N1	3FT deg		8-12	M0	M	26	CCC			
Economics with English Language Studies	L1Q1	3FT deg		8-12	M0	M	26	CCC			
Economics with European Studies	L1T2	3FT deg		8-12	M0	M	26	CCC			
Economics with Finance	L1N3	3FT deg		8-12	M0	M	26	CCC			
Economics with French	L1R1 ▼	3FT deg	* g	8-12	M0	M	26	CCC			
Economics with German	L1R2 ▼	3FT deg	* g	8-12	M0	M	26	CCC			
Economics with History	LV11	3FT deg		8-12	M0	M	26	CCC			
Economics with Information Management	L1P2	3FT deg		8-12	M0	M	26	CCC			
Economics with Information Systems	L1G5	3FT deg		8-12	M0	M	26	CCC			
Economics with International Studies	L1MX	3FT deg		8-12	M0	M	26	CCC			

Economics 18

course details				98 expected requirements						96 entry stats
TITLE	CODE	COURSE	SUBJECTS	A/AS	NO/C	AGNVQ	IB	SQA(H)	SQA	RATIO A/AS
Economics with Marketing	L1N5	3FT deg		8-12	MO	M	26	CCC		
Economics with Politics and International Rels	L1M1	3FT deg		8-12	MO	M	26	CCC		
Economics with Sociology	LL13	3FT deg		8-12	MO	M	26	CCC		
Economics with Spanish	L1R4▼	3FT deg	* g	8-12	MO	M	24	CCC		
Economics with Women's Studies	L1M9	3FT deg		8-12	MO	M	24	CCC		
Environmental Policy and Mgt with Business Econ	F9LC	3FT deg		8-12	MO	M	26	CCC		
Environmental Policy and Mgt with Economics	F9L1	3FT deg		8-12	MO	M	26	CCC		
European Studies with Economics	T2L1	3FT deg		8-12	MO	M	26	CCC		
Finance with Business Economics	N3LC	3FT deg		8-12	MO	M	26	CCC		
Finance with Economics	N3L1	3FT deg		8-12	MO	M	26	CCC		
French with Business Economics	R1LC	3FT deg		8-12	MO	M	26	CCC		
French with Economics	R1L1	3FT deg		8-12	MO	M	26	CCC		
German with Business Economics	R2LC	3FT deg		8-12	MO	M	26	CCC		
German with Economics	R2L1	3FT deg		8-12	MO	M	26	CCC		
History with Economics	V1L1	3FT deg		8-12	MO	M	26	CCC		
Human Resource Management with Economics	N6L1	3FT deg		8-12	MO	M	26	CCC		
Human Resource Mgt with Business Economics	N6LC	3FT deg		8-12	MO	M	26	CCC		
International Studies with Economics	M9L1	3FT deg		8-12	MO	M	26	CCC		
Law with Economics	M3L1	3FT deg		8-12	MO	M	26	CCC		
Politics & Int Relations with Business Economics	M1LC	3FT deg		8-12	MO	M	26	CCC		
Politics and International Relations with Econ	M1L1	3FT deg		8-12	MO	M	26	CCC		
Sociology with Economics	L3L1	3FT deg		8-12	MO	M	26	CCC		
Spanish with Business Economics	R4LC	3FT deg		8-12	MO	M	26	CCC		
Spanish with Economics	R4L1	3FT deg		8-12	MO	M	26	CCC		

Univ of ULSTER

TITLE	CODE	COURSE	SUBJECTS	A/AS	NO/C	AGNVQ	IB	SQA(H)	SQA	RATIO A/AS
Economics (4 Yr SW inc DIS)	L100▼	4SW deg	* g	CCC	MO+3D	D*6/^ gi	28	BBBB	Ind	17 18/22
Economics and Government (3 Yr Hons)	LM11▼	3FT deg	* g	CCC	MO+3D	D*6/^ gi	28	BBBB	Ind	14 18/18
Law and Economics	LM13▼	3FT deg	* g	BBC	MO+4D	D*6/^ gi	32	ABBB	Ind	17 18/26

UNIVERSITY COLL LONDON (Univ of London)

TITLE	CODE	COURSE	SUBJECTS	A/AS	NO/C	AGNVQ	IB	SQA(H)	SQA	RATIO A/AS
Economics	L100	3FT deg	g	ABB	3M	Ind	35$	BBBBC$ Ind		9 24/30
Economics and Geography	LL18	3FT deg	g	BBC-BBB	3M	Ind	30$	BBBCC$ Ind		7 24/28
Economics and History	LV11	3FT deg	g	BBC	3M	Ind	32$	BBBCC Ind		16 22/26
Economics and Statistics	LG14	3FT deg	M g	BCC	3M	Ind	30$	BBBCC$ Ind		6 18/28
Mathematics with Economics	G1L1	3FT deg	M g	ABC-ABB	MO $	Ind	30$	AAABB$ N$		4 18/26
Mathematics with Economics (MSci)	G1LC	4FT deg	M g	ABC-ABB	MO $	Ind	30$	AAABB$ N$		2
Philosophy and Economics	VL71	3FT deg	g	BBC	3M	X	30$	BBBBC Ind		6 22/28
Statistics,Computing,Operational Res & Economics	Y624	3FT deg	M g	BCC	MO $	Ind	30$	BBCCC$ N$		
Economics										

Univ of WARWICK

TITLE	CODE	COURSE	SUBJECTS	A/AS	NO/C	AGNVQ	IB	SQA(H)	SQA	RATIO A/AS
Applied Mathematics and Economics	LG11	3FT deg	M g	AAA-AAB	X	X	36$	CSYS$		14
Economics	L100	3FT deg	g	AAB	DO $	Ind	34	AAAAB		8 26/30
Economics and Economic History	LV13	3FT deg	g	AAB	DO $	Ind	34	AAAAB		12
Economics and International Studies	LM1C	3FT deg	g	AAB	DO $	Ind	34	AAAAB		13 26/30
Economics and Politics	LM11	3FT deg	g	AAB	DO $	Ind	34	AAAAB		13 26/30
Industrial Economics	L112	3FT deg	g	AAB	DO $	Ind	34	AAAAB		28
Mathematics and Economics	GL11	3FT deg	M g	AAA-AAB	X	X	36$	CSYS$		11 24/30
Maths-Operational Research-Statistics-Economics	Y602	3FT deg	M g	ABC	X	X	32$	AABBB$		
Economics										

Univ of WESTMINSTER

TITLE	CODE	COURSE	SUBJECTS	A/AS	NO/C	AGNVQ	IB	SQA(H)	SQA	RATIO A/AS
Economics	L100	3FT deg		14	MO+3D	D	26	BBB	Ind	
Economics for Business	LN11	3FT deg	*	BC	MO+3D	D	26	BBB	Ind	7 11/18

TITLE	CODE	COURSE	SUBJECTS	A/AS	ND/C	AGNVQ	IB	SQA(H)	SQA	RATIO A/AS
course details			**98 expected requirements**							**96 entry stats**

Univ of WOLVERHAMPTON

TITLE	CODE	COURSE	SUBJECTS	A/AS	ND/C	AGNVQ	IB	SQA(H)	SQA	RATIO A/AS
Business Economics	L1N1	3FT deg		14	4M	M	24	BBBB	Ind	6 6/14
Economics	L100	3FT deg	g	14	4M	M	24	BBBB$	Ind	14
Applied Sciences *Economics*	Y100	3FT/4SW deg	S g	12	4M	M	24	BBBB	Ind	
Combined Degrees *Economics*	Y401	3FT deg	g	12	4M	M	24	BBBB	Ind	

WORCESTER COLL of HE

TITLE	CODE	COURSE	SUBJECTS	A/AS	ND/C	AGNVQ	IB	SQA(H)	SQA	RATIO A/AS
Economy and Society/Biological Science	CL11	3FT deg	S	DD	Ind	M	Ind	Ind	Ind	
Economy and Society/Business Management	NL11	3FT deg		DD	Ind	M	Ind	Ind	Ind	2
Economy and Society/Drama	WL41	3FT deg		DD	Ind	M	Ind	Ind	Ind	
Education Studies/Economy and Society	LX19	3FT deg		DD	Ind	M	Ind	Ind	Ind	
English and Literary Studies/Economy and Society	LQ13	3FT deg		CC	Ind	M	Ind	Ind	Ind	4
Geography/Economy and Society	LL18	3FT deg		DD	Ind	M	Ind	Ind	Ind	
Health Studies/Economy and Society	LB19	3FT deg	g	DD	Ind	M	Ind	Ind	Ind	
History/Economy and Society	LV11	3FT deg		DD	Ind	M	Ind	Ind	Ind	2
Information Technology/Economy and Society	LG15	3FT deg		DD	Ind	M	Ind	Ind	Ind	
Psychology/Economy and Society	LL17	3FT deg	g	CC	Ind	M	Ind	Ind	Ind	
Sociology/Economy and Society	LL13	3FT deg		DD	Ind	M	Ind	Ind	Ind	9
Women's Studies/Economy and Society	LM19	3FT deg		DD	Ind	M	Ind	Ind	Ind	

Univ of YORK

TITLE	CODE	COURSE	SUBJECTS	A/AS	ND/C	AGNVQ	IB	SQA(H)	SQA	RATIO A/AS
Economics	L100	3FT deg	* g	BBC	DO	D*^	30	BBBC	Ind	20/28
Economics and Finance	L112	3FT deg	* g	BBC	DO	D*^	30	BBBB	Ind	20/28
Economics/Econometrics (Equal)	L144	3FT deg	M g	BBB	DO	D*^	30$	BBBB	Ind	28/28
Economics/Economic and Social History (Equal)	LV13	3FT deg	* g	BCC	DO	D*^	30	BBBC	Ind	
Economics/Education	L1X9	3FT deg	* g	BBC	DO	D*^	30	BBBB	Ind	
Economics/Philosophy (Equal)	LV17	3FT deg	* g	BBB	Ind	D$^ go	30	BBBBB	Ind	
Economics/Politics (Equal)	LM11	3FT deg	* g	BBB	Ind	D$^ go	30	BBBBB	Ind	22/30
Economics/Sociology (Equal)	LL13	3FT deg	* g	BBC	DO	D$^	30	BBBB	Ind	
Environmental Economics and Env Management	CL91	3FT deg	M/S g	BBC	Ind	DS^	28$	BBBB$	Ind	16/30
History/Economics	V1L1	3FT deg	H	ABC	Ind	D$6/^	32$	ABBB$	Ind	
Mathematics/Economics	G1L1	3FT deg	M	20-22	HN $	DS^	30$	CSYS$	HN$	24/26
Philosophy, Politics and Economics *Economics*	Y616	3FT deg	* g	BBB	Ind	D$^ go	32	BBBBB	Ind	

TITLE	CODE	COURSE	SUBJECTS	A/AS	ND/C	AGNVQ	IB	SQA(H)	SQA	RATIO A/AS
Univ of Wales, ABERYSTWYTH										
Education/American Studies	QX49	3FT deg	E/H g	18	1M+5D$	M^ g	29$	BBBCC$	Ind	
Education/Art	WX19	3FT deg	A/Ad g	18	1M+5D$	MA6 g	29$	BBBCC$	Ind	
Education/Art History	VX49	3FT deg	* g	18	1M+5D	MA6 g	29	BBBCC	Ind	
Education/Drama	WX49	3FT deg	* g	20	1M+5D	MQ6 g	30	BBBBC	Ind	
Education/Mathematics	GX19	3FT deg	M g	16	1M+5D$	M^ g	28$	BBCCC$	Ind	
Education/Statistics	GXK9	3FT deg	M g	16	1M+5D$	M^ g	28$	BBCCC$	Ind	
English/Education	QX39	3FT deg	El	20	1M+5D$	M^ g	30$	BBBBC$	Ind	
Environmental Earth Studies with Education	F6X9	3FT deg	2S g	18	2M+3D$	MS6 g	29$	BBBCC$	Ind	
Film and Television Studies/Education	WX59	3FT deg	* g	20	1M+5D	MQ6 g	30	BBBBC	Ind	
French/Education	RX19	4FT deg	F g	18	1M+5D$	M^ g	29$	BBBCC$	Ind	
Geography/Education	LX89	3FT deg	Gy g	20-22	3M+2D$	M^ g	31$	BBBBC$	Ind	
German/Education	RX29	4FT deg	G g	18	1M+5D$	M^ g	29$	BBBCC$	Ind	
History/Education	VX19	3FT deg	* g	18-20	1M+5D	M^ g	30	BBBCC	Ind	
Information and Library Studies/Education	PX29	3FT deg	* g	16	M0	M6 g	28	BBCCC	Ind	
Irish/Education	QXM9	4FT deg	* g	18	1M+5D$	M^ g	29$	BBBCC$	Ind	
Italian/Education	RX39	4FT deg	L g	18	1M+5D$	M^ g	29$	BBBCC$	Ind	
Mathematics with Education	G1X9	3FT deg	M g	16	1M+5D$	M^ g	28$	BBCCC$	Ind	
Physics with Education	F3X9	3FT deg	P+M g	14	3M $	MS^ g	27$	BBCCC$	Ind	
Spanish/Education	RX49	4FT deg	L g	18	1M+5D$	M^ g	29$	BBBCC$	Ind	
Welsh History/Education	VXC9	3FT deg	* g	18-20	1M+5D	M^ g	30	BBBCC	Ind	
Welsh/Education	QX59	3FT deg	W g	18	1M+5D$	M^ g	29$	BBBCC$	Ind	
Univ of Wales, BANGOR										
Education & Sports Science (Taught in Welsh)	BX6X	3FT deg	* g	BCC	5D $	D*^ go	30$	X	X	
Education and Mathematics (Taught in Welsh)	GXC9	3FT deg	M g	CCD	Ind	D*^ go	Ind	X	X	
History/Education (Taught in Welsh)	VX19	3FT deg	H g	CCD	Ind	D*^ go	28$	BBBC$	X	
Mathematics/Education (Taught in Welsh)	GX19	3FT deg	M g	CCD	Ind	D$^ go	Ind	X	X	
Physical Education/Education (Taught in Welsh)	XB96	3FT deg	* g	CCC	Ind	D*^ go	Ind	X	X	
Psychology/Education (Taught in Welsh)	CX89	3FT deg	* g	BCC	Ind	D$6/^ go	Ind	X	X	4
Religious Studies/Education (Taught in Welsh)	VX89	3FT deg	* g	CCD	Ind	D*6/^ go	Ind	X	X	3
Social Policy/Education (Taught in Welsh)	LX49	3FT deg	* g	16	Ind	D*6/^ go	Ind	X	X	
Sports Science/Education (Taught in Welsh)	BX69	3FT deg	* g	20	5D	D*6/^ go	30	X	X	
Welsh/Education	QX59	3FT/4FT deg	W g	CCD	Ind	D*^ go	Ind	X	X	7
BATH COLL of HE										
English and International Education	QX39	3FT deg	El	CD	Ind		Ind	$	$	3 10/18
Combined Awards *International Education*	Y400	3FT deg	*		N		Ind	$	$	
Modular Programme (DipHE) *International Education*	Y460	2FT Dip	*		N		Ind	$	$	
BELL COLLEGE OF TECHNOLOGY										
Sports Coaching with Sports Development	6B9X	2FT HND	Ap g	DD-D	N $	P$	Ind	CC$	12$	
BIRMINGHAM COLL of Food, Tourism & Creative St										
Early Childhood Studies	549X	2FT HND	*	4	3M	P$	Ind	Ind	Ind	
BRADFORD & ILKLEY Comm COLL										
Education and Community Studies	LX59	3FT deg	*	8	M0	M	Dip	CCC	Ind	
Early Childhood Studies	549X	2FT HND	*	4	M0	P	Ind	Ind	Ind	

course details			98 expected requirements							96 entry stats	
TITLE	CODE	COURSE	SUBJECTS	A/AS	ND/C	AGNVQ	IB	SQA(H)	SQA	RATIO	A/AS
BRETTON HALL											
Arts and Education (Art)	XW92	3FT deg	A	CC	MO		Ind	CCC	Ind	3	8/20
Arts and Education (Drama)	XW94	3FT deg	T	CC	MO		Ind	CCC	Ind	3	10/20
Arts and Education (Music)	XW93	3FT deg	Mu	CC	MO		Ind	CCC	Ind	7	
Child and Family Studies	LX39	3FT deg									4/16
Univ of BRISTOL											
Deaf Studies	X960	2FT Dip	* g	CC	Ind	D$^	Ind	Ind	Ind	6	4/16
Early Childhood Studies	L5X9	3FT deg	* g	BCC	Ind	D$^	28$	CSYS	Ind	10	20/26
BRISTOL, Univ of the W of England											
Joint Honours Programme Education and English	Y401	3FT deg	Ap g	14-16	5M $	M$ go	24	BCCC	Ind		
Joint Honours Programme Education and Science	Y401	3FT deg	S g	14-16	5M $	M$ go	24$	BCCC$	Ind		
CAMBRIDGE Univ											
Biological Sciences with Education Studies (BA)	C1X9▼	3FT deg	* g	AAB	Ind		Ind	CSYS	Ind		
English with Education Studies (BA)	Q3X9▼	3FT deg	* g	AAB	Ind		Ind	CSYS	Ind	7	
Geography with Education Studies (BA)	L8X9▼	3FT deg	* g	AAB	Ind		Ind	CSYS	Ind	8	
History with Education Studies (BA)	V1X9▼	3FT deg	* g	AAB	Ind		Ind	CSYS	Ind	10	
Music with Education Studies (BA)	W3X9▼	3FT deg	* g	AAB	Ind		Ind	CSYS	Ind	1	
Religious Studies with Education Studies (BA)	V8X9▼	3FT deg	* g	AAB	Ind		Ind	CSYS	Ind		
CANTERBURY CHRIST CHURCH COLL of HE											
Art with Early Childhood Studies	W1X9	3FT deg	A g	CC	MO	M	24	Ind	Ind		
Business Studies with Early Childhood Studies	N1X9	3FT deg	* g	CC	MO	M	24	Ind	Ind		
Early Childhood Studies and Art	XW91	3FT deg	A g	CC	MO	M	24	Ind	Ind	1	
Early Childhood Studies and Business Studies	XN91	3FT deg	* g	CC	MO	M	24	Ind	Ind		
Early Childhood Studies and Social Science	LX39	3FT deg	* g	CC	MO	M	24	Ind	Ind	1	
Early Childhood Studies with Art	X9W1	3FT deg	A g	CC	MO	M	24	Ind	Ind	4	
Early Childhood Studies with Business Studies	X9N1	3FT deg	* g	CC	MO	M	24	Ind	Ind	5	
Early Childhood Studies with English	X9Q3	3FT deg	E	CC	MO	M	24	Ind	Ind	7	
Early Childhood Studies with French	X9R1	3FT deg	F g	CC	MO	M	24	Ind	Ind		
Early Childhood Studies with Geography	X9L8	3FT deg	Gy g	CC	MO	M	24	Ind	Ind		
Early Childhood Studies with History	X9V1	3FT deg	H g	CC	MO	M	24	Ind	Ind	9	
Early Childhood Studies with Info Technology	X9G5	3FT deg	* g	CC	MO	M	24	Ind	Ind	1	
Early Childhood Studies with Mathematics	X9G1	3FT deg	M g	DD	Ind	Ind	24	Ind	Ind		
Early Childhood Studies with Music	X9W3	3FT deg	Mu g	CC	MO	M	24	Ind	Ind		
Early Childhood Studies with Psychology	X9L7	3FT deg	Ps g	CC	MO	M	24	Ind	Ind	33	
Early Childhood Studies with Radio, Film & TV St	X9W5	3FT deg	* g	CC	MO	M	24	Ind	Ind		
Early Childhood Studies with Religious Studies	X9V8	3FT deg	* g	CC	MO	M	24	Ind	Ind	3	
Early Childhood Studies with Science	X9Y1	3FT deg	S g	DD	Ind	Ind	24	Ind	Ind	3	
Early Childhood Studies with Social Sciences	X9L3	3FT deg	* g	CC	MO	M	24	Ind	Ind	1	10/18
Early Childhood Studies with Sport Science	X9B6	3FT deg	* g	CC	MO	M	24	Ind	Ind		
Early Childhood Studies with Statistics	X9G4	3FT deg	M g	DD	Ind	Ind	24	Ind	Ind		
English and Early Childhood Studies	XQ93	3FT deg	E	CC	MO	M	24	Ind	Ind		
English with Early Childhood Studies	Q3X9	3FT deg	E	CC	MO	M	24	Ind	Ind	7	
French and Early Childhood Studies	RX19	3FT deg	F g	CC	MO	M	24	Ind	Ind		
Geography and Early Childhood Studies	LX89	3FT deg	Gy g	CC	MO	M	24	Ind	Ind		
Geography with Early Childhood Studies	L8X9	3FT deg	Gy g	CC	MO	M	24	Ind	Ind	2	
History and Early Childhood Studies	XV91	3FT deg	H g	CC	MO	M	24	Ind	Ind		
History with Early Childhood Studies	V1X9	3FT deg	H g	CC	MO	M	24	Ind	Ind	4	
Informal Education	X900	2FT Dip	*	CC	MO	M	24	Ind	Ind		
Informal and Community Education	X920	3FT deg	*	CC	MO	M	24	Ind	Ind		

TITLE	CODE	COURSE	SUBJECTS	A/AS	ND/C	AGNVQ	IB	SQA(H)	SQA	RATIO A/AS
			98 expected requirements							**96 entry stats**
Information Technology and Early Childhood Studs	XG95	3FT deg	* g	CC	MO	M	24	Ind	Ind	
Information Technology with Early Childhood St	G5X9	3FT deg	* g	CC	MO	M	24	Ind	Ind	
Mathematics and Early Childhood Studies	XG91	3FT deg	M g	DD	Ind	Ind	24	Ind	Ind	3
Mathematics with Early Childhood Studies	G1X9	3FT deg	M g	DD	Ind	Ind	24	Ind	Ind	
Music and Early Childhood Studies	XW93	3FT deg	Mu g	CC	MO	M	24	Ind	Ind	
Music with Early Childhood Studies	W3X9	3FT deg	Mu g	CC	MO	M	24	Ind	Ind	4
Psychology and Early Childhood Studies	XL97	3FT deg	Ps g	CC	MO	M	24	Ind	Ind	23
Psychology with Early Childhood Studies	L7X9	3FT deg	Ps g	CC	MO	M	24	Ind	Ind	
Radio, Film & TV Studs with Early Childhood St	W5X9	3FT deg	* g	CC	MO	M	24	Ind	Ind	
Radio, Film and TV Studs and Early Childhood St	XW95	3FT deg	* g	CC	MO	M	24	Ind	Ind	
Religious Studies and Early Childhood Studies	XV98	3FT deg	* g	CC	MO	M	24	Ind	Ind	
Science and Early Childhood Studies	XY91	3FT deg	S g	DD	Ind	Ind	24	Ind	Ind	
Social Science with Early Childhood Studies	L3X9	3FT deg	* g	CC	MO	M	24	Ind	Ind	1
Sport Science and Early Childhood Studies	BX69	3FT deg	* g	CC	MO	M	24	Ind	Ind	
Sport Science with Early Childhood Studies	B6X9	3FT deg	* g	CC	MO	M	24	Ind	Ind	
Statistics and Early Childhood Studies	GX49	3FT deg	M g	DD	Ind	Ind	24	Ind	Ind	
Statistics with Early Childhood Studies	G4X9	3FT deg	M g	DD	Ind	Ind	24	Ind	Ind	

CARDIFF Univ of Wales

TITLE	CODE	COURSE	SUBJECTS	A/AS	ND/C	AGNVQ	IB	SQA(H)	SQA	RATIO A/AS
Education	X900	3FT deg	* g	BB-CCC	5M+3D	Ind	Ind	Ind	Ind	2 14/22
Education/Ancient History	XV91	3FT deg	*	BCC	Ind		Ind	AAABB		
Education/Archaeology	XV96	3FT deg		BCC	Ind		Ind	AABB	X	
Education/Economics	XL91	3FT deg	*	BBC-BBB	Ind	Ind	Ind	Ind	Ind	
English Literature/Education	QX39	3FT deg	E	ABB	Ind	Ind	Ind	AAABB	X	9
French/Education	RX19	4FT deg	F	BBC	Ind	Ind	Ind	ABBBB	Ind	4
German/Education	RX29	4FT deg	G	BCC	Ind	Ind	Ind	Ind	Ind	
History of Ideas/Education	VXD9	3FT deg	*	BBB	Ind	Ind	Ind	Ind	Ind	
Italian/Education	RX39	4FT deg	L	BCC	Ind	Ind	Ind	Ind	Ind	
Language Studies/Education	QX19	3FT deg	*	BBB	Ind		Ind	ABBBB		1
Music/Education	WX39	3FT deg	Mu	BCC	Ind		Ind	Ind	Ind	
Philosophy/Education	VX79	3FT deg	*	BBB	Ind	Ind	Ind	Ind	Ind	1
Politics/Education	MX19	3FT deg	*	BBB	Ind	Ind	Ind	ABBBB	Ind	2
Portuguese/Education	RX59	4FT deg	L	BBC-BCC	Ind	Ind	Ind	Ind	Ind	
Psychology/Education	LX79	3FT deg	*	BBB	MO+6D		Ind	AABBB	N	13 26/28
Pure Mathematics/Education	GX19	3FT deg	M	BCC	3M+2D$	Ind	Ind	BBBBC	Ind	5
Religious Studies/Education	VX89	3FT deg	*	BCC	Ind	Ind	Ind	Ind	Ind	4 18/24
Social Philosophy and Applied Ethics/Education	VX7X	3FT deg	*	BBB	Ind	Ind	Ind	Ind	Ind	
Sociology and Education	LX39	3FT deg	*	BCC	3M+2D	Ind	Ind	Ind	Ind	5 16/20
Spanish/Education	RX49	4FT deg	L	BBC-BCC	Ind	Ind	Ind	Ind	Ind	
Welsh History/Education	VXC9	3FT deg	H	BBC-BCC	X	Ind	Ind	AABBB	X	3
Welsh/Education	QX59	3FT deg	W	CCC	Ind	Ind	Ind	Ind	Ind	8

Univ of Wales INST, CARDIFF

TITLE	CODE	COURSE	SUBJECTS	A/AS	ND/C	AGNVQ	IB	SQA(H)	SQA	RATIO A/AS
Art and Aesthetics	EX19	3FT deg	Fa g	EE	N	MA go				
Art and Aesthetics	WX19	3FT deg	Fa g	EE	N	MA go	Ind	Ind	Ind	

Univ of CENTRAL LANCASHIRE

TITLE	CODE	COURSE	SUBJECTS	A/AS	ND/C	AGNVQ	IB	SQA(H)	SQA	RATIO A/AS
Combined Honours Programme Education Studies	Y400	3FT deg	*	14	MO+2D	M$6/^	26	BBCC	Ind	

CENTRAL SCHOOL of Speech & Drama

TITLE	CODE	COURSE	SUBJECTS	A/AS	ND/C	AGNVQ	IB	SQA(H)	SQA	RATIO A/AS
Drama and Education	XW94	3FT deg	g	BCC	Ind	Ind	30	BBBBC	Ind	

| | | | 98 expected requirements | | | | | | | 96 entry stats | |
course details			SUBJECTS	A/AS	NO/C	AGNVQ	IB	SQA(H)	SQA	RATIO	A/AS
TITLE	CODE	COURSE									
CHICHESTER INSTITUTE OF HIGHER EDUCATION											
Art with Education Studies (Opt. QTS) (P)	W1X9	3FT/4FT deg	A+Pf g	12	Ind	M$+^ go	Ind	Ind	Ind	6	6/18
Dance with Education Studies (Opt. QTS) (P)	W4X9	3FT/4FT deg	Pf g	12	Ind	M$+ go	Ind	Ind	Ind	9	8/20
English with Education Studies (Opt. QTS) (P)	Q3X9	3FT/4FT deg	E g	12	Ind	M^ go	Ind	Ind	Ind	3	6/18
Environmental Science with Educ. Stds (opt.QTS)	F9X9	3FT deg	* g	12		M$ go	Ind	Ind	Ind		
Geography with Education Studies (Opt. QTS) (P)	L8X9	3FT/4FT deg	Gy g	12	Ind	M$ go	Ind	Ind	Ind	4	6/12
History with Education Studies (Opt. QTS) (P)	V1X9	3FT/4FT deg	H g	12	Ind	M$ go	Ind	Ind	Ind	3	4/16
Mathematics with Education Studies (Opt. QTS)(P)	G1X9	3FT/4FT deg	M	12	Ind	M^	Ind	Ind	Ind	4	
Music with Education Studies (Opt. QTS) (P)	W3X9	3FT/4FT deg	Mu g	12	Ind	M$+ go	Ind	Ind	Ind	4	8/20
Study of Religions with Education Studs(Opt.QTS)	V8X9	3FT/4FT deg	* g	12	Ind	M$ go	Ind	Ind	Ind	3	5/16
DE MONTFORT Univ											
Humanities Combined Honours	Y300▼	3FT deg	* g	CCD	MO	M$^	26$	ABBB	Ind		
Education											
Univ of DERBY											
Credit Accumulation Modular Scheme	Y600	3FT deg		X	X	X	X	X	X		
Education (Yr 2 entry only)											
Univ of DURHAM											
Science and Childhood in Society	XY91▼	3FT deg	* g	EE	MO	Ind	Dip	CCCC	Ind		8/11
Sport in the Community	BX69	3FT deg	Pe/B	BBC	Ind	Ind	32$	AABBB$	Ind		14/20
Univ of EAST LONDON											
Archaeological Sciences and Educ & Community St	FX49	3FT deg	* g	12	MO	M	Ind	Ind	Ind		
Biology and Education & Community Studies	CX19	3FT deg	* g	12	MO	M	Ind	Ind	Ind	4	
Biology with Education & Community Studies	C1X9	3FT deg	* g	12	MO	M	Ind	Ind	Ind		
Business Studies and Education & Community St	NX19	3FT deg	* g	12	MO	M	Ind	Ind	Ind		
Business Studies with Education & Community St	N1X9	3FT deg	* g	14	MO	MB					
Communication Studies and Educ & Community St	PX39	3FT deg	* g	12	MO	M	Ind	Ind	Ind	1	
Communication Studies with Educ & Community St	P3X9	3FT deg	* g	12	MO	M	Ind	Ind			
Educ & Commun St & History of Art Design & Film	XV94	3FT deg	* g	12	MO	M					
Educ & Commun St w. History of Art Design & Film	X9V4	3FT deg	* g	12	MO	M					
Education & Commun St w. Third World & Devel St	X9M9	3FT deg	* g	12	MO	M	Ind				
Education & Community St & Maths, Stats & Comput	GX99	3FT deg	* g	12	MO	M$	Ind	Ind	Ind		
Education & Community St & Psychosocial Studies	LX79	3FT deg	* g	12	MO	M$	Ind	Ind	Ind	3	
Education & Community St & Third World & Dev St	MXY9	3FT deg	* g	12	MO	M	Ind	Ind	Ind		
Education & Community St w. Maths,Stats & Comput	X9G9	3FT deg	* g	12	MO	M					
Education & Community St with Psychosocial St	X9L7	3FT deg	* g	12	MO	M					
Education & Community Studies & Information Tech	GX59	3FT deg	* g	12	MO	M$	Ind	Ind	Ind	1	
Education & Community Studies and Environ Sci	FX99	3FT deg	* g	12	MO	MS	Ind	Ind	Ind		
Education & Community Studies and French	RX19	3FT deg	* g	12	MO	M^	Ind	Ind	Ind	3	
Education & Community Studies and German	RX29	3FT deg	* g	12	MO	M^	Ind	Ind	Ind		
Education & Community Studies and Health Studies	BX99	3FT deg	* g	12	MO	M$	Ind	Ind	Ind		
Education & Community Studies and History	VX19	3FT deg	H g	12	MO	M	Ind	Ind	Ind	2	
Education & Community Studies and Linguistics	QX19	3FT deg	* g	12	MO	X	Ind	Ind	Ind	1	
Education & Community Studies and Literature	QX39	3FT deg	* g	12	MO	X	Ind	Ind	Ind	1	
Education & Community Studies and Soc Pol Res	LX49	3FT deg	* g	12	MO	M					
Education & Community Studies and Sociology	LX39	3FT deg	* g	12	MO	M$	Ind	Ind	Ind	3	
Education & Community Studies and Spanish	RX49	3FT deg	* g	12	MO	M^	Ind	Ind	Ind		
Education & Community Studies and Women's St	MX99	3FT deg	* g	12	MO	M	Ind	Ind	Ind		
Education & Community Studies w. Archaeology Sci	X9F4	3FT deg	* g	12	MO	M					
Education & Community Studies with Biology	X9C1	3FT deg	* g	12	MO	M					
Education & Community Studies with Business St	X9N1	3FT deg	* g	12	MO	M					
Education & Community Studies with Comm Studies	X9P3	3FT deg	* g	12	MO	M					

| course details | | | 98 expected requirements | | | | | | | 96 entry stats |

TITLE	CODE	COURSE	SUBJECTS	A/AS	ND/C	AGNVQ	IB	SQA(H)	SQA	RATIO A/AS
Education & Community Studies with Environ Sci	X9F9	3FT deg	* g	12	MO	M				
Education & Community Studies with French	X9R1	3FT deg	* g	12	MO	M				
Education & Community Studies with German	X9R2	3FT deg	* g	12	MO	M				
Education & Community Studies with Health St	X9B9	3FT deg	* g	12	MO	M				
Education & Community Studies with History	X9V1	3FT deg	* g	12	MO	M				
Education & Community Studies with IT	X9G5	3FT deg	* g	12	MO	M				
Education & Community Studies with Italian	X9R3	3FT deg	* g	12	MO	M				
Education & Community Studies with Linguistics	X9Q1	3FT deg	* g	12	MO	M				
Education & Community Studies with Literature	X9Q3	3FT deg	* g	12	MO	M				
Education & Community Studies with Soc Pol Res	X9L4	3FT deg	* g	12	MO	M				
Education & Community Studies with Sociology	X9L3	3FT deg	* g	12	MO	M				
Education & Community Studies with Spanish	X9R4	3FT deg	* g	12	MO	M				
Education & Community Studies with Women's St	X9MX	3FT deg	* g	12	MO	M				
Education and Community Studies	XL95	3FT deg	* g	12	MO	M	Ind	Ind	Ind	6
Environmental Sciences with Educ & Commun St	F9X9	3FT deg	* g	12	MO	M	Ind	Ind	Ind	
French with Education & Community Studies	R1X9	3FT deg	* g	12	MO	M	Ind			
German with Education & Community Studies	R2X9	3FT deg	* g	12	MO	M	Ind			
Health Studies with Education & Community St	B9X9	3FT deg	* g	12	MO	M	Ind	Ind	Ind	
History of Art Design & Film w. Educ & Commun St	V4X9	3FT deg	* g	12	MO	M	Ind	Ind	Ind	
History with Education & Community Studies	V1X9	3FT deg	* g	12	MO	M	Ind	Ind		
Information Technology with Educ & Community St	G5X9	3FT deg	* g	12	MO	M	Ind	Ind	Ind	
Linguistics with Education & Community Studies	Q1X9	3FT deg	* g	12	MO	M				
Literature with Education & Community Studies	Q3X9	3FT deg	* g	12	MO	M	Ind			
Maths, Stats & Computing with Educ & Commun St	G9X9	3FT deg	* g	12	MO	M	Ind	Ind	Ind	
New Technology and Education	JX99	3FT deg	* g	12	MO	M	Ind	Ind	Ind	1
Psychosocial Studies with Ed & Community Studies	L7X9	3FT deg	* g	12	MO	M	Ind	Ind	Ind	
Social Policy Research with Educ & Community St	L4X9	3FT deg	* g	12	MO	M	Ind	Ind	Ind	
Sociology with Education & Community Studies	L3X9	3FT deg	* g	12	MO	M	Ind	Ind	Ind	
Spanish with Education & Community Studies	R4X9	3FT deg	* g	12	MO	M	Ind			
Third World & Development Stds with Ed & Comm St	M9X9	3FT deg	* g	12	MO	M	Ind	Ind		
Women's Studies with Education & Community St	M9XX	3FT deg	* g	12	MO	M	Ind			
Three-Subject Degree *Education and Community Studies*	Y600	3FT deg	* g	12	MO	M	Ind	Ind	Ind	

EDGE HILL Univ COLLEGE

Early Childhood Studies and English	QX39	3FT deg	E g	CC	X	P*^ go	Dip	BBCC$	Ind	
Early Childhood Studies and Mathematics	GX19	3FT deg	* g	CC	3M+3D	M*/ P*^ go	Dip	BBCC$	Ind	

HERIOT-WATT Univ

Mathematics with Education	G1X9	3FT/4FT deg	M	CDE	HN	M$^	28	BBCC	HN	
Physics with Education	F3X9	3FT/4FT deg	M+P	CC	Ind	M$^ go	26	BBBC	Ind	
Physics with Education (MPhys)	F3XX	4FT deg	M+P	BC	Ind	M$ go	30	AABB	Ind	

Univ of HERTFORDSHIRE

Educational Studies (1 Year)	X900	1FT deg	*	X	X	X	X	X	X	

Univ of HUDDERSFIELD

Community Education	X920	3FT deg	* g	10-14	Ind	Ind	Ind	Ind	Ind	

KEELE Univ

Biological and Medicinal Chemistry and Educ St	FXC9	3FT deg	C g	BCC	Ind	D$^	28$	CSYS	Ind	
Educational Studies and Ancient History (4 Yrs)	XV9D	4FT deg	*	BCC	Ind	Ind	28	BBBB	Ind	
Educational Studies and Applied Social Studies	LX59	3FT deg	*	BBC-BCC	Ind	Ind	28	CSYS	Ind	
Educational Studies and Astrophysics	FX59	3FT deg	P g	BCC	Ind	D$^	28$	CSYS	Ind	
Educational Studies and Astrophysics (4 Yrs)	XF95	4FT deg	*	BCC	Ind	Ind	28	BBBB	Ind	

| | | | 98 expected requirements | | | | | | | 96 entry stats |
| *course details* | | | | | | | | | | *96 entry stats* |

TITLE	CODE	COURSE	SUBJECTS	A/AS	ND/C	AGNVQ	IB	SQA(H)	SQA	RATIO A/AS	
Educational Studies and Biochemistry	CX79	3FT deg	C g	BCC	Ind	D$^	28$	CSYS	Ind		
Educational Studies and Biochemistry (4 Yrs)	XC97	4FT deg	*	BCC	Ind	Ind	28	BBBB	Ind		
Educational Studies and Biology	CX19	3FT deg	S g	BCC	Ind	D$^	28$	CSYS	Ind		
Educational Studies and Biology (4 Yrs)	XC91	4FT deg	*	BCC	Ind	Ind	28	BBBB	Ind	8	
Educational Studies and Business Admin (4 Yrs)	XN99	4FT deg	*	BBC-BCC	Ind	Ind	28	BBBB	Ind		
Educational Studies and Business Administration	NX99	3FT deg	*	BCC	Ind	Ind	28	CSYS	Ind	4	
Educational Studies and Chemistry	FX19	3FT deg	C g	BCC	Ind	D$^	28$	CSYS	Ind		
Educational Studies and Classical Studs (4 Yrs)	XQ98	4FT deg	*	BCC	Ind	Ind	28	BBBB	Ind		
Educational Studies and Criminology	MXH9	3FT deg	*	BBB	Ind	Ind	32	CSYS	Ind	5	
Educational Studies and Criminology (4 Yrs)	XM9H	4FT deg	*	BBB	Ind	Ind	32	ABBB	Ind		
Educational Studies and Economics	LX19	3FT deg	* g	BCC	Ind	Ind	28	CSYS	Ind		
Electronic Music and Educational Studies	WXJ9	3FT deg	Mu	BCC	Ind	D$^	28$	CSYS	Ind		
Electronic Music and Educational Studies (4 Yrs)	XW9J	4FT deg	*	BCC	Ind	Ind	28	BBBB	Ind		
English and Educational Studies	QX39	3FT deg	E	BBC	Ind	D$^	30$	CSYS	Ind	6	16/26
English and Educational Studies (4 Yrs)	XQ93	4FT deg	*	BBC	Ind	Ind	30	BBBB	Ind	11	
Environmental Management and Educational Studies	FXX9	3FT deg	* g	BCC	Ind	Ind	28	CSYS	Ind		
Finance and Educational Studies (4 Yrs)	XN93	4FT deg	* g	BCC	Ind	Ind	28	BBBB	Ind		
French and Educational Studies	RX19	3FT deg	F	BCC	Ind	D$^	28$	CSYS	Ind	8	
French/Russian or Russian Studies and Educ Studs	TXX9	3FT deg	F+R	BBC-BCC	Ind	D$^	28$	CSYS	Ind		
Geography and Education Studies (4 Yrs)	XL98	4FT deg	*	BCC	Ind	Ind	28	BBBB	Ind		
Geography and Educational Studies	LX89	3FT deg	Gy	BCC	Ind	D$^	28$	CSYS	Ind	10	
Geology and Educational Studies	FX69	3FT deg	S g	BCC	Ind	D$^	28$	CSYS	Ind		
Geology and Educational Studies (4 Yrs)	XF96	4FT deg	*	BCC	Ind	Ind	28	BBBB	Ind		
German and Educational Studies (4 Yrs)	XR92	4FT deg	* g	BCC	Ind	Ind	28	BBB	Ind		
History and Educational Studies	VX19	3FT deg	*	BCC	Ind	Ind	28	CSYS	Ind	6	
History and Educational Studies (4 Yrs)	XV91	4FT deg	*	BCC	Ind	Ind	28	BBBB	Ind	6	
Human Resource Management and Educational Studs	NX69	3FT deg	*	BCC	Ind	Ind	28	CSYS	Ind		
Human Resource Mgt and Educational Studs (4 Yrs)	XN96	4FT deg	*	BCC	Ind	Ind	28	BBBB	Ind		
International Hist and Educational Studs (4 Yrs)	XV9C	4FT deg	*	BCC	Ind	Ind	28	BBBB	Ind		
International History and Educational Studies	VXC9	3FT deg	*	BCC	Ind	Ind	28	CSYS	Ind	2	
International Politics and Educational Studies	MXC9	3FT deg	*	BCC	Ind	Ind	28	CSYS	Ind		
Latin and Educational Studies (4 Yrs)	XQ96	4FT deg	*	BCC	Ind	Ind	28	BBBB	Ind		
Law and Educational Studies	MX39	3FT deg	*	BBB	Ind	Ind	32	CSYS	Ind		
Law and Educational Studies (4 Yrs)	XM93	4FT deg	*	BBB	Ind	Ind	32	BBBB	Ind		
Marketing and Educational Studies	NX59	3FT deg	*	BCC	Ind	Ind	28	CSYS	Ind		
Mathematics and Educational Studies	GX19	3FT deg	M	BCC	Ind	D$^	28$	CSYS	Ind	3	
Mathematics and Educational Studies (4 Yrs)	XG91	4FT deg	*	BCC	Ind	Ind	28	BBBB	Ind		
Music and Educational Studies	WX39	3FT deg	Mu	BCC	Ind	D$^	28$	CSYS	Ind	7	
Music and Educational Studies (4 Yrs)	XW93	4FT deg	*	BCC	Ind	Ind	28	BBBB	Ind		
Philosophy and Educational Studies (4 Yrs)	XV97	4FT deg	*	BCC	Ind	Ind	28	BBBB	Ind		
Physics and Educational Studies	FX39	3FT deg	P	BCC	Ind	D$^	28$	CSYS	Ind		
Physics and Educational Studies (4 Yrs)	XF93	4FT deg	*	BCC	Ind	Ind	28	BBBB	Ind	1	
Politics and Educational Studies	MX19	3FT deg	*	BCC	Ind	Ind	28	CSYS	Ind		
Politics and Educational Studies (4 Yrs)	XM91	4FT deg	*	BCC	Ind	Ind	28	BBBB	Ind		
Psychology and Educational Studies	CX89	3FT deg	* g	BBB	Ind	Ind	32	CSYS	Ind	11	
Psychology and Educational Studies (4 Yrs)	XC98	4FT deg	*	BBB	Ind	Ind	32	ABBB	Ind	8	
Russian Studies and Educational Studies	RXV9	3FT deg	*	BCC	Ind	Ind	28	CSYS	Ind		
Russian Studies and Educational Studies (4 Yrs)	XR9V	4FT deg	*	BCC	Ind	Ind	28	BBBB	Ind		
Russian and Educational Studies	RX89	3FT deg	R	BCC	Ind	D$^	28$	CSYS	Ind		
Russian and Educational Studies (4 Yrs)	XR98	4FT deg	*	BCC	Ind	Ind	28	BBBB	Ind		
Sociology & Soc Anthrop and Educational St(4Yrs)	XL93	4FT deg	*	BBC-BCC	Ind	Ind	28	BBBB	Ind		
Statistics and Educational Studies	GX49	3FT deg	M	BCC	Ind	D$^	28$	CSYS	Ind		

TITLE	CODE	COURSE	SUBJECTS	A/AS	ND/C	RGNVQ	IB	SQA(H)	SQA	RATIO A/AS
course details			*98 expected requirements*							*96 entry stats*
Statistics and Educational Studies (4 Yrs)	XG94	4FT deg	*	BCC	Ind	Ind	28	BBBB	Ind	
Visual Arts and Educational Studies	XW91	4FT deg	*	BCC	Ind	Ind	28	BBBB	Ind	
KIDDERMINSTER COLL										
Performing Arts (Theatre and Education)	94XE	2FT HND	T	BC	Ind		Ind	Ind	Ind	
Performing Arts (Theatre and Education)	94XW	2FT HND	T	BC	Ind		Ind	Ind	Ind	4
KING ALFRED'S WINCHESTER										
Education Studies & Contemporary Cultural Studs	MX99	3FT deg	* g	14	6M	M	24	BCC	N	
Education Studies and Archaeology	FX49	3FT deg	* g	14	6M	M	24	BCC	N	
Education Studies and Dance Studies	WXK9	3FT deg	* g	14	6M	M	24	BCC	N	15
Education Studies and Design & Technology	JX99	3FT deg	Ds/Ad g	14	6M $	M	24$	BCC$	N$	1
Education Studies and Drama Studies	WX49	3FT deg	* g	14	6M	M	24	BCC	N	4
English Studies and Education Studies	QX39	3FT deg	E	14	X	X	24$	BCC$	X	3 8/18
Geography and Education Studies	LX89	3FT deg	Gy g	14	X	X	24$	BCC$	X	2
History and Education Studies	VX19	3FT deg	H g	14	X	X	24$	BCC$	X	6
Music (World) and Education Studies	WX39	3FT deg	* g	14	6M	M	24	BCC	N	
Philosophy and Education Studies	VX79	3FT deg	* g	14	6M	M	24	BCC	N	
Psychology and Education Studies	LX79	3FT deg	* g	14	6M	M	24	BCC	N	5 12/16
Religious Studies and Education Studies	VX89	3FT deg	* g	14	6M	M	24	BCC	N	1
Social Biology and Education Studies	CX19	3FT deg	B g	14	4M $	M	24$	CCC$	N$	
Sports Studies and Education Studies	LXH9	3FT deg	* g	14	6M	M	24	BCC	N	
Visual Studies and Education Studies	WX29	3FT deg								2
KING'S COLL LONDON (Univ of London)										
Mathematics and Education (4 Yrs)	GX19	4FT deg	M g	8	X		Ind	BBBCC$	X	7 8/10
Modern Foreign Langs with Education (4 Yrs)	T9X9	4FT deg	2L	BBC						5
Physics and Education (4 Yrs)	FX39	4FT deg	M+P g	8	3M		Ind	BBCCC	Ind	1 8/14
LANCASTER Univ										
Criminology and Educational Studies	MX39	3FT deg	*	CCC	M+D		30	ABBBB	Ind	
Educational Studies	X900	3FT deg	*	CCC	M+D		30	ABBB	Ind	
Educational Studies and Applied Social Science	LX49	3FT deg	*	CCC	Ind		30	BBBBB	Ind	
Educational Studies and English Language	QX39	3FT deg	* g	BBC	MO		30	BBBBB	Ind	
Educational Studies and History	XV91	3FT deg	H	BBC	Ind $		30$	ABBBB$	Ind	
Educational Studies and Mathematics	GX19	3FT deg	M	20	Ind $		30$	ABBBB$	Ind	
Educational Studies and Organisation Studies	XN91	3FT deg	*	BCC	MO		30	BBBBB	Ind	
Educational Studies and Psychology	XC98	3FT deg	* g	BCC	DO		30	ABBBB	Ind	
Educational Studies and Religious Studies	XV98	3FT deg	*	18	MO		30	ABBB	Ind	
Educational Studies and Sociology	XL93	3FT deg	*	BCC-CCC	Ind		30	BBBBB	Ind	
English Language and Teaching English as a Forei	QX3X	3FT deg								
French St and Teaching English as a Foreign Lang	RX1X	4SW deg	E+F g	BBC	Ind $		30$	BBBBB$	Ind	
French Studies and Educational Studies	RX19	4SW deg	F	BCC	Ind $		30$	BBBBB$	Ind	
German Studies and Educational Studies	RX29	4SW deg	G/L	BCC	MO $		30$	BBBBB$	Ind	
Independent Studies and Educational Studies	YX49	3FT deg	*	CCC	Ind		Ind	Ind	Ind	
Italian Studies and Educational Studies	RX39	4SW deg	I/L	BCC	MO $		30$	BBBBB$	Ind	
Spanish Studies and Educational Studies	RX49	4SW deg	Sp/L	BCC	MO $		30$	BBBBB$	Ind	
Theatre Studies and Educational Studies	WX49	3FT deg	*	BBC	Ind		32	BBBBB	Ind	
Women's Studies and Educational Studies	XM99	3FT deg	*	CCC	MO		30	ABBB	Ind	
LEEDS METROPOLITAN Univ										
Childhood Studies	X945	3FT deg								
Physical Education	X990	3FT deg	* g	20	2M+5D	DS go	28	BBBBB	Ind	
Rehabilitation Studies in Visual Impairment	X960	2FT Dip	* g		Ind	Ind go	Ind	Ind	Ind	1

course details			98 expected requirements							96 entry stats	
TITLE	CODE	COURSE	SUBJECTS	A/AS	NU/C	AGNVQ	IB	SQA(H)	SQA	RATIO	A/AS
Univ of LIVERPOOL											
Mathematics with Education	G1XX	3FT deg	<u>M</u> g	20	MO $	D$^ go	31$	BBBCC$	Ind	24	
BA Combined Honours *Education Studies*	Y200	3FT deg	* g	BBB	Ind	Ind	Ind	Ind	Ind		
LIVERPOOL JOHN MOORES Univ											
Childhood Studies	X945	2FT deg		18	N	M					
Coaching Science	BX69	3FT deg		BCC	MO+5D	MS^	Ind	BBBC		16	
LOUGHBOROUGH Univ											
Mathematics with Education	G1X9	3FT deg	<u>M</u>	BCC			28$	Ind			
Physical Education and Sports Science	BX69	3FT deg	* g	26	4D	DS6/^ go	30	Ind	Ind		
LUTON Univ											
Education Studies	X900	3FT deg									
Univ of MANCHESTER											
Combined Studies (Human Communication Studies)	X960	3FT deg		18	1M+4D	D^	26	CSYS	Ind	2	16/24
MANCHESTER METROPOLITAN Univ											
Early Childhood Studies	X945	3FT deg	*			Ind					8/16
MIDDLESEX Univ											
Joint Honours Degree *Education Studies*	Y400	3FT deg	* g	14-18	5M	M$ go	28	BCCCC	Ind		
Joint Honours Degree *Teaching English as a Foreign Language*	Y400	3FT deg	* g	12-16	5M	M$ go	28	CCCC	Ind		
Joint Honours Degree *Work-based Learning Studies*	Y400	3FT deg							Ind		
MORAY HOUSE Inst of Ed											
Community Education	X920	3FT/4FT deg			Ind	Ind			Ind	5	
Computer Science and Education	GX57	3FT/4FT deg	g	DD	Ind	Ind		CCC$	Ind		
NENE COLLEGE											
American Studies with Education	Q4X9	3FT deg		DD	5M	M	24	CCC	Ind		
Art and Design with Education	W2X9	3FT deg		DD	5M	M	24	CCC	Ind	6/12	
Economics with Education	L1X9	3FT deg	g	6	5M	M	24	CCC	Ind		
Education with American Studies	X9Q4	3FT deg		DD	5M	M	24	CCC	Ind		
Education with Art and Design	X9W2	3FT deg		DD	5M	M	24	CCC	Ind		
Education with Earth Science	X9F9	3FT deg		DD	5M	M	24	CCC	Ind		
Education with Economics	X9L1	3FT deg	g	DD	5M	M	24	CCC	Ind		
Education with English	X9Q3	3FT deg		DD	5M	M	24	CCC	Ind	6/12	
Education with French	X9R1	3FT deg	F	DD	5M	M	24	CCC	Ind		
Education with Geography	X9F8	3FT deg		DD	5M	M	24	CCC	Ind		
Education with Health Studies	X9L5	3FT deg		D	5M	M	24	CCC	Ind		
Education with History	X9V1	3FT deg		DD	5M	M	24	CCC	Ind		
Education with Human Biological Sciences	X9B1	3FT deg		DD	5M	M	24	CCC	Ind		
Education with Industry and Enterprise	X9H1	3FT deg	g	DD	5M	M	24	CCC	Ind		
Education with Information Systems	X9G5	3FT deg		DD	5M	M	24	CCC	Ind		
Education with Law	X9M3	3FT deg	g	DD	5M	M	24	CCC	Ind		
Education with Mathematics	X9G1	3FT deg	M	DD	5M	M	24	CCC	Ind		
Education with Media and Popular Culture	X9P4	3FT deg		DD	5M	M	24	CCC	Ind		
Education with Music	X9W3	3FT deg	Mu	DD	5M	M	24	CCC	Ind		
Education with Personal and Organisational Devel	X9N6	3FT deg		DD	5M	M	24	CCC	Ind		
Education with Politics	X9M1	3FT deg		DD	5M	M	24	CCC	Ind		
Education with Psychology	X9C8	3FT deg	g	DD	5M	M	24	CCC	Ind	8/14	
Energy Management with Education	J9X9	3FT deg	g	EE	3M	P	24	CCC	Ind		

				98 expected requirements						**96 entry stats**

course details / 98 expected requirements / 96 entry stats

TITLE	CODE	COURSE	SUBJECTS	A/AS	ND/C	AGNVQ	IB	SQA(H)	SQA	RATIO A/AS
English with Education	Q3X9	3FT deg		CC	4M+1D	M	24	CCC	Ind	8/18
French with Education	R1X9	3FT deg	F	DD	5M	Ind	24	CCC	Ind	
Geography with Education	F8X9	3 deg								
History with Education	V1X9	3FT deg		CD	5M	M	24	CCC	Ind	6/18
Human Biological Studies with Education	B1X9	3FT deg	S	DE	5M	M	24	CCC	Ind	
Industry and Enterprise with Education	H1X9	3FT deg	g	EE	3M	P	24	CCC	Ind	
Information Systems with Education	G5X9	3FT deg		6	5M	M	24	CCC	Ind	
Law with Education	M3X9	3FT deg	g	10	3M+2D	M	24	CCC	Ind	
Management Science with Education	G4X9	3FT deg	g	DD	5M	M	24	CCC	Ind	
Mathematics with Education	G1X9	3FT deg	M	DD	Ind	Ind	24	CCC	Ind	
Music with Education	W3X9	3FT deg	Mu	DD	5M	M	24	CCC	Ind	
Psychology with Education	C8X9	3FT deg	g	CC	5M+1D	M	24	CCC	Ind	12/18

Univ of NEWCASTLE

Combined Studies (BA) Education	Y400	3FT deg	*	ABC-BBB	5D	Ind	35$	AAAB	Ind	

NEWMAN COLLEGE OF HIGHER EDUCATION

English and Physical Education & Sports Studies	QX39	3FT deg	*	CC	3M	M*	Dip	CCC	Ind	
Expressive English & Physical Ed. & Sports Stds.	WX4X	3FT deg	*	CC	3M	M*	Dip	CCC	Ind	
History and PE and Sports Studies	VX19	3FT deg	*	CC	3M	M*	Dip	CCC	Ind	
Information Technology and PE & Sports Studies	GX59	3FT deg	*	CC	3M	M*	Dip	CCC	Ind	
PE & Sports Stds & Social & Applied Psychology	LX79	3FT deg	*	CC	3M	M*	Dip	CCC	Ind	
PE & Sports Studies and Biological Science	CX19	3FT deg	*	CC	3M	M*	Dip	CCC	Ind	
PE and Sports Studies and Geography	FX89	3FT deg	*	CC	3M	M*	Dip	CCC	Ind	
PE and Sports Studies and Theology	VX89	3FT deg	*	CC	3M	M*	Dip	CCC	Ind	

NORTHERN COLL

Community Education	X920▼	3FT deg	* g	CC				CCC$		3

Univ of NORTH LONDON

Biological Science and Education Studies	CX19	3FT/4SW/4EXT deg	B	12	Ind	Ind	Ind	Ind	Ind	
Chemistry and Education Studies	FX19	3FT/4SW/4EXT deg	C	CD	Ind	Ind	Ind	Ind	Ind	
Education St & Information & Communications Mgt	PX29	3FT deg	*	CD	Ind	Ind	Ind	Ind	Ind	
Education Studies & Communication & Cultural St	PX39	3FT deg	Me/Cm/E/So	CC	Ind	Ind	Ind	Ind	Ind	
Education Studies and Business	NX19	3FT deg	* G	12	MO+4D	D	Ind	Ind	Ind	
Education Studies and Politics	MX19	3FT deg	*	12	Ind	Ind	Ind	Ind	Ind	
Education Studies and Sociology	LX3X	3FT deg	*	CC	Ind	Ind	Ind	Ind	Ind	
Education Studies and Tourism	PX79	3FT deg	* g	12	Ind	Ind	Ind	Ind	Ind	
Mathematical Sciences and Educational Studies	GX19	3FT/4SW/4EXT deg	* g	CD	Ind	M* go	Ind	Ind	Ind	
Psychology (Applied) and Education Studies	LX79	3FT deg	* g	CC	Ind	Ind	Ind	Ind	Ind	
Public Administration and Education Studies	LX49	3FT deg	*	CC	Ind	Ind	Ind	Ind	Ind	
Social Research and Education	LX39	3FT deg	* g	CC	Ind	Ind	Ind	Ind	Ind	
Statistics and Education Studies	GX49	3FT/4SW/4EXT deg	* g	CD	Ind	M* go	Ind	Ind	Ind	
Combined Honours Education Studies	Y300	3FT/4FT deg	*	CC	Ind	Ind	Ind	Ind	Ind	

Univ of NORTHUMBRIA

Childhood Studies & Professional Practice Studs	X900	3FT deg	g	10	4M	M	24	CCC	Ind	11
Combined Honours Education Studies	Y400▼	3FT deg	g	12-20	MO+3D	D	26	BBCCC	Ind	

NOTTINGHAM TRENT Univ

Human and Education Studies	X920	3FT deg	* g	8	4M	M	Ind	BCCC	N	2 6/16
Sport (Coaching, Business and Exercise Science)	9X6B▼	2FT HND	* g	DD	N	Ind	Dip	C	$	

course details | 98 expected requirements | 96 entry stats

TITLE	CODE	COURSE	SUBJECTS	A/AS	ND/C	AGNVQ	IB	SQA(H)	SQA	RATIO A/AS
OXFORD BROOKES Univ										
Educational Studies/Accounting and Finance	NX49	3FT deg	* g	CC-BCC	Ind	M*3/D*3	Ind	Ind	Ind	
Educational Studies/Anthropology	LX69	3FT deg	*	CC-BCC	Ind	M*^/3	Ind	Ind	Ind	4
Educational Studies/Biological Chemistry	CX79	3FT deg								
Educational Studies/Biology	CX19	3FT deg	S g	DD-CC	Ind	MS/M*3	Ind	Ind	Ind	
Educational Studies/Business Admin & Management	NX19	3FT deg	* g	CC-BBC	Ind	M*3/MB4	Ind	Ind	Ind	
Educational Studies/Cartography	FX89	3FT deg	* g	CC-DDD	Ind	M*/M*3	Ind	Ind	Ind	
Educational Studies/Cell Biology	CXC9	3FT deg								
Educational Studies/Combined Studies	XY94	3FT deg	X			X	X	X		
Educational Studies/Computer Systems	GX69	3FT deg	* g	DDD-BC	Ind	M*/M*3	Ind	Ind	Ind	
Educational Studies/Computing	GX59	3FT deg	* g	CC-CDD	Ind	M*/M*3	Ind	Ind	Ind	
Educational Studies/Computing Mathematics	GX99	3FT deg	* g	CD-CC	Ind	M*/M*3	Ind	Ind	Ind	
Educational Studies/Ecology	CX99	3FT deg	* g	CD-CC	Ind	MS/M*3	Ind	Ind	Ind	
Educational Studies/Economics	LX19	3FT deg	* g	CC-BB	Ind	M*3	Ind	Ind	Ind	
Electronics/Educational Studies	HX69	3FT deg	S/M	CC-DDD	Ind	MS/M*3	Ind	Ind	Ind	
English Studies/Educational Studies	QX39	3FT deg	*	CC-AB	Ind	M*^/3	Ind	Ind	Ind	4 8/20
Environmental Chemistry/Educational Studies	XF91	3FT deg								
Environmental Policy/Educational Studies	KX39	3FT deg								
Environmental Sciences/Educational Studies	FXX9	3FT deg	S g	CD-CC	Ind	M*3/DS	Ind	Ind	Ind	
Exercise and Health/Educational Studies	XB96	3FT deg	S g	CD-CC	Ind	MS/M*3	Ind	Ind	Ind	
Fine Art/Educational Studies	WX19	3FT deg	Pf+A	BC-DDD	Ind	MA^/M*3	Ind	Ind	Ind	
Food Science and Nutrition/Educational Studies	DX49	3FT deg	S g	DD-CC	Ind	MS/M*3	Ind	Ind	Ind	
French Language and Contemp St/Educational St	RXC9	4SW deg	F	DDD-CC	Ind	M^/M*3	Ind	Ind	Ind	13
French Language and Literature/Educational St	RX19	4SW deg	S g	CC-CDD	Ind	M^m*3	Ind	Ind	Ind	3
Geography and the Phys Env/Educational Studies	FXV9	3FT deg								
Geography/Educational Studies	LX89	3FT deg	*	CC-BB	Ind	M*/M*3	Ind	Ind	Ind	19
Geology/Educational Studies	FX69	3FT deg	S/M g	DD-CC	Ind	PS/M*3	Ind	Ind	Ind	
Geotechnics/Educational Studies	HX29	3FT deg	S/M/Ds/Es	CC-DD	Ind	MS/M*3	Ind	Ind	Ind	
German Language and Contemp St/Educational Stud	RXF9	4SW deg	G	CC-DDD	Ind	M^/M*3	Ind	Ind	Ind	
German Language and Literature/Educational Studs	RX29	4SW deg	G	CC-DDD	Ind	M^/M*3	Ind	Ind	Ind	2
German Studies/Educational Studies	XR9G	4SW deg			Ind			Ind	Ind	
German Studies/Exercise and Health	XRXG	4SW deg			Ind			Ind	Ind	
Health Care/Educational Studies	BX79	3FT deg	X			X	X	X		
History of Art/Educational Studies	VX49	3FT deg	*	CC-BCC	Ind	M*^/3	Ind	Ind	Ind	
History/Educational Studies	VX19	3FT deg	*	CC-BB	Ind	M^/M*3	Ind	Ind	Ind	6
Hospitality Management Studies/Educational Studs	NX79	3FT deg	*	CC-DDD	Ind	M*3	Ind	Ind	Ind	
Human Biology/Educational Studies	BX19	3FT deg			Ind			Ind	Ind	
Information Systems/Educational Studies	GXM9	3FT deg	* g	CDD-BB	Ind	M*/M*3	Ind	Ind	Ind	
Intelligent Systems/Educational Studies	GX89	3FT deg	* g	CD-CC	Ind	M*/M*3	Ind	Ind	Ind	
Law/Educational Studies	MX39	3FT deg	*	CC-BBB	Ind	M*3/D*3	Ind	Ind	Ind	
Leisure Planning/Educational Studies	KXH9	3FT deg								
Marketing Management/Educational Studies	NXN9	3FT deg	* g	CC-BCC	Ind	M*3/D*3	Ind	Ind	Ind	
Mathematics/Educational Studies	GX19	3FT deg	M	DD-CC	Ind	M*3/M^	Ind	Ind	Ind	4
Music/Educational Studies	WX39	3FT deg	Mu	DD-CC	Ind	M/M*3	Ind	Ind	Ind	5
Palliative Care/Educational Studies (Post Exp)	BXR9	3FT deg	X			X	X	X		
Planning Studies/Educational Studies	KX49	3FT deg	* g	CC-DDD	Ind	M*/M*3	Ind	Ind	Ind	
Politics/Educational Studies	MX19	3FT deg	*	CC-AB	Ind	M^/M*3	Ind	Ind	Ind	2
Psychology/Educational Studies	CX89	3FT deg	* g	CC-BBC	Ind	M^/M*3	Ind	Ind	Ind	31
Publishing/Educational Studies	PX59	3FT deg	* g	CC-BB	Ind	M$3	Ind	Ind	Ind	5
Rehabilitation/Educational Studies (Post Exp)	BXT9	3FT deg	X			X	X	X		
Sociology/Educational Studies	LX39	3FT deg	*	CC-BCC	Ind	M*^/M*3	Ind	Ind	Ind	7
Software Engineering/Educational Studies	GX79	3FT deg	* g	CC-BC	Ind	M*/M*3	Ind	Ind	Ind	

				98 expected requirements						96 entry stats
TITLE	CODE	COURSE	SUBJECTS	A/AS	NO/C	AGNVQ	IB	SQA(H)	SQA	RATIO A/AS
Statistics/Educational Studies	GX49	3FT deg	* g	DD-CC	Ind	M*/M*3	Ind	Ind	Ind	
Telecommunications/Educational Studies	HXP9	3FT deg								
Tourism/Educational Studies	PX79	3FT deg	* g	CC-BC	Ind	M*3	Ind	Ind	Ind	
Transport Planning/Educational Studies	NX99	3FT deg	* g	CC-DDD	Ind	M*/M*3	Ind	Ind	Ind	
Water Resources/Educational Studies	HXF9	3FT deg								

Univ of PLYMOUTH

Art History with Education Studies	V4X9	3FT deg	Ap g	CCD	MO+3D	D$^	Ind	Ind	Ind	
Cultural Interpretation & Practice with Educ St	Y3X9	3FT deg	Ap g	CCD	MO+3D	D$^	Ind	Ind	Ind	
English with Education Studies	Q3X9	3FT deg	Ap g	BBC	MO+3D	D$^	Ind	Ind	Ind	7 16/22
Heritage and Landscape with Education Studies	W2XX	3FT deg	Ap g	CCD	MO+3D	DS^	Ind	Ind	Ind	
History with Education Studies	V1X9	3FT deg	Ap g	CCD	MO+3D	D$^	Ind	Ind	Ind	3
Mathematics with Education	G1X9	3FT deg	M g	10-15	MO $	M$^	Ind	BBCC	Ind	
Media Arts with Education Studies	W2XY	3FT deg	Ap g	CCD	MO+3D	D$^	Ind	Ind	Ind	5
Theatre and Performance St with Education St	W4X9	3FT deg	Ap g	CCD	MO+3D	D$^	Ind	Ind	Ind	4
Visual Arts with Education Studies	W2X9	3FT deg	Ap g	CCD	MO+3D	D$^	Ind	Ind	Ind	2

Univ of PORTSMOUTH

Geographical Science with Education	F8X9	3FT deg	Gy	16	4M	M$6/^	26	BBBB	Ind	

Univ College of RIPON & YORK ST JOHN

Communication Arts (Music, Dance, Drama) with Ed	P3X9	3FT deg		CC	M	M$	27	BBBC		
Cultural Studies with Education	L6X9	3FT deg		12	M	M*	27	BBBC		
Design & Technology/Education	W2X9	3FT deg	Pf g	CD	M	MA	27	BBBC		
Design & Technology/Education	WX29	3FT deg	Pf g	CD	M	MA	27	BBBC		
English Studies with Education	Q3X9	3FT deg	E	16	Ind	M*^	30	BBBB		
Environmental Science/Education	F9X9	3FT deg	g	CD	M	M*	27	BBCC		6/14
Environmental Science/Education	FX99	3FT deg	g	DD	M*	M	27	BBCC		
European Studies with Education	T2X9	3FT deg		12	M	M*	27	BBBC		
Theology/Education	VX89	3FT deg	g	12	M	M	27	BBBC		

ROEHAMPTON INST

Education	X900	3FT deg		DD	4M	P	24	CCC	N	
Education and Applied Consumer Studies	NX99▼	3FT deg	g	12	4M	P$ go	26	BCC	N$	
Education and Art for Community	WX19▼	3FT deg	*	DD	3M	P$	24	CCC	N	1 6/20
Education and Biology	CX19▼	3FT deg	B	12	3M $	P$ go	24	CCC	N$	2
Education and Business Computing	GX79▼	3FT deg	g	12	3D	M$ go	26	BCC	N$	
Education and Business Studies	NX19▼	3FT deg	g	DD	3D	M$ go	26	BCC	N	3
Education and Dance Studies	WX49▼	3FT deg	*	CC	2M+2D	M$^	30	BBC	Ind	5
Education and Drama & Theatre Studies	WXL9▼	3FT deg	T/E	16	3D	M$^	30	BBC	Ind	5
English Language & Linguistics and Education	XQ9H▼	3FT deg	E/L	CC	2M+2D	M$^	30	BBC	N$	1
English Literature and Education	XQ93▼	3FT deg	E	CC	2M+2D$	M^	28	BBC	Ind	2 4/14
Environmental Studies and Education	XF99▼	3FT deg	B/Gy	DD	4M $	P$ go	26	BCC	N$	
Film & Television Studies and Education	PX49▼	3FT deg	*	16	2M+2D$	M$^	30	BBC	N$	3
French and Education	XR91▼	4FT deg	F	12	4M $	P^	26	BCC	N$	3
Geography and Education	XL98▼	3FT deg	Gy	DD	4M $	P$ go	26	BCC	N$	2
Health Studies and Education	BX99▼	3FT deg	B	12	4M $	P$ go	26	BCC	N$	2
History and Education	XV91▼	3FT deg	H	DD	4M $	P^	26	BCC	N$	1 6/12
Human & Social Biology and Education	XC9C▼	3FT deg	B	12	3M	P$	24	CCC	N	2
Music and Education	XW93▼	3FT deg	Mu	DD	4M $	P^	26	BCC	N$	1 6/10
Natural Resource Studies and Education	DX29▼	3FT deg	g	DD	3M	P$ go	30	CCC	N$	
Psychology and Education	XL97▼	3FT deg	g	CC	3D	M$ go	30	BBC	Ind	16
Social Policy & Administration and Education	XL94▼	3FT deg	g	DD	3M	P$	24	CCC	N	3
Sociology and Education	XL93▼	3FT deg	g	DD	3M	P$ go	24	CCC	N	5

TITLE	CODE	COURSE	SUBJECTS	A/AS	ND/C	AGNVQ	IB	SQA(H)	SQA	RATIO A/AS
course details			**98 expected requirements**							**96 entry stats**
Spanish and Education	RX49▼	4FT deg	Sp	12	2M+2D$	P$ go	28	BBC	N$	
Sport Studies and Education	XB96▼	3FT deg	S g	12	3D	MS go	30	BBC	N$	
Theology & Religious Studies and Education	XV98▼	3FT deg	*	DD	3M	P$	24	CCC	N	4/10
Women's Studies and Education	XM99▼	3FT deg	*	DD	3M	P$	24	CCC	N	6

Univ College of St MARTIN, LANCASTER AND CUMBRIA

TITLE	CODE	COURSE	SUBJECTS	A/AS	ND/C	AGNVQ	IB	SQA(H)	SQA	RATIO A/AS
Applied Community Studies/Education Studies	LX59	3FT deg	*	CD-DDE	3M+2D	M*	28$	BCCC	Ind	2
English/Education Studies	QX39	3FT deg	E	BC-BDE	X	P^	28$	BBBC$	Ind	6
Geography/Education Studies	LX89	3FT deg	Gy	CD-DDE	X	P^	28$	BCCC$	Ind	
Health Studies/Education Studies	BX99	3FT deg	*	CD-DDE	3M+2D	M*	28$	BCCC	Ind	
History/Education Studies	VX19	3FT deg	H	CD-DDE	X	P^	28$	BCCC$	Ind	
Mathematics/Education Studies	GX19	3FT deg	M	DD-DEE	X	P^	28$	BCCC$	Ind	
Religious Studies/Education Studies	VX89	3FT deg	*	CD-DDE	3M+2D$	M*	28$	BCCC	Ind	
Science, Technology and Society/Education Studs	XY91	3FT deg	g	CD-DDE	3M+2D	M*	28	BCCC	Ind	

Univ of SOUTHAMPTON

TITLE	CODE	COURSE	SUBJECTS	A/AS	ND/C	AGNVQ	IB	SQA(H)	SQA	RATIO A/AS
Mathematics with Education	G1X9	3FT deg	M	BBC	Ind	Ind	30	ABBBB	Ind	4

ST HELENS COLL

TITLE	CODE	COURSE	SUBJECTS	A/AS	ND/C	AGNVQ	IB	SQA(H)	SQA	RATIO A/AS
Early Childhood Studies	549X	2FT HND	*	2	N	P*	Dip	Ind	N	

ST MARY'S Univ COLL

TITLE	CODE	COURSE	SUBJECTS	A/AS	ND/C	AGNVQ	IB	SQA(H)	SQA	RATIO A/AS
Education Studies and Biology	CX1X	3FT deg	B/C	4-8	Ind	Ind	Ind	BBBB$	Ind	
Education Studies and Drama	WX4X	3FT deg	*	8-12	Ind	Ind	Ind	BBBB	Ind	
English and Education Studies	QX3X	3FT deg	E	8-12	X	X	Ind	BBBB$	X	
Environmental Investigation St and Education St	FX9X	3FT deg	S/2S	4-8	Ind	Ind	Ind	BBBB	Ind	
Environmental Studies and Education Studies	FXXX	3FT deg	*	4-8	Ind	Ind	Ind	BBBB	Ind	
Gender Studies and Education Studies	MX99	3FT deg	*	4-8	Ind	Ind	Ind	BBBB	Ind	
Geography and Education Studies	FX8X	3FT deg	Gy	4-8	Ind	Ind	Ind	BBBB$	Ind	
Heritage Management and Education Studies	NX9X	3FT deg	*	4-8	Ind	Ind	Ind	BBBB	Ind	
History and Education Studies	VX1X	3FT deg	H	4-8	Ind	Ind	Ind	BBBB$	Ind	
Integrated Scientific Studies and Education St	XYX1	3FT deg	S/2S	4-8	Ind	Ind	Ind	BBBB$	Ind	
Irish Studies and Education Studies	QX5X	3FT deg	*	4-8	Ind	Ind	Ind	BBBB	Ind	
Mathematics and Education Studies	GX1X	3FT deg	M	4-8	X	X	Ind	BBBB$	X	
Media Arts and Education Studies	PX4X	3FT deg	*	4-8	Ind	Ind	Ind	BBBB	Ind	
Sport Rehabilitation and Education Studies	BX9X	3FT deg	B g	12-14	X	X	Ind	BBBB$	X	
Theology and Religious Studies and Education St	VX8X	3FT deg	*	4-8	Ind	Ind	Ind	BBBB	Ind	

Univ of STIRLING

TITLE	CODE	COURSE	SUBJECTS	A/AS	ND/C	AGNVQ	IB	SQA(H)	SQA	RATIO A/AS
English Language Teaching (General Degree only)	X910	3FT deg	g	CCD	Ind	Ind	28	BCCC	HN	

STOCKPORT COLL of F and HE

TITLE	CODE	COURSE	SUBJECTS	A/AS	ND/C	AGNVQ	IB	SQA(H)	SQA	RATIO A/AS
Prof St (Learning Difficulties-Adult) (18+exp)	X960	3FT deg	g	6	M+D	PG	Ind	Ind	Ind	
Professional Studies (Early Childhood Studies)	X945	4FT deg	g	4	N	PG				
Early Childhood Studies	549X	2FT HND	M+E g	4	N	PG				

Univ of STRATHCLYDE

TITLE	CODE	COURSE	SUBJECTS	A/AS	ND/C	AGNVQ	IB	SQA(H)	SQA	RATIO A/AS
Community Arts	WX99	3FT/4FT deg	g	CC	Ind		Ind	BBC$	HN	
Community Education	X920	3FT deg	E g	CC	3M		Ind	BCC$	HN	
Outdoor Education in the Community	X990	3FT/4FT deg	E g	CC	Ind		Ind	BBC$	Ind •	
Sport in the Community	BX69	3FT/4FT deg	E g	CC	Ind		Ind	BBC$	Ind	

UNIVERSITY COLLEGE SUFFOLK

TITLE	CODE	COURSE	SUBJECTS	A/AS	ND/C	AGNVQ	IB	SQA(H)	SQA	RATIO A/AS
Applied Biological Sci and Early Childhood Studs	CX19	3FT deg	S	ED	N $	PS	Ind	Ind	Ind	
Applied Biological Sci with Early Childhood St	C1X9	3FT deg	S	EE	N $	PS	Ind	Ind	Ind	
Applied Biological Science with Education Studs	C1XX	3FT deg	S	EE	N $	PS	Ind	Ind	Ind	

				98 expected requirements							96 entry stats	

course details　　　　　　　　　　　　　　**98 expected requirements**　　　　　　　　*96 entry stats*

TITLE	CODE	COURSE	SUBJECTS	A/AS	ND/C	AGNVQ	IB	SQA(H)	SQA	RATIO A/AS	
Art & Design and Early Childhood Studies	EW92	3FT deg	Pf	DE	N $	P$	Ind	Ind	Ind		
Art & Design and Early Childhood Studies	XW92	3FT deg	Pf	DE	N $	P$	Ind	Ind	Ind		
Art & Design with Early Childhood Studies	E2XX	3FT deg	Pf	EE	N $	P$	Ind	Ind	Ind		
Art & Design with Early Childhood Studies	W2XX	3FT deg	Pf	EE	N $	P$	Ind	Ind	Ind		
Art & Design with Education Studies	E2X9	3FT deg	Pf	EE	N $	P$	Ind	Ind	Ind		
Art & Design with Education Studies	W2X9	3FT deg	Pf	EE	N $	P$	Ind	Ind	Ind		
Behavioural Studies and Early Childhood Studies	LX79	3FT deg	*	DD	N $	P$	Ind	Ind	Ind		
Behavioural Studies with Early Childhood Studies	L7X9	3FT deg	*	DD	N $	P$	Ind	Ind	Ind		
Business Studies and Early Childhood Studies	NX19	3FT deg	*	DE	N $	P$	Ind	Ind	Ind		
Business Studies with Early Childhood Studies	N1XX	3FT deg	*	EE	N $	P$	Ind	Ind	Ind		
Business Studies with Education Studies	N1X9	3FT deg	*	EE	N $	P$	Ind	Ind	Ind		
Cultural Studies and Early Childhood Studies	YX39	3FT deg	*	CD	N $	P$	Ind	Ind	Ind		
Early Childhood Studies	X946	3FT deg	*	DD	N $	P*	Ind	Ind	Ind		
Early Childhood Studies and Environment Studies	XF99	3FT deg	*	DE	N $	P$	Ind	Ind	Ind		
Early Childhood Studies and Information Techn	XG95	3FT deg	*	DE	N $	P$	Ind	Ind	Ind		
Early Childhood Studies and Literary Studies	XQ92	3FT deg	E	CD	N $	P$	Ind	Ind	Ind		
Early Childhood Studies and Management	XN91	3FT deg	*	DE	N $	P$	Ind	Ind	Ind		
Early Childhood Studies and Media Studies	XP94	3FT deg	*	DC	N $	P$	Ind	Ind	Ind		
Early Childhood Studies with Applied Biol Sci	X9CC	3FT deg	S	DD	N $	P$	Ind	Ind	Ind		
Early Childhood Studies with Art & Design	X9W2	3FT deg	Pf	DD	N $	P$	Ind	Ind	Ind		
Early Childhood Studies with Behavioural Studies	X9LH	3FT deg	*	DD	N $	P$	Ind	Ind	Ind		
Early Childhood Studies with Business Studies	X9N1	3FT deg	*	DD	N $	P$	Ind	Ind	Ind		
Early Childhood Studies with Cultural Studies	X9Y3	3FT deg	*	DD	N $	P$	Ind	Ind	Ind		
Early Childhood Studies with Education Studies	X940	3FT deg	*	DD	N $	P$	Ind	Ind	Ind		
Early Childhood Studies with Environmental Studs	X9FX	3FT deg	S	DD	N $	PS	Ind	Ind	Ind		
Early Childhood Studies with Human Science	X9B1	3FT deg	S	DD	N $	P$	Ind	Ind	Ind		
Early Childhood Studies with Information Techn	X9GM	3FT deg	*	DD	N $	P$	Ind	Ind	Ind		
Early Childhood Studies with Literary Studies	X9Q2	3FT deg	*	DD	N $	P$	Ind	Ind	Ind		
Early Childhood Studies with Management	X9NC	3FT deg	*	DD	N $	P$	Ind	Ind	Ind		
Early Childhood Studies with Media Studies	X9P4	3FT deg	*	DD	N $	P$	Ind	Ind	Ind		
Early Childhood Studies with Social Policy	X9L4	3FT deg	*	DD	N $	P$	Ind	Ind	Ind		
Environmental Studies with Early Childhood Studs	F9XX	3FT deg	S/Gy	EE	N $	P$	Ind	Ind	Ind		
Environmental Studies with Education Studies	F9X9	3FT deg	S/Gy	EE	N $	P$	Ind	Ind	Ind		
Information Technology with Early Childhood St	G5XX	3FT deg	*	EE	N $	P$	Ind	Ind	Ind		
Information Technology with Education Studies	G5X9	3FT deg	*	EE	N $	P$	Ind	Ind	Ind		
Media Studies with Early Childhood Studies	P4XX	3FT deg	*	CE	N $	P$	Ind	Ind	Ind		
Media Studies with Education Studies	P4X9	3FT deg	*	CE	N $	P$	Ind	Ind	Ind		
Product Design & Manufacture & Early Child Studs	HX79	3FT deg	*	DE	N $	P$	Ind	Ind	Ind		
Product Design & Manufacture with Early Child St	H7XX	3FT deg	*	EE	N $	P$	Ind	Ind	Ind		
Product Design & Manufacture with Education St	H7X9	3FT deg	*	EE	N $	P$	Ind	Ind	Ind		

Univ of SUNDERLAND

Early Childhood Studies	X945	3FT deg	* g	12	3M+2D	M$	24	CCCCC	N$		

Univ of Wales SWANSEA

Early Childhood Studies	L5X9	3FT deg	*	BCC	1M+4D$	Ind	28	BBBBC	Ind		

Univ of WARWICK

Education and Psychology	XL97	3FT deg	* g	BBB	X	X	32	AABBB		9	24/30
Philosophy with Education	V7X9	3FT deg	* g	BBB	X	X	32	AABBB		10	
Sociology and Education	LX39	3FT deg	* g	BCC	Ind	Ind	30	ABBBC		26	

WEST HERTS COLL

Early Childhood Studies	549X	2FT HND									

course details			98 expected requirements							96 entry stats
TITLE	CODE	COURSE	SUBJECTS	A/AS	NO/C	AGNVQ	IB	SQA(H)	SQA	RATIO A/AS
WESTHILL COLL										
Humanities - Childhood Studies *Education Studies*	Y600	3FT deg	* g	CC	4M+2D	M^	Ind	Ind	Ind	
Humanities - Nineteenth and Twentieth Century St *Education Studies*	Y602	3FT deg	* g	CC	4M+2D	M^	Ind	Ind	Ind	
Univ of WOLVERHAMPTON										
Conductive Education	X961	3FT deg		10	4M	M	24	BBBB	Ind	
Combined Degrees *Conductive Education*	Y401	3FT deg	g	12-18	4M	M	24	BBBB	Ind	
Combined Degrees *Deaf Studies*	Y401	3FT deg	g	12	4M	M	24	BBBB	Ind	
Combined Degrees *Education Studies*	Y401	3FT deg		10	4M	M	24	BBBB	Ind	
Combined Degrees *Education Studies (3 Semesters in Holland)*	Y401	3FT deg		14	4M	M	24	BBBB	Ind	
Combined Degrees *Special Needs*	Y401	3FT deg		12	4M	M	24	BBBB	Ind	
Combined Degrees *Teaching of Engl for Speakers of other Langs*	Y401	3FT deg	g	12	4M	M	24	BBBB	Ind	
WORCESTER COLL of HE										
Education Studies/Art & Design	WX99	3FT deg	A	DD	Ind	M	Ind	Ind	Ind	2
Education Studies/Biological Science	CX19	3FT deg	<u>S</u>	DD	Ind	M	Ind	Ind	Ind	10
Education Studies/Business Management	NX19	3FT deg		DD	Ind	M	Ind	Ind	Ind	2
Education Studies/Economy and Society	LX19	3FT deg		DD	Ind	M	Ind	Ind	Ind	
English and Literary Studies/Education Studies	XQ93	3FT deg		CC	Ind	M	Ind	Ind	Ind	2 8/12
Environmental Science/Education Studies	XF99	3FT deg		DD	Ind	M	Ind	Ind	Ind	
History/Education Studies	XV91	3FT deg		DD	Ind	M	Ind	Ind	Ind	3
Information Technology/Education Studies	XG95	3FT deg		DD	Ind	M	Ind	Ind	Ind	
Psychology/Education Studies	XL97	3FT deg	g	CC	Ind	M	Ind	Ind	Ind	7
Sociology/Education Studies	XL93	3FT deg		DD	Ind	M	Ind	Ind	Ind	3
Sports Studies	B6X9	3FT deg		CC	Ind	M	Ind	Ind	Ind	
Sports Studies/Education Studies	XB96	3FT deg		CC	Ind	M	Ind	Ind	Ind	
Urban Studies/Education Studies	XL9V	3FT deg		DD	Ind	M	Ind	Ind	Ind	
Women's Studies/Education Studies	XM99	3FT deg		DD	Ind	M	Ind	Ind	Ind	
Univ of YORK										
Archaeology/Education	V6X9	3FT deg	*	BBC	M+D	D$^	30	BBBC	Ind	
Biology/Education	C1X9	3FT deg	B+C g	BCC	5M $	MS6/^	28$	BBBB$	N$	
Economic and Social History/Education	V3X9	3FT deg	* g	CCC	DO	D*^	30	BBBC	Ind	
Economics/Education	L1X9	3FT deg	* g	BBC	DO	D*^	30	BBBB	Ind	
Educational Studies	X900	3FT deg	*	CCC	MO	D*6/^ go	27$	BBCC	Ind	12/20
English/Education	Q3X9	3FT deg	E g	ABB-ABC	HN $	D$^	32$	AABB$	Ind	
History/Education	V1X9	3FT deg	<u>H</u>	ABC	Ind	D$6/^	32$	ABBB$	Ind	
Linguistics/Education	Q1X9	3FT/4FT deg	*/<u>L</u>	24	Ind	D$^	28$	BBCC$	Ind	
Mathematics/Education	G1X9	3FT deg	<u>M</u>	20-22	HN $	DS^	30$	CSYS$	HN$	16/26
Music/Education	W3X9	3FT deg	<u>Mu</u>	BBC	Ind	D$^	28$	BBBC$	Ind	
Philosophy/Education	V7X9	3FT deg	*	BBC	Ind	D$6/^	30	BBBC	Ind	
Physics/Education	F3X9	3FT deg	<u>M+P</u>	BCC	Ind	DS^	28$	CSYS$	Ind	
Physics/Education with a year in Europe	F3XX	4FT deg	<u>M+P</u> g	BCC	Ind	DS^	28$	CSYS$	Ind	
Politics/Education	M1X9	3FT deg	*	BBC	Ind	D*^	28	BBBB	Ind	
Sociology/Education	L3X9	3FT deg	*	BCC	Ind	D$6/^	28	BBBB	Ind	18/24

course details			98 expected requirements							96 entry stats	
TITLE	CODE	COURSE	SUBJECTS	A/AS	NQ/C	AGNVQ	IB	SQA(H)	SQA	RATIO	A/AS
Univ of BATH											
Aerospace Engineering (5 Yr SW)	H423	5SW deg	M+P g	ABB	Ind	Ind	30$	CSYS$	Ind		
Aerospace Engineering (MEng)	H420	4FT deg	M+P g	ABB	Ind	Ind	30$	CSYS$	Ind	8	20/30
Aerospace Engineering with French (5 Yr SW)	H424	5SW deg	M+P g	ABB	Ind	Ind	30$	CSYS$	Ind		
Aerospace Engineering with French (MEng)	H421	4FT deg	M+P g	ABB	Ind	Ind	30$	CSYS$	Ind	9	
Aerospace Engineering with German (5 Yr SW)	H425	5SW deg	M+P g	ABB	Ind	Ind	30$	CSYS$	Ind		
Aerospace Engineering with German (MEng)	H422	4FT deg	M+P g	ABB	Ind	Ind	30$	CSYS$	Ind	14	
BOLTON INST											
Control Engineering (Foundation)	964H	3FT HND	* g		Ind	Ind	Ind	Ind	Ind		
Univ of BRIGHTON											
Mech and Aeronautical Design Eng (Dip/BEng/MEng)	HH34	3FT/4SW/4FT/5SW deg	M+P/S g	18	5M $	ME/M$^	25$	BBBC$	Ind		
Univ of BRISTOL											
Aeronautical Eng with Study in C Eur(MEng)	H401	4FT deg	M+P g	AAB-BBB	HN	D$^	33$	CSYS	HN$	9	26/30
Aeronautical Engineering (MEng)	H400	4FT deg	M+P	AAB-BBB	HN	D$^	33$	CSYS	HN$	9	22/30
Avionic Systems	HH46	3FT deg	M+P	AAB-BBB	HN	D$^	33$	CSYS	HN$	9	22/28
Avionic Systems (MEng)	HH64	4FT deg	M+P	AAB-BBB	HN	D$^	33$	CSYS	HN$	7	20/30
BRISTOL, Univ of the W of England											
Aerospace Manufacturing Engineering	H420	3FT/4SW deg	M/P g	14	4M $	M$1 go	24$	BCCC$	N$		
Aerospace Manufacturing Engineering (MEng)	H421	4FT/5SW deg	M/P g	14	4M $	M$1 go	24$	BCCC$	N$		
Engineering (Aeronautical)	024H	2FT/3SW HND	M/P g	2-4	N $	P$1 go	24$	CD$	N$		
Engineering (Aircraft Maintenance)	004H▼	2FT/3SW HND	M/P g	2-4	N $	P$1 go	24$	CD$	N$		
BRUNEL Univ, West London											
Mech Eng w. Aeronautics (4/5 Yrs Thick SW)(MEng)	H3HL	4SW/5SW deg	M+P	BCC	4M+1D$	DE^	28$	BBBBB$	Ind	9	18/26
Mech Eng w. Aeronautics (4/5 Yrs Thin SW) (MEng)	H3H4	4SW/5SW deg	M+P	BCC	4M+1D$	DE^	28$	BBBBB$	Ind	8	
Mechanical Engineering with Aeronautics (MEng)	H3HK	3FT/4FT deg	M+P	BCC	4M+1D$	DE^	28$	BBBBB$	Ind	14	
CITY Univ											
Aeronautical Engineering	H400	3FT deg	M+P	BBC-BCC	4M+2D	DE6/^	28$	Ind	Ind	8	9/20
Aeronautical Engineering	H401	4SW deg	M+P	BBC-BCC	4M+2D	DE6/^	28$	Ind	Ind	9	14/22
Aeronautical Engineering (MEng)	H405	5SW deg	M+P	ABB-BBB	X		30$	Ind	X	35	
Aeronautical Engineering (MEng)	H403	4FT deg	M+P	ABB-BBB	X		30$	Ind	X	16	
Air Transport Engineering	H420	4SW deg	M+P	BCC-CCC	4M+2D	DE6/^	28$	Ind	Ind	20	
Air Transport Engineering	H422	3FT deg	M+P	BCC-CCC	4M+2D	DE6/^	28$	Ind	Ind	3	
Air Transport Engineering (Foundation)	H402	4EXT deg	M+P	6-8	N	P$	Dip	BC	N	3	
Air Transport Engineering (MEng)	H423	5SW deg	M+P	ABB-BBB	X		30$	Ind	X		
Air Transport Engineering (MEng)	H424	4FT deg	M+P	ABB-BBB	X		30$	Ind	X	7	
COVENTRY Univ											
Aerospace Systems Engineering	H400	3FT/4SW 4FT/5SW deg	M+S	12-18	3M $	M+	24$	BBCC$	Ind	9	6/14
Avionic Systems Engineering	HH46	3/4FT 4/5SW deg	M+S	12-18	3M $	M+	24$	BBCC$	Ind		
Aerospace Systems Engineering	004H	2FT/3SW HND	M/S		$	M	Ind	Ind	Ind	3	2/8
CRANFIELD Univ											
Aeromechanical Systems Engineering	H420	3FT deg	M+P g	BCC	3M+1D		Ind	Ind	Ind	9	14/24
FARNBOROUGH COLL of Technology											
Aerospace Engineering	H400	3FT deg	M/P	10	Ind	M*	Ind	Ind	Ind	10	6/20
Aerospace Studies	024H	2FT HND		E	N	P*	Ind	Ind	Ind	3	2/10
Univ of GLASGOW											
Aeronautical Engineering (MEng or BEng)	H400	4FT/5FT deg	M+S	BBB	HN $	Ind	28$	BBBBC$	HN$	6	20/24
Avionics (Aeronautical) (MEng or BEng)	HHK6	4FT/5FT deg	M+S	BB	HN $	Ind	28$	BBBBC$	HN$	13	
Avionics (Electronics) (BEng)	HHL6	4FT deg	M+P	CCD	MO	ME	24$	BBBBC$	N$	9	

			98 expected requirements							96 entry stats	
TITLE	CODE	COURSE	SUBJECTS	A/AS	ND/C	RGNVQ	IB	SQA(H)	SQA	RATIO	A/AS
Univ of HERTFORDSHIRE											
Aerospace Engineering	H400	3FT/4SW deg	M+P/S/Cs	18	3M $	Ind	$	Ind	Ind	7	8/20
Aerospace Engineering (MEng)	H401	4FT/5SW deg	M+2S	22	5M		Ind	Ind	Ind		
Aerospace Systems Engineering	H430	3FT/4SW deg	M+P/S/Cs	18	3M $	Ind	$	Ind	Ind	9	12/20
Aerospace Systems Engineering (Extended)	H438▼	4FT/5EXTSW deg	*	2	N	Ind	$	Ind	Ind	1	
Aerospace Systems Engineering (MEng)	H431	4FT/5SW deg	M+2S	22	5M		Ind	Ind	Ind		
IMPERIAL COLL (Univ of London)											
Aeronautical Engineering (MEng)	H401	4FT deg	M+P	AAB	X	X	$	CSYS	X	9	26/30
Aeronautical Engineering with a Yr in Eur (MEng)	H402	4FT deg	M+P	AAB	X	X	$	CSYS	X	6	28/30
Aerospace Materials	HJ45	4FT deg	M+P/C	22	Ind	Ind	Ind	Ind	Ind		22/30
KINGSTON Univ											
Aerospace Engineering	H420	3FT deg	2S	4-6	2M $	ME2	Ind	Ind	Ind		
Aerospace Engineering	H401	4SW deg	2S	4-6	2M	ME2	Ind	Ind	Ind		
Aerospace Engineering	H408	4EXT/5EXTSW deg	*	4-6	Ind		Ind	Ind	Ind	3	
Aerospace Engineering (BEng/MEng)	H424	4SW/5SW deg	M+S	10-12	3M $	Ind	Ind	Ind	Ind		6/16
Aerospace Engineering (BEng/MEng)	H423	3FT/4FT deg	M+S	10-12	3M $	Ind	Ind	Ind	Ind	1	6/20
Univ of LINCOLNSHIRE and HUMBERSIDE											
Engineering (Aircraft Structures)	H400	3FT deg	M+P/S g	18	1M+4D$	Ind	26	CCBBB$	Ind		
Engineering (Avionics)	HH46	3FT deg	M+P/S g	18	1M+4D$	Ind	26	BBBCC$	Ind		
Univ of LIVERPOOL											
Aerospace Engineering (BEng)	H420	4SW deg	M+P	24	4M+1D$		32$	BBBBB	Ind	15	
Aerospace Engineering (BEng)	H425	3FT deg	M+P	24	4M+1D$		32$	BBBBB	Ind	7	14/24
Aerospace Engineering (MEng)	H421	4SW deg	M+P	24	4M+1D$		32$	BBBBB	Ind	6	16/26
LOUGHBOROUGH Univ											
Aeronautical Engineering	H400	3FT deg	M+P	BBC	4D		30$	Ind	Ind	11	18/28
Aeronautical Engineering (4 Yr MEng)	H403	4FT deg	M+P	26	4D		30$	Ind	Ind	13	24/30
Aeronautical Engineering (4 Yr SW)	H401	4SW deg	M+P	BBC	4D		30$	Ind	Ind	7	20/30
Aeronautical Engineering (5 Yr SW MEng)	H402	5SW deg	M+P	26	4D		30$	Ind	Ind		
Univ of MANCHESTER											
Aerospace Engineering	H400	3FT deg	M+P g	24	1D $		32$	AAABB$	Ind	13	20/28
Aerospace Engineering (Int Eur Prog) (MEng)	H401	4FT deg	M+P g	24	1D $		32$	AAABB$	Ind	4	24/28
Aerospace Engineering (MEng)	H402	4FT deg	M+P g	24	1D $		32$	AAABB$	Ind	8	22/30
Aerospace Engineering with Systems (MEng)	H420	4FT deg	M+P g	24	1D $		32$	AAABB$	Ind	6	
Aerospace Materials Engineering (MEng)	HJ42	4FT deg	M+P g	CCC-BBB	1D $		32$	AAABB$	Ind		
UMIST (Manchester)											
Aerospace Engineering	H400	3FT deg	M+P g	BBB	MO+3D$	Ind	32$	CSYS$	Ind	29	
Aerospace Engineering (MEng)	H402	4FT deg	M+P g	BBB	MO+3D$	Ind	32$	CSYS$	Ind	14	20/26
Aerospace Engineering with French (MEng)	H4R1	4FT deg	M+P g	BBB	MO+3D$	Ind	32$	CSYS$	Ind		
NORTHBROOK COLLEGE Sussex											
Aeronautical Engineering	004H	2FT HND	*		N						
NORTH EAST WALES INST of HE											
Aeronautical & Mechanical Eng with Business Stds	H4N1	3FT deg		4-8	3M	M$	Ind	CCC	N$		
Aeronautical Electronics (Avionics)	HH46	3FT deg		4-8	3M	M$	Ind	CCC	N$		
Aeronautical/Mechanical Engineering	HH43	3FT deg		4-8	3M	M$	Ind	CCC	N$		
Aeronautical Electronics (Avionics)	64HH	2FT HND		2-4	2M	P$	Ind	CC	N$		
Aeronautical Engineering	004H	2FT HND		2-8	2M	P$	Ind	CC	N$		

Engineering – Aeronautical

course details			98 expected requirements							96 entry stats	
TITLE	CODE	COURSE	SUBJECTS	A/AS	NO/C	AGNVQ	IB	SQA(H)	SQA	RATIO	A/AS
NORWICH: City COLL											
Aerospace Studies	024H	3SW HND	M/P	DD	Ind		Ind	Ind	Ind		
QUEEN MARY & WESTFIELD COLL (Univ of London)											
Aerospace Engineering	H421	3FT deg	M	CCD-BCC	5M $	M$^	28$				
Aerospace Engineering (4 Yrs)	H422	4SW deg	M	CCD-BCC	5M	M$^	28				
Aerospace Engineering (MEng)	H420	4FT deg	M+P	BCC-BBB	5M $	M$^	28$				
Aerospace Materials Technology	J5H4	3FT deg	M+P	CCD	5M $	M$	28$				
Aerospace Materials Technology (MEng)	J5HK	4FT deg	M+P	BBB	X	X	28$				
Aerospace Systems (MEng)	H425	4FT deg	M+P	BCC-BBB	5M	M$^	28				
Avionics	HH45	3FT deg	M	CCD-BCC	5M $	M$^	28$				
Science and Engineering (4 yrs with Foundation) Aeronautical Engineering	Y157	4EXT deg		E	N	P					
QUEEN'S Univ Belfast											
Aeronautical Eng Extd (Dainton) Course (MEng)	H412	4FT deg	M+P g	BBB	X	X	32$	X	X	11	26/28
Aeronautical Engineering	H400	3FT/4FT deg	M+P g	BCC	Ind	Ind	29$	BBBC	Ind	13	20/26
Univ of SALFORD											
Aeronautical Engineering	H400	3FT/4SW deg		22	Ind	M	Ind	Ind	Ind	9	12/22
Aeronautical Engineering (MEng)	H404	4FT deg	M	22	Ind	M	Ind	Ind	Ind	13	13/20
Aeronautical Engineering (Stockport) (4 Yrs)	H402	4FT deg			Ind	M	Ind	Ind	Ind	5	
Aeronautical Systems	H422	4FT/5SW deg									
Aeronautical Systems (3 or 4 Yrs)	H420	3FT/4SW deg	M	18	Ind	M	Ind	Ind	Ind	10	12/16
Univ of SHEFFIELD											
Aerospace Engineering	H420	3FT/4FT deg									
Univ of SOUTHAMPTON											
Aerospace Engineering (MEng)	H401	4FT deg	M+P	28	Ind $	D^	34$	CSYS	Ind	12	26/30
Aerospace Engineering with European Studies	H425	4FT deg	M+P	28	Ind $	D^	34	CSYS	Ind		
STOCKPORT COLL of F and HE											
Aeronautical Engineering	H400	4FT deg	M/P	2	$		Ind	Ind	Ind		
Univ of STRATHCLYDE											
Mechanical Engineering with Aerodynamics	H3H4	5FT deg	M+P	BBB	HN		32$	AABBB$	HN		

TITLE	CODE	COURSE	SUBJECTS	A/AS	ND/C	AGNVQ	IB	SQA(H)	SQA	RATIO	A/AS
ASTON Univ											
Chemical Engineering	H804	4SW/5SW deg	C+M g	20	5M+5D$	D$6/^ go	31$	BBBBB$	Ind	6	12/24
Chemical Engineering	H803	3FT/4FT deg	C+M g	20	5M+5D$	D$6/^ go	31$	BBBBB$	Ind	7	14/20
Chemical Engineering (Steps)	H842	4FT/5SW deg	* g	20	4M	D$ go	31	BBBBB	Ind	7	
Chemical Engineering (Year Zero)	H808	4FT/5FT deg									
Chemical Engineering (Year Zero)	H805	5SW/6SW deg									
Chemical Engineering and App Chem (MEng)	FH18	4FT/5SW deg	C+M g	26	10D$	D$6/^ go	34$	AAABB$	Ind	3	20/30
Chemical Engineering with Euro St (MEng)	H8T2	4FT/5SW deg	C+M g	24	2M+8D$	D$6/^ go	33$	AABBB$	Ind	11	
Univ of BATH											
Chemical Engineering	H800	3FT deg	M+C	20-22	Ind	Ind	30	CSYS	Ind	10	16/20
Chemical Engineering (4 Yr SW)	H801	4SW deg	M+C	20-22	Ind	Ind	30	CSYS	Ind	5	16/28
Chemical Engineering and Environmental Mgt	H804	4FT deg	M+C	20-22	Ind	Ind	30	CSYS	Ind	7	24/28
Chemical Engineering and Environmental Mgt	H805	5SW deg	M+C	20-22	Ind	Ind	30	CSYS	Ind	3	18/26
Chemical and Bio Process Engineering	H840	3FT deg	M+C	20-22	Ind	Ind	30	CSYS	Ind	4	
Chemical and Bio Process Engineering (4 Yr SW)	H841	4SW deg	M+C	20-22	Ind	Ind	30	CSYS	Ind	2	
Univ of BIRMINGHAM											
Chemical Engineering	H800	3FT/4FT deg	M+C	BBC	4M+1D$	Ind	32$	Ind	Ind	5	16/30
Chemical Engineering w. Biochemical Engineering	H870	3FT/4FT deg	M+C	BBC	4M+1D$	Ind	32$	Ind	Ind	2	20/30
Chemical Engineering with Environmental Mgt	H8F9	4FT deg	M+C	BBC	4M+1D$	Ind	32$	Ind	Ind	15	
Chemical Engineering with Foundation Year	H892	4FT/5FT deg	* g	BBC	4M+1D$	Ind	30$	Ind	Ind	3	10/16
Chemical Engineering with Management (c)	H8N1	4FT deg	M+C	BBC	4M+1D$	Ind	32$	Ind	Ind	2	14/30
Chemical Engineering with Minerals Engineering	H8J1	3FT/4FT deg	M+C	BBC	4M+1D$	Ind	32$	Ind	Ind		
Univ of BRADFORD											
Chemical Engineering	H800	3FT deg	M+P/C	CCC	3M $	Ind	Ind	Ind	Ind	3	6/12
Chemical Engineering	H804	4SW deg	M+P/C	CCC	3M $	Ind	Ind	Ind	Ind	4	8/20
Chemical Engineering (Foundation Year)	H803	4FT/5SW deg	* g	4-6	N	PS	Ind	Ind	Ind	3	
Chemical Engineering (MEng)	H801	5SW deg	M+P+C	ABB-BBB	DO	Ind	Ind	Ind	Ind	15	
Chemical Engineering (MEng)	H802	4SW deg	M+P+C	ABB-BBB	DO	Ind	Ind	Ind	Ind		
Chemical Engineering with Management	H805	4SW deg	M+P+C	CCC	3M $	Ind	Ind	Ind	Ind	14	
Chemical Engineering with Management (MEng)	H814	5FT deg	M+P+C	ABB-BBB	DO	Ind	Ind	Ind	Ind		
Chemical Engineering with Process Control	H810	3FT deg	M+P+C	CCC	3M $	Ind	Ind	Ind	Ind		
Chemical Engineering with Process Control	H811	4SW deg	M+P+C	CCC	3M $	Ind	Ind	Ind	Ind		
Chemical Engineering with Process Control (MEng)	H813	5SW deg	M+P+C	ABB-BBB	DO	Ind	Ind	Ind	Ind		
Chemical Engineering with Process Control (MEng)	H812	4SW deg	M+P+C	ABB-BBB	DO	Ind	Ind	Ind	Ind		
European Chemical Engineering	H806	4SW deg	M+P/C	CCC	3M $	X	Ind	Ind	Ind		
European Chemical Engineering (MEng)	H815	5SW deg	M+P+C	BBB	DO	X	Ind	Ind	Ind		
Univ of BRIGHTON											
Energy & Environmental Sustainability (BSc Hons)	H8F9	3FT/4SW deg	M+P/S g	12	5M $	ME/M$^	25$	BBBC$	Ind$		
Energy Engineering (BEng Hons)	H862	3FT/4SW deg	M+P/S g	18	5M $	ME/M$^	25$	BBBC$	Ind$		
Univ of BRISTOL											
Mechanical Eng with Process Systems (MEng)	H3H8	4FT deg	M+P	ABB-CCC	HN $	D$^	28$	CSYS	HN $		
CAMBRIDGE Univ											
Natural Sciences *Chemical Engineering*	Y160▼	3FT/4FT deg	2(S/M) g	AAA-AAB	Ind		Ind	CSYS	Ind		
DUDLEY COLLEGE of Technology											
Engineering (Plant and Process Plant)	018H	2FT HND	* g	2	Ind	Ind					

course details			98 expected requirements							96 entry stats
TITLE	CODE	COURSE	SUBJECTS	A/AS	ND/C	AGNVQ	IB	SQA(H)	SQA	RATIO A/AS
Univ of EDINBURGH										
Chemical Engineering (BEng)	H800	4FT deg	M+C+P/B	CCC	MO $		Dip$	BBBB$	N$	8
Chemical Engineering (MEng)	H804	5FT deg	M+C+P/B	CCC	MO $		Dip$	BBBB$	N$	4	20/30
Chemical Engineering with European Studs (MEng)	H8T2	5FT deg	M+C+P/B	CCC	MO $		Dip$	BBBB$	N$	4
Chemical and Process Systems Engineering(MEng)	H810	5FT deg	C+M+P/B	CCC	MO $		Dip$	BBBB$	N$	6
Univ of GLAMORGAN										
Technology & Business Studies	H8N1	3FT deg	g	DD	N $	M$	Ind	Ind	Ind	6/10
HALTON COLL										
Chemical Process Engineering	048H	2FT HND	C/M	2	N	P	Ind	Ind	N	
HERIOT-WATT Univ										
Chem Eng with Brewing and Distilling Tech (MEng)	H8C9	5FT deg	C+M	CCD		M$ go	30	BBBB	$	
Chem Eng with Semiconductor Process Tech (MEng)	H810	5FT deg	C+M	CCD		M$ go	30	BBBB	$	
Chemical Engineering	H800	4FT deg	M+C g	CCD	$	M$ go	30	BBBB	$	
Chemical Engineering with Energy Resource Eng	H8J9	4FT deg	M+C g	CCD	$	M$ go	30	BBBB$	$	
Chemical Engineering with Environ Mgt (MEng)	H8F9	4FT/5FT deg	M+C	CCD	HN	M$ go	30	BBBB	Ind	
Chemical Engineering with Pharmaceutical Chemist	H8F1	5FT deg	C+M	CCD		M$ go	30	BBBB	$	
Combined Studies *Chemical Engineering*	Y100	4FT deg	M+C	DDE	Ind	M$ go	26	BCCC	Ind	
Univ of HUDDERSFIELD										
Chemistry with Chemical Engineering	F1H8	3FT/4SW deg	C g	10	3M $	MS gi	Ind	BCC	Ind	
Univ of HULL										
Chemistry with Quality Management	F1H8	3FT deg	C	CCD	MO $	M$^ gi	26$	BCCCC	Ind	13
Chemistry with Quality Management (MChem)	F1HV	4FT deg	C	BCC	MO+3D$	M$^ gi	26$	BBBCC		
IMPERIAL COLL (Univ of London)										
Chemical Engineering (MEng)	H801	4FT deg	M+C g	BBB	X		$	CSYS	HN	6	24/30
Chemical Engineering with a Year Abroad (MEng)	H802	4FT deg	M+C g	BBB	X		$	CSYS	X	5	24/30
Univ of LEEDS										
Chemical Engineering (3/4 Yrs)	H800	3FT/4FT deg	C+M/S g	BCC-BBC	4M+2D$	Ind	28$	BBBBC	Ind	10	14/28
Energy Engineering	H862	3FT/4FT deg	M+S g	CCD	1M+4D$	Ind	24$	BBCCC	Ind	2	8/18
Environmental Chemical Engineering	H8F9	3FT deg	C+S/M/Ec/Gy g	BCC	4M+2D$	Ind	28$	BBBBC	Ind	7
Environmental Energy Engineering	H8FX	3FT/4FT deg	M+S g	CCD	3M+2D$	Ind	24$	BBCCC	Ind	5	12/18
Fire Engineering	H860	3FT/4FT deg	M+S g	CCD	1M+3D$	Ind	24$	BBCCC	Ind	6	12/13
Fire Safety and Management	H866	3FT deg	C/P g	CCD	1M+3D$	Ind	24$	BBCCC	Ind	
Fire Science	H865	3FT deg	C/P g	CCD	1M+3D$	Ind	24$	BBCCC	Ind	4	10/18
Fuel and Combustion Science	H864	3FT deg	C/P g	CCD	1M+3D$	Ind	24$	BBCCC	Ind	3
LOUGHBOROUGH Univ										
Chemical Engineering	H800	3FT deg	M+C	22	3M+2D	DS6/^ go	28$	Ind	Ind	7	13/20
Chemical Engineering (4 Yr SW)	H801	4SW deg	M+C	22	3M+2D	DS6/^ go	28$	Ind	Ind	5	12/28
Chemical Engineering (4 Yr) (MEng)	H803	4FT deg	M+C	22	3M+2D	DS6/^ go	28$	Ind	Ind	54
Chemical Engineering (5 Yr SW) (MEng)	H802	5SW deg	M+C	22	3M+2D	DS6/^ go	28$	Ind	Ind	3	12/28
Chemical Engineering w. Environmental Protection	H880	3FT deg	M+C	22	3M+2D	DS6/^ go	28$	Ind	Ind	
Chemical Engineering with Bioprocessing	H872	3FT deg	M+C	22	3M+2D	DS6/^ go	28$	Ind	Ind	
Chemical Engineering with Bioprocessing (4Yr SW)	H873	4SW deg	M+C	22	3M+2D	DS6/^ go	28$	Ind	Ind	4
Chemical Engineering with Env Prot (4 Yr SW)	H881	4SW deg	M+C	22	3M+2D	DS6/^ go	28$	Ind	Ind	6
UMIST (Manchester)										
Chemical Eng and Environmental Techn (MEng)	H8F9	4FT deg	M+C g	BBC	MO+3D$	Ind	30$	CSYS$	Ind	4	18/30
Chemical Engineering	H800	3FT deg	M+C g	BBC	MO+3D$	Ind	30$	CSYS$	Ind	8	18/28
Chemical Engineering (MEng)	H801	4FT deg	M+C g	BBC	2M+2D$	Ind	30$	CSYS$	Ind	1	20/30

course details			98 expected requirements							96 entry stats	
TITLE	CODE	COURSE	SUBJECTS	A/AS	ND/C	RGNVQ	IB	SQA(H)	SQA	RATIO	A/AS
Chemical Engineering and Biotechnology (MEng)	HJ88	4FT deg	M+C g	BBC	MO+3D$	Ind	30$	CSYS$	Ind	6	20/30
Chemical Engineering with French (MEng)	H8RC	4FT deg	M+C g	BBC	MO+3D$	Ind	30$	CSYS$	Ind	3	20/30
Chemical Engineering with German (MEng)	H8RF	4FT deg	M+C g	BBC	MO+3D$	Ind	30$	CSYS$	Ind	3	
Chemical Engineering with Industrial Exp (MEng)	H803	4SW deg	M+C g	BBC	2M+2D$	Ind	30$	CSYS$	Ind		
Chemical Engineering with Spanish (MEng)	H8RK	4FT deg	M+C g	BBC	MO+3D$	Ind	30$	CSYS$	Ind		
Univ of NEWCASTLE											
Chemical and Process Engineering (BEng)	H800	3FT/4SW deg	M+C	BCC	Ind		Ind	CSYS$	Ind	4	16/28
Chemical and Process Engineering (BEng)	H801	4FT deg	* g	18	Ind	DE/S	Ind	BBBB	Ind	4	
Chemical and Process Engineering (MEng)	H840	4FT/5SW deg	M+C	BBB	Ind		Ind	CSYS$	Ind	5	24/30
Chemical and Process Engineering (MEng)	H841	5FT deg	* g	18	Ind	DE/S	Ind	BBBB	Ind	14	
Univ of NORTHUMBRIA											
Chemistry with Chemical Engineering	F1H8	3FT/4SW deg	C+S/M g	10	3M	MS gi	24$	CCCC$	Ind	10	
Univ of NOTTINGHAM											
Chemical Engineering	H800	3FT/4FT deg	M+C	BBC-BCC	Ind	Ind	28$	Ind	Ind	8	20/30
OXFORD Univ											
Chemical Engineering (4 Yrs)	H800	4FT deg	M+P	AAB	DO		36	AAAAA	Ind	6	
Univ of PAISLEY											
Chemical Engineering	H800	5SW deg	M+C/P g	CCC-EE	Ind	Ind	Ind	BCC	Ind	5	
QUEEN'S Univ Belfast											
Chemical Engineering	H800	3FT/4FT deg	M+C g	BCC	Ind	Ind	29$	BBBC	Ind	4	18/28
Chemical Engineering Extended Course (MEng)	H802	4FT deg	M+C g	BBB	X	X	32$	X	X	2	22/30
Chemical with Food Eng (Extended Course) (MEng)	H8DL	4FT deg	M+C g	BBB	X	X	32$	X	X		
Chemical with Food Engineering	H8D4	3FT/4FT deg	M+C g	BCC	Ind	Ind	29$	BBBC	Ind		
Univ of SHEFFIELD											
Chemical Eng with Fuel Technology (3/4 Yrs)	H840	3FT/4FT deg	M+C g	BBC-BCC	5M+1D$	X	30$	CSYS	Ind	3	18/30
Chemical Eng with a Modern Language (3/4 Yrs)	H8T9	3FT/4FT deg	M+C+L g	BBC-BCC	5M+1D$	X	30$	CSYS	Ind	6	18/30
Chemical Engineering (including Foundation Yr)	H841	4FT/5FT deg	* g	CCC-CCD	5M+1D$	X	26	BBBC	Ind	20	
Chemical Engineering with Biotechnology(3/4 Yrs)	H8J8	3FT/4FT deg	M+C g	BBC-BCC	5M+1D$	X	30$	CSYS	Ind	7	
Chemical Process Engineering	H800	3FT/4FT deg	M+C g	BBC-BCC	5M+1D$	X	30$	CSYS	Ind	8	16/30
SHEFFIELD HALLAM Univ											
Materials and Environment Engineering	HJ85	3FT/4SW deg	M/S	8	3M $	MS$	Ind	Ind	Ind		
Materials and Environment Engineering (Extended)	HJ8M▼	4EXT/5EXTSW deg									
SOUTH BANK Univ											
Chemical Engineering	H801	3FT/4SW deg	2(M/P/C/B) g	DE	2M	M go	Ind	Ind	Ind		
Chemical Engineering (MEng)	H802	4FT/5SW deg	2(M/P/C/B) g	DE	3M	M go	Ind	Ind	Ind		
Fire Engineering (3/4 years)	H860	3FT deg	S+M g	14-18	4M+2D	M go	Ind	Ind	Ind		
Foundation Chemical Engineering	H808	4EXT deg					Ind	Ind	Ind		
Chemical Engineering	008H	2FT HND	M/P/C/B	E	M $	P go	Ind	Ind	Ind		
Univ of STRATHCLYDE											
Chemical Engineering	H800	4FT deg	C+M+S	CCD			Ind	BBBB$			
Chemical Engineering	H801	5FT deg	C+M+S	ABB			Ind	AAABB$			
Chemical Engineering with Process Biotechnology	H8J8	4FT deg	C+M+P	CCD			Ind	BBBB$			
Univ of SURREY											
Chemical & Bioprocess Engineering with Found Yr	H841	4/5FT/5/6SW deg	* g	18-22	Ind	Ind	Ind	Ind	Ind	2	
Chemical Engineering	H802	3FT deg	M+C+P g	18-22	4M+2D$	X	28$	Ind	Ind	13	
Chemical Engineering	H800	4SW deg	M+C+P g	18-22	4M+2D$	X	28$	Ind	Ind	8	14/26
Chemical Engineering (MEng)	H801	4/5SW deg	M+C+P g	20-24	4M+2D	X	30$	Ind	Ind		

course details			98 expected requirements							96 entry stats	
TITLE	CODE	COURSE	SUBJECTS	R/AS	ND/C	RGNVQ	IB	SQA(H)	SQA	RATIO	R/AS
Chemical Engineering with European Lang (MEng)	H806	4/5SW deg	M+C+P g	20-24	4M+2D	X	30$	Ind	Ind		
Chemical Engineering with a European Language	H804	4SW deg	M+C+P g	18-22	4M+2D$	X	28$	Ind	Ind		
Chemical Engineering with a Foundation Year	H805	4FT/5SW deg	* g	18-22	Ind	Ind	Ind	Ind	Ind	14	
Chemical and Bioprocess Engineering	H840	3/4FT deg	M+C+P/B g	18-22	4M+2D$	X	28$	Ind	Ind		
Chemical and Bioprocess Engineering (MEng)	H842	4/5SW deg	M+C+P/B g	20-24	4M+2D$	X	30$	Ind	Ind	11	
Environmental Chemical Engineering	H813	3FT deg	M+C+P g	18-22	4M+2D$	X	28$	Ind	Ind		
Environmental Chemical Engineering	H810	4SW deg	M+C+P g	18-22	4M+2D$	X	28$	Ind	Ind		
Environmental Chemical Engineering (MEng)	H880	4/5SW deg	M+C+P g	20-24	4M+2D	X	30$	Ind	Ind		

Univ of Wales SWANSEA

Biochemical Engineering	H870	3FT deg	M+C	18-24	Ind	DS^	28$	Ind	Ind	9	
Biochemical Engineering	H873	4FT deg	M+C/2S g	12-16	Ind	DS	Ind	Ind	Ind	5	
Biochemical Engineering with a year in Industry	H872	4FT deg	M+C	20-24	Ind	DS^	28$	Ind	Ind	4	
Chemical Engineering	H800	3FT deg	M+C	20-24	Ind	DS^	28$	Ind	Ind	9	
Chemical Engineering	H803	4FT deg	M+C/2S g	12-16	Ind	DS	Ind	Ind	Ind	3	
Chemical Engineering (MEng)	H801	4FT deg	M+C	20-24	Ind	DS^	28$	Ind	Ind	3	20/24
Chemical Engineering with a year in Europe	H805	4FT deg	M+C g	20-24	Ind	DS^ go	28$	Ind	Ind	4	
Chemical Engineering with a year in Industry	H802	4FT deg	M+C	20-24	Ind	DS^	28$	Ind	Ind	6	

Univ of TEESSIDE

Chemical Engineering	H800	3FT/4SW deg	2(B/C/M/P)	12-20	3M $		Ind	CCC$	Ind	7	4/21
Modular Degree Scheme Chemical Engineering	Y401	3FT deg									
Science and Technology Combined Honours Scheme Chemical Engineering	Y108	3FT deg									
Chemical Engineering	008H	2FT HND	B/C/M/P	4	N		Ind	CD$	N	3	

UNIVERSITY COLL LONDON (Univ of London)

Biochemical Engineering (Process Biot) (MEng)	H871	4FT deg	M+C+P/B g	BBB-ABB	X	X	30$	BBBCC$	X	1	22/24
Biochemical Engineering (Process Biotechnology)	H870	3FT deg	M+C+P/B g	BBB-ABB	X	X	30$	BBBCC$	X	2	
Biochemical Engineering with Study Abroad (MEng)	H872	4FT deg	M+C+P/B g	BBB-ABB	X	X	30$	BBBCC$	X		
Biochemical and Environmental Engineering (MEng)	HH28	4FT deg	M+C+P/B g	BBB-ABB	X	X	30$	BBBCC$	X		
Chemical Engineering	H800	3FT deg	M+C+P/B g	BBB-ABB	X	X	30$	BBBCC$	X	8	18/22
Chemical Engineering (MEng)	H801	4FT deg	M+C+P/B g	BBB-ABB	X	X	30$	BBBCC$	X	5	20/30
Chemical Engineering with Study Abroad (MEng)	H802	4FT deg	M+C+P/B g	BBB-ABB	X	X	30$	BBBCC$	X	4	24/28
Chemical and Biochemical Engineering (MEng)	H875	4FT deg	M+C+P/B g	BBB-ABB	X	X	30$	BBBCC$	X	4	
Chemical and Environmental Engineering (MEng)	H811	4FT deg	M+C+P/B g	BBB-ABB	X	X	30$	BBBCC$	X		

	course details			*98 expected requirements*						*96 entry stats*
TITLE	CODE	COURSE	SUBJECTS	A/AS	ND/C	RGNVQ	IB	SQA(H)	SQA	RATIO A/AS
Univ of ABERDEEN										
Engineering (Civil and Structural)	H200	4FT deg	M+P/Ds g	CC	Ind	MS^ go	26$	BBBCC$	Ind	5
Engineering (Civil and Structural) (MEng)	H205	5FT deg	M+P/Ds g	BC	Ind	MS^ go	28$	AABB$	Ind	10
Univ of ABERTAY DUNDEE										
Civil Engineering	H200	4SW deg	M	CC	6M	Ind	Ind	BBB	Ind	
Civil Engineering (MEng)	H201	4FT deg								
Civil Engineering	002H	2FT HND	g	D	Ind	Ind	Ind	BC	Ind	
ANGLIA Poly Univ										
Law and Surveying	HM23▼	3FT deg	*	12	4M	M	Dip	BBCC	Ind	
Surveying	H260▼	3FT deg	g	8	2M	P go	Dip	CCCC	Ind	
Civil Engineering	002H▼	2FT HND	* g	4	N	P go	Dip	CCC	Ind	
ASTON Univ										
Civil Engineering	H200	3FT/4FT deg	M g	18	7M+3D$	D$6/^ go	29$	BBBBB$	Ind	14 14/16
Civil Engineering	H201	4SW/5SW deg	M g	18	7M+3D$	D$6/^ go	29$	BBBBB$	Ind	6 12/20
Civil Engineering (STEPS)	H202	4FT deg	* g	18	4M	D$ go	29	BBBBB	Ind	27
Civil Engineering with Euro St (MEng)	H2T2	4FT/5SW deg	M g	18	7M+3D$	D$6/^ go	29$	BBBBB$	Ind	8
Univ of BATH										
Civil Engineering	H201	4SW deg	M g	18	Ind	D^	28$	Ind	Ind	21 16/20
Civil and Architectural Engineering (4 Yrs)	H202	4FT deg	M	24	Ind	Ind	30$	Ind	Ind	1
Civil and Architectural Engineering (5 Yr SW)	H203	5SW deg	M	24	Ind	Ind	30$	Ind	Ind	
BELL COLLEGE OF TECHNOLOGY										
Civil Engineering	002H	2FT HND	* g	D	N $	PC	Ind	CC$	Ind	
Univ of BIRMINGHAM										
Civil Engineering	H200	3FT/4FT deg	M g	BBC-CCC	3M+2D$	D$	Ind	Ind	Ind	7 12/26
Civil Engineering with Computational Mechanics	H292	3FT deg	M g	BBC-CCC	3M+2D$	D$	Ind	Ind	Ind	5
Civil Engineering with Environmental Management	H293	3FT deg	M g	BBC-CCC	3M+2D$	D$	Ind	Ind	Ind	6
Civil Engineering with Foundation Year	H294	4FT/5FT deg	* g	BCC-CCC	3M+2D$	M$	Ind	Ind	Ind	6 10/18
Civil Engineering with Management	H291	4FT deg	M g	BBC-CCC	3M+2D$	D$	Ind	Ind	Ind	5 13/30
BOLTON INST										
Business Studies and Civil Engineering	HN21	3FT deg	M g	10	3M	M$	Ind	Ind	Ind	
Civil Engineering	H204	4FT deg	M/S g	4	N	P$	Ind	Ind	Ind	
Civil Engineering	H203	3FT deg	M/S g	4	N	P$	Ind	Ind	Ind	
Civil Engineering	H201	3FT/4SW deg	M g	10	3M $	M$	Ind	Ind	Ind	
Civil Engineering	H208	5EXTSW deg		Ind	Ind	Ind	Ind	Ind	Ind	
Civil Engineering	H200	3FT/4SW deg	M+P/C g	12	5M $	M$	Ind	Ind	Ind	
Civil Engineering (4 years)	H202	4FT deg	M/S g	4	N	P$	Ind	Ind	Ind	
Civil Engineering and Construction	HK22	3FT deg	M/S g	10	3M	M$	Ind	Ind	Ind	
Civil Engineering and Environmental Studies	HF29	3FT deg	M/S g	10	3M	M$	Ind	Ind	Ind	
Civil Engineering and French	HR21	3FT deg	F+M/S	10	3M	Ind	Ind	Ind	Ind	
Civil Engineering and German	HR22	3FT deg	G+M/S	10	3M	Ind	Ind	Ind	Ind	
Civil Engineering and Law	HM23	3FT deg	M/S g	10	3M	M$	Ind	Ind	Ind	
Civil Engineering and Occupational Hlth & Safety	HN26	3FT deg	M/S g	10	3M	M$	Ind	Ind	Ind	
Civil Engineering and Quantity Surveying	HK2F	3FT deg	M/S g	10	3M	M$	Ind	Ind	Ind	
Civil Engineering and Simulation/Virtual Environ	HG27	3FT deg	M/S g	10	3M	M$	Ind	Ind	Ind	
Civil Engineering and Transport Studies	HJ29	3FT deg	M/S g	10	3M	M$	Ind	Ind	Ind	
Civil Engineering Studies	002H	2FT/3SW HND	M/S g	4	N	Ind	Ind	Ind	Ind	

| | | | 98 expected requirements | | | | | | | 96 entry stats | |

TITLE	CODE	COURSE	SUBJECTS	A/AS	NO/C	AGNVQ	IB	SQA(H)	SQA	RATIO	A/AS
Univ of BRADFORD											
Civil and Environmental Engineering	H250	3FT deg	M g	CCC	5M $	M$^	Ind	CCCCD$	Ind		
Civil and Environmental Engineering	H251	4SW deg	M g	CCC	5M $	M$^	Ind	CCCCD$	Ind	1	
Civil and Structural Engineering	H220	3FT deg	M g	BB-CCD	5M $	M$^	Ind	Ind	Ind	8	
Civil and Structural Engineering	H221	4SW deg	M g	BB-CCD	5M $	M$^	Ind	Ind	Ind	6	12/20
Civil and Structural Engineering (Foundation Yr)	H223	4FT/5SW deg	* g	4-6	N	P$	Ind	Ind	Ind	2	4/16
Civil and Structural Engineering (MEng)	H222	4FT deg	M g	BCC	6M+1D$	M$^	Ind	CSYS$	Ind		
Civil and Structural Engineering (MEng)	H224	5SW deg	M g	BCC	6M+1D$	M$^	Ind	CSYS$	Ind		
Environmental Management and Technology	H2F9	3FT deg	S g	BB-CCC	3M $	MS4/^	Ind	Ind	Ind	3	16/18
Environmental Management and Technology	H2FX	4SW deg	S g	BB-CCC	3M $	MS4/^	Ind	Ind	Ind	4	
BRADFORD & ILKLEY Comm COLL											
Civil Engineering	002H	2FT HND	g	2	N$	P		Ind	Ind		
Univ of BRIGHTON											
Architectural Structures (MEng)	HK22	3FT/4SW/4FT/5SW deg	M g	18	2M+3D$	MC2/^ gi	26$	BBBB$	Ind		
Civil Engineering (BEng/MEng)	H200	3FT/4SW 4FT/5SW deg	M g	18	5M+1D$	MC2/^ gi	26$	BBBB$	Ind		
Environmental Engineering (BEng/MEng)	H250	3FT/4SW 4FT/5SW deg	M g	18	5M+1D$	MC2/^ gi	26$	BBBB$	Ind		
Univ of BRISTOL											
Civil Eng with Study in Continental Europe(MEng)	H201	4FT deg	M+P g	BBC	HN $	D$^	30$	CSYS	HN$	4	24/30
Civil Engineering (MEng)	H200	4FT deg	M+P	BBC	HN $	D$^	30$	CSYS	HN$	14	20/30
BRISTOL, Univ of the W of England											
Environmental Engineering	H251	1FT/1/2FT deg	g	X	HN $	X	X	X	Ind		
Environmental Engineering	H250	3FT/4SW deg	M/P g	12-14	MO $	M$1/^ go	24$	BCC$	Ind		
Tunnelling Technology (Bridgwater College)	002H▼	2FT HND	M/S g	2	Dip $	P$6/^ go	24	CD	N		
CARDIFF Univ of Wales											
Architectural Eng (with a Yr in France/Ger/Sp)	H233	5SW deg	M g	18-24	5M+1D		28	Ind	Ind		
Architectural Eng (with a Yr in France/Ger/Sp)	H232	4FT deg	M g	18-24	5M+1D		28	Ind	Ind		
Architectural Engineering	H239	5SW deg	M	18-24	5M+1D		28	Ind	Ind		
Architectural Engineering	H238	4FT deg	M	18-24	5M+1D		28	Ind	Ind		
Architectural Engineering	H237	4SW deg	M	18-24	5M+1D		28$	Ind	Ind	5	16/22
Architectural Engineering	H236	3FT deg	M	18-24	5M+1D$		28$	Ind	Ind	20	
Civil Eng (with a Yr in France/Germany/Spain)	H202	4FT deg	M g	18-24	5M+1D		28	Ind	Ind		
Civil Engineering	H201	4SW deg	M	18-24	5M+1D		28$	Ind	Ind	6	16/26
Civil Engineering	H200	3FT deg	M	18-24	5M+1D$		28$	Ind	Ind	8	18/20
Civil Engineering Design and Management	H222	4FT deg	M	18-24	5M+1D$		28$	Ind	Ind	3	20/30
Civil Engineering Design and Management	H223	5SW deg	M	18-24	5M+1D$		28$	Ind	Ind	3	18/26
Environmental Eng (with a Yr in France/Spain)	H252	4FT deg	M g	BBC-CCC	5M+1D$	Ind	Ind	Ind	Ind		
Environmental Engineering	H250	3FT deg	M	BBC-CCC	5M+1D$	Ind	Ind	Ind	Ind	3	14/24
CITY Univ											
Civil Engineering	H200	3FT deg	M	18	3M+2D$	D$^	27	ABBBB	HN	6	
Civil Engineering	H201	4SW deg	M	18	3M+2D$	D$^	27	ABBBB	HN	11	
Civil Engineering (Foundation)	H202	4EXT deg	*	6	3M	M$	Ind	ABB	N	7	
Civil Engineering (MEng)	H204	4FT deg	M	24	5D $	X	30	AABBB	X	6	
Civil Engineering (MEng)	H205	5SW deg	M	24	5D $	X	30	AABBB	X		
Civil Engineering with Surveying	H206	3FT deg	M	18	3M+2D$	D$	27	ABBBB	HN	13	
Civil Engineering with Surveying	H207	4SW deg	M	18	3M+2D$	D$	27	ABBBB	HN		
Civil Engineering with Surveying (MEng)	H208	4FT deg	M	22	4D $	X	30	AABBB	X	3	
Civil Engineering with Surveying (MEng)	H209	5SW deg	M	22	4D $	X	30	AABBB	X	2	

TITLE	CODE	COURSE	SUBJECTS	A/AS	NO/C	AGNVQ	IB	SQA(H)	SQA	RATIO A/AS
COVENTRY Univ										
Building Structures Engineering	KH22	3FT/4SW deg	M+S g	18	5M $	MC	Ind	Ind	Ind	13
Building Structures Engineering (Extended)	KHF2	4FT/5SW deg	* g	12	3M	M	Ind	Ind	Ind	2
Built Environment Studies	HK22	3FT/4SW deg	* g	10	4M	MC	Ind	Ind	Ind	
Civil Engineering	H200	3FT/4SW/5SW deg	M+S g	18	5M+1D$	MC	Ind	Ind	Ind	39
Civil Engineering	H203	3FT/4SW deg	* g		Ind	Ind	Ind	Ind	Ind	27
Civil Engineering (Extended)	H208	4FT/5SW deg	* g	12	3M	M	Ind	Ind	Ind	11
Civil Engineering Construction	H220	3FT/4SW deg	M g	10	4M	MC	Ind	Ind	Ind	5
Civil Engineering Construction (Extended)	H228	4FT/5SW deg	* g	8	3M	P	Ind	Ind	Ind	
Civil Engineering Construction with European St	H2T2	4FT deg	M g	10	4M	MC	Ind	Ind	Ind	
Civil Engineering with European Studies	H2TF	5FT/6FT deg	M+S g	18	5M+1D$	MC	Ind	Ind	Ind	14
Civil Engineering	002H	2FT/3SW HND	g	4	2M $	PC	Ind	Ind	Ind	9
CRANFIELD Univ										
Civil Engineering	H200	3FT deg	M+P g	CCC	3M+2D	DC/E	Ind	Ind	Ind	28
Environment Engineering (Land and Water)	H255	3FT/4SW deg	M+P g	CCC	4M $	M$6/^ go	30$	BBBB$	Ind	8
Univ of DERBY										
Civil Engineering (Management)	12NH	2FT HND	*	4	N	P	Dip	CCD	Ind	4 4/ 6
DONCASTER COLL										
Quarry and Road Surface Engineering	J1H2	3SW deg		CC	3M	Ind	Ind	Ind	Ind	
Univ of DUNDEE										
Civil Engineering	H200	4FT deg	M g	12	5M $	Ind	Ind	BBCC$	N$	8
Civil Engineering (MEng)	H201	4FT deg	M g	22	Ind	Ind	Ind	AABB$	Ind	
Civil Engineering and Building	HK22	4FT deg	M g	12	5M $	Ind	Ind	BBCC$	N$	6
Civil Engineering and Management	HN21	4FT deg	M g	12	5M $	Ind	Ind	BBCC$	N$	
Univ of DURHAM										
Engineering (Civil) (4 Yrs)	H200	4FT deg	M	22	2M+4D	Ind	30$	AAAAB$	Ind	10 22/30
Environmental Technology	F9H2▼	3FT/4SW deg	2S	DD	Ind	Ind	Dip	CCCCC	Ind	3
Univ of EAST LONDON										
Civil Engineering (BEng Honours)	H200	3FT/4SW deg	g	12	MO	ME	Ind	Ind	Ind	8
Civil Engineering (BEng Ordinary)	H201	3FT deg	* g	12	MO	ME				8
Civil Engineering (BSc Honours)	H203	3FT deg	g	12	MO	ME				8
Civil Engineering (Extended)	H208	4FT/5SW deg	* g	12	MO	ME	Ind	Ind	Ind	1
German/Civil Engineering	HR22	3FT deg	* g	12	MO	M^	Ind	Ind	Ind	
Surveying and Mapping Sciences	H264	3FT deg	* g	12	MO	MC	Ind	Ind	Ind	5
Three-Subject Degree *Civil Engineering*	Y600	3FT deg	* g	12	MO	M	Ind	Ind	Ind	
Civil Engineering	002H	2FT HND	* g	12	MO	ME	Ind	Ind	Ind	4
Land Surveying (FT)	462H	3FT HND	* g	12	MO	M	Ind	Ind	Ind	3 2/ 8
Univ of EDINBURGH										
Civil & Environmental Engineering (MEng)	H253	5FT deg	M+P/B	BCC	MO $			BBBBB$	N$	
Civil Engineering (BEng)	H200	4FT deg	M+P	CCC	MO $		Dip$	BBBB$	N$	8 14/30
Civil Engineering (MEng)	H203	5FT deg	M+P	BCC	MO $			BBBBB$	N$	2
Civil Engineering and Construction Mgt (BEng)	HK22	4FT deg	M+P	CCC	MO $		Dip$	BBBB$	N$	
Civil Engineering and Construction Mgt (MEng)	HK2F	5FT deg	M+P	BCC	MO $		Dip$	BBBB	N$	
Civil and Environmental Engineering (BEng)	H250	4FT deg	M+B/P/C	CCC	MO $		Dip$	BBBB	N$	6
Structural Engineering with Architecture	H2K1	4FT deg	M+P	ABB				BBBBB		
Structural Engineering with Architecture (MEng)	H2KC	4FT deg	M+P	ABB				BBBBB		

course details			98 expected requirements							96 entry stats	
TITLE	CODE	COURSE	SUBJECTS	A/AS	ND/C	AGNVQ	IB	SQA(H)	SQA	RATIO	A/AS
Univ of EXETER											
Civil Engineering (MEng)	H202	4FT deg	<u>M</u> g	BCC	MO+1D	M^	32$	Ind	Ind	6	10/22
Univ of GLAMORGAN											
Civil Engineering	H201	3FT deg	<u>M</u>+S g	6	MO $	M$	24$	CCC$	Ind	3	
Civil Engineering (MEng)	H202	3FT deg	<u>M</u>+S g	12	6M $	M$	Ind	Ind	Ind		
Civil Engineering (SW)	H200	3FT/4SW deg	<u>M</u>+S g	12	6M $	M$	Ind	Ind	Ind	18	
Civil Engineering Foundation Year	H208	3FT deg	g	E	Ind	Ind	Ind	Ind	Ind		
Civil Engineering	002H	2FT/3SW HND	M/P	2	N	P$	Ind	Ind	Ind	4	
Univ of GLASGOW											
Civil Eng with Architecture (MEng or BEng)	H2K1	4FT/5FT deg	M+P	CCD	4M $	M$	24$	BBBB$	N$		
Civil Engineering (MEng or BEng)	H200	4FT/5FT deg	M+P	CCD	4M $	M$	24$	BBBB$	N$	10	12/16
Civil Engineering with Geology (MEng or BEng)	H2F6	4FT/5FT deg	M+P	CCD	4M $	M$	24$	BBBB$	N$	9	
GLASGOW CALEDONIAN Univ											
Environmental Civil Engineering/Civil Eng	H200	3FT/4FT deg	<u>M</u>+P	EE	Ind		Ind	CCC$	Ind	5	
GLOUCESTERSHIRE COLLEGE of Arts and Technology											
Civil Engineering Studies	002H	2FT HND	* g	E	N	P			Ind		
Univ of GREENWICH											
Civil Eng with Water & Environmental Management	H2F9	3FT/4SW deg	M+S g	16	6M	M$2	Ind	Ind	Ind		
Civil Engineering	H200	3FT/4SW deg	<u>M</u>+S g	14-16	6M	M$2	Ind	Ind	Ind		
Civil Engineering	H202	3FT/4SW deg	M+S g	12	5M	M$2	Ind	Ind	Ind		
Civil Engineering (Extended)	H208	4FT/5SW deg	* g	E	N	P$	Ind	Ind	Ind		
Civil Engineering with Project Management	H2N1	3FT/4SW deg	<u>M</u>+S g	16	6M	M$2	24	Ind	Ind		
Civil Engineering with a European Language	H2T2	3FT/4SW deg	<u>M</u>+S g	16	6M	M$2 g	Ind	Ind	Ind		
European Civil Engineering (MEng)	H201	4FT/5SW deg	M+S g	20	M+D	D$2	Ind	Ind	Ind		
Civil Engineering Studies	002H	2FT/3SW HND	* g	E	N	P$	Ind	Ind	Ind		
HERIOT-WATT Univ											
Civil Engineering (MEng)	H200	4FT/5FT deg	M+P	CDD	HN	M$ go	30	BBBC	HN		
Civil Engineering with European Studies (MEng)	H2T2	4FT/5FT deg	M+P	CDD	HN	M$ go	30	BBBC	HN		
Civil and Environmental Engineering (MEng)	H250	4FT/5FT deg	M+P	CDD	HN	M$ go	30	BBBC	HN		
Structural Eng (opt in Architect Design) (MEng)	H240	5FT deg	M+P	CDD	HN	M$ go	30	BBBC	HN		
Combined Studies Civil Engineering	Y100	4FT deg	M+P	DDE	Ind	M$ go	26	BCCC	Ind		
Univ of HERTFORDSHIRE											
Civil Engineering	H200	3FT/4SW deg	<u>M</u>+S	16	5M $	Ind	$	Ind	Ind	9	
Civil Engineering (Extended)	H208▼	4FT/5SW deg	*	2	N	Ind	$	Ind	Ind	4	
Civil Engineering (MEng)	H201	4FT/5SW deg	M+2S	22	5M		Ind	Ind	Ind		
Civil Engineering and Environmental Tech (Ext)	H258▼	4FT/5SW deg	* g	2	N	Ind	Dip$	Ind	Ind		
Civil Engineering and Environmental Technology	H250	3FT/4SW deg	M/P/S/Cs	12	3M	Ind	Ind	Ind			4/10
IMPERIAL COLL (Univ of London)											
Civil Engineering (MEng)	H201	4FT deg	<u>M</u>+P	ABB			32$	CSYS$		7	24/30
Civil Engineering with a Yr in Europe (MEng)	H202	4FT deg	<u>M</u>+P g	ABB			32$	CSYS$		5	26/30
Civil and Environ Eng with a Yr in Eur (MEng)	H251	4FT deg	<u>M</u>+P g	ABB			32$	CSYS$		7	
Civil and Environmental Engineering (MEng)	H250	4FT deg	<u>M</u>+P	ABB			32$	CSYS$		10	
KINGSTON Univ											
Civil Engineering	H208	4EXT/5EXTSW deg	*	CC-DD	N	M	Ind	CSYS	Ind	4	
Civil Engineering (BEng/MEng)	H203	3FT/4FT deg	M+S	18	Ind	MC<u>3</u>	Ind	Ind	Ind		
Civil Engineering (BEng/MEng)	H204	4SW/5SW deg	M+S	18	Ind	MC<u>3</u>	Ind	Ind	Ind		
Civil Engineering Commercial Management	H262	4FT SW deg		10	3M	M	M				

| | | | | 98 expected requirements | | | | | | 96 entry stats | |
| | | | | | | | | | | | |

TITLE	CODE	COURSE	SUBJECTS	A/AS	NO/C	AGNVQ	IB	SQA(H)	SQA	RATIO A/AS	
Civil Engineering Commercial Management	H261	3FT deg		10	3M	Ind	M	CSYS	Ind	10	
Civil Engineering Studies	H202	3FT deg	M	10	3M	Ind	Ind	CSYS	Ind	5	
Civil Engineering Studies	H205	4SW deg	M	10	3M	Ind	Ind	CSYS	Ind		
Environmental Engineering	H250	3FT deg		10	3M	Ind	Ind	CSYS	Ind		
Civil Engineering Studies	002H	2FT/3SW HND		4	N	Ind	Ind	CSYS	Ind	2	2/8

Univ of LEEDS

TITLE	CODE	COURSE	SUBJECTS	A/AS	NO/C	AGNVQ	IB	SQA(H)	SQA	RATIO A/AS	
Architectural Engineering (4 Yrs)	H2KC	4FT deg	M g	CCC	3M+2D$	Ind	26$	BBBCC	Ind	5	12/26
Civil Engineering	H200	3FT/4FT deg	M g	CCC	3M+2D$	Ind	26$	BBBCC	Ind	6	12/24
Civil Engineering with Transport Engineering	H2J9	3FT deg	M g	CCC	Ind	Ind	Ind	Ind	Ind		
Civil Engineering with Architecture	H2K1	3FT/4FT deg	M g	CCC	3M+2D$	Ind	26$	BBBCC	Ind	6	14/22
Civil Engineering with Construction Mgt	H202	3FT/4FT deg	M g	CCC	3M+2D$	Ind	26$	BBBCC	Ind	7	16/24
Civil and Environmental Engineering	H2F9	3FT/4FT deg	M g	CCC	3M+2D$	Ind	26$	BBBCC	Ind	14	12/20

LEEDS METROPOLITAN Univ

TITLE	CODE	COURSE	SUBJECTS	A/AS	NO/C	AGNVQ	IB	SQA(H)	SQA	RATIO A/AS	
Civil Engineering	H200	3FT/4SW deg	M/S g	EE	2M $	M$3/^ go	Dip$	BCC$	Ind	7	4/13
Civil Engineering Commercial Management	H262	1FT deg								6	
Civil Engineering	002H	2FT/3SW HND	M/S g	E	N	PC go	20$	CC$	Ind	4	4/6

Univ of LIVERPOOL

TITLE	CODE	COURSE	SUBJECTS	A/AS	NO/C	AGNVQ	IB	SQA(H)	SQA	RATIO A/AS	
Civil Engineering (BEng Hons)	H221	4EXT deg	*	18	6M	Ind	26$	BBBCC	Ind	2	6/20
Civil Engineering (BEng)	H200	3FT deg	M	20	5M+2D$	Ind	30$	BBBBB$	Ind	16	14/26
Civil and Environmental Engineering (MEng)	HK23	4FT deg	M	20	5M+2D$	Ind	30$	BBBBB$	Ind	11	
Civil and Maritime Engineering (MEng)	HJ26	4FT deg	M	20	5M+2D$	Ind	30$	BBBBB$	Ind	6	
Civil and Structural Engineering (MEng)	H220	4FT deg	M	20	5M+2D$	Ind	30$	BBBBB$	Ind	12	

LIVERPOOL JOHN MOORES Univ

TITLE	CODE	COURSE	SUBJECTS	A/AS	NO/C	AGNVQ	IB	SQA(H)	SQA	RATIO A/AS	
Civil Engineering	H200	4SW deg	M	18	1M+3D	M4				20	
Civil Engineering (Extended)	H208▼	5EXTSW deg	M	12	1M+2D					25	
Civil Engineering (Ordinary)	H201	3FT deg									
Environmental Engineering	H250	3FT deg		10	5M	MC				7	
Civil Engineering Studies	002H	3SW HND	M	EE	N	MC				7	
Civil Engineering Studies (Extended)	802H▼	4FT HND	M	EE	N						

LOUGHBOROUGH Univ

TITLE	CODE	COURSE	SUBJECTS	A/AS	NO/C	AGNVQ	IB	SQA(H)	SQA	RATIO A/AS	
Civil Engineering	H200	3FT deg	M g	20	3M+2D	DE6/^ go	28$	Ind	Ind	6	14/22
Civil Engineering (4 Yr SW)	H201	4SW deg	M g	20	3M+2D	DE6/^ go	28$	Ind	Ind	5	14/24
Civil Engineering (4 Yr) (MEng)	H203	4FT deg	M g	22	3M+2D	DE6/^ go	28$	Ind	Ind	15	18/20
Civil Engineering (5 Yr SW) (MEng)	H202	5SW deg	M g	22	3M+2D	DE6/^ go	28$	CSYS	Ind	6	20/28
Civil and Building Engineering (4 Yr MEng)	H2K2	4FT deg	M g	22	3M+2D	DE6/^ go	28$	Ind	Ind		
Civil and Building Engineering (5 Yr SW MEng)	H2KF	5SW deg	M g	22	3M+2D	DE6/^ go	28$	Ind	Ind	6	
Commercial Mgt and Quantity Surveying (4 Yr SW)	HK22	4SW deg	* g	22	3M+2D	D*6/^ go	28	Ind	Ind	4	12/26

LUTON Univ

TITLE	CODE	COURSE	SUBJECTS	A/AS	NO/C	AGNVQ	IB	SQA(H)	SQA	RATIO A/AS	
Stage & Screen Technology and Digital Systs Des	PHK2	3FT deg		12-16	MO/DO	M/D	32	BBCC	Ind		

Univ of MANCHESTER

TITLE	CODE	COURSE	SUBJECTS	A/AS	NO/C	AGNVQ	IB	SQA(H)	SQA	RATIO A/AS	
Civil Engineering	H200	3FT deg	M+P	CCC	4M+2D$		30$	Ind	Ind	13	18/24
Civil Engineering (Classified)	H202	4FT deg	M+P	CCC						1	
Civil Engineering (Int Eur Prog)(MEng)	H210	4FT deg	M+P	CCC	4M+2D$		30$	Ind	Ind	12	
Civil Engineering (Int Japanese Programme)	H203	4SW deg									
Structural Eng with Arch (Int Eur Prog) (MEng)	H2KC	4FT deg		18	4M+2D$		30$	Ind	Ind	5	26/30
Structural Engineering with Arch (Japanese)	HK21	4SW deg									
Structural Engineering with Architecture	H2K1	4FT deg		18	4M+2D$		30$	Ind	Ind	9	16/18
Structural Engineering with Architecture (4 Yrs)	H2KD	4FT deg								3	

			98 expected requirements							**96 entry stats**

course details

TITLE	CODE	COURSE	SUBJECTS	A/AS	NO/C	AGNVQ	IB	SQA(H)	SQA	RATIO A/AS
UMIST (Manchester)										
Building Services Engineering (4 years)	H240	4FT deg	P g	18	2M+2D$	M$6/^ go	30$	ABB$	Ind	
Civil Engineering	H200	3FT deg	C g	BCC	3M+1D	Ind	30	CSYS	Ind	5
Civil Engineering (4 years)	H201	4FT deg	M+P g	BCC	3M+3D$	Ind	30$	CSYS	Ind	6 16/30
Civil Engineering and Environmental Mgt (MEng)	H2N8	4FT deg	M+P g	BCC	3M+3D$	Ind	30$	CSYS	Ind	2 18/22
Civil Engineering with French (MEng)	H2R1	4FT deg	M+P g	BBC	Ind	Ind	30$	CSYS	Ind	
Civil Engineering with German (MEng)	H2R2	4FT deg	M+P g	BBC	Ind	Ind	30$	CSYS	Ind	
Civil Engineering with N American Studies (MEng)	H2Q4	4FT deg	M+P g	BBC	Ind	Ind	30$	CSYS	Ind	
Civil and Structural Engineering (MEng)	H220	4FT deg	M+P g	BCC	3M+3D$	Ind	30$	CSYS	Ind	12 14/22
NAPIER Univ										
Civil Engineering	H200	3SW/4SW deg		DD	Ind	Ind	Ind	CCC	Ind	5
Civil and Transportation Engineering	HH23	3SW/4SW deg	M	CC	Ind	Ind	Ind	BBCC$	Ind	5
Civil Engineering	002H	2FT HND	*	D	Ind	Ind	Ind	CC	Ind	2
Univ of NEWCASTLE										
Civil Engineering	H200	3FT deg	M	CCC	MO $		Ind	CSYS	Ind	10 8/18
Civil Engineering	H201	4FT deg	g	CCC	MO $		Ind	BBBCC	Ind	10
Civil Engineering (MEng)	H291	5FT deg	g	BBC	MO $		Ind	BBBCC	Ind	3
Civil Engineering (MEng)	H290	4FT deg	M	BBC	MO $		Ind	CSYS	Ind	3 12/24
Civil and Environmental Engineering	H250	3FT deg	M	CCC	MO $		Ind	CSYS$	Ind	14
Civil and Environmental Engineering	H251	4FT deg	g	CCC	MO $		Ind	BBBCC	Ind	
Civil and Environmental Engineering (MEng)	H252	4FT deg	M	BBC	MO $		Ind	CSYS$	Ind	4 18/24
Civil and Environmental Engineering (MEng)	H253	5FT deg	g	BBC	MO $		Ind	BBBCC	Ind	
Computing Science and Surveying and Mapping Sci	GH5F	3FT deg	M	18	4M	Ind	28$	AABBB	Ind	5
Environmental and Ecological Engineering	HD2F	4FT deg	* g	CCC	3M $		26	BBCCC	Ind	10
Environmental and Ecological Engineering	HD22	3FT deg	M+C/P	CCC	MO $		28$	CSYS$	Ind	14
Geography and Surveying and Mapping Science	HF28	3FT deg	Gy+M	18	4M	Ind	28$	AABBB	Ind	12
Mathematics and Surveying and Mapping Science	GH12	3FT deg	M	18	4M	Ind	28$	AABBB	Ind	3
Structural Engineering	H240	3FT deg	M+P	BCC	MO $		Ind	CSYS	Ind	8
Structural Engineering	H241	4FT deg	g	CCC	MO $		Ind	BBBCC	Ind	7
Structural Engineering (MEng)	H242	4FT deg	M+P	BCC	MO $		Ind	CSYS	Ind	5
Structural Engineering (MEng)	H243	5FT deg	g	CCC	MO $		Ind	BBBCC	Ind	
Surveying and Mapping Science	H260	3FT deg	* g	CCC	Ind	M$ go	Ind	BBBB$	Ind	3 12/24
Combined Studies (BSc) *Surveying and Mapping Science*	Y100	3FT deg	M+S	18	4M	Ind	28$	AABBB	Ind	
NESCOT										
Environmental Engineering	H258	4FT deg	*							
Environmental Engineering	H250	3FT deg	*	EE	N	M	Dip	Ind	N$	
Civil Engineering	002H	2FT/3SW HND	*	E	N	P	Dip	Ind	N$	
Univ of NORTHUMBRIA										
Building Services Engineering	H250	4SW deg	M+P/S	12	5M $	MC/E2 gi	24$	CCCC$	Ind	3
Building Services Engineering	H258	5EXT deg	* g	2-4	N	P gi	24	CCC	Ind	2
Building Services Engineering	052H	2FT HND	M/P g	2-4	N	PC/E1 gi	Ind	C$	Ind	6
Univ of NOTTINGHAM										
Civil Engineering	H200	3FT/4FT deg	M+P	BBC-BCC	Ind	Ind	28$	Ind	Ind	7 22/30
Civil Engineering with French	H2R1	3FT/4FT deg	M+P g	BBC-BCC	Ind	Ind	28$	Ind	Ind	6 26/30
Civil Engineering with German	H2R2	3FT/4FT deg	M+P g	BBC-BCC	Ind	Ind	28$	Ind	Ind	7
Environmental Engineering and Resource Mgt	H250	3FT deg	M	BCC-CCC	Ind	Ind	28$	Ind	Ind	3 12/28

course details			98 expected requirements							96 entry stats
TITLE	CODE	COURSE	SUBJECTS	A/AS	ND/C	AGNVQ	IB	SQA(H)	SQA	RATIO A/AS
NOTTINGHAM TRENT Univ										
Civil Engineering	H200	3FT/4SW deg	M+P g	14	4M+1D$		Ind	$	Ind	7 8/16
Civil Engineering (BSc)	H202	3FT/4SW deg	M+S	8-10	3M	MC	Ind	Ind	Ind	4/10
Civil Engineering (Commercial Management) (Ext)	H209▼	4EXT/5EXTSW deg	* g		Ind	Ind	Ind	Ind	Ind	1
Civil Engineering (Extended)	H208▼	4EXT/5EXTSW deg	* g		Ind	Ind	Ind	Ind	Ind	16
Civil Engineering Commercial Management	H201	3FT/4SW deg	* g	12	5M $		Ind	CCC	Ind	5 8/14
Civil Engineering Geology	H265	3FT/4SW deg	M+S	8-10	3M	MC	Ind	Ind	Ind	
Civil Engineering Surveying	H260	3FT/4SW deg	M+P	14	4M+D	D/MC6	Ind	Ind	Ind	2
Civil Engineering Surveying (BSc)	H261	3FT/4SW deg	M+S	8-10	3M	MC	Ind	Ind	Ind	1
Civil Engineering with Management	H2N1	3FT/4SW deg	M+P	14	4M+D	D/MC6	Ind	Ind	Ind	
Civil and Environmental Engineering	H250	3FT/4SW deg	M+P	14	4M+D	D/MC6	Ind	Ind	Ind	
Engineering Surveying (Extended)	H268▼	4EXT/5EXTSW deg	* g		Ind	Ind	Ind	Ind	Ind	
Structural Engineering	H240	3FT/4SW deg	M+P	14	4M+D	D/MC6	Ind	Ind	Ind	
Civil Engineering	002H	2FT HND	* g	6	3M		Ind	Ind	Ind	5 4/7
Civil Engineering Commercial Management	462H	2FT/3SW HND	* g	4	3M $		Ind	Ind	Ind	2 4/6
OXFORD Univ										
Civil Engineering (4 Yrs)	H200	4FT deg	M+P	AAB	DO		36	AAAAA	Ind	8
OXFORD BROOKES Univ										
Civil Engineering	H201	3FT/4SW deg	M g	CD-DDE	Ind	M$^	Ind	Ind	Ind	
Civil Engineering (BEng)	H200	3FT/4SW deg	M+P g	CC-DDD	Ind	M$^	Ind	Ind	Ind	3 9/14
Civil Engineering (MEng)	H202	4FT/5SW deg	M+P g	CC-DDD	Ind	M$^	Ind	Ind	Ind	11
Civil Engineering Foundation	H208	4FT/5SW deg	* g	10	Ind	P*	Ind	Ind	Ind	1
Geography and the Phys Env/Geotechnics	FHV2	3FT deg								
Geotechnics/Accounting and Finance	HN24	3FT deg	S/M/Ds/Es	DD-BCC	Ind	M$/D*3	Ind	Ind	Ind	
Geotechnics/Anthropology	HL26	3FT deg	S/M/Ds/Es	DD-BCC	Ind	M$^	Ind	Ind	Ind	
Geotechnics/Biological Chemistry	CH72	3FT deg								
Geotechnics/Biology	CH12	3FT deg	S/M/Ds/Es g	DD-DDD	Ind	M$	Ind	Ind	Ind	
Geotechnics/Business Administration & Management	HN21	3FT deg	S/M/Ds/Es	DD-BBC	Ind	M$/MB4	Ind	Ind	Ind	
Geotechnics/Cartography	FH82	3FT deg	S/M/Ds/Es	CC-DD	Ind	M$	Ind	Ind	Ind	
Geotechnics/Cell Biology	CHC2	3FT deg								
Geotechnics/Combined Studies	HY24	3FT deg		X		X	X	X		
Geotechnics/Computer Systems	GH62	3FT deg	S/M/Ds/Es	DD-BC	Ind	M$	Ind	Ind	Ind	
Geotechnics/Computing	GH52	3FT deg	S/M/Ds/Es g	CC-DD	Ind	M$	Ind	Ind	Ind	1
Geotechnics/Computing Mathematics	GH92	3FT deg	S/M/Ds/Es	CC-DD	Ind	M$	Ind	Ind	Ind	
Geotechnics/Ecology	CH92	3FT deg	S/M/Ds/Es g	DD-CC	Ind	M$	Ind	Ind	Ind	
Geotechnics/Economics	HL21	3FT deg	S/M/Ds/Es	DD-BB	Ind	M$/M*3	Ind	Ind	Ind	
Geotechnics/Educational Studies	HX29	3FT deg	S/M/Ds/Es	CC-DD	Ind	M$/M*3	Ind	Ind	Ind	
Geotechnics/Electronics	HH26	3FT deg	S/M	CC-DD	Ind	M$	Ind	Ind	Ind	
Geotechnics/English Studies	HQ23	3FT deg	S/M/Ds/Es	DD-AB	Ind	M$^	Ind	Ind	Ind	
Geotechnics/Environmental Chemistry	HF21	3FT deg								
Geotechnics/Environmental Policy	KH32	3FT deg								
Geotechnics/Environmental Sciences	FHX2	3FT deg	S/M/Ds/Es g	CC-DD	Ind	M$/DS	Ind	Ind	Ind	
Geotechnics/Exercise and Health	HB26	3FT deg	S/M/Ds/Es	DD-CC	Ind	M$	Ind	Ind	Ind	
Geotechnics/Fine Art	HW21	3FT deg	Pf+S/M+A/Ds/Es	BC-DD	Ind	M$^	Ind	Ind	Ind	
Geotechnics/Food Science and Nutrition	DH42	3FT deg	S/M/Ds/Es g	DD-CC	Ind	M$	Ind	Ind	Ind	
Geotechnics/French Language and Contemp Studies	HR2C	4SW deg	F+S/M/Ds/Es	CC-DD	Ind	M$^	Ind	Ind	Ind	
Geotechnics/French Language and Literature	HR21	4SW deg	F+S/M/Ds/Es	CC-DD	Ind	M$^	Ind	Ind	Ind	
Geotechnics/Geography	HL28	3FT deg	S/M/Ds/Es	DD-BB	Ind	M$	Ind	Ind	Ind	
Geotechnics/Geology	FH62	3FT deg	S/M/Ds/Es	DD-CC	Ind	PS/M$	Ind	Ind	Ind	
German Language and Contemp Stud/Geotechnics	HR2F	4SW deg	G+S/M/Ds/Es	CC-DD	Ind	M$^	Ind	Ind	Ind	
German Language and Literature/Geotechnics	HR22	4SW deg	G+S/M/Ds/Es	CC-DD	Ind	M$^	Ind	Ind	Ind	

			98 expected requirements							96 entry stats

course details

TITLE	CODE	COURSE	SUBJECTS	A/AS	ND/C	AGNVQ	IB	SQA(H)	SQA	RATIO A/AS
German Studies/Geotechnics	HR2G	4SW deg			Ind		Ind	Ind	Ind	
Health Care/Geotechnics (Post Exp)	BH72	3FT deg		X		X	X	X		
History of Art/Geotechnics	HV24	3FT deg	S/M/Ds/Es	DD-BCC	Ind	M$/M*^	Ind	Ind	Ind	
History/Geotechnics	HV21	3FT deg	S/M	DD-BB	Ind	M$/M*^	Ind	Ind	Ind	
Hospitality Management Studies/Geotechnics	HN27	3FT deg	S/M	CC-DDD	Ind	M$/M$3	Ind	Ind	Ind	
Human Biology/Geotechnics	BH12	3FT deg								
Information Systems/Geotechnics	GHN2	3FT deg	S/M/Ds/Es g	DD-BC	Ind	M$	Ind	Ind	Ind	
Intelligent Systems/Geotechnics	GH82	3FT deg	S/M/Ds/Es	CC-DD	Ind	M$	Ind	Ind	Ind	
Law/Geotechnics	HM23	3FT deg	S/M/Ds/Es	DD-BBB	Ind	M$/D*3	Ind	Ind	Ind	
Leisure Planning/Geotechnics	KHH2	3FT deg								
Marketing Management/Geotechnics	HN2N	3FT deg	S/M/Ds/Es g	DD-BCC	Ind	M$/D*3	Ind	Ind	Ind	
Mathematics/Geotechnics	GH12	3FT deg	M	DD-CC	Ind	M$/M*_	Ind	Ind	Ind	
Music/Geotechnics	HW23	3FT deg	Mu+S/M/Ds/Es	DD-CC	Ind	M$	Ind	Ind	Ind	
Palliative Care/Geotechnics (Post Exp)	BHR2	3FT deg		X		X	X	X		
Planning Studies/Geotechnics	HK24	3FT deg	S/M/Ds/Es	DD-DDD	Ind	M$	Ind	Ind	Ind	
Politics/Geotechnics	HM21	3FT deg	S/M/Ds/Es	DD-AB	Ind	M$^	Ind	Ind	Ind	
Psychology/Geotechnics	CH82	3FT deg	S/M/Ds/Es g	DD-BBC	Ind	M$/M*^	Ind	Ind	Ind	
Publishing/Geotechnics	HP25	3FT deg	S/M/Ds/Es g	DD-BB	Ind	M$/M$3	Ind	Ind	Ind	
Rehabilitation/Geotechnics (Post Exp)	BHT2	3FT deg		X		X	X	X		
Retail Management/Geotechnics	HN25	3FT deg	S/M g	DD-CCD	Ind		Ind	Ind	Ind	
Sociology/Geotechnics	HL23	3FT deg	S/M/Ds/Es	DD-BCC	Ind	M$/M*^	Ind	Ind	Ind	
Software Engineering/Geotechnics	GH72	3FT deg	S/M/Ds/Es g	DD-BC	Ind	M$	Ind	Ind	Ind	
Statistics/Geotechnics	GH42	3FT deg	S/M/Ds/Es	DD-CC	Ind	M$	Ind	Ind	Ind	
Telecommunications/Geotechnics	HH2P	3FT deg								
Tourism/Geotechnics	HP27	3FT deg	S/M/Ds/Es	DD-BC	Ind	M$/M*3	Ind	Ind	Ind	
Transport Planning/Geotechnics	HN29	3FT deg	S/M/Ds/Es	CC-DD	Ind	M$	Ind	Ind	Ind	
Water Resources/Accounting and Finance	HNF4	3FT deg								
Water Resources/Anthropology	HLF6	3FT deg								
Water Resources/Biological Chemistry	CH7F	3FT deg								
Water Resources/Biology	CH1F	3FT deg								
Water Resources/Business Administration and Mgt	HNF1	3FT deg								
Water Resources/Cartography	FH8F	3FT deg								
Water Resources/Cell Biology	CHCF	3FT deg								
Water Resources/Combined Studies	HYF4	3FT deg		X		X	X	X		
Water Resources/Computer Systems	GH6F	3FT deg								
Water Resources/Computing	GH5F	3FT deg								
Water Resources/Computing Mathematics	GH9F	3FT deg								
Water Resources/Ecology	CH9F	3FT deg								
Water Resources/Economics	HLF1	3FT deg								
Water Resources/Educational Studies	HXF9	3FT deg								
Water Resources/Electronics	HH6F	3FT deg								
Water Resources/English Studies	HQF3	3FT deg								
Water Resources/Environmental Chemistry	FH1F	3FT deg								
Water Resources/Environmental Policy	HKF3	3FT deg								
Water Resources/Environmental Sciences	FHXF	3FT deg								
Water Resources/Exercise and Health	BH6F	3FT deg								
Water Resources/Fine Art	HWF1	3FT deg								
Water Resources/Food Science and Nutrition	DH4F	3FT deg								
Water Resources/French Language and Comtemp St	HRFC	3FT deg								
Water Resources/French Language and Literature	HRF1	3FT deg								
Water Resources/Geography	HLF8	3FT deg								
Water Resources/Geology	FH6F	3FT deg								

TITLE	CODE	COURSE	SUBJECTS	A/AS	ND/C	AGNVQ	IB	SQA(H)	SQA	RATIO A/AS
course details			98 expected requirements							96 entry stats
Water Resources/Geotechnics	HH2F	3FT deg								
Water Resources/German Language and Contemp Stud	HRFF	3FT deg								
Water Resources/German Language and Literature	HRF2	3FT deg								
Water Resources/German Studies	HRFG	3FT deg								
Water Resources/Health Care	BH7F	3FT deg		X		X	X	X		
Water Resources/History	HVF1	3FT deg								
Water Resources/History of Art	HVF4	3FT deg								
Water Resources/Hospitality Management Studies	HNF7	3FT deg								
Water Resources/Human Biology	BH1F	3FT deg								
Water Resources/Information Systems	HGFM	3FT deg								
Water Resources/Intelligent Systems	GH8F	3FT deg								
Water Resources/Law	HMF3	3FT deg								
Water Resources/Leisure Planning and Management	HKFH	3FT deg								
Water Resources/Marketing Management	HNFN	3FT deg								
Water Resources/Mathematics	GH1F	3FT deg								
Water Resources/Music	HWF3	3FT deg								
Water Resources/Palliative Care	BHRF	3FT deg		X		X	X	X		
Water Resources/Physical Geography	FHVF	3FT deg								
Water Resources/Planning Studies	HKF4	3FT deg								
Water Resources/Politics	HMF1	3FT deg								
Water Resources/Psychology	CH8F	3FT deg								
Water Resources/Publishing	HPF5	3 deg								
Water Resources/Rehabilitation	BHTF	3FT deg		X		X	X	X		
Water Resources/Sociology	HLF3	3FT deg								
Water Resources/Software Engineering	GH7F	3FT deg								
Water Resources/Statistics	GH4F	3FT deg								
Water Resources/Telecommunications	HHFP	3FT deg								
Water Resources/Tourism	HPF7	3FT deg								
Water Resources/Transport Planning	HNF9	3FT deg								
Civil Engineering Studies	002H	3SW HND	* g	E	Ind		Ind	Ind	Ind	4

Univ of PAISLEY

TITLE	CODE	COURSE	SUBJECTS	A/AS	ND/C	AGNVQ	IB	SQA(H)	SQA	RATIO A/AS
Civil Engineering	H200	4SW deg	M g	CDD	Ind	Ind	Ind	BBBC$	Ind	5
Civil Engineering	H201	3FT deg	M g	EE	Ind	Ind	Ind	CCC$	Ind	
Civil Engineering (MEng)	H202	5SW deg	M g	CCC	Ind	Ind	Ind	ABBC$	Ind	
Civil Engineering with Architectural Studies	H205	3FT deg	M g	EE	Ind	Ind	Ind	CCC$	SQA	
Civil Engineering with Environmental Studies	H252	3FT deg	M g	EE	Ind	Ind	Ind	CCC$	Ind	
Civil and Environmental Engineering	H251	5SW deg	M g	CCC	Ind	Ind	Ind	ABBC$	Ind	
Civil and Environmental Engineering	H250	4SW deg	M g	CDD	Ind	Ind	Ind	BBBC$	Ind	9
Structural Eng with Architectural Studies (MEng)	H2KD	5SW deg	M g	CCC	Ind	Ind	Ind	ABBC$	Ind	
Structural Engineering with Architectural Studs	H2K1	4SW deg	M g	CDD	Ind	Ind	Ind	BBBC$	Ind	9

Univ of PLYMOUTH

TITLE	CODE	COURSE	SUBJECTS	A/AS	ND/C	AGNVQ	IB	SQA(H)	SQA	RATIO A/AS
Civil Engineering (BSc)	H201	3FT/4SW deg	Ap g	4	MO $	P$	Ind	Ind	Ind	6/10
Civil Engineering (MEng Option)	H200	3FT/4SW 4FT/5SW deg	Ap g	14	MO $	M$^	Ind	BCCC $	Ind	7 10/16
Civil and Coastal Engineering	H256	3FT/4SW deg	Ap g	4	MO $	P$	Ind	Ind	Ind	
Civil and Coastal Engineering (MEng Option)	H255	3FT/4SW 4FT/5SW deg	Ap g	14	MO $	M$^	Ind	BCCC	Ind	
Environmental Design and Management	H250	3FT/4SW deg	Ap g		5M $	M$	Ind	Ind	Ind	
Civil Engineering Studies	002H	2FT/3SW HND	Ap g	2	N $	P$	Ind	Ind	Ind	4 4/7

Univ of PORTSMOUTH

TITLE	CODE	COURSE	SUBJECTS	A/AS	ND/C	AGNVQ	IB	SQA(H)	SQA	RATIO A/AS
Civil Engineering (BTech)	H201	3FT deg	M/P/S	4	N $	P$6/^	Dip$	Ind	Ind	6/10
Civil Engineering (MEng) (Ext Route Available)	H200	3FT/4SW deg	M+P/S	12-16	5M $	M$^	Dip$	BCCC	Ind	14
Civil Engineering with Engineering Geology(MEng)	H2F6	3FT/4SW deg	M+P/S	12-16	5M $	M$^	Dip	BCCC	Ind	1

course details			**98 expected requirements**							*96 entry stats*	
TITLE	CODE	COURSE	SUBJECTS	A/AS	ND/C	AGNVQ	IB	SQA(H)	SQA	RATIO	A/AS
Environmental Assessment (Construction Industry)	FH92	3FT deg	*	16	4M	M$6/^	26	BBBB	Ind	7	6/14
Environmental Engin (MEng) (Ext Route Avail)	H250	3FT/4SW deg	2(M/P/C/Es/Cs)	16	4M $	M$6/^	28$	BBBB	N$	5	8/12
Civil Engineering Studies	002H	2FT/3SW HND	M/P/S	4	N $	P$	Dip$	Ind	Ind	4	
QUEEN MARY & WESTFIELD COLL (Univ of London)											
Civil Engineering	H200	3FT deg	M	CCD-BCC	6M	D$^	28$	BBBCC			
Civil Engineering	H201	4SW deg	M	CCD-BCC	6M	D$^	28$	BBBCC			
Civil Engineering (MEng)	H202	4FT deg	M+P	BCC-BBB	6M $	D$^	28$	BBBCC			
Civil Engineering Systems (MEng)	H203	4FT deg	M+P	BCC-BBB	6M	D$^	28	BBBCC			
Science and Engineering (4 yrs with Foundation) *Civil Engineering*	Y157	4EXT deg		E	N	P					
QUEEN'S Univ Belfast											
Civil Engineering	H200	3FT/4FT deg	M+S	BCC	Ind	Ind	29$	BBBC	Ind	5	16/24
Civil Engineering Extended Course (MEng)	H202	4FT deg	M+S	BBB	X	X	32$	X	X	5	22/30
Environmental and Civil Engineering Extnd course	H252	4FT deg									
Univ of SALFORD											
Civil Engineering	H210	4FT/5SW deg									
Civil Engineering (3 or 4 Yrs)	H200	3FT/4SW deg	M	12	Ind	M$	Ind	Ind	Ind	20	10/16
Civil Engineering (Stockport)(4 Yrs)	H202	4FT deg			Ind	M	Ind	Ind	Ind		
Civil Engineering Technology (3/4 Yrs)	H208	3FT/4SW deg	M g	EEE	Ind	M$	Ind	Ind	Ind		
Civil Engineering with European Studies	H2TF	4FT deg	F/G/Sp	EEE		M^					
Civil Engineering with European Studies (4 Yrs)	H2T2	4SW deg	M g	EEE	Ind	M$	Ind	Ind	Ind	11	
Civil Engineering with Transport	H205	4FT deg		12	4M+1D	M					
Civil Engineering with Transport (3 or 4 Yrs)	H204	3FT/4SW deg	M g	12	Ind	M$	Ind	Ind	Ind	11	
Environmental Eng with European Studies (4 Yrs)	H207	4SW deg	M g	EEE	Ind	M$	Ind	Ind	Ind	3	
Environmental Engineering (3 or 4 Yrs)	H206	3FT/4SW deg	M g	12	Ind	M$	Ind	Ind	Ind	9	
Univ of SHEFFIELD											
Civil & Structural Eng (incl Found Yr)(4/5 Yrs)	H221	4FT/5FT deg	M+S g	BCC	X	M$^	28$	BBBC$	Ind	17	
Civil Engineering and Law	H2M3	4FT deg	M g	AAB	X	X	35$	AAAA$			
Civil Engineering with Architecture	H2K1	3FT/4FT deg	M+S+Pf g	BCC	5M+1D$	M$^	28$	BBBB$	Ind	10	18/24
Civil Engineering with a Modern Lang (3/4 Yrs)	H2T9	3FT/4FT deg	M+S g	BCC	X	M$^	28$	BBBB$	Ind	5	18/26
Civil and Environmental Engineering (3/4 Yrs)	H250	3FT/4FT deg	M+S g	BCC	5M+1D$	M$^	28$	BBBB$	Ind	10	18/24
Civil and Structural Engineering (3/4 Yrs)	H220	3FT/4FT deg	M+S g	BCC	5M+1D	M$^	28$	BBBB$	Ind	6	16/28
Structural Engineering and Architecture	HK21	4FT deg	M+S+Pf g	BBB	X	D^	32$	AABB$	Ind	4	20/30
SHEFFIELD HALLAM Univ											
Building Engineering	H240	4SW deg	S/M	16	6M $	M$2	Ind	BBBCC$	Ind		
Civil Engineering	H200	4SW deg	M+S	18	7M $	M$2	Ind	BBBBC$	Ind		
Civil and Environmental Engineering	H250	4SW deg	M+S	18	7M $	M$2	Ind	BBBBC$	Ind		
Combined Studies *Civil Engineering*	Y400	3FT deg	M+S	14	2M	M	Ind	Ind	Ind		
Combined Studies *Environmental and Mineral Management*	Y400	3FT deg	*	14	2M	M	Ind	Ind	Ind		
Civil Engineering Studies	002H	2FT HND	M/S	E	N	P$	Ind	Ind	Ind		
Univ of SOUTHAMPTON											
Civil Engineering	H200	3FT deg	M+P	BCC	Ind $	D^	30$	CSYS	Ind	6	14/22
Civil Engineering (MEng)	H201	4FT deg	M+P	24	Ind $	D^	32$	CSYS	Ind	25	
Civil Engineering with Euro St (MEng)	H204	4FT deg	M+P+F/G	24	Ind $	D^	32$	CSYS	Ind		
Environmental Engineering	H250	3FT deg	M+P	BCC	Ind $	D^	30$	CSYS	Ind	5	14/26
Environmental Engineering (MEng)	H251	4FT deg	M+P	24	Ind $	D^	32$	CSYS	Ind	13	
Environmental Engineering with Euro St (MEng)	H254	4FT deg	M+P+F/G	24	Ind $	D^	32$	CSYS	Ind		

			98 expected requirements							96 entry stats

TITLE	CODE	COURSE	SUBJECTS	A/AS	ND/C	RGNVQ	IB	SQR(H)	SQR	RATIO A/AS
SOUTH BANK Univ										
Civil Engineering	H200	3FT/4SW deg	M+S g	BC	4M $	D go	Ind	Ind	Ind	
Civil Engineering (MEng)	H202	4FT/5SW deg	M+S g	BC	4M $	D go	Ind	Ind	Ind	
Civil Engineering Design	H201	3FT/4SW deg	M+E g	DD	4M $	M go	Ind	Ind	Ind	
Environmental Engineering	HH23	3FT deg	* g	14-18	2M+4D	M go	Ind	Ind	Ind	
Foundation Civil Engineering	H208	4EXT deg					Ind	Ind	Ind	
Civil Engineering	002H	2FT/3SW HND	M/P g	C	2M $	P go	Ind	Ind	Ind	
ST HELENS COLL										
Civil Engineering	002H	2FT HND	M/Ph	2	N	PC	Ind	Ind	Ind	
STOCKPORT COLL of F and HE										
Civil Engineering	H200	4FT/5SW deg	M/P	EE	N $					
Civil Engineering	002H	2FT/3SW HND	M/P	2	N $					
Univ of STRATHCLYDE										
Civil Engineering	H200	4FT deg	M	CCC	HN		34$	BBBB$	HN	
Civil Engineering	H202	5FT deg	M	BBB			34$	AAAB$	Ind	
Environmental Health	CH92	4FT deg	M+C+P/B	CCC	HN		36$	BBBB$	HN	
Univ of SURREY										
Civil Engineering	H200	3FT deg	M g	CCC	3M+2D$	ME3/^	27	BBBB		8	12/19
Civil Engineering	H201	4SW deg	M+P g	CCC	3M+2D$	ME3/^	27	BBBB		6
Civil Engineering (MEng)	H206	4/5SW deg	M+P g	BBC	X	X	32	Ind		4	20/28
Civil Engineering with Computing	H202	3FT deg	M+P g	CCC	3M+2D$	ME3/^	27	BBBB		11
Civil Engineering with Computing	H203	4SW deg	M+P g	CCC	3M+2D$	ME3/^	27	BBBB		3
Civil Engineering with Computing (MEng)	H207	4/5SW deg	M+P g	BBC	X	X	32	Ind		6
Civil Engineering with a Euro Language (MEng)	H208	4/5SW deg	M+P g	BBC	X	X	32	Ind		2	22/28
Civil Engineering with a European Language	H204	4SW deg	M+P g	CCC	3M+2D$	Ind	27	BBBB		5
Civil Engineering with a Foundation Year	H205	4FT/5SW deg	* g	CCC	3M+2D$	M*	27	BBBB		4
Univ of Wales SWANSEA										
Civil Engineering	H200	3FT deg	M	BCD-CCC	4M+1D$	MC^	28$	BBBCC$	Ind	4	14/24
Civil Engineering	H203	4FT deg	* g	BCD-CCC	Ind	Ind	Ind	BBBCC	Ind	1	8/16
Civil Engineering (MEng)	H201	4FT deg	M	BCC	2M+3D$	Ind	32$	AABBB$	Ind	
Civil Engineering (with French)	H2R1	4FT deg	M g	BCD-CCC	4M+1D$	MC^ go	28$	BBBCC$	Ind	2	18/18
Civil Engineering (with German)	H2R2	4FT deg	M g	BCD-CCC	4M+1D$	MC^ go	28$	BBBCC$	Ind	
Civil Engineering (with Italian)	H2R3	4FT deg	M g	BCD-CCC	4M+1D$	MC^ go	28$	BBBCC$	Ind	
Civil Engineering (with Spanish)	H2R4	4FT deg	M g	BCD-CCC	4M+1D$	MC^ go	28$	BBBCC$	Ind	
SWANSEA INST of HE										
Civil Engineering Studies	002H	2FT HND		E	N	P	Ind	Ind	N	14
Univ of TEESSIDE										
Civil Engineering	H200	4SW deg	M+S	12	5M		Ind	Ind	Ind	8	14/18
Civil Engineering with Structural Design	H220	3FT deg	M+S	12	5M		Ind	Ind	Ind	
Modular Degree Scheme *Civil Engineering*	Y401	3FT deg								
Science and Technology Combined Honours Scheme *Civil Engineering*	Y108	3FT deg								
Civil Engineering Studies	002H▼	2FT HND	M/S	4	N		Ind	Ind	N	2	2/10
Univ of ULSTER										
Civil Engineering (4 Yr SW inc DIS)	H202▼	4SW deg	M+S	DDD	MO+1D	Ind	24	CCCC	Ind	7
Civil Engineering (4 Yr SW inc DIS)	H200▼	4SW deg	M+S	CCC	MO+3D	Ind	28	BBCC	Ind	20
Environmental Engineering (4 Yr SW inc DIS)	H250▼	4SW deg	S+M	BCC	MO+4D	Ind	30	BBBC		5	14/16
Civil Engineering (3 Yr SW inc CIS)	002H▼	3SW HND	M+S g		Ind	ME gi	Ind	Ind	Ind	7	4/10

course details			98 expected requirements							96 entry stats	
TITLE	CODE	COURSE	SUBJECTS	A/AS	NO/C	AGNVQ	IB	SQA(H)	SQA	RATIO	A/AS
UNIVERSITY COLL LONDON (Univ of London)											
Civil Engineering	H200	3FT deg	M+P g	BCC	3M+2D$	Ind	30$	BBBCC$	Ind	6	16/22
Civil Engineering (MEng)	H202	4FT deg	M+P g	BCC	3M+2D$	Ind	30$	BBBCC$	Ind	10	16/28
Civil Engineering, inc Foundation Yr (4 Yrs)	H201	4FT deg	* g	BCC	X	X	30	BBBCC	X	12	
Civil and Environmental Engineering	H250	3FT deg	M+P g	BCC	3M+2D$	Ind	30$	BBBCC$	Ind	12	
Structural Engineering	H240	3FT deg	M+P g	BCC	3M+2D$	Ind	30$	BBBCC$	Ind	5	
Univ of WARWICK											
Civil Engineering	H200	3FT deg	M+S g	CCC	5M+1D$	D$^	28$	BBBBC$		5	12/26
Civil Engineering	H202	4FT deg	M+S g	BBB	5M+1D$	D$^	32$	AABBB$			
Civil Engineering (European)	H204	4FT deg	M+S g	BBB	5M+1D$	D$^	32$	AABBB$		9	
Univ of WESTMINSTER											
Civil Engineering	H200	3FT/4SW deg	M	12	5M	M$	Ind	Ind	Ind	13	
Civil Engineering	H201	3FT deg	M	DD	3M		Ind	Ind	Ind	6	
Civil Engineering (with foundation)	H208	4EXT deg	M	D	N		Ind	Ind	Ind	14	
WIGAN and LEIGH COLL											
Civil Engineering	002H▼	2FT HND		DE	N	P$	Dip		N		
Univ of WOLVERHAMPTON											
Civil Engineering	H200	3FT/4SW deg	g	DD	N	M	24	CCCC	Ind		
Civil Engineering Management	H2NC	3FT/4SW deg	* g	DD	N	M	24	CCCC	Ind	37	
Civil Engineering Surveying (Quantities)	H260	3FT/4SW deg	* g	DD	N	M	24	CCCC	Ind	11	
European Civil Engineering Management	H2N1	3FT/4SW deg	* g	DD	N	M	24	CCCC	Ind	7	
Civil Engineering Studies	002H	2FT/3SW HND	* g	D	N	M	24	CCCC	Ind	5	

| | | | 98 expected requirements | | | | | | | 96 entry stats | |
| course details | | | | | | | | | | | |
TITLE	CODE	COURSE	SUBJECTS	A/AS	ND/C	AGNVQ	IB	SQA(H)	SQA	RATIO	A/AS
Univ of ABERDEEN											
Computing Science-Engineering	GH56	4FT deg	M+2S g	CCD	Ind	MS go	24$	BBBC$	Ind	14	
Electronic & Software Engineering	H6G7	4FT deg	M+P/Ds g	CC	Ind	M$ go	26$	BBBCC$	Ind	14	
Engineering (Electrical and Electronic)	H500	4FT deg	M+P/Ds g	CC	Ind	MS^ go	26$	BBBCC$	Ind	8	
Engineering (Electrical and Electronic) (MEng)	H505	5FT deg	M+P/Ds g	BC	Ind	MS^ go	28$	AABB$	Ind	4	
Univ of ABERTAY DUNDEE											
Electronic & Electrical Engineering	HH56	4FT/5SW deg	M+P/C/Ds	CD	Ind	Ind	Ind	BBCC	Ind		
Electronic & Electrical Systems	HH5P	3FT deg	g	E	Ind	Ind	Ind	CC	Ind		
Electronic & Photonic Engineering	H635	4FT/5SW deg	M+P/C/Ds	CD	Ind	Ind	Ind	BBCC	Ind		
Electronic Engineering	H600	4FT/5SW deg	M+P/C/Ds	CD	Ind	Ind	Ind	BBCC	Ind		
Electronic Engineering with French/Ger/Spanish	H6T2	4FT/5SW deg		CD	Ind	Ind	Ind	BBCC	Ind		
Electronic Product Design	H681	4FT/5SW deg	M+P/C/Ds	CD	Ind	Ind	Ind	BBCC	Ind		
Electronic Systems	H680	3FT deg	g	E	Ind	Ind	Ind	CC	Ind		
Marketing, Management & Consumer Electronics	H6N5	4FT/5SW deg	*	DD	Ind	Ind	Ind	BCC	Ind		
Marketing, Management & Consumer Electronics	N5H6	4FT/5SW deg	*	DD	Ind	Ind	Ind	BCC	Ind		
Mechatronics	HH63	3FT deg	g	D	Ind	Ind	Ind	BC	Ind		
Electronic & Electrical Systems	65HH	2FT HND	g	E	Ind	Ind	Ind	CC	Ind		
Electronic Systems	086H	2FT HND	g	E	Ind	Ind	Ind	CC	Ind		
Mechatronics	36HH	2FT HND	g	D	Ind	Ind	Ind	BC	Ind		
ANGLIA Poly Univ											
Audio and Music Technology	HW6J ▼	3FT deg	S	16	8M	D	Dip$	BBCCC	N	3	10/22
Audiotechnology and Biology	HC6C ▼	3FT deg	B	16	8M	D	Dip$	BBCCC	N		
Audiotechnology and Biomedical Science	HB6X ▼	3FT deg	S	16	8M	D	Dip$	BBCCC	N		
Audiotechnology and Business	HN6C ▼	3FT deg	S	16	8M	D	Dip$	BBCCC	N	4	
Audiotechnology and Chemistry	HF6C ▼	3FT deg	S	16	8M	D	Dip$	BBCCC	N		
Audiotechnology and Communication Studies	HP6H ▼	3FT deg	S	16	8M	D+/^	Dip$	BBCCC	N	6	
Audiotechnology and Computer Science	HGPM ▼	3FT deg	S	16	8M	D	Dip$	BBCCC	N	19	
Audiotechnology and Ecology and Conservation	HD6F ▼	3FT deg	S	16	8M	D	Dip$	BBCCC	N		
Audiotechnology and French	HR6C ▼	4FT deg	S g	16	8M	D+/^ go	Dip$	BBCCC	N		
Audiotechnology and Geography	HF6V ▼	3FT deg	S	16	8M	D	Dip$	BBCCC	N		
Audiotechnology and German	HR6F ▼	4FT deg	S g	16	8M	D+/^ go	Dip$	BBCCC	N		
Audiotechnology and Imaging Science	HW65 ▼	3FT deg	S	16	8M	D	Dip$	BBCCC	N		
Audiotechnology and Instrumentation Electronics	H606 ▼	3FT deg	S	16	8M	D	Dip$	BBCCC	N	5	
Audiotechnology and Italian	HR6H ▼	4FT deg	S g	16	8M	D+/^ go	Dip$	BBCCC	N	1	
Audiotechnology and Maths or Stats/Stat Mod.	HG6C ▼	3FT deg	S g	16	8M	D go	Dip$	BBCCC	N		
Audiotechnology and Music	HW6H ▼	3FT deg	S+M	16	8M	D+/^	Dip$	BBCCC	N	4	8/22
Audiotechnology and Real Time Computer Systems	HG6M ▼	3FT deg	S	16	8M	D	Dip$	BCCC	N	6	
Audiotechnology and Spanish	HR6K ▼	4FT deg	S g	16	8M	D+/^ go	Dip$	BBCCC	N		
Biology and Instrumentation Electronics	CH16 ▼	3FT deg	B	10	3M	P	Dip$	BCCC	N		
Biomedical Science & Instrumentation Electronics	BH96 ▼	3FT deg	B	10	3M	P go	Dip$	BCCC	N		
Business and Instrumentation Electronics	NH16 ▼	3FT deg	S g	10	3M	P go	Dip$	BCCC	Ind		
Chemistry and Instrumentation Electronics	FH16 ▼	3FT deg	S g	8	2M	P go	Dip$	CCCC	N		
Communication Systems Design and Product Design	HH6T ▼	3FT deg	g	10	3M	P go	Dip	BCCC			
Computer Science and Instrumentation Electronics	GH56 ▼	3FT deg	* g	10	3M	P go	Dip	BCCC	N	5	
Control Engineering Systems	H640 ▼	3FT deg	* g	10	3M	P go	Dip	BCCC	Ind		
Ecology and Conservation & Instrumentation Elect	DH26 ▼	3FT deg	S g	10	2M	M go	Dip$	BCCC	N		
Electronic Product Design	H680 ▼	3FT deg	S g	10	3M	P go	Dip$	BCCC	Ind		
Electronical Engineering Systems	H600 ▼	3FT deg	* g	10	3M	P go	Dip	BCCC	Ind		
Extended Science	H618 ▼	4EXT deg	*	2	N	P	Ind	CCC	Ind		4/14
Geography and Instrumentation Electronics	FH86 ▼	3FT deg	Gy+S g	12	4M	M go	Dip$	BCCC	N		
Imaging Science and Instrumentation Electronics	HW6M ▼	3FT deg	S	10	3M	P	Dip	BCCC	N		

Engineering – Electrical and Electronic   23

TITLE	CODE	COURSE	SUBJECTS	A/AS	NO/C	AGNVQ	IB	SQA(H)	SQA	RATIO A/AS
course details			**98 expected requirements**							**96 entry stats**
Instrumentation Electron & Maths or Stats/St Mod	GH16▼	3FT deg	S̲ g	10	3M	P go	Dip$	BCCC	N	
Instrumentation Electronics	H602▼	3FT deg	P̲ g	8	2M	P go	Dip$	CCCC	N	1
Instrumentation Electronics & Ophthalmic Dispens	BH56▼	3FT deg	S̲ g	10	3M	P go	Dip$	BCCC	N	
Instrumentation Electronics and Psychology	CH86▼	3FT deg	S̲ g	16	8M	D go	Dip$	BBCCC	N	
Instrumentation Elects & Real Time Comp Systems	HG65▼	3FT deg	S̲ g	10	3M	P go	Dip$	BCCC	N	2
Multimedia and Product Design	HH76▼	3FT deg	g	10	3M	P go	Dip	BCCC	Ind	
Telecommunication Engineering Systems	H620▼	3FT deg	* g	10	3M	P go	Dip	BCCC	Ind	

ASTON Univ

TITLE	CODE	COURSE	SUBJECTS	A/AS	NO/C	AGNVQ	IB	SQA(H)	SQA	RATIO A/AS
Communications Engineering	H621	4SW deg	M+Ph g	20	5M+5D$	D$6/^ go	30$	BBBBB$	Ind	
Communications Engineering	H620	3FT deg	M+Ph g	20	5M+5D$	D$6/^ go	30$	BBBBB$	Ind	
Electrical and Electronic Engineering	HHM6	4SW deg	M+Ph g	20	5M+5D$	D$6/^ go	30$	BBBBB$	Ind	9
Electrical and Electronic Engineering	HH56	3FT deg	M+Ph g	20	5M+5D$	D$6/^ go	30$	BBBBB$	Ind	5 12/24
Electrical and Electronic Engineering (STEPS)	HHMP	4FT/5SW deg	* g	20	4M	D$	30	BBBBB	Ind	2
Electromechanical Eng with European St (MEng)	H6T2	4FT/5SW deg	M̲ g	22	Ind $	D$6/^ go	31$	ABBBB$	Ind	
Electromechanical Engineering (BEng/MEng)	HH63	4SW/5SW deg	M̲ g	18	Ind $	D$6/^ go	29$	BBBBC$	Ind	4
Electromechanical Engineering (BEng/MEng)	HH36	3FT/4FT deg	M̲ g	18	Ind $	D$6/^ go	29$	BBBBC$	Ind	10
Electromechanical Engineering (STEPS)	HHH6	4FT/5SW deg	* g	18	4M	D$	30	BBBBC	Ind	5
Electronic Engineering and Computer Science	GH56	3FT/4SW deg	M+Ph/Cs g	20	5M+5D$	D$6/^ go	30$	BBBBB$	Ind	4 12/28
Electronic Engineering with Management Studies	H6N1	3FT deg	M+Ph g	20	5M+5D$	D$6/^ go	30$	BBBBB$	Ind	
Electronic Engineering with Management Studies	H6ND	4SW deg	M+Ph g	20	5M+5D$	D$6/^ go	30$	BBBBB$	Ind	
Electronic Systems Engineering (MEng)	HHN6	4FT deg	M+Ph g	24	2M+8D$	D$6/^ go	32$	AABBB$	Ind	7 26/28
Electronic Systems Engineering with Mgt Studies	H6NC	4FT deg	M+Ph g	24	1M+9D$	D$6/^ go	33$	AABBB$	Ind	
Electronics/Biology	HC61	3FT/4SW deg	B+M/P g	18	X	X	29$	BBBBC$	Ind	
Electronics/Business Administration	HN61	3FT/4SW deg	M/P g	20	5M+5D$	D$6/^ go	30$	BBBBB$	Ind	5
Electronics/Chemistry	HF61	3FT/4SW deg	C+M/P g	18	X	X	29$	BBBBC$	Ind	
Electronics/Computer Science	HG65	3FT/4SW deg	M/P g	18	5M+5D$	D$6/^ go	29$	BBBBC$	Ind	9
Engineering Management/Electronics	HH67	3FT/4SW deg	M̲/P g	18	5M+5D$	D$^ go	29$	BBBBC$	Ind	
French/Electronics	HR61	4SW deg	M/P+F g	20	X	X	30$	BBBBB$	Ind	
German/Electronics	HR62	4SW deg	G+M/P g	18	X	X	29$	BBBBC$	Ind	
Health & Safety Management/Electronics	HJ69	3FT/4SW deg	M/P g	18	5M+5D$	D$^ go	29$	BBBBC$	Ind	
Product Design (Engineering)/Electronics	HH76	3FT/4SW deg	M/P g	18	5M+5D$	D$^ go	29$	BBBBC$		
Public Policy & Management/Electronics	HM61	3FT/4SW deg	M/P g	20	5M+5D$	D$6/^ go	30$	BBBBB$	Ind	
Social Studies/Electronics	HL64	3FT/4SW deg	M/P g	18	5M+5D$	D$6/^ go	29$	BBBBC$	Ind	

Univ of Wales, BANGOR

TITLE	CODE	COURSE	SUBJECTS	A/AS	NO/C	AGNVQ	IB	SQA(H)	SQA	RATIO A/AS
Applied Physics and Electronics	FH36	3FT deg	M+P/Es/Cs̲ g	CC	3M $	M$^ go	26$	BBCC$	Ind	5
Computer Systems Engineering	H616	3FT deg	M+P/Es/Cs̲ g	CC	3M $	M$6/^ go	26$	CCCC$	Ind	5 8/18
Computer Systems Engineering (MEng)	H617	4FT deg	M+P/Es/Cs̲ g	BBB	Ind	D$6/^ go	30$	BBBB$	Ind	4
Computer Systems Engineering (Wide Entry)	H615	4FT deg	* g	DD	3M	M$6/^ go	26	CCCC	Ind	7
Computer Systems and Sports Science	BH66	3FT deg	M+P/Es/Cs̲ g	BDD	3M+1D$	D$6/^ go	30$	BBBC$	Ind	
Computer Systems with Business Studies	H6N1	3FT deg	* g	CC	3M	M$6/^ go	26	BBCC	Ind	5 8/16
Computer Systems with French (4 yrs)	H6R1	4FT deg	F̲ g	CC	X	M$^ go	26$	BBCC$	X	
Computer Systems with German (4 yrs)	H6R2	4FT deg	G̲ g	CC	3M	M$^ go	26	BBCC	Ind	
Computer Systems with Mathematics	H6G1	3FT deg	M+P/Es/Cs̲ g	CC	3M $	D$^ go	26$	CCCC$	Ind	4
Computer Systems with Psychology	H6C8	3FT deg	* g	CC	3M	M$6/^ go	26$	BBCC	Ind	
Electrical Engineering (Inc Power Electronics)	H500	3FT deg	M+P/Es/Cs̲ g	CC	3M $	M$6/^ go	26$	BBCC$	Ind	7
Electronic Engineering	H600	3FT deg	M+P/Es/Cs̲ g	CC	3M $	M$6/^ go	26$	BBCC$	Ind	6
Electronic Engineering	H602	2FT Dip	* g							
Electronic Engineering & Sports Science	HB66	3FT deg	M+P/Es/Cs̲ g	BDD	3M+1D$	D$6/^ go	30$	BBBC$	Ind	
Electronic Engineering (MEng)	H601	4FT deg	M+P/Es/Cs̲ g	BBB	Ind	D$6/^ go	30$	BBBB$	Ind	4
Electronic Engineering (Wide-Entry)	H605	4FT deg	* g	DD	3M	M$6/^ go	26	CCCC	Ind	2
Mathematics with Computer Systems	G1H6	3FT deg	M̲ g	14-18	3M $	D$^ go	26$	BBCC$	Ind	7

TITLE	CODE	COURSE	SUBJECTS	A/AS	ND/C	AGNVQ	IB	SQA(H)	SQA	RATIO A/AS
BARNSLEY COLL										
Electrical and Electronic Engineering	56HH	2FT HND	*	E	N	P*	Ind	Ind	Ind	
Media Technology	46PH	2FT HND	*	E	2M	P*	Ind	Ind	Ind	
Univ of BATH										
Elec Eng & App Elec for Euro Mkt (with St Abd)	H534	4FT deg	M+P	24	Ind	Ind	30$	CSYS$	Ind	5
Elec Eng & App Elec for Euro Mkt (with St Abd)	H535	5SW deg	M+P	24	Ind	Ind	30$	CSYS$	Ind	
Electrical & Electronic Eng for Euro Mkt(St Abd)	HH5Q	4FT deg	M+P	24	Ind	Ind	30$	CSYS	Ind	6
Electrical & Electronic Engineering	HH56	3FT deg	M+P	20	Ind	Ind	30$	CSYS	Ind	11	14/22
Electrical & Electronic Engineering (4 Yr SW)	HHM6	4SW deg	M+P	20	Ind	Ind	30$	CSYS	Ind	9	18/24
Electrical & Electronic Engineering (5 Yr SW)	HHP5	5SW deg	M+P	20	Ind	Ind	30$	CSYS	Ind	
Electrical & Electronic Engineering (MEng)	HH5P	4FT deg	M+P	24	Ind	Ind	30$	CSYS	Ind	5	18/30
Electrical & Electronic Engineering for Euro Mkt	HHQ5	5SW deg	M+P	20	Ind	Ind	30$	CSYS	Ind	
Electrical Engineering & App Electronics (MEng)	H532	4FT deg	M+P	24	Ind	Ind	30$	CSYS$	Ind	6
Electrical Engineering & App Electronics(4Yr SW)	H533	5SW deg	M+P	24	Ind	Ind	30$	CSYS$	Ind	
Electrical Engineering & App Electronics(4yr SW)	H531	4SW deg	M+P	20	Ind	Ind	30$	CSYS$	Ind	13
Electrical Engineering and App Electronics	H530	3FT deg	M+P	20	Ind	Ind	30$	CSYS$	Ind	8
Electronic & Comm Eng for Euro Mkt (with St Abd)	H624	4FT deg	M+P	24	Ind	Ind	30$	CSYS$	Ind	5
Electronic & Communication Eng for Euro Mkt	H625	5SW deg	M+P	24	Ind	Ind	30$	CSYS$	Ind	
Electronic & Communication Engineering	H620	3FT deg	M+P	20	Ind	Ind	30$	CSYS$	Ind	9
Electronic & Communication Engineering (4Yr SW)	H621	4SW deg	M+P	20	Ind	Ind	30$	CSYS$	Ind	9
Electronic & Communication Engineering (5 Yr SW)	H623	5SW deg	M+P	24	Ind	Ind	30$	CSYS$	Ind	
Electronic & Communication Engineering (MEng)	H622	4FT deg	M+P	24	Ind	Ind	30$	CSYS$	Ind	3	20/28
BELL COLLEGE OF TECHNOLOGY										
Electrical and Electronic Engineering	HH56	3FT deg	M/P	CD	Ind	Ind	Ind	BBC$	Ind	
Mechatronics	HH36	3FT deg	M/P	CD	Ind	Ind	Ind	BBC$	Ind	
Electronic and Electrical Engineering	65HH	2FT HND	* g	D	N $	P$	Ind	CC$	Ind	
Univ of BIRMINGHAM										
Electronic & Electrical Engineering with Mgt (e)	HH5P	4FT deg	M+P	BBB-BBC	2M+4D$	Ind	32$	Ind	Ind	5	14/24
Electronic Engineering	H601	3FT/4FT deg	M+P	BBB-BCC	2M+4D$	Ind	32$	Ind	Ind	6	12/30
Electronic and Communication Engineering	H620	3FT/4FT deg	M+P	BBB-BCC	2M+4D$	Ind	32$	Ind	Ind	7	12/30
Electronic and Computer Engineering	H610	3FT/4FT deg	M+P	BBB-BCC	2M+4D$	Ind	32$	Ind	Ind	7	12/30
Electronic and Control Engineering	H640	3FT/4FT deg	M+P	BBB-BCC	2M+4D$	Ind	32$	Ind	Ind	8
Electronic and Electrical Eng with Foundation Yr	HH5Q	4FT/5FT deg	* g	BBC-CCC	2M+4D$	Ind	28$	Ind	Ind	5	12/20
Electronic and Electrical Engineering	HH56	3FT/4FT deg	M+P	BBB-BCC	2M+4D$	Ind	32$	Ind	Ind	5	10/28
Electronic and Integrated Circuit Engineering	H616	3FT/4FT deg	M+P	BBB-BCC	2M+4D$	Ind	32$	Ind	Ind	11
Electronic and Software Engineering (e)	GH76	3FT/4FT deg	M+P	BBB-BCC	2M+4D$	Ind	32$	Ind	Ind	5	10/28
BLACKPOOL & FYLDE COLL										
Electronic Communications	026H	2FT HND	*	2	N	P*	Ind	Ind	Ind	
Mechatronics	63HH	2FT HND	*	2	N	P*	Ind	Ind	Ind	
BOLTON INST										
Computing and Electronics	GH5P	3FT deg	M/S g	10	3M	M$	Ind	Ind	Ind	
Consumer Electronics	H602	3FT deg	M/S g	10	3M	M$	Ind	Ind	Ind	
Electronic Engineering	H601	4FT deg	M/S	4	N	P$	Ind	Ind	Ind	
Electronic Engineering	H600	3FT deg	M+S	12	4M	M$	Ind	Ind	Ind	
Electronic Engineering (MEng)	H605	4FT deg	M+S	18	3M+1D	M3$	Ind	Ind	Ind	
Electronic and Computer Engineering	GH6Q	4FT deg	M/S	4	N	P$	Ind	Ind	Ind	
Electronic and Computer Engineering	GH66	3FT deg	M+S	12	4M	M$	Ind	Ind	Ind	
Electronic and Computer Engineering (MEng)	HG6Q	4FT deg	M+S	18	3M+1D	M3$	Ind	Ind	Ind	
Electronics and Computer Engineering (Found)	GH6P	4FT/5FT deg		Ind	Ind	Ind	Ind	Ind	Ind	
Electronics and French	HRP1	3FT deg	F+M/S	10	3M	Ind	Ind	Ind	Ind	

course details   **98 expected requirements**   **96 entry stats**

				98 expected requirements							96 entry stats	
course details													

TITLE	CODE	COURSE	SUBJECTS	A/AS	NO/C	AGNVQ	IB	SQA(H)	SQA	RATIO A/AS	
Electronics and German	HRP2	3FT deg	G+M/S	10	3M	Ind	Ind	Ind	Ind		
Electronics and Leisure Computing Technology	HG67	4FT deg	* g	4	N	P*	Ind	Ind	Ind		
Electronics and Manufacturing Systems Design	HHP7	3FT deg	M/S/Ds	10	3M	M$	Ind	Ind	Ind		
Electronics and Motor Vehicle Studies	HHQJ	4FT deg	M/S	4	N	P$	Ind	Ind	Ind		
Electronics and Motor Vehicle Studies	HHPJ	3FT deg	M/S	10	3M	M$	Ind	Ind	Ind		
Electronics and Occupational Health & Safety	HNP6	3FT deg	M/S	10	3M	M$	Ind	Ind	Ind		
Electronics and Product Design	HHPT	3FT deg	M/S/Ad/Ds	10	3M	M$	Ind	Ind	Ind		
Electronics and Simulation/Virtual Environment	HGP7	3FT deg	M/S	10	3M	M$	Ind	Ind	Ind		
Electronics and Technology Management	HNP9	3FT deg	M/S/Bu	10	3M	M$	Ind	Ind	Ind		
Electronics and Textiles	HJP4	3FT deg	M/S	10	3M	M$	Ind	Ind	Ind		
Occupational Health & Safety and Textiles	HJ64	3FT deg	* g	10	3M	M*	Ind	Ind	Ind		
Automobile Electronics	036H	2FT HND	M/S	4	N	P$	Ind	Ind	Ind		
Communication Engineering	126H	2FT HND	M/S	4	N	P$	Ind	Ind	Ind		
Control Engineering	046H	2FT HND	M/S	4	N	P$	Ind	Ind	Ind		
Electrical Engineering	005H	2FT HND	M/S	4	N	P$	Ind	Ind	Ind		
Electronic Engineering	006H	2FT HND	M/S	4	N	P$	Ind	Ind	Ind		
Microcomputer Engineering	016H	2FT HND	M/S	E	N	Ind	Ind	Ind	Ind		
Microelectronic Design	116H	2FT HND	M/S	E	N	Ind	Ind	Ind	Ind		

BOURNEMOUTH Univ

TITLE	CODE	COURSE	SUBJECTS	A/AS	NO/C	AGNVQ	IB	SQA(H)	SQA	RATIO A/AS	
Design Management	H680	4SW deg	S/M g	10	3M $	M$ go	Ind	CCCC	Ind	3	
Design Management Foundation	H688▼	1FT deg									
Electronic Systems Design (BEng/MEng)	H608▼	4EXT/5EXT deg	* g	DE	3M	M$ go	Ind	CCCC	Ind	3	
Electronic Systems Design (BEng/MEng)	H600	3FT/4FT deg	S/M g	10	3M $	M$ go	Ind	CCCC	Ind	3	
Medical Electronics Design	H671	4FT deg									
Medical Electronics Design Foundation	H678▼	1FT deg									
Microelectronics and Computing (BEng/MEng)	H618▼	5EXTSW/6EXTSW deg	* g	DE	3M	M$ go	Ind	CCCC	Ind	2	
Microelectronics and Computing (BEng/MEng)	H610	4SW/5SW deg	S/M g	10	3M $	M$ go	Ind	CCCC	Ind	2	6/20
Multi-media Communications (BEng/MEng)	H620	3FT/4FT deg	S/M g	10	3M $	M$ go	Ind	CCCC	Ind	6	6/12
Multi-media Communications (BEng/MEng)	H621▼	4EXT/5EXT deg	* g	10	3M $	M$ go	Ind	CCCC	Ind	1 •	

Univ of BRADFORD

TITLE	CODE	COURSE	SUBJECTS	A/AS	NO/C	AGNVQ	IB	SQA(H)	SQA	RATIO A/AS	
Electrical & Electronic Eng with Mgt (MEng)	H607	4SW deg	M+P g	ABB	4D $	DS^	Ind	Ind	Ind		
Electrical and Electronic Eng with Management	H606	4SW deg	M g	12	2M $	MS^	Ind	Ind	Ind	14	
Electrical and Electronic Eng with Management	H605	3FT deg	M g	12	2M $	MS^	Ind	Ind	Ind	6	
Electrical and Electronic Engineering	HH56	4SW deg	M g	12	2M $	MS^	Ind	Ind	Ind	8	
Electrical and Electronic Engineering	HHM6	3FT deg	M g	12	2M $	MS^	Ind	Ind	Ind	8	
Electrical and Electronic Engineering (Found Yr)	HH5P	4FT/5SW deg	* g	4-6	N	PS	Ind	Ind	Ind	1	6/11
Electrical and Electronic Engineering (MEng)	H691	4SW deg	M+P g	ABB	4D $	DS^	Ind	Ind	Ind	17	
Electronic Imaging and Media Comm (Found Yr)	H6PL	4FT deg	* g	CCC	3M $	M$^	Ind	Ind	Ind	1	10/20
Electronic Imaging and Media Communications	H6P4	3FT deg	* g	BCC	5M+1D	X	Ind	Ind	Ind	4	18/28
Electronic, Communication & Comp Eng (MEng)	H692	4SW deg	M+P g	ABB	4D $	DS^	Ind	Ind	Ind	3	
Electronic, Communication & Comp Engineering	H690	4SW deg	M g	12	2M $	MS^	Ind	Ind	Ind	4	10/16
Electronic, Communication & Computer Engineering	H695	3FT deg	M g	12	2M $	MS^	Ind	Ind	Ind	5	
Information Systems and Multimedia Tech (MEng)	H622	4FT deg	M+P g	ABB	5D $	DS^	Ind	Ind	Ind		
Information Systems and Multimedia Technology	H621	4SW deg	M	BBB	Ind	M$^	Ind	Ind	Ind	1	
Information Systems and Multimedia Technology	H620	3FT deg	M	BBB	Ind	M$^	Ind	Ind	Ind	3	
Media Technology and Production	HP64	3FT deg	* g	BCC	5M+1D	X	Ind	Ind	Ind	18	18/28

Univ of BRIGHTON

TITLE	CODE	COURSE	SUBJECTS	A/AS	NO/C	AGNVQ	IB	SQA(H)	SQA	RATIO A/AS	
Electrical & Electronic Engine (Dip/BEng/MEng)	HH56	3FT/4SW 4FT/5SW deg	M+P/S/Ds	18	5M $	M$^	25$	BBCC$	Ind		
Electrical Power Eng'ing (Dip Ing FH/BEng Hons)	H520	3FT/4SW deg	M+P/S/Ds	18	5M $	M$^	25$	BBCC$	Ind		
Electronic & Broadcast Engine (Dip/BEng/MEng)	H630	3FT/4SW 4FT/5SW deg	M+P/S/Ds	18	5M $	M$^	25$	BBCC$	Ind		
Electronic & Computer Engineering(Dip/BEng/MEng)	HG66	3FT/4SW 4FT/5SW deg	M+P/S/Ds	18	5M $	M$^	25$	BBCC$	Ind		

TITLE	CODE	COURSE	98 expected requirements SUBJECTS	A/AS	ND/C	RGNVQ	IB	SQA(H)	SQA	96 entry stats RATIO A/AS	
Electronic Engineering (Dip/BEng/MEng)	H600	3FT/4SW 4FT/5SW deg	M+P/S/Ds	18	5M $	M$_^	25$	BBCC$	Ind		
Engineering (Electronic)	106H▼	2FT HND	M/P/S/Ds	4	3M $	P$+	15$	CDD$	Ind		
Engineering (Electronics & Power)	65HH▼	2FT HND	M/P/S/Ds	4	3M $	P$+	15$	CDD$	Ind		
Engineering (Electronics for Broadcasting)	626H▼	2FT HND	M/P/S/Ds	4	3M $	P$+	15$	CDD$	Ind		
Engineering (Mechatronics)	63HH▼	2FT HND	M/P/S/Ds	4	3M $	P$+	15$	CDD$	Ind		

Univ of BRISTOL

TITLE	CODE	COURSE	SUBJECTS	A/AS	ND/C	RGNVQ	IB	SQA(H)	SQA	RATIO	A/AS
Avionic Systems	HH46	3FT deg	M+P	AAB-BBB	HN	D$^	33$	CSYS	HN$	9	22/28
Avionic Systems (MEng)	HH64	4FT deg	M+P	AAB-BBB	HN	D$^	33$	CSYS	HN$	7	20/30
Comp Syst Eng with Study in Cont Eur (MEng)	H621	4FT deg	M+P g	BBB	HN $	D$^	33$	CSYS	HN$	3	
Computer Systems Engineering (MEng)	H622	4FT deg	M+P	BBB	HN $	D$^	33$	CSYS	HN$	6	18/30
Electrical & Electron Eng with St in C Eur(MEng)	HH6M	4FT deg	M+P g	BBB	HN	D$^	33$	CSYS	HN$	9	
Electrical and Electronic Engineering	HH56	3FT deg	M+P	BBB	HN	D$^	32$	CSYS	HN$	43	
Electrical and Electronic Engineering (MEng)	HH65	4FT deg	M+P	BBB	HN	D$^	33$	CSYS	HN$	5	18/30
Electronic Engineering	H600	3FT deg	M+P	BBB	HN	D$^	33$	CSYS	HN$	71	
Electronic and Communications Engineering	H620	3FT deg	M+P	BBB	HN	D$^	33$	CSYS	HN$	10	22/28

BRISTOL, Univ of the W of England

TITLE	CODE	COURSE	SUBJECTS	A/AS	ND/C	RGNVQ	IB	SQA(H)	SQA	RATIO	A/AS
Digital Systems Engineering	H615	3FT/4SW deg	M/P g	14	4M $	M$1 go	24$	BCCC$	N$		
Digital Systems Engineering (MEng)	H616	4FT/5SW deg	M/P g	14	4M $	M$1 go	24$	BCCC$	N$		
Electrical and Electronic Engineering	HH56	3FT/4SW deg	M/P g	14	4M $	M$1 go	24$	BCCC$	N$		
Electrical and Electronic Engineering (MEng)	HH5P	4FT/5SW deg	M/P g	14	4M $	M$1 go	24$	BCCC$	N$		
Electronic Engineering	H600	3FT/4SW deg	M/P g	14	4M $	M$1 go	24$	BCCC$	N$		
Electronic Engineering (MEng)	H601	4FT/5SW deg	M/P g	14	4M $	M$1 go	24$	BCCC$	N$		
Engineering (Music Technology) (BSc)	HW63	3FT/4SW deg	M+S g	14-16	4M $	M$1 go	24$	BCCC$	Ind$		
Engineering (Electrical and Electronic)	65HH	2FT/3SW HND	M/P g	2-4	N $	P$1 go	24$	CD$	N$		
Engineering (Mechatronics)	63HH	2FT/3SW HND	M/P g	2-4	N $	P$1 go	24$	CD$	N$		
Environmental Engineering	025H	2FT/3SW HND	* g	2-4	N $	P$1 go	24	CD$	N		

BRUNEL Univ, West London

TITLE	CODE	COURSE	SUBJECTS	A/AS	ND/C	RGNVQ	IB	SQA(H)	SQA	RATIO	A/AS
Electronic & Elec Eng (Communication Sys) (MEng)	H621	4SW/5SW deg	M+S	BBC	4M+1D$	DE^	28$	CSYS$	Ind	6	
Electronic & Elec Eng (Communications Sys)(MEng)	H620	3FT/4FT deg	M+S	BBC	4M+1D$	DE^	28$	CSYS$	Ind	7	
Electronic & Elec Eng (Communications Sys)(MEng)	HH5P	4SW/5SW deg	M+S	BBC	4M+1D$	DE^	28$	CSYS$	Ind	7	
Electronic & Elec Eng (Computer Systems) (MEng)	HHM6	4SW/5SW deg	M+S	BBC	4M+1D$	DE^	28$	CSYS$	Ind	4	
Electronic & Elec Eng (Computer Systems) (MEng)	H616	4SW/5SW deg	M+S	BBC	4M+1D$	DE^	28$	CSYS$	Ind	16	
Electronic & Elec Eng (Computer Systems) (MEng)	H615	3FT/4FT deg	M+S	BBC	4M+1D$	DE^	28$	CSYS$	Ind	5	
Electronic & Elec Eng (Control Systems) (MEng)	H651	4SW/5SW deg	M+S	BBC	4M+1D$	DE^	28$	CSYS$	Ind		
Electronic & Elec Eng (Control Systems) (MEng)	HH5Q	4SW/5SW deg	M+S	BBC	4M+1D$	DE^	28$	CSYS$	Ind	6	
Electronic & Elec Eng (Control Systems) (MEng)	H650	3FT/4FT deg	M+S	BBC	4M+1D$	DE^	28$	CSYS$	Ind	10	
Electronic & Elec Eng (Electro & Aud Sys) (MEng)	HH6N	4SW/5SW deg	M+S	BBC	4M+1D$	DE^	28$	CSYS$	Ind	12	
Electronic & Elec Eng (Electro & Aud Sys) (MEng)	H622	3FT/4FT deg	M+S	BBC	4M+1D$	DE^	28$	CSYS$	Ind	47	
Electronic & Elec Eng (Electro & Aud Sys) (MEng)	H623	4SW/5SW deg	M+S	BBC	4M+1D$	DE^	28$	CSYS$	Ind	21	
Electronic & Elec Eng (Power Electro Sys) (MEng)	HH6M	4SW/5SW deg	M+S	BBC	4M+1D$	DE^	28$	CSYS$	Ind		
Electronic & Elec Eng (Power Electro Sys) (MEng)	H610	3FT/4FT deg	M+S	BBC	4M+1D$	DE^	28$	CSYS$	Ind	6	
Electronic & Elec Eng (Power Electro Sys) (MEng)	H611	4SW/5SW deg	M+S	BBC	4M+1D$	DE^	28$	CSYS$	Ind		
Electronic & Elec Engineering (MEng)	HH56	4SW/5SW deg	M+S	BBC	4M+1D$	DE^	28$	CSYS$	Ind	5	14/24
Electronic & Elec Engineering (MEng)	HHMP	4SW/5SW deg	M+S	BBC	4M+1D$	DE^	28$	CSYS$	Ind	7	
Electronic & Microelectronic Eng(4/5 Yr Thin SW)	H617	4SW/5SW deg	M+S	BBC	4M+1D$	DE^	28$	CSYS$	Ind	15	
Electronic & Microelectronic Eng(4/5Yr Thick SW)	H619	4SW/5SW deg	M+S	BBC	4M+1D$	DE^	28$	CSYS$	Ind	7	
Electronic and Elec Engineering (MEng)	HH65	3FT/4FT deg	M+S	BBC	4M+1D$	DE^	28$	CSYS$	Ind	9	
Electronic and Microelectronic Eng (3/4 Yrs)	H618	3FT/4FT deg	M+S	BBC	4M+1D$	DE^	28$	CSYS$	Ind	10	
Mech Eng with Elect Sys (4/5 Yrs Thick SW)(MEng)	H3HQ	4SW/5SW deg	M+P	BCC	4M+1D$	DE^	28$	BBBBB$	Ind		
Mech Eng with Elect Sys (4/5 Yrs Thin SW) (MEng)	H3H6	4SW/5SW deg	M+P	BCC	4M+1D$	DE^	28$	BBBBB$	Ind	4	
Mech Engineering with Electronic Systems (MEng)	H3HP	3FT/4FT deg	M+P	BCC	4M+1D$	DE^	28$	BBBBB$	Ind	14	

	course details		98 expected requirements							96 entry stats
TITLE	CODE	COURSE	SUBJECTS	A/AS	NO/C	AGNVQ	IB	SQA(H)	SQA	RATIO A/AS
CARDIFF Univ of Wales										
Computer Systems	GH56	3FT deg	M	18-20	MO+2D		Ind	AABBB		39
Computer Systems	HG66	3FT deg	M	18-24	5M $		28$	BBBC	Ind	5 14/16
Electrical and Electronic Engineering	HHM6	4SW deg	M	BCC-CCC	5M $		Ind			4
Electrical and Electronic Engineering	HH5Q	4FT deg	M	BBB						4 22/24
Electrical and Electronic Engineering	HH56	3FT deg	M	BCC-CCC	5M $		Ind			5
Electrical and Electronic Engineering	HH5P	5SW deg								
Electronic Engineering	H603	5SW deg								
Electronic Engineering	H602	4FT deg								
Electronic Engineering	H601	4SW deg	M	BCC-CCC	5M $		Ind			4
Electronic Engineering	H600	3FT deg	M	BCC-CCC	5M $		Ind			3
Univ of Wales INST, CARDIFF										
Electronics	H601	4FT deg	* g	E	N	P$ gi	Ind	Ind	Ind	1
Electronics Design	H602	3FT deg	* g	EE	N	M$ gi	Ind	Ind	Ind	5
Technology for Healthcare	H6B8	3FT deg	* g	4	N	P$ go	Ind	CCCC	Ind	
Communications	026H	2FT HND	* g	E	N	P$ gi	Ind	Ind	Ind	7
Design and Manufacture	006H	2FT HND	* g	E	N	P$ gi	Ind	Ind	Ind	
Electrical Power Systems	195H	2FT HND	* g	E	N	P$ gi	Ind	Ind	Ind	
Microelectronics	116H	2FT HND	* g	E	N	P$ gi	Ind	Ind	Ind	3
Univ of CENTRAL ENGLAND										
Electrical Power Engineering	H520	3FT/4SW deg	M g	12	3M $	ME1	24$	CCC$	Ind	14
Electrical Power Engineering Foundation year	H528▼	4FT/5SW deg	* g	2	N	P*	Ind	CC	Ind	1
Electronic & Communication Eng Foundation Year	H628▼	4FT/5SW deg	* g	2	N	P*	Ind	CC	Ind	4
Electronic & Control Eng Foundation Year	H648▼	4FT/5SW deg	* g	2	N	P*	Ind	CC	Ind	
Electronic Eng with French Foundation Year	H6RC▼	4FT/5SW deg	* g	2	N	P*	Ind	CC	Ind	
Electronic Eng with German Foundation Year	HR62▼	4FT/5SW deg	* g	2	N	P*	Ind	CC	Ind	
Electronic Engineering	H600	3FT/4SW deg	M g	12	3M $	ME1	24$	CCC$	Ind	11
Electronic Engineering Foundation Year	H608▼	4FT/5SW deg	* g	2	N	P*	Ind	CC	Ind	1
Electronic Engineering with French	H6R1	3FT/4SW deg	M g	12	3M $	ME1	24$	CCC$	Ind	
Electronic Engineering with German	H6RG	3FT/4SW deg	M g	12	3M $	ME1	24$	CCC$	Ind	
Electronic Engineering with German St Foun Yr	H6RF▼	5EXT deg	* g	2	$	P* go	Ind	CC$	Ind	
Electronic Engineering with German Studies	H6R2	4FT deg	M g	12	3M $	ME1 go	24$	CCC$	Ind	
Electronic and Communication Engineering	H620	3FT/4SW deg	M g	12	3M $	ME1	24$	CCC$	Ind	8
Electronic and Control Engineering	H640	3FT/4SW deg	M g	12	3M $	ME1	24$	CCC$	Ind	11
Engineering Systems	H641	3FT/4SW deg	M g	12	3M $	ME1	24$	CCC$	Ind	
Visual Communication (Time-Based Media)	EH26	3FT deg	FA/Pf	18	MO	M$	28	BBBB	Ind	
Visual Communication (Time-Based Media)	WH26	3FT deg	Fa/Pf	18	MO	M$	28	BBBB	Ind	
Engineering (Electronics and Communications)	126H	2FT/3SW HND	M/P	2	$	PE1	24	CC$	Ind	
Engineering (Electronics and Control)	046H	2FT/3SW HND	M/P	2	$	PE1	24	CC$	Ind	
Engineering (Electronics and Power)	125H	2FT/3SW HND	M/P	2	$	PE1	24	CC$	Ind	
Engineering (Electronics)	006H	2FT/3SW HND	M/P	2	$	PE1	24	CC$	Ind	8
Univ of CENTRAL LANCASHIRE										
Electronic Engineering	H600▼	3FT/4SW deg	M+P	DD	MO	M$	26	BCCC	Ind	
Electronic Engineering (Year 0)	H608	1FT deg	*	E	N	P	Ind	Ind	Ind	
Electronics	H612	3FT deg	* g	DD	MO	M$	26	BCCC	Ind	
Electronics (Year 0)	H618	4FT deg	*	E	N	P	Ind	Ind	Ind	
Media Technology	HP64	3FT deg	* g	14	MO	D	26	BCCC	Ind	
Combined Honours Programme *Electronics*	Y400	3FT deg	* g	4	N	P$	24	CCC	Ind	
Electronic Engineering	206H▼	2FT HND								
Electronics	106H▼	2FT HND								
Engineering (Electronic or Electrical and Elect)	006H	2FT HND	* g	E	N	P	Ind	Ind	Ind	

course details   98 expected requirements   96 entry stats

TITLE	CODE	COURSE	SUBJECTS	A/AS	ND/C	AGNVQ	IB	SQA(H)	SQA	RATIO A/AS
CITY Univ										
Electrical and Electronic Eng (Foundation)	HH65	4FT deg	M+P	EE	Ind $	M$	20$	ABB$	N$	3
Electrical and Electronic Eng (MEng)	H6HM	5SW deg	M+P	BBC	4D $		30$	AABBB$	X	
Electrical and Electronic Eng Specialisations	H640	3FT deg	M+P	CCD	3M+2D$	D$^	27$	BBBBB$	HN$	
Electrical and Electronic Eng Specialisations	H641	4SW deg	M+P	CCD	3M+2D$	D$^	27$	BBBBB$	HN$	20
Electrical and Electronic Engineering	H6H5	3FT deg	M+P	CCD	3M+2D$	D$^	27$	BBBBB$	HN$	20
Electrical and Electronic Engineering	HH56	3FT deg	M+P	DDE	5M $	M$^ | 24$	BBCCC$	N$	2	8/12
Electrical and Electronic Engineering	H680	4SW deg	M+P	CCD	3M+2D$	D$^	27$	BBBBB$	HN$	29
Electrical and Electronic Engineering (MEng)	H6HN	4FT deg	M+P	BBC	4D $		30$	AABBB$	X	
CITY of LIVERPOOL Comm COLL										
Electronics and Communications	026H	2FT HND								
Electronics, Power and Television	086H	2FT HND								
COVENTRY Univ										
Avionic Systems Engineering	HH46	3/4FT 4/5SW deg	M+S	12-18	3M $	M+	24$	BBCC$	Ind	
Communication Systems Engineering(MEng/BEng/BSc)	H620	3FT/4SW 4FT/5SW deg	M+S	12-18	3M $	M+	24$	BBCC$	Ind	37
Computer and Control Systems	GH66	4FT/5SW deg								
Electrical and Electronic Eng (MEng/BEng/BSc)	HH56	3FT/4SW 4FT/5SW deg	M+S	12-18	3M $	M+	24$	BBCC$	Ind	9	10/16
Electronic Product Engineering	H680	3FT/4SW 4FT/5SW deg	M/S/Ds g	8	3M $		24$	BBCC$	Ind	22
Engineering Systems with Mathematics	H6G1	3FT deg	M+S	14-18	5M $		24$	BBCC$	Ind	
Information Systems Engineering	H610	3FT/4SW 4FT/5SW deg	M+S	8-18	3M $	M+	24$	BBCC$	Ind	4
Medical Instrumentation	B8H6	3FT/4SW deg	P+C/B g	CC	Ind	Ind	Ind	Ind	Ind	4
Medical Instrumentation	H677	4FT/5SW deg	* g		Ind	Ind	Ind	Ind	Ind	
Medical Instrumentation with European Study	H679	4FT/5SW deg								
Systems and Control Engineering	H640	3FT/4SW 4FT/5SW deg	S/M	12-18	3M $	M+	24$	BBCC$	Ind	
Electrical and Electronic Engineering	65HH	2FT/3SW HND	M/S		$		X	X	Ind	3	2/8
CRANFIELD Univ										
Electrical Engineering	H500	3FT deg	M+P g	BC-BCC	4M $	D$	Ind	Ind	Ind	6
Electrical Engineering with Management	H510	3FT deg	M+P g	BC-CCC	4M $	D$	Ind	Ind	Ind	
Electronic Systems Engineering	H600	3FT deg	M+P g	BC-BCC	4M $	D$	Ind	Ind	Ind	9
CROYDON COLL										
Electrical and Electronic Engineering	65HH	2FT HND	*	E	N $	P$	Ind	Ind		
DE MONTFORT Univ										
Communication Engineering	H620▼	3FT/4SW deg	M+P g	16	4M+1D$	M	26$	BBBB	Ind	
Control System Design	H640▼	3FT/4SW deg	M+P g	16	4M+1D$	M	26$	BBBB	Ind	
Electrical Engineering	H500▼	3FT/4SW deg	M+P g	16	4M+1D$	M	26$	BBBB	Ind	33
Electronic Engineering	H600▼	3FT/4SW deg	M+P g	16	4M+1D$	M	26$	BBBB	Ind	4
Media Technology	HP64▼	3FT/4SW deg	g	16	4M	M	26	BBBB	Ind	
Univ of DERBY										
Electrical and Electronic Engineering	HH56	3FT deg	M/S	10	4M $	M$	26$	CCCD$	Ind	
Electrical and Electronic Engineering	HFC9	3FT deg	M+P	18	8M $	D+2	30$	BBBCC$	Ind	
Electronics Product Design	HH67	3FT deg	M/S	10	4M $	M$	26$	CCCD$	Ind	6
Music Technology and Audio Systems Design	H682	3FT deg	S/M	14	8M $	D$	28$	BBCC$	Ind	1	6/22
Electrical/Electronic Engineering	65HH	2FT HND	S/M	4	N $	P$	Dip$	CCD$	Ind	9
Electronics Product Design	086H	2FT HND	S/M	4	N $	P$	Dip$	CCD$	Ind	4
Electronics with Music Technology	286H	2FT HND	S	6	2M $	P$	Dip$	CCC$	Ind	4	2/16
DONCASTER COLL										
Mining and Electrical Engineering	JH15	3FT deg		CC	3M	Ind	Ind	Ind	Ind	
Electronic Engineering and Computing Technology	026H	2FT HND		E	N		Ind	Ind	Ind	

Engineering – Electrical and Electronic 23

	course details			98 expected requirements						96 entry stats	
TITLE	CODE	COURSE	SUBJECTS	A/AS	ND/C	AGNVQ	IB	SQA(H)	SQA	RATIO	A/AS
DUDLEY COLLEGE of Technology											
Engineering (Electrical/Electronics)	006H	2FT HND	* g	2	Ind	Ind					
Engineering (Instrumentation and Control)	046H	2FT HND									
Engineering (Mechatronics)	63HH	2FT HND	* g	2	Ind	Ind					
Univ of DUNDEE											
Applied Computing and Digital Microelectronics	GHM6	4FT deg	M+<u>S</u> g	14	5M $	M$^	25$	BBBC$	N$	5	
Electronic Eng and Microcomputer Systems (BEng)	HG66	3FT/4FT deg	M+<u>P/Ds</u> g	12	5M $	M$^	26$	BBCC$	N$		
Electronic Eng and Microcomputer Systems (MEng)	GH66	4FT/5FT deg	M+<u>P/Ds</u> g	12	5M $	M$^	26$	BBCC$	N$		
Electronic Engineering and Physics	HF63	3FT/4FT deg	M+<u>P/Ds</u> g	12	5M $	M$^	26$	BBCC$	N$	5	
Electronic Engineering and Physics (MEng)	FH3P	4FT/5FT deg	M+<u>P/Ds</u> g	12	5M $	M$^	26$	BBCC$	N$		
Electronic Engineering with Management	H6N1	3FT/4FT deg	M+<u>P/Ds</u> g	12	5M $	M$^	26$	BBCC$	N$	12	
Electronic Engineering with Management (MEng)	H6NC	4FT/5FT deg	M+<u>P/Ds</u> g	12	5M $	M$^	26$	BBCC$	N$		
Electronic and Electrical Engineering	HH56	3FT/4FT deg	M+<u>P/Ds</u> g	12	5M $	M$^	26$	BBCC$	N$	6	8/14
Electronic and Electrical Engineering (MEng)	HH65	4FT/5FT deg	M+<u>P/Ds</u> g	12	5M $	M$^	26$	BBCC$	N$		
Mathematics and Digital Microelectronics	GHC6	4FT deg	M+<u>S</u> g	14	5M $	M$^	25$	BBCC$	N$		
Semiconductor Engineering	H6F2	3FT/4FT deg	M+<u>P/Ds</u> g	12	5M $	M$^	26$	BBCC$	N$		
Semiconductor Engineering (MEng)	H6FF	4FT/5FT deg	M+<u>P/Ds</u> g	12	5M $	MS^	26$	BBCC$	N$		
Univ of DURHAM											
Engineering (Electrical) (4 Yrs)	H500	4FT deg	<u>M</u>	22	2M+4D	Ind	30$	AAAAB$	Ind	4	22/28
Engineering (Electronic) (4 Yrs)	H600	4FT deg	<u>M</u>	22	2M+4D	Ind	30$	AAAAB$	Ind	20	26/28
Engineering (Information Systems) (4 Yrs)	H610	4FT deg	<u>M</u>	22	2M+4D	Ind	30$	AAAAB$	Ind	22	
Natural Sciences *Electronic Engineering*	Y160	3FT deg	<u>M</u>+S	ABB	Ind	X	33$	CSYS$	X		
Univ of EAST ANGLIA											
Electronic Design and Technology	H608	3FT deg	<u>M</u>+S	CDD	4M $	M^	26$	BBCC	N$	2	
Electronic Eng (BEng) with a Yr in Europe(4 Yrs)	H604	4FT deg	<u>M</u>+S	CCC	4M $	M^	28$	BBBC	N$	5	
Electronic Eng (BEng) with a Yr in N Amer(3 Yrs)	H605	3FT deg	<u>M</u>+S	BBC	5D $	D^	30$	BBBBB	HN	8	
Electronic Engineering (4 years)	H600	4FT deg	<u>M</u>+S	ABB	7D $	X	30$	BBBBB	HN	1	
Electronic Engineering (BEng)	H602	3FT deg	<u>M</u>+S	CCD	4M $		28$	BBBC	N$	7	14/20
Electronic Engineering w a Yr in N Amer (4 yrs)	H601	4FT deg	<u>M</u>+S	ABB	7D $	X	30$	BBBBB	HN	1	
Electronic Systems Engineering (4 years)	H640	4FT deg	<u>S</u>								6/ 9
Electronics (BSc Tech)	H603	3FT deg	<u>M</u>+S	DD	3M $	M	24$	CCCC	N$		
Electronics with Business	H6N1	3FT deg	<u>M</u>+S	CCD	4M $	M^	28$	BBBC	N$		
Media Engineering	HP64	3FT deg		BBC							
Univ of EAST LONDON											
Computer and Control Engineering	GH66	3FT/4SW deg	* g	12	3M	ME	Ind	Ind	Ind	44	
Electrical & Electronic Engineering (Ext)	HH5Q▼	4FT/5SW deg	* g	12	MO	ME					
Electrical and Electronic Engineering	HH56▼	3FT/4SW deg	* g	12	3M	ME	Ind	Ind	Ind	6	
Integrated Electronic Systems Eng & Manufacture	H680	3FT/4SW deg	* g	12	3M	ME	Ind	Ind	Ind	4	
Integrated Manufacturing Syst Eng & Electronics	HH76	3FT/4SW deg	* g	12	3M	ME	Ind	Ind	Ind		
Telecommunications Engineering	H620	3FT/4SW deg	* g	12	MO	ME	Ind	Ind	Ind	17	
Electrical and Electronic Engineering	65HH	2FT/3SW HND	* g	12	MO	ME	Ind	Ind	Ind	6	
Electronics and Manufacturing Technology	76HH	2FT/3SW HND	* g	12	MO	ME	Ind	Ind	Ind		
Univ of EDINBURGH											
Computer Science and Electronics (BEng)	GH56	4FT deg	<u>M</u>+P	CCC	MO $		Dip$	BBBB$	N$	7	
Electrical & Mechanical Engineering (MEng)	HH3M	5FT deg	<u>M</u>+P	CCC	MO $		Dip$	BBBB$	N$		
Electrical and Mechanical Engineering (BEng)	HH35	4FT deg	<u>M</u>+P	CCC	MO $		Dip$	BBBB$	N$	11	
Electronics & Elec Eng (Communications) (BEng)	H620	4FT deg	<u>M</u>+P	CCC	MO $		Dip$	BBBB$	N$	12	
Electronics & Elec Eng (Microelectronics) (BEng)	H610	4FT deg	<u>M</u>+P	CCC	MO $		Dip$	BBBB$	N$	5	
Electronics (MEng)	H600	5FT deg	<u>M</u>+P	CCC	MO $		Dip$	BBBB$	N$	5	26/30

course details			**98 expected requirements**							**96 entry stats**	
TITLE	CODE	COURSE	SUBJECTS	A/AS	ND/C	AGNVQ	IB	SQA(H)	SQA	RATIO	A/AS
Electronics and Computer Science (BEng)	HG65	4FT deg	M+P	CCC	MO $		Dip$	BBBB$	N$	5	
Electronics and Electrical Engineering (BEng)	HH56	4FT deg	M+P	CCC	MO $		Dip$	BBBB$	N$	8	20/28
Electronics and Electrical Engineering (MEng)	HH5P	4FT deg	M+P	CCC	MO $		Dip$	BBBB$	N$		
Electronics and Physics (BEng)	HF63	4FT deg	M+P	CCC	MO $		Dip$	BBBB$	N$	12	
Physics and Electronics (BEng)	FH36	4FT deg	M+P	CCD	MO $		Dip$	BBBC$	N$	6	

Univ of ESSEX

TITLE	CODE	COURSE	SUBJECTS	A/AS	ND/C	AGNVQ	IB	SQA(H)	SQA	RATIO	A/AS
Audio Systems Engineering (BEng)	H603	3FT/4FT deg	P+M	14-18	MO $	D	28	BBCC	Ind		
Audio Systems Engineering (MEng)	H604	4FT deg	M+Cs/Es/P	BCC	MO $	Ind	28$	CSYS	Ind		
Computer Engineering	H616	3FT/4FT deg	(P+M)/*	14-18	MO $	D	28	BBCC	Ind	13	
Computers & Networks	H6G7	3FT/4FT deg	(P+M)/*	14-18	MO $	D	28	BBCC	Ind	6	
Electronic & Computer Systems Engineering (MEng)	H606	4FT deg	M+Cs/Es/P	BCC	MO $	Ind	28$	CSYS	Ind		
Electronic & Information Systems Eng (MEng)	H607	4FT deg	M+Cs/Es/P	BCC	MO $	Ind	28$	CSYS	Ind		
Electronic & Telecommunications Sys Eng (MEng)	H608	4FT deg	M+Cs/Es/P	BCC	MO $	Ind	28$	CSYS	Ind		
Electronic Engineering	H600	3FT/4FT deg	(P+M)/*	14-18	MO $	D	28	BBCC	Ind	5	
Electronic Engineering with a Modern Language	H6T9	3FT/4FT deg	(P+M)/*	14-18	MO $	D	28	BBCC	Ind		
Electronic Systems Eng with a Modern Lang (MEng)	H6TX	4FT deg	M+Cs/Es/P	BCC	MO $	Ind	28$	CSYS	Ind		
Electronic Systems Engineering (4 Yrs)(MEng)	H605	4FT deg	M+Cs/Es/P	20	HN $	Ind	28	BBBB	Ind	7	
Information Management Systems (4 years)	H630	4FT deg	g	14	MO	M$	26	BBCC	Ind	6	
Information Systems & Networks (MEng)	HG6P	4FT deg	M+Cs/Es/P	BCC	MO $	Ind	28$	CSYS	Ind		
Information Systems Engineering	H620	3FT/4FT deg	(P+M)/*	14-18	MO $	D	28	BBCC	Ind	6	
Multimedia Telecommunications (MEng)	H627	4FT deg	M+Cs/Es/P	BCC	MO $	Ind	28$	CSYS	Ind		
Optical Communications	H635	4FT deg	M+Cs/Es/P	BCC	MO $	Ind	28$	CSYS	Ind		
Telecommunications Engineering	H626	3FT/4FT deg	(P+M)/*	14-18	MO $	D	28	BBCC	Ind	6	

Univ of EXETER

TITLE	CODE	COURSE	SUBJECTS	A/AS	ND/C	AGNVQ	IB	SQA(H)	SQA	RATIO	A/AS
Electronic Engineering (MEng)	H601	4FT deg	M g	BCC	MO+1D	M$^	32$	Ind	Ind	8	14/26

FARNBOROUGH COLL of Technology

TITLE	CODE	COURSE	SUBJECTS	A/AS	ND/C	AGNVQ	IB	SQA(H)	SQA	RATIO	A/AS
Media Technology (Production)	HP64	3FT deg		12	Ind	D*	Ind	Ind	Ind	4	10/22
Electronic and Computer Systems Engineering	66HG	2FT HND		E	N	P*	Ind	Ind	Ind	3	
Media Technology (Production with Business)	46PH	2FT HND		6	Ind	M*	Ind	Ind	Ind	4	6/12

Univ of GLAMORGAN

TITLE	CODE	COURSE	SUBJECTS	A/AS	ND/C	AGNVQ	IB	SQA(H)	SQA	RATIO	A/AS
Design and Electronics	H602	3FT/4SW deg	S g	8	3M $	M$	Ind	Ind	Ind		
Electrical and Electronic Eng Found Year	HH6N	4EXT deg	* g	E	Ind	Ind	Ind	Ind	Ind	2	
Electrical and Electronic Engineering	HH5P	3FT/4SW deg	M+P/S/Cs g	CD	3M $	M$	Ind	Ind	Ind	11	
Electrical and Electronic Engineering	HH56▼	3FT/4SW deg	M+S/Cs g	4	N $	P$	Ind	Ind	Ind	11	
Electrical and Electronic Engineering (MEng)	HH5Q	5SW deg	M+P/S/Cs g	CD	3M $	M$	Ind	Ind	Ind	7	
Electromechanical Power Systems	H5H3	3FT/4SW deg	M+P/S/Cs g	CD	3M $	M$	Ind	Ind	Ind		
Electromechanical Systems	HH53	5SW deg	M+S/Cs g	CD	3M $	M$	Ind	Ind	Ind	2	
Electronic & Communication Engineering	H620	3FT/4SW deg	M+S/Cs g	CD	3M $	M$	Ind	Ind	Ind	5	
Electronic Engineering	H600	3FT/4SW deg	M+S/Cs g	CD	3M $	M$	Ind	Ind	Ind	22	
Electronics	H601	3FT/4SW deg	M/S/Cs g	8	3M $	M$	Ind	Ind	Ind	2	
Electronics with European Business Studies	H6N1	3FT/4SW deg	M+S/Cs g	8	3M $	M$	Ind	Ind	Ind		
Mechatronic Engineering	HH3P	3FT deg	M/Es g	CD	3M $	M$	Ind	Ind	Ind		
Mechatronic Engineering	HH36	3FT deg	M/Es g	CD	3M $	M$	Ind	Ind	Ind		
Combined Studies (Honours) *Electronics*	Y400	3FT deg	M/P g	8-16	Ind	Ind	Ind	Ind	Ind		
Combined Studies (Honours) *Image Processing*	Y400	3FT deg		8-16	Ind	Ind	Ind	Ind	Ind		
Combined Studies (Honours) *Media Electronics*	Y400	3FT deg	Es/P g	8-16	Ind	Ind	Ind	Ind	Ind		
Combined Studies (Honours) *Medical Electronics*	Y400	3FT deg	Es/P g	8-16	Ind	Ind	Ind	Ind	Ind		

			98 expected requirements							96 entry stats
TITLE	CODE	COURSE	SUBJECTS	A/AS	NO/C	AGNVQ	IB	SQA(H)	SQA	RATIO A/AS
Joint Honours *Electronics*	Y401	3FT deg	Es/P g	8-16	Ind	Ind	Ind	Ind	Ind	
Major/Minor Honours *Electronics*	Y402	3FT deg	P/M/Es g	8-16	Ind	Ind	Ind	Ind	Ind	
Major/Minor Honours *Image Processing*	Y402	3FT deg	* g	8-16	Ind	Ind	Ind	Ind	Ind	
Major/Minor Honours *Media Electronics*	Y402	3FT deg	Es/P g	8-16	Ind	Ind	Ind	Ind	Ind	
Major/Minor Honours *Medical Electronics*	Y402	3FT deg	Es/P g	8-16	Ind	Ind	Ind	Ind	Ind	
Electrical and Electronic Engineering	65HH	2FT/3SW HND	M+S/Cs g	D	$	P$	Ind	Ind	Ind	6
Mechatronic Engineering	63HH	3FT/4SW HND	M+S/Cs g	D	$	P$	Ind	BB$	N$	

Univ of GLASGOW

Avionics (Aeronautical) (MEng or BEng)	HHK6	4FT/5FT deg	M+S	BB	HN $	Ind	28$	BBBBC$	HN$	13
Avionics (Electronics) (BEng)	HHL6	4FT deg	M+P	CCD	MO	ME	24$	BBBBC$	N$	9
Electrical Power Engineering	HJ59	4FT deg	M+P	CCD	MO	ME	24$	BBBBC$	N$	10
Electronic Engineering and Physics	FH36	4FT deg	M+P	CCD	MO	ME	24$	BBBBC$	N$	17
Electronic Engineering with Optoelectronics	H6F3	4FT deg	M+P	CCD	MO	ME	24$	BBBBC$	N$	13
Electronic and Software Engineering	GH7P	4FT deg	M+P	CCD	MO	ME	24$	BBBBC$	N$	9
Electronic and Software Engineering	GH76	4FT deg	M+S	BBC-CCC	N	M	24$	BBBBB$	N	11
Electronics and Electrical Eng (European)(MEng)	HH65	5FT deg	M+P	BCC			30$	ABBBC$		
Electronics and Electrical Engineering	HH56	4FT deg	M+P	CCD	MO	ME	24$	BBBBC$	N$	10
Electronics with Music	H6W3	4FT deg	M+Mu	BCC	MO	ME	24$	ABBBB$	N$	3
Microcomputer Systems Engineering	GH66	4FT deg	M+P	CCD	MO	ME	24$	BBBBC$	N$	9
Physics/Electronic Engineering	FHH6	4FT deg	M+P	BBC-CCC	N	M	24$	BBBBB$	N	7

GLASGOW CALEDONIAN Univ

Electrical Power Engineering (BEngHons)	H520	4FT/5SW deg	M+P/C	CD	Ind		Ind	BCCC$	Ind	21
Electronic Engineering	H600	3FT deg	M/P/E	DEE	Ind		Ind	CCC$	Ind	2
Electronic Engineering BEng (Hons)	H601	4FT/5SW deg	M+E+S g	CD	Ind		Ind	BBC$	Ind	5
Manufacturing Systs Engineering BEng (Hons)	H7H6	4FT/5SW deg	M+P/C	CD	Ind		Ind	BBC$	Ind	4
Medical Engineering	H670	3FT deg								

Univ of GREENWICH

Electrical & Electronic Engineering (Extended)	HH5P▼	4EXT deg	* g	4	Ind	Ind	Ind	Ind	Ind	
Electrical Engineering	H500	3FT/4SW deg	M+P/S g	14	4M $	M+	24$	CCCC$	Ind	
Electrical Engineering (Extended)	H508▼	4EXT deg	* g	4	Ind	Ind	Ind	Ind	Ind	
Electrical and Electronic Engineering	HH56	3FT/4SW deg	M+P/S g	14	4M $	M+	24$	CCCC$	Ind	
Electronic Engineering	H600	3FT/4SW deg	M+P/S g	14	4M $	M+	24$	CCCC$	Ind	
Electronic Engineering (Extended)	H608▼	4EXT deg	* g	4	Ind	Ind	Ind	Ind	Ind	
Engineering (Electrical and Electronic)	HH5Q	3FT deg	* g	6	N	P	Ind	CC	Ind	
Electronic Engineering	006H▼	2FT HND	M/P/S g	6	N $	P+	Dip	CC	Ind	

HALTON COLL

Engineering (Mechatronics)	63HH	2FT HND	M+P	4	N	P	Ind	Ind	N	

HERIOT-WATT Univ

Computing and Electronics	GH56	4FT deg	M+P	CDD	MO	M$ go	28	BBBC	Ind	
Electrical & Electron Eng(Microwave & Optoelect)	HHN6	4FT deg	M+P	CDD	MO	M$ go	28	BBBC	Ind	
Electrical & Electronic Eng (2nd yr Ent) (MEng)	HHMP	4FT deg	M+P	CDD	MO	M$ go	28	BBBC	Ind	
Electrical & Electronic Eng (Automation System)	HH5P	4FT deg	M+P	CDD	MO	M$ go	28	BBBC	Ind	
Electrical & Electronic Eng (Communication Syst)	HH5Q	4FT deg	M+P	CDD	MO	M$ go	28	BBBC	Ind	
Electrical & Electronic Engineering (2nd yr Ent)	HH6M	3FT deg	M+P	CDD	MO	M$ go	28	BBBC	Ind	
Electrical & Electronic Engineering (Power Eng)	HHP5	4FT deg	M+P	CDD	MO	M$ go	28	BBBC	Ind	
Electrical and Electronic Eng (Computer Systems)	HHM6	4FT deg	M+P	CDD	MO	M$ go	28	BBBC	Ind	

course details			98 expected requirements							96 entry stats
TITLE	CODE	COURSE	SUBJECTS	A/AS	NO/C	AGNVQ	IB	SQA(H)	SQA	RATIO A/AS
Electrical and Electronic Engineering	HH56	4FT deg	M+P	CDD	MO	M$ go	28	BBBC	Ind	
Electrical and Electronic Engineering (MEng)	HH65	5FT deg	M+P	CDD	MO	M$ go	28	BBBC	Ind	
Electronics with Microelectronic Manuf Eng(MEng)	H6H7	5FT deg	P+M	CDD		M$ go	28	BBBC	Ind	
Information Systems Engineering	HG66	4FT deg	M+P	CDD	MO	M$^ go	28	BBBC	Ind	
Combined Studies *Electrical & Electronic Engineering*	Y100	4FT deg	M+P	DDE	Ind	M$ go	26	BCCC	Ind	

Univ of HERTFORDSHIRE

Applied Geology/Electronics	F6H6	3FT deg	* g	12	3M $	M$ gi	24$	CCCC$	Ind	
Applied Physics/Electronics	F3H6	3FT deg	M+P g	12	3M $	M$ gi	24$	CCCC$	Ind	
Business/Electronics	N1H6	3FT deg	* g	18	4M+4D	M$6 gi	26$	BBBC$	Ind	
Communication Systems	H620	3FT/4SW deg	M+P	16	3M $	Ind	Ind	CCC$	Ind	14
Communication Systems (Extended)	H628▼	4EXT/5EXTSW deg	*	2	N	Ind	Dip$	Ind	Ind	3
Computing/Electronics	G5H6	3FT deg	* g	12	3M $	M$ gi	24$	CCCC$	Ind	2
Digital Systems	H615	3FT/4SW deg	M+P	16	3M $	Ind	Ind	CCC$	Ind	4
Digital Systems (Extended)	H618▼	4FT/5EXTSW deg	*	2	N	Ind	Dip$	Ind	Ind	
Economics/Electronics	L1H6	3FT deg	* g	12	3M $	M$ gi	24$	CCCC$	Ind	2
Electrical Engineering	H500	3FT/4SW deg	M+P	16	3M $	Ind	Ind	CCC$	Ind	2
Electrical Engineering (Extended)	H508▼	4FT/5EXTSW deg	*	2	N	Ind	Dip$	Ind	Ind	
Electrical and Electronic Engineering	HH56	3FT/4SW deg	M+P	16	3M $	Ind	Ind	CCC$	Ind	6
Electrical and Electronic Engineering (Extended)	HH5P▼	4FT/5EXTSW deg	*	2	N	Ind	Dip$	Ind	Ind	
Electronic Eng with Medical Electronics	H670	3FT/4SW deg	M+P	16	3M $	Ind	Ind	CCC$	Ind	7
Electronic Eng with Medical Electronics (Ext)	H678▼	4FT/5EXTSW deg	*	2	N	Ind	Dip$	Ind	Ind	1
Electronic Engineering	H600	3FT/4SW deg	M+P	16	3M $	Ind	Ind	CCC$	Ind	5
Electronic Engineering (Extended)	H608▼	4FT/5EXTSW deg	*	2	N	Ind	Dip$	Ind	Ind	2
Electronic Engineering (MEng)	H601	4FT/5SW deg	M+2S	22	5M		Ind	Ind	Ind	
Electronic Music/Electronics	W3H6	3FT deg	Mu g	14	MO $	M$^ gi	26$	BCCC$	Ind	12
Electronics	H602	3FT deg	* g	12	3M $	M$ gi	24$	CCCC$	Ind	
Electronics Manufacture	H640	3FT/4SW deg	2(M/P/S/Cs)	16	3M$	Ind	$	Ind	Ind	6
Electronics Manufacture (Extended)	H648▼	4FT/5EXTSW deg	*	2	N	Ind	Dip$	Ind	Ind	
Electronics/Applied Geology	H6F6	3FT deg	* g	12	3M $	M$ gi	24$	CCCC$	Ind	
Electronics/Applied Physics	H6F3	3FT deg	M+P g	12	3M $	M$ gi	24$	CCCC$	Ind	
Electronics/Business	H6N1	3FT deg	* g	18	4M+4D	M$6 gi	26$	BBBC$	Ind	
Electronics/Computing	H6G5	3FT deg	* g	12	3M $	M$ gi	24$	CCCC$	Ind	6
Electronics/Economics	H6L1	3FT deg	* g	12	3M $	M$ gi	24$	CCCC$	Ind	
Electronics/Electronic Music	H6W3	3FT deg	Mu g	14	MO $	M$^ gi	26$	BCCC$	Ind	
Electronics/Environmental Science	H6F9	3FT deg	* g	14	MO $	M$ gi	26$	BCCC$	Ind	
Electronics/Human Biology	H6B1	3FT deg	S g	12	3M $	MS gi	24$	CCCC$	Ind	
Electronics/Law	H6M3	3FT deg	* g	20	4M+4D	D$ gi	26$	BBBC$	Ind	
Electronics/Linguistic Science	H6Q1	3FT deg	* g	14	MO $	M$ gi	26$	BCCC$	Ind	
Electronics/Manufacturing Systems	H6H7	3FT deg	* g	12	3M	M$ gi	24	CCCC		
Electronics/Mathematics	H6G1	3FT deg	M g	12	3M $	M$^ gi	24$	CCCC$	Ind	3
Electronics/Operational Research	H6N2	3FT deg	* g	12	3M $	M$ gi	24$	CCCC$	Ind	
Environmental Science/Electronics	F9H6	3FT deg	* g	14	MO $	M$ gi	26$	BCCC$	Ind	
Human Biology/Electronics	B1H6	3FT deg	S g	12	3M $	MS gi	24$	CCCC$	Ind	
Law/Electronics	M3H6	3FT deg	* g	20	4M+4D	D$ gi	26$	BBBC$	Ind	
Linguistic Science/Electronics	Q1H6	3FT deg	* g	14	MO $	M$ gi	26$	BCCC$	Ind	
Manufacturing Systems/Electronics	H7H6	3FT deg	* g	12	3M $	M$ gi	24$	CCCC$	Ind	
Mathematics/Electronics	G1H6	3FT deg	M g	12	3M $	M$^ gi	24$	CCCC$	Ind	
Medical Electronics	BH96	3FT/4SW deg	P/S	14	3M $	Ind	Dip$	Ind	Ind	2
Medical Electronics (Extended)	BH9P▼	4FT/5SW deg	*	2	N	Ind	Dip$	Ind	Ind	2
Medical Electronics with German Language	BH9Q	3FT/4SW deg	P/S	14	3M $		Dip$	Ind	Ind	
Operational Research/Electronics	N2H6	3FT deg	* g	12	3M $	M$ gi	24$	CCCC$	Ind	

Engineering – Electrical and Electronic 23

			98 expected requirements							96 entry stats
TITLE	CODE	COURSE	SUBJECTS	A/AS	NO/C	AGNVQ	IB	SQA(H)	SQA	RATIO A/AS
Power Electronics and Control	H641	3FT/4SW deg	M+P	16	3M $	Ind	Dip$	Ind	Ind	
Power Electronics and Control (Extended)	H649▼	4FT/5EXTSW deg	*	2	N	Ind	Dip$	Ind	Ind	
Combined Modular Scheme _Electronics_	Y100	3FT deg	* g	12	3M $	M$ gi	24$	CCCC$	Ind	
Mechatronics	63HH▼	2FT HND	M+P/S	2	N	Ind	$	Ind	Ind	

Univ of HUDDERSFIELD

Electronic & Communication Engineering (Extend)	H628	5SW deg	* g	DD	N	P go	Dip	CCC	Ind	
Electronic Design	H601	4SW deg	S g	12	4M $	M$ go	Ind	BBC	Ind	
Electronic Engineering	H600	4SW deg	M+S	12	4M $	M$ go	Ind	BBC	Ind	
Electronic Engineering (Extended)	H608	5SW deg	* g	DD	N	P go	Dip	CCC	Ind	
Electronic Engineering (MEng)	H602	5SW deg	M+S	CCC	3D $	M$3/^ go	Ind	Ind	Ind	
Electronic Engineering and Computer Systems	GH56	4SW deg	M+S	12	4M $	M$ go	Ind	BBC	Ind	
Electronic Engineering and Computer Systems(Ext)	GH5P	5SW deg	* g	DD	N	P go	Dip	CCC	Ind	
Electronic Engineering and Computer Systs (MEng)	GHM6	5SW deg	M+S	CCC	3D $	M$3/^ go	Ind	Ind	Ind	
Electronic and Communication Engineering	H620	4SW deg	M+S	12	4M $	M$ go	Ind	BBC	Ind	
Electronic and Communication Engineering (MEng)	H621	5SW deg	M+S	CCC	3D $	M$3/^ go	Ind	Ind	Ind	
Electronic and Electrical Engineering	HH56	4SW deg	M+S	12	4M $	M$ go	Ind	BBC	Ind	
Electronic and Electrical Engineering (Extended)	HH5P	5SW deg	* g	DD	N	P go	Dip	CCC	Ind	
Electronic and Electrical Engineering (MEng)	HHM6	5SW deg	M+S	CCC	3D $	M$3/^ go	Ind	Ind	Ind	
Engineering Systems: Control	H660	4SW deg	M+S	12	4M $	M$ go	Ind	Ind	Ind	
Engineering Systems: Control (Extended)	H668	5SW deg	* g	DD	N	P go	Dip	CCC	Ind	
Engineering Systems: Control (MEng)	H661	5SW deg	M+S	18	3D $	M$3/^ go	Ind	Ind	Ind	
Multimedia Technology	H6P4	4SW deg	S g	16-20	2D	M$ go	Ind	Ind	Ind	
Music Technology	HW63	3FT deg	S+Mu g	CC	4D	M$ go	Ind	Ind	Ind	
Electronic Engineering	006H	2FT HND	M/S	2	N	P$ go	Ind	CC	Ind	
Electronic and Electrical Engineering	65HH	2FT HND	M/S	2	N	P$ go	Ind	CC	Ind	
Industrial Measurement & Control	046H	2FT HND	M/S	2	N	P$ go	Ind	Ind	Ind	

Univ of HULL

Electronic Communications Engineering (MEng)	H620	4FT deg	S+M	BCC	MO+2D$	ME^ gi	26$	BCCC	Ind	5
Electronic Control and Robot Engineering (MEng)	H651	4FT deg	S+M	BCC	MO+2D$	ME^ gi	26$	BCCC	Ind	7 10/14
Electronic Engineering	H600	3FT deg	S+M	20	MO	M$+	25$	BCCC	Ind	
Electronic Engineering (Yr 1 Franchised)	H601	4FT deg	*	CD	N	PE	24	BCCC	Ind	5
Environmental Electronics (MEng)	H684	4FT deg	S+M	CCC	MO+2D$	M$^ gi	26$	BCCC	Ind	2
Mechatronics	HH3P	3FT deg	S+M	20	MO	M$+	26$	BCCC	Ind	
Mechatronics (MEng)	HH36	4FT deg	S+M	BCC	MO+2D$	ME^ gi	26$	BCCC	Ind	4 18/24
Mechatronics (Yr 1 Franchised)	HH63	4FT deg	* g	10	N	P*6/^ gi	24	CCCCD	Ind	
Microelectronic Systems Engineering (4 Yrs)	H610	4FT deg	S+M	CCC	MO+2D$	ME^ gi	26$	BCCC	Ind	2
Optoelectronic Systems Engineering (4 Yrs)	H635	4FT deg	S+M	CCC	MO+2D$	ME^ gi	26$	BCCC	Ind	4

IMPERIAL COLL (Univ of London)

Electrical & Elect Eng with a Yr Abroad (MEng)	H501	4FT deg	M+P g	AAB-BBB	HN/DO$	X	$	CSYS$	HN$	6 30/30
Electrical & Electronic Eng with Mgt (MEng)	H5NC	4FT deg	M+P g	AAB-BBB	HN/DO$	X	$	CSYS$	HN$	4 26/30
Electrical & Electronic Engineering (MEng)	HHM6	4FT deg	M+P g	AAB-BBB	HN/DO	X	$	CSYS$	HN$	4 26/30
Electrical and Electronic Engineering	HH56	3FT deg	M+P g	AAB-BBB	HN/DO	X	$	CSYS$	HN$	35 28/30
Information Systems Engineering	HG65	3FT deg	M+P	BBB	HN/DO	X	$	CSYS$	HN$	12
Information Systems Engineering (MEng)	GH56	4FT deg	M+P	BBB	HN/DO	X	$	CSYS$	HN$	4 26/30

Univ of KENT

Communications Engineering	H620	3FT deg	M+P	BB-BCC	MO $	Ind	28$	Ind	Ind	7
Computer Systems Eng including a foundation yr	H614	4FT deg	* g		N	Ind	Dip	Ind	Ind	1 6/14
Computer Systems Engineering	H610	3FT/4SW deg	M+P	BCC	MO $	Ind	28$	Ind	Ind	7 14/26
Computer Systems Engineering (MEng)	H611	4FT deg	M+P	BCC	MO $	Ind	28$	Ind	Ind	
Computer Systems Engineering with a year in Ind	H612	4FT deg	M+P	BCC	MO $	Ind	28$	Ind	Ind	

course details			98 expected requirements							96 entry stats	
TITLE	CODE	COURSE	SUBJECTS	A/AS	ND/C	RGNVQ	IB	SQA(H)	SQA	RATIO	A/AS
Digital Electronics	H616	3FT deg	M+P	BB-BCC	MO $	Ind	28$	Ind	Ind	4	
Electronic Engineering	H600	3FT deg	M+P	BB-BCC	MO $	Ind	28$	Ind	Ind	5	
Electronic Engineering including a foundation yr	H605	4FT deg	* g		N	Ind	Dip	Ind	Ind	2	4/18
Electronic Engineering with Medical Electronics	H673	3FT deg	M+P	BB-BCC	MO $	Ind	28$	Ind	Ind	12	
Electronic Engineering with a year in Europe	H601	4FT deg	M+P g	BB-BCC	MO $	Ind	28$	Ind	Ind	6	
Electronic Engineering with a year overseas	H602	4FT deg	M+P	BB-BCC	MO $	Ind	28$	Ind	Ind		

KING'S COLL LONDON (Univ of London)

Communications and Radio Engineering	H622	4FT deg									
Communications and Radio Engineering	H621	3FT deg	M+P	BBC	MO+3D		28	BBBCC$	Ind	10	
Communications and Radio Engineering with a year	H623	5FT deg									
Computer Science and Digital Electronics	GH56	3FT deg	M	20	X	X	30$	ABBBB$	X	9	
Computer Syst and Electronics with a yr Industry	GH6Q	5FT deg	M	20	X		30$	ABBBB$			
Computer Systems & Electronics with 1 Yr abroad	GH6P	4FT deg	M+P	BBC	MO+3D		28	BBBCC$	Ind	10	
Computer Systems and Electronics	GH66	3FT deg	M+P	BBC	MO+3D		28	BBBCC$	Ind	7	18/30
Computer Systems and Electronics	GHP6	4FT deg									
Electonic Engineering with a year in Industry	H604	5FT deg									
Electronic Engineering	H603	4FT deg									
Electronic Engineering	H602	3FT deg	M+P	BBC	MO+3D		28	BBBCC$		11	
Mechatronics	HH36	3FT deg	M+P	BCC	MO+1D		28	BBCCC$	Ind	7	16/26
Mechatronics and Manufacturing Systems	HH6T	4FT deg	M+P	BCC	MO+1D		28	BBCCC$	Ind	2	16/18

KINGSTON Univ

Electronic Engineering	H601	4SW deg		4-6							
Electronic Engineering	H600	3FT deg	M	4-6	Ind	PE	Ind	Ind	Ind		
Electronic Engineering with Computing	H6GM▼	4FT/5SW deg	*	4-6	Ind		Ind	Ind	Ind	2	
Electronic Engineering with Computing(BEng/MEng)	H6GN	3FT/4FT deg	M+S/Cs/Ec/Es/Ds	8	5M $	ME3	Ind	Ind	Ind	3	6/10
Electronic Engineering with Computing(BEng/MEng)	H6G5	4SW/5SW deg	M+S/Cs/Ec/Es/Ds	8	5M $	ME3	Ind	Ind	Ind	4	
Physics with Electronics & Computing	F3HP▼	4EXT deg	*		Ind		Ind	Ind	Ind	1	
Physics with Electronics and Computing	F3H6	3FT deg	P/M	12	2M $	Ind	Ind	CCC	Ind	5	
Electronic Engineering	006H▼	2FT HND	M	4	N	PE$	Ind	Ind	Ind	3	

LANCASTER Univ

Computer Systems Engineering (BEng)	GH66	3FT/4SW deg	M+P/Cs/Ds/Es g	20	MO+1D		30$	BBBBB$	Ind		
Computer Systems Engineering (MEng)	GH6P	4FT/5SW deg	M+P/Cs/Ds/Es g	20	MO+2D		30$	BBBBB$	Ind		
Electronic Communications Engineering (BEng)	H620	3FT deg	M+P/Cs/Es/Ds g	20	MO+1D		30$	BBBBB$	Ind		
Electronic Communications Engineering (MEng)	H621	4FT deg	M+P/Cs/Es/Ds g	20	MO+1D		30$	BBBBB$	Ind		
Electronic Engineering with Management Sci(MEng)	H6NC	4FT/5SW deg	M+P/Cs/Es/Ds g	20	MO+2D		30$	AABBB$	Ind		
Electronic Engineering with Management Science	H6N1	3FT/4SW deg	M+P/Cs/Es/Ds g	20	MO+1D		30$	BBBBB$	Ind		
Engineering (Electronic)	H600	3FT/4SW deg	M+P/Cs/Es/Ds g	20	MO+1D		30$	BBBBB$	Ind		
Engineering (Electronic) (MEng)	H606	4FT/5SW deg	M+P/Cs/Es/Ds g	20	MO+2D		30$	BBBBB$	Ind		
Engineering Physics	FH36	3FT/4SW deg	M+P g	CCE	MO $		22$	BBCCC$	Ind		
Mechatronics	HH63	3FT/4SW deg	M+P/Cs/Es/Ds g	20	MO+1D		30$	BBBBB$	Ind		
Mechatronics (MEng)	HH3Q	4FT/5SW deg	M+P/Cs/Es/Ds g	24	MO+2D		30$	BBBBB$	Ind		

Univ of LEEDS

Electronic Engineering	H600	3FT/4FT deg	M+P g	BBC	1M+5D$	Ind	30$	ABBBC	Ind	9	12/26
Electronic and Communications Engineering	H620	3FT/4FT deg	M+P g	BBC	1M+5D$	Ind	30$	CSYS	Ind		
Electronic and Computer Engineering	H6G6	3FT/4FT deg	M+P g	BBC	1M+5D$	Ind	30$	ABBBC	Ind	10	18/24
Electronic and Electrical Engineering	H6H5	3FT/4FT deg	M+P g	BBC	1M+5D$	Ind	30$	ABBBC	Ind	7	12/28
Mechanical with Medical Engineering	HH3P	4FT deg	M+P g	BBC	3M+3D$		30$	ABBBC	Ind		
Mechatronics	HH36	3FT/4FT deg	M+P g	BBC	4M+2D$ D$^ go		30$	ABBBC	Ind	5	18/24
Music-Electronic Engineering	WH36	3FT deg	Mu+P/M g	BBC	Ind	Ind	30$	CSYS	Ind	25	
Physics with Elect & Instrumentation	F3H6	3FT/4FT deg	P+M g	CCC	1M+4D$ DS^ go		26$	BBBCC	Ind	5	

TITLE	CODE	COURSE	SUBJECTS	A/AS	ND/C	RGNVQ	IB	SQA(H)	SQA	RATIO	A/AS
LEEDS METROPOLITAN Univ											
Electronic Media and Communications	H620	3FT/4SW deg									
Electronics, Music and Media Technology	H682	3FT/4SW deg								7	10/24
MultiMedia Technology	HP64	3FT/4SW deg	M/S g	8	3M $	P$ go	22$	BCC$	Ind	7	6/22
Electronic Media and Communications	026H	2FT/3SW deg									
Multimedia Technology	46PH	2FT/3SW HND									
Musical Instrument Technology.	65HJ	2FT HND									
Univ of LEICESTER											
Elec & Software Eng with Ind in Europe (MEng)	HG6R	5SW deg	M+P g	18	5M$	M$6^	30$	ABBBB$	Ind		
Electrical & Electronic w. Indust in Eur (MEng)	HH6N	5SW deg	M+P g	18	5M $	M$6^	30$	ABBBB$	Ind		
Electrical and Electronic (MEng)	HH65	4FT deg	M+P g	18	5M $	M$6^	30$	ABBBB$	Ind		
Electrical and Electronic Engineering	HH56	3FT deg	M+P g	18	4M $	M$6^	28$	BBBBC$	Ind		13/26
Electrical and Electronic w. Industry in Europe	HH5Q	4SW deg	M+P g	18	5M $	M$6^	28$	BBBBC$	Ind		
Electrical and Electronic with Industry	HH5P	4SW deg	M+P g	18	4M $	M$6^	28$	BBBBC$	Ind		
Electrical and Electronic with Industry (MEng)	HH6M	5SW deg	M+P g	18	5M $	M$6^	30$	ABBBB$	Ind		
Electronic & Software Eng with Ind in Europe	HGQR	4FT deg	M+P g	18	5M$	M$6^	28$	BBBBC$	Ind		
Electronic & Software Engineering with Industry	HG6T	4FT deg	M$6^	18	5M$	M$6^	28$	BBBBC$	Ind		
Electronic and Software Eng with Industry (MEng)	HGQ7	5SW deg	M+P g	18	5M $	M$6^	28$	ABBBB$	Ind		
Electronic and Software Engineering	HG67	3FT deg	M+P g	18	5M $	M$6^	28$	BBBBC$	Ind		12/20
Electronic and Software Engineering (MEng)	HGP7	4FT deg	M+P g	18	5M $	M$6^	28$	ABBBB$	Ind		
Univ of LINCOLNSHIRE and HUMBERSIDE											
Engineering (Avionics)	HH46	3FT deg	M+P/S g	18	1M+4D$	Ind	26	BBBCC$	Ind		
Engineering (Electrical and Electronic)	HH56	3FT deg	M+P/S	18	1M+4D	Ind	26	BBBCC$	Ind		
Engineering (Electronic Communication Systems)	H620	3FT deg	M+P/S g	18	1M+4D$	Ind	Ind	BBBCC$	Ind		
Engineering (Electronics and Communications)	H623	3FT deg	M+P/S g	8	3M $	Ind	Ind	CCC$	Ind		
Engineering (Electronics and Control)	H643	3FT deg	M+P/S g	18	1M+4D$	Ind	26	CCBB$	Ind		
Engineering (Mechanical and Electrical)	HH53	3FT deg	M+P/S	18	1M+4D$	Ind	26	BBBCC$	Ind		
Engineering (Electronics and Communications Eng)	026H▼	2FT HND	M+P/S g	4	Ind	Ind	Ind	Ind	Ind		
Univ of LIVERPOOL											
Computer Electronics and Robotics (BEng)	H651	3FT deg	M+P	22	3M+2D$		30$	BBBBB	Ind	28	
Computer and Microelectronic Systems	GH66	3FT deg	M+P/Cs	22	3M+2D		30$	BBBBB	Ind	8	
Electrical Engineering (BEng)	H500	3FT deg	M+P	22	3M+2D$		30$	BBBBB	Ind	17	
Electrical Engineering (MEng)	H501	4FT deg	M+P	22	3M+2D$		30$	BBBBB	Ind		
Electrical Engineering and Electronics (BEng)	HH5Q	4FT deg	*	18			25$	BBBCC	Ind	3	
Electrical Engineering and Electronics (BEng)	HH56	3FT deg	M+P	22	3M+2D$		30$	BBBBB	Ind	6	10/20
Electrical Engineering and Electronics (MEng)	HHM6	4FT deg	M+P	22	3M+2D$		30$	BBBBB	Ind	9	
Electrical and Electronic Engineering (BEngHons)	HH5P	4EXT deg	*	18			25$	BBBCC	Ind	2	8/18
Electronic and Communication Engineering (BEng)	H621	3FT deg	M+P	22	3M+2D$		30$	BBBBB	Ind	10	
Electronic and Integrated Circuit Eng (BEng)	H616	3FT deg	M+P	22	3M+2D$		30$	BBBBB	Ind	8	
Electronics (BEng)	H600	3FT deg	M+P	22	3M+2D$		30$	BBBBB	Ind	20	
Electronics (MEng)	H601	4FT deg	M+P	22	3M+2D$		30$	BBBBB	Ind	16	
Medical Electronics and Instrumentation (BEng)	H673	3FT deg	M+P	22	3M+2D$		30$	BBBBB	Ind	3	
THE LIVERPOOL INSTITUTE FOR PERORMING ARTS											
Sound Technology	HW63	3FT deg			Ind	Ind	Ind	Ind	Ind		
LIVERPOOL JOHN MOORES Univ											
Applied Electronics	H640	3FT deg	S	12	5M	M				3	
Applied Electronics (Foundation)	H648	4FT/5SW deg									
Broadcast Engineering	H680	3FT deg		12	5M	D$/M$6				5	10/15
Broadcast Engineering (Extended)	H688	4EXT deg			N					3	
Electrical & Electronic Engineering	HH56	3FT/4SW deg	M+P	12	5M	M				12	

course details · 98 expected requirements · 96 entry stats

TITLE	CODE	COURSE	SUBJECTS	A/AS	ND/C	AGNVQ	IB	SQA(H)	SQA	RATIO A/AS
Electrical and Electronic Engineering (Extended)	HH5P▼	4EXT/5EXTSW deg		4	N					7
Electronic Systems Engineering	H600	3FT/4SW deg	M+P	12	5M	M				11
Electronic Systems Engineering (Extended)	H608▼	4EXT/5EXTSW deg		4-8	N					4
Environmental Electronics	FH96	3FT/4SW deg		12	5M	M				
Environmental Electronics (Foundation)	FH9P	4FT/5SW deg								2
Electronics and Computers	6MHG	3EXT HND								
Engineering (Electrical and Electronic)	65HH	2FT HND	M/P	4	N					4
Engineering (Electrical and Electronic) (Ext)	56HH▼	3EXT HND		4	N					6
Engineering (Electronic)	006H	2FT HND	M/P	4	N					14
Engineering (Electronic) (Extended)	806H▼	3EXT HND		4	N					3
Engineering (Electronics & Communications) (Ext)	826H▼	3EXT HND		4	N					
Engineering (Electronics and Communications)	226H	2FT HND	M/P	4	N					10
Engineering (Electronics and Computers)	65HG	2FT/3SW HND								5
Engineering (Mechatronics)	63HH	2FT/3SW HND		E	N	P				
Engineering (Mechatronics) (Foundation)	6HHH▼	3FT/4SW HND								

LONDON GUILDHALL Univ

| Musical Instrument Technology | J5H6 | 3FT deg | M/P/Mu g | CC | N $ | | 24 | Ind | Ind | |
| Musical Instrument Technology | 65HJ | 2FT HND | M/P/Mu g | D | N $ | | Dip$ | Ind | Ind | |

LOUGHBOROUGH Univ

Electromechanical Power Eng (5 Yr SW) MEng	HHM3	5SW deg	M+P	BBC	3M+2D	DE6/^ go	28$	Ind	Ind	2	
Electromechanical Power Engineering	HH35	3FT deg	M+P	20	3M+2D	DE6/^ go	28$	Ind	Ind	11	
Electromechanical Power Engineering (4 Yr MEng)	HHN3	4FT deg	M+P	BBC	3M+2D	DE6/^ go	28$	Ind	Ind	3	
Electromechanical Power Engineering (4 Yr SW)	HH53	4SW deg	M+P	20	3M+2D	DE6/^ go	28$	Ind	Ind		
Electronic and Electrical Eng (5 Yr SW MEng)	HH6M	5SW deg	M+P	BBC	3M+2D	DE6/^ go	28$	Ind	Ind	8	20/26
Electronic and Electrical Engineering	HH56	3FT deg	M+P	BCC	3M+2D	DE6/^ go	28$	Ind	Ind	11	18/24
Electronic and Electrical Engineering (4 Yr MEng)	HH5P	4FT deg	M+P	BBC	3M+2D	DE6/^ go	28$	Ind	Ind	13	22/28
Electronic and Electrical Engineering (4 Yr SW)	HH65	4SW deg	M+P	BCC	3M+2D	DE6/^ go	28$	Ind	Ind	7	16/28
Electronic, Computer and Systems Eng (4 Yr SW)	H611	4SW deg	M+P	BCC	3M+2D	DE6/^ go	28$	Ind	Ind	6	14/24
Electronic, Computer and Systems Engineering	H610	3FT deg	M+P	BCC	3M+2D	DE6/^ go	28$	Ind	Ind	18	
Electronic, Computer and Systems Engineering	H613	4FT deg									
Electronic, Computer and Systems Engineering	H612	5SW deg									
Systems Engineering (4 Yr MEng)	H640	4FT deg	M+P	BCC	3M+2D		28$	Ind	Ind	4	20/28
Systems Engineering (5 Yr SW MEng)	H641	5SW deg	M+P	BCC	3M+2D		28$	Ind	Ind	2	22/30

LUTON Univ

Accounting with Digital System Design	NHKQ	3FT deg	g	12-16	MO/DO	M/D	32	BBCC	Ind	
Accounting with Electronic Systems Design	N4H6	3FT deg		12-16	MO/DO	M/D	32	BBCC	Ind	
Biology with Digital System Design	C1HP	3FT deg	g	12-16	MO/DO	M/D	32	BBCC	Ind	
Broadcasting & Media Tech with Commun Syst Des	H681	3FT deg		12-16	MO/DO	M/D	32	BBCC	Ind	
Broadcasting & Media Tech with Computer Syst Des	H6G6	3FT deg		12-16	MO/DO	M/D	32	BBCC	Ind	
Broadcasting & Media Tech with Digital Systs Des	H682	3FT deg		12-16	MO/DO	M/D	32	BBCC	Ind	
Broadcasting & Media Tech with Electron Syst Des	H683	3FT deg		12-16	MO/DO	M/D	32	BBCC	Ind	
Broadcasting & Media Tech with Mathematical Scis	H6GD	3FT deg		12-16	MO/DO	M/D	32	BBCC	Ind	
Broadcasting & Media Tech with Media Practices	H6PK	3FT deg		12-16	MO/DO	M/D	32	BBCC	Ind	
Broadcasting & Media Technology with Business	H6N1	3FT deg		12-16	MO/DO	M/D	32	BBCC	Ind	
Broadcasting & Media Technology with Geography	H6F8	3FT deg		12-16	MO/DO	M/D	32	BBCC	Ind	
Broadcasting & Media Technology with Health Sci	H6B9	3FT deg		12-16	MO/DO	M/D	32	BBCC	Ind	
Broadcasting & Media Technology with Linguistics	H6Q1	3FT deg		12-16	MO/DO	M/D	32	BBCC	Ind	
Broadcasting & Media Technology with Mapping Sci	H6FW	3FT deg		12-16	MO/DO	M/D	32	BBCC	Ind	
Broadcasting & Media Technology with Mathematics	H6G1	3FT deg		12-16	MO/DO	M/D	32	BBCC	Ind	
Broadcasting & Media Technology with Media Prod	H6PL	3FT deg		12-16	MO/DO	M/D	32	BBCC	Ind	
Broadcasting & Media Technology with Psychology	H6L7	3FT deg		12-16	MO/DO	M/D	32	BBCC	Ind	

Engineering – Electrical and Electronic

23

course details			98 expected requirements							96 entry stats
TITLE	CODE	COURSE	SUBJECTS	A/AS	NO/C	RGNVQ	IB	SQA(H)	SQA	RATIO A/AS
Broadcasting and Media Technology	H680	3FT deg		12-16	MO/DO	M/D	32	BBCC	Ind	
Business Systems with Communication Systs Design	N1HQ	3FT deg		12-16	MO/DO	M/D	32	BBCC	Ind	
Business with Digital Systems Design	N1HP	3FT deg	g	12-16	MO/DO	M/D	32	BBCC	Ind	
Business with Electronic Systems Design	N1H6	3FT deg		12-16	MO/DO	M/D	32	BBCC	Ind	
Communication Syst Des & Artificial Intelligence	GH8Q	3FT deg		12-16	MO/DO	M/D	32	BBCC	Ind	
Computer Applications and Communication Syst Des	GH6Q	3FT deg		12-16	MO/DO	M/D	32	BBCC	Ind	
Digital Systems Design	H615	3FT deg	g	12-16	MO/DO	M/D	32	BBCC	Ind	11
Digital Systems Design & Artificial Intelligence	GH8P	3FT deg		12-16	MO/DO	M/D	32	BBCC	Ind	
Digital Systems Design and Accounting	NHK6	3FT deg	g	12-16	MO/DO	M/D	32	BBCC	Ind	
Digital Systems Design and Business	NH1P	3FT deg	g	12-16	MO/DO	M/D	32	BBCC	Ind	
Digital Systems Design and Business Systems	NHCP	3FT deg	g	12-16	MO/DO	M/D	32	BBCC	Ind	
Digital Systems Design and Computer Applications	GH6P	3FT deg		12-16	MO/DO	M/D	32	BBCC	Ind	
Digital Systems Design and Computer Science	GH5P	3FT deg	g	12-16	MO/DO	M/D	32	BBCC	Ind	2
Digital Systems Design with Accounting	H6NL	3FT deg	g	12-16	MO/DO	M/D	32	BBCC	Ind	
Digital Systems Design with Animation	H6WG	3FT deg	g	12-16	MO/DO	M/D	32	BBCC	Ind	
Digital Systems Design with Business	H637	3FT deg	g	12-16	MO/DO	M/D	32	BBCC	Ind	
Digital Systems Design with Business Systems	H603	3FT deg	g	12-16	MO/DO	M/D	32	BBCC	Ind	
Digital Systems Design with Electronic Systs Des	H614	3FT deg		12-16	MO/DO	M/D	32	BBCC	Ind	
Digital Systems Design with Geographical Inf Sys	H618	3FT deg	g	12-16	MO/DO	M/D	32	BBCC	Ind	
Digital Systems Design with Management	HN6D	3FT deg	g	12-16	MO/DO	M/D	32	BBCC	Ind	
Digital Systems Design with Marketing	H6NM	3FT deg	g	12-16	MO/DO	M/D	32	BBCC	Ind	
Digital Systems Design with Mathematical Science	H6GC	3FT deg	g	12-16	MO/DO	M/D	32	BBCC	Ind	
Digital Systems Design with Media Production	H624	3FT deg	g	12-16	MO/DO	M/D	32	BBCC	Ind	
Digital Systems Design with Multimedia	H625	3FT deg	g	12-16	MO/DO	M/D	32	BBCC	Ind	
Digital Systems Design with Organisational Behav	H6LT	3FT deg	g	12-16	MO/DO	M/D	32	BBCC	Ind	
Digital Systems Design with Photography	H6WN	3FT deg	g	12-16	MO/DO	M/D	32	BBCC	Ind	
Digital Systems Design with Politics	H6MD	3FT deg	g	12-16	MO/DO	M/D	32	BBCC	Ind	
Digital Systems Design with Public Policy & Mgt	H636	3FT deg	g	12-16	MO/DO	M/D	32	BBCC	Ind	
Digital Systems Design with Social Studies	H6LH	3FT deg	g	12-16	MO/DO	M/D	32	BBCC	Ind	
Digital Systems Design with TV Studies	HW6N	3FT deg	g	12-16	MO/DO	M/D	32	BBCC	Ind	
Digital Systems Design with Video Production	H6WM	3FT deg	g	12-16	MO/DO	M/D	32	BBCC	Ind	
Electronic Sys Design with Digital System Design	GHM6	3FT deg	g	12-16	MO/DO	M/D	32	BBCC	Ind	
Electronic Syst Design & Artificial Intelligence	GH86	3FT deg		12-16	MO/DO	M/D	32	BBCC	Ind	
Electronic System Design	H646	3FT deg	g	12-16	MO/DO	M/D	32	BBCC	Ind	6
Electronic System Design and Accounting	NHKP	3FT deg	g	12-16	MO/DO	M/D	32	BBCC	Ind	
Electronic System Design and Business	HN61	3FT deg	g	12-16	MO/DO	M/D	32	BBCC	Ind	
Electronic System Design and Business Systems	HN6C	3FT deg	g	12-16	MO/DO	M/D	32	BBCC	Ind	
Electronic System Design and Computer Applic	GH66	3FT deg		12-16	MO/DO	M/D	32	BBCC	Ind	
Electronic System Design and Computer Science	HG65	3FT deg	g	12-16	MO/DO	M/D	32	BBCC	Ind	
Electronic System Design and Digital Systems Des	GH5Q	3FT deg	g	12-16	MO/DO	M/D	32	BBCC	Ind	
Electronic System Design and Media Production	HPPK	3FT deg	g	12-16	MO/DO	M/D	32	BBCC	Ind	
Electronic System Design with Accounting	HN6K	3FT deg	g	12-16	MO/DO	M/D	32	BBCC	Ind	
Electronic System Design with Animation	H6W2	3FT deg	g	12-16	MO/DO	M/D	32	BBCC	Ind	
Electronic System Design with Business	HN6P	3FT deg	g	12-16	MO/DO	M/D	32	BBCC	Ind	
Electronic System Design with Business Systems	HNP1	3FT deg	g	12-16	MO/DO	M/D	32	BBCC	Ind	
Electronic System Design with Japanese	H6T4	3FT deg	L g	12-16	MO/DO	M/D	32	BBCC	Ind	
Electronic System Design with Management	HNQ1	3FT deg	g	12-16	MO/DO	M/D	32	BBCC	Ind	
Electronic System Design with Marketing	HN6M	3FT deg	g	12-16	MO/DO	M/D	32	BBCC	Ind	
Electronic System Design with Multimedia	HP6K	3FT deg	g	12-16	MO/DO	M/D	32	BBCC	Ind	
Electronic System Design with Organis Behaviour	HL67	3FT deg	g	12-16	MO/DO	M/D	32	BBCC	Ind	
Electronic System Design with Photography	HW65	3FT deg	g	12-16	MO/DO	M/D	32	BBCC	Ind	
Electronic System Design with TV Studies	HWP5	3FT deg	g	12-16	MO/DO	M/D	32	BBCC	Ind	

course details			*98 expected requirements*							*96 entry stats*
TITLE	CODE	COURSE	SUBJECTS	A/AS	NQ/C	AGNVQ	IB	SQA(H)	SQA	RATIO A/AS
Electronic System Design with Video Production	HW6M	3FT deg	g	12-16	MQ/DQ	M/D	32	BBCC	Ind	
Electronic Systems Design with Leisure Studies	HN67	3FT deg	g	12-16	MQ/DQ	M/D	32	BBCC	Ind	
Electronics	H608	1FT deg			Ind	Ind	Ind	Ind	Ind	
Environmental Science with Electronic Systs Des	F9H6	3FT deg		12-16	MQ/DQ	M/D	32	BBCC	Ind	
European Language St with Electronic Systems Des	T2HQ	3FT deg		12-16	MQ/DQ	M/D	32	BBCC	Ind	
European Language Studies & Electronic Syst Des	HTP2	3FT deg	L g	12-16	MQ/DQ	M/D	32	BBCC	Ind	
Geology and Electronic System Design	FH66	3FT deg	g	12-16	MQ/DQ	M/D	32	BBCC	Ind	
Geology with Electronic Systems Design	F6HQ	3FT deg		12-16	MQ/DQ	M/D	32	BBCC	Ind	
Integrated Engineering with Digital Syst Design	H1HP	3FT deg	g	12-16	MQ/DQ	M/D	32	BBCC	Ind	
Leisure Studies and Electronic System Design	HNP7	3FT deg	g	12-16	MQ/DQ	M/D	32	BBCC	Ind	
Leisure Studies with Electronic Systems Design	N7HQ	3FT deg		12-16	MQ/DQ	M/D	32	BBCC	Ind	
Marketing and Digital Systems Design	HNP5	3FT deg	g	12-16	MQ/DQ	M/D	32	BBCC	Ind	
Marketing and Electronic System Design	HNP6	3FT deg	g	12-16	MQ/DQ	M/D	32	BBCC	Ind	
Marketing with Communication System Design	N5H6	3FT deg		12-16	MQ/DQ	M/D	32	BBCC	Ind	
Marketing with Digital Systems Design	N5HP	3FT deg	g	12-16	MQ/DQ	M/D	32	BBCC	Ind	
Marketing with Electronic Systems Design	N5HQ	3FT deg		12-16	MQ/DQ	M/D	32	BBCC	Ind	
Media Practices and Digital Systems Design	HPP4	3FT deg	g	12-16	MQ/DQ	M/D	32	BBCC	Ind	
Media Practices with Digital Systems Design	P4HP	3FT deg	g	12-16	MQ/DQ	M/D	32	BBCC	Ind	
Media Production and Digital Systems Design	HPPL	3FT deg	g	12-16	MQ/DQ	M/D	32	BBCC	Ind	
Media Technology	PH46	1FT deg			Ind	Ind	Ind	Ind	Ind	
Media Technology	HP64	3FT deg	g	12-16	MQ/DQ	M/D	32	BBCC	Ind	8/16
Organisational Behaviour and Digital Systs Des	HLP7	3FT deg	g	12-16	MQ/DQ	M/D	32	BBCC	Ind	
Software Engineering and Communication Syst Des	GH7Q	3FT deg		12-16	MQ/DQ	M/D	32	BBCC	Ind	
Software Engineering and Digitial Systems Design	GH7P	3FT deg		12-16	MQ/DQ	M/D	32	BBCC	Ind	
Broadcasting and Media Technology	086H	2FT HND	g	4-8	N/MQ	P/M	26	CCDD	Ind	
Electronics and Communications Engineering	026H	2FT HND	g	4-8	N/MQ	P/M	26	CCDD	Ind	9
Electronics and Computer Engineering	116H	2FT HND	g	4-8	N/MQ	P/M	26	CCDD	Ind	
Electronics and Control Engineering	046H	2FT HND	g	4-8	N/MQ	P/M	26	CCDD	Ind	5
Integrated Engineering (Mechatronics)	63HH	2FT HND	g	4-8	N/MQ	P/M	26	CCDD	Ind	1
Media Technology	64HP	2FT HND		12-16	MQ	M/D	26	CCDD	Ind	

Univ of MANCHESTER

Electronic Engineering	H608	4FT deg	M+P	BBB	6M $	DS^	30$	AABBB$	Ind	
Electronic Engineering	H600	3FT deg	M+P	BCC	6M $	DS^	30$	AABBB$	Ind	17
Electronic Engineering (Industrial Prog) (4 Yrs)	H604	4FT deg	M+P	BCC	4M+2D$	DS^	30$	AAABB$	Ind	8
Electronic Engineering (Int Eur Prog) (MEng)	H602	4FT deg	M+P	BBC	4M+2D$	DS^	30S	AAABB$	Ind	21
Electronic Engineering (Japan) (MEng)	H601	4FT deg	M+P	BBC	4M+2D$	DS^	30$	AAABB$	Ind	5
Electronic Engineering (Singapore)	H612	4FT deg	M+P	BBC	4M+2D$	DS^	30$	AAABB$	Ind	
Electronic Engineering (USA Prog)	H613	4FT deg	M+P	ABB	4M+2D$	DS^	30$	AAABB$	Ind	2
Electronic Systems Eng (Int Eur Prog) (MEng)	H603	4FT deg	M+P	BBC	4M+2D$	DS^	30$	AAABB$	Ind	16
Electronic Systems Engineering	H611	3FT deg	M+P	BCC	6M $	DS^	30$	AABBB$	Ind	4 16/22
Electronic Systems Engineering	H614	4FT deg	M+P	BBB	6M $	DS^	30$	AABBB$	Ind	
Electronic Systems Engineering (Ind Prog)	H605	4FT deg	M+P	BCC	4M+2D$	DS^	30$	AAABB$	Ind	5
Electronic Systems Engineering (Japan) (MEng)	H606	4FT deg	M+P	BBC	4M+2D$	DS^	30$	AAABB$	Ind	
Electronic Systems Engineering (Singapore)	H607	4FT deg	M+P	BBC	4M+2D$	DS^	30$	AAABB$	Ind	
Electronic Systems Engineering (USA Prog)	H609	4FT deg	M+P	ABB	4M+2D$	DS^	30$	AAABB$	Ind	1
Electronic and Electrical Eng (Euro) (MEng)	HHMP	4FT deg	M+P	BBC	4M+2D$	DS^	30$	AAABB$	Ind	10
Electronic and Electrical Eng (Ind Prog)	HHNP	4FT deg	M+P	BCC	4M+2D$	DS^	30$	AAABB$	Ind	15
Electronic and Electrical Eng (Japan) (MEng)	HHNQ	4FT deg	M+P	BBC	4M+2D$	DS^	30$	AAABB$	Ind	
Electronic and Electrical Eng (Singapore)	HH5Q	4FT deg	M+P	BBC	4M+2D$	DS^	30$	AAABB$	Ind	
Electronic and Electrical Engineering	HHN6	4FT deg	M+P	BBB	4M+2D$	DS^	30$	AAABB$	Ind	
Electronic and Electrical Engineering	HH56	3FT deg	M+P	BCC	M+D $	DS^	30$	AAABB$	Ind	10 14/20
Electronic and Electrical Engineering (USA Prog)	HHMQ	4FT deg	M+P	ABB	M+D $	DS^	30$	AAABB$	Ind	2

				98 expected requirements						96 entry stats	
course details											
TITLE	CODE	COURSE	SUBJECTS	A/AS	NQ/C	AGNVQ	IB	SQA(H)	SQA	RATIO	A/AS
UMIST (Manchester)											
Communication and Control Engineering	H645	3FT deg	M+P g	BCC	4M+3D	Ind	30$	AABB$	Ind	9	
Communication and Control Engineering (MEng)	H646	4FT deg	M+P g	BCC	4M+3D	Ind	30$	AABB$	Ind	2	
Computer Systems Engineering	GH66	3FT deg	M+P g	BBC	Ind	DE^	30$	AABBB$	Ind		
Computer Systems Engineering (MEng)	GH6P	4FT deg	M+P g	BBC	Ind	DE^	30$	AABBB$	Ind		
Electrical and Electronic Eng with French (MEng)	H5R1	4FT deg	M+P g	BCC	4M+3D	Ind	30$	AABB$	Ind	3	14/30
Electrical and Electronic Engineering	HH56	3FT deg	M+P g	BCC	4M+3D	Ind	30$	AABB$	Ind	7	16/28
Electrical and Electronic Engineering (MEng)	HH5P	4FT deg	M+P g	BCC	4M+3D	Ind	30$	AABB$	Ind	1	22/28
Electronic Engineering	H600	3FT deg	M+P g	BCC	4M+3D	Ind	30$	AABB$	Ind	5	12/28
Electronic Engineering (MEng)	H601	4FT deg	M+P g	BCC	4M+3D	Ind	30$	AABB$	Ind		18/30
Electronic Systems Engineering	H615	3FT deg	M+P g	BCC	Ind	DE^	30$	AABBB$	Ind	11	
Electronic Systems Engineering (MEng)	H619	4FT deg	M+P g	BCC	Ind	DE^	30$	AABBB$	Ind	8	14/28
Microelectronic Systems Engineering	HG66	3FT deg	M+P g	BBC	Ind	DE^	32$	AABBB$	Ind	6	
Microelectronic Systems Engineering (MEng)	HG6P	4FT deg	M+P g	BBC	Ind	DE^	32$	AABBB$	Ind	4	
Paper Science with Industrial Process Control	J5HP	3FT deg	M/P/C g	BCC	3M	DS^	30$	BBBC$	Ind	4	
MANCHESTER METROPOLITAN Univ											
Communication & Electronic Eng with Study in Eur	H621	4SW deg	M+P	10	MO $	ME2	24$	CCC$	Ind		
Communication and Electronic Engineering	H620	3FT/4SW deg	M+P	10	MO $	ME2	24$	CCC$	Ind		
Computer & Electronic Eng with Study in Eur	GH6P	4SW deg	M+P	10	MO $	ME2	24$	CCC$	Ind		
Computer and Electronic Engineering	GH66	3FT/4SW deg	M+P	10	MO $	ME2	24$	CCC$	Ind		
Electrical & Electronic Eng with Study in Eur	HH6M	4SW deg	M+P	10	MO $	ME2	24$	CCC$	Ind		
Electrical and Electronic Engineering	HH56	3FT/4SW deg	M+P	10	MO $	ME2	24$	CCC$	Ind		6/12
Electrical and Electronic Engineering (Found)	HH5P▼	4FT deg	M/P	E	2M $	P$	$	$	Ind		
Electronic Eng with Management with Study in Eur	H6NC	4SW deg	M+P	10	MO $	ME2	24$	CCC$	Ind		
Electronic Engineering (HND top-up)	H601	1FT deg									
Electronic Engineering with Management	H6N1	3FT/4SW deg	M+P	10	MO $	ME2	24$	CCC$	Ind		
Electronics	H600	3FT deg	* g	12-16	1M+3D	M$	28	BBBCC	Ind		
Electronics (Foundation)	H608▼	4FT deg	M/P	E	2M $	P$	$	$	Ind		
Electronics/Applied Physics	FH3P	3FT deg	M+P g	12	5M $	M$	27$	BCCC$	Ind		
Electronics/Biology	CH1P	3FT deg	* g	12	5M	M$	27	BCCC	Ind		
Electronics/Business Mathematics	GHCP	3FT deg	M/P/Ec g	12	5M $	M$	27$	BCCC$	Ind		
Electronics/Chemistry	FH1P	3FT deg	C g	12	5M $	M$	27$	BCCC$	Ind		
Electronics/Computer Technology	GHMP	3FT deg	* g	12	5M	M$	27	BCCC	Ind		
Electronics/Computing Science	GH5P	3FT deg	* g	12	5M	M$	27	BCCC	Ind		
Electronics/Economics	HLP1	3FT deg	* g	16	1M+3D	M$	28	BBBCC	Ind		
Geography/Electronics	HLP8	3FT deg	* g	14	MO	M$	28	BBCCC	Ind		
Languages/Electronics	HTP9	3FT deg	* g	14	MO	M$	28	BBCCC	Ind		
Manufacturing/Electronics	HHP7	3FT deg	* g	12	5M	M$	27	BCCC	Ind		
Mechatronics	HH36	3FT/4SW deg	M+P g	DDE	3M $	ME	24$	BB$	Ind		
Mechatronics (Foundation)	HH3P▼	4FT deg	M/P	E	2M $	P$	$	$	Ind		
Media Technology	HP64	3FT deg	*	10	N		Ind	Ind	Ind		
Physics Studies/Electronics	FHHP	3FT deg	M+P g	12	5M $	M$	27$	BCCC$	Ind		
Polymer Science/Electronics	HJP4	3FT deg	C g	12	5M $	M$	27$	BCCC$	Ind		
Scientific Instrumentation/Applicable Maths	GH16	3FT deg	M g	12	5M $	M$	27$	BCCC$	Ind		
Scientific Instrumentation/Applied Physics	FH36	3FT deg	M+P g	12	5M $	M$	27$	BCCC$	Ind		
Scientific Instrumentation/Business Mathematics	GHC6	3FT deg	M/P g	12	5M $	M$	27$	BCCC$	Ind		
Scientific Instrumentation/Chemistry	FH16	3FT deg	C+P/M g	12	4M $	M$	26$	CCCC$	Ind		
Scientific Instrumentation/Electronics	H680	3FT deg	M/P g	12	5M $	M$	27$	BCCC$	Ind		
Scientific Instrumentation/Environmental Studies	FH96	3FT deg	M+P g	16	1M+3D$	M$	28$	BBBCC$	Ind		
Scientific Instrumentation/Geography	HL68	3FT deg	M/P g	14	MO $	M$	28$	BBCCC$	Ind		
Scientific Instrumentation/Manufacturing	HH67	3FT deg	M/P g	12	5M $	M$	27$	BCCC$	Ind		
Scientific Instrumentation/Materials Science	FH26	3FT deg	M/P/C g	12	5M $	M$	27$	BCCC$	Ind		

course details			98 expected requirements							96 entry stats
TITLE	CODE	COURSE	SUBJECTS	A/AS	NO/C	AGNVQ	IB	SQA(H)	SQA	RATIO A/AS
Scientific Instrumentation/Physics Studies	HF63	3FT deg	M/P g	12	5M $	M$	27$	BCCCC$	Ind	
Scientific Instrumentation/Psychology	HL67	3FT deg	M/P g	18	1M+3D$	M$	28$	BBBCC$	Ind	
Social St of Technol/Scientific Instrumentation	HL63	3FT deg	M/P g	12	5M $	M$	27$	BCCCC$	Ind	
Social Studies of Technology/Electronics	HLP3	3FT deg	* g	12	5M	M$	27	BCCCC	Ind	
Combined Studies (Foundation) Electronics	Y108▼	4FT deg	M/P	E	2M $	P$	$	$	Ind	
Combined Studies (Foundation) Scientific Instrumentation	Y108	4FT deg	M/P	E	2M $	P$	P$	$	Ind	
Electronic Engineering	006H	2FT/3SW HND	M+P	2	N $		22$	DD$	Ind	
Mechanical Engineering and Mechatronics	63HH	2FT/3SW HND	M+P g	E	N	PE	Dip	Ind	N	

MIDDLESEX Univ

Computer Systems Engineering	H620▼	4SW deg	S g	10	3M	M$ go	24	CCCC	Ind	
Electronic Engineering	H600▼	3FT deg	M+P g	10	3M	M$ go	24	Ind	Ind	
Electronic Engineering and Management	H6N1▼	3FT/4SW deg	S g	10	3M	M$ go	24	Ind	Ind	
Electronics Foundation	H608▼	4EXT deg	* g	E	N	P* go	Ind	Ind	Ind	
Electronics and Business	HN61▼	3FT deg	S g	10	3M	M$ go	24	Ind	Ind	
Mechatronics	HH63▼	3FT/4SW deg	S g	10	3M	M$ go	24	CCCC	Ind	
Joint Honours Degree Telecommunications	Y400	3FT deg	S g	10-12	3M	M$ go	24	CCCC	Ind	
Electronic Engineering	006H▼	2FT/3SW HND	S g	E	N	P$ go	24	Ind	Ind	
Electronic Systems with Business Studies	16NH▼	2FT HND	S g	E	N	P$ go	24	Ind	Ind	

NAPIER Univ

Computing and Electronic Systems	GH5P	3FT/4FT deg						BBC		
Electronic and Communication Engineering	H620	4SW deg	*	DD	Ind	Ind	Ind	BBC	Ind	6
Electronic and Computer Engineering	GH56	4SW deg	*	DD	Ind	Ind	Ind	BBC	Ind	7
Electronic and Electrical Engineering	HH56	3FT/4FT deg	*	DE	Ind	Ind	Ind	BBC	Ind	4
Energy and Environmental Engineering	HJ59	3FT/4SW deg	M	DD	Ind	Ind	Ind	BBB$	Ind	3
Electronic and Electrical Engineering	65HH	2FT HND	*	D	Ind	Ind	Ind	CC	Ind	4

NENE COLLEGE

Electronic Systems	086H	2FT HND		2	N	P		CC	Ind	

Univ of NEWCASTLE

Electrical and Electronic Engineering	HHM6	4FT deg	* g	CCC	3M $	Ind	$	BCCCC$	$	15
Electrical and Electronic Engineering	HH56	3FT deg	M+P	BCC	6M $	Ind	$	CSYS$	$	7 14/16
Electrical and Electronic Engineering (MEng)	HH5Q	5FT deg	* g	CCC	3M $	Ind	$	BCCCC$	$	11
Electrical and Electronic Engineering (MEng)	HH5P	4FT deg	M+P	BBC	5M+1D$	Ind	$	CSYS$	$	10
Electronic Engineering	H600	3FT deg	M+P	BCC	6M $	Ind	$	CSYS$	$	7
Electronic Engineering	H601	4FT deg	* g	CCC	3M $	Ind	$	BCCCC$	$	6
Electronic Engineering (MEng)	H603	5FT deg	* g	CCC	3M $	Ind	$	BCCCC$	$	2
Electronic Engineering (MEng)	H602	4FT deg	M+P	BBC	5M+1D$	Ind	$	CSYS$	$	17
Mechanical Engineering and Mechatronics (4 years	HH36	4FT deg								
Mechanical Engineering and Mechatronics (5 yrs)	HH63	5FT deg								
Microelectronics and Software Engineering	HG67	4FT deg	* g	CCC	3M $	Ind	$	BCCCC$	$	7
Microelectronics and Software Engineering	GH76	3FT deg	M+P	BCC	6M $	Ind	$	CSYS$	$	12
Microelectronics and Software Engineering (MEng)	GHR6	5FT deg	* g	CCC	3M $	Ind	$	BCCCC$	$	
Microelectronics and Software Engineering (MEng)	GH7Q	4FT deg	M+P	BBC	5M+1D$	Ind	$	CSYS$	$	10

Univ of Wales COLLEGE, NEWPORT

Electrical and Instrumentation Systems	H641	3FT/4SW deg	*	4	N	M$	Ind	Ind	Ind	
Electronic and Instrumentation Systems	H642	3FT/4SW deg	*	4	N	M$	Ind	Ind	Ind	
Electrical Engineering	005H	2FT HND	*	2	N	P$	Ind	Ind	Ind	
Electronic Engineering	006H	2FT HND	*	2	N	P$	Ind	Ind	Ind	
Instrumentation and Control	046H	2FT HND		2	N	P$	Ind	Ind	Ind	
Mechatronics	63HH	2FT HND		2	N	P$	Ind	Ind	Ind	

Engineering – Electrical and Electronic 23

			98 expected requirements							96 entry stats	
course details											
TITLE	CODE	COURSE	SUBJECTS	A/AS	NO/C	AGNVQ	IB	SQA(H)	SQA	RATIO	A/AS
NORTHBROOK COLLEGE Sussex											
Engineering (Electronics)	006H	2FT HND	*		N						
NESCOT											
Electronic Imaging	086H	2FT HND	Py	C	MO	P	Dip	Ind	N$	1	5/6
NORTH EAST WALES INST of HE											
Aeronautical Electronics (Avionics)	HH46	3FT deg		4-8	3M	M$	Ind	CCC	N$		
Animation/Electronic and Digital Design	WH25	3FT deg	Pf		Ind	Ind	Ind	Ind	Ind		
Animation/Electronic and Digital Design	EH25	3FT deg	Pf		Ind	Ind	Ind	Ind	Ind		
Electrical and Electronic Eng with Bus Studies	H6N1	3FT deg		4-8	3M	M$	Ind	CCC	N$		
Electrical and Electronic Eng with European Stud	HH5Q	3FT deg		4-8	3M	M$	Ind	CCC	N$		
Electrical and Electronic Engineering	HH56	3FT deg		4-8	4M	M$	Ind	CCC	N$	6	
Graphic Design/Electronic and Digital Design	WH2M	3FT deg	Pf		Ind	Ind	Ind	Ind	Ind		
Graphic Design/Electronic and Digital Design	EH2M	3FT deg	Pf		Ind	Ind	Ind	Ind	Ind		
Sound/Broadcast Engineering	H688	3FT deg		4-8	3M	M$	Ind	CCC	N$		
Aeronautical Electronics (Avionics)	64HH	2FT HND		2-4	2M	P$	Ind	CC	N$		
Electrical Engineering (Power)	025H	2FT HND		2-6	2M	P$	Ind	CC	N$	2	
Electronic & Electrical Engineering	65HH	2FT HND		2-6	2M	P$	Ind	CC	N$	2	
Electronics and Micro Computing	016H	2FT HND		2-6	2M	P$	Ind	CC	N$		
Sound/Broadcast Engineering	886H	2FT HND		2-6	2M	P$	Ind	CC	N$		
NORTH LINCOLNSHIRE COLLEGE											
Electronics, Software and Systems Engineering	67HG	2FT HND	M/P g	2	$	P$	Ind	Ind	Ind		
Univ of NORTH LONDON											
Business and Communications Engineering	HN61	3FT/4SW/4EXT deg	M+P/Es/Cs/Ds	12	MO+4D	DE go	Ind	Ind	Ind		
Communications Engineering	H621	3FT/4SW/4EXT deg	M+P/Es/Cs/Ds	CC	3M $	ME go	$	Ind	Ind		
Computer Electronics and Business	HNP1	3FT/4SW/4EXT deg	M+P/Es/Cs/Ds	12	MO+4D	DE go	Ind	Ind	Ind		
Electronic & Communications Eng Foundation	H628▼	4FT/5SW deg			Ind	Ind	Ind	Ind	Ind	2	
Electronic Engineering	H601	3FT/4SW/4EXT deg	M+P/Es/Cs	CC	3M $	ME go	$	Ind	Ind	23	
Electronic and Communications Engineering	H620	3FT/4SW/4EXT deg	M+Cs/Es/P	CC	3M $	ME go	$	Ind	Ind	12	
Electronics	H600	3FT/4SW/4EXT deg	M+Es/Cs/Ds/S	CC	3M $	ME go	$	Ind	Ind		
Electronics and International Business	HN6C	3FT/4SW/4EXT deg	M+P/Es/Cs/Ds	12	MO+4D	DE go	Ind	Ind	Ind		
Combined Honours *Communications Engineering*	Y100	3FT/4SW/4EXT deg	P/Es/Ds/Cs+M	CC	3M $	ME go	$	Ind	Ind		
Combined Honours *Electronics*	Y100	3FT/4SW/4EXT deg	M+Es/Cs/Ds/P	CC	3M	ME	$	Ind	Ind		
Electronic and Communications Engineering	026H	2FT HND	M/P/Cs/Es	E	1M $	PE	$	Ind	Ind	7	
Univ of NORTHUMBRIA											
Communication and Electronic Engineering	H620	3FT/4SW deg	M+P/S g	18	Ind $	ME2 gi	Ind$	Ind$	Ind	7	
Communication and Electronic Engineering	H628	5EXT deg	* g	2-4	N	P	Ind$	Ind$	Ind	4	
Communication and Electronic Engineering	H621	4FT deg	M+P/S g	18	Ind$	ME2 gi	Ind$	Ind$	Ind		
Electrical & Electronic Engineering	HH56	3FT/4SW deg	M+P/S g	18	Ind $	ME2 gi	Ind	Ind	Ind	4	10/14
Electrical and Electronic Engineering	H588▼	5EXT deg	* g	2-4	Ind	Ind	Ind	Ind	Ind	1	
Electrical and Electronic Engineering	HH5Q	4FT deg	M+P/S g	18	Ind	ME2 gi	Ind	Ind	Ind		
Electronic Engineering for Europe	H601	4SW deg	M+P/S g	18	Ind	Ind	Ind	Ind$	Ind		
Electronic Systems Design Engineering	H614	1/2FT deg									
Integrated Circuit Design Engineering	H616	3FT deg	M+P/S g	18	Ind	ME2 gi	Ind	Ind	Ind		
Mechatronic Systems Design	HH36	3FT deg	M+P/S g	12	3M $	ME2 gi	24$	BBBC$	Ind		
Mechatronics System Design	HH3P	5EXT deg	* g	2-4	Ind	Ind	Ind	Ind	Ind		
Microelectronic Engineering	H612	4FT deg	M+P/S g	18	Ind $	ME2 gi	Ind	Ind	Ind		
Microelectronic Engineering	H611	3FT/4SW deg	M+P/S g	18	Ind $	ME2 gi	Ind	Ind	Ind	12	
Microelectronic Engineering	H618	5EXT deg	* g	2-4	Ind	Ind	Ind	Ind	Ind	4	

course details			98 expected requirements							96 entry stats	
TITLE	CODE	COURSE	SUBJECTS	A/AS	ND/C	AGNVQ	IB	SQA(H)	SQA	RATIO	A/AS
Optoelectronic Engineering	H635	3FT/4SW deg	M+S/P g	8	3M $	Ind	24$	CCC$	Ind	4	
Optoelectronic Engineering	H638	5EXT deg	* g	2-4	Ind	Ind	Ind	Ind	Ind	1	
Engineering (Electrical and Electronic)	65HH▼	2FT HND	M/P/S g	2-4	N	Ind	Ind	Ind$	Ind	5	
Mechatronics	63HH	2FT HND	M/P g	2-4	Ind	Ind	Ind	Ind	Ind		

NORWICH: City COLL

Engineering (Electrical/Electronic)	106H	3SW HND	*	E	Ind	PE go	Ind	Ind	Ind	3	

Univ of NOTTINGHAM

Electrical and Electronic Eng with French	H6R1	3FT/4FT deg	M+P g	BBC-BCC	Ind	Ind	28$	Ind	Ind	11	
Electrical and Electronic Eng with German	H6R2	3FT/4FT deg	M+P g	BBC-BCC	Ind	Ind	28$	Ind	Ind	3	
Electrical and Electronic Eng with Russian	H6R8	3FT/4FT deg	M+P	BBC-BCC	Ind	Ind	28$	Ind	Ind		
Electrical and Electronic Eng with Spanish	H6R4	3FT/4FT deg	M+P	BBC-BCC	Ind	Ind	28$	Ind	Ind	2	
Electrical and Electronic Engineering	HH56	3FT/4FT deg	M+P	BBC-BCC	Ind	Ind	28$	Ind	Ind	7	16/28
Electronic Engineering	H600	3FT/4FT deg	M+P	BBC-BCC	Ind	Ind	28$	Ind	Ind	7	16/30
Electronic Engineering and Mathematics	HG61	3FT deg	M+P	BBC-BCC	Ind	Ind	28$	Ind	Ind	5	22/30
Electronic Engineering with French	H6RC	3FT/4FT deg	M+P g	BBC-BCC	Ind	Ind	28$	Ind	Ind		
Electronic Engineering with German	H6RF	3FT/4FT deg	M+P g	BBC-BCC	Ind	Ind	28$	Ind	Ind	5	
Electronic Engineering with Russian	H6RV	3FT/4FT deg	M+P	BBC-BCC	Ind	Ind	28$	Ind	Ind		
Electronic Engineering with Spanish	H6RK	3FT/4FT deg	M+P	BBC-BCC	Ind	Ind	28$	Ind	Ind		

NOTTINGHAM TRENT Univ

Electrical and Electronic Engineering (Extended)	HH65▼	4EXT/5EXTSW deg	* g		Ind	Ind	Ind	$	$	2	8/10
Electrical and Electronic Engineering(BEng/MEng)	HH56	3FT/4SW deg	M+P g	14	4M $	Ind	Ind	AAB$	$	5	8/16
Electronic Engineering	H600	4FT/5SW deg	* g	14	4M $	Ind	Ind	Ind	Ind		
Electronics and Communications Engineering	H620	4FT/5SW deg	* g	14	4M $	Ind	Ind	Ind	Ind		
Electronics and Computing	GH56	3FT/4SW deg	* g	18	4M $	Ind	Ind	BBB$	$	6	8/20
Electronics and Computing (Extended)	GH5P▼	4EXT/5EXTSW deg	* g		Ind	Ind	Ind	$	Ind	2	
Engineering Systems and Computing (Extended)	H618▼	4EXT/5EXTSW deg	* g		Ind	Ind	Ind	Ind	Ind		
Mechatronics (BEng/MEng)	HH36	3FT/4SW deg	M g	14	3M $	Ind	Ind	Ind	Ind		
Mechatronics (Extended)	HH3P▼	4FT/5SW deg	* g		Ind	Ind	Ind	Ind	Ind		
Electrical and Electronic Engineering	65HH▼	2FT/3SW HND	M/P g	4	4M $		Ind	CC$	$	6	4/8
Electronics and Computing	65HG▼	2FT HND	* g	4	4M $	Ind	Ind	CC$	$	4	
Mechatronics	63HH	2FT HND	* g	4	Ind	Ind	Ind	Ind	Ind		

OXFORD Univ

Electrical Engineering (4 Yrs)	H500	4FT deg	M+P	AAB	DO		36	AAAAA	Ind	4	28/30
Information Engineering (4 Yrs)	H630	4FT deg	M+P	AAB	DO		36	AAAAA	Ind		

OXFORD BROOKES Univ

Computer Technology	H610	3FT deg	S/M g	CC	Ind	M$	Ind	Ind	Ind	4	
Electronic Engineering	H601	3FT/4SW deg	M+P/S g	12	Ind		Ind	Ind	Ind	6	
Electronic Engineering	H602	4FT/5SW deg									
Electronics	H600	3FT deg	* g	CC	Ind	M$	Ind	Ind	Ind	8	
Electronics/Accounting and Finance	HN64	3FT deg	S/M	CC-BCC	Ind	M$/D*3	Ind	Ind	Ind		
Electronics/Anthropology	HL66	3FT deg	S/M	CC-BCC	Ind	M$/M*^	Ind	Ind	Ind		
Electronics/Biological Chemistry	CH76	3FT deg									
Electronics/Business Administration & Management	HN61	3FT deg	S/M	CC-BBC	Ind	M$/MB4	Ind	Ind	Ind		
Electronics/Cartography	FH86	3FT deg	S/M	CC-DDD	Ind	M$	Ind	Ind	Ind		
Electronics/Cell Biology	CHC6	3FT deg									
Electronics/Combined Studies	HY64	3FT deg		X		X	X	X			
Electronics/Computer Systems	GH66	3FT deg	S/M	CC-BC	Ind	M$	Ind	Ind	Ind	4	
Electronics/Computing	GH56	2ACC/3FT deg	S/M	CDD-BB	Ind	M$	Ind	Ind	Ind	5	
Electronics/Computing Mathematics	GH96	3FT deg	M/S	CD-CC	Ind	M$	Ind	Ind	Ind		
Electronics/Economics	HL61	3FT deg	S/M	CC-BB	Ind	M$/M*3	Ind	Ind	Ind		

course details · 98 expected requirements · 96 entry stats

TITLE	CODE	COURSE	SUBJECTS	A/AS	NQ/C	AGNVQ	IB	SQA(H)	SQA	RATIO A/AS
Electronics/Educational Studies	HX69	3FT deg	S/M	CC-DDD	Ind	MS/M*3	Ind	Ind	Ind	
English Studies/Electronics	HQ63	3FT deg	S/M	CC-AB	Ind	M$/M*^	Ind	Ind	Ind	
Environmental Chemistry/Electronics	HF61	3FT deg								
Environmental Policy/Electronics	KH36	3FT deg								
Environmental Sciences/Electronics	FHX6	3FT deg	S/M g	CD-CC	Ind	M$/DS	Ind	Ind	Ind	
Exercise and Health/Electronics	HB66	3FT deg	S/M	DD-CC	Ind	MS	Ind	Ind	Ind	
Fine Art/Electronics	HW61	3FT deg	S/M+Pf+A	CC-BC	Ind	M$/MA^	Ind	Ind	Ind	
Food Science and Nutrition/Electronics	DH46	3FT deg	S/M g	DD-CC	Ind	MS	Ind	Ind	Ind	
French Language and Contemp Studies/Electronics	HR6C	4SW deg	F+S/M	CC-CDD	Ind	M$/M*^	Ind	Ind	Ind	
French Language and Literature/Electronics	HR61	4SW deg	F+S/M	CC-CDD	Ind	M$/M*^	Ind	Ind	Ind	
Geography and the Phys Env/Electronics	FHV6	3FT deg								
Geology/Electronics	FH66	3FT deg	S/M	DD-CC	Ind	M$/PS	Ind	Ind	Ind	
Geotechnics/Electronics	HH26	3FT deg	S/M	CC-DD	Ind	M$	Ind	Ind	Ind	
German Language and Contemp Stud/Electronics	HR6F	4SW deg	S/M+G	CC-DDD	Ind	M$/M*^	Ind	Ind	Ind	
German Language and Literature/Electronics	HR62	4SW deg	S/M+G	CC-DDD	Ind	M$/M*^	Ind	Ind	Ind	
German Studies/Electronics	HR6G	4SW deg	S/M+G	CC-DDD	Ind	M$/M*^	Ind	Ind	Ind	
Health Care/Electronics (Post Exp)	BH76	3FT deg		X		X	X	X		
History of Art/Electronics	HV64	3FT deg	S/M	CC-BCC	Ind	M$/M^	Ind	Ind	Ind	
History/Electronics	HV61	3FT deg	S/M	CC-BB	Ind	M$/M^	Ind	Ind	Ind	
Hospitality Management Studies/Electronics	HN67	3FT deg	S/M	CC-DDD	Ind	M$/M*3	Ind	Ind	Ind	
Human Biology/Electronics	BH16	3FT deg								
Information Systems/Electronics	GHM6	3FT deg	S/M	CC-BC	Ind	M$	Ind	Ind	Ind	
Intelligent Systems/Electronics	GH86	3FT deg	S/M	CD-CC	Ind	M$	Ind	Ind	Ind	
Law/Electronics	HM63	3FT deg	S/M	CC-BBB	Ind	M$/D*3	Ind	Ind	Ind	
Leisure Planning/Electronics	KHH6	3FT deg								
Marketing Management/Electronics	HN6N	3FT deg	S/M g	CC-BCC	Ind	M$/D*3	Ind	Ind	Ind	
Mathematics/Electronics	GH16	2ACC/3FT deg	M	DD-CC	Ind	M$/M*^	Ind	Ind	Ind	
Music/Electronics	HW63	3FT deg	Mu+S/M	DD-CC	Ind	M$	Ind	Ind	Ind	
Palliative Care/Electronics (Post Exp)	BHR6	3FT deg		X		X	X	X		
Politics/Electronics	MH16	3FT deg	S/M	CC-AB	Ind	M$	Ind	Ind	Ind	
Psychology/Electronics	CH86	3FT deg	S/M g	CC-BBC	Ind	M$/M*^	Ind	Ind	Ind	
Rehabilitation/Electronics (Post Exp)	BHT6	3FT deg		X		X	X	X		
Retail Management/Electronics	HN65	3FT deg	S/M g	CD-CCD	Ind		Ind	Ind	Ind	
Sociology/Electronics	HL63	3FT deg	S/M	CC-BCC	Ind	M$/M*^	Ind	Ind	Ind	
Software Engineering/Electronics	GH76	3FT deg	S/M	CC-BC	Ind	M$	Ind	Ind	Ind	
Statistics/Electronics	GH46	2ACC/3FT deg	S/M	DD-CC	Ind	M$	Ind	Ind	Ind	
Telecommunications/Accounting and Finance	HNP4	3FT deg								
Telecommunications/Anthropology	HLP6	3FT deg								
Telecommunications/Biological Chemistry	CH7P	3FT deg								
Telecommunications/Biology	CH1P	3FT deg								
Telecommunications/Business Administration & Mgt	NH1P	3FT deg								
Telecommunications/Cartography	FH8P	3FT deg								
Telecommunications/Cell Biology	CHCP	3FT deg								
Telecommunications/Combined Studies	HYP4	3FT deg		X		X	X	X		
Telecommunications/Computer Systems	GH6P	3FT deg								
Telecommunications/Computing	GH5P	3FT deg								
Telecommunications/Computing Mathematics	GH9P	3FT deg								
Telecommunications/Ecology	CH9P	3FT deg								
Telecommunications/Economics	LH1P	3FT deg								
Telecommunications/Educational Studies	HXP9	3FT deg								
Telecommunications/Electronics	H620	3FT deg								
Telecommunications/English Studies	HQP3	3FT deg								
Telecommunications/Environmental Chemistry	FH1P	3FT deg								
Telecommunications/Environmental Policy	HKP3	3FT deg								

TITLE	CODE	COURSE	SUBJECTS	A/AS	ND/C	AGNVQ	IB	SQA(H)	SQA	RATIO A/AS
Telecommunications/Environmental Sciences	FHXP	3FT deg								
Telecommunications/Exercise and Health	HBP6	3FT deg								
Telecommunications/Fine Art	HWP1	3FT deg								
Telecommunications/Food Science and Nutrition	DH4P	3FT deg								
Telecommunications/French Language & Contemp Std	HRPC	3FT deg								
Telecommunications/French Language and Lit	HRP1	3FT deg								
Telecommunications/Geography	HLP8	3FT deg								
Telecommunications/Geology	FH6P	3FT deg								
Telecommunications/Geotechnics	HH2P	3FT deg								
Telecommunications/German Language & Contemp St	HRPF	3FT deg								
Telecommunications/German Language and Lit	HRP2	3FT deg								
Telecommunications/German Studies	HRPG	3FT deg								
Telecommunications/Health Care (Post Exp)	BH7P	3FT deg		X		X	X	X		
Telecommunications/History	HVP1	3FT deg								
Telecommunications/History of Art	HVP4	3FT deg								
Telecommunications/Hospitality Management Studs	HNP7	3FT deg								
Telecommunications/Human Biology	BH1P	3FT deg								
Telecommunications/Information Systems	GHMP	3FT deg								
Telecommunications/Intelligent Systems	GH8P	3FT deg								
Telecommunications/Law	HMP3	3FT deg								
Telecommunications/Leisure Planning and Mgt	HKPH	3FT deg								
Telecommunications/Marketing Management	HNPN	3FT deg								
Telecommunications/Mathematics	GH1P	3FT deg								
Telecommunications/Music	HWP3	3FT deg								
Telecommunications/Palliative Care	BHRP	3FT deg								
Telecommunications/Physical Geography	FHVP	3FT deg								
Telecommunications/Planning Studies	HKP4	3FT deg								
Telecommunications/Politics	MH1P	3FT deg								
Telecommunications/Psychology	CH8P	3FT deg								
Telecommunications/Publishing	HPP5	3FT deg								
Telecommunications/Rehabilitation (Post Exp)	BHTP	3FT deg		X		X	X	X		
Telecommunications/Sociology	HLP3	3FT deg								
Telecommunications/Software Engineering	GH7P	3FT deg								
Telecommunications/Statistics	GH4P	3FT deg								
Tourism/Electronics	HP67	3FT deg	S/M	CC-BC	Ind	M$/M*3	Ind	Ind	Ind	
Tourism/Telecommunications	PH7P	3FT deg								
Transport Planning/Telecommunications	HNP9	3FT deg								
Water Resources/Electronics	HH6F	3FT deg								
Water Resources/Telecommunications	HHFP	3FT deg								
Extended Science *Electronics*	Y100	4FT deg	* g	EE	Ind	P*	Ind	Ind	Ind	
Extended Science *Microelectronics*	Y100	4FT deg	* g	EE	Ind	P*	Ind	Ind	Ind	
Electronic Engineering	006H	2FT/3SW HND	M+S/Ds/Es	E	Ind		Ind	Ind	Ind	3

Univ of PAISLEY

TITLE	CODE	COURSE	SUBJECTS	A/AS	ND/C	AGNVQ	IB	SQA(H)	SQA	RATIO A/AS
Computer Engineering	GH66	3FT/4FT/5SW deg	M+P g	DD	Ind	Ind	Ind	BBC$	Ind	12
Electronic & Electrical Engineering (MEng)	HH5P	5FT deg	M g	CCC	Ind	Ind	Ind	BBBB$	Ind	
Electronic Engineering	H641	2FT Dip	M g	EE	Ind	Ind	Ind	CCC$	Ind	1
Electronic Systems	H640	3FT deg	M g	EE	Ind	Ind	Ind	BCC$	Ind	2
Electronic and Electrical Engineering	HH56	4FT/5SW deg	M+P g	DD	Ind	Ind	Ind	BBC$	Ind	7
Media Technology	HP64	3FT/4FT deg	* g	CC	Ind	Ind	Ind	BBC$	Ind	1
Radio Frequency and Communication Engineering	H625	1FT deg		X	HN	X	X	X	HN	

Engineering – Electrical and Electronic 23

			98 expected requirements							96 entry stats	
course details											
TITLE	CODE	COURSE	SUBJECTS	A/AS	ND/C	AGNVQ	IB	SQA(H)	SQA	RATIO	A/AS
Univ of PLYMOUTH											
Communication Engineering	H621	3FT/4SW deg	Ap g	6	2M	ME	Ind	Ind	Ind		
Communication Engineering (MEng Option)	H620	3FT/4SW 4FT/5SW de	Ap g	4	MO $	ME^	Ind	Ind	Ind	4	10/14
Electrical and Electronic Engineering	HH5P	3FT deg	Ap g	6	2M	ME	Ind	Ind	Ind		
Electrical and Electronic Engineering (MEng Opt)	HH56	3FT/4SW 4FT/5SW de	Ap g	10	MO $	ME^	Ind	Ind	Ind	5	6/14
Electronic Engineering (MEng Option)	H603	3FT/4SW 4FT/5SW de	Ap g	10	MO $	ME^	Ind	Ind	Ind	9	14/26
Electronics and Business Management	HN6C	3FT deg	Ap g	6	2M	ME^	Ind	Ind	Ind		
Personal Communications Networks	H630	3FT deg	Ap g	4	MO $	ME^	Ind	Ind	Ind		
Robotics and Automated Systems	H650	3FT/4SW deg	Ap g	10	M $	ME^	Ind	Ind	Ind	6	
Satellite Communications	H625	3FT deg	2(M/P/Es)	4	MO $	ME^	Ind	Ind	Ind		
Communication Engineering	026H	2FT HND	Ap g		N $	Ind	Ind	Ind	Ind	4	
Electrical and Electronic Engineering	65HH	2FT/3SW HND	Ap g	4	N $	PE^	Ind	Ind	Ind	3	4/10
Electronic Business Management (Somerset)	16NH	2FT HND	*	4	N $	P$	Ind	Ind	Ind	3	
Electronics and Business Management	1PNH	2FT HND	Ap g	4	N $	PE^	Ind	Ind	Ind		
Electronics and Communications Eng (Bristol)	126H	2FT HND	*	8	N $	Ind	Ind	Ind	Ind	2	
Univ of PORTSMOUTH											
Communication Systems Engineering (Ext Rt Avail)	H620	3FT/4SW deg	M+P/Es	16	4M $	M$6/^	28$	BBBB	N$	10	
Communication Systems Engineering (MEng)	H621	4FT/5SW deg	M+P/Es	18	4M+1D$	D$6/^	30$	BBBBC	N$		
Communications and Media Technology	P4H6	3FT/4SW deg	M+P/Es	16	4M $	M$6/^	28$	BBBB	N$		
Communications and Media Technology	P4HP	4FT/5SW deg	M+P/Es	18	4M+1D$	D$6/^	30$	BBBBC	N$		
Electronic & Computer Engineering (MEng)	GH6P	4FT/5SW deg	2(M/P/Cs/Es)	16	4M $	M$6/^	28$	BBBB	N$		
Electronic and Computer Engin (Ext Route Avail)	GH66	3FT/4SW deg	2(M/P/Cs/Es)	14	4M $	M$6/^	26$	BBBC	N$	5	6/16
Electronic and Electrial Eng	HH56	3FT/4SW deg	M+P/Es	16	4M $	M$6/^	28$	BBBB	Ind	11	6/16
Electronic and Electrical Engineering (Eur Prog)	H602	4FT deg	M+P/Es g	18	4M $	M$6/^	28$	BBBB	Ind		
Electronic and Electrical Engineering (MEng)	HH5P	4FT/5SW deg	M+P/Es	18	4M+D $	D$6/^	30$	BBBBC	N$		
Electronics (1 year HND top-up)	H601	1ACC deg	Es	X	HN $	X	X	X	HN$		
Engineering (Electrical/Electronic)	65HH▼	2FT/3SW HND	M/P/Es	4	1M $	P$	Dip	CC	Ind	3	2/10
QUEEN MARY & WESTFIELD COLL (Univ of London)											
Avionics	HH45	3FT deg	M	CCD-BCC	5M $	M$^	28$				
Communication Engineering (4 Yrs) (MEng)	H621	4FT deg	M+P	18	5M $	M$^	26$	BBCCC			
Computer Engineering	H610	3FT deg	M+P	18	5M $	M$^	26$	BBCCC			
Computer Engineering (MEng)	H611	4FT deg	M+P	BCC	5M $	M	28$				
Electrical and Electronic Engineering	HH56	3FT deg	M+P	BCC	5M+2D$	M$^					
Electronic Engineering	H600	3FT deg	M+P	18	5M $	M$^	26$				
Electronic Engineering (MEng)	H601	4FT deg	M+P	BCC	5M $	M$^	28$				
Mechanical Systems Engineering (MEng)	HH36	4FT deg	M+P	BCC-BBB	3M+2D$	M$^	30$	AABBB			
Physics and Electronics	FH36	3FT deg	M+P	24		MS^					
Physics and Electronics (MSci)	FH3P	3FT deg	M+P	24		MS^					
Telecommunications	H626	3FT deg	M+P	18	5M $	M$^	26$	BBCCC			
Science and Engineering (4 yrs with Foundation) *Electronic Engineering*	Y157	4EXT deg		E	N	P					
QUEEN'S Univ Belfast											
Electrical & Electronic Eng Extended Crse (MEng)	HH5P	4FT deg	M+P g	BBB	X	X	32$	X	Ind	3	24/30
Electrical and Electronic Engineering	HH56	3FT/4FT deg	M+P g	BCC	Ind	Ind	29$	BBBC	Ind	5	18/26
Electronic and Software Eng (inc prof exp)	HG67	4SW deg	M+P g	BCC	Ind	Ind	29$	BBBC	Ind	13	18/26
RAVENSBOURNE COLLEGE of Design and Communication											
Broadcast Design	E2H6	3FT deg	M/P	E	N	PT	Ind	Ind	Ind		
Broadcast Engineering	H680	3FT deg	M/P	E	N	PT	Ind	Ind	Ind		
Professional Broadcasting	H685	2FT deg	M/P/Cs/Es	E	N	P	Ind	Ind	Ind		
Professional Broadcasting	586H	2FT HND	M/P/Cs/Es	E	N	PT	Ind	Ind	Ind		

course details

98 expected requirements

96 entry stats

TITLE	CODE	COURSE	SUBJECTS	A/AS	ND/C	AGNVQ	IB	SQA(H)	SQA	RATIO A/AS
Univ of READING										
Applied Computer Science and Cybernetics	GH5P	4SW deg	* g	20	3M+2D$	D$^ go	30$	BBBB	Ind	
Computer Science and Cybernetics	GH56	3FT deg	* g	20	3M+2D$	D$^ go	30$	BBBB$	Ind	8 14/28
Cybernetics & Control Engineering	H651	3FT deg	M+P g	18	4M+1D$	D$^ go	29$	BBBC$	Ind	5 16/26
Cybernetics (MEng)	H654	4FT deg	M+P g	24	2M+3D$	D$^ go	32$	ABBB$	Ind	10 22/28
Electronic Engineering	H600	3FT deg	M+P g	CCC	4M+1D$	DE^ go	29$	BBBC$	Ind	10 16/21
Electronic Engineering (Foundation)	H601	4EXT deg	* g	CDD	4M	M*6/^ go	27	BBBC	Ind	3 10/14
Electronic Engineering (MEng)	H603	4FT deg	M+P g	BBC	3M+2D$	DE^ go	31$	BBBB$	Ind	
Electronic and Optical Engineering	HF63	3FT deg	M+P g	CCC	4M+1D$	DE^ go	29$	BBBC$	Ind	
Human Cybernetics	H655	3FT deg	B/C/P/M g	18	4M+1D	D$^ go	29	BBBC	Ind	5 20/26
ROBERT GORDON Univ										
Electronic and Communications Engineering	H620	3FT/4FT deg	M+S	EE	N	Ind	Ind	BCC$	Ind	5
Electronic and Computer Engineering	GH66	3FT/4FT deg	M+S	EE	N	Ind	Ind	BCC$	Ind	6
Electronic and Electrical Engineering	HH5P	3FT deg	M+S	EE	N	Ind	Ind	CCC$	Ind	3
Electronic and Electrical Engineering	HH56	3FT/4FT deg	M+S	EE	N	Ind	Ind	BCC$	Ind	5
Electronic and Electrical Engineering	65HH	2FT HND	* g	E	N	Ind	Ind	CC$	Ind	5
ROYAL HOLLOWAY, Univ of London										
Applied Physics and Electronics	FH36	3FT deg	M+P	BBC-BCC	MO+2D	DS^	30$	BBBCC$		
Computer Science and Electronics	GH56	3FT/4SW deg	M+P/S	BCC-BBC	MO+2D	D^	30$	Ind		
Electronics	H600	3FT deg	M+P/S	BCC-BBC	MO+2D	D^	30$	Ind		6
Electronics with Management Studies	H6N1	3FT deg	M+P/S	BCC-BBC	MO+2D	D^	30	Ind		6
Science Foundation Year *Electronics*	Y100	4FT deg	*		Ind	Ind	Ind	Ind		
Univ of SALFORD										
Computers Management & Electronics (3 or 4 Yrs)	H6N1	3FT/4SW deg		CCC	Ind	Ind	Ind	Ind	Ind	2
Computers, Management and Electronics	H6NC	4FT deg								
Electroacoustics (3 or 4 Yrs)	H671	3FT/4SW deg	M/P	CCC	$	P$	Ind	Ind	Ind	9 12/26
Electronic & Electrical Eng (4 or 5yrs) (MEng)	HH5P	4FT/5SW deg	M+S	BCC-CCC	4M $	M	Ind	Ind	Ind	10
Electronic Computer Systems (3 or 4 Yrs)	H610	3FT/4SW deg	M+S	CCC	4M $	M	Ind	Ind	Ind	14
Electronic Computer Systems(4 or 5yrs) (MEng)	H611	4FT/5SW deg	M+S	BCC-CCC	4M $	M	Ind	Ind	Ind	
Electronic Engineering	H601	4FT/5SW deg	M+S	BCC-CCC	4M $	M	Ind	Ind	Ind	6
Electronic Engineering	H600▼	3FT/4SW deg	M+S	CCC	4M $	M	Ind	Ind	Ind	8 10/16
Electronic Engineering w. Studies in France MEng	H6R1	4SW deg	M g	CCC	4M $	M	Ind	Ind	Ind	
Electronic and Electrical Engineering (3/4 Yrs)	HH56	3FT/4SW deg	M+S	CCC	4M $	M	Ind	Ind	Ind	24
Electronic and Electrical Engineering (Oldham)	HHMN	4FT deg	M		Ind	M	Ind	Ind	Ind	
Electronic and Electrical Engineering (Priestly)	H605	4FT deg								
Electronic and Electrical Engineering (S Devon)	H606	4FT deg								
Mechatronics	HH6H	3FT/4SW deg	M+S/2S	18	Ind	M	Ind	Ind	Ind	11
Mechatronics (4FT or 5 yr SW)	HH63	4FT/5SW deg	M+S	BCC-CCC	Ind	M	Ind	Ind	Ind	6
Media Technology	HW64	3FT deg	M/P	18	4M	D3	28	CCCCC	Ind	19 10/24
Robotic & Electronic Eng (3 or 4Yrs) (BEng)	H651	3FT/4SW deg	M+S	BCC-CCC	4M $	M	Ind	Ind	Ind	3
Robotic & Electronic Engineering (4/5Yrs)(MEng)	H650	4FT/5SW deg	M+S	CCC	4M $	M	Ind	Ind	Ind	10
Telecommun & Network Eng (4 or 5yrs) (MEng)	H621	4FT/5SW deg	M+S	BCC-CCC	4M $	M	Ind	Ind	Ind	
Telecommunications & Network Eng (3/4 Yrs)	H620	3FT/4SW deg	M+S	CCC	4M $	M	Ind	Ind	Ind	22
Video Imaging and Communication Technology	H635	3FT deg	Ad	10-16	4M	M	24	CCCCC	Ind	10
Audio and Video Systems	706H	2FT HND	M/P	2-4	N	M	Ind	CCC	Ind	8 6/12
Professional Sound and Video Technology	806H	2FT HND		2-4	N	P	Ind	CC	Ind	4 4/17
SANDWELL COLL										
Electronic Engineering	006H	2FT HND	Ap	DD-EE	N	P$	Ind	Ind	Ind	
Professional Sound Engineering	086H	2FT HND	* g	BB-DD	N	P	Ind	Ind	Ind	

| | | | 98 expected requirements | | | | | | | 96 entry stats | |
TITLE	CODE	COURSE	SUBJECTS	A/AS	ND/C	RGNVQ	IB	SQA(H)	SQA	RATIO A/AS	
Univ of SHEFFIELD											
Control Systems Engineering (3/4 Yrs)	H640	3FT/4FT deg	M+P g	BBC-BCC	5M+1D$	D$^	31$	AABB	Ind	6	
Electrical Engineering (3/4 Yrs)	H500	3FT/4FT deg	M+P g	BBC-CCC	5M+1D$	D$^	30$	BBCC$	Ind	8	16/26
Electrical Engineering (incl Found Yr) (4/5 Yrs)	H501	4FT/5FT deg	* g	BBC-CCC	5M+1D$	D^/+	30	BBCC	Ind	8	
Electrical Engineering with a Modern Lang (MEng)	H5T9	4FT deg	M/P+L g	BBC-CCC	5M+1D$	D$^	30$	BBCC$	Ind		
Electronic Control and Systems Eng (3/4 Yrs)	H642	3FT/4FT deg	M+P g	BBB-BCC	5M+1D$	D$^	30$	ABBB$	Ind	8	
Electronic Eng (Solid State Dev) (3/4 Yrs)	H610	3FT/4FT deg	M+P g	BBC-CCC	5M+1D$	D$^	30$	BBCC$	Ind	4	
Electronic Eng (Systems) with a Mod Lang (MEng)	H6TX	4FT deg	M/P+L g	BBC-CCC	5M+1D$	D$^	30$	BBCC$	Ind	11	
Electronic Eng (incl Foundation Year) (4/5 Yrs)	H601	4FT/5FT deg	* g	BBC-CCC	5M+1D$	D^/+	30	BBCC	Ind	5	
Electronic Eng with a Modern Language (MEng)	H6T9	4FT deg	M/P+L g	BBC-CCC	5M+1D$	D$^	30$	BBCC$	Ind	7	
Electronic Engineering (3/4 Yrs)	H600	3FT/4FT deg	M+P g	BBC-CCC	5M+1D$	D$^	30$	BBCC$	Ind	8	16/30
Electronic Engineering (Communications)(3/4 Yrs)	H620	3FT/4FT deg	M+P g	BBC-CCC	5M+1D$	D$^	30$	BBCC$	Ind	6	16/26
Electronic Engineering (Computing) (3/4 Yrs)	H611	3FT/4FT deg	M+P g	BBC-CCC	5M+1D$	D$^	30$	BBCC$	Ind	6	18/26
Electronic Engineering (Systems) (3/4 Yrs)	H630	3FT/4FT deg	M+P g	BBC-CCC	5M+1D$	D$^	30$	BBCC$	Ind	25	
Medical Systems Engineering (3/4 Yrs)	H670	3/4 FT deg									
Systems Engineering (incl Foundation Year)	H641	4FT/5FT deg	* g	BBC-BCC	5M+1D	D^	30	ABBB	Ind	3	
SHEFFIELD HALLAM Univ											
Electronic Engineering	H600	3FT/4SW deg	M+S	8	3M $	M$	Ind	Ind	Ind		
Electronic Engineering (Extended)	H608▼	4EXT/5EXTSW deg									
Electronic Systems and Control Engineering	H660	3FT/4SW deg	M+S	8	3M $	M$	Ind	Ind	Ind		
Electronic Systems and Control Engineering (Ext)	H668▼	4EXT/5EXTSW deg									
Electronic Systems and Information Engineering	GH56	3FT/4SW deg	M+S	8	3M $	M$	Ind	Ind	Ind		
Electronic Systems and Information Engineering	GH5P▼	4EXT/5EXTSW deg									
Electronic and Computer Engineering	HG66	3FT/4SW deg	M+S	8	3M $	M$	Ind	Ind	Ind		
Electronic and Computer Engineering (Extended)	HG6P▼	4EXT/5EXTSW deg									
Mechatronics	HH63	4FT/SW deg	Cs/Es/M/Ph	8	3M $	M$	Ind	Ind	Ind		
Mechatronics	HH6H▼	5FT/SW deg									
Combined Studies *Electrical Systems Engineering*	Y400	3FT deg	M	8	2M	M	Ind	Ind	Ind		
Electrical and Electronic Engineering	65HH▼	2FT/3SW HND	Cs/Es/M/Ph	E	N $	P$	Ind	Ind	Ind		
Electronic Engineering	116H▼	2FT/3SW HND	Cs/Es/M/Ph	E	N $	P$	Ind	Ind	Ind		
Mechatronics	36HH▼	2FT/3SW HND	Cs/Es/M/Ph	E	N $	P$	Ind	Ind	Ind		
SHREWSBURY COLLEGE OF ARTS & TECHNOLOGY											
Electronics	006H	2FT HND									
Univ of SOUTHAMPTON											
Computer Engineering	H614	3FT deg	M+S	24	Ind $	D^	32$	CSYS	Ind	7	18/30
Computer Engineering (MEng)	H615	4FT deg	M+S	24	Ind $	D^	32$	CSYS	Ind	6	20/26
Electrical Engineering	H500	3FT deg	M+P	20	Ind $	D^	30$	CSYS	Ind	7	
Electrical Engineering (MEng)	H501	4FT deg	M+P	24	Ind $	D^	32$	CSYS	Ind	24	
Electrical Engineering with Euro St (MEng)	H504	4FT deg	M+P+F/G	24	Ind $	D^	32$	CSYS	Ind		
Electromechanical Engineering	HH35	3FT deg	M+P	24	Ind $	D^	32$	CSYS	Ind	4	14/20
Electromechanical Engineering (MEng)	HH3M	4FT deg	M+P	24	Ind $	D^	32$	CSYS	Ind	26	
Electromechanical Engineering with Euro St(MEng)	HH3N	4FT deg	M+P+F/G	24	Ind $	D^	32$	CSYS	Ind		
Electronic Engineering	H600	3FT deg	M+P	24	Ind $	D^	32$	CSYS	Ind	7	20/28
Electronic Engineering (Euro Tripartite)(MEng)	H602	5FT deg	M+P g	24	Ind $	D^	32$	CSYS	Ind		
Electronic Engineering (MEng)	H601	4FT deg	M+P	24	Ind $	D^	32$	CSYS	Ind	5	22/30
Electronic Engineering with Euro St (MEng)	H605	4FT deg	M+P+F/G	24	Ind $	D^	32$	CSYS	Ind	10	
Information Engineering (MEng)	H630	4FT deg	M+P	24	Ind $	D^	32$	CSYS	Ind	14	

TITLE	CODE	COURSE	SUBJECTS	A/AS	ND/C	AGNVQ	IB	SQA(H)	SQA	RATIO A/AS
SOUTHAMPTON INST										
Electronic Engineering	H600	3FT deg	M/P	4-10	MO	M$	Dip	CCCC	N	4
Electronic Engineering (with Foundation Year)	H608▼	4FT deg	*	2-4	N	P$	Dip	CCCC	N	1
Engineering (Electronics & Communications)	026H▼	2FT HND	M/P/E	2	N	P$	Dip	CCCC	N	4
Multimedia Electronics	586H	2FT HND	M/P/E	2	N	P$	Dip	CCCC	N	
SOUTH BANK Univ										
Electrical and Electronic Engineering	HH56	3FT/4SW deg	M+S g	DD	5M	M go	Ind	Ind	Ind	
Electrical and Electronic Engineering	HH65	1/2FT deg			HN		Ind	Ind	Ind	
Electrical and Electronic Engineering (MEng)	HH5Q	4FT/5SW deg	M+S g	DD	5M	M go	Ind	Ind	Ind	
Electronic Engineering Management	H6N1	3FT deg	M+S g	CC	5M	M go	Ind	Ind	Ind	
Electronic Engineering Management (top-up)	HN61	1/2FT deg			HN					
European Electronic Engineering	H6T2	3FT deg	L g	CD	MO	M go				
Foundation Electrical and Electronic Engineering	HH5P	4EXT deg					Ind	Ind	Ind	
Mechatronics	HH36	3FT deg	Ds/M g	DD	MO	M$ go	Ind	Ind	Ind	
Mechatronics (4/5 years)	HH3P	4FT deg	Ds/M g	DD	MO	M$ go	Ind	Ind	Ind	
Media Special Effects	HW62	3FT deg	2(Ar/Fa/Me/T) g	CC-CD	MO	M$ go	Ind	Ind	Ind	
Multi-Media Engineering	GH76	3FT/4SW deg	M g	CC	5M	M go	Ind	Ind	Ind	
Software Engineering for Real Time Systems	HG67	3FT deg	M+S	CD	M+D	M go	Ind	Ind	Ind	
Electrical and Electronic Engineering	65HH	2FT HND	M/P g	D	Ind	P go	Ind	Ind	Ind	
Univ of ST ANDREWS										
Laser Physics and Optoelectronics (MSci)	FH3P	4FT deg	M+P	CCC	Ind	Ind	28$	BBBC$	Ind	11
ST HELENS COLL										
Electrical/Electronic Engineering	HH56	3FT deg	M/P/Es	4-6	3M	M$	Ind	Ind	Ind	
Electrical/Electronic Engineering	65HH	2FT HND	M/P/Es/Cs	2-6	N	P$	Ind	Ind	Ind	
Mechatronics	36HH	2FT HND	M/P/Es/Cs/Ds	2-6	N	P$	Ind	Ind	Ind	
Telecommunications	626H	2FT HND	M/P/Es/Cs	2-6	N	P$	Ind	Ind	Ind	
STAFFORDSHIRE Univ										
Business Communications Technology	H629	4EXT deg	g	EE	P $	P$	Ind	Ind	Ind	
Computer & Electronics for Information Technol	HG65	4EXT deg	g	EE	P $	P$	Ind	Ind	Ind	
Computing and Electronics for Info Technology	GH5Q	3FT deg	g	8	3M $	M$	24	BCC	Ind	
Electrical Engineering (MEng)	H500	4FT/5SW deg	M+P	10	3M	M$	24	BCC	Ind	4
Electronic Engineering (MEng)	H600	4FT/5SW deg	M+P	10	3M	M$	24	BCC	Ind	6
Electronics and Applied Physics	FHH6	3FT deg	S g	8	3M	M	24	BCC	Ind	
Electronics and Applied Physics	HF6H	4FT deg								
Electronics/Applied Statistics	GH46	3FT deg	S g	8	3M	M	24	BCC	Ind	
Electronics/Biology	CH16	3FT deg	S	8	3M	M	24	BCC	Ind	
Electronics/Business Studies	HN61	3FT deg	S g	12	4M	M	24	BCC	Ind	
Electronics/Ceramic Science	HJ63	3FT deg	S g	8	3M	M	24	BCC	Ind	
Electronics/Chemistry	FH16	3FT deg	S	8	3M	M	24	BCC	Ind	
Electronics/Computing	GH56	3FT deg	S g	8	3M	M	24	BCC	Ind	5
Extended Electrical Engineering	H508	5EXT/6EXTSW deg	*	4	N	P$	24	CCC	Ind	3
Extended Electronic Engineering	H608	5EXT/6EXTSW deg	*	4	N	P$	24	CCC	Ind	5
Extended Mechatronics	HH3P	5EXT/6EXTSW deg	*	4	N	P$	24	CCC	Ind	
Foundation Biology and Electronics	CH1P▼	4EXT deg	*	4	N	P	24	CCC	Ind	
Foundation Chemistry and Electronics	FH1P▼	4EXT deg	*	4	N	P	24	CCC	Ind	
Foundation Electronics and Applied Physics	HF6J	4EXT deg	*	4	N	P	24	CCC		
Foundation Electronics and Computing	HG6M▼	4EXT deg	*	4	N	P	24	CCC	Ind	
Foundation Geology and Electronics	FH6P	4EXT deg	*	4	N	P	24	CCC		
Foundation Physics and Electronics	FH3P▼	4EXT deg	*	4	N	P	24	CCC	Ind	
Geology/Electronics	FH66	3FT deg	S	8	3M	M	24	BCC	Ind	

course details — *98 expected requirements* — *96 entry stats*

TITLE	CODE	COURSE	SUBJECTS	A/AS	NO/C	AGNVQ	IB	SQA(H)	SQA	RATIO A/AS
course details			98 expected requirements							96 entry stats
Health Technology	H670	3FT deg	g	8	3M $	M$	Ind	Ind	Ind	
Mechatronics	HH36	4FT/5SW deg	M+P	10	3M	M$	24	BCC	Ind	6
Microelectronics and Computer Engineering	HH6P	4EXT deg								
Microelectronics and Computer Engineering (MEng)	GH66	4FT/5SW deg	M+P	10	3M	M$	24	BCC	Ind	3	6/13
Physics and Electronics	FH3Q	4EXT deg	g	4	M	N	24	CCC	Ind	
Physics/Electronics	FH36	3FT deg	S	8	3M	M	24	BCC	Ind	
Physiology/Electronics	BH16	3FT deg								
Psychology/Electronics	LH76	3FT deg	S	8-18	4M	D	24	BBB	Ind	3
Sport Sciences and Electronics	BH66	3FT deg	S	14	Ind	D	Ind	BBCC	Ind	
Electrical Engineering	65HH	2FT HND	M/P g	2	N	P$	24	CCC	Ind	
Electronic Engineering	66HG	2FT HND	M/P g	2	N	P$	24	CCC	Ind	
Extended Electrical Engineering	6MHH	3EXT HND	g	2	N	P$	24	CCC	Ind	
Extended Electronic Engineering	6PHG	3EXT HND	g	2	N	P$	24	CCC	Ind	
Mechatronics	36HH▼	3EXT HND		2	N	P$				

STOCKPORT COLL of F and HE

TITLE	CODE	COURSE	SUBJECTS	A/AS	NO/C	AGNVQ	IB	SQA(H)	SQA	RATIO A/AS
Electronic and Electrical Engineering	HH56	4FT deg	M/P	2	N	PE/S	Dip	Ind	N	
Electrical and Electronic Engineering	65HH	2FT HND	M/P	2	N	PE/S	Dip	Ind	N	

Univ of STRATHCLYDE

TITLE	CODE	COURSE	SUBJECTS	A/AS	NO/C	AGNVQ	IB	SQA(H)	SQA	RATIO A/AS
Computer and Electronic Systems (BEng)	GH56	4FT deg	M+P	CCD	HN		Ind	ABBB$	HN	
Electrical and Mechanical Engineering	HH53	4FT deg	M+P g	BBC	Ind	Ind	36$	AABBC$	Ind	
Electronic & Electrical Eng with Business Stud	HHMP	5FT deg	M+P g	BBC			Ind	AAAB$		
Electronic & Electrical Eng with European Studs	HH6N	5FT deg	M+P+E/L	BBC			Ind	AAAB$		
Electronic and Electrical Eng (Communications)	HH6M	4FT deg	M+P	CCD	HN		32$	ABBB$	HN	
Electronic and Electrical Eng (Control Systems)	HH5P	4FT deg	M+P	CCD	HN		32$	ABBB$	HN	
Electronic and Electrical Eng (Electronic Systs)	HH65	4FT deg	M+P	CCD	HN		32$	ABBB$	HN	
Electronic and Electrical Eng (Power Eng)	HH5Q	4FT deg	M+P	CCD	HN		32$	ABBB$	HN	
Electronic and Electrical Engineering	HH56	4FT deg	M+P	CCD	HN		32$	ABBB$	HN	
Electronics Manufacture	H640	4FT/5FT deg								
Mechanical Engineering with Control Engineering	H3H6	5FT deg	M+P	BBB	HN		32$	AABBB$	HN	

UNIVERSITY COLLEGE SUFFOLK

TITLE	CODE	COURSE	SUBJECTS	A/AS	NO/C	AGNVQ	IB	SQA(H)	SQA	RATIO A/AS
Engineering (Electrical and Electronic)	65HH	2FT HND	*	E	N $	P$	Ind	Ind	Ind	

Univ of SUNDERLAND

TITLE	CODE	COURSE	SUBJECTS	A/AS	NO/C	AGNVQ	IB	SQA(H)	SQA	RATIO A/AS
Automation and Mechatronics	HH63	3FT/4SW deg	M+P/C g	12	3M $	ME	24$	CCC	N$	11
Automation and Mechatronics (Foundation)	HH36▼	4EXT/5EXTSW deg	*	2	N	P	24	CC	N	1
Communications Engineering	H620	3FT/4SW/4FT/5SW deg	M+P/C g	CC	N $	ME	24$	CCC$	N$	6
Communications Engineering (Foundation)	H628▼	4EXT/5EXTSW deg	*	2	N	P	24	CC	N	2
Computer Systems Engineering	H611	3FT/4SW deg	M+P g	DD	3M $	ME	24$	CCC$	N$	5
Computer Systems Engineering (Foundation)	H618▼	4EXT/5EXTSW deg	*	2	N	P	24	CC	N	
Electrical & Electronic Engineering (Foundation)	HH6P▼	4EXT/5EXTSW deg	*	2	N	P	24	CC	N	1
Electrical and Electronic Engineering	HH56	3FT/4SW deg	M/P/C/S g	DD	3M $	ME	24$	CCC$	N$	6
Electrical & Electronic Engineering (Foundation)	6MHH▼	3EXT/4EXTSW HND	*			P				
Electrical and Electronic Engineering	65HH	2FT/3SW HND	M/P g	2	N $	PE	24$	CC$	N$	4

Univ of SURREY

TITLE	CODE	COURSE	SUBJECTS	A/AS	NO/C	AGNVQ	IB	SQA(H)	SQA	RATIO A/AS
Electronic & Electrical Eng with Euro Lang(MEng)	HH5P	4/5SW deg	M+P g	20-24	2D $		$	Ind	X	7
Electronic & Electrical Eng with Euro Lang(MEng)	HHNP	4SW deg	M+P g	20-24	5M+2D$ X		28$	BBBBB	X	
Electronic & Electrical Eng with Euro Language	HH5Q	4SW deg	M+P g	18-22	5M+2D$ DE^ go		28$	BBBBC	X	6
Electronic & Electrical Engineering	HH56	3FT deg	M+P	18-22	5M+2D$ DE^ go		28$	BBBBC	X	6	16/22
Electronic & Electrical Engineering	HHM6	4SW deg	M+P	18-22	5M+2D$ DE^ go		28$	BBBBC	X	4	18/30
Electronic & Electrical Engineering (MEng)	HHMP	4/5SW deg	M+P	20-24	5M+2D$ X		28$	BBBBB	X	4	20/30
Electronic & Electrical Engineering (MEng)	HHMQ	4SW deg	M+P	20-24	5M+2D$ X		28$	BBBBB	X	4	20/26

course details			98 expected requirements							96 entry stats	
TITLE	CODE	COURSE	SUBJECTS	A/AS	ND/C	RGNVQ	IB	SQA(H)	SQA	RATIO	A/AS
Electronics & Info Systems Eng with Found Yr	HHP5	4FT/5SW deg	* g	16-20	Ind	Ind	Ind	Ind	Ind	4	
Information Systems Eng with a Euro Lang (MEng)	H635	4/5SW deg	M+P g	20-24	5M+2D$	X	28$	BBBBB	X		
Information Systems Eng with a Euro Lang (MEng)	H636	4SW deg	M+P g	20-24	5M+2D$	X	28$	BBBBB	X		
Information Systems Eng with a European Language	H634	4SW deg	M+P g	18-22	5M+2D$	DE^ go	28$	BBBBC	X		
Information Systems Engineering	H632	3FT deg	M+P	18-22	5M+2D$	DE^ go	28$	BBBBC	X	4	
Information Systems Engineering	H630	4SW deg	M+P	18-22	5M+2D$	DE^ go	28$	BBBBC	X	2	16/24
Information Systems Engineering (MEng)	H633	4SW deg	M+P	20-24	5M+2D$	X	28$	BBBBB	X	18	
Information Systems Engineering (MEng)	H631	4/5SW deg	M+P	20-24	5M+2D$		28$	BBBBB	X	6	

Univ of SUSSEX

Computer Systems Engineering	H610	3FT deg	M	BCC	MO $	MS^	$	Ind	Ind		
Computer Systems Engineering	H618	4FT deg									
Computer Systems Engineering (MEng)	H614	4FT deg	M	BCC	MO $	MS^	$	Ind	Ind		
Elec & Electronic Eng with N American St (MEng)	H5QK	4FT deg	M	BCC	MO $	MS^	$	Ind	Ind		
Electrical & Electronic Eng with Euro St (MEng)	HH5M	4FT deg	M g	BCC	MO $	MS^ go	$	Ind	Ind		
Electrical and Electronic Eng with Japanese	H5TK	4FT deg	M g	BCC	MO $	MS^ go	$	Ind	Ind		
Electrical and Electronic Engineering	HHQ5	4FT deg									
Electrical and Electronic Engineering	HH5P	3FT deg	M	BCC	MO $	MS^	$	Ind	Ind		
Electrical and Electronic Engineering	HH5Q	4FT deg	M	BCC	MO $	MS^	$	Ind	Ind		
Electromechanical Engineering	HH35	3FT deg	M	BCC	MO $	MS^	$	Ind	Ind		
Electronic Engineering	H600	3FT deg	M	BCC	MO $	MS^	$	Ind	Ind		
Electronic Engineering (MEng)	H601	4FT deg	M	BCC	MO $	MS^	$	Ind	Ind		
Electronic Engineering and Computer Science	H6G5	3FT deg	M	BCC	MO $	MS^	$	Ind	Ind		
Electronic Engineering with Business Management	H6N1	3FT deg	M	BCC	MO $	MS^	$	Ind	Ind		
Electronic Engineering with European St (MEng)	H6TF	4FT deg	M g	BCC	MO $	MS^ go	$	Ind	Ind		
Electronic Engineering with Japanese Studies	H6T4	4FT deg	M g	BCC	MO $	MS^ go	$	Ind	Ind		
Electronic Engineering with N Amer St (MEng)	H6QK	4FT deg	M	BCC	MO $	MS^	$	Ind	Ind		
Mechatronics	H3H6	3FT deg	M	BCC	MO $	MS^	$	Ind	Ind		
Physics with Elect & Optoelectronics (MPhys)	F3HP	4FT deg	M+P	CCC	MO $	MS^	$	Ind	Ind		
Physics with Electronics and Optoelectronics	F3HQ	3FT deg	M+P	CCC	MO $	MS^	$	Ind	Ind		
Robotics and Automated Manufacture	HH76	3FT deg	M	BCC	MO $	MS^	$	Ind	Ind		

Univ of Wales SWANSEA

Computer Science with Electronics	G5H6	3FT deg	M	BCC-BCC	5D $	Ind	30$	ABBBB$	Ind	7	
Electrical & Elect Eng(Eur.Austral.N.Am. or Ind)	HH5P	5FT deg	M+P g	BCC	1M+5D$	Ind	28$	BBBBB$	Ind		
Electrical and Electronic Engineering	HHM6	4FT deg	* g	CC	1M+4D	Ind	24	BCCCC	Ind	1	8/10
Electronic & Elect Eng (Eur.Austral.N.Am or Ind)	HH6M	4FT deg	M+P g	BCC	1M+5D$	Ind	28$	BBBBB$	Ind		
Electronic & Electrical Engineering (CCTA)	HH5Q	4FT deg	*	12-16	1M+3D	Ind	20	BBCCC	Ind	6	
Electronic and Electrical Engineering	HH65	3FT deg	M+P g	BCC	1M+5D$	Ind	28$	BBBBB$	Ind	4	10/22
Electronic and Electrical Engineering (MEng)	HH56	4FT deg	M+P g	BCC	1M+5D$	Ind	28$	BBBBB$	Ind	3	14/20
Electronics with Comm (Eur.Austral. N.Am or Ind)	H623	5FT deg	M+P g	BCC	1M+5D$	Ind	28$	BBBBB$	Ind		
Electronics with Commun(Eur.Austral.N.Am. o Ind)	H622	4FT deg	M+P g	BCC	1M+5D$	Ind	28$	BBBBB$	Ind		
Electronics with Communications	H620	3FT deg	M+P g	BCC	1M+5D$	Ind	28$	BBBBB$	Ind	5	14/18
Electronics with Communications (MEng)	H621	4FT deg	M+P g	BCC	1M+5D$	Ind	28$	BBBBB$	Ind	5	
Electronics with Comp Sci(Eur.Austral.N.Am o In)	H6GN	5FT deg	M+P g	BCC	1M+5D$	Ind	28$	BBBBB$	Ind		
Electronics with Comp Sci(Eur.Austral.N.Am.o In)	HG6M	4FT deg	M+P g	BCC	1M+5D$	Ind	28$	BBBBB$	Ind		
Electronics with Computing Science	H6G5	3FT deg	M+P g	BCC	1M+5D$	Ind	28$	BBBBB$	Ind	3	
Electronics with Computing Science (MEng)	H6GM	4FT deg	M+P g	BCC	1M+5D$	Ind	28$	BBBBB$	Ind		

SWANSEA INST of HE

Automotive Electronics Engineering	H6H3	3FT deg	2S	4	3M		Ind	Ind	Ind	4	
Automotive Electronics Engineering (Foundation)	H6HH	4EXT deg								2	
Electronic Engineering	H600	3FT deg	2S	4	3M		Ind	Ind	Ind	8	
Electronic Engineering (Foundation)	H608	4EXT deg								1	

		course details		98 expected requirements							96 entry stats	
TITLE	CODE	COURSE		SUBJECTS	A/AS	NO/C	AGNVQ	IB	SQA(H)	SQA	RATIO	A/AS
Mechatronics	HH36	3FT deg		2S	4	3M		Ind	Ind	Ind	2	
Mechatronics (Foundation)	HH3P	4EXT deg									2	
Electronic Engineering (Electronics)	016H	2FT HND		S	2	N		Ind	Ind	Ind	2	
Mechatronics	63HH	2FT HND		S	2	N		Ind	Ind	Ind	3	
Univ of TEESSIDE												
Computer Systems Engineering	H611	3FT/4SW deg		M+S	8	3M		Ind	CCC	Ind	6	
Electrical and Electronic Engineering	H500	3FT/4SW deg		M+S	10	3M $		Ind	Ind	N $	4	
Electronic Systems Engineering	H660	3FT deg		M+S	10	3M $		Ind	Ind	N$		
Instrumentation and Control Engineering	H640	3FT/4SW deg		M+S	10	3M $		Ind	Ind	N $	2	
Media Technology and Production	H620	3FT/4SW deg		* g	8	Ind		Ind	Ind	Ind	4	6/18
Telecommunication and Broadcast Engineering	H680	3FT deg		M+S	10	3M		Ind	Ind	Ind		
Modular Degree Scheme *Electronic Systems*	Y401	3FT deg										
Science and Technology Combined Honours Scheme *Electronic Systems*	Y108	3FT deg										
Electrical Engineering	005H	2FT HND		M/S	4	N		Ind	Ind	N	11	
Electronic and Communication Engineering	126H▼	2FT HND		M/S	4	N						
Electronic and Computer Engineering	116H	2FT HND		M/S	4	N		Ind	Ind	N	3	
Instrumentation and Control	046H	2FT HND		M/S	4	N		Ind	Ind	N	2	
Mechatronics	63HH▼	2FT HND		M/S	D	N		Ind	Ind	Ind	2	
Media Technology	026H▼	2FT HND			4	N					2	2/4
THAMES VALLEY Univ												
Digital Arts with Radio Broadcasting	W9H6	3FT deg			8-12	MO	M		CCC			
Media Arts with Radio Broadcasting	W9HP	3FT deg			8-12	MO	M	26	CCC			
Multi-Media Computing with Radio Broadcasting	G5H6	3FT deg			8-12	MO	M	26	CCC			
Sociology with Radio Broadcasting	L3H6	3FT deg			8-12	MO	M	26	CCC			
Univ of ULSTER												
Electronic Systems (4/5 Yr SW inc DIS)	H616▼	4SW/5SW deg		M	CCC	MO+3D	Ind	28	BBBC	Ind	6	14/24
Electronics & Computing (Hons) (4 Yr SW inc DIS)	GH76▼	4SW deg		S	CCC	MO+3D	Ind	28	BBBC	Ind	10	
Electronics and Computing (4 Yr SW inc DIS)	HG67▼	4SW deg		S	CDD	MO+1D	Ind	26	BCCC	Ind	7	
Eng (Electrical/Electronics) (3 Yr SW inc CIS)	56HH▼	3SW HND		M+S g	Ind	Ind	Ind	Ind	Ind	Ind	3	4/10
Eng (Electronics & Computing) (3 Yr SW inc CIS)	65HH▼	3SW HND		M+S g	Ind	Ind	Ind	Ind	Ind	Ind	3	
UNIVERSITY COLL LONDON (Univ of London)												
Computer Science with Electronic Eng (MSci)	G5HP	4FT deg		M g	BBB	MO $	Ind	32$	ABBBB$	Ind		
Computer Science with Electronic Engineering	G5H6	3FT deg		M g	BBB	MO $	Ind	32$	ABBBB$	Ind	6	22/26
Electronic Eng with Comp Sci for Eur (MEng)	H6GM	4FT deg		M+P g	ABB-AAB	DO $	X	30$	BBBCC$	Ind	7	
Electronic Eng with Optoelect for Eur (MEng)	H636	4FT deg		M+P g	ABB-AAB	DO $	X	30$	BBBCC$	Ind		
Electronic Eng with Optoelectronics	H635	3FT deg		M+P g	ABB-AAB	DO $	X	30$	BBBCC$	Ind		
Electronic Engineering	H600	3FT deg		M+P g	ABB-AAB	DO $	X	30$	BBBCC$	Ind		
Electronic Engineering (MEng)	H601	4FT deg		M+P g	ABB-AAB	DO $	X	30$	BBBCC$	Ind		
Electronic Engineering for Europe (MEng)	H603	4FT deg		M+P g	ABB-AAB	DO $	X	30$	BBBCC$	Ind		
Electronic Engineering with Computer Science	H6G5	3FT deg		M+P g	ABB-AAB	DO $	X	30$	BBBCC$	Ind	16	28/30
Electronic Engineering with Management Studies	H6N1	3FT deg		M+P g	ABB-AAB	DO $	X	30$	BBBCC$	Ind	6	
Electronic Engineering with Medical Electronics	H673	3FT deg		M+P g	ABB-AAB	DO $	X	30$	BBBCC$	Ind	7	
Electronic and Communications Engineering	H620	3FT deg		M+P g	ABB-AAB	DO $	X	30$	BBBCC$	Ind		
Electronic and Communications Engineering (MEng)	H621	4FT deg		M+P g	ABB-AAB	DO $	X	30$	BBBCC$	Ind		
Physics for Advanced Technologies	F3H6	3FT deg		M+P g	BCC-BBC	MO+2D$	Ind	32$	BBBCC$	N$		
Physics for Advanced Technologies (MSci)	F3HP	4FT deg		M+P g	BCC-BBC	MO+2D$	Ind	32$	BBBCC$	N$		

course details				**98 expected requirements**							**96 entry stats**
TITLE	CODE	COURSE	SUBJECTS	A/AS	NQ/C	AGNVQ	IB	SQA(H)	SQA	RATIO	A/AS
Univ of WARWICK											
Computer Systems Engineering	GH6P	4FT deg	M g	BBB	Ind	DS^	32$	AABBB$			
Computer Systems Engineering	GH66	3FT deg	M g	BBB	Ind	DS^	32$	AABBB$		6	22/30
Electrical Engineering	H500	3FT deg	M+S g	CCC	5M+1D$	DS^	28$	BBBBC$		5	14/26
Electrical Engineering	H502	4FT deg	M+S g	BBB	5M+1D$	DS^	32$	AABBB$			
Electrical Engineering (European)	H504	4FT deg	M+S g	BBB	5M+1D$	DS^	32$	AABBB$			
Electronic Engineering	H600	3FT deg	M+S g	CCC	5M+1D$	DS^	28$	BBBBC$		8	12/28
Electronic Engineering	H602	4FT deg	M+S g	BBB	5M+1D$	DS^	32$	AABBB$			
Electronic Engineering (European)	H604	4FT deg	M+S g	BBB	5M+1D$	DS^	32$	AABBB$		16	
Univ of WESTMINSTER											
Communication Systems Engineering (with found)	H628	4FT deg	M	D	N		Ind	Ind	Ind		
Communications Systems Engineering	H620	3FT deg	M	CD-DD	3M $	M	Ind	Ind	Ind		
Control and Computer Engineering	H640	3FT deg	M+P	CC	3M+1D	M	Ind	Ind	Ind	6	
Control and Computer Engineering (with found)	H648	4EXT deg	*	D-E	N	P	Ind	Ind	Ind	3	
Electronic Engineering	H600	3FT deg	M+P	CC	3M+1D	M	Ind	Ind	Ind	7	8/18
Electronic Engineering (with foundation)	H608	4EXT deg	*	D-E	N	P				3	
WIGAN and LEIGH COLL											
Electrical and Electronic Engineering	36HH▼	2FT HND	M/P/C	E	N	P$	Dip		N		
Univ of YORK											
Avionics	H640	4FT deg	M+S	BBB	MO+3D$	DS^	30$	CSYS$	Ind		22/26
Electronic Engineering	H602	4FT deg	M+S	BBB	MO+3D$	DS^	30$	CSYS$	Ind		22/30
Electronic Engineering	H600	3FT deg	M+S	BBB	MO+3D$	DS^	30$	CSYS$	Ind		16/30
Electronic Engineering	H603	4SW deg	M+S	BBB	MO+3D$	DS^	30$	CSYS$	Ind		
Electronic Engineering with Business Management	H6N1	3FT deg	M+S	BBB	MO+3D$	DS^	30$	CSYS$	Ind		
Electronic Engineering with Business Management	H6ND	4FT deg	M+S	BBB	MO+3D$	DS^	30$	CSYS$	Ind		
Electronic Engineering with Business Management	H6NC	4SW deg	M+S	BBB	MO+3D$	DS^	30$	CSYS$	Ind		
Electronic Engineering with Foundation Yr	H604	4FT deg	*		Ind	Ind	Ind	Ind	Ind		
Electronic Engineering with Music Technology Sys	H661	4SW deg	M+S	BBB	MO+3D$	DS^	30$	CSYS$	Ind		24/26
Electronic Engineering with Music Technology Sys	H662	4FT deg	M+S	BBB	MO+3D$	DS^	30$	CSYS$	Ind		18/30
Electronic Engineering with Music Technology Sys	H660	3FT deg	M+S	BBB	MO+3D$	DS^	30$	CSYS$	Ind		16/26
Electronic and Communication Engineering	H621	4SW deg	M+S	BBB	MO+3D$	DS^	30$	CSYS$	Ind		
Electronic and Communication Engineering	H620	3FT deg	M+S	BBB	MO+3D$	DS^	30$	CSYS$	Ind		
Electronic and Communication Engineering	H622	4FT deg	M+S	BBB	MO+3D$	DS^	30$	CSYS$	Ind		
Electronic and Computer Engineering	H633	3FT deg	M+S	BBB	MO+3D$	DS^	30$	CSYS$	Ind		
Electronic and Computer Engineering	H634	4SW deg	M+S	BBB	MO+3D$	DS^	30$	CSYS$	Ind		
Electronic and Computer Engineering	H636	4FT deg	M+S	BBB	MO+3D$	DS^	30$	CSYS$	Ind		
Music Technology	HW63	3FT/4FT deg	Mu+M g	BBC	Ind	DS^	28$	CSYS$	Ind		20/28

TITLE	CODE	COURSE	SUBJECTS	A/AS	ND/C	AGNVQ	IB	SQA(H)	SQA	RATIO A/AS	
course details			**98 expected requirements**							**96 entry stats**	

Univ of ABERDEEN

TITLE	CODE	COURSE	SUBJECTS	A/AS	ND/C	AGNVQ	IB	SQA(H)	SQA	RATIO A/AS	
Engineering	H100	4FT deg	M+P/Ds g	CC	Ind	MS^ go	26$	BBBCC$	Ind	5	
Engineering (Integrated)	H105	4FT deg	M+P/Ds g	CC	Ind	MS^ go	26$	BBBCC$	Ind	8	
Engineering (Integrated) (MEng)	H104	5FT deg	M+P/Ds g	BC	Ind	MS^ go	28$	AABB$	Ind		
Engineering with Foundation Studies	H101	3FT/4FT deg	* g	DD	Ind	M$ go	24$	BCCC$	Ind	3	

Univ of ABERTAY DUNDEE

TITLE	CODE	COURSE	SUBJECTS	A/AS	ND/C	AGNVQ	IB	SQA(H)	SQA	RATIO A/AS	
Business Engineering	HN11	4FT/5SW deg	M+P/C/Ds	CD	Ind	Ind	Ind	BBCC	Ind		
Business Engineering with French, German or Span	HN1C	4FT deg									
Business Engineering with French/German/Spanish	H1T2	4FT/5SW deg		CD	Ind	Ind	Ind	BBCC	Ind		
Engineering	H100	3FT deg	g	D	Ind	Ind	Ind	BC	Ind		
Engineering Management	HN1D	4FT deg									
Engineering	001H	2FT HND	g	D	Ind	Ind	Ind	BC	Ind		

ANGLIA Poly Univ

TITLE	CODE	COURSE	SUBJECTS	A/AS	ND/C	AGNVQ	IB	SQA(H)	SQA	RATIO A/AS	
Extended Design/Engineering	H108▼	3FT deg	*	2	N	D		CCC			

ASTON Univ

TITLE	CODE	COURSE	SUBJECTS	A/AS	ND/C	AGNVQ	IB	SQA(H)	SQA	RATIO A/AS	
Ergonomics/Biology	CJ1X	3FT/4SW deg	B g	20		D$^ go	30$	BBBBB$	Ind		
Ergonomics/Business Administration	JNX1	3FT/4SW deg	* g	20	5M+5D	D$6/^ go	30	BBBBB	Ind		
Ergonomics/Chemistry	FJ1X	3FT/4SW deg	C g	20		D$^ go	30$	BBBBB$	Ind		
Ergonomics/Computer Science	GJ5X	3FT/4SW deg	* g	20	5M+5D	D$6/^ go	30	BBBBB	Ind		
Ergonomics/Engineering Management	HJRX	3FT/4SW deg	S g	20	5M+5D	D$^ go	30	BBBBB	Ind		
French/Ergonomics	JRX1	4SW deg	F g	20	5M+5D$	D$6/^ go	30$	BBBBB$	Ind		
German/Ergonomics	JRX2	4SW deg	G g	20	5M+5D$	D$^ go	30$	BBBBB$	Ind		
Health & Safety Management/Biology	CJ19	3FT/4SW deg	B g	18	5M+5D$	D$^ go	29$	BBBBC$	Ind	2	
Health & Safety Management/Biology (Year Zero)	CJ9X	4FT/5SW deg									
Health & Safety Management/Chemistry	FJ19	3FT/4SW deg	C g	18	5M+5D$	D$^ go	29$	BBBBC$	Ind	2	
Health & Safety Management/Computer Science	GJ59	3FT/4SW deg	* g	18	5M+5D	D$6/^ go	29	BBBBC			
Health & Safety Management/Electronics	HJ69	3FT/4SW deg	M/P g	18	5M+5D$	D$^ go	29$	BBBBC$	Ind		
Health & Safety Management/Engineering Mgt	HJR9	3FT/4SW deg	S g	18	5M+5D$	D$^ go	29$	BBBBC$	Ind		
Health & Safety Management/Ergonomics	JJX9	3FT/4SW deg	* g	20	5M+5D	D$6/^ go	30	BBBBB	Ind	1	
Health & Safety Management/European Studies	JT92	3FT/4SW deg	* g	18	5M+5D	D$6/^ go	29	BBBBC	Ind		
Health & Safety Management/French	JR91	4SW deg	F g	20	X	D$^ go	30$	BBBBB$	Ind		
Health & Safety Management/German	JR92	4SW deg	G g	18	X	D$^ go	29$	BBBBC$	Ind	1	
Health & Safety Management/German (Year Zero)	JR9F	5SW deg									
Health & Safety Mgt/Chemistry (Year Zero)	JF91	4FT/5SW deg									
Health & Safety Mgt/Computer Science (Year Zero)	GJ5Y	4FT/5SW deg									
Health & Safety Mgt/Environ Sci & Tech (Yr Zero)	JF99	4FT/5SW deg									
Health & Safety Mgt/Environmental Science & Tech	FJ9Y	3FT/4SW deg	S g	18	5M+5D$	D$^ go	29	BBBBB$	Ind		
Health & Safety Mgt/European Studies (Year Zero)	JT9F	4FT/5SW deg									
Human Psychology/Health & Safety Management	JL97	3FT/4SW deg	* g	20	5M+5D	D$6/^ go	30	BBBBB	Ind		
Human Psychology/Health & Safety Mgt (Year Zero)	JL9R	4FT/5SW deg									
Logistics	J9N9	4SW deg	* g	18	8M+2D	D$6/^ go	29	BBBBC	Ind	2	13/20
Logistics	J9NX	3FT deg	* g	18	8M+2D	D$6/^ go	29	BBBBC	Ind	2	14/20
Mathematics/Health & Safety Management	GJ19	3FT/4SW deg	M g	20	X	D$^ go	31$	ABBBB$	Ind	2	
Medicinal Chemistry/Health & Safety Management	FJ1Y	3FT/4SW deg	C g	20	3M+7D$	D$^ go	30$	BBBBB$	Ind		
Product Design (Engineering)/Ergonomics	HJ7X	3FT/4SW deg	S g	20	5M+5D$	D$^ go	30$	BBBBB			
Product Design (Engineering)/Health & Safety Mgt	HJ79	3FT/4SW deg	S g	18	5M+5D$	D$^ go	29$	BBBBC$			
Public Policy & Management/Ergonomics	JMX1	3FT/4SW deg	* g	20	5M+5D	D$6/^ go	30	BBBBB	Ind		
Public Policy & Management/Health & Safety Mgt	JM91	3FT/4SW deg	* g	20	5M+5D	D$6/^ go	30	BBBBB	Ind	2	
Public Policy & Mgt/Health & Safety Mgt (Yr Z)	JM9C	4FT/5SW deg									
Social Studies/Ergonomics	JLX4	3FT/4SW deg	* g	20	5M+5D	D$6/^ go	30	BBBBB	Ind		
Social Studies/Health & Safety Management	JL94	3FT/4SW deg	* g	18	5M+5D	D$6/^ go	29	BBBBC	Ind	1	
Social Studies/Health & Safety Mgt (Year Zero)	JL9K	4FT/5SW deg									

course details			98 expected requirements							96 entry stats
TITLE	CODE	COURSE	SUBJECTS	A/AS	ND/C	AGNVQ	IB	SQA(H)	SQA	RATIO A/AS
BARNSLEY COLL										
Engineering Foundation	H100	4EXT deg								
Univ of BIRMINGHAM										
Engineering with Foundation Year	H100	4FT/5FT deg	* g	BBC	Ind	Ind	32	Ind	Ind	30
Mathematical Engineering	J920	4FT deg	3(M/P/C)	BBB	X	X	33$	CSYS	X	
BLACKBURN COLL										
Engineering	H100	4EXT deg			HN $					
BLACKPOOL & FYLDE COLL										
Computer Aided Engineering	061H	2FT HND		2	N	P*	Ind	Ind	Ind	
BOLTON INST										
Automotive Product Design	H160	3FT deg	M/S/Ds/Ad	10	3M	M$	Ind	Ind	Ind	
Automotive Product Design (4yrs)	H161	4FT deg	M/S/Ds/Ad	4	N	P$	Ind	Ind	Ind	
Civil Engineering and Transport Studies	HJ29	3FT deg	M/S g	10	3M	M$	Ind	Ind	Ind	
Environmental Technology and Transport Studies	KJ39	3FT deg	S g	10	3M	M$	Ind	Ind	Ind	
French and Transport Studies	RJ19	3FT deg	F+M/S g	10	3M	Ind	Ind	Ind	Ind	
German and Transport Studies	RJ29	3FT deg	G+M/S g	10	3M	Ind	Ind	Ind	Ind	
Motor Vehicle Studies and Transport Studies	HJJ9	3FT deg	M/S	10	3M	M$	Ind	Ind	Ind	
Motor Vehicle Studies and Transport Studies	HJJX	4FT deg	M/S	4	N	P$	Ind	Ind	Ind	
Motor Vehicle/Transport Studies (Foundation)	HJJY	4FT/5FT deg			Ind	Ind	Ind	Ind	Ind	
Simulation/Virtual Environment and Transport St	GJ79	3FT deg	M/S	10	3M	M$	Ind	Ind	Ind	
Technology Management and Transport Studies	JK93	3FT deg								
Technology Studies (Foundation)	J908	4FT/5FT deg			Ind	Ind	Ind	Ind	Ind	
Tourism Studies and Transport Studies	PJ79	3FT deg	* g	10	MO	M*	Ind	Ind	Ind	
Transport Studies	J930	3FT deg	M/S	10	3M	M$	Ind	Ind	Ind	
Transport Studies	J934	4FT deg	M/S	4	N	P$	Ind	Ind	Ind	
Design and Technology	92JW	2FT HND	M/S/Ad/Ds	4	N	P$	Ind	Ind	Ind	
BOURNEMOUTH Univ										
Engineering Business Development	H118▼	5EXTSW deg	* g	DD-DEE	4M	M$ go	Ind	CCCC	Ind	1
Engineering Business Development	H110	4SW deg	S/Ds g	DD-DEE	4M	M$ go	Ind	CCCC	Ind	3 6/11
Univ of BRADFORD										
Manufacturing Management and Technology	NJ1X	3FT deg	* g	BB-CCC	3M $	M$4/^	Ind	Ind	Ind	
Manufacturing Management and Technology	NJ19	4SW deg	* g	BB-CCC	3M $	M$4/^	Ind	Ind	Ind	
Medical Engineering	H1BC	4SW deg	2S g	22	5M $	M$4/^	Ind	Ind	Ind	
Medical Engineering	H1B1	3FT deg	2S g	22	5M $	M$4/^	Ind	Ind	Ind	
Medical Engineering (Foundation Yr)	H1BD	4FT/5SW deg	* g	18			Ind	Ind	Ind	6/12
Medical Engineering (MEng)	HBCD	4FT/5SW deg					Ind	Ind	Ind	
Technology and Management	JN91	4SW deg	* g	BB-CCC	3M $	M$4/^	Ind	Ind	Ind	1 4/16
Technology and Management (3 Years)	JN9C	3FT deg	* g	BB-CCC	3M $	M$4/^	Ind	Ind	Ind	2
BRADFORD & ILKLEY Comm COLL										
Industrial Technology	011H	2FT HND	* g	2	N $					
Univ of BRIGHTON										
Biology and Energy Studies	CJ19	3FT/4SW deg	S g	12	MO $	M$	Dip$	BBCC$	Ind	
Chemistry and Energy Studies	FJ19	3FT/4SW deg	S g	12	MO $	M$	Dip$	BBCC$	Ind	
Energy Science with Management	J9N1	3FT/4SW deg	M/S/P g	12	5M $	MS/M^	Dip$	BBBC$	Ind	
Energy Studies and Geography	JF98	3FT/4SW deg	S g	12	MO $	M$	Dip$	BBCC$	Ind	
Energy Studies and Mathematics	GJ19	3FT/4SW deg	M g	12	MO $	M$	Dip$	BBCC$	Ind	
Energy Studies and Physics	JF93	3FT/4SW deg	P g	12	MO $	M$	Dip$	BBCC$	Ind	
Energy Studies and Statistics	JG94	3FT/4SW deg	S g	12	MO $	M$	Dip$	BBCC$	Ind	

	course details				98 expected requirements						96 entry stats	
TITLE	CODE	COURSE	SUBJECTS	A/AS	ND/C	AGNVQ	IB	SQA(H)	SQA	RATIO	A/AS
Engineering & Construction/Surv (Foundation Yr)	H108	1FT/4EXT deg	*	2-6	Ind	P* go	Ind	Ind	Ind		
Engineering (Dip/BEng/MEng)	H100	3FT/4SW 4FT/5SW deg	M+P/S	18	5M	ME/M$^	25$	BBBC$	N$		
European Business with Technology	N1J9	4SW deg	* g	14	5M	M6/^$ go	Dip$	Ind	Ind		
Mech & Environmental Engineering (Dip/BEng/MEng)	HJ39	3FT/4SW/4FT/5SW deg	M+P/S g	18	5M$	ME/M$^	25$	BBBC$	Ind		
Engineering (General)	001H▼	2FT HND	M+P/S/Ds	6	3M $	P$+ gi	15$	CDD$	Ind		
Univ of BRISTOL											
Computational and Experimental Maths (MEng)	J921	4FT deg	M+P	BBB	HN $	D$^	30$	CSYS	HN$	3	
Engineering Mathematics (MEng)	J920	4FT deg	M+P	BBB	Ind	D$^	30$	CSYS	HN$	4	20/30
BRISTOL, Univ of the W of England											
Engineering (BSc)	H110	3FT/4SW deg	M g	10-14	3M $	M$1 go	24$	BC$	Ind		
Engineering Foundation Year	H108▼	4EXT/5EXTSW deg	* g	6-8	N	P* go	24	CCC	N		
BRUNEL Univ, West London											
Engineering Sci and Tech (MEng) (4 Yrs Thick SW)	H103	4SW/5SW deg	M+S	CCC	MO $	Ind	28$	BBBC$	Ind	1	8/12
Engineering Sci and Technology (4 Yr Thin SW)	H106	4SW/5SW deg	M+S	CCC	MO $	Ind	28$	BBBC$	Ind	2	10/16
Engineering Science and Technology (MEng)	H101	3FT/4FT deg	M+S	CCC	MO $	Ind	28$	BBBC$	Ind	2	12/16
Foundations of Eng (1 Yr Conv Prog) (MEng)	H100	4FT/5SW EXT deg	* g	CC	3M	Ind	24	Ind	Ind	2	8/18
Integrated Engineering	H111	4SW deg	M+P/S	BCC	4M+1D$ DE^		28$	BBCCC$	Ind		
Integrated Engineering	H112	4SW deg	M+P/S	BCC	4M+1D$ DE^		28$	BBCCC$	Ind		
Integrated Engineering	H110	3FT deg	M+P/S	BCC	4M+1D$ DE^		28$	BBCCC$	Ind		
Integrated Engineering (Computer Aided Eng)	H162	4SW deg	M+P/S	BCC	4M+1D$ DE^		28$	BBCCC$	Ind		
Integrated Engineering (Computer Aided Eng)	H160	3FT deg	M+P/S	BCC	4M+1D$ DE^		28$	BBCCC$	Ind		
Integrated Engineering (Computer Aided Eng)	H161	4SW deg	M+P/S	BCC	4M+1D$ DE^		28$	BBCCC$	Ind		
Integrated Engineering (Mechatronics)	H1HJ	4SW deg	M+P/S	BCC	4M+1D$ DE^		28$	BBCCC$	Ind		
Integrated Engineering (Mechatronics)	H1HH	4SW deg	M+P/S	BCC	4M+1D$ DE^		28$	BBCCC$	Ind		
Integrated Engineering (Mechatronics)	H1H3	3FT deg	M+P/S	BCC	4M+1D$ DE^		28$	BBCCC$	Ind		
Mathematics with Engineering	G1H1	3FT deg	M+P	BBC-BCC	3M+2D$ P^		29$	BBBC$	Ind	13	
Mathematics with Engineering (4 Yrs Thick SW)	G1HD	4SW deg	M+P	BBC-BCC	3M+2D$ P^		29$	BBBC$	Ind	4	
Mathematics with Engineering (4 Yrs Thin SW)	G1HC	4SW deg	M+P	BBC-BCC	3M+2D$ P^		29$	BBBC$	Ind	2	
Spec Eng Prog w. French (MEng) (4/5 Yrs Thin SW)	H1R1	4SW/5SW deg	M+P g	BBB	4M+1D$ DE^		30$	ABBBB$	Ind		
Spec Eng Prog w. French(MEng) (4/5 Yrs Thick SW)	H1RC	4SW/5SW deg	M+P g	BBB	4M+1D$ DE^		30$	ABBBB$	Ind		
Spec Eng Prog w. German (MEng) (4/5 Yrs Thin SW)	H1R2	4SW/5SW deg	M+P g	BBB	4M+1D$ DE^		30$	ABBBB$	Ind	1	
Spec Eng Prog w. German (MEng) (4/5Yrs Thick SW)	H1RF	4SW/5SW deg	M+P g	BBB	4M+1D$ DE^		30$	ABBBB$	Ind	4	
Special Eng Prog (SEP) (MEng) (4/5 Yrs Thin SW)	H102	4SW/5SW deg	M+P	BBB	4M+1D$ DE^		30$	ABBBB$	Ind	2	24/30
Special Eng Programme (4/5 Yrs Thick SW)	H104	4SW/5SW deg	M+P	BBB	4M+1D$ DE^		30$	ABBBB$	Ind	6	
Special Engineering Programme (MEng)	H105	3FT/4FT deg	M+P g	BBB	4M+1D$ DE^		30$	ABBBB$	Ind	8	
Special Engineering Programme with French (MEng)	H1RD	3FT/4FT deg	M+P g	BBB	4M+1D$ DE^		30$	ABBBB$	Ind		
Special Engineering Programme with German (MEng)	H1RG	3FT/4FT deg	M+P g	BBB	4M+1D$ DE^		30$	ABBBB$	Ind		
BUCKINGHAMSHIRE COLLEGE											
Computer Aided Design	H160	3FT deg		8-10	MO	M	Ind	CCC	Ind		
Computer Aided Design & Manufacture	H161	3FT deg		8-10	MO	M	Ind	CCC	Ind	2	6/12
Computer Aided Design & Manufacture(Conv to Deg)	H162	2FT deg			HN						
Computer Aided Design with Management	H1N1	3FT deg		8-10	MO	M	Ind	CCC	Ind		
Computer Aided Design with Marketing	H1N5	3FT deg		8-10	MO	M	Ind	CCC	Ind		
CAMBRIDGE Univ											
Engineering	H100▼	4FT deg	M+P g	AAA-AAB	Ind		Ind	CSYS	Ind	4	30/30
CARDIFF Univ of Wales											
Foundation Year	H101	4FT/5FT deg		CCC	Ind		Ind	Ind	Ind	2	14/24
Integrated Engineering	H110	3FT deg	M	18-24	5M+2D$ Ind		28$	ABCD	Ind	2	14/18
Integrated Engineering	H111	4SW deg	M	18-24	5M+2D$ Ind		28$	ABCD	Ind	2	20/28

			98 expected requirements							96 entry stats	
TITLE	CODE	COURSE	SUBJECTS	A/AS	ND/C	AGNVQ	IB	SQA(H)	SQA	RATIO	A/AS
Integrated Engineering	H113	4FT deg	M	18-24	5M+2D	Ind	28$	ABCD	Ind		
Integrated Engineering	H114	5SW deg	M	18-24	5M+2D	Ind	28$	ABCD	Ind		
Integrated Engineering (with a Yr in Germany)	H115	5SW deg	M g	18-24	5M+2D	Ind	28$	ABCD	Ind		
Integrated Engineering (with a Yr in Germany)	H112	4FT deg	M g	18-24	5M+2D	Ind	28$	ABCD	Ind		

Univ of Wales INST, CARDIFF

Design Engineering	HW12	3FT deg		EE	N	P$	Ind	CCCC	Ind		

Univ of CENTRAL ENGLAND

Computer Aided Design & Manufacture Found Year	H168▼	4FT/5SW deg	* g	2	N	P*	Ind	CC	Ind	1	
Computer Aided Design and Manufacture	H160	3FT/4SW deg	M g	12	3M $	ME1	24$	CCC$	Ind	8	
Engineering Systems & Management (MEng)	HN11	4FT/5SW deg	M g	12	3M $	ME1	24	CCC	Ind		
Engineering with Business Studies	H1N1	3FT/4SW deg	* g	12	3M	M* go	24	CCC	Ind	4	
Engineering with Business Studies Found Year	H1ND▼	4FT/5SW deg	*	2	N	P*	Ind	CC	Ind		
Technology with Business	J9N1	3FT/4SW deg	* g	12	3M	M* go	24	CCC	Ind		

Univ of CENTRAL LANCASHIRE

Computer-Aided Engineering	H160	3FT deg	M+S	8	3M	M$	24	BCCC	Ind		
Electrical Engineering Foundation Tech (Women)	J908▼	4FT deg	* g								
Engineering (Year Zero)	H108▼	4FT deg	* g								
Science Technology	FJ99	3FT deg	* g	CD	MO	MS	24	BCC	Ind		
Technology (Year 0)	J918▼	3FT deg									
Engineering (46 week course)	001H▼	1FT HND	* g	EE	N	P	Ind	CC	Ind		
Engineering (Computer-Aided Engineering)	061H	2FT/3SW HND	M	E	N	P$	Ind	Ind	Ind		
Engineering (Engineering Design)	101H	2FT/3SW HND	M	E	N	P$	Ind	Ind	Ind		

CITY Univ

Engineering and Energy Management	HJ39	3FT deg	M+P	BCD-CCD	4M+2D	DE6/^	28$	Ind	Ind		
Engineering and Energy Management (MEng)	JH93	4FT deg	M+P	BBB	X		30$	Ind	X		

CORNWALL COLLEGE WITH DUCHY COLLEGE

Engineering (Foundation)	H108	1FT deg	*								

COVENTRY Univ

Applied Science	H108▼	4FT/5SW deg					Ind	Ind	Ind		
Business and Technology	HN11▼	3FT deg	*	8	3M	M+	24	CCCC	Ind	2	4/13
Development and Health in Disaster Management	LJ49	3FT deg	* g	14	5M	M	Ind	Ind	Ind		6/12
Engineering	H100	3FT/4FT/5FT deg	M+S g	12-18	5M $	M+	24$	BBCC$	Ind	2	4/14
Engineering	H107	3FT deg									
Engineering with Modern Languages	H1TY	3FT deg									
European Business and Technology	HN1C▼	4FT deg	* g	8	3M	M+	24	CCCC	Ind	2	10/12
European Engineering Studies	H1TX	4FT/5FT deg	g	12-18	3M $	M+	24$	BBCC$	Ind	3	
International Disaster Engineering & Management	JN91	3FT/4SW deg	* g	14	5M	MC	Ind	Ind	Ind	2	6/22
International Disaster Engineering & Management	JN9C	4FT deg	* g	10	3M	P	Ind	Ind	Ind		
Sustainable Energy and the Environment	FJ99	3FT/4SW deg	*	16	6M $	Ind	Ind	Ind	Ind		
Sustainable Energy and the Environment	FJ9X	3FT deg									
Engineering Design (CAD)	061H	2FT/3SW HND									4/6

CRANFIELD Univ

Engineering Foundation Year	H101	1FT deg	*								

DE MONTFORT Univ

Engineering	H109▼	3FT/4SW deg	* g	2	N $	Ind	Dip	BB	Ind	2	4/14
Engineering (Extended)	H108▼	4FT/5SW deg	g		N	Ind	Dip	BB	Ind	1	8/9

course details					**98 expected requirements**					*96 entry stats*
TITLE	CODE	COURSE	SUBJECTS	A/AS	NO/C	RGNVQ	IB	SQA(H)	SQA	RATIO A/AS
Univ of DERBY										
Electrical and Electronic Engineering	HFC9	3FT deg	M+P	18	8M	D+2	30$	BBBCC$	Ind	
Mechanical and Manufacturing Engineering	HFD9	3FT/4FT deg	M+S	18	8M	D+2	30$	BBBCC$	Ind	
Tech Mgt, Innovation and Business Psychology	J9NC	3FT deg	*	10	4M	M$	26	CCCD	Ind	
Tech Mgt, Innovation and Human Resource Mgt	J9N1	3FT deg	*	10	4M	M$	26	CCCD	Ind	
Technology Management, Innovation and Marketing	J9N5	3FT deg	*	10	4M	M$	26	CCCD	Ind	
Credit Accumulation Modular Scheme *Technology Management*	Y600	3FT deg		8	MO	M	Ind	CCCC	Ind	
DONCASTER COLL										
Degree in Integrated Technology (1 Year top-up)	J900	1FT deg			HN		Ind	Ind	HN	
Univ of DUNDEE										
Engineering and Foreign Language (MEng)	HT19	4FT/5FT deg	M+P/Ds g	12	5M $	M$^	26$	BBCC$	N$	
Univ of DURHAM										
Engineering (Overseas Studies)	H101	4FT deg	M	22	2M+4D	Ind	30$	AAAAB$	Ind	
Engineering (Unified) (4 Yrs)	H100	4FT deg	M	22	2M+4D	Ind	30	AAAAB	Ind	4 24/30
Univ of EAST LONDON										
Combined Studies (Technology)	J900	3FT/4SW deg	* g	12	3M	M$	Ind	Ind	Ind	
Computer-Aided Engineering Design	H160	3FT/4SW deg	* g	12	3M	M	Ind	Ind	Ind	
Integrated Engineering	H110	3FT deg	* g	12	MO	M	Ind	Ind	Ind	
New Technology and Education	JX99	3FT deg	* g	12	MO	M	Ind	Ind	Ind	1
New Technology and Law	JM93	3FT deg	* g	12	MO	M	Ind	Ind	Ind	2
New Technology and Multimedia	JP9K	3FT deg	* g	12	MO	M				
New Technology, Media and Communications	JP94	3FT deg	* g	12	MO	M	Ind	Ind	Ind	2 8/16
Technology Management	JN91	4FT deg	* g	14	MO	M				
Women and New Technology	MJ99	3FT deg	* g	12	MO	M	Ind	Ind	Ind	3
Extended Science *Computer-Aided Engineering Design*	Y108	4SW deg	M+P	8-10	3M	M$	24$	B		
Univ of EDINBURGH										
Engineering (BEng)	H100	4FT deg	M+P	CCC	MO $		Dip$	BBBB$	N$	6 18/28
Univ of EXETER										
Engineering	H106	3FT deg	M g	BCC	MO+1D	M$^	32$	Ind	Ind	8
Engineering (BEng)	H103	4FT deg	M g	BCC	MO	M$^	32$	Ind	Ind	1
Engineering (MEng)	H104	4FT deg	M g	BCC	MO+1D	M$^	32$	Ind	Ind	6 12/30
Univ of GLAMORGAN										
Energy & Environmental Technology	JF9Y	4EXT deg								
Energy and Environmental Technology	FJ99	3FT/4SW deg	* g	DD	3M $	M$	Ind	Ind	Ind	4 6/12
Combined Studies (Honours) *Energy & Environmental Technology*	Y400	3FT deg	* g	8-16	Ind	Ind	Ind	Ind	Ind	
Joint Honours *Energy & Environmental Technology*	Y401	3FT deg	* g	8-16	Ind	Ind	Ind	Ind	Ind	
Major/Minor Honours *Energy & Environmental Technology*	Y402	3FT deg	* g	8-16	Ind	Ind	Ind	Ind	Ind	
Computer Aided Engineering	061H▼	2FT/3SW HND	M/P g	D	N	P$	Ind	Ind	Ind	13
Energy Resources Engineering - (Pembrokeshire)	059J▼	2FT HND		4-6	N	P$	Ind	Ind	Ind	5
Engineering Design	001H	2FT/3SW HND	M/P/S g	E	N $	P$	Ind	Ind	Ind	2
Univ of GLASGOW										
Electrical Power Engineering	HJ59	4FT deg	M+P	CCD	MO	ME	24$	BBBBC$	N$	10
Technological Education (BTech Ed)	H111	4FT deg	M g	CC	$		Dip$	BBC$	$	2

course details			98 expected requirements							96 entry stats	
TITLE	CODE	COURSE	SUBJECTS	A/AS	ND/C	AGNVQ	IB	SQA(H)	SQA	RATIO A/AS	
GLASGOW CALEDONIAN Univ											
Accident and Incident Investigation	J990	1FT Dip	*		Ind		Ind	Ind	Ind		
Computer Aided Engineering	H161	3FT deg	M+P	DE	Ind		Ind	CCC$	Ind	2	
Engineering for the Environment	H1F9	4FT deg	M+E	CD	Ind		Ind	BBC$	Ind		
Univ of GREENWICH											
Engineering and Business Management	HN1D	4EXT deg	* g	4	Ind	Ind	Ind	Ind	Ind		
Engineering and Business Management	HN11	3FT/4SW deg	* g	8	4M $	M	Dip	CCCC$	Ind		
Science and Technology (Extended)	Y1J9	4EXT deg	* g	EE	3M $	Ind	Ind	CCC$	Ind		
Technology and Design	JW92	3FT/4SW deg	* g	12	4M	M	24	BCC	Ind		
Computer-Aided Engineering	061H	2FT HND	* g	4	2M	P$ go	Ind	C	Ind		
Computer-Aided Manufacture	161H▼	2FT HND	* g	4	2M	P$ go	Ind	C	Ind		
HALTON COLL											
Engineering with Management Studies	1N1H	2FT HND	M/P	2	N	P	Ind	Ind	N		
HERIOT-WATT Univ											
Chemical Engineering with Energy Resource Eng	H8J9	4FT deg	M+C g	CCD	$	M$ go	30	BBBB$	$		
Mechanical Engineering with Computer Aided Engin	H3H1	3FT deg									
Mechanical Engineering with Energy Resource Eng	H3J9	4FT deg	M+P g	CDD	HN	M$^	28	BBB	HN		
Mechanical Engineering with Energy Resource Engi	H3JX	3FT deg									
Univ of HERTFORDSHIRE											
Computer Aided Engineering	H160	3FT/4SW deg	2(M/P/S/Cs)	16	3M $	Ind	$	Ind	Ind	7	
Computer Aided Engineering (Extended)	H168▼	4EXT/5EXTSW deg	*	2	N	Ind	Dip$	Ind	Ind	1	
Engineering Management	HN11	3FT/4SW deg	*	14	3M $	Ind	$	Ind	Ind	1	4/14
Engineering Management (Extended)	HN1C▼	4FT/5SW deg	*	2	N	Ind	Dip$	Ind	Ind	7	
Univ of HUDDERSFIELD											
Computer-Aided Design	H3H1	3FT/4SW deg	* g	14	4M	M	Ind	Ind	Ind		
Computer-Aided Engineering	H161	4SW deg	M+S	10	3M $	M$	Ind	Ind	Ind		
Computer-Aided Engineering (Extended)	H168	5SW deg	* g	DD	N	P go	Dip	CCC	Ind		
Computer-Aided Engineering (MEng)	H162	5SW deg	M+S	18	3D	M$3/^	Ind	Ind	Ind		
Engineering Foundation (General)	H108	5SW deg	* g	DD	N	P go	Dip	CCC	Ind		
Engineering with Technology Management (4 Yr SW)	H100	4SW deg	M/S	2	N	P$	Ind	CC	Ind		
Environmental Technology	FH91	4SW deg	S/Gy g	10-16	4M $	M$6/^ go	Ind	BBB	Ind		
Mechanical Engineering (Energy and Env) (Ext)	H3JX	5SW deg	* g	DD	N	P go	Dip	CCC	Ind		
Mechanical Engineering (Energy and Env) (MEng)	H3JY	5SW deg	M+S	CCC	3D $	M$3/^	Ind	Ind	Ind		
Mechanical Engineering (Energy and Environment)	H3J9	4SW deg	M+S	10-14	3M $	ME	Ind	Ind	Ind		
Technology with Business Studies	J9N1	4SW deg	S g	12	4M	M$ go	Ind	Ind	Ind		
Univ of HULL											
Computer Aided Engineering	H160	3FT deg	M	CCC	MO	M$^ gi	26$	BBCCC	Ind	8	
Computer Aided Engineering	H161	4FT deg	*	CD	N	P$ gi	24	BCCCC	Ind	2	
KING ALFRED'S WINCHESTER											
Design & Technology and Business Studies	JN91	3FT deg	Ds/Ad g	14	6M	M	24$	BCC$	N$		
Design & Technology and Computing	GJ59	3FT deg	Ds/Ad g	14	6M $	M	24$	BCC$	N$	1	
Design & Technology and Contemporary Cultural St	JM99	3FT deg	Ds/Ad g	14	6M	M	24$	BCC$	N$		
Education Studies and Design & Technology	JX99	3FT deg	Ds/Ad g	14	6M	M	24$	BCC$	N$	1	
KINGSTON Univ											
Music and Technology	JW93	3FT deg	Mu	CD	Ind	Ind^	Ind	Ind	Ind	10	10/22
Mechanical, Aerospace, Manuf Syst or Auto Eng	011H▼	2FT/3SW HND	M/S	2	N $	PE2	Ind	Ind	Ind	3	2/6

			course details		98 expected requirements						96 entry stats	
TITLE	CODE	COURSE	SUBJECTS	A/AS	ND/C	AGNVQ	IB	SQR(H)	SQR	RATIO	A/AS
LANCASTER Univ											
Engineering	H100	3FT/4SW deg	M+P/Cs/Es/Ds g	20	MO+1D		30$	BBBBB$	Ind		
Engineering (inc a year in USA or Canada)	H121	3FT/4SW deg	M+P/Cs/Es/Ds g	20	MO+1D		30$	BBBBB$	Ind		
Engineering (inc a year in USA or Canada)(MEng)	H104	4FT/5SW deg	M+P/Cs/Es/Ds g	20	MO+2D		30$	BBBBB$	Ind		
Environmental Systems Engineering	FH91	3FT/4SW deg	M+P/Cs/Es/Ds g	20	MO+1D		30$	BBBBB$	Ind		
Environmental Systems Engineering (MEng)	FH9C	4FT/5SW deg	M+P/Cs/Es/Ds g	20	MO+2D		30$	BBBBB$	Ind		
Combined Science *Engineering*	Y158	3FT deg	M+P/Cs/S g	CCD	MO $		28$	BBBBB$	Ind		
Combined Science (inc a year in USA or Canada) *Engineering*	Y155	3FT deg	M+P/Cs/S g	BBB	Ind $		32$	ABBBB$	Ind		
Univ of LEEDS											
Broadcast Journalism	PJ69	3FT deg	* g	BBB	Ind	Ind	33$	CSYS	Ind	1	22/28
Broadcasting Studies	PJ39	3FT/4FT deg	* g	ABB	Ind	Ind	33$	CSYS	Ind	13	24/30
Civil Engineering with Transport Engineering	H2J9	3FT deg	M g	CCC	Ind	Ind	Ind	Ind	Ind		
Civil Engineering with Transport Engineering	H3J9	3FT/4FT deg	M g	CCC	Ind	Ind	Ind	Ind	Ind		
Engineering with Foundation St (STEPS)	H101	4FT/5FT deg	g	18	1M+5D$	Ind	26$	BBBCC	Ind	3	10/22
LEEDS METROPOLITAN Univ											
Engineering	H108	3FT deg									
Univ of LEICESTER											
BEng Degree with integrated foundation (4 Yrs)	H101	4EXT deg	* g	8-16	N	*	24$	BBCCC	Ind		6/16
General Engineering	H100	3FT deg	M+P g	18	4M $	M$6^	30$	BBBBC$	Ind		
General Engineering (MEng)	H105	4FT deg	M+P g	18	5M $	M$6^	30$	ABBBB$	Ind		
General Engineering with Industry	H102	4SW deg	M+P g	18	4M $	M$6^	30$	BBBBC$	Ind		
General Engineering with Industry (MEng)	H107	5SW deg	M+P g	18	5M $	M$6^	30$	ABBBB$	Ind		
Univ of LINCOLNSHIRE and HUMBERSIDE											
Computing and Technology	GJ59	3FT deg	* g	12	3M+1D	M	24	CCCC	Ind		
Engineering Foundation	H108	1FT deg	* g		Ind	Ind	Ind	Ind	Ind		
Human Resource Management and Technology	JN96	3FT deg	* g	12	3M+1D	M	24	CCCC	Ind		
Media Technology and Technology	JP9K	3FT deg	* g	12	3M+1D	M	24	CCCC	Ind		
Computer-Aided Design	061H▼	2FT HND	g								
Engineering (Computer Integrated Engineering)	161H▼	2FT HND	g	4	Ind	Ind	Ind	Ind	Ind		
European Technology and Business	19NJ	2FT HND	* g	4		P					
European Technology and Finance	93JN	2FT HND	* g	4		P					
European Technology and Marketing	95JN	2FT HND	* g	4		P					
Finance and Technology	39NJ	2FT HND	* g	4		P					
Marketing and Technology	59NJ	2FT HND	* g								
Univ of LIVERPOOL											
Engineering with Mgt and a European Lang (MEng)	H1TF	4SW deg	M+P g	20	4M+1D$		30$	BBBBB	Ind	4	
Integrated Eng with Industrial Management (BEng)	H1ND	4EXT deg	*	18	3M $		30$	BBBCC	Ind	4	
Integrated Eng with Industrial Management (BEng)	H1N1	3FT deg	M+P	20	4M+1D$		30$	BBBBB	Ind	4	
Integrated Eng with Industrial Management (MEng)	H1NC	4SW deg	M+P	20	4M+1D$		30$	BBBBB	Ind	4	
Integrated Eng with Manufacturing Systems (BEng)	H1H7	3FT deg	M+P	20	4M+1D$		30$	BBBBB	Ind		
Integrated Engineering	H104	4FT deg									
Integrated Engineering	H103	3FT deg									
Integrated Engineering (BEng)	H100	3FT deg	M+P	20	4M+1D$		30$	BBBBB	Ind	5	16/20
Integrated Engineering (BEng)	H102	4EXT deg	*	18	3M $		30$	BBBCC	Ind	1	8/20
Integrated Engineering (MEng)	H101	4SW deg	M+P	20	4M+1D$		30$	BBBBB	Ind	8	
Integrated Engineering with a European Language	HT12	4SW deg	M+P g	20	4M+1D		30$	BBBBB	Ind		

course details			98 expected requirements							96 entry stats
TITLE	CODE	COURSE	SUBJECTS	A/AS	NO/C	AGNVQ	IB	SQA(H)	SQA	RATIO A/AS
LIVERPOOL JOHN MOORES Univ										
Combined Engineering Studies	H100	3FT/4SW deg		10	3M	M				10
Combined Engineering Studies (Extended)	H108▼	4EXT/5EXTSW deg		4-10	N					5
Computer Aided Engineering	H160	3FT/4SW deg		10	3M	M				12
Computer Aided Engineering (Extended)	H168▼	4EXT/5EXTSW deg		8	N					1
European Engineering Studies	H102▼	4FT deg		10	3M	M				
European Engineering Studies (MEng)	H101	4FT deg								
Engineering (Computer Aided)	161H	2FT/3SW HND		E	N	P				10
Engineering (Computer Aided) (Extended)	861H▼	3EXT HND								2
LOUGHBOROUGH Univ										
Engineering Science and Tech (5 Yr SW) (MEng)	H102	5SW deg	M+P	22	3M+2D	DE6/^ go	28$	Ind	Ind	1
Engineering Science and Technology	H100	3FT deg	M+P	22	3M+2D	DE6/^ go	28$	Ind	Ind	8
Engineering Science and Technology (4 Yr MEng)	H103	4FT deg	M+P	22	3M+2D	DE6/^ go	28$	Ind	Ind	
Engineering Science and Technology (4 Yr SW)	H101	4SW deg	M+P	22	3M+2D	DE6/^ go	28$	Ind	Ind	8
Ergonomics (Applied Human Sciences)	J960	3FT deg	*	18	5M	DI6/^ go	28	Ind	Ind	2 14/26
Ergonomics (Applied Human Sciences) (4 Yr SW)	J961	4SW deg	*	18	5M	DI6/^ go	28	Ind	Ind	2 12/20
Mathematical Engineering	J920	3FT deg	M	BCC	3M+2D		28$	Ind	Ind	10
Mathematical Engineering (4 Yr SW)	J921	4SW deg	M	BCC	3M+2D		28$	Ind	Ind	4
Psychology with Ergonomics	C8J9	3FT deg	* g	BBC		DS6/^ go	30	Ind		9
Psychology with Ergonomics (4 Yr SW)	C8JY	4SW deg	* g	BBC		DS6/^ go	30	Ind		3
Science and Eng Foundation Studs (4/5 Yrs)	HF19	4FT/5FT deg	* g	CC	5M	M*6/^ go	25	Ind	Ind	1 8/20
LUTON Univ										
CAD Technology and Industrial Design	H168	1FT deg			Ind	Ind	Ind	Ind	Ind	
Computer Aided Design Technology	H160	3FT deg	g	12-16	MO/DO	M/D	32	BBCC	Ind	6
Engineering	H108	1FT deg			Ind	Ind	Ind	Ind	Ind	
Integrated Engineering (Mechatronics)	H100	3FT deg	g	12-16	MO/DO	M/D	32	BBCC	Ind	2
Integrated Engineering with Animation	H1WF	3FT deg	g	12-16	MO/DO	M/D	32	BBCC	Ind	
Integrated Engineering with Business	H1N1	3FT deg	g	12-16	MO/DO	M/D	32	BBCC	Ind	
Integrated Engineering with Business Systems	H1NC	3FT deg	g	12-16	MO/DO	M/D	32	BBCC	Ind	
Integrated Engineering with Digital Syst Design	H1HP	3FT deg	g	12-16	MO/DO	M/D	32	BBCC	Ind	
Integrated Engineering with Environmental Sci	H1F9	3FT deg	g	12-16	MO/DO	M/D	32	BBCC	Ind	
Integrated Engineering with Geo Information Syst	H111	3FT deg	g	12-16	MO/DO	M/D	32	BBCC	Ind	1
Integrated Engineering with Mapping Science	H1F8	3FT deg	g	12-16	MO/DO	M/D	32	BBCC	Ind	
Integrated Engineering with Marketing	H1N5	3FT deg	g	12-16	MO/DO	M/D	32	BBCC	Ind	
Integrated Engineering with Media Production	H1PL	3FT deg	g	12-16	MO/DO	M/D	32	BBCC	Ind	
Integrated Engineering with Multimedia	H1PK	3FT deg	g	12-16	MO/DO	M/D	32	BBCC	Ind	
Integrated Engineering with Org Behaviour	H1L7	3FT deg	g	12-16	MO/DO	M/D	32	BBCC	Ind	
Integrated Engineering with Physical Geography	H1FV	3FT deg	g	12-16	MO/DO	M/D	32	BBCC	Ind	
Integrated Engineering with Politics	H1M1	3FT deg	g	12-16	MO/DO	M/D	32	BBCC	Ind	
Integrated Engineering with Psychology	H1LR	3FT deg	g	12-16	MO/DO	M/D	32	BBCC	Ind	
Integrated Engineering with Public Policy & Mgt	H1MC	3FT deg	g	12-16	MO/DO	M/D	32	BBCC	Ind	
Integrated Engineering with Video Production	H1W5	3FT deg	g	12-16	MO/DO	M/D	32	BBCC	Ind	
Organisational Behav & Integrated Engineering	HL17	3FT deg	g	12-16	MO/DO	M/D	32	BBCC	Ind	
Computer Aided Design and Manufacture	161H	2FT HND	g	4-8	N/MO	P/M	26	CCDD	Ind	
UMIST (Manchester)										
Integrated Engineering (4 Yrs)	H110	4FT deg	* g	20	5M	M6/^	28	BBCCC$	Ind	1 10/18
Textile Science and Tech with Ind Experience	JJ94	4SW deg	M+P/C g	20	4M+1D$	Ind	25	BBBBB	Ind	
Textile Science and Technology	JJ49	3FT deg	M+P/C g	20	4M+1D$	Ind	25	BBBBB	Ind	3
MANCHESTER METROPOLITAN Univ										
Engineering	H110	3FT/4SW deg	M/P g	DDE	3M $	ME	24	BB$	Ind	
Engineering (Foundation)	H108▼	4FT deg	M/P	E	2M $	P$	$	$	Ind	

| course details | | | 98 expected requirements | | | | | | | 96 entry stats |

TITLE	CODE	COURSE	SUBJECTS	A/AS	NO/C	AGNVQ	IB	SQA(H)	SQA	RATIO A/AS
MIDDLESEX Univ										
Computer Aided Engineering	H161▼	3FT deg	S g	10	3M	M$ go	24	CCCC	Ind	
Industrial and Business Systems	J9N1▼	3FT/4SW deg	S g	10	3M	M$ go	24	CCCC	Ind	
Sonic Arts	W3J9▼	3FT deg	* g	12-16	5M	X	26	Ind	Ind	
Joint Honours Degree _Technology_	Y400	3FT deg	* g	10	3M	M$ go				
Computer Aided Engineering	161H▼	2FT HND	S g	E	N	P$ go	Ind	CC	Ind	
Eurotechnology	009J▼	2FT HND	S g	4	N	P$ go	24	Ind	Ind	
NAPIER Univ										
Energy and Environmental Engineering	HJ59	3FT/4SW deg	M	DD	Ind	Ind	Ind	BBB$	Ind	3
Engineering with Management	H1N1	3FT/4SW deg	M	CD	Ind	Ind	Ind	BBB$	Ind	6
Management and Technology	HN11	3FT/4FT deg	*	DD	Ind	Ind	Ind	BBC	Ind	2
Mathematics with Technology	G1H1	4FT/5SW deg	M	CC	Ind	Ind	Ind	BBC	Ind	
Transport Studies	NJ99	3FT/4FT deg		CC	Ind	Ind	Ind	BBCC	Ind	
Engineering	001H	2FT HND	*	D	Ind	Ind	Ind	CC	Ind	3
NENE COLLEGE										
Art and Design with Industry and Enterprise	W2H1	3FT deg	g	DD	5M	M	24	CCC	Ind	
Business Admin with Industry and Enterprise	N1H1	3FT deg	g	10	M+1D	M	24	BCC	Ind	
Business Administration with Energy Management	N1J9	3FT deg	g	10	M+1D	M	24	BCC	Ind	
Earth Science with Energy Management	F9J9	3FT deg	g	DD	5M	M	24	CCC	Ind	
Earth Science with Industry and Enterprise	F9H1	3FT deg	g	DD	5M	M	24	CCC	Ind	
Ecology with Energy Management	C9J9	3FT deg		DD	5M	M	24	CCC	Ind	
Ecology with Industry and Enterprise	C9H1	3FT deg	g	DD	5M	M	24	CCC	Ind	
Economics with Energy Management	L1J9	3FT deg	g	6	5M	M	24	CCC	Ind	
Economics with Industry and Enterprise	L1H1	3FT deg	g	6	5M	M	24	CCC	Ind	
Education with Industry and Enterprise	X9H1	3FT deg	g	DD	5M	M	24	CCC	Ind	
Energy Management with Architectural Studies	J9V4	3FT deg	g	EE	3M	P	24	CCC	Ind	
Energy Management with Business Administration	J9N1	3FT deg	g	EE	3M	P	24	CCC	Ind	
Energy Management with Earth Science	J9F9	3FT deg	g	EE	3M	P	24	CCC	Ind	
Energy Management with Ecology	J9C9	3FT deg	g	EE	3M	P	24	CCC	Ind	
Energy Management with Economics	J9L1	3FT deg	g	EE	3M	P	24	CCC	Ind	
Energy Management with Education	J9X9	3FT deg	g	EE	3M	P	24	CCC	Ind	
Energy Management with Fossils and Evolution	J9F6	3FT deg	g	EE	3M	P	24	CCC	Ind	
Energy Management with Geography	J9F8	3FT deg	g	EE	3M	P	24	CCC	Ind	
Energy Management with Industrial Archaeology	J9V6	3FT deg	g	EE	3M	P	24	CCC	Ind	
Energy Management with Industry and Enterprise	J9H1	3FT deg	g	EE	3M	P	24	CCC	Ind	
Energy Management with Information Systems	J9G5	3FT deg	g	EE	3M	P	24	CCC	Ind	
Energy Management with Law	J9M3	3FT deg	g	EE	3M	P	24	CCC	Ind	
Energy Management with Property Management	J9N8	3FT deg	g	EE	3M	P	24	CCC	Ind	
Energy Management with Sport Studies	J9N7	3FT deg	g	EE	3M	P	24	CCC	Ind	
Energy Management with Wastes Mgt & the Environ	J9FX	3FT deg	g	EE	3M	P	24	CCC	Ind	
French with Industry and Enterprise	R1H1	3FT deg	F g	DD	5M	Ind	24	CCC	Ind	
Geography with Energy Management	F8J9	3FT deg	Gy g	8	5M	M	24	CCC	Ind	
Ind & Enterprise with Marketing Communication	H1N5	3FT deg	g	EE	3M	P	24	CCC	Ind	
Ind & Enterprise/Personal & Organisational Devel	H1N6	3FT deg	g	EE	3M	P	24	CCC	Ind	
Ind and Enterprise with Wastes Mgt & the Environ	H1FX	3FT deg		10	5M	M	24	CCC	Ind	
Industrial Archaeology with Energy Management	V6J9	3FT deg	g	10	5M	M	24	CCC	Ind	
Industrial Archaeology with Ind & Enterprise	V6H1	3FT deg	g	10	5M	M	24	CCC	Ind	
Industry & Enterprise with Business Admin	H1N1	3FT deg	g	EE	3M	P	24	CCC	Ind	4/7
Industry & Enterprise with Ind Archaeology	H1V6	3FT deg	g	EE	3M	P	24	CCC	Ind	
Industry and Enterprise with Art and Design	H1W2	3FT deg	g	EE	3M	P	24	CCC	Ind	

TITLE	CODE	COURSE	SUBJECTS	A/AS	ND/C	AGNVQ	IB	SQA(H)	SQA	RATIO A/AS	
Industry and Enterprise with Economics	H1L1	3FT deg	g	EE	3M	P	24	CCC	Ind		
Industry and Enterprise with Education	H1X9	3FT deg	g	EE	3M	P	24	CCC	Ind		
Industry and Enterprise with Energy Management	H1J9	3FT deg	g	EE	3M	P	24	CCC	Ind		
Industry and Enterprise with European Union St	H1T2	3FT deg									
Industry and Enterprise with French	H1R1	3FT deg	F g	EE	3M	P	24	CCC	Ind		
Industry and Enterprise with Information Systems	H1G5	3FT deg	g	EE	3M	P	24	CCC	Ind		
Industry and Enterprise with Mathematics	H1G1	3FT deg	M	EE	3M	P	24	CCC	Ind		
Industry and Enterprise with Property Management	H1N8	3FT deg	g	EE	3M	P	24	CCC	Ind		
Industry and Enterprise with Psychology	H1C8	3FT deg	g	EE	3M	P	24	CCC	Ind		
Information Systems with Energy Management	G5J9	3FT deg	g	6	5M	M	24	CCC	Ind		
Information Systems with Industry and Enterprise	G5H1	3FT deg	g	6	5M	M	24	CCC	Ind		
Law with Energy Management	M3J9	3FT deg	g	10	3M+2D	M	24	CCC	Ind		
Management Science with Energy Management	G4J9	3FT deg	g	DD	5M	M	24	CCC	Ind		
Mathematics with Industry and Enterprise	G1H1	3FT deg	M	DD	Ind	Ind	24	CCC	Ind		
Politics with Industry and Enterprise	M1H1	3FT deg	g	CD	5M	M	24	CCC	Ind		
Sport Studies with Industry and Enterprise	N7H1	3FT deg	Ss/Pe g	12	M+2D	M	24	BBB	Ind		
Engineering	001H	2FT HND		2	N	P	24	CC	Ind		

NEW COLLEGE DURHAM

| Engineering | 001H | 2FT HND | M/S | 2 | N | Ind | Ind | Ind | Ind | | |

Univ of Wales COLLEGE, NEWPORT

Technology	J908	3FT/4FT HND/deg									
Electronic Computer Aided Design	2W1H	2FT HND	*	2	N	P$	Ind	Ind	Ind		
Technology in Caring Contexts	59LJ▼	2FT HND									

Univ of NORTHUMBRIA

Computer Aided Engineering	H168	5EXT deg	* g	2-4	Ind	Ind	Ind	Ind	Ind		
Computer Aided Engineering	H160	3FT/4SW deg	M+P/S g	12	3M $	ME gi	24$	CCCC$	Ind	8	
Engineering with Business Studies	H1ND	3FT/4SW deg	* g	12	3M	M gi	24	CCCC	Ind	5	
International Business and Technology	H1NC	5EXT deg	* g	2-4	Ind	Ind	Ind	Ind	Ind	2	
International Business and Technology	H1N1	4FT deg	* g	12	MO	M gi	24	CCCC	Ind	2	10/16
Transportation Design	WJ29	3FT deg	Fa g	4	N $			Ind			
Transportation Design	EJ29	3FT deg	Fa g	4	N$			Ind			

NORWICH: City COLL

| Engineering (Computer Aided) | 061H | 3SW HND | * | E | Ind | P$6 gi | Ind | Ind | Ind | 3 | |

Univ of NOTTINGHAM

| Mathematics with Engineering | G1H1 | 3FT deg | M+P | BCC-BCD | Ind | Ind | 28$ | Ind | Ind | 5 | 20/30 |

NOTTINGHAM TRENT Univ

Engineering Systems and Computing	GH51	3FT/4SW deg	* g	18	3M $	Ind	Ind	Ind	Ind		
Integrated Engineering (BEng/MEng)	H110	3FT/4SW deg	M g	14	3M $	ME	24$	CCCC$	$	3	6/14
Integrated Engineering (Extended)	H118▼	4EXT/5EXTSW deg	* g		Ind	Ind	Ind	Ind	Ind	3	
Railway Infrastructure Engineering	J935	3FT/4SW deg	M g	18	3M $	Ind	Ind	Ind	Ind		
Integrated Engineering	011H▼	2FT HND	M g	4	2M $	PE	Ind	D$	$	4	

OXFORD Univ

Engineering (4 Yrs)	H100	4FT deg	M+P	AAB	DO		36	AAAAA	Ind	2	28/30
Engineering and Computing Science (4 Yrs)	GH51	4FT deg	M+P	AAB	DO		36	AAAAA	Ind	5	28/30
Engineering and Materials (4 Yrs)	HJ15	4FT deg	M+P	AAB-ABB	DO		36	AAAAA	Ind	3	
Engineering,Economics and Management	Y630	4FT deg	M+P	AAB	DO		36	AAAAA	Ind		
Engineering											

course details			98 expected requirements							96 entry stats	
TITLE	CODE	COURSE	SUBJECTS	A/AS	ND/C	RGNVQ	IB	SQA(H)	SQA	RATIO	A/AS
OXFORD BROOKES Univ											
Computer Aided Product Design	H160	3FT deg									
Engineering	H100	3FT/4SW deg	M+P/S g	12	Ind		Ind	Ind	Ind	15	
Engineering Foundation	H108	4FT/5SW deg	*	EE	Ind	P*	Ind	Ind	Ind	2	5/12
Technology Management	JN91	3FT/4SW deg	* g	DDD	Ind	M$	Ind	Ind	Ind	2	6/22
Univ of PAISLEY											
Computer Aided Design	H160	1FT deg		X	HN	Ind	X	X	HN		
Engineering - General	H100	3FT deg	* g	CD	Ind	Ind	Ind	CCC$	Ind		
Quality Management and Technology	J900	3FT/4FT deg	* g	DD	Ind	Ind	Ind	BCC	Ind	3	
Quality Management and Technology	J901	2FT Dip	* g	EE	Ind	Ind	Ind	CC	Ind		
Science and Technology	JY91	2FT Dip	* g	EE	Ind	Ind	Ind	CCC$	Ind		
Technology and Management	JN91	3FT/4SW/5SW deg	* g	DD	Ind	Ind	Ind	BCC	Ind	5	
Univ of PLYMOUTH											
Extended Engineering	H108▼	1FT/4EXT deg	* g	2	N $	P$	Ind	Ind	Ind	1	4/22
Fisheries Studies with Marine Navigation	J6J9	3FT deg	Ap g	14	5M $	M$	Ind	CCCC	Ind		
Hydrography with Marine Navigation	F8JY	3FT deg	2(M/P/C/Ap) g	14	5M $	M$	Ind	CCCC	Ind	6	
Marine Navigation	J930	3FT deg	2(M/P/C) g	14	5M $	M$	Ind	CCCC	Ind	5	8/16
Marine Navigation with Astronomy	J9FM	3FT deg	2(M/P/C) g	14	5M $	M$	Ind	CCCC	Ind		
Marine Navigation with Fisheries Business Studs	J9N9	3FT deg	2(M/P/C) g	14	5M $	M$	Ind	CCCC	Ind		
Marine Navigation with Fisheries Science	J9NX	3FT deg	2(M/P/C) g	14	5M $	M$	Ind	CCCC	Ind		
Marine Navigation with Fisheries Technology	J9JQ	3FT deg	2(M/P/C) g	14	5M $	M$	Ind	CCCC	Ind		
Marine Navigation with Hydrography	J9F8	3FT deg	2(M/P/C) g	14	5M $	M$	Ind	CCCC	Ind	7	
Marine Navigation with Marine Technology	J9J6	3FT deg	2(M/P/C) g	14	5M $	M$	Ind	CCCC	Ind		
Marine Navigation with Maritime Business	J9NY	3FT deg	2(M/P/C) g	14	5M $	M$	Ind	CCCC	Ind	1	
Marine Navigation with Maritime History	J9VD	3FT deg	2(M/P/C) g	14	5M $	M$	Ind	CCCC	Ind		
Marine Navigation with Underwater Studies	J9F9	3FT deg	2(M/P/C) g	14	5M $	M$	Ind	CCCC	Ind	2	
Marine Technology with Marine Navigation	J6JX	3FT deg	2(M/P/C) g	14	5M $	M$	Ind	CCCC	Ind	4	
Maritime Business with Marine Navigation	N1J9	3FT deg	* g	18	5M	M$	Ind	CCCC	Ind	8	
Ocean Science with Marine Navigation	F7J9	3FT deg	S g	14-16	5M $	M$	Ind	CCCC	Ind	8	
Underwater Studies with Marine Navigation	F9J9	3FT deg	Ap g	14-16	5M $	M$	Ind	CCCC	Ind	7	
Leisure Technology (Somerset)	009J	2FT HND	S g	2	N $	P$	Ind	Ind	Ind		
Univ of PORTSMOUTH											
Engineering (MEng)	H100	3FT/4SW deg	2(M/P/C/Cs/Es)	16	4M $	M$6/^	26	BBBB	N$	8	
Engineering Management	HN11	3FT deg	2(M/P/C/Cs/Es)	16	4M $	M$6/^	26	BBBB	N$		
Engineering with Business Management (BEng/MEng)	H1NC	3FT/4SW deg	2(M/P/C/Es/Cs)	16	4M $	M$6/^	26$	BBBB	N$	1	8/13
Extended Engineering Degree Scheme	H108	4FT/5SW deg	*	4	N	Ind	Ind	CC	Ind	1	4/14
QUEEN MARY & WESTFIELD COLL (Univ of London)											
Engineering (BSc(Eng))	H100	3FT deg	M+P	18	5M $	M$^	24$	BBBCC			
Engineering Science	H106	3FT deg	M	CCD-BCC	5M $	M$^	24$	BBBCC			
Engineering with Business Studies	H1N1	3FT deg	M	CDD-BCC	5M $	M$^	24$	BBBCC			
Engineering with Environmental Science	H1F9	3FT deg	M	CDD-BCC	4M $	M$^	24$	BBBCC			
Engineering with French Language	H1R1	3FT deg	M	CCD-BCC	4M $	M$^	24$	BBBCC			
Engineering with German Language	H1R2	3FT deg	M	CCD-BCC	4M $	M$^	24$	BBBCC			
Engineering with Spanish Language	H1R4	3FT deg	M	CCD-BCC	4M $	M$^	24$	BBBCC			
READING COLLEGE AND SCHOOL OF ART AND DESIGN											
Engineering	H100	3FT deg									
Engineering	001H	2FT deg									

TITLE	CODE	COURSE	SUBJECTS	A/AS	ND/C	AGNVQ	IB	SQR(H)	SQR	RATIO A/AS
Univ of READING										
Integrated Engineering	H110	3FT deg	M+P g	CCC	4M+1D$	DE^ go	29$	BBBC$	Ind	9
Integrated Engineering (Foundation)	H111	4EXT deg	* g	CDD	4M	M*6/^ go	27	BBCC	Ind	4
Integrated Engineering (MEng)	H103	4FT deg	M+P g	BBC	2M+3D$	DE^ go	31$	BBBB$	Ind	
ROBERT GORDON Univ										
Technology and Business	JN91	3FT/4FT deg	S g	EE	N	Ind	Ind	BCC$	Ind	1
ROYAL Agric COLL										
Farm Mechanization and Management (post HND)	DH21	1FT deg		X	HN		X	X	X	8
Univ of SALFORD										
Audio Technology (3 or 4 Yrs)	J975	3FT/4SW deg	M/S	CDD	3M $	P^	Ind	Ind	Ind	6 10/26
Audiotechnology with Foundation Year	J977	4FT deg								
Unified Engineering (4 Yrs)	H100	4FT deg	M		Ind	M	Ind	Ind	Ind	1 5/14
Video and Audio Engineering (3 or 4 yrs)	J985	3FT/4SW deg		CCC	Ind	M	Ind	Ind	Ind	
SANDWELL COLL										
Computer Aided Engineering	061H	2FT HND	Cs/Ds/M/P	DD-EE	N	P$	Ind	Ind	Ind	
SHEFFIELD HALLAM Univ										
Business and Technology	NJ19	4SW deg	* g	EE	3M	P	Ind	CCCC	Ind	
Computer Aided Engineering and Design	H161	3FT/4SW deg	M/P/C/Ph	8	3M $	M$	Ind	Ind	Ind	
Computer Aided Engineering and Design (Extended)	H168▼	4EXT/5EXTSW deg								
Engineering (1 Year top-up)	H100	1FT deg		X	HN	X	X	X	X	
Engineering Design	H761	3FT/4SW deg	M/S	8	3M $	M$	Ind	Ind	Ind	
Engineering Design (Extended)	H762▼	4EXT/5EXTSW deg								
Engineering with Business Studies	H1N1	3FT/4SW deg	M/P/C/Ph	8	3M $	M$	Ind	Ind	Ind	
Engineering with Business Studies (Extended)	H1NC▼	4EXTFT/5EXTSW deg								
Engineering with Environmental Studies	H1FX	3FT/4SW deg	M/P/C/Ph	8	3M $	M$	Ind	Ind	Ind	
Engineering with Environmental Studies (Ext)	H1FY▼	4EXT/5EXTSW deg								
Environmental Engineering and Entsorgungstechnik	HF29	4FT deg	M/P/C/Ph g	8	3M $	M$	Ind	Ind	Ind	
Integrated Engineering with Automotive Studies	H118▼	4EXT/5EXTSW deg								
Integrated Engineering with Automotive Studies	H110	3FT/4SW deg	M/P/C/Ph	8	3M $	M$	Ind	Ind	Ind	
Process Engineering (1 Year top-up)	J540	1FT deg		X	HN	X	X	X	X	
Combined Studies *Computer Aided Engineering and Design*	Y400	3FT deg	M	8	2M	M	Ind	Ind	Ind	
Combined Studies *Environmental Engineering*	Y400	3FT deg	M	8	2M	M	Ind	Ind	Ind	
Combined Studies *Transport Planning*	Y400	3FT deg	*	14	2M	M	Ind	Ind	Ind	
Environmental Engineering	9F1H▼	2FT/3SW HND	M/P/C/Ph	E	N	P	Ind	Ind	Ind	
SOLIHULL COLL										
Engineering	001H	2FT HND	*	E	N	P	Dip	Ind	Ind	
Univ of SOUTHAMPTON										
Engineering with Foundation Year	H103	4FT deg	*	18	3M	M	30	Ind	Ind	4 14/16
SOUTHAMPTON INST										
Business Technology Management	J9N1	3FT deg	*	4	MO	M$	Dip	CCCC	N	2 6/12
Business Technology Management (with Foundation)	J9NC▼	4FT deg	*	2-4	N	M$	Dip	CCCC	N	1
Engineering with Business	H1N1	3FT deg	M/P	4-10	MO	M$	Dip	CCCC	N	5
Engineering with Business (with Foundation)	H1NC▼	4FT deg	*	2-4	N	P$	Dip	CCCC	N	2

course details			98 expected requirements							96 entry stats
TITLE	CODE	COURSE	SUBJECTS	A/AS	NO/C	AGNVQ	IB	SQA(H)	SQA	RATIO A/AS
SOUTH BANK Univ										
Computer Aided Engineering	H161	3FT/4SW deg	M/P/C/Cs/Ds g	EE	5M	M go	Ind	Ind	Ind	
Computer Aided Engineering	H165	1/2FT deg			HN		Ind	Ind	Ind	
Energy Engineering	J950	3FT/4SW deg	M/P/C/Ds g	DD	3M $	M go	Ind	Ind	Ind	
Energy Engineering (MEng)	J955	4FT/5SW deg	M/P/C/Ds g	DD	3M $	M go	Ind	Ind	Ind	
Foundation Energy Engineering	J958	4EXT deg					Ind	Ind	Ind	
Technology and Accounting	JN94	3FT deg	Ac/Ec g	12-16	4M+2D	M go	Ind	Ind	Ind	
Technology and Computing	GJ59	3FT deg	M g	12-16	4M+2D	M go	Ind	Ind	Ind	
Technology and Economics	JL91	3FT deg	Ec/Bu g	12-16	4M+2D	M go	Ind	Ind	Ind	
Technology and European Studies	JT92	3FT deg	* g	14-18	2M+4D	M go	Ind	Ind	Ind	
Technology and Food Policy	DJ49	3FT deg	S g	12-16	4M+2D	M go	Ind	Ind	Ind	
Technology and French	JR91	3FT deg	F g	12-16	4M+2D	M^ go	Ind	Ind	Ind	
Technology and German - ab initio	JR92	3FT deg	* g	12-16	4M+2D	M go	Ind	Ind	Ind	
Technology and Health Studies	JL94	3FT deg	S g	12-16	4M+2D	M go	Ind	Ind	Ind	
Technology and History	JV91	3FT deg	H g	12-16	4M+2D	M^ go	Ind	Ind	Ind	
Technology and Housing	JK9K	3FT deg	* g	14-18	2M+4D	M go	Ind	Ind	Ind	
Technology and Human Biology	BJ19	3FT deg	S g	12-16	4M+2D	M go	Ind	Ind	Ind	
Technology and Human Resource Management	JN96	3FT deg	* g	14-18	2M+4D	M go	Ind	Ind	Ind	
Technology and Law	JM93	3FT deg	* g	14-18	2M+4D	D go	Ind	Ind	Ind	
Technology and Management	JN91	3FT deg	* g	12-16	4M+2D	M go	Ind	Ind	Ind	
Technology and Marketing	NJ59	3FT deg	* g	14-18	2M+4D	M go	Ind	Ind	Ind	
Technology and Media Studies	JP94	3FT deg	E g	14-18	2M+4D	D go	Ind	Ind	Ind	
Technology and Nutrition	BJ49	3FT deg	S g	12-16	4M+2D	M go	Ind	Ind	Ind	
Technology and Planning	JK94	3FT deg	* g	12-16	4M+2D	M go	Ind	Ind	Ind	
Technology and Social Policy	JL9K	3FT deg	* g	12-16	4M+2D	M go	Ind	Ind	Ind	
Technology and Sociology	JL93	3FT deg	* g	12-16	4M+2D	M go	Ind	Ind	Ind	
Technology and Spanish	JR9K	3FT deg	Sp g	14-18	2M+4D	M^ go	Ind	Ind	Ind	
Technology and Spanish - ab initio	JR94	3FT deg	Sp g	12-16	4M+2D	M go	Ind	Ind	Ind	
Technology and Sports Science	BJ69	3FT deg	S g	12-16	4M+2D	M go	Ind	Ind	Ind	
Tourism and Technology	JP97	3FT deg	L G	12-16	4M+2D	M go	Ind	Ind	Ind	
World Theatre and Technology	JW94	3FT deg	* g	14-18	2M+4D	M go	Ind	Ind	Ind	
Computer Aided Engineering	061H	2FT HND	M/P/C/Cs/Ds g	E	$	P go	Ind	Ind	Ind	
ST HELENS COLL										
Computer-Aided Engineering	061H	2FT HND	M/P/Cs/Ds	2-6	N	P$	Ind	Ind	Ind	
STAFFORDSHIRE Univ										
Computer Aided Engineering (MEng)	H110	4FT/5SW deg	M+P	10	3M	M$	24	BCC	Ind	11
Environmental Technology	FJ99	3FT deg	g	8	3M $	M$	Ind	Ind	Ind	
Extended Computer Aided Engineering	H169	5EXT/6EXTSW deg	*	4	N	P$	24	CCC	Ind	1
Extended Engineering	H107	4EXT deg								
Media Technology	J909	4EXT deg	g	EE	P $	P$	Ind	Ind	Ind	
Media Technology	J900	3FT deg	Ap	8	3M	M$	Ind	CCC	Ind	5 6/18
Occupational Health and Environment Technology	LJ59	3FT deg								
Sports Equipment Technology	J965	3FT deg	Ap g	8	3M	M$	24	BCC	Ind	
Transport Systems Technology	J930	3FT deg	Ap g	8	3M	M$	24	BCC	Ind	
Transportation Systems Technology	J939	4EXT deg	g	EE	P $	P$	Ind	Ind	Ind	
Computer Aided Engineering	061H	2FT HND	M/P	2	N	P	24	CCC	Ind	
Extended Computer Aided Engineering	961H	3EXT HND	g	2	N	P$	24	CCC	Ind	
Univ of STRATHCLYDE										
Eng with Business Mgt & Euro St(Int Euro Option)	H1N1	5FT deg	M+P g	CCC	HN		30$	BBBB$	HN	
Eng with Business Mgt & Euro St(Int Euro Option)	H1ND	5FT deg	M+P g	BBB	HN		32$	AAAA$	HN	
Eng with Business Mgt & Euro St(Int Euro Option)	H1NC	5FT deg	M+P g	BBB	HN		32$	AAAA$	HN	

course details			**98 expected requirements**							*96 entry stats*
TITLE	CODE	COURSE	SUBJECTS	A/AS	ND/C	AGNVQ	IB	SQA(H)	SQA	RATIO A/AS
Engineering with Business Mgt (Accounting)	H1N4	5FT deg	M+P g	BBB	HN		32$	AAAA$	HN	
Environmental Engineering	J974	5FT deg	M+P	BBB	HN		32$	AAAB$	HN	
Environmental Engineering	J972	4FT deg	M+P	CCC	HN		30$	ABBB$	HN	
Environmental Engineering	J973	5FT deg	M+P	BBB	HN		32$	AAAB$	HN	
Manufacturing Sciences and Engineering/Dip Mgt	H1NX	5SW deg	M+P	BCC			35$	AABBC$		
Materials Sciences and Engineering	JH21	4FT deg	M+P	CCC	HN		30$	ABBB$	HN	
Materials Sciences and Engineering (MEng)	JH2C	5FT deg	M+P	BBC	HN		32$	AAAB$	HN	
Mechanical Engineering with Energy Studies	H3J9	5FT deg	M+P	BBB	HN		32$	AABBB$	HN	
Mechanical Engineering with Environmental Eng	H3JX	5FT deg	M+P	BBB	HN		32$	AABBB$	HN	
Technology and Business Studies	HN19	3FT/4FT deg	M g	CCC	HN $		24$	BBBB$	HN$	
Technology and Business Studies with Accounting	HN14	3FT/4FT deg	M g	BBC	HN $		34$	AAABB$	HN$	

Univ of SUNDERLAND

Engineering	H110	3FT/4SW deg	M/P g	12	N $	ME	24$	CCC$	N$	
Engineering (Foundation)	H118▼	4EXT/5EXTSW deg	*	2	N	P	24	CC	N	2
Engineering Geology	J976	3FT/4SW deg	* g	8	3M $	M$	24$	CCCC	N$	6
Engineering Geology (Foundation)	J978▼	4EXT/5EXTSW deg	*		Ind	Ind	Ind	Ind	Ind	
Ergonomics and Biomechanics	BJ99	3FT/4SW deg	*	12	3M	P	24	CCC	N	
Technology Management	JN91▼	3FT/4SW deg	* g	10	N	M	24	CCCC	N	3

Univ of SURREY

Eng with Business Management & a Euro Language	H104	4FT/4/5SW deg	M+P g	18-22	MO+2D$	ME3/^	28$	BBBBC$	Ind	
Eng with Business Management & a Foundation Year	H105	4FT/5SW deg	* g	18-22	Ind	Ind	28$	BBBBC	Ind	3
Engineering with Business Management	H100	3FT/4/5SW deg	M+P	18-22	MO+2D$	ME3/^	28$	BBBBC$	Ind	13
Engineering with Business Management	H101	4FT/4/5SW deg	M+P	18-22	MO+2D$	ME3/^	28$	BBBBC$	Ind	4	16/18

Univ of Wales SWANSEA

Engineering (Integrated 4 Yrs, Deferred Spec)	H101	4FT deg	* g	12-16	1M+3D$	Ind	24	BBCCC	Ind	2
Engineering Foundation Year (4 yrs)	H102	4FT deg	* g	12	1M+4D	Ind	26	BBBCC	Ind	

SWANSEA INST of HE

Management of Innovation	HN11	3FT deg	g	10	MO+2D	M go	Ind	Ind	Ind	
Product Engineering	H100	3FT deg								
Design Technology	21WH	2FT HND		E	N		Ind	Ind	N	2
Design Technology	21WE	2FT HND		E	N		Ind	Ind	N	
Management of Innovation	11HN	2FT HND	g	E	MO	P go	Ind	Ind	Ind	

SWINDON COLL

Engineering	001H	2FT HND	M/P/Ds	2	N	PE/S	Ind	Ind	N	

Univ of TEESSIDE

Bio-Medical Engineering	BH91	3FT/4SW deg	S	12-14	Ind	M	Ind	CCCC	Ind	
Extended Computing or Mathematics	H109	4FT/5SW deg	* g	2	N	P	Dip	CCCC	N	
Extended Engineering	H108	4FT/5SW deg	* g	2	N	P	Dip	CCC	N	
Computer Aided Engineering	161H	2FT HND	M/S	4	N		Ind	Ind	N	4

Univ of ULSTER

Biomedical Engineering (4 Yr SW inc DIS)	BH91▼	4SW deg	P/C/B/M g	CCC	MO+3D	Ind	28	BBBB	Ind	
Engineering (4 Yr SW inc DIS)	H110▼	4SW deg	M+Ph g	BCC	MO+4D	Ind	30	BBBB	Ind	12	18/26
Engineering with Business (4 Yr SW inc DIS)	H1N1▼	4SW deg	S/M	CCC	MO+3D	Ind	28	BBBB	Ind	
Technology and Design	HW12▼	2FT/3FT/4SW Dip/deg	S/Cs/M	CCD	MO+2D	Ind	27	BBCC	Ind	7	14/22
Transportation (4 Yr SW inc DIS)	J930▼	4SW deg	* g	CCD	MO+2D	Ind	27	BBCC	Ind	5	12/16

UNIVERSITY COLL LONDON (Univ of London)

Engineering with Business Finance	H130	3FT deg	M g	BBC-ABB	Ind	Ind	32$	BBBBC$	Ind	5	22/28

course details			98 expected requirements							96 entry stats	
TITLE	CODE	COURSE	SUBJECTS	A/AS	ND/C	AGNVQ	IB	SQA(H)	SQA	RATIO	A/AS
Univ Col WARRINGTON											
Mechatronics	001H▼	2FT HND	* g	4-6	Ind	Ind	Ind	Ind	Ind		
Univ of WARWICK											
Engineering and Business Studies	H1N1	3FT deg	M+S g	CCC	5M+1D$	D$^	28$	BBBBC$		4	16/24
General Engineering	H100	3FT deg	M+S g	CCC	5M+1D$	D$^	28$	BBBBC$		14	10/26
General Engineering	H102	4FT deg	M+S g	BBB	5M+1D$	D$^	32$	AABBB$		6	
General Engineering (European)	H104	4FT deg	M+S g	BBB	5M+1D$	D$^	32$	AABBB$		6	
Univ of WESTMINSTER											
Industrial Systems & Business Mgt (with found)	HN11	5EXT deg	*	D-E	N	P				10	.
Univ of WOLVERHAMPTON											
Computer Aided Design & Construction	H1K2	3FT/4SW deg	* g	DD	N	M	24	CCCC	Ind	4	
Design & Technology	EJ29	3FT deg	A/Ds+Pf	8	N	M	24	CCCC	Ind		
Design and Technology	WJ29	3FT deg	A/Ds+Pf	8	N	M	24	CCCC	Ind	7	8/15
Engineering (MEng)	H103	4FT deg	S g	DD	N	M	24	CCCC	Ind		
Engineering Systems	H101	3FT/4SW deg	S g	DD	N	M	24	CCCC		5	
Applied Sciences *Engineering Systems*	Y100	3FT/4SW deg	g	DD	N	M	24	CCCC	Ind		
Applied Sciences (4 Yrs) *Computer Aided Design*	Y110▼	4FT deg	*								
Applied Sciences (4 yrs) *Engineering Systems*	Y110	4FT deg	*								
Combined Degrees *Computer Aided Design*	Y401	3FT/4SW deg	g	DD	N	M	24	CCCC	Ind		
Combined Degrees *Engineering Systems*	Y401	3FT/4SW deg	g	DD	N	M	24	CCCC	Ind		
WORCESTER COLLEGE of Technology											
Engineering	001H	2FT HND	*	2	N	P					

| | | | 98 expected requirements | | | | | | | 96 entry stats |
| course details | | | | | | | | | | |
TITLE	CODE	COURSE	SUBJECTS	A/AS	NO/C	AGNVQ	IB	SQA(H)	SQA	RATIO A/AS
Univ of ABERDEEN										
Engineering (Mechanical)	H300	4FT deg	M+P/Ds g	CC	Ind	MS△ go	24$	BBBCC$	Ind	6
Engineering (Mechanical) (MEng)	H305	5FT deg	M+P/Ds g	BC	Ind	MS△ go	28$	AABB$	Ind	53
Univ of ABERTAY DUNDEE										
Mechanical Engineering	H300	4FT/5SW deg	M+P/C/Ds	CD	Ind	Ind	Ind	BBCC	Ind	
Mechanical Engineering with French/Ger/Spanish	H3T2	4FT/5SW deg		CD	Ind	Ind	Ind	BBCC	Ind	
Mechatronics	HH63	3FT deg	g	D	Ind	Ind	Ind	BC	Ind	
Product Design Engineering	H770	4FT/5SW deg	M+P/C/Ds	CD	Ind	Ind	Ind	BBCC	Ind	
Product Design Engineering with French/German/Sp	H7T2	4FT/5SW deg		CD	Ind	Ind	Ind	BBCC	Ind	
Mechatronics	36HH	2FT HND	g	D	Ind	Ind	Ind	BC	Ind	
ANGLIA Poly Univ										
Business Studies and Product Design	NHC7▼	3FT deg	* g	14	6M	M go	Dip	BBCC	Ind	14
Engineering Management	H710▼	3FT deg	* g	10	3M	P go	Dip	BCCC	Ind	
Information Systems and Product Design	GH57▼	3FT deg	S g	10	3M	P go	Ind$	BCCC	Ind	
Law and Product Design	HM73▼	3FT deg	*	12	4M	M	Dip	BBCC	Ind	
Multimedia and Product Design	HH76▼	3FT deg	g	10	3M	P go	Dip	BCCC	Ind	
Product Design	H770▼	3FT deg								
Product Design - Management	H711▼	3FT deg	S g	10	3M	P go	Dip	BCCC	Ind	3 12/14
Product Design	007H▼	2FT HND	* g	4	N	P go	Ind	CCC	Ind	2 4/6
ASTON Univ										
Electromechanical Engineering (BEng/MEng)	HH63	4SW/5SW deg	M g	18	Ind $	D$6/△ go	29$	BBBBC$	Ind	4
Electromechanical Engineering (BEng/MEng)	HH36	3FT/4FT deg	M g	18	Ind $	D$6/△ go	29$	BBBBC$	Ind	10
Electromechanical Engineering (STEPS)	HHH6	4FT/5SW deg	* g	18	4M	D$	30	BBBBC	Ind	5
Engineering Management/Business Administration	HNR1	3FT/4SW deg	S g	20	5M+5D	D$6/△ go	30$	BBBBB$	Ind	
Engineering Management/Chemistry	FH1R	3FT/4SW deg	C g	18	X	D$△ go	29$	BBBBC$	Ind	
Engineering Management/Computer Science	GH57	3FT/4SW deg	S	18	5M+5D$	D$△ go	29$	BBBBC$	Ind	
Engineering Management/Electronics	HH67	3FT/4SW deg	M/P g	18	5M+5D$	D$△ go	29$	BBBBC$	Ind	
Engineering Product Design (BSc)	H770	3FT deg	M g	18	Ind$	D$6/△ go	29$	BBBBC$	Ind	
Environmental Sci & Technology/Engineering Mgt	FH9R	3FT/4SW deg	S g	18	5M+5D$	D$△ go	29$	BBBBC$	Ind	
Ergonomics/Engineering Management	HJRX	3FT/4SW deg	S g	20	5M+5D	D$△ go	30	BBBBB	Ind	
European Studies/Engineering Management	HTR2	3FT/4SW deg	S g	18	5M+5D$	D$△ go	29$	BBBBC		
Health & Safety Management/Engineering Mgt	HJR9	3FT/4SW deg	S g	18	5M+5D$	D$△ go	30$	BBBBC$	Ind	
Human Psychology/Engineering Management	LH7R	3FT/4SW deg	S g	20	5M+5D$	D$△ go	30$	BBBBB$		
Mathematics/Engineering Management	GH1R	3FT/4SW deg	M g	20	5M+5D$	D$△ go	30	BBBBB	Ind	
Mechanical Eng with European Studies (MEng)	H3T2	4FT/5SW deg	M g	22	Ind $	D$6/△ go	31$	ABBBB$	Ind	12
Mechanical Engineering (BEng/MEng)	H300	3FT/4FT deg	M g	18	Ind $	D$6/△ go	29$	BBBBC$	Ind	7 8/22
Mechanical Engineering (BEng/MEng)	H301	4SW/5SW deg	M g	18	Ind $	D$6/△ go	29$	BBBBC$	Ind	5 12/22
Mechanical Engineering (STEPS)	H302	4FT/5SW deg	* g	18	4M	D$ go	29	BBBBC	Ind	4 10/22
Medicinal Chemistry/Engineering Management	FH1T	3FT/4SW deg	C g	20	3M+7D$	D$△ go	30	BBBBB$	Ind	
Product Design (Engineering)/Biology	CH17	3FT/4SW deg	B g	18	5M+5D$	D$△ go	29	BBBBC$	Ind	
Product Design (Engineering)/Business Admin	HN71	3FT/4SW deg	S g	20	5M+5D$	D$△ go	30$	BBBBB		
Product Design (Engineering)/Electronics	HH76	3FT/4SW deg	M/P g	18	5M+5D$	D$△ go	29$	BBBBC$		
Product Design (Engineering)/Engineering Mgt	H710	3FT/4SW deg	S g	18	5M+5D$	D$△ go	29$	BBBBC		
Product Design (Engineering)/Environ Sci & Tech	FH97	3FT/4SW deg	S g	18	5M+5D$	D$△ go	29$	BBBBC		
Product Design (Engineering)/Ergonomics	HJ7X	3FT/4SW deg	S g	20	5M+5D$	D$△ go	30$	BBBBB		
Product Design (Engineering)/European Studies	HT72	3FT/4SW deg	S g	18	5M+5D$	D$△ go	29$	BBBBC		
Product Design (Engineering)/French	HR71	3FT/4SW deg	S+F g	20	X	X	30$	BBBBB$		
Product Design (Engineering)/German	HR72	3FT/4SW deg	S+G g	18	X	X	29$	BBBBC$		
Product Design (Engineering)/Health & Safety Mgt	HJ79	3FT/4SW deg	S g	18	5M+5D$	D$△ go	29$	BBBBC$		
Product Design (Engineering)/Human Psychology	LH77	3FT/4SW deg	S g	20	5M+5D$	D$△ go	30$	BBBBB$	Ind	

TITLE	CODE	COURSE	SUBJECTS	A/AS	ND/C	AGNVQ	IB	SQA(H)	SQA	RATIO A/AS
Product Design (Engineering)/Mathematics	GH17	3FT/4SW deg	M g	20	5M+5D$	D$^ go	30$	BBBBB$		
Product Design (Engineering)/Medicinal Chemistry	FH17	3FT/4SW deg	C g	20	5M+5D$	D$^ go	30$	BBBBB$		
Public Policy & Mgt/Product Design (Engineering)	HM71	3FT/4SW deg	S g	20	5M+5D	D$^ go	30$	BBBBB$	Ind	
Social Studies/Engineering Management	HL74	3FT/4SW deg	S g	18	5M+5D$	D$^ go	29$	BBBBC$	Ind	

BARKING COLL

Product Design (Extended)	H778	1EXT deg	M/P+Pf g	A	N	P				

BARNSLEY COLL

Engineering (Mechanical)	003H	2FT HND	*	E	N	P*	Ind	Ind	Ind	

Univ of BATH

Automotive Engineering (5 Yr SW)	H343	5SW deg	M+P g	ABB	Ind	Ind	30	CSYS$	Ind	
Automotive Engineering (MEng)	H340	4FT deg	M+P g	ABB	Ind	Ind	30	CSYS$	Ind	14 20/26
Automotive Engineering with French (5 Yr SW)	H344	5SW deg	M+P g	ABB	Ind	Ind	30$	CSYS$	Ind	
Automotive Engineering with French (MEng)	H341	4FT deg	M+P g	ABB	Ind	Ind	30$	CSYS$		
Automotive Engineering with German (5 Yr SW)	H345	5SW deg	M+P g	ABB	Ind	Ind	30$	CSYS$		
Automotive Engineering with German (MEng)	H342	4FT deg	M+P g	ABB	Ind	Ind	30$	CSYS$		
Innovation and Engineering Design (5 Yr SW)	H762	5SW deg	M+P	ABB	Ind	Ind	30	Ind	Ind	
Innovation and Engineering Design (MEng)	H761	4FT deg	M+P	ABB	Ind	Ind	30	Ind	Ind	6 20/28
Innovation and Engineering Design with French	H764	4FT deg	M+P g	ABB	Ind	Ind	30	Ind	Ind	
Innovation and Engineering Design with French	H766	5SW deg	M+P g	ABB	Ind	Ind	30	Ind	Ind	
Innovation and Engineering Design with German	H765	4FT deg	M+P g	ABB	Ind	Ind	30	Ind	Ind	
Innovation and Engineering Design with German	H767	5SW deg	M+P g	ABB	Ind	Ind	30	Ind	Ind	
Manufacturing Systems-Eng & Mgt with French	H714	5SW deg	M+P g	24	Ind	Ind	30$	CSYS$	Ind	
Manufacturing Systems-Eng & Mgt with German	H715	5SW deg	M+P g	24	Ind	Ind	30$	CSYS$	Ind	
Manufacturing Systems-Engineering & Mgt (5Yr SW)	H713	5SW deg	M+P g	ABB	Ind	Ind	30$	CSYS	Ind	
Manufacturing Systems-Engineering & Mgt (MEng)	H716	4FT deg	M+P	ABB	Ind	Ind	30$	CSYS	Ind	13
Manufacturing Systs-Eng & Mgt with French (MEng)	H717	4FT deg	M+P g	ABB	Ind	Ind	30$	CSYS	Ind	
Manufacturing Systs-Eng & Mgt with German (MEng)	H718	4FT deg	M+P g	ABB	Ind	Ind	30$	CSYS	Ind	
Mechanical Engineering (5 Yr SW)	H309	5SW deg	M+P g	ABB	Ind	Ind	30$	CSYS$	Ind	
Mechanical Engineering (MEng)	H306	4FT deg	M+P g	ABB	Ind	Ind	30$	CSYS$	Ind	9 22/30
Mechanical Engineering with French (5 Yr SW)	H304	5SW deg	M+P g	ABB	Ind	Ind	30$	CSYS$	Ind	
Mechanical Engineering with French (MEng)	H307	4FT deg	M+P g	ABB	Ind	Ind	30$	CSYS$	Ind	5 22/28
Mechanical Engineering with German (5 Yr SW)	H305	5SW deg	M+P g	ABB	Ind	Ind	30$	CSYS$	Ind	
Mechanical Engineering with German (MEng)	H308	4FT deg	M+P g	ABB	Ind	Ind	30$	CSYS$	Ind	8

BELL COLLEGE OF TECHNOLOGY

Automotive Engineering	H340	3FT deg	M/P	DD	Ind	Ind	Ind	CCC$	Ind	
Manufacturing Engineering and Management	HN71	3FT deg	* g	DD	Ind	Ind	Ind	CCC$	Ind	
Manufacturing Systems Engineering	H710	3FT deg	* g	DD	Ind	Ind	Ind	CCC$	Ind	
Mechatronics	HH36	3FT deg	M/P	CD	Ind	Ind	Ind	BBC$	Ind	
Engineering: Mechanical	003H	2FT HND	* g	D	N $	P$	Ind	CC$	Ind	
Manufacturing Engineering and Management	17NH	2FT HND	* g	D	N $	P$	Ind	CC$	Ind	
Manufacturing Systems Engineering	017H	2FT HND	* g	D	N $	P$	Ind	CC$	Ind	

Univ of BIRMINGHAM

Manufacturing Eng & Business St with Found Year	H7N1	4FT/5FT deg	* g	BBC	6M+D$	M*^ go	30$	BBBC$	Ind	3 14/22
Manufacturing Engineering	H700	3FT/4FT deg	M g	BCC	6M+1D$	M$^ go	30$	CSYS	Ind	5 16/22
Manufacturing Engineering and Business Studies	HN71	3FT/4FT deg	M g	BBC	6M+1D$	D$^ go	32$	CSYS	Ind	
Manufacturing Engineering and Commerce	H7NC	4FT deg	M	BBC	6M+1D$	D$^ go	32$	CSYS	Ind	2 18/28
Manufacturing Engineering with Foundation Year	H781	4FT/5FT deg	* g	BBC	6M+1D$	M*^ go	30$	BBBC$	Ind	6
Mechanical Engineering	H300	3FT/4FT deg	M+P	BBC	6M+1D$	D$^ go	32$	CSYS	Ind	7 20/28
Mechanical Engineering & Bus St with Found Yr	H3N1	4FT/5FT deg	* g	BBC	6M+1D$	M*^ go	30$	BBBC$	Ind	9
Mechanical Engineering and Business Studies	HN31	3FT/4FT deg	M+P	BBC	6M+1D$	D$^ go	32$	CSYS	Ind	

TITLE	CODE	COURSE	SUBJECTS	A/AS	ND/C	AGNVQ	IB	SQA(H)	SQA	RATIO A/AS
Mechanical Engineering with Foundation Year	H391	4FT/5FT deg	* g	BBC	6M+1D$	M*^ go	30$	BBBC$	Ind	23
Mechanical and Materials Engineering (b) (g)	HJ35	3FT/4FT deg	M+P g	BCC	6M+1D		32$	Ind	Ind	2 18/28
Mechanical Engineering, Manuf and Management *Manufacturing*	Y600	4FT deg	M+P	BBB	X	X	33$	CSYS	X	
Mechanical Engineering, Manuf and Management *Mechanical Engineering*	Y600	4FT deg	M+P	BBB	X	X	33$	CSYS	X	

BLACKBURN COLL

Mechanical/Plant Engineering	003H	1FT HND			N $	P$				

BLACKPOOL & FYLDE COLL

Engineering Design	067H	2FT HND		2	N	P*	Ind	Ind	Ind	
Mechanical Engineering	003H	2FT HND		2	N	P*	Ind	Ind	Ind	
Mechatronics	63HH	2FT HND		2	N	P*	Ind	Ind	Ind	
Production Engineering	007H	2FT HND		2	N	P*	Ind	Ind	Ind	

BOLTON INST

Automobile Engineering	H341	4FT deg	M/S	4	N	P$	Ind	Ind	Ind	
Automobile Engineering	H340	3FT deg	M+S	10	3M	M$	Ind	Ind	Ind	
Automobile Engineering (MEng)	H344	4FT deg	M+S	18	3M+1D	M3$	Ind	Ind	Ind	
Automobile/Mechanical Engineering (Foundation)	H318	4FT/5FT deg	* g		Ind	Ind	Ind	Ind	Ind	
Automobile/Mechanical Technology (Foundation)	H319	4FT/5FT deg	* g		Ind	Ind	Ind			
Computer Aided Product Design	HW72	3FT deg	M/S/Ad/Ds	10	3M	M$	Ind	Ind	Ind	
Computer Aided Product Design	HW7F	4FT deg	M/S/Ad/Ds	4	N	P$	Ind	Ind	Ind	
Computing and Manufacturing Systems	GH57	3FT deg	* g	10	3M	M$	Ind	Ind	Ind	
Computing and Motor Vehicle Studies	GH5J	3FT deg	M/S g	10	3M	M$	Ind	Ind	Ind	
Consumer Product Design	H770	3FT deg	M/S/Ad/Ds	10	3M	M$	Ind	Ind	Ind	
Consumer Product Design (4 yrs)	H771	4FT deg	* g	4	N	P*	Ind	Ind	Ind	
Electronics and Manufacturing Systems Design	HHP7	3FT deg	M/S/Ds	10	3M	M$	Ind	Ind	Ind	
Electronics and Motor Vehicle Studies	HHPJ	3FT deg	M/S	10	3M	M$	Ind	Ind	Ind	
Electronics and Motor Vehicle Studies	HHQJ	4FT deg	M/S	4	N	P$	Ind	Ind	Ind	
Electronics and Product Design	HHPT	3FT deg	M/S/Ad/Ds	10	3M	M$	Ind	Ind	Ind	
Environmental Studies and Motor Vehicle Studies	FH9J	3FT deg	M/S g	10	MO	M$	Ind	Ind	Ind	
French and Manufacturing Systems Design	RH17	3FT deg	F g	10	Ind	Ind	Ind	Ind	Ind	
French and Motor Vehicle Studies	RH1J	3FT deg	F+M/S g	10	Ind	Ind	Ind	Ind	Ind	
French and Product Design	RH1T	3FT deg	F g	CD	Ind	Ind	24	BBCC	Ind	
German and Manufacturing Systems Design	RH27	3FT deg	G g	10	3M	Ind	Ind	Ind	Ind	
German and Motor Vehicle Studies	RH2J	3FT deg	G+M/S g	10	3M	Ind	Ind	Ind	Ind	
German and Product Design	RH2T	3FT deg	G+Ds/Ad/M/S g	10	3M	Ind	Ind	Ind	Ind	
Man Systs Design & Occupational Health & Safety	HN76	3FT deg	M/S g	10	3M	M$	Ind	Ind	Ind	
Man Systs Design & Simulation/Virtual Environ	HG77	3FT deg	M/S g	10	3M	M$	Ind	Ind	Ind	
Man Systs Design & Simulation/Virtual Environ	HGRT	4FT deg	M/S g	4	N	P$	Ind	Ind	Ind	
Manufacturing Systems Design	H710	3FT deg	M/S g	10	3M	M$	Ind	Ind	Ind	
Manufacturing Systems Design	H711	4FT deg	M/S g	4	P	P$	Ind	Ind	Ind	
Manufacturing Systems Design & Motor Vehicle St	H7HJ	3FT deg								
Manufacturing Systems Design and Product Design	HHRT	4FT deg	M/S/Ad/Ds g	4	N	P$	Ind	Ind	Ind	
Manufacturing Systems Design and Product Design	HH7T	3FT deg	M/S/Ad/Ds g	10	3M	M$	Ind	Ind	Ind	
Manufacturing Systems Design and Technology Mgt	HNR9	4FT deg	M/S/Bu g	4	N	P$	Ind	Ind	Ind	
Manufacturing Systems Design and Technology Mgt	HN79	3FT deg								
Marketing and Motor Vehicle Studies	NH5J	3FT deg	M/S g	10	3M	M$	Ind	Ind	Ind	
Mechanical Engineering	H300	3FT deg	M+S	10	3M	M$	Ind	Ind	Ind	
Mechanical Engineering	H301	4FT deg	M/S	4	N	P$	Ind	Ind	Ind	
Mechanical Engineering (MEng)	H304	4FT deg	M+S	18	3M+1D	M3$	Ind	Ind	Ind	
Mechanical and Manufacturing Engineering	HH3R	4FT deg	M/S	E	N	Ind	Ind	Ind	Ind	

Engineering – Mechanical and Production 25

				98 expected requirements						96 entry stats
course details										
TITLE	CODE	COURSE	SUBJECTS	A/AS	NO/C	AGNVQ	IB	SQA(H)	SQA	RATIO A/AS
Mechanical and Manufacturing Engineering	HH37	3FT deg	M+S	EE	3M	Ind	Ind	Ind	Ind	
Motor Vehicle St & Occupational Health & Safety	HNJ6	3FT deg								
Motor Vehicle St and Simulation/Virtual Environ	HGJ7	3FT deg								
Motor Vehicle Studies	H342	3FT deg								
Motor Vehicle Studies	H346	4FT deg								
Motor Vehicle Studies and Product Design	HHJT	3FT deg								
Motor Vehicle Studies and Technology Management	HNJ9	3FT deg	M/S/Bu g	10	3M	M$	Ind	Ind	Ind	
Motor Vehicle Studies and Transport Studies	HJJX	4FT deg	M/S	4	N	P$	Ind	Ind	Ind	
Motor Vehicle Studies and Transport Studies	HJJ9	3FT deg	M/S	10	3M	M$	Ind	Ind	Ind	
Motor Vehicle/Transport Studies (Foundation)	HJJY	4FT/5FT deg		Ind	Ind	Ind	Ind	Ind		
Product Des/Simulation & Virtual Environ (Found)	HG7R	4FT/5FT deg		Ind	Ind	Ind	Ind	Ind		
Product Design and Simulation/Virtual Environ	HGT7	3FT deg	M/S/Ad/Ds	10	3M	M$	Ind	Ind	Ind	
Product Design and Simulation/Virtual Environ	HGTT	4FT deg	M/S/Ad/Ds	4	N	P$	Ind	Ind	Ind	
Product Design and Technology Management	HNTX	4FT deg	M/S/Ad/Ds/Bu	4	N	P$	Ind	Ind	Ind	
Product Design and Technology Management	HNT9	3FT deg	M/S/As/Ds/Bu	10	3M	M$	Ind	Ind	Ind	
Simulation and Virtual Environment	H7W2	3FT deg	M/S	10	3M	M$	Ind	Ind	Ind	
Simulation and Virtual Environment (4 yrs)	H7WF	4FT deg	M/S	4	N	P$	Ind	Ind	Ind	
Visual Arts and Product Design	WH17	3FT deg	* g	10	MO	M*	Ind	Ind	Ind	
Automobile Engineering	043H	2FT HND	M/S	4	N	P$	Ind	Ind	Ind	
Mechanical Engineering	003H	2FT HND	M/S	4	N	P$	Ind	Ind	Ind	
BOURNEMOUTH Univ										
Design Visualisation	H762	4SW deg	2(M/P/A/Ds) g	CC-CDD	Ind	M$^ go	Ind	CCCC	Ind	5
Design Visualisation Foundation	H768▼	1FT deg								
Product Design	H770	4SW deg	2(Ar/M/P) g	CC-CCE	MO	M$ go	Ind	CCCC	Ind	1 10/22
Univ of BRADFORD										
Manufacturing Engineering (MEng)	H700	4FT/5SW deg	M+S	14-20	3M $	M$^	Ind	Ind	Ind	
Manufacturing Systems with Management	H705	3FT deg	M+S	14-20	3M $	M$^	Ind	Ind	Ind	4
Manufacturing Systems with Management	H706	4SW deg	M+S	14-20	3M $	M$^	Ind	Ind	Ind	11
Manufacturing Systems with Mechanical Eng	HH7J	3FT deg	M+S	14-20	3M $	M$^	Ind	Ind	Ind	
Manufacturing Systems with Mechanical Eng	HH73	4SW deg	M+S	14-20	3M $	M$^	Ind	Ind	Ind	2
Mechanical Engineering	H301	4SW deg	M+S	14-20	3M $	M$^	Ind	Ind	Ind	18
Mechanical Engineering	H300	3FT deg	M+S	14-20	3M $	M$^	Ind	Ind	Ind	11 12/16
Mechanical Engineering (Foundation Year)	H303	4FT/5SW deg	* g	4-8	N	P$	Ind	Ind	Ind	2 4/12
Mechanical Engineering (MEng)	H305	4FT/5SW deg	M+S	14-20	3M $	M$^	Ind	Ind	Ind	
Mechanical Engineering with Management	H304	3FT deg	M+S	14-20	3M $	M$^	Ind	Ind	Ind	
Mechanical Engineering with Management	H302	4SW deg	M+S	14-20	3M $	M$^	Ind	Ind	Ind	10
Mechanical and Automotive Engineering	H341	4SW deg	M+S	14-20	3M $	M$^	Ind	Ind	Ind	
Mechanical and Automotive Engineering	H340	3FT deg	M+S	14-20	3M $	M$^	Ind	Ind	Ind	
BRADFORD & ILKLEY Comm COLL										
Process Systems	H750	3FT deg	g	2	P	P		Ind	Ind	
Process Control	157H	2FT HND	g	2	P	P		Ind	Ind	
Process Systems	057H	2FT HND	g	2	P	P		Ind	Ind	
Univ of BRIGHTON										
Engineering Systs Simul & Contr (Dip/BEng/MEng)	H650	3FT/4SW 4FT/5SWdeg	M+P/S g	18	5M $	ME/M$^	25$	BBBC$	N$	
Manufacturing Systems (Dip/BEng/MEng)	H710	3FT/4SW/4FT/5SW deg	M+P/S g	18	5M $	ME/M$^	25$	BBBC$	Ind	
Mech & Environmental Engineering (Dip/BEng/MEng)	HJ39	3FT/4SW/4FT/5SW deg	M+P/S g	18	5M $	ME/M$^	25$	BBBC$	Ind	
Mech and Aeronautical Design Eng (Dip/BEng/MEng)	HH34	3FT/4SW/4FT/5SW deg	M+P/S g	18	5M $	ME/M$^	25$	BBBC$	Ind	
Mechanical Engineering (Dip/BEng/MEng)	H300	3FT/4SW/4FT/5SW deg	M+P/S g	18	5M $	ME/M$^	25$	BBBC$	Ind	
Product Design (4 year sandwich)	W231	4SW deg	Pf+M+P/S g	18	5M $	ME/M$^	25$	BBBC$	Ind	
Engineering (Mechanical/Manufacture)	003H▼	2FT HND	M+P/S/Ds	6	3M $	P$+ gi	15$	CDD$	Ind	
Engineering (Mechatronics)	63HH▼	2FT HND	M/P/S/Ds	4	3M $	P$+	15$	CDD$	Ind	

TITLE	CODE	COURSE	SUBJECTS	A/AS	ND/C	RGNVQ	IB	SQA(H)	SQA	RATIO	A/AS
Univ of BRISTOL											
Mech Eng with Manufacturing Systems (MEng)	H3H7	4FT deg	M+P	ABB-CCC	HN $	D$^	28$	CSYS	HN $	13	24/28
Mech Engineering with Study in C Eur (MEng)	H301	4FT deg	M+P+L	ABB-CCC	HN $	D$^	28$	CSYS	HN $	8	26/30
Mechanical Eng with Process Systems (MEng)	H3H8	4FT deg	M+P	ABB-CCC	HN $	D$^	28$	CSYS	HN $		
Mechanical Engineering	H305	3FT deg	M+P	ABB-CCC	HN $	D$^	28$	CSYS	HN$		
Mechanical Engineering (MEng)	H300	4FT deg	M+P	ABB-CCC	HN $	D$^	28$	CSYS	HN $	8	22/30
BRISTOL, Univ of the W of England											
Building Production Engineering	H7K2	3FT/4SW deg	M/P g	10-12	5M $	P*3/^ go	24$	BC$	Ind		
Manufacturing Systems Engineering	H710	3FT/4SW deg	M/P g	14	4M $	M$1 go	24$	BCCC$	N$		
Manufacturing Systems Engineering (MEng)	H711	4FT/5SW deg	M/P g	14	4M $	M$1 go	24$	BCCC$	N$		
Mechanical Engineering	H300	3FT/4SW deg	M/P g	14	4M $	M$1 go	24$	BCCC$	N$		
Mechanical Engineering (MEng)	H301	4FT/5SW deg	M/P g	14	4M $	M$1 go	24$	BCCC$	N$		
Engineering (Mechanical)	003H	2FT/3SW HND	M/P g	2-4	N $	P$1 go	24$	CD$	N$		
Engineering (Mechatronics)	63HH	2FT/3SW HND	M/P g	2-4	N $	P$1 go	24$	CD$	N$		
Engineering (Production)	007H	2FT/3SW HND	M/P g	2-4	N $	P$1 go	24$	CD$	N$		
BRUNEL Univ, West London											
Industrial Design	H770	4SW deg	M	CCC	4M $	ME^	26$	CCCCC$	Ind	3	10/24
Industrial Design Engineering	H774	4SW/5SW deg	M+P/Ds	CCC	4M $	Ind	26$	CCCCC$	Ind	5	12/26
Industrial Design and Technology	HW72	3FT deg	Ds	CCC	4M $	Ind	26	CCCCC$	Ind		
Industrial Design and Technology (Thick SW)	HW7F	4SW deg	Ds	CCC	4M $	Ind	26	CCCCC$	Ind		
Integrated Engineering (Mechatronics)	H1HJ	4SW deg	M+P/S	BCC	4M+1D$	DE^	28$	BBCCC$	Ind		
Integrated Engineering (Mechatronics)	H1HH	4SW deg	M+P/S	BCC	4M+1D$	DE^	28$	BBCCC$	Ind		
Integrated Engineering (Mechatronics)	H1H3	3FT deg	M+P/S	BCC	4M+1D$	DE^	28$	BBCCC$	Ind		
Manu Eng w. Mgt & Bus Stud(MEng) (4Yrs Thick SW)	H7NC	4SW/5SW deg	M	CCC	4M+1D$	DE^	28$	AABBB$	Ind	4	
Manuf Eng with Mgt & Bus St(MEng)(4 Yrs Thin SW)	H7N1	4SW/5SW deg	M	CCC	4M+1D$	DE^	28$	AABBB$	Ind	1	6/15
Manufacturing Eng (BME) (MEng) (4 Yrs Thin SW)	H700	4SW/5SW deg	M	CCC	4M+1D$	DE^	28$	BBCCC$	Ind	2	
Manufacturing Eng (MEng) (4 Yrs Thick SW)	H703	4SW/5SW deg	M	CCC	4M+1D$	DE^	28$	BBCCC$	Ind	2	
Manufacturing Eng with Fr (MEng) (4Yrs Thin SW)	H7R1	4SW/5SW deg	M+F	CCC	4M+1D$	DE^	28$	AABBB$	Ind	2	
Manufacturing Eng with Ger (MEng) (4Yrs Thin SW)	H7R2	4SW/5SW deg	M+G	CCC	4M+1D$	DE^	28$	AABBB$	Ind		
Manufacturing Eng with Mgt and Bus Studs (MEng)	H7ND	3FT/4FT deg	M	CCC	4M+1D$	DE^	28$	AABBB$	Ind	4	
Manufacturing Engineering (3/4 Yrs) (MEng)	H704	3FT/4FT deg	M	CCC	4M+1D$	DE^	28$	BBCCC$	Ind		
Manufacturing Engineering with French (MEng)	H7RC	3FT/4FT deg	M+F	CCC	4M+1D$	DE^	28$	AABBB$	Ind		
Manufacturing Engineering with German (MEng)	H7RG	3FT/4FT deg	M+G	CCC	4M+1D$	DE^	28$	AABBB$	Ind		
Mech Eng w. Aeronautics (4/5 Yrs Thick SW)(MEng)	H3HL	4SW/5SW deg	M+P	BCC	4M+1D$	DE^	28$	BBBBB$	Ind	9	18/26
Mech Eng w. Aeronautics (4/5 Yrs Thin SW) (MEng)	H3H4	4SW/5SW deg	M+P	BCC	4M+1D$	DE^	28$	BBBBB$	Ind	8	
Mech Eng w. Automot Des (4/5 Yrs Thick SW)(MEng)	H342	4SW/5SW deg	M+P	BCC	4M+1D$	DE^	28$	BBBBB$	Ind	10	16/28
Mech Eng w. Automotive Des(4/5Yrs Thin SW)(MEng)	H341	4SW/5SW deg	M+P	BCC	4M+1D$	DE^	28$	BBBBB$	Ind	9	16/18
Mech Eng with Bld Serv (4/5 Yrs Thick SW) (MEng)	H3K2	4SW/5SW deg	M+P	BCC	4M+1D$	DE^	28$	BBBBB$	Ind	6	
Mech Eng with Build Serv (4/5 Yrs Thin SW)(MEng)	H3KF	4SW/5SW deg	M+P	BCC	4M+1D$	DE^	28$	BBBBB$	Ind		
Mech Eng with Elect Sys (4/5 Yrs Thick SW)(MEng)	H3HQ	4SW/5SW deg	M+P	BCC	4M+1D$	DE^	28$	BBBBB$	Ind		
Mech Eng with Elect Sys (4/5 Yrs Thin SW) (MEng)	H3H6	4SW/5SW deg	M+P	BCC	4M+1D$	DE^	28$	BBBBB$	Ind	4	
Mech Engineering with Automotive Design (MEng)	H340	3FT/4FT deg	M+P	BCC	4M+1D$	DE^	28$	BBBBB$	Ind	11	18/24
Mech Engineering with Building Services (MEng)	H3KG	3FT/4FT deg	M+P	BCC	4M+1D$	DE^	28$	BBBBB$	Ind		
Mech Engineering with Electronic Systems (MEng)	H3HP	3FT/4FT deg	M+P	BCC	4M+1D$	DE^	28$	BBBBB$	Ind	14	
Mechanical Engineering (4/5 Yrs Thick SW) (MEng)	H304	4SW/5SW deg	M+P	BCC	4M+1D$	DE^	28$	BBBBB$	Ind	12	20/24
Mechanical Engineering (4/5 Yrs Thin SW) (MEng)	H300	4SW/5SW deg	M+P	BCC	4M+1D$	DE^	28$	BBBBB$	Ind	7	16/24
Mechanical Engineering (MEng)	H303	3FT/4FT deg	M+P	BCC	4M+1D$	DE^	28$	BBBBB$	Ind	10	14/28
Mechanical Engineering and Design (5yr SW)(MEng)	HH3R	5SW deg	M+P	BBC	4M+1D	DE^	28$	BBBBB$	Ind		
Mechanical Engineering and Design (MEng)	HH37	4FT deg	M+P	BBC	4M+1D	DE^	28$	BBBBB$	Ind		
Mechanical Engineering with Aeronautics (MEng)	H3HK	3FT/4FT deg	M+P	BCC	4M+1D$	DE^	28$	BBBBB$	Ind	14	
Product Design	H772	4SW deg	M	CCC	4M $	MA/^	26$	CCCCC$	Ind	5	10/24

course details			98 expected requirements							96 entry stats
TITLE	CODE	COURSE	SUBJECTS	A/AS	NO/C	AGNVQ	IB	SQA(H)	SQA	RATIO A/AS
BUCKINGHAMSHIRE COLLEGE										
Computer Aided Design (Conversion to degree)	HW72	1FT/2FT deg			HN				HN	
Mechanical Engineering Design	HH37	3FT deg		8-10	MO	M	Ind	CCCC	Ind	
Product Design	H7W2	3FT deg		8-10	MO	M	Ind	CCC	Ind	
Product Design & Manufacture (Conv to Degree)	H771	1FT/2FT deg			HN					
Product Design (Conversion to degree)	H772	1FT/2FT deg			HN				HN	
Product Design Manufacture	H770	3FT deg		8-10	1D	M	27	CCCC	Ind	5	6/10
Product Design with Management	H7ND	3FT deg		8-10	MO	M	Ind	CCC	Ind	
Product Design with Marketing	H7N5	3FT deg		8-10	MO	M	Ind	CCC	Ind	
Product Design & Manufacture	077H	2FT HND		4	N	P	Ind	CC	Ind	4
CARDIFF Univ of Wales										
Manufacturing Engineering	H712	4FT deg	M	BBB	5M+1D$		30$	BBBB$	Ind	5
Manufacturing Engineering	H700	3FT deg	M	18-24	5M $		28$	BBBB$	Ind	3	14/16
Manufacturing Engineering	H701	4SW deg	M	18-24	5M $		28$	BBBB$	Ind	2
Mechanical Eng (Yr in France/Germany/Spain)	H304	4FT deg	M g	20-24	5M+2D$ Ind		28$	AABB	Ind	1
Mechanical Engineering	H307	5SW deg	M	20-24	5M+2D$ Ind		28$	AABB	Ind	
Mechanical Engineering	H302	4FT deg	M	20-24	5M+2D$ Ind		28$	AABB	Ind	4	20/30
Mechanical Engineering	H301	4SW deg	M	20-24	5M+2D$ Ind		28$	AABB	Ind	9	18/22
Mechanical Engineering	H300	3FT deg	M	20-24	5M+2D$ Ind		28$	AABB	Ind	8	10/24
Univ of Wales INST, CARDIFF										
Manufacturing Systems and Manufacturing Mgt	H7N1	4FT deg	* g	4	N	M$ gi	Ind	CCCC	Ind	8
Product Design and Manufacture	007H	2FT HND	* g	2	N	M$ go	Ind	CC	Ind	2	2/8
Univ of CENTRAL ENGLAND										
Automotive Engineering	H340	3FT/4SW deg	M g	12	3M $	ME1	24$	CCC$	Ind	30
Automotive Engineering Foundation Year	H348▼	4FT/5SW deg	* g	2	N	P*	Ind	CC	Ind	5
Engineering Product Design	H770	3FT/4SW deg	Ar+Pf g	12	Ind	Ind	24	CCC$	Ind	6	8/18
Engineering Product Design Foundation Year	H778▼	4FT/5SW deg	*	2	N	P*	Ind	CC	Ind	1
Management of Manufacturing Systems	H7N1	3FT/4SW deg	M g	12	3M $	ME1	24$	CCC$	Ind	
Management of Manufacturing Systems Found Year	H7NC▼	4FT/5SW deg	* g	2	N	P*	Ind	CC	Ind	
Manufacturing Technology & Mgt Foundation Year	HN7C▼	4FT/5SW deg	*	2	N	P*	Ind	CC	Ind	1
Manufacturing Technology and Management	HN71	3FT/4SW deg	* g	12	3M	M* go	24	CCC	Ind	20
Mechanical & Manufacturing Eng Foundation Yr	HH3R▼	4FT/5SW deg	* g	2	N	P*	Ind	CC	Ind	4
Mechanical Eng with German Studies Foundation Yr	H3RF▼	5EXT deg	* g	2	$	P* go	Ind	CC$	Ind	
Mechanical Engineering	H300	3FT/4SW deg	M g	12	3M $	ME1	24$	CCC$	Ind	9
Mechanical Engineering Foundation Year	H308▼	4FT/5SW deg	* g	2	N	P*	Ind	CC	Ind	4
Mechanical Engineering with French	H3R1	3FT/4SW deg	M g	12	3M $	ME1	24$		Ind	Ind
Mechanical Engineering with French Foundation Yr	H3RC▼	4FT/5SW deg	* g	2	N	P*	Ind	CC	Ind	
Mechanical Engineering with German	H3RG	3FT/4SW deg	M g	12	3M $	ME1	24$	CCC$	Ind	
Mechanical Engineering with German Foundation Yr	HR32▼	4FT/5SW deg	* g	2	N	P*	Ind	CC	Ind	
Mechanical Engineering with German Studies	H3R2	4FT deg	M g	8	3M $	ME1 go	24$	CCC$	Ind	
Mechanical and Manufacturing Engineering	HH37	3FT/4SW deg	M g	12	3M $	ME1	24$	CCC$	Ind	
Engineering (Automotive Engineering)	043H	2FT/3SW HND	M/P	2	$	PE1	24	CC$	Ind		2/2
Engineering (Manufacture)	007H	2FT/3SW HND	M/P	2	$	PE1	24	CC$	Ind	6
Engineering (Mechanical Engineering)	003H	2FT/3SW HND	M/P	2	$	PE1	24	CC$	Ind	5
Univ of CENTRAL LANCASHIRE										
Design and Manufacture	H770	4SW deg	M+P	14	3M	M$	26	BCCC	Ind	
Design and Manufacture (MEng)	H772	5FT deg	M+P	20	DO	D$6/^	30	BBBB	Ind	
Mechanical Engineering	H300	4SW deg	M+P	14	MO	D$	26	BCCC	Ind	
Mechanical Engineering (Year 0)	H308▼	1FT deg	* g	6	N	P$	24	CC	Ind	
Product Design	H771	3FT deg	Ds/Ad g	18	MO	D$	26	BCCC	Ind	

TITLE	CODE	COURSE	SUBJECTS	A/AS	ND/C	AGNVQ	IB	SQA(H)	SQA	RATIO A/AS
course details			98 expected requirements							96 entry stats
Product Design (Year Zero)	H778	4FT deg	* g	8	N	P	24	CC		
Engineering (Mechanical & Production)	73HH	2FT/3SW HND	M	E	N	P$	Ind	Ind	Ind	3
Machinery Management and Development	033H▼	2FT HND	* g	E	N $	P$	24$	CCC$	Ind	
Mechanical Engineering	003H▼	2FT HND								

CITY Univ

TITLE	CODE	COURSE	SUBJECTS	A/AS	ND/C	AGNVQ	IB	SQA(H)	SQA	RATIO A/AS
Design and Management in Engineering	HN71	3FT deg	*	18	3M+2D	D$^	27	BBBBB	HN	
Engineering and Energy Management	HJ39	3FT deg	M+P	BCD-CCD	4M+2D	DE6/^	28$	Ind	Ind	
Engineering and Energy Management (MEng)	JH93	4FT deg	M+P	BBB	X		30$	Ind	X	
Mechanical Engineering	H300	3FT deg	M+P	BCD-CCD	4M+2D	DE6/^	28$	Ind	Ind	4	10/18
Mechanical Engineering	H301	4SW deg	M+P	BCD-CCD	4M+2D	DE6/^	28$	Ind	Ind	12
Mechanical Engineering (Foundation)	H302	4EXT deg	M+P	6-8	N	P$	Dip	BC	N	10
Mechanical Engineering (MEng)	H305	5SW deg	M+P	ABB-BBB	X		30$	Ind	X	
Mechanical Engineering (MEng)	H304	4FT deg	M+P	ABB-BBB	X		30$	Ind	X	24

COVENTRY Univ

TITLE	CODE	COURSE	SUBJECTS	A/AS	ND/C	AGNVQ	IB	SQA(H)	SQA	RATIO A/AS
Advanced Product Engineering (MEng)	H705	3FT deg	M/P	20	3D		Ind	Ind	Ind	
Automotive Engineering	H343	3FT/4/5SW deg	M+S	12-18	3M					
Automotive Engineering Design (MEng/BEng/BSc)	H340	3FT/4SW 4FT/5SW deg	M+S+Pf	18	6D $	M+	30$	BBCC$	Ind	5	8/20
Automotive Manufacturing	H346	3FT deg	*	12-18		M+	24$	Ind	Ind	
Industrial Product Design	H770	3FT/4SW deg	* g	18	5M $	M+	27$	Ind$	Ind	6	6/22
Manufacturing Engineering	H710	3FT/4SW/4FT/5SW deg	M/S	12-18	3M $	M+	24$	BBCC$	Ind	10
Manufacturing Management and Business	H7N1	3FT/4SW/4FT/5SW deg	*	12-18	3M $	M+	24$	BBCC$	Ind	3
Manufacturing Management and Business	HN7D	3FT deg								
Materials Technology with Manufacturing	J5H7	3FT deg	* g	12	Ind	Ind	Ind	Ind	Ind	
Materials Technology with Manufacturing	J5HT	3FT deg	* g	12	Ind	Ind	Ind	Ind	Ind	
Mechanical Engineering (MEng/BEng/Bsc)	H300	3FT/4SW/4FT/5SW deg	M+S	12-18	3M $	M+	24$	BBCC$	Ind	8	6/16
Transport Design (MDes)	EH27	3FT/4SW deg	Pf g	X	Ind	Ind	Ind	Ind	Ind	
Transport Design (MDes)	WH27	3FT/4SW deg	Pf g	X	Ind	Ind	Ind	Ind	Ind	
Automotive Engineering	043H	2FT/3SW HND	M/S		$	M	X	X	Ind	4	2/8
Automotive Manufacturing	643H	2FT HND	M/S		$		Ind	Ind	Ind	
Manufacturing Engineering	007H	2FT/3SW HND	M/S		$	M	Ind	Ind	Ind	2
Manufacturing Management and Business	017H	2FT/3SW HND	M/S		$	M	Ind	Ind	Ind	1
Mechanical Engineering	003H	2FT/3SW HND	M/S		$	M	Ind	Ind	Ind	4	2/4

CRANFIELD Univ

TITLE	CODE	COURSE	SUBJECTS	A/AS	ND/C	AGNVQ	IB	SQA(H)	SQA	RATIO A/AS
Agricultural Engineering	H330	3FT/4SW deg	M+P g	CCC	4M $	M$6/^ go	30$	BBBB$	Ind	7
Mechanical Engineering	H300	3FT deg	M+P g	BCC	3M+1D		Ind	Ind	Ind	7	20/28
Mechanical Engineering with Management	H310	3FT deg	M+P g	BCC	3M+1D		Ind	Ind	Ind	

DE MONTFORT Univ

TITLE	CODE	COURSE	SUBJECTS	A/AS	ND/C	AGNVQ	IB	SQA(H)	SQA	RATIO A/AS
Industrial Design (Engineering)	H770▼	4SW deg	Fa+A+M+P g	14	3M+3D$ D		26$	BBBB	Ind	6	10/24
Industrial Design Engineering	E770▼	3FT deg	Fa+A+M+P g	14	3M+3D	D	26$	BBBB	Ind	
Industrial and Business Systems	N1H7▼	4SW deg	* g	14	4M	M	26	BBBB	Ind	3
Mechanical Engineering	H300▼	3FT/4SW deg	M+P g	16	4M $	M	26$	BBBB	Ind	8	10/20
Sports Engineering	H3B6▼	3FT/4SW deg	M+P g	16	4M	M^	26$	BBBB	Ind	
Engineering (Agricultural)	033H▼	2FT/3SW HND	S g	E	N	P	Dip	BB	Ind	

Univ of DERBY

TITLE	CODE	COURSE	SUBJECTS	A/AS	ND/C	AGNVQ	IB	SQA(H)	SQA	RATIO A/AS
Ecodesign	HW72	3FT deg		12-14	8M	D	28	BBCC	Ind	
Ecodesign	EW72	3FT deg		12-14	8M	D	28	BBCC	Ind	
Electronics Product Design	HH67	3FT deg	M/S	10	4M $	M$	26$	CCCD$	Ind	6
Mechanical and Manufacturing Engineering	HFD9	3FT/4FT deg	M+S	18	8M $	D+2	30$	BBBCC$	Ind	
Product Design Engineering	H771	3FT deg		18	8M $	D+2	30$	BBBCC$	Ind	
Product Design Innovation & Marketing	H770	3FT/4FT deg	*	12-14	8M	D$	28$	BBBC	Ind	3	6/22

course details			98 expected requirements							96 entry stats

TITLE	CODE	COURSE	SUBJECTS	A/AS	ND/C	RGNVQ	IB	SQA[H]	SQA	RATIO A/AS
Credit Accumulation Modular Scheme *Ecodesign*	Y600	3FT deg	*	8	MO	M	Ind	CCCC	Ind	
Credit Accumulation Modular Scheme *Product Design*	Y600	3FT deg	*	8	MO	M	Ind	CCCC	Ind	
Manufacturing Engineering	007H	2FT HND	M/S	4	N	P$	Dip$	CCD$	Ind	
Mechanical Engineering	003H	2FT HND	M/S	4	N $	P$	Dip$	CCD$	Ind	7
Mechanical and Manufacturing Engineering	73HH	2FT HND	M/S	4	N $	P$	Dip$	CCD$	Ind	10
Product Design	077H	2FT HND		6	2M	P$	Dip$	CCDD	Ind	3 2/4

DONCASTER COLL

TITLE	CODE	COURSE	SUBJECTS	A/AS	ND/C	RGNVQ	IB	SQA[H]	SQA	RATIO A/AS
Mining and Mechanical Engineering	JH13	3FT deg		CC	3M	Ind	Ind	Ind	Ind	

DUDLEY COLLEGE of Technology

TITLE	CODE	COURSE	SUBJECTS	A/AS	ND/C	RGNVQ	IB	SQA[H]	SQA	RATIO A/AS
Engineering (Mechanical/Manufacture)	007H	2FT HND	* g	2	Ind	Ind				
Engineering (Mechatronics)	63HH	2FT HND	* g	2	Ind	Ind				

Univ of DUNDEE

TITLE	CODE	COURSE	SUBJECTS	A/AS	ND/C	RGNVQ	IB	SQA[H]	SQA	RATIO A/AS
Manufacturing Engineering and Management	HN71	3FT/4FT deg	M+P/Ds g	8	5M $	M$^	26$	BBCC$	N$	14
Mechanical Engineering	H300	3FT/4FT deg	M+P/Ds g	8	5M $	M$^	26$	BBCC$	N$	6 10/12
Mechanical Engineering (MEng)	H301	4FT/5FT deg	M+P/Ds g	8-24	5M $	M$^	26$	BBCC$	N$	

Univ of DURHAM

TITLE	CODE	COURSE	SUBJECTS	A/AS	ND/C	RGNVQ	IB	SQA[H]	SQA	RATIO A/AS
Engineering (Manufacturing w. Management)(4 Yrs)	H700	4FT deg	M	22	2M+4D	Ind	30$	AAAAB$	Ind	10
Engineering (Mechanical) (4 Yrs)	H300	4FT deg	M	22	2M+4D	Ind	30$	AAAAB$	Ind	9 24/30

Univ of EAST LONDON

TITLE	CODE	COURSE	SUBJECTS	A/AS	ND/C	RGNVQ	IB	SQA[H]	SQA	RATIO A/AS
Integrated Manufacturing Syst Eng & Electronics	HH76	3FT/4SW deg	* g	12	3M	ME	Ind	Ind	Ind	
Manufacturing Engineering Technology	H700	3FT/4SW deg	* g	12	3M	ME	Ind	Ind	Ind	6
Manufacturing Systems Engineering	H710	3FT/4SW deg	* g	12	3M	ME	Ind	Ind	Ind	18
Manufacturing Systems Engineering	H701	4FT/5SW deg	* g	12	3M	ME	Ind	Ind	Ind	
Manufacturing Systems Engineering (Extended)	H718	5EXT deg	* g	8-10	MO	M				
Product Design	H764	4FT/5SW deg	* g	12	3M	M$	Ind	Ind	Ind	9 10/16
Product Design (Extended)	H765	4FT deg	* g	12	3M	M$				1
Electronics and Manufacturing Technology	76HH	2FT/3SW HND	* g	12	MO	ME	Ind	Ind	Ind	

Univ of EDINBURGH

TITLE	CODE	COURSE	SUBJECTS	A/AS	ND/C	RGNVQ	IB	SQA[H]	SQA	RATIO A/AS
Electrical & Mechanical Engineering (MEng)	HH3M	5FT deg	M+P	CCC	MO $		Dip$	BBBB$	N$	
Electrical and Mechanical Engineering (BEng)	HH35	4FT deg	M+P	CCC	MO $		Dip$	BBBB$	N$	11
Mechanical Eng with Management Techniques (BEng)	H3N1	4FT deg	M+P	CCC	MO $		Dip$	BBBB$	N$	8 18/26
Mechanical Engineering (BEng)	H300	4FT deg	M+P	CCC	MO $		Dip$	BBBB$	N$	13 16/30
Mechanical Engineering (MEng)	H303	5FT deg	M+P	CCC	MO $		Dip$	BBBB$		4
Mechanical Engineering with Mgt Techniques	H3NC	5FT deg	M+P	CCC	MO $		Dip$	BBBB$	N$	

Univ of EXETER

TITLE	CODE	COURSE	SUBJECTS	A/AS	ND/C	RGNVQ	IB	SQA[H]	SQA	RATIO A/AS
Engineering and Management (MEng)	H704	4FT deg	M g	BCC	MO+1D	M$^	32$	Ind	Ind	8
Mechanical Engineering (MEng)	H302	4FT deg	M g	BCC	MO+1D	M$^	32$	Ind	Ind	5 10/28
Engineering	173H	2FT HND	M/P/C g	D	MO	M$^	24$	Ind	Ind	

FARNBOROUGH COLL of Technology

TITLE	CODE	COURSE	SUBJECTS	A/AS	ND/C	RGNVQ	IB	SQA[H]	SQA	RATIO A/AS
Automotive Engineering	043H	2FT HND		E	N	P*	Ind	Ind	Ind	9

Univ of GLAMORGAN

TITLE	CODE	COURSE	SUBJECTS	A/AS	ND/C	RGNVQ	IB	SQA[H]	SQA	RATIO A/AS
Electromechanical Power Systems	H5H3	3FT/4SW deg	M+P/S/Cs g	CD	3M $	M$	Ind	Ind	Ind	
Electromechanical Systems	HH53	5SW deg	M+S/Cs g	CD	3M $	M$	Ind	Ind	Ind	2
Mechanical Engineering	H300	3FT/4SW deg	M g	DD	3M $	M$	Ind	Ind	Ind	40
Mechanical Engineering (Foundation Year)	H301	1FT deg	* g	E	Ind	Ind	Ind	Ind	Ind	1
Mechanical Engineering (MEng)	H302	3FT deg	M g	DD	Ind	Ind	Ind	Ind	Ind	

			98 expected requirements							96 entry stats	
course details											
TITLE	CODE	COURSE	SUBJECTS	A/AS	NO/C	RGNVQ	IB	SQA(H)	SQA	RATIO A/AS	
Mechanical and Manufacturing Engineering	H701▼	3FT/4SW deg									
Mechanical and Manufacturing Systems Engineering	H700	3FT/4SW deg	M g	DD	3M $	M$	Ind	Ind	Ind	16	
Mechatronic Engineering	HH36	3FT deg	M/Es g	CD	3M $	M$	Ind	Ind	Ind		
Mechatronic Engineering	HH3P	3FT deg	M/Es g	CD	3M $	M$	Ind	Ind	Ind		
Product Design	H770	3FT deg	A/Ad/Ds g	CC	Ind	Ind	Ind	Ind	Ind		
Product Design	H778	4EXT deg									
Product Design	W2H3	3FT deg	A/Ad/Ds g	CC	MO $	M$	Ind	Ind	Ind	15	
Product Design	H3W2	3FT deg	A/Ad/Ds g	CC	MO $	M$	Ind	Ind	Ind	9	10/11
Sports Equipment Design	H3B6	3FT deg									
Sports Equipment Design	E2HH	3FT deg									
Combined Studies (Honours) *Manufacturing*	Y400	3FT deg	* g	8-16	Ind	Ind	Ind	Ind	Ind		
Joint Honours *Manufacturing*	Y401	3FT deg	* g	8-16	Ind	Ind	Ind	Ind	Ind		
Engineering (Mechanical/Manufacture)	73HH	2FT/3SW HND	M/P g	D	N	P$	Ind	Ind	Ind	3	
Manufacturing and Business Studies	17NH	2FT HND	M/P/S g	D	N $	P$	Ind	Ind	Ind		
Mechatronic Engineering	63HH	3FT/4SW HND	M+S/Cs g	D	$	P$	Ind	BB$	N$		
Product Design	3H2E	2FT HND	A/Ad/Ds g		Ind	Ind	Ind	Ind	Ind		
Product Design	077H	2FT HND			Ind	Ind	Ind	Ind	Ind		

Univ of GLASGOW

Design: Product Design Eng (MEng or BEng)	H3W2	4FT/5FT deg	M	CDD	MO	Ind	24$	BBBB$	N$	5	
Mechanical Design Engineering (MEng or BEng)	HH37	4FT/5FT deg	M+P	CDD	MO	Ind	24$	BBBB$	N$	6	
Mechanical Eng/Computer Integration (MEng/BEng)	H305	4FT/5FT deg	M+P	CDD	MO	Ind	24$	BBBB$	N$	15	
Mechanical Engineering (European Curriculum)	H3T2	5FT deg	M+P+L	CCD	MO	Ind	30$	BBBBC	N$		
Mechanical Engineering (European Curriculum)	H3TF	4FT deg	M+P+L	CCD	MO	Ind	30$	BBBBC	N$		
Mechanical Engineering (MEng or BEng)	H300	4FT/5FT deg	M+P	CDD	MO	Ind	24$	BBBC$	N$	13	
Naval Architecture and Marine Engineering (MEng)	J6H3	5FT deg	M+P	BBC	M+D $	X	28$	ABBB$	Ind		

GLASGOW CALEDONIAN Univ

Business and Manufacturing Systems Eng (BEng)	HN71	4FT deg	M	CD	Ind		Ind	BBC$	Ind		
Industrial Engineering Management	H750	4FT deg	M	CD	Ind		Ind	BBC$	Ind		
Manufacturing Systs Engineering BEng (Hons)	H7H6	4FT/5SW deg	M+P/C	CD	Ind		Ind	BBC$	Ind	4	
Mechanical Electronic Systems Eng BEng (Hons)	H370	4FT/5SW deg	M+P/C	CD	Ind		Ind	BBC$	Ind	6	
Product Design	H770	3FT deg	X	Ind			Ind	X	Ind		

GLOUCESTERSHIRE COLLEGE of Arts and Technology

| | | | | | | | | | | | |
| Engineering (Mechanical Manufacture) | 067H | 2FT HND | M/P g | EE | N $ | P | | | Ind | | |

Univ of GREENWICH

Engineering (Mechanical)	H301	3FT deg	* g	6	N	P	Ind	CC	Ind		
Mechanical Engineering	H300	3FT/4SW deg	M+P/S g	14	4M $	M+	24$	CCCC$	Ind		
Mechanical Engineering (Extended)	H308▼	4EXT deg	* g	4	Ind	Ind	Ind	Ind	Ind		
Mechanical Engineering (MEng)	H305	4FT deg	M+P/S g	18	6M $	Ind	Ind	BBCC	Ind		
Motor Vehicle Engineering with Management (BEng)	H3N1	3FT deg	* g	6	2/3M	P	Ind	Ind	Ind		
Mechanical Engineering	003H▼	2FT HND	M/P/S g	6	N $	P+	Dip	CC	Ind		
Motor Vehicle Engineering Management	043H▼	2FT HND	M/P/S g	6	N $	Ind	Dip	CC	Ind		

HALTON COLL

| | | | | | | | | | | | |
| Engineering (Mechatronics) | 63HH | 2FT HND | M+P | 4 | N | P | Ind | Ind | N | | |

HARPER ADAMS Agric COLL

Agricultural Engineering	H330	4SW deg	M/P g	8-12	MO $	M$	Dip	CCCC$	Ind	3	8/24
Agricultural Engineering with Marketing and Mgt	H3N1	3FT/4SW deg	M/S g	8-12	MO $	M$	Dip	CCCC$	Ind	4	
Agricultural Engineering	033H	2FT/3SW HND	* g	2-8	N	P$	Ind	CC$	N	3	4/ 6

course details			**98 expected requirements**							*96 entry stats*
TITLE	CODE	COURSE	SUBJECTS	A/AS	ND/C	AGNVQ	IB	SQA(H)	SQA	RATIO A/AS
HERIOT-WATT Univ										
Applied Physics with Microelectro Manuf (MPhys)	F3H7	4FT deg	P+M	BC		M$ go	30	BBBB	Ind	
Electronics with Microelectronic Manuf Eng(MEng)	H6H7	5FT deg	P+M	CDD		M$ go	28	BBBC	Ind	
Industrial and Business Studies	HN71	4FT deg	M	CDD	HN	M$ go	28	BBB	HN	
Mechanical Engineering	H300	4FT deg	M+P g	CDD	HN	M$^	28	BBB	HN	
Mechanical Engineering (Computer-aided Eng)	H370	4FT deg	M+P g	CDD	HN	M$^	28	BBB	HN	
Mechanical Engineering (MEng)	H301	5FT deg	M+P	CDD	HN	M$ ^	28	BBB	Ind	
Mechanical Engineering with Computer Aided Engin	H3H1	3FT deg								
Mechanical Engineering with Energy Resource Eng	H3J9	4FT deg	M+P g	CDD	HN	M$^	28	BBB	HN	
Mechanical Engineering with Energy Resource Engi	H3JX	3FT deg								
Offshore Eng with Chemical & Process Eng (MEng)	H367	5FT deg	M+C g	CCD	$		30	BBBB	$	
Offshore Eng with Electrical and Elec Eng (MEng)	H365	5FT deg	M+P	CDD	MO		28	BBBC	Ind	
Offshore Engineering with Chemical & Process Eng	H366	4FT deg	M+C g	CCD	$		30	BBBB	$	
Offshore Engineering with Civil Eng (MEng)	H361	5FT deg	M+P	CDD	HN		30	BBBC	HN	
Offshore Engineering with Civil Engineering	H360	4FT deg	M+P	CDD	HN		30	BBBC	HN	
Offshore Engineering with Electrical & Elec Eng	H364	4FT deg	M+P	CDD	MO		28	BBBC	Ind	
Offshore Engineering with Mechanical Eng (MEng)	H363	5FT deg	M+P g	CDD	HN		28	BBB	HN	
Offshore Engineering with Mechanical Engineering	H362	4FT deg	M+P g	CDD	HN		28	BBB	HN	
Combined Studies *Mechanical Engineering*	Y100	4FT deg	M+P	DDE	Ind	M$ go	26	BCCC	Ind	
Univ of HERTFORDSHIRE										
Applied Physics/Manufacturing Systems	F3H7	3FT deg	M+P	12	3M $	M$ gi	24$	CCCC$	Ind	
Applied Statistics/Manufacturing Systems	G4H7	3FT deg	*	12	3M	M$ gi	24	CCCC	Ind	
Astronomy/Manufacturing Systems	F5H7	3FT deg	M g	12	3M $	M$ gi	24$	CCCC$	Ind	
Automotive Engineering	H340	3FT/4SW deg	M+P/S/Cs	18	3M $	Ind	$	Ind	Ind	11 8/16
Automotive Engineering (Extended)	H348▼	4EXT/5EXTSW deg	*	2	N	Ind	$	Ind	Ind	1 4/14
Automotive Engineering (MEng)	H341	4FT/5SW deg	M+2S	22	5M		Ind	Ind	Ind	
Business/Manufacturing Systems	N1H7	3FT deg	*	18	4M+4D	M$6 gi	26	BBBC	Ind	
Chemistry/Manufacturing Systems	F1H7	3FT deg	C g	12	3M $	MS gi	24$	CCCC$	Ind	
Computing/Manufacturing Systems	G5H7	3FT deg	*	12	3M	M$ gi	24	CCCC	Ind	2
Economics/Manufacturing Systems	L1H7	3FT deg	*	12	3M	M$ gi	24	CCCC	Ind	1
Electronics/Manufacturing Systems	H6H7	3FT deg	* g	12	3M	M$ gi	24	CCCC	Ind	
Environmental Science/Manufacturing Systems	F9H7	3FT deg	*	14	MO	M$ gi	26	BCCC	Ind	
European Studies/Manufacturing Systems	T2H7	3FT deg	*	14	MO	M$ gi	26	BCCC	Ind	
Human Biology/Manufacturing Systems	B1H7	3FT deg	S g	12	3M $	MS gi	24$	CCCC$	Ind	2
Innovation and Enterprise Technology (extended)	HN7C	4FT deg								
Linguistic Science/Manufacturing Systems	Q1H7	3FT deg	*	14	MO	M$ gi	26	BCCC	Ind	
Manufacturing Systems	H712	3FT deg	*	12	3M $	M$ gi	24	CCCC	Ind	
Manufacturing Systems Engineering	H710	3FT/4SW deg	2(M/P/S/Cs)	16	3M	Ind	$	Ind	Ind	5
Manufacturing Systems Engineering (Extended)	H718▼	4FT/5EXTSW deg	*	2	N	Ind	Dip$	Ind	Ind	3
Manufacturing Systems Engineering (MEng)	H711	4FT/5SW deg	3(M/P/S/Cs/Ds)	22	5M		Ind	Ind	Ind	
Manufacturing Systems Engineering with French	H7R1	3FT deg								
Manufacturing Systems Engineering with German	H7R2	3FT deg								
Manufacturing Systems/Applied Physics	H7F3	3FT deg	M+P	12	3M $	M$ gi	24$	CCCC$	Ind	
Manufacturing Systems/Applied Statistics	H7G4	3FT deg	*	12	3M	M$ gi	24	CCCC	Ind	
Manufacturing Systems/Astronomy	H7F5	3FT deg	M g	12	3M $	M$ gi	24$	CCCC$	Ind	
Manufacturing Systems/Business	H7N1	3FT deg	*	18	4M+4D	M$6 gi	26	BBBC	Ind	
Manufacturing Systems/Chemistry	H7F1	3FT deg	C g	12	3M $	MS gi	24$	CCCC$	Ind	
Manufacturing Systems/Computing	H7G5	3FT deg	*	12	3M	M$ gi	24	CCCC	Ind	
Manufacturing Systems/Economics	H7L1	3FT deg	*	12	3M	M$ gi	24	CCCC	Ind	1
Manufacturing Systems/Electronics	H7H6	3FT deg	* g	12	3M $	M$ gi	24$	CCCC$	Ind	
Manufacturing Systems/Environmental Science	H7F9	3FT deg	*	14	MO	M$ gi	26	BCCC	Ind	

course details			98 expected requirements							96 entry stats	
TITLE	CODE	COURSE	SUBJECTS	A/AS	ND/C	AGNVQ	IB	SQA(H)	SQA	RATIO	A/AS
Manufacturing Systems/European Studies	H7T2	3FT deg	*	14	MO	M$ gi	24	BCCC	Ind		
Manufacturing Systems/Human Biology	H7B1	3FT deg	S g	12	3M $	MS gi	24$	CCCC$	Ind		
Manufacturing Systems/Linguistic Science	H7Q1	3FT deg	*	14	MO	M$ gi	26	BCCC	Ind		
Manufacturing Systems/Operational Research	H7N2	3FT deg	*	12	3M	M$ gi	24	CCCC	Ind		
Manufacturing Systems/Philosophy	H7V7	3FT deg	*	14	MO	M$ gi	26	BCCC	Ind		
Mechanical Engineering	H300	3FT/4SW deg	M+P/S/Cs	18	3M $	Ind	Dip	Ind	Ind	7	6/16
Mechanical Engineering (Extended)	H308▼	4FT/5EXTSW deg	*	2	N	Ind	Dip$	Ind	Ind	1	
Mechanical Engineering (MEng)	H301	4FT/5SW deg	M+2S	22	5M		Ind	Ind	Ind		
Operational Research/Manufacturing Systems	N2H7	3FT deg	*	12	3M	M$ gi	24	CCCC	Ind		
Philosophy/Manufacturing Systems	V7H7	3FT deg	*	14	MO	M$ gi	26	BCCC	Ind		
Product Design	H772	3FT deg	Ad/Ds/Fa+Pf g	X	X	Ind	Ind	Ind	Ind		
Product Design	E772	3FT deg	Ad/Ds/Fa+Pf g	X	X	Ind	Ind	Ind	Ind		
Product Engineering	H700	3FT/4SW deg	2(M/P/S/Cs)	16	3M	Ind	Dip	Ind	Ind	4	
Product Engineering (Extended)	H708▼	4FT/5EXTSW deg	*	2	N	Ind	Dip$	Ind	Ind		
Combined Modular Scheme *Manufacturing Systems*	Y100	3FT deg	*	12	3M	M$ gi	24	CCCC	Ind		
Mechatronics	63HH▼	2FT HND	M+P/S	2	N	Ind	$	Ind	Ind		

Univ of HUDDERSFIELD

Automotive Engineering	H340	4SW deg	M+S	10-14	3M $	ME	Ind	Ind	Ind		
Automotive Engineering (Ext)	H348	5SW deg	* g	DD	N	P go	Dip	CCC	Ind		
Automotive Engineering (MEng)	H341	5SW deg	M+S	CCC	3D $	M$3/^	Ind	Ind	Ind		
Automotive Technology	H345	3FT/4SW deg	* g	14	4M	M	Ind	Ind	Ind		
Computer-Aided Design	H3H1	3FT/4SW deg	* g	14	4M	M	Ind	Ind	Ind		
Engineering Systems: Manufacture	H751	4SW deg	M+S	12	4M $	M$ go	Ind	Ind	Ind		
Engineering Systems: Manufacture (Extended)	H758	5SW deg	* g	DD	N	P go	Dip	CCC	Ind		
Engineering Systems: Manufacture (MEng)	H752	5SW deg	M+S	18	3D $	M$3/^ go	Ind	Ind	Ind		
Logistics and Supply Chain Management	N9H7	3FT/4SW deg	* g	14-18	Ind	Ind	Ind	BBB	Ind		
Manufacturing and Operations Management	HN71	4SW deg	* g	14	4M	M go	Ind	Ind	Ind		
Mechanical Engineering	H300	4SW deg	M+S	10-14	3M $	ME	Ind	Ind	Ind		
Mechanical Engineering (Energy and Env) (Ext)	H3JX	5SW deg	* g	DD	N	P go	Dip	CCC	Ind		
Mechanical Engineering (Energy and Env) (MEng)	H3JY	5SW deg	M+S	CCC	3D $	M$3/^	Ind	Ind	Ind		
Mechanical Engineering (Energy and Environment)	H3J9	4SW deg	M+S	10-14	3M $	ME	Ind	Ind	Ind		
Mechanical Engineering (Extended)	H308	5SW deg	* g	DD	N	P go	Dip	CCC	Ind		
Mechanical Engineering (MEng)	H303	5SW deg	M+S	CCC	3D $	M$3/^	Ind	Ind	Ind		
Mechanical and Automotive Design	HH37	4SW deg	M+S	10	3M $	ME	Ind	Ind	Ind		
Mechanical and Automotive Design (Extended)	HH3T	5SW deg	* g	DD	N	P go	Dip	CCC	Ind		
Mechanical and Automotive Design (MEng)	HH73	5SW deg	M+S	18	3D	M$3/^	Ind	Ind	Ind		
Product Design	HW72	4SW deg	Pf+Ar g	14	N	M$ gi	Ind	Ind	Ind		
Product Design	EW72	4SW deg	Pf+Ar g	14	N	M$ gi	Ind	Ind	Ind		
Product Development	H3N9	3FT/4SW deg	* g	14	4M	M	Ind	Ind	Ind		
Manufacturing Systems	157H	2FT HND	M/P	2	N	P$	Ind	Ind	Ind		
Mechanical Engineering	003H	2FT HND	M/P	2	N	PE	Ind	Ind	Ind		
Product Design	27WE	3SW HND	Pf+Ar g	8	N	P$ gi	Ind	Ind	Ind		
Product Design	27WH	3SW HND	Pf+Ar g	8	N	P$ gi	Ind	Ind	Ind		

Univ of HULL

Engineering Design & Manufacture (4 Yrs) (MEng)	H765	4FT deg	M	CCC	MO $	M$^ gi	26$	BCCCC	Ind	26	
Mechanical Design Engineering	HH37	3FT deg	M	CCC	MO $	M$6/^ gi	26$	BCCCC	Ind	5	
Mechanical Engineering	H300	3FT deg	M	CCC	MO $	M$6/^ gi	26$	BCCCC	Ind	6	8/20
Mechanical Engineering (4 Yrs) (MEng)	H301	4FT deg	M	CCC	MO $	M$6/^ gi	26$	BCCCC	Ind	9	
Mechanical Engineering (Yr 1 Franchised)	H302	4FT deg	*	CD	N	P*6/^ gi	24	BCCC	Indctn	2	
Mechanical and Manufacturing Engineering	H701	3FT deg	M	CCC	MO $	M$6/^ gi	26$	BCCCC	Ind	9	
Mechanical and Materials Engineering	HJ3M	3FT deg	M	CCC	MO $	M$6/^ gi	26$	BCCCC	Ind	7	

Engineering – Mechanical and Production 25

			98 expected requirements							96 entry stats	
TITLE	**CODE**	**COURSE**	**SUBJECTS**	**A/AS**	**NO/C**	**AGNVQ**	**IB**	**SQA(H)**	**SQA**	**RATIO**	**A/AS**
Mechatronics	HH3P	3FT deg	S+M	20	MO	M$+	26$	BCCCC	Ind		
Mechatronics (MEng)	HH36	4FT deg	S+M	BCC	MO+2D$	ME^ gi	26$	BCCCC	Ind	4	18/24
Mechatronics (Yr 1 Franchised)	HH63	4FT deg	* g	10	N	P*6/^ gi	24	CCCCD	Ind		
IMPERIAL COLL (Univ of London)											
Mechanical Eng (Inc Tot Tech a 1:4:1 SW) (MEng)	H301	4FT deg	M+P	ABB	HN $	X	$	CSYS$	HN$	5	26/30
Mechanical Engineering (Inc Tot Tech a 1:3:1 SW)	H300	3FT deg	M+P	ABB	HN $	X	$	CSYS$	HN$	50	
Mechanical Engineering with a Yr Abroad	H304	4FT deg	M+P	ABB	HN $	X	$	CSYS$	HN$	28	
KING'S COLL LONDON (Univ of London)											
Manufacturing Systems Engineering	H710	3FT deg	M+P	BCC	MO+1D		28	BBCCC$	Ind		
Manufacturing Systems Engineering with Mgt	H7N1	3FT deg	M+P	BCC	MO+1D		28	BBCCC$	Ind	6	18/18
Manufacturing Systems and Management	HN71	3FT deg	M+P	BCC	MO+1D		28	BBCCC$	Ind	5	
Mechatronics	HH36	3FT deg	M+P	BCC	MO+1D		28	BBCCC$	Ind	7	16/26
Mechatronics and Manufacturing Systems	HH6T	4FT deg	M+P	BCC	MO+1D		28	BBCCC$	Ind	2	16/18
KINGSTON Univ											
Automotive Systems Engineering	H340	3FT deg	2S	4-6	2M $	ME2	Ind	Ind	Ind	4	5/11
Automotive Systems Engineering	H341	4SW deg	2S	4-6	2M $	ME2	Ind	Ind	Ind		
Manufacturing Systems Engineering	H715	4FT SW deg	2S	4-6	2M $	ME2	Ind	Ind	Ind		
Manufacturing Systems Engineering	H714	3FT deg	2S	4-6	2M $	ME2	Ind	Ind	Ind		
Manufacturing Systems Engineering	H718	4EXT/5EXTSW deg	*	4-6	Ind	Ind	Ind	Ind	Ind	7	
Manufacturing Systems Engineering (BEng/MEng)	H712	3FT/4FT deg	M+S	6-8	3M $	Ind	Ind	Ind	Ind		
Manufacturing Systems Engineering (BEng/MEng)	H713	4SW/5SW deg	M+S	6-8	3M $	Ind	Ind	Ind	Ind		
Mechanical Engineering	H302	3FT deg	2S	4-6	2M $	ME2	Ind	Ind	Ind		
Mechanical Engineering	H305	4FT deg	2S	4-6	2M $	ME2	Ind	Ind	Ind		
Mechanical Engineering	H308	4EXT/5EXTSW deg	*	4-6	Ind	Ind	Ind	Ind	Ind	2	
Mechanical Engineering (BEng/MEng)	H304	4SW/5SW deg	M+S	6-8	Ind	Ind	Ind	Ind	Ind	1	
Mechanical Engineering (BEng/MEng)	H303	3FT/4FT deg	M+S	6-8	Ind	Ind	Ind	Ind	Ind	1	
LANCASTER Univ											
Engineering (Mechanical)	H300	3FT/4SW deg	M+P/Cs/Es/Ds g	20	MO+1D		30$	BBBBB$	Ind		
Engineering (Mechanical) (MEng)	H303	4FT/5SW deg	M+P/Cs/Es/Ds g	20	MO+2D		30$	BBBBB$	Ind		
Mechanical Engineering with Management Sci(MEng)	H3ND	4FT/5SW deg	M+P/Cs/Es/Ds g	20	MO+2D		30$	BBBBB$	Ind		
Mechanical Engineering with Management Science	H3N1	3FT/4SW deg	M+P/Cs/Es/Ds g	20	MO+1D		30$	BBBBB$	Ind		
Mechatronics	HH63	3FT/4SW deg	M+P/Cs/Es/Ds g	20	MO+1D		30$	BBBBB$	Ind		
Mechatronics (MEng)	HH3Q	4FT/5SW deg	M+P/Cs/Es/Ds g	24	MO+2D		30$	BBBBB$	Ind		
Univ of LEEDS											
Automative Engineering	H340	4FT deg	M+P g	BBC	4M+2D$ Ind		30$	ABBBC	Ind		
Civil Engineering with Transport Engineering	H3J9	3FT/4FT deg	M g	CCC	Ind	Ind	Ind	Ind	Ind		
Mathematical Engineering	H3G1	3FT/4FT deg	M+P+S g	BBC	4M+2D$ Ind		30$	ABBBC	Ind	5	14/26
Mechanical Engineering	H300	3FT/4FT deg	M+P g	BCC	4M+2D$ D$^ go		28$	BBBBC	HN$	6	12/26
Mechanical with Medical Engineering	HH3P	4FT deg	M+P g	BBC	3M+3D$		30$	ABBBC	Ind		
Mechatronics	HH36	3FT/4FT deg	M+P g	BBC	4M+2D$ D$^ go		30$	ABBBC	Ind	5	18/24
Mgt with Mechanical & Manufacturing Engineering	H3N1	3FT/4FT deg	M g	BBC	1M+5D$ D$^ go		30$	CSYS	Ind	10	16/28
LEEDS METROPOLITAN Univ											
Technology and Management	H700	3FT/4SW deg									
Technology and Management (2/3 years)	007H	2FT/3SW deg									
Univ of LEICESTER											
Mechanical	H300	3FT deg	M+P g	18	4M $	M$6^	28$	BBBBC$	Ind		10/24
Mechanical (MEng)	H305	4FT deg	M+P g	18	5M $	M$6^	28$	ABBBB$	Ind		
Mechanical with Industry	H302	4SW deg	M+P g	18	4M $	M$6^	28$	BBBBC$	Ind		
Mechanical with Industry (MEng)	H306	5SW deg	M+P g	18	5M $	M$6^	28$	ABBBB$	Ind		

course details			98 expected requirements							96 entry stats	
TITLE	CODE	COURSE	SUBJECTS	A/AS	NO/C	AGNVQ	IB	SQA(H)	SQA	RATIO	A/AS
Mechanical with Industry in Europe	H303	4SW deg	M+P g	18	5M $	M$6^	28$	BBBBC$	Ind		
Mechanical with Industry in Europe (MEng)	H304	5SW deg	M+P g	18	5M $	M$6^	28$	ABBBB$	Ind		

Univ of LINCOLNSHIRE and HUMBERSIDE

TITLE	CODE	COURSE	SUBJECTS	A/AS	NO/C	AGNVQ	IB	SQA(H)	SQA	RATIO	A/AS
Engineering (Manufacturing Systems)	H712	3FT deg	M+P/S g	18	1M+4D$	Ind	Ind	BBBCC$	Ind		
Engineering (Mechanical & Manufacturing Systems)	HH37	3FT deg	M+P/S g	18	1M+4D	Ind	Ind	CCCBB$	Ind		
Engineering (Mechanical Engineering)	H300	3FT/4SW deg	M+P/S g	18	1M+4D$	Ind	Ind	CCCBB$	Ind		
Engineering (Mechanical and Electrical)	HH53	3FT deg	M+P/S	18	1M+4D$	Ind	26	BBBCC$	Ind		
Engineering Refrigeration with Air Conditioning	073H▼	2FT HND	g		Ind	Ind	Ind	Ind	Ind		

Univ of LIVERPOOL

TITLE	CODE	COURSE	SUBJECTS	A/AS	NO/C	AGNVQ	IB	SQA(H)	SQA	RATIO	A/AS
Integrated Eng with Manufacturing Systems (BEng)	H1H7	3FT deg	M+P	20	4M+1D$		30$	BBBBB	Ind		
Manufacturing Engineering and Management (BEng)	H7N1	3FT deg	M+P	20	4M+1D$		30$	BBBBB	Ind	7	
Materials, Design and Manufacture	HJ35	3FT deg	M+P/C	18	4M+1D$		30$	BBBBB	Ind		
Mechanical Engineering (BEng Hons)	H310	4EXT deg	*	18	3M $		25$	BBBCC	Ind	3	8/18
Mechanical Engineering (BEng)	H385	4FT deg	*	18	3M $		25$	BBBCC	Ind		
Mechanical Engineering (BEng)	H300	3FT deg	M+P	20	4M+1D$		30$	BBBBB	Ind	9	12/28
Mechanical Engineering (MEng)	H301	4FT deg	M+P	20	4M+1D$		30$	BBBBB	Ind	7	14/26
Mechanical Engineering with Management (BEng)	H3N1	3FT deg	M+P	20	4M+1D$		30$	BBBBB	Ind		
Mechanical Engineering with Management (MEng)	H3NC	4FT deg	M+P	20	4M+1D$		30$	BBBBB	Ind	6	
Mechanical Systems and Design Engineering (BEng)	HH37	3FT deg	M+P	20	4M+1D$		30$	BBBBB	Ind	8	
Mechanical Systems and Design Engineering (MEng)	HH73	4FT deg	M+P	20	4M+1D$		30$	BBBBB	Ind	3	22/28
Mechanical with Maritime & Offshore Engineering	H3J6	3FT deg	M+P	20	4M+1D$		30$	BBBBB	Ind	18	

LIVERPOOL JOHN MOORES Univ

TITLE	CODE	COURSE	SUBJECTS	A/AS	NO/C	AGNVQ	IB	SQA(H)	SQA	RATIO	A/AS
Engineering (MEng)	HH37	4FT deg		16							
Engineering (MEng) foundation	HH3R▼	4FT deg									
Manufacturing Systems Engineering	H710	3FT/4SW deg	M+P	10	3M	M					
Manufacturing Systems Engineering (Extended)	H718▼	4EXT/5EXTSW deg		4-10							
Mechanical Engineering	H300	3FT/4SW deg	M+P	10	3M	M				9	6/14
Mechanical Engineering (Extended)	H308▼	4EXT/5EXTSW deg		4-10						3	
Mechanical and Manufacturing Tech (Foundation)	HH7H▼	4FT/5SW deg									
Mechanical and Manufacturing Technology	HH73	3FT/4SW deg								1	
Mechanical and Marine Engineering	H350	3FT/4SW deg	M+P	DDE	3M					3	6/18
Mechanical and Marine Engineering (Extended)	H358▼	4EXT/5EXTSW deg		8						3	
Product Design Engineering	H770	3FT deg	Pf+Ar	CC	2M+3D	D$/M6				10	8/20
Product Design and Business	NH17	3FT deg	Ar+Pf	14-16	5M+3D	D/M^	28$	BCCC			
Technology Management	HN71	3FT/4SW deg	* g	10	4M	M				2	6/18
Technology Management (Extended)	HN7C▼	4EXT/5EXTSW deg	* g	6	3M					4	
Visual Studies and Product Design	WH17	3FT deg	Pf/Fa	CC	5M+3D	D$/M$6^	28$	CCCC		1	8/14
Engineering (Mechanical & Manufacturing) (Ext)	37HH▼	3FT HND	E		N					2	
Engineering (Mechanical and Manufacturing)	73HH	2FT/3SW HND	E		N	P				8	
Engineering (Mechatronics)	63HH	2FT/3SW HND	E		N	P					
Engineering (Mechatronics) (Foundation)	6HHH▼	3FT/4SW HND									

LOUGHBOROUGH Univ

TITLE	CODE	COURSE	SUBJECTS	A/AS	NO/C	AGNVQ	IB	SQA(H)	SQA	RATIO	A/AS
Automotive Engineering	H340	3FT deg	M+P	BBC	4D		28$	Ind	Ind	12	18/30
Automotive Engineering (4 Yr MEng)	H343	4FT deg	M+P	26	4D		30$	Ind	Ind	6	24/30
Automotive Engineering (4 Yr SW)	H341	4SW deg	M+P	BBC	4D		28$	Ind	Ind	6	18/24
Automotive Engineering (5 Yr SW MEng)	H342	5SW deg	M+P	26	4D		30$	Ind	Ind		
Electromechanical Power Eng (5 Yr SW) MEng	HHM3	5SW deg	M+P	BBC	3M+2D	DE6/^ go	28$	Ind	Ind	2	
Electromechanical Power Engineering	HH35	3FT deg	M+P	20	3M+2D	DE6/^ go	28$	Ind	Ind	11	
Electromechanical Power Engineering (4 Yr MEng)	HHN3	4FT deg	M+P	BBC	3M+2D	DE6/^ go	28$	Ind	Ind	3	
Electromechanical Power Engineering (4 Yr SW)	HH53	4SW deg	M+P	20	3M+2D	DE6/^ go	28$	Ind	Ind		

			98 expected requirements							96 entry stats	
course details											
TITLE	CODE	COURSE	SUBJECTS	A/AS	ND/C	RGNVQ	IB	SQA(H)	SQA	RATIO	A/AS
Electronics Manufacture and Management	H790	3FT deg	M	18	3M+2D	DN6/^ go	28$	Ind	Ind		
Electronics Manufacture and Management (4 Yr SW)	H791	4SW deg	M	18	3M+2D	DN6/^ go	28$	Ind	Ind		
Electronics Manufacture and Mgt (4 Yr MEng)	H792	4FT deg	M	18	3M+2D	DN6/^ go	28$	Ind	Ind		
Electronics Manufacture and Mgt (5 Yr SW) (MEng)	H793	5SW deg	M	18	3M+2D	DN6/^ go	28$	Ind	Ind		
Industrial Design & Packaging Tech (4 Yr SW)	H777	4SW deg	* g	18	3M+2D		28$	Ind	Ind		
Industrial Design and Technology	H775	3FT deg	* g	18	3M+2D		28$	Ind	Ind	3	14/24
Industrial Design and Technology (4 Yr SW)	H776	4SW deg	* g	18	3M+2D		28$	Ind	Ind	4	16/24
Manufacturing Engineering and Management	H780	3FT deg	M+P	18	3M+2D	DN6/^ go	28$	Ind	Ind	6	14/18
Manufacturing Engineering and Management (MEng)	H782	4FT deg	M+P	18	3M+2D	DN6/^ go	28$	Ind	Ind		
Manufacturing Engineering and Mgt (4 Yr SW)	H781	4SW deg	M+P	18	3M+2D	DN6/^ go	28$	Ind	Ind	7	16/18
Manufacturing Engineering and Mgt(5 Yr SW)(MEng)	H783	5SW deg	M+P	18	3M+2D	DN6/^ go	28$	Ind	Ind	12	
Mechanical Engineering	H300	3FT deg	M+P	20	3M+2D	DE6/^ go	28$	Ind	Ind	9	16/28
Mechanical Engineering (4 Yr MEng)	H303	4FT deg	M+P	20	3M+2D	DE6/^ go	28$	Ind	Ind	10	18/30
Mechanical Engineering (4 Yr SW)	H301	4SW deg	M+P	20	3M+2D	DE6/^ go	28$	Ind	Ind	4	18/26
Mechanical Engineering (5 Yr SW MEng)	H302	5SW deg	M+P	20	3M+2D	DE6/^ go	28$	Ind	Ind	6	16/26
Product Design and Manufacture	H770	3FT deg	M	18	3M+2D	DN6/^ go	28$	Ind	Ind	7	14/26
Product Design and Manufacture (4 Yr MEng)	H772	4FT deg	M	18	3M+2D	DN6/^ go	28$	Ind	Ind		
Product Design and Manufacture (4 Yr SW)	H771	4SW deg	M	18	3M+2D	DN6/^ go	28$	Ind	Ind	4	14/28
Product Design and Manufacture (5 Yr SW MEng)	H773	5SW deg	M	18	3M+2D	DN6/^ go	28$	Ind	Ind		
LUTON Univ											
Computer Aided Manufacturing Technology	H765	3FT deg	g	12-16	MO/DO	M/D	32	BBCC	Ind		
Design and Manufacturing	HW72	3FT deg	g	12-16	MO/DO	M/D	32	BBCC	Ind	17	
Manufacturing Business Systems	H710	3FT deg	g	12-16	MO/DO	M/D	32	BBCC	Ind		
Manufacturing Quality Systems	H711	3FT deg	g	12-16	MO/DO	M/D	32	BBCC	Ind		
Integrated Engineering (Mechatronics)	63HH	2FT HND	g	4-8	N/MO	P/M	26	CCDD	Ind	1	
Mechanical and Production Engineering	003H	2FT HND	g	4-8	N/MO	P/M	26	CCDD	Ind		
Motor Vehicle Engineering and Management	043H	2FT HND	g	4-8	N/MO	P/M	26	CCDD	Ind	4	
Univ of MANCHESTER											
Engineering with Business	H1N1	3FT deg	M+P	18	Ind		30	AAAAA	Ind	10	
Engineering with Business	H1NC	4FT deg	M+P	18	Ind		30	AAAAA	Ind	5	
Engineering, Business and Management	HN11	3FT deg	M+P	18	Ind		30	AAAAA	Ind	14	
Mechanical Eng and Energy Systs(Integ Euro Prog)	H305	4FT deg	M+P	18	Ind		30	AAAAA	Ind	8	
Mechanical Engineering	H300	3FT deg	M+P	18	Ind		30	AAAAA	Ind	9	16/24
Mechanical Engineering	H303	4FT deg	M+P	18	Ind		30	AAAAA	Ind	10	20/28
Mechanical Engineering (Int Eur Prog) (MEng)	H302	4FT deg	M+P	18	Ind		30	AAAAA	Ind	9	20/26
Mechanical Engineering and Energy Systems	H304	4FT deg	M+P	18	Ind		30	AAAAA	Ind	16	
Mechanical Engineering and Energy Systems	H301	4FT deg	M+P	18	Ind		30	AAAAA	Ind		
UMIST (Manchester)											
Engineering Manufacture and Management (MEng)	H7N1	4FT deg	M+P g	BBB	DO $	Ind	32$	CSYS$	Ind	8	22/30
Manufacturing Systems Engineering	H716	3FT deg	M+P g	BCC	MO+3D$	Ind	30$	CSYS$	Ind	7	
Mechanical Eng with Design, Mats and Man (MEng)	HJ3M	4FT deg	M+P g	BCC	MO+3D$	Ind	30$	CSYS$	Ind		
Mechanical Engineering	H300	3FT deg	M+P g	BCC	MO+3D$	Ind	30$	CSYS$	Ind	8	16/28
Mechanical Engineering (MEng)	H301	4FT deg	M+P g	BCC	MO+3D$	Ind	30$	CSYS$	Ind	2	16/28
Mechanical Engineering with Design, Mats and Man	HJ35	3FT deg	M+P g	BCC	MO+3D$	Ind	30$	CSYS$	Ind		
Mechanical Engineering with Materials	H3J5	3FT deg	M+P g	BCC	MO+3D$	Ind	30$	CSYS$	Ind	6	14/28
Mechanical Engineering with Materials (MEng)	H3JM	4FT deg	M+P g	BCC	MO+3D$	Ind	30$	CSYS$	Ind	2	
MANCHESTER METROPOLITAN Univ											
Manufacturing Management	HN71	3FT deg	* g	DDD	3M	M$	24$	BB$	Ind		10/16
Manufacturing Management (Foundation)	HN7C▼	4FT deg	M/P	E	2M $	P$	$	$	Ind		
Manufacturing Systems Engineering	H710	4FT deg	M/P	DDE	3M	ME	24$	BB$	Ind		

course details | 98 expected requirements | 96 entry stats

TITLE	CODE	COURSE	SUBJECTS	A/AS	NO/C	AGNVQ	IB	SQA(H)	SQA	RATIO A/AS
Manufacturing/Applicable Mathematics	GH17	3FT deg	M g	12	5M $	M$	27$	BCCCC$	Ind	
Manufacturing/Applied Physics	FH37	3FT deg	M+P g	12	5M $	M$	27$	BCCCC$	Ind	
Manufacturing/Computer Technology	GHM7	3FT deg	* g	12	5M	M$	27	BCCCC	Ind	
Manufacturing/Computing Science	GH57	3FT deg	* g	12	5M	M$	27	BCCCC	Ind	
Manufacturing/Economics	HL71	3FT deg	* g	16	1M+3D	M$	28	BBBCC	Ind	
Manufacturing/Electronics	HHP7	3FT deg	* g	12	5M	M$	27	BCCCC	Ind	
Manufacturing/Languages	HT79	3FT deg	* g	14	MO	M$	28	BBCCC	Ind	
Materials Science/Manufacturing	FH27	3FT deg	M/P/C g	12	4M $	M$	26$	CCCCC$	Ind	
Mech Eng and Manufacturing Systems (Foundation)	HH37▼	4FT deg	M/P	E	2M $	P$	$	$	Ind	
Mechanical Engineering	H300	3FT/4SW deg	M+P g	DDE	3M $	ME	24$	BB$	Ind	6/20
Mechanical Engineering (Foundation)	H308▼	4FT deg	M/P	E	2M $	PE	$	$	Ind	
Mechanical Engineering and Manufacturing Systems	HH3R	3FT/4SW deg	M+P g	DDE	3M $	ME	24$	BB$	Ind	
Mechatronics	HH36	3FT/4SW deg	M+P g	DDE	3M $	ME	24$	BB$	Ind	
Mechatronics (Foundation)	HH3P▼	4FT deg	M/P	E	2M $	P$	$	$	Ind	
Physics Studies/Manufacturing	FHH7	3FT deg	M+P g	12	5M $		27$	BCCCC$	Ind	
Polymer Science/Manufacturing	HJ74	3FT deg	C g	10	4M $	M$	26$	CCCCC$	Ind	
Psychology/Manufacturing	HL77	3FT deg	* g	18	1M+3D	D$	28	BBBCC	Ind	
Scientific Instrumentation/Manufacturing	HH67	3FT deg	M/P g	12	5M $	M$	27$	BCCCC$	Ind	
Social Studies of Technology/Manufacturing	HL73	3FT deg	* g	12	5M	M$	27	BCCCC		
Combined Studies (Foundation) Manufacturing	Y108▼	4FT deg	M/P	E	2M $	P$	$	$	Ind	
Mechanical Engineering and Manufacture	73HH	2FT/3SW HND	M+P g	E	N	ME	Dip	Ind	N	2/8
Mechanical Engineering and Mechatronics	63HH	2FT/3SW HND	M+P g	E	N	PE	Dip	Ind	N	

MIDDLESEX Univ

TITLE	CODE	COURSE	SUBJECTS	A/AS	NO/C	AGNVQ	IB	SQA(H)	SQA	RATIO A/AS
European Product Engineering and Management	H779▼	3FT deg	S g	10	3M	M$ go	24	Ind	Ind	
Manufacturing Engineering and Management	HN71▼	3FT/4SW deg	S g	10	3M	M$ go	24	Ind	Ind	
Manufacturing Foundation	H708▼	4EXT deg	* g	E	N	P$ go	Ind	Ind	Ind	
Manufacturing Management	H7N1▼	3FT deg	S g	10	3M	M$ go	24	Ind	Ind	
Mechanical Engineering	H300▼	4SW deg	S g	10	3M	M$ go	24	CCCC	Ind	
Mechanical Engineering Foundation	H308▼	4EXT deg	* g	E	N	P$ go	Ind	CC	Ind	
Mechatronics	HH63▼	3FT/4SW deg	S g	10	3M	M$ go	24	CCCC	Ind	
Joint Honours Degree Manufacturing Management	Y400	3FT deg	S g	10	3M	M$ go	24	Ind	Ind	
Joint Honours Degree Mechanical Engineering	Y400	3FT deg	S g	10	3M	M$ go	24	Ind	Ind	
Mechanical, Energy and Manufacturing Engineering	73HH▼	2FT HND	S g	E	N	P$ go	24	CC	Ind	

NAPIER Univ

TITLE	CODE	COURSE	SUBJECTS	A/AS	NO/C	AGNVQ	IB	SQA(H)	SQA	RATIO A/AS
Civil and Transportation Engineering	HH23	3SW/4SW deg	M	CC	Ind	Ind	Ind	BBCC$	Ind	5
Industrial Design	H770	4SW deg	Pf	DD	Ind	Ind	Ind	CCC	Ind	7
Industrial Design	E770	4SW deg	Pf	DD	Ind	Ind	Ind	CCC	Ind	
Manufacturing Systems Engineering	H710	3FT/4SW deg	M	CD	Ind	Ind	Ind	BBB$	Ind	
Mechanical Engineering	H300	3FT/4SW deg	M	CD	Ind	Ind	Ind	BBB$	Ind	

NENE COLLEGE

TITLE	CODE	COURSE	SUBJECTS	A/AS	NO/C	AGNVQ	IB	SQA(H)	SQA	RATIO A/AS
Product Design (Route A)	HW72	3FT deg	g	4	3M	P	24	CCC	Ind	
Product Design (Route B)	EW72	3FT deg								
Product Design (Route A)	27WH	2FT HND	g	2	N	P		CC	Ind	
Product Design (Route B)	27WE	2FT HND								

Univ of NEWCASTLE

TITLE	CODE	COURSE	SUBJECTS	A/AS	NO/C	AGNVQ	IB	SQA(H)	SQA	RATIO A/AS
Marine Engineering	H350	3FT deg	M+P	BCC-CCC	Ind		34$	CSYS	Ind	4 12/22
Marine Engineering	H351	4FT deg	*	CCC-CCD	Ind		34$	BBBB	Ind	5
Marine Technology (MEng)	H352	4FT deg	M+P	BBC	Ind		34$	CSYS	Ind	3 18/26

Engineering – Mechanical and Production   25

TITLE	CODE	COURSE	SUBJECTS	A/AS	ND/C	AGNVQ	IB	SQA(H)	SQA	RATIO A/AS
Marine Technology (MEng)	H353	5FT deg	*	CCC-CCD	Ind		34$	BBBB	Ind	10
Materials Design and Engineering (MEng)	HJ75	4FT deg	M+P g	BCC	3M+2D$		30$	CSYS$	Ind	
Materials Design and Engineering (MEng)	JH57	5FT deg	* g	18	5M $		26$	BBBB$	Ind	
Materials Engineering	JH53	3FT deg	M+P	BCC	3M+2D$		30$	CSYS$	Ind	
Materials Engineering	HJ35	4FT deg	*	18	5M $		26$	BBBB$	Ind	3
Mechanical Engineering	H300	3FT deg	M+P	BCC	3M+2D$		30$	CSYS$	Ind	7 14/26
Mechanical Engineering	H301	4FT deg	*	18	5M $		26$	BBBB$	Ind	8 14/22
Mechanical Engineering	H304	4FT deg	*	18	5M $		26$	BBBB$	Ind	
Mechanical Engineering (5 years)	H305	5FT deg								
Mechanical Engineering (Europe) (MEng)	H302	4FT deg	M+P g	BCC	3M+2D$		30$	CSYS$	Ind	8 16/22
Mechanical Engineering (Europe) (MEng)	H303	5FT deg	* g	18	5M $		26$	BBBB$	Ind	
Mechanical Engineering and Mechatronics (4 years)	HH36	4FT deg								
Mechanical Engineering and Mechatronics (5 yrs)	HH63	5FT deg								
Mechanical and Automotive Engineering (MEng)	H341	4FT deg	M+P	BCC	3M+2D$		30$	CSYS$	Ind	9 18/26
Mechanical and Automotive Engineering (MEng)	H342	5FT deg	*	18	5M $		26$	BBBB$	Ind	9
Mechanical and Design Engineering (4 years)	H771	4FT deg								
Mechanical and Design Engineering (5 years)	H772	5FT deg								
Mechanical and Manufacturing Engineering (MEng)	HH37	4FT deg	M+P	BCC	3M+2D$		30$	CSYS$	Ind	3
Mechanical and Manufacturing Engineering (MEng)	HH73	5FT deg	*	18	5M $		26$	BBBB$	Ind	6
Offshore Engineering	HJ36	3FT deg	M+P	BCC-CCC	Ind			CSYS	Ind	5
Offshore Engineering	JH63	4FT deg	*	CCC-CCD	Ind			BBBB	Ind	7

NEWCASTLE COLL

TITLE	CODE	COURSE								
Engineering (Mechanical/Manufacture)	003H▼	2FT HND								

Univ of Wales COLLEGE, NEWPORT

TITLE	CODE	COURSE	SUBJECTS	A/AS	ND/C	AGNVQ	IB	SQA(H)	SQA	
Integrated Manufacturing Technology	H708	3FT deg		10	N	D$	Ind	Ind	Ind	
Manufacturing Engineering	007H	2FT HND		2	N	P$	Ind	Ind	Ind	
Mechanical Engineering	003H	2FT HND		2	N	P$	Ind	Ind	Ind	
Mechatronics	63HH	2FT HND		2	N	P$	Ind	Ind	Ind	

NORTHBROOK COLLEGE Sussex

TITLE	CODE	COURSE	SUBJECTS	A/AS						
Engineering (Mechanical/Manufacture)	37HH	2FT HND	*	N						
Motor Vehicle Engineering	043H	2FT HND	*	N						

NORTH EAST WALES INST of HE

TITLE	CODE	COURSE	SUBJECTS	A/AS	ND/C	AGNVQ	IB	SQA(H)	SQA	
Aeronautical/Mechanical Engineering	HH43	3FT deg		4-8	3M	M$	Ind	CCC	N$	
Manufacturing Engineering	H710	3FT deg		4-8	3M	M$	Ind	CCC	N$	
Manufacturing Systems Engineering with Bus St	H7ND	3FT deg		4-8	3M	M$	Ind	CCC	N$	
Manufacturing Engineering	007H	2FT HND		2-4	2M	P$	Ind	CC	N$	
Manufacturing Management	1N7H	2FT HND		2-4	2M	P$	Ind	CC	N$	
Mechanical Engineering	003H	2FT HND		2-4	2M	P$	Ind	CC	N$	

NORTH EAST WORCESTERSHIRE COLL

TITLE	CODE	COURSE								
Mechanical Engineering	003H	2FT HND								

Univ of NORTHUMBRIA

TITLE	CODE	COURSE	SUBJECTS	A/AS	ND/C	AGNVQ	IB	SQA(H)	SQA	RATIO A/AS
Engineering Technology (HND Top-up)	HH37	1/2FT deg	X	X	X	X	X	X	X	
Manufacturing Systems Engineering	H711	4FT deg	M+P/S g	12	3M $	ME2 gi	24$	BBBC$	Ind	
Manufacturing Systems Engineering	H710	3FT/4SW deg	M+P/S g	12	3M $	ME2 gi	24$	BBBC$	Ind	7
Manufacturing Systems Engineering	H718	5EXT deg	* g	2-4	Ind	Ind	Ind	Ind	Ind	3
Mechanical Engineering	H300	3FT/4SW deg	M+P/S g	12	3M $	ME2 gi	24$	BBBC$	Ind	8 8/18
Mechanical Engineering	H308▼	5EXT deg	* g	2-4	Ind	Ind	Ind	Ind	Ind	1 6/8
Mechanical Engineering	H301	3FT deg	M+P/S g	12	3M $	ME2 gi	24$	BBBC$	Ind	
Mechatronic Systems Design	HH36	3FT deg	M+P/S g	12	3M $	ME2 gi	24$	BBBC$	Ind	

course details			98 expected requirements							96 entry stats	
TITLE	CODE	COURSE	SUBJECTS	A/AS	NO/C	RGNVQ	IB	SQA(H)	SQA	RATIO	A/AS
Mechatronics System Design	HH3P	5EXT deg	* g	2-4	Ind	Ind	Ind	Ind	Ind		
Engineering (Mechanical and Production)	003H	2FT HND	M/P/S g	2-4	N	PE gi	Ind	Ind$	Ind	6	
Mechatronics	63HH	2FT HND	M/P g	2-4	Ind	Ind	Ind	Ind	Ind		

Univ of NOTTINGHAM

TITLE	CODE	COURSE	SUBJECTS	A/AS	NO/C	RGNVQ	IB	SQA(H)	SQA	RATIO	A/AS
Building Environment Engineering	H3K2	3FT deg	P+M	CCD-CDD	Ind	Ind	28$	Ind	Ind	3	16/24
Manufacturing Engineering & Mgt with Russian	H7R8	3FT/4FT deg	M g	CCC	Ind	Ind	28$	Ind	Ind		
Manufacturing Engineering and Management	H716	3FT/4FT deg	M	CCC	Ind	Ind	28$	Ind	Ind	3	17/28
Manufacturing Engineering and Mgt with French	H7R1	3FT/4FT deg	M g	CCC	Ind	Ind	28$	Ind	Ind	3	17/20
Manufacturing Engineering and Mgt with German	H7R2	3FT/4FT deg	M g	CCC	Ind	Ind	28$	Ind	Ind		
Manufacturing Engineering and Mgt with Japanese	H7TK	3FT/4FT deg	M	CCC	Ind	Ind	28$	Ind	Ind		
Manufacturing Engineering and Mgt with Spanish	H7R4	3FT/4FT deg	M g	CCC	Ind	Ind	28$	Ind	Ind	2	
Mechanical Design, Materials and Manufacture	HJ35	3FT/4FT deg	M+P	BCC-CCD	Ind	Ind	28$	Ind	Ind	4	14/28
Mechanical Engineering	H300	3FT/4FT deg	M+P	BBC-BCC	Ind	Ind	28$	Ind	Ind	12	20/30
Mechanical Engineering with French	H3R1	3FT/4FT deg	M+P g	BBC-BCC	Ind	Ind	28$	Ind	Ind	10	20/30
Mechanical Engineering with German	H3R2	3FT/4FT deg	M+P g	BBC-BCC	Ind	Ind	28$	Ind	Ind	9	22/25
Mechanical Engineering with Japanese	H3T4	3FT/4FT deg	M+P g	BBC-BCC	Ind	Ind	28$	Ind	Ind	7	
Mechanical Engineering with Mathematics	H3G1	3FT deg									
Mechanical Engineering with Russian	H3R8	3FT/4FT deg	M+P g	BBC-BCC	Ind	Ind	28$	Ind	Ind		
Mechanical Engineering with Spanish	H3R4	3FT/4FT deg	M+P g	BBC-BCC	Ind	Ind	28$	Ind	Ind		
Production and Operations Management	H711	3FT deg	M	CCC	Ind	Ind	28$	Ind	Ind	2	18/24
Production and Operations Management with French	H7RC	3FT deg	M g	CCC	Ind	Ind	28$	Ind	Ind	3	
Production and Operations Management with German	H7RF	3FT deg	M g	CCC	Ind	Ind	28$	Ind	Ind	3	
Production and Operations Mgt with Japanese	H7T4	3FT deg	M g	CCC	Ind	Ind	28$	Ind	Ind		
Production and Operations Mgt with Russian	H7RV	3FT deg	M g	CCC	Ind	Ind	28$	Ind	Ind		
Production and Operations Mgt with Spanish	H7RK	3FT deg	M g	CCC	Ind	Ind	28$	Ind	Ind	2	

NOTTINGHAM TRENT Univ

TITLE	CODE	COURSE	SUBJECTS	A/AS	NO/C	RGNVQ	IB	SQA(H)	SQA	RATIO	A/AS
Manufacturing Engineering (BEng/MEng)	H700	3FT/4SW deg	M g	14	3M $	Ind	Ind	DD$	Ind	3	6/12
Manufacturing Engineering (Extended)	H708▼	4EXT/5EXTSW deg	* g		Ind	Ind	Ind	Ind	Ind	1	
Mechanical Engineering (BEng/MEng)	H300	3FT/4SW deg	M g	14	3M $	ME	24$	CCCC$	N$	8	6/16
Mechanical Engineering (Extended)	H308▼	4EXT/5EXTSW deg	* g		Ind	Ind	Ind	Ind	Ind	2	6/17
Mechatronics (BEng/MEng)	HH36	3FT/4SW deg	M g	14	3M $	Ind	Ind	Ind	Ind		
Mechatronics (Extended)	HH3P▼	4FT/5SW deg	* g		Ind	Ind	Ind	Ind	Ind		
Manufacturing Engineering	007H▼	2FT HND	* g	4	N	Ind	Ind	D$	N	5	
Mechanical Engineering	003H▼	2FT HND	M g	4	2M $	PE	Ind	D$	Ind	5	4/8
Mechatronics	63HH	2FT HND	* g	4	Ind	Ind	Ind	Ind	Ind		

OXFORD Univ

TITLE	CODE	COURSE	SUBJECTS	A/AS	NO/C	RGNVQ	IB	SQA(H)	SQA	RATIO	A/AS
Mechanical Engineering (4 Yrs)	H300	4FT deg	M+P	AAB	DO		36	AAAAA	Ind	3	30/30

OXFORD BROOKES Univ

TITLE	CODE	COURSE	SUBJECTS	A/AS	NO/C	RGNVQ	IB	SQA(H)	SQA	RATIO	A/AS
Automotive Engineering	H340	3FT deg									
Mechanical Engineering	H302	4FT deg									
Mechanical Engineering	H300	3FT/4SW deg	M g	12	Ind	M$	Ind	Ind	Ind	6	6/18
Mechanical and Manufacturing Engineering	73HH	2FT/3SW HND	M g	12	Ind		Ind	Ind	Ind	2	

Univ of PAISLEY

TITLE	CODE	COURSE	SUBJECTS	A/AS	NO/C	RGNVQ	IB	SQA(H)	SQA	RATIO	A/AS
Manufacturing Systems with Management	H7N1	4SW/5SW deg	M g	DD	Ind	Ind	Ind	BCC$	Ind	3	
Manufacturing Systems with Management	H7NC	2FT Dip	M g	DD	Ind	Ind	Ind	CCC$	Ind		
Manufacturing Systems with Management (MEng)	H7ND	5SW deg	M g	CCC	Ind	Ind	Ind	BBC$	Ind		
Mechanical Engineering	H301	2FT Dip	M g	DD	Ind	Ind	Ind	CCC$	Ind		
Mechanical Engineering	H300	4SW/5SW deg	M+C/P g	DD	Ind	Ind	Ind	BCC$	Ind	4	
Mechanical Engineering (MEng)	H302	5SW deg	M+C/P g	CCC	Ind	Ind	Ind	BBBC$	Ind		

Engineering – Mechanical and Production   25

course details			98 expected requirements							96 entry stats	
TITLE	CODE	COURSE	SUBJECTS	A/AS	ND/C	AGNVQ	IB	SQA(H)	SQA	RATIO	A/AS
Univ of PLYMOUTH											
Design Technology and Business	H7N1	3FT/4SW deg	Ap g	10-11	5M $	M$	Ind	Ind	Ind	2	6/18
Manufacturing Systems Engineering (MEng Option)	H712	3FT/4SW 4FT/5SW deg	M+S/Ap g	10-11	MO $	ME	Ind	Ind	Ind	23	
Mechanical Engineering (MEng Option)	H300	3FT/4SW 4FT/5SW deg	M+S/Ap g	10-11	5M $	M$+	Ind	BBCC	Ind	8	6/18
Mechanical Engineering, Design and Manufacture	HH37	3FT deg			Ind	Ind	Ind		Ind		
Automotive Engineering (Somerset)	143H	2FT HND	Ap g	Ind	N	P$	Ind	Ind	Ind	3	
Mechanical Engineering, Design and Manufacture	73HH	2FT/3SW HND	M/S/Ds g	4-5	N $	P$	Ind	CCC	Ind	3	6/8
Univ of PORTSMOUTH											
Engineering Design & Materials	H770	3FT/4SW deg	2(M/P/C/Cs/Es)	16	4M $	M$6/^	26	BBBB	N$	9	
Manufacturing System Eng (MEng)(Ext Route Avail)	H700	3FT/4SW deg	2(M/P/C/Es/Cs)	16	4M $	M$6/^	26$	BBBB	Ind		
Mechanical Engineering (MEng) (Ext Route Avail)	H300	3FT/4SW deg	2(M/P/C/Es/Cs)	16	4M $	M$6/^	26$	BBBB	N$	6	4/18
Engineering (Mechanical/Manufacture)	73HH	2FT/3SW HND	M/P	4	1M	P$	Dip	CC	Ind	4	2/6
QUEEN MARY & WESTFIELD COLL (Univ of London)											
Mechanical Engineering	H300	3FT deg	M	CCD-BCC	4M $	M$^		BBBCC			
Mechanical Engineering	H303	4SW deg	M	CCD-BCC	4M	M$^		BBBCC			
Mechanical Engineering (MEng)	H301	4FT deg	M+P	BCC-BBB	5M $	M$^					
Mechanical Engineering and Materials (MEng)	JH53	4FT deg	M+P	22	3M+1D$ X			30$	BBBBB		
Mechanical Systems Engineering (MEng)	HH36	4FT deg	M+P	BCC-BBB	3M+2D$ M$^			30$	AABBB		
Science and Engineering (4 yrs with Foundation) Mechanical Engineering	Y157	4EXT deg	E		N	P					
QUEEN'S Univ Belfast											
Manufacturing Engineering	H780	3FT/4FT deg	M+P g	BCC	Ind	Ind	29$	BBBC	Ind	43	
Mech and Manuf Eng Exted (Dainton) Course (MEng)	HH37	4FT deg	M+P g	BBB	X	X	32$	X	X	3	24/30
Mechanical Engineering	H300	3FT/4FT deg	M+P g	BCC	Ind	Ind	29$	BBBC	Ind	5	16/28
Mechanical with Food Engineering	H3D4	3FT/4FT deg	M+P g	BCC	Ind	Ind	29$	BBBC	Ind		
Univ of READING											
Mechanical Engineering	H300	3FT deg	M+P g	CCC	4M+1D$ DE^ go		29$	BBBC$	Ind	10	12/26
Mechanical Engineering (Foundation)	H301	4EXT deg	* g	CDD	4M	M*6/^ go	27	BBCC	Ind	7	12/14
Mechanical Engineering (MEng)	H303	4FT deg	M+P g	BBC	3M+2D$ DE^ go		31$	BBBB$	Ind	1	
ROBERT GORDON Univ											
Mechanical Engineering	H300	3FT deg	M+S g	EE	N	Ind	Ind	CCC$	Ind	8	
Mechanical Engineering	H301	3FT/4FT deg	M+S g	EE	N	Ind	Ind	BCC$	Ind		
Mechanical and Offshore Engineering	H360	4FT deg	M+S g	EE	N	Ind	Ind	BCC$	Ind	4	
Mechanical Engineering	003H	2FT HND	* g	E	N	Ind	Ind	CC$	Ind	6	
RYCOTEWOOD COLL											
Engineering (Agriculture & the Environment)	033H	2FT HND	M/Ph/En	10	N	P	Ind	ABC	N		
Engineering (Construction Plant)	143H	2FT HND	M/Ph	10	N	P	Ind	ABC	N		
Engineering (Historic Vehicle Restoration)	543H	2FT HND	M/Ph/Ds	10	N	P	Ind	ABC	N		
SCOTTISH COLLEGE of TEXTILES											
Computing for Industry	GH57	4FT deg	* g	CC	Ind	M$	Dip	BBC	HN	1	
Univ of SALFORD											
Manufacturing Engineering	H702	4FT deg									
Manufacturing Engineering (3 or 4 Yrs)	H700	3FT/4SW deg	M+S/2S	18	3M+1D$ M		Ind	Ind	Ind	10	
Manufacturing Engineering with European Studies	H7T2	4SW deg									
Manufacturing Management	H7NC	4FT deg									
Manufacturing Management (NEWI) (4 Yrs)	H7N1	3FT/4SW deg	M/S	18	3M+1D$ M		Ind	Ind	Ind	11	
Manufacturing Management with European Studies	H7ND	4SW deg									
Mechanical Engineering	H306	4FT/5SW deg	M+S/2S	18	3M+1D M		Ind	Ind	Ind		

course details | 98 expected requirements | 96 entry stats

TITLE	CODE	COURSE	SUBJECTS	A/AS	NO/C	RGNVQ	IB	SQA(H)	SQA	RATIO	A/AS
Mechanical Engineering (Int) (4 Yrs)	H301	4SW deg	M+S/2S	18	3M+1D$	M	Ind	Ind	Ind	4	
Mechanical Engineering (MEng)	H300	3FT/4SW/5SW deg	M+S/2S	18	3M+1D$	M	Ind	Ind	Ind	11	12/22
Mechanical Engineering (Stockport)(4 Yrs)	H302	4FT deg		Ind	Ind		Ind	Ind	Ind	2	
Mechanical Engineering with European Studies	H3T2	4SW/5SW deg	M+S/2S g	18	3M+1D$	M	Ind	Ind	Ind	6	
Mechanical Engineering with European Studs(MEng)	H3TF	4FT deg	M+S/2S	18	Ind	M	Ind	Ind	Ind		
Mechatronics	HH6H	3FT/4SW deg	M+S/2S	18	Ind	M	Ind	Ind	Ind	11	
Mechatronics (4FT or 5 yr SW)	HH63	4FT/5SW deg	M+S	BCC-CCC	Ind	M	Ind	Ind	Ind	6	
Quality Management	H703▼	3FT deg		8	3M+2D	D	28	CCCC	Ind	3	8/14
Manufacturing Engineering	007H	2FT HND		2-4	N	P	24	CC	Ind	7	
Manufacturing Management	017H	2FT HND		2-4	N	P	24	CC	Ind	6	
Quality Management	307H▼	2FT HND		4	4M	M	24	CC	Ind	4	2/6

Univ of SHEFFIELD

TITLE	CODE	COURSE	SUBJECTS	A/AS	NO/C	RGNVQ	IB	SQA(H)	SQA	RATIO	A/AS
Mechanical Engineering	H300	4FT deg	M/P g	24	5M+1D$	DE^	32$	AABB$	Ind	6	20/30
Mechanical Engineering	H302	3FT deg	M/P g	24	5M+1D$	DE^	32$	AABB$	Ind		
Mechanical Engineering (incl Foundation Year)	H301	5FT deg	* g	20-22	5M+1D$	DE^	32	AABB	Ind	5	18/28
Mechanical Engineering with a Modern Language	H3T9	4FT deg	M/P g	24	5M+1D$	D^	32$	AABB$	Ind	6	20/30
Mechanical Systems Engineering (3/4 Yrs)	H370	3FT/4FT deg	M/P g	BBB-BCC	5M+1D$	D$6^	32$	AABB$	Ind	4	18/24

SHEFFIELD HALLAM Univ

TITLE	CODE	COURSE	SUBJECTS	A/AS	NO/C	RGNVQ	IB	SQA(H)	SQA	RATIO	A/AS
Automation	H340	3FT/4SW deg	M/S	8	3M $	M$	Ind	Ind	Ind		
Automation (Extended)	H348▼	5EXTSW deg									
Design and Manufacture with Management	H760	3FT/4SW deg	M/P/C/Ph	8	3M $	M$	Ind	Ind	Ind		
Design and Manufacture with Management (Ext)	H768▼	4EXT/5EXTSW deg									
Manufacturing Systems	H710	3FT/4SW deg	M/S	8	3M $	M$	Ind	Ind	Ind		
Manufacturing Systems (Extended)	H718▼	4EXT/5EXTSW deg									
Mechanical Engineering	H300	3FT/4SW deg	M/P/C/Ph	8	3M $	M$	Ind	Ind	Ind		
Mechanical Engineering (Extended)	H318▼	4EXT/5EXTSW deg									
Mechanical and Manufacturing Engineering	HH37	3FT/4SW deg	M/P/C/Ph	8	3M $	M$	Ind	Ind	Ind		
Mechanical and Manufacturing Engineering	HHH7	5SW deg	M/P/C/Ph g	8	3M $	M$	Ind	Ind	Ind		
Mechanical and Manufacturing Engineering (Ext)	HH3R▼	4EXT/5EXTSW deg									
Mechanical and Materials Engineering	HJ35	3FT/4SW deg	M/P/C/Ph	8	3M $	M$	Ind	Ind	Ind		
Mechanical and Materials Engineering (Extended)	HJ3M▼	4EXT/5EXTSW deg									
Mechatronics	HH63	4FT/SW deg	Cs/Es/M/Ph	8	3M $	M$	Ind	Ind	Ind		
Mechatronics	HH6H▼	5FT/SW deg									
Combined Studies _Manufacturing Engineering_	Y400	3FT deg	M	8	2M	M	Ind	Ind	Ind		
Combined Studies _Mechanical and Manufacturing Engineering_	Y400	3FT deg	M	8	2M	M	Ind	Ind	Ind		
Engineering (Mech,Manu & Computer Aided Eng)	003H▼	2FT/3SW HND	M/P/C/Ph	E	N	P	Ind	Ind	Ind		
Mechatronics	36HH▼	2FT/3SW HND	Cs/Es/M/Ph	E	N $	P$	Ind	Ind	Ind		

SHREWSBURY COLLEGE OF ARTS & TECHNOLOGY

TITLE	CODE	COURSE	SUBJECTS	A/AS	NO/C	RGNVQ	IB	SQA(H)	SQA	RATIO	A/AS
Manufacturing Technology	007H	2FT HND									

Univ of SOUTHAMPTON

TITLE	CODE	COURSE	SUBJECTS	A/AS	NO/C	RGNVQ	IB	SQA(H)	SQA	RATIO	A/AS
Acoustical Engineering	H723	3FT deg	M+P	20	Ind $	D^	30$	CSYS	Ind	5	14/24
Acoustical Engineering (MEng)	H722	4FT deg	M+P	24	Ind $	D^	32$	CSYS	Ind	3	22/30
Acoustical Engineering with European St (MEng)	H724	4FT deg	M+P+F/G	24	Ind $	D^	32$	CSYS	Ind		
Acoustics and Music	HW73	3FT deg	M+P+Mu	20	Ind $	D^	30$	CSYS	Ind	42	
Automotive Engineering	H340	3FT deg	M+P	26	Ind $	D^	34$	CSYS	Ind		
Automotive Engineering (MEng)	H341	4FT deg	M+P	26	Ind $	D^	34$	CSYS	Ind		
Electromechanical Engineering	HH35	3FT deg	M+P	24	Ind $	D^	32$	CSYS	Ind	4	14/20
Electromechanical Engineering (MEng)	HH3M	4FT deg	M+P	24	Ind $	D^	32$	CSYS	Ind	26	
Electromechanical Engineering with Euro St(MEng)	HH3N	4FT deg	M+P+F/G	24	Ind $	D^	32$	CSYS	Ind		

Engineering – Mechanical and Production 25

TITLE	CODE	COURSE	SUBJECTS	A/AS	ND/C	AGNVQ	IB	SQA(H)	SQA	RATIO A/AS
Mechanical Engineering	H300	3FT deg	M+P	24	Ind $	D^	32$	CSYS	Ind	11 14/28
Mechanical Engineering (MEng)	H301	4FT deg	M+P	26	Ind $	D^	34$	CSYS	Ind	11 18/30
Mechanical Engineering with Euro St (MEng)	H304	4FT deg	M+P+F/G	26	Ind $	D^	34$	CSYS	Ind	6 26/30
Oceanography with Acoustics	F7HR	3FT deg	M+S g	BCC-CCC	Ind	Ind	30$	BBBCC	Ind	

SOUTHAMPTON INST

TITLE	CODE	COURSE	SUBJECTS	A/AS	ND/C	AGNVQ	IB	SQA(H)	SQA	RATIO A/AS
Maritime Technology	H350	3FT deg	M	8-10	MO	M$	Dip	CCCC	N	8
Maritime Technology (with Foundation Year)	H358▼	4FT deg	g	2	N	P$	Dip	CCC	N	2
Mechanical Design	HH73	3FT deg	M/P	4-10	MO	M$	Dip	CCCC	N	2
Mechanical Design (with Foundation Year)	HH37▼	4FT deg	M/P	2-4	N	P$	Dip	CCCC	N	8
Engineering (Manufacturing and Design)	067H▼	2FT HND	S	2	N	P$	Dip	CCCC	N	

SOUTH BANK Univ

TITLE	CODE	COURSE	SUBJECTS	A/AS	ND/C	AGNVQ	IB	SQA(H)	SQA	RATIO A/AS
Engineering Product Design	H770	4SW deg	Ad/Ds/M/S g	DD	3M $	M go	Ind	Ind	Ind	
Environmental Engineering	HH23	3FT deg	* g	14-18	2M+4D	M go	Ind	Ind	Ind	
Foundation Engineering Product Design	H778	4EXT deg					Ind	Ind	Ind	
Foundation Mechanical Engineering	H308	4EXT deg					Ind	Ind	Ind	
Industrial Design	H760	3FT deg	Ad/Ds/M/S	DD	MO	M go	Ind	Ind	Ind	
Mechanical Engineering	H300	3FT/4SW deg	M/P/C/Ds g	DD	3M $	M go	Ind	Ind	Ind	
Mechanical Engineering	H305	4FT/5SW deg	M/P/C/Ds g	DD	3M $	M go	Ind	Ind	Ind	
Mechatronics	HH36	3FT deg	Ds/M g	DD	MO	M$ go	Ind	Ind	Ind	
Mechatronics (4/5 years)	HH3P	4FT deg	Ds/M g	DD	MO	M$ go	Ind	Ind	Ind	
Product Design & Business Information Technology	GH77	3FT deg	M+Ad g	12-16	4M+2D	M go	Ind	Ind	Ind	
Product Design and Computing	GH57	3FT deg	M+Ad g	12-16	4M+2D	M go	Ind	Ind	Ind	
Product Design and Economics	HL71	3FT deg	Ad+Ec/Bu g	12-16	4M+2D	M go	Ind	Ind	Ind	
Product Design and English Studies	HQ73	3FT deg	E+Ad g	14-18	X	M^ go	Ind	Ind	Ind	
Product Design and European Studies	HT72	3FT deg	Ad g	14-18	2M+4D	M go	Ind	Ind	Ind	
Product Design and Food Policy	DH47	3FT deg	S+Ad g	12-16	4M+2D	M go	Ind	Ind	Ind	
Product Design and French	HR71	3FT deg	F+Ad g	12-16	4M+2D	M go	Ind	Ind	Ind	
Product Design and German	HR7F	3FT deg	G+Ad g	14-18	2M+4D	M go	Ind	Ind	Ind	
Product Design and German - ab initio	HR72	3FT deg	Ad g	12-16	4M+2D	M go	Ind	Ind	Ind	
Product Design and History	HV71	3FT deg	Ad+H g	12-16	4M+2D	M^ go	Ind	Ind	Ind	
Product Design and Housing	HK7K	3FT deg	Ad g	14-18	2M+4D	M go	Ind	Ind	Ind	
Product Design and Human Biology	BH17	3FT deg	S+Ad/A g	12-16	4M+2D	M go	Ind	Ind	Ind	
Product Design and Human Resource Management	HN76	3FT deg	Ad g	14-18	2M+4D	M go	Ind	Ind	Ind	
Product Design and Management	HN71	3FT deg	Ad g	12-16	4M+2D	M go	Ind	Ind	Ind	
Product Design and Marketing	HN75	3FT deg	Ad g	14-18	2M+4D	M go	Ind	Ind	Ind	
Product Design and Nutrition	BH47	3FT deg	S+Ad/A g	12-16	4M+2D	M go	Ind	Ind	Ind	
Psychology and Product Design	CH87	3FT deg	Ad+S g	14-18	4M+2D	M go	Ind	Ind	Ind	
Spanish - ab initio and Product Design	HR74	3FT deg	Ad g	12-16	4M+2D	M go	Ind	Ind	Ind	
Spanish and Product Design	HR7K	3FT deg	Sp+Ad/A g	14-18	2M+4D	M^ go	Ind	Ind	Ind	
Sports Product Design	H7B6	3FT deg	S+Ad/A g	14-18	2M+4D	M go	Ind	Ind	Ind	
Urban Studies and Product Design	KH47	3FT deg	Ad g	14-18	2M+4D	M go	Ind	Ind	Ind	
World Theatre and Product Design	HW74	3FT deg	Ad g	14-18	2M+4D	M go	Ind	Ind	Ind	
Engineering Product Design	077H	2FT HND	Ad/Ds/M/S/Cm g	E	N	P go	Ind	Ind	Ind	

ST HELENS COLL

TITLE	CODE	COURSE	SUBJECTS	A/AS	ND/C	AGNVQ	IB	SQA(H)	SQA	RATIO A/AS
Mechanical Engineering	H300	3FT deg	M/P	4-10	3M	M$	Ind	Ind	Ind	
Mechanical Engineering	003H	2FT HND	M/P/Ds	2-6	N	P$	Ind	Ind	Ind	
Mechatronics	36HH	2FT HND	M/P/Es/Cs/Ds	2-6	N	P$	Ind	Ind	Ind	

STAFFORDSHIRE Univ

TITLE	CODE	COURSE	SUBJECTS	A/AS	ND/C	AGNVQ	IB	SQA(H)	SQA	RATIO A/AS
Engineering Design (MEng)	H770	4FT/5SW deg	M+P	10	3M	M$	24	BCC	Ind	7
Extended Engineering Design	H778	5EXT/6EXTSW deg	*	4	N	P$	24	CCC	Ind	3

course details				**98 expected requirements**						*96 entry stats*	
TITLE	CODE	COURSE	SUBJECTS	A/AS	NQ/C	RGNVQ	IB	SQA(H)	SQA	RATIO	A/AS
Extended Manufacturing Engineering with Business	H7ND	5EXT/6EXTSW deg	*	4	N	P$	24	CCC	Ind		
Extended Mechanical Engineering	H308	5EXT/6EXTSW deg	*	4	N	P$	24	CCC	Ind	4	
Extended Mechatronics	HH3P	5EXT/6EXTSW deg	*	4	N	P$	24	CCC	Ind		
Manufacturing Engineering with Business	H7NC	3FT deg		10	3M	M$					
Manufacturing Management	H710	3FT deg	g	8	3M	M$	24	BCC	Ind		
Manufacturing Management	H719	4EXT deg	g	EE	P$	P$	Ind	Ind	Ind		
Mechanical Engineering (MEng)	H300	4FT/5SW deg	M+P	10	3M	M$	24	BCC	Ind	3	
Mechatronics	HH36	4FT/5SW deg	M+P	10	3M	M$	24	BCC	Ind	6	
Product Design Technology	H771	4FT/5SW deg	Ds	12	3M	M$	24	BCC	Ind	1	8/22
Product Design Technology	H772	3FT deg									
Product Design Technology	H779	4EXT deg	g	EE	P$	P$	Ind	Ind	Ind		
Product Design Technology	H773	4EXT deg	g	EE	P$	P$	Ind	Ind	Ind		
Small Vehicle Design	H349	4EXT deg	g	EE	P$	P$	Ind	Ind	Ind		
Small Vehicle Design	H340	3FT deg	g	8	3M	M	Ind	Ind	Ind		
Small Vehicle Design	H348	4EXT deg	g	8	3M	M$					
Small Vehicle Design	H341	3FT deg									
Sports Equipment Technology	H3B6	4EXT deg	g	EE	P$	P$	Ind	Ind	Ind		
Extended Manufacturing Engineering with Business	817H	3EXT HND	g	2	N	P$	24	CCC	Ind	6	
Extended Mechanical Engineering	7HHH	3EXT HND	g	2	N	P$	24	CCC	Ind		
Manufacturing Engineering with Business	1N7H▼	2FT HND	M/P	2	N	P$	24	CCC	Ind		
Mechanical Engineering	73HH▼	2FT HND	M/P g	2	N	P$	24	CCC	Ind	5	
Mechatronics	36HH▼	3EXT HND		2	N	P$					

STOCKPORT COLL of F and HE

Manufacturing Engineering	H700	4FT deg	M	2	N	Ind	Ind	Ind	Ind		
Mechanical Engineering	H300	4FT deg	M	2	N	Ind	Ind	Ind	Ind		
Mechanical Engineering	003H	2FT HND	M/P	2	N	Ind	Ind	Ind	Ind		

Univ of STRATHCLYDE

Electrical & Mechanical Engineering with Euro St	H3T2	5FT deg	M+P+L g	BBC	Ind	Ind	36$	AABBC$	Ind		
Electrical and Mech Engineering with Business St	H3N1	5FT deg	M+P+E	BBC	Ind	Ind	36$	AABBC$	Ind		
Electrical and Mechanical Engineering	HH53	4FT deg	M+P g	BBC	Ind	Ind	36$	AABBC$	Ind		
Manufacturing Engineering and Management	HN71	4FT deg	M+P g	BCC	HN	Ind	34$	BBBBB$	HN		
Manufacturing Systems Engineering	H710	4FT deg	M+P	BCC	HN	Ind	34$	BBBBC$	HN		
Mechanical Engineering	H302	5FT deg	M+P	BBB	HN		32$	AABBB$	HN		
Mechanical Engineering	H301	5FT deg	M+P	BBB	HN		32$	AABBB$	HN		
Mechanical Engineering	H300	4FT deg	M+P	BCC	HN		30$	BBBBB$	HN		
Mechanical Engineering with Aerodynamics	H3H4	5FT deg	M+P	BBB	HN		32$	AABBB$	HN		
Mechanical Engineering with Control Engineering	H3H6	5FT deg	M+P	BBB	HN		32$	AABBB$	HN		
Mechanical Engineering with Energy Studies	H3J9	5FT deg	M+P	BBB	HN		32$	AABBB$	HN		
Mechanical Engineering with Environmental Eng	H3JX	5FT deg	M+P	BBB	HN		32$	AABBB$	HN		
Mechanical Engineering with Financial Management	H3N3	5FT deg	M+P	BBB	HN		32$	AABBB$	HN		
Mechanical Engineering with Materials Eng	H3J2	5FT deg	M+P	BBB	HN		32$	AABBB$	HN		
Product Design Engineering	H770	5FT deg	M+P/C	BCC	HN		34$	BBBBC$	HN		

UNIVERSITY COLLEGE SUFFOLK

Art & Design and Product Design and Manufacture	HW72	3FT deg	Pf	EE	N $	P$	Ind	Ind	Ind		
Art & Design and Product Design and Manufacture	EW72	3FT deg	Pf	EE	N $	P$	Ind	Ind	Ind		
Behavioural Studies and Product Design and Manuf	LH77	3FT deg	*	DE	N $	P$	Ind	Ind	Ind		
Behavioural Studies with Product Design & Manuf	L7H7	3FT deg	*	DD	N $	P$	Ind	Ind	Ind		
Media Studies with Product Design & Manufacture	P4H7	3FT deg	*	CE	N $	P$	Ind	Ind	Ind		
Product Design & Manuf with Applied Biol Science	H7C1	3FT deg	*	EE	N $	P$	Ind	Ind	Ind		
Product Design & Manufact with Information Techn	H7G5	3FT deg	*	EE	N $	P$	Ind	Ind	Ind		
Product Design & Manufacture & Applied Biol Sci	HC71	3FT deg	S	EE	N $	P$	Ind	Ind	Ind		

TITLE	CODE	COURSE	SUBJECTS	A/AS	NO/C	AGNVQ	IB	SQA(H)	SQA	RATIO A/AS
Product Design & Manufacture & Early Child Studs	HX79	3FT deg	*	DE	N $	P$	Ind	Ind	Ind	
Product Design & Manufacture & Environmental St	HF79	3FT deg	*	EE	N $	P$	Ind	Ind	Ind	
Product Design & Manufacture & Information Techn	HG75	3FT deg	*	EE	N $	P$	Ind	Ind	Ind	
Product Design & Manufacture and Business Studs	HN71	3FT deg	*	EE	N $	P$	Ind	Ind	Ind	
Product Design & Manufacture and Cultural Studs	HY73	3FT deg	*	CE	N $	P$	Ind	Ind	Ind	
Product Design & Manufacture and Literary Studs	HQ72	3FT deg	E	CE	N $	P$	Ind	Ind	Ind	
Product Design & Manufacture and Management	HN7C	3FT deg	*	EE	N $	P$	Ind	Ind	Ind	
Product Design & Manufacture and Media Studies	HP74	3FT deg	*	CE	N $	P$	Ind	Ind	Ind	
Product Design & Manufacture with Art & Design	H7N2	3FT deg	Pf	EE	N $	P$	Ind	Ind	Ind	
Product Design & Manufacture with Behavioural St	H7L3	3FT deg	*	DE	N $	P$	Ind	Ind	Ind	
Product Design & Manufacture with Business Studs	H7N1	3FT deg	*	EE	N $	P$	Ind	Ind	Ind	
Product Design & Manufacture with Cultural Studs	H7Y3	3FT deg	*	EE	N $	P$	Ind	Ind	Ind	
Product Design & Manufacture with Early Child St	H7XX	3FT deg	*	EE	N $	P$	Ind	Ind	Ind	
Product Design & Manufacture with Education St	H7X9	3FT deg	*	EE	N $	P$	Ind	Ind	Ind	
Product Design & Manufacture with Environ Studs	H7F9	3FT deg	*	EE	N $	P$	Ind	Ind	Ind	
Product Design & Manufacture with Human Science	H7B1	3FT deg	S	EE	N $	P$	Ind	Ind	Ind	
Product Design & Manufacture with Literary Studs	H7Q2	3FT deg	*	EE	N $	P$	Ind	Ind	Ind	
Product Design & Manufacture with Management	H7NC	3FT deg	*	EE	N $	P$	Ind	Ind	Ind	
Product Design & Manufacture with Media Studies	H7P4	3FT deg	*	EE	N $	P$	Ind	Ind	Ind	
Product Design & Manufacture with Social Policy	H7L4	3FT deg	*	EE	N $	P$	Ind	Ind	Ind	
Product Design and Manufacture	H770	3FT deg	*	EE	N $	P$	Ind	Ind	Ind	
Engineering (Motor Vehicle Studies)	043H	2FT HND	*	E	N $	P$	Ind	Ind	Ind	
Product Design and Manufacture	077H	2FT HND	*	E	N $	P$	Ind	Ind	Ind	

Univ of SUNDERLAND

TITLE	CODE	COURSE	SUBJECTS	A/AS	NO/C	AGNVQ	IB	SQA(H)	SQA	RATIO A/AS
Automation and Mechatronics	HH63	3FT/4SW deg	M+P/C g	12	3M $	ME	24$	CCC	N$	11	
Automation and Mechatronics (Foundation)	HH36▼	4EXT/5EXTSW deg	*	2	N	P	24	CC	N	1	
Automotive Design and Manufacture	H340	3FT/4SW deg	M+P/C/S g	12	3M $		24$	CCCCC	N$	5	6/18
Automotive Design and Manufacture (Foundation)	H348▼	4EXT/5EXTSW deg	*	2	N		24	CC	N	2	
European Studies in Mechanical Eng (Foundation)	HT3F▼	4EXT/5EXTSW deg	*	2	N	P	24	CC	N		
European Studies in Mechanical Engineering	HT32	3FT/4SW deg	M/P/C g	12	3M $	ME	24$	CCC$	N$	2	
Manufacturing Engineering	H700	3FT/4SW deg	M/P/C g	12	3M $	ME	24$	CCC	N$	3	
Manufacturing Engineering (Foundation)	H788▼	4EXT/5EXTSW deg	*	2	N	P	24	CC	N		
Manufacturing Operations Management	H7N1▼	3FT/4SW deg	* g	10	3M $	M	24	CCC	N $	2	
Manufacturing Operations Management (Foundation)	H7NC▼	4EXT/5EXTSW deg	*	2	N	P	24	CC	N		
Mechanical Engineering	H300	3FT/4SW deg	M/P/C	12	3M $	ME	24$	CCC	N$	7	
Mechanical Engineering (Foundation)	H308▼	4EXT/5EXTSW deg	*	2	N	P	24	CC	N	8	
Product Design	HW72	3FT deg	*	10	3M	M	24	CCC	N		
Product Design (Foundation)	HN7D	4FT deg	*								
Product Design Management	HN71▼	3FT deg	* g	10	3M $	M	24	CCC	N	3	6/12
Product Design Management (Foundation)	HN7C▼	4EXT deg	*	2	N	P	24	CC	N		
Mechanical and Manufacturing Eng (Foundation)	7JHH▼	3EXT HND	*			P					
Mechanical and Manufacturing Engineering	7HHH	2FT HND	M/P g	2	N $	PE	24$	CC$	N$	3	

Univ of SURREY

TITLE	CODE	COURSE	SUBJECTS	A/AS	NO/C	AGNVQ	IB	SQA(H)	SQA	RATIO A/AS
Mechanical Eng with Offshore and Maritime Eng	H351	4SW/4/5SW deg	M+P	18-22	MO+2D$	ME3/^	28$	BBBBC$	Ind	11	
Mechanical Eng with Offshore and Maritime Eng	H350	3FT/4/5SW deg	M+P	18-22	MO+2D$	ME3/^	28$	BBBBC$	Ind		
Mechanical Engineering	H301	4SW/4/5SW deg	M+P	18-22	MO+2D$	ME3/^	28$	BBBBC$	Ind	2	14/30
Mechanical Engineering	H300	3FT/4/5SW deg	M+P	18-22	MO+2D$	ME3/^	28$	BBBBC$	Ind		
Mechanical Engineering with Mechatronics	H340	3FT/4/5SW deg	M+P	18-22	MO+2D$	ME3/^	28$	BBBBC$	Ind	14	
Mechanical Engineering with Mechatronics	H341	4SW/4/5SW deg	M+P	18-22	MO+2D$	ME3/^	28$	BBBBC$	Ind	3	
Mechanical Engineering with Power/Aerospace Eng	H345	3FT/4/5SW deg	M+P	18-22	MO+2D$	ME3/^	28$	BBBBC$	Ind	43	
Mechanical Engineering with Power/Aerospace Eng	H346	4SW/4/5SW deg	M+P	18-22	MO+2D$	ME3/^	28$	BBBBC$	Ind	9	

course details — *98 expected requirements* — *96 entry stats*

TITLE	CODE	COURSE	98 expected requirements							96 entry stats	
			SUBJECTS	A/AS	ND/C	AGNVQ	IB	SQA(H)	SQA	RATIO	A/AS
Mechanical Engineering with a European Language	H304	4SW/4/5SW deg	M+P g	18-22	MO+2D$	ME3/^	28$	BBBBC$	Ind	18	
Mechanical Engineering with a Foundation Year	H305	4FT/5SW deg	* g	18-22	Ind	Ind	28$	BBBBC	Ind	14	

Univ of SUSSEX

TITLE	CODE	COURSE	SUBJECTS	A/AS	ND/C	AGNVQ	IB	SQA(H)	SQA	RATIO	A/AS
Electromechanical Engineering	HH35	3FT deg	M	BCC	MO $	MS^	$	Ind	Ind		
Mechanical Eng with North American St (MEng)	H3Q4	4FT deg	M	BCC	MO $	MS^	$	Ind	Ind		
Mechanical Engineering	H300	3FT deg	M	BCC	MO $	MS^	$	Ind	Ind		
Mechanical Engineering	H308	4FT deg	*	DD	N						
Mechanical Engineering (MEng)	H301	4FT deg	M	BCC	MO $	MS^	$	Ind	Ind		
Mechanical Engineering with Business Management	H3N1	3FT deg	M	BCC	MO $	MS^	$	Ind	Ind		
Mechanical Engineering with European St (MEng)	H3T2	4FT deg	M g	BCC	MO $	MS^ go	$	Ind	Ind		
Mechanical Engineering with Japanese Studies	H3T4	4FT deg	M	BCC	MO $	MS^ go	$	Ind	Ind		
Mechatronics	H3H6	3FT deg	M	BCC	MO $	MS^	$	Ind	Ind		
Robotics and Automated Manufacture	HH76	3FT deg	M	BCC	MO $	MS^	$	Ind	Ind		

Univ of Wales SWANSEA

TITLE	CODE	COURSE	SUBJECTS	A/AS	ND/C	AGNVQ	IB	SQA(H)	SQA	RATIO	A/AS
Mechanical Eng with a year in N America	H303	4FT deg	M+P	20	MO	Ind	28$	Ind	Ind	6	12/22
Mechanical Engineering	H301	4FT deg	* g	18	MO	Ind	Ind	Ind	Ind	3	
Mechanical Engineering	H300	3FT deg	M+P	18	MO	Ind	28$	Ind	Ind	4	10/28
Mechanical Engineering	H304	4FT deg	M+P	22	DO	Ind	Ind	Ind	Ind		
Mechanical Engineering (CCTA)	H305	4FT deg	M/P g	4	N	Ind	Ind	Ind	Ind		
Mechanical Engineering with a year in Europe	H302	4FT deg	M+P g	20	MO	Ind	28$	Ind	Ind	11	

SWANSEA INST of HE

TITLE	CODE	COURSE	SUBJECTS	A/AS	ND/C	AGNVQ	IB	SQA(H)	SQA	RATIO	A/AS
Automotive Electronics Engineering	H6H3	3FT deg	2S	4	3M		Ind	Ind	Ind	4	
Automotive Electronics Engineering (Foundation)	H6HH	4EXT deg								2	
Automotive Engineering	H340	3FT deg	2(M/P/S/C)	EE	Ind		Ind	Ind	Ind	5	
Automotive Engineering (Foundation)	H348	4EXT deg									
Engineering Design and Manufacture	H760	3FT deg									
Engineering Design and Manufacture (Foundation)	H768	4EXT deg									
Manufacturing Systems Engineering	H718	3FT deg									
Manufacturing Systems Engineering	H710	3FT deg									
Mechatronics	HH36	3FT deg	2S	4	3M		Ind	Ind	Ind	2	
Mechatronics (Foundation)	HH3P	4EXT deg								2	
Product Design	H770	3FT deg		DD	N		Ind	Ind	N	4	6/16
Product Design	E770	3FT deg		DD	N		Ind	Ind	N		
Product Design (Foundation)	E778▼	3FT deg									
Product Design (Foundation)	H778▼	4EXT deg								2	
Automotive Engineering	043H	2FT HND	S	2	N		Ind			5	
Mechanical and Manufacturing Engineering	37HH	2FT HND		E	N		Ind	Ind	Ind		
Mechatronics	63HH	2FT HND	S	2	N		Ind	Ind	Ind	3	

Univ of TEESSIDE

TITLE	CODE	COURSE	SUBJECTS	A/AS	ND/C	AGNVQ	IB	SQA(H)	SQA	RATIO	A/AS
Computer Aided Product Design Engineering	H7G5	3FT deg	M+S	8	3M		Ind	CCC	Ind		
Design Engineering	H760	4SW deg	M+S	8	3M		Ind	Ind	Ind	7	
Mechanical Engineering	H300	3FT/4SW deg	M+S	10	3M $		Ind	CCC	Ind	6	
Modular Degree Scheme *Design Engineering*	Y401	3FT deg									
Modular Degree Scheme *Mechanical Engineering*	Y401	3FT deg									
Science and Technology Combined Honours Scheme *Design Engineering*	Y108	3FT deg									
Science and Technology Combined Honours Scheme *Mechanical Engineering*	Y108	3FT deg									
Design for Manufacture	077H	2FT HND	M+S	4	N		Ind	Ind	Ind	4	

Engineering – Mechanical and Production 25

TITLE	CODE	COURSE	SUBJECTS	A/AS	NO/C	RGNVQ	IB	SQA(H)	SQA	RATIO	A/AS
course details			**98 expected requirements**							**96 entry stats**	
Fabrication & Welding Engineering	073H	2FT HND	M/S	4	N		Ind	Ind	Ind	1	
Mechanical and Production Engineering	73HH	2FT HND	M/S	4	N		Ind	Ind	Ind		
Mechatronics	63HH▼	2FT HND	M/S	D	N		Ind	Ind	Ind	2	
Univ of ULSTER											
Manufact Systems Management(4 Yr SW Inc DIS)	H710▼	4SW deg	S	CCC	MO+3D	Ind	28	BBBC	Ind	4	14/18
Mechanical Engineering	H300▼	3FT deg	M/S	CCD-DDD	MO+2D	Ind	24	CCCC	Ind	8	10/14
Eng (Mechanical Manuf, & Des) (3 Yr SW inc CIS)	73HH▼	3SW HND	M+S g		Ind	Ind	Ind	Ind	Ind	5	2/10
UNIVERSITY COLL LONDON (Univ of London)											
Mechanical Engineering	H300	3FT deg	M+P g	BCC-BBB	Ind	Ind	30$	BBBCC$	Ind	13	20/24
Mechanical Engineering (MEng)	H301	4FT deg	M+P g	BCC-BBB	Ind	Ind	30$	BBBCC$	Ind	7	16/28
Mechanical Engineering with Bioengineering	H370	3FT deg	M+S g	CCC-BCC	Ind	Ind	30$	BBBCC$	Ind	5	
Naval Architecture and Ocean Engineering	HJ36	3FT deg	M+P g	BCC-BBB	Ind	Ind	30$	BBBCC$	Ind	11	20/22
Univ of WARWICK											
Engineering (Design and Approp Technol) (Euro)	H764	4FT deg	M+S g	BBB	5M+1D$	D$^	32$	AABBB$			
Engineering (Design and Appropriate Technology)	H762	4FT deg	M+S g	BBB	5M+1D$	D$^	32$	AABBB$		7	18/26
Engineering (Design and Appropriate Technology)	H760	3FT deg	M+S g	CCC	5M+1D$	D$^	28$	BBBBC$			
Manufacturing Systems Engineering	H712	4FT deg	M+S g	BBB	5M+1D$	D$^	32$	AABBB$			
Manufacturing Systems Engineering	H710	3FT deg	M+S g	CCC	5M+1D$	D$^	28$	BBBBC$		4	12/28
Manufacturing Systems Engineering (European)	H714	4FT deg	M+S g	BBB	5M+1D$	D$^	32$	AABBB$		6	
Mechanical Engineering	H300	3FT deg	M+S g	CCC	5M+1D$	D$^	28$	BBBBC$		7	12/28
Mechanical Engineering	H302	4FT deg	M+S g	BBB	5M+1D$	D$^	32$	AABBB$			
Mechanical Engineering (European)	H304	4FT deg	M+S g	BBB	5M+1D$	D$^	32$	AABBB$		27	
Univ of WESTMINSTER											
Industrial Systems & Business Mgt (Sandwich)	HN71	4SW deg	*	12	6M	M	26	BBC		1	10/16
Manufacturing Systems Engineering	H710	3FT/4SW deg	M	8	3M $			BBC	Ind	4	
Manufacturing Systs Engineering(with foundation)	H718	4EXT deg	*	D-E	N				Ind		
Mechanical Design (Engineering)	H771	3FT/4SW deg	M	8	3M $	M	Ind	Ind	Ind	7	
Mechanical Design Engineering (with foundation)	H768	4EXT deg	*	D-E	N		Ind	Ind	Ind	2	
Mechanical Engineering	H300	3FT/4SW deg	M	8	3M $	M	Ind	Ind	Ind	8	
Mechanical Engineering (with foundation)	H308	4EXT deg	*	D-E	N		Ind	Ind	Ind	3	
Product Design Engineering	H770	3FT deg	*	CD	3M	M	Ind	Ind	Ind	4	10/17
Product Design Engineering with foundation	H778	4EXT deg	*	D-E	N	P	Ind	Ind	Ind	3	
WIGAN and LEIGH COLL											
Electrical and Electronic Engineering	36HH▼	2FT HND	M/P/C	E	N	P$	Dip		N		
Mechanical/Manufacturing Engineering	37HH▼	2FT HND	M/P/C	E	N	P$	Dip		N		
Univ of WOLVERHAMPTON											
Computer Aided Product Design	HW7F	3FT/4SW deg	g	8	2M		Ind	Ind	Ind		
Computer Aided Product Design	EW7F	3FT/4SW deg	g	8	2M		Ind	Ind	Ind		
Computer Aided Product Design	HW72	3FT/4SW deg	g	8	2M		Ind	Ind	Ind	3	6/17
Computer Aided Product Manufacture	H760	3FT/4SW deg	* g	DD	N	M	24	CCCC	Ind	6	
Manufacturing Engineering	H710	3FT/4SW deg	S g	DD	N	M	24	CCCC	Ind	4	
Product Engineering	H700	3FT/4SW deg	* g	DD	N	M	24	CCCC	Ind	4	
Applied Sciences *Manufacturing Studies*	Y100	3FT/4SW deg	S g	DD	N	M	24	CCCC	Ind		
Applied Sciences (4 Yrs) *Manufacturing Studies*	Y110▼	4FT deg	*								
Combined Degrees *Computer Aided Product Design*	Y401	3FT/4SW deg	g	DD	N	M	24	CCCC	Ind		
Combined Degrees *Manufacturing Studies*	Y401	3FT/4SW deg	g	DD	N	M	24	CCCC	Ind		

course details

TITLE	CODE	COURSE	SUBJECTS	A/AS	NO/C	AGNVQ	IB	SQA(H)	SQA	RATIO A/AS
WRITTLE COLL										
Agricultural Engineering	H331	3FT/4SW deg	M+S g	12	MO	M+	Ind	Ind	Ind	13
Agricultural Engineering with Business Mgt	H3N1	3FT/4SW deg	* g	12	MO	M+	Ind	Ind	Ind	3
Agricultural Engineering	133H	2FT/3SW HND	M g	6	N	M	Ind	Ind	Ind	3
Agriculture (Mechanisation)	32HD	2FT/3SW HND	Ap g	6	N	M	Ind	Ind	Ind	3

course details | 98 expected requirements | 96 entry stats

TITLE	CODE	COURSE	SUBJECTS	A/AS	NQ/C	RGNVQ	IB	SQA(H)	SQA	RATIO A/AS
Univ of ABERDEEN										
Celtic Civilisation-English	QQM3	4FT deg	* g	BBC	Ind	M$ go	30$	BBBB$	Ind	2
Celtic-English	QQ53	4FT deg	* g	BBC	Ind	M$ go	30$	BBBB$	Ind	3
Economics-English	LQ13	4FT deg	* g	BBC	Ind	M$ go	30$	BBBB$	Ind	
English	Q300	4FT deg	* g	BBC	Ind	M$ go	30$	BBBB$	Ind	3
English and Scottish Literature	Q314	4FT deg	* g	BBC	Ind	M$ go	30$	BBBB$	Ind	5
English with Film Studies	Q3W5	4FT deg	* g	BBC	Ind	M$ go	30$	BBBB$	Ind	5
English with Religious Studies	Q3V8	4FT deg	* g	BBC	Ind	M$ go	30$	BBBB$	Ind	
English with Womens Studies	Q3M9	4FT deg	* g	BBC	Ind	M$ go	30$	BBBB$	Ind	
English-Entrepreneurship	QN3C	4FT deg	* g	BBC	Ind	M$ go	30$	BBBB$	Ind	
English-French	QR31	4FT/5FT deg	* g	BBC	Ind	M$ go	30$	BBBB$	Ind	3
English-French (4 Yrs)	RQ13	4FT deg	* g	BBC	Ind	M$ go	30$	BBBB$	Ind	
English-German	QR32	4FT/5FT deg	* g	BBC	Ind	M$ go	30$	BBBB$	Ind	5
English-German (4 Yrs)	RQ23	4FT deg	* g	BBC	Ind	M$ go	30$	BBBB$	Ind	
English-Hispanic Studies	QR34	4FT/5FT deg	* g	BBC	Ind	M$ go	30$	BBBB$	Ind	2
English-Hispanic Studies (4Yrs)	RQ43	4FT deg	* g	BBC	Ind	M$ go	30$	BBBB$	Ind	
English-History	QV31	4FT deg	* g	BBC	Ind	M$ go	30$	BBBB$	Ind	3
English-History of Art	QV34	4FT deg	* g	BBC	Ind	M$ go	30$	BBBB$	Ind	16
English-International Relations	QM3C	4FT deg	* g	BBC	Ind	M$ go	30$	BBBB$	Ind	3
English-Management Studies	QN31	4FT deg	* g	BBC	Ind	M$ go	30$	BBBB$	Ind	3
English-Philosophy	QV37	4FT deg	* g	BBC	Ind	M$ go	30$	BBBB$	Ind	4
English-Religious Studies	QV38	4FT deg	* g	BBC	Ind	M$ go	30$	BBBB$	Ind	
English-Social Research	LQ33	4FT deg	* g	BBC	Ind	M$ go	30$	BBBB$	Ind	7
English-Sociology	QL33	4FT deg	* g	BBC	Ind	M$ go	30$	BBBB$	Ind	6
Univ of Wales, ABERYSTWYTH										
English	Q300	3FT deg	El	20	1M+5D$ M^ g		30$	BBBBC$	Ind	
English/American Studies	QQ34	3FT deg	El	20	1M+5D$ M^ g		30$	BBBBC$	Ind	
English/Art	QW31	3FT deg	El+A/Ad	20	1M+5D$ MA^ g		30$	BBBBC$	Ind	
English/Art History	QV34	3FT deg	El	20	1M+5D$ MA^ g		30$	BBBBC$	Ind	
English/Drama	QW34	3FT deg	El	20	1M+5D$ MQ^ g		30$	BBBBC$	Ind	
English/Education	QX39	3FT deg	El	20	1M+5D$ M^ g		30$	BBBBC$	Ind	
Film and Television Studies/English	QW35	3FT deg	El	20	1M+5D$ MQ^ g		30$	BBBBC$	Ind	
French/English	QR31	4FT deg	El+F	20	1M+5D$ M^ g		30$	BBBBC$	Ind	
Geography/English	LQ83	3FT deg	El+Gy	20-22	1M+5D$ M^ g		31$	BBBBC$	Ind	
German/English	QR32	4FT deg	El+G	20	1M+5D$ M^ g		30$	BBBBC$	Ind	
History/English	QV31	3FT deg	El	20	1M+5D$ M^ g		30$	BBBBC$	Ind	
Information and Library Studies/English	PQ23	3FT deg	El	20	1M+5D$ M^ g		30$	BBBBC$	Ind	
International Politics/English	MQ1H	3FT deg	El	20	1M+5D$ M^ g		30$	BBBBC$	Ind	
Irish/English	QQJ5	4FT deg	El	20	1M+5D$ M^ g		30$	BBBBC$	Ind	
Italian/English	QR33	4FT deg	El+L	20	1M+5D$ M^ g		30$	BBBBC$	Ind	
Politics/English	MQ13	3FT deg	El	20	1M+5D$ M^ g		30$	BBBBC$	Ind	
Spanish/English	QR34	4FT deg	El+L	20	1M+5D$ M^ g		30$	BBBBC$	Ind	
Welsh History/English	QVHC	3FT deg	El	20	1M+5D$ M^ g		30$	BBBBC$	Ind	
Welsh/English	QQH5	3FT deg	El+W	20	1M+5D$ M^ g		30$	BBBBC$	Ind	
ANGLIA Poly Univ										
Art History and English	QV34▼	3FT deg	E	14	6M	M+/^	Dip$	BBCC	Ind	4	10/24
Business and English	NQ13▼	3FT deg	E g	12	4M	M+/^ go	Dip$	BCCC	Ind	5	11/16
Communication Studies and English	PQ33▼	3FT deg	E+Ap	14	6M	M+/^	Dip$	BBCC	Ind	6	10/20
Economics and English	LQ13▼	3FT deg	E g	12	4M	M+/^ go	Dip$	BCCC	Ind	
English	Q300▼	3FT deg	E	16	8M	D^	Dip$	BBCCC	Ind	2	10/24
English Language Studies and Intercultural St	QL36▼	3FT deg	* g	12	4M	M go	Dip	BCCC		

course details			98 expected requirements							96 entry stats	
TITLE	CODE	COURSE	SUBJECTS	A/AS	NO/C	AGNVQ	IB	SQA(H)	SQA	RATIO	A/AS
English and English Language Studies	QQ13▼	3FT deg	E g	12	4M	M go	Dip$	BCCC			
English and European Philosophy and Literature	QV37▼	3FT deg	* g	12	4M	M+/^	Dip	BCCC	Ind	4	10/16
English and French	QR31▼	4FT deg	E g	12	4M	M+/^ go	Dip	BCCC	Ind	24	
English and Geography	LQ83▼	3FT deg	E+Gy	12	4M	M+/^ go	Dip$	BCCC	Ind	3	
English and German	QR32▼	4FT deg	E g	12	4M	M+/^ go	Dip$	BCCC	Ind	4	
English and Graphic Arts	QW32▼	3FT deg	A+E	14	6M	M+/^	Dip$	BBCC	Ind	11	
English and History	QV31▼	3FT deg	E	12	4M	M+/^	Dip$	BCCC	Ind	3	10/18
English and Italian	RQ33▼	4FT deg	E g	12	4M	M+/^	Dip$	BCCC	Ind	13	
English and Law	MQ33▼	3FT deg	E	14	6M	M+/^	Dip$	BBCC	Ind	11	
English and Maths or Stats/Statistical Modelling	QG31▼	3FT deg	E	12	4M	M+/^	Dip$	BCCC	Ind		
English and Music	QW33▼	3FT deg	E+Mu	12	4M	M+/^	Dip$	BCCC	Ind	2	14/16
English and Politics	QM31▼	3FT deg	E	14	6M	M+/^	Dip$	BBCC	Ind	10	
English and Social Policy	QL34▼	3FT deg	E	12	4M	M+/^	Dip$	BCCC	Ind	1	
English and Sociology	QL33▼	3FT deg	E	12	4M	M+/^	Dip$	BCCC	Ind	6	10/20
English and Spanish	QR34▼	4FT deg	E g	12	4M	M+/^	Dip$	BCCC	Ind		
English and Women's Studies	QM39▼	3FT deg	E	12	4M	M+/^	Dip$	BCCC	Ind	4	

Univ of Wales, BANGOR

English	Q300	3FT deg	E/El g	CCC	X	D*^ go	28$	BBBC$	X	4	14/24
English Literature with English Language	Q310	3FT deg	E/El g	CCC	X	D*^ go	28$	BBBC$	X		
English with Creative Writing	Q3W4	3FT deg	E/El g	CCC	X	D*^ go	28$	BBBC$	X		
English with Film Studies	Q3W5	3FT deg	E/El g	CCC	X	D*^ go	28$	BBBC$	X		
French (Syllabus A)/English	QR31	4FT deg	E+F g	CCC	X	D*^ go	28$	BBBC$	X	6	
French (Syllabus B)/English	QR3C	4FT deg	E+F g	CCC	X	D$^ go	28$	BBBC$	X	6	
German/English	QR32	4FT deg	E g	CCD	X	D*^ go	28$	BBBC$	X	10	
History/English	QV31	3FT deg	E+H g	CCC	X	D*^ go	28$	BBBC$	X	4	16/20
Linguistics with English Literature	Q1Q3	3FT deg	E/El g	CCD	X	D*^ go	28$	BBBC$	X		
Linguistics/English	QQ13	3FT deg	E g	CCC	X	D*^ go	28$	BBBC$	X	5	14/18
Religious Studies/English	QV38	3FT deg	E g	CCC	X	D*^ go	28$	BBBC$	X	5	
Russian/English	QR38	4FT deg	E g	CCC	X	D*^ go	28$	BBBC$	X		
Social Policy/English	LQ43	3FT deg	E g	CCC	X	D*^ go	28$	BBBC$	X		
Sociology/English	LQ33	3FT deg	E g	CCC	X	D*^ go	28$	BBBC$	X	5	18/20
Welsh/English	QQ35	3FT/4FT deg	E+W g	CCC	X	D*^ go	Ind	X	X	2	
Women's Studies and English	MQ93	3FT deg	E g	18	X	D*6/^ go	28$	BBBC$	X		

BATH COLL of HE

English and International Education	QX39	3FT deg	El	CD	Ind		Ind	$	$	3	10/18
Modern English Studies	Q300	3FT deg	E		Ind		Ind	$	$	7	8/26
Combined Awards *English Studies*	Y400	3FT deg	*	BC	N		Ind	$	$		
Modular Programme (DipHE) *English Studies*	Y460	2FT Dip	*	BC	N		Ind	$	$		

Univ of BIRMINGHAM

African Studies/English	QTH7	3FT deg		BBB	Ind	D*^	32	ABBB	Ind	4	24/30
American Studies/English	QQ34	3FT deg	*	BBB	Ind	D*^	32	ABBB	Ind	12	24/30
Ancient History & Archaeology/English	QV36	3FT deg	*	BBB	Ind	D*^	32	ABBB	Ind	11	
Artificial Intelligence/English	GQ83	3FT deg	* g	BBB	Ind	D*^	32	ABBB	Ind	4	
Computer Studies/English	GQ53	3FT deg	* g	BBB	Ind	D*^	32	ABBB	Ind	23	
Dance/English	WQ43	3FT deg	*	BBB	Ind	D*^	32	ABBB	Ind	35	
Drama/English	QW34	3FT deg	*	BBB	Ind	D*^	32	ABBB	Ind	38	26/30
East Mediterranean History/English	QVJ1	3FT deg	* g	BBB	Ind	D*^	32	ABBB	Ind	1	
English	Q300	3FT deg	* g	AAB/ABB	Ind	D*^	34	ABBB	Ind	9	24/30
English/Classical Literature and Civilisation	QQ38	3FT deg	*	BBB	Ind	D*^	32	ABBB	Ind		

English 26

course details			98 expected requirements							96 entry stats	
TITLE	CODE	COURSE	SUBJECTS	A/AS	ND/C	AGNVQ	IB	SQA(H)	SQA	RATIO	A/AS
English/French Studies	QR31	4FT deg	F	ABB	Ind	D*^	32$	ABBB	Ind	12	28/30
English/German Studies	QR32	4FT deg	G	BBB	Ind	D*^	32$	ABBB	Ind	11	
English/Hispanic Studies	QR34	4FT deg	*	BBB	Ind	D*^	32	ABBB	Ind	4	26/30
English/History	QV31	3FT deg	*	ABB	Ind	D*^	34	ABBB	Ind	13	26/30
English/History of Art	QV34	3FT deg	*	BBB	Ind	D*^	32	ABBB	Ind	6	24/30
English/Italian	QR33	4FT deg	*	BBB	Ind	D*^	32	ABBB	Ind	15	
English/Latin	QQ36	3FT deg	Ln	BBB	Ind	D*^	32$	ABBB	Ind		
English/Media & Cultural Studies	PQ43	3FT deg	*	BBB	Ind	D*^	32	ABBB	Ind	43	18/26
English/Modern Greek Studies	QTH2	4FT deg	* g	BBB	Ind	D*^	32	ABBB	Ind		
English/Music	QW33	3FT deg	Mu	AAB/ABB	Ind	D*^	32$	ABBB	Ind	9	26/28
English/Philosophy	QV37	3FT deg	*	ABB	Ind	D*^	32	ABBB	Ind	18	24/28
English/Portuguese	QR35	4FT deg	*	BBB	Ind	D*^	32	ABBB	Ind		
English/Russian	QR38	4FT deg	*	BBB	Ind	D*^	32	ABBB	Ind		
English/Sport & Recreation Studies	QB36	3FT deg	*	BBB	Ind	D*^	32	ABBB	Ind		
English/Theology	QV38	3FT deg	*	BBB	Ind	D*^	32	ABBB	Ind	19	
BLACKBURN COLL											
English (Language and Literary Studies)	Q300	3FT deg	E	18		M^					
BOLTON INST											
Creative Writing and French	RQ13	3FT deg	F g	CD	Ind	Ind	24	BBCC	Ind		
Creative Writing and German	RQ23	3FT deg	G g	CD	Ind	Ind	24	BBCC	Ind		
Visual Arts and Creative Writing	QW31	3FT deg	g	CD	MO	M*	24	BBCC	Ind		
BRETTON HALL											
English-Drama	Q3W4	3FT deg	E	CC-BB	MO $		Ind	CCC	Ind	7	8/26
English-Media Arts and Technology	Q3P4	3FT deg	E	CC-BB	MO $		Ind	CCC	Ind	4	10/22
Performing Arts (Drama/English)	W4Q3	3FT deg	T	BB	MO $		Ind	BBB	Ind	4	
Univ of BRISTOL											
Drama and English	WQ43	3FT deg	El g	BB	Ind	D$^	30$	AABBB	Ind	50	26/30
English	Q300	3FT deg	El	AAB	Ind	D$^	33$	AAABB	Ind	28	26/30
English and Latin	QQ36	3FT deg	El+Ln	BBC	Ind	D$^	32$	AABBB	Ind	4	
English and Philosophy	QV37	3FT deg	El g	AAB-ABB	Ind	D$^	33$	AAABB	Ind	20	20/30
BRISTOL, Univ of the W of England											
Drama and English	WQ43	3FT deg	Ap g	BBC	3M+3D	M$^ go	30	ABBB	Ind		
EFL and Business Systems	QN31	3FT deg	g	14-22	5M	M*^ go	24$	BCCC$	Ind		
EFL and European Studies	QT32	4FT deg	g	14-24	5M	M*^ go	24$	BCCC$	Ind		
EFL and Information Systems	QG35	3FT deg	g	14-22	5M	M*^ go	24$	BCCC$	Ind		
EFL and Law	QM33	4FT deg	g	16-24	6M	M*^ go	24$	BBCC$	Ind		
EFL, French and European Studies	QR31	4FT deg	g	14-24	5M	M*^ go	24$	BCCC$	Ind		
EFL, German and European Studies	QR32	4FT deg	g	14-24	5M	M*^ go	24$	BCCC$	Ind		
EFL, Spanish and European Studies	QR34	4FT deg	g	14-24	5M	M*^ go	24$	BCCC$	Ind		
English	Q300	3FT deg	El g	BBC	3M+3D	M$^ go	30$	ABBB$	Ind		
English and History	QV31	3FT deg	Ap g	CCC	4M+2D	M$^ go	26$	BBBC$	Ind$		
Information Systems, EFL and French	G5Q3	3FT deg	g	14-22	5M	M*^ go	24$	BCCC$	Ind		
Information Systems, EFL and German	G5QH	3FT deg	g	14-22	5M	M*^ go	24$	BCCC$	Ind		
Information Systems, EFL and Spanish	G5QJ	3FT deg	g	14-22	5M	M*^ go	24$	BCCC$	Ind		
Joint Honours Programme	Y401	3FT deg	Ap g	14-16	5M $	M$ go	24	BCCC	Ind		
Education and English											
BRUNEL Univ, West London											
English	Q300	3FT deg	El g	16	MO $	M$ go	26$	BCCC$	Ind		
English/American Studies	QQ34	3FT deg	E g	14	MO $	M* go	24$	BCCC$	Ind		

course details			**98 expected requirements**							*96 entry stats*
TITLE	CODE	COURSE	SUBJECTS	A/AS	NVQ/C	AGNVQ	IB	SQA(H)	SQA	RATIO A/AS
English/Art	Q3W1	3FT deg	E+A g	14	MO $	M* go	24$	BCCC$	Ind	
English/Drama	QW34	3FT deg	E+T g	CB	MO $	M* go	24$	BCCC$	Ind	
Film & TV Studies/English	Q3W5	3FT deg	Ap+E g	20	MO $	M* go	28$	BBCC$	Ind	
History/English	QV31	3FT deg	H+E g	14	MO $	M* go	22$	BCCC$	Ind	
Music/English	QW33	3FT deg								

Univ of BUCKINGHAM

Accounting and Finance with English Language St	N4Q3	2FT deg	* g	16	3M+2D	M	26	BCCC	Ind	
Economics with English Language Studies (EFL)	L1Q3	2FT deg	M g	14	3M+2D	M	26	BCCC	Ind	
English Language Studies (EFL) with Literature	Q1Q3	3FT deg		10	3M+2D	M	24	CCCC	Ind	
English Literature	Q300	2FT deg	E	10	5M	M	24	CCCC	Ind	
English Literature and History of Art	QV34	2FT deg	E g	10	5M	M	24	CCCC	Ind	
History and English Literature	QV31	2FT deg	E/H	10	5M	M	24	CCCC	Ind	
Psychology with English Language Studies (EFL)	C8Q3	3FT deg	*	14	5M	M	26	BCCC	Ind	

BUCKINGHAMSHIRE COLLEGE

English Studies and Visual Arts	QV34	3FT deg		12	2D	M	27	CCCC	Ind	2 6/12

CAMBRIDGE Univ

English	Q300▼	3FT deg	El g	AAA-AAB Ind			Ind	CSYS	Ind	4 28/30
English with Education Studies (BA)	Q3X9▼	3FT deg	* g	AAB	Ind		Ind	CSYS	Ind	7

CANTERBURY CHRIST CHURCH COLL of HE

American Studies with English	Q4Q3	4FT deg	E g	CC	MO	M	24	Ind	Ind	3 10/14
Art with English	W1Q3	3FT deg	E+A	CC	MO	M	24	Ind	Ind	4 12/16
Business Studies with English	N1Q3	3FT deg	E	CC	MO	M	24	Ind	Ind	10
Early Childhood Studies with English	X9Q3	3FT deg	E	CC	MO	M	24	Ind	Ind	7
English	Q300	3FT deg	E	CC	MO	M	24	Ind	Ind	
English and American Studies	QQ43	3FT deg	E	CC	MO	M	24	Ind	Ind	1 6/16
English and Art	WQ13	3FT deg	E+A	CC	MO	M	24	Ind	Ind	16
English and Business Studies	QN31	3FT deg	E	CC	MO	M	24	Ind	Ind	2
English and Early Childhood Studies	XQ93	3FT deg	E	CC	MO	M	24	Ind	Ind	
English and Social Science	LQ33	3FT deg	E	CC	MO	M	24	Ind	Ind	7
English with American Studies	Q3Q4	3FT deg	E	CC	MO	M	24	Ind	Ind	3 6/16
English with Art	Q3W1	3FT deg	E+A	CC	MO	M	24	Ind	Ind	4 10/20
English with Business Studies	Q3N1	3FT deg	E	CC	MO	M	24	Ind	Ind	5
English with Early Childhood Studies	Q3X9	3FT deg	E	CC	MO	M	24	Ind	Ind	7
English with French	Q3R1	3FT deg	E+F	CC	MO	M	24	Ind	Ind	
English with Geography	Q3L8	3FT deg	E+Gy							
English with History	Q3V1	3FT deg	E+H	CC	MO	M	24	Ind	Ind	6
English with Information Technology	Q3G5	3FT deg	E g	CC	MO	M	24	Ind	Ind	5
English with Marketing	Q3N5	3FT deg	E	CC	MO	M	24	Ind	Ind	4
English with Mathematics	Q3G1	3FT deg	E+M	DD	Ind	Ind	24	Ind	Ind	
English with Media Studies	Q3P4	3FT deg	E	CC	MO	M	24	Ind	Ind	
English with Music	Q3W3	3FT deg	E+Mu	CC	MO	M	24	Ind	Ind	4
English with Psychology	Q3L7	3FT deg	E+Ps	CC	MO	M	24	Ind	Ind	
English with Radio, Film and Television Studies	Q3W5	3FT deg	E	CC	MO	M	24	Ind	Ind	20 12/20
English with Religious Studies	Q3V8	3FT deg	E	CC	MO	M	24	Ind	Ind	3 10/12
English with Science	Q3Y1	3FT deg	E+S	DD	Ind	Ind	24	Ind	Ind	
English with Social Science	Q3L3	3FT deg	E	CC	MO	M	24	Ind	Ind	2 6/24
English with Sport Science	Q3B6	3FT deg	E	CC	MO	M	24	Ind	English	
English with Statistics	Q3G4	3FT deg	E+M	DD	Ind	Ind	24	Ind	Ind	
English with Tourism	Q3P7	3FT deg	E	CC	MO	M	24	Ind	Ind	
French and English	QR31	3FT deg	F+E g	CC	MO	M	24	Ind	Ind	

TITLE	CODE	COURSE	SUBJECTS	A/AS	ND/C	AGNVQ	IB	SQA(H)	SQA	RATIO A/AS	
course details			*98 expected requirements*							*96 entry stats*	
Geography and English	QL38	3FT deg	Gy+E	CC	MO	M	24	Ind	Ind		
Geography with English	L8Q3	3FT deg	Gy+E								
History and English	VQ13	3FT deg	H+E	CC	MO	M	24	Ind	Ind	3	
History with English	V1Q3	3FT deg	E+H	CC	MO	M	24	Ind	Ind	5	
Information Technology and English	QG35	3FT deg	E g	CC	MO	M	24	Ind	Ind		
Information Technology with English	G5Q3	3FT deg	E g	CC	MO	M	24	Ind	Ind		
Marketing and English	NQ53	3FT deg	E g	CC	MO	M	24	Ind	Ind	2	
Marketing with English	N5Q3	3FT deg	E g	CC	MO	M	24	Ind	Ind		
Mathematics and English	QG31	3FT deg	E+M	DD	Ind	Ind	24	Ind	Ind		
Mathematics with English	G1Q3	3FT deg	M+E g	DD	Ind	Ind	24	Ind	Ind		
Media Studies and English	PQ43	3FT deg	E g	CC	MO	M	24	Ind	Ind		
Media Studies with English	P4Q3	3FT deg	E g	CC	MO	M	24	Ind	Ind		
Music and English	WQ33	3FT deg	E+Mu g	CC	MO	M	24	Ind	Ind	2	
Music with English	W3Q3	3FT deg	E+Mu g	CC	MO	M	24	Ind	Ind	7	
Psychology and English	LQ73	3FT deg	Ps+E g	CC	MO	M	24	Ind	Ind		
Psychology with English	L7Q3	3FT deg	Ps+E g	CC	MO	M	24	Ind	Ind		
Radio, Film & Television Studies with English	W5Q3	3FT deg	E g	CC	MO	M	24	Ind	Ind	14	15/16
Radio, Film and Television Studies and English	QW35	3FT deg	E g	CC	MO	M	24	Ind	Ind	24	
Religious Studies and English	QV38	3FT deg	E g	CC	MO	M	24	Ind	Ind	3	
Religious Studies with English	V8Q3	3FT deg	E g	CC	MO	M	24	Ind	Ind		
Science and English	QY31	3FT deg	E+S	DD	Ind	Ind	24	Ind	Ind		
Science with English	Y1Q3	3FT deg	S+E	DD	Ind	Ind	24	Ind	Ind		
Social Science with English	L3Q3	3FT deg	E g	CC	MO	M	24	Ind	Ind	2	10/20
Sport Science and English	BQ63	3FT deg	E	CC	MO	M	24	Ind	Ind		
Sport Science with English	B6Q3	3FT deg	E g	CC	MO	M	24	Ind	Ind		
Statistics and English	GQ43	3FT deg	M+E	DD	Ind	Ind	24	Ind	Ind		
Statistics with English	G4Q3	3FT deg	M+E g	DD	Ind	Ind	24	Ind	Ind		
Tourism Studies with English	P7Q3	3FT deg	E g	CC	MO	M	24	Ind	Ind		
Tourism and English	QP37	3FT deg	E g	CC	MO	M	24	Ind	Ind		

CARDIFF Univ of Wales

TITLE	CODE	COURSE	SUBJECTS	A/AS	ND/C	AGNVQ	IB	SQA(H)	SQA	RATIO	A/AS
English Literature	Q306	3FT deg	E	ABB	X		Ind	AAABB	X	4	22/30
English Literature/Ancient History	QV3D	3FT deg	E	ABB			Ind	AAABB	X		
English Literature/Archaeology	QV36	3FT deg	E	ABB	X		Ind	AAAA	X		
English Literature/Cultural Criticism	MQ9H	3FT deg	E	ABB	X		Ind	AAABB	X		18/24
English Literature/Education	QX39	3FT deg	E	ABB	Ind	Ind	Ind	AAABB	X	9	
French/English Literature	RQ13	4FT deg	E+F	ABB	Ind		Ind	AAABB	Ind	8	24/28
German/English Literature	RQ23	4FT deg	E+G	ABB	X		Ind	AAABB	X	7	
History of Ideas/English Literature	VQD3	3FT deg	E	ABB			Ind	AAABB	X		
History/English Literature	VQ13	3FT deg	E+H	ABB	X		Ind	AAABB	X	4	24/30
Italian/English Literature	RQ33	4FT deg	E+L	ABB	Ind		Ind	AAAAB	Ind		
Language Studies/English Literature	QQ31	3FT deg	E	ABB	X		Ind	AAAA	X	7	
Modern English Studies	Q312	3FT deg	E	BBC			30	ABBBB		3	16/28
Music/English Literature	WQ33	3FT deg	E+Mu	ABB	X		Ind	AABBB	X	6	22/24
Philosophy/English Literature	VQ73	3FT deg	E	ABB	X		Ind	AAABB	X	5	20/28
Portuguese/English Literature	QR35	4FT deg	E+L	ABB	X		Ind	AAABB	X		
Psychology/English Literature	LQ73	3FT deg	E g	ABB	MO+6D		Ind	AABBB	N	6	24/30
Religious Studies/English Literature	VQ83	3FT deg	E	ABB	X		Ind	AAABB	X	18	
Social Philosophy and Applied Ethics/English Lit	VQ7J	3FT deg	E	ABB	X		Ind	AAABB	X		
Spanish/English Literature	QR34	4FT deg	E+L	ABB	X		Ind	AAABB	X	13	
Welsh History/English Literature	VQCH	3FT deg	E+H	ABB	X		Ind	AAABB	X		
Welsh/English Literature	QQ53	3FT deg	E+W	ABB	X		Ind	AAABB	X	7	

course details			98 expected requirements							96 entry stats	
TITLE	CODE	COURSE	SUBJECTS	A/AS	ND/C	AGNVQ	IB	SQA(H)	SQA	RATIO	A/AS
Univ of CENTRAL ENGLAND											
English Language and Literature	Q300	3FT deg	E g	16-18	Ind		Ind	Ind	Ind	4	8/22
Univ of CENTRAL LANCASHIRE											
English Language Studies	Q300	3FT deg	E	CCC	Ind	D$^	30$	BBBB$	Ind	5	12/22
English Literary Studies	Q306	3FT deg	E	CCC	Ind	D$^	30$	BBBB$	Ind	6	12/22
English for International Business (Yr 2 entry)	Q302	1FT dip	*				26				
English for International Business (Yr 3 entry)	Q301	1FT deg	*				26				
Combined Honours Programme English	Y400	3FT deg	EI	18	Ind	D*^	28$	BBBB$	Ind		
Combined Honours Programme English for International Business	Y400	3FT deg	*	10	MO	M	24	CCC	Ind		
CHELTENHAM & GLOUCESTER COLL of HE											
Countryside Planning and English Studies	DQ23	3FT deg	E	10-14	4M+3D	MK	26	CCCC	Ind		
Countryside Planning with English Studies	D2Q3	3FT deg	E	8-12	MO	MK	26	CCCC	Ind		
English Studies and Environmental Policy	QF39	3FT deg	E	12	4M+3D	M^	26	CCCC	Ind		
English Studies and Fashion	WQ23	3FT deg	E	12	4M+3D	M^	26	CCCC	Ind		
English Studies and Geography	LQ8H	3FT deg	E	12-14	MO	M3^	26	CCCC	Ind		
English Studies and History	QV31	3FT deg	E+H	12-16	4M+3D	M^	26	CCCC	Ind		
English Studies and Human Geography	LQ83	3FT deg	E	12-16	4M+3D	M^	26	CCCC	Ind		
English Studies and Media Communications	PQ43	3FT deg	E	12-16	4M+3D	M^	26	CCCC	Ind		
English Studies and Multimedia	QG35	3FT deg	E	12	4M+3D	M^	26	CCCC	Ind		
English Studies and Performance Arts	QW34	3FT deg	E	10-14	4M+3D	M3	26	CCCC	Ind		
English Studies and Physical Geography	FQ83	3FT deg	E	12-16	4M+3D	M^	26	CCCC	Ind		
English Studies and Psychology	LQ73	3FT deg	E g	12-16	4M+3D	M^	26	CCCC	Ind		
English Studies and Religious Studies	QV38	3FT deg	E	8-12	5M+2D	M^	26	CCCC	Ind		
English Studies and Sociological Studies	LQ33	3FT deg	E	12-16	4M+3D	M^	26	CCCC	Ind		
English Studies and Sport and Exercise Sciences	QB36	3FT deg	S+E	12-16	4M+3D	M^	26	CCCC	Ind		
English Studies and Tourism Management	PQ73	3FT deg	E	12-16	4M+3D	M^	26	CCCC	Ind		
English Studies and Visual Arts	QW31	3FT deg	E+A	10-14	4M+3D	MA3	26	CCCC	Ind		
English Studies and Women's Studies	MQ93	3FT deg	E	12	5M+2D	M^	26	CCCC	Ind		
English Studies with Combined Arts	Q3Y3	3FT deg	E	12-14	MO	M3^	26	CCCC	Ind		
English Studies with Countryside Planning	Q3D2	3FT deg	E	12	4M+3D	M^	26	CCCC	Ind		
English Studies with Environmental Policy	Q3F9	3FT deg	E	12	4M+3D	M^	26	CCCC	Ind		
English Studies with Fashion	Q3W2	3FT deg	E	12	4M+3D	M^	26	CCCC	Ind		
English Studies with Geography	Q3LV	3FT deg	E	12-14	MO	M3^	26	CCCC	Ind		
English Studies with History	Q3V1	3FT deg	E	12-14	4M+3D	M^	26	CCCC	Ind		
English Studies with Human Geography	Q3L8	3FT deg	E	12-14	4M+3D	M^	26	CCCC	Ind		
English Studies with Media Communications	Q3P4	3FT deg	E	12-14	4M+3D	M^	26	CCCC	Ind		
English Studies with Modern Languages (French)	Q3R1	3FT deg	E g	12-14	4M+3D	M^	26	CCCC	Ind		
English Studies with Multimedia	Q3G5	3FT deg	E	12	4M+3D	M^	26	CCCC	Ind		
English Studies with Performance Arts	Q3W4	3FT deg	E	10-14	4M+3D	M3	26	CCCC	Ind		
English Studies with Physical Geography	Q3F8	3FT deg	E	12	4M+3D	M^	26	CCCC	Ind		
English Studies with Psychology	Q3L7	3FT deg	E+M g	12-16	4M+3D	M^	26	CCCC	Ind		
English Studies with Religious Studies	Q3V8	3FT deg	E	12	4M+3D	M^	26	CCCC	Ind		
English Studies with Sociological Studies	Q3L3	3FT deg	E	12-16	4M+3D	M^	26	CCCC	Ind		
English Studies with Sport and Exercise Sciences	Q3B6	3FT deg	E+S g	12-16	4M+3D	M^	26	CCCC	Ind		
English Studies with Tourism Management	Q3P7	3FT deg	E	12-16	4M+3D	M^	26	CCCC	Ind		
English Studies with Visual Arts	Q3W1	3FT deg	E	10-14	4M+3D	MA3	26	CCCC	Ind		
English Studies with Women's Studies	Q3M9	3FT deg	E	12-14	4M+3D	M^	26	CCCC	Ind		
Environmental Policy with English Studies	F9Q3	3FT deg	E	8-12	MO	M3	26	CCCC	Ind		
Fashion with English Studies	W2Q3	3FT deg	*	10-14	MO	M^	26	CCCC	Ind		
Geography with English Studies	L8QH	3FT deg	E	12-14	MO	M3^	26	CCCC	Ind		

English   26

course details			*98 expected requirements*							*96 entry stats*
TITLE	CODE	COURSE	SUBJECTS	A/AS	ND/C	RGNVQ	IB	SQA(H)	SQA	RATIO A/AS
History with English Studies	V1Q3	3FT deg	H+E	12	4M+3D	M3_	26	CCCC	Ind	
Human Geography with English Studies	L8Q3	3FT deg	E	12-16	4M+3D	M3	26	CCCC	Ind	
Media Communications with English Studies	P4Q3	3FT deg	E	12-16	4M+3D	MP3	26	CCCC	Ind	
Multimedia with English Studies	G5Q3	3FT deg	E	8-12	MO	MI3	26	CCCC	Ind	
Multimedia with English Studies	G5QH	4SW deg	*	8-12	MO	MI3	24	CCCC	Ind	
Performance Arts with English Studies	W4Q3	3FT deg	*	10-14	5M+2D	M3	26	CCCC	Ind	
Physical Geography with English Studies	F8Q3	3FT deg	*	8-12	4M+3D	M3^	26	CCCC	Ind	
Psychology with English Studies	L7Q3	3FT deg	g	12-16	4M+3D	M3^	26	CCCC	Ind	
Religious Studies with English Studies	V8Q3	3FT deg	*	8-12	MO	M3_	26	CCCC	Ind	
Sociological Studies with English Studies	L3Q3	3FT deg	*	12-16	4M+3D	MG3	26	CCCC	Ind	
Sport & Exercise Sciences with English Studies	B6Q3	3FT deg	*	12-16	4M+3D	ML3	26	CCCC	Ind	
Tourism Management with English Studies	P7Q3	4SW deg	*	12-16	4M+3D	ML3	26	CCCC	Ind	
Visual Arts with English Studies	W1Q3	3FT deg	A	10-14	5M+2D	MA3	26	CCCC	Ind	
Women's Studies with English Studies	M9Q3	3FT deg	*	8-14	MO	M3	26	CCCC	Ind	

UNIVERSITY COLLEGE CHESTER

TITLE	CODE	COURSE	SUBJECTS	A/AS	ND/C	RGNVQ	IB	SQA(H)	SQA	RATIO A/AS
Art and English Literature	WQ93	3FT deg	E	CC	M	P^	Ind	CCCC	$	13
Art with English Literature	W9Q3	3FT deg	E	CC	M	P^	Ind	CCCC	$	6 18/20
Biology and English Literature	CQ13	3FT deg	B+E	CC	M	P^	Ind	CCCC	$	
Biology with English Literature	C1Q3	3FT deg	B+E	CC	M	P^	Ind	CCCC	$	
Computer Science/IT and English Literature	GQ53	3FT deg	E g	12	M	P^	Ind	CCCC	$	3
Computer Science/IT with English Literature	G5Q3	3FT deg	E g	12	M	P^	Ind	CCCC	$	5
Drama and Theatre Studies and English Lit	WQ43	3FT deg	E	12	M	P^	Ind	CCCC	$	16 16/26
Drama and Theatre Studies with English	W4Q3	3FT deg	E	CC	M	P^	Ind	CCCC	$	23 14/16
English Literature and Geography	QF38	3FT deg	E+Gy/Gl	CC	M	P^	Ind	CCCC	$	9
English Literature and History	QV31	3FT deg	E+H/Ec/So	CC	M	P^	Ind	CCCC	$	8 14/20
English Literature and Mathematics	QG31	3FT deg	E+M	12	M	P^	Ind	CCCC	$	1
English Literature and PE/Sports Science	QB36	3FT deg	E	CC	M	P^	Ind	CCCC	$	
English Literature and Psychology	QL37	3FT deg	E g	12	M	P^	Ind	CCCC	$	18 14/16
English Literature and Theology and Rel St	QV38	3FT deg	E	12	M	P^	Ind	CCCC	$	28
English Literature with French	Q3R1	3FT deg	E g	12	M	P^	Ind	CCCC	$	6 16/20
English Literature with German	Q3R2	3FT deg	E g	12	M	P^	Ind	CCCC	$	8
English with Art	Q3W9	3FT deg	E	CC	M	P^	Ind	CCCC	$	12
English with Biology	Q3C1	3FT deg	E+B	12	M	P^	Ind	CCCC	$	
English with Computer Science/IT	Q3G5	3FT deg	E g	12	M	P^	Ind	CCCC	$	5
English with Drama and Theatre Studies	Q3W4	3FT deg	E	CC	M	P^	Ind	CCCC	$	31
English with Geography	Q3F8	3FT deg	E+Gy/G1	CC	M	P^	Ind	CCCC	$	
English with History	Q3V1	3FT deg	E+H/Ec/So	CC	M	P^	Ind	CCCC	$	11
English with Mathematics	Q3G1	3FT deg	E+M	12	M	P^	Ind	CCCC	$	
English with Physical Education/Sports Science	Q3B6	3FT deg	E	CC	M	P^	Ind	CCCC	$	
English with Psychology	Q3L7	3FT deg	E g	12	M	P^	Ind	CCCC	$	15 12/16
English with Theology and Religious Studies	Q3V8	3FT deg	E	12	M	P^	Ind	CCCC	$	4
Geography with English Literature	F8Q3	3FT deg	E+Gy/Gl	CC	M	P^	Ind	CCCC	$	
History with English Literature	V1Q3	3FT deg	H/Ec/So+E	CC	M	P^	Ind	CCCC	$	10
Mathematics with English Literature	G1Q3	3FT deg	M+E	12	M	P^	Ind	CCCC	$	
PE/Sports Science with English Literature	B6Q3	3FT deg	E	CC	M	P^	Ind	CCCC	$	
Psychology with English Literature	L7Q3	3FT deg	E g	12	M	P^	Ind	CCCC	$	37
Theology and Religious Studies with English Lit	V8Q3	3FT deg	E	12	M	P^	Ind	CCCC	$	4

CHICHESTER INSTITUTE OF HIGHER EDUCATION

TITLE	CODE	COURSE	SUBJECTS	A/AS	ND/C	RGNVQ	IB	SQA(H)	SQA	RATIO A/AS
Art and English	WQ13	3FT deg	E+A+Pf	12	Ind	M$+^	Ind	Ind	Ind	7 14/22
Art with English	W1Q3	3FT deg	A+Pf	12	Ind	M$+^	Ind	Ind	Ind	
Art with English	E1Q3	3FT deg	A+Pf	12	Ind	M$+^	Ind	Ind	Ind	

course details | 98 expected requirements | 96 entry stats

TITLE	CODE	COURSE	SUBJECTS	A/AS	ND/C	AGNVQ	IB	SQA(H)	SQA	RATIO A/AS
English	Q300	3FT deg	E	12	Ind	M^	Ind	Ind	Ind	
English Language Teaching (EFL) and English	QQ13	3FT deg	E	12	Ind	M^	Ind	Ind	Ind	
English and Geography	QL38	3FT deg	E+Gy	12	Ind	M^	Ind	Ind	Ind	4
English and History	QV31	3FT deg	E+H	12	Ind	M^	Ind	Ind	Ind	4
English and Study of Religions	QV38	3FT deg	E	12	Ind	M^	Ind	Ind	Ind	7
English and Theology	QV3V	3FT deg	E	12	Ind	M$	Ind	Ind	Ind	
English with Art	Q3W1	3FT deg	E	12	Ind	M^	Ind	Ind	Ind	13
English with Education Studies (Opt. QTS) (P)	Q3X9	3FT/4FT deg	E g	12	Ind	M^ go	Ind	Ind	Ind	3	6/18
English with English Language Teaching (EFL)	Q3Q1	3FT deg	E	12	Ind	M^	Ind	Ind	Ind	4
English with Environmental Science	Q3F9	3FT deg	E g	12	Ind	M^	Ind	Ind	Ind	
English with Geography	Q3L8	3FT deg	E	12	Ind	M^	Ind	Ind	Ind	
English with History	Q3V1	3FT deg	E	12	Ind	M^	Ind	Ind	Ind	2	14/18
English with Mathematics	Q3G1	3FT deg	E g	12	Ind	M^	Ind	Ind	Ind	
English with Media Studies	Q3P4	3FT deg	E	12	Ind	M^	Ind	Ind	Ind	6	6/16
English with Music	Q3W3	3FT deg	E	12	Ind	M^	Ind	Ind	Ind	3
English with Related Arts	Q3W9	3FT deg	E	12	Ind	M^	Ind	Ind	Ind	3
English with Study of Religions	Q3V8	3FT deg	E	12	Ind	M^	Ind	Ind	Ind	4
English with Theology	Q3VV	3FT deg	E	12	Ind	M$	Ind	Ind	Ind	
English with Women's Studies	Q3M9	3FT deg	E	12	Ind	M^	Ind	Ind	Ind	2	10/10
Environmental Science and English	FQ93	3FT deg	E	12	Ind	M^	Ind	Ind	Ind	
Geography with English	L8Q3	3FT deg	Gy	12	Ind	M$	Ind	Ind	Ind	2
History with English	V1Q3	3FT deg	H	12	Ind	M$	Ind	Ind	Ind	12
Mathematics and English	GQ13	3FT deg	M+E	12	Ind	M^	Ind	Ind	Ind	
Mathematics with English	G1Q3	3FT deg	M	12	Ind	M^	Ind	Ind	Ind	
Media Studies and English	PQ43	3FT deg	E	12	Ind	M$	Ind	Ind	Ind	6	10/20
Music and English	QW33	3FT deg	E+Mu	12	Ind	M$+^	Ind	Ind	Ind	7
Music with English	W3Q3	3FT deg	Mu	12	Ind	M$+	Ind	Ind	Ind	
Related Arts and English	QW39	3FT deg	E	12	Ind	M+^	Ind	Ind	Ind	1	8/14
Study of Religions with English	V8Q3	3FT deg	*	12	Ind	M$	Ind	Ind	Ind	2
Theology and English	VQ83	3FT deg	E	12	Ind	M^	Ind	Ind	Ind	
Theology with English	V8QH	3FT deg	*	12	Ind	M$	Ind	Ind	Ind	
Women's Studies and English	MQ93	3FT deg	E	12	Ind	M$^	Ind	Ind	Ind	

COLCHESTER INST

TITLE	CODE	COURSE	SUBJECTS	A/AS	ND/C	AGNVQ	IB	SQA(H)	SQA	RATIO A/AS
Communications & Media Studies/English	PQ33	3FT deg		CC	Ind	Ind	Ind	Ind	Ind	5	14/18
English/History	QV31	3FT deg		CC	Ind	Ind	Ind	Ind	Ind	4
English/Sociology	QL33	3FT deg		CC	Ind	Ind	Ind	Ind	Ind	6

DE MONTFORT Univ

TITLE	CODE	COURSE	SUBJECTS	A/AS	ND/C	AGNVQ	IB	SQA(H)	SQA	RATIO A/AS
English	Q300▼	3FT deg	* g	BCD-CCC	D	D^	30$	AABB$	Ind	12	16/26
English and Cultural Studies	Q310▼	3FT deg	E/El	10	D	M^	Ind	BCCC	Ind	2	6/22
Humanities Combined Honours English	Y300▼	3FT deg	* g	CCC	MO	X	30$	ABBB	Ind	
Humanities Joint Honours English	Y301▼	3FT deg	* g	CCD	MO	X	28$	ABBB	Ind	

DONCASTER COLL

TITLE	CODE	COURSE	SUBJECTS	A/AS	ND/C	AGNVQ	IB	SQA(H)	SQA	RATIO A/AS
Combined Studies Social and Literary Studies	Y300	3FT deg		EE	N	Ind	Ind	Ind	Ind	

Univ of DUNDEE

TITLE	CODE	COURSE	SUBJECTS	A/AS	ND/C	AGNVQ	IB	SQA(H)	SQA	RATIO A/AS
American Studies and English	QQ34	4FT deg	E g	BCC	Ind	D$^	29$	BBBC$	Ind	7
Contemporary European Studies and English	QT32	4FT deg	E g	BCC	Ind	D$^	29$	BBBC$	Ind	4
English	Q300	4FT deg	E g	BCC	Ind	D$^ | 29$	BBBC$	Ind	6	18/29
English and Geography	LQ83	4FT deg	E g	BCC	Ind	D$^	29$	BBBC$	Ind	4

TITLE	CODE	COURSE	SUBJECTS	A/AS	NO/C	AGNVQ	IB	SQA(H)	SQA	RATIO	A/AS
English and Mathematics	GQ13	4FT deg	E+M g	BCC	Ind	D$^	29$	BBBC$	Ind	1	
English and Modern History	QV31	4FT deg	E g	BCC	Ind	D$^	29$	BBBC$	Ind	9	
English and Philosophy	QV37	4FT deg	E g	BCC	Ind	D$^	29$	BBBC$	Ind	5	
English and Political Science	MQ13	4FT deg	E g	BCC	Ind	D$^	29$	BBBC$	Ind	6	
English and Psychology	LQ73	4FT deg	E g	BCC	Ind	D$^	29$	BBBC$	Ind	5	
Arts and Social Sciences *English*	Y400	3FT deg	E g	BCC	Ind	D$^	29$	BBBC$	Ind		

Univ of DURHAM

TITLE	CODE	COURSE	SUBJECTS	A/AS	NO/C	AGNVQ	IB	SQA(H)	SQA	RATIO	A/AS
Classical Studies and English Literature	QQ38	3FT deg	E g	AAB	Ind	Ind	Ind	AAABB	Ind	21	
English Language & Linguistics	QQ13	3FT deg	*	BBB	Ind	Ind	Ind	AABBB	Ind	10	20/30
English Literature	Q300	3FT deg	E g	AAB	Ind	Ind	32	AAABB	Ind	15	26/30
English Literature and Latin	QQ36	3FT deg	E+Ln	AAB	Ind	Ind	32	AAABB	Ind		
English Literature and Linguistics	QQ1H	3FT deg	E g	AAB	Ind	Ind	32	AAABB	Ind	31	
English Literature and Music	QW33	3FT deg	E+Mu g	AAB	Ind	Ind	32	AAABB	Ind	28	
English Literature and Philosophy	QV37	3FT deg	E g	AAB	Ind	Ind	32	AAABB	Ind	20	26/28
Medieval Studies (English and History)	QV31	3FT deg	H/E g	AAB	Ind	Ind	Ind	Ind	Ind	22	
Arts Combined *English*	Y300	3FT deg	E g	24	MO	Ind	30	AAABB	Ind		

Univ of EAST ANGLIA

TITLE	CODE	COURSE	SUBJECTS	A/AS	NO/C	AGNVQ	IB	SQA(H)	SQA	RATIO	A/AS
American and English Literature (4 Yrs)	QQ43	4FT deg	E	BBB	X		28$	ABBBB	X	9	20/30
English Literature	Q306	3FT deg	E	ABB-BBB	X		30$	ABBBB	X	9	18/30
English Literature and Drama	WQ43	3FT deg	E	ABB-BBB	X		30$	AABBB	X	27	28/30
English Literature and Philosophy	VQ73	3FT deg	E	BBB	3M+3D		30	BBBBB	Ind	6	20/26
English Literature with Comparative Lit Minor	Q3QF	3FT deg	E	ABB-BBB	X		30$	ABBBB	X	14	
English Literature with Creative Writing Minor	Q3W9	3FT deg	E	ABB-BBB	X		30$	AABBB	X	50	22/24
English Literature with English History Minor	Q3V1	3FT deg	H+E	ABB-BBB	X		30	ABBBB	X	14	
English Studies (History and Literature)	QV31	3FT deg	H+E	BBB	X		30	ABBBB	X	7	8/30
English and American Literature	QQ34	3FT deg	E	ABB-BBB	X		30$	AABBB	X	6	22/30
Film and English Studies	QW35	3FT deg	E	BBB-BBC	X		30$	ABBBB	X	18	24/30

Univ of EAST LONDON

TITLE	CODE	COURSE	SUBJECTS	A/AS	NO/C	AGNVQ	IB	SQA(H)	SQA	RATIO	A/AS
Communication Studies and Literature	PQ33	3FT deg	* g	12	MO	X	Ind	Ind	Ind	5	
Communication Studies with Literature	P3Q3	3FT deg	* g	12	MO	M	Ind	Ind			
Cultural Studies and Literature	LQP3	3FT deg	* g	14	N	X	Ind	Ind	Ind	3	
Cultural Studies with Literature	L6Q3	3FT deg	* g	14	MO	M	Ind	Ind	Ind		
Education & Community Studies and Literature	QX39	3FT deg	* g	12	MO	X	Ind	Ind	Ind	1	
Education & Community Studies with Literature	X9Q3	3FT deg	* g	12	MO	M					
French and Literature	QR31	3FT deg	* g	12	MO	X	Ind	Ind	Ind	7	
French with Literature	R1Q3	3FT deg	* g	12	MO	M					
German and Literature	QR32	3FT deg	* g	12	MO	X	Ind	Ind	Ind		
German with Literature	R2Q3	3FT deg	* g	12	MO	M	Ind				
History and Literature	QV31	3FT deg	* g	12	MO	X	Ind	Ind	Ind	3	12/24
History of Art Design & Film and Literature	QV34	3FT deg	* g	12	MO	X	Ind	Ind	Ind	3	
History of Art Design & Film with Literature	V4Q3	3FT deg	* g	12	MO	M	Ind	Ind			
History with Literature	V1Q3	3FT deg	* g	12	MO	M	Ind	Ind			
Linguistics and Literature	QQ13	3FT deg	* g	14	MO	X	Ind	Ind	Ind	3	
Linguistics with Literature	Q1Q3	3FT deg	* g	12	MO	M	Ind				
Literature and Maths, Stats and Computing	GQ93	3FT deg	* g	6-14	N	M$	Ind	Ind	Ind		
Literature and Media Studies	PQ43	3FT deg	* g	12	N	D	Ind	Ind	Ind	16	
Literature and Politics	MQ13	3FT deg	* g	12	N	M	Ind	Ind	Ind	6	
Literature and Spanish	QR34	3FT deg	* g	6-14	N	M^	Ind	Ind	Ind		
Literature and Third World & Development Studies	MQY3	3FT deg	* g	12	N	M	Ind	Ind	Ind	1	

| course details | | | 98 expected requirements | | | | | | | 96 entry stats | |

TITLE	CODE	COURSE	SUBJECTS	A/AS	ND/C	AGNVQ	IB	SQA(H)	SQA	RATIO	A/AS
Literature and Women's Studies	QM39	3FT deg	* g	12	MO	M	Ind				
Literature with Communication Studies	Q3P3	3FT deg	* g	12	MO	M	Ind				
Literature with Cultural Studies	Q3L6	3FT deg	* g	12	MO	M	Ind				
Literature with Education & Community Studies	Q3X9	3FT deg	* g	12	MO	M	Ind				
Literature with French	Q3R1	3FT deg	* g	12	MO	M	Ind				
Literature with German	Q3R2	3FT deg	* g	12	MO	M	Ind				
Literature with History	Q3V1	3FT deg	* g	12	MO	M	Ind				
Literature with History of Art Design & Film	Q3V4	3FT deg	* g	12	MO	M	Ind				
Literature with Italian	Q3R3	3FT deg	* g	12	MO	M	Ind				
Literature with Law	Q3M3	3FT deg	* g	12	MO	M	Ind				
Literature with Linguistics	Q3Q1	3FT deg	* g	12	MO	M	Ind				
Literature with Maths, Stats & Computing	Q3G9	3FT deg	* g	12	MO	M	Ind				
Literature with Media Studies	Q3P4	3FT deg	* g	12	MO	M	Ind				
Literature with Politics	Q3MC	3FT deg	* g	12	MO	M	Ind				
Literature with Spanish	Q3R4	3FT deg	* g	12	MO	M	Ind				
Literature with Third World & Development St	Q3M9	3FT deg	* g	12	MO	M	Ind				
Literature with Women's Studies	Q3MX	3FT deg	* g	12	MO	M	Ind				
Maths, Stats & Computing with Literature	G9Q3	3FT deg	* g	12	MO	M	Ind	Ind	Ind		
Media Studies with Literature	P4Q3	3FT deg	* g	14	MO	M					
Politics with Literature	M1Q3	3FT deg	* g	12	MO	M	Ind				
Spanish with Literature	R4Q3	3FT deg	* g	12	MO	M	Ind				
Women's Studies with Literature	M9QH	3FT deg	* g	12	MO	M	Ind				
Three-Subject Degree *Literature*	Y600	3FT deg	* g	12	MO	M	Ind	Ind	Ind		

EDGE HILL Univ COLLEGE

TITLE	CODE	COURSE	SUBJECTS	A/AS	ND/C	AGNVQ	IB	SQA(H)	SQA	RATIO	A/AS
Art & Design and English	QW32	3FT deg	A+E	CC	X	X	Dip	BBCC$	X	2	7/18
Communication Studies and English	PQ33	3FT deg	E	CC	3M+3D	M* / P*_	Dip	BBCC	Ind		
Drama and English	QW34	3FT deg	E	CC	X	P*_^	Dip	BBCC$	X	7	8/20
Early Childhood Studies and English	QX39	3FT deg	E g	CC	X	P*_^ go	Dip	BBCC$	Ind		
English	Q301	3FT deg	E	CC	X	P*_^	Dip	BBCC$	X		
English	Q300	3FT deg	E	CC	X	P*_^	Dip	BBCC$	X	3	7/20
English and Applied Social Sciences	LQ33	3FT deg	E	CC	X	P*_^	Dip	BBCC$			
Geography and English	LQ83	3FT deg	(Gy/E) g	CC	X	X	Dip	BBCC$	X		
History and English	QV31	3FT deg	H/E	CC	X	X	Dip	BBCC$	Ind		
Modern European Studies and English	QT32	3FT deg	E	CD	X	P*_^	Dip	BBCC	Ind		
Women's Studies and English	MQ93	3FT deg	E	CC	X	P*_^	Dip	BBCC$	X	2	6/14

Univ of EDINBURGH

TITLE	CODE	COURSE	SUBJECTS	A/AS	ND/C	AGNVQ	IB	SQA(H)	SQA	RATIO	A/AS
English Language	Q302	4FT deg	E g	BBB	Ind	Ind	Dip$	BBBB$	Ind		
English Language and German	QR32	4FT deg	E+L g	BBB	Ind	Ind	Dip$	BBBB$	Ind		
English Language and History	QV31	4FT deg	E g	BBB	Ind	Ind	Dip$	BBBB$	Ind		
English Language and Linguistics	QQ31	4FT deg	g	BBB	Ind	Ind	Dip$	BBBB	Ind		
English Language and Literature	Q300	4FT deg	E g	AAB	Ind	Ind	Dip$	ABBB$	Ind		
English Language and Scandinavian Studies	QR37	4FT deg	L g	BBB	Ind	Ind	Dip$	BBBB$	Ind		
English Literature	Q306	4FT deg	E g	AAB	Ind	Ind	Dip$	ABBB$	Ind		
English Literature and Classics	QQ38	4FT deg	E g	BBB	Ind	Ind	Dip$	BBBB$	Ind		
English Literature and French	QR31	4FT deg	F+E g	AAB	Ind	Ind	Dip$	ABBB$	Ind		
English Literature and German	RQ23	4FT deg	L+E g	BBB	Ind	Ind	Dip$	BBBB$	Ind		
English Literature and History	QV3C	4FT deg	E g	AAB	Ind	Ind	Dip$	ABBB$	Ind		
English and Celtic	QQ35	4FT deg	L g	BBB	Ind	Ind	Dip$	BBBB$	Ind		
English and Scottish Literature	QQ32	4FT deg	E g	AAB	Ind	Ind	Dip$	ABBB$	Ind		
History of Art and English Literature	VQ43	4FT deg	E g	AAB	Ind	Ind	Dip$	ABBB$	Ind		
Italian and English Language	RQ33	4FT deg	L g	BBB	Ind	Ind	Dip$	BBBB$	Ind		

course details			98 expected requirements							96 entry stats
TITLE	CODE	COURSE	SUBJECTS	A/AS	ND/C	AGNVQ	IB	SQA(H)	SQA	RATIO A/AS
Italian and English Literature	RQ3H	4FT deg	L g	BBB	Ind	Ind	Dip$	BBBB$	Ind	
Philosophy and English Language	VQ7H	4FT deg	E g	BBB	Ind	Ind	Dip$	BBBB$	Ind	
Philosophy and English Literature	VQ73	4FT deg	E g	AAB	Ind	Ind	Dip$	ABBB$	Ind	
Scottish Ethnology and English Language	VQ93	4FT deg	g	BBB	Ind	Ind	Dip$	BBBB	Ind	
Scottish Ethnology and English Literature	VQ9H	4FT deg	E g	BBB	Ind	Ind	Dip$	BBBB$	Ind	
Univ of ESSEX										
English Language and English and European Lit	QQ23	3FT deg	*	22	MO+3D	Ind	28	AABB	Ind	11	22/26
English Language and Linguistics	QQ13	3FT deg	*	20	MO+2D	Ind	28	BBBB	Ind	8	16/24
English and European Literature	Q306	3FT deg	*	22	MO+3D	Ind	28	AABB	Ind	3	16/26
English and French (Language and Linguistics)	RQ13	4FT deg	F	20	MO+2D	Ind	28$	BBBB$	Ind	
English and German (Language and Linguistics)	RQ23	4FT deg	*	20	MO+2D	Ind	28	BBBB	Ind	
English and Russian (Language and Linguistics)	RQ83	FT deg	*	20	MO+2D	Ind	28	BBBB	Ind	
English and Spanish (Language and Linguistics)	RQ43	4FT deg	*	20	MO+2D	Ind	28	BBBB	Ind	
English as a Foreign Language	X910	3FT deg	*	20	MO+2D	Ind	28	BBBB	Ind	
Univ of EXETER										
English & American & Postcolonial St with Eur St	QQ34	4FT deg	E	BBB-BCC	MO	M/D$^	32$			
English Medieval Studies	QV31	3FT deg	E	BBB-BCC	MO	M/D$^	32$	Ind	Ind	
English Medieval Studies with European Study	QV3C	4FT deg	E+L	BBB-BCC	MO	M/D$^	32$	Ind	Ind	
English Studies	Q303	3FT deg	E	BBB-BCC	MO	M/D$^	32$			
English Studies with European Studies	Q304	4FT deg	E+L	BBB-BCC	MO	M/D$^	32$			
English and American & Postcolonial Studies	QQ43	3FT deg	E	BBB-BCC	MO	M/D$^	32$			
English and Drama	QW34	3FT deg	E	BBB-BCC	MO+3D	M/D$^ | 32$	Ind	Ind	27	24/28
English and Fine Art	QW31	3FT deg	E+Pf	BBB-BCC	MO	M/D$^ | 32$	Ind	Ind	9	18/30
English and German	QR32	4FT deg	E+G	BBB-BCC	MO	M/D$^ | 32$	Ind	Ind	8	
English and Greek & Roman Studies	QQ38	3FT deg	E	BBB-BCC	MO	M/D$^ | 32$	Ind	Ind	7	20/26
Univ of GLAMORGAN										
American Studies and English Studies	QQ43	3FT deg	* g	12	5M	M$	Ind	Ind	Ind	
American Studies with English Studies	Q4Q3	3FT deg	E g	12	5M	M$	Ind	Ind	Ind	
English Studies	Q301	3FT deg	E/EI g	16	Ind	Ind	Ind	Ind	Ind	7	8/24
English Studies and History	QV31	3FT deg	* g	12	Ind	Ind	Ind	Ind	Ind	
English Studies and Media Studies	QP34	3FT deg	Me/T/E g	14	Ind	Ind	Ind	Ind	Ind	
English Studies and Philosophy	QV37	3FT deg	* g	12	Ind	Ind	Ind	Ind	Ind	
English Studies and Psychology	LQ73	3FT deg	* g	CC	Ind	Ind	Ind	Ind	Ind	
English Studies and Religious Studies	QV38	3FT deg	* g	12	Ind	Ind	Ind	Ind	Ind	
English Studies and Sociology	LQ33	3FT deg	* g	12	Ind	Ind	Ind	Ind	Ind	
English Studies and Theatre & Media Drama	QW34	3FT deg	Me/T/E g	14	Ind	Ind	Ind	Ind	Ind	
English Studies and Visual Arts	QW31	3FT deg	A g	12	Ind	Ind	Ind	Ind	Ind	
English Studies and Welsh Studies	QQ35	3FT deg	* g	12	Ind	Ind	Ind	Ind	Ind	
English Studies with American Studies	Q3Q4	3FT deg	* g	12	Ind	Ind	Ind	Ind	Ind	
English Studies with Media Studies	Q3P4	3FT deg	* g	14	Ind	Ind	Ind	Ind	Ind	
English Studies with Philosophy	Q3V7	3FT deg	* g	12	Ind	Ind	Ind	Ind	Ind	
English Studies with Psychology	Q3L7	3FT deg	* g	CC	Ind	Ind	Ind	Ind	Ind	
English Studies with Sociology	Q3L3	3FT deg	* g	12	Ind	Ind	Ind	Ind	Ind	
English Studies with Theatre and Media Drama	Q3W4	3FT deg	Me/T/E g	14	Ind	Ind	Ind	Ind	Ind	
Geography and English Studies	LQ83	3FT deg	* g	12	Ind	Ind	Ind	Ind	Ind	
Humanities (English)	Q300	3FT deg	* g	CC	5M	M$	24	CCCC	HN	2	10/17
Law with English Studies	M3Q3	3FT deg	* g	18	Ind	Ind	Ind	Ind	Ind	
Media Studies with English Studies	P4Q3	3FT deg	Me/T/E g	14	Ind	Ind	Ind	Ind	Ind	
Combined Studies (Honours) *Creative Writing*	Y400	3FT deg	* g	8-16	Ind	Ind	Ind	Ind	Ind	
Combined Studies (Honours) *English Studies*	Y400	3FT deg	E g	8-16	Ind	Ind	Ind	Ind	Ind	

			98 expected requirements							96 entry stats
TITLE	CODE	COURSE	SUBJECTS	A/AS	ND/C	AGNVQ	IB	SQA(H)	SQA	RATIO A/AS
Joint Honours *English Studies*	Y401	3FT deg	E g	8-16	Ind	Ind	Ind	Ind	Ind	
Major/Minor Honours *English Studies*	Y402	3FT deg	E g	8-16	Ind	Ind	Ind	Ind	Ind	
Major/Minor Honours *English as a Foreign Language*	Y402	3FT deg	* g	8-16	Ind	Ind	Ind	Ind	Ind	

Univ of GLASGOW

TITLE	CODE	COURSE	SUBJECTS	A/AS	ND/C	AGNVQ	IB	SQA(H)	SQA	RATIO A/AS
Archaeology/English	QV36	4FT deg		BBC	HN	M	30	BBBB	Ind	4
Celtic Civilisation/English	QQ5H	4FT deg		BBC	HN	M	30	BBBB	Ind	
Celtic/English	QQ35	4FT deg		BBC	HN	M	30	BBBB	Ind	6
Classical Civilisation/English	QQ38	4FT deg		BBC	HN	M	30	BBBB	Ind	5
Classical Hebrew/English	QV3W	4FT deg		BBC	HN	M	30	BBBB	Ind	
Czech/English	QTH1	5FT deg		BBC	HN	M	30	BBBB	Ind	
Economic and Social History/English	QV33	4FT deg		BBC	HN	M	30	BBBB	Ind	3
Economic and Social History/Scottish Literature	QVH3	4FT deg		BBC	HN	M	30	BBBB	Ind	
English Language and Literature	Q300	4FT deg		BBC	HN	M	30	BBBB	Ind	6	22/28
English/Classical Hebrew	QQ39	4FT deg		BBC	HN	M	30	BBBB	Ind	
English/Economics	LQC3	4FT deg		BBC	HN	M	30	BBBB	Ind	
English/Film and Television Studies	QW35	4FT deg		BBB	HN	D	32	AABB	Ind	6	26/28
English/French	QR31	5FT deg		BBC	HN	M	30	BBBB	Ind	4	22/30
English/German	QR32	5FT deg		BBC	HN	M	30	BBBB	Ind	
English/Greek	QQ37	4FT deg		BBC	HN	M	30	BBBB	Ind	
English/Hispanic Studies	QR34	5FT deg		BBC	HN	M	30	BBBB	Ind	5
English/History	QV31	4FT deg		BBC	HN	M	30	BBBB	Ind	4	20/28
English/History of Art	QV34	4FT deg		BBC	HN	M	30	BBBB	Ind	6
English/Italian	QR33	5FT deg		BBC	HN	M	30	BBBB	Ind	15
English/Latin	QQ36	4FT deg		BBC	HN	M	30	BBBB	Ind	
English/Mathematics	QG31	4FT deg		BBC	HN	M	30	BBBB	Ind	
English/Music	QW33	4FT deg		BBC	HN	M	30	BBBB	Ind	6
English/Philosophy	QV37	4FT deg		BBC	HN	M	30	BBBB	Ind	7	22/30
English/Polish	QT31	5FT deg		BBC	HN	M	30	BBBB	Ind	
English/Politics	MQ13	4FT deg		BBC	HN	M	30	BBBB	Ind	6
English/Psychology	CQ83	4FT deg		BBC	HN	M	30	BBBB	Ind	5	24/26
English/Russian	QR38	5FT deg		BBC	HN	M	30	BBBB	Ind	5
English/Scottish History	QVHC	4FT deg		BBC	HN	M	30	BBBB	Ind	6
English/Scottish Literature	QQ23	4FT deg		BBC	HN	M	30	BBBB	Ind	6	22/28
English/Sociology	LQ33	4FT deg		BBC	HN	M	30	BBBB	Ind	6	22/24
Islamic Studies/English	TQ63	4FT deg		BBC	N	M	30	BBBB	Ind	
Management Studies/English	NQ1H	4FT deg		BBC	HN	M	30	BBBB	Ind	9
Social and Urban Policy/English	LQ43	4FT deg		BBC	HN	M	30	BBBB	Ind	
Theatre Studies/English	QW34	4FT deg		BBC	HN	M	30	BBBB	Ind	6	22/28
Theology & Religious Studies/English	QV3V	4FT deg		BBC	HN	M	30	BBBB	Ind	

GOLDSMITHS COLL (Univ of London)

TITLE	CODE	COURSE	SUBJECTS	A/AS	ND/C	AGNVQ	IB	SQA(H)	SQA	RATIO A/AS
English	Q300	3FT deg	E	BBC	MO	M	Dip	ABBBB	N	9	20/28
English and History	QV31	3FT deg	E	BCC	MO	M	Dip	BBBBC	N	6	18/30
English and History of Art	QV34	3FT deg	E	BCC	MO	M	Dip	BBBBC	N	6	10/30
English and Theatre Arts	QW34	3FT deg	E	BBC	MO	M	Dip	ABBBB	N	8	14/30

Univ of GREENWICH

TITLE	CODE	COURSE	SUBJECTS	A/AS	ND/C	AGNVQ	IB	SQA(H)	SQA	RATIO A/AS
English	Q300	3FT deg	* g	12	M	M	25	BBB	Ind	

| | | | 98 expected requirements | | | | | | | 96 entry stats | |
| course details | | | | | | | | | | | |

TITLE	CODE	COURSE	SUBJECTS	A/AS	ND/C	AGNVQ	IB	SQA(H)	SQA	RATIO	A/AS
Univ of HERTFORDSHIRE											
English Literature	Q300	3FT deg	*	18	M+D	Ind	28	CCCCC	Ind	6	12/22
Historical Studies/Literature	VQ13	3FT deg	*	14	M+D	Ind	28	CCCCC	Ind		
Linguistics/Literature	QQ13	3FT deg	*	14	M+D	Ind	28	CCCCC	Ind		
Literature	Q301	3FT deg	*	18	M+D	Ind	28	CCCCC	Ind		
Literature/Minor	Q302	3FT deg	*	14	M+D	Ind	28	CCCCC	Ind		
Literature/Minor/Minor	Q303	3FT deg	*	14	M+D	Ind	28	CCCCC	Ind		
Literature/Modern Language	QT39	3FT deg	Ap	14	M+D	Ind	28	CCCCC	Ind		
Literature/Philosophy	QV37	3FT deg	*	14	M+D	Ind	28	CCCCC	Ind		
Modern Literature in English	Q310	3FT deg	*	18	M+D	Ind	28	CCCCC	Ind	12	
Univ of HUDDERSFIELD											
English Studies	Q300	3FT deg	E	CCC	Ind	M$^	28	BBBB	Ind		
English and History	QV31	3FT deg	E/H	14-16	Ind	Ind	Ind	Ind	Ind		
English and Media	QP34	3FT deg	E	CCC	Ind	M$^	28	BBBB	Ind		
French with English	R1Q3	4FT deg	F+E	CCE	Ind	Ind	Ind	BBBC	Ind		
German with English	R2Q3	4FT deg	G+E	CCE	Ind	Ind	Ind	BBBC	Ind		
Music with English (Practical Quals Required)	W3Q3	3FT deg	Mu+E	CC	Ind	Ind	Ind	BBC	Ind		
Univ of HULL											
American Studies/English	QQ43	3FT deg	E	BBB-BCC	Ind	M$^/6 gi	28$	ABBCC	Ind	15	18/28
Drama/English	QW34	3FT deg	E	BBB-BCC	Ind	D$^ go	30	AAABB	Ind	19	24/30
English Language and Literature	Q300	3FT deg	E	BBB	Ind	M$6/^ gi	28	ABBCC	Ind	4	18/26
English/French	QR31	4FT deg	E+F	BBB-BCC	Ind	M$^ gi	28$	BBBCC	Ind	8	22/24
English/German	QR32	4FT deg	E+G	BBB-BCC	Ind	M$^ gi	28$	BBBCC	Ind	4	
English/History	QV31	3FT deg	E+H	BBB-BCC	Ind	M$^ gi	28$	BBBCC	Ind	19	24/28
English/Italian	QR33	4FT deg	E+L	BBB-BCC	Ind	M$^ gi	28$	BBBCC	Ind	3	
English/Music (Min Practical Standards Req)	QW33	3FT deg	E	BBB-BCC	Ind	M$^ gi	28$	BBCCC	Ind	11	
English/Philosophy	QV37	3FT deg	E	BBB-BCC	MO+D $	M$^ gi	28$	BBBCC	Ind	12	22/22
English/Scandinavian Studies	QRH7	4FT deg	E	BBB-CCC	Ind	M$^ gi	28$	BBBCC	Ind		
English/Spanish	QR34	4FT deg	E+L	BBB-CCC	MO+D $	M$^ gi	28$	BBBCC	Ind	25	
English/Theology	QV38	3FT deg	E	BBB-BC	MO+D $	M$^ gi	28$	BBBCC	Ind		
Gender Studies and English	MQ93	3FT deg	E	BBB-BCC	Ind	M$6/^ go	28	BBBCC	Ind	4	
International English	Q301	4FT deg	E	BBB	Ind	M$6/^ gi	28	ABBCC	Ind	5	
KEELE Univ											
Biological and Medicinal Chemistry and English	FQC3	3FT deg	C+E g	BBC-BCC	Ind	D$^	28$	CSYS	Ind		
English and American Studies	QQ34	3FT deg	E	BBC	Ind	D$^	30$	CSYS	Ind	9	20/30
English and American Studies (4 Yrs)	QQ43	4FT deg	*	BBC	Ind	Ind	30	BBBB	Ind	4	16/24
English and Ancient History	QV3D	3FT deg	E	BBC	Ind	D$^	30$	CSYS	Ind	7	
English and Ancient History (4 Yrs)	VQD3	4FT deg	*	BBC	Ind	Ind	30	BBBB	Ind	3	
English and Applied Social Studies	LQ53	3FT deg	E	BBB-BBC	Ind	D$^	30$	CSYS	Ind	5	
English and Applied Social Studies (4 Yrs)	QL35	4FT deg	*	BBB-BBC	Ind	Ind	30	BBBB	Ind		
English and Astrophysics	FQ53	3FT deg	E+P g	BCC	Ind	D$^	28$	CSYS	Ind		
English and Astrophysics (4 Yrs)	QF35	4FT deg	*	BCC	Ind	Ind	28	BBBB	Ind		
English and Biological & Medicinal Chem (4 Yrs)	QF3C	4FT deg	*	BCC	Ind	Ind	28	BBBB	Ind		
English and Biology	CQ13	3FT deg	S+E g	BCC	Ind	D$^	28$	CSYS	Ind	8	
English and Biology (4 Yrs)	QC31	4FT deg	*	BCC	Ind	Ind	28	BBBB	Ind	8	
English and Business Administration (4 Yrs)	QN39	4FT deg	*	BBC	Ind	Ind	30	BBBB	Ind		
English and Chemistry	FQ13	3FT deg	C+E g	BCC	Ind	D$^	28$	CSYS	Ind	1	
English and Chemistry (4 Yrs)	QF31	4FT deg	*	BCC	Ind	Ind	28	BBBB	Ind		
English and Classical Studies	QQ38	3FT deg	E	BBC	Ind	D$^	30$	CSYS	Ind	7	20/24
English and Classical Studies (4 Yrs)	QQ83	4FT deg	*	BBC	Ind	Ind	30	BBBB	Ind	16	
English and Computer Science	GQ53	3FT deg	E	BCC	Ind	D$^	28$	CSYS	Ind	13	

TITLE	CODE	COURSE	SUBJECTS	A/AS	NQ/C	RGNVQ	IB	SQA(H)	SQA	RATIO A/AS	
course details			**98 expected requirements**							*96 entry stats*	
Psychology with Modern English Studies	L7QH	3FT deg	g	12-16	MO/DO	M/D	32	BBCC	Ind	2	
Public Policy and Management and Modern Engl St	QM3C	3FT deg	g	12-16	MO/DO	M/D	32	BBCC	Ind		
Public Policy and Mgt with Modern English Studs	M1QH	3FT deg	g	12-16	MO/DO	M/D	32	BBCC	Ind		
Social Studies and Modern English Studies	QL33	3FT deg	g	12-16	MO/DO	M/D	32	BBCC	Ind	6	
Social Studies with Modern English Studies	L3Q3	3FT deg	g	12-16	MO/DO	M/D	32	BBCC	Ind	4	
Sociology and Modern English Studies	LQH3	3FT deg		12-16	MO/DO	M/D	32	BBCC	Ind		
Sociology with Modern English Studies	L3QH	3FT deg		12-16	MO/DO	M/D	32	BBCC	Ind		
Travel and Tourism and Modern English Studies	QP37	3FT deg	g	12-16	MO/DO	M/D	32	BBCC	Ind	7	
Travel and Tourism with Modern English Studies	P7Q3	3FT deg	g	12-16	MO/DO	M/D	32	BBCC	Ind		
Women's Studies and Modern English Studies	MQ93	3FT deg		12-16	MO/DO	M/D	32	BBCC	Ind		
Women's Studies with Modern English Studies	M9Q3	3FT deg		12-16	MO/DO	M/D	32	BBCC	Ind		

Univ of MANCHESTER

TITLE	CODE	COURSE	SUBJECTS	A/AS	NQ/C	RGNVQ	IB	SQA(H)	SQA	RATIO	A/AS
Drama with English	W4Q3	4FT deg	E	BBB	4M+6D		32	AAABB	HN$	33	26/30
English Language and Literature	Q300	3FT deg	E	ABB	Ind	X	32$	AABBB$		10	26/30
English and American Literature	QQ34	3FT deg	E	ABB	Ind		32$	AABBB$		11	26/30
English and Drama	WQ43	4FT deg	E	BBB	4M+6D		32	AAABB	HN$	25	26/30
English and Linguistics	QQ13	3FT deg	E	BBB	X		32$	AABBB		5	18/24
English and Philosophy	VQ73	3FT deg	E	ABB	Ind		32$	AABBB	Ind	11	26/30
English and a Modern Language (French)	RQ13	4FT deg	E+F	ABB				Ind	BBBBC	8	24/30
English and a Modern Language (German)	RQ23	4FT deg	E+G	ABB				Ind	BBBBC	7	24/30
English and a Modern Language (Italian)	RQ33	4FT deg	E	ABB				Ind	BBBBC	4	24/28
English and a Modern Language (Russian)	RQ83	4FT deg	E	ABB				Ind	BBBBC	3	
English and a Modern Language (Spanish)	RQ43	4FT deg	E+Sp	ABB				Ind	BBBBC	9	
Greek and English	QQ37	3FT deg	Gk+E	BBC	X	X	30	BBBBB	X		
Latin and English	QQ36	3FT deg	Ln+E	BBC	X	X	30$	BBBBB	X	8	
Mathematics and English	GQ13	3FT deg	M+E	24	Ind			30$	X	Ind	4
Mathematics with English	G1Q3	3FT deg	M+E	24	Ind			30$	CSYS	Ind	7

MANCHESTER METROPOLITAN Univ

TITLE	CODE	COURSE	SUBJECTS	A/AS	NQ/C	RGNVQ	IB	SQA(H)	SQA	RATIO A/AS	
Cultural Studies/American Studies	LQ3H	3FT deg	*	CC	M+D	D	28	CCCC	Ind		
English Studies	Q300	3FT deg	El/E	BC	Ind	Ind	Ind	Ind	Ind	12/24	
English/American Studies	QQ34	3FT deg	*	CC	M+D	D	28	CCCC	Ind		
English/Applied Social Studies	LQ33	3FT deg	*	CC	M+D	D	28	CCCC	Ind		
English/Business Studies	NQ13	3FT deg	*	CC	M+D	D	28	CCCC	Ind		
English/Cultural Studies	LQH3	3FT deg	*	CC	M+D	D	28	CCCC	Ind		
English/Dance	QW3K	3FT deg	*	CC	M+D	D	28	CCCC	Ind		
English/Design & Technology	QW3F	3FT deg	*	CD	M+D	D	28	CCCC	Ind		
English/Drama	QWH4	3FT deg	*	CC	M+D	D	28	CCCC	Ind		
Environmental Science/English	FQ93	3FT deg	*	CC	M+D	D	28	CCCC	Ind		
Geography/English	LQ83	3FT deg	*	CC	M+D	D	28	CCCC	Ind		
Health Studies/English	BQ93	3FT deg	*	CC	M+D	D	28	CCCC	Ind		
History/English	QV31	3FT deg	*	CC	M+D	D	28	CCCC	Ind		
Leisure Studies/English	LQ43	3FT deg	*	CC	M+D	D	28	CCCC	Ind		
Life Science/English	CQ13	3FT deg	*	CC	M+D	D	28	CCCC	Ind		
Music/English	QW33	3FT deg	*	CC	M+D	D	28	CCCC	Ind		
Philosophy/English	QV37	3FT deg	*	CC	M+D	D	28	CCCC	Ind		
Religious Studies/English	QV38	3FT deg	*	CC	M+D	D	28	CCCC	Ind		
Sport/English	BQ63	3FT deg	S	BC	M+D	DS	28	CCCC	Ind		
Visual Arts/English	QW31	3FT deg	*	CC	M+D	D	28	CCCC	Ind		
Writing/English	QW3L	3FT deg	*	CC	M+D	D	28	CCCC	Ind		
Humanities/Social Studies *English*	Y400	3FT deg	*	CDD	Ind	Ind	Ind	BBB	Ind		

course details			**98 expected requirements**							**96 entry stats**	
TITLE	CODE	COURSE	SUBJECTS	A/AS	ND/C	RGNVQ	IB	SQA(H)	SQA	RATIO A/AS	
MIDDLESEX Univ											
English	Q300▼	3FT deg	E g	12-16	X	X	28	Ind	Ind		
Joint Honours Degree *English Language and British Culture*	Y400	3FT deg	* g	12-16	5M	M$ go	26	X	X		
Joint Honours Degree *English and Literary Studies*	Y400	3FT deg	E g	16	X	X	28	Ind	Ind		
Joint Honours Degree *English for Business Communication*	Y400	3FT/4SW deg	* g	12-16	X	X	28	Ind	Ind		
NENE COLLEGE											
American Studies with English	Q4Q3	3FT deg		DD	5M	M	24	CCC	Ind	7/12	
Art and Design with English	W2Q3	3FT deg		DD	5M	M	24	CCC	Ind	6/20	
Business Administration with English	N1Q3	3FT deg	g	10	M+1D	M	24	BCC	Ind		
Drama with English	W4Q3	3FT deg		10	5M+1D	M	24	CCC	Ind	6/14	
Education with English	X9Q3	3FT deg		DD	5M	M	24	CCC	Ind	6/12	
English with American Studies	Q3Q4	3FT deg		CC	4M+1D	M	24	CCC	Ind	10/18	
English with Art and Design	Q3W2	3FT deg		CC	4M+1D	M	24	CCC	Ind		
English with Business Administration	Q3N1	3FT deg	g	CC	4M+1D	M	24	CCC	Ind		
English with Drama	Q3W4	3FT deg		CC	4M+1D	M	24	CCC	Ind	12/16	
English with Education	Q3X9	3FT deg		CC	4M+1D	M	24	CCC	Ind	8/18	
English with French	Q3R1	3FT deg	F	CC	4M+1D	M	24	CCC	Ind		
English with History	Q3V1▼	3FT deg		CC	4M+1D	M	24	CCC	Ind		
English with History of Art	Q3VK▼	3FT deg		CC	4M+1D	M	24	CCC	Ind		
English with Industrial Archaeology	Q3V6	3FT deg		CC	4M+1D	M	24	CCC	Ind		
English with Marketing Communications	Q3N5▼	3FT deg		CC	4M+1D	M	24	CCC	Ind		
English with Mathematics	Q3G1	3FT deg	M	CC	4M+1D	M	24	CCC	Ind		
English with Media and Popular Culture	Q3P4▼	3FT deg		CC	4M+1D	M	24	CCC	Ind	6/22	
English with Music	Q3W3	3FT deg	Mu	CC	4M+1D	M	24	CCC	Ind		
English with Personal and Organisational Develop	Q3N6▼	3FT deg		CC	4M+1D	M	24	CCC	Ind		
English with Philosophy	Q3V7▼	3FT deg		CC	4M+1D	M	24	CCC	Ind		
English with Psychology	Q3C8▼	3FT deg	g	CC	4M+1D	M	24	CCC	Ind	8/22	
English with Sociology	Q3L3▼	3FT deg		CC	4M+1D	M	24	CCC	Ind		
English with Sport Studies	Q3N7▼	3FT deg		CC	4M+1D	M	24	CCC	Ind		
French with English	R1Q3	3FT deg	F	DD	5M	Ind	24	CCC	Ind		
History with English	V1Q3▼	3FT deg		CD	5M	M	24	CCC	Ind	4/10	
Information Systems with English	G5Q3	3FT deg		6	5M	M	24	CCC	Ind		
Music with English	W3Q3	3FT deg	Mu	DD	5M	M	24	CCC	Ind		
Psychology with English	C8Q3▼	3FT deg	g	CC	5M+1D	M	24	CCC	Ind	6/20	
Sociology with English	L3Q3▼	3FT deg	g	10	5M	M	24	CCC	Ind	6/14	
Sport Studies with English	N7Q3▼	3FT deg	Ss/Pe	12	M+2D	M	24	BBB	Ind		
Univ of NEWCASTLE											
English Language	Q302	3FT deg	*	BBB	Ind		Ind	BBBBB	Ind	12	18/26
English Language and Literature	Q300	3FT deg	E	ABC	Ind		Ind	AABBB	Ind	12	22/28
English Literature	Q306	3FT deg	E	ABC	Ind		Ind	Ind	Ind	15	24/30
English Literature and Latin	QQ36	3FT deg	E+Ln	BBC	Ind		Ind	AABBB	Ind		
German and English Language	RQ23	4FT deg	G+E	22		X	$	AABBB$		12	
Combined Studies (BA) English Literature	Y400	3FT deg	E	ABC-BBB	5D	Ind	35$	AAAB	Ind		
NEWMAN COLLEGE OF HIGHER EDUCATION											
English and Biological Science	CQ13	3FT deg	*	CC	3M	M*	Dip	CCC	Ind		
English and Geography	FQ83	3FT deg	*	CC	3M	M*	Dip	CCC	Ind		
English and History	QV31	3FT deg	*	CC	3M	M*	Dip	CCC	Ind		
English and Physical Education & Sports Studies	QX39	3FT deg	*	CC	3M	M*	Dip	CCC	Ind		

Letts STUDY GUIDES
THE INDEPENDENT

course details			98 expected requirements							96 entry stats	
TITLE	CODE	COURSE	SUBJECTS	A/AS	ND/C	AGNVQ	IB	SQA(H)	SQA	RATIO	A/AS
Univ of Wales COLLEGE, NEWPORT											
English and Archaeology	QV36	3FT deg		10	M+D	D$	Ind	Ind	Ind		
European Studies and English	QT32	3FT deg		10	M+D	D$	Ind	Ind	Ind		
History and English	QV31	3FT deg		10	M+D	D$	Ind	Ind	Ind		
Information Technology and English	GQ53	3FT deg		10	M+D	D$	Ind	Ind	Ind		
Religious Studies and English	QV38	3FT deg		10	M+D	D$	Ind	Ind	Ind		
Sports Studies and English	BQ63	3FT deg		10	M+D	D$	Ind	Ind	Ind		
NORTH EAST WALES INST of HE											
English	Q300	3FT deg		6-12	4M	M$	Ind	BBB	N$		
English and History	QV31	3FT deg		6-12	4M	M$	Ind	BBB	N$		8/16
English and Media Studies	QP34	3FT deg		6-12	4M	M$	Ind	BBB	N$		10/16
English and Welsh Studies	QQ35	3FT deg		6-12	4M	M$	Ind	BBB	N$		
English with Geography	Q3F8	3FT deg		6-12	4M	M$	Ind	BBB	N$		
English with History	Q3V1	3FT deg		6-12	4M	M$	Ind	BBB	N$		
English with Media Studies	Q3P4	3FT deg		6-12	4M	M$	Ind	BBB	N$		
English with Psychology	Q3C8	3FT deg		6-12	4M	M$	Ind	BBB	N$		
English with Sociology	Q3L3	3FT deg		6-12	4M	M$	Ind	BBB	N$		
English/Geography	FQ83	3FT deg		6-12	3M	M$	Ind	CCC	N$		
English/Psychology	QC38	3FT deg		4-12	3M	M$	Ind	BBB	N$		
English/Sociology	QL33	3FT deg		6-12	3M	M$	Ind	CCC	N$		
History with English	V1Q3	3FT deg		6-12	4M	M$	Ind	BBB	N$		
Univ of NORTH LONDON											
English	Q300▼	3FT deg	E	BC	Ind	Ind	Ind	Ind	Ind	6	8/20
Combined Honours *Critical Theory*	Y300	3FT/4FT deg	E	CC	Ind	Ind	Ind	Ind	Ind		
Combined Honours *English*	Y300	3FT/4FT deg	E	CC	Ind	Ind	Ind	Ind	Ind		
Univ of NORTHUMBRIA											
English Studies	Q300	3FT deg	E	BBC	MO+5D		28	BBBBB	Ind	14	18/24
English and Film Studies	QW35	3FT deg	E	BBC	MO+4D		26	BBBCC	Ind	14	18/24
English and Women's Cultures	QM39	3FT deg	E	BCC	MO+4D		26	BBBCC	Ind	4	
NORWICH: City COLL											
Psychology with English	L7Q3	3FT deg	* g	12		X	Ind	Ind	Ind		
Combined Arts *English Literature*	Y300	3FT deg	* g	12	Ind		Ind	Ind	Ind		
Univ of NOTTINGHAM											
American and English Studies	QQ34	3FT deg	E	BBC						31	28/30
Archaeology and English Language	QV36	3FT deg	E	BBC						5	
Art History and English Studies	QV34	3FT deg	E	BBC						25	26/28
Classical Civilisation and English Studies	QQ83	3FT deg	E	BBC						43	
English Studies	Q300	3FT deg	E+L g	ABC						24	24/30
English Studies and Latin	QQ36	3FT deg	E+Ln	BBC							
English Studies and Philosophy	QV37	3FT deg	E	ABC						30	28/30
English Studies and Theology	QV38	3FT deg	E	BBC						8	26/30
NOTTINGHAM TRENT Univ											
English	Q300	3FT deg	E g	BBC	Ind	Ind	28	BBCC	Ind	10	16/26
English and Environmental Studies	QF3X	3FT deg	E g	12	Ind	M$ go	Ind	Ind	Ind	1	12/24
English and Urban Studies	QK34	3FT deg	E g	12	Ind	M$ go	Ind	Ind	Ind	2	10/16
Humanities *English*	Y301	3FT/4SW deg	* g	14-16	M+D	Ind	28	CCCC	Ind		

English 26

course details			98 expected requirements							96 entry stats	
TITLE	CODE	COURSE	SUBJECTS	A/AS	ND/C	AGNVQ	IB	SQA(H)	SQA	RATIO	A/AS
OXFORD Univ											
Classics and English	QQ38	3FT deg	E+Ln/Gk	AAB	DO		36	AAAAA	Ind	3	30/30
English Language and Literature	Q300	3FT deg	E	AAB	DO		36	AAAAA	Ind	4	26/30
English and Modern Languages (3 Yrs)	QT39	3FT deg	E+L	AAB	DO		36	AAAAA	Ind	9	
English and Modern Languages (4 Yrs)	TQ93	4FT deg	E+L	AAB	DO		36	AAAAA	Ind	4	30/30
Modern History and English	VQ13	3FT deg	E+H	AAB	DO		36	AAAAA	Ind	5	28/30
OXFORD WESTMINSTER COLLEGE											
Contemporary English Studies with Cultural St	Q3VX	2FT Dip	E	CE	MO	M	Ind	CCC	Ind		
Contemporary English Studies with Cultural St	Q3V9	3FT deg	E	CE	MO	M	Ind	CCC	Ind		
Contemporary English Studies with Development St	Q3LH	2FT Dip	E	CE	MO	M	Ind	CCC	Ind		
Contemporary English Studies with Development St	Q3L3	3FT deg	E	CE	MO	M	Ind	CCC	Ind		
Contemporary English Studies with Interfaith St	Q3VV	2FT Dip	E	CE	MO	M	Ind	CCC	Ind		
Contemporary English Studies with Interfaith St	Q3V8	3FT deg	E	CE	MO	M	Ind	CCC	Ind		
Contemporary English Studies with Language Studs	Q3T9	3FT deg	E	CE	MO	M	Ind	CCC	Ind		
Contemporary English Studies with Language Studs	Q3TX	2FT Dip	E	CE	MO	M	Ind	CCC	Ind		
Contemporary English Studies with World Studies	Q3M1	3FT deg	E	CE	MO	M	Ind	CCC	Ind		
Contemporary English Studies with World Studies	Q3MC	2FT Dip	E	CE	MO	M	Ind	CCC	Ind		
OXFORD BROOKES Univ											
English Studies	Q300	3FT deg			Ind		Ind	Ind	Ind		14/22
English Studies/Accounting and Finance	NQ43	3FT deg	* g	AB-BCC	Ind	M*^/D*3	Ind	Ind	Ind		
English Studies/Anthropology	LQ63	3FT deg	*	AB-BCC	Ind	M*^	Ind	Ind	Ind	9	
English Studies/Biological Chemistry	CQ73	3FT deg									
English Studies/Biology	CQ13	3FT deg	S g	DD-AB	Ind	M*^/MS	Ind	Ind	Ind		
English Studies/Business Administration & Mgt	NQ13	3FT deg	* g	AB-BCC	Ind	M*^/MB4	Ind	Ind	Ind	15	
English Studies/Cartography	FQ83	3FT deg	* g	DDD-AB	Ind	M*^	Ind	Ind	Ind		
English Studies/Cell Biology	CQC3	3FT deg									
English Studies/Combined Studies	QY34	3FT deg		X		X	X	X			
English Studies/Computer Systems	GQ63	3FT deg	* g	CDD-AB	Ind	M*^	Ind	Ind	Ind	1	
English Studies/Computing	GQ53	3FT deg	* g	CDD-AB	Ind	M*^	Ind	Ind	Ind	8	
English Studies/Computing Mathematics	GQ93	3FT deg	* g	CD-AB	Ind	M*^	Ind	Ind	Ind		
English Studies/Ecology	CQ93	3FT deg	* g	CD-AB	Ind	MS/M*^	Ind	Ind	Ind	10	
English Studies/Economics	LQ13	3FT deg	* g	CCD-AB	Ind	M*^M*3	Ind	Ind	Ind		
English Studies/Educational Studies	QX39	3FT deg	*	CC-AB	Ind	M*^/3	Ind	Ind	Ind	4	8/20
English Studies/Electronics	HQ63	3FT deg	S/M	CC-AB	Ind	M$/M*^	Ind	Ind	Ind		
Environmental Chemistry/English Studies	QF31	3FT deg									
Environmental Policy/English Studies	KQ33	3FT deg									
Environmental Sciences/English Studies	FQX3	3FT deg	S g	CD-AB	Ind	M*^/DS	Ind	Ind	Ind	5	
Exercise & Health/English Studies	QB36	3FT deg	S g	DD-AB	Ind	MS/M*^	Ind	Ind	Ind		
Fine Art/English Studies	QW31	3FT deg	Pf+A	BC-AB	Ind	MA^	Ind	Ind	Ind		
Food Science and Nutrition/English Studies	DQ43	3FT deg	S g	DD-AB	Ind	MS/M*^	Ind	Ind	Ind	5	
French Language and Contemp Studies/English St	QR3C	4SW deg	F	CDD-AB	Ind	M*^	Ind	Ind	Ind	16	
French Language and Literature/English Studies	QR31	4SW deg	F	CDD-AB	Ind	M*^	Ind	Ind	Ind	13	
Geography and the Phys Env/English Studies	FQV3	3FT deg									
Geography/English Studies	LQ83	3FT deg	*	CCD-AB	Ind	M*^	Ind	Ind	Ind	24	
Geotechnics/English Studies	HQ23	3FT deg	S/M/Ds/Es	DD-AB	Ind	M$^	Ind	Ind	Ind		
German Language and Contemp Stud/English Studies	QR3F	4SW deg	G	DDD-AB	Ind	M*^	Ind	Ind	Ind	4	
German Language and Literature/English Studies	QR32	4SW deg	G	DDD-AB	Ind	M*^	Ind	Ind	Ind	3	
German Studies/English Studies	QR3G	4SW deg			Ind		Ind	Ind	Ind		
Health Care/English Studies (Post Exp)	BQ73	3FT deg		X		X	X	X			
History of Art/English Studies	QV34	3FT deg	*	AB-BCC	Ind	M*^	Ind	Ind	Ind	4	10/22
History/English Studies	QV31	3FT deg	*	CCD-AB	Ind	M*^	Ind	Ind	Ind	7	14/20

course details			98 expected requirements							96 entry stats	
TITLE	CODE	COURSE	SUBJECTS	A/AS	NQ/C	RGNVQ	IB	SQA(H)	SQA	RATIO	A/AS
Hospitality Management Studies/English Studies	NQ73	3FT deg	*	DDD-AB	Ind	M*^/3	Ind	Ind	Ind		
Human Biology/English Studies	BQ13	3FT deg									
Information Systems/English Studies	GQM3	3FT deg	* g	CDD-BCC	Ind	M*^	Ind	Ind	Ind		
Intelligent Systems/English Studies	GQ83	3FT deg	* g	CD-AB	Ind	M*^	Ind	Ind	Ind		
Langs for Bus:Italian-Ab Initio/English-Post A	NQCJ	4FT deg									
Languages for Business:French/English-Post A	NQCH	4FT deg	F+E	BC-CDD	Ind	M*_^_	Ind	Ind	Ind		
Languages for Business:German/English-Post A	NQ1H	4FT deg	G+E	BC-CDD	Ind	M*_^_	Ind	Ind	Ind		
Languages for Business:Italian/English-Post A	NQ1J	4FT deg	I+E	BC-CDD	Ind	M*_^_	Ind	Ind	Ind		
Languages for Business:Spanish/English-Post A	NQC3	4FT deg	Sp+E	CDD-BC	Ind	M*_^_	Ind	Ind	Ind		
Law/English Studies	MQ33	3FT deg	*	AB-BCC	Ind	M*^/D*3	Ind	Ind	Ind	19	
Leisure Planning/English Studies	KQH3	3FT deg									
Marketing Management/English Studies	NQN3	3FT deg	* g	AB-BCC	Ind	M*^/D*3	Ind	Ind	Ind		
Music/English Studies	QW33	3FT deg	Mu	DD-AB	Ind	M*^	Ind	Ind	Ind	4	16/18
Palliative Care/English Studies (Post Exp)	BQR3	3FT deg		X		X	X	X			
Planning Studies/English Studies	KQ43	3FT deg	* g	DDD-AB	Ind	M*^	Ind	Ind	Ind		
Politics/English Studies	MQ13	3FT deg	*	AB-CCC	Ind	M*^	Ind	Ind	Ind	6	16/18
Psychology/English Studies	CQ83	3FT deg	* g	AB-BCC	Ind	M*^	Ind	Ind	Ind	28	
Publishing/English Studies	PQ53	3FT deg	* g	CCD-AB	Ind	M*^/M$3	Ind	Ind	Ind	3	12/26
Rehabilitation/English Studies (Post Exp)	BQT3	3FT deg		X		X	X	X			
Sociology/English Studies	LQ33	3FT deg	*	AB-BCC	Ind	M*^	Ind	Ind	Ind	15	
Software Engineering/English Studies	GQ73	3FT deg	* g	CD-AB	Ind	M*^	Ind	Ind	Ind		
Statistics/English Studies	GQ43	3FT deg	* g	DD-AB	Ind	M*^	Ind	Ind	Ind		
Telecommunications/English Studies	HQP3	3FT deg									
Transport Planning/English Studies	NQ93	3FT deg	* g	AB-DDD	Ind	M*^	Ind	Ind	Ind		
Water Resources/English Studies	HQF3	3FT deg									

Univ of PLYMOUTH

Art History with English	V4Q3	3FT deg	Ap g	CCD	MO+3D	D$^	Ind	Ind	Ind	7	
Cultural Interpretation & Practice with English	Y3Q3	3FT deg	Ap g	CCD	MO+3D	D$^	Ind	Ind	Ind		
English with Art History	Q3V4	3FT deg	Ap g	BBC	MO+3D	D$^	Ind	Ind	Ind	5	16/22
English with Cultural Interpretation & Practice	Q3Y3	3FT deg	E g	BBC	MO+3D	D$^	Ind	Ind	Ind		
English with Education Studies	Q3X9	3FT deg	Ap g	BBC	MO+3D	D$^	Ind	Ind	Ind	7	16/22
English with Heritage and Landscape	Q3WG	3FT deg	Ap g	BBC	MO+3D	D$^	Ind	Ind	Ind	2	
English with History	Q3V1	3FT deg	Ap g	BBC	MO+3D	D$^	Ind	Ind	Ind	5	12/18
English with Media Arts	Q3WF	3FT deg	Ap g	BBC	MO+3D	D$^	Ind	Ind	Ind	9	12/26
English with Music	Q3W3	3FT deg	Ap g	BBC	MO+3D	D$^	IB	Ind	Ind	2	
English with Theatre and Performance Studies	Q3W4	3FT deg	Ap g	BBC	MO+3D	D$^	Ind	Ind	Ind	8	14/22
English with Visual Arts	Q3W2	3FT deg	Ap g	BBC	MO+3D	D$^	Ind	Ind	Ind	2	12/18
Heritage and Landscape with English	W2QJ	3FT deg	Ap g	CCD	MO+3D	D$^	Ind	Ind	Ind		
History with English	V1Q3	3FT deg	Ap g	CCD	MO+3D	D$^	Ind	Ind	Ind	4	16/18
Media Arts with English	W2QH	3FT deg	Ap g	CCD	MO+3D	D$^	Ind	Ind	Ind	5	12/22
Theatre and Performance St with English	W4Q3	3FT deg	Ap g	CCD	MO+3D	D$^	Ind	Ind	Ind	7	10/24
Visual Arts with English	W2Q3	3FT deg	Ap g	CCD	MO+3D	D$^	Ind	Ind	Ind	3	

Univ of PORTSMOUTH

Art and English	WQ13	3FT deg	E+Fa/Pf	18	N	Ind	Dip	Ind	Ind		
Art and English	EQ13	3FT deg	E+Fa/Pf		N	Ind	Dip	Ind	Ind		
English and Creative Studies	QW39	3FT deg	E+Pf	BCC	X	D$6/^	Ind	AABBB	Ind	6	12/24

QUEEN MARY & WESTFIELD COLL (Univ of London)

English	Q300	3FT deg	E	22		M$^	30$				
English and Drama	QW34	3FT deg	E	22		M	30$				
English and French	QR3C	4FT deg	E+F	20		M^	30$				
English and German	RQ23	4FT deg	E+G	20		M^	30$				

English 26

			98 expected requirements							**96 entry stats**	
course details											
TITLE	CODE	COURSE	SUBJECTS	A/AS	ND/C	NGNVQ	IB	SQA(H)	SQA	RATIO	A/AS
English and Hispanic Studies	RQ4J	4FT deg	E	20		M	30$				
English and History	QV31	3FT deg	E	20		M	30$				
English and Russian	QRH8	4FT deg	E	20		M	30$				

QUEEN'S Univ Belfast

TITLE	CODE	COURSE	SUBJECTS	A/AS	ND/C	NGNVQ	IB	SQA(H)	SQA	RATIO	A/AS
English	Q300	3FT deg	E g	BCC	X	D*^ go	29$	ABBB	X	5	18/28
English/Ancient History	VQC3	3FT deg	E g	BCC	X	D*^ go	29$	ABBB	X	10	
English/Archaeology	VQ63	3FT deg	E g	BCC	X	D*^ go	29$	ABBB	X	6	
English/Biblical Studies	VQ83	3FT deg	E g	BCC	X	D*^ go	29$	ABBB	X	8	
English/Byzantine Studies	QQ38	3FT/4FT deg	E g	BCC	X	D*^ go	29$	ABBB	X	1	
English/Celtic	QQ53	3FT/4FT deg	E g	BCC	X	D*^ go	29$	ABBB	X	5	
English/Classical Studies	QQ83	3FT deg	E g	BCC	X	D*^ go	29$	ABBB	X	9	
English/Economics	LQ13	3FT deg									
French/English (4 years)	QR31	4FT deg	E+E g	BCC	X	X	29$	ABBB	X	5	20/26
German/English (4 years)	QR32	4FT deg	E g	BCC	X	D*^ go	29$	ABBB	X	3	
Greek/English	QQ37	3FT/4FT deg	E g	BCC	X	D*^ go	29$	ABBB	X		
Italian/English (4 years)	QR33	4FT deg	E g	BCC	X	D*^ go	29$	ABBB	X	9	
Latin/English	QQ36	3FT/4FT deg	E g	BCC	X	D*^ go	29$	ABBB	X	1	
Modern History/English	QV31	3FT deg	E g	BCC	X	D*^ go	29$	ABBB	X	6	18/28
Music/English	QW33	3FT deg	E g	BCC	X	D*^ go	29$	ABBB	X	11	
Philosophy/English	QV37	3FT deg	E g	BCC	X	D*^ go	29$	ABBB	X	8	20/26
Politics/English	QM31	3FT deg	E g	BCC	X	D*^ go	29$	ABBB	X	10	22/26
Psychology/English	CQ83	3FT deg	E g	BCC	X	D*^ go	29$	ABBB	X	8	20/28
Scholastic Philosophy/English	QV3R	3FT deg	E g	BCC	X	D*^ go	29$	ABBB	X	5	
Social Anthropology/English	QL36	3FT deg	E g	BCC	X	D*^ go	29$	ABBB	X	11	
Social Policy/English	QL34	3FT deg	E g	BCC	X	D*^ go	29$	ABBB	X		
Sociology/English	QL33	3FT deg	E g	BCC	X	D*^ go	29$	ABBB	X	10	20/28
Spanish/English (4 years)	QR34	4FT deg	E g	BCC	X	D*^ go	29$	ABBB	X	6	
Theology and English	QV38	3FT deg									
Women's Studies/English	QM39	3FT deg	E g	BCC	X	D*^ go	29$	ABBB	X		

Univ of READING

TITLE	CODE	COURSE	SUBJECTS	A/AS	ND/C	NGNVQ	IB	SQA(H)	SQA	RATIO	A/AS
Classical Studies with English Literature	Q8Q3	3FT deg	El	BCC	Ind	D*^	30$	BBBB$	Ind	8	
English Language & Literature	Q300	3FT deg	El	BBB	Ind	D*^	32$	ABBB$	Ind	12	20/28
English Literature & Modern English Language	QQ31	3FT deg	El	BBC	Ind	D*^	31$	BBBB$	Ind	10	20/30
English Literature and Classical Studies	QQ38	3FT deg	El	BCC	Ind	D*^	30$	BBBB$	Ind	10	20/22
English Literature and Film & Drama	QW34	3FT deg	El	BBC	Ind	D*^	31$	BBBB$	Ind	20	22/30
English Literature and French	QR31	3FT deg	El+F	BBC	Ind	D*^	31$	BBBB$	Ind	13	20/26
English Literature and German	QR32	4FT deg	El g	BBC	Ind	D$^ go	31$	BBBB$	Ind	6	
English Literature and History of Art	QV34	3FT deg	El	BBC	Ind	D$^	31$	BBBB$	Ind	25	
English Literature and Italian	QR33	4FT deg	El g	BBC	Ind	D$^ go	31$	BBBB$	Ind	29	
English Literature and Sociology	LQ33	3FT deg	El	BBC	Ind	D$^	31$	BBBB$	Ind	19	22/26
English Literature with Classical Studies	Q3Q8	3FT deg	El	BCC	Ind	D*^	30$	BBBB$	Ind	7	
English Literature with Latin	Q3Q6	3FT deg	El	BCC	Ind	D*^	30$	BBBB$	Ind		
French and English Literature	RQ13	4FT deg	El+F	BBC	Ind	D*^	31$	BBBB$	Ind	5	18/24
Greek and English Literature	QQ37	3FT deg	El g	BCC	Ind	D*^ go	30$	BBBB$	Ind		
History and English Literature	QV31	3FT deg	El	BBC	Ind	D*^	31$	BBBB$	Ind	14	22/28
Latin and English Literature	QQ36	3FT deg	El g	BCC	Ind	D*^ go	30$	BBBB$	Ind		
Music and English Literature	QW33	3FT deg	Mu+El	BBC	X	D*^	31$	BBBB$	Ind	8	
Philosophy and English Literature	VQ73	3FT deg	El	BBC	Ind	D*^	31$	BBBB$	Ind	15	22/26

Univ College of RIPON & YORK ST JOHN

TITLE	CODE	COURSE	SUBJECTS	A/AS	ND/C	NGNVQ	IB	SQA(H)	SQA	RATIO	A/AS
Art/English	W1Q3	3FT deg	A+E+Pf	BC-CCD	Ind	MA^	27	BBBB		3	10/24
Art/English	E1Q3	3FT deg	A+E+Pf	BC-CCD	Ind	MA^	27	BBBB			

			98 expected requirements							96 entry stats	
TITLE	CODE	COURSE	SUBJECTS	A/AS	ND/C	AGNVQ	IB	SQA(H)	SQA	RATIO	A/AS
Cultural Studies with English	L6Q3	3FT deg		12	M	M*	27	BBBC			
English Studies (Literature and Language)	QQ31	3FT deg	E	16	Ind	M*^	30	BBBB		5	10/22
English Studies with Cultural Studies	Q3L6	3FT deg	E	16	Ind	M*^	30	BBBB			
English Studies with Education	Q3X9	3FT deg	E	16	Ind	M*^	30	BBBB			
English Studies with European Studies	Q3T2	3FT deg	E	16	Ind	M*^	30	BBBB			
English/American Studies	Q3Q4	3FT deg	E	16	Ind	M*^	30	BBBB			
English/Art	Q3W1	3FT deg	E+A+Pf	16	Ind	Ind	30	BBBB		5	
English/History	Q3V1	3FT deg	E/H	16	Ind	Ind	30	BBBB		3	12/22
English/Language Studies (English)	Q3Q1	3FT deg	E	16	Ind	M*^	30	BBBB		4	8/24
English/Theology	Q3V8	3FT deg	E	16	Ind	M*^	27	BBBB			
English/Women's Studies	Q3M9	3FT deg	E	16	Ind	M*^	30	BBBB		5	14/22
History/English	V1Q3	3FT deg	H+E	14	X	Ind	30	BBBB		3	8/22
Language Studies (English)/English	Q1Q3	3FT deg	E	16	X	M*^	30	BBBB		5	12/18
Theology/English	V8Q3	3FT deg	E	12	M	M*	27	BBBC			

ROEHAMPTON INST

English Lang & Linguist and Business Computing	GQ7H▼	3FT deg	g	CC	2M+2D	M$^ go	30	BBC	N$		
English Lang & Linguistics and Art for Community	WQ1H▼	3FT deg	E/L	CC	2M+2D$	M$^	30	BBC	Ind	2	
English Language & Linguist & English Literature	Q310▼	3FT deg	E	CC	2M+2D$	M^	30	BBC	Ind	3	
English Language & Linguist and App Consumer St	QN39▼	3FT deg	E/L g	CC	2M+2D$	M$^	30	BBC	N$		
English Language & Linguist and Business Studies	QN31▼	3FT deg	E/Lg	CC	3D $	M$^ go	30	BBC	N$		
English Language & Linguist/Drama & Theatre St	WQLH▼	3FT deg	E/L+E/T	16	3D $	M$^	30	BBC	Ind	6	
English Language & Linguistics	Q340▼	3FT deg	E/L	CC	2M+2D$	M$^	30	BBC	N$	5	12/26
English Language & Linguistics and Biology	CQ1H▼	3FT deg	E/L+B	CC	2M+2D$	M$^ go	30	BBC	N$		
English Language & Linguistics and Education	XQ9H▼	3FT deg	E/L	CC	2M+2D	M$^	30	BBC	N$	1	
English Language & Linguistics/Dance Studies	WQ4H▼	3FT deg	E/L	CC	2M+2D$	M$^	30	BBC	Ind	3	
English Literature	Q300▼	3FT deg	E	CC	2M+2D$	M^	28	BBC	N$	4	10/20
English Literature and Applied Consumer Studies	NQ93▼	3FT deg	E g	CC	2M+2D$	M^ go	28	BBC	N$		
English Literature and Art for Community	WQ13▼	3FT deg	E	CC	2M+2D$	M^	28	BBC	Ind	4	
English Literature and Biology	CQ13▼	3FT deg	E+B	CC	2M+2D$	M^ go	28	BBC	Ind		
English Literature and Business Computing	GQ73▼	3FT deg	E g	CC	2M+2D	M^ go	30	BBC	N$		
English Literature and Business Studies	NQ13▼	3FT deg	E g	CC	3D $	M^ go	28	BBC	N$	4	12/16
English Literature and Dance Studies	WQ43▼	3FT deg	E	CC	2M+2D$	M^	30	BBC	Ind	7	16/18
English Literature and Drama & Theatre Studies	WQL3▼	3FT deg	E	16	3D $	M^	30	BBC	Ind	7	16/22
English Literature and Education	XQ93▼	3FT deg	E	CC	2M+2D$	M^	28	BBC	Ind	2	4/14
Environmental St and English Lang & Linguistics	QFH9▼	3FT deg	B/Gy+E/L	CC	2M+2D$	M$^ go	30	BBC			
Environmental Studies and English Literature	QF39▼	3FT deg	B/Gy+E	CC	2M+2D$	M^ go	28	BBC	Ind		
Film & Television Studies & English Lang & Ling	PQ4H▼	3FT deg	E/L	16	2M+2D$	M$^	30	BBC	N$	33	
Film & Television Studies and English Literature	PQ43▼	3FT deg	E	16	2M+2D$	M^	30	BBC	N$	10	14/20
French and English Language & Linguistics	QR3C▼	4FT deg	F+E/L	CC	2M+2D$	M^	30	BBC	Ind	4	
French and English Literature	QR31▼	4FT deg	F+E	CC	2M+2D$	M^	28	BBC	Ind	11	
Geography and English Language & Linguistics	QLH8▼	3FT deg	Gy+E/L	CC	2M+2D$	M$^	30	BBC	Ind		
Geography and English Literature	QL38▼	3FT deg	Gy+E	CC	2M+2D$	M^ go	28	BBC			
Health Studies and English Lang & Linguistics	BQ9H▼	3FT deg	E/L+B	CC	2M+2D$	M$^ go	30	BBC	N$		
Health Studies and English Literature	BQ93▼	3FT deg	E+B	CC	2M+2D$	M^ go	28	BBC	N$		
History and English Language & Linguistics	QV3C▼	3FT deg	H+E/L	CC	2M+2D$	M^	30	BBC	Ind	6	
History and English Literature	QV31▼	3FT deg	H+E	CC	2M+2D$	M^	28	BBC	Ind	4	6/20
Human & Social Biol and English Lang & Linguist	QCHC▼	3FT deg	B+E/L	CC	2M+2D$	M$	30	BBC	Ind		
Human & Social Biology and English Literature	QC3C▼	3FT deg	B+E	CC	2M+2D$	M^	28	BBC	Ind		
Music and English Language & Linguistics	QW3H▼	3FT deg	Mu+E/L	CC	2M+2D$	M^	30	BBC	Ind		
Music and English Literature	QW33▼	3FT deg	Mu+E	CC	2M+2D$	M^	28	BBC	Ind	3	
Natural Resource St and English Lang & Linguist	DQ2H▼	3FT deg	g	CC	2M+2D	M$^ go	30	BBC	N$		
Natural Resource Studies and English Literature	DQ23▼	3FT deg	E g	CC	2M+2D	M^ go	30	BBC	N$		

English 26

	course details		98 expected requirements							96 entry stats
TITLE	CODE	COURSE	SUBJECTS	A/AS	NO/C	RGNVQ	IB	SQA(H)	SQA	RATIO R/AS
Psychology and English Language & Linguistics	QLH7▼	3FT deg	E/L g	CC	3D $	M$^ go	30	BBC	Ind	5
Psychology and English Literature	QL37▼	3FT deg	E g	CC	3D $	M^ go	30	BBC	Ind	6 16/20
Social Policy & Admin and Eng Lang & Linguistics	QLH4▼	3FT deg	E/L g	CC	2M+2D$ M$^		30	BBC	Ind	
Social Policy & Administration & English Lit	QL34▼	3FT deg	E g	CC	2M+2D$ M^		28	BBC	Ind	6
Sociology and English Language & Linguistics	QL3H▼	3FT deg	E/L g	CC	2M+2D$ M$^ go		30	BBC	Ind	7
Sociology and English Literature	QL33▼	3FT deg	E g	CC	2M+2D$ M^ go		28	BBC	Ind	8 12/14
Spanish and English Language & Linguistics	QRH4▼	4FT deg	Sp	CC	2M+2D$ M$^		30	BBC	N$	9
Spanish and English Literature	QR34▼	4FT deg	Sp+E	CC	2M+2D$ M^		28	BBC	N$	2
Sport Studies and English Language & Linguistics	QBH6▼	3FT deg	S+E/L g	CC	3D $	MS go	30	BBC	Ind	
Sport Studies and English Literature	QB36▼	3FT deg	S+E g	CC	3D $	MS^ go	30	BBC	Ind	
Theology & Relig St and English Lang & Linguist	QVH8▼	3FT deg	E/L	CC	2M+2D$ M$^		30	BBC	Ind	3
Theology & Religious Studies and English Lit	QV38▼	3FT deg	E	CC	2M+2D$ M^		28	BBC	Ind	15
Women's Studies and English Lang & Linguistics	QM3Y▼	3FT deg	E/L	CC	2M+2D M$^		30	BBC	Ind	
Women's Studies and English Literature	QM39▼	3FT deg	E	CC	2M+2D$ M^		28	BBC	Ind	6
Humanities (English History Theol & Relig St) English	VY93▼	3FT deg	E/H	CC	2M+2D$ M^		30	BBC	Ind	

ROYAL HOLLOWAY, Univ of London

English	Q300	3FT deg	E g	ABC				Ind	Ind	5 22/28
English Language and Classical Studies	QQ3V	3FT deg	E g	BBC-ABC				30$	Ind	
English Language and Drama	QW3K	3FT deg	E g	ABC	Ind			30$	Ind	
English Language and French	QR3C	4FT deg	E+F	ABC				30$	Ind	4
English Language and German	QR3F	4FT deg	E+G	BBC-ABC				30$	Ind	6
English Language and Italian	QR3H	4FT deg	E+L/Ln	BBC-ABC				30$	Ind	
English Language and Latin	QQ3P	3FT deg	E g	BBC-ABC				30$	Ind	
English Language and Spanish	QR3L	4FT deg	E+Sp	ABC-BBC				Ind	Ind	
English and Classical Studies	QQ38	3FT deg	E g	BBC-ABC				30$	Ind	4 20/28
English and Drama	QW34	3FT deg	E g	ABC	Ind			30$	Ind	14 22/30
English and French	QR31	4FT deg	E+F	ABC				30$	Ind	7 24/28
English and German	QR32	4FT deg	E+G	BBC-ABC				30$	Ind	
English and Italian	QR33	4FT deg	E+L/Ln	BBC-ABC				30$	Ind	12
English and Latin	QQ36	3FT deg	E g	BBC-ABC				30$	Ind	
English and Spanish	QR34	4FT deg	E+Sp	ABC-BBC				Ind	Ind	
German Studies with English Language	R2Q3	3FT deg		BCC				28$	BBBBC$	
Foundation Programme English	Y408	4FT deg								

Univ of SALFORD

English & a Modern Lang-English/French (4 Yrs)	QR31	4FT deg	El+F	BCC	Ind	X		Ind	Ind	Ind	7
English & a Modern Lang-English/German (4 Yrs)	QR32	4FT deg	El+G	BCC	Ind	X		Ind	Ind	Ind	
English Language and Literature	Q300	3FT deg	El g	BBC	X	X		Ind	Ind	X	5 14/24
English and Cultural Studies	Q310	3FT deg	El g	BBC	X	X		Ind	Ind	X	5 14/26
English and History	Q3V1	3FT deg	El g	BBC	X	X		Ind	Ind	X	7 10/22
Info Tech with English for Professional Purposes	G5Q3	3FT deg			18	DO	M^/D	Ind	Ind	Ind	

SOAS:Sch of Oriental & African St (U of London)

Linguistics and Development Studies	MQ93	3FT deg
Linguistics and Economics	LQ13	3FT deg
Linguistics and Geography	LQ83	3FT deg
Linguistics and History	QV31	3FT deg
Linguistics and History of Art/Archaeology	QV36	3FT deg
Linguistics and Law	MQ33	3FT deg
Music and Linguistics	QW33	3FT deg
Politics and Linguistics	MQ13	3FT deg

				98 expected requirements						96 entry stats	

course details | | | | **98 expected requirements** | | | | | | *96 entry stats* |

TITLE	CODE	COURSE	SUBJECTS	A/AS	ND/C	AGNVQ	IB	SQA(H)	SQA	RATIO A/AS	
Psychology with Modern English Studies	L7QH	3FT deg	g	12-16	MO/DO	M/D	32	BBCC	Ind	2	
Public Policy and Management and Modern Engl St	QM3C	3FT deg	g	12-16	MO/DO	M/D	32	BBCC	Ind		
Public Policy and Mgt with Modern English Studs	M1QH	3FT deg	g	12-16	MO/DO	M/D	32	BBCC	Ind		
Social Studies and Modern English Studies	QL33	3FT deg	g	12-16	MO/DO	M/D	32	BBCC	Ind	6	
Social Studies with Modern English Studies	L3Q3	3FT deg	g	12-16	MO/DO	M/D	32	BBCC	Ind	4	
Sociology and Modern English Studies	LQH3	3FT deg		12-16	MO/DO	M/D	32	BBCC	Ind		
Sociology with Modern English Studies	L3QH	3FT deg		12-16	MO/DO	M/D	32	BBCC	Ind		
Travel and Tourism and Modern English Studies	QP37	3FT deg	g	12-16	MO/DO	M/D	32	BBCC	Ind	7	
Travel and Tourism with Modern English Studies	P7Q3	3FT deg	g	12-16	MO/DO	M/D	32	BBCC	Ind		
Women's Studies and Modern English Studies	MQ93	3FT deg		12-16	MO/DO	M/D	32	BBCC	Ind		
Women's Studies with Modern English Studies	M9Q3	3FT deg		12-16	MO/DO	M/D	32	BBCC	Ind		

Univ of MANCHESTER

TITLE	CODE	COURSE	SUBJECTS	A/AS	ND/C	AGNVQ	IB	SQA(H)	SQA	RATIO A/AS	
Drama with English	W4Q3	4FT deg	E	BBB	4M+6D		32	AAABB	HN$	33	26/30
English Language and Literature	Q300	3FT deg	E	ABB	Ind	X	32$	AABBB$		10	26/30
English and American Literature	QQ34	3FT deg	E	ABB	Ind		32$	AABBB$		11	26/30
English and Drama	WQ43	4FT deg	E	BBB	4M+6D		32	AAABB	HN$	25	26/30
English and Linguistics	QQ13	3FT deg	E	BBB	X		32$	AABBB		5	18/24
English and Philosophy	VQ73	3FT deg	E	ABB	Ind		32$	AABBB	Ind	11	26/30
English and a Modern Language (French)	RQ13	4FT deg	E+F	ABB				Ind	BBBBC	8	24/30
English and a Modern Language (German)	RQ23	4FT deg	E+G	ABB				Ind	BBBBC	7	24/30
English and a Modern Language (Italian)	RQ33	4FT deg	E	ABB				Ind	BBBBC	4	24/28
English and a Modern Language (Russian)	RQ83	4FT deg	E	ABB				Ind	BBBBC	3	
English and a Modern Language (Spanish)	RQ43	4FT deg	E+Sp	ABB				Ind	BBBBC	9	
Greek and English	QQ37	3FT deg	Gk+E	BBC	X	X	30	BBBBB	X		
Latin and English	QQ36	3FT deg	Ln+E	BBC	X	X	30$	BBBBB	X	8	
Mathematics and English	GQ13	3FT deg	M+E	24	Ind		30$	X	Ind	4	
Mathematics with English	G1Q3	3FT deg	M+E	24	Ind		30$	CSYS	Ind	7	

MANCHESTER METROPOLITAN Univ

TITLE	CODE	COURSE	SUBJECTS	A/AS	ND/C	AGNVQ	IB	SQA(H)	SQA	RATIO A/AS	
Cultural Studies/American Studies	LQ3H	3FT deg	*	CC	M+D	D	28	CCCC	Ind		
English Studies	Q300	3FT deg	El/E	BC	Ind	Ind	Ind	Ind	Ind	12/24	
English/American Studies	QQ34	3FT deg	*	CC	M+D	D	28	CCCC	Ind		
English/Applied Social Studies	LQ33	3FT deg	*	CC	M+D	D	28	CCCC	Ind		
English/Business Studies	NQ13	3FT deg	*	CC	M+D	D	28	CCCC	Ind		
English/Cultural Studies	LQH3	3FT deg	*	CC	M+D	D	28	CCCC	Ind		
English/Dance	QW3K	3FT deg	*	CC	M+D	D	28	CCCC	Ind		
English/Design & Technology	QW3F	3FT deg	*	CD	M+D	D	28	CCCC	Ind		
English/Drama	QWH4	3FT deg	*	CC	M+D	D	28	CCCC	Ind		
Environmental Science/English	FQ93	3FT deg	*	CC	M+D	D	28	CCCC	Ind		
Geography/English	LQ83	3FT deg	*	CC	M+D	D	28	CCCC	Ind		
Health Studies/English	BQ93	3FT deg	*	CC	M+D	D	28	CCCC	Ind		
History/English	QV31	3FT deg	*	CC	M+D	D	28	CCCC	Ind		
Leisure Studies/English	LQ43	3FT deg	*	CC	M+D	D	28	CCCC	Ind		
Life Science/English	CQ13	3FT deg	*	CC	M+D	D	28	CCCC	Ind		
Music/English	QW33	3FT deg	*	CC	M+D	D	28	CCCC	Ind		
Philosophy/English	QV37	3FT deg	*	CC	M+D	D	28	CCCC	Ind		
Religious Studies/English	QV38	3FT deg	*	CC	M+D	D	28	CCCC	Ind		
Sport/English	BQ63	3FT deg	S	BC	M+D	DS	28	CCCC	Ind		
Visual Arts/English	QW31	3FT deg	*	CC	M+D	D	28	CCCC	Ind		
Writing/English	QW3L	3FT deg	*	CC	M+D	D	28	CCCC	Ind		
Humanities/Social Studies English	Y400	3FT deg	*	CDD	Ind	Ind	Ind	BBB	Ind		

		course details		98 expected requirements							96 entry stats

TITLE	CODE	COURSE	SUBJECTS	A/AS	ND/C	AGNVQ	IB	SQA(H)	SQA	RATIO A/AS
MIDDLESEX Univ										
English	Q300▼ 3FT deg		E g	12-16	X	X	28	Ind	Ind	
Joint Honours Degree	Y400	3FT deg	* g	12-16	5M	M$ go	26	X	X	
English Language and British Culture										
Joint Honours Degree	Y400	3FT deg	E g	16	X	X	28	Ind	Ind	
English and Literary Studies										
Joint Honours Degree	Y400	3FT/4SW deg	* g	12-16	X	X	28	Ind	Ind	
English for Business Communication										
NENE COLLEGE										
American Studies with English	Q4Q3	3FT deg		DD	5M	M	24	CCC	Ind	7/12
Art and Design with English	W2Q3	3FT deg		DD	5M	M	24	CCC	Ind	6/20
Business Administration with English	N1Q3	3FT deg	g	10	M+1D	M	24	BCC	Ind	
Drama with English	W4Q3	3FT deg		10	5M+1D	M	24	CCC	Ind	6/14
Education with English	X9Q3	3FT deg		DD	5M	M	24	CCC	Ind	6/12
English with American Studies	Q3Q4	3FT deg		CC	4M+1D	M	24	CCC	Ind	10/18
English with Art and Design	Q3W2	3FT deg		CC	4M+1D	M	24	CCC	Ind	
English with Business Administration	Q3N1	3FT deg	g	CC	4M+1D	M	24	CCC	Ind	
English with Drama	Q3W4	3FT deg		CC	4M+1D	M	24	CCC	Ind	12/16
English with Education	Q3X9	3FT deg		CC	4M+1D	M	24	CCC	Ind	8/18
English with French	Q3R1	3FT deg	F	CC	4M+1D	M	24	CCC	Ind	
English with History	Q3V1▼ 3FT deg			CC	4M+1D	M	24	CCC	Ind	
English with History of Art	Q3VK▼ 3FT deg			CC	4M+1D	M	24	CCC	Ind	
English with Industrial Archaeology	Q3V6	3FT deg		CC	4M+1D	M	24	CCC	Ind	
English with Marketing Communications	Q3N5▼ 3FT deg			CC	4M+1D	M	24	CCC	Ind	
English with Mathematics	Q3G1	3FT deg	M	CC	4M+1D	M	24	CCC	Ind	
English with Media and Popular Culture	Q3P4▼ 3FT deg			CC	4M+1D	M	24	CCC	Ind	6/22
English with Music	Q3W3	3FT deg	Mu	CC	4M+1D	M	24	CCC	Ind	
English with Personal and Organisational Develop	Q3N6▼ 3FT deg			CC	4M+1D	M	24	CCC	Ind	
English with Philosophy	Q3V7▼ 3FT deg			CC	4M+1D	M	24	CCC	Ind	
English with Psychology	Q3C8▼ 3FT deg		g	CC	4M+1D	M	24	CCC	Ind	8/22
English with Sociology	Q3L3▼ 3FT deg			CC	4M+1D	M	24	CCC	Ind	
English with Sport Studies	Q3N7▼ 3FT deg			CC	4M+1D	M	24	CCC	Ind	
French with English	R1Q3	3FT deg	F	DD	5M	Ind	24	CCC	Ind	
History with English	V1Q3▼ 3FT deg			CD	5M	M	24	CCC	Ind	4/10
Information Systems with English	G5Q3	3FT deg		6	5M	M	24	CCC	Ind	
Music with English	W3Q3	3FT deg	Mu	DD	5M	M	24	CCC	Ind	
Psychology with English	C8Q3▼ 3FT deg		g	CC	5M+1D	M	24	CCC	Ind	6/20
Sociology with English	L3Q3▼ 3FT deg		g	10	5M	M	24	CCC	Ind	6/14
Sport Studies with English	N7Q3▼ 3FT deg		Ss/Pe	12	M+2D	M	24	BBB	Ind	
Univ of NEWCASTLE										
English Language	Q302	3FT deg	*	BBB	Ind		Ind	BBBBB	Ind	12 18/26
English Language and Literature	Q300	3FT deg	E	ABC	Ind		Ind	AABBB	Ind	12 22/28
English Literature	Q306	3FT deg	E	ABC	Ind		Ind	Ind	Ind	15 24/30
English Literature and Latin	QQ36	3FT deg	E+Ln	BBC	Ind		Ind	AABBB	Ind	
German and English Language	RQ23	4FT deg	G+E	22		X	$	AABBB$		12
Combined Studies (BA)	Y400	3FT deg	E	ABC-BBB	5D	Ind	35$	AAAB	Ind	
English Literature										
NEWMAN COLLEGE OF HIGHER EDUCATION										
English and Biological Science	CQ13	3FT deg	*	CC	3M	M*	Dip	CCC	Ind	
English and Geography	FQ83	3FT deg	*	CC	3M	M*	Dip	CCC	Ind	
English and History	QV31	3FT deg	*	CC	3M	M*	Dip	CCC	Ind	
English and Physical Education & Sports Studies	QX39	3FT deg	*	CC	3M	M*	Dip	CCC	Ind	

course details			98 expected requirements							96 entry stats	
TITLE	CODE	COURSE	SUBJECTS	A/AS	ND/C	AGNVQ	IB	SQA(H)	SQA	RATIO	A/AS
Univ of Wales COLLEGE, NEWPORT											
English and Archaeology	QV36	3FT deg		10	M+D	D$	Ind	Ind	Ind		
European Studies and English	QT32	3FT deg		10	M+D	D$	Ind	Ind	Ind		
History and English	QV31	3FT deg		10	M+D	D$	Ind	Ind	Ind		
Information Technology and English	GQ53	3FT deg		10	M+D	D$	Ind	Ind	Ind		
Religious Studies and English	QV38	3FT deg		10	M+D	D$	Ind	Ind	Ind		
Sports Studies and English	BQ63	3FT deg		10	M+D	D$	Ind	Ind	Ind		
NORTH EAST WALES INST of HE											
English	Q300	3FT deg		6-12	4M	M$	Ind	BBB	N$		
English and History	QV31	3FT deg		6-12	4M	M$	Ind	BBB	N$		8/16
English and Media Studies	QP34	3FT deg		6-12	4M	M$	Ind	BBB	N$		10/16
English and Welsh Studies	QQ35	3FT deg		6-12	4M	M$	Ind	BBB	N$		
English with Geography	Q3F8	3FT deg		6-12	4M	M$	Ind	BBB	N$		
English with History	Q3V1	3FT deg		6-12	4M	M$	Ind	BBB	N$		
English with Media Studies	Q3P4	3FT deg		6-12	4M	M$	Ind	BBB	N$		
English with Psychology	Q3C8	3FT deg		6-12	4M	M$	Ind	BBB	N$		
English with Sociology	Q3L3	3FT deg		6-12	4M	M$	Ind	BBB	N$		
English/Geography	FQ83	3FT deg		6-12	3M	M$	Ind	CCC	N$		
English/Psychology	QC38	3FT deg		4-12	3M	M$	Ind	BBB	N$		
English/Sociology	QL33	3FT deg		6-12	3M	M$	Ind	CCC	N$		
History with English	V1Q3	3FT deg		6-12	4M	M$	Ind	BBB	N$		
Univ of NORTH LONDON											
English	Q300▼	3FT deg	E	BC	Ind	Ind	Ind	Ind	Ind	6	8/20
Combined Honours Critical Theory	Y300	3FT/4FT deg	E	CC	Ind	Ind	Ind	Ind	Ind		
Combined Honours English	Y300	3FT/4FT deg	E	CC	Ind	Ind	Ind	Ind	Ind		
Univ of NORTHUMBRIA											
English Studies	Q300	3FT deg	E	BBC	MO+5D		28	BBBBB	Ind	14	18/24
English and Film Studies	QW35	3FT deg	E	BBC	MO+4D		26	BBBCC	Ind	14	18/24
English and Women's Cultures	QM39	3FT deg	E	BCC	MO+4D		26	BBBCC	Ind	4	
NORWICH: City COLL											
Psychology with English	L7Q3	3FT deg	* g	12		X	Ind	Ind	Ind		
Combined Arts English Literature	Y300	3FT deg	* g	12	Ind		Ind	Ind	Ind		
Univ of NOTTINGHAM											
American and English Studies	QQ34	3FT deg	E	BBC						31	28/30
Archaeology and English Language	QV36	3FT deg	E	BBC						5	
Art History and English Studies	QV34	3FT deg	E	BBC						25	26/28
Classical Civilisation and English Studies	QQ83	3FT deg	E	BBC						43	
English Studies	Q300	3FT deg	E+L g	ABC						24	24/30
English Studies and Latin	QQ36	3FT deg	E+Ln	BBC							
English Studies and Philosophy	QV37	3FT deg	E	ABC						30	28/30
English Studies and Theology	QV38	3FT deg	E	BBC						8	26/30
NOTTINGHAM TRENT Univ											
English	Q300	3FT deg	E g	BBC	Ind	Ind	28	BBCC	Ind	10	16/26
English and Environmental Studies	QF3X	3FT deg	E g	12	Ind	M$ go	Ind	Ind	Ind	1	12/24
English and Urban Studies	QK34	3FT deg	E g	12	Ind	M$ go	Ind	Ind	Ind	2	10/16
Humanities English	Y301	3FT/4SW deg	* g	14-16	M+D	Ind	28	CCCC	Ind		

English 26

| | | | 98 expected requirements | | | | | | | 96 entry stats | |

TITLE	CODE	COURSE	SUBJECTS	A/AS	ND/C	RGNVQ	IB	SQA(H)	SQA	RATIO	A/AS
OXFORD Univ											
Classics and English	QQ38	3FT deg	E+Ln/Gk	AAB	DO		36	AAAAA	Ind	3	30/30
English Language and Literature	Q300	3FT deg	E	AAB	DO		36	AAAAA	Ind	4	26/30
English and Modern Languages (3 Yrs)	QT39	3FT deg	E+L	AAB	DO		36	AAAAA	Ind	9	
English and Modern Languages (4 Yrs)	TQ93	4FT deg	E+L	AAB	DO		36	AAAAA	Ind	4	30/30
Modern History and English	VQ13	3FT deg	E+H	AAB	DO		36	AAAAA	Ind	5	28/30
OXFORD WESTMINSTER COLLEGE											
Contemporary English Studies with Cultural St	Q3VX	2FT Dip	E	CE	MO	M	Ind	CCC	Ind		
Contemporary English Studies with Cultural St	Q3V9	3FT deg	E	CE	MO	M	Ind	CCC	Ind		
Contemporary English Studies with Development St	Q3LH	2FT Dip	E	CE	MO	M	Ind	CCC	Ind		
Contemporary English Studies with Development St	Q3L3	3FT deg	E	CE	MO	M	Ind	CCC	Ind		
Contemporary English Studies with Interfaith St	Q3VV	2FT Dip	E	CE	MO	M	Ind	CCC	Ind		
Contemporary English Studies with Interfaith St	Q3V8	3FT deg	E	CE	MO	M	Ind	CCC	Ind		
Contemporary English Studies with Language Studs	Q3T9	3FT deg	E	CE	MO	M	Ind	CCC	Ind		
Contemporary English Studies with Language Studs	Q3TX	2FT Dip	E	CE	MO	M	Ind	CCC	Ind		
Contemporary English Studies with World Studies	Q3M1	3FT deg	E	CE	MO	M	Ind	CCC	Ind		
Contemporary English Studies with World Studies	Q3MC	2FT Dip	E	CE	MO	M	Ind	CCC	Ind		
OXFORD BROOKES Univ											
English Studies	Q300	3FT deg			Ind		Ind	Ind	Ind		14/22
English Studies/Accounting and Finance	NQ43	3FT deg	* g	AB-BCC	Ind	M*^/D*3	Ind	Ind	Ind		
English Studies/Anthropology	LQ63	3FT deg	*	AB-BCC	Ind	M*^	Ind	Ind	Ind	9	
English Studies/Biological Chemistry	CQ73	3FT deg									
English Studies/Biology	CQ13	3FT deg	S g	DD-AB	Ind	M*^/MS	Ind	Ind	Ind		
English Studies/Business Administration & Mgt	NQ13	3FT deg	* g	AB-BCC	Ind	M*^/MB4	Ind	Ind	Ind	15	
English Studies/Cartography	FQ83	3FT deg	* g	DDD-AB	Ind	M*^	Ind	Ind	Ind		
English Studies/Cell Biology	CQC3	3FT deg									
English Studies/Combined Studies	QY34	3FT deg		X		X	X	X			
English Studies/Computer Systems	GQ63	3FT deg	* g	CDD-AB	Ind	M*^	Ind	Ind	Ind	1	
English Studies/Computing	GQ53	3FT deg	* g	CDD-AB	Ind	M*^	Ind	Ind	Ind	8	
English Studies/Computing Mathematics	GQ93	3FT deg	* g	CD-AB	Ind	M*^	Ind	Ind	Ind		
English Studies/Ecology	CQ93	3FT deg	* g	CD-AB	Ind	MS/M*^	Ind	Ind	Ind	10	
English Studies/Economics	LQ13	3FT deg	* g	CCD-AB	Ind	M*^M*3	Ind	Ind	Ind		
English Studies/Educational Studies	QX39	3FT deg	*	CC-AB	Ind	M*^/3	Ind	Ind	Ind	4	8/20
English Studies/Electronics	HQ63	3FT deg	S/M	CC-AB	Ind	M$/M*^	Ind	Ind	Ind		
Environmental Chemistry/English Studies	QF31	3FT deg									
Environmental Policy/English Studies	KQ33	3FT deg									
Environmental Sciences/English Studies	FQX3	3FT deg	S g	CD-AB	Ind	M*^/DS	Ind	Ind	Ind	5	
Exercise & Health/English Studies	QB36	3FT deg	S g	DD-AB	Ind	MS/M*^	Ind	Ind	Ind		
Fine Art/English Studies	QW31	3FT deg	Pf+A	BC-AB	Ind	MA^	Ind	Ind	Ind		
Food Science and Nutrition/English Studies	DQ43	3FT deg	S g	DD-AB	Ind	MS/M*^	Ind	Ind	Ind	5	
French Language and Contemp Studies/English St	QR3C	4SW deg	F	CDD-AB	Ind	M*^	Ind	Ind	Ind	16	
French Language and Literature/English Studies	QR31	4SW deg	F	CDD-AB	Ind	M*^	Ind	Ind	Ind	13	
Geography and the Phys Env/English Studies	FQV3	3FT deg									
Geography/English Studies	LQ83	3FT deg	*	CCD-AB	Ind	M*^	Ind	Ind	Ind	24	
Geotechnics/English Studies	HQ23	3FT deg	S/M/Ds/Es	DD-AB	Ind	M$^	Ind	Ind	Ind		
German Language and Contemp Stud/English Studies	QR3F	4SW deg	G	DDD-AB	Ind	M*^	Ind	Ind	Ind	4	
German Language and Literature/English Studies	QR32	4SW deg	G	DDD-AB	Ind	M*^	Ind	Ind	Ind	3	
German Studies/English Studies	QR3G	4SW deg			Ind		Ind	Ind	Ind		
Health Care/English Studies (Post Exp)	BQ73	3FT deg		X		X	X	X			
History of Art/English Studies	QV34	3FT deg	*	AB-BCC	Ind	M*^	Ind	Ind	Ind	4	10/22
History/English Studies	QV31	3FT deg	*	CCD-AB	Ind	M*^	Ind	Ind	Ind	7	14/20

			98 expected requirements							**96 entry stats**	
TITLE	**CODE**	**COURSE**	**SUBJECTS**	**A/AS**	**NO/C**	**AGNVQ**	**IB**	**SQA(H)**	**SQA**	**RATIO**	**A/AS**
Hospitality Management Studies/English Studies	NQ73	3FT deg	*	DDD-AB	Ind	M*^/3	Ind	Ind	Ind		
Human Biology/English Studies	BQ13	3FT deg									
Information Systems/English Studies	GQM3	3FT deg	* g	CDD-BCC	Ind	M*^	Ind	Ind	Ind		
Intelligent Systems/English Studies	GQ83	3FT deg	* g	CD-AB	Ind	M*^	Ind	Ind	Ind		
Langs for Bus:Italian-Ab Initio/English-Post A	NQCJ	4FT deg									
Languages for Business:French/English-Post A	NQCH	4FT deg	F+E	BC-CDD	Ind	M*_^	Ind	Ind	Ind		
Languages for Business:German/English-Post A	NQ1H	4FT deg	G+E	BC-CDD	Ind	M*_^	Ind	Ind	Ind		
Languages for Business:Italian/English-Post A	NQ1J	4FT deg	I+E	BC-CDD	Ind	M*_^	Ind	Ind	Ind		
Languages for Business:Spanish/English-Post A	NQC3	4FT deg	Sp+E	CDD-BC	Ind	M*_^	Ind	Ind	Ind		
Law/English Studies	MQ33	3FT deg	*	AB-BCC	Ind	M*^/D*3	Ind	Ind	Ind	19	
Leisure Planning/English Studies	KQH3	3FT deg									
Marketing Management/English Studies	NQN3	3FT deg	* g	AB-BCC	Ind	M*^/D*3	Ind	Ind	Ind		
Music/English Studies	QW33	3FT deg	Mu	DD-AB	Ind	M*^	Ind	Ind	Ind	4	16/18
Palliative Care/English Studies (Post Exp)	BQR3	3FT deg		X		X	X	X			
Planning Studies/English Studies	KQ43	3FT deg	* g	DDD-AB	Ind	M*^	Ind	Ind	Ind		
Politics/English Studies	MQ13	3FT deg	*	AB-CCC	Ind	M*^	Ind	Ind	Ind	6	16/18
Psychology/English Studies	CQ83	3FT deg	* g	AB-BCC	Ind	M*^	Ind	Ind	Ind	28	
Publishing/English Studies	PQ53	3FT deg	* g	CCD-AB	Ind	M*^/M$3	Ind	Ind	Ind	3	12/26
Rehabilitation/English Studies (Post Exp)	BQT3	3FT deg		X		X	X	X			
Sociology/English Studies	LQ33	3FT deg	*	AB-BCC	Ind	M*^	Ind	Ind	Ind	15	
Software Engineering/English Studies	GQ73	3FT deg	* g	CD-AB	Ind	M*^	Ind	Ind	Ind		
Statistics/English Studies	GQ43	3FT deg	* g	DD-AB	Ind	M*^	Ind	Ind	Ind		
Telecommunications/English Studies	HQP3	3FT deg									
Transport Planning/English Studies	NQ93	3FT deg	* g	AB-DDD	Ind	M*^	Ind	Ind	Ind		
Water Resources/English Studies	HQF3	3FT deg									

Univ of PLYMOUTH

Art History with English	V4Q3	3FT deg	Ap g	CCD	MO+3D	D$^	Ind	Ind	Ind	7	
Cultural Interpretation & Practice with English	Y3Q3	3FT deg	Ap g	CCD	MO+3D	D$^	Ind	Ind	Ind		
English with Art History	Q3V4	3FT deg	Ap g	BBC	MO+3D	D$_^	Ind	Ind	Ind	5	16/22
English with Cultural Interpretation & Practice	Q3Y3	3FT deg	E g	BBC	MO+3D	D$_^	Ind	Ind	Ind		
English with Education Studies	Q3X9	3FT deg	Ap g	BBC	MO+3D	D$_^	Ind	Ind	Ind	7	16/22
English with Heritage and Landscape	Q3WG	3FT deg	Ap g	BBC	MO+3D	D$_^	Ind	Ind	Ind	2	
English with History	Q3V1	3FT deg	Ap g	BBC	MO+3D	D$_^	Ind	Ind	Ind	5	12/18
English with Media Arts	Q3WF	3FT deg	Ap g	BBC	MO+3D	D$_^	Ind	Ind	Ind	9	12/26
English with Music	Q3W3	3FT deg	Ap g	BBC	MO+3D	D$_^	Ind	Ind	Ind	2	
English with Theatre and Performance Studies	Q3W4	3FT deg	Ap g	BBC	MO+3D	D$_^	Ind	Ind	Ind	8	14/22
English with Visual Arts	Q3W2	3FT deg	Ap g	BBC	MO+3D	D$_^	Ind	Ind	Ind	2	12/18
Heritage and Landscape with English	W2QJ	3FT deg	Ap g	CCD	MO+3D	D$^	Ind	Ind	Ind		
History with English	V1Q3	3FT deg	Ap g	CCD	MO+3D	D$_^	Ind	Ind	Ind	4	16/18
Media Arts with English	W2QH	3FT deg	Ap g	CCD	MO+3D	D$_^	Ind	Ind	Ind	5	12/22
Theatre and Performance St with English	W4Q3	3FT deg	Ap g	CCD	MO+3D	D$_^	Ind	Ind	Ind	7	10/24
Visual Arts with English	W2Q3	3FT deg	Ap g	CCD	MO+3D	D$_^	Ind	Ind	Ind	3	

Univ of PORTSMOUTH

Art and English	WQ13	3FT deg	E+Fa/Pf	18	N	Ind	Dip	Ind	Ind		
Art and English	EQ13	3FT deg	E+Fa/Pf		N	Ind	Dip	Ind	Ind		
English and Creative Studies	QW39	3FT deg	E+Pf	BCC	X	D$6/^	Ind	AABBB	Ind	6	12/24

QUEEN MARY & WESTFIELD COLL (Univ of London)

English	Q300	3FT deg	E	22		M$^	30$				
English and Drama	QW34	3FT deg	E	22		M	30$				
English and French	QR3C	4FT deg	E+F	20		M^	30$				
English and German	RQ23	4FT deg	E+G	20		M^	30$				

course details			98 expected requirements							96 entry stats
TITLE	**CODE**	**COURSE**	**SUBJECTS**	**A/AS**	**ND/C**	**AGNVQ**	**IB**	**SQA(H)**	**SQA**	**RATIO A/AS**
English and Hispanic Studies	RQ4J	4FT deg	E	20		M	30$			
English and History	QV31	3FT deg	E	20		M	30$			
English and Russian	QRH8	4FT deg	E	20		M	30$			

QUEEN'S Univ Belfast

English	Q300	3FT deg	E g	BCC	X	D*^ go	29$	ABBB	X	5 18/28
English/Ancient History	VQC3	3FT deg	E g	BCC	X	D*^ go	29$	ABBB	X	10
English/Archaeology	VQ63	3FT deg	E g	BCC	X	D*^ go	29$	ABBB	X	6
English/Biblical Studies	VQ83	3FT deg	E g	BCC	X	D*^ go	29$	ABBB	X	8
English/Byzantine Studies	QQ38	3FT/4FT deg	E g	BCC	X	D*^ go	29$	ABBB	X	1
English/Celtic	QQ53	3FT/4FT deg	E g	BCC	X	D*^ go	29$	ABBB	X	5
English/Classical Studies	QQ83	3FT deg	E g	BCC	X	D*^ go	29$	ABBB	X	9
English/Economics	LQ13	3FT deg								
French/English (4 years)	QR31	4FT deg	E+F g	BCC	X	X	29$	ABBB	X	5 20/26
German/English (4 years)	QR32	4FT deg	E g	BCC	X	D*^ go	29$	ABBB	X	3
Greek/English	QQ37	3FT/4FT deg	E g	BCC	X	D*^ go	29$	ABBB	X	
Italian/English (4 years)	QR33	4FT deg	E g	BCC	X	D*^ go	29$	ABBB	X	9
Latin/English	QQ36	3FT/4FT deg	E g	BCC	X	D*^ go	29$	ABBB	X	1
Modern History/English	QV31	3FT deg	E g	BCC	X	D*^ go	29$	ABBB	X	6 18/28
Music/English	QW33	3FT deg	E g	BCC	X	D*^ go	29$	ABBB	X	11
Philosophy/English	QV37	3FT deg	E g	BCC	X	D*^ go	29$	ABBB	X	8 20/26
Politics/English	QM31	3FT deg	E g	BCC	X	D*^ go	29$	ABBB	X	10 22/26
Psychology/English	CQ83	3FT deg	E g	BCC	X	D*^ go	29$	ABBB	X	8 20/28
Scholastic Philosophy/English	QV3R	3FT deg	E g	BCC	X	D*^ go	29$	ABBB	X	5
Social Anthropology/English	QL36	3FT deg	E g	BCC	X	D*^ go	29$	ABBB	X	11
Social Policy/English	QL34	3FT deg	E g	BCC	X	D*^ go	29$	ABBB	X	
Sociology/English	QL33	3FT deg	E g	BCC	X	D*^ go	29$	ABBB	X	10 20/28
Spanish/English (4 years)	QR34	4FT deg	E g	BCC	X	D*^ go	29$	ABBB	X	6
Theology and English	QV38	3FT deg								
Women's Studies/English	QM39	3FT deg	E g	BCC	X	D*^ go	29$	ABBB	X	

Univ of READING

Classical Studies with English Literature	Q8Q3	3FT deg	El	BCC	Ind	D*^	30$	BBBB$	Ind	8
English Language & Literature	Q300	3FT deg	El	BBB	Ind	D*^	32$	ABBB$	Ind	12 20/28
English Literature & Modern English Language	QQ31	3FT deg	El	BBC	Ind	D*^	31$	BBBB$	Ind	10 20/30
English Literature and Classical Studies	QQ38	3FT deg	El	BCC	Ind	D*^	30$	BBBB$	Ind	10 20/22
English Literature and Film & Drama	QW34	3FT deg	El	BBC	Ind	D*^	31$	BBBB$	Ind	20 22/30
English Literature and French	QR31	3FT deg	El+F	BBC	Ind	D*^	31$	BBBB$	Ind	13 20/26
English Literature and German	QR32	4FT deg	El g	BBC	Ind	D$^ go	31$	BBBB$	Ind	6
English Literature and History of Art	QV34	3FT deg	El	BBC	Ind	D$^	31$	BBBB$	Ind	25
English Literature and Italian	QR33	4FT deg	El g	BBC	Ind	D$^ go	31$	BBBB$	Ind	29
English Literature and Sociology	LQ33	3FT deg	El	BBC	Ind	D$^	31$	BBBB$	Ind	19 22/26
English Literature with Classical Studies	Q3Q8	3FT deg	El	BCC	Ind	D*^	30$	BBBB$	Ind	7
English Literature with Latin	Q3Q6	3FT deg	El	BCC	Ind	D*^	30$	BBBB$	Ind	
French and English Literature	RQ13	4FT deg	El+F	BBC	Ind	D*^	31$	BBBB$	Ind	5 18/24
Greek and English Literature	QQ37	3FT deg	El g	BCC	Ind	D*^ go	30$	BBBB$	Ind	
History and English Literature	QV31	3FT deg	El	BBC	Ind	D*^	31$	BBBB$	Ind	14 22/28
Latin and English Literature	QQ36	3FT deg	El g	BCC	Ind	D*^ go	30$	BBBB$	Ind	
Music and English Literature	QW33	3FT deg	Mu+El	BBC	X	D*^	31$	BBBB$	Ind	8
Philosophy and English Literature	VQ73	3FT deg	El	BBC	Ind	D*^	31$	BBBB$	Ind	15 22/26

Univ College of RIPON & YORK ST JOHN

Art/English	W1Q3	3FT deg	A+E+Pf	BC-CCD	Ind	MA^	27	BBBB		3 10/24
Art/English	E1Q3	3FT deg	A+E+Pf	BC-CCD	Ind	MA^	27	BBBB		

course details			**98 expected requirements**							**96 entry stats**	
TITLE	CODE	COURSE	SUBJECTS	A/AS	ND/C	AGNVQ	IB	SQA(H)	SQA	RATIO	A/AS
Cultural Studies with English	L6Q3	3FT deg		12	M	M*	27	BBBC			
English Studies (Literature and Language)	QQ31	3FT deg	E	16	Ind	M*^	30	BBBB		5	10/22
English Studies with Cultural Studies	Q3L6	3FT deg	E	16	Ind	M*^	30	BBBB			
English Studies with Education	Q3X9	3FT deg	E	16	Ind	M*^	30	BBBB			
English Studies with European Studies	Q3T2	3FT deg	E	16	Ind	M*^	30	BBBB			
English/American Studies	Q3Q4	3FT deg	E	16	Ind	M*^	30	BBBB			
English/Art	Q3W1	3FT deg	E+A+Pf	16	Ind	Ind	30	BBBB		5	
English/History	Q3V1	3FT deg	E/H	16	Ind	Ind	30	BBBB		3	12/22
English/Language Studies (English)	Q3Q1	3FT deg	E	16	Ind	M*^	30	BBBB		4	8/24
English/Theology	Q3V8	3FT deg	E	16	Ind	M*^	27	BBBB			
English/Women's Studies	Q3M9	3FT deg	E	16	Ind	M*^	30	BBBB		5	14/22
History/English	V1Q3	3FT deg	H+E	14	X	Ind	30	BBBB		3	8/22
Language Studies (English)/English	Q1Q3	3FT deg	E	16	X	M*^	30	BBBB		5	12/18
Theology/English	V8Q3	3FT deg	E	12	M	M*	27	BBBC			

ROEHAMPTON INST

English Lang & Linguist and Business Computing	GQ7H▼	3FT deg	g	CC	2M+2D	M$^ go	30	BBC	N$		
English Lang & Linguistics and Art for Community	WQ1H▼	3FT deg	E/L	CC	2M+2D$	M$^	30	BBC	Ind	2	
English Language & Linguist & English Literature	Q310▼	3FT deg	E	CC	2M+2D$	M^	30	BBC	Ind	3	
English Language & Linguist and App Consumer St	QN39▼	3FT deg	E/L g	CC	2M+2D$	M$^	30	BBC	N$		
English Language & Linguist and Business Studies	QN31▼	3FT deg	E/Lg	CC	3D $	M$^ go	30	BBC	N$		
English Language & Linguist/Drama & Theatre St	WQLH▼	3FT deg	E/L+E/T	16	3D $	M$^	30	BBC	Ind	6	
English Language & Linguistics	Q340▼	3FT deg	E/L	CC	2M+2D$	M$^	30	BBC	N$	5	12/26
English Language & Linguistics and Biology	CQ1H▼	3FT deg	E/L+B	CC	2M+2D$	M$^ go	30	BBC	N$		
English Language & Linguistics and Education	XQ9H▼	3FT deg	E/L	CC	2M+2D	M$^	30	BBC	N$	1	
English Language & Linguistics/Dance Studies	WQ4H▼	3FT deg	E/L	CC	2M+2D$	M$^	30	BBC	Ind	3	
English Literature	Q300▼	3FT deg	E	CC	2M+2D$	M^	28	BBC	N$	4	10/20
English Literature and Applied Consumer Studies	NQ93▼	3FT deg	E g	CC	2M+2D$	M^ go	28	BBC	N$		
English Literature and Art for Community	WQ13▼	3FT deg	E	CC	2M+2D$	M^	28	BBC	Ind	4	
English Literature and Biology	CQ13▼	3FT deg	E+B	CC	2M+2D$	M^ go	28	BBC	N$		
English Literature and Business Computing	GQ73▼	3FT deg	E g	CC	2M+2D	M^ go	30	BBC	N$		
English Literature and Business Studies	NQ13▼	3FT deg	E g	CC	3D $	M^ go	28	BBC	N$	4	12/16
English Literature and Dance Studies	WQ43▼	3FT deg	E	CC	2M+2D$	M^	30	BBC	Ind	7	16/18
English Literature and Drama & Theatre Studies	WQL3▼	3FT deg	E	16	3D $	M^	30	BBC	Ind	7	16/22
English Literature and Education	XQ93▼	3FT deg	E	CC	2M+2D$	M^	28	BBC	Ind	2	4/14
Environmental St and English Lang & Linguistics	QFH9▼	3FT deg	B/Gy+E/L	CC	2M+2D$	M$^ go	30	BBC	Ind		
Environmental Studies and English Literature	QF39▼	3FT deg	B/Gy+E	CC	2M+2D$	M^ go	28	BBC	Ind		
Film & Television Studies & English Lang & Ling	PQ4H▼	3FT deg	E/L	16	2M+2D$	M$^	30	BBC	N$	33	
Film & Television Studies and English Literature	PQ43▼	3FT deg	E	16	2M+2D$	M^	30	BBC	N$	10	14/20
French and English Language & Linguistics	QR3C▼	4FT deg	F+E/L	CC	2M+2D$	M^	30	BBC	Ind	4	
French and English Literature	QR31▼	4FT deg	F+E	CC	2M+2D$	M^	28	BBC	Ind	11	
Geography and English Language & Linguistics	QLH8▼	3FT deg	Gy+E/L	CC	2M+2D$	M$^	30	BBC	Ind		
Geography and English Literature	QL38▼	3FT deg	Gy+E	CC	2M+2D$	M^ go	28	BBC	Ind		
Health Studies and English Lang & Linguistics	BQ9H▼	3FT deg	E/L+B	CC	2M+2D$	M$^ go	30	BBC	N$		
Health Studies and English Literature	BQ93▼	3FT deg	E+B	CC	2M+2D$	M^ go	28	BBC	N$		
History and English Language & Linguistics	QV3C▼	3FT deg	H+E/L	CC	2M+2D$	M^	30	BBC	Ind	6	
History and English Literature	QV31▼	3FT deg	H+E	CC	2M+2D$	M^	28	BBC	Ind	4	6/20
Human & Social Biol and English Lang & Linguist	QCHC▼	3FT deg	B+E/L	CC	2M+2D$	M$	30	BBC	Ind		
Human & Social Biology and English Literature	QC3C▼	3FT deg	B+E	CC	2M+2D$	M^	28	BBC	Ind		
Music and English Language & Linguistics	QW3H▼	3FT deg	Mu+E/L	CC	2M+2D$	M^	30	BBC	Ind		
Music and English Literature	QW33▼	3FT deg	Mu+E	CC	2M+2D$	M^	28	BBC	Ind	3	
Natural Resource St and English Lang & Linguist	DQ2H▼	3FT deg	g	CC	2M+2D	M$^ go	30	BBC	N$		
Natural Resource Studies and English Literature	DQ23▼	3FT deg	E g	CC	2M+2D	M^ go	30	BBC	N$		

course details		98 expected requirements							96 entry stats
TITLE	CODE COURSE	SUBJECTS	A/AS	NO/C	AGNVQ	IB	SQA(H)	SQA	RATIO A/AS
Psychology and English Language & Linguistics	QLH7▼ 3FT deg	E/L g	CC	3D $	M$^ go	30	BBC	Ind	5
Psychology and English Literature	QL37▼ 3FT deg	E g	CC	3D $	M^ go	30	BBC	Ind	6 16/20
Social Policy & Admin and Eng Lang & Linguistics	QLH4▼ 3FT deg	E/L g	CC	2M+2D$	M$^	30	BBC	Ind	
Social Policy & Administration & English Lit	QL34▼ 3FT deg	E g	CC	2M+2D$	M^	28	BBC	Ind	6
Sociology and English Language & Linguistics	QL3H▼ 3FT deg	E/L g	CC	2M+2D$	M$^ go	30	BBC	Ind	7
Sociology and English Literature	QL33▼ 3FT deg	E g	CC	2M+2D$	M^ go	28	BBC	Ind	8 12/14
Spanish and English Language & Linguistics	QRH4▼ 4FT deg	Sp	CC	2M+2D$	M$^	30	BBC	N$	9
Spanish and English Literature	QR34▼ 4FT deg	Sp+E	CC	2M+2D$	M^	28	BBC	N$	2
Sport Studies and English Language & Linguistics	QBH6▼ 3FT deg	S+E/L g	CC	3D $	MS go	30	BBC	Ind	
Sport Studies and English Literature	QB36▼ 3FT deg	S+E g	CC	3D $	MS^ go	30	BBC	Ind	
Theology & Relig St and English Lang & Linguist	QVH8▼ 3FT deg	E/L	CC	2M+2D$	M$^	30	BBC	Ind	3
Theology & Religious Studies and English Lit	QV38▼ 3FT deg	E	CC	2M+2D$	M^	28	BBC	Ind	15
Women's Studies and English Lang & Linguistics	QM3Y▼ 3FT deg	E/L	CC	2M+2D	M$^	30	BBC	Ind	
Women's Studies and English Literature	QM39▼ 3FT deg	E	CC	2M+2D$	M^	28	BBC	Ind	6
Humanities (English History Theol & Relig St) English	VY93▼ 3FT deg	E/H	CC	2M+2D$	M^	30	BBC	Ind	

ROYAL HOLLOWAY, Univ of London

English	Q300 3FT deg	E g	ABC				Ind	Ind	5 22/28
English Language and Classical Studies	QQ3V 3FT deg	E g	BBC-ABC				30$	Ind	
English Language and Drama	QW3K 3FT deg	E g	ABC	Ind			30$	Ind	
English Language and French	QR3C 4FT deg	E+F	ABC				30$	Ind	4
English Language and German	QR3F 4FT deg	E+G	BBC-ABC				30$	Ind	6
English Language and Italian	QR3H 4FT deg	E+L/Ln	BBC-ABC				30$	Ind	
English Language and Latin	QQ3P 3FT deg	E g	BBC-ABC				30$	Ind	
English Language and Spanish	QR3L 4FT deg	E+Sp	ABC-BBC				Ind	Ind	
English and Classical Studies	QQ38 3FT deg	E g	BBC-ABC				30$	Ind	4 20/28
English and Drama	QW34 3FT deg	E g	ABC	Ind			30$	Ind	14 22/30
English and French	QR31 4FT deg	E+F	ABC				30$	Ind	7 24/28
English and German	QR32 4FT deg	E+G	BBC-ABC				30$	Ind	
English and Italian	QR33 4FT deg	E+L/Ln	BBC-ABC				30$	Ind	12
English and Latin	QQ36 3FT deg	E g	BBC-ABC				30$	Ind	
English and Spanish	QR34 4FT deg	E+Sp	ABC-BBC				Ind	Ind	
German Studies with English Language	R2Q3 3FT deg		BCC				28$	BBBBC$	
Foundation Programme English	Y408 4FT deg								

Univ of SALFORD

English & a Modern Lang-English/French (4 Yrs)	QR31 4FT deg	El+F	BCC	Ind	X	Ind	Ind	Ind	7
English & a Modern Lang-English/German (4 Yrs)	QR32 4FT deg	El+G	BCC	Ind	X	Ind	Ind	Ind	
English Language and Literature	Q300 3FT deg	El g	BBC	X	X	Ind	Ind	X	5 14/24
English and Cultural Studies	Q310 3FT deg	El g	BBC	X	X	Ind	Ind	X	5 14/26
English and History	Q3V1 3FT deg	El g	BBC	X	X	Ind	Ind	X	7 10/22
Info Tech with English for Professional Purposes	G5Q3 3FT deg		18	DO	M^/D	Ind	Ind	Ind	

SOAS:Sch of Oriental & African St (U of London)

Linguistics and Development Studies	MQ93 3FT deg
Linguistics and Economics	LQ13 3FT deg
Linguistics and Geography	LQ83 3FT deg
Linguistics and History	QV31 3FT deg
Linguistics and History of Art/Archaeology	QV36 3FT deg
Linguistics and Law	MQ33 3FT deg
Music and Linguistics	QW33 3FT deg
Politics and Linguistics	MQ13 3FT deg

TITLE	CODE	COURSE	SUBJECTS	A/AS	NB/C	AGNVQ	IB	SQA(H)	SQA	RATIO A/AS
Univ College SCARBOROUGH										
English	Q300	3FT deg	E g	CC	Ind	M	28$	Ind	Ind	
English with Arts	Q3Y3	3FT deg	E g	CC	Ind	M	28$	Ind	Ind	
English with Social Sciences	Q3Y2	3FT deg	E g	CC	Ind	M	28$	Ind	Ind	
Univ of SHEFFIELD										
Biblical Studies and English	QV38	3FT deg	E g	BBB	X	X	32$	AABB$	Ind	
English Language and English Literature	Q304	3FT deg	E g	ABB	X	X	33$	AAAB$	Ind	
English Language and Sociology	QL33	3FT deg	E g	BBC	2M+4D$	D^	29$	BBBB$	Ind	36
English Language with Linguistics	Q3Q1	3FT deg	Ee g	BBC	X	X	30$	ABBB$	Ind	15 20/30
English Language with Medieval Literature	Q308	3FT deg	Ee g	BBC	X	X	30$	ABBB$	Ind	3 20/28
English Literature	Q306	3FT deg	El g	ABB	X	D^	33$	AAAB$	Ind	10 26/30
English and French	QR31	4FT deg	El+F g	ABB	X	X	33$	AAAB$	Ind	9 26/30
English and German	QR32	4FT deg	El+G g	BBB	X	X	32$	AABB$	Ind	22
English and Hispanic Studies	QR34	4FT deg	El+Sp g	BBB	X	X	32$	AABB$	Ind	19
English and History	QV31	3FT deg	El+H g	ABB	X	X	33$	AAAB$	Ind	14 24/30
English and Music	QW33	3FT deg	El+Mu g	BBB	X	X	32$	AABB$	Ind	35
English and Philosophy	QV37	3FT deg	El g	ABB	X	X	33$	AAAB$	Ind	12 26/30
English and Russian	QR38	4FT deg	El+L g	BBB	X	X	32$	AABB$	Ind	
SHEFFIELD HALLAM Univ										
English Studies	Q300	3FT deg	E	22	4M+2D	P^	Ind	BBBB	Ind	
Film and Literature	QW25	3FT deg	*	BB-BCC	3M+2D	P^	Ind	Ind	Ind	
Combined Studies English	Y400	3FT deg	E	18	2M	M	Ind	Ind	Ind	
Univ College of St MARTIN, LANCASTER AND CUMBRIA										
Art and Design/English	WQ1H	3FT deg	A+E	CC-CDE	3M+2D$	MA^	28$	BBCC$	Ind	10
Business Management Studies/English	NQ13	3FT deg	E	CD-CEE	3M+2D	M	28$	BCCC$		
English	Q300	3FT deg	E	BC-BDE	X	P^	28$	BBBC$	Ind	3 10/22
English/Art and Design	QW3C	3FT deg	E+A	BC-BDE	X	MA^	28$	BBBC$	Ind	12
English/Business Management Studies	QN31	3FT deg	E	BC-BDE	X	P^	28$	BBBC$		
English/Drama	QW34	3FT deg	E	BC-BDE	X	P^	28$	BBBC$	Ind	5 12/24
English/Education Studies	QX39	3FT deg	E	BC-BDE	X	P^	28$	BBBC$	Ind	6
English/Geography	QL3V	3FT deg	E+Gy	BC-BDE	X	X	28$	BBBC$	Ind	
English/Health Administration	QL34	3FT deg	E	BC-BDE	X	P^	28$	BBBC$	Ind	
English/Health Studies	QBH9	3FT deg	E	BC-BDE	X	P^	28$	BBBC$		
English/History	QV3C	3FT deg	E+H	BC-BDE	X	X	28$	BBBC$	Ind	7
English/Physical Education & Sports Studies	QX3X	3FT deg	E	BC-BDE	X	P^	28$	BBBC$		
English/Religious Studies	QV3V	3FT deg	E	BC-BDE	X	P^	28$	BBBC$	Ind	4
English/Science, Technology and Society	QY31	3FT deg	E g	BC-BDE	X	P^	28$	BBBC$	Ind	
English/Social Ethics	QV3R	3FT deg	E	BC-BDE	X	P^	28$	BBBC$	Ind	3
Geography/English	LQ8H	3FT deg	Gy+E	CD-DDE	X	X	28$	BCCC$	Ind	2
Health Studies/English	BQ9H	3FT deg	E	CD-DDE	X	P^	28$	BCCC$		
History/English	VQ1H	3FT deg	H+E	CD-DDE	X	X	28$	BCCC$	Ind	15
Religious Studies/English	VQ8H	3FT deg	E	CD-DDE	X	M^	28$	BCCC$	Ind	3
Science, Technology and Society/English	QY3C	3FT deg	E g	CD-DDE	X	M^	28$	BCCC$	Ind	
Social Ethics/English	VQ7H	3FT deg	E	CD-DDE	3M+2D	M^	28$	BCCC$	Ind	2
SOLIHULL COLL										
Cultural Studies	LQ33	3FT deg	*	EE	MO	M	Dip	Ind	Ind	
Univ of SOUTHAMPTON										
Contemporary Europe (English)	T2Q3	3FT deg			Ind	Ind	Ind	Ind	Ind	
English	Q300	3FT deg	E g	ABC-BBB	X	Ind	Ind	Ind	X	8 18/30

			98 expected requirements							96 entry stats	
TITLE	CODE	COURSE	SUBJECTS	A/AS	NO/C	AGNVQ	IB	SQA(H)	SQA	RATIO	A/AS
English and Film	QW35	3FT deg	E								
English and French	QR31	4FT deg	E+F	ABC-BBB	X	Ind	Ind	Ind	X	8	20/26
English and German	QR32	4FT deg	E+G	BBC	X	Ind	Ind	Ind	X	9	
English and History	QV31	3FT deg	E+H	BBC	X	Ind	Ind	Ind	X	8	20/28
English and Music	QW33	3FT deg	E+Mu	22	X	Ind	Ind	Ind	X	14	
English and Philosophy	QV37	3FT deg	E	BBC	X	Ind	Ind	Ind	X	10	16/28
English and Spanish	QR34	4FT deg	E+Sp	BBC	X	Ind	Ind	Ind	X	37	

SOUTH BANK Univ

English	Q300	3FT deg	E g	BCC	X	M go	Ind	Ind	Ind		
English Studies and Accounting	NQ43	3FT deg	E+Ac/Ec g	14-18	X	M^ go	Ind	Ind	Ind		
English Studies and Business Info Technology	GQ73	3FT deg	M+E g	14-18	X	M^ go	Ind	Ind	Ind		
English Studies and Economics	LQ13	3FT deg	Ec/Bu+E g	14-18	X	M^ go	Ind	Ind	Ind		
Environmental Policy and English Studies	FQ93	3FT deg	E g	14-18	X	M go	Ind	Ind	Ind		
European Studies and English Studies	QT32	3FT deg	E g	14-18	X	M^ go	Ind	Ind	Ind		
Food Policy and English Studies	DQ43	3FT deg	S+E g	14-18	X	M^ go	Ind	Ind	Ind		
French and English Studies	QR31	3FT deg	E+F g	14-18	X	M^ go	Ind	Ind	Ind		
German - ab initio and English Studies	QR32	3FT deg	E g	14-18	X	M^ go	Ind	Ind	Ind		
German and English Studies	QR3F	3FT deg	G+E g	16-18	X	M go	Ind	Ind	Ind		
Health Studies and English Studies	LQ43	3FT deg	E+S g	14-18	X	M^ go	Ind	Ind	Ind		
History and English Studies	QV31	3FT deg	E+H g	14-18	X	M^ go	Ind	Ind	Ind		
Housing and English Studies	KQ4J	3FT deg	E g	14-18	X	M^ go	Ind	Ind	Ind		
Human Biology and English Studies	BQ13	3FT deg	E+S g	14-18	X	M^ go	Ind	Ind	Ind		
Human Geography and English Studies	LQ83	3FT deg	E+Gy g	14-18	X	M^ go	Ind	Ind	Ind		
Human Resource Management and English Studies	QN36	3FT deg	E g	14-18	X	M^ go	Ind	Ind	Ind		
Law and English Studies	MQ33	3FT deg	E g	14-18	X	M^ go	Ind	Ind	Ind		
Marketing and English Studies	QN35	3FT deg	E g	14-18	X	M^ go	Ind	Ind	Ind		
Media Studies and English Studies	PQ43	3FT deg	E g	14-18	X	D^ go	Ind	Ind	Ind		
Nutrition and English Studies	BQ43	3FT deg	E+S g	14-18	X	M^ go	Ind	Ind	Ind		
Politics and English Studies	MQ13	3FT deg	E g	14-18	X	M^ go	Ind	Ind	Ind		
Product Design and English Studies	HQ73	3FT deg	E+Ad g	14-18	X	M^ go	Ind	Ind	Ind		
Psychology and English Studies	CQ83	3FT deg	E+S g	14-18	X	M^ go	Ind	Ind	Ind		
Social Policy and English Studies	QL34	3FT deg	E g	14-18	X	M^ go	Ind	Ind	Ind		
Sociology and English Studies	LQ3H	3FT deg	E g	14-18	X	M^ go	Ind	Ind	Ind		
Spanish - ab initio and English Studies	QR34	3FT deg	E g	14-18	X	M^ go	Ind	Ind	Ind		
Spanish and English Studies	QR3K	3FT deg	Sp+E g	14-18	X	M^ go	Ind	Ind	Ind		
Sports Science and English Studies	BQ63	3FT deg	E+S g	14-18	X	M^ go	Ind	Ind	Ind		
Urban Studies and English Studies	KQ4H	3FT deg	E g	14-18	X	M go	Ind	Ind	Ind		
World Theatre and English Studies	QW34	3FT deg	E g	14-18	X	M^ go	Ind	Ind	Ind		

Univ of ST ANDREWS

English	Q301	4FT deg	* g	BBB	X	Ind	30$	BBBB	Ind		
English-Arabic	TQ63	4FT deg	* g	BBB	X	Ind	30$	BBBB	Ind		
English-Art History	QV34	4FT deg	* g	BBB	X	Ind	30$	BBBB	Ind	3	24/30
English-Biblical Studies	QV3W	4FT deg	* g	BBB	X	Ind	30$	BBBB	Ind		
English-Classical Studies	QQ38	4FT deg	* g	BBB	X	Ind	30$	BBBB	Ind	6	
English-Economics	LQ13	4FT deg	* g	BBB	X	Ind	30$	BBBB	Ind		
French with Year Abroad-English	QRH1	4FT/5FT deg	F g	BBB	X	Ind	30$	BBBB$	Ind	5	26/30
French-English	QR31	4FT deg	F g	BBB	X	Ind	30$	BBBB$	Ind		
Geography-English	QL38	4FT deg	* g	BBB	X	Ind	30$	BBBB	Ind	9	
German with Year Abroad-English	QRH2	4FT/5FT deg	* g	BBB	X	Ind	30$	BBBB	Ind	9	
German-English	QR32	4FT deg	* g	BBB	X	Ind	30$	BBBB	Ind	2	
Greek-English	QQ37	4FT deg	* g	BBB	X	Ind	30$	BBBB	Ind		

| | | | | 98 expected requirements | | | | | | 96 entry stats |
| course details | | | | | | | | | | |

TITLE	CODE	COURSE	SUBJECTS	A/AS	ND/C	AGNVQ	IB	SQA(H)	SQA	RATIO A/AS
Hebrew-English	QQ39	4FT deg	* g	BBB	X	Ind	30$	BBBB	Ind	
Italian with Year Abroad-English	RQ33	4FT/5FT deg	* g	BBB	X	Ind	30$	BBBB	Ind	
Italian-English	QR33	4FT deg	* g	BBB	X	Ind	30$	BBBB	Ind	
Latin-English	QQ36	4FT deg	* g	BBB	X	Ind	30$	BBBB	Ind	9
Mediaeval History-English	QVH1	4FT deg	* g	BBB	X	Ind	30$	BBBB	Ind	6
Modern History-English	QV31	4FT deg	* g	BBB	X	Ind	30$	BBBB	Ind	11 26/28
Philosophy-English	QV37	4FT deg	* g	BBB	X	Ind	30$	BBBB	Ind	5 26/28
Psychology-English	LQ73	4FT deg	* g	ABB	X	Ind	32$	BBBBB	Ind	8
Russian with Year Abroad-English	QRH8	4FT/5FT deg	* g	BBB	X	Ind	30$	BBBB	Ind	
Russian-English	QR38	4FT deg	* g	BBB	X	Ind	30$	BBBB	Ind	
Scottish History-English	QV3D	4FT deg	* g	BBB	X	Ind	30$	BBBB	Ind	10
Social Anthropology-English	QL36	4FT deg	* g	BBB	X	Ind	30$	BBBB	Ind	6
Spanish with Year Abroad-English	QRH4	4FT/5FT deg	* g	BBB	X	Ind	32$	BBBB	Ind	
Spanish-English	QR34	4FT deg	* g	BBB	X	Ind	32$	BBBB	Ind	6
Theological Studies-English	QV38	4FT deg	* g	BBB	X	Ind	30$	BBBB	Ind	12
General Degree of MA English Language and Literature	Y450	3FT deg	* g	BBB	X	Ind	30$	BBBB	Ind	

THE UNIVERSITY COLLEGE OF ST MARK AND ST JOHN

TITLE	CODE	COURSE	SUBJECTS	A/AS	ND/C	AGNVQ	IB	SQA(H)	SQA	RATIO A/AS
English (Literary Studies)/English Language St	Q3Q1	3FT deg	El	12-16	Ind	M	Ind	Ind	Ind	
English (Literary Studies)/History	Q3V1	3FT deg	El	12-16	Ind	M	Ind	Ind	Ind	
English (Literary Studies)/Information Techno	Q3G5	3FT deg	El	12-16	Ind	M	Ind	Ind	Ind	
English (Literary Studies)/Media Studies	Q3P4	3FT deg	El	12-16	Ind	M	Ind	Ind	Ind	
English (Literary Studies)/Sociology	Q3L3	3FT deg	El	12-16	Ind	M	Ind	Ind	Ind	
English (Literary Studies)/Theology & Philosophy	Q3V8	3FT deg	El	12-16	Ind	M	Ind	Ind	Ind	
English Language Studies/English (Literary St)	Q1Q3	3FT deg		12	MO	M	Ind	Ind	Ind	
History/English (Literary Studies)	V1Q3	3FT deg	H	12	MO	M	Ind	Ind	Ind	
Information Technology/English (Literary St)	G5Q3	3FT deg		4	MO	M	Dip	CCCC	Ind	
Media Studies/English (Literary Studies)	P4Q3	3FT deg		16	MO	M	Ind	Ind	Ind	
Sociology/English (Literary Studies)	L3Q3	3FT deg	So	8	MO	M	Ind	Ind	Ind	
Theology & Philosophy/English (Literary Studies)	V8Q3	3FT deg	Re	4	MO	M	Dip	CCCC	Ind	

ST MARY'S Univ COLL

TITLE	CODE	COURSE	SUBJECTS	A/AS	ND/C	AGNVQ	IB	SQA(H)	SQA	RATIO A/AS
English	Q300	3FT deg	E	12-14	X	X	Ind	BBBB$	X	
English and Biology	QC31	3FT deg	E+B/C	8-12	X	X	Ind	BBBB$	X	
English and Classical Studies	QQ38	3FT deg	E	8-12	X	X	Ind	BBBB$	X	
English and Drama	QW34	3FT deg	E	12-14	X	X	Ind	BBBB$	X	
English and Education Studies	QX3X	3FT deg	E	8-12	X	X	Ind	BBBB$	X	
Geography and English	QF38	3FT deg	E+Gy	8-12	X	X	Ind	BBBB$	X	
Heritage Management and English	NQ93	3FT deg	E	8-12	X	X	Ind	BBBB$	X	
History and English	QV31	3FT deg	E+H	8-12	X	X	Ind	BBBB$	X	
Management Studies and English	NQ13	3FT deg	E g	8-12	X	X	Ind	BBBB$	X	
Media Arts and English	PQ43	3FT deg	E	8-12	X	X	Ind	BBBB$	X	
Sociology and English	QL33	3FT deg	E	8-12	X	X	Ind	BBBB$	X	
Sport Rehabilitation and English	BQ93	3FT deg	E+B g	12-14	X	X	Ind	BBBB$	X	
Sport Science and English	QB36	3FT deg	E+S g	12-14	X	X	Ind	BBBB$	X	
Theology and Religious Studies and English	QV38	3FT deg	E	8-12	X	X	Ind	BBBB$	X	

STAFFORDSHIRE Univ

TITLE	CODE	COURSE	SUBJECTS	A/AS	ND/C	AGNVQ	IB	SQA(H)	SQA	RATIO A/AS
European Culture/Literature	LQP3	3FT deg	g	CD	MO+2D	M	27	BBC	Ind	
Literature/American Studies	QQ34	3FT deg	El g	12	MO+2D	M	27	BBC	Ind	4 6/16
Literature/Cultural Studies	QL36	3FT deg	El g	CD	MO+2D	M	27	BBC	Ind	2 8/16
Literature/Development Studies	QM3Y	3FT deg	El g	12	MO+2D	M	27	BBC	Ind	
Literature/Environmental Studies	QF39	3FT deg	El g	CC	MO+2D	M	27	BBB	Ind	2

| course details | | | 98 expected requirements | | | | | | | 96 entry stats |

TITLE	CODE	COURSE	SUBJECTS	A/AS	NO/C	AGNVQ	IB	SQA(H)	SQA	RATIO A/AS
Literature/Film Studies	QW35	3FT deg	El g	CD	MO+2D	M	27	BBC	Ind	4 6/18
Literature/French	QR31	3FT/4SW deg	El+F g	CD	MO+2D	M^	27	BCC	Ind	6
Literature/German	QR32	3FT/4SW deg	El+G g	CD	MO+2D	M^	27	BCC	Ind	7
Literature/History	QV3C	3FT deg	El+H g	CD	MO+2D	M	27	BBC	Ind	4 6/16
Literature/History of Art and Design	QV34	3FT deg	El g	CD	MO+2D	M	27	BBC	Ind	4
Literature/Information Systems	QG35	3FT deg	El g	12	MO+2D	M	27	BBC	Ind	2
Literature/International Relations	QM3C	3FT deg	El g	12	MO+2D	M	27	BBC	Ind	1
Literature/Law	QM33	3FT deg	El g	CCC	HN	M^	27	BBBB	Ind	4 12/14
Literature/Legal Studies	QM3H	3FT deg	El g	CCC	HN	M^	27	BBBB	Ind	
Media Studies/Literature	PQ43	3FT deg	El g	CD	MO+2D	M	27	BBC	Ind	5 6/24
Philosophy/Literature	VQ73	3FT deg	El g	CD	MO+2D	M	27	BBBC	Ind	3 8/18
Psychology/Literature	LQ73	3FT deg	g	18	3M+3D	Ind	27	BBB	Ind	5 12/20
Sociology/Literature	LQ33	3FT deg	g	12	3M	M	24	BCC	Ind	3 8/18
Spanish/Literature	RQ43	3FT/4SW deg	El g	CD	MO+2D	M^	27	BBC	Ind	7
Women's Studies/Literature	MQ93	3FT deg	El g	12	MO+2D	M	27	BBC	Ind	4

Univ of STIRLING

TITLE	CODE	COURSE	SUBJECTS	A/AS	NO/C	AGNVQ	IB	SQA(H)	SQA	RATIO A/AS
Business Studies/English Studies	NQ13	4FT deg	g	BBC	HN	Ind	33	BBBB	HN	
English Studies	Q300	4FT deg	g	BBC	Ind	Ind	33	BBBB	HN	
English Studies/Commonwealth Literature	Q3QG	4FT deg	g	BBC	Ind	Ind	33	BBBB	HN	
English Studies/Film & Media Studies	QP34	4FT deg	g	BBC	Ind	Ind	35	ABBB	HN	
English Studies/French	QR31	4FT deg	g	CCC	Ind	Ind	31	BBBC	HN	
English Studies/German	QR32	4FT deg	g	CCC	Ind	Ind	31	BBBC	HN	
English Studies/History	QV31	4FT deg	g	BBC	Ind	Ind	33	BBBB	HN	
English Studies/Philosophy	QV37	4FT deg	g	BBC	Ind	Ind	33	BBBB	HN	
English Studies/Politics	QM31	4FT deg	g	BBC	Ind	Ind	33	BBBB	HN	
English Studies/Religious Studies	QV38	4FT deg	g	BBC	Ind	Ind	33	BBBB$	HN	
English Studies/Scottish Literature	Q3QF	4FT deg	g	BBC	Ind	Ind	33	BBBB	HN	
English Studies/Scottish Studies	Q3VC	4FT deg	g	BBC	Ind	Ind	33	BBBB	HN	
English Studies/Sociology	LQ33	4FT deg	g	BBC	Ind	Ind	33	BBBB	HN	
English Studies/Spanish	QR34	4FT deg	g	CCC	Ind	Ind	31	BBBC	HN	
English as a Foreign Lang(General Degree only)	Q316	3FT deg	g	CCD	Ind	Ind	28	BCCC	HN	
Japanese/English Studies	QT34	4FT deg	g	BCC	Ind	Ind	31	BBBC	HN	

Univ of STRATHCLYDE

TITLE	CODE	COURSE	SUBJECTS	A/AS	NO/C	AGNVQ	IB	SQA(H)	SQA	RATIO A/AS
Arts and Social Sciences *English*	Y440	3FT/4FT deg	g	CCC	Ind		28	BBBBB$	Ind	

Univ of SUNDERLAND

TITLE	CODE	COURSE	SUBJECTS	A/AS	NO/C	AGNVQ	IB	SQA(H)	SQA	RATIO A/AS
Biology and English	CQ13	3FT deg	B/C	10	4M	M	Ind	Ind	Ind	
Biology with English	C1Q3	3FT deg	B/C	10	4M	M	Ind	Ind	Ind	
Business Studies and English	NQ13	3FT/4SW deg	*	10	4M	M	Ind	Ind	Ind	
Business Studies with English	N1Q3	3FT/4SW deg	*	10	4M	M	Ind	Ind	Ind	
Chemistry and English	FQ13	3FT deg	C	10	4M	M	Ind	Ind	Ind	
Chemistry with English	F1Q3	3FT deg	C	10	4M	M	Ind	Ind	Ind	
Computer Studies and English	GQ53	3FT deg	El g	10	Ind	M	24$	CCCC$	Ind	4
Computer Studies with English	G5Q3	3FT/4SW deg	*	10	4M	M	Ind	Ind	Ind	
Economics and English	LQ13	3FT deg	*	10	4M	M	Ind	Ind	Ind	
Economics with English	L1Q3	3FT deg	*	10	4M	M	Ind	Ind	Ind	
English Studies	Q300	3FT deg	El g	CC	Ind	Ind	26$	BCCC$	Ind	2 6/18
English and French	QR31▼	4FT deg	F+El g	10	Ind	M	24$	CCCC$	Ind	3
English and Geography	QL38▼	3FT deg	El+Gy/Gl g	12	3M $	M	24$	BCCC$	N$	8
English and German	QR32▼	4FT deg	El+G g	10	N $	M	24$	CCCC$	N$	3
English and History	QV31▼	3FT deg	El+H g	12	Ind	M	24$	BCCC$	Ind	2 8/18

 *Letts* STUDY GUIDES
THE INDEPENDENT

course details   98 expected requirements   96 entry stats

TITLE	CODE	COURSE	SUBJECTS	A/AS	ND/C	AGNVQ	IB	SQA(H)	SQA	RATIO A/AS
English and History of Art and Design	QV34▼	3FT deg	El g	12	Ind	M	24$	BCCC$	Ind	11
English and Mathematics	QG31	3FT deg	M	8	3M	M	Ind	Ind	Ind	
English and Philosophy	QV37▼	3FT deg	El g	12	X	M	24$	BCCC$	X	5 6/14
English and Physiology	QB31	3FT deg	*	10	4M	M	Ind	Ind	Ind	
English and Politics	QM31▼	3FT deg	El g	12	Ind	M	24$	BCCC$	Ind	4
English and Religious Studies	QV38▼	3FT deg	El g	12	Ind	M	24$	BCCC$	Ind	4
English and Sociology	QL33▼	3FT deg	El g	12	Ind	M	24$	BCCC$	Ind	3 6/12
English with American Studies	Q3Q4	3FT deg	El g	12	Ind	M	24$	BCCC$	Ind	5 8/16
English with Biology	Q3C1	3FT deg	B/C	10	4M	M	Ind	Ind	Ind	
English with Business Studies	Q3N1	3FT/4SW deg	*	10	4M	M	Ind	Ind	Ind	
English with Chemistry	Q3F1	3FT deg	C	10	4M	M	Ind	Ind	Ind	
English with Comparative Literature	Q3Q2	3FT deg	El g	12	Ind	M	24$	BCCC$	Ind	4
English with Computer Studies	Q3G5	3FT deg	*	10	4M	M	Ind	Ind	Ind	
English with Economics	Q3L1	3FT deg	*	10	4M	M	Ind	Ind	Ind	
English with European Studies	Q3T2	3FT deg	El g	12	Ind	M	24$	BCCC$	N$	
English with French	Q3R1	3FT deg	F	10	4M	M	Ind	Ind	Ind	
English with Gender Studies	Q3M9	3FT deg	El g	12	Ind	M	24$	BCCC$	Ind	2
English with Geography	Q3L8	3FT deg	*	10	4M	M	Ind	Ind	Ind	
English with Geology	Q3F6	3FT deg	*	8	3M	M	Ind	Ind	Ind	
English with German	Q3R2	3FT deg	G	10	4M	M	Ind	Ind	Ind	
English with History	Q3V1	3FT deg	*	12	3M+1D	M	Ind	Ind	Ind	
English with History of Art and Design	Q3V4	3FT deg	*	10	4M	M	Ind	Ind	Ind	
English with Mathematics	Q3G1	3FT deg	M	10	4M	M	Ind	Ind	Ind	
English with Media Studies	Q3P4	3FT deg	*	20	Ind	Ind	Ind	Ind	Ind	
English with Philosophy	Q3V7	3FT deg	*	10	4M	M	Ind	Ind	Ind	
English with Physiology	Q3B1	3FT deg	*	10	4M	M	Ind	Ind	Ind	
English with Politics	Q3M1	3FT deg	*	10	4M	M	Ind	Ind	Ind	
English with Psychology	Q3C8	3FT deg	*	12	3M+1D	M^	Ind	Ind	Ind	
English with Religious Studies	Q3V8	3FT deg	*	10	4M	M	Ind	Ind	Ind	
English with Sociology	Q3L3	3FT deg	*	12	3M+1D	M	Ind	Ind	Ind	
English with Spanish	Q3R4▼	3FT deg	El+Sp g	10	Ind	M	24$	CCCC$	Ind	10
French with English	R1Q3	4FT deg	F	10	4M	M	Ind	Ind	Ind	
Geography with English	L8Q3	3FT deg	*	10	4M	M	Ind	Ind	Ind	
German with English	R2Q3	4SW deg	G	10	4M	M	Ind	Ind	Ind	
History with English	V1Q3	3FT deg	*	12	3M+1D	M	Ind	Ind	Ind	
Mathematics with English	G1Q3	3FT deg	M	10	4M	M	Ind	Ind	Ind	
Media Studies with English	P4Q3	3FT deg	*	26	Ind	Ind	Ind	Ind	Ind	
Philosophy with English	V7Q3	3FT deg	*	10	4M	Ind	Ind	Ind	Ind	
Politics with English	M1Q3	3FT deg	*	10	4M	M	Ind	Ind	Ind	
Religious Studies with English	V8Q3	3FT deg	*	10	4M	M	Ind	Ind	Ind	
Sociology with English	L3Q3	3FT deg	*	12	3M+1D	M	Ind	Ind	Ind	

Univ of SUSSEX

TITLE	CODE	COURSE	SUBJECTS	A/AS	ND/C	AGNVQ	IB	SQA(H)	SQA	RATIO A/AS
American Studies (Literature)	Q4Q3	4FT deg	*	BBB	MO	M*6	$	Ind	Ind	
English Language in English and American Studies	Q3QK	3FT deg	*	BBB	MO	M*6	$	Ind	Ind	
English Language in European Studies	Q3TF	4FT deg	g	BBB	MO	M*6 go	$	Ind	Ind	
English in African and Asian Studies	Q3T5	3FT deg	*	BBB	MO	M*6	$	Ind	Ind	
English in Cultural and Community Studies	Q3Y2	3FT deg	*	BBB	MO	M*6	$	Ind	Ind	
English in English and American Studies	Q3Q4	3FT deg	*	BBB	MO	M*6	$	Ind	Ind	
English in European Studies	Q3T2	4FT deg	* g	BBB	MO $	M*6 go	$	Ind	Ind	
English with Development Studies	Q3MY	3FT deg	*	BBB	MO	M*6	$	Ind	Ind	
English with Media Studies	Q3P4	3FT deg	*	BBB	MO	M*6	$	Ind	Ind	
Philosophy and English in Cultural & Commun St	VQ73	3FT deg	*	BBB	MO	M*6	$	Ind	Ind	

English   26

TITLE	CODE	COURSE	SUBJECTS	A/AS	NO/C	RGNVQ	IB	SQA(H)	SQA	RATIO A/AS
Philosophy and English in English & American St	VQ7H	3FT deg	*	BBB	MO	M*6	$	Ind	Ind	
Philosophy and English in European Studies	VQ7J	4FT deg	* g	BBB	MO $	M*6 go	$	Ind	Ind	

Univ of Wales SWANSEA

TITLE	CODE	COURSE	SUBJECTS	A/AS	NO/C	RGNVQ	IB	SQA(H)	SQA	RATIO A/AS
English	Q300	3FT deg	E	BBB	X	X	32$	AABBB$	X	3 16/28
English Language/Ancient History & Civilisation	QV3C	3FT deg	E	BBC	X	X	30$	ABBBB$	Ind	
English Language/French (with Business Studies)	QRH1	4FT deg	F	X	X	X	28	X	X	
English Language/German (with Business Studies)	QRH2	4FT deg	G	X	X	X	28	X	X	
English Language/Italian (with Business Studies)	QRH3	4FT deg	L	X	X	X	28	X	X	
English Language/Russian (with Business Studies)	QRH8	4FT deg	L	X	X	X	28	X	X	1
English Language/Spanish (with Business Studies)	QRH4	4FT deg	L	X	X	X	28	X	X	1
English/American Studies	QQ34	3FT deg	E	BBB-BBC	X	X	30$	ABBBB$	X	3 18/28
English/Ancient History and Civilisation	VQC3	3FT deg	E	BBC	X	X	30$	ABBBB$	X	3
English/Anthropology	LQ63	3FT deg	E	BBC	X	X	30$	ABBBB$	X	3 20/22
European History (with English)	V1Q3	4FT deg	E+H	BBB-BBC	X	Ind		ABBBB$	Ind	7
French/English	QR31	4FT deg	E+F	BBC	X	X	30$	ABBBB$	X	8 16/22
French/English Language	QR3C	3FT deg	E+F	BBC	X	X	30$	ABBBB$	Ind	
Geography/English	LQ83	3FT deg	E+Gy	BBB	X	X	32$	AABBB$	Ind	
German/English	QR32	4FT deg	E+G	BBC	1M+5D$	X	30$	ABBBB$	X	
German/English Language	QR3F	3FT deg	E+G	BBC	X	X	30$	ABBBB$	Ind	
Greek & Roman Studies/English Language	QQ38	3FT deg	E	BBC-BCC	X	X	30$	ABBBB$	Ind	
Greek and Roman Studies/English	QQ83	3FT deg	E	BBC	X	X	30$	ABBBB$	X	5
Greek/English	QQ37	3FT deg	Gk+E	BB-BCC	X	X	28$	BBBBB$	X	
Greek/English Language	QQ73	3FT deg	E+Gk	BBC-BCC	X	X	30$	ABBBB$	Ind	
History/English	QV31	3FT deg	E+H	BBB	X	Ind	32$	AABBB$	Ind	5 20/24
Italian/English	QR33	4FT deg	E+L	BBC	X	X	30$	ABBBB$	X	2
Italian/English Language	QR3H	3FT deg	E g	BBC	X	X	30$	ABBBB$	Ind	
Latin/English	QQ36	3FT deg	E+Ln	BBC	X	X	30$	ABBBB$	X	3
Latin/English Language	QQ63	3FT deg	E+Ln	BBC-BCC	X	X	30$	ABBBB$	X	
Medieval Studies/English	QVH1	3FT deg	E+H	BBC	X	X	30$	ABBBB$	X	
Philosophy/English	QV37	3FT deg	E	BBC	X	X	30$	ABBBB$	X	3 14/26
Politics/English	MQ13	3FT deg	E	BBB	X	X	32$	AABBB$	X	5 18/26
Russian/English	QR38	4FT deg	E+L	BB-BCC	X	X	28$	BBBBB$	X	
Russian/English Language	QR3V	3FT deg	E g	BBC	X	X	30$	ABBBB$	Ind	
Sociology/English	LQ33	3FT deg	E	BBC	X	X	30$	ABBBB$	X	5 20/24
Spanish/English	QR34	4FT deg	E+L	BBC	X	X	30$	ABBBB$	X	4
Spanish/English Language	QR3K	3FT deg	E g	BBC	X	X	30$	ABBBB$	Ind	
Welsh/English	QQH5	3FT/4FT deg	E+W	BBC	X	X	30$	ABBBB$	X	
Welsh/English Language	QQ35	3FT deg	E g	BBC	X	X	30$	ABBBB$	Ind	

SWANSEA INST of HE

TITLE	CODE	COURSE	SUBJECTS	A/AS	NO/C	RGNVQ	IB	SQA(H)	SQA	RATIO A/AS
Joint Honours English and Drama and Media	Y300	3FT deg		8	N				N	
Joint Honours English and Studies in Modern Society	Y300	3FT deg		8	N				N	

Univ of TEESSIDE

TITLE	CODE	COURSE	SUBJECTS	A/AS	NO/C	RGNVQ	IB	SQA(H)	SQA	RATIO A/AS
Cultural Studies and English	LQ33	3FT deg	*	14-16	Ind	M	Ind	Ind	Ind	
English (Jt Hons available)	Q306▼	3FT deg	*	14-16	Ind		Ind	Ind	Ind	3 8/22
English and History	QV31	3FT deg								
Politics and English	MQ1J	3FT deg	*	12-14	Ind		Ind	Ind	Ind	
Modular Degree Scheme English	Y401	3FT deg								

| | | | 98 expected requirements | | | | | | | 96 entry stats |
| | | | | | | | | | | |

TITLE	CODE	COURSE	SUBJECTS	A/AS	NO/C	AGNVQ	IB	SQA(H)	SQA	RATIO A/AS
THAMES VALLEY Univ										
American Studies with English	Q4Q3	3FT deg		8-12	MO	M	26	CCC		
English Language and Communications with English	Q1Q3	3FT deg		8-12	MO	M	26	CCC		
English with Advertising	Q3P3	3FT deg		8-12	MO	M	26	CCC		
English with American Studies	Q3Q4	3FT deg		8-12	MO	M	26	CCC		
English with English Language Studies	Q3Q1	3FT deg		8-12	MO	M	26	CCC		
English with French	Q3R1	3FT deg		8-12	MO	M	26	CCC		
English with German	Q3R2	3FT deg		8-12	MO	M	26	CCC		
English with History	Q3V1	3FT deg		8-12	MO	M	26	CCC		
English with Language and Communications	Q3PH	3FT deg		8-12	MO	M	26	CCC		
English with Media Studies	Q3W9	3FT deg		8-12	MO	M	26	CCC		
English with Music	Q3W3	3FT deg		8-12	MO	M	26	CCC		
English with Politics & International Relations	Q3M1	3FT deg		8-12	MO	M	26	CCC		
English with Psychology	Q3C8	3FT deg		8-12	MO	M	26	CCC		
English with Sociology	Q3L3	3FT deg		8-12	MO	M	26	CCC		
English with Spanish	Q3R4	3FT deg		8-12	MO	M	26	CCC		
English with Visual Cultures	Q3W1	3FT deg		8-12	MO	M	26	CCC		
English with Women's Studies	Q3M9	3FT deg		8-12	MO	M	26	CCC		
French with English	R1Q3	3FT deg		8-12	MO	M	26	CCC		
German with English	R2Q3	3FT deg		8-12	MO	M	26	CCC		
History with English	V1Q3	3FT deg		8-12	MO	M	26	CCC		
Media Arts with English	W9Q3	3FT deg		8-12	MO	M	26	CCC		
Multi-Media Computing with English	G5Q3	3FT deg		8-12	MO	M	26	CCC		
Psychology with English	C8Q3	3FT deg		8-12	MO	M	26	CCC		
Sociology with English	L3Q3	3FT deg		8-12	MO	M	26	CCC		
Spanish with English	R4Q3	3FT deg		8-12	MO	M	26	CCC		
TRINITY COLL Carmarthen										
English	Q300	3FT deg	E g	DD-CC	Ind		Ind	Ind	Ind	2 6/16
English/Archaeology	QV36	3FT deg	E g	DD-CC	Ind		Ind	Ind	Ind	
History/English	QV31	3FT deg	H+E g	DD-CC	Ind		Ind	Ind	Ind	7
Religious Studies/English	QV38	3FT deg	Re+E g	DD-CC	Ind		Ind	Ind	Ind	4
Saesneg/Astudiaethau Crefydd	QR3W	3FT deg	E+Re g	DD-CC	Ind		Ind	Ind	Ind	
Saesneg/Astudiaethau Theatr	WQ43	3FT deg	E+T g	DD-CC	Ind		Ind	Ind	Ind	
Saesneg/Cymraeg	QQ3N	3FT deg	W+E g	DD-CC	Ind		Ind	Ind	Ind	
Saesneg/Hanes	QV3C	3FT deg	E+H g	DD-CC	Ind		Ind	Ind	Ind	
Theatre Studies/English	QW34	3FT deg	T+E g	DD-CC	Ind		Ind	Ind	Ind	3
Welsh Studies/English	QQ35	3FT deg	E g	DD-CC	Ind		Ind	Ind	Ind	2
Humanities *English*	Y320	3FT deg	E g	DD-CC	Ind		Ind	Ind	Ind	
Univ of ULSTER										
English	Q300▼	3FT deg	*	BCC	MO+4D	D*6/△ gi	30	BBBB	Ind	19 14/22
Humanities Combined *English*	Y320▼	3FT/4SW deg	*	CCC	MO+3D	D*6/△ gi	28	BBBC	Ind	
UNIVERSITY COLL LONDON (Univ of London)										
English	Q300	3FT deg	El g	ABB	Ind	X	34$	AAABB$	Ind	13 26/30
English and German (4 Yrs)	QR32	4FT deg	El+G g	ABB	Ind	X	34$	AABBB$	Ind	12
English and History of Art	QV34	3FT deg	El g	ABB	Ind	X	34$	AAABB$	Ind	13 28/30
Univ of WARWICK										
English & German Literature (4 Yrs inc yr abrd)	QR32	4FT deg	E+G g	BBC	X	X	32$	ABBBB		9 20/24
English Literature	Q300	3FT deg	E g	ABB-BBB	X	X	34$	AAABB$		
English and American Literature	QQ34	3FT deg	E+H/L g	ABB-BBB	X	X	34$	AAABB$		9 24/30
English and European Literature	QQ32	3FT deg	E+H/L g	ABB-BBB	X	X	32$	AAABB$		11 24/30

					98 expected requirements						96 entry stats	

TITLE	CODE	COURSE	SUBJECTS	A/AS	NO/C	AGNVQ	IB	SQA(H)	SQA	RATIO	A/AS
English and French (4 Yrs inc yr abroad)	QR31	4FT deg	E+F g	BBB	X	X	32$	AABBB$		8	24/30
English and Italian Lit (4 Yrs inc yr abroad)	QR33	4FT deg	E g	BBC	X	X	30$	ABBBB$		7	22/26
English and Latin Literature	QQ36	3FT deg	Ln+E g	BBB	X	X	34	AABBB		4	
English and Spanish-American Literature	QR36	3FT deg	E+H/L g	BBB-BBC	X	X	32$	AABBB$		18	
English and Theatre Studies	QW34	3FT deg	E+H/L g	ABB	X	X	34	AAABB		14	24/30

WESTHILL COLL

TITLE	CODE	COURSE	SUBJECTS	A/AS	NO/C	AGNVQ	IB	SQA(H)	SQA	RATIO	A/AS
Humanities - English Lit, English Language & Art	Q3W1	3FT deg	* g	CC	4M+2D	M^	Ind	Ind	Ind		
Humanities - Childhood Studies English	Y600	3FT deg	* g	CC	4M+2D	M^	Ind	Ind	Ind		
Humanities - Nineteenth and Twentieth Century St English	Y602	3FT deg	* g	CC	4M+2D	M^	Ind	Ind	Ind		

Univ of WESTMINSTER

TITLE	CODE	COURSE	SUBJECTS	A/AS	NO/C	AGNVQ	IB	SQA(H)	SQA	RATIO	A/AS
English Language and Arabic	QTH6	4SW deg		CC	Ind		26$	BBB			
English Language and Chinese	T3QH	4SW deg		CC	Ind		26$	BBB			
English Studies	Q300	3FT deg	E	BCD	Ind		26$	BBB		7	10/22
English and Arabic	QT36	4SW deg	E	CC	Ind		26$	BBB		3	8/14
English and Chinese	T3Q3	4SW deg	E	CC	Ind		26$	BBB	Ind	2	
French and English	QR31	4SW deg	E+F	CC	Ind		26$	BBB		9	
French and English Language	QRH1	4SW deg		CC	Ind		26$	BBB			
German and English	QR32	4SW deg	E	CC	Ind		26$	BBB			
German and English Language	QRH2	4SW deg		CC	Ind		26$	BBB			
Italian and English	QR33	4SW deg	E	CC	Ind		26$	BBB			
Italian and English Language	QRH3	4SW deg		CC	Ind		26$	BBB			
Linguistics and English	QQ31	4SW deg	E	CC	Ind		26$	BBB		7	12/16
Russian and English	QR38	4SW deg	E	CC	Ind		26$	BBB		3	
Russian and English Language	QRH8	4SW deg		CC	Ind		26$	BBB			
Spanish and English	QR34	4SW deg	E	CC	Ind		26$	BBB		6	
Spanish and English Language	QRH4	4SW deg		CC	Ind		26$	BBB			

Univ of WOLVERHAMPTON

TITLE	CODE	COURSE	SUBJECTS	A/AS	NO/C	AGNVQ	IB	SQA(H)	SQA	RATIO	A/AS
English (Specialist Route)	Q300	3FT deg		18	4D	D	28	AAAA	Ind	6	10/24
Combined Degrees English	Y401	3FT/4SW deg		20	4D	D	28	AAAA	Ind		
Combined Degrees English (3 Semesters in Holland)	Y401	3FT deg		14	4M	M	24	BBBB	Ind		
Combined Degrees English as a Foreign Language	Y401	3FT deg		12	4M	M	24	BBBB	Ind		

WORCESTER COLL of HE

TITLE	CODE	COURSE	SUBJECTS	A/AS	NO/C	AGNVQ	IB	SQA(H)	SQA	RATIO	A/AS
English and Literary Studies	Q300	3FT deg		CC	3M	M	Ind	BCC	Ind	6	6/18
English and Literary Studies/Art and Design	WQ93	3 deg	A	CC	Ind	M	Ind	Ind	Ind		
English and Literary Studies/Drama	WQ43	3FT deg		CC	Ind	M	Ind	Ind	Ind	5	12/24
English and Literary Studies/Economy and Society	LQ13	3FT deg		CC	Ind	M	Ind	Ind	Ind	4	
English and Literary Studies/Education Studies	XQ93	3FT deg		CC	Ind	M	Ind	Ind	Ind	2	8/12
Environmental Science/English and Literary St	QF39	3FT deg	E	CC	Ind	M	Ind	Ind	Ind	2	
Geography/English and Literary Studies	QL38	3FT deg		CC	Ind	M	Ind	Ind	Ind	3	
Health Studies/English and Literary Studies	QB39	3FT deg	g	CC	Ind	M	Ind	Ind	Ind		
History/English and Literary Studies	QV31	3FT deg		CC	Ind	M	Ind	Ind	Ind	4	
Information Technology/English & Literary St	QG35	3FT deg		CC	Ind	M	Ind	Ind	Ind	5	
Psychology/English and Literary Studies	QL37	3FT deg	g	CC	Ind	M	Ind	Ind	Ind	5	12/18
Sociology/English and Literary Studies	QL33	3FT deg		CC	Ind	M	Ind	Ind	Ind	4	12/18
Sports Studies/English and Literary Studies	QB36	3FT deg		CC	Ind	M	Ind	Ind	Ind		
Urban Studies/English and Literary Studies	QL3V	3FT deg		CC	Ind	M	Ind	Ind	Ind		
Women's Studies/English and Literary Studies	QM39	3FT deg		CC	Ind	M	Ind	Ind	Ind	3	

course details			98 expected requirements							96 entry stats
TITLE	CODE	COURSE	SUBJECTS	A/AS	ND/C	AGNVQ	IB	SQA(H)	SQA	RATIO A/AS
Univ College SCARBOROUGH										
English	Q300	3FT deg	E g	CC	Ind	M	28$	Ind	Ind	
English with Arts	Q3Y3	3FT deg	E g	CC	Ind	M	28$	Ind	Ind	
English with Social Sciences	Q3Y2	3FT deg	E g	CC	Ind	M	28$	Ind	Ind	
Univ of SHEFFIELD										
Biblical Studies and English	QV38	3FT deg	E g	BBB	X	X	32$	AABB$	Ind	
English Language and English Literature	Q304	3FT deg	E g	ABB	X	X	33$	AAAB$	Ind	
English Language and Sociology	QL33	3FT deg	E g	BBC	2M+4D$	D^	29$	BBBB$	Ind	36
English Language with Linguistics	Q3Q1	3FT deg	Ee g	BBC	X	X	30$	ABBB$	Ind	15 20/30
English Language with Medieval Literature	Q308	3FT deg	Ee g	BBC	X	X	30$	ABBB$	Ind	3 20/28
English Literature	Q306	3FT deg	El g	ABB	X	D^	33$	AAAB$	Ind	10 26/30
English and French	QR31	4FT deg	El+F g	ABB	X	X	33$	AAAB$	Ind	9 26/30
English and German	QR32	4FT deg	El+G g	BBB	X	X	32$	AABB$	Ind	22
English and Hispanic Studies	QR34	4FT deg	El+Sp g	BBB	X	X	32$	AABB$	Ind	19
English and History	QV31	3FT deg	El+H g	ABB	X	X	33$	AAAB$	Ind	14 24/30
English and Music	QW33	3FT deg	El+Mu g	BBB	X	X	32$	AABB$	Ind	35
English and Philosophy	QV37	3FT deg	El g	ABB	X	X	33$	AAAB$	Ind	12 26/30
English and Russian	QR38	4FT deg	El+L g	BBB	X	X	32$	AABB$	Ind	
SHEFFIELD HALLAM Univ										
English Studies	Q300	3FT deg	E	22	4M+2D	P^	Ind	BBBB	Ind	
Film and Literature	QW25	3FT deg	*	BB-BCC	3M+2D	P^	Ind	Ind	Ind	
Combined Studies English	Y400	3FT deg	E	18	2M	M	Ind	Ind	Ind	
Univ College of St MARTIN, LANCASTER AND CUMBRIA										
Art and Design/English	WQ1H	3FT deg	A+E	CC-CDE	3M+2D$	MA^	28$	BBCC$	Ind	10
Business Management Studies/English	NQ13	3FT deg	E	CD-CEE	3M+2D	M	28$	BCCC$		
English	Q300	3FT deg	E	BC-BDE	X	P^	28$	BBBC$	Ind	3 10/22
English/Art and Design	QW3C	3FT deg	E+A	BC-BDE	X	MA^	28$	BBBC$	Ind	12
English/Business Management Studies	QN31	3FT deg	E	BC-BDE	X	P^	28$	BBBC$		
English/Drama	QW34	3FT deg	E	BC-BDE	X	P^	28$	BBBC$	Ind	5 12/24
English/Education Studies	QX39	3FT deg	E	BC-BDE	X	P^	28$	BBBC$	Ind	6
English/Geography	QL3V	3FT deg	E+Gy	BC-BDE	X	X	28$	BBBC$	Ind	
English/Health Administration	QL34	3FT deg	E	BC-BDE	X	P^	28$	BBBC$	Ind	
English/Health Studies	QBH9	3FT deg	E	BC-BDE	X	P^	28$	BBBC$		
English/History	QV3C	3FT deg	E+H	BC-BDE	X	X	28$	BBBC$	Ind	7
English/Physical Education & Sports Studies	QX3X	3FT deg	E	BC-BDE	X	P^	28$	BBBC$		
English/Religious Studies	QV3V	3FT deg	E	BC-BDE	X	P^	28$	BBBC$	Ind	4
English/Science, Technology and Society	QY31	3FT deg	E g	BC-BDE	X	P^	28$	BBBC$	Ind	
English/Social Ethics	QV3R	3FT deg	E	BC-BDE	X	P^	28$	BBBC$	Ind	3
Geography/English	LQ8H	3FT deg	Gy+E	CD-DDE	X	X	28$	BCCC$	Ind	2
Health Studies/English	BQ9H	3FT deg	E	CD-DDE	X	P^	28$	BCCC$		
History/English	VQ1H	3FT deg	H+E	CD-DDE	X	X	28$	BCCC$	Ind	15
Religious Studies/English	VQ8H	3FT deg	E	CD-DDE	X	M^	28$	BCCC$	Ind	3
Science, Technology and Society/English	QY3C	3FT deg	E g	CD-DDE	X	M^	28$	BCCC$	Ind	
Social Ethics/English	VQ7H	3FT deg	E	CD-DDE	3M+2D	M^	28$	BCCC$	Ind	2
SOLIHULL COLL										
Cultural Studies	LQ33	3FT deg	*	EE	MO	M	Dip	Ind	Ind	
Univ of SOUTHAMPTON										
Contemporary Europe (English)	T2Q3	3FT deg			Ind	Ind	Ind	Ind	Ind	
English	Q300	3FT deg	E g	ABC-BBB	X	Ind	Ind	Ind	X	8 18/30

| | | | 98 expected requirements | | | | | | | 96 entry stats | |
| course details | | | | | | | | | | | |
TITLE	CODE	COURSE	SUBJECTS	A/AS	ND/C	AGNVQ	IB	SQA(H)	SQA	RATIO	A/AS
English and Film	QW35	3FT deg	E								
English and French	QR31	4FT deg	E+F	ABC-BBB	X	Ind	Ind	Ind	X	8	20/26
English and German	QR32	4FT deg	E+G	BBC	X	Ind	Ind	Ind	X	9	
English and History	QV31	3FT deg	E+H	BBC	X	Ind	Ind	Ind	X	8	20/28
English and Music	QW33	3FT deg	E+Mu	22	X	Ind	Ind	Ind	X	14	
English and Philosophy	QV37	3FT deg	E	BBC	X	Ind	Ind	Ind	X	10	16/28
English and Spanish	QR34	4FT deg	E+Sp	BBC	X	Ind	Ind	Ind	X	37	

SOUTH BANK Univ

TITLE	CODE	COURSE	SUBJECTS	A/AS	ND/C	AGNVQ	IB	SQA(H)	SQA	RATIO	A/AS
English	Q300	3FT deg	E g	BCC	X	M go	Ind	Ind	Ind		
English Studies and Accounting	NQ43	3FT deg	E+Ac/Ec g	14-18	X	M^ go	Ind	Ind	Ind		
English Studies and Business Info Technology	GQ73	3FT deg	M+E g	14-18	X	M^ go	Ind	Ind	Ind		
English Studies and Economics	LQ13	3FT deg	Ec/Bu+E g	14-18	X	M^ go	Ind	Ind	Ind		
Environmental Policy and English Studies	FQ93	3FT deg	E g	14-18	X	M go	Ind	Ind	Ind		
European Studies and English Studies	QT32	3FT deg	E g	14-18	X	M^ go	Ind	Ind	Ind		
Food Policy and English Studies	DQ43	3FT deg	S+E g	14-18	X	M^ go	Ind	Ind	Ind		
French and English Studies	QR31	3FT deg	E+F g	14-18	X	M^ go	Ind	Ind	Ind		
German - ab initio and English Studies	QR32	3FT deg	E g	14-18	X	M^ go	Ind	Ind	Ind		
German and English Studies	QR3F	3FT deg	G+E g	16-18	X	M go	Ind	Ind	Ind		
Health Studies and English Studies	LQ43	3FT deg	E+S g	14-18	X	M^ go	Ind	Ind	Ind		
History and English Studies	QV31	3FT deg	E+H g	14-18	X	M^ go	Ind	Ind	Ind		
Housing and English Studies	KQ4J	3FT deg	E g	14-18	X	M^ go	Ind	Ind	Ind		
Human Biology and English Studies	BQ13	3FT deg	E+S g	14-18	X	M^ go	Ind	Ind	Ind		
Human Geography and English Studies	LQ83	3FT deg	E+Gy g	14-18	X	M^ go	Ind	Ind	Ind		
Human Resource Management and English Studies	QN36	3FT deg	E g	14-18	X	M^ go	Ind	Ind	Ind		
Law and English Studies	MQ33	3FT deg	E g	14-18	X	M^ go	Ind	Ind	Ind		
Marketing and English Studies	QN35	3FT deg	E g	14-18	X	M^ go	Ind	Ind	Ind		
Media Studies and English Studies	PQ43	3FT deg	E g	14-18	X	D^ go	Ind	Ind	Ind		
Nutrition and English Studies	BQ43	3FT deg	E+S g	14-18	X	M^ go	Ind	Ind	Ind		
Politics and English Studies	MQ13	3FT deg	E g	14-18	X	M^ go	Ind	Ind	Ind		
Product Design and English Studies	HQ73	3FT deg	E+Ad g	14-18	X	M^ go	Ind	Ind	Ind		
Psychology and English Studies	CQ83	3FT deg	E+S g	14-18	X	M^ go	Ind	Ind	Ind		
Social Policy and English Studies	QL34	3FT deg	E g	14-18	X	M^ go	Ind	Ind	Ind		
Sociology and English Studies	LQ3H	3FT deg	E g	14-18	X	M^ go	Ind	Ind	Ind		
Spanish - ab initio and English Studies	QR34	3FT deg	E g	14-18	X	M^ go	Ind	Ind	Ind		
Spanish and English Studies	QR3K	3FT deg	Sp+E g	14-18	X	M^ go	Ind	Ind	Ind		
Sports Science and English Studies	BQ63	3FT deg	E+S g	14-18	X	M^ go	Ind	Ind	Ind		
Urban Studies and English Studies	KQ4H	3FT deg	E g	14-18	X	M go	Ind	Ind	Ind		
World Theatre and English Studies	QW34	3FT deg	E g	14-18	X	M^ go	Ind	Ind	Ind		

Univ of ST ANDREWS

TITLE	CODE	COURSE	SUBJECTS	A/AS	ND/C	AGNVQ	IB	SQA(H)	SQA	RATIO	A/AS
English	Q301	4FT deg	* g	BBB	X	Ind	30$	BBBB	Ind		
English-Arabic	TQ63	4FT deg	* g	BBB	X	Ind	30$	BBBB	Ind		
English-Art History	QV34	4FT deg	* g	BBB	X	Ind	30$	BBBB	Ind	3	24/30
English-Biblical Studies	QV3W	4FT deg	* g	BBB	X	Ind	30$	BBBB	Ind		
English-Classical Studies	QQ38	4FT deg	* g	BBB	X	Ind	30$	BBBB	Ind	6	
English-Economics	LQ13	4FT deg	* g	BBB	X	Ind	30$	BBBB	Ind		
French with Year Abroad-English	QRH1	4FT/5FT deg	E g	BBB	X	Ind	30$	BBBB$	Ind	5	26/30
French-English	QR31	4FT deg	E g	BBB	X	Ind	30$	BBBB$	Ind		
Geography-English	QL38	4FT deg	* g	BBB	X	Ind	30$	BBBB	Ind	9	
German with Year Abroad-English	QRH2	4FT/5FT deg	* g	BBB	X	Ind	30$	BBBB	Ind	9	
German-English	QR32	4FT deg	* g	BBB	X	Ind	30$	BBBB	Ind	2	
Greek-English	QQ37	4FT deg	* g	BBB	X	Ind	30$	BBBB	Ind		

TITLE	CODE	COURSE	SUBJECTS	A/AS	ND/C	AGNVQ	IB	SQA(H)	SQA	RATIO A/AS
course details			**98 expected requirements**							**96 entry stats**
Hebrew-English	QQ39	4FT deg	* g	BBB	X	Ind	30$	BBBB	Ind	
Italian with Year Abroad-English	RQ33	4FT/5FT deg	* g	BBB	X	Ind	30$	BBBB	Ind	
Italian-English	QR33	4FT deg	* g	BBB	X	Ind	30$	BBBB	Ind	
Latin-English	QQ36	4FT deg	* g	BBB	X	Ind	30$	BBBB	Ind	9
Mediaeval History-English	QVH1	4FT deg	* g	BBB	X	Ind	30$	BBBB	Ind	6
Modern History-English	QV31	4FT deg	* g	BBB	X	Ind	30$	BBBB	Ind	11 26/28
Philosophy-English	QV37	4FT deg	* g	BBB	X	Ind	30$	BBBB	Ind	5 26/28
Psychology-English	LQ73	4FT deg	* g	ABB	X	Ind	32$	BBBBB	Ind	8
Russian with Year Abroad-English	QRH8	4FT/5FT deg	* g	BBB	X	Ind	30$	BBBB	Ind	
Russian-English	QR38	4FT deg	* g	BBB	X	Ind	30$	BBBB$	Ind	
Scottish History-English	QV3D	4FT deg	* g	BBB	X	Ind	30$	BBBB	Ind	10
Social Anthropology-English	QL36	4FT deg	* g	BBB	X	Ind	30$	BBBB	Ind	6
Spanish with Year Abroad-English	QRH4	4FT/5FT deg	* g	BBB	X	Ind	32$	BBBB	Ind	
Spanish-English	QR34	4FT deg	* g	BBB	X	Ind	32$	BBBB	Ind	6
Theological Studies-English	QV38	4FT deg	* g	BBB	X	Ind	30$	BBBB	Ind	12
General Degree of MA *English Language and Literature*	Y450	3FT deg	* g	BBB	X	Ind	30$	BBBB	Ind	

THE UNIVERSITY COLLEGE OF ST MARK AND ST JOHN

TITLE	CODE	COURSE	SUBJECTS	A/AS	ND/C	AGNVQ	IB	SQA(H)	SQA	RATIO A/AS
English (Literary Studies)/English Language St	Q3Q1	3FT deg	El	12-16	Ind	M	Ind	Ind	Ind	
English (Literary Studies)/History	Q3V1	3FT deg	El	12-16	Ind	M	Ind	Ind	Ind	
English (Literary Studies)/Information Techno	Q3G5	3FT deg	El	12-16	Ind	M	Ind	Ind	Ind	
English (Literary Studies)/Media Studies	Q3P4	3FT deg	El	12-16	Ind	M	Ind	Ind	Ind	
English (Literary Studies)/Sociology	Q3L3	3FT deg	El	12-16	Ind	M	Ind	Ind	Ind	
English (Literary Studies)/Theology & Philosophy	Q3V8	3FT deg	El	12-16	Ind	M	Ind	Ind	Ind	
English Language Studies/English (Literary St)	Q1Q3	3FT deg		12	MO	M	Ind	Ind	Ind	
History/English (Literary Studies)	V1Q3	3FT deg	H	12	MO	M	Ind	Ind	Ind	
Information Technology/English (Literary St)	G5Q3	3FT deg		4	MO	M	Dip	CCCC	Ind	
Media Studies/English (Literary Studies)	P4Q3	3FT deg		16	MO	M	Ind	Ind	Ind	
Sociology/English (Literary Studies)	L3Q3	3FT deg	So	8	MO	M	Ind	Ind	Ind	
Theology & Philosophy/English (Literary Studies)	V8Q3	3FT deg	Re	4	MO	M	Dip	CCCC	Ind	

ST MARY'S Univ COLL

TITLE	CODE	COURSE	SUBJECTS	A/AS	ND/C	AGNVQ	IB	SQA(H)	SQA	RATIO A/AS
English	Q300	3FT deg	E	12-14	X	X	Ind	BBBB$	X	
English and Biology	QC31	3FT deg	E+B/C	8-12	X	X	Ind	BBBB$	X	
English and Classical Studies	QQ38	3FT deg	E	8-12	X	X	Ind	BBBB$	X	
English and Drama	QW34	3FT deg	E	12-14	X	X	Ind	BBBB$	X	
English and Education Studies	QX3X	3FT deg	E	8-12	X	X	Ind	BBBB$	X	
Geography and English	QF38	3FT deg	E+Gy	8-12	X	X	Ind	BBBB$	X	
Heritage Management and English	NQ93	3FT deg	E	8-12	X	X	Ind	BBBB$	X	
History and English	QV31	3FT deg	E+H	8-12	X	X	Ind	BBBB$	X	
Management Studies and English	NQ13	3FT deg	E g	8-12	X	X	Ind	BBBB$	X	
Media Arts and English	PQ43	3FT deg	E	8-12	X	X	Ind	BBBB$	X	
Sociology and English	QL33	3FT deg	E	8-12	X	X	Ind	BBBB$	X	
Sport Rehabilitation and English	BQ93	3FT deg	E+B g	12-14	X	X	Ind	BBBB$	X	
Sport Science and English	QB36	3FT deg	E+S g	12-14	X	X	Ind	BBBB$	X	
Theology and Religious Studies and English	QV38	3FT deg	E	8-12	X	X	Ind	BBBB$	X	

STAFFORDSHIRE Univ

TITLE	CODE	COURSE	SUBJECTS	A/AS	ND/C	AGNVQ	IB	SQA(H)	SQA	RATIO A/AS
European Culture/Literature	LQP3	3FT deg	g	CD	MO+2D	M	27	BBC	Ind	
Literature/American Studies	QQ34	3FT deg	El g	12	MO+2D	M	27	BBC	Ind	4 6/16
Literature/Cultural Studies	QL36	3FT deg	El g	CD	MO+2D	M	27	BBC	Ind	2 8/16
Literature/Development Studies	QM3Y	3FT deg	El g	12	MO+2D	M	27	BBC	Ind	
Literature/Environmental Studies	QF39	3FT deg	El g	CC	MO+2D	M	27	BBB	Ind	2

	course details			98 expected requirements						96 entry stats	
TITLE		CODE	COURSE	SUBJECTS	A/AS	ND/C	AGNVQ	IB	SQA(H)	SQA	RATIO	A/AS
Literature/Film Studies		QW35	3FT deg	EL g	CD	MO+2D	M	27	BBC	Ind	4	6/18
Literature/French		QR31	3FT/4SW deg	El+F g	CD	MO+2D	M^	27	BCC	Ind	6	
Literature/German		QR32	3FT/4SW deg	El+G g	CD	MO+2D	M^	27	BCC	Ind	7	
Literature/History		QV3C	3FT deg	El+H g	CD	MO+2D	M	27	BBC	Ind	4	6/16
Literature/History of Art and Design		QV34	3FT deg	El g	CD	MO+2D	M	27	BBC	Ind	4	
Literature/Information Systems		QG35	3FT deg	El g	12	MO+2D	M	27	BBC	Ind	2	
Literature/International Relations		QM3C	3FT deg	El g	12	MO+2D	M	27	BBC	Ind	1	
Literature/Law		QM33	3FT deg	El g	CCC	HN	M^	27	BBBB	Ind	4	12/14
Literature/Legal Studies		QM3H	3FT deg	El g	CCC	HN	M^	27	BBBB	Ind		
Media Studies/Literature		PQ43	3FT deg	El g	CD	MO+2D	M	27	BBC	Ind	5	6/24
Philosophy/Literature		VQ73	3FT deg	El g	CD	MO+2D	M	27	BBBC	Ind	3	8/18
Psychology/Literature		LQ73	3FT deg	g	18	3M+3D	Ind	27	BBB	Ind	5	12/20
Sociology/Literature		LQ33	3FT deg	g	12	3M	M	24	BCC	Ind	3	8/18
Spanish/Literature		RQ43	3FT/4SW deg	El g	CD	MO+2D	M^	27	BBC	Ind	7	
Women's Studies/Literature		MQ93	3FT deg	El g	12	MO+2D	M	27	BBC	Ind	4	

Univ of STIRLING

Business Studies/English Studies		NQ13	4FT deg	g	BBC	HN	Ind	33	BBBB	HN		
English Studies		Q300	4FT deg	g	BBC	Ind	Ind	33	BBBB	HN		
English Studies/Commonwealth Literature		Q3QG	4FT deg	g	BBC	Ind	Ind	33	BBBB	HN		
English Studies/Film & Media Studies		QP34	4FT deg	g	BBC	Ind	Ind	35	ABBB	HN		
English Studies/French		QR31	4FT deg	g	CCC	Ind	Ind	31	BBBC	HN		
English Studies/German		QR32	4FT deg	g	CCC	Ind	Ind	31	BBBC	HN		
English Studies/History		QV31	4FT deg	g	BBC	Ind	Ind	33	BBBB	HN		
English Studies/Philosophy		QV37	4FT deg	g	BBC	Ind	Ind	33	BBBB	HN		
English Studies/Politics		QM31	4FT deg	g	BBC	Ind	Ind	33	BBBB	HN		
English Studies/Religious Studies		QV38	4FT deg	g	BBC	Ind	Ind	33	BBBB	HN		
English Studies/Scottish Literature		Q3QF	4FT deg	g	BBC	Ind	Ind	33	BBBB	HN		
English Studies/Scottish Studies		Q3VC	4FT deg	g	BBC	Ind	Ind	33	BBBB	HN		
English Studies/Sociology		LQ33	4FT deg	g	BBC	Ind	Ind	33	BBBB	HN		
English Studies/Spanish		QR34	4FT deg	g	CCC	Ind	Ind	31	BBBC	HN		
English as a Foreign Lang(General Degree only)		Q316	3FT deg	g	CCD	Ind	Ind	28	BCCC	HN		
Japanese/English Studies		QT34	4FT deg	g	BCC	Ind	Ind	31	BBBC	HN		

Univ of STRATHCLYDE

Arts and Social Sciences		Y440	3FT/4FT deg	g	CCC	Ind		28	BBBBB$	Ind		
English												

Univ of SUNDERLAND

Biology and English		CQ13	3FT deg	B/C	10	4M	M	Ind	Ind	Ind		
Biology with English		C1Q3	3FT deg	B/C	10	4M	M	Ind	Ind	Ind		
Business Studies and English		NQ13	3FT/4SW deg	*	10	4M	M	Ind	Ind	Ind		
Business Studies with English		N1Q3	3FT/4SW deg	*	10	4M	M	Ind	Ind	Ind		
Chemistry and English		FQ13	3FT deg	C	10	4M	M	Ind	Ind	Ind		
Chemistry with English		F1Q3	3FT deg	C	10	4M	M	Ind	Ind	Ind		
Computer Studies and English		GQ53	3FT deg	El g	10	Ind	M	24$	CCCC$	Ind	4	
Computer Studies with English		G5Q3	3FT/4SW deg	*	10	4M	M	Ind	Ind	Ind		
Economics and English		LQ13	3FT deg	*	10	4M	M	Ind	Ind	Ind		
Economics with English		L1Q3	3FT deg	*	10	4M	M	Ind	Ind	Ind		
English Studies		Q300	3FT deg	El g	CC	Ind	Ind	26$	BCCCC$	Ind	2	6/18
English and French		QR31▼	4FT deg	F+El g	10	Ind	M	24$	CCCC$	Ind	3	
English and Geography		QL38▼	3FT deg	El+Gy/Gl g	12	3M $	M	24$	BCCC$	N$	8	
English and German		QR32▼	4FT deg	El+G g	10	N $	M	24$	CCCC$	N$	3	
English and History		QV31▼	3FT deg	El+H g	12	Ind	M	24$	BCCC$	Ind	2	8/18

course details — 98 expected requirements — 96 entry stats

TITLE	CODE	COURSE	SUBJECTS	A/AS	NO/C	AGNVQ	IB	SQA(H)	SQA	RATIO A/AS
English and History of Art and Design	QV34▼	3FT deg	El g	12	Ind	M	24$	BCCC$	Ind	11
English and Mathematics	QG31	3FT deg	M	8	3M	M	Ind	Ind	Ind	
English and Philosophy	QV37▼	3FT deg	El g	12	X	M	24$	BCCC$	X	5 6/14
English and Physiology	QB31	3FT deg	*	10	4M	M	Ind	Ind	Ind	
English and Politics	QM31▼	3FT deg	El g	12	Ind	M	24$	BCCC$	Ind	4
English and Religious Studies	QV38▼	3FT deg	El g	12	Ind	M	24$	BCCC$	Ind	4
English and Sociology	QL33▼	3FT deg	El g	12	Ind	M	24$	BCCC$	Ind	3 6/12
English with American Studies	Q3Q4	3FT deg	El g	12	Ind	M	24$	BCCC$	Ind	5 8/16
English with Biology	Q3C1	3FT deg	B/C	10	4M	M	Ind	Ind	Ind	
English with Business Studies	Q3N1	3FT/4SW deg	*	10	4M	M	Ind	Ind	Ind	
English with Chemistry	Q3F1	3FT deg	C	10	4M	M	Ind	Ind	Ind	
English with Comparative Literature	Q3Q2	3FT deg	El g	12	Ind	M	24$	BCCC$	Ind	4
English with Computer Studies	Q3G5	3FT deg	*	10	4M	M	Ind	Ind	Ind	
English with Economics	Q3L1	3FT deg	*	10	4M	M	Ind	Ind	Ind	
English with European Studies	Q3T2	3FT deg	El g	12	Ind	M	24$	BCCC$	N$	
English with French	Q3R1	3FT deg	F	10	4M	M	Ind	Ind	Ind	
English with Gender Studies	Q3M9	3FT deg	El g	12	Ind	M	24$	BCCC$	Ind	2
English with Geography	Q3L8	3FT deg	*	10	4M	M	Ind	Ind	Ind	
English with Geology	Q3F6	3FT deg	*	8	3M	M	Ind	Ind	Ind	
English with German	Q3R2	3FT deg	G	10	4M	M	Ind	Ind	Ind	
English with History	Q3V1	3FT deg	*	12	3M+1D	M	Ind	Ind	Ind	
English with History of Art and Design	Q3V4	3FT deg	*	10	4M	M	Ind	Ind	Ind	
English with Mathematics	Q3G1	3FT deg	M	10	4M	M	Ind	Ind	Ind	
English with Media Studies	Q3P4	3FT deg	*	20	Ind	Ind	Ind	Ind	Ind	
English with Philosophy	Q3V7	3FT deg	*	10	4M	Ind	Ind	Ind	Ind	
English with Physiology	Q3B1	3FT deg	*	10	4M	M	Ind	Ind	Ind	
English with Politics	Q3M1	3FT deg	*	10	4M	M	Ind	Ind	Ind	
English with Psychology	Q3C8	3FT deg	*	12	3M+1D	M^	Ind	Ind	Ind	
English with Religious Studies	Q3V8	3FT deg	*	10	4M	M	Ind	Ind	Ind	
English with Sociology	Q3L3	3FT deg	*	12	3M+1D	M	Ind	Ind	Ind	
English with Spanish	Q3R4▼	3FT deg	El+Sp g	10	Ind	M	24$	CCCC$	Ind	10
French with English	R1Q3	4FT deg	F	10	4M	M	Ind	Ind	Ind	
Geography with English	L8Q3	3FT deg	*	10	4M	M	Ind	Ind	Ind	
German with English	R2Q3	4SW deg	G	10	4M	M	Ind	Ind	Ind	
History with English	V1Q3	3FT deg	*	12	3M+1D	M	Ind	Ind	Ind	
Mathematics with English	G1Q3	3FT deg	M	10	4M	M	Ind	Ind	Ind	
Media Studies with English	P4Q3	3FT deg	*	26	Ind	Ind	Ind	Ind	Ind	
Philosophy with English	V7Q3	3FT deg	*	10	4M	Ind	Ind	Ind	Ind	
Politics with English	M1Q3	3FT deg	*	10	4M	M	Ind	Ind	Ind	
Religious Studies with English	V8Q3	3FT deg	*	10	4M	M	Ind	Ind	Ind	
Sociology with English	L3Q3	3FT deg	*	12	3M+1D	M	Ind	Ind	Ind	

Univ of SUSSEX

TITLE	CODE	COURSE	SUBJECTS	A/AS	NO/C	AGNVQ	IB	SQA(H)	SQA	RATIO A/AS
American Studies (Literature)	Q4Q3	4FT deg	*	BBB	MO	M*6	$	Ind	Ind	
English Language in English and American Studies	Q3QK	3FT deg	*	BBB	MO	M*6	$	Ind	Ind	
English Language in European Studies	Q3TF	4FT deg	g	BBB	MO	M*6 go	$	Ind	Ind	
English in African and Asian Studies	Q3T5	3FT deg	*	BBB	MO	M*6	$	Ind	Ind	
English in Cultural and Community Studies	Q3Y2	3FT deg	*	BBB	MO	M*6	$	Ind	Ind	
English in English and American Studies	Q3Q4	3FT deg	*	BBB	MO	M*6	$	Ind	Ind	
English in European Studies	Q3T2	4FT deg	* g	BBB	MO $	M*6 go	$	Ind	Ind	
English with Development Studies	Q3MY	3FT deg	*	BBB	MO	M*6	$	Ind	Ind	
English with Media Studies	Q3P4	3FT deg	*	BBB	MO	M*6	$	Ind	Ind	
Philosophy and English in Cultural & Commun St	VQ73	3FT deg	*	BBB	MO	M*6	$	Ind	Ind	

			98 expected requirements							96 entry stats	
course details											
TITLE	CODE	COURSE	SUBJECTS	A/AS	ND/C	RGNVQ	IB	SQA(H)	SQA	RATIO	A/AS
Philosophy and English in English & American St	VQ7H	3FT deg	*	BBB	MO	M*6	$	Ind	Ind		
Philosophy and English in European Studies	VQ7J	4FT deg	* g	BBB	MO $	M*6 go	$	Ind	Ind		

Univ of Wales SWANSEA

TITLE	CODE	COURSE	SUBJECTS	A/AS	ND/C	RGNVQ	IB	SQA(H)	SQA	RATIO	A/AS
English	Q300	3FT deg	E	BBB	X	X	32$	AABBB$	X	3	16/28
English Language/Ancient History & Civilisation	QV3C	3FT deg	E	BBC	X	X	30$	ABBBB$	Ind		
English Language/French (with Business Studies)	QRH1	4FT deg	F	X	X	X	28	X	X		
English Language/German (with Business Studies)	QRH2	4FT deg	G	X	X	X	28	X	X		
English Language/Italian (with Business Studies)	QRH3	4FT deg	L	X	X	X	28	X	X		
English Language/Russian (with Business Studies)	QRH8	4FT deg	L	X	X	X	28	X	X	1	
English Language/Spanish (with Business Studies)	QRH4	4FT deg	L	X	X	X	28	X	X	1	
English/American Studies	QQ34	3FT deg	E	BBB-BBC	X	X	30$	ABBBB$	X	3	18/28
English/Ancient History and Civilisation	VQC3	3FT deg	E	BBC	X	X	30$	ABBBB$	X	3	
English/Anthropology	LQ63	3FT deg	E	BBC	X	X	30$	ABBBB$	X	3	20/22
European History (with English)	V1Q3	4FT deg	E+H	BBB-BBC	X	Ind	30$	ABBBB$	Ind	7	
French/English	QR31	4FT deg	E+F	BBC	X	X	30$	ABBBB$	X	8	16/22
French/English Language	QR3C	3FT deg	E+F	BBC	X	X	30$	ABBBB$	Ind		
Geography/English	LQ83	3FT deg	E+Gy	BBB	X	X	32$	AABBB$	Ind		
German/English	QR32	4FT deg	E+G	BBC	1M+5D$	X	30$	ABBBB$	X		
German/English Language	QR3F	3FT deg	E+G	BBC	X	X	30$	ABBBB$	Ind		
Greek & Roman Studies/English Language	QQ38	3FT deg	E	BBC-BCC	X	X	30$	ABBBB$	Ind		
Greek and Roman Studies/English	QQ83	3FT deg	E	BBC	X	X	30$	ABBBB$	X	5	
Greek/English	QQ37	3FT deg	Gk+E	BB-BCC	X	X	28$	BBBBB$	X		
Greek/English Language	QQ73	3FT deg	E+Gk	BBC-BCC	X	X	30$	ABBBB$	Ind		
History/English	QV31	3FT deg	E+H	BBB	X	Ind	32$	AABBB$	Ind	5	20/24
Italian/English	QR33	4FT deg	E+L	BBC	X	X	30$	ABBBB$	X	2	
Italian/English Language	QR3H	3FT deg	E g	BBC	X	X	30$	ABBBB$	Ind		
Latin/English	QQ36	3FT deg	E+Ln	BBC	X	X	30$	ABBBB$	X	3	
Latin/English Language	QQ63	3FT deg	E+Ln	BBC-BCC	X	X	30$	ABBBB$	X		
Medieval Studies/English	QVH1	3FT deg	E+H	BBC	X	X	30$	ABBBB$	X		
Philosophy/English	QV37	3FT deg	E	BBC	X	X	30$	ABBBB$	X	3	14/26
Politics/English	MQ13	3FT deg	E	BBB	X	X	32$	AABBB$	X	5	18/26
Russian/English	QR38	4FT deg	E+L	BB-BCC	X	X	28$	BBBBC$	X		
Russian/English Language	QR3V	3FT deg	E g	BBC	X	X	30$	ABBBB$	Ind		
Sociology/English	LQ33	3FT deg	E	BBC	X	X	30$	ABBBB$	X	5	20/24
Spanish/English	QR34	4FT deg	E+L	BBC	X	X	30$	ABBBB$	X	4	
Spanish/English Language	QR3K	3FT deg	E g	BBC	X	X	30$	ABBBB$	Ind		
Welsh/English	QQH5	3FT/4FT deg	E+W	BBC	X	X	30$	ABBBB$	X		
Welsh/English Language	QQ35	3FT deg	E g	BBC	X	X	30$	ABBBB$	Ind		

SWANSEA INST of HE

TITLE	CODE	COURSE	SUBJECTS	A/AS	ND/C	RGNVQ	IB	SQA(H)	SQA	RATIO	A/AS
Joint Honours English and Drama and Media	Y300	3FT deg		8	N				N		
Joint Honours English and Studies in Modern Society	Y300	3FT deg		8	N				N		

Univ of TEESSIDE

TITLE	CODE	COURSE	SUBJECTS	A/AS	ND/C	RGNVQ	IB	SQA(H)	SQA	RATIO	A/AS
Cultural Studies and English	LQ33	3FT deg	*	14-16	Ind	M	Ind	Ind	Ind		
English (Jt Hons available)	Q306▼	3FT deg	*	14-16	Ind		Ind	Ind	Ind	3	8/22
English and History	QV31	3FT deg									
Politics and English	MQ1J	3FT deg	*	12-14	Ind		Ind	Ind	Ind		
Modular Degree Scheme English	Y401	3FT deg									

	course details		98 expected requirements							96 entry stats	
TITLE	CODE	COURSE	SUBJECTS	A/AS	NO/C	AGNVQ	IB	SQA(H)	SQA	RATIO	A/AS
THAMES VALLEY Univ											
American Studies with English	Q4Q3	3FT deg		8-12	MO	M	26	CCC			
English Language and Communications with English	Q1Q3	3FT deg		8-12	MO	M	26	CCC			
English with Advertising	Q3P3	3FT deg		8-12	MO	M	26	CCC			
English with American Studies	Q3Q4	3FT deg		8-12	MO	M	26	CCC			
English with English Language Studies	Q3Q1	3FT deg		8-12	MO	M	26	CCC			
English with French	Q3R1	3FT deg		8-12	MO	M	26	CCC			
English with German	Q3R2	3FT deg		8-12	MO	M	26	CCC			
English with History	Q3V1	3FT deg		8-12	MO	M	26	CCC			
English with Language and Communications	Q3PH	3FT deg		8-12	MO	M	26	CCC			
English with Media Studies	Q3W9	3FT deg		8-12	MO	M	26	CCC			
English with Music	Q3W3	3FT deg		8-12	MO	M	26	CCC			
English with Politics & International Relations	Q3M1	3FT deg		8-12	MO	M	26	CCC			
English with Psychology	Q3C8	3FT deg		8-12	MO	M	26	CCC			
English with Sociology	Q3L3	3FT deg		8-12	MO	M	26	CCC			
English with Spanish	Q3R4	3FT deg		8-12	MO	M	26	CCC			
English with Visual Cultures	Q3W1	3FT deg		8-12	MO	M	26	CCC			
English with Women's Studies	Q3M9	3FT deg		8-12	MO	M	26	CCC			
French with English	R1Q3	3FT deg		8-12	MO	M	26	CCC			
German with English	R2Q3	3FT deg		8-12	MO	M	26	CCC			
History with English	V1Q3	3FT deg		8-12	MO	M	26	CCC			
Media Arts with English	W9Q3	3FT deg		8-12	MO	M	26	CCC			
Multi-Media Computing with English	G5Q3	3FT deg		8-12	MO	M	26	CCC			
Psychology with English	C8Q3	3FT deg		8-12	MO	M	26	CCC			
Sociology with English	L3Q3	3FT deg		8-12	MO	M	26	CCC			
Spanish with English	R4Q3	3FT deg		8-12	MO	M	26	CCC			
TRINITY COLL Carmarthen											
English	Q300	3FT deg	E g	DD-CC	Ind		Ind	Ind	Ind	2	6/16
English/Archaeology	QV36	3FT deg	E g	DD-CC	Ind		Ind	Ind	Ind		
History/English	QV31	3FT deg	H+E g	DD-CC	Ind		Ind	Ind	Ind	7	
Religious Studies/English	QV38	3FT deg	Re+E g	DD-CC	Ind		Ind	Ind	Ind	4	
Saesneg/Astudiaethau Crefydd	QR3W	3FT deg	E+Re g	DD-CC	Ind		Ind	Ind	Ind		
Saesneg/Astudiaethau Theatr	WQ43	3FT deg	E+T g	DD-CC	Ind		Ind	Ind	Ind		
Saesneg/Cymraeg	QQ3N	3FT deg	W+E g	DD-CC	Ind		Ind	Ind	Ind		
Saesneg/Hanes	QV3C	3FT deg	E+H g	DD-CC	Ind		Ind	Ind	Ind		
Theatre Studies/English	QW34	3FT deg	T+E g	DD-CC	Ind		Ind	Ind	Ind	3	
Welsh Studies/English	QQ35	3FT deg	E g	DD-CC	Ind		Ind	Ind	Ind	2	
Humanities *English*	Y320	3FT deg	E g	DD-CC	Ind		Ind	Ind	Ind		
Univ of ULSTER											
English	Q300▼	3FT deg	*	BCC	MO+4D	D*6/△ gi	30	BBBB	Ind	19	14/22
Humanities Combined *English*	Y320▼	3FT/4SW deg	*	CCC	MO+3D	D*6/△ gi	28	BBBC	Ind		
UNIVERSITY COLL LONDON (Univ of London)											
English	Q300	3FT deg	El g	ABB	Ind	X	34$	AAABB$	Ind	13	26/30
English and German (4 Yrs)	QR32	4FT deg	El+G g	ABB	Ind	X	34$	AABBB$	Ind	12	
English and History of Art	QV34	3FT deg	El g	ABB	Ind	X	34$	AAABB$	Ind	13	28/30
Univ of WARWICK											
English & German Literature (4 Yrs inc yr abrd)	QR32	4FT deg	E+G g	BBC	X	X	32$	ABBBB		9	20/24
English Literature	Q300	3FT deg	E g	ABB-BBB	X	X	34$	AAABB$			
English and American Literature	QQ34	3FT deg	E+H/L g	ABB-BBB	X	X	34$	AAABB$		9	24/30
English and European Literature	QQ32	3FT deg	E+H/L g	ABB-BBB	X	X	32$	AAABB$		11	24/30

 INDEPENDENT ON SUNDAY

course details			98 expected requirements							96 entry stats	
TITLE	CODE	COURSE	SUBJECTS	A/AS	ND/C	AGNVQ	IB	SQA(H)	SQA	RATIO	A/AS
English and French (4 Yrs inc yr abroad)	QR31	4FT deg	E+F g	BBB	X	X	32$	AABBB$		8	24/30
English and Italian Lit (4 Yrs inc yr abroad)	QR33	4FT deg	E g	BBC	X	X	30$	ABBBB$		7	22/26
English and Latin Literature	QQ36	3FT deg	Ln+E g	BBB	X	X	34	AABBB		4	
English and Spanish-American Literature	QR36	3FT deg	E+H/L g	BBB-BBC	X	X	32$	AABBB$		18	
English and Theatre Studies	QW34	3FT deg	E+H/L g	ABB	X	X	34	AAABB		14	24/30

WESTHILL COLL

Humanities - English Lit, English Language & Art	Q3W1	3FT deg	* g	CC	4M+2D	M^	Ind	Ind	Ind		
Humanities - Childhood Studies _English_	Y600	3FT deg	* g	CC	4M+2D	M^	Ind	Ind	Ind		
Humanities - Nineteenth and Twentieth Century St _English_	Y602	3FT deg	* g	CC	4M+2D	M^	Ind	Ind	Ind		

Univ of WESTMINSTER

English Language and Arabic	QTH6	4SW deg		CC	Ind		26$	BBB			
English Language and Chinese	T3QH	4SW deg		CC	Ind		26$	BBB			
English Studies	Q300	3FT deg	E	BCD	Ind		26$	BBB		7	10/22
English and Arabic	QT36	4SW deg	E	CC	Ind		26$	BBB		3	8/14
English and Chinese	T3Q3	4SW deg	E	CC	Ind		26$	BBB	Ind	2	
French and English	QR31	4SW deg	E+F	CC	Ind		26$	BBB		9	
French and English Language	QRH1	4SW deg		CC	Ind		26$	BBB			
German and English	QR32	4SW deg	E	CC	Ind		26$	BBB			
German and English Language	QRH2	4SW deg		CC	Ind		26$	BBB			
Italian and English	QR33	4SW deg	E	CC	Ind		26$	BBB			
Italian and English Language	QRH3	4SW deg		CC	Ind		26$	BBB			
Linguistics and English	QQ31	4SW deg	E	CC	Ind		26$	BBB		7	12/16
Russian and English	QR38	4SW deg	E	CC	Ind		26$	BBB		3	
Russian and English Language	QRH8	4SW deg		CC	Ind		26$	BBB			
Spanish and English	QR34	4SW deg	E	CC	Ind		26$	BBB		6	
Spanish and English Language	QRH4	4SW deg		CC	Ind		26$	BBB			

Univ of WOLVERHAMPTON

English (Specialist Route)	Q300	3FT deg		18	4D	D	28	AAAA	Ind	6	10/24
Combined Degrees _English_	Y401	3FT/4SW deg		20	4D	D	28	AAAA	Ind		
Combined Degrees _English (3 Semesters in Holland)_	Y401	3FT deg		14	4M	M	24	BBBB	Ind		
Combined Degrees _English as a Foreign Language_	Y401	3FT deg		12	4M	M	24	BBBB	Ind		

WORCESTER COLL of HE

English and Literary Studies	Q300	3FT deg		CC	3M	M	Ind	BCC	Ind	6	6/18
English and Literary Studies/Art and Design	WQ93	3 deg	A	CC	Ind	M	Ind	Ind	Ind		
English and Literary Studies/Drama	WQ43	3FT deg		CC	Ind	M	Ind	Ind	Ind	5	12/24
English and Literary Studies/Economy and Society	LQ13	3FT deg		CC	Ind	M	Ind	Ind	Ind	4	
English and Literary Studies/Education Studies	XQ93	3FT deg		CC	Ind	M	Ind	Ind	Ind	2	8/12
Environmental Science/English and Literary St	QF39	3FT deg	E	CC	Ind	M	Ind	Ind	Ind	2	
Geography/English and Literary Studies	QL38	3FT deg		CC	Ind	M	Ind	Ind	Ind	3	
Health Studies/English and Literary Studies	QB39	3FT deg	g	CC	Ind	M	Ind	Ind	Ind		
History/English and Literary Studies	QV31	3FT deg		CC	Ind	M	Ind	Ind	Ind	4	
Information Technology/English & Literary St	QG35	3FT deg		CC	Ind	M	Ind	Ind	Ind	5	
Psychology/English and Literary Studies	QL37	3FT deg	g	CC	Ind	M	Ind	Ind	Ind	5	12/18
Sociology/English and Literary Studies	QL33	3FT deg		CC	Ind	M	Ind	Ind	Ind	4	12/18
Sports Studies/English and Literary Studies	QB36	3FT deg		CC	Ind	M	Ind	Ind	Ind		
Urban Studies/English and Literary Studies	QL3V	3FT deg		CC	Ind	M	Ind	Ind	Ind		
Women's Studies/English and Literary Studies	QM39	3FT deg		CC	Ind	M	Ind	Ind	Ind	3	

TITLE	CODE	COURSE	SUBJECTS	A/AS	ND/C	AGNVQ	IB	SQA(H)	SQA	RATIO A/AS
Univ of DURHAM										
Environment and Development	L1F9▼	3FT deg	S	DD	Ind	Ind	Dip	CCCCC	Ind	2	6/16
Environmental Management	F900▼	3FT deg	2S	DD	Ind	Ind	Dip	CCCCC	Ind	6	10/20
Environmental Technology	F9H2▼	3FT/4SW deg	2S	DD	Ind	Ind	Dip	CCCCC	Ind	3	
Univ of EAST ANGLIA										
Environmental Chemistry	FF19	3FT deg	C+M/P	CCC	MO+1D$	Ind	27$	BBBB$	Ind	5	8/26
Environmental Chemistry with 1yr in Europe(4yrs)	FF1X	4FT deg	C+M/P g	BCC	MO+3D$	Ind	28$	ABBB$	Ind	1	
Environmental Sciences (Integrated or Spec Stud)	F900	3FT deg		BCC	Ind		29	BBBB	Ind	4	14/28
Environmental Sciences w a yr in N Amer(4 Yrs)	F901	4FT deg		AAB	Ind		32	AAAB	Ind	15	28/30
Environmental Sciences with a yr in Eur (4 Yrs)	F902	4FT deg		AAB	Ind		32	AAAB	Ind	5	26/30
Mathematics with Environmental Science	G1F9	3FT deg	M	BCC	Ind		32$	BBBC$	X		
Univ of EAST LONDON										
Anthropology and Environmental Sciences	FL96	3FT deg	* g	12	MO	M	Ind			
Anthropology with Environmental Sciences	L6F9	3FT deg	* g	12	MO	M	Ind	Ind	Ind	
Archaeological Sciences and Environmental Sci	FF4X	3FT deg	* g	12	MO	M				
Biology and Environmental Sciences	CF19	3FT deg	* g	12	MO	M	Ind	Ind	Ind	
Economics and Environmental Sciences	LF19	3FT deg	* g	12	MO	M				
Economics with Environmental Sciences	L1F9	3FT deg	* g	12	MO	M	Ind			
Education & Community Studies and Environ Sci	FX99	3FT deg	* g	12	MO	MS	Ind	Ind	Ind	
Education & Community Studies with Environ Sci	X9F9	3FT deg	* g	12	MO	M				
Environmental Sciences	F900	3FT/4SW deg	* g	12	MO	MS	Ind	Ind	Ind	5
Environmental Sciences and French	FR91	3FT deg	* g	12	MO	M				
Environmental Sciences and German	FR92	3FT deg	* g	12	MO	M				
Environmental Sciences and Health Studies	BF99	3FT deg	* g	12	MO	M$	Ind	Ind	Ind	
Environmental Sciences and Information Technol	GF59	3FT deg	* g	12	MO	M$	Ind	Ind	Ind	4
Environmental Sciences and Maths, Stats & Comput	GF99	3FT deg	* g	12	MO	M$	Ind	Ind	Ind	
Environmental Sciences and Sociology	FL9H	3FT deg	* g	12	MO	M				
Environmental Sciences and Spanish	FR94	3FT deg	* g	12	MO	M				
Environmental Sciences and Third World & Dev St	FM9Y	3FT deg	* g	12	MO	M	Ind	Ind	Ind	8
Environmental Sciences with Anthropology	F9L6	3FT deg	* g	12	MO	M	Ind	Ind	Ind	
Environmental Sciences with Archaeological Sci	F9F4	3FT deg	* g	12	MO	M				
Environmental Sciences with Biology	F9C1	3FT deg	* g	12	MO	M	Ind	Ind	Ind	
Environmental Sciences with Economics	F9L1	3FT deg	* g	12	MO	M	Ind	Ind	Ind	
Environmental Sciences with Educ & Commun St	F9X9	3FT deg	* g	12	MO	M	Ind	Ind	Ind	
Environmental Sciences with European Studies	F9T2	3FT deg	* g	12	MO	M	Ind	Ind	Ind	
Environmental Sciences with Health Studies	F9B9	3FT deg	* g	12	MO	M	Ind	Ind	Ind	
Environmental Sciences with Information Technol	F9G5	3FT deg	* g	12	MO	M	Ind	Ind	Ind	
Environmental Sciences with Maths,Stats & Comput	F9G9	3FT deg	* g	12	MO	M	Ind	Ind	Ind	
Environmental Sciences with Sociology	F9L3	3FT deg	* g	12	MO	M	Ind	Ind	Ind	
Environmental Sciences with Third World & Dev St	F9M9	3FT deg	* g	12	MO	M	Ind	Ind	Ind	
Environmental Studies	F911	3FT deg	* g	12	MO	MS	Ind	Ind	Ind	3
Geographical and Land Information Management	KP32	3FT deg	* g	12	MO	MC	Ind	Ind	Ind	5
Health Studies with Environmental Sciences	B9F9	3FT deg	* g	12	MO	M	Ind	Ind	Ind	
Information Technology with Environmental Sci	G5F9	3FT deg	* g	12	MO	M	Ind	Ind	Ind	
Maths, Stats & Computing with Environmental Sci	G9F9	3FT deg	* g	12	MO	M	Ind	Ind	Ind	
Sociology with Environmental Sciences	L3F9	3FT deg	* g	12	MO	M	Ind	Ind	Ind	
Third World & Development St with Environ Sci	M9F9	3FT deg	* g	12	MO	M	Ind	Ind		
Extended Science *Environmental Sciences*	Y108	4FT deg	* g	8-10	MO	M	Ind	Ind	Ind	
Three-Subject Degree *Environmental Sciences*	Y600	3FT deg	* g	12	MO	M	Ind	Ind	Ind	

Environmental Studies, Technology and Oceanography 27

| | | | 98 expected requirements | | | | | | | 96 entry stats | |
| course details | | | | | | | | | | | |

TITLE	CODE	COURSE	SUBJECTS	A/AS	NO/C	AGNVQ	IB	SQA(H)	SQA	RATIO	A/AS
EDGE HILL Univ COLLEGE											
Earth and Environmental Sciences	F900	3FT deg	B/Gy/En g	DD	3M+3D	MS / P*^	Dip	BBCC$	Ind	11	
Environmental Management and Information Systems	FG95	3FT deg	2(B/C/En/P) g	DD	3M+3D	MS / P*	Dip	BBCC	Ind		
Environmental Management and Mathematics	FG91	3FT deg	2(B/C/En/P) g	DD	3M+3D	MS / P*	Dip	BBCC	Ind		
Environmental Management and Sports Studies	BF69	3FT deg	2(B/C/En/P) g	CD	3M+3D	MS / P*	Dip	BBCC	Ind		
Univ of EDINBURGH											
Agricultural Science with Environmental Science	D8F9	4FT deg	C+B/M/P g	CCD	MO $		Dip$	BBBC$	N$	13	
Ecological Science with Environmental Science	C9F9	4FT deg	2(B/C/M/P) g	CCC	MO $		Dip$	BBBB$	N$	4	18/26
Economic and Social Hist with Environmental St	V3F9	4FT deg		BBB			34	ABBB			
Economics with Environmental Studies	L1F9	4FT deg		BBB			34	ABBB			
Geography with Environmental Studies	L8F9	4FT deg		ABB			36	AABB			
Politics with Environmental Studies	M1F9	4FT deg		ABB			36	AABB			
Social Anthropology with Environmental Studies	L6F9	4FT deg		AAB			38	ABBB			
Social Policy with Environmental Studies	L4F9	4FT deg		BBB			34	ABBB			
Sociology with Environmental Studies	L3F9	4FT deg		BBB			34	ABBB			
Univ of EXETER											
Environmental Science and Technology	F900	3FT deg	2S g	DD	MO	M$^	28$	Ind	Ind	3	10/14
Environmental and Minerals Science	FJ91	3FT deg	2S	DD	MO	M$^	28$	Ind	Ind		
Surveying and Earth Resources	FJ9C	3FT deg	S/E g	DD	MO	M$^	28$	Ind	Ind	5	
Environmental Science and Technology	139F	2FT HND	g	D	MO	M$	24	Ind	Ind		
FARNBOROUGH COLL of Technology											
Environmental Management and Business	F9N1	3FT deg		DE	4M	P* go	Ind	Ind	Ind		
Environmental Protection (Conservation Mgt)	F920	3FT deg	S	DE	4M	P* go	Ind	Ind	Ind	9	
Environmental Protection (Pollution Control)	F930	3FT deg	S	DE	4M	P* go	Ind	Ind	Ind	6	
Environmental Protection (Sustainable Developmen	F935	3FT deg									
Environmental Protection	019F	2FT HND	S	E	N	P*	Ind	Ind	Ind	3	
Univ of GLAMORGAN											
Biological Sci and Environmental Pollution Sci	CF19▼	3FT/4SW deg	M/S g	DD	5M $	M$	Ind	Ind	Ind	3	6/20
Biological Science with Environmental Pollution	C1F9	3FT/4SW deg	M/S g	DD	5M $	M$	Ind	Ind	Ind	3	
Chemical Sci with Environmental Pollution Sci	F1F9	3FT/4SW deg	M/S g	DD	5M $	M$	Ind	Ind	Ind	2	
Chemical Science and Environmental Pollution Sci	FF19	3FT/4SW deg	M/S g	DD	5M $	M$	Ind	Ind	Ind		
Coastal Zone and Marine Environment Studies	F910▼	3FT deg									
Energy & Environmental Technology	JF9Y	4EXT deg									
Energy and Environmental Technology	FJ99	3FT/4SW deg	* g	DD	3M $	M$	Ind	Ind	Ind	4	6/12
Environ Pollution Sci & Minerals Surveying Sci	FJ91	3FT/4SW deg	M/S g	DD	5M $	M$	Ind	Ind	Ind		
Environment and Social Values	FL93	3FT deg	* g	CD	3M $	M$	Ind	Ind	Ind	2	6/20
Environmental Pollution Sci w. Minerals Surv Sci	F9J1	3FT/4SW deg	M/S g	DD	5M $	M$	Ind	Ind	Ind		
Environmental Pollution Sci with Biological Sci	F9C1	3FT/4SW deg	M/S g	DD	5M $	M$	Ind	Ind	Ind		
Environmental Pollution Sci with Chemical Sci	F9F1	3FT/4SW deg	M/S g	DD	5M $	M$	Ind	Ind	Ind		
Environmental Pollution Science	F900	3FT/4SW deg	M/S g	DD	5M $	M$	Ind	Ind	Ind	7	8/14
Environmental Pollution Science and Sports Sci	BF69	3FT deg	M/S g	DD	5M $	M$	Ind	Ind	Ind		
Environmental Pollution Science with Geological	F9F6	3FT/4SW deg	M/S g	DD	5M $	M$	Ind	Ind	Ind		
Environmental Pollution Science with Sports Sci	F9B6	3FT deg	M/S g	DD	5M $	M$	Ind	Ind	Ind		
Geological Sci and Environmental Pollution Sci	FF69	3FT/4SW deg	M/S g	DD	5M $	M$	Ind	Ind	Ind	3	
Geological Sci with Environmental Pollution Sci	F6F9	3FT/4SW deg	M/S g	DD	5M $	M$	Ind	Ind	Ind		
Minerals Surveying with Enviro Pollution Science	J1F9	3FT/4SW deg	M/S g	DD	5M $	M$	Ind	Ind	Ind		
Sports Science with Environmental Pollution Sci	B6F9	3FT deg	M/S g	12	5M $	M$	Ind	Ind	Ind		
Combined Studies (Honours) *Energy Management*	Y400	3FT deg	* g	8-16	Ind	Ind	Ind	Ind	Ind		
Combined Studies (Honours) *Environmental Pollution Science*	Y400	3FT deg	M/S g	8-16	Ind	Ind	Ind	Ind	Ind		

TITLE	CODE	COURSE	SUBJECTS	A/AS	ND/C	RGNVQ	IB	SQA(H)	SQA	RATIO A/AS
course details			**98 expected requirements**							**96 entry stats**
Combined Studies (Honours) *Environmental Technology*	Y400	3FT deg	* g	8-16	Ind	Ind	Ind	Ind	Ind	
Joint Honours *Energy Management*	Y401	3FT deg	* g	8-16	Ind	Ind	Ind	Ind	Ind	
Joint Honours *Environmental Technology*	Y401	3FT deg	* g	8-16	Ind	Ind	Ind	Ind	Ind	
Major/Minor Honours *Astronomy*	Y402	3FT deg	M/S g	8-16	Ind	Ind	Ind	Ind	Ind	
Major/Minor Honours *Energy Management*	Y402	3FT deg	* g	8-16	Ind	Ind	Ind	Ind	Ind	
Major/Minor Honours *Environmental Pollution Science*	Y402	3FT deg	M/S g	8-16	Ind	Ind	Ind	Ind	Ind	
Coastal Zone and Marine Environment St (Pem Col)	019F▼	2FT HND	M/S	4-6	N $	P$	Ind	Ind	Ind	5
GLASGOW CALEDONIAN Univ										
Engineering for the Environment	H1F9	4FT deg	M+E	CD	Ind		Ind	BBC$	Ind	
Environment	F910	3FT/4FT deg	M+S	CD	Ind		Ind	BBC$	Ind	3
Environmental Toxicology	F930	3FT deg	M+S	DDD	Ind		Ind	BCCC	Ind	3
Univ of GREENWICH										
Civil Eng with Water & Environmental Management	H2F9	3FT/4SW deg	M+S g	16	6M	M$2	Ind	Ind	Ind	
Earth & Environmental Sciences	FF69	3FT/4SW deg	* g	12	3M	Ind	Dip	CCC	Ind	
Environmental Control	F9K3	3FT/4SW deg	g	12	3M	Ind	Ind	BCC$	Ind	
Environmental Control (Extended)	F9KH	4FT/5SW deg	g	4		Ind	Ind	Ind	Ind	
Environmental Geology	F925	3FT/4SW deg	* g	12	3M	Ind	Dip	CCC	Ind	
Environmental Geology (Extended)	F928	4FT/5SW deg	g	4		Ind	Ind	Ind	Ind	
Environmental Science (MSci)	F917	4FT deg	2S g	18	Ind	D$	30$	BBB	Ind	
Environmental Sciences (Extended)	F919	4FT/5SW deg	g	4	Ind	*	Ind	CC	Ind	
Environmental Sciences (Prof Acc)	F918	3FT/4SW deg	B/Gy/C/M/Ec g	12	MO	M$ go	Ind	BCC$	Ind	
Landscape Architecture	K300	3FT deg	* g	14	3M+5M	M	24	BBB		
Landscape Management (Land Use)	D2K3▼	4SW deg	* g	14	HN	M	24	BBB	HN	
Landscape Management (Land Use)	3K2D▼	2FT HND	* g	6			Dip	BB		
Science (Health Studies)	99FB▼	2FT HND	* g	6	N		Dip	Ind	Ind	
HALTON COLL										
Science (Environmental Sciences)	009F	2FT HND	B/C/Gy	2	N	P	Ind	Ind	N	
HARPER ADAMS Agric COLL										
Rural Environmental Protection	D260	3FT/4SW deg	S g	8-12	MO	M$	Dip	CCCC	Ind	6 8/22
HERIOT-WATT Univ										
Chemical Engineering with Environ Mgt (MEng)	H8F9	4FT/5FT deg	M+C	CCD	HN	M$ go	30	BBBB	Ind	
Environmental Management and Technology	FK93	4FT deg	*	CCD	MO	M$ go	26	BBBB	Ind	
Landscape Architecture	K300▼	4FT/5SW deg	*	CCC	6M	M$ go	33	ABBB	Ind	
Physics with Environmental Science	F3F9	3FT/4FT deg	M+P	CC	Ind	M$^ go	26	BBBC	Ind	
Physics with Environmental Science (MPhys)	F3FX	4FT deg	M+P	BC	Ind	M$ go	30	AABB	Ind	
Univ of HERTFORDSHIRE										
Applied Geology/Environmental Science	F6F9	3FT deg	* g	14	MO $	M$ gi	26$	BCCC$	Ind	6
Applied Physics/Environmental Science	F3F9	3FT deg	M+P	12	3M	M$ gi	24$	cCCC$	Ind	
Applied Statistics/Environmental Science	G4F9	3FT deg	*	14	MO	M$ gi	26	BCCC	Ind	
Astronomy/Environmental Science	F5F9	3FT deg	M g	12	3M	M$ gi	24$	CCCC$	Ind	
Business/Environmental Science	N1F9	3FT deg	*	18	4M+4D	M$6 gi	26	BBBC	Ind	13
Chemistry/Environmental Science	F1F9	3FT deg	C g	14	MO $	MS gi	26$	BCCC$	Ind	1
Conservation & Rec Mgt with a yr in N. America	F922	4FT deg	* g	14-18	4M	Ind	24	BBCCC	Ind	
Conservation & Recreational Mgt with a yr in Eur	F921	4FT deg	* g	14-18	4M	Ind	24	BBCCC	Ind	
Conservation and Recreational Management	F920	3FT/4SW deg	* g	14-18	4M	Ind	24	BBCCC	Ind	3 10/12

course details | 98 expected requirements | 96 entry stats

TITLE	CODE	COURSE	SUBJECTS	A/AS	NO/C	RGNVQ	IB	SQA(H)	SQA	RATIO A/AS
Electronic Music/Environmental Science	W3F9	3FT deg	Mu	14	MO $	M$^ gi	26$	BCCC$	Ind	
Electronics/Environmental Science	H6F9	3FT deg	* g	14	MO $	M$ gi	26$	BCCC$	Ind	
Environmental Change & Monitor with yr in Europe	F931	4FT deg	* g	14-18	4M	Ind	24	BBCCC	Ind	
Environmental Change & Monitor with yr in N.Amer	F932	4FT deg	* g	14-18	4M	Ind	24	BBCCC	Ind	
Environmental Change & Monitoring	F930	3FT/4SW deg	* g	14-18	4M	Ind	24	BBCCC	Ind	7
Environmental Science	F904	3FT deg	* g	14	4M	M$ gi	24	CCCC	Ind	
Environmental Science/Applied Geology	F9F6	3FT deg	* g	14	MO $	M$ gi	26$	BCCC$	Ind	
Environmental Science/Applied Physics	F9F3	3FT deg	M+P	12	3M	M$ gi	24$	CCCC$	Ind	1
Environmental Science/Applied Statistics	F9G4	3FT deg	*	14	MO	M$ gi	26	BCCC	Ind	
Environmental Science/Astronomy	F9F5	3FT deg	M g	12	3M	M$ gi	24$	CCCC$	Ind	
Environmental Science/Business	F9NC	3FT deg	*	18	4M+4D	M$^ gi	26	BBBC	Ind	
Environmental Science/Chemistry	F9F1	3FT deg	C g	14	MO $	MS gi	26$	BCCC$	Ind	
Environmental Science/Electronic Music	F9W3	3FT deg	Mu	14	MO $	M$^ gi	26$	BCCC	Ind	3
Environmental Science/Electronics	F9H6	3FT deg	* g	14	MO $	M$ gi	26$	BCCC$	Ind	
Environmental Science/European Studies	F9T2	3FT deg	*	14	MO	M$ gi	26	BCCC	Ind	2
Environmental Science/Human Biology	F9B1	3FT deg	S g	14	MO $	MS gi	26$	BCCC$	Ind	8
Environmental Science/Law	F9M3	3FT deg	*	20	4M+4D	D$ gi	26	BBBC	Ind	2
Environmental Science/Linguistic Science	F9Q1	3FT deg	*	14	MO	M$ gi	26	BCCC	Ind	
Environmental Science/Manufacturing Systems	F9H7	3FT deg	*	14	MO	M$ gi	26	BCCC	Ind	
Environmental Science/Mathematics	F9G1	3FT deg	M	14	MO $	M$^ gi	26$	BCCC$	Ind	
Environmental Science/Philosophy	F9V7	3FT deg	*	14	MO	M$ gi	26	BCCC	Ind	
Environmental Science/Psychology	F9C8	3FT deg	*	20	4M+4D	D$ gi	26	BBBC	Ind	
Environmental St with a year in North America	F902	4FT deg	* g	14-18	4M	Ind	24	BBCCC	Ind	4	12/14
Environmental St with deferred Choice of spec	F903	3FT/4SW deg	* g	14-18	4M	Ind	24	BBCCC	Ind	1
Environmental Studies	F910	3FT/4SW deg	* g	14-18	4M	Ind	24	BBCCC	Ind	4	8/18
Environmental Studies (Extended)	F918▼	4EXT/5EXTSW deg	* g	2	Ind	Ind	Ind	Ind	Ind	1
Environmental Studies with a year in Europe	F901	4FT deg	* g	14-18	4M	Ind	24	BBCCC	Ind	
European Studies/Environmental Science	T2F9	3FT deg	*	14	MO	M$ gi	26	BCCC	Ind	
Human Biology/Environmental Science	B1F9	3FT deg	S g	14	MO $	MS gi	26$	BCCC$	Ind	2
Law/Environmental Science	M3F9	3FT deg	*	20	4M+4D	D$ gi	26	BBBC	Ind	11
Linguistic Science/Environmental Science	Q1F9	3FT deg	*	14	MO	M$ gi	26	BCCC	Ind	
Manufacturing Systems/Environmental Science	H7F9	3FT deg	*	14	MO	M$ gi	26	BCCC	Ind	
Mathematics/Environmental Science	G1F9	3FT deg	M	14	MO $	M$^ gi	26$	BCCC$	Ind	
Philosophy/Environmental Science	V7F9	3FT deg	*	14	MO	M$ gi	26	BCCC	Ind	1
Psychology/Environmental Science	C8F9	3FT deg	*	20	4M+4D	D$ gi	26	BBBC	Ind	6
Combined Modular Scheme *Environmental Science*	Y100	3FT deg	*	14	MO	M$ gi	26	BCCC	Ind	
Combined Modular Scheme *Environmental Science (Extended)*	Y108▼	4EXT deg	*	4	N	Ind	Dip	DDDD	Ind	
Environmental Science	009F▼	2FT HND	S g	4	N $	Ind	Ind	Ind	Ind	

Univ of HUDDERSFIELD

Accountancy with Environmental Studies	N4F9	3FT deg	* g	12	3M+3D	M$ go	Ind	BBCC	Ind	
Business Studies with Environmental Management	N1F9	3FT/4SW deg	* g	16	MO+4D	M$ go	26	BBCC	Ind	
Chemistry with Environmental Science	F1F9	3FT/4SW deg	C g	10	3M $	MS gi	Ind	BCC	Ind	
Environment and Human Health	BF99	3FT/4SW deg	S/Gy g	10-16	4M $	M$6/^ go	Ind	BBB	Ind	
Environmental Analysis	F910	4SW deg	S/Gy g	10-16	4M $	M$6/^ go	Ind	BBB	Ind	
Environmental Sustainability	F9N1	3FT deg	* g	14-16	Ind	Ind	Ind	Ind	Ind	
Environmental Technology	FH91	4SW deg	S/Gy g	10-16	4M $	M$6/^ go	Ind	BBB	Ind	
Human Ecology	F901	4SW deg	S g	10-16	3M $	M$6/^ gi	26	BBB	Ind	
Science (Extended) *Environmental Analysis*	Y108	5SW deg	* g	EE	N	P$ gi	Ind	Ind	Ind	
Science (Extended) *Environmental Technology*	Y108	5SW deg	* g	EE	N	P$ gi	Ind	Ind	Ind	

Letts STUDY GUIDES
THE INDEPENDENT

course details			98 expected requirements							96 entry stats	
TITLE	CODE	COURSE	SUBJECTS	A/AS	ND/C	AGNVQ	IB	SQA(H)	SQA	RATIO	A/AS
Science (Extended)	Y108	5SW deg	* g	EE	N	P$ gi	Ind	Ind	Ind		
Human Ecology											

Univ of HULL

Chemistry with Environmental Toxicology	F1F9	3FT deg	C g	CCD	MO $	M$^ gi	26$	BCCCC	Ind		
Chemistry with Environmental Toxicology (MChem)	F1FX	4FT deg	C	BCC	MO+3D$	M$^ gi	26$	BBBCC			
Environmental and Resource Management	F920	3FT deg	*	BCC	Ind $	D$^ go	28$	BBBCC	Ind	8	16/20

IMPERIAL COLL (Univ of London)

Earth Resources (MSci)	F920	4FT deg	M/P/C/Gl/Gy	18	Ind	Ind	Ind	Ind	Ind	1	
Environ & Earth Res Eng with a Yr Abroad (MEng)	FJ9C	4FT deg	M/P+B/C/Gy	20	HN $		Ind$	BCCC$	HN$	1	
Environmental and Earth Resources Eng (MEng)	FJ91	4FT deg	M/P+B/C/Gy	20	HN $		Ind$	BCCCC$	HN$	7	
Environmental and Mining Engineering (e)	FJ9D	3FT deg	M/P/C/Gl/Gy	18	HN $		Ind$	BCCC$	HN$		

KEELE Univ

Biological & Medicinal Chem and Environment Mgt	FFCX	3FT deg	C g	BCC	Ind	D$^	28$	CSYS	Ind		
Environmental Management & Ancient Hist (4 Yrs)	VFDX	4FT deg	*	BCC	Ind	Ind	28	BBBB	Ind		
Environmental Management & Biochemistry (4 Yrs)	FCX7	4FT deg	* g	BCC	Ind	Ind	28	BBBB	Ind		
Environmental Management and American Studies	FQX4	3FT deg	* g	BCC	Ind	Ind	28	CSYS	Ind		
Environmental Management and Ancient History	FVXD	3FT deg	* g	BCC	Ind	Ind	28	CSYS	Ind		
Environmental Management and App Social Studies	FLX5	3FT deg	g	BBC-BCC	Ind	Ind	28	CSYS	Ind		
Environmental Management and Astrophysics(4 Yrs)	FFX5	4FT deg	* g	BCC-CCC	Ind	Ind	26	BBBB	Ind		
Environmental Management and Biochemistry	CF7X	3FT deg	C g	BCC	Ind	D$^	28$	BBBB	Ind		
Environmental Management and Biology	CF1X	3FT deg	S g	BCC	Ind	D$^	28$	CSYS	Ind	4	18/22
Environmental Management and Biology (4 Yrs)	FCX1	4FT deg	*	BCC	Ind	Ind	28	BBBB	Ind	3	
Environmental Management and Business Admin	FNX9	3FT deg	* g	BCC	Ind	Ind	28	CSYS	Ind	16	
Environmental Management and Chemistry	FFX1	3FT deg	C g	BCC	Ind	D$^	28$	CSYS	Ind		
Environmental Management and Classical St(4 Yrs)	QF8X	4FT deg	*	BCC	Ind	Ind	28	BBBB	Ind		
Environmental Management and Computer Science	FGX5	3FT deg	* g	BCC	Ind	Ind	28	CSYS	Ind		
Environmental Management and Criminology (4 Yrs)	MFHX	4FT deg	*	BBB	Ind	Ind	32	BBBB	Ind		
Environmental Management and Economics	FLX1	3FT deg	* g	BCC	Ind	Ind	28	BBBB	Ind		
Environmental Management and Educational Studies	FXX9	3FT deg	* g	BCC	Ind	Ind	28	CSYS	Ind		
Environmental Management and Elect Music (4 Yrs)	WFJX	4FT deg	*	BCC	Ind	Ind	28	BBBB	Ind		
Environmental Management and English	FQX3	3FT deg	E g	BBC	Ind	D$^	30$	CSYS	Ind		
Environmental Management and English (4 Yrs)	QF3X	4FT deg	*	BBC	Ind	Ind	30	BBBB	Ind		
Environmental Mgt and Business Admin (4 Yrs)	NF9X	4FT deg	*	BCC	Ind	Ind	28	BBBB	Ind	15	
Finance and Environmental Management	FNX3	3FT deg	* g	BCC	Ind	Ind	28	CSYS	Ind		
Finance and Environmental Management (4 Yrs)	NF3X	4FT deg	*	BCC	Ind	Ind	28	BBBB	Ind		
French and Environmental Management	FRX1	3FT deg	F g	BCC	Ind	D$^	28$	CSYS	Ind		
French/German and Environmental Management	FTX9	3FT deg	F+G g	BBC	Ind	D$^	30$	CSYS	Ind		
Geography and Environmental Management (4 Yrs)	FF8X	4FT deg	*	BCC	Ind	Ind	28	BBBB	Ind		
Geology and Environmental Management	FFX6	3FT deg	S g	BCC	Ind	D$^	28$	CSYS	Ind	5	
Geology and Environmental Management (4 Yrs)	FF6X	4FT deg	*	BCC	Ind	Ind	28	BBBB	Ind		
German and Environmental Management	FRX2	3FT deg	G g	BCC	Ind	D$^	28$	CSYS	Ind	1	
German and Environmental Management (4 Yrs)	RF2X	4FT deg	G	BCC	Ind	Ind	28$	BBBB	Ind		
History and Environmental Management	FVX1	3FT deg	* g	BCC	Ind	Ind	28	CSYS	Ind		
History and Environmental Management (4 Yrs)	VF1X	4FT deg	*	BCC	Ind	Ind	28	BBBB	Ind		
Human Resource Management and Env Mgt (4 Yrs)	NF6X	4FT deg	*	BCC	Ind	Ind	28	BBBB	Ind		
Human Resource Management and Environmental Mgt	FNX6	3FT deg	* g	BCC	Ind	Ind	28	CSYS	Ind	5	
International History and Env Mgt (4 Yrs)	VFCX	4FT deg	*	BCC	Ind	Ind	28	BBBB	Ind		
International History and Environmental Mgt	FVXC	3FT deg	* g	BCC	Ind	Ind	28	CSYS	Ind		
Latin and Environmental Management	FQX6	3FT deg	Ln g	BCC	Ind	D$^	28$	CSYS	Ind		
Latin and Environmental Management (4 Yrs)	QF6X	4FT deg	*	BCC	Ind	Ind	28	BBBB	Ind		
Marketing and Environmental Management	FNX5	3FT deg	* g	BCC	Ind	Ind	28	CSYS	Ind		

Environmental Studies, Technology and Oceanography   27

TITLE	CODE	COURSE	SUBJECTS	A/AS	NO/C	RGNVQ	IB	SQA(H)	SQA	RATIO A/AS
course details			**98 expected requirements**							**96 entry stats**
Mathematics and Environmental Management	FGX1	3FT deg	M g	BCC	Ind	D$^	28$	CSYS	Ind	
Mathematics and Environmental Mgt (4 Yrs)	GF1X	4FT deg	*	BCC	Ind	Ind	28	BBBB	Ind	1
Music and Environmental Management (4 Yrs)	WF3X	4FT deg	* g	BCC	Ind	Ind	28	BBBB	Ind	
Philosophy and Environmental Management (4 Yrs)	VF7X	4FT deg	*	BCC	Ind	Ind	28	BBBB	Ind	
Physics and Environmental Management (4 Yrs)	FFX3	4FT deg	* g	BCC	Ind	Ind	28	BBBB	Ind	
Politics and Environmental Management	FMX1	3FT deg	* g	BCC	Ind	D$^	28	CSYS	Ind	4
Politics and Environmental Management (4 Yrs)	MF1X	4FT deg	*	BCC	Ind	Ind	28	BBBB	Ind	
Psychology and Environmental Management	CF8X	3FT deg	* g	BBB	Ind	Ind	32$	CSYS	Ind	
Psychology and Environmental Management (4 Yrs)	FCX8	4FT deg	*	BBB	Ind	Ind	32	ABBB	Ind	
Russian Studies and Environmental Mgt (4 Yrs)	RFVX	4FT deg	* g	BCC	Ind	Ind	28	BBBB	Ind	
Russian and Environmental Management (4 Yrs)	RF8X	4FT deg	* g	BCC	Ind	Ind	28	BBBB	Ind	
Sociol & Soc Anthrop and Environment Mgt (4 Yrs)	LF3X	4FT deg	*	BCC	Ind	Ind	28	BBBB	Ind	
Sociol & Soc Anthropology and Environmental Mgt	FLX3	3FT deg	* g	BCC	Ind	Ind	28	CSYS	Ind	5
Statistics and Environmental Management (4 Yrs)	GF4X	4FT deg	*	BCC	Ind	Ind	28	BBBB	Ind	
Visual Arts and Environmental Management (4 Yrs)	WF1X	4FT deg	* g	BCC	Ind	Ind	28	BBBB	Ind	

Univ of KENT

TITLE	CODE	COURSE	SUBJECTS	A/AS	NO/C	RGNVQ	IB	SQA(H)	SQA	RATIO A/AS
Chemistry with Env Sci with Studies Abroad	F1FX	4FT deg	C g	16	MO $	Ind	24$	BBCC$	Ind	
Chemistry with Environ Sci with St Abrd (MChem)	F1FY	4FT deg	C g	16	MO $	Ind	24$	BBCC$	Ind	
Chemistry with Environmental Science	F1F9	3FT deg	C g	16	MO $	Ind	24$	BBCC$	Ind	14

KING ALFRED'S WINCHESTER

TITLE	CODE	COURSE	SUBJECTS	A/AS	NO/C	RGNVQ	IB	SQA(H)	SQA	RATIO A/AS
Business and Environmental Management	FN91	3FT deg	* g	14	6M	M	24	BCC	N	2

KING'S COLL LONDON (Univ of London)

TITLE	CODE	COURSE	SUBJECTS	A/AS	NO/C	RGNVQ	IB	SQA(H)	SQA	RATIO A/AS
Applied Environmental Science	F910	3FT/4SW deg	B+Gy	BCC	Ind	Ind	Ind	BCCC	Ind	3 14/26
Human Environmental Science	C1F9	3FT/4SW deg	B+C	BCC	Ind	Ind	Ind	BBCCC	Ind	11

KINGSTON Univ

TITLE	CODE	COURSE	SUBJECTS	A/AS	NO/C	RGNVQ	IB	SQA(H)	SQA	RATIO A/AS
Environmental Science	F900	3FT deg	S g	10-12	$	M$	Ind	CCC	Ind	3 4/20
Environmental Science	F908▼	4EXT/5EXTSW deg	*		Ind		Ind	Ind	Ind	1
Environmental Science	F901	4SW deg	S g	10-12	$	M$	Ind	CCC	Ind	3
Landscape Architecture	K300	3FT deg	*	18	5M	Ind^	24	Ind	Ind	6 12/20
Resources and the Environment	F928▼	4EXT deg	*		Ind		Ind	Ind	Ind	
Resources and the Environment	F921	3FT deg	S g	10	$	Ind	Ind	CCC	Ind	1 6/16

Univ of Wales, LAMPETER

TITLE	CODE	COURSE	SUBJECTS	A/AS	NO/C	RGNVQ	IB	SQA(H)	SQA	RATIO A/AS
Environment and Archaeology	FV96	3FT deg	* g	18	Ind	Ind	Ind	Ind	Ind	
Environmental Management and Resource Dev	F920	3FT deg		16	Ind	Ind	Ind	Ind	Ind	

LANCASTER Univ

TITLE	CODE	COURSE	SUBJECTS	A/AS	NO/C	RGNVQ	IB	SQA(H)	SQA	RATIO A/AS
Environmental Management	F920	3FT deg	Gy+S g	BCC	Ind		30	BBBBB	Ind	
Environmental Mathematics	GF19	3FT deg	M g	20	DO $		30$	Ind$	Ind	
Environmental Science	F900	3FT deg	M/P/C/S g	CCC	MO $		30$	BBBC$	Ind	
Environmental Science (inc yr in USA or Canada)	F902	3FT deg	M/P/C/S g	BBB	MO $		32$	AABB$	Ind	
Environmental Systems Engineering	FH91	3FT/4SW deg	M+P/Cs/Es/Ds g	20	MO+1D		30$	BBBBB$	Ind	
Environmental Systems Engineering (MEng)	FH9C	4FT/5SW deg	M+P/Cs/Es/Ds g	20	MO+2D		30$	BBBBB$	Ind	
Pollution Science	F930	3FT deg	M/P/C/S	18	MO $		30$	BBBC $	Ind	
Pollution Science (inc a year in USA/Canada)	F931	3FT deg	M/P/C/S	20	MO $		32$	AABB$	Ind	
Combined Science *Environmental Science*	Y158	3FT deg	M/P/C g	CCD	MO $		28$	BBBBB$	Ind	
Combined Science (inc a year in USA or Canada) *Environmental Science*	Y155	3FT deg	M/P/C g	BBB	Ind $		32$	ABBBB$	Ind	

	course details			98 expected requirements						96 entry stats	
TITLE	CODE	COURSE	SUBJECTS	A/AS	NO/C	AGNVQ	IB	SQA(H)	SQA	RATIO	A/AS
Univ of LEEDS											
Civil and Environmental Engineering	H2F9	3FT/4FT deg	M g	CCC	3M+2D$ Ind		26$	BBBCC	Ind	14	12/20
Environmental Chemical Engineering	H8F9	3FT deg	C+S/M/Ec/Gy g	BCC	4M+2D$ Ind		28$	BBBBC	Ind	7	
Environmental Energy Engineering	H8FX	3FT/4FT deg	M+S g	CCD	3M+2D$ Ind		24$	BBCCC	Ind	5	12/18
Environmental Management	F920	3FT deg	Gy/En g	BCC	1M+4D$ D$^ go		30$	ABBBB	Ind	6	16/26
Environmental Science: Bio-Geoscience Option	F900	3FT deg	B+Gy g	BCC	1M+5D$ D$^ go		28$	BBBBC	Ind	7	20/28
Environmental Science: Energy Option	F904	3FT deg	C/M g	CCC	1M+4D$ D$/^ go		26$	BBBCC	Ind	3	10/24
Environmental Science: Environ Chemistry Opt	F902	3FT deg	C g	CCC	1M+4D$ D$6/^ go		26$	BBCCC	Ind	5	14/30
Environmental Science: Environ Geology Option	F906	3FT deg	2(Gy/M/S) g	BCC	1M+5D$ D$6/^ go		28$	BBBBC	Ind	2	14/26
Environmental Science: General option	F910	3FT deg	En/Gy/M/S g	BCC	1M+4D$ D$6/^ go		28$	BBBBC	Ind	1	16/24
Mineral Industry Environmental Engineering	J1F9	3FT/4FT deg	C/M/P g	CDD	1M+2D$ Ind		24$	BBCCC	Ind		6/20
LEEDS METROPOLITAN Univ											
Health and Environment	FB99	3FT deg									
Landscape Architecture	K300	3FT deg	Pf g	CC	5M	M$ go	26	BBCC	Ind	3	8/22
Univ of LINCOLNSHIRE and HUMBERSIDE											
Environmental Science	F901	3FT deg	2(M/P/C/B/He) g	8	3M $	P	Ind	CCC$	Ind		
Environmental Science and Food Science	FD94	3FT deg	2(M/P/C/B/He) g	8	3M $	P	Ind	CCC$	Ind		
Environmental Science and Food Technology	FD9K	3FT deg	2(M/P/C/B/He) g	8	3M $	P	Ind	CCC$	Ind		
Environmental Science and Nutrition	FD9L	3FT deg	2(M/P/C/B/He) g	8	3M $	P	Ind	CCC$	Ind		
Environmental Studies	F900	3FT deg	* g	8	3M	P	Ind	CCC$	Ind		
Environmental Studies and Environmental Science	F910	3FT deg	* g	8	3M	P	Ind	CCC$	Ind		
Environmental Studies and Food Science	DF4Y	3FT deg	2(M/P/C/B/He) g	8	3M	P	Ind	CCC$	Ind		
Environmental Studies and Food Technology	DF4X	3FT deg	2(M/P/C/B/He) g	8	3M	P	Ind	CCC$	Ind		
Environmental Studies and Management	FN91	3FT deg	M/P/C/B/He g	8	3M	P	Ind	CCC$	Ind		
Univ of LIVERPOOL											
Chemistry with Oceanography	F1F7	3FT deg	C+S g	14	MO $	DS^ go	31$	BBBCC$	Ind	6	16/24
Civil and Environmental Engineering (MEng)	HK23	4FT deg	M	20	5M+2D$ Ind		30$	BBBBB$	Ind	11	
Environmental Physical Sciences	F900	3FT deg	C+P g	16	MO $	DS^ go	31$	BBBCC$	Ind	23	
Geophysics (Environmental Science)	F6F9	3FT deg	P+M g	18	MO $	DS^ go	31$	BBBCC$	Ind	7	
Mathematics with Ocean and Climate Studies	G1FR	3FT deg	M+S g	20	MO $	D$^ go	31$	BBBCC$	Ind		
Oceanography with Chemistry	F7F1	3FT deg	C+S g	16	MO $	DS^ go	31$	BBBCC$	Ind	15	
Radiation Physics and Environmental Science	F3F9	3FT deg	P+M g	12	MO $	DS^ go	31$	BBBCC$	Ind		
LIVERPOOL HOPE Univ COLL											
Environmental Studies/American Studies	QF49	3FT deg	B/Gy/En	12	8M	ML /P*^	Ind	Ind	Ind		
Environmental Studies/Art	WF99	3FT deg	B/Gy/En+A/Fa	12	8M	PA^	Ind	Ind	Ind	3	
Environmental Studies/English	QF39	3FT deg	El+B/Gy/En	12	8M	P$^	Ind	Ind	Ind	3	
European Studies/Environmental Studies	FT92	3FT deg	B/Gy/En	12	8M	M$	Ind	Ind	Ind		
Geography/Environmental Studies	FF98	3FT deg	Gy/En g	10	6M	M$ go	Ind	Ind	Ind	5	8/12
History/Environmental Studies	FV91	3FT deg	H+B/Gy/En	12	8M	P$^	Ind	Ind	Ind	6	
Human & Applied Biology/Environmental Studies	CF19	3FT deg	En/B g	10	6M	MS /P*^ go	Ind	Ind	Ind		
Information Technology/Environmental Studies	GF59	3FT deg	B/Gy/En g	10	6M	M$ go	Ind	Ind	Ind	3	
Mathematics/Environmental Studies	FG91	3FT deg	M+B/Gy/En	10	6M	P$^	Ind	Ind	Ind		
Music/Environmental Studies	FW93	3FT deg	B/Gy/En+Mu	12	8M	P$^	Ind	Ind	Ind		
Psychology/Environmental Studies	FC98	3FT deg	B/Gy/En g	10	6M	M$ go	Ind	Ind	Ind	6	
Sport, Recreation & P.E./Environmental Studies	FB96	3FT deg	B/Gy/En g	10	6M	M$ go	Ind	Ind	Ind		
Theology & Religious St/Environmental Studies	FV98	3FT deg	B/Gy/En	12	8M	M$	Ind	Ind	Ind		
LIVERPOOL JOHN MOORES Univ											
Earth Science	F920	3FT deg	S/Gy g	8	3M	M	Ind	CCCC		4	4/16
Earth Science and Countryside Management	FD92	3FT deg	S g	8	3M	M	Ind	CCCC		6	8/12
Environmental Electronics	FH96	3FT/4SW deg		12	5M	M					

Environmental Studies, Technology and Oceanography   27

course details			98 expected requirements							96 entry stats	
TITLE	CODE	COURSE	SUBJECTS	A/AS	ND/C	AGNVQ	IB	SQA(H)	SQA	RATIO	A/AS
Environmental Electronics (Foundation)	FH9P	4FT/5SW deg								2	
Environmental Science	F900	3FT deg	S/Gy	8	3M	M				8	8/16
Environmental Science and Policy	F910	3FT deg	S/Gy	12	3M	M				4	6/16
Environmental Technology Management	F911	3FT deg		10	3M	M					
Environmental Technology Management (Extended)	F918	3FT deg									
Maritime Environmental Studies	F710	3FT/4SW deg		10	3M	M				12	

LSE: LONDON Sch of Economics (Univ of London)

Environmental Management and Policy	F910	3FT deg	g	BBC	Ind	X	$	Ind	Ind		
Environmental Policy with Economics	F9L1	3FT deg	g	BBB	Ind	X	$	Ind	Ind		

LOUGHBOROUGH Univ

Physics with Environmental Sci & a yr in Europe	F3FY	4FT deg	M+P	BCC	3M+2D	DS6/^ go	28$	Ind	Ind		
Physics with Environmental Science	F3F9	3FT deg	M+P	BCC	3M+2D	DS6/^ go	28$	Ind	Ind		
Physics with Environmental Science (4 Yr SW)	F3FX	4SW deg	M+P	BCC	3M+2D	DS6/^ go	28$	Ind	Ind		
Science and Eng Foundation Studs (4/5 Yrs)	HF19	4FT/5FT deg	* g	CC	5M	M*6/^ go	25	Ind	Ind	1	8/20

LSU COLL of HE

Environment and Society (Combined)	F900	3FT deg									
Environment and Society with Politics	FM91	3FT deg									
Environment and Society with Psychology	FL97	3FT deg									
Environment and Society with Sports Science	BF69	3FT deg									
Environment and Society with Theology	FV98	3FT deg									

LUTON Univ

Biochemistry with Environmental Sciences	C7F9	3FT deg	g	12-16	MO/DO	M/D	32	BBCC	Ind		
Biology with Environmental Science	C1F9	3FT deg	g	12-16	MO/DO	M/D	32	BBCC	Ind	1	
Biology with Pollution Studies	CFC9	3FT deg	g	12-16	MO/DO	M/D	32	BBCC	Ind		
Biotechnology with Environmental Science	J8F9	3FT deg	g	12-16	MO/DO	M/D	32	BBCC	Ind		
Built Environment with Environmental Science	N8F9	3FT deg	g	12-16	MO/DO	M/D	32	BBCC	Ind		
Business with Environmental Science	N1F9	3FT deg	g	12-16	MO/DO	M/D	32	BBCC	Ind		
Business with Pollution Studies	NF1Y	3FT deg	g	12-16	MO/DO	M/D	32	BBCC	Ind		
Ecology (Eco Tech) with Environmental Science	C9F9	3FT deg	g	12-16	MO/DO	M/D	32	BBCC	Ind		
Environmental Management	F910	3FT deg	g	12-16	MO/DO	M/D	32	BBCC	Ind	15	
Environmental Sci with Comparative Literature	F9QF	3FT deg	g	12-16	MO/DO	M/D	32	BBCC	Ind		
Environmental Sci with Ecology & Biodiversity	F9C9	3FT deg	g	12-16	MO/DO	M/D	32	BBCC	Ind		
Environmental Sci with Geographical Info Systs	F999	3FT deg	g	12-16	MO/DO	M/D	32	BBCC	Ind		
Environmental Sci with Lang & Stylistics in Engl	F9QG	3FT deg	g	12-16	MO/DO	M/D	32	BBCC	Ind		
Environmental Sci with Literary St in English	F9Q2	3FT deg	g	12-16	MO/DO	M/D	32	BBCC	Ind		
Environmental Sci with Organisational Behaviour	F9L7	3FT deg	g	12-16	MO/DO	M/D	32	BBCC	Ind		
Environmental Sci with Regional Planning & Dev	F9K4	3FT deg	g	12-16	MO/DO	M/D	32	BBCC	Ind		
Environmental Science	F900	3FT deg	g	12-16	MO/DO	M/D	32	BBCC	Ind	8	8/12
Environmental Science & Artificial Intelligence	GF89	3FT deg		12-16	MO/DO	M/D	32	BBCC	Ind		
Environmental Science and Accounting	NFK9	3FT deg	g	12-16	MO/DO	M/D	32	BBCC	Ind		
Environmental Science and Applied Statistics	FG94	3FT deg	g	12-16	MO/DO	M/D	32	BBCC	Ind		
Environmental Science and Biochemistry	CF79	3FT deg	g	12-16	MO/DO	M/D	32	BBCC	Ind		
Environmental Science and Biology	CF19	3FT deg	g	12-16	MO/DO	M/D	32	BBCC	Ind	5	
Environmental Science and Biotechnology	FJ98	3FT deg	g	12-16	MO/DO	M/D	32	BBCC	Ind		
Environmental Science and Building Conservation	KF29	3FT deg		12-16	MO/DO	M/D	32	BBCC	Ind		
Environmental Science and Built Environment	NF89	3FT deg	g	12-16	MO/DO	M/D	32	BBCC	Ind		
Enviromental Science and Business	NF19	3FT deg	g	12-16	MO/DO	M/D	32	BBCC	Ind		
Environmental Science and Computer Science	GF59	3FT deg	g	12-16	MO/DO	M/D	32	BBCC	Ind		
Environmental Science and Ecology & Biodiversity	CF99	3FT deg	g	12-16	MO/DO	M/D	32	BBCC	Ind		
Environmental Science with Accounting	F9NK	3FT deg	g	12-16	MO/DO	M/D	32	BBCC	Ind		

				98 expected requirements							96 entry stats

course details · *98 expected requirements* · *96 entry stats*

TITLE	CODE	COURSE	SUBJECTS	A/AS	NO/C	RGNVQ	IB	SQA(H)	SQA	RATIO A/AS
Environmental Science with Animation	F9WF	3FT deg	g	12-16	MO/DO	M/D	32	BBCC	Ind	
Environmental Science with Applied Statistics	F9G4	3FT deg	g	12-16	MO/DO	M/D	32	BBCC	Ind	
Environmental Science with Biochemistry	F9C7	3FT deg	g	12-16	MO/DO	M/D	32	BBCC	Ind	
Environmental Science with Biology	F9C1	3FT deg	g	12-16	MO/DO	M/D	32	BBCC	Ind	3
Environmental Science with Biotechnology	F9J8	3FT deg	g	12-16	MO/DO	M/D	32	BBCC	Ind	
Environmental Science with Built Environment	F9N8	3FT deg	g	12-16	MO/DO	M/D	32	BBCC	Ind	
Environmental Science with Business	F9N1	3FT deg	g	12-16	MO/DO	M/D	32	BBCC	Ind	
Environmental Science with Electronic Systs Des	F9H6	3FT deg		12-16	MO/DO	M/D	32	BBCC	Ind	
Environmental Science with French	F9R1	3FT deg	F g	12-16	MO/DO	M/D	32	BBCC	Ind	
Environmental Science with Geology	F9F6	3FT deg	g	12-16	MO/DO	M/D	32	BBCC	Ind	
Environmental Science with Health Science	F9B9	3FT deg	g	12-16	MO/DO	M/D	32	BBCC	Ind	
Environmental Science with Human Biology	F9B1	3FT deg	g	12-16	MO/DO	M/D	32	BBCC	Ind	
Environmental Science with Journalism	F9P6	3FT deg	g	12-16	MO/DO	M/D	32	BBCC	Ind	
Environmental Science with Leisure Studies	F9N7	3FT deg	g	12-16	MO/DO	M/D	32	BBCC	Ind	
Environmental Science with Management	FN9D	3FT deg	g	12-16	MO/DO	M/D	32	BBCC	Ind	
Environmental Science with Mapping Science	F9F8	3FT deg	g	12-16	MO/DO	M/D	32	BBCC	Ind	
Environmental Science with Marketing	F9N5	3FT deg	g	12-16	MO/DO	M/D	32	BBCC	Ind	
Environmental Science with Mathematical Sciences	F9GC	3FT deg	g	12-16	MO/DO	M/D	32	BBCC	Ind	
Environmental Science with Mathematics	F9GD	3FT deg	g	12-16	MO/DO	M/D	32	BBCC	Ind	
Environmental Science with Modern English Studs	F9Q3	3FT deg	g	12-16	MO/DO	M/D	32	BBCC	Ind	
Environmental Science with Multimedia	F9PK	3FT deg	g	12-16	MO/DO	M/D	32	BBCC	Ind	
Environmental Science with Photography	F9W5	3FT deg	g	12-16	MO/DO	M/D	32	BBCC	Ind	
Environmental Science with Plant Biology	F9C2	3FT deg	g	12-16	MO/DO	M/D	32	BBCC	Ind	
Environmental Science with Psychology	F9LR	3FT deg	g	12-16	MO/DO	M/D	32	BBCC	Ind	
Environmental Science with Publishing	F9P5	3FT deg	g	12-16	MO/DO	M/D	32	BBCC	Ind	
Environmental Science with Social Studies	F9L3	3FT deg	g	12-16	MO/DO	M/D	32	BBCC	Ind	
Environmental St with Geographical Info Systems	F911	3FT deg		12-16	MO/DO	M/D	32	BBCC	Ind	
Environmental St with Organisational Behaviour	F906	3FT deg		12-16	MO/DO	M/D	32	BBCC	Ind	
Environmental St with Regional Planning & Dev	F9KK	3FT deg		12-16	MO/DO	M/D	32	BBCC	Ind	
Environmental Studies	F901	3FT deg	g	12-16	MO/DO	M/D	32	BBCC	Ind	17
Environmental Studies with Accounting	F9NL	3FT deg		12-16	MO/DO	M/D	32	BBCC	Ind	
Environmental Studies with Biochemistry	F9CR	3FT deg		12-16	MO/DO	M/D	32	BBCC	Ind	
Environmental Studies with Biology	F9CX	3FT deg		12-16	MO/DO	M/D	32	BBCC	Ind	
Environmental Studies with Biotechnology	F9JV	3FT deg		12-16	MO/DO	M/D	32	BBCC	Ind	
Environmental Studies with Built Environment	F9NV	3FT deg		12-16	MO/DO	M/D	32	BBCC	Ind	
Environmental Studies with Business	F9NC	3FT deg		12-16	MO/DO	M/D	32	BBCC	Ind	
Environmental Studies with Environmental Biology	F907	3FT deg		12-16	MO/DO	M/D	32	BBCC	Ind	
Environmental Studies with French	F9RC	3FT deg		12-16	MO/DO	M/D	32	BBCC	Ind	
Environmental Studies with Geology	F9FP	3FT deg		12-16	MO/DO	M/D	32	BBCC	Ind	
Environmental Studies with Health Science	F9BY	3FT deg		12-16	MO/DO	M/D	32	BBCC	Ind	
Environmental Studies with Human Biology	F9BC	3FT deg		12-16	MO/DO	M/D	32	BBCC	Ind	
Environmental Studies with Journalism	F9PP	3FT deg		12-16	MO/DO	M/D	32	BBCC	Ind	
Environmental Studies with Leisure Studies	F9NR	3FT deg		12-16	MO/DO	M/D	32	BBCC	Ind	
Environmental Studies with Management	F9NY	3FT deg		12-16	MO/DO	M/D	32	BBCC	Ind	
Environmental Studies with Mapping Science	F912	3FT deg		12-16	MO/DO	M/D	32	BBCC	Ind	
Environmental Studies with Marketing	F9NM	3FT deg		12-16	MO/DO	M/D	32	BBCC	Ind	
Environmental Studies with Mathematics	F9G1	3FT deg		12-16	MO/DO	M/D	32	BBCC	Ind	
Environmental Studies with Photography	F9WM	3FT deg		12-16	MO/DO	M/D	32	BBCC	Ind	
Environmental Studies with Plant Biology	F9CF	3FT deg		12-16	MO/DO	M/D	32	BBCC	Ind	
Environmental Studies with Psychology	F9LT	3FT deg		12-16	MO/DO	M/D	32	BBCC	Ind	
Environmental Studies with Social Studies	F9LH	3FT deg		12-16	MO/DO	M/D	32	BBCC	Ind	
Environmental Studs with Ecology & Biodiversity	F9CY	3FT deg		12-16	MO/DO	M/D	32	BBCC	Ind	

course details			***98 expected requirements***							*96 entry stats*
TITLE	CODE	COURSE	SUBJECTS	A/AS	ND/C	RGNVQ	IB	SQA(H)	SQA	RATIO A/AS
European Language Studies and Environmental Sci	FT92	3FT deg	L g	12-16	MO/DO	M/D	32	BBCC	Ind	
European Language Studies with Environmental Sci	T2F9	4FT deg	L g	12-16	MO/DO	M/D	32	BBCC	Ind	
Geography with Pollution Studies	FFY8	3FT deg	g	12-16	MO/DO	M/D	32	BBCC	Ind	
Geology and Environmental Science	FF96	3FT deg	g	12-16	MO/DO	M/D	32	BBCC	Ind	
Geology with Environmental Science	F6F9	3FT deg	g	12-16	MO/DO	M/D	32	BBCC	Ind	
Geology with Pollution Studies	FF69	3FT deg	g	12-16	MO/DO	M/D	32	BBCC	Ind	
Health Science and Environmental Science	FB99	3FT deg	g	12-16	MO/DO	M/D	32	BBCC	Ind	
Health Science with Environmental Science	B9F9	3FT deg	g	12-16	MO/DO	M/D	32	BBCC	Ind	
Health Science with Land Reclamation	B9K3	3FT deg	g	12-16	MO/DO	M/D	32	BBCC	Ind	
Health Science with Pollution Studies	BFXX	3FT deg	g	12-16	MO/DO	M/D	32	BBCC	Ind	
Human Biology and Environmental Science	BF19	3FT deg	g	12-16	MO/DO	M/D	32	BBCC	Ind	
Integrated Engineering with Environmental Sci	H1F9	3FT deg	g	12-16	MO/DO	M/D	32	BBCC	Ind	
Journalism and Environmental Science	PF69	3FT deg		12-16	MO/DO	M/D	32	BBCC	Ind	
Language & Stylistics in English & Environ Sci	QFG9	3FT deg	g	12-16	MO/DO	M/D	32	BBCC	Ind	
Law with Land Reclamation	M3K3	3FT deg	g	12-16	MO/DO	M/D	32	BBCC	Ind	
Law with Pollution Studies	M3FX	3FT deg	g	12-16	MO/DO	M/D	32	BBCC	Ind	
Leisure Studies and Ecology & Biodiversity	CF97	3FT deg		12-16	MO/DO	M/D	32	BBCC	Ind	
Leisure Studies and Environmental Science	FN97	3FT deg	g	12-16	MO/DO	M/D	32	BBCC	Ind	
Leisure Studies with Environmental Science	N7F9	3FT deg	g	12-16	MO/DO	M/D	32	BBCC	Ind	
Leisure Studies with Pollution Studies	N7FY	3FT deg	g	12-16	MO/DO	M/D	32	BBCC	Ind	
Mapping Science and Environmental Science	FF98	3FT deg	g	12-16	MO/DO	M/D	32	BBCC	Ind	
Mapping Science with Environmental Science	F8F9	3FT deg	g	12-16	MO/DO	M/D	32	BBCC	Ind	
Mapping Science with Land Reclamation	F8K3	3FT deg	g	12-16	MO/DO	M/D	32	BBCC	Ind	
Mapping Science with Pollution Studies	FFXY	3FT deg	g	12-16	MO/DO	M/D	32	BBCC	Ind	
Marketing and Environmental Science	FN95	3FT deg	g	12-16	MO/DO	M/D	32	BBCC	Ind	
Marketing with Environmental Science	N5F9	3FT deg	g	12-16	MO/DO	M/D	32	BBCC	Ind	
Marketing with Land Reclamation	N5K3	3FT deg	g	12-16	MO/DO	M/D	32	BBCC	Ind	
Mathematical Sciences and Environmental Science	FG91	3FT deg	g	12-16	MO/DO	M/D	32	BBCC	Ind	
Mathematical Sciences with Environmental Science	G1F9	3FT deg	g	12-16	MO/DO	M/D	32	BBCC	Ind	
Mathematics and Environmental Science	GF19	3FT deg	g	12-16	MO/DO	M/D	32	BBCC	Ind	
Media Practices and Environmental Science	FP94	3FT deg	g	12-16	MO/DO	M/D	32	BBCC	Ind	
Media Practices with Environmental Science	P4F9	3FT deg	g	12-16	MO/DO	M/D	32	BBCC	Ind	
Media Production and Environmental Science	FP9L	3FT deg	g	12-16	MO/DO	M/D	32	BBCC	Ind	
Modern English Studies and Environmental Science	FQ93	3FT deg	g	12-16	MO/DO	M/D	32	BBCC	Ind	
Modern English Studies with Environmental Sci	Q3F9	3FT deg	g	12-16	MO/DO	M/D	32	BBCC	Ind	
Modern History and Environmental Science	FV9C	3FT deg	g	12-16	MO/DO	M/D	32	BBCC	Ind	
Modern History with Environmental Science	V1FY	3FT deg	g	12-16	MO/DO	M/D	32	BBCC	Ind	
Organisational Behaviour and Environmental Sci	FL97	3FT deg	g	12-16	MO/DO	M/D	32	BBCC	Ind	
Physical Geography and Biotechnology	FJX8	3FT deg	g	12-16	MO/DO	M/D	32	BBCC	Ind	
Planning Studies and Environmental Science	KF49	3FT deg	g	12-16	MO/DO	M/D	32	BBCC	Ind	
Plant Biology and Environmental Science	CF29	3FT deg	g	12-16	MO/DO	M/D	32	BBCC	Ind	
Plant Biology with Environmental Science	C2F9	3FT deg	g	12-16	MO/DO	M/D	32	BBCC	Ind	
Politics and Environmental Science	FM91	3FT deg	g	12-16	MO/DO	M/D	32	BBCC	Ind	
Politics with Environmental Science	M1F9	3FT deg	g	12-16	MO/DO	M/D	32	BBCC	Ind	
Public Policy & Management with Land Reclamation	M1K3	3FT deg	g	12-16	MO/DO	M/D	32	BBCC	Ind	
Public Policy & Management with Pollution Studs	M1FY	3FT deg	g	12-16	MO/DO	M/D	32	BBCC	Ind	
Public Policy and Mgt and Environmental Science	FM9C	3FT deg	g	12-16	MO/DO	M/D	32	BBCC	Ind	
Regional Plan and Dev and Environmental Science	FK94	3FT deg	g	12-16	MO/DO	M/D	32	BBCC	Ind	
Regional Planning & Dev and Environmental Sci	FK9K	3FT deg	g	12-16	MO/DO	M/D	32	BBCC	Ind	
Regional Planning & Dev with Land Reclamation	K4K3	3FT deg	g	12-16	MO/DO	M/D	32	BBCC	Ind	
Regional Planning & Dev with Pollution Studies	KF4X	3FT deg	g	12-16	MO/DO	M/D	32	BBCC	Ind	
Regional Planning and Dev with Environmental Sci	K4F9	3FT deg	g	12-16	MO/DO	M/D	32	BBCC	Ind	

TITLE	CODE	COURSE	SUBJECTS	A/AS	NO/C	AGNVQ	IB	SQA(H)	SQA	RATIO A/AS
Social Policy with Environmental Science	L4F9	3FT deg		12-16	MO/DO	M/D	32	BBCC	Ind	
Social Studies and Environmental Science	FL93	3FT deg	g	12-16	MO/DO	M/D	32	BBCC	Ind	
Social Studies with Environmental Science	L3F9	3FT deg	g	12-16	MO/DO	M/D	32	BBCC	Ind	
Social Studies with Land Reclamation	L3K3	3FT deg	g	12-16	MO/DO	M/D	32	BBCC	Ind	
Travel and Tourism and Environmental Science	FP97	3FT deg	g	12-16	MO/DO	M/D	32	BBCC	Ind	
Travel and Tourism with Environmental Science	P7F9	3FT deg	g	12-16	MO/DO	M/D	32	BBCC	Ind	
Women's Studies and Environmental Science	MF99	3FT deg		12-16	MO/DO	M/D	32	BBCC	Ind	
Women's Studies with Environmental Science	M9F9	3FT deg		12-16	MO/DO	M/D	32	BBCC	Ind	
Environmental Science	009F	2FT HND	g	4-8	N/MO	P/M	26	CCDD	Ind	29

Univ of MANCHESTER

TITLE	CODE	COURSE	SUBJECTS	A/AS	NO/C	AGNVQ	IB	SQA(H)	SQA	RATIO A/AS
Environmental Management	F910	3FT deg		BCD	HN	D	26	BBBBC	Ind	
Environmental Science	F900	3FT deg	2S	BCC	HN	D^	28	BBBBB	Ind	5 14/22
Environmental Studies	F901	3FT deg		BCC	HN	D^	28	BBBBB	Ind	8

UMIST (Manchester)

TITLE	CODE	COURSE	SUBJECTS	A/AS	NO/C	AGNVQ	IB	SQA(H)	SQA	RATIO A/AS
Chemical Eng and Environmental Techn (MEng)	H8F9	4FT deg	M+C g	BBC	MO+3D$	Ind	30$	CSYS$	Ind	4 18/30
Physics with Environmental Science	F3F9	3FT deg	M+P g	BCD	4M+1D$	Ind	28$	CSYS	Ind	15
Physics with Environmental Science (MPhys)	F3FY	4FT deg	M+P g	BCD	4M+1D$	Ind	28$	CSYS	Ind	4

MANCHESTER METROPOLITAN Univ

TITLE	CODE	COURSE	SUBJECTS	A/AS	NO/C	AGNVQ	IB	SQA(H)	SQA	RATIO A/AS
Environmental Management	F910	3FT deg	* g	16	Ind		Ind	Ind	Ind	9/22
Environmental Management (Foundation)	F918▼	4FT deg	M/P	E	2M $	P$	$	$	Ind	
Environmental Mathematics and Modelling	FG91	3FT/4SW deg	M+S	12	3M	M$	Ind	Ind	Ind	
Environmental Mathematics and Modelling (Found)	FG9D	4FT deg	M/P	E	2M $	P$	$	$	Ind	
Environmental Science	F900	3FT deg	2S g	16	Ind		Ind	Ind	Ind	10/20
Environmental Science (Foundation)	F908▼	4FT deg	M/P	E	2M $	P$	$	$	Ind	
Environmental Science/Business Studies	FN91	3FT deg	*	CC	M+D	D	28	CCCC	Ind	
Environmental Science/English	FQ93	3FT deg	*	CC	M+D	D	28	CCCC	Ind	
Environmental Studies	F902	3FT deg	*	CD	Ind	M	24	CCC	Ind	8/18
Environmental Studies	F901	3FT deg	* g	14-18	Ind	M$	29	BBBBC	Ind	
Environmental Studies (Foundation)	F907▼	4FT deg	M/P	E	2M $	P$	$	$	Ind	
Environmental Studies/Biology	CF19	3FT deg	* g	14		M$				
Environmental Studies/Busines Mathematics	FG9C	3FT deg	M/P/Ec g	16	1M+3D$	M$	28$	BBBCC$	Ind	
Environmental Studies/Chemistry	FF19	3FT deg	C g	14	MO $	M$	28$	BBCCC$	Ind	
Environmental Studies/Computer Technology	FG9M	3FT deg	* g	16	1M+3D	M$	M$	BBBCC	Ind	
Environmental Studies/Computing Science	FG95	3FT deg	* g	16	1M+3D	M$	28	BBBCC	SQA	
Environmental Studies/Economics	FL91	3FT deg	* g	18	2M+4D	M$	29	BBBBC	Ind	
Geography/Environmental Science	FL9V	3FT deg	* g	DD	M+D	D	28	CCCC	Ind	
Geography/Environmental Studies	FL98	3FT deg	* g	CCC	2M+4D	M$	29	BBBBC	Ind	10/20
Health Studies/Environmental Science	BF99	3FT deg	*	CC	M+D	D	28	CCCC	Ind	
Landscape Design	K300	3FT deg	* g	14	5M	Ind	Ind	CCCCC	Ind	6/20
Languages/Environmental Studies	FT99	3FT deg	* g	18	2M+4D	M$	29	BBBBC	Ind	
Leisure Studies/Environmental Science	FL94	3FT deg	* g	DD	M+D	D	28	CCCC	Ind	
Life Science/Environmental Science	CF1X	3FT deg	* g	DD	M+D	D	28	CCCC	Ind	
Physics Studies/Environmental Studies	FF39	3FT deg	M/P g	16	1M+3D$	M$	28$	BBBCC$	Ind	
Polymer Science/Environmental Studies	FJ94	3FT deg	C g	16	1M+3D$	M$	28$	BBBCC$	Ind	
Scientific Instrumentation/Environmental Studies	FH96	3FT deg	M+P g	16	1M+3D$	M$	28$	BBBCC$	Ind	
Social Studies of Technology/Environmental Studs	FL93	3FT deg	* g	16	1M+3D	M$	28	BBBCC	Ind	
Sport/Environmental Science	BF69	3FT deg	S	BC	M+D	DS	28	CCCC	Ind	
Combined Studies (Foundation) Environmental Studies	Y108▼	4FT deg	M/P	E	2M $	P$	$	$	Ind	
Environmental Analysis and Monitoring	009F	2FT HND	* g	4	Ind	M	24	CC	Ind	2/2

TITLE	CODE	COURSE	SUBJECTS	A/AS	ND/C	AGNVQ	IB	SQA(H)	SQA	RATIO A/AS
MIDDLESEX Univ										
Applied Environmental Science	F911▼	3FT deg	* g	12	5M	M$ go	24	Ind	Ind	
Ecology and Ecotechnology	F940▼	3FT deg	* g	12	5M	M$ go	24	Ind	Ind	
Environment and Business Management	FNY1▼	3FT deg	* g	12-16	5M	M$ go	26	Ind	Ind	
Environmental Management and Policy	FNX1▼	3FT deg	* g	12-16	5M	M$ go	26	Ind	Ind	
Environmental Science Foundation	F908▼	4EXT deg	* g	E	N	P* go	Ind	Ind	Ind	
Environmental Science and Technology	F900▼	3FT/4SW deg	S g	12	5M	M$ go	24	Ind	Ind	
Water Science and Management	FN9C▼	3FT deg	* g	12-16	5M	M$ go	28	BBCC	Ind	
Joint Honours Degree _Environment and Society_	Y400	3FT deg	* g	12	5M	M$ go	24	CCCC	Ind	
Joint Honours Degree _Environmental Science_	Y400	3FT deg	* g	12-16	5M	M$ go	24	CCCC	Ind	
Joint Honours Degree _Physical Geography_	Y400	3FT deg	Gy g	10-12	5M	M$ go	24	Ind	Ind	
NENE COLLEGE										
Business Admin with Wastes Mgt & the Environment	N1FX	3FT deg	g	10	M+1D	M	24	BCC	Ind	
Earth Science with Business Administration	F9N1	3FT deg	g	DD	5M	M	24	CCC	Ind	
Earth Science with Chemistry and the Environment	F9F1	3FT deg		DD	5M	M	24	CCC	Ind	
Earth Science with Ecology	F9C9	3FT deg		DD	5M	M	24	CCC	Ind	
Earth Science with Energy Management	F9J9	3FT deg	g	DD	5M	M	24	CCC	Ind	
Earth Science with Fossils and Evolution	F9F6	3FT deg		DD	5M	M	24	CCC	Ind	
Earth Science with Geography	F9F8	3FT deg		DD	5M	M	24	CCC	Ind	
Earth Science with Human Biological Studies	F9B1	3FT deg		DD	5M	M	24	CCC	Ind	
Earth Science with Industrial Archaeology	F9V6	3FT deg		DD	5M	M	24	CCC	Ind	
Earth Science with Industry and Enterprise	F9H1	3FT deg	g	DD	5M	M	24	CCC	Ind	
Earth Science with Management Science	F9G4	3FT deg	g	DD	5M	M	24	CCC	Ind	
Earth Science with Mathematics	F9G1	3FT deg	M	DD	5M	M	24	CCC	Ind	
Earth Science with Personal & Organisational Dev	F9N6	3FT deg		DD	5M	M				
Earth Science with Sport Studies	F9N7	3FT deg		DD	5M	M	24	CCC	Ind	
Earth Science with Third World Development	F9M9	3FT deg		DD	5M	M	24	CCC	Ind	
Earth Science with Wastes Management and the Env	F9FX	3FT deg		EE	3M	P	24	CCC	Ind	
Ecology with Earth Science	C9F9	3FT deg		DD	5M	M	24	CCC	Ind	
Ecology with Wastes Management & the Environment	C9FX	3FT deg		DD	5M	M	24	CCC	Ind	
Economics with Wastes Management and the Environ	L1FX	3FT deg	g	6	5M	M	24	CCC	Ind	
Education with Earth Science	X9F9	3FT deg		DD	5M	M	24	CCC	Ind	
Energy Management with Earth Science	J9F9	3FT deg	g	EE	3M	P	24	CCC	Ind	
Energy Management with Wastes Mgt & the Environ	J9FX	3FT deg	g	EE	3M	P	24	CCC	Ind	
Environmental Science (Monitoring & Management)	F910	3FT deg	S	8	3M	M	24	CCC	Ind	8/14
Geography with Earth Science	F8F9	3FT deg	Gy	8	5M	M	24	CCC	Ind	
Human Biological St with Wastes Mgt & the Envir	B1FX	3FT deg	S	DE	5M	M	24	CCC	Ind	
Human Biological Studies with Earth Science	B1F9	3FT deg	S	DE	5M	M	24	CCC	Ind	
Ind Archaeology with Wastes Mgt & the Environ	V6FX	3FT deg		10	5M	M	24	CCC	Ind	
Ind and Enterprise with Wastes Mgt & the Environ	H1FX	3FT deg		10	5M	M	24	CCC	Ind	
Industrial Archaeology with Earth Science	V6F9	3FT deg		10	5M	M	24	CCC	Ind	
Mathematics with Wastes Management & the Environ	G1FX	3FT deg	M	DD	Ind	Ind	24	CCC	Ind	
Politics with Wastes Management & the Environ	M1FX	3FT deg		CD	5M	M	24	CCC	Ind	
Sport Studies with Earth Science	N7F9	3FT deg	Ss/Pe	12	M+2D	M	24	BBB	Ind	
Waste Management and Pollution Studies	F930	3FT deg		EE	3M	P	24	CCC	Ind	
Countryside Management	98FN	2FT HND		E	P	P	24	CC	Ind	
Univ of NEWCASTLE										
Ecological Resource Management	F9D2	3FT deg	2(S/Ec/Gy/M) g	CCD	4M	M$^ go	26$	BBBB$	Ind	
Environmental Protection	F910	3FT/4SW deg	C+M/P/B	BCC	Ind	Ind	Ind	AABBB	Ind	17
Environmental Science and Agricultural Ecology	DF29	3FT deg	2S g	CCC	Ind	Ind	Ind	ABBB	Ind	3 10/22

course details **98 expected requirements** **96 entry stats**

course details			98 expected requirements							96 entry stats
TITLE	CODE	COURSE	SUBJECTS	A/AS	ND/C	AGNVQ	IB	SQA(H)	SQA	RATIO A/AS
Univ of Wales COLLEGE, NEWPORT										
Environmental Studies	F908	3FT/4FT HND/deg								
Environmental Studies and Archaeology	FV96	3FT deg		10	M+D	D$	Ind	Ind	Ind	
European Studies and Environmental Studies	FT92	3FT deg		10	M+D	D$	Ind	Ind	Ind	
Geography and Environmental Studies	FL98	3FT deg		10	M+D	D$	Ind	Ind	Ind	
Information Technology and Environmental Studies	FG95	3FT deg		10	M+D	D$	Ind	Ind	Ind	
Sports Studies and Environmental Studies	BF69	3FT deg		10	M+D	D$	Ind	Ind	Ind	
NESCOT										
Environmental Management	F918	3FT deg	Ap	EE	N	M	Dip	Ind	N$	8
Environmental Management	F919	4FT deg	*							1
NORTH EAST WALES INST of HE										
Environmental Sciences	F900	3FT deg		4-8	4M	M$	Ind	CCC	N$	
Environmental Studies	F910	3FT deg		4-8	3M	M$	Ind	CCC	N$	
Environmental Sciences	009F	2FT HND		2-4	N	P$		CC	N$	
Univ of NORTH LONDON										
Ecology	CF99	3FT/4SW/4EXT deg	B/2S	CC	3M $	MS	$	Ind	Ind	4
Environmental Management	F900▼	3FT deg	*	CE	MO	M	Dip	CCCCC	Ind	19
Environmental Management and Ecological Science	CF9X	3FT/4SW/4EXT deg	B/2S	CC	3M $	MS	Ind	Ind	Ind	
International Environmental Management	F910▼	3FT deg	*	CE	MO	M	Dip	CCCCC	Ind	
Combined Honours Ecological Sciences	Y100	3FT/4SW/4EXT deg	B/2S	CC	3M $	MS	$	Ind	Ind	
Combined Honours Environmental Management	Y301	3FT deg	*	CC	MO	M	Dip	CCCCC	Ind	
Univ of NORTHUMBRIA										
Chemistry with Environmental Chemistry	F1F9	3FT/4SW deg	C+S/M g	10	3M	MS gi	24$	CCCC$	Ind	
Environment Protection Science	F900	3FT/4SW deg	* g	8	2M	M gi	24	CCC	Ind	
Environmental Management	F910	3FT deg	S/Gy g	12	3M	M$	26	CCCC	Ind	4 10/18
Environmental Studies	F901	3FT deg	S/Gy g	12	3M	M$	26	BBB$	Ind	
Geography and Environmental Management	FL98	3FT deg	Gy/B/C/En g	14	2M+2D	M	24	BCCC	Ind	33
Combined Honours Environmental Management	Y400▼	3FT deg	g	12-20	MO+3D	DK	26	BBCCC	Ind	
NORWICH: City COLL										
Combined Science Conservation Management	Y100	3FT/4FT deg	2S	10	5M		Ind	Ind	Ind	
Combined Science Ecosystems	Y100	3FT/4FT deg	2S	10	5M		Ind	Ind	Ind	
Combined Science Environmental Physiology	Y100	3FT/4FT deg	2S	10	5M		Ind	Ind	Ind	
Univ of NOTTINGHAM										
Environmental Science	F900	3FT deg	2(M/S/Gy)	CC-CDD	3M $	MS	24$	CSYS$	N$	15 12/20
Environmental Science with Euro Studies	F9T2	4FT deg	2(M/S/Gy) g	CC-CDD	3M $	MS	24$	CSYS$	N$	22
Environmental Technology	F901	3FT deg	2(P/C/B/G/L)	BCC	Ind	Ind	28$	Ind	Ind	
NOTTINGHAM TRENT Univ										
Business Administration & Environmental Studies	NF19▼	3FT deg	* g	12	Ind	M$ go	Ind	Ind	Ind	3 8/14
Chemistry & Environmental Systems & Monitoring	FF19	3FT deg	C g	DD	Ind	Ind	Dip	C	Ind	4
Computing and Environmental Systs and Monitoring	FGX5	3FT deg	S g	10	Ind	Ind	Dip	C	Ind	9
English and Environmental Studies	QF3X	3FT deg	E g	12	Ind	M$ go	Ind	Ind	Ind	1 12/24
Env Systems & Monitoring & Physics (Env Physics)	FF39	3FT deg	M/P g	10	Ind	Ind	Dip	C	Ind	4
Environment and Psychology	CF89	3FT deg	* g	12	Ind	Ind	Ind	Ind	Ind	10/16
Environmental Con & Mgt & Env Systs & Monitoring	F901	3FT deg	S g	12	Ind	Ind	Dip	C	Ind	8

TITLE	CODE	COURSE	SUBJECTS	A/AS	ND/C	RGNVQ	IB	SQA(H)	SQA	RATIO	A/AS
Environmental Conservation & Management & Maths	FG91	3FT deg	M g	10	Ind	Ind	Dip	C	Ind	3	
Environmental Conservation & Management and Chem	FF91	3FT deg	C g	10	Ind	Ind	Dip	C	Ind	5	
Environmental Conservation & Mgt & Biology	FC91	3FT deg	B g	10	Ind	Ind	Dip	C	Ind	10	10/20
Environmental Conservation & Mgt & Computing	FG95	3FT deg	S g	10	Ind	Ind	Dip	C	Ind	12	
Environmental Science	F900	4SW deg	S g	12	Ind		Dip	C	$	7	6/18
Environmental Systems & Monitoring & Mathematics	FGX1	3FT deg	M g	10	Ind	Ind	Dip	C	Ind		
Environmental Systs & Monitoring & IT for Sci's	FGXM	3FT deg	S g	10	Ind	Ind	Dip	C	Ind	5	
Information Technology for Scis & Env Cons & Mgt	GF59	3FT deg	S g	10	Ind	Ind	Dip	C	Ind		
Plant and Environmental Biology	CF29	4SW deg	S g	DDE	Ind	Ind	Dip	C	$	2	
Landscape Design	003K▼	3SW HND	S g	E	N	Ind	Dip	D	N	2	

OXFORD BROOKES Univ

TITLE	CODE	COURSE	SUBJECTS	A/AS	ND/C	RGNVQ	IB	SQA(H)	SQA	RATIO	A/AS
Environmental Policy/Accounting and Finance	KN34	3FT deg									
Environmental Policy/Anthropology	KL36	3FT deg									
Environmental Policy/Biological Chemistry	CK73	3FT deg									
Environmental Policy/Biology	CK13	3FT deg									
Environmental Policy/Business Admin & Mgt	KN31	3FT deg									
Environmental Policy/Cartography	FK83	3FT deg									
Environmental Policy/Cell Biology	CKC3	3FT deg									
Environmental Policy/Combined Studies	KY34	3FT deg		X		X	X				
Environmental Policy/Computer Systems	KG36	3FT deg									
Environmental Policy/Computing	KG35	3FT deg									
Environmental Policy/Computing Mathematics	KG39	3FT deg									
Environmental Policy/Ecology	CK93	3FT deg									
Environmental Policy/Economics	KL31	3FT deg									
Environmental Policy/Educational Studies	KX39	3FT deg									
Environmental Policy/Electronics	KH36	3FT deg									
Environmental Policy/English Studies	KQ33	3FT deg									
Environmental Policy/Environmental Chemistry	FK13	3FT deg									
Environmental Sciences/Accounting and Finance	FNX4	3FT deg	S g	CD-BCC	Ind	DS/D*3	Ind	Ind	Ind		
Environmental Sciences/Anthropology	FLX6	3FT deg	S g	CD-BCC	Ind	M*^/DS	Ind	Ind	Ind	3	
Environmental Sciences/Biological Chemistry	CF79	3FT deg									
Environmental Sciences/Biology	CF1X	3FT deg	S g	DD-CD	Ind	MS/DS	Ind	Ind	Ind		
Environmental Sciences/Business Admin & Mgt	FNX1	3FT deg	S g	CD-BBC	Ind	MB4/DS	Ind	Ind	Ind	6	
Environmental Sciences/Cartography	FF8X	3FT deg	S g	CC-DDD	Ind	M*/DS	Ind	Ind	Ind		
Environmental Sciences/Cell Biology	CFCX	3FT deg									
Environmental Sciences/Combined Studies	FYX4	3FT deg		X		X	X	X			
Environmental Sciences/Computer Systems	FGX6	3FT deg	S g	CD-BC	Ind	M*/DS	Ind	Ind	Ind		
Environmental Sciences/Computing	FGX5	3FT deg	S g	CD-CDD	Ind	M*/DS	Ind	Ind	Ind		
Environmental Sciences/Computing Mathematics	FGX9	3FT deg	S g	CD	Ind	M*/DS	Ind	Ind	Ind		
Environmental Sciences/Ecology	CF9X	3FT deg	S g	CD	Ind	MS/DS	Ind	Ind	Ind	10	
Environmental Sciences/Economics	FLX1	3FT deg	S g	CD-BB	Ind	M*3/DS	Ind	Ind	Ind	1	
Environmental Sciences/Educational Studies	FXX9	3FT deg	S g	CD-CC	Ind	M*3/DS	Ind	Ind	Ind		
Environmental Sciences/Electronics	FHX6	3FT deg	S/M g	CD-CC	Ind	MS$/DS	Ind	Ind	Ind		
Environmental Sciences/English Studies	FQX3	3FT deg	S g	CD-AB	Ind	M*^/DS	Ind	Ind	Ind	5	
Environmental Sciences/Environmental Chemistry	FF19	3FT deg									
Environmental Sciences/Environmental Policy	FKX3	3FT deg									
Exercise & Health/Environmental Sciences	FBX6	3FT deg	S g	DD-CD	Ind	MS/DS	Ind	Ind	Ind		
Exercise and Health/Environmental Policy	KB36	3FT deg									
Fine Art/Environmental Policy	KW31	3FT deg									
Fine Art/Environmental Sciences	FWX1	3FT deg	Pf+A+S g	CD-BC	Ind	MA^/DS	Ind	Ind	Ind		
Food Science and Nutrition/Environmental Policy	DK43	3FT deg									
Food Science and Nutrition/Environmental Sci	DF4X	3FT deg	S g	DD-CD	Ind	MS/DS	Ind	Ind	Ind	7	

			98 expected requirements							96 entry stats	
course details											
TITLE	CODE	COURSE	SUBJECTS	A/AS	ND/C	AGNVQ	IB	SQA(H)	SQA	RATIO	A/AS
French Language and Contemp St/Environ Policy	KR3C	3FT deg									
French Language and Contemp Studies/Environ Scis	FRXC	4SW deg	F+S g	CD-CDD	Ind	M^/DS	Ind	Ind	Ind		
French Language and Literature/Environmental Pol	KR31	3FT deg									
French Language and Literature/Environmental Sci	FRX1	4SW deg	F+S g	CD-CDD	Ind	M^/DS	Ind	Ind	Ind		
Geography and the Phys Env/Environmental Policy	FKV3	3FT deg									
Geography and the Phys Env/Environmental Scis	FFVX	3FT deg									
Geography and the Phys Env/Leisure Planning	FKVH	3FT deg									
Geography/Environmental Policy	KL38	3FT deg									
Geography/Environmental Sciences	FLX8	3FT deg	S g	CD-BB	Ind	M*/DS	Ind	Ind	Ind	10	15/18
Geology/Environmental Policy	FK63	3FT deg									
Geology/Environmental Sciences	FF6X	3FT deg	S/M g	DD-CD	Ind	PS/DS	Ind	Ind	Ind	4	
Geotechnics/Environmental Policy	KH32	3FT deg									
Geotechnics/Environmental Sciences	FHX2	3FT deg	S/M/Ds/Es g	CC-DD	Ind	M$/DS	Ind	Ind	Ind		
German Language and Contemp Stud/Environ Policy	KR3F	3FT deg									
German Language and Contemp Stud/Environ Science	FRXF	4SW deg	G+S g	CD-DDD	Ind	M^/DS	Ind	Ind	Ind		
German Language and Literature/Environmental Pol	KR32	3FT deg									
German Language and Literature/Environmental Sci	FRX2	4SW deg	G+S g	CD-DDD	Ind	M^/DS	Ind	Ind	Ind		
German Studies/Environmental Policy	KR3G	3FT deg									
German Studies/Environmental Sciences	FRXG	4SW deg			Ind		Ind	Ind	Ind		
Health Care/Environmental Policy (Post Exp)	BK73	3FT deg		X		X	X	X			
Health Care/Environmental Sciences (Post Exp)	BF7X	3FT deg		X		X	X	X			
History of Art/Environmental Policy	KV34	3FT deg									
History of Art/Environmental Sciences	FVX4	3FT deg	S g	CD-BCC	Ind	M*^/DS	Ind	Ind	Ind		
History/Environmental Policy	KV31	3FT deg									
History/Environmental Sciences	FVX1	3FT deg	S g	CD-BB	Ind	M^/DS	Ind	Ind	Ind		
Hospitality Management St/Environmental Sciences	FNX7	3FT deg	S/M g	CC-DDD	Ind	M*3/DS	Ind	Ind	Ind		
Hospitality Mgt Studies/Environmental Policy	KN37	3FT deg									
Human Biology/Environmental Policy	BK13	3FT deg									
Human Biology/Environmental Sciences	BF1X	3FT deg									
Information Systems/Environmental Policy	KG3M	3FT deg									
Information Systems/Environmental Sciences	FGXM	3FT deg	S g	CD-BC	Ind	M*/DS	Ind	Ind	Ind		
Intelligent Systems/Environmental Policy	KG38	3FT deg									
Intelligent Systems/Environmental Sciences	FGX8	3FT deg	S g	CD	Ind	M*/DS	Ind	Ind	Ind		
Law/Environmental Policy	KM33	3FT deg									
Law/Environmental Sciences	FMX3	3FT deg	S g	CD-BBB	Ind	DS/DS3	Ind	Ind	Ind	6	
Leisure Planning/Accounting and Finance	KNH4	3FT deg									
Leisure Planning/Anthropology	KLH6	3FT deg									
Leisure Planning/Biological Chemistry	CK7H	3FT deg									
Leisure Planning/Biology	CK1H	3FT deg									
Leisure Planning/Business Administration and Mgt	KNH1	3FT deg									
Leisure Planning/Cartography	FK8H	3FT deg									
Leisure Planning/Cell Biology	CKCH	3FT deg									
Leisure Planning/Combined Studies	KYH4	3FT deg		X		X	X	X			
Leisure Planning/Computer Systems	KGH6	3FT deg									
Leisure Planning/Computing	KGH5	3FT deg									
Leisure Planning/Computing Mathematics	KGH9	3FT deg									
Leisure Planning/Ecology	CK9H	3FT deg									
Leisure Planning/Economics	KLH1	3FT deg									
Leisure Planning/Educational Studies	KXH9	3FT deg									
Leisure Planning/Electronics	KHH6	3FT deg									
Leisure Planning/English Studies	KQH3	3FT deg									
Leisure Planning/Environmental Chemistry	FK1H	3FT deg									

Environmental Studies, Technology and Oceanography 27

course details

TITLE	CODE	COURSE	98 expected requirements							96 entry stats
			SUBJECTS	A/AS	NO/C	AGNVQ	IB	SQA(H)	SQA	RATIO A/AS
Leisure Planning/Environmental Policy	K310	3FT deg								
Leisure Planning/Environmental Sciences	FKXH	3FT deg								
Leisure Planning/Exercise and Health	KBH6	3FT deg								
Leisure Planning/Fine Art	KWH1	3FT deg								
Leisure Planning/Food Science & Nutrition	DK4H	3FT deg								
Leisure Planning/French Language and Contemp St	KRHC	3FT deg								
Leisure Planning/French Language and Literature	KRH1	3FT deg								
Leisure Planning/Geography	KLH8	3FT deg								
Leisure Planning/Geology	FK6H	3FT deg								
Leisure Planning/Geotechnics	KHH2	3FT deg								
Leisure Planning/German Language and Contemp St	KRHF	3FT deg								
Leisure Planning/German Language and Literature	KRH2	3FT deg								
Leisure Planning/German Studies	KRHG	3FT deg								
Leisure Planning/Health Care (Post Exp)	BK7H	3FT deg		X		X	X	X		
Leisure Planning/History	KVH1	3FT deg								
Leisure Planning/History of Art	KVH4	3FT deg								
Leisure Planning/Hospitality Management Studies	KNH7	3FT deg								
Leisure Planning/Human Biology	BK1H	3FT deg								
Leisure Planning/Information Systems	KGHM	3FT deg								
Leisure Planning/Intelligent Systems	KGH8	3FT deg								
Leisure Planning/Law	KMH3	3FT deg								
Marketing Management/Environmental Policy	KN3N	3FT deg								
Marketing Management/Environmental Sciences	FNXN	3FT deg	S g	CD-BCC	Ind	DS/DS3	Ind	Ind	Ind	3
Marketing Management/Leisure Planning and Mgt	KNHN	3FT deg								
Mathematics/Environmental Policy	KG31	3FT deg								
Mathematics/Environmental Sciences	FGX1	3FT deg	M g	DD-CD	Ind	DS/M^	Ind	Ind	Ind	
Mathematics/Leisure Planning and Management	KGH1	3FT deg								
Music/Environmental Policy	KW33	3FT deg								
Music/Environmental Sciences	FWX3	3FT deg	Mu+S g	DD-CD	Ind	M/DS	Ind	Ind	Ind	
Music/Leisure Planning and Management	KWH3	3FT deg								
Palliative Care/Environmental Policy (Post Exp)	BKR3	3FT deg		X		X	X	X		
Palliative Care/Environmental Sciences(Post Exp)	BFRX	3FT deg		X		X	X	X		
Palliative Care/Leisure Planning & Mgt(Post Exp)	BKRH	3FT deg		X		X	X	X		
Planning Studies/Environmental Policy	KK34	3FT deg								
Planning Studies/Environmental Sciences	FKX4	3FT deg	S g	CD-DDD	Ind	M*/DS	Ind	Ind	Ind	5
Planning Studies/Leisure Planning and Management	KKH4	3FT deg								
Politics/Environmental Policy	KM31	3FT deg								
Politics/Environmental Sciences	FMX1	3FT deg	S g	CD-AB	Ind	M^/DS	Ind	Ind	Ind	
Politics/Leisure Planning and Management	KMH1	3FT deg								
Psychology/Environmental Policy	CK83	3FT deg								
Psychology/Environmental Sciences	CF8X	3FT deg	S g	CD-BBC	Ind	M^/DS	Ind	Ind	Ind	4
Psychology/Leisure Planning and Management	CK8H	3FT deg								
Publishing/Environmental Policy	KP35	3FT deg								
Publishing/Environmental Sciences	FPX5	3FT deg	S g	CD-BB	Ind	DS/M$3	Ind	Ind	Ind	
Publishing/Leisure Planning and Management	KPH5	3FT deg								
Rehabilitation/Environmental Policy (Post Exp)	BKT3	3FT deg		X		X	X	X		
Rehabilitation/Environmental Sciences (Post Exp)	BFTX	3FT deg		X		X	X	X		
Rehabilitation/Leisure Planning & Mgt (Post Exp)	BKTH	3FT deg		X		X	X	X		
Retail Management/Environmental Policy	KN35	3FT deg								
Retail Management/Environmental Sciences	FNX5	3FT deg	S/M g	CD-CCD	Ind		Ind	Ind	Ind	
Sociology/Environmental Policy	KL33	3FT deg								
Sociology/Environmental Sciences	FLX3	3FT deg	S g	CD-BCC	Ind	M*^/DS	Ind	Ind	Ind	4

course details

TITLE	CODE	COURSE	SUBJECTS	A/AS	NO/C	AGNVQ	IB	SQA(H)	SQA	RATIO A/AS
Sociology/Leisure Planning and Management	KLH3	3FT deg								
Software Engineering/Environmental Policy	KG37	3FT deg								
Software Engineering/Environmental Sciences	FGX7	3FT deg	S g	CD-BC	Ind	M*/DS	Ind	Ind	Ind	
Software Engineering/Leisure Planning & Mgt	KGH7	3FT deg								
Statistics/Environmental Policy	KG34	3FT deg								
Statistics/Environmental Sciences	FGX4	3FT deg	S g	DD-CD	Ind	M*/DS	Ind	Ind	Ind	
Statistics/Leisure Planning and Management	KGH4	3FT deg								
Telecommunications/Environmental Policy	HKP3	3FT deg								
Telecommunications/Environmental Sciences	FHXP	3FT deg								
Telecommunications/Leisure Planning and Mgt	HKPH	3FT deg								
Tourism/Environmental Policy	KP37	3FT deg								
Tourism/Environmental Sciences	FPX7	3FT deg	S g	CD-BC	Ind	M*3/DS	Ind	Ind	Ind	
Tourism/Leisure Planning and Management	KPH7	3FT deg								
Transport Planning/Environmental Policy	KN39	3FT deg								
Transport Planning/Environmental Sciences	FNX9	3FT deg	S g	CD-CC	Ind	M*/DS	Ind	Ind	Ind	
Transport Planning/Leisure Planning & Management	KNH9	3FT deg								
Water Resources/Environmental Policy	HKF3	3FT deg								
Water Resources/Environmental Sciences	FHXF	3FT deg								
Water Resources/Leisure Planning and Management	HKFH	3FT deg								
Extended Science *Environmental Sciences*	Y100	4FT deg	* g	EE	Ind	P*	Ind	Ind	Ind	

Univ of PAISLEY

Construction and Environmental Management	FK92	4SW	M g	CD	Ind	Ind	Ind	BBC$	Ind	
Environmental Science and Technology	F900	3FT/4FT/5SW deg	B/C	CCC-EE	Ind	Ind	Ind	BCC$	Ind	7
Water and Environmental Management	F920	3FT deg	M g	CD	Ind	Ind	Ind	BBC$	Ind	

Univ of PLYMOUTH

Agriculture and the Environment	DF29	4SW deg	2(S/Gy/Ec) g	10	3M	M$	Ind	CCC	Ind	
Applied Economics with Res, Manuf & the Environ	L1F9	3FT deg	* g	CCD-CDD	MO	M$^	Ind	BCCC	Ind	
Business Econ with Resources Manu and the Env	L1FX	3FT deg	* g	CDD-CCD	MO	M$^	Ind	BCCC	Ind	
Chemistry with Ocean Science	F1F7	3FT deg	C g	CC	3M	M$^	Ind	CCCC	Ind	
Chemistry with Resources, Manufac & the Environ	F1F9	3FT deg	C g	CC	3M	M$^	Ind	CCCC	Ind	
Earth Sciences	FF69	3FT deg	Gl/Gy g	12	N $	MS	Ind	Ind	Ind	3	6/16
Environmental Science	F910	3FT deg	S g	12-18	MO	P$	Ind	Ind	Ind	4	8/20
European Economics with Resources,Manu & the Env	L1FY	3FT deg	* g	CDD-CCD	MO	M$^	Ind	BCCC	Ind	
Fisheries Studies with Ocean Science	J6F7	3FT deg	Ap g	14	5M $	M$	Ind	CCCC	Ind	7
Fisheries Studies with Underwater Studies	J6FX	3FT deg	Ap g	14	5M $	M$	Ind	CCCC	Ind	8
Geography with Ocean Science	F8F7	3FT deg	Gy+M/P/C g	16-18	X	M$^	Ind	ABBB	Ind	7	12/22
Geology with Ocean Science	F6F7	3FT deg	S g	14	4M	MS	Ind	CCC	Ind	8
Geology with Resources, Manuf & the Environment	F6FX	3FT deg	S g	12	4M	MS	Ind	CCC	Ind	9
Hydrography with Ocean Science	F8FR	3FT deg	2(M/P/C/Ap) g	14	5M $	M$	Ind	CCCC	Ind	3
Hydrography with Underwater Studies	F8F9	3FT deg	2(M/P/C/Ap) g	14	5M $	M$	Ind	CCCC	Ind	
Law with Resources, Manufacturing and the Env	M3F9	3FT deg	Ap g	BCC-BBC	DO	D12^	Ind	BBBB$	Ind	
Marine Biology with Ocean Science	C1F7	3FT deg	B+C g	CCC	4M $	M$^	Ind	BBBB	Ind	50
Marine Navigation with Underwater Studies	J9F9	3FT deg	2(M/P/C) g	14	5M $	M$	Ind	CCCC	Ind	2
Marine Technology with Ocean Science	J6FR	3FT deg	2(M/P/C) g	14	5M $	M$	Ind	CCCC	Ind	
Maritime Business with Ocean Science	N1F7	3FT deg	* g	18	5M	M$	Ind	CCCC	Ind	
Maritime Business with Underwater Studies	N1FX	3FT deg	M/P/C g	18	5M	M$	Ind	CCCC	Ind	
Mathematics with Ocean Science	G1F7	3FT deg	M g	10-15	MO $	M$^	Ind	BBCC	Ind	2
Ocean Science	F700	3FT deg	S g	14-16	5M $	M$	Ind	CCCC	Ind	5	8/28
Ocean Science with Astronomy	F7F5	3FT deg	S g	14-16	5M $	M$	Ind	CCCC	Ind	7
Ocean Science with Chemistry	F7F1	3FT deg	S g	14-16	5M $	M$	Ind	BBBB	Ind	
Ocean Science with Computing	F7G5	3FT deg	S g	14-16	5M $	M$	Ind	CCCC	Ind	5

Environmental Studies, Technology and Oceanography   27

course details			98 expected requirements							96 entry stats	
TITLE	CODE	COURSE	SUBJECTS	A/AS	ND/C	AGNVQ	IB	SQA(H)	SQA	RATIO	A/AS
Ocean Science with Fisheries Business Studies	F701	3FT deg	S g	14-16	5M $	M$	Ind	CCCC	Ind		
Ocean Science with Fisheries Science	F702	3FT deg	S g	14-16	5M $	M$	Ind	CCCC	Ind		
Ocean Science with Fisheries Technology	F7JP	3FT deg	S g	14-16	5M $	M$	Ind	CCCC	Ind		
Ocean Science with French	F7R1	3FT deg	S+F g	14-16	5M $	M$^	Ind	CCCC	Ind		
Ocean Science with Geography	F7F8	3FT deg	S g	14-16	5M $	M$^	Ind	CCCC	Ind	4	10/16
Ocean Science with Geology	F7F6	3FT deg	S g	14-16	5M $	M$	Ind	CCCC	Ind	16	
Ocean Science with Hydrography	F7FV	3FT deg	S g	14-16	5M $	M$	Ind	CCCC	Ind	6	
Ocean Science with Marine Biology	F7CC	3FT deg	S g	CCC	5M $	M$	Ind	CCCC	Ind	17	
Ocean Science with Marine Navigation	F7J9	3FT deg	S g	14-16	5M $	M$	Ind	CCCC	Ind	8	
Ocean Science with Marine Technology	F7J6	3FT deg	S g	14-16	5M $	M$	Ind	CCCC	Ind	9	
Ocean Science with Maritime Business	F7N1	3FT deg	S g	14-16	5M $	M$	Ind	CCCC	Ind		
Ocean Science with Maritime History	F7V1	3FT deg	S g	14-16	5M $	M$	Ind	CCCC	Ind		
Ocean Science with Maritime Law	F7M3	3FT deg	S g	14-16	5M $	M$	Ind	CCCC	Ind		
Ocean Science with Mathematics	F7G1	3FT deg	S g	14-16	5M $	M$	Ind	CCCC	Ind	2	
Ocean Science with Underwater Studies	F7F9	3FT deg	S g	14-16	5M $	M$	Ind	CCCC	Ind	5	10/20
Political Economy with Resources, Manu & the Env	LF1X	3FT deg	Ap g	CDD-CCD	MO $	M$^	Ind	BCCC	Ind		
Politics with Resources, Manuf and the Environ	M1F9	3FT deg	* g	14	3M	M$	Ind	BBBC$	Ind		
Psychology with Resources, Manuf and the Environ	C8F9	3FT/4SW deg	Ap g	BBC	MO+3D	M12^	Ind	BBBC$	Ind		
Underwater Studies	F900	3FT deg	Ap g	14-16	5M $	M$	Ind	CCCC	Ind	4	8/16
Underwater Studies with Astronomy	F9FM	3FT deg	Ap g	14-16	5M $	M$	Ind	CCCC	Ind		
Underwater Studies with Fisheries Business Studs	F960	3FT deg	Ap g	14-16	5M $	M$	Ind	CCCC	Ind		
Underwater Studies with Fisheries Science	F9JP	3FT deg	Ap g	14-16	5M $	M$	Ind	CCCC	Ind		
Underwater Studies with Fisheries Technology	F9J6	3FT deg	Ap g	14-16	5M $	M$	Ind	CCCC	Ind		
Underwater Studies with Hydrography	F9FW	3FT deg	Ap g	14-16	5M $	M$	Ind	Ind	Ind		
Underwater Studies with Marine Navigation	F9J9	3FT deg	Ap g	14-16	5M $	M$	Ind	CCCC	Ind	7	
Underwater Studies with Marine Technology	F9JQ	3FT deg	Ap g	14-16	5M $	M$	Ind	CCCC	Ind	6	
Underwater Studies with Maritime Business	F9NC	3FT deg	Ap g	14-16	5M $	M$	Ind	CCCC	Ind		
Underwater Studies with Maritime History	F9VC	3FT deg	Ap g	14-16	5M $	M$	Ind	CCCC	Ind		
Underwater Studies with Maritime Law	F9MH	3FT deg	Ap g	14-16	5M $	M$	Ind	CCCC	Ind		
Underwater Studies with Ocean Science	F9F7	3FT deg	Ap g	14-16	5M $	M$	Ind	CCCC	Ind	5	
Extended Science (Foundation Year) Environmental Science	Y108▼	1FT/4EXT deg	S	2	Ind	P$	Ind	Ind	Ind		
Extended Science (Foundation year) Marine Science	Y108▼	1FT/4EXT deg	S	2	Ind	P$	Ind	Ind	Ind		

Univ of PORTSMOUTH

Applied Environmental Science	F910	3FT/4SW deg	S g	8	3M $	M$6/^	Dip	CCCC	Ind	7	6/22
Applied Environmental Science	F918▼	4EXT/5EXTSW deg	*		Ind	P*	Ind	Ind	Ind	4	
Earth Resources Exploitation and Management	F920	3FT deg	S	14	3M	M$6/^	Dip	BBBB	Ind		
Ecological Chemical Monitoring (Extended)	CF9X	4FT deg	*	Ind	Ind	Ind	Ind	Ind	Ind		
Ecological and Chemical Monitoring	CF99	3FT deg	C+S	8	N $	M$6/^	Dip	Ind	Ind		
Environmental Assessment (Construction Industry)	FH92	3FT deg	*	16	4M	M$6/^	26	BBBB	Ind	7	6/14
Environmental Science	F900	3FT deg	2S	8	3M	M$6/^	Dip	BBB	Ind		4/10
Marine Environmental Science	F919	4FT deg	*	Ind	Ind	Ind	Ind	Ind	Ind		
Marine Environmental Science	F912	3FT deg	S g	10	3M $	M$6/^	Dip	BBCC	Ind		7/8

QUEEN MARY & WESTFIELD COLL (Univ of London)

Engineering with Environmental Science	H1F9	3FT deg	M	CDD-BCC	4M $	M$^	24$	BBBCC			
Environmental Science	F900	3FT deg	2(M/S/Gy/Gl)	18		M$	26$				

Univ of READING

Environmental Earth Sciences	F925	3FT deg	S g	18	4M+1D$	DS^ go	29$	BBBC$	Ind		
Environmental Science of the Earth & Atmosphere	F900	3FT deg	2S g	18	3M+2D$	DS^ go	29$	BBBC$	Ind	11	12/26
Mathematics and Meteorology	GF19	3FT deg	M	BCC	3M+2D$	D$^	30$	BBBB$	Ind	5	24/30

				98 expected requirements						96 entry stats	
course details											
TITLE	CODE	COURSE	SUBJECTS	A/AS	ND/C	AGNVQ	IB	SQA(H)	SQA	RATIO	A/AS
Meteorology	F950	3FT deg	M+P	BCC	3M+2D$	DS^	30$	BBBB$	Ind	3	18/30
Physics and Meteorology	FF39	3FT deg	M+P	BCD	4M+1D$	DS^	29$	BBBC$	Ind	6	
Soils and the Environment	F920	3FT deg	2S g	18	3M+2D$	DS^ go	29$	BBBC$	Ind		

Univ College of RIPON & YORK ST JOHN

TITLE	CODE	COURSE	SUBJECTS	A/AS	ND/C	AGNVQ	IB	SQA(H)	SQA	RATIO	A/AS
Applied Social Sciences/Environmental Science	L3F9	3FT deg	g	CC	M	M*	27	BBBC			
Environmental Science/Applied Social Sciences	F9L3	3FT deg	g	DD	M	M*	27	BBCC			
Environmental Science/Education	F9X9	3FT deg	g	CD	M	M*	27	BBCC			6/14
Environmental Science/Education	FX99	3FT deg	g	DD	M*	M	27	BBCC			
Environmental Science/Geography	F9L8	3FT deg	Gy g	DD	X	M*^	27	BBCC		4	10/14
Environmental Science/Management Studies	F9N1	3FT deg	g	DD	M	M*	27	BBCC		2	8/20
Geography/Environmental Science	L8F9	3FT deg	Gy g	CCD	X	M*^ g	30	BBBB		4	8/18

ROBERT GORDON Univ

TITLE	CODE	COURSE	SUBJECTS	A/AS	ND/C	AGNVQ	IB	SQA(H)	SQA	RATIO	A/AS
Applied Science and Management	FN91	3FT/4FT deg	S g	EE	N	Ind	Ind	BCC	Ind		
Environmental Science and Technology	F900	3FT/4FT deg	2(C/P/B)	EE	N	Ind	Ind	CCC$	Ind	5	
Applied Science (Analytical with Environ Sci)	9F1F	2FT HND	S g	E	N	Ind	Ind	CC$	Ind		

ROEHAMPTON INST

TITLE	CODE	COURSE	SUBJECTS	A/AS	ND/C	AGNVQ	IB	SQA(H)	SQA	RATIO	A/AS
Environmental St and English Lang & Linguistics	QFH9▼	3FT deg	B/Gy+E/L	CC	2M+2D$	M$^ go	30	BBC	Ind		
Environmental Studies	F900▼	3FT deg	B/Gy g	DD	3M $	M$ go	24	BCC	N$	8	6/12
Environmental Studies and Applied Consumer Studs	FN99▼	3FT deg	B/Gy g	12	4M $	P$ go	26	BCC	N$		
Environmental Studies and Art for Community	WF19▼	3FT deg	B/Gy	DD	4M $	P$ go	26	BCC	N$	3	
Environmental Studies and Biology	CF19▼	3FT deg	B g	12	4M $	P$ go	26	BCC	N$		
Environmental Studies and Business Computing	GF79▼	3FT deg	g	12	3D	M$ go	26	BCC	N$		
Environmental Studies and Business Studies	NF19▼	3FT deg	B/Gy g	DD	3D $	M$ go	26	BCC	N$	3	
Environmental Studies and Dance Studies	WF49▼	3FT deg	B/Gy	CC	2M+2D$	M$^ go	30	BBC	Ind		
Environmental Studies and Drama & Theatre St	WFL9▼	3FT deg	B/Gy+T/E	16	3D $	M$^ go	30	BBC	Ind		
Environmental Studies and Education	XF99▼	3FT deg	B/Gy	DD	4M $	P$ go	26	BCC	N$		
Environmental Studies and English Literature	QF39▼	3FT deg	B/Gy+E	CC	2M+2D$	M^ go	28	BBC			
Film & Television Studies & Environmental Studs	FP94▼	3FT deg	B/Gy	16	2M+2D$	M$^	30	BBC	N$		
French and Environmental Studies	FR91▼	4FT deg	F+B/Gy	12	4M $	P^ go	26	BCC	N$		
Geography and Environmental Studies	FL98▼	3FT deg	Gy g	DD	4M $	P$ go	26	BCC	N$	6	
Health Studies and Environmental Studies	BF99▼	3FT deg	B g	12	4M $	P$ go	26	BCC	N$	3	
History and Environmental Studies	FV91▼	3FT deg	H+B/Gy	DD	4M $	P^ go	26	BCC	N$		
Human & Social Biol and Environmental Studies	FC9C▼	3FT deg	B g	12	4M $	P$ go	26	BCC	N$		
Leisure Management Studies and Environmental Stu	FN97	3FT deg									
Music and Environmental Studies	FW93▼	3FT deg	Mu+B/Gy	DD	4M $	M^ go	26	BCC	N$	1	
Natural Resource Studies & Environmental Studies	DF29▼	3FT deg	B/Gy	DD	4M $	P$ go	24	CCC	N$		
Psychology and Environmental Studies	FL97▼	3FT deg	B/Gy g	CC	3D $	M$ go	30	BBC	Ind	11	
Social Policy & Administration & Enviro Studies	FL94▼	3FT deg	B/Gy g	DD	4M $	P$ go	26	BCC	N$		
Sociology and Environmental Studies	FL93▼	3FT deg	B/Gy g	DD	4M $	P$ go	26	BCC	N$		
Spanish and Environmental Studies	FR94▼	4FT deg	Sp+B/Gy	12	2M+2D$	P$ go	28	BBC	N$		
Sport Studies and Environmental Studies	FB96▼	3FT deg	B/Gy g	12	3D $	MS go	30	BBC	N$		
Theology & Religious Studs and Environmental St	FV98▼	3FT deg	B/Gy	DD	4M $	P$ go	26	BCC	N$		
Women's Studies and Environmental Studies	FM99▼	3FT deg	B/Gy	DD	4M $	P$ go	26	BCC	N$		

ROYAL HOLLOWAY, Univ of London

TITLE	CODE	COURSE	SUBJECTS	A/AS	ND/C	AGNVQ	IB	SQA(H)	SQA	RATIO	A/AS
Biology with Environmental Studies	C1F9	3FT deg	B+C/S g	BCC	4M	DS^	28$	BBBCC$		6	
Environmental Science	F900	3FT deg	*	BCC	Ind	DS^	Ind	Ind			
Geology with Environmental Studies	F6F9	3FT deg	S/2S g	CCC	Ind	D^	Ind	Ind		8	
Physics with Environmental Studies	F3F9	3FT deg	M+P	BCC-BBC	5M	DS^	30$	BBBCC$		5	
Social Policy with Environmental Studies	L4F9	3FT deg	*	BCC-BBC	Ind	D^	Ind	Ind		6	

course details			**98 expected requirements**							**96 entry stats**	
TITLE	CODE	COURSE	SUBJECTS	A/AS	NQ/C	AGNVQ	IB	SQA(H)	SQA	RATIO	A/AS
SCOTTISH Agric COLL											
Applied Environmental Science	F910▼	3FT/4FT deg	2S g	CDD	Ind	M$	Ind	BBBC$	Ind		
Environmental Protection and Management	KN38▼	3FT/4FT deg	2S g	CDD	Ind	M$	Ind	BBCC$	Ind	3	
Landscape Management and Design	D2K3▼	3FT/4FT deg	S/Gy	CD	Ind	M$	Ind	BCC$	Ind		
Environmental Protection and Management	83NK▼	2FT HND	S	D	N $	P$	Ind	CC$	Ind	1	
Univ of SALFORD											
Environ and Resource Sci with fur st in China	F9T3	4FT deg									
Environmental & Res Sci with fur st in Eu (4yrs)	F9T2	4FT deg	g	18-20	Ind	Ind	Ind	Ind	Ind	3	
Environmental Science	F902	4FT deg									
Environmental Sciences (3/4 Yrs)	F900	3FT/4SW deg	S g	CCD	MO	M	Ind	Ind	Ind	5	10/18
Environmental Technology and Management	K3N1	3FT/4SW deg	S g	EEE	Ind	M	Ind	Ind	Ind		
Environmental and Resource Sci with a Found Yr	F912▼	4FT/5SW deg	*		MO	M^	Ind	Ind	Ind	3	
Environmental and Resource Science (3/4 Yr)	F910	3FT/4SW deg	B/C/P/En/Gy/Gl	18	MO	M^	Ind	Ind	Ind	4	8/24
Environmental Health	009F	2FT HND	M/Gy/Gl/En	2	DO $	P$	24	CC	Ind		
SOAS:Sch of Oriental & African St (U of London)											
Environment and Environmental Management	F910	3FT deg									
Univ College SCARBOROUGH											
Environmental Science	F900	3FT deg	S g	DD	Ind	P	27$	Ind	Ind		
Environmental Science with Arts	F9Y3	3FT deg	Gy/B g	EE	Ind	P	27$	Ind	Ind		
Environmental Science with Sciences	F9Y1	3FT deg	Gy/B g	EE	Ind	P	27$	Ind	Ind		
Environmental Science with Social Sciences	F9Y2	3FT deg	Gy/B g	EE	Ind	P	27$	Ind	Ind		
Univ of SHEFFIELD											
Environmental Geosciences	F9F6	3FT deg	Gy g	BCC	5M+1D$	D^	29$	BBBB$	Ind	6	20/26
Integrated Physical Science	JF29	3/4EXT deg	2(C/M/P) g	BCC	5M $	D$^	29$	AABB$	Ind		
Landscape Design and Archaeology (Grad Dip Opt)	KF34	3FT/4FT deg	2S g	CCC	6M	D^	28$	BBBC$	Ind		
Landscape Design and Ecology (Grad Dip Opt)	KC39	3FT/4FT deg	B+S g	CCC	6M $	D^	28$	BBBC$	Ind		
Landscape with Planning	K3K4	3FT deg	g	CCC	6M	D^	28$	BBBC$	Ind	4	14/30
Natural Environmental Science	F900	3FT deg	Gy+S g	BCC	5M+1D	DS6/^	29$	BBBB$	Ind	9	20/28
SHEFFIELD HALLAM Univ											
Engineering with Environmental Studies	H1FX	3FT/4SW deg	M/P/C/Ph	8	3M $	M$	Ind	Ind	Ind		
Engineering with Environmental Studies (Ext)	H1FY▼	4EXT/5EXTSW deg									
Environmental Conservation	F912	3FT deg	*	14	8M+2D	M	Ind	Ind	Ind		
Environmental Engineering and Entsorgungstechnik	HF29	4FT deg	M/P/C/Ph g	8	3M $	M$	Ind	Ind	Ind		
Environmental Management	F910	3FT/4SW deg	M/S	16	6M	M$2	Ind	BBBCC$	Ind		
Environmental Science and Technology	F900	3FT deg									
Combined Studies *Environmental Planning*	Y400	3FT deg	S	8-14	2M	M	Ind	Ind	Ind		
Combined Studies *Environmental and Mineral Management*	Y400	3FT deg	*	14	2M	M	Ind	Ind	Ind		
Environmental Engineering	9F1H▼	2FT/3SW HND	M/P/C/Ph	E	N	P	Ind	Ind	Ind		
Environmental Land Management	552D	2FT HND	*	4	1M	P	Ind	Ind	Ind		
Univ of SOUTHAMPTON											
Biology with Oceanography	C1F7	3FT deg	B+M/C g	BCC	5M+1D$	Ind^	28$	BBBBC	Ind	4	16/28
Chemistry with Environmental Sciences	F1F9	3FT deg	C+S g	18	Ind	Ind	28$	CSYS	Ind	12	
Chemistry with Oceanography	F1F7	3FT deg	C+S g	18	Ind	Ind	28$	CSYS	Ind	3	18/24
Environmental Sciences	F900	3FT deg	2S g	BBC	1M+5D$	Ind	31$	ABBBB	Ind	7	18/28
Geography with Oceanography	F8F7	3FT deg	2S g	BBB	Ind	Ind	32	AABBB	Ind	15	
Geology with Oceanography	F6F7	3FT deg	M+P/C/B+S g	18-20	Ind	Ind	28$	BBBBC	Ind	3	14/25
Marine Environmental Chemistry	F7F1	3FT deg	C+S/M g	BCC	Ind	Ind	30$	BBBBC	Ind	11	
Marine Geosciences	FF67	3FT deg	2S g	18-20	Ind	Ind	28$	BBBCC$	Ind	3	12/16

course details				98 expected requirements						96 entry stats	
TITLE	CODE	COURSE	SUBJECTS	A/AS	NV/C	AGNVQ	IB	SQA(H)	SQA	RATIO	A/AS
Marine Sciences	F710	3FT deg	2S g	BBC-BCC	Ind	Ind	30$	BBBBC	Ind	14	14/18
Marine Sciences with French (4 Yrs)	F7R1	4FT deg	F+2S g	BCC	Ind	Ind	30$	BBBBC	Ind	4	
Mathematics with Oceanography	G1F7	3FT deg	M+P/B	BBC	Ind	Ind	30	ABBBB	Ind	5	
Oceanography with Acoustics	F7HR	3FT deg	M+S g	BCC-CCC	Ind	Ind	30$	BBBCC	Ind		
Oceanography with Geology	F7F6	3FT deg	2S g	BCC-CCC	Ind	Ind	30$	BBBCC	Ind	6	16/22
Oceanography with Marine Biology	F7CC	3FT deg	B+S/M g	BBB-BCC	Ind	Ind	30$	ABBBB	Ind	14	20/28
Oceanography with Mathematics	F7G1	3FT deg	M+S g	BCC	Ind	Ind	30$	BBBBC	Ind	3	
Oceanography with Physical Geography	F7F8	3FT deg	Gy+S/M g	BCC	Ind	Ind	30$	BBBCC	Ind	11	16/24
Oceanography with Physics	F7F3	3FT deg	P+S/M g	CCC	Ind	Ind	30$	BBBCC	Ind	6	
Physics with Oceanography	F3F7	3FT deg	M+P g	BC	Ind	Ind	28$	AAABB	Ind	6	
Physics with Space Science	F3F9	3FT deg	M+P	BC	Ind	Ind	28$	AAABB	Ind	12	
Physics with Space Science (4 Yrs) (MPhys)	F3FX	4FT deg	M+P	BC	Ind	Ind	28$	AAABB	Ind	7	14/26

SOUTHAMPTON INST

Landscape Architecture	K300	3FT deg	B	10-12	MO	M$	Dip	CCCC	N		
Landscape Architecture (with Foundation Year)	K308▼	4FT deg	*	2-4	N	P$	Dip	CCCC	N		
Maritime Environmental Management	F910	3FT deg	*	8	MO	M$	Dip	CCCC	N	2	6/16
Maritime Environmental Mgt (with Foundation Yr)	F918▼	4FT deg	*	2-4	N	P$	Dip	CCC	N	2	
Maritime Environmental Science	F900	3FT deg	*	8	MO	M$	Dip	CCCC	N	4	6/10
Maritime Environmental Science (with Foundation)	F909▼	4FT deg	*	2-4	N	P$	Dip	CCC	N	1	

SOUTH BANK Univ

Environmental Policy	F9L4	3 deg	* g	14-18	2M+4D	M go	Ind	Ind	Ind		
Environmental Policy & Business Info Technology	FG97	3FT deg	M g	12-16	4M+2D	M go	Ind	Ind	Ind		
Environmental Policy and Computing	FG95	3FT deg	M g	12-16	4M+2D	M go	Ind	Ind	Ind		
Environmental Policy and Economics	FL91	3FT deg	Ec/Bu g	12-16	4M+2D	M go	Ind	Ind	Ind		
Environmental Policy and English Studies	FQ93	3FT deg	E g	14-18	X	M go	Ind	Ind	Ind		
European Studies and Environmental Policy	FT92	3FT deg	* g	14-18	2M+4D	M go	Ind	Ind	Ind		
Food Policy and Environmental Policy	DF49	3FT deg	S g	14-18	4M+2D	M go	Ind	Ind	Ind		
History and Environmental Policy	FV91	3FT deg	H g	12-16	4M+2D	M go	Ind	Ind	Ind		
Housing and Environmental Policy	FK9K	3FT deg	* g	14-18	2M+4D	M go	Ind	Ind	Ind		
Human Biology and Environmental Policy	FB91	3FT deg	S g	12-16	4M+2D	M go	Ind	Ind	Ind		
Human Resource Management & Environmental Policy	FN96	3FT deg	* g	14-18	2M+4D	M go	Ind	Ind	Ind		
Management and Environmental Policy	FN91	3FT deg	* g	14-18	2M+4D	M go	Ind	Ind	Ind		
Marketing and Environmental Policy	FN95	3FT deg	* g	14-18	2M+4D	M go	Ind	Ind	Ind		
Nutrition and Environmental Policy	FB94	3FT deg	S g	14-18	2M+4D	M go	Ind	Ind	Ind		
Planning and Environmental Policy	FK94	3FT deg	* g	14-18	2M+4D	M go	Ind	Ind	Ind		
Social Policy and Environmental Policy	FL9K	3FT deg	* g	14-18	2M+4D	M go	Ind	Ind	Ind		
Sociology and Environmental Policy	FL93	3FT deg	* g	14-18	2M+4D	M go	Ind	Ind	Ind		
Sports Science and Environmental Policy	BF69	3FT deg	S g	14-18	4M+2D	M go	Ind	Ind	Ind		
Tourism and Environmental Policy	FP97	3FT deg	L g	14-18	4M+2D	M go	Ind	Ind	Ind		
Urban Studies and Environmental Policy	FK9L	3FT deg	* g	14-18	2M+4D	M go	Ind	Ind	Ind		
World Theatre and Environmental Policy	FW94	3FT deg	* g	14-18	2M+4D	M go	Ind	Ind	Ind		

ST HELENS COLL

Environmental Technology	003K	2FT HND	B/C/P/En/Gy	2	3M	M$	Ind	Ind	Ind		

ST MARY'S Univ COLL

Environmental Investigation St and Classical St	QF19	3FT deg	S/2S	4-8	Ind	Ind	Ind	BBBB	Ind		
Environmental Investigation St and Education St	FX9X	3FT deg	S/2S	4-8	Ind	Ind	Ind	BBBB	Ind		
Environmental Investigation Studies and Drama	FW94	3FT deg	S/2S	8-12	Ind	Ind	Ind	BBBB	Ind		
Environmental Science	F900	3FT/4SW deg	S/2S g	4-8	Ind	Ind	Ind	BBBB$	Ind		
Environmental Studies and Biology	CF1X	3FT deg	B/C	4-8	Ind	Ind	Ind	BBBB	Ind		
Environmental Studies and Classical Studies	QF1X	3FT deg	*	4-8	Ind	Ind	Ind	BBBB	Ind		

Environmental Studies, Technology and Oceanography   27

course details			98 expected requirements							96 entry stats
TITLE	CODE	COURSE	SUBJECTS	A/AS	NO/C	AGNVQ	IB	SQA(H)	SQA	RATIO A/AS
Environmental Studies and Drama	FWX4	3FT deg	*	8-12	Ind	Ind	Ind	BBBB	Ind	
Environmental Studies and Education Studies	FXXX	3FT deg	*	4-8	Ind	Ind	Ind	BBBB	Ind	
Geography and Environmental Investigation St	FF98	3FT deg	S/2S+Gy	4-8	Ind	Ind	Ind	BBBB	Ind	
Geography and Environmental Studies	FFX8	3FT deg	Gy	4-8	Ind	Ind	Ind	BBBB	Ind	
Heritage Management and Environ Investigation St	FN99	3FT deg	S/2S	4-8	Ind	Ind	Ind	BBBB$	Ind	
Heritage Management and Environmental Studies	FNX9	3FT deg	*	4-8	Ind	Ind	Ind	BBBB	Ind	
History and Environmental Investigation Studies	FV91	3FT deg	S/2S+H	4-8	Ind	Ind	Ind	BBBB	Ind	
History and Environmental Studies	FVX1	3FT deg	H	4-8	Ind	Ind	Ind	BBBB	Ind	
Management Studies and Environ Investigation St	FN91	3FT deg	S/2S g	4-8	Ind	Ind	Ind	BBBB$	Ind	
Management Studies and Environmental Studies	FNX1	3FT deg	* g	4-8	Ind	Ind	Ind	BBBB	Ind	
Media Arts and Environmental Investigation St	FP94	3FT deg	S/2S	4-8	Ind	Ind	Ind	BBBB$	Ind	
Media Arts and Environmental Studies	FPX4	3FT deg	*	4-8	Ind	Ind	Ind	BBBB	Ind	
Sociology and Environmental Investigation St	FL93	3FT deg	S/2S	4-8	Ind	Ind	Ind	BBBB	Ind	
Sociology and Environmental Studies	FLX3	3FT deg	*	4-8	Ind	Ind	Ind	BBBB	Ind	
Sport Rehabilitation and Environ Investig St	BF99	3FT deg	B g	10-14	X	X	Ind	BBBB$	X	
Sport Rehabilitation and Environmental Studies	BF9X	3FT deg	B g	10-14	X	X	Ind	BBBB$	X	
Sport Science and Environmental Investigation St	BF69	3FT deg	S/2S g	8-12	Ind	Ind	Ind	BBBB	Ind	
Sport Science and Environmental Studies	BF6X	3FT deg	S g	8-12	Ind	Ind	Ind	BBBB	Ind	
Theology and Religious St & Environ Investig St	FV98	3FT deg	S/2S	4-8	Ind	Ind	Ind	BBBB	Ind	
Theology and Religious Studies and Environ St	FVX8	3FT deg	S/2S	4-8	Ind	Ind	Ind	BBBB	Ind	

STAFFORDSHIRE Univ

TITLE	CODE	COURSE	SUBJECTS	A/AS	NO/C	AGNVQ	IB	SQA(H)	SQA	RATIO A/AS
Environmental Engineering	F900	3FT deg	M+P g	10	3M	M	Ind	Ind		
Environmental Engineering	F908	4EXT deg	g	4	P $	P$	Ind	Ind	Ind	
Environmental Science	F901	3FT deg	B/C/En/Gy	12	4M	M	24	BCC	Ind	7 8/16
Environmental Science and Biology	CF19	3FT deg	S g	8	3M	M	24	BCC	Ind	5
Environmental Science and Chemistry	FF19	3FT deg	S	8	3M	M	24	BCC	Ind	4
Environmental Studies	F902	3FT deg	*	14	4M+1D	M	Ind	BBB	Ind	
Environmental Studies/Applied Statistics	FG94	3FT deg	*	DD-CC	4M	M	Ind	BBB	Ind	
Environmental Studies/Cultural Studies	FL96	3FT deg	* g	CC	MO+2D	M	Ind	BBB	Ind	
Environmental Studies/Development Studies	FM9Y	3FT deg	* g	14	4M+1D	M	Ind	BBB	Ind	5
Environmental Studies/Economic Studies	FL91	3FT deg								
Environmental Technology	F919	4EXT deg	g	EE	P $	P$	Ind	Ind	Ind	
Environmental Technology	FJ99	3FT deg	g	8	3M $	M$	Ind	Ind	Ind	
Environmental Transportation Studies	FN99	4EXT deg	g	EE	P $	P$	Ind	Ind	Ind	
Extended Environmental Science (4 yr)	F907	4EXT deg	g	4	1M	M	24	CCC	Ind	1
Foundation Environmental Science	F909▼	4EXT deg	*	4	N	P	24	CCC	Ind	1
French/Environmental Studies	RF19	3FT/4SW deg	F g	14	4M+2D	M^	26	ABB	Ind	2
Geography/Environmental Studies	FL98	3FT deg								
German/Environmental Studies	RF29	3FT/4SW deg	G g	14	4M+2D	M^	26	ABB	Ind	
History/Environmental Studies	VF19	3FT deg	H g	CC	MO+2D	M	27	BBB	Ind	2
Information Systems/Environmental Studies	GF59	3FT deg	g	12	Ind	M	24	BBC	Ind	1
Law/Environmental Studies	MF39	3FT deg	g	16	HN	M^	26	BBBB	Ind	
Legal Studies/Environmental Studies	MF3X	3FT deg	g	16	HN	M^	26	BBBB	Ind	
Literature/Environmental Studies	QF39	3FT deg	El g	CC	MO+2D	M	27	BBB	Ind	2
Occupational Health and Environmental Technology	BF99	4EXT deg	g	EE	P $	P$	Ind	Ind	Ind	
Politics/Environmental Studies	MFC9	3FT deg	g	14	4M+1D	M	26	BBB	Ind	
Pollution Science	F939	4EXT deg	g	4	1M	P	24	CCC		
Pollution Science	F931	3FT deg	B g	12	4M	M	24	BCC		
Property Development and the Environment	K300	3FT deg	g	12	4M	M$	24	BBC	Ind	
Psychology/Environmental Studies	LF79	3FT deg	*	18	3M+3D	D	Ind	BBB	Ind	
Sociology/Environmental Studies	LF39	3FT deg	*	12-14	4M+1D	M	Ind	BBB	Ind	5
Spanish/Environmental Studies	RF49	3FT/4SW deg	g	14	4M+2D	M^	26	ABB	Ind	

course details — 98 expected requirements — 96 entry stats

TITLE	CODE	COURSE	SUBJECTS	A/AS	ND/C	AGNVQ	IB	SQA(H)	SQA	RATIO A/AS
Women's Studies/Environmental Studies	MF99	3FT deg	g	CC	3M+1D	M	24	BBB	Ind	
Environmental Science	109F	2FT HND	B/C g	2	N	P	24	CCC	Ind	3

Univ of STIRLING

TITLE	CODE	COURSE	SUBJECTS	A/AS	ND/C	AGNVQ	IB	SQA(H)	SQA	RATIO A/AS
Economics/Environmental Science	FL91	4FT deg	S g	CCC	Ind	Ind	31	BBBC	HN	
Environmental Analysis	FF19	4FT deg	S g	CCC	HN	Ind	31	BBBC	HN	
Environmental Science	F900	4FT deg	S g	CCC	Ind	Ind	31	BBBC	HN	
Environmental Science/Biology	CF19	4FT deg	S g	CCC	Ind	Ind	31	BBBC	HN	
Environmental Science/Computing Science	FG95	4FT deg	S g	CCC	Ind	Ind	31	BBBC	HN	
Environmental Science/Management Science	FN91	4FT deg	S g	CCC	Ind	Ind	31	BBBC	HN	
Mathematics and its Applications with Env Sci	G1F9	4FT deg	M+S g	CCC	Ind	Ind	28	BBCC	HN	

UNIVERSITY COLLEGE SUFFOLK

TITLE	CODE	COURSE	SUBJECTS	A/AS	ND/C	AGNVQ	IB	SQA(H)	SQA	RATIO A/AS
Applied Biological Science and Environmental St	CF19	3FT deg	S	EE	N $	PS	Ind	Ind	Ind	
Applied Biological Science with Environmental St	C1F9	3FT deg	S	EE	N $	PS	Ind	Ind	Ind	
Art & Design and Environmental Studies	FW9F	3FT deg	Pf	EE	N $	P$	Ind	Ind	Ind	
Behavioural Studies and Environmental Studies	FL97	3FT deg	S/Gy	DE	N $	P$	Ind	Ind	Ind	
Business Studies and Environmental Studies	FN91	3FT deg	S	EE	N $	P$	Ind	Ind	Ind	
Business Studies with Environmental Studies	N1F9	3FT deg	*	EE	N $	P$	Ind	Ind	Ind	
Cultural Studies and Environmental Studies	YF39	3FT deg	*	CE	N $	P$	Ind	Ind	Ind	
Early Childhood Studies and Environment Studies	XF99	3FT deg	*	DE	N $	P$	Ind	Ind	Ind	
Early Childhood Studies with Environmental Studs	X9FX	3FT deg	S	DD	N $	PS	Ind	Ind	Ind	
Environmental Studies	F900	3FT deg	S/Gy	EE	N $	P$	Ind	Ind	Ind	
Environmental Studies and Information Technology	FG95	3FT deg	S/Gy	EE	N $	P$	Ind	Ind	Ind	
Environmental Studies and Management	FN9C	3FT deg	S/Gy	EE	N $	P$	Ind	Ind	Ind	
Environmental Studies with Applied Biol Science	F9C1	3FT deg	S/Gy	EE	N $	P$	Ind	Ind	Ind	
Environmental Studies with Art & Design	F9W2	3FT deg	3/Gy	EE	N $	P$	Ind	Ind	Ind	
Environmental Studies with Business Studies	F9N1	3FT deg	S/Gy	EE	N $	P$	Ind	Ind	Ind	
Environmental Studies with Cultural Studies	F9Y3	3FT deg	S/Gy	EE	N $	P$	Ind	Ind	Ind	
Environmental Studies with Early Childhood Studs	F9XX	3FT deg	S/Gy	EE	N $	P$	Ind	Ind	Ind	
Environmental Studies with Education Studies	F9X9	3FT deg	S/Gy	EE	N $	P$	Ind	Ind	Ind	
Environmental Studies with Human Science	F9B1	3FT deg	S	EE	N $	P$	Ind	Ind	Ind	
Environmental Studies with Information Technol	F9GM	3FT deg	S	EE	N $	P$	Ind	Ind	Ind	
Environmental Studies with Leisure Studies	F9LH	3FT deg	S	EE	N $	P$	Ind	Ind	Ind	
Environmental Studies with Literary Studies	F9Q2	3FT deg	S/Gy	EE	N $	P$	Ind	Ind	Ind	
Environmental Studies with Management	F9NC	3FT deg	S/Gy	EE	N $	P$	Ind	Ind	Ind	
Environmental Studies with Media Studies	F9P4	3FT deg	S/Gy	EE	N $	P$	Ind	Ind	Ind	
Environmental Studies with Social Policy	F9L4	3FT deg	S	EE	N $	P$	Ind	Ind	Ind	
Environmental Studies with Tourism Studies	F9P7	3FT deg	S	EE	N $	P$	Ind	Ind	Ind	
Information Technology with Environmental Studs	G5F9	3FT deg	S/Gy	EE	N $	P$	Ind	Ind	Ind	
Literary Studies and Environmental Studies	QF29	3FT deg	E+S/Gy	CE	N $	P$	Ind	Ind	Ind	
Media Studies and Environmental Studies	FP94	3FT deg	S/Gy	CE	N $	P$	Ind	Ind	Ind	
Product Design & Manufacture & Environmental St	HF79	3FT deg	*	EE	N $	P$	Ind	Ind	Ind	
Product Design & Manufacture with Environ Studs	H7F9	3FT deg	*	EE	N $	P$	Ind	Ind	Ind	

Univ of SUNDERLAND

TITLE	CODE	COURSE	SUBJECTS	A/AS	ND/C	AGNVQ	IB	SQA(H)	SQA	RATIO	A/AS
Environmental Engineering (Foundation)	F919	3FT deg	*								
Environmental Production & Sustainability (Found)	F938	4EXT/5EXTSW deg	*		Ind	Ind	Ind	Ind	Ind	4	
Environmental Production and Sustainability	F930	3FT/4SW deg	* g	8	3M $	M$	24	CCCC	N$	4	6/11
Environmental Studies	F900	3FT/4SW deg	* g	8	3M $	M$	24	CCCC	N$	4	6/14
Environmental Studies (Foundation)	F918▼	4EXT/5EXTSW deg	*		Ind	Ind	Ind	Ind	Ind	1	
Environmental Technologies	F911	3FT deg	S g	8	3M $	M$	26$	CCCC	N$	3	6/14
Environmental Management	019F▼	2FT HND	S g	2	N $	P$	24$	CC$	N$	2	2/12
Environmental Management (Foundation)	819F▼	3EXT HND	*		Ind	Ind	Ind	Ind	Ind	1	

Environmental Studies, Technology and Oceanography 27

TITLE	CODE	COURSE	SUBJECTS	A/AS	ND/C	AGNVQ	IB	SQA(H)	SQA	RATIO A/AS
Univ of SUSSEX										
Environmental Science	F900	3FT deg	2(C/P/M) g	CCC	MO $	MS go	$	Ind	Ind	
Environmental Science with Development Studies	F9M9	3FT deg	2(C/P/M) g	CCC	MO $	MS go	$	Ind	Ind	
Environmental Science with Euro Studies (French)	F9R1	4FT deg	2(C/P/M) g	CCC	MO $	MS go	$	Ind	Ind	
Environmental Science with Euro Studies (German)	F9R2	4FT deg	2(C/P/M) g	CCC	MO $	MS go	$	Ind	Ind	
Environmental Science with Euro Studs (Spanish)	F9R4	4FT deg	2(C/P/M) g	CCC	MO $	MS go	$	Ind	Ind	
Environmental Science with Management Studies	F9N1	3FT deg	2(C/P/M) g	CCC	MO $	MS go	$	Ind	Ind	
Environmental Science with North American St	F9Q4	4FT deg	2(C/P/M) g	BCC	MO $	MS go	$	Ind	Ind	
Geography and Env St in African & Asian Studies	LF8X	3FT deg	*	BBC	MO	M*6	$	Ind	Ind	
Geography and Env St in Cult & Community St	LF8Y	3FT deg	*	BBC	MO	M*6	$	Ind	Ind	
Geography and Env Studies with Development St	LF89	3FT deg	*	BBC	MO	M*6	$	Ind	Ind	
Geography and Environmental Science	FF89	3FT deg	2(C/P/Ph) g	CCC	MO $	MS go	$	Ind	Ind	
Geography and Environmental St in European Studs	LFV9	4FT deg	* g	BBC	MO $	M*6 go	$	Ind	Ind	
Geography and Environmental St in Social Science	LFWY	3FT deg	*	BBC	MO	M*6	$	Ind	Ind	
Mathematics and Stats with Environ Sc(MMath)	G4FX	4FT deg	M	BCC	MO $	MS^	$	Ind	Ind	
Mathematics and Stats with Environmental Sci	G4F9	3FT deg	M	BCC	MO $	MS^	$	Ind	Ind	
Mathematics with Environmental Science	G1F9	3FT deg	M	BCC	MO $	MS^	$	Ind	Ind	
Mathematics with Environmental Science (MMath)	G1FX	4FT deg	M	BCC	MO $	MS^	$	Ind	Ind	
Physics with Environmental Science	F3F9	3FT deg	M+P+C	CCC	MO $	MS^	$	Ind	Ind	
Physics with Environmental Science (MPhys)	F3FX	4FT deg	M+P+C	CCC	MO $	MS^	$	Ind	Ind	
Univ of TEESSIDE										
Applied Science and Consumer Law	F9M3	3FT deg	* g	8-12	4M	M	Ind	CCC	Ind	1 8/12
Applied Science and Forensic Measurement	F9B9	3FT/4SW deg	M/S	12	4M	M	Ind	CCCC	Ind	3 6/20
THAMES VALLEY Univ										
Envir Policy & Mgt with Politics & Int Relations	F9M1	3FT deg		8-12	MO	M	26	CCC		
Environmental Policy & Mgt with English Lang St	F9Q1	3FT deg		8-12	MO	M	26	CCC		
Environmental Policy and Management with French	F9R1	3FT deg		8-12	MO	M	26	CCC		
Environmental Policy and Management with German	F9R2	3FT deg		8-12	MO	M	26	CCC		
Environmental Policy and Management with History	F9V1	3FT deg		8-12	MO	M	26	CCC		
Environmental Policy and Management with Law	F9M3	3FT deg		8-12	MO	M	26	CCC		
Environmental Policy and Management with Spanish	F9R4	3FT deg		8-12	MO	M	26	CCC		
Environmental Policy and Management with Tourism	F9P7	3FT deg		8-12	MO	M	26	CCC		
Environmental Policy and Mgt with Business	F9N1	3FT deg		8-12	MO	M	26	CCC		
Environmental Policy and Mgt with Business Econ	F9LC	3FT deg		8-12	MO	M	26	CCC		
Environmental Policy and Mgt with Economics	F9L1	3FT deg		8-12	MO	M	26	CCC		
Environmental Policy and Mgt with European St	F9T2	3FT deg		8-12	MO	M	26	CCC		
Environmental Policy and Mgt with Int Studies	F9MX	3FT deg		8-12	MO	M	26	CCC		
Environmental Policy and Mgt with Marketing	F9N5	3FT deg		8-12	MO	M	26	CCC		
Environmental Policy and Mgt with Recreation Mgt	F9N7	3FT deg		8-12	MO	M	26	CCC		
Environmental Policy and Mgt with Sociology	F9L3	3FT deg		8-12	MO	M	26	CCC		
European Studies with Environmental Policy & Mgt	T2F9	3FT deg		8-12	MO	M	26	CCC		
Health Studies with Environmental Policy and Mgt	L4F9	3FT deg		8-12	MO	M	26	CCC		
International St with Environmental Policy & Mgt	M9F9	3FT deg		8-12	MO	M	26	CCC		
Politics & Int Rels with Environ Policy & Mgt	M1F9	3FT deg		8-12	MO	M	26	CCC		
Sociology with Environmental Policy and Mgt	L3F9	3FT deg		8-12	MO	M	26	CCC		
Tourism with Environmental Policy and Management	P7F9	3FT deg		8-12	MO	M	26	CCC		
TRINITY COLL Carmarthen										
Rural Environment	DF29	3FT deg	S/Gy g	DD-CC	Ind		Ind	Ind	Ind	2 4/12

course details | 98 expected requirements | 96 entry stats

TITLE	CODE	COURSE	98 expected requirements							96 entry stats	
			SUBJECTS	A/AS	NO/C	AGNVQ	IB	SQA(H)	SQA	RATIO	A/AS
Univ of ULSTER											
Environmental Science (3 Yr)	F902▼	3FT deg	2S	CCD	MO+2D	MS6/△ gi	27	BBCC	Ind	10	12/14
Environmental Science Hons (3 Yr)	F900▼	3FT deg	2S	BCC	MO+4D	DS6/△ gi	30	BBBB	Ind	14	18/26
Environmental Science Hons (4 Yr SW inc DAS)	F901▼	4SW deg	2S g	BCC	MO+4D	DS6/△ gi	30	BBBB	Ind	27	
Univ of WESTMINSTER											
Environmental Science and Business Management	FN91	3FT deg	B	CD	3M	M	26$		Ind	5	6/12
WIGAN and LEIGH COLL											
Applied Environmental Science	019F▼	2FT HND									
Environmental Science	009F▼	2FT HND									
Univ of WOLVERHAMPTON											
Environmental Management	F910	3FT/4SW deg		DD	N	M	24	CCCC	Ind		
Environmental Science	F900	3FT/4SW deg	S g	DD	N	M	24	CCCC	Ind	3	7/16
Environmental Technology	K3F9	3FT/4SW deg	S/M g	DD	N	M	24	CCCC	Ind	2	
Applied Sciences Earth Science	Y100	3FT/4SW deg	S g	DD	N	M	24	CCCC	Ind		
Applied Sciences Environmental Animal Biology	Y100	3FT/4SW deg		DD	N	M	24	CCCC	Ind		
Applied Sciences Environmental Management	Y100	3FT/4SW deg	g	DD	N	M	24	CCCC	Ind		
Applied Sciences Environmental Science	Y100	3FT/4SW deg	S g	DD	N	M	24	CCCC	Ind		
Applied Sciences (4 Yrs) Environmental Animal Biology	Y110	4FT deg	*								
Applied Sciences (4 Yrs) Environmental Science	Y110▼	4FT deg	*								
Applied Sciences (4 yrs) Earth Science	Y110	4FT deg	*								
Applied Sciences (4 yrs) Environmental Management	Y110	4FT deg	*								
Combined Degrees Earth Science	Y401	3FT/4SW deg	S g	DD	N	M	24	CCCC	Ind		
Combined Degrees Environmental Animal Biology	Y401	3FT/4SW deg		DD	N	M	24	CCCC	Ind		
Combined Degrees Environmental Management	Y401	3FT deg	g	DD	N	M	24	CCCC	Ind		
Combined Degrees Environmental Science	Y401	3FT/4SW deg	S g	DD	N	M	24	CCCC	Ind		
Environmental Science	009F	2FT HND	g	D	N	P	24	CCCC	Ind	2	2/6
WORCESTER COLL of HE											
Environmental Science	F900	3FT deg		EE	N	P	Ind	Ind	Ind	10	
Environmental Science/Biological Science	CF19	3FT deg	S	EE	N	P	Ind	Ind	Ind	1	
Environmental Science/Business Management	NF19	3FT deg		DD	Ind	M	Ind	Ind	Ind	3	
Environmental Science/Drama	WF49	3FT deg		DD	Ind	M	Ind	Ind	Ind		
Environmental Science/Education Studies	XF99	3FT deg		DD	Ind	M	Ind	Ind	Ind		
Environmental Science/English and Literary St	QF39	3FT deg	E	CC	Ind	M	Ind	Ind	Ind	2	
Geography/Environmental Science	FL98	3FT deg		EE	N	P	Ind	Ind	Ind	2	6/12
Health Studies/Environmental Science	FB99	3FT deg	g	DD	Ind	M	Ind	Ind	Ind	3	
History/Environmental Science	FV91	3FT deg		DD	Ind	M	Ind	Ind	Ind		
Information Technology/Environmental Science	FG95	3FT deg		DD	Ind	M	Ind	Ind	Ind		
Psychology/Environmental Science	FL97	3FT deg	g	CC	Ind	M	Ind	Ind	Ind		
Sociology/Environmental Science	FL93	3FT deg		DD	Ind	M	Ind	Ind	Ind		
Women's Studies/Environmental Science	FM99	3FT deg		DD	Ind	M	Ind	Ind	Ind		
Environmental Management	019F▼	2FT HND		E	N	Ind	Ind	Ind	Ind		4/16

Environmental Studies, Technology and Oceanography   27

course details			**98 expected requirements**							**96 entry stats**	
TITLE	CODE	COURSE	SUBJECTS	A/AS	ND/C	RGNVQ	IB	SQA(H)	SQA	RATIO	A/AS
WRITTLE COLL											
Landscape and Garden Design	K300	3FT deg	Ap g	12	MO	M	Ind	Ind	Ind	5	9/18
Urban Landscape Management	K320	3FT deg	Ap g	12	MO	M	Ind	Ind	Ind		
Horticulture (Landscape Construction)	103K	2FT/3SW HND	Ap g	4	N	M	Ind	Ind	Ind	4	
Landscape and Garden Design	003K	2FT HND	Ap g	4	N	M	Ind	Ind	Ind		
Urban Landscape Management	023K	2FT/3SW HND	Ap g	16	N	M	Ind	Ind	Ind		
WYE COLL (Univ of London)											
Business and the Environment	N1F9	4FT deg									
Environmental Science	F910	3FT deg	B/C	14	2M+1D$	Ind		25$	BBCCC$	Ind	
Rural Environment Studies	F900	3FT deg	Gy+B/Ec	16	2M+1D$	Ind		25$	BBBCC$	Ind	
Univ of YORK											
Environmental Biology and Env Management	CC91	3FT deg	B+S/M/Ec g	BBC	Ind	DS^		28$	BBBB$	Ind	20/30

TITLE	CODE	COURSE	SUBJECTS	A/AS	ND/C	AGNVQ	IB	SQA(H)	SQA	RATIO A/AS
Univ of ABERDEEN										
European Languages	T201	4FT deg	* g	BBC	Ind	M$ go	30$	BBBB$	Ind	9
European Management Studies	N1T2	4FT deg	L g	BBC	Ind	M$^ go	30$	BBBB$	Ind	7
European Studies	T200	4FT deg	L g	BBC	Ind	M$^ go	30$	BBBB$	Ind	5
Univ of ABERTAY DUNDEE										
Applied Chemistry with a European Language	F1T2	4FT/5SW deg	C	DD	Ind	Ind	Ind	BCC	Ind	
Business Engineering with French/German/Spanish	H1T2	4FT/5SW deg		CD	Ind	Ind	Ind	BBCC	Ind	
Electronic Engineering with French/Ger/Spanish	H6T2	4FT/5SW deg		CD	Ind	Ind	Ind	BBCC	Ind	
Mechanical Engineering with French/Ger/Spanish	H3T2	4FT/5SW deg		CD	Ind	Ind	Ind	BBCC	Ind	
Product Design Engineering with French/German/Sp	H7T2	4FT/5SW deg		CD	Ind	Ind	Ind	BBCC	Ind	
Univ of Wales, ABERYSTWYTH										
Accounting and Finance with a European Language	N4T9	4FT deg	L g	18	3M+3D$ M^ g		29$	BBBCC$	Ind	
Business Studies with a Modern Language	N1T9	4FT deg	L g	18	3M+3D$ M^ g		29$	BBBCC$	Ind	
European Languages	T200	4FT deg	2L g	18	1M+5D$ M^ g		29$	BBBCC$	Ind	
European Studies and French	RT1F	4FT deg	F g	20	1M+5D$ M^ g		30$	BBBBC$	Ind	
European Studies and German	RT2F	4FT deg	G g	20	1M+5D$ M^ g		30$	BBBBC$	Ind	
European Studies and Italian	RT3F	4FT deg	L g	20	1M+5D$ M^ g		30$	BBBBC$	Ind	
European Studies and Spanish	RT4F	4FT deg	L g	20	1M+5D$ M^ g		30$	BBBBC$	Ind	
French/European Studies	RT12	4FT deg	F g	20	1M+5D$ M^ g		30$	BBBBC$	Ind	
German/European Studies	RT22	4FT deg	G g	20	1M+5D$ M^ g		30$	BBBBC$	Ind	
Italian/European Studies	RT32	4FT deg	L g	20	1M+5D$ M^ g		30$	BBBBC$	Ind	
Modern Languages with Business Studies	T9N1	4FT deg	L g	18	1M+5D$ M^ g		29$	BBBCC$	Ind	
Spanish/European Studies	RT42	4FT deg	L g	20	1M+5D$ M^ g		30$	BBBBC$	Ind	
ASTON Univ										
Chemical Engineering with Euro St (MEng)	H8T2	4FT/5SW deg	C+M g	24	2M+8D$ D$6/^ go		33$	AABBB$	Ind	11
Civil Engineering with Euro St (MEng)	H2T2	4FT/5SW deg	M g	18	7M+3D$ D$6/^ go		29$	BBBBB$	Ind	8
Computing Science with European St (MEng)	G5T2	4FT deg	* g	22	3M+7D D$6/^ go		32	ABBBB	Ind	
Electromechanical Eng with European St (MEng)	H6T2	4FT/5SW deg	M g	22	Ind $ D$6/^ go		31$	ABBBB$	Ind	
European Studies with French	T2R1	4SW deg	F g	BBC	3M+7D$ D$6/^ go		32$	AABBC$	Ind	3	14/26
European Studies with French and German	T200	4SW deg	F+G g	BBC	3M+7D$ D$6/^ go		32$	AABBC$	Ind	5	16/26
European Studies with German	T2R2	4SW deg	G g	BBC	5M+5D$ D$6/^ go		31$	ABBBC$	Ind	2	14/22
European Studies/Biology	CT12	3FT/4SW deg	B g	18	X D$^ go		29	BBBBC	Ind	
European Studies/Biology (Year Zero)	CT1F	4FT/5SW deg								
European Studies/Business Administration	NT12	3FT/4SW deg	* g	20	5M+5D D6/^ go		30	BBBBB	Ind	
European Studies/Chemistry	FT12	3FT/4SW deg	C g	18	X D$^ go		29	BBBBC	Ind	
European Studies/Chemistry (Year Zero)	FT1F	4FT/5SWdeg								
European Studies/Computer Science	GT52	3FT/4SW deg	* g	18	5M+5D D$6/^ go		29	BBBBC	Ind	
European Studies/Computer Science (Year Zero)	GT5F	4FT/5SW deg								
European Studies/Engineering Management	HTR2	3FT/4SW deg	S g	18	5M+5D$ D$^ go		29$	BBBBC		
Health & Safety Management/European Studies	JT92	3FT/4SW deg	* g	18	5M+5D D$6/^ go		29	BBBBC	Ind	
Health & Safety Mgt/European Studies (Year Zero)	JT9F	4FT/5SW deg								
International Business, French and German	NT1F	4SW deg	F+G g	BBB	3M+7D$ D$^ go		31$	AABBB$	Ind	
Mechanical Eng with European Studies (MEng)	H3T2	4FT/5SW deg	M g	22	Ind $ D$6/^ go		31$	ABBBB$	Ind	12
Modern Languages	T900	4SW deg	F/G g	BBC	3M+7D$ DB6/^ go		32$	AABBC$	Ind	14
Product Design (Engineering)/European Studies	HT72	3FT/4SW deg	S g	18	5M+5D$ D$^ go		29$	BBBBC		
Public Policy & Management/European Studies	MT12	3FT/4SW deg	* g	20	5M+5D D$6/^ go		30	BBBBB	Ind	
Social Studies/European Studies	LT42	3FT/4SWdeg	* g	18	5M+5D D$6/^ go		29	BBBBC	Ind	
Univ of Wales, BANGOR										
Biology with European Dimension	C1T2	4FT deg	B+F+S g	CDD	X DS^ go		28$	BBCC$	X	
European Cultural Studies and French	TR21	4FT deg	F g	CCD	X D*^ go		28$	BBBC$	X	
European Cultural Studies and French(Syllabus B)	TR2C	3FT deg	F g	CCD	X D*^ go		28$	BBBC$	X	

| | | | 98 expected requirements | | | | | | | 96 entry stats |
| | | | | | | | | | | |

TITLE	CODE	COURSE	SUBJECTS	A/AS	NO/C	AGNVQ	IB	SQA(H)	SQA	RATIO A/AS
European Cultural Studies and German	TR22	4FT deg	* g	CCD	5M	D*6/^ go	28	BBBC	Ind	
European Cultural Studies and Russian	TR28	4FT deg	* g	CCD	5M	D*6/^ go	28	BBBC	Ind	
French and German with Italian	T201	4FT deg	F g	BBC	X	D$^ go	30$	AABB$	X	
French and German with Russian	T200	4FT deg	F g	BBC	X	D$^ go	30$	AABB$	X	
French and Russian with German	T210	4FT deg	F g	BBC	X	D*^ go	30$	AABB$	X	
French and Russian with Italian	T211	4FT deg	F g	BBC	X	D*^ go	30$	AABB$	X	
German and Russian with French	T220	4FT deg	F/G g	BBC	X	D$^ go	30$	AABB$	X	
German and Russian with Italian	T221	4FT deg	G g	BBC	X	D$^ go	30$	AABB$		
Modern Languages/Accounting	NT49	4FT deg	F/G g	18	X	D$^ go	28$	BBBC$	X	
Modern Languages/Banking and Insurance	NT39	4FT deg	F/G g	18	X	D$^ go	28$	BBBC$	X	
Modern Languages/Economics	LT19	4FT deg	F/G g	18	X	D$^ go	28$	BBBC$	X	

BATH COLL of HE

| Combined Awards *Cultural Studies* | Y400 | 3FT deg | * | | N | | Ind | $ | $ | |
| Modular Programme (DipHE) *Cultural Studies* | Y460 | 2FT Dip | * | | N | | Ind | $ | $ | |

Univ of BIRMINGHAM

Ancient Hist & Archaeology/Modern Greek Studies	TV26	4FT deg	* g	BBB	Ind	D*^	32	ABBB	Ind	
Artificial Intelligence/Modern Greek Studies	GT82	4FT deg	* g	BBB	Ind	D*^	32	ABBB	Ind	
Classical Literature & Civilisation/Mod Greek St	QT82	4FT deg	* g	BBB	Ind	D*^	32	ABBB	Ind	
Computer Studies/Modern Greek Studies	GT52	4FT deg	* g	BBB	Ind	D*^	32	ABBB	Ind	
Dance/Modern Greek Studies	WT42	4FT deg	* g	BBB	Ind	D*^	32	ABBB	Ind	
Drama/Modern Greek Studies	TW24	4FT deg	* g	BBB	Ind	D*^	32	ABBB	Ind	
East Mediterranean History/Modern Greek Studies	TV21	4FT deg	g	BBB	Ind	D*^	32$	ABBB	Ind	
English/Modern Greek Studies	QTH2	4FT deg	* g	BBB	Ind	D*^	32	ABBB	Ind	
French Studies and Modern Greek Studies	RTC2	4FT deg	F g	BBB	Ind	D*^	32$	ABBB	Ind	3
German Studies and Modern Greek Studies	RTG2	4FT deg	G g	BBB	Ind	D*^	32$	ABBB	Ind	3
Hispanic Studies amd Modern Greek Studies	RTK2	4FT deg	* g	BBB	Ind	D*^	32	ABBB	Ind	
History of Art/Modern Greek Studies	TV24	4FT deg	* g	BBB	Ind	D*^	32	ABBB	Ind	
History/Modern Greek Studies	TVF1	4FT deg	* g	BBB	Ind	D*^	32	ABBB	Ind	
Italian and Modern Greek Studies	RTH2	4FT deg	* g	BBB	Ind	D*^	32	ABBB	Ind	
Latin/Modern Greek Studies	QT62	4FT deg	Ln g	BBB	Ind	D*^	32$	ABBB	Ind	
Mathematics/Modern Greek Studies	GT12	4FT deg	M g	ABB-ABC	Ind	D*^	32$	ABBB	Ind	
Media & Cultural Studies/Modern Greek Studies	PT42	4FT deg	* g	BBB	Ind	D*^	32	ABBB	Ind	
Modern Greek Studies	T240	4FT deg	L	BBB-BBC	Ind	D*^	32	ABBB	Ind	2
Modern Greek Studies and Portuguese	RT52	4FT deg	* g	BBB	Ind	D*^	32	ABBB	Ind	
Modern Greek Studies and Russian	RT82	4FT deg	* g	BBB	Ind	D*^	32	ABBB	Ind	
Modern Greek Studies/Music	TW23	4FT deg	Mu g	AAB-ABB	Ind	D*^	32$	ABBB	Ind	
Modern Greek Studies/Philosophy	TV27	4FT deg	* g	BBB	Ind	D*^	32	ABBB	Ind	
Modern Greek Studies/Political Science	MT12	4FT deg	* g	BBB	Ind	D*^	32	ABBB	Ind	
Modern Greek Studies/Sport & Recreation Studies	TB26	4FT deg	* g	BBB	Ind	D*^	32	ABBB	Ind	
Modern Greek Studies/Theology	TV28	4FT deg	* g	BBB	Ind	D*^	32	ABBB	Ind	

BOLTON INST

Art & Design History & European Cultural Studies	TV24	3FT deg	* g	CD	MO	M*	24	BBCC	Ind	
Biology and European Cultural Studies	TC21	3FT deg	* g	CD	MO	M*	24	BBCC	Ind	
Business Economics and European Cultural Studies	LT12	3FT deg	* g	CD	MO	M*	24	BBCC	Ind	
Business Info Systems and European Cultural St	GT52	3FT deg	* g	CD	MO	M*	24	BBCC	Ind	
Business Studies and European Cultural Studies	TN21	3FT deg	* g	CD	MO	M*	24	BBCC	Ind	
Community Studies and European Cultural Studies	LT52	3FT deg	* g	CD	MO	M*	24	BBCC	Ind	
Creative Writing and European Cultural Studies	WT92	3FT deg	* g	CD	MO	M*	24	BBCC	Ind	
Design and European Cultural Studies	TW22	3FT deg	* g	CD	MO	M*	24	BBCC	Ind	
European Cult St & Gender & Women's Studies	TM29	3FT deg	* g	CD	MO	M*	24	BBCC	Ind	

TITLE	CODE	COURSE	SUBJECTS	A/AS	NO/C	AGNVQ	IB	SQA(H)	SQA	RATIO A/AS
			98 expected requirements							*96 entry stats*
European Cult St & Urban & Cultural Studies	TL23	3FT deg	* g	CD	MO	M*	24	BBCC	Ind	
European Cultural & Social Studies and Sociology	LT32	3FT deg	* g	CD	MO	M	24	Ind	Ind	
European Cultural St & Organisations, Mgt & Work	NT72	3FT deg	* g	CD	MO	M*	24	BBCC	Ind	
European Cultural St and Peace & War Studies	TV2C	3FT deg	* g	CD	MO	M*	24	BBCC	Ind	
European Cultural Studies and Film & TV Studies	TW25	3FT deg	Me/T g	CD	Ind	Ind	24	BBCC	Ind	
European Cultural Studies and French	TR21	3FT deg	F g	CD	Ind	Ind	24	BBCC	Ind	
European Cultural Studies and French	RT12	3FT deg	F g	CD	Ind	Ind	24	BBCC	Ind	
European Cultural Studies and German	TR22	3FT deg	G g	CD	Ind	Ind	24	BBCC	Ind	
European Cultural Studies and History	TV21	3FT deg	* g	CD	MO	M*	24	BBCC	Ind	
European Cultural Studies and Human Resource Mgt	NT12	3FT deg	* g	CD	MO	M*	24	BBCC	Ind	
European Cultural Studies and Law	TM23	3FT deg	* g	CD	MO	M*	24	BBCC	Ind	
European Cultural Studies and Literature	TQ22	3FT deg	* g	CD	MO	M*	24	BBCC	Ind	
European Cultural Studies and Marketing	NT52	3FT deg	* g	CD	MO	M*	24	BBCC	Ind	
European Cultural Studies and Mathematics	TG21	3FT deg	M g	DD	MO	M*	24	BBCC	Ind	
European Cultural Studies and Operations Mgt	NT22	3FT deg	* g	CD	MO	M*	24	BBCC	Ind	
European Cultural Studies and Philosophy	TV27	3FT deg	* g	CD	MO	M*	24	BBCC	Ind	
European Cultural Studies and Psychology	TL27	3FT deg	* g	12	MO	D*	24	BBCC	Ind	
European Cultural Studies and Theatre Studies	TW24	3FT deg	Me/T g	CD	Ind	Ind	24	BBCC	Ind	
European Cultural Studies and Tourism Studies	TP27	3FT deg	* g	CD	10-12M	M*	24	BBCC	Ind	
Visual Arts and European Cultural Studies	TW21	3FT deg	* g	CD	MO	M*	24	BBCC	Ind	

BOURNEMOUTH Univ

Business Studies with Languages	N1T9	4SW deg								10/18

Univ of BRADFORD

Euro Area St (Opts French/Engl/German/Spanish)	T202	3FT deg	* g	BBB-BCC	4M+3D	M$4	Ind	Ind	Ind	3 10/15
European Studies (Options French/Ger/Russ/Sp)	T200	4SW deg	F/G/Sp g	BBB-BCC	Ind	M$^	Ind	Ind	Ind	6 10/24
History with a Modern Language	TV21	4SW deg	L g	BBB-BCC	Ind	M$^	Ind	Ind	Ind	
Politics with a Modern Language	TM21	4SW deg	L g	BBB-BCC	Ind	M$^	Ind	Ind	Ind	

BRISTOL, Univ of the W of England

EFL and European Studies	QT32	4FT deg	g	14-24	5M	M*^ go	24$	BCCC$	Ind	
EFL, French and Business Systems	TN91	3FT deg	g	14-22	5M	M*^ go	24$	BCCC$	Ind	
EFL, German and Business Systems	TN9C	3FT deg	g	14-22	5M	M*^ go	24$	BCCC$	Ind	
EFL, Spanish and Business Systems	TN9D	3FT deg	g	14-22	5M	M*^ go	24$	BCCC$	Ind	
European Languages & Law, EFL and French	MTH9	4FT deg	g	16-24	6M	M*^ go	24$	BBCC$	Ind	
European Languages & Law, EFL and German	MTHX	4FT deg	g	16-24	6M	M*^ go	24$	BBCC$	Ind	
European Languages & Law, EFL and Spanish	MTHY	4FT deg	g	16-24	6M	M*^ go	24$	BBCC$	Ind	
European Languages & Law, French & German (LLB)	MT39	4FT deg	F/G g	16-24	6M	M*^ go	24$	BBCC$	Ind	
European Languages & Law, French & Spanish (LLB)	MT3X	4FT deg	F/Sp g	16-24	6M	M*^ go	24$	BBCC$	Ind	
European Languages & Law, German & Spanish (LLB)	MT3Y	4FT deg	G/Sp g	16-24	6M	M*^ go	24$	BBCC$	Ind	
French and European Studies	RT12	4FT deg	F g	14-24	5M	M*^ go	24$	BCCC$	Ind	
French, German and Business Systems	TNX1	3FT deg	F/G g	14-22	5M	M*^ go	24$	BCCC$	Ind	
French, Spanish and Business Systems	TNXC	3FT deg	F/Sp g	14-22	5M	M*^ go	24$	BCCC$	Ind	
German and European Studies	RT22	4FT deg	G g	14-24	5M	M*^ go	24$	BCCC$	Ind	
German, Spanish and Business Systems	TNXD	3FT deg	G/Sp g	14-22	5M	M*^ go	24$	BCCC$	Ind	
Information Systems, French and German	G5T9	3FT deg	F/G g	14-22	5M	M*^ go	24$	BCCC$	Ind	
Information Systems, French and Spanish	G5TX	3FT deg	F/Sp g	14-22	5M	M*^ go	24$	BCCC$	Ind	
Information Systems, German and Spanish	G5TY	3FT deg	G/Sp g	14-22	5M	M*^ go	24$	BCCC$	Ind	
Spanish and European Studies	RT42	4FT deg	Sp g	14-24	5M	M*^ go	24$	BCCC$	Ind	
Joint Honours Programme *Geography and Languages*	Y401	4FT deg	Gy/En+L g	14-16	5M $	M$ go	24$	BCCC$	Ind	
Joint Honours Programme *Marketing and Languages*	Y401	4FT deg	L g	14-16	5M $	M$ go	24$	BCCC$	Ind	

European Studies and Languages 28

	course details			98 expected requirements						96 entry stats
TITLE	CODE	COURSE	SUBJECTS	A/AS	NO/C	AGNVQ	IB	SQA(H)	SQA	RATIO A/AS
BUCKINGHAMSHIRE COLLEGE										
Business Administration and Languages	NT1F	3FT deg		8	MO	M	27	CCCC	Ind	
Business Administration with European Studies	N1T2	3FT deg		8	2D	M	27	CCCC	Ind	
Business Studies and Languages	NT1G	4SW deg	L g	8	MO	M	27	CCCC	Ind	
Business Studies with European Studies	N1TF	4SW deg		8	M)+2D	M	27	CCCC	Ind	
Human Resources Management and Languages	NT62	3FT deg		8	MO	M	27	CCCC	Ind	
Human Resources Management with European Studies	N6T2	3FT deg		8	MO	M	27	CCCC	Ind	
Marketing and Languages	NT52	3FT deg		8	MO	M	27	CCCC	Ind	
CAMBRIDGE Univ										
Modern and Medieval Languages	T900▼	4FT deg	L g	AAB	Ind		Ind	CSYS	Ind	3 28/30
CARDIFF Univ of Wales										
European Union Studies	T202	4FT deg	L	BBB-BCC	Ind		Ind	ABCD	Ind	5 20/30
Univ of CENTRAL ENGLAND										
European Business and Languages	NT12	3FT deg	* g	14	M+3D	M	22	CCCC	Ind	21 12/14
Univ of CENTRAL LANCASHIRE										
European Politics and Culture	MT12	3FT deg								
European Studies	M1T2	3FT deg	*	12	MO	M$6/^	24	CCC	Ind	
International Business	NT19	3FT deg	* g	14	MO+2D	M$6/^	26	BBCC	Ind	
Languages for International Business	T9N1	4SW deg	L	14	Ind	M$^	26$	BBCC$	Ind	
Languages with Tourism	T9P7	4SW deg	L	14	Ind	M$^	26$	BBCC$	Ind	
Law and Languages	MT32	4FT deg	F/G	CCD	Ind	M$6/^	28$	BBBB$	Ind	
Modern Languages	T900	3FT deg	L	14	Ind	M$^	26$	BBCC$	Ind	
Combined Honours Programme *European Studies*	Y400	3FT deg	*	12	M	M$6/^	26	BCCC	Ind	
Business with Languages	9T1N	2FT HND	* g	8	MO	M$	24	CCC	Ind	
COVENTRY Univ										
Biochemistry with Study in Europe	C7T9	4FT/5SW deg			Ind	Ind	Ind	Ind	Ind	
Biochemistry with Study in Europe	C7T2	4FT deg	C+B g	10	3M $	Ind	Ind	CCC$	HN$	5
Biological Sciences with Study in Europe	C1T9	4FT/5SW deg			Ind	Ind	Ind	Ind	Ind	
Biological Sciences with Study in Europe	C1T2	4FT deg	B g	10	3M $	Ind	Ind	CCC$	HN$	
Building Surveying with European Studies	K2TG	3FT/4SW deg	* g	14	5M	MC	Ind	Ind	Ind	
Civil Engineering Construction with European St	H2T2	4FT deg	M g	10	4M	MC	Ind	Ind	Ind	
Civil Engineering with European Studies	H2TF	5FT/6FT deg	M+S g	18	5M+1D$	MC	Ind	Ind	Ind	14
Computing with European Studies	GT59	5FT deg								
Computing with European Studies	G5T2	4FT deg	L g	12	Ind	M	Ind	CCCC	Ind	8
Construction Management with European Studies	K2T2	4FT deg	* g	14	5M	MC	Ind	Ind	Ind	
Engineering with Modern Languages	H1TY	3FT deg								
European Engineering Studies	H1TX	4FT/5FT deg	g	12-18	3M $	M+	24$	BBCC$	Ind	3
European Studies	T200	3FT deg	*	CD	M	M	Ind	CCCC	Ind	9 8/18
European Studies with French (4 years)	TR21	4FT deg	F	CD	M	M	Ind	CCCC	Ind	
European Studies with German (4 years)	TR22	4FT deg	*	CD	M	M	Ind	CCCC	Ind	
European Studies with Italian (4 years)	TR23	4FT deg	*	CD	M	M	Ind	CCCC	Ind	
European Studies with Russian (4 years)	TR28	4FT deg	*	CD	M	M	Ind	CCCC	Ind	
European Studies with Spanish (4 years)	TR24	4FT deg	*	CD	M	M	Ind	CCCC	Ind	
Geography with European Study	F8T2	3FT deg								
Law and International Studies	MT32	3FT deg	*	CCC	D	D	Ind	BBBB	Ind	7 8/18
Materials Technology with European Languages	J5T2	3FT deg	* g	12	Ind	Ind	Ind	Ind	Ind	
Materials Technology with European Languages	J5TF	3FT deg	* g	12	Ind	Ind	Ind	Ind	Ind	
Pharmaceutical Sciences with Study in Europe	B302	3FT deg	B g	10	3M	Ind	Ind	Ind	Ind	
Pharmaceutical Sciences with Study in Europe	B303	3FT deg								

			98 expected requirements							96 entry stats	
TITLE	CODE	COURSE	SUBJECTS	A/AS	ND/C	AGNVQ	IB	SQA(H)	SQA	RATIO	A/AS
DE MONTFORT Univ											
European Studies	T200▼	3FT deg	g	10	D	M	Ind	BCCC	Ind	8	
Mathematics with a Language	G1T9▼	3FT deg	M g	12	3M+1D	M$ go	Ind	Ind	Ind		
Univ of DERBY											
European Studies	T200	3FT deg	F/G/Sp	12-14	MO	M^	28$	CCCC$	Ind	6	
Law with European Studies	M3T2	3FT deg	*	20	MO+4D	D$	30	BBBCC	Ind		
Law with a Modern Language	M3TF	3FT deg	F/G/Sp/R	20	MO+4D$	D$^	30$	BBBCC$	Ind		
Mathematical Studies with Ancillary Language	GT12	3FT deg	M	8	3M $	M^	Dip$	CCCD$	Ind		
Modern Languages	T900	4FT deg	F/G/Sp	12-14	MO $	M^	28$	CCCC$	Ind		
Credit Accumulation Modular Scheme *European Studies*	Y600	3FT deg	*	12	MO	M	Ind	CCCC	Ind		
Univ of DUNDEE											
American and Contemporary European Studies	QT42	4FT deg	* g	BCC	Ind	D$	29	BBBC	Ind	12	
Business Economics & Marketing & Contemp Euro St	Y601	4FT deg	* g	BCC	Ind	D$	29	BBBC	Ind	1	
Contemporary European St and Environmental Sci	FT92	4FT deg	* g	BCC	Ind	D$	29	BBBC	Ind		
Contemporary European St and Financial Economics	LTC2	4FT deg	* g	BCC	Ind	D$	29	BBBC	Ind		
Contemporary European St and Political Science	MT12	4FT deg	* g	BCC	Ind	D$	29	BBBC	Ind	9	
Contemporary European Studies	T200	4FT deg	* g	BCC	Ind	D$	29	BBBC	Ind	5	
Contemporary European Studies and Economics	LT12	4FT deg	* g	BCC	Ind	D$	29	BBBC	Ind		
Contemporary European Studies and English	QT32	4FT deg	E g	BCC	Ind	D$^	29$	BBBC$	Ind	4	
Contemporary European Studies and Geography	LT82	4FT deg	* g	BCC	Ind	D$	29	BBBC	Ind	2	
Contemporary European Studies and Modern History	TV21	4FT deg	* g	BCC	Ind	D$	29	BBBC	Ind	6	
Contemporary European Studies and Philosophy	TV27	4FT deg	* g	BCC	Ind	D$	29	BBBC	Ind		
Contemporary European Studies and Psychology	LT72	4FT deg	* g	BCC	Ind	D$	29	BBBC	Ind	6	
Engineering and Foreign Language (MEng)	HT19	4FT/5FT deg	M+P/Ds g	12	5M $	M$^	26$	BBCC$	N$		
Arts and Social Sciences *Contemporary European Studies*	Y400	3FT deg	* g	BCC	Ind	D$	29	BBBC	Ind		
Univ of DURHAM											
Arabic with European Languages	T6T9	4FT deg	L	BBC	Ind	Ind	31	AABBB	Ind	6	
Chinese with European Languages	T3T9	4FT deg	L	BBC	Ind	Ind	31	AABBB	Ind	20	
European Studies	T200▼	3FT deg	*	CD	Ind	Ind	Dip	BCCCC	Ind		
European Studies and French	RT12▼	4FT deg	*	CD	Ind	Ind	Dip	BCCCC	Ind		
European Studies and German	RT22▼	4FT deg	*	CD	Ind	Ind	Dip	BCCCC	Ind		
European Studies and Spanish	RT42▼	4FT deg	*	CD	Ind	Ind	Dip	BCCCC	Ind		
European Studies with French	T2R1▼	3FT deg	*	CD	Ind	Ind	Dip	BCCCC	Ind		
European Studies with German	T2R2▼	3FT deg	*	CD	Ind	Ind	Dip	BCCCC	Ind		
European Studies with Spanish	T2R4▼	3FT deg	*	CD	Ind	Ind	Dip	BCCCC	Ind		
Geography (European Studies)	LT82	3FT deg	Gy+L	BBC	MO	Ind	32	AAABB	Ind	10	
Geography (European Studies)	FT82	3FT deg	Gy+L+S	BBC	MO	Ind	32	AAABB	Ind	5	
Japanese with European Languages	T4T2	4FT deg	L	BBC	Ind	Ind	31	AABBB	Ind	4	24/30
Modern Languages	T900	4FT deg	L	24	Ind	Ind	33	AAABB	Ind	6	24/30
Modern Languages and Linguistics	QT19	4FT deg	L	24	Ind	Ind	33	AAABB	Ind	16	
Modern Languages and Music	TW93	4FT deg	L+Mu	BBB	Ind	Ind	33	AAABB	Ind	33	
Urban Studies and European Studies	KT42▼	3FT deg	*	CD	Ind	Ind	Dip	BCCCC	Ind		
Urban Studies with European Studies	K4T2▼	3FT deg	*	CD	Ind	Ind	Dip	BCCCC	Ind		
Arts Combined *Greek*	Y300	3FT deg	*	24	MO	Ind	30	AAABB	Ind		
Univ of EAST ANGLIA											
Contemporary European Studies with Honours Lang	T200	4FT deg	F/G	BBC	X		30$	AAABB	X	7	20/26
Contemporary European Studies with Optional Lang	T201	3FT deg	L	BCC	X		30$	AAABB	X	3	18/20
Development Studies with a Language	M9T9	3FT deg	*	BBC			Ind	Ind	Ind		

| | | | | 98 expected requirements | | | | | | | 96 entry stats | |
| course details | | | | | | | | | | | | |
TITLE	CODE	COURSE	SUBJECTS	A/AS	ND/C	GNVQ	IB	SQA(H)	SQA	RATIO	A/AS
Economic & Social History with Modern Euro Lang	V3T2	4FT deg	L/*	BBC	3M+3D		30	BBBBB	Ind		
Economics with a Modern European Language	L1T2	4FT deg	L/*	BBC	3M+3D		30	BBBBB	Ind	4	
Euro Bus Studs w Hons Lang-1 from Fr,Ger,Danish	T9N1	4FT deg	F/G	BBC	X		30	AAABB	X	4	18/28
European Cultural Studies	VT92	4FT deg		BCC			28$	AABB$	Ind		
European and Social Studies	TV29	3FT/4FT deg		BBC	X		29$	AAABB	X	5	12/22
History of Art and European Literature (4 Yrs)	VT49	4FT deg	L	BBC	X		29$	Ind	X	5	
History, European with French or German Language	V1T2	4FT deg	H+F/G	ABC-BCC	X		30	BBBBB	X	9	
History,European with Double Honours Language	V1TY	4FT deg	H+2L	ABC-BCC	X		30	BBBBB	X	3	
Honours Language with Management Studies	T2N1	4FT deg	L	BBC	X		30	AAABB	X	6	20/24
Linguistics with Honours Language	Q1TY	4FT deg	L	BCC	X		28$	AABBC	X	6	16/28
Media Studies with Honours Language	P4T9	4FT deg	F/G	BBC	X		30$	AAABC	X	4	14/28
Modern Languages (with Interp & Adv Translating)	T901	4FT deg	L	ABC-BCC	X		30$	AABBB	X	6	12/30
Philosophy with a Modern European Lang	V7T2	4FT deg	L/*	BBC	3M+3D		30	BBBBB	Ind	4	
Politics with a Modern European Language	M1T2	4FT deg	L/*	BBC	3M+3D		30	BBBBB	Ind	15	
Sociology with a Modern European Language	L3T2	4FT deg	L/*	BBC	3M+3D		30	BBBBB	Ind	12	

Univ of EAST LONDON

TITLE	CODE	COURSE	SUBJECTS	A/AS	ND/C	GNVQ	IB	SQA(H)	SQA	RATIO	A/AS
Accounting & Finance with European Studies	N4T2	3FT deg	* g	14	MO	M	Ind	Ind	Ind		
Communication Studies with European Studies	P3T2	3FT deg	* g	12							
Economics with European Studies	L1T2	3FT deg	* g	12	MO	M	Ind				
Environmental Sciences with European Studies	F9T2	3FT deg	* g	12	MO	M	Ind	Ind	Ind		
European Studies	T200	3FT/4SW deg	* g	12	MO	MB	Ind	Ind	Ind	13	
European Studies and French	TR21	3FT deg	* g	12	MO	M					
European Studies and German	TR22	3FT deg	* g	12	MO	M					
European Studies and Linguistics	QT12	3FT deg	* g	12	MO	X	Ind	Ind	Ind		
European Studies and Spanish	TR24	3FT deg	* g	12							
European Studies and Third World & Dev Studies	MTY2	3FT deg	* g	12	MO	M	Ind	Ind	Ind		
European Studies with Anthropology	T2L6	3FT deg	* g	12	MO	M	Ind	Ind			
European Studies with Archaeological Sciences	T2F4	3FT deg	* g	12	MO	M	Ind	Ind			
European Studies with Business Studies	T2N1	3FT deg	* g	12	MO	M	Ind	Ind			
European Studies with Communication Studies	T2P3	3FT deg	* g	12	MO	M	Ind	Ind			
European Studies with Economics	T2L1	3FT deg	* g	12	MO	M	Ind	Ind			
European Studies with French	T2R1	3FT deg	* g	12	MO	M					
European Studies with German	T2R2	3FT deg	* g	12	MO	M					
European Studies with Information Technology	T2G5	3FT deg	* g	12	MO	M	Ind	Ind			
European Studies with Italian	T2R3	3FT deg	* g	12	MO	M					
European Studies with Linguistics	T2Q1	3FT deg	* g	12	MO	M	Ind	Ind			
European Studies with Social Policy Research	T2L4	3FT deg	* g	12	MO	M	Ind	Ind			
European Studies with Sociology	T2L3	3FT deg	* g	12	MO	M	Ind	Ind			
European Studies with Spanish	T2R4	3FT deg	* g	12	MO	M					
European Studies with Third World & Dev Studies	T2MX	3FT deg	* g	12	MO	M	Ind	Ind			
French with European Studies	R1T2	3FT deg	* g	12	MO	M	Ind				
German with European Studies	R2T2	3FT deg	* g	12	MO	M	Ind				
History with European Studies	V1T2	3FT deg	* g	12	MO	M	Ind	Ind			
History/European Studies	TV21	3FT deg	* g	12	MO	M	Ind	Ind	Ind		
Information Technology with European Studies	G5T2	3FT deg	* g	12	MO	M	Ind	Ind	Ind		
Linguistics with European Studies	Q1T2	3FT deg	* g	12	MO	M	Ind	Ind			
Social Sciences with European Studies	L3T2	3FT deg	* g	12	MO	M	Ind	Ind	Ind		
Sociology with European Studies	L3TF	3FT deg	* g	12	MO	M	Ind	Ind	Ind		
Spanish with European Studies	R4T2	3FT deg	* g	12	MO	M	Ind				
Three-Subject Degree *European Studies*	Y600	3FT deg	* g	12	MO	M	Ind	Ind	Ind		

course details   98 expected requirements   96 entry stats

TITLE	CODE	COURSE	SUBJECTS	A/AS	ND/C	AGNVQ	IB	SQA(H)	SQA	RATIO	A/AS
EDGE HILL Univ COLLEGE											
Critical Criminology and Modern European Studies	MT32	3FT deg	*	CD	3M+3D	M* / P*^	Dip	BBCC	Ind		
Modern European Studies	T200	3FT deg	*	DD	3M+3D	M* / P*^	Dip	BBCC	Ind		
Modern European Studies	T204	3FT deg	*	DD	3M+3D · M* / P*^		Dip	BBCC	Ind	1	4/14
Modern European Studies and English	QT32	3FT deg	E	CD	X	P*^	Dip	BBCC	Ind		
Modern European Studies and Geography	LT82	3FT deg	Gv g	DD	X	P*^	Dip	BBCC	Ind		
Modern European Studies and History	TV21	3FT deg	H	DD	X	P*^	Dip	BBCC	Ind		
Modern European Studies and Urban Policy Studies	MTY2	3FT deg	*	DD	3M+3D	M* / P*^	Dip	BBCC	Ind		
Univ of EDINBURGH											
Chemical Engineering with European Studs (MEng)	H8T2	5FT deg	M+C+P/B	CCC	MO $		Dip$	BBBB$	N$	4	
Chemistry with a Year in Europe	F1T9	4FT deg	C+M+L	CCD	MO $		Dip$	BBBC$	N$	9	
Chemistry with a year in Europe	F1TX	5FT deg	C+M+L	CCD	MO $		Dip$	BBBC	N$		
Modern European Languages	T900	4FT deg	L g	BBB	Ind	Ind	Dip$	BBBB$	Ind		
Modern European Languages and Euro Union Studies	TM21	4FT deg	L g	BBB	Ind	Ind	Dip$	BBBB$	Ind		
Univ of ESSEX											
Electronic Engineering with a Modern Language	H6T9	3FT/4FT deg	(P+M)/*	14-18	MO $	D	28	BBCC	Ind		
Electronic Systems Eng with a Modern Lang (MEng)	H6TX	4FT deg	M+Cs/Es/P	BCC	MO $	Ind	28$	CSYS	Ind		
European Studies (4 Yrs)	T9Y4	4FT deg	F/*	20	MO+2D	Ind	28	BBBB	Ind	5	12/20
History of Art and Modern Languages	TV94	3FT deg									
Modern Languages and Linguistics (4 Yrs)	T900	4FT deg	F/*	20	MO+2D	Ind	28	BBBB	Ind	10	12/30
Physics with a European Language	F3T2	4FT deg	P+M g	16	MO $	X	26$	BBCC	Ind		
EUROPEAN Business School											
European Business Administration (Test+Int)	N1T2	4SW deg	L	12	Ind		Ind	Ind	Ind	5	
International Business Studies (2 languages)	N1TX	4FT deg									
International Business Studies (Test+Int)	N1T9	4SW deg	*	12	Ind		Ind	Ind	Ind	12	
Univ of EXETER											
Computer Science with European Study	G5T2	4FT deg	* g	20	MO+2D	M$	32	Ind	Ind	5	
Media Computing with European Study	G5TF	4FT deg	g	20	MO+2D	M$	32	Ind	Ind	2	
Sociology with European Study	LT32	4FT deg	* g	BBB-CCC	MO	M/D$	30				
Univ of GLAMORGAN											
Computer Studies with Foreign Lang & Business	G5T9	3FT/4SW deg	* g	12	7M	M$	Ind	Ind	Ind	16	
Marketing with Languages	N5T9	4SW deg	* g	14	MO+3D	M$	Ind	Ind	Ind	3	
Business Administration (European Languages)	002T	2FT HND	* g	6	MO	P$	Ind	Ind	Ind	6	
Univ of GLASGOW											
Accountancy with Languages	N4T9	4FT deg		BBB	HN		32	AAABB	X		
Mechanical Engineering (European Curriculum)	H3TF	4FT deg	M+P+L	CCD	MO	Ind	30$	BBBBC	N$		
Mechanical Engineering (European Curriculum)	H3T2	5FT deg	M+P+L	CCD	MO	Ind	30$	BBBBC	N$		
GLASGOW CALEDONIAN Univ											
Applicable Maths with Business and a Language	G1TX	3FT/4FT deg	M+L	CD	Ind		Ind	BBC$	Ind	6	
Applicable Maths with Languages	G1T9	3FT/4FT deg	M+L	CD	Ind		Ind	BBC$	Ind		
GOLDSMITHS COLL (Univ of London)											
European Languages, Culture and Society	T200	4FT deg		CC	MO	M	Dip	BCCC	N	6	8/22
Psychology with a European Language (4 Yrs)	C8T9	4FT deg	L	BBC	MO	M	Dip	ABBBB	N	10	
Univ of GREENWICH											
Business Administration/Language	NT1X	3FT deg	* g	16	MO+4D	M	24	CCC	Ind		
Business Studies/Language	NT1Y	4FT deg	* g	16	MO+4D	M	24	CCC	Ind		
Civil Engineering with a European Language	H2T2	3FT/4SW deg	M+S g	16	6M	M$2 g	Ind	Ind	Ind		
Heritage Management/Language	NT99	3FT deg	* g	16	MO+4D	M	24	CCC	Ind		

European Studies and Languages 28

course details | 98 expected requirements | 96 entry stats

TITLE	CODE	COURSE	SUBJECTS	A/AS	NO/C	AGNVQ	IB	SQA(H)	SQA	RATIO A/AS
International Business/Language	NT12	4SW deg	* g	16	MO+4D	M	24	CCC	Ind	
International Marketing/Language	NT52	4SW deg	* g	16	MO+4D	M	24	CCC	Ind	
Marketing Communications/Language	NT5X	3FT deg	* g	16	MO+4D	M	24	CCC	Ind	
Marketing/Language	TN95	3FT/4SW deg	* g	16	MO+4D	M	24	CCC	Ind	
Operations Management/Language	NT29	3FT/4SW deg	* g	16	MO+4D	M	24	CCC	Ind	
Personnel Management/Language	NT69	3FT/4SW deg	* g	16	MO+4D	M	24	CCC	Ind	
Tourism Management/Language	PT79	3FT deg	* g	16	MO+4D	M	24	CCC	Ind	

GYOSEI International COLL

| Business with Language Studies | N1T9 | 3FT/4FT deg | * | BCC | Ind | | Ind | Ind | Ind | |

HERIOT-WATT Univ

Chemistry with a European Language (MChem)	F1T2	5FT deg	C+S+L	CCD	$	Ind	28	BBB	Ind	
Civil Engineering with European Studies (MEng)	H2T2	4FT/5FT deg	M+P	CDD	HN	M$ go	30	BBBC	HN	
Economics and European Studies	LT12	4FT deg	L	BCC		M$ go	30	BBBB	Ind	
Economics and Languages: French/German	LT19	4FT deg	L	BBC	Ind	Ind	Ind	AABB	Ind	
Economics and Languages: French/Russian	LTCX	4FT deg	L	BBC	Ind	Ind	Ind	AABB	Ind	
Economics and Languages: French/Spanish	LTDX	4FT deg	L	BBC	Ind	Ind	Ind	AABB	Ind	
Economics and Languages: German/Russian	LTDY	4FT deg	L	BBC	Ind	Ind	Ind	AABB	Ind	
Economics and Languages: German/Spanish	LT1X	4FT deg	L	BBC	Ind	Ind	Ind	AABB	Ind	
Economics and Languages: Spanish/Russian	LTCY	4FT deg	L	BBC	Ind	Ind	Ind	AABB	Ind	
International Business and Langs:French/German	NT19	4FT deg	L	BBC	Ind	Ind	Ind	AABB	Ind	
International Business and Langs:French/Russian	NTC9	4FT deg	L	BBC	Ind	Ind	Ind	AABB	Ind	
International Business and Langs:French/Spanish	NTD9	4FT deg	L	BBC	Ind	Ind	Ind	AABB	Ind	
International Business and Langs:German/Russian	NTCX	4FT deg	L	BBC	Ind	Ind	Ind	AABB	Ind	
International Business and Langs:German/Spanish	NT1X	4FT deg	L	BBC	Ind	Ind	Ind	AABB	Ind	
International Business and Langs:Spanish/Russian	NT1Y	4FT deg	L	BBC	Ind	Ind	Ind	AABB	Ind	
Combined Studies Languages	Y300	4FT deg	L	CCC	Ind	M$^ go	30	BBBB	Ind	

Univ of HERTFORDSHIRE

Applied Geology/European Studies	F6T2	3FT deg	* g	14	MO $	M$ gi	26$	BCCC	Ind	
Applied Physics/European Studies	F3T2	3FT deg	M+P	12	3M	M$ gi	24$	CCCC$	Ind	
Business/European Studies	N1T2	3FT deg	*	18	4M+4D	M$6 gi	26	BBBC	Ind	3
Computer Science in Europe	G5T2	4SW deg	* g	18	MO	M$^ gi	30	Ind	Ind	7
Computing/European Studies	G5TF	3FT deg	*	14	MO	M$ gi	26	BCCC	Ind	2
Economics/European Studies	L1T2	3FT deg	*	14	MO	M$ gi	26	BCCC	Ind	2
Electronic Music/European Studies	W3T2	3FT deg	Mu	14	MO $	M$^ gi	26$	BCCC$	Ind	
Environmental Science/European Studies	F9T2	3FT deg	*	14	MO	M$ gi	26	BCCC	Ind	2
European Studies	L3T2	3FT deg	* g	14	M+D	Ind	26	BBCC	Ind	
European Studies	T200	3FT deg	*	14	MO	M$ gi	26	BCCC	Ind	
European Studies/Applied Geology	T2F6	3FT deg	* g	14	MO $	Ind	26$	BCCC$	Ind	
European Studies/Applied Physics	T2F3	3FT deg	M+P	12	3M	M$ gi	24$	CCCC$	Ind	
European Studies/Business	T2N1	3FT deg	*	18	4M+4D	M$6 gi	26	BBBC	Ind	10
European Studies/Computing	T2G5	3FT deg	*	14	MO	M$ gi	26	BCCC	Ind	
European Studies/Economics	T2L1	3FT deg	*	14	MO	M$ gi	26	BCCC	Ind	1
European Studies/Electronic Music	T2W3	3FT deg	Mu	14	MO $	M$^ gi	26$	BCCC$	Ind	
European Studies/Environmental Science	T2F9	3FT deg	*	14	MO	M$ gi	26	BCCC	Ind	
European Studies/Human Biology	T2B1	3FT deg	S g	14	MO $	MS gi	26$	BCCC$	Ind	
European Studies/Law	T2M3	3FT deg	*	20	4M+4D	D$ gi	26	BBBC	Ind	9
European Studies/Linguistic Science	T2Q1	3FT deg	*	14	MO	M$ gi	26	BCCC	Ind	
European Studies/Manufacturing Systems	T2H7	3FT deg	*	14	MO	M$ gi	26	BCCC	Ind	
European Studies/Mathematics	T2G1	3FT deg	M	14	MO $	M$^ gi	26$	BCCC$	Ind	
European Studies/Operational Research	T2N2	3FT deg	*	14	MO	M$ gi	26	BCCC	Ind	

course details			98 expected requirements							96 entry stats	
TITLE	CODE	COURSE	SUBJECTS	A/AS	ND/C	AGNVQ	IB	SQA(H)	SQA	RATIO	A/AS
Historical Studies/Modern Language	TV91	3FT deg	Ap	14	M+D	Ind	28	CCCC	Ind		
Human Biology/European Studies	B1T2	3FT deg	S g	14	MO $	MS gi	26$	BCCC$	Ind		
Law/European Studies	M3T2	3FT deg	*	20	4M+4D	D$ gi	26	BBBC	Ind	6	14/18
Linguistic Science/European Studies	Q1T2	3FT deg	*	14	MO	M$ gi	26	BCCC	Ind		
Linguistics/Modern Language	QT19	3FT deg	Ap	14	M+D	Ind	28	CCCCC	Ind		
Literature/Modern Language	QT39	3FT deg	Ap	14	M+D	Ind	28	CCCCC	Ind		
Manufacturing Systems/European Studies	H7T2	3FT deg	*	14	MO	M$ gi	24	BCCC	Ind		
Mathematics/European Studies	G1T2	3FT deg	M	14	MO $	M$^ gi	26$	BCCC$	Ind		
Operational Research/European Studies	N2T2	3FT deg	*	14	MO	M$ gi	26	BCCC	Ind		
Philosophy/Modern Language	TV98	3FT deg	Ap	14	M+D	Ind	28	CCCC	Ind		
Combined Modular Scheme *European Studies*	Y100	3FT deg	*	14	MO	M$ gi	26	BCCC	Ind		

Univ of HUDDERSFIELD

Business Studies with a Modern Language	N1T9	3FT/4SW deg	Ap g	16	MO+4D	M$ go	26	BBCC	Ind		
Computing with a Modern European Language	GT52	4SW deg	* g	14-16	MO	M go	Ind	BBB	Ind		
European Software Engineering	G7T2	1FT/2FT deg	g	X	HN	X	X	X	HN		
International Business with Modern Languages	N1TX	4FT/4SW deg	Ap g	16	MO+4D	M$ go	26	BBCC	Ind		
Marketing with a Modern Language	N5T9	4SW deg	* g	14	MO	M go	28	BBB	Ind		
Modern Languages	T900	4FT deg	F/G/Sp	CCE	Ind	Ind	Ind	BBBC	Ind		
Music with a Modern Lang (Practical Quals Req)	W3T2	3FT deg	Mu+F/G/Sp	CD	Ind	Ind	Ind	BBC	Ind		

Univ of HULL

Business Studies/Dutch	NT12	4FT deg	* g	BBC-BCC	Ind	D*^ go	26$	BCCCC	Ind	4	
Combined Honours in Languages	T900	4FT deg	L	BBC	Ind	Ind	28$	BBBCC	Ind	7	20/30
Dutch Studies	T220	4FT deg	* g	CCC-CCD	MO	Ind	26$	BBCCC	Ind	1	
Dutch/French	RTD2	4FT deg	F	BBB-BCD	Ind	Ind	26$	BBBCC	Ind		
Dutch/German	RTF2	4FT deg	G	BCC-CCC	Ind	Ind	26$	BBCCC	Ind	3	
Dutch/South-East Asian Studies	TT25	4FT deg	* g	BC	N	Ind	28$	BCCCC	Ind	4	
European International Studies	T202	3FT deg	L	BBC	Ind	Ind	28$	ABBCC	Ind		
European Studies	T200	4FT deg	L	ABC-BBC	Ind $	M$6/^ go	28$	BBBCC	Ind	4	12/28
Gender Studies and Dutch	MT92	4FT deg	* g	BBC-CCD	MO	M$6/^ go	26	BCCCC	Ind		
Statistics with a Mod Lang (Fr,Ger,Sp) (4 Yrs)	G4T2	4FT deg	M/L+M g	BCD	MO $	M$^ gi	26$	BBCCC	Ind		
Transnational Integrated European Studies	T201	4FT deg	F+G	ABC-BBC	Ind $	Ind	28$	BBBCC	Ind	4	20/26

KEELE Univ

Biol & Med Chem and German/Russian or Russian St	FTCY	3FT deg	G+R+P/C g	BBC-BCC	Ind	D$^	28$	CSYS	Ind		
French and European Studies	RT12	3FT deg	F	BCC	Ind	D$^	28$	CSYS	Ind	4	16/28
French and European Studies (4 Yrs)	TR21	4FT deg	*	BCC	Ind	Ind	28	BBBB	Ind	58	
French/German and Astrophysics	FT59	3FT deg	F+G+P g	BBC	Ind	D$^	30$	CSYS	Ind		
French/German and Biochemistry	CT79	3FT deg	F+G+C g	BBC	Ind	D$^	30$	CSYS	Ind		
French/German and Biochemistry (4 Yrs)	TC97	4FT deg	G	BBC	Ind	Ind	30$	BBBB	Ind		
French/German and Biology	CT19	3FT deg	F+G+S g	BBC	Ind	D$^	30$	CSYS	Ind		
French/German and Biology (4 Yrs)	TC91	4FT deg	g	BBC	Ind	Ind	30	BBBB	Ind		
French/German and Business Admin (4 Yrs)	TN99	4FT deg	g	BBC	Ind	Ind	30	BBBB	Ind		
French/German and Business Administration	NT99	3FT deg	F+G	BBC	Ind	D$^	30$	CSYS	Ind	2	
French/German and Economics	LT19	3FT deg	F+G g	BBC	Ind	D$^	30$	CSYS	Ind		
French/German and English	QT39	3FT deg	F+E+G	BBC	Ind	D$^	30$	CSYS	Ind		
French/German and English (4 Yrs)	TQ93	4FT deg	* g	BBC	Ind	Ind	30	BBBB	Ind		
French/German and Environmental Management	FTX9	3FT deg	F+G g	BBC	Ind	D$^	30$	CSYS	Ind		
French/German and European Studies	TT29	3FT deg	F+G	BBC	Ind	D$^	30$	CSYS	Ind	4	
French/German and European Studies (4 Yrs)	TT92	4FT deg	G g	BBC-BCC	Ind	Ind	28$	BBBB	Ind		
French/German and Geology (4 Yrs)	TF96	4FT deg	G g	BBC-BCC	Ind	Ind	28$	BBBB	Ind		
French/German and Latin	QT69	3FT deg	F+G+Ln	BBC	Ind	D$^	30$	CSYS	Ind		

European Studies and Languages

course details

98 expected requirements

96 entry stats

TITLE	CODE	COURSE	SUBJECTS	A/AS	ND/C	RGNVQ	IB	SQA(H)	SQA	RATIO A/AS
French/Russian and Electronic Music (4 Yrs)	WTJX	4FT deg	* g	BCC	Ind	Ind	28	BBBB	Ind	
French/Russian and English (4 Yrs)	TQX3	4FT deg	*	BBC	Ind	Ind	30	BBBB	Ind	
French/Russian and European Studies (4 Yrs)	TTX2	4FT deg	*	BCC	Ind	Ind	28	BBBB	Ind	
French/Russian or Russ St & Criminology (4 Yrs)	TMXH	4FT deg	*	BBB	Ind	Ind	32	BBBB	Ind	
French/Russian or Russ St and Classical Studies	QT8X	3FT deg	F+R	BBC	Ind	D$^	28$	CSYS	Ind	
French/Russian or Russ Studies and American St	QT4X	3FT deg	F+R	BBC	Ind	D$^	30$	CSYS	Ind	
French/Russian or Russian St and Biochem (4 Yrs)	TCX7	4FT deg	*	BCC	Ind	Ind	28	BBBB	Ind	
French/Russian or Russian St and Biology (4 Yrs)	TCX1	4FT deg	*	BCC	Ind	Ind	28	BBBB	Ind	
French/Russian or Russian St and Bus Admin(4Yrs)	TNX9	4FT deg	*	BBC	Ind	Ind	30	BBBB	Ind	
French/Russian or Russian Studies and Biology	CT1X	3FT deg	F+R+S g	BBC-BCC	Ind	D$^	28$	CSYS	Ind	
French/Russian or Russian Studies and Bus Admin	NT9X	3FT deg	F+R	BBC	Ind	D$^	30$	CSYS	Ind	
French/Russian or Russian Studies and Chemistry	FT1X	3FT deg	F+R+C g	BBC-BCC	Ind	D$^	28$	CSYS	Ind	
French/Russian or Russian Studies and Economics	LT1X	3FT deg	F+R g	BBC-BCC	Ind	D$^	28$	CSYS	Ind	
French/Russian or Russian Studies and Educ Studs	TXX9	3FT deg	F+R	BBC-BCC	Ind	D$^	28$	CSYS	Ind	
French/Russian or Russian Studies and English	QT3X	3FT deg	F+R+E	BBC	Ind	D$^	30$	CSYS	Ind	
French/Russian or Russian Studies and Euro St	TT2X	3FT deg	F+R	BBC-BCC	Ind	D$^	28$	CSYS	Ind	
French/Russian or Russian Studs and Biochemistry	CT7X	3FT deg	F+R+C g	BBC-BCC	Ind	D$^	28$	CSYS	Ind	
French/Russian or Russian Studs and Comp Science	GT5X	3FT deg	F+R	BBC-BCC	Ind	D$^	28$	CSYS	Ind	
Geography and French/German	LT89	3FT deg	F+G+Gy	BBC	Ind	D$^	30$	CSYS	Ind	
Geology and French/German	FT69	3FT deg	F+G+S g	BBC	Ind	D$^	30$	CSYS	Ind	
Geology and French/Russian or Russian St (4 Yrs)	TFX6	4FT deg	* g	BBC-BCC	Ind	Ind	28	BBBB	Ind	
Geology and French/Russian or Russian Studies	FT6X	3FT deg	F+R+S g	BBC-BCC	Ind	D$^	28$	CSYS	Ind	
German and European Studies	RT22	3FT deg	G	BCC	Ind	D$^	28$	CSYS	Ind	2 18/22
German and European Studies (4 Yrs)	TR22	4FT deg	G	BCC	Ind	Ind	28$	BBBB	Ind	
German and French/Russian (4 Yrs)	TRX2	4FT deg	* g	BBC-BCC	Ind	Ind	28	BBBB	Ind	
German and French/Russian or Russian Studies	RT2X	3FT deg	F+R+G	BBC-BCC	Ind	D$^	28$	CSYS	Ind	
German/Russian and English (4 Yrs)	TQY3	4FT deg	* g	BBC	Ind	Ind	30	BBBB	Ind	
German/Russian and European Studies (4 Yrs)	TTY2	4FT deg	G	BCC	Ind	Ind	28$	BBBB	Ind	
German/Russian and French	RT1Y	3FT deg	G+R+F	BBC-BCC	Ind	D$^	28$	CSYS	Ind	
German/Russian and French (4 Yrs)	TRY1	4FT deg	* g	BBC-BCC	Ind	Ind	28	BBBB	Ind	
German/Russian or Rus St & Applied Soc St (4Yrs)	TLY5	4FT deg	G	BBC-BCC	Ind	Ind	28$	BBBB	Ind	
German/Russian or Russ St and Applied Social St	LT5Y	3FT deg	G+R g	BBC	Ind	D$^	30$	CSYS	Ind	
German/Russian or Russ St and Bus Admin (4 Yrs)	TNY9	4FT deg	g	BCC	Ind	Ind	30	BBBB	Ind	
German/Russian or Russian St & Bio Med Chemistry	TFYC	4FT deg	G g	BCC	Ind	D$^	28$	BBBB	Ind	
German/Russian or Russian St and Biochem (4 Yrs)	TCY7	4FT deg	G	BCC	Ind	Ind	28$	BBBB	Ind	
German/Russian or Russian St and Biochemistry	CT7Y	3FT deg	G+R+C g	BBC-BCC	Ind	D$^	28$	CSYS	Ind	
German/Russian or Russian St and Biology (4 Yrs)	TCY1	4FT deg	g	BBC	Ind	Ind	30	BBBB	Ind	
German/Russian or Russian St and Business Admin	NT9Y	3FT deg	G+R	BBC	Ind	D$^	30$	CSYS	Ind	
German/Russian or Russian St and Chem (4 Yrs)	TFY1	4FT deg	G	BCC	Ind	Ind	28$	BBBB	Ind	
German/Russian or Russian St and Econ (4 Yrs)	TLY1	4FT deg	G	BCC	Ind	Ind	28$	BBBB	Ind	
German/Russian or Russian St and Geology	FT6Y	3FT deg	G+R+S g	BBC-BCC	Ind	D$^	28$	CSYS	Ind	
German/Russian or Russian St and Geology (4 Yrs)	TFY6	4FT deg	G	BCC	Ind	Ind	28$	BBBB	Ind	
German/Russian or Russian Studies and Biology	CT1Y	3FT deg	G+R+S g	BBC-BCC	Ind	D$^	28$	CSYS	Ind	
German/Russian or Russian Studies and Chemistry	FT1Y	3FT deg	G+R+C g	BBC-BCC	Ind	D$^	28$	CSYS	Ind	
German/Russian or Russian Studies and Economics	LT1Y	3FT deg	G+R g	BBC-BCC	Ind	D$^	28$	CSYS	Ind	
German/Russian or Russian Studies and English	QT3Y	3FT deg	G+R+E	BBC	Ind	D$^	30$	CSYS	Ind	
German/Russian or Russian Studies and Euro Studs	TT2Y	3FT deg	G+R	BBC-BCC	Ind	D$^	28$	CSYS	Ind	
History and French/German	TV91	3FT deg	F+G	BBC	Ind	D$^	30$	CSYS	Ind	
History and French/German (4 Yrs)	VT19	4FT deg	g	BBC	Ind	Ind	30	BBBB	Ind	
History and French/Russian (4 Yrs)	VT1X	4FT deg	*	BBC	Ind	Ind	30	BBBB	Ind	
History and French/Russian or Russian Studies	TVX1	3FT deg	F+R	BBC	Ind	D$^	30$	CSYS	Ind	
History and German/Russian or Russian St (4 Yrs)	VT1Y	4FT deg	g	BBC	Ind	Ind	30	BBBB	Ind	

course details

98 expected requirements

96 entry stats

TITLE	CODE	COURSE	SUBJECTS	A/AS	NQ/C	AGNVQ	IB	SQA(H)	SQA	RATIO A/AS
History and German/Russian or Russian Studies	TVY1	3FT deg	G+R	BBC-BCC	Ind	D$^	28$	BBBB	Ind	
Hum Res M and French/Russian or Russian St(4Yrs)	TNX6	4FT deg	*	BBC-BCC	Ind	D$^	28	BBBB	Ind	
Hum Res Mgt and German/Russ or Russ St (4 Yrs)	TNY6	4FT deg	G	BCC	Ind	Ind	28$	BBBB	Ind	
Human Res Mgt and French/Russian or Russian St	NT6X	3FT deg	F+R	BBC-BCC	Ind	D$^	28$	CSYS	Ind	
Human Res Mgt and German/Russian or Russian St	NT6Y	3FT deg	G+R	BBC-BCC	Ind	D$^	28$	CSYS	Ind	
Human Resource Management and French/German	NT69	3FT deg	F+G	BBC	Ind	D$^	30$	CSYS	Ind	
Human Resource Mgt and French/German (4 Yrs)	TN96	4FT deg	G	BCC	Ind	Ind	28$	BBBB	Ind	
Int History and French/Russian or Russian St	TVXC	3FT deg	F+R	BBC	Ind	D$^	30$	CSYS	Ind	
Int History and German/Russian or Russian St	TVYC	3FT deg	G	BCC	Ind	Ind	28$	BBBB	Ind	
Int Pol and German/Russian or Russian St (4 Yrs)	TMYC	4FT deg	G	BCC	Ind	Ind	30$	BBBB	Ind	
Int Politics and French/Russian or Russian Studs	MTCX	3FT deg	F+R	BBC	Ind	D$^	30$	CSYS	Ind	
Int Politics and German/Russian or Russian Studs	MTCY	3FT deg	G+R	BBC	Ind	D$^	30$	CSYS	Ind	
International History and French/German	TV9C	3FT deg	F+G	BBC	Ind	D$^	30$	CSYS	Ind	
International History and French/German (4 Yrs)	VTC9	4FT deg	* g	BBC-BCC	Ind	Ind	28	BBBB	Ind	
International History and French/Russian (4 Yrs)	VTCX	4FT deg	*	BBC-BCC	Ind	Ind	28	BBBB	Ind	
International History and German/Russian (4 Yrs)	VTCY	4FT deg	G	BCC	Ind	Ind	28$	BBBB	Ind	
International Politics and French/German	MTC9	3FT deg	F+G	BBC	Ind	D$^	30$	CSYS	Ind	
Management Sci & German/Russian or Russ (4 Yrs)	TNY1	4FT deg	*	BBC	Ind	Ind	30	BBBB	Ind	
Management Science and French/German (4 Yrs)	TN91	4FT deg	* g	BBC	Ind	Ind	30	BBBB	Ind	
Marketing and German/Russian or Russian Studies	NT5Y	3FT deg	G+R	BBC	Ind	D$^	30$	CSYS	Ind	
Mathematics and French/German	GT19	3FT deg	F+G+M	BBC	Ind	D$^	30$	CSYS	Ind	
Mathematics and French/German (4 Yrs)	TG91	4FT deg	G	BCC	Ind	Ind	28$	BBBB	Ind	
Mathematics and French/Russian or Russian Studs	GT1X	3FT deg	F+R+M	BBC-BCC	Ind	D$^	28$	CSYS	Ind	
Mathematics and German/Russian or Russian Studs	GT1Y	3FT deg	G+R+M	BBC-BCC	Ind	D$^	28$	CSYS	Ind	
Maths and French/Russian or Russian St (4 Yrs)	TGX1	4FT deg	*	BCC	Ind	Ind	28	BBBB	Ind	
Maths and German/Russian or Russian St (4 Yrs)	TGY1	4FT deg	G	BCC	Ind	Ind	28$	BBBB	Ind	
Mgt Science and German/Russian or Russian Studs	NT1Y	3FT deg	G+R g	BCC	Ind	D$^	28$	CSYS	Ind	
Music and French/German	TW93	3FT deg	F+G+Mu	BBC	Ind	D$^	30$	CSYS	Ind	
Music and French/German (4 Yrs)	WT39	4FT deg	g	BBC	Ind	Ind	30	BBBB	Ind	
Music and French/Russian (4 Yrs)	WT3X	4FT deg	*	BCC	Ind	Ind	28	BBBB	Ind	
Philosophy and French/German (4 Yrs)	VT79	4FT deg	g	BBC	Ind	Ind	30	BBBB	Ind	
Philosophy and French/Russian (4 Yrs)	VT7X	4FT deg	*	BBC	Ind	Ind	30	BBBB	Ind	
Philosophy and French/Russian or Russian Studies	TVX7	3FT deg	F+R	BBC-BCC	Ind	D$^	28$	CSYS	Ind	
Philosophy and German/Russian or Russ St (4 Yrs)	VT7Y	4FT deg	g	BBC	Ind	Ind	30	BBBB	Ind	
Physics and French/German	FT39	3FT deg	F+G+P	BBC	Ind	D$^	30$	CSYS	Ind	
Politics and French/German	MT19	3FT deg	F+G	BBC	Ind	D$^	30$	CSYS	Ind	
Politics and French/German (4 Yrs)	TM91	4FT deg	G g	BCC	Ind	Ind	28$	BBBB	Ind	
Politics and French/Russian or Russ St (4 Yrs)	TMX1	4FT deg	*	BCC	Ind	Ind	28	BBBB	Ind	
Politics and French/Russian or Russian Studies	MT1X	3FT deg	F+R	BBC	Ind	D$^	30$	CSYS	Ind	
Politics and German/Russian or Russian Studies	MT1Y	3FT deg	G+R	BBC	Ind	D$^	30$	CSYS	Ind	
Politics and German/Russian or Russian Studies	TMY1	4FT deg	G g	BCC	Ind	Ind	28$	BBBB	Ind	
Psychology and German/Russian or Russian Studies	CT8Y	3FT deg	G+R	BBB	Ind	D$^	32$	CSYS	Ind	
Russian Studies and European Studies	RTV2	3FT deg	*	BCC	Ind	Ind	28	CSYS	Ind	
Russian Studies and European Studies (4 Yrs)	TR2V	4FT deg	*	BCC	Ind	Ind	28	BBBB	Ind	
Russian Studies and French/German	RTV9	3FT deg	F+G	BBC	Ind	D$^	30$	CSYS	Ind	
Russian Studies and French/German (4 Yrs)	TR9V	4FT deg	* g	BBC-CCC	Ind	Ind	28	BBBB	Ind	
Russian and European Studies	RT82	3FT deg	R	BCC	Ind	D$^	28$	CSYS	Ind	
Russian and European Studies (4 Yrs)	TR28	4FT deg	*	BCC	Ind	Ind	28	BBBB	Ind	
Russian and French/German	RT89	3FT deg	F+R+G	BBC	Ind	D$^	30$	CSYS	Ind	
Russian and French/German (4 Yrs)	TR98	4FT deg	* g	BBC-BCC	Ind	Ind	28	BBBB	Ind	
Sociol & Soc Anthrop & French/Russian or Russ St	TLX3	4FT deg	*	BCC	Ind	Ind	28	BBBB	Ind	
Sociol & Soc Anthrop & French/Russian or Russ St	LT3X	3FT deg	F+R	BBC	Ind	D$^	30$	CSYS	Ind	
Statistics and French/Russian or Russ St (4 Yrs)	TGX4	4FT deg	* g	BCC	Ind	Ind	28	BBBB	Ind	

790

European Studies and Languages   28

| | | | 98 expected requirements | | | | | | | 96 entry stats | |
| course details | | | | | | | | | | | |
TITLE	CODE	COURSE	SUBJECTS	A/AS	NO/C	AGNVQ	IB	SQA(H)	SQA	RATIO	A/AS
Univ of KENT											
European Studies (4 Yrs)	T200	4FT deg		20	3M+3D	Ind	30	Ind		3	16/22
European Studies (Combined Languages)	T202	4FT deg	L	20-22	2M+4D	Ind	28	Ind	Ind	11	18/24
European Studies (Economics) (4 Yrs)	LTC2	4FT deg	L g	20	Ind	Ind	28$	BBBB$	Ind	5	
European Studies (History)	T205	4FT deg	L	22	2M+4D	Ind	30	Ind	Ind	5	
European Studies (Politics & Government) (4 Yrs)	MTC2	4FT deg	L	20	Ind	Ind	28$	BBBB$	Ind		
European Studies (Social Pol and Admin) (4 Yrs)	LTK2	4FT deg	L	20	Ind	Ind	28$	BBBB$	Ind		
European Studies (Sociology) (4 Yrs)	LT32	4FT deg	L	20	Ind	Ind	28$	BBBB$	Ind		
European Studies/Classical Studies	TQ28	4FT deg	L	20	3M+3D	Ind	28	Ind	Ind		
European Studies/Comparative Literary Studies	TQ22	4FT deg	L	20	3M+3D	Ind	28	Ind	Ind		
European Studies/Computing	TG25	4FT deg	L	20	3M+3D	Ind	28	Ind	Ind	3	
European Studies/Drama	TW24	4FT deg	L	22	2M+4D	Ind	30	Ind	Ind	3	
European Studies/English	TQ23	4FT deg	E+L	22	2M+4D	Ind	30	Ind	Ind		
European Studies/English (Post-Colonial Lits)	TQ2J	4FT deg	E+L	22	2M+4D	Ind	30	Ind	Ind		
European Studies/English Language	TQ2H	4FT deg	L+E	20	3M+3D	Ind	28	Ind	Ind	5	
Film Studies/European Studies	TW25	4FT deg	L	22	2M+4D	Ind	30	Ind	Ind		
Linguistics/European Studies	TQ21	4FT deg	L	20	3M+3D	Ind	28	Ind	Ind		
Philosophy/European Studies	TV27	4FT deg	L	20	3M+3D	Ind	28	Ind	Ind		
Theology/European Studies	TV28	4FT deg	L	20	3M+3D	Ind	28	Ind	Ind		
KING'S COLL LONDON (Univ of London)											
Biochemistry with a European Language	C7T9	4SW deg	C+S+L	BBC	Ind	Ind	Ind	BCCCC	Ind	4	18/22
Biological Sciences with a European Language	C1T9	3FT deg	B+S+L g	BCC	Ind	Ind	Ind	BBCCC	Ind	8	
Classical, Byzantine and Modern Greek Studies	QT72	4FT deg		BBC							
European Studies	T2Y3	4FT deg	L	ABB						7	26/30
French and Modern Greek	RTC2	4FT deg	F	BBC							
German and Modern Greek	RT22	4FT deg	G	BCC							
Hispanic Studies and Modern Greek	RT42	4FT deg	Sp	BBC-BCC						1	
Modern Foreign Langs with Education (4 Yrs)	T9X9	4FT deg	2L	BBC						5	
Modern Greek Studies	T240	3FT deg	E+H/L	BCC						2	
Modern Greek and Portuguese	TR25	4FT deg	E+H	BCC							
Modern Greek with Applied Computing	T2G5	4FT deg	*	BCC							
Modern Greek with English	T2Q3	4FT deg	E	BBC						8	
War Studies and Modern Greek	MT92	3FT deg	*	BBC							
KINGSTON Univ											
Business Studies (European Programme)	N1T9	4SW deg	L	CCC	3M+5D	Ind	30$	BBCC	Ind	12	14/22
Univ of Wales, LAMPETER											
European Languages and Management	T200	4FT deg		16	Ind	Ind	Ind	Ind	Ind		
Modern Languages (4 Yrs)	T900	4FT deg	F/G	16	Ind	Ind	Ind	Ind	Ind		
Translation Studies	T210	4FT deg		16	Ind	Ind	Ind	Ind	Ind		
LANCASTER Univ											
European Studies (4 years)	T200	4FT deg	2L g	BCC	Ind $		30$	BBBBB$	Ind		
Univ of LEEDS											
European Studies	T200	3FT deg	L g	BBC	Ind	Ind	30$	CSYS	Ind	11	20/30
European Union Studies	MT12	3FT deg	g	BBC	Ind	Ind	30	Ind	Ind		18/26
LEEDS METROPOLITAN Univ											
Professional Language Studies	T900	4FT deg									
Univ of LEICESTER											
Chemistry (Europe)	F1T9	4FT deg	C g	20	5M $	DS^ gi	30$	ABBBC	Ind		
European Studies	TM29	4FT deg	F g	BBC-BCC	2M+4D	DS^ gi	30$	ABBBB$	Ind		14/26

Letts STUDY GUIDES
THE INDEPENDENT

TITLE	CODE	COURSE	SUBJECTS	A/AS	NO/C	AGNVQ	IB	SQA(H)	SQA	RATIO A/AS
course details				*98 expected requirements*						*96 entry stats*
Modern Language Studies	T900	3FT deg	F/G/I g	BCD	X	D$^	28$	BBBB$	X	
Modern Language Studies with a yr in Europe	T901	4FT deg	F/G/I g	BCD	X	D$^	28$	BBBB$	X	14/28

Univ of LINCOLNSHIRE and HUMBERSIDE

TITLE	CODE	COURSE	SUBJECTS	A/AS	NO/C	AGNVQ	IB	SQA(H)	SQA	RATIO A/AS
Accountancy and Modern Languages	NT49	3FT deg	L g	12	3M+1D	M	24	CCCC	Ind	
Administration and Modern Languages	NT1Y	3FT deg	L g	12	3M+1D	M	24	CCCC	Ind	
Business and Modern Languages	NT19	3FT deg	L g	12	3M+1D		24	CCCC	Ind	
Computing and Modern Languages	GT5X	3FT deg	L g	12	3M+1D	M	24	CCCC	Ind	
Finance and Modern Languages	NT3X	3FT deg	L g	12	3M+1D	M	24	CCCC	Ind	
Human Resource Management and Modern Languages	NT62	3FT deg	L g	12	3M+1D	M	24	CCCC	Ind	
Information Systems and Modern Languages	GT5Y	3FT deg	L g	12	3M+1D	M	24	CCCC	Ind	
International Business Studies	N1T9	4FT deg	* g	16	1M+3D	D	24	BBCCC	Ind	
Marketing and Modern Languages	NT5X	3FT deg	L g	12	3M+1D	M	24	CCCC	Ind	
Media Technology and Modern Languages	PT42	3FT deg	L g	12	3M+1D	M	24	CCCC	Ind	

Univ of LIVERPOOL

TITLE	CODE	COURSE	SUBJECTS	A/AS	NO/C	AGNVQ	IB	SQA(H)	SQA	RATIO A/AS
Chemistry with a European Language	F1TF	4FT deg	C+S g	14	MO $	Ind	31$	BBBCC$	Ind	12
Chemistry with a European Language (MChem)	F1T2	4FT deg	C+S g	20	MO $	Ind	31$	BBBCC$	Ind	8
Computer Science with a European Language	G5T2	4FT deg	M g	18	MO $	Ind	31$	BBBCC$	Ind	5
Engineering with Mgt and a European Lang (MEng)	H1TF	4SW deg	M+P g	20	4M+1D$		30$	BBBBB	Ind	4
Geology with a European Language	F6TF	4FT deg	2S g	20	MO $	Ind	31$	BBBCC$	Ind	
Geophysics with a European Language	F6T2	4FT deg	M+P g	18	MO $	DS^ go	31$	BBBCC$	Ind	
Integrated Engineering with a European Language	HT12	4SW deg	M+P g	20	4M+1D		30$	BBBBB	Ind	
Life Sciences with a European Language	C1T2	4FT deg	B+S g	18	MO $	Ind	31$	BBBCC$	Ind	3 14/24
Materials Science with European Language	F2T2	3FT deg	M+P/C g	18	4M+1D$		30$	BBBBB	Ind	
Mathematical Sciences with a European Language	G1T2	4FT deg	M g	20	MO $	DS^ go	31$	BBBCC$	Ind	23
Modern European Languages	T900	4FT deg	2(F/G/Sp) g	ABB	X	D$^ 2	30$	AAABB$	Ind	9 26/30
Physics with a European Language	F3TF	4FT deg	P+M g	12	MO $	Ind	31$	BBBCC$	Ind	
Physics with a European Language (MPhys)	F3T2	4FT deg	P+M g	12	MO $	Ind	31$	BBBCC$	Ind	9
BA Combined Honours European Studies	Y200	3FT deg	* g	BBB	Ind	Ind	Ind	Ind	Ind	

LIVERPOOL HOPE Univ COLL

TITLE	CODE	COURSE	SUBJECTS	A/AS	NO/C	AGNVQ	IB	SQA(H)	SQA	RATIO A/AS
European Studies (Honours)	T200	4FT deg	F	8-12	6M-8M	P*^	Ind	Ind	Ind	4 6/16
European Studies and Music	TW23	3FT deg								
European Studies/Americal Studies	QT42	3FT deg	*	12	8M	M$	Ind	Ind	Ind	
European Studies/Art	WT92	3FT deg	A/Fa	12	8M	MA /P*^	Ind	Ind	Ind	
European Studies/Drama & Theatre Studies	WT42	3FT deg	g	12	8M	M* go	Ind	Ind	Ind	
European Studies/Environmental Studies	FT92	3FT deg	B/Gy/En	12	8M	M$	Ind	Ind	Ind	
French/European Studies	TR21	3FT deg	F	12	8M	P*^	Ind	Ind	Ind	
Geography/European Studies	TF28	3FT deg	Gy	12	8M	M$	Ind	Ind	Ind	
History/European Studies	TV21	3FT deg	H	12	8M	P$^	Ind	Ind	Ind	
Information Technology/European Studies	TG25	3FT deg	*	12	8M	M*	Ind	Ind	Ind	
Psychology/European Studies	TC28	3FT deg	* g	12	8M	M* go	Ind	Ind	Ind	
Sociology/European Studies	TL23	3FT deg	*	12	8M	M*	Ind	Ind	Ind	
Sport,Recreation & P.E./European Studies	TB26	3FT deg	*	12	8M	M*	Ind	Ind	Ind	
Theology & Religious Studies/European Studies	TV28	3FT deg	*	12	8M	M*	Ind	Ind	Ind	

LIVERPOOL JOHN MOORES Univ

TITLE	CODE	COURSE	SUBJECTS	A/AS	NO/C	AGNVQ	IB	SQA(H)	SQA	RATIO A/AS
European Studies	T200	4FT deg	L	16	5M+2D		Ind	BBCC		11 12/22
History and European Studies	TV21	3FT deg		14	5M+2D	P$	28$	BCCC		4 12/20
Human Geography and European Studies	LT82	3FT deg	Gy	14	5M+3D	P$	28$	BBCC		2 14/18
Politics and European Studies	MTC2	3FT deg		14	5M+2D	P$^	28$	BCCC		2 12/14
Tourism and Leisure with a Modern Foreign Langua	P7T9	3FT deg	L	16	3M+4D					

European Studies and Languages   28

TITLE	CODE	COURSE	SUBJECTS	A/AS	NO/C	AGNVQ	IB	SQA(H)	SQA	RATIO A/AS
LONDON GUILDHALL Univ										
3D/Spatial Design and European Studies	TW2F	3FT deg	Pf g	DD	MO	M$ go	24	Ind	Ind	
European Business Studies	N1T9	4FT deg	* g	CC-CDD	DO		26	Ind	Ind	
European St & Business Information Technology	GT72	3FT deg	* g	DD	MO	M$ go	24	Ind	Ind	
European St & Communications & Audio Vis Prod St	PT42	3FT deg	* g	CC-CDD	MO+4D	M$ go	26	Ind	Ind	
European Studies and Accounting	NT42	3FT deg	* g	DD	MO	M$ go	24	Ind	Ind	
European Studies and Business	NT12	3FT deg	* g	CC-CCD	MO+4D	M$ go	26	Ind	Ind	
European Studies and Business Economics	LTC2	3FT deg	* g	DD	MO	M$ go	24	Ind	Ind	
European Studies and Computing	GT52	3FT deg	* g	DD	MO	M$ go	24	Ind	Ind	
European Studies and Design Studies	TW22	3FT deg	* g	CD-DDD	MO+2D	M$ go	26	Ind	Ind	
European Studies and Development Studies	MT92	3FT deg	* g	DD	MO	M$ go	24	Ind	Ind	
European Studies and Economics	LT12	3FT deg	* g	DD	MO	M$ go	24	Ind	Ind	
European Studies and English	QT32	3FT deg	* g	CD-DDD	MO+2D	M$ go	26	Ind	Ind	
Financial Studies and European Studies	NT32	3FT deg	* g	DD	MO	M$ go	24	Ind	Ind	
Fine Art and European Studies	TW21	3FT deg	Pf g	CC-CDD	MO+2D	M$ go	26	Ind	Ind	
French and European Studies	RT12	4FT deg	* g	DD	MO	M$ go	24	Ind	Ind	
German and European Studies	RT22	4FT deg	* g	DD	MO	M$ go	24	Ind	Ind	
International Relations and European Studies	MTC2	3FT deg	* g	DD	MO	M$ go	24	Ind	Ind	
Law and European Studies	MT32	3FT deg	* g	CC-CDD	MO+2D	M$ go	26	Ind	Ind	
Marketing and European Studies	NT52	3FT deg	* g	CD-DDD	MO+2D	M$ go	26	Ind	Ind	
Mathematics and European Studies	GT12	3FT deg	* g	DD	MO	M$ go	24	Ind	Ind	
Modern History and European Studies	TV21	3FT deg	* g	DD	MO	M$ go	24	Ind	Ind	
Multimedia Systems and European Studies	GTM2	3FT deg	* g	DD	MO	M$ go	24	Ind	Ind	
Politics and European Studies	MT12	3FT deg	* g	DD	MO	M$ go	24	Ind	Ind	
Product Development & Manufacture & European St	JT42	3FT deg	* g	DD	MO	M$ go	24	Ind	Ind	
Psychology and European Studies	CT82	3FT deg	* g	CD-DDD	MO+2D	M$ go	26	Ind	Ind	
Social Policy & Management and European Studies	LT42	3FT deg	* g	CD-DDD	MO	M$ go	24	Ind	Ind	
Sociology and European Studies	LT32	3FT deg	* g	CD-DDD	MO	M$ go	24	Ind	Ind	
Spanish and European Studies	RT42	4FT deg	* g	DD	MO	M$ go	24	Ind	Ind	
Taxation and European Studies	NTH2	3FT deg	* g	DD	MO	M$ go	24	Ind	Ind	
Textile Furnishing Design and European Studies	TW2G	3FT deg	Pf g	DD	MO	M$ go	24	Ind	Ind	
Modular Programme *European Studies*	Y400	3FT deg	* g	CC-DD	MO	M$ go	24	Ind	Ind	
LOUGHBOROUGH Univ										
Chemistry with a European Language	F1T2	4SW deg	C	16	3M+2D	DS6/^ go	28$	Ind	Ind	
Chemistry with a European Language (MChem)	F1TF	5SW deg	C	16	3M+2D	DS6/^ go	28$	Ind	Ind	
Computing with a Modern Language (4 Yr SW)	G5T2	4SW deg	F/G	20		DI6/^ go	28	Ind		4
Modern European Studies	T206	3FT/4SW deg	F/G	20			30	Ind		2 12/22
LSU COLL of HE										
English with European Studies	Q3T2	3FT deg	E+Gy/H/Po	CD	Ind		Ind	Ind	Ind	2
European Studies (Combined)	T200	3FT deg								
European Studies and English	QT32	3FT deg								
European Studies with Ecology	T2D2	3FT deg								
European Studies with English	T2Q3	3FT deg								
European Studies with Sociology	T2L3	3FT deg	Gy/H/Po	DD	Ind		Ind	Ind	Ind	11
European Studies with Theology	T2V8	3FT deg								
Sociology and European Studies	TL23	3FT deg								
Sociology with European Studies	L3T2	3FT deg								
Theology with European Studies	V8T2	3FT deg								

TITLE	CODE	COURSE	SUBJECTS	A/AS	NO/C	AGNVQ	IB	SQA(H)	SQA	RATIO A/AS
LUTON Univ										
Euro Language St w Lang & Stylistics in English	T2QG	3FT deg	L g	12-16	MO/DO	M/D	32	BBCC	Ind	
European Lang St with Regional Planning & Dev	T2K4	3FT deg	L g	12-16	MO/DO	M/D	32	BBCC	Ind	
European Language St with Comparative Literature	T2QF	3FT deg	L g	12-16	MO/DO	M/D	32	BBCC	Ind	1
European Language St with Contemporary History	T2V1	3FT deg	L g	12-16	MO/DO	M/D	32	BBCC	Ind	
European Language St with Electronic Systems Des	T2HQ	3FT deg		12-16	MO/DO	M/D	32	BBCC	Ind	
European Language St with Geog Info Systems	T201	3FT deg	L g	12-16	MO/DO	M/D	32	BBCC	Ind	
European Language St with Literary St in English	T2Q2	3FT deg	L g	12-16	MO/DO	M/D	32	BBCC	Ind	
European Language St with Organisational Behav	T2L7	3FT deg	L g	12-16	MO/DO	M/D	32	BBCC	Ind	
European Language St with Public Policy and Mgt	T2MC	3FT deg	L g	12-16	MO/DO	M/D	32	BBCC	Ind	
European Language Stud with Physical Geography	T2FV	4FT deg	g	12-16	MO/DO	M/D	32	BBCC	Ind	
European Language Studies	T200	4SW deg	L g	12-16	MO/DO	M/D	32	BBCC	Ind	3 8/16
European Language Studies & Electronic Syst Des	HTP2	3FT deg	L g	12-16	MO/DO	M/D	32	BBCC	Ind	
European Language Studies and Accounting	NTK2	3FT deg	L g	12-16	MO/DO	M/D	32	BBCC	Ind	
European Language Studies and Biochemistry	CT72	3FT deg	L g	12-16	MO/DO	M/D	32	BBCC	Ind	
European Language Studies and Biology	CT12	3FT deg	L g	12-16	MO/DO	M/D	32	BBCC	Ind	
European Language Studies and Biotechnology	JT82	3FT deg	L g	12-16	MO/DO	M/D	32	BBCC	Ind	
European Language Studies and British Studies	VT92	3FT deg		12-16	MO/DO	M/D	32	BBCC	Ind	
European Language Studies and Business	NT12	3FT deg	L g	12-16	MO/DO	M/D	32	BBCC	Ind	
European Language Studies and Business Systems	NTC2	3FT deg	L g	12-16	MO/DO	M/D	32	BBCC	Ind	
European Language Studies and Computer Science	GT52	3FT deg	L g	12-16	MO/DO	M/D	32	BBCC	Ind	
European Language Studies and Contemporary Hist	VT12	3FT deg	L g	12-16	MO/DO	M/D	32	BBCC	Ind	
European Language Studies and Environmental Sci	FT92	3FT deg	L g	12-16	MO/DO	M/D	32	BBCC	Ind	
European Language Studies with Accounting	T2NK	4FT deg	L g	12-16	MO/DO	M/D	32	BBCC	Ind	
European Language Studies with Animation	T2WF	4FT deg	L g	12-16	MO/DO	M/D	32	BBCC	Ind	
European Language Studies with Biochemistry	T2C7	3FT deg	L g	12-16	MO/DO	M/D	32	BBCC	Ind	
European Language Studies with Biology	T2C1	4FT deg	L g	12-16	MO/DO	M/D	32	BBCC	Ind	
European Language Studies with Biotechnology	T2J8	3FT deg	L g	12-16	MO/DO	M/D	32	BBCC	Ind	
European Language Studies with British Studies	T2V9	3FT deg		12-16	MO/DO	M/D	32	BBCC	Ind	
European Language Studies with Business	T2N1	4FT deg	L g	12-16	MO/DO	M/D	32	BBCC	Ind	
European Language Studies with Business Systems	T2NC	4FT deg	L g	12-16	MO/DO	M/D	32	BBCC	Ind	
European Language Studies with Chinese	T2T3	3FT deg		12-16	MO/DO	M/D	32	BBCC	Ind	
European Language Studies with Environmental Sci	T2F9	4FT deg	L g	12-16	MO/DO	M/D	32	BBCC	Ind	
European Language Studies with Film Studies	T2WM	4FT deg	L g	12-16	MO/DO	M/D	32	BBCC	Ind	
European Language Studies with Geography	T2FW	4FT deg	L g	12-16	MO/DO	M/D	32	BBCC	Ind	
European Language Studies with Geology	T2F6	4FT deg	L g	12-16	MO/DO	M/D	32	BBCC	Ind	
European Language Studies with Health Science	T2B9	4FT deg	L g	12-16	MO/DO	M/D	32	BBCC	Ind	
European Language Studies with Health Studies	T2BX	3FT deg		12-16	MO/DO	M/D	32	BBCC	Ind	
European Language Studies with Human Biology	T2B1	4FT deg	L g	12-16	MO/DO	M/D	32	BBCC	Ind	
European Language Studies with Journalism	T2P6	4FT deg	L g	12-16	MO/DO	M/D	32	BBCC	Ind	
European Language Studies with Leisure Studies	T2N7	4FT deg	L g	12-16	MO/DO	M/D	32	BBCC	Ind	
European Language Studies with Management	T2ND	4FT deg	L g	12-16	MO/DO	M/D	32	BBCC	Ind	
European Language Studies with Mapping Science	T2F8	4FT deg	L g	12-16	MO/DO	M/D	32	BBCC	Ind	
European Language Studies with Marketing	T2N5	4FT deg	L g	12-16	MO/DO	M/D	32	BBCC	Ind	
European Language Studies with Media Practices	T2P4	4FT deg	L g	12-16	MO/DO	M/D	32	BBCC	Ind	
European Language Studies with Media Production	T2PL	4FT deg	L g	12-16	MO/DO	M/D	32	BBCC	Ind	
European Language Studies with Modern English St	T2Q3	4FT deg	L g	12-16	MO/DO	M/D	32	BBCC	Ind	
European Language Studies with Modern History	T2VC	4FT deg	L g	12-16	MO/DO	M/D	32	BBCC	Ind	
European Language Studies with Multimedia	T2PK	4FT deg	L g	12-16	EurO	M/D	32	BBCC	Ind	
European Language Studies with Photography	T2WN	4FT deg	L g	12-16	MO/DO	M/D	32	BBCC	Ind	
European Language Studies with Plant Biology	T2C2	4FT deg	L g	12-16	MO/DO	M/D	32	BBCC	Ind	
European Language Studies with Politics	T2M1	4FT deg	L g	12-16	MO/DO	M/D	32	BBCC	Ind	

course details			98 expected requirements							96 entry stats
TITLE	CODE	COURSE	SUBJECTS	A/AS	NO/C	AGNVQ	IB	SQA(H)	SQA	RATIO A/AS
European Language Studies with Publishing	T2P5	4FT deg	L g	12-16	MO/DO	M/D	32	BBCC	Ind	
European Language Studies with Social Studies	T2L3	4FT deg	L g	12-16	MO/DO	M/D	32	BBCC	Ind	
European Language Studies with Video Production	T2W5	4FT deg	L g	12-16	MO/DO	M/D	32	BBCC	Ind	
Geography and European Language Studies	FT82	3FT deg	L g	12-16	MO/DO	M/D	32	BBCC	Ind	
Geology and European Language Studies	TF26	3FT deg	g	12-16	MO/DO	M/D	32	BBCC	Ind	
Health Science and European Language Studies	TB29	3FT deg	L g	12-16	MO/DO	M/D	32	BBCC	Ind	
Health Studies and European Language Studies	TB2X	3FT deg	L g	12-16	MO/DO	M/D	32	BBCC	Ind	
Human Biology and European Language Studies	BT12	3FT deg	L g	12-16	MO/DO	M/D	32	BBCC	Ind	
Journalism and European Language Studies	PT62	3FT deg		12-16	MO/DO	M/D	32	BBCC	Ind	
Language & Stylistics in English & Euro Lang St	QTG2	3FT deg	L g	12-16	MO/DO	M/D	32	BBCC	Ind	
Law and European Language Studies	TM23	3FT deg	L g	12-16	MO/DO	M/D	32	BBCC	Ind	
Leisure Studies and European Language Studies	TN27	3FT deg	L g	12-16	MO/DO	M/D	32	BBCC	Ind	
Literary Studies in English and Euro Language St	TQ22	3FT deg	L g	12-16	MO/DO	M/D	32	BBCC	Ind	1
Mapping Science and European Language Studies	TF28	3FT deg	L g	12-16	MO/DO	M/D	32	BBCC	Ind	
Marketing and European Language Studies	TN25	3FT deg	L g	12-16	MO/DO	M/D	32	BBCC	Ind	3
Media Practices and European Language Studies	TP24	3FT deg	L g	12-16	MO/DO	M/D	32	BBCC	Ind	
Media Production and European Language Studies	TP2L	3FT deg	L g	12-16	MO/DO	M/D	32	BBCC	Ind	
Modern English Studies and European Language St	TQ23	3FT deg	L g	12-16	MO/DO	M/D	32	BBCC	Ind	2
Modern European Studies	T210	4FT deg	L g	12-16	MO/DO	M/D	32	BBCC	Ind	
Modern History and European Language Studies	TV2C	3FT deg	L g	12-16	MO/DO	M/D	32	BBCC	Ind	1
Organisational Behaviour and Euro Language Studs	TL27	3FT deg	L g	12-16	MO/DO	M/D	32	BBCC	Ind	
Physical Geography and European Language Studies	TF2V	3FT deg	L g	12-16	MO/DO	M/D	32	BBCC	Ind	
Plant Biology and European Language Studies	CT22	3FT deg	L g	12-16	MO/DO	M/D	32	BBCC	Ind	
Politics and European Language Studies	TM21	3FT deg	L g	12-16	MO/DO	M/D	32	BBCC	Ind	
Public Policy and Management and Euro Lang Studs	TM2C	3FT deg	g	12-16	MO/DO	M/D	32	BBCC	Ind	
Regional Planning and Dev and European Lang St	TK24	3FT deg	g	12-16	MO/DO	M/D	32	BBCC	Ind	
Social Studies and European Language Studies	TL23	3FT deg	L g	12-16	MO/DO	M/D	32	BBCC	Ind	
Sociology and European Language Studies	LTH2	3FT deg		12-16	MO/DO	M/D	32	BBCC	Ind	
Software Engineering and European Language Studs	GT72	3FT deg		12-16	MO/DO	M/D	32	BBCC	Ind	
Stage & Screen Technology and European Lang St	PTK2	3FT deg		12-16	MO/DO	M/D	32	BBCC	Ind	
Univ of MANCHESTER										
Computer Science with a Modern Language	G5T9	4FT deg	M+L	BBC	X	X	28$	BBBBB$	X	7
European Studies and Modern Langs (French)	RT12	4FT deg	F	ABB-BBB	Ind	D^	28$	AAABB$	Ind	5 22/30
European Studies and Modern Langs (German)	RT22	4FT deg	G	ABB-BBB	Ind	D^	28$	AAABB$	Ind	6 22/30
European Studies and Modern Langs (Italian)	RT32	4FT deg	L	ABB-BBB	Ind	D^	28$	AAABB$	Ind	9
European Studies and Modern Langs (Spanish)	RT42	4FT deg	Sp	ABB-BBB	Ind	D^	28$	AAABB$	Ind	7 22/28
Middle Eastern and Modern European Languages	TT62	3FT/4FT deg	L	BCC-BBC	2M+5D		30	ABBBB	Ind	5
UMIST (Manchester)										
Clothing Engineering and Mgt with a Mod Language	J4T9	4SW deg	M/P/C g	18	5M $	Ind	25	BBBCC	Ind	
Mathematics with Study in Europe	G1T2	4FT deg	M g	BBC	Ind	Ind	30$	CSYS	Ind	10
Textile Design and Des Mgt with a Mod Language	J4T2	4FT deg	* g	18	5M	Ind	28	BBBCC	Ind	6
Textile Science and Tech with a Mod Language	J4TX	3FT deg	M+P/C g	20	4M+1D$	Ind	25	BBBBB	Ind	1
Textile Technology and Mgt with a Modern Lang	J4TY	4FT deg	M/P/C g	18	5M $	Ind	25	BBBCC	Ind	
MANCHESTER METROPOLITAN Univ										
European Studies/Applied Physics	FT32	3FT deg	M+P g	12	5M $	M$	27$	BCCCC$	Ind	
European Studies/Business Mathematics	GTC2	3FT deg	M/P/Ec g	16	1M+3D$	M$	28$	BBBCC$	Ind	
European Studies/Chemistry	FT12	3FT deg	C g	14	MO $	M$	28$	BBCCC$	Ind	
European Studies/Computer Technology	GTM2	3FT deg	* g	16	1M+3D	M$	28	BBBCC	Ind	
European Studies/Computing Science	GT52	3FT deg	* g	16	1M+3D	M$	28	BBBCC	Ind	
European Studies/Economics	LT12	3FT deg	* g	18	2M+4D	M$	29	BBBBC	Ind	
Geography/European Studies	LT82	3FT deg	* g	CCC	2M+4D	M$	29	BBBBC	Ind	
Languages/Applicable Mathematics	GT19	3FT deg	M g	18	2M+4D$	M$	29$	BBBBC$	Ind	

course details | 98 expected requirements | 96 entry stats

TITLE	CODE	COURSE	SUBJECTS	A/AS	NO/C	RGNVQ	IB	SQA(H)	SQA	RATIO A/AS
Languages/Applied Physics	FT39	3FT deg	M+P g	14	MO $	M$	28$	BBCCC$	Ind	
Languages/Business Mathematics	GTC9	3FT deg	M/P/Ec g	18	2M+4D$	M$	29$	BBBBC$	Ind	
Languages/Chemistry	FT19	3FT deg	C g	14	MO $	M$	28$	BBCCC$	Ind	
Languages/Economics	LT19	3FT deg	* g	18	2M+4D	M$	29	BBBBC	Ind	
Languages/Electronics	HTP9	3FT deg	* g	14	MO	M$	28	BBCCC	Ind	
Languages/Environmental Studies	FT99	3FT deg	* g	18	2M+4D	M$	29	BBBBC	Ind	
Languages/European Studies	TT29	3FT deg	* g	18	2M+4D	M$	29	BBBBC	Ind	10/16
Languages/Geography	LT89	3FT deg	* g	CCC	2M+4D	M$	29	BBBBC	Ind	
Manufacturing/Languages	HT79	3FT deg	* g	14	MO	M$	28	BBCCC	Ind	
Materials Science/Languages	FT29	3FT deg	M/P/C g	14	MO $	M$	28$	BBCCC$	Ind	
Physics Studies/European Studies	TF23	3FT deg	M/P g	12	5M $		27$	BCCCC$	Ind	
Physics Studies/Languages	FTH9	3FT deg	P/M g	14	MO $		28$	BBCCC$	Ind	
Polymer Science/European Studies	JT42	3FT deg	C g	12	5M $	M$	27$	BCCCC$	Ind	
Psychology/Languages	LT79	3FT deg	* g	CCC	2M+4D	D$	29	BBBBC	Ind	
Social Studies of Technology/European Studies	LT32	3FT deg	* g	16	1M+3D	M$	28	BBBCC	Ind	
Social Studies of Technology/Languages	LT39	3FT deg	* g	18	2M+4D	M$	29	BBBBC	Ind	

MIDDLESEX Univ

TITLE	CODE	COURSE	SUBJECTS	A/AS	NO/C	RGNVQ	IB	SQA(H)	SQA	RATIO A/AS
Joint Honours Degree French Studies	Y400	3FT/4FT deg	F g	12-16	5M	Ind	28	Ind	Ind	
Joint Honours Degree German	Y400	3FT/4FT deg	* g	12-16	5M	Ind	28	Ind	Ind	
Joint Honours Degree Italian	Y400	3FT/4FT deg	* g	12-16	5M	M* go	28	Ind	Ind	
Joint Honours Degree Spanish	Y400	4FT deg	* g	12-16	5M	M$ go	28	BBCC	Ind	

NAPIER Univ

TITLE	CODE	COURSE	SUBJECTS	A/AS	NO/C	RGNVQ	IB	SQA(H)	SQA	RATIO A/AS
Business Studies and Languages	NT12	4SW/5SW deg	*	CDD	Ind	Ind	Ind	BBCC	Ind	
Hospitality and Languages	NT79	3FT/4FT deg	*	CC-DDD	Ind	Ind	Ind	BBCC	Ind	
Languages and Export Management	NT59	3FT/4FT deg	F/G	CDE	Ind	Ind	Ind	BBCC$	Ind	3 8/14
Languages and Marketing	NT5X	3FT/4FT deg	*	CCD	Ind	Ind	Ind	BBCC	Ind	
Languages and Tourism	PT79	3FT/4FT deg	*	CCD	Ind	Ind	Ind	BBCC	Ind	

NENE COLLEGE

TITLE	CODE	COURSE	SUBJECTS	A/AS	NO/C	RGNVQ	IB	SQA(H)	SQA	RATIO A/AS
American Studies with European Union Studies	Q4T2	3FT deg		DD	5M	M	24	CCC	Ind	
Business Administration with European Union St	N1T2	3FT deg	g	10	M+1D	M	24	BCC	Ind	
Economics with European Union Studies	L1T2	3FT deg	g	6	5M	M	24	CCC	Ind	
Geography with European Union Studies	F8T2	3FT deg	Gy	8	5M	M	24	CCC	Ind	
Industry and Enterprise with European Union St	H1T2	3FT deg								
Information Systems with European Union Studies	G5T2	3FT deg		6	5M	M	24	CCC	Ind	
Law with European Union Studies	M3T2	3FT deg	g	10	3M+2D	M	24	CCC	Ind	
Politics with European Union Studies	M1T2	3FT deg								

Univ of NEWCASTLE

TITLE	CODE	COURSE	SUBJECTS	A/AS	NO/C	RGNVQ	IB	SQA(H)	SQA	RATIO A/AS
Chemistry with European Studies (French)	F1TF	4FT deg	C g	BCC	Ind		Ind	ABBB$	Ind	
Chemistry with European Studies (German)	F1TG	4FT deg	C g	BCC	Ind		Ind	ABBB$	Ind	
Chemistry with European Studies (Spanish)	F1T2	4FT deg	C g	BCC	Ind		Ind	ABBB$	Ind	

Univ of Wales COLLEGE, NEWPORT

TITLE	CODE	COURSE	SUBJECTS	A/AS	NO/C	RGNVQ	IB	SQA(H)	SQA	RATIO A/AS
European Studies and Archaeology	VT62	3FT deg		10	M+D	D$	Ind	Ind	Ind	
European Studies and English	QT32	3FT deg		10	M+D	D$	Ind	Ind	Ind	
European Studies and Environmental Studies	FT92	3FT deg		10	M+D	D$	Ind	Ind	Ind	
Geography and European Studies	TL28	3FT deg		10	M+D	D$	Ind	Ind	Ind	
History and European Studies	TV21	3FT deg		10	M+D	D$	Ind	Ind	Ind	
Information Technology and European Studies	GT52	3FT deg		10	M+D	D$	Ind	Ind	Ind	
Religious Studies and European Studies	TV28	3FT deg		10	M+D	D$	Ind	Ind	Ind	

course details			98 expected requirements							96 entry stats	
TITLE	CODE	COURSE	SUBJECTS	A/AS	NQ/C	AGNVQ	IB	SQA(H)	SQA	RATIO	A/AS
NORTHBROOK COLLEGE Sussex											
Business Studies with Languages	2T1N	2FT HND	*	6-8	3M	Ind	Dip	Ind	Ind		
Univ of NORTH LONDON											
Combined Honours in European Studies	T201	3FT/4FT deg	*	CC	Ind	Ind	Ind	Ind	Ind		
European Studies	T200	4FT deg	*	CD	Ind	Ind	Ind	Ind	Ind	5	8/16
European Studies and Hospitality Management	NT72	3FT deg	* g	CD	MO+4D	D	Ind	Ind	Ind		
European Studies and International Business	NT12	3FT deg	* g	12	MO+4D	D	Ind	Ind	Ind		
European Studies and Politics	MT12	3FT deg	*	CC	Ind	Ind	Ind	Ind	Ind		
European Studies and Public Administration	LT42	3FT deg	*	CC	Ind	Ind	Ind	Ind	Ind		
European Studies and Sociology	LT32	3FT deg	*	CC	Ind	Ind	Ind	Ind	Ind		
Combined Honours Caribbean Studies	Y300	3FT/4FT deg	*	CC	Ind	Ind	Ind	Ind	Ind		
Univ of NORTHUMBRIA											
European Studies	T200	4FT deg	F/G g	14	Ind		24	BCCCC	Ind	6	10/20
International Business Studies	N1T9	4SW deg	* g	CCC	MO+4D	D4	26	BBBCC	Ind	4	14/26
Univ of NOTTINGHAM											
Agricultural Biochemistry with European Studies	D8T2	4FT deg	2(M/S/Gy) g	CC-CDD	3M $	MS	24$	CSYS$	N$	1	
Agriculture with European Studies	D2T2	4FT deg	2(M/S/Gy) g	CC-CDD	3M $	MS	24$	CSYS$	N$		
Animal Science with European Studies (4 Yrs)	D2TF	4FT deg	2(M/S/Gy) g	CC-CDD	3M $	MS	24$	CSYS$	N$	7	
Applied Biology with European Studies	D8TF	4FT deg	2(M/S/Gy) g	CC-CDD	3M $	MS	24$	CSYS$	N$	5	
Biotechnology in Agriculture with Euro Studies	D8TG	4FT deg	2(M/S/Gy) g	CC-CDD	3M $	MS	24$	CSYS$	N$		
Economics with European Union Studies	L1T2	3FT deg	* g	AAB-ABB	X		32	Ind	X	9	26/30
Environmental Biology with European Studies	C1T2	4FT deg	2(M/S/Gy) g	CC-CDD	3M $	MS	24$	CSYS$	N$	6	
Environmental Science with Euro Studies	F9T2	4FT deg	2(M/S/Gy) g	CC-CDD	3M $	MS	24$	CSYS$	N$	22	
Food Microbiology with European Studies	C5T2	4FT deg	2(M/S/Gy) g	CC-CDD	3M $	MS	24$	CSYS$	N$		
Food Science with European Studies	D4T2	4FT deg	2(M/S/Gy) g	CC-CDD	3M $	MS	24$	CSYS$	N$	15	
Horticulture with European Studies	D2TG	4FT deg	2(M/S/Gy) g	CC-CDD	3M $	MS	24$	CSYS$	N$		
Modern European Studies	T206	4FT deg	L/+H/So	BBB						15	26/30
Modern Language Studies	T900	4FT deg	2L	BBC						48	
Nutrition with European Studies	B4T2	4FT deg	2(M/S/Gy) g	CC-CDD	3M $	MS	24$	CSYS$	N$	7	
Nutritional Biochemistry with European Studies	C7T2	4FT deg	2(M/S/Gy) g	CC-CDD	3M $	MS	24$	CSYS$	N$		
Physics with European Language (4 Yrs)	F3T2	4FT deg	P+M g	BBB-BBC	Ind		Ind	Ind	Ind	9	
Physics with European Language (4 Yrs)	F3TF	4FT deg	P+M g	BB-BBC	Ind		Ind	CSYS	Ind		
Plant and Crop Science with European Studies	D2T9	4FT deg	2(M/S/Gy) g	CC-CDD	3M $	MS	24$	CSYS$	N$		
NOTTINGHAM TRENT Univ											
European Economics in the Netherlands	L1T2	4FT deg	* g	14-16	1M+3D	Ind	Ind	BBCC	Ind	8	
Modern European Studies	T200	3FT/4SW deg	* g	14-16	M+D	Ind	28	CCCC	Ind	3	10/20
Modern Languages with Communication Studies	T9P3	4FT deg	2L g	18	Ind	Ind	28	CCCC	Ind	4	12/20
OXFORD Univ											
Arabic with subsidiary language (4 Yrs)	T6T9	4FT deg	*	AAB-ABB	DO		36	AAAAA	Ind		
Classics and Modern Languages (3 Yrs)	QT89	3FT deg	Ln/Gk+L	AAB	DO		36	AAAAA	Ind	4	
Classics and Modern Languages (4 Yrs)	TQ98	4FT deg	Ln/Gk+L	AAB	DO		36	AAAAA	Ind	2	30/30
English and Modern Languages (3 Yrs)	QT39	3FT deg	E+L	AAB	DO		36	AAAAA	Ind	9	
English and Modern Languages (4 Yrs)	TQ93	4FT deg	E+L	AAB	DO		36	AAAAA	Ind	4	30/30
European and Middle Eastern Languages (3 Yrs)	TT26	3FT deg	L	AAB	DO		36	AAAAA	Ind		
European and Middle Eastern Languages (4 Yrs)	TT2P	4FT deg	L	AAB	DO		36	AAAAA	Ind	3	28/30
Modern History and Modern Languages (3 Yrs)	TV91	3FT deg	H+L	AAB	DO		36	AAAAA	Ind	2	
Modern History and Modern Languages (4 Yrs)	VT19	4FT deg	H+L	AAB	DO		36	AAAAA	Ind	3	30/30
Modern Languages (3 Yrs)	T900	3FT deg	L/2L	AAB	DO		36	AAAAA	Ind	6	
Modern Languages (4 Yrs)	T901	4FT deg	L/2L	AAB	DO		36	AAAAA	Ind	2	28/30

			98 expected requirements							96 entry stats	
TITLE	**CODE**	**COURSE**	**SUBJECTS**	**A/AS**	**ND/C**	**AGNVQ**	**IB**	**SQA(H)**	**SQA**	**RATIO**	**A/AS**
Persian with subsidiary language (4 Yrs)	T6TX	4FT deg	*	AAB-ABB	DO		36	AAAAA	Ind		
Philosophy and Modern Languages (3 Yrs)	TV97	3FT deg	L	AAB	DO		36	AAAAA	Ind	3	
Philosophy and Modern Languages (4 Yrs)	VT79	4FT deg	L	AAB	DO		36	AAAAA	Ind	2	26/30
Turkish with subsidiary language (4 Yrs)	T6TY	4FT deg	*	AAB-ABB	DO		36	AAAAA	Ind		

OXFORD WESTMINSTER COLLEGE

Contemporary English Studies with Language Studs	Q3T9	3FT deg	E	CE	MO	M	Ind	CCC	Ind		
Contemporary English Studies with Language Studs	Q3TX	2FT Dip	E	CE	MO	M	Ind	CCC	Ind		
Contemporary French Studies with Language Studs	R1T9	3FT deg	F	CE	MO	M	Ind	CCC	Ind		
Contemporary French Studies with Language Studs	R1TX	2FT Dip	F	CE	MO	M	Ind	CCC	Ind		
Contemporary Geography Studies with Language St	L8TX	2FT Dip	Gy	CE	MO	M	Ind	CCC	Ind		
Contemporary Geography Studies with Language St	L8T9	3FT deg	Gy	CE	MO	M	Ind	CCC	Ind		
Contemporary Historical Studies with Language St	V1T9	3FT deg	H	CE	MO	M	Ind	CCC	Ind		
Contemporary Historical Studies with Language St	V1TX	2FT Dip	H	CE	MO	M	Ind	CCC	Ind		

OXFORD BROOKES Univ

Lang for Bus:Italian-Ab Initio/Spanish-Post GCSE	TN91	4FT deg									
Langs for Bus:Italian-Ab Initio/French-Post A	TNGC	4FT deg									
Langs for Bus:Italian-Ab Initio/German-Post A	TNGD	4FT deg									
Langs for Bus:Italian-Ab Initio/German-Post GCSE	T2N1	4FT deg									
Langs for Bus:Italian-Ab Initio/Spanish-Post A	TNYD	4FT deg									
Languages for Business:English/French-Post A	NTCF	4FT deg	E+F	BC-CDD	Ind	M*^	Ind	Ind	Ind		
Languages for Business:English/French-Post GCSE	NT12	4FT deg	E g	BC-CDD	Ind	M*^	Ind	Ind	Ind	1	
Languages for Business:English/German-Post A	TNF1	4FT deg	E+G	BC-CDD	Ind	M*^	Ind	Ind	Ind		
Languages for Business:English/German-Post GCSE	NTDG	4FT deg	E g	BC-CDD	Ind	M*^	Ind	Ind	Ind		
Languages for Business:English/Italian-Post A	NTCX	4FT deg	E+I	BC-CDD	Ind	M*^	Ind	Ind	Ind		
Languages for Business:English/Italian-Post GCSE	NT19	4FT deg	E g	BC-CDD	Ind	M*^	Ind	Ind	Ind		
Languages for Business:English/Spanish-Post A	TNX1	4FT deg	E+Sp	BC-CDD	Ind	M*^	Ind	Ind	Ind	1	
Languages for Business:English/Spanish-Post GCSE	NTDY	4FT deg	E g	BC-CDD	Ind	M*^	Ind	Ind	Ind		
Languages for Business:French/German-Post A	TNFC	4FT deg	F+G	BC-CDD	Ind	M*^	Ind	Ind	Ind	6	
Languages for Business:French/German-Post GCSE	TN21	4FT deg	F g	BC-CDD	Ind	M*^	Ind	Ind	Ind	3	
Languages for Business:French/Italian-Post A	NTCY	4FT deg	F+I	BC-CDD	Ind	M*^	Ind	Ind	Ind	2	
Languages for Business:French/Italian-Post GCSE	NT1X	4FT deg	F g	BC-CDD	Ind	M*^	Ind	Ind	Ind	4	
Languages for Business:French/Spanish-Post A	TNXC	4FT deg	F+Sp	BC-CDD	Ind	M*^	Ind	Ind	Ind	4	18/22
Languages for Business:French/Spanish-Post GCSE	TNYC	4FT deg	F g	BC-CDD	Ind	M*^	Ind	Ind	Ind	5	
Languages for Business:German/French-Post A	NTCG	4FT deg	G+F	BC-CDD	Ind	M*^	Ind	Ind	Ind	5	
Languages for Business:German/French-Post GCSE	NT1F	4FT deg	G g	BC-CDD	Ind	M*^	Ind	Ind	Ind		
Languages for Business:German/Italian-Post A	NTD9	4FT deg	G+I	BC-CDD	Ind	M*^	Ind	Ind	Ind		
Languages for Business:German/Italian-Post GCSE	NT1Y	4FT deg	G g	BC-CDD	Ind	M*^	Ind	Ind	Ind		
Languages for Business:German/Spanish-Post A	TNXD	4FT deg	G+Sp	BC-CDD	Ind	M*^	Ind	Ind	Ind		
Languages for Business:German/Spanish-Post GCSE	TN9C	4FT deg	G g	BC-CDD	Ind	M*^	Ind	Ind	Ind		
Languages for Business:Italian/French-Post A	NTD2	4FT deg	I+F	BC-CDD	Ind	M*^	Ind	Ind	Ind		
Languages for Business:Italian/French-Post GCSE	NT1G	4FT deg	I	BC-CDD	Ind	M*^	Ind	Ind	Ind		
Languages for Business:Italian/German-Post A	TNFD	4FT deg	I+G	BC-CDD	Ind	M*^	Ind	Ind	Ind		
Languages for Business:Italian/German-Post GCSE	TN2C	4FT deg	I g	BC-CDD	Ind	M*^	Ind	Ind	Ind		
Languages for Business:Italian/Spanish-Post A	TNY1	4FT deg	I+Sp	BC-CDD	Ind	M*^	Ind	Ind	Ind		
Languages for Business:Italian/Spanish-Post GCSE	TN9D	4FT deg	I g	BC-CDD	Ind	M*^	Ind	Ind	Ind		
Languages for Business:Spanish/French-Post A	NTDF	4FT deg	Sp+F	BC-CDD	Ind	M*^	Ind	Ind	Ind	5	
Languages for Business:Spanish/French-Post GCSE	NTC2	4FT deg	Sp g	BC-CDD	Ind	M*^	Ind	Ind	Ind	8	
Languages for Business:Spanish/German-Post A	TNG1	4FT deg	Sp+G	BC-CDD	Ind	M*^	Ind	Ind	Ind		
Languages for Business:Spanish/German-Post GCSE	TN2D	4FT deg	Sp g	BC-CDD	Ind	M*^	Ind	Ind	Ind		
Languages for Business:Spanish/Italian-Post A	NTDX	4FT deg	Sp+I	BC-CDD	Ind	M*^	Ind	Ind	Ind		
Languages for Business:Spanish/Italian-Post GCSE	NTC9	4FT deg	Sp g	BC-CDD	Ind	M*^	Ind	Ind	Ind		

European Studies and Languages   28

	course details			98 expected requirements						96 entry stats
TITLE	CODE	COURSE	SUBJECTS	A/AS	ND/C	AGNVQ	IB	SQA(H)	SQA	RATIO A/AS
Univ of PAISLEY										
Biology with European Language	C1T2	3FT/4FT/5SW deg	* g	CCC-EE	Ind	Ind	Ind	BCC$	Ind	2
Business Info Technology and Euro Languages	GT72	4SW/5SW deg	* g	CC	Ind	Ind	Ind	BBCC$	Ind	
Mathematical Sciences with European Language	G1T2	3FT/4FT/5SW deg	M+S g	CCC-EE	Ind	Ind	Ind	BCC$	Ind	
Physics with European Language	F3T2	3FT/4FT/5SW deg	M+P g	CCC-EE	Ind	Ind	Ind	BCC$	Ind	
Univ of PLYMOUTH										
Applied Economics with Languages	L1T9	3FT deg	L g	CCD-CDD	MO	M$^	Ind	BCCC	Ind	5
Business Economics with Languages	L1TX	3FT deg	L g	CDD-CCD	MO	M$^	Ind	BCCC	Ind	
Chemistry with Languages	F1T9	3FT deg	C+L g	CC	3M	MS^	Ind	CCCC	Ind	
European Economics with Languages	L1TY	3FT deg	L g	CDD-CCD	MO	M$^	Ind	BCCC	Ind	
European Studies with French	T2R1	4FT deg	F g	18	Ind	Ind	Ind	Ind	Ind	
European Studies with German	T2R2	4FT deg	G g	18	Ind	Ind	Ind	Ind	Ind	
European Studies with Italian	T2R3	4FT deg	I g	18	Ind	Ind	Ind	Ind	Ind	
European Studies with Modern Languages	T2T9	4FT deg	F/G/I/Sp g	18	Ind	Ind	Ind	Ind	Ind	
European Studies with Spanish	T2R4	4FT deg	Sp g	18	Ind	Ind	Ind	Ind	Ind	
Geography with Languages	F8T9	3FT deg	Gy+L g	16-18	X	M$^	Ind	ABBB	Ind	6 12/20
Geology with Languages	F6T9	3FT deg	S+L g	12	4M	MS^	Ind	CCC	Ind	
International Business with Modern Languages	N1TX	4FT/4SW deg	L g	CCD-CCC	MO	M12^	Ind	BBCC	Ind	
Law with Languages	M3T9	3FT deg	L g	BCC-BBC	DO	D12^	Ind	BBBB$	Ind	
Modern Languages with Applied Economics	T9L1	3FT/4SW deg	L g	C	Ind	Ind	Ind	Ind	Ind	
Modern Languages with Business	T9N1	3FT/4SW deg	L g	C	Ind	Ind	Ind	Ind	Ind	
Modern Languages with Computing	T9G5	3FT/4SW deg	L g	C	Ind	Ind	Ind	Ind	Ind	
Modern Languages with Ecology	T9D2	3FT/4SW deg	L g	C	Ind	Ind	Ind	Ind	Ind	
Modern Languages with Geography	T9F8	3FT/4SW deg	L g	C	Ind	Ind	Ind	Ind	Ind	
Modern Languages with Geology	T9F6	3FT/4SW deg	L g	C	Ind	Ind	Ind	Ind	Ind	
Modern Languages with Human Biology	T9C9	3FT/4SW deg	L g	C	Ind	Ind	Ind	Ind	Ind	
Modern Languages with Law	T9M3	3FT/4SW deg	L g	C	Ind	Ind	Ind	Ind	Ind	
Modern Languages with Politics	T9M1	3FT/4SW deg	L g	C	Ind	Ind	Ind	Ind	Ind	
Modern Languages with Psychology	T9C8	3FT/4SW deg	L g	C	Ind	Ind	Ind	Ind	Ind	
Modern Languages with Social Policy	T9L4	3FT/4SW deg	L g	C	Ind	Ind	Ind	Ind	Ind	
Modern Languages with Sociology	T9L3	3FT/4SW deg	L g	C	Ind	Ind	Ind	Ind	Ind	
Political Economy with Languages	LT1X	3FT deg	L g	CDD-CCD	MO $	M$^	Ind	BCCC	Ind	
Politics with Languages	M1T9	3FT deg	L g	14	Ind	M$^	Ind	BBBC$	Ind	
Psychology with Languages	C8T9	3FT/4SW deg	L g	BBC	MO+3D	M12^	Ind	BBBC$	Ind	6 18/20
Social Policy with Languages	L4T9	3FT deg	L g	14	Ind	M$^	Ind	BBBC$	Ind	3
Sociology with Languages	L3T9	3FT deg	L g	14	3M	M$^	Ind	BBBC$	Ind	10
Statistics(App) and Mgt Sci with Languages	G4TX	3FT deg	M/St+L g	10	MO $	M$^	Ind	BBCC	Ind	
Statistics(App) with Languages	G4T9	3FT deg	M/St+L g	10	MO $	M$^	Ind	BBCC	Ind	
Univ of PORTSMOUTH										
European Studies	T200	4FT deg	L	12	5M	M/$6/^	25	BCCC	Ind	4 6/16
Languages and International Trade	TN21	4FT deg	L	12	5M	M*6/^	25	BCCC	Ind	5 4/14
QUEEN MARY & WESTFIELD COLL (Univ of London)										
French (European Studies)	RT1F	4FT deg	F	20		M^	30$			
French and German (European Studies)	TT92	4FT deg	F+G	18		M^	30$			
French and Hispanic Studies (European Studies)	TTX2	4FT deg	F	20		M^	30$			
French and Russian (European Studies)	TT9G	4FT deg	F	18		M^	30$			
German (European Studies)	RT2F	4FT deg	G	20		M^	30$			
German and Hispanic Studies (European Studies)	TTXF	4FT deg	G/Sp	18		M^	30$			
German and Russian (European Studies)	TTYG	4FT deg	G	20		M^	30$			
Hispanic Studies (European Studies)	RT4F	4FT deg	L	18		M^	30$			
Russian (European Studies)	RT8F	4FT deg	L	18		M^	30$			

TITLE	CODE	COURSE	SUBJECTS	A/AS	ND/C	AGNVQ	IB	SQA(H)	SQA	RATIO A/AS

course details · 98 expected requirements · 96 entry stats

QUEEN'S Univ Belfast

TITLE	CODE	COURSE	SUBJECTS	A/AS	ND/C	AGNVQ	IB	SQA(H)	SQA	RATIO A/AS
European Area Studies	M1T2	3FT deg	L/* g	BCC	3M+4D	D*6/^ go	29$	ABBB	Ind	
European Area Studies/Economics	LT1F	3FT deg								
European Studies	T203	4FT deg	L/* g	BCC	3M+4D	D*6/^ go	29$	ABBB	Ind	10 18/20
Geography with Extended Studies in Europe	F8TF	4FT deg	L+Gy g	BBC	X	X	30$	X	X	12
Geography with Studies in Europe	F8T2	3FT deg	L+Gy g	BBC	X	X	30$	X	X	
Management with European Area Studies	N1T2	3FT deg	L/* g	BBB	2M+5D	D*^ go	32$	AABBB	Ind	
Politics/European Area Studies	MT1F	3FT deg	L/* g	BCC	3M+4D	D*6/^ go	29$	ABBB	Ind	

Univ of READING

TITLE	CODE	COURSE	SUBJECTS	A/AS	ND/C	AGNVQ	IB	SQA(H)	SQA	RATIO A/AS
Agricultural Botany with International Studies	D8TX	4FT deg	2S g	CDD	MO	MS6/^ gi	28$	BBCC	Ind	2
Agricultural Botany with Studies in Europe	D8T2	4FT deg	2S g	CDD	MO	MS6/^ gi	28$	BBCC	Ind	
Crop Protection with Studies in Europe	D2TX	4FT deg	2S g	CCC	MO	MS6/^ gi	28$	BBBC	Ind	
Crop Science with International Studies	D2TY	4FT deg	2S g	CDD	MO	MS6/^ gi	28$	BBCC	Ind	
Crop Science with Studies in Europe	D2TF	4FT deg	2S g	CDD	MO	MS6/^ gi	28$	BBCC	Ind	
European Studies	T200	4FT deg	F/* g	BBC	Ind	DB6/^ go	31	BBBB	Ind	13 18/26
Horticulture with Studies in Europe	D2TG	4FT deg	B/C g	CDD	MO	MS6/^ gi	28$	BBCC	Ind	5
Landscape Management with Studies in Europe	D2T9	4FT deg	B/En/Gy g	CCD	MO	M$6/^ gi	28$	BBCC	Ind	7

Univ College of RIPON & YORK ST JOHN

TITLE	CODE	COURSE	SUBJECTS	A/AS	ND/C	AGNVQ	IB	SQA(H)	SQA	RATIO A/AS
Cultural Studies with European Studies	L6T2	3FT deg		12	M	M*	27	BBBC		
English Studies with European Studies	Q3T2	3FT deg	E	16	Ind	M*^	30	BBBB		
European Studies	T200	3FT deg		12	M	M*	27	BBBC		
European Studies with Education	T2X9	3FT deg		12	M	M*	27	BBBC		
European Studies with French	T2R1	3FT deg	F	12	Ind	M*^	27	BBBC		
European Studies with Language	T2Q1	3FT deg		12	M	M*	27	BBBC		

ROBERT GORDON Univ

TITLE	CODE	COURSE	SUBJECTS	A/AS	ND/C	AGNVQ	IB	SQA(H)	SQA	RATIO A/AS
Architecture with Languages	K1T2	5SW deg	E+F/G+M/S+Pf	CCD	N	Ind	Ind	BBCC$	Ind	4
Communication with Modern Languages	P3T9	3FT/4FT deg	E+F/G g	CC	Ind	Ind	Ind	BBC$	Ind	4
European Business Admin with Languages	N1T9	4FT deg	E+F/G g	CCC	Ind	Ind	Ind	BBBC$	Ind	4

ROEHAMPTON INST

TITLE	CODE	COURSE	SUBJECTS	A/AS	ND/C	AGNVQ	IB	SQA(H)	SQA	RATIO A/AS
Marketing French and Spanish	NT59▼	4FT deg	E g	12	2M+2D$	P^	26	BCC	N$	7 6/10

ROYAL HOLLOWAY, Univ of London

TITLE	CODE	COURSE	SUBJECTS	A/AS	ND/C	AGNVQ	IB	SQA(H)	SQA	RATIO A/AS
European Studies	T200	4FT deg	L	BBC-BBB			30$	Ind$		5 18/26
European Studies (Main language English)	T201	3FT deg	E	BBC-BBB			30$	Ind		1
Foundation Programme	Y408	4FT deg								
European Studies										

Univ of SALFORD

TITLE	CODE	COURSE	SUBJECTS	A/AS	ND/C	AGNVQ	IB	SQA(H)	SQA	RATIO A/AS
Civil Engineering with European Studies	H2TF	4FT deg	F/G/Sp	EEE		M^				
Civil Engineering with European Studies (4 Yrs)	H2T2	4SW deg	M g	EEE	Ind	M$	Ind	Ind	Ind	11
Environmental & Res Sci with fur st in Eu (4yrs)	F9T2	4FT deg	g	18-20	Ind	Ind	Ind	Ind	Ind	3
European Studies with a Modern Language	T2T9	3FT deg	g	CCC	MO+4D	M	Ind	Ind	X	8 8/20
Manufacturing Engineering with European Studies	H7T2	4SW deg								
Mechanical Engineering with European Studies	H3T2	4SW/5SW deg	M+S/2S g	18	3M+1D$	M	Ind	Ind	Ind	6
Mechanical Engineering with European Studs(MEng)	H3TF	4FT deg	M+S/2S	18	Ind	M	Ind	Ind	Ind	
Modern Languages and Marketing Studies (4 Yrs)	NT59	4SW deg	L g	ABC-BBC	X	X	Ind	Ind	X	3 18/28
Modern Languages with European Studies (4 Yrs)	T9T2	4SW deg	E g	CCC	M+4D	M	Ind	Ind	X	8 16/24

SOAS:Sch of Oriental & African St (U of London)

TITLE	CODE	COURSE	SUBJECTS	A/AS	ND/C	AGNVQ	IB	SQA(H)	SQA	RATIO A/AS
Georgian and Arabic	TT69	4FT deg		22	Ind		31	BBBBC	Ind	
Georgian and Development Studies	MT99	3FT deg		22	Ind		31	BBBBC	Ind	
Georgian and Economics	LT19	3FT deg	g	22	Ind		31	BBBBC	Ind	

course details			98 expected requirements							96 entry stats
TITLE	CODE	COURSE	SUBJECTS	A/AS	ND/C	AGNVQ	IB	SQA(H)	SQA	RATIO A/AS
Georgian and Geography	LT89	3FT deg		20	Ind		30	BBBCC	Ind	
Hebrew and Georgian	QT99	4FT deg		22	Ind		31	BBBBC	Ind	
History and Georgian	TV91	3FT deg		22	Ind		31	BBBBC	Ind	
History of Art/Archaeology and Georgian	TV96	3FT deg		22	Ind		31	BBBBC	Ind	
Indonesian and Dutch	TTM2	3FT/4FT deg		20	Ind		30	BBBCC	Ind	
Law and Georgian	MT39	3FT deg		24	Ind		32	BBBBB	Ind	
Linguistics and Georgian	QT19	3FT deg		22	Ind		31	BBBBC	Ind	
Music and Georgian	TW93	3FT deg		22	Ind		31	BBBBC	Ind	
Persian and Georgian	TTQ9	3FT deg		22	Ind		31	BBBBC	Ind	
Politics and Georgian	MT19	3FT deg		22	Ind		31	BBBBC	Ind	
Social Anthropology and Georgian	LT69	3FT deg		22	Ind		31	BBBBC	Ind	
Study of Religions and Georgian	TV98	3FT deg		22	Ind		31	BBBBC	Ind	
Turkish and Arabic	TT62	4FT deg		22	Ind		31	BBBBC	Ind	2
Turkish and Georgian	TTP9	4FT deg		22	Ind		31	BBBBC	Ind	

Univ of SHEFFIELD

TITLE	CODE	COURSE	SUBJECTS	A/AS	ND/C	AGNVQ	IB	SQA(H)	SQA	RATIO A/AS
Ceramic Science and Engineering with a Mod Lang	J3T9	4FT/5EXT deg	2(M/P/C) g	CCC	5M $	M$^	28$	BBBC$	Ind	
Chemical Eng with a Modern Language (3/4 Yrs)	H8T9	3FT/4FT deg	M+C+L g	BBC-BCC	5M+1D$	X	30$	CSYS	Ind	6 18/30
Civil Engineering with a Modern Lang (3/4 Yrs)	H2T9	3FT/4FT deg	M+S g	BCC	X	M$^	28$	BBBB$	Ind	5 18/26
Electrical Engineering with a Modern Lang (MEng)	H5T9	4FT deg	M/P+L g	BBC-CCC	5M+1D$	D$^	30$	BBCC$	Ind	
Electronic Eng (Systems) with a Mod Lang (MEng)	H6TX	4FT deg	M/P+L g	BBC-CCC	5M+1D$	D$^	30$	BBCC$	Ind	11
Electronic Eng with a Modern Language (MEng)	H6T9	4FT deg	M/P+L g	BBC-CCC	5M+1D$	D$^	30$	BBCC$	Ind	7
Glass Science and Engineering with a Modern Lang	J3TX	4FT/5EXT deg	2(M/P/C) g	CCC	5M $	M$^	28$	BBCC$	Ind	
Materials Science and Eng with a Modern Language	J5T9	3FT deg	2(M/P/C) g	CCC	5M$	M$^	28$	BBCC$	Ind	
Mechanical Engineering with a Modern Language	H3T9	4FT deg	M/P g	24	5M+1D$	D^	32$	AABB$	Ind	6 20/30
Metal Science and Engineering with a Modern Lang	J2T9	4FT/5EXT deg	2(M/P/C) g	CCC	5M $	M$^	28$	BBCC$	Ind	
Modern Languages	T900	4FT deg	2L g	BBC	X	X	30$	ABBB$	Ind	8 22/30
Polymer Science and Engineering with a Mod Lang	J4T9	4FT/5EXT deg	2(M/P/C) g	CCC	5M $	X	28$	BBBC$	Ind	

Univ of SOUTHAMPTON

TITLE	CODE	COURSE	SUBJECTS	A/AS	ND/C	AGNVQ	IB	SQA(H)	SQA	RATIO A/AS
Computer Science and Modern Languages (4 Yrs)	GT59	4FT deg	M+L	22	Ind $	D^	30$	CSYS	Ind	9
Contemporary Europe	T200	4FT deg	F/G/Sp	BBC	1M+4D	Ind	30$	Ind	Ind	6 14/28
Contemporary Europe (English)	T2Q3	3FT deg			Ind	Ind	Ind	Ind	Ind	
European Cultural Studies	T210	4FT deg	F/G/Sp	BBC						

SOUTH BANK Univ

TITLE	CODE	COURSE	SUBJECTS	A/AS	ND/C	AGNVQ	IB	SQA(H)	SQA	RATIO A/AS
Business Studies with Languages	N1T9	4SW deg	* g	CC	3D	M go	Ind	Ind	Ind	
European Electronic Engineering	H6T2	3FT deg	L g	CD	MO	M go	Ind	Ind	Ind	
European Studies	T200	3FT deg	* g	CC	4M+3D	M go	Ind	Ind	Ind	
European Studies and Accounting	NT42	3FT deg	Ac/Ec g	14-18	2M+4D	M go	Ind	Ind	Ind	
European Studies and Business Information Tech	GT72	3FT deg	M g	14-18	2M+4D	M go	Ind	Ind	Ind	
European Studies and Computing	GT52	3FT deg	M g	14-18	2M+4D	M go	Ind	Ind	Ind	
European Studies and Economics	LT1F	3FT deg	Ec/Bu g	14-18	2M+4D	M go	Ind	Ind	Ind	
European Studies and English Studies	QT32	3FT deg	E g	14-18	X	M^ go	Ind	Ind	Ind	
European Studies and Environmental Policy	FT92	3FT deg	* g	14-18	2M+4D	M go	Ind	Ind	Ind	
European Studies with French, German or Spanish	T201	3FT deg	F/G/Sp g	CC	Ind	M go	Ind	Ind	Ind	
Food Policy and European Studies	DT42	3FT deg	S g	14-18	2M+4D	M go	Ind	Ind	Ind	
Health Studies and European Studies	LT4F	3FT deg	S g	14-18	2M+4D	M go	Ind	Ind	Ind	
History and European Studies	TV21	3FT deg	H g	14-18	2M+4D	M go	Ind	Ind	Ind	
Housing and European Studies	KT42	3FT deg	* g	14-18	2M+4D	M go	Ind	Ind	Ind	
Human Biology and European Studies	BT12	3FT deg	S g	14-18	2M+4D	M go	Ind	Ind	Ind	
Human Geography and European Studies	LT82	3FT deg	Gy g	14-18	2M+4D	M go	Ind	Ind	Ind	
Human Resource Management and European Studies	NT62	3FT deg	* g	14-18	2M+4D	M go	Ind	Ind	Ind	
Law and European Studies	MT32	3FT deg	* g	14-18	2M+4D	D go	Ind	Ind	Ind	
Management and European Studies	NT12	3FT deg	* g	14-18	2M+4D	M go	Ind	Ind	Ind	

course details			98 expected requirements							96 entry stats	
TITLE	CODE	COURSE	SUBJECTS	A/AS	ND/C	AGNVQ	IB	SQA(H)	SQA	RATIO	A/AS
Marketing and European Studies	NT52	3FT deg	* g	14-18	2M+4D	M go	Ind	Ind	Ind		
Media Studies and European Studies	PT42	3FT deg	E g	14-18	2M+4D	D go	Ind	Ind	Ind		
Modern Languages and International Business	TN91	4SW deg	F/G/Sp g	CC	DO $	M go	Ind	Ind	Ind		
Modern Languages and International Studies	TN21	4SW deg	F/G/Sp	CC	DO	M go	Ind	Ind	Ind		
Modern Languages and International Tourism	PT7F	4SW deg	L g	CC	6M	M go	Ind	Ind	Ind		
Nutrition and European Studies	BT42	3FT deg	S g	14-18	2M+4D	M go	Ind	Ind	Ind		
Planning and European Studies	KT4F	3FT deg	* g	14-18	2M+4D	M go	Ind	Ind	Ind		
Product Design and European Studies	HT72	3FT deg	Ad g	14-18	2M+4D	M go	Ind	Ind	Ind		
Psychology and European Studies	CT82	3FT deg	S g	14-18	2M+4D	M go	Ind	Ind	Ind		
Social Policy and European Studies	LT42	3FT deg	* g	14-18	2M+4D	M go	Ind	Ind	Ind		
Sociology and European Studies	LT32	3FT deg	* g	14-18	2M+4D	M go	Ind	Ind	Ind		
Sports Science and European Studies	BT62	3FT deg	S g	14-18	2M+4D	M go	Ind	Ind	Ind		
Technology and European Studies	JT92	3FT deg	* g	14-18	2M+4D	M go	Ind	Ind	Ind		
Tourism and European Studies	PT72	3FT deg	L g	14-18	2M+4D	M^ go	Ind	Ind	Ind		
Urban Studies and European Studies	KT4G	3FT deg	* g	14-18	2M+4D	M go	Ind	Ind	Ind		
World Theatre and European Studies	TW24	3FT deg	* g	14-18	2M+4D	M go	Ind	Ind	Ind		
Univ of ST ANDREWS											
European Integration Studies (Modern Languages)	TT92	4FT deg	* g	BBB	X	Ind	30$	BBBB	Ind		
Modern Langs with Int Rels (with Int Yr Abroad)	T9M1	4FT/5FT deg	* g	AAB	X	Ind	36$	AAAB	Ind	4	
Modern Languages (Triple Subject)	T900	4FT deg	* g	BBB	X	Ind	30$	BBBB	Ind		
Modern Languages with Economics	T9LC	4FT deg	* g	BBB	X	Ind	30$	BBBB	Ind		
Modern Languages with Economics (Int Yr Abroad)	T9L1	4FT/5FT deg	* g	BBB	X	Ind	30$	BBBB	Ind		
Modern Languages with International Relations	T9MC	4FT deg	* g	AAB	X	Ind	36$	AAAB	Ind		
Modern Languages with Management	T9NC	4FT deg	* g	BBB	X	Ind	30$	BBBB	Ind		
Modern Languages with Mgt (Integ Year Abroad)	T9N1	4FT/5FT deg	* g	BBB	X	Ind	30$	BBBB	Ind	5	
Modern Languages(Triple Subject Integ Yr Abroad)	T901	4FT/5FT deg	* g	BBB	X	Ind	30$	BBBB	Ind	7	26/28
General Degree of MA *Modern Languages*	Y450	3FT deg	* g	BBB	X	Ind	30$	BBBB	Ind		
STAFFORDSHIRE Univ											
European Economics	LT12	3FT deg	g	12	4M	M$	24	BBC	Ind	2	
Univ of STIRLING											
European Studies	T201	4FT deg	L g	BCC	Ind	Ind	31	BBBC	HN		
Modern Languages/Business Studies	NT19	4FT deg	L g	CCC	Ind	Ind	31	BBBC	HN		
Modern Languages/Marketing	TN95	4FT deg	L g	CCC	Ind	Ind	31	BBBC	HN		
Univ of STRATHCLYDE											
Architectural Studies with European Studies	K1T2	4FT deg	M/P+L	BBC	HN		Ind	BBBBC$	HN		
Computer Science with Modern Languages	G5T9	4FT deg	E+M+L	CCC	HN		Ind	BBBBB$	HN		
Electrical & Mechanical Engineering with Euro St	H3T2	5FT deg	M+P+L g	BBC	Ind	Ind	36$	AABBC$	Ind		
International Business and Modern Languages	NT19	5FT deg	L g	BBC	Ind		32$	ABBBB$	Ind		
Law and a Modern Language	MT32	5FT deg	E+L g	BBB	Ind		30$	AAAAB$	Ind		
Mathematics with a Modern Language	G1T9	4FT deg	M+L g	CC	Ind		30$	BBCC$	Ind		
Arts and Social Sciences *European Studies*	Y440	3FT/4FT deg	g	CCC	Ind		28	BBBBB$	28		
UNIVERSITY COLLEGE SUFFOLK											
Business (European Environment)	21TN	2FT HND	*	E	*N	P*	Ind	Ind	Ind		
Univ of SUNDERLAND											
Biology with European Studies	C1T2	3FT deg	B/C	8	3M	M	Ind	Ind	Ind		
English with European Studies	Q3T2	3FT deg	El g	12	Ind	M	24$	BCCC$	N$		
European Studies	T200	3FT/4SW deg	g	12	2M+1D		24	CCCCC	N	7	4/14
European Studies in Mechanical Eng (Foundation)	HT3F▼	4EXT/5EXTSW deg	*	2	N	P	24	CC	N		

European Studies and Languages   28

course details					98 expected requirements						96 entry stats

TITLE	CODE	COURSE	SUBJECTS	R/AS	NO/C	AGNVQ	IB	SQA(H)	SQA	RATIO	R/AS
European Studies in Mechanical Engineering	HT32	3FT/4SW deg	M/P/C g	12	3M $	ME	24$	CCC$	N$	2	
French with European Studies	R1T2	4FT deg	F g	10	N $	M	24$	CCCC$	N$	5	
Geography with European Studies	L8T2	3FT deg	Gy/Gl g	12	3M $	M	24	BCCC$	N$	1	
German with European Studies	R2T2	4FT deg	G g	10	N $	M	24$	CCCC$	N$	6	
History with European Studies	V1T2	3FT deg	H g	12	Ind	M	24$	BCCC	Ind	1	
Philosophy with European Studies	V7T2	3FT deg	* g	12	Ind	M	24	BCCC	Ind	1	
Politics with European Studies	M1T2	3FT deg	* g	12	3M	M	24	BCCC	N	8	
Psychology with European Studies	C8T2	3FT deg	* g	14	MO	M	26$	BBCC$	N		
Religious Studies with European Studies	V8T2	3FT deg	* g	12	3M	M	24	BCCC	N		
Sociology with European Studies	L3T2	3FT deg	* g	12	3M	M	24	BCCC	N		

Univ of SURREY

Combined Languages	T900	4FT/SW deg	F/G/R	BBC-CCC	3M+3D$		30$	ABBCC	Ind		
French and European Studies	RT12	4SW deg	F	22	3M+3D$		30$	ABBCC	Ind	6	16/23
German and European Studies	RT22	4SW deg	G	22	3M+3D$		30$	ABBCC	Ind	5	8/26
Linguistic and International Studies	MT92	4SW deg	F/G/R	BBC-CCC	3M+3D$		30$	ABBCC	Ind		
Russian and European Studies	RT82	4SW deg	*	18	3M+3D$		30	ABBCC	Ind	2	

Univ of SUSSEX

Artificial Intelligence in European Studies	G8T2	4FT deg	* g	BBC	MO	M*6	$	Ind	Ind		
Contemporary History in European Studies	V1TF	4FT deg	* g	BBB	MO $	M*6 go	$	Ind	Ind		
Economics in European Studies	L1T2	4FT deg	* g	BBB	MO $	M*6 go	$	Ind	Ind		
Electronic Engineering with European St (MEng)	H6TF	4FT deg	M g	BCC	MO $	MS^ go	$	Ind	Ind		
English Language in European Studies	Q3TF	4FT deg	g	BBB	MO	M*6 go	$	Ind	Ind		
English in European Studies	Q3T2	4FT deg	* g	BBB	MO $	M*6 go	$	Ind	Ind		
European Drama in European Studies	W4T2	4FT deg	* g	BCC	MO $	M*6 go	$	Ind	Ind		
French in European Studies	R1T2	4FT deg	F	BCC	MO $	M*^	$	Ind	Ind		
Geography in European Studies	L8T2	4FT deg	* g	BBB	MO $	M*6 go	$	Ind	Ind		
History in European Studies	V1T2	4FT deg	* g	BBB	MO $	M*6 go	$	Ind	Ind		
History of Art in European Studies	V4T2	4FT deg	* g	BBB	MO $	M*6 go	$	Ind	Ind		
Intellectual History in European Studies	V1TG	4FT deg	* g	BBB	MO $	M*6 go	$	Ind	Ind		
International Relations in European Studies	M1TF	4FT deg	* g	BBC	MO $	M*6 go	$	Ind	Ind		
Law in European Studies	M3T2	4FT deg	L	BBB	MO $	M*^	$	Ind	Ind		
Linguistics in European Studies	Q1T2	4FT deg	* g	BBC	MO $	M*6 go	$	Ind	Ind		
Mechanical Engineering with European St (MEng)	H3T2	4FT deg	M g	BCC	MO $	MS^ go	$	Ind	Ind		
Media Studies in European Studies	P4T2	4FT deg	* g	BBB	MO $	M*6 go	$	Ind	Ind		
Philosophy in European Studies	V7T2	4FT deg	* g	BBB	MO $	M*6 go	$	Ind	Ind		
Politics in European Studies	M1TG	4FT deg	* g	BBC	MO $	M*6 go	$	Ind	Ind		
Social Anthropology in European Studies	L6T2	4FT deg	* g	BBC	MO $	M*6 go	$	Ind	Ind		

Univ of Wales SWANSEA

Euro Bus St with deferred choice of a Mod Lang	N1TX	4FT deg	L g	ABC-BBB	Ind	D$^ go	32$	AABBB$	Ind		
Euro Mgt Sci with deferred choice of a Mod Lang	N1TY	4FT deg	L+M	ABC-BBB	X	D$^ go	32$	AABBB$	Ind	2	
Geography with European Studies	F8T2	4FT deg	Gy	BBC	1M+5D$	Ind	30$	ABBBB$	Ind	3	20/28

SWANSEA INST of HE

European Languages and Leisure Management	NT72	3FT deg	2L	12		D	Ind	Ind	Ind		
Joint Honours Euro Social & Industrial St & St in Mod Society	Y300	3FT deg		8	N	P	Ind	Ind	N		
European Business	9T1N	2FT HND	L g	4	Ind	Ind	Ind	Ind	Ind	2	

Univ of TEESSIDE

Design with a Modern Language	E2T9	3FT deg	Pf g		N	M$	Ind	CCC	Ind		
Design with a Modern Language	W2T9	3FT deg	Pf g		N	M$	Ind	CCC	Ind		
Business and European St (incorp Kaufmann Awd)	12NT▼	2FT HND									
Business and European Studies	21TN▼	2FT HND									

course details | 98 expected requirements | 96 entry stats

TITLE	CODE	COURSE	SUBJECTS	A/AS	ND/C	AGNVQ	IB	SQA(H)	SQA	RATIO A/AS
THAMES VALLEY Univ										
American Studies with European Studies	Q4T2	3FT deg		8-12	MO	M	26	CCC		
Economics with European Studies	L1T2	3FT deg		8-12	MO	M	26	CCC		
English Lang and Communications with European St	Q1T2	3FT deg		8-12	MO	M	26	CCC		
Environmental Policy and Mgt with European St	F9T2	3FT deg		8-12	MO	M	26	CCC		
European St with Politics and Int Relations	T2M1	3FT deg		8-12	MO	M	26	CCC		
European Studies with American Studies	T2Q4	3FT deg		8-12	MO	M	26	CCC		
European Studies with Business	T2N1	3FT deg		8-12	MO	M	26	CCC		
European Studies with Economics	T2L1	3FT deg		8-12	MO	M	26	CCC		
European Studies with English Language Studies	T2Q1	3FT deg		8-12	MO	M	26	CCC		
European Studies with Environmental Policy & Mgt	T2F9	3FT deg		8-12	MO	M	26	CCC		
European Studies with European Law	T2MH	3FT deg		8-12	MO	M	26	CCC		
European Studies with French	T2R1	3FT deg		8-12	MO	M	26	CCC		
European Studies with German	T2R2	3FT deg		8-12	MO	M	26	CCC		
European Studies with History	T2V1	3FT deg		8-12	MO	M	26	CCC		
European Studies with International Studies	T2MX	3FT deg		8-12	MO	M	26	CCC		
European Studies with Law	T2M3	3FT deg		8-12	MO	M	26	CCC		
European Studies with Sociology	T2L3	3FT deg		8-12	MO	M	26	CCC		
European Studies with Spanish	T2R4	3FT deg		8-12	MO	M	26	CCC		
French with European Studies	R1T2	3FT deg		8-12	MO	M	26	CCC		
German with European Studies	R2T2	3FT deg		8-12	MO	M	26	CCC		
History with European Studies	V1T2	3FT deg		8-12	MO	M	26	CCC		
International Studies with European Studies	M9T2	3FT deg		8-12	MO	M	26	CCC		
Politics and Int Relations with European Studies	M1T2	3FT deg		8-12	MO	M	26	CCC		
Sociology with European Studies	L3T2	3FT deg		8-12	MO	M	26	CCC		
Spanish with European Studies	R4T2	3FT deg		8-12	MO	M	26	CCC		
Univ of ULSTER										
Applied Languages (two from French, German, Sp)	T901▼	4SW deg	L	BCC	MO+4D	D*△ gi	30	BBBB	Ind	7 16/26
International Business Communication	NT19▼	4SW deg	L g	CCC	MO+3D	D△ gi	28	BBBC	Ind	9 14/20
Humanities Combined *European Studies*	Y320▼	3FT/4SW deg	*	CCC	MO+3D	D*6/△ gi	28	BBBC	Ind	
UNIVERSITY COLL LONDON (Univ of London)										
Chemistry with a European Language	F1T2	3FT deg	C+M/P/B g	CCC-BBB	MO $	Ind	28$	BCCCC$	N$	
Chemistry with a European Language (MSci)	F1TF	4FT deg	C+M/P/B g	CCC-BBB	MO $	Ind	28$	BCCCC$	N$	3 14/26
Dutch (4 Yrs)	T220	4FT deg	g	BCC-BBC	3M	X	26$	BBBCC	Ind	3
Dutch and French (4 Yrs)	TR21	4FT deg	F g	BCC-BBC	3M	X	26$	BBBCC$	Ind	2
Dutch and German (4 Yrs)	TR22	4FT deg	G g	BCC-BBC	3M	X	28$	BBBCC$	Ind	
Dutch and History of Art (4 Yrs)	TV24	4FT deg	g	BBC	3M	X	26$	BBBCC$	Ind	2
Dutch and Italian (4 Yrs)	TR23	4FT deg	g	BCC-BBC	3M	X	26$	BBBCC$	Ind	2
Dutch and Scandinavian Studies (4 Yrs)	TR27	4FT deg	g	BCC-BBC	3M	X	26$	BBCCC$	Ind	
Dutch and Spanish (4 Yrs)	TR24	4FT deg	Sp g	BCC-BBC	3M	X	26$	BBBCC$	Ind	
Dutch with Management Studies (4 Yrs)	T2N1	4FT deg	g	BCC-BBC	3M	D$^ go	26$	BBBCC	Ind	2
French and an Asian or African Language (4 Yrs)	RT19	4FT deg	F g	BBC	3M	X	30$	BBBCC$	Ind	5 24/26
History with a European Language (4 Yrs)	V1T2	4FT deg	g	BBB	3M	Ind	32$	BBBCC	Ind	28
Mathematics with a European Language	G1T2	3FT deg	M g	ABC-ABB	MO $	Ind	30$	AAABB$	N$	
Mathematics with a European Language (MSci)	G1TF	4FT deg	M g	ABC-ABB	MO $	Ind	30$	AAABB$	N$	8
Modern European Studies (4 Yrs)	T207	4FT deg	F/Sp/G g	BBB-AAB	3M	X	33$	BBBBB$	Ind	10 20/28
Statistics with a European Language	G4T2	3FT deg	M g	BCC	MO $	Ind	30$	BBCCC$	N$	4
Statistics,Operational Res & a European Language *European Language*	Y625	3FT deg	M g	BCC	MO $	Ind	30$	BBCCC$	N$	

European Studies and Languages

course details			98 expected requirements							96 entry stats	
TITLE	CODE	COURSE	SUBJECTS	A/AS	ND/C	AGNVQ	IB	SQA(H)	SQA	RATIO A/AS	
Univ of WESTMINSTER											
International Business	N1T9	4FT deg	*	BC	MO+3D	D	26	BBB		11	12/18
Univ of WOLVERHAMPTON											
European Studies	T214	3FT deg		12-14	4M	M	24	BBBB	Ind		
Languages	T918	4FT deg		12	4M	M	24	BBBB			
Languages for Business (3 year)	T919	3FT deg		12	4M	M	24	BBBB	Ind		
Languages for Business (4 year)	T920	4FT deg		12	4M	M	24	BBBB	Ind		
Combined Degrees *European Cultural Studies*	Y401	3FT/4SW deg	L g	12	4M	M	24	BBBB	Ind		
Combined Degrees *European Studies*	Y401	3FT deg		12-14	4M	M	24	BBBB	Ind		
Univ of YORK											
Modern Languages and Linguistics	TQ91	4FT deg	*/L/2L	24	Ind	D$^	28$	BBCC$	Ind		

| | | | 98 expected requirements | | | | | | | 96 entry stats |
| course details | | | | | | | | | | |
TITLE	CODE	COURSE	SUBJECTS	A/AS	NO/C	AGNVQ	IB	SQA(H)	SQA	RATIO A/AS
ANGLIA Poly Univ										
Biology and Food Science	CD14▼	3FT deg	g	10	3M	P go	Dip	BCCC		
Biomedical Science and Food Science	BD94▼	3FT deg	g	10	3M	P go	Dip	BCCC		
Business and Food Science	DN41▼	3FT deg								
Chemistry and Food Science	DF41▼	3FT deg								
ASKHAM BRYAN COLL										
Food Production, Processing and Marketing	D430	3FT deg		2		M$	Ind	CCCC	Ind	
BATH COLL of HE										
Food Management	D450	3FT deg	S/Bu/Gy/Ec		Ind		Ind	$	$	8
Combined Awards	Y400	3FT deg			N		Ind	$	$	
Food Studies										
Modular Programme (DipHE)	Y460	2FT Dip			N		Ind	$	$	
Food Studies										
BIRMINGHAM COLL of Food, Tourism & Creative St										
Food and Consumer Management	DN49	3FT deg	* g	10	MO	M$ gi	Ind	Ind	Ind	4	4/22
Food and Retail Management	DN45	3FT/4SW deg	* g	10	MO	M$ gi	Ind	Ind	Ind	
Hospitality and Food Management	DN47	4SW deg	* g	10	MO	M$ gi	Ind	Ind	Ind	
Food and Consumer Management (Home Economics)	94ND	2FT HND	*	4	3M	P$	Ind	Ind	Ind	2	6/8
BLACKPOOL & FYLDE COLL										
Culinary Arts	N7B4	3FT deg	*	10	4M	M$	Ind	Ind	Ind	
Food Manufacturing Mgt (Conversion to Degree)	D430	2FT deg	*		HN		X	X	Ind	
Food (Baking Technology)	324D	2FT HND		2	2M	P$	Ind	Ind	Ind	
Food (Consumer Studies)	424D	2FT HND		2	2M	P$	Ind	Ind	Ind	
Food (Meat Technology & Management)	224D	2FT HND		2	2M	P$	Ind	Ind	Ind	
Food Safety Management	124D	2FT HND		2	2M	P$	Ind	Ind	Ind	
BOURNEMOUTH Univ										
Food Quality	D400	4SW deg	S/He g	8-10	MO	M$ go	Ind	BBC	Ind	3	6/22
Univ of Wales INST, CARDIFF										
Applied Human Nutrition (Dietetics)	B401	3FT/4SW deg	2S g	14	3M+2D	M$^ go	Ind	CCCC	Ind	5	11/22
Food Studies	D400	3FT/4SW deg	S g	10	MO	M$ go	Ind	CCCC	Ind	7	10/24
Food Studies with Catering Management	D4NT	3FT/4SW deg	S g	10-12	MO	M$ go	Ind	CCCC	Ind	
Food Studies with Hotel Management	D4NR	3FT/4SW deg	S g	10-12	MO	M$ go	Ind	CCCC	Ind	
Hotel Management with Food Studies	N7DK	3FT/4SW deg	S g	12	MO	M$ go	Ind	CCCC	Ind	9	
Technology of Food	124D	2FT HND	* g	2	N	P$ go	Ind	CC	Ind	2	2/4
UNIVERSITY COLLEGE CHESTER										
Food, Nutrition and Health	BD44	3FT/4FT deg	g	Ind	Ind	P	Ind	CCCC	$	
COVENTRY Univ										
Human Nutrition	B400	3FT deg								
CRANFIELD Univ										
Marketing and Food Management	N5D4	4SW deg	S g	CDD	4M	M$6/^ go | 27$	BBCC	Ind	8	
Univ of DUNDEE										
Food and Welfare Studies	D400	3FT/4FT deg	* g	DDD	6M $	M$	28	BBC	N$	2	6/20
Univ of GLAMORGAN										
Applied Food Sciences	D420	3FT deg	M/S g	DD	5M $	M$	Ind	Ind	Ind	
Univ of GLASGOW										
Physical Activity, Sports Science and Nutrition	BB46	4FT deg	C/M+S	BBC-CCC	N	M	24$	BBBB$	N	

TITLE	CODE	COURSE	98 expected requirements							96 entry stats	
			SUBJECTS	A/AS	ND/C	AGNVQ	IB	SQA(H)	SQA	RATIO	A/AS
GLASGOW CALEDONIAN Univ											
Consumer & Management St (Food Product Develop)	DN49	3SW/4SW deg	E g	CD	Ind		Ind	BBC$	Ind	3	
Food Technology	D420	2FT deg		X	Ind		Ind	X	HN	2	
Human Nutrition with options	B400	3FT/4SW deg	C+S/E/M	CC	Ind		Ind	BBC$	Ind	5	
Univ of GREENWICH											
Applied Nutrition	B400	3FT/4SW deg	C+B g	12	3M	Ind	Dip	BCC	Ind		
Applied Nutrition with European Study	B411	3FT/4SW deg	B+C	12	3M	Ind	Dip	BCC	Ind		
HARPER ADAMS Agric COLL											
Food Technology with Business Studies	024D▼	2FT/3SW HND	*	2-8	N	P$	Ind	CC	N	2	
Univ of HUDDERSFIELD											
Catering Management and Food Sciences	ND74	4SW deg	* g	10	6M	M$ go	Ind	BBC	Ind		
Catering Management and Nutrition	BN47	4SW deg	* g	10	6M	M$ go	Ind	BBC	Ind		
Chemistry with Food Science	F1D4	3FT/4SW deg	C g	10	3M $	MS gi	Ind	BCC	Ind		
Food Supply Chain Management	DN49	3FT/4SW deg	* g	14-18	Ind	Ind	Ind	BBB	Ind		
Food and Nutrition	DB44	4SW deg	* g	8-12	6M	M$ go	Ind	BBC	Ind		
Science (Extended) *Catering Management and Food Sciences*	Y108	5SW deg	* g	EE	N	P$ gi	Ind	Ind	Ind		
Science (Extended) *Catering Management and Nutrition*	Y108	5SW deg	* g	EE	N	P$ gi	Ind	Ind	Ind		
Science (Extended) *Food and Nutrition*	Y108	5SW deg	* g	EE	N	P$ gi	Ind	Ind	Ind		
KING'S COLL LONDON (Univ of London)											
Nutrition	B400	3FT deg	C+B	CCC			Ind	BBBBB	Ind	9	
Nutrition and Dietetics (4 Yrs)	B401	4FT deg	C+B	CCC			Ind	BBBBB		8	16/22
KINGSTON Univ											
Nutrition	B400	3FT deg									
Univ of LEEDS											
Biochemistry-Food Science	CD74	3FT/4FT deg	C+M/P/B g	CCC	1M+5D$ Ind		28$	BBBBC	Ind		
Food Science	D400	3FT/4FT deg	C+B/M/P g	CCD	2M+2D$ Ind		22$	BCCCC	Ind	4	12/26
Food Science-Microbiology	CD54	3FT deg	C+M/P/B g	CCC	1M+5D$ Ind		28$	BBBBC	Ind		
LEEDS METROPOLITAN Univ											
Applied Human Nutrition	B411	3FT/4SW deg	C+S g	CCD	3M $	X	26$	BBCC$	Ind	7	
Catering Technology	ND74	1FT deg									
Dietetics	B400	4SW deg	C+S g	CCD	3M $		26$	BBCC$	Ind	5	12/26
Univ of LINCOLNSHIRE and HUMBERSIDE											
Environmental Science and Food Science	FD94	3FT deg	2(M/P/C/B/He) g	8	3M $	P	Ind	CCC$	Ind		
Environmental Science and Food Technology	FD9K	3FT deg	2(M/P/C/B/He) g	8	3M $	P	Ind	CCC$	Ind		
Environmental Science and Nutrition	FD9L	3FT deg	2(M/P/C/B/He) g	8	3M $	P	Ind	CCC$	Ind		
Environmental Studies and Food Science	DF4Y	3FT deg	2(M/P/C/B/He) g	8	3M	P	Ind	CCC$	Ind		
Environmental Studies and Food Technology	DF4X	3FT deg	2(M/P/C/B/He) g	8	3M	P	Ind	CCC$	Ind		
Food Science	D400	3FT deg	2(M/P/C/B/He) g	8	3M	P	Ind	CCC$	Ind		
Food Science and Food Technology	D423	3FT deg	2(M/P/C/B/He) g	8	3M	P	Ind	CCC$	Ind		
Food Science and Management	DN41	3FT deg	M/P/C/B/He g	8	3M		Ind	CCC$	Ind		
Food Science and Nutrition	BD4K	3FT deg	2(M/P/C/B/He) g	8	3M	P	Ind	CCC$	Ind		
Food Studies Foundation	D408	1FT deg	g				Ind	Ind	Ind		
Food Technology	D421	3FT deg	2(M/P/C/B/He) g	8	3M	P	Ind	CCC$	Ind		
Food Technology and Management	DN4C	3FT deg	M/P/C/B/He g	8	3M	P	Ind	CCC$	Ind		
Food Technology and Nutrition	BD44	3FT deg	2(M/P/C/B/He) g	8	3M	P	Ind	CCC$	Ind		
Nutrition and Management	BN41	3FT deg	M/P/C/B/He g	8	3M		Ind	CC$	Ind		

course details			98 expected requirements							96 entry stats
TITLE	CODE	COURSE	SUBJECTS	A/AS	NO/C	RGNVQ	IB	SQA(H)	SQA	RATIO A/AS
Food Science	004D	2FT HND	M/S/He	4	1M	P	24	C		
Food Technology	124D	2FT HND	M/S/He g	4	1M	P	Ind	Ind	Ind	

LIVERPOOL JOHN MOORES Univ

Food and Nutrition	D420	3FT deg		CC	5M	M				5 8/19
Food and Nutrition and Business	DN41	3FT deg		14-16	5M+3D	D/M^	28$	BCCC		
Health and Food & Nutrition (F & N jt awd only)	BD94	3FT deg		CC	5M+2D	D$/M$6	28$	CCCC		2

LUTON Univ

Health Studies and Applied Statistics	BG49	3FT deg	g	12-16	MO/DO	M/D	32	BBCC	Ind	

MANCHESTER METROPOLITAN Univ

Food Manufacturing Management	D4N1	4SW deg	S g	8-10	Ind	M	24	CCCC	Ind	6/12
Food Manufacturing Management (Foundation)	D4NC	5SW deg	M/P	E	2M $	P$	$	$	Ind	
Food Technology	D421	4SW deg	S g	8-10	Ind	M	24	CCCC	Ind	4/12
Food Technology (Foundation)	D428	5SW deg	M/P	E	2M $	P$	$	$	Ind	
Food and Nutrition	BD44	3FT deg	* g	8-10	Ind	M	24	CCCC	Ind	
Food and Nutrition (Foundation)	BD4K	4FT deg	M/P	E	2M $	P$	$	$	Ind	
Food Technology	124D	2FT HND	* g	2-6	N	P	24	CC	Ind	2/ 4

Univ of NEWCASTLE

Agri-Business Management and Marketing	DN41	3FT deg	* g	CCC	Ind	Ind	Ind	BBBB	Ind	3 12/24
Food Marketing	D450	3FT deg	* g	CCC	Ind	Ind	Ind	BBBB	Ind	3 10/20
Food Marketing and Rural Economics	DL41	3FT deg	* g	CCC	Ind	Ind	Ind	BBBB	Ind	
Food Quality and Production	D420	3FT deg	B/C g	CCD	Ind	Ind	Ind	BBBB$	Ind	5
Food and Human Nutrition	B4D4	4SW deg	2S g	CCC	Ind	Ind	Ind	BBBB$	Ind	6 14/24
Rural Environmental Management and Marketing	DD24	3FT deg	* g	CCC	Ind	Ind	Ind	BBBB	Ind	

Univ of NORTH LONDON

Food & Consumer Studies	DN49	3FT/4SW/4EXT deg	He/M/Ec/Ph	CC	4M $	M$	24	Ind	Ind	6
Food & Nutritional Science	BD44	3FT/4SW/4EXT deg	B+C	CC	3M $	MS	24$	Ind	Ind	43
Health Studies and Nutrition	BB94	3FT/4SW/4EXT deg	C+B g	12	Ind	Ind	Ind	Ind	Ind	
Human Nutrition	B400	3FT/4SW/4EXT deg	B/C+S	CC	3M $	MS	$	Ind	Ind	
Human Nutrition & Dietetics	B401	4FT/5EXT deg	B+C	CCD	3M $	MS go	$	Ind	Ind	9 6/16
Human Nutrition and Sports Management	BB4P	3FT/4SW/4EXT deg	B/C g	12	MO+4D	DS	Ind	Ind	Ind	
Sports Science and Human Nutrition	BB46	3FT/4SW/4EXT deg	B/Ss	12	4M $	MS	$	Ind	Ind	
Combined Honours Nutrition	Y100	3FT/4SW/4EXT deg	C+B	CC	3M $	MS	$	Ind	Ind	

Univ of NORTHUMBRIA

Applied Consumer Sciences	JD44	3FT deg	* g	10	4M	M	24	CCCC	Ind	2 6/20
Applied Consumer Studies	N980	3FT deg	* g	10	4M	M	24	CCCC	Ind	
Food and Consumer Studies	DN28	3FT deg	* g	10	4M	M gi	24	CCCC	Ind	
Applied Consumer Sciences	44DJ	2FT HND	* g	4	N	P	24	CCC	Ind	
Applied Consumer Studies	089N	2FT HND	* g	4	N	P	24	CCC	Ind	
Food and Consumer Studies	054D	2FT HND	* g	4	N	P gi	24	CCC	Ind	2 2/ 6

Univ of NOTTINGHAM

Food Science (allows specialisation)	D400	3FT deg	2(M/S/Gy)	CC-CDD	3M $	MS	24$	CSYS$	N$	7 10/22
Food Science with European Studies	D4T2	4FT deg	2(M/S/Gy) g	CC-CDD	3M $	MS	24$	CSYS$	N$	15
Nutrition	B400	3FT deg	2(M/S/Gy)	CC-CDD	3M $	MS	24$	CSYS$	N$	9 16/22
Nutrition with European Studies	B4T2	4FT deg	2(M/S/Gy) g	CC-CDD	3M $	MS	24$	CSYS$	N$	7

NOTTINGHAM TRENT Univ

Applied Food Studies	004D ▼	3SW HND	S g	E	N	Ind	Dip	D	N	3

course details			98 expected requirements							96 entry stats	
TITLE	CODE	COURSE	SUBJECTS	A/AS	NO/C	AGNVQ	IB	SQA(H)	SQA	RATIO	A/AS
OXFORD BROOKES Univ											
Food Science and Nutrition/Accounting & Finance	DN44	3FT deg	S g	DD-BCC	Ind	MS/D*3	Ind	Ind	Ind		
Food Science and Nutrition/Anthropology	DL46	3FT deg	S g	DD-BCC	Ind	MS^	Ind	Ind	Ind	3	
Food Science and Nutrition/Biological Chemistry	CD74	3FT deg									
Food Science and Nutrition/Biology	CD14	3FT deg	S g	DD	Ind	MS	Ind	Ind	Ind	6	
Food Science and Nutrition/Bus Admin & Mgt	DN41	3FT deg	S g	DD-BBC	Ind	MS/MB4	Ind	Ind	Ind	8	
Food Science and Nutrition/Cartography	DF48	3FT deg	S g	DD-CC	Ind	MS	Ind	Ind	Ind		
Food Science and Nutrition/Cell Biology	CDC4	3FT deg									
Food Science and Nutrition/Combined Studies	DY44	3FT deg		X		X	X	X			
Food Science and Nutrition/Computer Systems	DG46	3FT deg	S g	DD-BC	Ind	MS	Ind	Ind	Ind		
Food Science and Nutrition/Computing	DG45	3FT deg	S g	DD-BC	Ind	MS	Ind	Ind	Ind		
Food Science and Nutrition/Computing Mathematics	DG49	3FT deg	S g	DD-CD	Ind	MS	Ind	Ind	Ind		
Food Science and Nutrition/Ecology	DC49	3FT deg	S g	DD-CD	Ind	MS	Ind	Ind	Ind		
Food Science and Nutrition/Economics	DL41	3FT deg	S g	DD-BB	Ind	MS/M*3	Ind	Ind	Ind		
Food Science and Nutrition/Educational Studies	DX49	3FT deg	S g	DD-CC	Ind	MS/M*3	Ind	Ind	Ind		
Food Science and Nutrition/Electronics	DH46	3FT deg	S/M g	DD-CC	Ind	MS	Ind	Ind	Ind		
Food Science and Nutrition/English Studies	DQ43	3FT deg	S g	DD-AB	Ind	MS/M*^	Ind	Ind	Ind	5	
Food Science and Nutrition/Environmental Chem	FD14	3FT deg									
Food Science and Nutrition/Environmental Policy	DK43	3FT deg									
Food Science and Nutrition/Environmental Sci	DF4X	3FT deg	S g	DD-CD	Ind	MS/DS	Ind	Ind	Ind	7	
Food Science and Nutrition/Exercise and Health	DB46	3FT deg	S g	DD	Ind	MS	Ind	Ind	Ind		
Food Science and Nutrition/Fine Art	DW41	3FT deg	Pf+A+S g	DD-BC	Ind	MS/MA^	Ind	Ind	Ind		
French Language and Contemp St/Food Sci and Nut	DR4C	4SW deg	F+S g	DD-CC	Ind	MS^	Ind	Ind	Ind		
French Language and Lit/Food Sci & Nutrition	DR41	4SW deg	F+S g	DD-CC	Ind	MS^	Ind	Ind	Ind		
Geography and the Phys Env/Food Sci & Nutrition	DF4V	3FT deg									
Geography/Food Science and Nutrition	DL48	3FT deg	S g	DD-BB	Ind	MS	Ind	Ind	Ind	2	
Geology/Food Science and Nutrition	DF46	3FT deg	S/M g	DD	Ind	PS/MS	Ind	Ind	Ind		
Geotechnics/Food Science and Nutrition	DH42	3FT deg	S/M/Ds/Es g	DD-CC	Ind	M$	Ind	Ind	Ind		
German Language and Contemp St/Food Sci and Nut	DR4F	4SW deg	G+S g	DD-CD	Ind	MS^	Ind	Ind	Ind		
German Language and Literature/Food Sci and Nutr	DR42	4SW deg	G+S g	DD-CD	Ind	MS^	Ind	Ind	Ind		
German Studies/Food Science and Nutrition	DR4G	4SW deg			Ind		Ind	Ind	Ind		
Health Care/Food Science and Nutrition(Post Exp)	BD74	3FT deg		X		X	X	X			
History of Art/Food Science and Nutrition	DV44	3FT deg	S g	DD-BCC	Ind	MS/M*^	Ind	Ind	Ind	1	
History/Food Science and Nutrition	DV41	3FT deg	M/S g	DD-BB	Ind	MS/M*^	Ind	Ind	Ind		
Hospitality Mgt Studies/Food Science & Nutrition	DN47	3FT deg	S g	DD-CC	Ind	MS/M*3	Ind	Ind	Ind	3	
Human Biology/Food Science and Nutrition	BD14	3FT deg									
Information Systems/Food Science and Nutrition	DG4M	3FT deg	S g	DD-BC	Ind	MS	Ind	Ind	Ind		
Intelligent Systems/Food Science and Nutrition	DG48	3FT deg	S g	DD-CD	Ind	MS	Ind	Ind	Ind		
Law/Food Science and Nutrition	DM43	3FT deg	S g	DD-BBB	Ind	MS/D*3	Ind	Ind	Ind	1	
Leisure Planning/Food Science & Nutrition	DK4H	3FT deg									
Marketing Management/Food Science and Nutrition	DN4N	3FT deg	S g	DD-BCC	Ind	MS/D*3	Ind	Ind	Ind		
Mathematics/Food Science and Nutrition	DG41	3FT deg	M g	DD-DDE	Ind	MS/M^	Ind	Ind	Ind		
Nutrition and Food Science	BD44	3FT deg	S g	DD	Ind	MS	Ind	Ind	Ind	6	6/10
Palliative Care/Food Sci and Nutrition(Post Exp)	BDR4	3FT deg		X		X	X	X			
Planning Studies/Food Science and Nutrition	DK44	3FT deg	S g	DD-CC	Ind	MS	Ind	Ind	Ind		
Politics/Food Science and Nutrition	DM41	3FT deg	S g	DD-AB	Ind	MS^	Ind	Ind	Ind		
Psychology/Food Science and Nutrition	CD84	3FT deg	S g	DD-BBC	Ind	MS/M*^	Ind	Ind			
Public Health Nutrition	B400	3FT deg									
Publishing/Food Science and Nutrition	DP45	3FT deg	S g	DD-BB	Ind	MS/M$3	Ind	Ind	Ind		
Rehabilitation/Food Sci and Nutrition (Post Exp)	BDT4	3FT deg		X		X	X	X			
Retail Management/Food Science and Nutrition	DN45	3FT deg	S/M g	DD-CCD	Ind		Ind	Ind	Ind		
Sociology/Food Science and Nutrition	DL43	3FT deg	S g	DD-BCC	Ind	MS/M*^	Ind	Ind	Ind		

course details			98 expected requirements							96 entry stats
TITLE	CODE	COURSE	SUBJECTS	A/AS	NO/C	AGNVQ	IB	SQA(H)	SQA	RATIO A/AS
Software Engineering/Food Science and Nutrition	DG47	3FT deg	S g	DD-BC	Ind	MS	Ind	Ind	Ind	
Telecommunications/Food Science and Nutrition	DH4P	3FT deg								
Tourism/Food Science and Nutrition	DP47	3FT deg	S g	DD-BC	Ind	MS/M*3	Ind	Ind	Ind	
Transport Planning/Food Science and Nutrition	DN49	3FT deg	S g	DD-CC	Ind	MS	Ind	Ind ·	Ind	
Water Resources/Food Science and Nutrition	DH4F	3FT deg								
Extended Science *Food Science & Nutrition*	Y100	4FT deg	* g	EE	Ind	P*	Ind	Ind	Ind	
Extended Science *Nutrition and Food Science*	Y100	4FT deg	* g	EE	Ind	P*	Ind	Ind	Ind	
Univ of PLYMOUTH										
Food Quality with Product Development	D400	4SW/3FT deg	He+S g	8	MO $	P$	Ind	Ind	Ind	3
Extended Science (Foundation year) *Food Resources*	Y108▼	1FT/4EXT deg	S	2	Ind	P$	Ind	Ind	Ind	
QUEEN MARGARET COLL										
Applied Food Science with Marketing	D4N5	3FT/4FT deg	* g	EE	M+D	P$ go	Dip	CCC	N	3
Applied Human Nutrition	B401	3FT/4FT deg	B+S g	CD	M+D	MS go	Ind$	BBC$	Ind$	5	10/12
Dietetics	B400	4FT deg	B+S g	CD	M+D	MS go	Ind$	BBC$	Ind$	6	14/18
Food Product Management	D420	3FT/4FT deg	* g	EE	M+D	P$ go	Dip	CCC	N	12
QUEEN'S Univ Belfast										
Chemical with Food Eng (Extended Course) (MEng)	H8DL	4FT deg	M+C g	BBB	X	X	32$	X	X	
Chemical with Food Engineering	H8D4	3FT/4FT deg	M+C g	BCC	Ind	Ind	29$	BBBC	Ind	
Food Science	D400	3FT/4FT deg	C+B/P/M g	CCD	Ind	Ind	27$	BBBC	Ind	10	18/20
Food Technology	D421	3FT/4FT deg	C+P/M/B g	CCD	Ind	Ind	27$	BBBC	Ind	15
Mechanical with Food Engineering	H3D4	3FT/4FT deg	M+P g	BCC	Ind	Ind	29$	BBBC	Ind	
Univ of READING										
Chemistry with Food Science	F1D4	3FT deg	C g	18	4M+1D$	DS^ go	29$	BBBC$	Ind	
Food Manufacture, Management & Marketing	D430	4SW deg	S g	CDD	MO	MS6/^ gi	28$	BBCC	Ind	6	16/22
Food Marketing Economics	D470	3FT deg	* g	CCD	MO	M*6/^ gi	28$	BBCC	Ind	1	12/22
Food Science	D400	3FT deg	2S g	CDD	MO	MS6/^ gi	28$	BBCC	Ind	5	12/28
Food Science, Food Economics & Marketing	D450	3FT deg	S g	CDD	MO	MS6/^ gi	28$	BBCC	Ind	3	18/26
Food Technology	D421	4SW deg	2S g	CDD	MO	MS6/^ gi	28$	BBCC	Ind	3	19/28
ROBERT GORDON Univ										
Food Science with Management	D4N1	3FT/4FT deg	S g	DE	N	Ind	Ind	BCC$	Ind	27
Nutrition	B400	3FT/4FT deg	C+S g	EE	N	Ind	Ind	BCC$	Ind	33
Nutrition & Dietetics with State Reg in Dietetic	B401	4FT deg	C+S g	EE	N	Ind	Ind	BCC$	Ind	8	12/14
Applied Science (Food Science)	004D	2FT HND	S g	E	N	Ind	Ind	CC$	Ind	
SCOTTISH Agric COLL										
Food Production, Manufacturing & Marketing	DD24▼	3FT/4FT deg	S	CC	Ind	MS	Ind	BCC$	Ind	6
Rural Business Management *Food Business Management*	Y400▼	3FT/4FT deg	S/M	CD	Ind	Ind	Ind	BBC$	Ind	
Food Technology	024D▼	2FT HND	S	D	N $	PS	Ind	CC$	Ind	2
Univ of SALFORD										
Food Industry Management	1N4D	2FT HND	* g	2	3M	P	24	CC	Ind	7
SHEFFIELD HALLAM Univ										
Food Marketing Management	DN45	3FT/4SW deg	g	10	10M	M	Ind	Ind	Ind	
Food and Catering Technology	D420	3FT/4SW deg	*	10	10M	M	Ind	Ind	Ind	
Food and Consumer Studies	DN47	3FT/4SW deg	g	10	10M	M	Ind	Ind	Ind	
Nutrition, Health and Lifestyle	L535	3FT/4SW deg	*	10	10M	M	Ind	Ind	Ind	

			98 expected requirements							96 entry stats
TITLE	CODE	COURSE	SUBJECTS	A/AS	ND/C	AGNVQ	IB	SQA(H)	SQA	RATIO A/AS
Univ of SOUTHAMPTON										
Biochemistry with Nutrition	C7B4	3FT deg	C+B/P/M/Gy g	BCC	$	M^	$	Ind	Ind	2
Nutritional Sciences	B400	3FT deg	C+B/P/M g	BCC	$	M^	$	Ind	Ind	
Physiology with Nutrition	B1B4	3FT deg	C+B/P/M/Gy g	BCC	$	M^	$	Ind	Ind	14
SOUTH BANK Univ										
Food Policy and Accounting	DN44	3FT deg	S+Ac/Ec g	12-16	4M+2D	M go	Ind	Ind	Ind	
Food Policy and Computing	DG45	3FT deg	S+M g	12-16	4M+2D	M go	Ind	Ind	Ind	
Food Policy and English Studies	DQ43	3FT deg	S+E g	14-18	X	M^ go	Ind	Ind	Ind	
Food Policy and Environmental Policy	DF49	3FT deg	S g	14-18	4M+2D	M go	Ind	Ind	Ind	
Food Policy and European Studies	DT42	3FT deg	S g	14-18	2M+4D	M go	Ind	Ind	Ind	
Food Science	D400	3FT/4SW deg	S/2S g	DD	4M	MS go	Ind	Ind	Ind	
Food Science with Nutrition	D4B4	3FT/4SW deg	S/2S g	DD	4M	MS go	Ind	Ind	Ind	
Food and Consumer Studies	DN49	3FT/4SW deg	S/2S g	DD	4M	MS go	Ind	Ind	Ind	
Foundation Food Sciences Scheme	D408	4EXT deg					Ind	Ind	Ind	
Health Studies and Food Policy	DL44	3FT deg	S g	12-16	4M+2D	M go	Ind	Ind	Ind	
Housing and Food Policy	DK4K	3FT deg	S g	14-18	2M+4D	M go	Ind	Ind	Ind	
Human Geography and Food Policy	DL48	3FT deg	S+Gy g	12-16	4M+2D	M go	Ind	Ind	Ind	
Human Resource Management and Food Policy	DN46	3FT deg	S g	14-18	2M+4D	M go	Ind	Ind	Ind	
Law and Food Policy	DM43	3FT deg	S g	14-18	2M+4D	D go	Ind	Ind	Ind	
Management and Food Policy	DN41	3FT deg	S g	12-16	4M+2D	M go	Ind	Ind	Ind	
Marketing and Food Policy	DN45	3FT deg	S g	14-18	2M+4D	M go	Ind	Ind	Ind	
Nutrition	B400	3FT/4SW deg	S g	CC	MO	M go	Ind	Ind	Ind	
Nutrition and Accounting	BN44	3FT deg	S+Ac/Ec g	12-16	4M+2D	M go	Ind	Ind	Ind	
Nutrition and Computing	BG45	3FT deg	S+M g	12-16	4M+2D	M go	Ind	Ind	Ind	
Nutrition and English Studies	BQ43	3FT deg	E+S g	14-18	X	M^ go	Ind	Ind	Ind	
Nutrition and Environmental Policy	FB94	3FT deg	S g	14-18	2M+4D	M go	Ind	Ind	Ind	
Nutrition and European Studies	BT42	3FT deg	S g	14-18	2M+4D	M go	Ind	Ind	Ind	
Nutrition and Health Studies	BL44	3FT deg	S g	12-16	4M+2D	M go	Ind	Ind	Ind	
Nutrition and Housing	BK4K	3FT deg	S g	14-18	2M+4D	M go	Ind	Ind	Ind	
Nutrition and Human Geography	BL48	3FT deg	S+Gy g	12-16	4M+2D	M go	Ind	Ind	Ind	
Nutrition and Human Resource Management	BN46	3FT deg	S g	14-18	2M+4D	M go	Ind	Ind	Ind	
Nutrition and Law	BM43	3FT deg	S g	14-18	2M+4D	D go	Ind	Ind	Ind	
Nutrition and Management	BN41	3FT deg	S g	12-16	4M+2D	M go	Ind	Ind	Ind	
Nutrition and Marketing	BN45	3FT deg	S g	14-18	2M+4D	M go	Ind	Ind	Ind	
Politics and Food Policy	DM41	3FT deg	S g	12-16	4M+2D	M go	Ind	Ind	Ind	
Politics and Nutrition	BM41	3FT deg	S g	12-16	4M+2D	M go	Ind	Ind	Ind	
Product Design and Food Policy	DH47	3FT deg	S+Ad g	12-16	4M+2D	M go	Ind	Ind	Ind	
Product Design and Nutrition	BH47	3FT deg	S+Ad/A g	12-16	4M+2D	M go	Ind	Ind	Ind	
Psychology and Food Policy	CD84	3FT deg	S g	14-18	2M+4D	M go	Ind	Ind	Ind	
Psychology and Nutrition	BC48	3FT deg	S g	14-18	4M+2D	M go	Ind	Ind	Ind	
Technology and Food Policy	DJ49	3FT deg	S g	12-16	4M+2D	M go	Ind	Ind	Ind	
Technology and Nutrition	BJ49	3FT deg	S g	12-16	4M+2D	M go	Ind	Ind	Ind	
Tourism and Food Policy	DP47	3FT deg	S+L g	12-16	4M+2D	M go	Ind	Ind	Ind	
Tourism and Nutrition	BP47	3FT deg	S+L g	12-16	4M+2D	M go	Ind	Ind	Ind	
Urban Studies and Food Policy	DK4L	3FT deg	S g	14-18	2M+4D	M go	Ind	Ind	Ind	
Urban Studies and Nutrition	BK4L	3FT deg	S g	14-18	2M+4D	M go	Ind	Ind	Ind	
World Theatre and Food Policy	DW44	3FT deg	S g	14-18	2M+4D	M go	Ind	Ind	Ind	
World Theatre and Nutrition	BW44	3FT deg	S g	14-18	2M+4D	M go	Ind	Ind	Ind	
STAFFORDSHIRE Univ										
Food Processing Technology	D429	4EXT deg	g	EE	P $	P$	Ind	Ind	Ind	
Food Processing Technology	D420	3FT deg	g	8	3M	M	24	BCC	Ind	

			98 expected requirements							96 entry stats	
course details											
TITLE	CODE	COURSE	SUBJECTS	A/AS	ND/C	RGNVQ	IB	SQA(H)	SQA	RATIO	A/AS
Univ of STRATHCLYDE											
Biochemistry and Food Science	CD74	4FT deg	C+B+M/P g	CCC	HN		Ind	BBC$	HN		
Univ of SURREY											
Food Science and Microbiology	CD54	3FT/4SW deg	C+B+M/P g	BCC-CCC	3M+2D$		28$	AABBB$	X	8	
Nutrition	B400	3FT/4SW deg	2S	BCC-CCC	3M+2D$		28$	AABBB$	X	6	14/16
Nutrition with Foundation Year	B405	4FT/5SW deg	* g	CCC	4M+1D$ D		28$	ABBBB	Ind	4	8/20
Nutrition/Dietetics	B401	4SW deg	2S	BCC-CCC	3M+2D$		30$	AABBB$	X	5	18/28
Nutrition/Food Science	BD44	3FT/4SW deg	C+S g	BCC-CCC	4M+1D$		28$	AABBB$	X	9	11/22
Univ of TEESSIDE											
Food Science and Nutrition	BD44	3FT/4SW deg	S	8	3M		Ind	CCC	3M	3	8/14
Food Technology	D421	3FT/4SW deg	S	8	3M		Ind	CCC	3M		
Nutrition and Health Sciences	BB49	3FT deg	S	8	3M		Ind	CCC	Ind		
Modular Degree Scheme *Food Science*	Y401	3FT deg									
Science and Technology Combined Honours Scheme *Food Science*	Y108	3FT deg									
THAMES VALLEY Univ											
Food and Drink Consumer St with Culinary Arts	D4C9	3FT deg		8-12	MO	M	26	CCC			
Food and Drink Consumer St with English Lang St	D4Q1	3FT deg		8-12	MO	M	26	CCC			
Food and Drink Consumer St with Food Servs Mgt	D4N9	3FT deg		8-12	MO	M	26	CCC			
Food and Drink Consumer St with Hospitality Mgt	D4N7	3FT deg		8-12	MO	M	26	CCC			
Food and Drink Consumer Studies with Business	D4N1	3FT deg		8-12	MO	M	26	CCC			
Food and Drink Consumer Studies with French	D4R1	3FT deg		8-12	MO	M	26	CCC			
Food and Drink Consumer Studies with German	D4R2	3FT deg		8-12	MO	M	26	CCC			
Food and Drink Consumer Studies with Health St	D4L4	3FT deg		8-12	MO	M	26	CCC			
Food and Drink Consumer Studies with Hotel Mgt	D4NR	3FT deg		8-12	MO	M	26	CCC			
Food and Drink Consumer Studies with Leisure Mgt	D4NT	3FT deg		8-12	MO	M	26	CCC			
Food and Drink Consumer Studies with Marketing	D4N5	3FT deg		8-12	MO	M	26	CCC			
Food and Drink Consumer Studies with Media St	D4W9	3FT deg		8-12	MO	M	26	CCC			
Food and Drink Consumer Studies with Retail Mgt	D4NM	3FT deg		8-12	MO	M	26	CCC			
Food and Drink Consumer Studies with Spanish	D4R4	3FT deg		8-12	MO	M	26	CCC			
Food and Drink Consumer Studies with Tourism	D4P7	3FT deg		8-12	MO	M	26	CCC			
Hospitality Mgt with Food and Drink Consumer St	N7D4	3FT deg		8-12	MO	M	26	CCC			
Leisure Mgt with Food and Drink Consumer Studies	N7DK	3FT deg		8-12	MO	M	26	CCC			
Tourism with Food and Drink Consumer Studies	P7D4	3FT deg		8-12	MO	M	26	CCC			
Univ of ULSTER											
Food Technology Management (4 Yr SW inc DIS)	D421▼	4SW deg	S/He g	CCD	MO+2D	D$6/△ gi	27	BBCC	Ind	9	
Human Nutrition (4 Yr SW inc DIS/Reg Dietetics)	B400▼	4SW deg	2S	CCC	MO+3D	DS6/△ gi	28	BBBC	Ind	12	18/24
Univ of WOLVERHAMPTON											
Biochemistry with Food Science	C7D4	3FT/4SW deg	C/B g	DD	N	M	24	CCCC	Ind		
Applied Sciences *Food Biology*	Y100	3FT/4SW deg		DD	N	M	24	CCCC	Ind		
Applied Sciences (4 Yrs) *Food Biology*	Y110	4FT deg	*								
Combined Degrees *Food Biology*	Y401	3FT/4SW deg		DD	N	M	24	CCCC	Ind		
Food Product Design (Stafford)	034D▼	2FT HND	S		N $				Ind	10	
WYE COLL (Univ of London)											
Food Marketing	D450	4FT deg									

Geography 30

TITLE	CODE	COURSE	SUBJECTS	A/AS	ND/C	RGNVQ	IB	SQA(H)	SQA	RATIO A/AS
Univ of ABERDEEN										
Accountancy-Geography	NL48	4FT deg	* g	BBC	Ind	M$ go	30$	BBBB$	Ind	6
Celtic-Geography	QL58	4FT deg	* g	BBC	Ind	M$ go	30$	BBBB$	Ind	
Economic History-Geography	VL38	4FT deg	* g	BBC	Ind	M$ go	30$	BBBB$	Ind	3
Economics-Geography	LL18	4FT deg	* g	BBC	Ind	M$ go	30$	BBBB$	Ind	
Entrepreneurship-Geography	LN8C	4FT deg	* g	BBC	Ind	M$ go	30$	BBBB$	Ind	
Environmental Geography	F830	4FT deg	* g	BBC	Ind	M$ go	30$	BBBB$	Ind	8
Environmental Geography	F832	4FT deg	3S/2S+M g	CCD	Ind	MS go	24$	BBBC$	Ind	3
French-Geography	LR81	4FT/5FT deg	* g	BBC	Ind	M$ go	30$	BBBB$	Ind	5
Geography	L800	4FT deg	* g	BBC	Ind	M$ go	30$	BBBB$	Ind	4
Geography	F800	4FT deg	3S/2S+M g	CCD	Ind	MS go	24$	BBBC$	Ind	5
Geography and Geology	FF86	4FT deg	3S/2S+M g	CCD	Ind	MS go	24$	BBBC$	Ind	4
Geography with Plant Science	F8C2	4FT deg	3S/2S+M g	CCD	Ind	MS go	24$	BBBC$	Ind	
Geography with Soil Science	F8D9	4FT deg	3S/2S+M g	CCD	Ind	MS go	24$	BBBC$	Ind	2
Geography-Celtic Civilisation	LQ85	4FT deg	* g	BBC	Ind	M$ go	30$	BBBB$	Ind	
Geography-Geoscience	FF68	4FT deg	3S/2S+M g	CCD	Ind	MS go	24$	BBBC$	Ind	
Geography-Hispanic Studies	LR84	4FT deg	* g	BBC	Ind	M$ go	30$	BBBB$	Ind	
Geography-History	LV81	4FT deg	* g	BBC	Ind	M$ go	30$	BBBB$	Ind	6
Geography-International Relations	LM81	4FT deg	* g	BBC	Ind	M$ go	30$	BBBB$	Ind	5
Geography-Management Studies	LN81	4FT deg	* g	BBC	Ind	M$ go	30$	BBBB$	Ind	11
Geography-Petroleum Geology	FF8P	4FT deg	3S/2S+M g	CCD	Ind	MS go	26$	BBBC$	Ind	6
Geography-Social Research	LL38	4FT deg	* g	BBC	Ind	M$ go	30$	BBBB$	Ind	
Geography-Sociology	LL83	4FT deg	* g	BBC	Ind	M$ go	30$	BBBB$	Ind	6
German-Geography	LR82	4FT/5FT deg	* g	BBC	Ind	M$ go	30$	BBBB$	Ind	
Human Geography	L822	4FT deg	* g	BBC	Ind	M$ go	30$	BBBB$	Ind	11
Human Geography	L824	4FT deg	3S/2S+M g	CCD	Ind	MS go	24$	BBBC$	Ind	5
Physical Geography	F842	4FT deg	* g	BBC	Ind	M$ go	30$	BBBB$	Ind	
Physical Geography	F840	4FT deg	3S/2S+M g	CCD	Ind	MS go	24$	BBBC$	Ind	6
Univ of Wales, ABERYSTWYTH										
Computer Science/Geography	FG85	3FT deg	Gy g	20	3M+2D$ M^ g		30$	BBBCC$	Ind	
Geography	L800	3FT deg	Gy g	20-22	3M+2D$ M^ g		31$	BBBBC$	Ind	
Geography	F800	3FT deg	Gy g	20	3M+2D$ M^ g		30$	BBBCC$	Ind	
Geography (Major)	L801	3FT deg	Gy g	20-22	3M+2D$ M^ g		31$	BBBBC$	Ind	
Geography (Major)	F801	3FT deg	Gy g	20	3M+2D$ M^ g		30$	BBBCC$	Ind	
Geography/American Studies	LQ84	3FT deg	Gy+E/H g	20-22	3M+2D$ M^ g		31$	BBBBC$	Ind	
Geography/Art	LW81	3FT deg	Gy+A/Ad g	20-22	3M+2D$ MA^ g		31$	BBBBC$	Ind	
Geography/Art History	LV84	3FT deg	Gy g	20-22	3M+2D$ MA^ g		31$	BBBBC$	Ind	
Geography/Drama	LW84	3FT deg	Gy g	20-22	1M+5D$ MQ^ g		31$	BBBBC$	Ind	
Geography/Economic & Social History	LV83	3FT deg	Gy g	20-22	3M+2D$ M^ g		31$	BBBBC$	Ind	
Geography/Education	LX89	3FT deg	Gy g	20-22	3M+2D$ M^ g		31$	BBBBC$	Ind	
Geography/English	LQ83	3FT deg	El+Gy	20-22	1M+5D$ M^ g		31$	BBBBC$	Ind	
Geography/Film and Television Studies	LW85	3FT deg	Gy g	20-22	1M+5D$ MQ^ g		30$	BBBBC$	Ind	
Geography/French	LR81	4FT deg	F+Gy g	20-22	1M+5D$ M^ g		31$	BBBBC$	Ind	
Geography/Geology	FF68	3FT deg	Gy+S g	20	3M+2D$ MS^ g		30$	BBBCC$	Ind	
Geography/Mathematics	FG81	3FT deg	M+Gy g	20	3M+2D$ MS^ g		30$	BBBCC$	Ind	
Geography/Physics	FF38	3FT deg	P+Gy+M g	20	3M+2D$ MS^ g		30$	BBBCC$	Ind	
Geography/Statistics	FG84	3FT deg	M+Gy g	20	3M+1D$ MS^ g		30$	BBBCC$	Ind	
German/Geography	LR82	4FT deg	Gy+G g	20-22	1M+5D$ M^ g		31$	BBBBC$	Ind	
History/Geography	LV81	3FT deg	Gy g	20-22	3M+2D$ M^ g		31$	BBBBC$	Ind	
Information and Library Studies/Geography	LP82	3FT deg	Gy g	20-22	3M+2D$ M^ g		31$	BBBBC$	Ind	
International Politics/Geography	LMW1	3FT deg	Gy g	20-22	3M+2D$ M^ g		31$	BBBBC$	Ind	
Italian/Geography	LR83	4FT deg	Gy+L g	20-22	1M+5D$ M^ g		31$	BBBBC$	Ind	

course details			98 expected requirements							96 entry stats	
TITLE	CODE	COURSE	SUBJECTS	A/AS	NO/C	AGNVQ	IB	SQA(H)	SQA	RATIO	A/AS
Politics/Geography	LMV1	3FT deg	Gy g	20-22	3M+2D$	M^ g	31$	BBBBC$	Ind		
Pure Mathematics/Geography	GLC8	3FT deg	M+Gy g	20-22	3M+2D$	M^ g	31$	BBBBC$	Ind		
Welsh History/Geography	LVVC	3FT deg	Gy g	20-22	3M+2D$	M^ g	31$	BBBBC$	Ind		
Welsh/Geography	LQ85	3FT deg	W+Gy g	20-22	3M+2D$	M^ g	31$	BBBBC$	Ind		
Information and Library St/an approved Sci Sub Geography	PY21	3FT deg	Gy g	20	3M+2D$	M^ g	30$	BBBCC$	Ind		

ANGLIA Poly Univ

Animal Behaviour and Geography	CF1V▼	3FT deg	Gy g	10	3M	P go	Dip	BCCC	N	5	
Art History and Geography	LV84▼	3FT deg	Gy g	14	6M	M+/^ go	Dip$	BBCC	Ind		
Audiotechnology and Geography	HF6V▼	3FT deg	S	16	8M	D	Dip$	BBCCC	N		
Biology and Geography	CF18▼	3FT deg	B+Gy	10	3M	P	Dip$	BCCC	N	13	
Biomedical Science and Geography	BF98▼	3FT deg	B+Gy g	10	3M	P go	Dip$	BCCC	N		
Business and Geography	NL18▼	3FT deg	Gy g	12	4M	M+/^ go	Dip$	BCCC	Ind	5	10/18
Chemistry and Geography	FF18▼	3FT deg	S+Gy g	12	4M	M go	Dip$	BCCC	N		
Communication Studies and Geography	PL38▼	3FT deg	Gy g	14	6M	M+/^ go	Dip$	BBCC	Ind		
Ecology and Conservation and Geography	DF28▼	3FT deg	Gy g	10	2M	M go	Dip$	BCCC	N	4	
Economics and Geography	LL18▼	3FT deg	Gy g	12	4M	M+/^ go	Dip	BCCC	Ind	11	
English Language Studies and Geography	QL18▼	3FT deg	* g	12	4M	M go	Dip	BCCC			
English and Geography	LQ83▼	3FT deg	E+Gy	12	4M	M+/^ go	Dip$	BCCC	Ind	3	
European Philosophy & Literature and Geography	VL78▼	3FT deg	Gy g	12	4M	M+/^ go	Dip$	BCCC	Ind		
French and Geography	LR81▼	4FT deg	Gy g	12 ·	4M	M+/^ go	Dip$	BCCC	Ind		
Geography	L800▼	3FT deg	Gy g	14	6M	M+/^ go	Dip$	BBCC	Ind	6	8/20
Geography	F800▼	3FT deg	Gy g	14	6M	M+/^ go	Dip$	BBCC	Ind	7	8/20
Geography and Geology	FF68▼	3FT deg	Gy g	10	3M	P go	Dip$	BCCC	N	5	8/10
Geography and German	LR82▼	4FT deg	Gy g	12	4M	M+/^ go	Dip$	BCCC	Ind	3	
Geography and Graphic Arts	LW82▼	3FT deg	A+Gy	14	6M	M	Dip$	BBCC			
Geography and History	LV81▼	3FT deg	Gy g	12	4M	M+/^ go	Dip$	BCCC	Ind		
Geography and Imaging Science	FW85▼	3FT deg	S+Gy g	12	4M	M go	Dip$	BCCC	N		
Geography and Instrumentation Electronics	FH86▼	3FT deg	Gy+S g	12	4M	M go	Dip$	BCCC	N		
Geography and Italian	LR83▼	4FT deg	Gy g	12	4M	M+/^ go	Dip$	BBCC	Ind		
Geography and Law	LM83▼	3FT deg	Gy g	14	6M	M go	Dip$	BBCC			
Geography and Maths or Stats/Stat Modelling	FG81▼	3FT deg	Gy g	12	4M	M go	Dip$	BCCC	N		
Geography and Music	LW83▼	3FT deg	Mu+Gy g	12	4M	M+/^ go	Dip$	BCCC	Ind	3	
Geography and Politics	LM81▼	3FT deg	Gy g	14	6M	M+/^	Dip$	BBCC	Ind		
Geography and Psychology	CF88▼	3FT deg	Gy g	16	8M	D go	Dip$	BBCCC	N		
Geography and Social Policy	LL84▼	3FT deg	Gy g	12	4M $	M+/^ go	Dip$	BCCC	Ind		
Geography and Sociology	LL83▼	3FT deg	Gy g	12	4M	M+/^ go	Dip$	BCCC	Ind		
Geography and Spanish	LR84▼	4FT deg	Gy g	12	4M	M+/^ go	Dip$	BCCC	Ind		

BARNSLEY COLL

Humanities Geographical St and Politics with Internat Rels	Y301	3FT deg	H/Gy/Po/E g	EE	4M	MB	Ind	Ind	Ind		
Humanities Geographical St and Politics with Internat Rels	Y302	4EXT deg									
Humanities History and Geographical Studies	Y302	4EXT deg									
Humanities History and Geographical Studies	Y301	3FT deg	H/Gy/Po/E g	EE	4M	MB	Ind	Ind	Ind		
Humanities Literature and Geographical Studies	Y302	4EXT deg									
Humanities Literature and Geographical Studies	Y301	3FT deg	H/Gy/Po/E g	EE	4M	MB	Ind	Ind	Ind		

| | | | 98 expected requirements | | | | | | | 96 entry stats | |
| course details | | | | | | | | | | | |
TITLE	CODE	COURSE	SUBJECTS	A/AS	NO/C	RGNVQ	IB	SQA(H)	SQA	RATIO	A/AS
BATH COLL of HE											
Geography	F800	3FT deg	Gy		Ind		Ind	$	$		
Combined Awards *Geography*	Y400	3FT deg	Gy		N		Ind	$	$		
Modular Programme (DipHE) *Geography*	Y460	2FT Dip	Gy		N		Ind	$	$		
Univ of BIRMINGHAM											
African Studies/Geography	LT87	3FT deg	Gy	BBB	Ind	D*^	32$	ABBB	Ind		
American Studies/Geography	LQ84	3FT deg	Gy	BBB	Ind	D*^	32$	ABBB	Ind	18	
Ancient History & Archaeology/Geography	LV86	3FT deg	Gy	BBB	Ind	D*^	32$	ABBB	Ind	11	
East Mediterranean History/Geography	LV8C	3FT deg	Gy g	BBB	Ind	D*^	32$	ABBB	Ind		
French Studies/Geography	LR81	4FT deg	F+Gy	BBB	Ind	D*^	32$	ABBB	Ind	11	
Geography	L800	3FT deg	Gy g	BBB	Ind	D*^	32$	ABBB	Ind	9	24/28
Geography	F800	3FT deg	Gy g	BBB	Ind	Ind	32	Ind	Ind	7	20/28
Geography and Economics	LL81	3FT deg	Gy	BBB	Ind	D+^	32	ABBBB	Ind	15	
Geography and Planning	LK84	3FT deg	Gy	BCC	DO $	D+^	30	BBBBB	Ind	5	18/26
Geography and Sports Science	BF68	3FT deg									
Geography/German Studies	LR82	4FT deg	Gy+G	BBB	Ind	D*^	32$	ABBB	Ind	4	
Geography/Hispanic Studies	LR84	4FT deg	Gy	BBB	Ind	D*^	32$	ABBB	Ind		
Geography/History	LV81	3FT deg	Gy	BBB	Ind	D*^	32$	ABBB	Ind	19	
Geography/Italian	LR83	4FT deg	Gy	BBB	Ind	D*^	32$	ABBB	Ind	3	
Geography/Portuguese	LR85	4FT deg	Gy	BBB	Ind	D*^	32$	ABBB	Ind		
Geography/Russian	LR88	4FT deg	Gy	BBB	Ind	D*^	32$	ABBB	Ind		
Geography/Theology	LV88	3FT deg	Gy	BBB	Ind	D*^	32$	ABBB	Ind	6	
Geology and Geography	FF68	3FT deg	Gy g	BCC	Ind	Ind	30	Ind	Ind	4	18/26
Univ of BRADFORD											
Environmental Science and Environmental Geog	FL98	4SW deg	Gy g	BB-CCC	3M	MS4/^	Ind	Ind	Ind	3	10/28
Environmental Science and Environmental Geog	FL9V	3FT deg	Gy g	BB-CCC	3M	MS4/^	Ind	Ind	Ind	7	10/18
Physical and Environmental Geography	F830	3FT deg	Gy/En g	BB-CCC	3M	MS4/^	Ind	Ind	Ind		
Physical and Environmental Geography (4 Yrs)	F831	4SW deg	Gy/En g	BB-CCC	3M	MS4/^	Ind	Ind	Ind		
Univ of BRIGHTON											
Biology and Geography	CF18	3FT/4SW deg	S g	12	MO $	M$	Dip$	BBCC$	Ind		
Computing and Geography	GF58	3FT/4SW deg	S g	12	MO $	M$	Dip$	BBCC$	Ind		
Energy Studies and Geography	JF98	3FT/4SW deg	S g	12	MO $	M$	Dip$	BBCC$	Ind		
Geography	F800	3FT/4SW deg	Gy g	16	Ind	Ind	26$	BBBB$	Ind		
Geography and Physics	FF83	3FT/4SW deg	S g	12	MO $	M$	Dip$	BBCC$	Ind		
Geography and Statistics	FG84	3FT/4SW deg	S g	12	MO $	M$	Dip$	BBCC$	Ind		
Univ of BRISTOL											
Biology and Geography	CF18	3FT deg	B+Gy g	BBC	Ind	D$^	32$	CSYS	Ind	7	22/30
Geography	L800	3FT deg	* g	ABB-BBB	Ind	D$^	32$	AABBB	Ind	10	26/30
Geography	F800	3FT deg	S g	ABB-BBB	Ind	D$^	32$	AABBB	Ind	11	24/30
Geography (MSci)	L803	4FT deg	* g	ABB-BBB	Ind	D$^	32$	AABBB	Ind		
Geography (MSci)	F803	4FT deg	S g	ABB-BBB	Ind	D$^	32$	AABBB	Ind		
Geography and Geology	FF86	3FT deg	Gy+S g	BBC-BCC	Ind	D$^	30$	BBBBB	Ind	12	20/28
BRISTOL, Univ of the W of England											
Geography	L800	3FT deg	* g	18-20	3M+3D	M*4/^ go	26$	BCCC$	Ind		
Geography & Environmental Management	FF89	3FT deg	* g	14-16	5M+1D	M*2/^ go	24$	BCCC	Ind		
Joint Honours Programme *Geography and Languages*	Y401	4FT deg	Gy/En+L g	14-16	5M $	M$ go	24$	BCCC$	Ind		
Joint Honours Programme *History and Geography*	Y401	3FT deg	Gy/En/H g	14-16	5M $	M$ go	24$	BCCC$	Ind		

			98 expected requirements							96 entry stats	
TITLE	CODE	COURSE	SUBJECTS	A/AS	NO/C	AGNVQ	IB	SQA(H)	SQA	RATIO	A/AS
BRUNEL Univ, West London											
Geography	F800	3FT deg	Gy/En/Gl g	18	1M+3D	M$ go	26$	BCCCC$	N		
Geology/Geography	FL68	3FT deg	Gy/Gl g	18	MO $	M* go	26$	BCCC$	Ind		
Human Geography/Earth Sciences	L8F9	3FT deg	Gy/Gl g	18	MO $	M* go	26$	BCCC$	Ind		
Human Geography/Geology	L8F6	3FT deg	Gy/Gl g	18	MO $	M* go	26$	BCCC$	Ind		
CAMBRIDGE Univ											
Geography	L800▼	3FT deg	* g	AAB	Ind		Ind	CSYS	Ind	3	28/30
Geography with Education Studies (BA)	L8X9▼	3FT deg	* g	AAB	Ind		Ind	CSYS	Ind	8	
CANTERBURY CHRIST CHURCH COLL of HE											
American Studies with Geography	Q4L8	4FT deg	Gy g	CC	MO	M	24	Ind	Ind	4	
Art with Geography	W1L8	3FT deg	A+Gy g	CC	MO	M	24	Ind	Ind	4	
Business Studies with Geography	N1L8	3FT deg	Gy g	CC	MO	M	24	Ind	Ind	4	18/20
Early Childhood Studies with Geography	X9L8	3FT deg	Gy g	CC	MO	M	24	Ind	Ind		
English with Geography	Q3L8	3FT deg	E+Gy								
Geography (BA)	L800	3FT deg	Gy g	CC	MO	M	24	Ind	Ind		
Geography and American Studies	QL48	3FT deg	Gy g	CC	MO	M	24	Ind	Ind	5	
Geography and Art	LW81	3FT deg	Gy+A g	CC	MO	M	24	Ind	Ind	3	
Geography and Business Studies	NL18	3FT deg	Gy g	CC	MO	M	24	Ind	Ind		
Geography and Early Childhood Studies	LX89	3FT deg	Gy g	CC	MO	M	24	Ind	Ind		
Geography and English	QL38	3FT deg	Gy+E	CC	MO	M	24	Ind	Ind		
Geography and French	LR81	3FT deg	F+G g	CC	MO	M	24	Ind	Ind		
Geography and Social Science	LL83	3FT deg	Gy g	CC	MO	M	24	Ind	Ind	1	
Geography with American Studies	L8Q4	3FT deg	Gy g	CC	MO	M	24	Ind	Ind	11	
Geography with Art	L8W1	3FT deg	Gy+A g	CC	MO	M	24	Ind	Ind	10	
Geography with Business Studies	L8N1	3FT deg	Gy g	CC	MO	M	24	Ind	Ind	5	12/20
Geography with Early Childhood Studies	L8X9	3FT deg	Gy g	CC	MO	M	24	Ind	Ind	2	
Geography with English	L8Q3	3FT deg	Gy+E								
Geography with History	L8V1	3FT deg	Gy+H g	CC	MO	M	24	Ind	Ind		
Geography with Information Technology	L8G5	3FT deg	Gy g	CC	MO	M	24	Ind	Ind	14	
Geography with Marketing	L8N5	3FT deg	Gy g	CC	MO	M	24	Ind	Ind		
Geography with Media Studies	L8P4	3FT deg	Gy g	CC	MO	M	24	Ind	Ind		
Geography with Music	L8W3	3FT deg	Gy+Mu g	CC	MO	M	24	Ind	Ind		
Geography with Psychology	L8L7	3FT deg	Gy+Ps g	CC	MO	M	24	Ind	Ind	1	
Geography with Radio, Film & Television Studies	L8W5	3FT deg	Gy g	CC	MO	M	24	Ind	Ind	11	
Geography with Religious Studies	L8V8	3FT deg	Gy g	CC	MO	M	24	Ind	Ind	2	
Geography with Science	L8Y1	3FT deg	Gy+S g	DD	Ind	Ind	24	Ind	Ind		
Geography with Social Science	L8L3	3FT deg	Gy g	CC	MO	M	24	Ind	Ind	2	
Geography with Sport Science	L8B6	3FT deg	Gy g	CC	MO	M	24	Ind	Ind		
Geography with Tourism Studies	L8P7	3FT deg	Gy g	CC	MO	M	24	Ind	Ind	3	
History and Geography	LV81	3FT deg	Gy+H g	CC	MO	M	24	Ind	Ind		
History with Geography	V1L8	3FT deg	Gy+H g	CC	MO	M	24	Ind	Ind	4	
Information Technology and Geography	GL58	3FT deg	Gy g	CC	MO	M	24	Ind	Ind	2	
Information Technology with Geography	G5L8	3FT deg	Gy g	CC	MO	M	24	Ind	Ind		
Marketing and Geography	LN85	3FT deg	Gy g	CC	MO	M	24	Ind	Ind		
Marketing with Geography	N5L8	3FT deg	Gy g	CC	MO	M	24	Ind	Ind	4	
Media Studies and Geography	LP84	3FT deg	Gy g	CC	MO	M	24	Ind	Ind		
Media Studies with Geography	P4L8	3FT deg	Gy g	CC	MO	M	24	Ind	Ind		
Music and Geography	WL38	3FT deg	Mu+Gy g	CC	MO	M	24	Ind	Ind		
Music with Geography	W3L8	3FT deg	Mu+Gy g	CC	MO	M	24	Ind	Ind		
Psychology and Geography	LL87	3FT deg	Ps+Gy g	CC	MO	M	24	Ind	Ind		
Psychology with Geography	L7L8	3FT deg	Ps+Gy g	CC	MO	M	24	Ind	Ind		

Geography   30

course details				98 expected requirements						96 entry stats	
TITLE	CODE	COURSE	SUBJECTS	A/AS	NO/C	AGNVQ	IB	SQA(H)	SQA	RATIO	A/AS
Radio, Film & Television Studies with Geography	W5L8	3FT deg	Gy g	CC	MO	M	24	Ind	Ind		
Radio, Film and Television Studies and Geography	WL58	3FT deg	Gy g	CC	MO	M	24	Ind	Ind		
Religious Studies and Geography	LV88	3FT deg	Gy g	CC	MO	M	24	Ind	Ind		
Religious Studies with Geography	V8L8	3FT deg	Gy g	CC	MO	M	24	Ind	Ind		
Science and Geography	LY81	3FT deg	Gy+S g	DD	Ind	Ind	24	Ind	Ind		
Science with Geography	Y1L8	3FT deg	S+Gy g	DD	Ind	Ind	24	Ind	Ind		
Social Science with Geography	L3L8	3FT deg	Gy g	CC	MO	M	24	Ind	Ind	1	
Sport Science and Geography	LB86	3FT deg	Gy g	CC	MO	M	24	Ind	Ind		
Sport Science with Geography	B6L8	3FT deg	Gy g	CC	MO	M	24	Ind	Ind		
Tourism Studies with Geography	P7L8	3FT deg	Gy g	CC	MO	M	24	Ind	Ind	1	
Tourism and Geography	LP87	3FT deg	Gy g	CC	MO	M	24	Ind	Ind	1	

CARDIFF Univ of Wales

Marine Geography	F820	3FT deg	*	BCC-CCC	3M+2D		Ind	BBBC		3	10/24
Marine Geography	F821	4SW deg	*	BCC-CCC	3M+2D		Ind	ABBBC		3	8/26

Univ of CENTRAL LANCASHIRE

Geography	FL88	3FT deg	Gy	14	MO+3D	M$6/^	26$	BBCC	$		
Combined Honours Programme Geography	Y400	3FT deg	Gy g	14	MO+3D	M*^	26	BBCC	Ind		

CHELTENHAM & GLOUCESTER COLL of HE

Business Computer Systems and Geography	GL5V	3FT deg	*	12	MO	M	24	CCCC	Ind		
Business Computer Systems and Physical Geography	FG8M	3FT deg	*	8-12	MO	M	26	CCCC	Ind		
Business Computer Systems with Geography	G5LW	3FT deg	*	8	MO	M	24	CCCC	Ind		
Business Computer Systs with Physical Geography	G5FW	3FT deg	*	8	MO	M	26	CCCC	Ind		
Business Management and Geography	LN8D	3FT deg	*	12	MO	MB3	26	CCCC	Ind		
Business Management and Human Geography	NL18	3FT deg	*	12-16	4M+3D	MB3	26	CCCC	Ind		
Business Management and Physical Geography	NF18	3FT deg	*	12	4M+3D	MB3	26	CCCC	Ind		
Business Management with Geography	N1LW	4SW deg	*	12	MO	MB3	24	CCCC	Ind		
Business Management with Human Geography	N1LV	4SW deg	*	12	4M+3D	MB3	26	CCCC	Ind		
Business Management with Physical Geography	N1FV	4SW deg	*	12	4M+3D	MB3	26	CCCC	Ind		
Computing and Geography	GL5W	3FT deg	*	8-12	MO	M	24	CCCC	Ind		
Computing and Human Geography	LG85	3FT deg	*	8-12	MO	M	26	CCCC	Ind		
Computing and Physical Geography	GF58	3FT deg	*	8-12	MO	M	26	CCCC	Ind		
Computing with Geography	GLMV	3FT deg	*	8	MO	M3	24	CCCC	Ind		
Computing with Human Geography	G5LV	3FT deg	*	8	MO	M	26	CCCC	Ind		
Computing with Physical Geography	G5FV	3FT deg	*	8	MO	M	26	CCCC	Ind		
Countryside Planning and Geography	DL2V	3FT deg	*	10-12	MO	M3	24	CCCC	Ind		
Countryside Planning and Human Geography	DL28	3FT deg	*	8-12	5M+2D	MK	26	CCCC	Ind		
Countryside Planning and Physical Geography	DF28	3FT deg	*	8-12	5M+2D	MK	26	CCCC	Ind		
Countryside Planning with Geography	D2LV	3FT deg	*	8	MO	M	24	CCCC	Ind		
Countryside Planning with Human Geography	D2L8	3FT deg	*	8-12	MO	MK	26	CCCC	Ind		
Countryside Planning with Physical Geography	D2F8	3FT deg	*	8-12	5M+2D	MK	26	CCCC	Ind		
English Studies and Geography	LQ8H	3FT deg	E	12-14	MO	M3^	26	CCCC	Ind		
English Studies and Human Geography	LQ83	3FT deg	E	12-16	4M+3D	M^	26	CCCC	Ind		
English Studies and Physical Geography	FQ83	3FT deg	E	12-16	4M+3D	M^	26	CCCC	Ind		
English Studies with Geography	Q3LV	3FT deg	E	12-14	MO	M3^	26	CCCC	Ind		
English Studies with Human Geography	Q3L8	3FT deg	E	12-14	4M+3D	M^	26	CCCC	Ind		
English Studies with Physical Geography	Q3F8	3FT deg	E	12	4M+3D	M^	26	CCCC	Ind		
Environmental Policy and Geography	FLX8	3FT deg	*	8-12	MO	M3	26	CCCC	Ind		
Environmental Policy and Human Geography	FL9V	3FT deg	*	8-12	5M+2D	M3	26	CCCC	Ind		
Environmental Policy and Physical Geography	FF89	3FT deg	*	8-12	MO	M3	26	CCCC	Ind		
Environmental Policy with Geography	F9L8	3FT deg	*	8-12	MO	M3	26	CCCC	Ind		

course details | 98 expected requirements | 96 entry stats

TITLE	CODE	COURSE	SUBJECTS	A/AS	ND/C	AGNVQ	IB	SQA(H)	SQA	RATIO A/AS
Environmental Policy with Human Geography	F9LW	3FT deg	*	10-14	5M+2D	M3	26	CCCC	Ind	
Environmental Policy with Physical Geography	F9F8	3FT deg	*	8-12	M0	M3	26	CCCC	Ind	
Geography and Geology	FL6V	3FT deg	*	10	M0	M3	26	CCCC	Ind	
Geography and History	LV8C	3FT deg	H	12-14	M0	M3^	26	CCCC	Ind	
Geography and Human Resource Management	LN8C	3FT deg	*	12	M0	MB3	26	CCCC	Ind	
Geography and Information Technology	GLM8	3FT deg	*	12	M0	M	24	CCCC	Ind	
Geography and Leisure Management	LN8R	3FT deg	*	12-14	M0	MB3	26	CCCC	Ind	
Geography and Marketing Management	LN8M	3FT deg	*	12	M0	MB3	26	CCCC	Ind	
Geography and Media Communications	LP8K	3FT deg	*	12	M0	M3^	26	CCCC	Ind	
Geography and Natural Resource Management	FL9W	3FT deg	*	10	M0	M3	24	CCCC	Ind	
Geography and Psychology	LL87	3FT deg	*	12-14	M0	M3^	26	CCCC	Ind	
Geography and Sociological Studies	LLH8	3FT deg	*	12	M0	M3^	26	CCCC	Ind	
Geography and Sport and Exercise Sciences	BL68	3FT deg	*	12-16	M0	ML3	26	CCCC	Ind	
Geography and Visual Arts	LW81	3FT deg	A	10-14	5M+2D	MA3	26	CCCC	Ind	
Geography and Women's Studies	LM8X	3FT deg	*	12	M0	M3^	26	CCCC	Ind	
Geography with Business Computer Systems	L8GN	3FT deg	*	12	M0	M3^	26	CCCC	Ind	
Geography with Business Management	L8ND	3FT deg	*	12	M0	M3^	26	CCCC	Ind	
Geography with Computing	LGVM	3FT deg	*	8-12	M0	M3^	26	CCCC	Ind	
Geography with Countryside Planning	L8DF	3FT deg	*	8-12	M0	M3^	26	CCCC	Ind	
Geography with English Studies	L8QH	3FT deg	E	12-14	M0	M3^	26	CCCC	Ind	
Geography with Environmental Policy	LFVX	3FT deg	*	8-12	M0	M3^	26	CCCC	Ind	
Geography with Geology	L8FP	3FT deg	*	8-12	M0	M3^	26	CCCC	Ind	
Geography with History	L8VC	3FT deg	*	12	M0	M3^	26	CCCC	Ind	
Geography with Human Resource Management	LNVC	3FT deg	*	12	M0	MB3	26	CCCC	Ind	
Geography with Information Technology	LGWM	3FT deg	*	8-12	M0	M	24	CCCC	Ind	
Geography with Leisure Management	L8NR	3FT deg	*	12-14	M0	ML3	26	CCCC	Ind	
Geography with Marketing Management	L8NM	3FT deg	*	12	M0	MB3	26	CCCC	Ind	
Geography with Media Communications	L8PK	3FT deg	*	12	M0	M3^	26	CCCC	Ind	
Geography with Modern Languages (French)	L8RC	3FT deg	F g	12	M0	M3^	26	CCCC	Ind	
Geography with Natural Resource Management	L8FY	3FT deg	*	10	M0	M3^	26	CCCC	Ind	
Geography with Psychology	L8LR	3FT deg	M g	12-14	M0	M3^	26	CCCC	Ind	
Geography with Sociological Studies	L8LH	3FT deg	*	12	M0	M3^	26	CCCC	Ind	
Geography with Sport and Exercise Sciences	L8BP	3FT deg	*	12-16	M0	ML3	26	CCCC	Ind	
Geography with Tourism Management	L8PR	3FT deg	*	12-16	M0	ML3	26	CCCC	Ind	
Geography with Visual Arts	L8W1	3FT deg	*	10-14	5M+2D	MA3	26	CCCC	Ind	
Geography with Women's Studies	L8MX	3FT deg	*	12	M0	M3^	26	CCCC	Ind	
Geology and Human Geography	FL68	3FT deg	S	8-12	M0	M3^	26	CCCC	Ind	
Geology and Physical Geography	FF68	3FT deg	S	8	M0	M3	26	CCCC	Ind	
Geology with Geography	F6LV	3FT deg	S	8-12	M0	M3^	24	CCCC	Ind	
Geology with Human Geography	F6L8	3FT deg	S	8-12	M0	M3	26	CCCC	Ind	
Geology with Physical Geography	F6F8	3FT deg	S	8-12	M0	M3	26	CCCC	Ind	
History and Human Geography	LV81	3FT deg	H	12	4M+3D	M3^	26	CCCC	Ind	
History and Physical Geography	FV81	3FT deg	H	12	5M+2D	M3^	26	CCCC	Ind	
History with Geography	V1LV	3FT deg	H	12	M0	M3^	26	CCCC	Ind	
History with Human Geography	V1L8	3FT deg	H	10-14	4M+3D	M3^	26	CCCC	Ind	
History with Physical Geography	V1F8	3FT deg	H	10-14	4M+3D	M3^	26	CCCC	Ind	
Hotel Management and Human Geography	LN8T	3FT deg	*	10-14	5M+2D	MH3	26	CCCC	Ind	
Hotel Management and Physical Geography	NF78	3FT deg	*	10-14	5M+2D	M$3	26	CCCC	Ind	
Hotel Management with Human Geography	N7FV	4SW deg	*	10-14	5M+2D	MH3	26	CCCC	Ind	
Hotel Management with Physical Geography	N7FW	4SW deg	*	10-14	5M+2D	MH3	26	CCC	Ind	
Human Geography and Human Resource Management	LN81	3FT deg	*	12	5M+2D	MB3	26	CCCC	Ind	
Human Geography and Information Technology	GL58	3FT/4SW deg	*	8-12	M0	M3	24	CCCC	Ind	

course details | 98 expected requirements | 96 entry stats

TITLE	CODE	COURSE	SUBJECTS	A/AS	ND/C	AGNVQ	IB	SQA(H)	SQA	RATIO A/AS
Human Geography and Leisure Management	LN87	3FT deg	*	12-16	5M+2D	ML3	26	CCCC	Ind	
Human Geography and Marketing Management	LN85	3FT deg	*	12	5M+2D	MB3	26	CCCC	Ind	
Human Geography and Media Communications	LP84	3FT deg	*	12	5M+2D	MT3	26	CCCC	Ind	
Human Geography and Multimedia	GLN8	3FT deg	*	10-14	5M+2D	M3	26	CCCC	Ind	
Human Geography and Natural Resource Management	FL98	3FT deg	*	8-12	M0	M3	26	CCCC	Ind	
Human Geography and Physical Geography	FL88	3FT deg	*	12	5M+2D	M3	26	CCCC	Ind	
Human Geography and Psychology	LL78	3FT deg	M g	12-16	4M+3D	M3	26	CCCC	Ind	
Human Geography and Religious Studies	LV88	3FT deg	*	8-12	5M+2D	M3	26	CCCC	Ind	
Human Geography and Sociological Studies	LL38	3FT deg	*	12-16	4M+3D	M3	26	CCCC	Ind	
Human Geography and Sport and Exercise Sciences	LB86	3FT deg	S	12-16	4M+3D	ML3	26	CCCC	Ind	
Human Geography and Tourism Management	LP87	3FT deg	*	12-16	4M+3D	ML3	26	CCCC	Ind	
Human Geography and Visual Arts	LW8C	3FT deg	*	10	M0	MA3	26	CCCC	Ind	
Human Geography and Women's Studies	LM89	3FT deg	*	12	5M+2D	M3	26	CCCC	Ind	
Human Geography with Business Management	L8NC	3FT deg	*	12	5M+2D	M3	26	CCCC	Ind	
Human Geography with Combined Arts	L8Y3	3FT deg	*	12	M0	M3^	26	CCCC	Ind	
Human Geography with Computing	L8GM	3FT deg	*	8-12	M0	M3	26	CCCC	Ind	
Human Geography with Countryside Planning	L8D2	3FT deg	*	12	5M+2D	M3	26	CCCC	Ind	
Human Geography with English Studies	L8Q3	3FT deg	E	12-16	4M+3D	M3	26	CCCC	Ind	
Human Geography with Environmental Policy	L8FX	3FT deg	*	12	4M+3D	M3	26	CCCC	Ind	
Human Geography with Geology	L8F6	3FT deg	*	10-12	4M+3D	M3	26	CCCC	Ind	
Human Geography with History	L8V1	3FT deg	H	12	4M+3D	M3	26	CCCC	Ind	
Human Geography with Hotel Management	L8NT	3FT deg	*	10-14	5M+2D	M3	26	CCCC	Ind	
Human Geography with Human Resource Management	L8N1	3FT deg	*	12	5M+2D	M3	26	CCCC	Ind	
Human Geography with Information Technology	L8G5	3FT deg	10-14	12	4M+3D	M3	26	CCCC	Ind	
Human Geography with Leisure Management	L8N7	3FT deg	Gy	12	5M+2D	M3	26	CCCC	Ind	
Human Geography with Marketing Management	L8N5	3FT deg	Gy	12	5M+2D	M3	26	CCCC	Ind	
Human Geography with Media Communications	L8P4	3FT deg	Gy	12	5M+2D	M3	26	CCCC	Ind	
Human Geography with Modern Languages (French)	L8R1	3FT deg	F g	12	4M+3D	M3	26	CCCC	Ind	
Human Geography with Multimedia	LG8M	3FT deg	*	10-14	5M+2D	M3	26	CCCC	Ind	
Human Geography with Natural Resource Management	L8F9	3FT deg	*	12	4M+3D	M3	26	CCCC	Ind	
Human Geography with Physical Geography	L8F8	3FT deg	*	12	5M+2D	M3	26	CCCC	Ind	
Human Geography with Psychology	L8L7	3FT deg	g	12-16	4M+3D	M3	26	CCCC	Ind	
Human Geography with Sociological Studies	L8L3	3FT deg	*	12	4M+3D	M3	26	CCCC	Ind	
Human Geography with Sport and Exercise Sciences	L8B6	3FT deg	S	12-16	4M+3D	M3	26	CCCC	Ind	
Human Geography with Tourism Management	L8P7	3FT deg	*	12-16	4M+3D	M3	26	CCCC	Ind	
Human Geography with Visual Arts	L8WC	3FT deg	*	10	M0	M3	26	CCCC	Ind	
Human Geography with Women's Studies	L8M9	3FT deg	*	10-14	4M+3D	M3	26	CCCC	Ind	
Human Resource Management and Physical Geography	FN81	3FT deg	*	8-12	5M+2D	MB3	26	CCCC	Ind	
Human Resource Mgt with Geography	NLCV	4SW deg	*	12	M0	MB3	26	CCCC	Ind	
Human Resource Mgt with Human Geography	N1L8	3FT deg	*	10	5M+2D	MB3	26	CCCC	Ind	
Human Resource Mgt with Physical Geography	N1F8	4SW deg	*	10-14	5M+2D	MB3	26	CCCC	Ind	
Information Technology and Physical Geography	FG85	3FT/4SW deg	*	8-12	M0	M3	24	CCCC	Ind	
Information Technology with Geography	GLMW	3FT deg	*	8-12	M0	M3	24	CCCC	Ind	
Information Technology with Human Geography	G5L8	3FT deg	*	8-12	M0	M3	24	CCCC	Ind	
Information Technology with Physical Geography	G5F8	3FT deg	*	8-12	M0	M3	24	CCCC	Ind	
Leisure Management and Physical Geography	FN87	3FT deg	*	12-16	5M+2D	ML3	26	CCCC	Ind	
Leisure Management with Geography	N7L8	4SW deg		12-16	M0	ML3	26	CCCC	Ind	
Leisure Management with Human Geography	N7LV	4SW deg	*	12-16	5M+2D	ML3	26	CCCC	Ind	
Leisure Management with Physical Geography	N7F8	4SW deg	*	12-16	5M+2D	ML3	26	CCCC	Ind	
Marketing Management and Physical Geography	FN85	3FT deg	*	12	5M+2D	MB3	26	CCCC	Ind	
Marketing Management with Geography	N5LV	4SW deg	*	12	M0	MB3	26	CCCC	Ind	
Marketing Management with Human Geography	N5L8	4SW deg	*	12	5M+2D	MB3	26	CCCC	Ind	

course details   98 expected requirements   96 entry stats

TITLE	CODE	COURSE	SUBJECTS	A/AS	ND/C	AGNVQ	IB	SQA(H)	SQA	RATIO A/AS
Marketing Management with Physical Geography	N5F8	4SW deg	*	12	5M+2D	MB3	26	CCCC	Ind	
Media Communications with Geography	P4L8	3FT deg	*	12	M0	M3^	26	CCCC	Ind	
Media Communications with Human Geography	P4LV	3FT deg	*	12	5M+2D	MP3	26	CCCC	Ind	
Multimedia and Physical Geography	GF5V	3FT deg	*	8-12	5M+2D	M3	26	CCCC	Ind	
Multimedia with Human Geography	GLNV	3FT deg	*	8-12	M0	MI3				
Multimedia with Human Geography	GLNW	4SW deg	*	8-12	M0	MI3				
Multimedia with Physical Geography	GFM8	4SW deg	*	8-12	M0	MI3	24	CCCC	Ind	
Multimedia with Physical Geography	GF5W	3FT deg	*	8-12	M0	MI3	24	CCCC	Ind	
Natural Resource Mgt and Physical Geography	FF8X	3FT deg	*	8-12	M0	M3	26	CCCC	Ind	
Natural Resource Mgt with Geography	FLXV	3FT deg	*	10	M0	M3	24	CCCC	Ind	
Natural Resource Mgt with Human Geography	F9LV	3FT deg	*	8	M0	M3	26	CCCC	Ind	
Natural Resource Mgt with Physical Geography	F9FV	3FT deg	*	8	M0	M3	26	CCCC	Ind	
Physical Geography and Sociological Studies	FL83	3FT deg	*	12	5M+2D	M3^	26	CCCC	Ind	
Physical Geography and Sport and Exercise Sci	FB86	3FT deg	S	12-16	5M+2D	ML3	26	CCCC	Ind	
Physical Geography and Tourism Management	FP87	3FT deg	*	12	5M+2D	ML3	26	CCCC	Ind	
Physical Geography with Business Computer Systs	F8GN	3FT deg	*	8-12	M0	M3^	26	CCCC	Ind	
Physical Geography with Business Management	F8NC	3FT deg	*	8-12	M0	M3^	26	CCCC	Ind	
Physical Geography with Computing	F8GM	3FT deg	*	8-12	M0	M3^	26	CCCC	Ind	
Physical Geography with Countryside Planning	F8D9	3FT deg	*	8-12	4M+3D	M3^	26	CCCC	Ind	
Physical Geography with English Studies	F8Q3	3FT deg	*	8-12	4M+3D	M3^	26	CCCC	Ind	
Physical Geography with Environmental Policy	F8FX	3FT deg	*	8-12	5M+2D	M3^	26	CCCC	Ind	
Physical Geography with Geology	F8F6	3FT deg	*	8-12	M0	M3^	26	CCCC	Ind	
Physical Geography with History	F8V1	3FT deg	*	8-12	4M+3D	M3^	26	CCCC	Ind	
Physical Geography with Hotel Management	F8NR	3FT deg	*	8-12	5M+2D	M3^	26	CCCC	Ind	
Physical Geography with Human Geography	F8L8	3FT deg	*	12	5M+2D	M3^	26	CCCC	Ind	
Physical Geography with Human Resource Mgt	F8N1	3FT deg	*	8-12	5M+2D	M3^	26	CCCC	Ind	
Physical Geography with Information Technology	F8G5	3FT deg	*	10	M0	M3^	26	CCCC	Ind	
Physical Geography with Leisure Management	F8N7	3FT deg	*	8-12	M0	M3^	26	CCCC	Ind	
Physical Geography with Marketing Management	F8N5	3FT deg	*	8-12	M0	M3^	26	CCCC	Ind	
Physical Geography with Multimedia	FG8N	3FT deg	*	8-12	M0	M3^	26	CCCC	Ind	
Physical Geography with Natural Resource Mgt	F8F9	3FT deg	*	8-12	M0	M3^	26	CCCC	Ind	
Physical Geography with Sociological Studies	F8L3	3FT deg	*	12	5M+2D	M3^	26	CCCC	Ind	
Physical Geography with Sport and Exercise Sci	F8B6	3FT deg	*	12	5M+2D	M3^	26	CCCC	Ind	
Physical Geography with Tourism Management	F8P7	3FT deg	*	12	5M+2D	M3^	26	CCCC	Ind	
Psychology with Geography	L7LV	3FT deg	g	12-16	M0	M3^	26	CCCC	Ind	
Psychology with Human Geography	L7L8	3FT deg	g	12-16	4M+3D	M3^	26	CCCC	Ind	
Religious Studies with Human Geography	V8L8	3FT deg	*	8-12	M0	M3^	26	CCCC	Ind	
Sociological Studies with Geography	L3LV	3FT deg	*	12	M0	M3^	26	CCCC	Ind	
Sociological Studies with Human Geography	L3L8	3FT deg	*	12	4M+3D	MG3	26	CCCC	Ind	
Sociological Studies with Physical Geography	L3F8	3FT deg	*	12	4M+3D	MG3	26	CCCC	Ind	
Sport & Exercise Sciences with Geography	B6LV	3FT deg	*	12-16	M0	M3^	26	CCCC	Ind	
Sport & Exercise Sciences with Human Geography	B6L8	3FT deg	*	12-16	4M+3D	ML3	26	CCCC	Ind	
Sport & Exercise Sciences with Physical Geog	B6F8	3FT deg	*	12-16	4M+3D	ML3	26	CCCC	Ind	
Tourism Management with Human Geography	P7L8	4SW deg	*	12-16	4M+3D	ML3	26	CCCC	Ind	
Tourism Management with Physical Geography	P7F8	4SW deg	*	12	4M+3D	ML3	26	CCCC	Ind	
Visual Arts with Geography	W1L8	3FT deg	A	10-14	5M+2D	MA3	26	CCCC	Ind	
Visual Arts with Human Geography	W1LV	3FT deg	A	10-14	5M+2D	MA3	26	CCCC	Ind	
Women's Studies with Geography	M9LV	3FT deg	*	8-12	M0	M3^	26	CCCC	Ind	
Women's Studies with Human Geography	M9L8	3FT deg	*	8-12	M0	M3	26	CCCC	Ind	

UNIVERSITY COLLEGE CHESTER

TITLE	CODE	COURSE	SUBJECTS	A/AS	ND/C	AGNVQ	IB	SQA(H)	SQA	RATIO A/AS
Art and Geography	WF98	3FT deg	Gy/Gl	CC	M	P^	Ind	CCCC	$	
Art with Geography	W9F8	3FT deg	Gy/Gl	CC	M	P^	Ind	CCCC	$	

Geography 30

course details			98 expected requirements							96 entry stats	
TITLE	CODE	COURSE	SUBJECTS	A/AS	ND/C	AGNVQ	IB	SQA(H)	SQA	RATIO	A/AS
Biology and Geography	CF18	3FT deg	B+Gy/Gl	CD	M	P^	Ind	CCCC	$	10	
Biology with Geography	C1F8	3FT deg	B+Gy/Gl	CD	M	P^	Ind	CCCC	$		
Computer Science/IT with Geography	G5F8	3FT deg	Gy/Gl g	CD	M	P^	Ind	CCCC	$		
Computer Studies/IT and Geography	GF58	3FT deg	Gy/Gl g	CD	3M	P^	Ind	CCCC	$	15	
Drama and Theatre Studies and Geography	WF48	3FT deg	Gy/Gl	CC	M	P^	Ind	CCCC	$		
Drama and Theatre Studies with Geography	W4F8	3FT deg	Gy/Gl	CC	M	P^	Ind	CCCC	$		
English Literature and Geography	QF38	3FT deg	E+Gy/Gl	CC	M	P^	Ind	CCCC	$	9	
English with Geography	Q3F8	3FT deg	E+Gy/G1	CC	M	P^	Ind	CCCC	$		
Geography and Geomatics	F8GM	3FT deg	Gy/Gl	10	M	P	Ind	CCCC	$		
Geography and History	FV81	3FT deg	Gy/Gl+H/Ec/So	CC	M	P^	Ind	CCCC	$		
Geography and Physical Education/Sports Science	FB86	3FT deg	Gy/Gl	CC	M	P^	Ind	CCCC	$		
Geography and Psychology	FL87	3FT deg	Gy/Gl g	12	M	P^	Ind	CCCC	$	7	
Geography and Theology and Religious Studies	FV88	3FT deg	Gy/Gl	12	M	P^	Ind	CCCC	$	5	
Geography with Art	F8W9	3FT deg	Gy/Gl	CC	M	P^	Ind	CCCC	$	6	
Geography with Biology	F8C1	3FT deg	Gy/Gl+B	CD	M	P^	Ind	CCCC	$	6	
Geography with Computer Science/IT	F8G5	3FT deg	Gy/Gl g	12	M	P^	Ind	CCCC	$	3	
Geography with Drama and Theatre Studies	F8W4	3FT deg	Gy/Gl	CC	M	P^	Ind	CCCC	$		
Geography with English Literature	F8Q3	3FT deg	E+Gy/Gl	CC	M	P^	Ind	CCCC	$		
Geography with French	F8R1	3FT deg	Gy/Gl g	12	M	P^	Ind	CCCC	$		
Geography with German	F8R2	3FT deg	Gy/Gl g	12	M	P^	Ind	CCCC	$	2	
Geography with History	F8V1	3FT deg	Gy/Gl+H/Ec/So	CC	M	P^	Ind	CCCC	$	11	
Geography with Mathematics	F8G1	3FT deg	Gy/Gl+M	CD	M	P^	Ind	CCCC	$	2	
Geography with Physical Education/Sports Science	F8B6	3FT deg	Gy/Gl	CC	M	P^	Ind	CCCC	$		
Geography with Psychology	F8L7	3FT deg	Gy/Gl g	10	M	P^	Ind	CCCC	$	12	
Geography with Social Science	F8L3	3FT deg	C g	10	M	P^	Ind	CCCC	$		
Geography with Theology and Religious Studies	F8V8	3FT deg	Gy/Gl	12	M	P^	Ind	CCCC	$		
History with Geography	V1F8	3FT deg	H/Ec/So+Gy/Gl	CC	M	P^	Ind	CCCC	$	6	
Mathematics and Geography	GF18	3FT deg	Gy/Gl+M	CD	M	P^	Ind	CCCC	$	7	
Mathematics with Geography	G1F8	3FT deg	M+Gy/Gl	10	M	P^	Ind	CCCC	$		
PE/Sports Science with Geography	B6F8	3FT deg	Gy/Gl	CC	M	P^	Ind	CCCC	$		
Psychology with Geography	L7F8	3FT deg	Gy/Gl g	10	M	P^	Ind	CCCC	$	19	
Theology and Religious Studies with Geography	V8F8	3FT deg	Gy/Gl	12	M	P^	Ind	CCCC	$		

CHICHESTER INSTITUTE OF HIGHER EDUCATION

Art and Geography	WL18	3FT deg	Gy+A+Pf	12	Ind	M$+^	Ind	Ind	Ind	6	
Art with Geography	E1L8	3FT deg	A+Pf	12	Ind	M$+^	Ind	Ind	Ind		
Art with Geography	W1L8	3FT deg	A+Pf	12	Ind	M$+^	Ind	Ind	Ind		
Dance and Geography	LW84	3FT deg	Gy+Pf	12	Ind	M$+	Ind	Ind	Ind		
Dance with Geography	W4L8	3FT deg	Pf	12	Ind	M$+	Ind	Ind	Ind		
English Language Teaching (EFL) and Geography	QL18	3FT deg	E	12	Ind	M^	Ind	Ind	Ind		
English and Geography	QL38	3FT deg	E+Gy	12	Ind	M^	Ind	Ind	Ind	4	
English with Geography	Q3L8	3FT deg	E	12	Ind	M^	Ind	Ind	Ind		
Environmental Science and Geography	LF89	3FT deg	Gy	12	Ind	M$	Ind	Ind	Ind	4	
Geography	L800	3FT deg	Gy	12	Ind	M$	Ind	Ind	Ind	9	4/13
Geography and Study of Religions	LV88	3FT deg	Gy	12	Ind	M$	Ind	Ind	Ind		
Geography and Theology	LV8V	3FT deg	Gy	12	Ind	M$	Ind	Ind	Ind		
Geography with Art	L8W1	3FT deg	Gy	12	Ind	M$	Ind	Ind	Ind		
Geography with Dance	L8W4	3FT deg	Gy	12	Ind	M$	Ind	Ind	Ind		
Geography with Education Studies (Opt. QTS) (P)	L8X9	3FT/4FT deg	Gy g	12	Ind	M$ go	Ind	Ind	Ind	4	6/12
Geography with English	L8Q3	3FT deg	Gy	12	Ind	M$	Ind	Ind	Ind	2	
Geography with English Language Teaching (EFL)	L8Q1	3FT deg	Gy	12	Ind	M$	Ind	Ind	Ind		
Geography with Environmental Science	L8F9	3FT deg	Gy g	12	Ind	M$	Ind	Ind	Ind		
Geography with History	L8V1	3FT deg	Gy	12	Ind	M$	Ind	Ind	Ind		

TITLE	CODE	COURSE	SUBJECTS	A/AS	ND/C	RGNVQ	IB	SQA(H)	SQA	RATIO A/AS
98 expected requirements colspan										**96 entry stats**
Geography with Mathematics	L8G1	3FT deg	Gy g	12	Ind	M$	Ind	Ind	Ind	
Geography with Media Studies	L8P4	3FT deg	Gy	12	Ind	M$	Ind	Ind	Ind	8
Geography with Music	L8W3	3FT deg	Gy	12	Ind	M$	Ind	Ind	Ind	
Geography with Related Arts	L8W9	3FT deg	Gy	12	Ind	M$	Ind	Ind	Ind	
Geography with Study of Religions	L8V8	3FT deg	Gy	12	Ind	M$	Ind	Ind	Ind	
Geography with Theology	L8VV	3FT deg	Gy	12	Ind	M$	Ind	Ind	Ind	
History and Geography	LV81	3FT deg	H/Gy	12	Ind	M$	Ind	Ind	Ind	
History with Geography	V1L8	3FT deg	H	12	Ind	M$	Ind	Ind	Ind	
Mathematics and Geography	GL18	3FT deg	M+Gy	12	Ind	M^	Ind	Ind	Ind	
Mathematics with Geography	G1L8	3FT deg	M	12	Ind	M^	Ind	Ind	Ind	
Media Studies and Geography	PL48	3FT deg	Gy	12	Ind	M$	Ind	Ind	Ind	5
Media Studies with Geography	P4L8	3FT deg	*	12	Ind	M$	Ind	Ind	Ind	
Music and Geography	LW83	3FT deg	Mu+Gy	12	Ind	M$+	Ind	Ind	Ind	
Music with Geography	W3L8	3FT deg	Mu	12	Ind	M$+	Ind	Ind	Ind	2
Related Arts and Geography	WL98	3FT deg	Gy	12	Ind	M$+	Ind	Ind	Ind	
Study of Religions with Geography	V8L8	3FT deg	*	12	Ind	M$	Ind	Ind	Ind	
Theology and Geography	VL88	3FT deg	Gy	12	Ind	M^	Ind	Ind	Ind	
Theology with Geography	V8LV	3FT deg	*	12	Ind	M$	Ind	Ind	Ind	

COVENTRY Univ

TITLE	CODE	COURSE	SUBJECTS	A/AS	ND/C	RGNVQ	IB	SQA(H)	SQA	RATIO A/AS
Biological Sciences and Geography	CF1V	4FT/5SW deg			Ind	Ind	Ind	Ind	Ind	
Chemistry and Geography	FL1W	4FT/5SW deg			Ind	Ind	Ind	Ind	Ind	
Geography	F800	3FT/4SW deg	Gy g	12-14	Ind	Ind	Ind	Ind	Ind	6 6/18
Geography and Biological Sciences	CL18	3FT/4SW deg								
Geography and Chemistry	FL18	3FT/4SW deg	C+Gy	10	3M	MS	Ind	Ind	Ind	4
Geography and Computing	LG85	3FT/4SW deg	* g	12	MO	M	Ind	Ind	Ind	4 8/14
Geography and Economics	LL18	3FT/4SW deg	Ec/Gy g	12	Ind	M	Ind	Ind	Ind	10
Geography and French	LR81	4SW deg	F+Gy g	12	Ind	M	Ind	Ind	Ind	6
Geography with European Study	F8T2	3FT deg								
German and Geography	LR82	4SW deg	G+Gy g	12	Ind	M+	Ind	Ind	Ind	2
History and Geography	LV81	3FT deg	*	CD	M	M	Ind	CCCC	Ind	
Mathematics and Geography	GL18	3FT/4SW deg	M/Gy g	14-18	3M $	M	Ind	Ind	Ind	9
Planning and Geography	LK84	3FT/4SW deg	Gy g	12	Ind	M	Ind	Ind	Ind	7 8/22
Politics and Geography	LM81	3FT/4SW deg	Po/Gy g	12	Ind	M	Ind	Ind	Ind	4 10/14
Statistics and Geography	GL48	3FT/4SW deg	Gy+St/M g	12-16	Ind	M	Ind	Ind	Ind	4
Third World Development Studies	L8M9	3FT deg	* g	12-14	Ind	M	Ind	Ind	Ind	8 8/16

CRANFIELD Univ

TITLE	CODE	COURSE	SUBJECTS	A/AS	ND/C	RGNVQ	IB	SQA(H)	SQA	RATIO A/AS
Physical Geography	F840	4SW deg	S/Gy g	BCD	4M	MS6/^ go	30$	BBBB	Ind	6

DE MONTFORT Univ

TITLE	CODE	COURSE	SUBJECTS	A/AS	ND/C	RGNVQ	IB	SQA(H)	SQA	RATIO A/AS
Human Geography	L822▼	3FT deg	Gy g	12	10M+2D M		Ind	BCCC	Ind	9 6/16

Univ of DERBY

TITLE	CODE	COURSE	SUBJECTS	A/AS	ND/C	RGNVQ	IB	SQA(H)	SQA	RATIO A/AS
Biology and Geography	CF18	3FT deg	S	10	N $	PS^	26$	CCCD$	Ind	9
Development Studies	M9L3	3FT deg		12	N $	M$	26$	CCCC	Ind	
Environmental Monitoring & Mgt and Geography	FF9V	3FT deg	S	10	N $	MS	26$	CCCD$	Ind	
Environmental Studies and Geography	FF98	3FT deg	S	10	N $	PS^	26$	CCCD	Ind	5 6/18
Geography	F800	3FT deg	Gy	10	N $	MS	26$	CCCD$	Ind	8 6/18
Geography	F801	4FT deg	Gy	10	N $	MS	26$	CCCD$	Ind	
Geography and Geology	FF86	3FT deg	Gy/Gl	10	N $	MS	26$	CCCD$	Ind	5 8/20
Geography and Heritage Conservation	FF81	3FT deg	Gy	10	N $	MS	26$	CCCD$	Ind	
Credit Accumulation Modular Scheme Geography	Y600	3FT deg	*	12	MO	M	Ind	CCCC	Ind	

course details			98 expected requirements							96 entry stats	
TITLE	CODE	COURSE	SUBJECTS	A/AS	NO/C	AGNVQ	IB	SQA(H)	SQA	RATIO	A/AS
Univ of DUNDEE											
American Studies and Geography	LQ84	4FT deg	* g	BCC	Ind	D$	29	BBBC	Ind	13	
Business Economics and Marketing and Geography	Y603	4FT deg	* g	BCC	Ind	D$	29	BBBC	Ind	1	
Contemporary European Studies and Geography	LT82	4FT deg	* g	BCC	Ind	D$	29	BBBC	Ind	2	
Economics and Geography	LL18	4FT deg	* g	BCC	Ind	D$	29	BBBC	Ind	10	
English and Geography	LQ83	4FT deg	E g	BCC	Ind	D$^	29$	BBBC$	Ind	4	
Environmental Science and Geography	FL98	4FT deg	* g	BCC	Ind	D$	29	BBBC	Ind	7	
Financial Economics and Geography	LLC8	4FT deg	* g	BCC	Ind	D$	29	BBBC	Ind		
Geography	L800	4FT deg	* g	BCC	Ind	D$	29	BBBC	Ind	9	22/26
Geography	F800	4FT deg	2S g	16	5M $	M$	25$	BBBC$	N$		
Geography and Modern History	LV81	4FT deg	* g	BCC	Ind	D$	29	BBBC	Ind	17	
Geography and Philosophy	LV87	4FT deg	* g	BCC	Ind	D$	29	BBBC	Ind	5	
Geography and Political Science	LM81	4FT deg	* g	BCC	Ind	D$	29	BBBC	Ind	4	
Geography and Psychology	LL78	4FT deg	* g	BCC	Ind	D$	29	BBBC	Ind	4	
Arts and Social Sciences *Geography*	Y400	3FT deg	* g	BCC	Ind	D$	29	BBBC	Ind		
Univ of DURHAM											
Arabic with Geography	T6L8	4FT deg	*	BBC	Ind	Ind	28	Ind	Ind		
Chinese with Geography	T3L8	4FT deg	*	BBC	Ind	Ind	31	AABBB	Ind		
Geography	F800	3FT deg	Gy+S	BBC	MO	Ind	32	AAABB	Ind	·8	22/30
Geography	L800	3FT deg	Gy	BBC	MO	Ind	32	AAABB	Ind	10	22/30
Geography (European Studies)	LT82	3FT deg	Gy+L	BBC	MO	Ind	32	AAABB	Ind	10	
Geography (European Studies)	FT82	3FT deg	Gy+L+S	BBC	MO	Ind	32	AAABB	Ind	5	
Japanese with Geography	T4L8	4FT deg	*	BBC	Ind	Ind	31	AABBB	Ind		
Natural Sciences *Geography*	Y160	3FT deg	Gy+S	ABB	Ind	X	33$	CSYS$	X		
Social Sciences Combined *Geography*	Y220	3FT deg	*	ABC	Ind	Ind	32	AAABB	Ind		
Univ of EAST LONDON											
Three-Subject Degree *Social Sciences*	Y600	3FT deg	* g	12	MO	M	Ind	Ind	Ind		
Geographical Information Systems	068F	2FT/3SW HND	* g	12	MO	MC	Ind	Ind	Ind	4	
EDGE HILL Univ COLLEGE											
Biology and Geography	CL18	3FT deg	S+Gy g	DD	X	PS^ go	Dip	BBCC$	Ind		
Geography	L801	3FT deg	Gy g	DD	X	P*^	Dip	BBCC$	Ind		
Geography	L800	3FT deg	Gy g	DD	X	P*^	Dip	BBCC$	X	3	4/16
Geography and Applied Social Sciences	LL83	3FT deg	Gy g	CD	X	X	Dip	BBCC$	X		
Geography and English	LQ83	3FT deg	(Gy/E) g	CC	X	X	Dip	BBCC$	X		
Geography and Information Systems	GL58	3FT deg	Gy g	CD	X	P*^	Dip	BBCC$	Ind	6	
Geography and Mathematics	GL18	3FT deg	Gy g	DD	3M+3D	P*^	Dip	BBCC	Ind	5	
Geography and Sports Studies	BL68	3FT deg	Gy g	CC	X	P*^	Dip	BBCC$	X		
Geography and Urban Policy Studies	LM8Y	3FT deg	Gy g	DD	X	P*^	Dip	BBCC$	X	20	
Geography and Women's Studies	LM89	3FT deg	Gy g	CD	X	P*^	Dip	BBCC$	X		
Human Geography	L820	3FT deg	Gy g	DD	X	P*^	Dip	BBCC$	Ind		
Human Geography	L822	3FT deg	Gy g	DD	X	P*^	Dip	BBCC$	Ind		
Modern European Studies and Geography	LT82	3FT deg	Gy g	DD	X	P*^	Dip	BBCC	Ind		
Physical Geography	F841	3FT deg	Gy g	DD	X	P*^ go	Dip	BBCC	Ind		
Physical Geography	F840	3FT deg	Gy g	DD	X	P*^ go	Dip	BBCC	Ind		
Science and Geography	LY81	3FT deg	S+Gy g	DD	X	PS^ go	Dip	BBCC$	Ind		

			98 expected requirements							96 entry stats
TITLE	CODE	COURSE	SUBJECTS	A/AS	ND/C	RGNVQ	IB	SQA(H)	SQA	RATIO A/AS
Univ of EDINBURGH										
Business Studies and Geography	NL18	4FT deg	M	ABB			36	AABB		
Geography	L800	4FT deg	*	ABB	Ind		36$	AABB	Ind	7
Geography	F800	4FT deg	Gy+2S g	BBC	MO $		Dip$	BBBB	N$	7	22/30
Geography and Archaeology	LV86	4FT deg	*	ABB	Ind		36$	AABB	Ind	12
Geography and Economic and Social History	LV83	4FT deg	*	ABB	Ind		36$	AABB	Ind	8
Geography and Economics	LL81	4FT deg	*	ABB	Ind		36$	AABB	Ind	31
Geography and Politics	LM81	4FT deg	*	ABB	Ind		36$	AABB	Ind	8
Geography and Social Anthropology	LL86	4FT deg	*	AAB	Ind		38$	AABB	Ind	7
Geography and Social Policy	LL84	4FT deg	*	ABB	Ind		36$	AABB	Ind	6
Geography and Sociology	LL83	4FT deg	*	ABB	Ind		36$	AABB	Ind	7
Geography with Environmental Studies	L8F9	4FT deg		ABB			36	AABB		
Geography with Gender Studies	L8M9	4FT deg	*	ABB	Ind		36$	AABB	Ind	
Geology and Physical Geography	FF68	4FT deg	2(Gy/S) g	CCC	MO $		Dip$	BBBB	N$	4	20/30
Social Science	Y200	3FT deg	*	ABB	Ind		36$	AABB	Ind	
Geography										
Univ of EXETER										
Biology and Geography	CF18	3FT deg	Gy+B g	22	4M	M$^ | 34$	Ind	Ind	6	12/26
Economics and Geography	LL18	3FT deg	Gy g	BBB	2M+3D	D$^ | 36$	Ind	Ind	6	20/26
Economics and Geography with European Study	LLC8	4FT deg	L+Gy g	BBB	2M+3D	D$^ | 36$	Ind	Ind	8	
Geography (Arts)	L802	3FT deg	Gy g	22-26	MO	M/D$^ | 34$	Ind	Ind	25	20/30
Geography (Earth Studies)	F801	3FT deg	Gy+S g	22-26	MO	M/D$^ | 34$	Ind	Ind		16/28
Geography (Science)	F800	3FT deg	Gy+S g	22-26	MO	M/D$^ | 34$	Ind	Ind	9	18/30
Geography (Social Studies)	L800	3FT deg	Gy g	22-26	MO	M/D$^ | 34$	Ind	Ind	9	18/30
Geography with European Study	L801	4FT deg	Gy+L g	22-26	MO	M/D$^ | 32$	Ind	Ind	11	24/28
Humanities in Contemporary Society	V9L8	3FT deg	*	BBC	MO	M/D$	34	Ind	Ind	
Univ of GLAMORGAN										
Geography	L801	3FT deg								
Geography and English Studies	LQ83	3FT deg	* g	12	Ind	Ind	Ind	Ind	Ind	
Geography and Geographical Systems	F800	3FT deg	M/S g	12	Ind	Ind	Ind	Ind	Ind	
Geography and History	LV81	3FT deg	* g	12	Ind	Ind	Ind	Ind	Ind	
Geography and Psychology	LL87	3FT deg	* g	CC	Ind	Ind	Ind	Ind	Ind	
Geography and Sociology	LL38	3FT deg	* g	12	Ind	Ind	Ind	Ind	Ind	
Geography and Visual Arts	LW81	3FT deg	A g	12	Ind	Ind	Ind	Ind	Ind	
Geological Science with Geography	F6L8	3FT deg	M/S g	12	Ind	Ind	Ind	Ind	Ind	
Humanities (Geography)	L800	3FT deg	* g	CC	5M	M$	24	CCCC	HN	11
Sports Science with Geography	B6L8	3FT deg	M/S g	12	Ind	Ind	Ind	Ind	Ind	
Urban Studies and Geography	KL48	3FT deg	* g	12	Ind	Ind	Ind	Ind	Ind	
Combined Studies (Honours) *Geographical Information Systems*	Y400	3FT deg	* g	8-16	Ind	Ind	Ind	Ind	Ind	
Combined Studies (Honours) *Geography*	Y400	3FT deg	* g	8-16	Ind	Ind	Ind	Ind	Ind	
Joint Honours *Geographical Information Systems*	Y401	3FT deg	* g	8-16	Ind	Ind	Ind	Ind	Ind	
Major/Minor Honours *Geographical Information Systems*	Y402	3FT deg	* g	8-16	Ind	Ind	Ind	Ind	Ind	
Major/Minor Honours *Geography*	Y402	3FT deg	* g	8-16	Ind	Ind	Ind	Ind	Ind	
Univ of GLASGOW										
Archaeology/Geography	FV86	4FT deg	2S	BBC-CCC N		M	24$	BBBB$	N	
Archaeology/Geography	LV86	4FT deg		BBC	HN	M	30	BBBB	Ind	7
Celtic Civilisation/Geography	LQ85	4FT deg		BBC	HN	M	30	BBBB	Ind	

Geography 30

course details			98 expected requirements							96 entry stats	
TITLE	CODE	COURSE	SUBJECTS	A/AS	NO/C	AGNVQ	IB	SQA(H)	SQA	RATIO A/AS	
Celtic/Geography	LQV5	4FT deg		BBC	HN	M	30	BBBB	Ind	1	
Classical Civilisation/Geography	LQ88	4FT deg		BBC	HN	M	30	BBBB	Ind		
Classical Hebrew/Geography	LV8W	4FT deg		BBC	HN	M	30	BBBB	Ind		
Computing Science/Geography	FG85	4FT deg	M+S	BBC-CCC	N	M	24$	BBBB$	N	7	
Czech/Geography	LTV1	5FT deg		BBC	HN	M	30	BBBB	Ind		
Economic and Social History/Geography	LV83	4FT deg		BBC	8M	M	30	BBBB	Ind	9	
Environmental Chemistry/Geography	FF18	4FT deg	C/M+S	BBC-CCC	N	M	24$	BBBB$	N		
Film and Television Studies/Geography	LW85	4FT deg		BBB	HN	D	32	AABB	HN		
French/Geography	LR81	5FT deg		BBC	HN	M	30	BBBB	Ind		
Geography	L802	4FT deg		BBC	HN	M	30	BBBB	Ind	48	
Geography	F800	4FT deg	2S	BBC-CCC	N	M	24$	BBBB$	N	7	18/22
Geography	L800	4FT deg		BBC	8M	M	30	BBBB	Ind	7	20/26
Geography with Celtic	L8Q5	4FT deg		BBC	8M	M	30	BBBB	Ind		
Geography with Czech	L8T1	4FT deg		BBC	8M	M	30	BBBB	Ind		
Geography with French	L8R1	4FT deg		BBC	8M	M	30	BBBB	Ind		
Geography with German	L8R2	4FT deg		BBC	8M	M	30	BBBB	Ind		
Geography with Hispanic Studies	L8R4	4FT deg		BBC	8M	M	30	BBBB	Ind		
Geography with Italian	L8R3	5FT deg		BBC	HN	8M	30	BBBB	Ind		
Geography with Polish	L8TC	4FT deg		BBC	8M	M	30	BBBB	Ind		
Geography with Russian	L8R8	4FT deg		BBC	8M	M	30	BBBB	Ind		
Geography/Archaeology	VL68	4FT deg		BBC	8M	M	30	BBBB	Ind		
Geography/Classical Civilisation	LQ8V	4FT deg		BBC	8M	M	30	BBBB	Ind	4	
Geography/Classical Hebrew	LQ89	4FT deg		BBC	HN	M	30	BBBB	Ind		
Geography/Computing Science	LG85	4FT deg		BBC	8M	M	30	BBBB	Ind	10	
Geography/Economics	LL18	4FT deg		BBC	8M	M	30	BBBB	Ind	13	
Geography/Geology	FF68	4FT deg	2S	BBC-CCC	N	M	24$	BBBB$	N	7	
Geography/German	LR82	5FT deg		BBC	HN	M	30	BBBB	Ind		
Geography/Hispanic Studies	LR84	5FT deg		BBC	HN	M	30	BBBB	Ind		
Geography/History	LV8C	4FT deg		BBC	HN	M	30	BBBB	Ind	8	
Geography/History of Art	LV84	4FT deg		BBC	HN	M	30	BBBB	Ind		
Geography/Italian	LR83	5FT deg		BBC	HN	M	30	BBBB	Ind		
Geography/Management Studies	LN81	4FT deg		BBC	8M	M	30	BBBB	Ind	9	
Geography/Music	LW83	4FT deg		BBC	HN	M	30	BBBB	Ind	6	
Geography/Philosophy	LV87	4FT deg		BBC	HN	M	30	BBBB	Ind	10	
Geography/Polish	LT81	5FT deg		BBC	HN	M	30	BBBB	Ind		
Geography/Politics	LM81	4FT deg		BBC	8M	M	30	BBBB	Ind	5	
Geography/Russian	LR88	5FT deg		BBC	HN	M	30	BBBB	Ind		
Geography/Scottish History	LVVC	4FT deg		BBC	HN	M	30	BBBB	Ind	5	
Geography/Scottish Literature	LQ82	4FT deg		BBC	HN	M	30	BBBB	Ind		
Geography/Social and Urban Policy	LL48	4FT deg		BBC	8M	M	30	BBBB	Ind	7	
Geography/Sociology	LL38	4FT deg		BBC	8M	M	30	BBBB	Ind	4	
Islamic Studies/Geography	TL68	4FT deg		BBC	N	M	30	BBBB	Ind		
Theatre Studies/Geography	LW84	4FT deg		BBC	HN	M	30	BBBB	Ind		
Theology & Religious Studies/Geography	LV8V	4FT deg		BBC	HN	M	30	BBBB	Ind		
Topographic Science	F862	4FT deg	2S	BBC-CCC	N	M	24$	BBBB$	N	5	

Univ of GREENWICH

Geographical Information Systems	FG85	3FT/4SW deg	* g	12	3M	Ind	Dip	CCC	Ind		
Geographical Information Systems (Extended)	FG8M	4FT/5SW deg	g	4		Ind	Ind	Ind	Ind		
Geography	L800	3FT/4SW deg	g	12	3M	Ind	Dip	CCC	Ind		
Geography	F800	3FT/4SW deg	g	12	3M	Ind	Dip	CCC	Ind		
Geography (Extended)	F808	4FT/5SW deg	g	4		Ind	Ind	Ind	Ind		
Geography, Cultural	L820	3FT deg	g	10	M	M	25	BBB	Ind		

			98 expected requirements							96 entry stats	

TITLE	CODE	COURSE	SUBJECTS	A/AS	ND/C	AGNVQ	IB	SQA(H)	SQA	RATIO A/AS	
Geology & Physical Geography	FF68	3FT/4SW deg	* g	12	3M	Ind	Dip	CCC	Ind		
Natural Resource Management (3FT/4SW)	FD82	3FT/4SW deg	* g	12	3M	Ind	Dip	CCC	Ind		
Natural Resource Management (Extended)	FD8F	4FT/5SW deg	g	4		Ind	Ind	Ind	Ind		
Remote Sensing	GF58	3FT/4SW deg	* g	12	3M	Ind	Dip	CCC	Ind		
Remote Sensing (Extended)	GF5V	4FT/5SW deg	g	4	N	Ind	Ind	Ind	Ind		

Univ of HERTFORDSHIRE

Geography	F800	3FT/4SW deg	* g	14-18	4M	Ind	24	BBCCC	Ind		
Geography with a year in Europe	F801	4FT deg	* g	14-18	4M	Ind	24	BBCCC	Ind		
Geography with a year in North America	F802	4FT deg	* g	14-18	4M	Ind	24	BBCCC	Ind		
Surveying and Mapping	068F▼	2FT HND	* g	2	N	P*	Dip	CC	N	7	

Univ of HUDDERSFIELD

Geography/Applied Geography	L800	3FT deg	G̲y̲ g	14-18	Ind	Ind	Ind	BBBC	Ind		

Univ of HULL

Economics/Geography	LL18	3FT deg	G̲y̲ g	BCC	Ind	M*^ go	28$	BBCCC	Ind	11	22/24
Environmental Biology and Geography	CF18	3FT deg	G̲y̲+S̲	BCC	MO $	M$^ gi	26	BBCCC	Ind	9	16/26
Environmental Physics	FF38	3FT deg	M̲+P̲	18	MO	M$^ gi	26$	BBBCC	Ind		
Geography	L800	3FT deg	G̲y̲	BBC-BCC	Ind	D$^ go	28$	BBBCC	Ind	8	18/26
Geography	F800	3FT deg	G̲y̲+S̲	20	Ind	D$^ go	28$	BBBCC	Ind	5	16/24
Geography/Sociology	LL38	3FT deg	G̲y̲	BBC-BCC	Ind	D$^ go	28$	BBBCC	Ind	10	24/24
Physical Geography	F840	3FT deg	G̲y̲	BCC	Ind	D$^ go	28$	BBBCC	Ind	8	14/26

KEELE Univ

Biological and Medicinal Chemistry and Geography	FLC8	3FT deg	C+G̲y̲ g	BCC	Ind	D$^	28$	CSYS	Ind		
Geography and American Studies	LQ84	3FT deg	G̲y̲	BCC	Ind	D$^	28$	CSYS	Ind	6	16/20
Geography and American Studies (4 Yrs)	QL48	4FT deg	*	BCC	Ind	Ind	28	BBBB	Ind	9	
Geography and Ancient History	LV8D	3FT deg	G̲y̲	BCC	Ind	D$^	28$	CSYS	Ind	2	
Geography and Applied Social Studies	LL58	3FT deg	G̲y̲	BCC	Ind	D$^	28$	CSYS	Ind		
Geography and Applied Social Studies (4 Yrs)	LL85	4FT deg	*	BCC	Ind	Ind	28	BBBB	Ind		
Geography and Biochemistry	CL78	3FT deg	G̲y̲+C g	BCC	Ind	D$^	28$	CSYS	Ind		
Geography and Biochemistry (4 Yrs)	LC87	4FT deg	*	BCC	Ind	Ind	28	BBBB	Ind		
Geography and Biological and Med Chem (4 Yrs)	LF8C	4FT deg	*	BCC	Ind	Ind	28	BBBB	Ind		
Geography and Biology	CL18	3FT deg	S+G̲y̲ g	BCC	Ind	D$^	28$	CSYS	Ind	11	
Geography and Biology (4 Yrs)	LC81	4FT deg	*	BCC	Ind	Ind	28	BBBB	Ind		
Geography and Business Administration (4 Yrs)	NF98	4FT deg	* g	BCC	Ind	Ind	28	BBBB	Ind		
Geography and Chemistry	FL18	3FT deg	G̲y̲+C g	BCC	Ind	D$^	28$	CSYS	Ind	2	
Geography and Chemistry (4 Yrs)	LF81	4FT deg	*	BCC	Ind	Ind	28	BBBB	Ind		
Geography and Classical Studies	LQ88	3FT deg	G̲y̲	BCC	Ind	D$^	28$	CSYS	Ind	3	
Geography and Computer Science	GL58	3FT deg	G̲y̲ g	BCC	Ind	D$^	28$	CSYS	Ind	4	15/18
Geography and Computer Science (4 Yrs)	LG85	4FT deg	*	BCC	Ind	Ind	28	BBBB	Ind		
Geography and Criminology (4 Yrs)	MFH8	4FT deg	*	BBB-BCC	Ind	Ind	28	BBBB	Ind		
Geography and Economics	LL18	3FT deg	G̲y̲ g	BCC	Ind	D$^	28$	CSYS	Ind	9	16/16
Geography and Economics (4 Yrs)	LL81	4FT deg	*	BCC	Ind	Ind	28	BBBB	Ind	10	
Geography and Education Studies (4 Yrs)	XL98	4FT deg	*	BCC	Ind	Ind	28	BBBB	Ind		
Geography and Educational Studies	LX89	3FT deg	G̲y̲	BCC	Ind	D$^	28$	CSYS	Ind	10	
Geography and Electronic Music (4 Yrs)	WFJ8	4FT deg	*	BCC	Ind	Ind	28	BBBB	Ind		
Geography and English	LQ83	3FT deg	G̲y̲+E̲	BBC	Ind	D$^	30$	CSYS	Ind	3	18/28
Geography and English (4 Yrs)	QL38	4FT deg	*	BBC	Ind	Ind	30	BBBB	Ind		
Geography and Environmental Management (4 Yrs)	FF8X	4FT deg	*	BCC	Ind	Ind	28	BBBB	Ind		
Geography and Finance	LN83	3FT deg	G̲y̲ g	BCC	Ind	D$^	28$	CSYS	Ind		
Geography and French	LR81	3FT deg	F̲+G̲y̲	BCC	Ind	D$^	28$	CSYS	Ind	5	
Geography and French (4 Yrs)	RL18	4FT deg	*	BCC	Ind	Ind	28	BBBB	Ind		

Geography 30

			98 expected requirements							96 entry stats	
TITLE	CODE	COURSE	SUBJECTS	A/AS	ND/C	AGNVQ	IB	SQA(H)	SQA	RATIO	A/AS
Geography and French/German	LT89	3FT deg	F+G+Gy	BBC	Ind	D$^	30$	CSYS	Ind		
Geography and Psychology	CL88	3FT deg	Gy g	BBB	Ind	D$^	32$	CSYS	Ind	11	
Geology and Geography	FL68	3FT deg	Gy g	BCC	Ind	M$^	28$	CSYS	Ind	4	14/26
Geology and Geography (4 Yrs)	LF86	4FT deg	*	BCC	Ind	Ind	28	BBBB	Ind	6	
German and Geography	LR82	3FT deg	G+Gy	BCC	Ind	D$^	28$	CSYS	Ind	5	
History and Geography	LV81	3FT deg	Gy	BCC	Ind	D$^	28$	CSYS	Ind	11	
History and Geography (4 Yrs)	VL18	4FT deg	*	BCC	Ind	Ind	28	BBBB	Ind		
Human Resource Management and Geography	LN86	3FT deg	Gy	BCC	Ind	D$^	28$	CSYS	Ind		
Human Resource Management and Geography (4 Yrs)	NL68	4FT deg	*	BCC	Ind	Ind	28	BBBB	Ind		
International History and Geography	LV8C	3FT deg	Gy	BCC	Ind	D$^	28$	CSYS	Ind	7	
International History and Geography (4 Yrs)	VLC8	4FT deg	*	BCC	Ind	Ind	28	BBBB	Ind		
International Politics and Geography	LM8C	3FT deg	Gy	BCC	Ind	D$^	28$	CSYS	Ind	2	16/22
International Politics and Geography (4 Yrs)	MLC8	4FT deg	*	BCC	Ind	Ind	28	BBBB	Ind		
Latin and Geography	LQ86	3FT deg	Gy+Ln	BCC	Ind	D$^	28$	CSYS	Ind		
Latin and Geography (4 Yrs)	QL68	4FT deg	*	BCC	Ind	Ind	28	BBBB	Ind		
Marketing and Geography	LN85	3FT deg	Gy	BCC	Ind	D$^	28$	CSYS	Ind	8	21/26
Mathematics and Geography	GL18	3FT deg	M+Gy	BCC	Ind	D$^	28$	CSYS	Ind	5	18/28
Mathematics and Geography (4 Yrs)	LG81	4FT deg	*	BCC	Ind	Ind	28	BBBB	Ind		
Music and Geography (4 Yrs)	WF38	4FT deg	*	BCC	Ind	Ind	28	BBBB	Ind		
Philosophy and Geography	LV87	3FT deg	Gy	BCC	Ind	D$^	28$	CSYS	Ind	6	
Philosophy and Geography (4 Yrs)	VL78	4FT deg	*	BCC	Ind	Ind	28	BBBB	Ind	3	
Politics and Geography	LM81	3FT deg	Gy	BCC	Ind	D$^	28$	CSYS	Ind	6	
Politics and Geography (4 Yrs)	ML18	4FT deg	*	BCC	Ind	Ind	28	BBBB	Ind		
Sociol & Soc Anthropology and Geography (4 Yrs)	LL83	4FT deg	*	BCC	Ind	Ind	28	BBBB	Ind	10	
Sociology & Social Anthropology and Geography	LL38	3FT deg	Gy	BCC	Ind	D$^	28$	CSYS	Ind	7	18/26
Statistics and Geography (4 Yrs)	GF48	4FT deg	*	BCC	Ind	Ind	28	BBBB	Ind		

KING ALFRED'S WINCHESTER

Geography and American Studies	LQ84	3FT deg	Gy g	14	X	X	24$	BCC$	X	4	
Geography and Archaeology	FL48	3FT deg	Gy g	14	X	X	24$	BCC$	X		
Geography and Computing	GL58	3FT deg	Gy g	14	X	X	24$	BCC$	X	5	
Geography and Contemporary Cultural Studies	LM89	3FT deg	Gy g	14	X	X	24$	BCC$	X		
Geography and Drama Studies	LW84	3FT deg	Gy g	14	X	X	24$	BCC$	X	6	
Geography and Education Studies	LX89	3FT deg	Gy g	14	X	X	24$	BCC$	X	2	
Geography and English Studies	LQ83	3FT deg	E+Gy	14	X	X	24$	BCC$	X		
History and Geography	LV81	3FT deg	Gy/H g	14	X	X	24$	BCC$	X	5	
Japanese Language and Geography	LT84	3FT deg	Gy+L g	14	X	X	24$	BCC$	X		
Philosophy and Geography	LV87	3FT deg	Gy g	14	X	X	24$	BCC$	X		
Social Biology and Geography	CL18	3FT deg	B+Gy g	14	X	X	24$	BCC$	N$	7	
Sports Studies and Geography	LL8H	3FT deg	Gy g	14	X	X	24$	BCC$	X		

KING'S COLL LONDON (Univ of London)

Geography	L800	3FT deg	Gy	BCC						5	18/26
Geography	F800	3FT deg	Gy	BCC						6	18/26
Geography and History	LV81	3FT deg	Gy/H	ABB-BBC						16	
Geography with Applied Computing	L8G5	3FT deg	Gy	BCC						6	
War Studies and Geography	ML98	3FT deg	Gy	BCC						23	

KINGSTON Univ

Applied Biology & Geography	CF18	3FT deg	Gy+B/C g	12	Ind	Ind	Ind	BCCC	Ind	4	
Geographical Information Systems	LG85▼	4EXT deg	*		Ind		Ind	Ind	Ind		
Geographical Information Systems	GL58	3FT deg	Gy	12	$	Ind	Ind	BCCC	Ind	2	6/20
Geography	F800	3FT deg	Gy	16-18	$	Ind	Ind	BCCC	Ind	5	8/19
Geography	F808▼	4EXT deg	*		Ind		Ind	Ind	Ind	1	

course details			98 expected requirements							96 entry stats	
TITLE	CODE	COURSE	SUBJECTS	A/AS	ND/C	AGNVQ	IB	SQA(H)	SQA	RATIO	A/AS
Geography	L800	3FT deg	Gy	16-18	$	Ind	Ind	BCCC	Ind	4	8/18
Geography & Computing	FG85	3FT deg	Gy g	12	$	Ind	Ind	BCCC	Ind	7	
Geography & Economics	FL81	3FT deg	Gy	12	N	Ind	Ind	BCCC	Ind	5	6/18
Geography & Geology	FF86	3FT deg	Gy/S g	12	$	Ind	Ind	BCCC	Ind	6	8/10
Geography & Mathematics	FG81	3FT deg	Gy/M g	12	$	Ind	Ind	BCCC	Ind	11	
Geography & Physics	FL38	3FT deg	Gy/P g	10	Ind	Ind	Ind	BCCC	Ind	4	
Geography & Statistics	FG84	3FT deg	Gy	12	$	Ind	Ind	BCCC	Ind		
Geography and French	FR81	4FT deg	Gy/F g	12	$	Ind	Ind	BCCC	Ind		
Geographical Information Systems	85LG	2FT HND	Gy	8	$	Ind	Ind	CC	Ind	2	

Univ of Wales, LAMPETER

TITLE	CODE	COURSE	SUBJECTS	A/AS	ND/C	AGNVQ	IB	SQA(H)	SQA	RATIO	A/AS
Cultural Studies in Geography	L800	3FT deg		16	Ind	Ind	Ind	Ind	Ind		
Cultural Studies in Geography & Ancient History	VLCW	3FT deg		16	Ind	Ind	Ind	Ind	Ind		
Cultural Studies in Geography and American Lit	LQ84	3FT deg			Ind	Ind	Ind	Ind	Ind		
Cultural Studies in Geography and Anthropology	LL6V	3FT deg	Gy	14	Ind	Ind	Ind	Ind	Ind		
Cultural Studies in Geography and Archaeology	LVVP	3FT deg	*	16	Ind	Ind	Ind	Ind	Ind		
Cultural Studies in Geography and Australian St	LL8P	3FT deg			Ind	Ind	Ind	Ind	Ind		
Cultural Studies in Geography and Church History	LVVD	3FT deg	*	16	Ind	Ind	Ind	Ind	Ind		
Cultural Studies in Geography and Classical St	LQVV	3FT deg	*	16	Ind	Ind	Ind	Ind	Ind		
English Literature and Cultural St in Geography	LQV3	3FT deg	E	16-18	Ind	Ind	Ind	Ind	Ind		
French and Cultural Studies in Geography	LR8C	3FT deg	F	16	Ind	Ind	Ind	Ind	Ind		
Geography	L8F8	3FT deg	Gy	16-18	Ind	Ind	Ind	Ind	Ind		
Geography and American Literature	LQ8K	3FT deg	Gy		Ind	Ind	Ind	Ind	Ind		
Geography and Ancient History	LV8D	3FT deg	Gy	16	Ind	Ind	Ind	Ind	Ind		
Geography and Anthropology	LL68	3FT deg	Gy	16	Ind	Ind	Ind	Ind	Ind		
Geography and Archaeology	LV86	3FT deg	Gy	16	Ind	Ind	Ind	Ind	Ind		
Geography and Australian Studies	LL86	3FT deg	Gy		Ind	Ind	Ind	Ind	Ind		
Geography and Church History	LVVC	3FT deg	Gy	16	Ind	Ind	Ind	Ind	Ind		
Geography and Classical Studies	LQV8	3FT deg	Gy	16	Ind	Ind	Ind	Ind	Ind		
Geography and Cultural Studies in Geography	L801	3FT deg	Gy	16	Ind	Ind	Ind	Ind	Ind		
Geography and English Literature	LQ83	3FT deg	Gy+E	16-18	Ind	Ind	Ind	Ind	Ind		
Geography and French	LR81	4FT deg	F+Gy	16	Ind	Ind	Ind	Ind	Ind		
German Studies and Cultural Studies in Geography	LRVF	4FT deg	Gy	16	Ind	Ind	Ind	Ind	Ind		
German Studies and Geography	LR8F	4FT deg	Gy	16	Ind	Ind	Ind	Ind	Ind		
German and Cultural Studies in Geography	LRV2	4FT deg	Gy+G	16	Ind	Ind	Ind	Ind	Ind		
German and Geography	LR82	4FT deg	Gy+G	16	Ind	Ind	Ind	Ind	Ind		
Greek and Cultural Studies in Geography	LQV7	3FT deg	* g	16	Ind	Ind	Ind	Ind	Ind		
Greek and Geography	LQ87	3FT deg	Gy g	16	Ind	Ind	Ind	Ind	Ind		
History and Cultural Studies in Geography	LVVC	3FT deg	Gy+H	16	Ind	Ind	Ind	Ind	Ind		
History and Geography	LV81	3FT deg	Gy+H	16	Ind	Ind	Ind	Ind	Ind		
Informatics and Cultural Studies in Geography	GL5V	3FT deg		16	Ind	Ind	Ind	Ind	Ind		
Informatics and Geography	GL58	3FT deg	Gy	16	Ind	Ind	Ind	Ind	Ind		
Islamic Studies and Cultural Studs in Geography	LTV6	3FT deg		16	Ind	Ind	Ind	Ind	Ind		
Islamic Studies and Geography	TL68	3FT deg	Gy	16	Ind	Ind	Ind	Ind	Ind		
Latin and Cultural Studies in Geography	LQV6	3FT deg	* g	16	Ind	Ind	Ind	Ind	Ind		
Latin and Geography	LQ86	3FT deg	Gy g	16	Ind	Ind	Ind	Ind	Ind		
Management Techniques and Geography	LN81	3FT deg	Gy	16	Ind	Ind	Ind	Ind	Ind		
Medieval Studies and Cultural Studs in Geography	VL1V	3FT deg		16	Ind	Ind	Ind	vq13	Ind		
Medieval Studies and Geography	VL18	3FT deg	Gy	16	Ind	Ind	Ind	Ind	Ind		
Modern Historical Studies & Cultural St in Geog	VL1W	3FT deg	*		Ind	Ind	Ind	Ind	Ind		
Modern Historical Studies and Geography	VLC8	3FT deg			Ind	Ind	Ind	Ind	Ind		
Philosophical Studies and Cultural St in Geog	LVV7	3FT deg	*	16	Ind	Ind	Ind	Ind	Ind		
Philosophical Studies and Geography	LV87	3FT deg	Gy	16	Ind	Ind	Ind	Ind	Ind		

Geography 30

course details			98 expected requirements							96 entry stats	
TITLE	CODE	COURSE	SUBJECTS	A/AS	ND/C	RGNVQ	IB	SQA(H)	SQA	RATIO	A/AS
Religious Studies and Cultural St in Geography	LVV	3FT deg	*	16	Ind	Ind	Ind	Ind	Ind		
Religious Studies and Geography	LVV8	3FT deg	Gy	16	Ind	Ind	Ind	Ind	Ind		
Theology and Cultural Studies in Geography	VL88	3FT deg	*	16	Ind	Ind	Ind	Ind	Ind		
Theology and Geography	LV88	3FT deg	Gy	16	Ind	Ind	Ind	Ind	Ind		
Victorian Studies and Cultural St in Geography	LVV1	3FT deg	*	16	Ind	Ind	Ind	Ind	Ind		
Victorian Studies and Geography	LV8C	3FT deg	Gy	16	Ind	Ind	Ind	Ind	Ind		
Welsh Studies and Cultural Studies in Geography	LQVM	3FT deg	*	16	Ind	Ind	Ind	Ind	Ind		
Welsh Studies and Geography	QLM8	3FT deg	Gy	16	Ind	Ind	Ind	Ind	Ind		
Welsh and Cultural Studies in Geography	LQV5	3FT/4FT deg	W	16	Ind	Ind	Ind	Ind	Ind		
Welsh and Geography	QL58	3FT/4FT deg	W+Gy	16	Ind	Ind	Ind	Ind	Ind		
Women's Studies and Cultural Studs in Geography	LM8X	3FT deg	*	16	Ind	Ind	Ind	Ind	Ind		
Women's Studies and Geography	LM89	3FT deg	Gy	16	Ind	Ind	Ind	Ind	Ind		
Combined Honours *Cultural Studies in Geography*	Y400	3FT deg	*	14-16	Ind	Ind	Ind	Ind	Ind		
Combined Honours *Geography, Physical*	Y400	3FT deg	Gy	14-16	Ind	Ind	Ind	Ind	Ind		

LANCASTER Univ

TITLE	CODE	COURSE	SUBJECTS	A/AS	ND/C	RGNVQ	IB	SQA(H)	SQA	RATIO	A/AS
Economics and Geography	LL81	3FT deg	Gy g	BBC	Ind $		32$	ABBBB$	Ind		
French Studies and Geography	LR81	4SW deg	F+Gy g	BBC	Ind $		30$	BBBBB$	Ind		
Geography	F800	3FT deg	Gy g	BBC	Ind $		30$	BBBBB$	Ind		
German Studies and Geography	LR82	4SW deg	G/L+Gy g	BBC	Ind $		30$	BBBBB$	Ind		
Human Geography	L820	3FT deg	Gy g	BBB	Ind $		30$	BBBBB$	Ind		
Italian Studies and Geography	LR83	4SW deg	I/L+Gy g	BBC	Ind $		30$	BBBBB$	Ind		
Physical Geography	F840	3FT deg	Gy+S g	BCC	Ind $		30$	BBBBB$	Ind		
Spanish Studies and Geography	LR84	4SW deg	Sp/L+Gy g	BBC	Ind $		30$	BBBBB$	Ind		
Combined Science *Geography*	Y158	3FT deg	Gy g	CCD	Ind $		30$	BBBBB$			
Combined Science (inc a year in USA or Canada) *Geography*	Y155	3FT deg	Gy g	BBB	Ind $		32$	ABBBB$	Ind		

Univ of LEEDS

TITLE	CODE	COURSE	SUBJECTS	A/AS	ND/C	RGNVQ	IB	SQA(H)	SQA	RATIO	A/AS
Chinese-Geography	LT83	4FT deg	Gy+L g	BBC	Ind	Ind	30$	CSYS	Ind		
Economic and Social History-Geography	LV83	3FT deg	Gy g	BBC	Ind	Ind	30$	CSYS	Ind		
Economics-Geography	LL18	3FT deg	Gy g	BBC	Ind	Ind	30$	CSYS	Ind	9	24/30
Geography	L800	3FT deg	Gy g	BBB	Ind	Ind	32$	CSYS	Ind	11	24/30
Geography	F800	3FT deg	Gy+M/S g	BBC	Ind	Ind	30$	CSYS	Ind	6	20/28
Geography-Geology	FF68	3FT/4FT deg	Gy+C/M/P g	BCC	1M+5D$	Ind	28$	BBBBC	Ind	10	18/24
Geography-History	VL18	3FT deg	Gy g	BBC	Ind	Ind	30$	CSYS	Ind	4	22/28
Geography-Italian	LR83	4FT deg	Gy+I g	BBC	Ind	Ind	Ind	Ind	Ind		
Geography-Italian B	LR8H	4FT deg	Gy+L g	BBC	Ind	Ind	Ind	Ind	Ind		
Geography-Management Studies	LN81	3FT deg	Gy g	ABB	Ind	Ind	33$	CSYS	Ind	14	26/30
Geography-Management Studies	FN81	3FT/4FT deg	Gy+C/B/M/P g	BBB	Ind	Ind	32$	CSYS	Ind	4	24/26
Geography-Mathematics	LG81	3FT deg	M+Gy g	BBC	1M+5D$	Ind	30$	ABBBB	Ind	21	
Geography-Mathematics	FG81	3FT/4FT deg	Gy+M g	BCC	1M+5D$	Ind	28$	BBBBC	Ind	11	
Geography-Politics	LM81	3FT deg	Gy g	BBB	Ind	Ind	32$	CSYS	Ind	11	
Geography-Russian Studies	RL88	4FT deg	R+Gy g	BBC	Ind	Ind	30$	CSYS	Ind		
Geography-Russian Studies B	RLV8	4FT deg	L+Gy g	BBC	Ind	Ind	30$	CSYS	Ind		
Geography-Social Policy	LL48	3FT deg	Gy g	BBC	Ind	D$^ go	30$	CSYS	Ind	4	
Geography-Sociology	LL38	3FT deg	Gy g	BBB	Ind	D$^ go	32$	CSYS	Ind	18	
Geography-Spanish	RL48	4FT deg	Sp+Gy g	BBC	Ind	Ind	30$	CSYS	Ind	5	
Geography-Statistics	FG84	3FT deg	Gy+M g	BBC	Ind	Ind	Ind	Ind	Ind		

LEEDS, TRINITY & ALL SAINTS Univ COLL

TITLE	CODE	COURSE	SUBJECTS	A/AS	ND/C	RGNVQ	IB	SQA(H)	SQA	RATIO	A/AS
Geography-Management	LN81	3FT deg	Gy g	CCD-CD	MO	X	24$	BBCCC	Ind	11	10/16
Geography-Media	LP84	3FT deg	Gy g	CCD-CC	MO	X	24$	BBCCC	Ind	7	8/14

course details			98 expected requirements							96 entry stats
TITLE	CODE	COURSE	SUBJECTS	A/AS	ND/C	AGNVQ	IB	SQA(H)	SQA	RATIO A/AS
LEEDS METROPOLITAN Univ										
Social Sciences - Human Geography	L822	3FT deg								
Univ of LEICESTER										
Geography	F800	3FT deg	Gy g	BCC	5D $	D$^	28$	ABBBB$	Ind	18/26
Geography	L800	3FT deg	Gy g	BBC-BCC	5D $	D$^	30$	AABBB$	Ind	16/28
Geography	L820	3FT deg	* g	BCC	1M+5D	D$^	28$	BBBBB	Ind	16/26
Geography and Archaeology	FF48	3FT deg	Gy g	BCD	5D $	D$^	28$	BBBBB$	Ind	16/24
Geography and Economic and Social History	LV83	3FT deg	* g	CCC	MO	D$^	28	BBBBC	Ind	16/22
Combined Arts *Geography*	Y300	3FT deg	Gy g	BCC	DO $	D$^	30$	Ind	Ind	
Combined Science *Geography*	Y100	3FT deg	Gy g	CCC	MO $	D$^	28$	BBBCC$	Ind	
Univ of LIVERPOOL										
Environment and Planning	K4L8	3FT deg		CCC	Ind	Ind	Ind	Ind	Ind	
Geography	L800	3FT deg		BBC-BBB	Ind	Ind	Ind	Ind	Ind	8 20/26
Geography (Science)	F800	3FT deg	S g	22	MO $	Ind	31$	BBBCC$	Ind	5 18/26
Geography and Archaeology	LV86	3FT deg	Gy g	BCC	MO $	Ind	Ind	Ind	Ind	6 20/24
Geography and Biology	CF18	3FT deg	B g	22	MO $	Ind	31$	BBBCC$	Ind	6 20/30
Geology and Physical Geography	F6F8	3FT deg	2S g	20	MO $	Ind	31$	BBBCC$	Ind	10 16/24
Arts Combined *Geography*	Y401	3FT deg	*	BBC-BBB	Ind	Ind	30$	ABBB	Ind	
BA Combined Honours *Geography*	Y200	3FT deg	g	BBB	Ind	Ind	Ind	Ind	Ind	
BSc Combined Honours *Geography*	Y100	3FT deg	S g	22	MO $	Ind	31$	BBBCC$	Ind	
LIVERPOOL HOPE Univ COLL										
Geography/American Studies	QF48	3FT deg	Gy	12	8M	P$^	Ind	Ind	Ind	
Geography/Art	WF98	3FT deg	A/Fa+Gy	12	8M	P$^	Ind	Ind	Ind	9
Geography/Drama & Theatre Studies	WF48	3FT deg	Gy g	12	8M	M$ go	Ind	Ind	Ind	3
Geography/English	QF38	3FT deg	El+Gy	12	8M	P$^	Ind	Ind	Ind	
Geography/Environmental Studies	FF98	3FT deg	Gy/En g	10	6M	M$ go	Ind	Ind	Ind	5 8/12
Geography/European Studies	TF28	3FT deg	Gy	12	8M	M$	Ind	Ind	Ind	
Geography/French	RF18	3FT deg	F+Gy	12	8M	P$^	Ind	Ind	Ind	
Human & Applied Biology/Geography	CF18	3FT deg	B+Gy g	10	6M	MS /P*^ go	Ind	Ind	Ind	
Information Technology/Geography	GF58	3FT deg	Gy g	10	6M	M$ go	Ind	Ind ·	Ind	
Mathematics/Geography	FG81	3FT deg	M+Gy	10	6M	P$^	Ind	Ind	Ind	3
Sociology/Geography	FL83	3FT deg	Gy	12	8M	M$ /P*^	Ind	Ind	Ind	5 6/10
Sport, Recreation & Physical Education/Geography	FB86	3FT deg	Gy g	10	6M	M$ go	Ind	Ind	Ind	
Theology & Religious Studies/Geography	FV88	3FT deg	Gy	12	8M	M$	Ind	Ind	Ind	7
LIVERPOOL JOHN MOORES Univ										
Geography	L800	3FT deg	Gy	16	5M+3D	P$		BBCC		19 12/20
Human Geography and Countryside Management	LD82	3FT deg	Gy+S g	12	5M+3D	PS^	28$	BBCC		9
Human Geography and Economics	LL18	3FT deg	Gy	12	5M+3D	PB	28$	BBCC		5 14/18
Human Geography and European Studies	LT82	3FT deg	Gy	14	5M+3D	P$	28$	BBCC		2 14/18
Human Geography and History	LV81	3FT deg	Gy	12	5M+3D	P$	28$	BBCC		6
Physical Geography	F840	3FT deg	Gy	8	3M	M				8/14
Politics and Human Geography	LM81	3FT deg	Gy	12-14	5M+3D	P$^	28$	BBCC		3
Urban Studies and Human Geography	KL48	3FT deg	Gy	12	5M+3D	P$	28$	BBCC		9 12/18
LONDON GUILDHALL Univ										
Modular Programme *Development Studies*	Y400	3FT deg	* g	CC-DD	MO	M$ go	24	Ind	Ind	

			98 expected requirements							96 entry stats	

course details

TITLE	CODE	COURSE	SUBJECTS	A/AS	ND/C	AGNVQ	IB	SQA(H)	SQA	RATIO	A/AS
LSE: LONDON Sch of Economics (Univ of London)											
Geography	L802	3FT deg	g	BBC	Ind	X	$	Ind	Ind		
Geography and Population Studies	L825	3FT deg	g	BBC	Ind	X	$	Ind	Ind	12	
Geography with Economics	L8L1	3FT deg	g	BBB	Ind	X	$	Ind	Ind	6	22/30
LOUGHBOROUGH Univ											
Economics with Geography	L1F8	3FT deg	Gy	20		D*6/^ go	30$	Ind		5	18/20
Geography	F800	3FT deg	Gy	BCC			30$	Ind		6	18/26
Geography & Physical Education and Sports Sci	FB86	3FT deg	Gy	24			30$	Ind			
Geography with Economics	LL18	3FT deg	Gy	BCC			30$	Ind		8	20/28
Politics with Geography	M1L8	3FT deg	* g	20	2M+3D	D*6/^ go	28	Ind	Ind		14/20
LSU COLL of HE											
English with Geography	Q3L8	3FT deg									
Geography (Combined)	L800	3FT deg									
Geography and Ecology	DL28	3FT deg									
Geography and English	LQ83	3FT deg									
Geography with English	L8Q3	3FT deg									
Geography with History	L8V1	3FT deg									
Geography with Politics	L8M1	3FT deg									
History and Geography	LV81	3FT deg									
History with Geography	V1L8	3FT deg									
Life Sciences and Geography	CL98	3FT deg									
Politics and Geography	LM81	3FT deg									
Politics with Geography	M1L8	3FT deg									
Sociology and Geography	LL83	3FT deg									
Sociology with Geography	L3L8	3FT deg									
Sport and Health Sciences with Geography	BL6V	3FT deg									
Sports Science and Geography	BL68	3FT deg									
LUTON Univ											
Biochemistry with Geography	C7F8	3FT deg	g	12-16	MO/DO	M/D	32	BBCC	Ind		
Biochemistry with Physical Geography	C7FV	3FT deg	g	12-16	MO/DO	M/D	32	BBCC	Ind		
Biology with Geography	CFDV	3FT deg	g	12-16	MO/DO	M/D	32	BBCC	Ind		
Biology with Mapping Science	C1F8	3FT deg	g	12-16	MO/DO	M/D	32	BBCC	Ind		
Biology with Physical Geography	C1FV	3FT deg	g	12-16	MO/DO	M/D	32	BBCC	Ind		
Biotechnology with Geography	J8F8	3FT deg	g	12-16	MO/DO	M/D	32	BBCC	Ind		
Biotechnology with Physical Geography	J8FV	3FT deg	g	12-16	MO/DO	M/D	32	BBCC	Ind		
Broadcasting & Media Technology with Geography	H6F8	3FT deg		12-16	MO/DO	M/D	32	BBCC	Ind		
Broadcasting & Media Technology with Mapping Sci	H6FW	3FT deg		12-16	MO/DO	M/D	32	BBCC	Ind		
Built Environment with Geography	NF8W	3FT deg	g	12-16	MO/DO	M/D	32	BBCC	Ind		
Built Environment with Mapping Science	N8F8	3FT deg		12-16	MO/DO	M/D	32	BBCC	Ind		
Built Environment with Physical Geography	N8FV	3FT deg	g	12-16	MO/DO	M/D	32	BBCC	Ind		
Business Systems with Geography	N1F8	3FT deg	g	12-16	MO/DO	M/D	32	BBCC	Ind		
Business with Geography	N1FW	3FT deg	g	12-16	MO/DO	M/D	32	BBCC	Ind		
Business with Physical Geography	N1FV	3FT deg	g	12-16	MO/DO	M/D	32	BBCC	Ind		
Contemp Br & Euro History with Mapping Science	V1F8	3FT deg	g	12-16	MO/DO	M/D	32	BBCC	Ind		
Contemp British & Euro History with Geography	V1FV	3FT deg	g	12-16	MO/DO	M/D	32	BBCC	Ind		
Ecology (Eco Tech) with Geography	C9F8	3FT deg	g	12-16	MO/DO	M/D	32	BBCC	Ind		
Ecology (Eco Tech) with Mapping Science	C9FV	3FT deg	g	12-16	MO/DO	M/D	32	BBCC	Ind		
Ecology (Eco Tech) with Physical Geography	C9FW	3FT deg	g	12-16	MO/DO	M/D	32	BBCC	Ind		
Ecology (Ecological Tech) and Mapping Science	CF9W	3FT deg	g	12-16	MO/DO	M/D	32	BBCC	Ind		
Environmental Science with Mapping Science	F9F8	3FT deg	g	12-16	MO/DO	M/D	32	BBCC	Ind		
European Language Stud with Physical Geography	T2FV	4FT deg	g	12-16	MO/DO	M/D	32	BBCC	Ind		

					98 expected requirements					96 entry stats

course details   *98 expected requirements*   *96 entry stats*

TITLE	CODE	COURSE	SUBJECTS	A/AS	NQ/C	AGNVQ	IB	SQA(H)	SQA	RATIO A/AS
European Language Studies with Geography	T2FW	4FT deg	L g	12-16	MQ/DQ	M/D	32	BBCC	Ind	
European Language Studies with Mapping Science	T2F8	4FT deg	L g	12-16	MQ/DQ	M/D	32	BBCC	Ind	
Geography	F800	3FT deg	g	12-16	MQ/DQ	M/D	32	BBCC	Ind	20 7/12
Geography and Artificial Intelligence	GF88	3FT deg		12-16	MQ/DQ	M/D	32	BBCC	Ind	
Geography and Biochemistry	CF78	3FT deg	g	12-16	MQ/DQ	M/D	32	BBCC	Ind	
Geography and Biology	FC81	3FT deg	g	12-16	MQ/DQ	M/D	32	BBCC	Ind	
Geography and Biotechnology	FJ88	3FT deg	g	12-16	MQ/DQ	M/D	32	BBCC	Ind	
Geography and British Studies	VF98	3FT deg		12-16	MQ/DQ	M/D	32	BBCC	Ind	
Geography and Built Environment	FN88	3FT deg	g	12-16	MQ/DQ	M/D	32	BBCC	Ind	
Geography and Business Systems	FN81	3FT deg	g	12-16	MQ/DQ	M/D	32	BBCC	Ind	
Geography and Computer Science	FG85	3FT deg	g	12-16	MQ/DQ	M/D	32	BBCC	Ind	
Geography and Contemporary History	FV81	3FT deg	g	12-16	MQ/DQ	M/D	32	BBCC	Ind	
Geography and Ecology & Biodiversity	CF98	3FT deg	g	12-16	MQ/DQ	M/D	32	BBCC	Ind	
Geography and European Language Studies	FT82	3FT deg	L g	12-16	MQ/DQ	M/D	32	BBCC	Ind	
Geography with Biochemistry	F8C7	3FT deg	g	12-16	MQ/DQ	M/D	32	BBCC	Ind	
Geography with Biology	F8CD	3FT deg	g	12-16	MQ/DQ	M/D	32	BBCC	Ind	
Geography with Biotechnology	F8J8	3FT deg	g	12-16	MQ/DQ	M/D	32	BBCC	Ind	
Geography with British Studies	F8V9	3FT deg		12-16	MQ/DQ	M/D	32	BBCC	Ind	
Geography with Built Environment	F8NW	3FT deg	g	12-16	MQ/DQ	M/D	32	BBCC	Ind	
Geography with Business Systems	FN8D	3FT deg	g	12-16	MQ/DQ	M/D	32	BBCC	Ind	
Geography with Chinese	F8T3	3FT deg		12-16	MQ/DQ	M/D	32	BBCC	Ind	
Geography with Contemporary History	F8VC	3FT deg	g	12-16	MQ/DQ	M/D	32	BBCC	Ind	
Geography with Ecology & Biodiversity	F8C9	3FT deg	g	12-16	MQ/DQ	M/D	32	BBCC	Ind	
Geography with French	F8R1	3FT deg	F g	12-16	MQ/DQ	M/D	32	BBCC	Ind	
Geography with Geology	F8FQ	3FT deg	g	12-16	MQ/DQ	M/D	32	BBCC	Ind	
Geography with German	F8R2	3FT deg	G g	12-16	MQ/DQ	M/D	32	BBCC	Ind	
Geography with Health Studies	F8BX	3FT deg		12-16	MQ/DQ	M/D	32	BBCC	Ind	
Geography with Human Biology	F8B1	3FT deg	g	12-16	MQ/DQ	M/D	32	BBCC	Ind	
Geography with Italian	F8R3	3FT deg	I g	12-16	MQ/DQ	M/D	32	BBCC	Ind	
Geography with Leisure Studies	F8NT	3FT deg	g	12-16	MQ/DQ	M/D	32	BBCC	Ind	
Geography with Plant Biology	F8C2	3FT deg	g	12-16	MQ/DQ	M/D	32	BBCC	Ind	
Geography with Politics	F8MD	3FT deg	g	12-16	MQ/DQ	M/D	32	BBCC	Ind	
Geography with Pollution Studies	FFY8	3FT deg	g	12-16	MQ/DQ	M/D	32	BBCC	Ind	
Geography with Psycology	F8LR	3FT deg	g	12-16	MQ/DQ	M/D	32	BBCC	Ind	
Geography with Public Policy & Management	FMWC	3FT deg	g	12-16	MQ/DQ	M/D	32	BBCC	Ind	
Geography with Publishing	F8P5	3FT deg	g	12-16	MQ/DQ	M/D	32	BBCC	Ind	
Geography with Social Studies	F8LJ	3FT deg	g	12-16	MQ/DQ	M/D	32	BBCC	Ind	
Geography with Spanish	F8R4	3FT deg	Sp g	12-16	MQ/DQ	M/D	32	BBCC	Ind	
Geography with Travel & Tourism	F8PT	3FT deg	g	12-16	MQ/DQ	M/D	32	BBCC	Ind	
Geology and Biotechnology	FJ86	3FT deg	g	12-16	MQ/DQ	M/D	32	BBCC	Ind	
Geology and Geography	FF86	3FT deg	g	12-16	MQ/DQ	M/D	32	BBCC	Ind	
Geology with Geography	FF6W	3FT deg	g	12-16	MQ/DQ	M/D	32	BBCC	Ind	
Geology with Mapping Science	F6F8	3FT deg	g	12-16	MQ/DQ	M/D	32	BBCC	Ind	
Geology with Physical Geography	F6FV	3FT deg	g	12-16	MQ/DQ	M/D	32	BBCC	Ind	
Health Science with Geographical Info Systems	B9F8	3FT deg	g	12-16	MQ/DQ	M/D	32	BBCC	Ind	
Health Science with Physical Geography	B9FV	3FT deg	g	12-16	MQ/DQ	M/D	32	BBCC	Ind	
Health Studies and Geography	FB89	3FT deg	g	12-16	MQ/DQ	M/D	32	BBCC	Ind	
Health Studies with Geography	BF98	3FT deg	g	12-16	MQ/DQ	M/D	32	BBCC	Ind	
Health Studies with Mapping Science	B9FW	3FT deg	g	12-16	MQ/DQ	M/D	32	BBCC	Ind	
Human Biology and Geography	BF18	3FT deg	g	12-16	MQ/DQ	M/D	32	BBCC	Ind	
Integrated Engineering with Mapping Science	H1F8	3FT deg	g	12-16	MQ/DQ	M/D	32	BBCC	Ind	
Integrated Engineering with Physical Geography	H1FV	3FT deg	g	12-16	MQ/DQ	M/D	32	BBCC	Ind	

			98 expected requirements							96 entry stats
course details										
TITLE	CODE	COURSE	SUBJECTS	A/AS	NO/C	RGNVQ	IB	SQA(H)	SQA	RATIO A/AS
Journalism and Geography	PF68	3FT deg		12-16	MO/DO	M/D	32	BBCC	Ind	
Law and Geography	FM83	3FT deg	g	12-16	MO/DO	M/D	32	BBCC	Ind	
Law with Geography	M3F8	3FT deg	g	12-16	MO/DO	M/D	32	BBCC	Ind	
Law with Mapping Science	M3FV	3FT deg	g	12-16	MO/DO	M/D	32	BBCC	Ind	
Law with Physical Geography	M3FW	3FT deg	g	12-16	MO/DO	M/D	32	BBCC	Ind	
Leisure Studies and Geography	FN87	3FT deg	g	12-16	MO/DO	M/D	32	BBCC	Ind	
Leisure Studies with Geographical Info Systems	N7F8	3FT deg	g	12-16	MO/DO	M/D	32	BBCC	Ind	
Leisure Studies with Geography	N7FW	3FT deg	g	12-16	MO/DO	M/D	32	BBCC	Ind	
Leisure Studies with Mapping Science	N7FV	3FT deg	g	12-16	MO/DO	M/D	32	BBCC	Ind	
Linguistics with Physical Geography	Q1FV	3FT deg	g	12-16	MO/DO	M/D	32	BBCC	Ind	
Mapping Sci with Language & Stylistics in Engl	F8QG	3FT deg	g	12-16	MO/DO	M/D	32	BBCC	Ind	
Mapping Science	F860	3FT deg	g	12-16	MO/DO	M/D	32	BBCC	Ind	22
Mapping Science & Language & Stylistics in Engl	QFG8	3FT deg	g	12-16	MO/DO	M/D	32	BBCC	Ind	
Mapping Science and Accounting	NFK8	3FT deg	g	12-16	MO/DO	M/D	32	BBCC	Ind	
Mapping Science and Applied Statistics	FG84	3FT deg	g	12-16	MO/DO	M/D	32	BBCC	Ind	
Mapping Science and Artificial Intelligence	GF8W	3FT deg		12-16	MO/DO	M/D	32	BBCC	Ind	
Mapping Science and Biology	CF18	3FT deg	g	12-16	MO/DO	M/D	32	BBCC	Ind	
Mapping Science and Building Conservation	KF2W	3FT deg		12-16	MO/DO	M/D	32	BBCC	Ind	
Mapping Science and Built Environment	NF88	3FT deg		12-16	MO/DO	M/D	32	BBCC	Ind	
Mapping Science and Business Systems	NFC8	3FT deg	g	12-16	MO/DO	M/D	32	BBCC	Ind	
Mapping Science and Computer Applications	GF6W	3FT deg		12-16	MO/DO	M/D	32	BBCC	Ind	
Mapping Science and Computer Science	GF58	3FT deg	g	12-16	MO/DO	M/D	32	BBCC	Ind	
Mapping Science and Contemporary History	VF18	3FT deg	g	12-16	MO/DO	M/D	32	BBCC	Ind	
Mapping Science and Environmental Science	FF98	3FT deg	g	12-16	MO/DO	M/D	32	BBCC	Ind	
Mapping Science and European Language Studies	TF28	3FT deg	L g	12-16	MO/DO	M/D	32	BBCC	Ind	
Mapping Science and Geology	FF68	3FT deg	g	12-16	MO/DO	M/D	32	BBCC	Ind	
Mapping Science and Health Studies	BFX8	3FT deg	g	12-16	MO/DO	M/D	32	BBCC	Ind	
Mapping Science and Human Biology	BF1V	3FT deg	g	12-16	MO/DO	M/D	32	BBCC	Ind	
Mapping Science and Law	MF38	3FT deg	g	12-16	MO/DO	M/D	32	BBCC	Ind	
Mapping Science and Leisure Studies	NF78	3FT deg	g	12-16	MO/DO	M/D	32	BBCC	Ind	
Mapping Science and Literary Studies in English	QF28	3FT deg	g	12-16	MO/DO	M/D	32	BBCC	Ind	
Mapping Science with Accounting	F8NL	3FT deg	g	12-16	MO/DO	M/D	32	BBCC	Ind	
Mapping Science with Animation	F8WF	3FT deg	g	12-16	MO/DO	M/D	32	BBCC	Ind	
Mapping Science with Applied Statistics	F8G4	3FT deg	g	12-16	MO/DO	M/D	32	BBCC	Ind	
Mapping Science with Biology	F8C1	3FT deg	g	12-16	MO/DO	M/D	32	BBCC	Ind	
Mapping Science with Built Environment	F8N8	3FT deg	g	12-16	MO/DO	M/D	32	BBCC	Ind	
Mapping Science with Business Systems	F8NC	3FT deg	g	12-16	MO/DO	M/D	32	BBCC	Ind	
Mapping Science with Contemporary History	F8V1	3FT deg	g	12-16	MO/DO	M/D	32	BBCC	Ind	
Mapping Science with Ecology & Biodiversity	F8CY	3FT deg	g	12-16	MO/DO	M/D	32	BBCC	Ind	
Mapping Science with Environmental Science	F8F9	3FT deg	g	12-16	MO/DO	M/D	32	BBCC	Ind	
Mapping Science with Geology	F8F6	3FT deg	g	12-16	MO/DO	M/D	32	BBCC	Ind	
Mapping Science with Human Biology	F8BC	3FT deg	g	12-16	MO/DO	M/D	32	BBCC	Ind	
Mapping Science with Japanese	F8T4	3FT deg	L g	12-16	MO/DO	M/D	32	BBCC	Ind	
Mapping Science with Journalism	F8P6	3FT deg	g	12-16	MO/DO	M/D	32	BBCC	Ind	
Mapping Science with Land Reclamation	F8K3	3FT deg	g	12-16	MO/DO	M/D	32	BBCC	Ind	
Mapping Science with Leisure Studies	F8N7	3FT deg	g	12-16	MO/DO	M/D	32	BBCC	Ind	
Mapping Science with Literary Studies in English	F8Q2	3FT deg	g	12-16	MO/DO	M/D	32	BBCC	Ind	
Mapping Science with Mathematical Sciences	F8GD	3FT deg	g	12-16	MO/DO	M/D	32	BBCC	Ind	
Mapping Science with Mathematics	FG8D	3FT deg	g	12-16	MO/DO	M/D	32	BBCC	Ind	
Mapping Science with Media Production	F8PL	3FT deg	g	12-16	MO/DO	M/D	32	BBCC	Ind	
Mapping Science with Multimedia	F8PK	3FT deg	g	12-16	MO/DO	M/D	32	BBCC	Ind	
Mapping Science with Physical Geography	F864	3FT deg	g	12-16	MO/DO	M/D	32	BBCC	Ind	

| | | | 98 expected requirements | | | | | | 96 entry stats |
| course details | | | | | | | | | | |

TITLE	CODE	COURSE	SUBJECTS	A/AS	NO/C	RGNVQ	IB	SQA(H)	SQA	RATIO A/AS
Mapping Science with Politics	F8M1	3FT deg	g	12-16	MO/DO	M/D	32	BBCC	Ind	
Mapping Science with Public Policy and Mgt	F8MC	3FT deg	g	12-16	MO/DO	M/D	32	BBCC	Ind	
Mapping Science with Regional Planning and Dev	F8K4	3FT deg	g	12-16	MO/DO	M/D	32	BBCC	Ind	
Mapping Science with Social Studies	F8L3	3FT deg	g	12-16	MO/DO	M/D	32	BBCC	Ind	
Mapping Science with Travel and Tourism	F8P7	3FT deg	g	12-16	MO/DO	M/D	32	BBCC	Ind	
Mapping Studies with Modern English Studies	F8Q3	3FT deg	g	12-16	MO/DO	M/D	32	BBCC	Ind	
Marketing with Geographical Information Systems	N5F8	3FT deg	g	12-16	MO/DO	M/D	32	BBCC	Ind	
Mathematical Sciences and Mapping Science	FG81	3FT deg	g	12-16	MO/DO	M/D	32	BBCC	Ind	
Mathematical Sciences with Mapping Science	G1F8	3FT deg	g	12-16	MO/DO	M/D	32	BBCC	Ind	
Mathematical Sciences with Physical Geography	GFC8	3FT deg	g	12-16	MO/DO	M/D	32	BBCC	Ind	
Mathematics and Mapping Science	GF18	3FT deg	g	12-16	MO/DO	M/D	32	BBCC	Ind	
Media Production and Mapping Science	FP8L	3FT deg	g	12-16	MO/DO	M/D	32	BBCC	Ind	
Media Production with Mapping Science	P4F8	3FT deg	g	12-16	MO/DO	M/D	32	BBCC	Ind	
Media Technology and Mapping Science	FP84	3FT deg	g	12-16	MO/DO	M/D	32	BBCC	Ind	
Modern English Studies and Mapping Science	FQ83	3FT deg	g	12-16	MO/DO	M/D	32	BBCC	Ind	
Modern English Studies with Mapping Science	Q3F8	3FT deg	g	12-16	MO/DO	M/D	32	BBCC	Ind	
Modern English Studies with Physical Geography	Q3FV	3FT deg	g	12-16	MO/DO	M/D	32	BBCC	Ind	
Modern History and Mapping Science	FV8C	3FT deg	g	12-16	MO/DO	M/D	32	BBCC	Ind	
New Media Technology with Mapping Science	P4FV	3FT deg	g	12-16	MO/DO	M/D	32	BBCC	Ind	
Physical Geog & Language & Stylistics in English	QFGV	3FT deg	g	12-16	MO/DO	M/D	32	BBCC	Ind	
Physical Geog with Language & Stylistics in Engl	F867	3FT deg	g	12-16	MO/DO	M/D	32	BBCC	Ind	
Physical Geography and Accounting	NFKV	3FT deg	g	12-16	MO/DO	M/D	32	BBCC	Ind	
Physical Geography and Applied Statistics	GF4V	3FT deg	g	12-16	MO/DO	M/D	32	BBCC	Ind	
Physical Geography and Biochemistry	CF7V	3FT deg	g	12-16	MO/DO	M/D	32	BBCC	Ind	
Physical Geography and Biology	CF1V	3FT deg	g	12-16	MO/DO	M/D	32	BBCC	Ind	
Physical Geography and Built Environment	NF8V	3FT deg	g	12-16	MO/DO	M/D	32	BBCC	Ind	
Physical Geography and Business	NF1V	3FT deg	g	12-16	MO/DO	M/D	32	BBCC	Ind	
Physical Geography and Computer Science	GF5V	3FT deg	g	12-16	MO/DO	M/D	32	BBCC	Ind	
Physical Geography and Ecology & Biodiversity	CF9V	3FT deg	g	12-16	MO/DO	M/D	32	BBCC	Ind	
Physical Geography and European Language Studies	TF2V	3FT deg	L g	12-16	MO/DO	M/D	32	BBCC	Ind	
Physical Geography and Geology	FF6V	3FT deg	g	12-16	MO/DO	M/D	32	BBCC	Ind	17
Physical Geography and Health Science	BF9V	3FT deg	g	12-16	MO/DO	M/D	32	BBCC	Ind	
Physical Geography and Human Biology	BF1W	3FT deg	g	12-16	MO/DO	M/D	32	BBCC	Ind	
Physical Geography and Law	MF3V	3FT deg	g	12-16	MO/DO	M/D	32	BBCC	Ind	
Physical Geography and Leisure Studies	NF7V	3FT deg	g	12-16	MO/DO	M/D	32	BBCC	Ind	
Physical Geography and Literary St in English	QF2V	3FT deg	g	12-16	MO/DO	M/D	32	BBCC	Ind	
Physical Geography and Mapping Science	F876	3FT deg	g	12-16	MO/DO	M/D	32	BBCC	Ind	11
Physical Geography and Marketing	NF5V	3FT deg	g	12-16	MO/DO	M/D	32	BBCC	Ind	
Physical Geography and Mathematical Sciences	FGV1	3FT deg	g	12-16	MO/DO	M/D	32	BBCC	Ind	
Physical Geography and Mathematics	GF1V	3FT deg	g	12-16	MO/DO	M/D	32	BBCC	Ind	
Physical Geography and Modern English Studies	QF3V	3FT deg	g	12-16	MO/DO	M/D	32	BBCC	Ind	
Physical Geography and Organisational Behaviour	LF7V	3FT deg	g	12-16	MO/DO	M/D	32	BBCC	Ind	
Physical Geography with Accounting	FN84	3FT deg	g	12-16	MO/DO	M/D	32	BBCC	Ind	
Physical Geography with Animation	F8WG	3FT deg	g	12-16	MO/DO	M/D	32	BBCC	Ind	
Physical Geography with Applied Statistics	F8GK	3FT deg	g	12-16	MO/DO	M/D	32	BBCC	Ind	
Physical Geography with Biochemistry	F8CR	3FT deg	g	12-16	MO/DO	M/D	32	BBCC	Ind	
Physical Geography with Biology	F8CC	3FT deg	g	12-16	MO/DO	M/D	32	BBCC	Ind	
Physical Geography with Biotechnology	F8JV	3FT deg	g	12-16	MO/DO	M/D	32	BBCC	Ind	
Physical Geography with Built Environment	F8NV	3FT deg	g	12-16	MO/DO	M/D	32	BBCC	Ind	
Physical Geography with Business	F8N1	3FT deg	g	12-16	MO/DO	M/D	32	BBCC	Ind	
Physical Geography with Comparative Literature	F8QF	3FT deg	g	12-16	MO/DO	M/D	32	BBCC	Ind	
Physical Geography with Ecology & Biodiversity	F8CX	3FT deg		12-16	MO/DO	M/D	32	BBCC	Ind	

course details

TITLE	CODE	COURSE	SUBJECTS	A/AS	ND/C	AGNVQ	IB	SQA(H)	SQA	RATIO A/AS
Physical Geography with Geographical Info Syst	F863	3FT deg	g	12-16	MO/DO	M/D	32	BBCC	Ind	
Physical Geography with Geology	F8FP	3FT deg	g	12-16	MO/DO	M/D	32	BBCC	Ind	
Physical Geography with Health Science	F8B9	3FT deg	g	12-16	MO/DO	M/D	32	BBCC	Ind	
Physical Geography with Human Biology	F8BD	3FT deg	g	12-16	MO/DO	M/D	32	BBCC	Ind	
Physical Geography with Leisure Studies	F8NR	3FT deg	g	12-16	MO/DO	M/D	32	BBCC	Ind	
Physical Geography with Literary St in English	F875	3FT deg	g	12-16	MO/DO	M/D	32	BBCC	Ind	
Physical Geography with Mapping Science	F873	3FT deg	g	12-16	MO/DO	M/D	32	BBCC	Ind	
Physical Geography with Marketing	F8N5	3FT deg	g	12-16	MO/DO	M/D	32	BBCC	Ind	
Physical Geography with Mathematical Sciences	FG8C	3FT deg	g	12-16	MO/DO	M/D	32	BBCC	Ind	
Physical Geography with Mathematics	FGVC	3FT deg	g	12-16	MO/DO	M/D	32	BBCC	Ind	
Physical Geography with Media Production	F870	3FT deg	g	12-16	MO/DO	M/D	32	BBCC	Ind	
Physical Geography with Modern English Studies	F8QH	3FT deg	g	12-16	MO/DO	M/D	32	BBCC	Ind	
Physical Geography with Multimedia	F871	3FT deg	g	12-16	MO/DO	M/D	32	BBCC	Ind	
Physical Geography with Organisational Behaviour	F8L7	3FT deg	g	12-16	MO/DO	M/D	32	BBCC	Ind	
Physical Geography with Plant Biology	F8CF	3FT deg	g	12-16	MO/DO	M/D	32	BBCC	Ind	
Physical Geography with Psychology	F8LT	3FT deg	g	12-16	MO/DO	M/D	32	BBCC	Ind	
Physical Geography with Public Policy and Mgt	F869	3FT deg	g	12-16	MO/DO	M/D	32	BBCC	Ind	
Physical Geography with Regional Plann and Dev	F8KK	3FT deg	g	12-16	MO/DO	M/D	32	BBCC	Ind	
Physical Geography with Social Studies	F8LH	3FT deg	g	12-16	MO/DO	M/D	32	BBCC	Ind	
Physical Geography with Travel and Tourism	F8PR	3FT deg	g	12-16	MO/DO	M/D	32	BBCC	Ind	6
Physical Geography with Video Production	F8WM	3FT deg	g	12-16	MO/DO	M/D	32	BBCC	Ind	
Planning Studies and Geography	KF48	3FT deg	g	12-16	MO/DO	M/D	32	BBCC	Ind	
Planning Studies and Physical Geography	KF4V	3FT deg	g	12-16	MO/DO	M/D	32	BBCC	Ind	
Plant Biology and Geography	CF28	3FT deg	Gy	12-16	MO/DO	M/D	32	BBCC	Ind	
Plant Biology and Physical Geography	CF2V	3FT deg	g	12-16	MO/DO	M/D	32	BBCC	Ind	
Plant Biology with Geography	C2F8	3FT deg	g	12-16	MO/DO	M/D	32	BBCC	Ind	
Plant Biology with Physical Geography	C2FV	3FT deg	g	12-16	MO/DO	M/D	32	BBCC	Ind	
Politics and Geography	FM8D	3FT deg	g	12-16	MO/DO	M/D	32	BBCC	Ind	
Politics and Mapping Science	FM81	3FT deg	g	12-16	MO/DO	M/D	32	BBCC	Ind	
Politics and Physical Geography	FMV1	3FT deg	g	12-16	MO/DO	M/D	32	BBCC	Ind	
Politics with Geography	M1FW	3FT deg	g	12-16	MO/DO	M/D	32	BBCC	Ind	
Politics with Mapping Science	M1F8	3FT deg	g	12-16	MO/DO	M/D	32	BBCC	Ind	
Politics with Physical Geography	M1FV	3FT deg	g	12-16	MO/DO	M/D	32	BBCC	Ind	
Psychology and Geography	FL87	3FT deg	g	12-16	MO/DO	M/D	32	BBCC	Ind	
Psychology and Mapping Science	FL8R	3FT deg	g	12-16	MO/DO	M/D	32	BBCC	Ind	
Psychology with Geography	L7FW	3FT deg		12-16	MO/DO	M/D	32	BBCC	Ind	
Public Policy & Management and Geography	MF18	3FT deg	g	12-16	MO/DO	M/D	32	BBCC	Ind	
Public Policy & Management with Geography	MF1V	3FT deg	g	12-16	MO/DO	M/D	32	BBCC	Ind	
Public Policy and Management and Mapping Science	FM8C	3FT deg	g	12-16	MO/DO	M/D	32	BBCC	Ind	
Regional Planning & Development & Mapping Sci	FK84	3FT deg	g	12-16	MO/DO	M/D	32	BBCC	Ind	4
Regional Planning and Dev and Physical Geography	FKV4	3FT deg	g	12-16	MO/DO	M/D	32	BBCC	Ind	
Regional Planning and Dev with Physical Geog	K4FV	3FT deg	g	12-16	MO/DO	M/D	32	BBCC	Ind	
Regional Planning and Develop with Mapping Sci	K4F8	3FT deg	g	12-16	MO/DO	M/D	32	BBCC	Ind	
Social Studies and Geography	LF38	3FT deg	g	12-16	MO/DO	M/D	32	BBCC	Ind	
Social Studies and Mapping Science	FL83	3FT deg	g	12-16	MO/DO	M/D	32	BBCC	Ind	
Social Studies and Physical Geography	FLV3	3FT deg	g	12-16	MO/DO	M/D	32	BBCC	Ind	
Social Studies with Geography	L3FW	3FT deg	g	12-16	MO/DO	M/D	32	BBCC	Ind	
Social Studies with Mapping Science	L3F8	3FT deg	g	12-16	MO/DO	M/D	32	BBCC	Ind	
Social Studies with Physical Geography	L3FV	3FT deg	g	12-16	MO/DO	M/D	32	BBCC	Ind	
Sociology and Geography	LFH8	3FT deg		12-16	MO/DO	M/D	32	BBCC	Ind	
Travel & Tourism with Geography	P7FW	3FT deg	g	12-16	MO/DO	M/D	32	BBCC	Ind	
Travel and Tourism and Geography	FP8R	3FT deg	g	12-16	MO/DO	M/D	32	BBCC	Ind	

				98 expected requirements							96 entry stats
course details											
TITLE	CODE	COURSE	SUBJECTS	A/AS	ND/C	AGNVQ	IB	SQA(H)	SQA	RATIO A/AS	

TITLE	CODE	COURSE	SUBJECTS	A/AS	ND/C	AGNVQ	IB	SQA(H)	SQA	RATIO	A/AS
Travel and Tourism and Mapping Science	FP87	3FT deg	g	12-16	MO/DO	M/D	32	BBCC	Ind		
Travel and Tourism and Physical Geography	FPV7	3FT deg	g	12-16	MO/DO	M/D	32	BBCC	Ind		
Travel and Tourism with Mapping Science	P7F8	3FT deg	g	12-16	MO/DO	M/D	32	BBCC	Ind		
Travel and Tourism with Physical Geography	P7FV	3FT deg	g	12-16	MO/DO	M/D	32	BBCC	Ind		
Geographical Information Systems	58GF	2FT HND	g	4-8	N/MO	P/M	26	CCDD	Ind		
Geographical Techniques	068F	2FT HND	g	4-8	N/MO	P/M	26	CCDD	Ind	1	2/ 4
Univ of MANCHESTER											
Geography	L800	3FT deg	Gy	BBC-BBB	MO	D^	30	ABBBB		14	22/30
Geography	F802	3FT deg	Gy	BBC-BBB	MO	D^	30	ABBBB		10	22/30
Geography and Archaeology	LV86	3FT deg	Gy	BBC-BBB	MO	D^	30	ABBBB	X	7	14/26
Geography and Geology	FF68	3FT deg	Gy	BCC	Ind	D^			Ind	4	12/24
MANCHESTER METROPOLITAN Univ											
Geography	L800	3FT deg	* g	14-18	2M+4D	M$	29	BBBBC	Ind		10/18
Geography	L801	3FT deg	Gy g	16	Ind		Ind	Ind	Ind		10/20
Geography/American Studies	LQ84	3FT deg	*	CC	M+D	D	28	CCCC	Ind		
Geography/Applicable Mathematics	GL18	3FT deg	M g	18	2M+4D$	M$	29$	BBBBC$	Ind		
Geography/Applied Physics	FL38	3FT deg	M+P g	14	MO $	M$	28$	BBCCC$	Ind		
Geography/Applied Social Studies	LL83	3FT deg	*	CC	M+D	D	28	CCCC	Ind		
Geography/Biology	CL18	3FT deg	Gy g	14	MO $	M$	28$	BBCCC$	Ind		
Geography/Business Studies	LN81	3FT deg	*	CC	M+D	D	28	CCCC	Ind		
Geography/Computer Technology	GLM8	3FT deg	* g	14	MO	M$	28	BBCCC	Ind		
Geography/Computing Science	GL58	3FT deg	* g	18	2M+4D	M$	29	BBBBC	Ind		
Geography/Cultural Studies	LL8H	3FT deg	*	CC	M+D	D	28	CCCC	Ind		
Geography/Design & Technology	LW82	3FT deg	*	CC	M+D	D	28	CCCC	Ind		
Geography/Drama	LW8K	3FT deg	*	CC	M+D	D	28	CCCC	Ind		
Geography/Economics	LL18	3FT deg	* g	CCC	2M+4D	M$	29	BBBBC	Ind		14/18
Geography/Electronics	HLP8	3FT deg	* g	14	MO	M$	28	BBCCC	Ind		
Geography/English	LQ83	3FT deg	*	CC	M+D	D	28	CCCC	Ind		
Geography/Environmental Science	FL9V	3FT deg	* g	DD	M+D	D	28	CCCC	Ind		
Geography/Environmental Studies	FL98	3FT deg	* g	CCC	2M+4D	M$	29	BBBBC	Ind		10/20
Geography/European Studies	LT82	3FT deg	* g	CCC	2M+4D	M$	29	BBBBC	Ind		
Health Studies/Geography	BL98	3FT deg	*	CC	M+D	D	28	CCCC	Ind		
History/Geography	LV81	3FT deg	*	CC	M+D	D	28	CCCC	Ind		
Languages/Geography	LT89	3FT deg	* g	CCC	2M+4D	M$	29	BBBBC	Ind		
Leisure Studies/Geography	LL84	3FT deg	* g	DD	M+D	D	28	CCCC	Ind		
Life Science/Geography	CL1V	3FT deg	* g	DD	M+D	D	28	CCCC	Ind		
Music/Geography	LW83	3FT deg	*	CC	M+D	D	28	CCCC	Ind		
Philosophy/Geography	LV87	3FT deg	*	CC	M+D	D	28	CCCC	Ind		
Physics Studies/Geography	LF83	3FT deg	M/P g	14	MO $		28$	BBCCC$	Ind		
Psychology/Geography	LL78	3FT deg	* g	CCC	2M+4D	D$	29	BBBBC	Ind		14/18
Religious Studies/Geography	LV88	3FT deg	*	CC	M+D	D	28	CCCC	Ind		
Scientific Instrumentation/Geography	HL68	3FT deg	M/P g	14	MO $	M$	28$	BBCCC$	Ind		
Social Studies of Technology/Geography	LL38	3FT deg	* g	18	2M+4D	M$	29	BBBBC	Ind		
Sport/Geography	BL68	3FT deg	S	BC	M+D	DS	28	CCCC	Ind		
Visual Arts/Geography	LW81	3FT deg	*	CC	M+D	D	28	CCCC	Ind		
Writing/Geography	LW8L	3FT deg	*	CC	M+D	D	28	CCCC	Ind		
MIDDLESEX Univ											
Geographical Information Technology	LG85▼	3FT deg	Gy g	12	5M	M$ go	24	Ind	Ind		
Geography	F800▼	3FT deg	Gy g	12-16	5M	M$ go	28	Ind	Ind		
Geography	L800▼	3FT deg	Gy g	12	5M	M$ go	28	Ind	Ind		
Heritage Studies	LV83▼	3FT deg	* g	12	5M	M$ go	24	Ind	Ind		

Geography 30

			98 expected requirements							96 entry stats

TITLE	CODE	COURSE	SUBJECTS	A/AS	NO/C	AGNVQ	IB	SQA(H)	SQA	RATIO A/AS
Urban and Rural Development	LK84▼	3FT deg	Gy g	12	5M	M$ go	24	Ind	Ind	
Joint Honours Degree *Geography*	Y400	3FT deg	Gy g	12-16	5M	M$ go	28	Ind	Ind	

NENE COLLEGE

TITLE	CODE	COURSE	SUBJECTS	A/AS	NO/C	AGNVQ	IB	SQA(H)	SQA	RATIO A/AS
American Studies with Geography	Q4F8	3FT deg		DD	5M	M	24	CCC	Ind	
Art and Design with Geography	W2F8	3FT deg		DD	5M	M	24	CCC	Ind	
Business Administration with Geography	N1F8	3FT deg	g	10	M+1D	M	24	CCC	Ind	
Drama with Geography	W4F8	3FT deg		10	5M+1D	M	24	CCC	Inma	
Earth Science with Geography	F9F8	3FT deg		DD	5M	M	24	CCC	Ind	
Ecology with Geography	C9F8	3FT deg		DD	5M	M	24	CCC	Ind	
Economics with Geography	L1F8	3FT deg	g	6	5M	M	24	CCC	Ind	
Education with Geography	X9F8	3FT deg		DD	5M	M	24	CCC	Ind	
Energy Management with Geography	J9F8	3FT deg	g	EE	3M	P	24	CCC	Ind	
French with Geography	R1F8	3FT deg	F	DD	5M	Ind	24	CCC	Ind	
Geography	F800	3FT deg	Gy g	8	5M	M	24	CCC	Ind	
Geography with American Studies	F8Q4	3FT deg	Gy	8	5M	M	24	CCC	Ind	
Geography with Business Administration	F8N1	3FT deg	Gy g	8	5M	M	24	CCC	Ind	8/24
Geography with Earth Science	F8F9	3FT deg	Gy	8	5M	M	24	CCC	Ind	
Geography with Ecology	F8C9	3FT deg	Gy	8	5M	M	24	CCC	Ind	
Geography with Economics	F8L1	3FT deg	Gy g	8	5M	M	24	CCC	Ind	
Geography with Education	F8X9	3 deg								
Geography with Energy Management	F8J9	3FT deg	Gy g	8	5M	M	24	CCC	Ind	
Geography with European Union Studies	F8T2	3FT deg	Gy	8	5M	M	24	CCC	Ind	
Geography with French	F8R1	3FT deg	F+Gy	8	5M	M	24	CCC	Ind	
Geography with Health Studies	F8L5	3FT deg	Gy	8	5M	M	24	CCC	Ind	
Geography with History	F8V1	3FT deg	Gy	8	5M	M	24	CCC	Ind	
Geography with Industrial Archaeology	F8V6	3FT deg	Gy	8	5M	M	24	CCC	Ind	
Geography with Information Systems	F8G5	3FT deg	Gy	8	5M	M	24	CCC	Ind	
Geography with Marketing Communications	F8N5	3FT deg	Gy	8	5M	M	24	CCC	Ind	
Geography with Personal and Organisational Devel	F8N6	3FT deg	Gy	8	5M	M	24	CCC	Ind	
Geography with Property Management	F8N8	3FT deg	Gy	8	5M	M	24	CCC	Ind	
Geography with Sociology	F8L3	3FT deg	Gy	8	5M	M	24	CCC	Ind	
Geography with Sport Studies	F8N7	3FT deg	Gy	8	5M	M	24	CCC	Ind	
Geography with Third World Development	F8M9	3FT deg	Gy	8	5M	M	24	CCC	Ind	
History with Geography	V1F8	3FT deg		CD	5M	M	24	CCC	Ind	
Industrial Archaeology with Geography	V6F8	3FT deg		10	5M	M	24	CCC	Ind	
Information Systems with Geography	G5F8	3FT deg		6	5M	M	24	CCC	Ind	
Mathematics with Geography	G1F8	3FT deg	M	DD	Ind	Ind	24	CCC	Ind	
Politics with Geography	M1F8	3FT deg		CD	5M	M	24	CCC	Ind	
Sociology with Geography	L3F8	3FT deg		10	5M	M	24	CCC	Ind	
Sport Studies with Geography	N7F8	3FT deg	Ss/Pe	12	M+2D	M	24	BBB	Ind	

Univ of NEWCASTLE

TITLE	CODE	COURSE	SUBJECTS	A/AS	NO/C	AGNVQ	IB	SQA(H)	SQA	RATIO A/AS
Economics and Geography	LL18	3FT deg	Gy g	BBB-BBC	Ind		32	AABBB	Ind	14
Geography	L800	3FT deg	Gy g	BBC	Ind		32	AABBB	Ind	7	18/28
Geography	F800	3FT deg	Gy g	BBC	Ind		32	AABBB	Ind	9	20/26
Geography and Mathematics	GF18	3FT deg	M+Gy	18	4M	Ind	28$	AABBB	Ind	7
Geography and Statistics	GF48	3FT deg	M+Gy	18	4M	Ind	28$	AABBB	Ind	5
Geography and Surveying and Mapping Science	HF28	3FT deg	Gy+M	18	4M	Ind	28$	AABBB	Ind	12
Mapping Information Science	F862	3FT deg	* g	CCC	Ind	M$ go	Ind	BBBB$	Ind	7
Combined Studies (BA) *Geography*	Y400	3FT deg	g	ABC-BBB	5D	Ind	35$	AAAB	Ind	

course details			98 expected requirements							96 entry stats
TITLE	CODE	COURSE	SUBJECTS	A/AS	ND/C	AGNVQ	IB	SQA(H)	SQA	RATIO A/AS
NEWMAN COLLEGE OF HIGHER EDUCATION										
Biological Science and Geography	CF18	3FT deg	*	CC	3M	M*	Dip	CCC	Ind	
English and Geography	FQ83	3FT deg	*	CC	3M	M*	Dip	CCC	Ind	
Expressive English and Geography	FW84	3FT deg	*	CC	3M	M*	Dip	CCC	Ind	
Geography and History	FV81	3FT deg	*	CC	3M	M*	Dip	CCC	Ind	
Geography and Information Technology	FG85	3FT deg	*	CC	3M	M*	Dip	CCC	Ind	
Geography and Social and Applied Psychology	LF78	3FT deg	*	CC	3M	M*	Dip	CCC	Ind	
PE and Sports Studies and Geography	FX89	3FT deg	*	CC	3M	M*	Dip	CCC	Ind	
Theology and Geography	FV88	3FT deg	*	CC	3M	M*	Dip	CCC	Ind	
Univ of Wales COLLEGE, NEWPORT										
Geography	L800	3FT/4FT HND/deg								
Geography and Archaeology	LV86	3FT deg		10	M+D	D$	Ind	Ind	Ind	
Geography and Environmental Studies	FL98	3FT deg		10	M+D	D$	Ind	Ind	Ind	
Geography and European Studies	TL28	3FT deg		10	M+D	D$	Ind	Ind	Ind	
History and Geography	LV81	3FT deg		10	M+D	D$	Ind	Ind	Ind	
Information Technology and Geography	GL58	3FT deg		10	M+D	D$	Ind	Ind	Ind	
Religious Studies and Geography	LV88	3FT deg		10	M+D	D$	Ind	Ind	Ind	
Sports Studies and Geography	BL68	3FT deg		10	M+D	D$	Ind	Ind	Ind	
NORTH EAST WALES INST of HE										
English with Geography	Q3F8	3FT deg		6-12	4M	M$	Ind	BBB	N$	
English/Geography	FQ83	3FT deg		6-12	3M	M$	Ind	CCC	N$	
Geography	F800	3FT deg		6-10	3M	M$	Ind	CCC	N$	
Geography, Planning and Development	FK84	3FT deg		6-12	3M	M$	Ind	CCC	N$	
History with Geography	V1F8	3FT deg		6-12	4M	M$	Ind	BBB	N$	
History/Geography	VF18	3FT deg		6-12	4M	M$	Ind	BBB	N$	
Univ of NORTH LONDON										
Geography	F800▼	3FT deg	*	CE	MO	M	Dip	CCCCC	Ind	12
History and Geography	FV81	3FT deg	*	CC	Ind	Ind	Ind	Ind	Ind	
Leisure Studies and Geography	LN87	3FT deg	* g	12	MO+4D	Ind	Ind	Ind	Ind	
Retail Management and Geography	NL18	3FT deg	* g	12-14	MO+4D	D	Ind	Ind	Ind	
Tourism Studies and Geography	FP87	3FT deg	* g	12-14	Ind	Ind	Ind	Ind	Ind	
Combined Honours	Y301	3FT deg	*	CC	MO	M	Dip	CCCCC	Ind	
Geography										
Univ of NORTHUMBRIA										
Geography	F800	3FT deg	Gy g	CDD	2M+2D$	M	24	BCCC$	Ind	14 12/18
Geography	L800	3FT deg	Gy g	CDD	2M+2D$	M	24	BCCC$	Ind	10 14/22
Geography and Environmental Management	FL98	3FT deg	Gy/B/C/En g	14	2M+2D	M	24	BCCC	Ind	33
Geography and Sport Studies	LB86	3FT deg	g	BCC	1M+5D	D+/^	28	BBBBC	Ind	
Univ of NOTTINGHAM										
Archaeology and Geography	LV86	3FT deg	Gy	BBB						14 24/28
Geography	F800	3FT deg	Gy+2S g	ABB	Ind	Ind	Ind	Ind	Ind	12 22/30
Geography	L800	3FT deg	Gy g	ABB	Ind		Ind	Ind	Ind	15 26/30
Geography with East European Studies	L8T1	3FT deg	Gy g	BBC	Ind		Ind	Ind	Ind	
NOTTINGHAM TRENT Univ										
Economics and Geography	LL18	3FT deg	* g	12	Ind	Ind	Ind	Ind	Ind	10/14
Geography and Human Sciences	BL18	3FT deg	* g	12	Ind	Ind	Ind	Ind	Ind	10/20
Human Geography	L822	3FT deg	Gy g	16-18	M+D	Ind	28	CCCC	Ind	
Humanities	Y301	3FT/4SW deg	Gy g	14-16	M+D	Ind	28	CCCC	Ind	
Geography										

Geography 30

				98 expected requirements						96 entry stats	
course details											
TITLE	CODE	COURSE	SUBJECTS	A/AS	ND/C	AGNVQ	IB	SQA(H)	SQA	RATIO	A/AS
OXFORD Univ											
Geography	L800	3FT deg	Gy	AAB-ABB DO			36	AAAAA	Ind	3	26/30
Human Sciences	Y400	3FT deg	*	AAB-ABB DO			36	AAAAA	Ind		
Human Population, Urban/Social Geography											
OXFORD WESTMINSTER COLLEGE											
Contemporary Geography Studies with Cultural St	L8V9	3FT deg	Gy	CE	MO	M	Ind	CCC	Ind		
Contemporary Geography Studies with Cultural St	L8VX	2FT Dip	Gy	CE	MO	M	Ind	CCC	Ind		
Contemporary Geography Studies with Language St	L8TX	2FT Dip	Gy	CE	MO	M	Ind	CCC	Ind		
Contemporary Geography Studies with Language St	L8T9	3FT deg	Gy	CE	MO	M	Ind	CCC	Ind		
Contemporary Geography Studies with World Studs	L8MC	2FT Dip	Gy	CE	MO	M	Ind	CCC	Ind		
Contemporary Geography Studies with World Studs	L8M1	3FT deg	Gy	CE	MO	M	Ind	CCC	Ind		
Contemporary Geography Studs with Development St	L8LH	2FT Dip	Gy	CE	MO	M	Ind	CCC	Ind		
Contemporary Geography Studs with Development St	L8L3	3FT deg	Gy	CE	MO	M	Ind	CCC	Ind		
Contemporary Geography Studs with Interfaith St	L8V8	3FT deg	Gy	CE	MO	M	Ind	CCC	Ind		
Contemporary Geography Studs with Interfaith St	L8VV	2FT Dip	Gy	CE	MO	M	Ind	CCC	Ind		
OXFORD BROOKES Univ											
Cartography/Accounting and Finance	FN84	3FT deg	* g	DDD-BCC Ind		M*/D*3	Ind	Ind	Ind		
Cartography/Anthropology	FL86	3FT deg	* g	DDD-BCC Ind		M*^	Ind	Ind	Ind		
Cartography/Biological Chemistry	CF78	3FT deg									
Cartography/Biology	CF18	3FT deg	S g	DD-DDD Ind		MS	Ind	Ind	Ind		
Cartography/Business Administration & Management	FN81	3FT deg	* g	CC-BBC Ind		MB/MB4	Ind	Ind	Ind		
Cell Biology/Cartography	CFC8	3FT deg									
Combined Studies/Cartography	FY84	3FT deg		X		X	X	X			
Computer Systems/Cartography	FG86	3FT deg	* g	DDD-BC Ind		M*	Ind	Ind	Ind		
Computing Mathematics/Cartography	FG89	3FT deg	* g	CC-DDD Ind		M*	Ind	Ind	Ind		
Computing/Cartography	FG85	3FT deg	* g	DDD-BC Ind		M*	Ind	Ind	Ind	2	
Ecology/Cartography	FC89	3FT deg	* g	DD-DDD Ind		MS	Ind	Ind	Ind		
Economics/Cartography	FL81	3FT deg	* g	DDD-BB Ind		M*/M*3	Ind	Ind	Ind		
Educational Studies/Cartography	FX89	3FT deg	* g	CC-DDD Ind		M*/M*3	Ind	Ind	Ind		
Electronics/Cartography	FH86	3FT deg	S/M	CC-DDD Ind		M$	Ind	Ind	Ind		
English Studies/Cartography	FQ83	3FT deg	* g	DDD-AB Ind		M*^	Ind	Ind	Ind		
Environmental Chemistry/Cartography	FF81	3FT deg									
Environmental Policy/Cartography	FK83	3FT deg									
Environmental Sciences/Cartography	FF8X	3FT deg	S g	CC-DDD Ind		M*/DS	Ind	Ind	Ind		
Exercise & Health/Cartography	FB86	3FT deg	S	DD-CC		MS	Ind	Ind	Ind		
Fine Art/Cartography	FW81	3FT deg	Pf+A g	BC-DDD Ind		MA^	Ind	Ind	Ind		
Food Science and Nutrition/Cartography	DF48	3FT deg	S g	DD-CC		MS	Ind	Ind	Ind		
French Language and Contemp Studies/Cartography	FR8C	4SW deg	F g	CC-DDD Ind		M*^	Ind	Ind	Ind		
French Language and Literature/Cartography	FR81	4SW deg	F g	CC-DDD Ind		M*^	Ind	Ind	Ind		
Geography & the Phy Env/French Lang & Contemp St	FRVC	3FT deg									
Geography and the Phys Env/Accounting & Finance	FNV4	3FT deg	* g	BB-BCC Ind		M*/D*3	Ind	Ind	Ind		
Geography and the Phys Env/Anthropology	FLV6	3FT deg									
Geography and the Phys Env/Biological Chemistry	FCV7	3FT deg									
Geography and the Phys Env/Biology	CF1V	3FT deg									
Geography and the Phys Env/Business Admin & Mgt	FNV1	3FT deg									
Geography and the Phys Env/Cartography	F860	3FT deg									
Geography and the Phys Env/Cell Biology	CFCV	3FT deg									
Geography and the Phys Env/Combined Studies	FYV4	3FT deg		X		X	X	X			
Geography and the Phys Env/Computer Systems	FGV6	3FT deg									
Geography and the Phys Env/Computing	FGV5	3FT deg									
Geography and the Phys Env/Computing Mathematics	FGV9	3FT deg									

course details

TITLE	CODE	COURSE	SUBJECTS	A/AS	ND/C	AGNVQ	IB	SQA(H)	SQA	RATIO A/AS	
Geography and the Phys Env/Ecology	CF9V	3FT deg									
Geography and the Phys Env/Economics	FLV1	3FT deg									
Geography and the Phys Env/Educational Studies	FXV9	3FT deg									
Geography and the Phys Env/Electronics	FHV6	3FT deg									
Geography and the Phys Env/English Studies	FQV3	3FT deg									
Geography and the Phys Env/Environmental Chem	FF1V	3FT deg									
Geography and the Phys Env/Environmental Policy	FKV3	3FT deg									
Geography and the Phys Env/Environmental Scis	FFVX	3FT deg									
Geography and the Phys Env/Exercise and Health	BF6V	3FT deg									
Geography and the Phys Env/Fine Art	FWV1	3FT deg									
Geography and the Phys Env/Food Sci & Nutrition	DF4V	3FT deg									
Geography and the Phys Env/French Lang and Lit	FRV1	3FT deg									
Geography and the Phys Env/Geography	FLV8	3FT deg									
Geography and the Phys Env/Geotechnics	FHV2	3FT deg									
Geography and the Phys Env/Ger Lang & Contemp St	FRVF	3FT deg									
Geography and the Phys Env/German Lang and Lit	FRV2	3FT deg									
Geography and the Phys Env/German Studies	FRVG	3FT deg									
Geography and the Phys Env/Health Care(Post Exp)	BF7V	3FT deg		X		X	X	X			
Geography and the Phys Env/History	FVV1	3FT deg									
Geography and the Phys Env/History of Art	FVV4	3FT deg									
Geography and the Phys Env/Hospitality Mgt St	FNV7	3FT deg									
Geography and the Phys Env/Human Biology	BF1V	3FT deg			Ind		Ind	Ind	Ind		
Geography and the Phys Env/Informatiion Systems	FGVM	3FT deg									
Geography and the Phys Env/Intelligent Systems	FGV8	3FT deg									
Geography and the Phys Env/Law	FMV3	3FT deg									
Geography and the Phys Env/Leisure Planning	FKVH	3FT deg									
Geography and the Phys Env/Marketing Management	FNVN	3FT deg									
Geography and the Phys Env/Mathematics	FGV1	3FT deg									
Geography and the Phys Env/Music	FWV3	3FT deg									
Geography and the Phys Env/Palliative Care	BFRV	3FT deg		X		X	X	X			
Geography and the Physical Environment/Geology	FFV6	3FT deg									
Geography/Accounting and Finance	LN84	3FT deg	* g	BB-BCC	Ind	M*/D*3	Ind	Ind	Ind		
Geography/Anthropology	LL68	3FT deg	*	BB-CCD	Ind	M*^	Ind	Ind	Ind	26	
Geography/Biological Chemistry	CL78	3FT deg									
Geography/Biology	CL18	3FT deg	S g	DD-CDD	Ind	MS	Ind	Ind	Ind	10	
Geography/Business Administration & Management	LN81	3FT deg	* g	CCD-BBC	Ind	M*/MB4	Ind	Ind	Ind	40	
Geography/Cartography	FL88	3FT deg	* g	DDD-BB	Ind	M*	Ind	Ind	Ind	5	6/18
Geography/Cell Biology	CLC8	3FT deg									
Geography/Combined Studies	LY84	3FT deg		X		X	X	X			
Geography/Computer Systems	GL68	3FT deg	* g	CDD-BB	Ind	M*	Ind	Ind	Ind		
Geography/Computing	GL58	3FT deg	* g	CDD-BB	Ind	M*	Ind	Ind	Ind		
Geography/Computing Mathematics	GL98	3FT deg	* g	CD-BB	Ind	M*	Ind	Ind	Ind		
Geography/Ecology	CL98	3FT deg	* g	CD-BB	Ind	MS	Ind	Ind	Ind		
Geography/Economics	LL18	3FT deg	* g	BB-CCD	Ind	M*/M*3	Ind	Ind	Ind	37	
Geography/Educational Studies	LX89	3FT deg	*	CC-BB	Ind	M*/M*3	Ind	Ind	Ind	19	
Geography/English Studies	LQ83	3FT deg	*	CCD-AB	Ind	M*^	Ind	Ind	Ind	24	
Geography/Environmental Chemistry	FF8C	3FT deg									
Geography/Environmental Policy	KL38	3FT deg									
Geography/Environmental Sciences	FLX8	3FT deg	S g	CD-BB	Ind	M*/DS	Ind	Ind	Ind	10	15/18
Geography/Exercise and Health	LB86	3FT deg	S	DD-BB	Ind	MS	Ind	Ind	Ind		
Geography/Fine Art	LW81	3FT deg	Pf+A g	BC-BB	Ind	MA^	Ind	Ind	Ind		
Geography/Food Science and Nutrition	DL48	3FT deg	S g	DD-BB	Ind	MS	Ind	Ind	Ind	2	

Geography 30

TITLE	CODE	COURSE	SUBJECTS	A/AS	NO/C	AGNVQ	IB	SQA(H)	SQA	RATIO A/AS	
Geography/French Language and Contemp Studies	LR8C	4SW deg	F	CDD-BB	Ind	M*^	Ind	Ind	Ind	8	
Geography/French Language and Literature	LR81	4SW deg	F	CDD-BB	Ind	M*^	Ind	Ind	Ind		
Geology/Cartography	FF68	3FT deg	S/M	DD-CC	Ind	PS/MS	Ind	Ind	Ind	3	
Geology/Geography	FL68	3FT deg	S/M g	DD-BB	Ind	PS/MS	Ind	Ind	Ind	10	
Geotechnics/Cartography	FH82	3FT deg	S/M/Ds/Es	CC-DD	Ind	M$	Ind	Ind	Ind		
Geotechnics/Geography	HL28	3FT deg	S/M/Ds/Es	DD-BB	Ind	M$	Ind	Ind	Ind		
German Language and Contemp Stud/Cartography	FR8F	4SW deg	G g	CC-DDD	Ind	M*^	Ind	Ind	Ind		
German Language and Contemp Stud/Geography	LR8F	4SW deg	G	DDD-BB	Ind	M*^	Ind	Ind	Ind		
German Language and Literature/Cartography	FR82	4SW deg	G g	CC-DDD	Ind	M*^	Ind	Ind	Ind		
German Language and Literature/Geography	LR82	4SW deg	G	DDD-BB	Ind	M*^	Ind	Ind	Ind		
German Studies/Cartography	FR8G	4SW deg			Ind		Ind	Ind	Ind		
German Studies/Geography	LR8G	4SW deg			Ind		Ind	Ind	Ind		
Health Care/Cartography (Post Exp)	BF78	3FT deg	X			X	X	X			
Health Care/Geography (Post Exp)	BL78	3FT deg	X			X	X	X			
History of Art/Cartography	FV84	3FT deg	* g	DDD-BCC	Ind	M*^	Ind	Ind	Ind		
History of Art/Geography	LV84	3FT deg	*	BB-CCD	Ind	M*^	Ind	Ind	Ind		
History/Cartography	FV81	3FT deg	* g	DDD-BB	Ind	M*^	Ind	Ind	Ind		
History/Geography	LV81	3FT deg	*	BB-CCD	Ind	M*^	Ind	Ind	Ind	10	
Hospitality Management Studies/Cartography	FN87	3FT deg	* g	CC-DDD	Ind	M*/M*3	Ind	Ind	Ind		
Hospitality Management Studies/Geography	LN87	3FT deg	*	DDD-BB	Ind	M*/M*3	Ind	Ind	Ind	8	
Human Biology/Cartography	BF18	3FT deg			Ind		Ind	Ind	Ind		
Human Biology/Geography	BL18	3FT deg									
Information Systems/Cartography	FG8M	3FT deg	* g	DDD-BC	Ind	M*	Ind	Ind	Ind	1	
Information Systems/Geography	GLM8	3FT deg	* g	BC-BB	Ind	M*	Ind	Ind	Ind		
Intelligent Systems/Cartography	FG88	3FT deg	* g	CC-DDD	Ind	M*	Ind	Ind	Ind		
Intelligent Systems/Geography	GL88	3FT deg	* g	CD-BB	Ind	M*	Ind	Ind	Ind		
Law/Cartography	FM83	3FT deg	* g	DDD-BBB	Ind	M*/D*3	Ind	Ind	Ind		
Law/Geography	LM83	3FT deg	*	CCD-BBB	Ind	M*/D*3	Ind	Ind	Ind	8	
Leisure Planning/Cartography	FK8H	3FT deg									
Leisure Planning/Geography	KLH8	3FT deg									
Marketing Management/Cartography	FN8N	3FT deg	* g	DDD-BCC	Ind	M*/D*3	Ind	Ind	Ind		
Marketing Management/Geography	LN8N	3FT deg	* g	BB-CCD	Ind	M*/D*3	Ind	Ind	Ind	25	
Mathematics/Cartography	FG81	3FT deg	M g	DD-CC	Ind	M*^	Ind	Ind	Ind		
Mathematics/Geography	GL18	3FT deg	M	DD-BB	Ind	M*^	Ind	Ind	Ind	9	
Music/Cartography	FW83	3FT deg	Mu g	DD-CC	Ind	M*	Ind	Ind	Ind		
Music/Geography	LW83	3FT deg	Mu	DD-BB	Ind	M*	Ind	Ind	Ind	4	
Palliative Care/Cartography (Post Exp)	BFR8	3FT deg	X			X	X	X			
Palliative Care/Geography (Post Exp)	BLR8	3FT deg	X			X	X	X			
Planning Studies/Cartography	FK84	3FT deg	* g	CC-DDD	Ind	M*	Ind	Ind	Ind	3	
Planning Studies/Geography	KL48	3FT deg	* g	DDD-BB	Ind	M*	Ind	Ind	Ind	4	8/20
Planning Studies/Physical Geography	FKV4	3FT deg									
Politics/Cartography	FM81	3FT deg	* g	DDD-AB	Ind	M*^	Ind	Ind	Ind		
Politics/Geography	LM81	3FT deg	*	CCD-AB	Ind	M*^	Ind	Ind	Ind	14	
Politics/Physical Geography	FMV1	3FT deg									
Psychology/Cartography	CF88	3FT deg	* g	DDD-BBC	Ind	M*^	Ind	Ind	Ind		
Psychology/Geography	CL88	3FT deg	* g	CCD-BBC	Ind	M*^	Ind	Ind	Ind		
Psychology/Physical Geography	CF8V	3FT deg									
Publishing/Cartography	FP85	3FT deg	* g	DDD-BB	Ind	M*/M$3	Ind	Ind	Ind		
Publishing/Physical Geography	FPV5	3FT deg									
Rehabilitation/Cartography (Post Exp)	BFT8	3FT deg	X			X	X	X			
Rehabilitation/Geography (Post Exp)	BLT8	3FT deg	X			X	X	X			
Rehabilitation/Physical Geography (Post Exp)	BFTV	3FT deg	X			X	X	X			

course details   98 expected requirements   96 entry stats

TITLE	CODE	COURSE	SUBJECTS	A/AS	ND/C	AGNVQ	IB	SQA(H)	SQA	RATIO A/AS	
Sociology/Cartography	FL83	3FT deg	* g	DDD-BCC	Ind	M*^	Ind	Ind	Ind		
Sociology/Geography	LL38	3FT deg	*	BB-CCD	Ind	M*^	Ind	Ind	Ind	34	
Sociology/Physical Geography	FLV3	3FT deg									
Software Engineering/Cartography	FG87	3FT deg	* g	DDD-CDD	Ind	M*	Ind	Ind	Ind		
Software Engineering/Geography	GL78	3FT deg	* g	CDD-BB	Ind	M*	Ind	Ind	Ind		
Software Engineering/Physical Geography	FGV7	3FT deg									
Statistics/Geography	GL48	3FT deg	* g	DD-BB	Ind	M*	Ind	Ind	Ind	3	
Statistics/Physical Geography	FGV4	3FT deg									
Telecommunications/Cartography	FH8P	3FT deg									
Telecommunications/Geography	HLP8	3FT deg									
Telecommunications/Physical Geography	FHVP	3FT deg									
Tourism/Cartography	FP87	3FT deg	* g	DDD-BC	Ind	M*/M*3	Ind	Ind	Ind	2	
Tourism/Geography	LP87	3FT deg	* g	BB-CCD	Ind	M*/M*3	Ind	Ind	Ind	14	
Tourism/Physical Geography	FPV7	3FT deg									
Transport Planning/Cartography	FN89	3FT deg	* g	CC-DDD	Ind	M*	Ind	Ind	Ind	2	
Transport Planning/Geography	LN89	3FT deg	* g	BB-DDD	Ind	M*	Ind	Ind	Ind	7	
Transport Planning/Physical Geography	FNV9	3FT deg									
Water Resources/Cartography	FH8F	3FT deg									
Water Resources/Geography	HLF8	3FT deg									
Water Resources/Physical Geography	FHVF	3FT deg									

Univ of PLYMOUTH

TITLE	CODE	COURSE	SUBJECTS	A/AS	ND/C	AGNVQ	IB	SQA(H)	SQA	RATIO A/AS	
Applied Economics with Geography	L1F8	3FT deg	* g	CCD	MO	M$^	Ind	BCCC	Ind	7	
Business Economics with Geography	L1FV	3FT deg	* g	CCD	MO	M$^	Ind	BCCC	Ind		
Ecology with Geography	D2F8	3FT deg	B g	16	4M $	MS^	Ind	BBC	Ind	4	
European Economics with Geography	L1FW	3FT deg	* g	CDD-CCD	MO	M$^	Ind	BCCC	Ind		
Fisheries Studies with Hydrography	J6F8	3FT deg	Ap g	14	5M $	M$	Ind	CCCC	Ind	1	
Geography	F800	3FT deg	Gy g	18	X	M$^	Ind	ABBB	Ind	6	12/22
Geography with Applied Economics	F8L1	3FT deg	Gy g	16-18	X	M$^	Ind	ABBB	Ind	16	
Geography with Astronomy	F8FM	3FT deg	Gy g	16-18	X	M$^	Ind	ABBB	Ind	8	
Geography with Computing	F8G5	3FT deg	Gy g	16-18	X	M$^	Ind	ABBB	Ind	12	14/16
Geography with Criminal Justice	FM8J	3FT deg	Gy g	16-18	X	M$^	Ind	ABBB	Ind		
Geography with Ecology	F8D2	3FT deg	Gy+B g	16-18	X	M$^	Ind	Ind	Ind	3	10/16
Geography with French	F8R1	3FT deg	Gy+F g	16-18	X	M$^	Ind	ABBB	Ind		
Geography with Geology	F8F6	3FT deg	Gy g	16-18	X	M$^	Ind	ABBB	Ind	15	14/20
Geography with German	F8R2	3FT deg	Gy+G g	16-18	X	M$^	Ind	ABBB	Ind		
Geography with International Relations	F8MC	3FT deg	Gy g	16-18	X	M$^	Ind	ABBB	Ind		
Geography with Italian	F8R3	3FT deg	Gy g	16-18	X	M$^	Ind	ABBB	Ind		
Geography with Languages	F8T9	3FT deg	Gy+L g	16-18	X	M$^	Ind	ABBB	Ind	6	12/20
Geography with Law	F8M3	3FT deg	Gy g	BCC	X	M$^	Ind	ABBB	Ind	17	
Geography with Ocean Science	F8F7	3FT deg	Gy+M/P/C g	16-18	X	M$^	Ind	ABBB	Ind	7	12/22
Geography with Politics	F8M1	3FT deg	Gy g	16-18	X	M$^	Ind	ABBB	Ind	8	
Geography with Social Policy	F8L4	3FT deg	Gy g	16-18	X	M$^	Ind	ABBB	Ind	15	
Geography with Social Research	F8LH	3FT deg	Gy g	16-18	X	M$^	Ind	Ind	Ind		
Geography with Sociology	F8L3	3FT deg	Gy g	16-18	X	M$^	Ind	Ind	Ind	22	
Geography with Spanish	F8R4	3FT deg	Gy+Sp g	16-18	X	M$^	Ind	ABBB	Ind		
Geography with Statistics	F8G4	3FT deg	Gy g	16-18	X	M$^	Ind	ABBB	Ind	6	
Geography with Transport	F8N9	3FT deg	Gy g	16-18	X	M$^	Ind	Ind	Ind	28	
Geology with Geography	F6F8	3FT deg	S+Gy g	16	4M	MS^	Ind	CCC	Ind	20	
Geology with Hydrography	F6FV	3FT deg	S+P/C/M g	14	4M	MS	Ind	CCC	Ind		
Hydrography	F870	3FT deg	2(M/P/C/Ap) g	14	5M $	M$	Ind	CCC	Ind	6	
Hydrography with Astronomy	F8F5	3FT deg	2(M/P/C/Ap) g	14	5M $	M$	Ind	CCCC	Ind		
Hydrography with Fisheries Business Studies	F871	3FT deg	2(M/P/C/Ap) g	14	5M $	M$	Ind	CCCC	Ind		

842

course details			98 expected requirements							96 entry stats	
TITLE	CODE	COURSE	SUBJECTS	A/AS	NO/C	NGNVQ	IB	SQA(H)	SQA	RATIO	A/AS
Hydrography with Fisheries Science	F8NX	3FT deg	2(M/P/C/Ap) g	14	5M $	M$	Ind	Ind	Ind		
Hydrography with Fisheries Technology	F8J6	3FT deg	2(M/P/C/Ap) g	14	5M $	M$	Ind	CCCC	Ind		
Hydrography with Marine Navigation	F8JY	3FT deg	2(M/P/C/Ap) g	14	5M $	M$	Ind	CCCC	Ind	6	
Hydrography with Marine Technology	F8JP	3FT deg	2(M/P/C/Ap) g	14	5M $	M$	Ind	CCCC	Ind		
Hydrography with Maritime Business	F8N1	3FT deg	2(M/P/C/Ap) g	14	5M $	M$	Ind	Ind	Ind		
Hydrography with Maritime History	F8V1	3FT deg	2(M/P/C/Ap) g	14	5M $	M$	Ind	CCCC	Ind		
Hydrography with Maritime Law	F8MH	3FT deg	2(M/P/C/Ap) g	14	5M $	M$	Ind	CCCC	Ind		
Hydrography with Ocean Science	F8FR	3FT deg	2(M/P/C/Ap) g	14	5M $	M$	Ind	CCCC	Ind	3	
Hydrography with Underwater Studies	F8F9	3FT deg	2(M/P/C/Ap) g	14	5M $	M$	Ind	CCCC	Ind		
Law with Geography	M3F8	3FT deg	Ap g	BCC-BBC	DO	D12^	Ind	BBBB$	Ind		
Marine Navigation with Hydrography	J9F8	3FT deg	2(M/P/C) g	14	5M $	M$	Ind	CCCC	Ind	7	
Marine Technology with Hydrography	J6FV	3FT deg	2(M/P/C) g	14	5M $	M$	Ind	CCCC	Ind	3	
Maritime Business with Hydrography	N1F8	3FT deg	* g	18	5M	M$	Ind	CCCC	Ind		
Modern Languages with Geography	T9F8	3FT/4SW deg	L g	C	Ind	Ind	Ind	Ind	Ind		
Ocean Science with Geography	F7F8	3FT deg	S g	14-16	5M $	M$^	Ind	CCCC	Ind	4	10/16
Ocean Science with Hydrography	F7FV	3FT deg	S g	14-16	5M $	M$	Ind	CCCC	Ind	6	
Political Economy with Geography	LF1V	3FT deg	Ap g	CDD-CCD	MO $	M$^	Ind	BCCC	Ind		
Politics with Geography	M1F8	3FT deg	Gy g	16	5M $	M$	Ind	BBBC$	Ind		
Social Policy with Geography	L4F8	3FT deg	Gy g	16	5M $	M$^	Ind	BBBC$	Ind		
Sociology with Geography	L3F8	3FT deg	Gy g	16	5M $	M$^	Ind	BBBC$	Ind	9	
Statistics (App) and Mgt Sci with Geography	G4FV	3FT deg	M/St g	10-15	MO $	M$^	Ind	BBCC	Ind		
Statistics (App) with Geography	G4F8	3FT deg	M/St g	10-15	MO $	M$^	Ind	BBCC	Ind		
Transport with Geography	N9FW	3FT deg	Gy g	16	5M	M$	Ind	Ind	Ind	8	
Underwater Studies with Hydrography	F9FW	3FT deg	Ap g	14-16	5M $	M$	Ind	Ind	Ind		

Univ of PORTSMOUTH

Chemistry and Geographical Science	FF18	3FT deg	C+Gy	14	4M	MS6/^	26	BBBB	Ind		
Chemistry and Geographical Science	FF1V▼	4FT deg	*	Ind	Ind	Ind	Ind	Ind	Ind		
Computing and Geographical Science	FG8M▼	4FT deg	*	Ind	Ind	Ind	Ind	Ind	Ind		
Economic History with Geography	V3L8	3FT deg	*	10	4M	M*	Dip	BBCC	Ind		
Economics and Geography	LL18	3FT deg	*	14	4M+2D	D$6/^	Dip	CCCCC	Ind	4	10/22
Geographical Science	F800	3FT deg	Gy	14-18	4M	M$6/^	26	BBBB	Ind	7	10/22
Geographical Science	F808▼	3FT deg	*		Ind	P*	Ind	Ind	Ind		
Geographical Science and Computing	FG85	3FT deg	Gy	16	3M	M$6/^	26	BBBB	Ind	5	
Geographical Science and Geology (Extended)	FF6V▼	4FT deg	*	Ind	Ind	Ind	Ind	Ind	Ind		
Geographical Science and Mathematics	FG81	3FT deg	Gy+M	16	4M	M$6/^	26$	BBBB	Ind		
Geographical Science and Mathematics (Extended)	FG8C▼	4FT deg	*	Ind	Ind	Ind	Ind	Ind	Ind		
Geographical Science and Physics (Extended)	FF3V▼	4FT deg	*	Ind	Ind	Ind	Ind	Ind	Ind		
Geographical Science and Statistics	FG8K▼	4FT deg	*	Ind	Ind	Ind	Ind	Ind	Ind		
Geographical Science and Statistics	FG84	3FT deg	Gy+M	16	4M	M$6/^	26$	BBBB	Ind		
Geographical Science with Education	F8X9	3FT deg	Gy	16	4M	M$6/^	26	BBBB	Ind		
Geography	L800	3FT deg	Gy	18	Ind	D$^	28	BBBCC	Ind	6	12/22
Geography with Economic History	L8V3	3FT deg	Gy+Ec/H	10	Ind	Ind	Dip	Ind	Ind		
Geology and Geographical Science	FF68	3FT deg	Gy+S	16	4M $	M$6/^	26	BBBB	Ind	4	6/14
Physics and Geographical Science	FF38	3FT deg	Gy+P	16	4M	MS6/^	26$	BBBB	Ind	3	
Urban Geoscience and Geohazard Assessment	FF86	3FT deg	S	14	3M $	M$6/^	Dip	BBBB	Ind		

QUEEN MARY & WESTFIELD COLL (Univ of London)

Environmental Geography	F830	3FT deg	Gy	18		M$^		30$			
French and Geography	LR81	4FT deg	F+Gy	BCC		M^		30$			
Geography	F800	3FT deg	Gy	18		M$^		30$			
Geography	L820	3FT deg	Gy	20		M$^		30$			
Geography	L800	3FT deg	Gy	18-20		M$^		30$			

			98 expected requirements							96 entry stats

course details

TITLE	CODE	COURSE	SUBJECTS	A/AS	NO/C	AGNVQ	IB	SQA(H)	SQA	RATIO A/AS
Geography and Economics	LL81	3FT deg	Gy g	BCC		M$^	30$	BBBBB		
Geography and Politics	LM81	3FT deg	Gy	BCC		M$^	30$			
German and Geography	LR8F	4FT deg	G+Gy	BCC		M^	30$			
Hispanic Studies and Geography	LR8K	4FT deg	L+Gy	BCC		M^	30$			
Human Geography	L822	3FT deg	Gy	18-20		M^	30$			
Physical Geography	F840	3FT deg	Gy	18		M$^	30$			
Russian and Geography	LRV8	4FT deg	L+Gy	BCC		M^	30$			

QUEEN'S Univ Belfast

Archaeology - Palaeoecology and Geography	VF68	3FT/4FT deg	Gy g	CCC	X	Ind	28$	BBBC	X	7 16/22
Geography	F800	3FT/4FT deg	Gy g	CCC	X	Ind	28$	BBBC	X	5 16/22
Geography	L800	3FT deg	Gy g	BCC	X	D*_ go	29$	X	X	12 20/28
Geography and Geology	FF86	3FT/4FT deg	Gy g	CCC	X	Ind	28$	BBBC	X	8 16/18
Geography with Extended Studies in Europe	F8TF	4FT deg	L+Gy g	BBC	X	X	30$	X	X	12
Geography with Studies in Europe	F8T2	3FT deg	L+Gy g	BBC	X	X	30$	X	X	
Human Geography	L822	3FT deg	* g	BCC	3M+4D	D*6/^ go	29$	ABBB	Ind	8 18/28
Human Geography/Economic & Social History	LV8H	3FT deg	* g	BCC	3M+4D	D*6/^ go	29$	ABBB	Ind	
Politics/Human Geography	LM8C	3FT deg	* g	BCC	3M+4D	D*6/^ go	29$	ABBB	Ind	
Social Anthropology/Geography	LL86	3FT deg	Gy g	BCC	X	D*_ go	29$	X	X	7 20/20
Social Policy/Human Geography	LL4V	3FT deg	* g	BCC	3M+4D	D*6/^ go	29$	ABBB	Ind	
Sociology/Human Geography	LL3V	3FT deg	* g	BCC	3M+4D	D*6/^ go	29$	ABBB	Ind	

Univ of READING

Geography (Human and Physical)	F820	3FT deg	Gy g	BBC	5M+3D	D$6/_ gi	31	BBBB	Ind	6 18/26
Geography (Human)	L822	3FT deg	Gy g	BBC	5M+3D	D$6/_ gi	31	BBBB	Ind	8 18/24
Geography (Physical)	F840	3FT deg	Gy g	BBC	5M+3D	D$6/_ gi	31	BBBB	Ind	17 18/26
Geography and Economics (Regional Science)	LL18	3FT deg	* g	BBC	5M+3D	D$6/_ gi	31	BBBB	Ind	7 20/26

Univ College of RIPON & YORK ST JOHN

Applied Social Sciences/Geography	L3L8	3FT deg	Gy	CC	X	M*_	27	BBBC		5
Environmental Science/Geography	F9L8	3FT deg	Gy g	DD	X	M*_	27	BBCC		4 10/14
Geography/Applied Social Sciences	L8L3	3FT deg	Gy	CCD	X	M*_	30	BBBB		4 18/20
Geography/Environmental Science	L8F9	3FT deg	Gy g	CCD	X	M*_ g	30	BBBB		4 8/18
Geography/History	L8V1	3FT deg	Gy+H	CCD	X	Ind	30	BBBB		
Geography/Management Studies	L8N1	3FT deg	Gy g	CCD	X	M*_ g	30	BBBB		5 10/22
Geography/Physical Education	L8B6	3FT deg	Gy	CCD	X	M*_	30	BBBB		
History/Geography	V1L8	3FT deg	H+Gy	14	X	Ind	30	BBBB		
Physical Education/Geography	B6L8	3FT deg	Gy	BB-CCC	X	D$_	30	ABBB		

ROEHAMPTON INST

Film & Television Studies and Geography	LP84▼	3FT deg	Gy	16	2M+2D$	M$^	30	BBC	N$	
Geography	L800▼	3FT deg	Gy	DD	3M $	P$ go	24	BCC	N$	10 6/12
Geography and Applied Consumer Studies	NL98▼	3FT deg	Gy g	12	4M $	P$ go	26	BCC	N$	
Geography and Art for Community	WL18▼	3FT deg	Gy	DD	4M $	P$ go	26	BCC	N$	5
Geography and Biology	CL18▼	3FT deg	B+Gy	12	4M $	P$ go	26	BCC	N$	3
Geography and Business Computing	GL78▼	3FT deg	Ge g	12	3D	M$ go	26	BCC	N$	
Geography and Business Studies	NL18▼	3FT deg	Gy g	DD	3D $	M$ go	26	BCC	N$	5
Geography and Dance Studies	WL48▼	3FT deg	Gy	CC	2M+2D$	M$^ go	30	BBC	Ind	
Geography and Drama & Theatre Studies	LW84▼	3FT deg	Gy+T/E	16	3D $	M$^ go	30	BBC	Ind	
Geography and Education	XL98▼	3FT deg	Gy	DD	4M $	P$ go	26	BCC	N$	2
Geography and English Language & Linguistics	QLH8▼	3FT deg	Gy+E/L	CC	2M+2D$	M$^	30	BBC	Ind	
Geography and English Literature	QL38▼	3FT deg	Gy+E	CC	2M+2D$	M^ go	28	BBC	Ind	
Geography and Environmental Studies	FL98▼	3FT deg	Gy g	DD	4M $	P$ go	26	BCC	N$	6
Geography and French	RL18▼	4FT deg	Gy+F	12	4M $	P^ go	26	BCC	N$	4

Geography 30

course details			98 expected requirements							96 entry stats
TITLE	CODE	COURSE	SUBJECTS	A/AS	NQ/C	AGNVQ	IB	SQA(H)	SQA	RATIO A/AS
Health Studies and Geography	BL98▼	3FT deg	B+Gy	12	4M $	P$^ go	26	BCC	N$	
History and Geography	LV81▼	3FT deg	H+Gy	DD	4M $	P^ go	26	BCC	N$	5
Human & Social Biology and Geography	LC8C▼	3FT deg	B+Gy	12	4M $	P$ go	26	BCC	N$	
Music and Geography	LW83▼	3FT deg	Mu+Gy	DD	4M $	P^ go	26	BCC	N$	
Natural Resource Studies and Geography	DL28▼	3FT deg	Gy g	DD	3M	P$ go	24	CCC	N$	
Psychology and Geography	LL87▼	3FT deg	Gy g	CC	3D $	M$ go	30	BBC	Ind	
Social Policy & Administration and Geography	LL84▼	3FT deg	Gy g	DD	4M $	P$ go	26	BCC	N$	2
Sociology and Geography	LL83▼	3FT deg	Gy g	DD	4M $	P$ go	26	BCC	N$	11
Spanish and Geography	LR84▼	4FT deg	Sp+Gy	12	2M+2D$	P$ go	28	BBC	N$	
Sport Studies and Geography	LB86▼	3FT deg	Gy g	12	3D $	MS go	30	BBC	N$	
Theology & Religious Studies and Geography	LV88▼	3FT deg	Gy	DD	4M $	P$ go	26	BCC	N$	
Women's Studies and Geography	LM89▼	3FT deg	Gy	DD	4M $	P$ go	26	BCC	N$	
ROYAL HOLLOWAY, Univ of London										
Biology and Geography	CF18	3FT deg	B+Gy+C/S g	BCC	Ind	DS^	28$	BBBBC$		8
Geography	F800	3FT deg	Gy	BCC-BBC	Ind	D^	30$	BBBBC$		4 14/26
Geography	L800	3FT deg	Gy	BCC-BBC	Ind	D^	30$	BBBBC$		4 16/26
Geography and Geology	FF68	3FT deg	Gy+S/2S g	CCC-BCC	Ind	D^	Ind	Ind		5 16/24
Geography and History	LV81	3FT deg	Gy g	BBC	Ind		30$	Ind		4
Geography and Mathematics	FG81	3FT deg	Gy+M	BCC-BBC	Ind	D^	Ind	Ind		6
Foundation Programme _Geography_	Y408	4FT deg								
Science Foundation Year _Geography_	Y100	4FT deg	*		Ind	Ind		Ind	Ind	
Univ of SALFORD										
Biochemistry & Geography (3 or 4 Yrs)	CF78	3FT/4SW deg	B/C+Gy	BBC-CCD	3M	M	Ind	Ind	Ind	
Biology and Geography (3 or 4 yr SW)	CF18	3FT/4SW deg	B/C+Gy g	BCC-CCD	3M	M	Ind	Ind	Ind	4
Economics & Geography (3 or 4 Yrs)	LF18	3FT/4SW deg	Gy	BCC-CCD	3M	M	Ind	Ind	Ind	2 14/18
Environmental Geography	F830	3FT deg								
Geography	F800	3FT deg	* g	BDD	Ind	Ind	Ind	Ind	Ind	3 8/22
Geography	L800	3FT deg	* g	BDD	Ind	Ind	Ind	Ind	Ind	4 10/22
Geography and Information Technology	GF58	3FT/4SW deg		BCC-CCD	3M	M	Ind	Ind	Ind	
Geography and Physics (3 or 4 Yrs)	FF83	3FT/4SW deg	Gy+P	BCC-BCD	3M	M	Ind	Ind	Ind	
Geography and Physiology	FC89	3FT/4SW deg		BCC-CCD	3M	M	Ind	Ind	Ind	
Urban Geography	F802	3FT deg								
SOAS:Sch of Oriental & African St (U of London)										
Geography	L870	3FT deg		20	Ind		30	BBBCC	Ind	6 20/22
Geography and African Studies	TL78	3FT deg		20	Ind		30	BBBCC	Ind	
Geography and Amharic	LT87	4FT deg		20	Ind		30	BBBCC	Ind	
Geography and Arabic	LT86	4FT deg		22	Ind		31	BBBBC	Ind	1
Geography and Bengali	LT85	3FT deg		20	Ind		30	BBBCC	Ind	
Geography and Burmese	LT8M	4FT deg		20	Ind		30	BBBCC	Ind	
Geography and Chinese	LT83	4FT deg		24	Ind		32	BBBBB	Ind	
Geography and Development Studies	ML98	3FT deg		22	Ind		31	BBBBC	Ind	1 16/24
Geography and Economics	LL18	3FT deg	g	22	Ind		31	BBBBC	Ind	14
Georgian and Geography	LT89	3FT deg		20	Ind		30	BBBCC	Ind	
Gujarati and Geography	TL58	3FT deg		20	Ind		30	BBBCC	Ind	
Hausa and Geography	LT8R	4FT deg		20	Ind		30	BBBCC	Ind	
Hebrew and Geography	LQ89	4FT deg		22	Ind		31	BBBBC	Ind	1
Hindi and Geography	TL5V	3FT/4FT deg		20	Ind		30	BBBCC	Ind	1
History and Geography	LV81	3FT deg		20	Ind		30	BBBCC	Ind	4
History of Art/Archaeology and Geography	LV86	3FT deg		20	Ind		30	BBBCC	Ind	

			98 expected requirements							96 entry stats	

course details | | | | **98 expected requirements** | | | | | | *96 entry stats* |

TITLE	CODE	COURSE	SUBJECTS	A/AS	ND/C	AGNVQ	IB	SQA(H)	SQA	RATIO A/AS
Indonesian and Geography	TLM8	3FT/4FT deg		20	Ind		30	BBBCC	Ind	
Japanese and Geography	LT84	4FT deg		24	Ind		32	BBBBB	Ind	
Korean and Geography	LT8N	4FT deg		20	Ind		30	BBBCC	Ind	
Law and Geography	LM83	3FT deg		24	Ind		32	BBBBB	Ind	
Linguistics and Geography	LQ83	3FT deg								
Music and Geography	LW83	3FT deg		20	Ind		30	BBBCC	Ind	
Nepali and Geography	LTV5	3FT deg		20	Ind		30	BBBCC	Ind	
Persian and Geography	LT8Q	3FT deg		22	Ind		31	BBBBC	Ind	
Politics and Geography	LM81	3FT deg		20	Ind		30	BBBCC	Ind	
Sanskrit and Geography	LQ8X	3FT deg		20	Ind		30	BBBCC	Ind	
Sinhalese and Geography	LTVM	3FT deg		20	Ind		30	BBBCC	Ind	
Social Anthropology and Geography	LL86	3FT deg		22	Ind		31	BBBBC	Ind	
South Asian Studies and Geography	TLMV	3FT deg								
Study of Religions and Geography	LV88	3FT deg		20	Ind		30	BBBCC	Ind	
Swahili and Geography	LT8T	4FT deg		20	Ind		30	BBBCC	Ind	
Tamil and Geography	LTVN	3FT deg		20	Ind		30	BBBCC	Ind	
Thai and Geography	LTW5	3FT/4FT deg		20	Ind		30	BBBCC	Ind	
Turkish and Geography	LT8P	4FT deg		22	Ind		31	BBBBC	Ind	
Urdu and Geography	LTWM	3FT deg		20	Ind		30	BBBCC	Ind	
Vietnamese and Geography	LTWN	4FT deg		20	Ind		30	BBBCC	Ind	1

Univ College SCARBOROUGH

TITLE	CODE	COURSE	SUBJECTS	A/AS	ND/C	AGNVQ	IB	SQA(H)	SQA	RATIO A/AS
Geographical Science	FD82	3FT deg	Gy g	DD	Ind	P	27$	Ind	Ind	

Univ of SHEFFIELD

TITLE	CODE	COURSE	SUBJECTS	A/AS	ND/C	AGNVQ	IB	SQA(H)	SQA	RATIO A/AS
Archaeological Science and Geography	FF48	3FT deg	Gy g	BBC	4M+2D	D6/^	30$	ABBB$	Ind	
Ecology and Geography	CF98	3FT/4EXT deg	Gy g	BBC	4M+2D$	DS^	30$	AABB$	Ind	9
Economics and Geography	LL18	3FT deg	Gy g	BBB	3M+3D$	D^	32$	AABB$	Ind	15 26/28
Geography	F800	3FT deg	Gy+S g	BBC-BBB	3M+3D$	DS^	31$	AABB$	Ind	11 24/30
Geography	L800	3FT deg	Gy g	BBB	3M+3D$	D^	32$	AABB$	Ind	7 22/30
Geography and Japanese Studies	LT84	4FT deg	Gy g	BBC	4M+2D$	D^	30$	ABBB$	Ind	
Geography and Mathematics	FG81	3FT deg	Gy+M g	BBB	3M+3D$	DS^	30$	AABB$	Ind	5 22/30
Geography and Politics	LM8C	3FT deg	Gy g	BBB	3M+3D$	D^	32$	AABB$	Ind	9
Geography and Social History	LV83	3FT deg	H+Gy g	BBB	3M+3D$	D^	32$	AABB$	Ind	
Geography and Sociology	LL83	3FT deg	Gy g	BBC	4D $	D^	30$	ABBB$	Ind	9 22/30

SHEFFIELD HALLAM Univ

TITLE	CODE	COURSE	SUBJECTS	A/AS	ND/C	AGNVQ	IB	SQA(H)	SQA	RATIO A/AS
European Urban and Regional Studies	K420	3FT deg	*	14	3M	M	Ind	Ind	Ind	
Urban and Regional Geography	LK84	3FT deg	*	16	4M	M	Ind	Ind	Ind	
Urban and Regional Studies	K462	4SW deg		14						
Urban and Regional Studies	K463	4SW deg		14						

Univ College of St MARTIN, LANCASTER AND CUMBRIA

TITLE	CODE	COURSE	SUBJECTS	A/AS	ND/C	AGNVQ	IB	SQA(H)	SQA	RATIO A/AS
Applied Community Studies/Geography	LL58	3FT deg	Gy	CD-DDE	3M+2D	M^	28$	BCCC$	Ind	
Art and Design/Geography	WL1V	3FT deg	A+Gy	CC-CDE	3M+2D$	MA^	28$	BBCC$	Ind	2
Business Management Studies/Geography	NL18	3FT deg	Gy	CD-DDE	X	M^	28$	BCCC$		
English/Geography	QL3V	3FT deg	E+Gy	BC-BDE	X	X	28$	BBBC$	Ind	
Geography	L800	3FT deg	Gy	CD-DDE	X	P^	28$	BCCC$	Ind	2 6/14
Geography/Applied Community Studies	LL8M	3FT deg	Gy	CD-DDE	X	P^	28$	BCCC$	Ind	
Geography/Art and Design	LW8C	3FT deg	Gy+A	CD-DDE	X	X	28$	BCCC$	Ind	
Geography/Business Management Studies	LN81	3FT deg	Gy	CD-DDE	X	P^	28$	BCCC$		
Geography/Education Studies	LX89	3FT deg	Gy	CD-DDE	X	P^	28$	BCCC$	Ind	
Geography/English	LQ8H	3FT deg	Gy+E	CD-DDE	X	X	28$	BCCC$	Ind	2
Geography/Health Studies	LB89	3FT deg	Gy	CD-DDE	X	P^	28$	BCCC$	Ind	

			course details							

course details — **98 expected requirements** — *96 entry stats*

TITLE	CODE	COURSE	SUBJECTS	A/AS	NO/C	AGNVQ	IB	SQA(H)	SQA	RATIO A/AS
Geography/History	LV8C	3FT deg	Gy+H	CD-DDE	X	X	28$	BCCC$	Ind	
Geography/Mathematics	LG81	3FT deg	Gy+M	CD-DDE	X	X	28$	BCCC$	Ind	
Geography/Physical Education & Sports Studies	LX8X	3FT deg	Gy	CD-DDE	X	P^	28$	BCCC$		
Geography/Science, Technology and Society	LY81	3FT deg	Gy g	CD-DDE	X	P^	28$	BCCC$	Ind	
Geography/Social Ethics	LV8R	3FT deg	Gy	CD-DDE	X	P^	28$	BCCC$	Ind	
Health Studies/Geography	BL98	3FT deg	Gy	CD-DDE	X	P^	28$	BCCC$	Ind	
History/Geography	VL1V	3FT deg	H+Gy	CD-DDE	X	X	28$	BCCC$	Ind	
Mathematics/Geography	GL18	3FT deg	M+Gy	DD-DEE	X	X	28$	BCCC$	Ind	
Science, Technology and Society/Geography	LY8C	3FT deg	Gy g	CD-DDE	X	M^	28$	BCCC$	Ind	
Social Ethics/Geography	VL7V	3FT deg	Gy	CD-DDE	3M+2D$	M^	28$	BCCC$	Ind	

Univ of SOUTHAMPTON

TITLE	CODE	COURSE	SUBJECTS	A/AS	NO/C	AGNVQ	IB	SQA(H)	SQA	RATIO A/AS
Archaeology and Geography	VL68	3FT deg	Gy	BCC	Ind	Ind	26	Ind	Ind	10 16/28
Geography	L800	3FT deg	Gy	BBB	Ind	Ind	32	AABBB	Ind	9 22/28
Geography	F800	3FT deg	Gy g	BBB	Ind	Ind	32	AABBB	Ind	9 20/28
Geography (MGeog)	F801	4FT deg	Gy	ABB	Ind	Ind	34	AAABB	Ind	
Geography with Geology	FF68	3FT deg	2S g	BBB	Ind	Ind	32	AABBB	Ind	
Geography with Oceanography	F8F7	3FT deg	2S g	BBB	Ind	Ind	32	AABBB	Ind	15
Geology with Physical Geography	F6F8	3FT deg	Gy+S g	18-20	Ind	Ind	28$	BBBBC	Ind	4 14/20
Mathematics with Geography	G1F8	3FT deg	M+Gy	BBC	Ind	Ind	30	ABBBB	Ind	6 20/24
Oceanography with Physical Geography	F7F8	3FT deg	Gy+S/M g	BCC	Ind	Ind	30$	BBBCC	Ind	11 16/24

SOUTH BANK Univ

TITLE	CODE	COURSE	SUBJECTS	A/AS	NO/C	AGNVQ	IB	SQA(H)	SQA	RATIO A/AS
Human Geography	L822	3FT deg	Gy g	14-18	2M+4D	M go	Ind	Ind	Ind	
Human Geography and Business Info Technology	GL78	3FT deg	M+Gy g	12-16	4M+2D	M go	Ind	Ind	Ind	
Human Geography and Computing	GL58	3FT deg	M+Gy g	12-16	4M+2D	M go	Ind	Ind	Ind	
Human Geography and Economics	LL18	3FT deg	Ec/Bu+Gy g	12-16	4M+2D	M go	Ind	Ind	Ind	
Human Geography and English Studies	LQ83	3FT deg	E+Gy g	14-18	X	M^ go	Ind	Ind	Ind	
Human Geography and European Studies	LT82	3FT deg	Gy g	14-18	2M+4D	M go	Ind	Ind	Ind	
Human Geography and Food Policy	DL48	3FT deg	S+Gy g	12-16	4M+2D	M go	Ind	Ind	Ind	
Human Geography and History	LV81	3FT deg	Gy+H g	12-16	4M+2D	M^ go	Ind	Ind	Ind	
Human Geography and Housing	KL4V	3FT deg	Gy g	14-18	2M+4D	M^ go	Ind	Ind	Ind	
Human Geography and Human Biology	BL18	3FT deg	S/Gy g	12-16	4M+2D	M go	Ind	Ind	Ind	
Human Resource Management and Human Geography	LN86	3FT deg	Gy	14-18	2M+4D	M go	Ind	Ind	Ind	
Management and Human Geography	LN81	3FT deg	Gy g	12-16	4M+2D	M go	Ind	Ind	Ind	
Marketing and Human Geography	LN85	3FT deg	Gy g	14-18	2M+4D	M go	Ind	Ind	Ind	
Nutrition and Human Geography	BL48	3FT deg	S+Gy g	12-16	4M+2D	M go	Ind	Ind	Ind	
Planning and Human Geography	KL48	3FT deg	Gy g	14-18	2M+4D	M go	Ind	Ind	Ind	
Social Policy and Human Geography	LL84	3FT deg	Gy g	12-16	4M+2D	M go	Ind	Ind	Ind	
Sociology and Human Geography	LL83	3FT deg	Gy g	12-16	4M+2D	M go	Ind	Ind	Ind	
Spanish and Psychology	LR8L	3FT deg	Sp+S g	14-18	2M+4D	D go	Ind	Ind	Ind	
Sports Science and Human Geography	BL68	3FT deg	Gy+S g	12-16	4M+2D	M go	Ind	Ind	Ind	
Tourism and Human Geography	LP87	3FT deg	Gy+L g	12-16	4M+2D	M go	Ind	Ind	Ind	
World Theatre and Human Geography	LW85	3FT deg	Gy g	14-18	2M+4D	M go	Ind	Ind	Ind	

Univ of ST ANDREWS

TITLE	CODE	COURSE	SUBJECTS	A/AS	NO/C	AGNVQ	IB	SQA(H)	SQA	RATIO A/AS
Environmental Biology-Geography	FC81	3FT/4FT deg	B/C/Gy/M/P g	BBB	Ind	Ind	30$	BBBB$	Ind	13
Environmental Geoscience	F840	3FT deg	B/C/Gy/M/P g	BCC	Ind	Ind	28$	BBBC	Ind	
Geography (Arts)	L800	4FT deg	* g	ABB	X	Ind	32$	BBBB	Ind	8
Geography (Science)	F800	3FT/4FT deg	B/C/Gy/M/P g	BBB	Ind	Ind	30$	BBBB$	Ind	12
Geography with French	F8R1	4FT deg	F+B/C/Gy/M/P g	BBB	Ind	Ind	30$	BBBB$	Ind	
Geography with French (with Integ Yr Abroad)	F8RC	4FT/5FT deg	F+B/C/Gy/M/P g	BBB	Ind	Ind	30$	BBBB$	Ind	
Geography with Spanish	L8R4	4FT deg	* g	ABB	X	Ind	32$	BBBB	Ind	
Geography-Art History	LV84	4FT deg	* g	BBB	X	Ind	32$	BBBB	Ind	

course details			98 expected requirements							96 entry stats
TITLE	CODE	COURSE	SUBJECTS	A/AS	NQ/C	AGNVQ	IB	SQA(H)	SQA	RATIO A/AS
Geography-Economics	LL18	4FT deg	* g	BBB	X	Ind	30$	BBBB	Ind	15
Geography-English	QL38	4FT deg	* g	BBB	X	Ind	30$	BBBB	Ind	9
Geography-French	LR81	4FT deg	F g	BBB	X	Ind	32$	BBBB$	Ind	
Geography-French with Year Abroad	LR8C	4FT/5FT deg	F g	BBB	X	Ind	32$	BBBB$	Ind	4
International Relations-Geography	LM81	4FT deg	* g	AAB	X	Ind	36$	AAAB	Ind	19
Management Sciences-Geography (Science)	FN81	4FT deg	M g	BBB	Ind	Ind	30$	BBBB$	Ind	14
Management-Geography (Arts)	NL18	4FT deg	* g	BBB	X	Ind	30$	BBBB	Ind	7
Management-Geography (Science)	FN8C	4FT deg	* g	BBB	X	Ind	30$	BBBB$	Ind	
Mathematics with Geography	G1F8	4FT deg	M g	BCC	Ind	Ind	28$	BBBC$	Ind	
Mathematics-Geography (Science)	GFC8	3FT/4FT deg	M g	BBB	Ind	Ind	30$	BBBB$	Ind	9
Mediaeval History-Geography	LVV1	4FT deg	* g	BBB	X	Ind	30$	BBBB	Ind	
Modern History-Geography	LV81	4FT deg	* g	BBB	X	Ind	30$	BBBB	Ind	7
Psychology-Geography	CL88	4FT deg	* g	ABB	X	Ind	32$	ABBB	Ind	
Scottish History-Geography	LV8D	4FT deg	* g	BBB	X	Ind	30$	BBBB	Ind	5
Social Anthropology with Geography	L6L8	4FT deg	* g	BBB	X	Ind	30$	BBBB	Ind	
Social Anthropology-Geography	LL68	4FT deg	* g	BBB	X	Ind	30$	BBBB	Ind	6
Spanish with Year Abroad-Geography	LR8K	4FT/5FT deg	* g	BBB	X	Ind	30$	BBBB	Ind	
Spanish-Geography	LR84	4FT deg	* g	BBB	X	Ind	30$	BBBB	Ind	
Statistics-Geography (Science)	FG84	3FT/4FT deg	M	BBB	Ind	Ind	30$	BBBB$	Ind	
Theological Studies-Geography	LV88	4FT deg								
General Degree of BSc Geography	Y100	3FT deg	B/C/Gy/M/P g	CCC	Ind	Ind	28$	BBBC$	Ind	
General Degree of MA Geography	Y450	3FT deg	* g	BBB	X	Ind	30$	BBBB	Ind	
THE UNIVERSITY COLLEGE OF ST MARK AND ST JOHN										
Development Studies/Geography	M9L8	3FT deg		8-10	MO	M	Ind	Ind	Ind	
Geography/Development Studies	L8M9	3FT deg	Gy	8-10	MO	M	Ind	Ind	Ind	
Geography/History	L8V1	3FT deg	Gy	10	MO	M	Ind	Ind	Ind	
Geography/Information Technology	L8G5	3FT deg	Gy	8-10	MO	M	Ind	Ind	Ind	
Geography/Leisure & Tourism Studies	L8P7	3FT deg	Gy	8-10	MO	M	Ind	Ind	Ind	
Geography/Physical Recreation Programmes	L8NR	3FT deg	Gy	8-10	MO	M	Ind	Ind	Ind	
Geography/Sociology	L8L3	3FT deg	Gy	8-10	MO	M	Ind	Ind	Ind	
Geography/Sports Science	L8B6	3FT deg	Gy	8-10	MO	M	Ind	Indd	Ind	
History/Geography	V1L8	3FT deg	H	12	MO	M	Ind	Ind	Ind	
Information Technology/Geography	G5L8	3FT deg		4	MO	M	Dip	CCCC	Ind	
Leisure & Tourism Studies/Geography	P7L8	3FT deg		8	MO	M	Ind	Ind	Ind	
Physical Recreation Programmes/Geography	N7LV	3FT deg		10	MO	M	Ind	Ind	Ind	
Sociology/Geography	L3L8	3FT deg	So	8	MO	M	Ind	Ind	Ind	
Sports Science/Geography	B6L8	3FT deg		8	MO	M	Ind	Ind	Ind	
ST MARY'S Univ COLL										
Environmental Investigation Studies and Biology	CF18	3FT deg	B/C	4-8	Ind	Ind	Ind	BBBB	Ind	
Geography	F800	3FT deg	Gy	10-14	Ind	Ind	Ind	BBBB	Ind	
Geography and Biology	FC81	3FT deg	Gy+B/C	4-8	Ind	Ind	Ind	BBBB$	Ind	
Geography and Classical Studies	FQ88	3FT deg	Gy	4-8	Ind	Ind	Ind	BBBB$	Ind	
Geography and Drama	FW84	3FT deg	Gy	8-12	Ind	Ind	Ind	BBBB$	Ind	
Geography and Education Studies	FX8X	3FT deg	Gy	4-8	Ind	Ind	Ind	BBBB$	Ind	
Geography and English	QF38	3FT deg	E+Gy	8-12	X	X	Ind	BBBB$	X	
Geography and Environmental Investigation St	FF98	3FT deg	S/2S+Gy	4-8	Ind	Ind	Ind	BBBB	Ind	
Geography and Environmental Studies	FFX8	3FT deg	Gy	4-8	Ind	Ind	Ind	BBBB	Ind	
Geography and Gender Studies	FM89	3FT deg	Gy	4-8	Ind	Ind	Ind	BBBB$	Ind	
History and Geography	FV81	3FT deg	Gy+H	8-10	Ind	Ind	Ind	BBBB$	Ind	
Irish Studies and Geography	FQ85	3FT deg	Gy	4-8	Ind	Ind	Ind	BBBB$	Ind	

			98 expected requirements							96 entry stats	
TITLE	CODE	COURSE	SUBJECTS	A/AS	ND/C	AGNVQ	IB	SQA(H)	SQA	RATIO	A/AS
Management Studies and Geography	FN81	3FT deg	Gy g	4-8	Ind	Ind	Ind	BBBB$	Ind		
Sociology and Geography	FL83	3FT deg	Gy	4-8	Ind	Ind	Ind	BBBB$	Ind		
Sport Science and Geography	FB86	3FT deg	Gy+S g	8-12	Ind	Ind	Ind	BBBB$	Ind		
STAFFORDSHIRE Univ											
Geography	F801	3FT deg	* g	16	4M+2D	M	28	AAB	Ind	8	8/20
Geography	F800	3FT deg	* g	16	4M+2D	M	28	AAB	Ind	8	10/18
Geography/American Studies	LQ84	3FT deg	g	CC	MO+2D	M	27	BBB	Ind	3	6/18
Geography/Applied Statistics	GL48	3FT deg	S	8	3M	M	24	BCC	Ind		
Geography/Biology	CL18	3FT deg	S/Gy	8	3M	M	24	BCC	Ind	9	
Geography/Business Studies	LN81	3FT deg	g	16	4M+2D	M	28	AAB	Ind	5	12/20
Geography/Chemistry	FL18	3FT deg	S g	8	3M	M	24	BCC	Ind		
Geography/Computing	GL58	3FT deg	*	8	3M	M	24	BBB	Ind	5	
Geography/Cultural Studies	LL86	3FT deg	g	CC	MO+2D	M	27	BBB	Ind	2	
Geography/Development Studies	LM8Y	3FT deg	g	14	4M+1D	M	26	ABB	Ind	6	8/14
Geography/Ecology	CL98	3FT deg									
Geography/Economic Studies	LL1V	3FT deg									
Geography/Environmental Studies	FL98	3FT deg									
Geography/French	LR81	3FT/4SW deg	F g	16	4M+2D	M^	28	AAB	Ind		
Geology/Geography	FL68	3FT deg	S g	8	3M	M	24	BCC	Ind	8	12/14
German/Geography	RL28	3FT/4SW deg	G g	16	4M+2D	M^	28	AAB	Ind	4	
History of Art and Design/Geography	VL48	3FT deg	g	16	MO+2D	M	28	AAB	Ind		
History/Geography	VL18	3FT deg	H g	CC	MO+2D	M	27	BBB	Ind	6	
Information Systems/Geography	GL5V	3FT deg	g	CC	4M+1D	M	24	BBB	Ind	2	
International Relations/Geography	ML1V	3FT deg	g	14	4M+1D	M	26	ABB	Ind	3	
Law/Geography	ML38	3FT deg	g	16	HN	M^	26	BBBB	Ind	4	
Legal Studies/Geography	ML3V	3FT deg	g	16	HN	M^	26d	BBBB	Ind		
Media Studies/Geography	FP84	3FT deg									
Philosophy/Geography	VL78	3FT deg	g	CC	MO+2D	M	27	BBB	Ind	2	
Physics/Geography	FL38	3FT deg	S g	8	3M	M	24	BCC	Ind		
Property with Geography	K2F8	3FT deg	g	12	4M	M$	24	BBC	Ind		
Psychology/Geography	LL78	3FT deg	g	18	3M+3D	Ind	30	AAA	Ind	9	
Recreation Geography and Environment	L830	3FT deg									
Sociology/Geography	LL38	3FT deg	g	CC	3M+1D	M	24	BBB	Ind	9	
Spanish/Geography	RL48	3FT/4SW deg	g	16	4M+2D	M^	28	AAB	Ind		
Sport Sciences and Geography	BF68	3FT deg	S	14	Ind	D	Ind	BBCC	Ind		
Women's Studies/Geography	ML98	3FT deg	g	CC	3M+1D	M	24	BBB	Ind		
Univ of STRATHCLYDE											
Geography and Planning	KL48	3FT/4FT deg	g	CCC	Ind		28	BBBBB$	Ind		
Arts and Social Sciences *Geography*	Y440	3FT/4FT deg	g	CCC	Ind		28	BBBBB$	Ind		
Univ of SUNDERLAND											
Biology and Geography	CL18▼	3FT deg	B+Gy/Gl g	10	N $	M	24$	CCCC$	N$	5	
Biology with Geography	C1L8	3FT deg	B/C	8	3M	M	Ind	Ind	Ind		
Business Studies and Geography	NL18	3FT deg	Gy/Gl g	12	3M $	M	24$	BCCC$	N$	6	
Business Studies with Geography	N1L8	3FT/4SW deg	*	8	3M	M	Ind	Ind	Ind		
Chemistry and Geography	FL18	3FT deg	C	8	3M	M	Ind	Ind	Ind		
Chemistry with Geography	F1L8	3FT deg	C	8	3M	M	Ind	Ind	Ind		
Computer Studies and Geography	GL58	3FT deg	Gy/Gl g	10	N $	M	24$	CCCC$	N$	5	
Computer Studies with Geography	G5L8	3FT/4SW deg	*	8	3M	M	Ind	Ind	Ind		
Economics and Geography	LL18	3FT deg	Gy/Gl g	10	N $	M	24$	CCCC$	N$	6	
Economics with Geography	L1L8	3FT deg	*	8	3M	M	Ind	Ind	Ind		

	course details		98 expected requirements							96 entry stats	
TITLE	CODE	COURSE	SUBJECTS	A/AS	ND/C	AGNVQ	IB	SQA(H)	SQA	RATIO A/AS	
English and Geography	QL38▼	3FT deg	El+Gy/Gl g	12	3M $	M	24$	BCCC$	N$	8	
English with Geography	Q3L8	3FT deg	*	10	4M	M	Ind	Ind	Ind		
French and Geography	RL18▼	4FT deg	F+Gy/Gl g	10	N $	M	24$	CCCC$	N$		
French with Geography	R1L8	4FT deg	F	8	3M	M	Ind	Ind	Ind		
Geography	L800	3FT deg	Gy g	12	MO	M	Ind	CCCC	N		
Geography and Geology	LF86	3FT deg	Gy/Gl g	10	N $	M	24$	CCCC$	N$	3	6/14
Geography and German	LR82▼	4FT deg	G+Gy/Gl g	10	N $	M	24$	CCCC$	N$		
Geography and History	LV81▼	3FT deg	H+Gy/Gl g	12	Ind	M	24$	BCCC	Ind	4	
Geography and History of Art and Design	LV84	3FT deg	*	8	3M	M	Ind	Ind	Ind		
Geography and Media Studies	LP84	3FT deg	*	24	Ind	Ind	Ind	Ind	Ind		
Geography and Philosophy	LV87▼	3FT deg	Gy/Gl g	12	3M	M	24$	BCCC	N	4	
Geography and Physiology	LB81	3FT deg	*	8	3M	M	Ind	Ind	Ind		
Geography and Politics	LM81▼	3FT deg	Gy/Gl g	12	Ind	M	24$	BCCC	Ind		
Geography and Psychology	LC88	3FT deg	Gy/Gl g	14	Ind	M	26$	BBCC$	Ind	6	
Geography and Sociology	LL83▼	3FT deg	Gy/Gl g	12	Ind	M	24	BCCC	Ind		
Geography with American Studies	L8Q4	3FT deg	Gy g	12	N $	M	24$	BCCC$	N$	5	
Geography with Biology	L8C1	3FT deg	*	8	3M	M	Ind	Ind	Ind		
Geography with Business Studies	L8N1	3FT deg	*	8	3M	M	Ind	Ind	Ind		
Geography with Chemistry	L8F1	3FT deg	*	8	3M	M	Ind	Ind	Ind		
Geography with Computer Studies	L8G5	3FT deg	*	8	3M	M	Ind	Ind	Ind		
Geography with Economics	L8L1	3FT deg	*	8	3M	M	Ind	Ind	Ind		
Geography with English	L8Q3	3FT deg	*	10	4M	M	Ind	Ind	Ind		
Geography with European Studies	L8T2	3FT deg	Gy/Gl g	12	3M $	M	24	BCCC$	N$	1	
Geography with French	L8R1	3FT deg	*	8	3M	M	Ind	Ind	Ind		
Geography with Gender Studies	L8M9	3FT deg	*	8	3M	M	Ind	Ind	Ind		
Geography with Geology	L8F6	3FT deg	*	8	3M	M	Ind	Ind	Ind		
Geography with German	L8R2	3FT deg	*	8	3M	M	Ind	Ind	Ind		
Geography with History	L8V1	3FT deg	*	10	4M	M	Ind	Ind	Ind		
Geography with History of Art and Design	L8V4	3FT deg	*	8	3M	M	Ind	Ind	Ind		
Geography with Media Studies	L8P4	3FT deg	*	24	Ind	Ind	Ind	Ind	Ind		
Geography with Philosophy	L8V7	3FT deg	*	8	3M	M	Ind	Ind	Ind		
Geography with Physiology	L8B1	3FT deg	*	8	3M	M	Ind	Ind	Ind		
Geography with Politics	L8M1	3FT deg	*	8	3M	M	Ind	Ind	Ind		
Geography with Psychology	L8C8	3FT deg	*	10	4M	M^	Ind	Ind	Ind		
Geography with Sociology	L8L3	3FT deg	*	10	4M	M	Ind	Ind	Ind		
Geography with Spanish	L8R4▼	3FT deg	*	8	3M	M	Ind	Ind	Ind	2	
Geology with Geography	F6L8	3FT deg	*	8	3M	M	Ind	Ind	Ind		
German with Geography	R2L8	4SW deg	G	8	3M	M	Ind	Ind	Ind		
History with Geography	V1L8	3FT deg	*	10	4M	M	Ind	Ind	Ind		
Media Studies with Geography	P4L8	3FT deg	*	24	Ind	Ind	Ind	Ind	Ind		
Philosophy with Geography	V7L8	3FT deg	*	8	3M	Ind	Ind	Ind	Ind		
Physiology with Geography	B1L8	3FT deg	*	8	3M	M	Ind	Ind	Ind		
Politics with Geography	M1L8	3FT deg	*	8	3M	M	Ind	Ind	Ind		
Psychology with Geography	C8L8	3FT deg	*	10	4M	M^	Ind	Ind	Ind		
Religious Studies and Geography	L8V8▼	3FT deg	Gy/Gl g	12	Ind	M	24	BCCC	Ind		
Sociology with Geography	L3L8	3FT deg	*	10	4M	M	Ind	Ind	Ind		

Univ of SUSSEX

Geography	F800	3FT deg	*	BBC	MO	M*6	$	Ind	Ind		
Geography and Env St in African & Asian Studies	LF8X	3FT deg	*	BBC	MO	M*6	$	Ind	Ind		
Geography and Env St in Cult & Community St	LF8Y	3FT deg	*	BBC	MO	M*6	$	Ind	Ind		
Geography and Env Studies with Development St	LF89	3FT deg	*	BBC	MO	M*6	$	Ind	Ind		
Geography and Environmental Science	FF89	3FT deg	2(C/P/Ph) g	CCC	MO $	MS go	$	Ind	Ind		

			98 expected requirements							96 entry stats	

TITLE	CODE	COURSE	SUBJECTS	A/AS	NO/C	AGNVQ	IB	SQA(H)	SQA	RATIO	A/AS
Geography and Environmental St in European Studs	LFV9	4FT deg	* g	BBC	MO $	M*6 go	$	Ind	Ind		
Geography and Environmental St in Social Science	LFWY	3FT deg	*	BBC	MO	M*6	$	Ind	Ind		
Geography in African and Asian Studies	L8T5	3FT deg	*	BBC	MO	M*6	$	Ind	Ind		
Geography in Cultural and Community Studies	L8Y2	3FT deg	*	BBC	MO	M*6	$	Ind	Ind		
Geography in European Studies	L8T2	4FT deg	* g	BBC	MO $	M*6 go	$	Ind	Ind		
Geography in Social Sciences	L8M9	3FT deg	*	BBC	MO	M*6	$	Ind	Ind		
Geography with Development Studies	L8MY	3FT deg	*	BBC	MO	M*6	$	Ind	Ind		

Univ of Wales SWANSEA

American Studies and Geography	LQ84	3FT deg	Gy	BBC	1M+5D$ Ind		30$	ABBBB$ Ind		12	
Anthropology and Geography	LL68	3FT deg	Gy	BBC	1M+5D$ Ind		30$	ABBBB$ Ind		4	
Biological Sciences and Geography	CL18	3FT deg	B+Gy	BBC-BCC	1M+5D$ Ind		28$	BBBBB$ Ind		6	16/24
Computer Science and Topographic Science	GF58	3FT deg	M+Gy	BCC	4D $ Ind		28$	BBBBC$ Ind		4	
Development Studies and Geography	LM89	3FT deg	Gy	BBC	1M+5D$ Ind		30$	ABBBB$ Ind		7	12/18
Economics and Geography	LL81	3FT deg	Gy g	BBC	1M+5D$ Ind		30$	ABBBB$ Ind			
Economics and Geography	LLC8	3FT deg	Gy g	BBC	1M+5D$ Ind		30$	ABBBB$ Ind		2	16/24
Geography	F800	3FT deg	Gy	BBC	1M+5D$ Ind		30$	ABBBB$ Ind		4	16/26
Geography	L820	3FT deg	Gy	BBC	1M+5D$ Ind		30$	ABBBB$ Ind		11	
Geography	L800	3FT deg	Gy	BBC	1M+5D$ Ind		30$	ABBBB$ Ind		4	16/28
Geography and Social Policy	LL48	3FT deg	Gy	BBC-BCC	1M+5D$ Ind		30$	BBBBB$ Ind		3	
Geography and Sociology	LL38	3FT deg	Gy	BBC	1M+5D$ Ind		30$	ABBBB$ Ind		7	
Geography and Topographic Science	F860	3FT deg	Gy	BCC	1M+4D$ Ind		28$	BBBBC$ Ind		4	16/26
Geography with European Studies	F8T2	4FT deg	Gy	BBC	1M+5D$ Ind		30$	ABBBB$ Ind		3	20/28
Geography/Economics	LL18	3FT deg	Gy g	BBC	1M+5D$ Ind		30$	ABBBB$ Ind		2	14/18
Geography/English	LQ83	3FT deg	E+Gy	BBB	X X		32$	AABBB$ Ind			
Geography/French	LR81	4FT deg	F+Gy	BBC	1M+5D$ Ind		30$	ABBBB$ Ind		13	
German/Geography	LR82	4FT deg	G+Gy	BBC	1M+5D$ Ind		30$	ABBBB$ Ind		4	
History/Geography	LV81	3FT deg	Gy	BBB-BBC	1M+5D$ Ind		30$	ABBBB$ Ind		8	
Italian/Geography	LR83	4FT deg	Gy+L	BBC	1M+5D$ Ind		30$	ABBBB$ Ind		1	
Mathematics and Topographic Science	GF18	3FT deg	M+Gy	20	Ind Ind		28$	BBBBC$ Ind		6	
Russian/Geography	LR8V	4FT deg	Gy+L	BBC-BCD	1M+5D$ Ind		28$	BBBBC$ Ind			
Welsh/Geography	LQ85	3FT/4FT deg	Gy+W	BBC-BCC	1M+5D$ X		30$	ABBBB$ Ind		4	
Joint Hons with defer choice of specialisation (inc Geography)	Y220	3FT deg	* g	20-22	1M+5D Ind		28	BBBBB Ind			

Univ of ULSTER

Geography (3 Yr)	F806▼	3FT deg	Gy g	CCD	MO+2D ML^ gi		27	BBCC Ind		47	
Geography Hons (3 Yr)	F800▼	3FT deg	Gy g	BCC	MO+4D DL^ gi		30	BBBB Ind		17	14/26
Geography Hons (4 Yr SW inc DAS)	F801▼	4SW deg	Gy g	BCC	MO+4D DL^ gi		30	BBBB Ind		12	18/26
Humanities Combined Geography	Y320▼	3FT/4SW deg	*	CCC	MO+3D D*6/^ gi		28	BBBC Ind			

UNIVERSITY COLL LONDON (Univ of London)

Anthropology and Geography BA	LL68	3FT deg	g	BBC	3M $ Ind		30$	BBBCC Ind		6	20/26
Anthropology and Geography BSc	LF68	3FT deg	g	BBC	3M $ Ind		30$	Ind Ind		3	
Economics and Geography	LL18	3FT deg	g	BBC-BBB	3M Ind		30$	BBBCC$ Ind		7	24/28
Environmental Geography	F830	3FT deg	Gy+S g	BBC-BBB	MO $ Ind		32$	BBBCC N$		6	20/26
Geography BA	L800	3FT deg	Gy g	BBC-BBB	MO $ Ind		32$	BBBCC$ N$		4	20/30
Geography BSc	F800	3FT deg	Gy+S g	BBC-BBB	MO $ Ind		32$	BBBCC$ N$		6	20/30

Univ of WESTMINSTER

Human Geography	L800	3FT deg	*	BC	MO+3D D		26	BBB			

Univ of WOLVERHAMPTON

Geography (Specialist Route)	F800	3FT deg		12	4M M		24	BBBB Ind		12	12/16

course details			98 expected requirements							96 entry stats	
TITLE	CODE	COURSE	SUBJECTS	A/AS	ND/C	AGNVQ	IB	SQA(H)	SQA	RATIO	A/AS
Geography (Specialist Route)	L800	3FT deg		12	4M	M	24	BBBB	Ind	9	10/18
Human Geography (Specialist Route)	L822	3FT deg		12	4M	M	24	BBBB	Ind	9	10/18
Physical Geography (Specialist Route)	F840	3FT/4SW deg	Gy g	DD	N	M	24	CCCC	Ind	6	6/12
Combined Degrees *Geography*	Y401	3FT/4SW deg		12	4M	M	24	BBBB	Ind		
Combined Degrees *Geography-Human*	Y401	3FT/4SW deg		12	4M	M	24	BBBB	Ind		

WORCESTER COLL of HE

Geography	L800	3FT deg		EE	N	P	Ind	Ind	Ind	7	4/16
Geography/Art & Design	WL98	3FT deg	A	DD	Ind	M	Ind	Ind	Ind	7	
Geography/Biological Science	CL18	3FT deg	S	EE	N	P	Ind	Ind	Ind		
Geography/Business Management	NL18	3FT deg		DD	Ind	M	Ind	Ind	Ind	12	
Geography/Economy and Society	LL18	3FT deg		DD	Ind	M	Ind	Ind	Ind		
Geography/English and Literary Studies	QL38	3FT deg		CC	Ind	M	Ind	Ind	Ind	3	
Geography/Environmental Science	FL98	3FT deg		EE	N	P	Ind	Ind	Ind	2	6/12
History/Geography	LV81	3FT deg		DD	Ind	M	Ind	Ind	Ind	5	
Information Technology/Geography	LG85	3FT deg		DD	Ind	M	Ind	Ind	Ind		
Psychology/Geography	LL87	3FT deg	g	CC	Ind	M	Ind	Ind	Ind		
Sociology/Geography	LL83	3FT deg		DD	Ind	M	Ind	Ind	Ind	5	
Sports Studies/Geography	LB86	3FT deg		CC	Ind	M	Ind	Ind	Ind		
Urban Studies/Biological Science	CL1V	3FT deg	S	DE	Ind	Ind	Ind	Ind	Ind		
Urban Studies/Business Management	NL1V	3FT deg		DD	Ind	M	Ind	Ind	Ind	3	
Urban Studies/Drama	WL4V	3FT deg		DD	Ind	M	Ind	Ind	Ind		
Urban Studies/Education Studies	XL9V	3FT deg		DD	Ind	M	Ind	Ind	Ind		
Urban Studies/English and Literary Studies	QL3V	3FT deg		CC	Ind	M	Ind	Ind	Ind		
Urban Studies/Geography	L822	3FT deg		DE	Ind	Ind	Ind	Ind	Ind		
Urban Studies/Health Studies	BL9V	3FT deg	g	DD	Ind	M	Ind	Ind	Ind		
Urban Studies/History	VL1V	3FT deg		DD	Ind	M	Ind	Ind	Ind		
Urban Studies/Information Technology	GL5V	3FT deg		DD	Ind	M	Ind	Ind	Ind		
Urban Studies/Psychology	LL7V	3FT deg	g	CC	Ind	M	Ind	Ind	Ind	4	
Urban Studies/Sociology	LL3V	3FT deg		DD	Ind	M	Ind	Ind	Ind	3	
Women's Studies/Geography	LM89	3FT deg		DD	Ind	M	Ind	Ind	Ind	2	
Women's Studies/Urban Studies	LMV9	3FT deg		DD	Ind	M	Ind	Ind	Ind		

Geological Sciences 31

course details			98 expected requirements							96 entry stats	
TITLE	CODE	COURSE	SUBJECTS	A/AS	ND/C	AGNVQ	IB	SQA(H)	SQA	RATIO	A/AS
Univ of ABERDEEN											
Geography and Geology	FF86	4FT deg	3S/2S+M g	CCD	Ind	MS go	24$	BBBC$	Ind	4	
Geography-Geoscience	FF68	4FT deg	3S/2S+M g	CCD	Ind	MS go	24$	BBBC$	Ind		
Geography-Petroleum Geology	FF8P	4FT deg	3S/2S+M g	CCD	Ind	MS go	26$	BBBC$	Ind	6	
Geology-Petroleum Geology	F602	4FT deg	3S/2S+M g	CCD	Ind	MS go	26$	BBBC$	Ind	4	
Geoscience	F610	4FT deg	3S/2S+M g	CCD	Ind	MS go	24$	BBBC$	Ind		
Physics with Geology	F3F6	4FT deg	2S+M g	CCD	Ind	MS go	24$	BBBC$	Ind		
Univ of Wales, ABERYSTWYTH											
Earth, Planetary and Space Science	FF65	3FT deg	P+M g	18	3M+2D$	M^ g	29$	BBBCC$	Ind		
Environmental Earth Studies with Education	F6X9	3FT deg	2S g	18	2M+3D$	MS6 g	29$	BBBCC$	Ind		
Geography/Geology	FF68	3FT deg	Gy+S g	20	3M+2D$	MS^ g	30$	BBBCC$	Ind		
Geology	F600	3FT deg	2S g	18	3M+2D$	MS6 g	29$	BBBCC$	Ind		
Geology/Physics	FF36	3FT deg	M+P g	18	3M+2D$	MS^ g	29$	BBBCC$	Ind		
Information and Library St/an approved Sci Sub _Geology_	PY21	3FT deg	2S g	18	3M+2D$	MS6 g	29$	BBBCC$	Ind		
ANGLIA Poly Univ											
Animal Behaviour and Geology	CF1P▼	3FT deg		10	3M	P	Dip	BCCC	N	1	
Applied Geology	F610▼	3FT deg		10	3M	P	Dip	BCCC	N	4	
Biology and Geology	CF16▼	3FT deg	B	10	3M	P	Dip$	BCCC	N	4	
Chemistry and Geology	FF16▼	3FT deg	S g	10	3M	P go	Dip$	CCCC	N		
Communication Studies and Geology	FP63▼	3FT deg	Ap	14	6M	M+/^ go	Dip$	BBCC	Ind		
Computer Science and Geology	GF56▼	3FT deg	* g	10	2M	P go	Dip	BCCC	N	4	
Ecology and Conservation and Geology	DF26▼	3FT deg	* g	10	2M	M go	Dip	BCCC	N	2	
French and Geology	RF16▼	4FT deg	S g	12	4M	M+/^ go	Dip$	BCCC	Ind		
Geochemistry	F670▼	3FT deg	S	8	2M	P	Dip$	CCCC	N		
Geography and Geology	FF68▼	3FT deg	Gy g	10	3M	P go	Dip$	BCCC	N	5	8/10
Geology	F600▼	3FT deg	*	10	3M	P go	Dip	BCCC	N	7	
Geology and German	FR62▼	4FT deg	* g	12	4M $	M go	Dip	BCCC	Ind		
Geology and Italian	FR63▼	4FT deg	* g	12	4M	M go	Dip	BCCC	Ind		
Geology and Maths or Stats/Statistical Modelling	FG61▼	3FT deg	* g	10	3M	P go	Dip	BCCC	N		
Geology and Psychology	CF86▼	3FT deg	S g	16	8M	D go	Dip$	BBCCC	N	2	
Geology and Spanish	FR64▼	4FT deg	* g	12	4M	M go	Dip	BCCC	Ind		
Univ of Wales, BANGOR											
Geological Oceanography	F646	3FT deg	3S g	CCD	4M $	DS^ go	28$	BBBC$	Ind	6	14/24
BATH COLL of HE											
Remote Sensing and Geographic Information Systs	F644	3FT deg	S/Gy		N		Ind	$	$	1	
Univ of BIRMINGHAM											
Environmental Geoscience	F630	3FT/4FT deg	2S g	BBC-CCC	Ind	Ind	30	Ind	Ind		
Geology	F600	3FT/4FT deg	2S g	BBC-CCC	Ind	Ind	30	Ind	Ind	4	14/24
Geology and Archaeology	FV64	3FT deg	S g	BBB-CCC	Ind	Ind	30	Ind	Ind		
Geology and Geography	FF68	3FT deg	Gy g	BCC	Ind	Ind	30	Ind	Ind	4	18/26
Geology with Biology	F6C1	3FT deg	B+S g	BBC-CCC	Ind	Ind	30	Ind	Ind		
Physics with Geophysics	F3F6	3FT/4FT deg	P+M	BCC	Ind	Ind	30	Ind	Ind	18	
Resource and Applied Geology	F611	3FT/4FT deg	2S g	BBC-CCC	Ind	Ind	30	Ind	Ind		
Univ of BRISTOL											
Archaeology and Geology	VF66	3FT deg	S	BBC	Ind	D$^	28$	BBBBB	Ind	44	
Environmental Geoscience	F630	3FT deg	S g	BBC	Ind	D$^	30$	ABBBB	Ind	4	
Geography and Geology	FF86	3FT deg	Gy+S g	BBC-BCC	Ind	D$^	30$	BBBBB	Ind	12	20/28
Geology	F600	3FT deg	3S g	BCC	Ind	D$^	28$	BBBCC	Ind	7	16/28

course details			98 expected requirements							96 entry stats	
TITLE	CODE	COURSE	SUBJECTS	A/AS	NO/C	RGNVQ	IB	SQA(H)	SQA	RATIO	A/AS
Geology (MSci)	F603	4FT deg	3S g	BCC	Ind	D$^	28$	BBBBC	Ind	3	14/30
Geology and Biology	FC61	3FT deg	B+S g	BBC	Ind	D$^	32$	CSYS	Ind	16	
Geology with a Preliminary Yr	F608	4FT deg	g			D$^				10	

BRUNEL Univ, West London

Geology/Geography	FL68	3FT deg	Gy/Gl g	18	MO $	M* go	26$	BCCC$	Ind		
Human Geography/Geology	L8F6	3FT deg	Gy/Gl g	18	MO $	M* go	26$	BCCC$	Ind		

CAMBRIDGE Univ

Natural Sciences *Geological Sciences*	Y160▼	3FT deg	2(S/M) g	AAA-AAB	Ind		Ind	CSYS	Ind		

CARDIFF Univ of Wales

Environmental Geoscience	F630	3FT deg	S g	18	3M	MS	Ind	Ind	Ind	5	16/28
Exploration Geology	F620	3FT deg	S g	18	3M	MS	Ind	Ind	Ind	4	16/24
Geology	F600	3FT deg	S g	18	3M	MS	Ind	Ind	Ind	5	14/24
Preliminary Year *Environmental Geoscience*	Y121	4FT deg	*		3M		Ind	Ind	Ind		
Preliminary Year *Exploration Geology*	Y121	4FT deg	*		3M		Ind	Ind	Ind		
Preliminary Year *Geology*	Y121	4FT deg	*		3M		Ind	Ind	Ind		

CHELTENHAM & GLOUCESTER COLL of HE

Business Computer Systems and Geology	GF5P	3FT deg	S	8	MO	M	26	CCCC	Ind		
Business Computer Systems with Geology	G5FQ	3FT deg	*	8	MO	M	26	CCCC	Ind		
Business Management and Geology	NF16	3FT deg	g	8-12	5M+2D	MB3	26	CCCC	Ind		
Business Management with Geology	N1F6	4SW deg	*	12	4M+3D	MB3	26	CCCC	Ind		
Computing and Geology	GF56	3FT deg	S	8	MO	P3	24	CCCC	Ind		
Computing with Geology	G5FP	3FT deg	*	8	MO	P3	24	CCCC	Ind		
Countryside Planning and Geology	DF26	3FT deg	S	8	MO	MK	26	CCCC	Ind		
Countryside Planning with Geology	D2F6	3FT deg	*	8	MO	MK	26	CCCC	Ind		
Environmental Policy and Geology	FF69	3FT deg	S	8-10	MO	MK	26	CCCC	Ind		
Environmental Policy with Geology	F9F6	3FT deg	S g	8-10	MO	M3	26	CCCC	Ind		
Financial Management and Geology	NF36	3FT deg	S	8-12	5M+2D	M3	26	CCCC	Ind		
Financial Management with Geology	N3F6	4SW deg	*	8-10	MO	M3	26	CCCC	Ind		
Geography and Geology	FL6V	3FT deg	*	10	MO	M3	26	CCCC	Ind		
Geography with Geology	L8FP	3FT deg	*	8-12	MO	M3^	26	CCCC	Ind		
Geology and History	FV61	3FT deg	H+S	8-12	5M+2D	M3^	26	CCCC	Ind		
Geology and Hotel Management	FN67	3FT deg	*	8-12	MO	M3	26	CCCC	Ind		
Geology and Human Geography	FL68	3FT deg	S	8-12	MO	M3^	26	CCCC	Ind		
Geology and Human Resource Management	FN61	3FT deg	*	8-12	5M+2D	MB3	26	CCCC	Ind		
Geology and Information Technology	FG65	3FT deg	S	8	MO	M3	26	CCCC	Ind		
Geology and Marketing Management	FN65	3FT deg	*	8-12	5M+2D	MB3	26	CCCC	Ind		
Geology and Multimedia	FG6M	3FT deg	*	8-12	MO	M3^	24	CCCC	Ind		
Geology and Natural Resource Management	FF6X	3FT deg	S	8	MO	MS	26	CCCC	Ind		
Geology and Physical Geography	FF68	3FT deg	S	8	MO	M3	26	CCCC	Ind		
Geology and Sport and Exercise Sciences	BF66	3FT deg	S	12-16	MO	ML3	24	CCCC	Ind		
Geology with Business Computer Systems	F6GN	3FT deg	S	8	MO	M3	26	CCCC	Ind		
Geology with Business Management	F6N1	3FT deg	*	8-12	5M+2D	M3	26	CCCC	Ind		
Geology with Computing	F6GM	3FT deg	S	8	MO	M3	26	CCCC	Ind		
Geology with Countryside Planning	F6D2	3FT deg	*	8	MO	M3	26	CCCC	Ind		
Geology with Environmental Policy	F6FX	3FT deg	*	8-10	MO	M3	26	CCCC	Ind		
Geology with Financial Management	F6N3	3FT deg	*	8	MO	M3	26	CCCC	Ind		
Geology with Geography	F6LV	3FT deg	S	8-12	MO	M3^	24	CCCC	Ind		

course details			98 expected requirements							96 entry stats	
TITLE	CODE	COURSE	SUBJECTS	A/AS	NO/C	AGNVQ	IB	SQA(H)	SQA	RATIO	A/AS
Geology with History	F6V1	3FT deg	H+S	8-12	MO	M3	26	CCCC	Ind		
Geology with Hotel Management	F6N7	3FT deg	*	8-12	MO	M3	26	CCCC	Ind		
Geology with Human Geography	F6L8	3FT deg	S	8-12	MO	M3	26	CCCC	Ind		
Geology with Human Resource Management	F6NC	3FT deg	*	8	MO	M3	26	CCCC	Ind		
Geology with Information Technology	F6G5	3FT deg	S	8	MO	M3	26	CCCC	Ind		
Geology with Marketing Management	F6N5	3FT deg	*	8	MO	M3	26	CCCC	Ind		
Geology with Modern Languages (French)	F6R1	3FT deg	S g	8	MO	M3	26	CCCC	Ind		
Geology with Multimedia	FGPM	3FT deg	*	8-12	MO	M3^	24	CCCC	Ind		
Geology with Natural Resource Management	F6F9	3FT deg	S	8	MO	M3	26	CCCC	Ind		
Geology with Physical Geography	F6F8	3FT deg	S	8-12	MO	M3	26	CCCC	Ind		
Geology with Religious Studies	F6V8	3FT deg	*	8	MO	M3	26	CCCC	Ind		
Geology with Sport and Exercise Sciences	F6B6	3FT deg	S	8-12	MO	M3	26	CCCC	Ind		
History with Geology	V1F6	3FT deg	H	8-12	5M+2D	M3^	26	CCCC	Ind		
Hotel Management with Geology	N7F6	4SW deg	*	10-14	5M-2D	MH3	26	CCCC	Ind		
Human Geography with Geology	L8F6	3FT deg	*	10-12	4M+3D	M3	26	CCCC	Ind		
Human Resource Mgt with Geology	N1FP	4SW deg	*	8-12	MO	MB3	26	CCCC	Ind		
Information Technology with Geology	G5F6	3FT/4SW deg	*	8	MO	M3	24	CCCC	Ind		
Marketing Management with Geology	N5F6	4SW deg	*	8-12	MO	MB3	26	CCCC	Ind		
Multimedia with Geology	GFMQ	4SW deg	*	8-12	MO	MI3	24	CCCC	Ind		
Multimedia with Geology	GFMP	3FT deg	*	8-12	MO	MI3	24	CCCC	Ind		
Natural Resource Mgt with Geology	F9FP	3FT deg	*	8	MO	MS	26	CCCC	Ind		
Physical Geography with Geology	F8F6	3FT deg	*	8-12	MO	M3^	26	CCCC	Ind		
Sport & Exercise Sciences with Geology	B6F6	3FT deg	*	12-16	MO	M3^	26	CCCC	Ind		

Univ of DERBY

TITLE	CODE	COURSE	SUBJECTS	A/AS	NO/C	AGNVQ	IB	SQA(H)	SQA	RATIO	A/AS
Applied Environmental Earth Science	F630	3FT deg	g	10	N $	MS	26	CCCC	Ind		
Biology and Geology	CF16	3FT deg	S	10	N $	MS	26$	CCCD$	Ind	8	
Chemistry and Geology	FF16	3FT deg	S	10	N $	MS	26$	CCCD$	Ind		
Environmental Monitoring & Management & Geology	FF9P	3FT deg	S	10	N $	MS	26$	CCCD$	Ind		
Environmental Studies and Geology	FF96	3FT deg	S	10	N $	MS	26$	CCCD	Ind		
Geography and Geology	FF86	3FT deg	Gy/Gl	10	N $	MS	26$	CCCD$	Ind	5	8/20
Geology	F600	3FT deg	*	10	N $	MS	26$	CCCD	Ind	4	4/16
Geology	F601	4FT deg		10	N $	MS	26$	CCCD	Ind		
Credit Accumulation Modular Scheme Geology	Y600	3FT deg	*	8	MO	M	Ind	CCCC	Ind		
Science (Combined Science/Geology)	16YF	2FT HND	S	4	N	PS	Dip$	DDD$	Ind	1	

Univ of DURHAM

TITLE	CODE	COURSE	SUBJECTS	A/AS	NO/C	AGNVQ	IB	SQA(H)	SQA	RATIO	A/AS
Environmental Geoscience	F630	3FT deg									
Geology	F600	3FT deg	2S	16-20	4M	Ind	28$	AABBB$	Ind	4	18/30
Geology/Geophysics	F640	3FT deg	M+P	16-20	4M	Ind	28$	AABBB$	Ind	11	22/26
Natural Sciences Geology	Y160	3FT deg	2S	ABB	Ind	X	33	CSYS	X		

Univ of EAST ANGLIA

TITLE	CODE	COURSE	SUBJECTS	A/AS	NO/C	AGNVQ	IB	SQA(H)	SQA	RATIO	A/AS
Environmental Earth Sciences	F630	3FT deg		BCC	Ind		29	BBBB	Ind	16	
Geophysical Sciences	F640	3FT deg	M+P	CCC	3M		29$	BBBB	Ind	8	18/22
Geophysical Sciences w a Yr in Europe(4 Yrs)	F642	4FT deg	M+P	AAA	DO		35$	AAAA	Ind		
Geophysical Sciences w a Yr in N America(4 Yrs)	F641	4FT deg	M+P	AAA	DO		35$	AAAA	Ind	13	

Univ of EDINBURGH

TITLE	CODE	COURSE	SUBJECTS	A/AS	NO/C	AGNVQ	IB	SQA(H)	SQA	RATIO	A/AS
Environmental Geoscience	F630	4FT deg	2S g	CCC	MO $		Dip$	BBBB$	N$	6	18/26
Geology	F600	4FT deg	2S g	CCC	MO $		Dip$	BBBB$	N$	6	18/30
Geology and Physical Geography	FF68	4FT deg	2(Gy/S) g	CCC	MO $		Dip$	BBBB	N$	4	20/30
Geophysics	F650	4FT deg	M+P	CCC	MO $		Dip$	BBBB	N$	5	20/30

				98 expected requirements						96 entry stats	
TITLE	CODE	COURSE	SUBJECTS	A/AS	NO/C	RGNVQ	IB	SQA(H)	SQA	RATIO	A/AS
Univ of EXETER											
Industrial Geology	F605	3FT deg	S g	CC	MO	M$^	28$	Ind	Ind	4	8/20
Industrial Geology	606F	2FT HND	S g	D	MO	M$^	24$	Ind	Ind		2/ 8
Univ of GLAMORGAN											
Biological Science with Geological Science	C1F6	3FT/4FT deg	M/S g	DD	5M $	M$	Ind	Ind	Ind		
Chemical Science and Geological Science	FF16	3FT/4SW deg	M/S g	DD	5M $	M$	Ind	Ind	Ind		
Chemical Science with Geological Science	F1F6	3FT/4SW deg	M/S g	DD	5M $	M$	Ind	Ind	Ind	2	
Environmental Pollution Science with Geological	F9F6	3FT/4SW deg	M/S g	DD	5M $	M$	Ind	Ind	Ind		
Geological Sci and Environmental Pollution Sci	FF69	3FT/4SW deg	M/S g	DD	5M $	M$	Ind	Ind	Ind	3	
Geological Sci with Environmental Pollution Sci	F6F9	3FT/4SW deg	M/S g	DD	5M $	M$	Ind	Ind	Ind		
Geological Science and Biological Science	FC61	3FT/4SW deg	M/S g	DD	5M $	M$	Ind	Ind	Ind		
Geological Science and Minerals Surveying Sci	FJ61	3FT/4SW deg	M/S g	DD	5M $	M$	Ind	Ind	Ind	13	
Geological Science and Sports Science	BF66	3FT deg	M/S g	DD	5M $	M$	Ind	Ind	Ind		
Geological Science with Biological Science	F6C1	3FT/4SW deg	M/S g	DD	5M $	M$	Ind	Ind	Ind		
Geological Science with Chemical Science	F6F1	3FT/4SW deg	M/S g	DD	5M $	M$	Ind	Ind	Ind		
Geological Science with Geography	F6L8	3FT deg	M/S g	12	Ind	Ind	Ind	Ind	Ind		
Geological Science with Minerals Surveying Sci	F6J1	3FT/4SW deg	M/S g	DD	5M $	M$	Ind	Ind	Ind	6	
Geological Science with Sports Science	F6B6	3FT deg	M/S g	DD	5M $	M$	Ind	Ind	Ind		
Geoscience	F630	3FT deg	M/S g	DD	5M $	M$	Ind	Ind	Ind		
Minerals Surveying with Geological Science	J1F6	3FT/4SW deg	M/S g	DD	5M $	M$	Ind	Ind	Ind	1	
Sports Science with Geological Science	B6F6	3FT deg	M/S g	DD	5M $	M$	Ind	Ind	Ind		
Combined Studies (Honours) _Geological Science_	Y400	3FT deg	M/S g	8-16	Ind	Ind	Ind	Ind	Ind		
Joint Honours _Geological Science_	Y401	3FT deg	M/S g	8-16	Ind	Ind	Ind	Ind	Ind		
Major/Minor Honours _Geological Science_	Y402	3FT deg	M/S g	8-16	Ind	Ind	Ind	Ind	Ind		
Univ of GLASGOW											
Archaeology/Geology	FV66	4FT deg	2S	BBC-CCC N	M		24$	BBBB$	N	8	
Chemistry/Geology	FF16	4FT deg	C/M+S	BBC-CCC N	M		24$	BBBB$	N	6	
Civil Engineering with Geology (MEng or BEng)	H2F6	4FT/5FT deg	M+P	CCD	4M $	M$	24$	BBBB$	N$	9	
Computing Science/Geology	FG65	4FT deg	M+S	BBC-CCC N	M		24$	BBBB$	N		
Environmental Biogeochemistry	CF76	4FT deg	C/M+S	BBC-CCC N	M		24$	BBBB$	N	7	
Geography/Geology	FF68	4FT deg	2S	BBC-CCC N	M		24$	BBBB$	N	7	
Geology and Applied Geology	F600	4FT deg	2S	BBC-CCC N	M		24$	BBBB$	Ind	6	
Physics with Geology	F3F6	4FT deg	M+P	BBC-CCC N	M		24$	BBBB$	N	13	
Univ of GREENWICH											
Applied Geochemistry	F670	3FT/4SW deg	S g	12	3M		Dip	CCC	Ind		
Applied Geochemistry (Extended)	F678	4FT/5SW deg	g	4	Ind		Ind	Ind	Ind		
Earth & Environmental Sciences	FF69	3FT/4SW deg	* g	12	3M	Ind	Dip	CCC	Ind		
Engineering Geology	F612	3FT/4SW deg	g	12	3M	Ind	Dip	CCC	Ind		
Engineering Geology (Extended)	F618	4FT/5SW deg	g	4		Ind	Ind	Ind	Ind		
Geology	F600	3FT/4SW deg	* g	12	3M	Ind	Dip	CCC	Ind		
Geology & Physical Geography	FF68	3FT/4SW deg	* g	12	3M	Ind	Dip	CCC	Ind		
Geology (Extended)	F608	4FT/5SW deg	g	4	Ind	Ind	Ind	Ind	Ind		
Geology (MSci)	F601	4FT deg	2S g	18	Ind	D$	30	BBB	Ind		
Univ of HERTFORDSHIRE											
Applied Geology	F610	3FT deg	* g	12	3M $	M$ gi	24$	CCCC$	Ind		
Applied Geology/Applied Physics	F6F3	3FT deg	M+P g	12	3M $	M$ gi	24$	CCCC$	Ind		
Applied Geology/Applied Statistics	F6G4	3FT deg	* g	12	3M $	M$ gi	24$	CCCC$	Ind		
Applied Geology/Astronomy	F6F5	3FT deg	M g	12	3M $	M$ gi	24$	CCCC$	Ind		

Geological Sciences 31

course details			98 expected requirements							96 entry stats
TITLE	CODE	COURSE	SUBJECTS	A/AS	ND/C	AGNVQ	IB	SQA(H)	SQA	RATIO A/AS
Applied Geology/Business	F6N1	3FT deg	* g	18	4M+4D	M$ gi	26$	BBBC	Ind	
Applied Geology/Chemistry	F6F1	3FT deg	C g	12	3M $	MS gi	24$	CCCC$	Ind	
Applied Geology/Computing	F6G5	3FT deg	* g	12	3M $	M$ gi	24$	CCCC$	Ind	4
Applied Geology/Economics	F6L1	3FT deg	* g	12	3M	M$ gi	24$	CCCC$	Ind	
Applied Geology/Electronics	F6H6	3FT deg	* g	12	3M $	M$ gi	24$	CCCC$	Ind	
Applied Geology/Environmental Science	F6F9	3FT deg	* g	14	MO $	M$ gi	26$	BCCC$	Ind	6
Applied Geology/European Studies	F6T2	3FT deg	* g	14	MO $	M$ gi	26$	BCCC	Ind	
Applied Geology/Human Biology	F6B1	3FT deg	S g	12	3M $	MS gi	24$	CCCC$	Ind	
Applied Geology/Linguistic Science	F6Q1	3FT deg	* g	14	MO $	M$ gi	26$	BCCC$	Ind	
Applied Geology/Operational Research	F6N2	3FT deg	S g	12	3M $	M$ gi	24$	CCCC$	Ind	
Applied Geology/Philosophy	F6V7	3FT deg	* g	14	MO $	M$ gi	26$	BCCC$	Ind	
Applied Physics/Applied Geology	F3F6	3FT deg	M+P g	12	3M $	M$ gi	24$	CCCC$	Ind	
Applied Statistics/Applied Geology	G4F6	3FT deg	* g	12	3M $	M$ gi	24$	CCCC$	Ind	
Astronomy/Applied Geology	F5F6	3FT deg	M+g	12	3M $	M$ gi	24$	CCCC$	Ind	3
Business/Applied Geology	N1F6	3FT deg	* g	18	4M+4D	M$6 gi	26$	BBBC$	Ind	
Chemistry/Applied Geology	F1F6	3FT deg	C g	12	3M $	MS gi	24$	CCCC$	Ind	
Computing/Applied Geology	G5F6	3FT deg	* g	12	3M $	M$ gi	24$	CCCC$	Ind	6
Economics/Applied Geology	L1F6	3FT deg	* g	12	3M $	M$ gi	24$	CCCC$	Ind	
Electronics/Applied Geology	H6F6	3FT deg	* g	12	3M $	M$ gi	24$	CCCC$	Ind	
Environmental Geology	F630	3FT/4SW deg	S g	14-18	4M	Ind	24	BBCCC	Ind	12
Environmental Geology (Extended)	F638▼	4EXT deg	* g	4	N $	Ind	Dip$	DDDD$	Ind	
Environmental Science/Applied Geology	F9F6	3FT deg	* g	14	MO $	M$ gi	26$	BCCC$	Ind	
European Studies/Applied Geology	T2F6	3FT deg	* g	14	MO $	Ind	26$	BCCC$	Ind	
Geology	F600	3FT/4SW deg	* g	14-18	4M	Ind	24	BBCCC	Ind	
Geology (Extended)	F608▼	4EXT/5EXTSW deg								
Geology with a year in Europe	F601	4FT deg	* g	14-18	4M	Ind	24	BBCCC	Ind	
Geology with a year in North America	F602	4FT deg	* g	14-18	4M	Ind	24	BBCCC	Ind	
Human Biology/Applied Geology	B1F6	3FT deg	S g	12	3M $	MS gi	24$	CCCC$	Ind	
Linguistic Science/Applied Geology	Q1F6	3FT deg	* g	14	MO $	M$ gi	26$	BCCC$	Ind	
Operational Research/Applied Geology	N2F6	3FT deg	* g	12	3M $	M$ gi	24$	CCCC$	Ind	
Philosophy/Applied Geology	V7F6	3FT deg	* g	14	MO $	M$ gi	26$	BCCC$	Ind	
Combined Modular Scheme *Applied Geology*	Y100	3FT deg	* g	12	3M $	M$ gi	24$	CCCC$	Ind	
Combined Modular Scheme *Applied Geology (Extended)*	Y108▼	4EXT deg	* g	4	N $	Ind	Dip$	DDDD$	Ind	

IMPERIAL COLL (Univ of London)

Environmental Geology	F631	4FT deg	M/P/C/Gl/Gy/En	22	Ind	Ind	Ind	Ind	Ind	1
Geological Sciences (MSci)	F640	4FT deg	M/P/C/Gl/Gy	18	Ind	Ind	Ind	Ind	Ind	6
Geology	F600	3FT deg	M/P/C/Gl/Gy	18	Ind		Ind	Ind	Ind	6 18/30
Geology and Geophysics (MSci)	F641	4FT deg	M/P/C/Gl/Gy	18	Ind	Ind	Ind	Ind	Ind	
Petroleum Geology (MSci)	FJ61	4FT deg	M/P/C/Gl/Gy	18	Ind	Ind	Ind	Ind	Ind	

KEELE Univ

Biological and Medicinal Chemistry and Geology	FF6C	3FT deg	C g	BCC-CCC	Ind	M$^	26$	CSYS	Ind	
Electronic Music and Geology	FW6J	3FT deg	Mu+S g	BCC	Ind	D$^	28$	CSYS	Ind	
Finance and Geology	FN63	3FT deg	S g	BCC	Ind	M$^	28$	CSYS	Ind	
French/German and Geology (4 Yrs)	TF96	4FT deg	G g	BBC-BCC	Ind	Ind	28$	BBBB	Ind	
Geology	F600	3FT deg	S g	BCC-CCC	Ind	M$^	26$	CSYS	Ind	27
Geology and American Studies (4 Yrs)	QF46	4FT deg	* g	BCC	Ind	Ind	28	BBBB	Ind	
Geology and Ancient History	FV6D	3FT deg	S g	BCC	Ind	D$^	28$	CSYS	Ind	
Geology and Ancient History (4 Yrs)	VFD6	4FT deg	*	BCC	Ind	Ind	28	BBBB	Ind	
Geology and Applied Social Studies	FL65	3FT deg	S g	BCC	Ind	D$^	28$	CSYS	Ind	
Geology and Applied Social Studies (4 Yrs)	LF56	4FT deg	*	BCC	Ind	Ind	28	BBBB	Ind	

course details | 98 expected requirements | 96 entry stats

TITLE	CODE	COURSE	SUBJECTS	A/AS	NO/C	AGNVQ	IB	SQA(H)	SQA	RATIO A/AS
Geology and Astrophysics	FF56	3FT deg	P g	BCC-CCC	Ind	M$^	26$	CSYS	Ind	
Geology and Astrophysics (4 Yrs)	FF65	4FT deg	*	BCC-CCC	Ind	Ind	26	BBBB	Ind	4
Geology and Astrophysics (MSci)	FF6M	4FT deg	P	BCC-CCC	Ind	M$^	26$	CSYS	Ind	
Geology and Biological & Medicinal Chem (4 Yrs)	FFC6	4FT deg	*	BCC-CCC	Ind	Ind	26	BBBB	Ind	
Geology and Biology	CF16	3FT deg	S g	BCC-CCC	Ind	M$^	26$	CSYS	Ind	
Geology and Biology (4 Yrs)	FC61	4FT deg	*	BCC-CCC	Ind	Ind	26	BBBB	Ind	1
Geology and Business Administration	FN69	3FT deg	S g	BCC	Ind	D$^	28$	CSYS	Ind	
Geology and Business Administration (4 Yrs)	NF96	4FT deg	*	BCC	Ind	Ind	28	BBBB	Ind	
Geology and Chemistry	FF16	3FT deg	C g	BCC-CCC	Ind	M$^	26$	CSYS	Ind	
Geology and Chemistry (4 Yrs)	FF61	4FT deg	*	BCC-CCC	Ind	Ind	26	BBBB	Ind	
Geology and Chemistry (MSci)	FF6D	4FT deg	C	BCC-CCC	Ind	M$^	26$	CSYS	Ind	
Geology and Classical Studies	FQ68	3FT deg	S g	BCC	Ind	D$^	28$	CSYS	Ind	
Geology and Classical Studies (4 Yrs)	QF86	4FT deg	*	BCC	Ind	Ind	28	BBBB	Ind	
Geology and Computer Science	FG65	3FT deg	S g	BCC-CCC	Ind	M$^	26$	CSYS	Ind	
Geology and Computer Science (4 Yrs)	GF56	4FT deg	*	BCC-CCC	Ind	Ind	26	BBBB	Ind	
Geology and Computer Science (MSci)	GF5P	4FT deg	S	BCC-CCC	Ind	M$^	26$	CSYS	Ind	
Geology and Economics	FL61	3FT deg	S g	BCC	Ind	D$^	28$	CSYS	Ind	
Geology and Economics (4 Yrs)	LF16	4FT deg	*	BCC	Ind	Ind	28	BBBB	Ind	
Geology and Educational Studies	FX69	3FT deg	S g	BCC	Ind	D$^	28$	CSYS	Ind	
Geology and Educational Studies (4 Yrs)	XF96	4FT deg	*	BCC	Ind	Ind	28	BBBB	Ind	
Geology and Electronic Music (4 Yrs)	WFJ6	4FT deg	*	BCC	Ind	Ind	28	BBBB	Ind	
Geology and Environmental Management	FFX6	3FT deg	S g	BCC	Ind	D$^	28$	CSYS	Ind	5
Geology and Environmental Management (4 Yrs)	FF6X	4FT deg	*	BCC	Ind	Ind	28	BBBB	Ind	
Geology and Finance (4 Yrs)	NF36	4FT deg	*	BCC	Ind	Ind	28	BBBB	Ind	
Geology and French	FR61	3FT deg	S+F g	BCC	Ind	D$^	28$	CSYS	Ind	1
Geology and French (4 Yrs)	RF16	4FT deg	*	BCC	Ind	Ind	28	BBBB	Ind	
Geology and French/German	FT69	3FT deg	F+G+S g	BBC	Ind	D$^	30$	CSYS	Ind	
Geology and French/Russian or Russian St (4 Yrs)	TFX6	4FT deg	* g	BBC-BCC	Ind	Ind	28	BBBB	Ind	
Geology and French/Russian or Russian Studies	FT6X	3FT deg	F+R+S g	BBC-BCC	Ind	D$^	28$	CSYS	Ind	
Geology and Geography	FL68	3FT deg	Gy g	BCC	Ind	M$^	28$	CSYS	Ind	4　14/26
Geology and Geography (4 Yrs)	LF86	4FT deg	*	BCC	Ind	Ind	28	BBBB	Ind	6
Geology and Latin	FQ66	3FT deg	Ln+S g	BCC	Ind	D$^	28$	CSYS	Ind	
Geology and Physics (MSci)	FF6H	4FT deg	P	BCC-CCC	Ind	M$^	26$	CSYS	Ind	
German and Geology	FR62	3FT deg	S+G g	BCC	Ind	D$^	28$	CSYS	Ind	
German and Geology (4 Yrs)	RF26	4FT deg	G	BCC	Ind	Ind	28$	BBBB	Ind	
German/Russian or Russian St and Geology	FT6Y	3FT deg	G+R+S g	BBC-BCC	Ind	D$^	28$	CSYS	Ind	
German/Russian or Russian St and Geology (4 Yrs)	TFY6	4FT deg	G	BCC	Ind	Ind	28$	BBBB	Ind	
History and Geology	FV61	3FT deg	S g	BCC	Ind	D$^	28$	CSYS	Ind	
History and Geology (4 Yrs)	VF16	4FT deg	*	BCC	Ind	Ind	28	BBBB	Ind	
International Politics and Geology	MFC6	4FT deg	*	BCC	Ind	Ind	28	BBBB	Ind	
International Politics and Geology	FM6C	3FT deg	S	BCC	Ind	D$^	28$	CSYS	Ind	
Latin and Geology (4 Yrs)	QF66	4FT deg	*	BCC	Ind	Ind	28	BBBB	Ind	
Law and Geology	FM63	3FT deg	S g	BBB	Ind	D$^	32$	CSYS	Ind	
Law and Geology (4 Yrs)	MF36	4FT deg	*	BBB	Ind	Ind	32	BBBB	Ind	
Marketing and Geology	FN65	3FT deg	S g	BCC	Ind	D$^	28$	CSYS	Ind	
Music and Geology	FW63	3FT deg	Mu+S g	BCC	Ind	D$^	28$	CSYS	Ind	
Music and Geology (4 Yrs)	WF36	4FT deg	*	BCC	Ind	Ind	28	BBBB	Ind	
Neuroscience and Geology	BF16	3FT deg	2S	BCC-CCC	Ind	M$^	26$	CSYS	Ind	
Neuroscience and Geology (4 Yrs)	BF1P	4FT deg	*	BCC-CCC	Ind	Ind	26	BBBB	Ind	
Philosophy and Geology	FV67	3FT deg	S g	BCC	Ind	D$^	28$	CSYS	Ind	
Philosophy and Geology (4 Yrs)	VF76	4FT deg	*	BCC	Ind	Ind	28	BBBB	Ind	
Physics and Geology	FF36	3FT deg	P g	BCC	Ind	M$^	28$	CSYS	Ind	

Geological Sciences 31

	course details			98 expected requirements						96 entry stats
TITLE	CODE	COURSE	SUBJECTS	A/AS	ND/C	AGNVQ	IB	SQA(H)	SQA	RATIO A/AS
Physics and Geology (4 Yrs)	FF63	4FT deg	*	BCC	Ind	Ind	28	BBBB	Ind	
Psychology and Geology	CF86	3FT deg	S g	BBB-BCC	Ind	D$^	28$	CSYS	Ind	
Psychology and Geology (4 Yrs)	FC68	4FT deg	*	BBB	Ind	Ind	32	ABBB	Ind	
Russian Studies and Geology	FRP8	3FT deg	S g	BCC	Ind	D$^	28$	CSYS	Ind	
Russian Studies and Geology (4 Yrs)	RF8P	4FT deg	*	BCC	Ind	Ind	28	BBBB	Ind	
Russian and Geology	FR68	3FT deg	R+S g	BCC	Ind	D$^	28$	CSYS	Ind	
Russian and Geology (4 Yrs)	RF86	4FT deg	*	BCC	Ind	Ind	28	BBBB	Ind	
Sociol & Social Anthropology and Geology (4 Yrs)	LF36	4FT deg	*	BCC	Ind	Ind	28	BBBB	Ind	
Sociology & Social Anthropology and Geology	FL63	3FT deg	S g	BCC	Ind	D$^	28$	CSYS	Ind	
Visual Arts and Geology	FW61	3FT deg	S	BCC	Ind	D$^	28$	CSYS	Ind	
Visual Arts and Geology (4 Yrs)	WF16	4FT deg	*	BCC	Ind	Ind	28	BBBB	Ind	

KINGSTON Univ

Applied Geology	F618▼	4EXT deg	*		Ind		Ind	Ind	Ind	
Applied Geology	F615	3FT deg	S g	10-12	N	Ind	Ind	Ind	Ind	9
Applied Geology with Business Management	F6ND	4FT deg								
Applied Geology with Business Management	F6N1	3FT deg		10-12	Ind	Ind	Ind	Ind	Ind	
Applied Geology with Business Management	F6NC▼	4EXT deg			Ind		Ind	Ind	Ind	
Earth Science	F640	3FT deg	S g	10-12	$	Ind	Ind	CCC	Ind	31
Earth Science	F648▼	4EXT deg	*		Ind		Ind	Ind	Ind	
Environmental Geology	F638▼	4EXT deg	*		Ind		Ind	Ind	Ind	1
Environmental Geology	F630	3FT deg	S g	10-12	$	Ind	Ind	CCC	Ind	5
Geography & Geology	FF86	3FT deg	Gy/S g	12	$	Ind	Ind	BCCC	Ind	6 8/10
Geology	F608▼	4EXT deg	*		Ind		Ind	Ind	Ind	4
Geology	F600	3FT deg	S g	10-12	$	Ind	Ind	CCC	Ind	3 6/18
Geology & Computing	FG65	3FT deg	S	10	3M $	Ind	Ind	CCC	Ind	3
Geology & Economics	FL61	3FT deg	S	10	N	Ind	Ind	CCC	Ind	
Geology & Physics	FF63	3FT deg	P g	10	3M $	Ind	Ind	CCC	Ind	
Geology and French	FR61	4FT deg	F/S g	10	$	Ind	Ind	CCC	Ind	

LANCASTER Univ

Geophysical Sciences	F640	3FT deg	M+P g	CCC	MO $		30$	BBBBB$	Ind	

Univ of LEEDS

Geography-Geology	FF68	3FT/4FT deg	Gy+C/M/P g	BCC	1M+5D$ Ind		28$	BBBBC	Ind	10 18/24
Geological Sciences	F600	3FT deg	2(Gy/M/S) g	BCC	1M+4D$ DS^ go		26$	BBBCC	Ind	5 12/26
Geophysical Sciences	F640	3FT deg	M+P g	BCC	1M+4D$ Ind		26$	BBBCC	Ind	7 20/26
Geophysical Sciences (North America)	F641	4FT deg	M+P g	AAB	Ind	Ind	Ind	Ind	Ind	1
Geosciences (North America)	F601	4FT deg	2(M/P/C)	AAB	Ind	Ind	Ind	Ind	Ind	

Univ of LEICESTER

Applied Geology	F611	4FT deg								
Applied Geology	F610	3FT deg	2S g	18	Ind	D$^ gi	28	BBBCC	Ind	11/20
Geology	F600	3FT deg	2S g	18	Ind	D$^	28$	BBBCC	Ind	10/22
Geology	F601	4FT deg								
Geophysics (Geological)	F641	4FT deg								
Geophysics (Geological)	F640	3FT deg	P+M g	18	Ind	D$^ gi	28$	BBBCC$	Ind	12/24
BSc with integrated foundation Geology	Y101	4EXT deg	* g		N	*			Ind	
Combined Science Geology	Y100	3FT deg	* g	CCC	MO $	D$^	28$	BBBCC$	HN	

Univ of LIVERPOOL

Geology	F600	3FT deg	2S g	20	MO $	Ind	31$	BBBCC$	Ind	6 12/26
Geology and Geophysics	F641	4FT deg	2S g	20	MO $	Ind	31$	BBBCC$	Ind	

	course details			98 expected requirements						96 entry stats	
TITLE	CODE	COURSE	SUBJECTS	A/AS	NO/C	AGNVQ	IB	SQA(H)	SQA	RATIO	A/AS
Geology and Physical Geography	F6F8	3FT deg	2S g	20	MO $	Ind	31$	BBBCC$	Ind	10	16/24
Geology with a European Language	F6TF	4FT deg	2S g	20	MO $	Ind	31$	BBBCC$	Ind		
Geophysics (Environmental Science)	F6F9	3FT deg	P+M g	18	MO $	DS^ go	31$	BBBCC$	Ind	7	
Geophysics (Geology)	F640	3FT deg	M+P g	18	MO $	DS^ go	31$	BBBCC$	Ind	6	14/20
Geophysics (Mathematics)	F6G1	3FT deg	M+P g	18	MO $	DS^ go	31$	BBBCC$	Ind	3	
Geophysics (Physics)	F656	3FT deg	P+M g	18	MO $	DS^ go	31$	BBBCC$	Ind	7	
Geophysics with Business Studies	F6N1	3FT deg	M+P g	18	MO $	DS^ go	31$	BBBCC$	Ind		
Geophysics with a European Language	F6T2	4FT deg	M+P g	18	MO $	DS^ go	31$	BBBCC$	Ind		
Arts Combined *Earth Sciences*	Y401	3FT deg	* g	BBC-BBB	Ind	Ind	30$	ABBB	Ind		
BSc Combined Honours *Earth Science*	Y100	3FT deg	2S	18	MO $	Ind	31$	BBBCC$	Ind		

LSU COLL of HE

Sport and Health Sciences with Ecology	BF66	3FT deg									

LUTON Univ

Biochemistry with Geology	C7F6	3FT deg	g	12-16	MO/DO	M/D	32	BBCC	Ind		
Biotechnology with Geology	J8F6	3FT deg	g	12-16	MO/DO	M/D	32	BBCC	Ind		
Built Environment with Geology	N8F6	3FT deg	g	12-16	MO/DO	M/D	32	BBCC	Ind		
Business Systems with Geology	N1FP	3FT deg	g	12-16	MO/DO	M/D	32	BBCC	Ind		
Business with Geology	N1F6	3FT deg	g	12-16	MO/DO	M/D	32	BBCC	Ind		
Contemp British & Euro History with Geology	V1F6	3FT deg	g	12-16	MO/DO	M/D	32	BBCC	Ind		
Ecology (Eco Tech) with Geology	C9F6	3FT deg	g	12-16	MO/DO	M/D	32	BBCC	Ind		
Environmental Geology	F630	3FT deg	g	12-16	MO/DO	M/D	32	BBCC	Ind		
Environmental Science with Geology	F9F6	3FT deg	g	12-16	MO/DO	M/D	32	BBCC	Ind		
Environmental Studies with Geology	F9FP	3FT deg		12-16	MO/DO	M/D	32	BBCC	Ind		
European Language Studies with Geology	T2F6	4FT deg	L g	12-16	MO/DO	M/D	32	BBCC	Ind		
Geography with Geology	F8FQ	3FT deg	g	12-16	MO/DO	M/D	32	BBCC	Ind		
Geological Technology	F645	3FT deg	g	12-16	MO/DO	M/D	32	BBCC	Ind		
Geology	F600	3FT deg	g	12-16	MO/DO	M/D	32	BBCC	Ind	28	
Geology and Applied Statistics	FG64	3FT deg	g	12-16	MO/DO	M/D	32	BBCC	Ind		
Geology and Biochemistry	CF76	3FT deg	g	12-16	MO/DO	M/D	32	BBCC	Ind		
Geology and Built Environment	NF86	3FT deg	g	12-16	MO/DO	M/D	32	BBCC	Ind		
Geology and Business	NF16	3FT deg	g	12-16	MO/DO	M/D	32	BBCC	Ind		
Geology and Business Systems	NFC6	3FT deg	g	12-16	MO/DO	M/D	32	BBCC	Ind		
Geology and Computer Science	GF56	3FT deg	g	12-16	MO/DO	M/D	32	BBCC	Ind		
Geology and Contemporary History	VF16	3FT deg	g	12-16	MO/DO	M/D	32	BBCC	Ind		
Geology and Ecology & Biodiversity	CF96	3FT deg	g	12-16	MO/DO	M/D	32	BBCC	Ind		
Geology and Electronic System Design	FH66	3FT deg	g	12-16	MO/DO	M/D	32	BBCC	Ind		
Geology and Environmental Science	FF96	3FT deg	g	12-16	MO/DO	M/D	32	BBCC	Ind		
Geology and European Language Studies	TF26	3FT deg	g	12-16	MO/DO	M/D	32	BBCC	Ind		
Geology and Geography	FF86	3FT deg	g	12-16	MO/DO	M/D	32	BBCC	Ind		
Geology with Animation	F6WF	3FT deg	g	12-16	MO/DO	M/D	32	BBCC	Ind		
Geology with Applied Statistics	F6G4	3FT deg	g	12-16	MO/DO	M/D	32	BBCC	Ind		
Geology with Biochemistry	F6C7	3FT deg	g	12-16	MO/DO	M/D	32	BBCC	Ind		
Geology with Biotechnology	F6J8	3FT deg	g	12-16	MO/DO	M/D	32	BBCC	Ind		
Geology with Built Environment	F6N8	3FT deg	g	12-16	MO/DO	M/D	32	BBCC	Ind		
Geology with Business	F6N1	3FT deg	g	12-16	MO/DO	M/D	32	BBCC	Ind		
Geology with Business Systems	F6NC	3FT deg	g	12-16	MO/DO	M/D	32	BBCC	Ind		
Geology with Comparative Literature	F6QF	3FT deg	g	12-16	MO/DO	M/D	32	BBCC	Ind		
Geology with Contemporary History	F6V1	3FT deg	g	12-16	MO/DO	M/D	32	BBCC	Ind		
Geology with Ecology & Biodiversity	F6C9	3FT deg	g	12-16	MO/DO	M/D	32	BBCC	Ind		
Geology with Electronic Systems Design	F6HQ	3FT deg		12-16	MO/DO	M/D	32	BBCC	Ind		

course details | 98 expected requirements | 96 entry stats

TITLE	CODE	COURSE	SUBJECTS	A/AS	NO/C	AGNVQ	IB	SQA(H)	SQA	RATIO A/AS
Geology with Environmental Science	F6F9	3FT deg	g	12-16	MO/DO	M/D	32	BBCC	Ind	
Geology with Geographical Information Systems	F644	3FT deg	g	12-16	MO/DO	M/D	32	BBCC	Ind	
Geology with Geography	FF6W	3FT deg	g	12-16	MO/DO	M/D	32	BBCC	Ind	
Geology with Health Science	F6B9	3FT deg	g	12-16	MO/DO	M/D	32	BBCC	Ind	
Geology with Human Biology	F6B1	3FT deg	g	12-16	MO/DO	M/D	32	BBCC	Ind	
Geology with Japanese	F6T4	3FT deg	L g	12-16	MO/DO	M/D	32	BBCC	Ind	
Geology with Journalism	F6P6	3FT deg	g	12-16	MO/DO	M/D	32	BBCC	Ind	
Geology with Leisure Studies	F6N7	3FT deg	g	12-16	MO/DO	M/D	32	BBCC	Ind	
Geology with Management	FN61	3FT deg	g	12-16	MO/DO	M/D	32	BBCC	Ind	
Geology with Mapping Science	F6F8	3FT deg	g	12-16	MO/DO	M/D	32	BBCC	Ind	
Geology with Marketing	F6N5	3FT deg	g	12-16	MO/DO	M/D	32	BBCC	Ind	
Geology with Mathematical Sciences	F6GC	3FT deg	g	12-16	MO/DO	M/D	32	BBCC	Ind	
Geology with Mathematics	F6GD	3FT deg	g	12-16	MO/DO	M/D	32	BBCC	Ind	
Geology with Media Production	F6PL	3FT deg	g	12-16	MO/DO	M/D	32	BBCC	Ind	
Geology with Multimedia	F6PK	3FT deg	g	12-16	MO/DO	M/D	32	BBCC	Ind	
Geology with Organisational Behaviour	F6L7	3FT deg	g	12-16	MO/DO	M/D	32	BBCC	Ind	
Geology with Physical Geography	F6FV	3FT deg	g	12-16	MO/DO	M/D	32	BBCC	Ind	
Geology with Plant Biology	F6C2	3FT deg	g	12-16	MO/DO	M/D	32	BBCC	Ind	
Geology with Politics	F6M1	3FT deg	g	12-16	MO/DO	M/D	32	BBCC	Ind	
Geology with Pollution Studies	FF69	3FT deg	g	12-16	MO/DO	M/D	32	BBCC	Ind	
Geology with Psychology	F6LR	3FT deg	g	12-16	MO/DO	M/D	32	BBCC	Ind	
Geology with Public Policy and Management	F6MC	3FT deg	g	12-16	MO/DO	M/D	32	BBCC	Ind	
Geology with Travel and Tourism	F6P7	3FT deg	g	12-16	MO/DO	M/D	32	BBCC	Ind	
Health Science and Geology	FB69	3FT deg	g	12-16	MO/DO	M/D	32	BBCC	Ind	
Human Biology and Geology	BF16	3FT deg	g	12-16	MO/DO	M/D	32	BBCC	Ind	
Law and Geology	FM63	3FT deg	g	12-16	MO/DO	M/D	32	BBCC	Ind	
Law with Geology	M3F6	3FT deg	g	12-16	MO/DO	M/D	32	BBCC	Ind	
Leisure Studies and Geology	FN67	3FT deg	g	12-16	MO/DO	M/D	32	BBCC	Ind	
Leisure Studies with Geology	N7F6	3FT deg	g	12-16	MO/DO	M/D	32	BBCC	Ind	
Literary Studies in English and Geology	FQ62	3FT deg	g	12-16	MO/DO	M/D	32	BBCC	Ind	
Literary Studies in English with Geology	Q2F6	3FT deg		12-16	MO/DO	M/D	32	BBCC	Ind	
Mapping Science and Geology	FF68	3FT deg	g	12-16	MO/DO	M/D	32	BBCC	Ind	
Mapping Science with Geology	F8F6	3FT deg	g	12-16	MO/DO	M/D	32	BBCC	Ind	
Marketing and Geology	FN65	3FT deg	g	12-16	MO/DO	M/D	32	BBCC	Ind	1
Marketing with Geology	N5F6	3FT deg	g	12-16	MO/DO	AGNVQ	32	BBCC	Ind	
Mathematical Sciences and Geology	FG61	3FT deg	g	12-16	MO/DO	M/D	32	BBCC	Ind	
Mathematical Sciences with Geology	G1F6	3FT deg	g	12-16	MO/DO	M/D	32	BBCC	Ind	
Mathematics and Geology	GF16	3FT deg	g	12-16	MO/DO	M/D	32	BBCC	Ind	
Media Production and Geology	FP6L	3FT deg	g	12-16	MO/DO	M/D	32	BBCC	Ind	
Modern History and Geology	FV6C	3FT deg	g	12-16	MO/DO	M/D	32	BBCC	Ind	
Modern History with Geology	V1FP	3FT deg	g	12-16	MO/DO	M/D	32	BBCC	Ind	
Organisational Behaviour and Geology	FL67	3FT deg	g	12-16	MO/DO	M/D	32	BBCC	Ind	
Physical Geography and Geology	FF6V	3FT deg	g	12-16	MO/DO	M/D	32	BBCC	Ind	17
Physical Geography with Geology	F8FP	3FT deg	g	12-16	MO/DO	M/D	32	BBCC	Ind	
Planning Studies and Geology	KF46	3FT deg	g	12-16	MO/DO	M/D	32	BBCC	Ind	
Plant Biology and Geology	CF26	3FT deg	g	12-16	MO/DO	M/D	32	BBCC	Ind	
Plant Biology with Geology	C2F6	3FT deg	g	12-16	MO/DO	M/D	32	BBCC	Ind	
Politics and Geology	FM61	3FT deg	g	12-16	MO/DO	M/D	32	BBCC	Ind	
Politics with Geology	M1F6	3FT deg	g	12-16	MO/DO	M/D	32	BBCC	Ind	
Psychology and Geology	FL6R	3FT deg	g	12-16	MO/DO	M/D	32	BBCC	Ind	
Psychology with Geology	L7FP	3FT deg	g	12-16	MO/DO	M/D	32	BBCC	Ind	
Public Policy and Management and Geology	FM6C	3FT deg	g	12-16	MO/DO	M/D	32	BBCC	Ind	

TITLE	CODE	COURSE	SUBJECTS	A/AS	NO/C	AGNVQ	IB	SQA(H)	SQA	RATIO A/AS
Public Policy and Management with Geology	M1FP	3FT deg	g	12-16	MO/DO	M/D	32	BBCC	Ind	
Travel and Tourism and Geology	FP67	3FT deg	g	12-16	MO/DO	M/D	32	BBCC	Ind	
Travel and Tourism with Geology	P7F6	3FT deg	g	12-16	MO/DO	M/D	32	BBCC	Ind	
Women's Studies and Geology	MF96	3FT deg		12-16	MO/DO	M/D	32	BBCC	Ind	
Women's Studies with Geology	M9F6	3FT deg		12-16	MO/DO	M/D	32	BBCC	Ind	
Geological Technology	446F	2FT HND	g	4-8	N/MO	P/M	26	CCDD	Ind	3

Univ of MANCHESTER

TITLE	CODE	COURSE	SUBJECTS	A/AS	NO/C	AGNVQ	IB	SQA(H)	SQA	RATIO A/AS
Biology and Geology	CF16	3FT deg	B g	BCD	3M+3D$	D^	26$	BBBCC$	Ind	9 18/22
Earth Sciences	F640	4FT deg								
Environmental and Resource Geology	F630	3FT deg	*	CCC	Ind	D^	24	BBBBB	Ind	3 14/20
Geochemistry	F670	3FT deg	C	CCC	Ind	D^	24	BBBBB	Ind	6
Geography and Geology	FF68	3FT deg	Gy	BCC	Ind	D^			Ind	4 12/24
Geology	F600	3FT deg	*	CCC	Ind	D^	24	BBBBB	Ind	5 14/26

MIDDLESEX Univ

TITLE	CODE	COURSE	SUBJECTS	A/AS	NO/C	AGNVQ	IB	SQA(H)	SQA	RATIO A/AS
Applied Earth Science	F640▼	3FT deg	* g	12	5M	M$ go	24	Ind	Ind	
Joint Honours Degree Geology	Y400	3FT deg	Gy g	12-16	5M	M$ go	28	Ind	Ind	
Joint Honours Degree Physical Geography	Y400	3FT deg	Gy g	10-12	5M	M$ go	24	Ind	Ind	

NENE COLLEGE

TITLE	CODE	COURSE	SUBJECTS	A/AS	NO/C	AGNVQ	IB	SQA(H)	SQA	RATIO A/AS
Earth Science with Fossils and Evolution	F9F6	3FT deg		DD	5M	M	24	CCC	Ind	
Ecology with Fossils and Evolution	C9F6	3FT deg		DD	5M	M	24	CCC	Ind	
Energy Management with Fossils and Evolution	J9F6	3FT deg	g	EE	3M	P	24	CCC	Ind	
Human Biological St with Fossils and Evolution	B1F6▼	3FT deg	S	DE	5M	M	24	CCC	Ind	
Ind Archaeology with Fossils and Evolution	V6F6	3FT deg		10	5M	M	24	CCC	Ind	

OXFORD Univ

TITLE	CODE	COURSE	SUBJECTS	A/AS	NO/C	AGNVQ	IB	SQA(H)	SQA	RATIO A/AS
Earth Sciences (4 Yrs)	F644	4FT deg	2S	ABB	DO		36	AAAAA	Ind	
Geology (3 Yrs)	F642	3FT deg	2S	ABB	DO		36	AAAAA	Ind	2 26/30

OXFORD BROOKES Univ

TITLE	CODE	COURSE	SUBJECTS	A/AS	NO/C	AGNVQ	IB	SQA(H)	SQA	RATIO A/AS
Applied Geology	F610	3FT deg	S/M g	DD	Ind	PS	Ind	Ind	Ind	5
Environmental Geotechnology	F644	3FT deg								
Geography and the Physical Environment/Geology	FFV6	3FT deg								
Geological Sciences	F600	3FT deg	S/M g	DD	Ind	PS	Ind	Ind	Ind	8 10/14
Geology/Accounting and Finance	FN64	3FT deg	S/M	DD-BCC	Ind	PS/D*3	Ind	Ind	Ind	
Geology/Biological Chemistry	CF76	3FT deg								
Geology/Biology	CF16	3FT deg	S/M g	DD	Ind	PS/MS	Ind	Ind	Ind	7
Geology/Business Administration and Management	FN61	3FT deg	S/M	DD-BBC	Ind	PS/MB4	Ind	Ind	Ind	
Geology/Cartography	FF68	3FT deg	S/M	DD-CC	Ind	PS/MS	Ind	Ind	Ind	3
Geology/Cell Biology	CFC6	3FT deg								
Geology/Combined Studies	FY64	3FT deg								
Geology/Computer Systems	FG66	3FT deg	* g	DD-BC	Ind	PS/MS	Ind	Ind	Ind	
Geology/Computing	FG65	3FT deg	S/M g	DD-BC	Ind	PS/MS	Ind	Ind	Ind	
Geology/Computing Mathematics	FG69	3FT deg	S/M g	DD-CD	Ind	PS/MS	Ind	Ind	Ind	
Geology/Ecology	FC69	3FT deg	S/M g	DD-CD	Ind	PS/MS	Ind	Ind	Ind	
Geology/Economics	FL61	3FT deg	S/M	DD-BB	Ind	PS/MS3	Ind	Ind	Ind	
Geology/Educational Studies	FX69	3FT deg	S/M g	DD-CC	Ind	PS/M*3	Ind	Ind	Ind	
Geology/Electronics	FH66	3FT deg	S/M	DD-CC	Ind	M$/PS	Ind	Ind	Ind	
Geology/Environmental Chemistry	FF61	3FT deg								
Geology/Environmental Policy	FK63	3FT deg								
Geology/Environmental Sciences	FF6X	3FT deg	S/M g	DD-CD	Ind	PS/DS	Ind	Ind	Ind	4

Geological Sciences 31

course details			98 expected requirements							96 entry stats	
TITLE	CODE	COURSE	SUBJECTS	A/AS	NO/C	AGNVQ	IB	SQA(H)	SQA	RATIO A/AS	
Geology/Exercise and Health	FB66	3FT deg	S/M g	DD	Ind	PS/MS	Ind	Ind	Ind		
Geology/Fine Art	FW61	3FT deg	S/M+Pf+A g	DD-BC	Ind	PS/MA^	Ind	Ind	Ind		
Geology/Food Science and Nutrition	DF46	3FT deg	S/M g	DD	Ind	PS/MS	Ind	Ind	Ind		
Geology/French Language and Contemp Studies	FR6C	4SW deg	F+S/M g	DD-CC	Ind	PS/M*^	Ind	Ind	Ind		
Geology/French Language and Literature	FR61	4SW deg	F g	DD-CC	Ind	PS/M*^	Ind	Ind	Ind		
Geology/Geography	FL68	3FT deg	S/M g	DD-BB	Ind	PS/MS	Ind	Ind	Ind	10	
Geotechnics/Geology	FH62	3FT deg	S/M/Ds/Es	DD-CC	Ind	PS/M$	Ind	Ind	Ind		
German Language and Contemp Stud/Geology	FR6F	4SW deg	S/M+G	DD-CD	Ind	PS/M*^	Ind	Ind	Ind		
German Studies/Geology	FR6G	4SW deg			Ind		Ind	Ind	Ind		
Health Care/Geology (Post Exp)	BF76	3FT deg		X		X	X	X			
History of Art/Geology	FV64	3FT deg	S/M g	DD-BCC	Ind	M*^/PS	Ind	Ind	Ind		
History/Geology	FV61	3FT deg	S/M	DD-BB	Ind	M*^/PS	Ind	Ind	Ind		
Hospitality Management Studies/Geology	FN67	3FT deg	S/M	DD-CC	Ind	M*3/PS	Ind	Ind	Ind		
Human Biology/Geology	BF16	3FT deg									
Information Systems/Geology	FG6N	3FT deg	M/S g	DD-BC	Ind	PS/M*	Ind	Ind	Ind		
Intelligent Systems/Geology	FG68	3FT deg	S/M	DD-CD	Ind	M*/PS	Ind	Ind	Ind		
International Applied Geology	F642	3FT deg	* g	DD	Ind	M$	Ind	Ind	Ind	2	
Law/Geology	FM63	3FT deg	S/M g	DD-BBB	Ind	PS/D*3	Ind	Ind	Ind	1	
Leisure Planning/Geology	FK6H	3FT deg									
Marketing Management/Geology	FN6N	3FT deg	S/M g	DD-BCC	Ind	PS/D*3	Ind	Ind	Ind	2	
Music/Geology	FW63	3FT deg	Mu+S/M g	DD	Ind	PS/M	Ind	Ind	Ind		
Palliative Care/Geology (Post Exp)	BFR6	3FT deg		X		X	X	X			
Planning Studies/Geology	FK64	3FT deg	S/M g	DD-CC	Ind	PS/M	Ind	Ind	Ind		
Politics/Geology	FM61	3FT deg	S/M g	DD-AB	Ind	PS/M*^	Ind	Ind	Ind		
Psychology/Geology	CF86	3FT deg	S/M g	DD-BBC	Ind	PS/M*^	Ind	Ind	Ind		
Publishing/Geology	FP65	3FT deg	S/M g	DD-BB	Ind	PS/M$3	Ind	Ind	Ind		
Rehabilitation/Geology (Post Exp)	BFT6	3FT deg		X		X	X	X			
Retail Management/Geology	FN65	3FT deg	S/M g	DD-CCD	Ind			Ind	Ind	Ind		
Sociology/Geology	FL63	3FT deg	S/M g	DD-BCC	Ind	PS/M*^	Ind	Ind	Ind		
Software Engineering/Geology	FG67	3FT deg	M/S g	DD-BC	Ind	PS/M*	Ind	Ind	Ind		
Statistics/Geology	FG64	3FT deg	S/M g	DD	Ind	M*/PS	Ind	Ind	Ind		
Telecommunications/Geology	FH6P	3FT deg									
Transport Planning/Geology	FN69	3FT deg	S/M g	DD-CC	Ind	PS/M*	Ind	Ind	Ind		
Water Resources/Geology	FH6F	3FT deg									
Extended Science 　Applied Geology	Y100	4FT deg	* g	EE	Ind	P*	Ind	Ind	Ind		
Extended Science 　Geological Sciences	Y100	4FT deg	* g	EE	Ind	P*	Ind	Ind	Ind		
Extended Science 　Geology	Y100	4FT deg	* g	EE	Ind	P*	Ind	Ind	Ind		

Univ of PAISLEY

Science with Geology	Y1F6	5SW deg	M g	CCC-EE	Ind	Ind	Ind	BCC$	Ind		

Univ of PLYMOUTH

Chemistry with Geology	F1F6	3FT deg	C g	CC	3M	MS^	Ind	CCCC	Ind		
Earth Sciences	FF69	3FT deg	Gl/Gy g	12	N $	MS	Ind	Ind	Ind	3	6/16
Ecology with Geology	D2F6	3FT deg	B g	14-16	4M $	MS^	Ind	BBC	Ind		
Geography with Geology	F8F6	3FT deg	Gy g	16-18	X	M$^	Ind	ABBB	Ind	15	14/20
Geological Sciences	F601	3FT deg	S g	12	4M	MS	Ind	CCC	Ind	6	12/18
Geology (Applied and Environmental)	F610	3FT deg	S g	Ind	N $	PS	Ind	Ind	Ind		
Geology with Astronomy	F6F5	3FT deg	S g	12	4M	MS	Ind	CCC	Ind	16	
Geology with Business	F6N1	3FT deg	S+Bu g	CCD	4M	MS	Ind	Ind	Ind		
Geology with Chemistry	F6F1	3FT deg	S+C g	12	4M	MS	Ind	CCC	Ind		

			98 expected requirements							96 entry stats
course details										
TITLE	CODE	COURSE	SUBJECTS	A/AS	NO/C	AGNVQ	IB	SQA(H)	SQA	RATIO A/AS
Geology with Computing	F6G5	3FT deg	S g	12	4M	MS	Ind	CCC	Ind	4
Geology with Ecology	F6D2	3FT deg	S+B g	12	4M	MS	Ind	Ind	Ind	2
Geology with French	F6R1	3FT deg	S+F g	12	4M	MS^	Ind	CCC	Ind	
Geology with Geography	F6F8	3FT deg	S+Gy g	16	4M	MS^	Ind	CCC	Ind	20
Geology with German	F6R2	3FT deg	S+G g	12	4M	MS^	Ind	CCC	Ind	
Geology with Hydrography	F6FV	3FT deg	S+P/C/M g	14	4M	MS	Ind	CCC	Ind	
Geology with Italian	F6R3	3FT deg	S g	12	4M	MS	Ind	CCC	Ind	
Geology with Languages	F6T9	3FT deg	S+L g	12	4M	MS^	Ind	CCC	Ind	
Geology with Ocean Science	F6F7	3FT deg	S g	14	4M	MS	Ind	CCC	Ind	8
Geology with Resources, Manuf & the Environment	F6FX	3FT deg	S g	12	4M	MS	Ind	CCC	Ind	9
Geology with Spanish	F6R4	3FT deg	S g	12	4M	MS^	Ind	CCC	Ind	
Geology with Statistics	F6G4	3FT deg	S g	12	4M	MS^	Ind	CCC	Ind	1
Mathematics with Geology	G1F6	3FT deg	M g	10-15	MO $	M$^	Ind	BBCC	Ind	
Modern Languages with Geology	T9F6	3FT/4SW deg	L g	C	Ind	Ind	Ind	Ind	Ind	
Ocean Science with Geology	F7F6	3FT deg	S g	14-16	5M $	M$	Ind	CCCC	Ind	16
Extended Science (Foundation year) Earth Sciences	Y108▼	1FT/4EXT deg	S	2	Ind	P$	Ind	Ind	Ind	
Extended Science (Foundation year) Geology	Y108▼	1FT/4EXT deg	S	2	Ind	P$	Ind	Ind	Ind	
Univ of PORTSMOUTH										
Applied Environmental Geology	F610	3FT deg	2S	12	3M	M$6/^	26	BBBB	Ind	4 8/16
Applied Environmental Geology	F618▼	4EXT deg	*		Ind	P*	Ind	Ind	Ind	1
Chemistry and Geology	FF16	3FT deg	C	10	3M	MS6/^	26	BBBB	Ind	
Chemistry and Geology	FF1P▼	4FT deg	*		Ind	Ind	Ind	Ind	Ind	
Civil Engineering with Engineering Geology(MEng)	H2F6	3FT/4SW deg	M+P/S	12-16	5M $	M$^	Dip	BCCC	Ind	1
Earth Sciences	F640	3FT deg	S	14	3M $	M$6/^	26	BBBB	Ind	
Earth Sciences (Extended)	F648▼	4FT deg								
Engineering Geology and Geotech (Ext Route Av)	F612	3FT deg	2S	12	3M	M$6/^	26	BBBB	Ind	2 6/22
Geographical Science and Geology (Extended)	FF6V▼	4FT deg	*		Ind	Ind	Ind	Ind	Ind	
Geology	F608▼	4EXT deg	*		Ind	P*	Ind	Ind	Ind	1
Geology	F600	3FT deg	S	14	3M $	M$6/^	26	BBBB	Ind	5 4/18
Geology and Geographical Science	FF68	3FT deg	Gy+S	16	4M $	M$6/^	26	BBBB	Ind	4 6/14
Palaeobiology and Evolution	F615	3FT deg	S	14	3M $	M$6/^	26$	BBBB	Ind	8/16
Palaeobiology and Evolution (Extended)	F616▼	4FT deg								
Urban Geoscience and Geohazard Assessment	FF86	3FT deg	S	14	3M $	M$6/^	Dip	BBBB	Ind	
QUEEN'S Univ Belfast										
Geography and Geology	FF86	3FT/4FT deg	Gy g	CCC	X	Ind	28$	BBBC	X	8 16/18
Geology	F600	3FT/4FT deg	* g	CCC	Ind	Ind	28$	BBBC	Ind	7 14/22
Physics with Geology	F3F6	3FT/4FT deg	P+M g	CCC	Ind	Ind	28$	BBBC	Ind	6
Univ of READING										
Environmental Geology	F630	3FT deg	M/C/P	18	4M+1D$	DS^ go	29$	BBBC$	Ind	
ROYAL HOLLOWAY, Univ of London										
Environmental Geology	F630	3FT deg	S/2S g	CCC	Ind	D^	Ind	Ind		4 12/18
Environmental Geoscience (MSci)	F631	4FT deg	S/2S	CCC	Ind	D^	Ind	Ind		
Geography and Geology	FF68	3FT deg	Gy+S/2S g	CCC-BCC	Ind	D^	Ind	Ind		5 16/24
Geology	F600	3FT deg	S/2S g	CCC	Ind	D^	Ind	Ind		3 12/24
Geology and Astrophysics	FF65	3FT deg	M+P	CCC-BCC	Ind	D^	Ind	Ind		6
Geology and Biology	FC61	3FT deg	B+C/S g	BBC-CCC	Ind	D^	28$	BBBCC$		8
Geology and Computing	FG65	3FT deg	M+S	BCC	Ind	D^	Ind	Ind		5
Geology and Mathematics	FG61	3FT deg	M	CCC-BCC	Ind	D^	Ind	Ind		
Geology with Environmental Studies	F6F9	3FT deg	S/2S g	CCC	Ind	D^	Ind	Ind		8

Geological Sciences 31

course details			98 expected requirements							96 entry stats	
TITLE	CODE	COURSE	SUBJECTS	A/AS	ND/C	AGNVQ	IB	SQA(H)	SQA	RATIO	A/AS
Geoscience (MSci)	F601	4FT deg	S/2S	CCC	Ind	D^	Ind	Ind			
Foundation Programme *Geology*	Y408	4FT deg									
Science Foundation Year *Geology*	Y100	4FT deg	*		Ind	Ind	Ind	Ind			
Univ of SHEFFIELD											
Archaeological Science and Geology	FF46	3FT deg	* g	BCC	5M+1D	D6/^	29	BBBB	Ind		
Environmental Geology	F600	3FT deg	2S g	CCC	6M $	DS^	28$	BBBC$	Ind	5	14/26
Environmental Geosciences	F9F6	3FT deg	Gy g	BCC	5M+1D$	D_^	29$	BBBB$	Ind	6	20/26
Univ of SOUTHAMPTON											
Chemistry with Geology	F1F6	3FT deg	C+S g	18	Ind	Ind	28$	CSYS	Ind	4	
Environmental Geology	F630	3FT deg	2S g	18-20	Ind	Ind	28$	BBBBC	Ind		
Geography with Geology	FF68	3FT deg	2S g	BBB	Ind	Ind	32	AABBB	Ind		
Geology	F600	3FT deg	2S g	18-20	Ind	Ind	28$	BBBBC$	Ind	7	12/28
Geology (MGeol)	F601	4FT deg	2S g	18-20	Ind	Ind	28$	BBBBC	Ind		
Geology with Biology	F6C1	3FT deg	B+S g	18-20	Ind	Ind	28$	BBBBC	Ind	3	12/24
Geology with Chemistry	F6F1	3FT deg	C+S g	18-20	Ind	Ind	28$	BBBBC$	Ind	2	
Geology with Computer Science	F6G5	3FT deg	M+S g	18-20	Ind	Ind	28$	BBBBC$	Ind		
Geology with Oceanography	F6F7	3FT deg	M+P/C/B+S g	18-20	Ind	Ind	28$	BBBBC	Ind	3	14/25
Geology with Physical Geography	F6F8	3FT deg	Gy+S g	18-20	Ind	Ind	28$	BBBBC	Ind	4	14/20
Geophysical Sciences	F640	3FT deg	M+P	CCC	Ind	Ind	26$	BBBCC	Ind	6	10/26
Marine Geosciences	FF67	3FT deg	2S g	18-20	Ind	Ind	28$	BBBCC$	Ind	3	12/16
Oceanography with Geology	F7F6	3FT deg	2S g	BCC-CCC	Ind	Ind	30$	BBBCC	Ind	6	16/22
Univ of ST ANDREWS											
Environmental Biology-Geology	CF16	3FT/4FT deg	B/C/Gy/M/P g	CCC	Ind	Ind	28$	BBBC$	Ind	6	
Environmental Geology	F630	3FT/4FT deg	B/C/Gy/M/P g	CCC	Ind	Ind	28$	BBBC	Ind	10	
Geochemistry	F670	3FT/4FT deg	C g	CCC	Ind	Ind	28$	BBBC$	Ind	5	
Geology	F600	3FT/4FT deg	B/C/Gy/M/P g	CCC	Ind	Ind	28$	BBBC$	Ind	9	20/22
Geology-Computer Science	FG65	3FT/4FT deg	M g	CCC	Ind	Ind	28$	BBCC$	Ind		
Geoscience	F640	3FT/4FT deg	B/C/Gy/M/P g	CCC	Ind	Ind	28$	BBBC$	Ind	23	
Management Sciences-Geology	FN61	4FT deg	M g	CCC	Ind	Ind	28$	BBBC$	Ind		
Management-Geology	FN6C	4FT deg	* g	CCC	X	Ind	28$	BBBC$	Ind		
General Degree of BSc *Geochemistry*	Y100	3FT deg	C g	CCC	Ind	Ind	28$	BBBC$	Ind		
General Degree of BSc *Geoscience*	Y100	3FT deg	B/C/Gy/M/P g	CCC	Ind	Ind	28$	BBBC$	Ind		
STAFFORDSHIRE Univ											
Applied Geology	F610	3FT deg	S g	12	4M	M^	24	BCC	Ind	4	4/16
Applied Geology	F619	4EXT deg	g	4	1M	P	24	CCC			
Earth Sciences	F640	3FT deg	Gy/Gl g	12	4M	M^	24	BCC	Ind		
Environmental Geology	F639	4EXT deg	g	4	1M	P	24	CCC			
Environmental Geology	F630	3FT deg	S g	12	4M	M^	24	BCC	Ind	10	
Foundation Applied Geology	F618	4EXT deg	*	4	N	P	24	CCC			
Foundation Biology and Geology	CF1P	4EXT deg	*	4	N	P	24	CCC			
Foundation Chemistry and Geology	FF1P	4EXT deg	*	4	N	P	24	CCC			
Foundation Environmental Geology	F638	4EXT deg	*	4	N	P	24	CCC			
Foundation Geology and Computing	FG6M	4EXT deg	*	4	N	P	24	CCC			
Foundation Geology and Electronics	FH6P	4EXT deg	*	4	N	P	24	CCC			
Foundation Geology and Physics	FF3P	4EXT deg	*	4	N	P	24	CCC			
Geology/Applied Statistics	FG64	3FT deg	S	8	3M	M	24	BCC	Ind		
Geology/Biology	CF16	3FT deg	S/Gy g	8	3M	M	24	BCC	Ind		

TITLE	CODE	COURSE	SUBJECTS	A/AS	ND/C	AGNVQ	IB	SQA(H)	SQA	RATIO A/AS	
			98 expected requirements							**96 entry stats**	
Geology/Ceramic Science	FJ63	3FT deg	S g	8	3M	M	24	BCC	Ind		
Geology/Chemistry	FF16	3FT deg	S	8	3M	M	24	BCC	Ind		
Geology/Computing	GF56	3FT deg	S	8	3M	M	24	BCC	Ind	26	
Geology/Ecology	CF96	3FT deg									
Geology/Electronics	FH66	3FT deg	S	8	3M	M	24	BCC	Ind		
Geology/Geography	FL68	3FT deg	S g	8	3M	M	24	BCC	Ind	8	12/14
Physics/Geology	FF63	3FT deg	S	8	3M	M	24	BCC	Ind		
Sport Sciences and Geology	BF66	3FT deg	S	14	Ind	D	Ind	BBCC	Ind		

Univ of SUNDERLAND

TITLE	CODE	COURSE	SUBJECTS	A/AS	ND/C	AGNVQ	IB	SQA(H)	SQA	RATIO	A/AS
Applied Geology	F611	3FT/4SW deg	* g	8	3M $	M$	24$	CCCC	N$	3	10/18
Applied Geology (Foundation)	F618▼	4EXT/5EXTSW deg	*		Ind	Ind	Ind	Ind	Ind		
Biology and Geology	CF16	3FT deg	B/C+Gy/Gl g	8	N $	M	24$	CCCC$	N$	2	
Biology with Geology	C1F6	3FT deg	B/C	8	3M	M	Ind	Ind	Ind		
Business Studies and Geology	NF16	3FT deg	Gy/Gl/S g	10	N $	M	24$	CCCC$	N$		
Business Studies with Geology	N1F6	3FT/4SW deg	*	8	3M	M	Ind	Ind	Ind		
Chemistry and Geology	FF16	3FT deg	C+Gy/Gl g	8	N $	M	24$	CCCC$	N$		
Chemistry with Geology	F1F6	3FT deg	C	8	3M	M	Ind	Ind	Ind		
Computer Studies and Geology	GF56	3FT deg	Gy/Gl g	8	N $	M	24	CCCC$	N$		
Computer Studies with Geology	G5F6	3FT/4SW deg	*	8	3M	M	Ind	Ind	Ind		
Economics and Geology	LF16	3FT deg	Gy/Gl g	8	N $	M	24	CCCC$	N$		
Economics with Geology	L1F6	3FT deg	*	8	3M	M	Ind	Ind	Ind		
English with Geology	Q3F6	3FT deg	*	8	3M	M	Ind	Ind	Ind		
Environmental Geology	F630	3FT/4SW deg	* g	8	3M $	M$	24$	CCCC	N$	4	6/14
Environmental Geology (Foundation)	F638▼	4EXT/5EXTSW deg	*		Ind	Ind	Ind	Ind	Ind		
French and Geology	RF16	4FT deg	F+Gy/Gl g	8	N $	M	24$	CCCC$	N$		
French with Geology	R1F6	4FT deg	F	8	3M	M	Ind	Ind	Ind		
Geography and Geology	LF86	3FT deg	Gy/Gl g	10	N $	M	24$	CCCC$	N$	3	6/14
Geography with Geology	L8F6	3FT deg	*	8	3M	M	Ind	Ind	Ind		
Geology and German	FR62	4FT deg	G+Gy/Gl/S g	8	N $	M	24$	CCCC$	N$		
Geology and History	FV61	3FT deg	*	10	4M	M	Ind	Ind	Ind		
Geology and History of Art and Design	FV64	3FT deg	*	8	3M	M	Ind	Ind	Ind		
Geology and Mathematics	FG61	3FT deg	M	8	3M	M	Ind	Ind	Ind		
Geology and Media Studies	FP64	3FT deg	*	24	Ind	Ind	Ind	Ind	Ind		
Geology and Philosophy	FV67	3FT deg	*	8	3M	M	Ind	Ind	Ind		
Geology and Physiology	FB61	3FT deg	*	8	3M	M	Ind	Ind	Ind		
Geology and Politics	FM61	3FT deg	*	8	3M	M	Ind	Ind			
Geology and Psychology	FC68	3FT deg	Gy/Gl g	12	3M $	M	24$	BCCC$	N$	1	
Geology and Religious Studies	FV68	3FT deg	*	8	3M	M	Ind	Ind			
Geology and Sociology	FL63	3FT deg	*	10	4M	M	Ind	Ind			
Geology and Spanish	FR64	4SW deg	*	8	3M	M	Ind	Ind			
Geology with American Studies	F6Q4	3FT deg	*	8	3M	M	Ind	Ind	Ind		
Geology with Biology	F6C1	3FT deg	*	8	3M	M	Ind	Ind	Ind		
Geology with Business Studies	F6N1	3FT deg	*	8	3M	M	Ind	Ind	Ind		
Geology with Chemistry	F6F1	3FT deg	*	8	3M	M	Ind	Ind	Ind		
Geology with Computer Studies	F6G5	3FT deg	*	8	3M	M	Ind	Ind	Ind		
Geology with Economics	F6L1	3FT deg	*	8	3M	M	Ind	Ind	Ind		
Geology with French	F6R1	3FT deg	*	8	3M	M	Ind	Ind	Ind		
Geology with Geography	F6L8	3FT deg	*	8	3M	M	Ind	Ind	Ind		
Geology with German	F6R2	3FT deg	*	8	3M	M	Ind	Ind	Ind		
Geology with History	F6V1	3FT deg	*	10	4M	M	Ind	Ind	Ind		
Geology with History of Art and Design	F6V4	3FT deg	*	8	3M	M	Ind	Ind	Ind		
Geology with Media Studies	F6P4	3FT deg	*	8	Ind	Ind	Ind	Ind	Ind		

course details			98 expected requirements							96 entry stats

TITLE	CODE	COURSE	SUBJECTS	A/AS	ND/C	AGNVQ	IB	SQA(H)	SQA	RATIO A/AS
Geology with Philosophy	F6V7	3FT deg	*	8	3M	M	Ind	Ind	Ind	
Geology with Physiology	F6B1	3FT deg	*	8	3M	M	Ind	Ind	Ind	
Geology with Politics	F6M1	3FT deg	*	8	3M	M	Ind	Ind	Ind	
Geology with Sociology	F6L3	3FT deg	*	10	4M	M	Ind	Ind	Ind	
Geology with Spanish	F6R4	3FT deg	*	8	3M	M	Ind	Ind	Ind	
German with Geology	R2F6	4SW deg	G	8	3M	M	Ind	Ind	Ind	
History with Geology	V1F6	3FT deg	*	10	4M	M	Ind	Ind	Ind	
Mathematics with Geology	G1F6	3FT deg	M	8	3M	M	Ind	Ind	Ind	
Media Studies with Geology	P4F6	3FT deg	*	24	Ind	Ind	Ind	Ind	Ind	
Philosophy with Geology	V7F6	3FT deg	*	8	3M	Ind	Ind	Ind	Ind	
Politics with Geology	M1F6	3FT deg	*	8	3M	M	Ind	Ind	Ind	
Religious Studies with Geology	V8F6	3FT deg	*	8	3M	M	Ind	Ind	Ind	
Sociology with Geology	L3F6	3FT deg	*	10	4M	M	Ind	Ind	Ind	

UNIVERSITY COLL LONDON (Univ of London)

TITLE	CODE	COURSE	SUBJECTS	A/AS	ND/C	AGNVQ	IB	SQA(H)	SQA	RATIO A/AS
Earth and Space Science	FF65	3FT deg	M+P g	BCC	MO $	Ind	30$	BBCCC$	N$	
Earth and Space Science (MSci)	FF6M	4FT deg	M+P g	BCC	MO $	Ind	30$	BBCCC$	N$	
Environmental Geophysics	F653	3FT deg	M+P g	BCC	MO $	Ind	30$	BBCCC$	N$	
Environmental Geophysics (MSci)	F652	4FT deg	M+P g	BCC	MO $	Ind	30$	BBCCC$	N$	
Environmental Geoscience	F630	3FT deg	2S g	BCC	MO $	Ind	30$	BBCCC$	N$	13
Environmental Geoscience (MSci)	F631	4FT deg	2S g	BCC	MO $	Ind	30$	BBCCC$	N$	18/22
Exploration Geophysics	F660	3FT deg	M+P g	BCC	MO $	Ind	30$	BBCCC$	N$	
Exploration Geophysics (MSci)	F661	4FT deg	M+P g	BCC	MO $	Ind	30$	BBCCC$	N$	
Geology	F600	3FT deg	2S g	BCC	MO $	Ind	30$	BBCCC$	N$	46
Geology (MSci)	F601	4FT deg	2S g	BCC	MO $	Ind	30$	BBCCC$	N$	16/30
Geophysics	F650	3FT deg	M+P g	BCC	MO $	Ind	30$	BBCCC$	N$	
Geophysics (MSci)	F651	4FT deg	M+P g	BCC	MO $	Ind	30$	BBCCC$	N$	
Palaeobiology	F610	3FT deg	2S g	BCC	MO $	Ind	30$	BBCCC$	N$	
Palaeobiology (MSci)	F611	4FT deg	2S g	BCC	MO $	Ind	30$	BBCCC$	N$	
Planetary Science	F654	3FT deg	2S g	BCC	MO $	Ind	30$	BBCCC$	N$	10
Planetary Science (MSci)	F655	4FT deg	2S g	BCC	MO $	Ind	30$	BBCCC$	N$	1 18/26
Physical Sciences *Geological Science*	Y100	3FT deg	S g	CCC-BCC $		Ind	28$	BCCCC$	N$	

			98 expected requirements							96 entry stats	
TITLE	CODE	COURSE	SUBJECTS	A/AS	ND/C	AGNVQ	IB	SQA(H)	SQA	RATIO	A/AS
Univ of ABERDEEN											
Biomedical Science (Molecular Biology)	B9C6	4FT deg	C+2S/C+M+S g	BBC	Ind	MS go	34$	AABB$	Ind		
Biomedical Science (Pharmacology)	B9B2	4FT deg	C+2S/C+M+S g	BBC	Ind	MS go	34$	AABB$	Ind		
Biomedical Science (Physiology)	B9B1	4FT deg	C+2S/C+M+S g	BBC	Ind	MS go	34$	AABB$	Ind		
Chemistry with Biomedical Sciences	F1B9	4FT deg	C+2S/C+M+S g	CCD	Ind	MS go	24$	BBBC$	Ind		
Health Science	B920	4FT deg	2S/M+S g	CCD	Ind	MS go	26$	BBBB$	Ind	2	
Human Life Sciences	B941	4FT deg	C+2S/C+M+S g	CCD	Ind	MS go	24$	BBBC$	Ind	4	
Univ of ABERTAY DUNDEE											
Medical Biotechnology	C9B9	4FT deg	B/C	DE	Ind	Ind	Ind	BCC	Ind		
ANGLIA Poly Univ											
Animal Behaviour and Biomedical Science	BC91▼	3FT deg	B	10	3M	P	Dip	BCCC	N	5	
Audiotechnology and Biomedical Science	HB6X▼	3FT deg	S	16	8M	D	Dip$	BBCCC	N		
Biology and Biomedical Science	CB19▼	3FT deg	B	10	3M	P	Dip$	BCCC	N	3	
Biology and Ophthalmic Dispensing	BC51▼	3FT deg	B	10	3M	P go	Dip$	BCCC	N	2	
Biomedical Science	B940▼	3FT deg	B	10	3M	P go	Dip$	BCCC	N	4	8/18
Biomedical Science & Instrumentation Electronics	BH96▼	3FT deg	B	10	3M	P go	Dip$	BCCC	N		
Biomedical Science and Chemistry	BF91▼	3FT deg	B	10	3M	P go	Dip$	BCCC	N	4	
Biomedical Science and Computer Science	BG95▼	3FT deg	B	10	3M	P go	Dip$	BCCC	N		
Biomedical Science and Ecology and Conservation	DB29▼	3FT deg	B	10	3M	P go	Dip$	BCCC	N		
Biomedical Science and Food Science	BD94▼	3FT deg	g	10	3M	P go	Dip	BCCC			
Biomedical Science and French	BR91▼	4FT deg	B g	12	4M	M+/^ go	Dip$	BCCC	N	1	
Biomedical Science and Geography	BF98▼	3FT deg	B+Gy g	10	3M	P go	Dip$	BCCC	N		
Biomedical Science and German	BR92▼	4FT deg	B g	12	4M $	M+/^ go	Dip$	BCCC	N		
Biomedical Science and Imaging Science	BW95▼	3FT deg	B g	10	3M	P go	Dip$	BCCC	N		
Biomedical Science and Italian	BR93▼	4FT deg	B g	12	4M	M+/^ go	Dip$	BCCC	N		
Biomedical Science and Maths or Stats/Stat Model	BG91▼	3FT deg	B g	10	3M	M go	Dip$	BCCC	N		
Biomedical Science and Ophthalmic Dispensing	BC59▼	3FT deg	B	10	3M	P go	Dip$	BCCC	N	3	
Biomedical Science and Psychology	BC98▼	3FT deg	B	16	8M	D go	Dip$	BBCCC	N		
Biomedical Science and Spanish	BR94▼	4FT deg	B g	12	4M	M+/^ go	Dip$	BCCC	N		
Business and Ophthalmic Dispensing	BN51▼	3FT deg	* g	10	3M	P go	Dip	BCCC	Ind	6	
Chemistry and Ophthalmic Dispensing	BF51▼	3FT deg	S g	10	3M	P	Dip$	BCCC	N		
Computer Science and Ophthalmic Dispensing	BG55▼	3FT deg	* g	10	3M	P go	Dip	BCCC	N		
Ecology & Conservation and Ophthalmic Dispensing	BD52▼	3FT deg	* g	10	3M	P go	Dip	BCCC	N		
French and Ophthalmic Dispensing	BR51▼	4FT deg	* g	12	4M	M+/^ go	Dip	BCCC	Ind		
German and Ophthalmic Dispensing	BR52▼	4FT deg	g	12	4M	M+/^ go	Dip	BCCC	Ind		
Imaging Science and Ophthalmic Dispensing	BW55▼	3FT deg	S	10	3M	P	Dip	BCCC	N		
Instrumentation Electronics & Ophthalmic Dispens	BH56▼	3FT deg	S g	10	3M	P go	Dip$	BCCC	N		
Italian and Ophthalmic Dispensing	BR53▼	4FT deg	* g	12	4M	M+/^ go	Dip$	BCCC	N		
Maths or Stats/Stat Mod. & Ophthalmic Dispensing	BG51▼	3FT deg	* g	10	3M	P go	Dip	BCCC	N	1	
Ophthalmic Dispensing and Psychology	BC58▼	3FT deg	S g	16	8M	D go	Dip$	BBCCC	N		
Ophthalmic Dispensing and Spanish	BR54▼	4FT deg	* g	12	4M	M go	Dip	BCCC	N		
Optical Management	BN5C▼	3FT deg	* g	10	3M	P go	Dip	BCCC			
ASTON Univ											
Optometry	B500	3FT deg	2S/S+M g	ABB-BBB	HN	X	32$	AABBB$	X	9	22/28
Optometry (Year Zero)	B508	4FT deg									
Univ of Wales, BANGOR											
Radiography and Diagnostic Imaging	B800	3FT deg	S g	14	5M+2D$	D$^ go	26$	BBCC$	Ind	6	
BARNSLEY COLL											
Health Studies	L450	3FT deg	* g	DD	5M	M*	Ind	Ind	Ind		
Health Studies	L451	2FT Dip	* g	D	5M	P*	Ind	Ind	Ind		

Health Care and Therapies 32

course details			98 expected requirements							96 entry stats	
TITLE	CODE	COURSE	SUBJECTS	A/AS	ND/C	AGNVQ	IB	SQA(H)	SQA	RATIO	A/AS
Science Foundation *Biomedical Science*	Y100	4EXT deg									
Univ of BIRMINGHAM											
Biomedical Materials Science	BJ95	3FT deg	2S g	BCC	6M+1D$	DS+^	32$	BBBBB	Ind	2	16/24
Medical Science	B900	3FT deg	2S g	BCC	7M $	DS+^	32$	BBBBB	Ind	6	20/28
Physiotherapy (Including State Registration)	B962	3FT deg	B g	BBB	DO	D$	32$	BBBBB$	Ind	19	22/30
BOURNEMOUTH Univ											
Health and Community Studies	B900	3FT deg	B/Ps g	10-12	MO	M$ go	Ind	CCCC	Ind	4	7/24
Health and Community Studies	B901	3FT deg	So/Ps g	10-12	MO	M$ go	Ind	CCCC	Ind	2	6/18
Univ of BRADFORD											
Biomedical Sciences	B940	3FT deg	2S g	BB-CCD	3M $	MS/M$4	Ind	Ind	Ind	3	12/22
Diagnostic Radiography (with State Registration)	B810▼	3FT deg	S g	CCC	3M+1D	D$	Ind	Ind	Ind		
Optometry	B500	3FT deg	2(P/B/C/M)	BBC	Ind	X	Ind	Ind	Ind	8	18/26
Physiotherapy (including State Registration)	B960	3FT deg	S g	BBC	MO+5D	D$^	Ind	Ind	Ind	15	18/28
BRADFORD & ILKLEY Comm COLL											
Consumer, Health & Community Studies	B900	3FT deg	*	8	MO	M	Dip	CCC	Ind		
Ophthalmic Dispensing	B502	2FT Dip									
Ophthalmic Dispensing	B503	3FT deg									
Ophthalmic Dispensing with Management	B5N1	3FT deg			Ind	P					
Beauty Therapy	018W	2FT HND	S	2	N	P		Ind	Ind		
Univ of BRIGHTON											
Biomedical Sciences	B940	3FT/4SW deg	Ap/B g	12	MO $	M$ go	Dip$	BBCC$	Ind		
Physiotherapy	B960	3FT deg	B	20-24	Ind	Ind	Ind	BBBCC$	Ind		
Podiatry	B985	3FT deg	S	12	3M $	M$	Ind	CCCC$	Ind		
BRISTOL, Univ of the W of England											
Environmental Health	B900	3FT/4SW deg	S g	12	4M $	MS go	24$	BCC$	Ind		
Physiotherapy	B960	3FT deg	B g	BBC	MO+3D	D6^ go	30$	BBBB$	Ind		
Professional Studies (1 Yr top-up post qual)	B999	1FT deg	g	X	X	X	X	X	X		
Psychology and Health Science	C8B9	3FT deg	* g	20	4M+2D$	M$6/^ go	28	BBBB	Ind		
Radiography (Diagnostic)	B810	3FT deg	S	12	4M $	M$ go	Ind	Ind	Ind		
Radiography (Therapeutic)	B820	3FT deg	S	12	4M $	M$ go	Ind	Ind	Ind		
Science Foundation Year *Environmental Health*	Y120	4EXT/5EXTSW deg	M/S g	E	N $	PS go	24$	Ind	N$		
BRITISH COLLEGE of NATUROPATHY and OSTEOPATHY											
Naturopathic Medicine	B111	4FT deg	B+C g	16	3M $			CCC	N$		
Osteopathic Medicine	B110	4FT deg	B+C g	16	3M $			CCC	N$		
BRUNEL Univ, West London											
Occupational Therapy	B970	3FT deg	B/M/So/Ps g	BCC	5D $	MG^	28$	BBBCC$	Ind		
Physiotherapy	B960	3FT deg	B g	BBB	DO $	D^ go	32$	AABBB$	Ind		
CANTERBURY CHRIST CHURCH COLL of HE											
Diagnostic Radiography	B810	3FT deg	* g	CC	MO	M	24	Ind	Ind	5	10/14
Health Science	B990	3FT deg	S g	CC	MO	M	24	Ind	Ind	5	
Health Science	B991	2FT dip	* g	D	Ind	Ind	24	Ind	Ind		
Occupational Therapy	B970	3FT deg	B/Ps/So g	CC	MO	M	24	Ind	Ind	10	8/24
Physical and Health Sciences	B900	3FT deg	S g	DD	Ind	Ind	24	Ind	Ind		
CARDIFF Univ of Wales											
Optometry	B500	3FT deg	2(M/P/B/C) g	ABB						13	20/30

TITLE	CODE	COURSE	SUBJECTS	A/AS	ND/C	AGNVQ	IB	SQA(H)	SQA	RATIO A/AS	

course details — **98 expected requirements** — *96 entry stats*

Univ of Wales INST, CARDIFF

Biomedical Sciences	B940	3FT/4SW deg	B+C g	10	3M	DS go	Ind	CCCC	Ind	3	6/16
Dental Technology	B920	3FT deg	S g	EE	N	MS go	Ind	CCCC	Ind		
Environmental Health	B900	3FT/4SW deg	S g	12	4M	MS go	Ind	CCCC	Ind	6	8/22
Podiatry	B985	3FT deg	S g	4	4M	D$ go	Ind	CCCC	Ind	3	6/18
Speech and Language Therapy	B950	4FT deg	* g	BCC	1M+5D	D$^ go	Ind	CCCC	Ind	19	18/26
Technology for Healthcare	H6B8	3FT deg	* g	4	N	P$ go	Ind	CCCC	Ind		
Biomedical Sciences	049B	2FT/3SW HND	B/C g	2	N	PS go	Ind	CC	Ind		2/ 8
Dental Technology	139B	2FT HND			N					2	

Univ of CENTRAL ENGLAND

Combined Health Studies	BL94	3FT deg	* g	8-12	4M	M$ gi	Ind	CCCCC	Ind	6	8/22
Diagnostic Radiography	B810	3FT deg	S g	12	4M+2D$	D$ gi	Ind	CCCCC	Ind	8	9/24
Podiatry	B985	3FT deg	g	12	4M $	DG/S gi	Ind	CCCC	Ind	9	10/14
Speech and Language Therapy	B950	3FT deg	S g	20	5M	M$ gi	Ind	CCCC	Ind	24	18/26
Therapeutic Radiography	B820	3FT deg	S g	12	4M+2D$	D$ gi	Ind	CCCCC	Ind	2	

Univ of CENTRAL LANCASHIRE

Biomedical Sciences	B940	3FT deg	C+S	DDD	MO $	MS6/^	26$	BCCC	$		
Health Sciences for Complementary Medicine	B990	3FT deg	S	14	MO+3D$	M$6/^	26$	BBCC	$		
Health Studies	LB49	3FT deg	*	12	MO	M$	24$	CCC	Ind		
Combined Honours Programme *Deaf Studies*	Y400	3FT deg	*	12	MO+2D	M$6/^	26	BCCC	Ind		

CENTRAL SCHOOL of Speech & Drama

| Clinical Communication Sciences | B950 | 4FT deg | * g | CCC | Ind | Ind | Ind | Ind | Ind | 7 | 10/26 |

CHICHESTER INSTITUTE OF HIGHER EDUCATION

| Health Studies | B990 | 3FT deg | * g | 12 | Ind | M^ | Ind | Ind | Ind | 2 | 4/18 |
| Recreation Studies | NB19 | 3FT deg | * | 12 | Ind | M$ | Ind | Ind | Ind | | |

CITY Univ

Clinical Communication St (Speech/Lang Therapy)	B950	4FT deg	* g	22	MO		30	AABBB	HN	9	10/24
Optometry	B500	3FT deg	2(M/B/P/C)	BBC	X	DS^	30$	BBBBB	Ind	10	16/24
Psychology and Health	BC98	3FT deg	* g	BCC	3M+4D	D*^	28$	BBBBC	Ind	22	
Radiography and Radiotherapy	B800	3FT deg	* g	16	3M+2D	D$	Ind	BBCCC	Ind	4	8/24

CITY COLLEGE Manchester

| Beauty Therapy | 018W | 2FT HND | | EE | N | | | | | | |

COVENTRY Univ

Biomedical Communications	B9P3	3FT deg									
Biomedical Communications	B9PH	3FT deg									
Health Sciences	B990	3FT deg	g	BD-CC	3M+3D	MG go	Ind	BBB	Ind		6/20
Medical Instrumentation	B8H6	3FT/4SW deg	P+C/B g	CC	Ind	Ind	Ind	Ind	Ind	4	
Occupational Therapy	B970	3FT deg	* g	BB-CCC	2M+6D	DG go	$	BBBBB	Ind	6	10/20
Physiotherapy	B960	3FT deg	* g	BBC	2M+6D	DG go	$	BBBBB	Ind	11	18/28

CRANFIELD Univ

| Diagnostic Radiography | B810 | 3FT deg | S g | 12-16 | 3M | | Ind | Ind | Ind | 5 | 10/22 |
| Therapeutic Radiography | B820 | 3FT deg | S g | 12-16 | 3M | | Ind | Ind | Ind | 6 | 13/14 |

DE MONTFORT Univ

| Health Studies | B991▼ | 3FT deg | * g | 10-12 | Ind | M | Ind | BBBBB | Ind | 5 | 6/14 |
| Human Communication(Speech and Language Therapy) | B950▼ | 3/4FT deg | * g | 20 | Ind | X | Ind | Ind | Ind | 14 | 14/24 |

Health Care and Therapies

course details			98 expected requirements								96 entry stats	
TITLE	CODE	COURSE	SUBJECTS	A/AS	ND/C	AGNVQ	IB	SQA(H)	SQA	RATIO	A/AS
Univ of DERBY											
Arts Therapies	W860	3FT deg	*	12	4M+1D	M$	26$	CCCC	Ind		
Diagnostic Radiography	B810	3FT deg	S	14	2M+3D$	D$	28$	BBCC	Ind	9	8/21
Occupational Therapy	B970	3FT deg	*	CCC	5D	MG^	30$	BBCCC	Ind	11	10/22
Therapeutic Radiography	B820	3FT deg	S	16	9M	D$	28$	BBCC	Ind	7	8/18
Credit Accumulation Modular Scheme *The Healing Arts*	Y600	3FT deg	*	12	MO	M	Ind	CCCC	Ind		
DUDLEY COLLEGE of Technology											
Health and Beauty Therapy	018W	2FT HND	* g	2	Ind	Ind					
Univ of DURHAM											
Biomedical Sciences	B940▼	3FT deg	B+C	12-18	3M+2D	Ind	Dip	BBBB	Ind	2	8/24
Health and Human Sciences	B991▼	3FT deg	*	12	Ind	Ind	Dip	CCCCC	Ind	2	4/18
Univ of EAST ANGLIA											
Occupational Therapy	B970	3FT deg		BCC	3M+4D		32$	AABBB	Ind	12	14/28
Physiotherapy	B960	3FT deg		BBB	3M+4D		35$	AABBB	Ind	19	20/30
Univ of EAST LONDON											
Anthropology with Health Studies	L6B9	3FT deg	* g	12	MO	M	Ind	Ind	Ind		
Biology and Health Studies	BC91	3FT deg	* g	12	MO	M$	Ind	Ind	Ind		
Biology with Health Studies	C1B9	3FT deg	* g	12	MO	M	Ind	Ind	Ind		
Biomedical Sciences	B940	4SW deg	* g	12	MO		Ind	Ind	Ind	6	6/12
Business Studies and Health Studies	BN91	3FT deg	* g	16	MO	M	Ind	Ind	Ind		
Business Studies with Health Studies	N1B9	3FT deg	* g	14	MO	MB					
Education & Community Studies and Health Studies	BX99	3FT deg	* g	12	MO	M$	Ind	Ind	Ind		
Education & Community Studies with Health St	X9B9	3FT deg	* g	12	MO	M					
Environmental Sciences and Health Studies	BF99	3FT deg	* g	12	MO	M$	Ind	Ind	Ind		
Environmental Sciences with Health Studies	F9B9	3FT deg	* g	12	MO	M	Ind	Ind	Ind		
Fitness and Health	B992	3FT deg	* g	12	MO	M$	Ind	Ind	Ind	4	8/16
French and Health Studies	BR91	3FT deg	* g	12	MO	M$	Ind	Ind	Ind		
French with Health Studies	R1B9	3FT deg	* g	12	MO	M	Ind				
German and Health Studies	BR92	3FT deg	* g	12	MO	M$	Ind	Ind	Ind		
German with Health Studies	R2B9	3FT deg	* g	12	MO	M	Ind				
Health Promotion	B990	3FT deg	* g	12	MO	M	Ind	Ind	Ind	3	
Health Services Management	B9N1	3FT deg	* g	12	MO	MG	Ind	Ind	Ind	3	
Health Studies	B991	3FT deg	* g	12	MO	MG	Ind	Ind	Ind	8	
Health Studies and Information Technology	BG95	3FT deg	* g	12	MO	M	Ind	Ind	Ind		
Health Studies and Psychosocial Studies	BL97	3FT deg	* g	12	MO	M	Ind	Ind	Ind		
Health Studies and Social Policy Research	BL94	3FT deg	* g	12	MO	M	Ind	Ind	Ind		
Health Studies and Sociology	BL93	3FT deg	* g	12	MO	M	Ind	Ind	Ind		
Health Studies and Spanish	BR94	3FT deg	* g	12	MO	M^	Ind	Ind	Ind		
Health Studies and Third World & Dev Studies	BM9Y	3FT deg	* g	12	MO	M	Ind	Ind	Ind		
Health Studies and Women's Studies	BM99	3FT deg	* g	14	MO	M	Ind	Ind	Ind		
Health Studies with Anthropology	B9L6	3FT deg	* g	12	MO	M	Ind	Ind	Ind		
Health Studies with Archaeological Sciences	BF9K	3FT deg	* g	12	MO	M					
Health Studies with Biology	B9C1	3FT deg	* g	12	MO	M	Ind	Ind	Ind		
Health Studies with Business Studies	B9NC	3FT deg	* g	12	MO	M	Ind	Ind	Ind		
Health Studies with Education & Community St	B9X9	3FT deg	* g	12	MO	M	Ind	Ind	Ind		
Health Studies with Environmental Sciences	B9F9	3FT deg	* g	12	MO	M	Ind	Ind	Ind		
Health Studies with French	B9R1	3FT deg	* g	12	MO	M	Ind	Ind	Ind		
Health Studies with German	B9R2	3FT deg	* g	12	MO	M	Ind	Ind	Ind		
Health Studies with Information Technology	B9G5	3FT deg	* g	12	MO	M	Ind	Ind	Ind		

TITLE	CODE	COURSE	SUBJECTS	A/AS	NO/C	RGNVQ	IB	SQA(H)	SQA	RATIO	A/AS
Health Studies with Italian	B9R3	3FT deg	* g	12	MO	M	Ind	Ind	Ind		
Health Studies with Psychosocial Studies	B9L7	3FT deg	* g	12	MO	M	Ind	Ind	Ind		
Health Studies with Social Policy Research	B9L4	3FT deg	* g	12	MO	M	Ind	Ind	Ind		
Health Studies with Sociology	B9L3	3FT deg	* g	12	MO	M	Ind	Ind	Ind		
Health Studies with Spanish	B9R4	3FT deg	* g	12	MO	M	Ind	Ind	Ind		
Health Studies with Third World & Dev Studies	B9M9	3FT deg	* g	12	MO	M	Ind	Ind	Ind		
Health Studies with Women's Studies	B9MX	3FT deg	* g	12	MO	M	Ind	Ind	Ind		
Information Technology with Health Studies	G5B9	3FT deg	* g	12	MO	M	Ind	Ind	Ind		
Physiotherapy	B960	3FT deg	* g	16	MO	DS6	Ind	Ind	Ind	10	16/24
Psychosocial Studies with Health Studies	L7B9	3FT deg	* g	12	MO	M	Ind	Ind	Ind		
Social Policy Research with Health Studies	L4B9	3FT deg	* g	12	MO	M	Ind	Ind	Ind		
Sociology with Health Studies	L3B9	3FT deg	* g	12	MO	M	Ind	Ind	Ind		
Spanish with Health Studies	R4B9	3FT deg	* g	12	MO	M	Ind				
Sports Development	B993	3FT deg	* g	12	MO	M	Ind	Ind	Ind		
Third World & Development Studies with Health St	M9B9	3FT deg	* g	12	MO	M	Ind	Ind			
Women's Studies with Health Studies	M9BX	3FT deg	* g	12	MO	M	Ind				
Extended Science	Y108	4FT deg	* g	8-10	MO	M	Ind	Ind	Ind		
Biomedical Sciences											
Immunology, Microbiology and Pharmacology	109B	2FT HND	* g	12	MO	M					

Univ of EDINBURGH

TITLE	CODE	COURSE	SUBJECTS	A/AS	NO/C	RGNVQ	IB	SQA(H)	SQA	RATIO	A/AS
Environmental Health	B900	4FT deg	C+1(B/M/P) g	CCC	Ind	X	Ind	BBBC	Ind	9	

Univ of GLAMORGAN

TITLE	CODE	COURSE	SUBJECTS	A/AS	NO/C	RGNVQ	IB	SQA(H)	SQA	RATIO	A/AS
Human Sciences (Chiropractic)	B965	3FT deg	M/S g	18	Ind	Ind	Ind	Ind	Ind		

Univ of GLASGOW

TITLE	CODE	COURSE	SUBJECTS	A/AS	NO/C	RGNVQ	IB	SQA(H)	SQA	RATIO	A/AS
Biomedical Sciences	B940	4FT deg	C/M+S	BBC-CCC	N	M	24$	BBBB$	N		
Sports Medicine	BB69	4FT deg	C/M+S	BBC-CCC	N	M	24$	BBBB$	N		

GLASGOW CALEDONIAN Univ

TITLE	CODE	COURSE	SUBJECTS	A/AS	NO/C	RGNVQ	IB	SQA(H)	SQA	RATIO	A/AS
Biomedical Sciences	B940	3FT/4FT deg	C+B/M/E	DDD	Ind		Ind	BCCC$	Ind	5	
Medical Engineering	B800	3FT/4FT deg	E+S	CCC	Ind		Ind	BBB$	Ind	1	
Medical Illustration	BW92	3FT/4FT deg		X	Ind		Ind	X	HN		
Occupational Therapy	B970	3FT/4SW deg	E+M	CC	Ind		Ind	BBCC$	Ind	14	
Ophthalmic Dispensing	B502	2FT Dip	E+M/P g	DE	Ind		Ind	BCCCC$	Ind	4	8/14
Optometry	B500	4SW deg	M+P+C+B g	BBC	Ind		Ind	BBBBC$	Ind	11	20/28
Orthoptics	B510	3FT deg	S+M+E	CC	Ind		Ind	BBCC$	Ind	7	14/16
Physiotherapy	B960	4SW deg	E+3S g	CCC	Ind		Ind	ABBB$	Ind	10	
Podiatry	B985	3FT/4SW deg	2S g	DD	Ind		Ind	BCC$	Ind	4	
Radiography-Diagnostic	B810	3FT/4SW deg	E+P+M	CCC	Ind		Ind	BBCC$	Ind	4	
Radiography-Therapeutic	B820	3FT/4SW deg	E+P+M	CCC	Ind		Ind	BBCC$	Ind	10	

Univ of GREENWICH

TITLE	CODE	COURSE	SUBJECTS	A/AS	NO/C	RGNVQ	IB	SQA(H)	SQA	RATIO	A/AS
Biomedical Sciences	B940▼	3FT/4SW deg	B+C g	10	3M	MS	Dip	BCC	Ind		
Environmental Health (Prof Acc)	B900	3FT/4SW deg	S g	CC	MO	M$ go	Ind	BBC$	Ind		
Health	B990	3FT deg	* g	12	N	M$	22	Ind	Ind		
Health and Learning Disabilities	BB97	3FT deg	*	12	N	M$	22	Ind	Ind		
Health and Management	BN91	3FT deg	* g	12	N	M$	22	Ind	Ind		
Health and Physiology	BB91	3FT deg	B g	12	N	X	22	Ind	Ind		
Health and Psychology	BC98	3FT deg	* g	16	N	M$	22	Ind	Ind		
Health and Sociology	BL93	3FT deg	* g	12	N	M$	22	Ind	Ind		
Health and Statistics	BG94	3FT deg	* g	12	N	M$	22	Ind	Ind		
Health with Learning Disabilities	B9B7	3FT deg	*	12	N	M$	22	Ind	Ind		
Health with Management	B9N1	3FT deg	* g	12	N	M$	22	Ind	Ind		

course details			98 expected requirements							96 entry stats	
TITLE	CODE	COURSE	SUBJECTS	A/AS	ND/C	AGNVQ	IB	SQA(H)	SQA	RATIO	A/AS
Health with Physiology	B9B1	3FT deg	S g	12	N	X	22	Ind	Ind		
Health with Psychology	B9C8	3FT deg	* g	12	N	M$	22	Ind	Ind		
Health with Sociology	B9L3	3FT deg	* g	12	N	M$	22	Ind	Ind		
Health with Statistics	B9G4	3FT deg	M g	12	N	X	22	Ind	Ind		
Public Health	B902	3FT/4SW deg	S/So g	8	Ind	M$ go	Ind	Ind	Ind		
Biomedical Sciences	049B▼	2FT HND	S	4	N	S					
Science (Health Studies)	99FB▼	2FT HND	* g	6	N		Dip	Ind	Ind		
Univ of HERTFORDSHIRE											
Diagnostic Radiography	B810	3FT deg	S	16	3M+3D	Ind	24	Ind	Ind	4	8/20
Medical Electronics	BH96	3FT/4SW deg	P/S	14	3M $	Ind	Dip$	Ind	Ind	2	
Medical Electronics (Extended)	BH9P▼	4FT/5SW deg	*	2	N	Ind	Dip$	Ind	Ind	2	
Medical Electronics with German Language	BH9Q	3FT/4SW deg	P/S	14	3M $		Dip$	Ind	Ind		
Paramedic Science with IHCD Paramedic Award	B910	3FT deg	Ap g	16-18	4M+3D	PG/S	Ind	Ind	Ind		
Physiotherapy	B960	3FT deg	B+2S	18-24	6D	D$	30$	BBBBB$	Ind	15	14/28
Therapeutic Radiography	B820	3FT deg	S	16	3M+3D	Ind	24	Ind	Ind	4	10/20
Univ of HUDDERSFIELD											
Environment and Human Health	BF99	3FT/4SW deg	S/Gv g	10-16	4M $	M$6/^ go	Ind	BBB	Ind		
Physiotherapy	B960	3FT deg	*	BCC	MO+6D	D$^	30	BBBB	Ind		
Podiatry	B985	3FT deg	B/C g	8-10	4M $	M$^ go	Ind	BBCC	Ind		
Science (Extended) Podiatry	Y108	4FT deg	* g	EE	N	P$ gi	Ind	Ind	Ind		
Univ of HULL											
Biomedical Sciences	B940	3FT deg	2S g	BBC-BCC	M+D$	D$^ go	26$	BBBBC	Ind	1	16/26
Health Sciences	B990	3FT deg	2S	18	MO	M$+	26$	BBBCC	Ind		
Health Sciences (4 Yrs)	B991	4FT deg	* g	CD	N	P*6/^ gi	24	CCCCD	Ind		
KEELE Univ											
Physiotherapy	B960	3FT deg	B/Pe g	BBB	Ind	D$^	32$	CSYS	Ind	12	24/30
KING'S COLL LONDON (Univ of London)											
Biomedical Science	BC99	3FT deg	C+S	BCC	MO+3D$	Ind	30	BBCCC	Ind	5	16/26
Clinical Sciences	B940	3FT deg	C+S	BCC		Ind	Ind	BCCCC	Ind	6	16/24
Environmental Health (4 Yrs)	B900	4FT deg	B/C	CCC			Ind	BBCCC	Ind	9	14/18
Environmental Health (MSci)	B901	4FT deg									
Physiotherapy (3 Yrs)	B960	3FT deg	2S(B/M/C/P)	BBB	DO		28	AABBB		15	18/28
Physiotherapy (MSci)	B961	4FT deg		BBB				AABBB			
KINGSTON Univ											
Biomedical Science	B948▼	4EXT deg	*		Ind		Ind	Ind	Ind	2	
Biomedical Science	B930	3FT deg	B g	12	$	Ind	Ind	CCC	Ind	3	4/20
Diagnostic Radiography	B810	3FT deg	S g	14	$	Ind	Ind	CCC	Ind	8	8/20
Therapeutic Radiography	B820	3FT deg	S	14	$	Ind	Ind	CCC	Ind	8	12/20
LANCASTER Univ											
Biological Sciences with Biomedicine	C1B9	3FT deg	2(M/P/C/B) g	CCC	MO $		28$	BBBCC$	Ind		
Biomedicine and Medical Statistics	BG91	3FT deg	2(M/P/C/B) g	BCC	MO $		30$	BBBBC$	Ind		
Univ of LEEDS											
Radiography (Diagnostic)	B810	3FT deg	S g	CC	Ind	Ind	Ind	Ind	Ind		
Radiography (Therapeutic)	B820	3FT deg	S g	CC	Ind	Ind	Ind	Ind	Ind		
LEEDS METROPOLITAN Univ											
Biosciences and Health	B940	3FT deg	S g	CD	3M $	MS2/^ go	26	BBC$	Ind	3	6/22
Clinical Language Sci (Speech and Lang Therapy)	B950	3FT deg	g	CCC	5M+3D	MG^ go	28	BBBBC	Ind	9	14/24

course details			98 expected requirements							96 entry stats	
TITLE	CODE	COURSE	SUBJECTS	A/AS	ND/C	AGNVQ	IB	SQA(H)	SQA	RATIO	A/AS
Environmental Health	B900	4SW deg	S g	18	2M+4D$	D$ go	28$	BBBCC$	Ind	6	6/20
Health and Environment	FB99	3FT deg									
Human Communication and Language Sciences	B952	3FT deg									16/20
Occupational Health and Safety	BN96	3FT deg	Ph g	12	1M+3D	MS/DG^ go	28$	CCCCC$	Ind	3	8/20
Physiotherapy	B960	3FT deg	B g	BBC	8D	Ind	30$	AABBB$	Ind	31	18/30
Physiotherapy Studies	B961	1FT deg									
Biosciences and Health	049B	2FT HND									

Univ of LINCOLNSHIRE and HUMBERSIDE

Caring Services (Social Care)	009B▼	2FT HND	* g		Ind	Ind	Ind	Ind	Ind		

Univ of LIVERPOOL

Clinical Engineering and Materials Science(BEng)	BF92	3FT deg	M+C/P	18	4M+1D$		30$	BBBBB	Ind	2	16/24
Diagnostic Radiography	B810	3FT deg	S g	CCC	MO+3D	DS^	30$	BBBCC	X	9	16/22
Occupational Therapy	B970	3FT deg	S	18	5M	D$+_^	Ind	BBBCC	Ind	12	10/26
Orthoptics	B510	3FT deg	B/M/P g	BCC	MO+2D		30	BBBCC	Ind	5	14/22
Physiotherapy	B960	3FT deg	B g	BBC	MO+4D$	DS^	30	BBBCC$	X	21	18/28
Therapy Radiography	B820	3FT deg	* g	CCC	MO	MS^ go	30$	BBBCC	Ind	4	10/22

LIVERPOOL HOPE Univ COLL

Health & Physical Recreation	BB96	3FT deg	* g	12	8M	M$ go	Ind	Ind	Ind		

LIVERPOOL JOHN MOORES Univ

Biomedical Sciences	B940	3FT/4SW deg	2S	10-20	3M	M				9	12/22
Biomedical Sciences (Foundation)	B948	4FT/5SW deg								13	
Health	B991	3FT deg	E/M/S	12	5M+2D	D$/M$6	28$	CCCC		3	
Health and Applied Psychology	BC98	3FT deg	* g	16	5M+3D	M$^ go	28$	BBCC		5	14/18
Health and Food & Nutrition (F & N jt awd only)	BD94	3FT deg		CC	5M+2D	D$/M$6	28$	CCCC		2	

LONDON INST

Beauty Sciences	B995	3FT deg									
Beauty Therapy	018W	2FT HND									
Fashion Styling (Hair and Make Up)	028E	2FT HND									
Fashion Styling and Photography	58WE	2FT HND									

LSU COLL of HE

Podiatry	B985	3FT deg	S	DD	Ind		Ind	Ind	Ind	3	4/14

LUTON Univ

Accounting with Health Studies	N4BX	3FT deg		12-16	MO/DO	M/D	32	BBCC	Ind		
Biochemistry with Health Science	C7B9	3FT deg	g	12-16	MO/DO	M/D	32	BBCC	Ind		
Biology with Health Science	C1B9	3FT deg	g	12-16	MO/DO	M/D	32	BBCC	Ind		
Biology with Health Studies	C1BX	3FT deg		12-16	MO/DO	M/D	32	BBCC	Ind		
Biotechnology with Health Science	J8B9	3FT deg	g	12-16	MO/DO	M/D	32	BBCC	Ind		
Broadcasting & Media Technology with Health Sci	H6B9	3FT deg		12-16	MO/DO	M/D	32	BBCC	Ind		
Built Environment with Health Studies	N8BX	3FT deg		12-16	MO/DO	M/D	32	BBCC	Ind		
Business Systems with Health Science	N1B9	3FT deg	g	12-16	MO/DO	M/D	32	BBCC	Ind		
Business with Health Studies	N1BX	3FT deg		12-16	MO/DO	M/D	32	BBCC	Ind		
Environmental Science with Health Science	F9B9	3FT deg	g	12-16	MO/DO	M/D	32	BBCC	Ind		
Environmental Studies with Health Science	F9BY	3FT deg		12-16	MO/DO	M/D	32	BBCC	Ind		
European Language Studies with Health Science	T2B9	4FT deg	L g	12-16	MO/DO	M/D	32	BBCC	Ind		
European Language Studies with Health Studies	T2BX	3FT deg		12-16	MO/DO	M/D	32	BBCC	Ind		
Geography with Health Studies	F8BX	3FT deg		12-16	MO/DO	M/D	32	BBCC	Ind		
Geology with Health Science	F6B9	3FT deg	g	12-16	MO/DO	M/D	32	BBCC	Ind		
Health & Social Studies	BLY3	1FT deg	*		Ind	Ind	Ind	Ind	Ind	1	
Health Science and Accounting	NBK9	3FT deg	g	12-16	MO/DO	M/D	32	BBCC	Ind		

Health Care and Therapies 32

TITLE	CODE	COURSE	SUBJECTS	A/AS	ND/C	AGNVQ	IB	SQA(H)	SQA	RATIO A/AS
Health Science and Artificial Intelligence	GB89	3FT deg		12-16	MD/DO	M/D	32	BBCC	Ind	
Health Science and Biochemistry	BC97	3FT deg	g	12-16	MD/DO	M/D	32	BBCC	Ind	
Health Science and Biology	CB19	3FT deg	g	12-16	MD/DO	M/D	32	BBCC	Ind	
Health Science and Biotechnology	BJ98	3FT deg	g	12-16	MD/DO	M/D	32	BBCC	Ind	
Health Science and Business Systems	NBC9	3FT deg	g	12-16	MD/DO	M/D	32	BBCC	Ind	
Health Science and Contemporary History	VB19	3FT deg	g	12-16	MD/DO	M/D	32	BBCC	Ind	
Health Science and Environmental Science	FB99	3FT deg	g	12-16	MD/DO	M/D	32	BBCC	Ind	
Health Science and European Language Studies	TB29	3FT deg	L g	12-16	MD/DO	M/D	32	BBCC	Ind	
Health Science and Geology	FB69	3FT deg	g	12-16	MD/DO	M/D	32	BBCC	Ind	
Health Science with Accounting	B9NL	3FT deg	g	12-16	MD/DO	M/D	32	BBCC	Ind	
Health Science with Biochemistry	B9C7	3FT deg	g	12-16	MD/DO	M/D	32	BBCC	Ind	
Health Science with Biology	B9C1	3FT deg	g	12-16	MD/DO	M/D	32	BBCC	Ind	4
Health Science with Biotechnology	B9J8	3FT deg	g	12-16	MD/DO	M/D	32	BBCC	Ind	
Health Science with Business Systems	B9NC	3FT deg	g	12-16	MD/DO	M/D	32	BBCC	Ind	
Health Science with Contemporary History	B9V1	3FT deg	g	12-16	MD/DO	M/D	32	BBCC	Ind	
Health Science with Environmental Science	B9F9	3FT deg	g	12-16	MD/DO	M/D	32	BBCC	Ind	
Health Science with French	B9R1	3FT deg	F g	12-16	MD/DO	M/D	32	BBCC	Ind	
Health Science with Geographical Info Systems	B9F8	3FT deg	g	12-16	MD/DO	M/D	32	BBCC	Ind	
Health Science with Geology	B906	3FT deg	g	12-16	MD/DO	M/D	32	BBCC	Ind	
Health Science with Human Biology	B9B1	3FT deg	g	12-16	MD/DO	M/D	32	BBCC	Ind	
Health Science with Japanese	B9T4	3FT deg	L g	12-16	MD/DO	M/D	32	BBCC	Ind	
Health Science with Journalism	B9P6	3FT deg	g	12-16	MD/DO	M/D	32	BBCC	Ind	
Health Science with Land Reclamation	B9K3	3FT deg	g	12-16	MD/DO	M/D	32	BBCC	Ind	
Health Science with Leisure Studies	B9N7	3FT deg	g	12-16	MD/DO	M/D	32	BBCC	Ind	
Health Science with Literary Studies in English	B9Q2	3FT deg	g	12-16	MD/DO	M/D	32	BBCC	Ind	
Health Science with Modern English Studies	B9Q3	3FT deg	g	12-16	MD/DO	M/D	32	BBCC	Ind	
Health Science with Multimedia	B9PK	3FT deg	g	12-16	MD/DO	M/D	32	BBCC	Ind	
Health Science with Pharmacology	B9B2	3FT deg	g	12-16	MD/DO	M/D	32	BBCC	Ind	
Health Science with Physical Geography	B9FV	3FT deg	g	12-16	MD/DO	M/D	32	BBCC	Ind	
Health Science with Plant Biology	B9C2	3FT deg	g	12-16	MD/DO	M/D	32	BBCC	Ind	
Health Science with Politics	B9M1	3FT deg	g	12-16	MD/DO	M/D	32	BBCC	Ind	
Health Science with Pollution Studies	BFXX	3FT deg	g	12-16	MD/DO	M/D	32	BBCC	Ind	
Health Science with Psychology	B9LR	3FT deg	g	12-16	MD/DO	M/D	32	BBCC	Ind	
Health Science with Public Policy and Management	B9MC	3FT deg	g	12-16	MD/DO	M/D	32	BBCC	Ind	
Health Science with Regional Planning and Dev	B9K4	3FT deg	g	12-16	MD/DO	M/D	32	BBCC	Ind	
Health Science with Social Studies	B9L3	3FT deg	g	12-16	MD/DO	M/D	32	BBCC	Ind	
Health Science with Travel and Tourism	B9P7	3FT deg	g	12-16	MD/DO	M/D	32	BBCC	Ind	
Health Studies and Accounting	NBKX	3FT deg	g	12-16	MD/DO	M/D	32	BBCC	Ind	
Health Studies and Artificial Intelligence	GB8X	3FT deg		12-16	MD/DO	M/D	32	BBCC	Ind	
Health Studies and Biochemistry	BCX7	3FT deg	g	12-16	MD/DO	M/D	32	BBCC	Ind	
Health Studies and Biology	CB1X	3FT deg	g	12-16	MD/DO	M/D	32	BBCC	Ind	
Health Studies and Biotechnology	BJX8	3FT deg	g	12-16	MD/DO	M/D	32	BBCC	Ind	
Health Studies and British Studies	VB9X	3FT deg		12-16	MD/DO	M/D	32	BBCC	Ind	
Health Studies and Built Environment	NB8X	3FT deg	g	12-16	MD/DO	M/D	32	BBCC	Ind	
Health Studies and Business	NB1X	3FT deg	g	12-16	MD/DO	M/D	32	BBCC	Ind	3
Health Studies and Computer Science	GB5X	3FT deg	g	12-16	MD/DO	M/D	32	BBCC	Ind	
Health Studies and Ecology and Biodiversity	BC99	3FT deg	g	12-16	MD/DO	M/D	32	BBCC	Ind	
Health Studies and European Language Studies	TB2X	3FT deg	L g	12-16	MD/DO	M/D	32	BBCC	Ind	
Health Studies and Geography	FB89	3FT deg	g	12-16	MD/DO	M/D	32	BBCC	Ind	
Health Studies and Health Science	B905	3FT deg	g	12-16	MD/DO	M/D	32	BBCC	Ind	5
Health Studies with Applied Statistics	B9G4	3FT deg	g	12-16	MD/DO	M/D	32	BBCC	Ind	
Health Studies with Biochemistry	B9CR	3FT deg	g	12-16	MD/DO	M/D	32	BBCC	Ind	

course details

98 expected requirements

96 entry stats

TITLE	CODE	COURSE	SUBJECTS	A/AS	ND/C	AGNVQ	IB	SQA(H)	SQA	RATIO A/AS
Health Studies with Biotechnology	B9JV	3FT deg	g	12-16	MO/DO	M/D	32	BBCC	Ind	
Health Studies with British Studies	B9V9	3FT deg		12-16	MO/DO	M/D	32	BBCC	Ind	
Health Studies with Chinese	B9T3	3FT deg		12-16	MO/DO	M/D	32	BBCC	Ind	
Health Studies with Ecology & Biodiversity	B9C9	3FT deg	g	12-16	MO/DO	M/D	32	BBCC	Ind	
Health Studies with Geography	BF98	3FT deg	g	12-16	MO/DO	M/D	32	BBCC	Ind	
Health Studies with Human Biology	B9BC	3FT deg	g	12-16	MO/DO	M/D	32	BBCC	Ind	
Health Studies with Leisure Studies	B9NR	3FT deg	g	12-16	MO/DO	M/D	32	BBCC	Ind	
Health Studies with Literary Studies in English	B903	3FT deg	g	12-16	MO/DO	M/D	32	BBCC	Ind	
Health Studies with Management	B9ND	3FT deg	g	12-16	MO/DO	M/D	32	BBCC	Ind	
Health Studies with Mapping Science	B9FW	3FT deg	g	12-16	MO/DO	M/D	32	BBCC	Ind	
Health Studies with Marketing	B9N5	3FT deg	g	12-16	MO/DO	M/D	32	BBCC	Ind	
Health Studies with Mathematical Sciences	B9GD	3FT deg	g	12-16	MO/DO	M/D	32	BBCC	Ind	
Health Studies with Mathematics	BG9C	3FT deg	g	12-16	MO/DO	M/D	32	BBCC	Ind	
Health Studies with Modern English Studies	B9QH	3FT deg	g	12-16	MO/DO	M/D	32	BBCC	Ind	
Health Studies with Modern History	B9VD	3FT deg	g	12-16	MO/DO	M/D	32	BBCC	Ind	
Health Studies with Multimedia	B901	3FT deg	g	12-16	MO/DO	M/D	32	BBCC	Ind	
Health Studies with Organisational Behaviour	B9L7	3FT deg	g	12-16	MO/DO	M/D	32	BBCC	Ind	
Health Studies with Pharmacology	B9BF	3FT deg	g	12-16	MO/DO	M/D	32	BBCC	Ind	
Health Studies with Plant Biology	B9CF	3FT deg	g	12-16	MO/DO	M/D	32	BBCC	Ind	
Health Studies with Politics	B9MD	3FT deg	g	12-16	MO/DO	M/D	32	BBCC	Ind	
Health Studies with Psychology	B9LT	3FT deg	g	12-16	MO/DO	M/D	32	BBCC	Ind	
Health Studies with Public Policy and Management	B997	3FT deg	g	12-16	MO/DO	M/D	32	BBCC	Ind	
Health Studies with Regional Planning and Dev	B9KK	3FT deg	g	12-16	MO/DO	M/D	32	BBCC	Ind	
Health Studies with Social Studies	B9LH	3FT deg	g	12-16	MO/DO	M/D	32	BBCC	Ind	
Health Studies with Travel and Tourism	B9PR	3FT deg	g	12-16	MO/DO	M/D	32	BBCC	Ind	
Human Biology and Health Science	BB19	3FT deg	g	12-16	MO/DO	M/D	32	BBCC	Ind	
Human Biology and Health Studies	BB1X	3FT deg	g	12-16	MO/DO	M/D	32	BBCC	Ind	
Journalism and Health Science	PB69	3FT deg		12-16	MO/DO	M/D	32	BBCC	Ind	
Journalism and Health Studies	PB6X	3FT deg		12-16	MO/DO	M/D	32	BBCC	Ind	
Law and Health Studies	BMX3	3FT deg	g	12-16	MO/DO	M/D	32	BBCC	Ind	
Leisure Studies and Health Science	BN97	3FT deg	g	12-16	MO/DO	M/D	32	BBCC	Ind	
Leisure Studies and Health Studies	BNX7	3FT deg	g	12-16	MO/DO	M/D	32	BBCC	Ind	
Leisure Studies with Health Science	N7B9	3FT deg	g	12-16	MO/DO	M/D	32	BBCC	Ind	
Leisure Studies with Health Studies	N7BX	3FT deg		12-16	MO/DO	M/D	32	BBCC	Ind	
Literary Studies in English and Health Studies	BQX2	3FT deg	g	12-16	MO/DO	M/D	32	BBCC	Ind	
Literary Studies in English with Health Studies	Q2BX	3FT deg		12-16	MO/DO	M/D	32	BBCC	Ind	
Mapping Science and Health Studies	BFX8	3FT deg	g	12-16	MO/DO	M/D	32	BBCC	Ind	
Marketing and Health Studies	BNX5	3FT deg	g	12-16	MO/DO	M/D	32	BBCC	Ind	
Marketing with Health Studies	N5BX	3FT deg		12-16	MO/DO	M/D	32	BBCC	Ind	
Mathematical Sciences and Health Studies	BG91	3FT deg	g	12-16	MO/DO	M/D	32	BBCC	Ind	
Mathematics and Health Studies	GB19	3FT deg	g	12-16	MO/DO	M/D	32	BBCC	Ind	
Media Practices and Health Studies	BPX4	3FT deg	g	12-16	MO/DO	M/D	32	BBCC	Ind	
Modern English Studies and Health Science	BQ93	3FT deg	g	12-16	MO/DO	M/D	32	BBCC	Ind	
Modern English Studies and Health Studies	BQX3	3FT deg	g	12-16	MO/DO	M/D	32	BBCC	Ind	2
Modern English Studies with Health Science	Q3B9	3FT deg	g	12-16	MO/DO	M/D	32	BBCC	Ind	
Modern English Studies with Health Studies	Q3BX	3FT deg		12-16	MO/DO	M/D	32	BBCC	Ind	
Modern History and Health Studies	BVXC	3FT deg	g	12-16	MO/DO	M/D	32	BBCC	Ind	
Modern History with Health Studies	V1BX	3FT deg		12-16	MO/DO	M/D	32	BBCC	Ind	
Organisational Behaviour and Health Studies	BLX7	3FT deg	g	12-16	MO/DO	M/D	32	BBCC	Ind	
Pharmacology and Health Science	BB29	3FT deg	g	12-16	MO/DO	M/D	32	BBCC	Ind	
Pharmacology and Health Studies	BB2X	3FT deg	g	12-16	MO/DO	M/D	32	BBCC	Ind	
Physical Geography and Health Science	BF9V	3FT deg	g	12-16	MO/DO	M/D	32	BBCC	Ind	

Health Care and Therapies 32

TITLE	CODE	COURSE	SUBJECTS	A/AS	NO/C	AGNVQ	IB	SQA(H)	SQA	RATIO A/AS
Physical Geography with Health Science	F8B9	3FT deg	g	12-16	MO/DO	M/D	32	BBCC	Ind	
Planning Studies and Health Studies	KB49	3FT deg	g	12-16	MO/DO	M/D	32	BBCC	Ind	
Plant Biology and Health Science	BC92	3FT deg	g	12-16	MO/DO	M/D	32	BBCC	Ind	
Plant Biology and Health Studies	BCX2	3FT deg	g	12-16	MO/DO	M/D	32	BBCC	Ind	
Plant Biology with Health Science	C2B9	3FT deg	g	12-16	MO/DO$	M/D	32	BBCC	Ind	
Plant Biology with Health Studies	C2BX	3FT deg		12-16	MO/DO	M/D	32	BBCC	Ind	
Politics and Health Science	BM91	3FT deg	g	12-16	MO/DO	M/D	32	BBCC	Ind	
Politics and Health Studies	BMX1	3FT deg	g	12-16	MO/DO	M/D	32	BBCC	Ind	
Politics with Health Science	M1B9	3FT deg	g	12-16	MO/DO	M/D	32	BBCC	Ind	
Psychology and Health Science	BL9R	3FT deg	g	12-16	MO/DO	M/D	32	BBCC	Ind	12
Psychology and Health Studies	BLXR	3FT deg	g	12-16	MO/DO	M/D	32	BBCC	Ind	6
Psychology with Health Science	L7B9	3FT deg	g	12-16	MO/DO	M/D	32	BBCC	Ind	3
Psychology with Health Studies	L7BX	3FT deg		12-16	MO/DO	M/D	32	BBCC	Ind	
Public Policy & Management with Health Studies	M1BX	3FT deg		12-16	MO/DO	M/D	32	BBCC	Ind	
Public Policy and Management and Health Science	BM9C	3FT deg	g	12-16	MO/DO	M/D	32	BBCC	Ind	
Public Policy and Management and Health Studies	BMXC	3FT deg	g	12-16	MO/DO	M/D	32	BBCC	Ind	
Regional Planning & Development and Health Sci	BK94	3FT deg	g	12-16	MO/DO	M/D	32	BBCC	Ind	
Regional Planning & Development and Health St	BKX4	3FT deg	g	12-16	MO/DO	M/D	32	BBCC	Ind	
Regional Planning & Development with Health Sci	K4B9	3FT deg	g	12-16	MO/DO	M/D	32	BBCC	Ind	
Regional Planning & Development with Health St	K4BX	3FT deg		12-16	MO/DO	M/D	32	BBCC	Ind	
Social Policy and Health Studies	LB4X	3FT deg		12-16	MO/DO	M/D	32	BBCC	Ind	
Social Policy with Health Studies	L4BX	3FT deg		12-16	MO/DO	M/D	32	BBCC	Ind	
Social Studies and Health Science	BL93	3FT deg	g	12-16	MO/DO	M/D	32	BBCC	Ind	
Social Studies and Health Studies	BLX3	3FT deg	g	12-16	MO/DO	M/D	32	BBCC	Ind	2
Social Studies with Health Science	L3B9	3FT deg	g	12-16	MO/DO	M/D	32	BBCC	Ind	
Sociology and Health Science	LBH9	3FT deg		12-16	MO/DO	M/D	32	BBCC	Ind	
Sociology and Health Studies	LBHX	3FT deg		12-16	MO/DO	M/D	32	BBCC	Ind	
Sociology with Health Science	L3BY	3FT deg		12-16	MO/DO	M/D	32	BBCC	Ind	
Sociology with Health Studies	L3BX	3FT deg		12-16	MO/DO	M/D	32	BBCC	Ind	
Travel and Tourism and Health Science	BP97	3FT deg	g	12-16	MO/DO	M/D	32	BBCC	Ind	
Travel and Tourism and Health Studies	BPX7	3FT deg	g	12-16	MO/DO	M/D	32	BBCC	Ind	
Travel and Tourism with Health Science	P7B9	3FT deg	g	12-16	MO/DO	M/D	32	BBCC	Ind	
Women's Studies and Health Studies	MB9X	3FT deg		12-16	MO/DO	M/D	32	BBCC	Ind	
Women's Studies with Health Studies	M9BX	3FT deg		12-16	MO/DO	M/D	32	BBCC	Ind	
Sport and Health Science	96BB	2FT HND	g	12-16	MO/DO	M/D	32	BBCC	Ind	

Univ of MANCHESTER

TITLE	CODE	COURSE	SUBJECTS	A/AS	NO/C	AGNVQ	IB	SQA(H)	SQA	RATIO A/AS
Biomedical Materials Sci with Ind Exp	J2BX	4SW deg	2(M/P/C) g	CCD	4M $	DS	28$	BBBBB$	Ind	5
Biomedical Materials Science	J2B9	3FT deg	2(M/P/C) g	CCD	4M $		26$	BBBBB$	Ind	3
Biomedical Materials Science with Industrial Exp	J2BY	4FT deg								
Biomedical Sciences	B940	3FT deg	B+C	BCC	2M+4D$	D^	28$	BBBBC$	Ind	15 19/28
Biomedical Sciences with Industrial Experience	B941	4SW deg	B+C	BCC	2M+4D$	D^	28$	BBBBC$	Ind	13 18/28
Physiotherapy	B960	3FT deg	B g	BBB	DO	D^	35$	AABBBB	Ind	10 22/28
Speech Pathology and Therapy	B950	4FT deg	g	BBC-BBB	M+D	D^	Ind	BBBBB	Ind	18 20/28

UMIST (Manchester)

TITLE	CODE	COURSE	SUBJECTS	A/AS	NO/C	AGNVQ	IB	SQA(H)	SQA	RATIO A/AS
Biomedical Materials Sci with Ind Exp (MMatSci)	J2BY	4SW deg	2(M/P/C) g	CCD	4M $	Ind	26$	BBBB$	Ind	
Biomedical Materials Science	J2B9	3FT deg	2(M/P/C) g	CCD	4M $	Ind	26$	BBBB$	Ind	17
Optometry	B500	3FT deg	B+M/P/C g	BBB	3M $	MS6/^	30$	AABBB$	X	14 24/30
Optometry (MOptom)	B501	4FT deg	B+M/P/C g	BBB	3M $	MS6/^	30$	AABBB$	X	

MANCHESTER METROPOLITAN Univ

TITLE	CODE	COURSE	SUBJECTS	A/AS	NO/C	AGNVQ	IB	SQA(H)	SQA	RATIO A/AS
Biomedical Science	B949	4FT deg								
Biomedical Science	B940	3FT deg	B+C g	12	5M	M	Dip$	BBB$	Ind	8/18

course details | 98 expected requirements | 96 entry stats

TITLE	CODE	COURSE	SUBJECTS	A/AS	ND/C	RGNVQ	IB	SQA(H)	SQA	RATIO A/AS
Dental Technology	B930	4FT deg	* g	CC	5M	M	Ind	Ind	Ind	8/16
Environmental Health	B900	3FT/4SW deg	B+S g	12	5M	M	Dip$	BBB$	Ind	8/20
Health Studies/American Studies	BQ94	3FT deg	*	CC	M+D	D	28	CCCC	Ind	
Health Studies/Applied Social Studies	BL93	3FT deg	*	CC	M+D	D	28	CCCC	Ind	
Health Studies/Business Studies	BN91	3FT deg	*	CC	M+D	D	28	CCCC	Ind	
Health Studies/Cultural Studies	BL9H	3FT deg	*	CC	M+D	D	28	CCCC	Ind	
Health Studies/Dance	BW94	3FT deg	*	CC	M+D	D	28	CCCC	Ind	
Health Studies/Drama	BW9K	3FT deg	*	CC	M+D	D	28	CCCC	Ind	
Health Studies/English	BQ93	3FT deg	*	CC	M+D	D	28	CCCC	Ind	
Health Studies/Environmental Science	BF99	3FT deg	*	CC	M+D	D	28	CCCC	Ind	
Health Studies/Geography	BL98	3FT deg	*	CC	M+D	D	28	CCCC	Ind	
History/Health Studies	BV91	3FT deg	*	CC	M+D	D	28	CCCC	Ind	
Leisure Studies/Health Studies	BL94	3FT deg	*	CC	M+D	D	28	CCCC	Ind	
Life Science/Health Studies	BC91	3FT deg	*	CC	M+D	D	28	CCCC	Ind	
Music/Health Studies	BW93	3FT deg	*	CC	M+D	D	28	CCCC	Ind	
Philosophy/Health Studies	BV97	3FT deg	*	CC	M+D	D	28	CCCC	Ind	
Psychology and Speech Pathology	BL97	4FT deg	* g	BCC	Ind	Ind	Ind	BBBB	Ind	20/22
Religious Studies/Health Studies	BV98	3FT deg	*	CC	M+D	D	28	CCCC	Ind	
Speech Pathology and Therapy	B950	3FT deg	* g	CCC	Ind	D	Ind	BBBC	Ind	16/24
Sport/Health Studies	BB69	3FT deg	S	BC	M+D	DS	28	CCCC	Ind	
Visual Arts/Health Studies	BW91	3FT deg	*	CC	M+D	D	28	CCCC	Ind	
Writing/Health Studies	BW9L	3FT deg	*	CC	M+D	D	28	CCCC	Ind	
Dental Technology	039B	2FT HND	* g		5M $		X	X	HN$	
MATTHEW BOULTON COLL of F & HE										
Podiatry	B985	3FT deg	B g	EE	N $		Ind	$	N$	10
Podiatry (with Foundation)	B988	4FT deg								
MIDDLESEX Univ										
Environmental Health	B900▼	4SW deg	S g	12-14	5M	M$ go	26	Ind	Ind	
Environmental Health	009B▼	2FT HND	S g	4	N	P$ go	24	Ind	Ind	
Health, Fitness and Beauty Therapies	86WB▼	2FT HND	* g	DD	N	P$ go	Dip	Ind		
NAPIER Univ										
Biomedical Sciences (common 1st year)	B940	4FT/5SW deg	B/C	DD	Ind	Ind	Ind	BBC	Ind	
NENE COLLEGE										
Occupational Therapy	B970	3FT deg	S	16	M+5D	M	Ind	Ind	Ind	8/18
Podiatry	B985	3FT deg	S g	8	6M	M	24	CCC	Ind	8/22
Univ of NEWCASTLE										
Speech	B950	4FT deg	*	BBB	Ind		Ind	BBBBB	Ind	13 20/30
NEW COLLEGE DURHAM										
Podiatry (with Foundn year & State Registration)	B988	4FT deg	*							
Podiatry (with State Registration)	B985	3FT deg	S g	4	4M	Ind	Dip	Ind	N	
NESCOT										
Biomedical Science	B940	3FT deg	S	EE	N	M	Dip	Ind	N$	10
Biomedical Science	B948	4FT deg	*							2
Osteopathic Medicine	B991	4FT deg	Ap	BB	MO	M	Ind	Ind	N$	
Univ of NORTH LONDON										
Biomedical Science	B940	3FT/4SW/4EXT deg	B+C	CC	3M $	MS go	$	Ind	Ind	
Health Studies	BL94▼	3FT deg	*	CC	MO	M	$	CCCCC	Ind	10
Health Studies and Nutrition	BB94	3FT/4SW/4EXT deg	C+B g	12	Ind	Ind	Ind	Ind	Ind	

Health Care and Therapies

32

TITLE	CODE	COURSE	SUBJECTS	A/AS	ND/C	AGNVQ	IB	SQA(H)	SQA	RATIO A/AS
					98 expected requirements					**96 entry stats**
Health Studies and Philosophy	BV97	3FT deg	* g	CC	MO	D	Ind	Ind	Ind	
Health Studies and Sports Management	BB96	3FT deg	* g	CC	Ind	Ind	Ind	Ind	Ind	
Health Studies and Women's Studies	BM99	3FT deg	* g	CC	MO	D	Ind	Ind	Ind	
Sports Science and Sports Therapy	BW68	3FT/4SW/4EXT deg	B/(Ss+S)	18	5M $	MS	$	Ind	Ind	12/16
Univ of NORTHUMBRIA										
Biomedical Sciences	B940	3FT/4SW deg	B+C/S g	14	6M $	MS gi	24$	CCCCC$	Ind	8 10/24
Chemistry with Biomedical Sciences	F1B9	3FT/4SW deg	C+S/M g	10	3M	MS gi	24$	CCCC$	Ind	3
European Health Sciences	B991	3FT deg	g	CC	3M+1D	M	24	CCCC	Ind	4
Occupational Therapy	B970	3FT deg	g	16	3M+1D	M	24	CCCC	Ind	25 12/20
Physiotherapy	B960	3FT deg	g	BCC	1M+4D	D	26	BBBCC	Ind	32 16/30
NORWICH: City COLL										
Environmental Health	B900	3FT deg	S g	6	5M	PS go	Ind	Ind	Ind	
Univ of NOTTINGHAM										
Medical Materials Science	BJ95	3FT deg	C+B/M/P	BCC	Ind	Ind	28$	Ind	Ind	5
Physiotherapy	B960	3FT deg	B	BBC	DO	D$^ go	32$	AABB$	Ind	39 22/28
NOTTINGHAM TRENT Univ										
Biomedical Science	B940	4SW deg	S g	DDE	Ind	Ind	Dip	C	$	7 8/18
Environmental Health	B900	4SW deg	S g	16-18	6M		Ind	$	Ind	5 12/24
Environmental Health (Extended)	B908▼	5EXTSW deg	* g		Ind	Ind	Ind	Ind	Ind	3
Sports Science and Sports Injuries	BB69▼	3FT deg	S/Pe/Ss g	CCC	Ind	Ind	Dip	BB	Ind	
Sport Science with Sports Injuries	9B6B▼	2FT HND	S/Pe/Ss g	DD	Ind	Ind	Dip	C	Ind	
OXFORD BROOKES Univ										
Occupational Therapy	B970	3FT deg	* g	CD	Ind	MG3	Ind	Ind	Ind	9 10/20
Physiotherapy	B960	3FT deg								
Univ of PAISLEY										
Biomedical Sciences	B940	4FT/5SW deg	* g	CCC-EE	Ind	Ind	Ind	BCC$	Ind	3
Univ of PLYMOUTH										
Podiatry	B985	3FT deg	B g	EE	3M $	M$	Ind	BBBC$	Ind	4 4/22
Univ of PORTSMOUTH										
Biomedical Sciences	B940	3FT deg	C+S	12	3M $	MS6/^	Dip	CCCC	Ind	4 8/16
Biomedical Sciences	B948▼	4EXT deg	*		Ind	P*	Ind	Ind	Ind	2
Exercise and Health Science	BB69	3FT deg	S	16	MO	D$6/^	26	BBBB	Ind	
Human Biology and Health Science	BB19	3FT deg	2S	14	3M $	MS6/^	Dip	BBB	Ind	
Radiography (Diagnostic)	B818▼	4EXT deg	*	Ind	Ind	P*	Ind	Ind	Ind	4 8/10
Radiography (Diagnostic)	B810	3FT deg	S	14	6M	M$^	Dip$	BBCCC	Ind	7 10/16
Radiography (Therapeutic)	B828▼	4EXT deg	*	Ind	Ind	P*	Ind	Ind	Ind	6
Radiography (Therapeutic)	B820	3FT deg	S	14	6M	M$^	Dip$	BBCCC	Ind	7 10/16
QUEEN MARGARET COLL										
Diagnostic Radiography	B810	3FT/4FT deg	M/S g	DD	M+D	M$^ go	Ind$	BCC$	Ind$	10
Health Sciences	B990	3FT/4FT deg	B+S g	CD	M+D	MS go	Ind$	BBC$	Ind$	4
Occupational Therapy	B970	3FT/4FT deg	B	CC	M+D	M$^ go	Ind$	BBB$	Ind$	11
Physiotherapy	B960	4FT deg	2S	ABB	X	DS^ go	Ind$	AAABB$	X	16 18/26
Podiatry	B985	3FT/4FT deg	S g	DD	M+D	M$^ go	Ind$	BCC$	Ind$	3 6/18
Social Sciences and Health	BL93	3FT/4FT deg	*	CC	M+D	D$ go	Ind	BBB	Ind	4 12/16
Speech Pathology and Therapy	B950	3FT/4FT deg	S g	BCC	M+D	DS^ go	Ind$	BBBB$	Ind$	12 20/24
Therapeutic Radiography	B820	3FT/4FT deg	M/S g	DD	M+D	M$^ go	Ind$	BCC$	Ind$	9

course details			98 expected requirements							96 entry stats	
TITLE	CODE	COURSE	SUBJECTS	A/AS	NO/C	AGNVQ	IB	SQA(H)	SQA	RATIO	A/AS
QUEEN MARY & WESTFIELD COLL *(Univ of London)*											
Basic Medical Science	B900	3FT deg	C+B	22		D$^	30$				
QUEEN'S Univ Belfast											
Biomedical Science	B940	3FT deg	2(S/B/C) g	CCC	X	Ind	28$	X	X	11	18/26
Podiatry	B985	3FT deg	C g	CCD-BC	X	Ind	25$	Ind	Ind	7	14/24
Univ of READING											
Linguistics and Language Pathology	B950	4FT deg	* g	24	Ind	D$6/^	32	ABBB	Ind	10	20/26
Univ College of RIPON & YORK ST JOHN											
Life Science and Health Studies	C9B9	3FT deg	g	DD	M	M	27	BBCC		3	6/12
Occupational Therapy inc Professional Reg	B970	3FT deg	g	CCC	M+D	D*6/^ g	30	ABBB		7	12/26
ROBERT GORDON Univ											
Occupational Therapy	B970	3FT/4FT deg	E+S g	BBC	Ind	Ind	Ind	BBCC$	Ind	14	
Physiotherapy	B960	4FT deg	E+2S	ABB	Ind	Ind	Ind	Ind	Ind	18	
Radiography	B810	3FT deg	E+S g	CD	Ind	Ind	Ind	BBC$	Ind	8	
ROEHAMPTON INST											
Film & Television Studies and Health Studies	BP94▼	3FT deg	g	16	2M+2D	M$^ go	30	BBC	N$		
Health Studies	B900▼	3FT deg	B	12	3M $	P$ go	24	BCC	N$	6	6/14
Health Studies and Applied Consumer Studies	NB99▼	3FT deg	B g	12	4M $	P$ go	26	BCC	N$		
Health Studies and Art for Community	BW91▼	3FT deg	g	12	3M	P$	24	CCC	N$		
Health Studies and Biology	BC91▼	3FT deg	B	12	4M $	P$ go	26	BCC	N$	4	
Health Studies and Business Computing	GB79▼	3FT deg	g	12	3D	M$ go	26	BCC	N$		
Health Studies and Business Studies	BN91▼	3FT deg	B g	12	3D	M$ go	26	BCC	Ind	8	
Health Studies and Dance Studies	BW94▼	3FT deg	B	CC	2M+2D$	M$^ go	30	BBC	N$		
Health Studies and Drama & Theatre Studies	BW9L▼	3FT deg	B+E/T	16	2M+2D$	M$^ go	30	BBC	N$		
Health Studies and Education	BX99▼	3FT deg	B	12	4M $	P$ go	26	BCC	N$	2	
Health Studies and English Lang & Linguistics	BQ9H▼	3FT deg	E/L+B	CC	2M+2D$	M$^ go	30	BBC	N$		
Health Studies and English Literature	BQ93▼	3FT deg	E+B	CC	2M+2D$	M^ go	28	BBC	N$		
Health Studies and Environmental Studies	BF99▼	3FT deg	B g	12	4M $	P$ go	26	BCC	N$	3	
Health Studies and French	BR91▼	4FT deg	F+B	12	4M $	P^ go	26	BCC	N$		
Health Studies and Geography	BL98▼	3FT deg	B+Gy	12	4M $	P$^ go	26	BCC	N$		
Health Studies and Spanish	BR94▼	4FT deg	Sp g	12	2M+2D	P$ go	28	BCC	N$		
History and Health Studies	BV91▼	3FT deg	H+B	12	4M $	P^ go	26	BCC	N$		
Human & Social Biology and Health Studies	CBC9▼	3FT deg	B	12	4M	P$ go	26	BCC	N$	1	
Music and Health Studies	BW93▼	3FT deg	Mu+B	12	4M $	P^ go	26	BCC	N$		
Natural Resource Studies and Health Studies	BD92▼	3FT deg	g	12	3M	P$^	24	CCC	N$		
Psychology and Health Studies	BL97▼	3FT deg	B g	CC	3D $	M$ go	30	BBC	N$	3	
Social Policy & Administration & Health Studies	BL9L▼	3FT deg	B g	12	4M	P$ go	26	BCC	N$	5	
Sociology and Health Studies	LB39▼	3FT deg	B g	12	4M	P$ go	26	BCC	N$	5	
Sport Studies and Health Studies	BB69▼	3FT deg	B g	12	3D	MS go	30	BBC	N$		
Theology & Religious Studies and Health Studies	BV98▼	3FT deg	B g	12	4M	P$ go	26	BCC	N$	1	
Women's Studies and Health Studies	BM99▼	3FT deg	B	12	4M $	P$ go	26	BCC	N$	5	
Univ of SALFORD											
Art Therapy	W860	3FT deg									
Biomedical Applications	B940	3 deg									
Complementary Therapy	B975	3FT deg									
Diagnostic Radiography	B810	3FT deg	2(B/P/M/Ps) g	8-12	6M+3D	M	Ind	CCCC	Ind	10	10/24
Exercise and Health Sciences	BB69	3FT deg									
Health Science	B990	3FT deg	g	4	N	P	Ind	Ind	Ind		
Health Science and Social Policy	BL94	3FT deg	g	12	6M	M					
Occupational Therapy	B970	3FT deg	So/B/Ps	8-16	5M+3D	DG^	Ind	BBBB	Ind	30	14/22

Health Care and Therapies 32

			98 expected requirements							96 entry stats	
TITLE	CODE	COURSE	SUBJECTS	A/AS	ND/C	AGNVQ	IB	SQA(H)	SQA	RATIO	A/AS
Physiotherapy	B960	3FT deg	S	20	Ind	D^	Ind	Ind	Ind	24	14/24
Podiatry	B985	3FT deg	B	12	5M	MG	Ind	CCCC	Ind	3	4/18
Prosthetics and Orthotics	B984	4FT deg	2(M/P/B/S)	14	4D	P8	Ind	Ind	Ind	5	16/20
Sports Rehabilitation	BB96	3FT deg									16/22

Univ of SHEFFIELD

Biomedical Science	B940	3FT deg	C+S g	20	4M+2D$	DS6/^	30$	BBBB$	Ind	8	20/30
Biomedical Sciences (including a Foundation Yr)	B941	4FT deg	g	20	4M+2D	DS6/^	30	BBBB	Ind		
Dental Technology	B930	3FT deg	* g	X	6M $	X	X	X	Ind	6	
Human Communication and its Disorders	B953	3FT deg	* g	BCC	6M	X	29	BBBB	Ind	14	22/26
Orthoptics	B510	3FT deg	* g	BCC	6M	X	29	BBBB	Ind	7	16/26
Paramedical Studies	B910	3FT deg	* g	BCC	X	X	29	BBBB	Ind	13	18/24
Speech Science	B950	4FT deg	* g	ABB	6M	D^	33	AAAB	Ind	15	26/30

SHEFFIELD HALLAM Univ

Diagnostic Radiography	B810	3FT deg	2S	CC	4M+2D	M$	Ind	CCCC$	Ind		
Occupational Therapy	B970	3FT deg	B/C	CCC	X	M^	Ind	Ind	Ind		
Physiotherapy	B960	3FT deg	B/C	CCC	X	M^	Ind	Ind	Ind		
Therapeutic Radiography	B820	3FT deg	2S	CC	4M+2D	M$	Ind	CCCC$	Ind		
Combined Studies Health Studies	Y400	3FT deg	*	14	2M	M	Ind	Ind	Ind		

Univ College of St MARTIN, LANCASTER AND CUMBRIA

Applied Community Studies/Health Studies	LB59	3FT deg	*	CD-DDE	3M+2D	M*	28$	BCCC	Ind	2	
Art and Design/Health Studies	WB19	3FT deg	A	CC-CDE	3M+2D	MA	28$	BBCC$	Ind	2	
Business Management Studies/Health Studies	NB19	3FT deg	*	CD-CEE	3M+2D	M*	28	BCCC			
English/Health Studies	QBH9	3FT deg	E	BC-BDE	X	P^	28$	BBBC$			
Geography/Health Studies	LB89	3FT deg	Gy	CD-DDE	X	P^	28$	BCCC$	Ind		
Health Studies	B900	3FT deg	*	CD-DDE	3M+2D	M*	28	BCCC	Ind	2	4/16
Health Studies/Applied Community Studies	BL95	3FT deg	*	CD-DDE	3M+2D	M*	28	BCCC	Ind	8	
Health Studies/Art and Design	BW91	3FT deg	A	CD-DDE	3M+2D$	MA	28$	BCCC$	Ind		
Health Studies/Business Management Studies	BN91	3FT deg	*	CD-DDE	3M+2D	M*	28	BCCC			
Health Studies/Drama	BW94	3FT deg	*	CD-DDE	3M+2D	M*	28	BCCC	Ind	1	
Health Studies/Education Studies	BX99	3FT deg	*	CD-DDE	3M+2D	M*	28$	BCCC	Ind		
Health Studies/English	BQ9H	3FT deg	E	CD-DDE	X	P^	28$	BCCC$			
Health Studies/Geography	BL98	3FT deg	Gy	CD-DDE	X	P^	28$	BCCC$	Ind		
Health Studies/Health Administration	BL94	3FT deg	*	CD-DDE	3M+2D	M*	28	BCCC	Ind	5	
Health Studies/Mathematics	BG91	3FT deg	M	CD-DDE	X	P^	28$	BCCC$			
Health Studies/Physical Education & Sports Stds	BX9X	3FT deg	*	CD-DDE	3M+2D	M	28	BCCC			
Health Studies/Religious Studies	BV98	3FT deg	*	CD-DDE	3M+2D	M*	28	BCCC	Ind		
Health Studies/Social Ethics	BV97	3FT deg	*	CD-DDE	3M+2D	M*	28$	BCCC	Ind	1	
Mathematics/Health Studies	GB19	3FT deg	M	DD-DEE	X	P^	28$	BCCC$			
Occupational Therapy (3 Yrs)	B970	3FT deg	* g	AA-BCC	2M+4D$	M^	28$	BBBB$	Ind	11	12/24
Radiography (Diagnostic)	B810	3FT deg	S g	AB-CCC	3M+3D$	MS^	28$	BBBB$	Ind	4	10/24
Religious Studies/Health Studies	VB89	3FT deg	*	CD-DDE	3M+2D	M*	28$	BCCC	Ind	1	
Social Ethics/Health Studies	VB79	3FT deg	*	CD-DDE	3M+2D	M*	28	BCCC	Ind		

SOLIHULL COLL

Sports Science with Health	B6B9	3FT deg	S/Pe/Ss	DD	M+2D $	MS$	Ind	Ind	Ind		

Univ of SOUTHAMPTON

Biomedical Sciences	B940	3FT deg	C+B/P/M/Gy g	BCC	$	M^	$	Ind	Ind		
Biomedical Sciences (MBioSci)	B941	4FT deg	C+B/P/M/Gy g	BCC	$	M^	$	Ind	Ind		
Occupational Therapy	B970	3FT deg	S g	BCC	Ind	D^	Ind	Ind	Ind	10	10/26
Physiotherapy	B960	3FT deg	S g	BCC	Ind	D^	Ind	Ind	Ind	23	18/28

course details			98 expected requirements							96 entry stats	
TITLE	CODE	COURSE	SUBJECTS	A/AS	ND/C	AGNVQ	IB	SQA(H)	SQA	RATIO	A/AS
SOUTH BANK Univ											
Foundation Occupational & Environmental Hygiene	BN9Q	4EXT deg					Ind	Ind	Ind		
Foundation Occupational Health and Safety	BNXQ	3FT deg					Ind	Ind	Ind		
Health Sciences	B900	3FT deg	S g	14-18	2M+4D	M go	Ind	Ind	Ind		
Occupational Health and Safety	BNY6	3FT deg	2S g	DD	N	M go	Ind	Ind	Ind		
Occupational and Environmental Hygiene	BNX6	3FT/4SW deg	2S g	DD	N	M go	Ind	Ind	Ind		
Radiography - Imaging	B810	3FT deg	S g	CC	MO	MG/S+ go	Ind	Ind	Ind		
Radiography - Radiotherapy	B820	3FT deg	S g	CC	MO	MG/S+ go	Ind	Ind	Ind		
ST LOYE'S SCHOOL of O T											
Health Sciences	B990	3FT deg	g	CC	X	M		CC	X	3	
Occupational Therapy	B970	3FT deg	g	CC	X	M		CC	X	8	12/24
THE UNIVERSITY COLLEGE OF ST MARK AND ST JOHN											
Human Communication Stud (Speech & Lang Therapy)	B950	3FT deg		14	Ind	M	Ind	Ind	Ind		
Physiotherapy	B960	3FT deg		14	Ind	M	Ind	Ind	Ind		
ST MARY'S Univ COLL											
Sport Rehabilitation & Integrated Scientific St	BY91	3FT deg	B g	12-14	X	X	Ind	BBBB$	X		
Sport Rehabilitation and Biology	BC91	3FT deg	B g	12-14	X	X	Ind	BBBB$	X		
Sport Rehabilitation and Classical Studies	BQ98	3FT deg	B g	12-14	X	X	Ind	BBBB$	X		
Sport Rehabilitation and Drama	BW94	3FT deg	B g	12-14	X	X	Ind	BBBB$	X		
Sport Rehabilitation and Education Studies	BX9X	3FT deg	B g	12-14	X	X	Ind	BBBB$	X		
Sport Rehabilitation and English	BQ93	3FT deg	E+B g	12-14	X	X	Ind	BBBB$	X		
Sport Rehabilitation and Environ Investig St	BF99	3FT deg	B g	10-14	X	X	Ind	BBBB$	X		
Sport Rehabilitation and Environmental Studies	BF9X	3FT deg	B g	10-14	X	X	Ind	BBBB$	X		
Sport Rehabilitation and Gender Studies	BM99	3FT deg	B g	12-14	X	X	Ind	BBBB$	X		
Sport Rehabilitation and History	BV91	3FT deg	B+H g	12-14	X	X	Ind	BBBB$	X		
Sport Rehabilitation and Irish Studies	BQ95	3FT deg	B g	12-14	X	X	Ind	BBBB$	X		
Sport Rehabilitation and Management Studies	BN91	3FT deg	B g	12-14	X	X	Ind	BBBB$	X		
Sport Rehabilitation and Sociology	BL93	3FT deg	B g	12-14	X	X	Ind	BBBB$	X		
Sport Rehabilitation and Sport Science	BB96	3FT deg	B g	12-14	X	X	Ind	BBBB$	X		
STAFFORDSHIRE Univ											
Exercise and Health	B991	3FT deg	S	14	Ind	D	Ind	BBCC	Ind	8	12/22
Health Technology	B999	4EXT deg	g	EE	P $	P$	Ind	Ind	Ind		
Medical Engineering	B808	4EXT deg	g	4	P $	P$	Ind	Ind	Ind	3	
Medical Engineering	B800	3FT deg	M+P g	10	3M	M	Ind	Ind	Ind		
Occupational Health and Environmental Technology	BF99	4EXT deg	g	EE	P $	P$	Ind	Ind	Ind		
Univ of STRATHCLYDE											
Forensic and Analytical Chemistry	F1B9	4FT deg	C+M+P	ABB	HN		30$	AABB$	HN		
Prosthetics and Orthotics	B984	4FT deg	M+C	CCC	HN		30$	BBBB$	HN		
Speech and Language Pathology	B950	3FT/4FT deg	g	BCC	Ind		24	BBBBB$	HN		
UNIVERSITY COLLEGE SUFFOLK											
Diagnostic Radiography	B810	3FT deg	S	DD	N $	P$	Ind	Ind	Ind		
Therapeutic Radiography	B820	3FT deg	S	DD	N $	P$	Ind	Ind	Ind		
Univ of SUNDERLAND											
Biomedical Sciences	B940▼	3FT/4SW deg	B+C g	10	3M $	MS	24	CCCC$	N$	4	6/18
Biomedical Sciences (Foundation)	B948▼	4EXT/5EXTSW deg	*							1	
Ergonomics and Biomechanics	BJ99	3FT/4SW deg	*	12	3M	P	24	CCC	N		
Health Studies	BL94▼	3FT deg	* g	12	MO$	MS	24$	BCCC$	N$	2	6/14
Health Studies (Foundation)	BL9K▼	4EXT deg	*							2	
Physiology and Biomedical Science	BB19	3FT/4SW deg	2S	8	N $	PS	24$	CCCC$	N$		
Sport, Physical Activity and Health	BB69	3FT/4SW deg	S g	18	3M+2D$	MS^	28	BBCCC	Ind		

Health Care and Therapies 32

		course details		98 expected requirements						96 entry stats	
TITLE	CODE	COURSE	SUBJECTS	A/AS	NO/C	AGNVQ	IB	SQA(H)	SQA	RATIO	A/AS
Univ of TEESSIDE											
Applied Science and Forensic Measurement	F9B9	3FT/4SW deg	M/S	12	4M	M	Ind	CCCC	Ind	3	6/20
Bio-Medical Engineering	BH91	3FT/4SW deg	S	12-14	Ind	M	Ind	CCCC	Ind		
Diagnostic Radiography	B810	3FT deg	S	12-14	Ind		Ind	Ind	Ind	7	10/18
Health Sciences (Generic)	B900	3FT deg									
Nutrition and Health Sciences	BB49	3FT deg	S	8	3M		Ind	CCC	Ind		
Occupational Therapy	B970	3FT deg	*	12-14	Ind		Ind	Ind	Ind	9	14/16
Physiotherapy	B960	3FT deg	B	20-22	Ind		Ind	Ind	Ind	10	18/26
THAMES VALLEY Univ											
Health Promotion	B991	2FT Dip		2-4	N	P	24	CC			
Health Promotion	B990	3FT deg		8-12	MO	M	26	CCC			
TRINITY COLL Carmarthen											
Health and Environment	B900	3FT deg	* g	DD-CC	Ind		Ind	Ind	Ind	1	
Univ of ULSTER											
Biomedical Engineering (4 Yr SW inc DIS)	BH91▼	4SW deg	P/C/B/M g	CCC	MO+3D	Ind	28	BBBB	Ind		
Biomedical Sciences (4 Yr SW inc DIS)	B940▼	4SW deg	2S	CCC	MO+3D	D*6/^ gi	28	BBBC	Ind	12	16/24
Clinical Science (4 Yr SW inc DIS)	B941▼	4SW deg	2S g	CCC	MO+3D	DS6/^ gi	28	BBBC	Ind	4	16/22
Environmental Health (4 Yr SW inc DIS)	B900▼	4SW deg	2(E/M/C/P/B) g	BBC	MO+4D	Ind	32	ABBB	Ind	9	20/30
Occupational Therapy inc State Reg (4 Yr)	B970▼	4FT deg	g	BBB	MO+5D	D*6/^ gi	33	AABB	Ind	14	24/30
Optometry (3 Yr)	B500▼	3FT deg	2S	ABB	MO+5D	DS6/^ gi	32	ABBB	Ind	10	16/28
Physiotherapy inc State Registration (4 Yr)	B960▼	4FT deg	2(S/M) g	ABB-AAB	MO+6D	DS6/^ gi	35	AAAB	Ind	17	24/30
Radiography (Inc Reg Diagnost or Therap) (4 Yr)	B800▼	4FT deg	S g	BBC	MO+4D	DS6/^ gi	32	ABBB	Ind	11	18/26
Speech and Lang Therapy inc prof recog (4 Yr)	B952▼	4FT deg	E/M/S/L g	BBB	MO+5D	D$6/^ gi	33	AABB	Ind	27	24/26
UNIVERSITY COLL LONDON (Univ of London)											
Podiatry	B986	3FT deg	C+S g	CDD-CCD 5M $	Ind		30$	Ind	Ind	4	10/18
Speech Communication	B951	3FT deg	S g	BBC	MO+2D$	Ind	32$	Ind	Ind		
Speech Sciences (4 Yrs)	B950	4FT deg	S g	BBC	MO+2D$	Ind	32$	Ind	Ind	5	16/26
Univ of WALES COLL of MEDICINE											
Occupational Therapy	B970	3FT deg	* g	BCC	MO+6D	M$6/^ go	Ind	BBBBB$	Ind		
Physiotherapy	B960	3FT deg	B g	BBC	DO $	D$^/DS6 go	Ind	AABBB$	Ind		
Radiography (Diagnostic)	B810	3FT deg	S g	BB-CCD	MO+2D	DS6/^ go	Ind	BBCC$	Ind		
Radiography (Therapeutic)	B820	3FT deg	S g	BB-CCD	MO+2D	DS6/^ go	Ind	BBCC$	Ind		
Univ of WESTMINSTER											
Biomedical Sciences	B940	3FT deg	B	CC-CD	3M	M			Ind	5	8/18
Biomedical Science	149B	2FT HND	B	C	2M					5	
Univ of WOLVERHAMPTON											
Biomedical Sciences	B940	3FT/4SW deg	S g	DD	N	M	24	CCCC	Ind	5	6/16
Interpreting (BSL)	BQ5C	3FT deg		12	4M	M	24	BBBB	Ind		
Public Health	B900	3FT/4SW deg		DD	N	M	24	CCCC	Ind		
Applied Sciences / Biomedical Science	Y100	3FT/4SW deg	S g	DD	N	M	24	CCCC$	Ind		
Applied Sciences / Health Sciences	Y100	3FT/4SW deg	S g	DD	N	M	24	CCCC	Ind		
Applied Sciences / Public Health	Y100	3FT/4SW deg		DD	N	M	24	CCCC	Ind		
Applied Sciences (4 Yrs) / Biomedical Science	Y110	4FT deg	*								
Combined Degrees / Biomedical Science	Y401	3FT/4SW deg	S g	DD	N	M	24	CCCC	Ind		

course details			.98 expected requirements							96 entry stats	
TITLE	CODE	COURSE	SUBJECTS	A/AS	ND/C	AGNVQ	IB	SQA(H)	SQA	RATIO A/AS	
Combined Degrees *Health Sciences*	Y401	3FT/4SW deg	S g	DD	N	M	24	CCCC	Ind		
Combined Degrees *Interpreting Brit Sign Lang (Stg2 CACDP Req)*	Y401	3FT/4SW deg	g	12	4M	M	24	BBBB	Ind		
Combined Degrees *Public Health*	Y401	3FT deg		DD	N	M	24	CCCC	Ind		
Biomedical Science	049B	2FT HND	S g	D	N	M	24	CCCC	Ind	3	2/10

WORCESTER COLL of HE

Health Studies/Art & Design	WB99	3FT deg	A g	DD	Ind	M	Ind	Ind	Ind	2	
Health Studies/Biological Science	CB19	3FT deg	S̲ g	DD	Ind	M	Ind	Ind	Ind	1	
Health Studies/Business Management	NB19	3FT deg	g	DD	Ind	M	Ind	Ind	Ind	3	
Health Studies/Economy and Society	LB19	3FT deg	g	DD	Ind	M	Ind	Ind	Ind		
Health Studies/English and Literary Studies	QB39	3FT deg	g	CC	Ind	M	Ind	Ind	Ind		
Health Studies/Environmental Science	FB99	3FT deg	g	DD	Ind	M	Ind	Ind	Ind	3	
History/Health Studies	BV91	3FT deg	g	DD	Ind	M	Ind	Ind	Ind		
Information Technology/Health Studies	BG95	3FT deg	g	DD	Ind	M	Ind	Ind	Ind		
Psychology/Health Studies	BL97	3FT deg	g	CC	Ind	M	Ind	Ind	Ind	7	
Sociology/Health Studies	BL93	3FT deg	g	DD	Ind	M	Ind	Ind	Ind	4	
Sports Studies/Health Studies	BB96	3FT deg	g	CC	Ind	M	Ind	Ind	Ind		
Urban Studies/Health Studies	BL9V	3FT deg	g	DD	Ind	M	Ind	Ind	Urdn		
Women's Studies/Health Studies	BM99	3FT deg	g	DD	Ind	M	Ind	Ind	Ind		

course details			98 expected requirements							96 entry stats
TITLE	CODE	COURSE	SUBJECTS	A/AS	ND/C	AGNVQ	IB	SQA(H)	SQA	RATIO A/AS
Univ of ABERDEEN										
Celtic Civilisation-History	QVM1	4FT deg	*g	BBC	Ind	M$ go	30$	BBBB$	Ind	4
Celtic-History	QV51	4FT deg	*g	BBC	Ind	M$ go	30$	BBBB$	Ind	7
Church History-Politics	MV11	4FT deg	*g	BBC	Ind	M$ go	30$	BBBB$	Ind	
Economic History-Geography	VL38	4FT deg	*g	BBC	Ind	M$ go	30$	BBBB$	Ind	3
Economic History-International Relations	VM3C	4FT deg	*g	BBC	Ind	M$ go	30$	BBBB$	Ind	
Economic History-Management Studies	NV13	4FT deg	*g	BBC	Ind	M$ go	30$	BBBB$	Ind	2
Economic History-Politics	VM31	4FT deg	*g	BBC	Ind	M$ go	30$	BBBB$	Ind	
Economic History-Social Research	LV33	4FT deg	*g	BBC	Ind	M$ go	30$	BBBB$	Ind	
Economic History-Sociology	VL33	4FT deg	*g	BBC	Ind	M$ go	30$	BBBB$	Ind	
Economics-Economic History	LV13	4FT deg	*g	BBC	Ind	M$ go	30$	BBBB$	Ind	
English-History	QV31	4FT deg	*g	BBC	Ind	M$ go	30$	BBBB$	Ind	3
Entrepreneurship-History	NVC1	4FT deg	*g	BBC	Ind	M$ go	30$	BBBB$	Ind	
French-History	RV11	4FT/5FT deg	*g	BBC	Ind	M$ go	30$	BBBB$	Ind	11
French-History (4 Yrs)	VR11	4FT deg	*g	BBC	Ind	M$ go	30$	BBBB$	Ind	
Geography-History	LV81	4FT deg	*g	BBC	Ind	M$ go	30$	BBBB$	Ind	6
German-History	RV21	4FT/5FT deg	*g	BBC	Ind	M$ go	30$	BBBB$	Ind	
German-History (4 Yrs)	VR12	4FT deg	*g	BBC	Ind	M$ go	30$	BBBB$	Ind	
Hispanic Studies-History	RV41	4FT/5FT deg	*g	BBC	Ind	M$ go	30$	BBBB$	Ind	
Hispanic Studies-History (4 Yrs)	VR14	4FT deg	*g	BBC	Ind	M$ go	30$	BBBB$	Ind	
Historical Studies	V105	4FT deg	*g	BBC	Ind	M$ go	30$	BBBB$	Ind	4
History	V100	4FT deg	*g	BBC	Ind	M$ go	30$	BBBB$	Ind	5
History with Film Studies	V1W5	4FT deg	*g	BBC	Ind	M$ go	30$	BBBB$	Ind	18
History with Women's Studies	V1M9	4FT deg	*g	BBC	Ind	M$ go	30$	BBBB$	Ind	
History-History of Art	VV14	4FT deg	*g	BBC	Ind	M$ go	30$	BBBB$	Ind	8
History-International Relations	VM1C	4FT deg	*g	BBC	Ind	M$ go	30$	BBBB$	Ind	7
History-Management Studies	NV11	4FT deg	*g	BBC	Ind	M$ go	30$	BBBB$	Ind	13
History-Mathematics	VG11	4FT deg	M g	BBC	Ind	M$ go	30$	BBBB$	Ind	
History-Philosophy	VV17	4FT deg	*g	BBC	Ind	M$ go	30$	BBBB$	Ind	8
History-Politics	VM11	4FT deg	*g	BBC	Ind	M$ go	30$	BBBB$	Ind	7
History-Religious Studies	VV18	4FT deg	*g	BBC	Ind	M$ go	30$	BBBB$	Ind	9
History-Social Research	LV31	4FT deg	*g	BBC	Ind	M$ go	30$	BBBB$	Ind	
History-Sociology	VL13	4FT deg	*g	BBC	Ind	M$ go	30$	BBBB$	Ind	4
Scottish Studies	V140	4FT deg	*g	BBC	Ind	M$ go	30$	BBBB$	Ind	4
Univ of Wales, ABERYSTWYTH										
Economic and Social History (Major)	V300	3FT deg	*g	18-20	1M+5D	M^ g	30	BBBCC	Ind	
Economic and Social History (Minor)	V301	3FT deg	*g	18-20	1M+5D	M^ g	30	BBBCC	Ind	
French/Economic & Social History	RV13	4FT deg	E g	18-20	1M+5D$	M^ g	30$	BBBBC$	Ind	
Geography/Economic & Social History	LV83	3FT deg	Gy g	20-22	3M+2D$	M^ g	31$	BBBBC$	Ind	
German/Economic & Social History	RV23	4FT deg	G g	18-20	1M+5D$	M^ g	30$	BBBBC$	Ind	
History	V100	3FT deg	*g	18-20	1M+5D	M^ g	30	BBBCC	Ind	
History/American Studies	QV41	3FT deg	E/H g	18-20	1M+5D$	M^ g	30$	BBBCC$	Ind	
History/Art	VW11	3FT deg	A/Ad g	18-20	1M+5D$	MA^ g	30$	BBBCC$	Ind	
History/Art History	VV14	3FT deg	*g	18-20	1M+5D	MA^ g	30	BBBCC	Ind	
History/Economic & Social History	VV13	3FT deg	*g	18-20	1M+5D	M^ g	30	BBBCC	Ind	
History/Education	VX19	3FT deg	*g	18-20	1M+5D	M^ g	30	BBBCC	Ind	
History/English	QV31	3FT deg	EI	20	1M+5D$	M^ g	30$	BBBBC$	Ind	
History/French	RV11	4FT deg	E g	18-20	1M+5D$	M^ g	30$	BBBBC$	Ind	
History/Geography	LV81	3FT deg	Gy g	20-22	3M+2D$	M^ g	31$	BBBBC$	Ind	
History/German	RV21	4FT deg	G g	18-20	1M+5D$	M^ g	30$	BBBBC$	Ind	
Information and Library Studies/History	PV21	3FT deg	*g	18-20	1M+5D	M^ g	30$	BBBCC	Ind	
International Politics/Economic and Soc Hist	MVC3	3FT deg	*g	20	1M+5D	M6 g	30	BBBCC	Ind	

		course details				98 expected requirements					96 entry stats

TITLE	CODE	COURSE	SUBJECTS	A/AS	NO/C	AGNVQ	IB	SQA(H)	SQA	RATIO A/AS
International Politics/History	MVDD	3FT deg	* g	20	1M+5D	M6 g	30	BBBCC	Ind	
Irish/History	QVND	4FT deg	* g	18-20	1M+5D$	M^ g	30$	BBBCC$	Ind	
Italian/Economic & Social History	RV33	4FT deg	L g	18-20	1M+5D$	M^ g	30$	BBBBC$	Ind	
Italian/History	RV31	4FT deg	L g	18-20	1M+5D$	M^ g	30$	BBBBC$	Ind	
Politics and Modern History	V135	3FT deg	* g	20	1M+5D	M6 g	30	BBBCC	Ind	
Politics/Economic and Social History	MV13	3FT deg	* g	20	1M+5D	M6 g	30	BBBCC	Ind	
Politics/History	MV1D	3FT deg	* g	20	1M+5D	M6 g	30	BBBCC	Ind	
Pure Mathematics/History	GV11	3FT deg	M g	18-20	1M+5D$	M^ g	30$	BBBCC$	Ind	
Spanish/Economic & Social History	RV43	4FT deg	L g	18-20	1M+5D$	M^ g	30$	BBBBC$	Ind	
Spanish/History	RV41	4FT deg	L g	18-20	1M+5D$	M^ g	30$	BBBBC$	Ind	
Welsh History/American Studies	QVK1	3FT deg	E/H g	18-20	1M+5D$	M^ g	30$	BBBCC$	Ind	
Welsh History/Art	VVC1	3FT deg	A/Ad g	18-20	1M+5D$	MA^ g	30$	BBBCC$	Ind	
Welsh History/Art History	VVC4	3FT deg	* g	18-20	1M+5D	MA^ g	30	BBBCC	Ind	
Welsh History/Drama	VWC4	3FT deg	* g	20	1M+5D	MQ^ g	30	BBBBC	Ind	
Welsh History/Economic & Social History	VVC3	3FT deg	* g	18-20	1M+5D	M^ g	30	BBBCC	Ind	
Welsh History/Education	VXC9	3FT deg	* g	18-20	1M+5D	M^ g	30	BBBCC	Ind	
Welsh History/English	QVHC	3FT deg	El	20	1M+5D$	M^ g	30$	BBBBC$	Ind	
Welsh History/Film and Television Studies	VW1M	3FT deg	* g	20	1M+5D	MQ6 g	30	BBBBC	Ind	
Welsh History/French	RV1D	4FT deg	F g	18-20	1M+5D$	M^ g	30$	BBBBC$	Ind	
Welsh History/Geography	LVVC	3FT deg	Gy g	20-22	3M+2D$	M^ g	31$	BBBBC$	Ind	
Welsh History/German	RVFC	4FT deg	G g	18-20	1M+5D$	M^ g	30$	BBBBC$	Ind	
Welsh History/History	V141	3FT deg	* g	18-20	1M+5D	M^ g	30	BBBCC	Ind	
Welsh History/Information and Library Studies	PV2C	3FT deg	* g	18-20	1M+5D	M^ g	30	BBBCC	Ind	
Welsh History/International Politics	MV1C	3FT deg	* g	20	1M+5D	M^ g	30	BBBCC	Ind	
Welsh History/Irish	QVNC	4FT deg	* g	18-20	1M+5D$	M^ g	30$	BBBCC$	Ind	
Welsh History/Italian	RVHC	4FT deg	L g	18-20	1M+5D$	M^ g	30$	BBBBC$	Ind	
Welsh History/Politics	MVCC	3FT deg	* g	20	1M+5D	M^ g	30	BBBCC	Ind	
Welsh History/Pure Mathematics	GVC1	3FT deg	M g	18-20	1M+5D$	M^ g	30$	BBBCC$	Ind	
Welsh History/Spanish	RVKC	4FT deg	L g	18-20	1M+5D$	M^ g	30$	BBBBC$	Ind	
Welsh History/Welsh	QV5C	3FT deg	W g	18-20	1M+5D$	M^ g	30$	BBBCC$	Ind	
Welsh/History	QV51	3FT deg	W g	18-20	1M+5D$	M^ g	30$	BBBCC$	Ind	

ANGLIA Poly Univ

TITLE	CODE	COURSE	SUBJECTS	A/AS	NO/C	AGNVQ	IB	SQA(H)	SQA	RATIO A/AS
Art History and History	VV14▼	3FT deg	*	14	6M	M+/^	Dip	BBCC	Ind	5
Business and History	NV11▼	3FT deg	* g	12	4M	M+/^ go	Dip	BCCC	Ind	19
Communication Studies and History	PV31▼	3FT deg	Ap	14	6M	M+/^	Dip$	BBCC	Ind	18
Economics and History	LV11▼	3FT deg	Ap g	12	4M	M+/^ go	Dip	BCCC	Ind	4
English Language Studies and History	QV11▼	3FT deg	* g	12	4M	M go	Dip	BCCC		
English and History	QV31▼	3FT deg	E	12	4M	M+/^	Dip$	BCCC	Ind	3	10/18
European Philosophy & Literature and History	VV17▼	3FT deg	*	12	4M	M+/^	Dip	BCCC	Ind	6
French and History	RV11▼	4FT deg	* g	12	4M	M+/^ go	Dip	BCCC	Ind	
Geography and History	LV81▼	3FT deg	Gy g	12	4M	M+/^ go	Dip$	BCCC	Ind	
German and History	RV21▼	4FT deg	* g	12	4M	M+/^ go	Dip	BCCC	Ind	5
Graphic Arts and History	VW12▼	3FT deg	A	14	6M	M+/^	Dip$	BBCC		
History	V130▼	3FT deg	H	14	6M	M+/^	Dip$	BBCC	Ind	4	6/18
History and Italian	VR13▼	4FT deg	* g	12	4M	M go	Dip	BCCC	Ind	
History and Law	MV31▼	3FT deg	*	14	6M	M	Dip	BBCC	Ind	7
History and Maths or Stats/Statistical Modelling	GV11▼	3FT deg	* g	12	4M	M+/^	Dip	BCCC	Ind	
History and Music	VW13▼	3FT deg	Mu	12	4M	M+/^	Dip$	BCCC	Ind	
History and Politics	VM11▼	3FT deg	*	14	6M	M	Dip$	BBCC	Ind	6
History and Social Policy	VL14▼	3FT deg	Ap	12	4M $	M+/^	Dip$	BCCC	Ind	3
History and Sociology	LV31▼	3FT deg	Ap	12	4M	M+/^	Dip$	BCCC	Ind	4	14/16
History and Spanish	RV41▼	4FT deg	Ap g	12	4M	M+/^ go	Dip$	BCCC	Ind	
History and Women's Studies	VM19▼	3FT deg	Ap	12	4M	M+/^	Dip$	BCCC	Ind	7

	course details			98 expected requirements						96 entry stats
TITLE	CODE	COURSE	SUBJECTS	A/AS	NO/C	AGNVQ	IB	SQA(H)	SQA	RATIO A/AS
Univ of Wales, BANGOR										
History	V100	3FT deg	H g	18	Ind	D*^ go	28$	BBBC$	Ind	4 10/26
History and Criminology	MV31	3FT deg	H g	CCC	X	D*^ go	28$	BBBC$	X	
History with Archaeology	V1V6	3FT deg	H g	18	Ind	D*^ go	28$	BBBC$	Ind	5 10/22
History/Economics	LV11	3FT deg	H g	18	Ind	D*^ go	28$	BBBC$	Ind	
History/Education (Taught in Welsh)	VX19	3FT deg	H g	CCD	Ind	D*^ go	28$	BBBC$	X	
History/English	QV31	3FT deg	E+H g	CCC	X	D*^ go	28$	BBBC$	X	4 16/20
History/French (Syllabus A)	RV11	4FT deg	F+H g	CCC	X	D*^ go	28$	BBBC$	X	
History/French (Syllabus B)	RVC1	4FT deg	F+H g	CCC	X	D*^ go	28$	BBBC$	X	
History/German	RV21	4FT deg	H g	CCC	X	D*^ go	28$	BBBC$	X	
Mediaeval and Early Modern History	V120	3FT deg	H g	18	Ind	D*^ go	28$	BBBC$	Ind	
Modern and Contemporary History	V130	3FT deg	H g	18	Ind	D*^ go	28$	BBBC$	Ind	
Religious Studies/History	VV18	3FT deg	H g	CCC	Ind	D*^ go	28$	BBBC$	Ind	2 16/22
Russian/History	RV81	4FT deg	H g	CCC	Ind	D*^ go	28$	BBBC$	Ind	
Social Policy/History	LV41	3FT deg	H g	18	Ind	D*^ go	28$	BBBC$	Ind	
Sociology/History	LV31	3FT deg	H g	CCC	Ind	D*^ go	28$	BBBC$	Ind	11
Welsh History with Archaeology	V1VQ	3FT deg	H g	CCD	Ind	D*^ go	28$	BBCC$	Ind	3 14/22
Welsh History/History	V141	3FT deg	H g	CCD	Ind	D*^ go	28$	BBBC$	Ind	12
Welsh History/Religious Studies	VVC8	3FT deg	H g	CCD	Ind	D*^ go	28$	BBBC$	Ind	
Welsh History/Social Policy	LV4C	3FT deg	H g	CCD	Ind	D*^ go	28$	BBBC$	Ind	
Welsh History/Sociology	LV3C	3FT deg	H g	CCD	Ind	D*^ go	28$	BBBC$	Ind	
Welsh History/Welsh	QV5C	3FT/4FT deg	H+W g	CCD	X	D*^ go	Ind	X	X	9
Welsh/History	QV51	3FT/4FT deg	H+W g	CCD	X	D*^ go	Ind	X	X	
Women's Studies and History	MV91	3FT deg	H g	18	Ind	D*6/^ go	28$	BBBC$	Ind	
BARNSLEY COLL										
Humanities *History and Geographical Studies*	Y302	4EXT deg								
Humanities *History and Geographical Studies*	Y301	3FT deg	H/Gy/Po/E g	EE	4M	MB	Ind	Ind	Ind	
Humanities *History and Literature*	Y301	3FT deg	H/Gy/Po/E g	EE	4M	MB	Ind	Ind	Ind	
Humanities *History and Literature*	Y302	4EXT deg								
Humanities *History and Politics with Internat Relations*	Y302	4EXT deg								
Humanities *History and Politics with Internat Relations*	Y301	3FT deg	H/Gy/Po/E g	EE	4M	MB	Ind	Ind	Ind	
BATH COLL of HE										
History	V100	3FT deg	*		Ind		Ind	$	$	11 12/25
Combined Awards *History*	Y400	3FT deg	*		N		Ind	$	$	
Modular Programme (DipHE) *History*	Y460	2FT Dip	*		N		Ind	$	$	
Univ of BIRMINGHAM										
African Studies/East Mediterranean History	TV71	3FT deg	* g	BBB	Ind	D*^	32	ABBB	Ind	
African Studies/History	TVR1	3FT deg	*	BBB	Ind	D*^	32	ABBB	Ind	
American Studies/History	QV41	3FT deg	*	BBB	Ind	D*^	32	ABBB	Ind	8 22/26
Ancient Hist & Archaeology/E Mediterranean Hist	VV1Q	3FT deg	* g	BBB	Ind	D*^	32	ABBB	Ind	
Ancient History	V110	3FT deg	* g	BBC	Ind	D*^	32	ABBB	Ind	21 22/26
Ancient History & Archaeology/History	VV16	3FT deg	*	BBB	Ind	D*^	32	ABBB	Ind	32
Ancient History and Archaeology	VVC6	3FT deg	* g	BBC	Ind	D*^	32	ABBB	Ind	6 18/28
Artificial Intelligence/East Medit History	GVV1	3FT deg	* g	BBB	Ind	D*^	32	ABBB	Ind	
Classical Literature and Civilisation/History	QV81	3FT deg	*	BBB	Ind	D*^	32	ABBB	Ind	

course details | 98 expected requirements | 96 entry stats

TITLE	CODE	COURSE	SUBJECTS	A/AS	NO/C	AGNVQ	IB	SQA(H)	SQA	RATIO A/AS
Computer Studies/East Mediterranean History	GVM1	3FT deg	* g	BBB	Ind	D*^	32	ABBB	Ind	
Dance/East Mediterranean History	WV41	3FT deg	* g	BBB	Ind	D*^	32	ABBB	Ind	
Dance/History	WV4C	3FT deg	*	BBB	Ind	D*^	32	ABBB	Ind	
Drama/East Mediterranean History	VWD4	3FT deg	* g	BBB	Ind	D*^	32	ABBB	Ind	
Drama/History	VW14	3FT deg	*	BBB	Ind	D*^	32	ABBB	Ind	
East Mediterranean History	V145	3FT deg	* g	BBB-BBC	Ind	D*^	32	ABBB	Ind	1	20/26
East Mediterranean History/Classical Lit & Civil	QV8C	3FT deg	* g	BBB	Ind	D*^	32	ABBB	Ind	
East Mediterranean History/English	QVJ1	3FT deg	* g	BBB	Ind	D*^	32	ABBB	Ind	1
East Mediterranean History/French Studies	RVCC	4FT deg	F g	BBB	Ind	D*_^	32	ABBB	Ind	
East Mediterranean History/Geography	LV8C	3FT deg	Gy g	BBB	Ind	D*_^	32$	ABBB	Ind	
East Mediterranean History/German Studies	RVG1	4FT deg	G g	BBB	Ind	D*_^	32$	ABBB	Ind	
East Mediterranean History/Hispanic Studies	RVL1	4FT deg	* g	BBB	Ind	D*^	32	ABBB	Ind	
East Mediterranean History/History	V122	3FT deg	* g	BBB	Ind	D*^	32	ABBB	Ind	4
East Mediterranean History/History of Art	VVD4	3FT deg	* g	BBB	Ind	D*^	32	ABBB	Ind	
East Mediterranean History/Italian	RVJ1	4FT deg	* g	BBB	Ind	D*^	32	ABBB	Ind	
East Mediterranean History/Latin	QV6C	3FT deg	Ln g	BBB	Ind	D*_^	32$	ABBB	Ind	
East Mediterranean History/Mathematics	GV1C	3FT deg	M g	ABB-ABC	Ind	D*_^	32$	ABBB	Ind	
East Mediterranean History/Modern Greek Studies	TV21	4FT deg	g	BBB	Ind	D*^	32$	ABBB	Ind	
East Mediterranean History/Music	VWD3	3FT deg	Mu g	AAB-ABB	Ind	D*_^	32$	ABBB	Ind	
East Mediterranean History/Philosophy	VVD7	3FT deg	* g	BBB	Ind	D*^	32	ABBB	Ind	
East Mediterranean History/Portuguese	RV51	4FT deg	* g	BBB	Ind	D*^	32	ABBB	Ind	
East Mediterranean History/Russian	RVW1	4FT deg	* g	BBB	Ind	D*^	32	ABBB	Ind	
East Mediterranean History/Sport & Recr Studies	VBD6	3FT deg	* g	BBB	Ind	D*^	32	ABBB	Ind	
East Mediterranean History/Theology	VVD8	3FT deg	* g	BBB	Ind	D*^	32	ABBB	Ind	2
Economic History and Political Science	MV13	3FT deg	*	BBC	Ind	D+^	32	ABBBB	Ind	
Economic and Social History	V300	3FT deg	*	BCC	Ind	D+^	30	BBBBB	Ind	5	20/26
Economics and Modern Economic History	LV13	3FT deg	*	BBC	Ind	D+^	32	ABBBB	Ind	7	24/28
English/History	QV31	3FT deg	*	ABB	Ind	D*^	34	ABBB	Ind	13	26/30
French Studies/History	RV11	4FT deg	F	BBB	Ind	D*_^	32	ABBB	Ind	8	28/30
Geography/History	LV81	3FT deg	Gy	BBB	Ind	D*_^	32$	ABBB	Ind	19
German Studies/History	RV21	4FT deg	G	BBB	Ind	D*_^	32$	ABBB	Ind	15
Hispanic Studies/History	RV41	4FT deg	*	BBB	Ind	D*^	32	ABBB	Ind	10
History (Modern)/Political Science	MV11	3FT deg	*	BBB	Ind	D*^	32	ABBB	Ind	15	26/26
History and Social Science	VL13	3FT deg	*	BCC	DO		30	BBBBB	Ind	4	20/26
History, Ancient and Medieval	V116	3FT deg	* g	BBB	Ind	D*^	32	ABBB	Ind	6	22/28
History, Medieval and Modern	V100	3FT deg	* g	AAB/ABB	Ind	D*^	34	ABBB	Ind	8	26/30
History/History of Art	VV14	3FT deg	*	BBB	Ind	D*^	32	ABBB	Ind	21
History/Italian	RV31	4FT deg	*	BBB	Ind	D*^	32	ABBB	Ind	
History/Latin	QV61	3FT deg	Ln	BBB	Ind	D*_^	32$	ABBB	Ind	
History/Mathematics	GV11	3FT deg	M	ABC/ABB	Ind	D*_^	32$	ABBB	Ind	
History/Media & Cultural Studies	PV41	3FT deg	*	BBB	Ind	D*^	32	ABBB	Ind	
History/Modern Greek Studies	TVF1	4FT deg	* g	BBB	Ind	D*^	32	ABBB	Ind	
History/Music	VW13	3FT deg	Mu	AAB-ABB	Ind	D*_^	32$	ABBB	Ind	4
History/Philosophy	VV17	3FT deg	*	BBB	Ind	D*^	32	ABBB	Ind	7	26/30
History/Portuguese	RV5C	4FT deg	*	BBB	Ind	D*^	32	ABBB	Ind	
History/Russian	RV81	4FT deg	*	BBB	Ind	D*^	32	ABBB	Ind	5
History/Sport & Recreation Studies	VB16	3FT deg	*	BBB	Ind	D*^	32	ABBB	Ind	
History/Theology	VV18	3FT deg	*	BBB	Ind	D*^	32	ABBB	Ind	8
Medieval Studies	V120	3FT deg	* g	BBB-BBC	Ind	D*^	32	ABBB	Ind	3	20/24
Russian & E Eur Stud and Economic & Social Hist	R8V3	3FT/4FT deg	R/*	BBC	Ind	D+^		ABBBB	Ind	3
Sociology and Economic History	LV33	3FT deg	*	BBC	Ind	D+^	32	ABBBB	Ind	14

course details			98 expected requirements							96 entry stats
TITLE	CODE	COURSE	SUBJECTS	A/AS	ND/C	AGNVQ	IB	SQA(H)	SQA	RATIO A/AS
BISHOP GROSSETESTE COLL										
Heritage Studies (3 Yrs)	V100	3FT deg	*	8	9M	M*^ go	Ind	Ind	Ind	
BOLTON INST										
Accountancy and History	NVK1	3FT deg	* g	CD	MO	M*	24	BBCC	Ind	
Accountancy and Peace and War Studies	NV41	3FT deg	* g	CD	MO	M*	24	BBCC	Ind	
Art & Design History & Peace and War Studies	VV4C	3FT deg	* g	CD	MO	M*	24	BBCC	Ind	
Art & Design History and History	VV1K	3FT deg	* g	CD	MO	M*	24	BBCC	Ind	
Biology and History	CV11	3FT deg	* g	CD	MO	M*	24	BBCC	Ind	
Biology and Peace and War Studies	CV1C	3FT deg	* g	CD	MO	M*	24	BBCC	Ind	
Business Economics and History	LV11	3FT deg	* g	CD	MO	M*	24	BBCC	Ind	
Business Economics and Peace and War Studies	LV1C	3FT deg	* g	CD	MO	M*	24	BBCC	Ind	
Business Info Systems and History	GVM1	3FT deg	* g	CD	MO	M*	24	BBCC	Ind	
Business Info Systems and Peace & War Studies	GVMC	3FT deg	* g	CD	MO	M*	24	BBCC	Ind	
Business Studies and History	NV11	3FT deg	* g	CD	MO	M*	24	BBCC	Ind	
Community Studies and History	LV51	3FT deg	* g	CD	MO	M*^ go	24	BBCC	Ind	
Community Studies and Peace & War Studies	LV5C	3FT deg	* g	CD	MO	M*	24	BBCC	Ind	
Computing and History	GV5C	3FT deg	* g	CD	MO	M*	24	BBCC	Ind	
Computing and Peace & War Studies	GV5D	3FT deg	* g	CD	MO	M*	24	BBCC	Ind	
Creative Writing and History	VW1X	3FT deg	* g	CD	MO	M*	24	BBCC	Ind	
Creative Writing and Peace and War Studies	WV9C	3FT deg	* g	CD	MO	M*	24	BBCC	Ind	
Design and History	VW12	3FT deg	* g	CD	MO	M*	24	BBCC	Ind	
Design and Peace & War Studies	VWC2	3FT deg	* g	CD	MO	M*	24	BBCC	Ind	
Environmental Studies and History	VF19	3FT deg	* g	CD	MO	M*	24	BBCC	Ind	
Environmental Studies and Peace & War Studies	FVX1	3FT deg	* g	CD	MO	M*	24	BBCC	Ind	
European Cultural St and Peace & War Studies	TV2C	3FT deg	* g	CD	MO	M*	24	BBCC	Ind	
European Cultural Studies and History	TV21	3FT deg	* g	CD	MO	M*	24	BBCC	Ind	
Film and TV Studies and History	WV51	3FT deg	Me/T g	CD	Ind	Ind	24	BBCC	Ind	
Film and TV Studies and Peace and War Studies	WV5C	3FT deg	Me/T g	CD	Ind	Ind	24	BBCC	Ind	
French and History	RV11	3FT deg	F g	CD	Ind	Ind	24	BBCC	Ind	
French and Peace and War Studies	RV1C	3FT deg	F g	CD	Ind	Ind	24	BBCC	Ind	
Gender & Women's Studies and History	MV9D	3FT deg	* g	CD	MO	M*	24	BBCC	Ind	
Gender & Women's Studies and Peace & War Studies	MVXC	3FT deg	* g	CD	MO	M*	24	BBCC	Ind	
German and History	RV21	3FT deg	G g	CD	Ind	Ind	24	BBCC	Ind	
German and Peace and War Studies	RV2C	3FT deg	G g	CD	Ind	Ind	24	BBCC	Ind	
History	V100	3FT deg	H g	CD	MO	M*	24	BBCC	Ind	
History and Human Resource Management	NV1C	3FT deg	* g	CD	MO	M*	24	BBCC	Ind	
History and Language Studies	VQ11	3FT deg	* g	CD	MO	M*^ go	24	BBCC	Ind	
History and Law	VM13	3FT deg	* g	CD	MO	M*	24	BBCC	Ind	
History and Leisure Studies	LV31	3FT deg	* g	CD	MO	M*	24	BBCC	Ind	
History and Literature	QV21	3FT deg	* g	CD	MO	M*	24	BBCC	Ind	
History and Marketing	NV51	3FT deg	* g	CD	MO	M*	24	BBCC	Ind	
History and Mathematics	GV11	3FT deg	M g	DD	Ind	Ind	24	BBCC	Ind	
History and Operations Management	NV21	3FT deg	* g	CD	MO	M*	24	BBCC	Ind	
History and Peace & War Studies	V101	3FT deg	* g	CD	MO	M*	24	BBCC	Ind	
History and Philosophy	VV17	3FT deg	* g	CD	MO	M*	24	BBCC	Ind	
History and Psychology	LV71	3FT deg	* g	12	MO	D*	24	BBCC	Ind	
History and Sociology	LV3D	3FT deg	* g	CD	MO	M	24	Ind	Ind	
History and Theatre Studies	WV41	3FT deg	Me/T g	CD	Ind	Ind	24	BBCC	Ind	
History and Tourism Studies	PV71	3FT deg	* g	CD	MO	M*	24	BBCC	Ind	
History and Urban & Cultural Studies	VL13	3FT deg	* g	CD	MO	M*	24	BBCC	Ind	
Human Resource Management and Peace and War St	NV1D	3FT deg	* g	CD	MO	M*	24	BBCC	Ind	
Law and Peace and War Studies	MV3C	3FT deg	* g	CD	MO	M*	24	BBCC	Ind	

course details — 98 expected requirements — 96 entry stats

TITLE	CODE	COURSE	SUBJECTS	A/AS	NO/C	AGNVQ	IB	SQA(H)	SQA	RATIO A/AS
Leisure Studies and Peace & War Studies	LV3C	3FT deg	* g	CD	MO	M*	24	BBCC	Ind	
Literature and Peace and War Studies	QV2C	3FT deg	* g	CD	MO	M*	24	BBCC	Ind	
Marketing and Peace & War Studies	NV5C	3FT deg	* g	CD	MO	M*	24	BBCC	Ind	
Mathematics and Peace and War Studies	GV1C	3FT deg	M g	CD	Ind	Ind	24	BBCC	Ind	
Operations Management and Peace and War Studies	NV2C	3FT deg	* g	CD	MO	M*	24	BBCC	Ind	
Organisations, Management & Work and Peace & War	NV7C	3FT deg	* g	CD	Ind	Ind	24	BBCC	Ind	
Peace & War Studies and Psychology	LV7C	3FT deg	* g	12	MO	D*	24	BBCC	Ind	
Peace & War Studies and Sociology	VL1H	3FT deg	* g	CD	MO	M	24	Ind	Ind	
Peace & War Studies and Theatre Studies	WV4C	3FT deg	Me/T g	CD	Ind	Ind	24	BBCC	Ind	
Peace & War Studies and Tourism Studies	PV7C	3FT deg	* g	CD	MO	M*	24	BBCC	Ind	
Peace & War Studies and Urban & Cultural Studies	VLC3	3FT deg	* g	CD	MO	M*	24	BBCC	Ind	
Philosophy and Peace & War Studies	VVC7	3FT deg	* g	CD	MO	M*	24	BBCC	Ind	
Visual Arts and History	VW11	3FT deg	* g	CD	MO	M*	24	BBCC	Ind	
Visual Arts and Peace & War Studies	VWC1	3FT deg	* g	CD	MO	M*	24	BBCC	Ind	

Univ of BRADFORD

TITLE	CODE	COURSE	SUBJECTS	A/AS	NO/C	AGNVQ	IB	SQA(H)	SQA	RATIO A/AS
Economics/History	LV11	3FT deg	*	BB-CCC	Ind	M*4	Ind	Ind	Ind	
History with a Modern Language	TV21	4SW deg	L g	BBB-BCC	Ind	M$^	Ind	Ind	Ind	
Politics/History	MV11	3FT deg	*	BB-CCC	Ind	M*4	Ind	Ind	Ind	3 8/22

Univ of BRIGHTON

TITLE	CODE	COURSE	SUBJECTS	A/AS	NO/C	AGNVQ	IB	SQA(H)	SQA	RATIO A/AS
Cultural and Historical Studies	LV61	3FT deg	*	CC	Ind	Ind	Ind	Ind	Ind	
Humanities 　　Modern History	Y300	3FT deg	*	CC	Ind	Ind	Ind	Ind	Ind	

Univ of BRISTOL

TITLE	CODE	COURSE	SUBJECTS	A/AS	NO/C	AGNVQ	IB	SQA(H)	SQA	RATIO A/AS
Ancient History	V110	3FT deg	H/Cl	BBC-BCC	Ind	D$^	28$	BBBBB	Ind	19 20/30
Economic and Social History	V300	3FT deg	* g	BBC	Ind	D$^	30$	AAABB	Ind	2 18/28
Economics and Economic History	LV13	3FT deg	* g	BBC	Ind	D$^	32$	CSYS	Ind	5 22/30
History	V100	3FT deg	*	ABB-BBC	Ind	D$^	33$	AAABB	Ind	15 24/30
History with Study in German	V1R2	4FT deg	G	BBC	Ind	D$^	30$	BBBBB	Ind	

BRISTOL, Univ of the W of England

TITLE	CODE	COURSE	SUBJECTS	A/AS	NO/C	AGNVQ	IB	SQA(H)	SQA	RATIO A/AS
Cultural & Media Studies and History	LV61	3FT deg	* g	CCC	2D+4M	M$^ go	26	BBBC	Ind	
Drama and History	WV41	3FT deg	Ap g	BCC	4M+2D	M$^ go	28	BBBB	Ind	
English and History	QV31	3FT deg	Ap g	CCC	4M+2D	M$^ go	26$	BBBC$	Ind$	
History	V100	3FT deg	H g	BCC	4M+2D	M$^ go	28$	BBBB$	Ind	
Joint Honours Programme 　　History and Geography	Y401	3FT deg	Gy/En/H g	14-16	5M $	M$ go	24$	BCCC$	Ind	

BRUNEL Univ, West London

TITLE	CODE	COURSE	SUBJECTS	A/AS	NO/C	AGNVQ	IB	SQA(H)	SQA	RATIO A/AS
History	V100	3FT deg	H g	BCC	5M	D^	28$	BBBCC	Ind	
History and Anthropology	LV61	3FT deg								
History and Law	MV31	3FT deg	*	BBB	DO	Ind				
History and Sociology	LV31	3FT deg	* g	BCC	5M	D^ go	28$	BBBCC	Ind	
History/American Studies	QV41	3FT deg	H g	14	MO $	M* go	22$	BCCC$	Ind	
History/Art	V1W1	3FT deg	H+A g	14	MO $	M* go	22$	BCCC$	Ind	
History/Drama	VW14	3FT deg	T+H g	BC	MO $	M* go	26$	BBCC$	Ind	
History/English	QV31	3FT deg	H+E g	14	MO $	M* go	22$	BCCC$	Ind	
History/Film & TV Studies	V1W5	3FT deg	H+Ap g	20	MO $	M* go	28$	BBCC$	Ind	
Music/History	VW13	3FT deg	H g	12	MO $	M* go	22$	BCCC$	Ind	
Politics and Contemporary Hist (4 Yrs Thick SW)	MV1D	4SW deg	*	BCC	5M	M^	28	BBBCC	Ind	
Politics and Contemporary History	MV1C	3FT deg	*	BCC	5M	M^	28	BBBCC	Ind	3 10/24
Politics and Contemporary History (4 Yr Thin SW)	MV11	4SW deg	*	BCC	5M	D^	28	BBBCC	Ind	3 8/26

course details			98 expected requirements							96 entry stats	
TITLE	CODE	COURSE	SUBJECTS	A/AS	ND/C	AGNVQ	IB	SQA(H)	SQA	RATIO	A/AS
Univ of BUCKINGHAM											
History	V130	2FT deg	H	10	5M	M	24	CCCC	Ind		
History and English Literature	QV31	2FT deg	E/H	10	5M	M	24	CCCC	Ind		
Politics and History	MV11	2FT deg	* g	12	5M	M	24	CCCC	Ind		
BUCKINGHAMSHIRE COLLEGE											
Leisure Management and Heritage Studies	NV71	3FT deg		8-10	1D	M	27	CCCC	Ind		
Leisure Management with Heritage Studies	N7V1	3FT deg		8-10	1D	M	27	CCCC	Ind		
Tourism and Heritage Studies	PV71	3FT deg									
Tourism with Heritage Studies	P7V1	3FT deg									
CAMBRIDGE Univ											
History	V100▼	3FT deg	* g	AAB	Ind		Ind	CSYS	Ind	3	28/30
History with Education Studies (BA)	V1X9▼	3FT deg	* g	AAB	Ind		Ind	CSYS	Ind	10	
CANTERBURY CHRIST CHURCH COLL of HE											
American Studies with History	Q4V1	4FT deg	H g	CC	MO	M	24	Ind	Ind	2	
Art with History	W1V1	3FT deg	A+H g	CC	MO	M	24	Ind	Ind	11	
Business Studies with History	N1V1	3FT deg	H g	CC	MO	M	24	Ind	Ind	6	
Early Childhood Studies with History	X9V1	3FT deg	H g	CC	MO	M	24	Ind	Ind	9	
English with History	Q3V1	3FT deg	E+H	CC	MO	M	24	Ind	Ind	6	
Geography with History	L8V1	3FT deg	Gy+H g	CC	MO	M	24	Ind	Ind		
History	V100	3FT deg	H g	CC	MO	M	24	Ind	Ind	7	8/20
History and American Studies	QV41	3FT deg	H g	CC	MO	M	24	Ind	Ind		
History and Art	VW11	3FT deg	A+H g	CC	MO	M	24	Ind	Ind	2	
History and Business Studies	VN11	3FT deg	H g	CC	MO	M	24	Ind	Ind	4	
History and Early Childhood Studies	XV91	3FT deg	H g	CC	MO	M	24	Ind	Ind		
History and English	VQ13	3FT deg	H+E	CC	MO	M	24	Ind	Ind	3	
History and French	RV11	3FT deg	F+H g	CC	MO	M	24	Ind	Ind		
History and Geography	LV81	3FT deg	Gy+H g	CC	MO	M	24	Ind	Ind		
History and Social Science	LV31	3FT deg	H g	CC	MO	M	24	Ind	Ind	5	
History with American Studies	V1Q4	3FT deg	H g	CC	MO	M	24	Ind	Ind	2	
History with Art	V1W1	3FT deg	A+H g	CC	MO	M	24	Ind	Ind		
History with Business Studies	V1N1	3FT deg	H g	CC	MO	M	24	Ind	Ind	12	
History with Early Childhood Studies	V1X9	3FT deg	H g	CC	MO	M	24	Ind	Ind	4	
History with English	V1Q3	3FT deg	E+H	CC	MO	M	24	Ind	Ind	5	
History with French	V1R1	3FT deg	H+F g	CC	MO	M	24	Ind	Ind		
History with Geography	V1L8	3FT deg	Gy+H g	CC	MO	M	24	Ind	Ind	4	
History with Information Technology	V1G5	3FT deg	H g	CC	MO	M	24	Ind	Ind	2	
History with Marketing	V1N5	3FT deg	H g	CC	MO	M	24	Ind	Ind		
History with Mathematics	V1G1	3FT deg	H+M g	DD	Ind	Ind	24	Ind	Ind		
History with Media Studies	V1P4	3FT deg	H g	CC	MO	M	24	Ind	Ind		
History with Music	V1W3	3FT deg	H+Mu g	CC	MO	M	24	Ind	Ind	2	
History with Psychology	V1L7	3FT deg	H+Ps g	CC	MO	M	24	Ind	Ind	6	
History with Radio, Film And Television Studies	V1W5	3FT deg	H g	CC	MO	M	24	Ind	Ind		
History with Religious Studies	V1V8	3FT deg	H g	CC	MO	M	24	Ind	Ind		
History with Science	V1Y1	3FT deg	H+S g	CC	MO	M	24	Ind	Ind		
History with Social Science	V1L3	3FT deg	H g	CC	MO	M	24	Ind	Ind	3	10/14
History with Sport Science	V1B6	3FT deg	H g	CC	MO	M	24	Ind	Ind		
History with Statistics	V1G4	3FT deg	H+M g	DD	Ind	Ind	24	Ind	Ind		
History with Tourism Studies	V1P7	3FT deg	H g	CC	MO	M	24	Ind	Ind		
Information Technology and History	VG15	3FT deg	H g	CC	MO	M	24	Ind	Ind		
Information Technology with History	G5V1	3FT deg	H g	CC	MO	M	24	Ind	Ind		
Marketing and History	NV51	3FT deg	H g	CC	MO	M	24	Ind	Ind		

course details			98 expected requirements							96 entry stats	
TITLE	CODE	COURSE	SUBJECTS	A/AS	ND/C	AGNVQ	IB	SQA(H)	SQA	RATIO R/AS	
Marketing with History	N5V1	3FT deg	H g	CC	MO	M	24	Ind	Ind		
Mathematics and History	GV11	3FT deg	M+H g	DD	Ind	Ind	24	Ind	Ind		
Mathematics with History	G1V1	3FT deg	M+H g	DD	Ind	Ind	24	Ind	Ind		
Media Studies and History	PV41	3FT deg	H g	CC	MO	M	24	Ind	Ind		
Media Studies with History	P4V1	3FT deg	H g	CC	MO	M	24	Ind	Ind		
Music and History	VW13	3FT deg	H+Mu g	CC	MO	M	24	Ind	Ind		
Music with History	W3V1	3FT deg	Mu+H g	CC	MO	M	24	Ind	Ind		
Psychology and History	LV71	3FT deg	Ps+H g	CC	MO	M	24	Ind	Ind		
Psychology with History	L7V1	3FT deg	Ps+H g	CC	MO	M	24	Ind	Ind		
Radio, Film and Television Studies and History	VW15	3FT deg	H g	CC	MO	M	24	Ind	Ind		
Radio,Film & Television Studies with History	W5V1	3FT deg	H g	CC	MO	M	24	Ind	Ind		
Religious Studies and History	VV18	3FT deg	H g	CC	MO	M	24	Ind	Ind		
Religious Studies with History	V8V1	3FT deg	H g	CC	MO	M	24	Ind	Ind		
Science and History	VY11	3FT deg	H+S g	DD	Ind	Ind	24	Ind	Ind		
Science with History	Y1V1	3FT deg	S+H g	DD	Ind	Ind	24	Ind	Ind		
Social Science with History	L3V1	3FT deg	H g	CC	MO	M	24	Ind	Ind	6	
Sport Science and History	BV61	3FT deg	H g	CC	MO	M	24	Ind	Ind		
Sport Science with History	B6V1	3FT deg	H g	CC	MO	M	24	Ind	Ind	2	
Statistics and History	GV41	3FT deg	M+H g	DD	Ind	Ind	24	Ind	Ind		
Statistics with History	G4V1	3FT deg	M+H g	DD	Ind	Ind	24	Ind	Ind		
Tourism Studies and History	PV71	3FT deg	H g	CC	MO	M	24	Ind	Ind	8	
Tourism Studies with History	P7V1	3FT deg	H g	CC	MO	M	24	Ind	Ind		

CARDIFF Univ of Wales

Ancient History	V110	3FT deg	*	BCC	Ind		Ind	AAABB		6	18/26
Ancient and Medieval History	V116	3FT deg	H	BBC-BCC	Ind		Ind	AABBB		7	18/22
Archaeology and Ancient History	VVC6	3FT deg	*	BCC	Ind		Ind	AAABB	X	6	18/26
Archaeology and Medieval History	VV1P	3FT deg	H	BBC-BCC	X		Ind	AABBB	X	9	
Cultural Criticism/Ancient History	MV91	3FT deg	E	ABC	Ind	Ind	Ind	Ind	Ind		
Education/Ancient History	XV91	3FT deg	*	BCC	Ind		Ind	AAABB			
English Literature/Ancient History	QV3D	3FT deg	E	ABB			Ind	AAABB	X		
French/Ancient History	RV11	4FT deg	F	BBC	Ind		Ind	ABBBB	Ind		
German/Ancient History	RV21	4FT deg	G	BCC			Ind				
History	V100	3FT deg	H	BBC	X		Ind	AABBB	X	5	18/28
History and Welsh History	V141	3FT deg	H	BBC	X		Ind	AABBB	X	7	18/22
History of Ideas and Philosophy	VVD7	3FT deg	*	BCC	3M+2D		Ind	AABB		2	16/22
History of Ideas/Ancient History	V176	3FT deg		BBC	Ind		Ind	AAABB			
History of Ideas/Archaeology	VVD6	3FT deg	*	BBC	Ind		Ind	AABB	X	1	
History of Ideas/Cultural Criticism	MV9D	3FT deg	E	ABC	X		Ind	AAABB	X		
History of Ideas/Economics	VLD1	3FT deg	*	BBC-BBB	7M+7D		Ind	AAAB	Ind		
History of Ideas/Education	VXD9	3FT deg	*	BBC	Ind	Ind	Ind	Ind	Ind		
History of Ideas/English Literature	VQD3	3FT deg	E	ABB			Ind	AAABB	X		
History of Ideas/French	VRD1	4FT deg	F	BBC	Ind		Ind	ABBBB	Ind		
History of Ideas/German	VRD2	4FT deg	G	BBC			Ind			1	
History of Ideas/History	V106	3FT deg	H	BCC	X		Ind	AABBB	X	5	
History/Ancient History	V117	3FT deg	H	BBC-BCC	Ind		Ind	AABBB	X	7	
History/Archaeology	VV16	3FT deg	H	BBC-BCC	X		Ind	AABBB	X	5	
History/Economics	VL11	3FT deg	H	BBC-BBB	X		Ind	AAABB	X	6	
History/English Literature	VQ13	3FT deg	E+H	ABB	X		Ind	AAABB	X	4	24/30
History/French	VR11	4FT deg	F+H	BBC	X		Ind	ABBBB	X	18	
History/German	VR12	4FT deg	H+G	BBC	X		Ind	AABBB	X		
Italian/Ancient History	RV3C	4FT deg	L	BCC	X		Ind	Ind	X		
Italian/History	RV31	4FT deg	H+L	BBC-BCC	X		Ind	ABBBB	X	5	

History 33

			SUBJECTS	A/AS	NQ/C	RGNVQ	IB	SQA(H)	SQA	RATIO A/AS
TITLE	**CODE**	**COURSE**								
Italian/History of Ideas	RV3D	4FT deg	L	BCC	X		Ind	ABBBB	X	
Music/History	WV31	3FT deg	H+Mu	BBC	X		Ind	AABBB	X	7
Philosophy/Ancient History	VV7C	3FT deg	*	BBC	Ind		Ind	AAABB		5
Philosophy/History	VVCR	3FT deg	H	BCC	X		Ind	AABBB	X	
Philosophy/History of Ideas	VVDT	3FT deg	*	BCC						
Politics and Modern History	MV11	3FT deg	H	BBB-BCC	X		Ind	AABBB	X	7 20/24
Politics/History of Ideas	MV1D	3FT deg	*	BBC			Ind	AABBB		
Portuguese/History of Ideas	RV5D	4FT deg	L	BBC						
Religious Studies/Ancient History	VV8C	3FT deg	*	BCC	Ind		Ind	AAABB		
Religious Studies/History	VV81	3FT deg	H	BBC-BCC	X		Ind	ABBBB	X	4 24/30
Religious Studies/History of Ideas	VV8D	3FT deg	*	BCC						
Social Philosophy & App Ethics/History of Ideas	VV7D	3FT deg	*	BCC						
Social Philosophy and App Ethics/Ancient History	VVR1	3FT deg	*	BBC	Ind		Ind	AAABB		
Social Philosophy and Applied Ethics/History	VVRC	3FT deg	H	BCC	X		Ind	AABBB	X	
Sociology/Ancient History	LV3C	3FT deg	*	BCC	3M+2D		Ind	Ind		
Sociology/History	LV31	3FT deg	H	BBC-BCC	X		Ind	ABBBB	X	12
Sociology/History of Ideas	LV3D	3FT deg	*	BCC			Ind			
Spanish/Ancient History	QR84	4FT deg	L	BBC-BCC	Ind		Ind	Ind	Ind	
Spanish/History	RV41	4FT deg	H+L	BBC-BCC	X		Ind	Ind	X	
Spanish/History of Ideas	RV4D	4FT deg	L	BBC						
Welsh History/Ancient History	V111	3FT deg	H	BBC-BCC	Ind		Ind	AAABB		1
Welsh History/Archaeology	VV6C	3FT deg	H	BBC-BCC	X		Ind	AABBB	X	
Welsh History/Cultural Criticism	MV9C	3FT deg	E	ABC	Ind	Ind	Ind	Ind	Ind	
Welsh History/Economics	VLCC	3FT deg	H	BBC-BBB	X		Ind	AAABB	X	
Welsh History/Education	VXC9	3FT deg	H	BBC-BCC	X	Ind	Ind	AABBB	X	3
Welsh History/English Literature	VQCH	3FT deg	E+H	ABB	X		Ind	AAABB	X	
Welsh History/History of Ideas	V108	3FT deg	H	BCC	X		Ind	AABBB	X	
Welsh History/Philosophy	VV1R	3FT deg	H	BCC	X		Ind	AABBB	X	
Welsh History/Religious Studies	VVC8	3FT deg	H	BBC-BCC	X		Ind	ABBBB	X	
Welsh History/Social Philosophy and App Ethics	VV1T	3FT deg	H	BCC	X		Ind	AABBB	X	
Welsh History/Sociology	VLC3	3FT deg	H	BBC-BCC	X		Ind	ABBBB	X	
Welsh History/Welsh	VQC5	3FT deg	H+W	BBC-BCC	X		Ind	X	X	6
Welsh/Ancient History	QV5C	3FT deg	W	BCC						
Welsh/History	QV51	3FT deg	H+W	BBC-BCC	X		Ind	X	X	

Univ of CENTRAL LANCASHIRE

History	V100	3FT deg	H	16	Ind	D$^	28$	BBBC$	Ind	
Combined Honours Programme _History_	Y400	3FT deg	*	14	Ind	M*6/^	28	BBBC	Ind	

CHELTENHAM & GLOUCESTER COLL of HE

Business Management and History	NV11	3FT deg	H	12-16	4M+3D	MB3	26	CCCC	Ind	
Business Management with History	N1V1	4SW deg	*	12	4M+3D	MB3	26	CCCC	Ind	
English Studies and History	QV31	3FT deg	E+H	12-16	4M+3D	M^	26	CCCC	Ind	
English Studies with History	Q3V1	3FT deg	E	12-14	4M+3D	M^	26	CCCC	Ind	
Geography and History	LV8C	3FT deg	H	12-14	M0	M3^	26	CCCC	Ind	
Geography with History	L8VC	3FT deg	*	12	M0	M3^	26	CCCC	Ind	
Geology and History	FV61	3FT deg	H+S	8-12	5M+2D	M3^	26	CCCC	Ind	
Geology with History	F6V1	3FT deg	H+S	8-12	M0	M3	26	CCCC	Ind	
History and Human Geography	LV81	3FT deg	H	12	4M+3D	M3^	26	CCCC	Ind	
History and Media Communications	PV41	3FT deg	H	12	M0	M3^	26	CCCC	Ind	
History and Natural Resource Management	FV91	3FT deg	H	10-12	M0	M3	26	CCCC	Ind	
History and Physical Geography	FV81	3FT deg	H	12	5M+2D	M3^	26	CCCC	Ind	
History and Psychology	LV71	3FT deg	H g	12-16	4M+3D	M3^	26	CCCC	Ind	

| | | | 98 expected requirements | | | | | | | 96 entry stats |
| course details | | | | | | | | | | |
TITLE	CODE	COURSE	SUBJECTS	A/AS	ND/C	AGNVQ	IB	SQA(H)	SQA	RATIO A/AS
History and Religious Studies	VV18	3FT deg	H	8-12	5M+2D	M3^	26	CCCC	Ind	
History and Sociological Studies	LV31	3FT deg	H	12-16	4M+3D	M3^	26	CCCC	Ind	
History and Sport & Exercise Sciences	VB16	3FT deg	H+S	12-16	5M+2D	M3^	26	CCCC	Ind	
History and Tourism Management	PV71	3FT deg	H	12-16	4M+3D	M3^	26	CCCC	Ind	
History and Visual Arts	VW11	3FT deg	A	10-14	5M+2D	MA3	26	CCCC	Ind	
History and Women's Studies	MV91	3FT deg	H	12	5M+2D	M3^	26	CCCC	Ind	
History with Business Management	V1N1	3FT deg	H	12	5M+2D	M3^	26	CCCC	Ind	
History with Combined Arts	V1Y3	3FT deg	H	12	MO	M3^	26	CCCC	Ind	
History with English Studies	V1Q3	3FT deg	H+E	12	4M+3D	M3^	26	CCCC	Ind	
History with Geography	V1LV	3FT deg	H	12	MO	M3^	26	CCCC	Ind	
History with Geology	V1F6	3FT deg	H	8-12	5M+2D	M3^	26	CCCC	Ind	
History with Human Geography	V1L8	3FT deg	H	10-14	4M+3D	M3^	26	CCCC	Ind	
History with Media Communications	V1P4	3FT deg	H	10-14	MO	M3^	26	CCCC	Ind	
History with Modern Languages (French)	V1R1	3FT deg	H g	12	5M+2D	M3^	26	CCCC	Ind	
History with Natural Resource Management	V1F9	3FT deg	H	10-14	4M+3D	M3^	26	CCCC	Ind	
History with Physical Geography	V1F8	3FT deg	H	10-14	4M+3D	M3^	26	CCCC	Ind	
History with Psychology	V1L7	3FT deg	H g	12-16	4M+3D	M3^	26	CCCC	Ind	
History with Religious Studies	V1V8	3FT deg	H	10-14	4M+3D	M3^	26	CCCC	Ind	
History with Sociological Studies	V1L3	3FT deg	H	10-14	4M+3D	M3^	26	CCCC	Ind	
History with Sport & Exercise Sciences	V1B6	3FT deg	H+S g	12-16	4M+3D	M3^	26	CCCC	Ind	
History with Tourism Management	V1P7	3FT deg	H	10-14	4M+3D	M3^	26	CCCC	Ind	
History with Visual Arts	V1W1	3FT deg	*	10-14	5M+2D	MA3	26	CCCC	Ind	
History with Women's Studies	V1M9	3FT deg	H	12	4M+3D	M3^	26	CCCC	Ind	
Human Geography with History	L8V1	3FT deg	H	12	4M+3D	M3	26	CCCC	Ind	
Media Communications with History	P4V1	3FT deg	*	12	MO	M3^	26	CCCC	Ind	
Natural Resource Mgt with History	F9VC	3FT deg	*	8-12	MO	M3	26	CCCC	Ind	
Physical Geography with History	F8V1	3FT deg	*	8-12	4M+3D	M3^	26	CCCC	Ind	
Psychology with History	L7V1	3FT deg	g	12-16	4M+3D	M3^	26	CCCC	Ind	
Religious Studies with History	V8V1	3FT deg	*	8-12	MO	M3^	26	CCCC	Ind	
Sociological Studies with History	L3V1	3FT deg	*	12-14	4M+3D	MG3	26	CCCC	Ind	
Sport & Exercise Sciences with History	B6V1	3FT deg	S	12-16	4M+3D	ML3	26	CCCC	Ind	
Tourism Management with History	P7V1	4SW deg	*	12-16	5M+2D	ML3	26	CCCC	Ind	
Visual Arts with History	W1V1	3FT deg	A	10-14	5M+2D	MA3	26	CCCC	Ind	
Women's Studies with History	M9V1	3FT deg	*	8-12	MO	M3	26	CCCC	Ind	

UNIVERSITY COLLEGE CHESTER

TITLE	CODE	COURSE	SUBJECTS	A/AS	ND/C	AGNVQ	IB	SQA(H)	SQA	RATIO A/AS
Art and History	WV91	3FT deg	H/Ec/So	CC	M	P^	Ind	CCCC	$	
Art with History	W9V1	3FT deg	H/Ec/So	CC	M	P^	Ind	CCCC	$	8
Biology and History	CV11	3FT deg	B+H/Ec/So	12	M	P^	Ind	CCCC	$	
Biology with History	C1V1	3FT deg	B+H/Ec/So	12	M	P^	Ind	CCCC	$	
Church and Society	VV38	3FT deg		12	MO	P	Ind	CCCC	$	
Computer Science/IT and History	GV51	3FT deg	H/Ec/So g	12	M	M	Ind	CCCC	$	8
Computer Science/IT with History	G5V1	3FT deg	H/Ec/So g	12	M	M	Ind	CCCC	$	2
Drama and Theatre Studies and History	WV41	3FT deg	H	CC	M	P^	Ind	CCCC	$	
Drama and Theatre Studies with History	W4V1	3FT deg	H/Ec/So	CC	M	P^	Ind	CCCC	$	
English Literature and History	QV31	3FT deg	E+H/Ec/So	CC	M	P^	Ind	CCCC	$	8 14/20
English with History	Q3V1	3FT deg	E+H/Ec/So	CC	M	P^	Ind	CCCC	$	11
Geography and History	FV81	3FT deg	Gy/Gl+H/Ec/So	CC	M	P^	Ind	CCCC	$	
Geography with History	F8V1	3FT deg	Gy/Gl+H/Ec/So	CC	M	P^	Ind	CCCC	$	11
History and Mathematics	VG11	3FT deg	H/Ec/So+M	12	M	P^	Ind	CCCC	$	1
History and Physical Education/Sports Science	VB16	3FT deg	H/Ec/So	CC	M	P^	Ind	CCCC	$	
History and Psychology	VL17	3FT deg	H/Ec/So g	12	M	P^	Ind	CCCC	$	11
History and Theology and Religious Studies	VV18	3FT deg	H/Ec/So	12	M	M	Ind	CCCC	$	5

| | | | 98 expected requirements | | | | | | | 96 entry stats |
| | | | | | | | | | | |

course details

TITLE	CODE	COURSE	SUBJECTS	A/AS	ND/C	RGNVQ	IB	SQA(H)	SQA	RATIO A/AS
History with Art	V1W9	3FT deg	H/Ec/So	CC	M	M	Ind	CCCC	$	
History with Biology	V1C1	3FT deg	H/Ec/So+B	12	M	P^	Ind	CCCC	$	
History with Computer Science/IT	V1G5	3FT deg	H/Ec/So g	12	M	M	Ind	CCCC	$	7
History with Drama and Theatre Studies	V1W4	3FT deg	H/Ec/So	CC	M	M	Ind	CCCC	$	7
History with English Literature	V1Q3	3FT deg	H/Ec/So+E	CC	M	P^	Ind	CCCC	$	10
History with French	V1R1	3FT deg	H/Ec/So g	12	M	P^	Ind	CCCC	$	4
History with Geography	V1F8	3FT deg	H/Ec/So+Gy/Gl	CC	M	P^	Ind	CCCC	$	6
History with German	V1R2	3FT deg	H/Ec/So g	12	M	P^	Ind	CCCC	$	
History with Mathematics	V1G1	3FT deg	H/Ec/So+M	12	M	P^	Ind	CCCC	$	
History with Physical Education/Sports Science	V1B6	3FT deg	H/Ec/So	CC	M	P^	Ind	CCCC	$	
History with Psychology	V1L7	3FT deg	H/Ec/So g	12	M	M	Ind	CCCC	$	5
History with Theology and Religious Studies	V1V8	3FT deg	H/Ec/So	12	M	M	Ind	CCCC	$	4
Mathematics with History	G1V1	3FT deg	M+H/Ec/So	12	M	P^	Ind	CCCC	$	
PE/Sports Science with History	B6V1	3FT deg	H/Ec/So	CC	M	P^	Ind	CCCC	$	
Psychology with History	L7V1	3FT deg	H/Ec/So g	12	M	M	Ind	CCCC	$	10
Theology and Religious Studies with History	V8V1	3FT deg	H/Ec/So	12	M	M	Ind	CCCC	$	8

CHICHESTER INSTITUTE OF HIGHER EDUCATION

TITLE	CODE	COURSE	SUBJECTS	A/AS	ND/C	RGNVQ	IB	SQA(H)	SQA	RATIO A/AS
Art and History	WV11	3FT deg	H+A+Pf	12	Ind	M$+^	Ind	Ind	Ind	
Art with History	W1V1	3FT deg	A+Pf	12	Ind	M$+^	Ind	Ind	Ind	
Art with History	E1V1	3FT deg	A+Pf	12	Ind	M$+^	Ind	Ind	Ind	
Dance and History	VW14	3FT deg	H+Pf	12	Ind	M$+	Ind	Ind	Ind	
Dance with History	W4V1	3FT deg	Pf	12	Ind	M$+	Ind	Ind	Ind	
English Language Teaching (EFL) and History	QV11	3FT deg	E	12	Ind	M^	Ind	Ind	Ind	
English and History	QV31	3FT deg	E+H	12	Ind	M^	Ind	Ind	Ind	4
English with History	Q3V1	3FT deg	E	12	Ind	M^	Ind	Ind	Ind	2	14/18
Environmental Science and History	VF19	3FT deg	H	12	Ind	M$	Ind	Ind	Ind	
Geography with History	L8V1	3FT deg	Gy	12	Ind	M$	Ind	Ind	Ind	
History	V100	3FT deg	H	12	Ind	M$	Ind	Ind	Ind	5	8/24
History and Geography	LV81	3FT deg	H/Gy	12	Ind	M$	Ind	Ind	Ind	
History and Study of Religions	VV18	3FT deg	H	12	Ind	M$	Ind	Ind	Ind	
History with Art	V1W1	3FT deg	H	12	Ind	M$	Ind	Ind	Ind	
History with Dance	V1W4	3FT deg	H	12	Ind	M$	Ind	Ind	Ind	2
History with Education Studies (Opt. QTS) (P)	V1X9	3FT/4FT deg	H g	12	Ind	M$ go	Ind	Ind	Ind	3	4/16
History with English	V1Q3	3FT deg	H	12	Ind	M$	Ind	Ind	Ind	12
History with English Language Teaching (EFL)	V1Q1	3FT deg	H	12	Ind	M$	Ind	Ind	Ind	
History with Environmental Science	V1F9	3FT deg	H g	12	Ind	M$	Ind	Ind	Ind	1
History with Geography	V1L8	3FT deg	H	12	Ind	M$	Ind	Ind	Ind	
History with Mathematics	V1G1	3FT deg	H g	12	Ind	M$	Ind	Ind	Ind	
History with Media Studies	V1P4	3FT deg	H	12	Ind	M$	Ind	Ind	Ind	6
History with Music	V1W3	3FT deg	H	12	Ind	M$	Ind	Ind	Ind	
History with Related Arts	V1W9	3FT deg	H	12	Ind	M$	Ind	Ind	Ind	
History with Study of Religions	V1V8	3FT deg	H	12	Ind	M$	Ind	Ind	Ind	
History with Theology	V1W	3FT deg	H	12	Ind	M$	Ind	Ind	Ind	
History with Women's Studies	V1M9	3FT deg	H	12	Ind	M$	Ind	Ind	Ind	1
Mathematics and History	GV11	3FT deg	M+H	12	Ind	M^	Ind	Ind	Ind	
Mathematics with History	G1V1	3FT deg	M	12	Ind	M^	Ind	Ind	Ind	
Media Studies and History	PV41	3FT deg	H	12	Ind	M$	Ind	Ind	Ind	3	10/14
Media Studies with History	P4V1	3FT deg	*	12	Ind	M$	Ind	Ind	Ind	
Music and History	VW13	3FT deg	H+Mu	12	Ind	M$+	Ind	Ind	Ind	
Music with History	W3V1	3FT deg	Mu	12	Ind	M$+	Ind	Ind	Ind	
Related Arts and History	WV91	3FT deg	H	12	Ind	M$+	Ind	Ind	Ind	
Study of Religions with History	V8V1	3FT deg	*	12	Ind	M$	Ind	Ind	Ind	6

course details			98 expected requirements							96 entry stats	
TITLE	CODE	COURSE	SUBJECTS	A/AS	NO/C	AGNVQ	IB	SQA(H)	SQA	RATIO	A/AS
Theology and History	VV81	3FT deg	H	12	Ind	M^	Ind	Ind	Ind		
Theology with History	V8VC	3FT deg	*	12	Ind	M$	Ind	Ind	Ind		
Women's Studies and History	MV91	3FT deg	H	12	Ind	M$	Ind	Ind	Ind		
COLCHESTER INST											
Communications & Media Studies/History	PV31	3FT deg		CC	Ind	Ind	Ind	Ind	Ind	3	
English/History	QV31	3FT deg		CC	Ind	Ind	Ind	Ind	Ind	4	
History/Sociology	VL13	3FT deg		CC	Ind	Ind	Ind	Ind	Ind	7	
COVENTRY Univ											
History and French	VR11	4FT deg	F	CD	M	M	Ind	CCCC$	Ind		
History and Geography	LV81	3FT deg	*	CD	M	M	Ind	CCCC	Ind		
History and German	VR12	4FT deg	*	CD	M	M	Ind	CCCC	Ind		
History and International Relations	MV11	3FT deg	*	CD	M	M	Ind	CCCC	Ind		
History and Politics	MV1C	3FT deg	*	CD	M	M	Ind	CCCC	Ind		
Italian and History	VR13	4FT deg	*	CD	M	M	Ind	CCCC	Ind		
Psychology and History	CV81	3FT deg	*	CD	M	M	Ind	CCCC	Ind		
Russian and History	VR18	4FT deg	*	CD	M	M	Ind	CCCC	Ind		
Sociology and History	LV31	3FT deg	* g	CC-CD	3M+3D	M go	Ind	BBB	Ind		
Spanish and History	VR14	4FT deg	*	CD	M	M	Ind	CCCC	Ind		
DE MONTFORT Univ											
History	V100▼	3FT deg	* g	CCD	MO	M$^	28$	ABBB	Ind	11	14/22
History	V101▼	3FT deg	H g	12	10M+2D	M^	Ind	BCCC	Ind	4	8/16
Humanities Combined Honours *History*	Y300▼	3FT deg	* g	CCD	MO	M$^	28$	ABBB	Ind		
Humanities Joint Honours *History*	Y301▼	3FT deg	* g	CCD	MO	M$^	26$	ABBB	Ind		
Univ of DERBY											
History	V100	3FT deg	H/Po	14	MO $	M$	28$	BBCC$	Ind		
Credit Accumulation Modular Scheme *Heritage and History*	Y600	3FT deg	*	12	MO	M	Ind	CCCC	Ind		
Credit Accumulation Modular Scheme *History*	Y600	3FT deg	*	12	MO	M	Ind	CCCC	Ind		
Credit Accumulation Modular Scheme *Local History*	Y600	3FT deg	*	12	MO	M	Ind	CCCC	Ind		
Univ of DUNDEE											
American Studies and Modern History	QV41	4FT deg	* g	BCC	Ind	D$	29	BBBC	Ind	6	
Business Economics & Marketing & Modern History	Y605	4FT deg	* g	BCC	Ind	D$	29	BBBC	Ind		
Contemporary European Studies and Modern History	TV21	4FT deg	* g	BCC	Ind	D$	29	BBBC	Ind	6	
Economics and Modern History	LV11	4FT deg	* g	BCC	Ind	D$	29	BBBC	Ind		
English and Modern History	QV31	4FT deg	E g	BCC	Ind	D$^	29$	BBBC$	Ind	9	
Environmental Science and Modern History	FV91	4FT deg	* g	BCC	Ind	D$	29	BBBC	Ind		
Financial Economics and Modern History	LVC1	4FT deg	* g	BCC	Ind	D$	29	BBBC	Ind		
Geography and Modern History	LV81	4FT deg	* g	BCC	Ind	D$	29	BBBC	Ind	17	
Modern History	V130	4FT deg	* g	BCC	Ind	D$	29	BBBC	Ind	12	
Modern History and Philosophy	VV17	4FT deg	* g	BCC	Ind	D$	29	BBBC	Ind	7	
Modern History and Political Science	MV11	4FT deg	* g	BCC	Ind	D$	29	BBBC	Ind	3	
Modern History and Psychology	LV71	4FT deg	* g	BCC	Ind	D$	29	BBBC	Ind	5	
Arts and Social Sciences *Modern History*	Y400	3FT deg	* g	BCC	Ind	D$	29	BBBC	Ind		
Univ of DURHAM											
Ancient History	V110	3FT deg	*	BCC	Ind	Ind	Ind	Ind	Ind		
Ancient History and Archaeology	VF14	3FT deg	*	BCC	MO	Ind	28	AAABB	Ind	8	22/26

TITLE	CODE	COURSE	SUBJECTS	A/AS	ND/C	AGNVQ	IB	SQA(H)	SQA	RATIO	A/AS
										96 entry stats	
Ancient, Medieval and Modern History	V101	3FT deg	*	ABC	Ind	Ind	Ind	Ind	Ind	12	24/30
Archaeology and History	FV41	3FT deg	*	BBC	MO	Ind	30	AAABB	Ind	12	
Chinese with History	T3V1	4FT deg	*	BBC	Ind	Ind	31	AABBB	Ind		
Economics and History	LV11	3FT deg	* g	ABC	Ind	X	32$	AAABB	Ind	9	26/28
History	V100	3FT deg	* g	ABB	Ind	Ind	Ind	Ind	Ind	9	26/30
History with French	V1R1	4FT deg	F	ABB	Ind	Ind	Ind	Ind	Ind	9	26/28
History with German	V1R2	4FT deg	G	ABB	Ind	Ind	Ind	Ind	Ind		
Japanese with History	T4V1	4FT deg	*	BBC	Ind	Ind	31	AABBB	Ind		
Medieval Studies (English and History)	QV31	3FT deg	H/E g	AAB	Ind	Ind	Ind	Ind	Ind	22	
Politics and History	MV11	3FT deg	*	ABC	Ind	Ind	Ind	Ind	Ind	27	28/30
Sociology and History	LV31	3FT deg	*	ABC	Ind	Ind	Ind	Ind	Ind		
Arts Combined *East Asian History*	Y300	3FT deg	*	24	MO	Ind	30	AAABB	Ind		
Social Sciences Combined *History*	Y220	3FT deg	*	ABC	MO	Ind	32	AAABB	Ind		

Univ of EAST ANGLIA

TITLE	CODE	COURSE	SUBJECTS	A/AS	ND/C	AGNVQ	IB	SQA(H)	SQA	RATIO	A/AS
Economic & Social History with Modern Euro Lang	V3T2	4FT deg	L/*	BBC	3M+3D		30	BBBBB	Ind		
Economic and Social History	V320	3FT deg	H	ABC-BCC	3M+3D		30	BBBBB	Ind	6	
Economic and Social History and Philosophy	VV37	3FT deg	*	BBC	3M+3D		30	BBBBB	Ind	12	
Economic and Social History and Politics	MV13	3FT deg	*	BBC	3M+3D		30	BBBBB	Ind	3	
Economics and Economic and Social History	LV13	3FT deg	*	BBC	3M+3D		30	BBBBB	Ind	18	
English Literature with English History Minor	Q3V1	3FT deg	H+E	ABB-BBB	X		30	ABBBB	X	14	
English Studies (History and Literature)	QV31	3FT deg	H+E	BBB	X		30	ABBBB	X	7	8/30
History	V100	3FT deg	H	ABC-BCC	X		30	BBBBB	X	6	16/28
History and Politics	MV11	3FT deg	H	BBB-BCC	X		30	BBBBB	X	11	18/24
History of Art and History	VV14	3FT deg	H	BBC-BCC	X		30	BBBBB	X	7	
History, American and English	V148	4FT deg	H	BBC-BCC	X		30	ABBBB	X	4	14/26
History, American with Politics	V1M1	4FT deg	H	BBC-BCC	X		30	ABBBB	Ind	5	
History, English	V140	3FT deg	H	ABC-BCC	X		30	BBBBB	X	11	16/22
History, English and American	V144	3FT deg	H	ABC-BCC	X		30	BBBBB	X	6	18/28
History, European	V145	3FT deg	H	ABC-BCC	X		30	BBBBB	X	4	18/22
History, European with French or German Language	V1T2	4FT deg	H+F/G	ABC-BCC	X		30	BBBBB	X	9	
History, Modern	V130	3FT deg	H	ABC-BCC	X		30	BBBBB	X	6	17/28
History,English,with Landscape Archaeology Minor	V1V6	3FT deg	H	ABC-BCC	X		30	BBBBB	X	4	18/26
History,European w Danish or Norw or Swed Lang	V1R7	4FT deg	M+L	ABC-BCC	X		30	BBBBB	X		
History,European with Double Honours Language	V1TY	4FT deg	H+2L	ABC-BCC	X		30	BBBBB	X	3	
Sociology and Economic and Social History	LV33	3FT deg	*	BBC	3M+3D		30	BBBBB	Ind	2	

Univ of EAST LONDON

TITLE	CODE	COURSE	SUBJECTS	A/AS	ND/C	AGNVQ	IB	SQA(H)	SQA	RATIO	A/AS
Archaeological Sciences and History	FV4C	3FT deg	* g	12	MO	M					
Cultural Studies and History	LVP1	3FT deg	* g	14	N	M	Ind	Ind	Ind	6	
Cultural Studies with History	L6V1	3FT deg	* g	14	MO	M	Ind	Ind	Ind		
Economics and History	LV11	3FT deg	* g	12	MO	M	Ind	Ind	Ind		
Economics with History	L1V1	3FT deg	* g	12	MO	M	Ind				
Education & Community Studies and History	VX19	3FT deg	* g	12	MO	M	Ind	Ind	Ind	2	
Education & Community Studies with History	X9V1	3FT deg	* g	12	MO	M					
History	V100	3FT deg	* g	12	MO	M$	Ind	Ind	Ind	6	6/14
History and History of Art Design & Film	VV14	3FT deg	* g	12	MO	M$	Ind	Ind	Ind		
History and Information Technology	GV51	3FT deg	* g	12	MO	M$	Ind	Ind	Ind		
History and Literature	QV31	3FT deg	* g	12	MO	X	Ind	Ind	Ind	3	12/24
History and Media Studies	PV4C	3FT deg	* g	12	MO	M	Ind	Ind	Ind		
History and Politics	MV11	3FT deg	* g	12	MO	M	Ind	Ind	Ind	26	
History and Psychosocial Studies	LV71	3FT deg	* g	12	MO	M$	Ind	Ind	Ind	2	

course details | 98 expected requirements | 96 entry stats

TITLE	CODE	COURSE	SUBJECTS	A/AS	NO/C	RGNVQ	IB	SQA(H)	SQA	RATIO A/AS
History and Sociology	LV31	3FT deg	*g	12	MO	M$	Ind	Ind	Ind	4
History and Third World & Development Studies	MVY1	3FT deg	*g	12	MO	M	Ind	Ind	Ind	2
History and Women's Studies	MV91	3FT deg	*g	12	MO	M	Ind	Ind	Ind	
History of Art Design & Film with History	V4V1	3FT deg	*g	12	MO	M	Ind	Ind		
History with Archaeological Sciences	V1F4	3FT deg	*g	12	MO	M				
History with Cultural Studies	V1L6	3FT deg	*g	12	MO	M				
History with Economics	V1L1	3FT deg	*g	12	MO	M	Ind	Ind		
History with Education & Community Studies	V1X9	3FT deg	*g	12	MO	M	Ind	Ind		
History with European Studies	V1T2	3FT deg	*g	12	MO	M	Ind	Ind		
History with History of Art Design & Film	V1V4	3FT deg	*g	12	MO	M	Ind	Ind		
History with Information Technology	V1G5	3FT deg	*g	12	MO	M	Ind	Ind		
History with Literature	V1Q3	3FT deg	*g	12	MO	M	Ind	Ind		
History with Politics	V1M1	3FT deg	*g	12	MO	M	Ind	Ind		
History with Sociology	V1L3	3FT deg	*g	12	MO	M	Ind	Ind		
History with Women's Studies	V1M9	3FT deg	*g	12	MO	M	Ind	Ind		
History/European Studies	TV21	3FT deg	*g	12	MO	M	Ind	Ind	Ind	
Information Technology with History	G5V1	3FT deg	*g	12	MO	M	Ind	Ind	Ind	
Literature with History	Q3V1	3FT deg	*g	12	MO	M	Ind			
Media Studies with History	P4V1	3FT deg	*g	14	MO	M				
Politics with History	M1V1	3FT deg	*g	12	MO	M	Ind			
Psychosocial Studies with History	L7V1	3FT deg	*g	12	MO	M	Ind	Ind	Ind	
Sociology with History	L3V1	3FT deg	*g	12	MO	M	Ind	Ind	Ind	
Third World & Development Studies with History	M9V1	3FT deg	*g	12	MO	M	Ind	Ind		
Women's Studies with History	M9VC	3FT deg	*g	12	MO	M	Ind			
Three-Subject Degree *History*	Y600	3FT deg	*g	12	MO	M	Ind	Ind	Ind	

EDGE HILL Univ COLLEGE

History	V101	3FT deg	H	DD	X	P*^	Dip	BBCC$	X	
History	V100	3FT deg	H	DD	X	P*^	Dip	BBCC$	X	3 6/16
History and Applied Social Sciences	LV31	3FT deg	H	CC	3M+3D	P*^	Dip	BBCC$	X	
History and Contemporary Religion & Beliefs	VV81	3FT deg	H	DD	3M+3D	P*^	Dip	BBCC$	Ind	
History and English	QV31	3FT deg	H/E	CC	X	X	Dip	BBCC$	Ind	
History and Sports Studies	BV61	3FT deg	H	CC	X	P*^	Dip	BBCC$	X	
History and Urban Policy Studies	MVY1	3FT deg	H	DD	X	P*^	Dip	BBCC$	X	
Modern European Studies and History	TV21	3FT deg	H	DD	X	P*^	Dip	BBCC	Ind	
Women's Studies and History	MV91	3FT deg	H	CD	X	P*^	Dip	BBCC$	X	2 10/14

Univ of EDINBURGH

Ancient Civilisations of the Med and Middle East	VV61	4FT deg	g	BBB	Ind	Ind	Dip$	BBBB	Ind	
Ancient History	V110	4FT deg	g	BBB	Ind	Ind	Dip$	BBBB	Ind	
Ancient History and Classical Archaeology	VV16	4FT deg	g	BBB	Ind	Ind	Dip$	BBBB	Ind	
Ancient History and Greek	VQ17	4FT deg	g	BBB	Ind	Ind	Dip$	BBBB	Ind	
Ancient History and Latin	VQ16	4FT deg	g	BBB	Ind	Ind	Dip$	BBBB	Ind	
Architectural History	VV41	4FT deg	*	BBB	Ind		34$	ABBB	Ind	3
Celtic and Scottish Historical Studies	QV51	4FT deg	L g	BBB	Ind	Ind	Dip$	BBBB$	Ind	
Classics and Medieval History	QV81	4FT deg	g	BBB	Ind	Ind	Dip$	BBBB	Ind	7
Economic History	V300	4FT deg	*	BBB	Ind		34	ABBB	Ind	7
Economic and Social Hist with Environmental St	V3F9	4FT deg		BBB			34	ABBB		
Economic and Social History	V340	4FT deg	*	BBB	Ind		34	ABBB	Ind	8
Economics and Economic History	LV13	4FT deg	g	BBB	Ind		34$	ABBB	Ind	11
English Language and History	QV31	4FT deg	E g	BBB	Ind	Ind	Dip$	BBBB$	Ind	
English Literature and History	QV3C	4FT deg	E g	AAB	Ind	Ind	Dip$	ABBB$	Ind	
French and European History	RV11	4FT deg	E g	BBB	Ind	Ind	Dip$	BBBB$	Ind	
Geography and Economic and Social History	LV83	4FT deg	*	ABB	Ind		36$	AABB	Ind	8

course details | 98 expected requirements | 96 entry stats

TITLE	CODE	COURSE	SUBJECTS	A/AS	ND/C	AGNVQ	IB	SQA(H)	SQA	RATIO A/AS
German and European History	RV21	4FT deg	L g	BBB	Ind	Ind	Dip$	BBBB$	Ind	
History	V100	4FT deg	g	BBB	Ind	Ind	Dip$	BBBB	Ind	
History and History of Art	VV14	4FT deg	g	BBB	Ind	Ind	Dip$	BBBB	Ind	
History and Scottish Historical Studies	V141	4FT deg	g	BBB	Ind	Ind	Dip$	BBBB	Ind	
History and Sociology	VL13	4FT deg	g	BBB	Ind	Ind	Dip$	BBBB	Ind	
Italian and European History	RV31	4FT deg	L g	BBB	Ind	Ind	Dip$	BBBB$	Ind	
Latin and Scottish Historical Studies	QV61	4FT deg	g	BBB	Ind	Ind	Dip$	BBBB	Ind	
Law and Economic History	MV33	4FT deg	g	ABB	X		32	AAABB	X	3
Law and History	MV31	4FT deg	g	ABB	X		32	AAABB	X	6
Politics and Economic and Social History	MV13	4FT deg	*	ABB	Ind		36$	AABB	Ind	5
Politics and Modern History	MV11	4FT deg	g	BBB	Ind	Ind	Dip$	BBBB	Ind	
Russian Studies and European History	RV81	4FT deg	L g	BBB	Ind	Ind	Dip$	BBBB$	Ind	
Scottish Ethnology and Scottish Historical Studs	VV91	4FT deg	g	BBB	Ind	Ind	Dip$	BBBB	Ind	
Scottish Historical Studies	V140	4FT deg	g	BBB	Ind	Ind	Dip$	BBBB	Ind	
Scottish Literature and Scottish Historical St	QV21	4FT deg	g	BBB	Ind	Ind	Dip$	BBBB	Ind	
Social Anthropology and Social History	LV63	4FT deg	*	AAB	Ind		38$	ABBB	Ind	10
Social Policy and Social and Economic History	LV43	4FT deg	*	BBB	Ind		34	ABBB	Ind	6
Social and Architectural History	VV34	4FT deg	*	BBB	Ind		34$	ABBB	Ind	2
Sociology and Social and Economic History	LV33	4FT deg	*	BBB	Ind		34$	ABBB	Ind	12
Spanish and European History	RV41	4FT deg	L g	BBB	Ind	Ind	Dip$	BBBB$	Ind	
Social Science Economic & Social History	Y200	3FT deg	*	BBB	Ind		34	ABBB	Ind	

Univ of ESSEX

History	V100	3FT deg	*	20	MO+2D	Ind	28	BBBB	Ind	5 14/20
History (European Exchange) (4 Yrs)	V105	4FT deg	L	20	MO+2D	Ind	28	BBBB	Ind	5
History and Economics	LV11	3FT deg	* g	20	MO+2D	Ind	28	BBBB	Ind	15
History and Literature	QV21	3FT deg	*	22	MO+3D	Ind	28	AABB	Ind	5 16/18
History and Music	VW13	3FT deg	*	20	MO+2D	Ind	28	BBBB	Ind	7
History and Politics	MV11	3FT deg	*	20	MO+2D	Ind	28	BBBB	Ind	9 16/20
History and Sociology	LV31	3FT deg	*	20	MO+2D	Ind	28	BBBB	Ind	7
Philosophy and History	VV17	3FT deg	*	20	MO+2D	Ind	28	BBBB	Ind	6

Univ of EXETER

Ancient History	V110	3FT deg	*	BCC	MO	M/D$	32	Ind	Ind	5 16/26
Ancient History and Archaeology	VVC6	3FT deg	*	BCC	MO	M/D$	30	Ind	Ind	14 18/22
Economic and Social History	V340	3FT deg	* g	BBB-CCC	MO	M/D$	30	Ind	Ind	2 16/22
Economic and Social History with European Study	V341	4FT deg	L g	BBB-CCC	MO	M/D$	30	Ind	Ind	2
English Medieval Studies	QV31	3FT deg	E	BBB-BCC	MO	M/D$^	32$	Ind	Ind	
English Medieval Studies with European Study	QV3C	4FT deg	E+L	BBB-BCC	MO	M/D$^	32$	Ind	Ind	
History	V100	3FT deg	*	ABB-BCC	MO	M/D$	32	Ind	Ind	11 20/30
History and Ancient History	V111	3FT deg	*	BBC-BCC	MO	M$	32	Ind	Ind	29
History and Archaeology	VV16	3FT deg	*	BBC-BCC	MO	M$	32	Ind	Ind	8 16/24
History and Archaeology with European Study	VV1P	4FT deg	L	BBC-BCC	MO	M/D$	32	Ind	Ind	
History and French	RV1C	4FT deg	F	ABB-BCC	MO	M/D$^	32$	Ind	Ind	
History and German	RV2C	4FT deg	G	ABB-BCC	MO	M/D$^	32$	Ind	Ind	
History and Italian	RV3C	4FT deg	L g	ABB-BCC	MO	M/D$	32	Ind	Ind	
History and Politics	MV11	3FT deg	*	ABB-BBC	MO	M/D$	34	Ind	Ind	8 22/30
History and Politics with European Study	VM11	4FT deg	L	ABB-BBC	MO	M/D$	34$	Ind	Ind	5
History and Russian	RV8C	4FT deg	* g	ABB-BCC	MO	M/D$	32	Ind	Ind	
History and Society	LV33	3FT deg	*	BBB-CCC	MO	M/D$	35	Ind	Ind	5 16/24
History and Spanish (Beginners Spanish avail)	RV4C	4FT deg	g	ABB-BCC	MO	M/D$^	32$	Ind	Ind	
History with European Study	V101	4FT deg	L	ABB-BBC	MO	M/D$	34	Ind	Ind	6
Russian and Economic History	RV83	4FT deg	* g	BBC-BDE	MO	M/D$	30	Ind	Ind	

course details			98 expected requirements							96 entry stats	
TITLE	CODE	COURSE	SUBJECTS	A/AS	NO/C	AGNVQ	IB	SQA(H)	SQA	RATIO	A/AS
Univ of GLAMORGAN											
American Studies and History	QV41	3FT deg	* g	12	5M	M$	Ind	Ind	Ind		
English Studies and History	QV31	3FT deg	* g	12	Ind	Ind	Ind	Ind	Ind		
Geography and History	LV81	3FT deg	* g	12	Ind	Ind	Ind	Ind	Ind		
Government and History	MV11	3FT deg	* g	12	Ind	Ind	Ind	Ind	Ind		
History	V100	3FT deg	* g	12	5M	M	Ind	Ind	Ind		
History and Philosophy	VV17	3FT deg	* g	12	5M	M	Ind	Ind	Ind		
History and Psychology	LV71	3FT deg	* g	CC	Ind	Ind	Ind	Ind	Ind		
History and Religious Studies	VV18	3FT deg	* g	12	5M	M	Ind	Ind	Ind		
History and Sociology	LV31	3FT deg	* g	12	5M	M	Ind	Ind	Ind		
History and Welsh Studies	QV51	3FT deg	* g	12	5M	M	Ind	Ind	Ind		
History with Anthropology	V1L6	3FT deg	* g	12	5M	M	Ind	Ind	Ind		
Humanities (History)	V101	3FT deg	* g	CC	5M	M$	24	CCCC	HN	4	8/14
Combined Studies (Honours) History	Y400	3FT deg	* g	8-16	Ind	Ind	Ind	Ind	Ind		
Joint Honours History	Y401	3FT deg	* g	8-16	Ind	Ind	Ind	Ind	Ind		
Major/Minor Honours History	Y402	3FT deg	* g	8-16	Ind	Ind	Ind	Ind	Ind		
Univ of GLASGOW											
Anthropology/History	LV61	4FT deg		BBC	N	M	30	BBBB	Ind		
Anthropology/Scottish History	LV6C	4FT deg		BBC	N	M	30	BBBB	Ind		
Anthropology/Sociology	LV63	4FT deg		BBC	N	M	30	BBBB	Ind		
Archaeology/Economic and Social History	VV36	4FT deg		BBC	HN	M	30	BBBB	Ind		
Archaeology/History	VV16	4FT deg		BBC	HN	M	30	BBBB	Ind	6	
Archaeology/Scottish History	VVCP	4FT deg		BBC	HN	M	30	BBBB	Ind		
Business Economics/History	LVC1	4FT deg		BBC	N	M	30	BBBB	N		
Business Economics/Scottish History	LVCD	4FT deg		BBC	N	M	30	BBBB	N		
Celtic Civilisation/Economic and Social History	QV5H	4FT deg		BBC	HN	M	30	BBBB	Ind		
Celtic Civilisation/History	QV5C	4FT deg		BBC	HN	M	30	BBBB	Ind		
Celtic Civilisation/Scottish History	QV5D	4FT deg		BBC	HN	M	30	BBBB	Ind	5	
Celtic/History	QV51	4FT deg		BBC	HN	M	30	BBBB	Ind	4	
Celtic/Scottish History	QVMC	4FT deg		BBC	HN	M	30	BBBB	Ind	4	
Classical Civilisation/History	QV81	4FT deg		BBC	HN	M	30	BBBB	Ind	4	
Classical Civilisation/Scottish History	QV8C	4FT deg		BBC	HN	M	30	BBBB	Ind	2	
Classical Hebrew/Economic and Social History	VV3W	4FT deg		BBC	HN	M	30	BBBB	Ind		
Classical Hebrew/Scottish History	VVWC	4FT deg		BBC	HN	M	30	BBBB	Ind		
Computing/Economic History	GV53	4FT deg		BBC	HN	M	30	BBBB	Ind		
Computing/History	GV51	4FT deg		BBC	HN	M	30	BBBB	Ind	7	
Computing/Scottish History	GV5C	4FT deg		BBC	HN	M	30	BBBB	Ind		
Czech/Economic History	TV13	5FT deg		BBC	HN	M	30	BBBB	Ind		
Czech/History	TV1D	5FT deg		BBC	HN	M	30	BBBB	Ind		
Czech/Scottish History	TV1C	5FT deg		BBC	HN	M	30	BBBB	Ind		
Economic & Social History/Classical Civilisation	QV83	4FT deg		BBC	HN	M	30	BBBB	Ind		
Economic and Social Hist/Social & Urban Policy	LV43	4FT deg		BBC	8M	M	30	BBBB	Ind		
Economic and Social History	V300	4FT deg		BBC	8M	M	30	BBBB	Ind	4	
Economic and Social History with Celtic	V3Q5	4FT deg		BBC	8M	M	30	BBBB	Ind		
Economic and Social History with Czech	V3T1	4FT deg		BBC	8M	M	30	BBBB	Ind		
Economic and Social History with French	V3R1	4FT deg		BBC	8M	M	30	BBBB	Ind		
Economic and Social History with German	V3R2	4FT deg		BBC	8M	M	30	BBBB	Ind		
Economic and Social History with Hispanic Studs	V3R4	4FT deg		BBC	8M	M	30	BBBB	Ind		
Economic and Social History with Italian	V3R3	4FT deg		BBC	8M	M	30	BBBB	Ind		

course details			***98 expected requirements***							*96 entry stats*
TITLE	CODE	COURSE	SUBJECTS	A/AS	ND/C	AGNVQ	IB	SQA(H)	SQA	RATIO A/AS
Economic and Social History with Polish	V3TC	4FT deg	BBC	8M	M	30	BBBB	Ind	
Economic and Social History/Archaeology	VV63	4FT deg	BBC	HN	M	30	BBBB	Ind	
Economic and Social History/Classical Hebrew	QV93	4FT deg	BBC	HN	M	30	BBBB	Ind	
Economic and Social History/Computing Science	VG35	4FT deg	BBC	8M	M	30	BBBB	Ind	
Economic and Social History/Economics	LV1H	4FT deg	BBC	8M	M	30	BBBB	Ind	3
Economic and Social History/English	QV33	4FT deg	BBC	HN	M	30	BBBB	Ind	3
Economic and Social History/French	RV13	5FT deg	BBC	HN	M	30	BBBB	Ind	4
Economic and Social History/Geography	LV83	4FT deg	BBC	8M	M	30	BBBB	Ind	9
Economic and Social History/German	RV23	5FT deg	BBC	HN	M	30	BBBB	Ind	
Economic and Social History/Greek	QV73	4FT deg	BBC	HN	M	30	BBBB	Ind	
Economic and Social History/History	VV1H	4FT deg	BBC	HN	M	30	BBBB	Ind	
Economic and Social History/History	VV13	4FT deg	BBC	8M	M	30	BBBB	Ind	3
Economic and Social History/Italian	RV33	5FT deg	BBC	HN	M	30	BBBB	Ind	
Economic and Social History/Latin	QV63	4FT deg	BBC	HN	M	30	BBBB	Ind	
Economic and Social History/Management Studies	NV13	4FT deg	BBC	8M	M	30	BBBB	Ind	
Economic and Social History/Mathematics	GV13	4FT deg	BBC	HN	M	30	BBBB	Ind	
Economic and Social History/Mathematics	VG31	4FT deg	BBC	8M	M	30	BBBB	Ind	
Economic and Social History/Medieval History	VV31	4FT deg	BBC	8M	M	30	BBBB	Ind	
Economic and Social History/Music	VW33	4FT deg	BBC	HN	M	30	BBBB	Ind	
Economic and Social History/Philosophy	VV37	4FT deg	BBC	8M	M	30	BBBB	Ind	1
Economic and Social History/Philosophy	VVH7	4FT deg	BBC	HN	M	30	BBBB	Ind	
Economic and Social History/Politics	MV13	4FT deg	BBC	8M	M	30	BBBB	Ind	6
Economic and Social History/Psychology	CV8H	4FT deg	BBC	HN	M	30	BBBB	Ind	7
Economic and Social History/Psychology	CV83	4FT deg	BBC	8M	M	30	BBBB	Ind	2
Economic and Social History/Scottish History	VVC3	4FT deg	BBC	HN	M	30	BBBB	X	3
Economic and Social History/Scottish History	VV3C	4FT deg	BBC	8M	M	30	BBBB	Ind	3
Economic and Social History/Scottish Literature	QVH3	4FT deg	BBC	HN	M	30	BBBB	Ind	
Economic and Social History/Sociology	LV33	4FT deg	BBC	8M	M	30	BBBB	Ind	7
Economics/History	LV11	4FT deg	BBC	8M	M	30	BBBB	Ind	
Economics/Scottish History	LV1C	4FT deg	BBC	HN	M	30	BBBB	Ind	
Economics/Scottish History	LVCC	4FT deg	BBC	8M	M	30	BBBB	Ind	
English/History	QV31	4FT deg	BBC	HN	M	30	BBBB	Ind	4 20/28
English/Scottish History	QVHC	4FT deg	BBC	HN	M	30	BBBB	Ind	6
Film and Television Studies/History	VW15	4FT deg	BBB	HN	D	32	AABB	HN	13
Film and Television Studies/Scottish History	VWC5	4FT deg	BBB	HN	D	32	AABB	HN	7
French/History	VR11	5FT deg	BBC	HN	M	30	BBBB	Ind	4
Geography/History	LV8C	4FT deg	BBC	HN	M	30	BBBB	Ind	8
Geography/Scottish History	LVVC	4FT deg	BBC	HN	M	30	BBBB	Ind	5
German/History	VR12	5FT deg	BBC	HN	M	30	BBBB	Ind	11
German/Scottish History	RV2C	5FT deg	BBC	HN	M	30	BBBB	Ind	
Greek/History	QV71	4FT deg	BBC	HN	M	30	BBBB	Ind	
Greek/Scottish History	QV7C	4FT deg	BBC	HN	M	30	BBBB	Ind	
Hispanic Studies/History	RV41	5FT deg	BBC	HN	M	30	BBBB	Ind	
Hispanic Studies/Scottish History	RV4C	5FT deg	BBC	HN	M	30	BBBB	Ind	
History (Medieval/Modern or Med/Mod/Scottish)	V100	4FT deg	BBC	HN	M	30	BBBB	Ind	8 24/28
History of Art/Scottish History	VVC4	4FT deg	BBC	HN	M	30	BBBB	Ind	5
History/Economics	LV1D	4FT deg	BBC	HN	M	30	BBBB	Ind	5
History/History of Art	VV14	4FT deg	BBC	HN	M	30	BBBB	Ind	11
History/Italian	RV31	5FT deg	BBC	HN	M	30	BBBB	Ind	
History/Latin	QV6D	4FT deg	BBC	HN	M	30	BBBB	Ind	
History/Mathematics	GV11	4FT deg	BBC	HN	M	30	BBBB	Ind	
History/Music	VW13	4FT deg	BBC	HN	M	30	BBBB	Ind	3

course details | 98 expected requirements | 96 entry stats

TITLE	CODE	COURSE	SUBJECTS	A/AS	NQ/C	AGNVQ	IB	SQA(H)	SQA	RATIO	A/AS
History/Philosophy	VV1R	4FT deg		BBC	HN	M	30	BBBB	Ind	4	
History/Polish	TVD1	5FT deg		BBC	HN	M	30	BBBB	Ind		
History/Politics	MVC1	4FT deg		BBC	HN	M	30	BBBB	Ind	9	22/26
History/Psychology	CV8C	4FT deg		BBC	HN	M	30	BBBB	Ind	13	
History/Russian	RVV1	5FT deg		BBC	HN	M	30	BBBB	Ind	3	
History/Scottish History	V146	4FT deg		BBC	HN	M	30	BBBB	Ind	18	
History/Scottish Literature	QVF1	4FT deg		BBC	HN	M	30	BBBB	Ind		
History/Sociology	LVH1	4FT deg		BBC	HN	M	30	BBBB	Ind	17	
History/Theology & Religious Studies	VV1V	4FT deg		BBC	HN	M	30	BBBB	Ind	4	
Islamic Studies/Economic History	TV63	4FT deg		BBC	N	M	30	BBBB	Ind		
Italian/Scottish History	RV3C	5FT deg		BBC	HN	M	30	BBBB	Ind		
Latin/Scottish History	QV6C	4FT deg		BBC	HN	M	30	BBBB	Ind		
Management Studies/History	NVC1	4FT deg		BBC	HN	M	30	BBBB	Ind	10	
Management Studies/History	NV11	4FT deg		BBC	8M	M	30	BBBB	Ind	6	
Management Studies/Scottish History	NVCC	4FT deg		BBC	8M	M	30	BBBB	Ind	4	
Management Studies/Scottish History	NV1C	4FT deg		BBC	HN	M	30	BBBB	Ind	4	
Mathematics/Scottish History	GV1C	4FT deg		BBC	HN	M	30	BBBB	Ind		
Modern History (American Studies)	V130	4FT deg		BBC	HN	M	30	BBBB	Ind	10	
Music/Scottish History	VWC3	4FT deg		BBC	HN	M	30	BBBB	Ind	4	
Philosophy/History	VV17	4FT deg		BBC	8M	M	30	BBBB	Ind	5	
Philosophy/Scottish History	VVC7	4FT deg		BBC	8M	M	30	BBBB	Ind		
Philosophy/Scottish History	VVCT	4FT deg		BBC	HN	M	30	BBBB	Ind		
Physics/Scottish History	FV3C	4FT deg	M+P	BBC	HN	M	30	BBBB	Ind	2	
Politics/History	MV1D	4FT deg		BBC	8M	M	30	BBBB	Ind	5	
Politics/Scottish History	MVCC	4FT deg		BBC	8M	M	30	BBBB	Ind	2	
Politics/Scottish History	MV1C	4FT deg		BBC	HN	M	30	BBBB	Ind	5	
Psychology/History	CV81	4FT deg		BBC	8M	M	30	BBBB	Ind	6	
Psychology/Scottish History	CVVC	4FT deg		BBC	8M	M	30	BBBB	Ind	5	
Psychology/Scottish History	CVV1	4FT deg		BBC	HN	M	30	BBBB	Ind	6	
Russian/Scottish History	RVVC	5FT deg		BBC	HN	M	30	BBBB	Ind		
Scottish History/Scottish Literature	QVG1	4FT deg		BBC	HN	M	30	BBBB	Ind	5	
Scottish History/Sociology	LV3C	4FT deg		BBC	HN	M	30	BBBB	Ind	8	
Scottish History/Theology & Religious Studies	VVCV	4FT deg		BBC	HN	M	30	BBBB	Ind		
Social and Urban Policy/History	LV41	4FT deg		BBC	8M	M	30	BBBB	Ind	4	
Sociology/History	LV31	4FT deg		BBC	8M	M	30	BBBB	Ind	7	
Sociology/Scottish History	LVJC	4FT deg		BBC	8M	M	30	BBBB	Ind	2	
Theatre Studies/Economic History	VW34	4FT deg		BBC	HN	M	30	BBBB	Ind		
Theatre Studies/History	VW14	4FT deg		BBC	HN	M	30	BBBB	Ind	3	
Theatre Studies/Scottish History	VWC4	4FT deg		BBC	HN	M	30	BBBB	Ind		
Theology & Religious Studies/Economic History	VV83	4FT deg		BBC	8M	M	30	BBBB	Ind		

GOLDSMITHS COLL (Univ of London)

TITLE	CODE	COURSE	SUBJECTS	A/AS	NQ/C	AGNVQ	IB	SQA(H)	SQA	RATIO	A/AS
English and History	QV31	3FT deg	E	BCC	MO	M	Dip	BBBBC	N	6	18/30
Historical Studies	V100	3FT deg	H	BCC	MO	M	Dip	BBBBC	N	3	9/22
History and History of Art	VV14	3FT deg	H	BCC	MO	M	Dip	BBBCC	N	4	18/26
History and Sociology	LV31	3FT deg		BCC	MO	M	Dip	BBBCC	N	6	16/20

Univ of GREENWICH

TITLE	CODE	COURSE	SUBJECTS	A/AS	NQ/C	AGNVQ	IB	SQA(H)	SQA	RATIO	A/AS
History	V100	3FT deg	*g	10	MO	M	25	BBB	Ind		
Humanities	Y301	3FT deg	*	12	MO	M	25	BBB	Ind		
Modern History											

History 33

TITLE	CODE	COURSE	SUBJECTS	A/AS	ND/C	AGNVQ	IB	SQA(H)	SQA	RATIO A/AS
Univ of HERTFORDSHIRE										
Historical Studies	V100	3FT deg	*	16	M+D	Ind	28	CCCCC	Ind	6 12/20
Historical Studies/Linguistics	VQ11	3FT deg	*	14	M+D	Ind	28	CCCCC	Ind	
Historical Studies/Literature	VQ13	3FT deg	*	14	M+D	Ind	28	CCCCC	Ind	
Historical Studies/Minor	V102	3FT deg	*	14	M+D	Ind	28	CCCCC	Ind	
Historical Studies/Minor/Minor	V103	3FT deg	*	14	M+D	Ind	28	CCCCC	Ind	
Historical Studies/Modern Language	TV91	3FT deg	Ap	14	M+D	Ind	28	CCCC	Ind	
Historical Studies/Philosophy	VV17	3FT deg	*	14	M+D	Ind	28	CCCCC	Ind	
Univ of HUDDERSFIELD										
English and History	QV31	3FT deg	E/H	14-16	Ind	Ind	Ind	Ind	Ind	
French with History	R1V1	4FT deg	F+H	CCE	Ind	Ind	Ind	BBBC	Ind	
History	V100	3FT deg	H	14-16	Ind	Ind	Ind	Ind	Ind	
History with Media	V1P4	3FT deg	H	14-16	Ind	Ind	Ind	Ind	Ind	
History with Sociology	V1L3	3FT deg	H	14-16	Ind	Ind	Ind	Ind	Ind	
Politics with Contemporary History	M1V1	3FT deg	*	14	M0+3D	M6/^	Ind	BBBC	Ind	
Univ of HULL										
American Studies/History	QV41	3FT deg	H	BBB-BCC	Ind	M*^ gi	28$	ABBCC	Ind	13 22/24
Economic and Social History	V340	3FT deg	* g	BCC	M0	M$6/^ go	26$	BBCCC	Ind	2 14/24
Economic and Social History/Sociology	LV33	3FT deg	*	BBC-BCC	M0	M$6/^ go	28	BBCCC	Ind	2 16/22
Economics and Economic History	VL31	3FT deg	* g	BBC-BCC	M0	M*^ go	26$	BBCCC	Ind	3
English/History	QV31	3FT deg	E+H	BBB-BCC	Ind	M$^ gi	28$	BBBCC	Ind	19 24/28
French/History	RV11	4FT deg	F+H	BBB-BCC	Ind	M$^ gi	28$	BBBCC	Ind	13
History, Medieval and Modern	V126	3FT deg	H	BCC	Ind	M*^ gi	28$	BBBCC	Ind	5 16/28
History/Italian	RV31	4FT deg	H+L	BBB-BCC	Ind	M$^ go	28$	BBBCC	Ind	
History/Politics	MV11	3FT deg	H	BBC-BCC	Ind	Ind	28	BBBCC	Ind	14 22/26
Humanities (History)	VV19	3FT deg	H	BCC	Ind	M*^ gi	26$	BBBCC	Ind	
KEELE Univ										
Ancient History and American Studies (4 Yrs)	QVK1	4FT deg	*	BCC	Ind	Ind	28	BBBB	Ind	
Applied Social Studies and Ancient History	LV5D	3FT deg	*	BBC-BCC	Ind	Ind	28	CSYS	Ind	4
Applied Social Studs and Ancient History (4 Yrs)	VLD5	4FT deg	*	BBC-BCC	Ind	Ind	28	BBBB	Ind	
Astrophysics and Ancient History	FV5D	3FT deg	P g	BCC	Ind	D$^	28$	CSYS	Ind	
Biochemistry and Ancient History	CV7D	3FT deg	C g	BCC	Ind	D$^	28$	CSYS	Ind	
Biochemistry and Ancient History (4 Yrs)	VCD7	4FT deg	*	BCC	Ind	Ind	28	BBBB	Ind	
Biological & Med Chem and Ancient Hist (4 Yrs)	VFDC	4FT deg	*	BCC	Ind	Ind	28	BBBB	Ind	
Biological and Med Chem and Ancient History	FVCD	3FT deg	C g	BCC	Ind	D$^	28$	CSYS	Ind	
Biological and Medicinal Chem and Int History	FVCC	3FT deg	C g	BCC	Ind	D$^	28$	CSYS	Ind	
Biological and Medicinal Chemistry and History	FVC1	3FT deg	C g	BCC	Ind	D$^	28$	CSYS	Ind	
Biology and Ancient History	CV1D	3FT deg	S g	BCC	Ind	D$^	28$	CSYS	Ind	
Biology and Ancient History (4 Yrs)	VCD1	4FT deg	*	BCC	Ind	Ind	28	BBBB	Ind	1
Business Administration and Ancient Hist (4 Yrs)	VND9	4FT deg	*	BCC	Ind	Ind	28	BBBB	Ind	
Business Administration and Ancient History	NV9D	3FT deg	*	BCC	Ind	Ind	28	CSYS	Ind	6
Chemistry and Ancient History	FV1D	3FT deg	C g	BCC	Ind	D$^	28$	CSYS	Ind	
Chemistry and Ancient History (4 Yrs)	VFD1	4FT deg	*	BCC	Ind	Ind	28	BBBB	Ind	
Computer Science and Ancient History (4 Yrs)	VGD5	4FT deg	*	BCC	Ind	Ind	28	BBBB	Ind	
Criminology and Ancient History	MVHD	3FT deg	*	BBB	Ind	Ind	32	CSYS		
Criminology and Ancient History (4 Yrs)	VMDH	4FT deg	*	BBB	Ind	Ind	32	ABBB		
Economics and Ancient History	LV1D	3FT deg	* g	BCC	Ind	Ind	28	CSYS	Ind	3
Economics and Ancient History (4 Yrs)	VLD1	4FT deg	*	BCC	Ind	Ind	28	BBBB	Ind	
Educational Studies and Ancient History (4 Yrs)	XV9D	4FT deg	*	BCC	Ind	Ind	28	BBBB	Ind	
Electronic Music and Ancient History (4 Yrs)	WVJD	4FT deg	*	BCC	Ind	Ind	28	BBBB	Ind	
English and Ancient History	QV3D	3FT deg	E	BBC	Ind	D$^	30$	CSYS	Ind	7

course details | 98 expected requirements | 96 entry stats

TITLE	CODE	COURSE	SUBJECTS	A/AS	ND/C	RGNVQ	IB	SQA(H)	SQA	RATIO A/AS	
English and Ancient History (4 Yrs)	VQD3	4FT deg	*	BBC	Ind	Ind	30	BBBB	Ind	3	
Environmental Management & Ancient Hist (4 Yrs)	VFDX	4FT deg	*	BCC	Ind	Ind	28	BBBB	Ind		
Environmental Management and Ancient History	FVXD	3FT deg	* g	BCC	Ind	Ind	28	CSYS	Ind		
Finance and History	NV31	3FT deg	* g	BBC-BCC	Ind	Ind	28	CSYS	Ind		
Finance and History (4 Yrs)	VN13	4FT deg	*	BBC-BCC	Ind	Ind	28	BBBB	Ind		
Finance and International History	NVHC	3FT deg	* g	BCC	Ind	Ind	28	CSYS	Ind		
French and Ancient History	RV1D	3FT deg	F	BCC	Ind	D$^	28$	CSYS	Ind		
French and Ancient History (4 Yrs)	VRD1	4FT deg	*	BCC	Ind	Ind	28	BBBB	Ind		
Geography and Ancient History	LV8D	3FT deg	Gy	BCC	Ind	D$^	28$	CSYS	Ind	2	
Geology and Ancient History	FV6D	3FT deg	S g	BCC	Ind	D$^	28$	CSYS	Ind		
Geology and Ancient History (4 Yrs)	VFD6	4FT deg	*	BCC	Ind	Ind	28	BBBB	Ind		
History and American Studies	QV41	3FT deg	*	BBC	Ind	Ind	30	CSYS	Ind	6	18/28
History and American Studies (4 Yrs)	VQ14	4FT deg	*	BBC	Ind	Ind	30	BBBB	Ind		
History and Ancient History	VV1D	3FT deg	*	BBC-BCC	Ind	Ind	30	CSYS	Ind	4	18/28
History and Ancient History (4 Yrs)	V103	4FT deg	*	BBC-BCC	Ind	Ind	30	BBBB	Ind	7	
History and Applied Social Studies	LV51	3FT deg	*	BBC	Ind	Ind	30	CSYS	Ind	3	
History and Applied Social Studies (4 Yrs)	VL15	4FT deg	*	BBC	Ind	Ind	30	BBBB	Ind		
History and Astrophysics	FV51	3FT deg	P g	BCC	Ind	D$^	28$	CSYS	Ind		
History and Astrophysics (4 Yrs)	VF15	4FT deg	*	BCC	Ind	Ind	28	BBBB	Ind		
History and Biochemistry	CV71	3FT deg	C g	BCC	Ind	D$^	28$	CSYS	Ind		
History and Biochemistry (4 Yrs)	VC17	4FT deg	*	BCC	Ind	Ind	28	BBBB	Ind		
History and Biological and Med Chemistry (4 Yrs)	VF1C	4FT deg	*	BCC	Ind	Ind	28	BBBB	Ind		
History and Chemistry	FV11	3FT deg	C g	BCC	Ind	D$^	28$	CSYS	Ind	4	
History and Chemistry (4 Yrs)	VF11	4FT deg	*	BCC	Ind	Ind	28	BBBB	Ind		
History and Classical Studies	QV81	3FT deg	*	BBC-BCC	Ind	Ind	28	CSYS	Ind		
History and Classical Studies (4 Yrs)	VQ18	4FT deg	*	BBC-BCC	Ind	Ind	28	BBBB	Ind	3	
History and Computer Science	GV51	3FT deg	* g	BCC	Ind	Ind	28	CSYS	Ind		
History and Computer Science (4 Yrs)	VG15	4FT deg	*	BCC	Ind	Ind	28	BBBB	Ind		
History and Criminology	MVH1	3FT deg	*	BBB	Ind	Ind	32	CSYS	Ind	16	
History and Criminology (4 Yrs)	VM1H	4FT deg	*	BBB	Ind	Ind	32	ABBB	Ind		
History and Economics (4 Yrs)	VL11	4FT deg	* g	BCC	Ind	Ind	28	BBBB	Ind		
History and Educational Studies	VX19	3FT deg	*	BCC	Ind	Ind	28	CSYS	Ind	6	
History and Educational Studies (4 Yrs)	XV91	4FT deg	*	BCC	Ind	Ind	28	BBBB	Ind	6	
History and Electronic Music	VW1J	3FT deg	Mu	BCC	Ind	D$^	28	CSYS	Ind		
History and English	QV31	3FT deg	E	BBC	Ind	D$^	30$	CSYS	Ind	11	12/26
History and English (4 Yrs)	VQ13	4FT deg	*	BBC	Ind	Ind	30	BBBB	Ind	4	16/20
History and Environmental Management	FVX1	3FT deg	* g	BCC	Ind	Ind	28	CSYS	Ind		
History and Environmental Management (4 Yrs)	VF1X	4FT deg	*	BCC	Ind	Ind	28	BBBB	Ind		
History and French	RV11	3FT deg	F	BBC-BCC	Ind	D$^	28$	CSYS	Ind	2	19/20
History and French (4 Yrs)	VR11	4FT deg	*	BBC-BCC	Ind	Ind	28	BBBB	Ind		
History and French/German	TV91	3FT deg	F+G	BBC	Ind	D$^	30$	CSYS	Ind		
History and French/German (4 Yrs)	VT19	4FT deg	g	BBC	Ind	Ind	30	BBBB	Ind		
History and French/Russian (4 Yrs)	VT1X	4FT deg	*	BBC	Ind	Ind	30	BBBB	Ind		
History and French/Russian or Russian Studies	TVX1	3FT deg	F+R	BBC	Ind	D$^	30$	CSYS	Ind		
History and Geography	LV81	3FT deg	Gy	BCC	Ind	D$^	28$	CSYS	Ind	11	
History and Geography (4 Yrs)	VL18	4FT deg	*	BCC	Ind	Ind	28	BBBB	Ind		
History and Geology	FV61	3FT deg	S g	BCC	Ind	D$^	28$	CSYS	Ind		
History and Geology (4 Yrs)	VF16	4FT deg	*	BCC	Ind	Ind	28	BBBB	Ind		
History and German	RV21	3FT deg	G	BCC	Ind	D$^	28$	CSYS	Hid	3	
History and German (4 Yrs)	VR12	4FT deg	* g	BCC	Ind	Ind	28	BBBB	Ind		
History and German/Russian or Russian St (4 Yrs)	VT1Y	4FT deg	g	BBC	Ind	Ind	30	BBBB	Ind		
History and German/Russian or Russian Studies	TVY1	3FT deg	G+R	BBC-BCC	Ind	D$^	28$	BBBB	Ind		

			98 expected requirements						96 entry stats	

course details

TITLE	CODE	COURSE	SUBJECTS	A/AS	ND/C	AGNVQ	IB	SQA(H)	SQA	RATIO A/AS	
Human Resource Management and Ancient History	NV6D	3FT deg	*	BCC	Ind	Ind	28	CSYS	Ind	2	
Human Resource Management and History	VN16	4FT deg	*	BBC-BCC	Ind	Ind	28	BBBB	Ind		
Human Resource Management and History	NV61	3FT deg	*	BBC-BCC	Ind	Ind	28	CSYS	Ind		
Human Resource Mgt and Ancient History (4 Yrs)	VND6	4FT deg	*	BCC	Ind	Ind	28	BBBB	Ind		
Int History and Biological and Med Chem (4 Yrs)	VFCC	4FT deg	*	BCC	Ind	Ind	28	BBBB	Ind		
Int History and French/Russian or Russian St	TVXC	3FT deg	F+R	BBC	Ind	D$^	30$	CSYS	Ind		
Int History and German/Russian or Russian St	TVYC	3FT deg	G	BCC	Ind	Ind	28$	BBBB	Ind		
International Hist and Educational Studs (4 Yrs)	XV9C	4FT deg	*	BCC	Ind	Ind	28	BBBB	Ind		
International History and American St (4 Yrs)	VQC4	4FT deg	*	BBC-BCC	Ind	Ind	28	BBBB	Ind	4	
International History and American Studies	QV4C	3FT deg	*	BBC-BCC	Ind	Ind	28	CSYS	Ind	4	20/22
International History and Ancient History	V100	3FT deg	*	BCC	Ind	Ind	28	CSYS	Ind	12	
International History and Ancient History (4Yrs)	V102	4FT deg	*	BCC	Ind	Ind	28	BBBB	Ind		
International History and Applied Social St	VLC5	4FT deg	*	BBC-BCC	Ind	Ind	28	BBBB	Ind	2	
International History and Applied Social Studies	LV5C	3FT deg	*	BBC-BCC	Ind	Ind	28	CSYS	Ind	4	
International History and Astrophysics	FV5C	3FT deg	P g	BCC	Ind	D$^	28$	CSYS	Ind		
International History and Astrophysics (4 Yrs)	VFC5	4FT deg	*	BCC	Ind	Ind	28	BBBB	Ind		
International History and Biology	CV1C	3FT deg	S g	BCC	Ind	D$^	28$	CSYS	Ind		
International History and Biology (4 Yrs)	VCC1	4FT deg	*	BCC	Ind	Ind	28	BBBB	Ind	2	
International History and Business Admin (4 Yrs)	VNC9	4FT deg	*	BCC	Ind	Ind	28	BBBB	Ind		
International History and Chemistry	FV1C	3FT deg	C g	BCC	Ind	D$^	28$	CSYS	Ind		
International History and Chemistry (4 Yrs)	VFC1	4FT deg	*	BCC	Ind	Ind	28	BBBB	Ind		
International History and Classical St (4 Yrs)	VQC8	4FT deg	*	BCC	Ind	Ind	28	BBBB	Ind		
International History and Classical Studies	QV8C	3FT deg	*	BCC	Ind	Ind	28	CSYS	Ind	3	
International History and Computer Sci (4 Yrs)	VGC5	4FT deg	*	BCC	Ind	Ind	28	BBBB	Ind		
International History and Computer Science	GV5C	3FT deg	* g	BCC	Ind	Ind	28	CSYS	Ind		
International History and Economics	LV1C	3FT deg	* g	BCC	Ind	Ind	28	CSYS	Ind	2	18/18
International History and Economics (4 Yrs)	VLC1	4FT deg	*	BCC	Ind	Ind	28	BBBB	Ind		
International History and Educational Studies	VXC9	3FT deg	*	BCC	Ind	Ind	28	CSYS	Ind	2	
International History and Electronic Music	VWCJ	3FT deg	Mu	BCC	Ind	D$^	28$	CSYS	Ind		
International History and Electronic Music(4Yrs)	WVJC	4FT deg	*	BCC	Ind	Ind	28	BBBB	Ind		
International History and Env Mgt (4 Yrs)	VFCX	4FT deg	*	BCC	Ind	Ind	28	BBBB	Ind		
International History and Environmental Mgt	FVXC	3FT deg	* g	BCC	Ind	Ind	28	CSYS	Ind		
International History and Finance (4 Yrs)	NV3D	4FT deg	*	BCC	Ind	Ind	28	BBBB	Ind		
International History and French	RV1C	3FT deg	F	BCC	Ind	D$^	28$	CSYS	Ind	5	
International History and French (4 Yrs)	VRC1	4FT deg	*	BCC	Ind	Ind	28	BBBB	Ind		
International History and French/German	TV9C	3FT deg	F+G	BBC	Ind	D$^	30$	CSYS	Ind		
International History and French/German (4 Yrs)	VTC9	4FT deg	* g	BBC-BCC	Ind	Ind	28	BBBB	Ind		
International History and French/Russian (4 Yrs)	VTCX	4FT deg	*	BBC-BCC	Ind	Ind	28	BBBB	Ind		
International History and Geography	LV8C	3FT deg	Gy	BCC	Ind	D$^	28$	CSYS	Ind	7	
International History and Geography (4 Yrs)	VLC8	4FT deg	*	BCC	Ind	Ind	28	BBBB	Ind		
International History and German	RV2C	3FT deg	G	BCC	Ind	D$^	28$	CSYS	Ind	3	
International History and German (4 Yrs)	VRC2	4FT deg	* g	BCC	Ind	Ind	28	BBBB	Ind		
International History and German/Russian (4 Yrs)	VTCY	4FT deg	G	BCC	Ind	Ind	28$	BBBB	Ind		
International History and History (4 Yrs)	VVC1	4FT deg	*	BCC	Ind	Ind	28	BBBB	Ind		
International History and Psychology	CV8C	3FT deg	* g	BBB	Ind	Ind	32	CSYS	Ind		
International Politics and Ancient Hist (4 Yrs)	VMDC	4FT deg	*	BCC	Ind	Ind	28	BBBB	Ind		
International Politics and Ancient History	MVCD	3FT deg	*	BCC	Ind	Ind	28	CSYS	Ind		
International Politics and History	MVC1	3FT deg	*	BCC	Ind	Ind	28	CSYS	Ind	6	18/24
International Politics and History (4 Yrs)	VM1C	4FT deg	*	BCC	Ind	Ind	28	BBBB	Ind	5	
International Politics and International History	VMCC	4FT deg	*	BCC	Ind	Ind	28	BBBB	Ind	7	
International Politics and International History	MVCC	3FT deg	*	BCC	Ind	Ind	28	CSYS	Ind		
Latin and Ancient History (4 Yrs)	VQD6	4FT deg	*	BCC	Ind	Ind	28	BBBB	Ind		

course details | 98 expected requirements | 96 entry stats

TITLE	CODE	COURSE	SUBJECTS	A/AS	ND/C	AGNVQ	IB	SQA(H)	SQA	RATIO A/AS	
Latin and History	QV61	3FT deg	Ln	BCC	Ind	D$^	28$	CSYS	Ind		
Latin and International History	QV6C	3FT deg	Ln	BCC	Ind	D$^	28$	CSYS	Ind		
Latin and International History (4 Yrs)	VQC6	4FT deg	*	BCC	Ind	Ind	28	BBBB	Ind		
Law and Ancient History	MV3D	3FT deg	*	BBB	Ind	Ind	32	CSYS	Ind	3	
Law and History	MV31	3FT deg	*	BBB	Ind	Ind	32	CSYS	Ind	33	
Law and History (4 Yrs)	VM13	4FT deg	*	BBB	Ind	Ind	32	BBBB	Ind		
Law and International History	MV3C	3FT deg	*	BBB	Ind	Ind	32	CSYS	Ind	3	
Law and International History (4 Yrs)	VMC3	4FT deg	*	BBB	Ind	Ind	32	BBBB	Ind		
Marketing and Ancient History	NV5D	3FT deg	*	BCC	Ind	Ind	28	CSYS	Ind		
Marketing and History	NV51	3FT deg	*	BBC	Ind	Ind	30	CSYS	Ind	9	
Marketing and International History	NV5C	3FT deg	*	BCC	Ind	Ind	28	CSYS	Ind	6	
Mathematics and Ancient History	GV1D	3FT deg	M	BCC	Ind	D$^	28$	CSYS	Ind		
Mathematics and Ancient History (4 Yrs)	VGD1	4FT deg	*	BCC	Ind	Ind	28	BBBB	Ind		
Mathematics and History	GV11	3FT deg	M	BCC	Ind	D$^	28$	CSYS	Ind	7	
Mathematics and History (4 Yrs)	VG11	4FT deg	*	BCC	Ind	Ind	28	BBBB	Ind		
Music and Ancient History (4 Yrs)	WV3D	4FT deg	*	BCC	Ind	Ind	28	BBBB	Ind		
Music and History	VW13	3FT deg	Mu	BBC	Ind	D$^	30	CSYS	Ind		
Music and International History	VWC3	3FT deg	Mu	BCC	Ind	D$^	28	CSYS	Ind		
Music and International History (4 Yrs)	WV3C	4FT deg	*	BCC	Ind	Ind	28	BBBB	Ind		
Philosophy and Ancient History (4 Yrs)	VVR1	4FT deg	*	BCC	Ind	Ind	28	BBBB	Ind		
Philosophy and History	VV17	3FT deg	*	BBC	Ind	Ind	30	CSYS	Ind		
Philosophy and International History	VV7C	3FT deg	*	BBC-BCC	Ind	Ind	28	CSYS	Ind		
Philosophy and International History (4 Yrs)	VVC7	4FT deg	*	BBC-BCC	Ind	Ind	28	BBBB	Ind		
Physics and Ancient History	FV3D	3FT deg	P	BCC	Ind	D$^	28$	CSYS	Ind		
Physics and History	FV31	3FT deg	P	BCC	Ind	D$^	28$	CSYS	Ind		
Physics and History (4 Yrs)	VF13	4FT deg	*	BCC	Ind	Ind	28	BBBB	Ind		
Physics and International History	FV3C	3FT deg	P	BCC	Ind	D$^	28$	CSYS	Ind		
Physics and International History (4 Yrs)	VFC3	4FT deg	*	BCC	Ind	Ind	28	BBBB	Ind		
Politics and Ancient History	MV1D	3FT deg	*	BCC	Ind	Ind	28	CSYS	Ind	4	
Politics and Ancient History (4 Yrs)	VMD1	4FT deg	*	BCC	Ind	Ind	28	BBBB	Ind		
Politics and History	MV11	3FT deg	*	BBC-BCC	Ind	Ind	28	CSYS	Ind	4	18/24
Politics and History (4 Yrs)	VM11	4FT deg	*	BBC-BCC	Ind	Ind	28	BBBB	Ind	9	
Psychology and Ancient History	CV8D	3FT deg	*g	BBB	Ind	Ind	32	CSYS	Ind		
Psychology and History	CV81	3FT deg	*g	BBB	Ind	Ind	32	CSYS	Ind	30	
Psychology and History (4 Yrs)	VC18	4FT deg	*	BBB	Ind	Ind	32	ABBB	Ind	5	
Psychology and International History (4 Yrs)	VCC8	4FT deg	*	BBB	Ind	Ind	32	ABBB	Ind		
Russian Studies and Ancient History	RVVD	3FT deg	*	BCC	Ind	Ind	28	CSYS	Ind		
Russian Studies and History	RV8C	3FT deg	*	BCC	Ind	Ind	28	CSYS	Ind		
Russian Studies and History (4 Yrs)	VRC8	4FT deg	*	BCC	Ind	Ind	28	BBBB	Ind		
Russian Studies and International History	RVVC	3FT deg	*	BCC	Ind	Ind	28	CSYS	Ind		
Russian Studies and International History(4 Yrs)	VRCV	4FT deg	*	BCC	Ind	Ind	28	BBBB	Ind		
Russian and Ancient History	RV8D	3FT deg	R	BCC	Ind	D$^	28$	CSYS	Ind		
Russian and History	RV81	3FT deg	R	BCC	Ind	D$^	28$	CSYS	Ind		
Russian and History (4 Yrs)	VR18	4FT deg	*	BCC	Ind	Ind	28	BBBB	Ind		
Russian and International History	RVWC	3FT deg	R	BCC	Ind	D$^	28$	CSYS	Ind		
Russian and International History (4 Yrs)	VRCW	4FT deg	*	BCC	Ind	Ind	28	BBBB	Ind		
Sociol & Soc Anthrop and Internat Hist (4 Yrs)	VLC3	4FT deg	*	BCC	Ind	Ind	28	BBBB	Ind		
Sociol & Soc Anthrop and International History	LV3C	3FT deg	*	BCC	Ind	Ind	28	CSYS	Ind	5	
Sociology & Social Anthrop & Ancient Hist(4 Yrs)	VLD3	4FT deg	*	BCC	Ind	Ind	28	BBBB	Ind		
Sociology & Social Anthropology and History	LV31	3FT deg	*	BCC	Ind	Ind	28	CSYS	Ind	7	
Statistics and Ancient History	GV4D	3FT deg	M	BCC	Ind	D$^	28$	CSYS	Ind		
Statistics and Ancient History (4 Yrs)	VGD4	4FT deg	*	BCC	Ind	Ind	28	BBBB	Ind		
Statistics and History (4 Yrs)	VG14	4FT deg	*	BCC	Ind	Ind	28	BBBB	Ind		
Visual Arts and Ancient History	VWD1	3FT deg	*	BBC	Ind	D$^	30	CSYS	Ind		

course details			98 expected requirements							96 entry stats	
TITLE	CODE	COURSE	SUBJECTS	A/AS	ND/C	AGNVQ	IB	SQA(H)	SQA	RATIO	A/AS
Visual Arts and History (4 Yrs)	VW11	4FT deg	*	BBC-BCC	Ind	Ind	28	BBBB	Ind		
Visual Arts and International History	VWC1	3FT deg	*	BCC	Ind	D$^	28	CSYS	Ind		
Visual Arts and International History (4 Yrs)	WV1C	4FT deg	*	BCC	Ind	Ind	28	BBBB	Ind		

Univ of KENT

History	V100	3FT deg	*	24	1M+5D	Ind	32	Ind	Ind	6	18/26
History and Heritage Studies	V321	3FT deg	*	24	1M+5D	Ind	32	Ind	Ind	4	
History and Law	MV31	3FT deg	*	22	2M+4D	Ind	30	Ind	Ind	6	20/28
History and Politics	MV11	3FT deg	*	22	2M+4D	Ind	30	Ind	Ind	6	18/26
History and Social Anthropology	LVP1	3FT deg	*	22	2M+4D	Ind	30	Ind	Ind	21	
History and Theory of Art/History	VV41	3FT deg	*	22	2M+4D	Ind	30	Ind	Ind	14	
History of Science/History	VV15	3FT deg	*	22	2M+4D	Ind	30	Ind	Ind	3	
History/Classical Studies	QV81	3FT deg	*	22	2M+4D	Ind	30	Ind	Ind		
History/Comparative Literary Studies	QV21	3FT deg	*	22	2M+4D	Ind	30	Ind	Ind		
History/Computing	VG15	3FT deg	*	22	2M+4D	Ind	30	Ind	Ind	7	
History/Drama	VW14	3FT deg	*	22	2M+4D	Ind	30	Ind	Ind	10	
History/English	QV31	3FT deg	E	24	1M+5D	Ind	32	Ind	Ind	11	20/24
History/English (Post-Colonial Literatures)	VQ1J	3FT deg	E	24	1M+5D	Ind	32	Ind	Ind		
History/English Language	VQ13	3FT deg	E	22	2M+4D	Ind	30	Ind	Ind	14	
History/Film Studies	VW15	3FT deg	*	24	1M+5D	Ind	32	Ind	Ind	8	
History/French	RV11	4FT deg	F	22	2M+4D	Ind	30	Ind	Ind	10	
History/German	RV21	4FT deg	G	22	2M+4D	Ind	30	Ind	Ind	9	
Italian/History	RV31	4FT deg	*	22	2M+4D	Ind	30	Ind	Ind		
Law and History	MVH1	3FT deg	*	26	6D	D$	33	AAAB	Ind	4	
Linguistics/History	QV11	3FT deg	*	22	2M+4D	Ind	30	Ind	Ind		
Philosophy/History	VV17	3FT deg	*	22	2M+4D	Ind	30	Ind	Ind	3	
Politics and Government and History	MVC1	3FT deg	*	BCC	3M+3D	M$	28	BBBB	Ind	23	
Social Anthropology and History	LV61	3FT deg	*	20	3M+3D	M$	28	BBBB	Ind	9	
Spanish/History	RV41	4FT deg	*	22	2M+4D	Ind	30	Ind	Ind		
Theology/History	VV18	3FT deg	*	22	2M+4D	Ind	30	Ind	Ind	6	

KING ALFRED'S WINCHESTER

History	V100	3FT deg	H g	14	X	X	24$	BCC$	X		
History and American Studies	QV41	3FT deg	H g	14	X	X	24$	BCC$	X	8	
History and Archaeology	FV4C	3FT deg	H g	14	X	X	24$	BCC$	X		
History and Computing	GV51	3FT deg	H g	14	X	X	24$	BCC$	X	2	
History and Contemporary Cultural Studies	MV91	3FT deg	H g	14	X	X	24$	BCC$	X		
History and Drama Studies	VW14	3FT deg	H g	14	X	X	24$	BCC$	X	20	
History and Education Studies	VX19	3FT deg	H g	14	X	X	24$	BCC$	X	6	
History and English Studies	QV31	3FT deg	E/H g	14	X	X	24$	BCC$	X	4	12/16
History and Geography	LV81	3FT deg	Gy/H g	14	X	X	24$	BCC$	X	5	
Music (World) and History	VW13	3FT deg	* g	14	6M	M	24	BCC	N		
Philosophy and History	VV17	3FT deg	* g	14	6M	M	24	BCC	N		
Psychology and History	LV71	3FT deg	* g	14	6M	M	24	BCC	N	3	
Religious Studies and History	VV18	3FT deg	* g	14	6M	M	24	BCC	N		
Sports Studies and History	VL1H	3FT deg	* g	14	6M	M	24	BCC	N		
Visual Studies and History	VW12	3FT deg	A/Ad/H g	14	6M $	M	24$	BCC$	X		

KING'S COLL LONDON (Univ of London)

Geography and History	LV81	3FT deg	Gy/H	ABB-BBC						16	
German and History	RV21	3FT deg	G+H	ABB-BBC							
History	V100	3FT deg	H	ABB-BBC						8	20/30
History and Portuguese and Brazilian Studies	VR15	3FT deg	H	ABB-BCC							
War Studies and History	MV91	3FT deg	H	ABB-BBC						13	24/28

course details			98 expected requirements							96 entry stats	
TITLE	CODE	COURSE	SUBJECTS	A/AS	NO/C	AGNVQ	IB	SQA(H)	SQA	RATIO	A/AS
KINGSTON Univ											
History	V100	3FT deg	H g	16	MO	Ind^	Ind	BBCCC	HN	4	8/20
History of Art, Architecture and Design/History	VV41	3FT deg	H g	16	MO	Ind^	Ind	BBCCC	HN		
History of Ideas/History	VV71	3FT deg	H g	16	MO	Ind^	Ind	BBCCC	HN	2	
History/Economics	VL11	3FT deg	H g	16	MO	Ind^	Ind	BBCCC	HN	2	
History/English Literature	VQ13	3FT deg	E+H	16	MO	Ind^	Ind	BBCCC	HN	8	
History/French	RV11	4FT deg	F+H g	14	MO	Ind^	Ind	BCCCC	HN	2	
History/German	RV21	4FT deg	H+G g	14	MO	Ind^	Ind	BCCCC	HN	4	
Politics/History	MV11	3FT deg	H g	16	MO	Ind^	Ind	BBCCC	HN	9	14/18
Psychology/History	LV71	3FT deg	H g	18	MO	Ind^	Ind	BBBCC	HN	9	
Social and Economic Hist/Hist of Art, Des & Arch	VV43	3FT deg	* g	16	MO	Ind^	Ind	BBCCC	HN		
Social and Economic History/Economics	LV13	3FT deg	* g	14	MO	Ind^	Ind	BCCCC	HN	8	
Social and Economic History/English Literature	QV33	3FT deg	E g	16	MO	Ind^	Ind	BBCCC	HN	1	
Social and Economic History/History	VV13	3FT deg	H g	14-16	MO	Ind^	Ind	BBCCC	HN	4	
Social and Economic History/Politics	MV13	3FT deg	* g	14	MO	Ind^	Ind	BCCCC	HN	1	
Sociology/History	LV31	3FT deg	H g	14	MO	Ind^	Ind	BCCCC	HN	4	
Sociology/Social and Economic History	LV33	3FT deg	* g	14	MO	Ind^	Ind	BCCCC	HN	2	
Spanish/History	RV41	4FT deg	H+Sp g	14	MO	Ind^	Ind	BCCCC	HN		
Women's Studies/Social and Economic History	MV93	3FT deg	* g	14	MO	Ind^	Ind	BCCC	HN	1	
Univ of Wales, LAMPETER											
Ancient History	V110	3FT deg	*	16	Ind		Ind	Ind	Ind		
Ancient History and American Literature	QV41	3FT deg			Ind	Ind	Ind	Ind	Ind		
Ancient History and Archaeology	VVC6	3FT deg		16	Ind	Ind	Ind	Ind	Ind		
Anthropology and Ancient History	LV61	3FT deg	*	16	Ind	Ind	Ind	Ind	Ind		
Archaeology and Ancient History	VV1Q	3FT deg	*	16	Ind	Ind	Ind	Ind	Ind		
Australian Studies and Ancient History	LVPC	3FT deg			Ind	Ind	Ind	Ind	Ind		
Church History and American Literature	QV4C	3FT deg			Ind	Ind	Ind	Ind	Ind		
Church History and Ancient History	V162	3FT deg	*	16	Ind	Ind	Ind	Ind	Ind		
Church History and Anthropology	LV6C	3FT deg	*	16	Ind	Ind	Ind	Ind	Ind		
Church History and Archaeology	VV1P	3FT deg	*	16	Ind	Ind	Ind	Ind	Ind		
Church History and Australian Studies	VLC6	3FT deg			Ind	Ind	Ind	Ind	Ind		
Classical Studies and Ancient History	QV8D	3FT deg	*	16	Ind	Ind	Ind	Ind	Ind		
Classical Studies and Church History	QVWC	3FT deg	*	16	Ind	Ind	Ind	Ind	Ind		
Cultural Studies in Geography & Ancient History	VLCW	3FT deg		16	Ind	Ind	Ind	Ind	Ind		
Cultural Studies in Geography and Church History	LVVD	3FT deg	*	16	Ind	Ind	Ind	Ind	Ind		
English Literature and Ancient History	QV3D	3FT deg	E	18	Ind	Ind	Ind	Ind	Ind		
English Literature and Church History	QVJC	3FT deg	E	14-18	Ind	Ind	Ind	Ind	Ind		
French and Ancient History	RV1D	4FT deg	F	16	Ind	Ind	Ind	Ind	Ind		
French and Church History	RVDC	4FT deg	F	16	Ind	Ind	Ind	Ind	Ind		
Geography and Ancient History	LV8D	3FT deg	Gy	16	Ind	Ind	Ind	Ind	Ind		
Geography and Church History	LVWC	3FT deg	Gy	16	Ind	Ind	Ind	Ind	Ind		
German Studies and Ancient History	RVG1	4FT deg	*	16	Ind	Ind	Ind	Ind	Ind		
German Studies and Church History	RVGC	4FT deg	*	14-16	Ind	Ind	Ind	Ind	Ind		
German and Ancient History	RVF1	4FT deg	G	16	Ind	Ind	Ind	Ind	Ind		
German and Church History	RVFD	4FT deg	G	14-16	Ind	Ind	Ind	Ind	Ind		
Greek and Ancient History	QV7D	3FT deg	* g	16	Ind	Ind	Ind	Ind	Ind		
Greek and Church History	QVTC	3FT deg	* g	16	Ind	Ind	Ind	Ind	Ind		
History	V100▼	3FT deg	H	16	Ind	Ind	Ind	Ind	Ind		
History and American Literature	QV4D	3FT deg	H		Ind	Ind	Ind	Ind	Ind		
History and Ancient History	V112	3FT deg	H	16	Ind	Ind	Ind	Ind	Ind		
History and Anthropology	LVP1	3FT deg	H	16	Ind	Ind	Ind	Ind	Ind		
History and Archaeology	VV16	3FT deg	H	16	Ind	Ind	Ind	Ind	Ind		

History 33

course details			98 expected requirements							96 entry stats
TITLE	CODE	COURSE	SUBJECTS	A/AS	ND/C	AGNVQ	IB	SQA(H)	SQA	RATIO A/AS
History and Australian Studies	VLCP	3FT deg	H		Ind	Ind	Ind	Ind	Ind	
History and Church History	V160	3FT deg	H	16	Ind	Ind	Ind	Ind	Ind	
History and Classical Studies	QV81	3FT deg	H	16	Ind	Ind	Ind	Ind	Ind	
History and Cultural Studies in Geography	LVVC	3FT deg	Gy+H	16	Ind	Ind	Ind	Ind	Ind	
History and English Literature	QV31▼	3FT deg	H+E	16-18	Ind	Ind	Ind	Ind	Ind	
History and French	RV11	4FT deg	H+F	16	Ind	Ind	Ind	Ind	Ind	
History and Geography	LV81	3FT deg	Gy+H	16	Ind	Ind	Ind	Ind	Ind	
History and German	RV21	4FT deg	H+G	16	Ind	Ind	Ind	Ind	Ind	
History and German Studies	RV2C	4FT deg	H	16	Ind	Ind	Ind	Ind	Ind	
History and Greek	QV71	3FT deg	H g	16	Ind	Ind	Ind	Ind	Ind	
Informatics and Ancient History	GV5C	3FT deg	*	14-16	Ind	Ind	Ind	Ind	Ind	
Informatics and Church History	GV51	3FT deg	*	14	Ind	Ind	Ind	Ind	Ind	
Informatics and History	GV5D	3FT deg	H	14-16	Ind	Ind	Ind	Ind	Ind	
Islamic Studies and Ancient History	TVP1	3FT deg	*	16	Ind	Ind	Ind	Ind	Ind	
Islamic Studies and Church History	TV61	3FT deg	*	14	Ind	Ind	Ind	Ind	Ind	
Islamic Studies and History	TV6C	3FT deg	H	16	Ind	Ind	Ind	Ind	Ind	
Latin and Ancient History	QV6D	3FT deg	* g	16	Ind	Ind	Ind	Ind	Ind	
Latin and Church History	QVQC	3FT deg	* g	16	Ind	Ind	Ind	Ind	Ind	
Latin and History	QV61	3FT deg	H g	16	Ind	Ind	Ind	Ind	Ind	
Management Techniques and Ancient History	NV11	3FT deg	*	16	Ind	Ind	Ind	Ind	Ind	
Management Techniques and Church History	NV1C	3FT deg	*	16	Ind	Ind	Ind	Ind	Ind	
Management Techniques and History	NVCC	3FT deg	H	16	Ind	Ind	Ind	Ind	Ind	
Medieval Studies	V120	3FT deg	*	16	Ind	Ind	Ind	Ind	Ind	
Medieval Studies and American Literature	VQ14	3FT deg			Ind	Ind	Ind	Ind	Ind	
Medieval Studies and Ancient History	V121	3FT deg		16	Ind	Ind	Ind	Ind	Ind	
Medieval Studies and Anthropology	VL16	3FT deg	*	16	Ind	Ind	Ind	Ind	Ind	
Medieval Studies and Archaeology	VV61	3FT deg	*	16	Ind	Ind	Ind	Ind	Ind	
Medieval Studies and Australian Studies	VLD6	3FT deg			Ind	Ind	Ind	Ind	Ind	
Medieval Studies and Church History	V122	3FT deg	*	16	Ind	Ind	Ind	Ind	Ind	
Medieval Studies and Classical Studies	VQ18	3FT deg	*	16	Ind	Ind	Ind	Ind	Ind	
Medieval Studies and Cultural Studs in Geography	VL1V	3FT deg		16	Ind	Ind	Ind	Ind	Ind	
Medieval Studies and English Literature	VQ13	3FT deg	E	18	Ind	Ind	Ind	Ind	Ind	
Medieval Studies and French	VR11	4FT deg	F	16	Ind	Ind	Ind	Ind	Ind	
Medieval Studies and Geography	VL18	3FT deg	Gy	16	Ind	Ind	Ind	Ind	Ind	
Medieval Studies and German	VR12	4FT deg	G	16	Ind	Ind	Ind	Ind	Ind	
Medieval Studies and German Studies	VR1F	4FT deg	*	16	Ind	Ind	Ind	Ind	Ind	
Medieval Studies and Greek	VQ17	3FT deg	g	16	Ind	Ind	Ind	Ind	Ind	
Medieval Studies and History	V123	3FT deg	H	16	Ind	Ind	Ind	Ind	Ind	
Medieval Studies and Informatics	VG1M	3FT deg	*	16	Ind	Ind	Ind	Ind	Ind	
Medieval Studies and Islamic Studies	VT16	3FT deg	*	16	Ind	Ind	Ind	Ind	Ind	
Medieval Studies and Latin	VQ16	3FT deg	g	16	Ind	Ind	Ind	Ind	Ind	
Medieval Studies and Management Techniques	NV1D	3FT deg	*	16	Ind	Ind	Ind	Ind	Ind	
Modern Historical Studies	V130	3FT deg	H		Ind	Ind	Ind	Ind	Ind	
Modern Historical Studies & American Literature	VQ1K	3FT deg	H		Ind	Ind	Ind	Ind	Ind	
Modern Historical Studies & Cultural St in Geog	VL1W	3FT deg	*		Ind	Ind	Ind	Ind	Ind	
Modern Historical Studies and Ancient History	V131	3FT deg			Ind	Ind	Ind	Ind	Ind	
Modern Historical Studies and Anthropology	VL1P	3FT deg			Ind	Ind	Ind	Ind	Ind	
Modern Historical Studies and Archaeology	VVCP	3FT deg			Ind	Ind	Ind	Ind	Ind	
Modern Historical Studies and Australian Studies	VLCQ	3FT deg			Ind	Ind	Ind	Ind	Ind	
Modern Historical Studies and Church History	V132	3FT deg			Ind	Ind	Ind	Ind	Ind	
Modern Historical Studies and Classical Studies	VVV1	3FT deg			Ind	Ind	Ind	Ind	Ind	
Modern Historical Studies and English Literature	VQ1H	3FT deg			Ind	Ind	Ind	Ind	Ind	

course details			**98 expected requirements**							*96 entry stats*
TITLE	CODE	COURSE	SUBJECTS	A/AS	ND/C	AGNVQ	IB	SQA(H)	SQA	RATIO A/AS
Modern Historical Studies and French	VR1C	3FT deg			Ind	Ind	Ind	Ind	Ind	
Modern Historical Studies and Geography	VLC8	3FT deg			Ind	Ind	Ind	Ind	Ind	
Modern Historical Studies and German	VRCF	3FT deg			Ind	Ind	Ind	Ind	Ind	
Modern Historical Studies and German Studies	VRCG	3FT deg			Ind	Ind	Ind	Ind	Ind	
Modern Historical Studies and Greek	VQ1R	3FT deg			Ind	Ind	Ind	Ind	Ind	
Modern Historical Studies and History	V133	3FT deg			Ind	Ind	Ind	Ind	Ind	
Modern Historical Studies and Informatics	VG1N	3FT deg			Ind	Ind	Ind	Ind	Ind	
Modern Historical Studies and Islamic Studies	VTCQ	3FT deg			Ind	Ind	Ind	Ind	Ind	
Modern Historical Studies and Latin	VQ1P	3FT deg			Ind	Ind	Ind	Ind	Ind	
Modern Historical Studies and Medieval Studies	V134	3FT deg			Ind	Ind	Ind	Ind	Ind	
Modern Historical Studies and Mgt Techniques	VN11	3FT deg			Ind	Ind	Ind	Ind	Ind	
Philosophical Studies and Ancient History	VV1R	3FT deg	*	16	Ind	Ind	Ind	Ind	Ind	
Philosophical Studies and Church History	VVCR	3FT deg	*	16	Ind	Ind	Ind	Ind	Ind	
Philosophical Studies and History	VV17	3FT deg	H	16	Ind	Ind	Ind	Ind	Ind	
Philosophical Studies and Medieval Studies	VV1T	3FT deg		16	Ind	Ind	Ind	Ind	Ind	
Philosophical Studies and Modern Historical St	VVCT	3FT deg			Ind	Ind	Ind	Ind	Ind	
Religious Studies and Ancient History	VVCV	3FT deg	*	16	Ind	Ind	Ind	Ind	Ind	
Religious Studies and Church History	VV1W	3FT deg	*	14	Ind	Ind	Ind	Ind	Ind	
Religious Studies and History	VVC8	3FT deg	H	16	Ind	Ind	Ind	Ind	Ind	
Religious Studies and Medieval Studies	VV81	3FT deg	*	16	Ind	Ind	Ind	Ind	Ind	
Religious Studies and Modern Historical Studies	VVVC	3FT deg			Ind	Ind	Ind	Ind	Ind	
Theology and Ancient History	VVDV	3FT deg	*	16	Ind	Ind	Ind	Ind	Ind	
Theology and Church History	VV1V	3FT deg	*	14	Ind	Ind	Ind	Ind	Ind	
Theology and History	VV18	3FT deg	H	16	Ind	Ind	Ind	Ind	Ind	
Theology and Medieval Studies	VV8C	3FT deg	*	16	Ind	Ind	Ind	Ind	Ind	
Theology and Modern Historical Studies	VVVD	3FT deg			Ind	Ind	Ind	Ind	Ind	
Victorian Studies	V128	3FT deg	*	16	Ind	Ind	Ind	Ind	Ind	
Victorian Studies and American Literature	QVK1	3FT deg			Ind	Ind	Ind	Ind	Ind	
Victorian Studies and Ancient History	V117	3FT deg	*	16	Ind	Ind	Ind	Ind	Ind	
Victorian Studies and Anthropology	LV6D	3FT deg	*	16	Ind	Ind	Ind	Ind	Ind	
Victorian Studies and Archaeology	VVD6	3FT deg	*	18	Ind	Ind	Ind	Ind	Ind	
Victorian Studies and Australian Studies	VLDP	3FT deg			Ind	Ind	Ind	Ind	Ind	
Victorian Studies and Church History	V129	3FT deg	*	14	Ind	Ind	Ind	Ind	Ind	
Victorian Studies and Classical Studies	QV8C	3FT deg	*	16	Ind	Ind	Ind	Ind	Ind	
Victorian Studies and Cultural St in Geography	LVV1	3FT deg	*	16	Ind	Ind	Ind	Ind	Ind	
Victorian Studies and English Literature	QV3C	3FT deg	E	18	Ind	Ind	Ind	Ind	Ind	
Victorian Studies and French	RV1C	4FT deg	F	16	Ind	Ind	Ind	Ind	Ind	
Victorian Studies and Geography	LV8C	3FT deg	Gy	16	Ind	Ind	Ind	Ind	Ind	
Victorian Studies and German	RVFC	4FT deg	G	16	Ind	Ind	Ind	Ind	Ind	
Victorian Studies and German Studies	RV2D	4FT deg	*	16	Ind	Ind	Ind	Ind	Ind	
Victorian Studies and Greek	QV7C	3FT deg	* g	16	Ind	Ind	Ind	Ind	Ind	
Victorian Studies and History	V127	3FT deg	H	16	Ind	Ind	Ind	Ind	Ind	
Victorian Studies and Informatics	VG15	3FT deg	*	14	Ind	Ind	Ind	Ind	Ind	
Victorian Studies and Islamic Studies	TV6D	3FT deg	*	14	Ind	Ind	Ind	Ind	Ind	
Victorian Studies and Latin	QV6C	3FT deg	* g	16	Ind	Ind	Ind	Ind	Ind	
Victorian Studies and Management Techniques	NVC1	3FT deg	*	14	Ind	Ind	Ind	Ind	Ind	
Victorian Studies and Medieval Studies	V124	3FT deg	*	16	Ind	Ind	Ind	Ind	Ind	
Victorian Studies and Modern Historical Studies	V118	3FT deg			Ind	Ind	Ind	Ind	Ind	
Victorian Studies and Philosophical Studies	VVC7	3FT deg	*	16	Ind	Ind	Ind	Ind	Ind	
Victorian Studies and Religious Studies	VVD8	3FT deg	*	14	Ind	Ind	Ind	Ind	Ind	
Victorian Studies and Theology	VVCW	3FT deg	*	14	Ind	Ind	Ind	Ind	Ind	
Welsh Studies and Ancient History	QVNC	3FT deg	*	16	Ind	Ind	Ind	Ind	Ind	

History 33

course details			98 expected requirements						96 entry stats

TITLE	CODE	COURSE	SUBJECTS	A/AS	NO/C	AGNVQ	IB	SQA(H)	SQA	RATIO A/AS
Welsh Studies and Church History	QVMD	3FT deg	*	14	Ind	Ind	Ind	Ind	Ind	
Welsh Studies and History	QV5D	3FT deg	H	16	Ind	Ind	Ind	Ind	Ind	
Welsh Studies and Medieval Studies	VQ1M	3FT deg	*	16	Ind	Ind	Ind	Ind	Ind	
Welsh Studies and Modern Historical Studies	Q5VC	3FT deg			Ind	Ind	Ind	Ind	Ind	
Welsh Studies and Victorian Studies	QVND	3FT deg	*	14	Ind	Ind	Ind	Ind	Ind	
Welsh and Ancient History	QVMC	3FT/4FT deg	W	16	Ind	Ind	Ind	Ind	Ind	
Welsh and Church History	QVN1	3FT/4FT deg	W	14	Ind	Ind	Ind	Ind	Ind	
Welsh and History	QV51	3FT/4FT deg	W+H	16	Ind	Ind	Ind	Ind	Ind	
Welsh and Medieval Studies	VQ15	3FT deg	W	16	Ind	Ind	Ind	Ind	Ind	
Welsh and Modern Historical Studies	Q5V1	3FT deg	W		Ind	Ind	Ind	Ind	Ind	
Welsh and Victorian Studies	QV5C	3FT/4FT deg	W	14	Ind	Ind	Ind	Ind	Ind	
Women's Studies and Ancient History	MV91	3FT deg	*	16	Ind	Ind	Ind	Ind	Ind	
Women's Studies and Church History	MV9C	3FT deg	*	14	Ind	Ind	Ind	Ind	Ind	
Women's Studies and History	MV9D▼	3FT deg	H	16	Ind	Ind	Ind	Ind	Ind	
Women's Studies and Medieval Studies	VM19	3FT deg	*	16	Ind	Ind	Ind	Ind	Ind	
Women's Studies and Modern Historical Studies	VM1X	3FT deg			Ind	Ind	Ind	Ind	Ind	
Women's Studies and Victorian Studies	VMC9	3FT deg	*	14	Ind	Ind	Ind	Ind	Ind	
Combined Honours *Ancient History*	Y400	3FT deg	*	14-16	Ind	Ind	Ind	Ind	Ind	
Combined Honours *Australian Studies*	Y400	3FT deg		14-16	Ind	Ind	Ind	Ind	Ind	
Combined Honours *Church History*	Y400	3FT deg	*	14-16	Ind	Ind	Ind	Ind	Ind	
Combined Honours *History*	Y400	3FT deg	H	14-16	Ind	Ind	Ind	Ind	Ind	
Combined Honours *Medieval Studies*	Y400	3FT deg		14-16	Ind	Ind	Ind	Ind	Ind	
Combined Honours *Victorian Studies*	Y400	3FT deg	*	14-16	Ind	Ind	Ind	Ind	Ind	
Religion, Ethics and Society *Society*	Y652	3FT deg	*	14	Ind	Ind	Ind	Ind	Ind	

LANCASTER Univ

TITLE	CODE	COURSE	SUBJECTS	A/AS	NO/C	AGNVQ	IB	SQA(H)	SQA	RATIO A/AS
Art History and History	WV11	3FT deg	H	BBC-BCC	Ind $		30$	BBBBB$	Ind	
Economics and Modern History	VL11	3FT deg	H g	BBC	MO+4D		32$	ABBBB$	Ind	
Educational Studies and History	XV91	3FT deg	H	BBC	Ind $		30$	ABBBB$	Ind	
English and History	QV31	3FT deg	E+H g	BBB-BCC	DO $		32$	ABBBB$	Ind	
French Studies and History	RV11	4SW deg	H+F	BCC	Ind $		30$	ABBBB$	Ind	
German Studies and History	RV21	4SW deg	G/L+H	BCC	Ind $		30$	BBBBB$	Ind	
History	V100	3FT deg	H	BBC	Ind $		30$	ABBBB$	Ind	
History and History of Science	VV15	3FT deg	H	BBC	Ind $		30$	ABBBB$	Ind	
History and International Relations	VM1C	3FT deg	H	BBC	Ind $		30$	ABBBB$	Ind	
History and Music	WV31	3FT deg	H+Mu	BBC	Ind $		30$	ABBBB$	Ind	
History and Philosophy	VV17	3FT deg	H	BBC	Ind $		30$	ABBBB$	Ind	
History and Politics	MV11	3FT deg	H	BBC	Ind $		30$	AABBB$	Ind	
History and Religious Studies	VV18	3FT deg	H	BBC	Ind $		30$	ABBBB$	Ind	
Italian Studies and History	RV31	4SW deg	I/L+H	BCC	Ind $		30$	BBBBB$	Ind	
Mediaeval and Renaissance Studies	V125	3FT deg	H g	BBC	Ind $		32$	Ind$	Ind	
Social History	V320	3FT deg	H	BBC	Ind $		32$	ABBBB$	Ind	
Spanish Studies and History	RV41	4SW deg	H+Sp/L	BBC	Ind $		30$	BBBBB$	Ind	
Women's Studies and History	VM19	3FT deg	H	BBC	Ind $		30$	ABBBB$	Ind	
History and Philosophy and Politics *History*	Y650	3FT deg	H	BBC	Ind $		30$	ABBBB$	Ind	

course details			98 expected requirements							96 entry stats	
TITLE	CODE	COURSE	SUBJECTS	A/AS	ND/C	AGNVQ	IB	SQA(H)	SQA	RATIO	A/AS
Univ of LEEDS											
Chinese-History	TV31	4FT deg	L g	BBC	Ind	Ind	30$	CSYS	Ind		
Classical Literature-History	QV81	3FT deg	* g	BBC	Ind	Ind	30	CSYS	Ind	4	
Economic and Social History	V340	3FT deg	* g	BCC	Ind	Ind	28$	CSYS	Ind	13	20/24
Economic and Social History-Gender Studies	MV93	3FT deg	* g	BCC	Ind	Ind	28$	CSYS	Ind		
Economic and Social History-Geography	LV83	3FT deg	Gy g	BBC	Ind	Ind	30$	CSYS	Ind		
Economic and Social History-History	VV13	3FT deg	g	BBC	Ind	Ind	30	CSYS	Ind	16	
Economic and Social History-Politics	MV13	3FT deg	* g	BBB	Ind	Ind	32	CSYS	Ind	12	
Economic and Social History-Social Policy	LV43	3FT deg	* g	BBC	Ind	Ind	30	CSYS	Ind		
Economic and Social History-Sociology	LV33	3FT deg	* g	BBC	Ind	Ind	30	CSYS	Ind		
Economics-Economic and Social History	LV13	3FT deg	g	BCC	Ind	Ind	28	CSYS	Ind	5	20/26
Economics-History	VL11	3FT deg	g	BBC	Ind	Ind	30	CSYS	Ind	12	26/30
Economics-History with North American Studies	VL1C	4FT deg	g	BBC	Ind	Ind	30	CSYS	Ind	6	
English-History	QV31	3FT deg	E g	ABB	Ind	Ind	33$	CSYS	Ind	23	28/30
French-History	RV11	4FT deg	F g	BBB	Ind	Ind	32$	CSYS	Ind	10	26/28
Geography-History	VL18	3FT deg	Gy g	BBC	Ind	Ind	30$	CSYS	Ind	4	22/28
German-History	RV21	4FT deg	G g	BBC	Ind	Ind	30$	CSYS	Ind	17	
Greek Civilisation-History	QVW1	3FT deg	* g	BBC	Ind	Ind	30	CSYS	Ind	14	
History	V100	3FT deg	* g	BBB	Ind	Ind	32	CSYS	Ind	7	22/30
History-History and Philosophy of Science	VV15	3FT deg	* g	BBC	Ind	Ind	30	CSYS	Ind	7	
History-History of Art	VV14	3FT deg	* g	BBB	Ind	Ind	32	CSYS	Ind	12	
History-Italian	RVH1	4FT deg	L g	BBC	Ind	Ind	30	CSYS	Ind		
History-Italian	RV31	4FT deg	I g	BBC	Ind	Ind	30$	CSYS	Ind		
History-Latin	QV61	3FT deg	Ln g	BBC	Ind	Ind	30$	CSYS	Ind	2	
History-Music	VW13	3FT deg	Mu g	BBC	Ind	Ind	30$	CSYS	Ind		
History-Philosophy	VV17	3FT deg	* g	BBC	Ind	Ind	30	CSYS	Ind	13	22/24
History-Portuguese	RV51	4FT deg	L g	BBC	Ind	Ind	30	CSYS	Ind		
History-Religious Studies	VV1V	3FT deg	* g	BBC	Ind	Ind	30	CSYS	Ind		
History-Roman Civilisation	QVV1	3FT deg	* g	BBC	Ind	Ind	30	CSYS	Ind	26	
History-Russian Studies	RV81	4FT deg	R g	BBC	Ind	Ind	30$	CSYS	Ind		
History-Russian Studies B	RVV1	4FT deg	L g	BBC	Ind	Ind	30	CSYS	Ind		
History-Social Policy	VL14	3FT deg	* g	BBC	Ind	Ind	30	CSYS	Ind	6	
History-Sociology	VL13	3FT deg	g	BBC	Ind	Ind	30	CSYS	Ind	12	22/26
History-Spanish	RV41	4FT deg	Sp g	BBC	Ind	Ind	30$	CSYS	Ind		
History-Theology	VV18	3FT deg	* g	BBC	Ind	Ind	30	CSYS	Ind	9	
International History and Politics	V134	3FT deg	* g	BBB	Ind	Ind	32	CSYS	Ind	6	22/30
LEEDS, TRINITY & ALL SAINTS Univ COLL											
History-Management	VN11	3FT deg	H g	BCC-BC	Ind	X	24	BBBCC	Ind	3	6/20
History-Media	VP14	3FT deg	H g	BB-BC	Ind	X	24	BBBCC	Ind	4	10/20
LEEDS METROPOLITAN Univ											
History and Literature	VQ12	3FT deg									
History and Politics	VM11	3FT deg	* g		Ind	Ind go	Ind	Ind	Ind		6/18
Univ of LEICESTER											
Ancient History and Archaeology	VV61	3FT deg	*	BCC	MO	D$^	30	BBBBB	Ind		20/26
Contemporary History	V130	3FT deg	* g	20	Ind	D$^	30	ABBBB	Ind		
Economic and Social History	V340	3FT deg	* g	BCC	MO	D$^	28	BBBBC	Ind		14/22
Economics and Economic History	LV13	3FT deg	* g	BCC	MO	D$^	28	BBBBC	Ind		14/16
Geography and Economic and Social History	LV83	3FT deg	* g	CCC	MO	D$^	28	BBBBC	Ind		16/22
History	V100	3FT deg	H g	BCC	X	D$_^	30$	ABBBC$	X		18/26
History and Archaeology	VV16	3FT deg	H g	20	MO	D$_^	28	BBBBB$	Ind		18/30
History and Politics	VM11	3FT deg	H g	BCC	Ind	D$_^	28	BBBB$	Ind		20/28

			98 expected requirements							96 entry stats	
TITLE	CODE	COURSE	SUBJECTS	A/AS	NVQ/C	AGNVQ	IB	SQA(H)	SQA	RATIO	A/AS
Politics and Economic and Social History	MV13	3FT deg	*g	BCC	2M+3D	D$^	28	BBBBC	Ind		16/22
Combined Arts _Ancient History_	Y300	3FT deg	*g	BCC	DO	D$^	30$	Ind	Ind		
Combined Arts _Economic & Social History_	Y300	3FT deg	*g	BCC	DO	D$^	30$	Ind	Ind		
Combined Arts _History_	Y300	3FT deg	H g	BCC	DO $	D$_^_	30$	Ind	Ind		
Combined Arts _History of Science_	Y300	3FT deg	*g	BCC	DO	D$^	30$	Ind	Ind		
Combined Science _History of Science_	Y100	3FT deg	*g	CCC	MO $	D$^	28$	BBBCC$	HN		

Univ of LIVERPOOL

Ancient History and Archaeology	VV16	3FT deg	*	BCC	Ind	Ind	30	BBBB	Ind	6	14/28
Economic and Social History	V340	3FT deg	*	BCC	Ind	Ind	Ind	Ind	Ind	3	14/24
Economics and Economic History	LV13	3FT deg	*g	BCC	Ind	Ind	Ind	Ind	Ind	8	
English and Modern History	QV31	3FT deg	E+H	BBB	Ind		30$	ABBBB$	Ind	12	22/28
History	V100	3FT deg	H	BCC-BBB	Ind	Ind	Ind	ABBBB$	Ind	13	22/28
Modern History and Politics	MV11	3FT deg	H	BBC	Ind			BBBBB$	Ind	8	22/28
Arts Combined _Ancient History_	Y401	3FT deg	*	BBC-BBB	Ind	Ind	30$	ABBB	Ind		
Arts Combined _Economic and Social History_	Y401	3FT deg	*g	BBC-BBB	Ind	Ind	30$	ABBB	Ind		
Arts Combined _History_	Y401	3FT deg	H	BBC-BBB	Ind	Ind	30$	ABBB	Ind		
BA Combined Honours _Economic and Social History_	Y200	3FT deg	*g	BBB	Ind	Ind	Ind	Ind	Ind		
BA Combined Honours _History_	Y200	3FT deg	H g	BBB	Ind	Ind	Ind	Ind	Ind		

LIVERPOOL HOPE Univ COLL

History/American Studies	QV41	3FT deg	H	12	8M	P$^	Ind	Ind	Ind	4	6/20
History/Art	WV91	3FT deg	H+A/Fa	12	8M	PA^	Ind	Ind	Ind	8	
History/Drama & Theatre Studies	WV41	3FT deg	H g	12	8M	P*^ go	Ind	Ind	Ind	16	
History/English	QV31	3FT deg	EI+H	12	8M	X	Ind	Ind	Ind	4	8/21
History/Environmental Studies	FV91	3FT deg	H+B/Gy/En	12	8M	P$^	Ind	Ind	Ind	6	
History/European Studies	TV21	3FT deg	H	12	8M	P$^	Ind	Ind	Ind		
History/French	RV11	3FT deg	H+F	12	8M	X	Ind	Ind	Ind		
Human & Applied Biology/History	CV11	3FT deg	H+B g	12	8M	PS^ go	Ind	Ind	Ind	5	
Information Technology/History	GV51	3FT deg	H	12	8M	P*^	Ind	Ind	Ind	4	
Mathematics/History	VG11	3FT deg	H+M	12	8M	X	Ind	Ind	Ind	4	
Sociology/History	VL13	3FT deg	H	12	8M	P*^	Ind	Ind	Ind	4	8/16
Sport, Recreation & Physical Education/History	VB16	3FT deg	H	12	8M	P*^	Ind	Ind	Ind		
Theology & Religious Studies/History	VV18	3FT deg	H	12	8M	P*^	Ind	Ind	Ind	3	

LIVERPOOL JOHN MOORES Univ

History and American Studies	QV41	3FT deg		12-20	5M+3D	PP^	28$				
History and Economics	LV11	3FT deg		12-14	5M+2D	PB	28$	CCCC		4	6/18
History and European Studies	TV21	3FT deg		14	5M+2D	P$	28$	BCCC		4	12/20
Human Geography and History	LV81	3FT deg	Gy	12	5M+3D	P$	28$	BBCC		6	
Literature, Life and Thought and History	QV31▼	3FT deg	E	12-20	5M+3D	PT^	28$	BBBC		4	16/20
Politics and History	MV1C▼	3FT deg		12-14	5M+2D	P$^	28$	CCCC		13	12/20
Sociology and History	LV31▼	3FT deg		12-14	MO+2D	D$/M$6	28$	BCCC		5	12/20

TITLE	CODE	COURSE	SUBJECTS	A/AS	ND/C	RGNVQ	IB	SQA(H)	SQA	RATIO	A/AS

LONDON GUILDHALL Univ

TITLE	CODE	COURSE	SUBJECTS	A/AS	ND/C	RGNVQ	IB	SQA(H)	SQA	RATIO	A/AS
3D/Spatial Design and Modern History	VW1F	3FT deg	Pf g	DD	MO	M$ go	24	Ind	Ind		
Mod History & Communications & Audio Vis Prod St	PV41	3FT deg	* g	CC-CDD	MO+4D	M$ go	26	Ind	Ind		
Modern History	V130	3FT deg	* g	CD-DDD	MO	M$ go	24	Ind	Ind		
Modern History & Business Information Technology	GV71	3FT deg	* g	DD	MO	M$ go	24	Ind	Ind		
Modern History and Accounting	NV41	3FT deg	* g	DD	MO	M$ go	24	Ind	Ind		
Modern History and Business	NV11	3FT deg	* g	CD-DDD	MO+2D	M$ go	26	Ind	Ind		
Modern History and Business Economics	LVC1	3FT deg	* g	DD	MO	M$ go	24	Ind	Ind		
Modern History and Computing	GV51	3FT deg	* g	DD	MO	M$ go	24	Ind	Ind		
Modern History and Design Studies	VW12	3FT deg	* g	CD-DDD	MO+2D	M$ go	24	Ind	Ind		
Modern History and Development Studies	MV91	3FT deg	* g	DD	MO	M$ go	24	Ind	Ind		
Modern History and Economics	LV11	3FT deg	* g	DD	MO	M$ go	24	Ind	Ind		
Modern History and English	QV31	3FT deg	* g	CC-CDD	MO+4D	M$ go	26	Ind	Ind		
Modern History and European Studies	TV21	3FT deg	* g	DD	MO	M$ go	24	Ind	Ind		
Modern History and Financial Services	NV31	3FT deg	* g	DD	MO	M$ go	24	Ind	Ind		
Modern History and Fine Art	VW11	3FT deg	* g	CC-CDD	MO+2D	M$ go	26	Ind	Ind		
Modern History and French	RV11	4FT deg	* g	DD	MO	M$ go	24	Ind	Ind		
Modern History and German	RV21	4FT deg	* g	DD	MO	M$ go	24	Ind	Ind		
Modern History and International Relations	MVC1	3FT deg	* g	DD	MO	M$ go	24	Ind	Ind		
Modern History and Law	MV31	3FT deg	* g	CC-CDD	MO+2D	M$ go	26	Ind	Ind		
Modern History and Marketing	NV51	3FT deg	* g	CD-DDD	MO+2D	M$ go	24	Ind	Ind		
Modern History and Mathematics	GV11	3FT deg	* g	DD	MO	M$ go	24	Ind	Ind		
Multimedia Systems and Modern History	GVM1	3FT deg	* g	DD	MO	M$ go	24	Ind	Ind		
Politics and Modern History	MV11	3FT deg	* g	DD	MO	M$ go	24	Ind	Ind		
Product Development & Manufacture & Modern Hist	JV41	3FT deg	* g	DD	MO	M$ go	24	Ind	Ind		
Psychology and Modern History	CV81	3FT deg	* g	CD-DDD	MO+2D	M$ go	26	Ind	Ind		
Social Policy & Management and Modern History	LV41	3FT deg	* g	CD-DDD	MO	M$ go	24	Ind	Ind		
Sociology and Modern History	LV31	3FT deg	* g	CD-DDD	MO	M$ go	24	Ind	Ind		
Spanish and Modern History	RV41	4FT deg	* g	DD	MO	M$ go	24	Ind	Ind		
Taxation and Modern History	NVH1	3FT deg	* g	DD	MO	M$ go	24	Ind	Ind		
Textile Furnishing Design and Modern History	VW1G	3FT deg	Pf g	DD	MO	M$ go	24	Ind	Ind		
Modular Programme *Modern History*	Y400	3FT deg	* g	CC-DD	MO	M$ go	24	Ind	Ind		

LSE: LONDON Sch of Economics (Univ of London)

TITLE	CODE	COURSE	SUBJECTS	A/AS	ND/C	RGNVQ	IB	SQA(H)	SQA	RATIO	A/AS
Economic History	V300	3FT deg	g	ABB	Ind	X	$	Ind	Ind	2	22/30
Economic History and Economics	VL31	3FT deg	g	ABB	Ind	X	$	Ind	Ind	6	24/28
Economic History with Economics	V3L1	3FT deg	g	ABB	Ind	X	$	Ind	Ind	12	
Economic History with Population Studies	V3LC	3FT deg	g	ABB	Ind	X	$	Ind	Ind	8	
Economics with Economic History	L1V3	3FT deg	g	AAB-ABB	Ind	X	$	Ind	Ind	8	28/30
Government and History	MV11	3FT deg	g	ABB	Ind	X	$	Ind	Ind	22	
History	V146	3FT deg	g	ABB	Ind	X	$	Ind	Ind	9	26/30
International History	V145	3FT deg	g	ABB	Ind	X	$	Ind	Ind	6	26/30
International Relations and History	VM11	3FT deg	g	ABB	Ind	X	$	Ind	Ind		

LSU COLL of HE

TITLE	CODE	COURSE	SUBJECTS	A/AS	ND/C	RGNVQ	IB	SQA(H)	SQA	RATIO	A/AS
Art and History	EV11	3FT deg									
Art with History	E1V1	3FT deg	A+H	CD	Ind		Ind	Ind	Ind		
Art with History	W1V1	3FT deg	A+H	CD	Ind		Ind	Ind	Ind		
English with History	Q3V1	3FT deg	E+H	CC	Ind		Ind	Ind	Ind	4	12/16
Geography with History	L8V1	3FT deg									
Historical and Political Studies	V1M1	3FT deg	H	CDD	Ind		Ind	Ind	Ind	3	6/14
History (Combined)	V100	3FT deg									

course details			98 expected requirements							96 entry stats	
TITLE	CODE	COURSE	SUBJECTS	A/AS	NO/C	AGNVQ	IB	SQA(H)	SQA	RATIO	A/AS
History and Art	WV11	3FT deg									
History and English	QV31	3FT deg									
History and Geography	LV81	3FT deg									
History with Art	V1W1	3FT deg									
History with English	V1Q3	3FT deg									
History with Geography	V1L8	3FT deg									
History with Psychology	V1L7	3FT deg	H	CD	Ind		Ind	Ind	Ind	9	
History with Sociology	V1L3	3FT deg	H	CD	Ind		Ind	Ind	Ind	4	8/16
History with Theology	V1V8	3FT deg	H	CD	Ind		Ind	Ind	Ind	6	
Politics and History	VM11	3FT deg									
Psychology and History	VL17	3FT deg									
Sociology and History	VL13	3FT deg									
Sociology with History	L3V1	3FT deg									
Theology and History	VV18	3FT deg									
Theology with History	V8V1	3FT deg									

LUTON Univ

Accounting with Contemporary History	N4VC	3FT deg	g	12-16	MO/DO	M/D	32	BBCC	Ind		
Biology with Contemporary History	C1V1	3FT deg	g	12-16	MO/DO	M/D	32	BBCC	Ind		
Built Environment with Contemporary History	N8V1	3FT deg	g	12-16	MO/DO	M/D	32	BBCC	Ind		
Business with Contemporary History	N1V1	3FT deg	g	12-16	MO/DO	M/D	32	BBCC	Ind	1	
Contemp Br & Euro Hist w Lang & Stylis in Engl	V1QG	3FT deg	g	12-16	MO/DO	M/D	32	BBCC	Ind		
Contemp Br & Euro Hist with Literary St in Engl	V1Q2	3FT deg	g	12-16	MO/DO	M/D	32	BBCC	Ind	1	
Contemp Br & Euro Hist with Modern English Studs	V1Q3	3FT deg	g	12-16	MO/DO	M/D	32	BBCC	Ind		
Contemp Br & Euro Hist with Organisational Behav	V1L7	3FT deg	g	12-16	MO/DO	M/D	32	BBCC	Ind		
Contemp Br & Euro Hist with Public Policy & Mgt	V1MC	3FT deg	g	12-16	MO/DO	M/D	32	BBCC	Ind		
Contemp Br & Euro Hist with Regional Plan & Dev	V1K4	3FT deg	g	12-16	MO/DO	M/D	32	BBCC	Ind		
Contemp Br & Euro Hist with Travel and Tourism	V1P7	3FT deg	g	12-16	MO/DO	M/D	32	BBCC	Ind		
Contemp Br & Euro History with Compar Literature	V1QF	3FT deg	g	12-16	MO/DO	M/D	32	BBCC	Ind		
Contemp Br & Euro History with Leisure Studies	V1N7	3FT deg	g	12-16	MO/DO	M/D	32	BBCC	Ind		
Contemp Br & Euro History with Mapping Science	V1F8	3FT deg	g	12-16	MO/DO	M/D	32	BBCC	Ind		
Contemp Br & Euro History with Media Practices	V1P4	3FT deg	g	12-16	MO/DO	M/D	32	BBCC	Ind		
Contemp Br & Euro History with Media Production	V1PL	3FT deg	g	12-16	MO/DO	M/D	32	BBCC	Ind		
Contemp Br & Euro History with Modern History	V131	3FT deg	g	12-16	MO/DO	M/D	32	BBCC	Ind		
Contemp Br & Euro History with Social Studies	V1L3	3FT deg	g	12-16	MO/DO	M/D	32	BBCC	Ind		
Contemp Br & Euro History with Video Production	V1W5	3FT deg	g	12-16	MO/DO	M/D	32	BBCC	Ind		
Contemp British & Euro History with Animation	V1WF	3FT deg	g	12-16	MO/DO	M/D	32	BBCC	Ind		
Contemp British & Euro History with Business	V1N1	3FT deg	g	12-16	MO/DO	M/D	32	BBCC	Ind		
Contemp British & Euro History with Film Studies	V1WM	3FT deg	g	12-16	MO/DO	M/D	32	BBCC	Ind		
Contemp British & Euro History with Geography	V1FV	3FT deg	g	12-16	MO/DO	M/D	32	BBCC	Ind		
Contemp British & Euro History with Geology	V1F6	3FT deg	g	12-16	MO/DO	M/D	32	BBCC	Ind		
Contemp British & Euro History with Journalism	V1P6	3FT deg	g	12-16	MO/DO	M/D	32	BBCC	Ind		
Contemp British & Euro History with Linguistics	V1Q1	3FT deg	g	12-16	MO/DO	M/D	32	BBCC	Ind		
Contemp British & Euro History with Management	V1ND	3FT deg	g	12-16	MO/DO	M/D	32	BBCC	Ind		
Contemp British & Euro History with Marketing	V1N5	3FT deg	g	12-16	MO/DO	M/D	32	BBCC	Ind		
Contemp British & Euro History with Multimedia	V1PK	3FT deg	g	12-16	MO/DO	M/D	32	BBCC	Ind		
Contemp British & Euro History with Politics	V1M1	3FT deg	g	12-16	MO/DO	M/D	32	BBCC	Ind	5	
Contemp British & Euro History with Psychology	V1LR	3FT deg	g	12-16	MO/DO	M/D	32	BBCC	Ind		
Contemp British & Euro History with Publishing	V1P5	3FT deg	g	12-16	MO/DO	M/D	32	BBCC	Ind		
Contemp British & Euro History with TV Studies	V1WN	3FT deg	g	12-16	MO/DO	M/D	32	BBCC	Ind		
Contemporary History	V130	3FT deg	g	12-16	MO/DO	M/D	32	BBCC	Ind	4	6/8
Contemporary History and Accounting	NVK1	3FT deg	g	12-16	MO/DO	M/D	32	BBCC	Ind		
Contemporary History and British Studies	VV9C	3FT deg		12-16	MO/DO	M/D	32	BBCC	Ind		

course details | 98 expected requirements | 96 entry stats

TITLE	CODE	COURSE	SUBJECTS	A/AS	NO/C	AGNVQ	IB	SQA(H)	SQA	RATIO A/AS
Contemporary History and Business	NV11	3FT deg	g	12-16	MO/DO	M/D	32	BBCC	Ind	2
Contemporary History and Computer Science	GV51	3FT deg	g	12-16	MO/DO	M/D	32	BBCC	Ind	2
Contemporary History with British Studies	V1V9	3FT deg		12-16	MO/DO	M/D	32	BBCC	Ind	
Contemporary History with Chinese	V1T3	3FT deg		12-16	MO/DO	M/D	32	BBCC	Ind	
European Language St with Contemporary History	T2V1	3FT deg	L g	12-16	MO/DO	M/D	32	BBCC	Ind	
European Language Studies and Contemporary Hist	VT12	3FT deg	L g	12-16	MO/DO	M/D	32	BBCC	Ind	
European Language Studies with Modern History	T2VC	4FT deg	L g	12-16	MO/DO	M/D	32	BBCC	Ind	
Geography and Contemporary History	FV81	3FT deg	g	12-16	MO/DO	M/D	32	BBCC	Ind	
Geography with Contemporary History	F8VC	3FT deg	g	12-16	MO/DO	M/D	32	BBCC	Ind	
Geology and Contemporary History	VF16	3FT deg	g	12-16	MO/DO	M/D	32	BBCC	Ind	
Geology with Contemporary History	F6V1	3FT deg	g	12-16	MO/DO	M/D	32	BBCC	Ind	
Health Science and Contemporary History	VB19	3FT deg	g	12-16	MO/DO	M/D	32	BBCC	Ind	
Health Science with Contemporary History	B9V1	3FT deg	g	12-16	MO/DO	M/D	32	BBCC	Ind	
Health Studies with Modern History	B9VD	3FT deg	g	12-16	MO/DO	M/D	32	BBCC	Ind	
History of Design & Architecture & Contemp Hist	VV4C	3FT deg		12-16	MO/DO	M/D	32	BBCC	Ind	
Journalism and Contemporary History	PV6C	3FT deg		12-16	MO/DO	M/D	32	BBCC	Ind	
Language & Stylistics in English & Contemp Hist	VQ1G	3FT deg	g	12-16	MO/DO	M/D	32	BBCC	Ind	
Law and Contemporary History	VM13	3FT deg	g	12-16	MO/DO	M/D	32	BBCC	Ind	6
Law with Contemporary History	M3V1	3FT deg	g	12-16	MO/DO	M/D	32	BBCC	Ind	
Law with Modern History	M3VC	3FT deg	g	12-16	MO/DO	M/D	32	BBCC	Ind	
Leisure Studies and Contemporary History	VN17	3FT deg	g	12-16	MO/DO	M/D	32	BBCC	Ind	
Leisure Studies with Contemporary History	N7V1	3FT deg	g	12-16	MO/DO	M/D	32	BBCC	Ind	
Leisure Studies with Modern History	N7VC	3FT deg	g	12-16	MO/DO	M/D	32	BBCC	Ind	
Linguistics and Contemporary History	VQ11	3FT deg	g	12-16	MO/DO	M/D	32	BBCC	Ind	
Linguistics with Contemporary History	Q1V1	3FT deg	g	12-16	MO/DO	M/D	32	BBCC	Ind	
Literary Studies in English & Contemporary Hist	VQ12	3FT deg	g	12-16	MO/DO	M/D	32	BBCC	Ind	3
Literary Studies in English with Contemp History	Q2VC	3FT deg		12-16	MO/DO	M/D	32	BBCC	Ind	
Literary Studies in English with Modern History	Q2V1	3FT deg		12-16	MO/DO	M/D	32	BBCC	Ind	
Mapping Science and Contemporary History	VF18	3FT deg	g	12-16	MO/DO	M/D	32	BBCC	Ind	
Mapping Science with Contemporary History	F8V1	3FT deg	g	12-16	MO/DO	M/D	32	BBCC	Ind	
Marketing and Contemporary History	VN15	3FT deg	g	12-16	MO/DO	M/D	32	BBCC	Ind	
Marketing with Contemporary History	N5V1	3FT deg	g	12-16	MO/DO	M/D	32	BBCC	Ind	
Media Practices and Contemporary History	VP14	3FT deg	g	12-16	MO/DO	M/D	32	BBCC	Ind	
Media Practices with Contemporary History	P4V1	3FT deg	g	12-16	MO/DO	M/D	32	BBCC	Ind	
Media Practices with Modern History	P4VC	3FT deg	g	12-16	MO/DO	M/D	32	BBCC	Ind	
Media Production and Contemporary History	VP1L	3FT deg	g	12-16	MO/DO	M/D	32	BBCC	Ind	
Media Production with Contemporary History	P4VD	3FT deg	g	12-16	MO/DO	M/D	32	BBCC	Ind	
Modern English Studies and Contemporary History	VQ13	3FT deg	g	12-16	MO/DO	M/D	32	BBCC	Ind	1
Modern English Studies with Contemporary History	Q3V1	3FT deg	g	12-16	MO/DO	M/D	32	BBCC	Ind	2
Modern English Studies with Modern History	Q3VC	3FT deg	g	12-16	MO/DO	M/D	32	BBCC	Ind	
Modern History	V100	3FT deg	g	12-16	MO/DO	M/D	32	BBCC	Ind	7	6/22
Modern History & Language & Stylistics in Engl	QVGC	3FT deg	g	12-16	MO/DO	M/D	32	BBCC	Ind	
Modern History and Accounting	NVKC	3FT deg	g	12-16	MO/DO	M/D	32	BBCC	Ind	
Modern History and Biology	CV1C	3FT deg	g	12-16	MO/DO	M/D	32	BBCC	Ind	
Modern History and British Studies	VV91	3FT deg		12-16	MO/DO	M/D	32	BBCC	Ind	
Modern History and Business	NV1C	3FT deg	g	12-16	MO/DO	M/D	32	BBCC	Ind	
Modern History and Business Systems	NVCC	3FT deg	g	12-16	MO/DO	M/D	32	BBCC	Ind	
Modern History and Contemporary History	V102	3FT deg	g	12-16	MO/DO	M/D	32	BBCC	Ind	4
Modern History and Environmental Science	FV9C	3FT deg	g	12-16	MO/DO	M/D	32	BBCC	Ind	
Modern History and European Language Studies	TV2C	3FT deg	L g	12-16	MO/DO	M/D	32	BBCC	Ind	1
Modern History and Geology	FV6C	3FT deg		12-16	MO/DO	M/D	32	BBCC	Ind	
Modern History and Health Studies	BVXC	3FT deg	g	12-16	MO/DO	M/D	32	BBCC	Ind	

History 33

course details — 98 expected requirements — 96 entry stats

TITLE	CODE	COURSE	SUBJECTS	A/AS	NO/C	AGNVQ	IB	SQA(H)	SQA	RATIO A/AS
Modern History and Law	MV3C	3FT deg	g	12-16	MO/DO	M/D	32	BBCC	Ind	14
Modern History and Linguistics	QV1C	3FT deg	g	12-16	MO/DO	M/D	32	BBCC	Ind	
Modern History and Literary Studies in English	QV2C	3FT deg	g	12-16	MO/DO	M/D	32	BBCC	Ind	6
Modern History and Mapping Science	FV8C	3FT deg	g	12-16	MO/DO	M/D	32	BBCC	Ind	
Modern History and Marketing	NV5C	3FT deg	g	12-16	MO/DO	M/D	32	BBCC	Ind	
Modern History and Media Practices	PV4C	3FT deg	g	12-16	MO/DO	M/D	32	BBCC	Ind	
Modern History and Modern English Studies	QV3C	3FT deg		12-16	MO/DO	M/D	32	BBCC	Ind	6
Modern History with Accounting	V1N4	3FT deg	g	12-16	MO/DO	M/D	32	BBCC	Ind	
Modern History with Biology	V1CC	3FT deg	g	12-16	MO/DO	M/D	32	BBCC	Ind	
Modern History with British Studies	V1VX	3FT deg		12-16	MO/DO	M/D	32	BBCC	Ind	
Modern History with Business	V142	3FT deg	g	12-16	MO/DO	M/D	32	BBCC	Ind	3
Modern History with Business Systems	V1NC	3FT deg	g	12-16	MO/DO	M/D	32	BBCC	Ind	
Modern History with Chinese	V1TH	3FT deg		12-16	MO/DO	M/D	32	BBCC	Ind	
Modern History with Comparative Literature	V132	3FT deg	g	12-16	MO/DO	M/D	32	BBCC	Ind	
Modern History with Contemporary History	V144	3FT deg	g	12-16	MO/DO	M/D	32	BBCC	Ind	
Modern History with Environmental Science	V1FY	3FT deg	g	12-16	MO/DO	M/D	32	BBCC	Ind	
Modern History with Geographical Info Syst	V101	3FT deg	g	12-16	MO/DO	M/D	32	BBCC	Ind	
Modern History with Geology	V1FP	3FT deg	g	12-16	MO/DO	M/D	32	BBCC	Ind	
Modern History with Health Studies	V1BX	3FT deg		12-16	MO/DO	M/D	32	BBCC	Ind	
Modern History with Lang & Stylistics in English	V133	3FT deg	g	12-16	MO/DO	M/D	32	BBCC	Ind	
Modern History with Linguistics	V1QC	3FT deg	g	12-16	MO/DO	M/D	32	BBCC	Ind	
Modern History with Literary Studies in English	V143	3FT deg	g	12-16	MO/DO	M/D	32	BBCC	Ind	3
Modern History with Mapping Science	V145	3FT deg	g	12-16	MO/DO	M/D	32	BBCC	Ind	
Modern History with Marketing	V1NM	3FT deg		12-16	MO/DO	M/D	32	BBCC	Ind	
Modern History with Media Practices	V139	3FT deg	g	12-16	MO/DO	M/D	32	BBCC	Ind	
Modern History with Modern English Studies	V1QH	3FT deg	g	12-16	MO/DO	M/D	32	BBCC	Ind	
Modern History with Organisational Behaviour	V1LT	3FT deg	g	12-16	MO/DO	M/D	32	BBCC	Ind	
Modern History with Psychology	V137	3FT deg	g	12-16	MO/DO	M/D	32	BBCC	Ind	
Modern History with Public Policy & Management	V1MD	3FT deg		12-16	MO/DO	M/D	32	BBCC	Ind	
Modern History with Publishing	V1PM	3FT deg	g	12-16	MO/DO	M/D	32	BBCC	Ind	
Modern History with Regional Planning and Dev	V1KK	3FT deg	g	12-16	MO/DO	M/D	32	BBCC	Ind	
Modern History with Social Studies	V1LH	3FT deg	g	12-16	MO/DO	M/D	32	BBCC	Ind	
Modern History with Travel and Tourism	V1PR	3FT deg	g	12-16	MO/DO	M/D	32	BBCC	Ind	
Organisational Behaviour and Contemporary Hist	VL17	3FT deg	g	12-16	MO/DO	M/D	32	BBCC	Ind	
Politics and Contemporary History	VM11	3FT deg	g	12-16	MO/DO	M/D	32	BBCC	Ind	14
Politics and Modern History	VMC1	3FT deg	g	12-16	MO/DO	M/D	32	BBCC	Ind	
Politics with Contemporary History	M1V1	3FT deg	g	12-16	MO/DO	M/D	32	BBCC	Ind	
Politics with Modern History	M1VC	3FT deg	g	12-16	MO/DO	M/D	32	BBCC	Ind	
Psychology and Contemporary History	VL1R	3FT deg	g	12-16	MO/DO	M/D	32	BBCC	Ind	6
Psychology with Contemporary History	L7VD	3FT deg	g	12-16	MO/DO	M/D	32	BBCC	Ind	
Public Policy & Management and Contemporary Hist	VM1C	3FT deg	g	12-16	MO/DO	M/D	32	BBCC	Ind	
Public Policy and Management and Modern History	VMCC	3FT deg	g	12-16	MO/DO	M/D	32	BBCC	Ind	
Public Policy and Mgt with Contemporary History	M1VD	3FT deg	g	12-16	MO/DO	M/D	32	BBCC	Ind	
Regional Planning & Dev and Contemporary History	VK14	3FT deg	g	12-16	MO/DO	M/D	32	BBCC	Ind	
Regional Planning and Dev with Contemp History	K4V1	3FT deg	g	12-16	MO/DO	M/D	32	BBCC	Ind	
Regional Planning and Dev with Modern History	K4VC	3FT deg		12-16	MO/DO	M/D	32	BBCC	Ind	
Regional Planning and Development & Modern Hist	VKC4	3FT deg	g	12-16	MO/DO	M/D	32	BBCC	Ind	
Social Policy and Contemporary History	LV4C	3FT deg		12-16	MO/DO	M/D	32	BBCC	Ind	
Social Policy and Modern History	LV41	3FT deg		12-16	MO/DO	M/D	32	BBCC	Ind	
Social Policy with Contemporary History	L4VC	3FT deg		12-16	MO/DO	M/D	32	BBCC	Ind	
Social Policy with Modern History	L4V1	3FT deg		12-16	MO/DO	M/D	32	BBCC	Ind	
Social Studies and Contemporary History	VL13	3FT deg	g	12-16	MO/DO	M/D	32	BBCC	Ind	3

TITLE	CODE	COURSE	SUBJECTS	A/AS	ND/C	RGNVQ	IB	SQA(H)	SQA	RATIO A/AS
course details			**98 expected requirements**							**96 entry stats**
Social Studies and Modern History	VLC3	3FT deg	g	12-16	MO/DO	M/D	32	BBCC	Ind	
Social Studies with Contemporary History	L3V1	3FT deg	g	12-16	MO/DO	M/D	32	BBCC	Ind	
Social Studies with Modern History	L3VC	3FT deg	g	12-16	MO/DO	M/D	32	BBCC	Ind	
Sociology and Contemporary History	LVHC	3FT deg		12-16	MO/DO	M/D	32	BBCC	Ind	
Sociology with Contemporary History	L3VD	3FT deg		12-16	MO/DO	M/D	32	BBCC	Ind	
Travel and Tourism and Contemporary History	VP17	3FT deg	g	12-16	MO/DO	M/D	32	BBCC	Ind	
Travel and Tourism with Contemp Br & Euro Hist	P7V1	3FT deg	g	12-16	MO/DO	M/D	32	BBCC	Ind	
Women's Studies and Contemporary History	MV9C	3FT deg		12-16	MO/DO	M/D	32	BBCC	Ind	
Women's Studies with Contemporary History	M9V1	3FT deg		12-16	MO/DO	M/D	32	BBCC	Ind	

Univ of MANCHESTER

TITLE	CODE	COURSE	SUBJECTS	A/AS	ND/C	RGNVQ	IB	SQA(H)	SQA	RATIO A/AS
Ancient History and Archaeology	VV16	3FT deg		BCD-BCC						9 14/22
Classics and Ancient History	QV81	3FT deg								
Economic History and Economics	LV13	3FT deg		BBC-BBB	Ind		30	CSYS$	Ind	7 22/26
Economic and Social History	V340	3FT deg	*g	BBC	M+6D	D^	32	AABBB	Ind	13 22/28
History	V100	3FT deg	*	BBC-BBB			30	CSYS$	Ind	10 22/30
History and French	VR11	4FT deg	F	BBC-BBB			30$	CSYS$		7 22/28
History and German	VR12	4FT deg	G+H	BBC			30	ABBBB		6 20/24
History and Italian	RV31	4FT deg	L	CCC			Ind	BBBCC		14
History and Sociology	VL13	3FT deg	*	BBC-BBB			30	CSYS$	Ind	5 18/26
History and Spanish	VR14	4FT deg	Sp	BBC			28$	ABBBB$		5
Medieval Studies	V120	3FT deg	g	BBC-BBB			30	CSYS$	Ind	6 22/26
Modern History with Economics	V136	3FT deg	*	BBC-BBB	Ind		Ind	CSYS$	Ind	3 20/26
Modern Middle Eastern History	V130	3FT deg	g	BCC-BBC	2M+5D		30d	ABBBB	Ind	2
Politics and Modern History	VM11	3FT deg		BBC-BBB	Ind		Dip	Ind	Ind	5 20/28

MANCHESTER METROPOLITAN Univ

TITLE	CODE	COURSE	SUBJECTS	A/AS	ND/C	RGNVQ	IB	SQA(H)	SQA	RATIO A/AS
Historical Studies	V100	3FT deg	H	BC	Ind	Ind	Ind	Ind	Ind	10/20
History/American Studies	QV41	3FT deg	*	CC	M+D	D	28	CCCC	Ind	
History/Applied Social Studies	LV31	3FT deg	*	CC	M+D	D	28	CCCC	Ind	
History/Business Studies	NV11	3FT deg	*	CC	M+D	D	28	CCCC	Ind	
History/Cultural Studies	LVH1	3FT deg	*	CC	M+D	D	28	CCCC	Ind	
History/Dance	VW14	3FT deg	*	CC	M+D	D	28	CCCC	Ind	
History/Design & Technology	VW12	3FT deg	*	CC	M+D	D	28	CCCC	Ind	
History/Drama	VW1K	3FT deg	*	CC	M+D	D	28	CCCC	Ind	
History/English	QV31	3FT deg	*	CC	M+D	D	28	CCCC	Ind	
History/Geography	LV81	3FT deg	*	CC	M+D	D	28	CCCC	Ind	
History/Health Studies	BV91	3FT deg	*	CC	M+D	D	28	CCCC	Ind	
Leisure Studies/History	LV41	3FT deg	*	CC	M+D	D	28	CCCC	Ind	
Music/History	VW13	3FT deg	*	CC	M+D	D	28	CCCC	Ind	
Philosophy/History	VV17	3FT deg	*	CC	M+D	D	28	CCCC	Ind	
Religious Studies/History	VV18	3FT deg	*	CC	M+D	D	28	CCCC	Ind	
Sport/History	BV61	3FT deg	S	BC	M+D	DS	28	CCCC	Ind	
Visual Arts/History	VW11	3FT deg	*	CC	M+D	D	28	CCCC	Ind	
Writing/History	VW1L	3FT deg	*	CC	M+D	D	28	CCCC	Ind	
Humanities/Social Studies History	Y400	3FT deg	*	CDD	Ind	Ind	Ind	BBB	Ind	
Humanities/Social Studies Social & Economic History	Y400	3FT deg	*	CDD	Ind	Ind	Ind	BBB	Ind	

TITLE	CODE	COURSE	SUBJECTS	A/AS	ND/C	AGNVQ	IB	SQA(H)	SQA	RATIO	A/AS
course details			**98 expected requirements**							**96 entry stats**	
MIDDLESEX Univ											
Cultural and Intellectual History	V175▼	3FT deg	* g	12-16	5M	M$ go	28	Ind	Ind		
Heritage Studies	LV83▼	3FT deg	* g	12	5M	M$ go	24	Ind	Ind		
History	V100▼	3FT deg	* g	12-16	5M	M$ go	28	Ind	Ind		
Joint Honours Degree *Asia-Pacific Studies*	Y400	3FT deg	* g	12-16	5M	M$ go	28	Ind	Ind		
Joint Honours Degree *Cultural and Intellectual History*	Y400	3FT deg	* g	12-16	5M	M$ go	28	Ind	Ind		
Joint Honours Degree *History*	Y400	3FT deg	H g	12-16	5M	Ind	28	Ind	Ind		
NENE COLLEGE											
American Studies with History	Q4V1	3FT deg		DD	5M	M	24	CCC	Ind		
Art and Design with History	W2V1	3FT deg		DD	5M	M	24	CCC	Ind		
Business Administration with History	N1V1	3FT deg	g	10	M+1D	M	24	BCC	Ind		
Drama with History	W4V1	3FT deg		10	5M+1D	M	24	CCC	Ind		
Education with History	X9V1	3FT deg		DD	5M	M	24	CCC	Ind		
English with History	Q3V1▼	3FT deg		CC	4M+1D	M	24	CCC	Ind		
Geography with History	F8V1	3FT deg	Gy	8	5M	M	24	CCC	Ind		
History	V100	3FT deg		CD	5M	M	24	CCC	Ind	8/16	
History with American Studies	V1Q4	3FT deg		CD	5M	M	24	CCC	Ind		
History with Architectural Studies	V1V4▼	3FT deg		CD	5M	M	24	CCC	Ind		
History with Art and Design	V1W2	3FT deg		CD	5M	M	24	CCC	Ind		
History with Business Administration	V1N1	3FT deg	g	CD	5M	M	24	CCC	Ind		
History with Drama	V1W4	3FT deg		CD	5M	M	24	CCC	Ind		
History with Economics	V1L1	3FT deg	g	CD	5M	M	24	CCC	Ind		
History with Education	V1X9	3FT deg		CD	5M	M	24	CCC	Ind	6/18	
History with English	V1Q3▼	3FT deg		CD	5M	M	24	CCC	Ind	4/10	
History with Geography	V1F8	3FT deg		CD	5M	M	24	CCC	Ind		
History with Health Studies	V1L5▼	3FT deg		CD	5M	M	24	CCC	Ind		
History with History of Art	V1VK▼	3FT deg		CD	5M	M	24	CCC	Ind		
History with Industrial Archaeology	V1V6	3FT deg		CD	5M	M	24	CCC	Ind		
History with Law	V1M3	3FT deg	g	CD	5M	M	24	CCC	Ind		
History with Marketing Communications	V1N5▼	3FT deg		CD	5M	M	24	CCC	Ind		
History with Music	V1W3	3FT deg	Mu	CD	5M	M	24	CCC	Ind		
History with Philosophy	V1V7▼	3FT deg		CD	5M	M	24	CCC	Ind		
History with Politics	V1M1	3FT deg		CD	5M	M	24	CCC	Ind		
History with Psychology	V1C8▼	3FT deg	g	CD	5M	M	24	CCC	Ind		
History with Sociology	V1L3▼	3FT deg		CD	5M	M	24	CCC	Ind		
History with Sport Studies	V1N7▼	3FT deg		CD	5M	M	24	CCC	Ind		
Industrial Archaeology with History	V6V1	3FT deg		10	5M	M	24	CCC	Ind		
Information Systems with History	G5V1	3FT deg		6	5M	M	24	CCC	Ind		
Law with History	M3V1	3FT deg	g	10	3M+2D	M	24	CCC	Ind		
Music with History	W3V1	3FT deg	Mu	DD	5M	M	24	CCC	Ind		
Politics with History	M1V1	3FT deg		CD	5M	M	24	CCC	Ind		
Psychology with History	C8V1▼	3FT deg	g	CC	5M+1D	M	24	CCC	Ind		
Sociology with History	L3V1▼	3FT deg		10	5M	M	24	CCC	Ind		
Sport Studies with History	N7V1▼	3FT deg	Ss/Pe	12	M+2D	M	24	BBB	Ind		
Univ of NEWCASTLE											
Ancient History	V110	3FT deg	*	20-22		Ind		AABBB		5	20/28
Ancient History and Archaeology	VV16	3FT deg	*	BCC-BBC	DO		Ind	Ind	Ind	8	18/28
History	V100	3FT deg	H	ABC-BBB	Ind		33$	Ind	Ind	9	22/28
Politics and History	VM11	3FT deg	H	BBB	Ind		30$	AABB	Ind	8	24/30

TITLE	CODE	COURSE	SUBJECTS	A/AS	NO/C	AGNVQ	IB	SQA(H)	SQA	RATIO A/AS
course details			**98 expected requirements**							**96 entry stats**
Combined Studies (BA) *Ancient History*	Y400	3FT deg	*	ABC-BBB	5D	Ind	35$	AAAB	Ind	
Combined Studies (BA) *English Medieval Studies*	Y400	3FT deg	*	ABC-BBB	5D	Ind	35$	AAAB	Ind	
Combined Studies (BA) *History*	Y400	3FT deg	*	ABC-BBB	5D	Ind	35$	AAAB	Ind	

NEWMAN COLLEGE OF HIGHER EDUCATION

TITLE	CODE	COURSE	SUBJECTS	A/AS	NO/C	AGNVQ	IB	SQA(H)	SQA	RATIO A/AS
Biological Science and History	CV11	3FT deg	*	CC	3M	M*	Dip	CCC	Ind	
English and History	QV31	3FT deg	*	CC	3M	M*	Dip	CCC	Ind	
Geography and History	FV81	3FT deg	*	CC	3M	M*	Dip	CCC	Ind	
History and Expressive English	WV41	3FT deg	*	CC	3M	M*	Dip	CCC	Ind	
History and PE and Sports Studies	VX19	3FT deg	*	CC	3M	M*	Dip	CCC	Ind	
History and Theology	VV18	3FT deg	*	CC	3M	M*	Dip	CCC	Ind	
Information Technology and History	GV51	3FT deg	*	CC	3M	M*	Dip	CCC	Ind	

Univ of Wales COLLEGE, NEWPORT

TITLE	CODE	COURSE	SUBJECTS	A/AS	NO/C	AGNVQ	IB	SQA(H)	SQA	RATIO A/AS
History and Archaeology	VV16	3FT deg		10	M+D	D$	Ind	Ind	Ind	
History and English	QV31	3FT deg		10	M+D	D$	Ind	Ind	Ind	
History and European Studies	TV21	3FT deg		10	M+D	D$	Ind	Ind	Ind	
History and Geography	LV81	3FT deg		10	M+D	D$	Ind	Ind	Ind	
Information Technology and History	GV51	3FT deg		10	M+D	D$	Ind	Ind	Ind	
Religious Studies and History	VV18	3FT deg		10	M+D	D$	Ind	Ind	Ind	
Sports Studies and History	BV61	3FT deg		10	M+D	D$	Ind	Ind	Ind	

NORTH EAST WALES INST of HE

TITLE	CODE	COURSE	SUBJECTS	A/AS	NO/C	AGNVQ	IB	SQA(H)	SQA	RATIO A/AS
English and History	QV31	3FT deg		6-12	4M	M$	Ind	BBB	N$	8/16
English with History	Q3V1	3FT deg		6-12	4M	M$	Ind	BBB	N$	
History	V100	3FT deg		6-12	4M	M$	Ind	BBB	N$	
History and Media Studies	VP14	3FT deg		6-12	4M	M$	Ind	BBB	N$	
History and Welsh Studies	VQ15	3FT deg		6-12	4M	M$	Ind	BBB	N$	
History with English	V1Q3	3FT deg		6-12	4M	M$	Ind	BBB	N$	
History with Geography	V1F8	3FT deg		6-12	4M	M$	Ind	BBB	N$	
History with Media Studies	V1P4	3FT deg		6-12	4M	M$	Ind	BBB	N$	
History with Psychology	V1C8	3FT deg		6-12	4M	M$	Ind	BBB	N$	
History with Sociology	V1L3	3FT deg		6-12	4M	M$	Ind	BBB	N$	
History with Welsh	V1Q5	3FT deg		6-12	4M	M$	Ind	BBB	N$	
History/Geography	VF18	3FT deg		6-12	4M	M$	Ind	BBB	N$	
History/Psychology	VC18	3FT deg		6-12	4M	M$	Ind	BBB	N$	
History/Sociology	VL13	3FT deg		6-12	4M	M$	Ind	BBB	N$	

Univ of NORTH LONDON

TITLE	CODE	COURSE	SUBJECTS	A/AS	NO/C	AGNVQ	IB	SQA(H)	SQA	RATIO A/AS
Economics and History	LV11	3FT deg	H g	CC	Ind	Ind	Ind	Ind	Ind	
History	V100	3FT deg	H	CC	Ind	Ind	Ind	Ind	Ind	7 8/16
History and Geography	FV81	3FT deg	*	CC	Ind	Ind	Ind	Ind	Ind	
History and Politics	VM11	3FT deg	*	CC	MO	M	Ind	Ind	Ind	9
Law and History	MV31	3FT deg	*	CC	Ind	Ind	Ind	Ind	Ind	
Sociology and History	LV31	3FT deg	*	CC	Ind	Ind	Ind	Ind	Ind	
Combined Honours *History*	Y300	3FT/4FT deg	H	CC	Ind	Ind	Ind	Ind	Ind	

Univ of NORTHUMBRIA

TITLE	CODE	COURSE	SUBJECTS	A/AS	NO/C	AGNVQ	IB	SQA(H)	SQA	RATIO A/AS
Historical Studies	V100	3FT deg	<u>H</u>	BBD	MO+5D		30	Ind	Ind	7 14/20
History and German	RV21	3FT deg	<u>H+G</u>	BCC	N		28	Ind	Ind	
History and Sociology	LV31	3FT deg	<u>H+So</u>	18	MO+4D		26	Ind	Ind	18
Combined Honours *History*	Y400▼	3FT deg	g	12-20	MO+3D	D	26	BBCCC	Ind	

course details			98 expected requirements							96 entry stats
TITLE	CODE	COURSE	SUBJECTS	A/AS	ND/C	RGNVQ	IB	SQA(H)	SQA	RATIO A/AS
NORWICH: City COLL										
Psychology with History	L7V1	3FT deg	* g	12		X	Ind	Ind	Ind	
Combined Arts *History*	Y300	3FT deg	* g	12	Ind		Ind	Ind	Ind	
Univ of NOTTINGHAM										
American Studies and History	QV41	3FT deg	H	BBC						14 24/28
Ancient History	V110	3FT deg		BCC						8 20/28
Ancient History and Archaeology	VVC6	3FT deg		BCC						28 22/28
Ancient History and History	V117	3FT deg	H	BCC						67
Ancient History and Latin	QV61	3FT deg	Ln	BCC						3
Archaeology and History	VV16	3FT deg	H	BBC						26
History	V100	3FT/4FT deg	H	ABB						17 26/30
History and Russian	VR18	4FT deg	H+R	BCC						
History and Russian (Beginners)	VR1V	4FT deg	H	BCC						6
NOTTINGHAM TRENT Univ										
History	V100	3FT deg	H g	18	Ind	Ind	28	CCCC	Ind	9 14/22
Humanities *Heritage Studies*	Y301	3FT/4SW deg	* g	14-16	M+D	Ind	28	CCCC	Ind	
Humanities *History*	Y301	3FT/4SW deg	* g	14-16	M+D	Ind	28	CCCC	Ind	
OXFORD Univ										
Ancient and Modern History	V118	3FT deg	H	AAB-ABB DO			36	AAAAA	Ind	3 24/30
Jewish Studies (3 Yrs)	QV91	3FT deg	*	AAB-ABB DO			36	AAAAA	Ind	
Modern History	V130	3FT deg	H	AAB-ABB DO			36	AAAAA	Ind	2 26/30
Modern History and Economics	LV11	3FT deg	H	AAB-ABB DO			36	AAAAA	Ind	3 26/30
Modern History and English	VQ13	3FT deg	E+H	AAB	DO		36	AAAAA	Ind	5 28/30
Modern History and Modern Languages (3 Yrs)	TV91	3FT deg	H+L	AAB	DO		36	AAAAA	Ind	2
Modern History and Modern Languages (4 Yrs)	VT19	4FT deg	H+L	AAB	DO		36	AAAAA	Ind	3 30/30
OXFORD WESTMINSTER COLLEGE										
Contemporary Historical Studies w. Interfaith St	V1V8	3FT deg	H	CE	MO	M	Ind	CCC	Ind	
Contemporary Historical Studies with Cultural St	V1V9	3FT deg	H	CE	MO	M	Ind	CCC	Ind	
Contemporary Historical Studies with Cultural St	V1VX	2FT Dip	H	CE	MO	M	Ind	CCC	Ind	
Contemporary Historical Studies with Dev Studies	V1L3	3FT deg	H	CE	MO	M	Ind	CCC	Ind	
Contemporary Historical Studies with Language St	V1T9	3FT deg	H	CE	MO	M	Ind	CCC	Ind	
Contemporary Historical Studies with Language St	V1TX	2FT Dip	H	CE	MO	M	Ind	CCC	Ind	
Contemporary Historical Studies with World St	V1MC	2FT Dip	H	CE	MO	M	Ind	CCC	Ind	
Contemporary Historical Studies with World St	V1M1	3FT deg	H	CE	MO	M	Ind	CCC	Ind	
Contemporary Historical Studs w. Development St	V1LH	2FT Dip	H	CE	MO	M	Ind	CCC	Ind	
Contemporary Historical Studs with Interfaith St	V1VV	2FT Dip	H	CE	MO	M	Ind	CCC	Ind	
OXFORD BROOKES Univ										
Geography and the Phys Env/History	FVV1	3FT deg								
History of Art/History	VV14	3FT deg	*	BB-CCD	Ind	M*^	Ind	Ind	Ind	7 16/18
History/Accounting and Finance	NV41	3FT deg	* g	BB-CCD	Ind	M^/D*3	Ind	Ind	Ind	6
History/Anthropology	LV61	3FT deg	*	BB-CCD	Ind	M*^	Ind	Ind	Ind	44
History/Biological Chemistry	CV71	3FT deg								
History/Biology	CV11	3FT deg	S g	DD-BB	Ind	MS/M^	Ind	Ind	Ind	2
History/Business Administration & Management	NV11	3FT deg	* g	BB-BBC	Ind	M^/MB4	Ind	Ind	Ind	15
History/Cartography	FV81	3FT deg	* g	DDD-BB	Ind	M*^	Ind	Ind	Ind	
History/Cell Biology	CVC1	3FT deg								
History/Combined Studies	VY14	3FT deg		X		X	X	X		

course details   98 expected requirements   96 entry stats

TITLE	CODE	COURSE	SUBJECTS	A/AS	ND/C	AGNVQ	IB	SQA(H)	SQA	RATIO A/AS
History/Computer Systems	GV61	3FT deg	* g	CDD-BB	Ind	M*^	Ind	Ind	Ind	
History/Computing	GV51	3FT deg	* g	CDD-BB	Ind	M*^	Ind	Ind	Ind	2
History/Computing Mathematics	GV91	3FT deg	* g	CD-BB	Ind	M*^	Ind	Ind	Ind	
History/Ecology	CV91	3FT deg	* g	CD-BB	Ind	MS/M^	Ind	Ind	Ind	
History/Economics	LV11	3FT deg	* g	BB-CCD	Ind	M^/M*3	Ind	Ind	Ind	9
History/Educational Studies	VX19	3FT deg	*	CC-BB	Ind	M^/M*3	Ind	Ind	Ind	6
History/Electronics	HV61	3FT deg	S/M	CC-BB	Ind	MS/M^	Ind	Ind	Ind	
History/English Studies	QV31	3FT deg	*	CCD-AB	Ind	M*^	Ind	Ind	Ind	7 14/20
History/Environmental Chemistry	VF11	3FT deg								
History/Environmental Policy	KV31	3FT deg								
History/Environmental Sciences	FVX1	3FT deg	S g	CD-BB	Ind	M^/DS	Ind	Ind	Ind	
History/Exercise and Health	VB16	3FT deg	S g	DD-BB	Ind	MS^	Ind	Ind	Ind	
History/Fine Art	VW11	3FT deg	Pf+A	BC-BB	Ind	MA^	Ind	Ind	Ind	
History/Food Science and Nutrition	DV41	3FT deg	M/S g	DD-BB	Ind	MS/M*^	Ind	Ind	Ind	
History/French Language and Contemp Studies	RVC1	4SW deg	F	CDD-BB	Ind	M*^	Ind	Ind	Ind	6
History/French Language and Literature	RV11	4SW deg	F	CDD-BB	Ind	M*^	Ind	Ind	Ind	
History/Geography	LV81	3FT deg	*	BB-CCD	Ind	M*^	Ind	Ind	Ind	10
History/Geology	FV61	3FT deg	S/M	DD-BB	Ind	M*^/PS	Ind	Ind	Ind	
History/Geotechnics	HV21	3FT deg	S/M	DD-BB	Ind	MS/M*^	Ind	Ind	Ind	
History/German Language and Contemp Stud	RVF1	4SW deg	G	DDD-BB	Ind	M*^	Ind	Ind	Ind	3
History/German Language and Literature	RV21	4SW deg	G	DDD-BB	Ind	M*^	Ind	Ind	Ind	
History/German Studies	VR1G	4SW deg	G	DDD-BB	Ind	M*^	Ind	Ind	Ind	
History/Health Care (Post Exp)	BV71	3FT deg		X		X	X	X		
Hospitality Management Studies/History	NV71	3FT deg	*	DDD-BB	Ind	M^/M*3	Ind	Ind	Ind	5
Human Biology/History	BV11	3FT deg								
Information Systems/History	GVN1	3FT deg	* g	BC-BB	Ind	M*	Ind	Ind	Ind	
Intelligent Systems/History	GV81	3FT deg	* g	BB-CD	Ind	M^	Ind	Ind	Ind	
Law/History	MV31	3FT deg	*	CCD-BBB	Ind	M^/D*3	Ind	Ind	Ind	11
Leisure Planning/History	KVH1	3FT deg								
Marketing Management/History	NVN1	3FT deg	* g	BB-BCC	Ind	M^/D*B	Ind	Ind	Ind	3
Mathematics/History	GV11	3FT deg	M	DD-BB	Ind	M*^	Ind	Ind	Ind	3
Modern History	V130	3FT deg			Ind		Ind	Ind	Ind	
Music/History	VW13	3FT deg	Mu	DD-BB	Ind	M^	Ind	Ind	Ind	7
Palliative Care/History	BVR1	3FT deg		X		X	X	X		
Planning Studies/History	KV41	3FT deg	* g	DDD-BB	Ind	M*^	Ind	Ind	Ind	
Politics/History	MV11	3FT deg	*	CCD-AB	Ind	M^	Ind	Ind	Ind	9 12/18
Psychology/History	CV81	3FT deg	* g	CCD-BBC	Ind	M*^	Ind	Ind	Ind	
Publishing/History	PV51	3FT deg	* g	BB-CCD	Ind	M^/M$3	Ind	Ind	Ind	3
Rehabilitation/History (Post Exp)	BVT1	3FT deg		X		X	X	X		
Sociology/History	LV31	3FT deg	*	BB-CCD	Ind	M*^	Ind	Ind	Ind	18
Software Engineering/History	GV71	3FT deg	* g	CDD-BB	Ind	M*^	Ind	Ind	Ind	
Statistics/History	GV41	3FT deg	* g	DD-BB	Ind	M*^	Ind	Ind	Ind	
Telecommunications/History	HVP1	3FT deg								
Tourism/History	PV71	3FT deg	* g	BB-CCD	Ind	M^/M*3	Ind	Ind	Ind	7
Transport Planning/History	NV91	3FT deg	* g	BB-DDD	Ind	M*^	Ind	Ind	Ind	1
Water Resources/History	HVF1	3FT deg								

Univ of PLYMOUTH

TITLE	CODE	COURSE	SUBJECTS	A/AS	ND/C	AGNVQ	IB	SQA(H)	SQA	RATIO A/AS
Art History with History	V4V1	3FT deg	Ap g	CCD	MO+3D	D$^	Ind	Ind	Ind	9
Cultural Interpretation & Practice with History	Y3V1	3FT deg	Ap g	CCD	MO+3D	D$^	Ind	Ind	Ind	
English with History	Q3V1	3FT deg	Ap g	BBC	MO+3D	D$^	Ind	Ind	Ind	5 12/18
Fisheries Studies with Maritime History	J6V1	3FT deg	Ap g	14	5M $	M$	Ind	CCCC	Ind	
Heritage and Landscape with History	W2VD	3FT deg	Ap g	CCD	MO+3D	D$^	Ind	Ind	Ind	16

course details | 98 expected requirements | 96 entry stats

TITLE	CODE	COURSE	SUBJECTS	A/AS	NO/C	AGNVQ	IB	SQA(H)	SQA	RATIO R/AS
History with Art History	V1V4	3FT deg	Ap g	CCD	MO+3D	D$_^	Ind	Ind	Ind	7
History with Cultural Interpretation & Practice	V1Y3	3FT deg	Ap g	CCD	MO+3D	D$_^	Ind	Ind	Ind	
History with Education Studies	V1X9	3FT deg	Ap g	CCD	MO+3D	D$_^	Ind	Ind	Ind	3
History with English	V1Q3	3FT deg	Ap g	CCD	MO+3D	D$_^	Ind	Ind	Ind	4 16/18
History with Heritage and Landscape	V1WG	3FT deg	Ap g	CCD	MO+3D	D$_^	Ind	Ind	Ind	11
History with Media Arts	V1WF	3FT deg	Ap g	CCD	MO+3D	D$_^	Ind	Ind	Ind	4
History with Music	V1W3	3FT deg	Ap g	CCD	MO+3D	D$_^	Ind	Ind	Ind	
History with Theatre and Performance Studies	V1W4	3FT deg	Ap g	CCD	MO+3D	D$_^	Ind	Ind	Ind	
History with Visual Arts	V1W2	3FT deg	Ap g	CCD	MO+3D	D$_^	Ind	Ind	Ind	
Hydrography with Maritime History	F8V1	3FT deg	2(M/P/C/Ap) g	14	5M $	M$	Ind	CCCC	Ind	
Marine Navigation with Maritime History	J9VD	3FT deg	2(M/P/C) g	14	5M $	M$	Ind	CCCC	Ind	
Marine Technology with Maritime History	J6VC	3FT deg	2(M/P/C) g	14	5M $	M$	Ind	CCCC	Ind	
Maritime Business with Maritime History	N1V1	3FT deg	* g	18	5M	M$	Ind	CCCC	Ind	5
Media Arts with History	W2V1	3FT deg	Ap g	CCD	MO+3D	D$_^	Ind	Ind	Ind	3
Ocean Science with Maritime History	F7V1	3FT deg	S g	14-16	5M $	M$	Ind	CCCC	Ind	
Theatre and Performance Studies with History	W4V1	3FT deg	Ap g	CCD	MO+3D	D$_^	Ind	Ind	Ind	3
Underwater Studies with Maritime History	F9VC	3FT deg	Ap g	14-16	5M $	M$	Ind	CCCC	Ind	
Visual Arts with History	W2VC	3FT deg	Ap g	CCD	MO+3D	D$_^	Ind	Ind	Ind	

Univ of PORTSMOUTH

TITLE	CODE	COURSE	SUBJECTS	A/AS	NO/C	AGNVQ	IB	SQA(H)	SQA	RATIO R/AS
Cultural and Historical Studies	LV31	3FT deg	E/H	12	Ind	M$6/^	26	BCCC	Ind	
Economic History with Geography	V3L8	3FT deg	*	10	4M	M*	Dip	BBCC	Ind	
Economic and Social History	V300	3FT deg	*	16	Ind	D$6/^	Dip	BBCC	Ind	4
Economics and Economic History	LV13	3FT deg	* g	16	4M+2D	D$6/^ go	Dip	CCCCC	Ind	1
Geography with Economic History	L8V3	3FT deg	Gy+Ec/H	10	Ind	Ind	Dip	Ind	Ind	
Historical Studies	V100	3FT deg	H	16	Ind	D$6/^	28	BBBC	Ind	4 8/19

QUEEN MARY & WESTFIELD COLL (Univ of London)

TITLE	CODE	COURSE	SUBJECTS	A/AS	NO/C	AGNVQ	IB	SQA(H)	SQA	RATIO R/AS
Economics and History	LV11	3FT deg	H g	BCC		M^	30$	BBBBB		
English and History	QV31	3FT deg	E	20		M	30$			
French and History	VR11	4FT deg	F	18		M^	30$			
History	V101	3FT deg	H	20		M^	30$			
History and German Language	VR1G	4FT deg	H+G	20		M^	30$			
History and Politics	MV11	3FT deg	H	BCC		M^	30$			
Medieval History	V120	3FT deg	H	20		M^	30$			
Modern and Contemporary History	V130	3FT deg	H	22		M^	30$			

QUEEN'S Univ Belfast

TITLE	CODE	COURSE	SUBJECTS	A/AS	NO/C	AGNVQ	IB	SQA(H)	SQA	RATIO R/AS
Ancient History	V110	3FT/4FT deg	* g	BCC	3M+4D	D*6/^ go	29$	ABBB	Ind	6 18/24
Archaeology/Ancient History	VVC6	3FT deg	* g	BCC	3M+4D	D*6/^ go	29$	ABBB	Ind	13
Biblical Studies/Ancient History	VVC8	3FT deg	* g	BCC	3M+4D	D*6/^ go	29$	ABBB	Ind	
Byzantine Studies/Ancient History	VQC8	3FT/4FT deg	* g	BCC	3M+4D	D*6/^ go	29$	ABBB	Ind	
Celtic/Ancient History	VQC5	3FT/4FT deg	* g	BCC	3M+4D	D*6/^ go	29$	ABBB	Ind	9
Classical Studies/Ancient History	QV8C	3FT/4FT deg	* g	BCC	3M+4D	D*6/^ go	29$	ABBB	Ind	7
Economic & Social History/Ancient History	VVC3	3FT deg	* g	BCC	3M+4D	D*6/^ go	29$	ABBB	Ind	
Economic & Social History/Biblical Studies	VV83	3FT deg	* g	BCC	3M+4D	D*6/^ go	29$	ABBB	Ind	
Economic & Social History/Byzantine Studies	QV83	3FT/4FT deg	* g	BCC	3M+4D	D*6/^ go	29$	ABBB	Ind	
Economic and Social History	V340	3FT deg	* g	BCC	3M+4D	D*6/^ go	29$	ABBB	Ind	7
Economics/Economic & Social History	LV13	3FT deg								
English/Ancient History	VQC3	3FT deg	E g	BCC	X	D*_^ go	29$	ABBB	X	10
Greek/Ancient History	VQC7	3FT/4FT deg	* g	BCC	3M+4D	D*6/^ go	29$	ABBB	Ind	
Greek/Economic & Social History	VQ37	3FT/4FT deg	* g	BCC	3M+4D	D*6/^ go	29$	ABBB	Ind	
History & Philosophy of Sci/Economic & Soc Hist	VV35	3FT deg	* g	BCC	3M+4D	D*6/^ go	29$	ABBB	Ind	
History & Philosophy of Science/Ancient History	VVC5	3FT deg	* g	BCC	3M+4D	D*6/^ go	29$	ABBB	Ind	

			98 expected requirements							96 entry stats	
course details											
TITLE	CODE	COURSE	SUBJECTS	A/AS	NO/C	AGNVQ	IB	SQA(H)	SQA	RATIO	A/AS
Human Geography/Economic & Social History	LV8H	3FT deg	* g	BCC	3M+4D	D*6/^ go	29$	ABBB	Ind		
Italian/Ancient History (4 years)	VRC3	4FT deg	* g	BCC	3M+4D	D*6/^ go	29$	ABBB	Ind		
Latin/Ancient History	VQC6	3FT/4FT deg	* g	BCC	3M+4D	D*6/^ go	29$	ABBB	Ind	3	
Latin/Economic & Social History	VQ36	3FT/4FT deg	* g	BCC	3M+4D	D*6/^ go	29$	ABBB	Ind		
Management with Economic and Social History	N1V3	3FT deg	* g	BBB	2M+5D	D*^ go	32$	AABBB	Ind		
Modern History	V130	3FT deg	* g	BCC	3M+4D	D*6/^ go	29$	ABBB	Ind	6	20/28
Modern History/Ancient History	V118	3FT deg	* g	BCC	3M+4D	D*6/^ go	29$	ABBB	Ind	37	
Modern History/Archaeology	VV61	3FT deg	* g	BCC	3M+4D	D*6/^ go	29$	ABBB	Ind	7	
Modern History/Economic & Social History	VV31	3FT deg	* g	BCC	3M+4D	D*6/^ go	29$	ABBB	Ind	37	
Modern History/Economics	LV11	3FT deg									
Modern History/English	QV31	3FT deg	E g	BCC	X	D*^ go	29$	ABBB	X	6	18/28
Modern History/French (4 years)	RV11	4FT deg	E g	BCC	X	D*^ go	29$	ABBB	X	6	
Philosophy/Ancient History	VVC7	3FT deg	* g	BCC	3M+4D	D*6/^ go	29$	ABBB	Ind	5	
Philosophy/Economic & Social History	VV37	3FT deg	* g	BCC	3M+4D	D*6/^ go	29$	ABBB	Ind	4	
Politics/Ancient History	VMC1	3FT deg	* g	BCC	3M+4D	D*6/^ go	29$	ABBB	Ind		
Politics/Economic & Social History	VM31	3FT deg	* g	BCC	3M+4D	D*6/^ go	29$	ABBB	Ind		
Politics/Modern History	VM11	3FT deg	* g	BCC	3M+4D	D*6/^ go	29$	ABBB	Ind	5	20/26
Psychology/Economic & Social History	CV83	3FT deg	* g	BCC	3M+4D	D*6/^ go	29$	ABBB	Ind		
Scholastic Philosophy/Ancient History	VVCR	3FT deg	* g	BCC	3M+4D	D*6/^ go	29$	ABBB	Ind		
Scholastic Philosophy/Economic & Social History	VV3R	3FT deg	* g	BCC	3M+4D	D*6/^ go	29$	ABBB	Ind		
Social Anthropology/Ancient History	VLC6	3FT deg	* g	BCC	3M+4D	D*6/^ go	29$	ABBB	Ind	7	
Social Anthropology/Economic & Social History	VL36	3FT deg	* g	BCC	3M+4D	D*6/^ go	29$	ABBB	Ind		
Social Anthropology/Modern History	VL16	3FT deg	* g	BCC	3M+4D	D*6/^ go	29$	ABBB	Ind	8	22/26
Social Policy/Economic & Social History	VL34	3FT deg	* g	BCC	3M+4D	D*6/^ go	29$	ABBB	Ind		
Social Policy/Modern History	VL14	3FT deg	* g	BCC	3M+4D	D*6/^ go	29$	ABBB	Ind		
Sociology/Economic & Social History	VL33	3FT deg	* g	BCC	3M+4D	D*6/^ go	29$	ABBB	Ind		
Sociology/Modern History	VL13	3FT deg	* g	BCC	3M+4D	D*6/^ go	29$	ABBB	Ind		
Spanish/Ancient History (4 years)	VRC4	4FT deg	* g	BCC	3M+4D	D*6/^ go	29$	ABBB	Ind		
Spanish/Economic & Social History (4 years)	VR34	4FT deg	* g	BCC	3M+4D	D*6/^ go	29$	ABBB	Ind		
Women's Studies/Economic & Social History	MV9H	3FT deg	* g	BCC	3M+4D	D*6/^ go	29$	ABBB	Ind		

Univ of READING

TITLE	CODE	COURSE	SUBJECTS	A/AS	NO/C	AGNVQ	IB	SQA(H)	SQA	RATIO	A/AS
Ancient History	V110	3FT deg	*	BCC	Ind	D*6/^	30	BBBB	Ind	7	14/22
Ancient History and Archaeology	VV61	3FT deg	*	BCC	Ind	D*6/^	30	BBBB	Ind	9	14/18
Ancient History and Sociology	VL13	3FT deg	*	BCC	Ind	D$^ go	30	BBBB	Ind	6	
Archaeology and History	VV16	3FT deg	*	BCC	Ind	D*6/^	30	BBBB	Ind	7	16/30
Classical and Medieval Studies	QV81	3FT deg	*	BCC	Ind	D*6/^	30	BBBB	Ind	8	
History	V100	3FT deg	*	BBC	Ind	D*6/^	31	BBBB	Ind	8	18/26
History and Ancient History	V117	3FT deg	*	BCC	Ind	D*6/^	30	BBBB	Ind	63	
History and Economics	LV11	3FT deg	* g	BBC	Ind	D$6/^ go	31	BBBB	Ind	5	
History and English Literature	QV31	3FT deg	EI	BBC	Ind	D*^	31$	BBBB$	Ind	14	22/28
History and French	RV11	4FT deg	F	BBC	Ind	D*^	31$	BBBB$	Ind	23	
History and German	RV21	4FT deg	* g	BBC	Ind	D$^ go	31	BBBB	Ind	9	
History and History of Art	VV14	3FT deg	*	BBC	Ind	D$6/^	31	BBBB	Ind	15	
History and Italian	RV31	4FT deg	* g	BBC	Ind	D$6/^ go	31	BBBB	Ind		
History and Philosophy	VV17	3FT deg	*	BBC	Ind	D*^	31	BBBB	Ind	7	
History and Sociology	LV31	3FT deg	*	BBC	Ind	D$^ go	31	BBBB	Ind	33	
History with Latin	V1Q6	3FT deg	* g	BBC	Ind	D*6/^ go	31	BBBB	Ind		
Latin and Medieval Studies	QV61	3FT deg	* g	BCC	Ind	D*6/^ go	30	BBBB	Ind		
Modern History and International Relations	VM11	3FT deg	*	BBC	Ind	D*6/^	31	BBBB	Ind	9	
Modern History and Politics	MV11	3FT deg	*	BBC	Ind	D*6/^	31	BBBB	Ind	10	18/24

course details			98 expected requirements							96 entry stats	
TITLE	CODE	COURSE	SUBJECTS	A/AS	NO/C	AGNVQ	IB	SQA(H)	SQA	RATIO	A/AS
Univ College of RIPON & YORK ST JOHN											
American Studies (History)	QV41	3FT deg		CDD	MO+2D	M+^	30	BBBB		4	10/20
Applied Social Sciences/History	L3V1	3FT deg	H	CC	M	M*^	27	BBBC			
Art/History	E1V1	3FT deg	A+H+Pf	BC-CCD	Ind	MA^	27	BBBB			
Art/History	W1V1	3FT deg	A+H+Pf	BC-CCD	Ind	MA^	27	BBBB		11	
English/History	Q3V1	3FT deg	E/H	16	Ind	Ind	30	BBBB		3	12/22
Geography/History	L8V1	3FT deg	Gy+H	CCD	X	Ind	30	BBBB			
History/American Studies	V1Q4	3FT deg	H	14	X	M*^	30	BBBB			
History/Applied Social Sciences	V1L3	3FT deg	H	14	X	M*^	30	BBBB			
History/Art	V1W1	3FT deg	A+H+Pf	14	X	MA^	30	BBBB		3	
History/English	V1Q3	3FT deg	H+E	14	X	Ind	30	BBBB		3	8/22
History/Geography	V1L8	3FT deg	H+Gy	14	X	Ind	30	BBBB			
History/Theology	V1V8	3FT deg	H	14	X	M*^	30	BBBB		6	
History/Women's Studies	V1M9	3FT deg	H	14	X	M*^	30	BBBB		3	
Theology/History	V8V1	3FT deg	H	12	X	M*^	27	BBBC		2	8/12
ROEHAMPTON INST											
Film & Television Studies and History	PV41▼	3FT deg	H	16	2M+2D$	M^	30	BBC	N$	31	
History	V100▼	3FT deg	H	DD	4M $	P^	26	BCC	N$	5	4/20
History and Applied Consumer Studies	NV91▼	3FT deg	H g	12	4M $	P^ go	26	BCC	N$		
History and Art for Community	WV11▼	3FT deg	H	DD	4M $	P^	26	BCC	N$	2	
History and Biology	CV11▼	3FT deg	B+H	12	4M $	P^ go	26	CCC	N$		
History and Business Computing	GV71▼	3FT deg	H g	12	3D	M^ go	26	BCC	N$		
History and Business Studies	NV11▼	3FT deg	H g	DD	3D $	M^ go	26	BCC	N$	5	
History and Dance Studies	WV41▼	3FT deg	H	CC	2M+2D$	M^	30	BBC	Ind		
History and Drama & Theatre Studies	WVL1▼	3FT deg	H+E/T	16	3D $	M^	30	BBC	Ind		
History and Education	XV91▼	3FT deg	H	DD	4M $	P^	26	BCC	N$	1	6/12
History and English Language & Linguistics	QV3C▼	3FT deg	H+E/L	CC	2M+2D$	M^	30	BBC	Ind	6	
History and English Literature	QV31▼	3FT deg	H+E	CC	2M+2D$	M^	28	BBC	Ind	4	6/20
History and Environmental Studies	FV91▼	3FT deg	H+B/Gy	DD	4M $	P^ go	26	BCC	N$		
History and French	RV11▼	4FT deg	F+H	12	4M $	P^	26	BCC	N$	2	
History and Geography	LV81▼	3FT deg	H+Gy	DD	4M $	P^ go	26	BCC	N$	5	
History and Health Studies	BV91▼	3FT deg	H+B	12	4M $	P^ go	26	BCC	N$		
Human & Social Biology and History	VC1C▼	3FT deg	B+H	12	4M $	P^	24	CCC	N$		
Music and History	VW13▼	3FT deg	Mu+H	DD	4M $	P^	26	BCC	N$	4	
Natural Resource Studies and History	DV21▼	3FT deg	H g	DD	3M	P^ go	24	CCC	N$		
Psychology and History	VL17▼	3FT deg	H g	CC	3D $	M^ go	30	BBC	Ind		
Social Policy & Administration and History	VL14▼	3FT deg	H g	DD	4M $	P^	26	BCC	N$	2	
Sociology and History	VL13▼	3FT deg	H g	DD	4M $	P^ go	26	BCC	N$	9	
Spanish and History	RV41▼	4FT deg	Sp+H	12	2M+2D$	P^	28	BBC	N$		
Sport Studies and History	VB16▼	3FT deg	H g	12	3D $	M^ go	30	BBC	N$		
Theology & Religious Studies and History	VV18▼	3FT deg	H	DD	4M $	P^	26	BCC	N$	5	
Women's Studies and History	VM19▼	3FT deg	H	DD	4M $	P^	26	BCC	N$	3	
Humanities (English History Theol & Relig St) History	VY93▼	3FT deg	E/H	CC	2M+2D$		30	BBC	Ind		
ROYAL HOLLOWAY, Univ of London											
Ancient History	V110	3FT deg	*	BCC	Ind		28	BBBB		5	14/24
Ancient History with Mathematics	V1G1	3FT deg	M	BCC	Ind		28	Ind			
Archaeology and Ancient History	VV16	3FT deg	*	BBC			30				
Archaeology and History	VV61	3FT deg	g	BBB-BBC			30				
Archaeology and History with a year in Europe	VV6C	4FT deg	L g	BBB-BBC			30$				
French and History	RV11	4FT deg	F g	BBC-ABC			30$	Ind		9	

			98 expected requirements							96 entry stats

course details

TITLE	CODE	COURSE	SUBJECTS	A/AS	NO/C	RGNVQ	IB	SQA(H)	SQA	RATIO A/AS
Geography and History	LV81	3FT deg	Gy g	BBC	Ind		30$	Ind		4
German and History	RV21	4FT deg	G g	BBC			30$	Ind		
German with History (4 years)	R2V1	4FT deg	G	BBC-BCC			28$	BBBBC$		
Greek and Ancient History	QV71	3FT deg		BCC			28	BBBBC		
History and Spanish	VR14	4FT deg	Sp g	ABC-BBC			Ind	Ind		
History with Japanese Studies	V1T4	3FT deg	L g	BBB-ABC			30	Ind		
History with Spanish	V1R4	3FT deg	L g	BBB-ABC			30	Ind		
History with a Year in Europe (4 Yrs)	V101	4FT deg	L g	BBB-ABC			30	Ind		5
History, Ancient and Medieval	V116	3FT deg	g	BBB-ABC			30	Ind		5	18/26
History, Medieval and Modern	V126	3FT deg	g	BBB-ABC			30	Ind		4	20/30
Latin and Ancient History	QV61	3FT deg	*	BCC			28	BBBBC		
Mod Hist, Econ Hist & Politics with a Yr in Eur	V137	4FT deg	L g	BBB-ABC			30	Ind		5
Modern History, Economic History and Politics	V136	3FT deg	g	BBB-ABC			30$	Ind		5	20/28
Foundation Programme	Y408	4FT deg								
History										

Univ of SALFORD

TITLE	CODE	COURSE	SUBJECTS	A/AS	NO/C	RGNVQ	IB	SQA(H)	SQA	RATIO A/AS
English and History	Q3V1	3FT deg	El g	BBC	X	X	Ind	Ind	X	7	10/22
Politics and Contemporary History	MV11	3FT deg	g	CCC	MO+4D	M	Ind	Ind	Ind	4	12/22

SOAS:Sch of Oriental & African St (U of London)

TITLE	CODE	COURSE	SUBJECTS	A/AS	NO/C	RGNVQ	IB	SQA(H)	SQA	RATIO A/AS
History	V100	3FT deg		20	Ind		30	BBBCC	Ind	3	14/28
History and African Studies	VT17	3FT deg		20	Ind		30	BBBCC	Ind	
History and Amharic	TV71	4FT deg		20	Ind		30	BBBCC	Ind	
History and Arabic	TV61	4FT deg		22	Ind		31	BBBBC	Ind	5
History and Bengali	TV51	3FT deg		20	Ind		30	BBBCC	Ind	2
History and Burmese	TVM1	4FT deg		20	Ind		30	BBBCC	Ind	
History and Chinese	TV31	4FT deg		24	Ind		32	BBBBB	Ind	6
History and Development Studies	MV9C	3FT deg		22	Ind		31	BBBBC	Ind	5
History and Economics	LV11	3FT deg	g	22	Ind		31	BBBBC	Ind	8
History and Geography	LV81	3FT deg		20	Ind		30	BBBCC	Ind	4
History and Georgian	TV91	3FT deg		22	Ind		31	BBBBC	Ind	
History and Gujarati	TV5C	3FT deg		20	Ind		30	BBBCC	Ind	
History and Hausa	TVR1	4FT deg		20	Ind		30	BBBCC	Ind	
History and Hebrew	QV91	4FT deg		22	Ind		31	BBBBC	Ind	
History and Hindi	VT15	3FT/4FT deg		20	Ind		30	BBBCC	Ind	
History of Art/Archaeology and History	VV16	3FT deg		20	Ind		30	BBBCC	Ind	6
Indonesian and History	VT1M	3FT/4FT deg		20	Ind		30	BBBCC	Ind	2
Japanese and History	TV41	4FT deg		24	Ind		32	BBBBB	Ind	
Korean and History	TVN1	4FT deg		16	Ind		28	BBCCC	Ind	
Law and History	MV31	3FT deg		24	Ind		32	BBBBB	Ind	
Linguistics and History	QV31	3FT deg								
Music and History	VW13	3FT deg		20	Ind		30	BBBCC	Ind	2
Nepali and History	VTC5	3FT deg		20	Ind		30	BBBCC	Ind	
Persian and History	TVQ1	3FT deg		22	Ind		31	BBBBC	Ind	
Politics and History	MV11	3FT deg		20	Ind		30	BBBCC	Ind	5
Sanskrit and History	QVX1	3FT deg		20	Ind		30	BBBCC	Ind	
Sinhalese and History	TVMC	3FT deg		20	Ind		30	BBBCC	Ind	
Social Anthropology and History	LV61	3FT deg		22	Ind		31	BBBBC	Ind	6
South Asian Studies and History	VT1N	3FT deg								
Study of Religions and History	VV18	3FT deg		20	Ind		30	BBBCC	Ind	1
Swahili and History	TVT1	4FT deg		20	Ind		30	BBBCC	Ind	
Tamil and History	TV5D	3FT deg		20	Ind		30	BBBCC	Ind	1
Thai and History	TVMD	3FT/4FT deg		20	Ind		30	BBBCC	Ind	

	course details			98 expected requirements						96 entry stats
TITLE	CODE	COURSE	SUBJECTS	A/AS	NQ/C	AGNVQ	IB	SQA(H)	SQA	RATIO A/AS
Turkish and History	TVP1	4FT deg		22	Ind		31	BBBBC	Ind	
Urdu and History	TVNC	3FT deg		20	Ind		30	BBBCC	Ind	
Vietnamese and History	TVND	4FT deg		20	Ind		30	BBBCC	Ind	

SSEES:Sch of Slavonic & E European St(U of London)

History	V100	3FT deg	H	BCC	3M $	Ind	28	BBBBB		3 14/20
History (Central & East European) and Jewish St	VV18	4FT deg	H	BCC	3M $	Ind	28	BBBBB		2
History and Russian	VR18	4FT deg	H	BCC		Ind	28			

Univ of SHEFFIELD

Archaeology and Prehistory and Medieval History	FV41	3FT deg	H g	BBB	4M+2D$ D^		32$	AABB$	Ind	
English and History	QV31	3FT deg	El+H g	ABB	X	X	33$	AAAB$	Ind	14 24/30
French and History	RV11	4FT deg	F+H g	BBB	X	X	32$	AABB$	Ind	12 24/28
Geography and Social History	LV83	3FT deg	H+Gy g	BBB	3M+3D$ D^		32$	AABB$	Ind	
German and History	RV21	4FT deg	G+H g	BBB	X	X	32$	AABB$	Ind	8
History	V100	3FT deg	H g	ABB	X	X	33$	AAAB$	Ind	8 24/30
History and Hispanic Studies	RV41	4FT deg	Sp+H g	BBB	X	X	32$	AABB$	Ind	7
History and Philosophy	VV17	3FT deg	H g	ABB	X	X	33$	AAAB$	Ind	7 28/28
History and Russian	RV81	4FT deg	H+L g	BBB	X	X	32$	AABB$	Ind	6
Modern History and Japanese	VT14	4FT deg	H g	BBC	X	X	30$	ABBB$	Ind	
Modern History and Politics	VM11	3FT deg	H+Po g	BBB	3M+3D$ D^		32$	AABB$	Ind	11 22/30
Social History	V320	3FT deg	H g	ABB	2M+4D$ D^		33$	AAAB$	Ind	8 16/28
Social and Political Studies Social History	Y220	3FT deg	* g	BBC	4D	D^	30	ABBB	Ind	

SHEFFIELD HALLAM Univ

Historical Studies	V100	3FT deg	H	CC-CDD	2M+2D	P^	Ind	Ind	Ind	
Combined Studies History	Y400	3FT deg	H	18	2M	M	24	CCCC	Ind	

Univ College of St MARTIN, LANCASTER AND CUMBRIA

Applied Community Studies/History	LV51	3FT deg	H	CD-DDE	3M+2D$ M^		28$	BCCC		
Art and Design/History	WV1C	3FT deg	A+H	CC-CDE	3M+2D$ MA		28$	BBCC$	Ind	
Business Management Studies/History	NV11	3FT deg	H	CD-CEE	X	M^	28$	BCCC$		
English/History	QV3C	3FT deg	E+H	BC-BDE	X	X	28$	BBBC$	Ind	7
Geography/History	LV8C	3FT deg	Gy+H	CD-DDE	X	X	28$	BCCC$	Ind	
History	V100	3FT deg	H	CD-DDE	X	P^	28$	BCCC$	Ind	2 4/18
History/Applied Community Studies	VL15	3FT deg	H	CD-DDE	X	P^	28$	BCCC$		
History/Art and Design	VW1C	3FT deg	H+A	CD-DDE	X	X	28$	BCCC$	Ind	
History/Business Management Studies	VN11	3FT deg	H	CD-DDE	3M+2D	P^	28$	BCCC$		
History/Drama	VW14	3FT deg	H	CD-DDE	X	P^	28$	BCCC$	Ind	
History/Education Studies	VX19	3FT deg	H	CD-DDE	X	P^	28$	BCCC$	Ind	
History/English	VQ1H	3FT deg	H+E	CD-DDE	X	X	28$	BCCC$	Ind	15
History/Geography	VL1V	3FT deg	H+Gy	CD-DDE	X	X	28$	BCCC$	Ind	
History/Health Administration	VL14	3FT deg	H	CD-DDE	X	P^	28$	BCCC$	Ind	
History/Mathematics	VG11	3FT deg	H+M	CD-DDE	X	X	28$	BCCC$	Ind	
History/Physical Education & Sports Studies	VX1X	3FT deg	H	CD-DDE	X	P^	28$	BCCC$		
History/Religious Studies	VV1V	3FT deg	H	CD-DDE	X	P^	28$	BCCC$	Ind	
History/Social Ethics	VV1R	3FT deg	H	CD-DDE	X	P^	28$	BCCC$	Ind	
Mathematics/History	GV11	3FT deg	M	DD-DEE	X		28$	BCCC$		
Religious Studies/History	VV8C	3FT deg	H	CD-DDE	3M+2D$ M^		28$	BCCC$	Ind	
Social Ethics/History	VV7C	3FT deg	H	CD-DDE	3M+2D M^		28$	BCCC$	Ind	

course details			98 expected requirements							96 entry stats	
TITLE	CODE	COURSE	SUBJECTS	A/AS	ND/C	AGNVQ	IB	SQA(H)	SQA	RATIO	R/AS
Univ of SOUTHAMPTON											
Archaeology and History	VV61	3FT deg	H	BCC	Ind	Ind	26	Ind	Ind	11	18/24
Economics and Economic History	LV13	3FT deg	* g	24	Ind	D$^ go	32	AABBB	Ind		
English and History	QV31	3FT deg	E+H	BBC	X	Ind	Ind	Ind	X	8	20/28
French and History	RV11	4FT deg	F+H	BBC	1M+4D	Ind	30$	Ind	Ind	7	20/28
German and History	RV21	4FT deg	H+G	BBC	X				X		
History	V100	3FT deg	H g	22	X	Ind	30$	ABBBB	X	8	18/26
History and Sociology	VL13	3FT deg	H g	22	X	Ind	30$	ABBBB	X	21	
Mod Hist&Pol with Econ/Phil/Quantitative Methods	VM11	3FT deg	H g	22	X	Ind	30$	ABBBB	X	8	20/30
Politics and Economic History	MV13	3FT deg	* g	20	Ind	D$^ go	28	BBBBC	Ind	5	20/22
Spanish and History	RV41	4FT deg	Sp+H	BBC		Ind		Ind	Ind		
SOUTH BANK Univ											
History and Accounting	NV41	3FT deg	H+Ac/Ec g	12-16	4M+2D	M^ go	Ind	Ind	Ind		
History and English Studies	QV31	3FT deg	E+H g	14-18	X	M^ go	Ind	Ind	Ind		
History and Environmental Policy	FV91	3FT deg	H g	12-16	4M+2D	M go	Ind	Ind	Ind		
History and European Studies	TV21	3FT deg	H g	14-18	2M+4D	M go	Ind	Ind	Ind		
History and French	RV11	3FT deg	F+H g	12-16	4M+2D	M^ go	Ind	Ind	Ind		
History and German	RV2C	3FT deg	H+G g	14-18	2M+4D	M^ go	Ind	Ind	Ind		
History and German - ab initio	RV21	3FT deg	H g	12-16	4M+2D	M^ go	Ind	Ind	Ind		
Housing and History	KV4D	3FT deg	H g	14-18	2M+4D	M go	Ind	Ind	Ind		
Human Geography and History	LV81	3FT deg	Gy+H g	12-16	4M+2D	M^ go	Ind	Ind	Ind		
Human Resource Management and History	NV61	3FT deg	H g	14-18	2M+4D	M go	Ind	Ind	Ind		
Law and History	MV31	3FT deg	H g	14-18	2M+4D	D^ go	Ind	Ind	Ind		
Management and History	NV11	3FT deg	H g	12-16	4M+2D	M^ go	Ind	Ind	Ind		
Marketing and History	NV51	3FT deg	H g	14-18	2M+4D	M^ go	Ind	Ind	Ind		
Media Studies and History	PV41	3FT deg	E+H g	14-18	2M+4D	D go	Ind	Ind	Ind		
Planning and Housing	KV4C	3FT deg	* g	14-18	2M+4D	M go	Ind	Ind	Ind		
Politics and History	MV11	3FT deg	H g	12-16	4M+2D	M^ go	Ind	Ind	Ind		
Product Design and History	HV71	3FT deg	Ad+H g	12-16	4M+2D	M^ go	Ind	Ind	Ind		
Psychology and History	CV81	3FT deg	S+H g	14-18	2M+4D	M^ go	Ind	Ind	Ind		
Spanish - ab initio and History	RV41	3FT deg	H g	12-16	4M+2D	M^ go	Ind	Ind	Ind		
Spanish and History	RV4C	3FT deg	Sp+H g	14-18	2M+4D	M^ go	Ind	Ind	Ind		
Technology and History	JV91	3FT deg	H g	12-16	4M+2D	M^ go	Ind	Ind	Ind		
Tourism and History	PV71	3FT deg	L+H g	12-16	4M+2D	M^ go	Ind	Ind	Ind		
Urban Studies and History	VK14	3FT deg	H g	14-18	2M+4D	M go	Ind	Ind	Ind		
World Theatre and History	WV41	3FT deg	H g	14-18	2M+4D	M go	Ind	Ind	Ind		
Univ of ST ANDREWS											
Ancient History	V110	4FT deg	* g	BBB	X	Ind	30$	BBBB	Ind	7	
Ancient History and Archaeology	VV16	3FT deg	* g	BBB	X	Ind	30$	BBBB	Ind		
Art History-Ancient History	VVD4	4FT deg	* g	BBB	X	Ind	30$	BBBB	Ind		
Biblical Studies-Ancient History	VV18	4FT deg	* g	BBB	X	Ind	30$	BBBB	Ind	4	
Economics-Ancient History	LV1D	4FT deg	* g	BBB	X	Ind	30$	BBBB	Ind		
French with Year Abroad-Ancient History	RV1D	4FT/5FT deg	F g	BBB	X	Ind	30$	BBBB$	Ind		
French-Ancient History	RVD1	4FT deg	F g	BBB	X	Ind	30$	BBBB$	Ind		
German with Year Abroad-Ancient History	RV2D	4FT/5FT deg	* g	BBB	X	Ind	30$	BBBB	Ind		
German-Ancient History	RVG1	4FT deg	* g	BBB	X	Ind	30$	BBBB	Ind		
Greek-Ancient History	QV71	4FT deg	* g	BBB	X	Ind	30$	BBBB	Ind	3	
History	V100	4FT deg	* g	BBB	X	Ind	30$	BBBB	Ind	6	24/30
Italian with Year Abroad-Ancient History	RVHD	4FT/5FT deg	* g	BBB	X	Ind	30$	BBBB	Ind		
Italian-Ancient History	RV31	4FT deg	* g	BBB	X	Ind	30$	BBBB	Ind		
Latin-Ancient History	QV61	4FT deg	* g	BBB	X	Ind	30$	BBBB	Ind		

course details | 98 expected requirements | 96 entry stats

TITLE	CODE	COURSE	SUBJECTS	A/AS	ND/C	AGNVQ	IB	SQA(H)	SQA	RATIO A/AS
Mathematics-Ancient History	GVC1	3FT/4FT deg	M g	BBB	X	Ind	30$	BBBB$	Ind	
Mediaeval History	V120	4FT deg	* g	BBB	X	Ind	30$	BBBB	Ind	7
Mediaeval History and Archaeology	VV1P	4FT deg	* g	BBB	X	Ind	30$	BBBB	Ind	
Mediaeval History-Arabic	TV6C	4FT deg	* g	BBB	X	Ind	30$	BBBB	Ind	
Mediaeval History-Art History	VV1K	4FT deg	* g	BBB	X	Ind	30$	BBBB	Ind	
Mediaeval History-Classical Studies	QV81	4FT deg	* g	BBB	X	Ind	30$	BBBB	Ind	
Mediaeval History-Economics	LVC1	4FT deg	* g	BBB	X	Ind	30$	BBBB	Ind	
Mediaeval History-English	QVH1	4FT deg	* g	BBB	X	Ind	30$	BBBB	Ind	6
Mediaeval History-French	RVC1	4FT deg	E g	BBB	X	Ind	30$	BBBB	Ind	
Mediaeval History-French with Year Abroad	RVCC	4FT/5FT deg	E g	BBB	X	Ind	30$	BBBB$	Ind	3
Mediaeval History-Geography	LVV1	4FT deg	* g	BBB	X	Ind	30$	BBBB	Ind	
Mediaeval History-German	RVF1	4FT deg	* g	BBB	X	Ind	30$	BBBB	Ind	
Mediaeval History-German with Year Abroad	RVFC	4FT/5FT deg	* g	BBB	X	Ind	30$	BBBB	Ind	3
Mediaeval History-International Relations	MV11	4FT deg	* g	AAB	X	Ind	36$	AAAB	Ind	
Mediaeval History-Italian	RV3C	4FT deg	* g	BBB	X	Ind	34$	BBBB	Ind	
Mediaeval History-Italian with Year Abroad	RVH1	4FT/5FT deg	* g	BBB	X	Ind	30$	BBBB	Ind	
Mediaeval History-Latin	QVP1	4FT deg	* g	BBB	X	Ind	30$	BBBB	Ind	
Mediaeval History-Mathematics	GV1D	4FT deg	M g	BBB	X	Ind	30$	BBBB$	Ind	1
Modern History	V130	4FT deg	* g	BBB	X	Ind	30$	BBBB	Ind	8 22/30
Modern History-Arabic	TV61	4FT deg	* g	BBB	X	Ind	30$	BBBB	Ind	
Modern History-Art History	VV1L	4FT deg	* g	BBB	X	Ind	30$	BBBB	Ind	8
Modern History-Classical Studies	QV8C	4FT deg	* g	BBB	X	Ind	30$	BBBB	Ind	2
Modern History-Economics	LV11	4FT deg	* g	BBB	X	Ind	30$	BBBB	Ind	5
Modern History-English	QV31	4FT deg	* g	BBB	X	Ind	30$	BBBB	Ind	11 26/28
Modern History-French	RV11	4FT deg	E g	BBB	X	Ind	30$	BBBB$	Ind	
Modern History-French with Year Abroad	RVCD	4FT/5FT deg	E g	BBB	X	Ind	30$	BBBB$	X	7
Modern History-Geography	LV81	4FT deg	* g	BBB	X	Ind	30$	BBBB	Ind	7
Modern History-German	RV21	4FT deg	* g	BBB	X	Ind	30$	BBBB	Ind	2
Modern History-German with Year Abroad	RVGC	4FT/5FT deg	* g	BBB	X	Ind	30$	BBBB	Ind	5
Modern History-International Relations	VM11	4FT deg	* g	AAB	X	Ind	36$	AAAB	Ind	4 30/30
Modern History-Italian	RV3D	4FT deg	* g	BBB	X	Ind	30$	BBBB	Ind	
Modern History-Italian with Year Abroad	RVHC	4FT/5FT deg	* g	BBB	X	Ind	30$	BBBB	Ind	
Modern History-Management	NV11	4FT deg	* g	BBB	X	Ind	30$	BBBB	Ind	
New Testament - Modern History	VV81	4FT deg	* g	BBB	X	Ind	30$	BBBB	Ind	
Philosophy-Ancient History	VV17	4FT deg	* g	BBB	X	Ind	30$	BBBB	Ind	9
Philosophy-Mediaeval History	VVC7	4FT deg	* g	BBB	X	Ind	30$	BBBB	Ind	4
Philosophy-Modern History	VVD7	4FT deg	* g	BBB	X	Ind	30$	BBBB	Ind	3
Psychology-Mediaeval History	LV71	4FT deg	* g	ABB	X	Ind	32$	ABBB	Ind	
Psychology-Modern History	LV7C	4FT deg	g	ABB	X	Ind	32$	ABBB$	Ind	
Russian with Year Abroad-Mediaeval History	RV8C	4FT/5FT deg	* g	BBB	X	Ind	30$	BBBB	Ind	
Russian with Year Abroad-Modern History	RVVC	4FT/5FT deg	* g	BBB	X	Ind	30$	BBBB	Ind	4
Russian-Mediaeval History	RVV1	4FT deg	* g	BBB	X	Ind	30$	BBBB	Ind	
Russian-Modern History	RV81	4FT deg	* g	BBB	X	Ind	30$	BBBB	Ind	4
Scottish History	V142	4FT deg	* g	BBB	X	Ind	30$	BBBB	Ind	10
Scottish History-English	QV3D	4FT deg	* g	BBB	X	Ind	30$	BBBB	Ind	10
Scottish History-Geography	LV8D	4FT deg	* g	BBB	X	Ind	30$	BBBB	Ind	5
Scottish History-International Relations	MV1C	4FT deg	* g	AAB	X	Ind	36$	AAAB	Ind	
Scottish History-Italian	VR13	4FT deg	* g	BBB	X	Ind	30$	BBBB	Ind	
Scottish History-Italian with Year Abroad	VR1H	4FT/5FT deg	* g	BBB	X	Ind	30$	BBBB	Ind	
Scottish History-Mathematics	GV11	4FT deg	M g	BBB	X	Ind	30$	BBBB$	Ind	
Scottish History-Philosophy	VV7C	4FT deg	* g	BBB	X	Ind	30$	BBBB	Ind	
Scottish Studies	V140	4FT deg	* g	BBB	X	Ind	30$	BBBB	Ind	3

Letts STUDY GUIDES
THE INDEPENDENT

course details			98 expected requirements							96 entry stats
TITLE	CODE	COURSE	SUBJECTS	A/AS	ND/C	AGNVQ	IB	SQA(H)	SQA	RATIO A/AS
Social Anthropology-Mediaeval History	LV61	4FT deg	* g	BBB	X	Ind	30$	BBBB	Ind	11
Social Anthropology-Modern History	LV6D	4FT deg	* g	BBB	X	Ind	30$	BBBB	Ind	
Social Anthropology-Scottish History	LV6C	4FT deg	* g	BBB	X	Ind	30$	BBBB	Ind	7
Spanish with Year Abroad-Ancient History	RV4D	4FT/5FT deg	* g	BBB	X	Ind	30$	BBBB	Ind	
Spanish with Year Abroad-Mediaeval History	RVLC	4FT/5FT deg	* g	BBB	X	Ind	30$	BBBB	Ind	
Spanish with Year Abroad-Modern History	RVK1	4FT/5FT deg	* g	BBB	X	Ind	30$	BBBB	Ind	
Spanish-Ancient History	VR14	4FT deg	* g	BBB	X	Ind	30$	BBBB	Ind	
Spanish-Mediaeval History	RV4C	4FT deg	* g	BBB	X	Ind	30$	BBBB	Ind	
Spanish-Modern History	RV41	4FT deg	* g	BBB	X	Ind	30$	BBBB	Ind	
Theological Studies-Modern History	VV1V	4FT deg	* g	BBB	X	Ind	30$	BBBB	Ind	
European Integration Studies Modern History	Y602	4FT deg	* g	BBB	X	Ind	30$	BBBB	Ind	
General Degree of MA Ancient History	Y450	3FT deg	* g	BBB	X	Ind	30$	BBBB	Ind	
General Degree of MA History	Y450	3FT deg	* g	BBB	X	Ind	30$	BBBB	Ind	
General Degree of MA Mediaeval History	Y450	3FT deg	* g	BBB	X	Ind	30$	BBBB	Ind	
General Degree of MA Modern History	Y450	3FT deg	* g	BBB	X	Ind	30$	BBBB	Ind	
General Degree of MA Scottish History	Y450	3FT deg	* g	BBB	X	Ind	30$	BBBB	Ind	

THE UNIVERSITY COLLEGE OF ST MARK AND ST JOHN

Art & Design/History	W1V1	3FT deg		4	MO	M	Dip	CCCC	Ind	
Development Studies/History	M9V1	3FT deg		8-10	MO	M	Ind	Ind	Ind	
English (Literary Studies)/History	Q3V1	3FT deg	El	12-16	Ind	M	Ind	Ind	Ind	
Geography/History	L8V1	3FT deg	Gy	10	MO	M	Ind	Ind	Ind	
History/Art & Design	V1W1	3FT deg	H	12	MO	M	Dip	Ind	Ind	
History/Development Studies	V1M9	3FT deg	H	12	MO	M	Ind	Ind	Ind	
History/English (Literary Studies)	V1Q3	3FT deg	H	12	MO	M	Ind	Ind	Ind	
History/Geography	V1L8	3FT deg	H	12	MO	M	Ind	Ind	Ind	
History/Media Studies	V1P4	3FT deg	H	12	MO	M	Ind	Ind	Ind	
History/Sociology	V1L3	3FT deg	H	12	MO	M	Ind	Ind	Ind	
History/Theology	V1VV	3FT deg	H	12	MO	M	Ind	Ind	Ind	
History/Theology & Philosophy	V1V8	3FT deg	H	12	MO	M	Ind	Ind	Ind	
Media Studies/History	P4V1	3FT deg		16	MO	M	Ind	Ind	Ind	
Sociology/History	L3V1	3FT deg	So	8	MO	M	Ind	Ind	Ind	
Theology & Philosophy/History	V8V1	3FT deg	Re	4	MO	M	Dip	CCCC	Ind	
Theology/History	V8VC	3FT deg	Re	4	MO	M	Dip	CCCC	Ind	

ST MARY'S Univ COLL

History	V100	3FT deg	H	8-12	Ind	Ind	Ind	BBBB$	Ind	
History and Classical Studies	VQ18	3FT deg	H	4-8	Ind	Ind	Ind	BBBB$	Ind	
History and Education Studies	VX1X	3FT deg	H	4-8	Ind	Ind	Ind	BBBB$	Ind	
History and English	QV31	3FT deg	E+H	8-12	X	X	Ind	BBBB$	X	
History and Environmental Investigation Studies	FV91	3FT deg	S/2S+H	4-8	Ind	Ind	Ind	BBBB	Ind	
History and Environmental Studies	FVX1	3FT deg	H	4-8	Ind	Ind	Ind	BBBB	Ind	
History and Gender Studies	MV91	3FT deg	H	4-8	Ind	Ind	Ind	BBBB$	Ind	
History and Geography	FV81	3FT deg	Gy+H	8-10	Ind	Ind	Ind	BBBB$	Ind	
History and Heritage Management	NV91	3FT deg	H	4-8	Ind	Ind	Ind	BBBB$	Ind	
Integrated Scientific Studies and History	VY11	3FT deg	S/2S+H	4-8	Ind	Ind	Ind	BBBB$	Ind	
Irish Studies and History	QV51	3FT deg	H	4-8	Ind	Ind	Ind	BBBB$	Ind	
Management Studies and History	NV11	3FT deg	H g	4-8	Ind	Ind	Ind	BBBB$	Ind	
Media Arts and History	PV41	3FT deg	H	4-8	Ind	Ind	Ind	BBBB	Ind	

	course details			*98 expected requirements*							*96 entry stats*
TITLE	CODE	COURSE	SUBJECTS	A/AS	NO/C	AGNVQ	IB	SQA(H)	SQA	RATIO A/AS	
Sociology and History	VL13	3FT deg	H	4-8	Ind	Ind	Ind	BBBB$	Ind		
Sport Rehabilitation and History	BV91	3FT deg	B+H g	12-14	X	X	Ind	BBBB$	X		
Sport Science and History	VB16	3FT deg	H+S g	8-12	Ind	Ind	Ind	BBBB$	Ind		
Theology and Religious Studies and History	VV81	3FT deg	H	4-8	Ind	Ind	Ind	BBBB$	Ind		

STAFFORDSHIRE Univ

TITLE	CODE	COURSE	SUBJECTS	A/AS	NO/C	AGNVQ	IB	SQA(H)	SQA	RATIO A/AS	
European Culture/History	LVP1	3FT deg	H g	CD	MO+2D	M	27	BBC	Ind		
Historical Studies	V100	3FT deg	H g	CD	MO+2D	M	27	BBC	Ind	7	6/16
History of Art and Design/History	VV41	3FT deg	H g	CD	MO+2D	M	27	BBC	Ind	2	
History/American Studies	VQ14	3FT deg	H g	CD	MO+2D	M	27	BBC	Ind	6	8/18
History/Cultural Studies	VL16	3FT deg	H g	CD	MO+2D	M	27	BBC	Ind	4	
History/Development Studies	VM1Y	3FT deg	H g	12	MO+2D	M	27	BBC	Ind	4	
History/Economic Studies	LV1C	3FT deg	H g	12	MO+2D	M	27	BBC			
History/Environmental Studies	VF19	3FT deg	H g	CC	MO+2D	M	27	BBB	Ind	2	
History/Film Studies	VW15	3FT deg	H g	CD	MO+2D	M	27	BBC	Ind	9	
History/French	VR11	3FT/4SW deg	F+H	CD	MO+2D	M^	27	BBC	Ind	5	
History/Geography	VL18	3FT deg	H g	CC	MO+2D	M	27	BBB	Ind	6	
History/German	VR12	3FT/4SW deg	G+H	CD	MO+2D	M^	27	BBC	Ind		
Information Systems/History	GV51	3FT deg	H g	12	Ind	M	27	BBB	Ind		
International Relations/History	MV11	3FT deg	H g	12	MO+2D	M	27	BBC	Ind	5	
Law/History	MV31	3FT deg	H g	CCC	HN	M^	26	BBB	Ind	4	10/16
Legal Studies/History	MV3C	3FT deg	H g	CCC	HN	M^	27	BBBB	Ind	6	
Literature/History	QV3C	3FT deg	El+H g	CD	MO+2D	M	27	BBC	Ind	4	6/16
Philosophy/History	VV71	3FT deg	H g	CD	MO+2D	M	27	BBC	Ind	3	7/8
Politics/History	MVC1	3FT deg	H g	12	MO+2D	M	27	BBC	Ind	8	10/14
Psychology/History	LV71	3FT deg	H g	18	3M+3D	Ind	27	BBB	Ind	4	12/24
Sociology/History	LV31	3FT deg	H g	12	MO+2D	M	27	BBC	Ind	6	12/20

Univ of STIRLING

TITLE	CODE	COURSE	SUBJECTS	A/AS	NO/C	AGNVQ	IB	SQA(H)	SQA	RATIO A/AS	
Economics/History	LV11	4FT deg	g	BCC	Ind	Ind	31	BBBC	HN		
English Studies/History	QV31	4FT deg	g	BBC	Ind	Ind	33	BBBB	HN		
English Studies/Scottish Studies	Q3VC	4FT deg	g	BBC	Ind	Ind	33	BBBB	HN		
Film & Media Studies/History	PV41	4FT deg	g	BBC	Ind	Ind	35	ABBB	HN		
French/History	RV11	4FT deg	g	CCC	Ind	Ind	31	BBBC	HN		
German/History	RV21	4FT deg	g	CCC	Ind	Ind	31	BBBC	HN		
History	V100	4FT deg	g	BCC	Ind	Ind	31	BBBC	HN		
History/Philosophy	VV17	4FT deg	g	CCC	Ind	Ind	28	BBCC	HN		
History/Politics	MV11	4FT deg	g	BCC	Ind	Ind	31	BBBC	HN		
History/Religious Studies	VV18	4FT deg	g	CCC	Ind	Ind	28	BBCC	HN		
History/Scottish Studies	V140	4FT deg	g	BCC	Ind	Ind	31	BBBC	HN		
History/Social Policy	LV4C	4FT deg	g	BCC	Ind	Ind	31	BBBC	HN		
History/Sociology	LV31	4FT deg	g	BCC	Ind	Ind	31	BBBC	HN		
History/Spanish	RV41	4FT deg	g	CCC	Ind	Ind	31	BBBC	HN		

Univ of STRATHCLYDE

TITLE	CODE	COURSE	SUBJECTS	A/AS	NO/C	AGNVQ	IB	SQA(H)	SQA	RATIO A/AS	
Arts and Social Sciences History (Economic and Social)	Y440	3FT/4FT deg	g	CCC	Ind		28	BBBBB$	Ind		
Arts and Social Sciences History (Modern)	Y440	3FT/4FT deg	g	CCC	Ind		28	BBBBB$	Ind		

Univ of SUNDERLAND

TITLE	CODE	COURSE	SUBJECTS	A/AS	NO/C	AGNVQ	IB	SQA(H)	SQA	RATIO A/AS	
Biology and History	CV11	3FT deg	B/C	10	4M	M	Ind	Ind	Ind		
Biology with History	C1V1	3FT deg	B/C	10	4M	M	Ind	Ind	Ind		
Business Studies and History	NV11	3FT/4SW deg	*	10	4M	M	Ind	Ind	Ind		
Business Studies with History	N1V1	3FT/4SW deg	*	10	4M	M	Ind	Ind	Ind		

course details   98 expected requirements   96 entry stats

TITLE	CODE	COURSE	SUBJECTS	A/AS	NQ/C	AGNVQ	IB	SQA(H)	SQA	RATIO A/AS
Computer Studies and History	GV51	3FT deg	H g	10	Ind	M	24$	CCCC	Ind	2	
Computer Studies with History	G5V1	3FT/4SW deg	*	10	4M	M	Ind	Ind	Ind	
Economics and History	LV11	3FT deg	H g	10	Ind	M	24$	CCCC	Ind	
Economics with History	L1V1	3FT deg	*	10	4M	M	Ind	Ind	Ind	
English and History	QV31▼	3FT deg	El+H g	12	Ind	M	24$	BCCC$	Ind	2 8/18
English with History	Q3V1	3FT deg	*	12	3M+1D	M	Ind	Ind	Ind	
French with History	R1V1	4FT deg	F	10	4M	M	Ind	Ind	Ind	
Geography and History	LV81▼	3FT deg	H+Gy/Gl g	12	Ind	M	24$	BCCC	Ind	4	
Geography with History	L8V1	3FT deg	*	10	4M	M	Ind	Ind	Ind	
Geology and History	FV61	3FT deg	*	10	4M	M	Ind	Ind	Ind	
Geology with History	F6V1	3FT deg	*	10	4M	M	Ind	Ind	Ind	
German and History	RV21▼	4FT deg	G+H g	10	Ind	M	24$	CCCC$	Ind	6	
German with History	R2V1	4SW deg	G	10	4M	M	Ind	Ind	Ind	
Historical Studies	V130	3FT deg	H g	CC	3M	M	24	CCCCC	N	5 6/20
History and History of Art and Design	VV14▼	3FT deg	H g	12	Ind	M	24$	BCCC	Ind	
History and Mathematics	VG11	3FT deg	M	10	4M	M	Ind	Ind		
History and Philosophy	VV17▼	3FT deg	H g	12	Ind	M	24	BCCC	Ind	3	
History and Physiology	VB11	3FT deg	*	10	4M	M	Ind	Ind		
History and Politics	VM11▼	3FT deg	H g	12	Ind	M	24	BCCC	Ind	3 4/24
History and Psychology	VC18	3FT deg	H g	14	Ind	M	26$	BBCC$	Ind	4	
History and Religious Studies	VV18▼	3FT deg	H g	12	Ind	M	24	BCCC	Ind	3	
History and Sociology	VL13▼	3FT deg	H g	12	Ind	M	24	BCCC	Ind	3 6/12
History with American Studies	V1Q4	3FT deg	H g	12	Ind	M	24	BCCC	Ind	4 6/10
History with Biology	V1C1	3FT deg	*	10	4M	M	Ind	Ind	Ind	
History with Business Studies	V1N1	3FT deg	*	10	4M	M	Ind	Ind	Ind	
History with Comparative Literature	V1Q2	3FT deg	E+H g	12	Ind	M	24$	BCCC$	Ind	3	
History with Computer Studies	V1G5	3FT deg	*	10	4M	M	Ind	Ind	Ind	
History with Economics	V1L1	3FT deg	*	10	4M	M	Ind	Ind	Ind	
History with English	V1Q3	3FT deg	*	12	3M+1D	M	Ind	Ind	Ind	
History with European Studies	V1T2	3FT deg	H g	12	Ind	M	24$	BCCC	Ind	1	
History with Gender Studies	V1M9	3FT deg	H g	12	Ind	M	24$	BCCC	Ind	
History with Geography	V1L8	3FT deg	*	10	4M	M	Ind	Ind	Ind	
History with Geology	V1F6	3FT deg	*	10	4M	M	Ind	Ind	Ind	
History with German	V1R2	3FT deg	*	10	4M	M	Ind	Ind	Ind	
History with History of Art and Design	V1V4	3FT deg	*	10	4M	M	Ind	Ind	Ind	
History with Mathematics	V1G1	3FT deg	*	10	4M	M	Ind	Ind	Ind	
History with Philosophy	V1V7	3FT deg	*	10	4M	M	Ind	Ind	Ind	
History with Physiology	V1B1	3FT deg	*	10	4M	M	Ind	Ind	Ind	
History with Politics	V1M1	3FT deg	*	10	4M	M	Ind	Ind	Ind	
History with Psychology	V1C8	3FT deg	*	12	3M+1D	M^	Ind	Ind	Ind	
History with Religious Studies	V1V8	3FT deg	*	10	4M	M	Ind	Ind	Ind	
History with Sociology	V1L3	3FT deg	*	12	3M+1D	M	Ind	Ind	Ind	
History with Spanish	V1R4▼	3FT deg	*	10	4M	M	Ind	Ind	Ind	
Mathematics with History	G1V1	3FT deg	M	10	4M	M	Ind	Ind	Ind	
Philosophy with History	V7V1	3FT deg	*	10	4M	Ind	Ind	Ind	Ind	
Physiology with History	B1V1	3FT deg	*	10	4M	M	Ind	Ind	Ind	
Politics with History	M1V1	3FT deg	*	10	4M	M	Ind	Ind	Ind	
Psychology with History	C8V1	3FT deg	*	12	3M+1D	M^	Ind	Ind	Ind	
Religious Studies with History	V8V1	3FT deg	*	10	4M	M	Ind	Ind	Ind	
Sociology with History	L3V1	3FT deg	*	12	3M+1D	M	Ind	Ind	Ind	

| | | | 98 expected requirements | | | | | | | 96 entry stats |
| course details | | | | | | | | | | |
TITLE	CODE	COURSE	SUBJECTS	A/AS	ND/C	AGNVQ	IB	SQA(H)	SQA	RATIO A/AS
Univ of SUSSEX										
American Studies (History)	Q4V1	4FT deg	*	BBB	MO	M*6	$	Ind	Ind	
Contemporary History in African & Asian Studies	V1TM	3FT deg	*	BBB	MO	M*6	$	Ind	Ind	
Contemporary History in European Studies	V1TF	4FT deg	* g	BBB	MO $	M*6 go	$	Ind	Ind	
Contemporary History in Social Sciences	V1MX	3FT deg	*	BBB	MO	M*6	$	Ind	Ind	
Economic History	V300	3FT deg	*	BBB	MO	M*6	$	Ind	Ind	
Economics with Economic History	L1V3	3FT deg	* g	BBB	MO $	M*6 go	$	Ind	Ind	
History in African and Asian Studies	V1T5	3FT deg	*	BBB	MO	M*6	$	Ind	Ind	
History in Cultural and Community Studies	V1Y2	3FT deg	*	BBB	MO	M*6	$	Ind	Ind	
History in English and American Studies	V1Q4	3FT deg	*	BBB	MO	M*6	$	Ind	Ind	
History in European Studies	V1T2	4FT deg	* g	BBB	MO $	M*6 go	$	Ind	Ind	
History with Development Studies	V1MY	3FT deg	*	BBB	MO	M*6	$	Ind	Ind	
Intellectual History in English & American St	V1QK	3FT deg	*	BBB	MO	M*6	$	Ind	Ind	
Intellectual History in European Studies	V1TG	4FT deg	* g	BBB	MO $	M*6 go	$	Ind	Ind	
Intellectural History in Social Sciences	V175	3FT deg	*	BBB	MO	M*6	$	Ind	Ind	
Univ of Wales SWANSEA										
American Studies and Economic History	VQ34	3FT deg	*	BBC	Ind	Ind	30	ABBBB	Ind	
American Studies and Social History	VQ3K	3FT deg	*	BBC	Ind	Ind	30	ABBBB	Ind	5
Ancient History and Civilisation	V112	3FT deg	*	BCC	Ind	X	30	ABBBB	X	3 14/22
Ancient History and Civilisation with Greek	V1Q7	3FT deg	*	BCC	X	X	28	BBBBC	X	
Ancient History and Civilisation with Latin	V1Q6	3FT deg	*	BCC	X	X	28	BBBBC	X	2
Ancient and Medieval History	V116	3FT deg	H	BBB-BBC	Ind	Ind	30	ABBBB	X	8 14/18
Anthropology and Social History	LV63	3FT deg	*	BBC	Ind	Ind	30	ABBBB	Ind	4
Anthropology/Ancient History & Civilisation	LV61	3FT deg	*	BBC-BCC	Ind	Ind	28	BBBBB	X	8
Economic History and Economics	LV13	3FT deg	* g	BBC	Ind	Ind	30	ABBBB	Ind	2
Economic History/Ancient Hist and Civilisation	VVCH	3FT deg	*	BBC	Ind	Ind	30	ABBBB	Ind	
Economic and Social History	V340	3FT deg	*	BBB-BBC	Ind	Ind	32	AABBB	Ind	7
English Language/Ancient History & Civilisation	QV3C	3FT deg	E	BBC	X	X	30$	ABBBB$	Ind	
English/Ancient History and Civilisation	VQC3	3FT deg	E	BBC	X	X	30$	ABBBB$	X	3
European History (with English)	V1Q3	4FT deg	E+H	BBB-BBC	X	Ind	30$	ABBBB$	Ind	7
European History (with French)	V1R1	4FT deg	F+H	BBB-BBC	Ind	Ind	30$	ABBBB$	Ind	4
European History (with German)	V1R2	4FT deg	G+H	BBB-BBC	Ind	Ind	30$	ABBBB$	Ind	
European History (with Italian)	V1R3	4FT deg	H+L	BBB-BBC	1M+5D$	Ind	30$	ABBBB$	Ind	
European History (with Spanish)	V1R4	4FT deg	H+L	BBB-BBC	Ind	Ind	30$	ABBBB$	Ind	
European History (with Welsh)	V1Q5	4FT deg	H+L	BBB-BBC	Ind	Ind	30$	ABBBB$	Ind	
French/Ancient History and Civilisation	VRC1	4FT deg	F	BBC	1M+5D$	X	30$	ABBBB$	X	
French/Economic History	RV13	4FT deg	F	BBC	1M+5D$	Ind	30$	ABBBB$	Ind	
German/Ancient History and Civilisation	VRC2	4FT deg	G	BBC	1M+5D$	X	30$	ABBBB$	X	
German/Economic History	RV23	4FT deg	G	BBC	1M+5D$	Ind	30$	ABBBB$	Ind	
Greek and Roman Studies/Economic History	QV83	3FT deg	*	BBC-BCC	Ind	X	28	BBBBB	X	
Greek/Ancient History and Civilisation	VQC7	3FT deg	Gk	BCC	X	X	28$	BBBBB$	X	
History	V100	3FT deg	*	BBB-BBC	Ind	Ind	32	AABBB	Ind	3 14/26
History/American Studies	VQ14	3FT deg	*	BBC	Ind	Ind	30	ABBBB	Ind	3 16/24
History/Ancient History and Civilisation	V110	3FT deg	*	BBC	Ind	Ind	30	ABBBB	X	5
History/Anthropology	VL16	3FT deg	*	BBC	Ind	Ind	30	ABBBB	Ind	7
History/Economic History	VV13	3FT deg	*	BBB-BBC	Ind	Ind	30	ABBBB	Ind	
History/Economics	LV11	3FT deg	* g	BBB-BBC	Ind	Ind	30	ABBBB	Ind	4
History/English	QV31	3FT deg	E+H	BBB	X	Ind	32$	AABBB$	Ind	5 20/24
History/French	RV11	4FT deg	F+H	BBC	1M+5D$	Ind	30$	ABBBB$	Ind	6
History/Geography	LV81	3FT deg	Gy	BBB-BBC	1M+5D$	Ind	30$	ABBBB$	Ind	8
History/German	RV21	4FT deg	G+H	BBC	1M+5D$	Ind	30$	ABBBB$	Ind	3
History/Greek	QV71	3FT deg	Gk	BBB-BBC	Ind	Ind	30$	ABBBB$	Ind	

TITLE	CODE	COURSE	SUBJECTS	A/AS	ND/C	AGNVQ	IB	SQA(H)	SQA	RATIO A/AS
course details → **98 expected requirements** → **96 entry stats**										
History/Greek and Roman Studies	QV81	3FT deg	*	BBB-BBC	Ind	Ind	30	ABBBB	Ind	
Italian/Ancient History and Civilisation	VRC3	4FT deg	L/*	BBC	1M+5D$	X	30$	ABBBB$	X	
Italian/Economic History	RV33	4FT deg	L/*	BBC	1M+5D$	Ind	30$	ABBBB$	Ind	
Italian/History	RV31	4FT deg	L/*	BBC	1M+5D$	Ind	30$	ABBBB$	Ind	1
Latin/Ancient History and Civilisation	VQC6	3FT deg	Ln	BCC	X	X	28$	BBBBC$	X	
Latin/History	QV61	3FT deg	Ln	BBC	Ind	Ind	28$	BBBBB$	Ind	
Medieval Studies/Ancient Hist and Civilisation	V115	3FT deg	H	BBC-BCC	X	X	28$	BBBBB$	X	9
Medieval Studies/Anthropology	LVP1	3FT deg	H	BBC	X	Ind	Ind	Ind	X	
Medieval Studies/English	QVH1	3FT deg	E+H	BBC	X	X	30$	ABBBB$	X	
Medieval Studies/French	RVC1	4FT deg	F+H	BBC-BCC	Ind	Ind	28$	BBBBB$	X	
Medieval Studies/Greek	QVR1	3FT deg	Gk+H	BBC-BCC	X	X	28$	BBBBB$	X	
Medieval Studies/Greek and Roman Studies	QV8C	3FT deg	H	BBC	X	X	30$	ABBBB$	X	
Medieval Studies/History	V120	3FT deg	H	BBB-BBC	X	Ind	30$	ABBBB$	X	11
Medieval Studies/Italian	RVH1	4FT deg	H+L	BCC	1M+5D$	Ind	28$	BBBBB$	X	
Medieval Studies/Latin	QVP1	3FT deg	Ln+H	BBC	X	X	30$	ABBBB$	X	
Philosophy/Ancient History and Civilisation	VV1R	3FT deg	*	BBC-BCC	1M+5D	X	28	BBBBB	X	3
Philosophy/History	VV17	3FT deg	*	BBC	1M+5D	Ind	30	ABBBB	Ind	5
Politics and Social History	VM31	3FT deg	*	BBC	1M+5D	Ind	30	ABBBB	Ind	
Politics/Ancient History and Civilisation	VMC1	3FT deg	*	BBC	1M+5D	X	30	ABBBB	X	
Politics/History	MV11	3FT deg	*	BBC	1M+5D	Ind	30	ABBBB	Ind	3 14/20
Russian Studies/History	RV8C	3FT deg	*	BBC	Ind	Ind	30	ABBBB	Ind	1
Russian/Economic History	RV83	4FT deg	L/*	BBC-BCC	1M+5D$	Ind	28$	BBBBC$	Ind	
Russian/History	RV81	4FT deg	L/*	BBC	1M+5D$	Ind	28$	BBBBC$	Ind	
Social History and Social Policy	LV43	3FT deg	*	BBC-BCC	1M+5D	Ind	28	BBBBB	Ind	5
Social History and Sociology	LV33	3FT deg	*	BBC	1M+5D	Ind	30	ABBBB	Ind	
Sociology/History	LV31	3FT deg	*	BBC	Ind	Ind	30	ABBBB	Ind	3 20/26
Sociology/Medieval Studies	VL13	3FT deg	H	BBC	X	Ind	Ind	Ind	X	
Spanish/Ancient History and Civilisation	VRC4	4FT deg	L/*	BBC	1M+5D$	X	30$	ABBBB$	X	2
Spanish/Economic History	RV43	4FT deg	L/*	BBC	1M+5D$	Ind	30$	ABBBB$	Ind	
Spanish/History	RV41	4FT deg	L/*	BBC	1M+5D$	Ind	30$	ABBBB$	Ind	3
Spanish/Medieval Studies	RVK1	4FT deg	H+L	BCC	1M+5D$	Ind	28$	BBBBB$	X	1
Welsh/Ancient History and Civilisation	VQC5	3FT/4FT deg	W	BCC	Ind	X	28$	BBBBB$	X	
Welsh/History	QV51	3FT/4FT deg	W	BBC	Ind	X	30$	ABBBB$	Ind	3
Welsh/Medieval Studies	QVM1	3FT/4FT deg	H+W	BCC	X	X	Ind	Ind	X	
Joint Hons with defer choice of specialisation (inc Economic History)	Y220	3FT deg	*	20-22	1M+5D	Ind	28	BBBBB	Ind	
Joint Hons with defer choice of specialisation (inc Social History)	Y220	3FT deg	*	20-22	1M+5D	Ind	28	BBBBB	Ind	

Univ of TEESSIDE

TITLE	CODE	COURSE	SUBJECTS	A/AS	ND/C	AGNVQ	IB	SQA(H)	SQA	RATIO A/AS
English and History	QV31	3FT deg								
History	V100	3FT deg	*	14	Ind		Ind	Ind	Ind	4 4/20
History and Law	MV31	3FT deg	*	14	Ind		Ind	Ind	Ind	
History and Politics	MV1C	3FT deg	*	14	Ind		Ind	Ind	Ind	
Politics and History	MV1D	3FT deg	*	12-14	Ind		Ind	Ind	Ind	
Modular Degree Scheme *History*	Y401	3FT deg								

THAMES VALLEY Univ

TITLE	CODE	COURSE	SUBJECTS	A/AS	ND/C	AGNVQ	IB	SQA(H)	SQA	RATIO A/AS
American Studies with History	Q4V1	3FT deg		8-12	M0	M	26	CCC		
Economics with History	LV11	3FT deg		8-12	M0	M	26	CCC		
English Language and Communications with History	Q1V1	3FT deg		8-12	M0	M	26	CCC		
English with History	Q3V1	3FT deg		8-12	M0	M	26	CCC		
Environmental Policy and Management with History	F9V1	3FT deg		8-12	M0	M	26	CCC		

| course details | | | | 98 expected requirements | | | | | | | 96 entry stats | |

TITLE	CODE	COURSE	SUBJECTS	A/AS	NO/C	AGNVQ	IB	SQA(H)	SQA	RATIO A/AS	
European Studies with History	T2V1	3FT deg		8-12	MO	M	26	CCC			
French with History	R1V1	3FT deg		8-12	MO	M	26	CCC			
German with History	R2V1	3FT deg		8-12	MO	M	26	CCC			
History with American Studies	V1Q4	3FT deg		8-12	MO	M	26	CCC			
History with Business	V1N1	3FT deg		8-12	MO	M	26	CCC			
History with Economics	V1L1	3FT deg		8-12	MO	M	26	CCC			
History with English	V1Q3	3FT deg		8-12	MO	M	26	CCC			
History with English Language Studies	V1Q1	3FT deg		8-12	MO	M	26	CCC			
History with European Studies	V1T2	3FT deg		8-12	MO	M	26	CCC			
History with French	V1R1	3FT deg		8-12	MO	M	26	CCC			
History with German	V1R2	3FT deg		8-12	MO	M	26	CCC			
History with International Studies	V1MX	3FT deg		8-12	MO	M	26	CCC			
History with Music	V1W3	3FT deg		8-12	MO	M	26	CCC			
History with Politics & International Relations	V1M1	3FT deg		8-12	MO	M	26	CCC			
History with Psychology	V1C8	3FT deg		8-12	MO	M	26	CCC			
History with Sociology	V1L3	3FT deg		8-12	MO	M	26	CCC			
History with Spanish	V1R4	3FT deg		8-12	MO	M	26	CCC			
History with Visual Cultures	V1W1	3FT deg		8-12	MO	M	26	CCC			
History with Women's Studies	V1M9	3FT deg		8-12	MO	M	26	CCC			
International Studies with History	M9V1	3FT deg		8-12	MO	M	26	CCC			
Politics and International Relations with Hist	M1V1	3FT deg		8-12	MO	M	26	CCC			
Sociology with History	L3V1	3FT deg		8-12	MO	M	26	CCC			
Spanish with History	R4V1	3FT deg		8-12	MO	M	26	CCC			

TRINITY COLL Carmarthen

Hanes	V102	3FT deg	H g	DD-CC	Ind		Ind	Ind	Ind	11	
Hanes/Astudiaethau Crefydd	VV1W	3FT deg	H g	DD-CC	Ind		Ind	Ind	Ind		
Hanes/Astudiaethau Theatr	WV41	3FT deg	H+T g	DD-CC	Ind		Ind	Ind	Ind		
Hanes/Cymraeg	QV5C	3FT deg	W+H g	DD-CC	Ind		Ind	Ind	Ind	4	
History	V100	3FT deg	H g	DD-CC	Ind		Ind	Ind	Ind	4	4/20
History/Archaeology	VV16	3FT deg	H g	DD-CC	Ind		Ind	Ind	Ind	8	
History/English	QV31	3FT deg	H+E g	DD-CC	Ind		Ind	Ind	Ind	7	
Religious Studies/History	VV18	3FT deg	Re+H g	DD-CC	Ind		Ind	Ind	Ind	4	
Saesneg/Hanes	QV3C	3FT deg	E+H g	DD-CC	Ind		Ind	Ind	Ind		
Theatre Studies/History	VW14	3FT deg	T+H g	DD-CC	Ind		Ind	Ind	Ind		
Welsh Studies/History	QV51	3FT deg	H g	DD-CC	Ind		Ind	Ind	Ind		
Dyniaethau *Hanes*	Y321	3FT deg	H g	DD-CC	Ind		Ind	Ind	Ind		
Humanities *History*	Y320	3FT deg	H g	DD-CC	Ind		Ind	Ind	Ind		

Univ of ULSTER

Irish History and Politics	V147▼	3FT deg	*	CCC	MO+3D	D*6/^ gi	28	BBBC	Ind	9	14/20
Modern and Contemporary History	V130▼	3FT deg	*	CCC	MO+3D	D*6/^ gi	28	BBBC	Ind	9	14/22
Humanities Combined *History*	Y320▼	3FT/4SW deg	*	CCC	MO+3D	D*6/^ gi	28	BBBC	Ind		

UNIVERSITY COLL LONDON (Univ of London)

Ancient History	V110	3FT deg	g	BBC	3M	Ind	30$	BBBCC	Ind	6	20/30
Ancient History and Egyptology	VQ19	3FT deg	g	BBB	3M	Ind	32$	BBBCC	Ind	10	22/28
Ancient History and Social Anthropology	VL16	3FT deg	* g	BCC-BBB	3M	Ind	30$	BBBCC	Ind	13	20/24
Economics and History	LV11	3FT deg	g	BBC	3M	Ind	32$	BBBCC	Ind	16	22/26
German and Jewish Studies (4 Yrs)	RV21	4FT deg	G g	BBC	3M	X	28$	BBCCC$	Ind		
History	V100	3FT deg	g	BBB-ABB	3M	Ind	32$	BBBCC	Ind	12	18/30
History and History of Art	VV14	3FT deg	g	BBC	3M	Ind	30$	BBBBB	Ind	9	

course details | 98 expected requirements | 96 entry stats

TITLE	CODE	COURSE	SUBJECTS	A/AS	NO/C	RGNVQ	IB	SQA(H)	SQA	RATIO A/AS
History of the Americas (4 Yrs)	V130	4FT deg	g	BBC	3M	Ind	32$	BBBCC	Ind	12
History with a European Language (4 Yrs)	V1T2	4FT deg	g	BBB	3M	Ind	32$	BBBCC	Ind	28
Italian and Jewish Studies (4 Yrs)	RV31	4FT deg	g	BCC	3M	X	28$	BBCCC$	Ind	
Jewish History (4 Yrs)	V149	4FT deg	* g	CCC	3M	X	28$	BBCCC$	Ind	1 6/26
Law and History (4 Yrs)	MV31	4FT deg	H g	ABB	Ind	Ind	35	AABBB	Ind	14

Univ of WARWICK

Ancient History and Classical Archaeology	VV16	3FT deg	* g	BCC	X	X	30	BBBBC		13 20/28
Economics and Economic History	LV13	3FT deg	g	AAB	DO $	Ind	34	AAAAB		12
French and History (4 Yrs inc yr abroad)	RV11	4FT deg	F+H g	BBC	X	X	32$	ABBBB$		7 24/26
History	V100	3FT deg	H+L g	ABB-BBB	X	X	34$	AAABB$		11 26/30
History and Politics	VM11	3FT deg	* g	ABB	X	X	32$	AAABB		9 24/30
History and Sociology	VL13	3FT deg	* g	BBB-BBC	X	X	29$	AABBB		14 22/30

WESTHILL COLL

Humanities - History:Islam & the Christian West	VV18	3FT deg	* g	CC	4M+2D	M^	Ind	Ind	Ind	
Humanities - Childhood Studies History	Y600	3FT deg	* g	CC	4M+2D	M^	Ind	Ind	Ind	
Humanities - Nineteenth and Twentieth Century St History	Y602	3FT deg	* g	CC	4M+2D	M^	Ind	Ind	Ind	

Univ of WESTMINSTER

Modern History	V100	3FT deg	*	BC	MO+3D	D	26	BBB		

Univ of WOLVERHAMPTON

History (Specialist Route)	V100	3FT deg		14	4M	D	24	BBBB	Ind	7 8/20
Social History (Specialist Route)	V320	3FT deg		14	4M	M	24	BBBB	Ind	17
Combined Degrees History	Y401	3FT/4SW deg		16	4M	D	24	BBBB	Ind	

WORCESTER COLL of HE

History	V100	3FT deg		DD	Ind	M	Ind	Ind	Ind	5 6/22
History/Art & Design	WV91	3FT deg	A	DD	Ind	M	Ind	Ind	Ind	4
History/Biological Science	CV11	3FT deg	S	DD	Ind	M	Ind	Ind	Ind	
History/Business Management	NV11	3FT deg		DD	Ind	M	Ind	Ind	Ind	11
History/Drama	WV41	3FT deg		DD	Ind	M	Ind	Ind	Ind	3
History/Economy and Society	LV11	3FT deg		DD	Ind	M	Ind	Ind	Ind	2
History/Education Studies	XV91	3FT deg		DD	Ind	M	Ind	Ind	Ind	3
History/English and Literary Studies	QV31	3FT deg		CC	Ind	M	Ind	Ind	Ind	4
History/Environmental Science	FV91	3FT deg		DD	Ind	M	Ind	Ind	Ind	
History/Geography	LV81	3FT deg		DD	Ind	M	32$	Ind	Ind	5
History/Health Studies	BV91	3FT deg	g	DD	Ind	M	Ind	Ind	Ind	
Information Technology/History	VG15	3FT deg		DD	Ind	M	Ind	Ind	Ind	
Sociology/History	VL13	3FT deg		DD	Ind	M	Ind	Ind	Ind	3
Sports Studies/History	VB16	3FT deg		CC	Ind	M	Ind	Ind	Ind	
Urban Studies/History	VL1V	3FT deg		DD	Ind	M	Ind	Ind	Ind	
Women's Studies/History	VM19	3FT deg		DD	Ind	M	Ind	Ind	Ind	8

Univ of YORK

Archaeology/History (Equal)	VV16	3FT deg	H	24	Ind	D$^	32$	BBBB$	Ind	
Economic and Social History	V340	3FT deg	* g	CCC	DO	D*^	30	BBBC	Ind	16/26
Economic and Social History/Education	V3X9	3FT deg	* g	CCC	DO	D*^	30	BBBC	Ind	
Economics/Economic and Social History (Equal)	LV13	3FT deg	* g	BCC	DO	D*^	30	BBBC	Ind	
English/History (Equal)	QV31	3FT deg	E+H g	ABB-ABC	HN $	D$^	32$	AABB$	Ind	24/28
History	V100	3FT deg	H	ABC	Ind	D$6/^	32$	ABBB$	Ind	22/28
History/Economics	V1L1	3FT deg	H	ABC	Ind	D$6/^	32$	ABBB$	Ind	

course details

TITLE	CODE	COURSE
History/Education	V1X9	3FT deg
History/French	V1R1	4FT deg
History/History of Art (Equal)	VV14	3FT deg
History/Philosophy (Equal)	VV17	3FT deg
History/Politics (Equal)	VM11	3FT deg
History/Sociology	V1L3	3FT deg
Politics/Economic and Social History (Equal)	MV13	3FT deg
Sociology/Economic and Social History (Equal)	LV33	3FT deg

98 expected requirements · 96 entry stats

SUBJECTS	A/AS	ND/C	AGNVQ	IB	SQA(H)	SQA	RATIO A/AS
H	ABC	Ind	D$6/^	32$	ABBB$	Ind	
H+F	ABC	Ind	D$6/^	32$	ABBB$	Ind	
H	ABC-BBB	Ind	D$^	32$	ABBB$	Ind	
H	ABC	Ind	D$6/^	32$	ABBB$	Ind	
H	ABC	Ind	D$6/^	32$	ABBB$	Ind	24/28
H	ABC	Ind	D$6/^	32$	ABBB$	Ind	
* g	BCC	DO	D*^	28	BBBC	Ind	
* g	BCC-CCC	Ind	D$^	28	BBBC	Ind	

			98 expected requirements							96 entry stats

TITLE	CODE	COURSE	SUBJECTS	A/AS	ND/C	AGNVQ	IB	SQA(H)	SQA	RATIO A/AS
Univ of ABERDEEN										
Celtic Civilisation-History of Art	QVM4	4FT deg	* g	BBC	Ind	M$ go	30$	BBBB$	Ind	
Celtic-History of Art	QV54	4FT deg	* g	BBC	Ind	M$ go	30$	BBBB$	Ind	
English-History of Art	QV34	4FT deg	* g	BBC	Ind	M$ go	30$	BBBB$	Ind	16
French-History of Art	RV14	4FT/5FT deg	* g	BBC	Ind	M$ go	30$	BBBB$	Ind	7
French-History of Art (4 Yrs)	VR41	4FT deg	* g	BBC	Ind	M$ go	30$	BBBB$	Ind	
German-History of Art	RV24	4FT/5FT deg	* g	BBC	Ind	M$ go	30$	BBBB$	Ind	
German-History of Art (4 Yrs)	VR42	4FT deg	* g	BBC	Ind	M$ go	30$	BBBB$	Ind	
Hispanic Studies-History of Art	RV44	4FT/5FT deg	* g	BBC	Ind	M$ go	30$	BBBB$	Ind	
Hispanic Studies-History of Art (4 Yrs)	VR44	4FT deg	* g	BBC	Ind	M$ go	30$	BBBB$	Ind	
History of Art	V400	4FT deg	* g	BBC	Ind	M$ go	30$	BBBB$	Ind	7
History of Art with Film Studies	V4W5	4FT deg	* g	BBC	Ind	M$ go	30$	BBBB$	Ind	5
History of Art with Women's Studies	V4M9	4FT deg	* g	BBC	Ind	M$ go	30$	BBBB$	Ind	
History of Art-Philosophy	VV47	4FT deg	* g	BBC	Ind	M$ go	30$	BBBB$	Ind	
History of Art-Religious Studies	VV48	4FT deg	* g	BBC	Ind	M$ go	30$	BBBB$	Ind	
History-History of Art	VV14	4FT deg	* g	BBC	Ind	M$ go	30$	BBBB$	Ind	8
Univ of Wales, ABERYSTWYTH										
Art History with Art	V4W1	3FT deg	A/Ad g	18	1M+5D$ MA6 g		29$	BBBCC$	Ind	
Art History/American Studies	QV44	3FT deg	E/H g	18	1M+5D$ MA^ g		29$	BBBCC$	Ind	
Art History/Art	VW41	3FT deg	A/Ad	18	1M+5D$ MA6 g		29$	BBBCC$	Ind	
Art with Art History	W1V4	3FT deg	A/Ad g	18	1M+5D$ MA6 g		29$	BBBCC$	Ind	
Drama/Art History	VW44	3FT deg	* g	20	1M+5D MQ/A6		30	BBBBC	Ind	
Education/Art History	VX49	3FT deg	* g	18	1M+5D MA6 g		29	BBBCC	Ind	
English/Art History	QV34	3FT deg	El	20	1M+5D$ MA^ g		30$	BBBBC$	Ind	
Film and Television Studies/Art History	VW45	3FT deg	* g	20	1M+5D MA/Q^ g		30	BBBBC	Ind	
French/Art History	RV14	4FT deg	F g	18	1M+5D$ MA^ g		29$	BBBCC$	Ind	
Geography/Art History	LV84	3FT deg	Gy g	20-22	3M+2D$ MA^ g		31$	BBBBC$	Ind	
History/Art History	VV14	3FT deg	* g	18-20	1M+5D MA^ g		30	BBBCC	Ind	
Information and Library Studies/Art History	PV24	3FT deg	* g	18	1M+5D MA6 g		29	BBBCC	Ind	
Irish/Art History	QVM4	4FT deg	* g	18	1M+5D$ MA6 g		29$	BBBCC$	Ind	
Italian/Art History	RV34	4FT deg	L g	18	1M+5D$ MA^ g		29$	BBBCC$	Ind	
Pure Mathematics/Art History	GVC4	3FT deg	M g	18	1M+5D$ MA^ g		29$	BBBCC$	Ind	
Spanish/Art History	RV44	4FT deg	L g	18	1M+5D$ MA^ g		29$	BBBCC$	Ind	
Welsh History/Art History	VVC4	3FT deg	* g	18-20	1M+5D MA^ g		30	BBBCC	Ind	
Welsh/Art History	QV54	3FT deg	W g	18	1M+5D$ MA^ g		29$	BBBCC$	Ind	
ANGLIA Poly Univ										
Art History	V400▼	3FT deg	*	14	6M	M	Dip	BBCC	Ind	4 8/18
Art History and Business	NV14▼	3FT deg	*	14	6M	M*	Dip	BBCC	Ind	5
Art History and Communication Studies	PV34▼	3FT deg	Ap	14	6M	M+/^	Dip$	BBCC	Ind	
Art History and English	QV34▼	3FT deg	E	14	6M	M+/^	Dip$	BBCC	Ind	4 10/24
Art History and English Language Studies	QV14▼	3FT deg	g	14	6M	M go	Dip			
Art History and European Philosophy & Literature	VV47▼	3FT deg	*	14	6M	M+/^	Dip	BBCC	Ind	6
Art History and French	RV14▼	4FT deg	* g	14	6M	M+/^ go	Dip	BBCC	Ind	3
Art History and Geography	LV84▼	3FT deg	Gy g	14	6M	M+/^ go	Dip$	BBCC	Ind	
Art History and German	RV24▼	4FT deg	g	14	6M	M+/^ go	Dip	BBCC	Ind	
Art History and Graphic Arts	WV24▼	3FT deg	A	16	6M	M+/^	Dip$	BBCC	Ind	4
Art History and History	VV14▼	3FT deg	*	14	6M	M+/^	Dip	BBCC	Ind	5
Art History and Italian	RV34▼	4FT deg	* g	14	6M	M+/^ go	Dip	BBCC	Ind	4
Art History and Law	MV34▼	3FT deg	*	14	6M	M+/^	Dip$	BBCC	Ind	
Art History and Music	VW43▼	3FT deg	*	14	6M	M+/^	Dip$	BBCC	Ind	
Art History and Politics	MV14▼	3FT deg	*	14	6M	M+/^	Dip	BBCC	Ind	

History of Art

				98 expected requirements						**96 entry stats**	
course details											
TITLE	CODE	COURSE	SUBJECTS	A/AS	ND/C	AGNVQ	IB	SQA(H)	SQA	RATIO A/AS	
Art History and Sociology	LV34▼	3FT deg	*	14	6M	M+/^	Dip	BBCC	Ind		
Art History and Spanish	RV44▼	4FT deg	*g	14	6M	M+/^ go	Dip	BBCC	Ind		
Art History and Studio Art	EV94▼	3FT deg	A	14	6M	M+/^	Dip$	BBCC	Ind		
Art History and Studio Art	WV94▼	3FT deg	A	14	6M	M+/^	Dip$	BBCC	Ind	2	10/20
Art History and Women's Studies	VM49▼	3FT deg	*	14	6M	M+/^	Dip	BBCC	Ind	3	

Univ of BIRMINGHAM

African Studies/History of Art	TV74	3FT deg	*	BBB	Ind	D*^	32	ABBB	Ind		
Ancient History & Archaeology/History of Art	VV46	3FT deg	*	BBB	Ind	D*^	32	ABBB	Ind		
Classical Lit and Civilisation/History of Art	QV84	3FT deg	*	BBB	Ind	D*^	32	ABBB	Ind		
Dance/History of Art	WV44	3FT deg	*	BBB	Ind	D*^	32	ABBB	Ind	5	
Drama/History of Art	VW44	3FT deg	*	BBB	Ind	D*^	32	ABBB	Ind		
East Mediterranean History/History of Art	VVD4	3FT deg	*g	BBB	Ind	D*^	32	ABBB	Ind		
English/History of Art	QV34	3FT deg	*	BBB	Ind	D*^	32	ABBB	Ind	6	24/30
French Studies/History of Art	RV14	4FT deg	F	BBB	Ind	D*^	32$	ABBB	Ind	25	
Geology and Archaeology	FV64	3FT deg	Sg	BBB-CCC	Ind	Ind	30	Ind	Ind		
German Studies/History of Art	RV24	4FT deg	G	BBB	Ind	D*^	32$	ABBB	Ind		
Hispanic Studies/History of Art	RV44	4FT deg	*	BBB	Ind	D*^	32	ABBB	Ind		
History of Art/Italian	RV34	4FT deg	*	BBB	Ind	D*^	32	ABBB	Ind	28	
History of Art/Latin	QV64	3FT deg	Ln	BBB	Ind	D*^	32$	ABBB	Ind		
History of Art/Modern Greek Studies	TV24	4FT deg	*g	BBB	Ind	D*^	32	ABBB	Ind		
History of Art/Music	VW43	3FT deg	Mu	AAB-ABB	Ind	D*^	32$	ABBB	Ind	4	
History of Art/Philosophy	VV47	3FT deg	*	BBB	Ind	D*^	32	ABBB	Ind	18	
History of Art/Portuguese	RV54	4FT deg	*	BBB	Ind	D*^	32	ABBB	Ind		
History of Art/Russian	RV84	4FT deg	*	BBB	Ind	D*^	32	ABBB	Ind		
History of Art/Theology	VV48	3FT deg	*	BBB	Ind	D*^	32	ABBB	Ind	6	
History/History of Art	VV14	3FT deg	*	BBB	Ind	D*^	32	ABBB	Ind	21	

BOLTON INST

Art & Design History	E490	3FT deg	*g	CD	MO	M*	24	BBCC	Ind		
Art & Design History & European Cultural Studies	TV24	3FT deg	*g	CD	MO	M*	24	BBCC	Ind		
Art & Design History & Peace and War Studies	VV4C	3FT deg	*g	CD	MO	M*	24	BBCC	Ind		
Art & Design History and Business Info Systems	GV54	3FT deg	*g	CD	MO	M*	24	BBCC	Ind		
Art & Design History and Business Studies	VN41	3FT deg	*g	CD	MO	M*	24	BBCC	Ind		
Art & Design History and Community Studies	LV54	3FT deg	*g	CD	MO	M*	24	BBCC	Ind		
Art & Design History and Computing	VG45	3FT deg	*g	CD	MO	M*	24	BBCC	Ind		
Art & Design History and Creative Writing	VW49	3FT deg	*g	CD	MO	M*	24	BBCC	Ind		
Art & Design History and Design	EV24	3FT deg	*g	CD	MO	M*	24	BBCC	Ind		
Art & Design History and Film & TV Studies	WV54	3FT deg	Me/T g	CD	Ind	Ind	24	BBCC	Ind		
Art & Design History and French	VR41	3FT deg	Fg	CD	Ind	Ind	24	BBCC	Ind		
Art & Design History and German	VR42	3FT deg	Gg	CD	Ind	Ind	24	BBCC	Ind		
Art & Design History and History	VV1K	3FT deg	*g	CD	MO	M*	24	BBCC	Ind		
Art & Design History and Leisure Studies	VL4H	3FT deg	*g	CD	MO	M*	24	BBCC	Ind		
Art & Design History and Literature	VQ41	3FT deg	*g	CD	MO	M*	24	BBCC	Ind		
Art & Design History and Mathematics	VG41	3FT deg	Mg	DD	Ind	Ind	24	BBCC	Ind		
Art & Design History and Philosophy	VV74	3FT deg	*g	CD	MO	M*	24	BBCC	Ind		
Art & Design History and Psychology	VL47	3FT deg	*g	12	MO	D*	24	BBCC	Ind		
Art & Design History and Sociology	LV3K	3FT deg	*g	CD	MO	M	24	Ind	Ind		
Art & Design History and Tourism Studies	VP47	3FT deg	*g	CD	MO	M*	24	BBCC	Ind		
Art & Design History and Urban & Cultural Studs	LV34	3FT deg	*g	CD	MO	M*	24	BBCC	Ind		
Art and Design Hist & Organisations, Mgt & Work	NV74	3FT deg	*g	CD	MO	M*	24	BBCC	Ind		
Art and Design History and Accountancy	NV44	3FT deg	*g	CD	MO	M*	24	BBCC	Ind		
Art and Design History and Biology	VC41	3FT deg	*g	CD	MO	M*	24	BBCC	Ind		

			98 expected requirements							96 entry stats
course details										
TITLE	CODE	COURSE	SUBJECTS	A/AS	ND/C	AGNVQ	IB	SQA(H)	SQA	RATIO A/AS
Art and Design History and Business Economics	LV14	3FT deg	* g	CD	MO	M*	24	BBCC	Ind	
Art and Design History and Environmental Studies	FV94	3FT deg	* g	CD	MO	M*	24	BBCC	Ind	
Art and Design History and Film and TV Studies	VW45	3FT deg	Me/T g	CD	MO	Ind	24	BBCC	Ind	
Art and Design History and Gender and Women's St	VM49	3FT deg	* g	CD	MO	M*	24	BBCC	Ind	
Art and Design History and Human Resource Mgt	NV14	3FT deg	* g	CD	MO	M*	24	BBCC	Ind	
Art and Design History and Law	MV34	3FT deg	* g	CD	MO	M*	24	BBCC	Ind	
Art and Design History and Marketing	NV54	3FT deg	* g	CD	MO	M*	24	BBCC	Ind	
Art and Design History and Operations Management	NV24	3FT deg	* g	CD	MO	M*	24	BBCC	Ind	
Art and Design History and Theatre Studies	VW44	3FT deg	Me/T g	CD	Ind	Ind	24	BBCC	Ind	
Sociology and Theatre Studies	LV3L	3FT deg	Me/T g	CD	MO	M	24	Ind	Ind	
Univ of BRIGHTON										
History of Decorative Arts and Crafts	V451	3FT deg	*	CC	Ind	Ind	Ind	Ind	Ind	
History of Design	V480	3FT deg	*	CC	Ind	Ind	Ind	Ind	Ind	
Visual Culture	V400	3FT deg	*	18	Ind	Ind	Ind	Ind	Ind	
Univ of BRISTOL										
History of Art	V400	3FT deg	* g	BBC	Ind	D$^	30$	BBBBB	Ind	12 22/30
History of Art and French	VR41	4FT deg	F	BBC	Ind	D$^	30$	BBBBB	Ind	5 24/28
History of Art and German	VR42	4FT deg	G	BBC	Ind	D$^	30$	BBBBB	Ind	8
History of Art and Italian	VR43	4FT deg	L	BBC	Ind	D$^	30$	BBBBB	Ind	12
History of Art and Russian	VR48	4FT deg	L	BBC	Ind	D$^	30$	BBBBB	Ind	
History of Art and Spanish	VR44	4FT deg	L	BBC	Ind	D$^	30$	BBBBB	Ind	
Univ of BUCKINGHAM										
English Literature and History of Art	QV34	2FT deg	E g	10	5M	M	24	CCCC	Ind	
History of Art and English Language Studies (EFL	VQ41	2FT deg	* g	10	5M	M	24	CCCC	Ind	
History of Art and Heritage Management	V440	2FT deg	*	12	5M	M	24	CCCC	Ind	9
BUCKINGHAMSHIRE COLLEGE										
English Studies and Visual Arts	QV34	3FT deg		12	2D	M	27	CCCC	Ind	2 6/12
Film and Visual Arts	VW45	3FT deg		12	2D	M	27	CCCC	Ind	
Media and Visual Arts	PV44	3FT deg		12	2D	M	27	CCCC	Ind	
Univ of Wales INST, CARDIFF										
History and Theory of Art and Design	V400	3FT deg	* g	4-6	N	DA^ go	Ind	CCCC	Ind	3 12/22
History and Theory of Art and Design	E400	3FT deg	* g	4-6	N	DA^ go	Ind	CCCC	Ind	
Univ of CENTRAL LANCASHIRE										
History and Theory of Art (year 2 entry)	V400	2FT deg	*		Ind					
Combined Honours Programme *Design History*	Y400	3FT deg	*	12	MO+2D	M$6/^	26	BCCC	Ind	
Combined Honours Programme *History and Theory of Art*	Y400	3FT deg	*	12	MO+2D	M$6/^	26	BCCC	Ind	
COURTAULD INST of Art (Univ of London)										
History of Art	V400	3FT deg		BBC						6 24/30
DE MONTFORT Univ										
History of Art and Design in the Modern Period	V480▼	3FT deg	* g	CDE-DDD	MO	M$^	26$	ABBB	Ind	3 6/18
Humanities Combined Honours *History of Art and Design*	Y300▼	3FT deg	* g	CCD	MO	M$^	26$			
Humanities Joint Honours *History of Art and Design*	Y301▼	3FT deg	* g	CCD	MO	M$^	26$	BBBB	Ind	

course details			98 expected requirements							96 entry stats	
TITLE	CODE	COURSE	SUBJECTS	A/AS	ND/C	AGNVQ	IB	SQA(H)	SQA	RATIO A/AS	
Univ of DERBY											
Visual Culture (Hist and Theory of Art and Des)	V400	3FT deg	*	16	Ind	Ind	Ind	BBCC	Ind	27	
Credit Accumulation Modular Scheme *History of Art and Photography*	Y600	3FT deg	*	12	MO	M	Ind	CCCC	Ind		
Credit Accumulation Modular Scheme *History of Design*	Y600	3FT deg	*	12	MO	M	Ind	CCCC	Ind		
Univ of EAST ANGLIA											
History of Art and Architecture	V440	3FT deg	*	BBC-BCC	Ind		30	BBBBB	Ind	3	14/26
History of Art and European Literature (3 Yrs)	VR43	3FT deg	L	BCC	X		30	BBBBB	X	3	12/24
History of Art and European Literature (4 Yrs)	VT49	4FT deg	L	BBC	X		29$	Ind	X	5	
History of Art and History	VV14	3FT deg	H	BBC-BCC	X		30	BBBBB	X	7	
Anthropology, Archaeology and Art History *Art History*	Y400	3FT deg	*	BBC	Ind		Ind	BBBBB	Ind		
Univ of EAST LONDON											
Business Studies and Hist of Art Design & Film	NV14	3FT deg	*g	12	MO	M$	Ind	Ind	Ind		
Business Studies with Hist of Art Design & Film	N1V4	3FT deg	*g	14	MO	MB					
Communication Studies and Hist of Art Des & Film	PV34	3FT deg	*g	12	MO	M$	Ind	Ind	Ind	1	
Communication Studies with Hist of Art Des&Film	P3V4	3FT deg	*g	12	MO	M	Ind	Ind			
Cultural Studies and Hist of Art Design & Film	LVP4	3FT deg	*g	14	MO	M				3	
Cultural Studies with Hist of Art Design & Film	L6V4	3FT deg	*g	12	MO	M	Ind	Ind	Ind		
Design - Visual Communic & Hist of Art Des &Film	VW42	3FT deg	*g	12	MO	M$	Ind	Ind	Ind		
Design - Visual Communic w. Hist of Art Des&Film	W2V4	3FT deg	*g	12	MO	M	Ind	Ind	Ind		
Educ & Commun St & History of Art Design & Film	XV94	3FT deg	*g	12	MO	M					
Educ & Commun St w. History of Art Design & Film	X9V4	3FT deg	*g	12	MO	M					
French and History of Art Design & Film	RV14	3FT deg	*g	12	MO	M$	Ind	Ind	Ind	2	
French with History of Art Design & Film	R1V4	3FT deg	*g	12	MO	M	Ind				
German and History of Art Design & Film	RV24	3FT deg	*g	12	MO	M$	Ind	Ind	Ind		
German with History of Art Design & Film	R2V4	3FT deg	*g	12	MO	M	Ind				
Hist of Art, Design & Film/Fash, Des & Marketing	JVK4	3FT deg	*g	12	MO	M	Ind	Ind	Ind		
History and History of Art Design & Film	VV14	3FT deg	*g	12	MO	M$	Ind	Ind	Ind		
History of Art Design & Film and IT	GV54	3FT deg	*g	12	MO	M$	Ind	Ind	Ind		
History of Art Design & Film and Literature	QV34	3FT deg	*g	12	MO	X	Ind	Ind	Ind	3	
History of Art Design & Film and Media Studies	PV4K	3FT deg	*g	12	MO	M					
History of Art Design & Film and Psychosocial St	LV74	3FT deg	*g	12	MO	M$	Ind	Ind	Ind		
History of Art Design & Film and Spanish	RV44	3FT deg	*g	12	MO	M^	Ind	Ind	Ind		
History of Art Design & Film and Women's Studies	MV94	3FT deg	*g	12	MO	M	Ind	Ind	Ind		
History of Art Design & Film w. Design-Text. Des	V4J4	3FT deg	*g	12	MO	M	Ind	Ind	Ind		
History of Art Design & Film w. Educ & Commun St	V4X9	3FT deg	*g	12	MO	M	Ind	Ind	Ind		
History of Art Design & Film w. Fashion Des&Mktg	V4JK	3FT deg	*g	12	MO	M	Ind	Ind			
History of Art Design & Film w. Psychosocial St	V4L7	3FT deg	*g	12	MO	M	Ind	Ind			
History of Art Design & Film w.Design-Vis Commun	V4W2	3FT deg	*g	12	MO	M	Ind	Ind			
History of Art Design & Film with Business St	V4N1	3FT deg	*g	12	MO	M	Ind	Ind			
History of Art Design & Film with Comm Studies	V4P3	3FT deg	*g	12	MO	M	Ind	Ind			
History of Art Design & Film with Cultural St	V4L6	3FT deg	*g	12	MO	M	Ind	Ind			
History of Art Design & Film with French	V4R1	3FT deg	*g	12	MO	M	Ind	Ind			
History of Art Design & Film with German	V4R2	3FT deg	*g	12	MO	M	Ind	Ind			
History of Art Design & Film with History	V4V1	3FT deg	*g	12	MO	M	Ind	Ind			
History of Art Design & Film with IT	V4G5	3FT deg	*g	12	MO	M	Ind	Ind			
History of Art Design & Film with Italian	V4R3	3FT deg	*g	12	MO	M	Ind	Ind			
History of Art Design & Film with Literature	V4Q3	3FT deg	*g	12	MO	M	Ind	Ind			
History of Art Design & Film with Media Studies	V4P4	3FT deg	*g	12	MO	M	Ind	Ind			
History of Art Design & Film with Spanish	V4R4	3FT deg	*g	12	MO	M	Ind	Ind			

			98 expected requirements							96 entry stats	
TITLE	CODE	COURSE	SUBJECTS	A/AS	NO/C	RGNVQ	IB	SQA(H)	SQA	RATIO	A/AS
History of Art Design & Film with Women's St	V4M9	3FT deg	*g	12	MO	M	Ind	Ind			
History of Art, Design & Film	V400	3FT deg	*g	12	MO	M$	Ind	Ind	Ind	4	6/20
History with History of Art Design & Film	V1V4	3FT deg	*g	12	MO	M	Ind	Ind			
Information Technology w. Hist of Art Des & Film	G5V4	3FT deg	*g	12	MO	M	Ind	Ind	Ind		
Literature with History of Art Design & Film	Q3V4	3FT deg	*g	12	MO	M	Ind				
Media Studies with History of Art Design & Film	P4V4	3FT deg	*g	14	MO	M					
Psychosocial Studies with Hist of Art Des & Film	L7V4	3FT deg	*g	12	MO	M	Ind	Ind	Ind		
Spanish with History of Art Design & Film	R4V4	3FT deg	*g	12	MO	M	Ind				
Women's Studies with History of Art Des & Film	M9VK	3FT deg	*g	12	MO	M	Ind				
Three-Subject Degree *History of Art, Design & Film*	Y600	3FT deg	*g	12	MO	M	Ind	Ind	Ind		

Univ of EDINBURGH

TITLE	CODE	COURSE	SUBJECTS	A/AS	NO/C	RGNVQ	IB	SQA(H)	SQA	RATIO	A/AS
Arabic and History of Art	TV64	4FT deg	g	BBB	Ind	Ind	Dip$	BBBB	Ind		
Architectural History	VV41	4FT deg	*	BBB	Ind		34$	ABBB	Ind	3	
French and History of Art	RV14	4FT deg	F g	BBB	Ind	Ind	Dip$	BBBB$	Ind		
German and History of Art	RV24	4FT deg	L g	BBB	Ind	Ind	Dip$	BBBB$	Ind		
History and History of Art	VV14	4FT deg	g	BBB	Ind	Ind	Dip$	BBBB	Ind		
History of Art	V400	4FT deg	g	BBB	Ind	Ind	Dip$	BBBB	Ind		
History of Art and Arabic	VT46	4FT deg	g	BBB	Ind	Ind	Dip$	BBBB	Ind		
History of Art and Chinese Studies	TV3L	4FT deg	L g	BBB	Ind	Ind	Dip$	BBBB$	Ind		
History of Art and English Literature	VQ43	4FT deg	E g	AAB	Ind	Ind	Dip$	ABBB$	Ind		
History of Art and French	VR41	4FT deg	F g	BBB	Ind	Ind	Dip$	BBBB$	Ind		
History of Art and German	VR42	4FT deg	L g	BBB	Ind	Ind	Dip$	BBBB$	Ind		
History of Art and History of Music	VW43	4FT deg	Mu g	BBB	Ind	Ind	Dip$	BBBB$	Ind		
History of Art and Italian	VR43	4FT deg	L g	BBB	Ind	Ind	Dip$	BBBB$	Ind		
History of Art and Spanish	VR44	4FT deg	L g	BBB	Ind	Ind	Dip$	BBBB$	Ind		
Italian and History of Art	RV34	4FT deg	L g	BBB	Ind	Ind	Dip$	BBBB$	Ind		
Social and Architectural History	VV34	4FT deg	*	BBB	Ind		34$	ABBB	Ind	2	
Spanish and History of Art	RV44	4FT deg	L g	BBB	Ind	Ind	Dip$	BBBB$	Ind		

Univ of ESSEX

TITLE	CODE	COURSE	SUBJECTS	A/AS	NO/C	RGNVQ	IB	SQA(H)	SQA	RATIO	A/AS
History of Art	V414	3FT deg	*	20	MO+2D	Ind	28	BBBB	Ind	5	10/22
History of Art and Modern Languages	TV94	3FT deg									
History of Art and Music	VW43	3FT deg	*	20	MO+2D	Ind	28	BBBB	Ind	1	
Literature and History of Art	QV24	3FT deg	*	20	MO+2D	Ind	28	BBBB	Ind	6	
Philosophy and History of Art	VV74	3FT deg	*	20	MO+2D	Ind	28	BBBB	Ind	6	
Sociology and History of Art	LV34	3FT deg	*	20	MO+2D	Ind	28	BBBB	Ind		
Spanish (Lang & Linguistics) & History of Art	RV44	4FT deg	*	20	MO+2D	Ind	28	BBBB	Ind	5	

FALMOUTH COLLEGE of Arts

TITLE	CODE	COURSE	SUBJECTS	A/AS	NO/C	RGNVQ	IB	SQA(H)	SQA	RATIO	A/AS
Visual Culture	V480	3FT deg	*	CC	N		24	CC	N	3	8/20

Univ of GLAMORGAN

TITLE	CODE	COURSE	SUBJECTS	A/AS	NO/C	RGNVQ	IB	SQA(H)	SQA	RATIO	A/AS
Visual Arts with Art History	W1V4	3FT deg	A g	12	5M	M	Ind	Ind	Ind		
Combined Studies (Honours) *Art History*	Y400	3FT deg	*g	8-16	Ind	Ind	Ind	Ind	Ind		

Univ of GLASGOW

TITLE	CODE	COURSE	SUBJECTS	A/AS	NO/C	RGNVQ	IB	SQA(H)	SQA	RATIO	A/AS
Archaeology/History of Art	VV46	4FT deg		BBC	HN	M	30	BBBB	Ind	16	
Celtic/History of Art	QVN4	4FT deg		BBC	HN	M	30	BBBB	Ind		
Classical Hebrew/History of Art	VV4W	4FT deg		BBC	HN	M	30	BBBB	Ind		
Computing/History of Art	GV54	4FT deg		BBC	HN	M	30	BBBB	Ind		
Czech/History of Art	TVC4	5FT deg		BBC	HN	M	30	BBBB	Ind		
English/History of Art	QV34	4FT deg		BBC	HN	M	30	BBBB	Ind	6	
Film and Television Studies/History of Art	VW45	4FT deg		BBB	HN	D	32	AABB	HN	47	

History of Art 34

TITLE	CODE	COURSE	SUBJECTS	A/AS	ND/C	RGNVQ	IB	SQA(H)	SQA	RATIO A/AS
French/History of Art	RV14	5FT deg		BBC	HN	M	30	BBBB	Ind	12
Geography/History of Art	LV84	4FT deg		BBC	HN	M	30	BBBB	Ind	
German/History of Art	RV24	5FT deg		BBC	HN	M	30	BBBB	Ind	
Greek/History of Art	QV74	4FT deg		BBC	HN	M	30	BBBB	Ind	
History of Art	V400	4FT deg		BBC	HN	M	30	BBBB	Ind	9
History of Art/Economics	LV14	4FT deg		BBC	HN	M	30	BBBB	Ind	
History of Art/Italian	RV34	5FT deg		BBC	HN	M	30	BBBB	Ind	14
History of Art/Latin	QV64	4FT deg		BBC	HN	M	30	BBBB	Ind	
History of Art/Mathematics	GV14	4FT deg		BBC	HN	M	30	BBBB	Ind	
History of Art/Music	VW43	4FT deg		BBC	HN	M	30	BBBB	Ind	5
History of Art/Philosophy	VV47	4FT deg		BBC	HN	M	30	BBBB	Ind	14
History of Art/Polish	TV14	5FT deg		BBC	HN	M	30	BBBB	Ind	
History of Art/Politics	MV14	4FT deg		BBC	HN	M	30	BBBB	Ind	
History of Art/Psychology	CV84	4FT deg		BBC	HN	M	30	BBBB	Ind	4
History of Art/Russian	RV84	5FT deg		BBC	HN	M	30	BBBB	Ind	
History of Art/Scottish History	VVC4	4FT deg		BBC	HN	M	30	BBBB	Ind	5
History of Art/Scottish Literature	QV24	4FT deg		BBC	HN	M	30	BBBB	Ind	5
History of Art/Sociology	LV34	4FT deg		BBC	HN	M	30	BBBB	Ind	
History/History of Art	VV14	4FT deg		BBC	HN	M	30	BBBB	Ind	11
Islamic Studies/History of Art	TV64	3FT deg		BBC	N	M	30	BBBB	Ind	
Management Studies/History of Art	NV14	4FT deg		BBC	HN	M	30	BBBB	Ind	
Social and Urban Policy/History of Art	LV44	4FT deg		BBC	HN	M	30	BBBB	Ind	
Theatre Studies/History of Art	VW44	4FT deg		BBC	HN	M	30	BBBB	Ind	6
Theology & Religious Studies/History of Art	VV4V	4FT deg		BBC	HN	M	30	BBBB	Ind	

GOLDSMITHS COLL (Univ of London)

TITLE	CODE	COURSE	SUBJECTS	A/AS	ND/C	RGNVQ	IB	SQA(H)	SQA	RATIO A/AS
Art (Studio Practice) and History of Art	VW41	3FT deg	Fa+Pf	BC	MO	M	Dip	BCCCC	N	12 20/30
Art History	V400	3FT deg		BCC	MO	M	Dip	BBBBC	N	
Art(Studio Prac)& Hist of Art-For O'seas Student	WV14	4EXT deg	Pf							5
English and History of Art	QV34	3FT deg	E	BCC	MO	M	Dip	BBBBC	N	6 10/30
History and History of Art	VV14	3FT deg	H	BCC	MO	M	Dip	BBBCC	N	4 18/26

Univ of HERTFORDSHIRE

TITLE	CODE	COURSE	SUBJECTS	A/AS	ND/C	RGNVQ	IB	SQA(H)	SQA	RATIO A/AS
Histories of Art and Visual Culture	WV14	3FT deg	Fa/Ap g	10	X	Ind	Ind	Ind	Ind	
Histories of Art and Visual Culture	EV14	3FT deg	Fa/Ap g	10	X	Ind	Ind	Ind	Ind	

Univ of KENT

TITLE	CODE	COURSE	SUBJECTS	A/AS	ND/C	RGNVQ	IB	SQA(H)	SQA	RATIO A/AS
European Arts (History & Theory of Art)	V490	3FT deg		26	6D	Ind	34	Ind	Ind	
Hist & Theory of Art/English (Post Colonial Lit)	VQ4J	3FT deg	E	22	2M+4D	Ind	30	Ind	Ind	
History & Theory of Art/Comparative Literary St	VQ42	3FT deg	*	20	3M+3D	Ind	28	Ind	Ind	3
History and Theory of Art	V400	3FT deg		22	2M+4D	Ind	30	Ind	Ind	3
History and Theory of Art/Classical Studies	VQ48	3FT deg	*	20	3M+3D	Ind	28	Ind	Ind	12
History and Theory of Art/Computing	VG45	3FT deg	*	20	3M+3D	Ind	28	Ind	Ind	1
History and Theory of Art/Drama	VW44	3FT deg	*	22	2M+4D	Ind	30	Ind	Ind	9
History and Theory of Art/English	VQ43	3FT deg	E	22	2M+4D	Ind	30	Ind	Ind	7
History and Theory of Art/English Language	VQ4H	3FT deg	E	20	3M+3D	Ind	28	Ind	Ind	4
History and Theory of Art/Film Studies	VW45	3FT deg	*	22	2M+4D	Ind	30	Ind	Ind	
History and Theory of Art/French	VR41	4FT deg	F	22	2M+4D	Ind	30	Ind	Ind	
History and Theory of Art/German	VR42	4FT deg	G	20	3M+3D	Ind	28	Ind	Ind	
History and Theory of Art/History	VV41	3FT deg	*	22	2M+4D	Ind	30	Ind	Ind	14
Italian/History and Theory of Art	VR43	4FT deg	*	22	2M+4D	Ind	30	Ind	Ind	6
Linguistics/History and Theory of Art	VQ41	3FT deg	*	20	3M+3D	Ind	28	Ind	Ind	
Philosophy/History and Theory of Art	VV47	3FT deg	*	22	4M+2D	Ind	30	Ind	Ind	15
Spanish/History and Theory of Art	VR44	4FT deg	*	20	3M+2D	Ind	28	Ind	Ind	
Theology/History and Theory of Art	VV48	3FT deg	*	20	2M+4D	Ind	28	Ind	Ind	

			98 expected requirements							96 entry stats
course details										
TITLE	CODE	COURSE	SUBJECTS	A/AS	ND/C	AGNVQ	IB	SQA(H)	SQA	RATIO A/AS
KINGSTON Univ										
History of Art, Architecture and Design	V440	3FT deg	* g	16	HN	Ind^	Ind	BBCCC	HN	1	8/18
History of Art, Architecture and Design/Eng Lang	VQ43	3FT deg	E g	16	MO	Ind^	Ind	BBCCC	HN	
History of Art, Architecture and Design/Eng Lit	VQ4H	3FT deg	E g	18	MO	Ind^	Ind	BBBCC	HN	
History of Art, Architecture and Design/French	VR41	3FT deg	F g	14-16	MO	Ind^	Ind	BBCCC	HN	
History of Art, Architecture and Design/German	VR42	3FT deg	G g	14-16	MO	Ind^	Ind	BBCCC	HN	
History of Art, Architecture and Design/History	VV41	3FT deg	H g	16	MO	Ind^	Ind	BBCCC	HN	
History of Ideas/History of Art, Arch & Design	VV47	3FT deg	* g	16	MO	Ind^	Ind	BBCCC	HN	
Social and Economic Hist/Hist of Art, Des & Arch	VV43	3FT deg	* g	16	MO	Ind^	Ind	BBCCC	HN	
Sociology/History of Art, Architecture & Design	VL43	3FT deg	* g	16	MO	Ind^	Ind	BBCCC	HN	
Spanish/History of Art, Architecture and Design	VR44	3FT deg	Sp g	14-16	MO	Ind^	Ind	BCCCC	HN	
Women's Studies/History of Art, Arch & Design	MV94	3FT deg	* g	16	MO	Ind^	Ind	BBCCC	HN	
Univ of LEEDS										
English-History of Art	QV34	3FT deg	E g	ABB	Ind	Ind	33$	CSYS	Ind	6	24/28
French-History of Art	RV14	4FT deg	F g	BBC	Ind	Ind	30$	CSYS	Ind	7	26/26
German-History of Art	RV24	4FT deg	G g	BBC	Ind	Ind	30$	CSYS	Ind	5	
History and Philosophy of Science-History of Art	VV45	3FT deg	* g	BBC	Ind	Ind	30	CSYS	Ind	
History of Art	V400	3FT deg	* g	BBC	Ind	Ind	30	CSYS	Ind	13	20/30
History of Art-Italian	RVH4	4FT deg	L g	BBC	Ind	Ind	30$	CSYS	Ind	13	
History of Art-Italian	RV34	4FT deg	I g	BBC	Ind	Ind	30$	CSYS	Ind	10	
History of Art-Music	VW43	3FT deg	Mu g	BBC	Ind	Ind	30$	CSYS	Ind	
History of Art-Religious Studies	VV4V	3FT deg	* g	BBC	Ind	Ind	30	CSYS	Ind	
History of Art-Sociology	VL43	3FT deg	g	BBC	Ind	Ind	30	CSYS	Ind	
History of Art-Spanish	RV44	4FT deg	Sp g	BBC	Ind	Ind	30$	CSYS	Ind	6	
History of Art-Theology	VV48	3FT deg	* g	BBC	Ind	Ind	30	CSYS	Ind	7	
History of the Fine and Decorative Arts	V450	4FT deg	* g	BBC	Ind	Ind	30	CSYS	Ind	3	20/26
History-History of Art	VV14	3FT deg	* g	BBB	Ind	Ind	32	CSYS	Ind	12	
Philosophy-History of Art	VV47	3FT deg	* g	BBC	Ind	Ind	30	CSYS	Ind	4	26/28
Univ of LEICESTER										
History of Art	V408	3FT deg	* g	BBC-BCC	Ind	D$^	30	ABBBB	Ind		14/24
Combined Arts *History of Art*	Y300	3FT deg	* g	BCC	DO	D$^	30$	Ind	Ind	
Univ of LIVERPOOL										
Arts Combined *History of Art and Architecture*	Y401	3FT deg	*	BBC-BBB	Ind	Ind	30$	ABBB	Ind	
BA Combined Honours *History of Art*	Y200	3FT deg	* g	BBB	Ind	Ind	Ind	Ind	Ind	
LIVERPOOL JOHN MOORES Univ										
Art History Studies	V490	3FT deg								
Art History Studies and Lit, Life and Thought	QV34	3FT deg	E	12-20	5M+3D	PT^	28$	BBBC	
History of Modern Design	V480	3FT deg								
Visual Studies and Art History Studies	VW41	3FT deg	Pf	12	5M+2D	M$	28$	CCCC	
LONDON INST										
History of Art & Design	V400	3FT deg								3	8/24
LOUGHBOROUGH COLLEGE of A & D										
History of Art and Design with Studio Practice	V480	3FT deg								
LOUGHBOROUGH Univ										
English and the History of Art and Design	QV34	3FT deg	E	BCC			30	Ind		3	20/24

History of Art 34

course details				98 expected requirements						96 entry stats
TITLE	CODE	COURSE	SUBJECTS	A/AS	NO/C	AGNVQ	IB	SQA(H)	SQA	RATIO A/AS
LUTON Univ										
History of Des & Arch & Artificial Intelligence	VG48	3FT deg		12-16	MO/DO	M/D	32	BBCC	Ind	
History of Des & Architecture & Building Conserv	KV24	3FT deg		12-16	MO/DO	M/D	32	BBCC	Ind	
History of Design & Architecture & Contemp Hist	VV4C	3FT deg		12-16	MO/DO	M/D	32	BBCC	Ind	
History of Design & Architecture & Creative Des	WV24	3FT deg		12-16	MO/DO	M/D	32	BBCC	Ind	
History of Design and Architecture	V440	3FT deg		12-16	MO/DO	M/D	32	BBCC	Ind	
History of Design and Architecture and Built Env	VN48	3FT deg		12-16	MO/DO	M/D	32	BBCC	Ind	
Planning St and History of Design & Architecture	VK44	3FT deg		12-16	MO/DO	M/D	32	BBCC	Ind	
Univ of MANCHESTER										
Art and Archaeology of the Ancient World	VW61	3FT deg		BBC	5M		28	BBBCC		8 18/20
History of Art and Architecture	V440	3FT deg		BBC	5M		28	BBBCC		5 20/26
History of Art and a Modern Language (French)	RV14	4FT deg		BBC	3M+3D		28	AABBB		
History of Art and a Modern Language (German)	RV24	4FT deg		BBC	3M+3D		28	AABBB		4
History of Art and a Modern Language (Italian)	RV34	4FT deg		BBC	3M+3D		28	AABBB		7
History of Modern Art	V401	3FT deg		BBC	3M+3D		28	AABBB		5 18/24
MANCHESTER METROPOLITAN Univ										
History of Art and Design	V480	3FT deg	*	18	N	Ind	Ind	Ind	Ind	8/20
History of Film, Photography and Graphic Media	VW45	3FT deg	*	18	N	Ind	Ind	Ind	Ind	6/22
MIDDLESEX Univ										
Visual Culture	V400▼	3FT deg	* g	12-16	5M	M$ go	28	Ind	Ind	
Joint Honours Degree Art & Design History	Y400	3FT deg	* g	12-16	MO	Ind	28	Ind	Ind	
Joint Honours Degree Pastoral Studies	Y400	3FT deg	* g	12-16	5M	Ind	28	BBCC	Ind	
NENE COLLEGE										
American Studies with Architectural Studies	Q4V4	3FT deg		DD	5M	M	24	CCC	Ind	
American Studies with History of Art	Q4VK	3FT deg		DD	5M	M	24	CCC	Ind	
Art and Design with Architectural Studies	W2V4	3FT deg		DD	5M	M	24	CCC	Ind	
Art and Design with History of Art	W2VK	3FT deg		DD	5M	M	24	CCC	Ind	
Business Administration with Architectural St	N1V4	3FT deg	g	10	M+1D	M	24	BCC	Ind	
Economics with Architectural Studies	L1V4	3FT deg	g	6	5M	M	24	CCC	Ind	
Energy Management with Architectural Studies	J9V4	3FT deg	g	EE	3M	P	24	CCC	Ind	
English with History of Art	Q3VK▼	3FT deg		CC	4M+1D	M	24	CCC	Ind	
French with Architectural Studies	R1V4	3FT deg	F	DD	5M	Ind	24	CCC	Ind	
French with History of Art	R1VK	3FT deg	F	DD	5M	Ind	24	CCC	Ind	
History with Architectural Studies	V1V4▼	3FT deg		CD	5M	M	24	CCC	Ind	
History with History of Art	V1VK▼	3FT deg		CD	5M	M	24	CCC	Ind	
Industrial Archaeology with Architectural St	V6V4	3FT deg		10	5M	M	24	CCC	Ind	
Information Systems with Architectural Studies	G5V4	3FT deg		6	5M	M	24	CCC	Ind	
Mathematics with Architectural Studies	G1V4	3FT deg	M	DD	Ind	Ind	24	CCC	Ind	
Music with Architectural Studies	W3V4	3FT deg	Mu	DD	5M	M	24	CCC	Ind	
Music with History of Art	W3VK	3FT deg	Mu	DD	5M	M	24	CCC	Ind	
Univ of NEWCASTLE										
Combined Studies (BA) History of Art	Y400	3FT deg	*	ABC-BBB	5D	Ind	35$	AAAB	Ind	
NORWICH School of A & D										
Cultural Studies	EV94	3FT deg	*	4	Ind		Ind	Ind	Ind	
Cultural Studies	WV94	3FT deg	*	4	Ind		Ind	Ind	Ind	8/22

course details			**98 expected requirements**							**96 entry stats**	
TITLE	CODE	COURSE	SUBJECTS	A/AS	ND/C	ADGNVQ	IB	SQA(H)	SQA	RATIO	A/AS
Univ of NOTTINGHAM											
Art History	V400	3FT deg	L g	BBC						11	22/28
Art History and English Studies	QV34	3FT deg	E	BBC						25	26/28
Art History and German	RV24	4FT deg	G	BBC							
OXFORD BROOKES Univ											
Geography and the Phys Env/History of Art	FVV4	3FT deg									
History of Art	V400	3FT deg									
History of Art/Accounting and Finance	NV44	3FT deg	* g	BCC	Ind	M^/D*3	Ind	Ind	Ind		
History of Art/Anthropology	LV64	3FT deg	*	BCC	Ind	M*^	Ind	Ind	Ind	7	16/20
History of Art/Biological Chemistry	CV74	3FT deg									
History of Art/Business Administration & Mgt	NV14	3FT deg	* g	BCC-BBC	Ind	M^/MB4	Ind	Ind	Ind	8	
History of Art/Cartography	FV84	3FT deg	* g	DDD-BCC	Ind	M*^	Ind	Ind	Ind		
History of Art/Cell Biology	CVC4	3FT deg									
History of Art/Combined Studies	VY44	3FT deg		X		X	X	X			
History of Art/Computer Systems	GV64	3FT deg	* g	CDD-BCC	Ind	M*^	Ind	Ind	Ind		
History of Art/Computing	GV54	3FT deg	* g	CDD-BCC	Ind	M*^	Ind	Ind	Ind		
History of Art/Economics	LV14	3FT deg	* g	BB-CCD	Ind	M*^/3	Ind	Ind	Ind		
History of Art/Educational Studies	VX49	3FT deg	*	CC-BCC	Ind	M*^/3	Ind	Ind	Ind		
History of Art/Electronics	HV64	3FT deg	S/M	CC-BCC	Ind	M$/M^	Ind	Ind	Ind		
History of Art/English Studies	QV34	3FT deg	*	AB-BCC	Ind	M*^	Ind	Ind	Ind	4	10/22
History of Art/Environmental Chemistry	VF41	3FT deg									
History of Art/Environmental Policy	KV34	3FT deg									
History of Art/Environmental Sciences	FVX4	3FT deg	S g	CD-BCC	Ind	M*^/DS	Ind	Ind	Ind		
History of Art/Exercise and Health	VB46	3FT deg	S g	DD-BCC	Ind	MS/M*^	Ind	Ind	Ind		
History of Art/Fine Art	VW41	3FT deg	Pf+A	BC-BCC	Ind	MA^	Ind	Ind	Ind	9	18/24
History of Art/Food Science and Nutrition	DV44	3FT deg	S g	DD-BCC	Ind	MS/M*^	Ind	Ind	Ind	1	
History of Art/French Language and Contemp Studs	RVC4	4SW deg	F	CDD-BCC	Ind	M*^	Ind	Ind	Ind		
History of Art/French Language and Literature	RV14	4SW deg	F	CDD-BCC	Ind	M*^	Ind	Ind	Ind		
History of Art/Geography	LV84	3FT deg	*	BB-CCD	Ind	M*^	Ind	Ind	Ind		
History of Art/Geology	FV64	3FT deg	S/M g	DD-BCC	Ind	M*^/PS	Ind	Ind	Ind		
History of Art/Geotechnics	HV24	3FT deg	S/M/Ds/Es	DD-BCC	Ind	M$/M*^	Ind	Ind	Ind		
History of Art/German Language and Contemp Stud	RVF4	4SW deg	G	DDD-BCC	Ind	M*^	Ind	Ind	Ind		
History of Art/German Language and Literature	RV24	4SW deg	G	DDD-BCC	Ind	M*^	Ind	Ind	Ind		
History of Art/German Studies	VR4G	4SW deg	G	BCC-CD	Ind	M*^	Ind	Ind	Ind		
History of Art/Health Care (Post Exp)	BV74	3FT deg		X		X	X	X			
History of Art/History	VV14	3FT deg	*	BB-CCD	Ind	M*^	Ind	Ind	Ind	7	16/18
Hospitality Management Studies/History of Art	NV74	3FT deg	*	DDD-BCC	Ind	M*/M*3	Ind	Ind	Ind	6	
Human Biology/History of Art	BV14	3FT deg									
Information Systems/History of Art	GVN4	3FT deg	* g	CDD-BCC	Ind	M^	Ind	Ind	Ind		
Intelligent Systems/History of Art	GV84	3FT deg	* g	BCC-CD	Ind	M^	Ind	Ind	Ind		
Leisure Planning/History of Art	KVH4	3FT deg									
Marketing Management/History of Art	NVN4	3FT deg	* g	BB-BCC	Ind	M^/D*3	Ind	Ind	Ind	2	14/20
Mathematics/History of Art	GV14	3FT deg	M	DD-BCC	Ind	M*^	Ind	Ind	Ind		
Music/History of Art	VW43	3FT deg	Mu	DD-BCC	Ind	M^	Ind	Ind	Ind	3	
Palliative Care/History of Art (Post Exp)	BVR4	3FT deg		X		X	X	X			
Planning Studies/History of Art	KV44	3FT deg	* g	DDD-BCC	Ind	M*^	Ind	Ind	Ind		
Psychology/History of Art	CV84	3FT deg	* g	BCC-BBC	Ind	M*^	Ind	Ind	Ind	6	
Publishing/History of Art	PV54	3FT deg	* g	BB-CCD	Ind	M^/M$3	Ind	Ind	Ind	5	
Rehabilitation/History of Art (Post Exp)	BVT4	3FT deg		X		X	X	X			
Sociology/History of Art	LV34	3FT deg	*	BCC	Ind	M*^	Ind	Ind	Ind	2	18/20
Software Engineering/History of Art	GV74	3FT deg	* g	CDD-BCC	Ind	M*^	Ind	Ind	Ind		
Statistics/History of Art	GV44	3FT deg	* g	DD-BCC	Ind	M*^	Ind	Ind	Ind		

			98 expected requirements							96 entry stats
course details										
TITLE	CODE	COURSE	SUBJECTS	A/AS	NO/C	RGNVQ	IB	SQA(H)	SQA	RATIO A/AS
Telecommunications/History of Art	HVP4	3FT deg								
Tourism/History of Art	PV74	3FT deg	* g	BCC-CCD	Ind	M^/M*3	Ind	Ind	Ind	6
Water Resources/History of Art	HVF4	3FT deg								
OXFORDSHIRE SCHOOL of A & D										
Fine Art and History of Art and Design	VW41	3FT deg	Fa+Pf	8	N	MA6 gi	Ind	Ind	Ind	
Fine Art and History of Art and Design	EW41	3FT deg	Fa+Pf	8	N	MA6 gi	Ind	Ind	Ind	
Univ of PLYMOUTH										
Art Hist with Cultural Interpretation & Practice	V4Y3	3FT deg	Ap g	CCD	MO+3D	D$^	Ind	Ind	Ind	
Art History with Education Studies	V4X9	3FT deg	Ap g	CCD	MO+3D	D$^	Ind	Ind	Ind	
Art History with English	V4Q3	3FT deg	Ap g	CCD	MO+3D	D$^	Ind	Ind	Ind	7
Art History with Heritage and Landscape	V4WF	3FT deg	Ap g	CCD	MO+3D	D$^	Ind	Ind	Ind	4
Art History with History	V4V1	3FT deg	Ap g	CCD	MO+3D	D$^	Ind	Ind	Ind	9
Art History with Media Arts	V4WG	3FT deg	Ap g	CCD	MO+3D	D$^	Ind	Ind	Ind	15
Art History with Music	V4W3	3FT deg	Ap g	CCD	MO+3D	D$^	Ind	Ind	Ind	
Art History with Theatre & Performance Studies	V4W4	3FT deg	Ap g	CCD	MO+3D	D$^	Ind	Ind	Ind	6
Art History with Visual Arts	V4W2	3FT deg	Ap g	CCD	MO+3D	D$^	Ind	Ind	Ind	5
Cultural Interpretation & Practice with Art Hist	Y3V4	3FT deg	Ap g	CCD	MO+3D	D$^	Ind	Ind	Ind	
English with Art History	Q3V4	3FT deg	Ap g	BBC	MO+3D	D$_^	Ind	Ind	Ind	5 16/22
Heritage and Landscape with Art History	W2VL	3FT deg	Ap g	CCD	MO+3D	D$^	Ind	Ind	Ind	3
History with Art History	V1V4	3FT deg	Ap g	CCD	MO+3D	D$_^	Ind	Ind	Ind	7
Media Arts with Art History	W2VK	3FT deg	Ap g	CCD	MO+3D	D$_^	Ind	Ind	Ind	7
Theatre & Performance Studs with Art History	W4V4	3FT deg	Ap g	CCD	MO+3D	D$_^	Ind	Ind	Ind	6
Visual Arts with Art History	W2V4	3FT deg	Ap g	CCD	MO+3D	D$_^	Ind	Ind	Ind	3
Univ of READING										
Archaeology and History of Art	VV64	3FT deg	*	BBC	Ind	D$6/^	31	BBBB	Ind	13
Art and History of Art	VW41	4FT deg	*	BBC	Ind	DA^	31	BBBB	Ind	20
Art and History of Art	EV14	4FT deg	*	BBC	Ind	DA^	31	BBBB	Ind	
Classical Studies and History of Art	QV84	3FT deg	*	BBC	Ind	D$6/^	31	BBBB	Ind	3
English Literature and History of Art	QV34	3FT deg	El	BBC	Ind	D$_^	31$	BBBB$	Ind	25
French and History of Art	RV14	4FT deg	F	BBC	Ind	D$_^	31$	BBBB$	Ind	7
German and History of Art	RV24	4FT deg	* g	BBC	Ind	DP^	31	BBBB	Ind	
History and History of Art	VV14	3FT deg	*	BBC	Ind	D$6/^	31	BBBB	Ind	15
History of Art and Architecture	V440	3FT deg	*	BBC	Ind	D$6/^ go	31	BBBB	Ind	3 8/26
Italian and History of Art	RV34	4FT deg	* g	BBC	Ind	D$6/^ go	31	BBBB	Ind	7
Music and History of Art	VW43	3FT deg	Mu	BBD	X	D*_^	30$	BBBB$	Ind	5
SOAS:Sch of Oriental & African St (U of London)										
History of Art (Asia,Africa,Europe)	V400	3FT deg		20	Ind		30	BBBCC	Ind	59
SHEFFIELD HALLAM Univ										
History of Art, Design and Film	V400	3FT deg	E/H/Ha	16	3M+1D	P^	Ind	Ind	Ind	
Combined Studies	Y400	3FT deg	*	18	2M	M	Ind	Ind	Ind	
History of Art, Design and Film										
Univ of SOUTHAMPTON										
History of Art (includes studio element)	V400▼	3FT deg								
Univ of ST ANDREWS										
Art History	V400	4FT deg	* g	BBC	X	Ind	30$	BBBB	Ind	5
Art History-Ancient History	VVD4	4FT deg	* g	BBB	X	Ind	30$	BBBB	Ind	
Art History-Arabic	TV64	4FT deg	* g	BBB	X	Ind	30$	BBBB	Ind	
Classical Studies-Art History	QV84	4FT deg	* g	BBC	X	Ind	30$	BBBB	Ind	3
English-Art History	QV34	4FT deg	* g	BBB	X	Ind	30$	BBBB	Ind	3 24/30

course details				98 expected requirements						96 entry stats

TITLE	CODE	COURSE	SUBJECTS	A/AS	NO/C	AGNVQ	IB	SQA(H)	SQA	RATIO A/AS
French with Year Abroad-Art History	RV1K	4FT/5FT deg	F g	BBB	X	Ind	30$	BBBB$	Ind	5
French-Art History	RV14	4FT deg	F g	BBB	X	Ind	30$	BBBB$	Ind	6
Geography-Art History	LV84	4FT deg	* g	BBB	X	Ind	32$	BBBB	Ind	
German with Year Abroad-Art History	RV2K	4FT/5FT deg	* g	BBC	X	Ind	30$	BBBB	Ind	
German-Art History	RV24	4FT deg	* g	BBC	X	Ind	30$	BBBB	Ind	
Hebrew-Art History	QV94	4FT deg	* g	BBC	X	Ind	30$	BBBB	Ind	
International Relations-Art History	MV14	4FT deg	* g	AAB	X	Ind	36$	AAAB	Ind	
Italian with Year Abroad-Art History	RV3K	4FT/5FT deg	* g	BBB	X	Ind	30$	BBBB	Ind	
Italian-Art History	RV34	4FT deg	* g	BBB	X	Ind	30$	BBBB	Ind	3
Mathematics-Art History	GV14	4FT deg	M g	BBB	X	Ind	30$	BBBB$	Ind	
Mediaeval History-Art History	VV1K	4FT deg	* g	BBB	X	Ind	30$	BBBB	Ind	
Modern History-Art History	VV1L	4FT deg	* g	BBB	X	Ind	30$	BBBB	Ind	8
Philosophy-Art History	VV47	4FT deg	* g	BBB	X	Ind	30$	BBBB	Ind	10
Psychology-Art History	LV74	4FT deg	* g	ABB	X	Ind	32$	BBBBB	Ind	
Russian with Year Abroad-Art History	RV8K	4FT/5FT deg	* g	BBC	X	Ind	30$	BBBB	Ind	
Russian-Art History	RV84	4FT deg	* g	BBC	X	Ind	30$	BBBB	Ind	
Social Anthropology-Art History	LV64	4FT deg	* g	BBB	X	Ind	30$	BBBB	Ind	5
Spanish with Year Abroad-Art History	RV4K	4FT/5FT deg	* g	BBB	X	Ind	30$	BBBB	Ind	
Spanish-Art History	RV44	4FT deg	* g	BBB	X	Ind	30$	BBBB	Ind	
Spanish-Scottish History	RV1L	4FT deg	* g	BBB	X	Ind	30$	BBBB	Ind	
General Degree of MA Art History	Y450	3FT deg	* g	BBB	X	Ind	30$	BBBB	Ind	

STAFFORDSHIRE Univ

TITLE	CODE	COURSE	SUBJECTS	A/AS	NO/C	AGNVQ	IB	SQA(H)	SQA	RATIO A/AS
European Culture/History of Art and Design	LVP4	3FT deg	g	CD	MO+2D	M	27	BBC	Ind	
History of Art and Design	V460	3FT deg	g	CD	MO+2D	M	27	BBC	Ind	3 6/16
History of Art and Design/American Studies	VQ44	3FT deg	g	CD	MO+2D	M	27	BBC	Ind	
History of Art and Design/Cultural Studies	VL46	3FT deg	g	CD	MO+2D	M	27	BBC	Ind	4
History of Art and Design/Development Studies	VM4Y	3FT deg	g	12	MO+2D	M	27	BBC	Ind	
History of Art and Design/Geography	VL48	3FT deg	g	16	MO+2D	M	28	AAB	Ind	
History of Art and Design/German	VR42	3FT/4SW deg	G	CD	MO+2D	M^	27	BBC	Ind	
History of Art and Design/History	VV41	3FT deg	H g	CD	MO+2D	M	27	BBC	Ind	2
Information Systems/History of Art and Design	GV54	3FT deg	g	12	Ind	M	27	BBB	Ind	
International Relations/History of Art & Design	MV1K	3FT deg	g	12	MO+2D	M	27	BBC	Ind	
Law/History of Art and Design	MV34	3FT deg	g	CCC	HN	M^	27	BBBB	Ind	
Legal Studies/History of Art and Design	MV3K	3FT deg	g	CCC	HN	M^	27	BBBB	Ind	
Literature/History of Art and Design	QV34	3FT deg	El g	CD	MO+2D	M	27	BBC	Ind	4
Media Studies/History of Art and Design	PV44	3FT deg	g	CD	MO+2D	M	27	BBC	Ind	2
Philosophy/History of Art and Design	VV74	3FT deg	g	CD	MO+2D	M	27	BBC	Ind	1
Politics/History of Art and Design	MVC4	3FT deg	g	12	MO+2D	M	27	BBC	Ind	
Psychology/History of Art and Design	LV74	3FT deg	g	18	3M+3D	Ind	27	BBB	Ind	
Spanish/History of Art and Design	RV44	3FT/4SW deg	g	CD	MO+2D	M^	27	BBC	Ind	2
Women's Studies/History of Art & Design	MV94	3FT deg	g	12	MO+2D	M	27	BBC	Ind	

Univ of SUNDERLAND

TITLE	CODE	COURSE	SUBJECTS	A/AS	NO/C	AGNVQ	IB	SQA(H)	SQA	RATIO A/AS
Biology and History of Art and Design	CV14	3FT deg	B/C	8	3M	M	Ind	Ind	Ind	
Biology with History of Art and Design	C1V4	3FT deg	B/C	8	3M	M	Ind	Ind	Ind	
Business Studies and History of Art and Design	NV14	3FT/4SW deg	*	8	3M	M	Ind	Ind	Ind	
Business Studies with History of Art and Design	N1V4	3FT/4SW deg	*	8	3M	M	Ind	Ind	Ind	
Chemistry and History of Art and Design	FV14	3FT deg	C	8	3M	M	Ind	Ind	Ind	
Chemistry with History of Art and Design	F1V4	3FT deg	C	8	3M	M	Ind	Ind	Ind	
Computer Studies and History of Art and Design	GV54	3FT/4SW deg	*	8	3M	M	Ind	Ind	Ind	
Computer Studies with History of Art and Design	G5V4	3FT/4SW deg	*	8	3M	M	Ind	Ind	Ind	
English and History of Art and Design	QV34▼	3FT deg	El g	12	Ind	M	24$	BCCC$	Ind	11

TITLE	CODE	COURSE	SUBJECTS	A/AS	ND/C	AGNVQ	IB	SQA(H)	SQA	RATIO A/AS
English with History of Art and Design	Q3V4	3FT deg	*	10	4M	M	Ind	Ind	Ind	
French with History of Art and Design	R1V4	4FT deg	F	8	3M	M	Ind	Ind	Ind	
Geography and History of Art and Design	LV84	3FT deg	*	8	3M	M	Ind	Ind	Ind	
Geography with History of Art and Design	L8V4	3FT deg	*	8	3M	M	Ind·	Ind	Ind	
Geology and History of Art and Design	FV64	3FT deg	*	8	3M	M	Ind	Ind	Ind	
Geology with History of Art and Design	F6V4	3FT deg	*	8	3M	M	Ind	Ind	Ind	
History and History of Art and Design	VV14▼	3FT deg	H g	12	Ind	M	24$	BCCC	Ind	
History of Art and Design and Mathematics	VG41	3FT deg	M	8	3M	M	Ind	Ind		
History of Art and Design and Media Studies	VP44	3FT deg	* g	12	Ind	M	24	BCCC	Ind	3
History of Art and Design and Physiology	VB41	3FT deg	*	8	3M	M	Ind	Ind		
History of Art and Design and Spanish	VR44	4SW deg	*	8	3M	M	Ind	Ind		
History with History of Art and Design	V1V4	3FT deg	*	10	4M	M	Ind	Ind	Ind	
Mathematics with History of Art and Design	G1V4	3FT deg	M	8	3M	M	Ind	Ind	Ind	
Philosophy with History of Art and Design	V7V4	3FT deg	*	8	3M	Ind	Ind	Ind	Ind	
Physiology with History of Art and Design	B1V4	3FT deg	*	8	3M	M	Ind	Ind	Ind	
Politics with History of Art and Design	M1V4	3FT deg	*	8	3M	M	Ind	Ind	Ind	
Psychology with History of Art and Design	C8V4	3FT deg	*	10	4M	M^	Ind	Ind	Ind	
Religious Studies with History of Art and Design	V8V4	3FT deg	*	8	3M	M	Ind	Ind	Ind	

SURREY INST of A & D

Design History	V480	3FT deg		12-16						
Design History	E480	3FT deg		12-16						

Univ of SUSSEX

History of Art in Cultural and Community Studs	V4Y2	3FT deg	*	BBB	MO	M*6	$	Ind	Ind	
History of Art in English and American Studies	V4Q4	3FT deg	*	BBB	MO	M*6	$	Ind	Ind	
History of Art in European Studies	V4T2	4FT deg	* g	BBB	MO $	M*6 go	$	Ind	Ind	

Univ of TEESSIDE

History of Design and Architecture	V480	3FT deg	g	8-12	N	M$	Ind	CCC	N	2

UNIVERSITY COLL LONDON (Univ of London)

Archaeology (Medieval) and History of Art	VV64	3FT deg	g	BBC	3M	Ind	30$	BBBCC	Ind	
Dutch and History of Art (4 Yrs)	TV24	4FT deg	g	BBC	3M	X	26$	BBBCC$	Ind	2
English and History of Art	QV34	3FT deg	El g	ABB	Ind	X	34$	AAABB$	Ind	13 28/30
French and History of Art (4 Yrs)	RV14	4FT deg	F g	BBC-BBB	3M	X	32$	BBBBB$	Ind	11
German and History of Art (4 Yrs)	RV24	4FT deg	G g	BBC	3M	X	30$	BBBCC$	Ind	3
History and History of Art	VV14	3FT deg	g	BBC	3M	Ind	30$	BBBBB	Ind	9
History of Art	V400	3FT deg	g	BBC-BBB	3M	Ind	30$	BBBBB	Ind	9 20/28
History of Art with Material Studies	V4F2	3FT deg	g	BBC-BBB	3M	Ind	30$	BBBBB	Ind	4 24/26
Italian and History of Art (4 Yrs)	RV34	4FT deg	g	BBB	3M	X	30$	BBBCC$	Ind	6 20/28
Philosophy and History of Art	VV74	3FT deg	g	BBC	3M	X	28	BBBBC	Ind	11
Spanish and History of Art (4 Yrs)	RV44	4FT deg	Sp g	BBC	3M	X	32$	BBBCC$	Ind	

Univ of WARWICK

History of Art	V400	3FT deg	* g	BBB-BBC	X	X	30	ABBBB		5 22/30

Univ of YORK

English/History of Art (Equal)	QV34	3FT deg	E g	ABB-ABC	HN $	D$^	32$	AABB$	Ind	20/28
History of Art	V400	3FT deg	Ha/E/H/L/A	BBC	Ind	D*^	32$	BBBB	Ind	20/26
History/History of Art (Equal)	VV14	3FT deg	H	ABC-BBB	Ind	D$^	32$	ABBB$	Ind	

Letts STUDY GUIDES
✕ THE INDEPENDENT

TITLE	CODE	COURSE	SUBJECTS	A/AS	NO/C	RGNVQ	IB	SQA(H)	SQA	RATIO A/AS
ANGLIA Poly Univ										
Business Administration (Leisure Management)	N700▼	3FT deg	* g	14	6M	M go	Dip	BBCC	N	
Business Studies (Leisure Management)	N701▼	3FT deg	* g	14	6M	M go	Dip	BBCC	Ind	
Leisure Planning and Development	N780▼	3FT deg	* g	8	2M	P	Dip	CCCC	Ind	
ASKHAM BRYAN COLL										
Leisure Management	N780	3FT deg	* g	DD	MO	M$	Ind	CCCC	Ind	
Univ of Wales, BANGOR										
Leisure and Tourism Resource Management	NP77	3FT deg	* g	10	4M	M$ go	Ind	Ind	Ind	
BARNSLEY COLL										
Hotel Catering and Institutional Management	027N	2FT HND	*	E	2M	P$	Ind	Ind	Ind	
Leisure Studies	087N	2FT HND	*	4	4M	M*	Ind	Ind	Ind	
BATH COLL of HE										
Human Ecology	N750	3FT deg	S		Ind		Ind	$	$	5 16/20
BELL COLLEGE OF TECHNOLOGY										
Leisure Management	N780	3FT deg	Ap g	DDEE-DE	Ind	Ind	Ind	CCC$	18$	
Leisure Management	N781	2FT Dip	Ap g	DDEE-DE	Ind	Ind	Ind	CCC$	18$	
Hospitality Management	017N	2FT HND	Ap g	DD-D	N $	P$	Ind	CC$	18$	
BIRMINGHAM COLL of Food, Tourism & Creative St										
Adventure Tourism Management	N735	3FT deg	* g	12	MO	M$ gi	Ind	Ind	Ind	
Hospitality Business Management	N720	4SW deg	* g	10	MO	M$ gi	Ind	Ind	Ind	4 6/18
Hospitality and Food Management	DN47	4SW deg	* g	10	MO	M$ gi	Ind	Ind	Ind	
Hospitality and Leisure Management	N730	4SW deg	* g	10	MO	M$ gi	Ind	Ind	Ind	
Hospitality and Tourism Management	NP77	4SW deg	* g	10	MO	M$ gi	Ind	Ind	Ind	
Leisure Management	N780	3FT deg	* g	12	MO	M$ gi	Ind	Ind	Ind	
Hotel, Catering and Institutional Management	027N	2SW/3SW HND	*	4	3M	P$	Ind	Ind	Ind	2 2/8
Leisure Management	087N	2FT HND	* g	4	4M	P$	Ind	Ind	Ind	
BLACKPOOL & FYLDE COLL										
Culinary Arts	N7B4	3FT deg	*	10	4M	M$	Ind	Ind	Ind	
Hospitality Management	N730	3FT deg	*	10	4M	M$	Ind	Ind	Ind	
Hospitality Management (International Hotel Mgt)	N745	4FT deg		10	4M	M$	Ind	Ind	Ind	
Hospitality Management (with Tourism)	N7PR	3FT deg		10	4M	M$	Ind	Ind	Ind	
Hotel and Catering Mgt (Conversion to degree)	N700	2FT deg	*		HN		X	X	Ind	
Leisure and Recreation Management	N780	3FT deg		10	4M	M$	Ind	Ind	Ind	
Business Studies (Leisure & Tourism)	77NP	2FT HND	*	4	3M	P$	Ind	Ind	Ind	
Contract Catering	127N	2FT HND		2	2M	P$	Ind	Ind	Ind	
Culinary Arts	107N	2FT HND	*	2	2M	P$	Ind	Ind	Ind	
Hotel and Catering Management	027N▼	2FT HND		2	2M	P$	Ind	Ind	Ind	
BOLTON INST										
Accountancy and Organisations, Mgt and Work	NN47	3FT deg	* g	CD	MO	M*	24	BBCC	Ind	
Art and Design Hist & Organisations, Mgt & Work	NV74	3FT deg	* g	CD	MO	M*	24	BBCC	Ind	
Biology and Organisations, Management & Work	CN17	3FT deg	* g	CD	MO	M*	24	BBCC	Ind	
Business Economics & Organisations, Mgt and Work	LN17	3FT deg	* g	CD	MO	M*	24	BBCC	Ind	
Business Info Systs & Organisations, Mgt & Work	GN57	3FT deg	* g	CD	MO	M*	24	BBCC	Ind	
Business Studies and Organisations, Mgt & Work	NNC7	3FT deg	* g	CD	MO	M*	24	BBCC	Ind	
Community Studies and Organisations, Mgt & Work	LN57	3FT deg	* g	CD	MO	M*	24	BBCC	Ind	
Computing and Human Resource Management	GN5T	3FT deg	* g	CD	MO	M*	24	BBCC	Ind	

course details			*98 expected requirements*							*96 entry stats*	
TITLE	CODE	COURSE	SUBJECTS	A/AS	ND/C	AGNVQ	IB	SQA(H)	SQA	RATIO A/AS	
Computing and Organisations, Management & Work	GN5R	3FT deg	* g	CD	MO	M*	24	BBCC	Ind		
Creative Writing and Organisations, Mgt & Work	NW74	3FT deg	* g	CD	MO	M*	24	BBCC	Ind		
Design and Organisations, Management & Work	NW72	3FT deg	* g	CD	MO	M*	24	BBCC	Ind		
Environmental St and Organisations, Mgt & Work	FN97	3FT deg	* g	CD	MO	M*	24	BBCC	Ind		
European Cultural St & Organisations, Mgt & Work	NT72	3FT deg	* g	CD	MO	M*	24	BBCC	Ind		
Film and TV St and Organisations, Mgt & Work	NW75	3FT deg	Me/T g	CD	Ind	Ind	24	BBCC	Ind		
French and Organisations, Management & Work	NR71	3FT deg	F g	CD	Ind	Ind	24	BBCC	Ind		
Gender & Women's St & Organisations, Mgt & Work	MN97	3FT deg	* g	CD	MO	M*	24	BBCC	Ind		
German and Organisations, Management & Work	NR72	3FT deg	G g	CD	Ind	Ind	24	BBCC	Ind		
Human Resource Mgt & Organisations, Mgt & Work	NN71	3FT deg	* g	CD	MO	M*	24	BBCC	Ind		
Law and Organisations, Management & Work	MNH7	3FT deg	* g	CD	MO	M*	24	BBCC	Ind		
Leisure Management	N780	3FT deg	* g	CD	MO	M*	24	BBCC	Ind		
Leisure Studies and Organisations, Mgt & Work	LN37	3FT deg	* g	CD	MO	M*	24	BBCC	Ind		
Literature and Organisations, Management & Work	NQ72	3FT deg	* g	CD	MO	M*	24	BBCC	Ind		
Marketing and Organisations, Management & Work	NN75	3FT deg	* g	CD	MO	M*	24	BBCC	Ind		
Mathematics and Organisations, Management & Work	GN17	3FT deg	M g	CD	Ind	Ind	24	BBCC	Ind		
Operations Mgt & Organisations, Mgt & Work	NN27	3FT deg	* g	CD	Ind	Ind	24	BBCC	Ind		
Organisations, Management & Work and Peace & War	NV7C	3FT deg	* g	CD	Ind	Ind	24	BBCC	Ind		
Organisations, Management & Work and Philosophy	NV77	3FT deg	* g	CD	Ind	Ind	24	BBCC	Ind		
Organisations, Management & Work and Psychology	NL77	3FT deg	* g	12	MO	D*	24	BBCC	Ind		
Organisations, Management & Work and Sociology	LN3T	3FT deg	* g	CD	MO	M	24	Ind	Ind		
Organisations, Management & Work and Tourism St	NP77	3FT deg	* g	CD	MO	M*	24	BBCC	Ind		
Organisations, Mgt & Work and Urban & Culture St	LN3R	3FT deg	* g	CD	MO	M*	24	BBCC	Ind		
Visual Arts and Organisations, Management & Work	NW71	3FT deg	* g	CD	MO	M*	24	BBCC	Ind		
BOURNEMOUTH Univ											
Food and Catering Management	N721	4SW deg	* g	12-14	MO	M$ go	24	BBCC	Ind	5	8/16
Hospitality Management	N720	4SW deg	* g	12-14	MO	M$ go	24	BBCC	Ind	5	10/20
Hotel, Catering and Institutional Management	027N	3FT HND	* g	8-10	MO	P$ go	24	BCC	Ind	4	6/12
BRADFORD & ILKLEY Comm COLL											
Hotel, Catering & Institutional Management(2 Yrs)	027N	2FT HND	*	6	MO	P	Ind	Ind	N		
Leisure Studies	087N	2FT HND	*	6	MO	P	Ind	Ind	N		
Univ of BRIGHTON											
Hospitality Management	N700	3FT/4SW deg	* g	12	MO	M go	Dip	BBCC	Ind		
International Hospitality Management	N720	4SW deg	* g	16	MO+2D	D go	Dip	BBBB	Ind		
Leisure and Sport Management	LN3R	3FT deg	* g	BC	3M+3D	M^ go/D go	26	BBBCC	Ind		
Leisure and Sport Studies	LN37	3FT deg	* g	BC	3M+3D	M^ go/D go	26	BBBCC	Ind		
Hotel, Catering and Institutional Management	027N▼	2SW HND	*	2	N	P	24	CC	Ind		
BRUNEL Univ, West London											
Leisure Management/Accounting	N7N4	3FT deg	* g	18	MO $	M* go	26$	BCCC$	Ind		
Leisure Management/Computer Studies	N7G5	3FT deg	* g	18	MO $	M* go	26$	BCCC$	Ind		
Sports Sciences/Leisure Management	BN67	3FT deg	* g	18	1M+3D	D	29	BBCC	Ind		
Univ of BUCKINGHAM											
Business Studies-International Hotel Management	N720	3FT deg	* g	12	3M+2D	M	26	BCCC	Ind		
BUCKINGHAMSHIRE COLLEGE											
Business Studies with Leisure Management	N1NR	3FT deg									
Entertainment Industry Management	N730	3FT deg		8-10	1D	M	27	CCCC	Ind		
Leisure Management	N780	3FT deg		8-10	1D	M	27	CCCC	Ind		
Leisure Management (1 yr conversion to Degree)	N781	1FT deg			HN						
Leisure Management and Heritage Studies	NV71	3FT deg		8-10	1D	M	27	CCCC	Ind		

TITLE	CODE	COURSE	SUBJECTS	A/AS	NO/C	RGNVQ	IB	SQA(H)	SQA	RATIO	A/AS
Leisure Management and Sports Studies	BN67	3FT deg		8-10	1D	M	27	CCCC	Ind		
Leisure Management with French	N7R1	3FT deg		8-10	1D	M	27	CCCC	Ind		
Leisure Management with German	N7R2	3FT deg		8-10	1D	M	27	CCCC	Ind		
Leisure Management with Heritage Studies	N7V1	3FT deg		8-10	1D	M	27	CCCC	Ind		
Leisure Management with Italian	N7R3	3FT deg		8-10	1D	M	27	CCCC	Ind		
Leisure Management with Marketing	N7N5	3FT deg		8-10	1D	M	27	CCCC	Ind		
Leisure Management with Outdoor Recreation St	N784	3FT deg		8-10	1D	M	27	CCCC	Ind		
Leisure Management with Spanish	N7R4	3FT deg		8-10	1D	M	27	CCCC	Ind		
Leisure Management with Sports Studies	N782	3FT deg		8-10	1D	M	27	CCCC	Ind		
Leisure Management with Tourism	N7P7	3FT deg		8-10	1D	M	27	CCCC	Ind		
Tourism and Leisure Management	PN77	3FT deg		8-10	1D	M	27	CCCC	Ind		
Tourism with Leisure Management	P7N7	3FT deg									
Travel and Tourism Management	NP77	3FT deg		8-10	1D	M	27	CCCC	Ind		
Leisure Studies	087N	2FT HND		8-10	MO	M	27	CCCC	Ind		

CANTERBURY CHRIST CHURCH COLL of HE

TITLE	CODE	COURSE	SUBJECTS	A/AS	NO/C	RGNVQ	IB	SQA(H)	SQA	RATIO	A/AS
Hotel, Catering and Institutional Management	047N	2FT HND	* g	D	N	P	24	Ind	Ind	9	

Univ of Wales INST, CARDIFF

TITLE	CODE	COURSE	SUBJECTS	A/AS	NO/C	RGNVQ	IB	SQA(H)	SQA	RATIO	A/AS
Catering Management	N722	3FT/4SW deg	* g	12	MO	M$ go	Ind	CCCC	Ind	18	
Consumer Science	N750	3FT deg	g	10	MO	M$ gi	Ind	CCCC	Ind	3	7/12
Food Studies with Catering Management	D4NT	3FT/4SW deg	S g	10-12	MO	M$ go	Ind	CCCC	Ind		
Food Studies with Hotel Management	D4NR	3FT/4SW deg	S g	10-12	MO	M$ go	Ind	CCCC	Ind		
Hotel Management	N720	3FT/4SW deg	* g	12	MO	M$ go	Ind	CCCC	Ind	10	14/20
Hotel Management with Catering Management	N721	3FT/4SW deg	* g	12	MO	M$ go	Ind	CCCC	Ind	11	10/16
Hotel Management with Food Studies	N7DK	3FT/4SW deg	S g	12	MO	M$ go	Ind	CCCC	Ind	9	
Hotel Management with Recreation and Leisure	N741	3FT/4SW deg	* g	12-14	MO	M$ go	Ind	CCCC	Ind	35	
Hotel Management with Tourism	N7PT	3FT/4SW deg	* g	12-16	MO	M$ go	Ind	CCCC	Ind	15	
International Hotel Management	N723	3FT/4SW deg	* g	12	MO	M$ go	Ind	CCCC	Ind	5	8/18
Recreation and Leisure Management	N780	3FT/4SW deg	* g	14	MO	D$^ go	Ind	CCCC	Ind	6	10/20
Recreation and Leisure and Hotel Management	N781	3FT/4SW deg	* g	12-14	MO	D$^ go	Ind	CCCC	Ind		
Recreation and Leisure with Catering Management	N782	3FT/4SW deg	* g	10-14	MO	D$^ go	Ind	CCCC	Ind		
Recreation and Leisure with Hotel Management	N783	3FT/4SW deg	* g	12-14	MO	D$^ go	Ind	CCCC	Ind		
Recreation and Leisure with Tourism	N7P7	3FT/4SW deg	* g	12-16	MO	D$^ go	Ind	CCCC	Ind	17	
Tourism and Hotel Management	NP77	3FT/4SW deg	* g	14-16	MO	D$^ go	Ind	CCCC	Ind	18	
Tourism and Recreation and Leisure	PN77	3FT/4SW deg	* g	14-16	MO	DL^ go	Ind	CCCC	Ind	7	
Tourism with Catering Management	P7NR	3FT/4SW deg	* g	12-16	MO	D$^ go	Ind	CCCC	Ind	5	
Tourism with Hotel Management	P7N7	3FT/4SW deg	* g	12-16	MO	D$^ go	Ind	CCCC	Ind	32	
Tourism with Recreation and Leisure	P7NT	3FT/4SW deg	* g	14-16	MO	DL^ go	Ind	CCCC	Ind	8	9/12
Hotel, Catering and Institutional Management	027N	3FT HND	* g	2	N	M$ gi	Ind	CC	Ind	3	2/9
Recreation and Leisure Management	087N	2FT HND	* g	8	MO	M$ go	Ind	CC	Ind	4	4/10

Univ of CENTRAL ENGLAND

TITLE	CODE	COURSE	SUBJECTS	A/AS	NO/C	RGNVQ	IB	SQA(H)	SQA	RATIO	A/AS
Hospitality Management	N720	4SW deg	* g	12	MO	M	24	CCC	Ind	7	6/20
Hospitality Management with Tourism	N7P7	4SW deg	* g	12	MO	M	24	CCC			

Univ of CENTRAL LANCASHIRE

TITLE	CODE	COURSE	SUBJECTS	A/AS	NO/C	RGNVQ	IB	SQA(H)	SQA	RATIO	A/AS
Hospitality Management/Int Hospitality Mgt	N700	4SW deg	*	12	MO+5D	M$6/^	26	BCCC	Ind		
Hospitality Studies (Year 3 Entry)	N721	1FT deg			HN $						
Leisure Studies (Year 3 Entry)	N730	1FT deg			HN $						
Tourism Studies (Year 3 Entry)	N731	1FT deg			HN $						
Hospitality Management	047N▼	2FT HND	*	EE	N	P	Ind	CC	Ind		
Hospitality and Tourism	77PN▼	2FT HND	* g	E	N	P$	24$	CCC	Ind		
Leisure Studies	087N▼	2FT HND	*	EE	2M	M$	24$	CCC	N$		

Hotel, Institutional and Recreation Management 35

course details			98 expected requirements						96 entry stats

TITLE	CODE	COURSE	SUBJECTS	A/AS	ND/C	AGNVQ	IB	SQA(H)	SQA	RATIO A/AS
CHELTENHAM & GLOUCESTER COLL of HE										
Business Computer Systems and Hotel Management	GN5R	3FT deg	*	8-12	M0	M	24	CCCC	Ind	
Business Computer Systems and Leisure Mgt	GN57	3FT deg	*	8-12	5M+2D	ML3	24	CCCC	Ind	
Business Computer Systems with Hotel Management	G5NR	3FT deg	*	8-12	M0	M	24	CCCC	Ind	
Business Computer Systems with Leisure Mgt	G5N7	3FT deg	*	8-12	M0	M	24	CCCC	Ind	
Business Info Technology and Catering Management	NG75	3FT deg	*	8	M0	M	24	CCCC	Ind	
Business Info Technology and Hotel Management	GNM7	3FT deg	*	10-14	M0	M	24	CCCC	Ind	
Business Info Technology and Leisure Mgt	NGR5	3FT/4SW deg	*	10-14	5M+2D	ML3	24	CCCC	Ind	
Business Info Technology with Catering Mgt	G5NT	3FT deg	*	8-12	M0	M	24	CCCC	Ind	
Business Info Technology with Leisure Management	GNNR	3FT/4SW deg	*	8-12	M0	M	24	CCCC	Ind	
Business Management and Catering Management	NN17	4SW deg	*	12	5M+2D	MB3	26	CCCC	Ind	
Business Management and Hotel Management	NN1R	4SW deg	*	12-16	4M+3D	MB3	26	CCCC	Ind	
Business Management and Leisure Management	NNR1	4SW deg	*	12-16	4M+3D	MB3	26	CCCC	Ind	
Business Management and Tourism Management	NN1T	4SW deg	*	12-16	4M+3D	MB3	26	CCCC	Ind	
Business Management with Catering Management	N1N7	4SW deg	*	12	4M+3D	MB3	26	CCCC	Ind	
Business Management with Hotel Management	N1NR	4SW deg	*	12-16	4M+3D	MB3	26	CCCC	Ind	
Business Management with Leisure Management	N1NT	4SW deg	*	12-16	4M+3D	MB3	26	CCCC	Ind	
Catering Management and Computing	GNNT	3FT deg	*	8	M0	MH3	24	CCCC	Ind	
Catering Management and Financial Management	NN37	4SW deg	*	8-12	M0	MH3	26	CCCC	Ind	
Catering Management and Financial Services Mgt	NN7H	4SW deg	*	8-12	M0	MH3	26	CCCC	Ind	
Catering Management and Hotel Management	N721	4SW deg	*	8-12	M0	MH3	24	CCCC	Ind	
Catering Management and Human Resource Mgt	NN7D	4SW deg	*	8-12	M0	MH3	26	CCCC	Ind	
Catering Management and Leisure Management	N780	4SW deg	*	8-12	5M+2D	MH3	24	CCCC	Ind	
Catering Management and Marketing Management	NN57	4SW deg	*	8-12	M0	MH3	26	CCCC	Ind	
Catering Management and Sport and Exercise Sci	NB76	3FT deg	S	8-12	5M+3D	MH3	26	CCCC	Ind	
Catering Management and Tourism Management	NP7T	4SW deg	*	8-12	5M+2D	MH3	24	CCCC	Ind	
Catering Management with Business Info Tech	N724	4SW deg	*	8	M0	MH3	24	CCCC	Ind	
Catering Management with Business Management	N7N1	4SW deg	*	8-12	5M+2D	MH3	24	CCCC	Ind	
Catering Management with Computing	NGTN	4SW deg	*	8	M0	MH3	24	CCCC	Ind	
Catering Management with Financial Management	N7NH	4SW deg	*	8	M0	MH3	26	CCCC	Ind	
Catering Management with Financial Services Mgt	N7NJ	4SW deg	*	8	M0	MH3	26	CCCC	Ind	
Catering Management with Hotel Management	N723	4SW deg	*	8-12	M0	MH3	24	CCCC	Ind	
Catering Management with Human Resource Mgt	N7NC	4SW deg	*	8	M0	MH3	26	CCCC	Ind	
Catering Management with Leisure Management	N781	4SW deg	*	8-12	5M+2D	MH3	24	CCCC	Ind	
Catering Management with Marketing Management	N7N5	4SW deg	*	8	M0	MH3	26	CCCC	Ind	
Catering Management with Modern Lang (French)	N7R1	4SW deg	g	8	M0	MH3	24	CCCC	Ind	
Catering Management with Sport and Exercise Sci	N7B6	4SW deg	S	8-12	5M+2D	MH3	24	CCCC	Ind	
Catering Management with Tourism Management	N7P7	4SW deg	*	8-12	5M+2D	MH3	24	CCCC	Ind	
Computing and Hotel Management	GN5T	3FT deg	*	8-12	M0	M	24	CCCC	Ind	
Computing with Catering Management	NGTM	3FT deg	*	8	M0	M	24	CCCC	Ind	
Countryside Planning and Leisure Management	DN2R	3FT deg	*	8-14	5M+2D	M$	26	CCCC	Ind	
Countryside Planning with Leisure Management	D2N7	3FT deg	*	8-14	M0	MK	26$	CCCC	Ind	
Environmental Policy and Leisure Management	FN97	3FT deg	*	12-16	5M+2D	M3	26	CCCC	Ind	
Environmental Policy with Hotel Management	F9NR	3FT deg	*	10	4M+2D	M3	26	CCCC	Ind	
Environmental Policy with Leisure Management	F9N7	3FT deg	*	10-14	5M+2D	M3	26	CCCC	Ind	
Financial Management and Hotel Management	NN73	4SW deg	*	8-12	5M+2D	M3	26	CCCC	Ind	
Financial Management and Leisure Management	NN3R	4SW deg	*	10-16	5M+2D	M3L	26	CCCC	Ind	
Financial Management with Catering Management	N3NR	4SW deg	*	10	5M+2D	M3	26	CCCC	Ind	
Financial Management with Hotel Management	N3N7	4SW deg	*	10	5M+2D	M3	26	CCCC	Ind	
Financial Management with Leisure Management	NN3T	4SW deg	*	10-16	5M+2D	M3	26	CCCC	Ind	
Financial Services Mgt and Hotel Management	NN7J	4SW deg	*	10-12	5M+2D	M3	26	CCCC	Ind	
Financial Services Mgt and Leisure Management	NNRH	4SW deg	*	10-14	5M+2D	ML3	26	CCCC	Ind	

course details

TITLE	CODE	COURSE	SUBJECTS	A/AS	ND/C	AGNVQ	IB	SQA(H)	SQA	RATIO A/AS
Financial Services Mgt with Catering Management	N3NT	4SW deg	*	8-12	5M+2D	M3	26	CCCC	Ind	
Financial Services Mgt with Hotel Management	NNT3	4SW deg	*	10-12	5M+2D	M3	26	CCCC	Ind	
Financial Services Mgt with Leisure Management	NNHT	4SW deg	*	10-14	5M+2D	M3	26	CCCC	Ind	
Geography and Leisure Management	LN8R	3FT deg	*	12-14	MO	MB3	26	CCCC	Ind	
Geography with Leisure Management	L8NR	3FT deg	*	12-14	MO	ML3	26	CCCC	Ind	
Geology and Hotel Management	FN67	3FT deg	*	8-12	MO	M3	26	CCCC	Ind	
Geology with Hotel Management	F6N7	3FT deg	*	8-12	MO	M3	26	CCCC	Ind	
Hotel Management and Human Geography	LN8T	3FT deg	*	10-14	5M+2D	MH3	26	CCCC	Ind	
Hotel Management and Human Resource Management	NN71	4SW deg	*	12	5M+2D	MH3	26	CCCC	Ind	
Hotel Management and Leisure Management	N740	4SW deg	*	12-16	4M+3D	M$3	26	CCCC	Ind	
Hotel Management and Marketing Management	NN75	4SW deg	*	12	5M+2D	M$3	26	CCCC	Ind	
Hotel Management and Physical Geography	NF78	3FT deg	*	10-14	5M+2D	M$3	26	CCCC	Ind	
Hotel Management and Sport and Exercise Sciences	NBR6	3FT deg	S	12	4M+3D	M$3	26	CCCC	Ind	
Hotel Management and Tourism Management	NPR7	4SW deg	*	12-16	4M+3D	M$3	26	CCCC	Ind	
Hotel Management with Business Computer Systems	N7GM	4SW deg	*	12	5M+2D	MH3	26	CCCC	Ind	
Hotel Management with Business Info Technology	N7GN	4SW deg	*	12	5M+2D	MH3	26	CCCC	Ind	
Hotel Management with Business Management	NNRC	4SW deg	*	12	4M+3D	MH3	26	CCCC	Ind	
Hotel Management with Catering Management	N722	4SW deg	*	12	5M+2D	MH3	26	CCCC	Ind	
Hotel Management with Computing	N7G5	4SW deg	*	8-12	5M+2D	MH3	26	CCCC	Ind	
Hotel Management with Financial Management	N7N3	4SW deg	*	12	5M+2D	MH3	26	CCCC	Ind	
Hotel Management with Financial Services Mgt	NNR3	4SW deg	*	12	5M+2D	MH3	26	CCCC	Ind	
Hotel Management with Geology	N7F6	4SW deg	*	10-14	5M-2D	MH3	26	CCCC	Ind	
Hotel Management with Human Geography	N7FV	4SW deg	*	10-14	5M+2D	MH3	26	CCCC	Ind	
Hotel Management with Human Resource Management	N7ND	4SW deg	*	12	5M+2D	MH3	26	CCCC	Ind	
Hotel Management with Leisure Management	N741	4SW deg	*	12	4M+3D	MH3	26	CCCC	Ind	
Hotel Management with Marketing Management	N7NM	4SW deg	*	12	5M+2D	MH3	26	CCCC	Ind	
Hotel Management with Modern Languages (French)	N7TX	4SW deg	g	12	5M+2D	MH3	26	CCCC	Ind	
Hotel Management with Physical Geography	N7FW	4SW deg	*	10-14	5M+2D	MH3	26	CCC	Ind	
Hotel Management with Sport and Exercise Sci	N7BQ	4SW deg	g	12	5M+2D	MH3	26	CCCC	Ind	
Hotel Management with Tourism Management	N7PT	4SW deg	*	12	4M+3D	MH3	26	CCCC	Ind	
Human Geography and Leisure Management	LN87	3FT deg	*	12-16	5M+2D	ML3	26	CCCC	Ind	
Human Geography with Hotel Management	L8NT	3FT deg	*	10-14	5M+2D	M3	26	CCCC	Ind	
Human Geography with Leisure Management	L8N7	3FT deg	Gy	12	5M+2D	M3	26	CCCC	Ind	
Human Resource Management and Leisure Mgt	NNCR	4SW deg	*	12-16	5M+2D	MB3	26	CCCC	Ind	
Human Resource Mgt with Catering Management	NN7C	4SW deg	*	8-12	MO	MB3	26	CCCC	Ind	
Human Resource Mgt with Hotel Management	NNC7	4SW deg	*	10	5M+2D	MB3	26	CCCC	Ind	
Human Resource Mgt with Leisure Management	NNRD	4SW deg	*	12-16	5M+2D	MB3	26	CCCC	Ind	
Leisure Management & Sport and Exercise Sciences	BN67	3FT deg	S	12-16	4M+3D	ML3	26	CCCC	Ind	
Leisure Management and Marketing Management	NN5R	4SW deg	*	12-16	5M+2D	M$3	26	CCCC	Ind	
Leisure Management and Multimedia	NGT5	3FT deg	*	12-16	5M+2D	ML3	26	CCCC	Ind	
Leisure Management and Physical Geography	FN87	3FT deg	*	12-16	5M+2D	ML3	26	CCCC	Ind	
Leisure Management and Tourism Management	PN77	4SW deg	*	12-16	4M+3D	ML3	26	CCCC	Ind	
Leisure Management with Business Computer Systs	N782	4SW deg	*	12	4M+3D	ML3	26	CCCC	Ind	
Leisure Management with Business Info Technology	N783	4SW deg	*	12	4M+3D	ML3	26	CCCC	Ind	
Leisure Management with Business Management	N784	4SW deg	*	12-16	4M+3D	ML3	26	CCCC	Ind	
Leisure Management with Catering Management	N785	4SW deg	*	12	4M+3D	ML3	26	CCCC	Ind	
Leisure Management with Countryside Planning	N7D2	4SW deg	*	12-16	4M+3D	ML3	26	CCCC	Ind	
Leisure Management with Financial Management	N786	4SW deg	*	12-16	5M+2D	ML3	26	CCCC	Ind	
Leisure Management with Financial Services Mgt	N787	4SW deg	*	12-16	5M+2D	ML3	26	CCCC	Ind	
Leisure Management with Geography	N7L8	4SW deg		12-16	MO	ML3	26	CCCC	Ind	
Leisure Management with Hotel Management	N788	4SW deg	*	12-16	4M+3D	ML3	26	CCCC	Ind	
Leisure Management with Human Geography	N7LV	4SW deg	*	12-16	5M+2D	ML3	26	CCCC	Ind	

Hotel, Institutional and Recreation Management 35

course details			98 expected requirements							96 entry stats	
TITLE	CODE	COURSE	SUBJECTS	A/AS	ND/C	AGNVQ	IB	SQA(H)	SQA	RATIO	A/AS
Leisure Management with Human Resource Mgt	N789	4SW deg	*	12-16	5M+2D	ML3	26	CCCC	Ind		
Leisure Management with Marketing Management	N7NN	4SW deg	*	12-16	5M+2D	ML3	26	CCCC	Ind		
Leisure Management with Modern Language (French)	N7RC	4SW deg	*	12-16	5M+2D	ML3	26	CCCC	Ind		
Leisure Management with Multimedia	N790	4SW deg	*	12-16	5M+2D	ML3	26	CCCC	Ind		
Leisure Management with Physical Geography	N7F8	4SW deg	*	12-16	5M+2D	ML3	26	CCCC	Ind		
Leisure Management with Sport and Exercise Sci	N7BP	4SW deg	*	12-16	4M+3D	ML3	26	CCCC	Ind		
Leisure Management with Tourism Management	N7PR	4SW deg	*	12-16	4M+3D	ML3	26	CCCC	Ind		
Marketing Management with Catering Management	N5N7	4SW deg	*	12	5M+2D	MB3	26	CCCC	Ind		
Marketing Management with Hotel Management	N5NR	4SW deg	*	12	5M+2D	MB3	26	CCCC	Ind		
Marketing Management with Leisure Management	N5NT	4SW deg	*	12-16	5M+2D	MB3	26	CCCC	Ind		
Multimedia with Leisure Management	GNN7	3FT deg	*	12	5M+2D	MI3	26	CCCC	Ind		
Multimedia with Leisure Management	GNMR	4SW deg	*	8-12	MO	MI3	24	CCCC	Ind		
Multimedia with Marketing Management	GNMT	4SW deg	*	8-12	MO	MI3	24	CCCC	Ind		
Physical Geography with Hotel Management	F8NR	3FT deg	*	8-12	5M+2D	M3^	26	CCCC	Ind		
Physical Geography with Leisure Management	F8N7	3FT deg	*	8-12	MO	M3^	26	CCCC	Ind		
Sport & Exercise Sciences with Catering Mgt	B6N7	3FT deg	S	12-16	4M+3D	ML3	26	CCCC	Ind		
Sport & Exercise Sciences with Hotel Management	B6NT	3FT deg	S	12-16	4M+3D	ML3	26	CCCC	Ind		
Sport & Exercise Sciences with Leisure Mgt	B6NR	3FT deg	S	12-16	4M+3D	ML3	26	CCCC	Ind		
Tourism Management with Catering Management	P7N7	4SW deg	*	12	4M+3D	ML3	26	CCCC	Ind		
Tourism Management with Hotel Management	P7NR	4SW deg	*	12-16	4M+3D	ML3	26	CCCC	Ind		
Tourism Management with Leisure Management	P7NT	4SW deg	*	12-16	4M+3D	ML3	26	CCCC	Ind		
Hotel, Catering and Institutional Mgt (2 Yrs)	007N	2FT HND	*	2	2M	Ind	Ind	Ind	Ind		
Hotel, Catering and Institutional Mgt (3 Yrs)	027N	3SW HND	*	2	2M	P	Ind	Ind	Ind		

CITY OF BRISTOL COLLEGE

Hotel, Catering and Institutional Management	027N	2FT HND									

CITY COLLEGE Manchester

Leisure and Tourism Management	77PN	2FT HND									

COLCHESTER INST

Business Studies (Hotel and Catering Management)	N720	4SW deg	* g	CC	6M	P$+	Dip	Ind	Ind	2	6/10
Leisure Studies	N780	3FT deg	* g	DD	6M	M$	Ind	Ind	Ind		
Hospitality Management	027N	2SW HND	* g	D	3M	P$	Ind	Ind	Ind	2	2/14
Leisure Studies (Sports and Recreation)	087N	2FT HND	* g	D	N	P$	Ind	Ind	Ind		

CORNWALL COLLEGE WITH DUCHY COLLEGE

Hotel, Catering and Institutional Operations Mgt	007N	2FT HND	*	D	N	P	Dip	Ind	N		
Marine Leisure Management	087N	2FT Dip	*	D	N	P	Ind	Ind	N		

COVENTRY Univ

Leisure Management	N780	3FT deg	* g	12	M+4D	D	Ind	CCC	Ind		
Recreation and the Countryside	N7D9	3FT/4SW deg	* g	12	Ind	M	Ind	Ind	Ind		
Sport Science with Human Resource Management	BN67▼	3FT deg	S g	8	5M	Ind	Ind	Ind	Ind		6/14

CROYDON COLL

Hospitality and Business Management (yr 3 entry)	NN17	3FT deg	*	6	MO $	P$2	Ind	Ind			
Hospitality and Business Management	027N	2FT HND	*	2	N $	P$	Ind	Ind			

DE MONTFORT Univ

Leisure and Recreation Studies	LN37▼	3FT deg	g	12-14	9M+3D	M	Ind	BBCCC	Ind	5	6/18
Golf & Leisure Management	087N▼	3SW HND	* g	4	N	P	Ind	BB	Ind		
Outdoor Recreation Management	037N▼	2FT HND									

Univ of DERBY

Hospitality Management	N725	3FT deg		14	MO+2D	D$	28	BBCC	Ind		
Hospitality Management	027N	2FT HND	*	4	MO	M$	Dip	CCD	Ind	4	2/6

TITLE	CODE	COURSE	SUBJECTS	A/AS	ND/C	AGNVQ	IB	SQA(H)	SQA	RATIO A/AS
Univ of DUNDEE										
Hotel and Catering Management	N720	3FT/4FT deg	* g	DDD	6M $	M$	27$	BBC	N$	3 8/22
EDGE HILL Univ COLLEGE										
Leisure Management	N780	3FT deg	* g	CC	3M+3D	M* / P*^	Dip	BBCC	Ind	
FARNBOROUGH COLL of Technology										
Leisure Management	N780	3FT deg	g	10	Ind	M*	Ind	Ind	Ind	6 6/12
Science and Management of Exercise and Health	BN67	3FT deg	g	10	Ind	M*	Ind	Ind	Ind	3 8/13
Hotel and Hospitality Management (Tourism)	77PN	2FT HND		6	N		Ind	Ind	Ind	11
Leisure Studies (Entertainment and Event Mgt)	17WN	2FT HND	g	6	Ind	P*	Ind	Ind	Ind	12
Leisure Studies (Sport and Recreation)	287N	2FT HND	g	6	Ind	P*	Ind	Ind	Ind	6 3/12
Leisure Studies (Travel and Tourism)	77NP	2FT HND	g	6	Ind	P*	Ind	Ind	Ind	7
Science and Management of Health and Fitness	67BN	2FT HND	g	4	Ind	P*	Ind	Ind	Ind	2 2/12
Univ of GLAMORGAN										
Hospitality Management	N711▼	3FT deg								
Leisure Management with Language	N700	3FT deg	* g	14	MO+3D	M$	Ind	Ind	Ind	
Leisure and Recreation Management	N780	3FT deg	* g	14	MO+3D	M$	Ind	Ind	Ind	
Leisure and Tourism Management	NP77	3FT deg	* g	14	MO+3D	M$	Ind	Ind	Ind	
Combined Studies (Honours) *Recreation Management*	Y400	3FT deg	* g	8-16	Ind	Ind	Ind	Ind	Ind	
Joint Honours *Recreation Management*	Y401	3FT deg	* g	8-16	Ind	Ind	Ind	Ind	Ind	
Major/Minor Honours *Recreation Management*	Y402	3FT deg	* g	8-16	Ind	Ind	Ind	Ind	Ind	
Business Administration (Leisure & Tourism)	007N▼	2FT HND	* g	6	N $	P$	Ind	Ind	Ind	2/ 6
Sports Sci (Outdoor Activities)-(Pembrokeshire)	76NB▼	2FT HND	S g	6	Ind	Ind	Ind	Ind	Ind	
GLASGOW CALEDONIAN Univ										
Consumer and Management Studies (Home Economics)	NN97	3FT/4FT deg	E g	CD	Ind		Ind	BBC$	Ind	3
Hospitality Management	N720	3FT/4SW deg	E+M/H/F/He	CC	Ind		Ind	BBCC$	Ind	4 14/24
Leisure Management	N7L3	4SW deg	E+M	CC	Ind		Ind	BBCC$	Ind	
Hospitality Management	127N	2FT HND	E+M/S	DD	Ind		Ind	CC$	Ind	4
Univ of GREENWICH										
Hospitality Management	087N▼	2FT HND	* g	6	MO	Ind		CC	Ind	
Leisure Management	037N▼	2FT HND	* g	6	MO	Ind		CC	Ind	
Tourism Management	77PN▼	2FT HND	* g	6	MO	Ind		CC	Ind	
HEREFORDSHIRE COLLEGE of Technology										
Hospitality Management	N710	3FT deg	*	8	Ind	M	Ind	CC	N	
Leisure Management	N700	3FT deg	*	8	Ind	M	Ind	CC	N	
Hospitality Management	017N	2FT HND	*	4	Ind	M	Ind	CC	N	
Leisure Management	087N	2FT HND	*	4	Ind	M	Ind	CC	N	6 2/ 4
Univ of HUDDERSFIELD										
Catering Management and Food Sciences	ND74	4SW deg	* g	10	6M	M$ go	Ind	BBC	Ind	
Catering Management and Nutrition	BN47	4SW deg	* g	10	6M	M$ go	Ind	BBC	Ind	
Hotel and Catering Business	N720	4SW deg	* g	12	MO	M$ gi	Ind	BBC	Ind	
Science (Extended) *Catering Management and Food Sciences*	Y108	5SW deg	* g	EE	N	P$ gi	Ind	Ind	Ind	
Science (Extended) *Catering Management and Nutrition*	Y108	5SW deg	* g	EE	N	P$ gi	Ind	Ind	Ind	
Hotel and Catering Management	027N	3SW HND	* g	2	N	P$ gi	Ind	BC	Ind	

Hotel, Institutional and Recreation Management   35

course details			98 expected requirements							96 entry stats	
TITLE	CODE	COURSE	SUBJECTS	A/AS	ND/C	AGNVQ	IB	SQA(H)	SQA	RATIO	A/AS
LEEDS METROPOLITAN Univ											
Catering Technology	ND74	1FT deg									
Hospitality Business Management	N720	3FT/4SW deg	* g	12	MO	D$ go	26	BBCC	Ind	9	10/18
International Hospitality Business Management	N722	3FT/4SW deg	L g	12	MO$	M$^ go	26$	BBCC$	Ind		10/18
Leisure and Sport Management	N780	3FT deg									
Licensed Retail Management	N740	3FT/4SW deg	* g	12	MO	M$ go	26	BBCC	Ind		
Sport and Recreation Development	B6N7	3FT deg	* g	20	2M+5D	D$ go	28	BBBBB	Ind	24	16/26
Hospitality Business Management (2/3 years)	027N	2FT/3SW HND	* g	6	4M	M$ go	22	CCC	Ind	5	2/8
Leisure and Sport Management	087N	2FT HND									
Univ of LINCOLNSHIRE and HUMBERSIDE											
Hospitality Management	027N▼	2FT/3SW HND	* g								
Leisure Management	037N▼	2FT HND	g								
LIVERPOOL JOHN MOORES Univ											
Dance and Community Sport/Dance	WN47	3FT deg		12	5D	M	28$	CCCC			
Home Economics	N750	3FT deg		CC	5M	M				5	8/18
LONDON INST											
International Travel and Tourism Management	NP77	3FT deg									
Travel and Tourism Management	047N	2FT HND								22	
LOUGHBOROUGH Univ											
Physical Education, Sports Science and Recr Mgt	BN67	3FT deg	* g	26	4D	DL6/^ go	30	Ind	Ind		
Recreation Management	N780	3FT deg	* g	22	4D	DL6/^ go	30	Ind	Ind		
LSU COLL of HE											
Sport Studies	LN37	3FT deg	S/Ss/Pe	CC							
LUTON Univ											
Biochemistry with Leisure Studies	C7N7	3FT deg	g	12-16	MO/DO	M/D	32	BBCC	Ind		
Biology with Leisure Studies	C1N7	3FT deg	g	12-16	MO/DO	M/D	32	BBCC	Ind		
Biotechnology with Leisure Studies	J8N7	3FT deg	g	12-16	MO/DO	M/D	32	BBCC	Ind		
Built Environment with Leisure Studies	N8N7	3FT deg	g	12-16	MO/DO	M/D	32	BBCC	Ind		
Business Systems with Leisure Studies	N1N7	3FT deg	g	12-16	MO/DO	M/D	32	BBCC	Ind		
Contemp Br & Euro History with Leisure Studies	V1N7	3FT deg	g	12-16	MO/DO	M/D	32	BBCC	Ind		
Ecology (Eco Tech) and Leisure Studies	CN97	3FT deg	g	12-16	MO/DO	M/D	32	BBCC	Ind		
Ecology (Eco Tech) with Leisure Studies	C9N7	3FT deg	g	12-16	MO/DO	M/D	32	BBCC	Ind		
Electronic Systems Design with Leisure Studies	HN67	3FT deg	g	12-16	MO/DO	M/D	32	BBCC	Ind		
Environmental Science with Leisure Studies	F9N7	3FT deg	g	12-16	MO/DO	M/D	32	BBCC	Ind		
Environmental Studies with Leisure Studies	F9NR	3FT deg		12-16	MO/DO	M/D	32	BBCC	Ind		
European Language Studies with Leisure Studies	T2N7	4FT deg	L g	12-16	MO/DO	M/D	32	BBCC	Ind		
Geography with Leisure Studies	F8NT	3FT deg	g	12-16	MO/DO	M/D	32	BBCC	Ind		
Geology with Leisure Studies	F6N7	3FT deg	g	12-16	MO/DO	M/D	32	BBCC	Ind		
Health Science with Leisure Studies	B9N7	3FT deg	g	12-16	MO/DO	M/D	32	BBCC	Ind		
Health Studies with Leisure Studies	B9NR	3FT deg	g	12-16	MO/DO	M/D	32	BBCC	Ind		
Hospitality Management	N730	4SW deg	g	12-16	MO/DO	M/D	32	BBCC	Ind		
Leisure St and Language & Stylistics in English	QNG7	3FT deg	g	12-16	MO/DO	M/D	32	BBCC	Ind		
Leisure St with Language & Stylistics in English	N7QG	3FT deg	g	12-16	MO/DO	M/D	32	BBCC	Ind		
Leisure Studies	N780	3FT deg	g	12-16	MO/DO	M/D	32	BBCC	Ind		
Leisure Studies and Biochemistry	CN77	3FT deg	g	12-16	MO/DO	M/D	32	BBCC	Ind		
Leisure Studies and Biology	CN17	3FT deg	g	12-16	MO/DO	M/D	32	BBCC	Ind		
Leisure Studies and Biotechnology	JN87	3FT deg	g	12-16	MO/DO	M/D	32	BBCC	Ind		
Leisure Studies and British Studies	VN97	3FT deg		12-16	MO/DO	M/D	32	BBCC	Ind		
Leisure Studies and Contemporary History	VN17	3FT deg	g	12-16	MO/DO	M/D	32	BBCC	Ind		

course details | 98 expected requirements | 96 entry stats

TITLE	CODE	COURSE	SUBJECTS	A/AS	ND/C	AGNVQ	IB	SQA(H)	SQA	RATIO A/AS
Leisure Studies and Electronic System Design	HNP7	3FT deg	g	12-16	MO/DO	M/D	32	BBCC	Ind	
Leisure Studies and Environmental Science	FN97	3FT deg	g	12-16	MO/DO	M/D	32	BBCC	Ind	
Leisure Studies and European Language Studies	TN27	3FT deg	L g	12-16	MO/DO	M/D	32	BBCC	Ind	
Leisure Studies and Geography	FN87	3FT deg	g	12-16	MO/DO	M/D	32	BBCC	Ind	
Leisure Studies and Geology	FN67	3FT deg	g	12-16	MO/DO	M/D	32	BBCC	Ind	
Leisure Studies and Health Science	BN97	3FT deg	g	12-16	MO/DO	M/D	32	BBCC	Ind	
Leisure Studies and Health Studies	BNX7	3FT deg	g	12-16	MO/DO	M/D	32	BBCC	Ind	
Leisure Studies and Human Biology	BN17	3FT deg	g	12-16	MO/DO	M/D	32	BBCC	Ind	
Leisure Studies and Law	MN37	3FT deg	g	12-16	MO/DO	M/D	32	BBCC	Ind	
Leisure Studies with Animation	N7WF	3FT deg	g	12-16	MO/DO	M/D	32	BBCC	Ind	
Leisure Studies with Biochemistry	N7C7	3FT deg	g	12-16	MO/DO	M/D	32	BBCC	Ind	
Leisure Studies with Biology	N7C1	3FT deg	g	12-16	MO/DO	M/D	32	BBCC	Ind	
Leisure Studies with Biotechnology	N7J8	3FT deg	g	12-16	MO/DO	M/D	32	BBCC	Ind	
Leisure Studies with British Studies	N7V9	3FT deg		12-16	MO/DO	M/D	32	BBCC	Ind	
Leisure Studies with Chinese	N7T3	3FT deg		12-16	MO/DO	M/D	32	BBCC	Ind	
Leisure Studies with Comparative Literature	N7QF	3FT deg	g	12-16	MO/DO	M/D	32	BBCC	Ind	
Leisure Studies with Contemporary History	N7V1	3FT deg	g	12-16	MO/DO	M/D	32	BBCC	Ind	
Leisure Studies with Ecology & Biodiversity	N7C9	3FT deg	g	12-16	MO/DO	M/D	32	BBCC	Ind	
Leisure Studies with Electronic Systems Design	N7HQ	3FT deg		12-16	MO/DO	M/D	32	BBCC	Ind	
Leisure Studies with Environmental Science	N7F9	3FT deg	g	12-16	MO/DO	M/D	32	BBCC	Ind	
Leisure Studies with French	N7R1	3FT deg	F g	12-16	MO/DO	M/D	32	BBCC	Ind	
Leisure Studies with Geographical Info Systems	N7F8	3FT deg	g	12-16	MO/DO	M/D	32	BBCC	Ind	
Leisure Studies with Geography	N7FW	3FT deg	g	12-16	MO/DO	M/D	32	BBCC	Ind	
Leisure Studies with Geology	N7F6	3FT deg	g	12-16	MO/DO	M/D	32	BBCC	Ind	
Leisure Studies with Health Science	N7B9	3FT deg	g	12-16	MO/DO	M/D	32	BBCC	Ind	
Leisure Studies with Health Studies	N7BX	3FT deg		12-16	MO/DO	M/D	32	BBCC	Ind	
Leisure Studies with Human Biology	N7B1	3FT deg	g	12-16	MO/DO	M/D	32	BBCC	Ind	
Leisure Studies with Japanese	N7T4	3FT deg	L g	12-16	MO/DO	M/D	32	BBCC	Ind	
Leisure Studies with Literary Studies in English	N7Q2	3FT deg	g	12-16	MO/DO	M/D	32	BBCC	Ind	
Leisure Studies with Mapping Science	N7FV	3FT deg	g	12-16	MO/DO	M/D	32	BBCC	Ind	
Leisure Studies with Marketing	N7N5	3FT deg	g	12-16	MO/DO	M/D	32	BBCC	Ind	
Leisure Studies with Media Practices	N7P4	3FT deg	g	12-16	MO/DO	M/D	32	BBCC	Ind	
Leisure Studies with Modern English Studies	N7Q3	3FT deg	g	12-16	MO/DO	M/D	32	BBCC	Ind	
Leisure Studies with Modern History	N7VC	3FT deg	g	12-16	MO/DO	M/D	32	BBCC	Ind	
Leisure Studies with Organisational Behaviour	N7L7	3FT deg	g	12-16	MO/DO	M/D	32	BBCC	Ind	
Leisure Studies with Photography	N7W5	3FT deg	g	12-16	MO/DO	M/D	32	BBCC	Ind	
Leisure Studies with Plant Biology	N7C2	3FT deg	g	12-16	MO/DO	M/D	32	BBCC	Ind	
Leisure Studies with Pollution Studies	N7FY	3FT deg	g	12-16	MO/DO	M/D	32	BBCC	Ind	
Leisure Studies with Psychology	N7LR	3FT deg	g	12-16	MO/DO	M/D	32	BBCC	Ind	
Leisure Studies with Publishing	N7P5	3FT deg	g	12-16	MO/DO	M/D	32	BBCC	Ind	
Leisure Studies with Regional Planning and Dev	N7K4	3FT deg	g	12-16	MO/DO	M/D	32	BBCC	Ind	
Leisure Studies with Social Studies	N7L3	3FT deg	g	12-16	MO/DO	M/D	32	BBCC	Ind	
Leisure Studies with Spanish	N7R4	3FT deg	Sp g	12-16	MO/DO	M/D	32	BBCC	Ind	
Leisure Studies with TV Studies	N7WM	3FT deg	g	12-16	MO/DO	M/D	32	BBCC	Ind	
Leisure Studies with Travel and Tourism	N7P7	3FT deg	g	12-16	MO/DO	M/D	32	BBCC	Ind	
Literary Studies in English and Leisure Studies	NQ72	3FT deg	g	12-16	MO/DO	M/D	32	BBCC	Ind	
Mapping Science and Leisure Studies	NF78	3FT deg	g	12-16	MO/DO	M/D	32	BBCC	Ind	
Mapping Science with Leisure Studies	F8N7	3FT deg	g	12-16	MO/DO	M/D	32	BBCC	Ind	
Marketing and Leisure Studies	NN57	3FT deg	3g	12-16	MO/DO	M/D	32	BBCC	Ind	
Marketing with Leisure Studies	N5N7	3FT deg	g	12-16	MO/DO	M/D	32	BBCC	Ind	
Media Practices and Leisure Studies	NP74	3FT deg	g	12-16	MO/DO	M/D	32	BBCC	Ind	
Media Practices with Leisure Studies	P4N7	3FT deg	g	12-16	MO/DO	M/D	32	BBCC	Ind	

Hotel, Institutional and Recreation Management   35

course details | 98 expected requirements | 96 entry stats

TITLE	CODE	COURSE	SUBJECTS	A/AS	NQ/C	AGNVQ	IB	SQA(H)	SQA	RATIO A/AS
Modern English Studies and Leisure Studies	NQ73	3FT deg	g	12-16	MO/DO	M/D	32	BBCC	Ind	
Modern English Studies with Leisure Studies	Q3N7	3FT deg	g	12-16	MO/DO	M/D	32	BBCC	Ind	
Organisational Behaviour and Leisure Studies	NL77	3FT deg	g	12-16	MO/DO	M/D	32	BBCC	Ind	
Physical Geography and Leisure Studies	NF7V	3FT deg	g	12-16	MO/DO	M/D	32	BBCC	Ind	
Physical Geography with Leisure Studies	F8NR	3FT deg	g	12-16	MO/DO	M/D	32	BBCC	Ind	
Planning Studies and Leisure Studies	KN47	3FT deg	G	12-16	MO/DO	M/D	32	BBCC	Ind	
Plant Biology and Leisure Studies	CN27	3FT deg	g	12-16	MO/DO	M/D	32	BBCC	Ind	
Plant Biology with Leisure Studies	C2N7	3FT deg	g	12-16	MO/DO	M/D	32	BBCC	Ind	
Psychology and Leisure Studies	NL7R	3FT deg	g	12-16	MO/DO	M/D	32	BBCC	Ind	
Psychology with Leisure Studies	L7NR	3FT deg	g	12-16	MO/DO	M/D	32	BBCC	Ind	
Regional Planning and Develop with Leisure St	K4N7	3FT deg	g	12-16	MO/DO	M/D	32	BBCC	Ind	
Regional Planning and Development & Leisure St	NK74	3FT deg	g	12-16	MO/DO	M/D	32	BBCC	Ind	
Social Policy and Leisure Studies	LN47	3FT deg		12-16	MO/DO	M/D	32	BBCC	Ind	
Social Policy with Leisure Studies	L4N7	3FT deg		12-16	MO/DO	M/D	32	BBCC	Ind	
Social Studies and Leisure Studies	NL73	3FT deg	g	12-16	MO/DO	M/D	32	BBCC	Ind	
Social Studies with Leisure Studies	L3N7	3FT deg	g	12-16	MO/DO	M/D	32	BBCC	Ind	
Sport and Fitness Studies	BN67	3FT deg	g	12-16	MO/DO	M/D	32	BBCC	Ind	
Sport and Recreation Facilities Management	N782	3FT deg		12-16	MO/DO	M/D	32	BBCC	Ind	
Sports & Leisure Facilities Management	N735	3FT deg	g	12-16	MO/DO	M/D	32	BBCC	Ind	
Sports and Fitness Science	B6N7	3FT deg	g	12-16	MO/DO	M/D	32	BBCC	Ind	1
Stage & Screen Technology and Leisure Studies	PNK7	3FT deg		12-16	MO/DO	M/D	32	BBCC	Ind	
Travel and Tourism and Leisure Studies	NP77	3FT deg	g	12-16	MO/DO	M/D	32	BBCC	Ind	
Travel and Tourism with Leisure Studies	P7N7	3FT deg	g	12-16	MO/DO	M/D	32	BBCC	Ind	
Women's Studies and Leisure Studies	MN97	3FT deg		12-16	MO/DO	M/D	32	BBCC	Ind	
Women's Studies with Leisure Studies	M9N7	3FT deg		12-16	MO/DO	M/D	32	BBCC	Ind	

Univ of MANCHESTER

Leisure Management	LN37	3FT deg	*	20-24	MO+5D	D^	28	ABBBB	Ind	

MANCHESTER METROPOLITAN Univ

Applied Consumer Science	N750	3FT/4SW deg	* g	10-12	Ind	M	24	CCCC	Ind	6/26
Business with Leisure (HND top-up)	N1NR	1FT deg								10/16
Business with Sport (HND top-up)	NN1R	1FT deg								
Hotel Management with Tourism	N7P7	4SW deg	* g	14	Ind	D	28	BBC	Ind	8/18
Hotel and Catering Management	N720	4SW deg	* g	14	Ind	D	28	BBC	Ind	8/18
International Hotel Management	N722	4SW deg	* g	14	Ind	D	28	BBC	Ind	8/18
Business with Leisure	71NN	2FT HND	* g	4	M+D	M	24	C	Ind	2/8
Business with Sport	17NN	2FT HND	* g	4	3M	M	24	C	Ind	2/8
Hotel Management with Tourism	7P7N	3SW HND	* g	6	Ind	M	24	CCC	Ind	4/8
Hotel and Catering Management	027N	3SW HND	* g	6	Ind	M	24	CCC	Ind	4/8

MIDDLESEX Univ

Hotel and Restaurant Management	N720▼	4SW deg	* g	CD	5M	M$ go	24	Ind	Ind	
Hospitality Management	047N▼	2FT HND	* g	2	N	PH go	Ind	Ind	Ind	
Hotel and Catering Management	027N▼	2FT HND	* g	2	N	PH go	Ind	Ind	Ind	

MORAY HOUSE Inst of Ed

Leisure Studies	N780	3FT/4FT deg	g	CCD	Ind	Ind		BBCC	Ind	10

NAPIER Univ

Hospitality (Hotel and Catering Management)	N720	4FT deg	*	CC-DDD	Ind	Ind	Ind	BBCC	Ind	12
Hospitality and Languages	NT79	3FT/4FT deg	*	CC-DDD	Ind	Ind	Ind	BBCC	Ind	
Hospitality and Marketing	NN57	3FT/4FT deg	*	CCD	Ind	Ind	Ind	BBCC	Ind	
Hotel Services Management	N740	3FT deg	*	C-DE	Ind	Ind	Ind	CCC	Ind	3 8/10

course details

TITLE	CODE	COURSE	SUBJECTS	A/AS	ND/C	AGNVQ	IB	SQA(H)	SQA	RATIO A/AS
NENE COLLEGE										
American Studies with Sport Studies	Q4N7	3FT deg		DD	5M	M	24	CCC	Ind	
Art and Design with Sport Studies	W2N7	3FT deg		DD	5M	M	24	CCC	Ind	
Earth Science with Sport Studies	F9N7	3FT deg		DD	5M	M	24	CCC	Ind	
Economics with Sport Studies	L1N7	3FT deg	g	6	5M	M	24	CCC	Ind	
Energy Management with Sport Studies	J9N7	3FT deg	g	EE	3M	P	24	CCC	Ind	
English with Sport Studies	Q3N7▼	3FT deg		CC	4M+1D	M	24	CCC	Ind	
French with Sport Studies	R1N7	3FT deg	F	DD	5M	Ind	24	CCC	Ind	
Geography with Sport Studies	F8N7	3FT deg	Gy	8	5M	M	24	CCC	Ind	
History with Sport Studies	V1N7▼	3FT deg		CD	5M	M	24	CCC	Ind	
Human Biological Studies with Sport Studies	B1N7▼	3FT deg	S	DE	5M	M	24	CCC	Ind	
Information Systems with Sport Studies	G5N7	3FT deg		6	5M	M	24	CCC	Ind	
Law with Sport Studies	M3N7	3FT deg	g	10	3M	M	24	CCC	Ind	
Management Science with Sport Studies	G4N7	3FT deg	g	DD	5M	M	24	CCC	Ind	
Mathematics with Sport Studies	G1N7	3FT deg	M	DD	Ind	Ind	24	CCC	Ind	
Music with Sport Studies	W3N7	3FT deg	Mu	EE	3M	P	24	CCC	Ind	
Politics with Sport Studies	M1N7	3FT deg		CD	5M	M	24	CCC	Ind	
Psychology with Sport Studies	C8N7▼	3FT deg	g	CC	5M+1D	M	24	CCC	Ind	
Sport St with Personal & Organisational Develop	N7N6▼	3FT deg	SS/Pe	12	M+2D	M	24		Ind	
Sport Studies with American Studies	N7Q4	3FT deg	Ss/Pe	12	M+2D	M	24	BBB	Ind	
Sport Studies with Art and Design	N7W2	3FT deg	Ss/Pe	12	M+2D	M	24	BBB	Ind	
Sport Studies with Chemistry and the Environment	N7F1	3FT deg	Ss/Pe	12	M+2D	M	24	BBB	Ind	
Sport Studies with Earth Science	N7F9	3FT deg	Ss/Pe	12	M+2D	M	24	BBB	Ind	
Sport Studies with Economics	N7L1	3FT deg	Ss/Pe g	12	M+2D	M	24	BBB	Ind	
Sport Studies with English	N7Q3▼	3FT deg	Ss/Pe	12	M+2D	M	24	BBB	Ind	
Sport Studies with French	N7R1	3FT deg	F+Ss/Pe	12	M+2D	M	24	BBB	Ind	
Sport Studies with Geography	N7F8	3FT deg	Ss/Pe	12	M+2D	M	24	BBB	Ind	
Sport Studies with Health Studies	N7L5▼	3FT deg	Ss/Pe	12	M+2D	M	24	BBB	Ind	
Sport Studies with History	N7V1▼	3FT deg	Ss/Pe	12	M+2D	M	24	BBB	Ind	
Sport Studies with Human Biological Studies	N7B1▼	3FT deg	Ss/Pe	12	M+2D	M	24	BBB	Ind	
Sport Studies with Industry and Enterprise	N7H1	3FT deg	Ss/Pe g	12	M+2D	M	24	BBB	Ind	
Sport Studies with Information Systems	N7G5	3FT deg	Ss/Pe	12	M+2D	M	24	BBB		
Sport Studies with Law	N7M3	3FT deg	Ss/Pe g	12	M+2D	M	24	BBB	Ind	
Sport Studies with Management Science	N7G4	3FT deg	Ss/Pe g	12	M+2D	M	24	BBB	Ind	
Sport Studies with Mathematics	N7G1	3FT deg	M+Ss/Pe	12	M+2D	M	24	BBB	Ind	
Sport Studies with Media and Popular Culture	N7P4▼	3FT deg	Ss/Pe	12	M+2D	M	24	BBB	Ind	
Sport Studies with Music	N7W3	3FT deg	Mu+Ss/Pe	12	M+2D	M	24	BBB	Ind	
Sport Studies with Philosophy	N7V7▼	3FT deg	Ss/Pe	12	M+2D	M	24	BBB	Ind	
Sport Studies with Property Management	N7N8	3FT deg	Ss/Pe	12	M+2D	M	24	BBB	Ind	
Sport Studies with Psychology	N7C8▼	3FT deg	Ss/Pe g	12	M+2D	M	24	BBB	Ind	
NEWCASTLE COLL										
Hotel, Catering & Institutional Management	047N▼	2FT/3FT HND								
NESCOT										
Leisure Management	087N	2FT HND	*	D	6M	P	Dip	Ind	N$	
Nature Conservation for Leisure and Tourism	7N2D	2FT HND	*	E	N	P	Dip	Ind	N$	
NORTH EAST WALES INST of HE										
Leisure Studies	77NP	2FT HND		2-6	N	P$	Ind	CC	N$	
NORTH EAST WORCESTERSHIRE COLL										
Hotel and Catering Management	027N	2FT HND								
Leisure Studies	087N	2FT HND								

Hotel, Institutional and Recreation Management   35

TITLE	CODE	COURSE	SUBJECTS	A/AS	NO/C	AGNVQ	IB	SQA(H)	SQA	RATIO A/AS
NORTH LINCOLNSHIRE COLLEGE										
Leisure and Hospitality Management	537N	2FT HND	* g	Ind	Ind	Ind	Ind	Ind	Ind	
Univ of NORTH LONDON										
Caribbean Studies and Leisure Studies	NT77	3FT deg	* g	CC	MO+4D	D	Ind	Ind	Ind	
European Studies and Hospitality Management	NT72	3FT deg	* g	CD	MO+4D	D	Ind	Ind	Ind	
Health Policy and Sports Management	LN47	3FT deg	* g	CC	MO+4D	Ind	Ind	Ind	Ind	
Hospitality Management	N721	3FT/4SW deg	* g	12	MO+4D	Ind	Ind	CCCC	Ind	25
Hospitality Management and Caribbean Studies	NT7T	3FT deg	* g	12	MO+4D	D	Ind	Ind	Ind	
International Hospitality Management	N720	4SW deg	* g	12	MO+4D	Ind	Ind	CCCC	Ind	23
International Leisure & Tourism Management	PN7R	4SW deg	* g	14	MO+4D	Ind	Ind	CCCC	Ind	
Leisure Studies and Geography	LN87	3FT deg	* g	12	MO+4D	Ind	Ind	Ind	Ind	
Leisure Studies and Social Research	LN37	3FT deg	* g	CC	MO+4D	Ind	Ind	Ind	Ind	
Leisure Studies and Sociology	LN3R	3FT deg	* g	12-14	MO+4D	Ind	Ind	Ind	Ind	
Leisure Studies and Urban Policy	KN47	3FT deg	* g	12	MO+4D	Ind	Ind	Ind	Ind	
Leisure and Tourism Management	PN77	4SW deg	* g	14	4D	Ind	Ind	CCCC	Ind	
Combined Honours Hospitality Management	Y400	3FT deg	* g	12-14	MO+4D	Ind	Ind	CCCC	Ind	
Combined Honours Human Resource Studies	Y400	3FT deg	* g	14	MO+4D	Ind	Ind	CCCC	Ind	
Combined Honours Leisure Studies	Y400	3FT deg	* g	14	MO+4D$	Ind	Ind	CCCC	Ind	
Hospitality and Business Management	17NN	2FT HND	* g	4	8M	Ind	Ind	CCC	Ind	
Sports and Leisure Management	007N	2FT HND	* g	6	10M	Ind	Ind	CCC	Ind	
Tourism Management	77PN	2FT HND	* g	6	10M	Ind	Ind	CCC	Ind	
Univ of NORTHUMBRIA										
Sport Studies	B6N7	3FT deg	g	BCC	1M+5D	D+/^	28	BBBBC	Ind	17 14/26
NORWICH: City COLL										
Hospitality Management	N710	1FT deg					Dip			
Hospitality and Tourism Management	N720	4SW deg	* g	6	M	PH/L go	Ind	Ind	Ind	4 6/10
Hotel, Catering and Institutional Management	107N	2FT HND	* g		5M $	PH go	Ind	Ind	N	5
Hotel, Catering and Institutional Management	007N	3SW HND	* g	E	MO	PB/H/L go	Ind	Ind	Ind	4 1/11
NOTTINGHAM TRENT Univ										
International Hospitality Management	N720	4SW deg	* g	14	M+D $		Ind	Ind	Ind	7 12/24
Sport (Administration & Science)	BN67	3FT deg	S/M g	BB	Ind	Ind	Dip	BBC	$	
Sport Science (Administration and Coaching)	B6N7▼	3FT deg	S g	CC	Ind	Ind	Dip	BB	$	
Hotel, Catering and Institutional Management	107N	3SW HND	* g	8	MO	M$	Ind	Ind	Ind	5 4/14
Hotel, Catering and Institutional Mgt(Full-Time)	007N	2FT HND	* g	8	MO	MH	Ind	Ind	Ind	20
Sport (Science and Recreation Management)	76NB▼	2FT HND	S/Pe/Ss g	6	MO	Ind	Dip	C	$	2/ 8
Sport Science (Administration & Coaching)	7N6B▼	2FT HND	S g	DD	Ind	Ind	Dip	C	$	
OXFORD BROOKES Univ										
Geography and the Phys Env/Hospitality Mgt St	FNV7	3FT deg								
Hospitality Management St/Accounting and Finance	NN47	3FT deg	* g	DDD-BCC	Ind	M*3/D*3	Ind	Ind	Ind	7
Hospitality Management St/Computing Mathematics	GN97	3FT deg	* g	CC-DDD	Ind	M*/M*3	Ind	Ind	Ind	
Hospitality Management St/Environmental Sciences	FNX7	3FT deg	S/M g	CC-DDD	Ind	M*3/DS	Ind	Ind	Ind	
Hospitality Management St/Health Care (Post Exp)	BN77	3FT deg		X		X	X	X		
Hospitality Management Stds/Environmental Chem	NF71	3FT deg								
Hospitality Management Studies/Anthropology	LN67	3FT deg	*	DDD-BCC	Ind	M*^/M*3	Ind	Ind	Ind	1
Hospitality Management Studies/Biological Chem	CN77	3FT deg								
Hospitality Management Studies/Biology	CN17	3FT deg	S/M g	DD-CC	Ind	MS/M*3	Ind	Ind	Ind	
Hospitality Management Studies/Cartography	FN87	3FT deg	* g	CC-DDD	Ind	M*/M*3	Ind	Ind	Ind	
Hospitality Management Studies/Cell Biology	CNC7	3FT deg								

course details | 98 expected requirements | 96 entry stats

TITLE	CODE	COURSE	SUBJECTS	A/AS	ND/C	AGNVQ	IB	SQA(H)	SQA	RATIO A/AS
Hospitality Management Studies/Combined Studies	NY74	3FT deg		X		X	X			
Hospitality Management Studies/Computer Systems	GN67	3FT deg	* g	DDD-BC	Ind	M*/M*3	Ind	Ind	Ind	
Hospitality Management Studies/Computing	GN57	3FT deg	* g	DDD-BC	Ind	M*/M*3	Ind	Ind	Ind	
Hospitality Management Studies/Ecology	CN97	3FT deg	* g	DD-DDD	Ind	MS/M*3	Ind	Ind	Ind	
Hospitality Management Studies/Economics	LN17	3FT deg	* g	DDD-BB	Ind	M*3	Ind	Ind	Ind	2
Hospitality Management Studies/Educational Studs	NX79	3FT deg	*	CC-DDD	Ind	M*3	Ind	Ind	Ind	
Hospitality Management Studies/Electronics	HN67	3FT deg	S/M	CC-DDD	Ind	MS/M*3	Ind	Ind	Ind	
Hospitality Management Studies/English Studies	NQ73	3FT deg	*	DDD-AB	Ind	M*^/3	Ind	Ind	Ind	
Hospitality Management Studies/Exercise & Health	NB76	3FT deg	S/M	DD-CC	Ind	MS/M*3	Ind	Ind	Ind	
Hospitality Management Studies/Fine Art	NW71	3FT deg	Pf+A	BC-DDD	Ind	MA^/M*3	Ind	Ind	Ind	
Hospitality Management Studies/Geography	LN87	3FT deg	*	DDD-BB	Ind	M*/M*3	Ind	Ind	Ind	8
Hospitality Management Studies/Geology	FN67	3FT deg	S/M	DD-CC	Ind	M*3/PS	Ind	Ind	Ind	
Hospitality Management Studies/Geotechnics	HN27	3FT deg	S/M	CC-DDD	Ind	MS/M$3	Ind	Ind	Ind	
Hospitality Management Studies/German Studies	NR7G	4SW deg	G	CC-DDD	Ind	M^/M*3	Ind	Ind	Ind	
Hospitality Management Studies/History	NV71	3FT deg	*	DDD-BB	Ind	M^/M*3	Ind	Ind	Ind	5
Hospitality Management Studies/History of Art	NV74	3FT deg	*	DDD-BCC	Ind	M*/M*3	Ind	Ind	Ind	6
Hospitality Mgt St/French Language & Literature	NR71	4SW deg	F	CC-DDD	Ind	M^/M*3	Ind	Ind	Ind	
Hospitality Mgt St/German Lang and Contemp Stud	NR7F	4SW deg	G	CC-DDD	Ind	M^/M*3	Ind	Ind	Ind	
Hospitality Mgt St/German Language & Literature	NR72	4SW deg	G	CC-DDD	Ind	M^/M*3	Ind	Ind	Ind	
Hospitality Mgt Studies/Environmental Policy	KN37	3FT deg								
Hospitality Mgt Studies/Food Science & Nutrition	DN47	3FT deg	S g	DD-CC	Ind	MS/M*3	Ind	Ind	Ind	3
Hospitality Mgt Studies/French Lang & Contemp St	NR7C	4SW deg	F	CC-DDD	Ind	M^/M*3	Ind	Ind	Ind	2
Hospitality Mgt Studs/Business Admin and Mgt	NN17	3FT deg	* g	DDD-BBC	Ind	M*3/MB4	Ind	Ind	Ind	8
Hotel and Restaurant Management	N720	4SW deg	*	CC-DDD	Ind	M*3	Ind	Ind	Ind	4	6/20
Human Biology/Hospitality Management Studies	BN17	3FT deg								
Information Systems/Hospitality Management Studs	GNM7	3FT deg	* g	CC-BC	Ind	M*/M*3	Ind	Ind	Ind	
Intelligent Systems/Hospitality Management Studs	GN87	3FT deg	* g	CC-DDD	Ind	M*/M*3	Ind	Ind	Ind	
Law/Hospitality Management Studies	MN37	3FT deg	*	DDD-BBB	Ind	M*3/D*3	Ind	Ind	Ind	
Leisure Planning/Hospitality Management Studies	KNH7	3FT deg								
Marketing Management/Hospitality Management St	NN7N	3FT deg	* g	DDD-BCC	Ind	M*3/D*3	Ind	Ind	Ind	4
Mathematics/Hospitality Management Studies	GN17	3FT deg	M g	DD-CC	Ind	M^/M*3	Ind	Ind	Ind	
Music/Hospitality Management Studies	NW73	3FT deg	Mu	DD-CC	Ind	M/M*3	Ind	Ind	Ind	
Palliative Care/Hospitality Mgt St (Post Exp)	BNR7	3FT deg		X		X	X	X		
Planning Studies/Hospitality Management Studies	KN47	3FT deg	* g	CC-DDD	Ind	M*/M*3	Ind	Ind	Ind	
Politics/Hospitality Management Studies	MN17	3FT deg	*	DDD-AB	Ind	M^/M*3	Ind	Ind	Ind	
Psychology/Hospitality Management Studies	CN87	3FT deg	* g	DDD-BBC	Ind	M^/M*3	Ind	Ind	Ind	12
Rehabilitation/Hospitality Mgt St (Post Exp)	BNT7	3FT deg		X		X	X	X		
Sociology/Hospitality Management Studies	LN37	3FT deg	* g	BCC	Ind	M*^/M*3	Ind	Ind	Ind	
Software Engineering/Hospitality Management Stds	GN77	3FT deg	* g	BB-BC	Ind	M*/M*3	Ind	Ind	Ind	
Statistics/Hospitality Management Studies	GN47	3FT deg	* g	DD-CC	Ind	M*/M*3	Ind	Ind	Ind	
Telecommunications/Hospitality Management Studs	HNP7	3FT deg								
Tourism/Hospitality Management Studies	NP77	3FT deg	* g	DDD-BC	Ind	M*3	Ind	Ind	Ind	9
Transport Planning/Hospitality Management Studs	NN79	3FT deg	* g	CC-DDD	Ind	M*/M*3	Ind	Ind	Ind	
Water Resources/Hospitality Management Studies	HNF7	3FT deg								

Univ of PLYMOUTH

TITLE	CODE	COURSE	SUBJECTS	A/AS	ND/C	AGNVQ	IB	SQA(H)	SQA	RATIO A/AS
Hospitality Management	N720	4SW deg	* g	10	4M $	M$	Ind	BCCC	Ind	4	4/16
Hospitality Mgt Stage one degree modules	N708	4SW deg	* g	10	4M $	M$	Ind	BCCC	Ind	
European Hospitality Management (PCFE)	007N	2FT HND	* g	2	MO	M$	Ind	Ind	Ind	4	2/12
Hotel,Catering and Inst Management (S Devon)	027N	2FT HND	* g	2	N	P$	Ind	Ind	Ind	4	2/10
Leisure Management (South Devon)	187N	2FT HND	* g	6	5M	M$	Ind	Ind	Ind	
Sports & Recreation Management (Exeter College)	087N	2FT HND	* g	6	MO	M$	Ind	Ind	Ind	
Tourist Attractions Management (Somerset)	047N	2FT HND	* g	6	MO	M$	Ind	Ind	Ind	3	4/16
Travel and Tourism Management (E Devon)	247N	2FT HND	* g	8	MO	M$	Ind	Ind	Ind	6	2/12

Hotel, Institutional and Recreation Management 35

TITLE	CODE	COURSE	SUBJECTS	A/AS	ND/C	AGNVQ	IB	SQA(H)	SQA	RATIO	A/AS
Univ of PORTSMOUTH											
Hospitality Management	N720	4SW deg	*	12	5M+1D	M$6/^ go	Dip	CCCCC	Ind	8	8/18
Hospitality Management with Tourism	NP77	3FT deg	*	12	5M+1D	M$6/^ go	Dip	CCCCC	Ind		
Leisure Resource Management	NN78	3FT deg	*	14	6M	M*6/^	Dip	BBCC	Ind		
Sports Management	N780	3FT deg	S	18	M0	D$6/^	26	BBBB	Ind		
QUEEN MARGARET COLL											
Hospitality and Tourism Management	NP77	3FT/4FT deg	* g	CD	M+D	M$ go	Ind	BBC	Ind	6	10/12
International Hospitality Management	N700	3FT/4FT deg	* g	DD	M+D	M$ go	Ind	BCC	Ind	9	
READING COLLEGE AND SCHOOL OF ART AND DESIGN											
Hotel Catering and Institutional Management	027N	2FT HND									
Univ College of RIPON & YORK ST JOHN											
Heritage St: Environmental, Leis & Heritage Mgt	N7P7	3FT deg		CD	M	M	27	BBBC			
Leisure and Tourism Management	N780	3FT deg		14	M	M	30				
ROBERT GORDON Univ											
Hospitality Management	N720	3FT/4FT deg	* g	DE	N	Ind	Ind	BCC$	Ind	5	
Tourism and Hospitality Management	PN77	3FT/4FT deg	* g	DE	N	Ind	Ind	BCC$	Ind		
Hospitality Management	027N	2FT HND	* g	D	N	Ind	Ind	BC$	Ind	3	
ROEHAMPTON INST											
Leisure Management Studies and Environmental Stu	FN97	3FT deg									
Leisure Managment Studies and Sports Studies	BN67	3FT deg									
SCOTTISH Agric COLL											
Leisure and Recreation Management	N780▼	3FT/4FT deg	*	CC	Ind	M$	Ind	BCC	Ind	3	
Leisure and Recreation Management	087N▼	2FT HND	*	D	N $	P$	Ind	CC	Ind	3	
Univ of SALFORD											
Applied Consumer Studies	N750	3FT deg		10	M0	M	28	BBB	Ind	17	
Food Industry Management	N721	3FT deg		8	M0	M					
Hospitality Management	N720	3FT deg		12	Ind	M	28	BBB	Ind	22	
Leisure Management	N780	3FT deg		12	M0	D	28	CCCCC	Ind	13	12/18
Applied Consumer Studies	057N	2FT HND	* g	2	5M	P	24	CC	Ind	3	4/6
Hotel, Catering and Institutional Management	027N	2FT HND		2	5M	M	24	DDD	Ind	6	2/8
Leisure Management	087N	2FT HND		6	5M	M	24	CC	Ind	6	4/8
Univ College SCARBOROUGH											
Leisure and Tourism Management	NP77	3FT deg	* g	DD	Ind	P	27$	Ind	Ind		
Leisure and Tourism with Arts	N7Y3	3FT deg	* g	DD	Ind	P	27$	Ind	Ind		
Leisure and Tourism with Sciences	N7Y1	3FT deg	* g	DD	Ind	P	27$	Ind	Ind		
Leisure and Tourism with Social Sciences	N7Y2	3FT deg	* g	DD	Ind	P	27$	Ind	Ind		
SHEFFIELD HALLAM Univ											
Countryside Recreation Management	DN27	3FT deg	*	14	8M+2D	M	Ind	Ind	Ind		
Food and Consumer Studies	DN47	3FT/4SW deg	g	10	10M	M	Ind	Ind	Ind		
Hotel and Catering Management	N720	3FT/4SW deg	*	12	8M+2D	M	Ind	Ind	Ind		
Hotel and Tourism Management	NP77	3FT/4SW deg	*	16	6M+4D	D	Ind	Ind	Ind		
Recreation Management	N780▼	3FT deg	*	16	6M+4D	D	Ind	Ind	Ind		
Tourism Management	PN7R	3FT deg	*	16	8M+2D	M	Ind	Ind	Ind		
Tourism and Recreation Management	PN77	3FT deg	*	16	6M+2D	D	Ind	Ind	Ind		
Combined Studies *Catering Systems*	Y400	3FT deg	*	14	2M	M	Ind	Ind	Ind		
Combined Studies *Countryside Management*	Y400	3FT deg	*	14	2M	M	Ind	Ind	Ind		

course details			98 expected requirements							96 entry stats	
TITLE	CODE	COURSE	SUBJECTS	A/AS	ND/C	AGNVQ	IB	SQA(H)	SQA	RATIO A/AS	
Combined Studies *Food and Consumer Studies*	Y400	3FT deg	*	14	2M	M	Ind	Ind	Ind		
Combined Studies *Hotel Management*	Y400	3FT deg	*	14	2M	M	Ind	Ind	Ind		
Combined Studies *Recreation Management*	Y400	3FT deg	*	14	2M	M	Ind	Ind	Ind		
Hotel, Catering and Institutional Management	027N▼	2FT/3SW HND	g	6	4M	P	Ind	Ind	Ind		
Leisure Studies	087N▼	2FT HND		E	N	P	Ind	Ind	Ind		

SOLIHULL COLL

Leisure Management	N730	2FT deg	*	X	HN	X	X	X	X		
Leisure Studies	037N	2FT HND	*	E	N	P	Dip	Ind	Ind		

SOUTHAMPTON INST

Maritime Leisure Management	N780▼	3FT deg	*	8	MO	M$	Dip	CCCC	N		
Sports Studies with Business	NN17	3FT deg	*	12	MO	M*4 gi	Dip	CCCC	N		8/16
Hotel, Catering and Institutional Management	007N▼	2FT HND	*	2	N	P$	Dip	CCCC	N	2	
Leisure Studies (Sport and Recreation)	187N	2FT HND	*	6	MO	M$	Dip	CCCC	N		
Leisure Studies (Water-based)	287N	2FT HND	*	6	MO	M$	Dip	CCCC	N		

SOUTH BANK Univ

Hotel Management	N720	4SW deg	* g	CC	6M	M go	Ind	Ind	Ind		
International Hotel and Tourism Management	PN77	3FT deg	L g	CC	6M	M go	Ind	Ind	Ind		
Leisure Management	N780	3FT/4SW deg	* g	CC	MO	M go	Ind	Ind	Ind		

SOUTHWARK COLL

Sports Coaching and Management	76NB	2FT HND	Bu/S/Ss/Pe/Ph	E	Ind	Ind	Ind	Ind	Ind		

THE UNIVERSITY COLLEGE OF ST MARK AND ST JOHN

Community Studies/Physical Recreation Progs	L5N7	3FT deg		10	MO	M	Dip	Ind	Ind		
Geography/Physical Recreation Programmes	L8NR	3FT deg	Gy	8-10	MO	M	Ind	Ind	Ind		
Leisure & Tourism Studies/Physical Recr Prog	P7N7	3FT deg		8	MO	M	Ind	Ind	Ind		
Physical Recreation Programmes/Community St	N7LM	3FT deg		10	MO	M	Ind	Ind	Ind		
Physical Recreation Programmes/Geography	N7LV	3FT deg		10	MO	M	Ind	Ind	Ind		
Physical Recreation Programmes/Leis & Tour St	N7P7	3FT deg		10	MO	M	Ind	Ind	Ind		

STAFFORDSHIRE Univ

Leisure Economics	L1N7	3FT deg	g	12	4M	M$		BBC			
Sport and Leisure Management	BN67	3FT deg	*	16	2M+4D	D	Ind	BBCC	Ind		

Univ of STRATHCLYDE

Hotel and Hospitality Management	N720	3FT/4FT deg	g	CCC	Ind		26	BBBCC$	HN		

UNIVERSITY COLLEGE SUFFOLK

Hotel, Catering and Institutional Management	027N	2FT HND	*	E	N	P*	Ind	Ind	Ind		
Leisure and Tourism Studies	77PN	2FT HND	*	E	N	P*	Ind	Ind	Ind		

Univ of SUNDERLAND

Countryside Recreation and Leisure	DN27	3FT deg	* g	12	M6	M	Ind	CCCC	N		
Countryside Recreation and Leisure (Foundation)	DN2T	4EXT deg	*		Ind	Ind	Ind	Ind	Ind		
Themed Leisure Management and Design	N7W2	3FT deg	* g	18	1M+4D	D	26	BBBCC	N$		

Univ of SURREY

Hotel and Catering Management	N720	4SW deg	* g	BCC-CCC	MO+3D	Ind	30$	BBBB	Ind	5	14/24
International Hospitality and Tourism Management	N730	3FT/4SW deg	* g	BCC-CCC	Ind	Ind	Ind	Ind	Ind	20	

Hotel, Institutional and Recreation Management   35

TITLE	CODE	COURSE	SUBJECTS	A/AS	ND/C	AGNVQ	IB	SQA(H)	SQA	RATIO A/AS
course details			**98 expected requirements**							**96 entry stats**
SWANSEA INST of HE										
European Languages and Leisure Management	NT72	3FT deg	2L	12		D	Ind	Ind	Ind	
Leisure Management	N780	3FT deg	*	DC		M	Ind	Ind	Ind	
Recreation Management	N730	3FT deg	*	10	6M	M	Ind	Ind	Ind	
Sports Studies	LN37	3FT deg	Pe+Ss	10	4M	M	Ind	Ind	Ind	
Univ of TEESSIDE										
Business and Hospitality	047N▼	2FT HND								
Business and Leisure	037N▼	2FT HND								
THAMES VALLEY Univ										
Environmental Policy and Mgt with Recreation Mgt	F9N7	3FT deg		8-12	MO	M	26	CCC		
Food and Drink Consumer St with Hospitality Mgt	D4N7	3FT deg		8-12	MO	M	26	CCC		
Food and Drink Consumer Studies with Hotel Mgt	D4NR	3FT deg		8-12	MO	M	26	CCC		
Food and Drink Consumer Studies with Leisure Mgt	D4NT	3FT deg		8-12	MO	M	26	CCC		
Hospitality Management with Business	N7N1	2FT/3FT Dip/deg		2-12	N/MO	P/M	24	CC		
Hospitality Management with Culinary Arts	N7C9	3FT deg		8-12	MO	M	26	CCC		
Hospitality Management with English Language St	N7Q1	3FT deg		8-12	MO	M	26	CCC		
Hospitality Management with Food Services Mgt	N7N9	3FT deg		8-12	MO	M	26	CCC		
Hospitality Management with French	N7R1	3FT deg		8-12	MO	M	26	CCC		
Hospitality Management with German	N7R2	3FT deg		8-12	MO	M	26	CCC		
Hospitality Management with Hotel Management	N701	3FT deg		8-12	MO	M	26	CCC		
Hospitality Management with Human Resource Mgt	N7N6	3FT deg		8-12	MO	M	26	CCC		
Hospitality Management with Leisure Management	N702	3FT deg		8-12	MO	M	26	CCC		
Hospitality Management with Marketing	N7N5	3FT deg		8-12	MO	M	26	CCC		
Hospitality Management with Recreation Mgt	N703	3FT deg		8-12	MO	M	26	CCC		
Hospitality Management with Retail Management	N7NM	3FT deg		8-12	MO	M	26	CCC		
Hospitality Management with Spanish	N7R4	3FT deg		8-12	MO	M	26	CCC		
Hospitality Management with Tourism	N7P7	3FT deg		8-12	MO	M	26	CCC		
Hospitality Mgt with Food and Drink Consumer St	N7D4	3FT deg		8-12	MO	M	26	CCC		
Leisure Management with Business	N7NC	3FT deg		8-12	MO	M	26	CCC		
Leisure Management with Culinary Arts	N7CX	3FT deg		8-12	MO	M	26	CCC		
Leisure Management with English Language Studies	N7QC	3FT deg		8-12	MO	M	26	CCC		
Leisure Management with Food Services Management	N7NX	3FT deg		8-12	MO	M	26	CCC		
Leisure Management with French	N7RC	3FT deg		8-12	MO	M	26	CCC		
Leisure Management with German	N7RF	3FT deg		8-12	MO	M	26	CCC		
Leisure Management with Health Studies	N7LK	3FT deg		8-12	MO	M	26	CCC		
Leisure Management with Hospitality Management	N704	3FT deg		8-12	MO	M	26	CCC		
Leisure Management with Hotel Management	N705	3FT deg		8-12	MO	M	26	CCC		
Leisure Management with Human Resource Mgt	N7NP	3FT deg		8-12	MO	M	26	CCC		
Leisure Management with Marketing	N7NN	3FT deg		8-12	MO	M	26	CCC		
Leisure Management with Recreation Management	N706	3FT deg		8-12	MO	M	26	CCC		
Leisure Management with Retail Management	N707	3FT deg		8-12	MO	M	26	CCC		
Leisure Management with Spanish	N7RK	3FT deg		8-12	MO	M	26	CCC		
Leisure Management with Tourism	N7PT	3FT deg		8-12	MO	M	26	CCC		
Leisure Mgt with Food and Drink Consumer Studies	N7DK	3FT deg		8-12	MO	M	26	CCC		
Recreation Management with Business	N7ND	3FT deg		8-12	MO	M	26	CCC		
Recreation Management with English Language St	N7QD	3FT deg		8-12	MO	M	26	CCC		
Recreation Management with French	N7RD	3FT deg		8-12	MO	M	26	CCC		
Recreation Management with German	N7RG	3FT deg		8-12	MO	M	26	CCC		
Recreation Management with Hospitality Mgt	N731	3FT deg		8-12	MO	M	26	CCC		
Recreation Management with Hotel Management	N740	3FT deg		8-12	MO	M	26	CCC		
Recreation Management with Leisure Management	N780	3FT deg		8-12	MO	M	26	CCC		

course details			98 expected requirements							96 entry stats	
TITLE	CODE	COURSE	SUBJECTS	A/AS	ND/C	AGNVQ	IB	SQA(H)	SQA	RATIO A/AS	
Recreation Management with Marketing	N708	3FT deg		8-12	MO	M	26	CCC			
Recreation Management with Retail Management	N709	3FT deg		8-12	MO	M	26	CCC			
Recreation Management with Spanish	N7RL	3FT deg		8-12	MO	M	26	CCC			
Recreation Management with Tourism	N7PR	3FT deg		8-12	MO	M	26	CCC			
Tourism with Hospitality Management	P7N7	3FT deg		8-12	MO	M	26	CCC			
Tourism with Leisure Management	P7NT	3FT deg		8-12	MO	M	26	CCC			
Tourism with Recreation Management	P7NR	3FT deg		8-12	MO	M	26	CCC			
Hospitality Management	027N▼	2SW/3SW HND	*	2-4	N	P	24	CC			
Univ of ULSTER											
Hospitality Management (3 Yr SW inc CIS)	N721▼	3SW Dip	* g	CDD	M+1D	D* gi	26	BCCC	Ind	17	12/16
Hospitality Management (4 Yr SW inc DIS)	N720▼	4SW deg	* g	CCC	MO+3D	D*6/^ gi	28	BBBC	Ind	21	18/26
Hotel and Tourism Mgt (4 Yr SW inc DIS)	NP77▼	4SW deg	* g	BCC	MO+4D	D*6/^ gi	30	BBBB	Ind	19	14/24
Sport and Leisure St (3 Yr or 4 Yr SW inc DIS)	BN67▼	3FT/4SW deg	* g	BBC	MO+4D	D*6/^ gi	32 ·	ABBB	Ind	22	20/26
Univ Col WARRINGTON											
Leisure Studies with Business Management and IT	NN71	3FT deg	* g	10-12	Ind	Ind	Ind	Ind	Ind		
Leisure Studies	73NL	2FT HND	* g	8	Ind	Ind	Ind	Ind	Ind		
WEST HERTS COLL											
Business Administration (Hospitality Management)	N710	1FT deg									
Business Administration (Leisure Management)	N780	1FT deg									
Hotel Catering and Leisure Management	77PN	2FT HND	*	2	N					2	2/8
Leisure Studies	087N	2FT HND	*	2							
Univ of WESTMINSTER											
Leisure Development & Strategic Mgt w.foundation	N788	4FT deg									
Leisure Development and Strategic Management	N780	3FT deg									
WESTMINSTER COLLEGE											
Hotel and Catering Management (1 yr top-up)	N740	1FT deg			HN						
Hotel, Catering and Institutional Management	007N	2FT HND	*	2	3M	P$	Ind	Ind	Ind		
WIGAN and LEIGH COLL											
Business with Hospitality, Leisure and Tourism	71NN▼	2FT HND		6	N	Ind	Dip		N		
WIRRAL METROPOLITAN COLLEGE											
Hotel, Catering and Institutional Management	007N	2FT HND			Ind	Ind	Ind	Ind	Ind		
Leisure Studies	087N	2FT HND			Ind	Ind	Ind	Ind	Ind		
Univ of WOLVERHAMPTON											
Hospitality Management (4 Year sandwich)	N741	4SW deg	g	12	4M	M	24	BBBB	Ind		
Licensed Retail Management (4 year sandwich)	N742	4SW deg	g	12	4M	M	24	BBBB	Ind		
Sports Studies (Specialist Route)	BN67	3FT deg		14	4M	M	24	BBBB	Ind		
Combined Degrees Leisure and Recreation Management	Y401	3FT deg		10	4M	M	24	BBBB	Ind		
Hotel, Catering & Institutional Management	007N▼	2FT HND		2	N	P	24	CCCC	Ind	6	2/4
WORCESTER COLLEGE of Technology											
Hotel Catering and Institutional Management	027N	3FT HND	*	2	N	P					
WRITTLE COLL											
Leisure Management	N780	3FT deg	Ap g	12	MO	M	Ind	Ind	Ind		
Leisure Management	087N	2FT/3SW HND	Ap g	6	N	M	Ind	Ind	Ind		
YORKSHIRE COAST COLLEGE of F and HE											
Leisure Studies	037N	2FT HND	*	6	4M	M	Ind	Ind	Ind		
Travel and Tourism Management	77NP	2FT HND	*	6	4M	M	Ind	Ind	Ind		

course details			98 expected requirements							96 entry stats	
TITLE	CODE	COURSE	SUBJECTS	A/AS	NO/C	AGNVQ	IB	SQA(H)	SQA	RATIO	A/AS
Univ of BIRMINGHAM											
African Studies	T700	3FT deg	*	BCC	Ind	D*^	30	ABBB	Ind	3	18/26
African Studies/American Studies	QT47	3FT deg	*	BBB	Ind	D*^	32	ABBB	Ind		
African Studies/Ancient History & Archaeology	TV76	3FT deg	*	BBB	Ind	D*^	32	ABBB	Ind		
African Studies/East Mediterranean History	TV71	3FT deg	* g	BBB	Ind	D*^	32	ABBB	Ind		
African Studies/English	QTH7	3FT deg		BBB	Ind	D*^	32	ABBB	Ind	4	24/30
African Studies/French Studies	RT17	4FT deg	F	BBB	Ind	D*^	32$	ABBB	Ind	5	
African Studies/Geography	LT87	3FT deg	Gy	BBB	Ind	D*^	32$	ABBB	Ind		
African Studies/German Studies	RT27	4FT deg	G	BBB	Ind	D*^	32$	ABBB	Ind	1	
African Studies/Hispanic Studies	RT47	4FT deg	*	BBB	Ind	D*^	32	ABBB	Ind		
African Studies/History	TVR1	3FT deg	*	BBB	Ind	D*^	32	ABBB	Ind		
African Studies/History of Art	TV74	3FT deg	*	BBB	Ind	D*^	32	ABBB	Ind		
African Studies/Media & Cultural Studies	PT47	3FT deg	*	BBB	Ind	D*^	32	ABBB	Ind		
African Studies/Portuguese	RT57	4FT deg	*	BBB	Ind	D*^	32	ABBB	Ind		
African Studies/Theology	TV78	3FT deg	*	BBB	Ind	D*^	32	ABBB	Ind		
BCom (Business Administration) with Japanese	NT14	4FT deg	L	BBC	Ind	D+^	32	ABBBB	Ind		
BRADFORD & ILKLEY Comm COLL											
South Asian Studies	T500	3FT deg	*	8	MO	M	Dip	CCC	Ind		
CARDIFF Univ of Wales											
Business Studies with Japanese	NT14	4FT deg	*	BBC-BBB	Ind	Ind	Ind	Ind	Ind	6	20/26
Japanese/French	TR41	4FT deg	F	BBC	Ind		Ind	ABBBB	Ind	6	26/30
Japanese/German	TR42	4FT deg	G	BBC	X		Ind	Ind	X	9	
Japanese/Italian	TR43	4FT deg	L	BCC	X		Ind	ABBBB	X		
Law and Japanese	MT34	4FT deg	*	BBB	Ind	Ind	Ind	Ind	Ind	6	22/28
Spanish/Japanese	TR44	4FT deg	L	BBC-BCC	X		Ind	Ind	X	10	
Univ of CENTRAL LANCASHIRE											
Asian Pacific Studies	T500	4SW deg	L	14	MO+3D$	M*^	26$	BCCC$	Ind		
Combined Honours Programme Japanese	Y400	3FT deg	L/* g	8	MO	M*^	26	BCCC	Ind		
DE MONTFORT Univ											
Humanities Joint Honours South Asian Studies	Y301▼	3FT deg	* g	CCD	MO	M$^	28$	ABBB	Ind		
Univ of DURHAM											
Chinese	T300	4FT deg	*	BBC	Ind	Ind	31	AABBB	Ind	42	
Chinese and Management Studies	TN31	4FT deg	*	BBC	Ind	Ind	31	AABBB	Ind	12	
Chinese with European Languages	T3T9	4FT deg	L	BBC	Ind	Ind	31	AABBB	Ind	20	
Chinese with Geography	T3L8	4FT deg	*	BBC	Ind	Ind	31	AABBB	Ind		
Chinese with History	T3V1	4FT deg	*	BBC	Ind	Ind	31	AABBB	Ind		
Chinese with Linguistics	T3Q1	4FT deg	*	BBC	Ind	Ind	31	AABBB	Ind		
Chinese with Philosophy	T3V7	4FT deg	*	BBC	Ind	Ind	31	AABBB	Ind		
Chinese with Politics	T3M1	4FT deg	*	BBC	Ind	Ind	31	AABBB	Ind	4	
Japanese Studies	T410	4FT deg	*	BBC	Ind	Ind	31	AABBB	Ind	8	24/26
Japanese and Management Studies	TN41	4FT deg	*	BBC	Ind	Ind	31	AABBB	Ind	8	22/30
Japanese with European Languages	T4T2	4FT deg	L	BBC	Ind	Ind	31	AABBB	Ind	4	24/30
Japanese with Geography	T4L8	4FT deg	*	BBC	Ind	Ind	31	AABBB	Ind		
Japanese with History	T4V1	4FT deg	*	BBC	Ind	Ind	31	AABBB	Ind		
Japanese with Linguistics	T4Q1	4FT deg	*	BBC	Ind	Ind	31	AABBB	Ind	3	
Japanese with Philosophy	T4V7	4FT deg	*	BBC	Ind	Ind	31	AABBB	Ind		
Japanese with Politics	T4M1	4FT deg	*	BBC	Ind	Ind	31	AABBB	Ind	4	

TITLE	CODE	COURSE	SUBJECTS	A/AS	ND/C	AGNVQ	IB	SQA(H)	SQA	RATIO A/AS	
Univ of EDINBURGH											
Chinese	T300	4FT deg	L g	BBB	Ind	Ind	Dip$	BBBB$	Ind		
History of Art and Chinese Studies	TV3L	4FT deg	L g	BBB	Ind	Ind	Dip$	BBBB$	Ind		
Japanese	T400	4FT deg	L g	BBB	Ind	Ind	Dip$	BBBB$	Ind		
Japanese and Linguistics	TQ41	4FT deg	L g	BBB	Ind	Ind	Dip$	BBBB$	Ind		
Social Anthropology with South Asian Studies	L6T5	4FT deg	*	AAB	Ind		38$	ABBB	Ind		
Sociology with South Asian Studies	L3T5	4FT deg	*	BBB	Ind		34$	ABBB	Ind	4	
EUROPEAN Business School											
International Bus St: Japan + one beginner lang	NT14	4FT deg									
International Bus Studs with Japanese (Test+Int)	N1T4	4SW deg		12	Ind		Ind	Ind	Ind		
International Business & Mgt Studs with Japanese	N1TL	4SW deg		12	Ind		Ind	Ind	Ind		
Univ of HULL											
Dutch/South-East Asian Studies	TT25	4FT deg	* g	BC	N	Ind	28$	BCCCC	Ind	4	
South-East Asian Studies (3 Yrs)	T500	3FT deg	*	BC	N	M$ gi	28	BCCCC	Ind	3	
South-East Asian Studies and Language (4 Yrs)	T501	4FT deg	*	BC	N	M$ gi	28	BCCCC	Ind	3	
KING ALFRED'S WINCHESTER											
Japanese Language and American Studies	QT44	3FT deg	L g	14	X	X	24$	BCC$	X		
Japanese Language and Business Culture	T4N1	3FT deg	L g	14	X	X	24$	BCC$	X		
Japanese Language and Business Studies	NT14	3FT deg	L g	14	X	X	24$	BCC$	X	3	
Japanese Language and Contemporary Cultural St	MT94	3FT deg	L g	14	X	X	24$	BCC$	X		
Japanese Language and English Studies	QT34	3FT deg	E+L	14	X	X	24$	BCC$	X	2	
Japanese Language and Geography	LT84	3FT deg	Gy+L g	14	X	X	24$	BCC$	X		
Media & Film Studies and Japanese Language	PT44	3FT deg	L g	14	X	X	24$	BCC$	X		
Psychology and Japanese Language	LT74	3FT deg	L g	14	X	X	24$	BCC$	X		
Univ of LEEDS											
Chinese Studies (Modern)	T300	4FT deg	L g	BBC	Ind	Ind	30$	CSYS	Ind	1	16/30
Chinese and Japanese Studies	TT34	4FT deg	L g	BBC	Ind	Ind	30$	CSYS	Ind	5	
Chinese-Economics	LT13	4FT deg	L g	BBC	Ind	Ind	30$	CSYS	Ind	4	
Chinese-English	QT33	4FT deg	E+L g	BBC	Ind	Ind	30$	CSYS	Ind	3	
Chinese-French	RT13	4FT deg	F g	BBC	Ind	Ind	30$	CSYS	Ind	3	22/30
Chinese-Geography	LT83	4FT deg	Gy+L g	BBC	Ind	Ind	30$	CSYS	Ind		
Chinese-German	RT23	4FT deg	G g	BBC	Ind	Ind	30$	CSYS	Ind	6	
Chinese-History	TV31	4FT deg	L g	BBC	Ind	Ind	30$	CSYS	Ind		
Chinese-Italian	RT33	4FT deg	I g	BBC	Ind	Ind	Ind	Ind	Ind		
Chinese-Italian B	RTH3	4FT deg	L g	BBC	Ind	Ind	Ind	Ind	Ind		
Chinese-Linguistics	QT13	4FT deg	L g	BBC	Ind	Ind	30$	CSYS	Ind	4	
Chinese-Management Studies	TN31	4FT deg	L g	BBC	Ind	Ind	30$	CSYS	Ind	10	
Chinese-Politics	MT13	4FT deg	L g	BBC	Ind	Ind	30$	CSYS	Ind		
Chinese-Portuguese	RT53	4FT deg	L g	BBC	Ind	Ind	30$	CSYS	Ind		
Chinese-Russian	RT83	4FT deg	R g	BBC	Ind	Ind	30$	CSYS	Ind	2	
Chinese-Russian B	RTV3	4FT deg	L g	BBC	Ind	Ind	30$	CSYS	Ind		
Chinese-Sociology	LT33	4FT deg	L g	BBC	Ind	Ind	30$	CSYS	Ind		
Chinese-Spanish	RT43	4FT deg	Sp g	BBC	Ind	Ind	30$	CSYS	Ind	7	
Economics-Japanese Studies	TL41	4FT deg	L g	BBB	Ind	Ind	32$	CSYS	Ind		
French-Japanese	RT14	4FT deg	F g	BBC	Ind	Ind	30$	CSYS	Ind		
German-Japanese	RT24	4FT deg	G g	BBC	Ind	Ind	30$	CSYS	Ind		
Italian-Japanese	RT34	4FT deg	I g	BBC	Ind	Ind	Ind	Ind	Ind		
Italian-Japanese B	RTH4	4FT deg	L g	BBC	Ind	Ind	Ind	Ind	Ind		
Japanese-Linguistics	QT14	4FT deg	L g	BBC	Ind	Ind	30$	CSYS	Ind		
Japanese-Management Studies	TN41	4FT deg	L g	BBB	Ind	Ind	32$	CSYS	Ind	10	26/30

course details   **98 expected requirements**   *96 entry stats*

Languages – African, Asian and Oriental 36

			98 expected requirements							96 entry stats

course details

TITLE	CODE	COURSE	SUBJECTS	A/AS	ND/C	RGNVQ	IB	SQA(H)	SQA	RATIO A/AS
Japanese-Russian	RT84	4FT deg	R g	BBC	Ind	Ind	30$	CSYS	Ind	3
Japanese-Russian B	RTV4	4FT deg	L g	BBC	Ind	Ind	30$	CSYS	Ind	5
Law-Chinese Studies	MT33	4FT deg	L g	ABB	Ind	Ind	33$	CSYS	Ind	11
Law-Japanese Studies	MT34	4FT deg	L g	ABB	Ind	Ind	33$	CSYS	Ind	13
LIVERPOOL JOHN MOORES Univ										
French and Japanese	RT14	4FT deg	L	14	3M+4D		Ind			6
German and Japanese	RT24	4FT deg	L	14	3M+4D		Ind			4
International Business Studies with Japanese	N1T4	4SW deg		16	3M+4D		Ind			40
LUTON Univ										
Accounting with Japanese	N4T4	3FT deg	L g	12-16	MO/DO	M/D	32	BBCC	Ind	
Biology with Japanese	C1T4	3FT deg	L g	12-16	MO/DO	M/D	32	BBCC	Ind	
Built Environment with Chinese	N8T3	3FT deg		12-16	MO/DO	M/D	32	BBCC	Ind	
Business with Japanese	N1T4	3FT deg	L g	12-16	MO/DO	M/D	32	BBCC	Ind	
Contemporary History with Chinese	V1T3	3FT deg		12-16	MO/DO	M/D	32	BBCC	Ind	
Electronic System Design with Japanese	H6T4	3FT deg	L g	12-16	MO/DO	M/D	32	BBCC	Ind	
European Language Studies with Chinese	T2T3	3FT deg		12-16	MO/DO	M/D	32	BBCC	Ind	
Geography with Chinese	F8T3	3FT deg		12-16	MO/DO	M/D	32	BBCC	Ind	
Geology with Japanese	F6T4	3FT deg	L g	12-16	MO/DO	M/D	32	BBCC	Ind	
Health Science with Japanese	B9T4	3FT deg	L g	12-16	MO/DO	M/D	32	BBCC	Ind	
Health Studies with Chinese	B9T3	3FT deg		12-16	MO/DO	M/D	32	BBCC	Ind	
Law with Chinese	M3T3	3FT deg		12-16	MO/DO	M/D	32	BBCC	Ind	
Law with Japanese	M3T4	3FT deg	L g	12-16	MO/DO	M/D	32	BBCC	Ind	
Leisure Studies with Chinese	N7T3	3FT deg		12-16	MO/DO	M/D	32	BBCC	Ind	
Leisure Studies with Japanese	N7T4	3FT deg	L g	12-16	MO/DO	M/D	32	BBCC	Ind	
Linguistics with Japanese	Q1T4	3FT deg	g	12-16	MO/DO	M/D	32	BBCC	Ind	
Literary Studies in English with Chinese	Q2T3	3FT deg		12-16	MO/DO	M/D	32	BBCC	Ind	
Mapping Science with Japanese	F8T4	3FT deg	L g	12-16	MO/DO	M/D	32	BBCC	Ind	
Marketing with Japanese	N5T4	3FT deg	g	12-16	MO/DO	M/D	32	BBCC	Ind	
Mathematical Sciences with Japanese	G1T4	3FT deg	L g	12-16	MO/DO	M/D	32	BBCC	Ind	
Media Practices with Japanese	P4T4	3FT deg	L g	12-16	MO/DO	M/D	32	BBCC	Ind	
Media Production with Japanese	P4TK	3FT deg	L g	12-16	MO/DO	M/D	32	BBCC	Ind	
Modern English Studies with Chinese	Q3T3	3FT deg		12-16	MO/DO	M/D	32	BBCC	Ind	
Modern English Studies with Japanese	Q3T4	3FT deg	L g	12-16	MO/DO	M/D	32	BBCC	Ind	
Modern History with Chinese	V1TH	3FT deg		12-16	MO/DO	M/D	32	BBCC	Ind	
Politics with Chinese	M1T3	3FT deg		12-16	MO/DO	M/D	32	BBCC	Ind	
Politics with Japanese	M1T4	3FT deg	L g	12-16	MO/DO	M/D	32	BBCC	Ind	
Psychology with Chinese	L7T3	3FT deg		12-16	MO/DO	M/D	32	BBCC	Ind	
Psychology with Japanese	L7T4	3FT deg	L g	12-16	MO/DO	M/D	32	BBCC	Ind	
Public Policy & Management with Chinese	M1TH	3FT deg		12-16	MO/DO	M/D	32	BBCC	Ind	
Public Policy & Management with Japanese	M1TK	3FT deg	L g	12-16	MO/DO	M/D	32	BBCC	Ind	
Regional Planning & Development with Chinese	K4T3	3FT deg		12-16	MO/DO	M/D	32	BBCC	Ind	
Regional Planning & Development with Japanese	K4T4	3FT deg	L g	12-16	MO/DO	M/D	32	BBCC	Ind	
Social Policy with Chinese	L4T3	3FT deg		12-16	MO/DO	M/D	32	BBCC	Ind	
Social Studies with Chinese	L3TH	3FT deg		12-16	MO/DO	M/D	32	BBCC	Ind	
Social Studies with Japanese	L3T4	3FT deg	L g	12-16	MO/DO	M/D	32	BBCC	Ind	
Sociology with Chinese	L3T3	3FT deg		12-16	MO/DO	M/D	32	BBCC	Ind	
Travel & Tourism with Japanese	P7T4	3FT deg	L g	12-16	MO/DO	M/D	32	BBCC	Ind	
Travel and Tourism with Chinese	P7T3	3FT deg		12-16	MO/DO	M/D	32	BBCC	Ind	
MIDDLESEX Univ										
Asia-Pacific Studies	T500▼	3FT deg	* g	12-16	5M	M$ go	28	Ind	Ind	
Traditional Chinese Medicine	BT23	3FT deg	S g	18-24	3D	D$ go	28	Ind	Ind	

TITLE	CODE	COURSE	SUBJECTS	A/AS	ND/C	AGNVQ	IB	SQA(H)	SQA	RATIO A/AS

Univ of NEWCASTLE

TITLE	CODE	COURSE	SUBJECTS	A/AS	ND/C	AGNVQ	IB	SQA(H)	SQA	RATIO A/AS
Politics and East Asian Studies	MTCM	4FT deg	*	BBC	Ind		Ind	AABB	Ind	2
Combined Studies (BA) *Chinese*	Y400	4FT deg	*	ABC-BBB	5D	Ind	35$	AAAB	Ind	
Combined Studies (BA) *East Asian Studies*	Y400	3FT deg	*	ABC-BBB	5D	Ind	35$	AAAB	Ind	
Combined Studies (BA) *Hindu Studies*	Y400	3FT deg	*	ABC-BBB	5D	Ind	35$	AAAB	Ind	
Combined Studies (BA) *Japanese*	Y400	4FT deg	*	ABC-BBB	5D	Ind	35$	AAAB	Ind	
Combined Studies (BA) *Korean*	Y400	4FT deg	*	ABC-BBB	5D		35$	AAAB	Ind	
Combined Studies (BA) *Sanskrit*	Y400	3FT deg	*	ABC-BBB	5D	Ind	35$	AAAB	Ind	

Univ of NORTH LONDON

TITLE	CODE	COURSE	SUBJECTS	A/AS	ND/C	AGNVQ	IB	SQA(H)	SQA	RATIO A/AS
Caribbean St & Information & Communications Mgt	PT27	3FT deg	*	CC	MO	M	Ind	Ind	Ind	
Caribbean Studies and Law	MT37	3FT deg	*	CC	Ind	Ind	Ind	BBCCC	Ind	
Caribbean Studies and Leisure Studies	NT77	3FT deg	* g	CC	MO+4D	D	Ind	Ind	Ind	
Hospitality Management and Caribbean Studies	NT7T	3FT deg	* g	12	MO+4D	D	Ind	Ind	Ind	
Social Research and Caribbean Studies	LT37	3FT deg	* g	CC	MO	M	Ind	Ind	Ind	5
Social Research and South Asian Studies	LT35	3FT deg	* g	CC	MO	M	Ind	Ind	Ind	
Sociology and South Asian Studies	LT3M	3FT deg	*	CC	Ind	Ind	Ind	Ind	Ind	
Tourism Studies and Caribbean Studies	PT77	3FT deg	* g	CC	MO+4D	D	Ind	Ind	Ind	27
Tourism and South Asian Studies	PT75	3FT deg	* g	CC	MO+4D	D	Ind	Ind	Ind	
Combined Honours *South Asian Studies*	Y300	3FT deg	*	CC	Ind	Ind	Ind	Ind	Ind	

Univ of NOTTINGHAM

TITLE	CODE	COURSE	SUBJECTS	A/AS	ND/C	AGNVQ	IB	SQA(H)	SQA	RATIO A/AS
Manufacturing Engineering and Mgt with Japanese	H7TK	3FT/4FT deg	M	CCC	Ind	Ind	28$	Ind	Ind	
Mechanical Engineering with Japanese	H3T4	3FT/4FT deg	M+P g	BBC-BCC	Ind	Ind	28$	Ind	Ind	7
Production and Operations Mgt with Japanese	H7T4	3FT deg	M g	CCC	Ind	Ind	28$	Ind	Ind	

OXFORD Univ

TITLE	CODE	COURSE	SUBJECTS	A/AS	ND/C	AGNVQ	IB	SQA(H)	SQA	RATIO A/AS
Chinese (4 Yrs)	T301	4FT deg	*	AAB-ABB	DO		36	AAAAA	Ind	2 26/30
Japanese (4 Yrs)	T401	4FT deg	*	AAB-ABB	DO		36	AAAAA	Ind	3 28/30

OXFORD BROOKES Univ

TITLE	CODE	COURSE	SUBJECTS	A/AS	ND/C	AGNVQ	IB	SQA(H)	SQA	RATIO A/AS
Langs for Bus:Italian-Ab Initio/Japanese-Ab Init	NTC4	4FT deg								
Langs for Business:English/Japanese-Ab Initio	NT14	4FT deg	E	BC-CDD	Ind	M*^	Ind	Ind	Ind	
Languages for Bus:Italian/Japanese-Ab Initio	NTCK	4FT deg	I	BC-CDD	Ind	M*^	Ind	Ind	Ind	
Languages for Business:French/Japanese-Ab Initio	NT1K	4FT deg	F	BC-CDD	Ind	M*^	Ind	Ind	Ind	12
Languages for Business:German/Japanese-Ab Initio	NT1L	4FT deg	G	BC-CDD	Ind	M*^	Ind	Ind	Ind	2
Languages for Business:Span/Japanese-Ab Initio	NTCL	4FT deg	Sp	BC-CDD	Ind	M*^	Ind	Ind	Ind	

Univ of READING

TITLE	CODE	COURSE	SUBJECTS	A/AS	ND/C	AGNVQ	IB	SQA(H)	SQA	RATIO A/AS
International Management with Japanese	N1T4	4FT deg	* g	BBB	Ind	DB^ go	32	ABBB	Ind	

ROYAL HOLLOWAY, Univ of London

TITLE	CODE	COURSE	SUBJECTS	A/AS	ND/C	AGNVQ	IB	SQA(H)	SQA	RATIO A/AS
Economics with Japanese Studies	L1T4	3FT deg	L g	BBB-BBC	Ind		32	Ind		6
German with Japanese Studies	R2T4	3FT deg								
History with Japanese Studies	V1T4	3FT deg	L g	BBB-ABC			30	Ind		
Management Studies with Japanese Studies	N1T4	3FT deg	L g	BBC-BBB	2M+3D	D^	30	Ind		
Music with Japanese Studies	W3T4	3FT deg	L+Mu g	BCC-BBC			Ind	ABBCC$		2
Social Policy with Japanese Studies	L4T4	3FT deg	L g	BCC-BBC	Ind	D^	Ind	Ind		
Sociology with Japanese Studies	L3T4	3FT deg	L g	BCC-BBC	Ind	D^	Ind	Ind		

course details			98 expected requirements							96 entry stats	
TITLE	CODE	COURSE	SUBJECTS	A/AS	ND/C	AGNVQ	IB	SQA(H)	SQA	RATIO	A/AS
Univ of SALFORD											
Environ and Resource Sci with fur st in China	F9T3	4FT deg									
Info Technology with Studies in Japan (4 Yrs)	G5T4	4SW deg	* g	20	DO	M/D^	Ind	Ind	Ind	10	
SOAS:Sch of Oriental & African St (U of London)											
African Language and Culture	T708	4FT deg		20	Ind		30	BBBCC	Ind	4	14/20
African Studies	T700	3FT deg		20	Ind		30	BBBCC	Ind	8	
Arabic and Amharic	TT67	4FT deg		22	Ind		31	BBBBC	Ind		
Chinese (Modern and Classical)	T300	4FT deg		24	Ind		32	BBBBB	Ind	8	
Development Studies and African Studies	TM79	3FT deg		22	Ind		31	BBBBC	Ind		
Development Studies and Amharic	MT97	4FT deg		22	Ind		31	BBBBC	Ind		
Development Studies and Bengali	MT95	3FT deg		22	Ind		31	BBBBC	Ind		
Development Studies and Burmese	TMM9	4FT deg		22	Ind		31	BBBBC	Ind		
Development Studies and Chinese	MT93	4FT deg		24	Ind		32	BBBBB	Ind		
Economics and African Studies	TL71	3FT deg	g	22	Ind		31	BBBBC	Ind		
Economics and Amharic	LT17	4FT deg	g	22	Ind		31	BBBBC	Ind		
Economics and Bengali	LT15	3FT deg	g	22	Ind		31	BBBBC	Ind		
Economics and Burmese	LT1M	4FT deg	g	22	Ind		31	BBBBC	Ind		
Economics and Chinese	LT13	4FT deg	g	24	Ind		32	BBBBB	Ind	11	
Geography and African Studies	TL78	3FT deg		20	Ind		30	BBBCC	Ind		
Geography and Amharic	LT87	4FT deg		20	Ind		30	BBBCC	Ind		
Geography and Bengali	LT85	3FT deg		20	Ind		30	BBBCC	Ind		
Geography and Burmese	LT8M	4FT deg		20	Ind		30	BBBCC	Ind		
Geography and Chinese	LT83	4FT deg		24	Ind		32	BBBBB	Ind		
Gujarati and Development Studies	TM59	3FT deg		22	Ind		31	BBBBC	Ind		
Gujarati and Economics	LT1N	3FT deg	g	22	Ind		31	BBBBC	Ind		
Gujarati and Geography	TL58	3FT deg		20	Ind		30	BBBCC	Ind		
Hausa and Arabic	TT6R	4FT deg		22	Ind		31	BBBBC	Ind		
Hausa and Development Studies	MT9R	4FT deg		22	Ind		31	BBBBC	Ind		
Hausa and Economics	LT1R	4FT deg	g	22	Ind		31	BBBBC	Ind		
Hausa and Geography	LT8R	4FT deg		20	Ind		30	BBBCC	Ind		
Hindi	T510	4FT deg		22	Ind		31	BBBBC	Ind		
Hindi and Development Studies	MT9M	3FT/4FT deg		22	Ind		31	BBBBC	Ind	3	
Hindi and Economics	LTC5	3FT/4FT deg	g	22	Ind		31	BBBBC	Ind	2	
Hindi and Geography	TL5V	3FT/4FT deg		20	Ind		30	BBBCC	Ind	1	
History and African Studies	VT17	3FT deg		20	Ind		30	BBBCC	Ind		
History and Amharic	TV71	4FT deg		20	Ind		30	BBBCC	Ind		
History and Bengali	TV51	3FT deg		20	Ind		30	BBBCC	Ind	2	
History and Burmese	TVM1	4FT deg		20	Ind		30	BBBCC	Ind		
History and Chinese	TV31	4FT deg		24	Ind		32	BBBBB	Ind	6	
History and Gujarati	TV5C	3FT deg		20	Ind		30	BBBCC	Ind		
History and Hausa	TVR1	4FT deg		20	Ind		30	BBBCC	Ind		
History and Hindi	VT15	3FT/4FT deg		20	Ind		30	BBBCC	Ind		
History of Art/Archaeology and African Studies	VT67	3FT deg		20	Ind		30	BBBCC	Ind		
History of Art/Archaeology and Amharic	TV76	4FT deg		20	Ind		30	BBBCC	Ind		
History of Art/Archaeology and Bengali	TV56	3FT deg		20	Ind		30	BBBCC	Ind		
History of Art/Archaeology and Burmese	TVM6	4FT deg		20	Ind		30	BBBCC	Ind		
History of Art/Archaeology and Chinese	TV36	4FT deg		24	Ind		32	BBBBB	Ind	7	
History of Art/Archaeology and Gujarati	TV5P	3FT deg		20	Ind		30	BBBCC	Ind		
History of Art/Archaeology and Hausa	TVR6	4FT deg		20	Ind		30	BBBCC	Ind		
History of Art/Archaeology and Hindi	TVMP	3FT/4FT deg		20	Ind		30	BBBCC	Ind		
Indonesian (single-subject language)	T541	4FT deg		20	Ind		30	BBBCC	Ind		
Indonesian and Arabic	TTM6	4FT deg		22	Ind		31	BBBBC	Ind		

course details | 98 expected requirements | 96 entry stats

TITLE	CODE	COURSE	SUBJECTS	A/AS	ND/C	AGNVQ	IB	SQA(H)	SQA	RATIO A/AS
Indonesian and Chinese	TT3M	4FT deg		24	Ind		32	BBBBB	Ind	
Indonesian and Development Studies	MT9N	3FT/4FT deg		22	Ind		31	BBBBC	Ind	
Indonesian and Dutch	TTM2	3FT/4FT deg		20	Ind		30	BBBCC	Ind	
Indonesian and Economics	LTCM	3FT/4FT deg	g	22	Ind		31	BBBBC	Ind	
Indonesian and Geography	TLM8	3FT/4FT deg		20	Ind		30	BBBCC	Ind	
Indonesian and History	VT1M	3FT/4FT deg		20	Ind		30	BBBCC	Ind	2
Indonesian and History of Art/Archaeology	TVMQ	3FT/4FT deg		20	Ind		30	BBBCC	Ind	1
Japanese	T400	4FT deg		24	Ind		32	BBBBB	Ind	5 16/30
Japanese and Economics	LT14	4FT deg	g	24	Ind		32	BBBBB	Ind	14
Japanese and Geography	LT84	4FT deg		24	Ind		32	BBBBB	Ind	
Japanese and History	TV41	4FT deg		24	Ind		32	BBBBB	Ind	
Japanese and History of Art/Archaeology	TV46	4FT deg		24	Ind		32	BBBBB	Ind	
Japanese and Indonesian	TT45	4FT deg		24	Ind		32	BBBBB	Ind	
Korean	T515	4FT deg		16	Ind		28	BBCCC		
Korean and Chinese	TT3N	4FT deg		24	Ind		32	BBBBB	Ind	
Korean and Development Studies	TM5Y	4FT deg		22	Ind		31	BBBBC	Ind	
Korean and Economics	LTCN	4FT deg	g	22	Ind		31	BBBBC	Ind	
Korean and Geography	LT8N	4FT deg		20	Ind		30	BBBCC	Ind	
Korean and History	TVN1	4FT deg		16	Ind		28	BBCCC	Ind	
Korean and History of Art/Archaeology	TVNP	4FT deg		16	Ind		28	BBCCC	Ind	
Korean and Indonesian	T518	4FT deg		20	Ind		30	BBBCC	Ind	
Korean and Japanese	TT4N	4FT deg		24	Ind		32	BBBBB	Ind	4
Law and Amharic	MT37	4FT deg		24	Ind		32	BBBBB	Ind	3
Law and Bengali	MT35	3FT deg		24	Ind		32	BBBBB	Ind	
Law and Burmese	MT3M	4FT deg		24	Ind		32	BBBBB	Ind	
Law and Chinese	MT33	4FT deg		24	Ind		32	BBBBB	Ind	5
Law and Gujarati	MTH5	3FT deg		24	Ind		32	BBBBB	Ind	
Law and Hausa	MT3R	4FT deg		24	Ind		32	BBBBB	Ind	
Law and Hindi	MT3N	3FT/4FT deg		24	Ind		32	BBBBB	Ind	
Law and Indonesian	MTHM	3FT/4FT deg		24	Ind		32	BBBBB	Ind	
Law and Japanese	MT34	4FT deg		24	Ind		32	BBBBB	Ind	9
Law and Korean	MTHN	4FT deg		24	Ind		32	BBBBB	Ind	
Linguistics and African Studies	TQ71	3FT deg		20	Ind		30	BBBCC	Ind	
Linguistics and Amharic	QT17	4FT deg		20	Ind		30	BBBCC	Ind	
Linguistics and Bengali	QT15	3FT deg		20	Ind		30	BBBCC	Ind	
Linguistics and Burmese	QT1M	4FT deg		20	Ind		30	BBBCC	Ind	
Linguistics and Chinese	QT13	4FT deg		24	Ind		32	BBBBB	Ind	
Linguistics and Gujarati	QTC5	3FT deg		20	Ind		30	BBBCC	Ind	
Linguistics and Hausa	QT1R	4FT deg		20	Ind		30	BBBCC	Ind	
Linguistics and Hindi	QT1N	3FT/4FT deg		20	Ind		30	BBBCC	Ind	
Linguistics and Indonesian	QTCM	3FT/4FT deg		20	Ind		30	BBBCC	Ind	
Linguistics and Japanese	QT14	4FT deg		24	Ind		32	BBBBB	Ind	
Linguistics and Korean	QTCN	4FT deg		16	Ind		28	BBCCC	Ind	
Management and Amharic	NT17	4FT deg	g	20	Ind		30	BBBCC	Ind	
Management and Bengali	NT15	3FT deg	g	20	Ind		30	BBBCC	Ind	
Management and Burmese	NT1M	4FT deg		20	Ind		30	BBBCC	Ind	
Management and Chinese	NT13	4FT deg	g	24	Ind		32	BBBBB	Ind	23
Management and Gujarati	NTC5	3FT deg	g	20	Ind		30	BBBCC	Ind	
Management and Hausa	NT1R	4FT deg		20	Ind		30	BBBCC	Ind	
Management and Hindi	NT1N	3FT/4FT deg	g	20	Ind		30	BBBCC	Ind	
Management and Indonesian	NTCM	3FT/4FT deg	g	20	Ind		30	BBBCC	Ind	
Management and Japanese	NT14	4FT deg	g	24	Ind		32	BBBBB	Ind	15

TITLE	CODE	COURSE	SUBJECTS	A/AS	ND/C	AGNVQ	IB	SQA(H)	SQA	RATIO A/AS
Management and Korean	NTCN	4FT deg	g	16	Ind		28	BBCCC	Ind	
Music and African Studies	WT37	3FT deg		20	Ind		30	BBBCC	Ind	1
Music and Amharic	TW73	4FT deg		20	Ind		30	BBBCC	Ind	1
Music and Bengali	TW53	3FT deg		20	Ind		30	BBBCC	Ind	
Music and Burmese	TWM3	4FT deg		20	Ind		30	BBBCC	Ind	
Music and Chinese	TW33	4FT deg		24	Ind		32	BBBBB	Ind	1
Music and Gujarati	TW5H	3FT deg		20	Ind		30	BBBCC	Ind	
Music and Hausa	TWR3	4FT deg		20	Ind		30	BBBCC	Ind	
Music and Hindi	TWN3	3FT deg		20	Ind		30	BBBCC	Ind	4
Music and Indonesian	TWMH	3FT/4FT deg		20	Ind		30	BBBCC	Ind	
Music and Japanese	TW43	4FT deg		24	Ind		32	BBBBB	Ind	
Music and Korean	TWNH	4FT deg		16	Ind		28	BBCCC	Ind	
Nepali and Development Studies	MTXN	3FT deg		22	Ind		31	BBBBC	Ind	
Nepali and Economics	LTD5	3FT deg	g	22	Ind		31	BBBBC	Ind	
Nepali and Geography	LTV5	3FT deg		20	Ind		30	BBBCC	Ind	
Nepali and History	VTC5	3FT deg		20	Ind		30	BBBCC	Ind	
Nepali and History of Art/Archaeology	TV5Q	3FT deg		20	Ind		30	BBBCC	Ind	
Nepali and Law	MTJ5	3FT deg		24	Ind		32	BBBBB	Ind	
Nepali and Linguistics	QTD5	3FT deg		20	Ind		30	BBBCC	Ind	
Nepali and Management	NTD5	3FT deg	g	20	Ind		30	BBBCC	Ind	
Nepali and Music	TW5J	3FT deg		20	Ind		30	BBBCC	Ind	
Politics and African Studies	TM71	3FT deg		20	Ind		30	BBBCC	Ind	
Politics and Amharic	MT17	4FT deg		20	Ind		30	BBBCC	Ind	
Politics and Bengali	MT15	3FT deg		20	Ind		30	BBBCC	Ind	
Politics and Burmese	MT1M	4FT deg	g	20	Ind		30	BBBCC	Ind	
Politics and Chinese	MT13	4FT deg		24	Ind		32	BBBBB	Ind	
Politics and Gujarati	MTC5	3FT deg		20	Ind		30	BBBCC	Ind	
Politics and Hausa	MT1R	4FT deg		20	Ind		30	BBBCC	Ind	
Politics and Hindi	MT1N	3FT/4FT deg		20	Ind		30	BBBCC	Ind	
Politics and Indonesian	MTCM	3FT/4FT deg		20	Ind		30	BBBCC	Ind	
Politics and Japanese	MT14	4FT deg		24	Ind		32	BBBBB	Ind	4
Politics and Korean	MTCN	4FT deg		20	Ind		30	BBBCC	Ind	
Politics and Nepali	MTDM	3FT deg		20	Ind		30	BBBCC	Ind	
Sinhalese and Development Studies	MTXM	3FT deg		22	Ind		31	BBBBC	Ind	
Sinhalese and Economics	LTDM	3FT deg	g	22	Ind		31	BBBBC	Ind	
Sinhalese and Geography	LTVM	3FT deg		20	Ind		30	BBBCC	Ind	
Sinhalese and History	TVMC	3FT deg		20	Ind		30	BBBCC	Ind	
Sinhalese and History of Art/Archaeology	TVN6	3FT deg		20	Ind		30	BBBCC	Ind	
Sinhalese and Law	MTJM	3FT deg		24	Ind		32	BBBBB	Ind	
Sinhalese and Linguistics	QTDM	3FT deg		20	Ind		30	BBBCC	Ind	
Sinhalese and Management	NTDM	3FT deg	g	20	Ind		30	BBBCC	Ind	
Sinhalese and Music	TWMJ	3FT deg		20	Ind		30	BBBCC	Ind	
Sinhalese and Politics	MTDN	3FT deg		20	Ind		30	BBBCC	Ind	
Social Anthropology and African Studies	TL76	3FT deg		22	Ind		31	BBBBC	Ind	10
Social Anthropology and Amharic	LT67	4FT deg		22	Ind		31	BBBBC	Ind	
Social Anthropology and Bengali	LT65	3FT deg		22	Ind		31	BBBBC	Ind	
Social Anthropology and Burmese	LT6M	4FT deg		22	Ind		31	BBBBC	Ind	
Social Anthropology and Chinese	LT63	4FT deg		24	Ind		32	BBBBB	Ind	10
Social Anthropology and Gujarati	LTP5	3FT deg		22	Ind		31	BBBBC	Ind	
Social Anthropology and Hausa	LT6R	4FT deg		22	Ind		31	BBBBC	Ind	
Social Anthropology and Hindi	LT6N	3FT/4FT deg		22	Ind		31	BBBBC	Ind	
Social Anthropology and Indonesian	LTPM	3FT/4FT deg		22	Ind		31	BBBBC	Ind	9

course details   **98 expected requirements**   **96 entry stats**

course details

98 expected requirements

96 entry stats

TITLE	CODE	COURSE	SUBJECTS	A/AS	NO/C	AGNVQ	IB	SQA(H)	SQA	RATIO A/AS
Social Anthropology and Japanese	LT64	4FT deg		24	Ind		32	BBBBB	Ind	
Social Anthropology and Korean	LTPN	4FT deg		22	Ind		31	BBBBC	Ind	1
Social Anthropology and Nepali	LTQM	3FT deg		22	Ind		31	BBBCC	Ind	
Social Anthropology and Sinhalese	TLM6	3FT deg		22	Ind		31	BBBBC	Ind	
South Asian Studies	T500	3FT deg		20	Ind		30	BBBCC	Ind	7
South Asian Studies and Development Studies	TMMX	3FT deg								
South Asian Studies and Economics	TLM1	3FT deg								
South Asian Studies and Geography	TLMV	3FT deg								
South Asian Studies and History	VT1N	3FT deg								
South Asian Studies and History of Art/Archaeol	VTP5	3FT deg								
South Asian Studies and Law	TM5H	3FT deg								
South Asian Studies and Linguistics	TQM1	3FT deg								
South Asian Studies and Management	TNM1	3FT deg								
South Asian Studies and Music	WTH5	3FT deg								
South Asian Studies and Politics	TMM1	3FT deg								
South Asian Studies and Social Anthropology	TL5Q	3FT deg								
South Asian Studies and Study of Religions	VT8N	3FT deg								
South-East Asian Studies	T502	3FT deg		20	Ind		30	BBBCC	Ind	3 12/22
Study of Religions and African Studies	VT87	3FT deg		20	Ind		30	BBBCC	Ind	
Study of Religions and Amharic	TV78	4FT deg		20	Ind		30	BBBCC	Ind	
Study of Religions and Bengali	TV58	3FT deg		20	Ind		30	BBBCC	Ind	
Study of Religions and Burmese	TVM8	4FT deg		20	Ind		30	BBBCC	Ind	
Study of Religions and Chinese	TV38	4FT deg		24	Ind		32	BBBBB	Ind	2
Study of Religions and Gujarati	TV5V	3FT deg		20	Ind		30	BBBCC	Ind	
Study of Religions and Hausa	TVR8	4FT deg		20	Ind		30	BBBCC	Ind	
Study of Religions and Hindi	TVN8	3FT/4FT deg		20	Ind		30	BBBCC	Ind	
Study of Religions and Indonesian	TV5W	3FT/4FT deg		20	Ind		30	BBBCC	Ind	
Study of Religions and Japanese	TV48	4FT deg		24	Ind		32	BBBBB	Ind	
Study of Religions and Korean	TVNV	4FT deg		20	Ind		30	BBBCC	Ind	
Study of Religions and Nepali	TVMV	3FT deg		20	Ind		30	BBBCC	Ind	
Study of Religions and Sinhalese	TVNW	3FT deg		20	Ind		30	BBBCC	Ind	
Swahili and Development Studies	MT9T	4FT deg		22	Ind		31	BBBBC	Ind	
Swahili and Economics	LT1T	4FT deg	g	22	Ind		31	BBBBC	Ind	
Swahili and Geography	LT8T	4FT deg		20	Ind		30	BBBCC	Ind	
Swahili and History	TVT1	4FT deg		20	Ind		30	BBBCC	Ind	
Swahili and History of Art/Archaeology	TVT6	4FT deg		20	Ind		30	BBBCC	Ind	
Swahili and Law	MT3T	4FT deg		24	Ind		32	BBBBB	Ind	
Swahili and Linguistics	QT1T	4FT deg		20	Ind		30	BBBCC	Ind	
Swahili and Management	NT1T	4FT deg	g	20	Ind		30	BBBCC	Ind	
Swahili and Music	TWT3	4FT deg		20	Ind		30	BBBCC	Ind	
Swahili and Politics	MT1T	4FT deg		20	Ind		30	BBBCC	Ind	
Swahili and Social Anthropology	LT6T	4FT deg		22	Ind		31	BBBBC	Ind	
Swahili and Study of Religions	TVT8	4FT deg		20	Ind		30	BBBCC	Ind	
Tamil and Development Studies	MTY5	3FT deg		22	Ind		31	BBBBC	Ind	
Tamil and Economics	LTDN	3FT deg	g	22	Ind		31	BBBBC	Ind	
Tamil and Geography	LTVN	3FT deg		20	Ind		30	BBBCC	Ind	
Tamil and History	TV5D	3FT deg		20	Ind		30	BBBCC	Ind	1
Tamil and History of Art/Archaeology	TVNQ	3FT deg		20	Ind		30	BBBCC	Ind	
Tamil and Law	MTJN	3FT deg		24	Ind		32	BBBBB	Ind	
Tamil and Linguistics	QTDN	3FT deg		20	Ind		30	BBBCC	Ind	
Tamil and Management	NTDN	3FT deg	g	20	Ind		30	BBBCC	Ind	
Tamil and Music	TWNJ	3FT deg		20	Ind		30	BBBCC	Ind	

Languages – African, Asian and Oriental   36

| course details | | | 98 expected requirements | | | | | | | 96 entry stats | |

TITLE	CODE	COURSE	SUBJECTS	A/AS	NQ/C	AGNVQ	IB	SQA(H)	SQA	RATIO	A/AS
Tamil and Politics	MTD5	3FT deg		20	Ind		30	BBBCC	Ind		
Tamil and Social Anthropology	LTQ5	3FT deg		22	Ind		31	BBBBC	Ind		
Tamil and Study of Religions	VT85	3FT deg		20	Ind		30	BBBCC	Ind		
Thai (single-subject language)	T553	4FT deg		20	Ind		30	BBBCC	Ind	1	
Thai and Chinese	TT53	3FT deg		24	Ind		32	BBBBB	Ind		
Thai and Development Studies	MTYM	3FT/4FT deg		22	Ind		31	BBBBC	Ind		
Thai and Economics	TL51	3FT/4FT deg	g	22	Ind		31	BBBBC	Ind		
Thai and Geography	LTW5	3FT/4FT deg		20	Ind		30	BBBCC	Ind		
Thai and History	TVMD	3FT/4FT deg		20	Ind		30	BBBCC	Ind		
Thai and History of Art/Archaeology	VT65	3FT/4FT deg		20	Ind		30	BBBCC	Ind		
Thai and Japanese	TT4M	4FT deg		24	Ind		32	BBBBB	Ind	4	
Thai and Korean	T554	4FT deg		22	Ind		31	BBBBC	Ind		
Thai and Law	TM53	3FT/4FT deg		24	Ind		32	BBBBB	Ind		
Thai and Linguistics	TQ51	3FT/4FT deg		20	Ind		30	BBBCC	Ind		
Thai and Management	TN51	3FT/4FT deg	g	20	Ind		30	BBBCC	Ind		
Thai and Music	WT35	3FT/4FT deg		20	Ind		30	BBBCC	Ind		
Thai and Politics	TM51	3FT/4FT deg		20	Ind		30	BBBCC	Ind		
Thai and Social Anthropology	LTQN	3FT/4FT deg		22	Ind		31	BBBBC	Ind		
Thai and Study of Religions	VT8M	3FT/4FT deg		20	Ind		30	BBBCC	Ind	4	
Tibetan and Development Studies	MTYN	3FT deg		22	Ind		31	BBBBC	Ind		
Tibetan and Study of Religions	V8TM	3FT deg		20	Ind		30	BBBCC	Ind		
Urdu and Arabic	TT56	4FT deg		22	Ind		31	BBBBC	Ind		
Urdu and Development Studies	MTX5	3FT deg		22	Ind		31	BBBBC	Ind		
Urdu and Economics	TL5C	3FT deg	g	22	Ind		31	BBBBC	Ind		
Urdu and Geography	LTWM	3FT deg		20	Ind		30	BBBCC	Ind		
Urdu and History	TVNC	3FT deg		20	Ind		30	BBBCC	Ind		
Urdu and History of Art/Archaeology	VT6M	3FT deg		20	Ind		30	BBBCC	Ind		
Urdu and Law	TMM3	3FT deg		24	Ind		32	BBBBB	Ind		
Urdu and Linguistics	TQ5C	3FT deg		20	Ind		30	BBBCC	Ind		
Urdu and Management	TN5C	3FT deg	g	20	Ind		30	BBBCC	Ind	3	
Urdu and Music	WT3M	3FT deg		20	Ind		30	BBBCC	Ind		
Urdu and Persian	TT5Q	3FT deg		22	Ind		31	BBBBC	Ind		
Urdu and Politics	TM5C	3FT deg		20	Ind		30	BBBCC	Ind		
Urdu and Social Anthropology	TL56	3FT deg		22	Ind		31	BBBBC	Ind		
Urdu and Study of Religions	VTV5	3FT deg		20	Ind		30	BBBCC	Ind		
Vietnamese and Development Studies	TM5X	4FT deg		20	Ind		30	BBBCC	Ind		
Vietnamese and Economics	TL5D	4FT deg	g	22	Ind		31	BBBBC	Ind		
Vietnamese and Geography	LTWN	4FT deg		20	Ind		30	BBBCC	Ind	1	
Vietnamese and History	TVND	4FT deg		20	Ind		30	BBBCC	Ind		
Vietnamese and History of Art/Archaeology	VT6N	4FT deg		20	Ind		30	BBBCC	Ind		
Vietnamese and Law	TMN3	4FT deg		24	Ind		32	BBBBB	Ind		
Vietnamese and Linguistics	TQ5D	4FT deg		20	Ind		30	BBBCC	Ind		
Vietnamese and Management	TN5D	4FT deg	g	20	Ind		30	BBBCC	Ind		
Vietnamese and Music	WT3N	4FT deg		20	Ind		30	BBBCC	Ind		
Vietnamese and Politics	TM5D	4FT deg		20	Ind		30	BBBCC	Ind	1	
Vietnamese and Social Anthropology	TL5P	4FT deg		22	Ind		31	BBBBC	Ind	1	
Vietnamese and Study of Religions	VTVM	4FT deg		20	Ind		30	BBBCC	Ind		

Univ of SHEFFIELD

TITLE	CODE	COURSE	SUBJECTS	A/AS	NQ/C	AGNVQ	IB	SQA(H)	SQA	RATIO	A/AS
Business Studies and Japanese Studies	NT14	4FT deg	* g	BBC	4M+2D	D^	30	ABBB	Ind	9	20/28
Chinese Studies	T310	4FT deg	* g	BBC	4M+2D	D^	30	ABBB	Ind	9	
Chinese Studies and Business Studies	TN31	4FT deg	* g	BBC	4M+2D	D^	30	ABBB	Ind	9	
East Asian Studies	T500	3FT deg	* g	BBC	4M+2D	D^	30	ABBB	Ind	4	

course details			98 expected requirements							96 entry stats	
TITLE	CODE	COURSE	SUBJECTS	A/AS	NO/C	RGNVQ	IB	SQA(H)	SQA	RATIO A/AS	
Economics and Japanese Studies	LT14	3FT deg	* g	BBC	4M+2D	D^	30	ABBB	Ind	6	
Geography and Japanese Studies	LT84	4FT deg	Gv g	BBC	4M+2D$	D^	30$	ABBB$	Ind		
Japanese Studies	T400	4FT deg	* g	BCC	5M+1D	D^	29	BBBB	Ind	5	16/24
Japanese Studies and Politics	TM41	4FT deg	* g	BBB	3M+3D	D^	32	AABB	Ind	7	
Japanese Studies and Sociology	TL43	4FT deg	* g	BBC	4D	D^	30	ABBB	Ind	4	
Japanese and Korean Studies	TT45	4FT deg	* g	BBC	4M+2D	D^	30	ABBB	Ind	1	
Korean Studies	T515	4FT deg	* g	BBC	4M+2D	D^	30	ABBB	Ind	5	
Korean Studies and Business Studies	TN51	4FT deg	* g	BBC	4M+2D	D^	30	ABBB	Ind		
Korean Studies and Economics	TL51	4FT deg	* g	BBC	4M+2D	D^	30	ABBB	Ind		
Linguistics and Japanese	QT14	4FT deg	Ee+L	BBC	X	X	30$	ABBB$	Ind		
Linguistics and Korean Studies	QT15	4FT deg	Ee+L	BBC	X	X	30$	ABBB$	Ind		
Modern History and Japanese	VT14	4FT deg	H g	BBC	X	X	30$	ABBB$	Ind		

Univ of STIRLING

TITLE	CODE	COURSE	SUBJECTS	A/AS	NO/C	RGNVQ	IB	SQA(H)	SQA	RATIO A/AS	
Business Studies/Japanese	N1T4	4FT deg	g	BCC	Ind	Ind	31	BBBC	HN		
Computing Science/Japanese	GT54	4FT deg	g	CCC	Ind	Ind	28	BBCC	HN		
Economics/Japanese	LT14	4FT deg	g	BCC	Ind	Ind	31	BBBC	HN		
Film & Media Studies/Japanese	PT4K	4FT deg	g	BBC	Ind	Ind	35	ABBB	HN		
Financial Studies/Japanese	NT34	4FT deg	g	BCC	Ind	Ind	31	BBBC	HN		
German/Japanese	RT24	4FT deg	g	CCC	Ind	Ind	31	BBBC	HN		
Japanese	T402	4FT deg	g	BCC	Ind	Ind	31	BBBC	HN		
Japanese/English Studies	QT34	4FT deg	g	BCC	Ind	Ind	31	BBBC	HN		
Japanese/French	TR41	4FT deg	g	BCC	Ind	Ind	31	BBBC	HN		
Japanese/Human Resources Management	NT1K	4FT deg	g	BCC	Ind	Ind	31	BBBC	HN		
Japanese/Philosophy	TV47	4FT deg	g	BCC	Ind	Ind	31	BBBC	HN		
Japanese/Politics	MT14	4FT deg	g	BCC	Ind	Ind	31	BBBC	HN		
Japanese/Sociology	LT34	4FT deg	g	BCC	Ind	Ind	31	BBBC	HN		
Management Science/Japanese	NT14	4FT deg	g	BCC	Ind	Ind	31	BBBC	HN		
Marketing/Japanese	N5T4	4FT deg	g	BCC	Ind	Ind	31	BBBC	HN		
Mathematics and its Applications with Japanese	G1T4	4FT deg	M g	CCC	Ind	Ind	28	BBCC	HN		
Spanish/Japanese	RT44	4FT deg	g	CCC	Ind	Ind	31	BBBC	HN		

Univ of SUNDERLAND

TITLE	CODE	COURSE	SUBJECTS	A/AS	NO/C	RGNVQ	IB	SQA(H)	SQA	RATIO A/AS	
International Business with Japanese	N1T4	3FT deg	* g	18	1M+4D$ D		26	BBBCC	N$		

Univ of SUSSEX

TITLE	CODE	COURSE	SUBJECTS	A/AS	NO/C	RGNVQ	IB	SQA(H)	SQA	RATIO A/AS	
Contemporary History in African & Asian Studies	V1TM	3FT deg	*	BBB	MO	M*6	$	Ind	Ind		
Economics in African & Asian Studies	L1T5	3FT deg	* g	BBB	MO $	M*6 go	$	Ind	Ind		
Electrical and Electronic Eng with Japanese	H5TK	4FT deg	M g	BCC	MO $	MS^ go	$	Ind	Ind		
Electronic Engineering with Japanese Studies	H6T4	4FT deg	M g	BCC	5M $	MS^ go	$	Ind	Ind		
English in African and Asian Studies	Q3T5	3FT deg	*	BBB	MO	M*6	$	Ind	Ind		
French in African and Asian Studies	R1T5	4FT deg	F	BCC	MO $	M*^	$	Ind	Ind		
Geography in African and Asian Studies	L8T5	3FT deg	*	BBC	MO	M*6	$	Ind	Ind		
History in African and Asian Studies	V1T5	3FT deg	*	BBB	MO	M*6	$	Ind	Ind		
International Relations in African & Asian St	M1TM	3FT deg	*	BBC	MO	M*6	$	Ind	Ind		
Mechanical Engineering with Japanese Studies	H3T4	4FT deg	M	BCC	MO $	MS^ go	$	Ind	Ind		
Politics in African and Asian Studies	M1T5	3FT deg	*	BBC	MO	M*6	$	Ind	Ind		
Social Anthropology in African & Asian Studies	L6T5	3FT deg	*	BBC	MO	M*6	$	Ind	Ind		
Sociology in African and Asian Studies	L3T5	3FT deg	*	BBB	MO	M*6	$	Ind	Ind		

Univ of ULSTER

TITLE	CODE	COURSE	SUBJECTS	A/AS	NO/C	RGNVQ	IB	SQA(H)	SQA	RATIO A/AS	
Business Studies with Japanese (4 Yr inc DAS)	N1T4▼	4SW deg	* g	CCC	MO+3D	D*6/^ gi	28	BBBC	Ind	9	16/20
Humanities Combined *Japanese Studies*	Y320▼	3FT/4FT deg	*	CCC	MO+3D	D*6/^ gi	28	BBBC	Ind		

Languages – African, Asian and Oriental 36

course details			98 expected requirements							96 entry stats	
TITLE	CODE	COURSE	SUBJECTS	A/AS	ND/C	AGNVQ	IB	SQA(H)	SQA	RATIO A/AS	
Univ of WESTMINSTER											
English Language and Chinese	T3QH	4SW deg		CC	Ind		26$	BBB			
English and Chinese	T3Q3	4SW deg	E	CC	Ind		26$	BBB	Ind	2	
French and Chinese	T3R1	4SW deg	F	CC	Ind		26$	BBB	Ind	2	11/22
German and Chinese	T3R2	4SW deg	G	CC	Ind		26$	BBB	Ind	2	
Italian and Chinese	T3R3	4SW deg	I	CC	Ind		26	BBB	Ind		
Linguistics and Chinese	T3Q1	4SW deg	L	CC	Ind		26	BBB	Ind	2	
Russian and Chinese	T3R8	4SW deg	R	CC	Ind		26	BBB	Ind	2	
Spanish and Chinese	T3R4	4SW deg	Sp	CC	Ind		26	BBB	Ind		
Univ of WOLVERHAMPTON											
Combined Degrees *Japanese Studies*	Y401	3FT/4SW deg	L g	12	4M $	M	24	BBBB	Ind		
Univ of YORK											
Hindi and Linguistics	QT15	4FT deg	*	24	Ind	D$^	28$	BBCC	Ind		
Linguistics with Chinese	Q1T3	3FT deg	*	24	Ind	D$^	28$	BBCC$	Ind		

			98 expected requirements							96 entry stats
TITLE	CODE	COURSE	SUBJECTS	A/AS	NO/C	RGNVQ	IB	SQA(H)	SQA	RATIO A/AS

Univ of ABERDEEN

Accountancy with Gaelic	N4Q5	4FT deg	* g	BBC	Ind	M$ go	30$	BBBB$	Ind	
Celtic Civilisation-English	QQM3	4FT deg	* g	BBC	Ind	M$ go	30$	BBBB$	Ind	2
Celtic Civilisation-German	QR5F	4FT/5FT deg	* g	BBC	Ind	M$ go	30$	BBBB$	Ind	
Celtic Civilisation-German (4 Yrs)	RQF5	4FT deg	* g	BBC	Ind	M$ go	30$	BBBB$	Ind	
Celtic Civilisation-History	QVM1	4FT deg	* g	BBC	Ind	M$ go	30$	BBBB$	Ind	4
Celtic Civilisation-History of Art	QVM4	4FT deg	* g	BBC	Ind	M$ go	30$	BBBB$	Ind	
Celtic Civilisation-Philosophy	QV57	4FT deg	* g	BBC	Ind	M$ go	30$	BBBB$	Ind	
Celtic Civilisation-Social Research	LQ3M	4FT deg	* g	BBC	Ind	M$ go	30$	BBBB$	Ind	
Celtic Civilisation-Sociology	LQ35	4FT deg	* g	BBC	Ind	M$ go	30$	BBBB$	Ind	
Celtic Studies	Q500	4FT deg	* g	BBC	Ind	M$ go	30$	BBBB$	Ind	4
Celtic-Economics	QL51	4FT deg	* g	BBC	Ind	M$ go	30$	BBBB$	Ind	
Celtic-English	QQ53	4FT deg	* g	BBC	Ind	M$ go	30$	BBBB$	Ind	3
Celtic-French	QR51	4FT/5FT deg	* g	BBC	Ind	M$ go	30$	BBBB$	Ind	
Celtic-French (4 Yrs)	RQ15	4FT deg	* g	BBC	Ind	M$ go	30$	BBBB$	Ind	
Celtic-Geography	QL58	4FT deg	* g	BBC	Ind	M$ go	30$	BBBB$	Ind	
Celtic-German	QR52	4FT/5FT deg	* g	BBC	Ind	M$ go	30$	BBBB$	Ind	
Celtic-German (4Yrs)	RQ25	4FT deg	* g	BBC	Ind	M$ go	30$	BBBB$	Ind	
Celtic-Hispanic Studies	QR54	4FT/5FT deg	* g	BBC	Ind	M$ go	30$	BBBB$	Ind	
Celtic-Hispanic Studies (4 Yrs)	RQ45	4FT deg	* g	BBC	Ind	M$ go	30$	BBBB$	Ind	
Celtic-History	QV51	4FT deg	* g	BBC	Ind	M$ go	30$	BBBB$	Ind	7
Celtic-History of Art	QV54	4FT deg	* g	BBC	Ind	M$ go	30$	BBBB$	Ind	
Celtic-Management Studies	QN51	4FT deg	* g	BBC	Ind	M$ go	30$	BBBB$	Ind	
Celtic-Social Research	LQ3N	4FT deg	* g	BBC	Ind	M$ go	30$	BBBB$	Ind	
Celtic-Sociology	QL53	4FT deg	* g	BBC	Ind	M$ go	30$	BBBB$	Ind	2
Gaelic Studies	Q502	4FT deg	* g	BBC	Ind	M$ go	30$	BBBB$	Ind	3
Geography-Celtic Civilisation	LQ85	4FT deg	* g	BBC	Ind	M$ go	30$	BBBB$	Ind	
Languages and Literature of Scotland	QQ52	4FT deg	* g	BBC	Ind	M$ go	30$	BBBB$	Ind	
Mathematics with Gaelic	G1Q5	4FT deg	2S+M g	CCD	Ind	MS go	24$	BBBC$	Ind	
Physics with Gaelic	F3Q5	4FT deg	2S+M g	CCD	Ind	MS go	24$	BBBC$	Ind	
Psychology with Gaelic	C8Q5	4FT deg	3S/2S+M g	CCD	Ind	MS go	24$	BBBC$	Ind	
Psychology with Gaelic (MA)	C8QM	4FT deg	* g	BBC	Ind	MS go	30$	BBBB$	Ind	
Religious Studies-Celtic	VQ85	5FT deg	* g	BBC	Ind	M$ go	30$	BBBB$	Ind	
Religious Studies-Celtic (4 Yrs)	QV58	4FT deg	* g	BBC	Ind	M$ go	30$	BBBB$	Ind	
Theology with Gaelic	V8Q5	3FT deg	* g	CC	Ind	M* go	24$	BBCC	Ind	

Univ of Wales, ABERYSTWYTH

Accounting and Finance with Welsh	N4Q5	3FT deg	W g	18	3M+3D$ M^ g	29$	BBBCC$	Ind		
Business Studies/Welsh	NQ15	3FT deg	W g	18	3M+3D$ M^ g	29$	BBBCC$	Ind		
Celtic Studies	Q500	4FT deg	* g	18	1M+5D$ M^ g	29$	BBBCC$	Ind		
Irish/American Studies	QQK5	4FT deg	E/H g	18	1M+5D$ M^ g	29$	BBBCC$	Ind		
Irish/Art	QWM1	4FT deg	A/Ad g	18	1M+5D$ MA6 g	29$	BBBCC$	Ind		
Irish/Art History	QVM4	4FT deg	* g	18	1M+5D$ MA6 g	29$	BBBCC$	Ind		
Irish/Drama	QWM4	4FT deg	* g	20	1M+5D$ MQ6 g	30$	BBBBC$	Ind		
Irish/Education	QXM9	4FT deg	* g	18	1M+5D$ M^ g	29$	BBBCC$	Ind		
Irish/English	QQJ5	4FT deg	EI	20	1M+5D$ M^ g	30$	BBBBC$	Ind		
Irish/Film and Television Studies	QW55	3FT deg	* g	20	1M+5D$ MQ6 g	30$	BBBBC$	Ind		
Irish/French	QRM1	4FT deg	F g	18	1M+5D$ M^ g	29$	BBBCC$	Ind		
Irish/German	QR5F	4FT deg	G g	18	1M+5D$ M^ g	29$	BBBCC$	Ind		
Irish/History	QVND	4FT deg	* g	18-20	1M+5D$ M^ g	30$	BBBCC$	Ind		
Irish/Information and Library Studies	PQ2M	4FT deg	* g	18	1M+5D$ M^ g	29$	BBBCC$	Ind		
Italian/Irish	QRM3	4FT deg	L g	18	1M+5D$ M^ g	29$	BBBCC$	Ind		
Literature and History of Wales	Q550	3FT deg	* g	18-20	1M+5D M^ g	30	BBBCC	Ind		

TITLE	CODE	COURSE	SUBJECTS	A/AS	NO/C	AGNVQ	IB	SQA(H)	SQA	RATIO A/AS
Pure Mathematics/Irish	GQC5	4FT deg	M g	18	1M+5D$	M^ g	29$	BBBCC$	Ind	
Welsh	Q520	3FT deg	W g	18	1M+5D$	M^ g	29$	BBBCC$	Ind	
Welsh History/Irish	QVNC	4FT deg	* g	18-20	1M+5D$	M^ g	30$	BBBCC$	Ind	
Welsh History/Welsh	QV5C	3FT deg	W g	18-20	1M+5D$	M^ g	30$	BBBCC$	Ind	
Welsh/American Studies	QQ45	3FT deg	E/H+W g	18	1M+5D$	M^ g	29$	BBBCC$	Ind	
Welsh/Art	QW51	3FT deg	W+A/Ad g	18	1M+5D$	MA^ g	29$	BBBCC$	Ind	
Welsh/Art History	QV54	3FT deg	W g	18	1M+5D$	MA^ g	29$	BBBCC$	Ind	
Welsh/Drama	QW54	3FT deg	W g	20	1M+5D$	MQ^ g	30$	BBBBC$	Ind	
Welsh/Education	QX59	3FT deg	W g	18	1M+5D$	M^ g	29$	BBBCC$	Ind	
Welsh/English	QQH5	3FT deg	El+W	20	1M+5D$	M^ g	30$	BBBBC$	Ind	
Welsh/Film and Television Studies	QW5M	3FT deg	W g	20	1M+5D$	MQ^ g	30$	BBBBC$	Ind	
Welsh/French	QR51	4FT deg	F+W g	18	1M+5D$	M^ g	29$	BBBCC$	Ind	
Welsh/Geography	LQ85	3FT deg	W+Gy g	20-22	3M+2D$	M^ g	31$	BBBBC$	Ind	
Welsh/German	QR52	4FT deg	W+G g	18	1M+5D$	M^ g	29$	BBBCC$	Ind	
Welsh/History	QV51	3FT deg	W g	18-20	1M+5D$	M^ g	30$	BBBCC$	Ind	
Welsh/Information and Library Studies	PQ25	3FT deg	W g	18	1M+5D$	M^ g	29$	BBBCC$	Ind	
Welsh/International Politics	MQ1M	3FT deg	W g	20	1M+5D$	M^ g	30$	BBBCC$	Ind	
Welsh/Italian	QR53	4FT deg	W+L g	18	1M+5D$	M^ g	29$	BBBCC$	Ind	
Welsh/Politics	MQ15	3FT deg	W g	20	1M+5D$	M^ g	30$	BBBBC$	Ind	
Welsh/Pure Mathematics	GQ15	3FT deg	M+W g	18	1M+5D$	M^ g	29$	BBBCC$	Ind	
Welsh/Spanish	QR54	4FT deg	W+L g	18	1M+5D$	M^ g	29$	BBBCC$	Ind	

Univ of Wales, BANGOR

TITLE	CODE	COURSE	SUBJECTS	A/AS	NO/C	AGNVQ	IB	SQA(H)	SQA	RATIO A/AS
Management/Welsh	NQ15	3FT deg	W g	18	X	D*^ go	Ind	X	X	
Welsh	Q520	3FT/4FT deg	W g	CCD	Ind	D*^ go	Ind	X	X	3 12/26
Welsh History/Welsh	QV5C	3FT/4FT deg	H+W g	CCD	X	D*^ go	Ind	X	X	9
Welsh Literature and Literature of the Media	Q5W4	3FT/4FT deg	W g	CCD	Ind	D*^ go	Ind	X	X	3 14/26
Welsh and Literature of the Media/Music	WQ35	3FT/4FT deg	Mu+W g	BB-BCD	X	D*^ go	Ind	X	X	
Welsh/Education	QX59	3FT/4FT deg	W g	CCD	Ind	D*^ go	Ind	X	X	7
Welsh/English	QQ35	3FT/4FT deg	E+W g	CCC	X	D*^ go	Ind	X	X	2
Welsh/French (Syllabus A)	QR51	4FT deg	F+W g	CCD	X	D*^ go	Ind	X	X	
Welsh/French (Syllabus B)	QR5C	4FT deg	F+W g	CCD	X	D*^ go	Ind	X	X	
Welsh/German	QR52	4FT deg	W g	CCD	X	D*^ go	Ind	X	X	1
Welsh/History	QV51	3FT/4FT deg	H+W g	CCD	X	D*^ go	Ind	X	X	
Welsh/Linguistics	QQ15	3FT/4FT deg	W g	CCD	Ind	D*^ go	Ind	X	X	
Welsh/Mathematics	GQ15	3FT/4FT deg	M+W g	CCD	Ind	D*^ go	Ind	X	X	1
Welsh/Music	QW53	3FT/4FT deg	Mu+W g	BB-BCD	X	D*^ go	Ind	X	X	9
Welsh/Physical Education	QB56	3FT/4FT deg	W g	CCC	Ind	D*^ go	Ind	X	X	
Welsh/Religious Studies	QV58	3FT/4FT deg	W g	CCD	Ind	D*^ go	Ind	X	X	4
Welsh/Russian	QR58	4FT deg	W g	CCD	Ind	D*^ go	Ind	X	X	
Welsh/Social Policy	LQ45	3FT/4FT deg	W g	CCD	Ind	D*^ go	Ind	X	X	
Welsh/Sociology	LQ35	3FT/4FT deg	W g	CCD	Ind	D*^ go	Ind	X	X	4
Welsh/Sports Science	BQ65	3FT/4FT deg	W g	CCC	Ind	D*^ go	Ind	X	X	

BATH COLL of HE

TITLE	CODE	COURSE	SUBJECTS	A/AS	NO/C	AGNVQ	IB	SQA(H)	SQA	RATIO A/AS
Combined Awards Irish Studies	Y400	3FT deg	*		N		Ind	$	$	
Modular Programme (DipHE) Irish Studies	Y460	2FT Dip	*		N		Ind	$	$	

CAMBRIDGE Univ

TITLE	CODE	COURSE	SUBJECTS	A/AS	NO/C	AGNVQ	IB	SQA(H)	SQA	RATIO A/AS
Anglo-Saxon, Norse and Celtic	QQ59▼	3FT deg	* g	AAB	Ind		Ind	CSYS	Ind	2 27/30

course details			98 expected requirements							96 entry stats	
TITLE	CODE	COURSE	SUBJECTS	A/AS	ND/C	AGNVQ	IB	SQA(H)	SQA	RATIO	A/AS
CARDIFF Univ of Wales											
Welsh	Q520	3FT deg	W	CCC	X		Ind	X		6	8/26
Welsh History/Welsh	VQC5	3FT deg	H+W	BBC-BCC	X		Ind	X	X	6	
Welsh/Ancient History	QV5C	3FT deg	W	BCC							
Welsh/Archaeology	QV56	3FT deg	W	BCC	X		Ind	X	X		
Welsh/Cultural Criticism	MQ95	3FT deg	E	ABC	X		Ind	AAABB	X		
Welsh/Economics	QL51	3FT deg	W	BBC-BBB	X		Ind	ABBBB	X		
Welsh/Education	QX59	3FT deg	W	CCC	Ind	Ind	Ind	Ind	Ind	8	
Welsh/English Literature	QQ53	3FT deg	E+W	ABB	X		Ind	AAABB	X	7	
Welsh/French	QR51	4FT deg	F+W	BBC	Ind		Ind	ABBBB	Ind		
Welsh/German	QR52	4FT deg	W+G	BBC			Ind				
Welsh/History	QV51	3FT deg	H+W	BBC-BCC	X		Ind	X	X		
Welsh/Italian	QR53	4FT deg	L+W	BCC	Ind		Ind	Ind	Ind		
Welsh/Language Studies	QQ15	3FT deg	W	BBC	X		Ind	X		1	
Welsh/Music	QW53	3FT deg	Mu+W	BCC	X		Ind	Ind	X	6	
Welsh/Philosophy	QV57	3FT deg	W	BCC							
Welsh/Politics	QM51	3FT deg	W	BBC							
Welsh/Pure Mathematics	QG51	3FT deg	M+W	BCC	X	Ind	Ind	X	X	1	
Welsh/Religious Studies	QV58	3FT deg	W	BCC						3	
Welsh/Sociology	QL53	3FT deg	W	BCC						3	
Welsh/Spanish	QR54	4FT deg	W+L	BBC-BCC	X		Ind	Ind	X		
Univ of EDINBURGH											
Celtic	Q500	4FT deg	L g	BBB	Ind	Ind	Dip$	BBBB$	Ind		
Celtic and Archaeology	QV56	4FT deg	L g	BBB	Ind	Ind	Dip$	BBBB$	Ind		
Celtic and German	QR52	4FT deg	L g	BBB	Ind	Ind	Dip$	BBBB$	Ind		
Celtic and Linguistics	QQ15	4FT deg	L g	BBB	Ind	Ind	Dip$	BBBB$	Ind		
Celtic and Scandinavian Studies	QR57	4FT deg	L g	BBB	Ind	Ind	Dip$	BBBB$	Ind		
Celtic and Scottish Historical Studies	QV51	4FT deg	L g	BBB	Ind	Ind	Dip$	BBBB$	Ind		
English and Celtic	QQ35	4FT deg	L g	BBB	Ind	Ind	Dip$	BBBB$	Ind		
Law and Celtic	MQ35	4FT deg	L g	ABB	X		32	AAABB	X		
Scottish Ethnology and Celtic	VQ95	4FT deg	L g	BBB	Ind	Ind	Dip$	BBBB$	Ind		
Univ of GLAMORGAN											
English Studies and Welsh Studies	QQ35	3FT deg	* g	12	Ind	Ind	Ind	Ind	Ind		
French with Welsh	R1Q5	3FT deg			Ind	Ind	Ind	Ind	Ind		
History and Welsh Studies	QV51	3FT deg	* g	12	5M	M	Ind	Ind	Ind		
Humanities (Welsh Studies)	Q520	3FT deg	* g	CC	5M	M$	24	CCCC	HN		
Religious Studies and Welsh Studies	QV58	3FT deg	* g	12	5M	M	Ind	Ind	Ind		
Welsh Studies with Welsh Language	Q521	3FT deg	* g	12	5M	M	Ind	Ind	Ind		
Combined Studies (Honours) *Welsh*	Y400	3FT deg	* g	8-16	Ind	Ind	Ind	Ind	Ind		
Combined Studies (Honours) *Welsh Studies*	Y400	3FT deg	* g	8-16	Ind	Ind	Ind	Ind	Ind		
Joint Honours *Welsh Studies*	Y401	3FT deg	* g	8-16	Ind	Ind	Ind	Ind	Ind		
Major/Minor Honours *Welsh*	Y402	3FT deg	* g	8-16	Ind	Ind	Ind	Ind	Ind		
Major/Minor Honours *Welsh Studies*	Y402	3FT deg	* g	8-16	Ind	Ind	Ind	Ind	Ind		
Univ of GLASGOW											
Anthropology with Celtic	LQ65	4FT deg		BBC	N	M	30	BBBB	Ind		
Archaeology/Celtic	QV56	4FT deg		BBC	HN	M	30	BBBB	Ind		
Business Economics with Celtic	L1QM	4FT deg		BBC	N	M	30	BBBB	N		

course details

TITLE	CODE	COURSE	SUBJECTS	A/AS	ND/C	AGNVQ	IB	SQA(H)	SQA	RATIO A/AS
Celtic Civilisation/Archaeology	QV5P	4FT deg		BBC	HN	M	30	BBBB	Ind	
Celtic Civilisation/Classical Hebrew	QV5V	4FT deg		BBC	HN	M	30	BBBB	Ind	
Celtic Civilisation/Computing Science	GQ5M	4FT deg		BBC	HN	M	30	BBBB	Ind	
Celtic Civilisation/Czech	QT5C	5FT deg		BBC	HN	M	30	BBBB	Ind	
Celtic Civilisation/Economic and Social History	QV5H	4FT deg		BBC	HN	M	30	BBBB	Ind	
Celtic Civilisation/English	QQ5H	4FT deg		BBC	HN	M	30	BBBB	Ind	
Celtic Civilisation/French	QR5C	5FT deg		BBC	HN	M	30	BBBB	Ind	2
Celtic Civilisation/Geography	LQ85	4FT deg		BBC	HN	M	30	BBBB	Ind	
Celtic Civilisation/German	QR52	5FT deg		BBC	HN	M	30	BBBB	Ind	
Celtic Civilisation/Greek	QQ57	4FT deg		BBC	HN	M	30	BBBB	Ind	
Celtic Civilisation/Hispanic Studies	QR54	5FT deg		BBC	HN	M	30	BBBB	Ind	
Celtic Civilisation/History	QV5C	4FT deg		BBC	HN	M	30	BBBB	Ind	
Celtic Civilisation/Italian	QR53	5FT deg		BBC	HN	M	30	BBBB	Ind	
Celtic Civilisation/Latin	QQ56	4FT deg		BBC	HN	M	30	BBBB	Ind	
Celtic Civilisation/Mathematics	GQ15	4FT deg		BBC	HN	M	30	BBBB	Ind	
Celtic Civilisation/Music	QW5H	4FT deg		BBC	HN	M	30	BBBB	Ind	
Celtic Civilisation/Philosophy	QV57	4FT deg		BBC	HN	M	30	BBBB	Ind	
Celtic Civilisation/Polish	QT5D	5FT deg		BBC	HN	M	30	BBBB	Ind	
Celtic Civilisation/Psychology	CQ8M	4FT deg		BBC	HN	M	30	BBBB	Ind	
Celtic Civilisation/Scottish History	QV5D	4FT deg		BBC	HN	M	30	BBBB	Ind	5
Celtic Civilisation/Scottish Literature	QQ2M	4FT deg		BBC	HN	M	30	BBBB	Ind	
Celtic Civilisation/Social and Urban Policy	LQLM	4FT deg		BBC	HN	M	30	BBBB	Ind	
Celtic Civilisation/Theology and Religious St	QV58	4FT deg		BBC	HN	M	30	BBBB	Ind	
Celtic Languages and Literatures	Q504	4FT deg		BBC	HN	M	30	BBBB	Ind	
Celtic/Classical Hebrew	QQM9	4FT deg		BBC	HN	M	30	BBBB	Ind	
Celtic/Computing	GQ55	4FT deg		BBC	HN	M	30	BBBB	Ind	1
Celtic/Czech	QT51	5FT deg		BBC	HN	M	30	BBBB	Ind	
Celtic/Economics	LQ15	4FT deg		BBC	8M	M	30	BBBB	Ind	
Celtic/English	QQ35	4FT deg		BBC	HN	M	30	BBBB	Ind	6
Celtic/Film and Television Studies	QW55	4FT deg		BBB	HN	D	32	AABB	Ind	4
Celtic/French	QRN1	5FT deg		BBC	HN	M	30	BBBB	Ind	
Celtic/Geography	LQV5	4FT deg		BBC	HN	M	30	BBBB	Ind	1
Celtic/German	QRN2	5FT deg		BBC	HN	M	30	BBBB	Ind	
Celtic/Greek	QQ5R	4FT deg		BBC	HN	M	30	BBBB	Ind	
Celtic/Hispanic Studies	QRM4	5FT deg		BBC	HN	M	30	BBBB	Ind	
Celtic/History	QV51	4FT deg		BBC	HN	M	30	BBBB	Ind	4
Celtic/History of Art	QVN4	4FT deg		BBC	HN	M	30	BBBB	Ind	
Celtic/Latin	QQM6	4FT deg		BBC	HN	M	30	BBBB	Ind	
Celtic/Mathematics	GQD5	4FT deg		BBC	HN	M	30	BBBB	Ind	
Celtic/Music	QW53	4FT deg		BBC	HN	M	30	BBBB	Ind	
Celtic/Philosophy	QVN7	4FT deg		BBC	HN	M	30	BBBB	Ind	
Celtic/Politics	MQ15	4FT deg		BBC	HN	M	30	BBBB	Ind	
Celtic/Psychology	CQ85	4FT deg		BBC	HN	M	30	BBBB	Ind	1
Celtic/Scottish History	QVMC	4FT deg		BBC	HN	M	30	BBBB	Ind	4
Celtic/Scottish Literature	QQ25	4FT deg		BBC	HN	M	30	BBBB	Ind	
Classical Civilisation/Celtic	QQ8M	4FT deg		BBC	HN	M	30	BBBB	Ind	
Classical Hebrew/Celtic	QV5W	4FT deg		BBC	HN	M	30	BBBB	Ind	
Economic and Social History with Celtic	V3Q5	4FT deg		BBC	8M	M	30	BBBB	Ind	
Economics with Celtic	L1Q5	4FT deg		BBC	8M	M	30	BBBB	Ind	
Geography with Celtic	L8Q5	4FT deg		BBC	8M	M	30	BBBB	Ind	
Islamic Studies/Celtic	TQ65	4FT deg		BBC	N	M	30	BBBB	Ind	
Management Studies with Celtic	N1Q5	4FT deg		BBC	8M	M	30	BBBB	Ind	

			98 expected requirements						96 entry stats
course details									
TITLE	CODE	COURSE	SUBJECTS	A/AS	ND/C	AGNVQ	IB	SQA(H)	SQA	RATIO A/AS
Management Studies/Celtic	NQ15	4FT deg		BBC	HN	M	30	BBBB	Ind	
Philosophy with Celtic	V7Q5	4FT deg		BBC	8M	M	30	BBBB	Ind	
Politics with Celtic	M1Q5	4FT deg		BBC	8M	M	30	BBBB	Ind	
Psychology with Celtic	C8Q5	4FT deg		BBC	8M	M	30	BBBB	Ind	5
Social and Urban Policy with Celtic	L4Q5	4FT deg		BBC	8M	M	30	BBBB	Ind	
Social and Urban Policy/Celtic	LQ45	4FT deg		BBC	HN	M	30	BBBB	Ind	
Sociology with Celtic	L3Q5	4FT deg		BBC	8M	M	30	BBBB	Ind	
Theology & Religious Studies/Celtic	QVM8	4FT deg		BBC	HN	M	30	BBBB	Ind	

Univ of Wales, LAMPETER

TITLE	CODE	COURSE	SUBJECTS	A/AS	ND/C	AGNVQ	IB	SQA(H)	SQA	RATIO A/AS
Welsh (3 or 4 Yrs)	Q520	3FT/4FT deg	W	10	Ind	Ind	Ind	Ind	Ind	
Welsh Studies	Q512	3FT deg	*	10	Ind	Ind	Ind	Ind	Ind	
Welsh Studies and American Literature	QQ5K	3FT deg			Ind	Ind	Ind	Ind	Ind	
Welsh Studies and Ancient History	QVNC	3FT deg	*	16	Ind	Ind	Ind	Ind	Ind	
Welsh Studies and Anthropology	LQ6M	3FT deg	*.	16	Ind	Ind	Ind	Ind	Ind	
Welsh Studies and Archaeology	QVN6	3FT deg	*	16	Ind	Ind	Ind	Ind	Ind	
Welsh Studies and Australian Studies	LQP5	3FT deg			Ind	Ind	Ind	Ind	Ind	
Welsh Studies and Church History	QVMD	3FT deg	*	14	Ind	Ind	Ind	Ind	Ind	
Welsh Studies and Classical Studies	QQM8	3FT deg	*	16	Ind	Ind	Ind	Ind	Ind	
Welsh Studies and Cultural Studies in Geography	LQVM	3FT deg	*	16	Ind	Ind	Ind	Ind	Ind	
Welsh Studies and English Literature	QQH5	3FT deg	E	18	Ind	Ind	Ind	Ind	Ind	
Welsh Studies and French	QR5C	4FT deg	F	16	Ind	Ind	Ind	Ind	Ind	
Welsh Studies and Geography	QLM8	3FT deg	Gy	16	Ind	Ind	Ind	Ind	Ind	
Welsh Studies and German	QRM2	4FT deg	G	16	Ind	Ind	Ind	Ind	Ind	
Welsh Studies and German Studies	QRMF	4FT deg	*	16	Ind	Ind	Ind	Ind	Ind	
Welsh Studies and Greek	QQM7	3FT deg	* g	16	Ind	Ind	Ind	Ind	Ind	
Welsh Studies and History	QV5D	3FT deg	H	16	Ind	Ind	Ind	Ind	Ind	
Welsh Studies and Informatics	GQ5N	3FT deg	*	14	Ind	Ind	Ind	Ind	Ind	
Welsh Studies and Islamic Studies	TQ6N	3FT deg	*	14	Ind	Ind	Ind	Ind	Ind	
Welsh Studies and Latin	QQ5P	3FT deg	* g	16	Ind	Ind	Ind	Ind	Ind	
Welsh Studies and Management Techniques	NQ1M	3FT deg	*	14	Ind	Ind	Ind	Ind	Ind	
Welsh Studies and Medieval Studies	VQ1M	3FT deg	*	16	Ind	Ind	Ind	Ind	Ind	
Welsh Studies and Modern Historical Studies	Q5VC	3FT deg			Ind	Ind	Ind	Ind	Ind	
Welsh Studies and Philosophical Studies	QV5R	3FT deg	*	16	Ind	Ind	Ind	Ind	Ind	
Welsh Studies and Religious Studies	QVMV	3FT deg	*	14	Ind	Ind	Ind	Ind	Ind	
Welsh Studies and Theology	QVM8	3FT deg	*	14	Ind	Ind	Ind	Ind	Ind	
Welsh Studies and Victorian Studies	QVND	3FT deg	*	14	Ind	Ind	Ind	Ind	Ind	
Welsh and American Literature	QQ45	3FT deg			Ind	Ind	Ind	Ind	Ind	
Welsh and Ancient History	QVMC	3FT/4FT deg	W	16	Ind	Ind	Ind	Ind	Ind	
Welsh and Anthropology	LQ65	3FT/4FT deg	W	16	Ind	Ind	Ind	Ind	Ind	
Welsh and Archaeology	QVM6	3FT/4FT deg	W	18	Ind	Ind	Ind	Ind	Ind	
Welsh and Australian Studies	LQ6N	3FT deg			Ind	Ind	Ind	Ind	Ind	
Welsh and Church History	QVN1	3FT/4FT deg	W	14	Ind	Ind	Ind	Ind	Ind	
Welsh and Classical Studies	QQ58	3FT/4FT deg	W	16	Ind	Ind	Ind	Ind	Ind	
Welsh and Cultural Studies in Geography	LQV5	3FT/4FT deg	W	16	Ind	Ind	Ind	Ind	Ind	
Welsh and English Literature	QQ3M	3FT/4FT deg	E+W	18	Ind	Ind	Ind	Ind	Ind	
Welsh and French	QR51	4FT deg	W+F	16	Ind	Ind	Ind	Ind	Ind	
Welsh and Geography	QL58	3FT/4FT deg	W+Gy	16	Ind	Ind	Ind	Ind	Ind	
Welsh and German	QR52	4FT deg	W+G	16	Ind	Ind	Ind	Ind	Ind	
Welsh and German Studies	QR5G	4FT deg	W	16	Ind	Ind	Ind	Ind	Ind	
Welsh and Greek	QQ57	3FT/4FT deg	W g	16	Ind	Ind	Ind	Ind	Ind	
Welsh and History	QV51	3FT/4FT deg	W+H	16	Ind	Ind	Ind	Ind	Ind	
Welsh and Informatics	GQ55	3FT/4FT deg	W	14	Ind	Ind	Ind	Ind	Ind	
Welsh and Islamic Studies	TQ65	3FT/4FT deg	W	14	Ind	Ind	Ind	Ind	Ind	

				98 expected requirements						96 entry stats
course details										
TITLE	CODE	COURSE	SUBJECTS	A/AS	ND/C	AGNVQ	IB	SQA(H)	SQA	RATIO A/AS
Welsh and Latin	QQ56	3FT/4FT deg	W g	16	Ind	Ind	Ind	Ind	Ind	
Welsh and Management Techniques	NQ15	3FT deg	W	14	Ind	Ind	Ind	Ind	Ind	
Welsh and Medieval Studies	VQ15	3FT deg	W	16	Ind	Ind	Ind	Ind	Ind	
Welsh and Modern Historical Studies	Q5V1	3FT deg	W		Ind	Ind	Ind	Ind	Ind	
Welsh and Philosophical Studies	QV57	3FT/4FT deg	W	16	Ind	Ind	Ind	Ind	Ind	
Welsh and Religious Studies	QVN8	3FT/4FT deg	W	14	Ind	Ind	Ind	Ind	Ind	
Welsh and Theology	QV58	3FT/4FT deg	W	14	Ind	Ind	Ind	Ind	Ind	
Welsh and Victorian Studies	QV5C	3FT/4FT deg	W	14	Ind	Ind	Ind	Ind	Ind	
Women's Studies and Welsh	MQ95	3FT deg	W	16	Ind	Ind	Ind	Ind	Ind	
Women's Studies and Welsh Studies	MQ9M	3FT deg	*	16	Ind	Ind	Ind	Ind	Ind	
Combined Honours Welsh	Y400	3FT deg	W	14-16	Ind	Ind	Ind	Ind	Ind	
Combined Honours Welsh Studies	Y400	3FT deg	W	14-16	Ind	Ind	Ind	Ind	Ind	
Univ of LIVERPOOL										
Irish Studies	Q530	3FT deg	*	BCC	Ind		29	BBBBB	Ind	6
Arts Combined Irish Studies	Y401	3FT deg	*	BBC-BBB	Ind	Ind	30$	ABBB	Ind	
BA Combined Honours Irish Studies	Y200	3FT deg	* g	BBB	Ind	Ind	Ind	Ind	Ind	
NORTH EAST WALES INST of HE										
English and Welsh Studies	QQ35	3FT deg		6-12	4M	M$	Ind	BBB	N$	
History and Welsh Studies	VQ15	3FT deg		6-12	4M	M$	Ind	BBB	N$	
History with Welsh	V1Q5	3FT deg		6-12	4M	M$	Ind	BBB	N$	
Media Studies/Welsh Studies	PQ45	3FT deg		6-12	4M	M$	Ind	BBB	N$	
Sociology/Welsh Studies	LQ35	3FT deg		6-12	4M	M$	Ind	BBB	N$	
Univ of NORTH LONDON										
Irish Studies and Politics	QM51	3FT deg	*	CC	MO	M	Ind	Ind	Ind	9
Social Research and Irish Studies	LQ35	3FT deg	* g	CC	MO	M	Ind	Ind	Ind	
Sociology and Irish Studies	LQ3M	3FT deg	*	CC	Ind	Ind	Ind	Ind	Ind	
Combined Honours Irish Studies	Y300	3FT deg	*	CC	Ind	Ind	Ind	Ind	Ind	
QUEEN'S Univ Belfast										
Celtic	Q504	3FT/4FT deg	* g	BCC	3M+4D	D*6/^ go	29$	ABBB	Ind	20
Celtic/Ancient History	VQC5	3FT/4FT deg	* g	BCC	3M+4D	D*6/^ go	29$	ABBB	Ind	9
Celtic/Archaeology	VQ65	3FT/4FT deg	* g	BCC	3M+4D	D*6/^ go	29$	ABBB	Ind	20
Celtic/Biblical Studies	VQ85	3FT/4FT deg	* g	BCC	3M+4D	D*6/^ go	29$	ABBB		
Celtic/Byzantine Studies	QQ85	3FT/4FT deg	* g	BCC	3M+4D	D*6/^ go	29$	ABBB		
Classical Studies/Celtic	QQ58	3FT/4FT deg	* g	BCC	3M+4D	D*6/^ go	29$	ABBB		
English/Celtic	QQ53	3FT/4FT deg	E g	BCC	X	D*_^ go	29$	ABBB	X	5
French/Celtic (4 years)	QR51	4FT deg	F g	BCC	X	D*_^ go	29$	ABBB	X	2
German/Celtic (4 years)	QR52	4FT deg	* g	BCC	3M+4D	D*6/^ go	29$	ABBB	Ind	1
Greek/Celtic	QQ57	3FT/4FT deg	* g	BCC	3M+4D	D*6/^ go	29$	ABBB	Ind	
Irish Studies	Q530	3FT deg	* g	BCC	3M+4D	D*6/^ go	29$	ABBB	Ind	22
Italian/Celtic (4 years)	QR53	4FT deg	* g	BCC	3M+4D	D*6/^ go	29$	ABBB	Ind	
Latin/Celtic	QQ56	3FT/4FT deg	* g	BCC	3M+4D	D*6/^ go	29$	ABBB	Ind	
Music/Celtic	QW53	3FT/4FT deg	* g	BCC	3M+4D	D*6/^ go	29$	ABBB	Ind	
Philosophy/Celtic	QV57	3FT/4FT deg	* g	BCC	3M+4D	D*6/^ go	29$	ABBB	Ind	
Politics/Celtic	QM51	3FT/4FT deg	* g	BCC	3M+4D	D*6/^ go	29$	ABBB	Ind	6
Scholastic Philosophy/Celtic	QV5R	3FT/4FT deg	* g	BCC	3M+4D	D*6/^ go	29$	ABBB	Ind	
Social Anthropology/Celtic	QL56	3FT/4FT deg	* g	BCC	3M+4D	D*6/^ go	29$	ABBB	Ind	7
Spanish/Celtic (4 years)	QR54	4FT deg	* g	BCC	3M+4D	D*6/^ go	29$	ABBB	Ind	

TITLE	CODE	COURSE	SUBJECTS	A/AS	NQ/C	AGNVQ	IB	SQA(H)	SQA	RATIO A/AS
ST MARY'S Univ COLL										
Irish Studies and Biology	CQ15	3FT deg	B/C	4-8	Ind	Ind	Ind	BBBB$	Ind	
Irish Studies and Classical Studies	QQ58	3FT deg	*	4-8	Ind	Ind	Ind	BBBB	Ind	
Irish Studies and Drama	QW54	3FT deg	*	8-12	Ind	Ind	Ind	BBBB	Ind	
Irish Studies and Education Studies	QX5X	3FT deg	*	4-8	Ind	Ind	Ind	BBBB	Ind	
Irish Studies and Geography	FQ85	3FT deg	Gy	4-8	Ind	Ind	Ind	BBBB$	Ind	
Irish Studies and Heritage Management	NQ95	3FT deg	*	4-8	Ind	Ind	Ind	BBBB	Ind	
Irish Studies and History	QV51	3FT deg	H	4-8	Ind	Ind	Ind	BBBB$	Ind	
Management Studies and Irish Studies	NQ15	3FT deg	* g	4-8	Ind	Ind	Ind	BBBB	Ind	
Media Arts and Irish Studies	PQ45	3FT deg	*	4-8	Ind	Ind	Ind	BBBB	Ind	
Sociology and Irish Studies	LQ35	3FT deg	*	4-8	Ind	Ind	Ind	BBBB	Ind	
Sport Rehabilitation and Irish Studies	BQ95	3FT deg	B g	12-14	X	X	Ind	BBBB$	X	
Sport Science and Irish Studies	QB56	3FT deg	S g	8-12	Ind	Ind	Ind	BBBB$	Ind	
Theology and Religious Studies and Irish Studies	QV58	3FT deg	*	4-8	Ind	Ind	Ind	BBBB	Ind	
Univ of Wales SWANSEA										
Computer Science (with Welsh)	G5Q5	4FT deg	*	BCC	4D	Ind	28	BBBBC	Ind	
European History (with Welsh)	V1Q5	4FT deg	H+L	BBB-BBC	Ind	Ind	30$	ABBBB$	Ind	
French/Welsh (with Business Studies)	RQ15	4FT deg	F+W g	BCC	1M+5D$	X	28$	BBBBC$	X	
French/Welsh (with Computer Studies)	RQ1N	4FT deg	F+W	BCC	1M+5D$	X	28$	BBBBC$	X	
French/Welsh (with Legal Studies)	RQC5	4FT deg	F+W	BCC	1M+5D$	X	28$	BBBBC$	X	
German/Welsh (with Business Studies)	RQ25	4FT deg	G+W g	BCC	1M+5D$	X	28$	BBBBC$	X	
German/Welsh (with Computer Studies)	RQ2N	4FT deg	G+W	BCC	1M+5D$	X	28$	BBBBC$	X	
German/Welsh (with Legal Studies)	RQ2M	4FT deg	G+W	BCC	1M+5D$	X	28$	BBBBC$	X	
Italian/Welsh (with Business Studies)	RQ35	4FT deg	I/W g	BCC	1M+5D$	X	28$	BBBBC$	X	
Italian/Welsh (with Computer Studies)	RQ3N	4FT deg	I/W	BCC	1M+5D$	X	28$	BBBBC$	X	
Italian/Welsh (with Legal Studies)	QR53	4FT deg	I/W	BCC	1M+5D$	X	28$	BBBBC$	X	
Law and Welsh	MQ35	3FT deg	W	BBB-BBC	1M+5D$	X	30$	Ind	Ind	4
Mathematics (with Welsh)	G1Q5	4FT deg	M+L/(M g)	BCC	X	Ind	26$	BBBBC$	Ind	
Russian/Welsh (with Business Studies)	RQ85	4FT deg	R/W g	BCC	1M+5D$	X	28$	BBBBB$	X	
Russian/Welsh (with Computer Studies)	RQ8N	4FT deg	R/W	BCC	1M+5D$	X	28$	BBBBB$	X	
Russian/Welsh (with Legal Studies)	QR58	4FT deg	R/W	BCC	1M+5D$	X	28$	BBBBB$	X	
Spanish/Welsh (with Business Studies)	RQ45	4FT deg	Sp/W g	BCC	1M+5D$	X	28$	BBBBB$	X	
Spanish/Welsh (with Computer Studies)	RQ4N	4FT deg	Sp/W	BCC	1M+5D$	X	28$	BBBBB$	X	
Spanish/Welsh (with Legal Studies)	RQK5	4FT deg	Sp/W	BCC	1M+5D$	X	28$	BBBBB$	X	
Welsh	Q520	3FT/4FT deg	W	CCC-CCD	1M+4D	X	Ind	Ind	Ind	5 10/24
Welsh (with Business Studies)	Q5N1	3FT/4FT deg	W	CCC-CCD	1M+4D$	X	Ind	Ind	Ind	3
Welsh (with Computer Studies)	Q5G5	3FT/4FT deg	W	CCC-CCD	1M+4D$	X	Ind	Ind	Ind	
Welsh (with Legal Studies)	Q5M3	3FT/4FT deg	W	CCC	1M+4D$	X	Ind	Ind	Ind	
Welsh and Psychology	LQ75	4FT deg	L/*	BBC	1M+5D$	Ind	30$	ABBBB$	Ind	
Welsh/American Studies	QQ45	4FT deg								
Welsh/American Studies	QQ54	3FT deg	W	BCC	1M+5D$	X	28$	BBBBB$	X	
Welsh/Ancient History and Civilisation	VQC5	3FT/4FT deg	W	BCC	Ind	X	28$	BBBBB$	X	
Welsh/Anthropology	LQ65	3FT/4FT deg	W	BCC	1M+5D$	X	28$	BBBBB$	Ind	
Welsh/English	QQH5	3FT/4FT deg	E+W	BBC	X	X	30$	ABBBB$	X	
Welsh/English Language	QQ35	3FT deg	E g	BBC	X	X	30$	ABBBB$	Ind	
Welsh/European Politics	MQ15	3FT/4FT deg	W	BBC-BCC	1M+5D$	X	28$	BBBBB$	X	
Welsh/French	QR51	4FT deg	F+W	BCC	1M+5D$	X	28$	BBBBB$	X	1
Welsh/Geography	LQ85	3FT/4FT deg	Gy+W	BBC-BCC	1M+5D$	X	30$	ABBBB$	Ind	4
Welsh/German	QR52	4FT deg	W g	BCC	1M+5D$	X	28$	BBBBB$	X	2
Welsh/Greek	QQ57	3FT/4FT deg	Gk+W	BCC	X	X	28$	BBBBB$	X	
Welsh/Greek and Roman Studies	QQ85	3FT/4FT deg	W	BCC	X	X	28$	BBBBB$	X	
Welsh/History	QV51	3FT/4FT deg	W	BBC	Ind	X	30$	ABBBB$	Ind	3

			98 expected requirements							96 entry stats
TITLE	CODE	COURSE	SUBJECTS	A/AS	ND/C	AGNVQ	IB	SQA(H)	SQA	RATIO A/AS
Welsh/Italian	QRM3	4FT deg	W/I	BCC	1M+5D$	X	28$	BBBBB$	X	
Welsh/Latin	QQ56	3FT/4FT deg	W+Ln	BCC	X	X	28$	BBBBB$	X	
Welsh/Medieval Studies	QVM1	3FT/4FT deg	H+W	BCC	X	X	Ind	Ind	X	
Welsh/Philosophy	QV57	3FT/4FT deg	W	BBC-BCC	Ind	X	28$	BBBBB$	X	
Welsh/Politics	MQC5	3FT/4FT deg	W	BBC-BCC	1M+5D$	X	28$	BBBBB$	X	
Welsh/Sociology	LQ35	3FT/4FT deg	W	BCC	1M+5D$	X	28	BBBBB$	Ind	6
Welsh/Spanish	QR54	4FT deg	Sp/W	BCC	1M+5D$	X	28$	BBBBB$	X	

TRINITY COLL Carmarthen

Cymraeg/Astudiaethau Crefydd	QV5W	3FT deg	W+Re g	DD-CC	Ind		Ind	Ind	Ind	3
Cymraeg/Astudiaethau Theatr	WQ45	3FT deg	W+T g	DD-CC	Ind		Ind	Ind	Ind	
Hanes/Cymraeg	QV5C	3FT deg	W+H g	DD-CC	Ind		Ind	Ind	Ind	4
Saesneg/Cymraeg	QQ3N	3FT deg	W+E g	DD-CC	Ind		Ind	Ind	Ind	
Welsh Studies	Q521	3FT deg	* g	DD-CC	Ind		Ind	Ind	Ind	
Welsh Studies/Archaeology	QV56	3FT deg	g	DD-CC	Ind		Ind	Ind	Ind	
Welsh Studies/English	QQ35	3FT deg	E g	DD-CC	Ind		Ind	Ind	Ind	2
Welsh Studies/History	QV51	3FT deg	H g	DD-CC	Ind		Ind	Ind	Ind	
Welsh Studies/Religious Studies	QV58	3FT deg	Re g	DD-CC	Ind		Ind	Ind	Ind	
Welsh Studies/Theatre Studies	QW54	3FT deg	g	DD-CC	Ind		Ind	Ind	Ind	
Dyniaethau *Cymraeg*	Y321	3FT deg	W g	DD-CC	Ind		Ind	Ind	Ind	
Humanities *Welsh Studies*	Y320	3FT deg	* g	DD-CC	Ind		Ind	Ind	Ind	

Univ of ULSTER

Irish Studies (DipHE or BA)	Q531▼	2FT/3FT Dip/deg	Ir	CCC	Ind	P gi	Ind	Ind	Ind	7
Irish Studies (Hons)	Q530▼	3FT deg	Ir	CCC	MO+3D	D^ gi	28	BBBC	Ind	12 14/24
Humanities Combined *Irish*	Y320▼	3FT/4SW deg	Ir	CCC	MO+3D	D*6/^ gi	28	BBBC	Ind	

TITLE	CODE	COURSE	SUBJECTS	A/AS	NO/C	AGNVQ	IB	SQA(H)	SQA	RATIO A/AS
course details			**98 expected requirements**							**96 entry stats**

Univ of BIRMINGHAM

TITLE	CODE	COURSE	SUBJECTS	A/AS	NO/C	AGNVQ	IB	SQA(H)	SQA	RATIO A/AS
Ancient History & Archaeology/Latin	QV66	3FT deg	Ln	BBB	Ind	D*^	32$	ABBB	Ind	
Artificial Intelligence/Latin	GQ86	3FT deg	Ln g	BBB	Ind	D*^	32$	ABBB	Ind	
Classical Lit and Civilisation/History of Art	QV84	3FT deg	*	BBB	Ind	D*^	32	ABBB	Ind	
Classical Literature & Civilisation/Hispanic St	QR84	4FT deg	*	BBB	Ind	D*^	32	ABBB	Ind	
Classical Literature & Civilisation/Mod Greek St	QT82	4FT deg	* g	BBB	Ind	D*^	32	ABBB	Ind	
Classical Literature and Civilisation	Q820	3FT deg	* g	BBC-BCC	Ind	D*^	30	ABBB	Ind	
Classical Literature and Civilisation/History	QV81	3FT deg	*	BBB	Ind	D*^	32	ABBB	Ind	
Classical Literature and Civilisation/Italian	QR83	4FT deg	*	BBB	Ind	D*^	32	ABBB	Ind	
Classical Literature and Civilisation/Music	QW83	3FT deg	Mu	AAB-ABB	Ind	D*^	32$	ABBB	Ind	
Classical Literature and Civilisation/Philosophy	QV87	3FT deg	*	BBB	Ind	D*^	32	ABBB	Ind	
Classical Literature and Civilisation/Portuguese	QR8M	4FT deg	*	BBB	Ind	D*^	32	ABBB	Ind	
Classical Literature and Civilisation/Russian	QR88	4FT deg	*	BBB	Ind	D*^	32	ABBB	Ind	
Classical Literature and Civilisation/Theology	QV88	3FT deg	*	BBB	Ind	D*^	32	ABBB	Ind	
Classics	Q800	3FT deg	Ln g	BBC	Ind	D*^	32$	ABBB	Ind	11	22/30
Classics and Classical Archaeology	QV86	3FT deg	*	BBC-BCC	Ind	D*^	32	ABBB	Ind	6	24/28
Computer Studies/Latin	GQ56	3FT deg	Ln g	BBB	Ind	D*^	32$	ABBB	Ind	
Dance/Latin	WQ46	3FT deg	Ln	BBB	Ind	D*^	32$	ABBB	Ind	
Drama/Classical Literature and Civilisation	QW84	3FT deg	*	BBB	Ind	D*^	32	ABBB	Ind	
Drama/Latin	QW64	3FT deg	Ln	BBB	Ind	D*^	32$	ABBB	Ind	
East Mediterranean History/Classical Lit & Civil	QV8C	3FT deg	* g	BBB	Ind	D*^	32	ABBB	Ind	
East Mediterranean History/Latin	QV6C	3FT deg	Ln g	BBB	Ind	D*^	32$	ABBB	Ind	
English/Classical Literature and Civilisation	QQ38	3FT deg	*	BBB	Ind	D*^	32	ABBB	Ind	
English/Latin	QQ36	3FT deg	Ln	BBB	Ind	D*^	32$	ABBB	Ind	
French Studies/Classical Lit and Civilisation	QR81	4FT deg	F	BBB	Ind	D*^	32$	ABBB	Ind	
French Studies/Latin	QR61	4FT deg	F+Ln	BBB	Ind	D*^	32$	ABBB	Ind	
German Studies/Classical Lit and Civilisation	QR82	4FT deg	G	BBB	Ind	D*^	32$	ABBB	Ind	
German Studies/Latin	QR62	4FT deg	G+Ln	BBB	Ind	D*^	32$	ABBB	Ind	
Hispanic Studies/Latin	QR64	4FT deg	Ln	BBB	Ind	D*^	32$	ABBB	Ind	
History of Art/Latin	QV64	3FT deg	Ln	BBB	Ind	D*^	32$	ABBB	Ind	
History/Latin	QV61	3FT deg	Ln	BBB	Ind	D*^	32$	ABBB	Ind	
International Studies with Greek	M1Q7	3FT deg	*	BBC	Ind	D+^	32	ABBBB	Ind	
Italian/Latin	QR63	4FT deg	Ln	BBB	Ind	D*^	32$	ABBB	Ind	4
Latin	Q600	3FT deg	Ln	BBC	Ind	D*^	32$	ABBB	Ind	
Latin/Mathematics	GQ16	3FT deg	Ln+M	ABB-ABC	Ind	D*^	32$	ABBB	Ind	
Latin/Modern Greek Studies	QT62	4FT deg	Ln g	BBB	Ind	D*^	32$	ABBB	Ind	
Latin/Music	QW63	3FT deg	Ln+Mu	AAB-ABB	Ind	D*^	32$	ABBB	Ind	
Latin/Philosophy	QV67	3FT deg	Ln	BBB	Ind	D*^	32$	ABBB	Ind	
Latin/Portuguese	QR65	4FT deg	Ln	BBB	Ind	D*^	32$	ABBB	Ind	
Latin/Russian	QR68	4FT deg	Ln	BBB	Ind	D*^	32$	ABBB	Ind	
Latin/Sport & Recreation Studies	QB66	3FT deg	Ln	BBB	Ind	D*^	32$	ABBB	Ind	
Latin/Theology	QV68	3FT deg	Ln	BBB	Ind	D*^	32$	ABBB	Ind	

Univ of BRISTOL

TITLE	CODE	COURSE	SUBJECTS	A/AS	NO/C	AGNVQ	IB	SQA(H)	SQA	RATIO A/AS
Classical Studies	Q810	3FT deg	H/Cl g	BBC-BCC	Ind	D$^ | 28$	BBBBB	Ind	12	20/30
Classical Studies with Study in Cont Europe	Q811	4FT deg	H/Cl g	BBC-BCC	Ind	D$^	28$	BBBBB	Ind	10
Classics	Q800	3FT deg	Cl	BBC-BCC	Ind	D$^ | 28$	BBBBB	Ind	10	22/30
Classics with Study in Continental Europe	Q801	4FT deg	Cl g	BBC-BCC	Ind	D$^	28$	BBBBB	Ind	6
English and Latin	QQ36	3FT deg	El+Ln	BBC	Ind	D$^	32$	AABBB	Ind	4
French and Latin	RQ16	4FT deg	F+Ln	BBC	Ind	D$^ | 30$	BBBBB	Ind	4	30/30
Greek and Philosophy	QV77	3FT deg	L	BBC	Ind	D$^	30$	BBBBB	Ind	

Languages – Classical and Ancient   38

TITLE	CODE	COURSE	SUBJECTS	A/AS	ND/C	RGNVQ	IB	SQA(H)	SQA	RATIO	A/AS
CAMBRIDGE Univ											
Anglo-Saxon, Norse and Celtic	QQ59▼	3FT deg	* g	AAB	Ind		Ind	CSYS	Ind	2	27/30
Classics: Greek and Latin	Q800▼	3FT deg	Ln/Gk g	AAB	Ind		Ind	CSYS	Ind	2	28/30
Oriental Studies	Q970▼	3FT/4FT deg	* g	AAB	Ind		Ind	CSYS	Ind	3	26/30
Univ of DURHAM											
Classical Studies	Q812	3FT deg	* g	BCC	Ind	Ind	Ind	AAABB	Ind	13	20/30
Classical Studies and English Literature	QQ38	3FT deg	E g	AAB	Ind	Ind	Ind	AAABB	Ind	21	
Classical Studies and Philosophy	QV87	3FT deg	*	BCC	Ind	Ind	Ind	AAABB	Ind	8	
Classics I	Q800	3FT deg	Gk+Ln	BCC	Ind	Ind	Ind	AAABB	Ind	12	24/30
Classics II	Q802	3FT deg	Ln	BCC	Ind	Ind	Ind	AAABB	Ind	6	22/30
Classics and Theology	QV88	3FT deg			Ind	Ind	Ind	Ind	Ind		
English Literature and Latin	QQ36	3FT deg	E+Ln	AAB	Ind	Ind	32	AAABB	Ind		
Latin	Q600	3FT deg	Ln	BCC	Ind	Ind	Ind	AAABB	Ind	6	
Latin and Music	QW63	3FT deg	Ln+Mu	24	X	Ind	30$	AAABB	X		
Arts Combined *Greek and Roman Civilisation*	Y300	3FT deg	*	24	MO	Ind	30	AAABB	Ind		
Arts Combined *Latin*	Y300	3FT deg	*	24	MO	Ind	30	AAABB	Ind		
Univ of EDINBURGH											
Ancient History and Greek	VQ17	4FT deg	g	BBB	Ind	Ind	Dip$	BBBB	Ind		
Ancient History and Latin	VQ16	4FT deg	g	BBB	Ind	Ind	Dip$	BBBB	Ind		
BA (Divinity)	QV88	3FT deg	L	BCC	Ind		Ind	BCCC	Ind	20	
Classical Archaeology and Greek or Latin	QV86	4FT deg	g	BBB	Ind	Ind	Dip$	BBBB	Ind		
Classical Studies	Q810	4FT deg	g	BBB	Ind	Ind	Dip$	BBBB	Ind	14	
Classics	Q800	4FT deg	Ln/Gk g	BBB	Ind	Ind	Dip$	BBBB$	Ind	11	24/30
Classics and Medieval History	QV81	4FT deg	g	BBB	Ind	Ind	Dip$	BBBB	Ind	7	
English Literature and Classics	QQ38	4FT deg	E g	BBB	Ind	Ind	Dip$	BBBB$	Ind		
French and Latin	RQ16	4FT deg	F g	BBB	Ind	Ind	Dip$	BBBB$	Ind		
German and Latin	RQ26	4FT deg	L g	BBB	Ind	Ind	Dip$	BBBB$	Ind		
Greek	Q700	4FT deg	g	BBB	Ind	Ind	Dip$	BBBB	Ind		
Greek and Arabic	QT76	4FT deg	g	BBB	Ind	Ind	Dip$	BBBB	Ind		
Greek and Linguistics	QQ71	4FT deg	g	BBB	Ind	Ind	Dip$	BBBB	Ind		
Italian and Greek	RQ37	4FT deg	L g	BBB	Ind	Ind	Dip$	BBBB$	Ind		
Italian and Latin	RQ36	4FT deg	L g	BBB	Ind	Ind	Dip$	BBBB$	Ind		
Latin Studies	Q600	4FT deg	g	BBB	Ind	Ind	Dip$	BBBB	Ind	7	
Latin and Scottish Historical Studies	QV61	4FT deg	g	BBB	Ind	Ind	Dip$	BBBB	Ind		
MA (Divinity)	QV8V	4FT deg	L	BCC	Ind		Ind	BCCC$	Ind	13	
Philosophy and Greek	QV77	4FT deg	g	BBB	Ind	Ind	Dip$	BBBB	Ind		
Sanskrit	Q950	4FT deg	g	BBB	Ind	Ind	Dip$	BBBB	Ind		
Sanskrit and Greek	QQ97	4FT deg	g	BBB	Ind	Ind	Dip$	BBBB	Ind		
Sanskrit and Latin	QQ96	4FT deg	g	BBB	Ind	Ind	Dip$	BBBB	Ind		
Sanskrit and Linguistics	QQ91	4FT deg	g	BBB	Ind	Ind	Dip$	BBBB	Ind		
Spanish and Latin	RQ46	4FT deg	L g	BBB	Ind	Ind	Dip$	BBBB$	Ind		
Univ of EXETER											
Classics	Q800	3FT deg	Ln	BCC	MO	M/D$	32	Ind	Ind	27	
English and Greek & Roman Studies	QQ38	3FT deg	E	BBB-BCC	MO	M/D$^	32$	Ind	Ind	7	20/26
French and Greek & Roman Studies	QR81	4FT deg	F	22-24	MO	M/D$^	34$	Ind	Ind	4	
French and Latin	QR61	4FT deg	F+Ln	22-24	MO	M/D$^	34$	Ind	Ind		
Greek & Roman Studies and Italian	QR83	4FT deg	L g	BCC	MO	M/D$	32	Ind	Ind	7	
Greek and Roman Studies	QQ78	3FT deg	*	BCC	MO	M$	32	Ind	Ind	6	16/26
Latin	Q600	3FT deg	Ln	BCC	MO	M$^	32	Ind	Ind	14	

course details

98 expected requirements

96 entry stats

TITLE	CODE	COURSE	SUBJECTS	A/AS	ND/C	AGNVQ	IB	SQA(H)	SQA	RATIO A/AS
Univ of GLASGOW										
Archaeology/Greek	QV76	4FT deg		BBC	HN	M	30	BBBB	Ind	
Archaeology/Latin	QV66	4FT deg		BBC	HN	M	30	BBBB	Ind	
Celtic Civilisation/Greek	QQ57	4FT deg		BBC	HN	M	30	BBBB	Ind	
Celtic Civilisation/Latin	QQ56	4FT deg		BBC	HN	M	30	BBBB	Ind	
Celtic/Classical Hebrew	QQM9	4FT deg		BBC	HN	M	30	BBBB	Ind	
Celtic/Greek	QQ5R	4FT deg		BBC	HN	M	30	BBBB	Ind	
Celtic/Latin	QQM6	4FT deg		BBC	HN	M	30	BBBB	Ind	
Classical Civilisation	Q820	4FT deg		BBC	HN	M	30	BBBB	Ind	
Classical Civilisation/Archaeology	QV86	4FT deg		BBC	HN	M	30	BBBB	Ind	24
Classical Civilisation/Celtic	QQ8M	4FT deg		BBC	HN	M	30	BBBB	Ind	.
Classical Civilisation/Classical Hebrew	QV88	4FT deg		BBC	HN	M	30	BBBB	Ind	
Classical Civilisation/Computing Science	GQ58	4FT deg		BBC	HN	M	30	BBBB	Ind	
Classical Civilisation/Czech	QT81	5FT deg		BBC	HN	M	30	BBBB	Ind	
Classical Civilisation/English	QQ38	4FT deg		BBC	HN	M	30	BBBB	Ind	5
Classical Civilisation/French	QR81	5FT deg		BBC	HN	M	30	BBBB	Ind	
Classical Civilisation/Geography	LQ88	4FT deg		BBC	HN	M	30	BBBB	Ind	
Classical Civilisation/German	QR82	5FT deg		BBC	HN	M	30	BBBB	Ind	
Classical Civilisation/Hebrew	QQ89	4FT deg		BBC	HN	M	30	BBBB	Ind	
Classical Civilisation/History	QV81	4FT deg		BBC	HN	M	30	BBBB	Ind	4
Classical Civilisation/Italian	QR83	5FT deg		BBC	HN	M	30	BBBB	Ind	2
Classical Civilisation/Mathematics	GQ18	4FT deg		BBC	HN	M	30	BBBB	Ind	
Classical Civilisation/Music	QW83	4FT deg		BBC	HN	M	30	BBBB	Ind	
Classical Civilisation/Philosophy	QV87	4FT deg		BBC	HN	M	30	BBBB	Ind	8
Classical Civilisation/Polish	QT8C	5FT deg		BBC	HN	M	30	BBBB	Ind	
Classical Civilisation/Politics	MQ18	4FT deg		BBC	HN	M	30	BBBB	Ind	
Classical Civilisation/Psychology	CQ88	4FT deg		BBC	HN	M	30	BBBB	Ind	3
Classical Civilisation/Russian	QR88	5FT deg		BBC	HN	M	30	BBBB	Ind	
Classical Civilisation/Scottish History	QV8C	4FT deg		BBC	HN	M	30	BBBB	Ind	2
Classical Civilisation/Scottish Literature	QQ28	4FT deg		BBC	HN	M	30	BBBB	Ind	
Classical Civilisation/Sociology	LQ38	4FT deg		BBC	HN	M	30	BBBB	Ind	
Classical Civilisation/Theology & Religious St	QV8V	4FT deg		BBC	HN	M	30	BBBB	Ind	
Classical Hebrew/Greek	QV7W	4FT deg		BBC	HN	M	30	BBBB	Ind	
Computing/Classical Hebrew	GQ59	4FT deg		BBC	HN	M	30	BBBB	Ind	
Computing/Greek	GQ57	4FT deg		BBC	HN	M	30	BBBB	Ind	
Computing/Latin	GQ56	4FT deg		BBC	HN	M	30	BBBB	Ind	
Czech/Classical Hebrew	QT91	5FT deg		BBC	HN	M	30	BBBB	Ind	
Czech/Greek	QTR1	5FT deg		BBC	HN	M	30	BBBB	Ind	
Czech/Latin	QTP1	5FT deg		BBC	HN	M	30	BBBB	Ind	
Economic & Social History/Classical Civilisation	QV83	4FT deg		BBC	HN	M	30	BBBB	Ind	
Economic and Social History/Classical Hebrew	QV93	4FT deg		BBC	HN	M	30	BBBB	Ind	
Economic and Social History/Greek	QV73	4FT deg		BBC	HN	M	30	BBBB	Ind	
Economic and Social History/Latin	QV63	4FT deg		BBC	HN	M	30	BBBB	Ind	
English/Classical Hebrew	QQ39	4FT deg		BBC	HN	M	30	BBBB	Ind	
English/Greek	QQ37	4FT deg		BBC	HN	M	30	BBBB	Ind	
English/Latin	QQ36	4FT deg		BBC	HN	M	30	BBBB	Ind	
Film and Television Studies/Classical Hebrew	QW95	4FT deg		BBB	HN	D	32	AABB	HN	
Film and Television Studies/Greek	QW75	4FT deg		BBB	HN	D	32	AABB	HN	
Film and Television Studies/Latin	QW65	4FT deg		BBB	HN	D	32	AABB	HN	
French/Classical Hebrew	QR91	5FT deg		BBC	HN	M	30	BBBB	Ind	
French/Greek	QR71	5FT deg		BBC	HN	M	30	BBBB	Ind	
French/Latin	QR61	5FT deg		BBC	HN	M	30	BBBB	Ind	

Languages – Classical and Ancient 38

course details			98 expected requirements							96 entry stats

TITLE	CODE	COURSE	SUBJECTS	A/AS	ND/C	RGNVQ	IB	SQA(H)	SQA	RATIO A/AS
Geography/Classical Civilisation	LQ8V	4FT deg		BBC	8M	M	30	BBBB	Ind	4
Geography/Classical Hebrew	LQ89	4FT deg		BBC	HN	M	30	BBBB	Ind	
Greek	Q700	4FT deg		BBC	HN	M	30	BBBB	Ind	
Greek/Classical Hebrew	QQ79	4FT deg		BBC	HN	M	30	BBBB	Ind	
Greek/Economics	LQ17	4FT deg		BBC	HN	M	30	BBBB	Ind	
Greek/Hispanic Studies	QR74	5FT deg		BBC	HN	M	30	BBBB	Ind	
Greek/History	QV71	4FT deg		BBC	HN	M	30	BBBB	Ind	
Greek/History of Art	QV74	4FT deg		BBC	HN	M	30	BBBB	Ind	
Greek/Italian	QR73	5FT deg		BBC	HN	M	30	BBBB	Ind	
Greek/Latin	QQ67	4FT deg		BBC	HN	M	30	BBBB	Ind	
Greek/Music	QW73	4FT deg		BBC	HN	M	30	BBBB	Ind	
Greek/Philosophy	QV77	4FT deg		BBC	HN	M	30	BBBB	Ind	
Greek/Polish	QT71	5FT deg		BBC	HN	M	30	BBBB	Ind	
Greek/Politics	MQ17	4FT deg		BBC	HN	M	30	BBBB	Ind	
Greek/Russian	QR78	5FT deg		BBC	HN	M	30	BBBB	Ind	
Greek/Scottish History	QV7C	4FT deg		BBC	HN	M	30	BBBB	Ind	
Greek/Scottish Literature	QQ27	4FT deg		BBC	HN	M	30	BBBB	Ind	
Greek/Sociology	LQ37	4FT deg		BBC	HN	M	30	BBBB	Ind	
Hispanic Studies/Latin	QR64	5FT deg		BBC	HN	M	30	BBBB	Ind	
History of Art/Latin	QV64	4FT deg		BBC	HN	M	30	BBBB	Ind	
History/Latin	QV6D	4FT deg		BBC	HN	M	30	BBBB	Ind	
Islamic Studies/Classical Hebrew	TQ69	4FT deg		BBC	N	M	30	BBBB	Ind	
Islamic Studies/Greek	TQ67	4FT deg		BBC	N	M	30	BBBB	Ind	
Islamic Studies/Latin	TQ66	4FT deg		BBC	N	M	30	BBBB	Ind	
Italian/Latin	QR63	5FT deg		BBC	HN	M	30	BBBB	Ind	
Latin	Q600	4FT deg		BBC	HN	M	30	BBBB	Ind	5
Latin/Economics	LQ16	4FT deg		BBC	HN	M	30	BBBB	Ind	
Latin/Mathematics	GQ16	4FT deg		BBC	HN	M	30	BBBB	Ind	
Latin/Music	QW63	4FT deg		BBC	HN	M	30	BBBB	Ind	
Latin/Philosophy	QV67	4FT deg		BBC	HN	M	30	BBBB	Ind	
Latin/Polish	QT61	5FT deg		BBC	HN	M	30	BBBB	Ind	
Latin/Politics	MQ16	4FT deg		BBC	HN	M	30	BBBB	Ind	
Latin/Russian	RQ86	5FT deg		BBC	HN	M	30	BBBB	Ind	
Latin/Scottish History	QV6C	4FT deg		BBC	HN	M	30	BBBB	Ind	
Latin/Scottish Literature	QQ26	4FT deg		BBC	HN	M	30	BBBB	Ind	
Latin/Sociology	LQ36	4FT deg		BBC	HN	M	30	BBBB	Ind	
Management Studies/Classical Civilisation	NQ1V	4FT deg		BBC	8M	M	30	BBBB	Ind	
Management Studies/Classical Civilisation	NQ18	4FT deg		BBC	HN	M	30	BBBB	Ind	2
Management Studies/Greek	NQ17	4FT deg		BBC	HN	M	30	BBBB	Ind	
Management Studies/Latin	NQ16	4FT deg		BBC	HN	M	30	BBBB	Ind	
Philosophy/Classical Civilisation	QV8R	4FT deg		BBC	8M	M	30	BBBB	Ind	2
Politics/Classical Civilisation	MQ1V	4FT deg		BBC	8M	M	30	BBBB	Ind	
Social and Urban Policy/Classical Civilisation	LQ4V	4FT deg		BBC	8M	M	30	BBBB	Ind	
Social and Urban Policy/Classical Civilisation	LQ48	4FT deg		BBC	HN	M	30	BBBB	Ind	
Social and Urban Policy/Greek	LQ47	4FT deg		BBC	HN	M	30	BBBB	Ind	
Social and Urban Policy/Latin	LQ46	4FT deg		BBC	HN	M	30	BBBB	Ind	
Theatre Studies/Classical Hebrew	QW94	4FT deg		BBC	HN	M	30	BBBB	Ind	
Theatre Studies/Greek	QW74	4FT deg		BBC	HN	M	30	BBBB	Ind	
Theatre Studies/Latin	QW64	4FT deg		BBC	HN	M	30	BBBB	Ind	1
Theology & Religious Studies/Classical Hebrew	QV9V	4FT deg		BBC	HN	M	30	BBBB	Ind	
Theology & Religious Studies/Greek	QV7V	4FT deg		BBC	HN	M	30	BBBB	Ind	
Theology & Religious Studies/Latin	QV68	4FT deg		BBC	HN	M	30	BBBB	Ind	

TITLE	CODE	COURSE	SUBJECTS	A/AS	ND/C	AGNVQ	IB	SQA(H)	SQA	RATIO A/AS
JEWS' COLL (Univ of London)										
Jewish Studies	Y400	3FT deg	*	18	Ind		Ind	CSYS	Ind	
Biblical Studies (Hebrew texts)										
KEELE Univ										
Biological and Medicinal Chemistry and Latin	FQC6	3FT deg	Ln+C g	BCC	Ind	D$^	28$	CSYS	Ind	
Classical St and Biological and Med Chem (4 Yrs)	QF8C	4FT deg	*	BCC	Ind	Ind	28	BBBB	Ind	
Classical Studies and American Studies (4 Yrs)	QQ84	4FT deg	*	BCC	Ind	Ind	28	BBBB		
Classical Studies and Applied Social St (4 Yrs)	QL85	4FT deg	*	BBC-BCC	Ind	Ind	28	BBBB	Ind	
Classical Studies and Applied Social Studies	LQ58	3FT deg	*	BCC	Ind	Ind	28	CSYS	Ind	
Classical Studies and Astrophysics	FQ58	3FT deg	P g	BCC	Ind	D$^	28$	CSYS	Ind	
Classical Studies and Biochemistry	CQ78	3FT deg	C g	BCC	Ind	D$^	28$	CSYS	Ind	
Classical Studies and Biochemistry (4 Yrs)	QC87	4FT deg	*	BCC	Ind	Ind	28	BBBB	Ind	
Classical Studies and Biology	CQ18	3FT deg	S g	BCC	Ind	D$^	28$	CSYS	Ind	
Classical Studies and Biology (4 Yrs)	QC81	4FT deg	*	BCC	Ind	Ind	28	BBBB	Ind	
Classical Studies and Business Admin (4 Yrs)	QN89	4FT deg	*	BCC	Ind	Ind	28	BBBB	Ind	
Classical Studies and Chemistry	FQ18	3FT deg	C g	BCC	Ind	D$^	28$	CSYS	Ind	
Classical Studies and Chemistry (4 Yrs)	QF81	4FT deg	*	BCC	Ind	Ind	28	BBBB	Ind	
Classical Studs and Biological & Medicinal Chem	FQC8	3FT deg	C g	BCC	Ind	D$^	28$	CSYS	Ind	
Computer Science and Classical Studies (4 Yrs)	QG85	4FT deg	*	BCC	Ind	Ind	28	BBBB	Ind	
Criminology and Classical Studies	MQH8	3FT deg	*	BBB	Ind	Ind	32	CSYS	Ind	5
Criminology and Classical Studies (4 Yrs)	QM8H	4FT deg	*	BBB	Ind	Ind	32	ABBB	Ind	
Economics and Classical Studies	LQ18	3FT deg	* g	BCC	Ind	Ind	28	CSYS	Ind	
Economics and Classical Studies (4 Yrs)	QL81	4FT deg	*	BCC	Ind	Ind	28	BBBB	Ind	
Educational Studies and Classical Studs (4 Yrs)	XQ98	4FT deg	*	BCC	Ind	Ind	28	BBBB	Ind	
Electronic Music and Classical Studies	QW8J	3FT deg	Mu	BCC	Ind	D$^	28	CSYS	Ind	
Electronic Music and Classical Studies (4 Yrs)	WQJ8	4FT deg	*	BCC	Ind	Ind	28	BBBB	Ind	
English and Classical Studies	QQ38	3FT deg	E	BBB	Ind	D$^	30$	CSYS	Ind	7 20/24
English and Classical Studies (4 Yrs)	QQ83	4FT deg	*	BBB	Ind	Ind	30	BBBB	Ind	16
Environmental Management and Classical St(4 Yrs)	QF8X	4FT deg	*	BCC	Ind	Ind	28	BBBB	Ind	
French and Classical Studies	QR81	3FT deg	F	BCC	Ind	D$^	28$	CSYS	Ind	
French and Classical Studies (4 Yrs)	RQ18	4FT deg	*	BCC	Ind	Ind	28	BBBB	Ind	
French/German and Latin	QT69	3FT deg	F+G+Ln	BBB	Ind	D$^	30$	CSYS	Ind	
French/Russian or Russ St and Classical Studies	QT8X	3FT deg	F+R	BBB	Ind	D$^	28$	CSYS	Ind	
Geography and Classical Studies	LQ88	3FT deg	Gy	BCC	Ind	D$^	28$	CSYS	Ind	3
Geology and Classical Studies	FQ68	3FT deg	S g	BCC	Ind	D$^	28$	CSYS	Ind	
Geology and Classical Studies (4 Yrs)	QF86	4FT deg	*	BCC	Ind	Ind	28	BBBB	Ind	
Geology and Latin	FQ66	3FT deg	Ln+S g	BCC	Ind	D$^	28$	CSYS	Ind	
History and Classical Studies	QV81	3FT deg	*	BBC-BCC	Ind	Ind	28	CSYS	Ind	
History and Classical Studies (4 Yrs)	VQ18	4FT deg	*	BBC-BCC	Ind	Ind	28	BBBB	Ind	3
Human Resource Management and Classical Studies	NQ68	3FT deg	*	BCC	Ind	Ind	28	CSYS	Ind	
Human Resource Management and Classical Studies	QN86	4FT deg	*	BCC	Ind	Ind	28	BBBB	Ind	
Int Politics and Classical Studies (4 Yrs)	QM8C	4FT deg	*	BCC	Ind	Ind	28	BBBB	Ind	
International History and Classical St (4 Yrs)	VQC8	4FT deg	*	BCC	Ind	Ind	28	BBBB	Ind	
International History and Classical Studies	QV8C	3FT deg	*	BCC	Ind	Ind	28	CSYS	Ind	3
International Politics and Classical Studies	MQC8	3FT deg	*	BCC	Ind	Ind	28	CSYS	Ind	
International Politics and Latin (4 Yrs)	QM6C	4FT deg	*	BCC	Ind	Ind	28	BBBB	Ind	
Latin and American Studies (4 Yrs)	QQ64	4FT deg	*	BCC	Ind	Ind	28	BBBB	Ind	
Latin and Ancient History (4 Yrs)	VQD6	4FT deg	*	BCC	Ind	Ind	28	BBBB	Ind	
Latin and Applied Social Studies	LQ56	3FT deg	Ln	BCC	Ind	D$^	28$	CSYS	Ind	
Latin and Applied Social Studies (4 Yrs)	QL65	4FT deg	*	BCC	Ind	Ind	28	BBBB	Ind	
Latin and Astrophysics	FQ56	3FT deg	Ln+P g	BCC	Ind	D$^	28$	CSYS	Ind	
Latin and Astrophysics (4 Yrs)	QF65	4FT deg	*	BCC	Ind	Ind	28	BBBB	Ind	

course details   98 expected requirements   96 entry stats

Languages – Classical and Ancient   38

course details			98 expected requirements							96 entry stats
TITLE	CODE	COURSE	SUBJECTS	A/AS	NO/C	AGNVQ	IB	SQA(H)	SQA	RATIO A/AS
Latin and Biochemistry	CQ76	3FT deg	C+Ln g	BCC	Ind	D$^	28$	CSYS	Ind	
Latin and Biochemistry (4 Yrs)	QC67	4FT deg	*	BCC	Ind	Ind	28	BBBB	Ind	
Latin and Biological and Medicinal Chem (4 Yrs)	QF6C	4FT deg	*	BCC	Ind	Ind	28	BBBB	Ind	
Latin and Biology	CQ16	3FT deg	S+Ln g	BCC	Ind	D$^	28$	CSYS	Ind	
Latin and Chemistry	FQ16	3FT deg	Ln+C g	BCC	Ind	D$^	28$	CSYS	Ind	
Latin and Chemistry (4 Yrs)	QF61	4FT deg	*	BCC	Ind	Ind	28	BBBB	Ind	
Latin and Classical Studies (4 Yrs)	QQ86	4FT deg	*	BCC	Ind	Ind	28	BBBB	Ind	
Latin and Computer Science (4 Yrs)	QG65	4FT deg	* g	BCC	Ind	Ind	28	BBBB	Ind	
Latin and Criminology (4 Yrs)	QM6H	4FT deg	*	BBB	Ind	Ind	32	BBBB	Ind	
Latin and Economics	LQ16	3FT deg	Ln g	BCC	Ind	D$^	28$	CSYS	Ind	
Latin and Economics (4 Yrs)	QL61	4FT deg	*	BCC	Ind	Ind	28	BBBB	Ind	
Latin and Educational Studies (4 Yrs)	XQ96	4FT deg	*	BCC	Ind	Ind	28	BBBB	Ind	
Latin and English	QQ36	3FT deg	E+Ln	BBC	Ind	D$^	30$	CSYS	Ind	
Latin and English (4 Yrs)	QQ63	4FT deg	*	BBC	Ind	Ind	30	BBBB	Ind	
Latin and Environmental Management	FQX6	3FT deg	Ln g	BCC	Ind	D$^	28$	CSYS	Ind	
Latin and Environmental Management (4 Yrs)	QF6X	4FT deg	*	BCC	Ind	Ind	28	BBBB	Ind	
Latin and Finance (4 Yrs)	QN63	4FT deg	*	BCC	Ind	Ind	28	BBBB	Ind	
Latin and French	QR61	3FT deg	F+Ln	BCC	Ind	D$^	28$	CSYS	Ind	
Latin and French (4 Yrs)	RQ16	4FT deg	*	BCC	Ind	Ind	28	BBBB	Ind	
Latin and Geography	LQ86	3FT deg	Gy+Ln	BCC	Ind	D$^	28$	CSYS	Ind	
Latin and Geography (4 Yrs)	QL68	4FT deg	*	BCC	Ind	Ind	28	BBBB	Ind	
Latin and Geology (4 Yrs)	QF66	4FT deg	*	BCC	Ind	Ind	28	BBBB	Ind	
Latin and History	QV61	3FT deg	Ln	BCC	Ind	D$^	28$	CSYS	Ind	
Latin and Human Resource Management (4 Yrs)	QN66	4FT deg	*	BCC	Ind	Ind	28	BBBB	Ind	
Latin and International History	QV6C	3FT deg	Ln	BCC	Ind	D$^	28$	CSYS	Ind	
Latin and International History (4 Yrs)	VQC6	4FT deg	*	BCC	Ind	Ind	28	BBBB	Ind	
Latin and International Politics	MQC6	3FT deg	Ln	BCC	Ind	D$^	28$	CSYS	Ind	
Law and Classical Studies	MQ38	3FT deg	*	BBB	Ind	Ind	32	CSYS	Ind	4
Law and Latin	MQ36	3FT deg	Ln	BBB	Ind	D$^	32$	CSYS	Ind	
Law and Latin (4 Yrs)	QM63	4FT deg	*	BBB	Ind	Ind	32	BBBB	Ind	
Marketing and Classical Studies	NQ58	3FT deg	*	BCC	Ind	Ind	28	CSYS	Ind	
Marketing and Latin	NQ56	3FT deg	Ln	BCC	Ind	D$^	28$	CSYS	Ind	
Mathematics and Classical Studies (4 Yrs)	QG81	4FT deg	*	BCC	Ind	Ind	28	BBBB	Ind	
Mathematics and Latin	GQ16	3FT deg	Ln+M	BCC	Ind	D$^	28$	CSYS	Ind	
Mathematics and Latin (4 Yrs)	QG61	4FT deg	*	BCC	Ind	Ind	28	BBBB	Ind	
Music and Classical Studies	QW83	3FT deg	Mu	BBC	Ind	D$^	30	CSYS	Ind	
Music and Classical Studies (4 Yrs)	WQ38	4FT deg	*	BCC	Ind	Ind	28	BBBB	Ind	
Philosophy and Classical Studies (4 Yrs)	VQ78	4FT deg	*	BCC	Ind	Ind	28	BBBB	Ind	
Physics and Classical Studies	FQ38	3FT deg	P	BCC	Ind	D$^	28$	CSYS	Ind	
Physics and Latin	FQ36	3FT deg	Ln+P	BCC	Ind	D$^	28$	CSYS	Ind	
Physics and Latin (4 Yrs)	QF63	4FT deg	*	BCC	Ind	Ind	28	BBBB	Ind	
Politics and Classical Studies	MQ18	3FT deg	*	BCC	Ind	Ind	28	CSYS	Ind	2
Politics and Classical Studies (4 Yrs)	QM81	4FT deg	*	BCC	Ind	Ind	28	BBBB	Ind	
Politics and Latin	MQ16	3FT deg	Ln	BCC	Ind	D$^	28$	CSYS	Ind	
Politics and Latin (4 Yrs)	QM61	4FT deg	*	BCC	Ind	Ind	28	BBBB	Ind	
Psychology and Classical Studies	CQ88	3FT deg	* g	BBB	Ind	Ind	32	CSYS	Ind	
Psychology and Latin	CQ86	3FT deg	Ln g	BBB	Ind	D$^	32$	CSYS	Ind	
Psychology and Latin (4 Yrs)	QC68	4FT deg	*	BBB	Ind	Ind	32	ABBB	Ind	
Russian Studies and Classical Studies	QR8V	3FT deg	*	BCC	Ind	Ind	28	CSYS	Ind	
Russian Studies and Latin	QR6V	3FT deg	Ln	BCC	Ind	D$^	28$	CSYS	Ind	
Russian and Classical Studies	QR88	3FT deg	R	BCC	Ind	D$^	28$	CSYS	Ind	
Russian and Latin	QR68	3FT deg	Ln+R	BCC	Ind	D$^	28$	CSYS	Ind	

TITLE	CODE	COURSE	SUBJECTS	A/AS	ND/C	AGNVQ	IB	SQA(H)	SQA	RATIO A/AS
Sociology and Soc Anthrop & Classical St (4 Yrs)	QL83	4FT deg	*	BCC	Ind	Ind	28	BBBB	Ind	
Statistics and Classical Studies (4 Yrs)	QG84	4FT deg	* g	BCC	Ind	Ind	28	BBBB	Ind	
Statistics and Latin (4 Yrs)	QG64	4FT deg	*	BCC	Ind	Ind	28	BBBB	Ind	
Visual Arts and Classical Studies	QW81	3FT deg	*	BCC	Ind	D$^	28	CSYS	Ind	

Univ of KENT

TITLE	CODE	COURSE	SUBJECTS	A/AS	ND/C	AGNVQ	IB	SQA(H)	SQA	RATIO A/AS
Classical Studies	Q820	3FT deg	*	20	3M+3D	Ind	28	Ind	Ind	5 14/22
Comparative Literary Studies/Classical Studies	QQ28	3FT deg	*	20	3M+3D	Ind	28	Ind	Ind	2
Computing/Classical Studies	QG85	3FT deg	*	20	3M+3D	Ind	28	Ind	Ind	
Drama/Classical Studies	QW84	3FT deg	*	22	2M+4D	Ind	30	Ind	Ind	
English (Post-Colonial Literatures)/Classical St	QQ8J	3FT deg	E	22	2M+4D	Ind	30$	Ind	Ind	
English Language/Classical Studies	QQ83	3FT deg	E	20	3M+3D	Ind	28	Ind	Ind	
English/Classical Studies	QQ38	3FT deg	E	22	2M+4D	Ind	30	Ind	Ind	10
European Studies/Classical Studies	TQ28	4FT deg	L	20	3M+3D	Ind	28	Ind	Ind	
Film Studies/Classical Studies	QW85	3FT deg	*	22	2M+4D	Ind	30	Ind	Ind	
French/Classical Studies	QR81	4FT deg	F	20	3M+3D	Ind	28	Ind	Ind	
German/Classical Studies	QR82	4FT deg	G	20	3M+3D	Ind	28	Ind	Ind	2
History and Theory of Art/Classical Studies	VQ48	3FT deg	*	20	3M+3D	Ind	28	Ind	Ind	12
History/Classical Studies	QV81	3FT deg	*	22	2M+4D	Ind	30	Ind	Ind	
Italian/Classical Studies	QR83	4FT deg	*	20	3M+3D	Ind	28	Ind	Ind	3
Linguistics/Classical Studies	QQ81	3FT deg	*	20	3M+3D	Ind	28	Ind	Ind	3
Philosophy/Classical Studies	QV87	3FT deg	*	20	3M+3D	Ind	28	Ind	Ind	4
Spanish/Classical Studies	QR84	4FT deg	*	20	3M+3D	Ind	28	Ind	Ind	
Theology/Classical Studies	QV88	3FT deg	*	20	3M+3D	Ind	28	Ind	

KING'S COLL LONDON (Univ of London)

TITLE	CODE	COURSE	SUBJECTS	A/AS	RATIO A/AS
Ancient History	Q806	3FT deg		BCC	8 20/24
Classical Studies	Q810	3FT deg		BCC	5 14/26
Classical Studies and French	QR81	4FT deg	F	BBC	4
Classical Studies and Portuguese	QR85	4FT deg		BBC	
Classical Studies with English	Q8Q3	3FT deg	E	BBC	4 20/30
Classical, Byzantine and Modern Greek Studies	QT72	4FT deg		BBC	
Classics	Q800	3FT deg	Ln/Gk	BBD-BCC	10 20/26
German and Classical Studies	QR82	3FT deg	G	BBC	
Greek and Philosophy	QV77	3FT deg	Gk	BBC-BCC	
Greek with English	Q7Q3	3FT deg	E+Gk	BBC	3
Hispanic and Classical Studies	QR84	4FT deg	Sp	BBC-BCC	
Latin with English	Q6Q3	3FT deg	Ln+E	BBC	
Philosophy with Greek	V7Q7	3FT deg	*	BBC-BCC	7
War Studies and Classical Studies	MQ98	3FT deg		BBC	

Univ of Wales, LAMPETER

TITLE	CODE	COURSE	SUBJECTS	A/AS	ND/C	AGNVQ	IB	SQA(H)	SQA
Classical Studies	Q810	3FT deg	*	16	Ind	Ind	Ind	Ind	Ind
Classical Studies and American Literature	QQ48	3FT deg			Ind	Ind	Ind	Ind	Ind
Classical Studies and Ancient History	QV8D	3FT deg	*	16	Ind	Ind	Ind	Ind	Ind
Classical Studies and Anthropology	LQ68	3FT deg	*	16	Ind	Ind	Ind	Ind	Ind
Classical Studies and Archaeology	QV86	3FT deg	*	16	Ind	Ind	Ind	Ind	Ind
Classical Studies and Australian Studies	LQP8	3FT deg			Ind	Ind	Ind	Ind	Ind
Classical Studies and Church History	QVWC	3FT deg	*	16	Ind	Ind	Ind	Ind	Ind
Classics	Q800	3FT deg	Ln g	16	Ind	Ind	Ind	Ind	Ind
Cultural Studies in Geography and Classical St	LQVV	3FT deg	*	16	Ind	Ind	Ind	Ind	Ind
English Literature and Classical Studies	QQ38	3FT deg	E	16-18	Ind	Ind	Ind	Ind	Ind
French and Classical Studies	QR81	4FT deg	F	16	Ind	Ind	Ind	Ind	Ind
Geography and Classical Studies	LQV8	3FT deg	Gy	16	Ind	Ind	Ind	Ind	Ind

			98 expected requirements							96 entry stats
course details										
TITLE	CODE	COURSE	SUBJECTS	A/AS	ND/C	AGNVQ	IB	SQA(H)	SQA	RATIO A/AS
German Studies and Classical Studies	QRW2	4FT deg	*	16	Ind	Ind	Ind	Ind	Ind	
German and Classical Studies	QR82	4FT deg	G	16	Ind	Ind	Ind	Ind	Ind	
Greek and American Literature	QQ74	3FT deg	g		Ind	Ind	Ind	Ind	Ind	
Greek and Ancient History	QV7D	3FT deg	* g	16	Ind	Ind	Ind	Ind	Ind	
Greek and Anthropology	LQ67	3FT deg	* g	16	Ind	Ind	Ind	Ind	Ind	
Greek and Archaeology	QV76	3FT deg	* g	16	Ind	Ind	Ind	Ind	Ind	
Greek and Australian Studies	LQ6R	3FT deg	* g		Ind	Ind	Ind	Ind	Ind	
Greek and Church History	QVTC	3FT deg	* g	16	Ind	Ind	Ind	Ind	Ind	
Greek and Classical Studies	QQ78	3FT deg	* g	16	Ind	Ind	Ind	Ind	Ind	
Greek and Cultural Studies in Geography	LQV7	3FT deg	* g	16	Ind	Ind	Ind	Ind	Ind	
Greek and English Literature	QQ37	3FT deg	E g	18	Ind	Ind	Ind	Ind	Ind	
Greek and French	QR71	4FT deg	F g	16	Ind	Ind	Ind	Ind	Ind	
Greek and Geography	LQ87	3FT deg	Gy g	16	Ind	Ind	Ind	Ind	Ind	
Greek and German	QR72	4FT deg	G g	16	Ind	Ind	Ind	Ind	Ind	
Greek and German Studies	QRR2	4FT deg	* g	16	Ind	Ind	Ind	Ind	Ind	
History and Classical Studies	QV81	3FT deg	H	16	Ind	Ind	Ind	Ind	Ind	
History and Greek	QV71	3FT deg	H g	16	Ind	Ind	Ind	Ind	Ind	
Informatics and Classical Studies	GQ58	3FT deg	*	16	Ind	Ind	Ind	Ind	Ind	
Informatics and Greek	GQ57	3FT deg	* g	14-16	Ind	Ind	Ind	Ind	Ind	
Islamic Studies and Classical Studies	TQ68	3FT deg	*	16	Ind	Ind	Ind	Ind	Ind	
Islamic Studies and Greek	TQ67	3FT deg	* g	16	Ind	Ind	Ind	Ind	Ind	
Latin	Q600	3FT deg	Ln	16	Ind	Ind	Ind	Ind	Ind	
Latin and American Literature	QQ64	3FT deg	Ln		Ind	Ind	Ind	Ind	Ind	
Latin and Ancient History	QV6D	3FT deg	* g	16	Ind	Ind	Ind	Ind	Ind	
Latin and Anthropology	LQ66	3FT deg	* g	16	Ind	Ind	Ind	Ind	Ind	
Latin and Archaeology	QV66	3FT deg	* g	16	Ind	Ind	Ind	Ind	Ind	
Latin and Australian Studies	QL66	3FT deg			Ind	Ind	Ind	Ind	Ind	
Latin and Church History	QVQC	3FT deg	* g	16	Ind	Ind	Ind	Ind	Ind	
Latin and Classical Studies	QQ68	3FT deg	* g	16	Ind	Ind	Ind	Ind	Ind	
Latin and Cultural Studies in Geography	LQV6	3FT deg	* g	16	Ind	Ind	Ind	Ind	Ind	
Latin and English Literature	QQ36	3FT deg	E g	18	Ind	Ind	Ind	Ind	Ind	
Latin and French	QR61	4FT deg	F g	16	Ind	Ind	Ind	Ind	Ind	
Latin and Geography	LQ86	3FT deg	Gy g	16	Ind	Ind	Ind	Ind	Ind	
Latin and German	QR62	4FT deg	G g	16	Ind	Ind	Ind	Ind	Ind	
Latin and German Studies	QRQ2	4FT deg	* g	16	Ind	Ind	Ind	Ind	Ind	
Latin and Greek	QQ67	3FT deg	* g	16	Ind	Ind	Ind	Ind	SQA	
Latin and History	QV61	3FT deg	H g	16	Ind	Ind	Ind	Ind	Ind	
Latin and Informatics	GQ56	3FT deg	* g	16	Ind	Ind	Ind	Ind	Ind	
Latin and Islamic Studies	TQ66	3FT deg	* g	16	Ind	Ind	Ind	Ind	Ind	
Management Techniques and Classical Studies	NQ18	3FT deg	*	16	Ind	Ind	Ind	Ind	Ind	
Management Techniques and Greek	NQ17	3FT deg	* g	16	Ind	Ind	Ind	Ind	Ind	
Management Techniques and Latin	NQ16	3FT deg	* g	16	Ind	Ind	Ind	Ind	Ind	
Medieval Studies and Classical Studies	VQ18	3FT deg	*	16	Ind	Ind	Ind	Ind	Ind	
Medieval Studies and Greek	VQ17	3FT deg	g	16	Ind	Ind	Ind	Ind	Ind	
Medieval Studies and Latin	VQ16	3FT deg	g	16	Ind	Ind	Ind	Ind	Ind	
Modern Historical Studies and Greek	VQ1R	3FT deg			Ind	Ind	Ind	Ind	Ind	
Modern Historical Studies and Latin	VQ1P	3FT deg			Ind	Ind	Ind	Ind	Ind	
Philosophical Studies and Classical Studies	QV87	3FT deg	*	16	Ind	Ind	Ind	Ind	Ind	
Philosophical Studies and Greek	QV77	3FT deg	* g	16	Ind	Ind	Ind	Ind	Ind	
Philosophical Studies and Latin	QV67	3FT deg	* g	16	Ind	Ind	Ind	Ind	Ind	
Religious Studies and Classical Studies	QVV8	3FT deg	*	16	Ind	Ind	Ind	Ind	Ind	
Religious Studies and Greek	QVR8	3FT deg	* g	16	Ind	Ind	Ind	Ind	Ind	

Letts STUDY GUIDES
THE INDEPENDENT

course details			**98 expected requirements**							*96 entry stats*
TITLE	CODE	COURSE	SUBJECTS	A/AS	ND/C	AGNVQ	IB	SQA(H)	SQA	RATIO A/AS
Religious Studies and Latin	QVP8	3FT deg	* g	16	Ind	Ind	Ind	Ind	Ind	
Theology and Classical Studies	QV88	3FT deg	*	16	Ind	Ind	Ind	Ind	Ind	
Theology and Greek	QV78	3FT deg	* g	16	Ind	Ind	Ind	Ind	Ind	
Theology and Latin	QV68	3FT deg	* g	16	Ind	Ind	Ind	Ind	Ind	
Victorian Studies and Classical Studies	QV8C	3FT deg	*	16	Ind	Ind	Ind	Ind	Ind	
Victorian Studies and Greek	QV7C	3FT deg	* g	16	Ind	Ind	Ind	Ind	Ind	
Victorian Studies and Latin	QV6C	3FT deg	* g	16	Ind	Ind	Ind	Ind	Ind	
Welsh Studies and Classical Studies	QQM8	3FT deg	*	16	Ind	Ind	Ind	Ind	Ind	
Welsh Studies and Greek	QQM7	3FT deg	* g	16	Ind	Ind	Ind	Ind	Ind	
Welsh Studies and Latin	QQ5P	3FT deg	* g	16	Ind	Ind	Ind	Ind	Ind	
Welsh and Classical Studies	QQ58	3FT/4FT deg	W	16	Ind	Ind	Ind	Ind	Ind	
Welsh and Greek	QQ57	3FT/4FT deg	W g	16	Ind	Ind	Ind	Ind	Ind	
Welsh and Latin	QQ56	3FT/4FT deg	W g	16	Ind	Ind	Ind	Ind	Ind	
Women's Studies and Classical Studies	MQ98	3FT deg	*	16	Ind	Ind	Ind	Ind	Ind	
Women's Studies and Greek	MQ97	3FT deg	g	16	Ind	Ind	Ind	Ind	Ind	
Women's Studies and Latin	MQ96	3FT deg	g	16	Ind	Ind	Ind	Ind	Ind	
Combined Honours *Classical Studies*	Y400	3FT deg	*	14-16	Ind	Ind	Ind	Ind	Ind	
Combined Honours *Greek*	Y400	3FT deg	g	14-16	Ind	Ind	Ind	Ind	Ind	
Combined Honours *Latin*	Y400	3FT deg	g	14-16	Ind	Ind	Ind	Ind	Ind	

Univ of LEEDS

TITLE	CODE	COURSE	SUBJECTS	A/AS	ND/C	AGNVQ	IB	SQA(H)	SQA	RATIO A/AS
Arabic-Classical Literature	QT86	4FT deg	Cl/L g	BBC	Ind	Ind	30$	CSYS	Ind	
Arabic-Greek Civilisation	QTW6	4FT deg	Cl/L g	BBC	Ind	Ind	30$	CSYS	Ind	
Arabic-Roman Civilisation	QTV6	4FT deg	C1/L g	BBC	Ind	Ind	30$	CSYS	Ind	
Classical Civilisation	Q820	3FT deg	* g	BCC	Ind	X	28	CSYS	Ind	4 18/26
Classical Literature-English	QQ38	3FT deg	E g	BBC	Ind	Ind	30$	CSYS	Ind	7 22/26
Classical Literature-French	QR81	4FT deg	F g	BBC	Ind	Ind	30$	CSYS	Ind	
Classical Literature-History	QV81	3FT deg	* g	BBC	Ind	Ind	30	CSYS	Ind	4
Classical Literature-Italian	QR83	4FT deg	I g	BBC	Ind	Ind	Ind	Ind	Ind	
Classical Literature-Italian B	QR8H	4FT deg	L g	BBC	Ind	Ind	Ind	Ind	Ind	
Classical Literature-Religious Studies	QV8V	3FT deg	* g	BBC	Ind	Ind	30	CSYS	Ind	
Classical Literature-Russian	QR88	4FT deg	R g	BBC	Ind	Ind	30$	CSYS	Ind	
Classical Literature-Russian B	QR8V	4FT deg	L g	BBC	Ind	Ind	30$	CSYS	Ind	
Classical Literature-Spanish	QR84	4FT deg	Sp g	BBC	Ind	Ind	30$	CSYS	Ind	
Classical Literature-Theology	QV88	3FT deg	* g	BBC	Ind	Ind	30	CSYS	Ind	
Classics	Q800	3FT/4FT deg	Gk/Ln g	BCC	Ind	X	28$	CSYS	Ind	15 22/28
English-Greek Civilisation	QQ3W	3FT deg	E g	BBC	Ind	Ind	30$	CSYS	Ind	35
English-Latin	QQ36	3FT/4FT deg	E+Ln/L g	BBC	Ind	Ind	30$	CSYS	Ind	13
English-Roman Civilisation	QQ3V	3FT deg	E g	BBC	Ind	Ind	30$	CSYS	Ind	19
French-Greek Civilisation	QRW1	4FT deg	F g	BBC	Ind	Ind	30$	CSYS	Ind	
French-Latin	RQ16	4FT deg	F+Ln g	BBC	Ind	Ind	30$	CSYS	Ind	20
French-Roman Civilisation	QRV1	4FT deg	F g	BBC	Ind	Ind	30$	CSYS	Ind	
Greek	Q700	3FT/4FT deg	Gk/L g	BCC	Ind	X	28$	CSYS	Ind	
Greek Civilisation with Greek	Q8QR	3FT deg	* g	BCC	Ind	Ind	28	CSYS	Ind	3
Greek Civilisation-History	QVW1	3FT deg	* g	BBC	Ind	Ind	30	CSYS	Ind	14
Greek Civilisation-Religious Studies	QVWV	3FT deg	* g	BBC	Ind	Ind	30	CSYS	Ind	
Greek Civilisation-Theology	QVW8	3FT deg	* g	BBC	Ind	Ind	30	CSYS	Ind	4
History-Latin	QV61	3FT deg	Ln g	BBC	Ind	Ind	30$	CSYS	Ind	2
History-Roman Civilisation	QVV1	3FT deg	* g	BBC	Ind	Ind	30	CSYS	Ind	26
Italian-Latin	QR63	4FT deg	Ln+I g	BBC	Ind	Ind	30$	CSYS	Ind	
Italian-Latin B	QR6H	4FT deg	Ln g	BBC	Ind	Ind	30$	CSYS	Ind	

TITLE	CODE	COURSE	SUBJECTS	A/AS	ND/C	AGNVQ	IB	SQA(H)	SQA	RATIO A/AS
			98 expected requirements							**96 entry stats**
Italian-Roman Civilisation	QRV3	4FT deg	I g	BBC	Ind	Ind	30$	CSYS	Ind	
Italian-Roman Civilisation B	QRVH	4FT deg	L g	BBC	Ind	Ind	30$	CSYS	Ind	
Latin	Q600	3FT/4FT deg	Ln/L g	BCC	Ind	X	28$	CSYS	Ind	
Latin with Ancient History	Q6Q8	3FT/4FT deg	Ln g	BCC	Ind	X	28$	CSYS	Ind	
Latin-Religious Studies	QV6V	3FT deg	Ln g	BBC	Ind	Ind	30$	CSYS	Ind	
Latin-Russian	QR68	4FT deg	Ln+R g	BBC	Ind	Ind	30$	CSYS	Ind	
Latin-Russian B	QR6V	4FT deg	Ln g	BBC	Ind	Ind	30$	CSYS	Ind	
Latin-Spanish	QR64	4FT deg	Sp+Ln g	BBC	Ind	Ind	30$	CSYS	Ind	1
Latin-Theology	QV68	3FT deg	Ln g	BBC	Ind	Ind	30$	CSYS	Ind	
Roman Civilisation with Latin	Q8QQ	3FT deg	* g	BCC	Ind	Ind	28$	CSYS	Ind	4
Roman Civilisation-Russian	QRV8	4FT deg	R g	BBC	Ind	Ind	30$	CSYS	Ind	
Roman Civilisation-Russian B	QRVV	4FT deg	L g	BBC	Ind	Ind	30$	CSYS	Ind	
Roman Civilisation-Spanish	QRV4	4FT deg	Sp g	BBC	Ind	Ind	30$	CSYS	Ind	

Univ of LIVERPOOL

TITLE	CODE	COURSE	SUBJECTS	A/AS	ND/C	AGNVQ	IB	SQA(H)	SQA	RATIO A/AS
Classical Studies	Q810	3FT deg	*	BCC-CCC	Ind		30	BBBB	Ind	4 14/22
Classics	Q800	3FT deg	Ln/Gk	CCC	Ind		30$	BBBB$	Ind	43
Arts Combined *Classics and Classical Studies*	Y401	3FT deg	*	BBC-BBB	Ind	Ind	30$	ABBB	Ind	
Arts Combined *Hebrew (Classical)*	Y401	3FT deg	* g	BBC-BBB	Ind	Ind	30$	ABBB	Ind	
BA Combined Honours *Classics*	Y200	3FT deg	g	BBB	Ind	Ind	Ind	Ind	Ind	

Univ of MANCHESTER

TITLE	CODE	COURSE	SUBJECTS	A/AS	ND/C	AGNVQ	IB	SQA(H)	SQA	RATIO A/AS
Classical Studies	Q810	3FT deg	g	CCC	X	X	26	BBBCC	X	4 16/28
Classics	Q800	3FT deg	Gk+Ln g	BBC	X	X	30	BBBCC	X	63
Classics and Ancient History	QV81	3FT deg								
French with Latin	R1Q6	4FT deg	F	BBC		D^	30$			2
Greek	Q700	3FT deg	Gk	BBC	X	X	30	BBBBB	X	
Greek and Archaeology	QV76	3FT deg	Gk	BBC	X	X	30	BBBBB	X	
Greek and English	QQ37	3FT deg	Gk+E	BBC	X	X	30	BBBBB	X	
Latin	Q600	3FT deg	Ln	BBC	X	X	30	BBBBB	X	
Latin and Archaeology	QV66	3FT deg	Ln	BBC	X	X	30$	BBBBB	X	
Latin and English	QQ36	3FT deg	Ln+E	BBC	X	X	30$	BBBBB	X	8
Latin and Italian	QR63	4FT deg	Ln	BBC	X	X	30	BBBBB	X	2
Latin and Linguistics	QQ61	3FT deg	Ln	BBC	X	X	30$	ABBBB	X	1
Latin and Spanish	QR64	4FT deg	Ln+Sp	BBC	X	X	30	BBBBB	X	
Latin with French	Q6R1	4FT deg	Ln+F	BBC	X	X	30	BBBBB	X	11

Univ of NEWCASTLE

TITLE	CODE	COURSE	SUBJECTS	A/AS	ND/C	AGNVQ	IB	SQA(H)	SQA	RATIO A/AS
Classical Studies	Q810	3FT deg	*	22				AABBB		9 20/26
Classics	Q800	3FT deg	Ln+Gk/Gk+Ln	22				AABBB		14 18/30
English Literature and Latin	QQ36	3FT deg	E+Ln	BBC	Ind		Ind	AABBB	Ind	
Greek (with Latin)	Q7Q6	3FT deg	Gk	22				AABBB		
Latin (with Greek)	Q6Q7	3FT deg	Ln	22				AABBB		14
Combined Studies (BA) *Greek (Classical)*	Y400	3FT deg	*	ABC-BBB	5D	Ind	35$	AAAB	Ind	
Combined Studies (BA) *Greek (New Testament)*	Y400	3FT deg	*	ABC-BBB	5D	Ind	35$	AAAB	Ind	
Combined Studies (BA) *Latin*	Y400	3FT deg	*	ABC-BBB	5D	Ind	35$	AAAB	Ind	

Univ of NORTH LONDON

TITLE	CODE	COURSE	SUBJECTS	A/AS	ND/C	AGNVQ	IB	SQA(H)	SQA	RATIO A/AS
Combined Honours *Classical Civilisation*	Y300	3FT/4FT deg	*	CC	Ind	Ind	Ind	Ind	Ind	

TITLE	CODE	COURSE	SUBJECTS	A/AS	ND/C	RGNVQ	IB	SQA(H)	SQA	RATIO A/AS
course details			**98 expected requirements**							*96 entry stats*
Univ of NOTTINGHAM										
Ancient History and Latin	QV61	3FT deg	Ln	BCC						3
Archaeology and Classical Civilisation	QVV6	3FT deg		BCC						15
Archaeology and Latin	QV66	3FT deg	Ln	BBC						
Classical Civilisation	Q820	3FT deg		BCC						18 22/28
Classical Civilisation and English Studies	QQ83	3FT deg	E	BBC						43
Classical Civilisation and French	QR81	4FT deg	F	BCC						7
Classical Civilisation and German	QR82	4FT deg	G	BCC						
Classical Civilisation and Philosophy	QV87	3FT deg		BBC						10
Classical Civilisation and Theology	QV88	3FT deg		CCC						
Classics (Greek and Latin)	Q802	3FT deg	Ln	BCC						11 22/28
English Studies and Latin	QQ36	3FT deg	E+Ln	BBC						
French and Latin	QR61	4FT deg	F+Ln	BCC						15
German and Greek	RQ27	4FT deg	G	BCC						
German and Latin	RQ26	4FT deg	G+Ln	BCC						
Greek and Philosophy	QV77	3FT deg		BBC						
Greek and Theology	QV78	3FT deg		BCC						
Latin	Q600	3FT deg	Ln	BCC						5
Latin and Theology	QV68	3FT deg	Ln	BCC						2
OXFORD Univ										
Arabic with Islamic Art and Archaeology (4 Yrs)	TQ6Y	4FT deg	*	AAB-ABB	DO		36	AAAAA	Ind	5
Arabic with Islamic Studies/History (4 Yrs)	TQ69	4FT deg	*	AAB-ABB	DO		36	AAAAA	Ind	5
Classics I	Q800	4FT deg	Ln/Gk	AAB	DO		36	AAAAA	Ind	2 28/30
Classics II	Q810	4FT deg	*	AAB	DO		36	AAAAA	Ind	3
Classics and English	QQ38	3FT deg	E+Ln/Gk	AAB	DO		36	AAAAA	Ind	3 30/30
Classics and Modern Languages (3 Yrs)	QT89	3FT deg	Ln/Gk+L	AAB	DO		36	AAAAA	Ind	4
Classics and Modern Languages (4 Yrs)	TQ98	4FT deg	Ln/Gk+L	AAB	DO		36	AAAAA	Ind	2 30/30
Egyptology (3 Yrs)	Q900	3FT deg	*	AAB-ABB	DO		36	AAAAA	Ind	3
Hebrew (3 Yrs)	Q960	3FT deg	*	AAB-ABB	DO		36	AAAAA	Ind	
Jewish Studies (3 Yrs)	QV91	3FT deg	*	AAB-ABB	DO		36	AAAAA	Ind	
Persian with Islamic Art and Archaeology (4 Yrs)	QT9P	4FT deg	*	AAB-ABB	DO		36	AAAAA	Ind	1
Persian with Islamic Studies/History (4 Yrs)	QT9Q	4FT deg	*	AAB-ABB	DO		36	AAAAA	Ind	
Sanskrit (3 Yrs)	Q950	3FT deg	*	AAB-ABB	DO		36	AAAAA	Ind	1
Turkish with Islamic Art and Archaeology (3 Yrs)	TQ6X	3FT deg	*	AAB-ABB	DO		36	AAAAA	Ind	
QUEEN'S Univ Belfast										
Byzantine Studies	Q860	3FT/4FT deg	* g	BCC	3M+4D	D*6/^ go	29$	ABBB	Ind	
Byzantine Studies/Ancient History	VQC8	3FT/4FT deg	* g	BCC	3M+4D	D*6/^ go	29$	ABBB	Ind	
Byzantine Studies/Archaeology	VQ68	3FT/4FT deg	* g	BCC	3M+4D	D*6/^ go	29$	ABBB	Ind	2
Byzantine Studies/Biblical Studies	VQ88	3FT/4FT deg	* g	BCC	3M+4D	D*6/^ go	29$	ABBB	Ind	
Celtic/Byzantine Studies	QQ85	3FT/4FT deg	* g	BCC	3M+4D	D*6/^ go	29$	ABBB	Ind	
Classical Studies	Q821	3FT deg	* g	BCC	3M+4D	D*6/^ go	29$	ABBB	Ind	13
Classical Studies/Ancient History	QV8C	3FT/4FT deg	* g	BCC	3M+4D	D*6/^ go	29$	ABBB	Ind	7
Classical Studies/Biblical Studies	QV88	3FT deg	* g	BCC	3M+4D	D*6/^ go	29$	ABBB	Ind	
Classical Studies/Celtic	QQ58	3FT/4FT deg	* g	BCC	3M+4D	D*6/^ go	29$	ABBB	Ind	
Classics	Q800	3FT/4FT deg	Gk/Ln g	BCC	X	D*⌐ go	29$	ABBB	X	4
Economic & Social History/Byzantine Studies	QV83	3FT/4FT deg	* g	BCC	3M+4D	D*6/^ go	29$	ABBB	Ind	
English/Byzantine Studies	QQ38	3FT/4FT deg	E g	BCC	X	D*⌐ go	29$	ABBB	X	1
English/Classical Studies	QQ83	3FT deg	E g	BCC	X	D*⌐ go	29$	ABBB	X	9
German/Classical Studies (4 years)	QR82	4FT deg	* g	BCC	3M+4D	D*6/^ go	29$	ABBB	Ind	
Greek/Ancient History	VQC7	3FT/4FT deg	* g	BCC	3M+4D	D*6/^ go	29$	ABBB	Ind	
Greek/Archaeology	VQ67	3FT/4FT deg	* g	BCC	3M+4D	D*6/^ go	29$	ABBB	Ind	

course details			98 expected requirements							96 entry stats
TITLE	CODE	COURSE	SUBJECTS	A/AS	ND/C	AGNVQ	IB	SQA(H)	SQA	RATIO A/AS
Greek/Biblical Studies	VQ87	3FT/4FT deg	* g	BCC	3M+4D	D*6/^ go	29$	ABBB	Ind	
Greek/Celtic	QQ57	3FT/4FT deg	* g	BCC	3M+4D	D*6/^ go	29$	ABBB	Ind	
Greek/Economic & Social History	VQ37	3FT/4FT deg	* g	BCC	3M+4D	D*6/^ go	29$	ABBB	Ind	
Greek/English	QQ37	3FT/4FT deg	E g	BCC	X	D*_ go	29$	ABBB	X	
Greek/French (4 years)	RQ17	4FT deg	E g	BCC	X	D*_ go	29$	ABBB	X	
Greek/German (4 years)	RQ27	4FT deg	* g	BCC	3M+4D	D*6/^ go	29$	ABBB	Ind	
History & Philosophy of Science/Byzantine Stds	QV85	3FT/4FT deg	* g	BCC	3M+4D	D*6/^ go	29$	ABBB	Ind	
History & Philosophy of Science/Classical Stds	VQ58	3FT deg	* g	BCC	3M+4D	D*6/^ go	29$	ABBB	Ind	
History & Philosophy of Science/Greek	QV75	3FT/4FT deg	* g	BCC	3M+4D	D*6/^ go	29$	ABBB	Ind	
Italian/Classical Studies (4 years)	QR83	4FT deg	* g	BCC	3M+4D	D*6/^ go	29$	ABBB	Ind	
Italian/Greek (4 years)	QR73	4FT deg	* g	BCC	3M+4D	D*6/^ go	29$	ABBB	Ind	
Latin/Ancient History	VQC6	3FT/4FT deg	* g	BCC	3M+4D	D*6/^ go	29$	ABBB	Ind	3
Latin/Biblical Studies	VQ86	3FT/4FT deg	* g	BCC	3M+4D	D*6/^ go	29$	ABBB	Ind	
Latin/Byzantine Studies	QQ86	3FT/4FT deg	* g	BCC	3M+4D	D*6/^ go	29$	ABBB	Ind	
Latin/Celtic	QQ56	3FT/4FT deg	* g	BCC	3M+4D	D*6/^ go	29$	ABBB	Ind	
Latin/Economic & Social History	VQ36	3FT/4FT deg	* g	BCC	3M+4D	D*6/^ go	29$	ABBB	Ind	
Latin/English	QQ36	3FT/4FT deg	E g	BCC	X	D*_ go	29$	ABBB	X	1
Latin/French (4 years)	RQ16	4FT deg	E g	BCC	X	D*_ go	29$	ABBB	X	6
Latin/German (4 years)	RQ26	4FT deg	* g	BCC	3M+4D	D*6/^ go	29$	ABBB	Ind	
Latin/History & Philosophy of Science	VQ56	3FT/4FT deg	* g	BCC	3M+4D	D*6/^ go	29$	ABBB	Ind	
Latin/Italian (4 years)	RQ36	4FT deg	* g	BCC	3M+4D	D*6/^ go	29$	ABBB	Ind	
Philosophy/Byzantine Studies	QV87	3FT/4FT deg	* g	BCC	3M+4D	D*6/^ go	29$	ABBB	Ind	
Philosophy/Classical Studies	VQ78	3FT deg	* g	BCC	3M+4D	D*6/^ go	29$	ABBB	Ind	6
Philosophy/Greek	QV77	3FT/4FT deg	* g	BCC	3M+4D	D*6/^ go	29$	ABBB	Ind	1
Philosophy/Latin	QV67	3FT/4FT deg	* g	BCC	3M+4D	D*6/^ go	29$	ABBB	Ind	
Politics/Byzantine Studies	QM81	3FT/4FT deg	* g	BCC	3M+4D	D*6/^ go	29$	ABBB	Ind	
Politics/Classical Studies	MQ18	3FT deg	* g	BCC	3M+4D	D*6/^ go	29$	ABBB	Ind	
Politics/Greek	QM71	3FT/4FT deg	* g	BCC	3M+4D	D*6/^ go	29$	ABBB	Ind	
Politics/Latin	QM61	3FT/4FT deg	* g	BCC	3M+4D	D*6/^ go	29$	ABBB	Ind	
Psychology/Byzantine Studies	CQ88	3FT/4FT deg	* g	BCC	3M+4D	D*6/^ go	29$	ABBB	Ind	
Psychology/Greek	CQ87	3FT/4FT deg	* g	BCC	3M+4D	D*6/^ go	29$	ABBB	Ind	
Psychology/Latin	CQ86	3FT/4FT deg	* g	BCC	3M+4D	D*6/^ go	29$	ABBB	Ind	
Scholastic Philosophy/Byzantine Studies	QV8R	3FT/4FT deg	* g	BCC	3M+4D	D*6/^ go	29$	ABBB	Ind	
Scholastic Philosophy/Classical Studies	VQR8	3FT deg	* g	BCC	3M+4D	D*6/^ go	29$	ABBB	Ind	
Scholastic Philosophy/Greek	QV7R	3FT/4FT deg	* g	BCC	3M+4D	D*6/^ go	29$	ABBB	Ind	
Scholastic Philosophy/Latin	QV6R	3FT/4FT deg	* g	BCC	3M+4D	D*6/^ go	29$	ABBB	Ind	
Social Anthropology/Byzantine Studies	QL86	3FT/4FT deg	* g	BCC	3M+4D	D*6/^ go	29$	ABBB	Ind	
Social Anthropology/Classical Studies	LQ68	3FT deg	* g	BCC	3M+4D	D*6/^ go	29$	ABBB	Ind	
Social Anthropology/Greek	QL76	3FT/4FT deg	* g	BCC	3M+4D	D*6/^ go	29$	ABBB	Ind	
Social Anthropology/Latin	QL66	3FT/4FT deg	* g	BCC	3M+4D	D*6/^ go	29$	ABBB	Ind	
Social Policy/Byzantine Studies	QL84	3FT/4FT deg	* g	BCC	3M+4D	D*6/^ go	29$	ABBB	Ind	
Social Policy/Greek	QL74	3FT/4FT deg	* g	BCC	3M+4D	D*6/^ go	29$	ABBB	Ind	
Social Policy/Latin	QL64	3FT/4FT deg	* g	BCC	3M+4D	D*6/^ go	29$	ABBB	Ind	
Sociology/Byzantine Studies	QL83	3FT/4FT deg	* g	BCC	3M+4D	D*6/^ go	29$	ABBB	Ind	
Sociology/Greek	QL73	3FT/4FT deg	* g	BCC	3M+4D	D*6/^ go	29$	ABBB	Ind	
Sociology/Latin	QL63	3FT/4FT deg	* g	BCC	3M+4D	D*6/^ go	29$	ABBB	Ind	
Spanish/Byzantine Studies (4 years)	QR84	4FT deg	* g	BCC	3M+4D	D*6/^ go	29$	ABBB	Ind	
Spanish/Greek (4 years)	QR74	4FT deg	* g	BCC	3M+4D	D*6/^ go	29$	ABBB	Ind	
Spanish/Latin (4 years)	QR64	4FT deg	* g	BCC	3M+4D	D*6/^ go	29$	ABBB	Ind	

Letts STUDY GUIDES
THE INDEPENDENT

course details | 98 expected requirements | 96 entry stats

TITLE	CODE	COURSE	SUBJECTS	A/AS	ND/C	AGNVQ	IB	SQA(H)	SQA	RATIO A/AS
Univ of READING										
Classical Studies	Q810	3FT deg	*	BCC	Ind	D*6/^	30	BBBB	Ind	8 14/26
Classical Studies and History of Art	QV84	3FT deg	*	BBC	Ind	D$6/^	31	BBBB	Ind	3
Classical Studies and Politics	QM81	3FT deg	*	BCC	Ind	D*6/^	30	BBBB	Ind	6
Classical Studies and Sociology	QL83	3FT deg	*	BCC	Ind	D$^ go	30	BBBB	Ind	
Classical Studies with English Literature	Q8Q3	3FT deg	El	BCC	Ind	D*_^	30$	BBBB$	Ind	8
Classical and Medieval Studies	QV81	3FT deg	*	BCC	Ind	D*6/^	30	BBBB	Ind	8
Classics	Q800	3FT deg	Ln/* g	BCC	Ind	D*6/^ go	30	BBBB	Ind	49
English Literature and Classical Studies	QQ38	3FT deg	El	BCC	Ind	D*_^	30$	BBBB$	Ind	10 20/22
English Literature with Classical Studies	Q3Q8	3FT deg	El	BCC	Ind	D*_^	30$	BBBB$	Ind	7
English Literature with Latin	Q3Q6	3FT deg	El	BCC	Ind	D*_^	30$	BBBB$	Ind	
Greek and English Literature	QQ37	3FT deg	El g	BCC	Ind	D*_^ go	30$	BBBB$	Ind	
Greek and Philosophy	QV77	3FT deg	* g	BCC	Ind	D*^ go	30	BBBB	Ind	
History with Latin	V1Q6	3FT deg	* g	BBC	Ind	D*6/^ go	31	BBBB	Ind	
Italian and Classical Studies	QR83	4FT deg	* g	BCC	Ind	D$6/^ go	30	BBBB	Ind	
Italian with Latin	R3Q6	4FT deg	* g	BCC	Ind	D$6/^ go	30	BBBB	Ind	
Latin and Archaeology	QV66	3FT deg	* g	BCC	Ind	D*6/^ go	30	BBBB	Ind	2
Latin and English Literature	QQ36	3FT deg	El g	BCC	Ind	D*_^ go	30$	BBBB$	Ind	
Latin and French	QR61	4FT deg	F g	BCC	Ind	D*_^ go	30$	BBBB$	Ind	
Latin and German	QR62	4FT deg	* g	BCC	Ind	D*_^ go	30	BBBB	Ind	
Latin and Italian	QR63	4FT deg	* g	BCC	Ind	D$6/^ go	30	BBBB	Ind	
Latin and Linguistics	QQ16	3FT deg	* g	BCC	Ind	D*6/^ go	30	BBBB	Ind	
Latin and Medieval Studies	QV61	3FT deg	* g	BCC	Ind	D*6/^ go	30	BBBB	Ind	
Latin and Philosophy	QV67	3FT deg	* g	BCC	Ind	D*^ go	30	BBBB	Ind	
Latin, Classical and Medieval	Q600	3FT deg	Ln	BCC	Ind	D*_^	30$	BBBB$	Ind	
Philosophy and Classical Studies	QV87	3FT deg	*	BCC	Ind	D*^	30	BBBB	Ind	17
ROYAL HOLLOWAY, Univ of London										
Classical Studies	Q810	3FT deg	*	BCC	Ind		28	BBBB		3 14/26
Classical Studies and Drama	QW84	3FT deg	E/T g	BBC-BCC	Ind		30		Ind	7
Classical Studies with Mathematics	Q8G1	3FT deg	M	BCC	Ind		28$	BBBB$		
Classics	Q800	3FT deg	* g	BCC	Ind		28	BBBB$		6 14/26
English Language and Classical Studies	QQ3V	3FT deg	E g	BBC-ABC			30$		Ind	
English Language and Latin	QQ3P	3FT deg	E g	BBC-ABC			30$		Ind	
English and Classical Studies	QQ38	3FT deg	E g	BBC-ABC			30$		Ind	4 20/28
English and Latin	QQ36	3FT deg	E g	BBC-ABC			30$		Ind	
French and Classical Studies	RQ18	4FT deg	F	BBC			28$		Ind	
French and Greek	RQ17	4FT deg	F	BBC			28$		Ind	
French and Latin	RQ16	4FT deg	F	BBC			28$		Ind	
German and Classical Studies	RQ28	4FT deg	G	BCC-BBC			28$		Ind	
German and Greek	RQ27	4FT deg	G	BCC-BBC			28$		Ind	
German and Latin	RQ26	4FT deg	G	BCC-BBC			28$		Ind	
Greek	Q700	3FT deg	*	BCC			28	BBBBC		
Greek and Ancient History	QV71	3FT deg		BCC			28	BBBBC		
Greek with Mathematics	Q7G1	3FT deg	M	BCC			28$	BBBBC$		
Latin	Q600	3FT deg	*	BCC			28	BBBBC		
Latin and Ancient History	QV61	3FT deg	*	BCC			28	BBBBC		
Latin with Mathematics	Q6G1	3FT deg	M	BCC			28$	BBBBC$		
Foundation Programme *Classics/Classical Studies*	Y408	4FT deg								

Languages – Classical and Ancient 38

			98 expected requirements							96 entry stats

course details

TITLE	CODE	COURSE	SUBJECTS	A/AS	ND/C	RGNVQ	IB	SQA(H)	SQA	RATIO A/AS
SOAS:Sch of Oriental & African St (U of London)										
Ancient Near Eastern Languages	Q901	4FT deg		22	Ind		31	BBBBC	Ind	
Ancient Near Eastern Studies	Q900	3FT deg		22	Ind		31	BBBBC	Ind	14
Arabic and Islamic Studies	QT96	4FT deg		22	Ind		31	BBBBC	Ind	7
Hebrew and Arabic	QT9P	4FT deg		22	Ind		31	BBBBC	Ind	
Hebrew and Economics	LQ19	4FT deg	g	22	Ind		31	BBBBC	Ind	
Hebrew and Geography	LQ89	4FT deg		22	Ind		31	BBBBC	Ind	1
Hebrew and Georgian	QT99	4FT deg		22	Ind		31	BBBBC	Ind	
Hebrew and Israeli Studies	QT9Q	4FT deg		22	Ind		31	BBBBC	Ind	
History and Hebrew	QV91	4FT deg		22	Ind		31	BBBBC	Ind	
History of Art/Archaeology and Hebrew	QV96	4FT deg		22	Ind		31	BBBBC	Ind	
Law and Hebrew	MQ39	4FT deg		24	Ind		32	BBBBB	Ind	
Linguistics and Hebrew	QQ19	4FT deg		22	Ind		31	BBBBC	Ind	
Management and Hebrew	NQ19	4FT deg	g	22	Ind		31	BBBBC	Ind	
Music and Hebrew	QW93	4FT deg		22	Ind		31	BBBBC	Ind	
Politics and Hebrew	MQ19	4FT deg		22	Ind		31	BBBBC	Ind	
Sanskrit and Economics	LQ1X	3FT deg	g	22	Ind		31	BBBBC	Ind	
Sanskrit and Geography	LQ8X	3FT deg		20	Ind		30	BBBCC	Ind	
Sanskrit and History	QVX1	3FT deg		20	Ind		30	BBBCC	Ind	
Sanskrit and History of Art/Archaeology	QVX6	3FT deg		20	Ind		30	BBBCC	Ind	
Sanskrit and Law	MQ3X	3FT deg		24	Ind		32	BBBBB	Ind	
Sanskrit and Linguistics	QQ1X	3FT deg		20	Ind		30	BBBCC	Ind	
Sanskrit and Management	NQ1X	3FT deg	g	20	Ind		30	BBBCC	Ind	
Sanskrit and Music	QWX3	3FT deg		20	Ind		30	BBBCC	Ind	
Sanskrit and Politics	MQ1X	3FT deg		20	Ind		30	BBBCC	Ind	
Social Anthropology and Hebrew	LQ69	4FT deg		22	Ind		31	BBBBC	Ind	
Social Anthropology and Sanskrit	LQ6X	3FT deg		22	Ind		31	BBBBC	Ind	
Study of Religions and Hebrew	QV98	4FT deg		22	Ind		31	BBBBC	Ind	
Study of Religions and Sanskrit	QVX8	3FT deg		20	Ind		30	BBBCC	Ind	1
Univ of ST ANDREWS										
Classical Studies	Q811	4FT deg	* g	BBC	X	Ind	30$	BBBB	Ind	4
Classical Studies-Art History	QV84	4FT deg	* g	BBC	X	Ind	30$	BBBB	Ind	3
Classical Studies-Biblical Studies	VQ88	4FT deg	* g	BBC	X	Ind	30$	BBBB	Ind	
Classics	Q810	4FT deg	* g	BBC	X	Ind	30$	BBBB	Ind	12
English-Classical Studies	QQ38	4FT deg	* g	BBB	X	Ind	30$	BBBB	Ind	6
Greek	Q700	4FT deg	* g	BBC	X	Ind	30$	BBBB	Ind	
Greek-Ancient History	QV71	4FT deg	* g	BBB	X	Ind	30$	BBBB	Ind	3
Greek-Biblical Studies	QV78	4FT deg	* g	BBC	X	Ind	30$	BBBB	Ind	
Greek-English	QQ37	4FT deg	* g	BBB	X	Ind	30$	BBBB	Ind	
Hebrew-Arabic	QT96	4FT deg	* g	BBC	X	Ind	30$	BBBB	Ind	
Hebrew-Art History	QV94	4FT deg	* g	BBC	X	Ind	30$	BBBB	Ind	
Hebrew-Biblical Studies	QV98	4FT deg	* g	BBC	X	Ind	30$	BBBB	Ind	
Hebrew-English	QQ39	4FT deg	* g	BBB	X	Ind	30$	BBBB	Ind	
Hebrew-French	QR91	4FT deg	E g	BBB	X	Ind	30$	BBBB	Ind	
Hebrew-French with Year Abroad	QR9C	4FT/5FT deg	E g	BBB	X	Ind	30$	BBBB$	Ind	
Hebrew-Greek	QQ79	4FT deg	* g	BBC	X	Ind	30$	BBBB	Ind	
International Relations-Classical Studies	MQ18	4FT deg	* g	AAB	X	Ind	36$	AAAB	Ind	
Italian with Year Abroad-Classical Studies	RQ3W	4FT/5FT deg	* g	BBB	X	Ind	30$	BBBB	Ind	
Italian with Year Abroad-Classics	RQ3V	4FT/5FT deg	* g	BBB	X	Ind	30$	BBBB	Ind	
Italian with Year Abroad-Greek	RQ37	4FT/5FT deg	* g	BBB	X	Ind	30$	BBBB	Ind	
Italian-Classical Studies	RQ38	4FT deg	* g	BBB	X	Ind	30$	BBBB	Ind	
Italian-Classics	QR83	4FT deg	* g	BBB	X	Ind	30$	BBB	Ind	
Italian-Greek	QR73	4FT deg	* g	BBB	X	Ind	30$	BBBB	Ind	

course details

TITLE	CODE	COURSE	SUBJECTS	A/AS	NO/C	RGNVQ	IB	SQA(H)	SQA	RATIO A/AS
Latin	Q600	4FT deg	* g	BBC	X	Ind	30$	BBBB	Ind	4
Latin-Ancient History	QV61	4FT deg	* g	BBB	X	Ind	30$	BBBB	Ind	
Latin-Arabic	QT66	4FT deg	* g	BBC	X	Ind	30$	BBBB	Ind	
Latin-English	QQ36	4FT deg	* g	BBB	X	Ind	30$	BBBB	Ind	9
Latin-French	QR61	4FT deg	F g	BBB	X	Ind	30$	BBBB$	Ind	3
Latin-French with Year Abroad	QR6C	4FT/5FT deg	F g	BBB	X	Ind	30$	BBBB$	Ind	
Latin-German	QR62	4FT deg	* g	BBC	X	Ind	30$	BBBB	Ind	
Latin-German with Year Abroad	QR6F	4FT/5FT deg	* g	BBC	X	Ind	30$	BBBB	Ind	
Latin-Greek	QQ67	4FT deg	* g	BBC	X	Ind	30$	BBBB	Ind	3
Latin-Italian	QR63	4FT deg	* g	BBB	X	Ind	30$	BBBB	Ind	
Latin-Italian with Year Abroad	RQ36	4FT/5FT deg	* g	BBB	X	Ind	30$	BBBB	Ind	
Management-Classics	NQ18	4FT deg		BBB	Ind	Ind	30$	BBBB$	Ind	
Mathematics-Hebrew	GQ19	4FT deg	M g	BBB	X	Ind	30$	BBBB$	Ind	
Mathematics-Latin	GQ16	4FT deg	M g	BBB	X	Ind	30$	BBBB$	Ind	
Mediaeval History-Classical Studies	QV81	4FT deg	* g	BBB	X	Ind	30$	BBBB	Ind	
Mediaeval History-Latin	QVP1	4FT deg	* g	BBB	X	Ind	30$	BBBB	Ind	
Modern History-Classical Studies	QV8C	4FT deg	* g	BBB	X	Ind	30$	BBBB	Ind	2
New Testament-Classical Studies	VQ78	4FT deg	* g	BBB	X	Ind	30$	BBC	Ind	
New Testament-Greek	QV7W	4FT deg	* g	BBC	X	Ind	30$	BBBB	Ind	
New Testament-Hebrew	QV9V	4FT deg	* g	BBC	X	Ind	30$	BBBB	Ind	
New Testament-Latin	QV6W	4FT deg	* g	BBC	X	Ind	30$	BBBB	Ind	
Philosophy-Greek	QV77	4FT deg	* g	BBB	X	Ind	30$	BBBB	Ind	
Philosophy-Latin	QV67	4FT deg	* g	BBB	X	Ind	30$	BBBB	Ind	
Russian with Year Abroad-Hebrew	QR9V	4FT/5FT deg	* g	BBC	X	Ind	30$	BBBB	Ind	
Russian with Year Abroad-Latin	QRP8	4FT/5FT deg	* g	BBC	X	Ind	30$	BBBB	Ind	
Russian-Hebrew	QR98	4FT deg	* g	BBC	X	Ind	30$	BBBB	Ind	
Russian-Latin	QR68	4FT deg	* g	BBC	X	Ind	30$	BBBB	Ind	
Social Anthropology-Classical Studies	LQ68	4FT deg	* g	BBB	X	Ind	30$	BBBB	Ind	
Spanish with Year Abroad-Latin	QRP4	4FT/5FT deg	* g	BBB	X	Ind	32$	BBBB	Ind	
Spanish-Latin	QR64	4FT deg	* g	BBB	X	Ind	32$	BBBB	Ind	
Theological Studies-Classical Studies	QV88	4FT deg	* g	BBC	X	Ind	30$	BBBB	Ind	
General Degree of MA *Classical Studies*	Y450	3FT deg	* g	BBB	X	Ind	30$	BBB	Ind	
General Degree of MA *Classics*	Y450	3FT deg	* g	BBB	X	Ind	30$	BBB	Ind	
General Degree of MA *Greek*	Y450	3FT deg	* g	BBB	X	Ind	30$	BBBB	Ind	
General Degree of MA *Hebrew*	Y450	3FT deg	* g	BBB	X	Ind	30$	BBBB	Ind	
General Degree of MA *Latin*	Y450	3FT deg	* g	BBB	X	Ind	30$	BBBB	Ind	

ST MARY'S Univ COLL

TITLE	CODE	COURSE	SUBJECTS	A/AS	NO/C	RGNVQ	IB	SQA(H)	SQA	RATIO A/AS
Classical Studies and Biology	CQ18	3FT deg	B/C	4-8	Ind	Ind	Ind	BBBB$	Ind	
Drama and Classical Studies	WQ48	3FT deg	*	8-12	Ind	Ind	Ind	BBBB	Ind	
English and Classical Studies	QQ38	3FT deg	E	8-12	X	X	Ind	BBBB$	X	
Gender Studies and Classical Studies	MQ98	3FT deg	*	4-8	Ind	Ind	Ind	BBBB	Ind	
Geography and Classical Studies	FQ88	3FT deg	Gy	4-8	Ind	Ind	Ind	BBBB$	Ind	
Heritage Management and Classical Studies	NQ98	3FT deg	*	4-8	Ind	Ind	Ind	BBBB	Ind	
History and Classical Studies	VQ18	3FT deg	H	4-8	Ind	Ind	Ind	BBBB$	Ind	
Integrated Scientific Studies and Classical St	QY81	3FT deg	S/2S	4-8	Ind	Ind	Ind	BBBB$	Ind	
Irish Studies and Classical Studies	QQ58	3FT deg	*	4-8	Ind	Ind	Ind	BBBB	Ind	
Media Arts and Classical Studies	PQ48	3FT deg	*	4-8	Ind	Ind	Ind	BBBB	Ind	
Sport Rehabilitation and Classical Studies	BQ98	3FT deg	B g	12-14	X	X	Ind	BBBB$	X	
Theology and Religious Studies and Classical St	VQ88	3FT deg	*	4-8	Ind	Ind	Ind	BBBB	Ind	

Languages – Classical and Ancient 38

			98 expected requirements							96 entry stats	

TITLE	CODE	COURSE	SUBJECTS	A/AS	ND/C	AGNVQ	IB	SQA(H)	SQA	RATIO	A/AS
Univ of Wales SWANSEA											
Ancient History and Civilisation with Greek	V1Q7	3FT deg	*	BCC	X	X	28	BBBBC	X		
Ancient History and Civilisation with Latin	V1Q6	3FT deg	*	BCC	X	X	28	BBBBC	X	2	
Classics	Q800	3FT deg	Ln/Gk	BCC	X	X	28$	BBBBC$	X	7	
Greek & Roman Studies/English Language	QQ38	3FT deg	E	BBC-BCC	X	X	30$	ABBBB	Ind		
Greek and Roman Studies with Greek	Q8Q7	3FT deg	*	BCC	X	X	28	BBBBB	X	1	
Greek and Roman Studies with Latin	Q8Q6	3FT deg	*	BCC	X	X	28	BBBBB	X	1	
Greek and Roman Studies/Economic History	QV83	3FT deg	*	BBC-BCC	Ind	X	28	BBBBB	X		
Greek and Roman Studies/English	QQ83	3FT deg	E	BBC	X	X	30$	ABBBB	X	5	
Greek and Roman Studies/French	QR81	4FT deg	F	BBC-BCC	1M+5D$	X	28$	BBBBB$	X	1	
Greek and Roman Studies/German	QR82	4FT deg	G	BBC-BCC	1M+5D$	X	28$	BBBBB$	X		
Greek and Roman Studies/Greek	QQ78	3									
Greek/Ancient History and Civilisation	VQC7	3FT deg	Gk	BCC	X	X	28$	BBBBB$	X		
Greek/English	QQ37	3FT deg	Gk+E	BB-BCC	X	X	28$	BBBBB$	X		
Greek/English Language	QQ73	3FT deg	E+Gk	BBC-BCC	X	X	30$	ABBBB$	Ind		
Greek/French	QR71	4FT deg	F+Gk	BBC-BCC	X	X	28$	BBBBB$	X		
Greek/German	QR72	4FT deg	Gk+G	BCC	X	X	28$	BBBBB$	X		
History/Greek	QV71	3FT deg	Gk	BBB-BBC	Ind	Ind	30$	ABBBB$	Ind		
History/Greek and Roman Studies	QV81	3FT deg	*	BBB-BBC	Ind	Ind	30	ABBBB	Ind		
Italian/Greek and Roman Studies	QR83	4FT deg	L/*	BBC-BCC	1M+5D$	X	28$	BBBBB$	X		
Latin	Q600	3FT deg	Ln	BCC	X	X	28$	BBBBC$	X		
Latin/Ancient History and Civilisation	VQC6	3FT deg	Ln	BCC	X	X	28$	BBBBC$	X		
Latin/English	QQ36	3FT deg	E+Ln	BBC	X	X	30$	ABBBB	X	3	
Latin/English Language	QQ63	3FT deg	E+Ln	BBC-BCC	X	X	30$	ABBBB$	X		
Latin/French	QR61	4FT deg	F+Ln	BBC-BCC	Ind	X	28$	BBBBB$	X		
Latin/German	QR62	4FT deg	G+Ln	BBC-BCC	Ind	X	28$	BBBBB$	X		
Latin/History	QV61	3FT deg	Ln	BBC	Ind	Ind	28$	BBBBB$	Ind		
Latin/Italian	QR63	4FT deg	Ln	BBC-BCC	Ind	X	28$	BBBBB$	X		
Medieval Studies/Greek	QVR1	3FT deg	Gk+H	BBC-BCC	X	X	28$	BBBBB$	X		
Medieval Studies/Greek and Roman Studies	QV8C	3FT deg	H	BBC	X	X	30$	ABBBB$	C		
Medieval Studies/Latin	QVP1	3FT deg	Ln+H	BBC	X	X	30$	ABBBB$	X		
Philosophy/Greek	QV77	3FT deg	Gk	BBC-BCC	X	X	28$	BBBBB$	X		
Philosophy/Greek and Roman Studies	QV87	3FT deg	*	BBC-BCC	1M+5D	X	28	BBBBB	X		
Spanish/Greek and Roman Studies	QR84	4FT deg	L/*	BBC-BCC	1M+5D$	X	28$	BBBBB$	X		
Spanish/Latin	QR64	4FT deg	Ln	BBC-BCC	Ind	X	28$	BBBBB$	X		
Welsh/Greek	QQ57	3FT/4FT deg	Gk+W	BCC	X	X	28$	BBBBB$	X		
Welsh/Greek and Roman Studies	QQ85	3FT/4FT deg	W	BCC	X	X	28$	BBBBB$	X		
Welsh/Latin	QQ56	3FT/4FT deg	W+Ln	BCC	X	X	28$	BBBBB$	X		
UNIVERSITY COLL LONDON (Univ of London)											
Ancient History and Egyptology	VQ19	3FT deg	g	BBB	3M	Ind	32$	BBBCC	Ind	10	22/28
Ancient World Studies	Q850	3FT deg	g	BCC-BBC	3M	X	30$	BBBCC$	Ind	6	20/26
Archaeology, Classics and Classical Art	VQ68	4FT deg	g	BCC-BBB	3M	Ind	30$	BBBCC	Ind	5	24/26
Classics	Q800	3FT deg	Ln/Gk g	BBC	3M	X	30$	BBBCC$	Ind	10	24/30
Greek (with Latin)	Q7Q6	3FT deg	Gk g	BBC	3M	X	30$	BBBCC$	Ind	4	
Hebrew (4 Yrs)	Q960	4FT deg	* g	CCC	3M	X	28$	BBCCC$	Ind	2	
Italian and Latin (4 Yrs)	RQ36	4FT deg	I/Ln g	BBC	3M	X	30$	BBBBC$	Ind		
Latin (with Greek)	Q6Q7	3FT deg	Ln g	BBC	3M	X	30$	BBBCC$	Ind		
Philosophy and Greek	VQ77	3FT deg	Gk g	BBC	3M	X	30$	BBBBC	Ind		

course details

TITLE	CODE	COURSE
Univ of WARWICK		
Classical Civilisation	Q820	3FT deg
Classical Civilisation with Philosophy	Q8V7	3FT deg
English and Latin Literature	QQ36	3FT deg
Philosophy with Classical Civilisation	V7Q8	3FT deg

98 expected requirements | 96 entry stats

SUBJECTS	A/AS	ND/C	AGNVQ	IB	SQA(H)	SQA	RATIO A/AS
* g	BCC	X	X	30	BBBBC		15 20/26
* g	BCC	X	X	30	BBBBC		6 20/24
Ln+E g	BBB	X	X	34	AABBB		4
* g	BBB	X	X	32	AABBB		14

course details			98 expected requirements							96 entry stats
TITLE	CODE	COURSE	SUBJECTS	A/AS	ND/C	AGNVQ	IB	SQA(H)	SQA	RATIO A/AS
Univ of GLASGOW										
Anthropology with Polish	LT61	4FT deg		BBC	N	M	30	BBBB	Ind	
Archaeology/Czech	TV16	5FT deg		BBC	HN	M	30	BBBB	Ind	
Business Economics with Czech	L1TD	4FT deg		BBC	N	M	30	BBBB	N	
Celtic Civilisation/Czech	QT5C	5FT deg		BBC	HN	M	30	BBBB	Ind	
Celtic Civilisation/Polish	QT5D	5FT deg		BBC	HN	M	30	BBBB	Ind	
Celtic/Czech	QT51	5FT deg		BBC	HN	M	30	BBBB	Ind	
Classical Civilisation/Czech	QT81	5FT deg		BBC	HN	M	30	BBBB	Ind	
Classical Civilisation/Polish	QT8C	5FT deg		BBC	HN	M	30	BBBB	Ind	
Classical Hebrew/Czech	TV1W	5FT deg		BBC	HN	M	30	BBBB	Ind	
Computing/Czech	GT51	5FT deg		BBC	HN	M	30	BBBB	Ind	
Czech/Classical Hebrew	QT91	5FT deg		BBC	HN	M	30	BBBB	Ind	
Czech/Economic History	TV13	5FT deg		BBC	HN	M	30	BBBB	Ind	
Czech/Economics	LTC1	5FT deg		BBC	HN	M	30	BBBB	Ind	
Czech/English	QTH1	5FT deg		BBC	HN	M	30	BBBB	Ind	
Czech/Film and Television Studies	WT51	5FT deg		BBB	HN	D	32	AABB	HN	
Czech/French	RTC1	5FT deg		BBC	HN	M	30	BBBB	Ind	
Czech/Geography	LTV1	5FT deg		BBC	HN	M	30	BBBB	Ind	
Czech/German	RT21	5FT deg		BBC	HN	M	30	BBBB	Ind	
Czech/Greek	QTR1	5FT deg		BBC	HN	M	30	BBBB	Ind	
Czech/Hispanic Studies	RTK1	5FT deg		BBC	HN	M	30	BBBB	Ind	
Czech/History	TV1D	5FT deg		BBC	HN	M	30	BBBB	Ind	
Czech/History of Art	TVC4	5FT deg		BBC	HN	M	30	BBBB	Ind	
Czech/Italian	RTJ1	5FT deg		BBC	HN	M	30	BBBB	Ind	
Czech/Latin	QTP1	5FT deg		BBC	HN	M	30	BBBB	Ind	
Czech/Mathematics	GT11	5FT deg		BBC	HN	M	30	BBBB	Ind	
Czech/Music	TWC3	5FT deg		BBC	HN	M	30	BBBB	Ind	
Czech/Philosophy	TVC7	5FT deg		BBC	HN	M	30	BBBB	Ind	
Czech/Polish	T144	5FT deg		BBC	HN	M	30	BBBB	Ind	
Czech/Politics	MT11	5FT deg		BBC	HN	M	30	BBBB	Ind	
Czech/Psychology	CT81	5FT deg		BBC	HN	M	30	BBBB	Ind	
Czech/Russian	RTV1	5FT deg		BBC	HN	M	30	BBBB	Ind	
Czech/Scottish History	TV1C	5FT deg		BBC	HN	M	30	BBBB	Ind	
Czech/Scottish Literature	QT21	5FT deg		BBC	HN	M	30	BBBB	Ind	
Czech/Sociology	LT31	5FT deg		BBC	HN	M	30	BBBB	Ind	
Czech/Theatre Studies	TW14	5FT deg		BBC	HN	M	30	BBBB	Ind	
Economic and Social History with Czech	V3T1	4FT deg		BBC	8M	M	30	BBBB	Ind	
Economic and Social History with Polish	V3TC	4FT deg		BBC	8M	M	30	BBBB	Ind	
Economics with Czech	L1T1	4FT deg		BBC	8M	M	30	BBBB	Ind	
Economics with Polish	L1TC	4FT deg		BBC	8M	M	30	BBBB	Ind	
English/Polish	QT31	5FT deg		BBC	HN	M	30	BBBB	Ind	
Film and Television Studies/Polish	TW15	5FT deg		BBB	HN	D	32	AABB	HN	
French/Polish	RTD1	5FT deg		BBC	HN	M	30	BBBB	Ind	
Geography with Czech	L8T1	4FT deg		BBC	8M	M	30	BBBB	Ind	
Geography with Polish	L8TC	4FT deg		BBC	8M	M	30	BBBB	Ind	
Geography/Polish	LT81	5FT deg		BBC	HN	M	30	BBBB	Ind	
German/Polish	RTF1	5FT deg		BBC	HN	M	30	BBBB	Ind	
Greek/Polish	QT71	5FT deg		BBC	HN	M	30	BBBB	Ind	
Hispanic Studies/Polish	RT41	5FT deg		BBC	HN	M	30	BBBB	Ind	
History of Art/Polish	TV14	5FT deg		BBC	HN	M	30	BBBB	Ind	
History/Polish	TVD1	5FT deg		BBC	HN	M	30	BBBB	Ind	
Islamic Studies/Czech	TT61	4FT deg		BBC	N	M	30	BBBB	Ind	

TITLE	CODE	COURSE	SUBJECTS	A/AS	ND/C	AGNVQ	IB	SQA(H)	SQA	RATIO A/AS
			98 expected requirements							**96 entry stats**
Islamic Studies/Polish	TT16	4FT deg		BBC	N	M	30	BBBB	Ind	
Italian/Polish	RTH1	5FT deg		BBC	HN	M	30	BBBB	Ind	
Latin/Polish	QT61	5FT deg		BBC	HN	M	30	BBBB	Ind	
Management Studies with Czech	N1T1	4FT deg		BBC	8M	M	30	BBBB	Ind	
Management Studies with Polish	N1TC	4FT deg		BBC	8M	M	30	BBBB	Ind	
Management Studies/Czech	NT11	5FT deg		BBC	HN	M	30	BBBB	Ind	
Management Studies/Polish	NT1C	5FT deg		BBC	HN	M	30	BBBB	Ind	
Music/Polish	TW13	5FT deg		BBC	HN	M	30	BBBB	Ind	
Philosophy with Czech	V7T1	4FT deg		BBC	8M	M	30	BBBB	Ind	
Philosophy with Polish	V7TC	4FT deg		BBC	8M	M	30	BBBB	Ind	
Philosophy/Polish	TV17	5FT deg		BBC	HN	M	30	BBBB	Ind	
Polish/Economics	LT11	5FT deg		BBC	HN	M	30	BBBB	Ind	
Polish/Politics	MTC1	5FT deg		BBC	HN	M	30	BBBB	Ind	
Polish/Russian	RT81	5FT deg		BBC	HN	M	30	BBBB	Ind	
Politics with Czech	M1T1	4FT deg		BBC	8M	M	30	BBBB	Ind	
Politics with Polish	M1TC	4FT deg		BBC	8M	M	30	BBBB	Ind	
Psychology with Czech	C8T1	4FT deg		BBC	8M	M	30	BBBB	Ind	
Psychology with Polish	C8TC	4FT deg		BBC	8M	M	30	BBBB	Ind	
Slavonic and East European Studies	T114	5FT deg		BBC	HN	M	30	BBBB	Ind	
Social and Urban Policy with Czech	L4T1	4FT deg		BBC	8M	M	30	BBBB	Ind	
Social and Urban Policy/Czech	LT41	5FT deg		BBC	HN	M	30	BBBB	Ind	
Social and Urban Policy/Polish	LT4C	5FT deg		BBC	HN	M	30	BBBB	Ind	
Sociology with Czech	L3T1	4FT deg		BBC	8M	M	30	BBBB	Ind	
Sociology with Polish	L3TC	4FT deg		BBC	8M	M	30	BBBB	Ind	
Theatre Studies/Polish	TWC4	5FT deg		BBC	HN	M	30	BBBB	Ind	
Theology & Religious Studies/Czech	TVD8	5FT deg		BBC	HN	M	30	BBBB	Ind	
Theology & Religious Studies/Polish	TVCV	5FT deg		BBC	HN	M	30	BBBB	Ind	

KING'S COLL LONDON (Univ of London)

| German and Czech | RT21 | 4FT deg | | | | | | | | |

Univ of NOTTINGHAM

Geography with East European Studies	L8T1	3FT deg	Gy g	BBC	Ind		Ind	Ind	Ind	
Management Studies with East European Studies	N1T1	3FT deg	g	BBB	Ind	D*6/△ go	32	AAABB	Ind	24/24
Politics with East European Studies	M1T1	3FT deg	*	BBB	Ind		32	Ind	Ind	
Russian and East European Area Studies	RT8C	4FT deg	H/So+L	BBC						10
Russian and Serbo-Croat	RT81	4FT deg	R	CCC						
Serbian and Croatian Studies	T180	3FT deg	g	CCC						
Social Policy with East European Studies	L4T1	3FT deg	*	BBC	Ind	Ind	30	Ind	Ind	
Sociology with East European Studies	L3T1	3FT deg	*	BBC	Ind	Ind	30	Ind	Ind	

SSEES:Sch of Slavonic & E European St(U of London)

Contemporary East European Studies	T118	3FT deg	*	CCC	3M $	Ind	28	BBBBB		1	14/24
East European Langs, Lit and Regional Studies	T191	4FT deg		BCC		Ind		BBBBB		
East European Langs, Lit and Regional Studies	T190	4FT deg		BCC		Ind		BBBBB		
Economics with East European Studies	L1T1	3FT deg		BCC		Ind	28	BBBBB		
Politics with East European Studies	M1T1	3FT deg		BCC		Ind	28	BBBBB		

Univ of SHEFFIELD

| Russian with Czech | R8T1 | 4FT deg | L g | BCC | X | X | 29$ | BBBB$ | Ind | |
| Russian with Polish | R8TC | 4FT deg | L g | BCC | X | X | 29$ | BBBB$ | Ind | |

Languages – French 40

Univ of ABERDEEN

TITLE	CODE	COURSE	SUBJECTS	A/AS	ND/C	AGNVQ	IB	SQA(H)	SQA	RATIO A/AS
Accountancy with French	N4R1	4FT deg	* g	BBC	Ind	M$ go	30$	BBBB$	Ind	13
Accountancy-French	NR41	4FT/5FT deg	* g	BBC	Ind	M$ go	30$	BBBB$	Ind	4
Celtic-French	QR51	4FT/5FT deg	* g	BBC	Ind	M$ go	30$	BBBB$	Ind	
Celtic-French (4 Yrs)	RQ15	4FT deg	* g	BBC	Ind	M$ go	30$	BBBB$	Ind	
Chemistry with French	F1R1	4FT deg	C+2S/C+M+S g	CCD	Ind	MS go	24$	BBBC$	Ind	7
Computing Science with French	G5R1	4FT deg	M+2S g	CCD	Ind	MS go	24$	BBBC$	Ind	2
Economics-French	LR11	4FT/5FT deg	* g	BBC	Ind	M$ go	30$	BBBB$	Ind	3
Economics-French (4 Yrs)	RL11	4FT deg	* g	BBC	Ind	M$ go	30$	BBBB$	Ind	
English-French	QR31	4FT/5FT deg	* g	BBC	Ind	M$ go	30$	BBBB$	Ind	3
English-French (4 Yrs)	RQ13	4FT deg	* g	BBC	Ind	M$ go	30$	BBBB$	Ind	
French Studies	R100	4FT/5FT deg	* g	BBC	Ind	M$ go	30$	BBBB$	Ind	6
French Studies (4 Yrs)	R101	4FT deg	* g	BBC	Ind	M$ go	30$	BBBB$	Ind	
French with Film Studies	R1W5	4FT/5FT deg	* g	BBC	Ind	M$ go	30$	BBBB$	Ind	17
French with Film Studies (4 Yrs)	R1WM	4FT deg	* g	BBC	Ind	M$ go	30$	BBBB$	Ind	
French with Women's Studies	R1M9	5FT deg	* g	BBC	Ind	M^ go	30$	BBBB$	Ind	
French with Women's Studies (4 Yrs)	R1MX	4FT deg	* g	BBC	Ind	M$ go	30$	BBBB$	Ind	
French-Entrepreneurship	RN1C	5FT deg	* g	BBC	Ind	M$ go	30$	BBBB$	Ind	
French-Entrepreneurship (4 Yrs)	NRC1	4FT deg	* g	BBC	Ind	M$ go	30$	BBBB$	Ind	
French-Geography	LR81	4FT/5FT deg	* g	BBC	Ind	M$ go	30$	BBBB$	Ind	5
French-German	RR12	4FT/5FT deg	* g	BBC	Ind	M$ go	30$	BBBB$	Ind	5
French-German with Education	RR21	5FT deg	* g	BBC	Ind	M$ go	30$	BBBB$	Ind	
French-Hispanic Studies	RR14	4FT/5FT deg	* g	BBC	Ind	M$ go	30$	BBBB$	Ind	6
French-Hispanic Studies with Education	RR41	5FT deg	* g	BBC	Ind	M$ go	30$	BBBB$	Ind	
French-History	RV11	4FT/5FT deg	* g	BBC	Ind	M$ go	30$	BBBB$	Ind	11
French-History (4 Yrs)	VR11	4FT deg	* g	BBC	Ind	M$ go	30$	BBBB$	Ind	
French-History of Art	RV14	4FT/5FT deg	* g	BBC	Ind	M$ go	30$	BBBB$	Ind	7
French-History of Art (4 Yrs)	VR41	4FT deg	* g	BBC	Ind	M$ go	30$	BBBB$	Ind	
French-International Relations	RM1C	4FT/5FT deg	* g	BBC	Ind	M$ go	30$	BBBB$	Ind	7
French-International Relations (4 Yrs)	MRC1	4FT deg	* g	BBC	Ind	M$ go	30$	BBBB$	Ind	
French-Management Studies	RN11	4FT/5FT deg	* g	BBC	Ind	M$ go	30$	BBBB$	Ind	13
French-Management Studies (4 Yrs)	NR11	4FT deg	* g	BBC	Ind	M$ go	30$	BBBB$	Ind	
French-Mathematics	RG11	5FT deg	* g	BBC	Ind	M$ go	30$	BBBB$	Ind	
French-Mathematics (4 Yrs)	GR11	4FT deg	* g	BBC	Ind	M$ go	30$	BBBB$	Ind	
French-Philosophy	RV17	4FT/5FT deg	* g	BBC	Ind	M$ go	30$	BBBB$	Ind	8
French-Philosophy (4 Yrs)	VR71	4FT deg	* g	BBC	Ind	M$ go	30$	BBBB$	Ind	
French-Politics	RM11	4FT/5FT deg	* g	BBC	Ind	M$ go	30$	BBBB$	Ind	5
French-Politics (4 Yrs)	MR11	4FT deg	* g	BBC	Ind	M$ go	30$	BBBB$	Ind	
French-Social Research	LR31	4FT/5FT deg	* g	BBC	Ind	M$ go	30$	BBBB$	Ind	
French-Social Research (4 Yrs)	LR3C	4FT deg	* g	BBC	Ind	M$ go	30$	BBBB$	Ind	
French-Sociology	RL13	4FT/5FT deg	* g	BBC	Ind	M$ go	30$	BBBB$	Ind	
French-Sociology (4 Yrs)	RL1H	4FT deg	* g	BBC	Ind	M$ go	30$	BBBB$	Ind	
Mathematics with French	G1R1	4FT deg	M+2S g	CCD	Ind	MS go	24$	BBBC$	Ind	
Physics with French	F3R1	4FT deg	2S+M g	CCD	Ind	MS go	24$	BBBC$	Ind	
Psychology with French	C8R1	4FT deg	3S/2S+M g	CCD	Ind	MS go	24$	BBBC$	Ind	
Psychology with French (MA)	C8RC	4FT deg	* g	BBC	Ind	M$ go	30$	BBBB$	Ind	
Religious Studies-French	VR81	4FT/5FT deg	* g	BBC	Ind	M$ go	30$	BBBB$	Ind	
Religious Studies-French (4 Yrs)	RV18	4FT deg	* g	BBC	Ind	M$ go	30$	BBBB$	Ind	
Theology with French	V8R1	3FT deg	* g	CC	Ind	M* go	24$	BBCC	Ind	

Univ of Wales, ABERYSTWYTH

Computer Science with French	G5R1	4FT deg	E g	20	1M+5D$ M^ g		30$	BBBBC$	Ind	
European Studies and French	RT1F	4FT deg	E g	20	1M+5D$ M^ g		30$	BBBBC$	Ind	

course details   98 expected requirements   *96 entry stats*

TITLE	CODE	COURSE	SUBJECTS	A/AS	NO/C	RGNVQ	IB	SQA(H)	SQA	RATIO A/AS
French	R100	4FT deg	F g	18	1M+5D$	M^ g	29$	BBBCC$	Ind	
French/American Studies	QR41	4FT deg	F+E/H g	18	1M+5D$	M^ g	29$	BBBCC$	Ind	
French/Art	RW11	4FT deg	F+A/Ad g	18	1M+5D$	MA^ g	29$	BBBCC$	Ind	
French/Art History	RV14	4FT deg	F g	18	1M+5D$	MA^ g	29$	BBBCC$	Ind	
French/Drama	RW14	4FT deg	F g	20	1M+5D$	MQ^ g	30$	BBBBC$	Ind	
French/Economic & Social History	RV13	4FT deg	F g	18-20	1M+5D$	M^ g	30$	BBBBC$	Ind	
French/Education	RX19	4FT deg	F g	18	1M+5D$	M^ g	29$	BBBCC$	Ind	
French/English	QR31	4FT deg	El+F	20	1M+5D$	M^ g	30$	BBBBC$	Ind	
French/European Studies	RT12	4FT deg	F g	20	1M+5D$	M^ g	30$	BBBBC$	Ind	
French/Film and Television Studies	RW15	4FT deg	F g	20	1M+5D$	MQ^ g	30$	BBBBC$	Ind	
Geography/French	LR81	4FT deg	F+Gy g	20-22	1M+5D$	M^ g	31$	BBBBC$	Ind	
German/French	RR12	4FT deg	G+F g	18	1M+5D$	M^ g	29$	BBBCC$	Ind	
History/French	RV11	4FT deg	F g	18-20	1M+5D$	M^ g	30$	BBBBC$	Ind	
Information and Library Studies/French	PR21	4FT deg	F g	18	1M+5D$	M^ g	29$	BBBCC$	Ind	
International Politics/French	MRD1	4FT deg	F g	20	1M+5D$	M^ g	30$	BBBBC$	Ind	
Irish/French	QRM1	4FT deg	F g	18	1M+5D$	M^ g	29$	BBBCC$	Ind	
Italian/French	RR13	4FT deg	F g	18	1M+5D$	M^ g	29$	BBBCC$	Ind	
Law with French (BA)	M3RD	4FT deg	F g	BBB	DO $	D^ g	32$	BBBCC$	Ind	
Law with French (LLB)	M3R1	4FT deg	F g	BBB	DO $	D^ g	32$	BBBCC$	Ind	
Politics/French	MR11	4FT deg	F g	20	1M+5D$	M^ g	30$	BBBBC$	Ind	
Pure Mathematics/French	GRC1	4FT deg	F+M g	18	1M+5D$	M^ g	29$	BBBCC$	Ind	
Spanish/French	RR14	4FT deg	F g	18	1M+5D$	M^ g	29$	BBBCC$	Ind	
Welsh History/French	RV1D	4FT deg	F g	18-20	1M+5D$	M^ g	30$	BBBBC$	Ind	
Welsh/French	QR51	4FT deg	F+W g	18	1M+5D$	M^ g	29$	BBBCC$	Ind	

ANGLIA Poly Univ

TITLE	CODE	COURSE	SUBJECTS	A/AS	NO/C	RGNVQ	IB	SQA(H)	SQA	RATIO A/AS
Animal Behaviour and French	CR1C▼	4FT deg	g	12	4M	P go	Dip	BCCC	N	
Art History and French	RV14▼	4FT deg	* g	14	6M	M+/^ go	Dip	BBCC	Ind	3
Audiotechnology and French	HR6C▼	4FT deg	S g	16	8M	D+/^ go	Dip$	BBCCC	N	
Biology and French	CR11▼	4FT deg	B g	12	4M	P+/^	Dip$	BCCC	N	
Biomedical Science and French	BR91▼	4FT deg	B g	12	4M	M+/^ go	Dip$	BCCC	N	1
Business and French	NR11▼	4FT deg	* g	12	4M	M+/^ go	Dip	BCCC	Ind	10
Chemistry and French	FR11▼	4FT deg	S g	12	4M	M go	Dip$	BCCC	Ind	
Communication Studies and French	PR31▼	4FT deg	Ap g	14	6M	M+/^ go	Dip$	BBCC	Ind	19
Computer Science and French	GR51▼	4FT deg	* g	12	4M	M go	Dip	BCCC	Ind	4
Ecology and Conservation and French	DR21▼	4FT deg	* g	12	4M	M+/^ go	Dip	BCCC	N	
Economics and French	LR11▼	4FT deg	* g	12	4M	M+/^ go	Dip	BCCC	Ind	
English Language Studies and French	QR11▼	4FT deg	* g	12	4M	M go	Dip	BCCC		
English and French	QR31▼	4FT deg	E g	12	4M	M+/^ go	Dip	BCCC	Ind	24
European Philosophy & Literature and French	RV17▼	4FT deg	* g	12	4M	M+/^ go	Dip	BCCC	Ind	6
French and Geography	LR81▼	4FT deg	Gy g	12	4M	M+/^ go	Dip$	BCCC	Ind	
French and Geology	RF16▼	4FT deg	S g	12	4M	M+/^ go	Dip$	BCCC	Ind	
French and German	RR12▼	4FT deg	F/G	12	4M	M	Dip$	BCCC	Ind	4
French and Graphic Arts	RW12▼	4FT deg	A g	14	6M	M+/^ go	Dip$	BBCC		
French and History	RV11▼	4FT deg	* g	12	4M	M+/^ go	Dip	BCCC	Ind	
French and Intercultural Studies	RL16▼	4FT deg	* g	12	4M	M go		BCCC		
French and Italian	RR13▼	4FT deg	F/I	12	4M	M	Ind$	BCCC	Ind	4
French and Law	MR31▼	4FT deg	* g	14	6M	M go	Dip	BBCC	Ind	
French and Maths or Stats/Statistical Modelling	GR11▼	4FT deg	* g	12	4M	M go	Dip	BCCC	Ind	
French and Music	RW13▼	4FT deg	Mu g	12	4M	M+/^ go	Dip$	BCCC	Ind	5
French and Ophthalmic Dispensing	BR51▼	4FT deg	* g	12	4M	M+/^ go	Dip	BCCC	Ind	
French and Politics	RM11▼	4FT deg	* g	14	6M	M go	Dip	BBCC	Ind	
French and Psychology	CR81▼	3FT deg	S g	16	8M	D go	Dip$	BBCC	Ind	

| | | | 98 expected requirements | | | | | | | 96 entry stats | |
| course details | | | | | | | | | | | |
TITLE	CODE	COURSE	SUBJECTS	A/AS	NO/C	RGNVQ	IB	SQA(H)	SQA	RATIO	A/AS
French and Social Policy	RL14▼	4FT deg	* g	12	4M	M	Dip	BCCC	Ind		
French and Sociology	LR31▼	4FT deg	* g	12	4M	M go	Dip	BCCC	Ind	8	
French and Spanish	RR14▼	4FT deg	F/Sp g	12	4M	M go	Ind$	BCCC	Ind	5	8/12
French and Women's Studies	RM19▼	4FT deg	* g	12	4M	M go	Dip	BCCC	Ind	2	

ASTON Univ

European Studies with French	T2R1	4SW deg	E g	BBC	3M+7D$	D$6/^ go	32$	AABBC$	Ind	3	14/26
French	R100	4SW deg	E g	BBC	3M+7D$		32$	AABBC$	Ind	2	16/20
French and German	RR12	4SW deg	F+G g	BBC	3M+7D$		32$	ABBBC$	Ind	6	18/26
French/Business Administration	NR11	4SW deg	F g	20	X	D$^ go	30$	BBBBB$	Ind	4	16/24
French/Chemistry	FR11	4SW deg	C+F g	20	X	X	30$	BBBBB$	Ind		
French/Computer Science	GR51	4SW deg	F g	20	X	D$6/^ go	30$	BBBBB$	Ind	7	
French/Electronics	HR61	4SW deg	M/P+F g	20	X	X	30$	BBBBB$	Ind		
French/Environmental Science & Technology	FR91	4SW deg	S+F g	20	X		30$	BBBBB$	Ind		
French/Ergonomics	JRX1	4SW deg	F g	20	5M+5D$	D$6/^ go	30$	BBBBB$	Ind		
Health & Safety Management/French	JR91	4SW deg	F g	20	X	D$^ go	30$	BBBBB$	Ind		
Human Psychology/French	LR71	4SW deg	F g	20	X	D$^ go	30$	BBBBB$	Ind	4	20/24
International Business and French	NRC1	4SW deg	E g	BBB	3M+7D$	D$^ go	31$	AABBB$	Ind	6	20/30
Mathematics/French	GR11	4SW deg	F+M g	20	X	X	31$	ABBBB$	Ind		
Medicinal Chemistry/French	FR1C	4SW deg	C+F g	20	3M+7D$	X		30$	BBBBB$	Ind	
Modern Languages with Translation Studies	RR1F	4FT deg	F+G g	BBC							
Product Design (Engineering)/French	HR71	3FT/4SW deg	S+F g	20	X	X	30$	BBBBB$			
Social Studies/French	LR41	4SW deg	F g	20	X	D$^ go	30$	BBBBB$	Ind	4	

Univ of Wales, BANGOR

Computer Systems with French (4 yrs)	H6R1	4FT deg	E g	CC	X	M$^ go	26$	BBCC$	X		
European Cultural Studies and French	TR21	4FT deg	E g	CCD	X	D*^ go	28$	BBBC$	X		
European Cultural Studies and French(Syllabus B)	TR2C	3FT deg	E g	CCD	X	D*^ go	28$	BBBC$	X		
French	R101	4FT deg	E g	CCD	X	D*^ go	28$	BBBC$	X	7	
French (Syllabus A) and Women's Studies	MR91	4FT deg	E g	18	X	D*^ go	28$	BBBC$	X		
French (Syllabus A)/Accounting	NR41	4FT deg	E g	18	X	D$^ go	28$	BBBC$	X		
French (Syllabus A)/Banking	NR31	4FT deg	E g	18	X	D$^ go	28$	BBBC$	X		
French (Syllabus A)/Economics	LR11	4FT deg	E g	18	X	D$^ go	28$	BBBC$	X		
French (Syllabus A)/English	QR31	4FT deg	E+F g	CCC	X	D*^ go	28$	BBBC$	X	6	
French (Syllabus B) and Women's Studies	MR9C	4FT deg	E g	18	X	D*^ go	28$	BBBC$	X		
French (Syllabus B)/Accounting	NR4C	4FT deg	E g	18	X	D$^ go	28$	BBBC$	X		
French (Syllabus B)/Banking	NR3C	4FT deg	E g	18	X	D$^ go	28$	BBBC$	X		
French (Syllabus B)/Economics	LR1C	4FT deg	E g	18	X	D$^ go	28$	BBBC$	X		
French (Syllabus B)/English	QR3C	4FT deg	E+F g	CCC	X	D$^ go	28$	BBBC$	X	6	
French A and Criminology	MR31	4FT deg	E g	18	X	D*^ go	28$	BBBC$	X		
French B and Criminology	MR3C	4FT deg	E g	18	X	D*^ go	28$	BBBC$	X		
French Language and Modern France	R112	4FT deg	E g	CCD	X	D*^ go	28$	BBBC$	X	2	10/20
French Syllabus (B) and Management	NR1C	4FT deg	E g	18	X	D$^ go	28$	BBBC$	X		
German/French (Syllabus A)	RR12	4FT deg	E g	CCD	X	D*^ go	28$	BBBC$	X	4	
German/French (Syllabus B)	RRC2	4FT deg	E g	CCD	X	D*^ go	28$	BBBC$	X	3	
History/French (Syllabus A)	RV11	4FT deg	F+H g	CCC	X	D*^ go	28$	BBBC$	X		
History/French (Syllabus B)	RVC1	4FT deg	F+H g	CCC	X	D*^ go	28$	BBBC$	X		
Linguistics/French (Syllabus A)	QR11	4FT deg	E g	CCD	X	D*^ go	28$	BBBC$	X	5	
Linguistics/French (Syllabus B)	QR1C	4FT deg	E g	CCD	X	D*^ go	28$	BBBC$	X	3	
Management and French Syllabus (A)	NR11	4FT deg	E g	18	X	D$^ go	28$	BBBC$	X		
Physical Education/French (Syllabus A)	RB16	4FT deg	E g	20	X	D*^ go	30$	BBBB$	X		
Physical Education/French (Syllabus B)	RBC6	4FT deg	E g	20	X	D*^ go	30$	BBBB$	X		
Russian/French (Syllabus A)	RR18	4FT deg	E g	CCD	X	D*^ go	28$	BBBC$	X		

TITLE	CODE	COURSE	SUBJECTS	A/AS	ND/C	AGNVQ	IB	SQA(H)	SQA	RATIO A/AS	
Russian/French (Syllabus B)	RRC8	4FT deg	F g	CCD	X	D*△ go	28$	BBBC$	X		
Sports Science/French (Syllabus A)	BR61	4FT deg	F g	20	X	D*△ go	30$	BBBB$	X		
Sports Science/French (Syllabus B)	BR6C	4FT deg	F g	20	X	D*△ go	30$	BBBB$	X		
Welsh/French (Syllabus A)	QR51	4FT deg	F+W g	CCD	X	D*△ go	Ind	X	X		
Welsh/French (Syllabus B)	QR5C	4FT deg	F+W g	CCD	X	D*△ go	Ind	X	X		

Univ of BATH

French and German (4 Yr SW)	RR12	4SW deg	F+G	BBC	Ind	Ind	30	Ind	Ind	5	18/28
French and Italian (4 Yr SW)	RR13	4SW deg	F+I	BBC	Ind	Ind	30	Ind	Ind	6	24/26
French and Russian (4 Yr SW)	RR18	4SW deg	F+R	BBC	Ind	Ind	30	Ind	Ind	3	
French and ab initio Italian or Russian(4 Yr SW)	R100	4SW deg	F	BBC	Ind	Ind	30	Ind	Ind	3	12/28
International Mgt and Modern Lang-French (4 Yr)	NR11	4SW deg	F	BBB	Ind	Ind	30	Ind	Ind	7	24/30

Univ of BIRMINGHAM

Accounting & Finance with French	N4R1	4FT deg	F	BBC	Ind	D+^	32	ABBBB	Ind	7	20/28
African Studies/French Studies	RT17	4FT deg	F	BBB	Ind	D*△	32$	ABBB	Ind	5	
American Studies/French Studies	QR41	4FT deg	F	BBB	Ind	D*△	32$	ABBB	Ind		
Ancient History & Archaeology/French Studies	RV16	4FT deg	F	BBB	Ind	D*△	32$	ABBB	Ind		
Artificial Intelligence/French Studies	GR81	4FT deg	F g	BBB	Ind	D*△	32$	ABBB	Ind		
BCom (Business Administration) with French	NR11	4FT deg	F	BBB	Ind	D+^	32	ABBBB	Ind	8	24/30
Business Studies/French Studies	RN11	4FT deg	F g	BBB	Ind	D*△	32$	ABBB	Ind	16	24/28
Chemistry with French	F1R1	3FT deg	C+M	BBB	Ind	Ind	34	Ind	Ind	6	
Computer Studies/French Studies	GR51	4FT deg	F g	BBB	Ind	D*△	32$	ABBB	Ind		
Dance/French Studies	WR41	4FT deg	F	BBB	Ind	D*△	32$	ABBB	Ind	3	
Drama/French Studies	RW14	4FT deg	F	BBB	Ind	D*△	32$	ABBB	Ind	17	
East Mediterranean History/French Studies	RVCC	4FT deg	F g	BBB	Ind	D*△	32	ABBB	Ind		
Economics with French	L1R1	4FT deg	F	BBB	Ind	D+^	32	ABBBB	Ind	7	22/28
English/French Studies	QR31	4FT deg	F	ABB	Ind	D*△	32$	ABBB	Ind	12	28/30
French Studies	R100	4FT deg	F	BBC	Ind	D*△	32$	ABBB	Ind	5	20/28
French Studies and German Studies	RR12	4FT deg	F+G	BBB	Ind	D*△	32$	ABBB	Ind	6	24/30
French Studies and Hispanic Studies	RR14	4FT deg	F	BBB	Ind	D*△	32$	ABBB	Ind	12	24/30
French Studies and Italian	RR13	4FT deg	F	BBB	Ind	D*△	32$	ABBB	Ind	13	24/28
French Studies and Modern Greek Studies	RTC2	4FT deg	F g	BBB	Ind	D*△	32$	ABBB	Ind	3	
French Studies and Portuguese	RR15	4FT deg	F	BBB	Ind	D*△	32$	ABBB	Ind	11	
French Studies and Russian	RR18	4FT deg	F	BBB	Ind	D*△	32$	ABBB	Ind	8	
French Studies/Classical Lit and Civilisation	QR81	4FT deg	F	BBB	Ind	D*△	32$	ABBB	Ind		
French Studies/Geography	LR81	4FT deg	F+Gy	BBB	Ind	D*△	32$	ABBB	Ind	11	
French Studies/History	RV11	4FT deg	F	BBB	Ind	D*△	32	ABBB	Ind	8	28/30
French Studies/History of Art	RV14	4FT deg	F	BBB	Ind	D*△	32$	ABBB	Ind	25	
French Studies/Latin	QR61	4FT deg	F+Ln	BBB	Ind	D*△	32$	ABBB	Ind		
French Studies/Mathematics	GR11	4FT deg	F+M	ABB-ABC	Ind	D*△	32$	ABBB	Ind	7	
French Studies/Media & Cultural Studies	PR41	4FT deg	F	BBB	Ind	D*△	32$	ABBB	Ind	68	
French Studies/Music	RW13	4FT deg	F+Mu	AAB-ABB	Ind	D*△	32$	ABBB	Ind	5	24/30
French Studies/Philosophy	RV17	4FT deg	F	BBB	Ind	D*△	32$	ABBB	Ind		
French Studies/Political Science	MR11	4FT deg	F	BBB	Ind	D*△	32$	ABBB	Ind	27	
French Studies/Sport & Recreation Studies	RB16	4FT deg	F	BBB	Ind	D*△	32$	ABBB	Ind		
French Studies/Theology	RV18	4FT deg	F	BBB	Ind	D*△	32$	ABBB	Ind		
International Studies with French	M1R1	4FT deg	F	BBC	Ind	D+^	32	ABBBB	Ind	7	22/30
Law with French	MR31	4FT deg	F	AAB	DO	X	35$	CSYS	Ind	8	26/30
Money, Banking and Finance with French	N3R1	4FT deg	F	BBB	Ind	D+^	33	ABBBB	Ind	6	26/26

BOLTON INST

Accountancy and French	NR41	3FT deg	F g	CD	Ind	Ind	24	BBCC	Ind		
Architectural Technology and French	KR21	3FT deg	F g	10	3M	Ind	Ind	Ind	Ind		

Languages – French   40

				98 expected requirements						96 entry stats

TITLE	CODE	COURSE	SUBJECTS	A/AS	ND/C	AGNVQ	IB	SQA(H)	SQA	RATIO A/AS
Art & Design History and French	VR41	3FT deg	E g	CD	Ind	Ind	24	BBCC	Ind	
Biology and French	CR11	3FT deg	E g	CD	Ind	Ind	24	BBCC	Ind	
Building Surveying and French	KRF1	3FT deg	E g	10	3M	Ind	Ind	Ind	Ind	
Business Economics and French	LR11	3FT deg	E g	CD	Ind	Ind	24	BBCC	Ind	
Business Information Systems and French	GR5C	3FT deg	E g	CD	Ind	Ind	24	BBCC	Ind	
Business Studies and French	NR11	3FT deg	E g	CD	Ind	Ind	24	BBCC	Ind	
Civil Engineering and French	HR21	3FT deg	F+M/S	10	3M	Ind	Ind	Ind	Ind	
Community Studies and French	LR51	3FT deg	E g	CD	Ind	Ind	24	BBCC	Ind	
Computing and French	GR51	3FT deg	E g	CD	Ind	Ind	24	BBCC	Ind	
Construction and French	KRG1	3FT deg	E g	10	3M	Ind	Ind	Ind	Ind	
Creative Writing and French	RQ13	3FT deg	E g	CD	Ind	Ind	24	BBCC	Ind	
Design and French	RW12	3FT deg	E g	CD	Ind	Ind	24	BBCC	Ind	
Electronics and French	HRP1	3FT deg	F+M/S	10	3M	Ind	Ind	Ind	Ind	
Environmental Studies and French	RF19	3FT deg	E g	CD	Ind	Ind	24	BBCC	Ind	
Environmental Technology and French	KR31	3FT deg	F+S g	10	3M	Ind	Ind	Ind	Ind	
European Cultural Studies and French	TR21	3FT deg	E g	CD	Ind	Ind	24	BBCC	Ind	
European Cultural Studies and French	RT12	3FT deg	E g	CD	Ind	Ind	24	BBCC	Ind	
Film and TV Studies and French	RW15	3FT deg	Me/T+F g	CD	Ind	Ind	24	BBCC	Ind	
French and Gender and Women's Studies	RM19	3FT deg	E g	CD	Ind	Ind	24	BBCC	Ind	
French and German	RR12	3FT deg	F+G	CD	Ind	Ind	24	BBCC	Ind	
French and History	RV11	3FT deg	E g	CD	Ind	Ind	24	BBCC	Ind	
French and Human Resource Management	NR1C	3FT deg	E g	CD	Ind	Ind	24	BBCC	Ind	
French and Law	RM13	3FT deg	E g	CD	Ind	Ind	24	BBCC	Ind	
French and Leisure Studies	RL1H	3FT deg	E g	CD	Ind	Ind	24	BBCC	Ind	
French and Literature	RQ12	3FT deg	E g	CD	Ind	Ind	24	BBCC	Ind	
French and Manufacturing Systems Design	RH17	3FT deg	E g	10	Ind	Ind	Ind	Ind	Ind	
French and Marketing	NR51	3FT deg	E g	CD	Ind	Ind	24	BBCC	Ind	
French and Mathematics	RG11	3FT deg	F+M g	CD	Ind	Ind	24	BBCC	Ind	
French and Motor Vehicle Studies	RH1J	3FT deg	F+M/S g	10	Ind	Ind	Ind	Ind	Ind	
French and Occupational Health & Safety	RN16	3FT deg	E g	10	Ind	Ind	Ind	Ind	Ind	
French and Operations Management	NR21	3FT deg	E g	CD	Ind	Ind	24	BBCC	Ind	
French and Organisations, Management & Work	NR71	3FT deg	E g	CD	Ind	Ind	24	BBCC	Ind	
French and Peace and War Studies	RV1C	3FT deg	E g	CD	Ind	Ind	24	BBCC	Ind	
French and Philosophy	RV17	3FT deg	E g	CD	Ind	Ind	24	BBCC	Ind	
French and Product Design	RH1T	3FT deg	E g	CD	Ind	Ind	24	BBCC	Ind	
French and Psychology	RL17	3FT deg	E g	12	Ind	Ind	24	BBCC	Ind	
French and Quantity Surveying	RK1F	3FT deg	E g	10	3M	Ind	Ind	Ind	Ind	
French and Simulation/Virtual Environment	RG17	3FT deg	E g	10	3M	Ind	Ind	Ind	Ind	
French and Sociology	LR31	3FT deg	E g	CD	Ind	Ind	24	Ind	Ind	
French and Technology Management	RN19	3FT deg	E g	10	3M	Ind	Ind	Ind	Ind	
French and Textiles	JR41	3FT deg	E g	10	3M	Ind	Ind	Ind	Ind	
French and Theatre Studies	RW14	3FT deg	F+Me/T g	CD	Ind	Ind	24	BBCC	Ind	
French and Tourism Studies	RP17	3FT deg	E g	CD	Ind	Ind	24	BBCC	Ind	
French and Transport Studies	RJ19	3FT deg	F+M/S g	10	3M	Ind	Ind	Ind	Ind	
French and Urban and Cultural Studies	RL13	3FT deg	E g	CD	Ind	Ind	24	BBCC	Ind	
International Business (French)	N1R1	3FT deg	* g	CD	MO	M*	24	BBCC	Ind	
International Tourism (French)	P7R1	3FT deg	* g	CD	MO	M*	24	BBCC	Ind	
Visual Arts and French	WR11	3FT deg	E g	CD	Ind	Ind	24	BBCC	Ind	

Univ of BRADFORD

French	R100	4SW deg	F	BCC	Ind	X	Ind	Ind	Ind	
French and German	RR12	4SW deg	2L	BCC	Ind	X	Ind	Ind	Ind	4 12/30
French and Russian	RR18	4SW deg	2L	BCC	Ind	X	Ind	Ind	Ind	5

course details			98 expected requirements							96 entry stats	
TITLE	CODE	COURSE	SUBJECTS	A/AS	ND/C	AGNVQ	IB	SQA(H)	SQA	RATIO	A/AS
French and Spanish	RR14	4SW deg	2L	BCC	Ind	X	Ind	Ind	Ind	5	10/30
International Management and French	N1R1	4SW deg	F g	22	DO $	D$^	Ind	Ind	Ind	5	16/28

Univ of BRIGHTON

Language Studies with Business	T9N1	3FT/4SW deg	F/G g	14	2M+3D$ Ind		Dip$	BBCC$	Ind		
Language Studies with Linguistics	T9Q1	3FT/4SW deg	F/G g	14	2M+3D$ Ind		Dip$	BBCC$	Ind		

Univ of BRISTOL

Computer Science and French	RG15	4FT deg	F g	BBC	Ind	D$^	30$	CSYS	Ind	13	
Drama and French	WR41	4FT deg	F	BC	Ind	D$^	28$	BBBBB	Ind	12	28/30
French	R100	4FT deg	F	BBC	Ind	D$^	30$	CSYS	Ind	9	22/30
French and German	RR12	4FT deg	F+G	ABB-BBB	Ind	D$^	30$	AABBB	Ind	13	24/30
French and Italian	RR13	4FT deg	F	ABB-BBB	Ind	D$^	30$	AABBB	Ind	7	24/30
French and Latin	RQ16	4FT deg	F+Ln	BBC	Ind	D$^	30$	BBBBB	Ind	4	30/30
French and Russian	RR18	4FT deg	F	BBB-BBC	Ind	D$^	30$	BBBBB	Ind	7	20/30
French and Spanish	RR14	4FT deg	F	ABB-BBB	Ind	D$^	30$	AABBB	Ind	9	24/30
History of Art and French	VR41	4FT deg	F	BBC	Ind	D$^	30$	BBBBB	Ind	5	24/28
Law and French	MR31	4FT deg	F	ABB	Ind	D$^	34$	AAABB	Ind	37	28/30
Music and French	WR31	4FT deg	Mu+F	BBC	Ind	D$^	30$	BBBBC	Ind		
Philosophy and French	RV17	4FT deg	F g	BBB	Ind	D$^	30$	CSYS	Ind	20	
Politics and French	RM11	4FT deg	F	ABB	Ind	D$^	33$	ABBBB	Ind	10	26/30

BRISTOL, Univ of the W of England

EFL, French and European Studies	QR31	4FT deg	g	14-24	5M	M*^ go	24$	BCCC$	Ind		
French and Business Systems	RN11	3FT deg	F g	14-22	5M	M*^ go	24$	BCCC$	Ind		
French and European Studies	RT12	4FT deg	F g	14-24	5M	M*^ go	24$	BCCC$	Ind		
French and Information Systems	RG15	3FT deg	F g	14-22	5M	M*^ go	24$	BCCC$	Ind		
French and Law	RM13	4FT deg	F g	16-24	MO	M*^ go	24$	BBCC$	Ind		
French, German and European Studies	RR12	4FT deg	F/G g	14-24	5M	M*^ go	24$	BCCC$	Ind		
French, Spanish and European Studies	RR14	4FT deg	F/Sp g	14-24	5M	M*^ go	24$	BCCC$	Ind		

BRITISH INST in Paris (Univ of London)

French Studies (3 years)	R100	3FT deg	F	ABB	X	X	Ind	Ind	X	4	20/22

BRUNEL Univ, West London

Business Mathematics with French	RG1C	3FT deg	M+F g	BBC-BCC	3M+2D$	D^+	29$	BBBC$	Ind		
Business Mathematics with French (4 Yrs Thin SW)	RG11	4SW deg	M+F g	BBC-BCC	3M+2D$	D^+	29$	BBBC$	Ind	2	
Business Mathematics with French(4 Yrs Thick SW)	G1RC	4SW deg	M+F g	BBC-BCC	3M+2D$	D^	29$	BBBC$	Ind	2	
Law with French (4 Yrs Thick SW)	M3R1	4SW deg	F	BBB	DO $	D^	30$	ABBBB$	Ind		
Manufacturing Eng with Fr (MEng) (4Yrs Thin SW)	H7R1	4SW/5SW deg	M+F	CCC	4M+1D$	DE^	28$	AABBB$	Ind	2	
Manufacturing Engineering with French (MEng)	H7RC	3FT/4FT deg	M+F	CCC	4M+1D$	DE^	28$	AABBB$	Ind		
Mathematics with French	GR11	3FT deg	M+F g	BBC-BCC	3M+2D$	P^	29$	BBBC$	Ind		
Mathematics with French (4 Yrs Thick SW)	G1R1	4SW deg	M+F g	BBC-BCC	3M+2D$	P^	29$	BBBC$	Ind		
Mathematics with French (4 Yrs Thin SW)	G1RD	4SW deg	M+F g	BBC-BCC	3M+2D$	P^	29$	BBBC$	Ind	2	
Spec Eng Prog w. French (MEng) (4/5 Yrs Thin SW)	H1R1	4SW/5SW deg	M+P g	BBB	4M+1D$	DE^	30$	ABBBB$	Ind		
Spec Eng Prog w. French(MEng) (4/5 Yrs Thick SW)	H1RC	4SW/5SW deg	M+P g	BBB	4M+1D$	DE^	30$	ABBBB$	Ind		
Special Engineering Programme with French (MEng)	H1RD	3FT/4FT deg	M+P g	BBB	4M+1D$	DE^	30$	ABBBB$	Ind		

Univ of BUCKINGHAM

Accounting and Finance with French	N4R1	2FT deg	* g	16	3M+2D	M	26	BCCC	Ind		
Economics with French	L1R1	2FT deg	F/M g	14	3M+2D	M	26	BCCC	Ind		
Law with French	M3R1	2FT deg	F	12	3M+2D	M	26	BCCC	Ind		
Marketing with French	N5R1	2FT deg	*	16	3M+2D	M	26	BCCC	Ind		
Politics with French	M1R1	2FT deg	F	12	3M+2D	M	26	BCCC	Ind		
Psychology with French	C8R1	2FT deg	*	14	5M	M	26	BCCC	Ind		

course details			*98 expected requirements*							*96 entry stats*
TITLE	CODE	COURSE	SUBJECTS	A/AS	ND/C	AGNVQ	IB	SQA(H)	SQA	RATIO A/AS
BUCKINGHAMSHIRE COLLEGE										
Business Administration with French	N1R1	3FT deg	F g	8	MO	M	27	CCCC	Ind	6
Business Studies with French	N1RD	4SW deg	F g	8	MO+2D	M	27	CCCC	Ind	
European Business Studies (French)	NR11	4SW deg	F g	8	MO	M	27	CCCC	Ind	
Human Resources Management with French	N6R1	3FT deg		8	MO	M	27	CCCC	Ind	
International Business Studies (French)	N1RC	4SW deg	L	8	MO	M	27	CCCC	Ind	
International Marketing with French	N5R1	3FT deg	F g	8	MO	M	27	CCCC	Ind	
Leisure Management with French	N7R1	3FT deg		8-10	1D	M	27	CCCC	Ind	
Tourism with French	P7R1	3FT deg		8-10	1D	M	27	CCCC	Ind	
Travel and Tourism Management with French	PR71	3FT deg	F	8-10	1D	M	27	CCCC	Ind	
Business Studies with French	11RN	2FT HND		4	3M	P	Ind	Ind	Ind	
CANTERBURY CHRIST CHURCH COLL of HE										
American Studies with French	Q4R1	4FT deg	F g	CC	MO	M	24	Ind	Ind	
Art with French	W1R1	3FT deg	A+F g	CC	MO	M	24	Ind	Ind	
Business Studies with French	N1R1	3FT deg	F g	CC	MO	M	24	Ind	Ind	
Early Childhood Studies with French	X9R1	3FT deg	F g	CC	MO	M	24	Ind	Ind	
English with French	Q3R1	3FT deg	E+F	CC	MO	M	24	Ind	Ind	
French and American Studies	QR41	3FT deg	F g	CC	MO	M	24	Ind	Ind	
French and Art	RW11	3FT deg	F+A g	CC	MO	M	24	Ind	Ind	
French and Business Studies	NR11	3FT deg	F g	CC	MO	M	24	Ind	Ind	
French and Early Childhood Studies	RX19	3FT deg	F g	CC	MO	M	24	Ind	Ind	
French and English	QR31	3FT deg	F+E g	CC	MO	M	24	Ind	Ind	
French and Social Science	LR31	3FT deg	F g	CC	MO	M	24	Ind	Ind	
Geography and French	LR81	3FT deg	F+G g	CC	MO	M	24	Ind	Ind	
History and French	RV11	3FT deg	F+H g	CC	MO	M	24	Ind	Ind	
History with French	V1R1	3FT deg	H+F g	CC	MO	M	24	Ind	Ind	
Information Technology and French	GR51	3FT deg	F g	CC	MO	M	24	Ind	Ind	
Information Technology with French	G5R1	3FT deg	F g	CC	MO	M	24	Ind	Ind	
Marketing and French	NR51	3FT deg	F g	CC	MO	M	24	Ind	Ind	
Marketing with French	N5R1	3FT deg	F g	CC	MO	M	24	Ind	Ind	
Media Studies and French	PR41	3FT deg	F g							
Media Studies with French	P4R1	3FT deg	F g	CC	MO	M	24	Ind	Ind	
Music and French	RW13	3FT deg	F+Mu g	CC	MO	M	24	Ind	Ind	
Music with French	W3R1	3FT deg	Mu+F g	CC	MO	M	24	Ind	Ind	
Psychology and French	LR71	3FT deg	Ps+F g	CC	MO	M	24	Ind	Ind	
Psychology with French	L7R1	3FT deg	Ps+F g	CC	MO	M	24	Ind	Ind	
Radio, Film & Television Studies with French	W5R1	3FT deg	F g	CC	MO	M	24	Ind	Ind	
Religious Studies and French	RV18	3FT deg	F g	CC	MO	M	24	Ind	Ind	
Religious Studies with French	V8R1	3FT deg	F g	CC	MO	M	24	Ind	Ind	
Science and French	RY11	3FT deg	F+S g	DD	Ind	Ind	24	Ind	Ind	
Science with French	Y1R1	3FT deg	S+F g	DD	Ind	Ind	24	Ind	Ind	
Social Science with French	L3R1	3FT deg	F g	CC	MO	M	24	Ind	Ind	
Sport Science and French	BR61	3FT deg	F g	CC	MO	M	24	Ind	Ind	
Sport Science with French	B6R1	3FT deg	F g	CC	MO	M	24	Ind	Ind	
Tourism Studies and French	PR71	3FT deg	F g	CC	MO	M	24	Ind	Ind	
Tourism Studies with French	P7R1	3FT deg	F g	CC	MO	M	24	Ind	Ind	
CARDIFF Univ of Wales										
Accounting with French	N4R1	4FT deg	F	BBC-BBB	Ind	Ind	Ind	Ind	Ind	7
Banking and Finance with French	N3R1	4FT deg	F	BBC-BBB	Ind	Ind	Ind	Ind	Ind	12
Business Administration with French	N1R1	4FT deg	F g	BBC-BBB	Ind	Ind	Ind	Ind	Ind	11 20/26
Business Economics with French	L1RC	4FT deg	F	BBC-BBB	Ind	Ind	Ind	Ind	Ind	20

course details | 98 expected requirements | 96 entry stats

TITLE	CODE	COURSE	SUBJECTS	A/AS	ND/C	AGNVQ	IB	SQA(H)	SQA	RATIO A/AS
Economics with French	L1R1	4FT deg	F	BBC-BBB	Ind	Ind	Ind	Ind	Ind	8
French	R100	4FT deg	F	BBC	Ind		Ind	ABBBB	Ind	8 22/24
French/Ancient History	RV11	4FT deg	F	BBC	Ind		Ind	ABBBB	Ind	
French/Archaeology	RV16	4FT deg	F	BBC	Ind		Ind	AABB	Ind	
French/Cultural Criticism	MR91	4FT deg	E	ABC	Ind	Ind	Ind	Ind	Ind	
French/Economics	RL11	4FT deg	F	BBC-BBB	X		Ind	ABBBB	Ind	
French/Education	RX19	4FT deg	F	BBC	Ind	Ind	Ind	ABBBB	Ind	4
French/English Literature	RQ13	4FT deg	E+F	ABB	Ind		Ind	AAABB	Ind	8 24/28
German/French	RR21	4FT deg	F+G	BBC	Ind		Ind	ABBBB	Ind	7 22/30
History of Ideas/French	VRD1	4FT deg	F	BBC	Ind		Ind	ABBBB	Ind	
History/French	VR11	4FT deg	F+H	BBC	X		Ind	ABBBB	X	18
Italian/French	RR31	4FT deg	F	BBC	Ind		Ind	ABBBB	Ind	8 22/26
Japanese/French	TR41	4FT deg	F	BBC	Ind		Ind	ABBBB	Ind	6 26/30
Language Studies/French	QR11	4FT deg	F	BBC	Ind		Ind	ABBBB		
Law and French	RM13	4FT deg	F	BBB	Ind	Ind	Ind	Ind	Ind	4 22/28
Music/French	WR31	4FT deg	F+Mu	BBC	Ind		Ind	ABBBB	Ind	7
Philosophy/French	VR71	4FT deg	F	BBC	Ind		Ind	ABBBB	Ind	10
Politics/French	MR11	4FT deg	F	BBC	Ind		Ind	ABBBB	Ind	15
Portuguese/French	RR15	4FT deg	F+L	BCC	Ind		Ind	ABBBB	Ind	
Pure Mathematics/French	GR11	4FT deg	F+M	BBC	Ind	Ind	Ind	ABBBB	Ind	
Social Philosophy and Applied Ethics/French	VR7C	4FT deg	F	BBC	Ind		Ind	ABBBB	Ind	
Sociology/French	LR31	4FT deg	F	BBC	Ind		Ind	ABBBB	Ind	12
Spanish/French	RR14	4FT deg	F+L	BBC	Ind		Ind	ABBBB	Ind	6 20/28
Welsh/French	QR51	4FT deg	F+W	BBC	Ind		Ind	ABBBB	Ind	

Univ of CENTRAL ENGLAND

TITLE	CODE	COURSE	SUBJECTS	A/AS	ND/C	AGNVQ	IB	SQA(H)	SQA	RATIO A/AS
Business Administration with French	N1R1	3FT deg	* g	14	M+3D	D	22	CCCC		
Business Systems Eng with French Found Yr	G5RC▼	4FT/5SW deg	*	2	N	P*	Ind	CC	Ind	
Business Systems Engineering with French	G5R1	3FT/4SW deg	* g	12	3M	M* go	24	CCC	Ind	1
Electronic Eng with French Foundation Year	H6RC▼	4FT/5SW deg	* g	2	N	P*	Ind	CC	Ind	
Electronic Engineering with French	H6R1	3FT/4SW deg	M g	12	3M $	ME1	24$	CCC$	Ind	
Marketing with French	N5R1	3FT deg	* g	16	M+3D	M	24	CCCCC		
Mechanical Engineering with French	H3R1	3FT/4SW deg	M g	12	3M $	ME1	24$	Ind	Ind	
Mechanical Engineering with French Foundation Yr	H3RC▼	4FT/5SW deg	* g	2	N	P*	Ind	CC	Ind	

Univ of CENTRAL LANCASHIRE

TITLE	CODE	COURSE	SUBJECTS	A/AS	ND/C	AGNVQ	IB	SQA(H)	SQA	RATIO A/AS
Combined Honours Programme *French/Business French*	Y400	4SW deg	L/* g	8	Ind	M*^	24$	CCC	Ind	

CHELTENHAM & GLOUCESTER COLL of HE

TITLE	CODE	COURSE	SUBJECTS	A/AS	ND/C	AGNVQ	IB	SQA(H)	SQA	RATIO A/AS
Business Computer Systems with Modern Languages	G5T9	3FT deg	g	8-12	M0	M	24	CCCC	Ind	
Business Management with Modern Lang (French)	N1R1	4SW deg	g	12-16	4M+3D	MB3	26	CCCC	Ind	
Catering Management with Modern Lang (French)	N7R1	4SW deg	g	8	M0	MH3	24	CCCC	Ind	
Computing with Modern Languages (French)	G5RD	3FT deg	g	8	M0	M	24	CCCC	Ind	
Countryside Planning with Modern Langs (French)	D2R1	3FT deg	g	8-12	M0	MK	26	CCCC	Ind	
English Studies with Modern Languages (French)	Q3R1	3FT deg	E g	12-14	4M+3D	M^	26	CCCC	Ind	
Environmental Policy with Modern Lang (French)	F9R1	3FT deg	g	10-14	5M+2D	M3	26	CCCC	Ind	
Financial Services Mgt with Mod Lang (French)	N3R1	4SW deg	g	8-10	M0	M3	26	CCCC	Ind	
Geography with Modern Languages (French)	L8RC	3FT deg	F g	12	M0	M3^	26	CCCC	Ind	
Geology with Modern Languages (French)	F6R1	3FT deg	S g	8	M0	M3	26	CCCC	Ind	
History with Modern Languages (French)	V1R1	3FT deg	H g	12	5M+2D	M3^	26	CCCC	Ind	
Hotel Management with Modern Languages (French)	N7TX	4SW deg	g	12	5M+2D	MH3	26	CCCC	Ind	
Human Geography with Modern Languages (French)	L8R1	3FT deg	F g	12	4M+3D	M3	26	CCCC	Ind	
Human Resource Mgt with Modern Languages(French)	N1RD	4SW deg	g	10	5M+2D	MB3	26	CCCC	Ind	

Languages – French 40

| course details | | | 98 expected requirements | | | | | | | 96 entry stats | |

TITLE	CODE	COURSE	SUBJECTS	A/AS	ND/C	AGNVQ	IB	SQA(H)	SQA	RATIO	A/AS
Information Technology with Modern Lang (French)	G5RC	3FT deg	F g	8	MO	M3	26	CCCC	Ind		
Leisure Management with Modern Language (French)	N7RC	4SW deg	*	12-16	5M+2D	ML3	26	CCCC	Ind		
Marketing Management with Modern Langs (French)	N5R1	4SW deg	g	12	5M+2D	MB3	26	CCCC	Ind		
Media Communications with Modern Langs (French)	P4R1	3FT deg	g	12	4M+3D	MP3	26	CCCC	Ind		
Multimedia with Modern Languages (French)	G5R1	3FT deg	g	8-12	MO	MI3	26	CCCC	Ind		
Multimedia with Modern Languages (French)	GRMC	4SW deg	F g	8-12	MO	MI3	24	CCCC	Ind		
Sport & Exercise Sciences with Mod Lang (French)	B6RD	3FT deg	F g	12-16	4M+3D	ML3	26	CCCC	Ind		
Tourism Management with Modern Languages(French)	P7R1	4SW deg	g	12-16	4M+3D	ML3	26	CCCC	Ind		
Visual Arts with Modern Languages (French)	W1T9	3FT deg	A g	10-14	5M+2D	MA3	26	CCCC	Ind		
Women's Studies with Modern Languages (French)	M9R1	3FT deg	g	8-12	MO	M3	26	CCCC	Ind		

UNIVERSITY COLLEGE CHESTER

Art with French	W9R1	3FT deg	g	12	M	P^	Ind	CCCC	$		
Biology with French	C1R1	3FT deg	B g	12	M	P^	Ind	CCCC	$	2	
Biosciences with a European Language (French)	C9R1	3FT deg	B g	12	MO	P^	Ind	CCCC	$		
Computer Science/IT with French	G5R1	3FT deg	g	12	M	M	Ind	CCCC	$	6	
Drama with French	W4R1	3FT deg	g	12	M	M	Ind	CCCC	$	9	
English Literature with French	Q3R1	3FT deg	E g	12	M	P^	Ind	CCCC	$	6	16/20
Geography with French	F8R1	3FT deg	Gy/Gl g	12	M	P^	Ind	CCCC	$		
History with French	V1R1	3FT deg	H/Ec/So g	12	M	P^	Ind	CCCC	$	4	
Mathematics with French	G1R1	3FT deg	M g	12	M	P^	Ind	CCCC	$	3	
Physical Education/Sports Science with French	B6R1	3FT deg	g	12	M	P^	Ind	CCCC	$		
Psychology with French	L7R1	3FT deg	g	12	M	M	Ind	CCCC	$	4	12/16
Theology and Religious Studies with French	V8R1	3FT deg	g	12	M	M	Ind	CCCC	$	6	

COVENTRY Univ

Business Studies with French	N1RC	4SW deg	F g	16	M+3D	M	Dip	CCC	Ind	25	16/24
European Studies with French (4 years)	TR21	4FT deg	F	CD	M	M	Ind	CCCC	Ind		
French and Economics	LR11	4FT deg	F g	12	M+D	M	Ind	Ind	Ind	12	
French and German	RR12▼	4FT deg	F	CD	M	M	Ind	CCCC$	Ind	7	6/18
French and Italian	RR13	4FT deg	F	CD	M	M	Ind	CCCC$	Ind	4	6/20
French and Russian	RR18	4FT deg	F	CD	M	M	Ind	CCCC$	Ind	10	
French and Spanish	RR14▼	4FT deg	F	CD	M	M	Ind	CCCC$	Ind	10	6/26
Geography and French	LR81	4SW deg	F+Gy g	12	Ind	M	Ind	Ind	Ind	6	
History and French	VR11	4FT deg	F	CD	M	M	Ind	CCCC$	Ind		
Mathematics and French	RG11	4FT deg	F+M	16-20	Ind	M	Ind	Ind	Ind		
Psychology and French	RC18	4FT deg	F	CD	M	M	Ind	CCCC$	Ind		
Sociology and French	RL13	3FT deg									
Statistics and French	GR41	4FT deg	F+M/St g	12-16	Ind	M	Ind	Ind	Ind		

DE MONTFORT Univ

European Studies-French	R100▼	3FT/4SW deg	F g	10	D	M	Ind	BCCC	Ind	8	
Law with French	M3R1▼	4FT deg	F g	BBC	6D	M^	30$	BBBBB$	X	10	
Combined Studies Language Studies-French	Y400▼	4SW deg	* g	12	2M+4D	M	30	BBB	X		
Humanities Combined Honours French Studies	Y300▼	3FT deg	F g	CCD	MO	X	26$	ABBB	Ind		
Humanities Joint Honours French Studies	Y301▼	3FT deg	F g	CCD	MO	X	26$	ABBB	Ind		

Univ of DERBY

Credit Accumulation Modular Scheme French	Y600	4FT deg	F	10	MO $	M$	Ind	CCCC$	Ind		

Univ of DUNDEE

Physics with French	F3R1	4FT deg	M+S g	10	5M $	M$^	25$	BBCC$	N$		

			98 expected requirements							96 entry stats	

TITLE	CODE	COURSE	SUBJECTS	A/AS	NO/C	AGNVQ	IB	SQA(H)	SQA	RATIO	A/AS
Univ of DURHAM											
Economics with French	L1R1	4FT deg	F g	ABC	Ind	X	32$	AAABB	Ind	10	28/28
European Studies and French	RT12▼	4FT deg	*	CD	Ind	Ind	Dip	BCCCC	Ind		
European Studies with French	T2R1▼	3FT deg	*	CD	Ind	Ind	Dip	BCCCC	Ind		
History with French	V1R1	4FT deg	F	ABB	Ind	Ind	Ind	Ind	Ind	9	26/28
Urban Studies with French	K4R1▼	3FT deg	*	CD	Ind	Ind	Dip	BCCCC	Ind		
Arts Combined	Y300	4FT deg	F	24	MO	Ind	30	AAABB	Ind		
French											
Univ of EAST ANGLIA											
French Studies with Hons Language	R100	4FT deg	F	BCD	X		28$	ABBCC	X	4	12/24
French and Germ Lang w Interpret and Translating	RR21	4FT deg	F+G	ABC	X		31$	AAAAA	X	6	20/30
Univ of EAST LONDON											
Anthropology and French	LR61	3FT deg	*	12	MO	M^	Ind				
Anthropology with French	L6R1	3FT deg	* g	12	MO	M	Ind	Ind	Ind		
Archaeological Sciences and French	FR41	3FT deg	* g	12	MO	M^	Ind	Ind	Ind		
Biology and French	CR11	3FT deg	* g	12	MO	M^	Ind	Ind	Ind		
Business Studies and French	NR11	3FT deg	* g	12	MO	M^	Ind	Ind	Ind		
Business Studies with French	N1R1	3FT deg	* g	14	MO	MB					
Communication Studies and French	PR31	3FT deg	* g	12	MO	M^	Ind	Ind	Ind	8	
Communication Studies with French	P3R1	3FT deg	* g	12	MO	M	Ind	Ind			
Computing & Business Info Systems and French	GR5C	3FT deg	* g	12	MO	M					
Cultural Studies and French	LRP1	3FT deg	* g	14	N	M^					
Design - Textile Design with French	J4R1	3FT deg	* g	12	MO	M	Ind	Ind	Ind		
Design - Visual Communication and French	RW12	3FT deg	* g	12	MO	M^	Ind	Ind	Ind		
Design - Visual Communication with French	W2R1	3FT deg	* g	12	MO	M	Ind	Ind	Ind		
Economics and French	LR11	3FT deg	* g	12	MO	M^	Ind	Ind	Ind	2	
Economics with French	L1R1	3FT deg	* g	12	MO	M	Ind				
Education & Community Studies and French	RX19	3FT deg	* g	12	MO	M^	Ind	Ind	Ind	3	
Education & Community Studies with French	X9R1	3FT deg	* g	12	MO	M					
Environmental Sciences and French	FR91	3FT deg	* g	12	MO	M					
European Studies and French	TR21	3FT deg	* g	12	MO	M					
European Studies with French	T2R1	3FT deg	* g	12	MO	M					
French and Health Studies	BR91	3FT deg	* g	12	MO	M$	Ind	Ind	Ind		
French and History of Art Design & Film	RV14	3FT deg	* g	12	MO	M$	Ind	Ind	Ind	2	
French and Information Technology	GR51	3FT deg	* g	12	MO	M$	Ind	Ind	Ind	1	
French and Law	MR31	3FT deg	* g	12	MO	D	Ind	Ind	Ind		
French and Linguistics	QR11	3FT deg	* g	12	MO	X	Ind	Ind	Ind	9	
French and Literature	QR31	3FT deg	* g	12	MO	X	Ind	Ind	Ind	7	
French and Maths, Stats & Computing	GR91	3FT deg	* g	12	MO	M$	Ind	Ind	Ind		
French and Media Studies	PR41	3FT deg	* g	12	MO	D	Ind	Ind	Ind	18	
French and Politics	MR11	3FT deg	* g	12	MO	M	Ind	Ind	Ind		
French and Psychosocial Studies	LR71	3FT deg	* g	12	MO	M$	Ind	Ind	Ind		
French and Social Policy Research	LR41	3FT deg	* g	12	MO	M	Ind	Ind	Ind		
French and Sociology	LR31	3FT deg	* g	12	MO	M$	Ind	Ind	Ind		
French and Third World & Development Studies	MR91	3FT deg	* g	12	MO	M	Ind	Ind	Ind		
French and Women's Studies	MRX1	3FT deg	* g	12	MO	M	Ind	Ind	Ind		
French with Anthropology	R1L6	3FT deg	* g	12	MO	M	Ind				
French with Biology	R1C6	3FT deg	* g	12	MO	M	Ind				
French with Business Studies	R1N1	3FT deg	* g	12	MO	M	Ind				
French with Communication Studies	R1P3	3FT deg	* g	12	MO	M	Ind				
French with Computing & Business Info Systems	R1G5	3FT deg	* g	12	MO	M	Ind				

Languages – French 40

course details			98 expected requirements							96 entry stats
TITLE	CODE	COURSE	SUBJECTS	A/AS	NO/C	AGNVQ	IB	SQA(H)	SQA	RATIO A/AS
French with Cultural Studies	R1LP	3FT deg	* g	12	MO	M	Ind			
French with Design - Textile Design	R1J4	3FT deg	* g	12	MO	M	Ind			
French with Design - Visual Communication	R1W2	3FT deg	* g	12	MO	M	Ind			
French with Economics	R1L1	3FT deg	* g	12	MO	M	Ind			
French with Education & Community Studies	R1X9	3FT deg	* g	12	MO	M	Ind			
French with European Studies	R1T2	3FT deg	* g	12	MO	M	Ind			
French with German	R1R2	3FT deg	* g	12	MO	M	Ind			
French with Health Studies	R1B9	3FT deg	* g	12	MO	M	Ind			
French with History of Art Design & Film	R1V4	3FT deg	* g	12	MO	M	Ind			
French with Information Technology	R1GN	3FT deg	* g	12	MO	M	Ind			
French with Italian	R1R3	3FT deg	* g	12	MO	M	Ind			
French with Law	R1M3	3FT deg	* g	12	MO	M	Ind			
French with Linguistics	R1Q1	3FT deg	* g	12	MO	M	Ind			
French with Literature	R1Q3	3FT deg	* g	12	MO	M				
French with Maths, Stats & Computing	R1GM	3FT deg	* g	12	MO	M				
French with Politics	R1M1	3FT deg	* g	12	MO	M				
French with Social Policy Research	R1L4	3FT deg	* g	12	MO	M				
French with Sociology	R1L3	3FT deg	* g	12	MO	M				
French with Spanish	R1R4	3FT deg	* g	12	MO	M				
French with Women's Studies	R1M9	3FT deg	* g	12	MO	M				
German with French	R2R1	3FT deg	* g	12	MO	M	Ind			
Health Studies with French	B9R1	3FT deg	* g	12	MO	M	Ind	Ind	Ind	
History of Art Design & Film with French	V4R1	3FT deg	* g	12	MO	M	Ind	Ind		
Information Technology with French	G5R1	3FT deg	* g	12	MO	M	Ind	Ind	Ind	
Law with French	M3R1	3FT deg	* g	14	MO	M				
Linguistics with French	Q1R1	3FT deg	* g	12	MO	M				
Literature with French	Q3R1	3FT deg	* g	12	MO	M	Ind			
Maths, Stats & Computing with French	G9R1	3FT deg	* g	12	MO	M	Ind	Ind	Ind	
Media Studies with French	P4R1	3FT deg	* g	14	MO	M				
Politics with French	M1R1	3FT deg	* g	12	MO	M	Ind			
Psychosocial Studies with French	L7R1	3FT deg	* g	12	MO	M	Ind	Ind	Ind	
Social Policy Research with French	L4R1	3FT deg	* g	12	MO	M	Ind	Ind	Ind	
Sociology with French	L3R1	3FT deg	* g	12	MO	M	Ind	Ind	Ind	
Spanish with French	R4R1	3FT deg	* g	12	MO	M	Ind			
Third World & Development Studies with French	M9R1	3FT deg	* g	12	MO	M	Ind	Ind		
Women's Studies with French	M9RC	3FT deg	* g	12	MO	M	Ind			
Three-Subject Degree French	Y600	3FT deg	* g	12	MO	M	Ind	Ind	Ind	

Univ of EDINBURGH

Arabic and French	TR61	4FT deg	E g	BBB	Ind	Ind	Dip$	BBBB$	Ind	
Business Studies and French	NR11	4FT deg	E g	BBB	Ind		34$	ABBB	Ind	7
English Literature and French	QR31	4FT deg	F+E g	AAB	Ind	Ind	Dip$	ABBB$	Ind	
French	R100	4FT deg	E g	BBB	Ind	Ind	Dip$	BBBB$	Ind	
French and Arabic	RT16	4FT deg	E g	BBB	Ind	Ind	Dip$	BBBB$	Ind	
French and Business Studies	RN11	4FT deg	E g	BBB	Ind	Ind	Dip$	BBBB$	Ind	
French and European History	RV11	4FT deg	E g	BBB	Ind	Ind	Dip$	BBBB$	Ind	
French and History of Art	RV14	4FT deg	E g	BBB	Ind	Ind	Dip$	BBBB$	Ind	
French and Latin	RQ16	4FT deg	E g	BBB	Ind	Ind	Dip$	BBBB$	Ind	
French and Linguistics	RQ11	4FT deg	E g	BBB	Ind	Ind	Dip$	BBBB$	Ind	
French and Philosophy	RV17	4FT deg	E g	BBB	Ind	Ind	Dip$	BBBB$	Ind	
French and Politics	RM11	4FT deg	E g	BBB	Ind	Ind	Dip$	BBBB$	Ind	
History of Art and French	VR41	4FT deg	E g	BBB	Ind	Ind	Dip$	BBBB$	Ind	
Law and French	MR31	4FT deg	E g	ABB	X		32	AAABB	X	4 26/30

			98 expected requirements							96 entry stats	

course details — *98 expected requirements* — *96 entry stats*

TITLE	CODE	COURSE	SUBJECTS	A/AS	ND/C	RGNVQ	IB	SQA(H)	SQA	RATIO	A/AS
Univ of ESSEX											
Computer Science with French (4 Yrs)	G5R1	4FT deg	F g	20	MO+2D	Ind	28$	CSYS	Ind		
English and French (Language and Linguistics)	RQ13	4FT deg	F	20	MO+2D	Ind	28$	BBBB$	Ind		
French (Language and Linguistics) (4 Yrs)	R1Q1	4FT deg	F	20	MO+2D	Ind	28$	BBBB$	Ind	8	
Mathematics and French (4 Yrs)	GR11	4FT deg	M+F	18	MO $	Ind	28$	CSYS	Ind	5	
EUROPEAN Business School											
Euro Bus Admin with French + one beginner lang	N1RC	4SW deg	L	12	Ind		Ind	Ind	Ind		
International Bus St: French + one beginner lang	NR11	4FT deg									
International Bus Studs with French (Test+Int)	N1R1	4SW deg		12	Ind		Ind	Ind	Ind		
International Business & Mgt Studies with French	N1RD	4SW deg		12	Ind		Ind	Ind	Ind		
Univ of EXETER											
French	R101	4FT deg	F	22-24	MO	M/D$^	34$				
French and Arabic	RT16	4FT deg	F	22-24	MO	M/D$^	34$	Ind	Ind	6	
French and Fine Art	RW11	4FT deg	F+Pf	22-24	MO	M/D$^	34$	Ind	Ind	7	26/30
French and German	RR1F	4FT deg	F+G	22-24	MO	M/D$^	34$				
French and Greek & Roman Studies	QR81	4FT deg	F	22-24	MO	M/D$^	34$		Ind	4	
French and Italian	RR1H	4FT deg	F	22-24	MO	M/D$^	34$				
French and Latin	QR61	4FT deg	F+Ln	22-24	MO	M/D$^	34$	Ind	Ind		
French and Mathematics	GR11	4FT deg	F+M	22-24	MO	M/D$^	34$	Ind	Ind	5	30/30
French and Russian	RR1V	4FT deg	F	22-24	MO	M/D$^	34$				
French and Spanish	RR1K	4FT deg	F	22-24	MO	M/D$^	34$				
History and French	RV1C	4FT deg	F	ABB-BCC	MO	M/D$^	32$	Ind	Ind		
Music and French	RW1H	4FT deg	F+Mu	BCC	MO	M/D$^	32$	Ind	Ind		
Univ of GLAMORGAN											
French and German	RR12	3FT deg			Ind	Ind	Ind	Ind	Ind		
French with German	R1R2	3FT deg			Ind	Ind	Ind	Ind	Ind		
French with Italian	R1R3	3FT deg			Ind	Ind	Ind	Ind	Ind		
French with Spanish	R1R4	3FT deg			Ind	Ind	Ind	Ind	Ind		
French with Welsh	R1Q5	3FT deg			Ind	Ind	Ind	Ind	Ind		
Mathematics with French	G1R1	3FT deg	M g	8	Ind	Ind	Ind	Ind	Ind		
Combined Studies (Honours) French	Y400	3FT deg	* g	8-16	Ind	Ind	Ind	Ind	Ind		
Major/Minor Honours French	Y402	3FT deg	* g	8-16	Ind	Ind	Ind	Ind	Ind		
Univ of GLASGOW											
Anthropology with French	LR61	4FT deg		BBC	N	M	30	BBBB	Ind		
Business Economics with French	L1RC	4FT deg		BBC	N	M	30	BBBB	N		
Celtic Civilisation/French	QR5C	5FT deg		BBC	HN	M	30	BBBB	Ind	2	
Celtic/French	QRN1	5FT deg		BBC	HN	M	30	BBBB	Ind		
Classical Civilisation/French	QR81	5FT deg		BBC	HN	M	30	BBBB	Ind		
Computing/French	GR51	5FT deg		BBC	HN	M	30	BBBB	Ind	17	
Czech/French	RTC1	5FT deg		BBC	HN	M	30	BBBB	Ind		
Economic and Social History with French	V3R1	4FT deg		BBC	8M	M	30	BBBB	Ind		
Economic and Social History/French	RV13	5FT deg		BBC	HN	M	30	BBBB	Ind	4	
Economics with French	L1R1	4FT deg		BBC	8M	M	30	BBBB	Ind		
English/French	QR31	5FT deg		BBC	HN	M	30	BBBB	Ind	4	22/30
Film and Television Studies/French	RW15	5FT deg		BBB	HN	D	32	AABB	HN	7	
French Language and Literature	R100	5FT deg		BBC	HN	M	30	BBBB	Ind	11	
French/Classical Hebrew	QR91	5FT deg		BBC	HN	M	30	BBBB	Ind		
French/Economics	LR11	5FT deg		BBC	HN	M	30	BBBB	Ind	4	
French/Geography	LR81	5FT deg		BBC	HN	M	30	BBBB	Ind		

Languages – French 40

					98 expected requirements					96 entry stats
TITLE	CODE	COURSE	SUBJECTS	A/AS	ND/C	RGNVQ	IB	SQA(H)	SQA	RATIO A/AS
French/German	RR12	5FT deg		BBC	HN	M	30	BBBB	Ind	5
French/Greek	QR71	5FT deg		BBC	HN	M	30	BBBB	Ind	
French/Hispanic Studies	RR14	5FT deg		BBC	HN	M	30	BBBB	Ind	9
French/History	VR11	5FT deg		BBC	HN	M	30	BBBB	Ind	4
French/History of Art	RV14	5FT deg		BBC	HN	M	30	BBBB	Ind	12
French/Italian	RR13	5FT deg		BBC	HN	M	30	BBBB	Ind	4
French/Latin	QR61	5FT deg		BBC	HN	M	30	BBBB	Ind	
French/Mathematics	GR11	5FT deg		BBC	HN	M	30	BBBB	Ind	10
French/Music	RW13	5FT deg		BBC	HN	M	30	BBBB	Ind	5
French/Philosophy	RV17	5FT deg		BBC	HN	M	30	BBBB	Ind	16
French/Polish	RTD1	5FT deg		BBC	HN	M	30	BBBB	Ind	
French/Politics	MR11	5FT deg		BBC	HN	M	30	BBBB	Ind	3
French/Psychology	CR81	5FT deg		BBC	HN	M	30	BBBB	Ind	7
French/Russian	RR18	5FT deg		BBC	HN	M	30	BBBB	Ind	
French/Scottish Literature	QR21	5FT deg		BBC	HN	M	30	BBBB	Ind	3
French/Sociology	LR31	5FT deg		BBC	HN	M	30	BBBB	Ind	8
Geography with French	L8R1	4FT deg		BBC	8M	M	30	BBBB	Ind	
Islamic Studies/French	TR61	4FT deg		BBC	N	M	30	BBBB	Ind	
Law with French Language	M3R1	4FT deg		ABB	X		34	AAAAB	X	3
Management Studies with French	N1R1	4FT deg		BBC	8M	M	30	BBBB	Ind	
Management Studies/French	NRC1	5FT deg		BBC	HN	M	30	BBBB	Ind	15
Philosophy with French	V7R1	4FT deg		BBC	8M	M	30	BBBB	Ind	
Politics with French	M1R1	4FT deg		BBC	8M	M	30	BBBB	Ind	7
Psychology with French	C8R1	4FT deg		BBC	8M	M	30	BBBB	Ind	6
Sociology with French	L3R1	4FT deg		BBC	8M	M	30	BBBB	Ind	1
Theatre Studies/French	RW14	5FT deg		BBC	HN	M	30	BBBB	Ind	3
Theology & Religious Studies/French	RV1V	5FT deg		BBC	HN	M	30	BBBB	Ind	

GOLDSMITHS COLL (Univ of London)

French Studies (4 Yrs)	R100	4FT deg	F	BCC	MO	M	Dip	BCCC	N	4 10/18

Univ of GREENWICH

Applied Biology with French	C1R1	3FT/4SW deg	B+C g	10	3M	MS	Dip	CCC	Ind	
Applied Chemistry with French	F1R1	3FT/4SW deg	C+S g	8	3M	MS	Dip	CCC	Ind	

HERIOT-WATT Univ

Accountancy with French	N4R1	4FT deg	L g	BCC	Ind		Ind	ABBB$	Ind	
Chemistry with French	F1R1	4FT deg	C+S+L	CCD	$	M$ go	28	BBB	$	
French/German	RR1F	4FT deg								
French/German (Interpreting and Translating)	RR12	4FT deg	2L	BBC	Ind		Ind	AABB	Ind	
French/Russian	RR1V	4FT deg								
French/Russian (Interpreting and Translating)	RR18	4FT deg	2L	BBC	Ind		Ind	AABB	Ind	
French/Spanish	RR1K	4FT deg								
French/Spanish (Interpreting and Translating)	RR14	4FT deg	2L	BBC	Ind		Ind	AABB	Ind	
Mathematics with French	G1R1	4FT deg	M+L	CDE	HN	M$^	28	BBB	HN	

Univ of HERTFORDSHIRE

Manufacturing Systems Engineering with French	H7R1	3FT deg								

Univ of HUDDERSFIELD

French and Media	RP14	4FT deg	F	CDD	Ind	Ind	Ind	BBBC	Ind	
French with English	R1Q3	4FT deg	F+E	CCE	Ind	Ind	Ind	BBBC	Ind	
French with History	R1V1	4FT deg	F+H	CCE	Ind	Ind	Ind	BBBC	Ind	

 *Letts* STUDY GUIDES
THE INDEPENDENT

			98 expected requirements							96 entry stats	
TITLE	CODE	COURSE	SUBJECTS	A/AS	ND/C	AGNVQ	IB	SQA(H)	SQA	RATIO	A/AS
Univ of HULL											
Business Studies/French	NR11	4FT deg	F g	BBC-BCC	Ind $	D*^ go	26$	BBCCC	Ind	11	18/24
Chemistry with French	F1R1	4FT deg	C g	CCD	MO $	M$^ go	26$	BCCCC	Ind		
Chemistry with French (MChem)	F1RC	4FT deg	C g	BCC	MO+3D$	M$^ gi	26$	BBBCC			
Drama/French	RW14	4FT deg	F	BBB-BCC	Ind	D$^ go	28$	ABBCC	Ind	27	
Dutch/French	RTD2	4FT deg	F	BBB-BCD	Ind	Ind	26$	BBBCC	Ind		
English/French	QR31	4FT deg	E+F	BBB-BCC	Ind	M$^ gi	28$	BBBCC	Ind	8	22/24
French	R100	4FT deg	F	BCC	Ind	Ind	28$	BBBCC	Ind	2	12/24
French/German	RR12	4FT deg	F+G	BCC	Ind	Ind	28$	BBBCC	Ind	10	16/26
French/History	RV11	4FT deg	F+H	BBB-BCC	Ind	M$^ gi	28$	BBBCC	Ind	13	
French/Italian	RR13	4FT deg	F	BCC	Ind	Ind	28$	BBBCC	Ind	9	16/30
French/Music (Min Practical Standards Req)	RW13	4FT deg	F	BCC-BCD	Ind	M$^ go	28$	BBCCC	Ind	18	
French/Philosophy	RV17	4FT deg	F	BCC	Ind	M$^ go	28$	BBBCC	Ind		
French/Politics	RM11	4FT deg	F	BBB-BCC	Ind	Ind	28$	BBBCC	Ind	12	
French/Scandinavian Studies	RRD7	4FT deg	F	BBB-BCD	Ind	Ind	28$	BBBCC	Ind	2	22/24
French/Spanish	RR14	4FT deg	F	BCC	Ind	Ind	28$	BBBCC	Ind	8	14/28
Gender Studies and French	MR91	4FT deg	F	BCC	Ind	M$6/^ go	28$	BBBCC	Ind	3	
Law with French	M3R1	4FT deg	F	BBB-BCC	M+D $	D$^ gi	28$	ABBBB	Ind	6	20/26
Mathematics with French	G1R1	4FT deg	M g	BCD	MO $	M$^ go	26$	BBCCC	Ind	15	
Mathematics with French (MMath)	G1RC	4FT deg	M g	BCC	MO $	M$^ go	26$	BBBCC	Ind	2	
KEELE Univ											
Finance and French	NR31	3FT deg	F	BBC-BCC	Ind	D$^	28$	CSYS	Ind		
French and American Studies	QR41	3FT deg	F	BBC-BCC	Ind	D$^	28$	CSYS	Ind	2	
French and Ancient History	RV1D	3FT deg	F	BCC	Ind	D$^	28$	CSYS	Ind		
French and Ancient History (4 Yrs)	VRD1	4FT deg	*	BCC	Ind	Ind	28	BBBB	Ind		
French and Astrophysics	FR51	3FT deg	P+F g	BCC	Ind	D$^	28$	CSYS	Ind		
French and Astrophysics (4 Yrs)	RF15	4FT deg	*	BCC	Ind	Ind	28	BBBB	Ind		
French and Biochemistry	CR71	3FT deg	C+F g	BCC	Ind	D$^	28$	CSYS	Ind		
French and Biochemistry (4 Yrs)	RC17	4FT deg	*	BCC	Ind	Ind	28	BBBB	Ind		
French and Biology	CR11	3FT deg	S+F g	BCC	Ind	D$^	28$	CSYS	Ind	3	
French and Biology (4 Yrs)	RC11	4FT deg	*	BCC	Ind	Ind	28	BBBB	Ind		
French and Business Administration	NR91	3FT deg	F	BBC-BCC	Ind	D$^	28$	CSYS	Ind	4	16/24
French and Business Administration (4 Yrs)	RN19	4FT deg	*	BBC-BCC	Ind	Ind	28	BBBB	Ind	63	
French and Classical Studies	QR81	3FT deg	F	BCC	Ind	D$^	28$	CSYS	Ind		
French and Classical Studies (4 Yrs)	RQ18	4FT deg	*	BCC	Ind	Ind	28	BBBB	Ind		
French and Computer Science	GR51	3FT deg	F g	BCC	Ind	D$^	28$	CSYS	Ind		
French and Criminology	MRH1	3FT deg	F	BBB	Ind	D$^	32$	CSYS	Ind	3	
French and Criminology (4 Yrs)	RM1H	4FT deg	*	BBB	Ind	Ind	32	ABBB	Ind		
French and Economics	LR11	3FT deg	F g	BCC	Ind	D$^	28$	CSYS	Ind		
French and Educational Studies	RX19	3FT deg	F	BCC	Ind	D$^	28$	CSYS	Ind	8	
French and Electronic Music	RW1J	3FT deg	Mu+F	BCC	Ind	D$^	28$	CSYS	Ind		
French and Electronic Music (4 Yrs)	WRJ1	4FT deg	*	BCC	Ind	Ind	28	BBBB	Ind		
French and English	QR31	3FT deg	E+F	BBC	Ind	D$^	30$	CSYS	Ind	4	18/26
French and English (4 Yrs)	RQ13	4FT deg	*	BBC	Ind	Ind	30	BBBB	Ind	11	
French and Environmental Management	FRX1	3FT deg	F g	BCC	Ind	D$^	28$	CSYS	Ind		
French and European Studies	RT12	3FT deg	F	BCC	Ind	D$^	28$	CSYS	Ind	4	16/28
French and European Studies (4 Yrs)	TR21	4FT deg	*	BCC	Ind	Ind	28	BBBB	Ind	58	
French and Finance (4 Yrs)	RN13	4FT deg	*	BCC	Ind	Ind	28	BBB	Ind		
Geography and French	LR81	3FT deg	F+Gy	BCC	Ind	D$^	28$	CSYS	Ind	5	
Geography and French (4 Yrs)	RL18	4FT deg	*	BCC	Ind	Ind	28	BBBB	Ind		
Geology and French	FR61	3FT deg	S+F g	BCC	Ind	D$^	28$	CSYS	Ind	1	
Geology and French (4 Yrs)	RF16	4FT deg	*	BCC	Ind	Ind	28	BBBB	Ind		

course details | 98 expected requirements | 96 entry stats

TITLE	CODE	COURSE	SUBJECTS	A/AS	NO/C	RGNVQ	IB	SQA(H)	SQA	RATIO	A/AS
German and French	RR12	3FT deg	F+G	BBC-BCC	Ind	D$^	28$	CSYS	Ind	5	20/20
German and French (4 Yrs)	RR21	4FT deg	* g	BCC	Ind	Ind	28	BBBB	Ind		
German/Russian and French	RT1Y	3FT deg	G+R+F	BBC-BCC	Ind	D$^	28$	CSYS	Ind		
German/Russian and French (4 Yrs)	TRY1	4FT deg	* g	BBC-BCC	Ind	Ind	28	BBBB	Ind		
History and French	RV11	3FT deg	F	BBC-BCC	Ind	D$^	28$	CSYS	Ind	2	19/20
History and French (4 Yrs)	VR11	4FT deg	*	BBC-BCC	Ind	Ind	28	BBBB	Ind		
Human Resource Management and French	NR61	3FT deg	F	BCC	Ind	D$^	28$	CSYS	Ind	2	
Human Resource Management and French (4 Yrs)	RN16	4FT deg	*	BCC	Ind	Ind	28	BBBB	Ind		
International History and French	RV1C	3FT deg	F	BCC	Ind	D$^	28$	CSYS	Ind	5	
International History and French (4 Yrs)	VRC1	4FT deg	*	BCC	Ind	Ind	28	BBBB	Ind		
Latin and French	QR61	3FT deg	F+Ln	BCC	Ind	D$^	28$	CSYS	Ind		
Latin and French (4 Yrs)	RQ16	4FT deg	*	BCC	Ind	Ind	28	BBBB	Ind		
Law and French	MR31	3FT deg	F	BBB	Ind	D$^	32$	CSYS	Ind	4	20/24
Law and French (4 Yrs)	RM13	4FT deg	*	BBB	Ind	Ind	32	BBBB	Ind	31	
Management Science and French (4 Yrs)	RN11	4FT deg	* g	BCC	Ind	Ind	28	BBBB	Ind		
Mathematics and French	GR11	3FT deg	F+M	BCC	Ind	D$^	28$	CSYS	Ind	5	
Mathematics and French (4 Yrs)	RG11	4FT deg	*	BCC	Ind	Ind	28	BBBB	Ind	9	
Music and French	RW13	3FT deg	Mu+F	BCC	Ind	D$^	28$	CSYS	Ind		
Music and French (4 Yrs)	WR31	4FT deg	*	BCC	Ind	Ind	28	BBBB	Ind		
Philosophy and French	RV17	3FT deg	F	BCC	Ind	D$^	28$	CSYS	Ind	1	
Philosophy and French (4 Yrs)	VR71	4FT deg	*	BBC-BCC	Ind	Ind	28	BBBB	Ind		
Physics and French	FR31	3FT deg	P+F	BCC	Ind	D$^	28$	CSYS	Ind		
Physics and French (4 Yrs)	RF13	4FT deg	*	BCC	Ind	Ind	28	BBBB	Ind	3	
Politics and French	MR11	3FT deg	F	BCC	Ind	D$^	28$	CSYS	Ind	4	
Politics and French (4 Yrs)	RM11	4FT deg	*	BCC	Ind	Ind	28	BBBB	Ind		
Psychology and French (4 Yrs)	RC18	4FT deg	* g	BBB	Ind	Ind	32	ABBB	Ind		
Russian Studies and French	RRC8	3FT deg	F	BCC	Ind	D$^	28$	CSYS	Ind		
Russian Studies and French (4 Yrs)	RR8C	4FT deg	*	BCC	Ind	Ind	28	BBBB	Ind		
Russian and French	RR18	3FT deg	R+F	BCC	Ind	D$^	28$	CSYS	Ind		
Russian and French (4 Yrs)	RR81	4FT deg	*	BCC	Ind	Ind	28	BBBB	Ind		
Sociol & Social Anthropology and French (4 Yrs)	RL13	4FT deg	*	BCC	Ind	Ind	28	BBBB	Ind		
Sociology & Social Anthropology and French	LR31	3FT deg	F	BCC	Ind	D$^	28$	CSYS	Ind		
Statistics and French (4 Yrs)	RG14	4FT deg	*	BCC	Ind	Ind	28	BBBB	Ind		
Visual Arts and French	RW11	3FT deg	F	BCC	Ind	D$^	28$	CSYS	Ind		
Visual Arts and French (4 Yrs)	WR11	4FT deg	*	BCC	Ind	Ind	28	BBBB	Ind		

Univ of KENT

TITLE	CODE	COURSE	SUBJECTS	A/AS	NO/C	RGNVQ	IB	SQA(H)	SQA	RATIO	A/AS
European Studies (French)	R141	4FT deg	F	22	2M+4D	Ind	30	Ind	Ind	6	18/25
French	R101	4FT deg	F	22	2M+4D	Ind	30	Ind	Ind	8	18/30
French (with Maitrise)	R110	4FT deg	F	26	6D	Ind	34	Ind	Ind	13	
French/Classical Studies	QR81	4FT deg	F	20	3M+3D	Ind	28	Ind	Ind		
French/Comparative Literary Studies	RQ12	4FT deg	F	20	3M+3D	Ind	28	Ind	Ind	2	
French/Computing	RG15	4FT deg	F	20	3M+3D	Ind	28	Ind	Ind	5	
French/Drama	RW14	4FT deg	F	22	2M+4D	Ind	30	Ind	Ind	20	
French/English	QR31	4FT deg	E+F	22	2M+4D	Ind	30	Ind	Ind	14	
French/English (Post-Colonial Literatures)	RQ1J	4FT deg	E+F	22	2M+4D	Ind	30	Ind	Ind		
French/English Language	RQ13	4FT deg	E+F	22	2M+4D	Ind	30	Ind	Ind	6	
French/Film Studies	RW15	4FT deg	F	22	2M+4D	Ind	30	Ind	Ind	21	
German/French	RR12	4FT deg	F+G	22	2M+4D	Ind	30	Ind	Ind	12	22/28
History and Theory of Art/French	VR41	4FT deg	F	22	2M+4D	Ind	30	Ind	Ind		
History of Science/French	RV15	4FT deg	F	20	3M+3D	Ind	28	Ind	Ind		
History/French	RV11	4FT deg	F	22	2M+4D	Ind	30	Ind	Ind	10	
Italian/French	RR13	4FT deg	F	22	2M+4D	Ind	30	Ind	Ind	11	20/24

course details			98 expected requirements							96 entry stats	
TITLE	CODE	COURSE	SUBJECTS	A/AS	NO/C	AGNVQ	IB	SQA(H)	SQA	RATIO	A/AS
Linguistics/French	RQ11	4FT deg	F	22	2M+4D	Ind	30	Ind	Ind	19	
Philosophy/French	RV17	4FT deg	F	22	2M+4D	Ind	30	Ind	Ind		
Politics and Government with French (4 Yrs)	MRC1	4FT deg	F	18	Ind	Ind	26$	BBBB$	Ind		
Spanish/French	RR14	4FT deg	F	22	2M+4D	Ind	30	Ind	Ind		
Theology/French	RV18	4FT deg	F	20	3M+3D	Ind	28	Ind	Ind	3	

KING'S COLL LONDON (Univ of London)

TITLE	CODE	COURSE	SUBJECTS	A/AS	NO/C	AGNVQ	IB	SQA(H)	SQA	RATIO	A/AS
Classical Studies and French	QR81	4FT deg	F	BBC						4	
French	R100	4FT deg	F	BBC						4	20/28
French (3 Yrs)	R102	3FT deg	F	BBB						29	
French and German	RR12	4FT deg	F+G	BBC						5	20/30
French and Hispanic Studies	RR14	4FT deg	F+Sp	BBC						6	20/28
French and Mathematics	RG11	4FT deg	F+M	BBC	X		30$	AABBB$ X		6	
French and Modern Greek	RTC2	4FT deg	F	BBC							
French and Philosophy	RV17	4FT deg	F	BBC						9	
French and Portuguese	RR15	4FT deg	F	BBC						5	
French with Applied Computing	R1G5	4FT deg	F	BCC						4	
French with English	R1Q3	4FT deg	F+E	BBC						8	22/28
French with Management	R1N1	4FT deg	F	BBC						7	20/26
Physics with French	F3R1	3FT deg	M+P g	18	2M+1D		28$	AABBB	Ind		
War Studies and French	MR91	4FT deg	F	BBC						3	
European Studies French	T2Y3	4FT deg	F	ABB							

KINGSTON Univ

TITLE	CODE	COURSE	SUBJECTS	A/AS	NO/C	AGNVQ	IB	SQA(H)	SQA	RATIO	A/AS
Applied Biology and French	CR11	4FT deg	2(B/C/F) g	10	Ind	Ind	Ind	CCC	Ind	5	
Chemistry and French	FR11	4FT deg	C/F g	8	Ind	Ind	Ind	CCC	Ind		
French	R100	4FT deg	F	14	MO	Ind^	Ind	BCCCC	HN	6	8/16
French/Economics	RL11	4FT deg	F g	14	MO	Ind^	Ind	BCCCC	HN	1	
French/English Language	RQ13	4FT deg	E+F	14	MO	Ind^	Ind	BCCCC	HN		8/14
French/English Literature	QR31	4FT deg	E+F	16	MO	Ind^	Ind	BBCCC	HN	2	10/20
Geography and French	FR81	4FT deg	Gy/F g	12	$	Ind	Ind	BCCC	Ind		
Geology and French	FR61	4FT deg	F/S g	10	$	Ind	Ind	CCC	Ind		
German/French	RR21	4FT deg	G+F	14	MO	Ind^	Ind	BCCCC	HN	7	
History of Art, Architecture and Design/French	VR41	3FT deg	F g	14-16	MO	Ind^	Ind	BBCCC	HN		
History/French	RV11	4FT deg	F+H g	14	MO	Ind^	Ind	BCCCC	HN	2	
Mathematics and French	GR11	4FT deg	M/F g	10	$	Ind	Ind	CCC	Ind	3	
Physics & French	FR31	4FT deg	P/F	10	Ind	Ind	Ind	CCC	Ind		
Politics/French	MR11	4FT deg	F g	14	MO	Ind^	Ind	BCCCC	HN	2	
Psychology/French	LR71	4FT deg	F g	16	MO	Ind^	Ind	BBCCC	HN	3	8/18
Spanish/French	RR41	4FT deg	F g	14	MO	Ind^	Ind	BCCCC	HN	5	6/16
Women's Studies/French	RM19	4FT deg	F g	14	MO	Ind^	Ind	BCCCC	HN	2	

Univ of Wales, LAMPETER

TITLE	CODE	COURSE	SUBJECTS	A/AS	NO/C	AGNVQ	IB	SQA(H)	SQA	RATIO	A/AS
French (4 Yrs)	R101	4FT deg	F	16	Ind	Ind	Ind	Ind	Ind		
French and American Literature	QR3C	3FT deg	F		Ind	Ind	Ind	Ind	Ind		
French and Ancient History	RV1D	4FT deg	F	16	Ind	Ind	Ind	Ind	Ind		
French and Anthropology	LR61	4FT deg	F	16	Ind	Ind	Ind	Ind	Ind		
French and Archaeology	RV16	4FT deg	F	16	Ind	Ind	Ind	Ind	Ind		
French and Australian Studies	LR6C	3FT deg	F		Ind	Ind	Ind	Ind	Ind		
French and Church History	RVDC	4FT deg	F	16	Ind	Ind	Ind	Ind	Ind		
French and Classical Studies	QR81	4FT deg	F	16	Ind	Ind	Ind	Ind	Ind		
French and Cultural Studies in Geography	LR8C	3FT deg	F	16	Ind	Ind	Ind	Ind	Ind		
French and English Literature	QR31	4FT deg	F+E	16-18	Ind	Ind	Ind	Ind	Ind		

Languages – French   40

course details			98 expected requirements							96 entry stats

TITLE	CODE	COURSE	SUBJECTS	A/AS	NO/C	AGNVQ	IB	SQA(H)	SQA	RATIO A/AS
Geography and French	LR81	4FT deg	F+Gy	16	Ind	Ind	Ind	Ind	Ind	
German Studies and French	RRC2	4FT deg	F	16	Ind	Ind	Ind	Ind	Ind	
German and French	RR12	4FT deg	F+G	16	Ind	Ind	Ind	Ind	Ind	
Greek and French	QR71	4FT deg	F g	16	Ind	Ind	Ind	Ind	Ind	
History and French	RV11	4FT deg	H+F	16	Ind	Ind	Ind	Ind	Ind	
Informatics and French	GR51	4FT deg	F	14-16	Ind	Ind	Ind	Ind	Ind	
Islamic Studies and French	TR61	4FT deg	F	16	Ind	Ind	Ind	Ind	Ind	
Latin and French	QR61	4FT deg	F g	16	Ind	Ind	Ind	Ind	Ind	
Management Techniques and French	NR11	3FT deg	F	16	Ind	Ind	Ind	Ind	Ind	
Medieval Studies and French	VR11	4FT deg	F	16	Ind	Ind	Ind	Ind	Ind	
Modern Historical Studies and French	VR1C	3FT deg			Ind	Ind	Ind	Ind	Ind	
Philosophical Studies and French	RV17	4FT deg	F	16	Ind	Ind	Ind	Ind	Ind	
Religious Studies and French	RVC8	4FT deg	F	16	Ind	Ind	Ind	Ind	Ind	
Theology and French	RV18	4FT deg	F	16	Ind	Ind	Ind	Ind	Ind	
Victorian Studies and French	RV1C	4FT deg	F	16	Ind	Ind	Ind	Ind	Ind	
Welsh Studies and French	QR5C	4FT deg	F	16	Ind	Ind	Ind	Ind	Ind	
Welsh and French	QR51	4FT deg	W+F	16	Ind	Ind	Ind	Ind	Ind	
Women's Studies and French	MR91	4FT deg	F	16	Ind	Ind	Ind	Ind	Ind	
Combined Honours French	Y400	3								

LANCASTER Univ

TITLE	CODE	COURSE	SUBJECTS	A/AS	NO/C	AGNVQ	IB	SQA(H)	SQA	RATIO A/AS
Chemistry with French Studies (4 years)	F1R1	4SW deg	C+F g	18	MO $		28$	BBBB$	Ind	
European Management (French)	N1R1	4FT/5SW deg	F g	ABB	MO+5D		32$	AABBB$	Ind	
French St and Teaching English as a Foreign Lang	RX1X	4SW deg	E+F g	BBC	Ind $		30$	BBBBB$	Ind	
French Studies	R100	4SW deg	F g	BCC	Ind $		30$	BBBBB$	Ind	
French Studies and Accounting and Finance	NR41	4SW deg	M+F g	BBC	DO $		32$	AABBB$	Ind	
French Studies and Art History	WR11	4SW deg	F	BCC	MO $		30$	BBBBB$	Ind	
French Studies and Computing	GR51	4FT deg	F g	BCC	Ind $		30$	BBBBB$	Ind	
French Studies and Economics	RL11	4SW deg	F g	BBC	Ind		32$	ABBBB$	Ind	
French Studies and Educational Studies	RX19	4SW deg	F	BCC	Ind $		30$	BBBBB$	Ind	
French Studies and English	RQ13	4SW deg	F+E	BBC	Ind $		32$	ABBBB$	Ind	
French Studies and Geography	LR81	4SW deg	F+Gy g	BBC	Ind $		30$	BBBBB$	Ind	
French Studies and German Studies	RR12	4SW deg	(F+G)/* g	BCC	Ind $		30$	BBBBB$	Ind	
French Studies and History	RV11	4SW deg	H+F	BCC	Ind $		30$	ABBBB$	Ind	
French Studies and Italian Studies	RR13	4SW deg	(F+I)/* g	BCC	Ind $		30$	BBBBB$	Ind	
French Studies and Linguistics	QR11	4SW deg	F g	BBC	MO $		30$	BBBBB$	Ind	
French Studies and Marketing	RN15	4SW deg	F g	BBC	MO+4D		32$	ABBBB$	Ind	
French Studies and Mathematics	GR11	4SW deg	F+M	20	MO $		30$	BBBBB$	Ind	
French Studies and Music	WR31	4SW deg	F+Mu	BCC	MO $		30$	BBBB$	Ind	
French Studies and Philosophy	RV17	4SW deg	F	BCC	Ind $		30$	BBBBB$	Ind	
French Studies and Politics	RM11	4SW deg	F	BCC	Ind $		30$	BBBBB$	Ind	
French Studies and Psychology	CR81	4SW deg	F g	BBC	DO $		32$	ABBBB$	Ind	
French Studies and Religious Studies	RV18	4SW deg	F	BCC	Ind $		30$	BBBBB$	Ind	
French Studies and Spanish Studies	RR14	4SW deg	(F+Sp)/* g	BCC	Ind $		30$	BBBBB$	Ind	
French Studies and Theatre Studies	WR41	4SW deg	F	BCC	MO $		30$	BBBBB$	Ind	
Physics with French Studies	F3R1	4SW deg	F+P+M	BCC	MO $		24$	BBCCC$	Ind	

Univ of LEEDS

TITLE	CODE	COURSE	SUBJECTS	A/AS	NO/C	AGNVQ	IB	SQA(H)	SQA	RATIO A/AS
Arabic-French	RT16	4FT deg	F g	BBC	Ind	Ind	30$	CSYS	Ind	
Chemistry-French	FR11	4FT deg	C+F+M/P	BBC	Ind	Ind	30$	CSYS	Ind	
Chinese-French	RT13	4FT deg	F g	BBC	Ind	Ind	30$	CSYS	Ind	3 22/30
Classical Literature-French	QR81	4FT deg	F g	BBC	Ind	Ind	30$	CSYS	Ind	
Computer Science-French	GR51	4FT deg	F+M g	BBC		Ind	30$	ABBBB	Ind	
Economics-French	RL11	4FT deg	F g	BBC	Ind	Ind	30$	CSYS	Ind	13

course details | 98 expected requirements | 96 entry stats

TITLE	CODE	COURSE	SUBJECTS	A/AS	ND/C	AGNVQ	IB	SQA(H)	SQA	RATIO	A/AS
English-French	QR31	4FT deg	E+F g	ABB	Ind	Ind	33$	CSYS	Ind	6	26/30
French	R100	4FT deg	F g	BBC	Ind	Ind	30$	BBBBC	Ind	4	18/30
French-German	RR12	4FT deg	F+G g	BBB	Ind	Ind	32$	CSYS	Ind	7	24/30
French-Greek Civilisation	QRW1	4FT deg	F g	BBC	Ind	Ind	30$	CSYS	Ind		
French-History	RV11	4FT deg	F g	BBB	Ind	Ind	32$	CSYS	Ind	10	26/28
French-History of Art	RV14	4FT deg	F g	BBC	Ind	Ind	30$	CSYS	Ind	7	26/26
French-Italian	RR13	4FT deg	F+I g	BBC	Ind	Ind	30$	CSYS	Ind	7	24/30
French-Italian B	RR1H	4FT deg	F g	BBC	Ind	Ind	30$	CSYS	Ind	6	20/30
French-Japanese	RT14	4FT deg	F g	BBC	Ind	Ind	30$	CSYS	Ind		
French-Latin	RQ16	4FT deg	F+Ln g	BBC	Ind	Ind	30$	CSYS	Ind	20	
French-Linguistics	QR11	4FT deg	F g	BBC	Ind	Ind	30$	CSYS	Ind	6	22/28
French-Management Studies	RN11	4FT deg	F g	BBB	Ind	Ind	32$	CSYS	Ind	14	24/30
French-Mathematics	RG11	4FT deg	F+M g	BBC	Ind	Ind	30$	CSYS	Ind	9	
French-Music	RW13	4FT deg	F+Mu g	BBC	Ind	Ind	30$	CSYS	Ind	14	
French-Philosophy	RV17	4FT deg	F g	BBB	Ind	Ind	32$	CSYS	Ind	5	24/30
French-Politics	RM11	4FT deg	F g	BBC	Ind	Ind	30$	CSYS	Ind	10	24/30
French-Politics and European Parliamentary St	RM1C	4FT deg	F g	BBB	Ind	Ind	Ind	Ind	Ind		
French-Portuguese	RR15	4FT deg	F g	BBC	Ind	Ind	30$	CSYS	Ind	6	
French-Religious Studies	RV1V	4FT deg	F g	BBC	Ind	Ind	30$	CSYS	Ind	3	
French-Roman Civilisation	QRV1	4FT deg	F g	BBC	Ind	Ind	30$	CSYS	Ind		
French-Russian	RR18	4FT deg	F+R g	BBC	Ind	Ind	30$	CSYS	Ind	6	
French-Russian B	RR1V	4FT deg	F g	BBC	Ind	Ind	30$	CSYS	Ind	7	20/26
French-Spanish	RR14	4FT deg	F+Sp g	BBB	Ind	Ind	32$	CSYS	Ind	6	24/30
French-Theology	RV18	4FT deg	F g	BBC	Ind	Ind	30$	CSYS	Ind		
Law-French	MR31	4FT deg	F g	ABB	Ind	Ind	33$	CSYS	Ind	36	
Mathematics-French	GR11	4FT deg	F+M g	BBC		Ind	30$	ABBBB	Ind		
Physics-French	FR31	4FT deg	M+P+F	BBC	Ind	Ind	30$	CSYS	Ind		
Statistics-French	GR41	4FT deg	F+M g	BBC		Ind	30$	ABBBB	Ind		

LEEDS, TRINITY & ALL SAINTS Univ COLL

TITLE	CODE	COURSE	SUBJECTS	A/AS	ND/C	AGNVQ	IB	SQA(H)	SQA	RATIO	A/AS
French-Management	RN11	4FT deg	F g	BCC-CCD	Ind	X	24$	BBCCC	Ind	6	8/17
French-Media	RP14	4FT deg	F g	BBC-CCD	Ind	X	24$	BBCCC	Ind	4	8/26

LEEDS METROPOLITAN Univ

TITLE	CODE	COURSE	SUBJECTS	A/AS	ND/C	AGNVQ	IB	SQA(H)	SQA	RATIO	A/AS
Public Relations (French)	P3R1	3FT deg									

Univ of LEICESTER

TITLE	CODE	COURSE	SUBJECTS	A/AS	ND/C	AGNVQ	IB	SQA(H)	SQA	RATIO	A/AS
French	R100	4FT deg	F g	BCD	X	D$^	28$	BBBB$	X		16/24
French and German	RR12	4FT deg	F+G g	BCD	X	D$^	26$	BBBB$	X		14/30
French and Italian	RR13	4FT deg	F g	BCD	X	D$^	28$	BBBB$	X		16/22
French and Politics	RM11	4FT deg	F g	BCD	X	D$^	28$	BBBB$	X		16/20
Law with French	M3R1	4FT deg	F g	26	X	D$^ gi	33$	AAABBB	X		22/30
Combined Arts	Y300	3FT deg	F g	BCC	DO $	D$^	30$	Ind	X		
French											

Univ of LINCOLNSHIRE and HUMBERSIDE

TITLE	CODE	COURSE	SUBJECTS	A/AS	ND/C	AGNVQ	IB	SQA(H)	SQA	RATIO	A/AS
Accountancy and French	NR41	3FT deg	F g	12	3M+1D	M	24	CCCC	Ind		
Administration and French	NR1D	3FT deg	F g	12	3M+1D	M	24	CCCC	Ind		
Business and French	RN11	3FT deg	F g	12	3M+1D	M	24	CCCC	Ind		
Computing and French	GR5C	3FT deg	F g	12	3M+1D	M	24	CCCC	Ind		
Finance and French	NR31	3FT deg	F g	12	3M+1D	M	24	CCCC	Ind		
French and Human Resource Management	NR61	3FT deg	F g	12	3M+1D	M	24	CCCC	Ind		
French and Media Technology	PR41	3FT deg	F g	12	3M+1D	M	24	CCCC	Ind		
Information Systems and French	GR51	3FT deg	F g	12	3M+1D	M	24	CCCC	Ind		
Marketing and French	NR51	3FT deg	F g	12	3M+1D	M	24	CCCC	Ind		

Languages – French   40

TITLE	CODE	COURSE	98 expected requirements							96 entry stats	
			SUBJECTS	A/AS	ND/C	AGNVQ	IB	SQA(H)	SQA	RATIO	A/AS
Univ of LIVERPOOL											
English and French	QR31	4FT deg	E+F	BBC	Ind		30$	ABBBB$	Ind	11	24/30
French	R100	4FT deg	F	BCC-BBC	Ind		30$	BBBBB$	Ind	5	16/24
French and German	RR12	4FT deg	F+G	BCC-BBC	Ind		30$	BBBBB$	Ind	9	20/26
French and Hispanic Studies	RR14	4FT deg	F+Sp	BBC	Ind		29$	BBBBB$	Ind	10	18/30
French and Pure Mathematics	GR11	4FT deg	F+M	BBD	Ind		29$	AABBC$	Ind	16	
Law and French	MR31	4FT deg	F	ABB	Ind	Ind	Ind	AAABB	X	13	26/30
Arts Combined French	Y401	4FT deg	F	BBC-BBB	Ind	Ind	30$	ABBB$	Ind		
BA Combined Honours French	Y200	3FT deg	F g	BBB	Ind	Ind	Ind	Ind	Ind		
LIVERPOOL HOPE Univ COLL											
French/American Studies	QR41	3FT deg	F	12	8M	P$^	Ind	Ind	Ind	11	
French/Art	WR91	3FT deg	A/Fa+F	12	8M	PA^	Ind	Ind	Ind	4	
French/English	QR31	3FT deg	EI+F	12	8M	X	Ind	Ind	Ind	8	
French/European Studies	TR21	3FT deg	F	12	8M	P*^	Ind	Ind	Ind		
Geography/French	RF18	3FT deg	F+Gy	12	8M	P$^	Ind	Ind	Ind		
History/French	RV11	3FT deg	H+F	12	8M	X	Ind	Ind	Ind		
Human & Applied Biology/French	RC11	3FT deg	B+F g	12	8M	P$^	Ind	Ind	Ind		
Information Technology/French	GR51	3FT deg	F	12	8M	P*^	Ind	Ind	Ind	2	
Mathematics/French	RG11	3FT deg	F+M	12	8M	X	Ind	Ind	Ind		
Music/French	RW13	3FT deg	F+Mu	12	8M	PQ^	Ind	Ind	Ind	3	
Psychology/French	RC18	3FT deg	F g	12	8M	P*^ go	Ind	Ind	Ind	6	
Sport, Recreation & Physical Education/French	RB16	3FT deg	F	12	8M	P*^	Ind	Ind	Ind		
Theology & Religious Studies/French	RV18	3FT deg	F	12	8M	P*^	Ind	Ind	Ind		
LIVERPOOL JOHN MOORES Univ											
French and German	RR12	4FT deg	L	14	3M+4D		Ind			8	10/18
French and Italian	RR13	4FT deg	L	14	3M+4D					17	
French and Japanese	RT14	4FT deg	L	14	3M+4D		Ind			6	
French and Russian	RR18	4FT deg	L	14	3M+4D		Ind			5	
French and Spanish	RR14	4FT deg	L	14	3M+4D		Ind			10	10/20
International Business Studies with French	N1R1	4SW deg	F	16	3M+4D					15	12/24
Literature, Life and Thought and French	QR31	4FT deg	F+E	16-20			28$	BBBC		6	
Media and Cultural Studies and French	PR41	4FT deg	F	16-18		X	28$	BBBC		10	14/18
LONDON GUILDHALL Univ											
3D/Spatial Design and French	RW1F	4FT deg	Pf g	DD	MO	M$ go	24	Ind	Ind		
French	R101	4FT deg									
French and Accounting	NR41	4FT deg	* g	DD	MO	M$ go	24	Ind	Ind		
French and Business	NR11	4FT deg	* g	CD-DDD	MO+2D	M$ go	26	Ind	Ind		
French and Business Economics	LRC1	4FT deg	* g	DD	MO	M$ go	24	Ind	Ind		
French and Business Information Technology	GR71	4FT deg	* g	DD	MO	M$ go	24	Ind	Ind		
French and Communications & Audio Visual Prod St	PR41	4FT deg	* g	CC-CDD	MO+2D	M$ go	26	Ind	Ind		
French and Computing	GR51	4FT deg	* g	DD	MO	M$ go	24	Ind	Ind		
French and Design Studies	RW12	4FT deg	* g	CD-DDD	MO+2D	M$ go	26	Ind	Ind		
French and Development Studies	MR91	4FT deg	* g	DD	MO	M$ go	24	Ind	Ind		
French and Economics	LR11	4FT deg	* g	DD	MO	M$ go	24	Ind	Ind		
French and English	QR31	4FT deg	* g	CD-DDD	MO+2D	M$ go	26	Ind	Ind		
French and European Studies	RT12	4FT deg	* g	DD	MO	M$ go	24	Ind	Ind		
French and Financial Services	NR31	4FT deg	* g	DD	MO	M$ go	24	Ind	Ind		
French and Fine Art	RW11	4FT deg	* g	CC-CDD	MO+2D	M$ go	26	Ind	Ind		
German and French	RR12	4FT deg	* g	DD	MO	M$ go	24	Ind			

			98 expected requirements							96 entry stats
course details										
TITLE	CODE	COURSE	SUBJECTS	A/AS	ND/C	AGNVQ	IB	SQA(H)	SQA	RATIO A/AS
International Relations and French	MRC1	4FT deg	* g	DD	MO	M$ go	24	Ind	Ind	
Law and French	MR31	4FT deg	* g	CC-CDD	MO+2D	M$ go	26	Ind	Ind	
Marketing and French	NR51	4FT deg	* g	CD-DDD	MO+2D	M$ go	26	Ind	Ind	
Mathematics and French	GR11	4FT deg	* g	DD	MO	M$ go	24	Ind	Ind	
Modern History and French	RV11	4FT deg	* g	DD	MO	M$ go	24	Ind	Ind	
Multimedia Systems and French	GRM1	4FT deg	* g	DD	MO	M$ go	24	Ind	Ind	
Politics and French	MR11	4FT deg	* g	DD	MO	M$ go	24	Ind	Ind	
Product Development & Manufacture and French	JR41	4FT deg	* g	DD	MO	M$ go	24	Ind	Ind	
Psychology and French	CR81	4FT deg	* g	CD-DDD	MO+2D	M$ go	26	Ind	Ind	
Social Policy & Management and French	LR41	4FT deg	* g	CD-DDD	MO	M$ go	24	Ind	Ind	
Sociology and French	LR31	4FT deg	* g	CD-DDD	MO	M$ go	24	Ind	Ind	
Spanish and French	RR14	4FT deg	* g	DD	MO	M$ go	24	Ind	Ind	
Taxation and French	NRH1	4FT deg	* g	DD	MO	M$ go	24	Ind	Ind	
Textile Furnishing Design and French	RW1G	4FT deg	Pf g	DD	MO	M$ go	24	Ind	Ind	
Modular Programme French	Y400	3FT/4FT deg	* g	CC-DD	MO	M$ go	24	Ind	Ind	

LOUGHBOROUGH Univ

Economics with French	L1R1	3FT deg	F g	20			30$	Ind		13
French and German Studies	RR12	3FT deg	F/G g	20			28$	Ind		
French and Politics	MR11	3FT deg	F	20			28$	Ind		
Politics with French	M1R1	3FT deg	F	20			28$	Ind		
Spanish and French Studies	RR41	3FT deg	Sp+F	20			28$	Ind		

LUTON Univ

Accounting with French	N4RC	3FT deg	F g	12-16	MO/DO	M/D	32	BBCC	Ind	
Biochemistry with French	C7R1	3FT deg	F g	12-16	MO/DO	M/D	32	BBCC	Ind	
Biology with French	C1R1	3FT deg	F g	12-16	MO/DO	M/D	32	BBCC	Ind	
Biotechnology with French	J8R1	3FT deg	F g	12-16	MO/DO	M/D	32	BBCC	Ind	
Business Systems with French	N1RC	3FT deg	F g	12-16	MO/DO	M/D	32	BBCC	Ind	
Business with French	N1R1	3FT deg	F g	12-16	MO/DO	M/D	32	BBCC	Ind	
Environmental Science with French	F9R1	3FT deg	F g	12-16	MO/DO	M/D	32	BBCC	Ind	
Environmental Studies with French	F9RC	3FT deg		12-16	MO/DO	M/D	32	BBCC	Ind	
Geography with French	F8R1	3FT deg	F g	12-16	MO/DO	M/D	32	BBCC	Ind	
Health Science with French	B9R1	3FT deg	F g	12-16	MO/DO	M/D	32	BBCC	Ind	
Law with French	M3R1	3FT deg		12-16	MO/DO	M/D	32	BBCC	Ind	
Leisure Studies with French	N7R1	3FT deg	F g	12-16	MO/DO	M/D	32	BBCC	Ind	
Linguistics with French	Q1R1	3FT deg	F g	12-16	MO/DO	M/D	32	BBCC	Ind	9
Literary Studies in English with French	Q2R1	3FT deg		12-16	MO/DO	M/D	32	BBCC	Ind	
Marketing with French	N5R1	3FT deg	F g	12-16	MO/DO	M/D	32	BBCC	Ind	
Mathematical Sciences with French	G1R1	3FT deg	F g	12-16	MO/DO	M/D	32	BBCC	Ind	
Media Practices with French	P4R1	3FT deg	F g	12-16	MO/DO	M/D	32	BBCC	Ind	
Modern English Studies with French	Q3R1	3FT deg	F g	12-16	MO/DO	M/D	32	BBCC	Ind	
Plant Biology with French	C2R1	3FT deg	F g	12-16	MO/DO	M/D	32	BBCC	Ind	
Psychology with French	L7R1	3FT deg	F g	12-16	MO/DO	M/D	32	BBCC	Ind	
Regional Planning & Development with French	K4R1	3FT deg	F g	12-16	MO/DO	M/D	32	BBCC	Ind	
Travel and Tourism with French	P7R1	3FT deg	F g	12-16	MO/DO	M/D	32	BBCC	Ind	

Univ of MANCHESTER

English and a Modern Language (French)	RQ13	4FT deg	E+F	ABB			Ind	BBBBC		8	24/30
European Studies and Modern Langs (French)	RT12	4FT deg	F	ABB-BBB Ind		D^	28$	AAABB$ Ind		5	22/30
French Studies (4 Yrs)	R110	4FT deg	F	ABB		D^		AAABB$		3	18/28
French and Linguistics	RQ11	4FT deg	F	BBB	X		32$	AABBB		6	18/28
French with Latin	R1Q6	4FT deg	F	BBC		D^	30$			2	

	course details			*98 expected requirements*						*96 entry stats*	
TITLE	CODE	COURSE	SUBJECTS	A/AS	ND/C	AGNVQ	IB	SQA(H)	SQA	RATIO	A/AS
French/German	RR12	4FT deg	F	ABB		D^	30$	AAABB$		12	18/28
French/German	RR1G	4FT deg	F	ABB		D^	30$	AABB$		9	
French/Italian	RR13	4FT deg	F	ABB		D^	30$	AABB$		6	18/28
French/Italian	RR1H	4FT deg	F	ABB		D^	30$	AABB$		5	
French/Portuguese	RR15	4FT deg	F	ABB		D^	30$	AABB$			
French/Russian	RR18	4FT deg	F	ABB		D^	30$	AABB$		4	22/28
French/Russian	RR1W	4FT deg	F	ABB		D^	30$	AABB$		4	
French/Spanish	RR1L	4FT deg	F	ABB		D^	30$	AABB$		5	20/30
French/Spanish	RR14	4FT deg	F	ABB		D^	30$	AABB$		5	18/30
German/French	RR2C	4FT deg	G+F	BBB			28	BBBBC		5	
History and French	VR11	4FT deg	F	BBC-BBB			30$	CSYS$		7	22/28
History of Art and a Modern Language (French)	RV14	4FT deg		BBC	3M+3D		28	AABBB			
Italian/French	RR3C	4FT deg	F	BBB-BCC			Ind	BBBCC		3	
Latin with French	Q6R1	4FT deg	Ln+F	BBC	X	X	30	BBBBB	X	11	
Russian/French	RR8C	4FT deg	R+F	BBC-CCC	Ind		28$	BBBCC	Ind		
Spanish/French	RR4C	4FT deg	Sp	BBB-BBC			28$	ABBBB$		4	

UMIST (Manchester)

Aerospace Engineering with French (MEng)	H4R1	4FT deg	M+P g	BBB	MO+3D$	Ind	32$	CSYS$	Ind		
Chemical Engineering with French (MEng)	H8RC	4FT deg	M+C g	BBC	MO+3D$	Ind	30$	CSYS$	Ind	3	20/30
Chemistry with French (MChem)	F1RC	4FT deg	C g	18	3M+1D	MS6/^ go	30	CSYS	Ind	7	
Civil Engineering with French (MEng)	H2R1	4FT deg	M+P g	BBB	Ind	Ind	30$	CSYS	Ind		
Electrical and Electronic Eng with French (MEng)	H5R1	4FT deg	M+P g	BCC	4M+3D	Ind	30$	AABB$	Ind	3	14/30
French Language Studies	R110	4FT deg	F g	20	X	Ind	28	BBBBB	Ind	5	
International Management with French	N1R1	4FT deg	F g	ABB	X	Ind	35$	CSYS$	Ind	4	20/30
Mathematics and Language Studies (French)	GRD1	4FT deg	M+F g	BBC	Ind	Ind	30$	CSYS	Ind	5	
Paper Science with French (4 Yrs)	J5R1	4FT deg	M/P/C g	CCD	3M	DS^ go	27$	BBBC$	Ind	2	
Physics with French (MPhys)	F3R1	4FT deg	M+P g	BCD	4M+1D$	Ind	28$	CSYS	Ind	12	

MANCHESTER METROPOLITAN Univ

Accounting and Finance in Europe (French)	N4R1	4FT deg	F g	18	MO+8D	D^	26$	BBBBC	Ind		
Business in Europe-French Route	N1R1	4FT deg	F g	BBC	Ind	DB	24$	Ind	Ind		14/24
French post A level/German ab initio	RR1F	4FT deg	F	CC	X		28$	AACCC$	X		
French post A level/German post A level	RR1G	4FT deg	F+G	CC	X		28$	AACCC$	X		10/14
French post A level/Spanish ab initio	RR1K	4FT deg	F	CC	X		28$	AACCC$	X		7/18
French post A level/Spanish post A level	RR1L	4FT deg	F+Sp	CC	X		28$	AACCC$	X		6/18
Health Studies with French	B6R1	4FT deg	F		M+D	M$	Ind	Ind	Ind		
Law with French	M3R1	4FT deg	F g	BBC	Ind	Ind	Ind	Ind	Ind		12/22
Humanities/Social Studies French	Y400	3FT/4FT deg	F	CDD	Ind	Ind	Ind	BBB	Ind		

MIDDLESEX Univ

French Studies	R110▼	3FT deg	F g	12-16	X	X	28	Ind	Ind		
Joint Honours Degree French Studies	Y400	3FT/4FT deg	F g	12-16	5M	Ind	28	Ind	Ind		

NENE COLLEGE

Art and Design with French	W2R1	3FT deg	F	DD	5M	M	24	CCC	Ind		
Drama with French	W4R1	3FT deg	F	10	5M+1D	M	24	CCC	Ind		
Economics with French	L1R1	3FT deg	F g	6	5M	M	24	CCC	Ind		
Education with French	X9R1	3FT deg	F	DD	5M	M	24	CCC	Ind		
English with French	Q3R1	3FT deg	F	CC	4M+1D	M	24	CCC	Ind		
European Business (French)	NR11	4SW deg	F g	8	M+D	M	24	CCC	Ind		
French with American Studies	R1Q4	3FT deg	F	DD	5M	In	24	CCC	Ind		
French with Architectural Studies	R1V4	3FT deg	F	DD	5M	Ind	24	CCC	Ind		

Letts STUDY GUIDES
THE INDEPENDENT

course details   98 expected requirements   96 entry stats

TITLE	CODE	COURSE	SUBJECTS	A/AS	NO/C	RGNVQ	IB	SQA(H)	SQA	RATIO A/AS
French with Art and Design	R1W2	3FT deg	F	DD	5M	Ind	24	CCC	Ind	
French with Drama	R1W4	3FT deg	F	DD	5M	Ind	24	CCC	Ind	
French with Economics	R1L1	3FT deg	F g	DD	5M	Ind	24	CCC	Ind	
French with Education	R1X9	3FT deg	F	DD	5M	Ind	24	CCC	Ind	
French with English	R1Q3	3FT deg	F	DD	5M	Ind	24	CCC	Ind	
French with Geography	R1F8	3FT deg	F	DD	5M	Ind	24	CCC	Ind	
French with History of Art	R1VK	3FT deg	F	DD	5M	Ind	24	CCC	Ind	
French with Industrial Archaeology	R1V6	3FT deg	F	DD	5M	Ind	24	CCC	Ind	
French with Industry and Enterprise	R1H1	3FT deg	F g	DD	5M	Ind	24	CCC	Ind	
French with Information Systems	R1G5	3FT deg	F	DD	5M	Ind	24	CCC	Ind	
French with Law	R1M3	3FT deg	F g	DD	5M	Ind	24	CCC	Ind	
French with Marketing Communications	R1N5	3FT deg		DD	5M	Ind	24	CCC	Ind	
French with Music	R1W3	3FT deg	Mu+F	DD	5M	Ind	24	CCC	Ind	
French with Philosophy	R1V7	3FT deg	F	DD	5M	Ind	24	CCC	Ind	
French with Politics	R1M1	3FT deg	F	DD	5M	Ind	24	CCC	Ind	
French with Psychology	R1C8	3FT deg	F g	DD	5M	Ind	24	CCC	Ind	
French with Sociology	R1L3	3FT deg	F	DD	5M	Ind	24	CCC	Ind	
French with Sport Studies	R1N7	3FT deg	F	DD	5M	Ind	24	CCC	Ind	
Geography with French	F8R1	3FT deg	F+Gy	8	5M	M	24	CCC	Ind	
Industrial Archaeology with French	V6R1	3FT deg	F	10	5M	M	24	CCC	Ind	
Industry and Enterprise with French	H1R1	3FT deg	F g	EE	3M	P	24	CCC	Ind	
Information Systems with French	G5R1	3FT deg	F	6	5M	M	24	CCC	Ind	
Law with French	M3R1	3FT deg	F g	10	3M+2D	M	24	CCC	Ind	
Management Science with French	G4R1	3FT deg	F g	DD	5M	M	24	CCC	Ind	
Music with French	W3R1	3FT deg	F+Mu	DD	5M	M	24	CCC	Ind	
Politics with French	M1R1	3FT deg	F	DD	5M	M	24	CCC	Ind	
Sociology with French	L3R1	3FT deg	F	10	5M	M	24	CCC	Ind	
Sport Studies with French	N7R1	3FT deg	F+Ss/Pe	12	M+2D	M	24	BBB	Ind	

Univ of NEWCASTLE

TITLE	CODE	COURSE	SUBJECTS	A/AS	NO/C	RGNVQ	IB	SQA(H)	SQA	RATIO A/AS
French	R100	4FT deg	F	BBC			$	AABBB$		9	22/28
French and German	RR12	4FT deg	F+G	BBC		X	$	AABBB$		9	22/30
French and Spanish	RR14	4FT deg	F+Sp	BBC			$	AABBB$		7	22/30
French with Accounting	R1N4	4FT deg	F+M/Ec	BBC			$	AABBB$		
French with German	R1R2	4FT deg	F	BBC		X	$	AABBB$		6	30/30
French with Politics	R1M1	4FT deg	F	BBC			$	AABBB$		8
French with Portuguese	R1R5	4FT deg	F	BBC		X	$	AABBB$		
French with Spanish	R1R4	4FT deg	F	BBC		X	$	AABBB$		5	22/30
German with French	R2R1	4FT deg	G g	20			$	ABBBB$		4
Law with French	M3R1	4FT deg	F	ABB	Ind	Ind	35	AABBB	Ind	7	22/30
Spanish with French	R4R1	4FT deg	Sp g	BCC		X	$	ABBBB$		20
Combined Studies (BA) French	Y400	3FT/4FT deg	F g	ABC-BBB	5D	Ind	35$	AAAB	Ind	

Univ of NORTH LONDON

TITLE	CODE	COURSE	SUBJECTS	A/AS	NO/C	RGNVQ	IB	SQA(H)	SQA	RATIO A/AS
Biological Science and French	CR11	4FT deg	B	CD	Ind	Ind	Ind	Ind	Ind	
Chemistry and French	FR11	4FT deg	C	CD	Ind	Ind	Ind	Ind	Ind	
French	R100	4FT deg	*	CC	Ind	Ind	Ind	Ind	Ind	10
French and Information Technology	GR51	4FT deg	M/Cs/P/Es/St	CD	Ind	Ind	Ind	Ind	Ind	
International Business and French	NR11	4FT deg	* g	CC	MO+4D	D	Ind	Ind	Ind	14
Marketing and French	NR51	4FT deg	* g	CC	MO+4D	D	Ind	Ind	Ind	
Combined Honours French	Y300	4FT deg	*	CC	Ind	Ind	Ind	Ind	Ind	

			98 expected requirements							96 entry stats	
course details											
TITLE	CODE	COURSE	SUBJECTS	A/AS	ND/C	RGNVQ	IB	SQA(H)	SQA	RATIO	A/AS
Univ of NORTHUMBRIA											
French	R100	3FT deg	F	CC	2M+2D	M^	24	BBCCC	Ind		
French and Economics	LR11	3FT deg	F	CC	2M+2D	M^	24	BBCCC	Ind		
French and German	RR12	3FT deg	F	CC	2M+2D	M^	24	BBCCC	Ind	4	8/20
French and Politics	MR11	3FT deg			2M+2D	M^	24	BBCCC	Ind		
French and Russian	RR18	3FT deg	F	CC	2M+2D	M^	24	BBCCC	Ind	5	
French and Spanish	RR14	3FT deg	F	CC	2M+2D	M^	24	BBCCC	Ind	5	10/20
Information Studies and French	PR21	3FT deg	F	CC	2M+2D	M^		BBCCC			
Univ of NOTTINGHAM											
Civil Engineering with French	H2R1	3FT/4FT deg	M+P g	BBC-BCC	Ind	Ind	28$	Ind	Ind	6	26/30
Classical Civilisation and French	QR81	4FT deg	F	BCC						7	
Economics with French	L1R1	4FT deg	F g	AAB-ABB	X		32$	Ind	X	10	26/30
Electrical and Electronic Eng with French	H6R1	3FT/4FT deg	M+P g	BBC-BCC	Ind	Ind	28$	Ind	Ind	11	
Electronic Engineering with French	H6RC	3FT/4FT deg	M+P g	BBC-BCC	Ind	Ind	28$	Ind	Ind		
French Studies (French/Hist or French/Politics)	R100	4FT deg	F	ABC						6	24/30
French and German	RR12	4FT deg	F+G	AAC						13	28/30
French and Hispanic Studies	RR1L	4FT deg	F+Sp	BBB						2	26/30
French and Latin	QR61	4FT deg	F+Ln	BCC						15	
French and Philosophy	RV17	4FT deg	F	ABC							
French and Portuguese (Beginners)	RR1M	4FT deg	F	BBC							
French and Russian	RR18	4FT deg	F+R	BBC						9	
French and Russian (Beginners)	RR1V	4FT deg	F	BBC						7	24/30
Law with French	M3R1	4FT deg	F	AAB	Ind		34$	Ind	Ind	20	28/30
Management Studies with French	N1R1	4FT deg	F g	BBB	Ind	D*^ go	32$	AAABB$	Ind	26	24/30
Manufacturing Engineering and Mgt with French	H7R1	3FT/4FT deg	M g	CCC	Ind	Ind	28$	Ind	Ind	3	17/20
Mechanical Engineering with French	H3R1	3FT/4FT deg	M+P g	BBC-BCC	Ind	Ind	28$	Ind	Ind	10	20/30
Production and Operations Management with French	H7RC	3FT deg	M g	CCC	Ind	Ind	28$	Ind	Ind	3	
NOTTINGHAM TRENT Univ											
European Business with French	N1R1	4SW deg	F g	18	M+D $		24$	Ind	Ind	11	14/24
European Economics with French	L1R1	4FT deg	F g	14-16	1M+3D	Ind	Ind	BBCC	Ind	5	12/18
Humanities French	Y301	3FT/4SW deg	F g	14-16	M+D	Ind	28	CCCC	Ind		
OXFORD WESTMINSTER COLLEGE											
Contemporary French Studies with Cultural St	R1V9	3FT deg	F	CE	MO	M	Ind	CCC	Ind		
Contemporary French Studies with Cultural Studs	R1VX	2FT Dip	F	CE	MO	M	Ind	CCC	Ind		
Contemporary French Studies with Development St	R1L3	3FT deg	F	CE	MO	M	Ind	CCC	Ind		
Contemporary French Studies with Development St	R1LH	2FT Dip	F	CE	MO	M	Ind	CCC	Ind		
Contemporary French Studies with Interfaith St	R1VV	2FT Dip	F	CE	MO	M	Ind	CCC	Ind		
Contemporary French Studies with Interfaith St	R1V8	3FT deg	F	CE	MO	M	Ind	CCC	Ind		
Contemporary French Studies with Language Studs	R1T9	3FT deg	F	CE	MO	M	Ind	CCC	Ind		
Contemporary French Studies with Language Studs	R1TX	2FT Dip	F	CE	MO	M	Ind	CCC	Ind		
Contemporary French Studies with World Studies	R1M1	3FT deg	F	CE	MO	M	Ind	CCC	Ind		
Contemporary French Studies with World Studies	R1MC	2FT Dip	F	CE	MO	M	Ind	CCC	Ind		
OXFORD BROOKES Univ											
French Language & Literature/Business Adm & Mgt	NR11	4SW deg	F g	CDD-BBC	Ind	M^/MB4	Ind	Ind	Ind	13	
French Language and Contemp St/Bus Adm & Mgt	NR1C	4SW deg	F g	CDD-BBC	Ind	MB^/4	Ind	Ind	Ind	10	
French Language and Contemp St/Educational St	RXC9	4SW deg	F	DDD-CC	Ind	M^/M*3	Ind	Ind	Ind	13	
French Language and Contemp St/Environ Policy	KR3C	3FT deg									
French Language and Contemp St/Exercise & Health	RBC6	4SW deg	F+S	DD-CC	Ind	MS	Ind	Ind	Ind		
French Language and Contemp St/Food Sci and Nut	DR4C	4SW deg	F+S g	DD-CC	Ind	MS^	Ind	Ind	Ind		

course details			*98 expected requirements*							*96 entry stats*	
TITLE	CODE	COURSE	SUBJECTS	A/AS	NO/C	AGNVQ	IB	SQA(H)	SQA	RATIO	A/AS
French Language and Contemp Studies/Acc and Fin	NR4C	4SW deg	F g	CDD-BCC	Ind	M^/D*3	Ind	Ind	Ind		
French Language and Contemp Studies/Anthropology	LR6C	4SW deg	F	CDD-BCC	Ind	M*^	Ind	Ind	Ind		
French Language and Contemp Studies/Bio Chem	CR7C	3FT deg									
French Language and Contemp Studies/Biology	CR1C	4SW deg	F+S g	DD-CC	Ind	MS^	Ind	Ind	Ind		
French Language and Contemp Studies/Cartography	FR8C	4SW deg	F g	CC-DDD	Ind	M*^	Ind	Ind	Ind		
French Language and Contemp Studies/Cell Biology	CRCC	3FT deg									
French Language and Contemp Studies/Combined St	RYC4	3FT deg		X		X	X	X			
French Language and Contemp Studies/Comp Maths	GR9C	4SW deg	F g	CD-CDD	Ind		Ind	Ind	Ind		
French Language and Contemp Studies/Comp Systs	GR6C	3FT deg	F g	CDD-BC	Ind	M*^	Ind	Ind	Ind		
French Language and Contemp Studies/Computing	GR5C	4SW deg	F g	BC-CDD	Ind	M*^	Ind	Ind	Ind		
French Language and Contemp Studies/Ecology	CR9C	4SW deg	F g	CD-CC	Ind	MS^	Ind	Ind	Ind		
French Language and Contemp Studies/Economics	LR1C	4SW deg	F g	CDD-BB	Ind	M^/M*3	Ind	Ind	Ind	2	
French Language and Contemp Studies/Electronics	HR6C	4SW deg	F+S/M	CC-CDD	Ind	MS/M*^	Ind	Ind	Ind		
French Language and Contemp Studies/English St	QR3C	4SW deg	F	CDD-AB	Ind	M*^	Ind	Ind	Ind	16	
French Language and Contemp Studies/Environ Chem	RF1C	3FT deg									
French Language and Contemp Studies/Environ Scis	FRXC	4SW deg	F+S g	CD-CDD	Ind	M^/DS	Ind	Ind	Ind		
French Language and Contemp Studies/Fine Art	RWC1	4SW deg	F+Pf+A	BC-DDD	Ind	MA^	Ind	Ind	Ind		
French Language and Lit/Food Sci & Nutrition	DR41	4SW deg	F+S g	DD-CC	Ind	MS^	Ind	Ind	Ind		
French Language and Lit/French Lang & Contemp St	R110	4SW deg	F	CC-CDD	Ind	M*^	Ind	Ind	Ind	3	18/22
French Language and Literature/Accounting & Fin	NR41	4SW deg	F g	CDD-BCC	Ind	M^/D*3	Ind	Ind	Ind		
French Language and Literature/Anthropology	LR61	4SW deg	F	CDD-BCC	Ind	M*^	Ind	Ind	Ind	1	
French Language and Literature/Biological Chem	CR71	3FT deg									
French Language and Literature/Cartography	FR81	4SW deg	F g	CC-DDD	Ind	M*^	Ind	Ind	Ind		
French Language and Literature/Cell Biology	CRC1	3FT deg									
French Language and Literature/Combined Studies	RY14	3FT deg		X		X	X	X			
French Language and Literature/Computer Systems	GR61	3FT deg	F g	CDD-BC	Ind	M*^	Ind	Ind	Ind		
French Language and Literature/Computing	GR51	4SW deg	F g	BC-CDD	Ind	M*^	Ind	Ind	Ind		
French Language and Literature/Computing Maths	GR91	4SW deg	F g	CD-CDD	Ind	M*^	Ind	Ind	Ind		
French Language and Literature/Economics	LR11	4SW deg	F g	CDD-BB	Ind	M^/M*3	Ind	Ind	Ind		
French Language and Literature/Educational St	RX19	4SW deg	S g	CC-CDD	Ind	M^m*3	Ind	Ind	Ind	3	
French Language and Literature/Electronics	HR61	4SW deg	F+S/M	CC-CDD	Ind	MS/M*^	Ind	Ind	Ind		
French Language and Literature/English Studies	QR31	4SW deg	F	CDD-AB	Ind	M*^	Ind	Ind	Ind	13	
French Language and Literature/Environ Chemistry	RF11	3FT deg									
French Language and Literature/Environmental Pol	KR31	3FT deg									
French Language and Literature/Environmental Sci	FRX1	4SW deg	F+S g	CD-CDD	Ind	M^/DS	Ind	Ind	Ind		
French Language and Literature/Exercise & Health	RB16	4SW deg	F+S	DD-CC	Ind	MS^	Ind	Ind	Ind		
French Language and Literature/Fine Art	RW11	4SW deg	F+Pf+A	BC-DDD	Ind	MA^	Ind	Ind	Ind	6	
Geography & the Phy Env/French Lang & Contemp St	FRVC	3FT deg									
Geography and the Phys Env/French Lang and Lit	FRV1	3FT deg									
Geography/French Language and Contemp Studies	LR8C	4SW deg	F	CDD-BB	Ind	M*^	Ind	Ind	Ind	8	
Geography/French Language and Literature	LR81	4SW deg	F	CDD-BB	Ind	M*^	Ind	Ind	Ind		
Geology/French Language and Contemp Studies	FR6C	4SW deg	F+S/M g	DD-CC	Ind	PS/M*^	Ind	Ind	Ind		
Geology/French Language and Literature	FR61	4SW deg	F g	DD-CC	Ind	PS/M*^	Ind	Ind	Ind		
Geotechnics/French Language and Contemp Studies	HR2C	4SW deg	F+S/M/Ds/Es	CC-DD	Ind	M$^	Ind	Ind	Ind		
Geotechnics/French Language and Literature	HR21	4SW deg	F+S/M/Ds/Es	CC-DD	Ind	M$^	Ind	Ind	Ind		
German Lang & Contemp St/French Lang& Contemp St	RRCF	4SW deg	F+G	CC-CDD	Ind	M*^	Ind	Ind	Ind	8	
German Language & Lit/French Lang & Contemp St	RR2C	4SW deg	G+F	CC-CDD	Ind	M*^	Ind	Ind	Ind		
German Language and Contemp St/French Lang & Lit	RR1F	4SW deg	G+F	CC-CDD	Ind	M*^	Ind	Ind	Ind		
German Language and Literature/French Lang & Lit	RR12	4SW deg	G+F	CC-CDD	Ind	M*^	Ind	Ind	Ind		
German Studies/French Language and Contemp Stds	RRCG	4SW deg			Ind		Ind	Ind	Ind		
German Studies/French Language and Literature	RR1G	4SW deg			Ind		Ind	Ind	Ind		
Health Care/French Lang and Contemp St(Post Exp)	BR7C	3FT deg		X		X	X	X			

	course details			98 expected requirements							96 entry stats
TITLE	CODE	COURSE	SUBJECTS	A/AS	ND/C	AGNVQ	IB	SQA(H)	SQA	RATIO A/AS
Health Care/French Lang and Literture (Post Exp)	BR71	3FT deg		X		X	X	X		
History of Art/French Language and Contemp Studs	RVC4	4SW deg	F	CDD-BCC	Ind	M*^	Ind	Ind	Ind	
History of Art/French Language and Literature	RV14	4SW deg	F	CDD-BCC	Ind	M*^	Ind	Ind	Ind	
History/French Language and Contemp Studies	RVC1	4SW deg	F	CDD-BB	Ind	M*^	Ind	Ind	Ind	6
History/French Language and Literature	RV11	4SW deg	F	CDD-BB	Ind	M*^	Ind	Ind	Ind	
Hospitality Mgt St/French Language & Literature	NR71	4SW deg	F	CC-DDD	Ind	M^/M*3	Ind	Ind	Ind	
Hospitality Mgt Studies/French Lang & Contemp St	NR7C	4SW deg	F	CC-DDD	Ind	M^/M*3	Ind	Ind	Ind	2
Human Biology/French Language and Contemp Stds	BR1C	3FT deg								
Human Biology/French Language and Literature	BR11	3FT deg								
Information Systems/French Lang & Contemp Studs	GRMC	3FT deg	F g	CC-BC	Ind	M*^	Ind	Ind	Ind	3
Information Systems/French Language & Literature	GRM1	3FT deg	F g	CC-BC	Ind	M*^	Ind	Ind	Ind	2
Intelligent Systems/French Lang & Contemp Studs	GR8C	4SW deg	F g	CD-CC	Ind	M*^	Ind	Ind	Ind	
Intelligent Systems/French Lang and Literature	GR81	4SW deg	F g	CD-CC	Ind	M*^	Ind	Ind	Ind	
Law/French Language & Contemporary Studies	MR3C	4SW deg	F	CDD-BBB	Ind	M^D*3	Ind	Ind	Ind	4
Law/French Language and Literature	MR31	4SW deg	F	CDD-BBB	Ind	M^/D*3	Ind	Ind	Ind	12
Leisure Planning/French Language and Contemp St	KRHC	3FT deg								
Leisure Planning/French Language and Literature	KRH1	3FT deg								
Marketing Management/French Lang and Contemp St	NRNC	4SW deg	F g	CC-BCC	Ind	M^/D*3	Ind	Ind	Ind	11
Marketing Management/French Language and Lit	NRN1	4SW deg	F g	CC-BCC	Ind	M^/D*3	Ind	Ind	Ind	
Mathematics/French Language and Contemp Studies	GR1C	4SW deg	M+F g	DD-CC	Ind	M*^	Ind	Ind	Ind	
Mathematics/French Language and Literature	GR11	4SW deg	M+F g	DD-CC	Ind	M*^	Ind	Ind	Ind	
Music/French Language and Contemporary Studies	RWC3	4SW deg	F+Mu	DD-CC	Ind	M*^	Ind	Ind	Ind	3
Palliative Care/French Lang & Cont St (Post Exp)	BRRC	3FT deg		X		X	X	X		
Palliative Care/French Lang and Lit (Post Exp)	BRR1	3FT deg		X		X	X	X		
Planning Studies/French Language and Contemp St	KR4C	4SW deg	F g	CDD-DDD	Ind	M*^	Ind	Ind	Ind	
Planning Studies/French Language and Literature	KR41	4SW deg	F g	CDD-DDD	Ind	M*^	Ind	Ind	Ind	
Politics/French Language and Contemp Studies	MR1C	4SW deg	F	CDD-AB	Ind	M*^	Ind	Ind	Ind	
Politics/French Language and Literature	MR11	4SW deg	F	CDD-AB	Ind	M*^	Ind	Ind	Ind	4
Psychology/French Language and Contemp Studies	CR8C	4SW deg	F g	CDD-BBC	Ind	M*^	Ind	Ind	Ind	11
Psychology/French Language and Literature	CR81	4SW deg	F g	CDD-BBC	Ind	M*^	Ind	Ind	Ind	11
Publishing/French Language and Contemp Studies	PR5C	4SW deg	F g	CDD-BB	Ind	M^M$3	Ind	Ind	Ind	2
Publishing/French Language and Literature	PR51	4SW deg	F g	CDD-BB	Ind	M^M$3	Ind	Ind	Ind	
Rehabilitation/French Lang & Cont St (Post Exp)	BRTC	3FT deg		X		X	X	X		
Rehabilitation/French Lang and Lit (Post Exp)	BRT1	3FT deg		X		X	X	X		
Sociology/French Language and Contemp Studies	LR3C	4SW deg	F	CDD-BCC	Ind	M*^	Ind	Ind	Ind	16
Sociology/French Language and Literature	LR31	4SW deg	F	CDD-BCC	Ind	M*^	Ind	Ind	Ind	5
Software Engineering/French Lang & Literature	GR71	4FT deg	F g	CDD-BC	Ind	M*^	Ind	Ind	Ind	
Software Engineering/French Lang and Contemp St	GR7C	4FT deg	F g	CDD-BC	Ind	M*^	Ind	Ind	Ind	
Statistics/French Language and Contemp Studies	GR4C	4SW deg	F g	DD-CC	Ind	M*^	Ind	Ind	Ind	
Statistics/French Language and Literature	GR41	4SW deg	F g	DD-CC	Ind	M*^	Ind	Ind	Ind	
Telecommunications/French Language & Contemp Std	HRPC	3FT deg								
Telecommunications/French Language and Lit	HRP1	3FT deg								
Tourism/French Language and Contemp Studies	PR7C	4SW deg	F g	CDD-BC	Ind	M^/M*3	Ind	Ind	Ind	
Tourism/French Language and Literature	PR71	4SW deg	F g	CDD-BC	Ind	M^/M*3	Ind	Ind	Ind	14
Transport Planning/French Language & Contemp St	NR9C	4SW deg	F g	CC-CDD	Ind	M*^	Ind	Ind	Ind	
Transport Planning/French Language & Literature	NR91	4SW deg	F g	CC-CDD	Ind	M*^	Ind	Ind	Ind	
Water Resources/French Language and Comtemp St	HRFC	3FT deg								
Water Resources/French Language and Literature	HRF1	3FT deg								

Univ of PLYMOUTH

Applied Economics with French	L1R1	3FT deg	E g	CCD-CDD	MO	M$^	Ind	BCCC	Ind	
Biotechnology with French	C9R1	3FT/4SW deg	B+F g	12-14	4M	MS^	Ind	BBBB	Ind	
Business Economics with French	L1RC	3FT deg	E g	CDD-CCD	MO	M$^	Ind	BCCC	Ind	

	course details			98 expected requirements							96 entry stats	
TITLE	CODE	COURSE	SUBJECTS	A/AS	ND/C	AGNVQ	IB	SQA(H)	SQA	RATIO	R/AS	
Cell Biology and Immunology with French	C1R1	3FT/4SW deg	B+F g	12-14	4M	MS^	Ind	BBBB	Ind		
Chemistry with French	F1R1	3FT deg	C+F g	CC	3M	MS^	Ind	CCCC	Ind		
European Economics with French	L1RD	3FT deg	F g	CDD-CCD	MO	M$^	Ind	BCCC	Ind		
European Studies with French	T2R1	4FT deg	F g	18	Ind	Ind	Ind	Ind	Ind		
Geography with French	F8R1	3FT deg	Gy+F g	16-18	X	M$^	Ind	ABBB	Ind		
Geology with French	F6R1	3FT deg	S+F g	12	4M	MS^	Ind	CCC	Ind		
Human Biology with French	C9RC	3FT/4SW deg	B+F g	BCC	4M $	M$^	Ind	BBBB	Ind		
International Business with French	N1R1	4SW deg	F g	CCD-CCC	MO	M12^	Ind	BBCC	Ind	10	16/22
Law with French	M3R1	3FT deg	F g	BCC-BBC	DO	D12^	Ind	BBBB$	Ind		
Mathematics with French	G1R1	3FT deg	M+F g	10-15	MO $	M$^	Ind	BBCC	Ind		
Microbiology with French	C5R1	3FT/4SW deg	B+F g	14-18	4M $	Ind	Ind	BBBB	Ind		
Ocean Science with French	F7R1	3FT deg	S+F g	14-16	5M $	M$^	Ind	CCCC	Ind		
Political Economy with French	LR1C	3FT deg	F g	CDD-CCD	MO $	M$^	Ind	BCCC	Ind		
Politics with French	M1R1	3FT deg	F g	14	Ind	M$^	Ind	BBBC$	Ind		
Psychology with French	C8R1	3FT/4SW deg	F g	BBC	MO+3D	M12^	Ind	BBBC$	Ind		
Social Policy with French	L4R1	3FT deg	F g	14	Ind	M$^	Ind	BBBC$	Ind		
Sociology with French	L3R1	3FT deg	F g	14	Ind	M$^	Ind	BBBC$	Ind		
Statistics (Applied) & Management Sc with French	G4RC	3FT deg	M/St+F g	10-15	MO $	M$^	Ind	BBCC	Ind		
Statistics (Applied) with French	G4R1	3FT deg	M/St+F g	10	MO $	M$^	Ind	BBCC	Ind		

Univ of PORTSMOUTH

French Studies	R110	4FT deg	F	14	5M $	M$6/^	25	BBBC	Ind	3	7/18
French and Italian Studies	RR13	4FT deg	F	14	5M $	M$6/^	25	BBBC	Ind	6	8/18
German and French Studies	RR12	4FT deg	G+F	12	5M $	M$6/^	25$	BBBC	Ind	5	8/14
Hispanic and French Studies	RR14	4FT deg	F	12	5M $	M$6/^	25	BBBC	Ind	5	10/18
Russian and French	RR18	3FT deg	F	12	5M $	M$6/^	Dip	BBBC	Ind		

QUEEN MARY & WESTFIELD COLL (Univ of London)

Engineering with French Language	H1R1	3FT deg	M	CCD-BCC	4M $	M$^	24$	BBBCC			
English and French	QR3C	4FT deg	E+F	20		M^	30$				
French	R100	4FT deg	F	20		M^	30$				
French (European Studies)	RT1F	4FT deg	F	20		M^	30$				
French and Drama	WR41	4FT deg	F	20		M^	30$				
French and Economics	LR11	4FT deg	F g	20		M^	30$	BBBBB			
French and Geography	LR81	4FT deg	F+Gy	BCC		M^	30$				
French and German	RR21	4FT deg	F+G	20		M^	30$				
French and Hispanic Studies	RR4C	4FT deg	F	20		M^	30$				
French and History	VR11	4FT deg	F	18		M^	30$				
French and Linguistics	RQ11	4FT deg	F	18		M^	30$				
French and Mathematics	GR11	4FT deg	F+M	18		M^	28$				
French and Politics	MR11	4FT deg	F	BCC		M^	30$				
French and Russian	RR18	4FT deg	F	18		M^	30$				
French with Business Studies	R1N1	4FT deg	F	18		M^	30$				
French, Linguistics and Computer Science	GR51	4FT deg	F	BBC-BCD	3D $	D^	28$				

QUEEN'S Univ Belfast

Accounting with French	N4R1	4FT deg	F g	ABB	X	D*^ go	34$	AAABB	X	4	24/30
Common and Civil Law with French	M3R1	4FT deg	F g	ABB	X	D*^ go	34$	AAABB	X	5	26/30
Economics with French	L1R1	3FT deg									
Finance with French	N3R1	4SW deg	F g	BBB	X	D*^ go	32$	AABBB	X	8	
French	R100	4FT deg	F g	BCC	X	D*^ go	29$	ABBB	X	8	20/30
French/Celtic (4 years)	QR51	4FT deg	F g	BCC	X	D*^ go	29$	ABBB	X	2	
French/Economics (4 years)	LR11	3FT deg									
French/English (4 years)	QR31	4FT deg	E+F g	BCC	X	X	29$	ABBB	X	5	20/26

| | | | 98 expected requirements | | | | | | | 96 entry stats |
| | | | | | | | | | | |

TITLE	CODE	COURSE	SUBJECTS	A/AS	ND/C	AGNVQ	IB	SQA(H)	SQA	RATIO A/AS
German/French (4 years)	RR12	4FT deg	F g	BCC	X	D*^ go	29$	ABBB	X	4	18/30
Greek/French (4 years)	RQ17	4FT deg	F g	BCC	X	D*^ go	29$	ABBB	X	
Information Management with French	P2R1	3FT deg	F g	BBC	X	D*^ go	30$	AABB	X	13
Italian/French (4 years)	RR13	4FT deg	F g	BCC	X	D*^ go	29$	ABBB	X	11
Latin/French (4 years)	RQ16	4FT deg	F g	BCC	X	D*^ go	29$	ABBB	X	6
Management with French	N1R1	3FT deg	F g	BBB	X	D*^ go	32$	AABBB	X	5	22/28
Modern History/French (4 years)	RV11	4FT deg	F g	BCC	X	D*^ go	29$	ABBB	X	6
Music/French (4 years)	RW13	4FT deg	F g	BCC	X	D*^ go	29$	ABBB	X	
Philosophy/French (4 years)	RV17	4FT deg	F g	BCC	X	D*^ go	29$	ABBB	X	
Politics/French (4 years)	RM11	4FT deg	F g	BCC	X	D*^ go	29$	ABBB	X	
Scholastic Philosophy/French (4 years)	RV1R	4FT deg	F g	BCC	X	D*^ go	29$	ABBB	X	
Social Anthropology/French (4 years)	RL16	4FT deg	F g	BCC	X	D*^ go	29$	ABBB	X	4
Spanish/French (4 years)	RR14	4FT deg	F g	BCC	X	D*^ go	29$	ABBB	X	3	18/30

Univ of READING

TITLE	CODE	COURSE	SUBJECTS	A/AS	ND/C	AGNVQ	IB	SQA(H)	SQA	RATIO A/AS
English Literature and French	QR31	3FT deg	El+F	BBC	Ind	D*^	31$	BBBB$	Ind	13	20/26
French	R100	4FT deg	F	BBC	Ind	D*^	31$	BBBB$	Ind	3	14/28
French B	R102	4FT deg	* g	BBC	Ind	D*^ go	31	BBBB	Ind	1
French and Economics	LR11	4FT deg	F g	BBC	Ind	D$^ go	31$	BBBB$	Ind	9
French and English Literature	RQ13	4FT deg	El+F	BBC	Ind	D*^	31$	BBBB$	Ind	5	18/24
French and German	RR12	4FT deg	F g	BBC	Ind	D$^ go	31$	BBBB$	Ind	29
French and History of Art	RV14	4FT deg	F	BBC	Ind	D$^	31$	BBBB$	Ind	7
French and International Relations	RM11	4FT deg	F	BBC	Ind	D*^	31$	BBBB$	Ind	
French and Italian	RR13	4FT deg	F	BBC	Ind	D$^	31$	BBBB$	Ind	17
French and Linguistics	QR11	4FT deg	F	BBC	Ind	D*^	31$	BBBB$	Ind	12
French and Management Studies	NR11	4FT deg	F g	BBC	Ind	DB^ go	31$	BBBB$	Ind	8	14/26
French and Politics	MR11	4FT deg	F	BBC	Ind	D*^	31$	BBBB$	Ind	7
French and Sociology	LR31	4FT deg	F	BBC	Ind	D$^ go | 31$	BBBB$	Ind	3	22/28
German and French	RR21	4FT deg	F g	BCC	Ind	D$^ go	30$	BBBB$	Ind	12
History and French	RV11	4FT deg	F	BBC	Ind	D*^	31$	BBBB$	Ind	23
International Management & Bus Admin with French	N1R1	4FT deg	F g	BBB	Ind	DB^ go	32$	ABBB$	Ind	
Italian and French	RR31	4FT deg	F	BBC	Ind	D$^	31$	BBBB$	Ind	
Latin and French	QR61	4FT deg	F g	BCC	Ind	D*^ go	30$	BBBB$	Ind	
Music and French	RW13	4FT deg	Mu+F	BBC	X	D*^	31$	BBBB$	Ind	14
Philosophy and French	RV17	4FT deg	F	BBC	Ind	D*^	31$	BBBB$	Ind	

Univ College of RIPON & YORK ST JOHN

TITLE	CODE	COURSE	SUBJECTS	A/AS	ND/C	AGNVQ	IB	SQA(H)	SQA	RATIO A/AS
European Studies with French	T2R1	3FT deg	F	12	Ind	M*^	27	BBBC		

ROEHAMPTON INST

TITLE	CODE	COURSE	SUBJECTS	A/AS	ND/C	AGNVQ	IB	SQA(H)	SQA	RATIO A/AS
Film & Television Studies and French	PR41▼	4FT deg	F	16	2M+2D$	M^	30	BBC	N$	
French and Applied Consumer Studies	NR91▼	4FT deg	F g	12	4M $	P^ go	26	BCC	N$	
French and Art for Community	WR11▼	4FT deg	F	12	4M $	P^	26	BCC	N$	
French and Biology	CR11▼	4FT deg	F+B	12	4M $	P^ go	26	BCC	N$	
French and Business Computing	GR71▼	4FT deg	F g	12	3D	M^ go	26	BCC	N$	
French and Business Studies	NR11▼	4FT deg	F g	12	3D $	M^ go	26	BCC	N$	6
French and Dance Studies	WR41▼	4FT deg	F	CC	2M+2D$	M^	30	BBC	Ind	
French and Drama & Theatre Studies	WRL1▼	4FT deg	F+E/T	16	3D $	M^	30	BBC	Ind	6
French and Education	XR91▼	4FT deg	F	12	4M $	P^	26	BCC	N$	3
French and English Language & Linguistics	QR3C▼	4FT deg	F+E/L	CC	2M+2D$	M^	30	BBC	Ind	4
French and English Literature	QR31▼	4FT deg	F+E	CC	2M+2D$	M^	28	BBC	Ind	11
French and Environmental Studies	FR91▼	4FT deg	F+B/Gy	12	4M $	P^ go	26	BCC	N$	
French: one year spent abroad	R100▼	4FT deg	F	12	4M $	P^	26	BCC	N$	6	8/15
Geography and French	RL18▼	4FT deg	Gy+F	12	4M $	P^ go	26	BCC	N$	4

course details			98 expected requirements							96 entry stats	
TITLE	CODE	COURSE	SUBJECTS	A/AS	NQ/C	AGNVQ	IB	SQA(H)	SQA	RATIO	A/AS
Health Studies and French	BR91▼	4FT deg	F+B	12	4M $	P^ go	26	BCC	N$		
History and French	RV11▼	4FT deg	F+H	12	4M $	P^	26	BCC	N$	2	
Human & Social Biology and French	CRC1▼	4FT deg	F+B	12	4M $	P^	26	BCC	N$		
Music and French	RW13▼	4FT deg	Mu+F	12	4M $	P^	26	BCC	N$	3	
Natural Resource Studies and French	DR21▼	4FT deg	F g	12	3M	P^ go	24	CCC	N$		
Psychology and French	LR71▼	4FT deg	F g	CC	3D $	M^ go	30	BBC	Ind	21	
Social Policy & Administration and French	RL14▼	4FT deg	F g	12	4M $	P^	26	BCC	N$		
Sociology and French	RL13▼	4FT deg	F g	12	4M $	P^	26	BCC	N$		
Spanish and French	RR14▼	4FT deg	Sp+F	12	2M+2D$	P$ go	28	BBC	N$	5	
Sport Studies and French	RB16▼	4FT deg	F+S g	12	3D	M^ go	30	BBC	N$		
Theology & Religious Studies and French	RV18▼	4FT deg	F	12	4M $	P^	26	BCC	N$		
Women's Studies and French	RM19▼	4FT deg	F	12	4M $	P^	26	BCC	N$		
ROYAL HOLLOWAY, Univ of London											
Computer Science with French	G5R1	3FT/4SW deg	M+F	BCC-BBC	MO+3D	D^	30$	Ind			
Economics with French	L1R1	3FT deg	F	BBB	Ind		32	Ind			
English Language and French	QR3C	4FT deg	E+F	ABC			30$	Ind		4	
English and French	QR31	4FT deg	E+F	ABC			30$	Ind		7	24/28
French	R100	4FT deg	F	BBC-ABC			30$	Ind		5	16/28
French and Classical Studies	RQ18	4FT deg	F	BBC			28$	Ind			
French and Drama	RW14	4FT deg	F+E/T g	ABC-BBC	Ind		30$	Ind		6	18/26
French and German	RR12	4FT deg	F+G	BBC			30$	Ind		27	
French and Greek	RQ17	4FT deg	F	BBC			28$	Ind			
French and History	RV11	4FT deg	F g	BBC-ABC			30$	Ind		9	
French and Italian	RR13	4FT deg	F	BBC			28$	Ind		20	
French and Latin	RQ16	4FT deg	F	BBC			28$	Ind			
French and Management Studies	RN11	4FT deg	F	BBC-ABC	Ind		30$	Ind		6	18/24
French and Music	RW13	4FT deg	F+Mu	BBC-ABC			Ind	Ind		7	
French and Spanish	RR14	4FT deg	F+Sp	ABC-BBC			Ind	Ind			
French with Economics	R1L1	4FT deg	F	BBC-ABC			28$	Ind			
French with German	R1R2	4FT deg	F+G	BBC-ABC			28$	Ind			
French with Italian	R1R3	4FT deg	F	BBC-ABC			28$	Ind			
French with Management Studies	R1N1	4FT deg	F	BBC-ABC			28$	Ind		1	14/16
French with Mathematics	R1G1	4FT deg	F+M	BBC-ABC			28$	Ind			
French with Music	R1W3	4FT deg	F+Mu	BBC-ABC			28$	Ind			
French with Political Studies	R1MC	4FT deg	F	BBC-ABC			28$	Ind		1	
French with Social Policy	R1L4	4FT deg	F	BBC-ABC			28$	Ind			
French with Sociology	R1L3	4FT deg	F	BBC-ABC			28$	Ind		6	
French with Spanish	R1R4	4FT deg	F	BBC-ABC			28$	Ind		4	22/26
German with French	R2R1	4FT deg	F+G	BCC			28$	BBBBC$			
Italian with French	R3R1	4FT deg	F	BBC			30	BBCCC$			
Management Studies with French	N1R1	3FT deg	F	BBB	2M+3D	D^	30	Ind		7	
Mathematics with French	G1R1	3FT deg	F+M	BCC-BBC	Ind	D^	Ind	Ind			
Music with French	W3R1	3FT deg	F+Mu	BCC-BBC			Ind	ABBCC$			
Sociology with French	L3R1	3FT deg	F	BCC-BBC	Ind	D^	Ind	Ind			
Foundation Programme French	Y408	4FT deg									
Univ of SALFORD											
Electronic Engineering w. Studies in France MEng	H6R1	4SW deg	M g	CCC	4M $	M	Ind	Ind	Ind		
English & a Modern Lang-English/French (4 Yrs)	QR31	4FT deg	El+F	BCC	Ind	X	Ind	Ind	Ind	7	
French/Arabic (4 Yrs)	RT16	4SW deg	L g	BBC	X	X	Ind	Ind	X		
French/German (4 Yrs)	RR12	4SW deg	L g	BCC	X	X	Ind	Ind	X	8	14/26
French/Hispanic Studies (4 Yrs)	RRC4	4SW deg	L g	BCC	X	X	Ind	Ind	X	16	

Languages – French 40

TITLE	CODE	COURSE	SUBJECTS	A/AS	ND/C	AGNVQ	IB	SQA(H)	SQA	RATIO	A/AS
				98 expected requirements							*96 entry stats*
French/Italian (4 Yrs)	RR13	4SW deg	L g	BCC	X	X	Ind	Ind	X	6	16/22
French/Spanish (4 Yrs)	RR14	4SW deg	L g	BCC	X	X	Ind	Ind	X	4	12/26
Info Technology with Language Training in French	G5R1	3FT deg	g	CCC	DO	D^	Ind	Ind	Ind	3	
Physics w. Addit Stud in France (4 Yrs)(M Phys)	F3RC	4FT deg	M+P g	4	Ind	Ind	Ind	CSYS	Ind		
Physics w. Additional Studies in France (4 Yrs)	F3R1	4SW deg	M+P g	4	Ind	Ind	Ind	CSYS	Ind		

SSEES:Sch of Slavonic & E European St(U of London)

TITLE	CODE	COURSE	SUBJECTS	A/AS	ND/C	AGNVQ	IB	SQA(H)	SQA	RATIO	A/AS
French and Russian	RR18	4FT deg	F	BBC	3M $	Ind	28	BBBBB		4	18/28

Univ of SHEFFIELD

TITLE	CODE	COURSE	SUBJECTS	A/AS	ND/C	AGNVQ	IB	SQA(H)	SQA	RATIO	A/AS
Computer Science and French	GR51	4FT deg	F+M g	BBC	4M+2D$	D^	30$	ABBB$	Ind	4	
English and French	QR31	4FT deg	El+F g	ABB	X	X	33$	AAAB$	Ind	9	26/30
French Language and Literature	R100	4FT deg	F g	BBC	X	D^	30$	ABBB$	Ind	8	22/30
French and Business Studies	RN11	4FT deg	F g	BBC	X	D^	30$	ABBB$	Ind	9	22/28
French and Economics	RL11	4FT deg	F g	BBC	X	D^	30$	ABBB$	Ind	22	
French and German	RR12	4FT deg	F+G g	BBC	X	X	30$	ABBB$	Ind	8	22/30
French and Hispanic Studies	RR14	4FT deg	F+L g	BBC	X	X	30$	ABBB$	Ind	16	22/30
French and History	RV11	4FT deg	F+H g	BBB	X	X	32$	AABB$	Ind	12	24/28
French and Linguistics	QR11	4FT deg	F g	BBC	X	X	30$	ABBB$	Ind	26	
French and Music	RW13	4FT deg	F+Mu g	BBC	X	X	30$	ABBB$	Ind	7	26/28
French and Philosophy	RV17	4FT deg	F g	BBB	X	X	32$	AABB$	Ind	5	26/28
French and Politics	RM11	4FT deg	F g	BBB	X	X	32$	AABB$	Ind	13	
French and Russian	RR18	4FT deg	F g	BCC	X	X	29$	BBBB$	Ind	24	
Law with French	MR31	4FT deg	F g	AAB	X	D^	35$	AAAA$	Ind	7	28/30

SHEFFIELD HALLAM Univ

TITLE	CODE	COURSE	SUBJECTS	A/AS	ND/C	AGNVQ	IB	SQA(H)	SQA	RATIO	A/AS
International Business with Language (French)	N1R1	4SW deg	F	16	X	M4/^	Ind	Ind	Ind		

Univ of SOUTHAMPTON

TITLE	CODE	COURSE	SUBJECTS	A/AS	ND/C	AGNVQ	IB	SQA(H)	SQA	RATIO	A/AS
Accounting and French	NR41	4FT deg	F g	22	Ind	D$^ go	30$	ABBBB$	Ind		
Economics and French	LR11	4FT deg	F g	24	Ind	D$^ go	32$	AABBB$	Ind	6	20/28
English and French	QR31	4FT deg	E+F	ABC-BBB	X	Ind	Ind	Ind	X	8	20/26
French	R100	4FT deg	F	BBB	1M+4D	Ind	30$	Ind	Ind	4	16/26
French (Cultural Studies)	R110	4FT deg	F	BBB		Ind		Ind	Ind		
French (Cultural Studies)	RR1F	4FT deg	F	BBC		Ind		Ind	Ind		
French (Linguistics and Language Studies)	R101	4FT deg	F	BBB		Ind		Ind	Ind		
French and Film	RW15	4FT deg	F	BBC		Ind		Ind	Ind		
French and German	RR12	4FT deg	F+G	BBC	1M+4D	Ind	30$	Ind	Ind	9	18/24
French and German (Linguistics & Language Stds)	RRC2	4FT deg	F+G	BBC		Ind		Ind	Ind		
French and German (Literary Studies)	RRCF	4FT deg	F+G	BBC		Ind		Ind	Ind		
French and German (Social and Political Studies)	RRCG	4FT deg	F+G	BBC		Ind		Ind	Ind		
French and History	RV11	4FT deg	F+H	BBC	1M+4D	Ind	30$	Ind	Ind	7	20/28
French and Music	RW13	4FT deg	F+Mu	22	1M+4D	Ind	30$	Ind	Ind		
French and Philosophy	RV17	4FT deg	F	BBC	1M+4D	Ind	30$	Ind	Ind	8	
French and Portuguese	RR15	4FT deg	F+Cl/L	BBC	1M+4D	Ind	30$	Ind	Ind		
French and Spanish	RR14	4FT deg	F+Sp	BBC	1M+4D	Ind	30$	Ind	Ind	8	15/26
French and Spanish (Linguistics & Language Stds)	RRC4	4FT deg	F+Sp	BBC							
French and Spanish (Literary Studies)	RRCK	4FT deg	F+Sp	BBC							
French and Spanish(Social and Political Studies)	RRCL	4FT deg	F+Sp	BBC							
Management Sciences and French	NRC1	4FT deg	F g	22	Ind	D$^ go	30$	ABBBB$	Ind	7	18/26
Marine Sciences with French (4 Yrs)	F7R1	4FT deg	F+2S g	BCC	Ind	Ind	30$	BBBBC	Ind	4	
Mathematics and French (4 Yrs)	GR11	4FT deg	M+F	BBC	Ind	Ind	30$	ABBBB	Ind	8	

	course details		98 expected requirements							96 entry stats
TITLE	CODE	COURSE	SUBJECTS	A/AS	ND/C	AGNVQ	IB	SQA(H)	SQA	RATIO A/AS
SOUTH BANK Univ										
French and Accounting	NR41	3FT deg	F+Ac/Ec g	12-16	4M+2D	M go	Ind	Ind	Ind	
French and Business Information Technology	GR71	3FT deg	M+F g	12-16	4M+2D	M go	Ind	Ind	Ind	
French and Computing	GR51	3FT deg	M+F g	12-16	4M+2D	M go	Ind	Ind	Ind	
French and Economics	LR11	3FT deg	Ec/Bu+F g	12-16	4M+2D	M go	Ind	Ind	Ind	
French and English Studies	QR31	3FT deg	E+F g	14-18	X	M^ go	Ind	Ind	Ind	
German - ab initio and French	RR12	3FT deg	F g	12-16	4M+2D	M go	Ind	Ind	Ind	
German and French	RR1F	3FT deg	G+F g	14-18	2M+4D	M go	Ind	Ind	Ind	
Health Studies and French	LR41	3FT deg	F+S g	12-16	4M+2D	M go	Ind	Ind	Ind	
History and French	RV11	3FT deg	F+H g	12-16	4M+2D	M^ go	Ind	Ind	Ind	
Housing and French	KR4C	3FT deg	F g	14-18	2M+4D	M go	Ind	Ind	Ind	
Human Resource Management and French	NR61	3FT deg	F g	14-18	2M+4D	M go	Ind	Ind	Ind	
Law and French	MR31	3FT deg	F g	14-18	2M+4D	D go	Ind	Ind	Ind	
Management and French	NR11	3FT deg	F g	12-16	4M+2D	M go	Ind	Ind	Ind	
Marketing and French	NR51	3FT deg	F g	12-16	2M+4D	M^ go	Ind	Ind	Ind	
Media Studies and French	PR41	3FT deg	E+F g	14-18	2M+4D	D go	Ind	Ind	Ind	
Product Design and French	HR71	3FT deg	F+Ad g	12-16	4M+2D	M go	Ind	Ind	Ind	
Psychology and French	CR81	3FT deg	F+S g	14-18	2M+4D	M go	Ind	Ind	Ind	
Social Policy and French	LR4C	3FT deg	F g	12-16	4M+2D	M go	Ind	Ind	Ind	
Sociology and French	LR31	3FT deg	F g	12-16	4M+2D	M go	Ind	Ind	Ind	
Spanish - ab initio and French	RR14	3FT deg	F g	12-16	4M+2D	M go	Ind	Ind	Ind	
Spanish and French	RR1K	3FT deg	Sp+F g	14-18	2M+4D	M^ go	Ind	Ind	Ind	
Technology and French	JR91	3FT deg	F g	12-16	4M+2D	M^ go	Ind	Ind	Ind	
Tourism and French	PR71	3FT deg	F g	12-16	4M+2D	M go	Ind	Ind	Ind	
Urban Studies and French	RK14	3FT deg	F g	14-18	2M+4D	M go	Ind	Ind	Ind	
World Theatre and French	RW14	3FT deg	F g	14-18	2M+4D	M go	Ind	Ind	Ind	
Univ of ST ANDREWS										
Biology with French (Science)	C1R1	4FT deg	B/C/Gy/M/P g	BBC	Ind	Ind	28$	BBBB$	Ind	3
Biology with French (with Integ Year Abroad)	C1RC	4FT/5FT deg	B/C/Gy/M/P g	BBC	Ind	Ind	28$	BBBB$	Ind	7
Chemistry with French	F1R1	4FT deg	C g	CCC	Ind	Ind	28$	BBBC$	Ind	
Chemistry with French (with Integ Year Abroad)	F1RC	4FT/5FT deg	C g	CCC	Ind	Ind	28$	BBBC$	Ind	
Economics with French	L1R1	4FT deg	M+F g	BCC	Ind	Ind	28$	BBBC$	Ind	
Economics with French (with Integ Year Abroad)	L1RC	4FT deg	M+F g	BCC	Ind	Ind	28$	BBBC$	Ind	
French with Year Abroad-Ancient History	RV1D	4FT/5FT deg	F g	BBB	X	Ind	30$	BBBB$	Ind	
French with Year Abroad-Arabic	RT1P	4FT/5FT deg	F g	BBB	X	Ind	30$	BBBB$	Ind	2
French with Year Abroad-Art History	RV1K	4FT/5FT deg	F g	BBB	X	Ind	30$	BBBB$	Ind	5
French with Year Abroad-Biblical Studies	RVC8	4FT/5FT deg	F g	BBB	X	Ind	30$	BBBB$	Ind	
French with Year Abroad-Economics	LRC1	4FT/5FT deg	F g	BBB	X	Ind	30$	BBBB	Ind	
French with Year Abroad-English	QRH1	4FT/5FT deg	F g	BBB	X	Ind	30$	BBBB$	Ind	5 26/30
French-Ancient History	RVD1	4FT deg	F g	BBB	X	Ind	30$	BBBB$	Ind	
French-Arabic	RT16	4FT deg	F g	BBB	X	Ind	30$	BBBB$	Ind	
French-Art History	RV14	4FT deg	F g	BBB	X	Ind	30$	BBBB$	Ind	6
French-Biblical Studies	RV18	4FT deg	F g	BBB	X	Ind	30$	BBBB$	Ind	
French-Economics	LR11	4FT deg	F g	BBB	X	Ind	30$	BBBB$	Ind	3
French-English	QR31	4FT deg	F g	BBB	X	Ind	30$	BBBB$	Ind	
Geography with French	F8R1	4FT deg	F+B/C/Gy/M/P g	BBB	Ind	Ind	30$	BBBB$	Ind	
Geography with French (with Integ Yr Abroad)	F8RC	4FT/5FT deg	F+B/C/Gy/M/P g	BBB	Ind	Ind	30$	BBBB$	Ind	
Geography-French	LR81	4FT deg	F g	BBB	X	Ind	32$	BBBB$	Ind	
Geography-French with Year Abroad	LR8C	4FT/5FT deg	F g	BBB	X	Ind	32$	BBBB$	Ind	4
German with Year Abroad-French	RRC2	4FT/5FT deg	F g	BBB	X	Ind	30$	BBBB	Ind	5 22/30
German-French	RR12	4FT deg	F g	BBB	X	Ind	30$	BBBB$	Ind	23
Hebrew-French	QR91	4FT deg	F g	BBB	X	Ind	30$	BBBB	Ind	

course details			98 expected requirements							96 entry stats	
TITLE	CODE	COURSE	SUBJECTS	A/AS	NQ/C	RGNVQ	IB	SQA(H)	SQA	RATIO A/AS	
Hebrew-French with Year Abroad	QR9C	4FT/5FT deg	F g	BBB	X	Ind	30$	BBBB$	Ind		
International Relations-French	MR11	4FT deg	F g	AAB	X	Ind	36$	AAAB$	Ind	6	
International Relations-French with Year Abroad	MR1C	4FT/5FT deg	F g	AAB	X	Ind	36$	AAAB$	Ind	9	
Italian-French	RR13	4FT deg	* g	BBB	X	Ind	30$	BBBB	Ind	1	
Italian-French with Year Abroad	RR31	4FT/5FT deg	F g	BBB	X	Ind	30$	BBBB$	Ind	4	
Latin-French	QR61	4FT deg	F g	BBB	X	Ind	30$	BBBB$	Ind	3	
Latin-French with Year Abroad	QR6C	4FT/5FT deg	F g	BBB	X	Ind	30$	BBBB$	Ind		
Management-French	NR11	4FT deg	F g	BBB	X	Ind	30	BBBB$	Ind		
Management-French with Year Abroad	NR1C	4FT/5FT deg	F g	BBB	X	Ind	30	BBBB$	Ind	8	
Mathematics with French	G1R1	4FT deg	F+M g	BCC	Ind	Ind	28$	BBBC$	Ind		
Mathematics with French (with Integ Yr Abroad)	G1RC	4FT/5FT deg	F+M g	BCC	Ind	Ind	28$	BBBC$	Ind	9	
Mediaeval History-French	RVC1	4FT deg	F g	BBB	X	Ind	30$	BBBB	Ind		
Mediaeval History-French with Year Abroad	RVCC	4FT/5FT deg	F g	BBB	X	Ind	30$	BBBB$	Ind	3	
Modern History-French	RV11	4FT deg	F g	BBB	X	Ind	30$	BBBB$	Ind		
Modern History-French with Year Abroad	RVCD	4FT/5FT deg	F g	BBB	X	Ind	30$	BBBB$	X	7	
Modern Languages (French with Integ Year Abroad)	R111	4FT/5FT deg	F g	BBB	X	Ind	30$	BBBB$	Ind	17	
Modern Languages (French)	R100	4FT deg	F g	BBB	X	Ind	30$	BBBB$	Ind		
Philosophy-French	RV17	4FT deg	F g	BBB	X	Ind	30$	BBBB$	Ind		
Philosophy-French with Year Abroad	RVDR	4FT/5FT deg	F g	BBB	X	Ind	30$	BBBB$	Ind	5	
Psychology with French	C8R1	4FT deg	F g	ABB	X	Ind	32$	ABBB$	Ind		
Psychology with French (with Integ Year Abroad)	C8RC	4FT/5FT deg	F g	ABB	X	Ind	32$	ABBB$	Ind		
Psychology-French	LR71	4FT deg	F g	ABB	X	Ind	32$	BBBBB$	Ind	4	
Psychology-French with Year Abroad	LR7C	4FT/5FT deg	F g	ABB	X	Ind	32$	BBBBB$	Ind	5	
Russian with Year Abroad-French	RRC8	4FT/5FT deg	F g	BBB	X	Ind	30$	BBBB$	Ind	7	
Russian-French	RR18	4FT deg	F g	BBB	X	Ind	30$	BBBB$	Ind	3	
Social Anthropology-French	LR61	4FT deg	F g	BBB	X	Ind	30$	BBBB$	Ind		
Social Anthropology-French with Year Abroad	LR6C	4FT/5FT deg	F g	BBB	X	Ind	30$	BBBB$	Ind	6	
Spanish with Year Abroad-French	RRC4	4FT/5FT deg	F g	BBB	X	Ind	30$	BBBB$	Ind	7	22/30
Spanish-French	RR14	4FT deg	F g	BBB	X	Ind	30$	BBBB$	Ind	13	
Spanish-Scottish History	RV1L	4FT deg	* g	BBB	X	Ind	30$	BBBB	Ind		
Statistics with French (Science)	G4R1	4FT deg	M g	BCC	Ind	Ind	28$	BBBC$	Ind		
Statistics with French (Science) (Int Yr Abroad)	G4RC	4FT/5FT deg	M g	BCC	Ind	Ind	28$	BBBC$	Ind	2	
Theological Studies-French	VR81	4FT deg	F g	BBB	X	Ind	30$	BBBB$	Ind		
Theological Studies-French with Year Abroad	VR8C	4FT/5FT deg	F g	BBB	X	Ind	30$	BBBB	Ind		
European Integration Studies *French*	Y602	4FT deg	F g	BBB	X	Ind	30$	BBBB	Ind		
General Degree of MA *Modern Languages (French)*	Y450	3FT deg	F g	BBB	X	Ind	30$	BBBB$	Ind		

STAFFORDSHIRE Univ

European Culture/French	LRP1	3FT deg	F g	CD	MO+2D	M^	27	BBC	Ind		
French with Language Studies	R1Q1	3FT deg	g	DD	4M+2D	M^	26	BCC			
French/American Studies	RQ14	3FT/4SW deg	F g	CD	MO+2D	M^	27	BBC	Ind		
French/Business Studies	RN11	3FT/4SW deg	F g	CCD	MO+2D	M$^	26	BBB	Ind	7	8/14
French/Cultural Studies	RL16	3FT/4SW deg	F g	CD	MO+2D	M^	26	BBC	Ind	8	
French/Development Studies	RM1Y	3FT/4SW deg	F g	12	4M+2D	M^	26	BCC	Ind		
French/Environmental Studies	RF19	3FT/4SW deg	F g	14	4M+2D	M^	26	ABB	Ind	2	
Geography/French	LR81	3FT/4SW deg	F g	16	4M+2D	M^	28	AAB	Ind		
German/French	RR21	4SW deg	G/F	DD	4M+2D	M^	26	BCC	Ind	10	
History/French	VR11	3FT/4SW deg	F+H	CD	MO+2D	M^	27	BBC	Ind	5	
Information Systems/French	GR51	3FT/4SW deg	F g	12	4M+2D	M^	26	BCC	Ind	2	
International Relations/French	MR1C	3FT/4SW deg	F g	12	4M+2D	M^	26	BCC	Ind	4	
Law/French	MR31	3FT/4SW deg	F g	18	HN	M^	26	BBBB	Ind	4	

TITLE	CODE	COURSE	SUBJECTS	A/AS	NO/C	AGNVQ	IB	SQA(H)	SQA	RATIO A/AS
Legal Studies/French	MR3C	3FT/4SW deg	F g	18	HN	M^	26	BBBB	Ind	
Literature/French	QR31	3FT/4SW deg	El+F g	CD	MO+2D	M^	27	BCC	Ind	6
Media Studies/French	PR41	3FT/4SW deg	F g	CD	MO+2D	M^	26	BCC	Ind	8
Philosophy/French	VR71	3FT/4SW deg	F	CD	MO+2D	M^	27	BBC	Ind	
Politics/French	MRC1	3FT/4SW deg	F g	12	4M+2D	M^	26	BCC	Ind	
Property with French	K2R1	3FT deg	g	12	4M	M$	24	BBC	Ind	
Psychology/French	LR71	3FT/4SW deg	F g	18	3M+3D	Ind	27	BBB	Ind	10
Spanish/French	RR41	4SW deg	F g	DD	4M+2D	M^	26	BCC	Ind	8
Women's Studies/French	MR91	3FT/4SW deg	F g	12	4M+2D	M^	26	BCC	Ind	

Univ of STIRLING

TITLE	CODE	COURSE	SUBJECTS	A/AS	NO/C	AGNVQ	IB	SQA(H)	SQA	RATIO A/AS
Accountancy/French Language	NR4C	4FT deg	g	BCC	HN	Ind	33	BBBB	HN	
Business Studies/French Language	NRCC	4FT deg	g	CCC	Ind	Ind	31	BBBC	HN	
Computing Science/French Language	GR51	4FT deg	g	CCC	Ind	Ind	28	BBCC	HN	
Economics/French Language	LR1C	4FT deg	g	CCC	Ind	Ind	31	BBBC	HN	
English Studies/French	QR31	4FT deg	g	CCC	Ind	Ind	31	BBBC	HN	
Financial Studies/French Language	N3R1	4FT deg	g	BCC	Ind	Ind	31	BBBC	HN	
French	R100	4FT deg	g	CCC	Ind	Ind	31	BBBC	HN	
French/Film & Media Studies	RP14	4FT deg	g	BBC	Ind	Ind	35	ABBB	HN	
French/German	RR12	4FT deg	g	CCC	Ind	Ind	31	BBBC	HN	
French/History	RV11	4FT deg	g	CCC	Ind	Ind	31	BBBC	HN	
French/Human Resources Management	NR1D	4FT deg	g	CCC	Ind	Ind	31	BBBC	HN	
French/Mathematics	GR11	4FT deg	M g	CCC	Ind	Ind	28	BBCC	HN	
French/Philosophy	RV17	4FT deg	g	CCC	Ind	Ind	31	BBBC	HN	
French/Politics	MR11	4FT deg	g	CCC	Ind	Ind	31	BBBC	HN	
French/Psychology	RC18	4FT deg	g	CCC	Ind	Ind	31	BBBC	HN	
French/Religious Studies	RV18	4FT deg	g	CCC	Ind	Ind	31	BBBC	HN	
French/Sociology	LR31	4FT deg	g	CCC	Ind	Ind	31	BBBC	HN	
French/Spanish	RR14	4FT deg	g	CCC	Ind	Ind	31	BBBC	HN	
Japanese/French	TR41	4FT deg	g	BCC	Ind	Ind	31	BBBC	HN	
Management Science/French Language	NR1C	4FT deg	g	CCC	Ind	Ind	31	BBBC	HN	
Marketing/French Language	N5R1	4FT deg	g	CCC	Ind	Ind	31	BBBC	HN	
Mathematics & its Applications with French Lang	G1R1	4FT deg	M g	CCC	Ind	Ind	28	BBCC	HN	

Univ of STRATHCLYDE

TITLE	CODE	COURSE	SUBJECTS	A/AS	NO/C	AGNVQ	IB	SQA(H)	SQA	RATIO A/AS
Arts and Social Sciences French	Y440	3FT/4FT deg	g	CCC	Ind		28	BBBBB$	Ind	

Univ of SUNDERLAND

TITLE	CODE	COURSE	SUBJECTS	A/AS	NO/C	AGNVQ	IB	SQA(H)	SQA	RATIO A/AS
Biology and French	CR11▼	4FT deg	B/C+F g	8	N $	M	24$	CCCC$	N$	
Biology with French	C1R1	3FT deg	B/C	8	3M	M	Ind	Ind	Ind	
Business Computing with French	G5R1	4SW deg	* g	4-8	4M	M* go	24	CCCC	N	5
Business Studies and French	NR11	4FT deg	F g	10	N $	M	24$	CCCC$	N$	5
Business Studies with French	N1R1	3FT/4SW deg	*	8	3M	M	Ind	Ind	Ind	
Computer Studies and French	GR51	4FT deg	F g	8	N $	M	24$	CCCC$	N$	
Economics and French	LR11	4FT deg	F g	8	N $	M	24$	CCCC$	N$	
Economics with French	L1R1	3FT deg	*	8	3M	M	Ind	Ind	Ind	
English and French	QR31▼	4FT deg	F+El g	10	Ind	M	24$	CCCC$	Ind	3
English with French	Q3R1	3FT deg	F	10	4M	M	Ind	Ind	Ind	
French and Geography	RL18▼	4FT deg	F+Gy/Gl g	10	N $	M	24$	CCCC$	N$	
French and Geology	RF16	4FT deg	F+Gy/Gl g	8	N $	M	24$	CCCC$	N$	
French and German	RR12▼	4FT deg	F+G g	8	N $	M	24$	CCCC$	N$	16
French and Mathematics	RG11	4FT deg	M+F g	8	N $	M	24$	CCCC$	N$	
French and Philosophy	RV17▼	4FT deg	F g	10	N $	M	24$	CCCC$	N$	4

Languages – French   40

	course details		98 expected requirements							96 entry stats

TITLE	CODE	COURSE	SUBJECTS	A/AS	ND/C	AGNVQ	IB	SQA(H)	SQA	RATIO A/AS
French and Physiology	RB11	4FT deg	B/C+F g	8	N $	M	24$	CCCC$	N$	
French and Politics	RM11▼	4FT deg	F g	10	N $	M	24$	CCCC$	N$	
French and Psychology	RC18	4FT deg	F g	12	3M $	M	24$	BCCC$	N$	6
French and Religious Studies	RV18▼	4FT deg	F g	10	N $	M	24$	CCCC$	N$	
French and Sociology	RL13▼	4FT deg	F g	10	N $	M	24$	CCCC$	N$	
French with American Studies	R1Q4	4FT deg	F g	10	Ind	M	24$	CCCC$	N$	3
French with Biology	R1C1	3FT deg	F+B/C	8	3M	M	Ind	Ind	Ind	
French with Business Studies	R1N1	4FT deg	F	8	3M	M	Ind	Ind	Ind	
French with Chemistry	R1F1	4FT deg								
French with Comparative Literature	R1Q2	4FT deg	F+EI g	10	Ind	M	24$	CCCC$	N$	
French with Computer Studies	R1G5	4FT deg	F	8	3M	M	Ind	Ind	Ind	
French with Economics	R1L1	4FT deg	F	8	3M	M	Ind	Ind	Ind	
French with English	R1Q3	4FT deg	F	10	4M	M	Ind	Ind	Ind	
French with European Studies	R1T2	4FT deg	F g	10	N $	M	24$	CCCC$	N$	5
French with Gender Studies	R1M9	4FT deg	F g	10	N $	M	24$	CCCC$	N$	
French with Geography	R1L8	4FT deg	F	8	3M	M	Ind	Ind	Ind	
French with Geology	R1F6	4FT deg	F	8	3M	M	Ind	Ind	Ind	
French with German	R1R2	4FT deg	F+G	8	3M	M	Ind	Ind	Ind	
French with History	R1V1	4FT deg	F	10	4M	M	Ind	Ind	Ind	
French with History of Art and Design	R1V4	4FT deg	F	8	3M	M	Ind	Ind	Ind	
French with Mathematics	R1G1	4FT deg	F+M	8	3M	M	Ind	Ind	Ind	
French with Media Studies	R1P4	4FT deg	F	20	Ind	Ind	Ind	Ind	Ind	
French with Philosophy	R1V7	4FT deg	F	8	3M	M	Ind	Ind	Ind	
French with Politics	R1M1	4FT deg	F	8	3M	M	Ind	Ind	Ind	
French with Psychology	R1C8	4FT deg	F	10	4M	M^	Ind	Ind	Ind	
French with Religious Studies	R1V8	4FT deg	F	8	3M	M	Ind	Ind	Ind	
French with Sociology	R1L3	4FT deg	F	10	4M	M	Ind	Ind	Ind	
French with Spanish	R1R4▼	4FT deg	F+Sp g	8	N $	M	24$	CCCC$	N$	9
Geography with French	L8R1	3FT deg	*	8	3M	M	Ind	Ind	Ind	
Geology with French	F6R1	3FT deg	*	8	3M	M	Ind	Ind	Ind	
German with French	R2R1	4SW deg	G	8	3M	M	Ind	Ind	Ind	
International Business with French	N1RC	3FT deg	* g	18	1M+4D$	D	26	BBBCC	N$	
Mathematics with French	G1R1	3FT deg	M	8	3M	M	Ind	Ind	Ind	
Philosophy with French	V7R1	3FT deg	*	8	3M	Ind	Ind	Ind	Ind	
Physiology with French	B1R1	3FT deg	*	8	3M	M	Ind	Ind	Ind	
Politics with French	M1R1	3FT deg	*	8	3M	M	Ind	Ind	Ind	
Psychology with French	C8R1	3FT deg	*	10	4M	M^	Ind	Ind	Ind	
Religious Studies with French	V8R1	3FT deg	*	8	3M	M	Ind	Ind	Ind	
Sociology with French	L3R1	3FT deg	*	10	4M	M	Ind	Ind	Ind	

Univ of SURREY

TITLE	CODE	COURSE	SUBJECTS	A/AS	ND/C	AGNVQ	IB	SQA(H)	SQA	RATIO	A/AS
French and Economics with International Business	RL11	4SW deg	F g	22	3M+3D$		30$	ABBCC	Ind	4	14/22
French and European Studies	RT12	4SW deg	F	22	3M+3D$		30$	ABBCC	Ind	6	16/23
French and German	RR12	4FT/SW deg	F+G	22	3M+3D$		30$	ABBCC	Ind		
French and Law	RM13	4SW deg	F	22	3M+3D$		30$	ABBCC	Ind	3	14/26
French and Russian	RR18	4FT/SW deg	F+R	20	3M+3D$		30$	ABBCC	Ind		

Univ of SUSSEX

TITLE	CODE	COURSE	SUBJECTS	A/AS	ND/C	AGNVQ	IB	SQA(H)	SQA	RATIO A/AS
Biochemistry with European Studies (French)	C7R1	4FT deg	C+S g	BCC	MO $	MS6 go	$	Ind	Ind	
Biology with European Studies (French)	C1R1	4FT deg	2S g	BCC	MO $	MS6 go	$	Ind	Ind	
Chemical Physics with Eur St (French) (MChem)	F3RD	4FT deg	C/P/Ph+M g	CCC	MO $	MS^ go	$	Ind	Ind	
Chemistry with European Studies (French)	F1R1	4FT deg	C+S g	CCC	MO $	MS go	$	Ind	Ind	
Chemistry with European Studies (French) (MChem)	F1RD	4FT deg	C+S g	CCC	MO $	MS go	$	Ind	Ind	

course details | 98 expected requirements | 96 entry stats

TITLE	CODE	COURSE	SUBJECTS	A/AS	NQ/C	AGNVQ	IB	SQA(H)	SQA	RATIO A/AS
Computer Science with European Studies (French)	G5R1	4FT deg	M g	BBC	MO $	M*^ go	$	Ind	Ind	
Economics with French/Maitrise Internationale	L1RC	4FT deg	F+Ec/M	BBC	MO $	M*6 go	$	Ind	Ind	
Environmental Science with Euro Studies (French)	F9R1	4FT deg	2(C/P/M) g	CCC	MO $	MS go	$	Ind	Ind	
French and German	RR12	4FT deg	F+G	BCC	MO $	M*^	$	Ind	Ind	
French and Italian	RR13	4FT deg	F	BCC	MO $	M*^	$	Ind	Ind	
French and Linguistics	RQ11	4FT deg	F	BCC	MO $	M*^	$	Ind	Ind	
French and Russian	RR18	4FT deg	F	BCC	MO $	M*^	$	Ind	Ind	
French in African and Asian Studies	R1T5	4FT deg	F	BCC	MO $	M*^	$	Ind	Ind	
French in European Studies	R1T2	4FT deg	F	BCC	MO $	M*^	$	Ind	Ind	
French with Development Studies	R1MY	4FT deg	F	BCC	MO $	M*^	$	Ind	Ind	
Mathematics & Stats with Eur St (French)(MMath)	G4RC	4FT deg	M g	BCC	MO $	MS^ go	$	Ind	Ind	
Mathematics and Statistics with Eur St (French)	G4R1	4FT deg	M g	BCC	MO $	MS^ go	$	Ind	Ind	
Mathematics with European St (French) (MMath)	G1RC	4FT deg	M g	BCC	MO $	MS^ go	$	Ind	Ind	
Mathematics with European Studies (French)	G1R1	4FT deg	M g	BCC	MO $	MS^ go	$	Ind	Ind	
Molecular Genetics in Biotechnology with French	C4R1	4FT deg	2S g	BCD	MO $	MS6 go	$	Ind	Ind	
Physics with European Studies (French)	F3R1	4FT deg	M+P g	CCC	MO $	MS^ go	$	Ind	Ind	
Physics with European Studies (French) (MPhys)	F3RC	4FT deg	M+P g	CCC	MO $	MS^ go	$	Ind	Ind	

Univ of Wales SWANSEA

TITLE	CODE	COURSE	SUBJECTS	A/AS	NQ/C	AGNVQ	IB	SQA(H)	SQA	RATIO A/AS
Biological Sciences (with French)	C1R1	4FT deg	B+F	BCC	X	X	28$	ABBCC$	Ind	5	
Civil Engineering (with French)	H2R1	4FT deg	M g	BCD-CCC	4M+1D$	MC^ go	28$	BBBCC$	Ind	2	18/18
Computer Science (with French)	G5R1	4FT deg	F	BBC	4D $	Ind	28$	BBBBB$	Ind	4	
English Language/French (with Business Studies)	QRH1	4FT deg	F	X	X	X	28	X	X		
European Business Studies (France)	N1R1	4FT deg	F g	ABC-BBB	Ind	D$^ go | 32$	AABBB$	Ind	3	18/26
European History (with French)	V1R1	4FT deg	F+H	BBB-BBC	Ind	Ind	30$	ABBBB$	Ind	4	
European Management Science (France)	N1RC	4FT deg	F+M	ABC-BBB	X	X	32$	AABBB$	Ind	2	12/26
French	R101	4FT deg	F	BBC	1M+5D$	Ind	30$	ABBBB$	Ind	5	14/26
French (with Business Studies)	R1N1	4FT deg	F g	BBC	1M+5D$	Ind	30$	ABBBB$	Ind	5	18/24
French (with Computer Studies)	R1G5	4FT deg	F	BBC	1M+5D$	Ind	28$	BBBBB$	Ind	2	
French (with Legal Studies)	R1M3	4FT deg	F	BBB-BBC	6D $	Ind	32$	AABBB$	Ind	5	
French/American Studies	QR41	4FT deg									
French/Ancient History and Civilisation	VRC1	4FT deg	F	BBC	1M+5D$	X	30$	ABBBB$	X		
French/Anthropology	LR61	4FT deg	F	BBC	1M+5D$	Ind	30$	ABBBB$	Ind		
French/Economic History	RV13	4FT deg	F	BBC	1M+5D$	Ind	30$	ABBBB$	Ind		
French/Economics	LR11	4FT deg	F g	BBC	1M+5D$	Ind	30$	ABBBB$	Ind	9	
French/English	QR31	4FT deg	E+F	BBC	X	X	30$	ABBBB$	X	8	16/22
French/English Language	QR3C	3FT deg	E+F	BBC	X	X	30$	ABBBB$	Ind		
French/European Politics	RM11	4FT deg	F	BBC	1M+5D$	Ind	30$	ABBBB$	Ind	4	
French/German (with Business Studies)	RR1F	4FT deg	F g	BBB-BBC	1M+5D$	Ind	30$	ABBBB$	Ind	6	18/28
French/German (with Computer Studies)	RR1G	4FT deg	F g	BBC	1M+5D$	Ind	30$	ABBBB$	Ind	2	
French/German (with Legal Studies)	RR21	4FT deg	F g	BBB-BBC	1M+5D$	Ind	30$	ABBBB$	Ind	3	
French/Italian (with Business Studies)	RR1H	4FT deg	F g	BBC	1M+5D$	Ind	30$	ABBBB$	Ind	3	
French/Italian (with Computer Studies)	RR1J	4FT deg	F	BBC	1M+5D$	Ind	30$	ABBBB$	Ind	2	
French/Italian (with Legal Studies)	RR31	4FT deg	F	BBC	1M+5D$	Ind	30$	ABBBB$	Ind	4	
French/Russian (with Business Studies)	RR1V	4FT deg	F g	BCC	1M+5D$	Ind	28$	BBBBC$	Ind	4	
French/Russian (with Computer Studies)	RR1W	4FT deg	F	BCC	1M+5D$	Ind	28$	BBBBC$	Ind		
French/Russian (with Legal Studies)	RR81	4FT deg	F	BBC-BCC	1M+5D$	Ind	28$	BBBBC$	Ind		
French/Spanish (with Business Studies)	RR1K	4FT deg	F g	BBB-BBC	1M+5D$	Ind	30$	ABBBB$	Ind	5	14/24
French/Spanish (with Computer Studies)	RR1L	4FT deg	F	BBC	1M+5D$	Ind	30$	ABBBB$	Ind	4	
French/Spanish (with Legal Studies)	RR41	4FT deg	F	BBB-BBC	1M+5D$	Ind	30$	ABBBB$	Ind	2	
French/Welsh (with Business Studies)	RQ15	4FT deg	F+W g	BCC	1M+5D$	X	28$	BBBBC$	X		
French/Welsh (with Computer Studies)	RQ1N	4FT deg	F+W	BCC	1M+5D$	X	28$	BBBBC$	X		
French/Welsh (with Legal Studies)	RQC5	4FT deg	F+W	BCC	1M+5D$	X	28$	BBBBC$	X		

course details

98 expected requirements

96 entry stats

TITLE	CODE	COURSE	SUBJECTS	A/AS	ND/C	AGNVQ	IB	SQA(H)	SQA	RATIO A/AS
Geography/French	LR81	4FT deg	F+Gy	BBC	1M+5D$	Ind	30$	ABBBB$	Ind	13
German/French	RR12	4FT deg	F+G/(E g)	BBC	1M+5D$	Ind	30$	ABBBB$	Ind	5	16/24
Greek and Roman Studies/French	QR81	4FT deg	F	BBC-BCC	1M+5D$	X	28$	BBBBB$	X	1
Greek/French	QR71	4FT deg	F+Gk	BBC-BCC	X	X	28$	BBBBB$	X	
History/French	RV11	4FT deg	F+H	BBC	1M+5D$	Ind	30$	ABBBB$	Ind	6
Italian/French	RR13	4FT deg	F	BBC	1M+5D$	Ind	30$	ABBBB$	Ind	4	14/24
Latin/French	QR61	4FT deg	F+Ln	BBC-BCC	Ind	X	28$	BBBBB$	X	
Law and French	MR31	4FT deg	F	BBB	6D $	Ind	32$	AABBB$	Ind	6	18/20
Mathematics (with French)	G1R1	4FT deg	F+M	BBC-BCC	X	Ind	28$	BBBBC$	Ind	11
Medieval Studies/French	RVC1	4FT deg	F+H	BBC-BCC	Ind	Ind	28$	BBBBB$	X	
Philosophy/French	RV17	4FT deg	F	BBC-BCC	1M+5D$	Ind	28$	BBBBB$	Ind	2
Politics/French	MR11	4FT deg	F	BBC-BCC	1M+5D$	Ind	28$	BBBBB$	Ind	4
Psychology and French	LR71	3FT deg	F g	BBC	1M+5D$	Ind	30$	ABBBB$	Ind	
Russian/French	RR18	4FT deg	F	BCC	1M+5D$	Ind	28$	BBBBC$	Ind	10
Sociology/French	LR31	4FT deg	F	BBC	1M+5D$	Ind	30$	ABBBB$	Ind	8
Spanish/French	RR14	4FT deg	F	BBC	1M+5D$	Ind	30$	ABBBB$	Ind	4	14/28
Welsh/French	QR51	4FT deg	F+W	BCC	1M+5D$	X	28$	BBBBB$	X	1

THAMES VALLEY Univ

TITLE	CODE	COURSE	SUBJECTS	A/AS	ND/C	AGNVQ	IB	SQA(H)
Accounting with French	N4R1	3FT deg		8-12	MO	M	26	CCC
American Studies with French	Q4R1	3FT deg		8-12	MO	M	26	CCC
Business Administration with French	N1RC	3FT deg		8-12	MO	M	26	CCC
Business Economics with French	L1RC	3FT deg		8-12	MO	M	26	CCC
Business Studies with French (Dip)	N1R1▼	3FT/4SW deg	* g	10-12	MO+2D	M	26	CCC
Economics with French	L1R1▼	3FT deg	* g	8-12	MO	M	26	CCC
English Language and Communications with French	Q1R1	3FT deg		8-12	MO	M	26	CCC
English with French	Q3R1	3FT deg		8-12	MO	M	26	CCC
Environmental Policy and Management with French	F9R1	3FT deg		8-12	MO	M	26	CCC
European Law with French	M3RC	3FT deg		8-12	MO	M	26	CCC
European Studies with French	T2R1	3FT deg		8-12	MO	M	26	CCC
Finance with French	N3R1	3FT deg		8-12	MO	M	26	CCC
Food and Drink Consumer Studies with French	D4R1	3FT deg		8-12	MO	M	26	CCC
French with Business	R1N1	3FT deg		8-12	MO	M	26	CCC
French with Business Economics	R1LC	3FT deg		8-12	MO	M	26	CCC
French with Economics	R1L1	3FT deg		8-12	MO	M	26	CCC
French with English	R1Q3	3FT deg		8-12	MO	M	26	CCC
French with English Language Studies	R1Q1	3FT deg		8-12	MO	M	26	CCC
French with European Law	R1M3	3FT deg		8-12	MO	M	26	CCC
French with European Studies	R1T2	3FT deg		8-12	MO	M	26	CCC
French with German	R1R2	3FT deg		8-12	MO	M	26	CCC
French with History	R1V1	3FT deg		8-12	MO	M	26	CCC
French with International Studies	R1MX	3FT deg		8-12	MO	M	26	CCC
French with Language and Communication	R1P3	3FT deg		8-12	MO	M	26	CCC
French with Media Studies	R1W9	3FT deg		8-12	MO	M	26	CCC
French with Music	R1W3	3FT deg		8-12	MO	M	26	CCC
French with Politics and International Relations	R1M1	3FT deg		8-12	MO	M	26	CCC
French with Spanish	R1R4	3FT deg		8-12	MO	M	26	CCC
French with Tourism	R1P7	3FT deg		8-12	MO	M	26	CCC
German with French	R2R1	3FT deg		8-12	MO	M	26	CCC
History with French	V1R1	3FT deg		8-12	MO	M	26	CCC
Hospitality Management with French	N7R1	3FT deg		8-12	MO	M	26	CCC
Human Resource Management with French	N6R1	3FT deg		8-12	MO	M	26	CCC
Information Management with French	P2R1	3FT deg		8-12	MO	M	26	CCC

course details				98 expected requirements						96 entry stats
TITLE	CODE	COURSE	SUBJECTS	A/AS	NO/C	AGNVQ	IB	SQA(H)	SQA	RATIO A/AS
International Studies with French	M9R1	3FT deg		8-12	MO	M	26	CCC		
Law with French	M3R1	3FT deg		8-12	MO	M	26	CCC		
Leisure Management with French	N7RC	3FT deg		8-12	MO	M	26	CCC		
Marketing with French	N5R1	3FT deg		8-12	MO	M	26	CCC		
Media Arts with French	W9R1	3FT deg		8-12	MO	M	26	CCC		
Politics and International Relations with French	M1R1	3FT deg		8-12	MO	M	26	CCC		
Psychology with French	C8R1	3FT deg		8-12	MO	M	26	CCC		
Recreation Management with French	N7RD	3FT deg		8-12	MO	M	26	CCC		
Sociology with French	L3R1	3FT deg		8-12	MO	M	26	CCC		
Spanish with French	R4R1	3FT deg		8-12	MO	M	26	CCC		
Tourism with French	P7R1	3FT deg		8-12	MO	M	26	CCC		

Univ of ULSTER

Humanities Combined French	Y320▼	3FT/4SW deg	F	CCC	MO+3D	D*6/△ gi	28	BBBC	Ind	

UNIVERSITY COLL LONDON (Univ of London)

Dutch and French (4 Yrs)	TR21	4FT deg	F g	BCC-BBC	3M	X	26$	BBBCC$	Ind	2
French (4 Yrs)	R100	4FT deg	F g	BBC	3M	X	32$	BBBCC$	Ind	4	16/26
French and German (4 Yrs)	RR12	4FT deg	F+G g	BBC	3M	X	32$	ABBBB$	Ind	6	20/30
French and History of Art (4 Yrs)	RV14	4FT deg	F g	BBC-BBB	3M	X	32$	BBBBB$	Ind	11	
French and Italian (4 Yrs)	RR13	4FT deg	F g	BBC	3M	X	30$	BBBBB$	Ind	5	24/30
French and Philosophy (4 Yrs)	RV17	4FT deg	F g	BBC-BBB	3M	X	32$	BBBBC$	Ind	4	24/26
French and Spanish (4 Yrs)	RR14	4FT deg	F+Sp g	BBC-BBB	3M	X	32$	ABBBB$	Ind	9	20/30
French and an Asian or African Language (4 Yrs)	RT19	4FT deg	F g	BBC	3M	X	30$	BBBCC$	Ind	5	24/26
Spanish with French (4 Yrs)	R4R1	4FT deg	F+Sp g	BBC	3M	X	32$	BBBBB$	Ind	17	

Univ of WARWICK

English and French (4 Yrs inc yr abroad)	QR31	4FT deg	E+F g	BBB	X	X	32$	AABBB$		8	24/30
French Studies (4 Yrs inc yr abroad)	R100	4FT deg	F g	BCC	X	X	30$	ABBBB$		6	18/26
French Studies with German (4 Yrs inc yr abroad)	R1R2	4FT deg	F+G g	BBC	X	X	30$	ABBBB$		4	
French Studies with Italian (4 Yrs inc yr abrd)	R1R3	4FT deg	F g	BBC	X	X	29$	ABBBC$		4	
French and German Studies (4 Yrs inc yr abroad)	RR12	4FT deg	F+G g	BBC	X	X	30$	ABBBB$			
French and History (4 Yrs inc yr abroad)	RV11	4FT deg	F+H g	BBC	X	X	32$	ABBBB$		7	24/26
French and Italian Studies (4 Yrs inc yr abroad)	RR13	4FT deg	F g	BCC	X	X	29$	ABBBB$			
French with Film Studies (4 Yrs inc yr abroad)	R1W5	4FT deg	F g	BCC	X	X	30$	ABBBB$		9	22/28
French with International St (4 Yrs inc yr abrd)	R1M1	4FT deg	F g	BBC	X	X	32$	AABBB$		7	20/30
German with French (4 Yrs inc yr abroad)	R2R1	4FT deg	G+F g	BCC	X	X	29$	ABBBB$			
Italian with French (4 Yrs inc yr abroad)	R3R1	4FT deg	E+F g	BCC	X	X	29$	ABBCC$			
Politics with French (4 Yrs inc year abroad)	M1R1	4FT deg	F g	ABB-BBB	X	X	32$	AAABB$		17	

Univ of WESTMINSTER

French and Arabic	RT16	4SW deg	F	CC	Ind		26$	BBB		4	
French and Chinese	T3R1	4SW deg	F	CC	Ind		26$	BBB	Ind	2	11/22
French and English	QR31	4SW deg	E+F	CC	Ind		26$	BBB		9	
French and English Language	QRH1	4SW deg		CC	Ind		26$	BBB			
German and French	RR12	4SW deg	F	CC	Ind		26$	BBB		4	
Italian and French	RR13	4SW deg	F	CC	Ind		26$	BBB		5	10/22
Law with French	M3R1	4FT deg	F	BCC	MO+2D	D	28	BBB		10	
Linguistics and French	RQ11	4SW deg	F	CC	Ind		26$	BBB		6	
Russian and French	RR18	4SW deg	F	CC	Ind		26$	BBB		5	
Spanish and French	RR14	4SW deg	F	CC	Ind		26$	BBB		8	12/18

course details			98 expected requirements							96 entry stats
TITLE	CODE	COURSE	SUBJECTS	A/AS	ND/C	AGNVQ	IB	SQA(H)	SQA	RATIO A/AS
Univ of WOLVERHAMPTON										
French	R100	3FT/4FT deg	L g	18	4D $	D	28	BBBB	Ind	
Combined Degrees	Y401	3FT/4SW deg	L g	12	4M $	M	24	BBBB	Ind	
French Studies										
Univ of YORK										
French and German (Language and Linguistics)	RR12	4FT deg	F+G	24	Ind	D$^	28$	BBCC$	Ind	20/28
French and Linguistics	RQ11	4FT deg	F	24	Ind	D$^	28$	BBCC$	Ind	24/30
History/French	V1R1	4FT deg	H+F	ABC	Ind	D$6/^	32$	ABBB$	Ind	

course details

96 entry stats

TITLE	CODE	COURSE	SUBJECTS	A/AS	ND/C	AGNVQ	IB	SQA(H)	SQA	RATIO A/AS
Univ of ABERDEEN										
Accountancy with German	N4R2	4FT deg	* g	BBC	Ind	M$ go	30$	BBBB$	Ind	
Accountancy-German	NR42	4FT/5FT deg	* g	BBC	Ind	M$ go	30$	BBBB$	Ind	
Celtic Civilisation-German	QR5F	4FT/5FT deg	* g	BBC	Ind	M$ go	30$	BBBB$	Ind	
Celtic Civilisation-German (4 Yrs)	RQF5	4FT deg	* g	BBC	Ind	M$ go	30$	BBBB$	Ind	
Celtic-German	QR52	4FT/5FT deg	* g	BBC	Ind	M$ go	30$	BBBB$	Ind	
Celtic-German (4Yrs)	RQ25	4FT deg	* g	BBC	Ind	M$ go	30$	BBBB$	Ind	
Chemistry with German	F1R2	4FT deg	C+2S/C+M+S g	CCD	Ind	MS go	24$	BBBC$	Ind	3
Computing Science with German	G5R2	4FT deg	M+2S g	CCD	Ind	MS go	24$	BBBC$	Ind	3
Economics-German	LR12	4FT/5FT deg	* g	BBC	Ind	M$ go	30$	BBBB$	Ind	
Economics-German (4 Yrs)	RL21	4FT deg	* g	BBC	Ind	M$ go	30$	BBBB$	Ind	
English-German	QR32	4FT/5FT deg	* g	BBC	Ind	M$ go	30$	BBBB$	Ind	5
English-German (4 Yrs)	RQ23	4FT deg	* g	BBC	Ind	M$ go	30$	BBBB$	Ind	
French-German	RR12	4FT/5FT deg	* g	BBC	Ind	M$ go	30$	BBBB$	Ind	5
French-German with Education	RR21	5FT deg	* g	BBC	Ind	M$ go	30$	BBBB$	Ind	
German Studies	R200	4FT/5FT deg	* g	BBC	Ind	M$ go	30$	BBBB$	Ind	2
German Studies (4 Yrs)	R201	4FT deg	* g	BBC	Ind	M$ go	30$	BBBB$	Ind	
German with Film Studies	R2W5	4FT/5FT deg	* g	BBC	Ind	M$ go	30$	BBBB$	Ind	2
German with Film Studies (4 Yrs)	R2WM	4FT deg	* g	BBC	Ind	M$ go	30$	BBBB$	Ind	
German with Women's Studies	R2M9	5FT deg	* g	BBC	Ind	M$ go	30$	BBBB$	Ind	
German with Women's Studies (4 Yrs)	R2MX	4FT deg	* g	BBC	Ind	M$ go	30$	BBBB$	Ind	
German-Geography	LR82	4FT/5FT deg	* g	BBC	Ind	M$ go	30$	BBBB$	Ind	
German-Hispanic Studies	RR24	4FT/5FT deg	* g	BBC	Ind	M$ go	30$	BBBB$	Ind	
German-Hispanic Studies with Education	RR42	5FT deg	* g	BBC	Ind	M$ go	30$	BBBB$	Ind	
German-History	RV21	4FT/5FT deg	* g	BBC	Ind	M$ go	30$	BBBB$	Ind	
German-History (4 Yrs)	VR12	4FT deg	* g	BBC	Ind	M$ go	30$	BBBB$	Ind	
German-History of Art	RV24	4FT/5FT deg	* g	BBC	Ind	M$ go	30$	BBBB$	Ind	
German-History of Art (4 Yrs)	VR42	4FT deg	* g	BBC	Ind	M$ go	30$	BBBB$	Ind	
German-International Relations	RM2C	4FT/5FT deg	* g	BBC	Ind	M$ go	30$	BBBB$	Ind	
German-International Relations (4 Yrs)	MRC2	4FT deg	* g	BBC	Ind	M$ go	30$	BBBB$	Ind	
German-Management Studies	RN21	4FT/5FT deg	* g	BBC	Ind	M$ go	30$	BBBB$	Ind	7
German-Management Studies (4 Yrs)	NR12	4FT deg	* g	BBC	Ind	M$ go	30$	BBBB$	Ind	
German-Mathematics	RG21	5FT deg	* g	BBC	Ind	M$ go	30$	BBBB$	Ind	
German-Mathematics (4 Yrs)	GR12	4FT deg	* g	BBC	Ind	M$ go	30$	BBBB$	Ind	
German-Philosophy	RV27	4FT/5FT deg	* g	BBC	Ind	M$ go	30$	BBBB$	Ind	
German-Philosophy (4 Yrs)	VR72	4FT deg	* g	BBC	Ind	M$ go	30$	BBBB$	Ind	
German-Politics	RM21	4FT/5FT deg	* g	BBC	Ind	M$ go	30$	BBBB$	Ind	
German-Politics (4 Yrs)	MR12	4FT deg	* g	BBC	Ind	M$ go	30$	BBBB$	Ind	
German-Social Research	LR32	4FT/5FT deg	* g	BBC	Ind	M$ go	30$	BBBB$	Ind	
German-Social Research (4 Yrs)	LR3F	4FT deg	* g	BBC	Ind	M$ go	30$	BBBB$	Ind	
German-Sociology	RL23	4FT/5FT deg	* g	BBC	Ind	M$ go	30$	BBBB$	Ind	
German-Sociology (4 Yrs)	RL2H	4FT deg	* g	BBC	Ind	M$ go	30$	BBBB$	Ind	
Mathematics with German	G1R2	4FT deg	M+2S g	CCD	Ind	MS go	24$	BBBC$	Ind	
Physics with German	F3R2	4FT deg	2S+M g	CCD	Ind	MS go	24$	BBBC$	Ind	
Psychology with German	C8R2	4FT deg	3S/2S+M g	CCD	Ind	M$ go	24$	BBBC$	Ind	
Psychology with German (MA)	C8RF	4FT deg	* g	BBC	Ind	M$ go	30$	BBBB$	Ind	
Religious Studies-German	VR82	4FT/5FT deg	* g	BBC	Ind	M$ go	30$	BBBB$	Ind	
Religious Studies-German (4 Yrs)	RV28	4FT deg	* g	BBC	Ind	M$ go	30$	BBBB$	Ind	
Theology with German	V8R2	3FT deg	* g	CC	Ind	M* go	24$	BBCC	Ind	
Univ of Wales, ABERYSTWYTH										
Computer Science with German	G5R2	4FT deg	G g	20	1M+5D$	M^ g	30$	BBBBC$	Ind	
European Studies and German	RT2F	4FT deg	G g	20	1M+5D$	M^ g	30$	BBBBC$	Ind	

Languages – German 41

course details			**98 expected requirements**							*96 entry stats*	
TITLE	CODE	COURSE	SUBJECTS	A/AS	ND/C	AGNVQ	IB	SQA(H)	SQA	RATIO	A/AS
German	R200	4FT deg	G g	18	1M+5D$	M^ g	29$	BBBCC$	Ind		
German/American Studies	QR42	4FT deg	E/H+G g	18	1M+5D$	M^ g	29$	BBBCC$	Ind		
German/Drama	RW24	4FT deg	G g	20	1M+5D$	MQ^ g	30$	BBBBC$	Ind		
German/Economic & Social History	RV23	4FT deg	G g	18-20	1M+5D$	M^ g	30$	BBBBC$	Ind		
German/Education	RX29	4FT deg	G g	18	1M+5D$	M^ g	29$	BBBCC$	Ind		
German/English	QR32	4FT deg	E!+G	20	1M+5D$	M^ g	30$	BBBBC$	Ind		
German/European Studies	RT22	4FT deg	G g	20	1M+5D$	M^ g	30$	BBBBC$	Ind		
German/Film and Television Studies	RW25	4FT deg	G g	20	1M+5D$	MQ^ g	30$	BBBBC$	Ind		
German/French	RR12	4FT deg	G+F g	18	1M+5D$	M^ g	29$	BBBCC$	Ind		
German/Geography	LR82	4FT deg	Gy+G g	20-22	1M+5D$	M^ g	31$	BBBBC$	Ind		
History/German	RV21	4FT deg	G g	18-20	1M+5D$	M^ g	30$	BBBBC$	Ind		
Information and Library Studies/German	PR22	4FT deg	G g	18	1M+5D$	M^ g	29$	BBBCC$	Ind		
International Politics/German	MRD2	4FT deg	G g	20	1M+5D$	M^ g	30$	BBBBC$	Ind		
Irish/German	QR5F	4FT deg	G g	18	1M+5D$	M^ g	29$	BBBCC$	Ind		
Italian/German	RR23	4FT deg	G g	18	1M+5D$	M^ g	29$	BBBCC$	Ind		
Law with German (BA)	M3RG	4FT deg	G g	BBB	DO $	D^ g	32$	BBBCC$	Ind		
Law with German (LLB)	M3R2	4FT deg	G g	BBB	DO $	D^ g	32$	BBBCC$	Ind		
Politics/German	MR12	4FT deg	G g	20	1M+5D$	M^ g	30$	BBBBC$	Ind		
Pure Mathematics/German	GRC2	4FT deg	M+G g	18	1M+5D$	M^ g	29$	BBBCC$	Ind		
Spanish/German	RR24	4FT deg	G g	18	1M+5D$	M^ g	29$	BBBCC$	Ind		
Welsh History/German	RVFC	4FT deg	G g	18-20	1M+5D$	M^ g	30$	BBBBC$	Ind		
Welsh/German	QR52	4FT deg	W+G g	18	1M+5D$	M^ g	29$	BBBCC$	Ind		

ANGLIA Poly Univ

TITLE	CODE	COURSE	SUBJECTS	A/AS	ND/C	AGNVQ	IB	SQA(H)	SQA	RATIO	A/AS
Animal Behaviour and German	CR1F▼	4FT deg	g	12	4M	P go	Dip	BCCC	N		
Art History and German	RV24▼	4FT deg	g	14	6M	M+/^ go	Dip	BBCC	Ind		
Audiotechnology and German	HR6F▼	4FT deg	S g	16	8M	D+/^ go	Dip$	BBCCC	N		
Biology and German	CR12▼	4FT deg	B g	12	4M	P+/^ go	Dip$	BCCC	N		
Biomedical Science and German	BR92▼	4FT deg	B g	12	4M $	M+/^ go	Dip$	BCCC	N		
Business and German	NR12▼	4FT deg	* g	12	4M	M+/^ go	Dip	BCCC	Ind	4	
Chemistry and German	FR12▼	4FT deg	S g	12	4M $	M go	Dip$	BCCC	Ind		
Communication Studies and German	PR32▼	4FT deg	Ap g	14	6M	M+/^ go	Dip$	BBCC	Ind		
Computer Science and German	GR52▼	4FT deg	* g	12	4M	M go	Dip	BCCC	N		
Ecology and Conservation and German	DR22▼	4FT deg	* g	12	4M $	M+/^	Dip	BCCC	N		
Economics and German	LR12▼	4FT deg	* g	12	4M	M+/^ go	Dip	BCCC	Ind		
English Language Studies and German	QR12▼	3FT deg	* g	12	4M	M go	Dip	BCCC			
English and German	QR32▼	4FT deg	E g	12	4M	M+/^ go	Dip$	BCCC	Ind	4	
European Business (German Programme)	N1R2▼	4FT deg	G g	10	3M	P go	Dip	BCCC	Ind	3	10/10
European Philosophy & Literature and German	RV27▼	4FT deg	* g	12	4M	M+/^ go	Dip	BCCC	Ind		
French and German	RR12▼	4FT deg	F/G	12	4M	M	Dip$	BCCC	Ind	4	
Geography and German	LR82▼	4FT deg	Gy g	12	4M	M+/^ go	Dip$	BCCC	Ind	3	
Geology and German	FR62▼	4FT deg	* g	12	4M $	M go	Dip	BCCC	Ind		
German and Graphic Arts	RW22▼	4FT deg	A g	14	6M	M+/^ go	Dip$	BBCCC	Ind		
German and History	RV21▼	4FT deg	* g	12	4M	M+/^ go	Dip	BCCC	Ind	5	
German and Intercultural Studies	RL26▼	4FT deg	* g	12	4M	M go	Dip	BCCC			
German and Italian	RR23▼	4FT deg	G/I	12	4M	M go	Dip$	BCCC	Ind	1	
German and Law	MR32▼	4FT deg	* g	14	6M	M go	Dip	BBCC	Ind	5	
German and Maths or Stats/Statistical Modelling	GR12▼	4FT deg	* g	12	4M	M+/^ go	Dip$	BCCC	Ind		
German and Music	RW23▼	4FT deg	Mu g	12	4M	M+/^ go	Dip$	BCCC	Ind		
German and Ophthalmic Dispensing	BR52▼	4FT deg	g	12	4M	M+/^ go	Dip	BCCC	Ind		
German and Politics	RM21▼	4FT deg	* g	14	6M	M+/^ go	Dip	BBCC	Ind		
German and Psychology	CR82▼	3FT deg	S g	16	8M	D go	Dip$	BBCCC	N		
German and Social Policy	RL24▼	4FT deg	* g	12	4M $	M+/^ go	Dip	BCCC	Ind		

course details			98 expected requirements							96 entry stats
TITLE	CODE	COURSE	SUBJECTS	A/AS	ND/C	AGNVQ	IB	SQA(H)	SQA	RATIO A/AS
German and Sociology	LR32▼	4FT deg	* g	12	4M	M+/^ go	Dip	BCCC	Ind	
German and Spanish	RR24▼	4FT deg	G/Sp	12	4M	M	Ind$	BCCC	Ind	
German and Women's Studies	RM29▼	4FT deg	* g	12	4M	M+/^ go	Dip	BCCC	Ind	

ASTON Univ

European Studies with German	T2R2	4SW deg	G g	BBC	5M+5D$	D$6/^ go | 31$	ABBBC$	Ind	2	14/22
French and German	RR12	4SW deg	F+G g	BBC	3M+7D$		32$	ABBBC$	Ind	6	18/26
German	R200	4SW deg	G g	BBC	5M+5D$	D$^ go | 31$	ABBBC$	Ind	4	
German/Business Administration	NR12	4SW deg	G g	20	X	D$^ go | 30$	BBBBB$	Ind	3	18/24
German/Chemistry	FR12	4SW deg	C+G g	18	X	X	29$	BBBBC$	Ind	6	
German/Chemistry (Year Zero)	FR1F	5SW deg								
German/Computer Science	GR52	4SW deg	G g	18	X	D$6/^ go | 29$	BBBBC$	Ind	2	
German/Computer Science (Year Zero)	GR5F	5SW deg								
German/Electronics	HR62	4SW deg	G+M/P g	18	X	X	29$	BBBBC$	Ind	
German/Environmental Science & Technology	FR92	4SW deg	S+G g	18	X		29$	BBBBC$	Ind	
German/Environmental Science (Year Zero)	FR9F	5SW deg								
German/Ergonomics	JRX2	4SW deg	G g	20	5M+5D$	D$^ go	30$	BBBBB$	Ind	
Health & Safety Management/German	JR92	4SW deg	G g	18	X	D$^ go	29$	BBBBC$	Ind	1
Health & Safety Management/German (Year Zero)	JR9F	5SW deg								
Human Psychology/German	LR72	4SW deg	G g	20	X	D$^ go	30$	BBBBB$	Ind	
Human Psychology/German (Year Zero)	LR7F	5SW deg								
International Business and German	NRD2	4SW deg	G g	BBB	3M+7D$	D$^ go | 31$	AABBB$	Ind	6	20/30
Mathematics/German	GR12	4SW deg	M+G g	20	X	X	31$	ABBBB$	Ind	
Medicinal Chemistry/German	FRC2	4SW deg	C+G g	20	3M+7D$	X	30$	BBBBB$	Ind	
Modern Languages with Translation Studies	RR1F	4FT deg	F+G g	BBC						
Product Design (Engineering)/German	HR72	3FT/4SW deg	S+G g	18	X	X	29$	BBBBC$		
Social Studies/German	LR42	4SW deg	G g	18	X	D$^ go	29$	BBBBC$	Ind	2

Univ of Wales, BANGOR

Computer Systems with German (4 yrs)	H6R2	4FT deg	G g	CC	3M	M$^ go	26	BBCC	Ind	
European Cultural Studies and German	TR22	4FT deg	* g	CCD	5M	D*6/^ go	28	BBBC	Ind	
German Language and Modern Germany	R224	4FT deg	G g	CCD	X	D*^ go	28$	BBBC$	X	3	12/16
German and Criminology	MR32	4FT deg	* g	18	X	D*^ go	28	BBBC	X	
German and Women's Studies	MR92	4FT deg	* g	18	X	D*^ go	28	BBBC	X	
German/Accounting	NR42	4FT deg	* g	18	X	D$^ go	28$	BBBC$	X	
German/Banking	NR32	4FT deg	* g	18	X	D$^ go	28$	BBBC$	X	
German/Economics	LR12	4FT deg	* g	18	X	D$^ go	28$	BBBC$	X	
German/English	QR32	4FT deg	E g	CCD	X	D*^ go	28$	BBBC$	X	10
German/French (Syllabus A)	RR12	4FT deg	F g	CCD	X	D*^ go	28$	BBBC$	X	4
German/French (Syllabus B)	RRC2	4FT deg	E g	CCD	X	D*^ go	28$	BBBC$	X	3
History/German	RV21	4FT deg	H g	CCC	X	D*^ go	28$	BBBC$	X	
Linguistics/German	QR12	4FT deg	* g	CCD	X	D*^ go	28$	BBBC$	X	2
Management and German	NR12	4FT deg	* g	18	X	D$^ go	28	BBBC	X	
Physical Education/German	RB26	4FT deg	* g	20	X	D*^ go	30$	BBBB$	X	
Religious Studies/German	RV28	4FT deg	* g	CCD	X	D*6/^ go	28$	BBBC$	X	
Russian/German	RR28	4FT deg	R g	CCD	X	D*^ go	28$	BBBC$	X	
Sports Science/German	BR62	4FT deg	* g	20	X	D*6/^ go	30	BBBB	X	
Welsh/German	QR52	4FT deg	W g	CCD	X	D*^ go	Ind	X	X	1

Univ of BATH

French and German (4 Yr SW)	RR12	4SW deg	F+G	BBC	Ind	Ind	30	Ind	Ind	5	18/28
German and Italian (4 Yr SW)	RR23	4SW deg	G+I	BBD	Ind	Ind	30	Ind	Ind	7
German and Russian (4 Yr SW)	RR28	4SW deg	G+R	BBD	Ind	Ind	30	Ind	Ind	5
German and ab initio Italian or Russian(4 Yr SW)	R200	4SW deg	G	BBD	Ind	Ind	30	Ind	Ind	3	14/28
International Mgt and Modern Lang-German (4 Yr)	NR12	4SW deg	G	BBB	Ind	Ind	30	Ind	Ind	5	22/30

course details   98 expected requirements   *96 entry stats*

TITLE	CODE	COURSE	SUBJECTS	A/AS	ND/C	RGNVQ	IB	SQA(H)	SQA	RATIO A/AS	
Univ of BIRMINGHAM											
Accounting and Finance with German	N4R2	4FT deg	G	BBC	Ind	D+^	32	ABBB	Ind		
African Studies/German Studies	RT27	4FT deg	G	BBB	Ind	D*^	32$	ABBB	Ind	1	
Ancient History & Archaeology/German Studies	RV26	4FT deg	G	BBB	Ind	D*^	32$	ABBB	Ind		
Artificial Intelligence/German Studies	GR82	4FT deg	G g	BBB	Ind	D*^	32$	ABBB	Ind	1	
BCom (Business Administration) with German	NR12	4FT deg	G	BBC	Ind	D+^	32	ABBBB	Ind	5	24/30
Business Studies/German Studies	RN21	4FT deg	G g	BBB	Ind	D*^	32$	ABBB	Ind	14	
Computer Studies/German Studies	GR52	4FT deg	G g	BBB	Ind	D*^	32$	ABBB	Ind		
Dance/German Studies	WR42	4FT deg	G	BBB	Ind	D*^	32$	ABBB	Ind		
Drama/German Studies	RW24	4FT deg	G	BBB	Ind	D*^	32$	ABBB	Ind		
East Mediterranean History/German Studies	RVG1	4FT deg	G g	BBB	Ind	D*^	32$	ABBB	Ind		
Economics with German	L1R2	4FT deg	G	BBC	Ind	D+^	32	ABBBB	Ind	7	
English/German Studies	QR32	4FT deg	G	BBB	Ind	D*^	32$	ABBB	Ind	11	
French Studies and German Studies	RR12	4FT deg	F+G	BBB	Ind	D*^	32$	ABBB	Ind	6	24/30
Geography/German Studies	LR82	4FT deg	Gy+G	BBB	Ind	D*^	32$	ABBB	Ind	4	
German Studies	R200	4FT deg	G	BCC	Ind	D*^	32$	ABBB	Ind	5	20/30
German Studies and Hispanic Studies	RR24	4FT deg	G	BBB	Ind	D*^	32$	ABBB	Ind	5	
German Studies and Italian	RR23	4FT deg	G	BBB	Ind	D*^	32$	ABBB	Ind	9	
German Studies and Modern Greek Studies	RTG2	4FT deg	G g	BBB	Ind	D*^	32$	ABBB	Ind	3	
German Studies and Portuguese	RR25	4FT deg	G	BBB	Ind	D*^	32$	ABBB	Ind		
German Studies and Russian	RR28	4FT deg	G	BBB	Ind	D*^	32$	ABBB	Ind	5	
German Studies/Classical Lit and Civilisation	QR82	4FT deg	G	BBB	Ind	D*^	32$	ABBB	Ind		
German Studies/History	RV21	4FT deg	G	BBB	Ind	D*^	32$	ABBB	Ind	15	
German Studies/History of Art	RV24	4FT deg	G	BBB	Ind	D*^	32$	ABBB	Ind		
German Studies/Latin	QR62	4FT deg	G+Ln	BBB	Ind	D*^	32$	ABBB	Ind		
German Studies/Mathematics	GR12	4FT deg	G+M	ABB-ABC	Ind	D*^	32$	ABBB	Ind		
German Studies/Media & Cultural Studies	PR42	4FT deg	G	BBB	Ind	D*^	32$	ABBB	Ind		
German Studies/Music	RW23	4FT deg	G+Mu	AAB-ABB	Ind	D*^	32$	ABBB	Ind	6	
German Studies/Philosophy	RV27	4FT deg	G	BBB	Ind	D*^	32$	ABBB	Ind		
German Studies/Political Science	MR12	4FT deg	G	BBB	Ind	D*^	32$	ABBB	Ind		
German Studies/Sport & Recreation Studies	RB26	4FT deg	G	BBB	Ind	D*^	32$	ABBB	Ind		
German Studies/Theology	RV28	4FT deg	G	BBB	Ind	D*^	32$	ABBB	Ind		
International Studies with German	M1R2	4FT deg	G	BBC	Ind	D+^	32	ABBBB	Ind	6	
Law with German	MR32	4FT deg	G	AAB	X	X	35$	CSYS	Ind		
Money, Banking and Finance with German	N3R2	4FT deg	G	BBB	Ind	D+^	33	ABBBB	Ind	3	24/30
BOLTON INST											
Accountancy and German	NR42	3FT deg	G g	CD	Ind	Ind	24	BBCC	Ind		
Architectural Technology and German	KR22	3FT deg	G g	10	3M	Ind	Ind	Ind	Ind		
Art & Design History and German	VR42	3FT deg	G g	CD	Ind	Ind	24	BBCC	Ind		
Biology and German	CR12	3FT deg	G g	CD	Ind	Ind	24	BBCC	Ind		
Building Surveying and German	KRF2	3FT deg	G g	10	3M	Ind	Ind	Ind	Ind		
Business Economics and German	LR12	3FT deg	G g	CD	Ind	Ind	24	BBCC	Ind		
Business Information Systems and German	GR5F	3FT deg	G g	CD	Ind	Ind	24	BBCC	Ind		
Business Studies and German	NR12	3FT deg	G g	CD	Ind	Ind	24	BBCC	Ind		
Civil Engineering and German	HR22	3FT deg	G+M/S	10	3M	Ind	Ind	Ind	Ind		
Community Studies and German	RL25	3FT deg	G g	CD	Ind	Ind	24	BBCC	Ind		
Computing and German	GR52	3FT deg	G g	CD	Ind	Ind	24	BBCC	Ind		
Construction and German	KRG2	3FT deg	G g	10	3M	Ind	Ind	Ind	Ind		
Creative Writing and German	RQ23	3FT deg	G g	CD	Ind	Ind	24	BBCC	Ind		
Design and German	RW22	3FT deg	G g	CD	Ind	Ind	24	BBCC	Ind		
Electronics and German	HRP2	3FT deg	G+M/S	10	3M	Ind	Ind	Ind	Ind		
Environmental Studies and German	RF29	3FT deg	G g	CD	Ind	Ind	24	BBCC	Ind		
Environmental Technology and German	KR32	3FT deg	G+S g	10	3M	Ind	Ind	Ind	Ind		

course details

TITLE	CODE	COURSE	SUBJECTS	A/AS	ND/C	AGNVQ	IB	SQA(H)	SQA	RATIO A/AS	
European Cultural Studies and German	TR22	3FT deg	G g	CD	Ind	Ind	24	BBCC	Ind		
Film & TV Studies and German	RW25	3FT deg	Me/T+G g	CD	Ind	Ind	24	BBCC	Ind		
French and German	RR12	3FT deg	F+G	CD	Ind	Ind	24	BBCC	Ind		
Gender and Women's Studies and German	RM29	3FT deg	G g	CD	Ind	Ind	24	BBCC	Ind		
German and History	RV21	3FT deg	G g	CD	Ind	Ind	24	BBCC	Ind		
German and Human Resource Management	NR1F	3FT deg	G g	CD	Ind	Ind	24	BBCC	Ind		
German and Law	RM23	3FT deg	G g	CD	Ind	Ind	24	BBCC	Ind		
German and Leisure Studies	RL2H	3FT deg	G g	CD	Ind	Ind	24	BBCC	Ind		
German and Literature	RQ22	3FT deg	G g	CD	Ind	Ind	24	BBCC	Ind		
German and Manufacturing Systems Design	RH27	3FT deg	G g	10	3M	Ind	Ind	Ind	Ind		
German and Marketing	NR52	3FT deg	G g	CD	Ind	Ind	24	BBCC	Ind		
German and Mathematics	RG21	3FT deg	G+M	CD	Ind	Ind	24	BBCC	Ind		
German and Motor Vehicle Studies	RH2J	3FT deg	G+M/S g	10	3M	Ind	Ind	Ind	Ind		
German and Occupational Health & Safety	RN26	3FT deg	G g	10	Ind	Ind	Ind	Ind	Ind		
German and Operations Management	NR22	3FT deg	G g	CD	Ind	Ind	Ind	Ind	Ind		
German and Organisations, Management & Work	NR72	3FT deg	G g	CD	Ind	Ind	24	BBCC	Ind		
German and Peace and War Studies	RV2C	3FT deg	G g	CD	Ind	Ind	24	BBCC	Ind		
German and Philosophy	RV27	3FT deg	G g	CD	Ind	Ind	24	BBCC	Ind		
German and Product Design	RH2T	3FT deg	G+Ds/Ad/M/S g	10	3M	Ind	Ind	Ind	Ind		
German and Psychology	RL27	3FT deg	G g	14	Ind	Ind	24	BBCC	Ind		
German and Quantity Surveying	RK2F	3FT deg	G g	10	3M	Ind	Ind	Ind	Ind		
German and Simulation/Virtual Environment	RG27	3FT deg	G g	10	3M	Ind	Ind	Ind	Ind		
German and Sociology	LR32	3FT deg	G g	CD	Ind	Ind	24	Ind	Ind		
German and Technology Management	RN29	3FT deg	G g	10	3M	Ind	Ind	Ind	Ind		
German and Textiles	JR42	3FT deg	G g	CD	Ind	Ind	24	BBCC	Ind		
German and Theatre Studies	RW24	3FT deg	G+Me/T g	CD	Ind	Ind	24	BBCC	Ind		
German and Tourism Studies	RP27	3FT deg	G g	CD	Ind	Ind	24	BBCC	Ind		
German and Transport Studies	RJ29	3FT deg	G+M/S g	10	3M	Ind	Ind	Ind	Ind		
German and Urban and Cultural Studies	RL23	3FT deg	G g	CD	Ind	Ind	24	BBCC	Ind		
International Business (German)	N1R2	3FT deg	* g	CD	MO	M*	24	BBCC	Ind		
International Tourism (German)	P7R2	3FT deg	* g	CD	MO	M*	24	BBCC	Ind		
Visual Arts and German	WR12	3FT deg	G g	CD	Ind	Ind	24	BBCC	Ind		

Univ of BRADFORD

TITLE	CODE	COURSE	SUBJECTS	A/AS	ND/C	AGNVQ	IB	SQA(H)	SQA	RATIO A/AS	
French and German	RR12	4SW deg	2L	BCC	Ind	X	Ind	Ind	Ind	4	12/30
German	R200	4SW deg	G	BCC	Ind	X	Ind	Ind	Ind		
German and Russian	RR28	4SW deg	2L	BCC	Ind	X	Ind	Ind	Ind	5	
German and Spanish	RR24	4SW deg	2L	BCC	Ind	X	Ind	Ind	Ind	4	
International Management and German	N1R2	4SW deg	G g	22	DO $	D$^	Ind	Ind	Ind	5	14/24

Univ of BRISTOL

TITLE	CODE	COURSE	SUBJECTS	A/AS	ND/C	AGNVQ	IB	SQA(H)	SQA	RATIO A/AS	
Computer Science and German	RG25	4FT deg	G g	BBB	Ind	D$^	30$	CSYS	Ind		
Drama and German	WR42	4FT deg	G	BC	Ind	D$^	28$	BBBBB	Ind		
French and German	RR12	4FT deg	F+G	ABB-BBB	Ind	D$^	30$	AABBB	Ind	13	24/30
German	R200	4FT deg	G g	BCC	Ind	D$^	28$	BBBBB	Ind	4	18/26
German and Italian	RR23	4FT deg	G	BBB	Ind	D$^	30$	BBBBB	Ind	7	28/28
German and Russian	RR28	4FT deg	G	BBB	Ind	D$^	30$	BBBBB	Ind	5	26/30
German and Spanish	RR24	4FT deg	G	BBB	Ind	D$^	30$	BBBBB	Ind	9	
History of Art and German	VR42	4FT deg	G	BBC	Ind	D$^	30$	BBBBB	Ind	8	
History with Study in German	V1R2	4FT deg	G	BBC	Ind	D$^	30$	BBBBB	Ind		
Law and German	MR32	4FT deg	G	ABB	Ind	D$^	34$	AAABB	Ind	20	
Music and German	WR32	4FT deg	Mu+G	BBC	Ind	D$^	30$	BBBBC	Ind	5	
Philosophy and German	RV27	4FT deg	G	BBB	Ind	D$^	30$	BBBBB	Ind	3	
Politics and German	RM21	4FT deg	G	BBB	Ind	D$^	32$	BBBBB	Ind	12	

Languages – German 41

course details			98 expected requirements							96 entry stats
TITLE	CODE	COURSE	SUBJECTS	A/AS	NO/C	AGNVQ	IB	SQA(H)	SQA	RATIO A/AS
BRISTOL, Univ of the W of England										
EFL, German and European Studies	QR32	4FT deg	g	14-24	5M	M*△ go	24$	BCCC$	Ind	
French, German and European Studies	RR12	4FT deg	F/G g	14-24	5M	M*△ go	24$	BCCC$	Ind	
German and Business Systems	RN21	3FT deg	G g	14-22	5M	M*△ go	24$	BCCC$	Ind	
German and European Studies	RT22	4FT deg	G g	14-24	5M	M*△ go	24$	BCCC$	Ind	
German and Information Systems	RG25	3FT deg	G g	14-22	5M	M*△ go	24$	BCCC$	Ind	
German and Law	RM23	4FT deg	G g	16-24	MO	M*△ go	24$	BBCC$	Ind	
German, Spanish and European Studies	RR24	4FT deg	G/Sp g	14-24	5M	M*△ go	24$	BCCC$	Ind	
BRUNEL Univ, West London										
Business Mathematics with German	RG2C	3FT deg	M+G g	BBC-BCC	3M+2D$	D△+	29$	BBBC$	Ind	1
Business Mathematics with German (4 Yrs Thin SW)	RG21	4SW deg	M+G g	BBC-BCC	3M+2D$	D△+	29$	BBBC$	Ind	3
Business Mathematics with German(4 Yrs Thick SW)	G1RF	4SW deg	M+G g	BBC-BCC	3M+2D$	D△+P△	29$	BBBC$	Ind	
Law with German (4 Yrs Thick SW)	M3R2	4SW deg	G	BBB	DO $	D△	30$	ABBBB$	Ind	
Manufacturing Eng with Ger (MEng) (4Yrs Thin SW)	H7R2	4SW/5SW deg	M+G	CCC	4M+1D$	DE△	28$	AABBB$	Ind	
Manufacturing Engineering with German (MEng)	H7RG	3FT/4FT deg	M+G	CCC	4M+1D$	DE△	28$	AABBB$	Ind	
Mathematics with German	GR12	3FT deg	M+G g	BBC-BCC	3M+2D$	P△	29$	BBBC$	Ind	
Mathematics with German (4 Yrs Thick SW)	G1R2	4SW deg	M+G g	BBC-BCC	3M+2D$	P△	29$	BBBC$	Ind	
Mathematics with German (4 Yrs Thin SW)	G1RG	4SW deg	M+G g	BBC-BCC	3M+2D$	D△	29$	BBBC$	Ind	
Spec Eng Prog w. German (MEng) (4/5 Yrs Thin SW)	H1R2	4SW/5SW deg	M+P g	BBB	4M+1D$	DE△	30$	ABBBB$	Ind	1
Spec Eng Prog w. German (MEng) (4/5Yrs Thick SW)	H1RF	4SW/5SW deg	M+P g	BBB	4M+1D$	DE△	30$	ABBBB$	Ind	4
Special Engineering Programme with German (MEng)	H1RG	3FT/4FT deg	M+P g	BBB	4M+1D$	DE△	30$	ABBBB$	Ind	
BUCKINGHAMSHIRE COLLEGE										
Business Administration with German	N1R2	3FT deg	G g	8	MO	M	27	CCCC	Ind	14
Business Studies with German	N1RG	4SW deg	G g	8	MO	M	27	CCCC	Ind	
European Business Studies (German)	NR12	4SW deg	G g	8	MO	M	27	CCCC	Ind	
Human Resources Management with German	N6R2	3FT deg		8	MO	M	27	CCCC	Ind	
International Business Studies (German)	N1RF	4SW deg	L	8	MO	M	27	CCCC	Ind	
International Marketing with German	N5R2	3FT deg	G g	8	MO	M	27	CCCC	Ind	
Leisure Management with German	N7R2	3FT deg		8-10	1D	M	27	CCCC	Ind	
Tourism with German	P7R2	3FT deg		8-10	1D	M	27	CCCC	Ind	
Travel and Tourism Management with German	PR72	3FT deg	G	8-10	1D	M	27	CCCC	Ind	
Business Studies with German	21RN	2FT HND		4	3M	P	Ind	Ind	Ind	
CARDIFF Univ of Wales										
Accounting with German	N4R2	4FT deg	L g	BBC-BBB	Ind	Ind	Ind	Ind	Ind	5
Banking and Finance with German	N3R2	4FT deg	G	BBC-BBB	Ind	Ind	Ind	Ind	Ind	8
Business Administration with German	N1R2	4FT deg	L g	BBC-BBB	Ind	Ind	Ind	Ind	Ind	9
Business Economics with German	L1RF	4FT deg	G	BBC-BBB	Ind	Ind	Ind	Ind	Ind	
Economics with German	L1R2	4FT deg	G	BBC-BBB	Ind	Ind	Ind	Ind	Ind	
German	R200	4FT deg	G	BBC			Ind			9
German/Ancient History	RV21	4FT deg	G	BCC			Ind			
German/Archaeology	RV26	4FT deg	G	BCC	Ind		Ind	AABB	X	
German/Cultural Criticism	MR92	4FT deg	E	ABC	Ind	Ind	Ind	Ind	Ind	
German/Economics	RL21	4FT deg	G	BBC-BBB	X		Ind	AABB	X	
German/Education	RX29	4FT deg	G	BCC	Ind	Ind	Ind	Ind	Ind	
German/English Literature	RQ23	4FT deg	E+G	ABB	X		Ind	AAABB	X	7
German/French	RR21	4FT deg	F+G	BBC	Ind		Ind	ABBBB	Ind	7	22/30
History of Ideas/German	VRD2	4FT deg	G	BBC			Ind			1
History/German	VR12	4FT deg	H+G	BBC	X		Ind	AABBB	X	
Italian/German	RR32	4FT deg	G	BBC-BCC	Ind		Ind	ABBBB	Ind	9
Japanese/German	TR42	4FT deg	G	BBC	X		Ind	Ind	X	9
Language Studies/German	QR12	4FT deg	G	BBC	Ind		Ind	ABBBB		4

course details

98 expected requirements

96 entry stats

TITLE	CODE	COURSE	SUBJECTS	A/AS	ND/C	AGNVQ	IB	SQA(H)	SQA	RATIO A/AS
Law and German	RM23	4FT deg	G	BBB	Ind	Ind	Ind	Ind	Ind	5　22/30
Music/German	WR32	4FT deg	Mu+G g	BBC	X		Ind	X	X	2
Politics/German	MR12	4FT deg	G	BCC	Ind		Ind	AABBB	X	
Pure Mathematics/German	GR12	4FT deg	M+G	BBC	Ind	Ind	Ind	AABBB	X	1
Religious Studies/German	VR82	4FT deg	G	BCC			Ind			
Sociology/German	LR32	4FT deg	G	BCC	3M+2D		Ind	Ind	X	
Spanish/German	RR24	4FT deg	L+G	BBC-BCC	Ind		Ind	Ind	Ind	6
Welsh/German	QR52	4FT deg	W+G	BBC			Ind			

Univ of CENTRAL ENGLAND

TITLE	CODE	COURSE	SUBJECTS	A/AS	ND/C	AGNVQ	IB	SQA(H)	SQA	RATIO A/AS
Business Administration with German	N1R2	3FT deg	* g	14	M+3D	D	22	CCCC		
Business Systems Eng with German Found Yr	G5RF▼	4FT/5SW deg	*	2	N	P*	Ind	CC	Ind	2
Business Systems Engineering with German	G5R2	3FT/4SW deg	* g	12	3M	M* go	24	CCC	Ind	
Electronic Eng with German Foundation Year	HR62▼	4FT/5SW deg	* g	2	N	P*	Ind	CC	Ind	
Electronic Engineering with German	H6RG	3FT/4SW deg	M g	12	3M $	ME1	24$	CCC$	Ind	
Electronic Engineering with German St Foun Yr	H6RF▼	5EXT deg	* g	2	$	P* go	Ind	CC$	Ind	
Electronic Engineering with German Studies	H6R2	4FT deg	M g	12	3M $	ME1 go	24$	CCC$	Ind	
Marketing with German	N5R2	3FT deg	* g	16	M+3D	M	24	CCCCC		
Mechanical Eng with German Studies Foundation Yr	H3RF▼	5EXT deg	* g	2	$	P* go	Ind	CC$	Ind	
Mechanical Engineering with German	H3RG	3FT/4SW deg	M g	12	3M $	ME1	24$	CCC$	Ind	
Mechanical Engineering with German Foundation Yr	HR32▼	4FT/5SW deg	* g	2	N	P*	Ind	CC	Ind	
Mechanical Engineering with German Studies	H3R2	4FT deg	M g	8	3M $	ME1 go	24$	CCC$	Ind	

Univ of CENTRAL LANCASHIRE

TITLE	CODE	COURSE	SUBJECTS	A/AS	ND/C	AGNVQ	IB	SQA(H)	SQA	RATIO A/AS
Combined Honours Programme 　German/Business German	Y400	4SW deg	L/* g	8	Ind	M*△	24$	CCC	Ind	

UNIVERSITY COLLEGE CHESTER

TITLE	CODE	COURSE	SUBJECTS	A/AS	ND/C	AGNVQ	IB	SQA(H)	SQA	RATIO A/AS
Art with German	W9R2	3FT deg	g	12	M	P^	Ind	CCCC	$	
Biology with German	C1R2	3FT deg	B g	12	M	P^	Ind	CCCC	$	
Biosciences with a European Language (German)	C9R2	3FT deg	B g	12	MO	P^	Ind	CCCC	$	
Computer Science/IT with German	G5R2	3FT deg	g	12	M	M	Ind	CCCC	$	3
Drama with German	W4R2	3FT deg	g	12	M	M	Ind	CCCC	$	3
English Literature with German	Q3R2	3FT deg	E g	12	M	P^	Ind	CCCC	$	8
Geography with German	F8R2	3FT deg	Gy/Gl g	12	M	P^	Ind	CCCC	$	2
History with German	V1R2	3FT deg	H/Ec/So g	12	M	P^	Ind	CCCC	$	
Mathematics with German	G1R2	3FT deg	M g	12	M	P^	Ind	CCCC	$	
Physical Education/Sports Science with German	B6R2	3FT deg	g	12	M	P^	Ind	CCCC	$	
Psychology with German	L7R2	3FT deg	g	12	M	M	Ind	CCCC	$	7
Theology and Religious Studies with German	V8R2	3FT deg	g	12	M	M	Ind	CCCC	$	

COVENTRY Univ

TITLE	CODE	COURSE	SUBJECTS	A/AS	ND/C	AGNVQ	IB	SQA(H)	SQA	RATIO A/AS
Business Studies with German	N1R2	4SW deg	* g	16	M+3D	M	Dip	CCC	Ind	9　12/18
European Studies with German (4 years)	TR22	4FT deg	*	CD	M	M	Ind	CCCC	Ind	
French and German	RR12▼	4FT deg	F	CD	M	M	Ind	CCCC$	Ind	7　6/18
German and Economics	LR12	4FT deg	G g	12	M+D	M	Ind	Ind	Ind	
German and Geography	LR82	4SW deg	G+Gy g	12	Ind	M+	Ind	Ind	Ind	2
German and Italian	RR23	4FT deg	G+I	CD	M	M	Ind	CCCC$	Ind	
German and Russian	RR28	4FT deg	G	CD	M		Ind	CCCC$	Ind	3
German and Spanish	RR24▼	4FT deg	G+Sp	CD	M	M	Ind	CCCC$	Ind	
History and German	VR12	4FT deg	*	CD	M	M	Ind	CCCC	Ind	
Mathematics and German	RG21	4FT deg	G+M g	16-20	Ind	M	Ind	Ind	Ind	8
Psychology and German	RC28	4FT deg	*	CD	M	M	Ind	CCCC	Ind	
Sociology and German	RL23	3FT deg								
Statistics and German	GR42	4FT deg	G+M/St g	12-16	Ind	M	Ind	Ind	Ind	

course details			98 expected requirements							96 entry stats	
TITLE	CODE	COURSE	SUBJECTS	A/AS	ND/C	AGNVQ	IB	SQA(H)	SQA	RATIO A/AS	
DE MONTFORT Univ											
European Studies-German	R200▼	3FT/4SW deg	G g	10	D	M	Ind	BCCC	Ind	4	
Law with German	M3R2▼	4FT deg	G g	BBC	6D	M^	30$	BBBBB$	X	3	18/18
Combined Studies *Language Studies-German*	Y400▼	3FT deg	* g	12	2M+4D	M	30	BBB	X		
Humanities Combined Honours *German Studies*	Y300▼	3FT deg	G g	CCD	MO	X	26$	ABBB	Ind		
Humanities Joint Honours *German Studies*	Y301▼	3FT deg	G g	CCD	MO	X	26$	ABBB	Ind		
Univ of DERBY											
Credit Accumulation Modular Scheme *German*	Y600	4FT deg	G	10	MO $	M$	Ind	CCCC$	Ind		
Univ of DUNDEE											
Physics with German	F3R2	4FT deg	M+S g	10	5M $	M$^	25$	BBCC$	N$		
Univ of DURHAM											
European Studies and German	RT22▼	4FT deg	*	CD	Ind	Ind	Dip	BCCC	Ind		
European Studies with German	T2R2▼	3FT deg	*	CD	Ind	Ind	Dip	BCCC	Ind		
History with German	V1R2	4FT deg	G	ABB	Ind	Ind	Ind	Ind	Ind		
Urban Studies with German	K4R2▼	3FT deg	*	CD	Ind	Ind	Dip	BCCC	Ind		
Arts Combined *German*	Y300	4FT deg	G	24	MO	Ind	30	AAABB	Ind		
Univ of EAST ANGLIA											
French and Germ Lang w Interpret and Translating	RR21	4FT deg	F+G	ABC	X		31$	AAAAA	X	6	20/30
German Studies with Honours Language	R200	4FT deg	G	BCD	X		28	ABBCC	X	6	
Univ of EAST LONDON											
Anthropology and German	LR62	3FT deg	* g	12	MO	M^					
Anthropology with German	L6R2	3FT deg	* g	12	MO	M^	Ind	Ind	Ind		
Archaeological Sciences and German	VR62	3FT deg	* g	12	MO	M	Ind	Ind	Ind		
Biology and German	CR12	3FT deg	* g	12	MO	M^	Ind	Ind	Ind		
Business Studies and German	NR12	3FT deg	* g	12	MO	M^	Ind	Ind	Ind		
Business Studies with German	N1R2	3FT deg	* g	14	MO	MB					
Communication Studies and German	PR32	3FT deg	* g	12	MO	M^	Ind	Ind	Ind		
Communication Studies with German	P3R2	3FT deg	* g	12	MO	M	Ind	Ind			
Computing & Business Info Systems and German	GR5F	3FT deg	* g	12	MO	M					
Cultural Studies and German	LRP2	3FT deg	* g	14	N	M^					
Design - Textile Design with German	J4R2	3FT deg	* g	12	MO	M	Ind	Ind	Ind		
Design - Visual Communication and German	RW22	3FT deg	* g	12	MO	M^	Ind	Ind	Ind		
Design - Visual Communication with German	W2R2	3FT deg	* g	12	MO	M	Ind	Ind	Ind		
Economics and German	LR12	3FT deg	* g	12	MO	M^	Ind	Ind	Ind		
Economics with German	L1R2	3FT deg	* g	12	MO	M	Ind				
Education & Community Studies and German	RX29	3FT deg	* g	12	MO	M^	Ind	Ind	Ind		
Education & Community Studies with German	X9R2	3FT deg	* g	12	MO	M					
Environmental Sciences and German	FR92	3FT deg	* g	12	MO	M					
European Studies and German	TR22	3FT deg	* g	12	MO	M					
European Studies with German	T2R2	3FT deg	* g	12	MO	M					
French with German	R1R2	3FT deg	* g	12	MO	M	Ind				
German and Health Studies	BR92	3FT deg	* g	12	MO	M$	Ind	Ind	Ind		
German and History of Art Design & Film	RV24	3FT deg	* g	12	MO	M$	Ind	Ind	Ind		
German and Information Technology	GR52	3FT deg	* g	12	MO	M$	Ind	Ind	Ind	2	
German and Law	MR32	3FT deg	* g	12	MO	D	Ind	Ind	Ind		
German and Linguistics	QR12	3FT deg	* g	12	MO	X	Ind	Ind	Ind	2	

course details

96 entry stats

TITLE	CODE	COURSE	SUBJECTS	A/AS	NO/C	AGNVQ	IB	SQA(H)	SQA	RATIO A/AS
German and Literature	QR32	3FT deg	* g	12	MO	X	Ind	Ind	Ind	
German and Maths, Stats & Computing	GR92	3FT deg	* g	12	MO	M$	Ind	Ind	Ind	
German and Media Studies	PR42	3FT deg	* g	12	MO	D	Ind	Ind	Ind	
German and Politics	MR12	3FT deg	* g	12	MO	M	Ind	Ind	Ind	
German and Psychosocial Studies	LR72	3FT deg	* g	12	MO	M$	Ind	Ind	Ind	
German and Sociology	LR32	3FT deg	* g	12	MO	M$	Ind	Ind	Ind	
German and Third World & Development Studies	MR92	3FT deg	* g	12	MO	M	Ind	Ind	Ind	
German and Women's Studies	MRX2	3FT deg	* g	12	MO	M	Ind	Ind	Ind	
German with Anthropology	R2L6	3FT deg	* g	12	MO	M				
German with Biology	R2C1	3FT deg	* g	12	MO	M				
German with Business Studies	R2N1	3FT deg	* g	12	MO	M				
German with Communication Studies	R2P3	3FT deg	* g	12	MO	M				
German with Computing & Business Info Systems	R2G5	3FT deg	* g	12	MO	M				
German with Cultural Studies	R2LP	3FT deg	* g	12	MO	M	Ind			
German with Design - Textile Design	R2J4	3FT deg	* g	12	MO	M	Ind			
German with Design - Visual Communication	R2W2	3FT deg	* g	12	MO	M	Ind			
German with Economics	R2L1	3FT deg	* g	12	MO	M	Ind			
German with Education & Community Studies	R2X9	3FT deg	* g	12	MO	M	Ind			
German with European Studies	R2T2	3FT deg	* g	12	MO	M	Ind			
German with French	R2R1	3FT deg	* g	12	MO	M	Ind			
German with Health Studies	R2B9	3FT deg	* g	12	MO	M	Ind			
German with History of Art Design & Film	R2V4	3FT deg	* g	12	MO	M	Ind			
German with Information Technology	R2GM	3FT deg	* g	12	MO	M	Ind			
German with Italian	R2R3	3FT deg	* g	12	MO	M	Ind			
German with Law	R2M3	3FT deg	* g	12	MO	M	Ind			
German with Linguistics	R2Q1	3FT deg	* g	12	MO	M	Ind			
German with Literature	R2Q3	3FT deg	* g	12	MO	M	Ind			
German with Maths, Stats & Computing	R2G9	3FT deg	* g	12	MO	M	Ind			
German with Politics	R2M1	3FT deg	* g	12	MO	M	Ind			
German with Social Policy Research	R2L4	3FT deg	* g	12	MO	M	Ind			
German with Sociology	R2L3	3FT deg	* g	12	MO	M	Ind			
German with Spanish	R2R4	3FT deg	* g	12	MO	M	Ind			
German with Women's Studies	R2M9	3FT deg	* g	12	MO	M	Ind			
German/Business Information Systems	GR72	3FT deg	* g	12	MO	M^	Ind			
German/Civil Engineering	HR22	3FT deg	* g	12	MO	M^	Ind	Ind	Ind	
Health Studies with German	B9R2	3FT deg	* g	12	MO	M	Ind	Ind	Ind	
History of Art Design & Film with German	V4R2	3FT deg	* g	12	MO	M	Ind	Ind		
Information Technology with German	G5R2	3FT deg	* g	12	MO	M	Ind	Ind	Ind	
Law with German	M3R2	3FT deg	* g	14	MO	M				
Linguistics with German	Q1R2	3FT deg	* g	12	MO	M				
Literature with German	Q3R2	3FT deg	* g	12	MO	M	Ind			
Maths, Stats & Computing with German	G9R2	3FT deg	* g	12	MO	M	Ind	Ind	Ind	
Media Studies with German	P4R2	3FT deg	* g	14	MO	M				
Politics with German	M1R2	3FT deg	* g	12	MO	M	Ind			
Psychosocial Studies with German	L7R2	3FT deg	* g	12	MO	M	Ind	Ind	Ind	
Social Policy Research with German	L4R2	3FT deg	* g	12	MO	M	Ind	Ind	Ind	
Sociology with German	L3R2	3FT deg	* g	12	MO	M	Ind	Ind	Ind	
Third World & Development Studies with German	M9R2	3FT deg	* g	12	MO	M	Ind	Ind		
Women's Studies with German	M9RF	3FT deg	* g	12	MO	M	Ind			
Three-Subject Degree German	Y600	3FT deg	* g	12	MO	M	Ind	Ind	Ind	

course details			98 expected requirements							96 entry stats
TITLE	CODE	COURSE	SUBJECTS	A/AS	NO/C	AGNVQ	IB	SQA(H)	SQA	RATIO A/AS
Univ of EDINBURGH										
Business Studies and German	NR12	4FT deg	L g	BBB	Ind		34$	ABBB$	Ind	10
Celtic and German	QR52	4FT deg	L g	BBB	Ind	Ind	Dip$	BBBB$	Ind	
English Language and German	QR32	4FT deg	E+L g	BBB	Ind	Ind	Dip$	BBBB$	Ind	
English Literature and German	RQ23	4FT deg	L+E g	BBB	Ind	Ind	Dip$	BBBB$	Ind	
German	R200	4FT deg	L g	BBB	Ind	Ind	Dip$	BBBB$	Ind	
German and Business Studies	RN21	4FT deg	L g	BBB	Ind	Ind	Dip$	BBBB$	Ind	
German and European History	RV21	4FT deg	L g	BBB	Ind	Ind	Dip$	BBBB$	Ind	
German and History of Art	RV24	4FT deg	L g	BBB	Ind	Ind	Dip$	BBBB$	Ind	
German and Latin	RQ26	4FT deg	L g	BBB	Ind	Ind	Dip$	BBBB$	Ind	
German and Linguistics	RQ21	4FT deg	L g	BBB	Ind	Ind	Dip$	BBBB$	Ind	
German and Philosophy	RV27	4FT deg	L g	BBB	Ind	Ind	Dip$	BBBB$	Ind	
German and Politics	RM21	4FT deg	L g	BBB	Ind	Ind	Dip$	BBBB$	Ind	
History of Art and German	VR42	4FT deg	L g	BBB	Ind	Ind	Dip$	BBBB$	Ind	
Law and German	MR32	4FT deg	L g	ABB	X		32	AAABB$	X	3
Philosophy and German	VR72	4FT deg	L g	BBB	Ind	Ind	Dip$	BBBB$	Ind	
Univ of ESSEX										
Computer Science with German (4 Yrs)	G5R2	4FT deg	* g	20	MO+2D	Ind	28	BBBB	Ind	12
English and German (Language and Linguistics)	RQ23	4FT deg	*	20	MO+2D	Ind	28	BBBB	Ind	
German (Language and Linguistics) (4 Yrs)	R2Q1	4FT deg	*	20	MO+2D	Ind	28	BBBB	Ind	
Mathematics and German (4 Yrs)	GR12	4FT deg	M	18	MO $	Ind	28$	CSYS	Ind	7
EUROPEAN Business School										
Euro Bus Admin with German + one beginner lang	N1RF	4SW deg	L	12	Ind		Ind	Ind	Ind	
International Bus St: German + one beginner lang	NR12	4FT deg								
International Bus Studs with German (Test+Int)	N1R2	4SW deg		12	Ind		Ind	Ind	Ind	
International Business & Mgt Studies with German	N1RG	4SW deg		12	Ind		Ind	Ind	Ind	
Univ of EXETER										
English and German	QR32	4FT deg	E+G	BBB-BCC	MO	M/D$^	32$	Ind	Ind	8
French and German	RR1F	4FT deg	F+G	22-24	MO	M/D$^	34$			
German	R201	4FT deg	G	BBB-BCC	MO	M/D$^	32$			
German and Drama	RW24	4FT deg	G	BBB-BCC	MO+3D	M/D$^	32$	Ind	Ind	
German and Italian	RR2H	4FT deg	G	BBB-BCC	MO	M/D$^	32$			
German and Mathematics	GR12	4FT deg	G+M	20-22	MO	M/D$^	32$			
German and Russian	RR2V	4FT deg	G	BBB-BCC	MO	M/D$^	32$			
German and Spanish	RR2K	4FT deg	G	BBB-BCC	MO	M/D$^	32$			
History and German	RV2C	4FT deg	G	ABB-BCC	MO	M/D$^	32$	Ind	Ind	
Music and German	RW2H	4FT deg	G+Mu	BCC	MO	M/D$^	32$	Ind	Ind	
Univ of GLAMORGAN										
French and German	RR12	3FT deg			Ind	Ind	Ind	Ind	Ind	
French with German	R1R2	3FT deg			Ind	Ind	Ind	Ind	Ind	
Mathematics with German	G1R2	3FT deg	M g	8	Ind	Ind	Ind	Ind	Ind	
Combined Studies (Honours) German	Y400	3FT deg	* g	8-16	Ind	Ind	Ind	Ind	Ind	
Univ of GLASGOW										
Anthropology with German	LR62	4FT deg		BBC	N	M	30	BBBB	Ind	
Archaeology/German	RV26	5FT deg		BBC	HN	M	30	BBBB	Ind	
Business Economics with German	L1RF	4FT deg		BBC	N	M	30	BBBB	N	
Celtic Civilisation/German	QR52	5FT deg		BBC	HN	M	30	BBBB	Ind	
Celtic/German	QRN2	5FT deg		BBC	HN	M	30	BBBB	Ind	
Classical Civilisation/German	QR82	5FT deg		BBC	HN	M	30	BBBB	Ind	

			98 expected requirements							96 entry stats
TITLE	CODE	COURSE	SUBJECTS	A/AS	ND/C	AGNVQ	IB	SQA(H)	SQA	RATIO A/AS
Czech/German	RT21	5FT deg		BBC	HN	M	30	BBBB	Ind	
Economic and Social History with German	V3R2	4FT deg		BBC	8M	M	30	BBBB	Ind	
Economic and Social History/German	RV23	5FT deg		BBC	HN	M	30	BBBB	Ind	
Economics with German	L1R2	4FT deg		BBC	8M	M	30	BBBB	Ind	
English/German	QR32	5FT deg		BBC	HN	M	30	BBBB	Ind	
Film and Television Studies/German	RW25	5FT deg		BBB	HN	D	32	AABB	HN	5
French/German	RR12	5FT deg		BBC	HN	M	30	BBBB	Ind	5
Geography with German	L8R2	4FT deg		BBC	8M	M	30	BBBB	Ind	
Geography/German	LR82	5FT deg		BBC	HN	M	30	BBBB	Ind	
German Language and Literature	R200	5FT deg		BBC	HN	M	30	BBBB	Ind	10
German/Economics	LRC2	5FT deg		BBC	HN	M	30	BBBB	Ind	
German/Hispanic Studies	RR24	5FT deg		BBC	HN	M	30	BBBB	Ind	6
German/History	VR12	5FT deg		BBC	HN	M	30	BBBB	Ind	11
German/History of Art	RV24	5FT deg		BBC	HN	M	30	BBBB	Ind	
German/Italian	RR23	5FT deg		BBC	HN	M	30	BBBB	Ind	7
German/Music	RW23	5FT deg		BBC	HN	M	30	BBBB	Ind	4
German/Philosophy	RV27	5FT deg		BBC	HN	M	30	BBBB	Ind	
German/Polish	RTF1	5FT deg		BBC	HN	M	30	BBBB	Ind	
German/Politics	MR12	5FT deg		BBC	HN	M	30	BBBB	Ind	
German/Psychology	CR82	5FT deg		BBC	HN	M	30	BBBB	Ind	4
German/Russian	RR28	5FT deg		BBC	HN	M	30	BBBB	Ind	
German/Scottish History	RV2C	5FT deg		BBC	HN	M	30	BBBB	Ind	
German/Scottish Literature	QR22	5FT deg		BBC	HN	M	30	BBBB	Ind	
German/Sociology	LR32	5FT deg		BBC	HN	M	30	BBBB	Ind	
Law with German Language	M3R2	4FT deg		ABB	X		34	AAAAB	X	3
Management Studies with German	N1R2	4FT deg		BBC	8M	M	30	BBBB	Ind	12
Management Studies/German	NR12	5FT deg		BBC	HN	M	30	BBBB	Ind	7
Philosophy with German	V7R2	4FT deg		BBC	8M	M	30	BBBB	Ind	
Politics with German	M1R2	4FT deg		BBC	8M	M	30	BBBB	Ind	
Psychology with German	C8R2	4FT deg		BBC	8M	M	30	BBBB	Ind	
Social and Urban Policy with German	L4R2	4FT deg		BBC	8M	M	30	BBBB	Ind	
Sociology with German	L3R2	4FT deg		BBC	8M	M	30	BBBB	Ind	
Theatre Studies/German	RW24	5FT deg		BBC	HN	M	30	BBBB	Ind	

GOLDSMITHS COLL (Univ of London)

German Studies (4 Yrs)	R200	4FT deg	G	CC	MO	M	Dip	BCCCC	N	3	12/16

Univ of GREENWICH

Applied Biology with German	C1R2	3FT/4SW deg	B+C g	10	3M	MS	Dip	CCC	Ind	
Applied Chemistry with German	F1R2	3FT/4SW deg	C+S g	8	3M	MS	Dip	CCC	Ind	

HERIOT-WATT Univ

Accountancy with German	N4R2	4FT deg	L g	BCC	Ind		Ind	ABBB$	Ind	
Chemistry with German	F1R2	4FT deg	C+S+L	CCD	$	M$ go	28	BBB	$	
French/German	RR1F	4FT deg								
French/German (Interpreting and Translating)	RR12	4FT deg	2L	BBC	Ind		Ind	AABB	Ind	
German/Russian	RR2V	4FT deg								
German/Russian (Interpreting and Translating)	RR28	4FT deg	2L	BBC	Ind		Ind	AABB	Ind	
German/Spanish	RR2K	4FT deg								
German/Spanish (Interpreting and Translating)	RR24	4FT deg	2L	BBC	Ind		Ind	AABB	Ind	
Mathematics with German	G1R2	4FT deg	M+L	CDE	HN	M$^	28	BBB	HN	

Univ of HERTFORDSHIRE

Manufacturing Systems Engineering with German	H7R2	3FT deg	

| course details | | | 98 expected requirements | | | | | | | 96 entry stats | |

TITLE	CODE	COURSE	SUBJECTS	A/AS	NO/C	AGNVQ	IB	SQA(H)	SQA	RATIO	A/AS
Univ of HUDDERSFIELD											
German and Media	RP24	4FT deg	G	CDD	Ind	Ind	Ind	BBBC	Ind		
German with English	R2Q3	4FT deg	G+E	CCE	Ind	Ind	Ind	BBBC	Ind		
German with Politics	R2M1	4FT deg	G	CCE	Ind	Ind	Ind	BBBC	Ind		
Univ of HULL											
Business Studies/German	NR12	4FT deg	G g	BBC-BCC	Ind $	D*^ go	26$	BBCCC	Ind	6	16/26
Chemistry with German	F1R2	4FT deg	C g	CCD	MO $	M$^ go	26$	BCCCC	Ind	8	
Chemistry with German (MChem)	F1RF	4FT deg	C g	BCC	MO+3D$	M$^ gi	26$	BBBCC			
Drama/German	RW24	4FT deg	G	BBB-BCC	Ind	D$^ go	28$	ABBCC	Ind		
Dutch/German	RTF2	4FT deg	G	BCC-CCC	Ind	Ind	26$	BBCCC	Ind	3	
English/German	QR32	4FT deg	E+G	BBB-BCC	Ind	M$^ gi	28$	BBBCC	Ind	4	
French/German	RR12	4FT deg	F+G	BCC	Ind	Ind	28$	BBBCC	Ind	10	16/26
Gender Studies and German	MR92	4FT deg	G	BCC-CCC	Ind	M$6/^ go	28$	BBBCC	Ind	2	
German	R200	4FT deg	G	BCC-CCC	Ind	Ind	28$	BBBCC	Ind	4	14/16
German/Italian	RR23	4FT deg	G	BCC	Ind	Ind	28$	BBBCC	Ind	9	
German/Scandinavian Studies	RRF7	4FT deg	G	BCC-CCC	Ind	Ind	28$	BBCCC	Ind	2	18/22
German/Spanish	RR24	4FT deg	G	BCC-CCC	Ind	Ind	28$	BBBCC	Ind	6	
Law with German	M3R2	4FT deg	G	BBB-CCC	M+D $	D$^ gi	28$	ABBBB	Ind	14	
Mathematics with German	G1R2	4FT deg	M g	BCD	MO $	M$^ go	26$	BBCCC	Ind		
Mathematics with German (MMath)	G1RF	4FT deg	M g	BCC	MO $	M$^ go	26$	BBBCC	Ind		
KEELE Univ											
Biological and Medicinal Chemistry and German	FRC2	3FT deg	G+C g	BCC	Ind	D$^	28$	CSYS	Ind		
German and American Studies (4 Yrs)	RQ24	4FT deg	* g	BCC	Ind	Ind	28	BBBB	Ind		
German and Applied Social Studies	LR52	3FT deg	G	BCC-BBC	Ind	D$^	28$	CSYS	Ind		
German and Applied Social Studies (4 Yrs)	RL25	4FT deg	G	BCC	Ind	Ind	28$	BBBB	Ind		
German and Astrophysics	FR52	3FT deg	G+P g	BCC	Ind	D$^	28$	CSYS	Ind		
German and Biochemistry	CR72	3FT deg	C+G g	BCC	Ind	D$^	28$	CSYS	Ind		
German and Biochemistry (4 Yrs)	RC27	4FT deg	G	BCC	Ind	Ind	28$	BBBB	Ind		
German and Biological and Medicine Chem (4 Yrs)	RF2C	4FT deg	* g	BCC	Ind	Ind	28	BBBB	Ind		
German and Biology	CR12	3FT deg	S+G g	BCC	Ind	D$^	28$	CSYS	Ind		
German and Biology (4 Yrs)	RC21	4FT deg	G	BCC	Ind	Ind	28$	BBBB	Ind		
German and Business Administration	NR92	3FT deg	G	BBC-BCC	Ind	D$^	28$	CSYS	Ind	6	
German and Business Administration (4 Yrs)	RN29	4FT deg	G	BBC-BCC	Ind	Ind	28$	BBBB	Ind	15	
German and Chemistry	FR12	3FT deg	C+G g	BCC	Ind	D$^	28$	CSYS	Ind	2	
German and Chemistry (4 Yrs)	RF21	4FT deg	G	BCC	Ind	Ind	28$	BBBB	Ind		
German and Computer Science (4 Yrs)	RG25	4FT deg	* g	BCC	Ind	Ind	28	BBBB	Ind		
German and Criminology (4 Yrs)	RM2H	4FT deg	* g	BBB-BCC	Ind	Ind	28	BBBB	Ind		
German and Economics	LR12	3FT deg	G g	BCC	Ind	D$^	28$	CSYS	Ind		
German and Economics (4 Yrs)	RL21	4FT deg	G	BCC	Ind	Ind	28$	BBBB	Ind		
German and Educational Studies (4 Yrs)	XR92	4FT deg	* g	BCC	Ind	Ind	28	BBB	Ind		
German and Electronic Music	RW2J	3FT deg	G+Mu	BCC	Ind	D$^	28$	CSYS	Ind		
German and Electronic Music (4 Yrs)	WRJ2	4FT deg	* g	BCC	Ind	Ind	28	BBBB	Ind		
German and English	QR32	3FT deg	E+G	BBC	Ind	D$^	30$	CSYS	Ind	3	
German and English (4 Yrs)	RQ23	4FT deg	* g	BBC	Ind	Ind	30	BBBB	Ind		
German and Environmental Management	FRX2	3FT deg	G g	BCC	Ind	D$^	28$	CSYS	Ind	1	
German and Environmental Management (4 Yrs)	RF2X	4FT deg	G	BCC	Ind	Ind	28$	BBBB	Ind		
German and European Studies	RT22	3FT deg	G	BCC	Ind	D$^	28$	CSYS	Ind	2	18/22
German and European Studies (4 Yrs)	TR22	4FT deg	G	BCC	Ind	Ind	28$	BBBB	Ind		
German and French	RR12	3FT deg	F+G	BBC-BCC	Ind	D$^	28$	CSYS	Ind	5	20/20
German and French (4 Yrs)	RR21	4FT deg	* g	BCC	Ind	Ind	28	BBBB	Ind		
German and French/Russian (4 Yrs)	TRX2	4FT deg	* g	BBC-BCC	Ind	Ind	28	BBBB	Ind		

course details   98 expected requirements   96 entry stats

TITLE	CODE	COURSE	SUBJECTS	A/AS	ND/C	AGNVQ	IB	SQA(H)	SQA	RATIO A/AS
German and French/Russian or Russian Studies	RT2X	3FT deg	F+R+G	BBC-BCC	Ind	D$^	28$	CSYS	Ind	
German and Geography	LR82	3FT deg	G+Gy	BCC	Ind	D$^	28$	CSYS	Ind	5
German and Geology	FR62	3FT deg	S+G̲ g	BCC	Ind	D$^	28$	CSYS	Ind	
German and Geology (4 Yrs)	RF26	4FT deg	G̲	BCC	Ind	Ind	28$	BBBB	Ind	
History and German	RV21	3FT deg	G̲	BCC	Ind	D$^	28$	CSYS	Ind	3
History and German (4 Yrs)	VR12	4FT deg	* g	BCC	Ind	Ind	28	BBBB	Ind	
Human Resource Management and German	NR62	3FT deg	G̲	BCC	Ind	D$^	28$	CSYS	Ind	
Human Resource Management and German (4 Yrs)	RN26	4FT deg	G̲	BCC	Ind	Ind	28$	BBBB	Ind	2
International History and German	RV2C	3FT deg	G̲	BCC	Ind	D$^	28$	CSYS	Ind	3
International History and German (4 Yrs)	VRC2	4FT deg	* g	BCC	Ind	Ind	28	BBBB	Ind	
International Politics and German	MRC2	3FT deg	G̲	BCC	Ind	D$^	28$	CSYS	Ind	
International Politics and German (4 Yrs)	RM2C	4FT deg	G̲	BCC	Ind	Ind	28$	BBBB	Ind	
Law and German	MR32	3FT deg	G̲	BBB	Ind	D$^	32$	CSYS	Ind	7
Management Science and German	NR12	3FT deg	G̲ g	BCC	Ind	D$^	28$	CSYS	Ind	5
Management Science and German (4 Yrs)	RN21	4FT deg	* g	BCC	Ind	Ind	28	BBBB	Ind	10
Marketing and German	NR52	3FT deg	G̲	BCC	Ind	D$^	28$	CSYS	Ind	6
Mathematics and German	GR12	3FT deg	G̲+M	BCC	Ind	D$^	28$	CSYS	Ind	
Mathematics and German (4 Yrs)	RG21	4FT deg	G̲	BCC	Ind	Ind	28$	BBBB	Ind	
Music and German	RW23	3FT deg	Mu+G̲	BCC	Ind	D$^	28$	CSYS	Ind	7
Music and German (4 Yrs)	WR32	4FT deg	* g	BCC	Ind	Ind	28	BBBB	Ind	
Philosophy and German	VR72	4FT deg	* g	BCC	Ind	Ind	28	BBBB	Ind	
Physics and German	FR32	3FT deg	G̲+P	BCC	Ind	D$^	28$	CSYS	Ind	
Politics and German	MR12	3FT deg	G̲	BCC	Ind	D$^	28$	CSYS	Ind	
Politics and German (4 Yrs)	RM21	4FT deg	G̲	BCC	Ind	Ind	28$	BBBB	Ind	
Psychology and German	CR82	3FT deg	G̲ g	BBB	Ind	D$^	32$	CSYS	Ind	
Russian Studies and German	RRF8	3FT deg	G̲	BCC	Ind	D$^	28$	CSYS	Ind	
Russian and German	RR28	3FT deg	G̲+R	BCC	Ind	D$^	28$	CSYS	Ind	
Sociology & Social Anthropol and German (4 Yrs)	RL23	4FT deg	g	BCC	Ind	Ind	28	BBBB	Ind	
Statistics and German (4 Yrs)	RG24	4FT deg	* g	BCC	Ind	Ind	28	BBBB	Ind	
Visual Arts and German	RW21	3FT deg	G̲	BCC	Ind	D$^	28$	CSYS	Ind	

Univ of KENT

TITLE	CODE	COURSE	SUBJECTS	A/AS	ND/C	AGNVQ	IB	SQA(H)	SQA	RATIO A/AS
European Studies (German)	R211	4FT deg	G	20	3M+3D	Ind	28	Ind	Ind	6
German	R200	4FT deg	G	20	3M+3D	Ind	28	Ind	Ind	12
German/Classical Studies	QR82	4FT deg	G	20	3M+3D	Ind	28	Ind	Ind	2
German/Comparative Literary Studies	RQ22	4FT deg	G	20	3M+3D	Ind	28	Ind	Ind	
German/Computing	RG25	4FT deg	G	20	3M+3D	Ind	28	Ind	Ind	
German/Drama	RW24	4FT deg	G	22	2M+4D	Ind	30	Ind	Ind	
German/English	QR32	4FT deg	E̲+G	22	2M+4D	Ind	30	Ind	Ind	
German/English (Post-Colonial Literatures)	RQ2J	4FT deg	E̲+G	22	2M+4D	Ind	30	Ind	Ind	
German/English Language	RQ23	4FT deg	G+E	20	3M+3D	Ind	28	Ind	Ind	
German/Film Studies	RW25	4FT deg	G	22	2M+4D	Ind	30	Ind	Ind	
German/French	RR12	4FT deg	F+G	22	2M+4D	Ind	30	Ind	Ind	12 22/28
History and Theory of Art/German	VR42	4FT deg	G	20	3M+3D	Ind	28	Ind	Ind	
History of Science/German	RV25	4FT deg	G	20	3M+3D	Ind	28	Ind	Ind	
History/German	RV21	4FT deg	G	22	2M+4D	Ind	30	Ind	Ind	9
Italian/German	RR23	4FT deg	G	20	3M+3D	Ind	28	Ind	Ind	
Linguistics/German	RQ21	4FT deg	G	20	3M+3D	Ind	28	Ind	Ind	7
Philosophy/German	RV27	4FT deg	G	20	3M+3D	Ind	28	Ind	Ind	
Politics and Government with German (4 Yrs)	MRC2	4FT deg	G	18	Ind	Ind	26$	BBBB$	Ind	
Spanish/German	RR24	4FT deg	G	20	3M+3D	Ind	28	Ind	Ind	
Theology/German	RV28	4FT deg	G	20	3M+3D	Ind	28	Ind	Ind	

			98 expected requirements							96 entry stats

course details

TITLE	CODE	COURSE	SUBJECTS	A/AS	ND/C	RGNVQ	IB	SQA(H)	SQA	RATIO A/AS
KING'S COLL LONDON (Univ of London)										
French and German	RR12	4FT deg	F+G	BBC						5 20/30
German	R200	4FT deg	G	BCC						4 18/22
German and Classical Studies	QR82	3FT deg	G	BBC						
German and Czech	RT21	4FT deg								
German and Hispanic Studies	RR24	4FT deg	G+Sp	BBC						5
German and History	RV21	3FT deg	G+H	ABB-BBC						
German and Modern Greek	RT22	4FT deg	G	BCC						
German and Music	RW23	4FT deg	G+Mu	BBC						2
German and Philosophy	RV27	3FT deg	G	BBC						4
German and Portuguese	RR25	4FT deg	G	BCC						2
German and Russian	RR28	3FT deg	G	BCC						
German with Applied Computing	R2G5	4FT deg	G	BCC						
German with English	R2Q3	4FT deg	G+E	BBC						3
War Studies and German	MR92	4FT deg	G	BCC						3
European Studies German	T2Y3	4FT deg	G	ABB						
KINGSTON Univ										
German/Economics	RL21	4FT deg	G g	14	MO	Ind^	Ind	BCCCC	HN	4
German/English Language	RQ23	4FT deg	E+G	14	MO	Ind^	Ind	BCCCC	HN	3
German/English Literature	QR32	4FT deg	E+G	16	MO	Ind^	Ind	BBCCC	HN	2
German/French	RR21	4FT deg	G+F	14	MO	Ind^	Ind	BCCCC	HN	7
History of Art, Architecture and Design/German	VR42	3FT deg	G g	14-16	MO	Ind^	Ind	BBCCC	HN	
History/German	RV21	4FT deg	H+G g	14	MO	Ind^	Ind	BCCCC	HN	4
Politics/German	MR12	4FT deg	G g	12-14	MO	Ind^	Ind	BCCCC	HN	7
Psychology/German	LR72	4FT deg	G g	16	MO	Ind^	Ind	BBCCC	HN	5
Univ of Wales, LAMPETER										
German (4 Yrs)	R200	4FT deg	G	16	Ind	Ind	Ind	Ind	Ind	
German Studies	R201	4FT deg		16	Ind	Ind	Ind	Ind	Ind	
German Studies and American Literature	QR4F	3FT deg			Ind	Ind	Ind	Ind	Ind	
German Studies and Ancient History	RVG1	4FT deg	*	16	Ind	Ind	Ind	Ind	Ind	
German Studies and Anthropology	LR6F	4FT deg	*	16	Ind	Ind	Ind	Ind	Ind	
German Studies and Archaeology	RVF6	4FT deg	*	16-18	Ind	Ind	Ind	Ind	Ind	
German Studies and Australian Studies	LRP2	3FT deg			Ind	Ind	Ind	Ind	Ind	
German Studies and Church History	RVGC	4FT deg	*	14-16	Ind	Ind	Ind	Ind	Ind	
German Studies and Classical Studies	QRW2	4FT deg	*	16	Ind	Ind	Ind	Ind	Ind	
German Studies and Cultural Studies in Geography	LRVF	4FT deg	Gy	16	Ind	Ind	Ind	Ind	Ind	
German Studies and English Literature	QRH2	4FT deg	E	16-18	Ind	Ind	Ind	Ind	Ind	
German Studies and French	RRC2	4FT deg	F	16	Ind	Ind	Ind	Ind	Ind	
German Studies and Geography	LR8F	4FT deg	Gy	16	Ind	Ind	Ind	Ind	Ind	
German and American Literature	QR42	3FT deg	G		Ind	Ind	Ind	Ind	Ind	
German and Ancient History	RVF1	4FT deg	G	16	Ind	Ind	Ind	Ind	Ind	
German and Anthropology	LR62	4FT deg	G	16	Ind	Ind	Ind	Ind	Ind	
German and Archaeology	RV26	4FT deg	G	16	Ind	Ind	Ind	Ind	Ind	
German and Australian Studies	LR6G	3FT deg	G		Ind	Ind	Ind	Ind	Ind	
German and Church History	RVFD	4FT deg	G	14-16	Ind	Ind	Ind	Ind	Ind	
German and Classical Studies	QR82	4FT deg	G	16	Ind	Ind	Ind	Ind	Ind	
German and Cultural Studies in Geography	LRV2	4FT deg	Gy+G	16	Ind	Ind	Ind	Ind	Ind	
German and English Literature	QR32	4FT deg	G+E	16-18	Ind	Ind	Ind	Ind	Ind	
German and French	RR12	4FT deg	F+G	16	Ind	Ind	Ind	Ind	Ind	
German and Geography	LR82	4FT deg	Gy+G	16	Ind	Ind	Ind	Ind	Ind	

course details | 98 expected requirements | 96 entry stats

TITLE	CODE	COURSE	SUBJECTS	A/AS	NQ/C	AGNVQ	IB	SQA(H)	SQA	RATIO A/AS
Greek and German	QR72	4FT deg	G g	16	Ind	Ind	Ind	Ind	Ind	
Greek and German Studies	QRR2	4FT deg	* g	16	Ind	Ind	Ind	Ind	Ind	
History and German	RV21	4FT deg	H+G	16	Ind	Ind	Ind	Ind	Ind	
History and German Studies	RV2C	4FT deg	H	16	Ind	Ind	Ind	Ind	Ind	
Informatics and German	GR52	4FT deg	G	14-16	Ind	Ind	Ind	Ind	Ind	
Informatics and German Studies	GR5F	4FT deg	*	14-16	Ind	Ind	Ind	Ind	Ind	
Islamic Studies and German	TR62	4FT deg	G	16	Ind	Ind	Ind	Ind	Ind	
Islamic Studies and German Studies	TR6F	4FT deg	*	16	Ind	Ind	Ind	Ind	Ind	
Latin and German	QR62	4FT deg	G g	16	Ind	Ind	Ind	Ind	Ind	
Latin and German Studies	QRQ2	4FT deg	* g	16	Ind	Ind	Ind	Ind	Ind	
Management Techniques and German	NR12	3FT deg	G	16	Ind	Ind	Ind	Ind	Ind	
Management Techniques and German Studies	NR1F	3FT deg	*	16	Ind	Ind	Ind	Ind	Ind	
Medieval Studies and German	VR12	4FT deg	G	16	Ind	Ind	Ind	Ind	Ind	
Medieval Studies and German Studies	VR1F	4FT deg	*	16	Ind	Ind	Ind	Ind	Ind	
Modern Historical Studies and German	VRCF	3FT deg			Ind	Ind	Ind	Ind	Ind	
Modern Historical Studies and German Studies	VRCG	3FT deg			Ind	Ind	Ind	Ind	Ind	
Philosophical Studies and German	RV27	4FT deg	G	16	Ind	Ind	Ind	Ind	Ind	
Philosophical Studies and German Studies	RVF7	4FT deg	*	16	Ind	Ind	Ind	Ind	Ind	
Religious Studies and German	RVF8	4FT deg	G	16	Ind	Ind	Ind	Ind	Ind	
Religious Studies and German Studies	RVG8	4FT deg	*	16	Ind	Ind	Ind	Ind	Ind	
Theology and German	RV28	4FT deg	G	16	Ind	Ind	Ind	Ind	Ind	
Theology and German Studies	RV2V	4FT deg	*	16	Ind	Ind	Ind	Ind	Ind	
Victorian Studies and German	RVFC	4FT deg	G	16	Ind	Ind	Ind	Ind	Ind	
Victorian Studies and German Studies	RV2D	4FT deg	*	16	Ind	Ind	Ind	Ind	Ind	
Welsh Studies and German	QRM2	4FT deg	G	16	Ind	Ind	Ind	Ind	Ind	
Welsh Studies and German Studies	QRMF	4FT deg	*	16	Ind	Ind	Ind	Ind	Ind	
Welsh and German	QR52	4FT deg	W+G	16	Ind	Ind	Ind	Ind	Ind	
Welsh and German Studies	QR5G	4FT deg	W	16	Ind	Ind	Ind	Ind	Ind	
Women's Studies and German	MR92	4FT deg	G	16	Ind	Ind	Ind	Ind	Ind	
Women's Studies and German Studies	RM29	4FT deg	*	16	Ind	Ind	Ind	Ind	Ind	

LANCASTER Univ

TITLE	CODE	COURSE	SUBJECTS	A/AS	NQ/C	AGNVQ	IB	SQA(H)	SQA	RATIO A/AS
Chemistry with German Studies (4 years)	F1R2	4SW deg	C+G/L g	18	MO $		28$	BBBB$	Ind	
English Language and French Studies	QR32	4FT deg	E+F g	BBC	DO $		32$	ABBBB$	Ind	
European Management (German)	N1R2	4FT/5SW deg	G/L g	ABB	MO+5D		32$	AABBB$	Ind	
French Studies and German Studies	RR12	4SW deg	(F+G)/* g	BCC	Ind $		30$	BBBBB$	Ind	
German Studies	R200	4SW deg	G/L g	CCC	Ind $		30$	BBBBB$	Ind	
German Studies and Accounting and Finance	NR42	4SW deg	M+G/L g	BBC	DO $		32$	AABBB$	Ind	
German Studies and Art History	WR12	4SW deg	G/L	BCC	MO $		30$	BBBBB$	Ind	
German Studies and Computing	GR52	4FT deg	G/L g	BCC	Ind $		30$	BBBBB$	Ind	
German Studies and Economics	RL21	4SW deg	G/L g	BBC	Ind $		32$	ABBBB$	Ind	
German Studies and Educational Studies	RX29	4SW deg	G/L	BCC	MO $		30$	BBBBB$	Ind	
German Studies and English	RQ23	4SW deg	E+G/L g	BBC	Ind $		32$	ABBBB$	Ind	
German Studies and Geography	LR82	4SW deg	G/L+Gy g	BBC	Ind $		30$	BBBBB$	Ind	
German Studies and History	RV21	4SW deg	G/L+H	BCC	Ind $		30$	BBBBB$	Ind	
German Studies and Italian Studies	RR23	4SW deg	G/I g	BCC	Ind $		30$	BBBBB$	Ind	
German Studies and Linguistics	QR12	4SW deg	G/L g	BBC	MO $		30$	BBBBB$	Ind	
German Studies and Marketing	RN25	4SW deg	G/L g	BBC	MO+4D		32$	ABBBB$	Ind	
German Studies and Mathematics	GR12	4SW deg	M+G/L	20	MO $		30$	BBBBB$	Ind	
German Studies and Music	WR32	4SW deg	G/L+Mu	BCC	MO $		30$	BBBB$	Ind	
German Studies and Philosophy	RV27	4SW deg	G/L	BCC	Ind $		30$	BBBBB$	Ind	

TITLE	CODE	COURSE	SUBJECTS	A/AS	NO/C	AGNVQ	IB	SQA(H)	SQA	RATIO A/AS
German Studies and Politics	RM21	4SW deg	G/L	BCC	Ind $		30$	BBBBB$	Ind	
German Studies and Psychology	CR82	4SW deg	G/L g	BBC	DO $		32$	ABBBB$	Ind	
German Studies and Religious Studies	RV28	4SW deg	G/L	BCC	Ind $		30$	BBBBB$	Ind	
German Studies and Spanish Studies	RR24	4SW deg	G/Sp	BCC	Ind $		30$	BBBBB$	Ind	
German Studies and Theatre Studies	WR42	4SW deg	G/L	BCC	MO $		30$	BBBBB$	Ind	
Physics with German Studies	F3R2	4SW deg	P+M+G/L	BCC	MO $		24$	BBCCC$	Ind	

Univ of LEEDS

TITLE	CODE	COURSE	SUBJECTS	A/AS	NO/C	AGNVQ	IB	SQA(H)	SQA	RATIO A/AS
Arabic-German	RT26	4FT deg	G g	BBC	Ind	Ind	30$	CSYS	Ind	
Chemistry-German	FR12	4FT deg	C+G+M/P	BBC	Ind	Ind	30$	CSYS	Ind	
Chinese-German	RT23	4FT deg	G g	BBC	Ind	Ind	30$	CSYS	Ind	6
Computer Science-German	GR52	4FT deg	G+M g	BBC		Ind	30$	ABBBB	Ind	
Economics-German	RL21	4FT deg	G g	BBC	Ind	Ind	30$	CSYS	Ind	8
English-German	QR32	4FT deg	E+G g	BBC	Ind	Ind	30$	CSYS	Ind	9	26/30
French-German	RR12	4FT deg	F+G g	BBB	Ind	Ind	32$	CSYS	Ind	7	24/30
German	R200	4FT deg	G g	BCC	Ind	Ind	28$	CSYS	Ind	3	20/26
German-History	RV21	4FT deg	G g	BBC	Ind	Ind	30$	CSYS	Ind	17
German-History of Art	RV24	4FT deg	G g	BBC	Ind	Ind	30$	CSYS	Ind	5
German-Italian	RR23	4FT deg	G+I g	BBC	Ind	Ind	30$	CSYS	Ind	4
German-Italian	RR2H	4FT deg	G g	BBC	Ind	Ind	30$	CSYS	Ind	7
German-Japanese	RT24	4FT deg	G g	BBC	Ind	Ind	30$	CSYS	Ind	
German-Linguistics	QR12	4FT deg	G g	BBC	Ind	Ind	30$	CSYS	Ind	10
German-Management Studies	RN21	4FT deg	G g	BBC	Ind	Ind	30$	CSYS	Ind	9	22/30
German-Music	RW23	4FT deg	G+Mu g	BBC	Ind	Ind	30$	CSYS	Ind	16
German-Philosophy	RV27	4FT deg	G g	BBC	Ind	Ind	30$	CSYS	Ind	
German-Religious Studies	RV2V	4FT deg	G g	BBC	Ind	Ind	30$	CSYS	Ind	
German-Russian	RR28	4FT deg	G+R g	BCC	Ind	Ind	28$	CSYS	Ind	5
German-Russian B	RR2V	4FT deg	G g	BCC	Ind	Ind	28$	CSYS	Ind	34
German-Spanish	RR24	4FT deg	G+Sp g	BBC	Ind	Ind	30$	CSYS	Ind	
German-Theology	RV28	4FT deg	G g	BBC	Ind	Ind	30$	CSYS	Ind	
Mathematics-German	GR12	4FT deg	G+M g	BBC		Ind	30$	ABBBB	Ind	
Physics-German	FR32	4FT deg	M+P+G	BBC	Ind	Ind	30$	CSYS	Ind	
Statistics-German	GR42	4FT deg	G+M g	BBC		Ind	30$	ABBBB	Ind	

LEEDS METROPOLITAN Univ

TITLE	CODE	COURSE	SUBJECTS	A/AS	NO/C	AGNVQ	IB	SQA(H)	SQA	RATIO A/AS
Public Relations (German)	P3R2	3FT deg								

Univ of LEICESTER

TITLE	CODE	COURSE	SUBJECTS	A/AS	NO/C	AGNVQ	IB	SQA(H)	SQA	RATIO A/AS
French and German	RR12	4FT deg	F+G g	BCD	X	D$^	26$	BBBB$	X	14/30
German	R200	4FT deg	G g	BC-BCD	X	D$^	28$	BBBB$	X	14/22
German and Italian	RR23	4FT deg	G g	BCD	X	D$^	Ind	BBBB$	X	
Combined Arts German	Y300	3FT deg	G g	BCC	DO $	D$^	30$	Ind	X	

Univ of LINCOLNSHIRE and HUMBERSIDE

TITLE	CODE	COURSE	SUBJECTS	A/AS	NO/C	AGNVQ	IB	SQA(H)	SQA	RATIO A/AS
Accountancy and German	NR42	3FT deg	G g	12	3M+1D	M	24	CCCC	Ind	
Administration and German	NR1G	3FT deg	G g	12	3M+1D	M	24	CCCC	Ind	
Business and German	RN21	3FT deg	G g	12	3M+1D	M	24	CCCC	Ind	
Computing and German	GR5F	3FT deg	G g	12	3M+1D	M	24	CCCC	Ind	
Finance and German	NR32	3FT deg	G g	12	3M+1D	M	24	CCCC	Ind	
German and Human Resource Management	NR62	3FT deg	G g	12	3M+1D	M	24	CCCC	Ind	
German and Media Technology	PR42	3FT deg	G g	12	3M+1D	M	24	CCCC	Ind	
Information Systems and German	GR52	3FT deg	G g	12	3M+1D	M	24	CCCC	Ind	
Marketing and German	NR52	3FT deg	G g	12	3M+1D	M	24	CCCC	Ind	

course details | **98 expected requirements** | *96 entry stats*

				98 expected requirements						96 entry stats

TITLE	CODE	COURSE	SUBJECTS	A/AS	ND/C	AGNVQ	IB	SQA(H)	SQA	RATIO A/AS
Univ of LIVERPOOL										
English and German	QR32	4FT deg	E+G	BBC	Ind		30$	ABBBB$	Ind	9
French and German	RR12	4FT deg	F+G	BCC-BBC	Ind		30$	BBBBB$	Ind	9 20/26
German	R200	4FT deg	G	BCC	Ind		30$	BBBBB$	Ind	5 16/24
German and Hispanic Studies	RR24	4FT deg	G+Sp	BCC	Ind		30$	BBBBB$	Ind	9
Arts Combined *German*	Y401	4FT deg	G	BBC-BBB	Ind	Ind	30$	ABBB$	Ind	
BA Combined Honours *German*	Y200	3FT deg	G g	BBB	Ind	Ind	Ind	Ind	Ind	
LIVERPOOL JOHN MOORES Univ										
French and German	RR12	4FT deg	L	14	3M+4D		Ind			8 10/18
German and Italian	RR23	4FT deg	L	14	3M+4D					6
German and Japanese	RT24	4FT deg	L	14	3M+4D		Ind			4
German and Russian	RR28	4FT deg	L	14	3M+4D		Ind			
German and Spanish	RR24	4FT deg	L	14	3M+4D					6
International Business Studies with German	N1R2	4SW deg		16	3M+4D					11 14/18
Media and Cultural Studs and German (Germ Jnt A)	PR42	4FT deg	G	16-18		X	28$	BBBC		4
Physics and German	F3R2	4SW deg		8	3M	D$/M$6				
LONDON GUILDHALL Univ										
3D/Spatial Design and German	RW2F	4FT deg	Pf g	DD	MO	M$ go	24	Ind	Ind	
German	R201	4FT deg								
German and Accounting	NR42	4FT deg	* g	DD	MO	M$ go	24	Ind	Ind	
German and Business	NR12	4FT deg	* g	CD-DDD	MO+2D	M$ go	24	Ind	Ind	
German and Business Economics	LRC2	4FT deg	* g	DD	MO	M$ go	24	Ind	Ind	
German and Business Information Technology	GR72	4FT deg	* g	DD	MO	M$ go	24	Ind	Ind	
German and Communications & Audio Visual Prod St	PR42	4FT deg	* g	CC-CDD	MO+2D	M$ go	26	Ind	Ind	
German and Computing	GR52	4FT deg	* g	DD	MO	M$ go	24	Ind	Ind	
German and Design Studies	RW22	4FT deg	* g	CD-DDD	MO+2D	M$ go	26	Ind	Ind	
German and Development Studies	MR92	4FT deg	* g	DD	MO	M$ go	24	Ind	Ind	
German and Economics	LR12	4FT deg	* g	DD	MO	M$ go	24	Ind	Ind	
German and English	QR32	4FT deg	* g	CD-DDD	MO+2D	M$ go	26	Ind	Ind	
German and European Studies	RT22	4FT deg	* g	DD	MO	M$ go	24	Ind	Ind	
German and Financial Services	NR32	4FT deg	* g	DD	MO	M$ go	24	Ind	Ind	
German and Fine Art	RW21	4FT deg	* g	CC-CDD	MO+2D	M$ go	26	Ind	Ind	
German and French	RR12	4FT deg	* g	DD	MO	M$ go	24	Ind	Ind	
International Relations and German	MRC2	4FT deg	* g	DD	MO	M$ go	24	Ind	Ind	
Law and German	MR32	4FT deg	* g	CC-CDD	MO+2D	M$ go	26	Ind	Ind	
Marketing and German	NR52	4FT deg	* g	CD-DDD	MO+2D	M$ go	26	Ind	Ind	
Mathematics and German	GR12	4FT deg	* g	DD	MO	M$ go	24	Ind	Ind	
Modern History and German	RV21	4FT deg	* g	DD	MO	M$ go	24	Ind	Ind	
Multimedia Systems and German	GRM2	4FT deg	* g	DD	MO	M$ go	24	Ind	Ind	
Politics and German	MR12	4FT deg	* g	DD	MO	M$ go	24	Ind	Ind	
Product Development & Manufacture and German	JR42	4FT deg	* g	DD	MO	M$ go	24	Ind	Ind	
Psychology and German	CR82	4FT deg	* g	CD-DDD	MO+2D	M$ go	26	Ind	Ind	
Social Policy & Management and German	LR42	4FT deg	* g	CD-DDD	MO	M$ go	24	Ind	Ind	
Sociology and German	LR32	4FT deg	* g	CD-DDD	MO	M$ go	24	Ind	Ind	
Spanish and German	RR24	4FT deg	* g	DD	MO	M$ go	24	Ind	Ind	
Taxation and German	NRH2	4FT deg	* g	DD	MO	Language$ go	24	Ind	Ind	
Textile Furnishing Design and German	RW2G	4FT deg	Pf g	DD	MO	M$ go	24	Ind	Ind	
Modular Programme *German*	Y400	3FT/4FT deg	* g	CC-DD	MO	M$ go	24	Ind	Ind	

			98 expected requirements							96 entry stats
TITLE	CODE	COURSE	SUBJECTS	A/AS	NO/C	RGNVQ	IB	SQA(H)	SQA	RATIO A/AS
LOUGHBOROUGH Univ										
Economics with German	L1R2	3FT deg	G g	20			30$	Ind		
French and German Studies	RR12	3FT deg	F/G g	20			28$	Ind		
German and Politics	MR12	3FT deg	G g	20			28$	Ind		
Politics with German	M1R2	3FT deg	G	20			28$	Ind		
Spanish and German Studies	RR42	3FT deg	Sp+G	20			28$	Ind		
LUTON Univ										
Accounting with German	N4RF	3FT deg	G g	12-16	MO/DO	M/D	32	BBCC	Ind	
Business Systems with German	N1RF	3FT deg	G g	12-16	MO/DO	M/D	32	BBCC	Ind	
Business with German	N1R2	3FT deg	G g	12-16	MO/DO	M/D	32	BBCC	Ind	
Geography with German	F8R2	3FT deg	G g	12-16	MO/DO	M/D	32	BBCC	Ind	
Linguistics with German	Q1R2	3FT deg	G g	12-16	MO/DO	M/D	32	BBCC	Ind	
Literary Studies in English with German	Q2R2	3FT deg		12-16	MO/DO	M/D	32	BBCC	Ind	
Marketing with German	N5R2	3FT deg	G g	12-16	MO/DO	M/D	32	BBCC	Ind	
Mathematical Sciences with German	G1R2	3FT deg	G g	12-16	MO/DO	M/D	32	BBCC	Ind	
Modern English Studies with German	Q3R2	3FT deg	G g	12-16	MO/DO	M/D	32	BBCC	Ind	
New Media Technology with German	P4R2	3FT deg	L g	12-16	MO/DO	M/D	32	BBCC	Ind	
Psychology with German	L7R2	3FT deg	G g	12-16	MO/DO	M/D	32	BBCC	Ind	4
Regional Planning & Development with German	K4R2	3FT deg	G g	12-16	MO/DO	M/D	32	BBCC	Ind	
Travel and Tourism with German	P7R2	3FT deg	G g	12-16	MO/DO	M/D	32	BBCC	Ind	12
Univ of MANCHESTER										
English and a Modern Language (German)	RQ23	4FT deg	E+G	ABB			Ind	BBBBC		7 · 24/30
European Studies and Modern Langs (German)	RT22	4FT deg	G	ABB-BBB Ind		D^	28$	AAABB$ Ind		6 · 22/30
French/German	RR1G	4FT deg	F	ABB		D^	30$	AABB$		9
French/German	RR12	4FT deg	F	ABB		D^	30$	AAABB$		12 · 18/28
German Studies	R210	4FT deg	G	BBB			28	BBBBC		3 · 16/26
German and Linguistics	RQ21	4FT deg	G	BBB	X		32$	AABBB		7
German and Philosophy	VR72	4FT deg	G	BBB	Ind		32$	AABBB$ Ind		
German/French	RR2C	4FT deg	G+F	BBB			28	BBBBC		5
German/Italian	RR2H	4FT deg	G	BBB			28	BBBBC		
German/Italian	RR23	4FT deg	G	BBB			28	BBBBC		4 · 22/30
German/Portuguese	RR25	4FT deg	G	BBB			28	BBBBC		1
German/Russian	RR28	4FT deg	G	BBB			28	BBBBC		12
German/Russian	RR2W	4FT deg	G	BBB			28	BBBBC		8
German/Spanish	RR2L	4FT deg	G	BBB			28	BBBBC		3
German/Spanish	RR24	4FT deg	G+Sp	BBB			28	BBBBC		15
History and German	VR12	4FT deg	G+H	BBC			30	ABBBB		6 · 20/24
History of Art and a Modern Language (German)	RV24	4FT deg		BBC	3M+3D		28	AABBB		4
Italian/German	RR3G	4FT deg	G	BBB-BCC			Ind	BBBCC		2
Russian/German	RR8G	4FT deg	R+G	BBC-CCC Ind			28$	BBBCC Ind		
Spanish/German	RR4G	4FT deg	Sp	BBB-BBC			28$	ABBBB$		
UMIST (Manchester)										
Biochemistry with German	C7R2	4FT deg	C+2S g	18-20	4M $	Ind	30$	CSYS	N$	4
Chemical Engineering with German (MEng)	H8RF	4FT deg	M+C g	BBC	MO+3D$ Ind		30$	CSYS$	Ind	3
Chemistry with German (MChem)	F1RF	4FT deg	C g	18	3M+1D	MS6/^ go	30	CSYS	Ind	19
Civil Engineering with German (MEng)	H2R2	4FT deg	M+P g	BBC	Ind	Ind	30$	CSYS	Ind	
German Language Studies	R220	4FT deg	G g	20	X	Ind	28	BBBBB	Ind	
International Management with German	N1R2	4FT deg	G g	BBC	X	Ind	30$	CSYS$	Ind	3 · 18/30
Mathematics and Language Studies (German)	GRD2	4FT deg	M+G g	BBC	Ind	Ind	30$	CSYS	Ind	2
Paper Science with German (4 Yrs)	J5R2	4FT deg	M/P/C g	CCD	3M	DS^ go	27$	BBBC$	Ind	
Physics with German (MPhys)	F3R2	4FT deg	M+P g	BCD	4M+1D$ Ind		28$	CSYS	Ind	3

Letts STUDY GUIDES
THE INDEPENDENT

course details			98 expected requirements							96 entry stats
TITLE	CODE	COURSE	SUBJECTS	A/AS	NO/C	AGNVQ	IB	SQA(H)	SQA	RATIO A/AS
MANCHESTER METROPOLITAN Univ										
Accounting and Finance in Europe (German)	N4R2	4FT deg	G g	18	MO+8D	D^	26$	BBBBC	Ind	
Business in Europe-German Route	N1R2	4FT deg	G g	BBC	Ind	DB	24$	Ind	Ind	14/18
French post A level/German ab initio	RR1F	4FT deg	F	CC	X		28$	AACCC$	X	
French post A level/German post A level	RR1G	4FT deg	F+G	CC	X		28$	AACCC$	X	10/14
German post A level/Spanish ab initio	RR2L	4FT deg	G	CC	X		28$	AACCC$	X	8/14
Law with German	M3R2	4FT deg	G g	BBC	Ind	Ind	Ind	Ind	Ind	14/20
Spanish post A level/German ab initio	RR2K	4FT deg	Sp	CC	X		28$	AACCC$	X	8/18
Humanities/Social Studies German	Y400	3FT/4FT deg	G	CDD	Ind	Ind	Ind	BBB	Ind	
MIDDLESEX Univ										
German	R200▼	3FT deg	* g	12-16	5M	M$ go	28	Ind	Ind	
Joint Honours Degree German	Y400	3FT/4FT deg	* g	12-16	5M	Ind	28	Ind	Ind	
NENE COLLEGE										
European Business (German)	NR12	4SW deg	G g	8	M+D	M	24	CCC	Ind	
Univ of NEWCASTLE										
French and German	RR12	4FT deg	F+G	BBC		X	$	AABBB$		9	22/30
French with German	R1R2	4FT deg	F	BBC		X	$	AABBB$		6	30/30
German	R200	4FT deg	G	20			$	ABBBB$		6	20/22
German and English Language	RQ23	4FT deg	G+E	22		X	$	AABBB$		12	
German with Accounting	R2N4	4FT deg	G+M/Ec	20			$	ABBBB$		
German with French	R2R1	4FT deg	G g	20			$	ABBBB$		4	
German with Politics	R2M1	4FT deg	G	20			$	ABBBB$		
German with Portuguese	R2R5	4FT deg	G	20			$	ABBBB$		
German with Spanish	R2R4	4FT deg	G	20			$	ABBBB$		6	
Spanish with German	R4R2	4FT deg	Sp	BCC		X	$	ABBBB$		2	
Combined Studies (BA) German	Y400	3FT deg	*	ABC-BBB	5D	Ind	35$	AAAB	Ind	
Univ of NORTH LONDON										
Biological Science and German	CR12	4FT deg	B	CC	Ind	Ind	Ind	Ind	Ind	
Chemistry and German	FR12	4FT deg	C	CC	Ind	Ind	Ind	Ind	Ind	
International Business and German	NR12	4FT deg	* g	CC	MO+4D	D	Ind	Ind	Ind	15
Combined Honours German	Y300	4FT deg	*	CC	Ind	Ind	Ind	Ind	Ind	
Univ of NORTHUMBRIA										
French and German	RR12	3FT deg	F	CC	2M+2D	M^	24	BBCCC	Ind	4	8/20
German and Economics	LR12	3FT deg		CG	2M+2D	M^	24	BBCCC	Ind	
German and Politics	MR12	3FT deg		CC	2M+2D	M^	24	BBCCC	Ind	
German and Russian	RR28	3FT deg	G	CC	2M+2D	M^	24	BBCCC	Ind	2	
German and Spanish	RR24	3FT deg	G	CC	2M+2D	M^	24	BBCCC	Ind	2	12/18
History and German	RV21	3FT deg	H+G	BCC	N		28	Ind	Ind	
Information Studies and German	PR22	3FT deg		CC	2M+2D	M^		BBCCC		
Russian and German	RR82	3FT deg	R	CC	2M+2D	M^	24	CCCC	Ind	
Spanish and German	RR42	3FT deg	Sp	CC	2M+2D	M^	24	BBCCC	Ind	
Univ of NOTTINGHAM										
Art History and German	RV24	4FT deg	G	BBC						
Civil Engineering with German	H2R2	3FT/4FT deg	M+P g	BBC-BCC	Ind	Ind	28$	Ind	Ind	7
Classical Civilisation and German	QR82	4FT deg	G	BCC						
Economics with German	L1R2	4FT deg	G g	AAB-ABB	X		32$	Ind	X	3	26/30

course details			**98 expected requirements**							**96 entry stats**	
TITLE	CODE	COURSE	SUBJECTS	A/AS	ND/C	AGNVQ	IB	SQA(H)	SQA	RATIO	A/AS
Electrical and Electronic Eng with German	H6R2	3FT/4FT deg	M+P g	BBC-BCC	Ind	Ind	28$	Ind	Ind	3	
Electronic Engineering with German	H6RF	3FT/4FT deg	M+P g	BBC-BCC	Ind	Ind	28$	Ind	Ind	5	
French and German	RR12	4FT deg	F+G	AAC						13	28/30
German (German/History or German/Politics)	R200	4FT deg	G	BCC						11	22/30
German and Greek	RQ27	4FT deg	G	BCC							
German and Hispanic Studies	RR2L	4FT deg	G+Sp	BBB						5	
German and Latin	RQ26	4FT deg	G+Ln	BCC							
German and Music	RW23	4FT deg	G+Mu	BBC							
German and Philosophy	RV27	4FT deg	G	BBC							
German and Portuguese (Beginners)	RR2M	4FT deg	G	BBC							
German and Russian	RR28	4FT deg	G+R	BBC							
German and Russian (Beginners)	RR2V	4FT deg	G	BBC						5	22/30
German and Theology	RV28	4FT deg	G	BBC-BCC						2	
Law with German	M3R2	4FT deg	G	ABB	Ind		34$	Ind	Ind	9	28/30
Management Studies with German	N1R2	4FT deg	G g	BBB	Ind	D*△ go	32$	AAABB$	Ind	24	24/28
Manufacturing Engineering and Mgt with German	H7R2	3FT/4FT deg	M g	CCC	Ind	Ind	28$	Ind	Ind		
Mechanical Engineering with German	H3R2	3FT/4FT deg	M+P g	BBC-BCC	Ind	Ind	28$	Ind	Ind	9	22/25
Production and Operations Management with German	H7RF	3FT deg	M g	CCC	Ind	Ind	28$	Ind	Ind	3	

NOTTINGHAM TRENT Univ

European Business with German	N1R2	4SW deg	G g	16	M+D $		24$	Ind	Ind	10	14/26
European Economics with German	L1R2	4FT deg	G g	14-16	1M+3D	Ind	Ind	BBCC	Ind	6	

OXFORD BROOKES Univ

Geography and the Phys Env/Ger Lang & Contemp St	FRVF	3FT deg									
Geography and the Phys Env/German Lang and Lit	FRV2	3FT deg									
Geography and the Phys Env/German Studies	FRVG	3FT deg									
German Lang & Contemp St/French Lang& Contemp St	RRCF	4SW deg	F+G	CC-DDD	Ind	M*△	Ind	Ind	Ind	8	
German Language & Lit/French Lang & Contemp St	RR2C	4SW deg	G+F	CC-DDD	Ind	M*△	Ind	Ind	Ind		
German Language & Literature/Exercise & Health	RB26	4SW deg	G+S/M	DD-DDD	Ind		Ind	Ind	Ind		
German Language and Contemp St/Educational Stud	RXF9	4SW deg	G	CC-DDD	Ind	M^/M*3	Ind	Ind	Ind		
German Language and Contemp St/Exercise & Health	RBF6	4SW deg	G+S g	DD-DDD	Ind	MS^	Ind	Ind	Ind		
German Language and Contemp St/Food Sci and Nut	DR4F	4SW deg	G+S g	DD-CD	Ind	MS^	Ind	Ind	Ind		
German Language and Contemp St/French Lang & Lit	RR1F	4SW deg	G+F	CC-DDD	Ind	M*△	Ind	Ind	Ind		
German Language and Contemp Stud/Acc & Finance	NR4F	4SW deg	G g	DDD-BCC	Ind	M^/D*3	Ind	Ind	Ind	3	
German Language and Contemp Stud/Anthropology	LR6F	4SW deg	G	DDD-BCC	Ind	M*△	Ind	Ind	Ind		
German Language and Contemp Stud/Biological Chem	CR7F	3FT deg									
German Language and Contemp Stud/Biology	CR1F	4SW deg	G+S g	DD-DDD	Ind	MS^	Ind	Ind	Ind	1	
German Language and Contemp Stud/Bus Admin & Mgt	NR1F	4SW deg	G g	DDD-BBC	Ind	M^/MB4	Ind	Ind	Ind		
German Language and Contemp Stud/Cartography	FR8F	4SW deg	G g	CC-DDD	Ind	M*△	Ind	Ind	Ind		
German Language and Contemp Stud/Cell Biology	CRCF	3FT deg									
German Language and Contemp Stud/Combined St	RYF4	3FT deg		X		X	X	X			
German Language and Contemp Stud/Computer System	GR6F	3FT deg	G g	DDD-BC	Ind	M*△	Ind	Ind	Ind		
German Language and Contemp Stud/Computing	GR5F	4SW deg	G g	DDD-BC	Ind	M*△	Ind	Ind	Ind		
German Language and Contemp Stud/Computing Maths	GR9F	4SW deg	G g	CD-DDD	Ind	M*△	Ind	Ind	Ind		
German Language and Contemp Stud/Ecology	CR9F	4SW deg	G g	CD-DDD	Ind	MS^	Ind	Ind	Ind		
German Language and Contemp Stud/Economics	LR1F	4SW deg	G g	DDD-BB	Ind	M^/M*3	Ind	Ind	Ind		
German Language and Contemp Stud/Electronics	HR6F	4SW deg	S/M+G	CC-DDD	Ind	MS$/M*△	Ind	Ind	Ind		
German Language and Contemp Stud/English Studies	QR3F	4SW deg	G	DDD-AB	Ind	M*△	Ind	Ind	Ind	4	
German Language and Contemp Stud/Environ Chem	RF2C	3FT deg									
German Language and Contemp Stud/Environ Policy	KR3F	3FT deg									
German Language and Contemp Stud/Environ Science	FRXF	4SW deg	G+S g	CD-DDD	Ind	M^/DS	Ind	Ind	Ind		
German Language and Contemp Stud/Fine Art	RWF1	4SW deg	G+Pf+A	BC-DDD	Ind	MA^	Ind	Ind	Ind		

course details

98 expected requirements

96 entry stats

TITLE	CODE	COURSE	SUBJECTS	A/AS	ND/C	AGNVQ	IB	SQA(H)	SQA	RATIO A/AS
German Language and Contemp Stud/Geography	LR8F	4SW deg	G	DDD-BB	Ind	M*△	Ind	Ind	Ind	
German Language and Contemp Stud/Geology	FR6F	4SW deg	S/M+G	DD-CD	Ind	PS/M*△	Ind	Ind	Ind	
German Language and Contemp Stud/Geotechnics	HR2F	4SW deg	G+S/M/Ds/Es	CC-DD	Ind	M$△	Ind	Ind	Ind	
German Language and Lit/Business Admin and Mgt	NR12	4SW deg	G g	DDD-BBC	Ind	M△/MB4	Ind	Ind	Ind	
German Language and Lit/German Lang & Contemp St	R210	3FT deg	G	CC-DDD	Ind	M*△	Ind	Ind	Ind	2
German Language and Literature/Accounting & Fin	NR42	4SW deg	G g	DDD-BCC	Ind	M△/D*3	Ind	Ind	Ind	2
German Language and Literature/Biological Chem	CR72	3FT deg								
German Language and Literature/Biology	CR12	4SW deg	G+S g	DD-DDD	Ind	MS△	Ind	Ind	Ind	
German Language and Literature/Cartography	FR82	4SW deg	G g	CC-DDD	Ind	M*△	Ind	Ind	Ind	
German Language and Literature/Cell Biology	CRC2	3FT deg								
German Language and Literature/Combined Studies	RY24	3FT deg		X		X	X	X		
German Language and Literature/Computer Systems	GR62	4FT deg	G g	DDD-BC	Ind	M*△	Ind	Ind	Ind	
German Language and Literature/Computing	GR52	4SW deg	G g	DDD-BC	Ind	M*△	Ind	Ind	Ind	
German Language and Literature/Computing Maths	GR92	4SW deg	G g	CD-DDD	Ind	M*△	Ind	Ind	Ind	
German Language and Literature/Ecology	CR92	4SW deg	G g	CD-DDD	Ind	MS△	Ind	Ind	Ind	
German Language and Literature/Economics	LR12	4SW deg	G g	DDD-BB	Ind	M△/M*3	Ind	Ind	Ind	
German Language and Literature/Educational Studs	RX29	4SW deg	G	CC-DDD	Ind	M△/M*3	Ind	Ind	Ind	2
German Language and Literature/Electronics	HR62	4SW deg	S/M+G	CC-DDD	Ind	M$/M*△	Ind	Ind	Ind	
German Language and Literature/English Studies	QR32	4SW deg	G	DDD-AB	Ind	M*△	Ind	Ind	Ind	3
German Language and Literature/Environmental Che	RF21	3FT deg								
German Language and Literature/Environmental Pol	KR32	3FT deg								
German Language and Literature/Environmental Sci	FRX2	4SW deg	G+S g	CD-DDD	Ind	M△/DS	Ind	Ind	Ind	
German Language and Literature/Fine Art	RW21	4SW deg	G+Pf+A	BC-DDD	Ind	MA△	Ind	Ind	Ind	
German Language and Literature/Food Sci and Nutr	DR42	4SW deg	G+S g	DD-CD	Ind	MS△	Ind	Ind	Ind	
German Language and Literature/French Lang & Lit	RR12	4SW deg	G+F	CC-DDD	Ind	M*△	Ind	Ind	Ind	
German Language and Literature/Geography	LR82	4SW deg	G	DDD-BB	Ind	M*△	Ind	Ind	Ind	
German Language and Literature/Geotechnics	HR22	4SW deg	G+S/M/Ds/Es	CC-DD	Ind	M$△	Ind	Ind	Ind	
German Studies/Accounting and Finance	NR4G	4SW deg	G g	DDD-BCC	Ind	M△/D*3	Ind	Ind	Ind	
German Studies/Anthropology	LR6G	4SW deg			Ind		Ind	Ind	Ind	
German Studies/Biological Chemistry	CR7G	3FT deg								
German Studies/Biology	CR1G	4SW deg			Ind		Ind	Ind	Ind	
German Studies/Business Administration and Mgt	RNG1	4SW deg			Ind		Ind	Ind	Ind	
German Studies/Cartography	FR8G	4SW deg			Ind		Ind	Ind	Ind	
German Studies/Cell Biology	CRCG	3FT deg								
German Studies/Combined Studies	RYG4	3FT deg		X		X	X	X		
German Studies/Computer Systems	GR6G	4SW deg			Ind		Ind	Ind	Ind	
German Studies/Computing	GR5G	4SW deg			Ind		Ind	Ind	Ind	
German Studies/Computing Mathematics	GR9G	4SW deg			Ind		Ind	Ind	Ind	
German Studies/Ecology	CR9G	4SW deg			Ind		Ind	Ind	Ind	
German Studies/Economics	LR1G	4SW deg			Ind		Ind	Ind	Ind	
German Studies/Educational Studies	XR9G	4SW deg			Ind		Ind	Ind	Ind	
German Studies/Electronics	HR6G	4SW deg	S/M+G	CC-DDD	Ind	M$/M*△	Ind	Ind	Ind	
German Studies/English Studies	QR3G	4SW deg			Ind		Ind	Ind	Ind	
German Studies/Environmental Chemistry	RF2D	3FT deg								
German Studies/Environmental Policy	KR3G	3FT deg								
German Studies/Environmental Sciences	FRXG	4SW deg			Ind		Ind	Ind	Ind	
German Studies/Exercise and Health	XRXG	4SW deg			Ind		Ind	Ind	Ind	
German Studies/Exercise and Health	BR6G	3FT deg								
German Studies/Fine Art	WR1G	4SW deg			Ind		Ind	Ind	Ind	
German Studies/Food Science and Nutrition	DR4G	4SW deg			Ind		Ind	Ind	Ind	
German Studies/French Language and Contemp Stds	RRCG	4SW deg			Ind		Ind	Ind	Ind	
German Studies/French Language and Literature	RR1G	4SW deg			Ind		Ind	Ind	Ind	

				98 expected requirements						96 entry stats

course details

TITLE	CODE	COURSE	SUBJECTS	A/AS	NC/C	AGNVQ	IB	SQA(H)	SQA	RATIO A/AS
German Studies/Geography	LR8G	4SW deg			Ind		Ind	Ind	Ind	
German Studies/Geology	FR6G	4SW deg			Ind		Ind	Ind	Ind	
German Studies/Geotechnics	HR2G	4SW deg			Ind		Ind	Ind	Ind	
Health Care/German Language and Contemp Stud	BR7F	3FT deg		X		X	X	X		
Health Care/German Language and Literature	BR72	3FT deg		X		X	X	X		
Health Care/German Studies (Post Exp)	BR7G	3FT deg		X		X	X	X		
History of Art/German Language and Contemp Stud	RVF4	4SW deg	G	DDD-BCC	Ind	M*_^_	Ind	Ind	Ind	
History of Art/German Language and Literature	RV24	4SW deg	G	DDD-BCC	Ind	M*_^_	Ind	Ind	Ind	
History of Art/German Studies	VR4G	4SW deg	G	BCC-CD	Ind	M*_^_	Ind	Ind	Ind	
History/German Language and Contemp Stud	RVF1	4SW deg	G	DDD-BB	Ind	M*_^_	Ind	Ind	Ind	3
History/German Language and Literature	RV21	4SW deg	G	DDD-BB	Ind	M*_^_	Ind	Ind	Ind	
History/German Studies	VR1G	4SW deg	G	DDD-BB	Ind	M*_^_	Ind	Ind	Ind	
Hospitality Management Studies/German Studies	NR7G	4SW deg	G	CC-DDD	Ind	M_^_/M*3	Ind	Ind	Ind	
Hospitality Mgt St/German Lang and Contemp Stud	NR7F	4SW deg	G	CC-DDD	Ind	M_^_/M*3	Ind	Ind	Ind	
Hospitality Mgt St/German Language & Literature	NR72	4SW deg	G	CC-DDD	Ind	M_^_/M*3	Ind	Ind	Ind	
Human Biology/German Language and Contemp Stud	BR1F	3FT deg								
Human Biology/German Language and Literature	BR12	3FT deg								
Human Biology/German Studies	BR1G	3FT deg								
Information Systems/German Lang and Contemp Stud	GRNF	3FT deg	G g	CD-BC	Ind	M*_^_	Ind	Ind	Ind	
Information Systems/German Language & Literature	GRN2	3FT deg	G g	CD-BC	Ind	M*_^_	Ind	Ind	Ind	
Information Systems/German Studies	GRMG	4SW deg	G g	CD-BC	Ind	M*_^_	Ind	Ind	Ind	
Intelligent Systems/German Lang & Contemp Stud	GR8F	4SW deg	G g	CD-DDD	Ind	M*_^_	Ind	Ind	Ind	
Intelligent Systems/German Lang and Literature	GR82	4SW deg	G g	CD-DDD	Ind	M*_^_	Ind	Ind	Ind	
Intelligent Systems/German Studies	GR8G	4SW deg		CD-DDD	Ind	M*_^_	Ind	Ind	Ind	
Langs for Bus:Italian-Ab Initio/German-Ab Initio	NRD2	4FT deg								
Languages for Business:English/German-Ab Initio	NR1G	4FT deg	E	BC-CDD	Ind	M*_^_	Ind	Ind	Ind	1
Languages for Business:French/German-Ab Initio	NRCF	4FT deg	F	BC-CDD	Ind	M*_^_	Ind	Ind	Ind	
Languages for Business:Italian/German-Ab Initio	NRCG	4FT deg	I	BC-CDD	Ind	M*_^_	Ind	Ind	Ind	6
Languages for Business:Spanish/German-Ab Initio	NRC2	4FT deg	Sp	BC-CDD	Ind	M*_^_	Ind	Ind	Ind	
Law/German Language and Contemp Stud	MR3F	4SW deg	G	DDD-BBB	Ind	M_^_/D*3	Ind	Ind	Ind	5
Law/German Language and Literature	MR32	4SW deg	G	DDD-BBB	Ind	M_^_/D*3	Ind	Ind	Ind	
Law/German Studies	MR3G	4SW deg	G	DDD-BBB	Ind	M_^_/D*3	Ind	Ind	Ind	
Leisure Planning/German Language and Contemp St	KRHF	3FT deg								
Leisure Planning/German Language and Literature	KRH2	3FT deg								
Leisure Planning/German Studies	KRHG	3FT deg								
Marketing Management/German Lang & Contemp Stud	NRNF	4SW deg	G g	DDD-BCC	Ind	M_^_/D*3	Ind	Ind	Ind	
Marketing Management/German Language and Lit	NRN2	4SW deg	G g	DDD-BCC	Ind	M_^_/D*3	Ind	Ind	Ind	
Marketing Management/German Studies	NRNG	4SW deg	G g	DDD-BCC	Ind	M_^_/D*3	Ind	Ind	Ind	
Mathematics/German Language and Contemp Stud	GR1F	4SW deg	M+G g	DD-CD	Ind	M*_^_	Ind	Ind	Ind	
Mathematics/German Studies	GR1G	4SW deg	M+G	DD-CD	Ind	M*_^_	Ind	Ind	Ind	
Music/German Language and Contemp Stud	RWF3	4SW deg	Mu+G	DD-CD	Ind	M*_^_	Ind	Ind	Ind	
Music/German Language and Literature	RW23	4SW deg	Mu+G	DD-CD	Ind	M*_^_	Ind	Ind	Ind	
Music/German Studies	WR3G	4SW deg	Mu+G	DD-CD	Ind	M*_^_	Ind	Ind	Ind	
Palliative Care/Ger Lang & Contemp St (Post Exp)	BRRF	3FT deg		X		X	X	X		
Palliative Care/German Lang and Lit (Post Exp)	BRR2	3FT deg		X		X	X	X		
Palliative Care/German Studies (Post Exp)	BRRG	3FT deg		X		X	X	X		
Planning Studies/German Language and Contemp St	KR4F	4SW deg	G g	CD-DDD	Ind	M*_^_	Ind	Ind	Ind	
Planning Studies/German Language and Literature	KR42	4SW deg	G g	CD-DDD	Ind	M*_^_	Ind	Ind	Ind	
Planning Studies/German Studies	KR4G	4SW deg	G g	DD-DDD	Ind	M*_^_	Ind	Ind	Ind	
Politics/German Language and Contemp Stud	MR1F	4SW deg	G	DDD-AB	Ind	M*_^_	Ind	Ind	Ind	1
Politics/German Language and Literature	MR12	4SW deg	G	DDD-AB	Ind	M*_^_	Ind	Ind	Ind	1
Politics/German Studies	MR1G	4SW deg	G	DDD-AB	Ind	M*_^_	Ind	Ind	Ind	

| | | | *98 expected requirements* | | | | | | | *96 entry stats* |

TITLE	CODE	COURSE	SUBJECTS	A/AS	NO/C	AGNVQ	IB	SQA(H)	SQA	RATIO A/AS
Psychology/German Language and Contemp Stud	CR8F	4SW deg	G g	DDD-BBC	Ind	M*^	Ind	Ind	Ind	
Psychology/German Language and Literature	CR82	4SW deg	G g	DDD-BBC	Ind	M*^	Ind	Ind	Ind	
Psychology/German Studies	CR8G	4SW deg		DDD-BBC	Ind	M*^	Ind	Ind	Ind	
Publishing/German Language and Contemp Stud	PR5F	4SW deg	G g	DDD-BB	Ind	M^M$3	Ind	Ind	Ind	
Publishing/German Language and Literature	PR52	4SW deg	G g	DDD-BB	Ind	M^M$3	Ind	Ind	Ind	
Publishing/German Studies	PR5G	4SW deg	* g	DDD-BB	Ind	M^/M$3	Ind	Ind	Ind	
Rehabilitation/Ger Lang & Contemp St (Post Exp)	BRTF	3FT deg		X		X	X	X		
Rehabilitation/German Language and Lit(Post Exp)	BRT2	3FT deg		X		X	X	X		
Rehabilitation/German Studies (Post Exp)	BRTG	3FT deg		X		X	X	X		
Sociology/German Language and Contemp Stud	LR3F	4SW deg	G	DDD-BCC	Ind	M*^	Ind	Ind	Ind	
Sociology/German Language and Literature	LR32	4SW deg	G	DDD-BCC	Ind	M*^	Ind	Ind	Ind	
Sociology/German Studies	LR3G	4SW deg	G	DDD-BCC	Ind	M*^	Ind	Ind	Ind	
Software Engineering/German Lang & Literature	GR72	4FT deg	G g	CDD-BC	Ind	M*^	Ind	Ind	Ind	
Software Engineering/German Lang and Contemp St	GR7F	4FT deg	G g	CDD-BC	Ind	M*^	Ind	Ind	Ind	
Software Engineering/German Studies	GR7G	4SW deg	G g	CDD-BC	Ind	M*^	Ind	Ind	Ind	
Statistics/German Language and Contemp Stud	GR4F	4SW deg	G g	DD-CD	Ind	M*^	Ind	Ind	Ind	
Statistics/German Language and Literature	GR42	4SW deg	G g	DD	Ind	M*^	Ind	Ind	Ind	
Statistics/German Studies	GR4G	4SW deg	G g	DD	Ind	M*^	Ind	Ind	Ind	
Telecommunications/German Language & Contemp St	HRPF	3FT deg								
Telecommunications/German Language and Lit	HRP2	3FT deg								
Telecommunications/German Studies	HRPG	3FT deg								
Tourism/German Language and Contemp Stud	PR7F	4SW deg	G g	DDD-BC	Ind	M^/M*3	Ind	Ind	Ind	
Tourism/German Language and Literature	PR72	4SW deg	G g	DDD-BC	Ind	M^/M*3	Ind	Ind	Ind	
Tourism/German Studies	PR7G	4SW deg	G g	DDD-BB	Ind	M^/M*3	Ind	Ind	Ind	
Transport Planning/German Language & Contemp St	NR9F	4SW deg	G	CD-CC	Ind	M*^	Ind	Ind	Ind	
Transport Planning/German Language & Literature	NR92	4SW deg	G	CD-CC	Ind	M*^	Ind	Ind	Ind	
Transport Planning/German Studies	NR9G	4SW deg	G	CD-CC	Ind	M*^	Ind	Ind	Ind	
Water Resources/German Language and Contemp Stud	HRFF	3FT deg								
Water Resources/German Language and Literature	HRF2	3FT deg								
Water Resources/German Studies	HRFG	3FT deg								

Univ of PLYMOUTH

TITLE	CODE	COURSE	SUBJECTS	A/AS	NO/C	AGNVQ	IB	SQA(H)	SQA	RATIO A/AS
Applied Economics with German	L1R2	3FT deg	G g	CCD-CDD	MO	M$^	Ind	BCCC	Ind	
Business Economics with German	L1RF	3FT deg	G g	CDD-CCD	MO	M$^	Ind	BCCC	Ind	
Chemistry with German	F1R2	3FT deg	C+G g	CC	3M	MS^	Ind	CCCC	Ind	
European Economics with German	L1RG	3FT deg	G g	CDD-CCD	MO	MS^	Ind	BCCC	Ind	
European Studies with German	T2R2	4FT deg	G g	18	Ind	Ind	Ind	Ind	Ind	
Geography with German	F8R2	3FT deg	Gy+G g	16-18	X	M$^	Ind	ABBB	Ind	
Geology with German	F6R2	3FT deg	S+G g	12	4M	MS^	Ind	CCC	Ind	
International Business with German	N1R2	4SW deg	G g	CCD-CCC	MO	M12^	Ind	BBCC	Ind	15 12/20
Law with German	M3R2	3FT deg	G g	BCC-BBC	DO	D12^	Ind	BBBB$	Ind	
Political Economy with German	LR1F	3FT deg	G g	CDD-CCD	MO $	M$^	Ind	BCCC	Ind	
Politics with German	M1R2	3FT deg	G g	14	Ind	M$^	Ind	BBBC$	Ind	
Psychology with German	C8R2	3FT/4SW deg	G g	BBC	MO+3D	M12^	Ind	BBBC$	Ind	
Social Policy with German	L4R2	3FT deg	G g	14	Ind	M$^	Ind	BBBC$	Ind	
Sociology with German	L3R2	3FT deg	G g	14	Ind	M$^	Ind	BBBC$	Ind	

Univ of PORTSMOUTH

TITLE	CODE	COURSE	SUBJECTS	A/AS	NO/C	AGNVQ	IB	SQA(H)	SQA	RATIO A/AS
German Studies	R210	4FT deg	G	10-12	5M $	M$6/^	25$	BBCC	Ind	3 6/16
German and French Studies	RR12	4FT deg	G+F	12	5M $	M$6/^	25$	BBBC	Ind	5 8/14
German and Italian	RR23	4FT deg	G	12	5M $	M$6/^	25$	BBCC	Ind	
German and Spanish	RR24	4FT deg	G	12	5M $	M$6/^	25$	BBCC	Ind	2
Russian and German	RR28	3FT deg	G	12	5M $	M$6/^	Dip	BBBC	Ind	

			98 expected requirements							**96 entry stats**
course details										
TITLE	CODE	COURSE	SUBJECTS	A/AS	NO/C	AGNVQ	IB	SQA(H)	SQA	RATIO A/AS
QUEEN MARY & WESTFIELD COLL (Univ of London)										
Chemistry and German	FR1F	4FT deg	C+G	BCC	5M $	DS^	26$	BBBCC		
Engineering with German Language	H1R2	3FT deg	M	CCD-BCC	4M $	M$^	24$	BBBCC		
English and German	RQ23	4FT deg	E+G	20		M^	30$			
French and German	RR21	4FT deg	F+G	20		M^	30$			
German	R201	4FT deg	G	18		M^	30$			
German (European Studies)	RT2F	4FT deg	G	20		M^	30$			
German and Drama	WR42	4FT deg	G	20		M^	30$			
German and Economics	LR1F	4FT deg	G	18		M^	30$	BBBBB		
German and Geography	LR8F	4FT deg	G+Gy	BCC		M^	30$			
German and Linguistics	RQ21	4FT deg	G	18		M^	30$			
German and Mathematics	GR1F	4FT deg	G+M	18		M^	30$			
German and Politics	MR1F	4FT deg	G	BCC		M^	30$			
German and Russian	RR82	4FT deg	G	20		M^	30$			
German with Business Studies	R2N1	4FT deg	G g	18		M^	30$			
German, Linguistics and Computer Science	GR52	4FT deg	G	BBC-BCD	3D $	D^	28$			
History and German Language	VR1G	4FT deg	H+G	20		M^	30$			
Law and German	MR32	4FT deg	G	ABB	DO	D^	32$	AABBB		
Law with German Language	M3R2	4FT deg	G	ABB	DO	D^	32$	AABBB		
Politics and German Language	MR1G	4FT deg	G	BCC		M	30$			
QUEEN'S Univ Belfast										
Accounting with German	N4R2	4FT deg	G g	ABB	X	D*^ go	34$	AAABB	X	
Economics with German	L1R2	3FT deg								
Finance with German	N3R2	4SW deg	G g	BBB	X	D*^ go	32$	AABBB	Ind	
German	R200	4FT deg	* g	BCC	3M+4D	D*6/^ go	29$	ABBB	Ind	
German/Celtic (4 years)	QR52	4FT deg	* g	BCC	3M+4D	D*6/^ go	29$	ABBB	Ind	1
German/Classical Studies (4 years)	QR82	4FT deg	* g	BCC	3M+4D	D*6/^ go	29$	ABBB	Ind	
German/Economics (4 years)	LR12	3FT deg								
German/English (4 years)	QR32	4FT deg	E g	BCC	X	D*^ go	29$	ABBB	X	3
German/French (4 years)	RR12	4FT deg	F g	BCC	X	D*^ go	29$	ABBB	X	4 18/30
Greek/German (4 years)	RQ27	4FT deg	* g	BCC	3M+4D	D*6/^ go	29$	ABBB	Ind	
Information Management with German	P2R2	3FT deg	G g	BBC	X	D*^ go	30$	AABB	X	
Italian/German (4 years)	RR23	4FT deg	* g	BCC	3M+4D	D*6/^ go	29$	ABBB	Ind	
Latin/German (4 years)	RQ26	4FT deg	* g	BCC	3M+4D	D*6/^ go	29$	ABBB	Ind	
Management with German	N1R2	3FT deg	G g	BBB	X	D*^ go	32$	AABBB	X	1
Music/German (4 years)	RW23	4FT deg	* g	BCC	3M+4D	D*6/^ go	29$	ABBB	Ind	
Philosophy/German (4 years)	RV27	4FT deg	* g	BCC	3M+4D	D*6/^ go	29$	ABBB	Ind	
Politics/German (4 years)	RM21	4FT deg	* g	BCC	3M+4D	D*6/^ go	29$	ABBB	Ind	
Scholastic Philosophy/German (4 years)	RV2R	4FT deg	* g	BCC	3M+4D	D*6/^ go	29$	ABBB	Ind	
Social Anthropology/German (4 years)	RL26	4FT deg	* g	BCC	3M+4D	D*6/^ go	29$	ABBB	Ind	
Spanish/German (4 years)	RR24	4FT deg	* g	BCC	3M+4D	D*6/^ go	29$	ABBB	Ind	
Univ of READING										
English Literature and German	QR32	4FT deg	El g	BBC	Ind	D$^ go	31$	BBBB$	Ind	6
French and German	RR12	4FT deg	F g	BBC	Ind	D$^ go	31$	BBBB$	Ind	29
German	R200	4FT deg	* g	BCC	Ind	D$^	30	BBBB	Ind	8
German and Economics	LR12	4FT deg	* g	BCC	Ind	D$^ go	30	BBBB	Ind	
German and Film & Drama	RW24	4FT deg	* g	BBC	Ind	D$^	31	BBBB	Ind	5
German and French	RR21	4FT deg	F g	BCC	Ind	D$^ go	30$	BBBB$	Ind	12
German and History of Art	RV24	4FT deg	* g	BBC	Ind	DP^	31	BBBB	Ind	
German and International Relations	RM21	4FT deg	* g	BCC	Ind	D$^	30	BBBB	Ind	
German and Italian	RR23	4FT deg	* g	BCC	Ind	D$^ go	30	BBBB	Ind	11

		course details		98 expected requirements						96 entry stats

TITLE	CODE	COURSE	SUBJECTS	A/AS	ND/C	AGNVQ	IB	SQA(H)	SQA	RATIO A/AS
German and Linguistics	QR12	4FT deg	* g	BCC	Ind	D$^	30	BBBB	Ind	7
German and Management Studies	NR12	4FT deg	* g	BBC	Ind	DB^ go	31	BBBB	Ind	28
German and Politics	MR12	4FT deg	* g	BCC	Ind	D$^	30	BBBB	Ind	
German and Sociology	LR32	4FT deg	* g	BCC	Ind	D$^ go	30	BBBB	Ind	3
History and German	RV21	4FT deg	* g	BBC	Ind	D$^ go	31	BBBB	Ind	9
International Management & Bus Admin with German	N1R2	4FT deg	* g	BBB	Ind	DB^ go	32	ABBB	Ind	
Latin and German	QR62	4FT deg	* g	BCC	Ind	D*^ go	30	BBBB	Ind	
Music and German	RW23	4FT deg	Mu g	BCC	X	D*^ go	30$	BBBB$	Ind	8
Philosophy and German	RV27	4FT deg	* g	BCC	Ind	D$^ go	30	BBBB	Ind	

ROYAL HOLLOWAY, Univ of London

TITLE	CODE	COURSE	SUBJECTS	A/AS	ND/C	AGNVQ	IB	SQA(H)	SQA	RATIO A/AS
Biochemistry with German	C7R2	3FT/4FT deg	C+G+B/M/P g	BCC	3M+2D	DS^	28$	BBBCC$		
Economics with German	L1R2	3FT deg	G	BBC-BBB	Ind		32	Ind		
English Language and German	QR3F	4FT deg	E+G	BBC-ABC			30$	Ind		6
English and German	QR32	4FT deg	E+G	BBC-ABC			30$	Ind		
French and German	RR12	4FT deg	F+G	BBC			30$	Ind		27
French with German	R1R2	4FT deg	F+G	BBC-ABC			28$	Ind		
German	R200	4FT deg	G	BCC			28$	BBBBC$		8
German Studies with English Language	R2Q3	3FT deg		BCC			28$	BBBBC$		
German and Classical Studies	RQ28	4FT deg	G	BCC-BBC			28$	Ind		
German and Greek	RQ27	4FT deg	G	BCC-BBC			28$	Ind		
German and History	RV21	4FT deg	G g	BBC			30$	Ind		
German and Italian	RR23	4FT deg	G	BBC-BCC			28$	Ind		6
German and Latin	RQ26	4FT deg	G	BCC-BBC			28$	Ind		
German and Management Studies	RN21	4FT deg	G	BBC	Ind		30$	BBBBC$		11
German and Music	RW23	4FT deg	G+Mu	BBC			Ind	Ind		4
German and Spanish	RR24	4FT deg	G+Sp	BBC-BCC			Ind	Ind		
German with Economics	R2L1	4FT deg	G	BCC			28$	BBBBC$		
German with French	R2R1	4FT deg	F+G	BCC			28$	BBBBC$		
German with History (4 years)	R2V1	4FT deg	G	BBC-BCC			28$	BBBBC$		
German with Italian	R2R3	4FT deg	G	BCC			28$	BBBBC$		
German with Japanese Studies	R2T4	3FT deg								
German with Management Studies	R2N1	4FT deg	G	BCC			28$	BBBBC$		
German with Mathematics	R2G1	4FT deg	G+M	BCC			28$	BBBBC$		
German with Music	R2W3	4FT deg	G+Mu	BCC			28$	BBBBC$		1
German with Political Studies	R2MC	4FT deg	G	BCC			28$	BBBBC$		
German with Social Policy	R2L4	4FT deg	G	BCC			28$	BBBBC$		
German with Sociology	R2L3	4FT deg	G	BCC			28$	BBBBC$		
German with Spanish	R2R4	4FT deg	G	BCC			28$	BBBBC$		5
Italian with German	R3R2	4FT deg	G	BBC			30	BBCCC$		
Management Studies with German	N1R2	3FT deg	G	BBC-BBB	2M+3D	D^	30	Ind		5
Mathematics with German	G1R2	3FT deg	G+M	BCC-BBC	Ind	D^	Ind	Ind		
Music with German	W3R2	3FT deg	G+Mu	BCC-BBC			Ind	ABBCC$		
Physics with German	F3R2	3FT deg	P+M+G	BCC-BBC	5M	DS^	30$	BBBCC$		
Sociology with German	L3R2	3FT deg	G	BCC-BBC	Ind	D^	Ind	Ind		2
Foundation Programme German	Y408	4FT deg								

Univ of SALFORD

TITLE	CODE	COURSE	SUBJECTS	A/AS	ND/C	AGNVQ	IB	SQA(H)	SQA	RATIO A/AS
English & a Modern Lang-English/German (4 Yrs)	QR32	4FT deg	EI+G	BCC	Ind	X	Ind	Ind	Ind	
French/German (4 Yrs)	RR12	4SW deg	L g	BCC	X	X	Ind	Ind	X	8 14/26
German/Arabic (4 Yrs)	RT26	4SW deg	L g	BCC	X	X	Ind	Ind	X	
German/Hispanic Studies (4 Yrs)	RRF4	4SW deg	L g	BCC	X	X	Ind	Ind	X	
German/Italian (4 Yrs)	RR23	4SW deg	L g	BCC	X	X	Ind	Ind	X	10

| | | | 98 expected requirements | | | | | | | 96 entry stats |

TITLE	CODE	COURSE	SUBJECTS	A/AS	ND/C	AGNVQ	IB	SQA(H)	SQA	RATIO A/AS
German/Spanish (4 Yrs)	RR24	4SW deg	L g	BCC	X	X	Ind	Ind	X	8
Info Technology with Language Training in German	G5R2	3FT deg	g	CCC	DO	D^	Ind	Ind	Ind	
Physics w. Addit Stud in Germany(4 Yrs)(M Phys)	F3RF	4FT deg	M+P g	4	Ind	Ind	Ind	CSYS	Ind	3
Physics w. Additional Studies in Germany (4 Yrs)	F3R2	4SW deg	M+P g	4	Ind	Ind	Ind	CSYS	Ind	

SSEES:Sch of Slavonic & E European St(U of London)

German and Russian	RR28	4FT deg	G	BBC	3M $	Ind	28	BBBBB		5

Univ of SHEFFIELD

Biblical Studies and German	RV28	4FT deg	G g	BBC	X	X	30$	ABBB$	Ind	
Computer Science and German	GR52	4FT deg	G+M g	BBC	4M+2D$	D^	30$	ABBB$	Ind	
English and German	QR32	4FT deg	EI+G g	BBB	X	X	32$	AABB$	Ind	22
French and German	RR12	4FT deg	F+G g	BBC	X	X	30$	ABBB$	Ind	8 22/30
German Studies	R200	4FT deg	G g	BBC	X	X	30$	ABBB$	Ind	7 20/28
German and Business Studies	RN21	4FT deg	G g	BBC	X	D^	30$	ABBB$	Ind	24
German and Economics	RL21	4FT deg	G g	BBC	X	D^	30$	ABBB$	Ind	8
German and Hispanic Studies	RR24	4FT deg	G+Sp g	BBC	X	X	30$	ABBB$	Ind	34
German and History	RV21	4FT deg	G+H g	BBB	X	X	32$	AABB$	Ind	8
German and Linguistics	QR12	4FT deg	G g	BBC	X	X	30$	ABBB$	Ind	16
German and Music	RW23	4FT deg	G+Mu g	BBC	X	X	30$	ABBB$	Ind	15
German and Philosophy	RV27	4FT deg	G g	BBB	X	X	32$	AABB$	Ind	
German and Politics	RM21	4FT deg	G g	BBC	X	X	30$	ABBB$	Ind	4
German and Russian	RR28	4FT deg	G g	BCC	X	X	29$	BBBB$	Ind	4 24/30
Law with German	MR32	4FT deg	G g	AAB	X	D^	35$	AAAA$	Ind	3 26/30

SHEFFIELD HALLAM Univ

International Business with Language (German)	N1R2	4SW deg	G	16	X	M4/^	Ind	Ind	Ind	

Univ of SOUTHAMPTON

Accounting and German	NR42	4FT deg	G g	22	Ind	D$^ go	30$	ABBBB$	Ind	8
Economics and German	LR12	4FT deg	G g	24	Ind	D$^ go	32$	AABBB$	Ind	13
English and German	QR32	4FT deg	E+G	BBC	X	Ind	Ind	Ind	X	9
French and German	RR12	4FT deg	F+G	BBC	1M+4D	Ind	30$	Ind	Ind	9 18/24
French and German (Linguistics & Language Stds)	RRC2	4FT deg	F+G	BBC		Ind		Ind	Ind	
French and German (Literary Studies)	RRCF	4FT deg	F+G	BBC		Ind		Ind	Ind	
French and German (Social and Political Studies)	RRCG	4FT deg	F+G	BBC		Ind		Ind	Ind	
German	R200	4FT deg	G	BBC	1M+4D	Ind	30$	Ind	Ind	6 14/24
German (Cultural Studies)	R210	4FT deg	G	BBC						
German (Linguistics and Language Studies)	R201	4FT deg	G	BBC						
German and Film	RW25	4FT deg	G	BBC						
German and History	RV21	4FT deg	H+G	BBC	X				X	
German and Music	RW23	4FT deg	Mu+G	22	1M+4D	Ind	30$	Ind	Ind	8
German and Philosophy	RV27	4FT deg	G	BCC	1M+4D	Ind	30$	Ind	Ind	
German and Spanish	RR24	4FT deg	G+Sp	BBC	1M+4D	Ind	30$	Ind	Ind	6
German and Spanish (Linguistics & Language Stds)	RRF4	4FT deg	G+Sp	BBC						
German and Spanish (Literary Studies)	RRFK	4FT deg	G+Sp	BBC						
German and Spanish(Social and Political Studies)	RRFL	4FT deg	G+Sp	BBC						
Management Sciences and German	NRC2	4FT deg	G g	22	Ind	D$^ go	30$	ABBBB$	Ind	4 20/20
Mathematics and German (4 Yrs)	GR12	4FT deg	M+G	BBC	Ind	Ind	30$	ABBBB	Ind	7

SOUTH BANK Univ

German - ab initio and Business Information Tech	GR72	3FT deg	M g	12-16	4M+2D	M go	Ind	Ind	Ind	
German - ab initio and Computing	GR52	3FT deg	M g	12-16	4M+2D	M go	Ind	Ind	Ind	
German - ab initio and Economics	LR12	3FT deg	Ec/Bu g	12-16	4M+2D	M go	Ind	Ind	Ind	
German - ab initio and English Studies	QR32	3FT deg	E g	14-18	X	M^ go	Ind	Ind	Ind	

			98 expected requirements							96 entry stats

course details

TITLE	CODE	COURSE	SUBJECTS	A/AS	NO/C	AGNVQ	IB	SQA(H)	SQA	RATIO A/AS
German - ab initio and French	RR12	3FT deg	F g	12-16	4M+2D	M go	Ind	Ind	Ind	
German and Business Information Technology	GR7F	3FT deg	M+G g	14-18	2M+4D	M go	Ind	Ind	Ind	
German and Computing	GR5F	3FT deg	M+G g	14-18	2M+4D	M go	Ind	Ind	Ind	
German and Economics	LR1F	3FT deg	G g	14-18	2M+4D	M go	Ind	Ind	Ind	
German and English Studies	QR3F	3FT deg	G+E g	16-18	X	M go	Ind	Ind	Ind	
German and French	RR1F	3FT deg	G+F g	14-18	2M+4D	M go	Ind	Ind	Ind	
Health Studies and German	RL24	3FT deg	S+G g	14-18	2M+4D	M go	Ind	Ind	Ind	
Health Studies and German - ab initio	LR42	3FT deg	S g	12-16	4M+2D	M go	Ind	Ind	Ind	
History and German	RV2C	3FT deg	H+G g	14-18	2M+4D	M^ go	Ind	Ind	Ind	
History and German - ab initio	RV21	3FT deg	H g	12-16	4M+2D	M^ go	Ind	Ind	Ind	
Housing and German	KR4F	3FT deg	G g	14-18	2M+4D	M go	Ind	Ind	Ind	
Housing and German - ab initio	KR4G	3FT deg	* g	14-18	2M+4D	M go	Ind	Ind	Ind	
Human Resource Management and German	NR62	3FT deg	G g	14-18	2M+4D	M^ go	Ind	Ind	Ind	
Human Resource Management and German - ab initio	NR6F	3FT deg	* g	14-18	2M+4D	M go	Ind	Ind	Ind	
Law and German	MR3F	3FT deg	G g	14-18	2M+4D	D go	Ind	Ind	Ind	
Law and German - ab initio	MR32	3FT deg	* g	14-18	2M+4D	D go	Ind	Ind	Ind	
Management and German	NR1F	3FT deg	G g	14-18	2M+4D	M go	Ind	Ind	Ind	
Management and German - ab initio	NR12	3FT deg	g	12-16	4M+2D	M go	Ind	Ind	Ind	
Marketing and German	NR52	3FT deg	G g	12-16	2M+4D	M^ go	Ind	Ind	Ind	
Marketing and German - ab initio	NR5F	3FT deg	* g	14-18	2M+4D	M go	Ind	Ind	Ind	
Media Studies and German	PR4F	3FT deg	E+G g	14-18	2M+4D	D go	Ind	Ind	Ind	
Media Studies and German - ab initio	PR42	3FT deg	E g	14-18	2M+4D	D go	Ind	Ind	Ind	
Product Design and German	HR7F	3FT deg	G+Ad g	14-18	2M+4D	M go	Ind	Ind	Ind	
Product Design and German - ab initio	HR72	3FT deg	Ad g	12-16	4M+2D	M go	Ind	Ind	Ind	
Social Policy and German	LR4G	3FT deg	G g	14-18	2M+4D	M go	Ind	Ind	Ind	
Social Policy and German - ab initio	LR4F	3FT deg	g	12-16	4M+2D	M go	Ind	Ind	Ind	
Sociology and German	LR3F	3FT deg	G g	14-18	2M+4D	M go	Ind	Ind	Ind	
Sociology and German - ab initio	LR32	3FT deg	G g	12-16	4M+2D	M go	Ind	Ind	Ind	
Spanish - ab initio and German	RR2L	3FT deg	G g	14-18	2M+4D	M go	Ind	Ind	Ind	
Spanish and German - ab initio	RR2K	3FT deg	Sp g	14-18	2M+4D	M^ go	Ind	Ind	Ind	
Sports Science and German	BR6F	3FT deg	S+G g	14-18	2M+4D	M^ go	Ind	Ind	Ind	
Technology and German - ab initio	JR92	3FT deg	* g	12-16	4M+2D	M go	Ind	Ind	Ind	
Tourism and German	PR7F	3FT deg	G g	12-16	4M+2D	M go	Ind	Ind	Ind	
Tourism and German - ab initio	PR72	3FT deg	g	12-16	4M+2D	M go	Ind	Ind	Ind	
Urban Studies and German	RK24	3FT deg	G g	14-18	2M+4D	M go	Ind	Ind	Ind	
Urban Studies and German - ab initio	RK2K	3FT deg	* g	14-18	2M+4D	M go	Ind	Ind	Ind	
World Theatre and German	RW24	3FT deg	G g	14-18	2M+4D	M go	Ind	Ind	Ind	
World Theatre and German - ab initio	RW2K	3FT deg	* g	14-18	2M+4D	M go	Ind	Ind	Ind	

Univ of ST ANDREWS

TITLE	CODE	COURSE	SUBJECTS	A/AS	NO/C	AGNVQ	IB	SQA(H)	SQA	RATIO A/AS
Biology with German (Science)	C1R2	4FT deg	B/C/Gy/M/P g	BBC	Ind	Ind	28$	BBBB$	Ind	1
Biology with German (with Integrated Yr Abroad)	C1RF	4FT/5FT deg	B/C/Gy/M/P g	BBC	X	Ind	28$	BBBB$	Ind	3
Chemistry with German	F1R2	4FT deg	C g	CCC	Ind	Ind	28$	BBBC		
Chemistry with German (with Integ Year Abroad)	F1RF	4FT/5FT deg	C g	CCC	Ind	Ind	28$	BBBC$	Ind	
German with Year Abroad-Ancient History	RV2D	4FT/5FT deg	* g	BBB	X	Ind	30$	BBBB	Ind	
German with Year Abroad-Arabic	RT2P	4FT/5FT deg	* g	BBC	X	Ind	30$	BBBB	Ind	
German with Year Abroad-Art History	RV2K	4FT/5FT deg	* g	BBC	X	Ind	30$	BBBB	Ind	
German with Year Abroad-Biblical Studies	RVFV	4FT/5FT deg	* g	BBC	X	Ind	30$	BBBB	Ind	
German with Year Abroad-Economics	LRC2	4FT/5FT deg	* g	BBB	X	Ind	30$	BBBB	Ind	3
German with Year Abroad-English	QRH2	4FT/5FT deg	* g	BBB	X	Ind	30$	BBBB	Ind	9
German with Year Abroad-French	RRC2	4FT/5FT deg	F g	BBB	X	Ind	30$	BBBB	Ind	5 22/30
German-Ancient History	RVG1	4FT deg	* g	BBB	X	Ind	30$	BBBB	Ind	
German-Arabic	RT26	4FT deg	* g	BBC	X	Ind	30$	BBBB	Ind	

TITLE	CODE	COURSE	SUBJECTS	A/AS	ND/C	AGNVQ	IB	SQA(H)	SQA	RATIO A/AS
German-Art History	RV24	4FT deg	* g	BBC	X	Ind	30$	BBBB	Ind	
German-Biblical Studies	RV28	4FT deg	* g	BBC	X	Ind	30$	BBBB	Ind	1
German-Economics	LR12	4FT deg	* g	BBB	X	Ind	30$	BBBB	Ind	
German-English	QR32	4FT deg	* g	BBB	X	Ind	30$	BBBB	Ind	2
German-French	RR12	4FT deg	F g	BBB	X	Ind	30$	BBBB$	Ind	23
International Relations-German	MR12	4FT deg	* g	AAB	X	Ind	36$	AAAB	Ind	
International Relations-German with Year Abroad	MR1F	4FT/5FT deg	* g	AAB	X	Ind	36$	AAAB	Ind	
Italian-German	RR23	4FT deg	* g	BBB	X	Ind	30$	BBBB	Ind	
Italian-German with Year Abroad	RR32	4FT/5FT deg	* g	BBB	X	Ind	30$	BBBB	Ind	
Latin-German	QR62	4FT deg	* g	BBC	X	Ind	30$	BBBB	Ind	
Latin-German with Year Abroad	QR6F	4FT/5FT deg	* g	BBC	X	Ind	30$	BBBB	Ind	
Management-German	NR12	4FT deg	* g	BBB	X	Ind	30$	BBBB	Ind	
Management-German with Year Abroad	NR1F	4FT/5FT deg	* g	BBB	X	Ind	30$	BBBB	Ind	8
Mathematics with German	G1R2	4FT deg	M g	BCC	Ind	Ind	28$	BBBC$	Ind	
Mathematics with German (with Integ Yr Abroad)	G1RF	4FT/5FT deg	M g	BCC	Ind	Ind	28$	BBBC$	Ind	
Mediaeval History-German	RVF1	4FT deg	* g	BBB	X	Ind	30$	BBBB	Ind	
Mediaeval History-German with Year Abroad	RVFC	4FT/5FT deg	* g	BBB	X	Ind	30$	BBBB	Ind	3
Modern History-German	RV21	4FT deg	* g	BBB	X	Ind	30$	BBBB	Ind	2
Modern History-German with Year Abroad	RVGC	4FT/5FT deg	* g	BBB	X	Ind	30$	BBBB	Ind	5
Modern Languages (German with Integ Year Abroad)	R211	4FT/5FT deg	* g	BBC	X	Ind	30$	BBBB	Ind	6
Modern Languages (German)	R200	4FT deg	* g	BBC	X	Ind	30$	BBBB	Ind	5
New Testament-German	RV2V	4FT deg	* g	BBC	X	Ind	30$	BBBB	Ind	
New Testament-German with Year Abroad	RVFW	4FT/5FT deg	* g	BBC	X	Ind	30$	BBBB	Ind	
Philosophy-German	RV27	4FT deg	* g	BBB	X	Ind	30$	BBBB	Ind	2
Philosophy-German with Year Abroad	RVG7	4FT/5FT deg	* g	BBB	X	Ind	30$	BBBB	Ind	
Psychology-German	LR72	4FT deg	* g	ABB	X	Ind	32$	ABBB	Ind	
Psychology-German with Year Abroad	LR7F	4FT/5FT deg	* g	ABB	X	Ind	32$	ABBB	Ind	7
Russian with Year Abroad-German	RRF8	4FT/5FT deg	* g	BBC	X	Ind	30$	BBBB	Ind	
Russian-German	RR28	4FT deg	* g	BBC	X	Ind	30$	BBBB	Ind	4
Spanish with Year Abroad-German	RRF4	4FT/5FT deg	* g	BBB	X	Ind	30$	BBBB	Ind	7
Spanish-German	RR24	4FT deg	* g	BBB	X	Ind	30$	BBBB	Ind	
Statistics with German (Science)	G4R2	4FT deg	M g	BCC	Ind	Ind	28$	BBBC$	Ind	
Statistics with German (Science) (Int Yr Abroad)	G4RF	4FT/5FT deg	M g	BCC	Ind	Ind	28$	BBBC$	Ind	
Theological Studies-German	RV2W	4FT deg	* g	BBC	X	Ind	30$	BBBB	Ind	
Theological Studies-German with Year Abroad	RVF8	4FT/5FT deg	* g	BBC	X	Ind	30$	BBBB	Ind	
European Integration Studies German	Y602	4FT deg	* g	BBB	X	Ind	30$	BBBB	Ind	
General Degree of MA Modern Languages (German)	Y450	3FT deg	* g	BBB	X	Ind	30$	BBBB	Ind	

STAFFORDSHIRE Univ

TITLE	CODE	COURSE	SUBJECTS	A/AS	ND/C	AGNVQ	IB	SQA(H)	SQA	RATIO A/AS
European Culture/German	LRP2	3FT deg	G g	CD	MO+2D	M^	27	BBC	Ind	
German/American Studies	RQ24	3FT/4SW deg	G g	CD	MO+2D	M^	27	BBC	Ind	
German/Business Studies	RN21	3FT/4SW deg	G g	CCD	MO+2D	M$^	26	BBB	Ind	
German/Environmental Studies	RF29	3FT/4SW deg	G g	14	4M+2D	M^	26	ABB	Ind	
German/Film Studies	RW25	3FT/4SW deg	G g	CD	MO+2D	M^	27	BBC	Ind	
German/French	RR21	4SW deg	G/F	DD	4M+2D	M^	26	BCC	Ind	10
German/Geography	RL28	3FT/4SW deg	G g	16	4M+2D	M^	28	AAB	Ind	4
History of Art and Design/German	VR42	3FT/4SW deg	G	CD	MO+2D	M^	27	BBC	Ind	
History/German	VR12	3FT/4SW deg	G+H	CD	MO+2D	M^	27	BBC	Ind	
Information Systems/German	GR52	3FT/4SW deg	G g	12	4M+2D	M^	26	BCC	Ind	2
International Relations/German	MR1F	3FT/4SW deg	G g	12	4M+2D	M^	26	BCC	Ind	
Literature/German	QR32	3FT/4SW deg	El+G g	CD	MO+2D	M^	27	BCC	Ind	7

| | | | 98 expected requirements | | | | | | | 96 entry stats |
| course details | | | | | | | | | | |

TITLE	CODE	COURSE	SUBJECTS	R/AS	NO/C	RGNVQ	IB	SQA(H)	SQA	RATIO R/AS
Media Studies/German	PR42	3FT/4SW deg	G g	CD	MO+2D	M^	26	BCC	Ind	
Philosophy/German	VR72	3FT/4SW deg	G	CD	MO+2D	M^	27	BBC	Ind	
Politics/German	MRC2	3FT/4SW deg	G g	12	4M+2D	M^	26	BCC	Ind	
Property with German	K2R2	3FT deg	g	12	4M	M$	24	BBC	Ind	
Psychology/German	LR72	3FT/4SW deg	G g	18	3M+3D	Ind	27	BBB	Ind	4
Sociology/German	LR32	3FT/4SW deg	G g	12	4M+2D	M^	26	BCC	Ind	
Spanish/German	RR42	4SW deg	G g	DD	4M+2D	M^	26	BCC	Ind	5
Women's Studies/German	MR92	3FT/4SW deg	G g	12	4M+2D	M^	26	BCC	Ind	

Univ of STIRLING

TITLE	CODE	COURSE	SUBJECTS	R/AS	NO/C	RGNVQ	IB	SQA(H)	SQA	RATIO R/AS
Accountancy/German Language	NR4F	4FT deg	g	BCC	HN	Ind	33	BBBB	HN	
Business Studies/German Language	NRCF	4FT deg	g	CCC	Ind	Ind	31	BBBC	HN	
Computing Science/German Language	GR52	4FT deg	g	CCC	Ind	Ind	28	BBCC	HN	
Economics/German Language	LR1F	4FT deg	g	CCC	Ind	Ind	31	BBBC	HN	
English Studies/German	QR32	4FT deg	g	CCC	Ind	Ind	31	BBBC	HN	
Film & Media Studies/German	RP24	4FT deg	g	BBC	Ind	Ind	35	ABBB	HN	
Financial Studies/German Language	N3R2	4FT deg	g	BCC	Ind	Ind	31	BBBC	HN	
French/German	RR12	4FT deg	g	CCC	Ind	Ind	31	BBBC	HN	
German	R200	4FT deg	g	CCC	Ind	Ind	31	BBBC	HN	
German/History	RV21	4FT deg	g	CCC	Ind	Ind	31	BBBC	HN	
German/Human Resources Management	NR1G	4FT deg	g	CCC	Ind	Ind	31	BBBC	HN	
German/Japanese	RT24	4FT deg	g	CCC	Ind	Ind	31	BBBC	HN	
German/Mathematics	R2G1	3FT deg	g	CCC		Ind	28	BBCC		
German/Philosophy	RV27	4FT deg	g	CCC	Ind	Ind	31	BBBC	HN	
German/Politics	MR12	4FT deg	g	CCC	Ind	Ind	31	BBBC	HN	
German/Religious Studies	RV28	4FT deg	g	CCC	Ind	Ind	31	BBBC	HN	
German/Sociology	LR32	4FT deg	g	CCC	Ind	Ind	31	BBBC	HN	
German/Spanish	RR24	4FT deg	g	CCC	Ind	Ind	31	BBBC	HN	
Management Science/German Language	NR1F	4FT deg	g	CCC	Ind	Ind	31	BBBC	HN	
Marketing/German Language	N5R2	4FT deg	g	CCC	Ind	Ind	31	BBBC	HN	
Mathematics & its Applications with German Lang	G1R2	4FT deg	M g	CCC	Ind	Ind	28	BBCC	HN	

Univ of STRATHCLYDE

TITLE	CODE	COURSE	SUBJECTS	R/AS	NO/C	RGNVQ	IB	SQA(H)	SQA	RATIO R/AS
Arts and Social Sciences German	Y440	3FT/4FT deg	g	CCC	Ind		28	BBBBB$	Ind	

Univ of SUNDERLAND

TITLE	CODE	COURSE	SUBJECTS	R/AS	NO/C	RGNVQ	IB	SQA(H)	SQA	RATIO R/AS
Biology and German	CR12▼	4FT deg	B/C+G g	8	N $	M	24$	CCCC$	N$	
Biology with German	C1R2	3FT deg	B/C	8	3M	M	Ind	Ind	Ind	
Business Computing with German	G5R2	4SW deg	* g	4-8	4M	M*	24	CCCC	N	
Business Studies and German	NR12	4FT deg	G g	10	N $	M	24$	CCCC$	N$	11
Business Studies with German	N1R2	3FT/4SW deg	*	8	3M	M	Ind	Ind	Ind	
Chemistry and German	FR12▼	4FT deg	G+C g	8	N $	M	24$	CCCC$	N$	1
Chemistry with German	F1R2	3FT deg	C	8	3M	M	Ind	Ind	Ind	
Computer Studies and German	GR52	4FT deg	G g	8	N $	M	24$	CCCC$	N$	
English and German	QR32▼	4FT deg	El+G g	10	N $	M	24$	CCCC$	N$	3
English with German	Q3R2	3FT deg	G	10	4M	M	Ind	Ind	Ind	
French and German	RR12▼	4FT deg	F+G g	8	N $	M	24$	CCCC$	N$	16
French with German	R1R2	4FT deg	F+G	8	3M	M	Ind	Ind	Ind	
Geography and German	LR82▼	4FT deg	G+Gy/Gl g	10	N $	M	24$	CCCC$	N$	
Geography with German	L8R2	3FT deg	*	8	3M	M	Ind	Ind	Ind	
Geology and German	FR62	4FT deg	G+Gy/Gl/S g	8	N $	M	24$	CCCC$	N$	
Geology with German	F6R2	3FT deg	*	8	3M	M	Ind	Ind	Ind	
German and History	RV21▼	4FT deg	G+H g	10	Ind	M	24$	CCCC$	Ind	6

Languages – German 41

course details			98 expected requirements							96 entry stats
TITLE	CODE	COURSE	SUBJECTS	A/AS	ND/C	AGNVQ	IB	SQA(H)	SQA	RATIO A/AS
German and Mathematics	RG21	4FT deg	M+G g	8	N $	M	24$	CCCC$	N$	
German and Media Studies	RP24	3FT deg	*	24	Ind	Ind	Ind	Ind		
German and Philosophy	RV27▼	4FT deg	G g	10	N $	M	24$	CCCC$	N$	
German and Politics	RM21▼	4FT deg	G g	10	N $	M	24$	CCCC$	N$	
German and Psychology	RC28	4FT deg	G g	12	3M $	M	24$	BCCC$	N$	2
German and Religious Studies	RV28▼	4FT deg	G g	10	N $	M	24$	CCCC$	N$	
German with Biology	R2C1	4SW deg	G	8	3M	M	Ind	Ind	Ind	
German with Business Studies	R2N1	4SW deg	G	8	3M	M	Ind	Ind	Ind	
German with Chemistry	R2F1	4SW deg	G	8	3M	M	Ind	Ind	Ind	
German with Comparative Literature	R2Q2	4FT deg	G+El g	10	Ind	M	24$	CCCC$		
German with Computer Studies	R2G5	4SW deg	G	8	3M	M	Ind	Ind	Ind	
German with English	R2Q3	4SW deg	G	10	4M	M	Ind	Ind	Ind	
German with European Studies	R2T2	4FT deg	G g	10	N $	M	24$	CCCC$	N$	6
German with French	R2R1	4SW deg	G	8	3M	M	Ind	Ind	Ind	
German with Geography	R2L8	4SW deg	G	8	3M	M	Ind	Ind	Ind	
German with Geology	R2F6	4SW deg	G	8	3M	M	Ind	Ind	Ind	
German with History	R2V1	4SW deg	G	10	4M	M	Ind	Ind	Ind	
German with Mathematics	R2G1	4SW deg	G	8	3M	M	Ind	Ind	Ind	
German with Media Studies	R2P4	4SW deg	G	24	Ind	Ind	Ind	Ind	Ind	
German with Philosophy	R2V7	4SW deg	G	8	3M	M	Ind	Ind	Ind	
German with Politics	R2M1	4SW deg	G	8	3M	M	Ind	Ind	Ind	
German with Psychology	R2C8	4SW deg	G	10	4M	M^	Ind	Ind	Ind	
German with Religious Studies	R2V8	4SW deg	G	8	3M	M	Ind	Ind	Ind	
German with Spanish	R2R4▼	4SW deg	G	10	4M	M	Ind	Ind	Ind	
History with German	V1R2	3FT deg	*	10	4M	M	Ind	Ind	Ind	
International Business with German	N1RF	3FT deg	* g	18	1M+4D$ D		26	BBBCC	N$	
Mathematics with German	G1R2	3FT deg	M	8	3M	M	Ind	Ind	Ind	
Media Studies with German	P4R2	3FT deg	*	24	Ind	Ind	Ind	Ind	Ind	
Philosophy with German	V7R2	3FT deg	*	8	3M	Ind	Ind	Ind	Ind	
Physiology with German	B1R2	3FT deg	*	8	3M	M	Ind	Ind	Ind	
Politics with German	M1R2	3FT deg	*	8	3M	M	Ind	Ind	Ind	
Psychology with German	C8R2	3FT deg	*	10	4M	M^	Ind	Ind	Ind	
Religious Studies with German	V8R2	3FT deg	*	8	3M	M	Ind	Ind	Ind	

Univ of SURREY

French and German	RR12	4FT/SW deg	F+G	22	3M+3D$		30$	ABBCC	Ind		
German and Economics with International Business	RL21	4SW deg	G g	22	3M+3D$		30$	ABBCC	Ind	2	16/28
German and European Studies	RT22	4SW deg	G	22	3M+3D$		30$	ABBCC	Ind	5	8/26
German and Law	RM23	4SW deg	G	22	3M+3D$		30$	ABBCC	Ind	5	
German and Russian	RR28	4FT/SW deg	G+R	20	3M+3D$		30$	ABBCC	Ind		

Univ of SUSSEX

Biochemistry with European Studies (German)	C7R2	4FT deg	C+S g	BCC	MO $	MS6 go	$	Ind	Ind	
Biology with European Studies (German)	C1R2	4FT deg	2S g	BCC	MO $	MS6 go	$	Ind	Ind	
Chemical Physics with Eur St (German) (MChem)	F3RG	4FT deg	C/P/Ph+M g	CCC	MO $	MS^ go	$	Ind	Ind	
Chemistry with European Studies (German)	F1R2	4FT deg	C+S g	CCC	MO $	MS go	$	Ind	Ind	
Chemistry with European Studies (German) (MChem)	F1RG	4FT deg	C+S g	CCC	MO $	MS go	$	Ind	Ind	
Computer Science with European Studies (German)	G5R2	4FT deg	M g	BBC	MO $	M*^ go	$	Ind	Ind	
Environmental Science with Euro Studies (German)	F9R2	4FT deg	2(C/P/M) g	CCC	MO $	MS go	$	Ind	Ind	
French and German	RR12	4FT deg	F+G	BCC	MO $	M*^	$	Ind	Ind	
German	R200	4FT deg	G	BCC	MO $	M*^	$	Ind	Ind	
German and Italian	RR23	4FT deg	G	BCC	MO $	M*^	$	Ind	Ind	
German and Linguistics	RQ21	4FT deg	G	BCC	MO $	M*^	$	Ind	Ind	

course details

98 expected requirements

96 entry stats

TITLE	CODE	COURSE	SUBJECTS	A/AS	ND/C	AGNVQ	IB	SQA(H)	SQA	RATIO A/AS
German and Russian	RR28	4FT deg	G	BCC	MO $	M*^	$	Ind	Ind	
Mathematics & Stats with Eur St (German)(MMath)	G4RF	4FT deg	M g	BCC	MO $	MS^ go	$	Ind	Ind	
Mathematics and Statistics with Eur St (German)	G4R2	4FT deg	M g	BCC	MO $	MS^ go	$	Ind	Ind	
Mathematics with European St (German) (MMath)	G1RF	4FT deg	M g	BCC	MO $	MS^ go	$	Ind	Ind	
Mathematics with European Studies (German)	G1R2	4FT deg	M g	BCC	MO $	MS^ go	$	Ind	Ind	
Molecular Genetics in Biotechnology with German	C4R2	4FT deg	2S g	BCD	MO $	MS6 $	$	Ind	Ind	
Physics with European Studies (German)	F3R2	4FT deg	M+P g	CCC	MO $	MS^ go	$	Ind	Ind	
Physics with European Studies (German)(MPhys)	F3RF	4FT deg	M+P g	CCC	MO $	MS^ go	$	Ind	Ind	

Univ of Wales SWANSEA

TITLE	CODE	COURSE	SUBJECTS	A/AS	ND/C	AGNVQ	IB	SQA(H)	SQA	RATIO A/AS
Biological Sciences (with German)	C1R2	4FT deg	B+G	BCC	X	X	28$	ABBCC$	Ind	12
Civil Engineering (with German)	H2R2	4FT deg	M g	BCD-CCC	4M+1D$	MC^ go	28$	BBBCC$	Ind	
Computer Science (with German)	G5R2	4FT deg	G	BBC	4D $	Ind	28$	BBBBB$	Ind	
English Language/German (with Business Studies)	QRH2	4FT deg	G	X	X	X	28	X	X	
European Business Studies (Germany)	N1R2	4FT deg	G g	ABC-BBB	Ind	D$^ go	32$	AABBB$	Ind	3
European History (with German)	V1R2	4FT deg	G+H	BBB-BBC	Ind	Ind	30$	ABBBB$	Ind	
European Management Science (Germany)	N1RF	4FT deg	G+M	ABC-BBB	X	X	32$	AABBB$	Ind	3
French/German (with Business Studies)	RR1F	4FT deg	F g	BBB-BBC	1M+5D$	Ind	30$	ABBBB$	Ind	6	18/28
French/German (with Computer Studies)	RR1G	4FT deg	F g	BBC	1M+5D$	Ind	30$	ABBBB$	Ind	2
French/German (with Legal Studies)	RR21	4FT deg	F g	BBB-BBC	1M+5D$	Ind	30$	ABBBB$	Ind	3
German	R200	4FT deg	G g	BBC	1M+5D$	Ind	30$	ABBBB$	Ind	2	10/20
German (with Business Studies)	R2N1	4FT deg	G g	BBC	1M+5D$	Ind	30$	ABBBB$	Ind	4	16/20
German (with Computer Studies)	R2G5	4FT deg	G	BBC	1M+5D$	Ind	30$	ABBBB$	Ind	
German (with Legal Studies)	R2M3	4FT deg	G	BBB-BBC	1M+5D$	Ind	32$	AABBB$	Ind	
German/American Studies	QR42	4FT deg								
German/Ancient History and Civilisation	VRC2	4FT deg	G	BBC	1M+5D$	X	30$	ABBBB$	X	
German/Anthropology	LR62	4FT deg	G	BBC	1M+5D$	Ind	30$	ABBBB$	Ind	
German/Economic History	RV23	4FT deg	G	BBC	1M+5D$	Ind	30$	ABBBB$	Ind	
German/Economics	LR12	4FT deg								
German/English	QR32	4FT deg	E+G	BBC	1M+5D$	X	30$	ABBBB$	X	
German/English Language	QR3F	3FT deg	E+G	BBC	X	X	30$	ABBBB$	Ind	
German/European Politics	RM21	4FT deg	G	BBC	1M+5D$	Ind	30$	ABBBB$	Ind	
German/French	RR12	4FT deg	F+G/(F g)	BBC	1M+5D$	Ind	30$	ABBBB$	Ind	5	16/24
German/Geography	LR82	4FT deg	G+Gy	BBC	1M+5D$	Ind	30$	ABBBB$	Ind	4
German/Italian (with Business Studies)	RR2H	4FT deg	G g	BBC	1M+5D$	Ind	30$	ABBBB$	Ind	4
German/Italian (with Computer Studies)	RR2J	4FT deg	G	BBC	1M+5D$	Ind	30$	ABBBB$	Ind	
German/Italian (with Legal Studies)	RR32	4FT deg	G	BBC	1M+5D$	Ind	30$	ABBBB$	Ind	
German/Russian (with Business Studies)	RR2V	4FT deg	G g	BCC	1M+5D$	Ind	28$	BBBBC$	Ind	8
German/Russian (with Computer Studies)	RR2W	4FT deg	G	BCC	1M+5D$	Ind	28$	BBBBC$	Ind	
German/Russian (with Legal Studies)	RR82	4FT deg	G	BBC-BCC	1M+5D$	Ind	28$	BBBBC$	Ind	
German/Spanish (with Business Studies)	RR2K	4FT deg	G g	BBB-BBC	1M+5D$	Ind	30$	ABBBB$	Ind	2
German/Spanish (with Computer Studies)	RR2L	4FT deg	G	BBC	1M+5D$	Ind	30$	ABBBB$	Ind	2
German/Spanish (with Legal Studies)	RR42	4FT deg	G	BBB-BBC	1M+5D$	Ind	30$	ABBBB$	Ind	
German/Welsh (with Business Studies)	RQ25	4FT deg	G+W g	BCC	1M+5D$	X	28$	BBBBC$	X	
German/Welsh (with Computer Studies)	RQ2N	4FT deg	G+W	BCC	1M+5D$	X	28$	BBBBC$	X	
German/Welsh (with Legal Studies)	RQ2M	4FT deg	G+W	BCC	1M+5D$	X	28$	BBBBC$	X	
Greek and Roman Studies/German	QR82	4FT deg	G	BBC-BCC	1M+5D$	X	28$	BBBBB$	X	
Greek/German	QR72	4FT deg	Gk+G	BCC	X	X	28$	BBBBB$	X	
History/German	RV21	4FT deg	G+H	BBC	1M+5D$	Ind	30$	ABBBB$	Ind	3
Italian/German	RR23	4FT deg	G/(I g)	BBC	1M+5D$	Ind	30$	ABBBB$	Ind	3
Latin/German	QR62	4FT deg	G+Ln	BBC-BCC	Ind	X	28$	BBBBB$	Ind	
Law and German	MR32	4FT deg	G	BBB	6D $	Ind	32$	AABBB$	Ind	11
Mathematics (with German)	G1R2	4FT deg	M+G	BBC-BCC	Ind	Ind	28$	BBBBC$	Ind	

course details

TITLE	CODE	COURSE	SUBJECTS	A/AS	NO/C	AGNVQ	IB	SQA(H)	SQA	RATIO A/AS
Philosophy/German	RV27	4FT deg	G	BBC-BCC	1M+5D$	Ind	28$	BBBBB$	Ind	
Politics/German	MR12	4FT deg	G	BBC-BCC	1M+5D$	Ind	28$	BBBBB$	Ind	
Psychology and German	LR72	4FT deg	G g	BBC	1M+5D$	Ind	30$	ABBBB$	Ind	
Russian/German	RR28	4FT deg	G/(R g)	BCC	1M+5D$	Ind	28$	BBBBC$	Ind	
Sociology/German	LR32	4FT deg	G	BBC	1M+5D$	Ind	30$	ABBBB$	Ind	2
Spanish/German	RR24	4FT deg	G/Sp g	BBC	1M+5D$	Ind	30$	ABBBB$	Ind	
Welsh/German	QR52	4FT deg	W g	BCC	1M+5D$	X	28$	BBBBB$	X	2

THAMES VALLEY Univ

TITLE	CODE	COURSE	SUBJECTS	A/AS	NO/C	AGNVQ	IB	SQA(H)
Accounting with German	N4R2	3FT deg		8-12	MO	M	26	CCC
American Studies with German	Q4R2	3FT deg		8-12	MO	M	26	CCC
Business Administration with German	N1RF	3FT deg		8-12	MO	M	26	CCC
Business Economics with German	L1RF	3FT deg		8-12	MO	M	26	CCC
Business Studies with German (Dip)	N1R2▼	3FT/4SW deg	* g	10-12	MO+2D	M	26	CCC
Economics with German	L1R2▼	3FT deg	* g	8-12	MO	M	26	CCC
English Language and Communications with German	Q1R2	3FT deg		8-12	MO	M	26	CCC
English with German	Q3R2	3FT deg		8-12	MO	M	26	CCC
Environmental Policy and Management with German	F9R2	3FT deg		8-12	MO	M	26	CCC
European Law with German	M3RF	3FT deg		8-12	MO	M	26	CCC
European Studies with German	T2R2	3FT deg		8-12	MO	M	26	CCC
Finance with German	N3R2	3FT deg		8-12	MO	M	26	CCC
Food and Drink Consumer Studies with German	D4R2	3FT deg		8-12	MO	M	26	CCC
French with German	R1R2	3FT deg		8-12	MO	M	26	CCC
German with Business	R2N1	3FT deg		8-12	MO	M	26	CCC
German with Business Economics	R2LC	3FT deg		8-12	MO	M	26	CCC
German with Economics	R2L1	3FT deg		8-12	MO	M	26	CCC
German with English	R2Q3	3FT deg		8-12	MO	M	26	CCC
German with English Language Studies	R2Q1	3FT deg		8-12	MO	M	26	CCC
German with European Law	R2M3	3FT deg		8-12	MO	M	26	CCC
German with European Studies	R2T2	3FT deg		8-12	MO	M	26	CCC
German with French	R2R1	3FT deg		8-12	MO	M	26	CCC
German with History	R2V1	3FT deg		8-12	MO	M	26	CCC
German with International Studies	R2MD	3FT deg		8-12	MO	M	26	CCC
German with Language and Communication	R2PH	3FT deg		8-12	MO	M	26	CCC
German with Media Studies	R2W9	3FT deg		8-12	MO	M	26	CCC
German with Music	R2W3	3FT deg		8-12	MO	M	26	CCC
German with Politics and International Relations	R2M1	3FT deg		8-12	MO	M	26	CCC
German with Spanish	R2R4	3FT deg		8-12	MO	M	26	CCC
History with German	V1R2	3FT deg		8-12	MO	M	26	CCC
Hospitality Management with German	N7R2	3FT deg		8-12	MO	M	26	CCC
Human Resource Management with German	N6R2	3FT deg		8-12	MO	M	26	CCC
Information Management with German	P2R2	3FT deg		8-12	MO	M	26	CCC
International Studies with German	M9R2	3FT deg		8-12	MO	M	26	CCC
Law with German	M3R2	3FT deg		8-12	MO	M	26	CCC
Leisure Management with German	N7RF	3FT deg		8-12	MO	M	26	CCC
Marketing with German	N5R2	3FT deg		8-12	MO	M	26	CCC
Media Arts with German	W9R2	3FT deg		8-12	MO	M	26	CCC
Politics and International Relations with German	M1R2	3FT deg		8-12	MO	M	26	CCC
Psychology with German	C8R2	3FT deg		8-12	MO	M	26	CCC
Recreation Management with German	N7RG	3FT deg		8-12	MO	M	26	CCC
Sociology with German	L3R2	3FT deg		8-12	MO	M	26	CCC
Spanish with German	R4R2	3FT deg		8-12	MO	M	26	CCC
Tourism with German	P7R2	3FT deg		8-12	MO	M	26	CCC

			98 expected requirements							*96 entry stats*	

TITLE	CODE	COURSE	SUBJECTS	A/AS	ND/C	AGNVQ	IB	SQA(H)	SQA	RATIO	A/AS
Univ of ULSTER											
Humanities Combined *German*	Y320▼	3FT/4SW deg	G	CCC	MO+3D	D*6/△ gi	28	BBBC	Ind		
UNIVERSITY COLL LONDON (Univ of London)											
Dutch and German (4 Yrs)	TR22	4FT deg	G g	BCC-BBC	3M	X	28$	BBBCC$	Ind		
English and German (4 Yrs)	QR32	4FT deg	El+G g	ABB	Ind	X	34$	AABBB$	Ind	12	
French and German (4 Yrs)	RR12	4FT deg	F+G g	BBC	3M	X	32$	ABBBB$	Ind	6	20/30
German (4 Yrs)	R200	4FT deg	G g	BBC	3M	X	30$	BBBCC$	Ind	3	12/24
German and History of Art (4 Yrs)	RV24	4FT deg	G g	BBC	3M	X	30$	BBBCC$	Ind	3	
German and Italian (4 Yrs)	RR23	4FT deg	G g	BBC	3M	X	30$	BBBCC$	Ind	3	22/24
German and Jewish Studies (4 Yrs)	RV21	4FT deg	G g	BBC	3M	X	28$	BBCCC$	Ind		
German and Scandinavian Studies (4 Yrs)	RR27	4FT deg	G g	BBC	3M	X	30$	BBCCC$	Ind	5	
Univ of WARWICK											
English & German Literature (4 Yrs inc yr abrd)	QR32	4FT deg	E+G g	BBC	X	X	32$	ABBBB		9	20/24
French Studies with German (4 Yrs inc yr abroad)	R1R2	4FT deg	F+G g	BBC	X	X	30$	ABBBB$		4	
French and German Studies (4 Yrs inc yr abroad)	RR12	4FT deg	F+G g	BBC	X	X	30$	ABBBB$			
German & Business Studies (4 Yrs inc yr abroad)	RN21	4FT deg	G g	BBB	X	X	32$	ABBBB$		6	22/30
German Studies (4 Yrs inc year abroad)	R200	4FT deg	G g	BCC	X	X	29$	ABBBB$		6	20/30
German Studies and Italian (4 Yrs inc year abrd)	RR23	4FT deg	G g	BCC	X	X	29$	ABBBB$			
German and Politics (4 Yrs inc yr abroad)	RM21	4FT deg	G g	BBC-BCC	X	X	29$	ABBBB$		8	
German with French (4 Yrs inc yr abroad)	R2R1	4FT deg	G+F g	BCC	X	X	29$	ABBBB$			
German with Int Studies (4 Yrs inc yr abroad)	R2M1	4FT deg	G g	BCC	X	X	28$	ABBBB$		7	20/26
German with Italian (4 Yrs inc year abroad)	R2R3	4FT deg	G g	BBC-BCC	X	X	29$	ABBBB$			
Italian with German (4 Yrs inc yr abroad)	R3R2	4FT deg	E+G g	BBC-BCC	X	X	29$	ABBBB$			
Univ of WESTMINSTER											
German and Arabic	RT26	4SW deg	G	CC	Ind		26$	BBB			
German and Chinese	T3R2	4SW deg	G	CC	Ind		26$	BBB	Ind	2	
German and English	QR32	4SW deg	E	CC	Ind		26$	BBB			
German and English Language	QRH2	4SW deg		CC	Ind		26$	BBB			
German and French	RR12	4SW deg	F	CC	Ind		26$	BBB		4	
Italian and German	RR23	4SW deg	G/I	CC	Ind		26$	BBB		7	
Linguistics and German	RQ21	4SW deg	L	CC	Ind		26$	BBB			
Russian and German	RR28	4SW deg	G/R	CC	Ind		26$	BBB		5	
Spanish and German	RR24	4SW deg	G/Sp	CC	Ind		26$	BBB		6	
Univ of WOLVERHAMPTON											
Combined Degrees *German Studies*	Y401	3FT/4SW deg	L g	12	4M $	M	24	BBBB	Ind		
Univ of YORK											
French and German (Language and Linguistics)	RR12	4FT deg	F+G	24	Ind	D$^	28$	BBCC$	Ind		20/28
German and Linguistics	RQ21	4FT deg	G	24	Ind	D$^	28$	BBCC$	Ind		

course details			98 expected requirements							96 entry stats
TITLE	CODE	COURSE	SUBJECTS	A/AS	ND/C	AGNVQ	IB	SQA(H)	SQA	RATIO A/AS
Univ of Wales, ABERYSTWYTH										
Computer Science with Italian	G5R3	4FT deg	L g	20	1M+5D$	M^ g	30$	BBBBC$	Ind	
European Studies and Italian	RT3F	4FT deg	L g	20	1M+5D$	M^ g	30$	BBBBC$	Ind	
Italian/Art	RW31	4FT deg	A/Ad+L g	18	1M+5D$	MA^ g	29$	BBBCC$	Ind	
Italian/Art History	RV34	4FT deg	L g	18	1M+5D$	MA^ g	29$	BBBCC$	Ind	
Italian/Drama	RW34	4FT deg	L g	20	1M+5D$	MQ^ g	30$	BBBBC$	Ind	
Italian/Economic & Social History	RV33	4FT deg	L g	18-20	1M+5D$	M^ g	30$	BBBBC$	Ind	
Italian/Education	RX39	4FT deg	L g	18	1M+5D$	M^ g	29$	BBBCC$	Ind	
Italian/English	QR33	4FT deg	El+L	20	1M+5D$	M^ g	30$	BBBBC$	Ind	
Italian/European Studies	RT32	4FT deg	L g	20	1M+5D$	M^ g	30$	BBBBC$	Ind	
Italian/Film and Television Studies	RW35	4FT deg	L g	20	1M+5D$	MQ^ g	30$	BBBBC$	Ind	
Italian/French	RR13	4FT deg	F g	18	1M+5D$	M^ g	29$	BBBCC$	Ind	
Italian/Geography	LR83	4FT deg	Gy+L g	20-22	1M+5D$	M^ g	31$	BBBBC$	Ind	
Italian/German	RR23	4FT deg	G g	18	1M+5D$	M^ g	29$	BBBCC$	Ind	
Italian/History	RV31	4FT deg	L g	18-20	1M+5D$	M^ g	30$	BBBBC$	Ind	
Italian/Information and Library Studies	PR23	4FT deg	L g	18	1M+5D$	M^ g	29$	BBBCC$	Ind	
Italian/International Politics	MRC3	4FT deg	L g	20	1M+5D$	M^ g	30$	BBBBC$	Ind	
Italian/Irish	QRM3	4FT deg	L g	18	1M+5D$	M^ g	29$	BBBCC$	Ind	
Law with Italian (BA)	M3RJ	4FT deg	L g	BBB	DO $	D^ g	32$	BBBCC$	Ind	
Law with Italian (LLB)	M3R3	4FT deg	L g	BBB	DO $	D^ g	32$	BBBCC$	Ind	
Politics/Italian	MR13	4FT deg	L g	20	1M+5D$	M^ g	30$	BBBBC$	Ind	
Pure Mathematics/Italian	GRC3	4FT deg	M+L g	18	1M+5D$	M^ g	29$	BBBCC$	Ind	
Spanish/Italian	RR34	4FT deg	L g	18	1M+5D$	M^ g	29$	BBBCC$	Ind	
Welsh History/Italian	RVHC	4FT deg	L g	18-20	1M+5D$	M^ g	30$	BBBBC$	Ind	
Welsh/Italian	QR53	4FT deg	W+L g	18	1M+5D$	M^ g	29$	BBBCC$	Ind	
ANGLIA Poly Univ										
Animal Behaviour and Italian	CR1H▼	4FT deg	g	12	4M	P go	Dip	BCCC	N	
Art History and Italian	RV34▼	4FT deg	* g	14	6M	M+/^ go	Dip	BBCC	Ind	4
Audiotechnology and Italian	HR6H▼	4FT deg	S g	16	8M	D+/^ go	Dip$	BBCC	N	1
Biology and Italian	CR13▼	4FT deg	B g	12	4M	P+/^ go	Dip$	BCCC	N	
Biomedical Science and Italian	BR93▼	4FT deg	B g	12	4M	M+/^ go	Dip$	BCCC	N	
Business and Italian	NR13▼	4FT deg	* g	12	4M	M go	Dip	BCCC	Ind	2
Chemistry and Italian	FR13▼	4FT deg	S g	12	4M	M go	Dip$	BCCC	Ind	
Communication Studies and Italian	PR33▼	4FT deg	Ap g	14	6M	M+/^ go	Dip$	BBCC	Ind	6
Computer Science and Italian	GR53▼	4FT deg	* g	12	4M	M go	Dip	BCCC	N	1
Ecology and Conservation and Italian	DR23▼	4FT deg	* g	12	4M	M+/^	Dip	BCCC	N	
Economics and Italian	LR13▼	4FT deg	* g	12	4M	M+/^ go	Dip	BCCC	Ind	
English Language Studies and Italian	QR13▼	3FT deg	* g	12	4M	M go	Dip	BCCC		
English and Italian	RQ33▼	4FT deg	E g	12	4M	M+/^	Dip$	BCCC	Ind	13
European Philosophy & Literature and Italian	RV37▼	4FT deg	* g	12	4M	M+/^ go	Dip	BCCC	Ind	
French and Italian	RR13▼	4FT deg	F/I	12	4M	M	Ind$	BCCC	Ind	4
Geography and Italian	LR83▼	4FT deg	Gy g	12	4M	M+/^ go	Dip$	BBCC	Ind	
Geology and Italian	FR63▼	4FT deg	* g	12	4M	M go	Dip	BCCC	Ind	
German and Italian	RR23▼	4FT deg	G/I	12	4M	M go	Dip$	BCCC	Ind	1
Graphic Arts and Italian	RW32▼	4FT deg	A g	14	6M	M+/^ go	Dip$	BBCC	Ind	
History and Italian	VR13▼	4FT deg	* g	12	4M	M go	Dip	BCCC	Ind	
Italian and Intercultural Studies	RL36▼	4FT deg	* g	12	4M	M go	Dip	BCCC		
Italian and Law	MR33▼	4FT deg	* g	14	6M	M go	Dip	BBCC	Ind	5
Italian and Maths or Stats/Stat Modelling	GR13▼	4FT deg	* g	12	4M	M+/^ go	Dip	BCCC	Ind	
Italian and Music	RW33▼	4FT deg	Mu g	12	4M	M+/^ go	Dip$	BCCC	Ind	
Italian and Ophthalmic Dispensing	BR53▼	4FT deg	* g	12	4M	M+/^ go	Dip$	BCCC	N	
Italian and Politics	RM31▼	4FT deg	* g	14	6M	M+/^ go	Dip	BBCC	Ind	1

				98 expected requirements						96 entry stats	

TITLE	CODE	COURSE	SUBJECTS	A/AS	ND/C	AGNVQ	IB	SQA(H)	SQA	RATIO	A/AS
Italian and Psychology	CR83▼	3FT deg	S g	16	8M	D go	Dip$	BBCCC	N	4	
Italian and Social Policy	RL34▼	4FT deg	* g	12	4M $	M+/^ go	Dip	BCCC	Ind		
Italian and Sociology	RL33▼	4FT deg	* g	12	4M	M+/^ go	Dip	BCCC	Ind		
Italian and Spanish	RR34▼	4FT deg	I/Sp	12	4M	M	Ind$	BCCC	Ind	18	
Italian and Women's Studies	RM39▼	4FT deg	* g	12	4M	M go	Dip	BCCC	Ind	1	

Univ of BATH

TITLE	CODE	COURSE	SUBJECTS	A/AS	ND/C	AGNVQ	IB	SQA(H)	SQA	RATIO	A/AS
French and Italian (4 Yr SW)	RR13	4SW deg	F+I	BBC	Ind	Ind	30	Ind	Ind	6	24/26
German and Italian (4 Yr SW)	RR23	4SW deg	G+I	BBD	Ind	Ind	30	Ind	Ind	7	

Univ of BIRMINGHAM

TITLE	CODE	COURSE	SUBJECTS	A/AS	ND/C	AGNVQ	IB	SQA(H)	SQA	RATIO	A/AS
Ancient History & Archaeology/Italian	RV36	4FT deg	*	BBB	Ind	D*^	32	ABBB	Ind		
Artificial Intelligence/Italian	GR83	4FT deg	* g	BBB	Ind	D*^	32	ABBB	Ind		
BCom (Business Administration) with Italian	NR13	4FT deg	L	BBC	Ind	D+^	32	ABBBB	Ind	16	
Business Studies/Italian	RN31	4FT deg	* g	BBB	Ind	D*^	32	ABBB	Ind	22	
Classical Literature and Civilisation/Italian	QR83	4FT deg	*	BBB	Ind	D*^	32	ABBB	Ind		
Computer Studies/Italian	GR53	4FT deg	* g	BBB	Ind	D*^	32	ABBB	Ind		
Dance/Italian	WR43	4FT deg	*	BBB	Ind	D*^	32	ABBB	Ind		
Drama/Italian	RW34	4FT deg	*	BBB	Ind	D*^	32	ABBB	Ind	3	
East Mediterranean History/Italian	RVJ1	4FT deg	* g	BBB	Ind	D*^	32	ABBB	Ind		
Economics with Italian	L1R3	4FT deg	*	BBC	Ind	D+^	32	ABBBB	Ind		
English/Italian	QR33	4FT deg	*	BBB	Ind	D*^	32	ABBB	Ind	15	
French Studies and Italian	RR13	4FT deg	F	BBB	Ind	D*_^	32$	ABBB	Ind	13	24/28
Geography/Italian	LR83	4FT deg	Gy	BBB	Ind	D*_^	32$	ABBB	Ind	3	
German Studies and Italian	RR23	4FT deg	G	BBB	Ind	D*_^	32$	ABBB	Ind	9	
History of Art/Italian	RV34	4FT deg	*	BBB	Ind	D*^	32	ABBB	Ind	28	
History/Italian	RV31	4FT deg	*	BBB	Ind	D*^	32	ABBB	Ind		
Italian Studies	R301	4FT deg	*	BBC/BCC	Ind	D*^	32	ABBB	Ind	3	18/26
Italian and Hispanic Studies	RR34	4FT deg	*	BBB	Ind	D*^	32	ABBB	Ind	11	
Italian and Modern Greek Studies	RTH2	4FT deg	* g	BBB	Ind	D*^	32	ABBB	Ind		
Italian and Portuguese	RR35	4FT deg	*	BBB	Ind	D*^	32	ABBB	Ind		
Italian and Russian	RR38	4FT deg	*	BBB	Ind	D*^	32	ABBB	Ind	2	
Italian/Latin	QR63	4FT deg	Ln	BBB	Ind	D*_^	32$	ABBB	Ind	4	
Italian/Mathematics	GR13	4FT deg	M	ABB-ABC	Ind	D*_^	32$	ABBB	Ind		
Italian/Media & Cultural Studies	PR43	4FT deg	*	BBB	Ind	D*^	32	ABBB	Ind		
Italian/Music	RW33	4FT deg	Mu	AAB-ABB	Ind	D*_^	32$	ABBB	Ind	2	
Italian/Philosophy	RV37	4FT deg	*	BBB	Ind	D*^	32	ABBB	Ind		
Italian/Political Science	MR13	4FT deg	*	BBB	Ind	D*^	32	ABBB	Ind		
Italian/Sport & Recreation Studies	RB36	4FT deg	*	BBB	Ind	D*^	32	ABBB	Ind		
Italian/Theology	RV38	4FT deg	*	BBB	Ind	D*^	32	ABBB	Ind		
Money, Banking and Finance with Italian	N3R3	4FT deg	L	BBB	Ind	D+^	33	ABBBB	Ind		

Univ of BRISTOL

TITLE	CODE	COURSE	SUBJECTS	A/AS	ND/C	AGNVQ	IB	SQA(H)	SQA	RATIO	A/AS
Computer Science and Italian	RG35	4FT deg	* g	BBC	Ind	D$^	30$	CSYS	Ind		
Drama and Italian	WR43	4FT deg		BC	Ind	D$^	28$	BBBBB	Ind		
French and Italian	RR13	4FT deg	F	ABB-BBB	Ind	D$^	30$	AABBB	Ind	7	24/30
German and Italian	RR23	4FT deg	G	BBB	Ind	D$^	30$	BBBBB	Ind	7	28/28
History of Art and Italian	VR43	4FT deg	L	BBC	Ind	D$^	30$	BBBBB	Ind	12	
Italian	R300	4FT deg	I/L	BCC	Ind	D$^	28$	BBBBB	Ind		
Italian and Russian	RR38	4FT deg	I/R	BBB-BBC	Ind	D$^	30$	AABBB	Ind		
Italian and Spanish	RR34	4FT deg	I/Sp	BBB	Ind	D$^	30$	AABBB	Ind	9	26/30
Music and Italian	WR33	4FT deg	Mu	BBC	Ind	D$^	30$	BBBBC	Ind		
Philosophy and Italian	RV37	4FT deg	I/L	BBC	Ind	D$^	30$	BBBBB	Ind		
Politics and Italian	RM31	4FT deg		BBB	Ind	D$^	32$	BBBBB	Ind	2	

Languages – Italian 42

			98 expected requirements							96 entry stats	
course details											
TITLE	CODE	COURSE	SUBJECTS	A/AS	ND/C	AGNVQ	IB	SQA(H)	SQA	RATIO	A/AS
BUCKINGHAMSHIRE COLLEGE											
Business Administration with Italian	N1R3	3FT deg	I g	8	MO+2D	M	27	CCCC	Ind	4	
Business Studies with Italian	N1RJ	4SW deg	I g	8	MO	M	27	CCCC	Ind		
European Business Studies (Italian)	NR13	4SW deg	I g	8	MO	M	27	CCCC	Ind		
Human Resources Management with Italian	N6R3	3FT deg		8	MO	M	27	CCCC	Ind		
International Business Studies (Italian)	N1RH	4SW deg	L	8	MO	M	27	CCCC	Ind		
International Marketing with Italian	N5R3	3FT deg	I g	8	MO	M	27	CCCC	Ind		
Leisure Management with Italian	N7R3	3FT deg		8-10	1D	M	27	CCCC	Ind		
Tourism with Italian	P7R3	3FT deg		8-10	1D	M	27	CCCC	Ind		
Travel and Tourism Management with Italian	PR73	3FT deg	I	8-10	1D	M	27	CCCC	Ind		
Business Studies with Italian	31RN	2FT HND		4	3M	P	Ind	Ind	Ind		
CARDIFF Univ of Wales											
Accounting with Italian	N4R3	4FT deg	L g	BBC-BBB	Ind	Ind	Ind	Ind	Ind		
Banking and Finance with Italian	N3R3	4FT deg	L	BBC-BBB	Ind	Ind	Ind	ABBBB	Ind		
Business Administration with Italian	N1R3	4FT deg	L g	BBC-BBB	Ind	Ind	Ind	Ind	Ind	6	
Business Economics with Italian	L1RH	4FT deg	L	BBC-BBB	Ind	Ind	Ind	Ind	Ind		
Economics with Italian	L1R3	4FT deg	L	BBC-BBB	Ind	Ind	Ind	Ind	Ind		
Italian	R300	4FT deg	L	BCC	Ind		Ind	Ind	Ind	3	
Italian/Ancient History	RV3C	4FT deg	L	BCC	X		Ind	Ind	X		
Italian/Archaeology	RV36	4FT deg	L	BCC	Ind		Ind	Ind	Ind		
Italian/Cultural Criticism	MR93	4FT deg	E	ABC	Ind	Ind	Ind	Ind	Ind		
Italian/Economics	RL31	4FT deg	L	BBC-BBB	X		Ind	AAAAB	X		
Italian/Education	RX39	4FT deg	L	BCC	Ind	Ind	Ind	Ind	Ind		
Italian/English Literature	RQ33	4FT deg	E+L	ABB	Ind		Ind	AAAAB	Ind		
Italian/French	RR31	4FT deg	F	BBC	Ind		Ind	ABBBB	Ind	8	22/26
Italian/German	RR32	4FT deg	G	BBC-BCC	Ind		Ind	ABBBB	Ind	9	
Italian/History	RV31	4FT deg	H+L	BBC-BCC	X		Ind	ABBBB	X	5	
Italian/History of Ideas	RV3D	4FT deg	L	BCC	X		Ind	ABBBB	X		
Japanese/Italian	TR43	4FT deg	L	BCC	X		Ind	ABBBB	X		
Language Studies/Italian	QR13	4FT deg	L	BBC	Ind		Ind	ABBBB			
Law and Italian	RM33	4FT deg	L	BBB	Ind	Ind	Ind	Ind	Ind	3	21/28
Music/Italian	WR33	4FT deg	L+Mu	BBC	X		Ind	ABBBB	X	1	
Philosophy/Italian	VR73	4FT deg	L	BBC	Ind		Ind	ABBBB	Ind		
Politics/Italian	MR13	4FT deg	L	BCC	X		Ind	Ind	X		
Portuguese/Italian	RR35	4FT deg	I/Pt	BBC-BCC	Ind		Ind	Ind	Ind	1	
Religious Studies/Italian	VR83	4FT deg	L	BCC	Ind		Ind	Ind	Ind		
Sociology/Italian	LR33	4FT deg	L	BCC	Ind		Ind	Ind	Ind	3	
Spanish/Italian	RR34	4FT deg	Sp/I	BCC	Ind		Ind	ABBBB	Ind	4	22/28
Welsh/Italian	QR53	4FT deg	L+W	BCC	Ind		Ind	Ind	Ind		
Univ of CENTRAL LANCASHIRE											
Combined Honours Programme *Italian*	Y400	3FT deg	L/* g	8	Ind	M*^	24$	BCCC	Ind		
COVENTRY Univ											
Business Studies with Italian	N1R3	4SW deg	* g	16	M+3D	M	Dip	CCC	Ind		
European Studies with Italian (4 years)	TR23	4FT deg	*		CD	M	M	Ind	CCCC	Ind		
French and Italian	RR13	4FT deg	F		CD	M	M	Ind	CCCC$	Ind	4	6/20
German and Italian	RR23	4FT deg	G+I		CD	M	M	Ind	CCCC$	Ind		
Italian and History	VR13	4FT deg	*		CD	M	M	Ind	CCCC	Ind		
Italian and Russian	RR38	4FT deg	I		CD	M	M	Ind	CCCC	Ind		
Psychology and Italian	RC38	4FT deg	*		CD	M	M	Ind	CCCC	Ind		
Social Policy and Italian	RL34	3FT deg									

course details			98 expected requirements							96 entry stats	
TITLE	CODE	COURSE	SUBJECTS	A/AS	ND/C	AGNVQ	IB	SQA(H)	SQA	RATIO	A/AS
Sociology and Italian	RL33	3FT deg									
Spanish and Italian	RR43	4FT deg	Sp+I	CD	M	M	Ind	CCCC$	Ind	5	10/14

Univ of DURHAM

Arts Combined	Y300	4FT deg	*	24	MO	Ind	30	AAABB	Ind		
Italian											

Univ of EAST ANGLIA

History of Art and European Literature (3 Yrs)	VR43	3FT deg	L	BCC	X		30	BBBBB	X	3	12/24

Univ of EAST LONDON

Anthropology with Italian	LR63	3FT deg	* g	12	MO	M^	Ind	Ind	Ind
Business Studies with Italian	N1R3	3FT deg	* g	14	MO	MB			
Communication Studies with Italian	P3R3	3FT deg	* g	12	MO	M	Ind	Ind	
Design - Textile Design with Italian	J4R3	3FT deg	* g	12	MO	M	Ind	Ind	Ind
Design - Visual Communication with Italian	W2R3	3FT deg	* g	12	MO	M	Ind	Ind	Ind
Economics with Italian	L1R3	3FT deg	* g	12	MO	M	Ind		
Education & Community Studies with Italian	X9R3	3FT deg	* g	12	MO	M			
European Studies with Italian	T2R3	3FT deg	* g	12	MO	M			
French with Italian	R1R3	3FT deg	* g	12	MO	M	Ind		
German with Italian	R2R3	3FT deg	* g	12	MO	M	Ind		
Health Studies with Italian	B9R3	3FT deg	* g	12	MO	M	Ind	Ind	Ind
History of Art Design & Film with Italian	V4R3	3FT deg	* g	12	MO	M	Ind	Ind	
Information Technology with Italian	G5R3	3FT deg	* g	12	MO	M	Ind	Ind	Ind
Law with Italian	M3R3	3FT deg	* g	14	MO	M			
Linguistics with Italian	Q1R3	3FT deg	* g	12	MO	M			
Literature with Italian	Q3R3	3FT deg	* g	12	MO	M	Ind		
Maths, Stats & Computing with Italian	G9R3	3FT deg	* g	12	MO	M	Ind	Ind	Ind
Media Studies with Italian	P4R3	3FT deg	* g	14	MO	M			
Politics with Italian	M1R3	3FT deg	* g	12	MO	M	Ind		
Psychosocial Studies with Italian	L7R3	3FT deg	* g	12	MO	M	Ind	Ind	Ind
Social Policy Research with Italian	L4R3	3FT deg	* g	12	MO	M	Ind	Ind	Ind
Sociology with Italian	L3R3	3FT deg	* g	12	MO	M	Ind	Ind	Ind
Spanish with Italian	R4R3	3FT deg	* g	12	MO	M	Ind		
Third World & Development Studies with Italian	M9R3	3FT deg	* g	12	MO	M	Ind	Ind	
Women's Studies with Italian	M9RH	3FT deg	* g	12	MO	M	Ind		
Three-Subject Degree	Y600	4FT deg	* g	12	MO	M	Ind	Ind	Ind
Italian									

Univ of EDINBURGH

History of Art and Italian	VR43	4FT deg	L g	BBB	Ind	Ind	Dip$	BBBBB$	Ind
Italian	R300	4FT deg	L g	BBB	Ind	Ind	Dip$	BBBBB$	Ind
Italian and Business Studies	RN31	4FT deg	L g	BBB	Ind		Dip$	BBBBB$	Ind
Italian and English Language	RQ33	4FT deg	L g	BBB	Ind	Ind	Dip$	BBBBB$	Ind
Italian and English Literature	RQ3H	4FT deg	L g	BBB	Ind	Ind	Dip$	BBBBB$	Ind
Italian and European History	RV31	4FT deg	L g	BBB	Ind	Ind	Dip$	BBBBB$	Ind
Italian and Greek	RQ37	4FT deg	L g	BBB	Ind	Ind	Dip$	BBBBB$	Ind
Italian and History of Art	RV34	4FT deg	L g	BBB	Ind	Ind	Dip$	BBBBB$	Ind
Italian and Latin	RQ36	4FT deg	L g	BBB	Ind	Ind	Dip$	BBBBB$	Ind
Italian and Linguistics	RQ31	4FT deg	L g	BBB	Ind	Ind	Dip$	BBBBB$	Ind

EUROPEAN Business School

Euro Bus Admin with Italian + one beginner lang	N1RH	4SW deg	L	12	Ind		Ind	Ind	Ind
International Bus St: Italian +one beginner lang	NR13	4FT deg							
International Bus Studs with Italian (Test+Int)	N1R3	4SW deg		12	Ind		Ind	Ind	Ind
International Business & Mgt Studs with Italian	N1RJ	4SW deg		12	Ind		Ind	Ind	Ind

Languages – Italian 42

			98 expected requirements							96 entry stats

TITLE	CODE	COURSE	SUBJECTS	A/AS	NO/C	AGNVQ	IB	SQA(H)	SQA	RATIO A/AS
Univ of EXETER										
American & Postcolonial Studies and Italian	QR4H	3FT deg	L g	BBB-BCC		D$	34			
French and Italian	RR1H	4FT deg	F	22-24	MO	M/D$^	'34$			
German and Italian	RR2H	4FT deg	G	BBB-BCC	MO	M/D$^	32$			
Greek & Roman Studies and Italian	QR83	4FT deg	L g	BCC	MO	M/D$	32	Ind	Ind	7
History and Italian	RV3C	4FT deg	L g	ABB-BCC	MO	M/D$	32	Ind	Ind	
Italian	R301	4FT deg	L g	20-22	MO	M$	32			
Italian and Fine Art	RW31	4FT deg	L+Pf g	20-22	MO	M$	32$	Ind	Ind	5
Italian and Politics	MR13	4FT deg	L g	20-22	MO	M$	32	Ind	Ind	
Italian and Spanish (Beginners Spanish avail)	RR3K	4FT deg	L/Sp g	20-22	MO	M$	32$			
Music and Italian	RW3H	4FT deg	L+Mu g	BCC	MO	MD$^	32$	Ind	Ind	
Univ of GLAMORGAN										
French with Italian	R1R3	3FT deg			Ind	Ind	Ind	Ind	Ind	
Major/Minor Honours *Italian*	Y402	3FT deg	* g	8-16	Ind	Ind	Ind	Ind	Ind	
Univ of GLASGOW										
Anthropology with Italian	LR63	4FT deg		BBC	N	M	30	BBBB	Ind	
Archaeology/Italian	RV36	5FT deg		BBC	HN	M	30	BBBB	Ind	
Business Economics with Italian	L1RH	4FT deg		BBC	N	M	30	BBBB	N	
Celtic Civilisation/Italian	QR53	5FT deg		BBC	HN	M	30	BBBB	Ind	
Classical Civilisation/Italian	QR83	5FT deg		BBC	HN	M	30	BBBB	Ind	2
Czech/Italian	RTJ1	5FT deg		BBC	HN	M	30	BBBB	Ind	
Economic and Social History with Italian	V3R3	4FT deg		BBC	8M	M	30	BBBB	Ind	
Economic and Social History/Italian	RV33	5FT deg		BBC	HN	M	30	BBBB	Ind	
Economics with Italian	L1R3	4FT deg		BBC	8M	M	30	BBBB	Ind	
English/Italian	QR33	5FT deg		BBC	HN	M	30	BBBB	Ind	15
Film and Television Studies/Italian	RW35	5FT deg		BBB	HN	D	32	AABB	HN	15
French/Italian	RR13	5FT deg		BBC	HN	M	30	BBBB	Ind	4
Geography with Italian	L8R3	5FT deg		BBC	HN	8M	30	BBBB	Ind	
Geography/Italian	LR83	5FT deg		BBC	HN	M	30	BBBB	Ind	
German/Italian	RR23	5FT deg		BBC	HN	M	30	BBBB	Ind	7
Greek/Italian	QR73	5FT deg		BBC	HN	M	30	BBBB	Ind	
Hispanic Studies/Italian	RR34	5FT deg		BBC	HN	M	30	BBBB	Ind	10
History of Art/Italian	RV34	5FT deg		BBC	HN	M	30	BBBB	Ind	14
History/Italian	RV31	5FT deg		BBC	HN	M	30	BBBB	Ind	
Italian Language and Literature	R300	5FT deg		BBC	HN	M	30	BBBB	Ind	
Italian/Latin	QR63	5FT deg		BBC	HN	M	30	BBBB	Ind	
Italian/Mathematics	GR13	5FT deg		BBC	HN	M	30	BBBB	Ind	
Italian/Music	RW33	5FT deg		BBC	HN	M	30	BBBB	Ind	
Italian/Philosophy	RV37	5FT deg		BBC	HN	M	30	BBBB	Ind	
Italian/Polish	RTH1	5FT deg		BBC	HN	M	30	BBBB	Ind	
Italian/Politics	MR13	5FT deg		BBC	HN	M	30	BBBB	Ind	
Italian/Psychology	CR83	5FT deg		BBC	HN	M	30	BBBB	Ind	4
Italian/Russian	RR38	5FT deg		BBC	HN	M	30	BBBB	Ind	
Italian/Scottish History	RV3C	5FT deg		BBC	HN	M	30	BBBB	Ind	
Italian/Scottish Literature	QR23	5FT deg		BBC	HN	M	30	BBBB	Ind	1
Italian/Sociology	LR33	5FT deg		BBC	HN	M	30	BBBB	Ind	
Management Studies with Italian	N1R3	4FT deg		BBC	8M	M	30	BBBB	Ind	
Management Studies/Italian	NR13	5FT deg		BBC	HN	M	30	BBBB	Ind	
Philosophy with Italian	V7R3	4FT deg		BBC	8M	M	30	BBBB	Ind	
Politics with Italian	M1R3	4FT deg		BBC	8M	M	30	BBBB	Ind	

| | | | | 98 expected requirements | | | | | | 96 entry stats | |

TITLE	CODE	COURSE	SUBJECTS	A/AS	NQ/C	AGNVQ	IB	SQA(H)	SQA	RATIO A/AS	
Psychology with Italian	C8R3	4FT deg		BBC	8M	M	30	BBBB	Ind		
Social and Urban Policy with Italian	L4R3	4FT deg		BBC	8M	M	30	BBBB	Ind		
Sociology with Italian	L3R3	4FT deg		BBC	8M	M	30	BBBB	Ind		
Theatre Studies/Italian	RW34	5FT deg		BBC	HN	M	30	BBBB	Ind		

Univ of HULL

Business Studies/Italian	NR13	4FT deg	L g	BBC-BCC	Ind $	D*^ go	26$	BBCCC	Ind	5	20/22
Drama/Italian	RW34	4FT deg	L	BBB-BCC	Ind	D$^ go	28$	ABBCC	Ind		
English/Italian	QR33	4FT deg	E+L	BBB-BCC	Ind	M$^ gi	28$	BBBCC	Ind	3	
French/Italian	RR13	4FT deg	F	BCC	Ind	Ind	28$	BBBCC	Ind	9	16/30
Gender Studies and Italian	MR93	4FT deg	L	BCC-CCC	Ind	M$6/^ go	28$	BBBCC	Ind		
German/Italian	RR23	4FT deg	G	BCC	Ind	Ind	28$	BBBCC	Ind	9	
History/Italian	RV31	4FT deg	H+L	BBB-BCC	Ind	M$^ go	28$	BBBCC	Ind		
Italian	R300	4FT deg	L	CCC	Ind	Ind	28$	BBBCC	Ind	2	8/18

Univ of KENT

European Studies (Italian)	R311	4FT deg	*	20	3M+3D	Ind	28	Ind	Ind	7	
Italian/Classical Studies	QR83	4FT deg	*	20	3M+3D	Ind	28	Ind	Ind	3	
Italian/Comparative Literary Studies	QRF3	4FT deg	*	20	3M+3D	Ind	28	Ind	Ind		
Italian/Computing	RG35	4FT deg	*	20	3M+3D	Ind	28	Ind	Ind	1	
Italian/Drama	RW34	4FT deg	*	22	2M+4D	Ind	30	Ind	Ind	8	
Italian/English	QR33	4FT deg	E	22	2M+4D	Ind	30	Ind	Ind	15	
Italian/English (Post-Colonial Literatures)	QR3J	4FT deg	E	22	2M+4D	Ind	30	Ind	Ind		
Italian/English Language	RQ33	4FT deg	E	20	3M+3D	Ind	28	Ind	Ind	8	
Italian/Film Studies	RW35	4FT deg	*	22	2M+4D	Ind	30	Ind	Ind		
Italian/French	RR13	4FT deg	F	22	2M+4D	Ind	30	Ind	Ind	11	20/24
Italian/German	RR23	4FT deg	G	20	3M+3D	Ind	28	Ind	Ind		
Italian/History	RV31	4FT deg	*	22	2M+4D	Ind	30	Ind	Ind		
Italian/History and Theory of Art	VR43	4FT deg	*	22	2M+4D	Ind	30	Ind	Ind	6	
Italian/History of Science	RV35	4FT deg	*	20	3M+3D	Ind	28	Ind	Ind		
Linguistics/Italian	RQ31	4FT deg	*	20	3M+3D	Ind	28	Ind	Ind		
Philosophy/Italian	RV37	4FT deg	*	20	3M+3D	Ind	28	Ind	Ind		
Politics and Government with Italian (4 Yrs)	M1R3	4FT deg	* g	18	4M+2D	Ind	26	BBBB	Ind		
Spanish/Italian	RR43	4FT deg	*	20	3M+3D	Ind	28	Ind	Ind		
Theology/Italian	RV38	4FT deg	*	20	3M+3D	Ind	28	Ind	Ind	1	

LANCASTER Univ

Chemistry with Italian Studies (4 years)	F1R3	4SW deg	C+I/L g	18	MO $		28$	BBBB$	Ind		
European Management (Italian)	N1R3	4FT/5SW deg	I/L g	ABB	MO+5D		32$	AABBB$	Ind		
French Studies and Italian Studies	RR13	4SW deg	(F+I)/* g	BCC	Ind $		30$	BBBBB$	Ind		
German Studies and Italian Studies	RR23	4SW deg	G/I g	BCC	Ind $		30$	BBBBB$	Ind		
Italian Studies and Accounting and Finance	NR43	4SW deg	M+I/L g	BBC	DO $		32$	AABBB$	Ind		
Italian Studies and Art History	WR13	4SW deg	I/L	BCC	MO $		30$	BBBBB$	Ind		
Italian Studies and Computing	GR53	4FT deg	I/L g	BCC	Ind $		30$	BBBBB$	Ind		
Italian Studies and Economics	RL31	4SW deg	I/L g	BBC	MO+4D		32$	ABBBB$	Ind		
Italian Studies and Educational Studies	RX39	4SW deg	I/L	BCC	MO $		30$	BBBBB$	Ind		
Italian Studies and English	RQ33	4SW deg	I/L+E	BBC	DO $		32$	ABBBB$	Ind		
Italian Studies and Geography	LR83	4SW deg	I/L+Gy g	BBC	Ind $		30$	BBBBB$	Ind		
Italian Studies and History	RV31	4SW deg	I/L+H	BCC	Ind $		30$	BBBBB$	Ind		
Italian Studies and Linguistics	QR13	4SW deg	I/L g	BBC	MO $		30$	BBBBB$	Ind		
Italian Studies and Marketing	RN35	4SW deg	I/L g	BBC	MO+4D		32$	ABBBB$	Ind		
Italian Studies and Mathematics	GR13	4SW deg	I/L+M	20	MO $		30$	BBBBB$	Ind		
Italian Studies and Music	WR33	4SW deg	I/L+Mu	BCC	Ind $		30$	BBBBB$	Ind		
Italian Studies and Philosophy	RV37	4SW deg	I/L	BCC	Ind $		30$	BBBBB$	Ind		

Languages – Italian 42

TITLE	CODE	COURSE	SUBJECTS	A/AS	NO/C	AGNVQ	IB	SQA(H)	SQA	RATIO A/AS
course details			**98 expected requirements**							**96 entry stats**
Italian Studies and Politics	RM31	4SW deg	I/L	BCC	Ind $		30$	BBBBB$	Ind	
Italian Studies and Psychology	CR83	4SW deg	I/L g	BBC	DO $		32$	ABBBB$	Ind	
Italian Studies and Religious Studies	RV38	4SW deg	I/L	BCC	Ind $		30$	BBBBB$	Ind	
Italian Studies and Spanish Studies	RR34	4SW deg	I/Sp/L	BCC	Ind $		30$	BBBBB$	Ind	
Italian Studies and Theatre Studies	WR43	4SW deg	I/L	BCC	MO $		30$	BBBBB$	Ind	
Physics with Italian Studies	F3R3	4SW deg	P+M+I/L	BCC	MO $		24$	BBCCC$	Ind	

Univ of LEEDS

TITLE	CODE	COURSE	SUBJECTS	A/AS	NO/C	AGNVQ	IB	SQA(H)	SQA	RATIO A/AS
Arabic-Italian	RT36	4FT deg	I g	BCC	Ind	Ind	28$	CSYS	Ind	
Chinese-Italian	RT33	4FT deg	I g	BBC	Ind	Ind	Ind	Ind	Ind	
Chinese-Italian B	RTH3	4FT deg	L g	BBC	Ind	Ind	Ind	Ind	Ind	
Classical Literature-Italian	QR83	4FT deg	I g	BBC	Ind	Ind	Ind	Ind	Ind	
Classical Literature-Italian B	QR8H	4FT deg	L g	BBC	Ind	Ind	Ind	Ind	Ind	
Economics and Italian B	LR1H	4FT deg	L g	BBC						
Economics-Italian	LR13	4FT deg	I g	BBC	Ind	Ind	Ind	Ind	Ind	
English-Italian	QR33	4FT deg	E+I g	BBC	Ind	Ind	30$	CSYS	Ind	
English-Italian B	QR3H	4FT deg	E+L g	BBC	Ind	Ind	30$	CSYS	Ind	5 24/30
French-Italian	RR13	4FT deg	F+I g	BBC	Ind	Ind	30$	CSYS	Ind	7 24/30
French-Italian B	RR1H	4FT deg	F g	BBC	Ind	Ind	30$	CSYS	Ind	6 20/30
Geography-Italian	LR83	4FT deg	Gy+I g	BBC	Ind	Ind	Ind	Ind	Ind	
Geography-Italian B	LR8H	4FT deg	Gy+L g	BBC	Ind	Ind	Ind	Ind	Ind	
German-Italian	RR23	4FT deg	G+I g	BBC	Ind	Ind	30$	CSYS	Ind	4
German-Italian	RR2H	4FT deg	G g	BBC	Ind	Ind	30$	CSYS	Ind	7
History and Philosophy of Science-Italian	RV35	4FT deg	I g	BBC	Ind	Ind	Ind	Ind	Ind	
History and Philosophy of Science-Italian B	RVH5	4FT deg	L g	BBC	Ind	Ind	Ind	Ind	Ind	
History of Art-Italian	RV34	4FT deg	I g	BBC	Ind	Ind	30$	CSYS	Ind	10
History of Art-Italian	RVH4	4FT deg	L g	BBC	Ind	Ind	30$	CSYS	Ind	13
History-Italian	RV31	4FT deg	I g	BBC	Ind	Ind	30$	CSYS	Ind	
History-Italian	RVH1	4FT deg	L g	BBC	Ind	Ind	30	CSYS	Ind	
Italian	R300	4FT deg	I g	BCC	Ind	Ind	28$	CSYS	Ind	4
Italian B	R305	4FT deg	L g	BCC	Ind	Ind	28$	CSYS	Ind	2 16/22
Italian-Japanese	RT34	4FT deg	I g	BBC	Ind	Ind	Ind	Ind	Ind	
Italian-Japanese B	RTH4	4FT deg	L g	BBC	Ind	Ind	Ind	Ind	Ind	
Italian-Latin	QR63	4FT deg	Ln+I g	BBC	Ind	Ind	30$	CSYS	Ind	
Italian-Latin B	QR6H	4FT deg	Ln g	BBC	Ind	Ind	30$	CSYS	Ind	
Italian-Linguistics	QR13	4FT deg	I g	BCC	Ind	Ind	28$	CSYS	Ind	
Italian-Linguistics B	QR1H	4FT deg	L g	BCC	Ind	Ind	28$	CSYS	Ind	7
Italian-Management Studies	RN31	4FT deg	I g	BBC	Ind	Ind	30$	CSYS	Ind	15
Italian-Management Studies B	RNH1	4FT deg	L g	BBC	Ind	Ind	30$	CSYS	Ind	
Italian-Music	RW33	4FT deg	Mu+I g	BBC	Ind	Ind	30$	CSYS	Ind	
Italian-Music B	RWH3	4FT deg	Mu+L g	BBC	Ind	Ind	30$	CSYS	Ind	4
Italian-Philosophy	RV37	4FT deg	I g	BBC	Ind	Ind	Ind	Ind	Ind	
Italian-Philosophy B	RVH7	4FT deg	L g	BBC	Ind	Ind	Ind	Ind	Ind	
Italian-Politics A	MR13	4FT deg	I g	BBC	Ind	Ind	Ind	Ind	Ind	
Italian-Politics B	MR1H	4FT deg	L g	BBC	Ind	Ind	Ind	Ind	Ind	
Italian-Portuguese	RR35	4FT deg	I g	BCC	Ind	Ind	Ind	Ind	Ind	
Italian-Portuguese B	RRH5	4FT deg	L g	BCC	Ind	Ind	Ind	Ind	Ind	
Italian-Religious Studies	RV38	4FT deg	I g	BBC	Ind	Ind	Ind	Ind	Ind	
Italian-Religious Studies B	RVH8	4FT deg	L g	BBC	Ind	Ind	Ind	Ind	Ind	
Italian-Roman Civilisation	QRV3	4FT deg	I g	BBC	Ind	Ind	30$	CSYS	Ind	
Italian-Roman Civilisation B	QRVH	4FT deg	L g	BBC	Ind	Ind	30$	CSYS	Ind	
Italian-Russian	RR38	4FT deg	I+R g	BCC	Ind	Ind	28$	CSYS	Ind	
Italian-Russian B	RRHV	4FT deg	I/R g	BCC	Ind	Ind	28$	CSYS	Ind	

Letts STUDY GUIDES
THE INDEPENDENT

course details			98 expected requirements							96 entry stats	
TITLE	CODE	COURSE	SUBJECTS	A/AS	NO/C	AGNVQ	IB	SQA(H)	SQA	RATIO	A/AS
Italian-Spanish	RR34	4FT deg	Sp+I g	BCC	Ind	Ind	28$	CSYS	Ind	5	
Italian-Spanish B	RRH4	4FT deg	Sp g	BCC	Ind	Ind	28$	CSYS	Ind	4	18/28
Italian-Theology	RV3V	4FT deg	I g	BBC	Ind	Ind	Ind	Ind	Ind		
Italian-Theology B	RVHV	4FT deg	L g	BBC	Ind	Ind	Ind	Ind	Ind		

LEEDS METROPOLITAN Univ

Public Relations (Italian)	P3R3	3FT deg									

Univ of LEICESTER

French and Italian	RR13	4FT deg	F g	BCD	X	D$^	28$	BBBB$	X		16/22
German and Italian	RR23	4FT deg	G g	BCD	X	D$^	Ind	BBBB$	X		
Combined Arts Italian	Y300	3FT deg	L g	BCC	DO $	D$^ gi	30$	Ind	Ind		

LIVERPOOL JOHN MOORES Univ

French and Italian	RR13	4FT deg	L	14	3M+4D					17	
German and Italian	RR23	4FT deg	L	14	3M+4D					6	
International Business Studies with Italian	N1R3	4SW deg		16	3M+4D					5	10/14

LUTON Univ

Business Systems with Italian	N1RH	3FT deg	I g	12-16	MO/DO	M/D	32	BBCC	Ind		
Business with Italian	N1R3	3FT deg	I g	12-16	MO/DO	M/D	32	BBCC	Ind		
Geography with Italian	F8R3	3FT deg	I g	12-16	MO/DO	M/D	32	BBCC	Ind		
Linguistics with Italian	Q1R3	3FT deg	I g	12-16	MO/DO	M/D	32	BBCC	Ind		
Marketing with Italian	N5R3	3FT deg	I g	12-16	MO/DO	M/D	32	BBCC	Ind		
Mathematical Sciences with Italian	G1R3	3FT deg	I g	12-16	MO/DO	M/D	32	BBCC	Ind		
Regional Planning & Development with Italian	K4R3	3FT deg	I g	12-16	MO/DO	M/D	32	BBCC	Ind		
Travel and Tourism with Italian	P7R3	3FT deg	I g	12-16	MO/DO	M/D	32	BBCC	Ind		

Univ of MANCHESTER

English and a Modern Language (Italian)	RQ33	4FT deg	E	ABB			Ind	BBBBC		4	24/28
European Studies and Modern Langs (Italian)	RT32	4FT deg	L	ABB-BBB	Ind	D^	28$	AAABB$	Ind	9	
French/Italian	RR1H	4FT deg	F	ABB		D^	30$	AABB$		5	
French/Italian	RR13	4FT deg	F	ABB		D^	30$	AABB$		6	18/28
German/Italian	RR2H	4FT deg	G	BBB			28	BBBBC			
German/Italian	RR23	4FT deg	G	BBB			28	BBBBC		4	22/30
History and Italian	RV31	4FT deg	L	CCC			Ind	BBBCC		14	
History of Art and a Modern Language (Italian)	RV34	4FT deg		BBC	3M+3D		28	AABBB		7	
Italian Studies	R310	4FT deg	L	BBB-BCC			Ind	AAABB		3	16/26
Italian and Linguistics	RQ31	4FT deg	L	BBB	X		32$	AABBB			
Italian/French	RR3C	4FT deg	F	BBB-BCC			Ind	BBBCC		3	
Italian/German	RR3G	4FT deg	G	BBB-BCC			Ind	BBBCC		2	
Italian/Portuguese	RR35	4FT deg	I/Pt	BBB-BCC			Ind	BBBCC			
Italian/Russian	RR3W	4FT deg	I/R	BBB-BCC			Ind	BBBCC			
Italian/Russian	RR38	4FT deg	I/R	BBB-BCC			Ind	BBBCC			
Italian/Spanish	RR34	4FT deg	Sp	BBB-BCC			Ind	BBBCC		8	
Italian/Spanish	RR3L	4FT deg	I/Sp	BBB-BCC			Ind	BBBCC			
Latin and Italian	QR63	4FT deg	Ln	BBC	X	X	30	BBBBB	X	2	
Russian/Italian	RR8H	4FT deg	R	CCC-BBC	Ind		26$	BBBCC	Ind		
Spanish/Italian	RR4H	4FT deg	Sp	BBB-BBC			28$	ABBBB$			

MANCHESTER METROPOLITAN Univ

Business in Europe-Italian Route	N1R3	4FT deg	* g	BBC	Ind	DB	24$	Ind	Ind		14/20

MIDDLESEX Univ

Joint Honours Degree Italian	Y400	3FT deg	* g	12-16	5M	M* go	28	Ind	Ind		

course details			98 expected requirements							96 entry stats	
TITLE	CODE	COURSE	SUBJECTS	A/AS	NO/C	RGNVQ	IB	SQA(H)	SQA	RATIO	A/AS
NENE COLLEGE											
European Business (Italian)	NR13	4SW deg	I g	8	M+D	M	24	CCC	Ind		
Univ of NOTTINGHAM											
Manufacturing Engineering & Management with Ital	H7R3	4FT deg									
Production and Operations Management with Ital	H7RH	3FT deg									
NOTTINGHAM TRENT Univ											
European Economics with Italian	L1R3	4FT deg	I g	14-16	1M+3D	Ind	Ind	BBCC	Ind		
OXFORD BROOKES Univ											
Languages for Business:English/Italian Ab Initio	NR13	4FT deg	E	BC-CDD	Ind	M*^	Ind	Ind	Ind		
Languages for Business:French/Italian-Ab Initio	NR1H	4FT deg	F	BC-CDD	Ind	M*^	Ind	Ind	Ind	5	14/22
Languages for Business:German/Italian-Ab Initio	NR1J	4FT deg	G	BC-CDD	Ind	M*^	Ind	Ind	Ind	2	
Languages for Business:Spanish/Italian-Ab Initio	NRC3	4FT deg	Sp	BC-CDD	Ind	M*^	Ind	Ind	Ind	5	
Univ of PLYMOUTH											
Applied Economics with Italian	L1R3	3FT deg	* g	CDD-CCD	MO	M$^	Ind	BCCC	Ind		
Business Economics with Italian	L1RH	3FT deg	* g	CDD-CCD	MO	M$^	Ind	BCCC	Ind		
Chemistry with Italian	F1R3	3FT deg	C g	CC	3M	MS^	Ind	CCCC	Ind		
Design and Italian	WR23	3FT deg	Fa+Ap g	Ind	MO	MA go	Ind	Ind	Ind		
Design and Italian	ER23	3FT deg	Fa+Ap g	Ind	MO	MA go	Ind	Ind	Ind		
European Economics with Italian	L1RJ	3FT deg	* g	CDD-CCD	MO	M$^	Ind	BCCC	Ind		
European Studies with Italian	T2R3	4FT deg	I g	18	Ind	Ind	Ind	Ind	Ind		
Geography with Italian	F8R3	3FT deg	Gy g	16-18	X	M$^	Ind	ABBB	Ind		
Geology with Italian	F6R3	3FT deg	S g	12	4M	MS	Ind	CCC	Ind		
International Business with Italian	N1R3	4SW deg	I g	CCD-CCC	MO	M12^	Ind	BBCC	Ind		
Law with Italian	M3R3	3FT deg	Ap g	BCC-BBC	DO	D12^	Ind	BBBB$	Ind		
Political Economy with Italian	LR1H	3FT deg	Ap g	CDD-CCD	MO $	M$^	Ind	BCCC	Ind		
Politics with Italian	M1R3	3FT deg	* g	14	3M $	M$	Ind	BBBC$	Ind		
Psychology with Italian	C8R3	3FT/4SW deg	Ap g	BBC	MO+3D	M12^	Ind	BBBC$	Ind		
Social Policy with Italian	L4R3	3FT deg	* g	14	3M $	M$	Ind	BBBC$	Ind		
Sociology with Italian	L3R3	3FT deg	* g	14	3M $	M$	Ind	BBBC$	Ind		
Univ of PORTSMOUTH											
French and Italian Studies	RR13	4FT deg	F	14	5M $	M$6/^	25	BBBC	Ind	6	8/18
German and Italian	RR23	4FT deg	G	12	5M $	M$6/^	25$	BBCC	Ind		
Russian and Italian	RR83	4FT deg	*	10-12	5M	M*6/^ go	Dip	BBCC	Ind		
Spanish and Italian Studies	RR34	4FT deg	Sp	12	5M $	M$6/^	25	BBBC	Ind	4	10/12
QUEEN'S Univ Belfast											
Accounting with Italian	N4R3	4FT deg	* g	ABB	7D	D*^ go	34$	AAABB	Ind		
Common and Civil Law with Italian	M3R3	4FT deg									
Economics with Italian	L1R3	3FT deg									
Finance with Italian	N3R3	4SW deg	* g	BBB	1M+6D	D*^ go	32$	AABBB	Ind		
Information Management with Italian	P2R3	3FT deg	* g	BBC	2M+5D	D*6/^ go	30$	AABB	Ind		
Italian	R300	4FT deg	* g	BCC	3M+4D	D*6/^ go	29$	ABBB	Ind		
Italian/Ancient History (4 years)	VRC3	4FT deg	* g	BCC	3M+4D	D*6/^ go	29$	ABBB	Ind		
Italian/Celtic (4 years)	QR53	4FT deg	* g	BCC	3M+4D	D*6/^ go	29$	ABBB	Ind		
Italian/Classical Studies (4 years)	QR83	4FT deg	* g	BCC	3M+4D	D*6/^ go	29$	ABBB	Ind		
Italian/Economics (4 years)	LR13	3FT deg									
Italian/English (4 years)	QR33	4FT deg	E g	BCC	X	D*^ go	29$	ABBB	X	9	
Italian/French (4 years)	RR13	4FT deg	E g	BCC	X	D*^ go	29$	ABBB	X	11	
Italian/German (4 years)	RR23	4FT deg	* g	BCC	3M+4D	D*6/^ go	29$	ABBB	Ind		
Italian/Greek (4 years)	QR73	4FT deg	* g	BCC	3M+4D	D*6/^ go	29$	ABBB	Ind		
Latin/Italian (4 years)	RQ36	4FT deg	* g	BCC	3M+4D	D*6/^ go	29$	ABBB	Ind		

			98 expected requirements							96 entry stats

course details ... *98 expected requirements* ... *96 entry stats*

TITLE	CODE	COURSE	SUBJECTS	A/AS	NO/C	AGNVQ	IB	SQA(H)	SQA	RATIO A/AS
Management with Italian	N1R3	3FT deg	*g	BBB	2M+5D	D*^ go	32$	AABBB	Ind	
Music/Italian (4 years)	RW33	4FT deg	*g	BCC	3M+4D	D*6/^ go	29$	ABBB	Ind	
Philosophy/Italian (4 years)	RV37	4FT deg	*g	BCC	3M+4D	D*6/^ go	29$	ABBB	Ind	
Politics/Italian (4 years)	RM31	4FT deg	*g	BCC	3M+4D	D*6/^ go	29$	ABBB	Ind	
Scholastic Philosophy/Italian (4 years)	RV3R	4FT deg	*g	BCC	3M+4D	D*6/^ go	29$	ABBB	Ind	
Social Anthropology/Italian (4 years)	RL36	4FT deg	*g	BCC	3M+4D	D*6/^ go	29$	ABBB	Ind	
Spanish/Italian (4 years)	RR34	4FT deg	*g	BCC	3M+4D	D*6/^ go	29$	ABBB	Ind	9

Univ of READING

TITLE	CODE	COURSE	SUBJECTS	A/AS	NO/C	AGNVQ	IB	SQA(H)	SQA	RATIO A/AS
Archaeology and Italian	VR63	4FT deg	*g	BCC	Ind	D$6/^ go	30	BBBB	Ind	2
English Literature and Italian	QR33	4FT deg	El g	BBC	Ind	D$^ go	31$	BBBB$	Ind	29
Film & Drama and Italian	RW34	4FT deg	*g	BBC	Ind	D*^ go	31	BBBB	Ind	
French and Italian	RR13	4FT deg	F	BBC	Ind	D$^	31$	BBBB$	Ind	17
German and Italian	RR23	4FT deg	*g	BCC	Ind	D$^ go	30	BBBB	Ind	11
History and Italian	RV31	4FT deg	*g	BBC	Ind	D$6/^ go	31	BBBB	Ind	
International Management & Bus Admin with Ital	N1R3	4FT deg	*g	BBB	Ind	DB^ go	32	ABBB	Ind	
Italian	R300	4FT deg	*g	BCC	2M	D$6/^ go	30	BBBB	Ind	6
Italian and Classical Studies	QR83	4FT deg	*g	BCC	Ind	D$6/^ go	30	BBBB	Ind	
Italian and Economics	LR13	4FT deg	*g	BCC	Ind	D$6/^ go	30	BBBB	Ind	2
Italian and French	RR31	4FT deg	F	BBC	Ind	D$^	31$	BBBB$	Ind	
Italian and History of Art	RV34	4FT deg	*g	BBC	Ind	D$6/^ go	31	BBBB	Ind	7
Italian and International Relations	RM31	4FT deg	*g	BCC	Ind	D$6/^ go	30	BBBB	Ind	5
Italian and Linguistics	QR13	4FT deg	*g	BCC	Ind	D$6/^ go	30	BBBB	Ind	3
Italian and Management Studies	NR13	4FT deg	*g	BCC	Ind	DB^ go	30	BBBB	Ind	9
Italian and Politics	MR13	4FT deg	*g	BCC	Ind	D$6/^ go	30	BBBB	Ind	
Italian with Film Studies	R3W5	4FT deg	*g	BCC	Ind	D$6/^ go	30	BBBB	Ind	8
Italian with Latin	R3Q6	4FT deg	*g	BCC	Ind	D$6/^ go	30	BBBB	Ind	
Latin and Italian	QR63	4FT deg	*g	BCC	Ind	D$6/^ go	30	BBBB	Ind	
Music and Italian	RW33	4FT deg	Mu g	BCC	X	D*^ go	30$	BBBB$	Ind	
Philosophy and Italian	RV37	4FT deg	*g	BCC	Ind	D$^ go	30	BBBB	Ind	

ROYAL HOLLOWAY, Univ of London

TITLE	CODE	COURSE	SUBJECTS	A/AS	NO/C	AGNVQ	IB	SQA(H)	SQA	RATIO A/AS
Economics with Italian	L1R3	3FT deg	L/Ln	BBC-BBB	Ind		32	Ind		
English Language and Italian	QR3H	4FT deg	E+L/Ln	BBC-ABC			30$	Ind		
English and Italian	QR33	4FT deg	E+L/Ln	BBC-ABC			30$	Ind		12
French and Italian	RR13	4FT deg	F	BBC			28$	Ind		20
French with Italian	R1R3	4FT deg	F	BBC-ABC			28$	Ind		
German and Italian	RR23	4FT deg	G	BBC-BCC			28$	Ind		6
German with Italian	R2R3	4FT deg	G	BCC			28$	BBBBC$		
Italian	R300	4FT deg	L/Ln	BBC			30	BBCCC$		4
Italian and Management Studies	RN31	4FT deg	L/Ln	BBC	Ind		30	Ind		12
Italian and Music	RW33	4FT deg	Mu+L/Ln	BBC			Ind	Ind		
Italian and Spanish	RR34	4FT deg	Sp	BBC-BCC			Ind	Ind		
Italian with Economics	R3L1	4FT deg	L/Ln	BBC			30	BBCCC$		
Italian with French	R3R1	4FT deg	F	BBC			30	BBCCC$		
Italian with German	R3R2	4FT deg	G	BBC			30	BBCCC$		
Italian with Management Studies	R3N1	4FT deg	L/Ln	BBC			30	BBCCC$		3
Italian with Mathematics	R3G1	4FT deg	M+L/Ln	BBC			30	BBCCC$		
Italian with Music	R3W3	4FT deg	L/Ln+Mu	BBC			30	BBCCC$		
Italian with Political Studies	R3MC	4FT deg	L/Ln	BBC			30	BBCCC$		
Italian with Social Policy	R3L4	4FT deg	L/Ln	BBC			30	BBCCC$		
Italian with Sociology	R3L3	4FT deg	L/Ln	BBC			30	BBCCC$		1
Italian with Spanish	R3R4	4FT deg	L/Ln	BBC			30	BBCCC$		
Management Studies with Italian	N1R3	3FT deg	L/Ln	BBC-BBB	2M+3D	D^	30	Ind		
Mathematics with Italian	G1R3	3FT deg	M+L/Ln	BCC-BBC	Ind	D^	Ind	Ind		

TITLE	CODE	COURSE	SUBJECTS	A/AS	NO/C	AGNVQ	IB	SQA(H)	SQA	RATIO A/AS
Music with Italian	W3R3	3FT deg	Mu+L/Ln	BCC-BBC			Ind	ABBCC$		
Sociology with Italian	L3R3	3FT deg	L/Ln	BCC-BBC	Ind	D^	Ind	Ind		
Foundation Programme *Italian*	Y408	4FT deg								

Univ of SALFORD

TITLE	CODE	COURSE	SUBJECTS	A/AS	NO/C	AGNVQ	IB	SQA(H)	SQA	RATIO A/AS
French/Italian (4 Yrs)	RR13	4SW deg	L g	BCC	X	X	Ind	Ind	X	6 16/22
German/Italian (4 Yrs)	RR23	4SW deg	L g	BCC	X	X	Ind	Ind	X	10
Italian/Arabic (4 Yrs)	RT36	4SW deg	L g	BCC	X	X	Ind	Ind	X	
Italian/Hispanic Studies (4 Yrs)	RRH4	4SW deg	L g	BCC	X	X	Ind	Ind	X	
Italian/Spanish (4 Yrs)	RR34	4SW deg	L g	BCC	X	X	Ind	Ind	X	3 18/24

SHEFFIELD HALLAM Univ

TITLE	CODE	COURSE	SUBJECTS	A/AS	NO/C	AGNVQ	IB	SQA(H)	SQA	RATIO A/AS
International Business with Language (Italian)	N1R3	4SW deg	g	16	M+D	M gi	Ind	Ind	Ind	

Univ of ST ANDREWS

TITLE	CODE	COURSE	SUBJECTS	A/AS	NO/C	AGNVQ	IB	SQA(H)	SQA	RATIO A/AS
Italian with Year Abroad-Ancient History	RVHD	4FT/5FT deg	* g	BBB	X	Ind	30$	BBBB	Ind	
Italian with Year Abroad-Art History	RV3K	4FT/5FT deg	* g	BBB	X	Ind	30$	BBBB	Ind	
Italian with Year Abroad-Classical Studies	RQ3W	4FT/5FT deg	* g	BBB	X	Ind	30$	BBBB	Ind	
Italian with Year Abroad-Classics	RQ3V	4FT/5FT deg	* g	BBB	X	Ind	30$	BBBB	Ind	
Italian with Year Abroad-Economics	LR1H	4FT/5FT deg	* g	BBB	X	Ind	30$	BBBB	Ind	
Italian with Year Abroad-English	RQ33	4FT/5FT deg	* g	BBB	X	Ind	30$	BBBB	Ind	
Italian with Year Abroad-Greek	RQ37	4FT/5FT deg	* g	BBB	X	Ind	30$	BBBB	Ind	
Italian with Year Abroad-International Relations	MR1H	4FT/5FT deg	* g	AAB	X	Ind	36$	AAAB	Ind	
Italian-Ancient History	RV31	4FT deg	* g	BBB	X	Ind	30$	BBBB	Ind	
Italian-Arabic	RT36	4FT deg	* g	BBB	X	Ind	30$	BBBB	Ind	
Italian-Art History	RV34	4FT deg	* g	BBB	X	Ind	30$	BBBB	Ind	3
Italian-Classical Studies	RQ38	4FT deg	* g	BBB	X	Ind	30$	BBBB	Ind	
Italian-Classics	QR83	4FT deg	* g	BBB	X	Ind	30$	BBB	Ind	
Italian-English	QR33	4FT deg	* g	BBB	X	Ind	30$	BBBB	Ind	
Italian-French	RR13	4FT deg	* g	BBB	X	Ind	30$	BBBB	Ind	1
Italian-French with Year Abroad	RR31	4FT/5FT deg	E g	BBB	X	Ind	30$	BBBB$	Ind	4
Italian-German	RR23	4FT deg	* g	BBB	X	Ind	30$	BBBB	Ind	
Italian-German with Year Abroad	RR32	4FT/5FT deg	* g	BBB	X	Ind	30$	BBBB	Ind	
Italian-Greek	QR73	4FT deg	* g	BBB	X	Ind	30$	BBBB	Ind	
Italian-International Relations	MR13	4FT deg	* g	AAB	X	Ind	36$	AAAB	Ind	
Latin-Italian	QR63	4FT deg	* g	BBB	X	Ind	30$	BBBB	Ind	
Latin-Italian with Year Abroad	RQ36	4FT/5FT deg	* g	BBB	X	Ind	30$	BBBB	Ind	
Management-Italian	NR13	4FT deg	* g	BBB	X	Ind	34$	BBBB	Ind	
Management-Italian with Year Abroad	NR1H	4FT/5FT deg	* g	BBB	X	Ind	30$	BBBB	Ind	
Mediaeval History-Italian	RV3C	4FT deg	* g	BBB	X	Ind	34$	BBBB	Ind	
Mediaeval History-Italian with Year Abroad	RVH1	4FT/5FT deg	* g	BBB	X	Ind	30$	BBBB	Ind	
Modern History-Italian	RV3D	4FT deg	* g	BBB	X	Ind	30$	BBBB	Ind	
Modern History-Italian with Year Abroad	RVHC	4FT/5FT deg	* g	BBB	X	Ind	30$	BBBB	Ind	
Philosophy-Italian	RV37	4FT deg	* g	BBB	X	Ind	30$	BBBB	Ind	
Philosophy-Italian with Year Abroad	RV3R	4FT/5FT deg	* g	BBB	X	Ind	30$	BBBB	Ind	
Russian with Year Abroad-Italian	RR83	4FT/5FT deg	* g	BBB	X	Ind	30$	BBBB	Ind	
Russian-Italian	RR38	4FT deg	* g	BBB	X	Ind	30$	BBBB	Ind	
Scottish History-Italian	VR13	4FT deg	* g	BBB	X	Ind	30$	BBBB	Ind	
Scottish History-Italian with Year Abroad	VR1H	4FT/5FT deg	* g	BBB	X	Ind	30$	BBBB	Ind	
Social Anthropology-Italian	LR63	4FT deg	* g	BBB	X	Ind	30$	BBBB	Ind	
Social Anthropology-Italian with Year Abroad	RL36	4FT/5FT deg	* g	BBB	X	Ind	30$	BBBB	Ind	
Spanish with Year Abroad-Italian	RR34	4FT/5FT deg	* g	BBB	X	Ind	30$	BBBB	Ind	
Spanish-Italian	RR43	4FT/5FT deg	* g	BBB	X	Ind	30$	BBBB	Ind	

			98 expected requirements							96 entry stats
TITLE	CODE	COURSE	SUBJECTS	A/AS	NO/C	AGNVQ	IB	SQA(H)	SQA	RATIO A/AS
Univ of STRATHCLYDE										
Arts and Social Sciences	Y440	3FT/4FT deg	g	CCC	Ind		28	BBBBB$	Ind	
Italian										
Univ of SUSSEX										
Computer Science with European Studs (Italian)	G5R3	4FT deg	M g	BBC	MO $	M*^ go	$	Ind	Ind	
French and Italian	RR13	4FT deg	F	BCC	MO $	M*^	$	Ind	Ind	
German and Italian	RR23	4FT deg	G	BCC	MO $	M*^	$	Ind	Ind	
Italian Studies	R300	4FT deg	g	BCC	MO $	M*6 go	$	Ind	Ind	
Italian and Linguistics	RQ31	4FT deg	g	BCC	MO $	M*6 go	$	Ind	Ind	
Mathematics & Stats with Eur St(Italian) (MMath)	G4RH	4FT deg	M g	BCC	MO $	MS^ go	$	Ind	Ind	
Mathematics and Stats with Eur Studies (Ital)	G4R3	4FT deg	M g	BCC	MO $	MS^ go	$	Ind	Ind	
Mathematics with European St (Italian) (MMath)	G1RH	4FT deg	M g	BCC	MO $	MS^ go	$	Ind	Ind	
Mathematics with European Studies (Italian)	G1R3	4FT deg	M g	BCC	MO $	MS^ go	$	Ind	Ind	
Physics with European Studies (Italian)	F3R3	4FT deg	M+P g	CCC	MO $	MS^ go	$	Ind	Ind	
Univ of Wales SWANSEA										
Biochemistry (with Italian)	C7R3	4FT deg	C	BCC-CCC	2M+3D$	X	28$	BBBCC$	Ind	
Biological Sciences (with Italian)	C1R3	4FT deg	B	BCC	X	X	28$	ABBCC$	Ind	5
Civil Engineering (with Italian)	H2R3	4FT deg	M g	BCD-CCC	4M+1D$	MC^ go	28$	BBBCC$	Ind	
Computer Science (with Italian)	G5R3	4FT deg	L	BBC	4D	Ind	28	BBBBB	Ind	
English Language/Italian (with Business Studies)	QRH3	4FT deg	L	X	X	X	28	X	X	
European Business Studies (Italy)	N1R3	4FT deg	I g	ABC-BBB	Ind	D$^ go	32$	AABBB$	Ind	2
European History (with Italian)	V1R3	4FT deg	H+L	BBB-BBC	1M+5D$	Ind	30$	ABBBB$	Ind	
European Management Science (Italy)	N1RH	4FT deg	I+M	ABC-BBB	X	D$^ go	32$	AABBB$	Ind	
French/Italian (with Business Studies)	RR1H	4FT deg	F g	BBC	1M+5D$	Ind	30$	ABBBB$	Ind	3
French/Italian (with Computer Studies)	RR1J	4FT deg	F	BBC	1M+5D$	Ind	30$	ABBBB$	Ind	2
French/Italian (with Legal Studies)	RR31	4FT deg	F	BBC	1M+5D$	Ind	30$	ABBBB$	Ind	4
German/Italian (with Business Studies)	RR2H	4FT deg	G g	BBC	1M+5D$	Ind	30$	ABBBB$	Ind	4
German/Italian (with Computer Studies)	RR2J	4FT deg	G	BBC	1M+5D$	Ind	30$	ABBBB$	Ind	
German/Italian (with Legal Studies)	RR32	4FT deg	G	BBC	1M+5D$	Ind	30$	ABBBB$	Ind	
Italian	R300	4FT deg	I/L	BBC	1M+5D$	Ind	30$	ABBBB$	Ind	3
Italian (with Business Studies)	R3N1	4FT deg	I/L g	BBC	1M+5D$	Ind	30$	ABBBB$	Ind	6
Italian (with Computer Studies)	R3G5	4FT deg	L	BBC	1M+5D$	Ind	30$	ABBBB$	Ind	
Italian (with Legal Studies)	R3M3	4FT deg	L	BBB-BBC	1M+5D$	Ind	30$	ABBBB$	Ind	
Italian/American Studies	QR43	4FT deg								
Italian/Ancient History and Civilisation	VRC3	4FT deg	L/*	BBC	1M+5D$	X	30$	ABBBB$	X	
Italian/Anthropology	LR63	4FT deg	L/*	BBC	1M+5D$	Ind	30$	ABBBB$	Ind	
Italian/Economic History	RV33	4FT deg	L/*	BBC	1M+5D$	Ind	30$	ABBBB$	Ind	
Italian/Economics	LR13	4FT deg								
Italian/English	QR33	4FT deg	E+L	BBC	X	X	30$	ABBBB$	X	2
Italian/English Language	QR3H	3FT deg	E g	BBC	X	X	30$	ABBBB$	Ind	
Italian/European Politics	MR1H	4FT deg	L/*	BBC	1M+5D$	Ind	30$	ABBBB$	Ind	
Italian/French	RR13	4FT deg	F	BBC	1M+5D$	Ind	30$	ABBBB$	Ind	4 14/24
Italian/Geography	LR83	4FT deg	Gy+L	BBC	1M+5D$	Ind	30$	ABBBB$	Ind	1
Italian/German	RR23	4FT deg	G/(I g)	BBC	1M+5D$	Ind	30$	ABBBB$	Ind	3
Italian/Greek and Roman Studies	QR83	4FT deg	L/*	BBC-BCC	1M+5D$	X	28$	BBBBB$	X	
Italian/History	RV31	4FT deg	L/*	BBC	1M+5D$	Ind	30$	ABBBB$	Ind	1
Italian/Russian (with Business Studies)	RR3V	4FT deg	I/R g	BCC	1M+5D$	Ind	28$	BBBBC$	Ind	
Italian/Russian (with Computer Studies)	RR3W	4FT deg	I/R	BCC	1M+5D$	Ind	28$	BBBBC$	Ind	
Italian/Russian (with Legal Studies)	RR83	4FT deg	I/R	BCC	1M+5D$	Ind	28$	BBBBC$	Ind	
Italian/Spanish (with Business Studies)	RR3K	4FT deg	I/Sp g	BBB-BBC	1M+5D$	Ind	30$	ABBBB$	Ind	
Italian/Spanish (with Computer Studies)	RR3L	4FT deg	I/Sp	BBC	1M+5D$	Ind	30$	ABBBB$	Ind	

| | | | | 98 expected requirements | | | | | | 96 entry stats | |

course details

TITLE	CODE	COURSE	SUBJECTS	A/AS	NO/C	AGNVQ	IB	SQA(H)	SQA	RATIO A/AS	
Italian/Spanish (with Legal Studies)	RR43	4FT deg	I/Sp	BBB-BBC	1M+5D$	Ind	30$	ABBBB$	Ind		
Italian/Welsh (with Business Studies)	RQ35	4FT deg	I/W g	BCC	1M+5D$	X	28$	BBBBC$	X		
Italian/Welsh (with Computer Studies)	RQ3N	4FT deg	I/W	BCC	1M+5D$	X	28$	BBBBC$	X		
Italian/Welsh (with Legal Studies)	QR53	4FT deg	I/W	BCC	1M+5D$	X	28$	BBBBC$	X		
Latin/Italian	QR63	4FT deg	Ln	BBC-BCC	Ind	X	28$	BBBBB$	X		
Law and Italian	MR33	4FT deg	L/*	BBB	6D $	Ind	32$	AABBB$	Ind		
Mathematics (with Italian)	G1R3	4FT deg	M+L	BBC-BCC	X	Ind	28$	BBBBC$	Ind		
Medieval Studies/Italian	RVH1	4FT deg	H+L	BCC	1M+5D$	Ind	28$	BBBBB$	X		
Philosophy/Italian	RV37	4FT deg	L/*	BBC-BCC	1M+5D$	Ind	28$	BBBBB$	Ind		
Politics/Italian	MR13	4FT deg	L/*	BBC-BCC	1M+5D	Ind	28	BBBBB	Ind		
Psychology and Italian	LR73	4FT deg	L/*	BBC	1M+5D$	Ind	30$	ABBBB$	Ind		
Russian/Italian	RR38	4FT deg	I/R	BCC	1M+5D$	Ind	28$	BBBBC$	Ind		
Sociology/Italian	LR33	4FT deg	L/*	BBC	1M+5D$	Ind	30$	ABBBB$	Ind		
Spanish/Italian	RR34	4FT deg	I/Sp	BBC	1M+5D$	Ind	30$	ABBBB$	Ind	2	
Welsh/Italian	QRM3	4FT deg	W/I	BCC	1M+5D$	X	28$	BBBBB$	X		

UNIVERSITY COLL LONDON (Univ of London)

Dutch and Italian (4 Yrs)	TR23	4FT deg	g	BCC-BBC	3M	X	26$	BBBCC$	Ind	2	
French and Italian (4 Yrs)	RR13	4FT deg	F g	BBC	3M	X	30$	BBBBC$	Ind	5	24/30
German and Italian (4 Yrs)	RR23	4FT deg	G g	BBC	3M	X	30$	BBBCC$	Ind	3	22/24
Italian (4 Yrs)	R300	4FT deg	g	BCC	3M	X	30	BBBCC$	Ind	2	14/26
Italian and Business Studies (4 Yrs)	RN31	4FT deg	g	BCC-BBC	3M	M$^ go	30	BBBCC$	Ind	6	16/26
Italian and Design (4 Yrs)	RW32	4FT deg	g	BCC	3M	MA^ go	30$	BBBCC$	Ind	4	18/26
Italian and History of Art (4 Yrs)	RV34	4FT deg	g	BBB	3M	X	30$	BBBCC$	Ind	6	20/28
Italian and Jewish Studies (4 Yrs)	RV31	4FT deg	g	BCC	3M	X	28$	BBCCC$	Ind		
Italian and Latin (4 Yrs)	RQ36	4FT deg	I/Ln g	BBC	3M	X	30$	BBBBC$	Ind		
Italian and Linguistics (4 Yrs)	RQ31	4FT deg	g	BBC	3M	X	30	BBBCC$	Ind	6	

Univ of WARWICK

English and Italian Lit (4 Yrs inc yr abroad)	QR33	4FT deg	E g	BBC	X	X	30$	ABBBB$		7	22/26
French Studies with Italian (4 Yrs inc yr abrd)	R1R3	4FT deg	F g	BBC	X	X	29$	ABBBC$		4	
French and Italian Studies (4 Yrs inc yr abroad)	RR13	4FT deg	F g	BCC	X	X	29$	ABBBB$			
German Studies and Italian (4 Yrs inc year abrd)	RR23	4FT deg	G g	BCC	X	X	29$	ABBBB$			
German with Italian (4 Yrs inc year abroad)	R2R3	4FT deg	G g	BBC-BCC	X	X	29$	ABBBB$			
Italian and European Lit (4 Yrs inc yr abroad)	RQ32	4FT deg	E/L g	BCC	X	X	29$	ABBCC$		9	
Italian with Film Studies (4 Yrs inc yr abroad)	R3W5	4FT deg	E/L g	BBC	X	X	29$	ABBCC$		13	
Italian with French (4 Yrs inc yr abroad)	R3R1	4FT deg	E+F g	BCC	X	X	29$	ABBCC$			
Italian with German (4 Yrs inc yr abroad)	R3R2	4FT deg	E+G g	BBC-BCC	X	X	29$	ABBBB$			
Italian with Int Studies (4 Yrs inc yr abroad)	R3M1	4FT deg	E/L g	BCC	X	X	29$	ABBCC$		32	
Italian with Theatre Studies (4 Yrs inc yr abrd)	R3W4	4FT deg	E/L g	BCC	X	X	29$	ABBCC$			

Univ of WESTMINSTER

Italian and Arabic	RT36	4SW deg	I	CC	Ind		26	BBB			
Italian and Chinese	T3R3	4SW deg	I	CC	Ind		26	BBB	Ind		
Italian and English	QR33	4SW deg	E	CC	Ind		26$	BBB			
Italian and English Language	QRH3	4SW deg		CC	Ind		26$	BBB			
Italian and French	RR13	4SW deg	F	CC	Ind		26$	BBB		5	10/22
Italian and German	RR23	4SW deg	G/I	CC	Ind		26$	BBB		7	
Linguistics and Italian	RQ31	4SW deg	L	CC	Ind		26	BBB		5	
Russian and Italian	RR38	4SW deg	I/R	CC	Ind		26	BBB			
Spanish and Italian	RR34	4SW deg	I/Sp	CC	Ind		26	BBB		4	10/18

Univ of WOLVERHAMPTON

Combined Degrees *Italian Studies*	Y401	3FT/4SW deg	L g	12	4M $	M	24	BBBB	Ind		

course details			98 expected requirements							96 entry stats	
TITLE	CODE	COURSE	SUBJECTS	A/AS	ND/C	AGNVQ	IB	SQA(H)	SQA	RATIO A/AS	
Univ of DURHAM											
Arabic with Anthropology	T6L6	4FT deg	*	BBC	Ind	Ind	28	Ind	Ind		
Arabic with Economics	T6L1	4FT deg	* g	BBB	Ind	Ind	28	Ind	Ind	5	
Arabic with European Languages	T6T9	4FT deg	L	BBC	Ind	Ind	31	AABBB	Ind	6	
Arabic with Geography	T6L8	4FT deg	*	BBC	Ind	Ind	28	Ind	Ind		
Arabic with Mid-East and Islamic Studies	TM69	4FT deg	*	BBC	Ind	Ind	28	Ind	Ind	4	14/24
Arabic with Politics	T6M1	4FT deg	*	BBB	Ind	Ind	28	Ind	Ind	8	
Arabic with Sociology and Social Policy	T6L3	4FT deg	*	BBC	Ind	Ind	28	Ind	Ind	4	
Islamic Studies and Arabic	T600	3FT deg									
Politics and History of Middle East with Arabic	M1T6	3FT deg		BBC	Ind	Ind	28	Ind	Ind		
Politics and History of Middle East with Persian	M1TP	3FT deg		BBC	Ind	Ind	28	Ind	Ind		
Politics and History of Middle East with Turkish	M1TQ	3FT deg		BBC	Ind	Ind	28	Ind	Ind		
Social Sciences Combined *Islamic Studies*	Y220	3FT deg	*	ABC	MO	Ind	32	AAABB	Ind		
Univ of EDINBURGH											
Arabic	T620	4FT deg	g	BBB	Ind	Ind	Dip$	BBBB	Ind		
Arabic and Business Studies	TN61	4FT deg	g	BBB	Ind	Ind	Dip$	BBBB	Ind		
Arabic and Economics	TL61	4FT deg	g	BBB	Ind	Ind	Dip$	BBBB	Ind		
Arabic and French	TR61	4FT deg	F g	BBB	Ind	Ind	Dip$	BBBB$	Ind		
Arabic and History of Art	TV64	4FT deg	g	BBB	Ind	Ind	Dip$	BBBB	Ind		
Arabic and Linguistics	TQ61	4FT deg	g	BBB	Ind	Ind	Dip$	BBBB	Ind		
Arabic and Persian	T621	4FT deg	g	BBB	Ind	Ind	Dip$	BBBB	Ind		
Arabic and Politics	TM61	4FT deg	g	BBB	Ind	Ind	Dip$	BBBB	Ind		
Arabic and Social Anthropology	LT66	4FT deg	g	BBB	Ind	Ind	Dip$	BBBB	Ind		
Arabic and Spanish	TR64	4FT deg	Sp g	BBB	Ind	Ind	Dip$	BBBB$	Ind		
French and Arabic	RT16	4FT deg	F g	BBB	Ind	Ind	Dip$	BBBB$	Ind		
Greek and Arabic	QT76	4FT deg	g	BBB	Ind	Ind	Dip$	BBBB	Ind		
History of Art and Arabic	VT46	4FT deg	g	BBB	Ind	Ind	Dip$	BBBB	Ind		
Persian and Politics	MT16	4FT deg	g	BBB	Ind	Ind	Dip$	BBBB$	Ind		
Spanish and Arabic	RT46	4FT deg	Sp g	BBB	Ind	Ind	Dip$	BBBB$	Ind		
Univ of EXETER											
Arabic Studies	T622	4FT deg	*	BCC	MO	D$	30	Ind	Ind		
French and Arabic	RT16	4FT deg	F	22-24	MO	M/D$^	34$	Ind	Ind	6	
Spanish and Arabic (Beginners Spanish available)	RT46	4FT deg	Sp	BBC	MO	M/D$^	34$	Ind	Ind		
Univ of GLASGOW											
Islamic Studies/Archaeology	TV66	4FT deg		BBC	N	M	30	BBBB	Ind		
Islamic Studies/Celtic	TQ65	4FT deg		BBC	N	M	30	BBBB	Ind		
Islamic Studies/Classical Hebrew	TQ69	4FT deg		BBC	N	M	30	BBBB	Ind		
Islamic Studies/Czech	TT61	4FT deg		BBC	N	M	30	BBBB	Ind		
Islamic Studies/Economic History	TV63	4FT deg		BBC	N	M	30	BBBB	Ind		
Islamic Studies/Economics	TL61	4FT deg		BBC	N	M	30	BBBB	Ind		
Islamic Studies/English	TQ63	4FT deg		BBC	N	M	30	BBBB	Ind		
Islamic Studies/French	TR61	4FT deg		BBC	N	M	30	BBBB	Ind		
Islamic Studies/Geography	TL68	4FT deg		BBC	N	M	30	BBBB	Ind		
Islamic Studies/Greek	TQ67	4FT deg		BBC	N	M	30	BBBB	Ind		
Islamic Studies/Hispanic Studies	TR64	4FT deg		BBC	N	M	30	BBBB	Ind		
Islamic Studies/History of Art	TV64	3FT deg		BBC	N	M	30	BBBB	Ind		
Islamic Studies/Latin	TQ66	4FT deg		BBC	N	M	30	BBBB	Ind		
Islamic Studies/Mathematics	TG61	4FT deg		BBC	N	M	30	BBBB	Ind		
Islamic Studies/Music	TW63	4FT deg		BBC	N	M	30	BBBB	Ind		
Islamic Studies/Philosophy	TV67	4FT deg		BBC	N	M	30	BBBB	Ind		

course details | 98 expected requirements | 96 entry stats

TITLE	CODE	COURSE	SUBJECTS	A/AS	ND/C	AGNVQ	IB	SQA(H)	SQA	RATIO A/AS
Islamic Studies/Polish	TT16	4FT deg		BBC	N	M	30	BBBB	Ind	
Islamic Studies/Politics	TM61	4FT deg		BBC	N	M	30	BBBB	Ind	
Islamic Studies/Psychology	TC68	4FT deg		BBC	N	M	30	BBBB	Ind	
Islamic Studies/Russian	TR68	4FT deg		BBC	N	M	30	BBBB	Ind	
Islamic Studies/Sociology	TL63	4FT deg		BBC	N	M	30	BBBB	Ind	
Islamic Studies/Theatre Studies	TW64	4FT deg		BBC	N	M	30	BBBB	Ind	

Univ of Wales, LAMPETER

TITLE	CODE	COURSE	SUBJECTS	A/AS	ND/C	AGNVQ	IB	SQA(H)	SQA	RATIO A/AS
Islamic Studies and American Literature	QT4P	3FT deg			Ind	Ind	Ind	Ind	Ind	
Islamic Studies and Ancient History	TVP1	3FT deg	*	16	Ind	Ind	Ind	Ind	Ind	
Islamic Studies and Anthropology	LT66	3FT deg	*	14	Ind	Ind	Ind	Ind	Ind	
Islamic Studies and Archaeology	TV66	3FT deg	*	16	Ind	Ind	Ind	Ind	Ind	
Islamic Studies and Australian Studies	TL66	3FT deg			Ind	Ind	Ind	Ind	Ind	
Islamic Studies and Church History	TV61	3FT deg	*	14	Ind	Ind	Ind	Ind	Ind	
Islamic Studies and Classical Studies	TQ68	3FT deg	*	16	Ind	Ind	Ind	Ind	Ind	
Islamic Studies and Cultural Studs in Geography	LTV6	3FT deg		16	Ind	Ind	Ind	Ind	Ind	
Islamic Studies and English Literature	TQ63	3FT deg	E	18	Ind	Ind	Ind	Ind	Ind	
Islamic Studies and French	TR61	4FT deg	F	16	Ind	Ind	Ind	Ind	Ind	
Islamic Studies and Geography	TL68	3FT deg	Gy	16	Ind	Ind	Ind	Ind	Ind	
Islamic Studies and German	TR62	4FT deg	G	16	Ind	Ind	Ind	Ind	Ind	
Islamic Studies and German Studies	TR6F	4FT deg	*	16	Ind	Ind	Ind	Ind	Ind	
Islamic Studies and Greek	TQ67	3FT deg	* g	16	Ind	Ind	Ind	Ind	Ind	
Islamic Studies and History	TV6C	3FT deg	H	16	Ind	Ind	Ind	Ind	Ind	
Islamic Studies and Informatics	GT56	3FT deg	*	14	Ind	Ind	Ind	Ind	Ind	
Latin and Islamic Studies	TQ66	3FT deg	* g	16	Ind	Ind	Ind	Ind	Ind	
Management Techniques and Islamic Studies	NT16	3FT deg	*	16	Ind	Ind	Ind	Ind	Ind	
Medieval Studies and Islamic Studies	VT16	3FT deg	*	16	Ind	Ind	Ind	Ind	Ind	
Modern Historical Studies and Islamic Studies	VTCQ	3FT deg			Ind	Ind	Ind	Ind	Ind	
Philosophical Studies and Islamic Studies	TV67	3FT deg	*	16	Ind	Ind	Ind	Ind	Ind	
Religious Studies and Islamic Studies	TV68	3FT deg	*	14	Ind	Ind	Ind	Ind	Ind	
Theology and Islamic Studies	TV6V	3FT deg	*	14	Ind	Ind	Ind	Ind	Ind	
Victorian Studies and Islamic Studies	TV6D	3FT deg	*	14	Ind	Ind	Ind	Ind	Ind	
Welsh Studies and Islamic Studies	TQ6N	3FT deg	*	14	Ind	Ind	Ind	Ind	Ind	
Welsh and Islamic Studies	TQ65	3FT/4FT deg	W	14	Ind	Ind	Ind	Ind	Ind	
Women's Studies and Islamic Studies	MT96	3FT deg	*	14	Ind	Ind	Ind	Ind	Ind	
Combined Honours *Arabic*	Y400	3FT deg	*	14-16	Ind	Ind	Ind	Ind	Ind	
Combined Honours *Islamic Studies*	Y400	3FT deg	*	14-16	Ind	Ind	Ind	Ind	Ind	

Univ of LEEDS

TITLE	CODE	COURSE	SUBJECTS	A/AS	ND/C	AGNVQ	IB	SQA(H)	SQA	RATIO A/AS
Arabic Studies	T626	4FT deg	CI/L g	BBC	Ind	Ind	30	CSYS	Ind	1	14/22
Arabic and Islamic Studies	TVP8	4FT deg	CI/L g	BBC	Ind	Ind	30$	CSYS	Ind	15
Arabic-Classical Literature	QT86	4FT deg	CI/L g	BBC	Ind	Ind	30$	CSYS	Ind	
Arabic-English	QT36	4FT deg	E+CI/L g	BBC	Ind	Ind	30$	CSYS	Ind	
Arabic-French	RT16	4FT deg	F g	BBC	Ind	Ind	30$	CSYS	Ind	
Arabic-German	RT26	4FT deg	G g	BBC	Ind	Ind	30$	CSYS	Ind	
Arabic-Greek Civilisation	QTW6	4FT deg	CI/L g	BBC	Ind	Ind	30$	CSYS	Ind	
Arabic-Italian	RT36	4FT deg	I g	BCC	Ind	Ind	28$	CSYS	Ind	
Arabic-Linguistics	QT16	4FT deg	C1/L g	BCC	Ind	Ind	28$	CSYS	Ind	4
Arabic-Management Studies	TN61	4FT deg	CI/L g	BBC	Ind	Ind	30$	CSYS	Ind	
Arabic-Politics	TM61	4FT deg	CI/L g	BBC	Ind	Ind	30$	CSYS	Ind	
Arabic-Portuguese	RT56	4FT deg	CI/L g	BBC	Ind	Ind	30$	CSYS	Ind	
Arabic-Religious Studies	TV6V	4FT deg	CI/L g	BBC	Ind	Ind	30	CSYS	Ind	

			98 expected requirements							96 entry stats	
course details											
TITLE	CODE	COURSE	SUBJECTS	A/AS	NO/C	AGNVQ	IB	SQA(H)	SQA	RATIO	A/AS
Arabic-Roman Civilisation	QTV6	4FT deg	C1/L g	BBC	Ind	Ind	30$	CSYS	Ind		
Arabic-Russian B	RT86	4FT deg	R g	BCC	Ind	Ind	28$	CSYS	Ind		
Arabic-Russian B	RTV6	4FT deg	Cl/L g	BCC	Ind	Ind	28$	CSYS	Ind		
Arabic-Spanish	RT46	4FT deg	Sp g	BBC	Ind	Ind	30$	CSYS	Ind		
Arabic-Theology	TV68	4FT deg	Cl/L g	BBC	Ind	Ind	30	CSYS	Ind		

Univ of MANCHESTER

TITLE	CODE	COURSE	SUBJECTS	A/AS	NO/C	AGNVQ	IB	SQA(H)	SQA	RATIO	A/AS
Linguistics and Middle Eastern Languages	QT16	4FT deg	L	BBB	X		32$	AABBB		4	
Middle Eastern Langs and Comparative Religion	TV68	3FT/4FT deg	g	BCC-BBC	2M+5D		30	ABBBB	Ind	4	
Middle Eastern Studies	T608	3FT/4FT deg	g	BCC-BBC	2M+5D		30	ABBBB	Ind	2	10/18
Middle Eastern and Modern European Languages	TT62	3FT/4FT deg	L	BCC-BBC	2M+5D		30	ABBBB	Ind	5	

OXFORD Univ

TITLE	CODE	COURSE	SUBJECTS	A/AS	NO/C	AGNVQ	IB	SQA(H)	SQA	RATIO	A/AS
Arabic (4 Yrs)	T621	4FT deg	*	AAB-ABB	DO		36	AAAAA	Ind	2	
Arabic with Islamic Art and Archaeology (4 Yrs)	TQ6Y	4FT deg	*	AAB-ABB	DO		36	AAAAA	Ind	5	
Arabic with Islamic Studies/History (4 Yrs)	TQ69	4FT deg	*	AAB-ABB	DO		36	AAAAA	Ind	5	
Arabic with Modern Middle Eastern Studs (4 Yrs)	T610	4FT deg	*	AAB-ABB	DO		36	AAAAA	Ind		
Arabic with subsidiary language (4 Yrs)	T6T9	4FT deg	*	AAB-ABB	DO		36	AAAAA	Ind		
European and Middle Eastern Languages (3 Yrs)	TT26	3FT deg	L	AAB	DO		36	AAAAA	Ind		
European and Middle Eastern Languages (4 Yrs)	TT2P	4FT deg	L	AAB	DO		36	AAAAA	Ind	3	28/30
Persian with Islamic Art and Archaeology (4 Yrs)	QT9P	4FT deg	*	AAB-ABB	DO		36	AAAAA	Ind	1	
Persian with Islamic Studies/History (4 Yrs)	QT9Q	4FT deg	*	AAB-ABB	DO		36	AAAAA	Ind		
Persian with subsidiary language (4 Yrs)	T6TX	4FT deg	*	AAB-ABB	DO		36	AAAAA	Ind		
Turkish with Islamic Art and Archaeology (3 Yrs)	TQ6X	3FT deg	*	AAB-ABB	DO		36	AAAAA	Ind		
Turkish with subsidiary language (4 Yrs)	T6TY	4FT deg	*	AAB-ABB	DO		36	AAAAA	Ind		

OXFORD BROOKES Univ

TITLE	CODE	COURSE	SUBJECTS	A/AS	NO/C	AGNVQ	IB	SQA(H)	SQA	RATIO	A/AS
Langs for Bus:Italian-Ab Initio/French-Post GCSE	NT1Q	4FT deg									

Univ of SALFORD

TITLE	CODE	COURSE	SUBJECTS	A/AS	NO/C	AGNVQ	IB	SQA(H)	SQA	RATIO	A/AS
French/Arabic (4 Yrs)	RT16	4SW deg	L g	BBC	X	X	Ind	Ind	X		
German/Arabic (4 Yrs)	RT26	4SW deg	L g	BCC	X	X	Ind	Ind	X		
Italian/Arabic (4 Yrs)	RT36	4SW deg	L g	BCC	X	X	Ind	Ind	X		
Spanish/Arabic (4 Yrs)	RT46	4SW deg	L g	BCC	X	X	Ind	Ind	X		

SOAS:Sch of Oriental & African St (U of London)

TITLE	CODE	COURSE	SUBJECTS	A/AS	NO/C	AGNVQ	IB	SQA(H)	SQA	RATIO	A/AS
Arabic	T620	4FT deg		22	Ind		31	BBBBC	Ind	3	20/28
Arabic and Amharic	TT67	4FT deg		22	Ind		31	BBBBC	Ind		
Arabic and Islamic Studies	QT96	4FT deg		22	Ind		31	BBBBC	Ind	7	
Development Studies and Arabic	MT96	4FT deg		22	Ind		31	BBBBC	Ind	2	
Economics and Arabic	LT16	4FT deg	g	22	Ind		31	BBBBC	Ind	2	
Geography and Arabic	LT86	4FT deg		22	Ind		31	BBBBC	Ind	1	
Georgian and Arabic	TT69	4FT deg		22	Ind		31	BBBBC	Ind		
Hausa and Arabic	TT6R	4FT deg		22	Ind		31	BBBBC	Ind		
Hebrew and Arabic	QT9P	4FT deg		22	Ind		31	BBBBC	Ind		
Hebrew and Israeli Studies	QT9Q	4FT deg		22	Ind		31	BBBBC	Ind		
History and Arabic	TV61	4FT deg		22	Ind		31	BBBBC	Ind	5	
History of Art/Archaeology and Arabic	TV66	4FT deg		22	Ind		31	BBBBC	Ind	5	
Indonesian and Arabic	TTM6	4FT deg		22	Ind		31	BBBBC	Ind		
Law and Arabic	MT36	4FT deg		24	Ind		32	BBBBB	Ind	17	
Linguistics and Arabic	QT16	4FT deg		22	Ind		31	BBBBC	Ind		
Management and Arabic	NT16	4FT deg	g	22	Ind		31	BBBBC	Ind	16	
Music and Arabic	TW63	4FT deg		22	Ind		31	BBBBC	Ind		
Persian	T660	3FT deg		22	Ind		31	BBBBC	Ind	11	
Persian and Arabic	T621	4FT deg		22	Ind		31	BBBBC	Ind	4	
Persian and Development Studies	MT9Q	3FT deg		22	Ind		31	BBBBC	Ind		

Languages – Middle Eastern 43

TITLE	CODE	COURSE	SUBJECTS	A/AS	ND/C	AGNVQ	IB	SQA(H)	SQA	RATIO A/AS
Persian and Economics	LT1Q	3FT deg	g	22	Ind		31	BBBBC	Ind	
Persian and Geography	LT8Q	3FT deg		22	Ind		31	BBBBC	Ind	
Persian and Georgian	TTQ9	3FT deg		22	Ind		31	BBBBC	Ind	
Persian and History	TVQ1	3FT deg		22	Ind		31	BBBBC	Ind	
Persian and History of Art/Archaeology	TVQ6	3FT deg		22	Ind		31	BBBBC	Ind	
Persian and Law	MT3Q	3FT deg		24	Ind		32	BBBBB	Ind	
Persian and Linguistics	QT1Q	3FT deg		22	Ind		31	BBBBC	Ind	
Persian and Management	NT1Q	3FT deg	g	22	Ind		31	BBBBC	Ind	
Persian and Music	TWQ3	3FT deg		22	Ind		31	BBBBC	Ind	
Politics and Arabic	MT16	4FT deg		22	Ind		31	BBBBC	Ind	5
Politics and Persian	MT1Q	3FT deg		22	Ind		31	BBBBC	Ind	
Social Anthropology and Arabic	LT66	4FT deg		22	Ind		31	BBBBC	Ind	
Social Anthropology and Persian	LT6Q	3FT deg		22	Ind		31	BBBBC	Ind	
Study of Religions and Arabic	TV68	4FT deg		22	Ind		31	BBBBC	Ind	5
Study of Religions and Persian	TVQ8	3FT deg		22	Ind		31	BBBBC	Ind	
Turkish	T680	4FT deg		22	Ind		31	BBBBC$	Ind	2
Turkish and Arabic	TT62	4FT deg		22	Ind		31	BBBBC	Ind	2
Turkish and Development Studies	MT9P	4FT deg		22	Ind		31	BBBBC	Ind	
Turkish and Economics	LT1P	4FT deg	g	22	Ind		31	BBBBC	Ind	
Turkish and Geography	LT8P	4FT deg		22	Ind		31	BBBBC	Ind	
Turkish and Georgian	TTP9	4FT deg		22	Ind		31	BBBBC	Ind	
Turkish and History	TVP1	4FT deg		22	Ind		31	BBBBC	Ind	
Turkish and History of Art/Archaeology	TVP6	4FT deg		22	Ind		31	BBBBC	Ind	
Turkish and Law	MT3P	4FT deg		24	Ind		32	BBBBB	Ind	
Turkish and Linguistics	QT1P	4FT deg		22	Ind		31	BBBBC	Ind	1
Turkish and Management	NT1P	4FT deg	g	22	Ind		31	BBBBC	Ind	
Turkish and Music	TWP3	4FT deg		22	Ind		31	BBBBC	Ind	
Turkish and Persian	T661	4FT deg		22	Ind		31	BBBBC	Ind	1
Turkish and Politics	MT1P	3FT deg		22	Ind		31	BBBBC	Ind	
Turkish and Social Anthropology	LT6P	4FT deg		22	Ind		31	BBBBC	Ind	
Turkish and Study of Religions	VT8P	4FT deg		22	Ind		31	BBBBC	Ind	
Urdu and Arabic	TT56	4FT deg		22	Ind		31	BBBBC	Ind	
Urdu and Persian	TT5Q	3FT deg		22	Ind		31	BBBBC	Ind	

Univ of ST ANDREWS

TITLE	CODE	COURSE	SUBJECTS	A/AS	ND/C	AGNVQ	IB	SQA(H)	SQA	RATIO A/AS
Art History-Arabic	TV64	4FT deg	* g	BBB	X	Ind	30$	BBBB	Ind	
Economics-Arabic	LT16	4FT deg	* g	BBB	X	Ind	30$	BBBB	Ind	
English-Arabic	TQ63	4FT deg	* g	BBB	X	Ind	30$	BBBB	Ind	
French with Year Abroad-Arabic	RT1P	4FT/5FT deg	£ g	BBB	X	Ind	30$	BBBB$	Ind	2
French-Arabic	RT16	4FT deg	£ g	BBB	X	Ind	30$	BBBB$	Ind	
German with Year Abroad-Arabic	RT2P	4FT/5FT deg	* g	BBC	X	Ind	30$	BBBB	Ind	
German-Arabic	RT26	4FT deg	* g	BBC	X	Ind	30$	BBBB	Ind	
Hebrew-Arabic	QT96	4FT deg	* g	BBC	X	Ind	30$	BBBB	Ind	
International Relations-Arabic	MT16	4FT deg	* g	AAB	X	Ind	36$	AAAB	Ind	6
Italian-Arabic	RT36	4FT deg	* g	BBB	X	Ind	30$	BBBB	Ind	
Latin-Arabic	QT66	4FT deg	* g	BBC	X	Ind	30$	BBBB	Ind	
Management-Arabic	NT1P	4FT deg	* g	BBB	X	Ind	30$	BBBB	Ind	
Mediaeval History-Arabic	TV6C	4FT deg	* g	BBB	X	Ind	30$	BBBB	Ind	
Modern History-Arabic	TV61	4FT deg	* g	BBB	X	Ind	30$	BBBB	Ind	
Social Anthropology-Arabic	LT66	4FT deg	* g	BBB	X	Ind	30$	BBBB	Ind	
Spanish with Year Abroad-Arabic	RT4P	4FT/5FT deg	* g	BBB	X	Ind	30$	BBBB	Ind	
Spanish-Arabic	RT46	4FT deg	* g	BBB	X	Ind	30$	BBBB	Ind	
General Degree of MA Modern Languages (Arabic)	Y450	3FT deg	* g	BBB	X	Ind	30$	BBBB	Ind	

Letts STUDY GUIDES · THE INDEPENDENT

course details			98 expected requirements							96 entry stats	
TITLE	CODE	COURSE	SUBJECTS	A/AS	NO/C	RGNVQ	IB	SQA(H)	SQA	RATIO	A/AS
Univ of WESTMINSTER											
English Language and Arabic	QTH6	4SW deg		CC	Ind		26$	BBB			
English and Arabic	QT36	4SW deg	E	CC	Ind		26$	BBB		3	8/14
French and Arabic	RT16	4SW deg	F	CC	Ind		26$	BBB		4	
German and Arabic	RT26	4SW deg	G	CC	Ind		26$	BBB			
Italian and Arabic	RT36	4SW deg	I	CC	Ind		26	BBB			
Linguistics and Arabic	TQ61	4SW deg	L	CC	Ind		26	BBB		2	
Russian and Arabic	RT86	4SW deg	R	CC	Ind		26	BBB			
Spanish and Arabic	RT46	4SW deg	Sp	CC	Ind		26	BBB			

Languages – Russian 44

TITLE	CODE	COURSE	SUBJECTS	A/AS	NQ/C	RGNVQ	IB	SQA(H)	SQA	RATIO A/AS
Univ of Wales, BANGOR										
European Cultural Studies and Russian	TR28	4FT deg	* g	CCD	5M	D*6/^ go	28	BBBC	Ind	
Russian	R800	4FT deg	* g	CCD	Ind	D*6/^ go	28	BBBC	Ind	8
Russian and Criminology	MR38	4FT deg	* g	18	X	D*^ go	28	BBBC	X	
Russian and Women's Studies	MR98	4FT deg	* g	18	X	D*^ go	28	BBBC	X	
Russian/Accounting	NR48	4FT deg	* g	18	3M+3D	D$6/^ go	28	BBBC	Ind	
Russian/Banking	NR38	4FT deg	* g	18	3M+2D	D$6/^ go	28	BBBC	Ind	
Russian/Economics	LR18	4FT deg	* g	18	3M+2D	D$6/^ go	28	BBBC	Ind	
Russian/English	QR38	4FT deg	E g	CCC	X	D*^ go	28$	BBBC$	X	
Russian/French (Syllabus A)	RR18	4FT deg	E g	CCD	X	D*_ go	28$	BBBC$	X	
Russian/French (Syllabus B)	RRC8	4FT deg	E g	CCD	X	D*_ go	28$	BBBC$	X	
Russian/German	RR28	4FT deg	R g	CCD	X	D*^ go	28$	BBBC$	X	
Russian/History	RV81	4FT deg	H g	CCC	Ind	D*^ go	28$	BBBC$	Ind	
Russian/Linguistics	QR18	4FT deg	* g	CCD	3M $	D*^ go	28	BBBC	Ind	
Russian/Physical Education	RB86	4FT deg	* g	CCC	5D	D*6/^ go	28	BBBC	Ind	
Russian/Religious Studies	RV88	4FT deg	* g	CCD	Ind	D*6/^ go	28	BBBC	Ind	
Sports Science/Russian	BR68	4FT deg	* g	20	5D	D*6/^ go	30	BBBC	Ind	
Welsh/Russian	QR58	4FT deg	W g	CCD	Ind	D*_ go	Ind	X	X	
Univ of BATH										
French and Russian (4 Yr SW)	RR18	4SW deg	F+R	BBC	Ind	Ind	30	Ind	Ind	3
German and Russian (4 Yr SW)	RR28	4SW deg	G+R	BBD	Ind	Ind	30	Ind	Ind	5
Russian and Politics (4 Yr SW)	RM81	4SW deg	R	22	Ind	Ind	30	Ind	Ind	3
Univ of BIRMINGHAM										
Ancient History & Archaeology/Russian	RV86	4FT deg	*	BBB	Ind	D*^	32	ABBB	Ind	
Artificial Intelligence/Russian	GR88	4FT deg	* g	BBB	Ind	D*^	32	ABBB	Ind	
BCom (Russian Studies)	NR98	3FT/4FT deg	R/*	BBC	Ind	D+^	32	ABBBB	Ind	
Classical Literature and Civilisation/Russian	QR88	4FT deg	*	BBB	Ind	D*^	32	ABBB	Ind	
Computer Studies/Russian	GR58	4FT deg	* g	BBB	Ind	D*^	32	ABBB	Ind	
Dance/Russian	WR48	4FT deg	*	BBB	Ind	D*^	32	ABBB	Ind	
Drama/Russian	RW84	4FT deg	*	BBB	Ind	D*^	32	ABBB	Ind	
East Mediterranean History/Russian	RVW1	4FT deg	* g	BBB	Ind	D*^	32	ABBB	Ind	
English/Russian	QR38	4FT deg	*	BBB	Ind	D*^	32	ABBB	Ind	
French Studies and Russian	RR18	4FT deg	F	BBB	Ind	D*_	32$	ABBB	Ind	8
Geography/Russian	LR88	4FT deg	Gy	BBB	Ind	D*_	32$	ABBB	Ind	
German Studies and Russian	RR28	4FT deg	G	BBB	Ind	D*_	32$	ABBB	Ind	5
History of Art/Russian	RV84	4FT deg	*	BBB	Ind	D*^	32	ABBB	Ind	
History/Russian	RV81	4FT deg	*	BBB	Ind	D*^	32	ABBB	Ind	5
International Studies with Russian	M1R8	3FT deg	R	BBC	Ind	D+^	32	ABBBB	Ind	3
Italian and Russian	RR38	4FT deg	*	BBB	Ind	D*^	32	ABBB	Ind	2
Latin/Russian	QR68	4FT deg	Ln	BBB	Ind	D*_	32$	ABBB	Ind	
Mathematics/Russian	GR18	4FT deg	M	ABB-ABC	Ind	D*_	32$	ABBB	Ind	
Media & Cultural Studies/Russian	PR48	4FT deg	*	BBB	Ind	D*^	32	ABBB	Ind	
Modern Greek Studies and Russian	RT82	4FT deg	* g	BBB	Ind	D*^	32	ABBB	Ind	
Music/Russian	RW83	4FT deg	Mu	AAB-ABB	Ind	D*_	32$	ABBB	Ind	
Philosophy/Russian	RV87	4FT deg	*	BBB	Ind	D*^	32	ABBB	Ind	4
Political Science/Russian	MR18	4FT deg	*	BBB	Ind	D*^	32	ABBB	Ind	4
Portuguese and Russian	RR58	4FT deg	*	BBB	Ind	D*^	32	ABBB	Ind	
Russian	R801	4FT deg	*	BBC-BCC	Ind	D*^	30	ABBB	Ind	1
Russian	R800	4FT deg	R	BBC-BCC	Ind	D*_	30$	ABBB	Ind	4
Russian & E Eur Stud and Economic & Social Hist	R8V3	3FT/4FT deg	R/*	BBC	Ind	D+^		ABBBB	Ind	3
Russian & E Eur Studs and Politics & Internat St	R8M1	3FT/4FT deg	R/*	BBC	Ind	D+^		ABBBB	Ind	7

| course details | | | 98 expected requirements | | | | | | | 96 entry stats |

TITLE	CODE	COURSE	SUBJECTS	A/AS	NQ/C	AGNVQ	IB	SQA(H)	SQA	RATIO A/AS
Russian & East European Studies & Social Policy	RL84	3FT/4FT deg	R/*	BBC	Ind	D+^		ABBBB	Ind	
Russian and East European Studies and Economics	RL81	3FT/4FT deg	R/*	BBC	Ind	D+^		ABBBB	Ind	
Russian and East European Studies and Sociology	R8L3	3FT/4FT deg	R/*	BBC	Ind	D+^		ABBBB	Ind	
Russian and Hispanic Studies	RR48	4FT deg	*	BBB	Ind	D*^	32	ABBB	Ind	
Russian/Russian Studies	R814	4FT deg	*	BBB	Ind	D*^	32	ABBB	Ind	
Russian/Sport & Recreation Studies	RB86	4FT deg	*	BBB	Ind	D*^	32	ABBB	Ind	
Russian/Theology	RV88	4FT deg	*	BBB	Ind	D*^	32	ABBB	Ind	
Univ of BRADFORD										
French and Russian	RR18	4SW deg	2L	BCC	Ind	X	Ind	Ind	Ind	5
German and Russian	RR28	4SW deg	2L	BCC	Ind	X	Ind	Ind	Ind	5
Russian	R800	4SW deg	R	BCC	Ind	X	Ind	Ind	Ind	
Russian and Spanish	RR48	4SW deg	2L	BCC	Ind	X	Ind	Ind	Ind	1
Univ of BRISTOL										
Computer Science and Russian	RG85	4FT deg	* g	BBC-BBD	Ind	D$^	30$	CSYS	Ind	2
French and Russian	RR18	4FT deg	F	BBB-BBC	Ind	D$^	30$	BBBBB	Ind	7 20/30
German and Russian	RR28	4FT deg	G	BBB	Ind	D$^	30$	BBBBB	Ind	5 26/30
History of Art and Russian	VR48	4FT deg	L	BBC	Ind	D$^	30$	BBBBB	Ind	
Italian and Russian	RR38	4FT deg	I/R	BBB-BBC	Ind	D$^	30$	AABBB	Ind	
Philosophy and Russian	RV87	4FT deg	L	BB	Ind	D$^	30$	ABBBB	Ind	
Politics and Russian	RM81	4FT deg		BBB	Ind	D$^	32$	AABBB	Ind	
Russian	R800	4FT deg	L	BCC	Ind	D$^	28$	ABBBB	Ind	6
Spanish and Russian	RR48	4FT deg	Sp/R	BBB-BBC	Ind	D$^	30$	ABBBB	Ind	4
BUCKINGHAMSHIRE COLLEGE										
Business Studies with Russian	81RN	2FT HND		4	3M	P	Ind	Ind	Ind	
COVENTRY Univ										
Business Studies with Russian	N1R8	4SW deg	* g	16	M+3D	M	Dip	CCC	Ind	
European Studies with Russian (4 years)	TR28	4FT deg	*	CD	M	M	Ind	CCCC	Ind	
French and Russian	RR18	4FT deg	F	CD	M	M	Ind	CCCC$	Ind	10
German and Russian	RR28	4FT deg	G	CD	M		Ind	CCCC$	Ind	3
Italian and Russian	RR38	4FT deg	I	CD	M	M	Ind	CCCC	Ind	
Russian and History	VR18	4FT deg	*	CD	M	M	Ind	CCCC	Ind	
Russian and Psychology	RC88	4FT deg	*	CD	M	M	Ind	CCCC	Ind	
Social Policy and Russian	RL84	3FT deg								
Sociology and Russian	RL83	3FT deg								
Spanish and Russian	RR48	4FT deg	Sp	CD	M	M	Ind	CCCC$	Ind	
Univ of DURHAM										
Russian and Politics	MR18	4FT deg	*	24	Ind	Ind	33	AAABB	Ind	4
Arts Combined *Russian*	Y300	4FT deg	*	24	MO	Ind	30	AAABB	Ind	
Univ of EDINBURGH										
Russian Studies and Business Studies	RN81	4FT deg	L g	BBB	Ind	Ind	Dip$	BBBB$	Ind	
Russian Studies and European History	RV81	4FT deg	L g	BBB	Ind	Ind	Dip$	BBBB$	Ind	
Russian Studies and Linguistics	RQ81	4FT deg	L g	BBB	Ind	Ind	Dip$	BBBB$	Ind	
Univ of ESSEX										
Computer Science with Russian (4 Yrs)	G5R8	4FT deg	R g	20	MO+2D	Ind	28$	CSYS	Ind	
English and Russian (Language and Linguistics)	RQ83	FT deg	*	20	MO+2D	Ind	28	BBBB	Ind	
Mathematics and Russian (4 Yrs)	GR18	4FT deg	M	18	MO $	Ind	28$	CSYS	Ind	
Russian (Language and Linguistics) (4 Yrs)	R8Q1	4FT deg	*	20	MO+2D	Ind	28	BBBB	Ind	
Russian Studies (4 Yrs)	R810	4FT deg	*	20	MO+2D	Ind	28	BBBB	Ind	21

			98 expected requirements							96 entry stats

course details | *98 expected requirements* | *96 entry stats*

TITLE	CODE	COURSE	SUBJECTS	A/AS	ND/C	AGNVQ	IB	SQA(H)	SQA	RATIO A/AS
EUROPEAN Business School										
Euro Bus Admin with Russian + one beginner lang	N1RV	4SW deg	L	12	Ind		Ind	Ind	Ind	
International Bus St: Russian +one beginner lang	NR18	4FT deg			Ind					
International Bus Studs with Russian (Test+Int)	N1R8	4SW deg		12	Ind		Ind	Ind	Ind	
International Business & Mgt Studs with Russian	N1RW	4SW deg		12	Ind		Ind	Ind	Ind	
Univ of EXETER										
French and Russian	RR1V	4FT deg	F	22-24	MO	M/D$^	34$			
German and Russian	RR2V	4FT deg	G	BBB-BCC	MO	M/D$^	32$			
History and Russian	RV8C	4FT deg	* g	ABB-BCC	MO	M/D$	32	Ind	Ind	
Music and Russian	RW8H	4FT deg	Mu g	BCC	MO	M/D$^	32$	Ind	Ind	
Russian	R801	4FT deg	*	BBC-BDE	MO	M/D$	30			
Russian and Economic History	RV83	4FT deg	* g	BBC-BDE	MO	M/D$	30	Ind	Ind	
Univ of GLASGOW										
Anthropology with Russian	LR68	4FT deg		BBC	N	M	30	BBBB	Ind	
Archaeology/Russian	RV86	5FT deg		BBC	HN	M	30	BBBB	Ind	
Business Economics with Russian	L1RV	4FT deg		BBC	N	M	30	BBBB	N	
Classical Civilisation/Russian	QR88	5FT deg		BBC	HN	M	30	BBBB	Ind	
Computing/Russian	GR58	5FT deg		BBC	HN	M	30	BBBB	Ind	
Czech/Russian	RTV1	5FT deg		BBC	HN	M	30	BBBB	Ind	
Economics with Russian	L1R8	4FT deg		BBC	8M	M	30	BBBB	Ind	
Economics/Russian	LRD8	5FT deg		BBC	HN	M	30	BBBB	Ind	
English/Russian	QR38	5FT deg		BBC	HN	M	30	BBBB	Ind	5
Film and Television Studies/Russian	RW85	5FT deg		BBB	HN	D	32	AABB	HN	
French/Russian	RR18	5FT deg		BBC	HN	M	30	BBBB	Ind	
Geography with Russian	L8R8	4FT deg		BBC	8M	M	30	BBBB	Ind	
Geography/Russian	LR88	5FT deg		BBC	HN	M	30	BBBB	Ind	
German/Russian	RR28	5FT deg		BBC	HN	M	30	BBBB	Ind	
Greek/Russian	QR78	5FT deg		BBC	HN	M	30	BBBB	Ind	
Hispanic Studies/Russian	RR48	5FT deg		BBC	HN	M	30	BBBB	Ind	
History of Art/Russian	RV84	5FT deg		BBC	HN	M	30	BBBB	Ind	
History/Russian	RVV1	5FT deg		BBC	HN	M	30	BBBB	Ind	3
Islamic Studies/Russian	TR68	4FT deg		BBC	N	M	30	BBBB	Ind	
Italian/Russian	RR38	5FT deg		BBC	HN	M	30	BBBB	Ind	
Latin/Russian	RQ86	5FT deg		BBC	HN	M	30	BBBB	Ind	
Management Studies with Russian	N1R8	3FT deg		BBC	8M	M	30	BBBB	Ind	5
Management Studies/Russian	NR18	5FT deg		BBC	HN	M	30	BBBB	Ind	
Mathematics/Russian	GR18	5FT deg		BBC	HN	M	30	BBBB	Ind	
Music/Russian	RW83	5FT deg		BBC	HN	M	30	BBBB	Ind	1
Philosophy with Russian	V7R8	4FT deg		BBC	8M	M	30	BBBB	Ind	
Philosophy/Russian	RV87	5FT deg		BBC	HN	M	30	BBBB	Ind	
Polish/Russian	RT81	5FT deg		BBC	HN	M	30	BBBB	Ind	
Politics with Russian	M1R8	4FT deg		BBC	8M	M	30	BBBB	Ind	
Politics/Russian	MR18	5FT deg		BBC	HN	M	30	BBBB	Ind	
Psychology with Russian	C8R8	4FT deg		BBC	8M	M	30	BBBB	Ind	
Psychology/Russian	CR88	5FT deg		BBC	8M	M	30	BBBB	Ind	
Russian Language and Literature	R800	5FT deg		BBC	HN	M	30	BBBB	Ind	
Russian/Scottish History	RVVC	5FT deg		BBC	HN	M	30	BBBB	Ind	
Russian/Scottish Literature	QR28	5FT deg		BBC	HN	M	30	BBBB	Ind	
Russian/Sociology	LR38	5FT deg		BBC	HN	M	30	BBBB	Ind	
Social and Urban Policy with Russian	L4R8	4FT deg		BBC	8M	M	30	BBBB	Ind	
Social and Urban Policy/Russian	LR48	5FT deg		BBC	HN	M	30	BBBB	Ind	

| | | | | | 98 expected requirements | | | | | | 96 entry stats |
| course details | | | | | | | | | | | |
TITLE	CODE	COURSE	SUBJECTS	A/AS	ND/C	AGNVQ	IB	SQA(H)	SQA	RATIO A/AS
Sociology with Russian	L3R8	4FT deg		BBC	8M	M	30	BBBB	Ind	
Theatre Studies/Russian	RW84	5FT deg		BBC	HN	M	30	BBBB	Ind	
Theology & Religious Studies/Russian	RV88	5FT deg		BBC	HN	M	30	BBBB	Ind	

HERIOT-WATT Univ

TITLE	CODE	COURSE	SUBJECTS	A/AS	ND/C	AGNVQ	IB	SQA(H)	SQA	RATIO A/AS
French/Russian	RR1V	4FT deg								
French/Russian (Interpreting and Translating)	RR18	4FT deg	2L	BBC	Ind		Ind	AABB	Ind	
German/Russian	RR2V	4FT deg								
German/Russian (Interpreting and Translating)	RR28	4FT deg	2L	BBC	Ind		Ind	AABB	Ind	
Russian/Spanish (Interpreting and Translating)	RR48	4FT deg	2L	BBC	Ind		Ind	AABB	Ind	
Spanish/Russian	RR4V	4FT deg								

KEELE Univ

TITLE	CODE	COURSE	SUBJECTS	A/AS	ND/C	AGNVQ	IB	SQA(H)	SQA	RATIO A/AS
Finance and Russian	NR38	3FT deg	R g	BCC	Ind	D$^	28$	CSYS	Ind	
Finance and Russian Studies	NR3W	3FT deg	* g	BCC	Ind	D$	28	CSYS	Ind	
Russian Studies & Business Administration(4 Yrs)	RNV9	4FT deg	*	BCC	Ind	Ind	28	BBBB	Ind	
Russian Studies and American Studies	QRK8	3FT deg	*	BCC	Ind	Ind	28	CSYS	Ind	
Russian Studies and American Studies (4 Yrs)	RQ8K	4FT deg	*	BCC	Ind	Ind	28	BBBB	Ind	
Russian Studies and Ancient History	RVVD	3FT deg	*	BCC	Ind	Ind	28	CSYS	Ind	
Russian Studies and Applied Social Studies	LR5V	3FT deg	*	BCC	Ind	Ind	28	CSYS	Ind	
Russian Studies and Applied Social Studs (4 Yrs)	RLV5	4FT deg	*	BCC	Ind	Ind	28	BBBB	Ind	
Russian Studies and Biochemistry	CRR8	3FT deg	C g	BCC	Ind	D$^	28$	CSYS	Ind	
Russian Studies and Biochemistry (4 Yrs)	RC8R	4FT deg	*	BCC	Ind	Ind	28	BBBB	Ind	
Russian Studies and Biolgical & Med Chem (4 Yrs)	RFVC	4FT deg	*	BCC	Ind	Ind	28	BBBB	Ind	
Russian Studies and Biology	CRC8	3FT deg	S g	BCC	Ind	D$^	28$	CSYS	Ind	
Russian Studies and Biology (4 Yrs)	RC8C	4FT deg	*	BCC	Ind	Ind	28	BBBB	Ind	
Russian Studies and Business Administration	NR9V	3FT deg	*	BCC	Ind	Ind	28	CSYS	Ind	
Russian Studies and Chemistry	FRC8	3FT deg	C g	BCC	Ind	D$^	28$	CSYS	Ind	
Russian Studies and Chemistry (4 Yrs)	RF8C	4FT deg	*	BCC	Ind	Ind	28	BBBB	Ind	
Russian Studies and Classical Studies	QR8V	3FT deg	*	BCC	Ind	Ind	28	CSYS	Ind	
Russian Studies and Computer Science	GRM8	3FT deg	* g	BCC	Ind	Ind	28	CSYS	Ind	
Russian Studies and Computer Science (4 Yrs)	RG8M	4FT deg	*	BCC	Ind	Ind	28	BBBB	Ind	
Russian Studies and Criminology (4 Yrs)	RMVH	4FT deg	*	BBB-BCC	Ind	Ind	32	BBBB	Ind	
Russian Studies and Economics	LRC8	3FT deg	* g	BCC	Ind	Ind	28	CSYS	Ind	
Russian Studies and Economics (4 Yrs)	RL8C	4FT deg	*	BCC	Ind	Ind	28	BBBB	Ind	
Russian Studies and Educational Studies	RXV9	3FT deg	*	BCC	Ind	Ind	28	CSYS	Ind	
Russian Studies and Educational Studies (4 Yrs)	XR9V	4FT deg	*	BCC	Ind	Ind	28	BBBB	Ind	
Russian Studies and Electronic Music (4 Yrs)	WRJV	4FT deg	*	BCC	Ind	Ind	28	BBBB	Ind	
Russian Studies and English	QRH8	3FT deg	E	BBC	Ind	D$^	30$	CSYS	Ind	
Russian Studies and English (4 Yrs)	RQ8H	4FT deg	*	BBC	Ind	Ind	30	BBBB	Ind	
Russian Studies and Environmental Mgt (4 Yrs)	RFVX	4FT deg	* g	BCC	Ind	Ind	28	BBBB	Ind	
Russian Studies and European Studies	RTV2	3FT deg	*	BCC	Ind	Ind	28	CSYS	Ind	
Russian Studies and European Studies (4 Yrs)	TR2V	4FT deg	*	BCC	Ind	Ind	28	BBBB	Ind	
Russian Studies and French	RRC8	3FT deg	F	BCC	Ind	D$^	28$	CSYS	Ind	
Russian Studies and French (4 Yrs)	RR8C	4FT deg	*	BCC	Ind	Ind	28	BBBB	Ind	
Russian Studies and French/German	RTV9	3FT deg	F+G	BBC	Ind	D$^	30$	CSYS	Ind	
Russian Studies and French/German (4 Yrs)	TR9V	4FT deg	* g	BBC-CCC	Ind	Ind	28	BBBB	Ind	
Russian Studies and Geology	FRP8	3FT deg	S g	BCC	Ind	D$^	28$	CSYS	Ind	
Russian Studies and Geology (4 Yrs)	RF8P	4FT deg	*	BCC	Ind	Ind	28	BBBB	Ind	
Russian Studies and German	RRF8	3FT deg	G	BCC	Ind	D$^	28$	CSYS	Ind	
Russian Studies and History	RV8C	3FT deg	*	BCC	Ind	Ind	28	CSYS	Ind	
Russian Studies and History (4 Yrs)	VRC8	4FT deg	*	BCC	Ind	Ind	28	BBBB	Ind	
Russian Studies and Human Resource Management	NR6V	3FT deg	*	BCC	Ind	Ind	28	CSYS	Ind	

course details			*98 expected requirements*							*96 entry stats*
TITLE	CODE	COURSE	SUBJECTS	A/AS	ND/C	AGNVQ	IB	SQA(H)	SQA	RATIO A/AS
Russian Studies and Human Resource Mgt (4 Yrs)	RNV6	4FT deg	*	BCC	Ind	Ind	28	BBBB	Ind	
Russian Studies and International History	RVVC	3FT deg	*	BCC	Ind	Ind	28	CSYS	Ind	
Russian Studies and International History(4 Yrs)	VRCV	4FT deg	*	BCC	Ind	Ind	28	BBBB	Ind	
Russian Studies and International Pol (4 Yrs)	RMVC	4FT deg	*	BCC	Ind	Ind	28	BBBB	Ind	
Russian Studies and International Politics	MRCV	3FT deg	*	BCC	Ind	Ind	28	CSYS	Ind	
Russian Studies and Latin	QR6V	3FT deg	Ln	BCC	Ind	D$^	28$	CSYS	Ind	
Russian Studies and Management Science	NR1V	3FT deg	* g	BCC	Ind	Ind	28	CSYS	Ind	
Russian Studies and Management Science (4 Yrs)	RN8C	4FT deg	*	BCC	Ind	Ind	28	BBBB	Ind	
Russian Studies and Marketing	NR5V	3FT deg	*	BCC	Ind	Ind	28	CSYS	Ind	
Russian Studies and Mathematics	GRC8	3FT deg	M	BCC	Ind	D$^	28$	CSYS	Ind	
Russian Studies and Mathematics (4 Yrs)	RG8C	4FT deg	*	BCC	Ind	Ind	28	BBBB	Ind	
Russian Studies and Music (4 Yrs)	WR3V	4FT deg	*	BCC	Ind	Ind	28	BBBB	Ind	
Russian Studies and Philosophy	RVV7	3FT deg	*	BCC	Ind	Ind	28	CSYS	Ind	
Russian Studies and Philosophy (4 Yrs)	VR7V	4FT deg	*	BCC	Ind	Ind	28	BBBB	Ind	
Russian Studies and Politics	MRC8	3FT deg	*	BCC	Ind	Ind	28	CSYS	Ind	
Russian Studies and Politics (4 Yrs)	RM8C	4FT deg	*	BCC	Ind	Ind	28	BBBB	Ind	
Russian Studies and Psychology	CR8V	3FT deg	* g	BBB	Ind	Ind	32	CSYS	Ind	
Russian Studies and Sociology & Soc Anthropology	LR3V	3FT deg	*	BCC	Ind	Ind	28	CSYS	Ind	
Russian Studs and Biological and Medicinal Chem	FRCV	3FT deg	C g	BCC	Ind	D$^	28$	CSYS	Ind	
Russian and American Studies	QR48	3FT deg	R	BCC	Ind	D$^	28$	CSYS	Ind	
Russian and American Studies (4 Yrs)	RQ84	4FT deg	*	BCC	Ind	Ind	28	BBBB	Ind	
Russian and Ancient History	RV8D	3FT deg	R	BCC	Ind	D$^	28$	CSYS	Ind	
Russian and Applied Social Studies	LR58	3FT deg	R	BCC	Ind	D$^	28$	CSYS	Ind	
Russian and Applied Social Studies (4 Yrs)	RL85	4FT deg	*	BCC	Ind	Ind	28	BBBB	Ind	
Russian and Biochemistry	CR78	3FT deg	C+R g	BCC	Ind	D$^	28$	CSYS	Ind	
Russian and Biochemistry (4 Yrs)	RC87	4FT deg	*	BCC	Ind	Ind	28	BBBB	Ind	
Russian and Biological and Medicinal Chem(4 Yrs)	RFWC	4FT deg	*	BCC	Ind	Ind	28	BBBB	Ind	
Russian and Biological and Medicinal Chemistry	FRCW	3FT deg	R/C g	BCC	Ind	D$^	28$	CSYS	Ind	
Russian and Biology	CR18	3FT deg	S+R g	BCC	Ind	D$^	28$	CSYS	Ind	
Russian and Biology (4 Yrs)	RC81	4FT deg	*	BCC	Ind	Ind	28	BBBB	Ind	
Russian and Business Administration	NR98	3FT deg	R	BCC	Ind	D$^	28$	CSYS	Ind	3
Russian and Business Administration (4 Yrs)	RN89	4FT deg	*	BCC	Ind	Ind	28	BBBB	Ind	
Russian and Chemistry	FR18	3FT deg	C+R g	BCC	Ind	D$^	28$	CSYS	Ind	
Russian and Chemistry (4 Yrs)	RF81	4FT deg	*	BCC	Ind	Ind	28	BBBB	Ind	
Russian and Classical Studies	QR88	3FT deg	R	BCC	Ind	D$^	28$	CSYS	Ind	
Russian and Computer Science	GR58	3FT deg	R	BCC	Ind	D$^	28$	CSYS	Ind	
Russian and Computer Science (4 Yrs)	RG85	4FT deg	*	BCC	Ind	Ind	28	BBBB	Ind	
Russian and Criminology (4 Yrs)	RM8H	4FT deg	* g	BBB	Ind	Ind	32	ABBB	Ind	
Russian and Economics	LR18	3FT deg	R g	BCC	Ind	D$^	28$	CSYS	Ind	
Russian and Economics (4 Yrs)	RL81	4FT deg	*	BCC	Ind	Ind	28	BBBB	Ind	
Russian and Educational Studies	RX89	3FT deg	R	BCC	Ind	D$^	28$	CSYS	Ind	
Russian and Educational Studies (4 Yrs)	XR98	4FT deg	*	BCC	Ind	Ind	28	BBBB	Ind	
Russian and Electronic Music (4 Yrs)	WRJ8	4FT deg	*	BCC	Ind	Ind	28	BBBB	Ind	
Russian and English	QR38	3FT deg	R+E	BBC	Ind	D$^	30$	CSYS	Ind	
Russian and English (4 Yrs)	RQ83	4FT deg	*	BBC	Ind	Ind	30	BBBB	Ind	
Russian and Environmental Management (4 Yrs)	RF8X	4FT deg	* g	BCC	Ind	Ind	28	BBBB	Ind	
Russian and European Studies	RT82	3FT deg	R	BCC	Ind	D$^	28$	CSYS	Ind	
Russian and European Studies (4 Yrs)	TR28	4FT deg	*	BCC	Ind	Ind	28	BBBB	Ind	
Russian and French	RR18	3FT deg	R+F	BCC	Ind	D$^	28$	CSYS	Ind	
Russian and French (4 Yrs)	RR81	4FT deg	*	BCC	Ind	Ind	28	BBBB	Ind	
Russian and French/German	RT89	3FT deg	F+R+G	BBC	Ind	D$^	30$	CSYS	Ind	
Russian and French/German (4 Yrs)	TR98	4FT deg	* g	BBC-BCC	Ind	Ind	28	BBBB	Ind	

			98 expected requirements							96 entry stats

course details

TITLE	CODE	COURSE	SUBJECTS	A/AS	ND/C	AGNVQ	IB	SQA(H)	SQA	RATIO A/AS
Russian and Geology	FR68	3FT deg	R+S g	BCC	Ind	D$^	28$	CSYS	Ind	
Russian and Geology (4 Yrs)	RF86	4FT deg	*	BCC	Ind	Ind	28	BBBB	Ind	
Russian and German	RR28	3FT deg	G+R	BCC	Ind	D$^	28$	CSYS	Ind	
Russian and History	RV81	3FT deg	R	BCC	Ind	D$^	28$	CSYS	Ind	
Russian and History (4 Yrs)	VR18	4FT deg	*	BCC	Ind	Ind	28	BBBB	Ind	
Russian and Human Resource Management	NR68	3FT deg	R	BCC	Ind	D$^	28$	CSYS	Ind	
Russian and Human Resource Management (4 Yrs)	RN86	4FT deg	*	BCC	Ind	Ind	28	BBBB	Ind	
Russian and International History	RVWC	3FT deg	R	BCC	Ind	D$^	28$	CSYS	Ind	
Russian and International History (4 Yrs)	VRCW	4FT deg	*	BCC	Ind	Ind	28	BBBB	Ind	
Russian and International Politics	MRDV	3FT deg	R	BCC	Ind	D$^	28$	CSYS	Ind	
Russian and International Politics (4 Yrs)	RMWC	4FT deg	*	BCC	Ind	Ind	28	BBBB	Ind	
Russian and Latin	QR68	3FT deg	Ln+R	BCC	Ind	D$^	28$	CSYS	Ind	
Russian and Management Science	NR18	3FT deg	R g	BCC	Ind	D$^	28$	CSYS	Ind	
Russian and Management Science (4 Yrs)	RN81	4FT deg	*	BCC	Ind	Ind	28	BBBB	Ind	
Russian and Marketing	NR58	3FT deg	R	BCC	Ind	D$^	28$	CSYS	Ind	
Russian and Mathematics	GR18	3FT deg	R+M	BCC	Ind	D$^	28$	CSYS	Ind	
Russian and Mathematics (4 Yrs)	RG81	4FT deg	*	BCC	Ind	Ind	28	BBBB	Ind	
Russian and Music (4 Yrs)	WR38	4FT deg	* g	BCC	Ind	Ind	28	BBBB	Ind	
Russian and Philosophy	RV87	3FT deg	R	BCC	Ind	D$^	28$	CSYS	Ind	
Russian and Philosophy (4 Yrs)	VR78	4FT deg	*	BCC	Ind	Ind	28	BBBB	Ind	2
Russian and Politics	MR18	3FT deg	R	BCC	Ind	D$^	28$	CSYS	Ind	
Russian and Politics (4 Yrs)	RM81	4FT deg	*	BCC	Ind	Ind	28	BBBB	Ind	
Russian and Psychology	CR88	3FT deg	R g	BBB	Ind	D$^	32$	CSYS	Ind	
Sociol & Soc Anthropology and Russian St (4 Yrs)	RLV3	4FT deg	*	BCC	Ind	Ind	28	BBBB	Ind	
Sociol & Social Anthropology and Russian (4 Yrs)	RL83	4FT deg	*	BCC	Ind	Ind	28	BBBB	Ind	
Sociology & Social Anthropology and Russian	LR38	3FT deg	R	BCC	Ind	D$^	28$	CSYS	Ind	
Statistics and Russian (4 Yrs)	RG84	4FT deg	*	BCC	Ind	Ind	28	BBBB	Ind	
Statistics and Russian Studies (4 Yrs)	RGV4	4FT deg	*	BCC	Ind	Ind	28	BBBB	Ind	
Visual Arts and Russian	RW81	3FT deg	R	BCC	Ind	D$^	28$	CSYS	Ind	
Visual Arts and Russian Studies	RWV1	3FT deg	*	BCC	Ind	D$^	28	D$^	Ind	

KING'S COLL LONDON (Univ of London)

German and Russian	RR28	3FT deg	G	BCC						

Univ of LEEDS

Arabic-Russian B	RTV6	4FT deg	Cl/L g	BCC	Ind	Ind	28$	CSYS	Ind	
Arabic-Russian B	RT86	4FT deg	R g	BCC	Ind	Ind	28$	CSYS	Ind	
Chinese-Russian	RT83	4FT deg	R g	BBC	Ind	Ind	30$	CSYS	Ind	2
Chinese-Russian B	RTV3	4FT deg	L g	BBC	Ind	Ind	30$	CSYS	Ind	
Classical Literature-Russian	QR88	4FT deg	R g	BBC	Ind	Ind	30$	CSYS	Ind	
Classical Literature-Russian B	QR8V	4FT deg	L g	BBC	Ind	Ind	30$	CSYS	Ind	
Economics-Russian	RL81	4FT deg	R g	BBC	Ind	Ind	30$	CSYS	Ind	
Economics-Russian B	RLV1	4FT deg	L g	BBC	Ind	Ind	30$	CSYS	Ind	
English-Russian	QR38	4FT deg	E+R g	BBC	Ind	Ind	30$	CSYS	Ind	5
English-Russian B	QR3V	4FT deg	E+L g	BBC	Ind	Ind	30$	CSYS	Ind	
French-Russian	RR18	4FT deg	F+R g	BBC	Ind	Ind	30$	CSYS	Ind	6
French-Russian B	RR1V	4FT deg	F g	BBC	Ind	Ind	30$	CSYS	Ind	7 20/26
Geography-Russian Studies	RL88	4FT deg	R+Gy g	BBC	Ind	Ind	30$	CSYS	Ind	
Geography-Russian Studies B	RLV8	4FT deg	L+Gy g	BBC	Ind	Ind	30$	CSYS	Ind	
German-Russian	RR28	4FT deg	G+R g	BCC	Ind	Ind	28$	CSYS	Ind	5
German-Russian B	RR2V	4FT deg	G g	BCC	Ind	Ind	28$	CSYS	Ind	34
History-Russian Studies	RV81	4FT deg	R g	BBC	Ind	Ind	30$	CSYS	Ind	
History-Russian Studies B	RVV1	4FT deg	L g	BBC	Ind	Ind	30	CSYS	Ind	

Languages – Russian 44

TITLE	CODE	COURSE	SUBJECTS	A/AS	NO/C	AGNVQ	IB	SQA(H)	SQA	RATIO A/AS
Italian-Russian	RR38	4FT deg	I+R g	BCC	Ind	Ind	28$	CSYS	Ind	
Italian-Russian B	RRHV	4FT deg	I/R g	BCC	Ind	Ind	28$	CSYS	Ind	
Japanese-Russian	RT84	4FT deg	R g	BBC	Ind	Ind	30$	CSYS	Ind	3
Japanese-Russian B	RTV4	4FT deg	L g	BBC	Ind	Ind	30$	CSYS	Ind	5
Latin-Russian	QR68	4FT deg	Ln+R g	BBC	Ind	Ind	30$	CSYS	Ind	
Latin-Russian B	QR6V	4FT deg	Ln g	BBC	Ind	Ind	30$	CSYS	Ind	
Linguistics-Russian	QR18	4FT deg	R g	BCC	Ind	Ind	28$	CSYS	Ind	
Linguistics-Russian B	QR1V	4FT deg	L g	BCC	Ind	Ind	28$	CSYS	Ind	
Management Studies-Russian	RN81	4FT deg	R g	BBC	Ind	Ind	30$	CSYS	Ind	
Management Studies-Russian B	RNV1	4FT deg	L g	BBC	Ind	Ind	30$	CSYS	Ind	
Mathematics-Russian	RG81	4FT deg	M+R g	BBC	Ind	Ind	30$	CSYS	Ind	
Mathematics-Russian B	RGV1	4FT deg	M+L g	BBC	Ind	Ind	30$	CSYS	Ind	
Philosophy-Russian	RV87	4FT deg	R g	BBC	Ind	Ind	30$	CSYS	Ind	
Philosophy-Russian B	RVV7	4FT deg	L g	BBC	Ind	Ind	30$	CSYS	Ind	
Politics and Parliamentary Studies-Russian St	MR18	4FT deg								
Politics-Russian Studies	RM81	4FT deg	R g	BBC	Ind	Ind	30$	CSYS	Ind	
Portuguese-Russian	RR58	4FT deg	R g	BBC	Ind	Ind	30$	CSYS	Ind	
Portuguese-Russian B	RR5V	4FT deg	L g	BBC	Ind	Ind	30$	CSYS	Ind	
Religious Studies-Russian	RV8V	4FT deg	R g	BBC	Ind	Ind	30$	CSYS	Ind	
Religious Studies-Russian B	RVVV	4FT deg	L g	BBC	Ind	Ind	30	CSYS	Ind	
Roman Civilisation-Russian	QRV8	4FT deg	R g	BBC	Ind	Ind	30$	CSYS	Ind	
Roman Civilisation-Russian B	QRVV	4FT deg	L g	BBC	Ind	Ind	30$	CSYS	Ind	
Russian Studies	R800	4FT deg	R g	BCC	Ind	Ind	28$	CSYS	Ind	2 14/20
Russian Studies B	R805	4FT deg	* g	BCC	Ind	Ind	28$	CSYS	Ind	3
Russian-Sociology	RL83	4FT deg	R g	BBC	Ind	Ind	30$	CSYS	Ind	
Russian-Sociology B	RLV3	4FT deg	L g	BBC	Ind	Ind	30$	CSYS	Ind	
Russian-Spanish	RR48	4FT deg	Sp+R g	BCC	Ind	Ind	28$	CSYS	Ind	
Russian-Spanish B	RR4V	4FT deg	Sp g	BCC	Ind	Ind	28$	CSYS	Ind	
Russian-Theology	RV88	4FT deg	R g	BBC	Ind	Ind	30$	CSYS	Ind	
Russian-Theology B	RVV8	4FT deg	L g	BBC	Ind	Ind	30	CSYS	Ind	

Univ of LIVERPOOL

TITLE	CODE	COURSE	SUBJECTS	A/AS	NO/C	AGNVQ	IB	SQA(H)	SQA	RATIO A/AS
Arts Combined *Russian and Soviet Studies*	Y401	3FT deg	*	BBC-BBB	Ind	Ind	30$	ABBB	Ind	

LIVERPOOL JOHN MOORES Univ

TITLE	CODE	COURSE	SUBJECTS	A/AS	NO/C	AGNVQ	IB	SQA(H)	SQA	RATIO A/AS
French and Russian	RR18	4FT deg	L	14	3M+4D		Ind			5
German and Russian	RR28	4FT deg	L	14	3M+4D		Ind			
International Business Studies with Russian	N1R8	4SW deg		16	3M+4D					

LSE: LONDON Sch of Economics (Univ of London)

TITLE	CODE	COURSE	SUBJECTS	A/AS	NO/C	AGNVQ	IB	SQA(H)	SQA	RATIO A/AS
Russian Joint Studies	MR18	3FT deg	L g	BBB	X	X	$	X	X	8

Univ of MANCHESTER

TITLE	CODE	COURSE	SUBJECTS	A/AS	NO/C	AGNVQ	IB	SQA(H)	SQA	RATIO A/AS
English and a Modern Language (Russian)	RQ83	4FT deg	E	ABB			Ind	BBBBC		3
French/Russian	RR1W	4FT deg	F	ABB		D^	30$	AABB$		4
French/Russian	RR18	4FT deg	F	ABB		D^	30$	AABB$		4 22/28
German/Russian	RR28	4FT deg	G	BBB			28	BBBBC		12
German/Russian	RR2W	4FT deg	G	BBB			28	BBBBC		8
Italian/Russian	RR38	4FT deg	I/R	BBB-BCC			Ind	BBBCC		
Italian/Russian	RR3W	4FT deg	I/R	BBB-BCC			Ind	BBBCC		
Linguistics and Russian	QR18	4FT deg	R	BBB	X		32$	AABBB		1
Russian Studies	R810	4FT deg		BBC-CCC	Ind		28$	BBBB	Ind	10
Russian/French	RR8C	4FT deg	R+F	BBC-CCC	Ind		28$	BBBCC	Ind	
Russian/German	RR8G	4FT deg	R+G	BBC-CCC	Ind		28$	BBBCC	Ind	

| | | | | 98 expected requirements | | | | | | | 96 entry stats |
| course details | | | | | | | | | | | |

TITLE	CODE	COURSE	SUBJECTS	A/AS	NO/C	AGNVQ	IB	SQA(H)	SQA	RATIO A/AS
Russian/Italian	RR8H	4FT deg	R	CCC-BBC	Ind		26$	BBBCC	Ind	
Russian/Portuguese	RR85	4FT deg	R	CCC-BBC	Ind		26$	BBBCC	Ind	
Russian/Spanish	RR84	4FT deg	Sp	CCC-BBC	Ind		26$	BBBCC	Ind	
Russian/Spanish	RR8L	4FT deg	R	CCC-BBC	Ind		26$	BBBCC	Ind	
Spanish/Russian	RR4W	4FT deg	Sp	BBB-BBC	Ind		28$	ABBBB$		1

Univ of NORTHUMBRIA

TITLE	CODE	COURSE	SUBJECTS	A/AS	NO/C	AGNVQ	IB	SQA(H)	SQA	RATIO A/AS
French and Russian	RR18	3FT deg	F	CC	2M+2D	M^	24	BBCCC	Ind	5
German and Russian	RR28	3FT deg	G	CC	2M+2D	M^	24	BBCCC	Ind	2
Russian and Economics	LR18	3FT deg		CC	2M+2D	M^	24	BBCCC	Ind	
Russian and German	RR82	3FT deg	R	CC	2M+2D	M^	24	CCCC	Ind	
Russian and Politics	MR18	3FT deg		CC	2M+2D	M^	24	BBCCC	Ind	
Russian and Spanish	RR84	3FT deg	R	CC	MO+1D		24	CCCC	Ind	
Spanish and Russian	RR48	3FT deg	Sp	CC	2M+2D	M^	24	BBCCC	Ind	

Univ of NOTTINGHAM

TITLE	CODE	COURSE	SUBJECTS	A/AS	NO/C	AGNVQ	IB	SQA(H)	SQA	RATIO A/AS
Economics with Russian	L1R8	4FT deg	L g	AAB-ABB	X		32$	Ind	X	8
Electrical and Electronic Eng with Russian	H6R8	3FT/4FT deg	M+P	BBC-BCC	Ind	Ind	28$	Ind	Ind	
Electronic Engineering with Russian	H6RV	3FT/4FT deg	M+P	BBC-BCC	Ind	Ind	28$	Ind	Ind	
French and Russian	RR18	4FT deg	F+R	BBB						9
French and Russian (Beginners)	RR1V	4FT deg	F	BBC						7	24/30
German and Russian	RR28	4FT deg	G+R	BBC						
German and Russian (Beginners)	RR2V	4FT deg	G	BBC						5	22/30
Hispanic Studies and Russian	RRL8	4FT deg	Sp+R	BBC						
Hispanic Studies and Russian (Beginners)	RRLV	4FT deg	Sp	BBC						1
History and Russian	VR18	4FT deg	H+R	BCC						
History and Russian (Beginners)	VR1V	4FT deg	H	BCC						6
Manufacturing Engineering & Mgt with Russian	H7R8	3FT/4FT deg	M g	CCC	Ind	Ind	28$	Ind	Ind	
Mechanical Engineering with Russian	H3R8	3FT/4FT deg	M+P g	BBC-BCC	Ind	Ind	28$	Ind	Ind	
Portuguese (Beginners) and Russian	RRM8	4FT deg	R	BBC						
Production and Operations Mgt with Russian	H7RV	3FT deg	M g	CCC	Ind	Ind	28$	Ind	Ind	
Russian Studies	R810	4FT deg	R	CCC						6
Russian Studies (Beginners)	R812	4FT deg	L	CCC						4	18/22
Russian and East European Area Studies	RT8C	4FT deg	H/So+L	BBC						10
Russian and Serbo-Croat	RT81	4FT deg	R	CCC						

Univ of PORTSMOUTH

TITLE	CODE	COURSE	SUBJECTS	A/AS	NO/C	AGNVQ	IB	SQA(H)	SQA	RATIO A/AS
Russian and French	RR18	3FT deg	F	12	5M $	M$6/^	Dip	BBBC	Ind	
Russian and German	RR28	3FT deg	G	12	5M $	M$6/^	Dip	BBBC	Ind	
Russian and Italian	RR83	4FT deg	*	10-12	5M	M*6/^ go	Dip	BBCC	Ind	
Russian and Soviet Studies	R810	4FT deg	*	10-12	5M	M*6/^ go	Dip	BBCC	Ind	2	8/14
Russian and Spanish	RR84	4FT deg	*	10-12	5M	M*6/^ go	Dip	BBCC	Ind	

QUEEN MARY & WESTFIELD COLL (Univ of London)

TITLE	CODE	COURSE	SUBJECTS	A/AS	NO/C	AGNVQ	IB	SQA(H)	SQA	RATIO A/AS
English and Russian	QRH8	4FT deg	E	20		M	30$			
French and Russian	RR18	4FT deg	F	18		M^	30$			
German and Russian	RR82	4FT deg	G	20		M^	30$			
Hispanic Studies and Russian (European Studies)	RR8L	4FT deg	L	20		M^	30$			
Russian	R800	4FT deg	L	22		M^	30$			
Russian (European Studies)	RT8F	4FT deg	L	18		M^	30$			
Russian and Drama (European Studies)	WR48	4FT deg	L	20		M^	30$			
Russian and Economics	LR1V	4FT deg	L g	BCC		M^	30$	BBBBB		
Russian and Geography	LRV8	4FT deg	L+Gy	BCC		M^	30$			
Russian and Linguistics	QR18	4FT deg	L	18		M^	30$			

			98 expected requirements							96 entry stats	
course details											
TITLE	CODE	COURSE	SUBJECTS	A/AS	ND/C	AGNVQ	IB	SQA(H)	SQA	RATIO	A/AS
Russian and Mathematics	GRD8	4FT deg	L+M	18		M^	30$				
Russian and Politics	MR18	4FT deg		BCC		M^					
Russian with Business Studies	R8N1	4FT deg	g	18		M^					
Russian, Linguistics and Computer Science	GR58	4FT deg	L	BBC-BCD	3D $	D^	28$				
SSEES:Sch of Slavonic & E European St(U of London)											
French and Russian	RR18	4FT deg	F	BBC	3M $	Ind	28	BBBBB		4	18/28
German and Russian	RR28	4FT deg	G	BBC	3M $	Ind	28	BBBBB		5	
History and Russian	VR18	4FT deg	H	BCC		Ind	28				
Russian Studies	R810	4FT deg		BCC	3M $	Ind	28	BBBBB		4	20/24
Univ of SHEFFIELD											
Computer Science and Russian	GR58	4FT deg	L+M g	BBC	4M+2D$	D^	30$	ABBB$	Ind		
English and Russian	QR38	4FT deg	El+L g	BBB	X	X	32$	AABB$	Ind		
French and Russian	RR18	4FT deg	F g	BCC	X	X	29$	BBBB$	Ind	24	
German and Russian	RR28	4FT deg	G g	BCC	X	X	29$	BBBB$	Ind	4	24/30
History and Russian	RV81	4FT deg	H+L g	BBB	X	X	32$	AABB$	Ind	6	
Linguistics and Russian	QR18	4FT deg	Ee+L g	BBC	X	X	30$	ABBB$	Ind		
Russian Studies	R800	4FT deg	L g	BCD	X	X	28$	BBBC$	Ind	6	
Russian and Business Studies	RN81	4FT deg	L g	BBC	X	D^	30$	ABBB$	Ind		
Russian and Economics	RL81	4FT deg	L g	BBC	X	D^	30	ABBB	Ind	2	
Russian and Hispanic Studies	RR48	4FT deg	L g	BCC	X	X	30$	ABBB$	Ind		
Russian and Politics	RM81	4FT deg	L g	BBC	X	X	30$	ABBB$	Ind	6	
Russian with Czech	R8T1	4FT deg	L g	BCC	X	X	29$	BBBB$	Ind		
Russian with Polish	R8TC	4FT deg	L g	BCC	X	X	29$	BBBB$	Ind		
Univ of ST ANDREWS											
Modern Languages (Russian with Integ Yr Abroad)	R811	4FT/5FT deg	* g	BBB	X	Ind	30$	BBBB	Ind		
Modern Languages (Russian)	R800	4FT deg	* g	BBC	X	Ind	30$	BBBB	Ind		
Russian with Year Abroad-Art History	RV8K	4FT/5FT deg	* g	BBB	X	Ind	30$	BBBB	Ind		
Russian with Year Abroad-Economics	LRC8	4FT/5FT deg	* g	BBB	X	Ind	30$	BBBB	Ind		
Russian with Year Abroad-English	QRH8	4FT/5FT deg	* g	BBB	X	Ind	30$	BBBB	Ind		
Russian with Year Abroad-French	RRC8	4FT/5FT deg	F g	BBB	X	Ind	30$	BBBB$	Ind	7	
Russian with Year Abroad-German	RRF8	4FT/5FT deg	* g	BBC	X	Ind	30$	BBBB	Ind		
Russian with Year Abroad-Hebrew	QR9V	4FT/5FT deg	* g	BBC	X	Ind	30$	BBBB	Ind		
Russian with Year Abroad-International Relations	MRC8	4FT/5FT deg	* g	AAB	X	Ind	36$	AAAB	Ind		
Russian with Year Abroad-Italian	RR83	4FT/5FT deg	* g	BBB	X	Ind	30$	BBBB	Ind		
Russian with Year Abroad-Latin	QRP8	4FT/5FT deg	* g	BBC	X	Ind	30$	BBBB	Ind		
Russian with Year Abroad-Management	NRC8	4FT/5FT deg	* g	BBB	X	Ind	30$	BBBB	Ind		
Russian with Year Abroad-Mediaeval History	RV8C	4FT/5FT deg	* g	BBB	X	Ind	30$	BBBB	Ind		
Russian with Year Abroad-Modern History	RVVC	4FT/5FT deg	* g	BBB	X	Ind	30$	BBBB	Ind	4	
Russian with Year Abroad-Philosophy	RVV7	4FT/5FT deg	* g	BBB	X	Ind	30$	BBBB	Ind		
Russian-Art History	RV84	4FT deg	* g	BBB	X	Ind	30$	BBBB	Ind		
Russian-Economics	LR18	4FT deg	* g	BBB	X	Ind	30$	BBBB	Ind		
Russian-English	QR38	4FT deg	* g	BBB	X	Ind	30$	BBBB	Ind		
Russian-French	RR18	4FT deg	F g	BBB	X	Ind	30$	BBBB$	Ind	3	
Russian-German	RR28	4FT deg	* g	BBC	X	Ind	30$	BBBB	Ind	4	
Russian-Hebrew	QR98	4FT deg	* g	BBC	X	Ind	30$	BBBB	Ind		
Russian-International Relations	MR18	4FT deg	* g	AAB	X	Ind	36$	AAAB	Ind	2	
Russian-Italian	RR38	4FT deg	* g	BBB	X	Ind	30$	BBBB	Ind		
Russian-Latin	QR68	4FT deg	* g	BBC	X	Ind	30$	BBBB	Ind		
Russian-Management	NR18	4FT deg	* g	BBB	X	Ind	30$	BBBB	Ind		
Russian-Mediaeval History	RVV1	4FT deg	* g	BBB	X	Ind	30$	BBBB	Ind		
Russian-Modern History	RV81	4FT deg	* g	BBB	X	Ind	30$	BBBB	Ind	4	

| | | | 98 expected requirements | | | | | | | 96 entry stats |

course details

TITLE	CODE	COURSE	SUBJECTS	A/AS	NO/C	AGNVQ	IB	SQA(H)	SQA	RATIO A/AS
Russian-Philosophy	RV87	4FT deg	* g	BBB	X	Ind	30$	BBBB	Ind	
Social Anthropology-Russian	LR68	4FT deg	* g	BBB	X	Ind	30$	BBBB	Ind	
Social Anthropology-Russian with Year Abroad	LR6V	4FT/5FT deg	* g	BBB	X	Ind	30$	BBBB	Ind	
Spanish with Year Abroad-Russian	RR4V	4FT/5FT deg	* g	BBB	X	Ind	30$	BBBB	Ind	
Spanish-Russian	RR48	4FT deg	* g	BBB	X	Ind	30$	BBBB	Ind	
European Integration Studies Russian	Y602	4FT deg	* g	BBB	X	Ind	30$	BBBB	Ind	
General Degree of MA Modern Languages (Russian)	Y450	3FT deg	* g	BBB	X	Ind	30$	BBBB	Ind	

Univ of STRATHCLYDE

Arts and Social Sciences Russian	Y440	3FT/4FT deg	g	CCC	Ind		28	BBBBB$		
Arts and Social Sciences Russian and East European Studies	Y440	3FT deg	g	CCC	Ind		28	BBBBB$	Ind	

Univ of SURREY

French and Russian	RR18	4FT/SW deg	F+R	20	3M+3D$		30$	ABBCC	Ind	
German and Russian	RR28	4FT/SW deg	G+R	20	3M+3D$		30$	ABBCC	Ind	
Russian and Economics w International Business	RL81	4SW deg	* g	18	3M+3D$		30	ABBCC	Ind	2 10/12
Russian and European Studies	RT82	4SW deg	*	18	3M+3D$		30	ABBCC	Ind	2
Russian and Law	RM83	4SW deg	*	18	3M+3D$		30$	ABBCC	Ind	2 12/22

Univ of SUSSEX

Computer Science with European Studies (Russian)	G5R8	4FT deg	M g	BBC	MO $	M*△ go	$	Ind	Ind	
French and Russian	RR18	4FT deg	F	BCC	MO $	M*△	$	Ind	Ind	
German and Russian	RR28	4FT deg	G	BCC	MO $	M*△	$	Ind	Ind	
Mathematics & Stats with Eur St(Russian) (MMath)	G4RV	4FT deg	M g	BCC	MO $	MS△ go	$	Ind	Ind	
Mathematics and Stats with Eur Studies (Russ)	G4R8	4FT deg	M g	BCC	MO $	MS△ go	$	Ind	Ind	
Mathematics with European St (Russian) (MMath)	G1RV	4FT deg	M g	BCC	MO $	MS△ go	$	Ind	Ind	
Mathematics with European Studies (Russian)	G1R8	4FT deg	M g	BCC	MO $	MS△ go	$	Ind	Ind	
Physics with European Studies (Russian)	F3R8	4FT deg	M+P g	CCC	MO $	MS△ go	$	Ind	Ind	
Russian and East European Studies	R809	4FT deg	* g	BCC	MO $	M*6 go	$	Ind	Ind	
Russian and Linguistics	RQ81	4FT deg	* g	BCC	MO $	M*6 go	$	Ind	Ind	

Univ of Wales SWANSEA

Computer Science (with Russian)	G5R8	4FT deg	L	BBD-BCC	4D	Ind	28	BBBBB	Ind	
English Language/Russian (with Business Studies)	QRH8	4FT deg	L	X	X	X	28	X	X	1
French/Russian (with Business Studies)	RR1V	4FT deg	F g	BCC	1M+5D$	Ind	28$	BBBBC$	Ind	4
French/Russian (with Computer Studies)	RR1W	4FT deg	F	BCC	1M+5D$	Ind	28$	BBBBC$	Ind	
French/Russian (with Legal Studies)	RR81	4FT deg	F	BBC-BCC	1M+5D$	Ind	28$	BBBBC$	Ind	
German/Russian (with Business Studies)	RR2V	4FT deg	G g	BCC	1M+5D$	Ind	28$	BBBBC$	Ind	8
German/Russian (with Computer Studies)	RR2W	4FT deg	G	BCC	1M+5D$	Ind	28$	BBBBC$	Ind	
German/Russian (with Legal Studies)	RR82	4FT deg	G	BBC-BCC	1M+5D$	Ind	28$	BBBBC$	Ind	
Italian/Russian (with Business Studies)	RR3V	4FT deg	I/R g	BCC	1M+5D$	Ind	28$	BBBBC$	Ind	
Italian/Russian (with Computer Studies)	RR3W	4FT deg	I/R	BCC	1M+5D$	Ind	28$	BBBBC$	Ind	
Italian/Russian (with Legal Studies)	RR83	4FT deg	I/R	BCC	1M+5D$	Ind	28$	BBBBC$	Ind	
Law and Russian	MR38	4FT deg	L/*	BBB	6D	Ind	30$	ABBBB$	Ind	
Mathematics (with Russian)	G1R8	4FT deg	M+L	BCC	X	Ind	26$	BBBBC$	Ind	
Russian (with Business Studies)	R8N1	4FT deg	L/* g	BBC-BCD	1M+5D$	Ind	26$	BBBBC$	Ind	2
Russian (with Computer Studies)	R8G5	4FT deg	L/*	BBC-BCD	1M+5D$	Ind	26$	BBBBC$	Ind	
Russian (with Legal Studies)	R8M3	4FT deg	L/*	BBC-BCC	1M+5D$	Ind	28$	BBBBC$	Ind	
Russian Studies	R810	4FT deg	L/*	BCC	1M+5D	Ind	28	BBBBC	Ind	
Russian Studies/Economics	LRC8	3FT deg	* g	BBB-BBC	1M+5D	Ind	30$	ABBBB$	Ind	
Russian Studies/History	RV8C	3FT deg	*	BBC	Ind	Ind	30	ABBBB	Ind	1

course details			98 expected requirements							96 entry stats
TITLE	CODE	COURSE	SUBJECTS	A/AS	NO/C	AGNVQ	IB	SQA(H)	SQA	RATIO A/AS
Russian Studies/Politics	MRC8	3FT deg	*	BBC	1M+5D	Ind	30	ABBBB	Ind	
Russian and Psychology	LR78	4FT deg	L g							
Russian/American Studies	QR48	4FT deg								
Russian/Anthropology	RL86	4FT deg	L/*	BCC	1M+5D$	Ind	28$	BBBBC$	Ind	
Russian/Economic History	RV83	4FT deg	L/*	BBC-BCC	1M+5D$	Ind	28$	BBBBC$	Ind	
Russian/Economics	LR18	4FT deg								
Russian/English	QR38	4FT deg	E+L	BB-BCC	X	X	28$	BBBBC$	X	
Russian/English Language	QR3V	3FT deg	E g	BBC	X	X	30$	ABBBB$	Ind	
Russian/European Politics	MR1V	4FT deg	L/*	BBC-BCD	1M+5D	Ind	28$	BBBBC$	Ind	
Russian/French	RR18	4FT deg	F	BCC	1M+5D$	Ind	28$	BBBBC$	Ind	10
Russian/Geography	LR8V	4FT deg	Gy+L	BBC-BCD	1M+5D$	Ind	28$	BBBBC$	Ind	
Russian/German	RR28	4FT deg	G/(R g)	BCC	1M+5D$	Ind	28$	BBBBC$	Ind	
Russian/History	RV81	4FT deg	L/*	BBC	1M+5D$	Ind	28$	BBBBC$	Ind	
Russian/Italian	RR38	4FT deg	I/R	BCC	1M+5D$	Ind	28$	BBBBC$	Ind	
Russian/Politics	MR18	4FT deg	L/*	BBC-BCC	1M+5D$	Ind	28$	BBBBB$	Ind	2
Russian/Spanish (with Computer Studies)	RRWK	4FT deg	R/Sp	BCC	1M+5D$	Ind	28$	BBBBC$	Ind	
Russian/Spanish (with Legal Studies)	RR84	4FT deg	R/Sp	BCC	1M+5D$	Ind	28$	BBBBC$	Ind	
Russian/Welsh (with Business Studies)	RQ85	4FT deg	R/W g	BCC	1M+5D$	X	28$	BBBBB$	X	
Russian/Welsh (with Computer Studies)	RQ8N	4FT deg	R/W	BCC	1M+5D$	X	28$	BBBBB$	X	
Russian/Welsh (with Legal Studies)	QR58	4FT deg	R/W	BCC	1M+5D$	X	28$	BBBBB$	X	
Sociology/Russian	RL83	4FT deg	L/*	BCC	1M+5D$	Ind	28$	BBBBC$	Ind	
Spanish/Russian	RR48	4FT deg	R/Sp	BCC	1M+5D$	Ind	28$	BBBBC$	Ind	

TRINITY COLL Carmarthen

Saesneg/Astudiaethau Crefydd	QR3W	3FT deg	E+Re g	DD-CC	Ind		Ind	Ind	Ind	

Univ of WESTMINSTER

Russian and Arabic	RT86	4SW deg	R	CC	Ind		26	BBB		
Russian and Chinese	T3R8	4SW deg	R	CC	Ind		26	BBB	Ind	2
Russian and English	QR38	4SW deg	E	CC	Ind		26$	BBB		3
Russian and English Language	QRH8	4SW deg		CC	Ind		26$	BBB		
Russian and French	RR18	4SW deg	F	CC	Ind		26$	BBB		5
Russian and German	RR28	4SW deg	G/R	CC	Ind		26$	BBB		5
Russian and Italian	RR38	4SW deg	I/R	CC	Ind		26	BBB		
Russian and Linguistics	RQ81	4SW deg	L	CC	Ind		26	BBB		1
Spanish and Russian	RR48	4SW deg	R/Sp	CC	Ind		26	BBB		4

Univ of WOLVERHAMPTON

Combined Degrees Russian Studies	Y401	3FT/4SW deg	L g	12	4M $	M	24	BBBB	Ind	

			98 expected requirements							96 entry stats	
course details											
TITLE	CODE	COURSE	SUBJECTS	A/AS	ND/C	RGNVQ	IB	SQA(H)	SQA	RATIO	A/AS
Univ of EAST ANGLIA											
History,European w Danish or Norw or Swed Lang	V1R7	4FT deg	M+L	ABC-BCC	X		30	BBBBB	X		
Scandiv Studs w Hons Lang-1 of Danish, Nor, Swed	R700	4FT deg	* g	CC-CCC	X		25	BBBB	X	7	
Univ of EDINBURGH											
Celtic and Scandinavian Studies	QR57	4FT deg	L g	BBB	Ind	Ind	Dip$	BBBB$	Ind		
English Language and Scandinavian Studies	QR37	4FT deg	L g	BBB	Ind	Ind	Dip$	BBBB$	Ind		
Law with Scandanavian Studies	MR37	4FT deg	g	ABB			32	AAABB	X		
Scandinavian Studies	R700	4FT deg	L g	BBC	Ind	Ind	Dip$	BBBC$	Ind	7	
Scandinavian Studies and Linguistics	RQ71	4FT deg	L g	BBC	Ind	Ind	Dip$	BBBC$	Ind		
Scandinavian Studies and Politics	RM71	4FT deg	L g	BBC	Ind	Ind	Dip$	BBBC$	Ind		
Scandinavian Studies and Social Policy	RL74	4FT deg	L g	BBC	Ind	Ind	Dip$	BBBC$	Ind		
Scottish Ethnology and Scandinavian Studies	VR97	4FT deg	L g	BBB	Ind	Ind	Dip$	BBBB$	Ind		
Univ of HULL											
Business Studies/Scandinavian Studies	NR17	4FT deg	* g	BBC-BCC	Ind	D*^ go	26$	BCCC	Ind		
English/Scandinavian Studies	QRH7	4FT deg	E	BBB-CCC	Ind	M$^ gi	28$	BBBCC	Ind		
French/Scandinavian Studies	RRD7	4FT deg	F	BBB-BCD	Ind	Ind	28$	BBBCC	Ind	2	22/24
Gender Studies and Scandinavian Studies	MR97	4FT deg	*	BCC-CCC	MO	M$6/^ go	28$	BBCCC	Ind		
German/Scandinavian Studies	RRF7	4FT deg	G	BCC-CCC	Ind	Ind	28$	BBCCC	Ind	2	18/22
Scandinavian Studies	R700	4FT deg	*	CC	Ind	Ind	28$	BBCCC	Ind	2	8/12
UNIVERSITY COLL LONDON (Univ of London)											
Dutch and Scandinavian Studies (4 Yrs)	TR27	4FT deg	g	BCC-BBC	3M	X	26$	BBCCC$	Ind		
German and Scandinavian Studies (4 Yrs)	RR27	4FT deg	G g	BBC	3M	X	30$	BBCCC$	Ind	5	
Icelandic (4 Yrs)	R760	4FT deg	* g	CCC	3M	X	26$	BBBCC	Ind		
Scandinavian Studies (4 Yrs)	R700	4FT deg	* g	CC	3M	X	26$	BBCCC	Ind	2	6/26
Scandinavian Studies with Management St (4 Yrs)	R7N1	4FT deg	* g	CC	3M	X	26$	BBCCC	Ind	2	12/14

course details			98 expected requirements							96 entry stats
TITLE	CODE	COURSE	SUBJECTS	A/AS	ND/C	AGNVQ	IB	SQA(H)	SQA	RATIO A/AS
Univ of ABERDEEN										
Accountancy with Spanish	N4R4	4FT deg	* g	BBC	Ind	M$ go	30$	BBBB$	Ind	
Celtic-Hispanic Studies	QR54	4FT/5FT deg	* g	BBC	Ind	M$ go	30$	BBBB$	Ind	
Celtic-Hispanic Studies (4 Yrs)	RQ45	4FT deg	* g	BBC	Ind	M$ go	30$	BBBB$	Ind	
Chemistry with Spanish	F1R4	4FT deg	C+2S/C+M+S g	CCD	Ind	MS go	24$	BBBC$	Ind	
Computing Science with Spanish	G5R4	4FT deg	M+2S g	CCD	Ind	MS go	24$	BBBC$	Ind	
Economics-Hispanic Studies	LR14	5FT deg	* g	BBC	Ind	M$ go	30$	BBBB$	Ind	
Economics-Hispanic Studies (4Yrs)	RL41	4FT deg	* g	BBC	Ind	M$ go	30$	BBBB$	Ind	
English-Hispanic Studies	QR34	4FT/5FT deg	* g	BBC	Ind	M$ go	30$	BBBB$	Ind	2
English-Hispanic Studies (4Yrs)	RQ43	4FT deg	* g	BBC	Ind	M$ go	30$	BBBB$	Ind	
Entrepreneurship-Hispanic Studies	NRC4	4FT deg	* g	BBC	Ind	M$ go	30$	BBBB$	Ind	
Entrepreneurship-Hispanic Studies (4 Yrs)	NRCK	4FT deg	* g	BBC	Ind	M$ go	30$	BBBB$	Ind	
French-Hispanic Studies	RR14	4FT/5FT deg	* g	BBC	Ind	M$ go	30$	BBBB$	Ind	6
French-Hispanic Studies with Education	RR41	5FT deg	* g	BBC	Ind	M$ go	30$	BBBB$	Ind	
Geography-Hispanic Studies	LR84	4FT deg	* g	BBC	Ind	M$ go	30$	BBBB$	Ind	
German-Hispanic Studies	RR24	4FT/5FT deg	* g	BBC	Ind	M$ go	30$	BBBB$	Ind	
German-Hispanic Studies with Education	RR42	5FT deg	* g	BBC	Ind	M$ go	30$	BBBB$	Ind	
Hispanic Studies (Latin American)	R600	4FT/5FT deg	* g	BBC	Ind	M$ go	30$	BBBB$	Ind	5
Hispanic Studies (Latin American) (4 Yrs)	R601	4FT deg	* g	BBC	Ind	M$ go	30$	BBBB$	Ind	
Hispanic Studies (Spanish)	R400	4FT/5FT deg	* g	BBC	Ind	M$ go	30$	BBBB$	Ind	1
Hispanic Studies (Spanish) (4 Yrs)	R401	4FT deg	* g	BBC	Ind	M$ go	30$	BBBB$	Ind	
Hispanic Studies with Film Studies	R4W5	4FT/5FT deg	* g	BBC	Ind	M$ go	30$	BBBB$	Ind	3
Hispanic Studies with Film Studies (4 Yrs)	R4WM	4FT deg	* g	BBC	Ind	M$ go	30$	BBBB$	Ind	
Hispanic Studies with Women's Studies	R4M9	5FT deg	* g	BBC	Ind	M$ go	30$	BBBB$	Ind	
Hispanic Studies with Women's Studies (4 Yrs)	R4MX	4FT deg	* g	BBC	Ind	M$ go	30$	BBBB$	Ind	
Hispanic Studies-History	RV41	4FT/5FT deg	* g	BBC	Ind	M$ go	30$	BBBB$	Ind	
Hispanic Studies-History (4 Yrs)	VR14	4FT deg	* g	BBC	Ind	M$ go	30$	BBBB$	Ind	
Hispanic Studies-History of Art	RV44	4FT/5FT deg	* g	BBC	Ind	M$ go	30$	BBBB$	Ind	
Hispanic Studies-History of Art (4 Yrs)	VR44	4FT deg	* g	BBC	Ind	M$ go	30$	BBBB$	Ind	
Hispanic Studies-International Relations	RM4C	4FT/5FT deg	* g	BBC	Ind	M$ go	30$	BBBB$	Ind	
Hispanic Studies-International Relations (4 Yrs)	MRC4	4FT deg	* g	BBC	Ind	M$ go	30$	BBBB$	Ind	
Hispanic Studies-Management Studies	RN41	4FT/5FT deg	* g	BBC	Ind	M$ go	30$	BBBB$	Ind	2
Hispanic Studies-Management Studies (4 Yrs)	NR14	4FT deg	* g	BBC	Ind	M$ go	30$	BBBB$	Ind	
Hispanic Studies-Mathematics	RG41	5FT deg	* g	BBC	Ind	M$ go	30$	BBBB$	Ind	
Hispanic Studies-Mathematics (4 Yrs)	GR14	4FT deg	* g	BBC	Ind	M$ go	30$	BBBB$	Ind	
Hispanic Studies-Philosophy	RV47	5FT deg	* g	BBC	Ind	M$ go	30$	BBBB$	Ind	
Hispanic Studies-Philosophy (4 Yrs)	VR74	4FT deg	* g	BBC	Ind	M$ go	30$	BBBB$	Ind	
Hispanic Studies-Politics	RM41	4FT/5FT deg	* g	BBC	Ind	M$ go	30$	BBBB$	Ind	
Hispanic Studies-Politics (4 Yrs)	MR14	4FT deg	* g	BBC	Ind	M$ go	30$	BBBB$	Ind	
Hispanic Studies-Social Research	LR34	4FT/5FT deg	* g	BBC	Ind	M$ go	30$	BBBB$	Ind	
Hispanic Studies-Social Research (4 Yrs)	LR3K	4FT deg	* g	BBC	Ind	M$ go	30$	BBBB$	Ind	
Hispanic Studies-Sociology	RL43	4FT/5FT deg	* g	BBC	Ind	M$ go	30$	BBBB$	Ind	
Hispanic Studies-Sociology (4 Yrs)	RL4H	4FT deg	* g	BBC	Ind	M$ go	30$	BBBB$	Ind	
Mathematics with Spanish	G1R4	4FT deg	M+S g	CCD	Ind	MS go	24$	BBBC$	Ind	
Physics with Hispanic Studies	F3R4	4FT deg	2S+M g	CCD	Ind	MS go	24$	BBBC$	Ind	
Psychology with Spanish	C8R4	4FT deg	3S/2S+M g	CCD	Ind	MS go	24$	BBBC$	Ind	
Psychology with Spanish (MA)	C8RK	4FT deg	* g	BBC	Ind	MS go	30$	BBBB$	Ind	
Religious Studies-Hispanic Studies	VR84	4FT/5FT deg	* g	BBC	Ind	M$ go	30$	BBBB$	Ind	
Religious Studies-Hispanic Studies (4 Yrs)	RV48	4FT deg	* g	BBC	Ind	M$ go	30$	BBBB$	Ind	
Theology with Spanish	V8R4	3FT deg	* g	CC	Ind	M* go	24$	BBCC	Ind	

			98 expected requirements							96 entry stats

TITLE	CODE	COURSE	SUBJECTS	A/AS	ND/C	AGNVQ	IB	SQA(H)	SQA	RATIO A/AS
Univ of Wales, ABERYSTWYTH										
Computer Science with Spanish	G5R4	4FT deg	L g	20	1M+5D$	M^ g	30$	BBBBC$	Ind	
European Studies and Spanish	RT4F	4FT deg	L g	20	1M+5D$	M^ g	30$	BBBBC$	Ind	
Law with Spanish (BA)	M3RL	4FT deg	L g	BBB	DO $	D^ g	32$	BBBCC$	Ind	
Law with Spanish (LLB)	M3R4	4FT deg	L g	BBB	DO $	D^ g	32$	BBBCC$	Ind	
Spanish	R400	4FT deg	L g	18	1M+5D$	M^ g	29$	BBBCC$	Ind	
Spanish/American Studies	QR44	4FT deg	E/H+L g	18	1M+5D$	M^ g	29$	BBBCC$	Ind	
Spanish/Art	RW41	4FT deg	A/Ad+L g	18	1M+5D$	MA^ g	29$	BBBCC$	Ind	
Spanish/Art History	RV44	4FT deg	L g	18	1M+5D$	MA^ g	29$	BBBCC$	Ind	
Spanish/Drama	RW44	4FT deg	L g	20	1M+5D$	MQ^ g	30$	BBBBC$	Ind	
Spanish/Economic & Social History	RV43	4FT deg	L g	18-20	1M+5D$	M^ g	30$	BBBBC$	Ind	
Spanish/Education	RX49	4FT deg	L g	18	1M+5D$	M^ g	29$	BBBCC$	Ind	
Spanish/English	QR34	4FT deg	El+L	20	1M+5D$	M^ g	30$	BBBBC$	Ind	
Spanish/European Studies	RT42	4FT deg	L g	20	1M+5D$	M^ g	30$	BBBBC$	Ind	
Spanish/Film and Television Studies	RW45	4FT deg	L g	20	1M+5D$	MQ^ g	30$	BBBBC$		
Spanish/French	RR14	4FT deg	F g	18	1M+5D$	M^ g	29$	BBBCC$	Ind	
Spanish/German	RR24	4FT deg	G g	18	1M+5D$	M^ g	29$	BBBCC$	Ind	
Spanish/History	RV41	4FT deg	L g	18-20	1M+5D$	M^ g	30$	BBBBC$	Ind	
Spanish/Information and Library Studies	PR24	4FT deg	L g	18	1M+5D$	M^ g	29$	BBBCC$	Ind	
Spanish/International Politics	MRC4	4FT deg	L g	20	1M+5D$	M^ g	30$	BBBBC$	Ind	
Spanish/Italian	RR34	4FT deg	L g	18	1M+5D$	M^ g	29$	BBBCC$	Ind	
Spanish/Politics	MR14	4FT deg	L g	20	1M+5D$	M^ g	30$	BBBBC$	Ind	
Spanish/Pure Mathematics	GRC4	4FT deg	M+L g	18	1M+5D$	M^ g	29$	BBBCC$	Ind	
Welsh History/Spanish	RVKC	4FT deg	L g	18-20	1M+5D$	M^ g	30$	BBBBC$	Ind	
Welsh/Spanish	QR54	4FT deg	W+L g	18	1M+5D$	M^ g	29$	BBBCC$	Ind	
ANGLIA Poly Univ										
Animal Behaviour and Spanish	CR1K▼	4FT deg	g	12	4M	P go	Dip	BCCC	N	
Art History and Spanish	RV44▼	4FT deg	* g	14	6M	M+/^ go	Dip	BBCC	Ind	
Audiotechnology and Spanish	HR6K▼	4FT deg	S g	16	8M	D+/^ go	Dip$	BBCCC	N	
Biology and Spanish	CR14▼	4FT deg	B g	12	4M	M+/^ go	Dip$	BCCC	N	
Biomedical Science and Spanish	BR94▼	4FT deg	B g	12	4M	M+/^ go	Dip$	BCCC	N	
Business and Spanish	NR14▼	4FT deg	* g	12	4M	M+/^ go	Dip	BCCC	Ind	4
Chemistry and Spanish	FR14▼	4FT deg	S g	12	4M	M go	Dip$	BCCC	Ind	
Communication Studies and Spanish	PR34▼	4FT deg	Ap g	14	6M	M+/^	Dip$	BBCC	Ind	4
Computer Science and Spanish	GR54▼	4FT deg	* g	12	4M	M go	Dip	BCCC	N	
Ecology and Conservation and Spanish	DR24▼	4FT deg	* g	12	4M	M+/^ go	Dip	BCCC	N	
Economics and Spanish	LR14▼	4FT deg	* g	12	4M	M go	Dip$	BCCC	Ind	
English Language Studies and Spanish	QR14▼	3FT deg	* g	12	4M	M go	Dip	BCCC		
English and Spanish	QR34▼	4FT deg	E g	12	4M	M+/^	Dip$	BCCC	Ind	
European Philosophy & Literature and Spanish	RV47▼	4FT deg	* g	12	4M	M+/^ go	Dip	BCCC	Ind	3
French and Spanish	RR14▼	4FT deg	F/Sp g	12	4M	M go	Ind$	BCCC	Ind	5 8/12
Geography and Spanish	LR84▼	4FT deg	Gy g	12	4M	M+/^ go	Dip$	BCCC	Ind	
Geology and Spanish	FR64▼	4FT deg	* g	12	4M	M go	Dip	BCCC	Ind	
German and Spanish	RR24▼	4FT deg	G/Sp	12	4M	M	Ind$	BCCC	Ind	
Graphic Arts and Spanish	RW42▼	4FT deg	A g	14	6M	M+/^ go	Dip$	BBCC	Ind	1
History and Spanish	RV41▼	4FT deg	Ap g	12	4M	M+/^ go	Dip$	BCCC	Ind	
Italian and Spanish	RR34▼	4FT deg	I/Sp	12	4M	M	Ind$	BCCC	Ind	18
Law and Spanish	MR34▼	4FT deg	* g	14	6M	M go	Dip	BBCC	Ind	3
Mathematics or Stats/Stat Modelling and Spanish	GR14▼	4FT deg	* g	12	4M	M go	Dip	BCCC	Ind	
Music and Spanish	RW43▼	4FT deg	Mu g	12	4M	M+/^ go	Dip$	BCCC	Ind	2
Ophthalmic Dispensing and Spanish	BR54▼	4FT deg	* g	12	4M	M go	Dip	BCCC	N	
Politics and Spanish	MR14▼	4FT deg	* g	14	6M	M+/^ go	Dip$	BBCC	Ind	

	course details			98 expected requirements							96 entry stats
TITLE	CODE	COURSE	SUBJECTS	A/AS	NO/C	AGNVQ	IB	SQA(H)	SQA	RATIO A/AS	
Psychology and Spanish	CR84▼	4FT deg	S g	16	8M	D go	Dip$	BBCCC	N		
Social Policy and Spanish	LR44▼	4FT deg	* g	12	4M	M go	Dip	BCCC	Ind		
Sociology and Spanish	LR34▼	4FT deg	* g	12	4M	M go	Dip	BCCC	Ind		
Spanish and Intercultural Studies	RL46▼	4FT deg	* g	12	4M	M go	Dip	BCCC			
Spanish and Women's Studies	RM49▼	4FT deg	* g	12	4M	M go	Dip	BCCC	Ind	2	

Univ of BIRMINGHAM

TITLE	CODE	COURSE	SUBJECTS	A/AS	NO/C	AGNVQ	IB	SQA(H)	SQA	RATIO	A/AS
African Studies/Hispanic Studies	RT47	4FT deg	*	BBB	Ind	D*^	32	ABBB	Ind		
African Studies/Portuguese	RT57	4FT deg	*	BBB	Ind	D*^	32	ABBB	Ind		
American Studies/Hispanic Studies	QR44	4FT deg	*	BBB	Ind	D*^	32	ABBB	Ind	17	
American Studies/Portuguese	QR45	4FT deg	*	BBB	Ind	D*^	32	ABBB	Ind		
Ancient History & Archaeology/Hispanic Studies	RV46	4FT deg	*	BBB	Ind	D*^	32	ABBB	Ind		
Ancient History & Archaeology/Portuguese	RV56	4FT deg	*	BBB	Ind	D*^	32	ABBB	Ind		
Artificial Intelligence/Hispanic Studies	GR84	4FT deg	* g	BBB	Ind	D*^	32	ABBB	Ind		
Artificial Intelligence/Portuguese	GR85	4FT deg	* g	BBB	Ind	D*^	32	ABBB	Ind		
BCom (Business Administration) with Portuguese	NR15	4FT deg	L	BBC	Ind	D+^	32	ABBBB	Ind		
BCom (Business Administration) with Spanish	NR14	4FT deg	L	BBC	Ind	D+^	32	ABBBB	Ind	10	22/28
Business Studies/Hispanic Studies	RN41	4FT deg	* g	BBB	Ind	D*^	32	ABBB	Ind	5	24/28
Business Studies/Portuguese	RN51	4FT deg	* g	BBB	Ind	D*^	32	ABBB	Ind	6	
Classical Literature & Civilisation/Hispanic St	QR84	4FT deg	*	BBB	Ind	D*^	32	ABBB			
Classical Literature and Civilisation/Portuguese	QR8M	4FT deg	*	BBB	Ind	D*^	32	ABBB			
Computer Studies/Hispanic Studies	GR54	4FT deg	* g	BBB	Ind	D*^	32	ABBB	Ind		
Computer Studies/Portuguese	GR55	4FT deg	* g	BBB	Ind	D*^	32	ABBB	Ind		
Dance/Hispanic Studies	WR44	4FT deg	*	BBB	Ind	D*^	32	ABBB			
Dance/Portuguese	WR45	4FT deg	*	BBB	Ind	D*^	32	ABBB			
Drama/Hispanic Studies	RW44	4FT deg	*	BBB	Ind	D*^	32	ABBB	Ind	11	
Drama/Portuguese	RW54	4FT deg	*	BBB	Ind	D*^	32	ABBB	Ind		
East Mediterranean History/Hispanic Studies	RVL1	4FT deg	* g	BBB	Ind	D*^	32	ABBB	Ind		
East Mediterranean History/Portuguese	RV51	4FT deg	* g	BBB	Ind	D*^	32	ABBB	Ind		
Economics with Portuguese	L1R5	4FT deg	*	BBC	Ind	D+^	32	ABBBB	Ind		
Economics with Spanish	L1R4	4FT deg	*	BBC	Ind	D+^	32	ABBBB	Ind	4	
English/Hispanic Studies	QR34	4FT deg	*	BBB	Ind	D*^	32	ABBB	Ind	4	26/30
English/Portuguese	QR35	4FT deg	*	BBB	Ind	D*^	32	ABBB	Ind		
French Studies and Hispanic Studies	RR14	4FT deg	F	BBB	Ind	D*^_	32$	ABBB	Ind	12	24/30
French Studies and Portuguese	RR15	4FT deg	F	BBB	Ind	D*^_	32$	ABBB	Ind	11	
Geography/Hispanic Studies	LR84	4FT deg	Gy	BBB	Ind	D*^_	32$	ABBB	Ind		
Geography/Portuguese	LR85	4FT deg	Gy	BBB	Ind	D*^_	32$	ABBB	Ind		
German Studies and Hispanic Studies	RR24	4FT deg	G	BBB	Ind	D*^_	32$	ABBB	Ind	5	
German Studies and Portuguese	RR25	4FT deg	G	BBB	Ind	D*^_	32$	ABBB	Ind		
Hispanic Studies	R400	4FT deg	Sp	BBB	Ind	D*^_	32$	ABBB	Ind	5	20/28
Hispanic Studies amd Modern Greek Studies	RTK2	4FT deg	* g	BBB	Ind	D*^	32	ABBB	Ind		
Hispanic Studies and Portuguese	RR45	4FT deg	*	BBB	Ind	D*^	32	ABBB	Ind	7	
Hispanic Studies/History	RV41	4FT deg	*	BBB	Ind	D*^	32	ABBB	Ind	10	
Hispanic Studies/History of Art	RV44	4FT deg	*	BBB	Ind	D*^	32	ABBB	Ind		
Hispanic Studies/Latin	QR64	4FT deg	Ln	BBB	Ind	D*^_	32$	ABBB	Ind		
Hispanic Studies/Mathematics	GR14	4FT deg	M	ABB-ABC	Ind	D*^_	32$	ABBB	Ind		
Hispanic Studies/Media & Cultural Studies	PR44	4FT deg	*	BBB	Ind	D*^	32	ABBB	Ind	18	
Hispanic Studies/Music	RW43	4FT deg	Mu	AAB-ABB	Ind	D*^_	32$	ABBB	Ind	3	
Hispanic Studies/Philosophy	RV47	4FT deg	*	BBB	Ind	D*^	32	ABBB	Ind		
Hispanic Studies/Political Science	MR14	4FT deg	*	BBB	Ind	D*^	32	ABBB	Ind		
Hispanic Studies/Sport & Recreation Studies	RB46	4FT deg	*	BBB	Ind	D*^	32	ABBB	Ind		
Hispanic Studies/Theology	RV48	4FT deg	*	BBB	Ind	D*^	32	ABBB	Ind		
History of Art/Portuguese	RV54	4FT deg	*	BBB	Ind	D*^	32	ABBB	Ind		

| course details | | | 98 expected requirements | | | | | | | 96 entry stats | |

TITLE	CODE	COURSE	SUBJECTS	A/AS	NO/C	AGNVQ	IB	SQA(H)	SQA	RATIO A/AS	
History/Portuguese	RV5C	4FT deg	*	BBB	Ind	D*^	32	ABBB	Ind		
International Studies with Spanish	M1R4	4FT deg	L	BBC	Ind	D+^	32	ABBBB	Ind	10	22/24
Italian and Hispanic Studies	RR34	4FT deg	*	BBB	Ind	D*^	32	ABBB	Ind	11	
Italian and Portuguese	RR35	4FT deg	*	BBB	Ind	D*^	32	ABBB	Ind		
Latin/Portuguese	QR65	4FT deg	Ln	BBB	Ind	D*_	32$	ABBB	Ind		
Mathematics/Portuguese	GR15	4FT deg	M	ABB-ABC	Ind	D*_	32$	ABBB	Ind		
Media & Cultural Studies/Portuguese	PR45	4FT deg	*	BBB	Ind	D*^	32	ABBB	Ind		
Modern Greek Studies and Portuguese	RT52	4FT deg	* g	BBB	Ind	D*^	32	ABBB	Ind		
Money, Banking and Finance with Portuguese	N3R5	4FT deg	*	BBB	Ind	D+^	33	ABBBB	Ind		
Money, Banking and Finance with Spanish	N3R4	4FT deg	L	BBB	Ind	D+^	33	ABBBB	Ind	8	
Music/Portuguese	RW53	4FT deg	Mu	AAB-ABB	Ind	D*_	32$	ABBB	Ind		
Philosophy/Portuguese	RV57	4FT deg	*	BBB	Ind	D*^	32	ABBB	Ind		
Political Science/Portuguese	MR15	4FT deg	*	BBB	Ind	D*^	32	ABBB	Ind		
Portuguese and Russian	RR58	4FT deg	*	BBB	Ind	D*^	32	ABBB	Ind		
Portuguese/Sport & Recreation Studies	RB56	4FT deg	*	BBB	Ind	D*^	32	ABBB	Ind		
Portuguese/Theology	RV58	4FT deg	*	BBB	Ind	D*^	32	ABBB	Ind		
Russian and Hispanic Studies	RR48	4FT deg	*	BBB	Ind	D*^	32	ABBB	Ind		
BOLTON INST											
International Business (Spanish)	N1R4	3FT deg	* g	CD	MO	M*	24	BBCC	Ind		
International Tourism (Spanish)	P7R4	3FT deg	* g	CD	MO	M*	24	BBCC	Ind		
Univ of BRADFORD											
French and Spanish	RR14	4SW deg	2L	BCC	Ind	X	Ind	Ind	Ind	5	10/30
German and Spanish	RR24	4SW deg	2L	BCC	Ind	X	Ind	Ind	Ind	4	
International Management and Spanish	N1R4	4SW deg	Sp g	22	DO $	D$^	Ind	Ind	Ind	11	
Russian and Spanish	RR48	4SW deg	2L	BCC	Ind	X	Ind	Ind	Ind	1	
Spanish	R400	4SW deg	Sp	BCC	Ind	X	Ind	Ind	Ind		
Univ of BRISTOL											
Computer Science and Spanish	RG45	4FT deg	* g	BBB-BBC	Ind	D$^	30$	CSYS	Ind		
Drama and Spanish	WR44	4FT deg		BC	Ind	D$^	28$	BBBBB	Ind		
French and Spanish	RR14	4FT deg	F	ABB-BBB	Ind	D$^	30$	AABBB	Ind	9	24/30
German and Spanish	RR24	4FT deg	G	BBB	Ind	D$^	30$	BBBBB	Ind	9	
Hispanic Studies	RR45	4FT deg	Sp	BCC	Ind	D$^	28$	ABBBB	Ind	6	20/30
History of Art and Spanish	VR44	4FT deg	L	BBC	Ind	D$^	30$	BBBBB	Ind		
Italian and Spanish	RR34	4FT deg	I/Sp	BBB	NO/C	D$^	30$	AABBB	Ind	9	26/30
Philosophy and Spanish	RV47	4FT deg	L	BBB-BBC	Ind	D$^	30$	ABBBB	Ind	15	
Politics and Spanish	RM41	4FT deg		BBB-BBC	Ind	D$^	32$	ABBBB	Ind	10	
Spanish	R400	4FT deg	Sp/L	BCC	Ind	D$^	28$	ABBBB	Ind	6	20/30
Spanish and Russian	RR48	4FT deg	Sp/R	BBB-BBC	Ind	D$^	30$	ABBBB	Ind	4	
BRISTOL, Univ of the W of England											
EFL, Spanish and European Studies	QR34	4FT deg	g	14-24	5M	M*_ go	24$	BCCC$	Ind		
French, Spanish and European Studies	RR14	4FT deg	F/Sp g	14-24	5M	M*_ go	24$	BCCC$	Ind		
German, Spanish and European Studies	RR24	4FT deg	G/Sp g	14-24	5M	M*_ go	24$	BCCC$	Ind		
Spanish and Business Systems	RN41	3FT deg		14-22	5M	M*_ go	24$	BCCC$	Ind		
Spanish and European Studies	RT42	4FT deg	Sp g	14-24	5M	M*_ go	24$	BCCC$	Ind		
Spanish and Information Systems	RG45	3FT deg	Sp g	14-22	5M	M*_ go	24$	BCCC$	Ind		
Spanish and Law	RM43	4FT deg	Sp g	16-24	MO	M*_ go	24$	BBCC$	Ind		
Univ of BUCKINGHAM											
Accounting and Finance with Spanish	N4R4	2FT deg	* g	16	3M+2D	M	26	BCCC	Ind		
Economics with Spanish	L1R4	2FT deg	Sp g	14	3M+2D	M	26	BCCC	Ind		
Law with Spanish	M3R4	2FT deg	Sp	12	3M+2D	M	26	BCCC	Ind		

TITLE	CODE	COURSE	SUBJECTS	A/AS	ND/C	AGNVQ	IB	SQA(H)	SQA	RATIO A/AS
course details			*98 expected requirements*							*96 entry stats*
Marketing with Spanish	N5R4	2FT deg	*	16	3M+2D	M	26	BCCC	Ind	
Politics with Spanish	M1R4	2FT deg	Sp	12	3M+2D	M	26	BCCC	Ind	
Psychology with Spanish	C8R4	2FT deg	*	14	5M	M	26	BCCC	Ind	

BUCKINGHAMSHIRE COLLEGE

TITLE	CODE	COURSE	SUBJECTS	A/AS	ND/C	AGNVQ	IB	SQA(H)	SQA	RATIO A/AS
Business Administration with Spanish	N1R4	3FT deg	Sp g	8	MO+2D	M	27	CCCC	Ind	3
Business Studies with Spanish	N1RL	4SW deg	Sp g	8	MO	M	27	CCCC	Ind	
European Business Studies (Spanish)	NR14	4SW deg	Sp g	8	MO	M	27	CCCC	Ind	
Human Resources Management with Spanish	N6R4	3FT deg		8	MO	M	27	CCCC	Ind	
International Business Studies (Spanish)	N1RK	4SW deg	L	8	MO	M	27	CCCC	Ind	
International Marketing with Spanish	N5R4	3FT deg	Sp g	8	MO	M	27	CCCC	Ind	
Leisure Management with Spanish	N7R4	3FT deg		8-10	1D	M	27	CCCC	Ind	
Tourism with Spanish	P7R4	3FT deg	g	8-10	1D	M	27	CCCC	Ind	
Travel and Tourism Management with Spanish	PR74	3FT deg	Sp	8-10	1D	M	27	CCCC	Ind	
Business Studies with Spanish	41RN	2FT HND		4	3M	P	Ind	Ind	Ind	

CARDIFF Univ of Wales

TITLE	CODE	COURSE	SUBJECTS	A/AS	ND/C	AGNVQ	IB	SQA(H)	SQA	RATIO A/AS
Accounting with Spanish	N4R4	4FT deg	Sp	BBC-BBB	Ind	Ind	Ind	Ind	Ind	
Banking and Finance with Spanish	N3R4	4FT deg	Sp	BBC-BBB	Ind	Ind	Ind	Ind	Ind	
Business Administration with Spanish	N1R4	4FT deg	Sp g	BBC-BBB	Ind	Ind	Ind	Ind	Ind	10
Business Economics with Spanish	L1RK	4FT deg	Sp	BBC-BBB	Ind	Ind	Ind	Ind	Ind	4
Economics with Spanish	L1R4	4FT deg	Sp	BBC-BBB	Ind	Ind	Ind	Ind	Ind	
Hispanic Studies	RR45	4FT deg	Sp/Pt	BBC-BCC	Ind		Ind	Ind	Ind	22
Law and Spanish	RM43	4FT deg	Sp	BBB	Ind	Ind	Ind	Ind	Ind	4 22/28
Portuguese/Cultural Criticism	MR95	4FT deg	E	ABC	Ind	Ind	Ind	Ind	Ind	
Portuguese/Economics	LR15	4FT deg	L	BBC-BBB	X		Ind	AAAB	X	
Portuguese/Education	RX59	4FT deg	L	BBC-BCC	Ind	Ind	Ind	Ind	Ind	
Portuguese/English Literature	QR35	4FT deg	E+L	ABB	X		Ind	AAABB	X	
Portuguese/French	RR15	4FT deg	F+L	BCC	Ind		Ind	ABBBB	Ind	
Portuguese/History of Ideas	RV5D	4FT deg	L	BBC						
Portuguese/Italian	RR35	4FT deg	I/Pt	BBC-BCC	Ind		Ind	Ind	Ind	1
Portuguese/Language Studies	QR15	4FT deg	L	BBC	Ind		Ind	ABBBB		
Portuguese/Politics	MR15	4FT deg	L	BBC-BCC	X		Ind	Ind	X	
Religious Studies/Portuguese	RV58	4FT deg	L	BBC-BCC						
Sociology/Portuguese	LR35	4FT deg	L	BBC-BCC						
Spanish	R400	4FT deg	L	BBC-BCC	Ind		Ind	Ind	Ind	4 20/24
Spanish/Ancient History	QR84	4FT deg	L	BBC-BCC	Ind		Ind	Ind	Ind	
Spanish/Cultural Criticism	MR94	4FT deg	E	ABC	Ind	Ind	Ind	Ind	Ind	
Spanish/Economics	LR14	4FT deg	L	BBC-BBB	X		Ind	AAAB	X	
Spanish/Education	RX49	4FT deg	L	BBC-BCC	Ind	Ind	Ind	Ind	Ind	
Spanish/English Literature	QR34	4FT deg	E+L	ABB	X		Ind	AAABB	X	13
Spanish/French	RR14	4FT deg	F+L	BBC	Ind		Ind	ABBBB	Ind	6 20/28
Spanish/German	RR24	4FT deg	L+G	BBC-BCC	Ind		Ind	Ind	Ind	6
Spanish/History	RV41	4FT deg	H+L	BBC-BCC	X		Ind	Ind	X	
Spanish/History of Ideas	RV4D	4FT deg	L	BBC						
Spanish/Italian	RR34	4FT deg	Sp/I	BCC	Ind		Ind	ABBBB	Ind	4 22/28
Spanish/Japanese	TR44	4FT deg	L	BBC-BCC	X		Ind	Ind	X	10
Spanish/Language Studies	QR14	4FT deg	L	BBC	Ind		Ind	ABBBB		3
Spanish/Philosophy	RV47	4FT deg	L	BBC						
Spanish/Politics	MR14	4FT deg	L	BBC-BCC	X		Ind	Ind	X	
Spanish/Portuguese	RR54	4FT deg	Sp+Pt	BBC-BCC	Ind		Ind	Ind	Ind	2
Spanish/Religious Studies	RV48	4FT deg	L	BBC-BCC						
Spanish/Social Philosophy and Applied Ethics	RV4T	4FT deg	L	BBC						1

course details			98 expected requirements							96 entry stats	
TITLE	CODE	COURSE	SUBJECTS	A/AS	NO/C	AGNVQ	IB	SQA(H)	SQA	RATIO	A/AS
Spanish/Sociology	LR34	4FT deg	L	BBC-BCC	3M+2D		Ind	Ind	Ind		
Welsh/Spanish	QR54	4FT deg	W+L	BBC-BCC	X		Ind	Ind	X		

Univ of CENTRAL ENGLAND

Business Administration with Spanish	N1R4	3FT deg	Sp g	14	M+3D	D	22	CCCC			
Marketing with Spanish	N5R4	3FT deg	* g	16	M+3D	M	24	CCCCC			

Univ of CENTRAL LANCASHIRE

Combined Honours Programme *Spanish/Business Spanish*	Y400	4SW deg	L/* g	8	MO $	M*^	24$	CCC	Ind		

COVENTRY Univ

Business Studies with Portuguese	N1R5	4SW deg	* g	16	M+3D	M	Dip	CCC	Ind		
Business Studies with Spanish	N1R4	4SW deg	* g	16	M+3D	M	Dip	CCC	Ind	13	
European Studies with Spanish (4 years)	TR24	4FT deg	*	CD	M	M	Ind	CCCC	Ind		
French and Spanish	RR14▼	4FT deg	F	CD	M	M	Ind	CCCC$	Ind	10	6/26
German and Spanish	RR24▼	4FT deg	G+Sp	CD	M	M	Ind	CCCC$	Ind		
Spanish and History	VR14	4FT deg	*	CD	M	M	Ind	CCCC	Ind		
Spanish and Italian	RR43	4FT deg	Sp+I	CD	M	M	Ind	CCCC$	Ind	5	10/14
Spanish and Psychology	RC48	4FT deg	*	CD	M	M	Ind	CCCC	Ind		
Spanish and Russian	RR48	4FT deg	Sp	CD	M	M	Ind	CCCC$	Ind		
Spanish and Sociology	RL43	3FT deg									

DE MONTFORT Univ

Humanities Combined Honours *Hispanic Studies*	Y300▼	3FT deg	Sp g	CCD	MO	X	26$	ABBB	Ind		
Humanities Joint Honours *Hispanic Studies*	Y301▼	3FT deg	Sp g	CCD	MO	X	26$	ABBB	Ind		

Univ of DERBY

Credit Accumulation Modular Scheme *Spanish*	Y600	4FT deg	Sp	10	MO $	M$	Ind	CCCC$	Ind		

Univ of DUNDEE

Physics with Spanish	F3R4	4FT deg	M+S g	10	5M $	M$^	25$	BBCC$	N$		

Univ of DURHAM

European Studies and Spanish	RT42▼	4FT deg	*	CD	Ind	Ind	Dip	BCCC	Ind		
European Studies with Spanish	T2R4▼	3FT deg	*	CD	Ind	Ind	Dip	BCCC	Ind		
Urban Studies with Spanish	K4R4▼	3FT deg	*	CD	Ind	Ind	Dip	BCCC	Ind		
Arts Combined *Spanish*	Y300	4FT deg	*	24	MO	Ind	30	AAABB	Ind		

Univ of EAST LONDON

Anthropology and Spanish	LR64	3FT deg	* g	12	MO	M^	Ind	Ind	Ind		
Anthropology with Spanish	L6R4	3FT deg	* g	12	MO	M	Ind	Ind	Ind		
Archaeological Sciences and Spanish	FR44	3FT deg	* g	12	MO	M^	Ind	Ind	Ind		
Biology and Spanish	CR14	3FT deg	* g	12	MO	M^	Ind	Ind	Ind		
Business Studies and Spanish	RN41	3FT deg	* g	12	MO	M^	Ind	Ind	Ind	7	
Business Studies with Spanish	N1R4	3FT deg	* g	14	MO	MB					
Communication Studies and Spanish	PR34	3FT deg	* g	12	MO	M^	Ind	Ind	Ind		
Communication Studies with Spanish	P3R4	3FT deg	* g	12	MO	M	Ind	Ind			
Computing & Business Info Systems and Spanish	GR5K	3FT deg	* g	12	MO	M					
Cultural Studies and Spanish	LRP4	3FT deg	* g	14	N	M^					
Design - Textile Design with Spanish	J4R4	3FT deg	* g	12	MO	M	Ind	Ind	Ind		
Design - Visual Communication and Spanish	RW42	3FT deg	* g	12	MO	M^	Ind	Ind	Ind		
Design - Visual Communication with Spanish	W2R4	3FT deg	* g	12	MO	M	Ind	Ind	Ind		
Economics and Spanish	LR14	3FT deg	* g	12	MO	M^	Ind	Ind	Ind		

Languages – Spanish/Latin American

course details

98 expected requirements

96 entry stats

TITLE	CODE	COURSE	SUBJECTS	A/AS	ND/C	RGNVQ	IB	SQA(H)	SQA	RATIO A/AS
Economics with Spanish	L1R4	3FT deg	*g	12	MO	M	Ind			
Education & Community Studies and Spanish	RX49	3FT deg	*g	12	MO	M^	Ind	Ind	Ind	
Education & Community Studies with Spanish	X9R4	3FT deg	*g	12	MO	M				
Environmental Sciences and Spanish	FR94	3FT deg	*g	12	MO	M				
European Studies and Spanish	TR24	3FT deg	*g	12						
European Studies with Spanish	T2R4	3FT deg	*g	12	MO	M				
French with Spanish	R1R4	3FT deg	*g	12	MO	M				
German with Spanish	R2R4	3FT deg	*g	12	MO	M	Ind			
Health Studies and Spanish	BR94	3FT deg	*g	12	MO	M^	Ind	Ind	Ind	
Health Studies with Spanish	B9R4	3FT deg	*g	12	MO	M	Ind	Ind	Ind	
History of Art Design & Film and Spanish	RV44	3FT deg	*g	12	MO	M^	Ind	Ind	Ind	
History of Art Design & Film with Spanish	V4R4	3FT deg	*g	12	MO	M	Ind	Ind		
Information Technology and Spanish	GR54	3FT deg	*g	12	MO	M^	Ind	Ind	Ind	1
Information Technology with Spanish	G5R4	3FT deg	*g	12	MO	M	Ind	Ind	Ind	
Law and Spanish	MR34	3FT deg	*g	14	MO	M^	Ind	Ind	Ind	
Law with Spanish	M3R4	3FT deg	*g	14	MO	M				
Linguistics and Spanish	QR14	3FT deg	*g	12	MO	M^	Ind	Ind	Ind	
Linguistics with Spanish	Q1R4	3FT deg	*g	12	MO	M				
Literature and Spanish	QR34	3FT deg	*g	6-14	N	M^	Ind	Ind	Ind	
Literature with Spanish	Q3R4	3FT deg	*g	12	MO	M	Ind			
Maths, Stats & Computing and Spanish	GR94	3FT deg	*g	12	MO	M^	Ind	Ind	Ind	
Maths, Stats & Computing with Spanish	G9R4	3FT deg	*g	12	MO	M	Ind	Ind	Ind	
Media Studies and Spanish	PR44	3FT deg	*g	14	N	M^	Ind	Ind	Ind	6
Media Studies with Spanish	P4R4	3FT deg	*g	14	MO	M				
Politics and Spanish	MR14	3FT deg	*g	12	MO	M^	Ind	Ind	Ind	
Politics with Spanish	M1R4	3FT deg	*g	12	MO	M	Ind			
Psychosocial Studies and Spanish	LR74	3FT deg	*g	12	MO	M^	Ind	Ind	Ind	
Psychosocial Studies with Spanish	L7R4	3FT deg	*g	12	MO	M	Ind	Ind	Ind	
Social Policy Research and Spanish	LR44	3FT deg	*g	12	MO	M^	Ind	Ind	Ind	
Social Policy Research with Spanish	L4R4	3FT deg	*g	12	MO	M	Ind	Ind	Ind	
Sociology and Spanish	LR34	3FT deg	*g	12	MO	M^	Ind	Ind	Ind	3
Sociology with Spanish	L3R4	3FT deg	*g	12	MO	M	Ind	Ind	Ind	
Spanish and Third World & Development Studies	RM49	3FT deg	*g	12	MO	M	Ind			
Spanish and Women's Studies	RM4X	3FT deg	*g	12	MO	M	Ind			
Spanish with Anthropology	R4L6	3FT deg	*g	12	MO	M	Ind			
Spanish with Biology	R4C1	3FT deg	*g	12	MO	M	Ind			
Spanish with Business Studies	R4N1	3FT deg	*g	12	MO	M	Ind			
Spanish with Communication Studies	R4P3	3FT deg	*g	12	MO	M	Ind			
Spanish with Computing & Business Info Systems	R4G5	3FT deg	*g	12	MO	M	Ind			
Spanish with Cultural Studies	R4LP	3FT deg	*g	12	MO	M	Ind			
Spanish with Design - Textile Design	R4J4	3FT deg	*g	12	MO	M	Ind			
Spanish with Design - Visual Communication	R4W2	3FT deg	*g	12	MO	M	Ind			
Spanish with Economics	R4L1	3FT deg	*g	12	MO	M	Ind			
Spanish with Education & Community Studies	R4X9	3FT deg	*g	12	MO	M	Ind			
Spanish with European Studies	R4T2	3FT deg	*g	12	MO	M	Ind			
Spanish with French	R4R1	3FT deg	*g	12	MO	M	Ind			
Spanish with Health Studies	R4B9	3FT deg	*g	12	MO	M	Ind			
Spanish with History of Art Design & Film	R4V4	3FT deg	*g	12	MO	M	Ind			
Spanish with Information Technology	R4GM	3FT deg	*g	12	MO	M	Ind			
Spanish with Italian	R4R3	3FT deg	*g	12	MO	M	Ind			
Spanish with Law	R4M3	3FT deg	*g	12	MO	M	Ind			
Spanish with Linguistics	R4Q1	3FT deg	*g	12	MO	M	Ind			
Spanish with Literature	R4Q3	3FT deg	*g	12	MO	M	Ind			

TITLE	CODE	COURSE	SUBJECTS	A/AS	NO/C	AGNVQ	IB	SQA(H)	SQA	RATIO A/AS
Spanish with Maths, Stats & Computing	R4G9	3FT deg	* g	12	MO	M	Ind			
Spanish with Politics	R4M1	3FT deg	* g	12	MO	M	Ind			
Spanish with Social Policy Research	R4L4	3FT deg	* g	12	MO	M	Ind			
Spanish with Sociology	R4L3	3FT deg	* g	12	MO	M	Ind			
Third World & Development Studies with Spanish	M9R4	3FT deg	* g	12	MO	M	Ind	Ind		
Women's Studies with Spanish	M9RK	3FT deg	* g	12	MO	M	Ind			
Three-Subject Degree _Spanish_	Y600	3FT deg	* g	12	MO	D	Ind	Ind	Ind	

Univ of EDINBURGH

TITLE	CODE	COURSE	SUBJECTS	A/AS	NO/C	AGNVQ	IB	SQA(H)	SQA	RATIO A/AS
Arabic and Spanish	TR64	4FT deg	Sp g	BBB	Ind	Ind	Dip$	BBBB$	Ind	
Business Studies and Spanish	NR14	4FT deg	L g	BBB	Ind		34$	ABBB$	Ind	10
History of Art and Spanish	VR44	4FT deg	L g	BBB	Ind	Ind	Dip$	BBBB$	Ind	
Law and Spanish	MR34	4FT deg	L g	ABB	X		32	AAABB	X	7
Spanish	R400	4FT deg	L g	BBB	Ind	Ind	Dip$	BBBB$	Ind	
Spanish and Arabic	RT46	4FT deg	Sp g	BBB	Ind	Ind	Dip$	BBBB$	Ind	
Spanish and Business Studies	RN41	4FT deg	L g	BBB	Ind	Ind	Dip$	BBBB$	Ind	
Spanish and European History	RV41	4FT deg	L g	BBB	Ind	Ind	Dip$	BBBB$	Ind	
Spanish and History of Art	RV44	4FT deg	L g	BBB	Ind	Ind	Dip$	BBBB$	Ind	
Spanish and Latin	RQ46	4FT deg	L g	BBB	Ind	Ind	Dip$	BBBB$	Ind	
Spanish and Linguistics	RQ41	4FT deg	L g	BBB	Ind	Ind	Dip$	BBBB$	Ind	
Spanish and Politics	RM41	4FT deg	L g	BBB	Ind	Ind	Dip$	BBBB$	Ind	
Spanish and Portuguese	RR45	4FT deg	L g	BBB	Ind	Ind	Dip$	BBBB$	Ind	
Spanish and Portuguese with European Union Studs	RM61	4FT deg	L g	BBB	Ind	Ind	Dip$	BBBB$	Ind	

Univ of ESSEX

TITLE	CODE	COURSE	SUBJECTS	A/AS	NO/C	AGNVQ	IB	SQA(H)	SQA	RATIO A/AS
Computer Science with Spanish (4 Yrs)	G5R4	4FT deg	* g	20	MO+2D	Ind	28	BBBB	Ind	
English and Spanish (Language and Linguistics)	RQ43	4FT deg	*	20	MO+2D	Ind	28	BBBB	Ind	
Latin American Studies (4 Yrs)	R600	4FT deg	*	20	MO+2D	Ind	28	BBBB	Ind	4
Mathematics and Spanish (4 Yrs)	GR14	4FT deg	M	18	MO $	Ind	28$	CSYS	Ind	
Spanish (Lang & Linguistics) & History of Art	RV44	4FT deg	*	20	MO+2D	Ind	28	BBBB	Ind	5
Spanish (Language & Linguistics) with Portuguese	R4R5	4FT deg	*	20	MO+2D	Ind	28	BBBB	Ind	7
Spanish (Language and Linguistics) (4 Yrs)	R4Q1	4FT deg	*	20	MO+2D	Ind	28	BBBB	Ind	10

EUROPEAN Business School

TITLE	CODE	COURSE	SUBJECTS	A/AS	NO/C	AGNVQ	IB	SQA(H)	SQA	RATIO A/AS
Euro Bus Admin with Spanish + one beginner lang	N1RK	4SW deg	L	12	Ind		Ind	Ind	Ind	
International Bus St: Spanish +one beginner lang	NR14	4FT deg								
International Bus Studs with Spanish (Test+Int)	N1R4	4SW deg		12	Ind		Ind	Ind	Ind	
International Business & Mgt Studs with Spanish	N1RL	4SW deg		12	Ind		Ind	Ind	Ind	

Univ of EXETER

TITLE	CODE	COURSE	SUBJECTS	A/AS	NO/C	AGNVQ	IB	SQA(H)	SQA	RATIO A/AS
French and Spanish	RR1K	4FT deg	F	22-24	MO	M/D$^	34$			
German and Spanish	RR2K	4FT deg	G	BBB-BCC	MO	M/D$^	32$			
History and Spanish (Beginners Spanish avail)	RV4C	4FT deg	g	ABB-BCC	MO	M/D$^	32$	Ind	Ind	
Italian and Spanish (Beginners Spanish avail)	RR3K	4FT deg	L/Sp g	20-22	MO	M$	32$			
Music and Spanish (Beginners Spanish available)	RW4H	4FT deg	Mu+Sp	BCC	MO	M$^	34$	Ind	Ind	
Spanish (4 years) (Beginners Spanish available)	R401	4FT deg	Sp	BBC/BCC	MO	M/D$^	32$			
Spanish and Arabic (Beginners Spanish available)	RT46	4FT deg	Sp	BBC	MO	M/D$^	34$	Ind	Ind	
Spanish and Drama (Beginners Spanish available)	RW44	4FT deg	Sp	BBC	MO+3D	M/D$^	34$	Ind	Ind	18

Univ of GLAMORGAN

TITLE	CODE	COURSE	SUBJECTS	A/AS	NO/C	AGNVQ	IB	SQA(H)	SQA	RATIO A/AS
French with Spanish	R1R4	3FT deg			Ind	Ind	Ind	Ind	Ind	
Combined Studies (Honours) _Spanish_	Y400	3FT deg	* g	8-16	Ind	Ind	Ind	Ind	Ind	
Major/Minor Honours _Spanish_	Y402	3FT deg	* g	8-16	Ind	Ind	Ind	Ind	Ind	

TITLE	CODE	COURSE	SUBJECTS	A/AS	ND/C	AGNVQ	IB	SQA(H)	SQA	RATIO A/AS
Univ of GLASGOW										
Anthropology with Hispanic Studies	LR64	4FT deg		BBC	N	M	30	BBBB	Ind	
Archaeology/Hispanic Studies	RV46	5FT deg		BBC	HN	M	30	BBBB	Ind	2
Business Economics with Hispanic Studies	L1RK	4FT deg		BBC	N	M	30	BBBB	N	
Celtic Civilisation/Hispanic Studies	QR54	5FT deg		BBC	HN	M	30	BBBB	Ind	
Celtic/Hispanic Studies	QRM4	5FT deg		BBC	HN	M	30	BBBB	Ind	
Czech/Hispanic Studies	RTK1	5FT deg		BBC	HN	M	30	BBBB	Ind	
Economic and Social History with Hispanic Studs	V3R4	4FT deg		BBC	8M	M	30	BBBB	Ind	
Economics with Hispanic Studies	L1R4	4FT deg		BBC	8M	M	30	BBBB	Ind	
English/Hispanic Studies	QR34	5FT deg		BBC	HN	M	30	BBBB	Ind	5
Film and Television Studies/Hispanic Studies	RW45	5FT deg		BBB	HN	D	32	AABB	HN	6
French/Hispanic Studies	RR14	5FT deg		BBC	HN	M	30	BBBB	Ind	9
Geography with Hispanic Studies	L8R4	4FT deg		BBC	8M	M	30	BBBB	Ind	
Geography/Hispanic Studies	LR84	5FT deg		BBC	HN	M	30	BBBB$	Ind	
German/Hispanic Studies	RR24	5FT deg		BBC	HN	M	30	BBBB	Ind	6
Greek/Hispanic Studies	QR74	5FT deg		BBC	HN	M	30	BBBB	Ind	
Hispanic Studies	RR45	5FT deg		BBC	HN	M	30	BBBB	Ind	7
Hispanic Studies/Economics	LRC4	5FT deg		BBC	HN	M	30	BBBB	Ind	
Hispanic Studies/History	RV41	5FT deg		BBC	HN	M	30	BBBB	Ind	
Hispanic Studies/Italian	RR34	5FT deg		BBC	HN	M	30	BBBB	Ind	10
Hispanic Studies/Latin	QR64	5FT deg		BBC	HN	M	30	BBBB	Ind	
Hispanic Studies/Music	RW43	5FT deg		BBC	HN	M	30	BBBB	Ind	6
Hispanic Studies/Philosophy	RV47	5FT deg		BBC	HN	M	30	BBBB	Ind	
Hispanic Studies/Polish	RT41	5FT deg		BBC	HN	M	30	BBBB	Ind	
Hispanic Studies/Politics	MR14	5FT deg		BBC	HN	M	30	BBBB	Ind	4
Hispanic Studies/Psychology	CR84	5FT deg		BBC	HN	M	30	BBBB	Ind	8
Hispanic Studies/Russian	RR48	5FT deg		BBC	HN	M	30	BBBB	Ind	
Hispanic Studies/Scottish History	RV4C	5FT deg		BBC	HN	M	30	BBBB	Ind	
Hispanic Studies/Scottish Literature	QR24	5FT deg		BBC	HN	M	30	BBBB	Ind	
Hispanic Studies/Sociology	LR34	5FT deg		BBC	HN	M	30	BBBB	Ind	
Islamic Studies/Hispanic Studies	TR64	4FT deg		BBC	N	M	30	BBBB	Ind	
Law with Spanish Language	M3R4	4FT deg		ABB	X		34	AAAAB	X	5
Management Studies/Hispanic Studies	NR14	5FT deg		BBC	HN	M	30	BBBB	Ind	7
Philosophy with Hispanic Studies	V7R4	4FT deg		BBC	8M	M	30	BBBB	Ind	
Politics with Hispanic Studies	M1R4	4FT deg		BBC	8M	M	30	BBBB	Ind	
Psychology with Hispanic Studies	C8R4	4FT deg		BBC	8M	M	30	BBBB	Ind	9
Social and Urban Policy with Hispanic Studies	L4R4	4FT deg		BBC	8M	M	30	BBBB	Ind	
Social and Urban Policy/Hispanic Studies	LR44	5FT deg		BBC	HN	M	30	BBBB	Ind	
Sociology with Hispanic Studies	L3R4	4FT deg		BBC	8M	M	30	BBBB	Ind	
Theatre Studies/Hispanic Studies	RW44	5FT deg		BBC	HN	M	30	BBBB	Ind	
Theology & Religious Studies/Hispanic Studies	RV4V	5FT deg		BBC	HN	M	30	BBBB	Ind	
GOLDSMITHS COLL (Univ of London)										
Spanish and Latin American Studies (4 Yrs)	RR46	4FT deg		BCD	MO	M	Dip	BBBBC	N	6 8/22
Univ of GREENWICH										
Applied Biology with Spanish	C1R4	3FT/4SW deg	B+C g	10	3M	MS	Dip	CCC	Ind	
Applied Chemistry with Spanish	F1R4	3FT/4SW deg	C+S g	8	3M	MS	Dip	CCC	Ind	
HERIOT-WATT Univ										
Accountancy with Spanish	N4R4	4FT deg	L g	BCC	Ind		Ind	ABBB$	Ind	
Chemistry with Spanish	F1R4	4FT deg	C+S+L	CCD	$	MS^ go	28	BBB	$	
French/Spanish	RR1K	4FT deg								
French/Spanish (Interpreting and Translating)	RR14	4FT deg	2L	BBC	Ind		Ind	AABB	Ind	

			98 expected requirements							**96 entry stats**	
TITLE	CODE	COURSE	SUBJECTS	A/AS	ND/C	AGNVQ	IB	SQA(H)	SQA	RATIO	A/AS
German/Spanish	RR2K	4FT deg									
German/Spanish (Interpreting and Translating)	RR24	4FT deg	2L	BBC	Ind		Ind	AABB	Ind		
Mathematics with Spanish	G1R4	4FT deg	M+L	CDE	HN	M$^	28	BBB	HN		
Russian/Spanish (Interpreting and Translating)	RR48	4FT deg	2L	BBC	Ind		Ind	AABB	Ind		
Spanish/Russian	RR4V	4FT deg									

Univ of HUDDERSFIELD

Spanish and Media	RP44	4FT deg	Sp	CDD	Ind	Ind	Ind	BBBC	Ind		
Spanish with Politics	R4M1	4FT deg	Sp	CCE	Ind	Ind	Ind	BBBC	Ind		

Univ of HULL

Business Studies/Spanish	NR14	4FT deg	L g	BBC-BCC	Ind $	D*^ go	26$	BBCCC	Ind	4	18/24
English/Spanish	QR34	4FT deg	E+L	BBB-CCC	MO+D $	M$^ gi	28$	BBBCC	Ind	25	
French/Spanish	RR14	4FT deg	F	BCC	Ind	Ind	28$	BBBCC	Ind	8	14/28
Gender Studies and Spanish	MR94	4FT deg	L	BCC-CCC	MO	M$6/^ go	28$	BBCCC	Ind	2	
German/Spanish	RR24	4FT deg	G	BCC-CCC	Ind	Ind	28$	BBBCC	Ind	6	
Mathematics with Spanish	G1R4	4FT deg	M/L+M g	BCD	MO $	M$^ go	26$	BBCCC	Ind	2	20/24
Mathematics with Spanish (MMath)	G1RK	4FT deg	M/L+M g	BCC	MO $	M$^ go	26$	BBBCC	Ind		
Philosophy/Spanish	RV47	4FT deg	L	BBB-CCC	Ind	M$^ go	28$	BBBCC	Ind		
Spanish	R401	4FT deg	Sp	BBB-CCC	Ind	Ind	28$	BBCCC	Ind	3	12/20

Univ of KENT

European Studies (Spanish)	R411	4FT deg	*	20	3M+3D	Ind	28	Ind	Ind		
Spanish/Classical Studies	QR84	4FT deg	*	20	3M+3D	Ind	28	Ind	Ind		
Spanish/Comparative Literary Studies	QR24	4FT deg	*	20	3M+3D	Ind	28	Ind	Ind		
Spanish/Computing	GR54	4FT deg	*	20	3M+3D	Ind	28	Ind	Ind		
Spanish/Drama	WR44	4FT deg	*	22	2M+4D	Ind	30	Ind	Ind		
Spanish/English	QR34	4FT deg	E	22	2M+4D	Ind	30	Ind	Ind		
Spanish/English (Post-Colonial Literatures)	QRJ4	4FT deg	E	22	2M+4D	Ind	30	Ind	Ind		
Spanish/English Language	QRH4	4FT deg	E	20	3M+3D	Ind	28	Ind	Ind		
Spanish/Film Studies	WR54	4FT deg	*	22	2M+4D	Ind	30	Ind	Ind		
Spanish/French	RR14	4FT deg	F	22	2M+4D	Ind	30	Ind	Ind		
Spanish/German	RR24	4FT deg	G	20	3M+3D	Ind	28	Ind	Ind		
Spanish/History	RV41	4FT deg	*	22	2M+4D	Ind	30	Ind	Ind		
Spanish/History and Theory of Art	VR44	4FT deg	*	20	3M+2D	Ind	28	Ind	Ind		
Spanish/History of Science	RV45	4FT deg	*	20	3M+3D	Ind	28	Ind	Ind		
Spanish/Italian	RR43	4FT deg	*	20	3M+3D	Ind	28	Ind	Ind		
Spanish/Linguistics	RQ41	4FT deg	*	20	3M+3D	Ind	28	Ind	Ind		
Spanish/Philosophy	RV47	4FT deg	*	20	3M+3D	Ind	28	Ind	Ind		
Theology/Spanish	RV48	4FT deg	*	20	3M+3D	Ind	28	Ind	Ind		

KING'S COLL LONDON (Univ of London)

Classical Studies and Portuguese	QR85	4FT deg		BBC							
French and Hispanic Studies	RR14	4FT deg	F+Sp	BBC						6	20/28
French and Portuguese	RR15	4FT deg	F	BBC						5	
German and Hispanic Studies	RR24	4FT deg	G+Sp	BBC						5	
German and Portuguese	RR25	4FT deg	G	BCC						2	
Hispanic Studies	R400	4FT deg	Sp	ABB-BBC						6	20/24
Hispanic Studies and Modern Greek	RT42	4FT deg	Sp	BBC-BCC						1	
Hispanic Studies with Applied Computing	R4G5	4FT deg	Sp	BBC							
Hispanic Studies with English	R4Q3	4FT deg	Sp+E	BBC						6	
Hispanic and Classical Studies	QR84	4FT deg	Sp	BBC-BCC							
Hispanic and Portuguese Studies	R610	4FT deg	Sp	BBC						14	
History and Portuguese and Brazilian Studies	VR15	3FT deg	H	ABB-BCC							

course details			98 expected requirements							96 entry stats	
TITLE	CODE	COURSE	SUBJECTS	A/AS	NO/C	AGNVQ	IB	SQA(H)	SQA	RATIO	A/AS
Modern Greek and Portuguese	TR25	4FT deg	E+H	BCC							
Philosophy and Hispanic Studies	RV47	4FT deg	Sp	BBC-BCC						3	
Portuguese and Brazilian Studies	RR56	3FT deg	E+H/L	BCC						5	
Portuguese with Applied Computing	R5G5	3FT deg	E+H/L	BCC							
Portuguese with English	R5Q3	3FT deg	E/L	BBC							
War Studies and Portuguese	MR95	3FT deg		BBC							
Afro-Portuguese, Brazilian and Religious Studies _Afro Portuguese_	Y654	3FT/4FT deg	*	BCC							
Afro-Portuguese, Brazilian and Religious Studies _Brazilian Studies_	Y654	3FT/4FT deg	*	BCC							

KINGSTON Univ

TITLE	CODE	COURSE	SUBJECTS	A/AS	NO/C	AGNVQ	IB	SQA(H)	SQA	RATIO	A/AS
Spanish/Economics	RL41	4FT deg	Sp g	14	MO	Ind^	Ind	BCCCC	HN	2	
Spanish/English Language	QR34	4FT deg	Sp+E	16	MO	Ind^	Ind	BBCCC	HN	3	
Spanish/English Literature	RQ43	4FT deg	E+Sp	14	MO	Ind^	Ind	BCCCC	HN	3	
Spanish/French	RR41	4FT deg	F g	14	MO	Ind^	Ind	BCCCC	HN	5	6/16
Spanish/History	RV41	4FT deg	H+Sp g	14	MO	Ind^	Ind	BCCCC	HN		
Spanish/History of Art, Architecture and Design	VR44	3FT deg	Sp g	14-16	MO	Ind^	Ind	BCCCC	HN		
Spanish/Politics	MR14	4FT deg	Sp g	12-14	MO	Ind^	Ind	BCCCC	HN	1	
Spanish/Psychology	LR74	4FT deg	Sp g	16	MO	Ind^	Ind	BBCCC	HN	17	

LANCASTER Univ

TITLE	CODE	COURSE	SUBJECTS	A/AS	NO/C	AGNVQ	IB	SQA(H)	SQA	RATIO	A/AS
Chemistry with Spanish Studies (4 years)	F1R4	4SW deg	C+Sp/L g	18	MO $		28$	BBBB$	Ind		
European Management (Spanish)	N1R4	4FT/5SW deg	Sp/* g	ABB	MO+5D		32$	AABBB$	Ind		
French Studies and Spanish Studies	RR14	4SW deg	(F+Sp)/* g	BCC	Ind $		30$	BBBBB$	Ind		
German Studies and Spanish Studies	RR24	4SW deg	G/Sp	BCC	Ind $		30$	BBBBB$	Ind		
Italian Studies and Spanish Studies	RR34	4SW deg	I/Sp/L	BCC	Ind $		30$	BBBBB$	Ind		
Physics with Spanish Studies	F3R4	4SW deg	(M+P)+Sp/*	BCC	MO $		24$	BBCCC$	Ind		
Spanish Studies and Accounting and Finance	NR44	4SW deg	M+Sp/L g	BBC	DO $		30$	AABBB$	Ind		
Spanish Studies and Art History	WR14	4SW deg	Sp/L	BCC	MO $		30$	BBBBB$	Ind		
Spanish Studies and Computing	GR54	4FT deg	Sp/L	BCC	Ind $		30$	BBBBB$	Ind		
Spanish Studies and Economics	RL41	4SW deg	Sp/L g	BBC	MO+4D		32$	ABBBB$	Ind		
Spanish Studies and Educational Studies	RX49	4SW deg	Sp/L	BCC	MO $		30$	BBBBB$	Ind		
Spanish Studies and English	RQ43	4SW deg	Sp/L+E g	BBC	Ind $		32$	ABBBB$	Ind		
Spanish Studies and Geography	LR84	4SW deg	Sp/L+Gy g	BBC	Ind $		30$	BBBBB$	Ind		
Spanish Studies and History	RV41	4SW deg	H+Sp/L	BBC	Ind $		30$	BBBBB$	Ind		
Spanish Studies and Linguistics	QR14	4SW deg	Sp/L g	BBC	MO $		30$	BBBBB$	Ind		
Spanish Studies and Marketing	RN45	4SW deg	Sp/L g	BBC	MO+4D		32$	ABBBB$	Ind		
Spanish Studies and Mathematics	GR14	4SW deg	M+Sp/L	20	MO $		30$	BBBBB$	Ind		
Spanish Studies and Music	WR34	4SW deg	Sp/L+Mu	BCC	Ind $		Ind$	BBBB$	Ind		
Spanish Studies and Philosophy	RV47	4SW deg	Sp/L	BCC	Ind $		30$	BBBBB$	Ind		
Spanish Studies and Politics	RM41	4SW deg	Sp/L	BCC	Ind $		30$	BBBBB$	Ind		
Spanish Studies and Psychology	CR84	4SW deg	Sp/L g	BBC	DO $		32$	ABBBB$	Ind		
Spanish Studies and Religious Studies	RV48	4SW deg	Sp/L	BCC	Ind $		30$	BBBBB$	Ind		
Spanish Studies and Theatre Studies	WR44	4SW deg	Sp/L	BCC	MO $		30$	BBBBB$	Ind		

Univ of LEEDS

TITLE	CODE	COURSE	SUBJECTS	A/AS	NO/C	AGNVQ	IB	SQA(H)	SQA	RATIO	A/AS
Arabic-Portuguese	RT56	4FT deg	Cl/L g	BBC	Ind	Ind	30$	CSYS	Ind		
Arabic-Spanish	RT46	4FT deg	Sp g	BBC	Ind	Ind	30$	CSYS	Ind		
Chinese-Portuguese	RT53	4FT deg	L g	BBC	Ind	Ind	30$	CSYS	Ind		
Chinese-Spanish	RT43	4FT deg	Sp g	BBC	Ind	Ind	30$	CSYS	Ind	7	
Classical Literature-Spanish	QR84	4FT deg	Sp g	BBC	Ind	Ind	30$	CSYS	Ind		
Economics-Spanish	RL41	4FT deg	Sp g	BBC	Ind	Ind	30$	CSYS	Ind	9	
English-Portuguese	QR35	4FT deg	E+L g	BBC	Ind	Ind	30$	CSYS	Ind		

course details   98 expected requirements   96 entry stats

TITLE	CODE	COURSE	SUBJECTS	A/AS	ND/C	AGNVQ	IB	SQA(H)	SQA	RATIO	A/AS
English-Spanish	QR34	4FT deg	E+Sp g	BBC	Ind	Ind	30$	CSYS	Ind	8	24/28
French-Portuguese	RR15	4FT deg	F g	BBC	Ind	Ind	30$	CSYS	Ind	6	
French-Spanish	RR14	4FT deg	F+Sp g	BBB	Ind	Ind	32$	CSYS	Ind	6	24/30
Geography-Spanish	RL48	4FT deg	Sp+Gy g	BBC	Ind	Ind	30$	CSYS	Ind	5	
German-Spanish	RR24	4FT deg	G+Sp g	BBC	Ind	Ind	30$	CSYS	Ind		
History of Art-Spanish	RV44	4FT deg	Sp g	BBC	Ind	Ind	30$	CSYS	Ind	6	
History-Portuguese	RV51	4FT deg	L g	BBC	Ind	Ind	30	CSYS	Ind		
History-Spanish	RV41	4FT deg	Sp g	BBC	Ind	Ind	30$	CSYS	Ind		
Ibero-American Studies	R4R5	4FT deg	Sp g	BCC	Ind	Ind	28$	CSYS	Ind	4	20/26
Italian-Portuguese	RR35	4FT deg	I g	BCC	Ind	Ind	Ind	Ind	Ind		
Italian-Portuguese B	RRH5	4FT deg	L g	BCC	Ind	Ind	Ind	Ind	Ind		
Italian-Spanish	RR34	4FT deg	Sp+I g	BCC	Ind	Ind	28$	CSYS	Ind	5	
Italian-Spanish B	RRH4	4FT deg	Sp g	BCC	Ind	Ind	28$	CSYS	Ind	4	18/28
Latin-Spanish	QR64	4FT deg	Sp+Ln g	BBC	Ind	Ind	30$	CSYS	Ind	1	
Linguistics-Spanish	QR14	4FT deg	Sp g	BBC	Ind	Ind	30$	CSYS	Ind	9	
Management Studies-Portuguese	RN51	4FT deg	L g	BBC	Ind	Ind	30$	CSYS	Ind	8	
Management Studies-Spanish	RN41	4FT deg	Sp g	BBC	Ind	Ind	30$	CSYS	Ind	11	22/30
Politics and Parliamentary Studies-Portuguese	MR15	4FT deg									
Politics-Spanish	RM41	4FT deg	Sp g	BBC	Ind	Ind	30$	CSYS	Ind	8	
Portuguese-Russian	RR58	4FT deg	R g	BBC	Ind	Ind	30$	CSYS	Ind		
Portuguese-Russian B	RR5V	4FT deg	L g	BBC	Ind	Ind	30$	CSYS	Ind		
Portuguese-Spanish	RR45	4FT deg	Sp g	BBC	Ind	Ind		CSYS	Ind	5	
Roman Civilisation-Spanish	QRV4	4FT deg	Sp g	BBC	Ind	Ind	30$	CSYS	Ind		
Russian-Spanish	RR48	4FT deg	Sp+R g	BCC	Ind	Ind	28$	CSYS	Ind		
Russian-Spanish B	RR4V	4FT deg	Sp g	BCC	Ind	Ind	28$	CSYS	Ind		
Spanish	R400	4FT deg	Sp g	BCC	Ind	Ind	28$	CSYS	Ind	6	20/30

LEEDS, TRINITY & ALL SAINTS Univ COLL

TITLE	CODE	COURSE	SUBJECTS	A/AS	ND/C	AGNVQ	IB	SQA(H)	SQA	RATIO	A/AS
Spanish-Management	RN41	4FT deg	Sp g	BCC-CCD	Ind	X	24$	BBCCC	Ind	8	
Spanish-Media	RP44	4FT deg	Sp g	BCC-CCD	Ind	X	24$	BBCCC	Ind	3	8/20

LEEDS METROPOLITAN Univ

TITLE	CODE	COURSE	SUBJECTS	A/AS	ND/C	AGNVQ	IB	SQA(H)	SQA	RATIO	A/AS
Public Relations (Spanish)	P3R4	3FT deg									

Univ of LINCOLNSHIRE and HUMBERSIDE

TITLE	CODE	COURSE	SUBJECTS	A/AS	ND/C	AGNVQ	IB	SQA(H)	SQA	RATIO	A/AS
Accountancy and Spanish	NR44	3FT deg	Sp g	12	3M+1D	M	24	CCCC	Ind		
Administration and Spanish	NR1K	3FT deg	Sp g	12	3M+1D	M	24	CCCC	Ind		
Business and Spanish	RN41	3FT deg	Sp g	12	3M+1D		24	CCCC	Ind		
Computing and Spanish	G5RK	3FT deg									
Finance and Spanish	NR34	3FT deg	Sp g	12	3M+1D	M	24	CCCC	Ind		
Human Resource Management and Spanish	NR64	3FT deg	Sp g	12	3M+1D	M	24	CCCC	Ind		
Information Systems and Spanish	GR54	3FT deg	Sp g	12	3M+1D	M	24	CCCC	Ind		
Marketing and Spanish	NR54	3FT deg	Sp g	12	3M+1D	M	24	CCCC	Ind		
Media Technology and Spanish	PR44	3FT deg	Sp g	12	3M+1D	M	24	CCCC	Ind		

Univ of LIVERPOOL

TITLE	CODE	COURSE	SUBJECTS	A/AS	ND/C	AGNVQ	IB	SQA(H)	SQA	RATIO	A/AS
French and Hispanic Studies	RR14	4FT deg	F+Sp	BBC	Ind		29$	BBBBB$	Ind	10	18/30
German and Hispanic Studies	RR24	4FT deg	G+Sp	BCC	Ind		30$	BBBBB$	Ind	9	
Hispanic Studs (Span,Catalan,Port,Latin Amer St)	RR45	4FT deg	Sp	BBC	Ind		30$	BBBBC$	Ind	4	12/28
Latin American Studies	R601	4FT deg	*	BCC	Ind		30	BBBBC	Ind	3	14/26
Arts Combined *Catalan*	Y401	4FT deg	L	BBC-BBB	Ind	Ind	30$	ABBB$	Ind		
Arts Combined *Latin American Studies*	Y401	3FT deg	*	BBC-BBB	Ind	Ind	30$	ABBB	Ind		

| | | | 98 expected requirements | | | | | | | 96 entry stats |
TITLE	CODE	COURSE	SUBJECTS	A/AS	NO/C	AGNVQ	IB	SQA(H)	SQA	RATIO A/AS
Arts Combined *Portuguese*	Y401	4FT deg	L	BBC-BBB	Ind	Ind	30$	ABBB$	Ind	
Arts Combined *Spanish*	Y401	4FT deg	Sp	BBC-BBB	Ind	Ind	30$	ABBB$	Ind	
BA Combined Honours *Hispanic Studies*	Y200	3FT deg	* g	BBB	Ind	Ind	Ind	Ind	Ind	
LIVERPOOL JOHN MOORES Univ										
French and Spanish	RR14	4FT deg	L	14	3M+4D		Ind			10 10/20
German and Spanish	RR24	4FT deg	L	14	3M+4D					6
International Business Studies with Spanish	N1R4	4SW deg	*	16	3M+4D					6 12/20
LONDON GUILDHALL Univ										
3D/Spatial Design and Spanish	RW4F	4FT deg	Pf g	DD	MO	M$ go	24	Ind	Ind	
Spanish & Communications & Audio Visual Prod St	PR44	4FT deg	* g	CC-CDD	MO+2D	M$ go	26	Ind	Ind	
Spanish and Accounting	NR44	4FT deg	* g	DD	MO	M$ go	24	Ind	Ind	
Spanish and Business	NR14	4FT deg	* g	CD-DDD	MO+2D	M$ go	24	Ind	Ind	
Spanish and Business Economics	LRC4	4FT deg	* g	DD	MO	M$ go	24	Ind	Ind	
Spanish and Business Information Technology	GR74	4FT deg	* g	DD	MO	M$ go	24	Ind	Ind	
Spanish and Computing	GR54	4FT deg	* g	DD	MO	M$ go	24	Ind	Ind	
Spanish and Design Studies	RW42	4FT deg	* g	CD-DDD	MO+2D	M$ go	26	Ind	Ind	
Spanish and Development Studies	MR94	4FT deg	* g	DD	MO	M$ go	24	Ind	Ind	
Spanish and Economics	LR14	4FT deg	* g	DD	MO	M$ go	24	Ind	Ind	
Spanish and English	QR34	4FT deg	* g	CD-DDD	MO+2D	M$ go	26	Ind	Ind	
Spanish and European Studies	RT42	4FT deg	* g	DD	MO	M$ go	24	Ind	Ind	
Spanish and Financial Services	NR34	4FT deg	* g	DD	MO	M$ go	24	Ind	Ind	
Spanish and Fine Art	RW41	4FT deg	* g	CC-CDD	MO+2D	M$ go	24	Ind	Ind	
Spanish and French	RR14	4FT deg	* g	DD	MO	M$ go	24	Ind	Ind	
Spanish and German	RR24	4FT deg	* g	DD	MO	M$ go	24	Ind	Ind	
Spanish and International Relations	MRC4	4FT deg	* g	DD	MO	M$ go	24	Ind	Ind	
Spanish and Law	MR34	4FT deg	* g	CC-CDD	MO+2D	M$ go	26	Ind	Ind	
Spanish and Marketing	NR54	4FT deg	* g	CD-DDD	MO+2D	M$ go	26	Ind	Ind	
Spanish and Mathematics	GR14	4FT deg	* g	DD	MO	M$ go	24	Ind	Ind	
Spanish and Modern History	RV41	4FT deg	* g	DD	MO	M$ go	24	Ind	Ind	
Spanish and Multimedia Systems	GRM4	4FT deg	* g	DD	MO	M$ go	24	Ind	Ind	
Spanish and Politics	MR14	4FT deg	* g	DD	MO	M$ go	24	Ind	Ind	
Spanish and Product Development & Manufacture	JR44	4FT deg	* g	DD	MO	M$ go	24	Ind	Ind	
Spanish and Psychology	CR84	4FT deg	* g	CD-DDD	MO+2D	M$ go	26	Ind	Ind	
Spanish and Social Policy & Management	LR44	4FT deg	* g	CD-DDD	MO	M$ go	24	Ind	Ind	
Spanish and Sociology	LR34	4FT deg	* g	CD-DDD	MO	M$ go	24	Ind	Ind	
Taxation and Spanish	NRH4	4FT deg	* g	DD	MO	M$ go	24	Ind	Ind	
Textile Furnishing Design and Spanish	RW4G	4FT deg	Pf g	DD	MO	M$ go	24	Ind	Ind	
Modular Programme *Spanish*	Y400	3FT/4FT deg	* g	CC-DD	MO	M$ go	24	Ind	Ind	
LOUGHBOROUGH Univ										
Economics with Spanish	L1R4	3FT deg	Sp g	20			30$	Ind		
Politics with Spanish	M1R4	3FT deg	Sp	20			28$	Ind		
Spanish and French Studies	RR41	3FT deg	Sp+F	20			28$	Ind		
Spanish and German Studies	RR42	3FT deg	Sp+G	20			28$	Ind		
Spanish and Politics	RM41	3FT deg	Sp	20			28$	Ind		
LUTON Univ										
Business Systems with Spanish	N1RK	3FT deg	Sp g	12-16	MO/DO	M/D	32	BBCC	Ind	
Business with Spanish	N1R4	3FT deg	Sp g	12-16	MO/DO	M/D	32	BBCC	Ind	

course details

TITLE	CODE	COURSE	SUBJECTS	A/AS	NO/C	RGNVQ	IB	SQA(H)	SQA	RATIO A/AS
Geography with Spanish	F8R4	3FT deg	Sp g	12-16	MO/DO	M/D	32	BBCC	Ind	
Leisure Studies with Spanish	N7R4	3FT deg	Sp g	12-16	MO/DO	M/D	32	BBCC	Ind	
Linguistics with Spanish	Q1R4	3FT deg	Sp g	12-16	MO/DO	M/D	32	BBCC	Ind	
Marketing with Spanish	N5R4	3FT deg	Sp g	12-16	MO/DO	M/D	32	BBCC	Ind	
Mathematical Sciences with Spanish	G1R4	3FT deg	Sp g	12-16	MO/DO	M/D	32	BBCC	Ind	
Media Practices with Spanish	P4R4	3FT deg	Sp g	12-16	MO/DO	M/D	32	BBCC	Ind	
Modern English Studies with Spanish	Q3R4	3FT deg	Sp g	12-16	MO/DO	M/D	32	BBCC	Ind	
Psychology with Spanish	L7R4	3FT deg	Sp g	12-16	MO/DO	M/D	32	BBCC	Ind	2
Regional Planning & Development with Spanish	K4R4	3FT deg	Sp g	12-16	MO/DO	M/D	32	BBCC	Ind	
Travel and Tourism with Spanish	P7R4	3FT deg	Sp g	12-16	MO/DO	M/D	32	BBCC	Ind	8

Univ of MANCHESTER

TITLE	CODE	COURSE	SUBJECTS	A/AS	NO/C	RGNVQ	IB	SQA(H)	SQA	RATIO A/AS
American and Latin-American Studies	QR46	4FT deg	Sp	BBC			28$	ABBBB$		10
English and a Modern Language (Spanish)	RQ43	4FT deg	E+Sp	ABB			Ind	BBBBC		9
European Studies and Modern Langs (Spanish)	RT42	4FT deg	Sp	ABB-BBB Ind	D^		28$	AAABB$ Ind		7	22/28
French/Portuguese	RR15	4FT deg	F	ABB	D^		30$	AABB$		
French/Spanish	RR14	4FT deg	F	ABB	D^		30$	AABB$		5	18/30
French/Spanish	RR1L	4FT deg	F	ABB	D^		30$	AABB$		5	20/30
German/Portuguese	RR25	4FT deg	G	BBB			28	BBBBC		1
German/Spanish	RR2L	4FT deg	G	BBB			28	BBBBC		3
German/Spanish	RR24	4FT deg	G+Sp	BBB			28	BBBBC		15
Hispanic Studies (Span,Port,Latin American St)	RR45	4FT deg	Sp	BBB-BBC			28$	ABBBB$		7	14/26
History and Spanish	VR14	4FT deg	Sp	BBC			28$	ABBBB$		5
Italian/Portuguese	RR35	4FT deg	I/Pt	BBB-BCC			Ind	BBBCC		
Italian/Spanish	RR34	4FT deg	Sp	BBB-BCC			Ind	BBBCC		8
Italian/Spanish	RR3L	4FT deg	I/Sp	BBB-BCC			Ind	BBBCC		
Latin and Spanish	QR64	4FT deg	Ln+Sp	BBC	X	X	30	BBBBB	X	
Linguistics and Spanish	QR14	4FT deg	Sp	BBB	X		32$	AABBB		10
Russian/Portuguese	RR85	4FT deg	R	CCC-BBC Ind			26$	BBBCC	Ind	
Russian/Spanish	RR84	4FT deg	Sp	CCC-BBC Ind			26$	BBBCC	Ind	
Russian/Spanish	RR8L	4FT deg	R	CCC-BBC Ind			26$	BBBCC	Ind	
Spanish/French	RR4C	4FT deg	Sp	BBB-BBC			28$	ABBBB$		4
Spanish/German	RR4G	4FT deg	Sp	BBB-BBC			28$	ABBBB$		
Spanish/Italian	RR4H	4FT deg	Sp	BBB-BBC			28$	ABBBB$		
Spanish/Russian	RR4W	4FT deg	Sp	BBB-BBC Ind			28$	ABBBB$		1

UMIST (Manchester)

TITLE	CODE	COURSE	SUBJECTS	A/AS	NO/C	RGNVQ	IB	SQA(H)	SQA	RATIO A/AS
Chemical Engineering with Spanish (MEng)	H8RK	4FT deg	M+C g	BBC	MO+3D$ Ind		30$	CSYS$	Ind	
Chemistry with Spanish (MChem)	F1RL	4FT deg	C g	18	3M+1D	MS6/^ go	30	CSYS	Ind	8

MANCHESTER METROPOLITAN Univ

TITLE	CODE	COURSE	SUBJECTS	A/AS	NO/C	RGNVQ	IB	SQA(H)	SQA	RATIO A/AS
Accounting and Finance in Europe (Spanish)	N4R4	4FT deg	Sp g	18	MO+8D	D^	26$	BBBBC	Ind	
Business in Europe-Spanish Route	N1R4	4FT deg	* g	BBC	Ind	DB	24$	Ind	Ind	10/22
French post A level/Spanish ab initio	RR1K	4FT deg	F	CC	X		28$	AACCC$ X		7/18
French post A level/Spanish post A level	RR1L	4FT deg	F+Sp	CC	X		28$	AACCC$ X		6/18
German post A level/Spanish ab initio	RR2L	4FT deg	G	CC	X		28$	AACCC$ X		8/14
Spanish post A level/German ab initio	RR2K	4FT deg	Sp	CC	X		28$	AACCC$ X		8/18
Humanities/Social Studies *Spanish*	Y400	3FT/4FT deg	Sp	CDD	Ind	Ind	Ind	BBB	Ind	

MIDDLESEX Univ

TITLE	CODE	COURSE	SUBJECTS	A/AS	NO/C	RGNVQ	IB	SQA(H)	SQA	RATIO A/AS
Latin American Studies	R600▼	4FT deg	* g	12-16	5M	M$ go		Ind	Ind	
Spanish	R400▼	3FT/4FT deg	* g	12-16	5M	M$ go	28	Ind	Ind	
Joint Honours Degree *Spanish*	Y400	4FT deg	* g	12-16	5M	M$ go	28	BBCC	Ind	

Languages – Spanish/Latin American   46

TITLE	CODE	COURSE	SUBJECTS	A/AS	NO/C	RGNVQ	IB	SQA(H)	SQA	RATIO A/AS
NENE COLLEGE										
European Business (Spanish)	NR14	4SW deg	Sp g	8	M+D	M	24	CCC	Ind	
Univ of NEWCASTLE										
French and Spanish	RR14	4FT deg	F+Sp	BBC			$	AABBB$		7 22/30
French with Portuguese	R1R5	4FT deg	F	BBC		X	$	AABBB$		
French with Spanish	R1R4	4FT deg	F	BBC		X	$	AABBB$		5 22/30
German with Portuguese	R2R5	4FT deg	G	20			$	ABBBB$		
German with Spanish	R2R4	4FT deg	G	20			$	ABBBB$		6
Latin American Studies	R600	4FT deg	Sp	18		X	$	ABBBB$		13
Spanish with Accounting	R4N4	4FT deg	Sp+M/Ec	BCC			$	ABBBB$		
Spanish with French	R4R1	4FT deg	Sp g	BCC		X	$	ABBBB$		20
Spanish with German	R4R2	4FT deg	Sp	BCC		X	$	ABBBB$		2
Spanish with Politics	R4M1	4FT deg	Sp	BCC			$	ABBBB$		
Spanish with Portuguese	R4R5	4FT deg	Sp	BCC		X	$	ABBBB$		11
Spanish, Portuguese and Latin American Studies	R400	4FT deg	Sp	BCC			$	ABBBB$		7 20/28
Combined Studies (BA) *Portugese*	Y400	3FT deg	*	ABC-BBB	5D	Ind	35$	AAAB	Ind	
Combined Studies (BA) *Spanish and Latin American Studies*	Y400	3FT deg	*	ABC-BBB	5D	Ind	35$	AAAB	Ind	
Univ of NORTH LONDON										
International Business and Spanish	NR14	4FT deg	* g	CC	MO+4D	D	Ind	Ind	Ind	7
Marketing and Spanish & Latin American Studies	NR54	4FT deg	* g	CC	MO+4D	D	Ind	Ind	Ind	
Combined Honours *Spanish and Latin American Studies*	Y300	4FT deg	*	CC	Ind	Ind	Ind	Ind	Ind	
Univ of NORTHUMBRIA										
French and Spanish	RR14	3FT deg	F	CC	2M+2D	M^	24	BBCCC	Ind	5 10/20
German and Spanish	RR24	3FT deg	G	CC	2M+2D	M^	24	BBCCC	Ind	2 12/18
Information Studies and Spanish	PR24	3FT deg		CC	2M+2D	M^		BBCCC		
Russian and Spanish	RR84	3FT deg	R	CC	MO+1D		24	CCCC	Ind	
Spanish and Economics	LR14	3FT deg		CC	2M+2D	M^	24	BBCCC	Ind	
Spanish and German	RR42	3FT deg	Sp	CC	2M+2D	M^	24	BBCCC	Ind	
Spanish and Politics	MR14	3FT deg		CC	2M+2D	M^	24	BBCCC	Ind	
Spanish and Russian	RR48	3FT deg	Sp	CC	2M+2D	M^	24	BBCCC	Ind	
Univ of NOTTINGHAM										
Economics with Hispanic Studies	L1R4	4FT deg	L g	AAB-ABB	X		32$	Ind	X	11
Electrical and Electronic Eng with Spanish	H6R4	3FT/4FT deg	M+P	BBC-BCC	Ind	Ind	28$	Ind	Ind	2
Electronic Engineering with Spanish	H6RK	3FT/4FT deg	M+P	BBC-BCC	Ind	Ind	28$	Ind	Ind	
French and Hispanic Studies	RR1L	4FT deg	F+Sp	BBB						2 26/30
French and Portuguese (Beginners)	RR1M	4FT deg	F	BBC						
German and Hispanic Studies	RR2L	4FT deg	G+Sp	BBB						5
German and Portuguese (Beginners)	RR2M	4FT deg	G	BBC						
Hispanic Studies	R400	4FT deg	Sp	BBC						7 22/30
Hispanic Studies and Russian	RRL8	4FT deg	Sp+R	BBC						
Hispanic Studies and Russian (Beginners)	RRLV	4FT deg	Sp	BBC						1
Management Studies with Portuguese	N1R5	4FT deg	L g	BBB	Ind	D*6/^ go	32	AAABB	Ind	4
Management Studies with Spanish	N1R4	4FT deg	S g	BBB	Ind	D*^ go	32$	AAABB$	Ind	13 26/28
Manufacturing Engineering and Mgt with Spanish	H7R4	3FT/4FT deg	M g	CCC	Ind	Ind	28$	Ind	Ind	2
Mechanical Engineering with Spanish	H3R4	3FT/4FT deg	M+P g	BBC-BCC	Ind	Ind	28$	Ind	Ind	
Portuguese (Beginners) and Russian	RRM8	4FT deg	R	BBC						
Portuguese (Beginners) and Spanish	RRM4	4FT deg	Sp	BBC						7
Production and Operations Mgt with Spanish	H7RK	3FT deg	M g	CCC	Ind	Ind	28$	Ind	Ind	2

| | | | 98 expected requirements | | | | | | | 96 entry stats | |

TITLE	CODE	COURSE	SUBJECTS	A/AS	ND/C	RGNVQ	IB	SQA(H)	SQA	RATIO	A/AS
NOTTINGHAM TRENT Univ											
European Business with Spanish	N1R4	4SW deg	Sp g	16	M+D $		24$	Ind	Ind	24	20/23
European Economics with Spanish	L1R4	4FT deg	Sp g	14-16	1M+3D	Ind		Ind	BBCC	Ind	2	10/16
OXFORD BROOKES Univ											
Langs for Bus:Italian-Ab Initio/Spanish-Ab Init	NRCK	4FT deg									
Languages for Business:English/Spanish-Ab Initio	NR14	4FT deg	E	BC-CDD	Ind	M*^	Ind	Ind	Ind		
Languages for Business:French/Spanish-Ab Initio	NR1K	4FT deg	F	BC-CDD	Ind	M*^	Ind	Ind	Ind	8	
Languages for Business:German/Spanish-Ab Initio	NR1L	4FT deg	G	BC-CDD	Ind	M*^	Ind	Ind	Ind	2	
Languages for Business:Italian/Spanish-Ab Initio	NRC4	4FT deg	I	BC-CDD	Ind	M*^	Ind	Ind	Ind	2	
Univ of PLYMOUTH											
Applied Economics with Spanish	L1R4	3FT deg	Sp g	CCD-CDD	MO	M$^	Ind	BCCC	Ind		
Business Economics with Spanish	L1RK	3FT deg	Sp g	CDD-CCD	MO	M$^	Ind	BCCC	Ind		
Chemistry with Spanish	F1R4	3FT deg	C+Sp g	CC	3M	MS^	Ind	CCCC	Ind		
European Economics with Spanish	L1RL	3FT deg	Sp g	CDD-CCD	MO	M$^	Ind	BCCC	Ind		
European Studies with Spanish	T2R4	4FT deg	Sp g	18	Ind	Ind	Ind	Ind	Ind		
Geography with Spanish	F8R4	3FT deg	Gy+Sp g	16-18	X	M$^	Ind	ABBB	Ind		
Geology with Spanish	F6R4	3FT deg	S g	12	4M	MS^	Ind	CCC	Ind		
International Business with Spanish	N1R4	4FT/4SW deg	Sp g	CCD-CCC	MO	M12^	Ind	BBCC	Ind	12	14/22
Law with Spanish	M3R4	3FT deg	Sp g	BCC-BBC	DO	D12^	Ind	BBBB$	Ind		
Mathematics with Spanish	G1R4	3FT deg	M+Sp g	10-15	MO $	M$^	Ind	BBCC	Ind		
Political Economy with Spanish	LR1K	3FT deg	Sp g	CDD-CCD	MO $	M$^	Ind	BCCC	Ind		
Politics with Spanish	M1R4	3FT deg	Sp g	14	Ind	M$^	Ind	BBBC$	Ind		
Psychology with Spanish	C8R4	3FT/4SW deg	Sp g	BBC	MO+3D	M12^	Ind	BBBC$	Ind		
Social Policy with Spanish	L4R4	3FT deg	Sp g	14	Ind	M$^	Ind	BBBC$	Ind		
Sociology with Spanish	L3R4	3FT deg	Sp g	14	Ind	M$^	Ind	BBBC$	Ind		
Statistics (Applied) & Mgt Science with Spanish	G4RK	3FT deg	M/St+Sp g	10-15	MO $	M$^	Ind	BBCC	Ind		
Statistics (Applied) with Spanish	G4R4	3FT deg	M/St+Sp g	10	MO $	M$^	Ind	BBCC	Ind		
Univ of PORTSMOUTH											
German and Spanish	RR24	4FT deg	G	12	5M $	M$6/^	25$	BBCC	Ind	2	
Hispanic and French Studies	RR14	4FT deg	F	12	5M $	M$6/^	25	BBBC	Ind	5	10/18
Latin American Development Studies	R601	4FT deg	*	12	5M	M*6/^	25	BBCC	Ind	4	
Latin American Studies	R600	4FT deg	*	12	5M	M*6/^	25	BBCC	Ind	2	8/18
Russian and Spanish	RR84	4FT deg	*	10-12	5M	M*6/^ go	Dip	BBCC	Ind		
Spanish Studies	R410	4FT deg	*	12	5M	M*6/^ go	25	BBCC	Ind	3	10/14
Spanish and Italian Studies	RR34	4FT deg	Sp	12	5M $	M$6/^	25	BBBC	Ind	4	10/12
Spanish and Latin American Studies	RR46	4FT deg	*	12	5M	M*6/^ go	25	BBCC	Ind	3	6/18
Spanish and Portuguese Studies	RR45	4FT deg	*	12	5M	M*6/^ go	25	BBCC	Ind	2	6/10
QUEEN MARY & WESTFIELD COLL (Univ of London)											
Engineering with Spanish Language	H1R4	3FT deg	M	CCD-BCC	4M $	M$^	24$	BBBCC			
English and Hispanic Studies	RQ4J	4FT deg	E	20		M	30$				
French and Hispanic Studies	RR4C	4FT deg	F	20		M^	30$				
Hispanic Studies (4 Yrs)	R451	4FT deg	L	18		M^	30$				
Hispanic Studies (European Studies)	RT4F	4FT deg	L	18		M^	30$				
Hispanic Studies and Drama	WRK4	4FT deg	L	20		M^	30$				
Hispanic Studies and Economics	LR1K	4FT deg	L g	BCC		M^	30$	BBBBB			
Hispanic Studies and Geography	LR8K	4FT deg	L+Gy	BCC		M^	30$				
Hispanic Studies and Linguistics	RQ4C	4FT deg	L	20		M^	30$				
Hispanic Studies and Mathematics	GR1K	4FT deg	L+M	20		M^	30$				
Hispanic Studies and Politics	MR14	4FT deg		BCC		M^					
Hispanic Studies and Russian (European Studies)	RR8L	4FT deg	L	20		M^	30$				

			98 expected requirements							96 entry stats
course details										
TITLE	CODE	COURSE	SUBJECTS	A/AS	ND/C	AGNVQ	IB	SQA(H)	SQA	RATIO A/AS
Hispanic Studies with Business Studies	R4N1	4FT deg	g	18		M^				
Hispanic Studs, Linguistics and Computer Science	GR5K	4FT deg	L	BBC-BCD	3D $	D^	28$			
QUEEN'S Univ Belfast										
Accounting with Spanish	N4R4	4FT deg	*g	ABB	7D	D*^ go	34$	AAABB	Ind	9
Common and Civil Law with Spanish	M3R4	4FT deg	*g	ABB	7D	D*^ go	34$	AAABB	Ind	5 28/30
Finance with Spanish	N3R4	4SW deg	*g	BBB	1M+6D	D*^ go	32$	AABBB	Ind	
Information Management with Spanish	P2R4	3FT deg	*g	BBC	2M+5D	D*6/^ go	30$	AABB	Ind	3
Management with Spanish	N1R4	3FT deg	*g	BBB	2M+5D	D*^ go	32$	AABBB	Ind	2
Spanish	R400	4FT deg	*g	BCC	3M+4D	D*6/^ go	29$	ABBB	Ind	8 22/24
Spanish/Ancient History (4 years)	VRC4	4FT deg	*g	BCC	3M+4D	D*6/^ go	29$	ABBB	Ind	
Spanish/Byzantine Studies (4 years)	QR84	4FT deg	*g	BCC	3M+4D	D*6/^ go	29$	ABBB	Ind	
Spanish/Celtic (4 years)	QR54	4FT deg	*g	BCC	3M+4D	D*6/^ go	29$	ABBB	Ind	
Spanish/Economic & Social History (4 years)	VR34	4FT deg	*g	BCC	3M+4D	D*6/^ go	29$	ABBB	Ind	
Spanish/English (4 years)	QR34	4FT deg	E g	BCC	X	D*^ go	29$	ABBB	X	6
Spanish/French (4 years)	RR14	4FT deg	E g	BCC	X	D*^ go	29$	ABBB	X	3 18/30
Spanish/German (4 years)	RR24	4FT deg	*g	BCC	3M+4D	D*6/^ go	29$	ABBB	Ind	
Spanish/Greek (4 years)	QR74	4FT deg	*g	BCC	3M+4D	D*6/^ go	29$	ABBB	Ind	
Spanish/Italian (4 years)	RR34	4FT deg	*g	BCC	3M+4D	D*6/^ go	29$	ABBB	Ind	9
Spanish/Latin (4 years)	QR64	4FT deg	*g	BCC	3M+4D	D*6/^ go	29$	ABBB	Ind	
Spanish/Music (4 years)	WR34	4FT deg	*g	BCC	3M+4D	D*6/^ go	29$	ABBB	Ind	
Spanish/Philosophy (4 years)	VR74	4FT deg	*g	BCC	3M+4D	D*6/^ go	29$	ABBB	Ind	
Spanish/Politics (4 years)	MR14	4FT deg	*g	BCC	3M+4D	D*6/^ go	29$	ABBB	Ind	
Spanish/Scholastic Philosophy (4 years)	VRR4	4FT deg	*g	BCC	3M+4D	D*6/^ go	29$	ABBB	Ind	
Spanish/Social Anthropology (4 years)	LR64	4FT deg	*g	BCC	3M+4D	D*6/^ go	29$	ABBB	Ind	6
ROEHAMPTON INST										
Health Studies and Spanish	BR94▼	4FT deg	Sp g	12	2M+2D	P$ go	28	BCC	N$	
Spanish and Applied Consumer Studies	NR94▼	4FT deg	Sp g	12	2M+2D$	P$ go	28	BBC	N$	1
Spanish and Biology	CR14▼	4FT deg	Sp+B	12	2M+2D$	P$ go	28	BBC	N$	
Spanish and Business Computing	GR74▼	3FT deg	Sp g	12	3D	M^ go	26	BCC	N$	
Spanish and Business Studies	NR14▼	4FT deg	Sp g	12	3D	M$ go	28	BBC	N$	3
Spanish and Dance Studies	RW44▼	4FT deg	Sp	CC	2M+2D$	M$^	30	BBC	N$	2
Spanish and Drama & Theatre Studies	RW4L▼	4FT deg	Sp+E/T	16	2M+2D$	M$^	30	BBC	N$	3
Spanish and Education	RX49▼	4FT deg	Sp	12	2M+2D$	P$ go	28	BBC	N$	
Spanish and English Language & Linguistics	QRH4▼	4FT deg	Sp	CC	2M+2D$	M$^	30	BBC	N$	9
Spanish and English Literature	QR34▼	4FT deg	Sp+E	CC	2M+2D$	M^	28	BBC	N$	2
Spanish and Environmental Studies	FR94▼	4FT deg	Sp+B/Gy	12	2M+2D$	P$ go	28	BBC	N$	
Spanish and French	RR14▼	4FT deg	Sp+F	12	2M+2D$	P$ go	28	BBC	N$	5
Spanish and Geography	LR84▼	4FT deg	Sp+Gy	12	2M+2D$	P$ go	28	BBC	N$	
Spanish and History	RV41▼	4FT deg	Sp+H	12	2M+2D$	P^	28	BBC	N$	
Spanish and Human & Social Biology	CRC4▼	4FT deg	Sp+B	12	2M+2D$	P$ go	28	BBC	N$	
Spanish and Music	RW43▼	4FT deg	Sp+Mu	12	2M+2D$	P^	28	BBC	N$	2
Spanish and Natural Resource Studies	DR24▼	4FT deg	Sp g	12	3M	P$ go	24	CCC	N$	
Spanish and Psychology	LR74▼	4FT deg	Sp g	CC	3D	M$ go	30	BBC	N$	
Spanish and Social Policy & Administration	LR44▼	4FT deg	Sp	12	2M+2D$	P$ go	28	BBC	N$	
Spanish and Sociology	LR34▼	4FT deg	Sp g	12	2M+2D$	P$ go	28	BBC	N$	
Sport Studies and Spanish	RB46▼	4FT deg	Sp+S g	12	3D	MS go	30	BBC	N$	
Theology & Religious Studies and Spanish	RV48▼	4FT deg	Sp	12	2M+2D$	P$ go	28	BBC	N$	
Women's Studies and Spanish	RM49▼	4FT deg	Sp	12	2M+2D$	P$ go	28	BBC	N$	

course details   98 expected requirements   96 entry stats

TITLE	CODE	COURSE	SUBJECTS	A/AS	ND/C	AGNVQ	IB	SQA(H)	SQA	RATIO	A/AS
ROYAL HOLLOWAY, *Univ of London*											
Economics with Spanish	L1R4	3FT deg	L	BBC-BBB	Ind		32	Ind			
English Language and Spanish	QR3L	4FT deg	E+Sp	ABC-BBC			Ind	Ind			
English and Spanish	QR34	4FT deg	E+Sp	ABC-BBC			Ind	Ind			
French and Spanish	RR14	4FT deg	F+Sp	ABC-BBC			Ind	Ind			
French with Spanish	R1R4	4FT deg	F	BBC-ABC			28$	Ind		4	22/26
German and Spanish	RR24	4FT deg	G+Sp	BBC-BCC			Ind	Ind			
German with Spanish	R2R4	4FT deg	G	BCC			28$	BBBBC$		5	
History and Spanish	VR14	4FT deg	Sp g	ABC-BBC			Ind	Ind			
History with Spanish	V1R4	3FT deg	L g	BBB-ABC			30	Ind			
Italian and Spanish	RR34	4FT deg	Sp	BBC-BCC			Ind	Ind			
Italian with Spanish	R3R4	4FT deg	L/Ln	BBC			30	BBCCC$			
Management Studies and Spanish	NR14	4FT deg	Sp	BBB-BBC	Ind	D^	Ind	Ind			
Management Studies with Spanish	N1R4	3FT deg	L	BBC-BBB	2M+3D	D^	30	Ind		8	
Mathematics with Spanish	G1R4	3FT deg	M+L	BCC-BBC	Ind	D^	Ind	Ind			
Music with Spanish	W3R4	3FT deg	L+Mu	BCC-BBC			Ind	ABBCC$			
Social Policy with Spanish	L4R4	3FT deg	L	BCC-BBC	Ind	D^	Ind	Ind			
Sociology with Spanish	L3R4	3FT deg	L	BCC-BBC	Ind	D^	Ind	Ind			
Univ of SALFORD											
French/Hispanic Studies (4 Yrs)	RRC4	4SW deg	L g	BCC	X	X	Ind	Ind	X	16	
French/Spanish (4 Yrs)	RR14	4SW deg	L g	BCC	X	X	Ind	Ind	X	4	12/26
German/Hispanic Studies (4 Yrs)	RRF4	4SW deg	L g	BCC	X	X	Ind	Ind	X		
German/Spanish (4 Yrs)	RR24	4SW deg	L g	BCC	X	X	Ind	Ind	X	8	
Italian/Hispanic Studies (4 Yrs)	RRH4	4SW deg	L g	BCC	X	X	Ind	Ind	X		
Italian/Spanish (4 Yrs)	RR34	4SW deg	L g	BCC	X	X	Ind	Ind	X	3	18/24
Spanish/Arabic (4 Yrs)	RT46	4SW deg	L g	BCC	X	X	Ind	Ind	X		
Univ of SHEFFIELD											
Computer Science and Spanish	GR54	4FT deg	M+L g	BBC	4M+2D$	D^	30$	ABBB$	Ind		
English and Hispanic Studies	QR34	4FT deg	El+Sp g	BBB	X	X	32$	AABB$	Ind	19	
French and Hispanic Studies	RR14	4FT deg	F+L g	BBC	X	X	30$	ABBB$	Ind	16	22/30
German and Hispanic Studies	RR24	4FT deg	G+Sp g	BBC	X	X	30$	ABBB$	Ind	34	
Hispanic Studies	R400	4FT deg	Sp g	BBC-BCC	X	X	30$	ABBB$	Ind	7	20/30
Hispanic Studies and Business Studies	RN41	4FT deg	Sp g	BBC	X	D^	30$	ABBB$	Ind	13	22/26
Hispanic Studies and Economics	RL41	4FT deg	Sp g	BBC	X	D^	30$	ABBB$	Ind		
Hispanic Studies and Politics	RM41	4FT deg	Sp g	BBC	X	X	30$	ABBB$	Ind	6	
History and Hispanic Studies	RV41	4FT deg	Sp+H g	BBB	X	X	32$	AABB$	Ind	7	
Law with Spanish	MR34	4FT deg	Sp g	ABB	X	D^	33$	AAAB$	Ind	11	26/28
Linguistics and Hispanic Studies	QR14	4FT deg	Ee+L	BBC	X	X	30$	ABBB$	Ind		
Music and Hispanic Studies	RW43	4FT deg	Mu+Sp g	BBC	X	X	30$	ABBB$	Ind		
Philosophy and Hispanic Studies	RV47	4FT deg	L g	BBB	X	X	32$	AABB$	Ind		
Russian and Hispanic Studies	RR48	4FT deg	L g	BBC	X	X	30$	ABBB$	Ind		
SHEFFIELD HALLAM Univ											
International Business with Language (Spanish)	N1R4	4SW deg	g	16	M+D	M gi	Ind	Ind	Ind		
Univ of SOUTHAMPTON											
Accounting and Spanish	NR44	4FT deg	Sp g	22	Ind	D$^ go	30$	ABBBB$	Ind		
Archaeology and Iberian Studies	VR64	4FT deg	Sp/Pt	BCD-CCC	Ind	Ind	26	Ind	Ind	5	
English and Spanish	QR34	4FT deg	E+Sp	BBC	X	Ind	Ind	Ind	X	37	
French and Portuguese	RR15	4FT deg	F+Cl/L	BBC	1M+4D	Ind	30$	Ind	Ind		
French and Spanish	RR14	4FT deg	F+Sp	BBC	1M+4D	Ind	30$	Ind	Ind	8	15/26
French and Spanish (Linguistics & Language Stds)	RRC4	4FT deg	F+Sp	BBC							

course details			98 expected requirements							96 entry stats	
TITLE	CODE	COURSE	SUBJECTS	A/AS	ND/C	AGNVQ	IB	SQA(H)	SQA	RATIO	A/AS
French and Spanish (Literary Studies)	RRCK	4FT deg	F+Sp	BBC							
French and Spanish(Social and Political Studies)	RRCL	4FT deg	F+Sp	BBC							
German and Spanish	RR24	4FT deg	G+Sp	BBC	1M+4D	Ind	30$	Ind	Ind	6	
German and Spanish (Linguistics & Language Stds)	RRF4	4FT deg	G+Sp	BBC							
German and Spanish (Literary Studies)	RRFK	4FT deg	G+Sp	BBC							
German and Spanish(Social and Political Studies)	RRFL	4FT deg	G+Sp	BBC							
Iberian and Latin American Studies	RR46	4FT deg	Sp	BBC	2M+4D	Ind	30$	Ind	Ind	4	16/20
Management Sciences and Spanish	NRC4	4FT deg	Sp g	22	Ind	D$^ go	30$	ABBBB$	Ind	11	
Mathematics and Spanish (4 Yrs)	GR14	4FT deg	M+Sp	BBC	Ind	Ind	30	ABBBB	Ind	8	
Pol & Spanish(or Portuguese)& Latin American St	RM4C	4FT deg	Sp/Pt g	BBC	1M+4D	Ind	30$	Ind	Ind	3	16/24
Spanish (Linguistics and Language Studies)	R401	4FT deg	Sp	BBC							
Spanish (Social and Political Studies)	R410	4FT deg	Sp	BBC							
Spanish (beginners) and Latin American Studies	RRK6	4FT deg	* g	BBC	1M+4D	Ind	30	Ind	Ind	7	
Spanish (including Portuguese or Catalan)	R400	4FT deg	Sp	BBC	1M+4D	Ind	30$	Ind	Ind	3	14/26
Spanish and Film	RW45	4FT deg	Sp	BBC							
Spanish and History	RV41	4FT deg	Sp+H	BBC	Ind		Ind	Ind			
Spanish and Portuguese	RR45	4FT deg	Sp+L	BBC	1M+4D	Ind	30$	Ind	Ind	5	14/20

SOUTH BANK Univ

Spanish - ab initio and Accounting	NR44	3FT deg	Ec/Ac g	12-16	4M+2D	M go	Ind	Ind	Ind		
Spanish - ab initio and Business Information Tec	GR74	3FT deg	M g	12-16	4M+2D	M go	Ind	Ind	Ind		
Spanish - ab initio and Computing	GR54	3FT deg	M g	12-16	4M+2D	M go	Ind	Ind	Ind		
Spanish - ab initio and Economics	LR14	3FT deg	Ec/Bu g	12-16	4M+2D	M go	Ind	Ind	Ind		
Spanish - ab initio and English Studies	QR34	3FT deg	E g	14-18	X	M^ go	Ind	Ind	Ind		
Spanish - ab initio and French	RR14	3FT deg	F g	12-16	4M+2D	M go	Ind	Ind	Ind		
Spanish - ab initio and German	RR2L	3FT deg	G g	14-18	2M+4D	M go	Ind	Ind	Ind		
Spanish - ab initio and Health Studies	LR44	3FT deg	S g	12-16	4M+2D	M go	Ind	Ind	Ind		
Spanish - ab initio and History	RV41	3FT deg	H g	12-16	4M+2D	M^ go	Ind	Ind	Ind		
Spanish - ab initio and Housing	RK4K	3FT deg	* g	14-18	2M+4D	M go	Ind	Ind	Ind		
Spanish - ab initio and Human Resource Mgt	NR6K	3FT deg	* g	14-18	2M+4D	M go	Ind	Ind	Ind		
Spanish - ab initio and Law	MR34	3FT deg	* g	14-18	2M+4D	D go	Ind	Ind	Ind		
Spanish - ab initio and Management	NR14	3FT deg	* g	12-16	4M+2D	M go	Ind	Ind	Ind		
Spanish - ab initio and Media Studies	PR44	3FT deg	E g	14-18	2M+4D	D go	Ind	Ind	Ind		
Spanish - ab initio and Product Design	HR74	3FT deg	Ad g	12-16	4M+2D	M go	Ind	Ind	Ind		
Spanish - ab initio and Psychology	CR84	3FT deg	S g	14-18	2M+4D	M go	Ind	Ind	Ind		
Spanish - ab initio and Social Policy	LR4K	3FT deg	* g	12-16	4M+2D	M go	Ind	Ind	Ind		
Spanish - ab initio and Sociology	LR34	3FT deg	* g	12-16	4M+2D	M go	Ind	Ind	Ind		
Spanish and Accounting	NR4K	3FT deg	Sp+Ac/Ec g	14-18	2M+4D	M go	Ind	Ind	Ind		
Spanish and Business Information Technology	GR7K	3FT deg	Sp+M g	14-18	2M+4D	M go	Ind	Ind	Ind		
Spanish and Computing	GR5K	3FT deg	Sp+M g	14-18	2M+4D	M go	Ind	Ind	Ind		
Spanish and Economics	LR1K	3FT deg	Sp+Ec/Bu g	14-18	2M+4D	M go	Ind	Ind	Ind		
Spanish and English Studies	QR3K	3FT deg	Sp+E g	14-18	X	M^ go	Ind	Ind	Ind		
Spanish and French	RR1K	3FT deg	Sp+F g	14-18	2M+4D	M^ go	Ind	Ind	Ind		
Spanish and German - ab initio	RR2K	3FT deg	Sp g	14-18	2M+4D	M^ go	Ind	Ind	Ind		
Spanish and Health Studies	RL44	3FT deg	Sp+S g	14-18	2M+4D	M^ go	Ind	Ind	Ind		
Spanish and History	RV4C	3FT deg	Sp+H g	14-18	2M+4D	M^ go	Ind	Ind	Ind		
Spanish and Housing	KR4L	3FT deg	Sp g	14-18	2M+4D	M^ go	Ind	Ind	Ind		
Spanish and Human Resource Management	NR64	3FT deg	Sp g	14-18	2M+4D	M^ go	Ind	Ind	Ind		
Spanish and Law	MR3K	3FT deg	Sp g	14-18	2M+4D	M^ go	Ind	Ind	Ind		
Spanish and Management	NR1K	3FT deg	Sp g	14-18	2M+4D	M^ go	Ind	Ind	Ind		
Spanish and Marketing	NR54	3FT deg	Sp g	14-18	2M+4D	M^ go	Ind	Ind	Ind		
Spanish and Media Studies	PR4K	3FT deg	Sp+E	14-18	2M+4D	D go	Ind	Ind	Ind		
Spanish and Product Design	HR7K	3FT deg	Sp+Ad/A g	14-18	2M+4D	M^ go	Ind	Ind	Ind		

course details   98 expected requirements   96 entry stats

TITLE	CODE	COURSE	SUBJECTS	A/AS	NO/C	AGNVQ	IB	SQA(H)	SQA	RATIO A/AS
Spanish and Psychology	LR8L	3FT deg	Sp+S g	14-18	2M+4D	D go	Ind	Ind	Ind	
Spanish and Social Policy	LR4L	3FT deg	Sp g	14-18	2M+4D	M^ go	Ind	Ind	Ind	
Spanish and Sociology	LR3K	3FT deg	Sp g	14-18	2M+4D	M^ go	Ind	Ind	Ind	
Technology and Spanish	JR9K	3FT deg	Sp g	14-18	2M+4D	M^ go	Ind	Ind	Ind	
Technology and Spanish - ab initio	JR94	3FT deg	Sp g	12-16	4M+2D	M go	Ind	Ind	Ind	
Tourism and Spanish	PR7K	3FT deg	Sp g	14-18	2M+4D	M^ go	Ind	Ind	Ind	
Tourism and Spanish - ab initio	PR74	3FT deg	g	12-16	4M+2D	M go	Ind	Ind	Ind	
Urban Studies and Spanish	RK44	3FT deg	S g	14-18	2M+4D	M go	Ind	Ind	Ind	
Urban Studies and Spanish - ab initio	RK4L	3FT deg	* g	14-18	2M+4D	M go	Ind	Ind	Ind	
World Theatre and Spanish	RW44	3FT deg	S g	14-18	2M+4D	M^ go	Ind	Ind	Ind	
World Theatre and Spanish - ab initio	RW4K	3FT deg	* g	14-18	2M+4D	M go	Ind	Ind	Ind	

Univ of ST ANDREWS

TITLE	CODE	COURSE	SUBJECTS	A/AS	NO/C	AGNVQ	IB	SQA(H)	SQA	RATIO A/AS
Geography with Spanish	L8R4	4FT deg	* g	ABB	X	Ind	32$	BBBB	Ind	
Modern Languages (Spanish with Integ Yr Abroad)	R411	4FT/5FT deg	* g	BBB	X	Ind	30$	BBBB	Ind	
Modern Languages (Spanish)	R400	4FT deg	* g	BBB	X	Ind	30$	BBBB	Ind	
Spanish with Year Abroad-Ancient History	RV4D	4FT/5FT deg	* g	BBB	X	Ind	30$	BBBB	Ind	
Spanish with Year Abroad-Arabic	RT4P	4FT/5FT deg	* g	BBB	X	Ind	30$	BBBB	Ind	
Spanish with Year Abroad-Art History	RV4K	4FT/5FT deg	* g	BBB	X	Ind	30$	BBBB	Ind	
Spanish with Year Abroad-Economics	LRC4	4FT/5FT deg	* g	BBB	X	Ind	30$	BBBB	Ind	
Spanish with Year Abroad-English	QRH4	4FT/5FT deg	* g	BBB	X	Ind	32$	BBBB	Ind	
Spanish with Year Abroad-French	RRC4	4FT/5FT deg	F g	BBB	X	Ind	30$	BBBB$	Ind	7 22/30
Spanish with Year Abroad-Geography	LR8K	4FT/5FT deg	* g	BBB	X	Ind	30$	BBBB	Ind	
Spanish with Year Abroad-German	RRF4	4FT/5FT deg	* g	BBB	X	Ind	30$	BBBB	Ind	7
Spanish with Year Abroad-International Relations	MRC4	4FT/5FT deg	* g	AAB	X	Ind	36$	AAAB	Ind	6
Spanish with Year Abroad-Italian	RR34	4FT/5FT deg	* g	BBB	X	Ind	30$	BBBB	Ind	
Spanish with Year Abroad-Latin	QRP4	4FT/5FT deg	* g	BBB	X	Ind	32$	BBBB	Ind	
Spanish with Year Abroad-Management	NRC4	4FT/5FT deg	* g	BBB	X	Ind	30	BBBB	Ind	11
Spanish with Year Abroad-Mediaeval History	RVLC	4FT/5FT deg	* g	BBB	X	Ind	30$	BBBB	Ind	
Spanish with Year Abroad-Modern History	RVK1	4FT/5FT deg	* g	BBB	X	Ind	30$	BBBB	Ind	
Spanish with Year Abroad-Philosophy	RVL7	4FT/5FT deg	* g	BBB	X	Ind	30$	BBBB	Ind	
Spanish with Year Abroad-Russian	RR4V	4FT/5FT deg	* g	BBB	X	Ind	30$	BBBB	Ind	
Spanish with Year Abroad-Social Anthropology	LR6K	4FT/5FT deg	* g	BBB	X	Ind	30$	BBBB	Ind	
Spanish-Ancient History	VR14	4FT deg	* g	BBB	X	Ind	30$	BBBB	Ind	
Spanish-Arabic	RT46	4FT deg	* g	BBB	X	Ind	30$	BBBB	Ind	
Spanish-Art History	RV44	4FT deg	* g	BBB	X	Ind	30$	BBBB	Ind	
Spanish-Economics	LR14	4FT deg	* g	BBB	X	Ind	32$	BBBB	Ind	
Spanish-English	QR34	4FT deg	* g	BBB	X	Ind	32$	BBBB	Ind	6
Spanish-French	RR14	4FT deg	F g	BBB	X	Ind	30$	BBBB$	Ind	13
Spanish-Geography	LR84	4FT deg	* g	BBB	X	Ind	30$	BBBB	Ind	
Spanish-German	RR24	4FT deg	* g	BBB	X	Ind	30$	BBBB	Ind	
Spanish-International Relations	MR14	4FT deg	* g	AAB	X	Ind	36$	AAAB	Ind	4
Spanish-Italian	RR43	4FT/5FT deg	* g	BBB	X	Ind	30$	BBBB	Ind	
Spanish-Latin	QR64	4FT deg	* g	BBB	X	Ind	32$	BBBB	Ind	
Spanish-Management	NR14	4FT deg	* g	BBB	X	Ind	32$	BBBB	Ind	
Spanish-Mediaeval History	RV4C	4FT deg	* g	BBB	X	Ind	30$	BBBB	Ind	
Spanish-Modern History	RV41	4FT deg	* g	BBB	X	Ind	30$	BBBB	Ind	
Spanish-Philosophy	RV47	4FT deg	* g	BBB	X	Ind	30$	BBBB	Ind	
Spanish-Russian	RR48	4FT deg	* g	BBB	X	Ind	30$	BBBB	Ind	
Spanish-Social Anthropology	LR64	4FT deg	* g	BBB	X	Ind	32$	BBBB	Ind	
European Integration Studies Spanish	Y602	4FT deg	* g	BBB	X	Ind	30$	BBBB	Ind	
General Degree of MA Modern Languages (Spanish)	Y450	3FT deg	* g	BBB	X	Ind	30$	BBBB	Ind	

Languages – Spanish/Latin American 46

TITLE	CODE	COURSE	SUBJECTS	A/AS	NO/C	AGNVQ	IB	SQA(H)	SQA	RATIO A/AS
STAFFORDSHIRE Univ										
European Culture/Spanish	LRP4	3FT deg	g	CD	MO+2D	M	27	BBC	Ind	1
Property with Spanish	K2R4	3FT deg	g	12	4M	M$	24	BBC	Ind	
Spanish/American Studies	RQ44	3FT/4SW deg	g	CD	MO+2D	M^	27	BBC	Ind	2
Spanish/Business Studies	RN41	3FT/4SW deg	g	CCD	MO+2D	M$^	26	BBB	Ind	
Spanish/Cultural Studies	RL46	3FT/4SW deg	g	CD	MO+2D	M^	27	BBC	Ind	7
Spanish/Development Studies	RM4Y	3FT/4SW deg	g	12	3M	M^	26	BCC	Ind	
Spanish/Environmental Studies	RF49	3FT/4SW deg	g	14	4M+2D	M^	26	ABB	Ind	
Spanish/Film Studies	RW45	3FT/4SW deg	g	CD	MO+2D	M^	27	BBC	Ind	
Spanish/French	RR41	4SW deg	F g	DD	4M+2D	M^	26	BCC	Ind	8
Spanish/Geography	RL48	3FT/4SW deg	g	16	4M+2D	M^	28	AAB	Ind	
Spanish/German	RR42	4SW deg	G g	DD	4M+2D	M^	26	BCC	Ind	5
Spanish/History of Art and Design	RV44	3FT/4SW deg	g	CD	MO+2D	M^	27	BBC	Ind	2
Spanish/Information Systems	RG45	3FT/4SW deg		12	Ind	M^	27	BCC	Ind	
Spanish/International Relations	RM4C	3FT/4SW deg	g	12	3M	M^	26	BCC	Ind	7
Spanish/Law	RM43	3FT/4SW deg	g	18	HN	M^	26	BBBB	Ind	5
Spanish/Legal Studies	RM4H	3FT/4SW deg	g	18	HN	M^	26	BCC	Ind	
Spanish/Literature	RQ43	3FT/4SW deg	El g	CD	MO+2D	M^	27	BBC	Ind	7
Spanish/Philosophy	RV47	3FT/4SW deg	g	CD	MO+2D	M^	27	BBC	Ind	
Spanish/Politics	RMK1	3FT/4SW deg	g	12	3M	M^	26	BCC	Ind	
Spanish/Psychology	RL47	3FT/4SW deg	g	18	3M+3D	Ind	27	BBB	Ind	
Spanish/Sociology	RL43	3FT/4SW deg	g	12	3M	M^	26	BCC	Ind	
Univ of STIRLING										
Accountancy/Spanish Language	NR4K	4FT deg	g	BCC	HN	Ind	33	BBBB	HN	
Business Studies/Spanish Language	NRCK	4FT deg	g	CCC	Ind	Ind	31	BBBC	HN	
Computing Science/Spanish Language	GR54	4FT deg	g	CCC	Ind	Ind	28	BBCC	HN	
Economics/Spanish Language	LR1K	4FT deg	g	CCC	Ind	Ind	31	BBBC	HN	
English Studies/Spanish	QR34	4FT deg	g	CCC	Ind	Ind	31	BBBC	HN	
Film & Media Studies/Spanish	RP44	4FT deg	g	BBC	Ind	Ind	35	ABBB	HN	
Financial Studies/Spanish Language	N3R4	4FT deg	g	BCC	Ind	Ind	31	BBBC	HN	
French/Spanish	RR14	4FT deg	g	CCC	Ind	Ind	31	BBBC	HN	
German/Spanish	RR24	4FT deg	g	CCC	Ind	Ind	31	BBBC	HN	
Hispanic Studies	RR46	4FT deg	g	CCC	Ind	Ind	31	BBBC	HN	
History/Spanish	RV41	4FT deg	g	CCC	Ind	Ind	31	BBBC	HN	
Management Science/Spanish Language	NR1K	4FT deg	g	CCC	Ind	Ind	31	BBBC	HN	
Marketing/Spanish Language	N5R4	4FT deg	g	CCC	Ind	Ind	31	BBBC	HN	
Mathematics and its Applications with Span Lang	G1R4	4FT deg	M g	CCC	Ind	Ind	28	BBCC	HN	
Religious Studies/Spanish	RV48	4FT deg	g	CCC	Ind	Ind	31	BBBC	HN	
Scottish Literature/Spanish	RQ42	4FT deg	g	CCC	HN	Ind	31	BBBC	HN	
Spanish	R400	4FT deg	g	CCC	Ind	Ind	31	BBBC	HN	
Spanish Language/Human Resources Management	NR14	4FT deg	g	CCC	Ind	Ind	31	BBBC	HN	
Spanish/Business Law	MR34	4FT deg	g	BCC	HN	Ind	33	BBBB	HN	
Spanish/Japanese	RT44	4FT deg	g	CCC	Ind	Ind	31	BBBC	HN	
Spanish/Philosophy	RV47	4FT deg	g	CCC	Ind	Ind	31	BBBC	HN	
Spanish/Politics	MR14	4FT deg	g	CCC	Ind	Ind	31	BBBC	HN	
Spanish/Sociology	LR34	4FT deg	g	CCC	Ind	Ind	31	BBBC	HN	
Univ of STRATHCLYDE										
Arts and Social Sciences *Spanish*	Y440	3FT/4FT deg	g	CCC	Ind		28	BBBBB$	Ind	

course details — 98 expected requirements — 96 entry stats

TITLE	CODE	COURSE	SUBJECTS	A/AS	ND/C	AGNVQ	IB	SQA(H)	SQA	RATIO A/AS
Univ of SUNDERLAND										
Business Computing with Spanish	G5R4	4SW deg	* g	4-8	4M	M*	24	CCCC	N	2
Chemistry and Spanish	FR14	4FT deg	C	8	3M	M	Ind	Ind	Ind	
Chemistry with Spanish	F1R4	3FT deg	C	8	3M	M	Ind	Ind	Ind	
Computer Studies and Spanish	GR54	3FT/4SW deg	*	8	3M	M	Ind	Ind	Ind	
Economics and Spanish	LR14	4FT deg	*	8	3M	M	Ind	Ind	Ind	
Economics with Spanish	L1R4	3FT deg	*	8	3M	M	Ind	Ind	Ind	
English with Spanish	Q3R4▼	3FT deg	El+Sp g	10	Ind	M	24$	CCCC$	Ind	10
French with Spanish	R1R4▼	4FT deg	F+Sp g	8	N $	M	24$	CCCC$	N$	9
Geography with Spanish	L8R4▼	3FT deg	*	8	3M	M	Ind	Ind		2
Geology and Spanish	FR64	4SW deg	*	8	3M	M	Ind	Ind		
Geology with Spanish	F6R4	3FT deg	*	8	3M	M	Ind	Ind	Ind	
German with Spanish	R2R4▼	4SW deg	G	10	4M	M	Ind	Ind	Ind	
History of Art and Design and Spanish	VR44	4SW deg	*	8	3M	M	Ind	Ind		
History with Spanish	V1R4▼	3FT deg	*	10	4M	M	Ind	Ind	Ind	
International Business with Spanish	N1RK	3FT deg	* g	18	1M+4D$	D	26	BBBCC	N$	
Mathematics and Spanish	GR14	4SW deg	M	8	3M	M	Ind	Ind		
Mathematics with Spanish	G1R4	3FT deg	M	8	3M	M	Ind	Ind	Ind	
Media Studies with Spanish	P4R4	3FT deg	*	24	Ind	Ind	Ind	Ind	Ind	
Physiology and Spanish	BR14	4SW deg	*	8	3M	M	Ind	Ind		
Physiology with Spanish	B1R4	3FT deg	*	8	3M	M	Ind	Ind	Ind	
Psychology with Spanish	C8R4	3FT deg	*	10	4M	M^	Ind	Ind	Ind	
Religious Studies and Spanish	VR84	4SW deg	*	8	3M	M	Ind	Ind		
Religious Studies with Spanish	V8R4	3FT deg	*	8	3M	M	Ind	Ind	Ind	
Sociology with Spanish	L3R4▼	3FT deg	*	10	4M	M	Ind	Ind	Ind	2
Univ of SUSSEX										
Biochemistry with European Studies (Spanish)	C7R4	4FT deg	C+S g	BCC	MO $	MS6 go	$	Ind	Ind	
Biology with European Studies (Spanish)	C1R4	4FT deg	2S g	BCC	MO $	MS6 go	$	Ind	Ind	
Chemical Physics with Eur St (Spanish) (MChem)	F3RL	4FT deg	C/P/Ph+M g	CCC	MO $	MS^ go	$	Ind	Ind	
Chemistry with European Studies (Spanish)	F1R4	4FT deg	C+S g	CCC	MO $	MS go	$	Ind	Ind	
Chemistry with European Studs (Spanish) (MChem)	F1RL	4FT deg	C+S g	CCC	MO $	MS go	$	Ind	Ind	
Computer Science with European Studies (Spanish)	G5R4	4FT deg	M g	BBC	MO $	M*^ go	$	Ind	Ind	
Environmental Science with Euro Studs (Spanish)	F9R4	4FT deg	2(C/P/M) g	CCC	MO $	MS go	$	Ind	Ind	
Mathematics & Stats with Eur St(Spanish) (MMath)	G4RK	4FT deg	M g	BCC	MO $	MS^ go	$	Ind	Ind	
Mathematics and Stats with Eur Studies (Span)	G4R4	4FT deg	M g	BCC	MO $	MS^ go	$	Ind	Ind	
Mathematics with European St (Spanish) (MMath)	G1RK	4FT deg	M g	BCC	MO $	MS^ go	$	Ind	Ind	
Mathematics with European Studies (Spanish)	G1R4	4FT deg	M g	BCC	MO $	MS^ go	$	Ind	Ind	
Molecular Genetics in Biotechnology with Spanish	C4R4	4FT deg	2S g	BCD	MO $	MS6 go	$	Ind	Ind	
Physics with European Studies (Spanish)	F3R4	4FT deg	M+P g	CCC	MO $	MS^ go	$	Ind	Ind	
Physics with European Studies (Spanish) (MPhys)	F3RK	4FT deg	M+P g	CCC	MO $	MS^ go	$	Ind	Ind	
Univ of Wales SWANSEA										
Biological Sciences (with Spanish)	C1R4	4FT deg	B+Sp	BCC	X	X	28$	ABBCC$	Ind	3
Catalan/Spanish (with Business Studies)	R4NC	4FT deg	Sp g	BBC	1M+5D$	Ind	30$	ABBBB$	Ind	
Civil Engineering (with Spanish)	H2R4	4FT deg	M g	BCD-CCC	4M+1D$	MC^ go	28$	BBBCC$	Ind	
Computer Science (with Spanish)	G5R4	4FT deg	L	BBC	4D	Ind	28	BBBBB	Ind	
Development Studies and Spanish	MR94	4FT deg	L/*	BBC	1M+5D$	Ind	30$	ABBBB$	Ind	1
English Language/Spanish (with Business Studies)	QRH4	4FT deg	L	X	X	X	28	X	X	1
European Business Studies (Spain)	N1R4	4FT deg	Sp g	ABC-BBB	Ind	D$^ go	32$	AABBB$	Ind	2
European History (with Spanish)	V1R4	4FT deg	H+L	BBB-BBC	Ind	Ind	30$	ABBBB$	Ind	
European Management Science (Spain)	N1RK	4FT deg	Sp+M	ABC-BBB	X	D$^ go	32$	AABBB$	Ind	1 14/18
French/Spanish (with Business Studies)	RR1K	4FT deg	F g	BBB-BBC	1M+5D$	Ind	30$	ABBBB$	Ind	5 14/24

course details

98 expected requirements

96 entry stats

TITLE	CODE	COURSE	SUBJECTS	A/AS	NO/C	AGNVQ	IB	SQA(H)	SQA	RATIO A/AS	
French/Spanish (with Computer Studies)	RR1L	4FT deg	F	BBC	1M+5D$	Ind	30$	ABBBB$	Ind	4	
French/Spanish (with Legal Studies)	RR41	4FT deg	F	BBB-BBC	1M+5D$	Ind	30$	ABBBB$	Ind	2	
German/Spanish (with Business Studies)	RR2K	4FT deg	G g	BBB-BBC	1M+5D$	Ind	30$	ABBBB$	Ind	2	
German/Spanish (with Computer Studies)	RR2L	4FT deg	G	BBC	1M+5D$	Ind	30$	ABBBB$	Ind	2	
German/Spanish (with Legal Studies)	RR42	4FT deg	G	BBB-BBC	1M+5D$	Ind	30$	ABBBB$	Ind		
Italian/Spanish (with Business Studies)	RR3K	4FT deg	I/Sp g	BBB-BBC	1M+5D$	Ind	30$	ABBBB$	Ind		
Italian/Spanish (with Computer Studies)	RR3L	4FT deg	I/Sp	BBC	1M+5D$	Ind	30$	ABBBB$	Ind		
Italian/Spanish (with Legal Studies)	RR43	4FT deg	I/Sp	BBB-BBC	1M+5D$	Ind	30$	ABBBB$	Ind		
Law and Spanish	MR34	4FT deg	L/*	BBB	6D	Ind	32$	AABBB$	Ind	4	
Mathematics (with Spanish)	G1R4	4FT deg	M+L	BBC-BCC	X	Ind	28$	BBBBC$	Ind		
Russian/Spanish (with Business Studies)	RRQK	4FT deg	R/Sp g	BCC	1M+5D$	Ind	28$	BBBBC$	Ind		
Russian/Spanish (with Computer Studies)	RRWK	4FT deg	R/Sp	BCC	1M+5D$	Ind	28$	BBBBC$	Ind		
Russian/Spanish (with Legal Studies)	RR84	4FT deg	R/Sp	BCC	1M+5D$	Ind	28$	BBBBC$	Ind		
Spanish	R400	4FT deg	Sp/L	BBC	1M+5D$	Ind	30$	ABBBB$	Ind	8	
Spanish (with Business Studies)	R4N1	4FT deg	L/* g	BBC	1M+5D$	Ind	30$	ABBBB$	Ind	4	12/22
Spanish (with Catalan)	R420	4FT deg	Sp	BBC	1M+5D$	Ind	30$	ABBBB$	Ind	5	
Spanish (with Computer Studies)	R4G5	4FT deg	L/*	BBC	1M+5D$	Ind	30$	ABBBB$	Ind		
Spanish (with Legal Studies)	R4M3	4FT deg	L/*	BBB-BBC	1M+5D$	Ind	30$	ABBBB$	Ind	1	
Spanish and Psychology	LR74	4FT deg	L/* g	BBC	1M+5D$	Ind	30$	ABBBB$	Ind		
Spanish/American Studies	QR44	4FT deg									
Spanish/Ancient History and Civilisation	VRC4	4FT deg	L/*	BBC	1M+5D$	X	30$	ABBBB$	X	2	
Spanish/Anthropology	RL46	4FT deg	L/*	BBC	1M+5D$	Ind	30$	ABBBB$	Ind	3	
Spanish/Economic History	RV43	4FT deg	L/*	BBC	1M+5D$	Ind	30$	ABBBB$	Ind		
Spanish/Economics	LR14	4FT deg	L/* g	BBC	1M+5D$	Ind	30$	ABBBB$	Ind	4	
Spanish/English	QR34	4FT deg	E+L	BBC	X	X	30$	ABBBB$	X	4	
Spanish/English Language	QR3K	3FT deg	E g	BBC	X	X	30$	ABBBB$	Ind		
Spanish/European Politics	MR1K	4FT deg	L/*	BBC	1M+5D$	Ind	30$	ABBBB$	Ind		
Spanish/French	RR14	4FT deg	F	BBC	1M+5D$	Ind	30$	ABBBB$	Ind	4	14/28
Spanish/German	RR24	4FT deg	G/Sp g	BBC	1M+5D$	Ind	30$	ABBBB$	Ind		
Spanish/Greek and Roman Studies	QR84	4FT deg	L/*	BBC-BCC	1M+5D$	X	28$	BBBBB$	X		
Spanish/History	RV41	4FT deg	L/*	BBC	1M+5D$	Ind	30$	ABBBB$	Ind	3	
Spanish/Italian	RR34	4FT deg	I/Sp	BBC	1M+5D$	Ind	30$	ABBBB$	Ind	2	
Spanish/Latin	QR64	4FT deg	Ln	BBC-BCC	Ind	X	28$	BBBBB$	X		
Spanish/Medieval Studies	RVK1	4FT deg	H+L	BCC	1M+5D$	Ind	28$	BBBBB$	X	1	
Spanish/Philosophy	RV47	4FT deg	L/*	BBC-BCC	1M+5D$	Ind	28	BBBBB	Ind		
Spanish/Politics	MR14	4FT deg	L/*	BBC-BCC	1M+5D	Ind	28	BBBBB	Ind	5	
Spanish/Russian	RR48	4FT deg	R/Sp	BCC	1M+5D$	Ind	28$	BBBBC$	Ind		
Spanish/Sociology	LR34	4FT deg	L/*	BBC	1M+5D$	Ind	30$	ABBBB$	Ind		
Spanish/Welsh (with Business Studies)	RQ45	4FT deg	Sp/W g	BCC	1M+5D$	X	28$	BBBBB$	X		
Spanish/Welsh (with Computer Studies)	RQ4N	4FT deg	Sp/W	BCC	1M+5D$	X	28$	BBBBB$	X		
Spanish/Welsh (with Legal Studies)	RQK5	4FT deg	Sp/W	BCC	1M+5D$	X	28$	BBBBB$	X		
Welsh/Spanish	QR54	4FT deg	Sp/W	BCC	1M+5D$	X	28$	BBBBB$	X		

THAMES VALLEY Univ

TITLE	CODE	COURSE	SUBJECTS	A/AS	NO/C	AGNVQ	IB	SQA(H)	SQA	RATIO A/AS
Accounting with Spanish	N4R4	3FT deg		8-12	MO	M	26	CCC		
American Studies with Spanish	Q4R4	3FT deg		8-12	MO	M	26	CCC		
Business Administration with Spanish	N1RK	3FT deg		8-12	MO	M	26	CCC		
Business Economics with Spanish	L1RK	3FT deg		8-12	MO	M	26			
Business Studies with Spanish	N1R4▼	3FT/4SW deg	* g	10-12	MO+2D	M	26	CCC		
Economics with Spanish	L1R4▼	3FT deg	* g	8-12	MO	M	24	CCC		
English Language and Communications with Spanish	Q1R4	3FT deg		8-12	MO	M	26	CCC		
English with Spanish	Q3R4	3FT deg		8-12	MO	M	26	CCC		
Environmental Policy and Management with Spanish	F9R4	3FT deg		8-12	MO	M	26	CCC		

course details
98 expected requirements
96 entry stats

TITLE	CODE	COURSE	SUBJECTS	A/AS	ND/C	AGNVQ	IB	SQA(H)	SQA	RATIO A/AS
European Law with Spanish	M3RK	3FT deg		8-12	MO	M	26	CCC		
European Studies with Spanish	T2R4	3FT deg		8-12	MO	M	26	CCC		
Finance with Spanish	N3R4	3FT deg		8-12	MO	M	26	CCC		
Food and Drink Consumer Studies with Spanish	D4R4	3FT deg		8-12	MO	M	26	CCC		
French with Spanish	R1R4	3FT deg		8-12	MO	M	26	CCC		
German with Spanish	R2R4	3FT deg		8-12	MO	M	26	CCC		
History with Spanish	V1R4	3FT deg		8-12	MO	M	26	CCC		
Hospitality Management with Spanish	N7R4	3FT deg		8-12	MO	M	26	CCC		
Human Resource Management with Spanish	N6R4	3FT deg		8-12	MO	M	26	CCC		
Information Management with Spanish	P2R4	3FT deg		8-12	MO	M	26	CCC		
International Studies with Spanish	M9R4	3FT deg		8-12	MO	M	26	CCC		
Law with Spanish	M3R4	3FT deg		8-12	MO	M	26	CCC		
Leisure Management with Spanish	N7RK	3FT deg		8-12	MO	M	26	CCC		
Marketing with Spanish	N5R4	3FT deg		8-12	MO	M	26	CCC		
Media Arts with Spanish	W9R4	3FT deg		8-12	MO	M	26	CCC		
Politics & International Relations with Spanish	M1R4	3FT deg		8-12	MO	M	26	CCC		
Psychology with Spanish	C8R4	3FT deg		8-12	MO	M	26	CCC		
Recreation Management with Spanish	N7RL	3FT deg		8-12	MO	M	26	CCC		
Sociology with Spanish	L3R4	3FT deg		8-12	MO	M	26	CCC		
Spanish with American Studies	R4Q4	3FT deg		8-12	MO	M	26	CCC		
Spanish with Business	R4N1	3FT deg		8-12	MO	M	26	CCC		
Spanish with Business Economics	R4LC	3FT deg		8-12	MO	M	26	CCC		
Spanish with Economics	R4L1	3FT deg		8-12	MO	M	26	CCC		
Spanish with English	R4Q3	3FT deg		8-12	MO	M	26	CCC		
Spanish with English Language Studies	R4Q1	3FT deg		8-12	MO	M	26	CCC		
Spanish with European Law	R4M3	3FT deg		8-12	MO	M	26	CCC		
Spanish with European Studies	R4T2	3FT deg		8-12	MO	M	26	CCC		
Spanish with French	R4R1	3FT deg		8-12	MO	M	26	CCC		
Spanish with German	R4R2	3FT deg		8-12	MO	M	26	CCC		
Spanish with History	R4V1	3FT deg		8-12	MO	M	26	CCC		
Spanish with International Studies	R4MX	3FT deg		8-12	MO	M	26	CCC		
Spanish with Language and Communications	R4PH	3FT deg		8-12	MO	M	26	CCC		
Spanish with Media Studie	R4W9	3FT deg		8-12	MO	M	26	CCC		
Spanish with Music	R4W3	3FT deg		8-12	MO	M	26	CCC		
Spanish with Politics & International Relations	R4M1	3FT deg		8-12	MO	M	26	CCC		
Spanish with Visual Cultures	R4W1	3FT deg		8-12	MO	M	26	CCC		
Tourism with Spanish	P7R4	3FT deg		8-12	MO	M	26	CCC		

Univ of ULSTER

TITLE	CODE	COURSE	SUBJECTS	A/AS	ND/C	AGNVQ	IB	SQA(H)	SQA	RATIO A/AS
Humanities Combined *Spanish*	Y320▼	3FT/4SW deg	Sp	CCC	MO+3D	D*6/^ gi	28	BBBC	Ind	

UNIVERSITY COLL LONDON (Univ of London)

TITLE	CODE	COURSE	SUBJECTS	A/AS	ND/C	AGNVQ	IB	SQA(H)	SQA	RATIO A/AS
Dutch and Spanish (4 Yrs)	TR24	4FT deg	Sp g	BCC-BBC	3M	X	26$	BBBCC$	Ind	
French and Spanish (4 Yrs)	RR14	4FT deg	F+Sp g	BBC-BBB	3M	X	32$	ABBBB$	Ind	9	20/30
Hispanic Studies (4 Yrs)	R400	4FT deg	Sp g	BBC	3M	X	32$	BBBCC$	Ind	4	16/26
Modern Iberian and Latin American Reg St (4 Yrs)	RR46	4FT deg	Sp g	BBC	3M	X	32$	BBBCC$	Ind	9	
Spanish and History of Art (4 Yrs)	RV44	4FT deg	Sp g	BBC	3M	X	32$	BBBCC$	Ind		
Spanish with French (4 Yrs)	R4R1	4FT deg	F+Sp g	BBC	3M	X	32$	BBBBB$	Ind	17	

Univ of WARWICK

TITLE	CODE	COURSE	SUBJECTS	A/AS	ND/C	AGNVQ	IB	SQA(H)	SQA	RATIO A/AS
English and Spanish-American Literature	QR36	3FT deg	E+H/L g	BBB-BBC	X	X	32$	AABBB$		18

course details			98 expected requirements							96 entry stats	
TITLE	CODE	COURSE	SUBJECTS	A/AS	NO/C	AGNVQ	IB	SQA(H)	SQA	RATIO	A/AS
Univ of WESTMINSTER											
Law with Spanish	M3R4	4FT deg	Sp	BCC	MO+2D	D	28	BBB		3	
Spanish and Arabic	RT46	4SW deg	Sp	CC	Ind		26	BBB			
Spanish and Chinese	T3R4	4SW deg	Sp	CC	Ind		26	BBB	Ind		
Spanish and English	QR34	4SW deg	E	CC	Ind		26$	BBB		6	
Spanish and English Language	QRH4	4SW deg		CC	Ind		26$	BBB			
Spanish and French	RR14	4SW deg	F	CC	Ind		26$	BBB		8	12/18
Spanish and German	RR24	4SW deg	G/Sp	CC	Ind		26$	BBB		6	
Spanish and Italian	RR34	4SW deg	I/Sp	CC	Ind		26	BBB		4	10/18
Spanish and Linguistics	RQ41	4SW deg	L	CC	Ind		26	BBB		8	
Spanish and Russian	RR48	4SW deg	R/Sp	CC	Ind		26	BBB		4	
Univ of WOLVERHAMPTON											
Latin American Studies	R600	4FT deg	L g	18	4D $	D	28	BBBB	Ind		
Spanish	R400	3FT/4FT deg	L g	18	4D $	D	28	BBBB	Ind		
Combined Degrees *Latin American Studies*	Y401	3FT deg	L g	18	4D $	D	28	BBBB	Ind		
Combined Degrees *Spanish Studies*	Y401	3FT/4SW deg	L g	12	4M $	M	24	BBBB	Ind		

course details			98 expected requirements							96 entry stats
TITLE	CODE	COURSE	SUBJECTS	A/AS	ND/C	AGNVQ	IB	SQA(H)	SQA	RATIO A/AS
Univ of ABERDEEN										
Jurisprudence-International Relations	MMHC	4FT deg	* g	BBC	Ind	M$ go	30$	BBBBB$	Ind	
Jurisprudence-Politics	MMH1	4FT deg	* g	BBC	Ind	M$ go	30$	BBBB$	Ind	3
Jurisprudence-Social Research	LM33	4FT deg	* g	BBC	Ind	M$ go	30$	BBBB$	Ind	
Jurisprudence-Sociology	MLH3	4FT deg	* g	BBC	Ind	M$ go	30$	BBBB$	Ind	
Law (LLB)	M320	3FT/4FT deg	* g	BBB	Ind	X	34$	ABBBB$	Ind	4
Law (with Belgian Law) (LLB)	M333	3FT/4FT deg	F g	BBB	Ind	X	34$	ABBBB$	Ind	7
Law (with French Law) (LLB)	M351	3FT/4FT deg	* g	BBB	Ind	X	34$	ABBBB$	Ind	4
Law (with German Law) (LLB)	M361	3FT/4FT deg	* g	BBB	Ind	X	34$	ABBBB$	Ind	10
Law (with Options in Economics) (LLB)	M3L1	3FT/4FT deg	* g	BBB	Ind	X	34$	ABBBB$	Ind	5
Law (with Options in French) (LLB)	M355	3FT/4FT deg	F g	BBB	Ind	X	34$	ABBBB$	Ind	5
Law (with Options in German) (LLB)	M360	3FT/4FT deg	G g	BBB	Ind	X	34$	ABBBB$	Ind	9
Law (with Spanish Law) (LLB)	M381	5FT deg	* g	BBB	Ind	X	34$	ABBBB$	Ind	
Law (with options in Accountancy) (LLB)	M3N4	3FT/4FT deg	* g	BBB	Ind	X	34$	ABBBB$	Ind	4
Law (with options in Management Studies) (LLB)	M3N1	3FT/4FT deg	* g	BBB	Ind	X	34$	ABBBB$	Ind	3
Law (with options in Spanish) (LLB)	M380	3FT/4FT deg	Sp g	BBB	Ind	X	34$	ABBBB$	Ind	4
Philosophy-Jurisprudence	VM7H	4FT deg	* g	BBC	Ind	M$ go	30$	BBBB$	Ind	
Univ of ABERTAY DUNDEE										
Conveyancing and Executry Law	M393	4FT Dip	*	CD	Ind	Ind	Ind	BBC	Ind	
European Business Law	M310	4FT deg		CC	Ind	Ind	Ind	BBCC	Ind	
Law	M390	4FT deg	*	CD	Ind	Ind	Ind	BBC	Ind	
Univ of Wales, ABERYSTWYTH										
Accounting and Finance/Law	MN34	3FT deg	* g	BBB	DO $	D g	32$	BBBCC$	Ind	
Business/Law	MN31	3FT deg	* g	BBB	DO $	D g	32$	BBBCC$	Ind	
Law	M300	3FT deg	* g	BBB	DO $	D g	32$	BBBCC$	Ind	
Law (3 yrs)	M303	3FT deg	* g	BBB	DO $	D g	32$	BBBCC$	Ind	
Law with French (BA)	M3RD	4FT deg	F g	BBB	DO $	D^ g	32$	BBBCC$	Ind	
Law with French (LLB)	M3R1	4FT deg	F g	BBB	DO $	D^ g	32$	BBBCC$	Ind	
Law with German (BA)	M3RG	4FT deg	G g	BBB	DO $	D^ g	32$	BBBCC$	Ind	
Law with German (LLB)	M3R2	4FT deg	G g	BBB	DO $	D^ g	32$	BBBCC$	Ind	
Law with Italian (BA)	M3RJ	4FT deg	L g	BBB	DO $	D^ g	32$	BBBCC$	Ind	
Law with Italian (LLB)	M3R3	4FT deg	L g	BBB	DO $	D^ g	32$	BBBCC$	Ind	
Law with Spanish (BA)	M3RL	4FT deg	L g	BBB	DO $	D^ g	32$	BBBCC$	Ind	
Law with Spanish (LLB)	M3R4	4FT deg	L g	BBB	DO $	D^ g	32$	BBBCC$	Ind	
Political Studies/Law	MM13	3FT deg	* g	BBB	DO	D g	32	BBBBCC	Ind	
ANGLIA Poly Univ										
Art History and Law	MV34▼	3FT deg	*	14	6M	M+/^	Dip$	BBCC	Ind	
Business Law	M340▼	3FT deg	g	14	6M	M go	Dip	BBCC	N	
Business and Law	NM13▼	3FT deg	* g	14	6M	M go	Dip	BBCC	Ind	11 14/18
Communication Studies and Law	PM33▼	3FT deg	Ap	14	6M	M	Dip$	BBCC	Ind	5
Countryside Management and Law	DM23▼	3FT deg	* g	8	2M	P go	Dip	CCCC	Ind	
Criminology and Forensic Science	BM13▼	3FT deg	g	12	4M	M go	Dip	BCCC	Ind	
Criminology and Law	M331▼	3FT deg	g	14	6M	M go	Dip	BBCC	Ind	
Criminology and Psychology	CM8H▼	3FT deg	g	16	8M	D go	Dip	BBCCC	Ind	
Criminology and Social Policy	LM43▼	3FT deg	g	12	4M	M go	Dip	BCCC	Ind	
Criminology and Sociology	ML33▼	3FT deg	g	12	4M	M go	Dip	BCCC	Ind	
Economics and Law	LM13▼	3FT deg	* g	14	6M	M go	Dip	BBCC	Ind	12
English Language Studies and Law	QM13▼	3FT deg	* g	14	4M	M go	Dip	BCCC		
English and Law	MQ33▼	3FT deg	E	14	6M	M+/^	Dip$	BBCC	Ind	11
Environmental Planning and Law	FM93▼	3FT deg	* g	8	2M	P gi	Dip	CCCC	Ind	
European Philosophy & Literature and Law	MV37▼	3FT deg	*	14	6M	M	Dip	BBCC	Ind	1

course details | 98 expected requirements | 96 entry stats

TITLE	CODE	COURSE	SUBJECTS	A/AS	NO/C	AGNVQ	IB	SQA(H)	SQA	RATIO A/AS
Facilities Management and Law	KM23▼	3FT deg	g	10	3M	P go	Dip	BCCC	Ind	
Forensic Science and Law	MB31▼	3FT deg	g	14	6M	M go	Dip	BBCC	Ind	
French and Law	MR31▼	4FT deg	* g	14	6M	M go	Dip	BBCC	Ind	
Geography and Law	LM83▼	3FT deg	Gy g	14	6M	M go	Dip$	BBCC	Ind	
German and Law	MR32▼	4FT deg	* g	14	6M	M go	Dip$	BBCC	Ind	5
Graphic Arts and Law	MW32▼	3FT deg	A	14	6M	M	Dip$	BBCC	Ind	
History and Law	MV31▼	3FT deg	*	14	6M	M	Dip	BBCC	Ind	7
Housing and Law	KM43▼	3FT deg	* g	8	2M	P	Dip	CCCC	Ind	
Italian and Law	MR33▼	4FT deg	* g	14	6M	M go	Dip	BBCC	Ind	5
Law	M300▼	3FT deg	* g	12	4M	M go	Dip	BCCC	Ind	2 6/22
Law and Mathematics or Stats/Stat Modelling	MG31▼	3FT deg	* g	14	6M	M go	Dip	BBCC	Ind	3
Law and Music	MW33▼	3FT deg	Mu	14	6M	M	Dip$	BBCC	Ind	
Law and Politics	MM31▼	3FT deg	*	14	6M	M	Dip	BBCC	Ind	12
Law and Product Design	HM73▼	3FT deg	*	12	4M	M	Dip	BBCC	Ind	
Law and Property Management	MK34▼	3FT deg								
Law and Psychology	CM83▼	3FT deg	S g	16	8M	D go	Dip$	BBCCC	Ind	9 10/18
Law and Social Policy	ML34▼	3FT deg	*	14	6M	M	Dip	BBCC	Ind	9
Law and Sociology	LM33▼	3FT deg	*	14	6M	M	Dip	BBCC	Ind	8 14/16
Law and Spanish	MR34▼	4FT deg	* g	14	6M	M go	Dip	BBCC	Ind	3
Law and Surveying	HM23▼	3FT deg	*	12	4M	M	Dip	BBCC	Ind	
Law and Women's Studies	MM39▼	3FT deg	*	14	6M	M	Dip	BBCC	Ind	12

ASTON Univ

TITLE	CODE	COURSE	SUBJECTS	A/AS	NO/C	AGNVQ	IB	SQA(H)	SQA	RATIO A/AS
Law with Legal Practice Management	M340	3FT/4SW deg	* g	BBB-BBC	3M+7D	DB6/^ go	31	ABBBB	Ind	10 20/28

Univ of Wales, BANGOR

TITLE	CODE	COURSE	SUBJECTS	A/AS	NO/C	AGNVQ	IB	SQA(H)	SQA	RATIO A/AS
Criminology and Criminal Justice	M330	3FT deg	* g	18	M0	D*^ go	28	BBBC	Ind	1
Criminology and Psychology	MC38	3FT deg	* g	BBB	M0	D*^ go	30$	BBBB$	Ind	
French A and Criminology	MR31	4FT deg	F g	18	X	D*△ go	28$	BBBC$	X	
French B and Criminology	MR3C	4FT deg	F g	18	X	D*△ go	28$	BBBC$	X	
German and Criminology	MR32	4FT deg	* g	18	X	D*^ go	28	BBBC	X	
History and Criminology	MV31	3FT deg	H g	CCC	X	D*△ go	28$	BBBC$	X	
Russian and Criminology	MR38	4FT deg	* g	18	X	D*^ go	28	BBBC	X	
Social Policy/Criminology	LM43	3FT deg	* g	18	5M	D*6/^ go	28	BBBC	Ind	8 16/18
Sociology/Criminology	LM33	3FT deg	* g	18	5M	D*6/^ go	28	BBBC	Ind	5 12/22
Women's Studies and Criminology	MM39	3FT deg	* g	18	5M	D*6/^ go	28	BBBC	Ind	

BELL COLLEGE OF TECHNOLOGY

TITLE	CODE	COURSE	SUBJECTS	A/AS	NO/C	AGNVQ	IB	SQA(H)	SQA	RATIO A/AS
Legal Services	093M	2FT HND	Ap g	DD-D	N $	P$	Ind	CC$	12$	

Univ of BIRMINGHAM

TITLE	CODE	COURSE	SUBJECTS	A/AS	NO/C	AGNVQ	IB	SQA(H)	SQA	RATIO A/AS
Law	M300	3FT deg		AAB	D0	D$^ go	34$	CSYS	Ind	7 24/30
Law and Business Studies	MN31	3FT deg	g	AAB	D0	D$^ go	34$	CSYS	Ind	27 28/30
Law and Politics	MM31	3FT deg		AAB	D0	D$^ go	34$	CSYS	Ind	13 28/30
Law with French	MR31	4FT deg	F	AAB	D0	X	35$	CSYS	Ind	8 26/30
Law with German	MR32	4FT deg	G	AAB	X	X	35$	CSYS	Ind	
Legal Studies	M390	2FT deg		X	X	X	X	X	X	

BLACKBURN COLL

TITLE	CODE	COURSE	SUBJECTS	A/AS	NO/C	AGNVQ	IB	SQA(H)	SQA	RATIO A/AS
Criminology	M330	3FT deg		12	M	M	X	X		
Employment Law	M310	3FT deg		12	M	M				
Law: Multimode (3 years)	M300	3FT deg	* g	18	11M+3D	D$	Ind	Ind	Ind	
Law: Part 1 (1 year)	M301	3FT deg	g	24	10M+4D	D				
Paralegal Studies	M320	3FT deg		12	M	M				
Legal Studies	003M	2FT HND	* g	12	8M+2D	M$	Ind	Ind	Ind	

course details			98 expected requirements							96 entry stats	
TITLE	CODE	COURSE	SUBJECTS	A/AS	NO/C	AGNVQ	IB	SQA(H)	SQA	RATIO	A/AS
BOLTON INST											
Accountancy and Law	NM43	3FT deg	* g	CD	MO	M*	24	BBCC	Ind		
Architectural Technology and Law	KM23	3FT deg	* g	10	3M	M*	Ind	Ind	Ind		
Art and Design History and Law	MV34	3FT deg	* g	CD	MO	M*	24	BBCC	Ind		
Biology and Law	CM13	3FT deg	* g	CD	MO	M*	24	BBCC	Ind		
Building Surveying and Law	KMF3	3FT deg	* g	10	3M	M*	Ind	Ind	Ind		
Business Economics and Law	LM13	3FT deg	* g	CD	MO	M*	24	BBCC	Ind		
Business Information Systems and Law	GM5H	3FT deg	* g	CD	MO	M*	24	BBCC	Ind		
Business Studies and Law	NM13	3FT deg	* g	CD	MO	M g	24	BBCC	Ind		
Civil Engineering and Law	HM23	3FT deg	M/S g	10	3M	M$	Ind	Ind	Ind		
Community Studies and Law	LM53	3FT deg	* g	CD	MO	M*	24	BBCC	Ind		
Computing and Law	GM53	3FT deg	* g	CD	MO	M*	24	BBCC	Ind		
Construction and Law	KMG3	3FT deg	* g	10	3M	M*	Ind	Ind	Ind		
Creative Writing and Law	MW3X	3FT deg	* g	CD	MO	M*	24	BBCC	Ind		
Design and Law	MW32	3FT deg	* g	CD	MO	M*	24	BBCC	Ind		
Environmental Studies and Law	FM93	3FT deg	* g	CD	MO	M*	24	BBCC	Ind		
European Cultural Studies and Law	TM23	3FT deg	* g	CD	MO	M*	24	BBCC	Ind		
Film and TV Studies and Law	MW35	3FT deg	Me/T g	CD	Ind	Ind	24	BBCC	Ind		
French and Law	RM13	3FT deg	F g	CD	Ind	Ind	24	BBCC	Ind		
Gender and Women's Studies and Law	MM39	3FT deg	* g	CD	MO	M*	24	BBCC	Ind		
German and Law	RM23	3FT deg	G g	CD	Ind	Ind	24	BBCC	Ind		
History and Law	VM13	3FT deg	* g	CD	MO	M*	24	BBCC	Ind		
Human Resource Management and Law	MN31	3FT deg	* g	CD	MO	M*	24	BBCC	Ind		
Law and Literature	MQ32	3FT deg	* g	CD	MO	M*	24	BBCC	Ind		
Law and Marketing	MN35	3FT deg	* g	CD	MO	M*	24	BBCC	Ind		
Law and Mathematics	MG31	3FT deg	M g	CD	Ind	Ind	24	BBCC	Ind		
Law and Operations Management	MN32	3FT deg	* g	CD	MO	M*	24	BBCC	Ind		
Law and Organisations, Management & Work	MNH7	3FT deg	* g	CD	MO	M*	24	BBCC	Ind		
Law and Peace and War Studies	MV3C	3FT deg	* g	CD	MO	M*	24	BBCC	Ind		
Law and Philosophy	MV37	3FT deg	* g	CD	MO	M g	24	BBCC	Ind		
Law and Psychology	ML37	3FT deg	* g	12	MO	D*	24	BBCC	Ind		
Law and Quantity Surveying	MK3F	3FT deg	* g	10	3M	Ind	Ind	Ind	Ind		
Law and Sociology	LM3H	3FT deg	* g	CD	MO	M	24	Ind	Ind		
Law and Theatre Studies	MW34	3FT deg	Me/T g	CD	Ind	Ind	24	BBCC	Ind		
Law and Tourism Studies	MP37	3FT deg	* g	CD	MO	M g	24	BBCC	Ind		
Law and Urban and Cultural Studies	LM33	3FT deg	* g	CD	MO	M*	24	BBCC	Ind		
Visual Arts and Law	MW31	3FT deg	* g	CD	MO	M*	24	BBCC	Ind		
BOURNEMOUTH Univ											
Business Law	M340	4SW deg	*	18	MO+3D	D$	32	BBBB	Ind	2	10/20
Law	M300	3FT deg	*	18	MO+3D	D$	32	BBBB	Ind		
Taxation and Revenue Law	M345	3FT deg	* g	14	MO+3D	Ind go	30	BBBB	Ind	2	6/18
BRADFORD & ILKLEY Comm COLL											
Law	M300	3FT deg	g	16	DO	D	Ind	Ind	Ind		
Law and European Business	MN31	3FT deg		6	DO	M+	Ind	Ind	Ind		
Univ of BRIGHTON											
Accountancy with Law	NM43	3FT/4SW deg	* g	18	2M+4D	M$6/^/D$go Dip		BBBB	Ind		
Business Studies with Law	N1M3	3FT/4SW deg	* g	18	MO+5D	D$ go	28$	BBBB$	Ind		
Univ of BRISTOL											
Chemistry and Law	FM13	4FT deg	C g	ABB	Ind	D$^	33$	AAABB	Ind	4	24/30
Law	M300	3FT deg	*	ABB	Ind	D$^	34$	AAABB	Ind	15	24/30

course details			98 expected requirements						96 entry stats	

TITLE	CODE	COURSE	SUBJECTS	A/AS	NO/C	AGNVQ	IB	SQA(H)	SQA	RATIO A/AS	
Law and French	MR31	4FT deg	F	ABB	Ind	D$^	34$	AAABB	Ind	37	28/30
Law and German	MR32	4FT deg	G	ABB	Ind	D$^	34$	AAABB	Ind	20	

BRISTOL, Univ of the W of England

EFL and Law	QM33	4FT deg	g	16-24	6M	M*^ go	24$	BBCC$	Ind	
European Languages & Law, EFL and French	MTH9	4FT deg	g	16-24	6M	M*^ go	24$	BBCC$	Ind	
European Languages & Law, EFL and German	MTHX	4FT deg	g	16-24	6M	M*^ go	24$	BBCC$	Ind	
European Languages & Law, EFL and Spanish	MTHY	4FT deg	g	16-24	6M	M*^ go	24$	BBCC$	Ind	
European Languages & Law, French & German (LLB)	MT39	4FT deg	F/G g	16-24	6M	M*^ go	24$	BBCC$	Ind	
European Languages & Law, French & Spanish (LLB)	MT3X	4FT deg	F/Sp g	16-24	6M	M*^ go	24$	BBCC$	Ind	
European Languages & Law, German & Spanish (LLB)	MT3Y	4FT deg	G/Sp g	16-24	6M	M*^ go	24$	BBCC$	Ind	
French and Law	RM13	4FT deg	F g	16-24	MO	M*^ go	24$	BBCC$	Ind	
German and Law	RM23	4FT deg	G g	16-24	MO	M*^ go	24$	BBCC$	Ind	
Law	M300	3FT deg	* g	BBC-BBB	MO+3D	D*^ go	30	AABB	Ind	
Law (English and European)	M333	3FT deg	* g	CCC-BCC	MO+2D	M*^ go	26$	BBBC$	Ind	
Spanish and Law	RM43	4FT deg	Sp g	16-24	MO	M*^ go	24$	BBCC$	Ind	
Joint Honours Programme _Law and Science_	Y401	3FT deg	S g	14-16	5M $	M$ go	24$	BCCC$	Ind	

BRUNEL Univ, West London

Business and Finance Law	M342	3FT deg	*	BBB	DO	Ind/^	30	ABBBB	Ind	11	20/26
Business and Finance Law (4 Yrs Thin SW)	M341	4SW deg	*	BBB	DO	Ind/^	30	ABBBB	Ind	6	20/28
Economics and Law	LMC3	3FT deg	* g	22-24	M+D	D^	30$	Ind	Ind	13	
Economics and Law (4 Yrs Thick SW)	LMD3	4SW deg	* g	22-24	M+D	D^	30$	Ind	Ind		
Economics and Law (4 Yrs Thin SW)	LM13	4SW deg	* g	22-24	M+D	D^	30$	Ind	Ind	11	
Ethico Legal Issues in Health Care	L4M3	3FT deg	B	12-20	Ind	MG	Ind	Ind	Ind		
History and Law	MV31	3FT deg	*	BBB	DO	Ind					
Law	M303	3FT deg	*	BBB	DO	Ind^	30	ABBBB	Ind	11	20/26
Law (4 Yrs Thin SW)	M300	4SW deg	*	BBB	DO	Ind^	30	ABBBB	Ind	6	20/26
Law with French (4 Yrs Thick SW)	M3R1	4SW deg	F	BBB	DO $	D^	30$	ABBBB$	Ind		
Law with German (4 Yrs Thick SW)	M3R2	4SW deg	G	BBB	DO $	D^	30$	ABBBB$	Ind		
Management Studies and Law	NM13	3FT deg	*	20-24	5D	D^	28	Ind	Ind	11	20/24
Management Studies and Law (4 Yrs Thick SW)	NM1J	4SW deg	*	20-24	5D	D^	28	Ind	Ind		
Management Studies and Law (4 Yrs Thin SW)	NM1H	4SW deg	*	20-24	5D	D^	28	Ind	Ind	10	

Univ of BUCKINGHAM

Law	M300	2FT deg	*	18	3M+2D	M	26	BCCC	Ind	13
Law (July)	M302	2FT deg	*	18	3M+2D	M	26	BCCC	Ind	
Law and Politics	MM13	2FT deg	*	16	3M+2D	M	26	CCCC	Ind	
Law with Accounting and Finance	M3N4	2FT deg	*	18	3M+2D	M	26	BCCC	Ind	
Law with Business Studies	M3N1	2FT deg	M* g	18	3M+2D	M	26	BCCC	Ind	
Law with Finance	M3N3	2FT deg	M* g	18	3M+2D	M	26	BCCC	Ind	
Law with French	M3R1	2FT deg	F	12	3M+2D	M	26	BCCC	Ind	
Law with Spanish	M3R4	2FT deg	Sp	12	3M+2D	M	26	BCCC	Ind	
Politics, Economics and Law _Law_	Y618	2FT deg	* g	12	5M	M	24	CCCC	Ind	

BUCKINGHAMSHIRE COLLEGE

Business Administration and Law	MN31	3FT deg		8	MO	M	27	CCCC	Ind	
Business Administration with Law	N1M3	3FT deg		8	MO+2D	M	27	CCCC	Ind	
Business Studies and Law	MN3C	4SW deg			MO	M	27	CCCC	Ind	
Business Studies with Law	N1MH	4SW deg		8	MO	M	27	CCCC	Ind	
Criminology	M330	3FT deg		16	2D	M	27	CCCC	Ind	
Criminology with Social Policy	M3L4	3FT deg		12	2D	M	27	CCCC	Ind	
Human Resources Management and Law	MN36	3FT deg		8	MO	M	27	CCCC	Ind	

TITLE	CODE	COURSE	SUBJECTS	A/AS	ND/C	AGNVQ	IB	SQA(H)	SQA	RATIO	A/AS
Human Resources Management with Law	N6M3	3FT deg		8	MO	M	27	CCCC	Ind		
Marketing and Law	MN35	3FT deg		8	MO	M	27	CCCC	Ind		
Psychology and Criminology	LM73	3FT deg		14	2D	M	27	CCCC	Ind	11	9/22
Sociology and Criminology	LM33	3FT deg		12	2D	M	27	CCCC	Ind	5	6/16
CAMBRIDGE Univ											
Law	M300▼	3FT deg	* g	AAA	Ind		Ind	CSYS	Ind	4	28/30
CAMBRIDGE BUSINESS COLLEGE											
Law	M300	3FT deg									
CARDIFF Univ of Wales											
Law	M300	3FT deg		AA-BBB	Ind		Ind	AABB	Ind	5	22/28
Law and French	RM13	4FT deg	F	BBB	Ind	Ind	Ind	Ind	Ind	4	22/28
Law and German	RM23	4FT deg	G	BBB	Ind	Ind	Ind	Ind	Ind	5	22/30
Law and Italian	RM33	4FT deg	L	BBB	Ind	Ind	Ind	Ind	Ind	3	21/28
Law and Japanese	MT34	4FT deg	*	BBB	Ind	Ind	Ind	Ind	Ind	6	22/28
Law and Politics	MM31	3FT deg	*	BBB	Ind	Ind	Ind	Ind	Ind	11	22/28
Law and Sociology	ML33	3FT deg	*	BBB	Ind	Ind	Ind	Ind	Ind	8	20/30
Law and Spanish	RM43	4FT deg	Sp	BBB	Ind	Ind	Ind	Ind	Ind	4	22/28
Univ of CENTRAL ENGLAND											
Business Administration with Law	N1M3	3FT deg	* g	14	M+3D	D	24	CCCCC	Ind	9	12/18
Criminal Justice and Policing	M390	3FT deg		18	MO	M	24	CCC		9	10/18
Economics with Law	L1M3	3FT deg	* g	14	M+3D	D	24	CCCC	Ind	4	8/14
Finance with Law	N3M3	3FT deg	* g	14	M+3D	D6	24	CCCC			
Law (LLB)	M300	3FT deg	*	CCC	M+5D	M	30	BBCC	Ind	10	14/24
Law with Politics	M3M1	3FT deg	*	CCC	M+5D	M	30	BBCC	Ind	2	10/18
Politics with Law	M1M3	3FT deg	*	14	MO	M	24	CCCC	Ind	4	8/14
Univ of CENTRAL LANCASHIRE											
Law	M300	3FT deg	*	CCC	3M+5D$	D$6/^	30$	AABB	Ind		
Law and Languages	MT32	4FT deg	F/G	CCD	Ind	M$6/^	28$	BBBB$	Ind		
Combined Honours Programme Law	Y400	3FT deg	* g	16	MO+4D	D$6/^	28	BBBC	Ind		
CITY Univ											
Business Law	M340	3FT deg	* g	BBB	3M+5D	D*^	Ind	AAABB	Ind	31	20/26
Law	M300	3FT deg	* g	BBB	3M+5D	D*^	Ind	AAABB	Ind	14	18/24
COVENTRY Univ											
Economics and Law	LM13	3FT deg	* g	12-16	M+2D	M	Ind	CCC	Ind		
European Law (4 years)	M333	4FT deg	F/G/Sp/R/I	BCC	D	D	Ind	BBBBC	Ind	9	16/18
Law (Senior Status)	M305	2FT deg		X		X	X	X			
Law and International Studies	MT32	3FT deg	*	CCC	D	D	Ind	BBBB	Ind	7	8/18
Law and Social Policy	LM43	3FT deg	*	CCC	D	D	Ind	BBBB	Ind		
Law/Business Law/Criminal Justice	M300▼	3FT deg	*	BCC	D	D	Ind	BBBBC	Ind		14/22
CROYDON COLL											
Business St (Business & Law) (yr 3 entry opt)	NM13	3FT deg	*	6	MO $	M$/P$3	Ind	Ind			
Law	M300	3FT deg	*	CC	Ind	M$	Ind	Ind			
Business Studies (Business and Law)	31MN	2FT HND	*	E	N $	P$	Ind	Ind			
DE MONTFORT Univ											
Law	M300▼	3FT deg	* g	BBC	6D	D^	30	BBBBB	X	8	14/22
Law and Human Resource Management	M3N1▼	3FT deg	* g	BBC	6D	M^	30	BBBBB	X		
Law and Marketing	M3N5▼	3FT deg	* g	BBC	6D	M^	30	BBBBB	X		

Law   47

course details			98 expected requirements							96 entry stats
TITLE	CODE	COURSE	SUBJECTS	A/AS	NO/C	RGNVQ	IB	SQA(H)	SQA	RATIO A/AS
Law and Public Policy	M3L4▼	3FT deg	* g	BBC	6D	M^	30	BBBBB	X	
Law with French	M3R1▼	4FT deg	F g	BBC	6D	M^	30$	BBBBB$	X	10
Law with German	M3R2▼	4FT deg	G g	BBC	6D	M^	30$	BBBBB$	X	3 18/18
Law/Accounting	MN34▼	3FT deg	* g	BBC	6D	M^	30$	BBBBB$	X	
Law/Business	MN31▼	3FT deg	* g	BBC	6D	M^	30$	BBBBB$	X	
Law/Business Economics	LM13▼	3FT deg	* g	BBC	6D	M^	30$	BBBBB$	X	
Law/Finance	MN33▼	3FT deg	* g	BBC	6D	M^	30$	BBBBB$	X	
Management/Law	MN3C▼	3FT deg	* g	18	3M+3D	M	32	AABB	X	
Combined Studies Law	Y400▼	3FT deg	* g	14	2M+4D	D	30	BBB	Ind	
Combined Studies Law-Qualifying	Y400▼	3FT deg	* g	14	2M+4D	D	30	BBB	Ind	
Univ of DERBY										
Law	M300	3FT deg	*	18-20	MO+4D	D$	30	BBBCC	Ind	12 12/20
Law with European Studies	M3T2	3FT deg	*	20	MO+4D	D$	30	BBBCC	Ind	
Law with a Modern Language	M3TF	3FT deg	F/G/Sp/R	20	MO+4D$	D$^	30$	BBBCC$	Ind	
Credit Accumulation Modular Scheme Law	Y600	3FT deg	*	14	MO	M	28	CCCC	Ind	
Univ of DUNDEE										
LLB (English Law)	M300	2FT/3FT/4FT deg	* g	BBC	Ind	D$	28	ABBBC	Ind	5 16/26
Scots Law (LLB)	M320	2FT/3FT/4FT deg	* g	BBC	Ind	D$	28	ABBBC	Ind	5
Univ of DURHAM										
Economics and Law	LM13	3FT deg	* g	ABB	DO	X	32$	AAABB	HN	13
Law	M300	3FT deg	*	AAB	DO	Ind	32	AAABB	HN	17 26/30
Law and Politics	MM13	3FT deg	*	ABB	DO	Ind	32	AAABB	HN	11
Law and Sociology	LM33	3FT deg	*	ABB	DO	Ind	32	AAABB	HN	
Law with Economics	M3L1	3FT deg	* g	AAB	DO	X	32	AAABB	HN	16
Law with Politics	M3M1	3FT deg	*	AAB	DO	Ind	32	AAABB	HN	34
Law with Sociology	M3L3	3FT deg	*	AAB	DO	Ind	32	AAABB	HN	
Politics with Law	M1M3	3FT deg	*	BBB	Ind	Ind	Ind	Ind	Ind	
Sociology with Law	L3M3	3FT deg	*	BCC	Ind	Ind	30	Ind	Ind	11
Univ of EAST ANGLIA										
Accountancy with Law	N4M3	3FT deg	* g	BBB-BBC	HN		30$	ABBBB	X	4 18/21
Law	M300	3FT deg	*	BBB	1M+4D		30$	AAABB	X	7 20/28
Law (American Legal Systems) (4 Yrs)	M374	4FT deg	*	AAA	X		X	X	X	15 30/30
Law with European Legal Systems (4 Yrs)	M333	4FT deg	*	BBB	1M+4D		30$	AAABB	X	9 24/30
Law with French Law and Language (4 Yrs)	M350	4FT deg	F	BBB	X		30$	AAABB	X	8 22/28
Law with German Law and Language (4 Yrs)	M360	4FT deg	G	BBB	X		30$	AAABB	X	10 24/28
Univ of EAST LONDON										
Accounting & Finance and Law	NM43	3FT deg	* g	14	MO	D	Ind	Ind	Ind	7
Accounting & Finance with Law	N4M3	3FT deg	* g	14	MO	MB	Ind	Ind	Ind	
Criminology and Criminal Justice	M330	3FT deg	* g	16	MO	M				
Economics and Law	LM13	3FT deg	* g	12	MO	D	Ind	Ind	Ind	5
Economics with Law	L1M3	3FT deg	* g	12	MO	M	Ind			
French and Law	MR31	3FT deg	* g	12	MO	D	Ind	Ind	Ind	
French with Law	R1M3	3FT deg	* g	12	MO	M	Ind			
German and Law	MR32	3FT deg	* g	12	MO	D	Ind	Ind	Ind	
German with Law	R2M3	3FT deg	* g	12	MO	M	Ind			
Information Technology and Law	GM53	3FT deg	* g	12	MO	D	Ind	Ind	Ind	4
Information Technology with Law	G5M3	3FT deg	* g	12	MO	M	Ind			
Law	M300	3FT deg	* g	14	MO	D	Ind	Ind	Ind	5 8/20

TITLE	CODE	COURSE	SUBJECTS	A/AS	NO/C	RGNVQ	IB	SQA(H)	SQA	RATIO A/AS
course details			**98 expected requirements**							**96 entry stats**
Law and Psychosocial Studies	LM73	3FT deg	* g	14	M0	M$	Ind	Ind	Ind	7
Law and Social Sciences	LMH3	3FT deg	* g	14	M0	MB	Ind	Ind	Ind	4
Law and Sociology	LM33	3FT deg	* g	14	M0	M$	Ind	Ind	Ind	15
Law and Spanish	MR34	3FT deg	* g	14	M0	M^	Ind	Ind	Ind	
Law and Third World & Development Studies	MM93	3FT deg	* g	14	M0	M				
Law with Accounting & Finance	M3N4	3FT deg	* g	14	M0	M				
Law with Business Studies	M3N1	3FT deg	* g	14	M0	M				
Law with French	M3R1	3FT deg	* g	14	M0	M				
Law with German	M3R2	3FT deg	* g	14	M0	M				
Law with Italian	M3R3	3FT deg	* g	14	M0	M				
Law with Psychosocial Studies	M3L7	3FT deg	* g	14	M0	M				
Law with Social Sciences	M3L3	3FT deg	* g	14	M0	M				
Law with Spanish	M3R4	3FT deg	* g	14	M0	M				
Law with Third World & Development Studies	M3M9	3FT deg	* g	14	M0	M				
Law, Culture and Society	LM3H	3FT deg	* g	14	M0	M				
Literature with Law	Q3M3	3FT deg	* g	12	M0	M	Ind			
New Technology and Law	JM93	3FT deg	* g	12	M0	M	Ind	Ind	Ind	2
Psychosocial Studies with Law	L7M3	3FT deg	* g	12	M0	M	Ind	Ind	Ind	
Social Sciences with Law	L3M3	3FT deg	* g	12	M0	M	Ind	Ind	Ind	
Sociology with Law	L3MH	3FT deg	* g	12	M0	M	Ind	Ind	Ind	
Spanish with Law	R4M3	3FT deg	* g	12	M0	M	Ind			
Third World & Development Studies with Law	M9M3	3FT deg	* g	12	M0	M				
Three-Subject Degree Law	Y600	3FT deg	* g	12	M0	M	Ind	Ind	Ind	
EDGE HILL Univ COLLEGE										
Critical Criminology & Disability & Community St	MM9H	3FT deg	* g	CD	3M+3D	M*/ P*^ go	Dip	BBCC$	Ind	
Critical Criminology and Applied Social Sciences	LM33	3FT deg	*	CC	3M+3D	M*/ P*^	Dip	BBCC	Ind	
Critical Criminology and Community & Race Rel	MM39	3FT deg	*	CD	3M+3D	M*/ P*^	Dip	BBCC	Ind	
Critical Criminology and Modern European Studies	MT32	3FT deg	*	CD	3M+3D	M*/ P*^	Dip	BBCC	Ind	
Critical Criminology and Urban Policy Studies	MM93	3FT deg	*	CD	3M+3D	M*/ P*^	Dip	BBCC	Ind	
Critical Criminology and Women's Studies	MM3X	3FT deg	*	CD	3M+3D	M*/ P*^	Dip	BBCC	Ind	
Univ of EDINBURGH										
Business Studies and Law	NM13	4FT deg	g	ABB	Ind		36$	AABB	Ind	16
Economics and Law	LM13	4FT deg	g	ABB	Ind		36$	AABB	Ind	33
Law (LLB)	M320	3FT/4FT deg	g	ABB	X		32	AAABB	X	4 26/30
Law and Accountancy	MN34	4FT deg	g	ABB	X		32	AAABB	X	5
Law and Business Studies	MN31	4FT deg	g	ABB	X		32	AAABB	X	9
Law and Celtic	MQ35	4FT deg	L g	ABB	X		32	AAABB	X	
Law and Economic History	MV33	4FT deg	g	ABB	X		32	AAABB	X	3
Law and Economics	ML31	4FT deg	g	ABB	X		32	AAABB	X	7
Law and French	MR31	4FT deg	F g	ABB	X		32	AAABB	X	4 26/30
Law and German	MR32	4FT deg	L g	ABB	X		32	AAABB$	X	3
Law and History	MV31	4FT deg	g	ABB	X		32	AAABB	X	6
Law and Philosophy	MV37	4FT deg	g	ABB	X		32	AAABB	X	7
Law and Politics	MM31	4FT deg	g	ABB	X		32	AAABB	X	8
Law and Social Policy	ML34	4FT deg	g	ABB	X		32	AAABB	X	
Law and Sociology	ML33	4FT deg	g	ABB	X		32	AAABB	X	17
Law and Spanish	MR34	4FT deg	L g	ABB	X		32	AAABB	X	7
Law with Scandanavian Studies	MR37	4FT deg	g	ABB			32	AAABB	X	

Law 47

course details			98 expected requirements							96 entry stats	
TITLE	CODE	COURSE	SUBJECTS	A/AS	ND/C	AGNVQ	IB	SQA(H)	SQA	RATIO	A/AS
Univ of ESSEX											
English and European Laws (4 Yrs)	M333	4FT deg	L	24	MO+4D	Ind	30$	AAABB	Ind	7	18/24
English and French Law (4 Yrs)	M351	4FT deg	F	ABC	MO+4D	Ind	30$	AAABB	Ind	13	
Law	M300	3FT deg	*	ABB	MO+4D	Ind	30	AAABB	Ind	7	18/28
Univ of EXETER											
Chemistry and Law	FM13	3FT deg	C/S g	BCC	DO	M/D$^	32$	Ind	Ind	6	14/18
Law	M300	3FT deg	*	ABB	DO	D$^	36$	Ind	Ind	7	26/30
Law (European)	M301	4FT deg	F/G	ABB	DO	D$^	36$	Ind	Ind	11	26/30
Law and Society	LM33	3FT deg	*	BBC	MO	M/D$^	34$	Ind	Ind	14	22/26
Law with European Study	M303	4FT deg	L	ABB	DO	D$^	36$	Ind	Ind	17	
Univ of GLAMORGAN											
Criminal Justice	M330	3FT deg	Lw/Ps/So g	18	Ind	Ind	Ind	Ind	Ind	10	16/24
Forensic Measurement with Criminal Justice	FM13	3FT deg	M/S+Lw/Ps/So g	14	Ind	Ind	Ind	Ind	Ind		
Government and Law	MM13	3FT deg	* g	18	MO+3D	D	Ind	Ind	Ind		
Law	M300	3FT deg	* g	18	MO+3D	D$	Ind	Ind	Ind	3	12/20
Law and Business Studies	MN31	3FT deg	* g	18	MO+3D	D$	Ind	Ind	Ind		
Law with Accounting and Finance	M3N4	3FT deg	* g	18	Ind	Ind	Ind	Ind	Ind		
Law with Business Studies	M3N1	3FT deg	* g	18	Ind	Ind	Ind	Ind	Ind		
Law with Criminal Justice	M3MH	3FT deg	Lw/Ps/So g	18	Ind	Ind	Ind	Ind	Ind		
Law with English Studies	M3Q3	3FT deg	* g	18	Ind	Ind	Ind	Ind	Ind		
Paralegal Studies	M391	4SW deg	* g	14	Ind	Ind	Ind	Ind	Ind		
Psychology with Criminal Justice	L7M3	3FT deg	Lw/Ps/So g	14	Ind	Ind	Ind	Ind	Ind		
Psychology with Criminology	L7MH	3FT deg	Lw/Ps/So g	14	Ind	Ind	Ind	Ind	Ind		
Sociology with Criminal Justice	L3M3	3FT deg	Lw/Ps/So g	14	Ind	Ind	Ind	Ind	Ind		
Sociology with Criminology	L3MH	3FT deg	Lw/Ps/So g	14	Ind	Ind	Ind	Ind	Ind		
Combined Studies (Honours) Criminal Justice	Y400	3FT deg	Lw/Ps/So g	8-16	Ind	Ind	Ind	Ind	Ind		
Combined Studies (Honours) Criminology	Y400	3FT deg	Lw/Ps/So g	8-16	Ind	Ind	Ind	Ind	Ind		
Combined Studies (Honours) Law	Y400	3FT deg	* g	8-16	Ind	Ind	Ind	Ind	Ind		
Joint Honours Law	Y401	3FT/4SW deg	* g	8-16	Ind	Ind	Ind	Ind	Ind		
Major/Minor Honours Criminal Justice	Y402	3FT deg	Lw/Ps/So g	8-16	Ind	Ind	Ind	Ind	Ind		
Major/Minor Honours Criminology	Y402	3FT deg	Lw/Ps/So g	8-16	Ind	Ind	Ind	Ind	Ind		
Major/Minor Honours Law	Y402	3FT deg	* g	8-16	Ind	Ind	Ind	Ind	Ind		
Legal Studies	003M▼	2FT HND	* g	12	MO+1D	P$	Ind	Ind	Ind	1	4/10
Univ of GLASGOW											
Financial and Legal Studies	MN34	4FT deg		BBB	HN		32	AAABB	X		
Law Ordinary/Honours	M320	4FT deg		ABB	X		34	AAAAB	X	4	24/28
Law with French Language	M3R1	4FT deg		ABB	X		34	AAAAB	X	3	
Law with French Legal Studies	M351	4FT deg		ABB	X		34	AAAAB	X	4	
Law with German Language	M3R2	4FT deg		ABB	X		34	AAAAB	X	3	
Law with German Legal Studies	M360	4FT deg		ABB	X		34	AAAAB	X	3	
Law with Spanish Language	M3R4	4FT deg		ABB	X		34	AAAAB	X	5	
Law with Spanish Legal Studies	M381	4FT deg		ABB	X		34	AAAAB	X	3	
GLASGOW CALEDONIAN Univ											
Accountancy with Law	N4M3	3FT/4FT deg	E+M	BC	Ind		Ind	BBBC$	Ind		
Law with Administrative Studies	M3N1	3FT/4FT deg	E+M	BC-CC	Ind		Ind	BBBC$	Ind	3	
Legal Studies	M390	2FT Dip	E+Ec/M	CD	Ind		Ind	BCC$	Ind	3	

TITLE	CODE	COURSE	SUBJECTS	A/AS	ND/C	AGNVQ	IB	SQA(H)	SQA	RATIO A/AS
Univ of GREENWICH										
Applied Biology and Law	CM13	3FT deg	B+C g	12	M+D	M	Dip	Ind	Ind	
Applied Biology with Law	C1M3	3FT deg	B+C g	12	M+D	M	Dip	Ind	Ind	
Applied Chemistry and Law	FM13	3FT deg	B+C g	12	M+D	M	Dip	Ind	Ind	
Applied Chemistry with Law	F1M3	3FT deg	B+C g	12	M+D	M	Dip	Ind	Ind	
Law	M300	3FT deg	* g	18	DO	Ind	28	BBBBC	Ind	
Law (Graduate Entry Direct to year 2)	M301	3FT deg								
Law with Sociology	M3L3	3FT deg	* g	18	DO	Ind	28	BBBBC	Ind	
Pharmaceutical Sciences with Law	B3M3	3FT deg	B+C g	12	M+D	M	Dip	Ind	Ind	
HERIOT-WATT Univ										
Management with Business Law	N1M3	4FT deg	*	CCC		M$ go	30	BBBB	Ind	
Univ of HERTFORDSHIRE										
Accounting and Law	NM43	3FT/4SW deg	* g	18	DO	DB	28	BBBC	Ind	
Applied Physics/Law	F3M3	3FT deg	M+P	18	4M+4D	D$ gi	26$	BBBC$	Ind	
Applied Statistics/Law	G4M3	3FT deg	*	20	4M+4D	D$ gi	26	BBBC	Ind	
Astronomy/Law	F5M3	3FT deg	M g	18	4M+4D	D$ gi	26$	BBBC$	Ind	
Business/Law	N1M3	3FT deg	*	20	4M+4D	D$ gi	26	BBBC	Ind	7 14/20
Chemistry/Law	F1M3	3FT deg	C g	20	4M+4D	DS gi	26$	BBBC$	Ind	4
Computing/Law	G5M3	3FT deg	*	20	4M+4D	D$ gi	26	BBBC	Ind	
Economics/Law	L1M3	3FT deg	*	20	4M+4D	D$ gi	26	BBBC	Ind	9
Electronics/Law	H6M3	3FT deg	* g	20	4M+4D	D$ gi	26$	BBBC$	Ind	
Environmental Science/Law	F9M3	3FT deg	*	20	4M+4D	D$ gi	26	BBBC	Ind	2
European Studies/Law	T2M3	3FT deg	*	20	4M+4D	D$ gi	26	BBBC	Ind	9
Human Biology/Law	B1M3	3FT deg	S g	20	4M+4D	DS gi	26$	BBBC$	Ind	6
Law	M300	3FT deg	* g	20	M+6D	Ind	26	BBBBB	Ind	4 12/22
Law	M302	3FT deg	* g	20	4M+4D	D$ gi	26	BBBC	Ind	
Law (2 Yr Accelerated Programme)	M307	2ACC deg	* g	20	M+6D	Ind	26	BBBBB	Ind	2 6/20
Law/Applied Physics	M3F3	3FT deg	M+P	18	4M+4D	D$ gi	26$	BBBC$	Ind	
Law/Applied Statistics	M3G4	3FT deg	*	20	4M+4D	D$ gi	26	BBBC	Ind	
Law/Astronomy	M3F5	3FT deg	M g	18	4M+4D	D$ gi	26$	BBBC$	Ind	
Law/Business	M3N1	3FT deg	*	20	4M+4D	D$ gi	26	BBBC	Ind	19
Law/Chemistry	M3F1	3FT deg	C g	20	4M+4D	D$ gi	26$	BBBC$	Ind	
Law/Computing	M3G5	3FT deg	*	20	4M+4D	D$ gi	26	BBBC	Ind	7
Law/Economics	M3L1	3FT deg	*	20	4M+4D	D$ gi	26	BBBC	Ind	16
Law/Electronics	M3H6	3FT deg	* g	20	4M+4D	D$ gi	26$	BBBC$	Ind	
Law/Environmental Science	M3F9	3FT deg	*	20	4M+4D	D$ gi	26	BBBC	Ind	11
Law/European Studies	M3T2	3FT deg	*	20	4M+4D	D$ gi	26	BBBC	Ind	6 14/18
Law/Human Biology	M3B1	3FT deg	S g	20	4M+4D	D$ gi	26$	BBBC$	Ind	5
Law/Linguistic Science	M3Q1	3FT deg	*	20	4M+4D	D$ gi	28	BBBC	Ind	
Law/Operational Research	M3N2	3FT deg	*	20	4M+4D	D$ gi	26	BBBC	Ind	
Linguistic Science/Law	Q1M3	3FT deg	*	20	4M+4D	D$ gi	28	BBBC	Ind	
Operational Research/Law	N2M3	3FT deg	*	20	4M+4D	D$ gi	26	BBBC	Ind	
Combined Modular Scheme _Law_	Y100	3FT deg	*	20	4M+4D	D$ gi	26	BBBC	Ind	
HOLBORN COLL										
Law (Univ of London External Programme)	M301	3FT deg	*	EE	3M	M	Dip	BCCCC		
Law (in conjunction with Univ of Wolverhampton)	M300	3FT deg	*	EE	Ind	M	24	Ind	Ind	32
Univ of HUDDERSFIELD										
Law and Accountancy	MN34	3FT deg	* g	16	3M+3D	M go	Ind	BBCC	Ind	
Law/Business Law/European Studies	M300	3FT deg	* g	CCC	4M+6D	M$4/^ go	Ind	BBBB	Ind	

Law 47

| | | | | 98 expected requirements | | | | | | 96 entry stats | |
TITLE	CODE	COURSE	SUBJECTS	A/AS	NO/C	AGNVQ	IB	SQA(H)	SQA	RATIO	A/AS
Univ of HULL											
Law (Honours)	M300	3FT deg	*	BBB	Ind	D$^ gi	28	ABBBB	Ind	6	20/27
Law and Politics	MM13	3FT deg	*	BBB	MO	D$^ gi	28$	ABBBB	Ind	4	22/28
Law and Sociology	LM33	3FT deg	*	22	MO	D$^ gi	28$	ABBBB	Ind	25	
Law with French	M3R1	4FT deg	F	BBB-BCC	M+D $	D$^ gi	28$	ABBBB	Ind	6	20/26
Law with German	M3R2	4FT deg	G	BBB-CCC	M+D $	D$^ gi	28$	ABBBB	Ind	14	
Law with Philosophy	M3V7	3FT deg	*	BBB	DO	D$	28	AABBB	Ind		
KEELE Univ											
Biological and Medicinal Chemistry and Law	FMC3	3FT deg	C g	BBB-BBC	Ind	D$^	30$	CSYS	Ind	3	
Criminology and American Studies	MQH4	3FT deg	*	BBB	Ind	Ind	32	CSYS	Ind	27	
Criminology and American Studies (4 Yrs)	QM4H	4FT deg	*	BBB	Ind	Ind	32	BBBB	Ind	7	
Criminology and Ancient History	MVHD	3FT deg	*	BBB	Ind	Ind	32	CSYS	Ind		
Criminology and Ancient History (4 Yrs)	VMDH	4FT deg	*	BBB	Ind	Ind	32	ABBB	Ind		
Criminology and Applied Social Studies	LM5H	3FT deg	*	BBB	Ind	Ind	32	CSYS	Ind	7	22/26
Criminology and Applied Social Studies (4 Yrs)	MLH5	4FT deg	*	BBB	Ind	Ind	32	ABBB	Ind	5	
Criminology and Astrophysics	FM5H	3FT deg	P	BBB-BCC	Ind	D$^	28$	CSYS	Ind		
Criminology and Astrophysics (4 Yrs)	MFH5	4FT deg	*	BBB	Ind	Ind	32	ABBB	Ind		
Criminology and Biological & Med Chem (4 yrs)	MFHC	4FT deg	*	BBB-BCC	Ind	Ind	28	BBB			
Criminology and Biology (4 Yrs)	MCH1	4FT deg	*	BBB-BCC	Ind	Ind	28	BBBB			
Criminology and Business Administration (4 Yrs)	NM9H	4FT deg	*	BBB-BCC	Ind	Ind	28	BBBB			
Criminology and Chemistry (4 Yrs)	MFH1	4FT deg	*	BBB-BCC	Ind	Ind	28	BBBB			
Criminology and Classical Studies	MQH8	3FT deg	*	BBB	Ind	Ind	32	CSYS	Ind	5	
Criminology and Classical Studies (4 Yrs)	QM8H	4FT deg	*	BBB	Ind	Ind	32	ABBB	Ind		
Criminology and Computer Science	GM5H	3FT deg	* g	BBB-BCC	Ind	D$^	28	CSYS	Ind		
Criminology and Computer Science (4 Yrs)	MGH5	4FT deg	*	BBB	Ind	Ind	32	ABBB	Ind	2	
Economics and Criminology	LM1H	3FT deg	* g	BBB	Ind	Ind	32	CSYS	Ind	6	
Economics and Criminology (4 Yrs)	MLH1	4FT deg	*	BBB	Ind	Ind	32	ABBB	Ind		
Educational Studies and Criminology	MXH9	3FT deg	*	BBB	Ind	Ind	32	CSYS	Ind	5	
Educational Studies and Criminology (4 Yrs)	XM9H	4FT deg	*	BBB	Ind	Ind	32	ABBB	Ind		
Electronic Music and Criminology	MWHJ	3FT deg	Mu	BBB	Ind	D$^	32$	CSYS	Ind		
Electronic Music and Criminology (4 Yrs)	WMJH	4FT deg	*	BBB	Ind	Ind	32	ABBB	Ind		
Environmental Management and Criminology (4 Yrs)	MFHX	4FT deg	*	BBB	Ind	Ind	32	BBBB	Ind		
Finance and Criminology	MNH3	3FT deg	* g	BBB	Ind	Ind	32	CSYS	Ind		
Finance and Criminology (4 Yrs)	MNHH	4FT deg	*	BBB	Ind	Ind	32	BBBB	Ind		
French and Criminology	MRH1	3FT deg	F	BBB	Ind	D$^	32$	CSYS	Ind	3	
French and Criminology (4 Yrs)	RM1H	4FT deg	*	BBB	Ind	Ind	32	ABBB	Ind		
French/Russian or Russ St & Criminology (4 Yrs)	TMXH	4FT deg	*	BBB	Ind	Ind	32	BBBB	Ind		
Geography and Criminology (4 Yrs)	MFH8	4FT deg	*	BBB-BCC	Ind	Ind	28	BBBB	Ind		
German and Criminology (4 Yrs)	RM2H	4FT deg	* g	BBB-BCC	Ind	Ind	28	BBBB	Ind		
History and Criminology	MVH1	3FT deg	*	BBB	Ind	Ind	32	CSYS	Ind	16	
History and Criminology (4 Yrs)	VM1H	4FT deg	*	BBB	Ind	Ind	32	ABBB	Ind		
International Politics and Criminology	MMHC	3FT deg	*	BBB	Ind	Ind	32	CSYS	Ind		
International Politics and Criminology (4 Yrs)	MMCH	4FT deg	*	BBB	Ind	Ind	32	BBBB	Ind		
Latin and Criminology (4 Yrs)	QM6H	4FT deg	*	BBB	Ind	Ind	32	BBBB	Ind		
Law and American Studies	MQ34	3FT deg	*	BBB	Ind	Ind	32	CSYS	Ind	7	22/24
Law and American Studies	QM43	4FT deg	*	BBB	Ind	Ind	32	BBBB	Ind	9	
Law and Ancient History	MV3D	3FT deg	*	BBB	Ind	Ind	32	CSYS	Ind	3	
Law and Applied Social Studies	LM53	3FT deg	*	BBB	Ind	Ind	32	CSYS	Ind		
Law and Applied Social Studies (4 Yrs)	ML35	4FT deg	*	BBB	Ind	Ind	32	BBBB	Ind		
Law and Biochemistry	CM73	3FT deg	C g	BBB	Ind	D$^	32$	CSYS	Ind	2	
Law and Biochemistry (4 Yrs)	MC37	4FT deg	*	BBB	Ind	Ind	32	BBBB	Ind		
Law and Biological and Medicinal Chem (4 Yrs)	MF3C	4FT deg	*	BBB	Ind	Ind	32	ABBB	Ind		

course details | 98 expected requirements | 96 entry stats

TITLE	CODE	COURSE	SUBJECTS	A/AS	ND/C	AGNVQ	IB	SQA(H)	SQA	RATIO	A/AS
Law and Biology	CM13	3FT deg	S g	BBB	Ind	D$^	32$	CSYS	Ind		
Law and Biology (4 Yrs)	MC31	4FT deg	*	BBB	Ind	Ind	32	BBBB	Ind		
Law and Business Administration	MN39	3FT deg	*	BBB	Ind	Ind	32	CSYS	Ind	8	22/26
Law and Business Administration (4 Yrs)	NM93	4FT deg	*	BBB	Ind	Ind	32	BBBB	Ind	8	
Law and Chemistry	FM13	3FT deg	C g	BBB-BBC	Ind	D$^	30$	CSYS	Ind	4	
Law and Chemistry (4 Yrs)	MF31	4FT deg	*	BBB	Ind	Ind	32	BBBB	Ind		
Law and Classical Studies	MQ38	3FT deg	*	BBB	Ind	Ind	32	CSYS	Ind	4	
Law and Computer Science	GM53	3FT deg	*	BBB-BBC	Ind	Ind	30	CSYS	Ind	14	
Law and Computer Science (4 Yrs)	MG35	4FT deg	*	BBB	Ind	Ind	32	BBBB	Ind		
Law and Criminology	M330	3FT deg	*	ABB	Ind	Ind	32	CSYS	Ind	12	24/30
Law and Criminology (4 Yrs)	M331	4FT deg	*	ABB	Ind	Ind	32	BBBB	Ind	11	
Law and Economics	LM13	3FT deg	* g	BBB	Ind	Ind	32	CSYS	Ind	4	20/28
Law and Economics (4 Yrs)	ML31	4FT deg	*	BBB	Ind	Ind	32	BBBB	Ind		
Law and Educational Studies	MX39	3FT deg	*	BBB	Ind	Ind	32	CSYS	Ind		
Law and Educational Studies (4 Yrs)	XM93	4FT deg	*	BBB	Ind	Ind	32	BBBB	Ind		
Law and Electronic Music (4 Yrs)	WMJ3	4FT deg	*	BBB	Ind	Ind	32	BBBB	Ind		
Law and English	MQ33	3FT deg	E	BBB	Ind	D$^	32$	CSYS	Ind	8	24/28
Law and English (4 Yrs)	QM33	4FT deg	*	BBB	Ind	Ind	32	BBBB	Ind	2	20/22
Law and Finance	MN33	3FT deg	* g	BBB	Ind	Ind	32	CSYS	Ind		
Law and French	MR31	3FT deg	F	BBB	Ind	D$^	32$	CSYS	Ind	4	20/24
Law and French (4 Yrs)	RM13	4FT deg	*	BBB	Ind	Ind	32	BBBB	Ind	31	
Law and Geology	FM63	3FT deg	S g	BBB	Ind	D$^	32$	CSYS	Ind		
Law and Geology (4 Yrs)	MF36	4FT deg	*	BBB	Ind	Ind	32	BBBB	Ind		
Law and German	MR32	3FT deg	G	BBB	Ind	D$^	32$	CSYS	Ind	7	
Law and History	MV31	3FT deg	*	BBB	Ind	Ind	32	CSYS	Ind	33	
Law and History (4 Yrs)	VM13	4FT deg	*	BBB	Ind	Ind	32	BBBB	Ind		
Law and Human Resource Management	MN36	3FT deg	*	BBB	Ind	Ind	32	CSYS	Ind	5	
Law and Human Resource Management (4 Yrs)	NM63	4FT deg	*	BBB	Ind	Ind	32	BBBB	Ind		
Law and International History	MV3C	3FT deg	*	BBB	Ind	Ind	32	CSYS	Ind	3	
Law and International History (4 Yrs)	VMC3	4FT deg	*	BBB	Ind	Ind	32	BBBB	Ind		
Law and International Politics	MMC3	3FT deg	*	BBB	Ind	Ind	32	BBBB	Ind	3	
Law and International Politics (4 Yrs)	MM3C	4FT deg	*	BBB	Ind	Ind	32	CSYS	Ind		
Law and Latin	MQ36	3FT deg	Ln	BBB	Ind	D$^	32$	CSYS	Ind		
Law and Latin (4 Yrs)	QM63	4FT deg	*	BBB	Ind	Ind	32	BBBB	Ind		
Law and Mathematics	GM13	3FT deg	M	BBB	Ind	D$^	32$	CSYS	Ind	4	
Law and Mathematics (4 Yrs)	MG31	4FT deg	*	BBB	Ind	Ind	32	BBBB	Ind	1	
Management Science and Law	MN31	3FT deg	* g	BBB	Ind	Ind	32	CSYS	Ind		
Marketing and Criminology	MNH5	3FT deg	*	BBB	Ind	Ind	32	CSYS	Ind		
Marketing and Law	MN35	3FT deg	*	BBB	Ind	Ind	32	CSYS	Ind	30	
Music and Criminology	MWH3	3FT deg	Mu	BBB	Ind	D$^	32$	CSYS	Ind		
Music and Criminology (4 Yrs)	WM3H	4FT deg	*	BBB	Ind	Ind	32	ABBB	Ind		
Music and Law (4 Yrs)	WM33	4FT deg	*	BBB	Ind	Ind	32	BBBB	Ind		
Philosophy and Criminology	MVH7	3FT deg	*	BBB	Ind	Ind	32	CSYS	Ind		
Philosophy and Criminology (4 Yrs)	VM7H	4FT deg	*	BBB	Ind	Ind	32	ABBB	Ind		
Philosophy and Law	MV37	3FT deg	*	BBB	Ind	Ind	32	CSYS	Ind	6	
Philosophy and Law (4 Yrs)	VM73	4FT deg	*	BBB	Ind	Ind	32	BBBB	Ind		
Physics and Criminology	FM3H	3FT deg	P g	BBB-BCC	Ind	D$^	28$	CSYS	Ind		
Physics and Criminology (4 Yrs)	MFH3	4FT deg	*	BBB-BCC	Ind	Ind	28	ABBB	Ind		
Politics and Law	MM13	3FT deg	*	BBB	Ind	Ind	32	CSYS	Ind	21	
Politics and Law (4 Yrs)	MM31	4FT deg	*	BBB	Ind	Ind	32	ABBB	Ind		
Psychology and Criminology	CM8H	3FT deg	* g	ABB	Ind	Ind	32	CSYS	Ind	14	24/28
Psychology and Criminology (4 Yrs)	MCH8	4FT deg	*	ABB	Ind	Ind	32	ABBB	Ind	4	14/30

TITLE	CODE	COURSE	SUBJECTS	A/AS	ND/C	AGNVQ	IB	SQA(H)	SQA	RATIO	A/AS
				98 expected requirements						**96 entry stats**	
Psychology and Law	CM83	3FT deg	*	BBB	Ind	Ind	32	CSYS	Ind	14	24/28
Russian Studies and Criminology (4 Yrs)	RMVH	4FT deg	*	BBB-BCC	Ind	Ind	32	BBBB	Ind		
Russian and Criminology (4 Yrs)	RM8H	4FT deg	* g	BBB	Ind	Ind	32	ABBB	Ind		
Sociol & Soc Anthrop and Criminology (4 Yrs)	ML3J	4FT deg	*	BBB	Ind	Ind	32	ABBB	Ind	4	
Sociology & Social Anthropology and Criminology	LM3J	3FT deg	*	BBB	Ind	Ind	32	CSYS	Ind	23	26/26
Sociology & Social Anthropology and Law	LM33	3FT deg	*	BBB	Ind	Ind	32	CSYS	Ind	20	
Sociology & Social Anthropology and Law (4 Yrs)	ML33	4FT deg	*	BBB	Ind	Ind	32	BBBB	Ind		
Statistics and Law (4 Yrs)	MG34	4FT deg	*	BBB-BCC	Ind	Ind	28	BBBB	Ind		
Visual Arts and Criminology (4 Yrs)	WM1H	4FT deg	*	BBB	Ind	Ind	32	BBBB	Ind		

Univ of KENT

TITLE	CODE	COURSE	SUBJECTS	A/AS	ND/C	AGNVQ	IB	SQA(H)	SQA	RATIO	A/AS
English and French Law (4 Yrs)	M351	4FT deg	F	ABC	Ind	Ind	32$	AABB$	Ind	4	20/30
English and German Law (4 Yrs)	M361	4FT deg	G	22	Ind	Ind	30$	ABBB$	Ind	5	20/26
English and Italian Law (4 Yrs)	M363	4FT deg	* g	22	2M+4D	Ind	30	ABBB	Ind	6	
English and Spanish Law (4 Yrs)	M380	4FT deg	Sp	22	Ind	Ind	30$	ABBB$	Ind	6	
European Legal Studies (4 Yrs)	M333	4FT deg	*	BBB	1M+5D	D$	32	AABB	Ind	6	
History and Law	MV31	3FT deg	*	22	2M+4D	Ind	30	Ind	Ind	6	20/28
Industrial Relations & Human Resource Mgt (Law)	MN36	3FT deg	* g	26	6D	D$ go	33	AAAB	Ind	7	
Law	M300▼	3FT deg	*	26	6D	D$	33	AAAB	Ind	5	20/30
Law and History	MVH1	3FT deg	*	26	6D	D$	33	AAAB	Ind	4	
Law and Philosophy	MV37	3FT deg	*	26	6D	D$	33	AAAB	Ind	9	
Law and Welfare	LM43	3FT deg	*	22	2M+4D	D$	30	ABBB	Ind	6	
Law with a Language	M364	3FT deg	F/G	22	Ind	Ind	30$	ABBB$	Ind	7	20/26
Law/Economics	LM13	3FT deg	* g	26	6D	D$ go	33	AAAB	Ind	25	
Philosophy and Law	MVH7	3FT deg	*	22	2M+4D	Ind	30	Ind	Ind	6	
Politics & Government/Law	MM13	3FT deg	*	26	6D	D$	33	AAAB	Ind	15	
Social Anthropology/Law	LM63	3FT deg	*	26	6D	D$	33	AAAB	Ind		
Sociology/Law	LM33	3FT deg	*	26	6D	D$	33	AAAB	Ind	24	

KING'S COLL LONDON (Univ of London)

TITLE	CODE	COURSE	SUBJECTS	A/AS	ND/C	AGNVQ	IB	SQA(H)	SQA	RATIO	A/AS
LLB Honours	M300	3FT deg	*	ABB	DO		36	AAABB		14	24/30
LLB Honours English and French Law (4 Yrs)	M350	4FT deg	F	AAB	DO		36	AAABB		12	26/30
LLB Honours Law with German Law (4 Yrs)	M361	4FT deg	G	ABB	DO		36	AAABB		5	26/30
LLB with European Legal Studies (4 Yrs)	M355	4FT deg	F/G/I	AAB	DO		36	AAABB		27	30/30

KINGSTON Univ

TITLE	CODE	COURSE	SUBJECTS	A/AS	ND/C	AGNVQ	IB	SQA(H)	SQA	RATIO	A/AS
Accounting and Law	MN34	3FT deg	*	CCC	3M+5D	Ind	Ind	CCCCC	Ind	5	14/20
Criminal Justice Studies	M390	3FT deg				Ind					
LLB Honours with French Law	M350	4FT deg	F	BBC	Ind		Ind	Ind	Ind	8	14/20
LLB Honours with German Law	M360	4FT deg	G	BBC	Ind		Ind	Ind	Ind	3	
Law	M300	3FT deg	*	BBC	Ind		Ind	Ind	Ind	11	18/24

LANCASTER Univ

TITLE	CODE	COURSE	SUBJECTS	A/AS	ND/C	AGNVQ	IB	SQA(H)	SQA	RATIO	A/AS
Criminology	M330	3FT deg	*	CCC	M+D		30	ABBBB	Ind		
Criminology and Applied Social Science	LM43	3FT deg	*	CCC	M+D		30	ABBBB	Ind		
Criminology and Educational Studies	MX39	3FT deg	*	CCC	M+D		30	ABBBB	Ind		
Criminology and Independent Studies	MY34	3FT deg	*	CCC	M+D		30	ABBBB	Ind		
Criminology and Women's Studies	MM39	3FT deg	*	CCC	M+D		30	ABBBB	Ind		
European Legal Studies	M355	4SW deg	F/G/I/Sp g	ABB	4D $		32$	AABBB$	Ind		
Law	M300	3FT deg	* g	ABB	4D		30	AABBB	Ind		

LANSDOWNE COLLEGE

TITLE	CODE	COURSE	SUBJECTS	A/AS	ND/C	AGNVQ	IB	SQA(H)	SQA	RATIO	A/AS
Law	M300	3FT deg		4		M					

TITLE	CODE	COURSE	SUBJECTS	A/AS	ND/C	AGNVQ	IB	SQA(H)	SQA	RATIO	A/AS
course details			**98 expected requirements**							**96 entry stats**	
Univ of LEEDS											
Law	M300	3FT deg	*g	ABB	Ind	D$^ go	33	CSYS	Ind	11	24/30
Law-Chinese Studies	MT33	4FT deg	L g	ABB	Ind	Ind	33$	CSYS	Ind	11	
Law-French	MR31	4FT deg	E g	ABB	Ind	Ind	33$	CSYS	Ind	36	
Law-Japanese Studies	MT34	4FT deg	L g	ABB	Ind	Ind	33$	CSYS	Ind	13	
LEEDS METROPOLITAN Univ											
Law	M300	3FT deg	*g	BBC	4M+3D	DB^ go	28	BBBBB	Ind	13	16/24
Univ of LEICESTER											
Economics and Law	LM13	3FT deg	*g	BBB	6D	D$^	32	AABBB	Ind		20/26
Law	M300	3FT deg	*g	26	DO	D$^ gi	33$	AAABBB	X		20/28
Law with French	M3R1	4FT deg	E g	26	X	D$^ gi	33$	AAABBB	X		22/30
Univ of LINCOLNSHIRE and HUMBERSIDE											
Communications and Criminology	MP33▼	3FT deg	*g	16	1M+3D		24	BBCCC	Ind		
Communications and Law	MP3H▼	3FT deg	*g	16	1M+3D	D	24	BBCCC	Ind		
Criminology	M331▼	3FT deg	g	16	1M+3D	D	24	BBCCC	Ind		
Criminology and Economics	LM1H▼	3FT deg	*g	16	1M+3D	D	24	BBCCC	Ind		
Criminology and Health Studies	LMKH▼	3FT deg	*g	16	1M+3D	D	24	BBCCC	Ind		
Criminology and International Relations	MM1H▼	3FT deg	*g	16	1M+3D	D	24	BBCCC	Ind		
Criminology and Journalism	MP36▼	3FT deg	*g	18	1M+4D	D	26	BBBCC	Ind		
Criminology and Law	M330▼	3FT deg	*g	18	1M+4D	D	26	BBBCC	Ind		
Criminology and Management	MNH1▼	3FT deg	*g	16	1M+3D	D	24	BBCCC	Ind		
Criminology and Media	MPH4▼	3FT deg	*g	18	1M+4D	D	26	BBBCC	Ind		
Criminology and Politics	MM1J▼	3FT deg	*g	16	1M+3D	D	24	BBCCC	Ind		
Criminology and Psychology	CM83▼	3FT deg	*g	18	1M+4D	D	26	BBBCC	Ind		
Criminology and Social Policy	LM43▼	3FT deg	*g	16	1M+3D	D	24	BBCCC	Ind		
Criminology and Tourism	MPH7▼	3FT deg	*g	16	1M+3D	D	24	BBCCC	Ind		
Economics and Law	LM13▼	3FT deg	*g	16	1M+3D	D	24	BBCCC	Ind		
Health Studies and Law	LMK3▼	3FT deg	*g	16	1M+3D	D	24	BBCCC	Ind		
International Relations and Law	MM13▼	3FT deg	*g	16	1M+3D	D	24	BBCCC	Ind		
Journalism and Law	MP3P▼	3FT deg	g	18	1M+4D	D	26	BBBCC	Ind		
Law	M300	3FT deg	g								
Law and Management	MN3D▼	3FT deg	*g	16	1M+3D	D	24	BBCCC	Ind		
Law and Media	MP34▼	3FT deg	*g	18	1M+4D	D	26	BBBCC	Ind		
Law and Politics	MM31▼	3FT deg	*g	16	1M+3D	D	24	BBCCC	Ind		
Law and Social Policy	LM4H▼	3FT deg	*g	16	1M+3D	D	24	BBCCC	Ind		
Law and Tourism	MP37▼	3FT deg	*g	16	1M+3D	D	24	BBCCC	Ind		
Univ of LIVERPOOL											
English and German Laws	M360	4FT deg	G	ABB	Ind	Ind	Ind	AAABB	X		
Law (LLB) Honours	M300	3FT deg	*	ABB	DO	D$^	33	AAABB	X	8	24/30
Law and French	MR31	4FT deg	E	ABB	Ind	Ind	Ind	AAABB	X	13	26/30
BA Combined Honours _Law_	Y200	3FT deg	*g	BBB	Ind	Ind	Ind	Ind	Ind		
LIVERPOOL JOHN MOORES Univ											
Criminal Justice and Applied Psychology	CM83	3FT deg	*g	16	5M+3D	X	28$	BBCC		30	14/26
Law	M300	3FT deg		BCC	MO+5D	D^	Ind	BBBC		10	16/24
Law and Business	MN3D	3FT deg		CCC	MO+5D	D^	28$	BBBC		11	16/24
Law and Criminal Justice (Law Joint Award only)	M301	3FT deg		CCC	MO+5D	X	28$	BBBC		16	18/26
Politics and Criminal Justice	MM13	3FT deg		16	5M+3D	X	28$	BCCC		11	14/20
Sociology and Criminal Justice	LM3H	3FT deg		16	MO+3D	X	28$	BCCC		21	14/20
Women's Studies and Criminal Justice	MM3Y	3FT deg		16	5M+3D	X	28$	BCCC		5	

				98 expected requirements						96 entry stats	
course details											
TITLE	CODE	COURSE	SUBJECTS	A/AS	NQ/C	AGNVQ	IB	SQA(H)	SQA	RATIO A/AS	

LONDON GUILDHALL Univ											
3D/Spatial Design and Law	MW3F	3FT deg	Pf g	CC-CDD	MO+5D	D$ go	26	Ind	Ind		
Business Law	M340	3FT deg	* g	BCC	DO	D$ go	24	Ind	Ind		
Law	M300	3FT deg	* g	BCC	DO	D$ go	24	Ind	Ind		
Law and Accounting	MN34	3FT deg	* g	CC-CDD	MO+4D	M$ go	26	Ind	Ind		
Law and Business	MN31	3FT deg	* g	CC-CDD	MO+4D	M$ go	26	Ind	Ind		
Law and Business Economics	LMC3	3FT deg	* g	CC-CDD	MO+2D	M$ go	26	Ind	Ind		
Law and Business Information Technology	GM73	3FT deg	* g	CC-CDD	MO+2D	M$ go	26	Ind	Ind		
Law and Communications & Audio Visual Prod Studs	MP34	3FT deg	* g	BC-CCC	MO+6D	D$ go	28	Ind	Ind		
Law and Computing	GM53	3FT deg	* g	CC-CDD	MO+2D	M$ go	26	Ind	Ind		
Law and Design Studies	MW32	3FT deg	* g	CC-DDD	MO+4D	M$ go	26	Ind	Ind		
Law and Development Studies	MM39	3FT deg	* g	CC-CDD	MO+2D	M$ go	26	Ind	Ind		
Law and Economics	LM13	3FT deg	* g	CC-CDD	MO+2D	M$ go	26	Ind	Ind		
Law and English	MQ33	3FT deg	* g	CC-CDD	MO+4D	D$ go	26	Ind	Ind		
Law and European Studies	MT32	3FT deg	* g	CC-CDD	MO+2D	M$ go	26	Ind	Ind		
Law and Financial Services	MN33	3FT deg	* g	CC-CDD	MO+2D	M$ go	26	Ind	Ind		
Law and Fine Art	MW31	3FT deg	* g	BC-CCC	MO+6D	D$ go	28	Ind	Ind		
Law and French	MR31	4FT deg	* g	CC-CDD	MO+2D	M$ go	26	Ind	Ind		
Law and German	MR32	4FT deg	* g	CC-CDD	MO+2D	M$ go	26	Ind	Ind		
Law and International Relations	MM3C	3FT deg	* g	CC-CDD	MO+2D	M$ go	26	Ind	Ind		
Legal Studies	M301	3FT deg									
Legal and Economic St/Licence D'Administration	M3L1	3FT deg	F g	CCD	MO	X	24	Ind	Ind		
Marketing and Law	MN35	3FT deg	* g	CC-CDD	MO+4D	M$ go	26	Ind	Ind		
Mathematics and Law	GM13	3FT deg	* g	CC-CDD	MO+2D	M$ go	26	Ind	Ind		
Modern History and Law	MV31	3FT deg	* g	CC-CDD	MO+2D	M$ go	26	Ind	Ind		
Multimedia Systems and Law	GMM3	3FT deg	* g	CC-CDD	MO+2D	M$ go	26	Ind	Ind		
Politics and Law	MM13	3FT deg	* g	CC-CDD	MO+4D	M$ go	26	Ind	Ind		
Product Development & Manufacture and Law	JM43	3FT deg	* g	CC-CDD	MO+2D	M$ go	26	Ind	Ind		
Psychology and Law	CM83	3FT deg	* g	CC	MO+3D	M$ go	26	Ind	Ind		
Social Policy & Management and Law	LM43	3FT deg	* g	CC-CDD	MO+2D	M$ go	26	Ind	Ind		
Sociology and Law	LM33	3FT deg	* g	CC	MO+4D	M$ go	26	Ind	Ind		
Spanish and Law	MR34	4FT deg	* g	CC-CDD	MO+2D	M$ go	26	Ind	Ind		
Taxation and Law	MN3H	3FT deg	* g	CC-CDD	MO+2D	M$ go	26	Ind	Ind		
Textile Furnishing Design and Law	MW3G	3FT deg	Pf g	CC-CDD	MO	M$ go	24	Ind	Ind		
Modular Programme *Law*	Y400	3FT deg	* g	BB-CC	MO+4D	D/M$ go	26	Ind	Ind		

LSE: LONDON Sch of Economics (Univ of London)											
Anthropology and Law	ML36	3FT deg		BBB	Ind	X	$	Ind	Ind		
Law	M300	3FT deg		ABB	Ind	X	$	Ind	Ind	33	24/30
Law with French Law (4 Yrs)	M351	4FT deg	F	ABB	Ind	X	$	Ind	Ind	21	

LUTON Univ											
Law	M300	3FT deg	g	12-16	MO/DO	M/D	32	BBCC	Ind	8	10/18
Law and Accounting	NMK3	3FT deg	g	12-16	MO/DO	M/D	32	BBCC	Ind		
Law and Biology	CM13	3FT deg	g	12-16	MO/DO	M/D	32	BBCC	Ind		
Law and British Studies	VM93	3FT deg		12-16	MO/DO	M/D	32	BBCC	Ind		
Law and Building Conservation	KM23	3FT deg	g	12-16	MO/DO	M/D	32	BBCC	Ind		
Law and Business	NM13	3FT deg	g	12-16	MO/DO	M/D	32	BBCC	Ind	25	
Law and Business Systems	NMC3	3FT deg	g	12-16	MO/DO	M/D	32	BBCC	Ind		
Law and Computer Science	GM53	3FT deg	g	12-16	MO/DO	M/D	32	BBCC	Ind	9	
Law and Contemporary History	VM13	3FT deg	g	12-16	MO/DO	M/D	32	BBCC	Ind	6	
Law and European Language Studies	TM23	3FT deg	L g	12-16	MO/DO	M/D	32	BBCC	Ind		

			98 expected requirements							96 entry stats

course details

TITLE	CODE	COURSE	SUBJECTS	A/AS	ND/C	AGNVQ	IB	SQA(H)	SQA	RATIO A/AS
Law and Geography	FM83	3FT deg	g	12-16	MO/DO	M/D	32	BBCC	Ind	
Law and Geology	FM63	3FT deg	g	12-16	MO/DO	M/D	32	BBCC	Ind	
Law and Health Studies	BMX3	3FT deg	g	12-16	MO/DO	M/D	32	BBCC	Ind	
Law and Housing Studies	KM4H	3FT deg	g	12-16	MO/DO	M/D	32	BBCC	Ind	
Law and Human Biology	BM13	3FT deg	g	12-16	MO/DO	M/D	32	BBCC	Ind	
Law and Journalism	PM63	3FT deg		12-16	MO/DO	M/D	32	BBCC	Ind	
Law and Language & Stylistics in English	QMG3	3FT deg	g	12-16	MO/DO	M/D	32	BBCC	Ind	
Law with Accounting	M3N4	3FT deg	g	12-16	MO/DO	M/D	32	BBCC	Ind	
Law with Biology	M3C1	3FT deg	g	12-16	MO/DO	M/D	32	BBCC	Ind	
Law with British Studies	M3V9	3FT deg		12-16	MO/DO	M/D	32	BBCC	Ind	
Law with Business	MN31	3FT deg	g	12-16	MO/DO	M/D	32	BBCC	Ind	
Law with Business Systems	M3NC	3FT deg	g	12-16	MO/DO	M/D	32	BBCC	Ind	
Law with Chinese	M3T3	3FT deg		12-16	MO/DO	M/D	32	BBCC	Ind	
Law with Comparative Literature	M3Q2	3FT deg	g	12-16	MO/DO	M/D	32	BBCC	Ind	
Law with Contemporary History	M3V1	3FT deg	g	12-16	MO/DO	M/D	32	BBCC	Ind	
Law with French	M3R1	3FT deg		12-16	MO/DO	M/D	32	BBCC	Ind	
Law with Geography	M3F8	3FT deg	g	12-16	MO/DO	M/D	32	BBCC	Ind	
Law with Geology	M3F6	3FT deg	g	12-16	MO/DO	M/D	32	BBCC	Ind	
Law with Human Biology	M3B1	3FT deg	g	12-16	MO/DO	M/D	32	BBCC	Ind	
Law with Japanese	M3T4	3FT deg	L g	12-16	MO/DO	M/D	32	BBCC	Ind	
Law with Journalism	M3P6	3FT deg	g	12-16	MO/DO	M/D	32	BBCC	Ind	
Law with Land Reclamation	M3K3	3FT deg	g	12-16	MO/DO	M/D	32	BBCC	Ind	
Law with Management	M3ND	3FT deg	g	12-16	MO/DO	M/D	32	BBCC	Ind	
Law with Mapping Science	M3FV	3FT deg	g	12-16	MO/DO	M/D	32	BBCC	Ind	
Law with Marketing	M3N5	3FT deg	g	12-16	MO/DO	M/D	32	BBCC	Ind	
Law with Media Production	M3P4	3FT deg	g	12-16	MO/DO	M/D	32	BBCC	Ind	
Law with Modern English Studies	M3Q3	3FT deg	g	12-16	MO/DO	M/D	32	BBCC	Ind	
Law with Modern History	M3VC	3FT deg	g	12-16	MO/DO	M/D	32	BBCC	Ind	
Law with Organisational Behaviour	M3L7	3FT deg	g	12-16	MO/DO	M/D	32	BBCC	Ind	
Law with Pharmacology	M3B2	3FT deg	g	12-16	MO/DO	M/D	32	BBCC	Ind	
Law with Physical Geography	M3FW	3FT deg	g	12-16	MO/DO	M/D	32	BBCC	Ind	
Law with Politics	M3M1	3FT deg	g	12-16	MO/DO	M/D	32	BBCC	Ind	
Law with Pollution Studies	M3FX	3FT deg	g	12-16	MO/DO	M/D	32	BBCC	Ind	
Law with Public Policy & Management	M3MC	3FT deg	g	12-16	MO/DO	M/D	32	BBCC	Ind	
Law with Publishing	M3P5	3FT deg	g	12-16	MO/DO	M/D	32	BBCC	Ind	
Law with Regional Planning & Development	M3K4	3FT deg	g	12-16	MO/DO	M/D	32	BBCC	Ind	
Law with Social Studies	M3L3	3FT deg	g	12-16	MO/DO	M/D	32	BBCC	Ind	
Law with TV Studies	M3W5	3FT deg	g	12-16	MO/DO	M/D	32	BBCC	Ind	
Leisure Studies and Law	MN37	3FT deg	g	12-16	MO/DO	M/D	32	BBCC	Ind	
Mapping Science and Law	MF38	3FT deg	g	12-16	MO/DO	M/D	32	BBCC	Ind	
Marketing and Law	MN35	3FT deg	g	12-16	MO/DO	M/D	32	BBCC	Ind	6
Media Practices and Law	MP34	3FT deg	g	12-16	MO/DO	M/D	32	BBCC	Ind	
Media Production and Law	MP3L	3FT deg	g	12-16	MO/DO	M/D	32	BBCC	Ind	
Media Technology and Law	MP3K	3FT deg	g	12-16	MO/DO	M/D	32	BBCC	Ind	
Modern English Studies and Law	MQ33	3FT deg	g	12-16	MO/DO	M/D	32	BBCC	Ind	
Modern History and Law	MV3C	3FT deg	g	12-16	MO/DO	M/D	32	BBCC	Ind	14
Organisational Behaviour and Law	ML37	3FT deg	g	12-16	MO/DO	M/D	32	BBCC	Ind	
Pharmacology and Law	BM23	3FT deg	g	12-16	MO/DO	M/D	32	BBCC	Ind	
Physical Geography and Law	MF3V	3FT deg	g	12-16	MO/DO	M/D	32	BBCC	Ind	
Planning Studies and Law	KM43	3FT deg	g	12-16	MO/DO	M/D	32	BBCC	Ind	
Politics and Law	MM31	3FT deg	g	12-16	MO/DO	M/D	32	BBCC	Ind	19
Property Studies and Law	KM2H	3FT deg	g	12-16	MO/DO	M/D	32	BBCC	Ind	

course details			98 expected requirements						96 entry stats	
TITLE	CODE	COURSE	SUBJECTS	A/AS	ND/C	AGNVQ	IB	SQA(H)	SQA	RATIO A/AS
Psychology and Law	ML3R	3FT deg		12-16	MO/DO	M/D	32	BBCC	Ind	
Public Policy and Management and Law	MM3C	3FT deg	g	12-16	MO/DO	M/D	32	BBCC	Ind	
Regional Planning and Development and Law	MK34	3FT deg	g	12-16	MO/DO	M/D	32	BBCC	Ind	
Social Policy and Law	LM43	3FT deg		12-16	MO/DO	M/D	32	BBCC	Ind	
Social Studies and Law	ML33	3FT deg	g	12-16	MO/DO	M/D	32	BBCC	Ind	25
Sociology and Law	LMH3	3FT deg		12-16	MO/DO	M/D	32	BBCC	Ind	
Sociology and Social Policy	LM4H	3FT deg		12-16	MO/DO	M/D	32	BBCC	Ind	
Public Administration (Legal Studies)	3M1M	2FT HND	g	4-8	N/MO	P/M	26	CCDD	Ind	1 2/6

Univ of MANCHESTER

Accounting and Law	MN34	4FT deg	g	ABB	Ind	D^	32$	CSYS	X	7 24/30
Chemistry with Patent Law	F1M3	4SW deg	C	ABB	X		35$	CSYS	X	5
English Law and French Law	M355	4FT deg	F	AAB	X	D^	32$	CSYS	X	13 28/30
Government and Law	MM13	3FT deg		ABB	Ind	D^	32$	CSYS	Ind	9 24/30
Law	M300	3FT deg		AAB	Ind	D^	32$	CSYS	X	11 26/30

MANCHESTER METROPOLITAN Univ

Law	M300	3FT deg	* g	BBC	Ind	Ind	Ind	Ind	Ind	14/24
Law with French	M3R1	4FT deg	F g	BBC	Ind	Ind	Ind	Ind	Ind	12/22
Law with German	M3R2	4FT deg	G g	BBC	Ind	Ind	Ind	Ind	Ind	14/20

MIDDLESEX Univ

Law	M300▼	3FT deg	* g	18	D	M$ go	28	Ind	Ind	
Joint Honours Degree Law	Y400	3FT deg	* g	16	3D	D$ go	28	Ind	Ind	

NAPIER Univ

Law	M320	3FT/4FT deg	E	CCC	Ind	Ind	Ind	BBCC	Ind	

NENE COLLEGE

American Studies with Law	Q4M3	3FT deg		DD	5M	M	24	CCC	Ind	
Art and Design with Law	W2M3	3FT deg	g	DD	5M	M	24	CCC	Ind	
Business Administration with Law	N1M3	3FT deg	g	10	M+1D	M	24	BCC	Ind	10/15
Drama with Law	W4M3	3FT deg								
Economics with Law	L1M3	3FT deg	g	6	5M	M	24	CCC	Ind	
Education with Law	X9M3	3FT deg	g	DD	5M	M	24	CCC	Ind	
Energy Management with Law	J9M3	3FT deg	g	EE	3M	P	24	CCC	Ind	
French with Law	R1M3	3FT deg	F g	DD	5M	Ind	24	CCC	Ind	
History with Law	V1M3	3FT deg	g	CD	5M	M	24	CCC	Ind	
Information Systems with Law	G5M3	3FT deg	g	6	5M	M	24	CCC	Ind	4/ 9
Law (LLB Hons)	M300	3FT deg	g	14	M+3D	M	Ind	Ind	Ind	10/18
Law with American Studies	M3Q4	3FT deg	g	10	3M+2D	M	24	CCC	Ind	
Law with Business Administration	M3N1	3FT deg	g	10	3M+2D	M	24	CCC	Ind	6/20
Law with Ecology	M3C9	3FT deg	g	10	3M+2D	M	24	CCC	Ind	
Law with Economics	M3L1	3FT deg	g	10	3M+2D	M	24	CCC	Ind	
Law with Education	M3X9	3FT deg	g	10	3M+2D	M	24	CCC	Ind	
Law with Energy Management	M3J9	3FT deg	g	10	3M+2D	M	24	CCC	Ind	
Law with European Union Studies	M3T2	3FT deg	g	10	3M+2D	M	24	CCC	Ind	
Law with French	M3R1	3FT deg	F g	10	3M+2D	M	24	CCC	Ind	
Law with History	M3V1	3FT deg	g	10	3M+2D	M	24	CCC	Ind	
Law with Industrial Archaeology	M3V6	3FT deg	g	10	3M+2D	M	24	CCC	Ind	
Law with Information Systems	M3G5	3FT deg	g	10	3M+2D	M	24	CCC	Ind	
Law with Marketing Communications	M3N5	3FT deg	g	10	3M+2D	M	24	CCC	Ind	
Law with Mathematics	M3G1	3FT deg	g	10	M3+2D	M	24	CCC	Ind	
Law with Media and Popular Culture	M3P4	3FT deg	g	10	3M+2D	M	24	CCC	Ind	

course details | 98 expected requirements | 96 entry stats

TITLE	CODE	COURSE	SUBJECTS	R/AS	NO/C	AGNVQ	IB	SQA(H)	SQA	RATIO	R/AS
Law with Music	M3W3	3FT deg	Mu g	10	3M+2D	M	24	CCC	Ind		
Law with Personal and Organisational Development	M3N6	3FT deg	g	10	3M+2D	M	24	CCC	Ind		
Law with Philosophy	M3V7	3FT deg	g	10	3M+2D	M	24	CCC	Ind		
Law with Politics	M3M1	3FT deg	g	10	3M+2D	M	24	CCC	Ind		
Law with Property Management	M3N8	3FT deg	g	10	3M+2D	M	24	CCC	Ind		
Law with Psychology	M3C8	3FT deg	g	10	3M+2D	M	24	CCC	Ind		7/12
Law with Sociology	M3L3	3FT deg	g	10	3M+2D	M	24	CCC	Ind		6/18
Law with Sport Studies	M3N7	3FT deg	g	10	3M	M	24	CCC	Ind		
Mathematics with Law	G1M3	3FT deg	M g	DD	Ind	Ind	24	CCC	Ind		
Politics with Law	M1M3	3FT deg	g	CD	5M	M	24	CCC	Ind		
Psychology with Law	C8M3	3FT deg	g	CC	5M+1D	M	24	CCC	Ind		12/22
Sociology with Law	L3M3	3FT deg	g	10	5M	M	24	CCC	Ind		
Sport Studies with Law	N7M3	3FT deg	Ss/Pe g	12	M+2D	M	24	BBB	Ind		

Univ of NEWCASTLE

TITLE	CODE	COURSE	SUBJECTS	R/AS	NO/C	AGNVQ	IB	SQA(H)	SQA	RATIO	R/AS
Accounting and Law	NM43	3FT deg	* g	BBB	5D		30	AAAAB	Ind	21	26/28
Law	M300	3FT deg	*	ABB	Ind	Ind	35	AABBB	Ind	7	22/30
Law with French	M3R1	4FT deg	F	ABB	Ind	Ind	35	AABBB	Ind	7	22/30

Univ of Wales COLLEGE, NEWPORT

TITLE	CODE	COURSE	SUBJECTS	R/AS	NO/C	AGNVQ	IB	SQA(H)	SQA	RATIO	R/AS
Accounting and Legal Studies	MN34	3FT deg	*	8-10	MO	D$	24	CCCC	Ind		
Business and Legal Studies	MN31	3FT deg	*	8-10	MO	D$	24	CCCC	Ind		
Social Welfare and Legal Studies	LM43	3FT deg		8	M	M					
Business and Legal Studies	093M	2FT HND	*	4	4M	M$	Ind	Ind	Ind		

NORTH EAST WALES INST of HE

TITLE	CODE	COURSE	SUBJECTS	R/AS	NO/C	AGNVQ	IB	SQA(H)	SQA	RATIO	R/AS
Legal Services	003M	2FT HND		4-8	2M	P$	Ind	CC	N$		

Univ of NORTH LONDON

TITLE	CODE	COURSE	SUBJECTS	R/AS	NO/C	AGNVQ	IB	SQA(H)	SQA	RATIO	R/AS
Business and Law	MN31	3FT deg	* g	CC	Ind	Ind	Ind	Ind	Ind		
Caribbean Studies and Law	MT37	3FT deg	*	CC	Ind	Ind	Ind	BBCCC	Ind		
Law	M300	3FT deg	*	BCC	MO	M	$	BBCCC	Ind	11	10/18
Law and History	MV31	3FT deg	*	CC	Ind	Ind	Ind	Ind	Ind		
Law and Philosophy	MV37	3FT deg	*	CC	Ind	Ind	Ind	Ind	Ind		
Women's Studies and Law	MM39	3FT deg	*	CC	Ind	Ind	Ind	Ind	Ind		
Combined Honours Law	Y301	3FT deg	*	CC	MO	M	$	BBCCC	Ind		
Combined Honours Law in Business	Y400	3FT deg	* g	14	MO+4D	Ind	Ind	CCCC	Ind		

Univ of NORTHUMBRIA

TITLE	CODE	COURSE	SUBJECTS	R/AS	NO/C	AGNVQ	IB	SQA(H)	SQA	RATIO	R/AS
Criminology And Social Research	LM43	4FT deg	So g	BC	2M+2D	M	24	BCCC	Ind		
Criminology And Sociology	LM33	3FT deg	So g	BC	2M+2D	M	24	BCCC	Ind		
Law	M300	3FT/4FT deg	g	BBB	DO		32	AABBB	Ind	6	18/26
Law(Exempting) with French Law	M352	4FT deg	F g	BBB	DO		32	AABBB	Ind	5	20/28

Univ of NOTTINGHAM

TITLE	CODE	COURSE	SUBJECTS	R/AS	NO/C	AGNVQ	IB	SQA(H)	SQA	RATIO	R/AS
Law	M300	3FT deg	*	AAB	Ind		36$	Ind	Ind	18	28/30
Law and Politics	MM13	3FT deg	*	ABB	Ind		34	Ind	Ind	17	24/30
Law with French	M3R1	4FT deg	F	AAB	Ind		34$	Ind	Ind	20	28/30
Law with German	M3R2	4FT deg	G	ABB	Ind		34$	Ind	Ind	9	28/30

NOTTINGHAM TRENT Univ

TITLE	CODE	COURSE	SUBJECTS	R/AS	NO/C	AGNVQ	IB	SQA(H)	SQA	RATIO	R/AS
Law	M300	3FT deg	* g	BBC	1M+5D		Ind	ABBBB	Ind	10	18/26
Law (Europe with French)	M312	4FT deg	F g	BBC	1M+5D		Ind	ABBBB	Ind	4	18/26
Law (Europe with German)	M313	4FT deg	G g	BBC	1M+5D		Ind	ABBBB	Ind	3	18/22
Law (Sandwich)	M301	4SW deg	* g	BBC	1M+5D		Ind	ABBBB	Ind	6	18/28

Law 47

			98 expected requirements							96 entry stats	
TITLE	**CODE**	**COURSE**	**SUBJECTS**	**A/AS**	**NO/C**	**AGNVQ**	**IB**	**SQA(H)**	**SQA**	**RATIO**	**A/AS**
OXFORD Univ											
Law	M300	3FT deg	*	AAB	DO		36	AAAAA	Ind	4	26/30
Law with Law Studies in Europe (4 Yrs)	M355	4FT deg	L	AAB	DO		36	AAAAA	Ind	11	28/30
OXFORD BROOKES Univ											
Geography and the Phys Env/Law	FMV3	3FT deg									
Law	M300	3FT deg	*	BBC	Ind	D*3	Ind	Ind	Ind	13	15/24
Law/Accounting and Finance	MN34	3FT deg	* g	BCC-BBB	Ind	D*3	Ind	Ind	Ind	17	
Law/Anthropology	LM63	3FT deg	*	BCC-BBB	Ind	M*^/D*	Ind	Ind	Ind		
Law/Biological Chemistry	CM73	3FT deg									
Law/Business Administration & Management	MN31	3FT deg	* g	BBC-BBB	Ind	MB4/D*3	Ind	Ind	Ind	14	
Law/Cartography	FM83	3FT deg	* g	DDD-BBB	Ind	M*/D*3	Ind	Ind	Ind		
Law/Cell Biology	CMC3	3FT deg									
Law/Combined Studies	MY34	3FT deg		X		X	X	X			
Law/Computer Systems	GM63	3FT deg	* g	CDD-BBB	Ind	M*/D*3	Ind	Ind	Ind		
Law/Computing	GM53	3FT deg	* g	CDD-BBB	Ind	M*/D*3	Ind	Ind	Ind	3	
Law/Computing Mathematics	GM93	3FT deg	* g	CD-BBB	Ind	M*/D*3	Ind	Ind	Ind		
Law/Economics	LM13	3FT deg	* g	CCD-BBB	Ind	M*3/D*3	Ind	Ind	Ind	5	14/16
Law/Educational Studies	MX39	3FT deg	*	CC-BBB	Ind	M*3/D*3	Ind	Ind	Ind		
Law/Electronics	HM63	3FT deg	S/M	CC-BBB	Ind	M$/D*3	Ind	Ind	Ind		
Law/English Studies	MQ33	3FT deg	*	AB-BCC	Ind	M*^/D*3	Ind	Ind	Ind	19	
Law/Environmental Chemistry	MF31	3FT deg									
Law/Environmental Policy	KM33	3FT deg									
Law/Environmental Sciences	FMX3	3FT deg	S g	CD-BBB	Ind	DS/DS3	Ind	Ind	Ind	6	
Law/Exercise and Health	MB36	3FT deg	S g	DD-BBB	Ind	MS/D*3	Ind	Ind	Ind		
Law/Fine Art	MW31	3FT deg	Pf+A	BC-BBB	Ind	MA^/D*3	Ind	Ind	Ind		
Law/Food Science and Nutrition	DM43	3FT deg	S g	DD-BBB	Ind	MS/D*3	Ind	Ind	Ind	1	
Law/French Language & Contemporary Studies	MR3C	4SW deg	F	CDD-BBB	Ind	M^D*3	Ind	Ind	Ind	4	
Law/French Language and Literature	MR31	4SW deg	F	CDD-BBB	Ind	M^/D*3	Ind	Ind	Ind	12	
Law/Geography	LM83	3FT deg	*	CCD-BBB	Ind	M*/D*3	Ind	Ind	Ind	8	
Law/Geology	FM63	3FT deg	S/M g	DD-BBB	Ind	PS/D*3	Ind	Ind	Ind	1	
Law/Geotechnics	HM23	3FT deg	S/M/Ds/Es	DD-BBB	Ind	M$/D*3	Ind	Ind	Ind		
Law/German Language and Contemp Stud	MR3F	4SW deg	G	DDD-BBB	Ind	M^/D*3	Ind	Ind	Ind	5	
Law/German Language and Literature	MR32	4SW deg	G	DDD-BBB	Ind	M^/D*3	Ind	Ind	Ind		
Law/German Studies	MR3G	4SW deg	G	DDD-BBB	Ind	M^/D*3	Ind	Ind	Ind		
Law/Health Care (Post Exp)	BM73	3FT deg		X		X	X	X			
Law/History	MV31	3FT deg	*	CCD-BBB	Ind	M^/D*3	Ind	Ind	Ind	11	
Law/Hospitality Management Studies	MN37	3FT deg	*	DDD-BBB	Ind	M*3/D*3	Ind	Ind	Ind		
Law/Human Biology	BM13	3FT deg									
Law/Information Systems	GMM3	3FT deg	* g	CDD-BBB	Ind	M*/D*3	Ind	Ind	Ind	1	
Law/Intelligent Systems	GM83	3FT deg	* g	CD-BBB	Ind	M*/D*3	Ind	Ind	Ind		
Leisure Planning/Law	KMH3	3FT deg									
Marketing Management/Law	MN3N	3FT deg	* g	BCC-BBB	Ind	D*3	Ind	Ind	Ind	13	
Mathematics/Law	GM13	3FT deg	M	DD-BBB	Ind	M^/D*3	Ind	Ind	Ind	7	
Music/Law	MW33	3FT deg	Mu	DD-BBB	Ind	M/D*3	Ind	Ind	Ind		
Palliative Care/Law (Post Exp)	BMR3	3FT deg		X		X	X	X			
Planning Studies/Law	KM43	3FT deg	* g	DDD-BBB	Ind	M*/D*3	Ind	Ind	Ind		
Politics/Law	MM31	3FT deg	*	CCC-AB	Ind	M^/D*3	Ind	Ind	Ind	31	
Psychology/Law	CM83	3FT deg	* g	BBB-BBC	Ind	M^/D*3	Ind	Ind	Ind	37	
Publishing/Law	MP35	3FT deg	* g	CCD-BBB	Ind	M$/D*3	Ind	Ind	Ind		
Rehabilitation/Law (Post Exp)	BMT3	3FT deg		X		X	X	X			
Sociology/Law	LM33	3FT deg	*	BCC-BBB	Ind	M*^/D*3	Ind	Ind	Ind	20	
Software Engineering/Law	GM73	3FT deg	* g	CDD-BBB	Ind	M*/D*3	Ind	Ind	Ind		

TITLE	CODE	COURSE	SUBJECTS	A/AS	ND/C	AGNVQ	IB	SQA(H)	SQA	RATIO	A/AS
Statistics/Law	GM43	3FT deg	* g	DD-BBB	Ind	M*/D*3	Ind	Ind	Ind		
Telecommunications/Law	HMP3	3FT deg									
Tourism/Law	MP37	3FT deg	* g	CCD-BBB	Ind	M*3/D*3	Ind	Ind	Ind		
Water Resources/Law	HMF3	3FT deg									

Univ of PAISLEY

European Business Law	M335	3FT deg	* g	CC	Ind	Ind	Ind	BCCC	Ind		

Univ of PLYMOUTH

TITLE	CODE	COURSE	SUBJECTS	A/AS	ND/C	AGNVQ	IB	SQA(H)	SQA	RATIO	A/AS
Applied Economics with Law	L1M3	3FT deg	* g	BCC-BBC	MO	M$^	Ind	BBBB	Ind	12	
Applied Economics with Maritime Law	LM1J	3FT deg	* g	CDD-CCD	MO	M$^	Ind	BCCC	Ind		
Business Economics with Law	L1MH	3FT deg	* g	BCC-BBC	MO	M$^	Ind	BBBB	Ind		
Business Economics with Maritime Law	MLH1	3FT deg	* g	CDD-CCD	MO	M$^	Ind	BCCC	Ind		
European Economics with Law	L1MJ	3FT deg	* g	BCC-BBC	MO	M$^	Ind	BBBB	Ind		
European Economics with Maritime Law	MLHC	3FT deg	* g	CDD-CCD	MO	M$^	Ind	BCCC	Ind		
Fisheries Studies with Maritime Law	J6M3	3FT deg	Ap g	14	5M $	M$	Ind	CCCC	Ind		
Geography with Criminal Justice	FM8J	3FT deg	Gy g	16-18	X	M$^	Ind	ABBB	Ind		
Geography with Law	F8M3	3FT deg	Gy g	BCC	X	M$^	Ind	ABBB	Ind	17	
Hydrography with Maritime Law	F8MH	3FT deg	2(M/P/C/Ap) g	14	5M $	M$	Ind	CCCC	Ind		
Law	M300	3FT deg	Ap g	BCC-BBC	DO	D12^	Ind	BBBB$	Ind	10	18/26
Law with Applied Economics	M3L1	3FT deg	Ap g	BCC-BBC	DO	D12^	Ind	BBBB$	Ind		
Law with Business	M3N1	3FT deg	Ap g	BCC-BBC	DO	D12^	Ind	BBBB$	Ind	20	16/22
Law with Computing	M3G5	3FT deg	Ap g	BCC-BBC	DO	D12^	Ind	BBBB$	Ind		
Law with French	M3R1	3FT deg	E g	BCC-BBC	DO	D12^	Ind	BBBB$	Ind		
Law with Geography	M3F8	3FT deg	Ap g	BCC-BBC	DO	D12^	Ind	BBBB$	Ind		
Law with German	M3R2	3FT deg	G g	BCC-BBC	DO	D12^	Ind	BBBB$	Ind		
Law with International Relations	M3MC	3FT deg	Ap g	BCC-BBC	DO	D12^	Ind	BBBB$	Ind		
Law with Italian	M3R3	3FT deg	Ap g	BCC-BBC	DO	D12^	Ind	BBBB$	Ind		
Law with Languages	M3T9	3FT deg	L g	BCC-BBC	DO	D12^	Ind	BBBB$	Ind		
Law with Politics	M3M1	3FT deg	Ap g	BCC-BBC	DO	D12^	Ind	BBBB$	Ind	31	
Law with Psychology	M3C8	3FT deg	Ap g	BCC-BBC	DO	D12^	Ind	BBBB$	Ind	31	
Law with Resources, Manufacturing and the Env	M3F9	3FT deg	Ap g	BCC-BBC	DO	D12^	Ind	BBBB$	Ind		
Law with Social Policy	M3L4	3FT deg	Ap g	BCC-BBC	DO	D12^	Ind	BBBB$	Ind		
Law with Sociology	M3L3	3FT deg	Ap g	BCC-BBC	DO	D12^	Ind	BBBB$	Ind	46	
Law with Spanish	M3R4	3FT deg	Sp g	BCC-BBC	DO	D12^	Ind	BBBB$	Ind		
Law with Transport	M3N9	3FT deg	Ap g	BCC-BBC	DO	D12^	Ind	BBBB$	Ind		
Marine Technology with Maritime Law	J6MH	3FT deg	2(M/P/C) g	14	5M $	M$	Ind	CCCC	Ind		
Maritime Business with Maritime Law	N1M3	3FT deg	* g	18	5M	M$	Ind	CCCC	Ind	4	
Modern Languages with Law	T9M3	3FT/4SW deg	L g	C	Ind	Ind	Ind	Ind	Ind		
Ocean Science with Maritime Law	F7M3	3FT deg	S g	14-16	5M $	M$	Ind	CCCC	Ind		
Political Economy with Law	LM1H	3FT deg	Ap g	BCC-BBC	MO $	M$^	Ind	BBBB	Ind		
Political Economy with Maritime Law	MLHD	3FT deg	Ap g	CDD-CCD	MO $	M$^	Ind	BCCC	Ind		
Politics with Criminal Justice	M1MJ	3FT deg	* g	16	3M	M$	Ind	BBBC$	Ind	4	10/20
Politics with Law	M1M3	3FT deg	* g	BCC	Ind	D12^	Ind	BBBC$	Ind	9	
Psychology with Criminal Justice	C8MH	3FT/4SW deg	Ap g	BBB	4D	M12^	Ind	BBBC$	Ind	25	12/20
Psychology with Law	C8M3	3FT/4SW deg	Ap g	BBC	MO+3D	M12^	Ind	BBBC$	Ind	7	20/26
Social Policy with Criminal Justice	L4MH	3FT deg	* g	16	3M	M$	Ind	BBBC$	Ind	5	6/18
Social Policy with Law	L4M3	3FT deg	* g	BCC	Ind	D12^	Ind	BBBC$	Ind		
Sociology with Criminal Justice	L3M3	3FT deg	* g	16	3M	M$	Ind	BBBC$	Ind	5	8/18
Sociology with Law	L3MH	3FT deg	* g	BCC	Ind	D12^	Ind	BBBC$	Ind	28	
Transport with Maritime Law	N9MH	3FT deg	* g	14	5M	M$	Ind	CCCC	Ind	5	
Underwater Studies with Maritime Law	F9MH	3FT deg	Ap g	14-16	5M $	M$	Ind	CCCC	Ind		

Law 47

| | | | 98 expected requirements | | | | | | | 96 entry stats | |
| course details | | | | | | | | | | | |
TITLE	CODE	COURSE	SUBJECTS	A/AS	NO/C	AGNVQ	IB	SQA(H)	SQA	RATIO	A/AS
Univ of PORTSMOUTH											
Criminology and Criminal Justice	M330	3FT deg	So+Ps/Lw	16-20	1M+4D	M*$6/^	26	BBBB	Ind		6/16
Law and Accounting	MN34	3FT/4SW deg	*	18	MO+2D	D$6/^ go	Dip	BBBCC	Ind		
Law and Business	MN31	3FT deg	*	18	MO+2D	D$6/^ go	Dip	BBBCC	Ind		
Law and Economics	ML31	3FT deg	*	18	MO+2D	D$6/^ go	Dip	BBBCC	Ind		
QUEEN MARY & WESTFIELD COLL (Univ of London)											
English and European Law	M301	4FT deg		25	DO	D	32$	AABBB			
Law	M300	3FT deg		ABB	DO	D^	32$	AABBB			
Law and Economics	LM13	3FT deg	g	ABB	DO	D^	32$	AABBB			
Law and German	MR32	4FT deg	G	ABB	DO	D^	32$	AABBB			
Law and Politics	MM13	3FT deg		ABB	DO	D^	32$	AABBB			
Law with German Language	M3R2	4FT deg	G	ABB	DO	D^	32$	AABBB			
QUEEN'S Univ Belfast											
Common and Civil Law with French	M3R1	4FT deg	F g	ABB	X	D*_^ go	34$	AAABB	X	5	26/30
Common and Civil Law with Italian	M3R3	4FT deg									
Common and Civil Law with Spanish	M3R4	4FT deg	* g	ABB	7D	D*^ go	34$	AAABB	Ind	5	28/30
Law	M300	3FT deg	* g	ABB	7D	D*^ go	34$	AAABB	Ind	4	26/30
Law and Accounting	MN34	4FT deg	* g	AAB	7D	D*^ go	35$	AAABB	Ind	8	26/30
Law with Politics	M3M1	3FT deg	* g	ABB	7D	D*^ go	34$	AAABB	Ind	7	26/30
Univ of READING											
Law	M300	3FT deg	*	ABB	Ind	DB^	33	ABBBB	Ind	16	20/27
Law with French Law	M351	4FT deg	F	ABB	Ind	DB_^	33$	ABBBB$	Ind	16	
Law with Legal Studies in Europe	M355	4FT deg	*	ABB	Ind	DB^	33	ABBBB	Ind		
ROBERT GORDON Univ											
Law and Management	M390	3FT/4FT deg	* g	CE	N	Ind	Ind	BBCC$	Ind	4	
SOAS:Sch of Oriental & African St (U of London)											
Law	M300	3FT deg		24	Ind		32	BBBBB	Ind	9	22/26
Law and Amharic	MT37	4FT deg		24	Ind		32	BBBBB	Ind	3	
Law and Arabic	MT36	4FT deg		24	Ind		32	BBBBB	Ind	17	
Law and Bengali	MT35	3FT deg		24	Ind		32	BBBBB	Ind		
Law and Burmese	MT3M	4FT deg		24	Ind		32	BBBBB	Ind		
Law and Chinese	MT33	4FT deg		24	Ind		32	BBBBB	Ind	5	
Law and Development Studies	MM93	3FT deg		24	Ind		32	BBBBB	Ind	2	
Law and Economics	LM13	3FT deg	g	24	Ind		32	BBBBB	Ind	8	
Law and Geography	LM83	3FT deg		24	Ind		32	BBBBB	Ind		
Law and Georgian	MT39	3FT deg		24	Ind		32	BBBBB	Ind		
Law and Gujarati	MTH5	3FT deg		24	Ind		32	BBBBB	Ind		
Law and Hausa	MT3R	4FT deg		24	Ind		32	BBBBB	Ind		
Law and Hebrew	MQ39	4FT deg		24	Ind		32	BBBBB	Ind		
Law and Hindi	MT3N	3FT/4FT deg		24	Ind		32	BBBBB	Ind		
Law and History	MV31	3FT deg		24	Ind		32	BBBBB	Ind		
Law and Indonesian	MTHM	3FT/4FT deg		24	Ind		32	BBBBB	Ind		
Law and Japanese	MT34	4FT deg		24	Ind		32	BBBBB	Ind	9	
Law and Korean	MTHN	4FT deg		24	Ind		32	BBBBB	Ind		
Linguistics and Law	MQ33	3FT deg									
Nepali and Law	MTJ5	3FT deg		24	Ind		32	BBBBB	Ind		
Persian and Law	MT3Q	3FT deg		24	Ind		32	BBBBB	Ind		
Politics and Law	MM13	3FT deg		24	Ind		32	BBBBB	Ind	5	
Sanskrit and Law	MQ3X	3FT deg		24	Ind		32	BBBBB	Ind		
Sinhalese and Law	MTJM	3FT deg		24	Ind		32	BBBBB	Ind		

				98 expected requirements						96 entry stats
course details										
TITLE	CODE	COURSE	SUBJECTS	A/AS	ND/C	AGNVQ	IB	SQA(H)	SQA	RATIO A/AS
Social Anthropology and Law	LM63	3FT deg		24	Ind		32	BBBBB	Ind	
South Asian Studies and Law	TM5H	3FT deg								
Study of Religions and Law	MV38	3FT deg		24	Ind		32	BBBBB	Ind	2
Swahili and Law	MT3T	4FT deg		24	Ind		32	BBBBB	Ind	
Tamil and Law	MTJN	3FT deg		24	Ind		32	BBBBB	Ind	
Thai and Law	TM53	3FT/4FT deg		24	Ind		32	BBBBB	Ind	
Turkish and Law	MT3P	4FT deg		24	Ind		32	BBBBB	Ind	
Urdu and Law *	TMM3	3FT deg		24	Ind		32	BBBBB	Ind	
Vietnamese and Law	TMN3	4FT deg		24	Ind		32	BBBBB	Ind	

Univ of SHEFFIELD

TITLE	CODE	COURSE	SUBJECTS	A/AS	ND/C	AGNVQ	IB	SQA(H)	SQA	RATIO A/AS
Civil Engineering and Law	H2M3	4FT deg	M g	AAB	X	X	35$	AAAA$		
Law	M300	3FT deg	* g	AAB	1M+5D	D^	35	AAAA	Ind	8	26/30
Law and Criminology	M330	3FT deg	* g	AAB	1M+5D	D^	35	AAAA	Ind	11	24/30
Law with French	MR31	4FT deg	F g	AAB	X	D^	35$	AAAA$	Ind	7	28/30
Law with German	MR32	4FT deg	G g	AAB	X	D^	35$	AAAA$	Ind	3	26/30
Law with Spanish	MR34	4FT deg	Sp g	ABB	X	D^	33$	AAAB$	Ind	11	26/28
Software Engineering and Law (MEng)	GM73	4FT deg	M g	ABB	2M+4D$	X	33$	AAAB$		

SHEFFIELD HALLAM Univ

TITLE	CODE	COURSE	SUBJECTS	A/AS	ND/C	AGNVQ	IB	SQA(H)	SQA	RATIO A/AS
International Financial and Legal Studies	MN33	4FT deg	F/G	14	3M+3D	M	Ind	Ind	Ind	
LLB (Canada)	M3T9	3FT deg	*	20	DO	M4	Ind	Ind	Ind	
LLB (Law)	M300	3FT deg	*	20	DO	M4	Ind	Ind	Ind	
LLB/Maitrise En Droit (Francaise)	M301	3FT deg	F	20	DO	4M	Ind	Ind	Ind	
Combined Studies *Law*	Y400	3FT deg	*	18	2M	M	Ind	Ind	Ind	

Univ of SOUTHAMPTON

TITLE	CODE	COURSE	SUBJECTS	A/AS	ND/C	AGNVQ	IB	SQA(H)	SQA	RATIO A/AS
Accounting and Law	NM43	4FT deg	* g	24	Ind	D$^ go	32	AABBB	Ind	7	20/28
Law	M300	3FT deg	*	ABB	2M+6D	D$^ go	32	AAABB	Ind	4	22/30
Politics and Law	MM13	3FT deg	* g	24	Ind	D$^ go	32	AABBB	Ind	13	20/28

SOUTHAMPTON INST

TITLE	CODE	COURSE	SUBJECTS	A/AS	ND/C	AGNVQ	IB	SQA(H)	SQA	RATIO A/AS
Accountancy and Law	NM43	3FT deg	*	10	MO	M$	Dip	CCCC	N	6	7/10
Business and Law	NM13	3FT deg	*	10	MO	M$	Dip	CCCC	N	3	8/14
Criminology	M330	3FT deg	*	16	MO	M$	Dip	BBBB	N	
Law	M300	3FT deg	*	16-18	M+D $	M$	32$	BBBB	N	3	12/20
Legal Studies	M301	3FT deg	*	12	MO	M$	Dip	CCCC	N	

SOUTH BANK Univ

TITLE	CODE	COURSE	SUBJECTS	A/AS	ND/C	AGNVQ	IB	SQA(H)	SQA	RATIO A/AS
Law	M300	3FT deg	* g	BCC	6D	D go	Ind	Ind	Ind	
Law and Accounting	MN34	3FT deg	Ec/Ac g	14-18	2M+4D	D go	Ind	Ind	Ind	
Law and Business Information Technology	GM73	3FT deg	M g	14-18	2M+4D	D go	Ind	Ind	Ind	
Law and Computing	GM53	3FT deg	M g	14-18	2M+4D	D go	Ind	Ind	Ind	
Law and Economics	LM13	3FT deg	Ec/Bu g	14-18	2M+4D	D go	Ind	Ind	Ind	
Law and English Studies	MQ33	3FT deg	E g	14-18	X	M^ go	Ind	Ind	Ind	
Law and European Studies	MT32	3FT deg	* g	14-18	2M+4D	D go	Ind	Ind	Ind	
Law and Food Policy	DM43	3FT deg	S g	14-18	2M+4D	D go	Ind	Ind	Ind	
Law and French	MR31	3FT deg	F g	14-18	2M+4D	D go	Ind	Ind	Ind	
Law and German	MR3F	3FT deg	G g	14-18	2M+4D	D go	Ind	Ind	Ind	
Law and German - ab initio	MR32	3FT deg	* g	14-18	2M+4D	D go	Ind	Ind	Ind	
Law and History	MV31	3FT deg	H g	14-18	2M+4D	D^ go	Ind	Ind	Ind	
Law and Housing	KM4H	3FT deg	* g	14-18	2M+4D	D^ go	Ind	Ind	Ind	
Law and Human Biology	BM13	3FT deg	S g	14-18	2M+4D	M go	Ind	Ind	Ind	
Law and Human Resource Management	MN36	3FT deg	* g	14-18	2M+4D	M go	Ind	Ind	Ind	

Law 47

	course details			98 expected requirements						96 entry stats
TITLE	CODE	COURSE	SUBJECTS	A/AS	ND/C	RGNVQ	IB	SQA(H)	SQA	RATIO A/AS
Management and Law	MN31	3FT deg	* g	14-18	2M+4D	D go	Ind	Ind	Ind	
Marketing and Law	MN35	3FT deg	* g	14-18	2M+4D	D go	Ind	Ind	Ind	
Nutrition and Law	BM43	3FT deg	S g	14-18	2M+4D	D go	Ind	Ind	Ind	
Politics and Housing	MK34	3FT deg	* g	14-18	2M+4D	M go	Ind	Ind	Ind	
Politics and Law	MM31	3FT deg	g	14-18	2M+4D	D go	Ind	Ind	Ind	
Psychology and Law	CM83	3FT deg	S g	14-18	2M+4D	M go	Ind	Ind	Ind	
Social Policy and Law	LM4H	3FT deg	* g	14-18	2M+4D	D go	Ind	Ind	Ind	
Sociology and Law	LM33	3FT deg	* g	14-18	2M+4D	D go	Ind	Ind	Ind	
Spanish - ab initio and Law	MR34	3FT deg	* g	14-18	2M+4D	D go	Ind	Ind	Ind	
Spanish and Law	MR3K	3FT deg	Sp g	14-18	2M+4D	M^ go	Ind	Ind	Ind	
Sports Science and Law	BM63	3FT deg	S g	14-18	2M+4D	M go	Ind	Ind	Ind	
Technology and Law	JM93	3FT deg	* g	14-18	2M+4D	D go	Ind	Ind	Ind	
Tourism and Law	MP37	3FT deg	L g	14-18	2M+4D	D go	Ind	Ind	Ind	
Urban Studies and Law	KM4J	3FT deg	* g	14-18	2M+4D	D go	Ind	Ind	Ind	
World Theatre and Law	MW34	3FT deg	* g	14-18	2M+4D	D go	Ind	Ind	Ind	

STAFFORDSHIRE Univ

TITLE	CODE	COURSE	SUBJECTS	A/AS	ND/C	RGNVQ	IB	SQA(H)	SQA	RATIO A/AS
Advice Work and Law	M391	2FT Dip	g	12	3M	M	24	BCC	Ind	3
Law	M300	3FT deg	g	18	HN	M^	26	BBBB	Ind	3	8/19
Law/Accounting	MN34	3FT deg	g	16	MO+2D	M$	24	BBB	Ind	3	8/18
Law/American Studies	MQ34	3FT deg	g	CCC	HN	M^	27	BBBB	Ind	4	6/22
Law/Business Studies	MN31	3FT deg	g	18	HN	M^	26	BBBB	Ind	6	10/24
Law/Environmental Studies	MF39	3FT deg	g	16	HN	M^	26	BBBB	Ind	
Law/French	MR31	3FT/4SW deg	F g	18	HN	M^	26	BBBB	Ind	4
Law/Geography	ML38	3FT deg	g	16	HN	M^	26	BBBB	Ind	4
Law/History	MV31	3FT deg	H g	CCC	HN	M^	26	BBB	Ind	4	10/16
Law/History of Art and Design	MV34	3FT deg	g	CCC	HN	M^	27	BBBB	Ind	
Law/Information Systems	MG35	3FT deg	g	14	3D	M^	26	BBBB	Ind	6
Law/International Relations	MM3C	3FT deg	g	18	HN	M^	26	BBBB	Ind	6
Legal Studies/American Studies	MQ3K	3FT deg	g	CCC	HN	M^	27	BBBB	Ind	
Legal Studies/Business Studies	MN3C	3FT deg	g	18	HN	M^	26	BBBB	Ind	9
Legal Studies/Computing	GM53	3FT deg	g	18	HN	M^	Ind	BBB	Ind	
Legal Studies/Economic Studies	LMCH	3FT deg								
Legal Studies/Environmental Studies	MF3X	3FT deg	g	16	HN	M^	26	BBBB	Ind	
Legal Studies/French	MR3C	3FT/4SW deg	F g	18	HN	M^	26	BBBB	Ind	
Legal Studies/Geography	ML3V	3FT deg	g	16	HN	M^	26d	BBBB	Ind	
Legal Studies/History	MV3C	3FT deg	H g	CCC	HN	M^	27	BBBB	Ind	6
Legal Studies/History of Art and Design	MV3K	3FT deg	g	CCC	HN	M^	27	BBBB	Ind	
Legal Studies/Information Systems	MG3M	3FT deg	g	14	3D	M^	26	BBBB	Ind	
Legal Studies/International Relations	MM3D	3FT deg	g	18	HN	M^	26	BBBB	Ind	
Literature/Law	QM33	3FT deg	El g	CCC	HN	M^	27	BBBB	Ind	4	12/14
Literature/Legal Studies	QM3H	3FT deg	El g	CCC	HN	M^	27	BBBB	Ind	
Media Studies/Law	MP34	3FT deg	g	18	HN	M^	27	BBBB	Ind	13
Media Studies/Legal Studies	MPH4	3FT deg	g	18	HN	M^	27	BBBB	Ind	6
Philosophy/Law	VM73	3FT deg	g	CCC	HN	M^	27	BBBB	Ind	4
Philosophy/Legal Studies	VM7H	3FT deg	g	CCC	HN	M^	27	BBBB	Ind	
Politics/Law	MMC3	3FT deg	g	18	HN	M^	26	BBBB	Ind	3	12/20
Politics/Legal Studies	MMCH	3FT deg	g	18	HN	M^	26d	BBBB	Ind	
Psychology and Criminology	CM83	3FT deg								
Psychology/Law	LM73	3FT deg	g	18	3D	M^	26	BBBB	Ind	5	12/18
Psychology/Legal Studies	LM7H	3FT deg	g	18	3D	M^	26	BBBB	Ind	18
Sociology/Law	LM33	3FT deg	g	18	3D	M^	26	BBBB	Ind	5	10/20
Sociology/Legal Studies	LM3H	3FT deg	g	18	3D	M^	26	BBBB	Ind	4

TITLE	CODE	COURSE	SUBJECTS	A/AS	NO/C	RGNVQ	IB	SQA(H)	SQA	RATIO A/AS
Spanish/Law	RM43	3FT/4SW deg	g	18	HN	M^	26	BBBB	Ind	5
Spanish/Legal Studies	RM4H	3FT/4SW deg	g	18	HN	M^	26	BCC	Ind	
Women's Studies/Law	MM93	3FT deg	g	18	HN	M^	26d	BBBB	Ind	7
Women's Studies/Legal Studies	MM9H	3FT deg	g	18	HN	M^	26	BBBB	Ind	

Univ of STIRLING

TITLE	CODE	COURSE	SUBJECTS	A/AS	NO/C	RGNVQ	IB	SQA(H)	SQA	RATIO A/AS
Accountancy/Business Law	MN34	4FT deg	g	BCC	HN	Ind	33	BBBB	HN	
Business Law (General only)	M340	4FT deg	g	BCC	Ind	Ind	33	BBBB	HN	
Business Studies/Business Law	MN31	4FT deg	g	BCC	Ind	Ind	33	BBBB	HN	
Economics/Business Law	L1M3	4FT deg	g	CCC	Ind	Ind	28	BBCC	HN	
Human Resources Management/Business Law	MN36	4FT deg	g	BCC	Ind	Ind	33	BBBB	HN	
Management Science/Business Law	NM13	4FT deg	g	BCC	Ind	Ind	33	BBBB	HN	
Marketing/Business Law	MN35	4FT deg	g	BCC	Ind	Ind	33	BBBB	HN	
Politics/Business Law	MM13	4FT deg	g	BCC	HN	Ind	33	BBBB	HN	
Spanish/Business Law	MR34	4FT deg	g	BCC	HN	Ind	33	BBBB	HN	

Univ of STRATHCLYDE

TITLE	CODE	COURSE	SUBJECTS	A/AS	NO/C	RGNVQ	IB	SQA(H)	SQA	RATIO A/AS
Computer Science with Law	G5M3	4FT deg	M+E	CCC	HN		Ind	AABB$	HN	
European Law	M333	5FT deg	E+M+L g	BBB	Ind		30$	AAAAB$	Ind	
Law (Based on Scots Law)	M320	3FT/4FT deg	E+M g	BBB	Ind		30	AAAAB$	Ind	
Law and a Modern Language	MT32	5FT deg	E+L g	BBB	Ind		30$	AAAAB$	Ind	

UNIVERSITY COLLEGE SUFFOLK

TITLE	CODE	COURSE	SUBJECTS	A/AS	NO/C	RGNVQ	IB	SQA(H)	SQA	RATIO A/AS
Business (Law)	31MN	2FT HND	*	E	N	P*	Ind	Ind	Ind	

Univ of SUNDERLAND

TITLE	CODE	COURSE	SUBJECTS	A/AS	NO/C	RGNVQ	IB	SQA(H)	SQA	RATIO A/AS
Business and Legal Studies	MN31	3FT deg	* g	18	1M+4D	D	26	BBBCC	N	6 10/16

Univ of SURREY

TITLE	CODE	COURSE	SUBJECTS	A/AS	NO/C	RGNVQ	IB	SQA(H)	SQA	RATIO A/AS
French and Law	RM13	4SW deg	F	22	3M+3D$		30$	ABBCC	Ind	3 14/26
German and Law	RM23	4SW deg	G	22	3M+3D$		30$	ABBCC	Ind	5
Russian and Law	RM83	4SW deg	*	18	3M+3D$		30$	ABBCC	Ind	2 12/22

Univ of SUSSEX

TITLE	CODE	COURSE	SUBJECTS	A/AS	NO/C	RGNVQ	IB	SQA(H)	SQA	RATIO A/AS
European Commercial Law	M310	3FT deg	*	BBB	MO	M*6	$	Ind	Ind	
European Commercial Law with a Language (4 Yrs)	M333	4FT deg	L	BBB	MO $	M*^	$	Ind	Ind	
Law	M300	3FT deg	*	BBB	MO	M*6	$	Ind	Ind	
Law in English and American Studies	M3QK	3FT deg	*	BBB	MO	M*6	$	Ind	Ind	
Law in European Studies	M3T2	4FT deg	L	BBB	MO $	M*^	$	Ind	Ind	
Law with North American Studies	M3Q4	4FT deg	*	BBB	MO	M*6	$	Ind	Ind	
Law with a Language (4 Yrs)	M301	4FT deg	L	BBB	MO $	M*^	$	Ind	Ind	

Univ of Wales SWANSEA

TITLE	CODE	COURSE	SUBJECTS	A/AS	NO/C	RGNVQ	IB	SQA(H)	SQA	RATIO A/AS
Business, Economics and Law	LM13	3FT deg	* g	BBB	1M+5D$	Ind	30$	BBBBBS	Ind	
Chemistry with Law with a year abroad	F1MH	4FT deg	C	BBC-BCC	2M+3D$	DS^	30$	ABBBB$	Ind	4
Chemistry with Law with a year in Industry	F1MJ	4FT deg	C	BCD-CCC	3M+2D$	MS^/DS	26$	BBBCC$	Ind	5
French (with Legal Studies)	R1M3	4FT deg	F	BBB-BBC	6D $	Ind	32$	AABBB$	Ind	5
German (with Legal Studies)	R2M3	4FT deg	G	BBB-BBC	1M+5D$	Ind	32$	AABBB$	Ind	
Italian (with Legal Studies)	R3M3	4FT deg	L	BBB-BBC	1M+5D$	Ind	30$	ABBBB$	Ind	
Law	M300	3FT deg	*	ABC-BBB	6D	Ind	32	AABBB	Ind	3 16/26
Law and American Studies	MQ34	3FT deg	*	BBB	Ind	Ind	32	ABBBB	Ind	
Law and Business Studies	MN31	3FT deg	* g	BBB	6D	Ind	32	AABBB	Ind	6 16/24
Law and Economics	ML31	3FT deg	* g	BBB-BBC	1M+5D	Ind	30$	ABBBB$	Ind	3 14/26
Law and French	MR31	4FT deg	F	BBB	6D $	Ind	32$	AABBB$	Ind	6 18/20
Law and German	MR32	4FT deg	G	BBB	6D $	Ind	32$	AABBB$	Ind	11
Law and Italian	MR33	4FT deg	L/*	BBB	6D $	Ind	32$	AABBB$	Ind	

Law 47

	course details			98 expected requirements						96 entry stats	
TITLE	CODE	COURSE	SUBJECTS	A/AS	ND/C	RGNVQ	IB	SQR(H)	SQR	RATIO	A/AS
Law and Politics	MM13	3FT deg	*	BBB-BBC	1M+5D	Ind	30	ABBBB	Ind	4	14/24
Law and Psychology	LM73	3FT deg	*g	BBB-BCC	1M+5D	Ind	30$	ABBBB$	Ind		
Law and Russian	MR38	4FT deg	L/*	BBB	6D	Ind	30$	ABBBB$	Ind		
Law and Spanish	MR34	4FT deg	L/*	BBB	6D	Ind	32$	AABBB$	Ind	4	
Law and Welsh	MQ35	3FT deg	W	BBB-BBC	1M+5D$	X	30$	Ind	Ind	4	
Psychology and Law	LM7H	3FT deg	*g	BBC	1M+5D	Ind	30$	ABBBB$	Ind		
Russian (with Legal Studies)	R8M3	4FT deg	L/*	BBC-BCC	1M+5D$	Ind	28$	BBBBC$	Ind		
Spanish (with Legal Studies)	R4M3	4FT deg	L/*	BBB-BBC	1M+5D$	Ind	30$	ABBBB$	Ind	1	
Welsh (with Legal Studies)	Q5M3	3FT/4FT deg	W	CCC	1M+4D$	X	Ind	Ind	Ind		

SWANSEA INST of HE

Law	M300	3FT deg		EE						3	8/18

Univ of TEESSIDE

Applied Science and Consumer Law	F9M3	3FT deg	*g	8-12	4M	M	Ind	CCC	Ind	1	8/12
Criminology (Jt Hons available)	L3M3	3FT deg	*	16-18	MO	M	Ind	BBCCC	Ind	7	10/18
History and Law	MV31	3FT deg	*	14	Ind		Ind	Ind	Ind		
Law	M300	3FT deg	*	18	DO	D	Ind	Ind	Ind	4	10/22
Law and Politics	MM31	3FT deg	*	18	DO	D	Ind	Ind	Ind		
Psychology and Criminology	LM3J	3FT deg	S	14-16	Ind	Ind	Ind	BBCCC	Ind		
Modular Degree Scheme Criminology	Y401	3FT deg									
Modular Degree Scheme Law	Y401	3FT deg									

THAMES VALLEY Univ

Accounting with Law	N4M3	3FT deg		8-12	MO	M	26	CCC			
Business Economics with Law	L1MH	3FT deg		8-12	MO	M	26	CCC			
Business Studies with Law (Dip)	N1M3	3FT/4SW deg		8-12	MO	M	26	CCC			
Criminal Justice with Community Law	M301	3FT deg		8-12	MO	M	26	CCC			
Criminal Justice with Law	M302	3FT deg		8-12	MO	M		CCC			
English Language and Communications with Eur Law	Q1MH	3FT deg		8-12	MO	M	26	CCC			
English Language and Communications with Law	Q1M3	3FT deg		8-12	MO	M	26	CCC			
Environmental Policy and Management with Law	F9M3	3FT deg		8-12	MO	M	26	CCC			
European Law with English Language Studies	M3QC	3FT deg		8-12	MO	M	26	CCC			
European Law with French	M3RC	3FT deg		8-12	MO	M	26	CCC			
European Law with German	M3RF	3FT deg		8-12	MO	M	26	CCC			
European Law with Law	M333	3FT deg		8-12	MO	M	26	CCC			
European Law with Spanish	M3RK	3FT deg		8-12	MO	M	26	CCC			
European Studies with European Law	T2MH	3FT deg		8-12	MO	M	26	CCC			
European Studies with Law	T2M3	3FT deg		8-12	MO	M	26	CCC			
French with European Law	R1M3	3FT deg		8-12	MO	M	26	CCC			
German with European Law	R2M3	3FT deg		8-12	MO	M	26	CCC			
Health Studies with Community Law	L4M3	3FT deg		8-12	MO	M	26	CCC			
Human Resource Management with Community Law	N6MH	3FT deg		8-12	MO	M	26	CCC			
Law (LLB)	M300▼	3FT deg	*	12	MO	M	26	CCC			
Law with Business	M3N1	3FT deg		8-12	MO	M	26	CCC			
Law with Community Law	M303	3FT deg		8-12	MO	M	26	CCC			
Law with Criminal Justice	M304	3FT deg		8-12	MO	M	26	CCC			
Law with Economics	M3L1	3FT deg		8-12	MO	M	26	CCC			
Law with English Language Studies	M3Q1	3FT deg		8-12	MO	M	26	CCC			
Law with French	M3R1	3FT deg		8-12	MO	M	26	CCC			
Law with German	M3R2	3FT deg		8-12	MO	M	26	CCC			
Law with Spanish	M3R4	3FT deg		8-12	MO	M	26	CCC			

course details			98 expected requirements								96 entry stats

TITLE	CODE	COURSE	SUBJECTS	A/AS	ND/C	AGNVQ	IB	SQA(H)	SQA	RATIO	A/AS
Politics and International Relations with Law	M1M3	3FT deg		8-12	MO	M	26	CCC			
Psychology with Community Law	C8MH	3FT deg		8-12	MO	M	26	CCC			
Psychology with Criminal Justice	C8MJ	3FT deg		8-12	MO	M	26	CCC			
Sociology with Community Law	L3MH	3FT deg		8-12	MO	M	26	CCC			
Sociology with Criminal Justice	L3MJ	3FT deg		8-12	MO	M	26	CCC			
Sociology with Law	L3M3	3FT deg		8-12	MO	M	26	CCC			
Spanish with European Law	R4M3	3FT deg		8-12	MO	M	26	CCC			

Univ of ULSTER

TITLE	CODE	COURSE	SUBJECTS	A/AS	ND/C	AGNVQ	IB	SQA(H)	SQA	RATIO	A/AS
Government and Law	MM13▼	3FT deg	* g	BBC	MO+4D	D*6/^ gi	32	ABBB	Ind	15	22/26
Law and Economics	LM13▼	3FT deg	* g	BBC	MO+4D	D*6/^ gi	32	ABBB	Ind	17	18/26

UNIVERSITY COLL LONDON (Univ of London)

TITLE	CODE	COURSE	SUBJECTS	A/AS	ND/C	AGNVQ	IB	SQA(H)	SQA	RATIO	A/AS
Law	M300	3FT deg	* g	ABB	Ind	Ind	35	AABBB	Ind	17	26/30
Law and History (4 Yrs)	MV31	4FT deg	H g	ABB	Ind	Ind	35	AABBB	Ind	14	
Law with Advanced Studies (4 Yrs)	M301	4FT deg	* g	ABB	Ind	Ind	35	AABBB	Ind	26	
Law with French Law (4 Yrs)	M351	4FT deg	F g	AAB	Ind	Ind	36	AAABB	Ind	8	26/30
Law with German Law (4 Yrs)	M361	4FT deg	G g	AAB	Ind	Ind	36	AAABB	Ind	11	
Law with Hispanic Law (4 Yrs)	M380	4FT deg	Sp g	AAB	Ind	Ind	36	AAABB	Ind		
Law with Italian Law (4 Yrs)	M363	4FT deg	I g	AAB	Ind	Ind	36	AAABB	Ind	20	

Univ of WARWICK

TITLE	CODE	COURSE	SUBJECTS	A/AS	ND/C	AGNVQ	IB	SQA(H)	SQA	RATIO	A/AS
European Law (4 Yrs inc year abroad)	M355	4FT deg	F/G g	AAB	X	Ind	36$	AAAAB$		7	28/30
Law	M300	3FT deg	* g	ABB	Ind	Ind	34	AAABB		19	22/30
Law (4 Yrs)	M301	4FT deg	* g	ABB	Ind	Ind	34	AAABB		23	
Law and Business Studies (3/4 years)	MN31	3FT/4FT deg	* g	ABB-BBB	Ind	Ind	34	AAABB			
Law and Sociology (4 Yrs)	ML33	4FT deg	* g	ABB-BBB	X	Ind	34	AAABB		9	24/30

Univ of WESTMINSTER

TITLE	CODE	COURSE	SUBJECTS	A/AS	ND/C	AGNVQ	IB	SQA(H)	SQA	RATIO	A/AS
European Legal Studies	M355	3FT deg	*	BCC	MO+2D		28	BBB		13	18/22
Law	M300	3FT deg	*	BC-BCC	MO+2D	D	32	BBB		9	14/24
Law with French	M3R1	4FT deg	F	BCC	MO+2D	D	28	BBB		10	
Law with Spanish	M3R4	4FT deg	Sp	BCC	MO+2D	D	28	BBB		3	

Univ of WOLVERHAMPTON

TITLE	CODE	COURSE	SUBJECTS	A/AS	ND/C	AGNVQ	IB	SQA(H)	SQA	RATIO	A/AS
Law	M300	3FT deg		BCC	4D	D	28	AAAA	Ind	5	12/22
Combined Degrees Business Law	Y401	3FT deg	g	12	4M	M	24	BBBB	Ind		
Combined Degrees Environmental Law	Y401	3FT deg		12	4M	M	24	BBBB	Ind		
Combined Degrees European, and International Law	Y401	3FT deg		12	4M	M	24	CCCC	Ind		
Combined Degrees Law	Y401	3FT deg	g	14	4M	M	24	BBBB	Ind		
Combined Degrees Social Welfare Law	Y401	3FT deg		12	4M	M	24	BBBB	Ind		
Legal Studies	093M	2FT HND		8	N	M	24	CCCC	Ind		

course details			98 expected requirements							96 entry stats
TITLE	CODE	COURSE	SUBJECTS	A/AS	NO/C	AGNVQ	IB	SQA(H)	SQA	RATIO A/AS
Univ of ABERTAY DUNDEE										
Information Management	P200	4FT deg	g	CD	Ind	Ind	Ind	BBC	Ind	
Univ of Wales, ABERYSTWYTH										
Information and Library St/an approved Sci Sub	PY21	3FT deg	* g	BCC	Ind	Ind	Ind		Ind	
Information and Library Studies	P200	3FT deg	* g	14	MO	M6 g	27	BBCCC	Ind	
Information and Library Studies/American Studies	PQ24	3FT deg	E/H g	18	1M+5D$	M^ g	29$	BBBCC$	Ind	
Information and Library Studies/Art	PW21	3FT deg	A/Ad g	18	1M+5D$	MA6 g	29$	BBBCC$	Ind	
Information and Library Studies/Art History	PV24	3FT deg	* g	18	1M+5D	MA6 g	29	BBBCC	Ind	
Information and Library Studies/Drama	PW24	3FT deg	* g	20	1M+5D	MQ6 g	30	BBBBC	Ind	
Information and Library Studies/Education	PX29	3FT deg	* g	16	MO	M6 g	28	BBCCC	Ind	
Information and Library Studies/English	PQ23	3FT deg	EI	20	1M+5D$	M^ g	30$	BBBBC$	Ind	
Information and Library Studies/Film & TV St	PW25	3FT deg	* g	20	1M+5D	MQ6 g	30	BBBBC	Ind	
Information and Library Studies/French	PR21	4FT deg	F g	18	1M+5D$	M^ g	29$	BBBCC$	Ind	
Information and Library Studies/Geography	LP82	3FT deg	Gy g	20-22	3M+2D$	M^ g	31$	BBBBC$	Ind	
Information and Library Studies/German	PR22	4FT deg	G g	18	1M+5D$	M^ g	29$	BBBCC$	Ind	
Information and Library Studies/History	PV21	3FT deg	* g	18-20	1M+5D	M^ g	30$	BBBCC	Ind	
Information and Library Studies/Int Politics	PM11	3FT deg	* g	20	1M+5D	M6 g	30	BBBCC	Ind	
Information and Library Studies/Politics	PM1C	3FT deg	* g	20	1M+5D	M6 g	30	BBBCC	Ind	
Irish/Information and Library Studies	PQ2M	4FT deg	* g	18	1M+5D$	M^ g	29$	BBBCC$	Ind	
Italian/Information and Library Studies	PR23	4FT deg	L g	18	1M+5D$	M^ g	29$	BBBCC$	Ind	
Spanish/Information and Library Studies	PR24	4FT deg	L g	18	1M+5D$	M^ g	29$	BBBCC$	Ind	
Welsh History/Information and Library Studies	PV2C	3FT deg	* g	18-20	1M+5D	M^ g	30	BBBCC	Ind	
Welsh/Information and Library Studies	PQ25	3FT deg	W g	18	1M+5D$	M^ g	29$	BBBCC$	Ind	
BELL COLLEGE OF TECHNOLOGY										
Administration and Information Management	12NP	2FT HND	Ap g	DD-D	N $	P$	Ind	CC$	N$	
Univ of BRIGHTON										
Information and Library Studies	PP12	3FT deg	*	16	DO	D	27	BBBC	Ind	
Information and Media Studies	PP42	3FT deg	*	18	DO	D	28	BBBB	Ind	
Univ of CENTRAL ENGLAND										
Information and Library Studies	P210	3FT deg	* g	12	MO	M	24	Ind		2 8/12
Information and Media	PP24	3FT deg	* g	12	MO	M	24	Ind		1 12/22
Univ of EAST LONDON										
Geographical and Land Information Management	KP32	3FT deg	* g	12	MO	MC	Ind	Ind	Ind	5
GLOUCESTERSHIRE COLLEGE of Arts and Technology										
Publishing and Information Management	25PP	2FT HND	* g	E	N $	P			Ind	
Univ of Wales, LAMPETER										
Information Management Informatics	GP52	2FTDip/3FTdeg	*	14	Ind	Ind	Ind	Ind	Ind	
LEEDS METROPOLITAN Univ										
Business Information Management	GP52	3FT/4SW deg	*/L g	12	Ind	D$^/D$ go	26	BBCC	Ind	
Information and Library Studies	P100	3FT deg	* g	12	N	M* go	26	BBCC	Ind	4 7/22
Univ of LINCOLNSHIRE and HUMBERSIDE										
Museum and Exhibition Design	PW12	3FT deg	* g	10	4M	M	24	CCC	Ind	
LIVERPOOL JOHN MOORES Univ										
Information and Library Management	PP12	3FT deg		10	3M	M				

TITLE	CODE	COURSE	SUBJECTS	A/AS	NO/C	AGNVQ	IB	SQA(H)	SQA	RATIO	A/AS
course details			**98 expected requirements**							**96 entry stats**	
LOUGHBOROUGH Univ											
Information & Library Studs Joint Hons (4 Yr SW)	P203	4SW deg	* g	20	3M+2D	D*6/^ go	28	Ind	Ind	5	
Information Studies	P210	3FT deg	* g	18	3M+2D	D*6/^ go	28	Ind	Ind	1	
Information Studies (4 Yr SW)	P211	4SW deg	* g	18	3M+2D	D*6/^ go	28	Ind	Ind		
Information Studies Joint Hons	P212	3FT deg	* g	20	3M+2D	D*6/^ go	28	Ind	Ind	2	
Information Studies Joint Hons (4 Yr SW)	P213	4SW deg	* g	20	3M+2D	D*6/^ go	28	Ind	Ind	1	
Information and Library Studies	P200	3FT deg	* g	18	3M+2D	D*6/^ go	28	Ind	Ind	5	10/26
Information and Library Studies (4 Yr SW)	P201	4SW deg	* g	18	3M+2D	D*6/^ go	28	Ind	Ind	2	14/20
Information and Library Studies Joint Hons	P202	3FT deg	* g	20	3M+2D	D*6/^ go	28	Ind	Ind		
Information and Management	PN21	3FT deg	* g	22	2M+3D	D*6/^ go	28	Ind	Ind		
Information and Management (4 Yr SW)	PN2C	4SW deg	* g	22	2M+3D	D*6/^ go	28	Ind	Ind		
MANCHESTER METROPOLITAN Univ											
Information Management	P100	3FT deg	* g	10	Ind	Ind	Ind	CCC	Ind		
Information and Library Management	PP12	3FT deg	* g	10	Ind	Ind	Ind	CCC	Ind		4/18
NAPIER Univ											
Accounting and Information Management	NP42	3FT/4FT deg	*	CDE	Ind	Ind	Ind	BCCC$	Ind		
Librarianship	P100	3FT deg									
Transport Studies with Information Management	N9P2	3FT/4FT deg	CC	Ind	Ind	Ind	BBCC	Ind			
Univ of NORTH LONDON											
Caribbean St & Information & Communications Mgt	PT27	3FT deg	*	CC	MO	M	Ind	Ind	Ind		
Education St & Information & Communications Mgt	PX29	3FT deg	*	CD	Ind	Ind	Ind	Ind	Ind		
Information and Communications Management	PP2H!	3FT deg	*	CC	MO	M	$	CCCCC	Ind		
Combined Honours *Humanities IT*	Y300	3FT deg	*	CC	Ind	Ind	Ind	Ind	Ind		
Combined Honours *Information and Communication Management*	Y301	3FT deg	*	CC	MO	M	Dip	CCCCC	Ind		
Univ of NORTHUMBRIA											
Information Studies and French	PR21	3FT deg	F	CC	2M+2D	M^		BBCCC			
Information Studies and German	PR22	3FT deg		CC	2M+2D	M^		BBCCC			
Information Studies and Spanish	PR24	3FT deg		CC	2M+2D	M^		BBCCC			
Information and Library Management	P200	3FT deg		10	4M	M	24	CCC	Ind	3	4/20
QUEEN MARGARET COLL											
Information Management	P200	3FT/4FT deg	*	CD	M+D	M$ go	Ind	BBC	Ind	2	
Combined Studies *Information Management*	Y600	3FT/4FT deg	*	BC	M+D	M/D$^ go	Ind	BBBC	Ind		
QUEEN'S Univ Belfast											
Information Management	P2N4	3FT deg	* g	BBC	2M+5D	D*6/^ go	30$	AABB	Ind	8	20/24
Information Management	P202	3FT deg	* g	BCC	3M+4D	D*6/^ go	29$	ABBB	Ind	4	18/20
Information Management with French	P2R1	3FT deg	F g	BBC	X	D*^ go	30$	AABB	X	13	
Information Management with German	P2R2	3FT deg	G g	BBC	X	D*^ go	30$	AABB	X		
Information Management with Italian	P2R3	3FT deg	* g	BBC	2M+5D	D*6/^ go	30$	AABB	Ind		
Information Management with Spanish	P2R4	3FT deg	* g	BBC	2M+5D	D*6/^ go	30$	AABB	Ind	3	
ROBERT GORDON Univ											
Information and Library Studies	P2P1	3FT/4FT deg	E	DD	N	Ind	Ind	BCC$	Ind	3	
Univ of SHEFFIELD											
Accounting & Financial Management and Info Mgt	NP42	3FT deg	* g	24	3M+3D	D6/^	32	AABB	Ind	20	
Business Studies and Information Management	NP12	3FT deg	* g	24	3M+3D	D^	32	AABB	Ind	14	22/26

Librarianship and Information Science 48

course details			98 expected requirements							96 entry stats
TITLE	CODE	COURSE	SUBJECTS	A/AS	ND/C	AGNVQ	IB	SQA(H)	SQA	RATIO A/AS
THAMES VALLEY Univ										
Business Administration with Information Mgt	N1PF	3FT deg		8-12	MO	M	26	CCC		
Business Studies with Information Mgt (Dip)	N1P2	3FT/4SW deg		8-12	MO	M	26	CCC		
Digital Arts with Information Management	W9P2!	3FT deg		8-12	MO	M		CCC		
Economics with Information Management	L1P2	3FT deg		8-12	MO	M	26	CCC		
Finance with Information Management	N3P2	3FT deg		8-12	MO	M	26	CCC		
Information Management with Accounting	P2N4	3FT deg		8-12	MO	M	26	CCC		
Information Management with Business	P2N1	3FT deg		8-12	MO	M	26	CCC		
Information Management with Digital Arts	P2W9	3FT deg		8-12	MO	M	26	CCC		
Information Management with English Language St	P2Q1	3FT deg		8-12	MO	M	26	CCC		
Information Management with French	P2R1	3FT deg		8-12	MO	M	26	CCC		
Information Management with German	P2R2	3FT deg		8-12	MO	M	26	CCC		
Information Management with Information Systems	P2G5	3FT deg		8-12	MO	M	26	CCC		
Information Management with Lang & Communication	P2PH	3FT deg		8-12	MO	M	26	CCC		
Information Management with Media Studies	P2WX	3FT deg		8-12	MO	M	26	CCC		
Information Management with Retail Management	P2NM	3FT deg		8-12	MO	M	26	CCC		
Information Management with Spanish	P2R4	3FT deg		8-12	MO	M	26	CCC		
Information Mgt with Multi-Media Computing	P2GM	3FT deg		8-12	MO	M	26	CCC		
Information Mgt with Sound and Music Recording	P2WH	3FT deg		8-12	MO	M	26	CCC		
Multi-Media Computing with Information Mgt	G5P2	3FT deg		8-12	MO	M	26	CCC		
Psychology with Information Management	C8P2	3FT deg		8-12	MO	M	26	CCC		
Tourism with Information Management	P7P2	3FT deg		8-12	MO	M	26	CCC		
UNIVERSITY COLL LONDON (Univ of London)										
Information Management	P2G5	3FT deg	g	BBC	MO $	Ind	30$	BBCCC$	N$	6 20/26
WEST HERTS COLL										
Media Production	24PE	2FT HND	*	2						
Univ of WOLVERHAMPTON										
Business Information Management	P200	3FT deg	g	14	4M	M	24	BBBB	Ind	7
Combined Degrees	Y401	3FT deg	g	14	4M	M	24	BBBB	Ind	
Business Information Management										

course details			98 expected requirements							96 entry stats
TITLE	CODE	COURSE	SUBJECTS	A/AS	NQ/C	AGNVQ	IB	SQA(H)	SQA	RATIO A/AS
Univ of ABERDEEN										
Languages and Literature of Scotland	QQ52	4FT deg	* g	BBC	Ind	M$ go	30$	BBBB$	Ind	
ANGLIA Poly Univ										
Art History and English Language Studies	QV14▼	3FT deg	g	14	6M	M go	Dip			
Business and English Language Studies	NQ11▼	3FT deg	g	10	3M	P go	Dip	BCCC		
Communication Studies and English Language Studs	PQ31▼	3FT deg	Ap g	14	6M	M go	Dip$	BBCC	Ind	
Economics and English Language Studies	LQ11▼	3FT deg	* g	12		go	Dip$	BCCC	Ind	
English Language Studies and Euro Phil. & Lit.	QV17▼	3FT deg	* g	12	4M	M go	Dip	BCCC		
English Language Studies and French	QR11▼	4FT deg	* g	12	4M	M go	Dip	BCCC		
English Language Studies and Geography	QL18▼	3FT deg	* g	12	4M	M go	Dip	BCCC		
English Language Studies and German	QR12▼	3FT deg	* g	12	4M	M go	Dip	BCCC		
English Language Studies and History	QV11▼	3FT deg	* g	12	4M	M go	Dip	BCCC		
English Language Studies and Italian	QR13▼	3FT deg	* g	12	4M	M go	Dip	BCCC		
English Language Studies and Law	QM13▼	3FT deg	* g	14	4M	M go	Dip	BCCC		
English Language Studies and Music	QW13▼	3FT deg	Mu g	12	4M	M go	Dip$	BCCC		
English Language Studies and Politics	QM11▼	3FT deg	* g	14	4M	M go	Dip	BCCC		
English Language Studies and Social Policy	LQ41▼	3FT deg	* g	12	4M	M go	Dip	BCCC		
English Language Studies and Sociology	QL13▼	3FT deg	* g	12	4M	M go	Dip	BCCC		
English Language Studies and Spanish	QR14▼	3FT deg	* g	12	4M	M go	Dip	BCCC		
English Language Studies and Women's Studies	QM19▼	3FT deg	* g	12	4M	M go	Dip	BCCC		
English and English Language Studies	QQ13▼	3FT deg	E g	12	4M	M go	Dip$	BCCC		
Univ of Wales, BANGOR										
Linguistics	Q100	3FT deg	* g	CCD	3M $	D*^ go	28	BBBC	Ind	3 8/20
Linguistics and the English Language	Q140	3FT deg	E g	CCD	X	D*^ go	28$	BBBC$	X	4 10/24
Linguistics with English Literature	Q1Q3	3FT deg	E/El g	CCD	X	D*^_ go	28$	BBBC$	X	
Linguistics/English	QQ13	3FT deg	E g	CCC	X	D*^_ go	28$	BBBC$	X	5 14/18
Linguistics/French (Syllabus A)	QR11	4FT deg	E g	CCD	X	D*^_ go	28$	BBBC$	X	5
Linguistics/French (Syllabus B)	QR1C	4FT deg	E g	CCD	X	D*^_ go	28$	BBBC$	X	3
Linguistics/German	QR12	4FT deg	* g	CCD	X	D*^ go	28$	BBBC$	X	2
Physical Education/Linguistics	QB16	3FT deg	* g	20	5D	D*^ go	28	BBBC	Ind	
Psychology/Linguistics	CQ81	3FT deg	* g	BCC	MO	D$6/^ go	30	BBBB	Ind	13
Russian/Linguistics	QR18	4FT deg	* g	CCD	3M $	D*^ go	28	BBBC	Ind	
Sociology/Linguistics	LQ31	3FT deg	* g	CCD	5M	D*6/^ go	28	BBBC	Ind	7
Sports Science/Linguistics	BQ61	3FT deg	* g	20	5D	D*6/^ go	30	BBBC	Ind	
Welsh/Linguistics	QQ15	3FT/4FT deg	W g	CCD	Ind	D*^_ go	Ind	X	X	
Women's Studies and Linguistics	MQ91	3FT deg	* g	18	Ind	D*6/^ go	28	BBBC	Ind	
BARNSLEY COLL										
Humanities *History and Literature*	Y301	3FT deg	H/Gy/Po/E g	EE	4M	MB	Ind	Ind	Ind	
Humanities *History and Literature*	Y302	4EXT deg								
Humanities *Literature and Geographical Studies*	Y301	3FT deg	H/Gy/Po/E g	EE	4M	MB	Ind	Ind	Ind	
Humanities *Literature and Geographical Studies*	Y302	4EXT deg								
Humanities *Literature and Politics with Internat Relations*	Y301	3FT deg								
Humanities *Literature and Politics with Internat Relations*	Y302	3FT deg								

Linguistics and Literature 49

	course details			98 expected requirements							96 entry stats
TITLE	CODE	COURSE	SUBJECTS	A/AS	NO/C	RGNVQ	IB	SQA(H)	SQA	RATIO A/AS

BOLTON INST

TITLE	CODE	COURSE	SUBJECTS	A/AS	NO/C	RGNVQ	IB	SQA(H)	SQA	RATIO A/AS
Accountancy and Literature	NQ42	3FT deg	* g	CD	MO	M*	24	BBCC	Ind	
Art & Design History and Literature	VQ41	3FT deg	* g	CD	MO	M*	24	BBCC	Ind	
Biology and Literature	CQ12	3FT deg	* g	CD	MO	M*	24	BBCC	Ind	
Business Economics and Literature	LQ12	3FT deg	* g	CD	MO	M*	24	BBCC	Ind	
Business Info Systems and Literature	GQ5F	3FT deg	* g	CD	MO	M*	24	BBCC	Ind	
Business Studies and Literature	NQ12	3FT deg	* g	CD	MO	M*	24	BBCC	Ind	
Community Studies and Literature	LQ52	3FT deg	* g	CD	MO	M*	24	BBCC	Ind	
Computing and Literature	GQ52	3FT deg	* g	CD	MO	M*	24	BBCC	Ind	
Creative Writing and Literature	WQ92	3FT deg	* g	CD	MO	M*	24	BBCC	Ind	
Design and Literature	QW22	3FT deg	* g	CD	MO	M*	24	BBCC	Ind	
Environmental Studies and Literature	FQ92	3FT deg	* g	CD	MO	M*	24	BBCC	Ind	
European Cultural Studies and Literature	TQ22	3FT deg	* g	CD	MO	M*	24	BBCC	Ind	
Film and TV Studies and Literature	WQ52	3FT deg	Me/T g	CD	Ind	Ind	24	BBCC	Ind	
French and Literature	RQ12	3FT deg	F g	CD	Ind	Ind	24	BBCC	Ind	
Gender & Women's Studies and Literature	MQ92	3FT deg	* g	CD	10-12M	M*	24	BBCC	Ind	
German and Literature	RQ22	3FT deg	G g	CD	Ind	Ind	24	BBCC	Ind	
History and Language Studies	VQ11	3FT deg	* g	CD	MO	M*	24	BBCC	Ind	
History and Literature	QV21	3FT deg	* g	CD	MO	M*	24	BBCC	Ind	
Human Resource Management and Literature	NQ1F	3FT deg	* g	CD	MO	M*	24	BBCC	Ind	
Language Studies and Literature	QQ12	3FT deg	* g	CD	MO	M*	24	BBCC	Ind	
Language Studies and Philosophy	QV17	3FT deg	* g	CD	MO	M*	24	BBCC	Ind	
Law and Literature	MQ32	3FT deg	* g	CD	MO	M*	24	BBCC	Ind	
Leisure Studies and Literature	LQ31	3FT deg	* g	CD	MO	M*	24	BBCC	Ind	
Literature	Q202	3FT deg	E g	CD	MO	M*	24	BBCC	Ind	
Literature and Marketing	NQ52	3FT deg	* g	CD	MO	M*	24	BBCC	Ind	
Literature and Mathematics	GQ12	3FT deg	M g	DD	Ind	Ind	24	BBCC	Ind	
Literature and Operations Management	NQ22	3FT deg	* g	CD	MO	M*	24	BBCC	Ind	
Literature and Organisations, Management & Work	NQ72	3FT deg	* g	CD	MO	M*	24	BBCC	Ind	
Literature and Peace and War Studies	QV2C	3FT deg	* g	CD	MO	M*	24	BBCC	Ind	
Literature and Philosophy	QV27	3FT deg	* g	CD	MO	M g	24	BBCC	Ind	
Literature and Psychology	QL27	3FT deg	* g	12	MO	D*	24	BBCC	Ind	
Literature and Sociology	LQ32	3FT deg	* g	CD	MO	M	24	Ind	Ind	
Literature and Theatre Studies	WQ42	3FT deg	Me/T g	CD	Ind	Ind	24	BBCC	Ind	
Literature and Tourism Studies	PQ72	3FT deg	* g	CD	MO	M*	24	BBCC	Ind	
Literature and Urban & Cultural Studies	QL23	3FT deg	* g	CD	MO	M*	24	BBCC	Ind	
Visual Arts and Literature	QW21	3FT deg	* g	10	MO	M*	24	BBCC	Ind	

Univ of BRADFORD

TITLE	CODE	COURSE	SUBJECTS	A/AS	NO/C	RGNVQ	IB	SQA(H)	SQA	RATIO A/AS
Literature	Q200	3FT deg	* g	BB-CCC	4M+3D	D*^	Ind	Ind	Ind	10
Interdisciplinary Human Studies Literature	Y402	3FT deg	* g	BB-CCC	4M+3D	D*^	Ind	Ind	Ind	

Univ of BRIGHTON

TITLE	CODE	COURSE	SUBJECTS	A/AS	NO/C	RGNVQ	IB	SQA(H)	SQA	RATIO A/AS
Language Studies with Linguistics	T9Q1	3FT/4SW deg	F/G g	14	2M+3D$	Ind	Dip$	BBCC$	Ind	

BRISTOL, Univ of the W of England

TITLE	CODE	COURSE	SUBJECTS	A/AS	NO/C	RGNVQ	IB	SQA(H)	SQA	RATIO A/AS
Joint Honours Programme Psychology and Linguistics	Y401	3FT deg	* g	14-16	5M	M$ go	24	BCCC	Ind	
Joint Honours Programme Sociology and Linguistics	Y401	3FT deg	* g	14-16	5M	M$ go	24	BCCC	Ind	

Univ of BUCKINGHAM

TITLE	CODE	COURSE	SUBJECTS	A/AS	NO/C	RGNVQ	IB	SQA(H)	SQA	RATIO A/AS
English Language Studies (EFL) with Literature	Q1Q3	3FT deg		10	3M+2D	M	24	CCCC	Ind	
History of Art and English Language Studies (EFL	VQ41	2FT deg	* g	10	5M	M	24	CCCC	Ind	

| | | | 98 expected requirements | | | | | | | 96 entry stats |

course details — **98 expected requirements** — **96 entry stats**

TITLE	CODE	COURSE	SUBJECTS	A/AS	ND/C	RGNVQ	IB	SQA(H)	SQA	RATIO A/AS
BUCKINGHAMSHIRE COLLEGE										
Film and English Studies	QW25	3FT deg		12	2D	M	27	CCCC	Ind	
Media and English Studies	PQ42	3FT deg		12	2D	M	27	CCCC	Ind	
CARDIFF Univ of Wales										
Language Studies/Cultural Criticism	MQ91	3FT deg	E	ABC	X		Ind	AAABB	X	
Language Studies/Education	QX19	3FT deg	*	BBC	Ind		Ind	ABBBB		1
Language Studies/English Literature	QQ31	3FT deg	E	ABB	X		Ind	AAAA	X	7
Language Studies/French	QR11	4FT deg	F	BBC	Ind		Ind	ABBBB		
Language Studies/German	QR12	4FT deg	G	BBC	Ind		Ind	ABBBB		4
Language Studies/Italian	QR13	4FT deg	L	BBC	Ind		Ind	ABBBB		
Language and Communication	PQ31	3FT deg	*	ABC			30	Ind		2	16/28
Philosophy/Language Studies	QV17	3FT deg	*	BBC	Ind		Ind	ABBBB		
Portuguese/Language Studies	QR15	4FT deg	L	BBC	Ind		Ind	ABBBB		
Spanish/Language Studies	QR14	4FT deg	L	BBC	Ind		Ind	ABBBB		3
Welsh/Language Studies	QQ15	3FT deg	W	BBC	X		Ind	X		1
Univ of CENTRAL LANCASHIRE										
Combined Honours Programme *Linguistics*	Y400	3FT deg	E	14	Ind	M*^	26	BBCC	Ind	
CHICHESTER INSTITUTE OF HIGHER EDUCATION										
Art and English Language Teaching (EFL)	WQ11	3FT deg	A+Pf	12	Ind	M^+	Ind	Ind	Ind	
Art with English Language Teaching (EFL)	E1Q1	3FT deg	A+Pf	12	Ind	M$+^	Ind	Ind	Ind	
Art with English Language Teaching (EFL)	W1Q1	3FT deg	A+Pf	12	Ind	M$+^	Ind	Ind	Ind	
Dance and English Language Teaching (EFL)	WQ41	3FT deg	Pf	12	Ind	M$+	Ind	Ind	Ind	
Dance with English Language Teaching (EFL)	W4Q1	3FT deg	Pf g	12	Ind	M$+	Ind	Ind	Ind	
English Lang Teaching (EFL) and St of Religions	QV18	3FT deg	E	12	Ind	M^	Ind	Ind	Ind	
English Language Teaching (EFL) and English	QQ13	3FT deg	E	12	Ind	M^	Ind	Ind	Ind	
English Language Teaching (EFL) and Geography	QL18	3FT deg	E	12	Ind	M^	Ind	Ind	Ind	
English Language Teaching (EFL) and History	QV11	3FT deg	E	12	Ind	M^	Ind	Ind	Ind	
English Language Teaching (EFL) and Mathematics	QG11	3FT deg	E+M	12	Ind	M^	Ind	Ind	Ind	
English Language Teaching (EFL) and Women's St	QM19	3FT deg	E	12	Ind	M^	Ind	Ind	Ind	
English Language Teaching (EFL)and Media Studies	QP14	3FT deg	E	12	Ind	M^	Ind	Ind	Ind	
English with English Language Teaching (EFL)	Q3Q1	3FT deg	E	12	Ind	M^	Ind	Ind	Ind	4
Environmental Sci and English Language Teaching	FQ91	3FT deg	E	12	Ind	M^	Ind	Ind	Ind	
Geography with English Language Teaching (EFL)	L8Q1	3FT deg	Gy	12	Ind	M$	Ind	Ind	Ind	
History with English Language Teaching (EFL)	V1Q1	3FT deg	H	12	Ind	M$	Ind	Ind	Ind	
Mathematics with English Language Teaching (EFL)	G1Q1	3FT deg	M	12	Ind	M^	Ind	Ind	Ind	
Music with English Language Teaching (EFL)	W3Q1	3FT deg	Mu	12	Ind	M$+	Ind	Ind	Ind	
Study of Religions with Eng Lang Teaching(EFL)	V8Q1	3FT deg	* g	12	Ind	M$	Ind	Ind	Ind	
Univ of DERBY										
Credit Accumulation Modular Scheme *Experience of Writing*	Y600	3FT deg								
Credit Accumulation Modular Scheme *Literature*	Y600	3FT deg	*	12	MO	M	Ind	CCCC	Ind	
Univ of DURHAM										
Chinese with Linguistics	T3Q1	4FT deg	*	BBC	Ind	Ind	31	AABBB	Ind	
English Language & Linguistics	QQ13	3FT deg	*	BBB	Ind	Ind	Ind	AABBB	Ind	10	20/30
English Literature and Linguistics	QQ1H	3FT deg	E g	AAB	Ind	Ind	32	AAABB	Ind	31
Japanese with Linguistics	T4Q1	4FT deg	*	BBC	Ind	Ind	31	AABBB	Ind	3
Modern Languages and Linguistics	QT19	4FT deg	L	24	Ind	Ind	33	AAABB	Ind	16
Arts Combined *Linguistics*	Y300	3FT deg	*	24	MO	Ind	30	AAABB	Ind	

Linguistics and Literature · 49

	course details		98 expected requirements							96 entry stats
TITLE	CODE	COURSE	SUBJECTS	A/AS	NO/C	RGNVQ	IB	SQA(H)	SQA	RATIO R/AS
Univ of EAST ANGLIA										
English Literature with Comparative Lit Minor	Q3QF	3FT deg	E	ABB-BBB	X		30$	ABBBB	X	14
English and Comparative Lit with Hons Lang	Q200	4FT deg	F/G	BBC	X		30	AAABC	X	2 · 14/22
Linguistics	Q100	3FT deg	*	BBC-BCC	4M+2D		28$	AAABC	X	4 · 12/28
Linguistics and Philosophy	VQ71	3FT deg	F/G	BBC	4M+2D		30	AAAAB	Ind	
Linguistics with Honours Language	Q1TY	4FT deg	L	BCC	X		28$	AABBC	X	6 · 16/28
Univ of EAST LONDON										
Anthropology and Linguistics	LQ6C	3FT deg	* g	12	MO	X	Ind	Ind	Ind	4
Anthropology with Linguistics	L6Q1	3FT deg	* g	12	MO	M	Ind	Ind	Ind	
Communication Studies and Linguistics	PQ31	3FT deg	* g	12	MO	X				
Communication Studies with Linguistics	P3Q1	3FT deg	* g	12	MO	M	Ind	Ind		
Cultural Studies and Linguistics	LQ61	3FT deg	* g	12	MO	M				
Cultural Studies with Linguistics	L6QC	3FT deg	* g	12	MO	M				
Education & Community Studies and Linguistics	QX19	3FT deg	* g	12	MO	X	Ind	Ind	Ind	1
Education & Community Studies with Linguistics	X9Q1	3FT deg	* g	12	MO	M				
European Studies and Linguistics	QT12	3FT deg	* g	12	MO	X	Ind	Ind	Ind	
European Studies with Linguistics	T2Q1	3FT deg	* g	12	MO	M	Ind	Ind		
French and Linguistics	QR11	3FT deg	* g	12	MO	X	Ind	Ind	Ind	9
French with Linguistics	R1Q1	3FT deg	* g	12	MO	M	Ind			
German and Linguistics	QR12	3FT deg	* g	12	MO	X	Ind	Ind	Ind	2
German with Linguistics	R2Q1	3FT deg	* g	12	MO	M	Ind			
Information Technology and Linguistics	GQ51	3FT deg	* g	12	MO	X	Ind	Ind	Ind	
Information Technology with Linguistics	G5Q1	3FT deg	* g	12	MO	M	Ind	Ind	Ind	
Linguistics and Literature	QQ13	3FT deg	* g	14	MO	X	Ind	Ind	Ind	3
Linguistics and Sociology	LQ31	3FT deg	* g	14	MO	M$	Ind	Ind	Ind	3
Linguistics and Spanish	QR14	3FT deg	* g	12	MO	M^	Ind	Ind	Ind	
Linguistics with Anthropology	Q1L6	3FT deg	* g	12	MO	M				
Linguistics with Communication Studies	Q1P3	3FT deg	* g	12	MO	M				
Linguistics with Cultural Studies	Q1LP	3FT deg	* g	12	MO	M				
Linguistics with Education & Community Studies	Q1X9	3FT deg	* g	12	MO	M				
Linguistics with European Studies	Q1T2	3FT deg	* g	12	MO	M				
Linguistics with French	Q1R1	3FT deg	* g	12	MO	M				
Linguistics with German	Q1R2	3FT deg	* g	12	MO	M				
Linguistics with Information Technology	Q1G5	3FT deg	* g	12	MO	M				
Linguistics with Italian	Q1R3	3FT deg	* g	12	MO	M				
Linguistics with Literature	Q1Q3	3FT deg	* g	12	MO	M				
Linguistics with Sociology	Q1L3	3FT deg	* g	12	MO	M				
Linguistics with Spanish	Q1R4	3FT deg	* g	12	MO	M				
Literature with Linguistics	Q3Q1	3FT deg	* g	12	MO	M	Ind			
Sociology with Linguistics	L3Q1	3FT deg	* g	12	MO	M	Ind	Ind	Ind	
Spanish with Linguistics	R4Q1	3FT deg	* g	12	MO	M	Ind			
Three-Subject Degree *Linguistics*	Y600	3FT deg	* g	12	MO	M	Ind	Ind	Ind	
Univ of EDINBURGH										
Arabic and Linguistics	TQ61	4FT deg	g	BBB	Ind	Ind	Dip$	BBBB	Ind	
Celtic and Linguistics	QQ15	4FT deg	L g	BBB	Ind	Ind	Dip$	BBBB$	Ind	
English Language and Linguistics	QQ31	4FT deg	g	BBB	Ind	Ind	Dip$	BBBB	Ind	
English and Scottish Literature	QQ32	4FT deg	E g	AAB	Ind	Ind	Dip$	ABBB$	Ind	
French and Linguistics	RQ11	4FT deg	F g	BBB	Ind	Ind	Dip$	BBBB$	Ind	
German and Linguistics	RQ21	4FT deg	L g	BBB	Ind	Ind	Dip$	BBBB$	Ind	
Greek and Linguistics	QQ71	4FT deg	g	BBB	Ind	Ind	Dip$	BBBB	Ind	

TITLE	CODE	COURSE	SUBJECTS	A/AS	NO/C	RGNVQ	IB	SQA(H)	SQA	RATIO	A/AS
Italian and Linguistics	RQ31	4FT deg	L g	BBB	Ind	Ind	Dip$	BBBB$	Ind		
Japanese and Linguistics	TQ41	4FT deg	L g	BBB	Ind	Ind	Dip$	BBBB$	Ind		
Linguistics	Q100	4FT deg	g	BBB	Ind	Ind	Dip$	BBBB	Ind		
Linguistics and Artificial Intelligence	QG18	4FT deg	g	BBB	Ind	Ind	Dip$	BBBB	Ind		
Linguistics and Scottish Ethnology	QV19	4FT deg	g	BBB	Ind	Ind	Dip$	BBBB	Ind		
Linguistics and Social Anthropology	QL16	4FT deg	g	BBB	Ind	Ind	Dip$	BBBB	Ind		
Philosophy and Linguistics	VQ71	4FT deg	g	BBB	Ind	Ind	Dip$	BBBB	Ind		
Psychology and Linguistics	LQ71	4FT deg	g	AAB	Ind		38	AABB	Ind	11	
Russian Studies and Linguistics	RQ81	4FT deg	L g	BBB	Ind	Ind	Dip$	BBBB$	Ind		
Sanskrit and Linguistics	QQ91	4FT deg	g	BBB	Ind	Ind	Dip$	BBBB	Ind		
Scandinavian Studies and Linguistics	RQ71	4FT deg	L g	BBC	Ind	Ind	Dip$	BBBC$	Ind		
Scottish Ethnology and Scottish Literature	VQ92	4FT deg	E g	BBB	Ind	Ind	Dip$	BBBB$	Ind		
Scottish Literature	Q210	4FT deg	E g	BBB	Ind	Ind	Dip$	BBBB$	Ind		
Scottish Literature and Scottish Historical St	QV21	4FT deg	g	BBB	Ind	Ind	Dip$	BBBB	Ind		
Social Anthropology and Linguistics	LQ61	4FT deg	*	AAB	Ind		38$	ABBB	Ind	20	
Spanish and Linguistics	RQ41	4FT deg	L g	BBB	Ind	Ind	Dip$	BBBB$	Ind		

Univ of ESSEX

TITLE	CODE	COURSE	SUBJECTS	A/AS	NO/C	RGNVQ	IB	SQA(H)	SQA	RATIO	A/AS
English Language and British Studies	QV19	3FT deg	*	20			28	BBBB			
English Language and English and European Lit	QQ23	3FT deg	*	22	MO+3D	Ind	28	AABB	Ind	11	22/26
English Language and Linguistics	QQ13	3FT deg	*	20	MO+2D	Ind	28	BBBB	Ind	8	16/24
French (Language and Linguistics) (4 Yrs)	R1Q1	4FT deg	F	20	MO+2D	Ind	28$	BBBB$	Ind	8	
German (Language and Linguistics) (4 Yrs)	R2Q1	4FT deg	*	20	MO+2D	Ind	28	BBBB	Ind		
History and Literature	QV21	3FT deg	*	22	MO+3D	Ind	28	AABB	Ind	5	16/18
Language Studies	Q140	3FT deg	*	20	MO+2D	Ind	28	BBBB	Ind	2	
Linguistics	Q100	3FT deg	*	20	MO+2D	Ind	28	BBBB	Ind		
Linguistics and Music	QW13	3FT deg	*	20	MO+2D	Ind	28	BBBB	Ind	3	
Linguistics and Philosophy	QV17	3FT deg	*	20	MO+2D	Ind	28	BBBB	Ind		
Literature and History of Art	QV24	3FT deg	*	20	MO+2D	Ind	28	BBBB	Ind	6	
Literature and Music	QW23	3FT deg	*	20	MO+2D	Ind	28	BBBB	Ind	9	
Literature and Sociology	LQ32	3FT deg	*	20	MO+2D	Ind	28	BBBB	Ind	10	
Philosophy and Literature	QV27	3FT deg	*	20	MO+2D	Ind	28	BBBB	Ind	5	14/24
Psycholinguistics	Q160	3FT deg	*	20	MO+2D	Ind	28	BBBB	Ind	5	18/24
Russian (Language and Linguistics) (4 Yrs)	R8Q1	4FT deg	*	20	MO+2D	Ind	28	BBBB	Ind		
Spanish (Language and Linguistics) (4 Yrs)	R4Q1	4FT deg	*	20	MO+2D	Ind	28	BBBB	Ind	10	

Univ of GLAMORGAN

TITLE	CODE	COURSE	SUBJECTS	A/AS	NO/C	RGNVQ	IB	SQA(H)	SQA	RATIO	A/AS
Combined Studies (Honours) *English as a Foreign Language*	Y400	3FT deg	* g	8-16	Ind	Ind	Ind	Ind	Ind		

Univ of GLASGOW

TITLE	CODE	COURSE	SUBJECTS	A/AS	NO/C	RGNVQ	IB	SQA(H)	SQA	RATIO	A/AS
Celtic Civilisation/Scottish Literature	QQ2M	4FT deg		BBC	HN	M	30	BBBB	Ind		
Celtic/Scottish Literature	QQ25	4FT deg		BBC	HN	M	30	BBBB	Ind		
Classical Civilisation/Scottish Literature	QQ28	4FT deg		BBC	HN	M	30	BBBB	Ind		
Classical Hebrew/Scottish Literature	QV2W	4FT deg		BBC	HN	M	30	BBBB	Ind		
Computing/Scottish Literature	GQ52	4FT deg		BBC	HN	M	30	BBBB	Ind		
Czech/Scottish Literature	QT21	5FT deg		BBC	HN	M	30	BBBB	Ind		
Economics/Scottish Literature	LQ12	4FT deg		BBC	HN	M	30	BBBB	Ind		
English/Scottish Literature	QQ23	4FT deg		BBC	HN	M	30	BBBB	Ind	6	22/28
Film and Television Studies/Scottish Literature	QW25	4FT deg		BBB	HN	D	32	AABB	HN	16	
French/Scottish Literature	QR21	5FT deg		BBC	HN	M	30	BBBB	Ind	3	
Geography/Scottish Literature	LQ82	4FT deg		BBC	HN	M	30	BBBB	Ind		
German/Scottish Literature	QR22	5FT deg		BBC	HN	M	30	BBBB	Ind		
Greek/Scottish Literature	QQ27	4FT deg		BBC	HN	M	30	BBBB	Ind		

Linguistics and Literature 49

course details | 98 expected requirements | 96 entry stats

TITLE	CODE	COURSE	SUBJECTS	A/AS	NO/C	AGNVQ	IB	SQA(H)	SQA	RATIO A/AS
Hispanic Studies/Scottish Literature	QR24	5FT deg		BBC	HN	M	30	BBBB	Ind	
History of Art/Scottish Literature	QV24	4FT deg		BBC	HN	M	30	BBBB	Ind	5
History/Scottish Literature	QVF1	4FT deg		BBC	HN	M	30	BBBB	Ind	
Italian/Scottish Literature	QR23	5FT deg		BBC	HN	M	30	BBBB	Ind	1
Latin/Scottish Literature	QQ26	4FT deg		BBC	HN	M	30	BBBB	Ind	
Management Studies/Scottish Literature	NQ12	4FT deg		BBC	HN	M	30	BBBB	Ind	
Mathematics/Scottish Literature	GQ12	4FT deg		BBC	HN	M	30	BBBB	Ind	
Music/Scottish Literature	QW23	4FT deg		BBC	HN	M	30	BBBB	Ind	
Philosophy/Scottish Literature	QVG7	4FT deg		BBC	HN	M	30	BBBB	Ind	
Politics/Scottish Literature	MQ12	4FT deg		BBC	HN	M	30	BBBB	Ind	
Psychology/Scottish Literature	CQ82	4FT deg		BBC	HN	M	30	BBBB	Ind	
Russian/Scottish Literature	QR28	5FT deg		BBC	HN	M	30	BBBB	Ind	
Scottish History/Scottish Literature	QVG1	4FT deg		BBC	HN	M	30	BBBB	Ind	5
Scottish Language and Literature	Q201	4FT deg		BBC	HN	M	30	BBBB	Ind	
Scottish Literature/Sociology	LQH2	4FT deg		BBC	HN	M	30	BBBB	Ind	
Theatre Studies/Scottish Literature	QW24	4FT deg		BBC	HN	M	30	BBBB	Ind	5

Univ of HERTFORDSHIRE

TITLE	CODE	COURSE	SUBJECTS	A/AS	NO/C	AGNVQ	IB	SQA(H)	SQA	RATIO A/AS
Applied Geology/Linguistic Science	F6Q1	3FT deg	* g	14	MO $	M$ gi	26$	BCCC$	Ind	
Applied Statistics/Linguistic Science	G4Q1	3FT deg	*	14	MO $	M$ gi	26	BCCC	Ind	
Astronomy/Linguistic Science	F5Q1	3FT deg	M g	12	MO $	M$ gi	26$	BCCC$	Ind	
Chemistry/Linguistic Science	F1Q1	3FT deg	C g	12	MO $	MS gi	26$	BCCC$	Ind	
Computing/Linguistic Science	G5Q1	3FT deg	*	14	MO	M$ gi	26	BCCC	Ind	
Economics/Linguistic Science	L1Q1	3FT deg	*	14	MO $	M$ gi	26	BCCC	Ind	
Electronic Music/Linguistic Science	W3Q1	3FT deg	Mu	14	MO $	M$^ gi	26$	BCCC$	Ind	
Electronics/Linguistic Science	H6Q1	3FT deg	* g	14	MO $	M$ gi	26$	BCCC$	Ind	
Environmental Science/Linguistic Science	F9Q1	3FT deg	*	14	MO	M$ gi	26	BCCC	Ind	
European Studies/Linguistic Science	T2Q1	3FT deg	*	14	MO	M$ gi	26	BCCC	Ind	
Historical Studies/Linguistics	VQ11	3FT deg	*	14	M+D	Ind	28	CCCCC	Ind	
Law/Linguistic Science	M3Q1	3FT deg	*	20	4M+4D	D$ gi	28	BBBC	Ind	
Linguistic Science	Q101	3FT deg	*	14	MO	M$ gi	26	BCCC	Ind	
Linguistic Science/Applied Geology	Q1F6	3FT deg	* g	14	MO $	M$ gi	26$	BCCC$	Ind	
Linguistic Science/Applied Statistics	Q1G4	3FT deg	*	14	MO $	M$ gi	26	BCCC	Ind	
Linguistic Science/Astronomy	Q1F5	3FT deg	M g	12	MO $	M$ gi	26$	BCCC$	Ind	
Linguistic Science/Chemistry	Q1F1	3FT deg	C g	12	MO $	MS gi	26$	BCCC$	Ind	
Linguistic Science/Computing	Q1G5	3FT deg	*	14	MO	M$ gi	26	BCCC	Ind	
Linguistic Science/Economics	Q1L1	3FT deg	*	14	MO $	M$ gi	26	BCCC	Ind	
Linguistic Science/Electronic Music	Q1W3	3FT deg	Mu	14	MO $	M$^ gi	26$	BCCC$	Ind	
Linguistic Science/Electronics	Q1H6	3FT deg	* g	14	MO $	M$ gi	26$	BCCC$	Ind	
Linguistic Science/Environmental Science	Q1F9	3FT deg	*	14	MO	M$ gi	26	BCCC	Ind	
Linguistic Science/European Studies	Q1T2	3FT deg	*	14	MO	M$ gi	26	BCCC	Ind	
Linguistic Science/Law	Q1M3	3FT deg	*	20	4M+4D	D$ gi	28	BBBC	Ind	
Linguistic Science/Manufacturing Systems	Q1H7	3FT deg	*	14	MO	M$ gi	26	BCCC	Ind	
Linguistic Science/Mathematics	Q1G1	3FT deg	M	14	MO $	M$^ gi	26$	BCCC$	Ind	
Linguistic Science/Operational Research	Q1N2	3FT deg	*	14	MO $	M$ gi	26	BCCC	Ind	
Linguistic Science/Psychology	Q1C8	3FT deg	*	20	4M+4D	D$ gi	28	BBBC	Ind	
Linguistics	Q100	3FT deg	*	16	M+D	Ind	28	CCCCC	Ind	5 10/22
Linguistics/Literature	QQ13	3FT deg	*	14	M+D	Ind	28	CCCCC	Ind	
Linguistics/Minor	Q102	3FT deg	*	14	M+D	Ind	28	CCCCC	Ind	
Linguistics/Minor/Minor	Q103	3FT deg	*	14	M+D	Ind	28	CCCCC	Ind	
Linguistics/Modern Language	QT19	3FT deg	Ap	14	M+D	Ind	28	CCCCC	Ind	
Linguistics/Philosophy	QV17	3FT deg	*	14	M+D	Ind	28	CCCCC	Ind	
Manufacturing Systems/Linguistic Science	H7Q1	3FT deg	*	14	MO	M$ gi	26	BCCC	Ind	

course details			98 expected requirements							96 entry stats	
TITLE	CODE	COURSE	SUBJECTS	A/AS	NO/C	RGNVQ	IB	SQA(H)	SQA	RATIO	A/AS
Mathematics/Linguistic Science	G1Q1	3FT deg	M	14	MO $	M$_ gi	26$	BCCC$	Ind		
Operational Research/Linguistic Science	N2Q1	3FT deg	*	14	MO $	M$ gi	26	BCCC	Ind		
Psychology/Linguistic Science	C8Q1	3FT deg	*	20	4M+4D	D$ gi	28	BBBC	Ind		
Combined Modular Scheme	Y100	3FT deg									
Linguistic Science											

JEWS' COLL (Univ of London)

Jewish Studies	Y400	3FT deg	*	18	Ind		Ind	CSYS	Ind		
Rabbinical Literature											

Univ of KENT

Comparative Literary Studies/Classical Studies	QQ28	3FT deg	*	20	3M+3D	Ind	28	Ind	Ind	2	
Computing/Comparative Literary Studies	QG25	3FT deg	*	20	3M+3D	Ind	28	Ind	Ind		
Drama/Comparative Literary Studies	QWF4	3FT deg	*	22	2M+4D	Ind	30	Ind	Ind	3	
English (Post-Colonial Lits)/Comparative Lit St	QQ2J	3FT deg	E	24	1M+5D	Ind	32$	Ind	Ind		
English Language/Comparative Literary Studies	QQ23	3FT deg	E	20	3M+3D	Ind	28	Ind	Ind	2	18/22
English/Comparative Literary Studies	QQF3	3FT deg	E	24	1M+5D	Ind	32	Ind	Ind	3	18/24
European Studies/Comparative Literary Studies	TQ22	4FT deg	L	20	3M+3D	Ind	28	Ind	Ind		
Film Studies/Comparative Literary Studies	WQ52	3FT deg	*	22	2M+4D	Ind	30	Ind	Ind		
French/Comparative Literary Studies	RQ12	4FT deg	F	20	3M+3D	Ind	28	Ind	Ind	2	
German/Comparative Literary Studies	RQ22	4FT deg	G	20	3M+3D	Ind	28	Ind	Ind		
History & Theory of Art/Comparative Literary St	VQ42	3FT deg	*	20	3M+3D	Ind	28	Ind	Ind	3	
History/Comparative Literary Studies	QV21	3FT deg	*	22	2M+4D	Ind	30	Ind	Ind		
Italian/Comparative Literary Studies	QRF3	4FT deg	*	20	3M+3D	Ind	28	Ind	Ind		
Linguistics/Classical Studies	QQ81	3FT deg	*	20	3M+3D	Ind	28	Ind	Ind	3	
Linguistics/Comparative Literary Studies	QQ21	3FT deg	*	20	3M+3D	Ind	28	Ind	Ind		
Linguistics/Computing	QG15	3FT deg	*	20	3M+3D	Ind	28	Ind	Ind		
Linguistics/Drama	WQ41	3FT deg	*	22	2M+4D	Ind	30	Ind	Ind		
Linguistics/English	QQ31	3FT deg	E	24	1M+5D	Ind	32	Ind	Ind	7	
Linguistics/English (Post-Colonial Literatures)	QQJ1	3FT deg	E	24	1M+5D	Ind	32	Ind	Ind		
Linguistics/European Studies	TQ21	4FT deg	L	20	3M+3D	Ind	28	Ind	Ind		
Linguistics/Film Studies	WQ51	3FT deg	*	22	2M+4D	Ind	30	Ind	Ind		
Linguistics/French	RQ11	4FT deg	F	22	2M+4D	Ind	30	Ind	Ind	19	
Linguistics/German	RQ21	4FT deg	G	20	3M+3D	Ind	28	Ind	Ind	7	
Linguistics/History	QV11	3FT deg	*	22	2M+4D	Ind	30	Ind	Ind		
Linguistics/History and Theory of Art	VQ41	3FT deg	*	20	3M+3D	Ind	28	Ind	Ind		
Linguistics/Italian	RQ31	4FT deg	*	20	3M+3D	Ind	28	Ind	Ind		
Philosophy/Comparative Literary Studies	VQ72	3FT deg	*	20	3M+3D	Ind	28	Ind	Ind		
Philosophy/Linguistics	VQ71	3FT deg	*	20	3M+3D	Ind	28	Ind	Ind	9	
Spanish/Comparative Literary Studies	QR24	4FT deg	*	20	3M+3D	Ind	28	Ind	Ind		
Spanish/Linguistics	RQ41	4FT deg	*	20	3M+3D	Ind	28	Ind	Ind		
Theology/Comparative Literary Studies	VQ82	3FT deg	*	20	3M+3D	Ind	28	Ind	Ind	1	
Theology/Linguistics	VQ81	3FT deg	*	20	3M+3D	Ind	28	Ind	Ind		

Univ of Wales, LAMPETER

Management Techniques and American Literature	NQ41	3FT deg			Ind	Ind	Ind	Ind	Ind		

LANCASTER Univ

Computer Science and Linguistics	GQ51	3FT deg	* g	BBC	Ind		30	ABBBB	Ind		
English Literature and Linguistics	QQ13	3FT deg	E g	BBC	Ind $		30$	ABBBB$	Ind		
French Studies and Linguistics	QR11	4SW deg	F g	BBC	MO $		30$	BBBBB$	Ind		
German Studies and Linguistics	QR12	4SW deg	G/L g	BBC	MO $		30$	BBBBB$	Ind		
Human Communication	PQ31	3FT deg	* g	BBC	MO		30	ABBBB	Ind		
Italian Studies and Linguistics	QR13	4SW deg	I/L g	BBC	MO $		30$	BBBBB$	Ind		
Linguistics	Q100	3FT deg	* g	BBC	MO		30	ABBBB	Ind		

			98 expected requirements							96 entry stats	
course details											
TITLE	CODE	COURSE	SUBJECTS	A/AS	NO/C	AGNVQ	IB	SQA(H)	SQA	RATIO	A/AS
Linguistics and English Language	QQ1H	3FT deg	E/L/Cl g	BBC	MO		30	ABBBB	Ind		
Linguistics and Philosophy	QV17	3FT deg	* g	BBC	MO		30$	BBBBB$	Ind		
Linguistics and Psychology	CQ81	3FT deg	* g	BBC	DO		32	ABBBB	Ind		
Spanish Studies and Linguistics	QR14	4SW deg	Sp/L g	BBC	MO $		30$	BBBBB$	Ind		
Univ of LEEDS											
Arabic-Linguistics	QT16	4FT deg	C1/L g	BCC	Ind	Ind	28$	CSYS	Ind	4	
Chinese-Linguistics	QT13	4FT deg	L g	BBC	Ind	Ind	30$	CSYS	Ind	4	
English-Linguistics	QQ13	3FT deg	E	BBC	Ind	Ind	Ind	Ind	Ind		
French-Linguistics	QR11	4FT deg	F g	BBC	Ind	Ind	30$	CSYS	Ind	6	22/28
German-Linguistics	QR12	4FT deg	G g	BBC	Ind	Ind	30$	CSYS	Ind	10	
Italian-Linguistics	QR13	4FT deg	I g	BCC	Ind	Ind	28$	CSYS	Ind		
Italian-Linguistics B	QR1H	4FT deg	L g	BCC	Ind	Ind	28$	CSYS	Ind	7	
Japanese-Linguistics	QT14	4FT deg	L g	BBC	Ind	Ind	30$	CSYS	Ind		
Linguistics	Q100	3FT deg	* g	BCC-BBC	Ind	Ind	28$	CSYS	Ind	15	20/24
Linguistics and Language Learning	Q140	3 deg	* g	BCC	Ind	Ind	28$	CSYS	Ind		
Linguistics-Computing	QG15	3FT deg	L g	BBC	Ind	Ind	30$	ABBBB	Ind	6	
Linguistics-Russian	QR18	4FT deg	R g	BCC	Ind	Ind	28$	CSYS	Ind		
Linguistics-Russian B	QR1V	4FT deg	L g	BCC	Ind	Ind	28$	CSYS	Ind		
Linguistics-Spanish	QR14	4FT deg	Sp g	BBC	Ind	Ind	30$	CSYS	Ind	9	
LEEDS METROPOLITAN Univ											
History and Literature	VQ12	3FT deg									
Literature	Q200	3FT deg									
LUTON Univ											
Broadcasting & Media Technology with Linguistics	H6Q1	3FT deg		12-16	MO/DO	M/D	32	BBCC	Ind		
Built Environment w Lang & Stylistics in English	N8QG	3FT deg	g	12-16	MO/DO	M/D	32	BBCC	Ind		
Business Systems with Comparative Literature	N1QF	3FT deg	g	12-16	MO/DO	M/D	32	BBCC	Ind		
Business with Language & Stylistics in English	N1QG	3FT deg	g	12-16	MO/DO	M/D	32	BBCC	Ind		
Business with Linguistics	N1Q1	3FT deg	g	12-16	MO/DO	M/D	32	BBCC	Ind		
Business with Literary Studies in English	N1Q2	3FT deg	g	12-16	MO/DO	M/D	32	BBCC	Ind		
Contemp Br & Euro Hist w Lang & Stylis in Engl	V1QG	3FT deg	g	12-16	MO/DO	M/D	32	BBCC	Ind		
Contemp Br & Euro Hist with Literary St in Engl	V1Q2	3FT deg	g	12-16	MO/DO	M/D	32	BBCC	Ind	1	
Contemp Br & Euro History with Compar Literature	V1QF	3FT deg	g	12-16	MO/DO	M/D	32	BBCC	Ind		
Contemp British & Euro History with Linguistics	V1Q1	3FT deg	g	12-16	MO/DO	M/D	32	BBCC	Ind		
Contemporary English Language Studies	Q140	3FT deg		12-16	MO/DO	AGNVQ	32	BBCC	Ind		
Environmental Sci with Comparative Literature	F9QF	3FT deg	g	12-16	MO/DO	M/D	32	BBCC	Ind		
Environmental Sci with Lang & Stylistics in Engl	F9QG	3FT deg	g	12-16	MO/DO	M/D	32	BBCC	Ind		
Environmental Sci with Literary St in English	F9Q2	3FT deg	g	12-16	MO/DO	M/D	32	BBCC	Ind		
Euro Language St w Lang & Stylistics in English	T2QG	3FT deg	L g	12-16	MO/DO	M/D	32	BBCC	Ind		
European Language St with Comparative Literature	T2QF	3FT deg	L g	12-16	MO/DO	M/D	32	BBCC	Ind	1	
European Language St with Literary St in English	T2Q2	3FT deg	L g	12-16	MO/DO	M/D	32	BBCC	Ind		
Geology with Comparative Literature	F6QF	3FT deg	g	12-16	MO/DO	M/D	32	BBCC	Ind		
Health Science with Literary Studies in English	B9Q2	3FT deg	g	12-16	MO/DO	M/D	32	BBCC	Ind		
Language & Stylistics in Engl and Business Syst	NQCG	3FT deg	g	12-16	MO/DO	M/D	32	BBCC	Ind		
Language & Stylistics in English & Built Environ	NQ8G	3FT deg	g	12-16	MO/DO	M/D	32	BBCC	Ind		
Language & Stylistics in English & Computer Sci	GQ5G	3FT deg	g	12-16	MO/DO	M/D	32	BBCC	Ind		
Language & Stylistics in English & Contemp Hist	VQ1G	3FT deg	g	12-16	MO/DO	M/D	32	BBCC	Ind		
Language & Stylistics in English & Environ Sci	QFG9	3FT deg	g	12-16	MO/DO	M/D	32	BBCC	Ind		
Language & Stylistics in English & Euro Lang St	QTG2	3FT deg	L g	12-16	MO/DO	M/D	32	BBCC	Ind		
Language & Stylistics in English and Business	NQ1G	3FT deg	g	12-16	MO/DO	M/D	32	BBCC	Ind		
Law and Language & Stylistics in English	QMG3	3FT deg	g	12-16	MO/DO	M/D	32	BBCC	Ind		
Law with Comparative Literature	M3Q2	3FT deg	g	12-16	MO/DO	M/D	32	BBCC	Ind		

course details | 98 expected requirements | 96 entry stats

TITLE	CODE	COURSE	SUBJECTS	A/AS	NO/C	AGNVQ	IB	SQA(H)	SQA	RATIO A/AS
Leisure St and Language & Stylistics in English	QNG7	3FT deg	g	12-16	MO/DO	M/D	32	BBCC	Ind	
Leisure St with Language & Stylistics in English	N7QG	3FT deg	g	12-16	MO/DO	M/D	32	BBCC	Ind	
Leisure Studies with Comparative Literature	N7QF	3FT deg	g	12-16	MO/DO	M/D	32	BBCC	Ind	
Leisure Studies with Literary Studies in English	N7Q2	3FT deg	g	12-16	MO/DO	M/D	32	BBCC	Ind	
Linguistics	Q101	3FT deg	g	12-16	MO/DO	M/D	32	BBCC	Ind	5 10/14
Linguistics and Accounting	NQK1	3FT deg	g	12-16	MO/DO	M/D	32	BBCC	Ind	
Linguistics and Artificial Intelligence	GQ81	3FT deg		12-16	MO/DO	M/D	32	BBCC	Ind	
Linguistics and Biology	CQ11	3FT deg	g	12-16	MO/DO	M/D	32	BBCC	Ind	
Linguistics and Business	NQ11	3FT deg	g	12-16	MO/DO	M/D	32	BBCC	Ind	
Linguistics and Computer Science	GQ51	3FT deg	g	12-16	MO/DO	M/D	32	BBCC	Ind	
Linguistics and Contemporary History	VQ11	3FT deg	g	12-16	MO/DO	M/D	32	BBCC	Ind	
Linguistics and Journalism	PQ61	3FT deg		12-16	MO/DO	M/D	32	BBCC	Ind	
Linguistics and Language & Stylistics in English	QQG1	3FT deg	g	12-16	MO/DO	M/D	32	BBCC	Ind	
Linguistics with Accounting	Q1NK	3FT deg	g	12-16	MO/DO	M/D	32	BBCC	Ind	
Linguistics with Animation	Q1WF	3FT deg	g	12-16	MO/DO	M/D	32	BBCC	Ind	
Linguistics with Biology	Q1C1	3FT deg	g	12-16	MO/DO	M/D	32	BBCC	Ind	
Linguistics with Business	Q1N1	3FT deg	g	12-16	MO/DO	M/D	32	BBCC	Ind	
Linguistics with Comparative Literature	Q1QF	3FT deg	g	12-16	MO/DO	M/D	32	BBCC	Ind	
Linguistics with Contemporary History	Q1V1	3FT deg	g	12-16	MO/DO	M/D	32	BBCC	Ind	
Linguistics with French	Q1R1	3FT deg	F g	12-16	MO/DO	M/D	32	BBCC	Ind	9
Linguistics with Geographical Info Systems	Q102	3FT deg	g	12-16	MO/DO	M/D	32	BBCC	Ind	
Linguistics with German	Q1R2	3FT deg	G g	12-16	MO/DO	M/D	32	BBCC	Ind	
Linguistics with Italian	Q1R3	3FT deg	I g	12-16	MO/DO	M/D	32	BBCC	Ind	
Linguistics with Japanese	Q1T4	3FT deg	g	12-16	MO/DO	M/D	32	BBCC	Ind	
Linguistics with Journalism	Q1P6	3FT deg	g	12-16	MO/DO	M/D	32	BBCC	Ind	
Linguistics with Lang & Stylistics in English	Q1QG	3FT deg	g	12-16	MO/DO	M/D	32	BBCC	Ind	
Linguistics with Marketing	Q1N5	3FT deg	g	12-16	MO/DO	M/D	32	BBCC	Ind	
Linguistics with Media Practices	Q1P4	3FT deg	g	12-16	MO/DO	M/D	32	BBCC	Ind	
Linguistics with Media Production	Q1PL	3FT deg	g	12-16	MO/DO	M/D	32	BBCC	Ind	
Linguistics with Multimedia	Q1PK	3FT deg	g	12-16	MO/DO	M/D	32	BBCC	Ind	
Linguistics with Organisational Behaviour	Q1L7	3FT deg	g	12-16	MO/DO	M/D	32	BBCC	Ind	
Linguistics with Physical Geography	Q1FV	3FT deg	g	12-16	MO/DO	M/D	32	BBCC	Ind	
Linguistics with Politics	Q1M1	3FT deg	g	12-16	MO/DO	M/D	32	BBCC	Ind	
Linguistics with Public Policy and Management	Q1MC	3FT deg	g	12-16	MO/DO	M/D	32	BBCC	Ind	
Linguistics with Publishing	Q1P5	3FT deg	g	12-16	MO/DO	M/D	32	BBCC	Ind	
Linguistics with Social Studies	Q1L3	3FT deg	g	12-16	MO/DO	M/D	32	BBCC	Ind	
Linguistics with Spanish	Q1R4	3FT deg	Sp g	12-16	MO/DO	M/D	32	BBCC	Ind	
Linguistics with TV Studies	Q1W5	3FT deg	g	12-16	MO/DO	M/D	32	BBCC	Ind	
Lit St in English with Lang & Stylistics in Engl	Q203	3FT deg		12-16	MO/DO	M/D	32	BBCC	Ind	
Literary St in Engl & Lang & Stylistics in Engl	Q206	3FT deg		12-16	MO/DO	M/D	32	BBCC	Ind	
Literary St in English with Public Policy & Mgt	Q2MC	3FT deg		12-16	MO/DO	M/D	32	BBCC	Ind	
Literary Studies in English	Q200	3FT deg	g	12-16	MO/DO	M/D	32	BBCC	Ind	5 8/18
Literary Studies in English & Contemporary Hist	VQ12	3FT deg	g	12-16	MO/DO	M/D	32	BBCC	Ind	3
Literary Studies in English and British Studies	VQ92	3FT deg		12-16	MO/DO	M/D	32	BBCC	Ind	
Literary Studies in English and Business	NQ12	3FT deg	g	12-16	MO/DO	M/D	32	BBCC	Ind	
Literary Studies in English and Computer Science	GQ52	3FT deg	g	12-16	MO/DO	M/D	32	BBCC	Ind	
Literary Studies in English and Euro Language St	TQ22	3FT deg	L g	12-16	MO/DO	M/D	32	BBCC	Ind	1
Literary Studies in English and Geology	FQ62	3FT deg	g	12-16	MO/DO	M/D	32	BBCC	Ind	
Literary Studies in English and Health Studies	BQX2	3FT deg	g	12-16	MO/DO	M/D	32	BBCC	Ind	
Literary Studies in English and Journalism	PQ62	3FT deg		12-16	MO/DO	M/D	32	BBCC	Ind	
Literary Studies in English and Leisure Studies	NQ72	3FT deg	g	12-16	MO/DO	M/D	32	BBCC	Ind	
Literary Studies in English and Linguistics	QQ12	3FT deg	g	12-16	MO/DO	M/D	32	BBCC	Ind	1

Linguistics and Literature 49

course details | 98 expected requirements | 96 entry stats

TITLE	CODE	COURSE	SUBJECTS	A/AS	ND/C	AGNVQ	IB	SQA(H)	SQA	RATIO A/AS
Literary Studies in English with British Studies	Q2V9	3FT deg		12-16	MO/DO	M/D	32	BBCC	Ind	
Literary Studies in English with Business	Q2N1	3FT deg		12-16	MO/DO	M/D	32	BBCC	Ind	
Literary Studies in English with Chinese	Q2T3	3FT deg		12-16	MO/DO	M/D	32	BBCC	Ind	
Literary Studies in English with Comparative Lit	Q201	3FT deg		12-16	MO/DO	M/D	32	BBCC	Ind	
Literary Studies in English with Contemp History	Q2VC	3FT deg		12-16	MO/DO	M/D	32	BBCC	Ind	
Literary Studies in English with Film Studies	Q2W5	3FT deg		12-16	MO/DO	M/D	32	BBCC	Ind	
Literary Studies in English with French	Q2R1	3FT deg		12-16	MO/DO	M/D	32	BBCC	Ind	
Literary Studies in English with Geology	Q2F6	3FT deg		12-16	MO/DO	M/D	32	BBCC	Ind	
Literary Studies in English with German	Q2R2	3FT deg		12-16	MO/DO	M/D	32	BBCC	Ind	
Literary Studies in English with Health Studies	Q2BX	3FT deg		12-16	MO/DO	M/D	32	BBCC	Ind	
Literary Studies in English with Journalism	Q2P6	3FT deg		12-16	MO/DO	M/D	32	BBCC	Ind	
Literary Studies in English with Linguistics	Q2Q1	3FT deg		12-16	MO/DO	M/D	32	BBCC	Ind	
Literary Studies in English with Marketing	Q2N5	3FT deg		12-16	MO/DO	M/D	32	BBCC	Ind	
Literary Studies in English with Media Practices	Q2P4	3FT deg		12-16	MO/DO	M/D	32	BBCC	Ind	
Literary Studies in English with Mod English St	Q2Q3	3FT deg		12-16	MO/DO	M/D	32	BBCC	Ind	
Literary Studies in English with Modern History	Q2V1	3FT deg		12-16	MO/DO	M/D	32	BBCC	Ind	
Literary Studies in English with Org Behaviour	Q2LT	3FT deg		12-16	MO/DO	M/D	32	BBCC	Ind	
Literary Studies in English with Politics	Q2M1	3FT deg		12-16	MO/DO	M/D	32	BBCC	Ind	
Literary Studies in English with Psychology	Q2L7	3FT deg		12-16	MO/DO	M/D	32	BBCC	Ind	
Literary Studies in English with Publishing	Q2P5	3FT deg		12-16	MO/DO	M/D	32	BBCC	Ind	
Literary Studies in English with TV Studies	Q2WM	3FT deg		12-16	MO/DO	M/D	32	BBCC	Ind	
Literary Studs in English with Media Production	Q2PL	3FT deg		12-16	MO/DO	M/D	32	BBCC	Ind	
Mapping Sci with Language & Stylistics in Engl	F8QG	3FT deg	g	12-16	MO/DO	M/D	32	BBCC	Ind	
Mapping Science & Language & Stylistics in Engl	QFG8	3FT deg	g	12-16	MO/DO	M/D	32	BBCC	Ind	
Mapping Science and Literary Studies in English	QF28	3FT deg	g	12-16	MO/DO	M/D	32	BBCC	Ind	
Mapping Science with Literary Studies in English	F8Q2	3FT deg	g	12-16	MO/DO	M/D	32	BBCC	Ind	
Marketing and Language & Stylistics in English	QNG5	3FT deg	g	12-16	MO/DO	M/D	32	BBCC	Ind	
Marketing and Linguistics	QN15	3FT deg	g	12-16	MO/DO	M/D	32	BBCC	Ind	
Marketing and Literary Studies in English	QN25	3FT deg	g	12-16	MO/DO	M/D	32	BBCC	Ind	
Marketing with Language & Stylistics in English	N5QG	3FT deg	L g	12-16	MO/DO	M/D	32	BBCC	Ind	
Marketing with Linguistics	N5Q1	3FT deg	g	12-16	MO/DO	M/D	32	BBCC	Ind	
Marketing with Literary Studies in English	N5Q2	3FT deg	g	12-16	MO/DO	M/D	32	BBCC	Ind	
Media Practices & Language & Stylistics in Engl	QPG4	3FT deg	g	12-16	MO/DO	M/D	32	BBCC	Ind	
Media Practices and Linguistics	QP14	3FT deg	g	12-16	MO/DO	M/D	32	BBCC	Ind	
Media Practices and Literary Studies in English	QP24	3FT deg	g	12-16	MO/DO	M/D	32	BBCC	Ind	18
Media Practices w Lang & Stylistics in English	P4QG	3FT deg	g	12-16	MO/DO	M/D	32	BBCC	Ind	
Media Practices with Linguistics	P4Q1	3FT deg	g	12-16	MO/DO	M/D	32	BBCC	Ind	
Media Practices with Literary Studies in English	P4Q2	3FT deg	g	12-16	MO/DO	M/D	32	BBCC	Ind	
Media Production and Linguistics	QP1L	3FT deg	g	12-16	MO/DO	M/D	32	BBCC	Ind	
Media Production and Literary Studies in English	QP2L	3FT deg	g	12-16	MO/DO	M/D	32	BBCC	Ind	
Media Production with Comparative Literature	P4QF	3FT deg		12-16	MO/DO	M/D	32	BBCC	Ind	
Media Production with Linguistics	P4QC	3FT deg		12-16	MO/DO	M/D	32	BBCC	Ind	
Modern English St & Language & Stylistics in Eng	QQG3	3FT deg	g	12-16	MO/DO	M/D	32	BBCC	Ind	
Modern English Studies & Literary St in English	QQ23	3FT deg		12-16	MO/DO	M/D	32	BBCC	Ind	
Modern English Studies with Comparative Lit	Q3QF	3FT deg	g	12-16	MO/DO	M/D	32	BBCC	Ind	
Modern History & Language & Stylistics in Engl	QVGC	3FT deg	g	12-16	MO/DO	M/D	32	BBCC	Ind	
Modern History and Linguistics	QV1C	3FT deg	g	12-16	MO/DO	M/D	32	BBCC	Ind	
Modern History and Literary Studies in English	QV2C	3FT deg	g	12-16	MO/DO	M/D	32	BBCC	Ind	6
Modern History with Linguistics	V1QC	3FT deg		12-16	MO/DO	M/D	32	BBCC	Ind	
Org Behaviour and Language & Stylistics in Engl	QLG7	3FT deg	g	12-16	MO/DO	M/D	32	BBCC	Ind	
Organisational Behaviour & Literary St in Engl	QL27	3FT deg	g	12-16	MO/DO	M/D	32	BBCC	Ind	
Organisational Behaviour and Linguistics	QL17	3FT deg	g	12-16	MO/DO	M/D	32	BBCC	Ind	

			98 expected requirements							96 entry stats

course details / **98 expected requirements** / **96 entry stats**

TITLE	CODE	COURSE	SUBJECTS	A/AS	NO/C	RGNVQ	IB	SQA(H)	SQA	RATIO A/AS
Physical Geog & Language & Stylistics in English	QFGV	3FT deg	g	12-16	MO/DO	M/D	32	BBCC	Ind	
Physical Geography and Literary St in English	QF2V	3FT deg	g	12-16	MO/DO	M/D	32	BBCC	Ind	
Physical Geography with Comparative Literature	F8QF	3FT deg	g	12-16	MO/DO	M/D	32	BBCC	Ind	
Politics and Language & Stylistics in English	QMG1	3FT deg	g	12-16	MO/DO	M/D	32	BBCC	Ind	
Politics and Literary Studies in English	QM21	3FT deg	g	12-16	MO/DO	M/D	32	BBCC	Ind	
Politics with Comparative Literature	M1QF	3FT deg	g	12-16	MO/DO	M/D	32	BBCC	Ind	
Politics with Language & Stylistics in English	M1QG	3FT deg	g	12-16	MO/DO	M/D	32	BBCC	Ind	
Politics with Literary Studies in English	M1Q2	3FT deg	g	12-16	MO/DO	M/D	32	BBCC	Ind	
Psychology and Language & Stylistics in English	QLGR	3FT deg	g	12-16	MO/DO	M/D	32	BBCC	Ind	2
Psychology and Literary Studies in English	QL2T	3FT deg		12-16	MO/DO	M/D	32	BBCC	Ind	
Psychology with Comparative Literature	L7QF	3FT deg	g	12-16	MO/DO	M/D	32	BBCC	Ind	
Public Policy & Management with Linguistics	M1QC	3FT deg	g	12-16	MO/DO	M/D	32	BBCC	Ind	
Public Policy & Mgt and Literary St in English	QM2C	3FT deg	g	12-16	MO/DO	M/D	32	BBCC	Ind	
Public Policy and Management and Linguistics	QM1C	3FT deg	g	12-16	MO/DO	M/D	32	BBCC	Ind	
Regional Plan & Dev & Lang & Stylistics in Engl	QKG4	3FT deg	g	12-16	MO/DO	M/D	32	BBCC	Ind	
Social Policy and Linguistics	LQ41	3FT deg		12-16	MO/DO	M/D	32	BBCC	Ind	
Social Policy with Linguistics	L4Q1	3FT deg		12-16	MO/DO	M/D	32	BBCC	Ind	
Social Studies & Language & Stylistics in Engl	QLG3	3FT deg	g	12-16	MO/DO	M/D	32	BBCC	Ind	
Social Studies and Linguistics	QL13	3FT deg	g	12-16	MO/DO	M/D	32	BBCC	Ind	
Social Studies with Comparative Literature	L3QF	3FT deg	g	12-16	MO/DO	M/D	32	BBCC	Ind	
Social Studies with Lang & Stylistics in English	L3QG	3FT deg	g	12-16	MO/DO	M/D	32	BBCC	Ind	
Social Studies with Linguistics	L3Q1	3FT deg	g	12-16	MO/DO	M/D	32	BBCC	Ind	
Sociology and Linguistics	LQH1	3FT deg		12-16	MO/DO	M/D	32	BBCC	Ind	
Sociology and Literary Studies in English	LQH2	3FT deg		12-16	MO/DO	M/D	32	BBCC	Ind	
Sociology with Linguistics	L3QC	3FT deg		12-16	MO/DO	M/D	32	BBCC	Ind	
Sociology with Literary Studies in English	L3Q2	3FT deg		12-16	MO/DO	M/D	32	BBCC	Ind	
Travel & Tourism with Lang & Stylistics in Engl	P7QG	3FT deg	g	12-16	MO/DO	M/D	32	BBCC	Ind	
Travel and Tourism and Lang & Stylistics in Engl	QPG7	3FT deg	g	12-16	MO/DO	M/D	32	BBCC	Ind	
Travel and Tourism with Comparative Literature	P7QF	3FT deg	g	12-16	MO/DO	M/D	32	BBCC	Ind	

Univ of MANCHESTER

TITLE	CODE	COURSE	SUBJECTS	A/AS	NO/C	RGNVQ	IB	SQA(H)	SQA	RATIO A/AS
English and Linguistics	QQ13	3FT deg	E	BBB	X		32$	AABBB		5	18/24
French and Linguistics	RQ11	4FT deg	F	BBB	X		32$	AABBB		6	18/28
German and Linguistics	RQ21	4FT deg	G	BBB	X		32$	AABBB		7	
Italian and Linguistics	RQ31	4FT deg	L	BBB	X		32$	AABBB			
Latin and Linguistics	QQ61	3FT deg	Ln	BBC	X	X	30$	ABBBB	X	1	
Linguistics	Q100	3FT deg		BBB	X		32$	AABBB		6	18/28
Linguistics and Middle Eastern Languages	QT16	4FT deg	L	BBB	X		32$	AABBB		4	
Linguistics and Philosophy	QV17	3FT deg		BBB	X		32$	AABBB		3	
Linguistics and Russian	QR18	4FT deg	R	BBB	X		32$	AABBB		1	
Linguistics and Social Anthropology	QL16	3FT deg		BBB	X		32$	AABBB		3	22/24
Linguistics and Sociology	QL13	3FT deg		BBB	X		32$	AABBB		15	
Linguistics and Spanish	QR14	4FT deg	Sp	BBB	X		32$	AABBB		10	

UMIST (Manchester)

TITLE	CODE	COURSE	SUBJECTS	A/AS	NO/C	RGNVQ	IB	SQA(H)	SQA	RATIO A/AS
Computational Linguistics	G5Q1	3FT deg	* g	20	MO+3D	Ind	28	BBBBB	Ind	
Computational Linguistics (MLang Eng)	G5QC	4FT deg	* g	20	MO+3D	Ind	28	BBBBB	Ind	

NENE COLLEGE

TITLE	CODE	COURSE	SUBJECTS	A/AS	NO/C	RGNVQ	IB	SQA(H)	SQA	RATIO A/AS
English and Cultural Studies	Q202	3FT deg	E	CC	5M	M	24	CCC	Ind	6/18

Univ of NEWCASTLE

TITLE	CODE	COURSE	SUBJECTS	A/AS	NO/C	RGNVQ	IB	SQA(H)	SQA	RATIO A/AS
Linguistics	Q100	3FT deg	*	BBC	2M+1D		Ind	BBBBC	Ind	5	18/28
Combined Studies (BA) *English Linguistic Studies*	Y400	3FT deg	*	ABC-BBB	5D	Ind	35$	AAAB	Ind	

Linguistics and Literature 49

| | | | 98 expected requirements | | | | | | | 96 entry stats | |
TITLE	CODE	COURSE	SUBJECTS	A/AS	ND/C	AGNVQ	IB	SQA(H)	SQA	RATIO	A/AS
Univ of NORTHUMBRIA											
Combined Honours *English*	Y400▼	3FT deg	g	12-20	MO+3D	DT	26	BBCCC	Ind		
NOTTINGHAM TRENT Univ											
Humanities *Language and Linguistics*	Y301	3FT/4SW deg									
Univ of PORTSMOUTH											
Applied Languages	Q140	4FT deg	L	10-12	5M	M$6/^	25	BCCC	Ind	3	8/20
Literary Studies	Q210	3FT deg	E/EI	14-16	5M	M$^	25	BBBB	Ind	2	8/22
QUEEN MARY & WESTFIELD COLL (Univ of London)											
French and Linguistics	RQ11	4FT deg	F	18		M^	30$				
German and Linguistics	RQ21	4FT deg	G	18		M^	30$				
Hispanic Studies and Linguistics	RQ4C	4FT deg	L	20		M^	30$				
Russian and Linguistics	QR18	4FT deg	L	18		M^	30$				
Univ of READING											
English Literature & Modern English Language	QQ31	3FT deg	EI	BBC	Ind	D*^	31$	BBBB$	Ind	10	20/30
French and Linguistics	QR11	4FT deg	F	BBC	Ind	D*^	31$	BBBB$	Ind	12	
German and Linguistics	QR12	4FT deg	*g	BCC	Ind	D$^	30	BBBB	Ind	7	
Italian and Linguistics	QR13	4FT deg	*g	BCC	Ind	D$6/^ go	30	BBBB	Ind	3	
Latin and Linguistics	QQ16	3FT deg	*g	BCC	Ind	D*6/^ go	30	BBBB	Ind		
Linguistics	Q101	3FT deg	*	18	Ind	D*6/^	29	BBBC	Ind	6	16/22
Linguistics with a Foreign Language	Q102	4FT deg	*	18	Ind	D*6/^ go	29	BBBC	Ind	6	
Philosophy and Linguistics	QV17	3FT deg	*	BCC	Ind	D*^	30	BBBB	Ind	7	
Psychology and Linguistics	CQ81	3FT deg	*g	BCC	Ind	D*6/^ go	30	BBBB	Ind	11	
Univ College of RIPON & YORK ST JOHN											
American Studies (Literature)	QQ42	3FT deg	E	CDD	MO	M*^	30	BBBB		6	8/20
Applied Social Sciences/Language Studs (English)	L3Q1	3FT deg		CC	M	M	27	BBBC		3	10/20
English Studies (Literature and Language)	QQ31	3FT deg	E	16	Ind	M*^	30	BBBB		5	10/22
English/Language Studies (English)	Q3Q1	3FT deg	E	16	Ind	M*^	30	BBBB		4	8/24
European Studies with Language	T2Q1	3FT deg		12	M	M*	27	BBBC			
Film, TV, Literature & Theatre Studies	WQ42	3FT deg		AB-BBC	MO+3D	D$6/^	30	ABBBB		6	16/28
Language Studies (English)/English	Q1Q3	3FT deg	E	16	X	M*^	30	BBBB		5	12/18
Language Studies (English)/Psychology	Q1L7	3FT deg	g	16	M	M*^	30	BBBB			
Language Studies (English)/Women's Studies	Q1M9	3FT deg		16	M	M*^	30	BBBB			
Language Studs (Engl)/Applied Social Sciences	Q1L3	3FT deg		16	M	M*^	30	BBBB		2	8/22
Psychology/Language Studies (English)	L7Q1	3FT deg	g	16	M	M	30	BBBB			
Univ of SALFORD											
Media, Language and Business	WQ41	3FT deg	L g	18-24	6M	M/D^	28	BBBB	Ind	7	14/22
SOAS:Sch of Oriental & African St (U of London)											
Linguistics	Q100	3FT deg		20	Ind		30	BBBCC	Ind	6	
Linguistics and African Studies	TQ71	3FT deg		20	Ind		30	BBBCC	Ind		
Linguistics and Amharic	QT17	4FT deg		20	Ind		30	BBBCC	Ind		
Linguistics and Arabic	QT16	4FT deg		22	Ind		31	BBBBC	Ind		
Linguistics and Bengali	QT15	3FT deg		20	Ind		30	BBBCC	Ind		
Linguistics and Burmese	QT1M	4FT deg		20	Ind		30	BBBCC	Ind		
Linguistics and Chinese	QT13	4FT deg		24	Ind		32	BBBBB	Ind		
Linguistics and Georgian	QT19	3FT deg		22	Ind		31	BBBBC	Ind		
Linguistics and Gujarati	QTC5	3FT deg		20	Ind		30	BBBCC	Ind		
Linguistics and Hausa	QT1R	4FT deg		20	Ind		30	BBBCC	Ind		

TITLE	CODE	COURSE	SUBJECTS	A/AS	ND/C	AGNVQ	IB	SQA(H)	SQA	RATIO A/AS
Linguistics and Hebrew	QQ19	4FT deg		22	Ind		31	BBBBC	Ind	
Linguistics and Hindi	QT1N	3FT/4FT deg		20	Ind		30	BBBCC	Ind	
Linguistics and Indonesian	QTCM	3FT/4FT deg		20	Ind		30	BBBCC	Ind	
Linguistics and Japanese	QT14	4FT deg		24	Ind		32	BBBBB	Ind	
Linguistics and Korean	QTCN	4FT deg		16	Ind		28	BBCCC	Ind	
Nepali and Linguistics	QTD5	3FT deg		20	Ind		30	BBBCC	Ind	
Persian and Linguistics	QT1Q	3FT deg		22	Ind		31	BBBBC	Ind	
Sanskrit and Linguistics	QQ1X	3FT deg		20	Ind		30	BBBCC	Ind	
Sinhalese and Linguistics	QTDM	3FT deg		20	Ind		30	BBBCC	Ind	
Social Anthropology and Linguistics	LQ61	3FT deg		22	Ind		31	BBBBC	Ind	4
South Asian Studies and Linguistics	TQM1	3FT deg								
Study of Religions and Linguistics	QV18	3FT deg		20	Ind		30	BBBCC	Ind	
Swahili and Linguistics	QT1T	4FT deg		20	Ind		30	BBBCC	Ind	
Tamil and Linguistics	QTDN	3FT deg		20	Ind		30	BBBCC	Ind	
Thai and Linguistics	TQ51	3FT/4FT deg		20	Ind		30	BBBCC	Ind	
Turkish and Linguistics	QT1P	4FT deg		22	Ind		31	BBBBC	Ind	1
Urdu and Linguistics	TQ5C	3FT deg		20	Ind		30	BBBCC	Ind	
Vietnamese and Linguistics	TQ5D	4FT deg		20	Ind		30	BBBCC	Ind	

Univ of SHEFFIELD

TITLE	CODE	COURSE	SUBJECTS	A/AS	ND/C	AGNVQ	IB	SQA(H)	SQA	RATIO A/AS
Biblical Studies and Linguistics	QV18	3FT deg	Ee g	BBC	X	X	30	ABBB	Ind	
English Language with Linguistics	Q3Q1	3FT deg	Ee g	BBC	X	X	30$	ABBB$	Ind	15 20/30
French and Linguistics	QR11	4FT deg	F g	BBC	X	X	30$	ABBB$	Ind	26
German and Linguistics	QR12	4FT deg	G g	BBC	X	X	30$	ABBB$	Ind	16
Linguistics and Hispanic Studies	QR14	4FT deg	Ee+L	BBC	X	X	30$	ABBB$	Ind	
Linguistics and Japanese	QT14	4FT deg	Ee+L	BBC	X	X	30$	ABBB$	Ind	
Linguistics and Korean Studies	QT15	4FT deg	Ee+L	BBC	X	X	30$	ABBB$	Ind	
Linguistics and Philosophy	QV17	3FT deg	Ee g	BBB	X	X	32$	AABB$	Ind	
Linguistics and Russian	QR18	4FT deg	Ee+L g	BBC	X	X	30$	ABBB$	Ind	

THE UNIVERSITY COLLEGE OF ST MARK AND ST JOHN

TITLE	CODE	COURSE	SUBJECTS	A/AS	ND/C	AGNVQ	IB	SQA(H)	SQA	RATIO A/AS
English (Literary Studies)/English Language St	Q3Q1	3FT deg	El	12-16	Ind	M	Ind	Ind	Ind	
English Language Studies/English (Literary St)	Q1Q3	3FT deg		12	MO	M	Ind	Ind	Ind	
English Language Studies/Information Technology	Q1G5	3FT deg		12	MO	M	Ind	Ind	Ind	
English Language Studies/Media Studies	Q1P4	3FT deg		12	MO	M	Ind	Ind	Ind	
English Language Studies/Public Relations	Q1P3	3FT deg		12	MO	M	Ind	Ind	Ind	
English Language Studies/Sociology	Q1L3	3FT deg		12	MO	M	Ind	Ind	Ind	
Info Technology/English Language Studies	G5Q1	3FT deg		4 ·	MO	M	Dip	CCCC	Ind	
Media Studies/English Language Studies	P4Q1	3FT deg		16	MO	M	Ind	Ind	Ind	
Public Relations/English Language Studies	P3QD	3FT deg		16	MO	M	Ind	Ind	Ind	
Sociology/English Language Studies	L3Q1	3FT deg	So	8	MO	M	Ind	Ind	Ind	

ST MARY'S Univ COLL

TITLE	CODE	COURSE	SUBJECTS	A/AS	ND/C	AGNVQ	IB	SQA(H)	SQA	RATIO A/AS
Environmental Investigation St and Classical St	QF19	3FT deg	S/2S	4-8	Ind	Ind	Ind	BBBB	Ind	
Environmental Studies and Classical Studies	QF1X	3FT deg	*	4-8	Ind	Ind	Ind	BBBB	Ind	

STAFFORDSHIRE Univ

TITLE	CODE	COURSE	SUBJECTS	A/AS	ND/C	AGNVQ	IB	SQA(H)	SQA	RATIO A/AS
French with Language Studies	R1Q1	3FT deg	g	DD	4M+2D	M^	26	BCC		
Literary Studies	Q202	3FT deg	El g	CD	MO+2D	M	27	BBC	Ind	3 8/20

Univ of STIRLING

TITLE	CODE	COURSE	SUBJECTS	A/AS	ND/C	AGNVQ	IB	SQA(H)	SQA	RATIO A/AS
English Studies/Commonwealth Literature	Q3QG	4FT deg	g	BBC	Ind	Ind	33	BBBB	HN	
English Studies/Scottish Literature	Q3QF	4FT deg	g	BBC	Ind	Ind	33	BBBB	HN	
Scottish Literature	Q210	4FT deg	g	BBC	Ind	Ind	33	BBBB	HN	
Scottish Literature/Spanish	RQ42	4FT deg	g	CCC	HN	Ind	31	BBBC	HN	

Linguistics and Literature
49

course details			98 expected requirements							96 entry stats
TITLE	CODE	COURSE	SUBJECTS	A/AS	NO/C	RGNVQ	IB	SQA(H)	SQA	RATIO A/AS
UNIVERSITY COLLEGE SUFFOLK										
Applied Biological Science with Literary Studies	C1Q2	3FT deg	S	EE	N $	PS	Ind	Ind	Ind	
Art & Design and Literary Studies	WQ22	3FT deg	E+Pf	EC	N $	P$	Ind	Ind	Ind	
Art & Design and Literary Studies	EQ22	3FT deg	E+Pf	EC	N $	P$	Ind	Ind	Ind	
Art & Design with Literary Studies	E2Q2	3FT deg	Pf	EE	N $	P$	Ind	Ind	Ind	
Art & Design with Literary Studies	W2Q2	3FT deg	Pf	EE	N $	P$	Ind	Ind	Ind	
Behavioural Studies and Literary Studies	LQ72	3FT deg	E	DC	N $	P$	Ind	Ind	Ind	
Behavioural Studies with Literary Studies	L7Q2	3FT deg	E	DD	N $	P$	Ind	Ind	Ind	
Business Studies and Literary Studies	NQ12	3FT deg	E	EC	N $	P$	Ind	Ind	Ind	
Business Studies with Literary Studies	N1Q2	3FT deg	*	EE	N $	P$	Ind	Ind	Ind	
Cultural Studies and Literary Studies	YQ32	3FT deg	E	CE	N $	P$	Ind	Ind	Ind	
Early Childhood Studies and Literary Studies	XQ92	3FT deg	E	CD	N $	P$	Ind	Ind	Ind	
Early Childhood Studies with Literary Studies	X9Q2	3FT deg	*	DD	N $	P$	Ind	Ind	Ind	
Environmental Studies with Literary Studies	F9Q2	3FT deg	S/Gy	EE	N $	P$	Ind	Ind	Ind	
Literary Studies and Applied Biological Science	QC21	3FT deg	E/S	CE	N $	P$	Ind	Ind	Ind	
Literary Studies and Environmental Studies	QF29	3FT deg	E+S/Gy	CE	N $	P$	Ind	Ind	Ind	
Literary Studies and Information Technology	QG25	3FT deg	E	CE	N $	P$	Ind	Ind	Ind	
Literary Studies and Management	QN2C	3FT deg	E	CE	N $	P$	Ind	Ind	Ind	
Literary Studies and Media Studies	QP24	3FT deg	E	CE	N $	P$	Ind	Ind	Ind	
Media Studies with Literary Studies	P4Q2	3FT deg	E	CE	N $	P$	Ind	Ind	Ind	
Product Design & Manufacture and Literary Studs	HQ72	3FT deg	E	CE	N $	P$	Ind	Ind	Ind	
Product Design & Manufacture with Literary Studs	H7Q2	3FT deg	*	EE	N $	P$	Ind	Ind	Ind	
Univ of SUNDERLAND										
Biology with Comparative Literature	C1Q2	3FT deg	B/C	8	3M	M	Ind	Ind	Ind	
English with Comparative Literature	Q3Q2	3FT deg	El g	12	Ind	M	24$	BCCC$	Ind	4
French with Comparative Literature	R1Q2	4FT deg	F+El g	10	Ind	M	24$	CCCC$	N$	
German with Comparative Literature	R2Q2	4FT deg	G+El g	10	Ind	M	24$	CCCC$	Ind	
History with Comparative Literature	V1Q2	3FT deg	E+H g	12	Ind	M	24$	BCCC$	Ind	3
Media Studies with Comparative Literature	P4Q2	3FT deg	El g	12	X	M	24$	BCCC$	$	2
Philosophy with Comparative Literature	V7Q2	3FT deg	El g	12	X	M	24$	BCCC$	X	1
Physiology with Comparative Literature	B1Q2	3FT deg	*	8	3M	M	Ind	Ind	Ind	
Politics with Comparative Literature	M1Q2	3FT deg	*	8	3M	M	Ind	Ind	Ind	
Psychology with Comparative Literature	C8Q2	3FT deg	*	10	4M	M^	Ind	Ind	Ind	
Religious Studies with Comparative Literature	V8Q2	3FT deg	El g	12	Ind	M	24$	BCCC$	Ind	
Sociology with Comparative Literature	L3Q2	3FT deg	El g	12	Ind	M	24$	BCCC$	Ind	1
Univ of SUSSEX										
French and Linguistics	RQ11	4FT deg	F	BCC	MO $	M*^	$	Ind	Ind	
German and Linguistics	RQ21	4FT deg	G	BCC	MO $	M*^	$	Ind	Ind	
Italian and Linguistics	RQ31	4FT deg	g	BCC	MO $	M*6 go	$	Ind	Ind	
Linguistics in Cognitive and Computing Sciences	Q1G5	3FT deg	*	BBC	MO	M*6	$	Ind	Ind	
Linguistics in European Studies	Q1T2	4FT deg	* g	BBC	MO $	M*6 go	$	Ind	Ind	
Russian and Linguistics	RQ81	4FT deg	* g	BCC	MO $	M*6 go	$	Ind	Ind	
THAMES VALLEY Univ										
Accounting with English Language Studies	N4Q1	3FT deg		8-12	MO	M	26	CCC		
American Studies with English Language Studies	Q4Q1	3FT deg		8-12	MO	M	26	CCC		
Business Administration with English Language St	N1QC	3FT deg		8-12	MO	M	26	CCC		
Business Economics with English Language Studies	L1QC	3FT deg		8-12	MO	M	26	CCC		
Business Studies with English Language St (Dip)	N1Q1	3FT/4SW deg		12	MO	M	26			
Economics with English Language Studies	L1Q1	3FT deg		8-12	MO	M	26	CCC		
English Lang & Communs with Politics & Int Rels	Q1M1	3FT deg		8-12	MO	M	24	CCC		
English Lang and Communications with American St	Q1Q4	3FT deg		8-12	MO	M	24	CCC		

course details | 98 expected requirements | 96 entry stats

TITLE	CODE	COURSE	SUBJECTS	A/AS	ND/C	AGNVQ	IB	SQA(H)	SQA	RATIO A/AS
English Lang and Communications with Business	Q1N1	3FT deg		8-12	MO	M	24	CCC		
English Lang and Communications with European St	Q1T2	3FT deg		8-12	MO	M	26	CCC		
English Lang and Communications with Psychology	Q1C8	3FT deg		8-12	MO	M	26	CCC		
English Lang and Communications with Sociology	Q1L3	3FT deg		8-12	MO	M	26	CCC		
English Language and Communications with English	Q1Q3	3FT deg		8-12	MO	M	26	CCC		
English Language and Communications with Eur Law	Q1MH	3FT deg		8-12	MO	M	26	CCC		
English Language and Communications with French	Q1R1	3FT deg		8-12	MO	M	26	CCC		
English Language and Communications with German	Q1R2	3FT deg		8-12	MO	M	26	CCC		
English Language and Communications with History	Q1V1	3FT deg		8-12	MO	M	26	CCC		
English Language and Communications with Int St	Q1MX	3FT deg		8-12	MO	M	26	CCC		
English Language and Communications with Law	Q1M3	3FT deg		8-12	MO	M	26	CCC		
English Language and Communications with Spanish	Q1R4	3FT deg		8-12	MO	M	26	CCC		
English Languages & Communications with Media St	Q1W9	3FT deg		8-12	MO	M	26	CCC		
English with English Language Studies	Q3Q1	3FT deg		8-12	MO	M	26	CCC		
Environmental Policy & Mgt with English Lang St	F9Q1	3FT deg		8-12	MO	M	26	CCC		
European Law with English Language Studies	M3QC	3FT deg		8-12	MO	M	26	CCC		
European Studies with English Language Studies	T2Q1	3FT deg		8-12	MO	M	26	CCC		
Finance with English Language Studies	N3Q1	3FT deg		8-12	MO	M	26	CCC		
Food and Drink Consumer St with English Lang St	D4Q1	3FT deg		8-12	MO	M	26	CCC		
French with English Language Studies	R1Q1	3FT deg		8-12	MO	M	26	CCC		
German with English Language Studies	R2Q1	3FT deg		8-12	MO	M	26	CCC		
Health Studies with English Language Studies	L4Q1	3FT deg		8-12	MO	M	26	CCC		
History with English Language Studies	V1Q1	3FT deg		8-12	MO	M	26	CCC		
Hospitality Management with English Language St	N7Q1	3FT deg		8-12	MO	M	26	CCC		
Human Resource Mgt with English Language Studies	N6Q1	3FT deg		8-12	MO	M	26	CCC		
Information Management with English Language St	P2Q1	3FT deg		8-12	MO	M	26	CCC		
International Studies with English Language St	M9Q1	3FT deg		8-12	MO	M	26	CCC		
Law with English Language Studies	M3Q1	3FT deg		8-12	MO	M	26	CCC		
Leisure Management with English Language Studies	N7QC	3FT deg		8-12	MO	M	26	CCC		
Marketing with English Language Studies	N5Q1	3FT deg		8-12	MO	M	26	CCC		
Media Arts with English Language Studies	W9Q1	3FT deg		8-12	MO	M	26	CCC		
Multi-Media Computing with English Language St	G5Q1	3FT deg		8-12	MO	M	26	CCC		
Politics and Int Relations with English Lang St	M1Q1	3FT deg		8-12	MO	M	26	CCC		
Psychology with English Language Studies	C8Q1	3FT deg		8-12	MO	M	26	CCC		
Recreation Management with English Language St	N7QD	3FT deg		8-12	MO	M	26	CCC		
Sociology with English Language Studies	L3Q1	3FT deg		8-12	MO	M	26	CCC		
Spanish with English Language Studies	R4Q1	3FT deg		8-12	MO	M	26	CCC		
Tourism with English Language Studies	P7Q1	3FT deg		8-12	MO	M	26	CCC		

Univ of ULSTER

TITLE	CODE	COURSE	SUBJECTS	A/AS	ND/C	AGNVQ	IB	SQA(H)	SQA	RATIO A/AS
Computing & Linguistics (4 Yr SW inc DIS or DAS)	GQ51▼	4SW deg	* g	BCC	MO+4D	D*6/^ gi	30	BBBB	Ind	4 14/16
Linguistic Science	Q100▼	3FT deg	* g	CCC	MO+3D	D*6/^ gi	28	BBBC	Ind	6 14/20
Modern Studies in the Humanities _Literature, Culture & Society_	Y321▼	3FT deg	*	CCC	MO+3D	D*6/^ gi	28	BBBC	Ind	

UNIVERSITY COLL LONDON (Univ of London)

TITLE	CODE	COURSE	SUBJECTS	A/AS	ND/C	AGNVQ	IB	SQA(H)	SQA	RATIO A/AS
Anthropology and Linguistics	LQ61	3FT deg	* g	BBC	3M	D$^ go	34$	BBBCC	Ind	9 26/28
Italian and Linguistics (4 Yrs)	RQ31	4FT deg	g	BBC	3M	X	30	BBBCC$	Ind	6
Linguistics	Q100	3FT deg	* g	BBC	3M	Ind	28	BBBCG	Ind	4 16/30
Linguistics with Cognitive Science	Q1C8	3FT deg	* g	BBC	3M	Ind	28	BBBCC	Ind	8
Philosophy and Linguistics	VQ71	3FT deg	* g	BBC	3M	X	28	BBBBC	Ind	21

Linguistics and Literature 49

course details			98 expected requirements							96 entry stats	
TITLE	CODE	COURSE	SUBJECTS	A/AS	ND/C	AGNVQ	IB	SQA(H)	SQA	RATIO	A/AS
Univ of WARWICK											
English and European Literature	QQ32	3FT deg	E+H/L g	ABB-BBB	X	X	32$	AAABB$		11	24/30
Film and Literature	QW25	3FT deg	EI/L g	AAB	X	X	36$	AAAAB$		10	24/30
Italian and European Lit (4 Yrs inc yr abroad)	RQ32	4FT deg	E/L g	BCC	X	X	29$	ABBCC$		9	
Philosophy and Literature	VQ72	3FT deg	E g	BBB	X	X	32$	AABBB$		7	22/30
Univ of WESTMINSTER											
English Language Studies and Linguistics	Q140	3FT deg									
Linguistics and Arabic	TQ61	4SW deg	L	CC	Ind		26	BBB		2	
Linguistics and Chinese	T3Q1	4SW deg	L	CC	Ind		26	BBB	Ind	2	
Linguistics and English	QQ31	4SW deg	E	CC	Ind		26$	BBB		7	12/16
Linguistics and French	RQ11	4SW deg	F	CC	Ind		26$	BBB		6	
Linguistics and German	RQ21	4SW deg	L	CC	Ind		26$	BBB			
Linguistics and Italian	RQ31	4SW deg	L	CC	Ind		26	BBB		5	
Russian and Linguistics	RQ81	4SW deg	L	CC	Ind		26	BBB		1	
Spanish and Linguistics	RQ41	4SW deg	L	CC	Ind		26	BBB		8	
Univ of WOLVERHAMPTON											
Interpreting (BSL)	BQ5C	3FT deg		12	4M	M	24	BBBB	Ind		
Language and Communication	PQ31	4FT deg	L g	18	4D	D	28	BBBB	Ind		
Combined Degrees *Interpreting Brit Sign Lang (Stg2 CACDP Req)*	Y401	3FT/4SW deg	g	12	4M	M	24	BBBB	Ind		
Combined Degrees *Linguistics*	Y401	3FT deg	g	12	4M	M	24	BBBB	Ind		
Univ of YORK											
English/Linguistics (Equal)	QQ31	3FT deg	E g	ABB-ABC	HN $	D$^	32$	AABB$	Ind		
French and Linguistics	RQ11	4FT deg	F	24	Ind	D$^	28$	BBCC$	Ind		24/30
German and Linguistics	RQ21	4FT deg	G	24	Ind	D$^	28$	BBCC$	Ind		
Hindi and Linguistics	QT15	4FT deg	*	24	Ind	D$^	28$	BBCC	Ind		
Languages and Linguistics	Q100	3FT deg	*/L	24	Ind	D$^	28$	BBCC$	Ind		
Linguistics with Chinese	Q1T3	3FT deg	*	24	Ind	D$^	28$	BBCC$	Ind		
Linguistics/Education	Q1X9	3FT/4FT deg	*/L	24	Ind	D$^	28$	BBCC$	Ind		
Linguistics/Literature	Q1Q3	3FT/4FT deg	E g	24	HN $	D$^	30$	ABBB$	Ind		
Linguistics/Philosophy	Q1V7	3FT/4FT deg	*/L	24	Ind	D$^	28$	BBCC$	Ind		
Mathematics/Linguistics	G1Q1	3FT deg	M	20-22	HN $	DS^	30$	CSYS$	HN$		
Mathematics/Linguistics (MMath)	G1QC	4FT deg	M	20-22	HN $	DS^	30$	CSYS$	HN$		
Modern Languages and Linguistics	TQ91	4FT deg	*/L/2L	24	Ind	D$^	28$	BBCC$	Ind		
Philosophy/Linguistics	V7Q1	3FT deg	*	22	Ind	D$6/^	30	BBBC	Ind		
Philosophy/Linguistics (Equal)	VQ71	3FT deg	*	24	Ind	D$^	28$	BBBC	Ind		

TITLE	CODE	COURSE	SUBJECTS	A/AS	ND/C	AGNVQ	IB	SQA(H)	SQA	RATIO A/AS
CORNWALL COLLEGE WITH DUCHY COLLEGE										
Marine Studies	006J	2FT Dip	*		D	N	P	Ind	Ind	N
Univ of GLAMORGAN										
Leisure Boat Design	346J▼	2FT HND	g	4-6	N $	P$	Ind	Ind	Ind	
Univ of GLASGOW										
Naval Architecture and Marine Engineering (MEng)	J6H3	5FT deg	M+P	BBC	M+D $	X	28$	ABBB$	Ind	
Naval Architecture and Ocean Eng/Eur St (MEng)	J627	5FT deg	M+P	BBC	M+D $	X	28$	ABBB$	Ind	
Naval Architecture and Ocean Engineering	J625	4FT/3ACC deg	M+P	BCC-CDD	5M $	Ind	24$	BBBC$	N$	8
Naval Architecture with Fast Ship Design (MEng)	J620	5FT deg	M+P	BBC	M+D $	X	28$	ABBB$	Ind	
Offshore Engineering (MEng)	J650	5FT deg	M+P	BBC	M+D $	X	28$	ABBB$	Ind	
Univ of LIVERPOOL										
Civil and Maritime Engineering (MEng)	HJ26	4FT deg	M	20	5M+2D$	Ind	30$	BBBBB$	Ind	6
Mechanical with Maritime & Offshore Engineering	H3J6	3FT deg	M+P	20	4M+1D$		30$	BBBBB	Ind	18
LIVERPOOL JOHN MOORES Univ										
Marine Operations	J630	3FT/4SW deg		10	3M					
Maritime Engineering	J603	3FT deg								
Maritime Engineering	J608	4FT deg								
Maritime Studies	J601	3FT/4SW deg		6-10	3M					7
Maritime Technology	J602	3FT/4SW deg		10	3M					
Nautical Science (Seafaring)	J604	3FT/4SW deg		10	3M	M				
Marine Operations (2 Yrs/3 Yr SW)	036J	2FT/3SW HND		8	N					1	3/4
Marine Technology (Extended)	806J▼	3EXT HND		E	N					4
Marine Technology (Seafaring) (3 Yrs)	206J	3FT HND		8	N					7
Maritime Engineering	406J	3EXT HND								
Maritime Engineering	106J	2FT HND		E	N	P				14
Nautical Science (Seafaring) (3 Yrs)	056J	3FT HND		E	N	P				
LUTON Univ										
Geology and Biotechnology	FJ86	3FT deg	g	12-16	MO/DO	M/D	32	BBCC	Ind	
Univ of NEWCASTLE										
Naval Architecture	J621	4FT deg	*	CCC-CCD	Ind			BBBB	Ind	4
Naval Architecture	J620	3FT deg	M+P	BCC-CCC	Ind			CSYS	Ind	6
Offshore Engineering	HJ36	3FT deg	M+P	BCC-CCC	Ind			CSYS	Ind	5
Offshore Engineering	JH63	4FT deg	*	CCC-CCD	Ind			BBBB	Ind	7
Small Craft Technology	J611	4FT deg	*	CCC-CCD	Ind			BBBB	Ind	6
Small Craft Technology	J610	3FT deg	M+P	BCC-CCC	Ind			CSYS	Ind	4	12/26
Univ of PLYMOUTH										
Fisheries Studies	J602	3FT deg	Ap g	14	5M $	M$	Ind	CCCC	Ind	25
Fisheries Studies with Astronomy	J6FM	3FT deg	Ap g	14	5M $	M$	Ind	CCCC	Ind	
Fisheries Studies with Hydrography	J6F8	3FT deg	Ap g	14	5M $	M$	Ind	CCCC	Ind	1
Fisheries Studies with Marine Navigation	J6J9	3FT deg	Ap g	14	5M $	M$	Ind	CCCC		
Fisheries Studies with Marine Technology	J660	3FT deg	Ap g	14	5M $	M$	Ind	CCCC	Ind	
Fisheries Studies with Maritime Business	J6N1	3FT deg	Ap g	14	5M $	M$	Ind	Ind	Ind	
Fisheries Studies with Maritime History	J6V1	3FT deg	Ap g	14	5M $	M$	Ind	CCCC	Ind	
Fisheries Studies with Maritime Law	J6M3	3FT deg	Ap g	14	5M $	M$	Ind	CCCC	Ind	
Fisheries Studies with Ocean Science	J6F7	3FT deg	Ap g	14	5M $	M$	Ind	CCCC	Ind	7
Fisheries Studies with Underwater Studies	J6FX	3FT deg	Ap g	14	5M $	M$	Ind	CCCC	Ind	8
Hydrography with Fisheries Technology	F8J6	3FT deg	2(M/P/C/Ap) g	14	5M $	M$	Ind	CCCC		
Hydrography with Marine Technology	F8JP	3FT deg	2(M/P/C/Ap) g	14	5M $	M$	Ind	CCCC		
Marine Navigation with Fisheries Technology	J9JQ	3FT deg	2(M/P/C) g	14	5M $	M$	Ind	CCCC	Ind	

| | | | 98 expected requirements | | | | | | | 96 entry stats | |
| *course details* | | | | | | | | | | | |
TITLE	CODE	COURSE	SUBJECTS	A/AS	NO/C	AGNVQ	IB	SQA(H)	SQA	RATIO	A/AS
Marine Navigation with Marine Technology	J9J6	3FT deg	2(M/P/C) g	14	5M $	M$	Ind	CCCC	Ind		
Marine Systems Technology	J612	3FT deg	2(M/P/C) g	14	5M $	M$	Ind	CCCC	Ind	1	
Marine Technology	J600	3FT deg	2(M/P/C) g	14	5M $	M$	Ind	CCCC	Ind	5	12/20
Marine Technology with Astronomy	J6F5	3FT deg	2(M/P/C) g	14	5M $	M$	Ind	CCCC	Ind		
Marine Technology with Fisheries Business Studs	J6NY	3FT deg	2(M/P/C) g	14	5M $	M$	Ind	CCCC	Ind		
Marine Technology with Fisheries Science	J697	3FT deg	2(M/P/C) g	14	5M $	M$	Ind	CCCC	Ind		
Marine Technology with Fisheries Technology	J601	3FT deg	2(M/P/C) g	12	5M $	M$	Ind	CCCC	Ind		
Marine Technology with Hydrography	J6FV	3FT deg	2(M/P/C) g	14	5M $	M$	Ind	CCCC	Ind	3	
Marine Technology with Marine Navigation	J6JX	3FT deg	2(M/P/C) g	14	5M $	M$	Ind	CCCC	Ind	4	
Marine Technology with Maritime Business	J6NC	3FT deg	2(M/P/C) g	14	5M $	M$	Ind	CCCC	Ind		
Marine Technology with Maritime History	J6VC	3FT deg	2(M/P/C) g	14	5M $	M$	Ind	CCCC	Ind		
Marine Technology with Maritime Law	J6MH	3FT deg	2(M/P/C) g	14	5M $	M$	Ind	CCCC	Ind		
Marine Technology with Ocean Science	J6FR	3FT deg	2(M/P/C) g	14	5M $	M$	Ind	CCCC	Ind		
Marine Technology with Underwater Studies	J605	3FT deg	2(M/P/C) g	14	5M $	M$	Ind	CCCC	Ind	6	
Maritime Business with Fisheries Technology	N1J6	3FT deg	* g	18	5M	M$	Ind	CCCC	Ind		
Nautical Studies	J611	3FT deg	S g	14	5M $	M$	Ind	CCCC	Ind		
Ocean Science with Fisheries Technology	F7JP	3FT deg	S g	14-16	5M $	M$	Ind	CCCC	Ind		
Ocean Science with Marine Technology	F7J6	3FT deg	S g	14-16	5M $	M$	Ind	CCCC	Ind	9	
Underwater Studies with Fisheries Science	F9JP	3FT deg	Ap g	14-16	5M $	M$	Ind	CCCC	Ind		
Underwater Studies with Fisheries Technology	F9J6	3FT deg	Ap g	14-16	5M $	M$	Ind	CCCC	Ind		
Underwater Studies with Marine Technology	F9JQ	3FT deg	Ap g	14-16	5M $	M$	Ind	CCCC	Ind	6	

Univ of SOUTHAMPTON

Ship Science	J640	3FT deg	M+P	20	Ind $	D^	28$	CSYS	Ind	6	16/26
Ship Science with European Studies (MEng)	J645	4FT deg	M+P+F/G	24	Ind $	D^	32$	CSYS	Ind		
Ship Science/Advanced Materials (MEng)	J644	4FT deg	M+P	24	Ind $	D^	32$	CSYS	Ind		
Ship Science/Multi-disciplinary	J641	4FT deg	M+P	24	Ind $	D^	32$	CSYS	Ind	9	
Ship Science/Naval Architecture (MEng)	J642	4FT deg	M+P	24	Ind $	D^	32$	CSYS	Ind	8	
Ship Science/Yacht and Small Craft (MEng)	J643	4FT deg	M+P	24	Ind $	D^	32$	CSYS	Ind	6	20/22

SOUTHAMPTON INST

Maritime Studies	J600▼	3FT deg	*	8	MO	M$	Dip	CCCC	N		
Maritime Studies (with Foundation Year)	J608▼	4FT deg	*	2	N	P$	Dip	CCC	N		
Shipping Operations	J640	3FT deg	*	8	MO	M$	Dip	CCCC	N		
Yacht and Powercraft Design	J610	3FT deg	*	8-10	MO	M$	Dip	CCCC	N	4	6/16
Yacht and Powercraft Design (with Foundation)	J618▼	4FT deg	*	2	N	P$	Dip	CCC	N	2	8/10
Yacht Design and Operation	046J	2FT HND	*	2	N	P$	Dip	CCC	N	3	
Yacht Manufacture and Management	216J	3FT HND	*	2	N	P$	Dip	CCC	N	2	2/11

Univ of STRATHCLYDE

Naval Architecture	J621	5FT deg	M+P g	BBC				AAAB$			
Naval Architecture and Offshore Engineering	J600	4FT deg	M+P	CCC			36$	BBBB$			
Naval Architecture and Small Craft Engineering	J610	4FT deg	M+P	CCC	HN		36$	BBBB$	HN		

UNIVERSITY COLL LONDON (Univ of London)

Naval Architecture and Ocean Engineering	HJ36	3FT deg	M+P g	BCC-BBB Ind		Ind	30$	BBBCC$ Ind		11	20/22

course details			98 expected requirements							96 entry stats	
TITLE	CODE	COURSE	SUBJECTS	A/AS	NO/C	AGNVQ	IB	SQA(H)	SQA	RATIO	A/AS
Univ of ABERDEEN											
Chemistry with New Materials Technology	F1J5	4FT deg	C+2S/C+S+M g	CCD	Ind	MS go	24$	BBBC$	Ind	5	
Univ of ABERTAY DUNDEE											
Materials Engineering	J502	4FT/5SW deg	M+P/C/Ds	CD	Ind	Ind	Ind	BBCC	Ind		
Univ of Wales, BANGOR											
Natural Products and Materials	J500	3FT deg	B/C+S g	CCD	3M $	MS6/^ go	26$	BBBC$			
Natural Products and Materials	J501	4FT deg	B/C+S g	CCD	3M $	MS6/^ go	26$	BBBC$			
Univ of BATH											
Materials Science and Engineering	J500	3FT deg	M+P/C	CCC	Ind	D	28$	CSYS	N$	8	
Materials Science and Engineering (4 Yr SW)	J502	4SW deg	M+P/C	CCC	Ind	D	28$	CSYS	N$	2	14/24
Materials Science and Engineering (MEng)	J520	5SW deg	M+P/C	CCC	Ind	D	28$	CSYS	N$	3	
Materials Science and Engineering (MEng)	J501	4FT deg	M+P/C	CCC	Ind	D	28$	CSYS	N$	9	
Materials Science and Engineering (Yr Abd)(MEng)	J525	4FT deg	M+P/C	CCC	Ind	Ind	28$	CSYS	N$	12	
Natural Sciences *Material Science*	Y161	4SW deg	S/M+S/M g	20	Ind	DS	30	Ind	Ind		
Natural Sciences *Materials Science*	Y160	3FT deg	S/M+S/M g	20	Ind	DS	30	Ind	Ind		
Univ of BIRMINGHAM											
Biomedical Materials Science	BJ95	3FT deg	2S g	BCC	6M+1D$	DS+^	32$	BBBBB	Ind	2	16/24
Chemical Engineering with Minerals Engineering	H8J1	3FT/4FT deg	M+C	BBC	4M+1D$	Ind	32$	Ind	Ind		
Materials Science and Tech/Materials Engineering	J5F2	3FT/4FT deg	M+P/C g	CCC	6M+1D	Ind	30$	Ind	Ind	3	10/24
Mechanical and Materials Engineering (b) (g)	HJ35	3FT/4FT deg	M+P g	BCC	6M+1D		32$	Ind	Ind	2	18/28
Metallurgy/Materials Engineering	JJ25	3FT/4FT deg	M+P/C g	CCC	6M+1D	Ind	30$	Ind	Ind	2	14/26
Metallurgy/Materials Engineering w. Found Year	JJF5	4FT/5FT deg	* g	CCC	6M+1D	Ind	30$	Ind	Ind	2	
BOLTON INST											
Business Information Systems and Textiles	GJ54	3FT deg	* g	CD	MO	M*	24	BBCC	Ind		
Electronics and Textiles	HJP4	3FT deg	M/S	10	3M	MS$	Ind	Ind	Ind		
Environmental Studies and Textiles	FJ94	3FT deg	* g	CD	MO	M*	24	BBCC	Ind		
Environmental Technology and Textiles	KJ34	3FT deg									
French and Textiles	JR41	3FT deg	F g	10	3M	Ind	Ind	Ind	Ind		
German and Textiles	JR42	3FT deg	G g	CD	Ind	Ind	24	BBCC	Ind		
Occupational Health & Safety and Textiles	HJ64	3FT deg	* g	10	3M	M*	Ind	Ind	Ind		
Simulation/Virtual Environment and Textiles	GJ74	3FT deg	M/S	10	3M	MS$	Ind	Ind	Ind		
Textile Technology	J462	4FT deg	* g	4	N	P*	Ind	Ind	Ind		
Textile Technology	J461	3FT deg	* g	10	3M	M*	Ind	Ind	Ind		
Textiles (Technology and Design)	JW42	3FT deg	* g	10	3M	M*	Ind	Ind	Ind		
Textiles (Technology and Design)	JW4F	4FT deg	* g	4	N	P*	Ind	Ind	Ind		
Textiles (Technology and Management)	JN4C	4FT deg	* g	4	N	P*	Ind	Ind	Ind		
Textiles (Technology and Management)	JN41	3FT deg	* g	10	3M	M*	Ind	Ind	Ind		
Textiles (Technology and Marketing)	JN4M	4FT deg	* g	4	N	P*	Ind	Ind	Ind		
Textiles (Technology and Marketing)	JN45	3FT deg	* g	10	3M	M*	Ind	Ind	Ind		
Textiles and Theatre Studies	JW44	3FT deg	Me/T g	10	Ind	Ind	Ind	Ind	Ind		
Textile Studies	064J	2FT HND	* g	4	N	P*	Ind	Ind	Ind		
BRADFORD & ILKLEY Comm COLL											
Metallurgy and Materials	25JJ	2FT HND	*	2	N $	P		Ind	Ind		
BRUNEL Univ, West London											
Materials Engineering with Management (3/4 Yrs)	J5ND	3FT/4FT deg	2(M/P/C/Ds)	CCC-DDD	3M $	ME/S^	26$	CCCCC$	Ind	2	
Materials Engineering with Management (4/5 Yrs)	J5N1	4SW/5SW deg	2(M/P/C/Ds)	CCC-DDD	3M $	ME/S^	26$	CCCCC$	Ind		
Materials Engineering with Management (4/5 Yrs)	J5NC	4SW/5SW deg	2(M/P/C/Ds)	CC-DD	3M $	ME/S^	26$	CCCC$	Ind		

Materials/Minerals Sciences and Technologies 51

| | | | 98 expected requirements | | | | | | | 96 entry stats |
| course details | | | | | | | | | | |
TITLE	CODE	COURSE	SUBJECTS	A/AS	NO/C	AGNVQ	IB	SQA(H)	SQA	RATIO A/AS
Materials Engineering with Mgt (4/5 Yr Thick SW)	J521	4SW/5SW deg	2(M/P/C/Ds)	CCC-DDD	3M $	ME/S^	26$	CCCCC$	Ind	
Materials Science and Eng (4/5 Yr Thick SW)	J526	4SW/5SW deg	2(M/P/C/Ds)	CCC-DDD	3M $	ME/S^	26$	CCCCC$	Ind	2
Materials Science and Engineering (3/4 Yrs)	J522	3FT/4FT deg	2(M/P/C/Ds)	CCC-DDD	3M $	ME/S^	26$	CCCCC$	Ind	2
Materials Science and Engineering (4/5 Yrs)	J520	4SW/5SW deg	2(M/P/C/Ds)	CCC-DDD	3M $	ME/S^	26$	CCCCC$	Ind	5
Materials Science and Engineering (4/5 Yrs)	J525	4SW/5SW deg	2(M/P/C/Ds)	CC-DD	3M $	ME/S^	26$	CCCC$	Ind	6/8
Metallurgy (4 Yrs Thin SW)	J205	4SW/5SW deg	2(M/P/C/Ds)	CC-DD	3M $	ME/S^	26$	CCCC$	Ind	
Metallurgy (4/5 Yrs Thick SW) (BSc/MEng)	J201	4SW/5SW	2(M/P/C/Ds)	CCC-DDD	3M $	ME/S^	26$	CCCCC$	Ind	
Metallurgy (4/5 Yrs Thin SW) (BSc/MEng)	J200	4SW/5SW deg	2(M/P/C/Ds)	CCC-DDD	3M $	ME/S^	26$	CCCCC$	Ind	1
Metallurgy (BSc/MEng)	J202	3FT/4FT deg	2(M/P/C/Ds)	CCC-DDD	3M $	ME/S^	26$	CCCCC$	Ind	3

BUCKINGHAMSHIRE COLLEGE

Ceramics with Glass	EJ23	3FT deg		CC	1D		Ind	Ind	Ind	
Ceramics with Glass	WJ23	3FT deg								
Forest Products Technology	J501	3FT deg		8-10	MO	M	Ind	CCC	Ind	4
Forest Products Technology with Management	J5N1	3FT deg		8-10	MO	M	Ind	CCC	Ind	
Forest Products Technology with Marketing	J5N5	3FT deg		8-10	MO	M	Ind	CCC	Ind	
Furniture & Related Product Design	EJ24	3FT deg		CC	1D		Ind	Ind	Ind	
Furniture & Related Product Design	WJ24	3 deg								
Furniture Production Management	J450	4FT deg		EE	Ind		Ind	CCC	Ind	1
Furniture Production Management	E450	4FT deg		EE	Ind		Ind	CCC	Ind	
Furniture Studies	42JE	2FT HND								
Furniture Studies	42JW	2FT HND								

CAMBRIDGE Univ

Natural Sciences Crystalline State	Y160▼	3FT deg	2(S/M) g	AAA-AAB	Ind		Ind	CSYS	Ind	
Natural Sciences Materials Science & Metallurgy	Y160▼	3FT deg	2(S/M) g	AAA-AAB	Ind		Ind	CSYS	Ind	
Natural Sciences Materials and Mineral Science	Y160▼	3FT deg	2(S/M) g	AAA-AAB	Ind		Ind	CSYS	Ind	
Natural Sciences Mineralogy and Petrology	Y160▼	3FT deg	2(S/M) g	AAA-AAB	Ind		Ind	CSYS	Ind	

CANTERBURY CHRIST CHURCH COLL of HE

Ceramics	J300	3FT deg	A g	CC	MO	M	24	Ind	Ind	

Univ of CENTRAL ENGLAND

Three-Dimensional Design (Ceramics with Glass)	EJ23	3FT deg	Fa/Pf	18	MO	M$	28	BBBB	Ind	
Three-Dimensional Design (Ceramics with Glass)	WJ23	3FT deg	Fa/Pf	18	MO	M$	28	BBBB	Ind	12

Univ of CENTRAL LANCASHIRE

Fashion	EJ24	4SW deg	Pf							
Fashion Promotion	EJ2K	4SW deg	Pf							
Furniture Design	24WJ▼	2FT HND	Ar	E	N $	P$	Ind	CC$	Ind	

CITY of LIVERPOOL Comm COLL

Clothing Technology	24WJ	2FT HND								

CORDWAINERS COLL

Design, Marketing & Prod Dev (Footwear & Access)	JW42	3FT deg			N	PA	Dip	Ind	Ind	
Design (Footwear and Accessories)	24WJ	2FT HND			N		Ind	Ind	Ind	
Footwear Technology	534J	2FT HND			N		Ind	Ind	Ind	

COVENTRY Univ

Applied Chemistry with Polymer Science	F1J4	3FT/4SW deg	C	DD	3M	MS	Ind	Ind	Ind	7
Applied Chemistry with Polymer Science	F1J5	4FT/5SW deg			Ind	Ind	Ind	Ind	Ind	
Chemistry and Materials Technology	JF51	4FT/5SW deg			Ind	Ind	Ind	Ind	Ind	
Materials Technology	J529	4FT/5SW deg	* g		Ind	Ind	Ind	Ind	Ind	

TITLE	CODE	COURSE	SUBJECTS	A/AS	ND/C	AGNVQ	IB	SQA(H)	SQA	RATIO A/AS
Materials Technology	J520	3FT/4SW deg	M/P+C	CC	Ind	Ind	Ind	Ind	Ind	
Materials Technology and Chemistry	FJ15	3FT/4SW deg	C+D/M	CC	Ind	Ind	Ind	Ind	Ind	
Materials Technology with European Languages	J5T2	3FT deg	* g	12	Ind	Ind	Ind	Ind	Ind	
Materials Technology with European Languages	J5TF	3FT deg	* g	12	Ind	Ind	Ind	Ind	Ind	
Materials Technology with Management	J5N1	3FT deg	* g	12	Ind	Ind	Ind	Ind	Ind	
Materials Technology with Management	J5NC	3FT deg	* g	12	Ind	Ind	Ind	Ind	Ind	
Materials Technology with Manufacturing	J5HT	3FT deg	* g	12	Ind	Ind	Ind	Ind	Ind	
Materials Technology with Manufacturing	J5H7	3FT deg	* g	12	Ind	Ind	Ind	Ind	Ind	
Materials Technology with Sports Science	J5B6	3FT deg	S g	12	Ind	Ind	Ind	Ind	Ind	
Materials Technology with Sports Science	J5BP	3FT deg	S g	12	Ind	Ind	Ind	Ind	Ind	
Mathematics and Materials Technology	JG51	3FT/4SW deg	M+P/C	CC	Ind	Ind	Ind	Ind	Ind	
Polymer Science and Technology	J400	3FT/4SW deg	C/P/M	CC	3M	Ind	Ind	Ind	Ind	
Polymer Science and Technology	J401	4FT/5SW deg	* g		Ind	Ind	Ind	Ind	Ind	
Materials Technology	025J	2FT HND	P/C/M	2	Ind	Ind	Ind	DDDD$	N	
Materials Technology	825J	3FT HND	* g		Ind	Ind	Ind	Ind	Ind	

CROYDON COLL

Fine Art (Printmaking & Book Arts)	JW56	3FT deg	Fa+Pf		N $	PA2				

DE MONTFORT Univ

Textiles Design and Production	J461▼	4SW deg	g	12	6M $	M	24$	BBB	N	2	12/20
Clothing	074J▼	2FT HND	Fa g	6	N $	P	Dip	BB	$	3	4/6
Textiles	164J▼	2FT HND	Fa g	6	N $	P	Dip	BB	$	2	4/10
Textiles	164E▼	2F HND	Fa g	6	N$	P	Dip	BB	$	

DONCASTER COLL

Mining and Electrical Engineering	JH15	3FT deg		CC	3M	Ind	Ind	Ind	Ind	
Mining and Mechanical Engineering	JH13	3FT deg		CC	3M	Ind	Ind	Ind	Ind	
Quarry and Road Surface Engineering	J1H2	3SW deg		CC	3M	Ind	Ind	Ind	Ind	

Univ of DUNDEE

Semiconductor Engineering	H6F2	3FT/4FT deg	M+P/Ds g	12	5M $	M$^	26$	BBCC$	N$	
Semiconductor Engineering (MEng)	H6FF	4FT/5FT deg	M+P/Ds g	12	5M $	MS^	26$	BBCC$	N$	

Univ of EAST LONDON

Business Studies with Fashion Design & Marketing	N1J4	3FT deg	* g	14	MO	MB				
Design - Textile Design with Business Studies	J4N1	3FT deg	* g	12	MO	M	Ind	Ind	Ind	
Design - Textile Design with Communication St	J4P3	3FT deg	* g	12	MO	M	Ind	Ind	Ind	
Design - Textile Design with Fashion Des & Mktg	J400	3FT deg	* g	12	MO	M	Ind	Ind	Ind	
Design - Textile Design with French	J4R1	3FT deg	* g	12	MO	M	Ind	Ind	Ind	
Design - Textile Design with German	J4R2	3FT deg	* g	12	MO	M	Ind	Ind	Ind	
Design - Textile Design with Information Technol	J4G5	3FT deg	* g	12	MO	M	Ind	Ind	Ind	
Design - Textile Design with Italian	J4R3	3FT deg	* g	12	MO	M	Ind	Ind	Ind	
Design - Textile Design with Spanish	J4R4	3FT deg	* g	12	MO	M	Ind	Ind	Ind	
Design - Visual Communication with Fash Des&Mktg	W2J4	3FT deg	* g	12	MO	M	Ind	Ind		
French with Design - Textile Design	R1J4	3FT deg	* g	12	MO	M	Ind			
German with Design - Textile Design	R2J4	3FT deg	* g	12	MO	M	Ind			
Hist of Art, Design & Film/Fash, Des & Marketing	JVK4	3FT deg	* g	12	MO	M	Ind	Ind	Ind	
History of Art Design & Film w. Design-Text. Des	V4J4	3FT deg	* g	12	MO	M	Ind	Ind	Ind	
History of Art Design & Film w. Fashion Des&Mktg	V4JK	3FT deg	* g	12	MO	M	Ind	Ind	Ind	
Information Technology with Design - Textile Des	G5J4	3FT deg	* g	12	MO	M	Ind	Ind	Ind	
Spanish with Design - Textile Design	R4J4	3FT deg	* g	12	MO	M	Ind			

Univ of EXETER

Environmental and Minerals Science	FJ91	3FT deg	2S	DD	MO	M$^	28$	Ind	Ind	
Mine and Quarry Engineering	J101	3FT deg	M/P+S	DD	MO	M$^	28$	Ind	Ind	11

course details			98 expected requirements							96 entry stats	
TITLE	CODE	COURSE	SUBJECTS	A/AS	NO/C	AGNVQ	IB	SQA(H)	SQA	RATIO	A/AS
Minerals Engineering	J120	3FT deg	M/P/C g	DD	MO	M$^	28$	Ind	Ind	6	
Minerals Surveying & Resource Mgt with Euro St	J152	4FT deg	S/E g	DD	MO	M$^	28$	Ind	Ind		
Minerals Surveying and Resource Management	J150	3FT deg	S/E g	DD	MO	M$^	28$	Ind	Ind	2	
Mining Engineering	J100	3FT deg	M/P/C g	DD	MO	M$^	28$	Ind	Ind	2	13/22
Surveying and Earth Resources	FJ9C	3FT deg	S/E g	DD	MO	M$^	28$	Ind	Ind	5	
Surveying and Environmental Management	J151	3FT deg	S/E g	DD	MO	M$^	28$	Ind	Ind	7	
Minerals Surveying and Resource Management	151J	2FT HND	S/E g	D	MO	M$^	24$	Ind	Ind		
Mining and Minerals Engineering	121J	2FT HND	M/P/C g	D	MO	M$^	24$	Ind	Ind	1	

FARNBOROUGH COLL of Technology

Antiques and Collection Management	1N4J	2FT HND		6	Ind	P*	Ind	Ind	Ind	2	2/4

Univ of GLAMORGAN

Biological Science and Minerals Surveying Sci	CJ11	3FT/4SW deg	M/S g	DD	5M $	M$	Ind	Ind	Ind		
Biological Science with Minerals Surveying Sci	C1J1	3FT/4SW deg	M/S g	DD	5M $	M$	Ind	Ind	Ind		
Chemical Science and Minerals Surveying Science	FJ11	3FT/4SW deg	M/S g	DD	5M $	M$	Ind	Ind	Ind		
Chemical Science with Minerals Surveying Science	F1J1	3FT/4SW deg	M/S g	DD	5M $	M$	Ind	Ind	Ind		
Environ Pollution Sci & Minerals Surveying Sci	FJ91	3FT/4SW deg	M/S g	DD	5M $	M$	Ind	Ind	Ind		
Environmental Pollution Sci w. Minerals Surv Sci	F9J1	3FT/4SW deg	M/S g	DD	5M $	M$	Ind	Ind	Ind		
Geological Science and Minerals Surveying Sci	FJ61	3FT/4SW deg	M/S g	DD	5M $	M$	Ind	Ind	Ind	13	
Geological Science with Minerals Surveying Sci	F6J1	3FT/4SW deg	M/S g	DD	5M $	M$	Ind	Ind	Ind	6	
Minerals Resource Development	J153	3FT deg	M/S g	DD	5M $	M$	Ind	Ind	Ind	5	
Minerals Surveying and Resource Development	J152	3FT/4SW deg	M/S g	DD	5M $	M$	Ind	Ind	Ind	3	
Minerals Surveying and Sports Science	JB16	3FT deg	M/S g	DD	5M $	M$	Ind	Ind	Ind		
Minerals Surveying with Biological Science	J1C1	3FT/4SW deg	M/S g	DD	5M $	M$	Ind	Ind	Ind		
Minerals Surveying with Chemical Science	J1F1	3FT/4SW deg	M/S g	DD	5M $	M$	Ind	Ind	Ind		
Minerals Surveying with Enviro Pollution Science	J1F9	3FT/4SW deg	M/S g	DD	5M $	M$	Ind	Ind	Ind		
Minerals Surveying with Geological Science	J1F6	3FT/4SW deg	M/S g	DD	5M $	M$	Ind	Ind	Ind	1	
Minerals Surveying with Sports Science	J1B6	3FT deg	M/S g	DD	5M $	M$	Ind	Ind	Ind		
Minerals and Process Engineering	J140	3FT deg	M/S g	DD	5M $	M$	Ind	Ind	Ind		
Sports Science with Minerals Surveying Science	B6J1	3FT deg	M/S g	DD	5M $	M$	Ind	Ind	Ind		
Combined Studies (Honours) *Minerals Surveying*	Y400	3FT deg	M/S g	8-16	Ind	Ind	Ind	Ind	Ind		
Joint Honours *Minerals Surveying*	Y401	3FT deg	M/S g	8-16	Ind	Ind	Ind	Ind	Ind		
Major/Minor Honours *Minerals Surveying*	Y402	3FT deg	M/S g	8-16	Ind	Ind	Ind	Ind	Ind		
Graphic Design and Print Technology	52JW▼	2FT HND		Ind	Ind	Ind	Ind	Ind		
Minerals Surveying (Surveying for Resource Dev)	251J	2FT HND	M/S g	2	N	P$	Ind	Ind	Ind	2	2/4

GLASGOW CALEDONIAN Univ

Consumer & Management St (Fashion with Business)	JN49	3SW/4SW deg	E g	CD	Ind		Ind	BBC$	Ind	5	

HANDSWORTH COLL

Clothing	2W4E	2FT HND	*	E		M					

Univ of HUDDERSFIELD

Modern Developments for Textile Production	J461	3FT/4SW deg	* g	8-10	Ind	Ind	Ind	Ind	Ind		
Textile Design	EJ24	2FT Dip	Pf+A/Ad/Fa g	6-8	Ind	Ind	Ind	Ind	Ind		
Textile Design	JW42	3FT/4SW deg	Pf+A/Ad/Fa g	8-12	Ind	Ind	Ind	Ind	Ind		
Textile Design	WJ24	2FT Dip	Pf+A/Ad/Fa g	6-8	Ind	Ind	Ind	Ind	Ind		
Textile Design	EW42	3FT/4SW deg	Pf+A/Ad/Fa g	8-12	Ind	Ind	Ind	Ind	Ind		

Univ of HULL

Mechanical and Materials Engineering	HJ3M	3FT deg	M	CCC	MO $	M$6/^ gi	26$	BCCCC	Ind	7	

course details			98 expected requirements							96 entry stats	
TITLE	CODE	COURSE	SUBJECTS	A/AS	NO/C	AGNVQ	IB	SQA(H)	SQA	RATIO	A/AS
IMPERIAL COLL (Univ of London)											
Aerospace Materials	HJ45	4FT deg	M+P/C	22	Ind	Ind	Ind	Ind	Ind		22/30
Environ & Earth Res Eng with a Yr Abroad (MEng)	FJ9C	4FT deg	M/P+B/C/Gy	20	HN $		Ind$	BCCC$	HN$	1	
Environmental and Earth Resources Eng (MEng)	FJ91	4FT deg	M/P+B/C/Gy	20	HN $		Ind$	BCCCC$	HN$	7	
Environmental and Mining Engineering (e)	FJ9D	3FT deg	M/P/C/Gl/Gy	18	HN $		Ind$	BCCC$	HN$		
Materials Sci and Engineering (Specialisations)	JF52	3FT deg	M+P/C	18	HN		$	BBBB	$	4	
Materials Science and Engineering (MEng)	JF5F	4FT deg	M+P/C	22	HN		$	BBBB	$	5	22/28
Materials with Management	J5N1	3FT deg	M+P/C	18	HN		$	BBBB	$	5	
Materials with Management and a Year Abroad	J5NC	4FT deg	M+P/C g	18	HN		$	BBBB	$		
Materials with a Year Abroad	J526	4FT deg	M+P/C g	18	HN		$	BBBB	$	6	
Mining and Environmental Engineering (MEng)	J101	4FT deg	M/P+B/B/C/Gy	20	HN $	Ind	Ind$	BCCC$	HN$		
Petroleum Engineering (MEng)	J171	4FT deg	M+P	20	HN $		Ind$	BCCCC$	HN$	4	
Petroleum Geology (MSci)	FJ61	4FT deg	M/P/C/Gl/Gy	18	Ind	Ind	Ind	Ind	Ind		
Univ of LEEDS											
Ceramics Science and Engineering	J300	3FT/4FT deg	M+P/C g	CCC	5M $	Ind	24$	BBCCC	Ind		
Industrial Minerals Technology	J122	2FT Dip	2S g	EE	Ind	Ind	Ind	Ind	Ind	1	
Materials Science and Engineering	J500	3FT/4FT deg	M+P/C g	CCC	3M+2D$	Ind	26$	BBBCC	Ind	4	8/16
Materials Science and Technology	J502	2FT Dip	g	4	Ind	Ind	Ind	Ind	Ind	1	
Metallurgy	J200	3FT/4FT deg	M+P/C g	CCC	3M+2D$	Ind	26$	BBBCC	Ind		
Mineral Engineering	J120	3FT/4FT deg	C+M+S g	CDD	4M $	Ind	Ind	CSYS	Ind	1	8/20
Mineral Industry Environmental Engineering	J1F9	3FT/4FT deg	C/M/P g	CDD	1M+2D$	Ind	24$	BBCCC	Ind		6/20
Mining Engineering	J100	3FT/4FT deg	P+M+S g	CDD	4M $	Ind	Ind	CSYS	Ind	1	6/15
Textile Design	WJ24	3FT deg	A g	BCC	Ind	Ind	28$	BBBBC	Ind	7	14/26
Textile Management	J4N1	3FT deg	* g	CCC	Ind	Ind	26$	BBBCC	Ind	3	10/22
Textile Manufacturing	J461	4FT deg	g		Ind	Ind	Ind	Ind	Ind		
Textile Studies (Options)	J460	3FT deg	C/M/P g	CCC	Ind	Ind	26	BBBCC	Ind	5	14/24
LEEDS METROPOLITAN Univ											
Print Management	J531	3FT/4FT deg									
Musical Instrument Technology	65HJ	2FT HND									
LEICESTER SOUTH FIELDS COLL											
Footwear Fashion and Technology	534E	2FT HND	Fa g	4	N	P$	Dip	CSYS	N		
Footwear Fashion and Technology	534J	2FT HND	Fa g	4	N	P$	Dip	CSYS	N		
Univ of LIVERPOOL											
Chemistry with Materials Science	FF12	3FT deg	C+S g	14	MO $	DS^ go	31$	BBBCC$	Ind	15	
Clinical Engineering and Materials Science(BEng)	BF92	3FT deg	M+C/P	18	4M+1D$		30$	BBBBB	Ind	2	16/24
Materials Engineering (MEng)	J500	4FT deg	M+P/C	20	4M+2D$		30$	BBBBB	Ind	5	
Materials Science (BEng Hons)	J520	4EXT deg	*	12	3M $		25$	BBBCC	Ind	1	
Materials Science (BEng)	F200	3FT deg	M+P/C	18	4M+1D$		30$	BBBBB	Ind	8	
Materials Science and Management Studies	F2N1	3FT deg	M+P/C	18	4M+1D$		30$	BBBBB	Ind		
Materials Science with European Language	F2T2	3FT deg	M+P/C g	18	4M+1D$		30$	BBBBB	Ind		
Materials, Design and Manufacture	HJ35	3FT deg	M+P/C	18	4M+1D$		30$	BBBBB	Ind		
Mathematics with Materials Science	FG21	3FT deg	M+P/C g	20	MO $	DS^ go	31$	BBBCC$	Ind		
Metallurgy and Materials Science (BEng)	J200	3FT deg	M+P/C	18	4M+1D$		30$	BBBBB	Ind	4	
Physics with Materials Science	FF23	3FT deg	P+M g	12	MO $	DS^ go	31$	BBBCC$	Ind	12	
BSc Combined Honours _Materials Science_	Y100	3FT deg	M+P	18	MO $	Ind	31$	BBBCC$	Ind		
LONDON GUILDHALL Univ											
3D/Spatial Design & Product Development & Manuf	JW4F	3FT deg	Pf g	CD-DDD	MO+3D	M$ go	24	Ind	Ind		
Furniture Design and Technology	EW4F	3FT deg	Fa+Pf g		3M		X	Ind	Ind		
Furniture Manufacture and Innovation	J452	3FT deg	g	DD	3M		24	Ind	Ind		

course details			98 expected requirements							96 entry stats	
TITLE	CODE	COURSE	SUBJECTS	A/AS	NO/C	AGNVQ	IB	SQA(H)	SQA	RATIO	A/AS
Interior Design and Technology	EW42	3FT deg	Fa+Pf g		3M	Ind	X	Ind	Ind		
Musical Instrument Technology	J5H6	3FT deg	M/P/Mu g	CC	N $		24	Ind	Ind		
Prod Devel & Manuf & Commun & Audio Vis Prod St	JP44	3FT deg	* g	CC-CDD	MO+2D	M$ go	24	Ind	Ind		
Product Development & Manuf & Development Studs	JM49	3FT deg	* g	DD	MO	M$ go	24	Ind	Ind		
Product Development & Manuf & Financial Services	JN43	3FT deg	* g	DD	MO	M$ go	24	Ind	Ind		
Product Development & Manuf & Internat Relations	JM4C	3FT deg	* g	DD	MO	M$ go	24	Ind	Ind		
Product Development & Manuf and Multimedia Systs	GJM4	3FT deg	* g	DD	MO	M$ go	24	Ind	Ind		
Product Development & Manufacture & Accounting	JN44	3FT deg	* g	DD	MO	M$ go	24	Ind	Ind		
Product Development & Manufacture & Bus Econ	JL4C	3FT deg	* g	DD	MO	M$ go	24	Ind	Ind		
Product Development & Manufacture & Business IT	GJ74	3FT deg	* g	DD	MO	M$ go	24	Ind	Ind		
Product Development & Manufacture & Design Studs	JW42	3FT deg	* g	CD-DDD	MO	M$ go	24	Ind	Ind		
Product Development & Manufacture & European St	JT42	3FT deg	* g	DD	MO	M$ go	24	Ind	Ind		
Product Development & Manufacture & Mathematics	GJ14	3FT deg	* g	DD	MO	M$ go	24	Ind	Ind		
Product Development & Manufacture & Modern Hist	JV41	3FT deg	* g	DD	MO	M$ go	24	Ind	Ind		
Product Development & Manufacture and Business	JN41	3FT deg	* g	CD-DDD	MO+2D	M$ go	24	Ind	Ind		
Product Development & Manufacture and Computing	GJ54	3FT deg	* g	DD	MO	M$ go	24	Ind	Ind		
Product Development & Manufacture and Economics	JL41	3FT deg	* g	DD	MO	M$ go	24	Ind	Ind		
Product Development & Manufacture and English	JQ43	3FT deg	* g	CD-DDD	MO+2D	M$ go	26	Ind	Ind		
Product Development & Manufacture and Fine Art	JW41	3FT deg	* g	CD-DDD	MO+2D	M$ go	26	Ind	Ind		
Product Development & Manufacture and French	JR41	4FT deg	* g	DD	MO	M$ go	24	Ind	Ind		
Product Development & Manufacture and German	JR42	4FT deg	* g	DD	MO	M$ go	24	Ind	Ind		
Product Development & Manufacture and Law	JM43	3FT deg	* g	CC-CDD	MO+2D	M$ go	26	Ind	Ind		
Product Development & Manufacture and Marketing	JN45	3FT deg	* g	CD-DDD	MO+2D	M$ go	24	Ind	Ind		
Product Development & Manufacture and Politics	JM41	3FT deg	* g	DD	MO	M$ go	24	Ind	Ind		
Psychology and Product Development & Manufacture	CJ84	3FT deg	* g	CD-DDD	MO+2D	M$ go	26	Ind	Ind		
Restoration and Conservation	JJ45	3FT deg	* g	CC	Ind	M$ go	24	Ind	Ind		
Social Policy & Mgt and Product Develop & Manuf	JL44	3FT deg	* g	CD-DDD	MO	M$ go	24	Ind	Ind		
Sociology and Product Development & Manufacture	JL43	3FT deg	* g	CD-DDD	MO	M$ go	24	Ind	Ind		
Spanish and Product Development & Manufacture	JR44	4FT deg	* g	DD	MO	M$ go	24	Ind	Ind		
Taxation and Product Development & Manufacture	JN4H	3FT deg	* g	DD	MO	M$ go	24	Ind	Ind		
Modular Programme *Product Development and Manufacture*	Y400	3FT deg	* g	CC-DD	MO	M$ go	24	Ind	Ind		
Furniture (Design and Realisation)	024J	2FT HND	Pf g	D	Ind	Ind	Dip	Ind	Ind		
Furniture (Design and Realisation)	024E	2FT HND	Pf g	D	Ind	Ind	Dip	Ind	Ind		
Furniture (Manufacture and Management)	1N4J	2FT HND	g	D	Ind	Ind	Dip	Ind	Ind		
Furniture (Restoration)	54JJ	2FT HND	g	D	Ind	Ind	Dip	Ind	Ind		
Musical Instrument Technology	65HJ	2FT HND	M/P/Mu g	D	N $		Dip$	Ind	Ind		
LONDON INST											
Conservation	J560	3FT deg								4	12/24
Conservation	E560	3FT deg								15	
Printing Management	J530	3FT deg								15	
Product Development for the Fashion Industries	J470	4SW deg								3	6/14
Publishing	JP55	3FT deg								6	
Fashion Design and Technology	074E	2FT HND									
Printing, Publishing and Packaging Production	035J	2FT HND								3	
LOUGHBOROUGH Univ											
Materials Engineering	J500	3FT deg	M	20	5M	DE6/^ go	28$	Ind	Ind	1	10/18
Materials Engineering (4 Yr SW)	J501	4SW deg	M	20	5M	DE6/^ go	28$	Ind	Ind	5	
Materials with Business Studies	J5N1	3FT deg	M	20	5M	DE6/^ go	28$	Ind	Ind	2	14/16
Materials with Business Studies (4 Yr SW)	J5NC	4SW deg	M	20	5M	DE6/^ go	28$	Ind	Ind	4	

			98 expected requirements							*96 entry stats*
TITLE	CODE	COURSE	SUBJECTS	A/AS	ND/C	RGNVQ	IB	SQA(H)	SQA	RATIO A/AS
MANCHESTER COLLEGE OF ARTS AND TECHNOLOGY										
Furniture Design and Making	WJ24	3FT deg								
Furniture Design and Making	EJ24	3FT deg								
Univ of MANCHESTER										
Aerospace Materials Engineering (MEng)	HJ42	4FT deg	M+P g	CCC-BBB	1D $		32$	AAABB$	Ind	
Biomedical Materials Sci with Ind Exp	J2BX	4SW deg	2(M/P/C) g	CCD	4M $	DS	28$	BBBBB$	Ind	5
Biomedical Materials Science	J2B9	3FT deg	2(M/P/C) g	CCD	4M $		26$	BBBBB$	Ind	3
Biomedical Materials Science with Industrial Exp	J2BY	4FT deg								
Materials Sci & Engineering (Pol) with Ind Exp	J5JK	4FT deg								
Materials Science & Eng (Ceramics) with Ind Exp	J5JH	4FT deg								
Materials Science & Eng (Metals) with Ind Exp	J5JF	4FT deg								
Materials Science and Engineering	J500	3FT deg	2(M/P/C) g	CCD	4M $	DS	28	BBBBB$	Ind	
Materials Science and Engineering	J501	4FT deg								
Materials Science and Engineering (Ceramics)	J5J3	4FT deg								
Materials Science and Engineering (Metals)	J5J2	4FT deg								
Materials Science and Engineering (Polymers)	J5J4	4FT deg								
Materials Science and Engineering with Ind Exp	J503	4FT deg								
Materials Science with Business & Mgt (MMatSci)	J5N9	4FT deg	2(M/P/C) g	CCC	4M+1D	DS	28$	CSYS	Ind	
UMIST (Manchester)										
Biomedical Materials Sci with Ind Exp (MMatSci)	J2BY	4SW deg	2(M/P/C) g	CCD	4M $	Ind	26$	BBBB$	Ind	
Biomedical Materials Science	J2B9	3FT deg	2(M/P/C) g	CCD	4M $	Ind	26$	BBBB$	Ind	17
Chemistry and Polymer Science and Tech (MChem)	FJ14	4FT deg	C g	18	3M+1D	MS6/^ go	30	CSYS	Ind	2 20/24
Chemistry with Polymer Science	F1J4	3FT deg	C g	18	3M+1D	MS6/^ go	30	CSYS	Ind	4
Clothing Engineering and Management (4 Yrs)	J4N9	4SW deg	M/P/C g	18	5M	Ind	25	BBBCC	Ind	
Clothing Engineering and Mgt with a Mod Language	J4T9	4SW deg	M/P/C g	18	5M $	Ind	25	BBBCC	Ind	
Management & Marketing of Textiles with Ind Exp	J4NM	4SW deg	* g	BCC	4M+1D	MS6/^ go	30	BBBCC	Ind	
Management & Mkting of Textiles with a Mod Lang	J4N5	4FT deg	* g	BCC	X	Ind	Ind	BBBCC	Ind	5
Management and Marketing of Textiles	J4N1	3FT deg	* g	BCC	4M+1D	D$6/^ go	30	BBBCC	Ind	2 10/22
Materials Sci & Eng (Metals) w.Ind Exp (MMatSci)	J5JF	4SW deg	2(M/P/C) g	CCD	4M $	Ind	26$	BBBB$	Ind	
Materials Sci & Eng(Ceramics)w.Ind Exp (MMatSci)	J5JC	4SW deg	2(M/P/C) g	CCD	4M $	Ind	26$	BBBB$	Ind	
Materials Sci & Eng(Polymers)w.Ind Exp (MMatSci)	J5JK	4SW deg	M/P/C g	CCD	4M $	Ind	26$	BBBB$	Ind	
Materials Sci & Engineering (Ceramics) (MMatSci)	J5J3	4FT deg	2(M/P/C) g	CCD	4M $	Ind	26$	BBBB$	Ind	
Materials Sci & Engineering (Polymers) (MMatSci)	J5J4	3FT deg	M/P/C g	CCD	4M $	Ind	26$	BBBB$	Ind	
Materials Science and Eng (Metals) (MMatSci)	J5J2	4FT deg	2(M/P/C) g	CCD	4M $	Ind	26$	BBBB$	Ind	
Materials Science and Eng with Ind Exp (MMatSci)	J503	4SW deg	2(M/P/C) g	CCD	4M $	Ind	26$	BBBB$	Ind	
Materials Science and Engineering	J500	3FT deg	2(M/P/C) g	CCD	4M $	Ind	26$	BBBB$	Ind	
Materials Science and Engineering (MMatSci)	J501	4FT deg	2(M/P/C) g	CCD	4M $	Ind	26$	BBBB$	Ind	
Materials Science with Business and Mgt (4 Yrs)	J5N9	4FT deg	2(M/P/C) g	CCC	4M+1D$	Ind	28$	CSYS	Ind	
Mechanical Eng with Design, Mats and Man (MEng)	HJ3M	4FT deg	M+P g	BCC	MO+3D$	Ind	30$	CSYS$	Ind	
Mechanical Engineering with Design, Mats and Man	HJ35	3FT deg	M+P g	BCC	MO+3D$	Ind	30$	CSYS$	Ind	
Mechanical Engineering with Materials	H3J5	3FT deg	M+P g	BCC	MO+3D$	Ind	30$	CSYS$	Ind	6 14/28
Mechanical Engineering with Materials (MEng)	H3JM	4FT deg	M+P g	BCC	MO+3D$	Ind	30$	CSYS$	Ind	2
Paper Science	J560	3FT deg	M/P/C g	CCD	3M	DS^	27$	BBBC$	Ind	4
Paper Science with American Studies	J563	4SW deg	M/P/C g	CCC	3M	DS^	27$	BBBC$	Ind	
Paper Science with French (4 Yrs)	J5R1	4FT deg	M/P/C g	CCD	3M	DS^ go	27$	BBBC$	Ind	2
Paper Science with German (4 Yrs)	J5R2	4FT deg	M/P/C g	CCD	3M	DS^ go	27$	BBBC$	Ind	
Paper Science with Industrial Exp (4 Yrs)	J561	4SW deg	M/P/C g	CCD	3M	DS^	27$	BBBC$	Ind	
Paper Science with Industrial Process Control	J5HP	3FT deg	M/P/C g	BCC	3M	DS^	30$	BBBC$	Ind	4
Paper Science with Management	J5N1	3FT deg	M/P/C g	CCD	3M	DS^	27$	BBBC$	Ind	6
Paper Science with foundation year (4 years)	J565	4FT deg	M/P/C g	EE	3M	PS	25$	BCCC$	Ind	8/10
Textile Design and Des Mgt with a Mod Language	J4T2	4FT deg	* g	18	5M	Ind	28	BBBCC	Ind	6

				98 expected requirements						96 entry stats	

TITLE	CODE	COURSE	SUBJECTS	A/AS	ND/C	RGNVQ	IB	SQA(H)	SQA	RATIO	A/AS
Textile Design and Design Management	J4W2	3FT deg	* g	18	5M	Ind	28	BBBCC	Ind	4	12/24
Textile Design and Design Management with Ind	J4WG	3FT deg	* g	18	5M	Ind	28	BBBCC	Ind		
Textile Science and Tech with Ind Experience	JJ94	4SW deg	M+P/C g	20	4M+1D$	Ind	25	BBBBB	Ind		
Textile Science and Tech with a Mod Language	J4TX	3FT deg	M+P/C g	20	4M+1D$	Ind	25	BBBBB	Ind	1	
Textile Science and Technology	JJ49	3FT deg	M+P/C g	20	4M+1D$	Ind	25	BBBBB	Ind	3	
Textile Technology and Management	J4NC	3FT deg	M/P/C g	18	5M $	Ind	25	BBBCC	Ind	13	
Textile Technology and Mgt with Industrial Exp	J4ND	4SW deg	M/P/C	18	5M $	Ind	25	BBBCC	Ind		
Textile Technology and Mgt with a Modern Lang	J4TY	4FT deg	M/P/C g	18	5M $	Ind	25	BBBCC	Ind		

MANCHESTER METROPOLITAN Univ

TITLE	CODE	COURSE	SUBJECTS	A/AS	ND/C	RGNVQ	IB	SQA(H)	SQA	RATIO	A/AS
Clothing	J470	3FT/4SW deg	* g	8-12	Ind	M	26	CCCC	Ind		8/20
Fashion	J471	3FT deg	Fa+Pf g	4	N		Ind	CCCC	N		
Fashion Design with Technology	JW42	4SW deg	Fa/A+Pf g	12	Ind	M	Ind	Ind	Ind		10/20
Materials Science	F200	3FT deg	M/P/C g	12-16	3M $	M$	28$	BBBCC$	Ind		
Materials Science (Foundation)	F208▼	4FT deg	M/P	E	2M $	P$	$	$	Ind		
Materials Science/Applied Physics	FF23	3FT deg	M g	12	5M $	M$	27$	BCCCC$	Ind		
Materials Science/Biology	CF12	3FT deg	M/P/C g	12	4M $	M$	26$	CCCCC$	Ind		
Materials Science/Business Mathematics	GFC2	3FT deg	M/P g	12	5M $	M$	27$	BCCCC$	Ind		
Materials Science/Chemistry	FF12	3FT deg	C g	12	N $	M$	24$	CCCC$	Ind		
Materials Science/Computer Technology	FG2M	3FT deg	M/P/C g	12	5M $	M$	27$	BCCCC$	Ind		
Materials Science/Computing Science	FG25	3FT deg	M/P/C g	12	5M $	M$	27$	BCCCC$	Ind		
Materials Science/Economics	FL21	3FT deg	M/P/C g	16	1M+3D$	M$	28$	BBBCC$	Ind		
Materials Science/Languages	FT29	3FT deg	M/P/C g	14	MO $	M$	28$	BBCCC$	Ind		
Materials Science/Manufacturing	FH27	3FT deg	M/P/C g	12	4M $	M$	26$	CCCCC$	Ind		
Materials Science/Polymer Science	FJ24	3FT deg	C g	8	3M $	M$	27$	BCCCC$	Ind		
Photography	JW55	3FT deg	Pf	CC	Ind		Ind	Ind	Ind		8/22
Physics Studies/Materials Science	FF32	3FT deg	M/P/C g	12	5M $		27$	BCCCC$	Ind		
Polymer Science and Technology	J400	3FT deg	C g	12-16	3M $	M$	27$	BCCCC$	Ind		
Polymer Science and Technology (Foundation)	J408▼	4FT deg	M/P/C	E	2M $	P$	$	$	Ind		
Polymer Science/Applicable Mathematics	GJ14	3FT deg	M+C g	12	5M $	M$	27$	BCCCC$	Ind		
Polymer Science/Applied Physics	FJ34	3FT deg	C+P/M g	12	5M $	M$	27$	BCCCC$	Ind		
Polymer Science/Business Mathematics	GJC4	3FT deg	C+M/P/Ec g	12	5M $	M$	27$	BCCCC$	Ind		
Polymer Science/Chemistry	FJ14	3FT deg	C g	12	N $	M$	24$	CCCC$	Ind		
Polymer Science/Economics	JL41	3FT deg	C g	16	1M+3D$	M$	28$	BBBCC$	Ind		
Polymer Science/Electronics	HJP4	3FT deg	C g	12	5M $	M$	27$	BCCCC$	Ind		
Polymer Science/Environmental Studies	FJ94	3FT deg	C g	16	1M+3D$	M$	28$	BBBCC$	Ind		
Polymer Science/European Studies	JT42	3FT deg	C g	12	5M $	M$	27$	BCCCC$	Ind		
Polymer Science/Manufacturing	HJ74	3FT deg	C g	10	4M $	M$	26$	CCCCC$	Ind		
Polymer Science/Physics Studies	FJH4	3FT deg	C g	12	5M $	M$	27$	BCCCC$	Ind		
Scientific Instrumentation/Materials Science	FH26	3FT deg	M/P/C g	12	5M $	M$	27$	BCCCC$	Ind		
Social Studies of Technology/Materials Science	FL23	3FT deg	M/P/C g	12	5M $	M$	27$	BCCCC$	Ind		
Social Studies of Technology/Polymer Science	JL43	3FT deg	C g	12	5M $	M$	27$	BCCCC$	Ind		
Textiles	E410	3FT deg	Fa+Pf g	4	N		Ind	CCCC	N		
Textiles	J410	3FT deg	Fa+Pf g	4	N		Ind	CCCC	N		
Clothing	074J	2FT HND	* g	4	Ind	P	24	Ind	Ind		4/6
Design (Fashion with Technology)	24WJ	2FT HND	Pf g	4	Ind	P	Ind	Ind	Ind		4/20
Materials Science	002F	2FT HND	S	2	N	P$	Dip		Ind		

NAPIER Univ

TITLE	CODE	COURSE	SUBJECTS	A/AS	ND/C	RGNVQ	IB	SQA(H)	SQA	RATIO	A/AS
Polymer Engineering	J400	3FT deg								4	

NENE COLLEGE

TITLE	CODE	COURSE	SUBJECTS	A/AS	ND/C	RGNVQ	IB	SQA(H)	SQA	RATIO	A/AS
Leather Technology	J430	3FT deg	S	EE	3M	M	24	CCC	Ind		

course details			98 expected requirements							96 entry stats	
TITLE	CODE	COURSE	SUBJECTS	A/AS	NO/C	AGNVQ	IB	SQA(H)	SQA	RATIO	A/AS
Univ of NEWCASTLE											
Materials Design and Engineering (MEng)	JH57	5FT deg	* g	18	5M $		26$	BBBB$	Ind		
Materials Design and Engineering (MEng)	HJ75	4FT deg	M+P g	BCC	3M+2D$		30$	CSYS$	Ind		
Materials Engineering	HJ35	4FT deg	*	18	5M $		26$	BBBB$	Ind	3	
Materials Engineering	JH53	3FT deg	M+P	BCC	3M+2D$		30$	CSYS$	Ind		
NESCOT											
Biological Imaging	CJ1M	3FT deg	*	EE	N	M	Dip	Ind	N$		
NORTH EAST WALES INST of HE											
Ceramics/Glass	WJ23	3FT deg	Pf		Ind	Ind	Ind	Ind	Ind		
Ceramics/Glass	EJ23	3 deg	Pf		Ind	Ind	Ind	Ind	Ind		
Ceramics/Jewellery Metalwork	EJ63	3FT deg	Pf		Ind	Ind	Ind	Ind	Ind		
Ceramics/Jewellery Metalwork	WJ63	3 deg	Pf		Ind	Ind	Ind	Ind	Ind		
Ceramics/Small Business Practice	EJ13	3 deg	Pf		Ind	Ind	Ind	Ind	Ind		
Ceramics/Small Business Practice	WJ13	3FT deg	Pf		Ind	Ind	Ind	Ind	Ind		
Glass/Jewellery Metalwork	WJ6H	3FT deg	Pf		Ind	Ind	Ind	Ind	Ind		
Glass/Jewellery Metalwork	EJ6H	3FT deg	Pf		Ind	Ind	Ind	Ind	Ind		
Illustration/Glass	WJ2H	3FT deg	Pf		Ind	Ind	Ind	Ind	Ind		
Illustration/Glass	EJ2H	3FT deg	Pf		Ind	Ind	Ind	Ind	Ind		
Univ of NORTH LONDON											
Business and Polymer Engineering	JN41	3FT/4SW/4EXT deg	M/Ph	CD	MO+4D	DE	Ind	Ind	Ind		
International Business and Polymers	NJ1K	3FT deg	M/Ph	CC	MO+4D	D$	Ind	Ind	Ind		
Polymer Engineering	J440	3FT/4SW/4EXT deg	M/Ph	CC	3M $	ME	$	Ind	Ind	1	
Polymer Engineering Foundation	J448▼	4FT/5SW deg			Ind	Ind	Ind	INd	Ind		
Combined Honours Polymers	Y100	3FT/4SW/4EXT deg	M/Ph	CC	3M $	ME	$	Ind	Ind		
Polymer Science and Engineering	044J	2FT/3SW HND	M/P/C/Ds	E	N $	P$	$	Ind	Ind		
Univ of NORTHUMBRIA											
Materials Engineering	J500	3FT/4SW deg	M+P/S g	12	3M $	ME2 gi	24$	BBBC$	Ind	9	
Materials Engineering	J508	5EXT deg	* g	2-4	Ind	Ind	Ind	Ind	Ind		
Univ of NOTTINGHAM											
Chemistry of Materials	FJ15	3FT deg	C+P/M g	CCD	HN		28$	CSYS	HN	7	14/20
Chemistry of Materials (MSci) (4 Yrs)	FJC5	4FT deg	C+P/M g	CCD	HN		28$	CSYS	HN		
Materials Design and Processing	J540	3FT/4FT deg	M+C	BCC-CCD	Ind	Ind	28$	Ind	Ind		
Mechanical Design, Materials and Manufacture	HJ35	3FT/4FT deg	M+P	BCC-CCD	Ind	Ind	28$	Ind	Ind	4	14/28
Medical Materials Science	BJ95	3FT deg	C+B/M/P	BCC	Ind	Ind	28$	Ind	Ind	5	
Mine Environmental Engineering	J102	3FT deg	M+P/C	CCC-CDD	Ind	Ind	28$	Ind	Ind		
Mining Engineering	J100	3FT/4FT deg	M+P/C	CCC-CDD	Ind	Ind	28$	Ind	Ind	2	14/22
Mining and Minerals Engineering	J125	3FT deg	M+P/C	CCC-CDD	Ind	Ind	28$	Ind	Ind		
NOTTINGHAM TRENT Univ											
Clothing Studies with Textiles	JW42	4SW deg	Fa g	12	Ind	Ind	Ind	Ind	Ind	4	12/24
Printing and Publishing Media	P5J5	3FT/4SW deg									
Print Media Management	035J	3SW HND	Fa g	6-8	Ind	Ind	Ind	Ind	Ind	4	4/18
Textiles with Clothing	164J	2FT HND	g	4-6	Ind	Ind	Ind	Ind	Ind	3	4/20
OXFORD Univ											
Engineering and Materials (4 Yrs)	HJ15	4FT deg	M+P	AAB-ABB DO			36	AAAAA	Ind	3	
Metallurgy and Science of Materials (4 Yrs)	FJ22	4FT deg	2S	AAB-ABB DO			36	AAAAA	Ind	2	30/30
Materials, Economics and Management Metallurgy	Y634	4FT deg	2S	AAB-ABB DO			36	AAAAA	Ind		

Materials/Minerals Sciences and Technologies 51

			98 expected requirements							96 entry stats
TITLE	CODE	COURSE	SUBJECTS	A/AS	NO/C	AGNVQ	IB	SQA(H)	SQA	RATIO A/AS
Univ of PLYMOUTH										
Composite Materials Engineering (MEng Option)	J520	3FT/4SW 4FT/5SW deg	Ap g	10-11	5M $	ME+	Ind	Ind	Ind	4
Product Design and Manufacture (Somerset)	045J	2FT HND	Ds g	E	N $	P$	Ind	Ind	Ind	6
QUEEN MARY & WESTFIELD COLL (Univ of London)										
Aerospace Materials Technology	J5H4	3FT deg	M+P	CCD	5M $	M$	28$			
Aerospace Materials Technology (MEng)	J5HK	4FT deg	M+P	BBB	X	X	28$			
Biomedical Materials Sci and Engineering (MEng)	J502	4FT deg	2(B/C/M/P)	BBB	X	X	28$			
Biomedical Materials Science and Engineering	J501	3FT deg	B+C/M/P	CCC	5M $	M$^	24$			
Materials Science and Engineering	J550	3FT deg	M+P/C/B	CCD	3M	M$	24$	BCCCC		
Mechanical Engineering and Materials (MEng)	JH53	4FT deg	M+P	22	3M+1D$	X	30$	BBBBB		
Physics and Materials Science	FF23	3FT deg	M+P	24		MS^				
Polymer Science and Engineering	J400	3FT deg	C+B/P/M	CCD	3M	M$^	24$	BCCCC		
Science and Engineering (4 yrs with Foundation) Materials	Y157	4EXT deg		E	N	P				
QUEEN'S Univ Belfast										
Physics with Materials Science	F3J5	3FT/4FT deg	M+P g	CCC	Ind	Ind	28$	BBBC	Ind	
Physics with Materials Science	F3F2	3FT deg								
SCOTTISH COLLEGE of TEXTILES										
Clothing Design and Manufacture	J470	4FT deg	* g	CC	N	M$	Dip	BBC	HN	2
Textiles	J400	4FT deg	* g	CC	Ind	M$	Dip	BBC	HN	10
Textiles and Fashion Design Management	J4NM	4FT deg	* g	CC	Ind	M$	Dip	BBC	HN	5
Textiles with Marketing	J4N5	4FT deg	* g	CC	Ind	M$	Dip	BBC	HN	8
SANDWELL COLL										
Metals Technology	002J	2FT HND	Ap	DD-EE	N	P$	Ind	Ind	Ind	
Univ of SHEFFIELD										
Ceramic Science and Engineering	J320	4FT/5EXT deg	2(M/P/C) g	CCC	5M $	M$^	28$	BBBC$	Ind	
Ceramic Science and Engineering with a Mod Lang	J3T9	4FT/5EXT deg	2(M/P/C) g	CCC	5M $	M$^	28$	BBBC$	Ind	
Chemistry and Materials Science	FJ15	3FT/4EXT deg	C+M/P g	BCC	5M+1D$	DS^	29$	BBBB$	Ind	5
Glass Science and Engineering	J340	4FT/5EXT deg	2(M/P/C) g	CCC	5M $	M$^	28$	BBCC$	Ind	
Glass Science and Engineering with a Modern Lang	J3TX	4FT/5EXT deg	2(M/P/C) g	CCC	5M $	M$^	28$	BBCC$	Ind	
Integrated Physical Science	JF29	3/4EXT deg	2(C/M/P) g	BCC	5M $	D$^	29$	AABB$	Ind	
Materials Science & Eng (inc Found Yr) (4/5 Yrs)	J501	4FT/5FT deg	* g	CCC	5M	M	28	BBCC	Ind	1 6/16
Materials Science and Eng with a Modern Language	J5T9	3FT deg	2(M/P/C) g	CCC	5M$	M$^	28$	BBCC$	Ind	
Materials Science and Engineering (3/4 Yrs)	J500	3FT/4FT deg	2(M/P/C) g	CCC	5M $	M$^	28$	BBCC$	Ind	3 12/26
Materials Science and Physics	JF53	3FT/4EXT deg	P+M g	BCD	6M $	D$^	28$	BBBC$	Ind	
Medical Materials Science and Engineering	J510	3FT deg	2(M/P/C) g	CCC	5M $	M$^	28	BBBC		
Metal Science and Engineering	J200	4FT/5EXT deg	2(M/P/C) g	CCC	5M $	M$^	28$	BBCC$	Ind	6
Metal Science and Engineering with a Modern Lang	J2T9	4FT/5EXT deg	2(M/P/C) g	CCC	5M $	M$^	28$	BBCC$	Ind	
Physics with Materials Science (4Yrs)	F3J5	4FT/5EXT deg	P+S g	BCD	6M $	DS^	28$	BBBC$	Ind	
Polymer Science and Engineering	J440	4FT/5EXT deg	2(M/P/C) g	CCC	5M $	X	28$	BBBC$	Ind	
Polymer Science and Engineering with a Mod Lang	J4T9	4FT/5EXT deg	2(M/P/C) g	CCC	5M $	X	28$	BBBC$	Ind	
SHEFFIELD HALLAM Univ										
Materials Engineering	J500	3FT/4SW deg	M/P/C/Ph	8	3M $	M$	Ind	Ind	Ind	
Materials Engineering (Extended)	J508▼	4EXT/5EXTSW deg								
Materials Engineering with Management	J501	3FT/4SW deg	M/P/C/Ph	8	3M $	M$	Ind	Ind	Ind	
Materials Engineering with Management (Extended)	J518▼	4EXT/5EXTSW deg								
Materials and Environment Engineering	HJ85	3FT/4SW deg	M/S	8	3M $	M$	Ind	Ind	Ind	
Materials and Environment Engineering (Extended)	HJ8M▼	4EXT/5EXTSW deg								
Mechanical and Materials Engineering	HJ35	3FT/4SW deg	M/P/C/Ph	8	3M $	M$	Ind	Ind	Ind	

			98 expected requirements							96 entry stats	
course details											
TITLE	CODE	COURSE	SUBJECTS	A/AS	ND/C	AGNVQ	IB	SQA(H)	SQA	RATIO	A/AS
Mechanical and Materials Engineering (Extended)	HJ3M▼	4EXT/5EXTSW deg									
Combined Studies	Y400	3FT deg	*	8	2M	M	Ind	Ind	Ind		
Materials Engineering											
Materials Engineering	005J▼	2FT/3SW HND	M/P/C/Ph	E	N	P	Ind	Ind	Ind		

SHREWSBURY COLLEGE OF ARTS & TECHNOLOGY

Furniture Design	EJ24	3FT deg	Fa+Pf		N $	Ind			N$		
Design (Furniture)	42JE	2FT HND	Fa+Pf		N $	Ind			N$		

SOLIHULL COLL

Fashion/Knitwear	24WE	2FT HND	Fa+Pf		N	PA	Ind	Ind	Ind		
Fashion/Knitwear	24WJ	2FT HND	Fa+Pf		N	PA	Ind	Ind	Ind		

SOMERSET COLLEGE of Arts and Technology

Design (Packaging)	JW52	1ACC deg		X	HN	X	X	X	HN		
Design (Product Design and Manufacture)	045J	2FT HND	Ad/Ds/Fa+Pf			Ind	Ind	Ind	Ind		

SOUTH BANK Univ

Urban Studies and Technology	KJ94	3FT deg	* g	14-18	2M+4D	M go	Ind	Ind	Ind		

STAFFORDSHIRE Univ

Ceramic Science/Applied Statistics	JG34	3FT deg	g	8	3M	M$	24	BCC	Ind		
Ceramic Technology	J320	3FT deg	P/C/Gl	8	3M	M	24	BCC	Ind	1	
Chemistry/Ceramic Science	FJ13	3FT deg	S g	8	3M	M	24	BCC	Ind		
Computing/Ceramic Science	JG35	3FT deg	g	8	3M	M$	24	BCC	Ind		
Electronics/Ceramic Science	HJ63	3FT deg	S g	8	3M	M	24	BCC	Ind		
Geology/Ceramic Science	FJ63	3FT deg	S g	8	3M	M	24	BCC	Ind		
Physics/Ceramic Science	FJ33	3FT deg	S g	8	3M	M	24	BCC	Ind		
Ceramic Technology	023J	2FT HND	*	2	N	P	24	CCC	Ind		

Univ of STRATHCLYDE

Materials Sciences and Engineering	JH21	4FT deg	M+P	CCC	HN			30$	ABBB$	HN	
Materials Sciences and Engineering (MEng)	JH2C	5FT deg	M+P	BBC	HN			32$	AAAB$	HN	
Mechanical Engineering with Materials Eng	H3J2	5FT deg	M+P	BBB	HN			32$	AABBB$	HN	

Univ of SURREY

Materials Sci & Eng w. European Language (MEng)	J526	4/5SW deg	C+P+M g	22-26	Ind	Ind	Ind	Ind	Ind		
Materials Science & Eng with European Language	J524	4SW deg	2(M/P/C) g	16-20	Ind	X	28$	Ind	Ind		
Materials Science & Eng with a Foundation Year	J525	4FT/5SW deg	* g	8-20	Ind	Ind	$	Ind	Ind	1	
Materials Science & Engineering (MEng)	J523	3/4FT deg	C+P+M	22-26	Ind	Ind	Ind	Ind	Ind		
Materials Science and Engineering	J521	4SW deg	2(M/P/C) g	16-20	Ind	M$^	28$	Ind	Ind	1	6/14
Materials Science and Engineering	J520	3FT deg	2(M/P/C) g	16-20	Ind	M$^	28$	Ind	Ind		
Materials Science and Engineering (MEng)	J522	4/5SW deg	C+P+M	22-26	Ind	Ind	Ind	Ind	Ind		
Metallurgy	J200	3FT deg	2(M/P/C) g	16-20	Ind	M$^	28$	Ind	Ind		
Metallurgy	J201	4SW deg	2(M/P/C) g	16-20	Ind	M$^	28$	Ind	Ind		
Metallurgy with European Language	J204	4SW deg	2(M/P/C) g	16-20	Ind	X	28$	Ind	Ind		

SURREY INST of A & D

Fashion	W2J4▼	3FT deg	Fa		N					12	14/18
Fashion	E2J4▼	3FT deg	Fa		N						
Packaging Design	E2J5	3FT deg	Fa		N						
Packaging Design	W2J5	3FT deg	Fa		N					4	

Univ of SUSSEX

Chemistry with Polymer Science	F1J4	3FT deg	C+S g	CCC	MO $	MS go	$	Ind	Ind		
Chemistry with Polymer Science (MChem)	F1JK	4FT deg	C+S g	CCC	MO $	MS go	$	Ind	Ind		
Polymer Science	F1JL	4SW deg	C+S g	CCC	MO $	MS go	$	Ind	Ind		

Materials/Minerals Sciences and Technologies 51

TITLE	CODE	COURSE	SUBJECTS	A/AS	ND/C	AGNVQ	IB	SQA(H)	SQA	RATIO	A/AS
Univ of Wales SWANSEA											
Materials Science & Eng with a year in N America	J510	4FT deg	M/P/C/Ds	18	3M+3D$	Ind	26$	Ind	Ind	2	14/22
Materials Science & Engineering	J500	3FT deg	M/P/C/Ds	18	3M+3D$	Ind	26$	Ind	Ind	2	6/26
Materials Science & Engineering	J501	4FT deg	*	4	N	Ind	Ind	Ind	Ind	1	
Materials Science & Engineering (CCTA)	J503	4FT deg	M/P/C/Ds	4	N	Ind	Ind	Ind	Ind	1	
Materials Science and Engineering (MEng)	J504	4FT deg	M/P/C/Ds	18	3M+3D$	Ind	26$	Ind	Ind	2	12/24
UNIVERSITY COLL LONDON (Univ of London)											
Chemistry with Materials Science	F1F2	3FT deg	C+M+P g	BCC-BBB	MO $	Ind	30$	BBCCC$	N$		
Chemistry with Materials Science (MSci)	F1FF	4FT deg	C+M+P g	BCC-BBB	MO $	Ind	30$	BBCCC$	N$	2	
History of Art with Material Studies	V4F2	3FT deg	g	BBC-BBB	3M	Ind	30$	BBBBB	Ind	4	24/26
WEST HERTS COLL											
Graphic Media Studies	PJ55	4SW deg	*	4	N					2	8/18
Graphic Arts Technical Mgt (Print, Pub & Pkg)	55JP	2FT/3SW HND	*	2	N						
Univ of WESTMINSTER											
Photographic and Electronic Imaging Sciences	WJ55▼	3FT deg	P/C/M	DE	N	M	Ind	Ind	Ind	4	8/20
WIGAN and LEIGH COLL											
Fashion Design	24WE▼	2FT HND	Ad		N	P$		Ind	Ind		
Univ of WOLVERHAMPTON											
Applied Chemistry with Polymer Science	F1J4	3FT/4SW deg	C g	DD	N	M	24	CCCC	Ind		
Ceramics	EJ23	3FT deg	A/Ad/Ds+Pf	12	4M	M	24	BBBB	Ind		
Ceramics	WJ23	3FT deg	A/Ad/Ds+Pf	12	4M	M	24	BBBB	Ind	3	
Furniture Design	WJ24	3FT deg	A/Ad/Ds+Pf	12	4M	M	24	BBBB	Ind		
Furniture Design	EJ24	3FT deg	A/Ad/Ds+Pf	12	4M	M	24	BBBB	Ind		
Applied Sciences _Materials Technology_	Y100	3FT/4SW deg	S g	DD	N	M	24	CCCC	Ind		
Applied Sciences (4 Yrs) _Materials Technology_	Y110	4FT deg	*								
Combined Degrees _Ceramics_	Y401	3FT deg	A/Ad/Ds	12	4M	M	24	BBBB	Ind		
Combined Degrees _Ceramics_	E401	3FT deg	A/Ad/Ds	12	4M	M	24	BBBB	Ind		
Combined Degrees _Furniture Design_	E401	3FT deg	A/Ad/Ds+Pf	12	4M	M	24	BBBB	Ind		
Combined Degrees _Furniture Design_	Y401	3FT deg	A/Ad/Ds+Pf	12	4M	M	24	BBBB	Ind		
Combined Degrees _Materials Technology_	Y401	3FT/4SW deg	g	DD	N	M	24	CCCC	Ind		
Design (Furniture)	42JW▼	2FT HND	A/Ds+Pf	E	N	P	24	CCCC	Ind		
Design (Furniture)	42JE	2FT HND	A/Ds+Pf	E	N	P	24	CCCC	Ind		

| course details | | | 98 expected requirements | | | | | | | 96 entry stats |

TITLE	CODE	COURSE	SUBJECTS	A/AS	ND/C	AGNVQ	IB	SQA(H)	SQA	RATIO A/AS
Univ of ABERDEEN										
Accountancy-Statistics	NG44	4FT deg	M g	BBC	Ind	M$ go	30$	BBBB$	Ind	7
Computing Science-Mathematics	GGMC	4FT deg	M+2S g	CCD	Ind	MS go	24$	BBBC$	Ind	6
Computing Science-Statistics	GG54	4FT deg	M+2S g	CCD	Ind	MS go	24$	BBBC$	Ind	
Computing-Mathematics	GG51	4FT deg	M g	BBC	Ind	M$ go	30$	BBBB$	Ind	5
Computing-Statistics	GG4M	4FT deg	M g	BBC	Ind	M$ go	30$	BBBB$	Ind	
Economics-Mathematics	LG11	4FT deg	M g	BBC	Ind	M$ go	30$	BBBB$	Ind	
Economics-Statistics	LG14	4FT deg	M g	BBC	Ind	M$ go	30$	BBBB$	Ind	
Entrepreneurship-Mathematics	GN1C	4FT deg	* g	BBC	Ind	M$ go	30$	BBBB$	Ind	
French-Mathematics	RG11	5FT deg	* g	BBC	Ind	M$ go	30$	BBBB$	Ind	
French-Mathematics (4 Yrs)	GR11	4FT deg	* g	BBC	Ind	M$ go	30$	BBBB$	Ind	
German-Mathematics	RG21	5FT deg	* g	BBC	Ind	M$ go	30$	BBBB$	Ind	
German-Mathematics (4 Yrs)	GR12	4FT deg	* g	BBC	Ind	M$ go	30$	BBBB$	Ind	
Hispanic Studies-Mathematics	RG41	5FT deg	* g	BBC	Ind	M$ go	30$	BBBB$	Ind	
Hispanic Studies-Mathematics (4 Yrs)	GR14	4FT deg	* g	BBC	Ind	M$ go	30$	BBBB$	Ind	
History-Mathematics	VG11	4FT deg	M g	BBC	Ind	M$ go	30$	BBBB$	Ind	
Mathematics	G102	4FT deg	M g	BBC	Ind	M$ go	30$	BBBB$	Ind	9
Mathematics	G100	4FT deg	M+2S g	CCD	Ind	MS go	24$	BBBC$	Ind	7
Mathematics with French	G1R1	4FT deg	M+2S g	CCD	Ind	MS go	24$	BBBC$	Ind	
Mathematics with Gaelic	G1Q5	4FT deg	2S+M g	CCD	Ind	MS go	24$	BBBC$	Ind	
Mathematics with German	G1R2	4FT deg	M+2S g	CCD	Ind	MS go	24$	BBBC$	Ind	
Mathematics with Spanish	G1R4	4FT deg	M+S g	CCD	Ind	MS go	24$	BBBC$	Ind	
Mathematics with Theoretical Physics	G182	4FT deg	M g	BBC	Ind	M$ go	30$	BBBB$	Ind	7
Mathematics with Theoretical Physics	G180	4FT deg	M+2S g	CCD	Ind	MS go	24$	BBBC$	Ind	8
Mathematics-Management Studies	GN11	4FT deg	M g	BBC	Ind	M$ go	30$	BBBB$	Ind	
Mathematics-Philosophy	GV17	4FT deg	M g	BBC	Ind	M$ go	30$	BBBB$	Ind	10
Mathematics-Physics	FG31	3FT/4FT deg	M+S g	CCD	Ind	MS go	24$	BBBC$	Ind	7
Mathematics-Physics	GF13	4FT deg	* g	BBC	Ind	M$ go	30$	BBBB$	Ind	
Mathematics-Statistics	GG1K	4FT deg	M+2S g	CCD	Ind	MS go	24$	BBBC$	Ind	7
Mathematics-Statistics	GG14	4FT deg	M g	BBC	Ind	M$ go	30$	BBBB$	Ind	12
Mathematics-Zoology	CG31	4FT deg	M+2S g	CCD	Ind	MS go	24$	BBBC$	Ind	5
Psychology-Statistics	CG84	4FT deg	3S/2S+M g	CCD	Ind	M$ go	24$	BBBC$	Ind	
Psychology-Statistics (MA)	CG8K	4FT deg	* g	BBC	Ind	M$ go	30$	BBBB$	Ind	
Statistics	G400	4FT deg	M+2S g	CCD	Ind	MS go	24$	BBBC$	Ind	
Statistics	G402	4FT deg	M g	BBC	Ind	M$ go	30$	BBBB$	Ind	
Statistics (Economics)	G404	4FT deg	M g	BBC	Ind	M$ go	30$	BBBB$	Ind	1
Statistics with Economics	G408	4FT deg	M+2S g	CCD	Ind	MS go	24$	BBBC$	Ind	
Statistics-Management Studies	GN41	4FT deg	M g	BBC	Ind	M$ go	30$	BBBB$	Ind	
Univ of ABERTAY DUNDEE										
Applied Statistics	G410	4FT/5SW deg	M	CD	Ind	Ind	Ind	BBC	Ind	
Chemistry & Mathematics	FG11	4FT/5SW deg	C+M	CD	Ind	Ind	Ind	BBC	Ind	
Computing & Mathematics	GG51	4FT/5SW deg	M	CD	Ind	Ind	Ind	BBC	Ind	
Management & Mathematics	GN11	4FT/5SW deg	M	CD	Ind	Ind	Ind	BBC	Ind	
Mathematical Sciences	G1G5	4FT/5SW deg	M	CD	Ind	Ind	Ind	BBC	Ind	
Mathematics with Business Methods	G1N1	4FT/5SW deg	M	CD	Ind	Ind	Ind	BBC	Ind	
Psychology with Mathematics	CG81	4FT/5SW deg	E	CD	Ind	Ind	Ind	BBC	Ind	
Univ of Wales, ABERYSTWYTH										
Accounting/Mathematics	GN14	3FT deg	M g	18	3M+3D$ M^ g		29$	BBBCC$	Ind	
Accounting/Statistics	GN44	3FT deg	M g	18	3M+3D$ M^ g		29$	BBBCC$	Ind	
Applied Mathematics	G110	3FT deg	M g	16	1M+5D$ M^ g		28$	BBCCC$	Ind	
Applied Mathematics/Pure Mathematics	G130	3FT deg	M g	16	1M+5D$ M^ g		28$	BBCCC$	Ind	

Mathematics and Statistics

course details			*98 expected requirements*							*96 entry stats*
TITLE	CODE	COURSE	SUBJECTS	A/AS	NO/C	AGNVQ	IB	SQA(H)	SQA	RATIO A/AS
Applied Mathematics/Statistics	GGC4	3FT deg	M g	16	1M+5D$	M^ g	28$	BBCCC$	Ind	
Computer Science/Mathematics	GG15	3FT deg	M g	20	3M+2D$	M^ g	30$	BBBCC$	Ind	
Computer Science/Statistics	GG45	3FT deg	M g	20	3M+2D$	M^ g	30$	BBBCC$	Ind	
Education/Mathematics	GX19	3FT deg	M g	16	1M+5D$	M^ g	28$	BBCCC$	Ind	
Education/Statistics	GXK9	3FT deg	M g	16	1M+5D$	M^ g	28$	BBCCC$	Ind	
Financial Mathematics	G1N3	3FT deg	M g	16	1M+5D$	M^ g	28$	BBCCC$	Ind	
Geography/Mathematics	FG81	3FT deg	M+Gy g	20	3M+2D$	MS^ g	30$	BBBCC$	Ind	
Geography/Statistics	FG84	3FT deg	M+Gy g	20	3M+1D$	MS^ g	30$	BBBCC$	Ind	
Mathematics	G100	3FT deg	M g	16	1M+5D$	M^ g	28$	BBCC$	Ind	
Mathematics (MMath)	G103	4FT deg	M g	16	1M+5D$	M^ g	28$	BBCC$	Ind	
Mathematics (Ordinary)	G102	3FT deg	M g	4	N $	P g	Dip$	DD$	Ind	
Mathematics with Education	G1X9	3FT deg	M g	16	1M+5D$	M^ g	28$	BBCCC$	Ind	
Mathematics/Physics	FG31	3FT deg	M+P g	16	1M+5D$	MS^ g	28$	BBCC$	Ind	
Pure Mathematics	G120	3FT deg	M g	16	1M+5D$	M^ g	28$	BBCCC$	Ind	
Pure Mathematics/American Studies	GQ14	3FT deg	M+E/H g	18	1M+5D$	M^ g	29$	BBBCC$	Ind	
Pure Mathematics/Art	GW11	3FT deg	M+A/Ad g	18	1M+5D$	MA^ g	29$	BBBCC$	Ind	
Pure Mathematics/Art History	GVC4	3FT deg	M g	18	1M+5D$	MA^ g	29$	BBBCC$	Ind	
Pure Mathematics/Drama	GW14	3FT deg	M g	20	1M+5D$	MQ^ g	30$	BBBBC$	Ind	
Pure Mathematics/Film and Television Studies	GW15	3FT deg	M g	20	1M+5D$	MQ^ g	30$	BBBBC$	Ind	
Pure Mathematics/French	GRC1	4FT deg	F+M g	18	1M+5D$	M^ g	29$	BBBCC$	Ind	
Pure Mathematics/Geography	GLC8	3FT deg	M+Gy g	20-22	3M+2D$	M^ g	31$	BBBBC$	Ind	
Pure Mathematics/German	GRC2	4FT deg	M+G g	18	1M+5D$	M^ g	29$	BBBCC$	Ind	
Pure Mathematics/History	GV11	3FT deg	M g	18-20	1M+5D$	M^ g	30$	BBBCC$	Ind	
Pure Mathematics/Irish	GQC5	4FT deg	M g	18	1M+5D$	M^ g	29$	BBBCC$	Ind	
Pure Mathematics/Italian	GRC3	4FT deg	M+L g	18	1M+5D$	M^ g	29$	BBBCC$	Ind	
Pure Mathematics/Statistics	GGD4	3FT deg	M g	16	1M+5D$	M^ g	28$	BBCCC$	Ind	
Spanish/Pure Mathematics	GRC4	4FT deg	M+L g	18	1M+5D$	M^ g	29$	BBBCC$	Ind	
Statistics	G400	3FT deg	M g	16	1M+5D$	M^ g	28$	BBCCC$	Ind	
Welsh History/Pure Mathematics	GVC1	3FT deg	M g	18-20	1M+5D$	M^ g	30$	BBBCC$	Ind	
Welsh/Pure Mathematics	GQ15	3FT deg	M+W g	18	1M+5D$	M^ g	29$	BBBCC$	Ind	
Information and Library St/an approved Sci Sub *Applied Mathematics*	PY21	3FT deg	M g	16	1M+5D$	M^ g	28$	BBCCC$	Ind	
Information and Library St/an approved Sci Sub *Mathematics*	PY21	3FT deg	M g	16	1M+5D$	M^ g	28$	BBCCC$	Ind	
Information and Library St/an approved Sci Sub *Pure Mathematics*	PY21	3FT deg	M g	16	1M+5D$	M^ g	28$	BBCCC$	Ind	
Information and Library St/an approved Sci Sub *Statistics*	PY21	3FT deg	M g	16	1M+5D$	M^ g	28$	BBCCC$	Ind	

ANGLIA Poly Univ

TITLE	CODE	COURSE	SUBJECTS	A/AS	NO/C	AGNVQ	IB	SQA(H)	SQA	RATIO A/AS
Animal Behaviour and Maths or Stats/Stat Mod.	CG1C▼	3FT deg	g	10	3M	P go	Dip	BCCC	N	
Audiotechnology and Maths or Stats/Stat Mod.	HG6C▼	3FT deg	S g	16	8M	D go	Dip$	BBCCC	N	
Biology and Maths or Stats/Statistical Mod.	CG11▼	3FT deg	B g	10	3M	P go	Dip$	BCCC	N	
Biomedical Science and Maths or Stats/Stat Model	BG91▼	3FT deg	B g	10	3M	M go	Dip$	BCCC	N	
Business and Maths or Stats/Statistical Mod.	NG11▼	3FT deg	* g	10	3M	P go	Dip	BCCC	Ind	3
Chemistry and Maths or Stats/Stat Modelling	FG11▼	3FT deg	S g	8	2M	P go	Dip$	CCCC	N	3
Computer Science and Maths or Stats/Stat Mod.	GG51▼	3FT deg	* g	10	3M	P go	Dip	BCCC	N	4
Ecology and Conservation & Maths or Stats/St.Mod.	DG21▼	3FT deg	g	10	2M	M go	Dip	BCCC	N	
Economics and Maths or Statistics/Stat Modelling	LG11▼	3FT deg	* g	10	3M	P go	Dip	BCCC	Ind	
English and Maths or Stats/Statistical Modelling	QG31▼	3FT deg	E	12	4M	M+/^	Dip$	BCCC	Ind	
European Philosophy & Lit&Maths or Stats/St Mod.	GV17▼	3FT deg	*	12	4M	M+/^	Dip	BCCC	Ind	
French and Maths or Stats/Statistical Modelling	GR11▼	4FT deg	* g	12	4M	M go	Dip	BCCC	Ind	
Geography and Maths or Stats/Stat Modelling	FG81▼	3FT deg	Gy g	12	4M	M go	Dip$	BCCC	N	
Geology and Maths or Stats/Statistical Modelling	FG61▼	3FT deg	* g	10	3M	P go	Dip	BCCC	N	

course details | 98 expected requirements | 96 entry stats

TITLE	CODE	COURSE	SUBJECTS	A/AS	NO/C	AGNVQ	IB	SQA(H)	SQA	RATIO A/AS
German and Maths or Stats/Statistical Modelling	GR12▼	4FT deg	* g	12	4M	M+/^ go	Dip$	BCCC	Ind	
Graphic Arts and Maths or Stats/Stat Modelling	GW12▼	3FT deg	A g	14	6M	M go	Dip$	BBCC	Ind	3
History and Maths or Stats/Statistical Modelling	GV11▼	3FT deg	* g	12	4M	M+/^	Dip	BCCC	Ind	
Imaging Science and Maths or Stats/Stat Mod.	GWC5▼	3FT deg	S g	10	3M	P	Dip	BCCC	N	
Instrumentation Electron & Maths or Stats/St Mod	GH16▼	3FT deg	S g	10	3M	P go	Dip$	BCCC	N	
Italian and Maths or Stats/Stat Modelling	GR13▼	4FT deg	* g	12	4M	M+/^ go	Dip	BCCC	Ind	
Law and Mathematics or Stats/Stat Modelling	MG31▼	3FT deg	* g	14	6M	M go	Dip	BBCC	Ind	3
Mathematics or Stats/Stat Mod. and Politics	GM11▼	3FT deg	* g	14	6M	M go	Dip	BBCC	Ind	
Mathematics or Stats/Stat Mod. and Psychology	CG81▼	3FT deg	S g	16	8M	D go	Dip$	BBCCC	N	5
Mathematics or Stats/Stat Mod. and Social Policy	GL14▼	3FT deg	* g	12	4M	M go	Dip	BCCC	N	
Mathematics or Stats/Stat Modelling and Music	GW13▼	3FT deg	Mu g	12	4M	M+/^ go	Dip$	BCCC	Ind	6
Mathematics or Stats/Stat Modelling and Spanish	GR14▼	4FT deg	* g	12	4M	M go	Dip	BCCC	Ind	
Maths or Stats/Stat Mod. & Ophthalmic Dispensing	BG51▼	3FT deg	* g	10	3M	P go	Dip	BCCC	N	1
Maths or Stats/Stat Mod.& Real Time Comp.Systems	GG15▼	3FT deg	* g	10	3M	P go	Dip	BCCC	N	

ASTON Univ

TITLE	CODE	COURSE	SUBJECTS	A/AS	NO/C	AGNVQ	IB	SQA(H)	SQA	RATIO A/AS
Mathematics/Biology	CG11	3FT/4SW deg	B+M g	20	X	X	31$	ABBBB$	Ind	9
Mathematics/Business Administration	GN11	3FT/4SW deg	M g	20	X	D$^ go	31$	ABBBB$	Ind	12
Mathematics/Chemistry	FG11	3FT/4SW deg	C+M g	20	X	X	31$	ABBBB$	Ind	7
Mathematics/Computer Science	GG15	3FT/4SW deg	M g	20	X	D$^ go	31$	ABBBB$	Ind	7 14/22
Mathematics/Engineering Management	GH1R	3FT/4SW deg	M g	20	5M+5D$	D$^ go	30	BBBBB	Ind	
Mathematics/French	GR11	4SW deg	F+M g	20	X	X	31$	ABBBB$	Ind	
Mathematics/German	GR12	4SW deg	M+G g	20	X	X	31$	ABBBB$	Ind	
Mathematics/Health & Safety Management	GJ19	3FT/4SW deg	M g	20	X	D$^ go	31$	ABBBB$	Ind	2
Product Design (Engineering)/Mathematics	GH17	3FT/4SW deg	M g	20	5M+5D$	D$^ go	30$	BBBBB$		
Public Policy & Management/Mathematics	GM1C	3FT/4SW deg	M g	20	X	D$^ go	30$	BBBBB$	Ind	5
Social Studies/Mathematics	GL14	3FT/4SW deg	M g	22	X	D$6/^ go	31$	ABBBB$	Ind	4

Univ of Wales, BANGOR

TITLE	CODE	COURSE	SUBJECTS	A/AS	NO/C	AGNVQ	IB	SQA(H)	SQA	RATIO A/AS
Computer Systems with Mathematics	H6G1	3FT deg	M+P/Es/Cs g	CC	3M $	D$^ go	26$	CCCC$	Ind	4
Education and Mathematics (Taught in Welsh)	GXC9	3FT deg	M g	CCD	Ind	D*^ go	Ind	X	X	
Information Technology and Applied Statistics	GG54	2FT dip	* g							
MMath (4 Yrs)	G103	4FT deg	M g	20-24	3M+2D$	D$^ go	30$	BBBB$	HN	3 22/30
Management and Mathematics	NG11	3FT deg	M g	18	5M $	D$^ go	28$	BBBC$	Ind	
Mathematics	G100	3FT deg	M g	14-18	3M $	D$^ go	28$	BBCC$	Ind	7 8/18
Mathematics	G102	3FT deg	M g	14-18	3M $	D$^ go	28$	BBCC$	Ind	
Mathematics and Physical Education	GBC6	3FT deg	M g	CCC	2M+2D$	D$^ go	30$	BBBC$	Ind	
Mathematics and Physical Oceanography	FG71	3FT deg	M+S g	CD	Ind	D$^ go	28$	BCCC$	Ind	9
Mathematics and Psychology	CG81	3FT deg	M g	18	MO	D$^ go	28$	BBBC$	Ind	12
Mathematics and Sports Science	BG6C	3FT deg	M g	CCC	2M+2D$	D$^ go	30$	BBBC$	Ind	
Mathematics with Computer Systems	G1H6	3FT deg	M g	14-18	3M $	D$^ go	26$	BBCC$	Ind	7
Mathematics with Insurance	G1N3	3FT deg	M g	CCC	3M+2D$	D$^ go	28$	BBBC$	Ind	
Mathematics/Accounting	GN14	3FT deg	M g	CCC	3M+2D	D$^ go	28$	BBBC$	Ind	8
Mathematics/Banking	GN13	3FT deg	M g	CCC	3M+2D$	D$^ go	28$	BBBC$	Ind	6
Mathematics/Economics	GL11	3FT deg	M g	18	3M+2D$	D$^ go	28$	BBBC$	Ind	3
Mathematics/Education (Taught in Welsh)	GX19	3FT deg	M g	CCD	Ind	D$^ go	Ind	X	X	
Psychology/Mathematics	CGV1	3FT deg	M g	18	MO	D$6/^ go	28$	BBBC$	Ind	
Pure Mathematics	G122	3FT deg	M g	14-18	3M $	D$^ go	28$	BBCC$	Ind	
Welsh/Mathematics	GQ15	3FT/4FT deg	M+W g	CCD	Ind	D*^ go	Ind	X	X	1

BARNSLEY COLL

TITLE	CODE	COURSE
Science Foundation	Y100	4EXT deg
Mathematics		

TITLE	CODE	COURSE	SUBJECTS	A/AS	ND/C	AGNVQ	IB	SQA(H)	SQA	RATIO A/AS
Univ of BATH										
Mathematical Sciences	G141	4SW deg	M	22	Ind	Ind	30$	AABBC$	Ind	4
Mathematical Sciences	G140	3FT deg	M	22	Ind	Ind	30$	AABBC$	Ind	10
Mathematics	G100	3FT deg	M	22-24	Ind	Ind	30$	AABBC$	Ind	7 18/30
Mathematics	G101	4SW deg	M	22-24	Ind	Ind	30$	AABBC$	Ind	6 20/26
Mathematics (MMath)	G103	4FT deg	M	24	Ind	Ind	30$	AABBC$	Ind	6 20/30
Mathematics (MMath) (inc 1 year abroad)	G104	4FT deg	M	24	Ind	Ind	30$	AABBC$	Ind	2 24/30
Mathematics and Computing	G5GC	3FT deg	M	22	Ind	Ind	30$	AABBC$	Ind	8 22/26
Mathematics and Computing	G5G1	4SW deg	M	22	Ind	Ind	30$	AABBC$	Ind	3 20/28
Mathematics and Statistics	GG14	3FT deg	M	22	Ind	Ind	30$	AABBC$	Ind	8 24/26
Mathematics and Statistics (4 Yr SW)	GG41	4SW deg	M	22	Ind	Ind	30$	AABBC$	Ind	4 24/28
Statistics	G401	4SW deg	M	22	Ind	Ind	30$	AABBC$		
Statistics	G400	3FT deg	M	22	Ind	Ind	30$	AABBC$	Ind	7
Natural Sciences *Mathematics*	Y161	4SW deg	S/M+S/M	20	Ind	DS	30	Ind	Ind	
Natural Sciences *Mathematics*	Y160	3FT deg	S/M+S/M	20	Ind	DS	30	Ind	Ind	
BATH COLL of HE										
Combined Awards *Applicable Mathematics*	Y400	3FT deg	g		N		Ind	$	$	
Modular Programme (DipHE) *Applicable Mathematics*	Y460	2FT Dip	g		N		Ind	$	$	
BELL COLLEGE OF TECHNOLOGY										
Applicable Mathematics	G110	3FT deg	M g	DD	Ind	Ind	Ind	BCC$	20$	
Applicable Mathematics with Computing	5G1G	2FT HND	M	D-E	Ind	Ind	Ind	CC$	18$	
Univ of BIRMINGHAM										
Ancient History & Archaeology/Mathematics	GV16	3FT deg	M	ABB-ABC Ind		D*^	32$	ABBB	Ind	3
East Mediterranean History/Mathematics	GV1C	3FT deg	M g	ABB-ABC Ind		D*^	32$	ABBB	Ind	
Economics and Statistics	GL41	3FT deg	M	BBC	Ind	D+^	32	ABBBB	Ind	17
French Studies/Mathematics	GR11	4FT deg	F+M	ABB-ABC Ind		D*^	32$	ABBB	Ind	7
German Studies/Mathematics	GR12	4FT deg	G+M	ABB-ABC Ind		D*^	32$	ABBB	Ind	
Hispanic Studies/Mathematics	GR14	4FT deg	M	ABB-ABC Ind		D*^	32$	ABBB	Ind	
History/Mathematics	GV11	3FT deg	M	ABC/ABB Ind		D*^	32$	ABBB	Ind	
Italian/Mathematics	GR13	4FT deg	M	ABB-ABC Ind		D*^	32$	ABBB	Ind	
Latin/Mathematics	GQ16	3FT deg	Ln+M	ABB-ABC Ind		D*^	32$	ABBB	Ind	
Mathematical Sci w. Study in Continental Europe	G141	4FT deg	M g	ACC	Ind	Ind	30	Ind	Ind	3 22/30
Mathematical Sciences	G103	3FT/4FT deg	M	ACC	Ind	Ind	30	Ind	Ind	6 20/30
Mathematics and Artificial Intelligence	GG18	3FT deg	M	ABC	Ind	Ind	30	Ind	Ind	17
Mathematics and Computer Science	GG15	3FT deg	M	ACC	Ind	Ind	30	Ind	Ind	10 20/28
Mathematics and Psychology	CG81	3FT deg	M	ABC	Ind	Ind	30	Ind	Ind	5 22/30
Mathematics and Sports Science	GC17	3FT deg	M+B/C/P	ABB-ABC Ind		Ind	30	Ind	Ind	12 24/30
Mathematics/Modern Greek Studies	GT12	4FT deg	M g	ABB-ABC Ind		D*^	32$	ABBB	Ind	
Mathematics/Music	GW13	3FT deg	M+Mu	AAB-ABB Ind		D*^	32$	ABBB	Ind	5 28/30
Mathematics/Philosophy	GV17	3FT deg	M	ABB-ABC Ind		D*^	32$	ABBB	Ind	12
Mathematics/Portuguese	GR15	4FT deg	M	ABB-ABC Ind		D*^	32$	ABBB	Ind	
Mathematics/Russian	GR18	4FT deg	M	ABB-ABC Ind		D*^	32$	ABBB	Ind	
Mathematics/Theology	GV18	3FT deg	M g	ABB-ABC Ind		D*^	32$	ABBB	Ind	
Theoretical Physics and Applied Mathematics	FG31	3FT/4FT deg	P+M	BBC	Ind	Ind	30	Ind	Ind	7 18/30

course details — *98 expected requirements* — *96 entry stats*

TITLE	CODE	COURSE	SUBJECTS	A/AS	NO/C	AGNVQ	IB	SQA(H)	SQA	RATIO A/AS
BOLTON INST										
Accountancy and Mathematics	GN14	3FT deg	M g	DD	Ind	Ind	24	BBCC	Ind	
Accountancy and Statistics	GN44	3FT deg	* g	CD	MO	M	24	Ind	Ind	
Art & Design History and Mathematics	VG41	3FT deg	M g	DD	Ind	Ind	24	BBCC	Ind	
Biology and Mathematics	CG11	3FT deg	M g	DD	Ind	Ind	24	BBCC	Ind	
Biology and Statistics	CG14	3FT deg	* g	CD	MO	M	24	Ind	Ind	
Business Economics and Mathematics	LG11	3FT deg	M g	DD	Ind	Ind	24	BBCC	Ind	
Business Info Systems and Mathematics	GG51	3FT deg	M g	DD	Ind	Ind	24	BBCC	Ind	
Business Information Systems and Statistics	GG54	3FT deg	* g	CD	MO	M	24	Ind	Ind	
Business Studies and Mathematics	GN11	3FT deg	M g	DD	Ind	Ind	24	BBCC	Ind	
Business Studies and Statistics	GN41	3FT deg	* g	CD	MO	M	24	Ind	Ind	
Community Studies and Mathematics	GL15	3FT deg	M g	DD	Ind	Ind	24	BBCC	Ind	
Computing and Mathematics	GG15	3FT deg	M g	DD	Ind	Ind	24	BBCC	Ind	
Computing and Statistics	GG5K	3FT deg	* g	CD	MO	M	24	Ind	Ind	
Design and Mathematics	GW12	3FT deg	* g	CD	MO	M*	24	BBCC	Ind	
Environmental Studies and Mathematics	FG91	3FT deg	M g	DD	Ind	Ind	24	BBCC	Ind	
European Cultural Studies and Mathematics	TG21	3FT deg	M g	DD	MO	M*	24	BBCC	Ind	
Film & TV Studies and Mathematics	GW15	3FT deg	M g	CD	MO	M*	24	BBCC	Ind	
French and Mathematics	RG11	3FT deg	F+M g	CD	Ind	Ind	24	BBCC	Ind	
Gender and Women's Studies and Mathematics	MG91	3FT deg	M g	CD	Ind	Ind	24	BBCC	Ind	
German and Mathematics	RG21	3FT deg	G+M	CD	Ind	Ind	24	BBCC	Ind	
History and Mathematics	GV11	3FT deg	M g	DD	Ind	Ind	24	BBCC	Ind	
Human Resource Management and Mathematics	NG11	3FT deg	M g	CD	Ind	Ind	24	BBCC	Ind	
Human Resource Management and Statistics	GN4C	3FT deg	* g	CD	MO	M	24	Ind	Ind	
Law and Mathematics	MG31	3FT deg	M g	CD	Ind	Ind	24	BBCC	Ind	
Leisure Studies and Mathematics	GL13	3FT deg	M g	CD	Ind	Ind	24	BBCC	Ind	
Leisure Studies and Statistics	GL4H	3FT deg	* g	CD	MO	M	24	Ind	Ind	
Literature and Mathematics	GQ12	3FT deg	M g	DD	Ind	Ind	24	BBCC	Ind	
Marketing and Mathematics	GN15	3FT deg	M g	CD	Ind	Ind	24	BBCC	Ind	
Marketing and Statistics	GN45	3FT deg	* g	CD	MO	M	24	Ind	Ind	
Mathematics	G100	3FT deg	M g	DD	Ind	Ind	24	BBCC	Ind	
Mathematics and Operations Management	GN12	3FT deg	M g	CD	Ind	Ind	24	BBCC	Ind	
Mathematics and Organisations, Management & Work	GN17	3FT deg	M g	CD	Ind	Ind	24	BBCC	Ind	
Mathematics and Peace and War Studies	GV1C	3FT deg	M g	CD	Ind	Ind	24	BBCC	Ind	
Mathematics and Philosophy	GV17	3FT deg	M g	DD	Ind	Ind	24	BBCC	Ind	
Mathematics and Psychology	GL17	3FT deg	M g	DD	Ind	Ind	24	BBCC	Ind	
Mathematics and Sociology	GL1H	3FT deg	M g	CD	MO	Ind	24	Ind	Ind	
Mathematics and Statistics	GG14	3FT deg	M g	CD	MO	Ind	24	Ind	Ind	
Mathematics and Theatre Studies	WG41	3FT deg	M+Me/T g	CD	Ind	Ind	24	BBCC	Ind	
Mathematics and Tourism Studies	GP17	3FT deg	M g	CD	Ind	Ind	24	BBCC	Ind	
Mathematics and Urban and Cultural Studies	GK14	3FT deg	M g	CD	Ind	Ind	24	BBCC	Ind	
Psychology and Statistics	GL47	3FT deg	* g	12	MO	M	24	Ind	Ind	
Tourism Studies and Statistics	GP47	3FT deg	* g	CD	MO	M	24	Ind	Ind	
Visual Arts and Mathematics	GW11	3FT deg	* g	DD	MO	M*	24	BBCC	Ind	
Univ of BRIGHTON										
Biology and Mathematics	CG11	3FT/4SW deg	M g	12	MO $	M$	Dip$	BBCC$	Ind	
Chemistry and Statistics	FG14	3FT/4SW deg	C/St g	12	MO $	M$	Dip$	BBCC$	Ind	
Computing and Mathematics	GG51	3FT/4SW deg	M g	12	MO $	M$	Dip$	BBCC$	Ind	
Computing and Statistics	GG54	3FT/4SW deg	S g	12	MO $	M$	Dip$	BBCC$	Ind	
Energy Studies and Mathematics	GJ19	3FT/4SW deg	M g	12	MO $	M$	Dip$	BBCC$	Ind	
Energy Studies and Statistics	JG94	3FT/4SW deg	S g	12	MO $	M$	Dip$	BBCC$	Ind	
Geography and Statistics	FG84	3FT/4SW deg	S g	12	MO $	M$	Dip$	BBCC$	Ind	

Mathematics and Statistics — 52

course details			98 expected requirements							96 entry stats
TITLE	CODE	COURSE	SUBJECTS	A/AS	ND/C	AGNVQ	IB	SQA(H)	SQA	RATIO A/AS
Mathematics	G101	3FT/4SW deg	M g	12	Ind	Ind	Dip$	BBCC$	Ind	
Mathematics and Operational Research	GN12	3FT/4SW deg	M g	12	MO $	M$	Dip$	BBCC$	Ind	
Mathematics and Physics	GF13	3FT/4SW deg	M g	12	MO $	M$	Dip$	BBCC$	Ind	
Mathematics and Statistics	GG14	3FT/4SW deg	M g	12	MO $	M$	Dip$	BBCC$	Ind	
Mathematics for Computing	G170	3FT/4SW deg	M g	12	Ind	Ind	Dip$	BBCC$	Ind	
Mathematics for Management	G1N1	3FT/4SW deg	M g	12	Ind	Ind	Dip$	BBCC$	Ind	
Statistics for Management	G4N1	3FT/4SW deg	M g	12	Ind	Ind	Dip$	BBCC$	Ind	
Mathematical Studies (Business Applications)	1N1G	2FT HND	M g	4	Ind	Ind	24$	CC$	Ind	

Univ of BRISTOL

Computational and Experimental Maths (MEng)	J921	4FT deg	M+P	BBB	HN $	D$^	30$	CSYS	HN$	3
Computer Science with Mathematics	G5G1	3FT deg	M	ABB	HN $	D$^	32$	CSYS	HN$	12 20/24
Economics and Mathematics	LG11	3FT deg	M	ABC	Ind	D$^	32$	CSYS	Ind	7 24/30
Engineering Mathematics (MEng)	J920	4FT deg	M+P	BBB	Ind	DS^	30$	CSYS	HN$	4 20/30
Mathematics	G100	3FT deg	M	ABB	Ind	D$^	32$	CSYS	Ind	8 21/30
Mathematics (MSci)	G103	4FT deg	M	ABB	Ind	D$^	32$	CSYS	Ind	9 24/30
Mathematics and Physics	GF13	3FT deg	M+P	ABC-BBC	Ind	D$^	32$	CSYS	Ind	20
Mathematics and Physics (MSci)	GF1H	4FT deg	M+P	ABC-BBC	Ind	D$^	32$	CSYS	Ind	11
Mathematics and Physics with St in Cont Europe	FG31	4FT deg	M+P	ABC-BBC	Ind	D$^	32$	CSYS	Ind	9
Mathematics with Statistics	G1G4	3FT deg	M	ABB	Ind	D$^	32$	CSYS	Ind	8 24/30
Mathematics with Statistics (MSci)	G1GK	4FT deg	M	ABB	Ind	D$^	32$	CSYS	Ind	7
Mathematics with Study in Continental Eur (MSci)	G104	4FT deg	M	ABB	Ind	D$^	32$	CSYS	Ind	
Mathematics with Study in Continental Europe	G101	4FT deg	M g	ABB	Ind	D$^	32$	CSYS	Ind	6 22/28
Philosophy and Mathematics	VG71	3FT deg	M	ABC	Ind	D$^	32$	CSYS	Ind	6 24/28

BRISTOL, Univ of the W of England

Mathematical Sciences	G900	3FT/4SW deg	M g	14	3M $	M$^ go	24$	BCCC$	N$	
Mathematics and Computing	GG15	3FT/4SW deg	M g	14	MO $	M$^ go	24$	BCCC$	N$	
Statistics	G400	3FT/4SW deg	M/St g	14	3M $	M*^ go	24$	BCCC$	N$	
Statistics and Computing	G4GM	3FT/4SW deg	M/St g	14	3M $	M*^ go	24$	BCCC$	N$	
Statistics and Information Systems	GG45	3FT/4SW deg	M/St g	14	MO	M*^ go	24$	BCCC$	N$	
Joint Honours Programme *Accounting and Statistics*	Y401	3FT deg	* g	14-16	5M	M$ go	24	BCCC	Ind	
Joint Honours Programme *Economics and Mathematics*	Y401	3FT deg	M g	14-16	5M $	M$ go	24$	BCCC$	Ind	
Joint Honours Programme *Marketing and Statistics*	Y401	3FT deg	M g	14-16	5M $	M$ go	24$	BCCC$	Ind	

BRUNEL Univ, West London

Business Mathematics with French	RG1C	3FT deg	M+F g	BBC-BCC	3M+2D$	D^+	29$	BBBC$	Ind	
Business Mathematics with French (4 Yrs Thin SW)	RG11	4SW deg	M+F g	BBC-BCC	3M+2D$	D^+	29$	BBBC$	Ind	2
Business Mathematics with French(4 Yrs Thick SW)	G1RC	4SW deg	M+F g	BBC-BCC	3M+2D$	D^	29$	BBBC$	Ind	2
Business Mathematics with German	RG2C	3FT deg	M+G g	BBC-BCC	3M+2D$	D^+	29$	BBBC$	Ind	1
Business Mathematics with German (4 Yrs Thin SW)	RG21	4SW deg	M+G g	BBC-BCC	3M+2D$	D^+	29$	BBBC$	Ind	3
Business Mathematics with German(4 Yrs Thick SW)	G1RF	4SW deg	M+G g	BBC-BCC	3M+2D$	D^+P^	29$	BBBC$	Ind	
Mathematical & Management Studs (4 Yrs Thick SW)	GN1D	4SW deg	M	BBC-BCC	3M+2D$	P^	29$	BBBC$	Ind	7
Mathematical and Management St (4 Yrs Thin SW)	GN11	4SW deg	M	BBC-BCC	3M+2D$	P^	29$	BBBC$	Ind	2 16/18
Mathematical and Management Studies	GN1C	3FT deg	M	BBC-BCC	3M+2D$	P^	29$	BBBC$	Ind	23
Mathematics	G103	3FT deg	M	BBC-BCC	3M+2D$	P^	29$	BBBC$	Ind	12
Mathematics & Statistics with Mgt(4 Yrs Thin SW)	G1N1	4SW deg	M	BBC-BCC	3M+2D$	P^	29$	BBBC$	Ind	2 12/20
Mathematics & Statistics with Mgt(4Yrs Thick SW)	G1ND	4SW deg	M	BBC-BCC	3M+2D$	P^	29$	BBBC$	Ind	9
Mathematics (4 Yrs Thick SW)	G104	4SW deg	M	BBC-BCC	3M+2D$	P^	29$	BBBC$	Ind	
Mathematics (4 Yrs Thin SW)	G100	4SW deg	M	BBC-BCC	3M+2D$	P^	29$	BBBC$	Ind	6
Mathematics and Statistics with Management	G1NC	3FT deg	M	BBC-BCC	3M+2D$	P^	29$	BBBC$	Ind	5 14/18
Mathematics with Computer Sci (4 Yrs Thick SW)	G1GN	4SW deg	M	BBC-BCC	3M+2D$	P^	29$	BBBC$	Ind	11
Mathematics with Computer Sci (4 Yrs Thin SW)	G1G5	4SW deg	M	BBC-BCC	3M+2D$	P^	29$	BBBC$	Ind	6

course details — 98 expected requirements — 96 entry stats

TITLE	CODE	COURSE	SUBJECTS	A/AS	ND/C	AGNVQ	IB	SQA(H)	SQA	RATIO A/AS
Mathematics with Computer Science	G1GM	3FT deg	M	BBC-BCC	3M+2D$	P^	29$	BBBC$	Ind	9
Mathematics with Engineering	G1H1	3FT deg	M+P	BBC-BCC	3M+2D$	P^	29$	BBBC$	Ind	13
Mathematics with Engineering (4 Yrs Thick SW)	G1HD	4SW deg	M+P	BBC-BCC	3M+2D$	P^	29$	BBBC$	Ind	4
Mathematics with Engineering (4 Yrs Thin SW)	G1HC	4SW deg	M+P	BBC-BCC	3M+2D$	P^	29$	BBBC$	Ind	2
Mathematics with French	GR11	3FT deg	M+F g	BBC-BCC	3M+2D$	P^	29$	BBBC$	Ind	
Mathematics with French (4 Yrs Thick SW)	G1R1	4SW deg	M+F g	BBC-BCC	3M+2D$	P^	29$	BBBC$	Ind	
Mathematics with French (4 Yrs Thin SW)	G1RD	4SW deg	M+F g	BBC-BCC	3M+2D$	P^	29$	BBBC$	Ind	2
Mathematics with German	GR12	3FT deg	M+G g	BBC-BCC	3M+2D$	P^	29$	BBBC$	Ind	
Mathematics with German (4 Yrs Thick SW)	G1R2	4SW deg	M+G g	BBC-BCC	3M+2D$	P^	29$	BBBC$	Ind	
Mathematics with German (4 Yrs Thin SW)	G1RG	4SW deg	M+G g	BBC-BCC	3M+2D$	D^	29$	BBBC$	Ind	
Statistics and Mathematics	GG4C	3FT deg	M	BBC-BCC	4M+2D$	D^	28$	BBBC$	Ind	13
Statistics and Mathematics (4 Yrs Thick SW)	GG4D	4SW deg	M	BBC-BCC	4M+2D$	P^	29$	BBBC$	Ind	
Statistics and Mathematics (4 Yrs Thin SW)	GG41	4SW deg	M	BBC-BCC	4M+2D$	D^	28$	BBBC$	Ind	

CAMBRIDGE Univ

TITLE	CODE	COURSE	SUBJECTS	A/AS	ND/C	AGNVQ	IB	SQA(H)	SQA	RATIO A/AS
Mathematics, Pure and Applied	G100▼	3FT/4FT deg	M g	AAA-AAB	Ind		Ind	CSYS	Ind	3 30/30
Natural Sciences _Fluid Mechanics_	Y160▼	3FT deg	2(S/M) g	AAA-AAB	Ind		Ind	CSYS	Ind	

CANTERBURY CHRIST CHURCH COLL of HE

TITLE	CODE	COURSE	SUBJECTS	A/AS	ND/C	AGNVQ	IB	SQA(H)	SQA	RATIO A/AS
American Studies with Mathematics	Q4G1	4FT deg	M g	DD	Ind	Ind	24	Ind	Ind	
American Studies with Statistics	Q4G4	4FT deg	M g	DD	Ind	Ind	24	Ind	Ind	
Art with Mathematics	W1G1	3FT deg	A+M g	DD	Ind	Ind	24	Ind	Ind	
Art with Statistics	W1G4	3FT deg	A+M g	DD	Ind	Ind	24	Ind	Ind	
Business Studies with Mathematics	N1G1	3FT deg	M g	DD	Ind	Ind	24	Ind	Ind	5
Business Studies with Statistics	N1G4	3FT deg	M g	DD	Ind	Ind	24	Ind	Ind	
Early Childhood Studies with Mathematics	X9G1	3FT deg	M g	DD	Ind	Ind	24	Ind	Ind	
Early Childhood Studies with Statistics	X9G4	3FT deg	M g	DD	Ind	Ind	24	Ind	Ind	
English with Mathematics	Q3G1	3FT deg	E+M	DD	Ind	Ind	24	Ind	Ind	
English with Statistics	Q3G4	3FT deg	E+M	DD	Ind	Ind	24	Ind	Ind	
History with Mathematics	V1G1	3FT deg	H+M g	DD	Ind	Ind	24	Ind	Ind	
History with Statistics	V1G4	3FT deg	H+M g	DD	Ind	Ind	24	Ind	Ind	
Information Technology with Mathematics	G5G1	3FT deg	M g	DD	Ind	Ind	24	Ind	Ind	2
Information Technology with Statistics	G5G4	3FT deg	M g	DD	Ind	Ind	24	Ind	Ind	
Marketing with Mathematics	N5G1	3FT deg	M g	DD	Ind	Ind	24	Ind	Ind	
Marketing with Statistics	N5G4	3FT deg	M g	DD	Ind	Ind	24	Ind	Ind	
Mathematics and American Studies	GQ14	3FT deg	M g	DD	Ind	Ind	24	Ind	Ind	1
Mathematics and Art	WG11	3FT deg	A+M g	DD	Ind	Ind	24	Ind	Ind	4
Mathematics and Business Studies	NG11	3FT deg	M g	DD	Ind	Ind	24	Ind	Ind	
Mathematics and Early Childhood Studies	XG91	3FT deg	M g	DD	Ind	Ind	24	Ind	Ind	3
Mathematics and English	QG31	3FT deg	E+M	DD	Ind	Ind	24	Ind	Ind	
Mathematics and History	GV11	3FT deg	M+H g	DD	Ind	Ind	24	Ind	Ind	
Mathematics and Information Technology	GG15	3FT deg	M g	DD	Ind	Ind	24	Ind	Ind	1
Mathematics and Marketing	NG51	3FT deg	M g	DD	Ind	Ind	24	Ind	Ind	
Mathematics and Social Science	GL13	3FT deg	M g	DD	Ind	Ind	24	Ind	Ind	
Mathematics with American Studies	G1Q4	3FT deg	M g	DD	Ind	Ind	24	Ind	Ind	
Mathematics with Art	G1W1	3FT deg	M+A g	DD	Ind	Ind	24	Ind	Ind	
Mathematics with Business Studies	G1N1	3FT deg	M g	DD	Ind	Ind	24	Ind	Ind	4
Mathematics with Early Childhood Studies	G1X9	3FT deg	M g	DD	Ind	Ind	24	Ind	Ind	
Mathematics with English	G1Q3	3FT deg	M+E g	DD	Ind	Ind	24	Ind	Ind	
Mathematics with History	G1V1	3FT deg	M+H g	DD	Ind	Ind	24	Ind	Ind	
Mathematics with Information Technology	G1G5	3FT deg	M g	DD	Ind	Ind	24	Ind	Ind	11
Mathematics with Marketing	G1N5	3FT deg	M g	DD	Ind	Ind	24	Ind	Ind	
Mathematics with Media Studies	G1P4	3FT deg	M g	DD	Ind	Ind	24	Ind	Ind	
Mathematics with Music	G1W3	3FT deg	M+Mu g	DD	Ind	Ind	24	Ind	Ind	

Mathematics and Statistics

course details

TITLE	CODE	COURSE

98 expected requirements

96 entry stats

TITLE	CODE	COURSE	SUBJECTS	A/AS	ND/C	AGNVQ	IB	SQA(H)	SQA	RATIO A/AS
Mathematics with Psychology	G1L7	3FT deg	M+Ps g	DD	Ind	Ind	24	Ind	Ind	
Mathematics with Radio, Film & Television Studs	G1W5	3FT deg	M g	DD	Ind	Ind	24	Ind	Ind	
Mathematics with Religious Studies	G1V8	3FT deg	M g	DD	Ind	Ind	24	Ind	Ind	3
Mathematics with Science	G1Y1	3FT deg	M+S g	DD	Ind	Ind	24	Ind	Ind	3
Mathematics with Social Science	G1L3	3FT deg	M g	DD	Ind	Ind	24	Ind	Ind	2
Mathematics with Sport Science	G1B6	3FT deg	M g	DD	Ind	Ind	24	Ind	Ind	
Mathematics with Tourism	G1P7	3FT deg	M g	DD	Ind	Ind	24	Ind	Ind	
Media Studies and Mathematics	GP14	3FT deg	M g	DD	Ind	Ind	24	Ind	Ind	
Media Studies with Mathematics	P4G1	3FT deg	M g	DD	Ind	Ind	24	Ind	Ind	
Media Studies with Statistics	P4G4	3FT deg	M g	DD	Ind	Ind	24	Ind	Ind	
Music and Mathematics	WG31	3FT deg	M+Mu g	DD	Ind	Ind	24	Ind	Ind	
Music with Mathematics	W3G1	3FT deg	M+Mu g	DD	Ind	Ind	24	Ind	Ind	
Music with Statistics	W3G4	3FT deg	Mu+M g	DD	Ind	Ind	24	Ind	Ind	
Psychology and Mathematics	LG71	3FT deg	Ps+M g	DD	Ind	Ind	24	Ind	Ind	
Psychology with Mathematics	L7G1	3FT deg	Ps+M g	DD	Ind	Ind	24	Ind	Ind	
Psychology with Statistics	L7G4	3FT deg	Ps+M g	DD	Ind	Ind	24	Ind	Ind	
Radio, Film & Television Studies with Statistics	W5G4	3FT deg	M g	CC	MO	M	24	Ind	Ind	
Radio, Film and Television Studs and Mathematics	GW15	3FT deg	M g	DD	Ind	Ind	24	Ind	Ind	
Radio,Film & Television Studies with Mathematics	W5G1	3FT deg	M g	CC	MO	M	24	Ind	Ind	
Religious Studies and Mathematics	VG81	3FT deg	M g	DD	Ind	Ind	24	Ind	Ind	
Religious Studies with Mathematics	V8G1	3FT deg	M g	DD	Ind	Ind	24	Ind	Ind	
Religious Studies with Statistics	V8G4	3FT deg	M g	DD	Ind	Ind	24	Ind	Ind	
Science and Mathematics	GY11	3FT deg	M+S g	DD	Ind	Ind	24	Ind	Ind	
Science with Mathematics	Y1G1	3FT deg	M+S g	DD	Ind	Ind	24	Ind	Ind	
Science with Statistics	Y1G4	3FT deg	S+M g	DD	Ind	Ind	24	Ind	Ind	
Social Science with Mathematics	L3G1	3FT deg	M g	DD	Ind	Ind	24	Ind	Ind	
Social Science with Statistics	L3G4	3FT deg	M g	DD	Ind	Ind	24	Ind	Ind	
Sport Science and Mathematics	GB16	3FT deg	M g	DD	Ind	Ind	24	Ind	Ind	
Sport Science with Mathematics	B6G1	3FT deg	M g	DD	Ind	Ind	24	Ind	Ind	
Sport Science with Statistics	B6G4	3FT deg	M g	DD	Ind	Ind	24	Ind	Ind	
Statistics and American Studies	GQ44	3FT deg	M g	DD	Ind	Ind	24	Ind	Ind	
Statistics and Art	GW41	3FT deg	M+A g	DD	Ind	Ind	24	Ind	Ind	
Statistics and Business Studies	GN41	3FT deg	M g	DD	Ind	Ind	24	Ind	Ind	
Statistics and Early Childhood Studies	GX49	3FT deg	M g	DD	Ind	Ind	24	Ind	Ind	
Statistics and English	GQ43	3FT deg	M+E	DD	Ind	Ind	24	Ind	Ind	
Statistics and History	GV41	3FT deg	M+H g	DD	Ind	Ind	24	Ind	Ind	
Statistics and Information Technology	GG45	3FT deg	M g	DD	Ind	Ind	24	Ind	Ind	
Statistics and Marketing	GN45	3FT deg	M g	DD	Ind	Ind	24	Ind	Ind	
Statistics and Media Studies	PG44	3FT deg	M g	DD	Ind	Ind	24	Ind	Ind	
Statistics and Music	GW43	3FT deg	M+Mu g	DD	Ind	Ind	24	Ind	Ind	
Statistics and Psychology	GL47	3FT deg	M+Ps g	DD	Ind	Ind	24	Ind	Ind	
Statistics and Radio, Film and Television Studs	GW45	3FT deg	M g	DD	Ind	Ind	24	Ind	Ind	
Statistics and Religious Studies	GV48	3FT deg	M g	DD	Ind	Ind	24	Ind	Ind	
Statistics and Science	GY41	3FT deg	S+M g	DD	Ind	Ind	24	Ind	Ind	
Statistics and Social Science	GL43	3FT deg	M g	DD	Ind	Ind	24	Ind	Ind	
Statistics and Sport Science	BG64	3FT deg	M g	DD	Ind	Ind	24	Ind	Ind	
Statistics with American Studies	G4Q4	3FT deg	M g	DD	Ind	Ind	24	Ind	Ind	
Statistics with Art	G4W1	3FT deg	M+A g	DD	Ind	Ind	24	Ind	Ind	
Statistics with Business Studies	G4N1	3FT deg	M g	DD	Ind	Ind	24	Ind	Ind	
Statistics with Early Childhood Studies	G4X9	3FT deg	M g	DD	Ind	Ind	24	Ind	Ind	
Statistics with English	G4Q3	3FT deg	M+E g	DD	Ind	Ind	24	Ind	Ind	
Statistics with History	G4V1	3FT deg	M+H g	DD	Ind	Ind	24	Ind	Ind	

course details			98 expected requirements							96 entry stats	
TITLE	CODE	COURSE	SUBJECTS	A/AS	ND/C	AGNVQ	IB	SQA(H)	SQA	RATIO A/AS	
Statistics with Information Technology	G4G5	3FT deg	M g	DD	Ind	Ind	24	Ind	Ind		
Statistics with Marketing	G4N5	3FT deg	M g	DD	Ind	Ind	24	Ind	Ind		
Statistics with Media Studies	G4P4	3FT deg	M g	DD	Ind	Ind	24	Ind	Ind		
Statistics with Music	G4W3	3FT deg	M+Mu g	DD	Ind	Ind	24	Ind	Ind		
Statistics with Psychology	G4L7	3FT deg	M+Ps g	DD	Ind	Ind	24	Ind	Ind		
Statistics with Radio, Film & Television Studies	G4W5	3FT deg	M g	DD	Ind	Ind	24	Ind	Ind		
Statistics with Religious Studies	G4V8	3FT deg	M g	DD	Ind	Ind	24	Ind	Ind		
Statistics with Science	G4Y1	3FT deg	M+S g	DD	Ind	Ind	24	Ind	Ind		
Statistics with Social Science	G4L3	3FT deg	M g	DD	Ind	Ind	24	Ind	Ind		
Statistics with Sport Science	G4B6	3FT deg	M g	DD	Ind	Ind	24	Ind	Ind		
Statistics with Tourism Studies	G4P7	3FT deg	M g	CC	MO	M	24	Ind	Ind		
Tourism Studies and Mathematics	GP17	3FT deg	M g	DD	Ind	Ind	24	Ind	Ind		
Tourism Studies and Statistics	GP47	3FT deg	M g	DD	Ind	Ind	24	Ind	Ind		
Tourism Studies with Mathematics	P7G1	3FT deg	M g	DD	Ind	Ind	24	Ind	Ind		
Tourism Studies with Statistics	P7G4	3FT deg	M g	DD	Ind	Ind	24	Ind	Ind		

CARDIFF Univ of Wales

Mathematics	G100	3FT deg	M	20	3M+2D$	Ind	Ind	BBBBC$	Ind	2	10/28
Mathematics and its Applications	G110	3FT deg	M	20	3M+2D$	Ind	Ind	BBBBC$	Ind	2	18/30
Mathematics and its Applications	G111	4SW deg	M	20	3M+2D$	Ind	Ind	BBBBC$	Ind	2	10/28
Mathematics, Operational Research & Statistics	G434	3FT deg	M	20	3M+2D$	Ind	Ind	BBBBC	Ind		
Mathematics, Operational Research & Statistics	G435	4SW deg	M	20	3M+2D$	Ind	Ind	BBBBC	Ind		
Physics and Mathematics	FG3D	3FT deg	M+P	CCC	Ind	Ind	Ind	Ind	Ind	3	16/24
Pure Mathematics/Computing	GG15	3FT deg	M	BCC	3M+2D$	Ind	Ind	AABB	Ind	17	
Pure Mathematics/Education	GX19	3FT deg	M	BCC	3M+2D$	Ind	Ind	BBBBC	Ind	5	
Pure Mathematics/French	GR11	4FT deg	F+M	BBC	Ind	Ind	Ind	ABBBB	Ind		
Pure Mathematics/German	GR12	4FT deg	M+G	BBC	Ind	Ind	Ind	AABBB	X	1	
Pure Mathematics/Music	GW13	3FT deg	M+Mu	BCC	X	Ind	Ind	ABBBB	X	9	
Pure Mathematics/Philosophy	GV17	3FT deg	M	BCC	3M+2D$	Ind	Ind	AABB	Ind		
Religious Studies/Pure Mathematics	VG81	3FT deg	M	BCC	Ind	Ind	Ind	BBBBC	Ind		
Welsh/Pure Mathematics	QG51	3FT deg	M+W	BCC	X	Ind	Ind	X	X	1	
Preliminary Year *Mathematics*	Y121	4FT deg	*		Ind	Ind	Ind	Ind	Ind		
Preliminary Year *Mathematics and its Applications*	Y121	4FT/5SW deg	*		Ind	Ind	Ind	Ind	Ind		
Preliminary Year *Mathematics, Operational Research & Statistics*	Y121	4FT/5SW deg	*		Ind	Ind	Ind	Ind	Ind		

Univ of CENTRAL LANCASHIRE

Mathematical Sciences	G140	3FT deg	M	CCD	MO+5D	DS6/^	28$	BBBB$	$		
Mathematics	G100	3FT deg	M	CCD	MO+5D	DS6/^	28$	BBBB$	$		
Combined Honours Programme *Mathematics*	Y400	3FT deg	M	8	3M $	P$_^	24$	CCC	Ind		
Combined Honours Programme *Statistics*	Y400	3FT deg	* g	8	MO $	P$	24$	CCC	Ind		

UNIVERSITY COLLEGE CHESTER

Art and Mathematics	WG91	3FT deg	M	12	M	P^	Ind	CCCC	$	4	
Art with Mathematics	W9G1	3FT deg	M	12	M	P^	Ind	CCCC	$		
Biology with Mathematics	C1G1	3FT deg	B+M	10	M	P^	Ind	CCCC	$		
Computational Mathematics	G170	3FT deg	M	10	M	P^	Ind	CCCC	$		
Computer Science/IT with Mathematics	G5G1	3FT deg	M	10	M	P^	Ind	CCCC	$	4	
Computer Studies/IT and Mathematics	GG51	3FT deg	M	10	M	P^	Ind	CCCC	$	7	
Drama and Theatre Studies and Mathematics	WG41	3FT deg	M	12	M	P^	Ind	CCCC	$	2	
Drama and Theatre Studies with Mathematics	W4G1	3FT deg	M	12	M	P^	Ind	CCCC	$		

Mathematics and Statistics 52

course details			98 expected requirements							96 entry stats
TITLE	CODE	COURSE	SUBJECTS	A/AS	ND/C	AGNVQ	IB	SQA(H)	SQA	RATIO A/AS
English Literature and Mathematics	QG31	3FT deg	E+M	12	M	P^	Ind	CCCC	$	1
English with Mathematics	Q3G1	3FT deg	E+M	12	M	P^	Ind	CCCC	$	
Geography with Mathematics	F8G1	3FT deg	Gy/Gl+M	CD	M	P^	Ind	CCCC	$	2
History and Mathematics	VG11	3FT deg	H/Ec/So+M	12	M	P^	Ind	CCCC	$	1
History with Mathematics	V1G1	3FT deg	H/Ec/So+M	12	M	P^	Ind	CCCC	$	
Mathematics and Biology	GC11	3FT deg	B+M	10	M	P^	Ind	CCCC	$	6
Mathematics and Geography	GF18	3FT deg	Gy/Gl+M	CD	M	P^	Ind	CCCC	$	7
Mathematics and PE/Sports Science	GB16	3FT deg	M	10	M	P^	Ind	CCCC	$	
Mathematics and Psychology	GL17	3FT deg	M g	10	M	P^	Ind	CCCC	$	6
Mathematics and Theology and Religious Studies	GV18	3FT deg	M	12	M	P^	Ind	CCCC	$	1
Mathematics with Art	G1W9	3FT deg	M	12	M	P^	Ind	CCCC	$	1
Mathematics with Biology	G1C1	3FT deg	M+B	10	M	P^	Ind	CCCC	$	
Mathematics with Computer Science/IT	G1G5	3FT deg	M	10	M	P^	Ind	CCCC	$	7
Mathematics with Drama and Theatre Studies	G1W4	3FT deg	M	12	M	P^	Ind	CCCC	$	2
Mathematics with English Literature	G1Q3	3FT deg	M+E	12	M	P^	Ind	CCCC	$	
Mathematics with French	G1R1	3FT deg	M g	12	M	P^	Ind	CCCC	$	3
Mathematics with Geography	G1F8	3FT deg	M+Gy/Gl	10	M	P^	Ind	CCCC	$	
Mathematics with German	G1R2	3FT deg	M g	12	M	P^	Ind	CCCC	$	
Mathematics with History	G1V1	3FT deg	M+H/Ec/So	12	M	P^	Ind	CCCC	$	
Mathematics with PE/Sports Science	G1B6	3FT deg	M	10	M	P^	Ind	CCCC	$	
Mathematics with Psychology	G1L7	3FT deg	M	10	M	P^	Ind	CCCC	$	5
Mathematics with Social Science	G1L3	3FT deg	M g	10	M	P^	Ind	CCCC	$	
Mathematics with Theology and Religious Studies	G1V8	3FT deg	M	12	M	P^	Ind	CCCC	$	1
Mathematics, Statistics and Computing	G900	3FT deg	E	10	M	P^	Ind	CCCC	$	
PE/Sports Science with Mathematics	B6G1	3FT deg	M	10	M	P^	Ind	CCCC	$	
Psychology with Mathematics	L7G1	3FT deg	M	10	M	P^	Ind	CCCC	$	
Theology and Religious Studies with Mathematics	V8G1	3FT deg	M	12	M	P^	Ind	CCCC	$	

CHICHESTER INSTITUTE OF HIGHER EDUCATION

Art and Mathematics	GW11	3FT deg	M+A+Pf	12	Ind	M$+^	Ind	Ind	Ind	
Art with Mathematics	E1G1	3FT deg	A+Pf g	12	Ind	M$+^	Ind	Ind	Ind	
Art with Mathematics	W1G1	3FT deg	A+Pf g	12	Ind	M$+^	Ind	Ind	Ind	
Dance and Mathematics	GW14	3FT deg	M+Pf	12	Ind	M$+^	Ind	Ind	Ind	
Dance with Mathematics	W4G1	3FT deg	Pf g	12	Ind	M$+	Ind	Ind	Ind	2
English Language Teaching (EFL) and Mathematics	QG11	3FT deg	E+M	12	Ind	M^	Ind	Ind	Ind	
English with Mathematics	Q3G1	3FT deg	E g	12	Ind	M^	Ind	Ind	Ind	
Environmental Science and Mathematics	FG91	3FT deg	E+M	12	Ind	M^	Ind	Ind	Ind	
Geography with Mathematics	L8G1	3FT deg	Gy g	12	Ind	M$	Ind	Ind	Ind	
History with Mathematics	V1G1	3FT deg	H g	12	Ind	M$	Ind	Ind	Ind	
Mathematics and English	GQ13	3FT deg	M+E	12	Ind	M^	Ind	Ind	Ind	
Mathematics and Geography	GL18	3FT deg	M+Gy	12	Ind	M^	Ind	Ind	Ind	
Mathematics and History	GV11	3FT deg	M+H	12	Ind	M^	Ind	Ind	Ind	
Mathematics and Media Studies	GP14	3FT deg	M	12	Ind	M^	Ind	Ind	Ind	
Mathematics and Study of Religions	GV18	3FT deg	M	12	Ind	M^	Ind	Ind	Ind	
Mathematics and Theology	GV1V	3FT deg	A+Pf	12	Ind	M$	Ind	Ind	Ind	
Mathematics with Dance	G1W4	3FT deg	M	12	Ind	M^	Ind	Ind	Ind	
Mathematics with Education Studies (Opt. QTS)(P)	G1X9	3FT/4FT deg	M	12	Ind	M^	Ind	Ind	Ind	4
Mathematics with English	G1Q3	3FT deg	M	12	Ind	M^	Ind	Ind	Ind	
Mathematics with English Language Teaching (EFL)	G1Q1	3FT deg	M	12	Ind	M^	Ind	Ind	Ind	
Mathematics with Environmental Science	G1F9	3FT deg	M	12	Ind	M^	Ind	Ind	Ind	
Mathematics with Geography	G1L8	3FT deg	M	12	Ind	M^	Ind	Ind	Ind	
Mathematics with History	G1V1	3FT deg	M	12	Ind	M^	Ind	Ind	Ind	
Mathematics with Media Studies	G1P4	3FT deg	M	12	Ind	M^	Ind	Ind	Ind	

| | | | 98 expected requirements | | | | | | | 96 entry stats | |
| course details | | | | | | | | | | | |
TITLE	CODE	COURSE	SUBJECTS	A/AS	ND/C	AGNVQ	IB	SQA(H)	SQA	RATIO	A/AS
Mathematics with Music	G1W3	3FT deg	M	12	Ind	M^	Ind	Ind	Ind		
Mathematics with Study of Religions	G1V8	3FT deg	M	12	Ind	M^	Ind	Ind	Ind		
Mathematics with Theology	G1VV	3FT deg	M	12	Ind	M^	Ind	Ind	Ind		
Music and Mathematics	GW13	3FT deg	M+Mu	12	Ind	M$+^	Ind	Ind	Ind		
Music with Mathematics	W3G1	3FT deg	Mu g	12	Ind	M$+	Ind	Ind	Ind		
Study of Religions with Mathematics	V8G1	3FT deg	* g	12	Ind	M$	Ind	Ind	Ind		
Theology and Mathematics	VG81	3FT deg	M	12	Ind	M^	Ind	Ind	Ind		
Theology with Mathematics	V8GC	3FT deg	* g	12	Ind	M$	Ind	Ind	Ind		

CITY Univ

Actuarial Science	G422	3FT deg	M	BBB	Ind		28$	AABBB	Ind	6	18/26
Actuarial Science (Foundation)	G420	4EXT deg			Ind	Ind	Ind	Ind	Ind		
Actuarial Science (with Study Abroad)	G421	4FT deg	M	BBB	Ind		28$	AABBB	Ind	2	20/28
Mathematical Sci with Computer Sci (Foundation)	G1GM	4EXT Deg	*		Ind	Ind	Ind	Ind	Ind		
Mathematical Science	G100	3FT/4SW deg	M	BCD-CDD	Ind	D*^	26$	Ind	Ind	13	
Mathematical Science (Foundation)	G105	4EXT deg	*		Ind	Ind	Ind	Ind	Ind	1	
Mathematical Science with Computer Science	G1G5	3FT/4SW deg	M	BCD-CDD	Ind	D*^	26$	Ind	Ind	25	
Mathematical Science with Finance and Economics	G1L1	3FT/4SW deg	M	BBC-BCD	Ind	D*^	28$	Ind	Ind	4	12/16
Mathematical Science with Stats	G1G4	3FT/4SW deg	M	BCD-CDD	Ind	D*^	26$	Ind	Ind	7	
Statistical Sci with Management St (Foundation)	G4ND	4EXT deg	M		Ind		Ind	Ind	Ind	4	
Statistical Science with Management Studies	G4N1	3FT deg	M	BCC	Ind		Ind	ABBBB	Ind	6	
Statistical Science with Mgt St(with Study Abrd)	G4NC	4SW deg	M	BCC	Ind		Ind	ABBBB	Ind	1	

COVENTRY Univ

Business Decision Methods	GN41	3FT/4SW deg	*	12-16	Ind		Ind	Ind	Ind	16	
Business Decision Methods	NG14	4FT/5SW deg	*	2	N	P	Ind	Ind	Ind	3	
Chemistry and Mathematics	FG1D	4FT/5SW deg			Ind	Ind	Ind	Ind	Ind		
Chemistry and Statistics	FG1L	4FT/5SW deg			Ind	Ind	Ind	Ind	Ind		
Engineering Systems with Mathematics	H6G1	3FT deg	M+S	14-18	5M $		24$	BBCC$	Ind		
Mathematical Sciences	G901	4FT/5SW deg	g	2	N	P	Ind	Ind	Ind	2	
Mathematical Sciences	G140	3FT/4SW deg	M g	10-14	3M $	M	Ind	Ind	Ind		
Mathematical Studies & Accounting	GN94	3FT/4SW deg	M g	14-18	Ind	Ind	Ind	Ind	Ind		
Mathematical Studies & Finance	GN93	3FT/4SW deg	M g	14-18	Ind	Ind	Ind	Ind	Ind		
Mathematical Studies & Sports Science	GB96	3FT/4SW deg	M+B	14-18	Ind	Ind	Ind	Ind	Ind		
Mathematics	G100	3FT/4SW deg	M g	16-20	4M $	M	Ind	Ind	Ind	23	
Mathematics (MMATH)	G103	4FT deg	M g	20-24	5D $	X	Ind	Ind	Ind		
Mathematics and Biological Sciences	CG11	3FT/4SW deg	M+B/C	12-18	3M $	Ind	Ind	Ind	Ind		
Mathematics and Chemistry	FG11	3FT/4SW deg	C+M	DD	Ind	Ind	Ind	Ind	Ind	10	
Mathematics and Computing	GG15	3FT/4SW deg	M/Cs	12-16	3M $		Ind	Ind	Ind	13	
Mathematics and Economics	GL1C	4FT/5SW deg	*	2	N	P	Ind	Ind	Ind		
Mathematics and Economics	GL11	3FT/4SW deg	M/E g	14-18	3M $	M	M	Ind	Ind	7	
Mathematics and French	RG11	4FT deg	F+M	16-20	Ind	M	Ind	Ind	Ind		
Mathematics and Geography	GL18	3FT/4SW deg	M/Gy g	14-18	3M $	M	Ind	Ind	Ind	9	
Mathematics and German	RG21	4FT deg	G+M g	16-20	Ind	M	Ind	Ind	Ind	8	
Mathematics and Materials Technology	JG51	3FT/4SW deg	M+P/C	CC	Ind	Ind	Ind	Ind	Ind		
Mathematics, Statistics and Computing (4 years)	G900	4FT deg	M							3	6/18
Statistics and Biological Sciences	GC41	3FT/4SW deg	M/St+B/C g	12-16	3M $	M	Ind	Ind	Ind	4	
Statistics and Biological Sciences	GC4C	4FT/5SW deg		2	N $	P	Ind	Ind	Ind		
Statistics and Chemistry	FG14	3FT/4SW deg	C	CD	3M	MS	Ind	Ind	Ind		
Statistics and Computing	GG45	3FT/4SW deg	M/Cs/St g	12-16	3M $	M	Ind	Ind	Ind		
Statistics and Economics	LG14	3FT/4SW deg	M/E g	12-16	3M $	M	Ind	Ind	Ind	18	
Statistics and French	GR41	4FT deg	F+M/St g	12-16	Ind	M	Ind	Ind	Ind		
Statistics and Geography	GL48	3FT/4SW deg	Gy+St/M g	12-16	Ind	M	Ind	Ind	Ind	4	

			98 expected requirements							96 entry stats	
TITLE	CODE	COURSE	SUBJECTS	A/AS	ND/C	AGNVQ	IB	SQA(H)	SQA	RATIO	A/AS
Statistics and German	GR42	4FT deg	G+M/St g	12-16	Ind	M	Ind	Ind	Ind		
Statistics and Mathematics	GG14	4FT deg	M g	12-16	3M $	M	Ind	Ind	Ind	10	
Statistics and Operational Research	GN4F	4FT/5SW deg	*	2	N	P	Ind	Ind	Ind		
Statistics and Operational Research	GN42	3FT deg	M/St g	12-16	Ind	M	Ind	Ind	Ind	20	
Statistics and Psychology	CG84	3FT/4SW deg	* g	CC	3M+3D	M^ go	Ind	BBB	Ind	3	
Mathematical Sciences	809G	3FT HND									
Mathematics and Computing	51GG	2FT HND	M	2	N $	P	Ind	Ind	Ind		
Mathematics and Statistics	41GG	2FT HND	M	2	N $	P	Ind	Ind	Ind		
Mathematics, Statistics and Computing	009G	2FT HND	M							3	
Statistics and Computing	54GG	2FT HND	M/St/Cs	2	N $	P	Ind	Ind	Ind		

DE MONTFORT Univ

Computer-based Mathematics	G170▼	3FT deg	M	12	3M+1D	M$ go	Ind	Ind	Ind		
Economics and Management Science	L1G9▼	4SW deg	* g	12	3M+1D	M$ go	Ind	Ind	Ind		
Management Science	G9N1▼	4SW deg	* g	12	3M+1D	M$ go	Ind	Ind	Ind	1	4/16
Management Science and Economics	GL91▼	4SW deg	* g	12	3M+1D	M$ go	Ind	Ind	Ind		
Mathematics	G100▼	4SW deg	M	12	3M+1D	M$ go	Ind	Ind	Ind	9	8/12
Mathematics and Statistics	G1G4▼	4SW deg	M	12	3M+1D	M$ go	Ind	Ind	Ind	15	
Mathematics with Computing	G1G5▼	4SW deg	M	12	3M+1D	M$ go	Ind	Ind	Ind	7	
Mathematics with a Language	G1T9▼	3FT deg	M g	12	3M+1D	M$ go	Ind	Ind	Ind		
Medical Statistics and Biophysics	CG64▼	3FT deg	P g		Ind	Ind	Ind	Ind	Ind		
Medical and Health Statistics	GG54▼	3FT/4SW deg	*	10-14	MO	M	Ind	Ind	Ind		6/14
Combined Sciences *Maths*	Y108▼	3FT deg	g	2	N	P	Dip	CC	Ind		
Combined Studies *Mathematical Science*	Y400▼	3FT/4SW deg	M g	10	MO	M	30	BBB			
Management Science	1N9G▼	2FT HND	* g	4	2M	P$ go	Ind	Ind	Ind	3	1/5
Mathematics	009G▼	2FT HND	M	4	2M	P$ go	Ind	Ind	Ind		

Univ of DERBY

Applicable Mathematics and Computing	GG15	4SW deg	M	8	3M $	M^	Dip$	CCCD$	Ind	13	
Mathematical & Computer Studies	GG51	3FT deg	M	8	3M $	M^	Dip$	CCCD$	Ind		
Mathematical Studies	G110	4SW deg	M	8	3M $	M^	Dip$	CCCD$	Ind	7	
Mathematical Studies with Ancillary Language	GT12	3FT deg	M	8	3M $	M^	Dip$	CCCD$	Ind		
Mathematics, Statistics and Computing	G900	3FT/4SW deg	M	8	3M $	M^	Dip$	CCCD$	Ind	3	
Operational Research	G434	3FT deg	M	8	3M $	M^	Dip$	CCCD$	Ind		
Credit Accumulation Modular Scheme *Applicable Mathematics*	Y600	3FT deg	*	8	MO	M	Ind	CCCC	Ind		
Credit Accumulation Modular Scheme *Statistics*	Y600	3FT deg		8	MO	M	Ind	CCCC	Ind		

Univ of DUNDEE

Accountancy and Mathematics	GN14	4FT deg	M g	14	5M $	M$^	25$	BBBC$	N$	9	
Applied Mathematics	G110	4FT deg	M g	14	5M $	M$^	25$	BBBC$	N$	7	
Business Econ, Marketing and Operational Res	GL4D	4FT deg	M g	14	5M $	M$^	25$	BBBC$	N$		
Business Economics and Marketing and Mathematics	Y604	4FT deg	M g	BCC	Ind	D$^	29	BBBC	Ind		
Business and Financial Mathematics	G140	4FT deg	M g	14	5M $	M$^	25$	BBBC$	N$		
Chemistry and Mathematics	FG11	4FT deg	M+S g	14	5M $	M$^	25$	BBCC$	N$		
Chemistry and Statistics	FG14	4FT deg	M+S g	14	5M $	M$^	25$	BBCC$	N$		
Economics and Mathematics	LG11	4FT deg	M g	BCC	Ind	D$^	29$	BBBC$	Ind		
English and Mathematics	GQ13	4FT deg	E+M g	BCC	Ind	D$^	29$	BBBC$	Ind	1	
Environmental Science and Mathematics	FG91	4FT deg	M g	BCC	Ind	D$^	29$	BBBC$	Ind		
Financial Economics and Mathematics	GLC1	4FT deg	M g	BCC	Ind	D$^	29$	BBBC$	Ind		
Mathematics	G100	4FT deg	M g	14	5M $	M$^	25$	BBBC$	N$	7	
Mathematics	G101	3FT deg	M g	10	5M $	M$^	25$	BBC$	N$		

course details			98 expected requirements							96 entry stats	
TITLE	CODE	COURSE	SUBJECTS	R/AS	NO/C	RGNVQ	IB	SQA(H)	SQA	RATIO	R/AS
Mathematics and Applied Computing	GG51	3FT deg	M g	10	5M $	M$^	25$	BBCC$	N$	6	
Mathematics and Applied Computing	GG15	4FT deg	M g	14	5M $	M$^	25$	BBBC$	N$	7	
Mathematics and Digital Microelectronics	GHC6	4FT deg	M+S g	14	5M $	M$^	25$	BBCC$	N$		
Mathematics and Economics	GL11	4FT deg	M g	14	5M $	M$^	25$	BBBC$	N$	2	
Mathematics and Financial Economics	GL1C	4FT deg	M g	14	5M $	M$^	25$	BBBC$	N$		
Mathematics and Numerical Analysis	GG19	4FT deg	M g	14	5M $	M$^	25$	BBBC$	N$		
Mathematics and Philosophy	GV17	4FT deg	M g	BCC	Ind	D$^	29$	BBBB$	Ind		
Mathematics and Physics	FG31	4FT deg	M+S g	14	5M $	M$^	25$	BBCC$	N$	5	
Mathematics and Psychology	GL17	4FT deg	M g	BCC	Ind	D$^	29$	BBBC$	Ind	10	
Mathematics and Psychology	LG71	4FT deg	M g	14	5M $	M$^	25$	BBCC$	N$		
Mathematics and Statistics	GG14	4FT deg	M g	14	5M $	M$^	25$	BBBC$	N$	13	
Psychology and Statistics	LG74	4FT deg	M g	14	5M $	M$^	25$	BBBC$	N$		
Statistics and Economics	GL41	4FT deg	M g	14	5M $	M$^	25$	BBBC$	N$		
Statistics and Financial Economics	GL4C	4FT deg	M g	14	5M $	M$^	25$	BBBC$	N$		
Arts and Social Sciences *Mathematics*	Y400	3FT deg	M g	BCC	Ind	D$^	29$	BBBC$	Ind		

Univ of DURHAM

Computer Science and Mathematics	GG51	3FT deg	M+S	24	X	X	32$	CSYS$	X	10	26/30
Economics with Mathematics	L1G1	3FT deg	M	ABC	Ind	X	32$	Ind	Ind		
Mathematics (BA)	G102	3FT deg	M	24	X	X	32$	CSYS$	X	10	
Mathematics (BSc)	G100	3FT deg	M+S	24	X	X	32$	CSYS$	X	8	26/30
Mathematics (European Studies)	G104	4FT deg	M	24	X	X	32$	CSYS$	X	5	26/30
Mathematics (European Studies)	G105	4FT deg	M	24	X	X	32$	CSYS$	X		
Mathematics (MMath)	G103	4FT deg	M+S	24	X	X	32$	CSYS$	X	5	26/30
Mathematics and Economics	GL11	3FT deg	M	ABC	Ind	X	32$	AAABB$	Ind	9	26/30
Mathematics and Physics	FG31	3FT deg	M+P	24	X	X	32$	CSYS$	X	5	26/30
Mathematics and Physics (MSci)	FG3C	4FT deg	M+P	24	X	X	32$	CSYS$	X		
Arts Combined *Mathematics (Applied)*	Y300	3FT deg	M	24	MO	X	30	AAABB	Ind		
Arts Combined *Mathematics (Pure)*	Y300	3FT deg	M	24	MO	X	30	AAABB	Ind		
Natural Sciences *Mathematics*	Y160	3FT deg	M+S	ABB	Ind	X	33$	CSYS$	X		

Univ of EAST ANGLIA

(MMaths) with a Year in Canada (4 Yrs)	G102	4FT deg	M	ABB	X		32$	AAAB$	X	8	
Chemistry & Mathematics with 1yr in Europe(4Yrs)	FG1C	4FT deg	M+C g	BCC	MO+3D$	Ind	28$	ABBB$	Ind	2	
Chemistry and Mathematics	FG11	3FT deg	M+C	BCC	MO+3D$	Ind	28$	ABBB$	Ind	18	
Chemistry with Mathematics	F1G1	3FT deg	C+M	CCC	MO+1D$		27$	BBBB$	Ind		
Chemistry with Mathematics and 1yr in Eur(4 Yrs)	F1GC	4FT deg	C+M g	BCC	MO+3D$		28$	ABBB$	Ind		
Computing and Mathematics	GG51	3FT deg	M	BC-CCC	Ind		32$	BBBC$	X	6	
Mathematics	G104	3FT deg	M	BD-CC	Ind		32$	BBBC$	X	2	
Mathematics	G100	3FT deg	M	BCC	Ind		32$	AABB$	X	5	10/28
Mathematics Hons (4 Yrs) (MMaths)	G103	4FT deg	M	BBC	X		32$	AABB$	X	23	
Mathematics with Computing	G1G5	3FT deg	M	BCC	Ind		32$	BBBC$	X	3	12/20
Mathematics with Economics	G1L1	3FT deg	M	BCC	Ind		32$	BBBC$	X	8	
Mathematics with Environmental Science	G1F9	3FT deg	M	BCC	Ind		32$	BBBC$	X		
Mathematics with Management Studies	G1N1	3FT deg	M	BCC	Ind		32$	BBBC$	X	6	12/20
Mathematics with Philosophy	G1V7	3FT deg	M	BCC	Ind		32$	BBBC$	X		
Mathematics with Statistics	G1G4	3FT deg	M	BCC	Ind		32$	BBBC$	X	8	
Mathematics with a year in Europe	G105	4FT deg	M								
Mathematics with a year in Europe (4 Yrs)	G101	4FT deg	M g	BCC	Ind		32$	BBBC$	X	10	

course details | 98 expected requirements | 96 entry stats

TITLE	CODE	COURSE	SUBJECTS	A/AS	ND/C	AGNVQ	IB	SQA(H)	SQA	RATIO A/AS
Univ of EAST LONDON										
Accounting & Finance and Maths, Stats & Comp	NG49	3FT deg	*g	14	MO	M$	Ind	Ind	Ind	
Accounting & Finance with Maths, Stats & Comp	N4G9	3FT deg	*g	14	MO	MB	Ind	Ind	Ind	
Archaeological Sciences and Maths, Stats & Comp	FG49	3FT deg	*g	12	MO	M$	Ind	Ind	Ind	
Biology and Maths, Stats & Computing	CG19	3FT deg	*g	12	MO	M$	Ind	Ind	Ind	
Biology with Maths, Stats & Computing	C1G9	3FT deg	*g	12	MO	M	Ind	Ind	Ind	
Business Studies and Maths, Stats & Computing	GN91	3FT deg	*g	12	MO	M$	Ind	Ind	Ind	
Business Studies with Maths Stats & Computing	N1G9	3FT deg	*g	14	MO	MB				
Economics and Maths, Stats & Computing	GL91	3FT deg	*g	12	MO	M$	Ind	Ind	Ind	
Economics with Maths, Stats & Computing	L1G9	3FT deg	*g	12	MO	M	Ind			
Education & Community St & Maths, Stats & Comput	GX99	3FT deg	*g	12	MO	M$	Ind	Ind	Ind	
Education & Community St w. Maths,Stats & Comput	X9G9	3FT deg	*g	12	MO	M				
Environmental Sciences and Maths, Stats & Comput	GF99	3FT deg	*g	12	MO	M$	Ind	Ind	Ind	
Environmental Sciences with Maths,Stats & Comput	F9G9	3FT deg	*g	12	MO	M	Ind	Ind	Ind	
French and Maths, Stats & Computing	GR91	3FT deg	*g	12	MO	M$	Ind	Ind	Ind	
German and Maths, Stats & Computing	GR92	3FT deg	*g	12	MO	M$	Ind	Ind	Ind	
German with Maths, Stats & Computing	R2G9	3FT deg	*g	12	MO	M	Ind			
Health Studies and Maths, Stats & Computing	LG49	3FT deg	*g	12	MO	M				
Health Studies with Maths, Stats & Computing	L4G9	3FT deg	*g	12	MO	M				
Information Technology and Maths, Stats & Comput	GG59	3FT deg	*g	12	MO	M	Ind	Ind	Ind	
Information Technology with Maths Stats & Comput	G5G9	3FT deg	*g	12	MO	M	Ind	Ind	Ind	
Literature and Maths, Stats and Computing	GQ93	3FT deg	*g	6-14	N	M$	Ind	Ind	Ind	
Literature with Maths, Stats & Computing	Q3G9	3FT deg	*g	12	MO	M	Ind			
Mathematics & Computing	GG15	3/4FT deg	*g	12	MO	M$	Ind	Ind	Ind	9
Mathematics, Statistics and Computing	G900	3FT deg	*g	12	MO	M	Ind	Ind	Ind	3
Maths, Stats & Computing and Spanish	GR94	3FT deg	*g	12	MO	M^	Ind	Ind	Ind	
Maths, Stats & Computing with Acc & Finance	G9N4	3FT deg	*g	12	MO	M	Ind	Ind	Ind	
Maths, Stats & Computing with Archaeological Sci	G9F4	3FT deg	*g	12	MO	M	Ind	Ind	Ind	
Maths, Stats & Computing with Biology	G9C1	3FT deg	*g	12	MO	M	Ind	Ind	Ind	
Maths, Stats & Computing with Business Studies	G9N1	3FT deg	*g	12	MO	M	Ind	Ind	Ind	
Maths, Stats & Computing with Economics	G9L1	3FT deg	*g	12	MO	M	Ind	Ind	Ind	
Maths, Stats & Computing with Educ & Commun St	G9X9	3FT deg	*g	12	MO	M	Ind	Ind	Ind	
Maths, Stats & Computing with Environmental Sci	G9F9	3FT deg	*g	12	MO	M	Ind	Ind	Ind	
Maths, Stats & Computing with French	G9R1	3FT deg	*g	12	MO	M	Ind	Ind	Ind	
Maths, Stats & Computing with German	G9R2	3FT deg	*g	12	MO	M	Ind	Ind	Ind	
Maths, Stats & Computing with Health Studies	G9L4	3FT deg	*g	12	MO	M				
Maths, Stats & Computing with IT	G9G5	3FT deg	*g	12	MO	M	Ind	Ind	Ind	
Maths, Stats & Computing with Italian	G9R3	3FT deg	*g	12	MO	M	Ind	Ind	Ind	
Maths, Stats & Computing with Literature	G9Q3	3FT deg	*g	12	MO	M	Ind	Ind	Ind	
Maths, Stats & Computing with Psychology	G9L7	3FT deg	*g	12	MO	M				
Maths, Stats & Computing with Spanish	G9R4	3FT deg	*g	12	MO	M	Ind	Ind	Ind	
Psychology with Maths, Stats & Computing	L7G9	3FT deg	*g	12	MO	M				
Spanish with Maths, Stats & Computing	R4G9	3FT deg	*g	12	MO	M	Ind			
Statistics and Computing	G440	3FT deg	*g	12	MO	M	Ind	Ind	Ind	
Statistics and Mathematics	GG14	3FT deg	*g	12	MO	M	Ind	Ind	Ind	15
Extended Science *Mathematics and Computing*	Y108	4FT deg	*g	8-10	MO	M	Ind	Ind	Ind	
Extended Science *Mathematics, Statistics and Computing*	Y108	4FT deg	*g	8-10	MO	M	Ind	Ind	Ind	
Extended Science *Statistics and Computing*	Y108	4FT deg	*g	8-10	MO	M	Ind	Ind	Ind	
Extended Science *Statistics and Mathematics*	Y108	4FT deg	*g	8-10	MO	M	Ind	Ind	Ind	
Three-Subject Degree *Maths, Statistics and Computing*	Y600	3FT deg	*g	12	MO	M	Ind	Ind	Ind	

TITLE	CODE	COURSE	SUBJECTS	A/AS	NO/C	AGNVQ	IB	SQA(H)	SQA	RATIO A/AS
EDGE HILL Univ COLLEGE										
Biology and Mathematics	CG11	3FT deg	<u>S</u> g	DD	3M+3D	PS^ go	Dip	BBCC$	Ind	
Early Childhood Studies and Mathematics	GX19	3FT deg	* g	CC	3M+3D	M* / P*^ go	Dip	BBCC$	Ind	
Environmental Management and Mathematics	FG91	3FT deg	2(B/C/En/P) g	DD	3M+3D	MS / P*	Dip	BBCC	Ind	
Geography and Mathematics	GL18	3FT deg	<u>G</u>y g	DD	3M+3D	P*^	Dip	BBCC	Ind	5
Information Systems and Mathematics	GG15	3FT deg	* g	CD	3M+3D	M* / P*^	Dip	BBCC	Ind	2
Science and Mathematics	GY11	3FT deg	2(B/C/En/P) g	DD	3M+3D	MS / P*^	Dip	BBCC$	Ind	
Sports Studies and Mathematics	BG61	3FT deg	* g	CD	3M+3D	M* / P*^	Dip	BBCC	Ind	
Univ of EDINBURGH										
Artificial Intelligence and Mathematics	GG18	4FT deg	<u>M</u>	BCC	MO $		Dip$	ABBC$	N$	4 22/30
Business Studies and Mathematics	NG11	4FT deg	<u>M</u>	BBB	Ind		34$	ABBB	Ind	10
Business Studies and Statistics	NG14	4FT deg	<u>M</u>	BBB	Ind		34	ABBB	Ind	
Computer Science and Mathematics	GG15	4FT deg	<u>M</u>	BCC	MO $		Dip$	ABBC$	N$	9
Economics and Mathematics	LG11	4FT deg	<u>M</u>	BBB	Ind		34$	ABBB	Ind	29
Economics and Statistics	LG14	4FT deg	<u>M</u>	BBB	Ind		34$	ABBB	Ind	6
Mathematics	G102	4FT deg	<u>M</u> g	BBB	Ind	Ind	Dip$	ABBC$	Ind	
Mathematics	G100	4FT deg	<u>M</u>	BCC	MO $		Dip$	ABBC$	N$	7 18/30
Mathematics and Business Studies	GN11	4FT deg	<u>M</u>	BBC	MO $		Dip$	ABBC$	N$	5 20/30
Mathematics and Physics	GF13	4FT deg	<u>M+P</u>	BCC	MO $		Dip$	ABBC$	N$	10
Mathematics and Statistics	GG14	4FT deg	<u>M</u>	BCC	MO $		Dip$	ABBC$	N$	5
Philosophy and Mathematics	VG71	4FT deg	<u>M</u> g	BBB	Ind	Ind	Dip$	ABBC$	Ind	
Statistics and Business Studies	GN41	4FT deg	<u>M</u>	BBB	MO $		Dip$	ABBB	N$	
Univ of ESSEX										
Master of Mathematical Sciences (4 years)	G141	4FT deg	<u>M</u>	24	MO+4D	X	30	CSYS	Ind	
Mathematical Sciences (4 Yrs)	G101	4FT deg	* g	4	N	M	28$	BBCC	Ind	2
Mathematics	G100	3FT deg	<u>M</u>	18	MO $	D^	28$	CSYS	Ind	12
Mathematics and Computing	GG15	3FT deg	<u>M</u>	18	MO $	D^	28$	CSYS	Ind	25
Mathematics and Finance	GN13	3FT deg	<u>M</u>	BBC	MO+4D	D^	30$	CSYS	Ind	11
Mathematics and French (4 Yrs)	GR11	4FT deg	<u>M+F</u>	18	MO $	Ind	28$	CSYS	Ind	5
Mathematics and German (4 Yrs)	GR12	4FT deg	<u>M</u>	18	MO $	Ind	28$	CSYS	Ind	7
Mathematics and Music	GW13	3FT deg	<u>M</u>	18	MO $	Ind	28$	CSYS	Ind	13
Mathematics and Operational Research	GN12	3FT deg	<u>M</u>	18	MO $	D^	28$	CSYS	Ind	8
Mathematics and Russian (4 Yrs)	GR18	4FT deg	<u>M</u>	18	MO $	Ind	28$	CSYS	Ind	
Mathematics and Spanish (4 Yrs)	GR14	4FT deg	<u>M</u>	18	MO $	Ind	28$	CSYS	Ind	
Mathematics and Statistics	GG14	3FT deg	<u>M</u>	18	MO $	D^	28$	CSYS	Ind	6 14/20
Mathematics with Economics	G1L1	3FT deg	<u>M</u>	CCC	MO $	Ind	28$	CSYS	Ind	
Mathematics, Operational Research and Economics	G4L1	3FT deg	<u>M</u>	18	MO $	D^	28	CSYS	Ind	14
Statistics and Economics	GL41	3FT deg	<u>M</u>	CCC	MO $	Ind	28$	CSYS	Ind	
Univ of EXETER										
Computational Mathematics	G170	3FT deg	<u>M</u>	22	MO	M$^	34$	Ind	Ind	9
Computational Mathematics (MMath)	G171	4FT deg	<u>M</u>	22	MO	M$^	34$	Ind	Ind	3
Computer Science with Mathematics	G5G1	3FT deg	<u>M</u>	20	MO+2D	M$^	32$	Ind	Ind	13
Computer Science with Statistics	G5G4	3FT deg	<u>M</u>/St	20	MO+2D	M$^	32$	Ind	Ind	5
French and Mathematics	GR11	4FT deg	<u>F+M</u>	22-24	MO	M/D$^	34$	Ind	Ind	5 30/30
German and Mathematics	GR12	4FT deg	<u>G+M</u>	20-22	MO	M/D$^	32$			
Mathematical Statistics (MStat)	G431	4FT deg	<u>M</u>	22	MO	M/D$^	34$	Ind	Ind	
Mathematical Statistics and Operational Research	GN42	3FT deg	<u>M</u>/St	22	MO	M/D$^	34$	Ind	Ind	3 13/28
Mathematical Stats & Op Research with Euro Studs	GN4F	4FT deg	<u>M</u>/St g	22	MO	M/D$^	34$	Ind	Ind	5
Mathematics	G100	3FT deg	<u>M</u>	22	MO	M/D$^	34$	Ind	Ind	6 12/28
Mathematics (MMath)	G102	4FT deg	<u>M</u>	22	MO	M/D$^	34$	Ind	Ind	14 18/30
Mathematics and Physics	FG31	3FT deg	<u>M</u>+P/Es	20	MO	M$^	32$	Ind	Ind	12

Mathematics and Statistics 52

	course details			98 expected requirements							96 entry stats	
TITLE	CODE	COURSE	SUBJECTS	A/AS	ND/C	RGNVQ	IB	SQA(H)	SQA	RATIO A/AS		
Mathematics and Theoretical Physics	FGH1	3FT deg	M+P	20	MO	M$^	32$	Ind	Ind	12	
Mathematics with Accounting	G1N4	3FT deg	M	22	MO	M/D$^	34$	Ind	Ind		
Mathematics with Computer Science	G1G5	3FT deg	M	22	MO	M/D$^	34$	Ind	Ind	14	
Mathematics with Economics	G1L1	3FT deg	M	22	2M+3D	M/D$^	34$	Ind	Ind	7	16/30
Mathematics with European Study	G101	4FT deg	M g	22	MO	M/D$^	34$	Ind	Ind	11	
Mathematics with Media Computing	G1GM	3FT deg	M	22	MO	M/D$^	34$	Ind	Ind	2	
Media Computing with Mathematics	G5GC	3FT deg	M	20	MO+2D	M$^	32$	Ind	Ind		
Media Computing with Statistics	G5GK	3FT deg	M/St	20	MO+2D	M$^	32$	Ind	Ind		
Pure Mathematics & Mathematical Stats (MMath)	GGDK	4FT deg	M	22	MO	M/D$^	34$	Ind	Ind		
Pure Mathematics and Mathematical Statistics	GGD4	3FT deg	M	22	MO	M/D$^	34$	Ind	Ind	10	22/22
Pure and Applied Mathematics	G130	3FT deg	M	22	MO	M/D$^	34$	Ind	Ind	10	
Pure and Applied Mathematics (MMath)	G131	4FT deg	M	22	MO	M/D$^	34$	Ind	Ind	4	
Statistical Science with Information Technology	GGK5	3FT deg	M/St	22	MO+2D	M/D$^	34$	Ind	Ind	4	
Statistics with Media Computing	G4GM	3FT deg	M/St	22	MO+2D	M/D$^	34$	Ind	Ind	4	

Univ of GLAMORGAN

TITLE	CODE	COURSE	SUBJECTS	A/AS	ND/C	RGNVQ	IB	SQA(H)	SQA	RATIO A/AS	
Accounting & Finance and Mathematics	GN14	3FT deg	M g	12	Ind	M$	Ind	Ind	Ind		
Mathematics	G100	3FT deg	M g	8	Ind	Ind	Ind	Ind	Ind		
Mathematics (MMath)	G101	4FT deg	M g	CD	Ind	M$	Ind	Ind	Ind	2	
Mathematics and Accounting & Finance	GN1K	3FT deg									
Mathematics and Business Studies	GN1C	3FT deg									
Mathematics and Psychology	GL17	3FT deg	M g	CC	5M $	M$	Ind	Ind	Ind		
Mathematics and Sports Science	BG61	3FT deg	M/S g	12	Ind	Ind	Ind	Ind	Ind		
Mathematics with Accounting & Finance	G1NK	3FT deg									
Mathematics with Art	G1W1	3FT deg	M/A g	12	Ind	Ind	Ind	Ind	Ind		
Mathematics with Business Studies	G1N1	3FT deg	M g	14	Ind	Ind	Ind	Ind	Ind		
Mathematics with French	G1R1	3FT deg	M g	8	Ind	Ind	Ind	Ind	Ind		
Mathematics with German	G1R2	3FT deg	M g	8	Ind	Ind	Ind	Ind	Ind		
Mathematics with Psychology	G1L7	3FT deg	M g	12	Ind	Ind	Ind	Ind	Ind		
Mathematics with Sports Science	G1B6	3FT deg	M/S g	12	Ind	Ind	Ind	Ind	Ind		
Psychology with Statistics	L7G4	3FT deg									
Public Management and Statistics	GM4D	3FT deg									
Public Policy and Statistics	GM4C	3FT deg									
Statistics and Business Studies	GN41	3FT deg	M g	14	Ind	Ind	Ind	Ind	Ind		
Statistics with Psychology	G4L7	3FT deg	M g	CC	Ind	Ind	Ind	Ind	Ind		
Combined Studies (Honours) Mathematics	Y400	3FT deg	M g	8-16	Ind	Ind	Ind	Ind	Ind		
Combined Studies (Honours) Statistics	Y400	3FT deg	M g	8-16	Ind	Ind	Ind	Ind	Ind		
Joint Honours Mathematics	Y401	3FT deg	M g	8-16	Ind	Ind	Ind	Ind	Ind		
Joint Honours Statistics	Y401	3FT deg	M g	8-16	Ind	Ind	Ind	Ind	Ind		
Major/Minor Honours Mathematics	Y402	3FT deg	M g	8-16	Ind	Ind	Ind	Ind	Ind		
Major/Minor Honours Statistics	Y402	3FT deg	M g	8-16	Ind	Ind	Ind	Ind	Ind		

Univ of GLASGOW

TITLE	CODE	COURSE	SUBJECTS	A/AS	ND/C	RGNVQ	IB	SQA(H)	SQA	RATIO A/AS	
Archaeology/Mathematics	GV16	4FT deg		BBC	HN	M	30	BBBB	Ind		
Astronomy/Mathematics (MSci)	FG51	4FT deg	M+P	BBC-CCC	N	M	24$	BBBB$	N	6	
Business Economics/Mathematics	LGC1	4FT deg		BBC	N	M	30	BBBB	N		
Business Economics/Statistics	LGC4	4FT deg		BBC	N	M	30	BBBB	N		
Celtic Civilisation/Mathematics	GQ15	4FT deg		BBC	HN	M	30	BBBB	Ind		
Celtic/Mathematics	GQD5	4FT deg		BBC	HN	M	30	BBBB	Ind		

course details			98 expected requirements							96 entry stats	
TITLE	CODE	COURSE	SUBJECTS	A/AS	ND/C	AGNVQ	IB	SQA(H)	SQA	RATIO A/AS	
Classical Civilisation/Mathematics	GQ18	4FT deg		BBC	HN	M	30	BBBB	Ind		
Classical Hebrew/Mathematics	GV1W	4FT deg		BBC	HN	M	30	BBBB	Ind		
Computing Science/Statistics	GG45	4FT deg	M+S	BBC-CCC	N	M	24$	BBBB$	N	8	
Czech/Mathematics	GT11	5FT deg		BBC	HN	M	30	BBBB	Ind		
Economic and Social History/Mathematics	GV13	4FT deg		BBC	HN	M	30	BBBB	Ind		
Economic and Social History/Mathematics	VG31	4FT deg		BBC	8M	M	30	BBBB	Ind		
Economics/Mathematics	GL11	4FT deg		BBC	8M	M	30	BBBB	Ind		
Economics/Statistics	LG14	4FT deg		BBC	HN	M	30	BBBB	Ind	3	
English/Mathematics	QG31	4FT deg		BBC	HN	M	30	BBBB	Ind		
Film and Television Studies/Mathematics	GW15	4FT deg		BBB	HN	D	32	AABB	HN	4	
French/Mathematics	GR11	5FT deg		BBC	HN	M	30	BBBB	Ind	10	
History of Art/Mathematics	GV14	4FT deg		BBC	HN	M	30	BBBB	Ind		
History/Mathematics	GV11	4FT deg		BBC	HN	M	30	BBBB	Ind		
Islamic Studies/Mathematics	TG61	4FT deg		BBC	N	M	30	BBBB	Ind		
Italian/Mathematics	GR13	5FT deg		BBC	HN	M	30	BBBB	Ind		
Latin/Mathematics	GQ16	4FT deg		BBC	HN	M	30	BBBB	Ind		
Management Studies/Mathematics	GNC1	4FT deg		BBC	HN	M	30	BBBB	Ind	11	
Management Studies/Mathematics	GN1C	4FT deg		BBC	8M	M	30	BBBB	Ind	11	
Management Studies/Statistics	GN41	4FT deg		BBC	8M	M	30	BBBB	Ind	8	
Mathematics	G100	4FT deg	M+S	BBC-CCC	N	M	24$	BBBB$	N	6	
Mathematics	G102	4FT deg		BBC	HN	M	30	BBBB	Ind		
Mathematics/Computing Science	GG15	4FT deg	M+S	BBC-CCC	N	M	24$	BBBB$	N	7	
Mathematics/Economics	GL1C	4FT deg		BBC	HN	M	30	BBBB	Ind		
Mathematics/Management Studies	NG11	4FT deg	M+S	BBC-CCC	N	M	24$	BBBB$	N	11	
Mathematics/Music	GW13	4FT deg		BBC	HN	M	30	BBBB	Ind	11	
Mathematics/Philosophy	GV17	4FT deg		BBC	HN	M	30	BBBB	Ind		
Mathematics/Philosophy	GV1R	4FT deg	M+S	BBC-CCC	N	M	24$	BBBB$	N		
Mathematics/Physics	FGH1	4FT deg	M+P	BBC-CCC	N	M	24$	BBBB$	N	5	
Mathematics/Politics	GM11	4FT deg		BBC	HN	M	30	BBBB	Ind		
Mathematics/Russian	GR18	5FT deg		BBC	HN	M	30	BBBB	Ind		
Mathematics/Scottish History	GV1C	4FT deg		BBC	HN	M	30	BBBB	Ind		
Mathematics/Scottish Literature	GQ12	4FT deg		BBC	HN	M	30	BBBB	Ind		
Mathematics/Statistics	GG14	4FT deg	M+S	BBC-CCC	N	M	24$	BBBB$	N	5	
Philosophy/Mathematics	VG71	4FT deg		BBC	8M	M	30	BBBB	Ind		
Politics/Mathematics	MG11	4FT deg		BBC	8M	M	30	BBBB	Ind	1	
Statistics	G400	4FT deg	M+S	BBC-CCC	N	M	24$	BBBB$	N	1	
Theatre Studies/Mathematics	GWC4	4FT deg		BBC	HN	M	30	BBBB	Ind		
Theology & Religious Studies/Mathematics	GV1V	4FT deg		BBC	HN	M	30	BBBB	Ind		

GLASGOW CALEDONIAN Univ

TITLE	CODE	COURSE	SUBJECTS	A/AS	ND/C	AGNVQ	IB	SQA(H)	SQA	RATIO A/AS	
Applicable Maths with Business and a Language	G1TX	3FT/4FT deg	M+L	CD	Ind		Ind	BBC$	Ind	6	
Applicable Maths with Languages	G1T9	3FT/4FT deg	M+L	CD	Ind		Ind	BBC$	Ind		
Applied Statistics	G400	3FT/4FT deg	M+E	CD	Ind		Ind	BBC$	Ind		
Computational Mathematics	G170	3FT/4FT deg	M+E	CD	Ind		Ind	BBC$	Ind	5	
Financial Mathematics	GN13	3FT deg	M	CD	Ind		Ind	BBC	Ind	2	
Mathematics for Business Analysis	G1NC	4FT/5SW deg	M+E	CD	Ind		Ind	BBC$	Ind	4	

GOLDSMITHS COLL (Univ of London)

TITLE	CODE	COURSE	SUBJECTS	A/AS	ND/C	AGNVQ	IB	SQA(H)	SQA	RATIO A/AS	
Computer Science and Statistics	GG54	3FT deg	M	DD	MO	M	Dip	BBBBC	N		
Mathematics	G140	3FT deg	M	DD	MO	M	Dip	BCCCC	N	6	
Mathematics & Computer Sci with Wk Exp (4 Yrs)	GG1M	4FT deg	M	DD	MO	M	Dip	BCCCC	N		
Mathematics (4-Yrs extension degree)	G147	4FT deg	*		Ind		Ind	Ind	Ind	2	
Mathematics and Computer Science	GG15	3FT deg	M	DD	MO	M	Dip	BCCCC	N	4	14/16

Mathematics and Statistics   52

| | | | | 98 expected requirements | | | | | | 96 entry stats |
| course details | | | | | | | | | | |
TITLE	CODE	COURSE	SUBJECTS	A/AS	ND/C	AGNVQ	IB	SQA(H)	SQA	RATIO A/AS
Mathematics and Psychology	CG81	3FT deg	M	CCC	MO	M	Dip	BBBCC	N	
Mathematics and Statistics	GG14	3FT deg	M	DD	MO	M	Dip	BCCCC	N	16
Mathematics and Statistics with Work Exp (4 Yrs)	GG41	4FT deg	M	DD	MO	M	Dip	BCCCC	N	
Mathematics with Computer Sci with Wk Ex (4 Yrs)	G1GM	4FT deg	M	DD	MO	M	Dip	BCCCC	N	9
Mathematics with Computer Science	G1G5	3FT deg	M	DD	MO	M	Dip	BCCCC	N	8
Mathematics with Statistics	G1G4	3FT deg	M	DD	MO	M	Dip	BCCCC	N	
Mathematics with Statistics with Wk Exp (4 Yrs)	G1GK	4FT deg	M	DD	MO	M	Dip	BCCCC	N	
Mathematics with work experience (4 Yrs)	G141	4FT deg	M	DD	MO	M	Dip	BCCCC	N	
Statistics, Computer Science & Applicable Maths	GG45	3FT deg	M	DD	MO	M	Dip	BCCCC	N	3

Univ of GREENWICH

Applied Statistics	G411	3FT/4SW deg	*g	CE	3M	Ind	24	CCC	Ind	
Applied Statistics with Accounting and Finance	G4N4	3FT/4SW deg	*g	CE	3M	Ind	Ind	CCC	Ind	
Applied Statistics with Business Management	G4N1	3FT/4SW deg	*g	CE	3M	Ind	Ind	CCC$	Ind	
Applied Statistics with Computing	G4G5	3FT/4SW deg	*g	CE	3M	Ind	Ind	CCC$	Ind	
Applied Statistics with Social Science	G4M9	3FT/4SW deg	*g	CE	Ind	Ind	Ind	Ind	Ind	
Business Systems Modelling	G9N1	3FT/4SW deg	*g	CE	3M	Ind	Ind	CCC$	Ind	
Health and Statistics	BG94	3FT deg	*g	12	N	M$	22	Ind	Ind	
Health with Statistics	B9G4	3FT deg	M g	12	N	X	22	Ind	Ind	
Management Science	GN11	3FT/4SW deg	M g	CE	3M $	Ind	Ind	CCC$	Ind	
Mathematical Studies (Extended)	G148▼	4FT/5SW deg	*g	4	Ind	Ind	Ind	Ind	Ind	
Mathematics for Finance and Accountancy	G1G4	3FT/4SW deg	M g	CE	3M $	Ind	Ind	CCC$	Ind	
Mathematics with Computing	GG15	3FT/4SW deg	M g	CE	3M $	Ind	Ind	CCC$	Ind	
Mathematics, Statistics and Computing	G900	3FT/4SW deg	M g	CE	3M $	Ind	Ind	CCC$	Ind	
Psychology with Statistics	C8G4	3FT/4SW deg	M g	16	1M+1D	Ind	24	Ind	Ind	
Mathematical St (Statistics & Management Sci)	109G	2FT HND	*g	2	1M	Ind	Ind	C	Ind	
Mathematical Studs (Maths, Stats & Computing)	009G	2FT HND	M g	2	1M $	Ind	Ind	C$	Ind	

HERIOT-WATT Univ

Actuarial Mathematics and Statistics	GG14	4FT deg	M	BBC	Ind	M$^	36	AABB$	Ind	
General Mathematics (Ordinary)	G102	3FT deg	M	CDE	HN	M$ go	28	BBCC	HN	
Mathematics	G100	4FT deg	M	CDE	HN	M$^	28	BBB	HN	
Mathematics with Applied Mechanics	G104	4FT deg	M	CDE	HN	M$^	28	BBB	HN	
Mathematics with Computer Science	G1G5	4FT deg	M	CDE	HN	M$^	28	BBB	HN	
Mathematics with Economics	G1L1	4FT deg	M	CDE	HN	M$^	28	BBB	HN	
Mathematics with Education	G1X9	3FT/4FT deg	M	CDE	HN	M$^	28	BBCC	HN	
Mathematics with Finance	G1N3	4FT deg	M	CDE		M$^				
Mathematics with French	G1R1	4FT deg	M+L	CDE	HN	M$^	28	BBB	HN	
Mathematics with German	G1R2	4FT deg	M+L	CDE	HN	M$^	28	BBB	HN	
Mathematics with Physics	G1F3	4FT deg	M+P	CDE	HN	M$^	28	BBB	HN	
Mathematics with Spanish	G1R4	4FT deg	M+L	CDE	HN	M$^	28	BBB	HN	
Mathematics with Statistics	G1GK	4FT deg	M	CDE	HN	M$^	28	BBB	HN	
Statistics	G400	4FT deg	M	BBC	Ind	M$^	36	AABB	Ind	
Combined Studies *Actuarial Mathematics with Statistics*	Y100	4FT deg	M	CCC	Ind	M$^ go	30	BBBB	Ind	
Combined Studies *Mathematics*	Y100	4FT deg	M	DDE	Ind	M$ go	26	BCCC	Ind	

Univ of HERTFORDSHIRE

Applicable Mathematics	G110	3FT/4SW deg	M g	12	MO+D	M$	26	Ind	Ind	
Applied Geology/Applied Statistics	F6G4	3FT deg	*g	12	3M $	M$ gi	24$	CCCC$	Ind	
Applied Physics/Applied Statistics	F3G4	3FT deg	M+P	12	3M $	M$ gi	24$	CCCC$	Ind	
Applied Physics/Mathematics	F3G1	3FT deg	M+P	12	3M $	M$^ gi	24$	CCCC$	Ind	
Applied Statistics	G410	3FT deg	*g	12	3M	M$ gi	24	CCCC	Ind	

course details | 98 expected requirements | 96 entry stats

TITLE	CODE	COURSE	SUBJECTS	A/AS	NO/C	AGNVQ	IB	SQA(H)	SQA	RATIO A/AS
Applied Statistics/Applied Geology	G4F6	3FT deg	* g	12	3M $	M$ gi	24$	CCCC$	Ind	
Applied Statistics/Applied Physics	G4F3	3FT deg	M+P	12	3M $	M$ gi	24$	CCCC$	Ind	
Applied Statistics/Business	G4N1	3FT deg	*	18	4M+4D	M$6 gi	26	BBBC	Ind	
Applied Statistics/Computing	G4G5	3FT deg	*	12	3M	M$ gi	24	CCCC	Ind	1
Applied Statistics/Economics	G4L1	3FT deg	*	12	3M	M$ gi	24	CCCC	Ind	
Applied Statistics/Electronic Music	G4W3	3FT deg	Mu	14	MO $	M$^ gi	26$	BCCC$	Ind	
Applied Statistics/Environmental Science	G4F9	3FT deg	*	14	MO	M$ gi	26	BCCC	Ind	
Applied Statistics/Human Biology	G4B1	3FT deg	S g	12	3M $	MS gi	24$	CCCC$	Ind	
Applied Statistics/Law	G4M3	3FT deg	*	20	4M+4D	D$ gi	26	BBBC	Ind	
Applied Statistics/Linguistic Science	G4Q1	3FT deg	*	14	MO $	M$ gi	26	BCCC	Ind	
Applied Statistics/Manufacturing Systems	G4H7	3FT deg	*	12	3M	M$ gi	24	CCCC	Ind	
Applied Statistics/Mathematics	G4G1	3FT deg	M	12	3M $	M$^ gi	24$	CCCC$	Ind	2
Applied Statistics/Operational Research	G4N2	3FT deg	*	12	3M	M$ gi	24	CCCC	Ind	6
Astronomy/Mathematics	F5G1	3FT deg	M g	12	3M $	M$^ gi	24$	CCCC$	Ind	
Business Decision Sciences	GN42	3FT/4SW deg	g	12	MO	Ind $	24$	Ind		1 4/14
Business/Applied Statistics	N1G4	3FT deg	*	18	4M+4D	M$6 gi	26	BBBC	Ind	
Business/Mathematics	N1G1	3FT deg	M	18	4M+4D	M$^ gi	26$	BBBC$	Ind	7
Chemistry/Mathematics	F1G1	3FT deg	C+M g	12	3M $	MS^ gi	24$	CCCC$	Ind	
Computing Mathematics	GG15	3FT/4SW deg	M g	12	MO+D	M$^ gi	26	Ind	Ind	6
Computing/Applied Statistics	G5G4	3FT deg	* g	12	3M	M$ gi	24	CCCC	Ind	
Computing/Mathematics	G5G1	3FT deg	M	12	3M $	M$^ gi	24$	CCCC$	Ind	13
Economics/Applied Statistics	L1G4	3FT deg	*	12	3M $	M$ gi	24	CCCC	Ind	3
Economics/Mathematics	L1G1	3FT deg	M	12	3M $	M$^ gi	24$	CCCC$	Ind	
Electronic Music with Mathematics	W3GC	3FT deg	* g	14	Ind	Ind	Ind	Ind	Ind	
Electronic Music/Applied Statistics	W3G4	3FT deg	Mu	14	MO $	M$^ gi	26$	BCCC$	Ind	
Electronics/Mathematics	H6G1	3FT deg	M g	12	3M $	M$^ gi	24$	CCCC$	Ind	3
Environmental Science/Applied Statistics	F9G4	3FT deg	*	14	MO	M$ gi	26	BCCC	Ind	
Environmental Science/Mathematics	F9G1	3FT deg	M	14	MO $	M$^ gi	26$	BCCC$	Ind	
European Studies/Mathematics	T2G1	3FT deg	M	14	MO $	M$^ gi	26$	BCCC$	Ind	
Human Biology/Applied Statistics	B1G4	3FT deg	S g	12	3M $	MS gi	24$	CCCC$	Ind	1
Human Biology/Mathematics	B1G1	3FT deg	S+M g	12	3M $	MS^ gi	24$	CCCC$	Ind	2
Law/Applied Statistics	M3G4	3FT deg	*	20	4M+4D	D$ gi	26	BBBC	Ind	
Linguistic Science/Applied Statistics	Q1G4	3FT deg	*	14	MO $	M$ gi	26	BCCC	Ind	
Linguistic Science/Mathematics	Q1G1	3FT deg	M	14	MO $	M$^ gi	26$	BCCC$	Ind	
Manufacturing Systems/Applied Statistics	H7G4	3FT deg	*	12	3M	M$ gi	24	CCCC	Ind	
Mathematics	G100	3FT/4SW deg	M g	12	MO+D	M*+	26	Ind	Ind	4 6/18
Mathematics	G101	3FT deg	M g	12	MO+D	M$^ gi	24	BCCC$	Ind	
Mathematics for Business Analysis	G1NF	3FT deg								
Mathematics/Applied Physics	G1F3	3FT deg	M+P	12	3M $	M$^ gi	24$	CCCC$	Ind	
Mathematics/Applied Statistics	G1G4	3FT deg	M	12	3M $	M$^ gi	24$	CCCC$	Ind	6
Mathematics/Astronomy	G1F5	3FT deg	M g	12	3M $	M$^ gi	24$	CCCC$	Ind	9
Mathematics/Business	G1N1	3FT deg	M	18	4M+4D	M$^ gi	26$	BBBC$	Ind	6
Mathematics/Chemistry	G1F1	3FT deg	M+C g	12	3M $	MS^ gi	24$	CCCC$	Ind	
Mathematics/Computing	G1G5	3FT deg	M	12	3M $	M$^ gi	24$	CCCC$	Ind	17
Mathematics/Economics	G1L1	3FT deg	M	12	3M $	M$^ gi	24$	CCCC$	Ind	12
Mathematics/Electronics	G1H6	3FT deg	M g	12	3M $	M$^ gi	24$	CCCC$	Ind	
Mathematics/Environmental Science	G1F9	3FT deg	M	14	MO $	M$^ gi	26$	BCCC$	Ind	
Mathematics/European Studies	G1T2	3FT deg	M	14	MO $	M$^ gi	26$	BCCC$	Ind	
Mathematics/Human Biology	G1B1	3FT deg	M+S	12	3M $	MS^ gi	24$	CCCC$	Ind	3
Mathematics/Linguistic Science	G1Q1	3FT deg	M	14	MO $	M$^ gi	26$	BCCC$	Ind	
Mathematics/Operational Research	G1N2	3FT deg	M	12	3M $	M$^ gi	24$	CCCC$	Ind	
Mathematics/Philosophy	G1V7	3FT deg	M	14	MO $	M$^ gi	26$	BCCC$	Ind	8

Mathematics and Statistics 52

TITLE	CODE	COURSE	SUBJECTS	A/AS	NO/C	AGNVQ	IB	SQA(H)	SQA	RATIO A/AS
Operational Research/Applied Statistics	N2G4	3FT deg	*	12	3M	M$ gi	24	CCCC	Ind	1
Operational Research/Mathematics	N2G1	3FT deg	M	12	3M $	M$^ gi	24$	CCCC$	Ind	
Philosophy/Mathematics	V7G1	3FT deg	M	14	MO $	M$^ gi	26$	BCCC$	Ind	
Combined Modular Scheme Applied Statistics	Y100	3FT deg	*	12	3M	M$ gi	24	CCCC	Ind	
Combined Modular Scheme Applied Statistics (Extended)	Y109▼	4EXT deg	*	4	N	P$ gi	Dip	DDDD	Ind	
Combined Modular Scheme Mathematics	Y100	3FT deg	M	12	3M $	M$^ gi	24$	CCCC$	Ind	
Combined Modular Scheme Mathematics (Extended)	Y109▼	4EXT deg	* g	4	N $	P$ gi	Dip$	DDDD$	Ind	

Univ of HUDDERSFIELD

TITLE	CODE	COURSE	SUBJECTS	A/AS	NO/C	AGNVQ	IB	SQA(H)	SQA	RATIO A/AS
Computing and Mathematics	GG51	3FT/4SW deg	M g	18-20	MO+1D$	M^ go	Ind	BBB	Ind	
Computing and Statistics	GG54	3FT deg	* g	14-16	MO	M go	Ind	BBB	Ind	
Mathematical Sciences	G140	3FT deg	M g	18-20	MO+1D$	M^ go	Ind	BBB	Ind	
Scientific Computing	GG15	4SW deg	M g	18-20	MO+1D$	M^ go	Ind	BBB	Ind	

Univ of HULL

TITLE	CODE	COURSE	SUBJECTS	A/AS	NO/C	AGNVQ	IB	SQA(H)	SQA	RATIO A/AS
Computer Graphics and Mathematical Modelling	GG5D	4FT deg	* g	10	N	P	24	CCCCD	Ind	
Computer Graphics and Mathematical Modelling	GG5C	3FT deg	S+M	18	MO	M$+	26$	BBBCC	Ind	
Mathematical Statistics	G430	3FT deg	M	BCD	MO $	M$^ go	26$	BBCCC	Ind	10
Mathematics	G100	3FT deg	M	BCD	MO $	M$^ go	26$	BCCCC	Ind	5 12/28
Mathematics	G101	4FT deg	*	CD	N	P*6/^ gi	24	BCCCC	Ind	2
Mathematics (4 Yrs) (MMath)	G103	4FT deg	M	BCC	MO $	M$^ go	26$	BBCCC	Ind	6 22/26
Mathematics and Economics	GL11	3FT deg	M	BCC-BCD	MO $	M$^ go	26$	BBCCC	Ind	12
Mathematics and Management Sciences	NG11	3FT deg	M	BBC-BCD	MO $	M$^ go	28$	Ind	Ind	7 16/20
Mathematics and Philosophy	GV17	3FT deg	M	BCC-BCD	MO $	M$^ go	28$	BBBCC	Ind	4
Mathematics and Philosophy (4 Yrs)	GV1R	4FT deg	*	CD	N	P*^ gi	24	BCCCC	Ind	
Mathematics with French	G1R1	4FT deg	M g	BCD	MO $	M$^ go	26$	BBCCC	Ind	15
Mathematics with French (MMath)	G1RC	4FT deg	M g	BCC	MO $	M$^ go	26$	BBBCC	Ind	2
Mathematics with German	G1R2	4FT deg	M g	BCD	MO $	M$^ go	26$	BBCCC	Ind	
Mathematics with German (MMath)	G1RF	4FT deg	M g	BCC	MO $	M$^ go	26$	BBBCC	Ind	
Mathematics with Spanish	G1R4	4FT deg	M/L+M g	BCD	MO $	M$^ go	26$	BBCCC	Ind	2 20/24
Mathematics with Spanish (MMath)	G1RK	4FT deg	M/L+M g	BCC	MO $	M$^ go	26$	BBBCC	Ind	
Mathematics, Pure	G120	3FT deg	M	BCD	MO $	M$^ go	26$	BCCCC	Ind	6
Physical Education and Sports Science with Maths	B6G1	3FT deg	M	18-20	3M $	M$^ gi	25$	BBBCC	Ind	
Statistics and Economics	GL41	3FT deg	M	18-20	MO $	M$^ gi	26$	BBCCC	Ind	
Statistics with a Mod Lang (Fr,Ger,Sp) (4 Yrs)	G4T2	4FT deg	M/L+M g	BCD	MO $	M$^ gi	26$	BBCCC	Ind	

IMPERIAL COLL (Univ of London)

TITLE	CODE	COURSE	SUBJECTS	A/AS	NO/C	AGNVQ	IB	SQA(H)	SQA	RATIO A/AS
Mathematics	G100	3FT deg	M	BBC-ACC	Ind	X	Ind	Ind	Ind	7 24/30
Mathematics (MSci)	G103	4FT deg	M	AAB	Ind	X	Ind	Ind	Ind	4 24/30
Mathematics and Computer Science	GG15	3FT deg	M	BBC-ACC	Ind	X	Ind	Ind	Ind	11 26/30
Mathematics and Computer Science (MSci)	GG51	4FT deg	M	AAB	Ind	X	Ind	Ind	Ind	3 24/30
Mathematics with Management	G1N1	3FT deg	M	BBC-ACC	Ind	X	Ind	Ind	Ind	10 24/30
Mathematics with Mathematical Computation	G102	3FT deg	M	BBC-ACC	Ind	X	Ind	Ind	Ind	4
Mathematics with Statistics	G1G4	3FT deg	M	BBC-ACC	Ind	X	Ind	Ind	Ind	32
Mathematics with a Year in Europe (4 Yrs)	G101	4FT deg	M	BBC-ACC	Ind	X	Ind	Ind	Ind	5
Mathematics with a Year in Europe (MSci)	G104	4FT deg	M	AAB	Ind	X	Ind	Ind	Ind	3
Mathematics, Optimisation and Statistics	GG41	3FT deg	M	BBC-ACC	Ind	X	Ind	Ind	Ind	
Maths (Pure Mathematics)	G125	3FT deg	M	BBC-ACC	Ind	X	Ind	Ind	Ind	11
Maths with Applied Maths/Mathematical Physics	G1F3	3FT deg	M	BBC-ACC	Ind	X	Ind	Ind	Ind	15

course details | 98 expected requirements | 96 entry stats

TITLE	CODE	COURSE	SUBJECTS	A/AS	ND/C	AGNVQ	IB	SQA(H)	SQA	RATIO A/AS	
KEELE Univ											
Biological and Medicinal Chem and Mathematics	FGC1	3FT deg	M+C g	BCC-CCC	Ind	M$^	26$	CSYS	Ind	1	
Biology and Mathematics (MSci)	CG1C	4FT deg	S+M	BCC-CCC	Ind	M$^	26$	CSYS	Ind		
Computer Science and Mathematics (MSci)	GG5C	4FT deg	M	BCC-CCC	Ind	M$^	26$	CSYS	Ind		
Finance and Mathematics	GN13	3FT deg	M	BCC	Ind	M$^	28$	CSYS	Ind		
Finance and Statistics	GN43	3FT deg	M	BCC	Ind	M$^	28$	CSYS	Ind		
International Politics and Mathematics	GM1C	3FT deg	M	BCC	Ind	D$^	28$	CSYS	Ind		
International Politics and Statistics	GM4C	3FT deg	M	BCC	Ind	D$^	28$	CSYS	Ind		
Law and Mathematics	GM13	3FT deg	M	BBB	Ind	D$^	32$	CSYS	Ind	4	
Law and Mathematics (4 Yrs)	MG31	4FT deg	*	BBB	Ind	Ind	32	BBBB	Ind	1	
Mathematics	G100	3FT deg	M	BCC-CCC	Ind	M$^	26$	CSYS	Ind	61	
Mathematics and American Studies (4 Yrs)	QG41	4FT deg	* g	BCC	Ind	Ind	28	BBBB	Ind		
Mathematics and Ancient History	GV1D	3FT deg	M	BCC	Ind	D$^	28$	CSYS	Ind		
Mathematics and Ancient History (4 Yrs)	VGD1	4FT deg	*	BCC	Ind	Ind	28	BBBB	Ind		
Mathematics and Applied Social Studies	GL15	3FT deg	M	BCC	Ind	D$^	28$	CSYS	Ind	1	
Mathematics and Applied Social Studies (4 Yrs)	LG51	4FT deg	*	BCC	Ind	Ind	28	BBBB	Ind		
Mathematics and Astrophysics	FG51	3FT deg	P+M g	BCC-CCC	Ind	M$^	26$	CSYS	Ind	5	
Mathematics and Astrophysics (4 Yrs)	GF15	4FT deg	*	BCC-CCC	Ind	Ind	26	BBBB	Ind		
Mathematics and Astrophysics (MSci)	GF1M	4FT deg	P+M g	BCC-CCC	Ind	M$^	26$	CSYS	Ind		
Mathematics and Biology	CG11	3FT deg	S+M g	BCC-CCC	Ind	M$^	26$	CSYS	Ind		
Mathematics and Biology (4 Yrs)	GC11	4FT deg	*	BCC-CCC	Ind	Ind	26	BBBB	Ind		
Mathematics and Business Administration (4 Yrs)	NG91	4FT deg	*	BCC	Ind	Ind	28	BBBB	Ind		
Mathematics and Chemistry	FG11	3FT deg	M+C g	BCC-CCC	Ind	M$^	26$	CSYS	Ind	6	
Mathematics and Chemistry (4 Yrs)	GF11	4FT deg	*	BCC-CCC	Ind	Ind	26	BBBB	Ind	4	
Mathematics and Chemistry (MSci)	GFC1	4FT deg	M+C	BCC-CCC	Ind	M$^	26$	CSYS	Ind		
Mathematics and Classical Studies (4 Yrs)	QG81	4FT deg	*	BCC	Ind	Ind	28	BBBB	Ind		
Mathematics and Computer Science	GG15	3FT deg	M	BCC-CCC	Ind	M$^	26$	CSYS	Ind	3	16/24
Mathematics and Computer Science (4 Yrs)	GG51	4FT deg	*	BCC-CCC	Ind	Ind	26	BBBB	Ind		
Mathematics and Economics	GL11	3FT deg	M g	BCC	Ind	D$^	28$	CSYS	Ind	4	14/20
Mathematics and Economics (4 Yrs)	LG11	4FT deg	*	BCC	Ind	Ind	28	BBBB	Ind		
Mathematics and Educational Studies	GX19	3FT deg	M	BCC	Ind	D$^	28$	CSYS	Ind	3	
Mathematics and Educational Studies (4 Yrs)	XG91	4FT deg	*	BCC	Ind	Ind	28	BBBB	Ind		
Mathematics and Electronic Music	GW1J	3FT deg	M+Mu	BCC	Ind	D$^	28$	CSYS	Ind		
Mathematics and Electronic Music (4 Yrs)	WGJ1	4FT deg	*	BCC	Ind	Ind	28	BBBB	Ind		
Mathematics and Environmental Management	FGX1	3FT deg	M g	BCC	Ind	D$^	28$	CSYS	Ind		
Mathematics and Environmental Mgt (4 Yrs)	GF1X	4FT deg	*	BCC	Ind	Ind	28	BBBB	Ind	1	
Mathematics and Finance (4 Yrs)	NG31	4FT deg	*	BCC	Ind	Ind	28	BBBB	Ind		
Mathematics and French	GR11	3FT deg	F+M	BCC	Ind	D$^	28$	CSYS	Ind	5	
Mathematics and French (4 Yrs)	RG11	4FT deg	*	BCC	Ind	Ind	28	BBBB	Ind	9	
Mathematics and French/German	GT19	3FT deg	F+G+M	BBC	Ind	D$^	30$	CSYS	Ind		
Mathematics and French/German (4 Yrs)	TG91	4FT deg	G	BCC	Ind	Ind	28$	BBBB	Ind		
Mathematics and French/Russian or Russian Studs	GT1X	3FT deg	F+R+M	BBC-BCC	Ind	D$^	28$	CSYS	Ind		
Mathematics and Geography	GL18	3FT deg	M+Gy	BCC	Ind	D$^	28$	CSYS	Ind	5	18/28
Mathematics and Geography (4 Yrs)	LG81	4FT deg	*	BCC	Ind	Ind	28	BBBB	Ind		
Mathematics and German	GR12	3FT deg	G+M	BCC	Ind	D$^	28$	CSYS	Ind		
Mathematics and German (4 Yrs)	RG21	4FT deg	G	BCC	Ind	Ind	28$	BBBB	Ind		
Mathematics and German/Russian or Russian Studs	GT1Y	3FT deg	G+R+M	BBC-BCC	Ind	D$^	28$	CSYS	Ind		
Mathematics and History	GV11	3FT deg	M	BCC	Ind	D$^	28$	CSYS	Ind	7	
Mathematics and History (4 Yrs)	VG11	4FT deg	*	BCC	Ind	Ind	28	BBBB	Ind		
Mathematics and International Politics	MGC1	4FT deg	*	BCC	Ind	Ind	28	BBBB	Ind		
Mathematics and Latin	GQ16	3FT deg	Ln+M	BCC	Ind	D$^	28$	CSYS	Ind		
Mathematics and Latin (4 Yrs)	QG61	4FT deg	*	BCC	Ind	Ind	28	BBBB	Ind		

Mathematics and Statistics

52

course details

TITLE	CODE	COURSE	SUBJECTS	A/AS	ND/C	AGNVQ	IB	SQA(H)	SQA	RATIO A/AS
Mathematics and Management Science	GN11	3FT deg	M g	BCC	Ind	D$^	28$	CSYS	Ind	6
Mathematics and Management Science (4 Yrs)	NG11	4FT deg	*	BCC	Ind	Ind	28	BBBB	Ind	
Mathematics and Marketing	GN15	3FT deg	M	BCC	Ind	D$^	28$	CSYS	Ind	
Maths and Biological & Medicinal Chem (4 Yrs)	GF1C	4FT deg	*	BCC-CCC	Ind	Ind	26	BBBB	Ind	
Maths and French/Russian or Russian St (4 Yrs)	TGX1	4FT deg	*	BCC	Ind	Ind	28	BBBB	Ind	
Maths and German/Russian or Russian St (4 Yrs)	TGY1	4FT deg	G	BCC	Ind	Ind	28$	BBBB	Ind	
Music and Mathematics	GW13	3FT deg	M+Mu	BCC	Ind	D$^	28$	CSYS	Ind	5
Music and Mathematics (4 Yrs)	WG31	4FT deg	*	BCC	Ind	Ind	28	BBBB	Ind	2
Neuroscience and Mathematics	BG11	3FT deg	S+M	BCC-CCC	Ind	M$^	26$	CSYS	Ind	
Neuroscience and Mathematics (4 Yrs)	BG1C	4FT deg	*	BCC-CCC	Ind	Ind	26	BBBB	Ind	
Neuroscience and Statistics	BG14	3FT deg	S+M	BCC-CCC	Ind	M$^	26$	CSYS	Ind	
Philosophy and Mathematics	GV17	3FT deg	M	BCC	Ind	D$^	28$	CSYS	Ind	
Philosophy and Mathematics (4 Yrs)	VG71	4FT deg	*	BCC	Ind	Ind	28	BBBB	Ind	
Physics and Mathematics	FG31	3FT deg	M+P	BCC-CCC	Ind	M$^	26$	CSYS	Ind	5
Physics and Mathematics (4 Yrs)	GF13	4FT deg	*	BCC-CCC	Ind	Ind	26	BBBB	Ind	1
Physics and Mathematics (MSci)	GF1H	4FT deg	M+P	BCC-CCC	Ind	M$^	26$	CSYS	Ind	
Psychology and Mathematics	CG81	3FT deg	M g	BBB	Ind	D$^	32$	CSYS	Ind	16
Psychology and Mathematics (4 Yrs)	GC18	4FT deg	*	BBB	Ind	Ind	32	ABBB	Ind	
Russian Studies and Mathematics	GRC8	3FT deg	M	BCC	Ind	D$^	28$	CSYS	Ind	
Russian Studies and Mathematics (4 Yrs)	RG8C	4FT deg	*	BCC	Ind	Ind	28	BBBB	Ind	
Russian and Mathematics	GR18	3FT deg	R+M	BCC	Ind	D$^	28$	CSYS	Ind	
Russian and Mathematics (4 Yrs)	RG81	4FT deg	*	BCC	Ind	Ind	28	BBBB	Ind	
Sociol & Soc Anthropology and Maths (4 Yrs)	LG31	4FT deg	*	BCC	Ind	Ind	28	BBBB	Ind	
Sociology & Social Anthropology and Mathematics	GL13	3FT deg	M	BCC	Ind	D$^	28$	CSYS	Ind	
Statistics and American Studies (4 Yrs)	QG44	4FT deg	* g	BCC	Ind	Ind	28	BBBB	Ind	
Statistics and Ancient History	GV4D	3FT deg	M	BCC	Ind	D$^	28$	CSYS	Ind	
Statistics and Ancient History (4 Yrs)	VGD4	4FT deg	*	BCC	Ind	Ind	28	BBBB	Ind	
Statistics and Applied Social Studies	GL45	3FT deg	M	BCC	Ind	D$^	28$	CSYS	Ind	
Statistics and Applied Social Studies (4 Yrs)	LG54	4FT deg	*	BCC	Ind	Ind	28	BBBB	Ind	
Statistics and Astrophysics (4 Yrs)	GF45	4FT deg	* g	BCC-CCC	Ind	Ind	26	BBBB	Ind	
Statistics and Biological & Medicinal Chem(4Yrs)	GF4C	4FT deg	*	BCC-CCC	Ind	Ind	26	BBBB	Ind	
Statistics and Biological and Medicinal Chem	FGC4	3FT deg	M/C g	BCC-CCC	Ind	M$^	26$	CSYS	Ind	
Statistics and Biology	CG14	3FT deg	S+M g	BCC-CCC	Ind	M$^	26$	CSYS	Ind	
Statistics and Biology (4 Yrs)	GC41	4FT deg	*	BCC-CCC	Ind	Ind	26	BBBB	Ind	
Statistics and Business Administration (4 Yrs)	NG94	4FT deg	* g	BCC	Ind	Ind	28	BBBB	Ind	
Statistics and Chemistry	FG14	3FT deg	M+C g	BCC-CCC	Ind	M$^	26$	CSYS	Ind	
Statistics and Chemistry (4 Yrs)	GF41	4FT deg	*	BCC-CCC	Ind	Ind	26	BBBB	Ind	
Statistics and Classical Studies (4 Yrs)	QG84	4FT deg	* g	BCC	Ind	Ind	28	BBBB	Ind	
Statistics and Computer Science	GG45	3FT deg	M	BCC-CCC	Ind	M$^	26$	CSYS	Ind	3
Statistics and Computer Science (4 Yrs)	GG54	4FT deg	*	BCC-CCC	Ind	Ind	26	BBBB	Ind	
Statistics and Economics	GL41	3FT deg	M g	BCC	Ind	D$^	28$	CSYS	Ind	8
Statistics and Economics (4 Yrs)	LG14	4FT deg	*	BCC	Ind	Ind	28	BBBB	Ind	
Statistics and Educational Studies	GX49	3FT deg	M	BCC	Ind	D$^	28$	CSYS	Ind	
Statistics and Educational Studies (4 Yrs)	XG94	4FT deg	*	BCC	Ind	Ind	28	BBBB	Ind	
Statistics and Electronic Music (4 Yrs)	WGJ4	4FT deg	*	BCC	Ind	Ind	28	BBBB	Ind	
Statistics and Environmental Management (4 Yrs)	GF4X	4FT deg	*	BCC	Ind	Ind	28	BBBB	Ind	
Statistics and Finance (4 Yrs)	NG34	4FT deg	*	BCC	Ind	Ind	28	BBBB	Ind	
Statistics and French (4 Yrs)	RG14	4FT deg	*	BCC	Ind	Ind	28	BBBB	Ind	
Statistics and French/Russian or Russ St (4 Yrs)	TGX4	4FT deg	* g	BCC	Ind	Ind	28	BBBB	Ind	
Statistics Geography (4 Yrs)	GF48	4FT deg	*	BCC	Ind	Ind	28	BBBB	Ind	
Statistics and German (4 Yrs)	RG24	4FT deg	* g	BCC	Ind	Ind	28	BBBB	Ind	
Statistics and History (4 Yrs)	VG14	4FT deg	*	BCC	Ind	Ind	28	BBBB	Ind	
Statistics and International Politics	MGC4	4FT deg	*	BCC	Ind	Ind	28	BBBB	Ind	
Statistics and Latin (4 Yrs)	QG64	4FT deg	*	BCC	Ind	Ind	28	BBBB	Ind	

course details

TITLE	CODE	COURSE	SUBJECTS	A/AS	ND/C	RGNVQ	IB	SQA(H)	SQA	RATIO A/AS
Statistics and Law (4 Yrs)	MG34	4FT deg	*	BBB-BCC	Ind	Ind	28	BBBB	Ind	
Statistics and Management Science	GN41	3FT deg	M g	BCC	Ind	D$^	28$	CSYS	Ind	13
Statistics and Management Science (4 Yrs)	NG14	4FT deg	*	BCC	Ind	Ind	28	BBBB	Ind	
Statistics and Marketing	GN45	3FT deg	M	BCC	Ind	D$^	28$	CSYS	Ind	
Statistics and Music (4 Yrs)	WG34	4FT deg	*	BCC	Ind	Ind	28	BBBB	Ind	
Statistics and Neurosciences (4 Yrs)	BG1K	4FT deg	*	BCC-CCC	Ind	Ind	26	BBBB	Ind	
Statistics and Philosophy (4 Yrs)	VG74	4FT deg	*	BCC	Ind	Ind	28	BBBB	Ind	
Statistics and Physics (4 Yrs)	GF43	4FT deg	*	BCC-CCC	Ind	Ind	26	BBBB	Ind	
Statistics and Psychology	CG84	3FT deg	M g	BBB	Ind	D$^	32$	CSYS	Ind	
Statistics and Psychology (4 Yrs)	GC48	4FT deg	*	BBB	Ind	Ind	32	ABBB	Ind	
Statistics and Russian (4 Yrs)	RG84	4FT deg	*	BCC	Ind	Ind	28	BBBB	Ind	
Statistics and Russian Studies (4 Yrs)	RGV4	4FT deg	*	BCC	Ind	Ind	28	BBBB	Ind	
Statistics and Sociol & Soc Anthropology (4 Yrs)	LG34	4FT deg	*	BCC	Ind	Ind	28	BBBB	Ind	
Statistics and Sociology & Social Anthropology	GL43	3FT deg	M	BCC	Ind	D$^	28$	CSYS	Ind	
Visual Arts and Mathematics	GW11	3FT deg	M	BCC	Ind	D$^	28$	CSYS	Ind	
Visual Arts and Mathematics	WG11	4FT deg	*	BCC	Ind	Ind	28	BBBB	Ind	
Visual Arts and Statistics	WG14	4FT deg	*	BCC	Ind	Ind	28	BBBB	Ind	
Visual Arts and Statistics	GW41	3FT deg	M	BCC	Ind	D$^	28$	CSYS	Ind	

Univ of KENT

TITLE	CODE	COURSE	SUBJECTS	A/AS	ND/C	RGNVQ	IB	SQA(H)	SQA	RATIO A/AS
Business Mathematics	G1N1	3FT/4SW deg	M	20	Ind	Ind	28$	BBBB$	Ind	12
Computing and Social Statistics	GG54	3FT deg	M	20	Ind	Ind	28$	BBBB$	Ind	
European Mathematics (MMath)	G147	4FT deg	M	22	Ind	Ind	30	ABBB$	Ind	
Mathematics	G100	3FT/4SW deg	M	22	Ind	Ind	30	ABBB$	Ind	5 16/28
Mathematics & Computer Science with a Yr in Ind	GG1M	4SW deg	M	20	Ind	Ind	28$	BBBB$	Ind	
Mathematics (Foundation - 4 Yrs)	G108	4FT deg		Ind	Ind	Ind	Ind	Ind	Ind	4/16
Mathematics (MMath)	G101	4FT deg	M	24	Ind	Ind	32	ABBB$	Ind	5 16/18
Mathematics and Accounting	GNC4	3FT/4SW deg	M	22	Ind	Ind	30$	ABBB$	Ind	7 20/26
Mathematics and Computer Science	GG15	3FT deg	M	20	Ind	Ind	28$	BBBB$	Ind	7 12/24
Mathematics and Economics	GLC1	3FT/4SW deg	M	20	Ind	Ind	28$	BBBB$	Ind	4 18/26
Mathematics and Management Science	GN11	3FT/4SW deg	M	20	Ind	Ind	28$	BBBB$	Ind	13
Mathematics and Philosophy	GV17	3FT/4SW deg	M	20	Ind	Ind	28	BBBB$	Ind	
Mathematics and Statistics	GG14	3FT/4SW deg	M	20	Ind	Ind	28	BBBB$	Ind	4 12/24
Mathematics with Management Science	G1NC	3FT/4SW deg	M	20	Ind	Ind	28$	BBBB$	Ind	
Statistics and Computer Science (3/4 Yrs)	GG45	3FT/4FT deg	M	20	Ind	Ind	28$	Ind	Ind	
Statistics and Economics	GL41	3FT/4SW deg	M	20	Ind	Ind	28$	BBBB$	Ind	

KING'S COLL LONDON (Univ of London)

TITLE	CODE	COURSE	SUBJECTS	A/AS	ND/C	RGNVQ	IB	SQA(H)	SQA	RATIO A/AS
Chemistry and Mathematics	FG11	3FT deg	C+M	BCC	X	Ind	28$	BBBCC	X	21
Chemistry and Mathematics (4 years) (MSci)	FG1C	4FT deg	C+M	BCC	X	Ind	28$	BBBCC	X	1
French and Mathematics	RG11	4FT deg	F+M	BBC	X		30$	AABBB$	X	6
Mathematics	G100	3FT deg	M	20	X		28$	AABBB$	X	11 16/30
Mathematics (4 Yrs)	G103	4FT deg	M	20	X		28$	AABBB$	X	3 18/28
Mathematics and Computer Science	GG15	3FT deg	M	20	X		28	ABBBB$	X	4 12/24
Mathematics and Computer Science (Management)	GG1N	3FT deg	M	20	X		28	ABBBB$	X	4 16/26
Mathematics and Education (4 Yrs)	GX19	4FT deg	M g	8	X		Ind	BBBCC$	X	7 8/10
Mathematics and Management	GN11	3FT deg	M	20	X		28$	AABBB$	X	4 16/28
Mathematics and Philosophy	GV17	3FT deg	M	24	X		30$	AAABB$	X	10
Mathematics and Physics	FG31	3FT deg	M+P	20	X		28$	AABBB$	X	14
Mathematics and Physics (4 years)	FG3D	4FT deg	M+P	20	X		28$	AABBB$	X	1
Mathematics and Physics with Astrophysics	FG3C	3FT deg	M+P	20	X		28$	AABBB	X	17
Mathematics with Philosophy of Mathematics	G1V5	3FT deg	M	20	X		28$	AABBB$	X	4 18/30
Mathematics with Philosophy of Maths (4Yr)(MSci)	G1VM	4FT deg	M	20	X		28$	AABBB$	X	

			98 expected requirements							96 entry stats	
course details											
TITLE	CODE	COURSE	SUBJECTS	A/AS	NO/C	RGNVQ	IB	SQA(H)	SQA	RATIO	A/AS

KINGSTON Univ

TITLE	CODE	COURSE	SUBJECTS	A/AS	NO/C	RGNVQ	IB	SQA(H)	SQA	RATIO	A/AS
Computing & Mathematics	GG15	3FT deg	M	10	3M $	Ind	Ind	CCC	Ind	5	12/16
Computing & Statistics	GG54	3FT deg	* g	10	3M $	Ind	Ind	CCC	Ind	3	
Geography & Mathematics	FG81	3FT deg	Gy/M g	12	$	Ind	Ind	BCCC	Ind	11	
Geography & Statistics	FG84	3FT deg	Gy	12	$	Ind	Ind	BCCC	Ind		
Mathematical Sciences	G100	3FT deg	M	10	3M $	Ind	Ind	CCC	Ind	13	
Mathematical Sciences	G108▼	4EXT deg	*		Ind		Ind	Ind	Ind	2	
Mathematics & Economics	GL11	3FT deg	M g	10	N	Ind	Ind	CCC	Ind	6	
Mathematics & Physics	FG31	3FT deg	P+M g	10	3M $	Ind	Ind	CCC	Ind	2	
Mathematics and French	GR11	4FT deg	M/F g	10	$	Ind	Ind	CCC	Ind	3	
Mathematics with Business Management	G1ND▼	4EXT deg			Ind		Ind	Ind	Ind	3	
Mathematics with Business Management	G1NC	4SW deg	M g	10	Ind	Ind	Ind	Ind	Ind	2	6/14
Mathematics with Business Management	G1N1	3FT deg	M g	10	Ind	Ind	Ind	Ind	Ind	10	
Statistics & Economics	GL41	3FT deg	M g	10	N	Ind	Ind	CCC	Ind	4	
Statistics & Mathematics	GG41	3FT deg	M	10	3M $	Ind	Ind	CCC	Ind	4	
Statistics with Business Management	G4N1	3FT deg	M g	10	Ind	Ind	Ind	Ind	Ind	4	
Statistics with Business Management	G4ND▼	4EXT deg			Ind	Ind	Ind	Ind	Ind	4	
Statistics with Business Management	G4NC	4SW deg	M g	10	Ind	Ind	Ind	Ind	Ind	2	6/10
Mathematical Studies	009G	2FT HND	M	2	$	Ind	Ind	DD	Ind	1	1/6

LANCASTER Univ

TITLE	CODE	COURSE	SUBJECTS	A/AS	NO/C	RGNVQ	IB	SQA(H)	SQA	RATIO	A/AS
Accounting, Finance and Mathematics	NG41	3FT deg	M g	BBC	DO $		30$	ABBBB$	Ind		
Biomedicine and Medical Statistics	BG91	3FT deg	2(M/P/C/B) g	BCC	MO $		30$	BBBBC$	Ind		
Computer Science and Mathematics	GG15	3FT deg	M g	20	Ind $		30$	BBBBB$	Ind		
Economics and Mathematics	GL11	3FT deg	M	BCC	Ind $		30$	BBBBB$	Ind		
Educational Studies and Mathematics	GX19	3FT deg	M	20	Ind $		30$	ABBBB$	Ind		
Environmental Mathematics	GF19	3FT deg	M g	20	DO $		30$	Ind$	Ind		
French Studies and Mathematics	GR11	4SW deg	F+M	20	MO $		30$	BBBBB$	Ind		
German Studies and Mathematics	GR12	4SW deg	M+G/L	20	MO $		30$	BBBBB$	Ind		
Italian Studies and Mathematics	GR13	4SW deg	I/L+M	20	MO $		30$	BBBBB$	Ind		
Mathematics	G100	3FT deg	M	20	MO+D $		30$	Ind$	Ind$		
Mathematics (inc a year in USA or Canada)	G103	3/4FT deg	M	24	DO $		34$	Ind$	Ind		
Mathematics and Operational Research	NG21	3FT deg	M	22	MO $		30$	ABBBB$	Ind		
Mathematics and Philosophy	GV17	3FT deg	M	20	MO $		30$	Ind$	Ind		
Mathematics with Statistics	G1G4	3FT deg	M	20	DO $		30$	Ind$	Ind$		
Spanish Studies and Mathematics	GR14	4SW deg	M+Sp/L	20	MO $		30$	BBBBB$	Ind		
Statistics	G400	3FT/4FT deg	M	20	DO $		30$	Ind$	Ind		
Statistics (inc a year in USA or Canada)	G401	4FT deg	M	24	DO $		30$	Ind$	Ind		
Combined Science *Mathematics*	Y158	3FT deg	M	CCD	MO $		30$	BBBB$	Ind		
Combined Science (inc a year in USA or Canada) *Mathematics*	Y155	3FT deg	M	BBB	Ind $		32$	ABBBB$	Ind		
Economics & Mathematics & Operational Research *Mathematics*	Y642	3FT deg	M	BCC	DO $		30$	BBBBB$	Ind		

Univ of LEEDS

TITLE	CODE	COURSE	SUBJECTS	A/AS	NO/C	RGNVQ	IB	SQA(H)	SQA	RATIO	A/AS
Artificial Intelligence-Mathematics	GG18	3FT/4FT deg	M g	BBC	1M+5D$	Ind	30$	ABBBC	Ind	12	
Astronomy-Mathematics	FG51	3FT deg	M+P g	BBC	1M+5D$	Ind	30$	ABBBB	Ind		
Biology-Mathematics	CG11	3FT/4FT deg	B+M g	BCC	1M+5D$	Ind	28$	BBBBC	Ind	11	
Biology-Statistics	CG14	3FT/4FT deg	B+M g	BCC	1M+5D$	Ind	28$	BBBBC	Ind	3	
Chemistry-Mathematics	FG11	3FT/4FT deg	C+M g	BBC	1M+5D$	Ind	30$	ABBBC	Ind	13	
Computer Science-Mathematics	GG15	3FT/4FT deg	M g	BBC	1M+5D$	Ind	30$	ABBBC	Ind	10	20/24
Computer Science-Statistics	GG45	3FT/4FT deg	M g	BCC	1M+5D$	Ind	28$	BBBBC	Ind	4	
Economics-Mathematics	GL11	3FT/4FT deg	M g	BBC	1M+5D$	Ind	30$	ABBBB	Ind	10	22/28

				98 expected requirements						*96 entry stats*

course details / 98 expected requirements / 96 entry stats

TITLE	CODE	COURSE	SUBJECTS	A/AS	ND/C	AGNVQ	IB	SQA(H)	SQA	RATIO A/AS
Economics-Statistics	GL41	3FT/4FT deg	M g	BBB	Ind	Ind	32$	CSYS	Ind	7
French-Mathematics	RG11	4FT deg	F+M g	BBC	Ind	Ind	30$	CSYS	Ind	9
Geography-Mathematics	FG81	3FT/4FT deg	Gy+M g	BCC	1M+5D$	Ind	28$	BBBBC	Ind	11
Geography-Mathematics	LG81	3FT deg	M+Gy g	BBC	1M+5D$	Ind	30$	ABBBB	Ind	21
Geography-Statistics	FG84	3FT deg	Gy+M g	BBC	Ind	Ind	Ind	Ind	Ind	
Management Studies-Mathematics	GN11	3FT/4FT deg	M g	BBC	1M+5D$	Ind	30$	CSYS	Ind	6	20/28
Management Studies-Statistics	GN41	3FT/4FT deg	M g	BBC	1M+5D$	Ind	30$	CSYS	Ind	25
Mathematical Engineering	H3G1	3FT/4FT deg	M+P+S g	BBC	4M+2D$	Ind	30$	ABBBC	Ind	5	14/26
Mathematical Studies	G150	3FT/4FTdeg	M g	20	1M+5D$	Ind	28$	CSYS	Ind	2	12/24
Mathematics	G100	3FT/4FT deg	M g	22	1M+5D$	Ind	30$	CSYS	Ind	7	16/30
Mathematics with Finance	G1N3	3FT deg	M g	24	Ind	Ind	32$	CSYS	Ind	
Mathematics-French	GR11	4FT deg	F+M g	BBC		Ind	30$	ABBBB	Ind	
Mathematics-German	GR12	4FT deg	G+M g	BBC		Ind	30$	ABBBB	Ind	
Mathematics-History and Philosophy of Science	GV15	3FT/4FT deg	M g	BBB	1M+5D$	Ind	32$	ABBBB	Ind	2
Mathematics-Music	GW13	3FT/4FT deg	M+Mu g	BBB	1M+5D$	Ind	32$	ABBBB	Ind	9
Mathematics-Philosophy	GV17	3FT/4FT deg	M g	BBB	1M+5D$	Ind	32$	ABBBB	Ind	13
Mathematics-Philosophy	VG71	3FT deg	M g	BBC	1M+5D$	Ind	30$	ABBBB	Ind	7
Mathematics-Physics	FG31	3FT/4FT deg	M+P g	BBC	1M+5D$	Ind	30$	ABBBC	Ind	13	20/28
Mathematics-Russian	RG81	4FT deg	M+R g	BBC	Ind	Ind	30$	CSYS	Ind	
Mathematics-Russian B	RGV1	4FT deg	M+L g	BBC	Ind	Ind	30$	CSYS	Ind	
Mathematics-Statistics	GG14	3FT/4FT deg	M g	BBC	1M+5D$	Ind	30$	ABBBC	Ind	12	22/26
Statistics-French	GR41	4FT deg	F+M g	BBC		Ind	30$	ABBBB	Ind	
Statistics-German	GR42	4FT deg	G+M g	BBC		Ind	30$	ABBBB	Ind	

LEEDS, TRINITY & ALL SAINTS Univ COLL

TITLE	CODE	COURSE	SUBJECTS	A/AS	ND/C	AGNVQ	IB	SQA(H)	SQA	RATIO A/AS
Mathematics-Management	GN11	3FT deg	M g	CCC-DE	Ind	X	24	BBCCC	Ind	5	10/14

Univ of LEICESTER

TITLE	CODE	COURSE	SUBJECTS	A/AS	ND/C	AGNVQ	IB	SQA(H)	SQA	RATIO A/AS
Mathematics	G100	3FT deg	M g	20	Ind	D$^	28$	BBBBC$	Ind	14/24
Mathematics	G102	3FT deg	M g	20	Ind	D$^	28$	BBBBC$	Ind	
Mathematics (Europe)	G101	4FT deg	M g	20	Ind	D$^	28$	BBBBC$	Ind	
Mathematics (MMath)	G105	4FT deg	M g	20	Ind	D$^	28$	BBBBC$	Ind	18/28
Mathematics (USA)	G103	3FT deg	M g	20	Ind	D$^	28$	BBBBC$	Ind	
Mathematics (USA) (MMath)	G107	4FT deg	M g	20	Ind	D$^	28$	BBBBC$		16/24
Mathematics and Computer Science	GG15	3FT deg	M g	20	Ind	D$^	28$	BBBBC$	Ind	12/24
Mathematics and Computer Science (Europe)	GG1M	4FT deg	M g	20	Ind	D$^	28$	BBBBC$	Ind	
Mathematics with Astronomy	G1F5	3FT deg	M g	20	Ind	D$^	28$	BBBBC$	Ind	
Mathematics with Astronomy	G1FN	4FT deg	M g	20	Ind	D$^	28$	BBBBS	Ind	
Mathematics with Astronomy (European Union)	G1FM	4FT deg	M g	20	Ind	D$^	28$	BBBBC$	Ind	
BSc with integrated foundation *Mathematics*	Y101	4EXT deg	* g		N	*			Ind	
Combined Arts *Pure Mathematics*	Y300	3FT deg	M g	BCC	DO $	D$^	30$	Ind	Ind	
Combined Science *Applied Mathematics*	Y100	3FT deg	M g	CCC	MO $	D$^	28$	BBBCC$	Ind	
Combined Science *Mathematical Statistics*	Y100	3FT deg	M	CCC	MO $	D$^	28 $	BBBCC$	Ind	
Combined Science *Pure Mathematics*	Y100	3FT deg	M g	CCC	MO $	D$^	28$	BBBCC$	HN	

Univ of LIVERPOOL

TITLE	CODE	COURSE	SUBJECTS	A/AS	ND/C	AGNVQ	IB	SQA(H)	SQA	RATIO A/AS
Economics and Mathematics	GL11	3FT deg	M	BCC	Ind	Ind	Ind	Ind	Ind	7	20/26
French and Pure Mathematics	GR11	4FT deg	F+M	BBD	Ind		29$	AABBC$	Ind	16
Geophysics (Mathematics)	F6G1	3FT deg	M+P g	18	MO $	DS^ go	31$	BBBCC$	Ind	3
Mathematical Physics (MMath)	FG3C	4FT deg	P+M	20	MO $	Ind	31$	BBBCC$	Ind	9

Mathematics and Statistics 52

TITLE	CODE	COURSE	SUBJECTS	A/AS	ND/C	AGNVQ	IB	SQA(H)	SQA	RATIO	A/AS
course details			*98 expected requirements*							*96 entry stats*	
Mathematical Sciences	G140	3FT deg	M g	20	MO $	D$^ go	31$	BBBCC$	Ind	6	
Mathematical Sciences	G142	4FT deg	* g	12	Ind	Ind	Dip	Ind	Ind	6	
Mathematical Sciences with Physics	G1F3	4FT deg	* g	12	Ind	Ind	Dip	Ind	Ind		
Mathematical Sciences with a European Language	G1T2	4FT deg	M g	20	MO $	D$^ go	31$	BBBCC$	Ind	23	
Mathematical Statistics	G400	3FT deg	M g	20	MO $	D$^ go	31$	BBBCC$	Ind	12	
Mathematics	G100	3FT deg	M g	20	MO $	D$^ go	31$	BBBCC$	Ind	6	12/24
Mathematics (MMath)	G101	4FT deg	M g	20	MO $	D$^ go	31$	BBBCC$	Ind	6	12/26
Mathematics and Computer Science	GG15	3FT deg	M g	20	MO $	D$^ go	31$	BBBCC$	Ind	7	16/30
Mathematics and Philosophy	GV17	3FT deg	M	BCC-BBC	Ind	Ind		BBBBB$	Ind	6	
Mathematics and Statistics	GG14	3FT deg	M g	20	MO $	D$^ go	31$	BBBCC$	Ind	5	18/24
Mathematics with Education	G1XX	3FT deg	M g	20	MO $	D$^ go	31$	BBBCC$	Ind	24	
Mathematics with Management	G1N1	3FT deg	M g	20	MO $	D$^ go	31$	BBBCC$	Ind	5	14/28
Mathematics with Materials Science	FG21	3FT deg	M+P/C g	20	MO $	D$^ go	31$	BBBCC$	Ind		
Mathematics with Ocean and Climate Studies	G1FR	3FT deg	M+S g	20	MO $	D$^ go	31$	BBBCC$	Ind		
Physics and Mathematics	FG31	3FT deg	M+P g	12	MO $	DS^ go	31$	BBBCC$	Ind	11	
Pure Mathematics	G120	3FT deg	M g	20	MO $	D$^ go	31	BBBCC	Ind	20	
Arts Combined *Mathematics*	Y401	3FT deg	M	BBC-BBB	Ind	Ind	30$	ABBB$	Ind		
Arts Combined *Pure Mathematics*	Y401	3FT deg	M	BBC-BBB	Ind	Ind	30$	ABBB$	Ind		
BA Combined Honours *Mathematics*	Y200	3FT deg	M g	BBB	Ind	Ind	Ind	Ind	Ind		
BSc Combined Honours *Mathematics*	Y100	3FT deg		20	MO $	Ind	31$	BBBCC$	Ind		

LIVERPOOL HOPE Univ COLL

TITLE	CODE	COURSE	SUBJECTS	A/AS	ND/C	AGNVQ	IB	SQA(H)	SQA	RATIO	A/AS
Mathematics/American Studies	QG41	3FT deg	M	12	8M	P*^	Ind	Ind	Ind	4	
Mathematics/Art	WG91	3FT deg	A/Fa+M	12	8M	PA^	Ind	Ind	Ind		
Mathematics/Drama & Theatre Studies	WG41	3FT deg	M g	12	8M	P*^ go	Ind	Ind	Ind		
Mathematics/Environmental Studies	FG91	3FT deg	M+B/Gy/En	10	6M	P$^	Ind	Ind	Ind		
Mathematics/French	RG11	3FT deg	F+M	12	8M	X	Ind	Ind	Ind		
Mathematics/Geography	FG81	3FT deg	M+Gy	10	6M	P$^	Ind	Ind	Ind	3	
Mathematics/History	VG11	3FT deg	H+M	12	8M	X	Ind	Ind	Ind	4	
Mathematics/Information Technology	GG51	3FT deg	M	10	6M	P*^	Ind	Ind	Ind	5	
Music/Mathematics	GW13	3FT deg	M+Mu	12	8M	PQ^	Ind	Ind	Ind	4	
Psychology/Mathematics	GC18	3FT deg	M	10	6M	P*^	Ind	Ind	Ind	17	
Sociology/Mathematics	GL13	3FT deg	M	12	8M	P*^	Ind	Ind	Ind	5	
Sport, Recreation & Physical Educ/Mathematics	GB16	3FT deg	M	10	6M	P*^	Ind	Ind	Ind		
Theology & Religious Studies/Mathematics	GV18	3FT deg	M	12	8M	P*^	Ind	Ind	Ind	3	

LIVERPOOL JOHN MOORES Univ

TITLE	CODE	COURSE	SUBJECTS	A/AS	ND/C	AGNVQ	IB	SQA(H)	SQA	RATIO	A/AS
Applied Statistics and Computing	G440	4SW deg	M g	10	3M	D$				1	
Mathematics, Statistics and Computing	G920	4SW deg	M	10	MO	D$				5	6/16

LONDON GUILDHALL Univ

TITLE	CODE	COURSE	SUBJECTS	A/AS	ND/C	AGNVQ	IB	SQA(H)	SQA	RATIO	A/AS
3D/Spatial Design and Mathematics	GW1F	3FT deg	Pf g	DD	MO	M$ go	24	Ind	Ind		
Mathematics & Communications & Audio Vis Prod St	GP14	3FT deg	* g	CC-CDD	MO+2D	M$ go	26	Ind	Ind		
Mathematics and Accounting	GN14	3FT deg	* g	DD	MO	M$ go	24	Ind	Ind		
Mathematics and Business	GN11	3FT deg	* g	CD-DDD	MO+2D	M$ go	24	Ind	Ind		
Mathematics and Business Economics	GL1C	3FT deg	* g	DD	MO	M$ go	24	Ind	Ind		
Mathematics and Business Information Technology	GG17	3FT deg	* g	DD	MO	M$ go	24	Ind	Ind		
Mathematics and Computing	GG15	3FT deg	* g	DD	MO	M$ go	24	Ind	Ind		
Mathematics and Design Studies	GW12	3FT deg	* g	CD-DDD	MO	M$ go	24	Ind	Ind		
Mathematics and Development Studies	GM19	3FT deg	* g	DD	MO	M$ go	24	Ind	Ind		
Mathematics and Economics	GL11	3FT deg	* g	DD	MO	M$ go	24	Ind	Ind		

				98 expected requirements						96 entry stats

course details — 98 expected requirements — 96 entry stats

TITLE	CODE	COURSE	SUBJECTS	A/AS	NO/C	AGNVQ	IB	SQA(H)	SQA	RATIO A/AS
Mathematics and English	GQ13	3FT deg	* g	CD-DDD	MO+2D	M$ go	26	Ind	Ind	
Mathematics and European Studies	GT12	3FT deg	* g	DD	MO	M$ go	24	Ind	Ind	
Mathematics and Financial Services	GN13	3FT deg	* g	DD	MO	M$ go	24	Ind	Ind	
Mathematics and Fine Art	GW11	3FT deg	* g	CC-CDD	MO+2D	M$ go	26	Ind	Ind	
Mathematics and French	GR11	4FT deg	* g	DD	MO	M$ go	24	Ind	Ind	
Mathematics and German	GR12	4FT deg	* g	DD	MO	M$ go	24	Ind	Ind	
Mathematics and International Relations	GM1C	3FT deg	* g	DD	MO	M$ go	24	Ind	Ind	
Mathematics and Law	GM13	3FT deg	* g	CC-CDD	MO+2D	M$ go	26	Ind	Ind	
Mathematics and Marketing	GN15	3FT deg	* g	CD-DDD	MO+2D	M$ go	26	Ind	Ind	
Mathematics with Business Applications	G1N1	3FT deg	M g	DE-EE	MO	P$ go	24	Ind	Ind	
Modern History and Mathematics	GV11	3FT deg	* g	DD	MO	M$ go	24	Ind	Ind	
Multimedia Systems and Mathematics	GG1M	3FT deg	* g	DD	MO	M$ go	24	Ind	Ind	
Politics and Mathematics	GM11	3FT deg	* g	DD	MO	M$ go	24	Ind	Ind	
Product Development & Manufacture & Mathematics	GJ14	3FT deg	* g	DD	MO	M$ go	24	Ind	Ind	
Psychology and Mathematics	CG81	3FT deg	* g	CD-DDD	MO+2D	M$ go	26	Ind	Ind	
Social Policy & Management and Mathematics	GL14	3FT deg	* g	CD-DDD	MO	M$ go	24	Ind	Ind	
Sociology and Mathematics	GL13	3FT deg	* g	CD-DDD	MO	M$ go	24	Ind	Ind	
Spanish and Mathematics	GR14	4FT deg	* g	DD	MO	M$ go	24	Ind	Ind	
Taxation and Mathematics	GN1H	3FT deg	* g	DD	MO	M$ go	24	Ind	Ind	
Textile Furnishing Design and Mathematics	GW1G	3FT deg	Pf g	DD	MO	M$ go	24	Ind	Ind	
Modular Programme _Mathematics_	Y400	3FT deg	* g	CC-DD	MO	M$ go	24	Ind	Ind	

LSE: LONDON Sch of Economics (Univ of London)

TITLE	CODE	COURSE	SUBJECTS	A/AS	NO/C	AGNVQ	IB	SQA(H)	SQA	RATIO A/AS
Mathematics and Economics	GL11	3FT deg	M	ABB	Ind	X	$	Ind	Ind	6 28/30
Philosophy and Mathematics	GV17	3FT deg	M	BBB	Ind	X	$	Ind	Ind	9
Business Mathematics and Statistics _Applicable Mathematics_	Y240	3FT deg	M	BBB-AAB	Ind	X	$	Ind	Ind	
Business Mathematics and Statistics _Applied Statistics_	Y240	3FT deg	M	BBB-AAB	Ind	X	$	Ind	Ind	

LOUGHBOROUGH Univ

TITLE	CODE	COURSE	SUBJECTS	A/AS	NO/C	AGNVQ	IB	SQA(H)	SQA	RATIO A/AS
Industrial Mathematics	G167	3FT deg	M	BCC			28$	Ind		3
Industrial Mathematics (4 Yr SW)	G168	4SW deg	M	BCC			28$	Ind		2
Mathematical Engineering	J920	3FT deg	M	BCC	3M+2D		28$	Ind	Ind	10
Mathematical Engineering (4 Yr SW)	J921	4SW deg	M	BCC	3M+2D		28$	Ind	Ind	4
Mathematics	G100	3FT deg	M	BCC			28$	Ind		5 14/26
Mathematics (4 Yr MMath)	G103	4FT deg	M	BCC			28$	Ind		7
Mathematics (4 Yr SW)	G101	4SW deg	M	BCC			28$	Ind		5
Mathematics and Computing	GG15	3FT deg	M	BCC			28$	Ind		4 14/24
Mathematics and Computing (4 Yr SW)	GG51	4SW deg	M	BCC			28$	Ind		3 14/26
Mathematics with Accountancy	G1N4	3FT deg	M	BCC			28$	Ind		
Mathematics with Accountancy (4 Yr SW)	G1NK	4SW deg	M	BCC			28$	Ind		
Mathematics with Economics	G1L1	3FT deg	M	BCC			28$	Ind		6 16/24
Mathematics with Economics (4 Yr SW)	G1LC	4SW deg	M	BCC			28$	Ind		4
Mathematics with Education	G1X9	3FT deg	M	BCC			28$	Ind		
Mathematics with Management	G1N1	3FT deg	M	BCC			28$	Ind		
Mathematics with Management (4 Yr SW)	G1NC	4SW deg	M	BCC			28$	Ind		
Physical Education and Sports Science and Maths	BG61	3FT deg	M	24			30$	Ind		
Physics and Mathematics	FG31	3FT deg	M+P	BBC			28$	Ind		7 20/22
Physics and Mathematics (4 Yr SW)	GF13	4SW deg	M+P	BBC			28$	Ind		3
Physics and Mathematics with a year in Europe	FG3C	4SW deg	M+P	BBC	3M+2D		28$	Ind		

			98 expected requirements							96 entry stats

course details

TITLE	CODE	COURSE	SUBJECTS	A/AS	ND/C	AGNVQ	IB	SQA(H)	SQA	RATIO A/AS
LUTON Univ										
Accounting with Applied Statistics	N4G4	3FT deg	g	12-16	MO/DO	M/D	32	BBCC	Ind	
Accounting with Mathematical Sciences	N4GC	3FT deg	g	12-16	MO/DO	M/D	32	BBCC	Ind	
Accounting with Mathematics	N4GD	3FT deg	g	12-16	MO/DO	M/D	32	BBCC	Ind	
Applied Statistics and Accounting	GN4K	3FT deg	g	12-16	MO/DO	M/D	32	BBCC	Ind	
Biology and Applied Statistics	CG14	3FT deg	g	12-16	MO/DO	M/D	32	BBCC	Ind	
Biology with Applied Statistics	C1G4	3FT deg	g	12-16	MO/DO	M/D	32	BBCC	Ind	
Biology with Mathematical Sciences	C1GC	3FT deg	g	12-16	MO/DO	M/D	32	BBCC	Ind	
Biology with Mathematics	C1GD	3FT deg	g	12-16	MO/DO	M/D	32	BBCC	Ind	
Broadcasting & Media Tech with Mathematical Scis	H6GD	3FT deg		12-16	MO/DO	M/D	32	BBCC	Ind	
Broadcasting & Media Technology with Mathematics	H6G1	3FT deg		12-16	MO/DO	M/D	32	BBCC	Ind	
Built Environment and Applied Statistics	GN48	3FT deg	g	12-16	MO/DO	M/D	32	BBCC	Ind	
Built Environment with Applied Statistics	N8G4	3FT deg	g	12-16	MO/DO	M/D	32	BBCC	Ind	
Built Environment with Mathematical Sciences	N8G1	3FT deg	g	12-16	MO/DO	M/D	32	BBCC	Ind	
Built Environment with Mathematics	N8GC	3FT deg	g	12-16	MO/DO	M/D	32	BBCC	Ind	
Business Systems and Applied Statistics	GN4C	3FT deg	g	12-16	MO/DO	M/D	32	BBCC	Ind	
Business Systems with Applied Statistics	N1GK	3FT deg	g	12-16	MO/DO	M/D	32	BBCC	Ind	
Business Systems with Mathematical Sciences	N1GD	3FT deg	g	12-16	MO/DO	M/D	32	BBCC	Ind	
Business Systems with Mathematics	NG1D	3FT deg	g	12-16	MO/DO	M/D	32	BBCC	Ind	
Business and Applied Statistics	GN41	3FT deg	g	12-16	MO/DO	M/D	32	BBCC	Ind	
Business with Applied Statistics	N1G4	3FT deg	g	12-16	MO/DO	M/D	32	BBCC	Ind	
Business with Mathematical Sciences	N1GC	3FT deg	g	12-16	MO/DO	M/D	32	BBCC	Ind	
Business with Mathematics	NGCD	3FT deg	g	12-16	MO/DO	M/D	32	BBCC	Ind	
Computer Science and Applied Statistics	GG45	3FT deg	g	12-16	MO/DO	M/D	32	BBCC	Ind	
Digital Systems Design with Mathematical Science	H6GC	3FT deg	g	12-16	MO/DO	M/D	32	BBCC	Ind	
Environmental Science and Applied Statistics	FG94	3FT deg	g	12-16	MO/DO	M/D	32	BBCC	Ind	
Environmental Science with Applied Statistics	F9G4	3FT deg	g	12-16	MO/DO	M/D	32	BBCC	Ind	
Environmental Science with Mathematical Sciences	F9GC	3FT deg	g	12-16	MO/DO	M/D	32	BBCC	Ind	
Environmental Science with Mathematics	F9GD	3FT deg	g	12-16	MO/DO	M/D	32	BBCC	Ind	
Environmental Studies with Mathematics	F9G1	3FT deg		12-16	MO/DO	M/D	32	BBCC	Ind	
Geology and Applied Statistics	FG64	3FT deg	g	12-16	MO/DO	M/D	32	BBCC	Ind	
Geology with Applied Statistics	F6G4	3FT deg	g	12-16	MO/DO	M/D	32	BBCC	Ind	
Geology with Mathematical Sciences	F6GC	3FT deg	g	12-16	MO/DO	M/D	32	BBCC	Ind	
Geology with Mathematics	F6GD	3FT deg	g	12-16	MO/DO	M/D	32	BBCC	Ind	
Health Studies and Applied Statistics	BG49	3FT deg	g	12-16	MO/DO	M/D	32	BBCC	Ind	
Health Studies with Applied Statistics	B9G4	3FT deg	g	12-16	MO/DO	M/D	32	BBCC	Ind	
Health Studies with Mathematical Sciences	B9GD	3FT deg	g	12-16	MO/DO	M/D	32	BBCC	Ind	
Health Studies with Mathematics	BG9C	3FT deg	g	12-16	MO/DO	M/D	32	BBCC	Ind	
Mapping Science and Applied Statistics	FG84	3FT deg	g	12-16	MO/DO	M/D	32	BBCC	Ind	
Mapping Science with Applied Statistics	F8G4	3FT deg	g	12-16	MO/DO	M/D	32	BBCC	Ind	
Mapping Science with Mathematical Sciences	F8GD	3FT deg	g	12-16	MO/DO	M/D	32	BBCC	Ind	
Mapping Science with Mathematics	FG8D	3FT deg	g	12-16	MO/DO	M/D	32	BBCC	Ind	
Marketing and Applied Statistics	GN45	3FT deg	g	12-16	MO/DO	M/D	32	BBCC	Ind	
Marketing with Applied Statistics	N5G4	3FT deg	g	12-16	MO/DO	M/D	32	BBCC	Ind	
Marketing with Mathematics	NG5C	3FT deg	g	12-16	MO/DO	M/D	32	BBCC	Ind	
Mathematical Sciences	G140	3FT deg	g	12-16	MO/DO	M/D	32	BBCC	Ind	
Mathematical Sciences & Artificial Intelligence	GG8C	3FT deg		12-16	MO/DO	M/D	32	BBCC	Ind	
Mathematical Sciences and Accounting	GN14	3FT deg	g	12-16	MO/DO	M/D	32	BBCC	Ind	
Mathematical Sciences and Biology	CG11	3FT deg	g	12-16	MO/DO	M/D	32	BBCC	Ind	
Mathematical Sciences and Building Conservation	KG2C	3FT deg		12-16	MO/DO	M/D	32	BBCC	Ind	
Mathematical Sciences and Built Environment	GN18	3FT deg	g	12-16	MO/DO	M/D	32	BBCC	Ind	
Mathematical Sciences and Business	GN11	3FT deg	g	12-16	MO/DO	M/D	32	BBCC	Ind	

course details   98 expected requirements   *96 entry stats*

TITLE	CODE	COURSE	SUBJECTS	A/AS	ND/C	AGNVQ	IB	SQA(H)	SQA	RATIO A/AS
Mathematical Sciences and Business Systems	GN1C	3FT deg	g	12-16	MO/DO	M/D	32	BBCC	Ind	
Mathematical Sciences and Computer Applications	GG6C	3FT deg		12-16	MO/DO	M/D	32	BBCC	Ind	
Mathematical Sciences and Computer Science	GG15	3FT deg	g	12-16	MO/DO	M/D	32	BBCC	Ind	
Mathematical Sciences and Environmental Science	FG91	3FT deg	g	12-16	MO/DO	M/D	32	BBCC	Ind	
Mathematical Sciences and Geology	FG61	3FT deg	g	12-16	MO/DO	M/D	32	BBCC	Ind	
Mathematical Sciences and Health Studies	BG91	3FT deg	g	12-16	MO/DO	M/D	32	BBCC	Ind	
Mathematical Sciences and Mapping Science	FG81	3FT deg	g	12-16	MO/DO	M/D	32	BBCC	Ind	
Mathematical Sciences and Marketing	GN15	3FT deg	g	12-16	MO/DO	M/D	32	BBCC	Ind	
Mathematical Sciences with Accounting	G1N4	3FT deg	g	12-16	MO/DO	M/D	32	BBCC	Ind	
Mathematical Sciences with Biology	G1C1	3FT deg	g	12-16	MO/DO	M/D	32	BBCC	Ind	
Mathematical Sciences with Built Environment	G1N8	3FT deg	g	12-16	MO/DO	M/D	32	BBCC	Ind	
Mathematical Sciences with Business	G1N1	3FT deg	g	12-16	MO/DO	M/D	32	BBCC	Ind	
Mathematical Sciences with Business Systems	G1NC	3FT deg	g	12-16	MO/DO	M/D	32	BBCC	Ind	
Mathematical Sciences with Environmental Science	G1F9	3FT deg	g	12-16	MO/DO	M/D	32	BBCC	Ind	
Mathematical Sciences with French	G1R1	3FT deg	F g	12-16	MO/DO	M/D	32	BBCC	Ind	
Mathematical Sciences with Geographical Info Sys	G120	3FT deg	g	12-16	MO/DO	M/D	32	BBCC	Ind	
Mathematical Sciences with Geology	G1F6	3FT deg	g	12-16	MO/DO	M/D	32	BBCC	Ind	
Mathematical Sciences with German	G1R2	3FT deg	G g	12-16	MO/DO	M/D	32	BBCC	Ind	
Mathematical Sciences with Italian	G1R3	3FT deg	I g	12-16	MO/DO	M/D	32	BBCC	Ind	
Mathematical Sciences with Japanese	G1T4	3FT deg	L g	12-16	MO/DO	M/D	32	BBCC	Ind	
Mathematical Sciences with Management	G1ND	3FT deg	g	12-16	MO/DO	M/D	32	BBCC	Ind	
Mathematical Sciences with Mapping Science	G1F8	3FT deg	g	12-16	MO/DO	M/D	32	BBCC	Ind	
Mathematical Sciences with Marketing	G1N5	3FT deg	g	12-16	MO/DO	M/D	32	BBCC	Ind	
Mathematical Sciences with Org Behaviour	G1L7	3FT deg	g	12-16	MO/DO	M/D	32	BBCC	Ind	
Mathematical Sciences with Physical Geography	GFC8	3FT deg	g	12-16	MO/DO	M/D	32	BBCC	Ind	
Mathematical Sciences with Public Policy & Mgt	G1M1	3FT deg	g	12-16	MO/DO	M/D	32	BBCC	Ind	
Mathematical Sciences with Social Studies	G1L3	3FT deg	g	12-16	MO/DO	M/D	32	BBCC	Ind	
Mathematical Sciences with Spanish	G1R4	3FT deg	Sp g	12-16	MO/DO	M/D	32	BBCC	Ind	
Mathematics and Accounting	NG41	3FT deg	g	12-16	MO/DO	M/D	32	BBCC	Ind	
Mathematics and Applied Statistics	GG14	3FT deg		12-16	MO/DO	M/D	32	BBCC	Ind	
Mathematics and Artificial Intelligence	GG81	3FT deg		12-16	MO/DO	M/D	32	BBCC	Ind	
Mathematics and Biology	GC11	3FT deg	g	12-16	MO/DO	M/D	32	BBCC	Ind	
Mathematics and Building Conservation	KG21	3FT deg		12-16	MO/DO	M/D	32	BBCC	Ind	
Mathematics and Built Environment	NG81	3FT deg	g	12-16	MO/DO	M/D	32	BBCC	Ind	
Mathematics and Business	NG11	3FT deg	g	12-16	MO/DO	M/D	32	BBCC	Ind	
Mathematics and Business Systems	NGC1	3FT deg	g	12-16	MO/DO	M/D	32	BBCC	Ind	
Mathematics and Computer Science	GG51	3FT deg	g	12-16	MO/DO	M/D	32	BBCC	Ind	
Mathematics and Environmental Science	GF19	3FT deg	g	12-16	MO/DO	M/D	32	BBCC	Ind	
Mathematics and Geology	GF16	3FT deg	g	12-16	MO/DO	M/D	32	BBCC	Ind	
Mathematics and Health Studies	GB19	3FT deg	g	12-16	MO/DO	M/D	32	BBCC	Ind	
Mathematics and Mapping Science	GF18	3FT deg	g	12-16	MO/DO	M/D	32	BBCC	Ind	
Mathematics and Marketing	NG51	3FT deg	g	12-16	MO/DO	M/D	32	BBCC	Ind	
Mathematics with Social Studies	G1LH	3FT deg	g	12-16	MO/DO	M/D	32	BBCC	Ind	
Organisational Behaviour & Mathematical Sciences	GL17	3FT deg	g	12-16	MO/DO	M/D	32	BBCC	Ind	
Organisational Behaviour and Applied Statistics	GL47	3FT deg	g	12-16	MO/DO	M/D	32	BBCC	Ind	
Organisational Behaviour and Mathematics	LG71	3FT deg	g	12-16	MO/DO	M/D	32	BBCC	Ind	
Physical Geography and Applied Statistics	GF4V	3FT deg	g	12-16	MO/DO	M/D	32	BBCC	Ind	
Physical Geography and Mathematical Sciences	FGV1	3FT deg	g	12-16	MO/DO	M/D	32	BBCC	Ind	
Physical Geography and Mathematics	GF1V	3FT deg	g	12-16	MO/DO	M/D	32	BBCC	Ind	
Physical Geography with Applied Statistics	F8GK	3FT deg	g	12-16	MO/DO	M/D	32	BBCC	Ind	
Physical Geography with Mathematical Sciences	FG8C	3FT deg	g	12-16	MO/DO	M/D	32	BBCC	Ind	
Physical Geography with Mathematics	FGVC	3FT deg	g	12-16	MO/DO	M/D	32	BBCC	Ind	

Mathematics and Statistics 52

| | course details | | | 98 expected requirements | | | | | | 96 entry stats |

TITLE	CODE	COURSE	SUBJECTS	A/AS	ND/C	AGNVQ	IB	SQA(H)	SQA	RATIO A/AS
Public Policy & Management and Mathematics	MG11	3FT deg	g	12-16	M0/D0	M/D	32	BBCC	Ind	
Public Policy & Management with Mathematical Sci	M1GD	3FT deg	g	12-16	M0/D0	M/D	32	BBCC	Ind	
Public Policy & Management with Mathematics	MG1C	3FT deg	g	12-16	M0/D0	M/D	32	BBCC	Ind	
Public Policy & Mgt and Mathematical Sciences	GM11	3FT deg	g	12-16	M0/D0	M/D	32	BBCC	Ind	
Public Policy & Mgt with Applied Statistics	M1G4	3FT deg	g	12-16	M0/D0	M/D	32	BBCC	Ind	
Public Policy and Mgt and Applied Statistics	GM4C	3FT deg	g	12-16	M0/D0	M/D	32	BBCC	Ind	
Social Policy and Applied Statistics	LG44	3FT deg		12-16	M0/D0	M/D	32	BBCC	Ind	
Social Policy with Applied Statistics	L4G4	3FT deg		12-16	M0/D0	M/D	32	BBCC	Ind	
Social Studies and Applied Statistics	GL43	3FT deg	g	12-16	M0/D0	M/D	32	BBCC	Ind	
Social Studies and Mathematical Sciences	GL13	3FT deg	g	12-16	M0/D0	M/D	32	BBCC	Ind	
Social Studies and Mathematics	LG31	3FT deg	g	12-16	M0/D0	M/D	32	BBCC	Ind	
Social Studies with Applied Statistics	L3G4	3FT deg	g	12-16	M0/D0	M/D	32	BBCC	Ind	
Social Studies with Mathematical Sciences	L3GC	3FT deg	g	12-16	M0/D0	M/D	32	BBCC	Ind	
Social Studies with Mathematics	L3GD	3FT deg	g	12-16	M0/D0	M/D	32	BBCC	Ind	
Software Engineering and Mathematical Sciences	GG7C	3FT deg		12-16	M0/D0	M/D	32	BBCC	Ind	
Software Engineering and Mathematics	GG71	3FT deg		12-16	M0/D0	M/D	32	BBCC	Ind	

Univ of MANCHESTER

TITLE	CODE	COURSE	SUBJECTS	A/AS	ND/C	AGNVQ	IB	SQA(H)	SQA	RATIO A/AS
Computer Science and Mathematics	GG15	3FT deg	M	BBC	X	D$^	30$	CSYS$	X	10 18/30
Mathematics	G100	3FT deg	M	22-24	Ind		30$	CSYS	Ind	6 18/28
Mathematics (MMath)	G103	4FT deg	M	22-24	Ind		30$	CSYS	Ind	5 18/30
Mathematics and English	GQ13	3FT deg	M+E	24	Ind		30$	X	Ind	4
Mathematics and Philosophy	GV17	3FT deg	M	22-24	Ind		30$	CSYS	Ind	13
Mathematics and Physics (BSc/MMath & Phys)	FG3C	3FT/4FT deg	M+P	BBC	4M+2D$	D^	30$	CSYS	Ind	20
Mathematics with Business and Management	G1N1	3FT deg	M	22-24	Ind		30$	CSYS	Ind	6 21/30
Mathematics with English	G1Q3	3FT deg	M+E	24	Ind		30$	CSYS	Ind	7
Mathematics with a Modern Language	G101	4FT deg	M+L	24	Ind		30$	CSYS	Ind	4 20/30

UMIST (Manchester)

TITLE	CODE	COURSE	SUBJECTS	A/AS	ND/C	AGNVQ	IB	SQA(H)	SQA	RATIO A/AS
Mathematical Physics	F3G1	3FT deg	M+P g	BBD	Ind	Ind	30$	CSYS	Ind	
Mathematical Physics (MPhys)	F3GC	4FT deg	M+P g	BBD	Ind	Ind	30$	CSYS	Ind	
Mathematics	G100	3FT deg	M g	BBC	Ind	Ind	30$	CSYS	Ind	10 16/30
Mathematics (MMath)	G101	4FT deg	M g	BBC	Ind	Ind	30$	CSYS	Ind	5 16/30
Mathematics and Language Studies (French)	GRD1	4FT deg	M+F g	BBC	Ind	Ind	30$	CSYS	Ind	5
Mathematics and Language Studies (German)	GRD2	4FT deg	M+G g	BBC	Ind	Ind	30$	CSYS	Ind	2
Mathematics and Management Sciences	GN11	3FT deg	M g	BBC	Ind	M*^ go	30$	CSYS	Ind	4 16/26
Mathematics with Astrophysics	G1F5	3FT deg	M g	BBC	Ind	Ind	30$	CSYS	Ind	8 22/28
Mathematics with Study in Europe	G1T2	4FT deg	M g	BBC	Ind	Ind	30$	CSYS	Ind	10
Mathematics with Study in Europe (MMath)	G102	4FT deg	M g	BBC	Ind	Ind	30$	CSYS	Ind	11
Mathematics, Statistics and Operational Research	G434	3FT deg	M g	BBC	Ind	Ind	30$	CSYS	Ind	3 16/24

MANCHESTER METROPOLITAN Univ

TITLE	CODE	COURSE	SUBJECTS	A/AS	ND/C	AGNVQ	IB	SQA(H)	SQA	RATIO A/AS
Applicable Mathematics	G110	3FT deg	M g	12	2M+4D$	M$	29$	BBBBC$	Ind	
Applicable Mathematics (Foundation)	G108▼	4FT deg	M/P	E	2M $	P$	$	$	Ind	
Applied Physics/Applicable Mathematics	FG31	3FT deg	M+P g	12	5M $	M$	27$	BCCCC$	Ind	
Biology/Applicable Mathematics	CG11	3FT deg	M g	12	5M $	M$	27$	BCCCC$	Ind	
Business Mathematics	G190	3FT deg	M/P/Ec g	12-18	2M+2D$	M$	28	BBBCC$	Ind	
Business Mathematics (Foundation)	G198▼	4FT deg	M/P	E	2M $	P$	$	$	Ind	
Business Mathematics/Applicable Mathematics	G140	3FT deg	M g	12	5M $	M$	27$	BCCCC$	Ind	10/16
Business Mathematics/Applied Physics	FG3C	3FT deg	M+P g	12	5M $	M$	27$	BCCCC$	Ind	
Business Mathematics/Biology	CG1C	3FT deg	M/P/Ec g	12	5M $	M$	27$	BCCCC$	Ind	
Chemistry/Applicable Mathematics	FG11	3FT deg	M+C g	12	4M $	M$	26$	CCCCC$	Ind	
Computer Technology/Applicable Mathematics	GGM1	3FT deg	M g	12	5M $	M$	27	BCCCC$	Ind	
Computer Technology/Business Mathematics	GGMC	3FT deg	M/P/Ec g	12	5M $	M$	27$	BCCCC$	Ind	

course details			98 expected requirements							96 entry stats

TITLE	CODE	COURSE	SUBJECTS	A/AS	ND/C	AGNVQ	IB	SQA(H)	SQA	RATIO A/AS
Computing Science/Applicable Mathematics	GG15	3FT deg	M g	16	1M+3D$	M$	28$	BBBCC$	Ind	
Computing Science/Business Mathematics	GGC5	3FT deg	M/P/Ec g	16	1M+3D$	M$	28$	BBBCC$	Ind	
Economics/Applicable Mathematics	GL11	3FT deg	M g	16	1M+3D$	M$	28$	BBBCC$	Ind	
Economics/Business Mathematics	GLC1	3FT deg	M/P/Ec g	16	1M+3D$	M$	28$	BBBCC$	Ind	
Electronics/Business Mathematics	GHCP	3FT deg	M/P/Ec g	12	5M $	M$	27$	BCCCC$	Ind	
Environmental Mathematics and Modelling	FG91	3FT/4SW deg	M+S	12	3M	M$	Ind	Ind	Ind	
Environmental Mathematics and Modelling (Found)	FG9D	4FT deg	M/P	E	2M $	P$	$	$	Ind	
Environmental Studies/Busines Mathematics	FG9C	3FT deg	M/P/Ec g	16	1M+3D$	M$	28$	BBBCC$	Ind	
European Studies/Business Mathematics	GTC2	3FT deg	M/P/Ec g	16	1M+3D$	M$	28$	BBBCC$	Ind	
Geography/Applicable Mathematics	GL18	3FT deg	M g	18	2M+4D$	M$	29$	BBBBC$	Ind	
Languages/Applicable Mathematics	GT19	3FT deg	M g	18	2M+4D$	M$	29$	BBBBC$	Ind	
Languages/Business Mathematics	GTC9	3FT deg	M/P/Ec g	18	2M+4D$	M$	29$	BBBBC$	Ind	
Manufacturing/Applicable Mathematics	GH17	3FT deg	M g	12	5M $	M$	27$	BCCCC$	Ind	
Materials Science/Business Mathematics	GFC2	3FT deg	M/P g	12	5M $	M$	27$	BCCCC$	Ind	
Physics Studies/Applicable Mathematics	FGH1	3FT deg	M g	12	5M $	M$	27$	BCCCC$	Ind	
Physics Studies/Business Mathematics	FGHC	3FT deg	P/M/Ec g	12	5M $	M$	27$	BCCCC$	Ind	
Polymer Science/Applicable Mathematics	GJ14	3FT deg	M+C g	12	5M $	M$	27$	BCCCC$	Ind	
Polymer Science/Business Mathematics	GJC4	3FT deg	C+M/P/Ec g	12	5M $	M$	27$	BCCCC$	Ind	
Psychology/Business Mathematics	GLC7	3FT deg	M/P/Ec g	18	2M+4D$	D$	29$	BBBBC$	Ind	
Scientific Instrumentation/Applicable Maths	GH16	3FT deg	M g	12	5M $	M$	27$	BCCCC$	Ind	
Scientific Instrumentation/Business Mathematics	GHC6	3FT deg	M/P g	12	5M $	M$	27$	BCCCC$	Ind	
Social Studies of Technology/Applicable Maths	GL13	3FT deg	M g	12	5M $	M$	27$	BCCCC$	Ind	
Social Studs of Technology/Business Mathematics	GLC3	3FT deg	M/P/Ec g	12	5M $	M$	27$	BCCCC$	Ind	
Combined Studies (Foundation) *Applicable Mathematics*	Y108▼	4FT deg	M/P	E	2M $	P$	$	$	Ind	
Combined Studies (Foundation) *Business Mathematics*	Y108▼	4FT deg	M/P	E	2M $	P$	$	$	Ind	
Mathematical Studies	009G	2FT HND	M	E	1M $		Ind	D$	Ind$	3/9

MIDDLESEX Univ

Mathematical Sciences	G140▼	3FT deg	M g	8	5M	X	24	Ind	Ind	
Mathematics Foundation	G108▼	4EXT deg	* g	E	N	P$ go	Ind	CC	Ind	
Mathematics for Business	G1N1▼	4SW deg	M g	8	MO	M$^ go	24	CCCC	Ind	
Joint Honours Degree *Mathematics*	Y400	3FT deg	M g	10	5M	X	Ind	CCCC	Ind	
Joint Honours Degree *Statistics*	Y400	3FT deg	* g	10	3M	M$ go	24	CCCC	Ind	

NAPIER Univ

Mathematical Sciences	G140	4FT/5SW deg	M	CC	Ind	Ind	Ind	BBC	Ind	
Mathematics with Computing	G1G5	4FT/5SW deg	M	CC	Ind	Ind	Ind	BBC	Ind	
Mathematics with Financial Studies	G1N3	4FT/5SW deg	M	CC	Ind	Ind	Ind	BBC	Ind	
Mathematics with Technology	G1H1	4FT/5SW deg	M	CC	Ind	Ind	Ind	BBC	Ind	

NENE COLLEGE

Business Administration with Management Science	N1G4	3FT deg	g	10	M+1D	M	24	BCC	Ind	
Business Administration with Mathematics	N1G1	3FT deg	M	10	M+1D	M	24	BCC	Ind	
Earth Science with Management Science	F9G4	3FT deg	g	DD	5M	M	24	CCC	Ind	
Earth Science with Mathematics	F9G1	3FT deg	M	DD	5M	M	24	CCC	Ind	
Ecology with Management Science	C9G4	3FT deg	g	DD	5M	M	24	CCC	Ind	
Economics with Management Science	L1G4	3FT deg	g	6	5M	M	24	CCC	Ind	
Economics with Mathematics	L1G1	3FT deg	M	6	5M	M	24	CCC	Ind	
Education with Mathematics	X9G1	3FT deg	M	DD	5M	M	24	CCC	Ind	
English with Mathematics	Q3G1	3FT deg	M	CC	4M+1D	M	24	CCC	Ind	
Industrial Archaeology with Management Science	V6G4	3FT deg	g	10	5M	M	24	CCC	Ind	

Mathematics and Statistics   52

course details			**98 expected requirements**							**96 entry stats**
TITLE	CODE	COURSE	SUBJECTS	A/AS	ND/C	AGNVQ	IB	SQA(H)	SQA	RATIO A/AS
Industry and Enterprise with Mathematics	H1G1	3FT deg	M	EE	3M	P	24	CCC	Ind	
Information Systems with Management Science	G5G4	3FT deg	g	6	5M	M	24	CCC	Ind	
Information Systems with Mathematics	G5G1	3FT deg	M	6	5M	M	24	CCC	Ind	
Law with Mathematics	M3G1	3FT deg	g	10	M3+2D	M	24	CCC	Ind	
Management Science with Business Administration	G4N1	3FT deg	g	DD	5M	M	24	CCC	Ind	
Management Science with Economics	G4L1	3FT deg	g	DD	5M	M	24	CCC	Ind	
Management Science with Education	G4X9	3FT deg	g	DD	5M	M	24	CCC	Ind	
Management Science with Energy Management	G4J9	3FT deg	g	DD	5M	M	24	CCC	Ind	
Management Science with French	G4R1	3FT deg	F g	DD	5M	M	24	CCC	Ind	
Management Science with Industrial Archaeology	G4V6	3FT deg	g	DD	5M	M	24	CCC	Ind	
Management Science with Information Systems	G4G5	3FT deg	g	DD	5M	M	24	CCC	Ind	
Management Science with Marketing Communications	G4N5	3FT deg	g	DD	5M	M	24	CCC	Ind	
Management Science with Mathematics	G4G1	3FT deg	M	DD	5M	M	24	CCC	Ind	
Management Science with Property Management	G4N8	3FT deg	g	DD	5M	M	24	CCC	Ind	
Management Science with Psychology	G4C8	3FT deg	g	DD	5M	M	24	CCC	Ind	
Management Science with Sociology	G4L3	3FT deg	g	DD	5M	M	24	CCC	Ind	
Management Science with Sport Studies	G4N7	3FT deg	g	DD	5M	M	24	CCC	Ind	
Mathematics with Architectural Studies	G1V4	3FT deg	M	DD	Ind	Ind	24	CCC	Ind	
Mathematics with Art and Design	G1W2	3FT deg	M	DD	Ind	Ind	24	CCC	Ind	
Mathematics with Business Administration	G1N1	3FT deg	M	DD	Ind	Ind	24	CCC	Ind	
Mathematics with Chemistry and the Environment	G1F1	3FT deg	M	DD	Ind	Ind	24	CCC	Ind	
Mathematics with Ecology	G1C9	3FT deg	M	DD	Ind	Ind	24	CCC	Ind	
Mathematics with Economics	G1L1	3FT deg	M	DD	Ind	Ind	24	CCC	Ind	
Mathematics with Education	G1X9	3FT deg	M	DD	Ind	Ind	24	CCC	Ind	
Mathematics with Geography	G1F8	3FT deg	M	DD	Ind	Ind	24	CCC	Ind	
Mathematics with Industry and Enterprise	G1H1	3FT deg	M	DD	Ind	Ind	24	CCC	Ind	
Mathematics with Information Systems	G1G5	3FT deg	M	DD	Ind	Ind	24	CCC	Ind	
Mathematics with Law	G1M3	3FT deg	M g	DD	Ind	Ind	24	CCC	Ind	
Mathematics with Management Science	G1G4	3FT deg	M	DD	Ind	Ind	24	CCC	Ind	
Mathematics with Marketing Communications	G1N5	3FT deg	M	DD	Ind	Ind	24	CCC	Ind	
Mathematics with Music	G1W3	3FT deg	Mu+M	DD	Ind	Ind	24	CCC	Ind	
Mathematics with Philosophy	G1V7	3FT deg	M	DD	Ind	Ind	24	CCC	Ind	
Mathematics with Psychology	G1C8	3FT deg	M	DD	Ind	Ind	24	CCC	Ind	
Mathematics with Sport Studies	G1N7	3FT deg	M	DD	Ind	Ind	24	CCC	Ind	
Mathematics with Wastes Management & the Environ	G1FX	3FT deg	M	DD	Ind	Ind	24	CCC	Ind	
Mgt Sci with Personal & Organisational Develop	G4N6	3FT deg	g	EE	5M	M	24	CCC	Ind	
Music with Mathematics	W3G1	3FT deg	Mu+M	DD	5M	M	24	CCC	Ind	
Psychology with Management Science	C8G4	3FT deg	g	CC	5M+1D	M	24	CCC	Ind	
Psychology with Mathematics	C8G1	3FT deg	M	CC	5M+1D	M	24	CCC	Ind	
Sport Studies with Management Science	N7G4	3FT deg	Ss/Pe g	12	M+2D	M	24	BBB	Ind	
Sport Studies with Mathematics	N7G1	3FT deg	M+Ss/Pe	12	M+2D	M	24	BBB	Ind	

Univ of NEWCASTLE

Accounting and Mathematics	NG41	3FT deg	<u>M</u>	20	4M+1D	Ind	30$	AAABB	Ind	10 20/24
Accounting and Statistics	NG44	3FT deg	<u>M</u>	20	4M+1D	Ind	30$	AAABB	Ind	11
Applied Mathematics	G110	3FT deg	<u>M</u>	18-20	Ind		28$	AAAB$	Ind	6
Applied Mathematics and Statistics	GG1L	3FT deg	<u>M</u>	18-20	Ind		28$	AAAB$	Ind	
Chemistry and Mathematics	FG11	3FT deg	<u>C+M</u>	18	4M	Ind	28$	AABBB	Ind	8
Chemistry and Statistics	FG14	3FT deg	<u>C+M</u>	18	4M	Ind	28$	AABBB	Ind	
Computing Science and Mathematics	GG15	3FT deg	<u>M</u>	18-20	Ind		28$	AAAB$	Ind	5 16/22
Computing Science and Statistics	GG45	3FT deg	<u>M</u>	18-20	Ind		28$	AAAB$	Ind	3
Economics and Mathematics	GL11	3FT deg	<u>M</u>	20	4M+1D	Ind	28$	AAABB	Ind	5 22/28
Economics and Statistics	GL41	3FT deg	<u>M</u>	20	4M+1D	Ind	28$	AAABB	Ind	4

course details | 98 expected requirements | 96 entry stats

TITLE	CODE	COURSE	SUBJECTS	A/AS	ND/C	AGNVQ	IB	SQA(H)	SQA	RATIO A/AS
Geography and Mathematics	GF18	3FT deg	M+Gy	18	4M	Ind	28$	AABBB	Ind	7	
Geography and Statistics	GF48	3FT deg	M+Gy	18	4M	Ind	28$	AABBB	Ind	5	
Mathematical Sciences	G140	3FT deg	M	18-20	Ind		28$	AAAB$	Ind	4	20/20
Mathematical Sciences	G141	4FT deg	* g	Ind	Ind		Ind	Ind	Ind	3	
Mathematics	G100	3FT deg	M	18-20	Ind		28$	AAAB$	Ind	6	16/26
Mathematics (MMaths)	G103	4FT deg	M	18-20	Ind		28$	AAAB$	Ind		
Mathematics and Physics	FG31	3FT deg	M+P	18	4M	Ind	28$	AABBB	Ind	8	
Mathematics and Psychology	CG81	3FT deg	M	24	Ind	Ind	30$	AAABB	Ind	5	20/26
Mathematics and Statistics	GG14	3FT deg	M	18-20	Ind		28$	AAAB$	Ind	9	
Mathematics and Surveying and Mapping Science	GH12	3FT deg	M	18	4M	Ind	28$	AABBB	Ind	3	
Psychology and Statistics	CG84	3FT deg	M	24	Ind	Ind	30$	AAABB	Ind		
Pure Mathematics	G120	3FT deg	M	18-20	Ind		28$	AAAB$	Ind	4	16/26
Pure Mathematics and Statistics	GG1K	3FT deg	M	18-20	Ind		28$	AAAB$	Ind	2	18/28
Statistics	G400	3FT deg	M	18-20	Ind		28$	AAAB$	Ind	11	
Combined Studies (BA) *Mathematics*	Y400	3FT deg	* g	ABC-BBB	5D	Ind	35$	AAAB	Ind		
Combined Studies (BSc) *Mathematics*	Y100	3FT deg	M+S	18	4M	Ind	28$	AABBB	Ind		
Combined Studies (BSc) *Statistics*	Y100	3FT deg	M+S	18	4M	Ind	28$	AABBB	Ind		

Univ of NORTH LONDON

TITLE	CODE	COURSE	SUBJECTS	A/AS	ND/C	AGNVQ	IB	SQA(H)	SQA	RATIO A/AS
Computer Science & Discrete Maths	GG5C	3FT/4SW/4EXT deg	M/Cs/P/Es/St	CC	4M $	M* go	$	Ind	Ind	5	
Computing/Mathematics Foundation	GGN1▼	4FT/5SW deg		Ind	Ind	Ind	Ind	Ind	1	
Mathematical Modelling	G116	3FT/4SW/4EXT deg	M	CC	X	M*^	$	Ind	Ind		
Mathematical Sciences	G140	3FT/4SW/4EXT deg	* g	CC	4M $	M* go	Dip	Ind	Ind	3	
Mathematical Sciences and Business	GN11	3FT/4SW/4EXT deg	* g	10-12	MO+4D	Ind	Ind	Ind	Ind		
Mathematical Sciences and Educational Studies	GX19	3FT/4SW/4EXT deg	* g	CD	Ind	M* go	Ind	Ind	Ind		
Mathematics	G100	3FT/4SW/4EXT deg	M	CC	X	M*^	$	Ind	Ind	27	
Mathematics and Business	GN1C	3FT/4SW/4EXT deg	M g	12	X	Ind	Ind	Ind	Ind		
Mathematics and Computing	GG5D	3FT/4SW/4EXT deg	M	CC	X	M*^	$	Ind	Ind	40	
Mathematics and Philosophy	GV17	3FT/4SW/4EXT deg	M	CD	X	M*^	Ind	Ind	Ind		
Social Research and Statistics	LG34	3FT deg	* g	CD	4M $	M	Ind	Ind	Ind	3	
Statistics (Applied)	G411	3FT/4SW/4EXT deg	M	CC	X	X	$	Ind	Ind	8	
Statistics and Business	GN41	3FT/4SW/4EXT deg	* g	12	4M-2D$	Ind	Ind	Ind	Ind		
Statistics and Computing	GGL5	3FT/4SW/4EXT deg	M/Cs/P/Es/St	CC	4M $	M* go	$	Ind	Ind	4	
Statistics and Education Studies	GX49	3FT/4SW/4EXT deg	* g	CD	Ind	M* go	Ind	Ind	Ind		
Combined Honours *Decision Systems*	Y100	3FT/4SW/4EXT deg	Ap	CC	4M $	M$ go	$	Ind	Ind		
Combined Honours *Mathematical Sciences*	Y100	3FT/4SW/4EXT deg	* g	CC	4M $	M* go	Dip	Ind	Ind		
Combined Honours *Mathematics*	Y100	3FT/4SW/4EXT deg	M	CC	X	M*^	$	Ind	Ind		
Combined Honours *Statistics*	Y100	3FT/4SW/4EXT deg	* g	CC	4M $	M* go	Dip				
Computing and Mathematical Sciences	009G	2FT HND	* g	E	$	P* go	Dip	Ind	Ind		
Mathematics and its Applications	031G	2FT HND	M	E	X	X	$	Ind	Ind		

Univ of NORTHUMBRIA

TITLE	CODE	COURSE	SUBJECTS	A/AS	ND/C	AGNVQ	IB	SQA(H)	SQA	RATIO A/AS
Applied Statistics and Life Sciences	GC49	3FT deg	B+M/S g	12	Ind	Ind	24$	CCCC$	Ind		
Applied Statistics and Scientific Computing	GG45	3FT deg	M/S g	12	3M	Ind	24	CCCC	Ind		
Applied Statistics for Business and Industry	G408	5EXT deg	* g	2-4	Ind	Ind	Ind	Ind	Ind		
Applied Statistics for Business and Industry	G400	4SW deg	* g	12	3M	Ind	24	CCCC	Ind	3	8/16
Business Systems and Information Technology	GN15	3FT deg	* g	12	MO+2D	D	26	BCCC	Ind		
Mathematics	G101	4FT deg	M g	8-14	Ind	Ind	24$	BBC$	Ind		

Mathematics and Statistics 52

TITLE	CODE	COURSE	SUBJECTS	A/AS	ND/C	RGNVQ	IB	SQA(H)	SQA	RATIO	A/AS
Mathematics	G100	3FT/4SW deg	M g	8-12	Ind	Ind	24$	BBC$	Ind	4	6/20
Mathematics	G108	5EXT deg	* g		Ind	Ind	Ind	Ind	Ind	1	
Mathematics and Scientific Computing	GG15	3FT deg	M g	8-12	Ind	Ind	24$	BBC$	Ind		
Mathematics and Statistics	GG14	3FT/4SW deg	M g	8-12	Ind	Ind	24$	BBC$	Ind	5	
Mathematics and Statistics (Extended)	GG1K	4EXT/5EXTSW deg	* g	2-4	Ind	Ind	Ind	Ind	Ind		
Mathematics with Business Administration	G1N1	3FT/4SW deg	M g	8-12	Ind	Ind	24$	BBC$	Ind	2	10/20
Mathematics with Business Administration (Ext)	G1NC	4EXT/5EXTSW deg	* g	2-4	Ind	Ind	Ind	Ind	Ind		
Mathematics with Mathematical Finance	G1N3	3FT/4SW deg	M g	8-12	Ind	Ind	24$	BBC$	Ind		

Univ of NOTTINGHAM

TITLE	CODE	COURSE	SUBJECTS	A/AS	ND/C	RGNVQ	IB	SQA(H)	SQA	RATIO	A/AS
Electronic Engineering and Mathematics	HG61	3FT deg	M+P	BBC-BCC	Ind	Ind	28$	Ind	Ind	5	22/30
Mathematics (BSc) (3 Yrs)	G100	3FT deg	M	AAB-ABB	Ind	Ind	Ind	Ind	Ind	8	26/30
Mathematics (MMath 4 Yrs)	G103	4FT deg	M	AAB-ABB	Ind	Ind	Ind	Ind	Ind	7	26/30
Mathematics and Computer Science	GG51	3FT deg	M	AAB-ABB	Ind	Ind	Ind	Ind	Ind	9	26/30
Mathematics and Economics	GL11	3FT deg	M	AAB-ABB	Ind	Ind	Ind	Ind	Ind	13	28/30
Mathematics and Management Studies	GN11	3FT deg	M	AAB-ABB	Ind	Ind	Ind	Ind	Ind	10	28/30
Mathematics and Philosophy	GV17	3FT deg	M	AAB-ABB	Ind	Ind	Ind	Ind	Ind	7	26/30
Mathematics with Engineering	G1H1	3FT deg	M+P	BCC-BCD	Ind	Ind	28$	Ind	Ind	5	20/30
Mechanical Engineering with Mathematics	H3G1	3FT deg									

NOTTINGHAM TRENT Univ

TITLE	CODE	COURSE	SUBJECTS	A/AS	ND/C	RGNVQ	IB	SQA(H)	SQA	RATIO	A/AS
Biology and Mathematics	CG11	3FT deg	B+M	10	Ind	Ind	Dip	C	Ind	3	8/10
Chemistry and Mathematics	FG11	3FT deg	C+M	10	Ind	Ind	Dip	C	Ind		
Environmental Conservation & Management & Maths	FG91	3FT deg	M g	10	Ind	Ind	Dip	C	Ind	3	
Environmental Systems & Monitoring & Mathematics	FGX1	3FT deg	M g	10	Ind	Ind	Dip	C	Ind		
Information Technology for Sciences & Maths	GG51	3FT deg	M g	10	Ind	Ind	Dip	C	Ind		
Mathematical Methods for Information Tech (Ext)	G1GM▼	5EXTSW deg	* g		Ind	Ind	Ind	Ind	Ind	1	
Mathematical Methods for Information Technology	G1G5	4SW deg	M g	DD	Ind	Ind	Dip	C	$	3	6/16
Mathematics	G100	3FT/4SW deg	M g	DD	Ind	Ind	Dip	C	Ind		
Mathematics & Statistics and Economics	GL11	3FT deg	M/Ec	12	Ind	M go	Ind	Ind	Ind		
Mathematics & Statistics and Psychology	CG81	3FT deg	M/Ps	12	Ind	M go	Ind	Ind	Ind		
Mathematics and Computing	GG15	3FT deg	M g	10	Ind	Ind	Dip	C	Ind	6	6/14
Mathematics and Physics	FG31	3FT deg	M/P g	10	Ind	Ind	Dip	C	Ind	5	
Sport & Exercise Science and Mathematics	BG61	3FT deg	M+B/Pe/Ss g	16	Ind	Ind	Dip	B	Ind		
Statistics	G400	4SW deg	M/St	DD	Ind	Ind	Dip	C	Ind	2	8/14

OXFORD Univ

TITLE	CODE	COURSE	SUBJECTS	A/AS	ND/C	RGNVQ	IB	SQA(H)	SQA	RATIO	A/AS
Mathematics (3 Yrs)	G100	3FT deg	M	AAB	DO		36	AAAAA	Ind	3	28/30
Mathematics (4 Yrs)	G101	4FT deg	M	AAB	DO		36	AAAAA	Ind	2	28/30
Mathematics and Computation	GG15	3FT deg	M	AAB	DO		36	AAAAA	Ind	2	28/30
Mathematics and Philosophy (4 Yrs)	GV17	4FT deg	M	AAB	DO		36	AAAAA	Ind	2	30/30

OXFORD BROOKES Univ

TITLE	CODE	COURSE	SUBJECTS	A/AS	ND/C	RGNVQ	IB	SQA(H)	SQA	RATIO	A/AS
Computing Mathematics/Accounting and Finance	GN94	3FT deg	* g	CD-BCC	Ind	M*/D*3	Ind	Ind	Ind		
Computing Mathematics/Anthropology	GL96	3FT deg	* g	CD-BCC	Ind	M*^	Ind	Ind	Ind		
Computing Mathematics/Biological Chemistry	CG79	3FT deg									
Computing Mathematics/Business Admin & Mgt	GN91	3FT deg	* g	CD-BBC	Ind	M*/MB4	Ind	Ind	Ind		
Computing Mathematics/Cartography	FG89	3FT deg	* g	CC-DDD	Ind	M*	Ind	Ind	Ind		
Computing Mathematics/Cell Biology	CGC9	3FT deg									
Computing Mathematics/Combined Studies	GY94	3FT deg		X		X	X	X			
Computing Mathematics/Computer Systems	GG69	3FT deg	* g	CD-BC	Ind	M*	Ind	Ind	Ind	3	
Computing Mathematics/Computing	GG59	3FT deg	* g	CD-CDD	Ind	M*	Ind	Ind	Ind		
Economics/Computing Mathematics	GL91	3FT deg	* g	CD-BB	Ind	M*/M*3	Ind	Ind	Ind	5	
Educational Studies/Computing Mathematics	GX99	3FT deg	* g	CD-CC	Ind	M*/M*3	Ind	Ind	Ind		

course details — 98 expected requirements — 96 entry stats

TITLE	CODE	COURSE	SUBJECTS	A/AS	ND/C	AGNVQ	IB	SQA(H)	SQA	RATIO A/AS
Electronics/Computing Mathematics	GH96	3FT deg	M/S	CD-CC	Ind	M$	Ind	Ind	Ind	
English Studies/Computing Mathematics	GQ93	3FT deg	* g	CD-AB	Ind	M*^	Ind	Ind	Ind	
Environmental Chemistry/Computing Mathematics	GF91	3FT deg								
Environmental Policy/Computing Mathematics	KG39	3FT deg								
Environmental Sciences/Computing Mathematics	FGX9	3FT deg	S g	CD	Ind	M*/DS	Ind	Ind	Ind	
Exercise and Health/Computing Mathematics	GB96	3FT deg	S g	DD-CD	Ind	MS	Ind	Ind	Ind	
Fine Art/Computing Mathematics	GW91	3FT deg	Pf+A g	CD-BC	Ind	MA^	Ind	Ind	Ind	
Food Science and Nutrition/Computing Mathematics	DG49	3FT deg	S g	DD-CD	Ind	MS	Ind	Ind	Ind	
French Language and Contemp Studies/Comp Maths	GR9C	4SW deg	F g	CD-CDD	Ind		Ind	Ind	Ind	
French Language and Literature/Computing Maths	GR91	4SW deg	F g	CD-CDD	Ind	M*^	Ind	Ind	Ind	
Geography and the Phys Env/Computing Mathematics	FGV9	3FT deg								
Geography and the Phys Env/Mathematics	FGV1	3FT deg								
Geography/Computing Mathematics	GL98	3FT deg	* g	CD-BB	Ind	M*	Ind	Ind	Ind	
Geology/Computing Mathematics	FG69	3FT deg	S/M g	DD-CD	Ind	PS/MS	Ind	Ind	Ind	
Geotechnics/Computing Mathematics	GH92	3FT deg	S/M/Ds/Es	CC-DD	Ind	M$	Ind	Ind	Ind	
German Language and Contemp Stud/Computing Maths	GR9F	4SW deg	G g	CD-DDD	Ind	M*^	Ind	Ind	Ind	
German Language and Literature/Computing Maths	GR92	4SW deg	G g	CD-DDD	Ind	M*^	Ind	Ind	Ind	
German Studies/Computing Mathematics	GR9G	4SW deg			Ind		Ind	Ind	Ind	
Health Care/Computing Mathematics (Post Exp)	BG79	3FT deg		X		X	X	X		
History/Computing Mathematics	GV91	3FT deg	* g	CD-BB	Ind	M*^	Ind	Ind	Ind	
Hospitality Management St/Computing Mathematics	GN97	3FT deg	* g	CC-DDD	Ind	M*/M*3	Ind	Ind	Ind	
Human Biology/Computing Mathematics	BG19	3FT deg			Ind		Ind	Ind	Ind	
Information Systems/Computing Mathematics	GGM9	3FT deg	* g	CD-BC	Ind	M*	Ind	Ind	Ind	
Intelligent Systems/Computing Mathematics	GG89	3FT deg	* g	CD	Ind	M*	Ind	Ind	Ind	
Law/Computing Mathematics	GM93	3FT deg	* g	CD-BBB	Ind	M*/D*3	Ind	Ind	Ind	
Leisure Planning/Computing Mathematics	KGH9	3FT deg								
Marketing Management/Computing Mathematics	GN9N	3FT deg	* g	CD-BCC	Ind	M*/D*3	Ind	Ind	Ind	
Mathematical Sciences	G140	3FT deg	M g	DD	Ind	M^	Ind	Ind	Ind	14
Mathematics/Accounting and Finance	GN14	3FT deg	M	DD-BCC	Ind	M^D*3	Ind	Ind	Ind	8 16/18
Mathematics/Biological Chemistry	CG71	3FT deg								
Mathematics/Biology	CG11	2ACC/3FT deg	M g	DD-DDE	Ind	MS^	Ind	Ind	Ind	
Mathematics/Business Administration & Management	GN11	3FT deg	M	DD-BBC	Ind	MB4/M^	Ind	Ind	Ind	13
Mathematics/Cartography	FG81	3FT deg	M g	DD-CC	Ind	M*^	Ind	Ind	Ind	
Mathematics/Cell Biology	CGC1	3FT deg								
Mathematics/Combined Studies	GY14	3FT deg		X		X	X	X		
Mathematics/Computer Systems	GG61	3FT deg	M g	DD-BC	Ind	M*^	Ind	Ind	Ind	
Mathematics/Computing	GG15	2ACC/3FT deg	M	DD-BC	Ind	M*^	Ind	Ind	Ind	11
Mathematics/Computing Mathematics	GG19	3FT deg	M	DD-CD	Ind	M*^	Ind	Ind	Ind	9
Mathematics/Ecology	CG91	3FT deg	M g	DD-CD	Ind	MS/M^	Ind	Ind	Ind	
Mathematics/Economics	GL11	3FT deg	M	DD-BB	Ind	M*3/M^	Ind	Ind	Ind	11
Mathematics/Educational Studies	GX19	3FT deg	M	DD-CC	Ind	M*3/M^	Ind	Ind	Ind	4
Mathematics/Electronics	GH16	2ACC/3FT deg	M	DD-CC	Ind	M$/M*^	Ind	Ind	Ind	
Mathematics/Environmental Chemistry	GF11	3FT deg								
Mathematics/Environmental Policy	KG31	3FT deg								
Mathematics/Environmental Sciences	FGX1	3FT deg	M g	DD-CD	Ind	DS/M^	Ind	Ind	Ind	
Mathematics/Exercise and Health	GB16	3FT deg	M g	DD-DDE	Ind	MS/M^	Ind	Ind	Ind	
Mathematics/Fine Art	GW11	3FT deg	M+Pf+A	DD-BC	Ind	MA^	Ind	Ind	Ind	
Mathematics/Food Science and Nutrition	DG41	3FT deg	M g	DD-DDE	Ind	MS/M^	Ind	Ind	Ind	
Mathematics/French Language and Contemp Studies	GR1C	4SW deg	M+F g	DD-CC	Ind	M*^	Ind	Ind	Ind	
Mathematics/French Language and Literature	GR11	4SW deg	M+F g	DD-CC	Ind	M*^	Ind	Ind	Ind	
Mathematics/Geography	GL18	3FT deg	M	DD-BB	Ind	M*^	Ind	Ind	Ind	9
Mathematics/Geotechnics	GH12	3FT deg	M	DD-CC	Ind	M$/M*^	Ind	Ind	Ind	

course details

98 expected requirements

96 entry stats

TITLE	CODE	COURSE	SUBJECTS	A/AS	ND/C	AGNVQ	IB	SQA(H)	SQA	RATIO A/AS	
Mathematics/German Language and Contemp Stud	GR1F	4SW deg	M+G g	DD-CD	Ind	M*_	Ind	Ind	Ind		
Mathematics/German Studies	GR1G	4SW deg	M+G	DD-CD	Ind	M*_	Ind	Ind	Ind		
Mathematics/Health Care (Post Exp)	BG71	3FT deg		X		X		X	X		
Mathematics/History	GV11	3FT deg	M	DD-BB	Ind	M*_	Ind	Ind	Ind	3	
Mathematics/History of Art	GV14	3FT deg	M	DD-BCC	Ind	M*_	Ind	Ind	Ind		
Mathematics/Hospitality Management Studies	GN17	3FT deg	M g	DD-CC	Ind	M^/M*3	Ind	Ind	Ind		
Mathematics/Human Biology	BG11	3FT deg									
Mathematics/Information Systems	GGM1	3FT deg	M	DD-BC	Ind	M*_	Ind	Ind	Ind		
Mathematics/Intelligent Systems	GG18	3FT deg	M	DD-BC	Ind	M*_	Ind	Ind	Ind	5	
Mathematics/Law	GM13	3FT deg	M	DD-BBB	Ind	M^/D*3	Ind	Ind	Ind	7	
Mathematics/Leisure Planning and Management	KGH1	3FT deg									
Mathematics/Marketing Management	GN1N	3FT deg	M g	DD-BCC	Ind	M^/D*3	Ind	Ind	Ind	8	
Music/Computing Mathematics	GW93	3FT deg	Mu g	DD-CD	Ind	M*	Ind	Ind	Ind		
Music/Mathematics	GW13	3FT deg	M+Mu	DD-DDE	Ind	M*_	Ind	Ind	Ind		
Palliative Care/Computing Mathematics (Post Exp)	BGR9	3FT deg		X		X		X	X		
Palliative Care/Mathematics (Post Exp)	BGR1	3FT deg		X		X		X	X		
Planning Studies/Computing Mathematics	GK94	3FT deg	* g	BC-DDD	Ind	M*	Ind	Ind	Ind		
Planning Studies/Mathematics	GK14	3FT deg	M	DD-CC	Ind	M*_	Ind	Ind	Ind		
Politics/Computing Mathematics	GM91	3FT deg	* g	CD-AB	Ind	M*^	Ind	Ind	Ind		
Politics/Mathematics	MG11	3FT deg	M	DD-AB	Ind	M*^	Ind	Ind	Ind		
Psychology/Computing Mathematics	CG89	3FT deg	* g	CD-BBC	Ind	M*^	Ind	Ind	Ind	3	
Psychology/Mathematics	CG81	3FT deg	M g	DD-BBC	Ind	M*^	Ind	Ind	Ind	4	14/20
Publishing/Computing Mathematics	GP95	3FT deg	* g	CD-BB	Ind	M*/M$3	Ind	Ind	Ind		
Publishing/Mathematics	GP15	3FT deg	M g	DD-BB	Ind	M*^/M$3	Ind	Ind	Ind		
Rehabilitation/Computing Mathematics (Post Exp)	BGT9	3FT deg		X		X		X	X		
Rehabilitation/Mathematics (Post Exp)	BGT1	3FT deg		X		X		X	X		
Retail Management/Computing Mathematics	GN95	3FT deg	* g	CD-CCD	Ind			Ind	Ind		
Retail Management/Mathematics	GN15	3FT deg	M g	DD-CCD	Ind			Ind	Ind		
Sociology/Computing Mathematics	GL93	3FT deg	* g	CD-BCC	Ind	M*^	Ind	Ind	Ind		
Sociology/Mathematics	GL13	3FT deg	M	DD-BCC	Ind	M*^	Ind	Ind	Ind		
Software Engineering/Computing Mathematics	GG79	3FT deg	* g	CD-BC	Ind	M*	Ind	Ind	Ind		
Software Engineering/Mathematics	GG71	3FT deg	M g	DD-BC	Ind	M*_	Ind	Ind	Ind		
Statistics/Accounting and Finance	GN44	3FT deg	* g	DD-BCC	Ind	M*/D*3	Ind	Ind	Ind	5	
Statistics/Anthropology	GL46	3FT deg	* g	DD-BCC	Ind	M*^	Ind	Ind	Ind		
Statistics/Biological Chemistry	CG74	3FT deg									
Statistics/Biology	CG14	2ACC/3FT deg	S/M g	DD	Ind	MS	Ind	Ind	Ind	4	
Statistics/Business Administration & Management	GN41	3FT deg	* g	DD-BBC	Ind	M*/MB4	Ind	Ind	Ind	14	
Statistics/Cell Biology	CGC4	3FT deg									
Statistics/Combined Studies	GY44	3FT deg		X		X		X	X		
Statistics/Computer Systems	GG64	3FT deg	* g	DD-BC	Ind	M*	Ind	Ind	Ind		
Statistics/Computing	GG45	2ACC/3FT deg	* g	DD-BC	Ind	M*	Ind	Ind	Ind	4	
Statistics/Computing Mathematics	GG49	3FT deg	* g	DD-CD	Ind	M*	Ind	Ind	Ind		
Statistics/Ecology	CG94	3FT deg	S g	DD-CD	Ind	MS	Ind	Ind	Ind		
Statistics/Economics	GL41	3FT deg	* g	DD-BB	Ind	M*/M*3	Ind	Ind	Ind	3	
Statistics/Educational Studies	GX49	3FT deg	* g	DD-CC	Ind	M*/M*3	Ind	Ind	Ind		
Statistics/Electronics	GH46	2ACC/3FT deg	S/M	DD-CC	Ind	M$	Ind	Ind	Ind		
Statistics/English Studies	GQ43	3FT deg	* g	DD-AB	Ind	M*^	Ind	Ind	Ind		
Statistics/Environmental Chemistry	GF41	3FT deg									
Statistics/Environmental Policy	KG34	3FT deg									
Statistics/Environmental Sciences	FGX4	3FT deg	S g	DD-CD	Ind	M*/DS	Ind	Ind	Ind		
Statistics/Exercise and Health	GB46	3FT deg	S g	DD	Ind	MS	Ind	Ind	Ind		
Statistics/Fine Art	GW41	3FT deg	Pf+A g	DD-BC	Ind	MA^	Ind	Ind	Ind		

course details   98 expected requirements   96 entry stats

TITLE	CODE	COURSE	SUBJECTS	A/AS	ND/C	AGNVQ	IB	SQA(H)	SQA	RATIO A/AS
Statistics/French Language and Contemp Studies	GR4C	4SW deg	F g	DD-CC	Ind	M*^	Ind	Ind	Ind	
Statistics/French Language and Literature	GR41	4SW deg	F g	DD-CC	Ind	M*^	Ind	Ind	Ind	
Statistics/Geography	GL48	3FT deg	* g	DD-BB	Ind	M*	Ind	Ind	Ind	3
Statistics/Geology	FG64	3FT deg	S/M g	DD	Ind	M*/PS	Ind	Ind	Ind	
Statistics/Geotechnics	GH42	3FT deg	S/M/Ds/Es	DD-CC	Ind	M$	Ind	Ind	Ind	
Statistics/German Language and Contemp Stud	GR4F	4SW deg	G g	DD-CD	Ind	M*^	Ind	Ind	Ind	
Statistics/German Language and Literature	GR42	4SW deg	G g	DD	Ind	M*^	Ind	Ind	Ind	
Statistics/German Studies	GR4G	4SW deg	G g	DD	Ind	M*^	Ind	Ind	Ind	
Statistics/Health Care (Post Exp)	BG74	3FT deg		X		X	X	X		
Statistics/History	GV41	3FT deg	* g	DD-BB	Ind	M*^	Ind	Ind	Ind	
Statistics/History of Art	GV44	3FT deg	* g	DD-BCC	Ind	M*^	Ind	Ind	Ind	
Statistics/Hospitality Management Studies	GN47	3FT deg	* g	DD-CC	Ind	M*/M*3	Ind	Ind	Ind	
Statistics/Human Biology	BG14	3FT deg								
Statistics/Information Systems	GGM4	3FT deg	* g	DD-BC	Ind	M*	Ind	Ind	Ind	
Statistics/Intelligent Systems	GG48	3FT deg	* g	DD-CD	Ind	M*	Ind	Ind	Ind	
Statistics/Law	GM43	3FT deg	* g	DD-BBB	Ind	M*/D*3	Ind	Ind	Ind	
Statistics/Leisure Planning and Management	KGH4	3FT deg								
Statistics/Marketing Management	GN4N	3FT deg	* g	DD-BCC	Ind	M*/D*3	Ind	Ind	Ind	3
Statistics/Mathematics	GG14	2ACC/3FT deg	M	DD-DDE	Ind	M*^	Ind	Ind	Ind	4
Statistics/Music	GW43	3FT deg	Mu g	DD	Ind	M*	Ind	Ind	Ind	
Statistics/Palliative Care (Post Exp)	BGR4	3FT deg		X		X	X	X		
Statistics/Physical Geography	FGV4	3FT deg								
Statistics/Planning Studies	GK44	3FT deg	* g	DD-CC	Ind	M*	Ind	Ind	Ind	
Statistics/Politics	GM41	3FT deg	* g	DD-AB	Ind	M*^	Ind	Ind	Ind	
Statistics/Psychology	CG84	3FT deg	* g	DD-BBC	Ind	M*^	Ind	Ind	Ind	14
Statistics/Publishing	GP45	3FT deg	* g	DD-BB	Ind	M*/M$3	Ind	Ind	Ind	
Statistics/Rehabilitation (Post Exp)	BGT4	3FT deg		X		X	X	X		
Statistics/Sociology	GL43	3FT deg	* g	DD-BCC	Ind	M*^	Ind	Ind	Ind	
Statistics/Software Engineering	GG74	3FT deg	* g	DD-BC	Ind	M*	Ind	Ind	Ind	
Telecommunications/Computing Mathematics	GH9P	3FT deg								
Telecommunications/Mathematics	GH1P	3FT deg								
Telecommunications/Statistics	GH4P	3FT deg								
Tourism/Computing Mathematics	GP97	3FT deg	* g	CD-BC	Ind	M*/M*3	Ind	Ind	Ind	
Tourism/Statistics	GP47	3FT deg	* g	DD-BC	Ind	M*/M*3	Ind	Ind	Ind	
Transport Planning/Computing Mathematics	GN99	3FT deg	* g	CD-CC	Ind	M*	Ind	Ind	Ind	
Transport Planning/Mathematics	GN19	3FT deg	M	DD-CC	Ind	M*^	Ind	Ind	Ind	
Transport Planning/Statistics	GN49	3FT deg	* g	DD-CC	Ind	M*	Ind	Ind	Ind	
Water Resources/Computing Mathematics	GH9F	3FT deg								
Water Resources/Mathematics	GH1F	3FT deg								
Water Resources/Statistics	GH4F	3FT deg								

Univ of PAISLEY

Applicable Mathematics with Computing	GG15	3FT/4FT/5SW deg	M+S g	CCC-EE	Ind	Ind	Ind	BCC$	Ind	14
Computing Science, Stats & Operational Research	GG54	3FT/4SW/5SW deg	M g	CC	Ind	Ind	Ind	BCCC$	Ind	
Mathematical Sciences	G150	3FT/4FT/5SW deg	M+S g	CCC-EE	Ind	Ind	Ind	BCC$	Ind	4
Mathematical Sciences with European Language	G1T2	3FT/4FT/5SW deg	M+S g	CCC-EE	Ind	Ind	Ind	BCC$	Ind	
Mathematical Sciences with Finance	G1N3	3FT/4FT/5SW deg	M+S g	CCC-EE	Ind	Ind	Ind	BCC$	Ind	7
Mathematical Sciences with Management	G1N1	3FT/4FT/5SW deg	M+S g	CCC-EE	Ind	Ind	Ind	BCC$	Ind	

Univ of PLYMOUTH

Applied Economics with Statistics	L1G4	3FT deg	* g	CCD-CDD	MO	M$^	Ind	BCCC	Ind	14
Biotechnology with Mathematics	C9G1	3FT/4SW deg	B g	12-14	4M	MS^	Ind	BBBB	Ind	2
Business Economics with Statistics	L1GK	3FT deg	* g	CDD-CCD	MO	M$^	Ind	BCCC	Ind	

course details   98 expected requirements   96 entry stats

TITLE	CODE	COURSE	SUBJECTS	A/AS	NO/C	AGNVQ	IB	SQA(H)	SQA	RATIO A/AS	
Cell Biology and Immunology with Statistics	C1G4	3FT/4SW deg	B g	10-14	4M	MS^	Ind	BBBB	Ind		
Chemistry with Mathematics	F1G1	3FT deg	C+M g	CC	3M	MS^	Ind	CCCC	Ind	5	
Chemistry with Statistics	F1G4	3FT deg	C g	CC	3M	MS^	Ind	CCCC	Ind		
European Economics with Statistics	L1GL	3FT deg	* g	CDD-CCD	MO	M$^	Ind	BCCC	Ind		
Geography with Statistics	F8G4	3FT deg	Gy g	16-18	X	M$^	Ind	ABBB	Ind	6	
Geology with Statistics	F6G4	3FT deg	S g	12	4M	MS^	Ind	CCC	Ind	1	
Human Biology with Statistics	C9GL	3FT/4SW deg	B g	10-14	4M $	M$^	Ind	BBBB	Ind	2	
Mathematical Studies	G150	3FT deg	M g	10-15	MO	M$^	Ind	Ind	Ind	4	10/12
Mathematics with Astronomy	G1F5	3FT deg	M g	10-15	MO $	M$^	Ind	Ind	Ind	8	
Mathematics with Chemistry	G1F1	3FT deg	M g	10-15	MO $	M$^	Ind	Ind	Ind		
Mathematics with Computing	G1G5	3FT deg	M g	10-15	MO $	M$^	Ind	Ind	Ind	10	
Mathematics with Ecology	G1D2	3FT deg	M g	10-15	MO $	M$^	Ind	Ind	Ind		
Mathematics with Education	G1X9	3FT deg	M g	10-15	MO $	M$^	Ind	BBCC	Ind		
Mathematics with French	G1R1	3FT deg	M+F g	10-15	MO $	M$^	Ind	BBCC	Ind		
Mathematics with Geology	G1F6	3FT deg	M g	10-15	MO $	M$^	Ind	BBCC	Ind		
Mathematics with Human Biology	G1C9	3FT deg	M g	10-15	MO $	M$^	Ind	BBCC	Ind		
Mathematics with Microbiology	G1C5	3FT deg	M g	10-15	MO $	M$^	Ind	BBCC	Ind		
Mathematics with Ocean Science	G1F7	3FT deg	M g	10-15	MO $	M$^	Ind	BBCC	Ind	2	
Mathematics with Spanish	G1R4	3FT deg	M+Sp g	10-15	MO $	M$^	Ind	BBCC	Ind		
Mathematics/MMath	G100	3FT/4FT deg	M g	10-15	MO $	M$^	Ind	BBCC	Ind	5	12/18
Microbiology with Mathematics	C5G1	3FT/4SW deg	B g	10-14	4M $	MS	Ind	BBBB	Ind	5	
Ocean Science with Mathematics	F7G1	3FT deg	S g	14-16	5M $	M$	Ind	CCCC	Ind	2	
Political Economy with Statistics	LG1K	3FT deg	Ap g	CDD-CCD	MO $	M$^	Ind	BCCC	Ind		
Politics with Statistics	M1G4	3FT deg	* g	14	Ind	M$	Ind	BBBC$	Ind		
Psychology with Statistics	C8G4	3FT/4SW deg	Ap g	BCC	MO+3D	M12^	Ind	BBBC$	Ind	6	
Social Policy with Statistics	L4G4	3FT deg	* g	14	Ind	M$	Ind	BBBC$	Ind		
Sociology with Statistics	L3G4	3FT deg	* g	14	Ind	M$^	Ind	BBBC$	Ind		
Statistics (App) & Mgt Sci with App Economics	G4LC	3FT deg	M/St g	10-15	MO $	M$	Ind	BBCC	Ind		
Statistics (App) and Mgt Sci with Geography	G4FV	3FT deg	M/St g	10-15	MO $	M$^	Ind	BBCC	Ind		
Statistics (App) with Applied Economics	G4L1	3FT deg	M/St g	10	MO $	M$	Ind	BBCC	Ind		
Statistics (App) with Chemistry	G4F1	3FT deg	M/St g	10	MO $	M$	Ind	BBCC	Ind		
Statistics (App) with Geography	G4F8	3FT deg	M/St g	10-15	MO $	M$^	Ind	BBCC	Ind		
Statistics (App) with Human Biology	G4C9	3FT deg	M/St g	10	MO $	M$^	Ind	BBCC	Ind	1	
Statistics (App) with Management Science	G4N1	3FT deg	M/St g	10	MO $	M$	Ind	BBCC	Ind	2	10/16
Statistics (App) with Mathematics	G4G1	3FT deg	M/St g	10	MO $	M$	Ind	BBCC	Ind	11	
Statistics (App) with Microbiology	G4C5	3FT deg	M/St g	10-14	MO $	M$	Ind	BBCC	Ind		
Statistics (Applied)	G411	3FT deg	M/St g	10	MO $	M$	Ind	BBCC	Ind	3	
Statistics (Applied) & Management Sc with French	G4RC	3FT deg	M/St+F g	10-15	MO $	M$^	Ind	BBCC	Ind		
Statistics (Applied) & Mgt Science with Spanish	G4RK	3FT deg	M/St+Sp g	10-15	MO $	M$^	Ind	BBCC	Ind		
Statistics (Applied) and Business	GN41	3FT deg	M/St g	10-15	MO $	M$	Ind	BBCC	Ind		
Statistics (Applied) with Business	G4NC	3FT deg	M/St g	10	MO $	M$	Ind	BBCC	Ind		
Statistics (Applied) with Ecology	G4D2	3FT deg	M/St g	10	MO $	M$	Ind	BBCC	Ind		
Statistics (Applied) with French	G4R1	3FT deg	M/St+F g	10	MO $	M$^	Ind	BBCC	Ind		
Statistics (Applied) with Spanish	G4R4	3FT deg	M/St+Sp g	10	MO $	M$^	Ind	BBCC	Ind		
Statistics(App) and Mgt Sci with Computing	G4GM	3FT deg	M/St g	10	MO $	M$	Ind	BBCC	Ind	3	
Statistics(App) and Mgt Sci with Languages	G4TX	3FT deg	M/St g	10	MO $	M$^	Ind	BBCC	Ind		
Statistics(App) and Mgt Sci with Transport	G4N9	3FT deg	M/St g	10	MO $	M$	Ind	BBCC	Ind		
Statistics(App) with Computing	G4G5	3FT deg	M/St g	10	MO $	M$	Ind	BBCC	Ind	2	
Statistics(App) with Languages	G4T9	3FT deg	M/St+L g	10	MO $	M$^	Ind	BBCC	Ind		
Statistics(App) with Psychology	G4C8	3FT deg	M/St g	10	MO $	M$	Ind	BBCC	Ind	6	
Statistics(App) with Transport	G4NX	3FT deg	M/St g	10	MO $	M$	Ind	BBCC	Ind		

course details			98 expected requirements							96 entry stats	
TITLE	CODE	COURSE	SUBJECTS	A/AS	ND/C	RGNVQ	IB	SQA(H)	SQA	RATIO A/AS	

Univ of PORTSMOUTH

Chemistry and Mathematics	FG11	3FT deg	C+M	10	1M $	MS6/^	Dip	BCCC	Ind	9	
Chemistry and Mathematics	FG1C▼	4FT deg	*	Ind	Ind	Ind	Ind	Ind	Ind		
Chemistry and Statistics	FG1K▼	4FT deg	*	Ind	Ind	Ind	Ind	Ind	Ind		
Chemistry and Statistics	FG14	3FT deg	C+M	10	N $	MS6/^	Dip	Ind	Ind		
Computing and Mathematics	GG15	3FT deg	M	8	1M $	M*6/^	Dip	BCCC	Ind	7	
Computing and Mathematics	GG1M▼	4FT deg	*	Ind	Ind	Ind	Ind	Ind	Ind		
Computing and Statistics	GG4M▼	4FT deg	*	Ind	Ind	Ind	Ind	Ind	Ind		
Computing and Statistics	GG45	3FT deg	M	8	1M $	M*6/^	Dip	BCCC	Ind	8	
Geographical Science and Mathematics	FG81	3FT deg	Gy+M	16	4M	M$6/^	26$	BBBB	Ind		
Geographical Science and Mathematics (Extended)	FG8C▼	4FT deg	*	Ind	Ind	Ind	Ind	Ind	Ind		
Geographical Science and Statistics	FG8K▼	4FT deg	*	Ind	Ind	Ind	Ind	Ind	Ind		
Geographical Science and Statistics	FG84	3FT deg	Gy+M	16	4M	M$6/^	26$	BBBB	Ind		
Mathematical Sciences	G140	3FT deg	M	12	4M $	M$6/^	Dip$	BCCC	Ind	15	
Mathematics	G100	4SW deg	M	12	4M $	M$6/^	Dip$	BCCC	Ind	11	
Mathematics (4 years)	G103	4SW deg	M	20	4M+2D	D$6/^	Dip	BBBB	Ind		
Mathematics and Statistics	GG14	3FT deg	M	12	1M $	M$6/^	Dip$	BCCC	Ind		
Mathematics for Finance and Management	G161	4SW deg	M	12	4M $	M$6/^	Dip$	BCCC	Ind	3	6/16
Mathematics with Astronomy	G1F5	3FT deg	M	10	4M $	M$6/^	Dip$	BCCC	Ind		
Mathematics with Computing	G900	4SW deg	M	12	4M $	M$6/^	Dip$	BCCC	Ind	4	8/15
Mathematics with Computing	G908▼	5EXTSW deg	*	Ind	N $	P*	Ind	Ind	Ind	1	
Physics and Mathematics	FG31	3FT deg	M+P	8	1M $	MS6/^	Dip$	BCCC	Ind	9	
Physics and Statistics	FG34	3FT deg	M+P	8	1M $	MS6/^	Dip$	BCCC	Ind		
Statistics	G400	3FT deg	M/St	12	4M $	M$6/^	Dip$	BBCC	Ind		
Mathematical Studies (with Comp & Bus Applics)	009G	2FT HND	M	4	N $	P$3/^	Dip	CC	Ind	1	2/4

QUEEN MARY & WESTFIELD COLL (Univ of London)

Applied Mathematics	G110	3FT deg	M			MS^					
Astronomy and Mathematics	FG51	3FT deg	M+P	24		MS^					
Chemistry and Mathematics	FG11	3FT deg	C+M	CCC	6M $	DS^	26$	BBBCC			
Computer Science and Mathematics	GG15	3FT deg	M	BCC	3M+2D	D^	28$				
Economics/Statistics and Mathematics	LG1C	3FT deg	M g	BCC	5M	M$^	30$	BBBBB			
French and Mathematics	GR11	4FT deg	F+M	18		M^	28$				
German and Mathematics	GR1F	4FT deg	G+M	18		M^	30$				
Hispanic Studies and Mathematics	GR1K	4FT deg	L+M	20		M^	30$				
Mathematical Sci for Business, Ind and Finance	G140	3FT deg	M			M$^					
Mathematics	G100	3FT deg	M			M$^					
Mathematics (Europe) (MSci)	G103	4FT deg	M	18		M$^	30$				
Mathematics (MSci)	G102	4FT deg	M			M$^					
Mathematics and Astrophysics	GF15	3FT deg	M+P	CCC		M$^					
Mathematics and Business Economics	GL11	3FT deg	M	BCC		M$^	30$	BBBBB			
Mathematics and Computing	GG51	3FT deg	M			M$^					
Mathematics and Physics	FG31	3FT deg	M+P	CCC		M$^					
Mathematics and Statistics	GG41	3FT deg	M	BC		M$^					
Mathematics with Astrophysics (MSci)	G1FM	4FT deg	M+P	BCC		M$^					
Mathematics with Business Studies	G1N1	3FT deg	M			M$^					
Mathematics with Statistics (MSci)	G1G4	4FT deg	M			M$^					
Pure Mathematics	G120	3FT deg	M			M$^					
Russian and Mathematics	GRD8	4FT deg	L+M	18		M^	30$				
Statistics	G400	3FT deg	M	BCC		M$^	26$				
Statistics, Computing, Operational Res and Maths	G900	3FT deg	M			M$^					
Statistics, Mathematics and Business Economics	GL41	3FT deg	M	BCC		M$^	30$	BBBBB			

Mathematics and Statistics 52

			98 expected requirements							**96 entry stats**	
course details			SUBJECTS	A/AS	ND/C	AGNVQ	IB	SQA(H)	SQA	RATIO	A/AS
TITLE	CODE	COURSE									
QUEEN'S Univ Belfast											
Applied Mathematics and Physics	GF13	3FT/4FT deg	M+P g	CCC	Ind	Ind	28$	BBBC	Ind	5	18/28
Applied Mathematics and Physics (MSci)	GF1H	4FT deg	M+P g	CCC	X	X	28$	X	Ind	6	
Computational Mathematics	G176	3FT/4FT deg	M g	CCC	Ind	D*^ go	28$	BBBC	Ind	18	
Computer Sci & Stats and Operational Research	GG54	3FT/4FT deg	M g	CCC	Ind	D*^ go	28$	BBBC	Ind	3	
Computer Science and Mathematics	GG51	3FT/4FT deg	M g	CCC	Ind	D*^ go	28$	BBBC	Ind	5	18/24
Mathematics (MSci)	G103	4FT deg	M g	BCC	X	D*^ go	28$	X	Ind	3	18/30
Mathematics (Pure and Applied)	G130	3FT/4FT deg	M g	BCC	Ind	D*^ go	28$	BBBC	Ind	12	
Mathematics (Pure and/or Applied)	G100	3FT/4FT deg	M g	BCC	Ind	D*^ go	28$	BBBC	Ind	4	18/28
Mathematics and Statistics and Operational Res	GG14	3FT/4FT deg	M g	BCC	Ind	D*^ go	28$	BBBC	Ind	6	21/26
Mathematics with Extended Studies in Europe	G104	4FT deg	M g	BCC	X	D*^ go	28$	X	Ind	14	
Statistics and Operational Research	GN42	3FT/4FT deg	M g	CCC	Ind	D*^ go	28$	BBBC	Ind	12	
Univ of READING											
Analytical Computer Science	G5G1	3FT deg	M g	20	3M+2D$	D$^	30$	BBBB$	Ind		
Applied Analytical Computer Science	G5GC	4SW deg	M g	20	3M+2D$	D$^	30$	BBBB$	Ind		
Applied Mathematics (MMath)	G113	4FT deg	M	BCC	3M+2D$	D*^	30$	BBBB$	Ind	9	
Applied Statistics	G401	4SW deg	* g	20	3M+2D	D*^ go	30	BBBB	Ind	4	
Computational Mathematics	G1G5	3FT deg	M g	BCC	3M+2D$	D$^	30$	BBBB$	Ind		
Mathematical Studies	G152	3FT deg	M	CDD	4M $	D$^	27$	BBBC$	Ind	4	11/20
Mathematics	G100	3FT deg	M	BCC	3M+2D$	D$^	30$	BBBB$	Ind	14	16/24
Mathematics (MMath)	G103	4FT deg	M	BCC	3M+2D$	D$^	30$	BBBB$	Ind	7	18/22
Mathematics and Applied Statistics	GG1K	4SW deg	M	BCC	3M+2D$	D$^	30$	BBBB$	Ind	3	
Mathematics and Economics	GL11	3FT deg	M	BCC	3M+2D$	D$^	30$	BBBB$	Ind	11	
Mathematics and Meteorology	GF19	3FT deg	M	BCC	3M+2D$	D$^	30$	BBBB$	Ind	5	24/30
Mathematics and Physics	GF13	3FT deg	M+P	BCC	3M+2D$	D$^	30$	BBBB$	Ind	31	
Mathematics and Psychology	GC18	3FT deg	M	BCC	3M+2D$	D$^	30$	BBBB$	Ind	10	24/24
Mathematics and Statistics	GG14	3FT deg	M	BCC	3M+2D$	D$^	30$	BBBB$	Ind	63	
Physics and Mathematics (MPhys/MMath)	FG31	4FT deg	M+P	BCC	3M+2D$	DS^	30$	BBBB$	Ind		
Psychology and Statistics	CG84	3FT deg	* g	BCC	3M+2D	D$^ go	30	BBBB$	Ind	3	18/22
Pure Mathematics (MMath)	G123	4FT deg	M	BCC	3M+2D$	D$^	30$	BBBB$	Ind	7	
Statistics	G400	3FT deg	* g	BCC	3M+2D	D$^ go	30	BBBB	Ind	5	
ROBERT GORDON Univ											
Mathematics and Computing	G1G5	3FT/4FT deg	M g	DE	N	Ind	Ind	BCC$	Ind	6	
ROYAL HOLLOWAY, Univ of London											
Ancient History with Mathematics	V1G1	3FT deg	M	BCC	Ind		28	Ind			
Classical Studies with Mathematics	Q8G1	3FT deg	M	BCC	Ind		28$	BBBB$			
Computer Science and Discrete Mathematics	GG5C	3FT/4SW deg	M	BCC-BBC	MO+3D	D^	Ind	Ind			
Computer Science and Mathematics	GG51	3FT/4SW deg	M	BCC-BBC	MO+3D	D^	Ind	Ind		5	15/24
Economics and Mathematics	LG11	3FT deg	M	BBC-BBB	Ind		Ind	Ind			
Economics with Mathematics	L1G1	3FT deg	M	BBC-BBB	Ind		32$	Ind		6	
French with Mathematics	R1G1	4FT deg	F+M	BBC-ABC			28$	Ind			
Geography and Mathematics	FG81	3FT deg	Gy+M	BCC-BBC	Ind	D^	Ind	Ind		6	
Geology and Mathematics	FG61	3FT deg	M	CCC-BCC	Ind	D^	Ind	Ind			
German with Mathematics	R2G1	4FT deg	G+M	BCC			28$	BBBBC$			
Greek with Mathematics	Q7G1	3FT deg	M	BCC			28$	BBBBC$			
Italian with Mathematics	R3G1	4FT deg	M+L/Ln	BBC			30	BBCCC$			
Latin with Mathematics	Q6G1	3FT deg	M	BCC			28$	BBBBC$			
Management Studies with Mathematics	N1G1	3FT deg	M	BBC-BBB	2M+3D	D^	30	Ind			
Mathematics	G100	3FT deg	M	BCC-BBC	Ind	D^	Ind	Ind		4	14/28
Mathematics (MSci)	G103	4FT deg	M	ABC-ACC	Ind	D^	Ind	Ind		26	
Mathematics and Management Studies	GN11	3FT deg	M	BCC-BBC	Ind	D^	Ind	Ind		17	

| | | | 98 expected requirements | | | | | | | 96 entry stats | |
| course details | | | | | | | | | | | |
TITLE	CODE	COURSE	SUBJECTS	A/AS	ND/C	AGNVQ	IB	SQA(H)	SQA	RATIO	A/AS
Mathematics and Music	GW13	3FT deg	M+Mu	BCC-BBC	Ind	D^	Ind	Ind		20	
Mathematics and Physics	GF13	3FT deg	M+P	BCC	Ind	D^	Ind	Ind		9	
Mathematics and Psychology	GC18	3FT deg	M	BBC	Ind	D^	Ind	Ind		8	
Mathematics with Economics	G1L1	3FT deg	M	BCC	Ind	D^	Ind	Ind			
Mathematics with Economics and Management	G1LC	3FT deg	M	BCC-BBC	Ind	D^	Ind	Ind		20	
Mathematics with French	G1R1	3FT deg	F+M	BCC-BBC	Ind	D^	Ind	Ind			
Mathematics with German	G1R2	3FT deg	G+M	BCC-BBC	Ind	D^	Ind	Ind			
Mathematics with Italian	G1R3	3FT deg	M+L/Ln	BCC-BBC	Ind	D^	Ind	Ind			
Mathematics with Management Studies	G1N1	3FT deg	M	BCC-BBC	Ind	D^	Ind	Ind		1	16/22
Mathematics with Music	G1W3	3FT deg	M+Mu	BCC-BBC	Ind	D^	Ind	Ind			
Mathematics with Operational Research	G1N2	3FT deg	M	BCC-BBC	Ind	D^	Ind	Ind			
Mathematics with Political Studies	G1MC	3FT deg	M	BCC-BBC	Ind	D^	Ind	Ind			
Mathematics with Social Policy	G1L4	3FT deg	M	BCC-BBC	Ind	D^	Ind	Ind			
Mathematics with Spanish	G1R4	3FT deg	M+L	BCC-BBC	Ind	D^	Ind	Ind			
Mathematics with Statistics	G1G4	3FT deg	M	BCC-BBC	Ind	D^	Ind	Ind		4	16/26
Music with Mathematics	W3G1	3FT deg	M+Mu	BCC-BBC			Ind	ABBCC$			
Social Policy with Mathematics	L4G1	3FT deg	M	BCC-BBC	Ind	D^	Ind	Ind			
Sociology with Mathematics	L3G1	3FT deg	M	BCC-BBC	Ind	D^	Ind	Ind			
Foundation Programme *Mathematics*	Y408	4FT deg									
Science Foundation Year *Mathematics*	Y100	4FT deg	*		Ind	Ind	Ind	Ind			

Univ of SALFORD

TITLE	CODE	COURSE	SUBJECTS	A/AS	ND/C	AGNVQ	IB	SQA(H)	SQA	RATIO	A/AS
Business Operation & Contr (inc Maths & Mgt Sci)	G4N1	3FT/4SW deg	M	BCC	X	X	Ind	Ind	Ind	2	12/28
Business Operation & Control with St in N Amer	G4NC	3FT/4SW deg	M	BBB	X	X	Ind	Ind	Ind	5	
Computer Science & Applied Mathematics (3/4 yr)	GG51	3FT/4SW deg	M	16	X	X	Ind	Ind	Ind		
Computer Science and O R and Applied Statistics	GG54	3FT/4SW deg	M	16	X	X					
Mathematics	G102	4SW deg	M g	24	X	X					
Mathematics	G100	3FT/4SW deg	M g	20	X	X	Ind	Ind	Ind	7	14/24
Mathematics with Professional Studies (4 yr SW)	G101	4SW deg	M g	20	X	X	Ind	Ind	Ind	5	

Univ of SHEFFIELD

TITLE	CODE	COURSE	SUBJECTS	A/AS	ND/C	AGNVQ	IB	SQA(H)	SQA	RATIO	A/AS
Accounting & Financial Management and Maths	NG4D	3FT deg	M g	24	3M+3D$	D^	32$	AABB$	Ind	7	20/28
Chemistry and Mathematics	FG1D	3FT/4EXT deg	C+M g	BBC	5M+1D$	DS^	29$	ABBC$	Ind	6	26/30
Computer Science and Mathematics	GG51	3FT/4EXT deg	M g	24	3M+3D$	D^	32$	AABB$	Ind	9	20/28
Economics and Mathematics	LG1D	3FT deg	M g	24	3M+3D$	D^	32$	AABB$	Ind	4	20/30
Economics and Statistics	LG14	3FT deg	M g	24	3M+3D$	D^	32$	AABB$	Ind	19	
Geography and Mathematics	FG81	3FT deg	Gy+M g	BBB	3M+3D$	DS^	30$	AABB$	Ind	5	22/30
Management and Mathematics	NG11	3FT deg	M g	24	3M+3D$	D^	32$	AABB$	Ind	13	22/24
Mathematics	G100	3FT/4FT deg	M g	22-24	4M+2D$	D^	30$	ABBB$	Ind	6	20/30
Mathematics Foundation Year (4 or 5 Yrs)	G101	4FT/5FT deg	g	22-24	4M+2D	D^	30	ABBB	Ind		
Mathematics and Astronomy	GF15	3FT deg	M+P g	BBC	4M+2D$	D^	30$	AABC$	Ind	8	
Mathematics and Philosophy	VG7D	3FT deg	M g	BBB	X	X	32$	AABB$	Ind	4	22/30
Mathematics and Physics	GF13	3FT/4EXT deg	M+P g	24	4M+2D$	D^	28$	ABBC$	Ind	9	22/26
Mathematics with Study in Europe (MMaths)	G102	4FT deg	M+L g	22	4M+2D$	D^	30$	ABBB$	Ind	8	20/30
Physics with Mathematics (MPhys)	F3G1	4FT/5EXT deg	M+P g	BBC	4M+2D$	DS^	28$	ABBC$	Ind	9	
Economics with Mathematics and Statistics *Mathematics*	Y620	3FT deg	M g	22	4M+2D$	D^	30$	ABBB$	Ind		
Economics with Mathematics and Statistics *Statistics*	Y620	3FT deg	M g	22	4M+2D$	D^	30$	ABBB$	Ind		

Mathematics and Statistics · 52

| | | | 98 expected requirements | | | | | | | 96 entry stats | |
| course details | | | | | | | | | | | |
TITLE	CODE	COURSE	SUBJECTS	A/AS	ND/C	AGNVQ	IB	SQA(H)	SQA	RATIO	A/AS
SHEFFIELD HALLAM Univ											
Applied Statistics	G411	4SW deg	*	12	5M	M	Ind	Ind	Ind		
Business Systems Modelling	G932	4SW deg	*	12	5M	M	Ind	Ind	Ind		
Computing Mathematics	G170	3FT/4SW deg	M/St	12	5M	M	Ind	Ind	Ind		
Computing Mathematics with Business Studies	GN11	4SW deg	M/St	12	5M	M	Ind	Ind	Ind		
Mathematics	G100	3FT/4SW deg	M/St	DD	M$	P	Ind	Ind	Ind		
Mathematics and Technology	GJ19	3FT/4SW deg	M/St/P								
Mathematics with Biomedical Sciences	G1B9	3FT/4SW deg	M/St/B	EE	3M	P	Ind	Ind	Ind		
Mathematics with Women's Studies	G1M9	3FT/4SW deg	M/St	EE	3M	P	Ind	Ind	Ind		
Combined Studies *Computing Mathematics*	Y400	3FT deg	M	14	2M	M	Ind	Ind	Ind		
Combined Studies *Mathematics*	Y400	3FT deg	M	8-10	2M	M	Ind	Ind	Ind		
Combined Studies *Statistics*	Y400	3FT deg	M	14	2M	M	Ind	Ind	Ind		
Computing Mathematics	071G	2FT/3SW HND	M/St	E	M$	P	Ind	Ind	Ind		
Univ College of St MARTIN, LANCASTER AND CUMBRIA											
Art and Design/Mathematics	WG11	3FT deg	A+M	CC-CDE	3M+2D$	MA^	28$	BBCC$	Ind		
Business Management Studies/Mathematics	NG11	3FT deg	M	CD-CEE	3M+2D	M^	28$	BCCC$			
Geography/Mathematics	LG81	3FT deg	Gy+M	CD-DDE	X	X	28$	BCCC$	Ind		
Health Studies/Mathematics	BG91	3FT deg	M	CD-DDE	X	P^	28$	BCCC$			
History/Mathematics	VG11	3FT deg	H+M	CD-DDE	X	X	28$	BCCC$	Ind		
Mathematics/Art and Design	GW1C	3FT deg	A+M	DD-DEE	X	X	28$	BCCC$	Ind		
Mathematics/Business Management Studies	GN11	3FT deg	M	DD-DEE	X	P^	28$	BCCC$			
Mathematics/Drama	GW14	3FT deg	M	DD-DEE	X	P^	28$	BCCC$	Ind		
Mathematics/Education Studies	GX19	3FT deg	M	DD-DEE	X	P^	28$	BCCC$	Ind		
Mathematics/Geography	GL18	3FT deg	M+Gy	DD-DEE	X	X	28$	BCCC$	Ind		
Mathematics/Health Administration	GL14	3FT deg	M	DD-DEE	X	P^	28$	BCCC$	Ind		
Mathematics/Health Studies	GB19	3FT deg	M	DD-DEE	X	P^	28$	BCCC$			
Mathematics/History	GV11	3FT deg	M	DD-DEE	X		28$	BCCC$			
Mathematics/Physical Education & Sports Studies	GX1X	3FT deg	M	DD-DEE	X	P^	28$	BCCC$			
Mathematics/Religious Studies	GV18	3FT deg	M	DD-DEE	X	X	28$	BCCC$	Ind		
Mathematics/Science, Technology and Society	GY11	3FT deg	M g	DD-DEE	X	P^	28$	BCCC$	Ind		
Mathematics/Social Ethics	GV17	3FT deg	M	DD-DEE	X	P^	28$	BCCC$	Ind		
Religious Studies/Mathematics	VG81	3FT deg	M	CD-DDE	3M+2D$	M^	28$	BCCC$	Ind		
Science, Technology and Society/Mathematics	GY1C	3FT deg	M g	CD-DDE	X	M^	28$	BCCC$	Ind		
Social Ethics/Mathematics	VG71	3FT deg	M	CD-DDE	3M+2D$	M^	28$	BCCC$	Ind		
Univ of SOUTHAMPTON											
Chemistry and Mathematics (4 Yrs)	FG11	4FT deg	C+M g	BBC	Ind	Ind	30$	CSYS	Ind	3	20/30
Chemistry with Mathematics	F1G1	3FT deg	C+M	18	Ind	Ind	28$	CSYS	Ind	4	
Economics and Mathematics	LG11	3FT deg	M	24	Ind	D$^ go	32$	AABBB$	Ind	29	
Industrial Applied Mathematics	G168	3FT deg	M	BBC	Ind	Ind	30	ABBBB	Ind	15	
Mathematical Studies	G110	3FT deg	M	BBC	Ind	Ind	30	ABBBB	Ind	8	
Mathematics	G100	3FT deg	M	BBC	Ind	Ind	30	ABBBB	Ind	7	18/28
Mathematics (4 Yrs) (MMath)	G103	4FT deg	M	ABB	Ind	Ind	30	ABBBB	Ind	12	16/28
Mathematics and French (4 Yrs)	GR11	4FT deg	M+F	BBC	Ind	Ind	30$	ABBBB	Ind	8	
Mathematics and German (4 Yrs)	GR12	4FT deg	M+G	BBC	Ind	Ind	30$	ABBBB	Ind	7	
Mathematics and Music	GW13	3FT deg	M+Mu	BBC	Ind	Ind	30	ABBBB	Ind	6	
Mathematics and Philosophy	GV17	3FT deg	M	BBC	Ind	Ind	30	ABBBB	Ind	7	
Mathematics and Spanish (4 Yrs)	GR14	4FT deg	M+Sp	BBC	Ind	Ind	30	ABBBB	Ind	8	
Mathematics with Actuarial Studies	G1N3	3FT deg	M	BBC	Ind	Ind	30	ABBBB	Ind	6	14/30
Mathematics with Chemistry	G1F1	3FT deg	M+C	BBC	Ind	Ind	30	ABBBB	Ind	8	

			98 expected requirements							96 entry stats	
course details											
TITLE	CODE	COURSE	SUBJECTS	A/AS	ND/C	AGNVQ	IB	SQA(H)	SQA	RATIO	A/AS
Mathematics with Computer Science	G1G5	3FT deg	M	BBC	Ind	Ind	30	ABBBB	Ind	7	16/26
Mathematics with Economics	G1L1	3FT deg	M	BBC	Ind	Ind	30	ABBBB	Ind	7	20/30
Mathematics with Education	G1X9	3FT deg	M	BBC	Ind	Ind	30	ABBBB	Ind	4	
Mathematics with Finance	G1NH	3FT deg	M	BBC	Ind	Ind	30	ABBBB	Ind	8	18/28
Mathematics with Geography	G1F8	3FT deg	M+Gy	BBC	Ind	Ind	30	ABBBB	Ind	6	20/24
Mathematics with Oceanography	G1F7	3FT deg	M+P/B	BBC	Ind	Ind	30	ABBBB	Ind	5	
Mathematics with Operational Research	G1N2	3FT deg	M	BBC	Ind	Ind	30	ABBBB	Ind	12	
Mathematics with Physics	G1F3	3FT deg	M+P	BBC	Ind	Ind	30	ABBBB	Ind	7	
Mathematics with Statistics	G1G4	3FT deg	M	BBC	Ind	Ind	30	ABBBB	Ind	7	16/20
Oceanography with Mathematics	F7G1	3FT deg	M+S g	BCC	Ind	Ind	30$	BBBBC	Ind	3	
Philosophy and Mathematics	VG71	3FT deg	M	BCC-BCD	1M+4D	Ind	26	Ind	Ind	4	
Physics and Mathematics (4 Yrs)	FG31	4FT deg	M+P	BC	Ind	Ind	28$	AAABB	Ind	8	
Physics with Mathematics	F3G1	3FT deg	M+P	BC	Ind	Ind	28$	AAABB	Ind	3	
Univ of ST ANDREWS											
Applied Mathematics (Arts)	G112	4FT deg	M g	BBB	X	Ind	30$	BBBB$	Ind		
Applied Mathematics (Science) (BSc/MSci)	G110	3FT/4FT deg	M g	BCC	Ind	Ind	28$	BBBC$	Ind	4	
Computer Science and Mathematics (BSc/MSci)	GG15	3FT/4FT deg	M g	CCC	Ind	Ind	28$	BBBC$	Ind	5	
Mathematics (Arts)	G102	4FT deg	M g	BBB	X	Ind	30$	BBBB$	Ind	4	
Mathematics (Science) (BSc/MSci)	G100	3FT/4FT deg	M g	BCC	Ind	Ind	28$	BBBC$	Ind	7	22/30
Mathematics with French	G1R1	4FT deg	F+M g	BCC	Ind	Ind	28$	BBBC$	Ind		
Mathematics with French (with Integ Yr Abroad)	G1RC	4FT/5FT deg	F+M g	BCC	Ind	Ind	28$	BBBC$	Ind	9	
Mathematics with Geography	G1F8	4FT deg	M g	BCC	Ind	Ind	28$	BBBC$	Ind		
Mathematics with German	G1R2	4FT deg	M g	BCC	Ind	Ind	28$	BBBC$	Ind		
Mathematics with German (with Integ Yr Abroad)	G1RF	4FT/5FT deg	M g	BCC	Ind	Ind	28$	BBBC$	Ind		
Mathematics-Ancient History	GVC1	3FT/4FT deg	M g	BBB	X	Ind	30$	BBBB$	Ind		
Mathematics-Art History	GV14	4FT deg	M g	BBB	X	Ind	30$	BBBB$	Ind		
Mathematics-Chemistry	FG11	3FT/4FT deg	C+M	CCC	Ind	Ind	28$	BBCC$	Ind	5	
Mathematics-Economics (Arts)	GL11	4FT deg	M g	BBB	X	Ind	30$	BBBB$	Ind	4	
Mathematics-Economics (Science)	GLC1	3FT/4FT deg	M g	BCC	Ind	Ind	28$	BBBC$	Ind	4	
Mathematics-Geography (Science)	GFC8	3FT/4FT deg	M g	BBB	Ind	Ind	30$	BBBB$	Ind	9	
Mathematics-Hebrew	GQ19	4FT deg	M g	BBB	X	Ind	30$	BBBB$	Ind		
Mathematics-Latin	GQ16	4FT deg	M g	BBB	X	Ind	30$	BBBB$	Ind		
Mathematics-Logic and Philosophy of Science	GV1R	3FT/4FT deg	M g	CCC	Ind	Ind	28$	BBBC$	Ind	6	
Mathematics-Management Sciences	GN11	4FT deg	M g	BBB	Ind	Ind	28$	BBBB$	Ind	6	
Mathematics-Theoretical Physics	FG3D	4FT deg	M+P g	CCC	X	Ind	28$	BBCC	Ind		
Mediaeval History-Mathematics	GV1D	4FT deg	M g	BBB	X	Ind	30$	BBBB$	Ind	1	
Philosophy-Mathematics	GV17	4FT deg	M g	BBB	X	Ind	30$	BBBB$	Ind	3	
Physics-Mathematics	FG3C	4FT deg	M+P g	CCC	X	Ind	28$	BBCC	Ind		
Psychology-Mathematics (Arts)	LG71	4FT deg	M g	ABB	X	Ind	32$	ABBB$	Ind		
Psychology-Mathematics (Science)	GC18	3FT/4FT deg	M g	ABB	Ind	Ind	34$	ABBB$	Ind	6	
Pure Mathematics (Arts)	G122	4FT deg	M g	BBB	X	Ind	30$	BBBB$	Ind	2	
Pure Mathematics (Science) (BSc/MSci)	G120	3FT/4FT deg	M g	BCC	Ind	Ind	28$	BBBC$	Ind		
Scottish History-Mathematics	GV11	4FT deg	M g	BBB	X	Ind	30$	BBBB$	Ind		
Statistics (Arts)	G402	4FT deg	M g	BBB	X	Ind	30$	BBBB$	Ind		
Statistics (Science) (BSc/MSci)	G400	3FT/4FT deg	M g	BCC	Ind	Ind	28$	BBBC$	Ind	3	
Statistics with French (Science)	G4R1	4FT deg	M g	BCC	Ind	Ind	28$	BBBC$	Ind		
Statistics with French (Science) (Int Yr Abroad)	G4RC	4FT/5FT deg	M g	BCC	Ind	Ind	28$	BBBC$	Ind	2	
Statistics with German (Science)	G4R2	4FT deg	M g	BCC	Ind	Ind	28$	BBBC$	Ind		
Statistics with German (Science) (Int Yr Abroad)	G4RF	4FT/5FT deg	M g	BCC	Ind	Ind	28$	BBBC$	Ind		
Statistics-Computer Science	GG45	3FT/4FT deg	M g	BCC	Ind	Ind	28$	BBBC$	Ind		
Statistics-Economics (Arts)	GLK1	4FT deg	M g	BBB	X	Ind	30$	BBBB$	Ind		
Statistics-Economics (Science)	GL41	4FT deg	M g	BCC	Ind	Ind	28$	BBBC$	Ind	6	

Mathematics and Statistics

52

course details | 98 expected requirements | 96 entry stats

TITLE	CODE	COURSE	SUBJECTS	A/AS	NO/C	AGNVQ	IB	SQA(H)	SQA	RATIO A/AS
Statistics-Geography (Science)	FG84	3FT/4FT deg	M	BBB	Ind	Ind	30$	BBBB$	Ind	
Statistics-Logic and Philosophy of Science	GV4R	3FT/4FT deg	M g	CCC	Ind	Ind	28$	BBBC$	Ind	
Statistics-Management Sciences	GN41	4FT deg	M g	BBB	Ind	Ind	28$	BBBB$	Ind	6
Statistics-Mathematics (Arts)	GG14	3FT/4FT deg	M g	BBB	Ind	Ind	28$	BBBB$	Ind	4
Statistics-Mathematics (Science)	GGC4	3FT/4FT deg	M g	BCC	Ind	Ind	28$	BBBC$	Ind	9
Statistics-Philosophy	GV47	4FT deg	M g	BBB	X	Ind	30$	BBBB$	Ind	
Statistics-Psychology (Science)	CG84	3FT/4FT deg	M g	ABB	Ind	Ind	32$	ABBB$	Ind	
General Degree of BSc Applied Mathematics (Science)	Y100	3FT deg	M g	CCC	Ind	Ind	28$	BBBC$	Ind	
General Degree of BSc Mathematics (Science)	Y100	3FT deg	M g	CCC	Ind	Ind	28$	BBBC$	Ind	
General Degree of BSc Pure Mathematics (Science)	Y100	3FT deg	M g	CCC	Ind	Ind	28$	BBBC$	Ind	
General Degree of BSc Statistics (Science)	Y100	3FT deg	M g	CCC	Ind	Ind	28$	BBBC$	Ind	
General Degree of MA Applied Mathematics (Arts)	Y450	3FT deg	M g	BBB	X	Ind	30$	BBBB$	Ind	
General Degree of MA Pure Mathematics (Arts)	Y450	3FT deg	M g	BBB	X	Ind	30$	BBBB$	Ind	
General Degree of MA Statistics (Arts)	Y450	3FT deg	M g	BBB	X	Ind	30$	BBBB$	Ind	

ST MARY'S Univ COLL

TITLE	CODE	COURSE	SUBJECTS	A/AS	NO/C	AGNVQ	IB	SQA(H)	SQA	RATIO A/AS
Mathematics and Education Studies	GX1X	3FT deg	M	4-8	X	X	Ind	BBBB$	X	
Mathematics and Heritage Management	GN19	3FT deg	M	4-8	X	X	Ind	BBBB$	X	
Mathematics and Management Studies	GN11	3FT deg	M	4-8	X	X	Ind	BBBB$	X	
Mathematics and Media Arts	GP14	3FT deg	M	4-8	X	X	Ind	BBBB$	X	

STAFFORDSHIRE Univ

TITLE	CODE	COURSE	SUBJECTS	A/AS	NO/C	AGNVQ	IB	SQA(H)	SQA	RATIO A/AS
Applied Statistics/Accounting	GN44	3FT deg	g	12	Ind	M	27	CCC	Ind	
Biology/Applied Statistics	CG14	3FT deg	S	8	3M	M^	24	BCC	Ind	2
Business Studies/Applied Statistics	NG14	3FT deg	g	16	Ind	M	24	BBC	Ind	
Ceramic Science/Applied Statistics	JG34	3FT deg	g	8	3M	M$	24	BCC	Ind	
Chemistry/Applied Statistics	FG14	3FT deg	S	8	3M	M	24	BCC	Ind	
Computing and Applicable Mathematics	GG15	4SW deg	g	12	Ind	M	27	CCC	Ind	5
Computing/Applied Statistics	GG54	3FT deg	g	10	Ind	Ind	Ind	Ind	Ind	4
Electronics/Applied Statistics	GH46	3FT deg	S g	8	3M	M	24	BCC	Ind	
Environmental Studies/Applied Statistics	FG94	3FT deg	*	DD-CC	4M	M	Ind	BBB	Ind	
Foundation Computing and Applicable Mathematics	GG1M▼	4EXT/5SW deg		Ind	Ind	Ind	Ind	Ind	Ind	
Geography/Applied Statistics	GL48	3FT deg	S	8	3M	M	24	BCC	Ind	
Geology/Applied Statistics	FG64	3FT deg	S	8	3M	M	24	BCC	Ind	
Information Systems/Applied Statistics	GG45	3FT deg	g	10	Ind	Ind	Ind	Ind	Ind	1
Mathematics for Information Technology	G150	3FT deg	g	12	Ind	M	27	CCC		
Mathematics for Information Technology	G151	3FT deg								
Physics/Applied Statistics	FG34	3FT deg	S	8	3M	M	24	BCC	Ind	
Psychology/Applied Statistics	GL47	3FT deg	g	18	3M+3D	D/M^	27	BBB	Ind	
Sociology/Applied Statistics	GL43	3FT deg	g	12	3M	M	24	BCC	Ind	
Sport Sciences and Applied Statistics	BG14	3FT deg	S	14	Ind	D	Ind	BBCC	Ind	

Univ of STIRLING

TITLE	CODE	COURSE	SUBJECTS	A/AS	NO/C	AGNVQ	IB	SQA(H)	SQA	RATIO A/AS
Accountancy/Mathematics	GN14	4FT deg	M g	BCC	HN	Ind	33	BBBB	HN	
Biology/Mathematics	CG11	4FT deg	S+M	CCC	Ind	Ind	28	BBCC	HN	
Business Studies/Mathematics	GN11	4FT deg	M g	CCC	Ind	Ind	28	BBCC	HN	
Computing Science/Mathematics	G5G1	4FT deg	M g	CCC	Ind	Ind	28	BBCC	HN	
Economics/Mathematics	GL11	4FT deg	M g	CCC	Ind	Ind	28	BBCC	HN	
Financial Studies/Mathematics	GN13	4FT deg	M g	CCC	Ind	Ind	28	BBCC	HN	

	course details			98 expected requirements						96 entry stats
TITLE	CODE	COURSE	SUBJECTS	A/AS	NO/C	AGNVQ	IB	SQA(H)	SQA	RATIO A/AS
French/Mathematics	GR11	4FT deg	M g	CCC	Ind	Ind	28	BBCC	HN	
German/Mathematics	R2G1	3FT deg	g	CCC		Ind	28	BBCC		
Management Science/Mathematics	GN12	4FT deg	M g	CCC	Ind	Ind	28	BBCC	HN	
Mathematics & its Applications with Comp Science	G1G5	4FT deg	M g	CCC	Ind	Ind	28	BBCC	HN	
Mathematics & its Applications with French Lang	G1R1	4FT deg	M g	CCC	Ind	Ind	28	BBCC	HN	
Mathematics & its Applications with German Lang	G1R2	4FT deg	M g	CCC	Ind	Ind	28	BBCC	HN	
Mathematics (General Degree only)	G100	4FT deg	M g	CCC		Ind	28	BBCC	HN	
Mathematics and its Applications	G110	4FT deg	M g	CCC	Ind	Ind	28	BBCC	HN	
Mathematics and its Applications with Biology	G1C1	4FT deg	M+S g	CCC	Ind	Ind	28	BBCC	HN	
Mathematics and its Applications with Economics	G1L1	4FT deg	M g	CCC	Ind	Ind	28	BBCC	HN	
Mathematics and its Applications with Env Sci	G1F9	4FT deg	M+S g	CCC	Ind	Ind	28	BBCC	HN	
Mathematics and its Applications with Fin St	G1N3	4FT deg	M g	CCC	Ind	Ind	28	BBCC	HN	
Mathematics and its Applications with Japanese	G1T4	4FT deg	M g	CCC	Ind	Ind	28	BBCC	HN	
Mathematics and its Applications with Mgt Sci	G1N1	4FT deg	M g	CCC	Ind	Ind	28	BBCC	HN	
Mathematics and its Applications with Span Lang	G1R4	4FT deg	M g	CCC	Ind	Ind	28	BBCC	HN	
Mathematics/Psychology	CG81	4FT deg	M g	CCC	Ind	Ind	28	BBCC	HN	
Mathematics/Social Policy	GL14	4FT deg	M g	CCC	Ind	Ind	28	BBCC	HN	
Mathematics/Sociology	GL13	4FT deg	M g	CCC	Ind	Ind	28	BBCC	HN	

Univ of STRATHCLYDE

Mathematical Biology	GC11	4FT deg	M+C g	CD	Ind		30$	BBCC$	Ind	
Mathematics	G100	4FT deg	M g	CD	Ind		30$	BBCC$	Ind	
Mathematics and Computer Science	GG15	4FT deg	M g	CD	Ind		30$	BBBC$	Ind	
Mathematics and Physics	GF13	4FT deg	M+P g	CD	Ind		30$	BBCC$	Ind	
Mathematics with a Modern Language	G1T9	4FT deg	M+L g	CC	Ind		30$	BBCC$	Ind	
Mathematics, Statistics and Accounting	GN44	4FT deg	M g	BBC	Ind		36$	AAABB$	Ind	
Mathematics, Statistics and Economics	G1L1	4FT deg	M g	CD	Ind		30$	BBCC$	Ind	
Mathematics, Statistics and Finance	GN43	4FT deg	M g	CD	HN		30$	BBBC$	Ind	
Mathematics, Statistics and Management Science	GN11	4FT deg	M g	CD	Ind		30$	BBCC$	Ind	
Statistics	G400	4FT deg	M g	CD	Ind		30$	BBCC$	Ind	
Science Studies (Pass Degree) *Mathematics*	Y100	3FT deg	M+S	DD	Ind		Ind	CCC$	Ind	
Science Studies (Pass Degree) *Statistics*	Y100	3FT deg	g	DD	Ind		Ind	CCC$	Ind	

Univ of SUNDERLAND

Accounting and Mathematics	NG41	3FT/4SW deg	M g	4-8	4M $	M*△	24	CCCC	N	6 6/12
Biology and Mathematics	CG11	3FT deg	B/C+M g	8	N $	M	24$	CCCC$	N$	
Biology with Mathematics	C1G1	3FT deg	B/C	8	3M	M	Ind	Ind	Ind	
Business Studies and Mathematics	NG11	3FT/4SW deg	M	8	3M	M	Ind	Ind	Ind	
Business Studies with Mathematics	N1G1	3FT/4SW deg	*	8	3M	M	Ind	Ind	Ind	
Chemistry and Mathematics	FG11	3FT deg	M+C g	8	N $	M	24$	CCCC$	N$	
Chemistry with Mathematics	F1G1	3FT deg	C	8	3M	M	Ind	Ind	Ind	
Computer Studies and Mathematics	GG51	3FT deg	M g	8	N $	M	24$	CCCC$	N$	
Computer Studies with Mathematics	G5G1	3FT/4SW deg	*	8	3M	M	Ind	Ind	Ind	
Economics and Mathematics	LG11	3FT deg	M g	8	N $	M	24$	CCCC$	N$	
Economics with Mathematics	L1G1	3FT deg	*	8	3M	M	Ind	Ind	Ind	
English and Mathematics	QG31	3FT deg	M	8	3M	M	Ind	Ind	Ind	
English with Mathematics	Q3G1	3FT deg	M	10	4M	M	Ind	Ind	Ind	
French and Mathematics	RG11	4FT deg	M+F g	8	N $	M	24$	CCCC$	N$	
French with Mathematics	R1G1	4FT deg	F+M	8	3M	M	Ind	Ind	Ind	
Geology and Mathematics	FG61	3FT deg	M	8	3M	M	Ind	Ind	Ind	
German and Mathematics	RG21	4FT deg	M+G g	8	N $	M	24$	CCCC$	N$	
German with Mathematics	R2G1	4SW deg	G	8	3M	M	Ind	Ind	Ind	

Mathematics and Statistics 52

TITLE	CODE	COURSE	SUBJECTS	A/AS	ND/C	AGNVQ	IB	SQA(H)	SQA	RATIO A/AS
History and Mathematics	VG11	3FT deg	M	10	4M	M	Ind	Ind		
History of Art and Design and Mathematics	VG41	3FT deg	M	8	3M	M	Ind	Ind		
History with Mathematics	V1G1	3FT deg	*	10	4M	M	Ind	Ind	Ind	
Mathematics and Media Studies	GP14	3FT deg	M	24	Ind	Ind	Ind	Ind		
Mathematics and Philosophy	GV17	3FT deg	M	8	3M	M	Ind	Ind		
Mathematics and Physiology	GB11	3FT deg	M	8	3M	M	Ind	Ind		
Mathematics and Politics	GM11	3FT deg	M	8	3M	M	Ind	Ind		
Mathematics and Psychology	GC18	3FT deg	M g	12	3M $	M	24$	BCCC$	N$	2
Mathematics and Sociology	GL13	3FT deg	M	10	4M	M	Ind	Ind		
Mathematics and Spanish	GR14	4SW deg	M	8	3M	M	Ind	Ind		
Mathematics with Biology	G1C1	3FT deg	M	8	3M	M	Ind	Ind	Ind	
Mathematics with Business Studies	G1N1	3FT deg	M	8	3M	M	Ind	Ind	Ind	
Mathematics with Chemistry	G1F1	3FT deg	M	8	3M	M	Ind	Ind	Ind	
Mathematics with Computer Studies	G1G5	3FT deg	M	8	3M	M	Ind	Ind	Ind	
Mathematics with Economics	G1L1	3FT deg	M	8	3M	M	Ind	Ind	Ind	
Mathematics with English	G1Q3	3FT deg	M	10	4M	M	Ind	Ind	Ind	
Mathematics with French	G1R1	3FT deg	M	8	3M	M	Ind	Ind	Ind	
Mathematics with Geology	G1F6	3FT deg	M	8	3M	M	Ind	Ind	Ind	
Mathematics with German	G1R2	3FT deg	M	8	3M	M	Ind	Ind	Ind	
Mathematics with History	G1V1	3FT deg	M	10	4M	M	Ind	Ind	Ind	
Mathematics with History of Art and Design	G1V4	3FT deg	M	8	3M	M	Ind	Ind	Ind	
Mathematics with Media Studies	G1P4	3FT deg	M	24	Ind	Ind	Ind	Ind	Ind	
Mathematics with Philosophy	G1V7	3FT deg	M	8	3M	M	Ind	Ind	Ind	
Mathematics with Physiology	G1B1	3FT deg	M	8	3M	M	Ind	Ind	Ind	
Mathematics with Politics	G1M1	3FT deg	M	8	3M	M	Ind	Ind	Ind	
Mathematics with Psychology	G1C8	3FT deg	M	10	4M	M^	Ind	Ind	Ind	
Mathematics with Sociology	G1L3	3FT deg	M	10	4M	M	Ind	Ind	Ind	
Mathematics with Spanish	G1R4	3FT deg	M	8	3M	M	Ind	Ind	Ind	
Media Studies with Mathematics	P4G1	3FT deg	*	24	Ind	Ind	Ind	Ind	Ind	
Philosophy with Mathematics	V7G1	3FT deg	*	8	3M	Ind	Ind	Ind	Ind	
Physiology with Mathematics	B1G1	3FT deg	*	8	3M	M	Ind	Ind	Ind	
Politics with Mathematics	M1G1	3FT deg	*	8	3M	M	Ind	Ind	Ind	
Psychology with Mathematics	C8G1	3FT deg	*	10	4M	M^	Ind	Ind	Ind	
Sociology with Mathematics	L3G1	3FT deg	*	10	4M	M	Ind	Ind	Ind	

Univ of SURREY

Mathematics	G101	3FT deg	M	18-20	Ind	Ind	Ind	CSYS	Ind	20
Mathematics	G102	4SW deg	M	18-20	Ind	Ind	Ind	CSYS	Ind	11
Mathematics (MMath)	G104	4FT deg	M	18-20	Ind	Ind	Ind	Ind	Ind	
Mathematics and Computing Science	GG1M	3FT deg	M	18-20	Ind	Ind	Ind	CSYS	Ind	9
Mathematics and Computing Science	GG15	4SW deg	M	18-20	Ind	Ind	Ind	CSYS	Ind	5 14/20
Mathematics and Statistics	GG1L	4SW deg	M	18-20	Ind	Ind	Ind	CSYS	Ind	3
Mathematics and Statistics	GG1K	3FT deg	M	18-20	Ind	Ind	Ind	CSYS	Ind	28
Mathematics with Business Studies	G1NC	4SW deg	M	18-20	Ind	Ind	Ind	CSYS	Ind	5 18/20
Mathematics with Business Studies	G1N1	3FT deg	M	18-20	Ind	Ind	Ind	CSYS	Ind	6 14/20
Mathematics with a Foundation Year	G105	4FT/5SW deg	M	CCC	Ind	Ind	Ind	CSYS	Ind	6/ 8

Univ of SUSSEX

Economics with Mathematics	L1G1	3FT deg	M/St	BBB	MO $	M*^ go	$	Ind	Ind	
Mathematical Science	G140▼	4FT deg								
Mathematics	G100	3FT deg	M	BCC	MO $	MS^	$	Ind	Ind	
Mathematics & Stats with Eur St (French)(MMath)	G4RC	4FT deg	M g	BCC	MO $	MS^ go	$	Ind	Ind	
Mathematics & Stats with Eur St (German)(MMath)	G4RF	4FT deg	M g	BCC	MO $	MS^ go	$	Ind	Ind	

course details

TITLE	CODE	COURSE	SUBJECTS	A/AS	NO/C	AGNVQ	IB	SQA(H)	SQA	RATIO A/AS
Mathematics & Stats with Eur St(Italian) (MMath)	G4RH	4FT deg	M g	BCC	MO $	MS△ go	$	Ind	Ind	
Mathematics & Stats with Eur St(Russian) (MMath)	G4RV	4FT deg	M g	BCC	MO $	MS△ go	$	Ind	Ind	
Mathematics & Stats with Eur St(Spanish) (MMath)	G4RK	4FT deg	M g	BCC	MO $	MS△ go	$	Ind	Ind	
Mathematics & Stats with Management St (MMath)	G4NC	4FT deg	M	BCC	MO $	MS△	$	Ind	Ind	
Mathematics & Stats with North Amer St (MMath)	G4QK	4FT deg	M	BCC	MO $	MS△	$	Ind	Ind	
Mathematics (MMath)	G103	4FT deg	M	BCC	MO $	MS△	$	Ind	Ind	
Mathematics and Artificial Intelligence	GG51	3FT deg	M	BCC	MO $	MS△	$	Ind	Ind	
Mathematics and Computer Science	GG15	3FT deg	M	BCC	MO $	MS△	$	Ind	Ind	
Mathematics and Economics	GL11	3FT deg	M	BCC	MO $	MS△	$	Ind	Ind	
Mathematics and Statistics	G406	3FT deg	M	BCC	MO $	MS△	$	Ind	Ind	
Mathematics and Statistics (MMath)	GG14	4FT deg	M	BCC	MO $	MS△	$	Ind	Ind	
Mathematics and Statistics with Economics	G4L1	3FT deg	M	BCC	MO $	MS△	$	Ind	Ind	
Mathematics and Statistics with Eur St (French)	G4R1	4FT deg	M g	BCC	MO $	MS△ go	$	Ind	Ind	
Mathematics and Statistics with Eur St (German)	G4R2	4FT deg	M g	BCC	MO $	MS△ go	$	Ind	Ind	
Mathematics and Statistics with N Amer Studies	G4Q4	4FT deg	M	BCC	MO $	MS△	$	Ind	Ind	
Mathematics and Statistics with Physics	G4F3	3FT deg	M+P	BCC	MO $	MS△	$	Ind	Ind	
Mathematics and Statistics with Physics (MMath)	G4FH	4FT deg	M+P	BCC	MO $	MS△	$	Ind	Ind	
Mathematics and Stats with Computer Sc(MMat)	G4GM	4FT deg	M	BCC	MO $	MS△	$	Ind	Ind	
Mathematics and Stats with Computer Science	G4G5	3FT deg	M	BCC	MO $	MS△	$	Ind	Ind	
Mathematics and Stats with Economics (MMath)	G4LC	4FT deg	M	BCC	MO $	MS△	$	Ind	Ind	
Mathematics and Stats with Environ Sc(MMath)	G4FX	4FT deg	M	BCC	MO $	MS△	$	Ind	Ind	
Mathematics and Stats with Environmental Sci	G4F9	3FT deg	M	BCC	MO $	MS△	$	Ind	Ind	
Mathematics and Stats with Eur Studies (Ital)	G4R3	4FT deg	M g	BCC	MO $	MS△ go	$	Ind	Ind	
Mathematics and Stats with Eur Studies (Russ)	G4R8	4FT deg	M g	BCC	MO $	MS△ go	$	Ind	Ind	
Mathematics and Stats with Eur Studies (Span)	G4R4	4FT deg	M g	BCC	MO $	MS△ go	$	Ind	Ind	
Mathematics and Stats with Management Studs	G4N1	3FT deg	M	BCC	MO $	MS△	$	Ind	Ind	
Mathematics with Computer Science	G1G5	3FT deg	M	BCC	MO $	MS△	$	Ind	Ind	
Mathematics with Computer Science (MMath)	G1GM	4FT deg	M	BCC	MO $	MS△	$	Ind	Ind	
Mathematics with Economics	G1L1	3FT deg	M	BCC	MO $	MS△	$	Ind	Ind	
Mathematics with Economics (MMath)	G1LC	4FT deg	M	BCC	MO $	MS△	$	Ind	Ind	
Mathematics with Environmental Science	G1F9	3FT deg	M	BCC	MO $	MS△	$	Ind	Ind	
Mathematics with Environmental Science (MMath)	G1FX	4FT deg	M	BCC	MO $	MS△	$	Ind	Ind	
Mathematics with European St (French) (MMath)	G1RC	4FT deg	M g	BCC	MO $	MS△ go	$	Ind	Ind	
Mathematics with European St (German) (MMath)	G1RF	4FT deg	M g	BCC	MO $	MS△ go	$	Ind	Ind	
Mathematics with European St (Italian) (MMath)	G1RH	4FT deg	M g	BCC	MO $	MS△ go	$	Ind	Ind	
Mathematics with European St (Russian) (MMath)	G1RV	4FT deg	M g	BCC	MO $	MS△ go	$	Ind	Ind	
Mathematics with European St (Spanish) (MMath)	G1RK	4FT deg	M g	BCC	MO $	MS△ go	$	Ind	Ind	
Mathematics with European Studies (French)	G1R1	4FT deg	M g	BCC	MO $	MS△ go	$	Ind	Ind	
Mathematics with European Studies (German)	G1R2	4FT deg	M g	BCC	MO $	MS△ go	$	Ind	Ind	
Mathematics with European Studies (Italian)	G1R3	4FT deg	M g	BCC	MO $	MS△ go	$	Ind	Ind	
Mathematics with European Studies (Russian)	G1R8	4FT deg	M g	BCC	MO $	MS△ go	$	Ind	Ind	
Mathematics with European Studies (Spanish)	G1R4	4FT deg	M g	BCC	MO $	MS△ go	$	Ind	Ind	
Mathematics with Management Studies	G1N1	3FT deg	M	BCC	MO $	MS△	$	Ind	Ind	
Mathematics with Management Studies (MMath)	G1ND	4FT deg	M	BCC	MO $	MS△	$	Ind	Ind	
Mathematics with North American Studies	G1Q4	4FT deg	M	BCC	MO $	MS△	$	Ind	Ind	
Mathematics with North American Studies (MMath)	G1QK	4FT deg	M	BCC	MO $	MS△	$	Ind	Ind	
Mathematics with Physics	G1F3	3FT deg	M+P	BCC	MO $	MS△	$	Ind	Ind	
Mathematics with Physics (MMath)	G1FH	4FT deg	M+P	BCC	MO $	MS△	$	Ind	Ind	
Physics and Mathematics	FG31	3FT deg	M+P	CCC	MO $	MS△	$	Ind	Ind	
Physics and Mathematics	FG3C	4FT deg	M+P	CCC	MO $	MS△	$	Ind	Ind	
Physics with Mathematics	F3G1	3FT deg	M+P	CCC	MO $	MS△	$	Ind	Ind	

Mathematics and Statistics 52

	course details			98 expected requirements							96 entry stats	
TITLE	CODE	COURSE	SUBJECTS	A/AS	ND/C	RGNVQ	IB	SQA(H)	SQA	RATIO A/AS		
Univ of Wales SWANSEA												
Actuarial Studies	G4N3	3FT deg	M	BBB	X	D$^ go	32$	AABBB$	X			
Actuarial Studies with a year abroad	G4NH	4FT deg	M	BBB	X	D$^ go	32$	AABBB$	X			
Applied Mathematics	G110	3FT deg	M	BCC	Ind	Ind	28$	Ind	Ind	11		
Computing Mathematics	G5G1	3FT deg	M	BBC-BCC	5D $	Ind	30$	ABBBB$	Ind	20		
Economics and Mathematics	GLD1	3FT deg	M g	BBC-BCC	Ind	Ind	28$	BBBBB$	Ind	4		
Management Sci and Statistics with a year abroad	GN4C	4FT deg	M	BBC	X	D$^ go	32$	AABBB$	Ind	1		
Management Science (with Mathematics)	G1N1	3FT deg	M	BBC	X	D$^ go	32$	AABBB$	Ind	8		
Management Science and Statistics	GN41	3FT deg	M	BBC	X	D$^ go	32$	AABBB$	Ind	5		
Management Science with Maths (with a yr abroad)	G1NC	4FT deg	M	BBC	X	D$^ go	32$	AABBB$	Ind			
Mathematics	G141	4FT deg	*	12-16	N	Ind	26	Ind	Ind	1		
Mathematics (MMath)	G103	4FT deg	M	BBC	X	Ind	30$	Ind	Ind			
Mathematics (with French)	G1R1	4FT deg	F+M	BBC-BCC	X	Ind	28$	BBBBB$	Ind	11		
Mathematics (with German)	G1R2	4FT deg	M+G	BBC-BCC	Ind	Ind	28$	BBBBB$	Ind			
Mathematics (with Italian)	G1R3	4FT deg	M+L	BBC-BCC	X	Ind	28$	BBBBC$	Ind			
Mathematics (with Russian)	G1R8	4FT deg	M+L	BCC	X	Ind	26$	BBBBC$	Ind			
Mathematics (with Spanish)	G1R4	4FT deg	M+L	BBC-BCC	X	Ind	28$	BBBBC$	Ind			
Mathematics (with Welsh)	G1Q5	4FT deg	M+L/(M g)	BCC	X	Ind	26$	BBBBC$	Ind			
Mathematics and Physics	FG31	3FT deg	M+P	BCC	Ind	Ind	28$	BBBBC$	Ind	14		
Mathematics and Topographic Science	GF18	3FT deg	M+Gy	20	Ind	Ind	28$	BBBBC$	Ind	6		
Maths with deferred choice of specialisation	G100	3FT deg	M	BCC	Ind	Ind	28$	Ind	Ind	3	12/24	
Pure Mathematics	G122	3FT deg	M	BCC	Ind	Ind	28$	Ind	Ind			
Pure Mathematics	G120	3FT deg	M	BCC	Ind	Ind	28$	Ind	Ind	15		
Pure Mathematics and Statistics	GG14	3FT deg	M	BCC	Ind	Ind	28$	Ind	Ind	11		
Statistics	G400	3FT deg	M	BCC	X	D$^ go	28$	BBBBB$	X	5		
Statistics with a year abroad (4 Yrs)	G401	4FT deg	M	BCC	X	D$^ go	28$	BBBBB$	X	1		
Univ of TEESSIDE												
Applied Statistics for Business	GN41	3FT/4SW deg	* g	8-12	Ind	M	Ind	CCCC	Ind	2	8/22	
Business Informatics (HND top-up)	NG14	1FT deg		X	HN	M		X		5		
Computational Mathematics for Industry	G110	3FT/4SW deg	M	8-12	Ind	M	Ind	CCCC	Ind	2		
Computing and Mathematics	GG15	3FT/4SW deg	M	8-12	Ind	M	Ind	CCCC	Ind	4	6/10	
Computing and Statistics	GG54	3FT/4SW deg	* g	8-12	Ind	M	Ind	CCCC	Ind	7		
Mathematics	G100	3FT/4SW deg	M	8-12	Ind	M	Ind	CCCC	Ind	5	14/26	
Sport Science and Mathematics	BG61	3FT/4SW deg	*	16	Ind		Ind	Ind	Ind			
Sports Science and Mathematics	GB16	3FT deg										
Statistics and Operational Research	GN42	3FT/4SW deg	M	8-12	Ind	M	Ind	CCCC	Ind			
Modular Degree Scheme *Mathematics*	Y401	3FT deg										
Applied Statistics for Business	4G1N	2FT HND	* g	4	N	P	Ind	CC	Ind			
Univ of ULSTER												
Mathematics,Stats & Comp (Hons)(4 Yr SW inc DIS)	G920▼	4SW deg	M	BCC	MO+4D	D*^ gi	30	BBBB	Ind			
Mathematics,Stats and Comp (4 Yr SW inc DIS)	G921▼	4SW deg	M	CDD	MO+1D	M*^ gi	26	BCCC	Ind			
Mathematical Studies (Maths, Stats & Computing)	009G▼	2FT HND	M g		Ind	M*^ gi	Ind	Ind	Ind	5	6/12	
UNIVERSITY COLL LONDON (Univ of London)												
Chemistry with Mathematics	F1G1	3FT deg	C+M g	BCC-BBB	MO $	Ind	30$	BBCCC$	N$			
Chemistry with Mathematics (MSci)	F1GC	4FT deg	C+M g	BCC-BBB	MO $	Ind	30$	BBCCC$	N$	2		
Economics and Statistics	LG14	3FT deg	M g	BCC	3M	Ind	30$	BBBCC$	Ind	6	18/28	
Mathematics	G100	3FT deg	M g	ABC-ABB	MO $	Ind	30$	AAABB$	N$	9	20/28	
Mathematics (MSci)	G107	4FT deg	M g	ABC-ABB	MO $	Ind	30$	AAABB$	N$	3	20/30	
Mathematics and Astronomy	GF15	3FT deg	M+P g	ABC-ABB	MO $	Ind	30$	AAABB$	N$			
Mathematics and Astronomy (MSci)	GF1M	4FT deg	M+P g	ABC-ABB	MO $	Ind	30$	AAABB$	N$	3		

TITLE	CODE	COURSE	SUBJECTS	A/AS	NO/C	AGNVQ	IB	SQA(H)	SQA	RATIO	A/AS
Mathematics and Computer Science	GG15	3FT deg	M g	ABC-ABB	MO $	Ind	30$	AAABB$	N$	12	24/26
Mathematics and Computer Science (MSci)	GG1M	4FT deg	M g	ABC-ABB	MO $	Ind	30$	AAABB$	N$	4	24/30
Mathematics and Physics	GF13	3FT deg	M+P g	ABC-ABB	MO $	Ind	30$	AAABB$	N$		
Mathematics and Physics (MSci)	GF1H	4FT deg	M+P g	ABC-ABB	MO $	Ind	30$	AAABB$	N$	9	
Mathematics and Statistical Science	GG14	3FT deg	M g	ABC-ABB	MO $	Ind	30$	AAABB$	N$	8	
Mathematics and Statistical Science (MSci)	GG1K	4FT deg	M g	ABC-ABB	MO $	Ind	30$	AAABB$	N$	1	
Mathematics with Economics	G1L1	3FT deg	M g	ABC-ABB	MO $	Ind	30$	AAABB$	N$	4	18/26
Mathematics with Economics (MSci)	G1LC	4FT deg	M g	ABC-ABB	MO $	Ind	30$	AAABB$	N$	2	
Mathematics with Management Studies	G1N1	3FT deg	M g	ABC-ABB	MO $	Ind	30$	AAABB$	N$	9	24/28
Mathematics with Management Studies (MSci)	G1NC	4FT deg	M g	ABC-ABB	MO $	Ind	30$	AAABB$	N$	4	
Mathematics with Theoretical Physics	G1F3	3FT deg	M+P g	ABC-ABB	MO $	Ind	30$	AAABB$	N$	14	
Mathematics with Theoretical Physics (MSci)	G1FH	4FT deg	M+P g	ABC-ABB	MO $	Ind	30$	AAABB$	N$	2	26/30
Mathematics with a European Language	G1T2	3FT deg	M g	ABC-ABB	MO $	Ind	30$	AAABB$	N$		
Mathematics with a European Language (MSci)	G1TF	4FT deg	M g	ABC-ABB	MO $	Ind	30$	AAABB$	N$	8	
Statistics	G400	3FT deg	M g	BCC	MO $	Ind	30$	BBCCC$	N$		
Statistics and Operational Research with Mgt St	G4N1	3FT deg	M g	BCC	MO $	Ind	30$	BBCCC$	N$	7	22/24
Statistics with a European Language	G4T2	3FT deg	M g	BCC	MO $	Ind	30$	BBCCC$	N$	4	
Physical Sciences *Mathematics*	Y100	3FT deg	S g	CCC-BCC	$	Ind	28$	BCCCC$	N$		
Physical Sciences *Statistical Science*	Y100	3FT deg	S g	CCC-BCC	$	Ind	28$	BCCCC$	N$		
Statistics,Computing,Operational Res & Economics *Statistics*	Y624	3FT deg	M g	BCC	MO $	Ind	30$	BBCCC$	N$		
Statistics,Operational Res & a European Language *Statistics*	Y625	3FT deg	M g	BCC	MO $	Ind	30$	BBCCC$	N$		

Univ of WARWICK

TITLE	CODE	COURSE	SUBJECTS	A/AS	NO/C	AGNVQ	IB	SQA(H)	SQA	RATIO	A/AS
Applied Mathematics	G110	3FT deg	M g	AAA-AAB	X	X	36$	CSYS$		5	28/30
Applied Mathematics (MMath)	G113	4FT deg	M g	AAA-AAB	X	X	36$	CSYS$		5	
Applied Mathematics and Business Studies	G1N1	3FT deg	M g	AAA-AAB	X	X	36$	CSYS$			
Applied Mathematics and Economics	LG11	3FT deg	M g	AAA-AAB	X	X	36$	CSYS$		14	
Applied Mathematics with Computing	G1G5	3FT deg	M g	AAA-AAB	X	X	36$	CSYS$		4	
Mathematics	G100	3FT deg	M g	AAA-AAB	X	X	36$	CSYS$		5	26/30
Mathematics (MMath)	G103	4FT deg	M g	AAA-AAB	X	X	36$	CSYS$		6	26/30
Mathematics and Business Studies	G1NC	3FT deg	M g	AAA-AAB	X	X	36$	CSYS$		11	26/30
Mathematics and Economics	GL11	3FT deg	M g	AAA-AAB	X	X	36$	CSYS$		11	24/30
Mathematics and Philosophy	GV17	3FT deg	M g	AAA-AAB	X	X	36$	CSYS$		7	30/30
Mathematics and Physics	GF13	3FT deg	M+P g	ABB	X	X	32$	AAABB$		6	24/30
Mathematics and Physics (MPhys)	FG31	4FT deg	M+P g	ABB	X	X	32$	AAABB$		3	24/30
Mathematics and Statistics	GG14	3FT deg	M g	ABC	X	X	32$	AAABB$		7	24/30
Mathematics and Statistics (MMathStat)	GGCK	4FT deg	M g	ABC	X	X	32$	AAABB$		5	
Mathematics with Computing	G1GN	3FT deg	M g	AAA-AAB	X	X	36$	CSYS$		6	26/30
Maths-Operational Research-Statistics-Economics *Mathematics*	Y602	3FT deg	M g	ABC	X	X	32$	AABBB$			
Maths-Operational Research-Statistics-Economics *Statistics*	Y602	3FT deg	M g	ABC	X	X	32$	AABBB$			

WESTHILL COLL

TITLE	CODE	COURSE	SUBJECTS	A/AS	NO/C	AGNVQ	IB	SQA(H)	SQA	RATIO	A/AS
Humanities - Mathematics, Science and Psychology *Mathematics*	Y601	3FT deg	M g	CC	4M+2D	M^	Ind	Ind	Ind		

Univ of WESTMINSTER

TITLE	CODE	COURSE	SUBJECTS	A/AS	NO/C	AGNVQ	IB	SQA(H)	SQA	RATIO	A/AS
Computational Mathematics	GG15	3FT deg	M	CD	N	M	Ind	Ind	Ind	6	4/10
Mathematical Sciences	G100	3FT deg	M	CD	3M	M	Ind	BBC		9	
Operational Research and Information Systems	GG45	3FT deg	M	CD		M	Ind	Ind	Ind		
Statistics and Operational Research	GN42	3FT deg	M	CD		M	Ind	Ind	Ind		

Mathematics and Statistics

course details			98 expected requirements							96 entry stats

TITLE	CODE	COURSE	SUBJECTS	A/AS	ND/C	AGNVQ	IB	SQA(H)	SQA	RATIO A/AS
Univ of WOLVERHAMPTON										
Mathematical Business Analysis	GN12	4SW deg	M	12	4M	M	24	BBBB	Ind	2 8/18
Applied Sciences *Decision Sciences*	Y100	3FT/4SW deg	S g	DD	N	M	24	CCCC	Ind	
Applied Sciences *Mathematical Sciences*	Y100	3FT/4SW deg	M g	DD	N	M	24	CCCC	Ind	
Applied Sciences (4 Yrs) *Decision Sciences*	Y110▼	4FT deg	*							
Applied Sciences (4 Yrs) *Mathematical Sciences*	Y110▼	4FT deg	*							
Combined Degrees *Decision Sciences*	Y401	3FT/4SW deg	S g	DD	N	M	24	CCCC	Ind	
Combined Degrees *Mathematical Sciences*	Y401	3FT/4SW deg	M g	DD	N	M	24	CCCC	Ind	
Univ of YORK										
Computer Science/Mathematics (Equal)	GG51	3FT deg	M	24	HN $	D$^	32$	CSYS$	HN$	22/30
Computer Science/Mathematics (Equal)	GG5C	4SW deg	M	24	HN $	D$^	32$	CSYS$	HN$	
Mathematics	G100	3FT deg	M	22	HN $	DS^	30$	CSYS$	HN$	18/28
Mathematics (MMath)	G102	4FT deg	M	22	HN $	DS^	30$	CSYS$	HN$	20/30
Mathematics with a year in Europe	G101	4FT deg	M	22	HN $	DS^ go	30$	CSYS$	HN$	18/26
Mathematics/Biostatistics	G1CX	3FT deg	M	22	HN$	D$^	30$	CSYS$	HN$	
Mathematics/Computer Science (Equal) (MMath)	GG15	4FT deg	M	24	HN $	D$^	32$	CSYS$	HN$	
Mathematics/Economics	G1L1	3FT deg	M	20-22	HN $	DS^	30$	CSYS$	HN$	24/26
Mathematics/Education	G1X9	3FT deg	M	20-22	HN $	DS^	30$	CSYS$	HN$	16/26
Mathematics/Linguistics	G1Q1	3FT deg	M	20-22	HN $	DS^	30$	CSYS$	HN$	
Mathematics/Linguistics (MMath)	G1QC	4FT deg	M	20-22	HN $	DS^	30$	CSYS$	HN$	
Mathematics/Philosophy (Equal)	GV17	3FT deg	M	22	HN $	DS^	30$	CSYS$	HN$	
Mathematics/Physics	G1F3	3FT deg	M+P	20-22	HN $	DS^	30$	CSYS$	HN$	
Mathematics/Physics (Equal)	GF13	3FT deg	M+P	20-22	HN $	DS^	30$	CSYS$	HN$	
Mathematics/Physics (Equal) (MMath)	GF1H	4FT deg	M+P	20-22	HN $	DS^	30$	CSYS$	HN$	
Mathematics/Physics (Equal) with a yr in Europe	GF1J	4FT deg	M+P	20-22	HN $	DS^	30$	CSYS$	HN $	
Mathematics/Physics (MMath)	G1FH	4FT deg	M+P	20-22	HN $	DS^	30$	CSYS$	HN$	
Mathematics/Physics with a year in Europe	G1FJ	4FT deg	M+P	20-22	HN $	DS^	30$	CSYS$	HN $	
Mathematics/Statistics	G1G4	3FT deg	M	22	HN$	D$^	30$	CSYS$	HN$	

TITLE	CODE	COURSE	SUBJECTS	A/AS	ND/C	AGNVQ	IB	SQA(H)	SQA	RATIO A/AS
ANGLIA Poly Univ										
Art History and Communication Studies	PV34▼	3FT deg	Ap	14	6M	M+/^	Dip$	BBCC	Ind	
Audiotechnology and Communication Studies	HP6H▼	3FT deg	S	16	8M	D+/^	Dip$	BBCCC	N	6
Business and Communication Studies	PN31▼	3FT deg	Ap	14	6M	M+/^ go	Dip$	BBCC	Ind	8
Communication Studies	P300▼	3FT deg	Ap	14	6M	M+/^	Dip$	BBCC	Ind	
Communication Studies & Real Time Computer Systs	PG35▼	3FT deg	Ap g	14	6M	M+/^ go	Dip$	BBCC	Ind	
Communication Studies and Computer Science	GP53▼	3FT deg	Ap g	14	6M	M+/^ go	Dip$	BBCC	Ind	
Communication Studies and Ecology & Conservation	DP23▼	3FT deg	Ap	14	6M	M+/^ go	Dip$	BBCC	Ind	2
Communication Studies and Economics	PL31▼	3FT deg	Ap g	14	6M	M+/^ go	Dip$	BBCC	Ind	4
Communication Studies and English	PQ33▼	3FT deg	E+Ap	14	6M	M+/^	Dip$	BBCC	Ind	6 10/20
Communication Studies and English Language Studs	PQ31▼	3FT deg	Ap g	14	6M	M go	Dip$	BBCC	Ind	
Communication Studies and French	PR31▼	4FT deg	Ap g	14	6M	M+/^ go	Dip$	BBCC	Ind	19
Communication Studies and Geography	PL38▼	3FT deg	Gy g	14	6M	M+/^ go	Dip$	BBCC	Ind	
Communication Studies and Geology	FP63▼	3FT deg	Ap	14	6M	M+/^ go	Dip$	BBCC	Ind	
Communication Studies and German	PR32▼	4FT deg	Ap g	14	6M	M+/^ go	Dip$	BBCC	Ind	
Communication Studies and Graphic Arts	PW32▼	3FT deg	Ap	14	6M	M+/^	Dip$	BBCC	Ind	4 12/20
Communication Studies and History	PV31▼	3FT deg	Ap	14	6M	M+/^	Dip$	BBCC	Ind	18
Communication Studies and Italian	PR33▼	4FT deg	Ap g	14	6M	M+/^ go	Dip$	BBCC	Ind	6
Communication Studies and Law	PM33▼	3FT deg	Ap	14	6M	M	Dip$	BBCC	Ind	5
Communication Studies and Music	PW33▼	3FT deg	Mu	14	6M	M+/^	Dip$	BBCC	Ind	11
Communication Studies and Politics	PM31▼	3FT deg	Ap	14	6M	M+/^	Dip$	BBCC	Ind	
Communication Studies and Social Policy	PL34▼	3FT deg	Ap	14	6M	M+/^	Dip$	BBCC	Ind	
Communication Studies and Sociology	PL33▼	3FT deg	Ap	14	6M	M+/^	Dip$	BBCC	Ind	6 14/16
Communication Studies and Spanish	PR34▼	4FT deg	Ap g	14	6M	M+/^	Dip$	BBCC	Ind	4
Communication Studies and Women's Studies	PM39▼	3FT deg	Ap	14	6M	M+/^	Dip$	BBCC	Ind	4
Communication Studs & European Philosophy & Lit	PV37▼	3FT deg	Ap	14	6M	M+/^	Dip$	BBCC	Ind	2
Univ of Wales, BANGOR										
Communication (taught in Welsh)	P300	3FT deg	g	12	4M	M$ go	Ind	Ind	Ind	
BARNSLEY COLL										
Combined Studies *Journalism*	Y400	3FT deg	* g	CC	4M	M*	Ind	Ind	Ind	
Combined Studies *Media*	Y400	3FT deg	* g	CC	4M	M*	Ind	Ind	Ind	
Media (Journalism)	006P	2FT HND	*	C	4M	P*	Ind	Ind	Ind	
Media Technology	46PH	2FT HND	*	E	2M	P*	Ind	Ind	Ind	
BELL COLLEGE OF TECHNOLOGY										
Communication	003P	2FT HND	E/Ee g	DDD-DE	Ind	Ind	Ind	CCC$	N$	
Journalism	006P	2FT HND	E/Ee g	DD	Ind	Ind	Ind	BCC$	Ind	
Univ of BIRMINGHAM										
African Studies/Media & Cultural Studies	PT47	3FT deg	*	BBB	Ind	D*^	32	ABBB	Ind	
American Studies/Media & Cultural Studies	PQ44	3FT deg	*	BBB	Ind	D*^	32	ABBB	Ind	44
Dance/Media & Cultural Studies	WP44	3FT deg	*	BBB	Ind	D*^	32	ABBB	Ind	
Drama/Media & Cultural Studies	PW44	3FT deg	*	BBB	Ind	D*^	32	ABBB	Ind	103
English/Media & Cultural Studies	PQ43	3FT deg	*	BBB	Ind	D*^	32	ABBB	Ind	43 18/26
French Studies/Media & Cultural Studies	PR41	4FT deg	F	BBB	Ind	D*^	32$	ABBB	Ind	68
German Studies/Media & Cultural Studies	PR42	4FT deg	G	BBB	Ind	D*^	32$	ABBB	Ind	
Hispanic Studies/Media & Cultural Studies	PR44	4FT deg	*	BBB	Ind	D*^	32	ABBB	Ind	18
History/Media & Cultural Studies	PV41	3FT deg	*	BBB	Ind	D*^	32	ABBB	Ind	
Italian/Media & Cultural Studies	PR43	4FT deg	*	BBB	Ind	D*^	32	ABBB	Ind	
Media & Cultural Studies/Modern Greek Studies	PT42	4FT deg	* g	BBB	Ind	D*^	32	ABBB	Ind	
Media & Cultural Studies/Music	PW43	3FT deg	Mu	AAB-ABB	Ind	D*^	32$	ABBB	Ind	

Media Studies – Communications, 53
Journalism, Publishing

course details			98 expected requirements							96 entry stats	
TITLE	CODE	COURSE	SUBJECTS	A/AS	ND/C	AGNVQ	IB	SQA(H)	SQA	RATIO	A/AS
Media & Cultural Studies/Philosophy	PV47	3FT deg	*	BBB	Ind	D*^	32	ABBB	Ind	84	
Media & Cultural Studies/Portuguese	PR45	4FT deg	*	BBB	Ind	D*^	32	ABBB	Ind		
Media & Cultural Studies/Russian	PR48	4FT deg	*	BBB	Ind	D*^	32	ABBB	Ind		
Media & Cultural Studies/Theology	PV48	3FT deg	*	BBB	Ind	D*^	32	ABBB	Ind		
Media, Culture and Society	P400	3FT deg	*	BBC	Ind	D+^	32	ABBBB	Ind	12	16/26
BLACKBURN COLL											
Telecommunications	053P	2FT HND		N $	P						
BLACKPOOL & FYLDE COLL											
Design (Publications)	62PE	2FT HND	*	10	4M		Ind	Ind	Ind		
Design (Publications)	62PW	2FT HND	*	10	4M		Ind	Ind	Ind		
BOURNEMOUTH Univ											
Communication	P300	3FT deg	2Ap g	BB-BBC	MO+5D	Ind go	28	BBBBC	Ind	8	16/24
Media Production	PP34	3FT deg	* g	18-22	MO+4D	D$ go	Ind	ABBBB	Ind	46	18/26
Multi-media Journalism	P600	3FT deg	* g	BBC	MO+5D	D$^ go	30	AABBB	Ind	19	20/26
Public Relations	P340	4SW deg	* g	18-20	MO+4D	D$ go	28	BBBB	Ind	7	14/22
Univ of BRADFORD											
Communications	P300	3FT deg	* g	BB-CCC	4M+3D	D*^	Ind	Ind	Ind	10	14/18
Electronic Imaging and Media Comm (Found Yr)	H6PL	4FT deg	* g	CCC	3M $	M$^	Ind	Ind	Ind	1	10/20
Electronic Imaging and Media Communications	H6P4	3FT deg	* g	BCC	5M+1D	X	Ind	Ind	Ind	4	18/28
Media Technology and Production	HP64	3FT deg	* g	BCC	5M+1D	X	Ind	Ind	Ind	18	18/28
Interdisciplinary Human Studies Communications	Y402	3FT deg	* g	BB-CCC	4M+3D	D*^	Ind	Ind	Ind		
BRADFORD & ILKLEY Comm COLL											
Electronic Imaging and Media Communication	PW45	2FT HND									
BRETTON HALL											
English-Media Arts and Technology	Q3P4	3FT deg	E	CC-BB	MO $		Ind	CCC	Ind	4	10/22
Univ of BRIGHTON											
Information and Media Studies	PP42	3FT deg	*	18	DO	D	28	BBBB	Ind		
BRISTOL, Univ of the W of England											
Cultural & Media Studies	L6P3	3FT deg	* g	BBC	3M+3D	M$^ go	30	ABBB	Ind		
Science, Society and the Media	F9P4	3FT deg	* g	12	4M	M* go	24	BCC	Ind		
BRUNEL Univ, West London											
Communication and Media Studies (4 Yr Thin SW)	P310	4SW deg	* g	BCC	5M	D^ go	28	BBBCC	Ind	6	12/24
Soc Anthrop and Communications (4 Yrs Thin SW)	LP63	4SW deg	* g	BCC	5M	D^ go	28	BBBCC	Ind	9	
Sociology and Communication (4 Yrs Thin SW)	LP33	4SW deg	* g	BCC	5M	D^ go	28	BBBCC	Ind	9	12/14
Computing (Multi-Media Production)	45PG	2FT HND	* g	6	MO $	P go	24$	BCCC$	Ind		
BUCKINGHAMSHIRE COLLEGE											
Business Information Technology with Multimedia	G7P4	3FT deg		8-10	MO	M	Ind	CCC	Ind		
Computer Engineering with Multimedia	G6P4	3FT deg		8-10	MO	M	Ind	CCC	Ind		
Computing with Multimedia	G5P4	3FT deg		8-10	MO	M	Ind	CCC	Ind		
Film and Media	PW45	3FT deg		12	2D	M	27	CCCC	Ind	3	10/18
Film with Media & Video Production	W5P4	3FT deg		12	2D	M	27	CCCC	Ind		
Graphic Design & Advertising	W2P3	3FT deg									
Graphic Design & Advertising	E2P3	3FT deg		CC	1D		Ind	Ind	Ind		
Media and English Studies	PQ42	3FT deg		12	2D	M	27	CCCC	Ind		
Media and Visual Arts	PV44	3FT deg		12	2D	M	27	CCCC	Ind		
Media with Film & Video Production	P4W5	3FT deg		12	2D	M	27	CCCC	Ind		

			98 expected requirements							96 entry stats
TITLE	CODE	COURSE	SUBJECTS	A/AS	ND/C	RGNVQ	IB	SQA(H)	SQA	RATIO R/AS
CANTERBURY CHRIST CHURCH COLL of HE										
Art with Media Studies	W1P4	3FT deg	A g	CC	MO	M	24	Ind	Ind	
Business Studies with Media Studies	N1P4	3FT deg	* g	CC	MO	M	24	Ind	Ind	
English with Media Studies	Q3P4	3FT deg	E	CC	MO	M	24	Ind	Ind	
Geography with Media Studies	L8P4	3FT deg	Gy g	CC	MO	M	24	Ind	Ind	
History with Media Studies	V1P4	3FT deg	H g	CC	MO	M	24	Ind	Ind	
Information Technology with Media Studies	G5P4	3FT deg	* g	CC	MO	M	24	Ind	Ind	
Mathematics with Media Studies	G1P4	3FT deg	M g	DD	Ind	Ind	24	Ind	Ind	
Media Studies and Art	PW41	3FT deg	A g	CC	MO	M	24	Ind	Ind	
Media Studies and Business Studies	PN41	3FT deg	* g	CC	MO	M	24	Ind	Ind	
Media Studies and English	PQ43	3FT deg	E g	CC	MO	M	24	Ind	Ind	
Media Studies and French	PR41	3FT deg	F g							
Media Studies and Geography	LP84	3FT deg	Gy g	CC	MO	M	24	Ind	Ind	
Media Studies and History	PV41	3FT deg	H g	CC	MO	M	24	Ind	Ind	
Media Studies and Information Technology	GP54	3FT deg	* g	CC	MO	M	24	Ind	Ind	
Media Studies and Mathematics	GP14	3FT deg	M g	DD	Ind	Ind	24	Ind	Ind	
Media Studies and Social Science	LP34	3FT deg	* g	CC	MO	M	24	Ind	Ind	
Media Studies with Art	P4W1	3FT deg	A g	CC	MO	M	24	Ind	Ind	
Media Studies with Business Studies	P4N1	3FT deg	* g	CC	MO	M	24	Ind	Ind	
Media Studies with English	P4Q3	3FT deg	E g	CC	MO	M	24	Ind	Ind	
Media Studies with French	P4R1	3FT deg	F g	CC	MO	M	24	Ind	Ind	
Media Studies with Geography	P4L8	3FT deg	Gy g	CC	MO	M	24	Ind	Ind	
Media Studies with History	P4V1	3FT deg	H g	CC	MO	M	24	Ind	Ind	
Media Studies with Information Technology	P4G5	3FT deg	* g	CC	MO	M	24	Ind	Ind	
Media Studies with Mathematics	P4G1	3FT deg	M g	DD	Ind	Ind	24	Ind	Ind	
Media Studies with Music	P4W3	3FT deg	Mu g	CC	MO	M	24	Ind	Ind	
Media Studies with Psychology	P4L7	3FT deg	Ps g	CC	MO	M	24	Ind	Ind	
Media Studies with Radio, Film & Television St	P4W5	3FT deg	* g	CC	MO	M	24	Ind	Ind	
Media Studies with Religious Studies	P4V8	3FT deg	* g	CC	MO	M	24	Ind	Ind	
Media Studies with Science	P4Y1	3FT deg	S g	DD	Ind	Ind	24	Ind	Ind	
Media Studies with Social Science	P4L3	3FT deg	* g	CC	MO	M	24	Ind	Ind	
Media Studies with Sport Science	P4B6	3FT deg	* g	CC	MO	M	24	Ind	Ind	
Media Studies with Statistics	P4G4	3FT deg	M g	DD	Ind	Ind	24	Ind	Ind	
Music and Media Studies	PW43	3FT deg	Mu g	CC	MO	M	24	Ind	Ind	
Music with Media Studies	W3P4	3FT deg	Mu g	CC	MO	M	24	Ind	Ind	
Psychology and Media Studies	LP74	3FT deg	Ps g	CC	MO	M	24	Ind	Ind	
Psychology with Media Studies	L7P4	3FT deg	Ps g	CC	MO	M	24	Ind	Ind	
Radio, Film & Television Studies and Media Studs	PW45	3FT deg	* g	CC	MO	M	24	Ind	Ind	
Radio, Film & Television Studies with Media St	W5P4	3FT deg	* g	CC	MO	M	24	Ind	Ind	
Religious Studies and Media Studies	PV48	3FT deg	* g	CC	MO	M	24	Ind	Ind	
Religious Studies with Media Studies	V8P4	3FT deg	* g	CC	MO	M	24	Ind	Ind	
Science and Media Studies	PY41	3FT deg	S	DD	Ind	Ind	24	Ind	Ind	
Social Science with Media Studies	L3P4	3FT deg	* g	CC	MO	M	24	Ind	Ind	
Sport Science and Media Studies	BP64	3FT deg	* g	CC	MO	M	24	Ind	Ind	
Sport Science with Media Studies	B6P4	3FT deg	* g	CC	MO	M	24	Ind	Ind	
Statistics and Media Studies	PG44	3FT deg	M g	DD	Ind	Ind	24	Ind	Ind	
Statistics with Media Studies	G4P4	3FT deg	M g	DD	Ind	Ind	24	Ind	Ind	
CARDIFF Univ of Wales										
Communication	P300	3FT deg		BBC	Ind		30	ABBBB		4 18/28
Journalism, Film & Broadcasting	PW65	3FT deg	*	BBC	Ind	Ind	30	ABBBB	Ind	11 20/26
Language and Communication	PQ31	3FT deg	*	ABC			30	Ind		2 16/28
Social Policy/Journalism, Film and Broadcasting	LP43	3FT deg	*	BBC	Ind	Ind	30	ABBBB	Ind	
Sociology/Journalism, Film and Broadcasting	LP33	3FT deg	*	BBC	Ind	Ind	30	ABBBB	Ind	

Media Studies – Communications, 53 Journalism, Publishing

| | | | | 98 expected requirements | | | | | | 96 entry stats | |
TITLE	CODE	COURSE	SUBJECTS	A/AS	ND/C	AGNVQ	IB	SQA(H)	SQA	RATIO	A/AS
Univ of CENTRAL ENGLAND											
Human Communication	P301	3FT deg	* g	12	4M	M$ go	Ind	CCCC	Ind	5	10/18
Information and Media	PP24	3FT deg	* g	12	MO	M	24	Ind		1	12/22
Media and Communication	P300	3FT deg	*	BBC	Ind		Ind	Ind	Ind	10	12/26
Multimedia Technology	P410	3FT/4SW deg	* g	12	3M	M* go	24	CCC	Ind		4/12
Multimedia Technology Foundation Year	P418▼	4FT/5SW deg	*	2	N	P*	Ind	CC	Ind		
Visual Communication	PW32	3FT deg	Fa/Pf	18	MO	M$	28	BBBB	Ind	20	
Visual Communication	EW32	3FT deg	Fa/Pf	18	MO	M$	28	BBBB	Ind		
Visual Communication (Information Media)	EP23	3FT deg	Fa/Pf	18	MO	M$	28	BBBB	Ind		
Visual Communication (Information Media)	WP23	3FT deg	Fa/Pf	18	MO	M$	28	BBBB	Ind		
Univ of CENTRAL LANCASHIRE											
Film and Media Studies	PW45	3FT deg	*	16	MO+5D	D$6/^	28	BBBB$	Ind		
Journalism	P600	3FT deg	*	22-24	Ind	Ind	32	AABB	Ind		
Media Technology	HP64	3FT deg	* g	14	MO	D	26	BCCC	Ind		
Public Relations	P360	3FT deg	*	18	MO+4D	D*6/^	28	BBBB	Ind		
Combined Honours Programme Audio Visual Media Studies	Y400	3FT deg	A/Ad/Fa	14	MO+3D	MA6/^	26$	BBCC	Ind		
Combined Honours Programme Fashion Promotion & Media Studies	Y400	3FT deg	A/Ad/Fa	12	MO	M$	26	BCCC	Ind		
Combined Honours Programme Journalism	Y400	3FT deg	*	16	MO+3D	D$6/^	28	BBBC	Ind		
CHELTENHAM & GLOUCESTER COLL of HE											
Business Computer Systems and Media Communicat	GP54	3FT deg	*	8-12	MO	M	24	CCCC	Ind		
Business Computer Systems with Media Communic	G5P4	3FT deg	*	8-12	MO	M	24	CCCC	Ind		
Computing and Media Communications	GP5L	3FT deg	*	8-12	5M+2D	M	24	CCCC	Ind		
Computing with Media Communications	G5PL	3FT deg	*	8-12	MO	M	24	CCCC	Ind		
English Studies and Media Communications	PQ43	3FT deg	E	12-16	4M+3D	M^	26	CCCC	Ind		
English Studies with Media Communications	Q3P4	3FT deg	E	12-14	4M+3D	M^	26	CCCC	Ind		
Fashion and Media Communications	WP24	3FT deg	*	10-14	MO	MT3	26	CCCC	Ind		
Fashion with Media Communications	W2P4	3FT deg	*	10-14	MO	MT3	26	CCCC	Ind		
Geography and Media Communications	LP8K	3FT deg	*	12	MO	M3^	26	CCCC	Ind		
Geography with Media Communications	L8PK	3FT deg	*	12	MO	M3^	26	CCCC	Ind		
History and Media Communications	PV41	3FT deg	H	12	MO	M3^	26	CCCC	Ind		
History with Media Communications	V1P4	3FT deg	H	10-14	MO	M3^	26	CCCC	Ind		
Human Geography and Media Communications	LP84	3FT deg	*	12	5M+2D	MT3	26	CCCC	Ind		
Human Geography with Media Communications	L8P4	3FT deg	Gy	12	5M+2D	M3	26	CCCC	Ind		
Information Technology and Media Communications	GP5K	3FT deg	*	8-12	5M+2D	MT3	24	CCCC	Ind		
Information Technology with Media Communications	G5PK	3FT deg	*	8-12	MO	M3	24	CCCC	Ind		
Media Communication with Fashion	P4W2	3FT deg	*	12	5M+2D	MT3	26	CCCC	Ind		
Media Communications and Multimedia	PG45	3FT deg	*	12	5M+2D	MT3	26	CCCC	Ind		
Media Communications and Performance Arts	PW44	3FT deg	*	12	5M+2D	M3	26	CCCC	Ind		
Media Communications and Religious Studies	PV48	3FT deg	*	8-14	MO	MT3	26	CCCC	Ind		
Media Communications and Visual Arts	PW41	3FT deg	*	12	5M+2D	MA3	26	CCCC	Ind		
Media Communications and Women's Studies	MP94	3FT deg	*	10-14	5M+2D	MT3	26	CCCC	Ind		
Media Communications with Business Computer Syst	P4GM	3FT deg	*	12	5M+2D	MT3	26	CCCC	Ind		
Media Communications with Combined Arts	P4Y3	3FT deg	*	12	MO	M3^	26	CCCC	Ind		
Media Communications with Computing	P4GN	3FT deg	*	12	5M+2D	MT3	26	CCCC	Ind		
Media Communications with English Studies	P4Q3	3FT deg	E	12-16	4M+3D	MT3	26	CCCC	Ind		
Media Communications with Geography	P4L8	3FT deg	*	12	MO	M3^	26	CCCC	Ind		
Media Communications with History	P4V1	3FT deg	*	12	MO	M3^	26	CCCC	Ind		
Media Communications with Human Geography	P4LV	3FT deg	*	12	5M+2D	MT3	26	CCCC	Ind		
Media Communications with Information Tech	P4G5	3FT deg	*	12	5M+2D	MT3	26	CCCC	Ind		

course details			98 expected requirements							96 entry stats	
TITLE	CODE	COURSE	SUBJECTS	A/AS	ND/C	RGNVQ	IB	SQA(H)	SQA	RATIO A/AS	
Media Communications with Modern Langs (French)	P4R1	3FT deg	g	12	4M+3D	MT3	26	CCCC	Ind		
Media Communications with Multimedia	PGK5	3FT deg	*	12	5M+2D	MT3	26	CCCC	Ind		
Media Communications with Performance Arts	P4W4	3FT deg	*	12	5M+2D	M3	26	CCCC	Ind		
Media Communications with Religious Studies	P4V8	3FT deg	*	12	4M+3D	MT3	26	CCCC	Ind		
Media Communications with Visual Arts	P4W1	3FT deg	*	12	5M+2D	M3	26	CCCC	Ind		
Media Communications with Women's Studies	P4M9	3FT deg	*	12	4M+3D	MT3	26	CCCC	Ind		
Multimedia with Media Communications	PGL5	3FT deg	*	12	5M+2D	MI3	26	CCCC	Ind		
Multimedia with Media Communications	GPMK	4SW deg	*	8-12	M0	MI3	24	CCCC	Ind		
Performance Arts with Media Communications	W4P4	3FT deg	*	10-14	5M+2D	M3	26	CCCC	Ind		
Psychology with Media Communications	L7P4	3FT deg	g	12-16	M0	M3^	26	CCCC	Ind		
Religious Studies with Media Communications	V8P4	3FT deg	*	8-14	M0	M3^	26	CCCC	Ind		
Visual Arts with Media Communications	W1P4	3FT deg	A	10-14	5M+2D	MA3	26	CCCC	Ind		
Women's Studies with Media Communications	M9P4	3FT deg	*	8-12	M0	M3	26	CCCC	Ind		

CHICHESTER INSTITUTE OF HIGHER EDUCATION

TITLE	CODE	COURSE	SUBJECTS	A/AS	ND/C	RGNVQ	IB	SQA(H)	SQA	RATIO A/AS	
Art and Media Studies	PW41	3FT deg	A+Pf	12	Ind	M$+^	Ind	Ind	Ind	11	
Dance and Media Studies	PW44	3FT deg	Pf	12	Ind	M$+	Ind	Ind	Ind	14	
Dance with Media Studies	W4P4	3FT deg	Pf	12	Ind	M$+	Ind	Ind	Ind		
English Language Teaching (EFL) and Media Studies	QP14	3FT deg	E	12	Ind	M^	Ind	Ind	Ind		
English with Media Studies	Q3P4	3FT deg	E	12	Ind	M^	Ind	Ind	Ind	6	6/16
Environmental Science and Media Studies	FP94	3FT deg	*	12	Ind	M^	Ind	Ind	Ind		
Geography with Media Studies	L8P4	3FT deg	Gy	12	Ind	M$	Ind	Ind	Ind	8	
History with Media Studies	V1P4	3FT deg	H	12	Ind	M$	Ind	Ind	Ind	6	
Mathematics and Media Studies	GP14	3FT deg	M	12	Ind	M^	Ind	Ind	Ind		
Mathematics with Media Studies	G1P4	3FT deg	M	12	Ind	M^	Ind	Ind	Ind		
Media Studies and English	PQ43	3FT deg	E	12	Ind	M$	Ind	Ind	Ind	6	10/20
Media Studies and Geography	PL48	3FT deg	Gy	12	Ind	M$	Ind	Ind	Ind	5	
Media Studies and History	PV41	3FT deg	H	12	Ind	M$	Ind	Ind	Ind	3	10/14
Media Studies and Study of Religions	PV48	3FT deg	*	12	Ind	M$	Ind	Ind	Ind	7	
Media Studies and Theology	PV4V	3FT deg	*	12	Ind	M$	Ind	Ind	Ind		
Media Studies with Art	P4W1	3FT deg		12							
Media Studies with Dance	P4W4	3FT deg		12							
Media Studies with Geography	P4L8	3FT deg	*	12	Ind	M$	Ind	Ind	Ind		
Media Studies with History	P4V1	3FT deg	*	12	Ind	M$	Ind	Ind	Ind		
Media Studies with Music	P4W3	3FT deg		12							
Media Studies with Related Arts	P4W9	3FT deg		12							
Media Studies with Study of Religions	P4V8	3FT deg	*	12	Ind	M$	Ind	Ind	Ind		
Media Studies with Theology	P4VV	3FT deg	*	12	Ind	M$	Ind	Ind	Ind		
Music and Media Studies	PW43	3FT deg	Mu	12	Ind	M$+	Ind	Ind	Ind	6	
Music with Media Studies	W3P4	3FT deg	Mu	12	Ind	M$+	Ind	Ind	Ind	8	
Related Arts and Media Studies	WP94	3FT deg	Pf	12	Ind	M$+	Ind	Ind	Ind		
Study of Religions with Media Studies	V8P4	3FT deg	*	12	Ind	M$	Ind	Ind	Ind		
Theology and Media Studies	VP84	3FT deg	*	12	Ind	M$	Ind	Ind	Ind		
Theology with Media Studies	V8PK	3FT deg	*	12	Ind	M$	Ind	Ind	Ind		
Women's Studies and Media Studies	MP94	3FT deg	*	12	Ind	M$	Ind	Ind	Ind		

CITY Univ

TITLE	CODE	COURSE	SUBJECTS	A/AS	ND/C	RGNVQ	IB	SQA(H)	SQA	RATIO A/AS	
Journalism/Economics	LP16	3FT/4SW deg	* g	BBC-CCC	Ind	D*^	Ind	Ind	Ind	18	
Journalism/Philosophy	PV67	3FT/4SW deg	* g	BBC-CCC	Ind	D*^	Ind	Ind	Ind	26	
Journalism/Psychology	LP76	3FT/4SW deg	* g	BBC-CCC	Ind	D*^	Ind	Ind	Ind	26	18/22
Journalism/Sociology	LP36	3FT/4SW deg	* g	BBC-CCC	Ind	D*^	Ind	Ind	Ind	22	18/28
Sociology/Media Studies	PL43	3FT deg	* g	BCC	3M+4D	D*^	28$	BBBBC	Ind	13	16/24

Media Studies – Communications, 53 Journalism, Publishing

TITLE	CODE	COURSE	SUBJECTS	A/AS	ND/C	AGNVQ	IB	SQA(H)	SQA	RATIO A/AS
CITY COLLEGE Manchester										
Multimedia	005E	2FT HND	Pf							
Multimedia	005P	2FT HND	Pf							
COLCHESTER INST										
Communications & Media Studies/English	PQ33	3FT deg		CC	Ind	Ind	Ind	Ind	Ind	5 14/18
Communications & Media Studies/History	PV31	3FT deg		CC	Ind	Ind	Ind	Ind	Ind	3
Communications & Media Studies/Sociology	PL33	3FT deg		CC	Ind	Ind	Ind	Ind	Ind	6
COVENTRY Univ										
Biomedical Communications	B9P3	3FT deg								
Biomedical Communications	B9PH	3FT deg								
Communication Culture and Media	P300	3FT deg	*	16-22	DO	Ind	25	Ind	Ind	7 12/22
Technical Communication	P310	3FT deg	*	10-20	Ind	Ind	Ind	Ind	Ind	1 6/14
CUMBRIA COLL of A & D										
Media	P430	3FT deg		CC	5M+2D	M	$	BB	Ind	7 10/20
Media	E430	3FT deg	*	CC	5M+2D	M	$	BB	Ind	
Media (Creative Digital Technology)	055P	2FT HND		C	N	M	$	B	Ind	
DE MONTFORT Univ										
Film & Popular Culture	PL43▼	3FT deg	g	12	10M+2D	M	Ind	BCCC	Ind	
Media Studies	P400▼	3FT deg	* g	BBC	D $	D^	32$	AABB	Ind	20 18/24
Media Technology	HP64▼	3FT/4SW deg	g	16	4M	M	26	BBBB	Ind	
Humanities Combined Honours *Media Studies*	Y300▼	3FT deg	* g	CCC	MO	M$^	30$	ABBB	Ind	
Humanities Joint Honours *Media Studies*	Y301▼	3FT deg	* g	CCD	MO	M$^	30$	ABBB	Ind	
DONCASTER COLL										
Design (Advertising)	32PE	2FT HND								
Univ of EAST ANGLIA										
Media Engineering	HP64	3FT deg		BBC						
Media Studies with Honours Language	P4T9	4FT deg	F/G	BBC	X		30$	AAABC	X	4 14/28
Univ of EAST LONDON										
Communication Studies	P300	3FT deg	* g	12	MO	M				1 6/18
Communication Studies and Design-Visual Commun	PW32	3FT deg	* g	12	MO	MA	Ind	Ind	Ind	
Communication Studies and Educ & Community St	PX39	3FT deg	* g	12	MO	M	Ind	Ind	Ind	1
Communication Studies and French	PR31	3FT deg	* g	12	MO	M^	Ind	Ind	Ind	8
Communication Studies and German	PR32	3FT deg	* g	12	MO	M^	Ind	Ind	Ind	
Communication Studies and Health Studies	PL34	3FT deg	* g	12	MO	M				
Communication Studies and Hist of Art Des & Film	PV34	3FT deg	* g	12	MO	M$	Ind	Ind	Ind	1
Communication Studies and Information Technology	GP53	3FT deg	* g	12	MO	M$	Ind	Ind	Ind	1
Communication Studies and Linguistics	PQ31	3FT deg	* g	12	MO	X				
Communication Studies and Literature	PQ33	3FT deg	* g	12	MO	X	Ind	Ind	Ind	5
Communication Studies and Psychosocial Studies	LP73	3FT deg	* g	12	MO	MG	Ind	Ind	Ind	3
Communication Studies and Sociology	LP33	3FT deg	* g	12	MO	M$	Ind	Ind	Ind	5
Communication Studies and Spanish	PR34	3FT deg	* g	12	MO	M^	Ind	Ind	Ind	
Communication Studies and Third World & Dev St	MPY3	3FT deg	* g	12	MO	M	Ind	Ind	Ind	
Communication Studies and Women's Studies	MP93	3FT deg	* g	12	MO	M	Ind	Ind	Ind	2
Communication Studies with Design-Visual Commun	P3WF	3FT deg	* g	12	MO	M	Ind	Ind		
Communication Studies with Educ & Community St	P3X9	3FT deg	* g	12	MO	M	Ind	Ind		
Communication Studies with European Studies	P3T2	3FT deg	* g	12						
Communication Studies with French	P3R1	3FT deg	* g	12	MO	M	Ind	Ind		

TITLE	CODE	COURSE	SUBJECTS	A/AS	ND/C	AGNVQ	IB	SQA(H)	SQA	RATIO A/AS	
			course details		*98 expected requirements*					*96 entry stats*	
Communication Studies with German	P3R2	3FT deg	* g	12	MO	M	Ind	Ind			
Communication Studies with Health Studies	P3L4	3FT deg	* g	12	MO	M					
Communication Studies with Hist of Art Des&Film	P3V4	3FT deg	* g	12	MO	M	Ind	Ind			
Communication Studies with Information Technol	P3G5	3FT deg	* g	12	MO	M	Ind	Ind			
Communication Studies with Italian	P3R3	3FT deg	* g	12	MO	M	Ind	Ind			
Communication Studies with Linguistics	P3Q1	3FT deg	* g	12	MO	M	Ind	Ind			
Communication Studies with Literature	P3Q3	3FT deg	* g	12	MO	M	Ind	Ind			
Communication Studies with Psychosocial Studies	P3L7	3FT deg	* g	12	MO	M	Ind	Ind			
Communication Studies with Sociology	P3L3	3FT deg	* g	12	MO	M	Ind	Ind			
Communication Studies with Spanish	P3R4	3FT deg	* g	12	MO	M	Ind	Ind			
Communication Studies with Third World & Dev St	P3M9	3FT deg	* g	12	MO	M	Ind	Ind			
Communication Studies with Women's Studies	P3MX	3FT deg	* g	12	MO	M	Ind	Ind			
Cultural Studies and Media Studies	LPP4	3FT deg	* g	14	N	D	Ind	Ind	Ind	14	
Cultural Studies with Media Studies	L3P4	3FT deg	* g	14	MO	M	Ind	Ind	Ind		
Design - Textile Design with Communication St	J4P3	3FT deg	* g	12	MO	M	Ind	Ind	Ind		
Design - Visual Communication with Comm Studies	W2P3	3FT deg	* g	12	MO	M	Ind	Ind	Ind		
Education & Community Studies with Comm Studies	X9P3	3FT deg	* g	12	MO	M					
European Studies with Communication Studies	T2P3	3FT deg	* g	12	MO	M	Ind	Ind			
French and Media Studies	PR41	3FT deg	* g	12	MO	D	Ind	Ind	Ind	18	
French with Communication Studies	R1P3	3FT deg	* g	12	MO	M	Ind				
German and Media Studies	PR42	3FT deg	* g	12	MO	D	Ind	Ind	Ind		
German with Communication Studies	R2P3	3FT deg	* g	12	MO	M					
Health Studies with Communication Studies	L4P3	3FT deg	* g	12	MO	M					
History and Media Studies	PV4C	3FT deg	* g	12	MO	M					
History of Art Design & Film and Media Studies	PV4K	3FT deg	* g	12	MO	M					
History of Art Design & Film with Comm Studies	V4P3	3FT deg	* g	12	MO	M	Ind	Ind			
History of Art Design & Film with Media Studies	V4P4	3FT deg	* g	12	MO	M	Ind	Ind			
Information Technology with Communication St	G5P3	3FT deg	* g	12	MO	M	Ind	Ind	Ind		
Information Technology with Media Studies	G5P4	3FT deg	* g	12	MO	M	Ind	Ind	Ind		
Linguistics with Communication Studies	Q1P3	3FT deg	* g	12	MO	M					
Literature and Media Studies	PQ43	3FT deg	* g	12	N	D	Ind	Ind	Ind	16	
Literature with Communication Studies	Q3P3	3FT deg	* g	12	MO	M	Ind				
Literature with Media Studies	Q3P4	3FT deg	* g	12	MO	M	Ind				
Media Studies	P400	3FT deg	* g	14	N	D	Ind	Ind	Ind	18	12/20
Media Studies and Spanish	PR44	3FT deg	* g	14	N	M^	Ind	Ind	Ind	6	
Media Studies and Women's Studies	P4MX	3FT deg	* g	14	MO	M					
Media Studies with Cultural Studies	P4L6	3FT deg	* g	14	MO	M					
Media Studies with French	P4R1	3FT deg	* g	14	MO	M					
Media Studies with German	P4R2	3FT deg	* g	14	MO	M					
Media Studies with History	P4V1	3FT deg	* g	14	MO	M					
Media Studies with History of Art Design & Film	P4V4	3FT deg	* g	14	MO	M					
Media Studies with Information Technology	P4G5	3FT deg	* g	14	MO	M					
Media Studies with Italian	P4R3	3FT deg	* g	14	MO	M					
Media Studies with Literature	P4Q3	3FT deg	* g	14	MO	M					
Media Studies with Spanish	P4R4	3FT deg	* g	14	MO	M					
Media Studies with Women's Studies	P4M9	3FT deg	* g	14	MO	M					
New Technology and Multimedia	JP9K	3FT deg	* g	12	MO	M					
New Technology, Media and Communications	JP94	3FT deg	* g	12	MO	M	Ind	Ind	Ind	2	8/16
Psychosocial Studies with Communication Studies	L7P3	3FT deg	* g	12	MO	M	Ind	Ind	Ind		
Sociology with Communication Studies	L3P3	3FT deg	* g	12	MO	M	Ind	Ind	Ind		
Spanish with Communication Studies	R4P3	3FT deg	* g	12	MO	M	Ind				
Women's Studies with Communication Studies	M9PH	3FT deg	* g	12	MO	M	Ind				
Women's Studies with Media Studies	M9PK	3FT deg	* g	12	MO	M	Ind				

Media Studies – Communications, 53
Journalism, Publishing

TITLE	CODE	COURSE	SUBJECTS	A/AS	ND/C	AGNVQ	IB	SQA(H)	SQA	RATIO	A/AS
Three-Subject Degree *Communication Studies*	Y600	3FT deg	* g	12	MO	M	Ind	Ind	Ind		
Three-Subject Degree *Media Studies*	Y600	3FT deg	* g	12	MO	M	Ind	Ind	Ind		
EDGE HILL Univ COLLEGE											
Art & Design and Communication Studies	PW32	3FT deg	A	CC	3M+3D	MA / P*^	Dip	BBCC	Ind	2	10/14
Communication Studies	PP34	3FT deg	*	CC	3M+3D	M* / P*^	Dip	BBCC	Ind	3	6/18
Communication Studies	PP3K	3FT deg	*	CC	3M+3D	M* / P*^	Dip	BBCC	Ind		
Communication Studies & Applied Social Sciences	LP33	3FT deg		CC	3M+3D	M* / P*^	Dip	BBCC	Ind		
Communication Studies and Drama	PW34	3FT deg	*	CC	3M+3D	M* / P*^	Dip	BBCC	Ind	4	8/16
Communication Studies and English	PQ33	3FT deg	E	CC	3M+3D	M* / P*^	Dip	BBCC	Ind		
Information Systems and Communication Studies	GP53	3FT deg	* g	CC	3M+3D	M* / P*^	Dip	BBCC	Ind	5	6/20
Music and Media Production	PW43	3FT deg	*	CC	3M+3D	M* / P*^	Dip	BBCC	Ind		
Women's Studies and Communication Studies	MP93	3FT deg	*	CC	3M+3D	M* / P*^	Dip	BBCC	Ind	5	
FALMOUTH COLLEGE of Arts											
Broadcasting Studies	P430	3FT deg	*	CC	N		24	CC	N	7	8/22
Journalism Studies	P600	3FT deg	*	CC	N		24	CC	N	14	13/23
FARNBOROUGH COLL of Technology											
Media Technology (Production)	HP64	3FT deg		12	Ind	D*	Ind	Ind	Ind	4	10/22
Media Technology (Production with Business)	46PH	2FT HND		6	Ind	M*	Ind	Ind	Ind	4	6/12
Univ of GLAMORGAN											
American Studies and Media Studies	QP44	3FT deg	Me/T/E g	14	5M	M$	Ind	Ind	Ind		
American Studies with Media Studies	Q4P4	3FT deg	Me/T/E g	14	5M	M$	Ind	Ind	Ind		
Communication Studies	P300	3FT deg	* g	CC	5M+2D	M$	Ind	Ind	Ind	3	8/18
English Studies and Media Studies	QP34	3FT deg	Me/T/E g	14	Ind	Ind	Ind	Ind	Ind		
English Studies with Media Studies	Q3P4	3FT deg	* g	14	Ind	Ind	Ind	Ind	Ind		
Media Studies and Psychology	PL47	3FT deg	Me/T/E g	14	Ind	Ind	Ind	Ind	Ind		
Media Studies and Sociology	LP34	3FT deg	Me/T/E g	14	Ind	Ind	Ind	Ind	Ind		
Media Studies and Theatre & Media Drama	PW44	3FT deg	Me/T/E g	14	Ind	Ind	Ind	Ind	Ind		
Media Studies and Visual Arts	PW41	3FT deg	Me/T/E g	14	Ind	Ind	Ind	Ind	Ind		
Media Studies with American Studies	P4Q4	3FT deg	Me/T/E g	14	Ind	Ind	Ind	Ind	Ind		
Media Studies with English Studies	P4Q3	3FT deg	Me/T/E g	14	Ind	Ind	Ind	Ind	Ind		
Media Studies with Psychology	P4L7	3FT deg	Me/T/E g	14	Ind	Ind	Ind	Ind	Ind		
Media Studies with Sociology	P4L3	3FT deg	Me/T/E g	14	Ind	Ind	Ind	Ind	Ind		
Media Studies with Theatre and Media Drama	P4W4	3FT deg	Me/T/E g	14	Ind	Ind	Ind	Ind	Ind		
Media Technology	P420	3FT deg	* g	8	Ind	Ind	Ind	Ind	Ind		
Media Technology	P421▼	3FT deg									
Media Technology and Media Studies	P415	3FT deg	Me/T/E	14	Ind	Ind	Ind	Ind	Ind		
Theatre and Media Drama with Media Studies	W4P4	3FT deg	T/E/Me g	14	Ind	Ind	Ind	Ind	Ind		
Combined Studies (Honours) *Media Studies*	Y400	3FT deg	Me/T/E g	8-16	Ind	Ind	Ind	Ind	Ind		
Combined Studies (Honours) *Multimedia*	Y400	3FT deg	* g	8-16	Ind	Ind	Ind	Ind	Ind		
Joint Honours *Media Studies*	Y401	3FT deg	Me/T/E g	8-16	Ind	Ind	Ind	Ind	Ind		
Joint Honours *Multimedia*	Y401	3FT deg	* g	8-16	Ind	Ind	Ind	Ind	Ind		
Major/Minor Honours *Media Studies*	Y402	3FT deg	Me/T/E g	8-16	Ind	Ind	Ind	Ind	Ind		
Major/Minor Honours *Multimedia*	Y402	3FT deg	* g	8-16	Ind	Ind	Ind	Ind	Ind		
Media Technology	024P▼	2FT HND	* g	D	Ind	Ind	Ind	Ind	Ind		
Multimedia	53GP	2FT HND	* g	D	Ind	P$	Ind	Ind	Ind		

course details / *98 expected requirements* / *96 entry stats*

TITLE	CODE	COURSE	98 expected requirements							96 entry stats	
			SUBJECTS	A/AS	NO/C	RGNVQ	IB	SQA(H)	SQA	RATIO	A/AS
GLASGOW CALEDONIAN Univ											
Communication and Mass Media	PP34	3FT/4FT deg	E+M	BCC	Ind		Ind	ABBB$	Ind	11	16/18
Information Management Systems	NP14	4FT deg	M+E+Cs	CC-DDD	Ind		Ind	BCCC	Ind	1	
Marketing and Communication	NP53	3FT/4SW deg	E+L	CC	Ind		Ind	BBC$	Ind	8	12/24
Media Technology Management	PN41	2FT deg		X	Ind		Ind	X	Ind		
Multimedia Technology	P421	3FT deg		X	Ind		Ind	X	HN		
GLOUCESTERSHIRE COLLEGE of Arts and Technology											
Electronic Publishing Technology	024P	2FT HND	* g	E	MO $	P			Ind		
Publishing and Information Management	25PP	2FT HND	* g	E	N $	P			Ind		
Univ of GREENWICH											
Media and Communication	PP43▼	3FT deg	*	BC	MO	Ind	Ind	Ind	Ind		
Media and Society	LP34	3FT deg	* g	10	MO	M	25	BBB	Ind		
Univ of HERTFORDSHIRE											
Multimedia Systems	G5P4	3FT deg									
Univ of HUDDERSFIELD											
English and Media	QP34	3FT deg	E	CCC	Ind	M$^	28	BBBB	Ind		
French and Media	RP14	4FT deg	F	CDD	Ind	Ind	Ind	BBBC	Ind		
German and Media	RP24	4FT deg	G	CDD	Ind	Ind	Ind	BBBC	Ind		
History with Media	V1P4	3FT deg	H	14-16	Ind	Ind	Ind	Ind	Ind		
Interactive Media	G5P4	4SW deg	* g	18-20	MO	M go	Ind	BBB	Ind		
Media	P400	3FT deg	E/Cm/Me/So/T	CCC	Ind	M$^	28	BBBB	Ind		
Multimedia Technology	H6P4	4SW deg	S g	16-20	2D	M$ go	Ind	Ind	Ind		
Politics with Media Studies	M1P4	3FT deg	*	14	MO+3D	M6/^	Ind	BBBC	Ind		
Spanish and Media	RP44	4FT deg	Sp	CDD	Ind	Ind	Ind	BBBC	Ind		
Theatre Studies and Media	WP44	3FT deg	*	CCC	3M+4D	M$^	Ind	BBBC	Ind		
Multimedia	4P5G	3SW HND	* g	4	N	P go	Ind	CCC	Ind		
KING ALFRED'S WINCHESTER											
Business Communications	PN31	3FT deg	* g	14	6M $	M	24$	CCC$	N$		
Media & Film Studies & Contemporary Cultural St	MP94	3FT deg	* g	14	6M	M	24	BCC	N	7	8/20
Media & Film Studies and American Studies	PQ44	3FT deg	* g	14	6M	M	24	BCC	N	7	8/16
Media & Film Studies and Business Studies	NP14	3FT deg	* g	14	6M	M	24	BCC	N	5	10/12
Media & Film Studies and Dance Studies	PW4K	3FT deg	* g	14	6M	M	24	BCC	N	9	
Media & Film Studies and Drama Studies	PW44	3FT deg	* g	14	6M	M	24	BCC	N	5	10/18
Media & Film Studies and English Studies	PQ43	3FT deg	E	14	X	X	24$	BCC$	X	15	
Media & Film Studies and Japanese Language	PT44	3FT deg	L g	14	X	X	24$	BCC$	X		
Media and Film Studies	P4W5	3FT deg	* g	14	6M	M	24	BCC	N		
Music (World) and Media & Film Studies	PW43	3FT deg	* g	14	6M	M	24	BCC	N		
Psychology and Media & Film Studies	LP74	3FT deg	* g	14	6M	M	24	BCC	N	10	10/12
Religious Studies and Media & Film Studies	PV48	3FT deg	* g	14	6M	M	24	BCC	N	3	
Social Biology and Media & Film Studies	CP14	3FT deg	B g	14	6M $	M	24$	BCC$	N$		
Sports Studies and Media & Film Studies	PL4H	3FT deg	* g	14	6M	M	24	BCC	N		
Visual Studies and Media & Film Studies	PW42	3FT deg	A/Ad g	14	6M $	M	24$	BCC$	N$	9	12/20
LANCASTER Univ											
Computer Science with Multimedia Systems	G5P4	3FT deg	* g	BCC	M+D $		30	BBBBB	Ind		
Human Communication	PQ31	3FT deg	* g	BBC	MO		30	ABBBB	Ind		
Culture, Media and Communication Media	Y400	3FT deg	*	BBB-BBC	M+D		30	ABBBB	Ind		

Media Studies – Communications, 53 Journalism, Publishing

| | | | 98 expected requirements | | | | | | | 96 entry stats | |
| course details | | | | | | | | | | | |
TITLE	CODE	COURSE	SUBJECTS	A/AS	ND/C	AGNVQ	IB	SQA(H)	SQA	RATIO	A/AS
Univ of LEEDS											
Broadcast Journalism	PJ69	3FT deg	* g	BBB	Ind	Ind	33$	CSYS	Ind	1	22/28
Broadcasting Studies	PJ39	3FT/4FT deg	* g	ABB	Ind	Ind	33$	CSYS	Ind	13	24/30
Communications	P300	3FT deg	* g	ABB	Ind	Ind	33$	CSYS	Ind	10	24/30
LEEDS, TRINITY & ALL SAINTS Univ COLL											
Communication and Cultural Studies-Media	PP34	3FT deg	* g	BBB-CCC	MO	Ind	26	AABBB	Ind	7	10/22
English-Media	QP34	3FT deg	g	BBB-CDD	Ind	X	26$	BBBCC	Ind	19	12/22
French-Media	RP14	4FT deg	F g	BBC-CCD	Ind	X	24$	BBCCC	Ind	4	8/26
Geography-Media	LP84	3FT deg	Gy g	CCD-CC	MO	X	24$	BBCCC	Ind	7	8/14
History-Media	VP14	3FT deg	H g	BB-BC	Ind	X	24	BBBCC	Ind	4	10/20
Media Information Technology-Information Culture	GP54	3FT deg	* g	BBB-CCC	MO	Ind	26	AABBB	Ind		
Media-Management	PN41	3FT deg	* g	BCC-CC	MO	$	24	BBCCC	Ind	11	8/24
Psychology-Media	LP74	3FT deg	* g	BBC-BD	MO	X	24	BBCCC	Ind	15	8/22
Sociology-Media	LP34	3FT deg	* g	BCC-CCD	MO	X	24	BBCCC	Ind	6	8/24
Spanish-Media	RP44	4FT deg	Sp g	BCC-CCD	Ind	X	24$	BBCCC	Ind	3	8/20
Sport, Health and Leisure-Media	BP64	3FT deg	* g	BBB-CCC	MO+3D	Ind	26	AABBB	Ind		
LEEDS METROPOLITAN Univ											
Events Management	P3N5	3FT/4SW deg	* g	12	MO	M$ go	26	BBCC	Ind		10/16
Health Studies with Communications	L4P3	3FT deg									
MultiMedia Technology	HP64	3FT/4SW deg	M/S g	8	3M $	P$ go	22$	BCC$	Ind	7	6/22
Public Relations	P360	3FT/4SW deg	* g	BBC	4M+3D	M$ go	28	BBBBB	Ind		
Public Relations (French)	P3R1	3FT deg									
Public Relations (German)	P3R2	3FT deg									
Public Relations (Italian)	P3R3	3FT deg									
Public Relations (Spanish)	P3R4	3FT deg									
Multimedia Technology	46PH	2FT/3SW HND									
Univ of LEICESTER											
Communications and Society	P300	3FT deg	* g	BBB	DO	D$^	32	AABBB	HN		18/28
Univ of LINCOLNSHIRE and HUMBERSIDE											
Accountancy and Media Technology	NP44	3FT deg	* g	12	3M+1D	M	24	CCCC	Ind		
Administration and Media Technology	NP1K	3FT deg	* g	12	3M+1D	M	24	CCCC	Ind		
Business and Media Technology	NP1L	3FT deg	* g	12	3M+1D		24	CCCC	Ind		
Communications	P300▼	3FT deg	* g	16	1M+3D	M	24	BBCCC	Ind		
Communications and Criminology	MP33▼	3FT deg	* g	16	1M+3D		24	BBCCC	Ind		
Communications and Economics	LP13▼	3FT deg	* g	16	1M+3D	D	24	BBCCC	Ind		
Communications and Health Studies	LP43▼	3FT deg	* g	16	1M+3D	D	24	BBCCC	Ind		
Communications and International Relations	MP13▼	3FT deg	* g	16	1M+3D	D	24	BBCCC	Ind		
Communications and Journalism	PP36▼	3FT deg	g	18	1M+4D	D	26	BBBCC	Ind		
Communications and Law	MP3H▼	3FT deg	* g	16	1M+3D	D	24	BBCCC	Ind		
Communications and Management	NP13▼	3FT deg	* g	16	1M+3D	D	24	BBCCC	Ind		
Communications and Media	PP34▼	3FT deg	* g	18	1M+4D	D	26	BBBCC	Ind		
Communications and Politics	MP1H▼	3FT deg	* g	16	1M+3D	D	24	BBCCC	Ind		
Communications and Psychology	CP83▼	3FT deg	* g	18	1M+4D	D	26	BBBCC	Ind		
Communications and Social Policy	LP4H▼	3FT deg	* g	14	2M+2D	M	24	BCCC	Ind		
Communications and Tourism	PP37▼	3FT deg	* g	14	2M+2D	M	24	BCCC	Ind		
Computing and Media Technology	GP54	3FT deg	* g	12	3M+1D	M	24	CCCC	Ind		
Criminology and Journalism	MP36▼	3FT deg	* g	18	1M+4D	D	26	BBBCC	Ind		
Criminology and Media	MPH4▼	3FT deg	* g	18	1M+4D	D	26	BBBCC	Ind		
Economics and Journalism	LP16▼	3FT deg	* g	18	1M+4D	D	26	BBBCC	Ind		
Economics and Media	LP14▼	3FT deg	* g	18	1M+4D	D	26	BBBCC	Ind		

Letts STUDY GUIDES THE INDEPENDENT

course details			**98 expected requirements**						**96 entry stats**	
TITLE	CODE	COURSE	SUBJECTS	A/AS	NO/C	RGNVQ	IB	SQA(H)	SQA	RATIO A/AS
European Media	P471▼	3FT deg	F/Sp g	18	1M+4D	D	26	BBBCC$	Ind	
Finance and Media Technology	NP34	3FT deg	* g	12	3M+1D	M	24	CCCC	Ind	
French and Media Technology	PR41	3FT deg	F g	12	3M+1D	M	24	CCCC	Ind	
German and Media Technology	PR42	3FT deg	G g	12	3M+1D	M	24	CCCC	Ind	
Health Studies and Journalism	LP46▼	3FT deg	* g	18	1M+4D	D	26	BBBCC	Ind	
Health Studies and Media	LPK4▼	3FT deg	* g	18	1M+4D	D	26	BBBCC	Ind	
Information Systems and Media Technology	GP5K	3FT deg	* g	12	3M+1D	M	24	CCCC	Ind	
International Relations and Journalism	MP1P▼	3FT deg	* g	18	1M+4D	D	26	BBBCC	Ind	
International Relations and Media	MP14▼	3FT deg	* g	18	1M+4D	D	26	BBBCC	Ind	
Journalism	P600▼	3FT deg	g	18	1M+4D	D	26	BBBCC	Ind	
Journalism and Law	MP3P▼	3FT deg	g	18	1M+4D	D	26	BBBCC	Ind	
Journalism and Management	NP16▼	3FT deg	* g	18	1M+4D	D	26	BBBCC	Ind	
Journalism and Media	PP64▼	3FT deg	* g	18	1M+4D	D	26	BBBCC	Ind	
Journalism and Politics	MP16▼	3FT deg	g	18	1M+4D	D	26	BBBCC	Ind	
Journalism and Psychology	CP86▼	3FT deg	* g	18	1M+4D	D	26	BBBCC	Ind	
Journalism and Social Policy	LP4P▼	3FT deg	* g	18	1M+4D	D	26	BBBCC	Ind	
Journalism and Tourism	PP67▼	3FT deg	* g	18	1M+4D	D	26	BBBCC	Ind	
Law and Media	MP34▼	3FT deg	* g	18	1M+4D	D	26	BBBCC	Ind	
Management and Media	NP14▼	3FT deg	* g	18	1M+4D	D	26	BBBCC	Ind	
Marketing and Media Technology	NP54	3FT deg	* g	12	3M+1D	M	24	CCCC	Ind	
Media	P401▼	3FT deg	* g	18	1M+4D	D	26	BBBCC	Ind	
Media Technology	P400	3FT deg	* g							
Media Technology and Modern Languages	PT42	3FT deg	L g	12	3M+1D	M	24	CCCC	Ind	
Media Technology and Spanish	PR44	3FT deg	Sp g	12	3M+1D	M	24	CCCC	Ind	
Media Technology and Technology	JP9K	3FT deg	* g	12	3M+1D	M	24	CCCC	Ind	
Media and Politics	MP1K▼	3FT deg	* g	18	1M+4D	D	26	BBBCC	Ind	
Media and Psychology	CP84▼	3FT deg	* g	18	1M+4D	D	26	BBBCC	Ind	
Media and Social Policy	LP44▼	3FT deg	* g	18	1M+4D	D	26	BBBCC	Ind	
Media and Tourism	PP47▼	3FT deg	* g	18	1M+4D	D	26	BBBCC	Ind	
Media Production	024P▼	2FT HND	g	6	2M	M	Ind	CCC	Ind	
Media Technology	004P	2FT HND	g							

Univ of LIVERPOOL

English and Communication Studies	QP33	3FT deg	E	ABB	Ind		30$	AABBB$	Ind	28	26/30
Politics and Communication Studies	MP13	3FT deg	*	ABB	Ind	Ind	Ind	Ind	Ind	5	26/30
BA Combined Honours Communication Studies	Y200	3FT deg	* g	BBB	Ind	Ind	Ind	Ind	Ind	

LIVERPOOL JOHN MOORES Univ

Journalism	P600	3FT deg		BC	5M+3D	P$		BBBC		
Media Professional Studies	P400	3FT deg		BB	5M+3D	D$^ | 28$	BBCC		39	18/26
Media and Cultural St & Marketing (Mkt Jnt Awd)	NP54	3FT deg		14-18	5M+3D	X	28$	BBBC		6	14/26
Media and Cultural St and Lit, Life and Thought	PQ43▼	3FT deg	E/H	14-20	5M+3D	X	28$	BBBC		3	12/22
Media and Cultural Studies	LP64	3FT deg		14-18	5M+3D	X	28$	BBBC		28	14/24
Media and Cultural Studies and French	PR41	4FT deg	F	16-18		X	28$	BBBC		10	14/18
Media and Cultural Studs and Applied Psychology	CP84	3FT deg	* g	16-18	5M+3D	X	28$	BBBC		7	18/22
Media and Cultural Studs and German (Germ Jnt A)	PR42	4FT deg	G	16-18		X	28$	BBBC		4	
Screen Studies and Media and Cultural Studies	PW45	3FT deg	E	BB-BCC	5M+3D	X	28$	BBBC		7	20/28
Sociology and Media and Cultural Studies	LP34▼	3FT deg		14-18	MO+3D	X	28$	BBBB		10	14/24
Theatre St and Media & Cultural St(Th St Jt Awd)	PW44	3FT deg	T	BB	7D	X	28$	BBBC		9	14/20

Media Studies – Communications, 53 Journalism, Publishing

course details			98 expected requirements							96 entry stats
TITLE	CODE	COURSE	SUBJECTS	A/AS	ND/C	AGNVQ	IB	SQA(H)	SQA	RATIO A/AS
LONDON GUILDHALL Univ										
3D/Spatial Des & Communs & Audio Visual Prod St	PW4F	3FT deg	Pf g	CC-CDD	MO+4D	M$ go	26	Ind	Ind	
Communications & Audio Vis Prod St & Accounting	NP44	3FT deg	* g	CC-CDD	MO+6D	D$ go	26	Ind	Ind	
Communications & Audio Vis Prod St & Business	NP14	3FT deg	* g	CC-CDD	MO+6D	D$ go	26	Ind	Ind	
Communications & Audio Vis Prod St & Business IT	GP74	3FT deg	* g	CC-CDD	MO+6D	D$ go	26	Ind	Ind	
Communications & Audio Visual Prod St & Bus Econ	LPC4	3FT deg	* g	CC-CDD	MO+6D	D$ go	26	Ind	Ind	
Communications and Audio Visual Production Studs	PW45	3FT deg	* g	BC-CCD	MO+2D		24	Ind	Ind	
Computing & Communications & Audio Vis Prod St	GP54	3FT deg	* g	CC-CDD	MO+6D	D$ go	26	Ind	Ind	
Design St and Communications & Audio Vis Prod St	PW42	3FT deg	* g	CC	MO+4D	D$ go	26	Ind	Ind	
Development St & Commun & Audio Visual Prod St	MP94	3FT deg	* g	CC-CDD	MO+4D	M$ go	26	Ind	Ind	
Economics & Communications & Audio Vis Prod St	LP14	3FT deg	* g	CC-CDD	MO+4D	M$ go	26	Ind	Ind	
English & Communications & Audio Visual Prod St	PQ43	3FT deg	* g	CC-CDD	MO+4D	D$ go	26	Ind	Ind	
European St & Communications & Audio Vis Prod St	PT42	3FT deg	* g	CC-CDD	MO+4D	M$ go	26	Ind	Ind	
Financial Servs & Commun & Audio Visual Prod St	NP34	3FT deg	* g	CC-CDD	MO+4D	M$ go	26	Ind	Ind	
Fine Art & Communications & Audio Visual Prod St	PW41	3FT deg	Pf g	BC-CCC	MO+6D	D$ go	28	Ind	Ind	
French and Communications & Audio Visual Prod St	PR41	4FT deg	* g	CC-CDD	MO+2D	M$ go	26	Ind	Ind	
German and Communications & Audio Visual Prod St	PR42	4FT deg	* g	CC-CDD	MO+2D	M$ go	26	Ind	Ind	
Int Relations and Commun & Audio Visual Prod St	MPC4	3FT deg	* g	CD-DDD	MO+2D	M$ go	26	Ind	Ind	
Law and Communications & Audio Visual Prod Studs	MP34	3FT deg	* g	BC-CCC	MO+6D	D$ go	28	Ind	Ind	
Marketing and Communications & Audio Vis Prod St	NP54	3FT deg	* g	CC-CDD	MO+4D	D$ go	26	Ind	Ind	
Mathematics & Communications & Audio Vis Prod St	GP14	3FT deg	* g	CC-CDD	MO+2D	M$ go	26	Ind	Ind	
Mod History & Communications & Audio Vis Prod St	PV41	3FT deg	* g	CC-CDD	MO+4D	M$ go	26	Ind	Ind	
Multimedia Systs and Communs & Audio Vis Prod St	GPM4	3FT deg	* g	CC-CDD	MO+2D	M$ go	26	Ind	Ind	
Politics and Communications & Audio Vis Prod St	MP14	3FT deg	* g	CC-CDD	MO+2D	M$ go	26	Ind	Ind	
Prod Devel & Manuf & Commun & Audio Vis Prod St	JP44	3FT deg	* g	CC-CDD	MO+2D	M$ go	24	Ind	Ind	
Psychology & Communications & Audio Vis Prod St	CP84	3FT deg	* g	CC	MO+4D	M$ go	26	Ind	Ind	
Social Policy & Mgt & Commun & Audio Vis Prod St	LP44	3FT deg	* g	CC	MO+3D	M$ go	26	Ind	Ind	
Sociology & Communications & Audio Vis Prod St	LP34	3FT deg	* g	CC	MO+4D	M$ go	26	Ind	Ind	
Spanish & Communications & Audio Visual Prod St	PR44	4FT deg	* g	CC-CDD	MO+2D	M$ go	26	Ind	Ind	
Taxation & Communications & Audio Visual Prod St	NPH4	3FT deg	* g	CC-CDD	MO+3D	M$ go	26	Ind	Ind	
Textile Furnish Des & Commun & Audio Vis Prod St	PW4G	3FT deg	Pf g	CC-CDD	MO	M$ go	24	Ind	Ind	
Modular Programme *Communications and Audio Visual Production Studs*	Y400	3FT deg	* g	BB-CC	MO+4D	D/M$ go	26	Ind	Ind	
LONDON INST										
Business Communication	NP13	3FT deg								3 6/20
Fashion Promotion	PP63	3FT deg								14 10/24
Journalism	P600	3FT deg								21 12/26
Marketing and Advertising	NP53	3FT deg								34 10/20
Media and Cultural Studies	P400	3FT deg								36 14/26
Publishing	JP55	3FT deg								6
Journalism	006P	2FT HND								12 6/22
Marketing and Advertising	35PN	2FT HND								26
LOUGHBOROUGH Univ										
Communication and Media Studies	P350	3FT deg	*	24		DT6/^ go	30	Ind		6 20/28
Information and Publishing Studies (3 Yrs)	P360	3FT deg	* g	18	2M+3D	D*6/^ go	28	Ind	Ind	3 12/20
Information and Publishing Studies (4 Yr SW)	P361	4SW deg	* g	18	2M+3D	D*6/^ go	28	Ind	Ind	2 14/20
Politics with Communication and Media Studies	M1P4	3FT deg	* g	20	2M+3D	D*6/^ go	28	Ind	Ind	14/20
LUTON Univ										
Accounting with Journalism	N4PP	3FT deg	g	12-16	MO/DO	M/D	32	BBCC	Ind	
Accounting with Media Practices	NPKK	3FT deg	g	12-16	MO/DO	M/D	32	BBCC	Ind	
Accounting with Media Production	NPLK	3FT deg	g	12-16	MO/DO	M/D	32	BBCC	Ind	

| | | | 98 expected requirements | | | | | | | 96 entry stats |
| course details | | | | | | | | | | |

TITLE	CODE	COURSE	SUBJECTS	A/AS	NO/C	AGNVQ	IB	SQA(H)	SQA	RATIO A/AS
Accounting with Multimedia	NPLL	3FT deg	g	12-16	MO/DO	M/D	32	BBCC	Ind	
Biology with Journalism	C1P6	3FT deg	g	12-16	MO/DO	M/D	32	BBCC	Ind	
Biology with Media Production	C1PL	3FT deg	g	12-16	MO/DO	M/D	32	BBCC	Ind	
Biology with Multimedia	C1PK	3FT deg	g	12-16	MO/DO	M/D	32	BBCC	Ind	
Biology with Publishing	C1P5	3FT deg	g	12-16	MO/DO	M/D	32	BBCC	Ind	
Broadcasting & Media Tech with Media Practices	H6PK	3FT deg		12-16	MO/DO	M/D	32	BBCC	Ind	
Broadcasting & Media Technology with Media Prod	H6PL	3FT deg		12-16	MO/DO	M/D	32	BBCC	Ind	
Built Environment with Journalism	N8P6	3FT deg	g	12-16	MO/DO	M/D	32	BBCC	Ind	
Built Environment with Media Production	N8PL	3FT deg	g	12-16	MO/DO	M/D	32	BBCC	Ind	
Business Systems with Journalism	N1PP	3FT deg	g	12-16	MO/DO	M/D	32	BBCC	Ind	
Business Systems with Media Practices	N1P4	3FT deg	g	12-16	MO/DO	M/D	32	BBCC	Ind	
Business Systems with Media Production	N1PK	3FT deg	g	12-16	MO/DO	M/D	32	BBCC	Ind	
Business with Journalism	N1P6	3FT deg	g	12-16	MO/DO	M/D	32	BBCC	Ind	
Business with Media Production	N1PL	3FT deg	g	12-16	MO/DO	M/D	32	BBCC	Ind	
Contemp Br & Euro History with Media Practices	V1P4	3FT deg	g	12-16	MO/DO	M/D	32	BBCC	Ind	
Contemp Br & Euro History with Media Production	V1PL	3FT deg	g	12-16	MO/DO	M/D	32	BBCC	Ind	
Contemp British & Euro History with Journalism	V1P6	3FT deg	g	12-16	MO/DO	M/D	32	BBCC	Ind	
Contemp British & Euro History with Multimedia	V1PK	3FT deg	g	12-16	MO/DO	M/D	32	BBCC	Ind	
Contemp British & Euro History with Publishing	V1P5	3FT deg	g	12-16	MO/DO	M/D	32	BBCC	Ind	
Electronic System Design and Media Production	HPPK	3FT deg	g	12-16	MO/DO	M/D	32	BBCC	Ind	
Electronic System Design with Multimedia	HP6K	3FT deg	g	12-16	MO/DO	M/D	32	BBCC	Ind	
Environmental Science with Journalism	F9P6	3FT deg	g	12-16	MO/DO	M/D	32	BBCC	Ind	
Environmental Science with Multimedia	F9PK	3FT deg	g	12-16	MO/DO	M/D	32	BBCC	Ind	
Environmental Science with Publishing	F9P5	3FT deg	g	12-16	MO/DO	M/D	32	BBCC	Ind	
Environmental Studies with Journalism	F9PP	3FT deg		12-16	MO/DO	M/D	32	BBCC	Ind	
European Language Studies with Journalism	T2P6	4FT deg	L g	12-16	MO/DO	M/D	32	BBCC	Ind	
European Language Studies with Media Practices	T2P4	4FT deg	L g	12-16	MO/DO	M/D	32	BBCC	Ind	
European Language Studies with Media Production	T2PL	4FT deg	L g	12-16	MO/DO	M/D	32	BBCC	Ind	
European Language Studies with Multimedia	T2PK	4FT deg	L g	12-16	MO/DO	M/D	32	BBCC	Ind	
European Language Studies with Publishing	T2P5	4FT deg	L g	12-16	MO/DO	M/D	32	BBCC	Ind	
Geography with Publishing	F8P5	3FT deg	g	12-16	MO/DO	M/D	32	BBCC	Ind	
Geology with Journalism	F6P6	3FT deg	g	12-16	MO/DO	M/D	32	BBCC	Ind	
Geology with Media Production	F6PL	3FT deg	g	12-16	MO/DO	M/D	32	BBCC	Ind	
Geology with Multimedia	F6PK	3FT deg	g	12-16	MO/DO	M/D	32	BBCC	Ind	
Health Science with Journalism	B9P6	3FT deg	g	12-16	MO/DO	M/D	32	BBCC	Ind	
Health Science with Multimedia	B9PK	3FT deg	g	12-16	MO/DO	M/D	32	BBCC	Ind	
Humanities/Media (Foundation)	YP34	1FT deg			Ind	Ind	Ind	Ind	Ind	
Integrated Engineering with Media Production	H1PL	3FT deg	g	12-16	MO/DO	M/D	32	BBCC	Ind	
Integrated Engineering with Multimedia	H1PK	3FT deg	g	12-16	MO/DO	M/D	32	BBCC	Ind	
Journalism and Accounting	PN64	3FT deg		12-16	MO/DO	M/D	32	BBCC	Ind	
Journalism and British Studies	VP96	3FT deg		12-16	MO/DO	M/D	32	BBCC	Ind	
Journalism and Building Conservation	PK62	3FT deg		12-16	MO/DO	M/D	32	BBCC	Ind	
Journalism and Business	PN61	3FT deg		12-16	MO/DO	M/D	32	BBCC	Ind	
Journalism and Business Systems	PN6C	3FT deg		12-16	MO/DO	M/D	32	BBCC	Ind	
Journalism and Computer Applications	PG66	3FT deg		12-16	MO/DO	M/D	32	BBCC	Ind	
Journalism and Contemporary History	PV6C	3FT deg		12-16	MO/DO	M/D	32	BBCC	Ind	
Journalism and Creative Design	PW62	3FT deg		12-16	MO/DO	M/D	32	BBCC	Ind	
Journalism and Environmental Science	PF69	3FT deg		12-16	MO/DO	M/D	32	BBCC	Ind	
Journalism and European Language Studies	PT62	3FT deg		12-16	MO/DO	M/D	22	BBCC	Ind	
Journalism and Geography	PF68	3FT deg		12-16	MO/DO	M/D	32	BBCC	Ind	
Journalism and Health Science	PB69	3FT deg		12-16	MO/DO	M/D	32	BBCC	Ind	
Journalism and Health Studies	PB6X	3FT deg		12-16	MO/DO	M/D	32	BBCC	Ind	

Media Studies – Communications, 53 Journalism, Publishing

course details			98 expected requirements							96 entry stats	
TITLE	CODE	COURSE	SUBJECTS	A/AS	ND/C	AGNVQ	IB	SQA(H)	SQA	RATIO A/AS	
Law and Journalism	PM63	3FT deg		12-16	MO/DO	M/D	32	BBCC	Ind		
Law with Journalism	M3P6	3FT deg	g	12-16	MO/DO	M/D	32	BBCC	Ind		
Law with Media Production	M3P4	3FT deg	g	12-16	MO/DO	M/D	32	BBCC	Ind		
Law with Publishing	M3P5	3FT deg	g	12-16	MO/DO	M/D	32	BBCC	Ind		
Leisure Studies with Media Practices	N7P4	3FT deg	g	12-16	MO/DO	M/D	32	BBCC	Ind		
Leisure Studies with Publishing	N7P5	3FT deg	g	12-16	MO/DO	M/D	32	BBCC	Ind		
Linguistics and Journalism	PQ61	3FT deg		12-16	MO/DO	M/D	32	BBCC	Ind		
Linguistics with Journalism	Q1P6	3FT deg	g	12-16	MO/DO	M/D	32	BBCC	Ind		
Linguistics with Media Practices	Q1P4	3FT deg	g	12-16	MO/DO	M/D	32	BBCC	Ind		
Linguistics with Media Production	Q1PL	3FT deg	g	12-16	MO/DO	M/D	32	BBCC	Ind		
Linguistics with Multimedia	Q1PK	3FT deg	g	12-16	MO/DO	M/D	32	BBCC	Ind		
Linguistics with Publishing	Q1P5	3FT deg	g	12-16	MO/DO	M/D	32	BBCC	Ind		
Literary Studies in English and Journalism	PQ62	3FT deg		12-16	MO/DO	M/D	32	BBCC	Ind		
Literary Studies in English with Journalism	Q2P6	3FT deg		12-16	MO/DO	M/D	32	BBCC	Ind		
Literary Studies in English with Media Practices	Q2P4	3FT deg		12-16	MO/DO	M/D	32	BBCC	Ind		
Literary Studies in English with Publishing	Q2P5	3FT deg		12-16	MO/DO	M/D	32	BBCC	Ind		
Literary Studs in English with Media Production	Q2PL	3FT deg		12-16	MO/DO	M/D	32	BBCC	Ind		
Mapping Science with Journalism	F8P6	3FT deg	g	12-16	MO/DO	M/D	32	BBCC	Ind		
Mapping Science with Media Production	F8PL	3FT deg	g	12-16	MO/DO	M/D	32	BBCC	Ind		
Mapping Science with Multimedia	F8PK	3FT deg	g	12-16	MO/DO	M/D	32	BBCC	Ind		
Marketing and Journalism	PN65	3FT deg		12-16	MO/DO	M/D	32	BBCC	Ind		
Marketing with Journalism	N5P6	3FT deg	g	12-16	MO/DO	M/D	32	BBCC	Ind		
Marketing with Media Production	N5PL	3FT deg	g	12-16	MO/DO	M/D	32	BBCC	Ind	16	
Marketing with Multimedia	N5PK	3FT deg	g	12-16	MO/DO	M/D	32	BBCC	Ind		
Media Performance with Journalism	W4P6	3FT deg	Pf g	12-16	MO/DO	M/D	32	BBCC	Ind		
Media Performance with Scriptwriting	W4PP	3FT deg		12-16	MO/DO	M/D	32	BBCC	Ind		
Media Practices	P400	3FT deg	Pf g	12-16	MO/DO	M/D	32	BBCC	Ind	5	8/20
Media Practices & Language & Stylistics in Engl	QPG4	3FT deg	g	12-16	MO/DO	M/D	32	BBCC	Ind		
Media Practices and Accounting	NPK4	3FT deg	g	12-16	MO/DO	M/D	32	BBCC	Ind		
Media Practices and Artificial Intelligence	GP84	3FT deg		12-16	MO/DO	M/D	32	BBCC	Ind		
Media Practices and Biology	CP14	3FT deg	g	12-16	MO/DO	M/D	32	BBCC	Ind		
Media Practices and Computer Science	GP54	3FT deg	g	12-16	MO/DO	M/D	32	BBCC	Ind		
Media Practices and Contemporary History	VP14	3FT deg	g	12-16	MO/DO	M/D	32	BBCC	Ind		
Media Practices and Digital Systems Design	HPP4	3FT deg	g	12-16	MO/DO	M/D	32	BBCC	Ind		
Media Practices and Environmental Science	FP94	3FT deg	g	12-16	MO/DO	M/D	32	BBCC	Ind		
Media Practices and European Language Studies	TP24	3FT deg	L g	12-16	MO/DO	M/D	32	BBCC	Ind		
Media Practices and Health Studies	BPX4	3FT deg	g	12-16	MO/DO	M/D	32	BBCC	Ind		
Media Practices and Journalism	PP64	3FT deg		12-16	MO/DO	M/D	32	BBCC	Ind		
Media Practices and Law	MP34	3FT deg		12-16	MO/DO	M/D	32	BBCC	Ind		
Media Practices and Leisure Studies	NP74	3FT deg	g	12-16	MO/DO	M/D	32	BBCC	Ind		
Media Practices and Linguistics	QP14	3FT deg	g	12-16	MO/DO	M/D	32	BBCC	Ind		
Media Practices and Literary Studies in English	QP24	3FT deg	g	12-16	MO/DO	M/D	32	BBCC	Ind	18	
Media Practices w Lang & Stylistics in English	P4QG	3FT deg	g	12-16	MO/DO	M/D	32	BBCC	Ind		
Media Practices with Accounting	P4NL	3FT deg	g	12-16	MO/DO	M/D	32	BBCC	Ind		
Media Practices with Animation	P4WF	3FT deg	g	12-16	MO/DO	M/D	32	BBCC	Ind		
Media Practices with Biology	P4C1	3FT deg	g	12-16	MO/DO	M/D	32	BBCC	Ind		
Media Practices with Contemporary History	P4V1	3FT deg	g	12-16	MO/DO	M/D	32	BBCC	Ind		
Media Practices with Digital Systems Design	P4HP	3FT deg	g	12-16	MO/DO	M/D	32	BBCC	Ind		
Media Practices with Environmental Science	P4F9	3FT deg	g	12-16	MO/DO	M/D	32	BBCC	Ind		
Media Practices with Film Studies	WP54	3FT deg		12-16	MO/DO	M/D	32	BBCC	Ind		
Media Practices with French	P4R1	3FT deg	F g	12-16	MO/DO	M/D	32	BBCC	Ind		
Media Practices with Geographical Info Systems	P447	3FT deg	g	12-16	MO/DO	M/D	32	BBCC	Ind		

STUDY GUIDES
THE INDEPENDENT

course details			98 expected requirements							96 entry stats
TITLE	CODE	COURSE	SUBJECTS	A/AS	NO/C	AGNVQ	IB	SQA(H)	SQA	RATIO A/AS
Media Practices with Japanese	P4T4	3FT deg	L g	12-16	MO/DO	M/D	32	BBCC	Ind	
Media Practices with Journalism	P4P6	3FT deg	g	12-16	MO/DO	M/D	32	BBCC	Ind	22
Media Practices with Leisure Studies	P4N7	3FT deg	g	12-16	MO/DO	M/D	32	BBCC	Ind	
Media Practices with Linguistics	P4Q1	3FT deg	g	12-16	MO/DO	M/D	32	BBCC	Ind	
Media Practices with Literary Studies in English	P4Q2	3FT deg	g	12-16	MO/DO	M/D	32	BBCC	Ind	
Media Practices with Media Production	P433	3FT deg	g	12-16	MO/DO	M/D	32	BBCC	Ind	14
Media Practices with Modern English Studies	P4Q3	3FT deg	g	12-16	MO/DO	M/D	32	BBCC	Ind	
Media Practices with Modern History	P4VC	3FT deg	g	12-16	MO/DO	M/D	32	BBCC	Ind	
Media Practices with Multimedia	P434	3FT deg	g	12-16	MO/DO	M/D	32	BBCC	Ind	
Media Practices with Performance Management	P4N9	3FT deg		12-16	MO/DO	M/D	32	BBCC	Ind	
Media Practices with Photography	WP5K	3FT deg		12-16	MO/DO	M/D	32	BBCC	Ind	
Media Practices with Politics	P4M1	3FT deg	g	12-16	MO/DO	M/D	32	BBCC	Ind	
Media Practices with Psychology	P4LR	3FT deg	g	12-16	MO/DO	M/D	32	BBCC	Ind	3
Media Practices with Public Policy & Management	P4MC	3FT deg	g	12-16	MO/DO	M/D	32	BBCC	Ind	
Media Practices with Publishing	P4PM	3FT deg		12-16	MO/DO	M/D	32	BBCC	Ind	
Media Practices with Radio	WP5L	3FT deg		12-16	MO/DO	M/D	32	BBCC	Ind	
Media Practices with Regional Planning and Dev	P4K4	3FT deg	g	12-16	MO/DO	M/D	32	BBCC	Ind	
Media Practices with Scriptwriting	P4PQ	3FT deg		12-16	MO/DO	M/D	32	BBCC	Ind	
Media Practices with Social Studies	P4L3	3FT deg	g	12-16	MO/DO	M/D	32	BBCC	Ind	
Media Practices with Spanish	P4R4	3FT deg	Sp g	12-16	MO/DO	M/D	32	BBCC	Ind	
Media Practices with TV Studies	PW4M	3FT deg		12-16	MO/DO	M/D	32	BBCC	Ind	
Media Practices with Travel and Tourism	P4P7	3FT deg	g	12-16	MO/DO	M/D	32	BBCC	Ind	
Media Practices with Video Production	P4W5	3FT deg	g	12-16	MO/DO	M/D	32	BBCC	Ind	
Media Prod & Computer Visualisation & Animation	GPNL	3FT deg		12-16	MO/DO	M/D	32	BBCC	Ind	
Media Production	P410	3FT deg	g	12-16	MO/DO	M/D	32	BBCC	Ind	
Media Production and Accounting	NPKL	3FT deg	g	12-16	MO/DO	M/D	32	BBCC	Ind	
Media Production and Artificial Intelligence	GP8L	3FT deg		12-16	MO/DO	M/D	32	BBCC	Ind	
Media Production and Biology	CP1L	3FT deg	g	12-16	MO/DO	M/D	32	BBCC	Ind	
Media Production and Business	NP1L	3FT deg	g	12-16	MO/DO	M/D	32	BBCC	Ind	
Media Production and Business Systems	NPCL	3FT deg	g	12-16	MO/DO	M/D	32	BBCC	Ind	
Media Production and Computer Applications	GP6L	3FT deg		12-16	MO/DO	M/D	32	BBCC	Ind	
Media Production and Contemporary History	VP1L	3FT deg	g	12-16	MO/DO	M/D	32	BBCC	Ind	
Media Production and Digital Systems Design	HPPL	3FT deg	g	12-16	MO/DO	M/D	32	BBCC	Ind	
Media Production and Environmental Science	FP9L	3FT deg	g	12-16	MO/DO	M/D	32	BBCC	Ind	
Media Production and European Language Studies	TP2L	3FT deg	L g	12-16	MO/DO	M/D	32	BBCC	Ind	
Media Production and Geology	FP6L	3FT deg	g	12-16	MO/DO	M/D	32	BBCC	Ind	
Media Production and Human Centred Computing	GPML	3FT deg		12-16	MO/DO	M/D	32	BBCC	Ind	
Media Production and Law	MP3L	3FT deg	g	12-16	MO/DO	M/D	32	BBCC	Ind	
Media Production and Linguistics	QP1L	3FT deg	g	12-16	MO/DO	M/D	32	BBCC	Ind	
Media Production and Literary Studies in English	QP2L	3FT deg	g	12-16	MO/DO	M/D	32	BBCC	Ind	
Media Production and Mapping Science	FP8L	3FT deg	g	12-16	MO/DO	M/D	32	BBCC	Ind	
Media Production and Marketing	NP5L	3FT deg	g	12-16	MO/DO	M/D	32	BBCC	Ind	
Media Production and Media Practices	PG46	3FT deg	g	12-16	MO/DO	M/D	32	BBCC	Ind	16
Media Production with Accounting	PN44	3FT deg	g	12-16	MO/DO	M/D	32	BBCC	Ind	
Media Production with Animation	PW42	3FT deg								
Media Production with Biology	P4CC	3FT deg	g	12-16	MO/DO	M/D	32	BBCC	Ind	
Media Production with Business	P4N1	3FT deg	g	12-16	MO/DO	M/D	32	BBCC	Ind	7
Media Production with Business Systems	P435	3FT deg	g	12-16	MO/DO	M/D	32	BBCC	Ind	
Media Production with Comparative Literature	P4QF	3FT deg	g	12-16	MO/DO	M/D	32	BBCC	Ind	
Media Production with Contemporary History	P4VD	3FT deg	g	12-16	MO/DO	M/D	32	BBCC	Ind	
Media Production with Design	P4WG	3FT deg								
Media Production with Digital Systems Design	P437	3FT deg	g	12-16	MO/DO	M/D	32	BBCC	Ind	

Media Studies – Communications, 53 Journalism, Publishing

course details			**98 expected requirements**							**96 entry stats**	
TITLE	CODE	COURSE	SUBJECTS	A/AS	NO/C	AGNVQ	IB	SQA(H)	SQA	RATIO A/AS	
Media Production with Environmental Science	P440	3FT deg	g	12-16	MO/DO	M/D	32	BBCC	Ind		
Media Production with Film Studies	P4WM	3FT deg	g	12-16	MO/DO	M/D	32	BBCC	Ind		
Media Production with Geographical Info Systems	P431	3FT deg	g	12-16	MO/DO	M/D	32	BBCC	Ind		
Media Production with Japanese	P4TK	3FT deg	L g	12-16	MO/DO	M/D	32	BBCC	Ind		
Media Production with Journalism	PP4P	3FT deg									
Media Production with Lang & Stylistics in Engl	P436	3FT deg	g	12-16	MO/DO	M/D	32	BBCC	Ind		
Media Production with Linguistics	P4QC	3FT deg	g	12-16	MO/DO	M/D	32	BBCC	Ind		
Media Production with Literary Studies in Engl	P445	3FT deg	g	12-16	MO/DO	M/D	32	BBCC	Ind		
Media Production with Mapping Science	P4F8	3FT deg	g	12-16	MO/DO	M/D	32	BBCC	Ind		
Media Production with Marketing	P4N5	3FT deg	g	12-16	MO/DO	M/D	32	BBCC	Ind		
Media Production with Media Practices	P442	3FT deg	g	12-16	MO/DO	M/D	32	BBCC	Ind	29	
Media Production with Modern English Studies	P4QH	3FT deg	g	12-16	MO/DO	M/D	32	BBCC	Ind		
Media Production with Modern History	P443	3FT deg	g	12-16	MO/DO	M/D	32	BBCC	Ind		
Media Production with Multimedia	P411	3FT deg									
Media Production with Organisational Behaviour	P4L7	3FT deg	g	12-16	MO/DO	M/D	32	BBCC	Ind		
Media Production with Performance Management	P4NX	3FT deg									
Media Production with Photography	P4W9	3FT deg	g	12-16	MO/DO	M/D	32	BBCC	Ind		
Media Production with Physical Geography	P441	3FT deg	g	12-16	MO/DO	M/D	32	BBCC	Ind		
Media Production with Psychology	P4LT	3FT deg	g	12-16	MO/DO	M/D	32	BBCC	Ind		
Media Production with Publishing	P4P5	3FT deg	g	12-16	MO/DO	M/D	32	BBCC	Ind		
Media Production with Radio	WPM4	3FT deg									
Media Production with Scriptwriting	PP46	3FT deg									
Media Production with Social Studies	P4LH	3FT deg	g	12-16	MO/DO	M/D	32	BBCC	Ind		
Media Production with TV Studies	PW45	3FT deg	g	12-16	MO/DO	M/D	32	BBCC	Ind		
Media Production with Video Production	PW4N	3FT deg									
Media Tech & Computer Visualisation & Animation	GPNK	3FT deg		12-16	MO/DO	M/D	32	BBCC	Ind		
Media Technology	PH46	1FT deg			Ind	Ind	Ind	Ind	Ind		
Media Technology	HP64	3FT deg	g	12-16	MO/DO	M/D	32	BBCC	Ind	8/16	
Media Technology and Computer Science	GP5K	3FT deg	g	12-16	MO/DO	M/D	32	BBCC	Ind		
Media Technology and Human Centred Computing	GPMK	3FT deg		12-16	MO/DO	M/D	32	BBCC	Ind		
Media Technology and Law	MP3K	3FT deg	g	12-16	MO/DO	M/D	32	BBCC	Ind		
Media Technology and Mapping Science	FP84	3FT deg	g	12-16	MO/DO	M/D	32	BBCC	Ind		
Media Technology and Media Practices	P415	3FT deg	g	12-16	MO/DO	M/D	32	BBCC	Ind		
Media Technology and Media Production	P417	3FT deg	g	12-16	MO/DO	M/D	32	BBCC	Ind		
Media Technology with Photography	P4WN	3FT deg		12-16	MO/DO	M/D	32	BBCC	Ind		
Modern English Studies and Journalism	PQ63	3FT deg		12-16	MO/DO	M/D	32	BBCC	Ind		
Modern English Studies and Media Practices	PQ43	3FT deg	g	12-16	MO/DO	M/D	32	BBCC	Ind		
Modern English Studies and Media Production	PQL3	3FT deg	g	12-16	MO/DO	M/D	32	BBCC	Ind		
Modern English Studies with Journalism	Q3P6	3FT deg	g	12-16	MO/DO	M/D	32	BBCC	Ind	22	
Modern English Studies with Media Practices	Q3P4	3FT deg	g	12-16	MO/DO	M/D	32	BBCC	Ind		
Modern English Studies with Media Production	Q3PL	3FT deg		12-16	MO/DO	M/D	32	BBCC	Ind		
Modern English Studies with Multimedia	Q3PK	3FT deg	g	12-16	MO/DO	M/D	32	BBCC	Ind		
Modern English Studies with Publishing	Q3P5	3FT deg	g	12-16	MO/DO	M/D	32	BBCC	Ind		
Modern History and Media Practices	PV4C	3FT deg	g	12-16	MO/DO	M/D	32	BBCC	Ind		
Modern History with Publishing	V1PM	3FT deg	g	12-16	MO/DO	M/D	32	BBCC	Ind		
New Media Technology with Animation	P4W2	3FT deg	g	12-16	MO/DO	M/D	32	BBCC	Ind		
New Media Technology with Geographical Info Syst	P404	3FT deg	g	12-16	MO/DO	M/D	32	BBCC	Ind		
New Media Technology with German	P4R2	3FT deg	L g	12-16	MO/DO	M/D	32	BBCC	Ind		
New Media Technology with Journalism	P4PP	3FT deg	g	12-16	MO/DO	M/D	32	BBCC	Ind		
New Media Technology with Mapping Science	P4FV	3FT deg	g	12-16	MO/DO	M/D	32	BBCC	Ind		
New Media Technology with Media Practices	P403	3FT deg	g	12-16	MO/DO	M/D	32	BBCC	Ind		
New Media Technology with Media Production	P402	3FT deg	g	12-16	MO/DO	M/D	32	BBCC	Ind		

course details | 98 expected requirements | 96 entry stats

TITLE	CODE	COURSE	SUBJECTS	A/AS	NO/C	RGNVQ	IB	SQA(H)	SQA	RATIO A/AS
New Media Technology with Multimedia	P405	3FT deg	g	12-16	MO/DO	M/D	32	BBCC	Ind	
Organisational Behaviour and Media Production	PLL7	3FT deg	g	12-16	MO/DO	M/D	32	BBCC	Ind	
Planning Studies and Journalism	PK64	3FT deg		12-16	MO/DO	M/D	32	BBCC	Ind	
Politics with Publishing	M1P5	3FT deg	g	12-16	MO/DO	M/D	32	BBCC	Ind	
Psychology and Journalism	PL67	3FT deg		12-16	MO/DO	M/D	32	BBCC	Ind	
Psychology and Media Practices	PL4R	3FT deg	g	12-16	MO/DO	M/D	32	BBCC	Ind	
Psychology and Media Production	PLLR	3FT deg	g	12-16	MO/DO	M/D	32	BBCC	Ind	
Psychology with Journalism	L7PP	3FT deg	g	12-16	MO/DO	M/D	32	BBCC	Ind	
Psychology with Media Practices	L7P4	3FT deg	g	12-16	MO/DO	M/D	32	BBCC	Ind	
Psychology with Publishing	L7P5	3FT deg	g	12-16	MO/DO	M/D	32	BBCC	Ind	
Public Policy & Management with Publishing	M1PM	3FT deg	g	12-16	MO/DO	M/D	32	BBCC	Ind	
Public Policy and Management and Media Practices	PM4C	3FT deg	g	12-16	MO/DO	M/D	32	BBCC	Ind	
Public Policy and Mgt with Media Practices	M1PL	3FT deg	g	12-16	MO/DO	M/D	32	BBCC	Ind	
Regional Planning & Development with Journalism	K4P6	3FT deg	g	12-16	MO/DO	M/D	32	BBCC	Ind	
Regional Planning and Develop with Multimedia	K4PK	3FT deg	g	12-16	MO/DO	M/D	32	BBCC	Ind	
Social Policy and Journalism	PL64	3FT deg		12-16	MO/DO	M/D	32	BBCC	Ind	
Social Policy with Journalism	L4P6	3FT deg		12-16	MO/DO	M/D	32	BBCC	Ind	
Social Studies and Journalism	PL63	3FT deg		12-16	MO/DO	M/D	32	BBCC	Ind	
Social Studies with Journalism	L3P6	3FT deg	g	12-16	MO/DO	M/D	32	BBCC	Ind	
Social Studies with Multimedia	L3PK	3FT deg	g	12-16	MO/DO	M/D	32	BBCC	Ind	
Social Studies with Publishing	L3P5	3FT deg	g	12-16	MO/DO	M/D	32	BBCC	Ind	
Sociology and Media Practices	LPH4	3FT deg		12-16	MO/DO	M/D	32	BBCC	Ind	
Sociology with Media Practices	L3P4	3FT deg		12-16	MO/DO	M/D	32	BBCC	Ind	
Stage & Screen Technol & Comp Visual & Animation	GPN4	3FT deg		12-16	MO/DO	M/D	32	BBCC	Ind	
Stage & Screen Technology and Business	PNK1	3FT deg		12-16	MO/DO	M/D	32	BBCC	Ind	
Stage & Screen Technology and Creative Design	WP24	3FT deg		12-16	MO/DO	M/D	32	BBCC	Ind	
Stage & Screen Technology and Digital Systs Des	PHK2	3FT deg		12-16	MO/DO	M/D	32	BBCC	Ind	
Stage & Screen Technology and European Lang St	PTK2	3FT deg		12-16	MO/DO	M/D	32	BBCC	Ind	
Stage & Screen Technology and Human Centred Comp	GPM4	3FT deg		12-16	MO/DO	M/D	32	BBCC	Ind	
Stage & Screen Technology and Leisure Studies	PNK7	3FT deg		12-16	MO/DO	M/D	32	BBCC	Ind	
Stage & Screen Technology and Marketing	PNK5	3FT deg		12-16	MO/DO	M/D	32	BBCC	Ind	
Stage & Screen Technology and Media Practices	PPK4	3FT deg		12-16	MO/DO	M/D	32	BBCC	Ind	
Stage and Screen Technology	P432	3FT deg		12-16	MO/DO	M/D	32	BBCC	Ind	
Travel and Tourism and Journalism	PP67	3FT deg		12-16	MO/DO	M/D	32	BBCC	Ind	
Travel and Tourism and Media Practices	PP47	3FT deg	g	12-16	MO/DO	M/D	32	BBCC	Ind	5
Travel and Tourism and Media Production	PPL7	3FT deg	g	12-16	MO/DO	M/D	32	BBCC	Ind	
Travel and Tourism with Journalism	P7P6	3FT deg	g	12-16	MO/DO	M/D	32	BBCC	Ind	
Travel and Tourism with Media Practices	P7P4	3FT deg	g	12-16	MO/DO	M/D	32	BBCC	Ind	
Travel and Tourism with Media Production	P7PL	3FT deg	g	12-16	MO/DO	M/D	32	BBCC	Ind	
Travel and Tourism with Multimedia	P7PK	3FT deg	g	12-16	MO/DO	M/D	32	BBCC	Ind	
Women's Studies and Journalism	PM69	3FT deg		12-16	MO/DO	M/D	32	BBCC	Ind	
Media Technology	64HP	2FT HND		12-16	MO	M/D	26	CCDD	Ind	

MANCHESTER METROPOLITAN Univ

TITLE	CODE	COURSE	SUBJECTS	A/AS	NO/C	RGNVQ	IB	SQA(H)	SQA	RATIO A/AS
Applied Human Communication	P310	3FT deg	* g	Ind	Ind	Ind	Ind	Ind	Ind	8/20
Interactive and Broadcast Media	EW42	3FT deg	Fa+Pf	CC	Ind		Ind	Ind	Ind	
Interactive and Broadcast Media	PW42	3FT deg	Fa+Pf	CC	Ind		Ind	Ind	Ind	
Media Technology	HP64	3FT deg	*	10	N		Ind	Ind	Ind	

MIDDLESEX Univ

TITLE	CODE	COURSE	SUBJECTS	A/AS	NO/C	RGNVQ	IB	SQA(H)	SQA	RATIO A/AS
Communication Studies	P300▼	3FT deg	* g	12-16	5M	M$ go	28	Ind	Ind	
Media and Cultural Studies	LP64▼	3FT deg	* g	12-16	5M	M$ go	28	Ind	Ind	
Writing and Publishing Studies	PP65▼	3FT deg	* g	12-16	5M	M$ go	28	Ind	Ind	

Media Studies – Communications, 53
Journalism, Publishing

	course details			98 expected requirements						96 entry stats	
TITLE	CODE	COURSE	SUBJECTS	A/AS	NO/C	AGNVQ	IB	SQA(H)	SQA	RATIO	A/AS
Joint Honours Degree *Communication Studies*	Y400	3FT deg	* g	14-18	5M	M$ go	28	BCCCC	Ind		
Joint Honours Degree *Media and Cultural Studies*	Y400	3FT deg	* g	14-18	MO+2D	MT go	28	BCCCC	Ind		
Joint Honours Degree *Writing & Publishing Studies*	Y400	3FT deg	E g	12-16	5M	M$ go	28	BBCC	Ind		
Journalism	006P▼	2FT HND	* g	12	5M	MT go	26	Ind	Ind	11	4/20

NAPIER Univ

TITLE	CODE	COURSE	SUBJECTS	A/AS	NO/C	AGNVQ	IB	SQA(H)	SQA	RATIO	A/AS
Communication	P300	3FT deg	E	CCD	Ind	Ind	Ind	BBCCC	Ind	9	10/26
Journalism Studies	P600	3FT deg	E g	CCC	Ind	Ind	Ind	BBBC	Ind	17	16/26
Publishing	P500	3FT/4FT deg	E	BC	Ind	Ind	Ind	BBB	Ind	3	14/22

NENE COLLEGE

TITLE	CODE	COURSE	SUBJECTS	A/AS	NO/C	AGNVQ	IB	SQA(H)	SQA	RATIO	A/AS
American Studies with Media and Popular Culture	Q4P4	3FT deg		DD	5M	M	24	CCC	Ind		6/16
Art and Design with Media and Popular Culture	W2P4	3FT deg		DD	5M	M	24	CCC	Ind		8/22
Business Admin with Media and Popular Culture	N1P4	3FT deg	g	10	M+1D	M	24	BCC	Ind		
Drama with Media and Popular Culture	W4P4	3FT deg		10	5M+1D	M	24	CCC	Ind		6/22
Economics with Media and Popular Culture	L1P4	3FT deg	g	6	5M	M	24	CCC	Ind		
Education with Media and Popular Culture	X9P4	3FT deg		DD	5M	M	24	CCC	Ind		
English with Media and Popular Culture	Q3P4▼	3FT deg		CC	4M+1D	M	24	CCC	Ind		6/22
Information Systems with Media & Popular Culture	G5P4	3FT deg		6	5M	M	24	CCC	Ind		
Law with Media and Popular Culture	M3P4	3FT deg	g	10	3M+2D	M	24	CCC	Ind		
Music with Media and Popular Culture	W3P4	3FT deg	Mu	DD	5M	M	24	CCC	Ind		
Politics with Media and Popular Culture	M1P4	3FT deg		CD	5M	M	24	CCC	Ind		4/8
Psychology with Media and Popular Culture	C8P4▼	3FT deg	g	CC	5M+1D	M	24	CCC	Ind		10/16
Sociology with Media and Popular Culture	L3P4▼	3FT deg		10	5M	M	24	CCC	Ind		10/12
Sport Studies with Media and Popular Culture	N7P4▼	3FT deg	Ss/Pe	12	M+2D	M	24	BBB	Ind		
Media Studies	004P▼	2FT HND									

Univ of Wales COLLEGE, NEWPORT

TITLE	CODE	COURSE	SUBJECTS	A/AS	NO/C	AGNVQ	IB	SQA(H)	SQA	RATIO	A/AS
Telecommunications	053P	2FT HND		2	N	P$	Ind	Ind	Ind		

NORTH EAST WALES INST of HE

TITLE	CODE	COURSE	SUBJECTS	A/AS	NO/C	AGNVQ	IB	SQA(H)	SQA	RATIO	A/AS
Biology and Media Practice	CP14	3FT deg		4-8	3M	M$	Ind	CCC	N$		
Business and Media Studies	NP14	3FT deg		6-12	3M	M$		CCC	N$		
English and Media Studies	QP34	3FT deg		6-12	4M	M$	Ind	BBB	N$		10/16
English with Media Studies	Q3P4	3FT deg		6-12	4M	M$	Ind	BBB	N$		
History and Media Studies	VP14	3FT deg		6-12	4M	M$	Ind	BBB	N$		
History with Media Studies	V1P4	3FT deg		6-12	4M	M$	Ind	BBB	N$		
Media Studies/Psychology	PC48	3FT deg		6-12	4M	M$	Ind	BBB	N$		
Media Studies/Sociology	PL43	3FT deg		6-12	3M	M$	Ind	CCC	N$		
Media Studies/Welsh Studies	PQ45	3FT deg		6-12	4M	M$	Ind	BBB	N$		

NORTH EAST WORCESTERSHIRE COLL

TITLE	CODE	COURSE	SUBJECTS	A/AS	NO/C	AGNVQ	IB	SQA(H)	SQA	RATIO	A/AS
Media (Design-Electronic Media)	42PE	2FT HND	Pf		N	Ind	Ind	Ind	Ind		

Univ of NORTH LONDON

TITLE	CODE	COURSE	SUBJECTS	A/AS	NO/C	AGNVQ	IB	SQA(H)	SQA	RATIO	A/AS
Communication and Cultural Studies	LP63▼	3FT deg	*	CC	MO	M	$	CCCCC	Ind	6	8/20
Critical Theory and Communication & Cultural St	LP6H	3FT deg	Me/Cm/E/So	CC	Ind	Ind	Ind	Ind	Ind		
Education Studies & Communication & Cultural St	PX39	3FT deg	Me/Cm/E/So	CC	Ind	Ind	Ind	Ind	Ind		
Information and Communications Management	PP2H▼	3FT deg	*	CC	MO	M	$	CCCCC	Ind		
Combined Honours *Communication and Cultural Studies*	Y301	3FT deg	*	CC	MO	M	Dip	CCCC	Ind		

Letts STUDY GUIDES
THE INDEPENDENT

course details			98 expected requirements							96 entry stats	
TITLE	CODE	COURSE	SUBJECTS	A/AS	ND/C	AGNVQ	IB	SQA(H)	SQA	RATIO	A/AS
Univ of NORTHUMBRIA											
Multi Media Design	WP25	3FT deg			N	Ind	Ind	Ind	X		
Multimedia Design	EP25	3FT deg			N	Ind	Ind	Ind	X		
NOTTINGHAM TRENT Univ											
Broadcast Journalism	P600	3FT deg	* g	22	M+D	Ind	28	CCCC	Ind	25	14/26
Communication Studies	P300	3FT deg	* g	BBC	M+D	Ind	28	CCCC	Ind	13	14/26
Media and Cultural Studies	LP64	3FT deg	* g	16-18	M+D	Ind	28	CCCC	Ind	1	14/22
Modern Languages with Communication Studies	T9P3	4FT deg	2L g	18	Ind	Ind	28	CCCC	Ind	4	12/20
Printing and Publishing Media	P5J5	3FT/4SW deg									
OXFORD BROOKES Univ											
Publishing/Accounting and Finance	NP45	3FT deg	* g	BB-CCD	Ind	M$3/D*3	Ind	Ind	Ind		
Publishing/Anthropology	LP65	3FT deg	* g	BB-CCD	Ind	M*^/M$	Ind	Ind	Ind	3	
Publishing/Biological Chemistry	CP75	3FT deg									
Publishing/Biology	CP15	3FT deg	S g	DD-BB	Ind	MS/M$3	Ind	Ind	Ind		
Publishing/Business Administration & Management	NP15	3FT deg	* g	BB-CCD	Ind	MB4/M$3	Ind	Ind	Ind	2	
Publishing/Cartography	FP85	3FT deg	* g	DDD-BB	Ind	M*/M$3	Ind	Ind	Ind		
Publishing/Cell Biology	CPC5	3FT deg									
Publishing/Combined Studies	PY54	3FT deg		X		X	X	X			
Publishing/Computer Systems	GP65	3FT deg	* g	CDD-CCC	Ind	M*/M$3	Ind	Ind	Ind		
Publishing/Computing	GP55	3FT deg	* g	CDD-BB	Ind	M*/M$3	Ind	Ind	Ind	2	
Publishing/Computing Mathematics	GP95	3FT deg	* g	CD-BB	Ind	M*/M$3	Ind	Ind	Ind		
Publishing/Ecology	CP95	3FT deg	* g	CD-BB	Ind	MS/M$3	Ind	Ind	Ind		
Publishing/Economics	LP15	3FT deg	* g	BB-CCD	Ind	M$3	Ind	Ind	Ind	1	
Publishing/Educational Studies	PX59	3FT deg	* g	CC-BB	Ind	M$3	Ind	Ind	Ind	5	
Publishing/English Studies	PQ53	3FT deg	* g	CCD-AB	Ind	M*^/M$3	Ind	Ind	Ind	3	12/26
Publishing/Environmental Chemistry	FP15	3FT deg									
Publishing/Environmental Policy	KP35	3FT deg									
Publishing/Environmental Sciences	FPX5	3FT deg	S g	CD-BB	Ind	DS/M$3	Ind	Ind	Ind		
Publishing/Exercise and Health	PB56	3FT deg	S g	DD-BB	Ind	MS/M$3	Ind	Ind	Ind		
Publishing/Fine Art	PW51	3FT deg	Pf+A g	BC-BB	Ind	MA^/M$3	Ind	Ind	Ind		
Publishing/Food Science and Nutrition	DP45	3FT deg	S g	DD-BB	Ind	MS/M$3	Ind	Ind	Ind		
Publishing/French Language and Contemp Studies	PR5C	4SW deg	F g	CDD-BB	Ind	M^M$3	Ind	Ind	Ind	2	
Publishing/French Language and Literature	PR51	4SW deg	F g	CDD-BB	Ind	M^M$3	Ind	Ind	Ind		
Publishing/Geology	FP65	3FT deg	S/M g	DD-BB	Ind	PS/M$3	Ind	Ind	Ind		
Publishing/Geotechnics	HP25	3FT deg	S/M/Ds/Es g	DD-BB	Ind	M$/M$3	Ind	Ind	Ind		
Publishing/German Language and Contemp Stud	PR5F	4SW deg	G g	DDD-BB	Ind	M^M$3	Ind	Ind	Ind		
Publishing/German Language and Literature	PR52	4SW deg	G g	DDD-BB	Ind	M^M$3	Ind	Ind	Ind		
Publishing/German Studies	PR5G	4SW deg	* g	DDD-BB	Ind	M^/M$3	Ind	Ind	Ind		
Publishing/Health Care (Post Exp)	BP75	3FT deg		X		X	X	X			
Publishing/History	PV51	3FT deg	* g	BB-CCD	Ind	M^/M$3	Ind	Ind	Ind	3	
Publishing/History of Art	PV54	3FT deg	* g	BB-CCD	Ind	M^/M$3	Ind	Ind	Ind	5	
Publishing/Human Biology	BP15	3FT deg									
Publishing/Information Systems	GPM5	3FT deg	* g	CDD-BB	Ind	M*/M$3	Ind	Ind	Ind		
Publishing/Intelligent Systems	GP85	3FT deg	* g	CDD-BB	Ind	M*/M$3	Ind	Ind	Ind		
Publishing/Law	MP35	3FT deg	* g	CCD-BBB	Ind	M$3/D*3	Ind	Ind	Ind		
Publishing/Leisure Planning and Management	KPH5	3FT deg									
Publishing/Marketing Management	NPN5	3FT deg	* g	BB-CCD	Ind	M$3/D*3	Ind	Ind	Ind	17	
Publishing/Mathematics	GP15	3FT deg	M g	DD-BB	Ind	M*^/M$3	Ind	Ind	Ind		
Publishing/Music	PW53	3FT deg	Mu g	DD-BB	Ind	M/M$3	Ind	Ind	Ind	4	
Publishing/Palliative Care (Post Exp)	BPR5	3FT deg		X		X	X	X			
Publishing/Physical Geography	FPV5	3FT deg									

Media Studies – Communications, 53
Journalism, Publishing

course details			98 expected requirements							96 entry stats	
TITLE	CODE	COURSE	SUBJECTS	A/AS	ND/C	AGNVQ	IB	SQA(H)	SQA	RATIO	A/AS
Publishing/Planning Studies	KP45	3FT deg	* g	DDD-BB	Ind	M*/M$3	Ind	Ind	Ind	1	
Publishing/Politics	MP15	3FT deg	* g	CCD-AB	Ind	M^/M$3	Ind	Ind	Ind	3	
Publishing/Psychology	CP85	3FT deg	* g	CCD-BBC	Ind	M^/M$3	Ind	Ind	Ind	12	
Rehabilitation/Publishing (Post Exp)	BPT5	3FT deg	X		X		X	X			
Sociology/Publishing	LP35	3FT deg	* g	BB-CCD	Ind	M*^/M$3	Ind	Ind	Ind	3	
Software Engineering/Publishing	GP75	3FT deg	* g	CDD-CCC	Ind	M*/M$3	Ind	Ind	Ind		
Statistics/Publishing	GP45	3FT deg	* g	DD-BB	Ind	M*/M$3	Ind	Ind	Ind		
Telecommunications/Publishing	HPP5	3FT deg									
Tourism/Publishing	PP75	3FT deg	* g	CCC-CCD	Ind	M$3	Ind	Ind	Ind	4	
Transport Planning/Publishing	NP95	3FT deg	* g	BB-DDD	Ind	M*/M$3	Ind	Ind	Ind		
Water Resources/Publishing	HPF5	3 deg									

OXFORDSHIRE SCHOOL of A & D

Media Production	014P	2FT HND			N	M$ gi	Ind	Ind	Ind		
Media Production	014E	2FT HND			N	M$ gi	Ind	Ind	Ind		

Univ of PAISLEY

Media Technology	HP64	3FT/4FT deg	* g	CC	Ind	Ind	Ind	BBC$	Ind	1	
Media Theory and Production	P400▼	3FT/4FT deg	E g	BC	Ind	Ind	Ind	BBC$	Ind	3	12/14

PLYMOUTH COLLEGE of A & D

Media Production	034E	2FT HND	Fa/Ad		N	P	Ind	Ind	Ind		
Media Production	034P	2FT HND	Fa/Ad		N	P	Ind	Ind	Ind		

Univ of PORTSMOUTH

Communications and Media Technology	P4HP	4FT/5SW deg	M+P/Es	18	4M+1D$	D$6/^	30$	BBBBC	N$		
Communications and Media Technology	P4H6	3FT/4SW deg	M+P/Es	16	4M $	M$6/^	28$	BBBB	N$		
Economics and Media Studies	LP14	3FT deg	*	16	4M+2D	D$6/^	Dip	CCCCC	Ind		

QUEEN MARGARET COLL

Communication Studies	P300	3FT/4FT deg	* g	BC	M+D	M/D$^ go	Ind	BBBC	Ind	4	12/22
Corporate Communication	P301	3FT/4FT deg	* g	BC	M+D	M/D$^ go	Ind	BBBC	Ind	6	
Combined Studies Human and Professional Communication	Y600	3FT/4FT deg	*	BC	M+D	M/D$^ go	Ind	BBBC	Ind		
Combined Studies Media and Cultural Studies	Y600	3FT/4FT deg	*	BC	M+D	M/D$^ go	Ind	BBBC	Ind		

Univ College of RIPON & YORK ST JOHN

Communication Arts (Music, Dance, Drama) with Ed	P3X9	3FT deg		CC	M	M$	27	BBBC			
Communication Arts - Image and Text	P3P4	3FT deg		CC	M	M	27	BBBC		3	6/22
Dance: Performance and Communication Arts	PW3K	3FT deg		CC	M	M$	27	BBBC			
Drama: Performance and Communication Arts	PW34	3FT deg		CC	M	M$	27	BBBC			
Music: Performance and Communication Arts	PW33	3FT deg		CC	M	M$	27	BBBC			

ROBERT GORDON Univ

Communication with Modern Languages	P3T9	3FT/4FT deg	E+F/G g	CC	Ind	Ind	Ind	BBC$	Ind	4	
Corporate Communication	P300	3/4FT deg	E g	CC	Ind	Ind	Ind	BCC$	Ind		
Publishing Studies	P500	3FT/4FT deg	E g	DD	N	Ind	Ind	BBB$	Ind	4	

ROEHAMPTON INST

Calligraphy & Bookbinding	PW52▼	3FT deg	g	DD	4M	P$	26	BCC	N	2	
Film & Television Studies & English Lang & Ling	PQ4H▼	3FT deg	E/L	16	2M+2D$	M$^	30	BBC	N$	33	
Film & Television Studies & Environmental Studs	FP94▼	3FT deg	B/Gy	16	2M+2D$	M$^	30	BBC	N$		
Film & Television Studies & Human & Social Biol	CPC4▼	3FT deg	B	16	2M+2D$	M$^	30	BBC	N$		
Film & Television Studies and Biology	CP14▼	3FT deg	B g	16	2M+2D$	M$^	30	BBC	N$		
Film & Television Studies and Business Computing	GP74▼	3FT deg	g	16	2M+2D	M$^ go	30	BBC	N$		
Film & Television Studies and Business Studies	NP14▼	3FT deg	g	16	3D	M$^ go	30	BBC	N$	15	

course details			98 expected requirements							96 entry stats	
TITLE	CODE	COURSE	SUBJECTS	A/AS	NO/C	RGNVQ	IB	SQA(H)	SQA	RATIO	A/AS
Film & Television Studies and Dance Studies	PW44▼	3FT deg	*	16	2M+2D$	M$^	30	BBC	N$	14	
Film & Television Studies and Drama & Theatre St	PW4K▼	3FT deg	E/T	16	2M+2D$	M$^	30	BBC	N$	10	16/20
Film & Television Studies and Education	PX49▼	3FT deg	*	16	2M+2D$	M$^	30	BBC	N$	3	
Film & Television Studies and English Literature	PQ43▼	3FT deg	E	16	2M+2D$	M^	30	BBC	N$	10	14/20
Film & Television Studies and French	PR41▼	4FT deg	F	16	2M+2D$	M^	30	BBC	N$		
Film & Television Studies and Geography	LP84▼	3FT deg	Gy	16	2M+2D$	M$^	30	BBC	N$		
Film & Television Studies and Health Studies	BP94▼	3FT deg	g	16	2M+2D	M$^ go	30	BBC	N$		
Film & Television Studies and History	PV41▼	3FT deg	H	16	2M+2D$	M^	30	BBC	N$	31	
Film & Television Studs & Applied Consumer Studs	NP94▼	3FT deg	g	16	2M+2D$	M$^ go	30	BBC	N$		
Music and Film & Television Studies	PW43▼	3FT deg	Mu	16	2M+2D$	M^	30	BBC	N$		
Natural Resource Studs & Film & Television Studs	DP24▼	3FT deg	g	16	2M+2D	M$^ go	30	BBC	N$		
Psychology and Film & Television Studies	LP74▼	3FT deg	g	16	3D	M$^ go	30	BBC	N$	35	
Social Policy & Admin and Film & Television St	LP44▼	3FT deg	*	16	2M+2D$	M$^	30	BBC	N$	5	
Sociology and Film & Television Studies	LP34▼	3FT deg	g	16	2M+2D$	M$^ go	30	BBC	N$	17	
Sport Studies and Film & Television Studies	PB46▼	3FT deg	S g	16	3D	M$^ go	30	BBC	N$		
Theology & Religious St and Film & Television St	PV48▼	3FT deg	*	16	2M+2D$	M$^	30	BBC	N$		
Women's Studies and Film & Television Studies	MP94▼	3FT deg	*	16	2M+2D$	M$^	30	BBC	N$	18	

ROYAL HOLLOWAY, Univ of London

| Science and the Media | Y1P4 | 3FT deg | S | BBC-CCC | Ind | DS^ | 28$ | Ind | | 6 | |

Univ of SHEFFIELD

| Journalism Studies | P600 | 3FT deg | * g | BBB | 3M+3D | D^ | 32 | AABB | Ind | 18 | 24/30 |

SHEFFIELD HALLAM Univ

Communication Studies	P300	3FT deg	*	20	DO	P^	Ind	BBBB	Ind		
Media Science	P405	3FT/4SW deg	g	14	4M	M	Ind	Ind	Ind		
Media Studies	P400	3FT deg	*	BCC	3M+4D	M^	Ind	Ind	Ind		
Combined Studies — Communication Studies	Y400	3FT deg	*	18	2M	M	Ind	Ind	Ind		
Combined Studies — Media Studies	Y400	3FT deg	*	18	2M	M	Ind	Ind	Ind		
Combined Studies — Science in the Media	Y400	3FT deg	S	8-10	2M	M	Ind	Ind	Ind		

SOLIHULL COLL

| Media Production | E430 | 3FT deg | Fa+Pf g | DD | N | P go | Dip | Ind | Ind | | |
| Media Production | P430 | 3FT deg | Fa+Pf g | DD | N | P go | Dip | Ind | Ind | | |

SOUTHAMPTON INST

Advertising (HND top-up)	P340	1FT deg	Pf	X	HN $	X	X	X	HN$		
Corporate Communication	P300	3FT deg	*	14	MO	M$	Dip	BBCC	$	3	12/18
Journalism	P600	3FT deg	*	20-22	MO	M/D	Dip	BBBBB	N	9	18/26
Media Technology	P430	3FT deg	M/P	8-10	MO	M$	Dip	CCCC	N	6	8/18
Media Technology (with Foundation Year)	P438▼	4FT deg	*	2-4	MO	P$	Dip	CCCC	N	3	4/16
Media with Cultural Studies	P400	3FT deg	*	18	M	M$	Dip	BBBBC	N	4	12/24
Visual Culture	P440	3FT deg	*	12	MO	M$	Dip	CCCC	N		

SOUTH BANK Univ

Media Studies & Business Information Technology	GP74	3FT deg	M+E g	14-18	4M+2D	D go	Ind	Ind	Ind		
Media Studies and Computing	GP54	3FT deg	M+E g	14-18	2M+4D	D go	Ind	Ind	Ind		
Media Studies and Economics	LP14	3FT deg	Ec/Bu+E g	14-18	2M+4D	D go	Ind	Ind	Ind		
Media Studies and English Studies	PQ43	3FT deg	E g	14-18	X	D^ go	Ind	Ind	Ind		
Media Studies and European Studies	PT42	3FT deg	E g	14-18	2M+4D	D go	Ind	Ind	Ind		
Media Studies and French	PR41	3FT deg	E+F g	14-18	2M+4D	D go	Ind	Ind	Ind		
Media Studies and German	PR4F	3FT deg	E+G g	14-18	2M+4D	D go	Ind	Ind	Ind		
Media Studies and German - ab initio	PR42	3FT deg	E g	14-18	2M+4D	D go	Ind	Ind	Ind		

Media Studies – Communications, Journalism, Publishing, 53

			98 expected requirements							96 entry stats
TITLE	CODE	COURSE	SUBJECTS	A/AS	ND/C	RGNVQ	IB	SQA(H)	SQA	RATIO A/AS
Media Studies and History	PV41	3FT deg	E+H g	14-18	2M+4D	D go	Ind	Ind	Ind	
Media Studies and Housing	KP4K	3FT deg	E g	14-18	2M+4D	D go	Ind	Ind	Ind	
Media Studies and Human Biology	BP14	3FT deg	S+E g	14-18	2M+4D	M go	Ind	Ind	Ind	
Media Studies and Human Resource Management	NP64	3FT deg	E g	14-18	2M+4D	D go	Ind	Ind	Ind	
Media Studies and Management	NP14	3FT deg	E g	14-18	2M+4D	D go	Ind	Ind	Ind	
Media Studies and Marketing	NP54	3FT deg	E g	14-18	2M+4D	D go	Ind	Ind	Ind	
Media and Society	PL43	3FT deg	El/Ee	BCC	4D	D go	Ind	Ind	Ind	
Politics and Media Studies	MP14	3FT deg	E g	14-18	2M+4D	D go	Ind	Ind	Ind	
Psychology and Media Studies	CP84	3FT deg	E+S g	14-18	2M+4D	M go	Ind	Ind	Ind	
Social Policy and Media Studies	LP4K	3FT deg	E g	14-18	2M+4D	D go	Ind	Ind	Ind	
Sociology and Media Studies	LP34	3FT deg	E g	14-18	2M+4D	D go	Ind	Ind	Ind	
Spanish - ab initio and Marketing	NP5K	3FT deg	* g	14-18	2M+4D	M go	Ind	Ind	Ind	
Spanish - ab initio and Media Studies	PR44	3FT deg	E g	14-18	2M+4D	D go	Ind	Ind	Ind	
Spanish and Media Studies	PR4K	3FT deg	Sp+E	14-18	2M+4D	D go	Ind	Ind	Ind	
Sports Science and Media Studies	BP64	3FT deg	E+S g	14-18	2M+4D	M go	Ind	Ind	Ind	
Technology and Media Studies	JP94	3FT deg	E g	14-18	2M+4D	D go	Ind	Ind	Ind	
Tourism and Media Studies	PP47	3FT deg	E+L g	14-18	2M+4D	D go	Ind	Ind	Ind	
Urban Studies and Media Studies	KP4L	3FT deg	E g	14-18	2M+4D	D go	Ind	Ind	Ind	
World Theatre and Media Studies	PW44	3FT deg	E g	14-18	2M+4D	D go	Ind	Ind	Ind	

ST HELENS COLL

TITLE	CODE	COURSE	SUBJECTS	A/AS	ND/C	RGNVQ	IB	SQA(H)	SQA	RATIO A/AS
Media Production	P410	3FT deg								
Media Production	204P	2FT HND	*	2	N	M*	Ind	Ind	Ind	
Media Technology	104P	2FT HND	*	2	N	M*	Ind	Ind	Ind	

THE UNIVERSITY COLLEGE OF ST MARK AND ST JOHN

TITLE	CODE	COURSE	SUBJECTS	A/AS	ND/C	RGNVQ	IB	SQA(H)	SQA	RATIO A/AS
Art & Design/Public Relations	W1P3	3FT deg		4	MO	M	Dip	CCCC	Ind	
Art and Design/Media Studies	W1P4	3FT deg		4	MO	M	Dip	CCCC	Ind	
Community Studies/Public Relations	L5P3	3FT deg		10	MO	M	Dip	CCCC	Ind	
Development Studies/Public Relations	M9P3	3FT deg		8-10	MO	M	Ind	Ind	Ind	
English (Literary Studies)/Media Studies	Q3P4	3FT deg	El	12-16	Ind	M	Ind	Ind	Ind	
English Language Studies/Media Studies	Q1P4	3FT deg		12	MO	M	Ind	Ind	Ind	
English Language Studies/Public Relations	Q1P3	3FT deg		12	MO	M	Ind	Ind	Ind	
History/Media Studies	V1P4	3FT deg	H	12	MO	M	Ind	Ind	Ind	
Information Technology/Media Studies	G5P4	3FT deg		4	MO	M	Dip	CCCC	Ind	
Information Technology/Public Relations	G5P3	3FT deg		4	MO	M	Dip	CCCC	Ind	
Leisure & Tourism Studies/Public Relations	P7P3	3FT deg		8	MO	M	Ind	Ind	Ind	
Media Studies/Art and Design	P4W1	3FT deg		16	MO	M	Ind	Ind	Ind	
Media Studies/English (Literary Studies)	P4Q3	3FT deg		16	MO	M	Ind	Ind	Ind	
Media Studies/English Language Studies	P4Q1	3FT deg		16	MO	M	Ind	Ind	Ind	
Media Studies/History	P4V1	3FT deg		16	MO	M	Ind	Ind	Ind	
Media Studies/Information Technology	P4G5	3FT deg		16	MO	M	Ind	Ind	Ind	
Media Studies/Public Relations	P4P3	3FT deg		16	MO	M	Ind	Ind	Ind	
Media Studies/Sociology	P4L3	3FT deg		16	MO	M	Ind	Ind	Ind	
Public Relations/Art & Design	P3W1	3FT deg		16	MO	M	Ind	Ind	Ind	
Public Relations/Community Studies	P3L5	3FT deg		16	MO	M	Ind	Ind	Ind	
Public Relations/Development Studies	P3M9	3FT deg		16	MO	M	Ind	Ind	Ind	
Public Relations/English Language Studies	P3Q1	3FT deg		16	MO	M	Ind	Ind	Ind	
Public Relations/Information Technology	P3GN	3FT deg		16	MO	M	Ind	Ind	Ind	
Public Relations/Leisure & Tourism Studies	P3P7	3FT deg		16	MO	M	Ind	Ind	Ind	
Public Relations/Media Studies	P3P4	3FT deg		16	MO	M	Ind	Ind	Ind	
Public Relations/Sports Science	P3B6	3FT deg		16	MO	M	Ind	Ind	Ind	
Sociology/Media Studies	L3P4	3FT deg	So	8	MO	M	Ind	Ind	Ind	
Sports Science/Public Relations	B6P3	3FT deg		8	MO	M	Ind	Ind	Ind	

TITLE	CODE	COURSE	SUBJECTS	A/AS	NO/C	RGNVQ	IB	SQA(H)	SQA	RATIO A/AS
ST MARY'S Univ COLL										
Management Studies and Media Arts	NP14	3FT deg	* g	8-12	Ind	Ind	Ind	BBBB	Ind	
Mathematics and Media Arts	GP14	3FT deg	M	4-8	X	X	Ind	BBBB$	X	
Media Arts and Biology	CP14	3FT deg	B/C	4-8	Ind	Ind	Ind	BBBB	Ind	
Media Arts and Classical Studies	PQ48	3FT deg	*	4-8	Ind	Ind	Ind	BBBB	Ind	
Media Arts and Drama	PW44	3FT deg	*	8-12	Ind	Ind	Ind	BBBB	Ind	
Media Arts and Education Studies	PX4X	3FT deg	*	4-8	Ind	Ind	Ind	BBBB	Ind	
Media Arts and English	PQ43	3FT deg	E	8-12	X	X	Ind	BBBB$	X	
Media Arts and Environmental Investigation St	FP94	3FT deg	S/2S	4-8	Ind	Ind	Ind	BBBB$	Ind	
Media Arts and Environmental Studies	FPX4	3FT deg	*	4-8	Ind	Ind	Ind	BBBB	Ind	
Media Arts and Gender Studies	MP94	3FT deg	*	4-8	Ind	Ind	Ind	BBBB	Ind	
Media Arts and History	PV41	3FT deg	H	4-8	Ind	Ind	Ind	BBBB	Ind	
Media Arts and Integrated Scientific Studies	PY41	3FT deg	S/2S	4-8	Ind	Ind	Ind	BBBB$	Ind	
Media Arts and Irish Studies	PQ45	3FT deg	*	4-8	Ind	Ind	Ind	BBBB	Ind	
Sociology and Media Arts	LP34	3FT deg	*	4-8	Ind	Ind	Ind	BBBB	Ind	
Sport Science and Media Arts	BP64	3FT deg	S g	8-12	Ind	Ind	Ind	BBBB$	Ind	
STAFFORDSHIRE Univ										
Design: Media Production	P430	3FT deg	Pf		Ind	MA	Ind	Ind	Ind	54
European Culture/Media Studies	LPP4	3FT deg	g	CD	MO+2D	M	27	BBC	Ind	
European Media, Culture and Politics	PL43	3FT deg	g	CD	MO+2D	M	27	BBC		
Foundation Enterprise,Innovation & Communication	NP1H▼	3FT/4FT deg	g							
Foundation Interactive Systems Design	GP5K▼	4EXT/5EXTSW deg	g	4	N	P	24	CCC	Ind	
Interactive Systems Design	GP54	4SW deg	g	12	Ind	M	Ind	CCC	Ind	4 8/12
Media Studies	P400	3FT deg	g	CD	MO+2D	M	27	BBC		
Media Studies/American Studies	PQ44	3FT deg	g	CD	MO+2D	M	27	BBC	Ind	6 8/18
Media Studies/Cultural Studies	PL46	3FT deg	g	CD	MO+2D	M	27	BBC	Ind	5 6/16
Media Studies/Development Studies	MPY4	3FT deg	g	12	MO+2D	M	27	BBC	Ind	
Media Studies/Film Studies	PW45	3FT deg	g	CD	MO+2D		27	BBC		
Media Studies/French	PR41	3FT/4SW deg	F g	CD	MO+2D	M^	26	BCC	Ind	8
Media Studies/Geography	FP84	3FT deg								
Media Studies/German	PR42	3FT/4SW deg	G g	CD	MO+2D	M^	26	BCC	Ind	
Media Studies/History of Art and Design	PV44	3FT deg	g	CD	MO+2D	M	27	BBC	Ind	2
Media Studies/Information Systems	PG45	3FT deg	g	12	MO+2D	M	27	BBC	Ind	4
Media Studies/International Relations	MPC4	3FT deg	g	12	MO+2D	M	27	BBC	Ind	9
Media Studies/Law	MP34	3FT deg	g	18	HN	M^	27	BBBB	Ind	13
Media Studies/Legal Studies	MPH4	3FT deg	g	18	HN	M^	27	BBBB	Ind	6
Media Studies/Literature	PQ43	3FT deg	El g	CD	MO+2D	M	27	BBC	Ind	5 6/24
Philosophy/Media Studies	PV47	3FT deg	g	CD	MO+2D	M	27	BBC	Ind	6
Politics/Media Studies	MPCK	3FT deg	g	12	MO+2D	D	27	BBC	Ind	25
Psychology/Media Studies	LP74	3FT deg	g	18	3M+3D	Ind	27	BBB	Ind	17
Sociology/Media Studies	LP34	3FT deg	g	12	MO+2D	M	27	BBC	Ind	12
Univ of STIRLING										
Business Studies/Film & Media Studies	NP14	4FT deg	g	BBC	Ind	Ind	35	ABBB	HN	
Computing Science/Film & Media Studies	GW55	4FT deg	g	BBC	HN	Ind	35	ABBB	HN	
English Studies/Film & Media Studies	QP34	4FT deg	g	BBC	Ind	Ind	35	ABBB	HN	
Film & Media Studies	P400	4FT deg	g	BBC	Ind	Ind	35	ABBB	HN	
Film & Media Studies/German	RP24	4FT deg	g	BBC	Ind	Ind	35	ABBB	HN	
Film & Media Studies/History	PV41	4FT deg	g	BBC	Ind	Ind	35	ABBB	HN	
Film & Media Studies/Japanese	PT4K	4FT deg	g	BBC	Ind	Ind	35	ABBB	HN	
Film & Media Studies/Marketing	PN45	4FT deg	g	BBC	Ind	Ind	35	ABBB	HN	
Film & Media Studies/Philosophy	VP74	4FT deg	g	BBC	Ind	Ind	35	ABBB	HN	

Media Studies – Communications, 53 Journalism, Publishing

			98 expected requirements						96 entry stats	

course details

TITLE	CODE	COURSE	SUBJECTS	A/AS	ND/C	RGNVQ	IB	SQA(H)	SQA	RATIO A/AS
Film & Media Studies/Politics	PM41	4FT deg	g	BBC	Ind	Ind	35	ABBB	HN	
Film & Media Studies/Psychology	CP84	4FT deg	g	BBC	Ind	Ind	35	ABBB	HN	
Film & Media Studies/Social Policy	PL44	4FT deg	g	BBC	Ind	Ind	35	ABBB	HN	
Film & Media Studies/Spanish	RP44	4FT deg	g	BBC	Ind	Ind	35	ABBB	HN	
French/Film & Media Studies	RP14	4FT deg	g	BBC	Ind	Ind	35	ABBB	HN	
Religious Studies/Film & Media Studies	VP84	4FT deg	g	BBC	Ind	Ind	35	ABBB	HN	
Sociology/Film & Media Studies	LP34	4FT deg	g	BBC	Ind	Ind	35	ABBB	HN	

UNIVERSITY COLLEGE SUFFOLK

TITLE	CODE	COURSE	SUBJECTS	A/AS	ND/C	RGNVQ	IB	SQA(H)	SQA	RATIO A/AS
Applied Biological Science with Media Studies	C1P4	3FT deg	S	EE	N $	PS	Ind	Ind	Ind	
Art & Design and Media Studies	PW42	3FT deg	Pf	CE	N $	P$	Ind	Ind	Ind	
Art & Design and Media Studies	EW42	3FT deg	Pf	CE	N $	P$	Ind	Ind	Ind	
Art & Design with Media Studies	E2P4	3FT deg	Pf	EE	N $	P$	Ind	Ind	Ind	
Art & Design with Media Studies	W2P4	3FT deg	Pf	EE	N $	P$	Ind	Ind	Ind	
Behavioural Studies and Media Studies	LP74	3FT deg	*	DC	N $	P$	Ind	Ind	Ind	
Behavioural Studies with Media Studies	L7P4	3FT deg	*	DD	N $	P$	Ind	Ind	Ind	
Business Studies with Media Studies	N1P4	3FT deg	*	EE	N $	P$	Ind	Ind	Ind	
Cultural Studies and Media Studies	YP34	3FT deg	*	CE	N $	P$	Ind	Ind	Ind	
Early Childhood Studies and Media Studies	XP94	3FT deg	*	DC	N $	P$	Ind	Ind	Ind	
Early Childhood Studies with Media Studies	X9P4	3FT deg	*	DD	N $	P$	Ind	Ind	Ind	
Environmental Studies with Media Studies	F9P4	3FT deg	S/Gy	EE	N $	P$	Ind	Ind	Ind	
Information Technology with Media Studies	G5P4	3FT deg	*	EE	N $	P$	Ind	Ind	Ind	
Literary Studies and Media Studies	QP24	3FT deg	E	CE	N $	P$	Ind	Ind	Ind	
Media Studies and Applied Biological Science	CP14	3FT deg	S	CE	N $	P$	Ind	Ind	Ind	
Media Studies and Business Studies	PN41	3FT deg	*	CE	N $	P$	Ind	Ind	Ind	
Media Studies and Environmental Studies	FP94	3FT deg	S/Gy	CE	N $	P$	Ind	Ind	Ind	
Media Studies and Information Technology	P4G5	3FT deg	*	CE	N $	P$	Ind	Ind	Ind	
Media Studies and Management	PN4C	3FT deg	*	CE	N $	P$	Ind	Ind	Ind	
Media Studies with Applied Biological Science	P4C1	3FT deg	*	CE	N $	P$	Ind	Ind	Ind	
Media Studies with Art & Design	P4W2	3FT deg	Pf	CE	N $	P$	Ind	Ind	Ind	
Media Studies with Behavioural Studies	P4L3	3FT deg	*	CE	N $	P$	Ind	Ind	Ind	
Media Studies with Business Studies	P4NC	3FT deg	*	CE	N $	P$	Ind	Ind	Ind	
Media Studies with Cultural Studies	P4Y3	3FT deg	*	CE	N $	P$	Ind	Ind	Ind	
Media Studies with Early Childhood Studies	P4XX	3FT deg	*	CE	N $	P$	Ind	Ind	Ind	
Media Studies with Education Studies	P4X9	3FT deg	*	CE	N $	P$	Ind	Ind	Ind	
Media Studies with Human Science	P4B1	3FT deg	S	CE	N $	P$	Ind	Ind	Ind	
Media Studies with Information Technology	P4GM	3FT deg	*	CE	N $	P$	Ind	Ind	Ind	
Media Studies with Leisure Studies	P4LH	3FT deg	*	CE	N $	P$	Ind	Ind	Ind	
Media Studies with Literary Studies	P4Q2	3FT deg	E	CE	N $	P$	Ind	Ind	Ind	
Media Studies with Product Design & Manufacture	P4H7	3FT deg	*	CE	N $	P$	Ind	Ind	Ind	
Media Studies with Social Policy	P4L4	3FT deg	*	CE	N $	P$	Ind	Ind	Ind	
Media Studies with Tourism Studies	P4P7	3FT deg	*	CE	N $	P$	Ind	Ind	Ind	
Product Design & Manufacture and Media Studies	HP74	3FT deg	*	CE	N $	P$	Ind	Ind	Ind	
Product Design & Manufacture with Media Studies	H7P4	3FT deg	*	EE	N $	P$	Ind	Ind	Ind	

Univ of SUNDERLAND

TITLE	CODE	COURSE	SUBJECTS	A/AS	ND/C	RGNVQ	IB	SQA(H)	SQA	RATIO A/AS
Biology and Media Studies	CP14	3FT deg	B/C	24	Ind	Ind	Ind	Ind	Ind	
Biology with Media Studies	C1P4	3FT deg	B/C	24	6M	X	Ind	Ind	Ind	
Business Studies with Media Studies	N1P4	3FT/4SW deg	*	24	Ind	Ind	Ind	Ind	Ind	
Communication Studies	P300	3FT deg	* g	14-18	3M	Ind	26	ABBBB	N	4 8/20
Computer Studies and Media Studies	GP54	3FT/4SW deg	*	24	Ind	Ind	Ind	Ind	Ind	
Computer Studies with Media Studies	G5P4	3FT deg	*	24	Ind	Ind	Ind	Ind	Ind	
Economics and Media Studies	LP14	3FT deg	*	24	Ind	Ind	Ind	Ind	Ind	

TITLE	CODE	COURSE	SUBJECTS	A/AS	NO/C	AGNVQ	IB	SQA(H)	SQA	RATIO	A/AS
course details			**98 expected requirements**							**96 entry stats**	
Economics with Media Studies	L1P4	3FT deg	*	24	Ind	Ind	Ind	Ind	Ind		
English with Media Studies	Q3P4	3FT deg	*	20	Ind	Ind	Ind	Ind	Ind		
French with Media Studies	R1P4	4FT deg	F	20	Ind	Ind	Ind	Ind	Ind		
Geography and Media Studies	LP84	3FT deg	*	24	Ind	Ind	Ind	Ind	Ind		
Geography with Media Studies	L8P4	3FT deg	*	24	Ind	Ind	Ind	Ind	Ind		
Geology and Media Studies	FP64	3FT deg	*	24	Ind	Ind	Ind	Ind	Ind		
Geology with Media Studies	F6P4	3FT deg	*	8	Ind	Ind	Ind	Ind	Ind		
German and Media Studies	RP24	3FT deg	*	24	Ind	Ind	Ind	Ind			
German with Media Studies	R2P4	4SW deg	G	24	Ind	Ind	Ind	Ind	Ind		
History of Art and Design and Media Studies	VP44	3FT deg	* g	12	Ind	M	24	BCCC	Ind	3	
Mathematics and Media Studies	GP14	3FT deg	M	24	Ind	Ind	Ind	Ind			
Mathematics with Media Studies	G1P4	3FT deg	M	24	Ind	Ind	Ind	Ind			
Media Studies and Philosophy	PV47	3FT deg	*	24	Ind	Ind	Ind	Ind			
Media Studies and Physiology	PB41	3FT deg	*	24	Ind	Ind	Ind	Ind			
Media Studies and Politics	PM41	3FT deg	* g	12	3M	M	24	BCCC	N		
Media Studies and Psychology	PC48	3FT deg	* g	14	MO	M	26$	BBCC$	N	5	13/18
Media Studies and Religious Studies	PV48	3FT deg	*	24	Ind	Ind	Ind	Ind			
Media Studies and Sociology	PL43	3FT deg	* g	12	3M	M	24$	BCCC$	N	18	
Media Studies with American Studies	P4Q4	3FT deg	* g	12	Ind	M	24	BCCC	Ind	15	
Media Studies with Biology	P4C1	3FT deg	*	24	Ind	Ind	Ind	Ind	Ind		
Media Studies with Business Studies	P4N1	3FT deg	*	24	Ind	Ind	Ind	Ind	Ind		
Media Studies with Comparative Literature	P4Q2	3FT deg	EI g	12	X	M	24$	BCCC$	$	2	
Media Studies with Computer Studies	P4G5	3FT deg	*	24	Ind	Ind	Ind	Ind	Ind		
Media Studies with Economics	P4L1	3FT deg	*	24	Ind	Ind	Ind	Ind	Ind		
Media Studies with English	P4Q3	3FT deg	*	26	Ind	Ind	Ind	Ind	Ind		
Media Studies with Gender Studies	P4M9	3FT deg	* g	12	Ind	M	24	BCCC	Ind	11	
Media Studies with Geography	P4L8	3FT deg	*	24	Ind	Ind	Ind	Ind	Ind		
Media Studies with Geology	P4F6	3FT deg	*	24	Ind	Ind	Ind	Ind	Ind		
Media Studies with German	P4R2	3FT deg	*	24	Ind	Ind	Ind	Ind	Ind		
Media Studies with Mathematics	P4G1	3FT deg	*	24	Ind	Ind	Ind	Ind	Ind		
Media Studies with Philosophy	P4V7	3FT deg	*	24	Ind	Ind	Ind	Ind	Ind		
Media Studies with Physiology	P4B1	3FT deg	*	24	Ind	Ind	Ind	Ind	Ind		
Media Studies with Politics	P4M1	3FT deg	*	24	Ind	Ind	Ind	Ind	Ind		
Media Studies with Psychology	P4C8	3FT deg	*	26	Ind	Ind	Ind	Ind	Ind		
Media Studies with Religious Studies	P4V8	3FT deg	*	24	Ind	Ind	Ind	Ind	Ind		
Media Studies with Sociology	P4L3	3FT deg	*	26	Ind	Ind	Ind	Ind	Ind		
Media Studies with Spanish	P4R4	3FT deg	*	24	Ind	Ind	Ind	Ind	Ind		
Media Systems	PP34	3FT/4SW deg	* g	14	3M $	M	24	CCC	N	1	6/16
Media Systems (Foundation)	PP3K	3FT deg	*			P		CC			
Media and Cultural Studies	P400	3FT deg	* g	18-22	DO	Ind	28	AABBB	X	8	12/22
Philosophy with Media Studies	V7P4	3FT deg	*	24	Ind	Ind	Ind	Ind	Ind		
Physiology with Media Studies	B1P4	3FT deg	*	24	Ind	Ind	Ind	Ind	Ind		
Politics with Media Studies	M1P4	3FT deg	*	24	Ind	Ind	Ind	Ind	Ind		
Psychology with Media Studies	C8P4	3FT deg	*	26	Ind	Ind	Ind	Ind	Ind		
Religious Studies with Media Studies	V8P4	3FT deg	*	24	Ind	Ind	Ind	Ind	Ind		
Sociology with Media Studies	L3P4	3FT deg	*	26	Ind	Ind	Ind	Ind	Ind		

SURREY INST of A & D

TITLE	CODE	COURSE	SUBJECTS	A/AS	NO/C	AGNVQ	IB	SQA(H)	SQA	RATIO	A/AS
Journalism	P601	3FT deg		12-16	N					10	10/20
Journalism	E601	3FT deg		12-16	N						
Media Studies	E400	3FT deg		14-18	N						
Media Studies	P400	3FT deg		14-18	N					11	8/18

Media Studies – Communications, 53 Journalism, Publishing

			.98 expected requirements							96 entry stats	
TITLE	CODE	COURSE	SUBJECTS	A/AS	ND/C	AGNVQ	IB	SQA(H)	SQA	RATIO	A/AS
Univ of SUSSEX											
English with Media Studies	Q3P4	3FT deg	*	BBB	MO	M*6	$	Ind	Ind		
Media Studies in Cultural and Community Studs	P4Y2	3FT deg	*	BBB	MO	M*6	$	Ind	Ind		
Media Studies in European Studies	P4T2	4FT deg	* g	BBB	MO $	M*6 go	$	Ind	Ind		
Music and Media Studies	WP34	3FT deg	Mu	BBC	MO $	M*_^	$	Ind	Ind		
SWANSEA INST of HE											
Multi Media	PG45	3FT deg		DD	N			Ind	N	4	8/18
Multi Media	EG45	3FT deg		DD	N			Ind	N		
Multi Media (Foundation)	EG4M▼	4EXT deg									
Multi Media (Foundation)	PG4M▼	4EXT deg								2	
Photojournalism	E5P6	3FT deg		12		M	Ind	Ind	Ind		
Photojournalism	W5P6	3FT deg		12		M	Ind	Ind	Ind	85	
Univ of TEESSIDE											
Journalism	P600▼	3FT deg	*	12	Ind		Ind	Ind	Ind	17	10/24
Modular Degree Scheme *Multimedia*	Y401	3FT deg									
THAMES VALLEY Univ											
American Studies with Language and Communication	Q4PH	3FT deg		8-12	MO	M	26	CCC			
Business Administration with Advertising	N1PH	3FT deg		8-12	MO	M	26	CCC			
Business Studies with Advertising (Dip)	N1P3	3FT/4SW deg		12	MO	M	26				
Digital Arts with Advertising	W9P3	3FT deg		8-12	MO	M		CCC			
English with Advertising	Q3P3	3FT deg		8-12	MO	M	26	CCC			
English with Language and Communications	Q3PH	3FT deg		8-12	MO	M	26	CCC			
French with Language and Communication	R1P3	3FT deg		8-12	MO	M	26	CCC			
German with Language and Communication	R2PH	3FT deg		8-12	MO	M	26	CCC			
Information Management with Lang & Communication	P2PH	3FT deg		8-12	MO	M	26	CCC			
Marketing with Advertising	N5P3	3FT deg		8-12	MO	M	26	CCC			
Media Arts with Advertising	W9PH	3FT deg		8-12	MO	M	26	CCC			
Multi-Media Computing with Advertising	G5P3	3FT deg		8-12	MO	M	26	CCC			
Multi-Media Computing with Lang & Communication	G5PH	3FT deg		8-12	MO	M	26	CCC			
Psychology with Advertising	C8P3	3FT deg		8-12	MO	M	26	CCC			
Psychology with Language and Communication	C8PH	3FT deg		8-12	MO	M	26	CCC			
Sociology with Advertising	L3P3	3FT deg		8-12	MO	M	26	CCC			
Spanish with Language and Communications	R4PH	3FT deg		8-12	MO	M	26	CCC			
Tourism with Advertising	P7P3	3FT deg		8-12	MO	M	26	CCC			
Media Technology	004P	2FT HND		2-4	N	P	24	CC			
Multi-Media Computing	1N4P	2FT HND	* g	2-4	N	P	24	CC			
Univ of ULSTER											
Communication Studies (3 Years)	P300▼	3FT deg	* g	CCC	MO+3D	D*6/^ gi	28	BBBC	Ind	26	18/24
Communication Studies (Fast Track)	P301▼	2ACC deg	* g	CCC	MO+3D	D*6/^ gi	28	BBBC	Ind		
Communication, Advert and Mkt (4 Yr inc DIS)	P340▼	4SW deg	* g	BBB	MO+5D	D*6/^ gi	33	AABB	Ind	20	24/30
Media Studies	P400▼	3FT deg	*	BBC	MO+4D	DT^ gi	32	ABBB	Ind	19	24/26
Humanities Combined *Media Studies*	Y320▼	3FT/4SW deg	*	CCC	MO+3D	D*6/^ gi	28	BBBC	Ind		
Univ Col WARRINGTON											
Media St with Bus Mgt & IT (Multi-Media Journal)	NP1K	3FT deg	* g	16	Ind	Ind	Ind	Ind	Ind	3	8/16
Media St with Bus Mgt and IT (Music Record Prod)	NP1L	3FT deg	* g	16	Ind	Ind	Ind	Ind	Ind		
Media Studs with Bus Mgt & IT (Radio Production)	NPD4	3FT deg	* g	16	Ind	Ind	Ind	Ind	Ind	4	10/24
Media Studs with Bus Mgt & IT (Television Prod)	NPC4	3FT deg	* g	16	Ind	Ind	Ind	Ind	Ind	4	9/22
Media and Cultural Studies	P400	3FT deg	* g	18	Ind	Ind	Ind	Ind	Ind		

course details			98 expected requirements							96 entry stats	
TITLE	CODE	COURSE	SUBJECTS	A/AS	ND/C	AGNVQ	IB	SQA(H)	SQA	RATIO	A/AS
WEST HERTS COLL											
Graphic Media Studies	PJ55	4SW deg	*	4	N					2	8/18
Media Production Management	EP14	3FT deg	*	4	N						
Graphic Arts Technical Mgt (Print, Pub & Pkg)	55JP	2FT/3SW HND	*	2	N						
Media Production	24PE	2FT HND	*	2							
Univ of WESTMINSTER											
Broadcast Journalism	P610	3FT deg									
Computer Communications and Networks	PG35	3FT deg	M/P/Cs	CC	3M	M	Ind	Ind	Ind		
Media Studies	P400▼	3FT deg	*	BB-BC	4M+3D	D	28	BBB		28	10/26
Mixed-Media Art	WP24▼	3FT deg	*	14-16	4M+3D	D	28	BBB		14	
Multimedia Computing	GP54▼	3FT deg		BC	4M	M	Ind	Ind	Ind	1	
Print Journalism	P600	3FT deg									
WIRRAL METROPOLITAN COLLEGE											
Media Studies	P400	3FT deg			Ind	Ind	Ind	Ind	Ind		
Univ of WOLVERHAMPTON											
Communication Studies	P302	3FT deg		20-24	4D	D	28	AAAA	Ind		
Electronic Media	P420	3FT deg	A/Ds	12	4M	M	24	BBBB	Ind		
Electronic Media	E420	3FT deg	A/Ds	12	4M	M	24	BBBB	Ind		
Interactive Multimedia Comm (Specialist Route)	P300	4SW deg		18	4D	D	28	BBBB	Ind	4	8/20
Language and Communication	PQ31	4FT deg	L g	18	4D	D	28	BBBB	Ind		
Media and Cultural Studies (Specialist Route)	PL46	3FT deg		12-14	4M	D	24	BBBB	Ind		
Combined Degrees Communication Studies	Y401	3FT/4SW deg	*	20-24	4D	D	28	AAAA	Ind		
Combined Degrees Electronic Media	Y401	3FT/4SW deg	A/Ad/Ds	12	4M	M	24	BBBB	Ind		
Combined Degrees Electronic Media	E401	3FT/4SW deg	A/Ad/Ds	12	4M	M	24	BBBB	Ind		
Combined Degrees Interactive Multimedia Communication	Y401	4SW deg		18	4D	D	28	BBBB	Ind		
Combined Degrees Media and Cultural Studies	Y401	3FT/4SW deg		12	4M	M	24	BBBB	Ind		
Design	42PW	2FT HND	A/Ds+Pf	E	N	P	24	CCCC	Ind	9	
Design	42PE	2FT HND	A/Ds+Pf	E	N	P	24	CCCC	Ind		
WORCESTER COLL of HE											
Media	P401	1FT deg									
Media Studies	004P▼	2FT HND		DD	Ind	Ind	Ind	Ind	Ind	10	2/10

| | | | 98 expected requirements | | | | | | | 96 entry stats | |
TITLE	CODE	COURSE	SUBJECTS	A/AS	ND/C	AGNVQ	IB	SQA(H)	SQA	RATIO	A/AS
Univ of ABERDEEN											
Medicine (MB/ChB)	A100	5FT deg	C+2S/C+S+M g	ABB	Ind	X	36$	AAAAB$	Ind	6	
Univ of BIRMINGHAM											
Medicine (MB,ChB)	A100	5FT deg	C+S g	AAB	X		36$	CSYS	X	8	26/30
Univ of BRISTOL											
Medicine - First MB/ChB (pre-medical) entry	A104	6FT deg	* g	ABB	Ind	D$^	32$	AAAAB	Ind	28	28/30
Medicine - Second MB/ChB Entry	A106	5FT deg	C+2(M/P/B) g	ABB	Ind	X	32$	AAAAB	Ind	12	26/30
CAMBRIDGE Univ											
Medical Sciences	A100▼	5FT/6FT deg	C+S/M g	AAA	X		Ind	CSYS	X	4	30/30
Univ of DUNDEE											
Medicine (MB,ChB)	A100	5FT deg	C+2(B/M/P) g	ABB	Ind	Ind	34$	AAABB$	Ind	9	26/30
Medicine MB,ChB (Pre-medical year)	A104	6FT deg	* g	ABB	Ind	Ind	34	AAABB	Ind	91	
Univ of EDINBURGH											
Medicine MB,ChB (5 Yrs)	A100	5FT deg	C+2(B/M/P) g	AAB	X	X	37	AAAAB$	Ind	9	28/30
Medicine MB,ChB (6 Yrs)	A104	6FT deg	g	AAB	X	X	37	AAAAB	Ind	59	
Univ of GLASGOW											
Medicine (MB,ChB)	A100	5FT deg	C+B/M/P g	AAB	X		36$	AAAAB$	X	5	24/30
IMPERIAL COLL (Univ of London)											
Medicine	A100	6FT deg	C g	ABB	X	X	$	CSYS	X	18	24/30
KING'S COLL LONDON (Univ of London)											
Foundation Course in Natural Sciences/Medicine	A103	6FT deg	*	ABB	X	X	$	AAABB	X		
Medicine	A100	5FT deg	C+2(M/S)/M/S+Ap	ABB	X	X	$	AAABB$	X	19	26/30
Univ of LEEDS											
Medical Sciences	A108	3FT deg	C+B/M/P g	BBB	Ind	Ind	32$	CSYS	Ind	8	22/28
Medicine	A100	5FT deg	C g	AAB-ABB	Ind	X	33$	CSYS	Ind	12	26/30
Univ of LEICESTER											
Medicine, MB,ChB	A100	5FT deg	C+B/P/M g	ABB	Ind	Ind	34$	CSYS$	Ind		24/30
Univ of LIVERPOOL											
Medicine, MB,ChB	A100	5FT deg	C+S	ABB	X		36	CSYS	X	8	26/30
Univ of MANCHESTER											
Medicine	A106	5FT deg	C+P/B/M	ABB	X		34	X		9	26/30
Medicine MB,ChB	A104	6FT deg		ABB	X		34	AAABB		15	30/30
Univ of NEWCASTLE											
Medicine (pre-medical)	A104	6FT deg	* g	AAB	Ind	X	Ind	AAAAB$	Ind		
Medicine (stage 1 entry)	A106	5FT deg	C g	AAB	Ind	X	Ind	AAAAB$	Ind	10	26/30
Univ of NOTTINGHAM											
Medicine, BM, BS	A100	5FT deg	C+S g	ABB	Ind		32$	CSYS		16	26/30
OXFORD Univ											
Medicine	A100	6FT deg	C+S	AAA-AAB	DO		36	AAAAA	Ind	6	28/30
QUEEN MARY & WESTFIELD COLL (Univ of London)											
Medicine	A100▼	5FT deg	C+(S/2S) g	BBB	X	X	34$	X	X		
QUEEN'S Univ Belfast											
Medicine MB,BCh,BAO	A100	5FT deg	C+2(P/M/B) g	AAB	X	X	35$	AAAAB	X	3	28/30

course details			98 expected requirements							96 entry stats	
TITLE	CODE	COURSE	SUBJECTS	A/AS	NO/C	AGNVQ	IB	SQA(H)	SQA	RATIO	A/AS
ROYAL FREE Hosp School of Med (Univ of London)											
Medicine	A100	5FT deg	C+B/P g	ABB	X	X	34$	CSYS	X	16	26/30
Univ of SHEFFIELD											
Medicine (First-Year Entry)	A104	6FT deg	* g	ABB	6M+5D	D^	33	AAAAB	Ind	26	26/30
Medicine (Second-Year Entry)	A106	5FT deg	C+S g	ABB	6M+5D$	DS^	33$	CSYS	Ind	14	26/30
Medicine (Sheffield Asean Medical College)	A107	4FT deg	C+S g	ABB			33$				
Univ of SOUTHAMPTON											
Medicine (BM)	A100	5FT deg	C g	ABB	Ind	D^	33$	BBBBB$	Ind	13	26/30
Univ of ST ANDREWS											
Degree of BSc (Medical Sci) (Ordinary and Hons)	A108	3FT/4FT deg	C+M/P g	ABB	X	Ind	36$	AAABB$	Ind	6	24/30
ST GEORGE'S HOSP MED SCHOOL (Univ of London)											
Medicine	A100	5FT deg	C/(B+C) g	AAA-ABB	X	X	Ind	CSYS	X	10	24/30
UMDS of Guy's & St Thomas's (Univ of London)											
Medicine	A100	5FT deg	C+S/M g	ABB	X	X	35$	CSYS$	X	13	24/30
UNIVERSITY COLL LONDON (Univ of London)											
MB BS Medicine	A100	5FT deg	C g	AAB-ABB	Ind	X	36$	CSYS	X	19	26/30
Univ of WALES COLL of MEDICINE											
Medicine (First-year entry) (Foundation Course)	A104	6FT deg	* g	AAB	MO+5D$	DS^ go	34	AAAAB$	Ind	14	26/30
Medicine (Second-year entry)	A106	5FT deg	C+B/P g	AAB	HN+5D$	X	34$	CSYS$	Ind	6	26/30

TITLE	CODE	COURSE	SUBJECTS	A/AS	ND/C	AGNVQ	IB	SQA(H)	SQA	RATIO A/AS
Univ of ABERDEEN										
Biochemistry-Microbiology	CC75	4FT deg	C+2S/C+S+M g	CCD	Ind	MS go	24$	BBBC$	Ind	9
Biochemistry-Microbiology with Indust Placement	CC57	5FT deg	C+2S/C+S+M g	CCD	Ind	MS go	24$	BBBC$	Ind	
Environmental Microbiology (Micr & Soil Science)	CD59	4FT deg	C+2S/C+S+M g	CCD	Ind	MS go	24$	BBBC$	Ind	
Environmental Microbiology with Indust Placement	DC95	5FT deg	C+2S/C+S+M g	CCD	Ind	MS go	24$	BBBC$	Ind	
Microbiology	C500	4FT deg	3S/2S+M g	CCD	Ind	MS go	24$	BBBC$	Ind	15
Microbiology with Industrial Placement	C501	5FT deg	3S/2S+M g	CCD	Ind	MS go	24$	BBBC$	Ind	
Microbiology-Genetics	CC54	4FT deg	3S/2S+M g	CCD	Ind	MS go	24$	BBBC$	Ind	7
Microbiology-Genetics with Industrial Placement	CC45	5FT deg	3S/2S+M g	CCD	Ind	MS go	24$	BBBC$	Ind	
Molecular Microbiology	C550	4FT deg	3S/2S+M g	CCD	Ind	MS go	24$	BBBC$	Ind	
Molecular Microbiology with Industrial Placement	C551	5FT deg	3S/2S+M g	CCD	Ind	MS go	24$	BBBC$	Ind	
Univ of ABERTAY DUNDEE										
Microbial Biotechnology	C9C5	4FT deg	B/C	DE	Ind	Ind	Ind	BCC	Ind	
Univ of Wales, ABERYSTWYTH										
Microbiology	C500	3FT deg	B/C g	16-18	3M $	MS6/^ g	29$	BBBCC$	Ind	
Microbiology and Biochemistry	CC57	3FT deg	B/C g	16-18	3M $	MS6/^ g	29$	BBBCC$	Ind	
Zoology and Microbiology	CC35	3FT deg	B/C g	16-18	3M $	MS6/^ g	29$	BBBCC$	Ind	
ANGLIA Poly Univ										
Microbiology	C500▼	3FT deg	B	10	3M	P	Dip$	CCCC	N	9
BARNSLEY COLL										
Science Foundation *Microbiology*	Y100	4EXT deg								
Univ of BIRMINGHAM										
Biological Sciences (Microbiology)	C500	3FT deg	B+S/M/Gy/Gl/Ps g	BCC	Ind	Ind	30	Ind	Ind	13 18/24
Univ of BRADFORD										
Medical Microbiology	C500	3FT deg	2S g	BB-CCD	3M $	MS4	Ind	Ind	$	12
Univ of BRISTOL										
Microbiology	C500	3FT deg	C+2(B/M/P) g	BCC	Ind	D$^	28$	CSYS	Ind	7 20/24
Pathology and Microbiology	C550	3FT deg	C+2(B/M/P) g	BCC	Ind	D$^	28$	CSYS	Ind	7 18/26
BRISTOL, Univ of the W of England										
Applied Microbiology	C510	4SW deg	B+C g	12	4M $	MS go	24$	BCC$	Ind	
CARDIFF Univ of Wales										
Microbiology	C500	3FT deg	B+C/M/P g	BBB-BCC	MO $	Ind	30$	BBBB$	Ind	9
Microbiology	C501	4SW deg	B+C/M/P g	BBB-BCC	MO $	Ind	30$	BBBB$	Ind	3
Preliminary Year *Microbiology*	Y101	4FT/5SW deg	* g		Ind	Ind	Ind	Ind	Ind	
Univ of CENTRAL LANCASHIRE										
Microbiology	C500	3FT deg	C+S	DDD	MO $	MS6/^	26$	BBCC		
Combined Honours Programme *Applied Microbiology*	Y400	3FT deg	B+C g	8	MO $	MS	26$	BCCC	Ind	
Univ of DUNDEE										
Chemistry and Microbiology	CF51	4FT deg	C+S/2S g	16	5M $	M$	25$	BBBC$	N$	1
Microbiology	C500	4FT deg	C+S/2S g	16	5M $	M$	25$	BBBC$	N$	8
Univ of EAST ANGLIA										
Microbiology	C500	3FT deg	C+P/M/B	CCC	3D $		28$	BBBCC$	Ind	22

course details

98 expected requirements   *96 entry stats*

course details			98 expected requirements							96 entry stats	
TITLE	CODE	COURSE	SUBJECTS	A/AS	NO/C	AGNVQ	IB	SQA(H)	SQA	RATIO	A/AS
Univ of EAST LONDON											
Microbiology	C500	4SW deg	* g	12	MO	MS	Ind	Ind	Ind	6	
Extended Science *Microbiology*	Y108	4FT deg	* g	8-10	MO	M	Ind	Ind	Ind		
Univ of EDINBURGH											
Medical Microbiology	C530	4FT deg	C+2(M/B/P) g	BBC	MO $		Dip$	BBBB$	N$	11	
Microbiology	C500	4FT deg	C+2(B/M/P) g	BBC	MO $		Dip$	BBBB$	N$	9	
Virology	C540	4FT deg	C+2(B/P/M) g	BBC	MO $		Dip$	BBBB$	NS		
Univ of GLASGOW											
Microbiology	C500	4FT deg	C/M+S	BBC-CCC	N	M	24$	BBBB$	N	5	
Microbiology (with work placement)	C501	4FT deg	C/M+S	BBC-CCC	N	M	24$	BBBB$	N		
HERIOT-WATT Univ											
Microbiology	C500	4FT deg	C	DDD	MO	MS go	28	BBB	Ind		
Univ of HERTFORDSHIRE											
Microbiology	C1C5	3FT/4SW deg	2S g	14-16	4M $	Ind	24	BCCC	Ind	9	
Microbiology with a year in Europe	C501	4FT deg	2S g	14-16	4M $	Ind	24	BCCC	Ind		
Microbiology with a year in North America	C502	4FT deg	2S g	14-16	4M $	Ind	24	BCCC	Ind		
Univ of HUDDERSFIELD											
Microbial Sciences	C500	3FT/4SW deg	S g	10-18	3M $	MS go	Ind	Ind	Ind		
Science (Extended) *Microbial Sciences*	Y108	4FT/5SW deg	* g	EE	N	P$ gi	Ind	Ind	Ind		
IMPERIAL COLL (Univ of London)											
Biology with Microbiology	C1C5	3FT deg	B+C/M/P	BCC	MO+2D	Ind	30$	Ind	Ind	7	
Microbiology	C500	3FT deg	B+C/M/P	BCC	MO+2D	Ind	30$	Ind	Ind	13	
Univ of KENT											
Microbiology	C500	3FT deg	C g	BCC	MO $	Ind	28$	BBBB$	Ind	11	
Microbiology	C502	4SW deg	C g	BCC	MO $	Ind	28$	BBBB$	Ind	6	
Microbiology with Biotechnology	C580	3FT deg	C g	BCC	MO $	Ind	28$	BBBB$	Ind	2	
Microbiology with Medical Biosciences	C520	3FT deg	C g	BCC	MO $	Ind	28$	BBBB$	Ind	8	
Microbiology with a year in Europe	C501	4FT deg	C g	BCC	MO $	Ind	28$	BBBB$	Ind		
KING'S COLL LONDON (Univ of London)											
Biochemistry and Microbiology	CC57	3FT deg	C+S	BCC	5M	M	Ind	BCCCC	Ind	7	
Microbiology	C500	3FT deg	C+S	BCC	5M	M	Ind	BCCCC	Ind	6	16/24
LANCASTER Univ											
Biochemistry with Microbiology	C7C5	3FT deg	C+B/M/P g	BCC	5M $		30$	BBBBC$	Ind		
Univ of LEEDS											
Biochemistry-Microbiology	CC57	3FT/4FT deg	C+B g	BCC	1M+5D$	Ind	28$	BBBBC	Ind	8	
Food Science-Microbiology	CD54	3FT deg	C+M/P/B g	CCC	1M+5D$	Ind	28$	BBBBC	Ind		
Genetics-Microbiology	CC45	3FT/4FT deg	C+B g	BCC	1M+5D$	Ind	28$	BBBBC	Ind	22	
Medical Microbiology	C530	3FT deg	2S g	BCD	1M+3D$	Ind	24$	BBCCC	Ind	6	18/30
Microbiology	C500	3FT deg	2S g	BCD	1M+4D$	Ind	26$	BBBCC	Ind	9	18/26
Microbiology with Immunology	C5C9	3FT deg	2S g	BBC	3M+2D$	Ind	30$	ABBBC	Ind		
Microbiology-Zoology	CC35	3FT/4FT deg	C+B g	BCC	1M+5D$	Ind	28$	BBBBC	Ind	9	
Univ of LEICESTER											
Biological Sciences (Microbiology)	C500	3FT deg	B+C g	18-20	DO $	D$4/^ gi	28$	BBBCC	Ind		14/20

course details			98 expected requirements							96 entry stats	
TITLE	CODE	COURSE	SUBJECTS	A/AS	ND/C	AGNVQ	IB	SQA(H)	SQA	RATIO	A/AS
Univ of LIVERPOOL											
Microbial Biotechnology	C5J8	3FT deg	B+S g	18	MO $	DS^ go	31$	BBBCC$	Ind	5	
Microbiology	C500	3FT deg	B+S g	18	MO $	DS^ go	31$	BBBCC$	Ind	8	16/20
BSc Combined Honours	Y100	3FT deg	B	18	MO $	Ind	31$	BBBCC$	Ind		
Microbiology											
LIVERPOOL JOHN MOORES Univ											
App Biochemistry & App Microbiology (Foundation)	CC7M	4FT/5SW deg									
Applied Biochemistry & Applied Microbiology	CC75	3FT/4SW deg		8	3M	M				6	10/14
Applied Microbiology	C510	3FT/4SW deg		8	3M	M				4	8/14
Applied Microbiology (Foundation)	C518	4FT/5SW deg									
Univ of MANCHESTER											
Microbiology	C500	3FT deg	B+C	BCD	3M+3D$ D^		26$	BBBCC$	Ind	19	
Microbiology with Biotechnology	C5J8	4SW deg	B+C	BCD	3M+3D$ D^		26$	BBBBC$	Ind	17	
Microbiology with Industrial Experience	C501	4SW deg	B+C	BCD	3M+3D$ D^		26$	BBBCC$	Ind	9	
Microbiology with a Modern Language	C502	4FT deg	B+C+L	BCD	3M+3D$ D^		26$	BBBCC$	Ind		
NAPIER Univ											
Applied Microbiology & Biotechnology (comm Yr 1)	CJ58	4FT/5SW deg	B/C	DD	Ind	Ind	Ind	BBC	Ind		
Univ of NEWCASTLE											
Medical Microbiology	C530	3FT deg	B+C	CCC	Ind		26$	BBBB$	Ind	4	18/26
Microbiology	C500	3FT deg	B+C	CCC	Ind		26$	BBBB$	Ind	4	14/24
NESCOT											
Microbiology	C500	3FT deg	S	EE	N	M	Dip	Ind	N$	6	
Microbiology	C508	4FT deg	*								
Univ of NORTH LONDON											
Microbiology	C500	3FT/4SW/4EXT deg	B+C	CC	3M $	MS	$	Ind	Ind	8	
Combined Honours	Y100	3FT/4SW/4EXT deg	B+C	CC	3M $	MS	$	Ind	Ind		
Microbiology											
Univ of NOTTINGHAM											
Food Microbiology	C560	3FT deg	2(M/S/Gy)	CC-CDD	3M $	MS	24$	CSYS$	N$	6	
Food Microbiology with European Studies	C5T2	4FT deg	2(M/S/Gy) g	CC-CDD	3M $	MS	24$	CSYS$	N$		
Microbiology	C501	3FT deg	B+C g	BBC	Ind	Ind	Ind	Ind	Ind	12	22/30
Plant Life Science	C2C5	3FT deg	B+C/M g	BCC	Ind	Ind	Ind	Ind	Ind	14	
NOTTINGHAM TRENT Univ											
Biochemistry and Microbiology	CC57	4SW deg	S g	DDE	Ind	Ind	Dip	C	$	8	6/10
Univ of PAISLEY											
Biochemistry and Microbiology	CC75	4FT/5SW deg	* g	CCC-EE	Ind	Ind	Ind	BCC$	Ind		
Immunology and Microbiology	CC59	3FT/4FT deg	* g	CCC-EE	Ind	Ind	Ind	BCC$	Ind		
Univ of PLYMOUTH											
Chemistry with Microbiology	F1C5	3FT deg	C+B g	CC	3M	MS^	Ind	CCCC	Ind	2	
Food Biology	C560	3FT deg	Ap g	8	N $	MS	Ind	CCC$	Ind	1	
Marine Biology with Microbiology	C1C5	3FT deg	B+C g	CCC	4M $	MS^	Ind	BBBB	Ind	21	
Mathematics with Microbiology	G1C5	3FT deg	M g	10-15	MO $	M$^	Ind	BBCC	Ind		
Microbial and Cellular Biology	C510	3FT/4SW deg	B g	10-14	4M $	MS	Ind	BBC	Ind	11	
Microbiology with Chemistry	C5F1	3FT/4SW deg	B+C g	12-16	4M $	MS	Ind	BBBB	Ind	3	
Microbiology with Computing	C5G5	3FT/4SW deg	B g	10-14	4M $	MS	Ind	BBBB	Ind		
Microbiology with French	C5R1	3FT/4SW deg	B+F g	14-18	4M $	Ind	Ind	BBBB	Ind		
Microbiology with Mathematics	C5G1	3FT/4SW deg	B g	10-14	4M $	MS	Ind	BBBB	Ind	5	
Statistics (App) with Microbiology	G4C5	3FT deg	M/St g	10-14	MO $	M$	Ind	BBCC	Ind		

course details			98 expected requirements							96 entry stats	
TITLE	CODE	COURSE	SUBJECTS	A/AS	ND/C	AGNVQ	IB	SQA(H)	SQA	RATIO	A/AS
Univ of PORTSMOUTH											
Applied Microbiology	C510	3FT deg	2S	10	3M $	M$6/^	Dip	BBB	Ind		
QUEEN MARY & WESTFIELD COLL (Univ of London)											
Biochemistry/Microbiology	C7C5	3FT deg	C+B/P/M	16	6M $	MS^/DS	26$	BBBCC			
Genetics/Microbiology	C4C5	3FT deg	B+C/P/M	16	6M $	MS^/DS	26$	BBBCC			
QUEEN'S Univ Belfast											
Microbiology	C500	3FT/4FT deg	B+C g	CCC	Ind	Ind	28$	BBBC	Ind	7	20/24
Microbiology	C510	3FT/4FT deg	B+C g	CCC	Ind	Ind	28$	BBBC	Ind	11	
Univ of READING											
Microbiology	C500	3FT deg	B/C g	18	4M+1D$	DS^ go	29$	BBBC$	Ind	8	15/24
Univ of SHEFFIELD											
Biochemistry and Microbiology	CC75	3FT deg	C+S g	BCC	5M+1D$	DS^	29$	BBBB$	Ind	15	
Biotechnology and Microbiology	JC85	3FT/4EXT deg	C+S g	18	6M $	DS^	28$	BBBC$	Ind	11	
Genetics and Microbiology	CC45	3FT deg	C+S g	BCD	6M $	DS^	28$	BBBC$	Ind	7	20/22
Microbiology	C500	3FT deg	C+S g	18	6M $	D^	28$	BBBC$	Ind	19	
SOUTH BANK Univ											
Microbiology	C500	3FT/4SW deg	S g	CC	MO	M go	Ind	Ind	Ind		
Univ of ST ANDREWS											
Biochemistry with Microbiology	C7C5	3FT/4FT deg	C g	CCC	Ind	Ind	28	BBCC	Ind	7	
STAFFORDSHIRE Univ											
Applied Microbiology	C519	4EXT deg	g	4	1M	P	24	CCC			
Applied Microbiology	C510	3FT deg									
Biochemistry and Microbiology	CC75	3FT deg	B	12	4M	M^	24	BCC	Ind	9	8/10
Extended Biochemistry and Microbiology (4 yr)	CC5T	4EXT deg	g	4	1M	P	24	CCC	Ind	1	
Foundation Biochemistry and Microbiology	CC5R▼	4EXT deg	*	4	N	P	24	CCC	Ind		
Microbiology/Computing	CG55	3FT deg									
Univ of STRATHCLYDE											
Biochemistry and Microbiology	CC75	4FT deg	C+B/M+P g	CCC	HN		Ind	BBC$	HN		
Immunology and Microbiology	CC59	4FT deg	C+B+M/P g	CCC	Ind		Ind	BBC$	Ind		
Science Studies (Pass Degree) Microbiology	Y100	3FT deg	M+S	DD	Ind		Ind	CCC$	Ind		
Univ of SUNDERLAND											
Applied Microbiology	C510▼	3FT/4SW deg	B+C g	10	N $	PS	24$	CCCC$	N$	4	7/10
Applied Microbiology (Foundation)	C518▼	4EXT/5EXTSW deg	*							2	
Medical Microbiology	C530	3FT/4SW deg	B+C g	10	N $	PS	24$	CCCC$	N$		
Univ of SURREY											
Environmental Microbiology	C510	3FT/4SW deg	C+B+M/P g	BCC-CCC	3M+2D$	DS	28$	ABBBB$	Ind	9	
Food Science and Microbiology	CD54	3FT/4SW deg	C+B+M/P g	BCC-CCC	3M+2D$		28$	AABBB$	X	8	
Microbiology (Biotechnology)	C500	3FT/4SW deg	C+B+M/P g	BCC-CCC	3M+2D$	DS	28$	ABBBB$	Ind	5	6/8
Microbiology (Medical)	C502	3FT/4SW deg	C+B+M/P g	BCC-CCC	3M+2D$	DS	28$	ABBBB$	Ind	2	8/26
Microbiology with a Foundation Year	C505	4FT/5SW deg	* g	CCC	4M+1D$	D	28$	ABBBB	Ind	9	
Univ of TEESSIDE											
Microbiology	C500	3FT deg	C+S	8	3M		Ind	CCC	3M		
UNIVERSITY COLL LONDON (Univ of London)											
Medical Microbiology	C530	3FT deg	C+B/M/P g	BCC-BBB	3M+2D$	Ind	32$	Ind	Ind	26	
Microbiology	C500	3FT deg	C+B/M/P g	BCC-BBB	3M+2D$	Ind	32$	Ind	Ind	11	
Microbiology and Genetics	CC54	3FT deg	C+B/M/P g	BCC-BBB	3M+2D$	Ind	32$	Ind	Ind	24	

course details			98 expected requirements							96 entry stats	
TITLE	CODE	COURSE	SUBJECTS	A/AS	ND/C	AGNVQ	IB	SQA(H)	SQA	RATIO	A/AS
Univ of WARWICK											
Microbiology/Virology	C520	3FT deg	C/S+B g	20-22	DO $	D$^	28$	BBBBC$		8	16/28
Univ of WESTMINSTER											
Biochemistry & Microbiology	CC75	3FT deg	B/C	CC-CD	3M	M			Ind	6	4/10
Univ of WOLVERHAMPTON											
Food Biology	C560	3FT/4SW deg		DD	N	M	24	CCCC	Ind		
Microbiology	C501	3FT/4SW deg		DD	N	M	24	CCCC	Ind		
Applied Sciences *Food Biology*	Y100	3FT/4SW deg		DD	N	M	24	CCCC	Ind		
Applied Sciences *Microbiology*	Y110	4FT deg	*								
Applied Sciences *Microbiology*	Y100	3FT/4SW deg	B g	DD	N	M	24	CCCC	Ind		
Applied Sciences (4 Yrs) *Food Biology*	Y110	4FT deg	*								
Combined Degrees *Food Biology*	Y401	3FT/4SW deg		DD	N	M	24	CCCC	Ind		
Combined Degrees *Microbiology*	Y401	3FT/4SW deg	B g	DD	N	M	24	CCCC	Ind		

			98 expected requirements							96 entry stats
course details										
TITLE	CODE	COURSE	SUBJECTS	A/AS	ND/C	RGNVQ	IB	SQA(H)	SQA	RATIO A/AS
ANGLIA Poly Univ										
Art History and Music	VW43▼	3FT deg	*	14	6M	M+/^	Dip$	BBCC	Ind	
Audio and Music	HW6J▼	3FT deg	S	16	8M	D	Dip$	BBCCC	N	3 10/22
Audiotechnology and Music	HW6H▼	3FT deg	S+M	16	8M	D+/^	Dip$	BBCCC	N	4 8/22
Business and Music	NW13▼	3FT deg	Mu g	12	4M	M+/^ go	Dip$	BCCC	Ind	2 14/14
Communication Studies and Music	PW33▼	3FT deg	Mu	14	6M	M+/^	Dip$	BBCC	Ind	11
Economics and Music	LW13▼	3FT deg	Mu g	12	4M	M+/^	Dip$	BCCC	Ind	
English Language Studies and Music	QW13▼	3FT deg	Mu g	12	4M	M go	Dip$	BCCC		
English and Music	QW33▼	3FT deg	E+Mu	12	4M	M+/^	Dip$	BCCC	Ind	2 14/16
European Philosophy & Literature and Music	VW73▼	3FT deg	Mu	12	4M	M+/^	Dip$	BCCC	Ind	1
French and Music	RW13▼	4FT deg	Mu g	12	4M	M+/^ go	Dip$	BCCC	Ind	5
Geography and Music	LW83▼	3FT deg	Mu+Gy g	12	4M	M+/^ go	Dip$	BCCC	Ind	3
German and Music	RW23▼	4FT deg	Mu g	12	4M	M+/^ go	Dip$	BCCC	Ind	
Graphic Arts and Music	WW32▼	3FT deg	Mu+A	14	6M	M+/^	Dip$	BBCC	Ind	
History and Music	VW13▼	3FT deg	Mu	12	4M	M+/^	Dip$	BCCC	Ind	
Italian and Music	RW33▼	4FT deg	Mu g	12	4M	M+/^ go	Dip$	BCCC	Ind	
Law and Music	MW33▼	3FT deg	Mu	14	6M	M	Dip$	BBCC	Ind	
Mathematics or Stats/Stat Modelling and Music	GW13▼	3FT deg	Mu g	12	4M	M+/^ go	Dip$	BCCC	Ind	6
Music	W300▼	3FT deg	Mu	12	4M	M+	Dip$	BCCC	Ind	4 6/22
Music and Psychology	CW83▼	3FT deg	Mu g	16	8M	D	Dip	BB	Ind	5
Music and Spanish	RW43▼	4FT deg	Mu g	12	4M	M+/^ go	Dip$	BCCC	Ind	2
Univ of Wales, BANGOR										
Music	W300	3FT deg	Mu g	BB-BCD	Ind	D*^ go	28$	BBBC$	Ind	7 14/28
Music (BMus)	W302	3FT deg	Mu g	BB-BCD	Ind	D*^ go	28$	BBBC$	Ind	4 16/29
Welsh and Literature of the Media/Music	WQ35	3FT/4FT deg	Mu+W g	BB-BCD	X	D*^ go	Ind	X	X	
Welsh/Music	QW53	3FT/4FT deg	Mu+W g	BB-BCD	X	D*^ go	Ind	X	X	9
BARNSLEY COLL										
Band Studies	W303	3FT deg	Mu	EE	4M	M*	Ind	Ind	Ind	
Creative Music Technology	W350	3FT deg	*	EE	4M	M*	Ind	Ind	Ind	
Popular Music Studies	W311	4EXT deg	Mu	EE	4M	P*	Ind	Ind	Ind	
Popular Music Studies	W310	3FT deg	Mu	EE	4M	P*	Ind	Ind	Ind	
Combined Studies *Performing Arts*	Y400	3FT deg	* g	DD	4M	M*	Ind	Ind	Ind	
Performing Arts (Creative Music Technology)	053W	2FT HND	*	E	2M	M*	Ind	Ind	Ind	
BATH COLL of HE										
Music	W300	3FT deg	Mu		N		Ind	$	$	5 8/20
Combined Awards *Music*	Y400	3FT deg	Mu		N		Ind	$	$	
Modular Programme (DipHE) *Music*	Y460	2FT Dip	Mu		N		Ind	$	$	
Univ of BIRMINGHAM										
Artificial Intelligence/Music	GW83	3FT deg	Mu g	AAB-ABB Ind		D*^	32$	ABBB	Ind	1
Classical Literature and Civilisation/Music	QW83	3FT deg	Mu	AAB-ABB Ind		D*^	32$	ABBB	Ind	
Computer Studies/Music	GW53	3FT deg	Mu g	AAB-ABB Ind		D*^	32$	ABBB	Ind	7
Dance/Music	WW43	3FT deg	Mu	AAB-ABB Ind		D*^	32$	ABBB	Ind	14
Drama/Music	WW34	3FT deg	Mu	AAB-ABB Ind		D*^	32$	ABBB	Ind	
East Mediterranean History/Music	VWD3	3FT deg	Mu g	AAB-ABB Ind		D*^	32$	ABBB	Ind	
English/Music	QW33	3FT deg	Mu	AAB/ABB Ind		D*^	32$	ABBB	Ind	9 26/28
French Studies/Music	RW13	4FT deg	F+Mu	AAB-ABB Ind		D*^	32$	ABBB	Ind	5 24/30
German Studies/Music	RW23	4FT deg	G+Mu	AAB-ABB Ind		D*^	32$	ABBB	Ind	6
Hispanic Studies/Music	RW43	4FT deg	Mu	AAB-ABB Ind		D*^	32$	ABBB	Ind	3

				98 expected requirements							96 entry stats	
TITLE	CODE	COURSE		SUBJECTS	A/AS	ND/C	AGNVQ	IB	SQA(H)	SQA	RATIO	A/AS
History of Art/Music	VW43	3FT deg		Mu	AAB-ABB	Ind	D*^	32$	ABBB	Ind	4	
History/Music	VW13	3FT deg		Mu	AAB-ABB	Ind	D*^	32$	ABBB	Ind	4	
Italian/Music	RW33	4FT deg		Mu	AAB-ABB	Ind	D*^	32$	ABBB	Ind	2	
Latin/Music	QW63	3FT deg		Ln+Mu	AAB-ABB	Ind	D*^	32$	ABBB	Ind		
Mathematics/Music	GW13	3FT deg		M+Mu	AAB-ABB	Ind	D*^	32$	ABBB	Ind	5	28/30
Media & Cultural Studies/Music	PW43	3FT deg		Mu	AAB-ABB	Ind	D*^	32$	ABBB	Ind		
Modern Greek Studies/Music	TW23	4FT deg		Mu g	AAB-ABB	Ind	D*^	32$	ABBB	Ind		
Music (BMus Honours)	W302	3FT deg		Mu	AAB-ABB	Ind	D*^	32$	ABBB	Ind	9	24/30
Music/Philosophy	VW73	3FT deg		Mu	AAB-ABB	Ind	D*^	32$	ABBB	Ind	7	
Music/Portuguese	RW53	4FT deg		Mu	AAB-ABB	Ind	D*^	32$	ABBB	Ind		
Music/Russian	RW83	4FT deg		Mu	AAB-ABB	Ind	D*^	32$	ABBB	Ind		
Music/Sport & Recreation Studies	WB36	3FT deg		Mu	AAB-ABB	Ind	D*^	32$	ABBB	Ind		
Music/Theology	VW83	3FT deg		Mu	AAB-ABB	Ind	D*^	32$	ABBB	Ind		
BRETTON HALL												
Arts and Education (Music)	XW93	3FT deg		Mu	CC	MO		Ind	CCC	Ind	7	
Contemporary Musics	W300	3FT deg		Mu	CC	MO $		Ind	CCC	Ind	3	8/24
Music: Performance Studies	W304	3FT deg		Mu	CC	MO		Ind	CCC	Ind	7	8/18
Popular Music Studies	W310	3FT deg		*	CD	MO		Ind	CCC	Ind	12	8/23
Univ of BRIGHTON												
Music with Visual Practice	E3W1	3FT deg		Fa+Pf g		N $	Ind$ go	Ind$	Ind$	Ind$		
Music with Visual Practice	W3W1	3FT deg		Fa+Pf g		N $	Ind$ go	Ind$	Ind$	Ind$		
Univ of BRISTOL												
Music	W300	3FT deg		Mu	BCC	Ind	D$^	28$	BBBCC	Ind	10	20/30
Music and French	WR31	4FT deg		Mu+F	BBC	Ind	D$^	30$	BBBBC	Ind		
Music and German	WR32	4FT deg		Mu+G	BBC	Ind	D$^	30$	BBBBC	Ind	5	
Music and Italian	WR33	4FT deg		Mu	BBC	Ind	D$^	30$	BBBBC	Ind		
BRISTOL, Univ of the W of England												
Engineering (Music Technology) (BSc)	HW63	3FT/4SW deg		M+S g	14-16	4M $	M$1 go	24$	BCCC$	Ind$		
BRUNEL Univ, West London												
Music	W300	3FT deg		* g	16	MO $	M* go	26$	BCCC$	Ind		
Music/American Studies	QW43	3FT deg		* g	14	MO $	M* go	26$	BCCC$	Ind		
Music/Art	W3W1	3FT deg		A g	14	MO $	M* go	26$	BCCC$	Ind		
Music/Drama	WW34	3FT deg		T g	BC	MO $	M* go	22$	BCCC$	Ind		
Music/English	QW33	3FT deg										
Music/Film & TV Studies	W3W5	3FT deg		Ap g	20	MO $	M* go	28$	BBCC$	Ind		
Music/History	VW13	3FT deg		H g	12	MO $	M* go	22$	BCCC$	Ind		
BUCKINGHAMSHIRE COLLEGE												
Music Industry Management	W3N1	3FT deg			8-10	1D	M	27	CCCC	Ind	3	8/20
CAMBRIDGE Univ												
Music	W300▼	3FT deg		Mu g	AAB	Ind		Ind	CSYS	Ind	3	26/30
Music with Education Studies (BA)	W3X9▼	3FT deg		* g	AAB	Ind		Ind	CSYS	Ind	1	
CANTERBURY CHRIST CHURCH COLL of HE												
American Studies with Music	Q4W3	4FT deg		Mu g	CC	MO	M	24	Ind	Ind		
Art with Music	W1W3	3FT deg		A+Mu g	CC	MO	M	24	Ind	Ind		
Business Studies with Music	N1W3	3FT deg		Mu g	CC	MO	M	24	Ind	Ind	3	
Early Childhood Studies with Music	X9W3	3FT deg		Mu g	CC	MO	M	24	Ind	Ind		
English with Music	Q3W3	3FT deg		E+Mu	CC	MO	M	24	Ind	Ind	4	
Geography with Music	L8W3	3FT deg		Gy+Mu g	CC	MO	M	24	Ind	Ind		
History with Music	V1W3	3FT deg		H+Mu g	CC	MO	M	24	Ind	Ind	2	

course details

TITLE	CODE	COURSE	SUBJECTS	A/AS	ND/C	AGNVQ	IB	SQA(H)	SQA	RATIO A/AS
Information Technology with Music	G5W3	3FT deg	Mu g	CC	MO	M	24	Ind	Ind	
Marketing with Music	N5W3	3FT deg	Mu g	CC	MO	M	24	Ind	Ind	
Mathematics with Music	G1W3	3FT deg	M+Mu g	DD	Ind	Ind	24	Ind	Ind	
Media Studies with Music	P4W3	3FT deg	Mu g	CC	MO	M	24	Ind	Ind	
Music	W300	3FT deg	Mu g	CC	MO	M	24	Ind	Ind	3 6/20
Music and American Studies	WQ34	3FT deg	Mu g	CC	MO	M	24	Ind	Ind	1
Music and Art	WW13	3FT deg	A+Mu g	CC	MO	M	24	Ind	Ind	2
Music and Business Studies	WN31	3FT deg	Mu g	CC	MO	M	24	Ind	Ind	2
Music and Early Childhood Studies	XW93	3FT deg	Mu g	CC	MO	M	24	Ind	Ind	
Music and English	WQ33	3FT deg	E+Mu g	CC	MO	M	24	Ind	Ind	2
Music and French	RW13	3FT deg	F+Mu g	CC	MO	M	24	Ind	Ind	
Music and Geography	WL38	3FT deg	Mu+Gy g	CC	MO	M	24	Ind	Ind	
Music and History	VW13	3FT deg	H+Mu g	CC	MO	M	24	Ind	Ind	
Music and Information Technology	WG35	3FT deg	Mu g	CC	MO	M	24	Ind	Ind	
Music and Marketing	NW53	3FT deg	Mu g	CC	MO	M	24	Ind	Ind	
Music and Mathematics	WG31	3FT deg	M+Mu g	DD	Ind	Ind	24	Ind	Ind	
Music and Media Studies	PW43	3FT deg	Mu g	CC	MO	M	24	Ind	Ind	
Music and Social Science	LW33	3FT deg	Mu g	CC	MO	M	24	Ind	Ind	1
Music with American Studies	W3Q4	3FT deg	Mu g	CC	MO	M	24	Ind	Ind	2
Music with Art	W3W1	3FT deg	Mu+A g	CC	MO	M	24	Ind	Ind	
Music with Business Studies	W3N1	3FT deg	Mu g	CC	MO	M	24	Ind	Ind	6
Music with Early Childhood Studies	W3X9	3FT deg	Mu g	CC	MO	M	24	Ind	Ind	4
Music with English	W3Q3	3FT deg	E+Mu g	CC	MO	M	24	Ind	Ind	7
Music with French	W3R1	3FT deg	Mu+F g	CC	MO	M	24	Ind	Ind	
Music with Geography	W3L8	3FT deg	Mu+Gy g	CC	MO	M	24	Ind	Ind	
Music with History	W3V1	3FT deg	Mu+H g	CC	MO	M	24	Ind	Ind	
Music with Information Technology	W3G5	3FT deg	Mu g	CC	MO	M	24	Ind	Ind	
Music with Marketing	W3N5	3FT deg	Mu g	CC	MO	M	24	Ind	Ind	3
Music with Mathematics	W3G1	3FT deg	M+Mu g	DD	Ind	Ind	24	Ind	Ind	
Music with Media Studies	W3P4	3FT deg	Mu g	CC	MO	M	24	Ind	Ind	
Music with Psychology	W3L7	3FT deg	Mu+Ps g	CC	MO	M	24	Ind	Ind	
Music with Radio, Film and Television Studies	W3W5	3FT deg	Mu g	CC	MO	M	24	Ind	Ind	
Music with Religious Studies	W3V8	3FT deg	Mu g	CC	MO	M	24	Ind	Ind	
Music with Science	W3Y1	3FT deg	Mu+S g	DD	Ind	Ind	24	Ind	Ind	
Music with Social Science	W3L3	3FT deg	Mu g	CC	MO	M	24	Ind	Ind	1 14/26
Music with Sport Science	W3B6	3FT deg	Mu g	CC	MO	M	24	Ind	Ind	
Music with Statistics	W3G4	3FT deg	Mu+M g	DD	Ind	Ind	24	Ind	Ind	
Music with Tourism Studies	W3P7	3FT deg	Mu g	CC	MO	M	24	Ind	Ind	
Psychology and Music	LW73	3FT deg	Ps+Mu g	CC	MO	M	24	Ind	Ind	
Psychology with Music	L7W3	3FT deg	Ps+Mu g	CC	MO	M	24	Ind	Ind	
Radio, Film and Television Studies and Music	WW53	3FT deg	Mu g	CC	MO	M	24	Ind	Ind	19
Radio, Film and Television Studies with Music	W5W3	3FT deg	Mu g	CC	MO	M	24	Ind	Ind	
Religious Studies and Music	VW83	3FT deg	Mu g	CC	MO	M	24	Ind	Ind	2
Religious Studies with Music	V8W3	3FT deg	Mu g	CC	MO	M	24	Ind	Ind	
Science and Music	WY31	3FT deg	Mu+S g	DD	Ind	Ind	24	Ind	Ind	
Science with Music	Y1W3	3FT deg	Mu+S g	DD	Ind	Ind	24	Ind	Ind	
Social Science with Music	L3W3	3FT deg	Mu g	CC	MO	M	24	Ind	Ind	
Sport Science and Music	BW63	3FT deg	Mu g	CC	MO	M	24	Ind	Ind	
Sport Science with Music	B6W3	3FT deg	Mu g	CC	MO	M	24	Ind	Ind	
Statistics and Music	GW43	3FT deg	M+Mu g	DD	Ind	Ind	24	Ind	Ind	
Statistics with Music	G4W3	3FT deg	M+Mu g	DD	Ind	Ind	24	Ind	Ind	
Tourism Studies and Music	PW73	3FT deg	Mu g	CC	MO	M	24	Ind	Ind	
Tourism Studies with Music	P7W3	3FT deg	Mu g	CC	MO	M	24	Ind	Ind	

98 expected requirements   96 entry stats

Music 56

	course details			98 expected requirements							96 entry stats	
TITLE	CODE	COURSE	SUBJECTS	A/AS	ND/C	AGNVQ	IB	SQA(H)	SQA	RATIO A/AS	

CARDIFF Univ of Wales

TITLE	CODE	COURSE	SUBJECTS	A/AS	ND/C	AGNVQ	IB	SQA(H)	SQA	RATIO	A/AS
Music	W302	3FT deg	Mu	BBC-BCC	X		Ind	X	X	2	12/26
Music	W300	3FT deg	Mu	BBC-BCC	X		Ind	X	X	18	16/26
Music/Cultural Criticism	MW93	3FT deg	Mu+E	ABC	X		Ind	AAABB	X		
Music/Education	WX39	3FT deg	Mu	BCC	Ind		Ind	Ind	Ind		
Music/English Literature	WQ33	3FT deg	E+Mu	ABB	X		Ind	AABBB	X	6	22/24
Music/French	WR31	4FT deg	F+Mu	BBC	Ind		Ind	ABBBB	Ind	7	
Music/German	WR32	4FT deg	Mu+G g	BBC	X		Ind	X	X	2	
Music/History	WV31	3FT deg	H+Mu	BBC	X		Ind	AABBB	X	7	
Music/Italian	WR33	4FT deg	L+Mu	BBC	X		Ind	ABBBB	X	1	
Philosophy/Music	VW73	3FT deg	Mu	BCC	X		Ind	Ind	X		
Physics and Music	FW33	3FT deg	Mu+P+M	BCC	Ind		Ind	Ind	Ind	2	20/28
Pure Mathematics/Music	GW13	3FT deg	M+Mu	BCC	X	Ind	Ind	ABBBB	X	9	
Religious Studies/Music	VW83	3FT deg	Mu	BCC	X		Ind	Ind	X		
Social Philosophy and Applied Ethics/Music	VW7H	3FT deg	Mu	BBC	X		Ind	Ind	X	1	
Sociology/Music	LW33	3FT deg	Mu	BBC							
Welsh/Music	QW53	3FT deg	Mu+W	BCC	X		Ind	Ind	X	6	

CHICHESTER INSTITUTE OF HIGHER EDUCATION

TITLE	CODE	COURSE	SUBJECTS	A/AS	ND/C	AGNVQ	IB	SQA(H)	SQA	RATIO	A/AS
Art and Music	WW13	3FT deg	A+Mu+Pf	12	Ind	M$+^	Ind	Ind	Ind	5	
Art with Music	E1W3	3FT deg	A+Pf	12	Ind	M$+^	Ind	Ind	Ind		
Art with Music	W1W3	3FT deg	A+Pf	12	Ind	M$+^	Ind	Ind	Ind		
Dance with Music	W4W3	3FT deg	Pf	12	Ind	M$+	Ind	Ind	Ind		
English with Music	Q3W3	3FT deg	E	12	Ind	M^	Ind	Ind	Ind	3	
Geography with Music	L8W3	3FT deg	Gy	12	Ind	M$	Ind	Ind	Ind		
History with Music	V1W3	3FT deg	H	12	Ind	M$	Ind	Ind	Ind		
Mathematics with Music	G1W3	3FT deg	M	12	Ind	M^	Ind	Ind	Ind		
Media Studies with Music	P4W3	3FT deg		12							
Music	W300	3FT deg	Mu+Pf	12	Ind	M^+	Ind	Ind	Ind		
Music and English	QW33	3FT deg	E+Mu	12	Ind	M$+^	Ind	Ind	Ind	7	
Music and Geography	LW83	3FT deg	Mu+Gy	12	Ind	M$+	Ind	Ind	Ind		
Music and History	VW13	3FT deg	H+Mu	12	Ind	M$+	Ind	Ind	Ind		
Music and Mathematics	GW13	3FT deg	M+Mu	12	Ind	M$+^	Ind	Ind	Ind		
Music and Media Studies	PW43	3FT deg	Mu	12	Ind	M$+	Ind	Ind	Ind	6	
Music and Study of Religions	VW83	3FT deg	Mu	12	Ind	M$+	Ind	Ind	Ind	1	
Music and Theology	WV38	3FT deg	Mu+Pf	12	Ind	M^+	Ind	Ind	Ind		
Music with Art	W3W1	3FT deg	Mu	12	Ind	M$+	Ind	Ind	Ind	3	
Music with Dance	W3W4	3FT deg	Mu	12	Ind	M$+	Ind	Ind	Ind	3	
Music with Education Studies (Opt. QTS) (P)	W3X9	3FT/4FT deg	Mu g	12	Ind	M$+ go	Ind	Ind	Ind	4	8/20
Music with English	W3Q3	3FT deg	Mu	12	Ind	M$+	Ind	Ind	Ind		
Music with English Language Teaching (EFL)	W3Q1	3FT deg	Mu	12	Ind	M$+	Ind	Ind	Ind		
Music with Environmental Science	W3F9	3FT deg	Mu g	12	Ind	M$+	Ind	Ind	Ind		
Music with Geography	W3L8	3FT deg	Mu	12	Ind	M$+	Ind	Ind	Ind	2	
Music with History	W3V1	3FT deg	Mu	12	Ind	M$+	Ind	Ind	Ind		
Music with Mathematics	W3G1	3FT deg	Mu g	12	Ind	M$+	Ind	Ind	Ind		
Music with Media Studies	W3P4	3FT deg	Mu	12	Ind	M$+	Ind	Ind	Ind	8	
Music with Related Arts	W3W9	3FT deg	Mu	12	Ind	M$+	Ind	Ind	Ind	5	
Music with Study of Religions	W3V8	3FT deg	Mu	12	Ind	M$+	Ind	Ind	Ind	4	
Music with Theology	W3VV	3FT deg	Mu+Pf	12	Ind	M^+	Ind	Ind	Ind		
Related Arts and Music	WW39	3FT deg	Mu	12	Ind	M$+	Ind	Ind	Ind		6/8
Study of Religions with Music	V8W3	3FT deg	*	12	Ind	M$	Ind	Ind	Ind		
Theology with Music	V8WH	3FT deg	*	12	Ind	M$	Ind	Ind	Ind		

course details			98 expected requirements							96 entry stats	
TITLE	CODE	COURSE	SUBJECTS	A/AS	ND/C	AGNVQ	IB	SQA(H)	SQA	RATIO	A/AS
CITY Univ											
Music	W300	3FT deg	* g	BBC-BCC	Ind	D*^	Ind	Ind	Ind	5	16/28
CITY COLLEGE Manchester											
Jazz	013W	2FT HND									
Music Technology	053W	2FT HND									
CITY of LIVERPOOL Comm COLL											
Music	003E	2FT HND									
Music	003W	2FT HND									
CLARENDON COLL											
Community Performance	503W	2FT HND	*	4	Ind	Ind	Ind	Ind	Ind		
COLCHESTER INST											
Music	W300	3FT deg	*	CD	N	P$	Dip	CCCC	Ind	3	6/24
COVENTRY Univ											
Music Compostion and Professional Practice	W303	3FT deg	Pa g	8	4M $	Ind	Ind	Ind	Ind		
DARTINGTON COLL of Arts											
Music	W300	3FT deg	Mu	CD	10M	Ind	26$	CCCC$	Ind	3	6/22
Music with Arts Management	W3N1	3FT deg	Mu	CD	10M	Ind	26$	CCCC$	Ind	5	
Univ of DERBY											
Popular Music and Music Technology	W310	3FT deg	*	12	Ind	Ind	Ind	CCCC	Ind	1	
Credit Accumulation Modular Scheme *Music*	Y600	3FT deg	Mu	12	MO	M	Ind	CCCC	Ind		
Credit Accumulation Modular Scheme *Music Technology*	Y600	3FT deg	M/P/Es/Ds	8	MO $	M$	Ind	CCCC$	Ind		
Univ of DURHAM											
English Literature and Music	QW33	3FT deg	E+Mu g	AAB	Ind	Ind	32	AAABB	Ind	28	
Latin and Music	QW63	3FT deg	Ln+Mu	24	X	Ind	30$	AAABB	X		
Modern Languages and Music	TW93	4FT deg	L+Mu	BBB	Ind	Ind	33	AAABB	Ind	33	
Music	W300	3FT deg	Mu g	BBC	Ind	Ind	30$	Ind	Ind	5	20/30
Music and Theology	VW83	3FT deg	Mu	BBC	Ind	Ind	Ind	Ind	Ind		
Arts Combined *Music*	Y300	3FT deg	Mu	24	MO	Ind	30	AAABB	Ind		
Univ of EAST ANGLIA											
Music	W300	3FT deg	Mu	BBC-BCC	Ind		Ind	BBC	Ind	6	10/24
EDGE HILL Univ COLLEGE											
Music and Media Production	PW43	3FT deg	*	CC	3M+3D	M* / P*^	Dip	BBCC	Ind		
Univ of EDINBURGH											
History of Art and History of Music	VW43	4FT deg	Mu g	BBB	Ind	Ind	Dip$	BBBB$	Ind		
Music (BMus)	W302	3FT/4FT deg	Mu g	BC				BBC$		9	20/28
Music Technology (BMus)	W351	3FT/4FT deg	Mu+M g	BC	Ind		30$	BBC$	Ind	62	
Univ of ESSEX											
History and Music	VW13	3FT deg	*	20	MO+2D	Ind	28	BBBB	Ind	7	
History of Art and Music	VW43	3FT deg	*	20	MO+2D	Ind	28	BBBB	Ind	1	
Linguistics and Music	QW13	3FT deg	*	20	MO+2D	Ind	28	BBBB	Ind	3	
Literature and Music	QW23	3FT deg	*	20	MO+2D	Ind	28	BBBB	Ind	9	
Mathematics and Music	GW13	3FT deg	M	18	MO $	Ind	28$	CSYS	Ind	13	
Philosophy and Music	VW73	3FT deg	*	20	MO+2D	Ind	28	BBBB	Ind		
Sociology and Music	LW33	3FT deg	*	20	MO+2D	Ind	28	BBBB	Ind		

	course details			98 expected requirements							96 entry stats
TITLE	**CODE**	**COURSE**	**SUBJECTS**	**A/AS**	**ND/C**	**AGNVQ**	**IB**	**SQA(H)**	**SQA**	**RATIO A/AS**
Univ of EXETER										
Music	W300	3FT deg	Mu	BCC	MO	M/D$^	32$	Ind	Ind	12	14/28
Music and American & Postcolonial Studies	QW4H	3FT deg	Mu	BCC	MO	M/D$^	32$			
Music and French	RW1H	4FT deg	F+Mu	BCC	MO	M/D$^	32$	Ind	Ind	
Music and German	RW2H	4FT deg	G+Mu	BCC	MO	M/D$^	32$	Ind	Ind	
Music and Italian	RW3H	4FT deg	L+Mu g	BCC	MO	MD$^	32$	Ind	Ind	
Music and Russian	RW8H	4FT deg	Mu g	BCC	MO	M/D$^	32$	Ind	Ind	
Music and Spanish (Beginners Spanish available)	RW4H	4FT deg	Mu+Sp	BCC	MO	M$^	34$	Ind	Ind	
Univ of GLASGOW										
Archaeology/Music	VW63	4FT deg		BBC	HN	M	30	BBBB	Ind	
Celtic Civilisation/Music	QW5H	4FT deg		BBC	HN	M	30	BBBB	Ind	
Celtic/Music	QW53	4FT deg		BBC	HN	M	30	BBBB	Ind	
Classical Civilisation/Music	QW83	4FT deg		BBC	HN	M	30	BBBB	Ind	
Classical Hebrew/Music	VWW3	4FT deg		BBC	HN	M	30	BBBB	Ind	
Computing/Music	GW53	4FT deg		BBC	HN	M	30	BBBB	Ind	3
Czech/Music	TWC3	5FT deg		BBC	HN	M	30	BBBB	Ind	
Economic and Social History/Music	VW33	4FT deg		BBC	HN	M	30	BBBB	Ind	
Electronics with Music	H6W3	4FT deg	M+Mu	BCC	MO	ME	24$	ABBBB$	N$	3
English/Music	QW33	4FT deg		BBC	HN	M	30	BBBB	Ind	6
Film and Television Studies/Music	WW35	4FT deg		BBB	HN	D	32	AABB	HN	14
French/Music	RW13	5FT deg		BBC	HN	M	30	BBBB	Ind	5
Geography/Music	LW83	4FT deg		BBC	HN	M	30	BBBB	Ind	6
German/Music	RW23	5FT deg		BBC	HN	M	30	BBBB	Ind	4
Greek/Music	QW73	4FT deg		BBC	HN	M	30	BBBB	Ind	
Hispanic Studies/Music	RW43	5FT deg		BBC	HN	M	30	BBBB	Ind	6
History of Art/Music	VW43	4FT deg		BBC	HN	M	30	BBBB	Ind	5
History/Music	VW13	4FT deg		BBC	HN	M	30	BBBB	Ind	3
Islamic Studies/Music	TW63	4FT deg		BBC	N	M	30	BBBB	Ind	
Italian/Music	RW33	5FT deg		BBC	HN	M	30	BBBB	Ind	
Latin/Music	QW63	4FT deg		BBC	HN	M	30	BBBB	Ind	
Mathematics/Music	GW13	4FT deg		BBC	HN	M	30	BBBB	Ind	11
Music	W300	4FT deg		BBC	HN	M	30	BBBB	Ind	6
Music (BMus)	W302	4FT deg		BBC	HN	Ind	30	BBBB	Ind	10
Music/Economics	LWC3	4FT deg		BBC	HN	M	30	BBBB	Ind	
Music/Philosophy	VW73	4FT deg		BBC	HN	M	30	BBBB	Ind	7
Music/Physics	FW33	4FT deg		BBC	HN	M	30	BBBB	Ind	
Music/Polish	TW13	5FT deg		BBC	HN	M	30	BBBB	Ind	
Music/Politics	MW13	4FT deg		BBC	HN	M	30	BBBB	Ind	
Music/Psychology	CW83	4FT deg		BBC	HN	M	30	BBBB	Ind	17
Music/Russian	RW83	5FT deg		BBC	HN	M	30	BBBB	Ind	1
Music/Scottish History	VWC3	4FT deg		BBC	HN	MD	30	BBBB	Ind	4
Music/Scottish Literature	QW23	4FT deg		BBC	HN	M	30	BBBB	Ind	
Music/Sociology	LW33	4FT deg		BBC	HN	M	30	BBBB	Ind	
Physics/Music	FWH3	4FT deg	M+P	BBC-CCC	N	M	24$	BBBB$	N	
Social and Urban Policy/Music	LW43	4FT deg		BBC	HN	M	30	BBBB	Ind	
Theatre Studies/Music	WW34	4FT deg		BBC	HN	M	30	BBBB	Ind	12
Theology & Religious Studies/Music	VWV3	4FT deg		BBC	HN	M	30	BBBB	Ind	
GLASGOW CALEDONIAN Univ										
Music Technology with Electronics	W350	3FT/4FT deg		X	Ind		Ind	X	HN	4

TITLE	CODE	COURSE	SUBJECTS	A/AS	NQ/C	RGNVQ	IB	SQA(H)	SQA	RATIO A/AS
course details			*98 expected requirements*							*96 entry stats*
GOLDSMITHS COLL (Univ of London)										
Music	W302	3FT deg	Mu	BBE	MO	M	Dip	BBBCC	N	8 12/28
Music (4 Yrs Ext Degree)-For O'Seas Students	W303	4FT deg				M				4
Univ of HERTFORDSHIRE										
Applied Physics/Electronic Music	F3W3	3FT deg	M+P+Mu	12	3M	M$^ gi	24$	CCCC$	Ind	
Applied Statistics/Electronic Music	G4W3	3FT deg	Mu	14	MO $	M$^ gi	26$	BCCC$	Ind	
Astronomy/Electronic Music	F5W3	3FT deg	M+Mu g	12	3M	M$^ gi	24$	CCCC$	Ind	
Business/Electronic Music	N1W3	3FT deg	Mu	18	4M+4D	M$^ gi	26$	BBBC	Ind	
Chemistry/Electronic Music	F1W3	3FT deg	C+Mu g	14	MO $	MS^ gi	26$	BCCC$	Ind	
Computing/Electronic Music	G5W3	3FT deg	Mu	14	MO $	M$^ gi	26$	BCCC$	Ind	8
Economics/Electronic Music	L1W3	3FT deg	Mu	14	MO $	M$^ gi	26$	BCCC$	Ind	
Electronic Music	W350	3FT deg	* g	14	Ind	Ind	Ind	Ind	Ind	
Electronic Music with Mathematics	W3GC	3FT deg	* g	14	Ind	Ind	Ind	Ind	Ind	
Electronic Music/Applied Physics	W3F3	3FT deg	Mu+M+P	12	3M $	M$^ gi	24$	CCCC$	Ind	2
Electronic Music/Applied Statistics	W3G4	3FT deg	Mu	14	MO $	M$^ gi	26$	BCCC$	Ind	
Electronic Music/Astronomy	W3F5	3FT deg	Mu+M g	12	3M $	M$^ gi	24$	CCCC$	Ind	6
Electronic Music/Business	W3N1	3FT deg	Mu	18	4M+4D	M$^ gi	26$	BBBC$	Ind	2
Electronic Music/Chemistry	W3F1	3FT deg	Mu+C g	14	MO $	MS^ gi	26$	BCCC$	Ind	
Electronic Music/Computing	W3G5	3FT deg	Mu	14	MO $	M$^ gi	26$	BCCC$	Ind	3
Electronic Music/Economics	W3L1	3FT deg	Mu	14	MO $	M$^ gi	26$	BCCC$	Ind	
Electronic Music/Electronics	W3H6	3FT deg	Mu g	14	MO $	M$^ gi	26$	BCCC$	Ind	12
Electronic Music/Environmental Science	W3F9	3FT deg	Mu	14	MO $	M$^ gi	26$	BCCC$	Ind	
Electronic Music/European Studies	W3T2	3FT deg	Mu	14	MO $	M$^ gi	26$	BCCC$	Ind	
Electronic Music/Human Biology	W3B1	3FT deg	Mu+S	14	MO $	MS^ gi	26$	BCCC$	Ind	2
Electronic Music/Linguistic Science	W3Q1	3FT deg	Mu	14	MO $	M$^ gi	26$	BCCC$	Ind	
Electronic Music/Operational Research	W3N2	3FT deg	Mu	14	MO $	M$^ gi	26$	BCCC$	Ind	
Electronic Music/Philosophy	W3V7	3FT deg	Mu	14	MO $	M$^ gi	26$	BCCC$	Ind	4
Electronics/Electronic Music	H6W3	3FT deg	Mu g	14	MO $	M$^ gi	26$	BCCC$	Ind	
Environmental Science/Electronic Music	F9W3	3FT deg	Mu	14	MO $	M$^ gi	26$	BCCC	Ind	3
European Studies/Electronic Music	T2W3	3FT deg	Mu	14	MO $	M$^ gi	26$	BCCC$	Ind	
Human Biology/Electronic Music	B1W3	3FT deg	S+Mu g	14	MO $	MS^ gi	26$	BCCC$	Ind	
Linguistic Science/Electronic Music	Q1W3	3FT deg	Mu	14	MO $	M$^ gi	26$	BCCC$	Ind	
Operational Research/Electronic Music	N2W3	3FT deg	Mu	14	MO $	M$^ gi	26$	BCCC	Ind	
Philosophy/Electronic Music	V7W3	3FT deg	Mu	14	MO $	M$^ gi	26$	BCCC$	Ind	
Combined Modular Scheme *Electronic Music*	Y100	3FT deg	Mu	14	MO $	M$^ gi	26$	BCCC$	Ind	
Univ of HUDDERSFIELD										
Music (Practical Quals. required)	W300	3FT deg	Mu	CE	Ind	Ind	Ind	BCC	Ind	
Music Technology	HW63	3FT deg	S+Mu g	CC	4D	M$ go	Ind	Ind	Ind	
Music with English (Practical Quals Required)	W3Q3	3FT deg	Mu+E	CC	Ind	Ind	Ind	BBC	Ind	
Music with Theatre Studies (Practical Quals Req)	W3W4	3FT deg	Mu	CC	Ind	Ind	Ind	BBC	Ind	
Music with a Modern Lang (Practical Quals Req)	W3T2	3FT deg	Mu+F/G/Sp	CD	Ind	Ind	Ind	BBC	Ind	
Theatre Studies with Music	W4W3	3FT deg	Mu	CCC	3M+4D	Ind	Ind	BBBC	Ind	
Univ of HULL										
BMus (Honours) (Practical Standards Req)	W302	3FT deg	Mu	BCC-BCD	Ind	M$^ go	28$	BBCCC	Ind	7 10/24
Drama/Music (Practical Standards Req)	WW34	3FT deg	Mu	BBB-BCC	Ind	D$^ go	28$	BBCCC	Ind	10
English/Music (Min Practical Standards Req)	QW33	3FT deg	E	BBB-BCC	Ind	M$^ gi	28$	BBCCC	Ind	11
French/Music (Min Practical Standards Req)	RW13	4FT deg	F	BCC-BCD	Ind	M$^ go	28$	BBCCC	Ind	18
Music (Prac Standard Req)	W300	3FT deg	Mu	BCD-BCC	Ind	M$^ go	28$	BBCCC	Ind	19

| | | | 98 expected requirements | | | | | | | 96 entry stats |
| | | | | | | | | | | |

TITLE	CODE	COURSE	SUBJECTS	A/AS	NO/C	AGNVQ	IB	SQA(H)	SQA	RATIO A/AS
IMPERIAL COLL (Univ of London)										
Physics with Studies in Musical Performance	F3W3	4FT deg	M+P	BCC-CC	HN	Ind	$	CSYS	Ind	7
KEELE Univ										
Biological & Medicinal Chem and Electronic Music	FWCJ	3FT deg	Mu+C	BCC	Ind	D$^	28$	CSYS	Ind	
Electronic Music & Applied Social Studs (4 Yrs)	WLJ5	4FT deg	*	BBC-BCC	Ind	Ind	28	BBBB	Ind	
Electronic Music and American Studies	QW4J	3FT deg	Mu	BCC	Ind	D$^	28$	CSYS	Ind	
Electronic Music and American Studies (4 Yrs)	WQJ4	4FT deg	*	BCC	Ind	Ind	28	BBBB	Ind	
Electronic Music and Ancient History (4 Yrs)	WVJD	4FT deg	*	BCC	Ind	Ind	28	BBBB	Ind	
Electronic Music and Applied Social Studies	LW5J	3FT deg	Mu	BCC	Ind	D$^	28$	CSYS	Ind	
Electronic Music and Astrophysics (4 Yrs)	WFJ5	4FT deg	*	BCC	Ind	Ind	28	BBBB	Ind	
Electronic Music and Biochemistry	CW7J	3FT deg	Mu+C g	BCC	Ind	D$^	28$	CSYS	Ind	
Electronic Music and Biochemistry (4 Yrs)	WCJ7	4FT deg	*	BCC	Ind	Ind	28	BBBB	Ind	
Electronic Music and Biol and Med Chem (4 Yrs)	WFJC	4FT deg	*	BCC	Ind	Ind	28	BBBB	Ind	
Electronic Music and Biology	CW1J	3FT deg	Mu+S g	BCC	Ind	D$^	28$	CSYS	Ind	
Electronic Music and Chemistry	FW1J	3FT deg	Mu+C g	BCC	Ind	D$^	28$	CSYS	Ind	
Electronic Music and Chemistry (4 Yrs)	WFJ1	4FT deg	*	BCC	Ind	Ind	28	BBBB	Ind	
Electronic Music and Classical Studies	QW8J	3FT deg	Mu	BCC	Ind	D$^	28	CSYS	Ind	
Electronic Music and Classical Studies (4 Yrs)	WQJ8	4FT deg	*	BCC	Ind	Ind	28	BBBB	Ind	
Electronic Music and Computer Science	GW5J	3FT deg	Mu	BCC	Ind	D$^	28$	CSYS	Ind	6
Electronic Music and Computer Science (4 Yrs)	WGJ5	4FT deg	*	BCC	Ind	Ind	28	BBBB	Ind	5
Electronic Music and Criminology	MWHJ	3FT deg	Mu	BBB	Ind	D$^	32$	CSYS	Ind	
Electronic Music and Criminology (4 Yrs)	WMJH	4FT deg	*	BBB	Ind	Ind	32	ABBB	Ind	
Electronic Music and Economics	LW1J	3FT deg	Mu g	BCC	Ind	D$^	28$	CSYS	Ind	
Electronic Music and Economics (4 Yrs)	WLJ1	4FT deg	*	BCC	Ind	Ind	28	BBBB	Ind	
Electronic Music and Educational Studies	WXJ9	3FT deg	Mu	BCC	Ind	D$^	28$	CSYS	Ind	
Electronic Music and Educational Studies (4 Yrs)	XW9J	4FT deg	*	BCC	Ind	Ind	28	BBBB	Ind	
Electronic Music and Geology	FW6J	3FT deg	Mu+S g	BCC	Ind	D$^	28$	CSYS	Ind	
English and Electronic Music	QW3J	3FT deg	Mu+E	BBC	Ind	D$^	30$	CSYS	Ind	
English and Electronic Music (4 Yrs)	WQJ3	4FT deg	*	BBC	Ind	Ind	30	BBBB	Ind	
Environmental Management and Elect Music (4 Yrs)	WFJX	4FT deg	*	BCC	Ind	Ind	28	BBBB	Ind	
Finance and Electronic Music	NW3J	3FT deg	Mu g	BCC	Ind	D$^	28$	CSYS	Ind	
Finance and Electronic Music (4 Yrs)	WNJ3	4FT deg	*	BCC	Ind	Ind	28	BBBB	Ind	
Finance and Music	NW33	3FT deg	Mu g	BCC	Ind	D$^	28$	CSYS	Ind	
French and Electronic Music	RW1J	3FT deg	Mu+F	BCC	Ind	D$^	28$	CSYS	Ind	
French and Electronic Music (4 Yrs)	WRJ1	4FT deg	*	BCC	Ind	Ind	28	BBBB	Ind	
French/Russian and Electronic Music (4 Yrs)	WTJX	4FT deg	* g	BCC	Ind	Ind	28	BBBB	Ind	
Geography and Electronic Music (4 Yrs)	WFJ8	4FT deg	*	BCC	Ind	Ind	28	BBBB	Ind	
Geology and Electronic Music (4 Yrs)	WFJ6	4FT deg	*	BCC	Ind	Ind	28	BBBB	Ind	
German and Electronic Music	RW2J	3FT deg	G+Mu	BCC	Ind	D$^	28$	CSYS	Ind	
German and Electronic Music (4 Yrs)	WRJ2	4FT deg	* g	BCC	Ind	Ind	28	BBBB	Ind	
History and Electronic Music	VW1J	3FT deg	Mu	BCC	Ind	D$^	28	CSYS	Ind	
Human Resource Management and Electronic Music	NW6J	3FT deg	Mu	BCC	Ind	D$^	28$	CSYS	Ind	
Human Resource Mgt and Electronic Music (4 Yrs)	WNJ1	4FT deg	*	BCC	Ind	Ind	28	BBBB	Ind	
International History and Electronic Music	VWCJ	3FT deg	Mu	BCC	Ind	D$^	28$	CSYS	Ind	
International History and Electronic Music(4Yrs)	WVJC	4FT deg	*	BCC	Ind	Ind	28	BBBB	Ind	
International Politics and Elect Music (4 Yrs)	WMJC	4FT deg	*	BCC	Ind	Ind	28	BBBB	Ind	2
International Politics and Electronic Music	MWCJ	3FT deg	Mu	BCC	Ind	D$^	28$	CSYS	Ind	
Law and Electronic Music (4 Yrs)	WMJ3	4FT deg	*	BBB	Ind	Ind	32	BBBB	Ind	
Marketing and Electronic Music	NW5J	3FT deg	Mu	BCC	Ind	D$^	28	CSYS	Ind	
Mathematics and Electronic Music	GW1J	3FT deg	M+Mu	BCC	Ind	D$^	28$	CSYS	Ind	
Mathematics and Electronic Music (4 Yrs)	WGJ1	4FT deg	*	BCC	Ind	Ind	28	BBBB	Ind	
Music and American Studies	QW43	3FT deg	Mu	BBC	Ind	D$^	30	CSYS	Ind	

course details

98 expected requirements

96 entry stats

TITLE	CODE	COURSE	SUBJECTS	A/AS	ND/C	AGNVQ	IB	SQA(H)	SQA	RATIO A/AS
Music and American Studies (4 Yrs)	WQ34	4FT deg	*	BBC	Ind	Ind	30	BBBB	Ind	
Music and Ancient History (4 Yrs)	WV3D	4FT deg	*	BCC	Ind	Ind	28	BBBB	Ind	
Music and Applied Social Studies	LW53	3FT deg	Mu	BBC	Ind	D$^	30$	CSYS	Ind	
Music and Applied Social Studies (4 Yrs)	WL35	4FT deg	*	BBC	Ind	Ind	30	BBBB	Ind	
Music and Astrophysics (4 Yrs)	WF35	4FT deg	* g	BCC	Ind	Ind	28	BBBB	Ind	
Music and Biochemistry	CW73	3FT deg	Mu+C g	BCC	Ind	D$^	28$	CSYS	Ind	
Music and Biochemistry (4 Yrs)	WC37	4FT deg	*	BCC	Ind	Ind	28	BBBB	Ind	
Music and Biological & Medicinal Chemistry	FWC3	3FT deg	Mu/C g	BCC	Ind	D$^	28$	CSYS	Ind	
Music and Biological and Medicinal Chem (4 Yrs)	WF3C	4FT deg	*	BCC	Ind	Ind	28	BBBB	Ind	
Music and Biology	CW13	3FT deg	Mu+S g	BCC	Ind	D$^	28$	CSYS	Ind	3
Music and Chemistry	FW13	3FT deg	Mu+C g	BCC	Ind	D$^	28$	CSYS	Ind	
Music and Chemistry (4 Yrs)	WF31	4FT deg	*	BCC	Ind	Ind	28	BBBB	Ind	
Music and Classical Studies	QW83	3FT deg	Mu	BBC	Ind	D$^	30	CSYS	Ind	
Music and Classical Studies (4 Yrs)	WQ38	4FT deg	*	BCC	Ind	Ind	28	BBBB	Ind	
Music and Computer Science	GW53	3FT deg	Mu g	BCC	Ind	D$^	28$	CSYS	Ind	9
Music and Computer Science (4 Yrs)	WG35	4FT deg	*	BCC	Ind	Ind	28	BBBB	Ind	
Music and Criminology	MWH3	3FT deg	Mu	BBB	Ind	D$^	32$	CSYS	Ind	
Music and Criminology (4 Yrs)	WM3H	4FT deg	*	BBB	Ind	Ind	32	ABBB	Ind	
Music and Economics	LW13	3FT deg	Mu g	BCC	Ind	D$^	28$	CSYS	Ind	
Music and Economics (4 Yrs)	WL31	4FT deg	*	BCC	Ind	Ind	28	BBBB	Ind	
Music and Educational Studies	WX39	3FT deg	Mu	BCC	Ind	D$^	28$	CSYS	Ind	7
Music and Educational Studies (4 Yrs)	XW93	4FT deg	*	BCC	Ind	Ind	28	BBBB	Ind	
Music and English	QW33	3FT deg	Mu+E	BBC	Ind	D$^	30$	CSYS	Ind	8
Music and English (4 Yrs)	WQ33	4FT deg	*	BBC	Ind	Ind	30	BBBB	Ind	6
Music and Environmental Management (4 Yrs)	WF3X	4FT deg	* g	BCC	Ind	Ind	28	BBBB	Ind	
Music and Finance (4 Yrs)	WN33	4FT deg	*	BBC-BCC	Ind	Ind	28	BBBB	Ind	
Music and French	RW13	3FT deg	Mu+F	BCC	Ind	D$^	28$	CSYS	Ind	
Music and French (4 Yrs)	WR31	4FT deg	*	BCC	Ind	Ind	28	BBBB	Ind	
Music and French/German	TW93	3FT deg	F+G+Mu	BBC	Ind	D$^	30$	CSYS	Ind	
Music and French/German (4 Yrs)	WT39	4FT deg	g	BBC	Ind	Ind	30	BBBB	Ind	
Music and French/Russian (4 Yrs)	WT3X	4FT deg	*	BCC	Ind	Ind	28	BBBB	Ind	
Music and Geography (4 Yrs)	WF38	4FT deg	*	BCC	Ind	Ind	28	BBBB	Ind	
Music and Geology	FW63	3FT deg	Mu+S g	BCC	Ind	D$^	28$	CSYS	Ind	
Music and Geology (4 Yrs)	WF36	4FT deg	*	BCC	Ind	Ind	28	BBBB	Ind	
Music and German	RW23	3FT deg	Mu+G	BCC	Ind	D$^	28$	CSYS	Ind	7
Music and German (4 Yrs)	WR32	4FT deg	* g	BCC	Ind	Ind	28	BBBB	Ind	
Music and History	VW13	3FT deg	Mu	BBC	Ind	D$^	30	CSYS	Ind	
Music and Human Resource Management (4 Yrs)	WN36	4FT deg	*	BCC	Ind	Ind	28	BBBB	Ind	
Music and International History	VWC3	3FT deg	Mu	BCC	Ind	D$^	28	CSYS	Ind	
Music and International History (4 Yrs)	WV3C	4FT deg	*	BCC	Ind	Ind	28	BBBB	Ind	
Music and International Politics	MWC3	3FT deg	Mu	BCC	Ind	D$^	28$	CSYS	Ind	
Music and International Politics (4 Yrs)	WM3C	4FT deg	*	BCC	Ind	Ind	28	BBBB	Ind	
Music and Law (4 Yrs)	WM33	4FT deg	*	BBB	Ind	Ind	32	BBBB	Ind	
Music and Marketing	NW53	3FT deg	Mu	BCC	Ind	D$^	28$	CSYS	Ind	
Music and Mathematics	GW13	3FT deg	M+Mu	BCC	Ind	D$^	28$	CSYS	Ind	5
Music and Mathematics (4 Yrs)	WG31	4FT deg	*	BCC	Ind	Ind	28	BBBB	Ind	2
Philosophy and Electronic Music	VW7J	3FT deg	Mu	BCC	Ind	D$^	28$	CSYS	Ind	
Philosophy and Music	VW73	3FT deg	Mu	BBC-BCC	Ind	D$^	28$	CSYS	Ind	
Physics and Electronic Music (4 Yrs)	WFJ3	4FT deg	* g	BCC	Ind	Ind	28	BBBB	Ind	
Physics and Music (4 Yrs)	WF33	4FT deg	* g	BCC	Ind	Ind	28	BBBB	Ind	
Politics and Electronic Music	MW1J	3FT deg	Mu	BCC	Ind	D$^	28$	CSYS	Ind	
Politics and Electronic Music (4 Yrs)	WMJ1	4FT deg	*	BCC	Ind	Ind	28	BBBB	Ind	

TITLE	CODE	COURSE	SUBJECTS	A/AS	ND/C	RGNVQ	IB	SQA(H)	SQA	RATIO A/AS	
Politics and Music (4 Yrs)	WM31	4FT deg	*	BCC	Ind	Ind	28	BBBB	Ind		
Psychology and Electronic Music	CW8J	3FT deg	Mu g	BBB	Ind	D$^	32$	CSYS	Ind	2	
Psychology and Electronic Music (4 Yrs)	WCJ8	4FT deg	*	BBB	Ind	Ind	32	ABBB	Ind		
Psychology and Music	CW83	3FT deg	Mu g	BBB	Ind	D$^	32$	CSYS	Ind	14	
Psychology and Music (4 Yrs)	WC38	4FT deg	*	BBB	Ind	Ind	32	ABBB	Ind	3	
Russian Studies and Electronic Music (4 Yrs)	WRJV	4FT deg	*	BCC	Ind	Ind	28	BBBB	Ind		
Russian Studies and Music (4 Yrs)	WR3V	4FT deg	*	BCC	Ind	Ind	28	BBBB	Ind		
Russian and Electronic Music (4 Yrs)	WRJ8	4FT deg	*	BCC	Ind	Ind	28	BBBB	Ind		
Russian and Music (4 Yrs)	WR38	4FT deg	* g	BCC	Ind	Ind	28	BBBB	Ind		
Sociology & Social Anthropology and Elect Music	LW3J	3FT deg	Mu	BCC	Ind	D$^	28$	CSYS	Ind		
Sociology & Social Anthropology and Music	LW33	3FT deg	Mu	BBC-BCC	Ind	D$^	28$	CSYS	Ind		
Statistics and Electronic Music (4 Yrs)	WGJ4	4FT deg	*	BCC	Ind	Ind	28	BBBB	Ind		
Statistics and Music (4 Yrs)	WG34	4FT deg	*	BCC	Ind	Ind	28	BBBB	Ind		
Visual Arts and Electronic Music	WW1J	3FT deg	Mu	BCC	Ind	D$^	28	CSYS	Ind		
Visual Arts and Electronic Music (4 Yrs)	WWJ1	4FT deg	*	BCC	Ind	Ind	28	BBBB	Ind		
Visual Arts and Music	WW31	3FT deg	Mu	BCC	Ind	D$^	28$	BBBB	Ind		
Visual Arts and Music (4 Yrs)	WW13	4FT deg	*	BCC	Ind	Ind	28	BBBB	Ind		
KING ALFRED'S WINCHESTER											
Music (World) and Archaeology	FW43	3FT deg	* g	14	6M	M	24	BCC	N		
Music (World) and Computing	GW53	3FT deg	* g	14	6M	M	24	BCC	N	1	
Music (World) and Dance Studies	WW3K	3FT deg	* g	14	6M	M	24	BCC	N	2	
Music (World) and Drama Studies	WW34	3FT deg	* g	14	6M	M	24	BCC	N	2	
Music (World) and Education Studies	WX39	3FT deg	* g	14	6M	M	24	BCC	N		
Music (World) and History	VW13	3FT deg	* g	14	6M	M	24	BCC	N		
Music (World) and Media & Film Studies	PW43	3FT deg	* g	14	6M	M	24	BCC	N		
Psychology and Music (World)	LW73	3FT deg	* g	14	6M	M	24	BCC	N	2	
Religious Studies and Music (World)	VW83	3FT deg	* g	14	6M	M	24	BCC	N	1	
KING'S COLL LONDON (Univ of London)											
German and Music	RW23	4FT deg	G+Mu	BBC						2	
Music	W302	3FT deg	Mu	ABB						15	20/30
Music with Applied Computing	W3G5	3FT deg	Mu	BBC						17	
KINGSTON Univ											
Music	W300	3FT deg	Mu	CD	Ind	Ind^	Ind	Ind	Ind	9	10/22
Music and Technology	JW93	3FT deg	Mu	CD	Ind	Ind^	Ind	Ind	Ind	10	10/22
LANCASTER Univ											
Computer Science and Music	GW53	3FT deg	Mu g	BCC	Ind $		30$	ABBBB$	Ind		
English and Music	WQ33	3FT deg	E+Mu g	BBC-BCC	Ind $		32$	ABBBB$	Ind		
French Studies and Music	WR31	4SW deg	F+Mu	BCC	MO $		30$	BBBB$	Ind		
German Studies and Music	WR32	4SW deg	G/L+Mu	BCC	MO $		30$	BBBB$	Ind		
History and Music	WV31	3FT deg	H+Mu	BBC	Ind $		30$	ABBBB$	Ind		
Italian Studies and Music	WR33	4SW deg	I/L+Mu	BCC	Ind $		30$	BBBBB$	Ind		
Music	W302	3FT deg	*	BB-CC	Ind $		Ind$	BBBB$	Ind		
Music	W300	3FT deg	*	BBB-BCD	Ind $		Ind$	BBBB$	Ind		
Musicology	W340	3FT deg	Mu	BBB-BCD	Ind $		Ind$	BBBB$	Ind		
Spanish Studies and Music	WR34	4SW deg	Sp/L+Mu	BCC	Ind $		Ind$	BBBB$	Ind		
Univ of LEEDS											
Computer Science-Music	GW53	3FT/4FT deg	M+Mu g	BBC	1M+5D$	Ind	30$	ABBBB	Ind	12	
English-Music	QW33	3FT deg	E+Mu g	BBC	Ind	Ind	30$	CSYS	Ind	9	22/28
French-Music	RW13	4FT deg	F+Mu g	BBC	Ind	Ind	30$	CSYS	Ind	14	
German-Music	RW23	4FT deg	G+Mu g	BBC	Ind	Ind	30$	CSYS	Ind	16	

course details — *98 expected requirements* — *96 entry stats*

| | | | 98 expected requirements | | | | | | | 96 entry stats | |
| course details | | | | | | | | | | | |

TITLE	CODE	COURSE	SUBJECTS	A/AS	NO/C	AGNVQ	IB	SQA(H)	SQA	RATIO A/AS	
History of Art-Music	VW43	3FT deg	Mu g	BBC	Ind	Ind	30$	CSYS	Ind		
History-Music	VW13	3FT deg	Mu g	BBC	Ind	Ind	30$	CSYS	Ind		
Italian-Music	RW33	4FT deg	Mu+I g	BBC	Ind	Ind	30$	CSYS	Ind		
Italian-Music B	RWH3	4FT deg	Mu+L g	BBC	Ind	Ind	30$	CSYS	Ind	4	
Mathematics-Music	GW13	3FT/4FT deg	M+Mu g	BBB	1M+5D$	Ind	32$	ABBBB	Ind	9	
Music	W300	3FT/4FT deg	Mu g	BCC	Ind	Ind	28$	CSYS	Ind	14	19/28
Music-Electronic Engineering	WH36	3FT deg	Mu+P/M g	BBC	Ind	Ind	30$	CSYS	Ind	25	
Music-Philosophy	VW73	3FT deg	Mu g	BBC	Ind	Ind	30$	CSYS	Ind	6	
Music-Religious Studies	VWV3	3FT deg	Mu g	BBC	Ind	Ind	30$	CSYS	Ind		
Music-Theology	VW83	3FT deg	Mu g	BBC	Ind	Ind	30$	CSYS	Ind		

LEEDS METROPOLITAN Univ

Music Technology	W350	3FT deg	Mu+S	DD	3M$	P$ go	26$	BCC	Ind		10/24

LEEDS COLL of MUSIC

Jazz Studies	W310	3FT deg	g	CC	N			CCCC		9	10/22
Music	W304	3FT deg	g	EE	N			CCCC			

Univ of LIVERPOOL

Music	W300	3FT deg	Mu	BB-BCC	Ind		30$	BBBBB$	Ind	7	10/26
Music/Popular Music	W320	3FT deg	Mu	BB-BBC	Ind		30$	BBBBB$	Ind	14	16/28
Arts Combined Music	Y401	3FT deg	Mu	BBC-BBB	Ind	Ind	30$	ABBB$	Ind		
Arts Combined Popular Music	Y401	3FT deg	Mu	BBC-BBB	Ind	Ind	30$	ABBB$	Ind		

LIVERPOOL HOPE Univ COLL

European Studies and Music	TW23	3FT deg									
Human & Applied Biology and Music	CW13	3FT deg									
Music/American Studies	QW43	3FT deg	Mu	12	8M	P$^	Ind	Ind	Ind		
Music/Art	WW93	3FT deg	A/Fa+Mu	12	8M	PQ^	Ind	Ind	Ind	2	
Music/Drama & Theatre Studies	WW43	3FT deg	Mu g	12	8M	MQ /P*^ go	Ind	Ind	Ind	3	10/20
Music/English	QW33	3FT deg	El+Mu	12	8M	PQ^	Ind	Ind	Ind	3	
Music/Environmental Studies	FW93	3FT deg	B/Gy/En+Mu	12	8M	P$^	Ind	Ind	Ind		
Music/French	RW13	3FT deg	F+Mu	12	8M	PQ^	Ind	Ind	Ind	3	
Music/Information Technology	GW53	3FT deg	Mu	12	8M	MQ /P*^	Ind	Ind	Ind	2	
Music/Mathematics	GW13	3FT deg	M+Mu	12	8M	PQ^	Ind	Ind	Ind	4	
Sociology/Music	WL33	3FT deg	Mu	12	8M	P*^	Ind	Ind	Ind	3	
Sport, Recreation & Physical Education/Music	WB36	3FT deg	Mu	12	8M	P*^	Ind	Ind	Ind		
Theology & Religious Studies/Music	WV38	3FT deg	Mu	12	8M	P*^	Ind	Ind	Ind	2	

THE LIVERPOOL INSTITUTE FOR PERORMING ARTS

Sound Technology	HW63	3FT deg			Ind	Ind	Ind	Ind	Ind		

Univ of MANCHESTER

Music	W302	3FT deg	Mu	22			30$	BBBBC		7	18/30
Music and Drama	WW34	3FT deg	Mu+E	BBC-BBB			30$	BBBBB		17	

MANCHESTER METROPOLITAN Univ

Music/American Studies	QW43	3FT deg	*	CC	M+D	D	28	CCCC	Ind		
Music/Applied Social Studies	LW33	3FT deg	*	CC	M+D	D	28	CCCC	Ind		
Music/Business Studies	NW13	3FT deg	*	CC	M+D	D	28	CCCC	Ind		
Music/Cultural Studies	LWH3	3FT deg	*	CC	M+D	D	28	CCCC	Ind		
Music/Dance	WW34	3FT deg	*	DD	M+D	D	28	CCCC	Ind		
Music/Drama	WW3K	3FT deg	*	DD	M+D	D	28	CCCC	Ind		
Music/English	QW33	3FT deg	*	CC	M+D	D	28	CCCC	Ind		

	course details			98 expected requirements							96 entry stats	
TITLE	CODE	COURSE	SUBJECTS	A/AS	NQ/C	RGNVQ	IB	SQA(H)	SQA		RATIO	A/AS
Music/Geography	LW83	3FT deg	*	CC	M+D	D	28	CCCC	Ind			
Music/Health Studies	BW93	3FT deg	*	CC	M+D	D	28	CCCC	Ind			
Music/History	VW13	3FT deg	*	CC	M+D	D	28	CCCC	Ind			
Music/Leisure Studies	LW43	3FT deg	*	CC	M+D	D	28	CCCC	Ind			
Philosophy/Music	VW73	3FT deg	*	CC	M+D	D	28	CCCC	Ind			
Religious Studies/Music	VW83	3FT deg	*	CC	M+D	D	28	CCCC	Ind			
Sport/Music	BW63	3FT deg	S	BC	M+D	DS	28	CCCC	Ind			
Visual Arts/Music	WW13	3FT deg	*	DD	M+D	DQ/A	28	CCCC	Ind			
Writing/Music	WW3L	3FT deg	*	DD	M+D	DQ/A	28	CCCC	Ind			
MIDDLESEX Univ												
Music	W300▼	3FT deg	Mu	12-16	5M	X	Ind	Ind	Ind			
Music (Jazz)	W311▼	3FT deg	Mu	12-16	5M	X	Ind	Ind	Ind			
Performing Arts - Music	WW34▼	3FT deg	Mu	12-16	3M+2D	MQ go	Ind	Ind	Ind			
Sonic Arts	W3J9▼	3FT deg	* g	12-16	5M	X	26	Ind	Ind			
Theatre Dance	W4W3▼	3FT deg	D		Ind	Ind	Ind	Ind	Ind			
Joint Honours Degree Music	Y400	3FT deg	Mu g	12-16	5M	X	Ind	Ind	Ind			
NAPIER Univ												
Music	W302	3FT deg	Mu	BC	Ind	Ind	Ind	ABB	Ind		9	
Music Studies	003W	2FT HND	Mu	CD	Ind	Ind	Ind	BB	Ind		3	
NENE COLLEGE												
Art and Design with Music	W2W3	3FT deg	Mu	DD	5M	M	24	CCC	Ind			
Drama with Music	W4W3	3FT deg	Mu	10	5M+1D	M	24	CCC	Ind			
Education with Music	X9W3	3FT deg	Mu	DD	5M	M	24	CCC	Ind			
English with Music	Q3W3	3FT deg	Mu	CC	4M+1D	M	24	CCC	Ind			
French with Music	R1W3	3FT deg	Mu+F	DD	5M	Ind	24	CCC	Ind			
History with Music	V1W3	3FT deg	Mu	CD	5M	M	24	CCC	Ind			
Law with Music	M3W3	3FT deg	Mu g	10	3M+2D	M	24	CCC	Ind			
Mathematics with Music	G1W3	3FT deg	Mu+M	DD	Ind	Ind	24	CCC	Ind			
Music	W300	3FT deg	Mu	DD	5M	M	24	CCC	Ind			
Music with Architectural Studies	W3V4	3FT deg	Mu	DD	5M	M	24	CCC	Ind			
Music with Art and Design	W3W2	3FT deg	Mu	DD	5M	M	24	CCC	Ind			
Music with Business Administration	W3N1	3FT deg	Mu g	DD	5M	M	24	CCC	Ind			
Music with Drama	W3W4	3FT deg	Mu	DD	5M	M	24	CCC	Ind			
Music with Education	W3X9	3FT deg	Mu	DD	5M	M	24	CCC	Ind			
Music with English	W3Q3	3FT deg	Mu	DD	5M	M	24	CCC	Ind			
Music with French	W3R1	3FT deg	F+Mu	DD	5M	M	24	CCC	Ind			
Music with History	W3V1	3FT deg	Mu	DD	5M	M	24	CCC	Ind			
Music with History of Art	W3VK	3FT deg	Mu	DD	5M	M	24	CCC	Ind			
Music with Mathematics	W3G1	3FT deg	Mu+M	DD	5M	M	24	CCC	Ind			
Music with Media and Popular Culture	W3P4	3FT deg	Mu	DD	5M	M	24	CCC	Ind			
Music with Personal & Organisational Development	W3N6	3FT deg	Mu	DD	5M	M	24	CCC	Ind			
Music with Philosophy	W3V7	3FT deg	Mu	DD	5M	M	24	CCC	Ind			
Music with Sociology	W3L3	3FT deg	Mu	DD	5M	M	24	CCC	Ind			
Music with Sport Studies	W3N7	3FT deg	Mu	EE	3M	P	24	CCC	Ind			
Sport Studies with Music	N7W3	3FT deg	Mu+Ss/Pe	12	M+2D	M	24	BBB	Ind			
Univ of NEWCASTLE												
Music	W300	3FT deg	Mu	BB-BCC	X		31$	AABB$	X		6	16/22
Combined Studies (BA) Music	Y400	3FT deg	*	ABC-BBB	5D	Ind	35$	AAAB	Ind			

			98 expected requirements							96 entry stats	
course details											
TITLE	CODE	COURSE	SUBJECTS	A/AS	ND/C	AGNVQ	IB	SQA(H)	SQA	RATIO	A/AS
NEWCASTLE COLL											
Jazz, Popular and Commercial Music	W310▼	3FT deg									
Music Production	403W▼	2FT HND									
Music Technology	053W▼	2FT HND									
Performing Arts (Jazz, Popular & Comm Music)	013W▼	2FT HND									
NORTHERN COLL											
Expressive Arts	W300▼	4FT deg	g	CD				CCC$			
Univ of NORTHUMBRIA											
Music	W300	3FT deg	Mu	EE	N		24	CCC	Ind	5	4/14
Univ of NOTTINGHAM											
German and Music	RW23	4FT deg	G+Mu	BBC							
Music	W300	3FT deg	Mu	ABC						20	22/30
OXFORD Univ											
Music	W300	3FT deg	Mu	AAB-ABB	DO		36	AAAAA	Ind	2	22/30
OXFORD BROOKES Univ											
Geography and the Phys Env/Music	FWV3	3FT deg									
Music	W300	3FT deg									
Music/Accounting and Finance	NW43	3FT deg	Mu g	DD-BCC	Ind	M/D*3	Ind	Ind	Ind		
Music/Anthropology	LW63	3FT deg	Mu	DD-BCC	Ind	M/M*^	Ind	Ind	Ind	3	
Music/Biological Chemistry	CW73	3FT deg									
Music/Biology	CW13	3FT deg	Mu+S g	DD	Ind	MS	Ind	Ind	Ind	1	
Music/Business Administration & Management	NW13	3FT deg	Mu g	DD-BBC	Ind	M/MB4	Ind	Ind	Ind	16	
Music/Cartography	FW83	3FT deg	Mu g	DD-CC	Ind	M*	Ind	Ind	Ind		
Music/Cell Biology	CWC3	3FT deg									
Music/Combined Studies	WY34	3FT deg		X		X	X	X			
Music/Computer Systems	GW63	3FT deg	Mu g	DD-BC	Ind	M*	Ind	Ind	Ind		
Music/Computing	GW53	3FT deg	Mu g	DD-BC	Ind	M*	Ind	Ind	Ind		
Music/Computing Mathematics	GW93	3FT deg	Mu g	DD-CD	Ind	M*	Ind	Ind	Ind		
Music/Ecology	CW93	3FT deg	Mu+S g	DD-CD	Ind	MS	Ind	Ind	Ind		
Music/Economics	LW13	3FT deg	Mu g	DD-BB	Ind	M/M*3	Ind	Ind	Ind	2	
Music/Educational Studies	WX39	3FT deg	Mu	DD-CC	Ind	M/M*3	Ind	Ind	Ind	5	
Music/Electronics	HW63	3FT deg	Mu+S/M	DD-CC	Ind	M$	Ind	Ind	Ind		
Music/English Studies	QW33	3FT deg	Mu	DD-AB	Ind	M*^	Ind	Ind	Ind	4	16/18
Music/Environmental Chemistry	WF31	3FT deg									
Music/Environmental Policy	KW33	3FT deg									
Music/Environmental Sciences	FWX3	3FT deg	Mu+S g	DD-CD	Ind	M/DS	Ind	Ind	Ind		
Music/Exercise and Health	WB36	3FT deg	Mu+S g	DD	Ind	MS	Ind	Ind	Ind		
Music/Fine Art	WW13	3FT deg	Mu+Pf+A	DD-BC	Ind	MA^	Ind	Ind	Ind	11	
Music/French Language and Contemporary Studies	RWC3	4SW deg	F+Mu	DD-CC	Ind	M*^	Ind	Ind	Ind	3	
Music/Geography	LW83	3FT deg	Mu	DD-BB	Ind	M*	Ind	Ind	Ind	4	
Music/Geology	FW63	3FT deg	Mu+S/M g	DD	Ind	PS/M	Ind	Ind	Ind		
Music/Geotechnics	HW23	3FT deg	Mu+S/M/Ds/Es	DD-CC	Ind	M$	Ind	Ind	Ind		
Music/German Language and Contemp Stud	RWF3	4SW deg	Mu+G	DD-CD	Ind	M*^	Ind	Ind	Ind		
Music/German Language and Literature	RW23	4SW deg	Mu+G	DD-CD	Ind	M*^	Ind	Ind	Ind		
Music/German Studies	WR3G	4SW deg	Mu+G	DD-CD	Ind	M*^	Ind	Ind	Ind		
Music/Health Care (Post Exp)	BW73	3FT deg		X		X	X	X			
Music/History	VW13	3FT deg	Mu	DD-BB	Ind	M^	Ind	Ind	Ind	7	
Music/History of Art	VW43	3FT deg	Mu	DD-BCC	Ind	M^	Ind	Ind	Ind	3	
Music/Hospitality Management Studies	NW73	3FT deg	Mu	DD-CC	Ind	M/M*3	Ind	Ind	Ind		
Music/Human Biology	BW13	3FT deg									

TITLE	CODE	COURSE	SUBJECTS	A/AS	ND/C	AGNVQ	IB	SQA(H)	SQA	RATIO	A/AS
Music/Information Systems	GWM3	3FT deg	Mu g	DD-BC	Ind	M*	Ind	Ind	Ind		
Music/Intelligent Systems	GW83	3FT deg	Mu g	DD-CD	Ind	M*	Ind	Ind	Ind		
Music/Law	MW33	3FT deg	Mu	DD-BBB	Ind	M/D*3	Ind	Ind	Ind		
Music/Leisure Planning and Management	KWH3	3FT deg									
Music/Marketing Management	NWN3	3FT deg	Mu g	DD-BCC	Ind	M/D*3	Ind	Ind	Ind		
Music/Mathematics	GW13	3FT deg	M+Mu	DD-DDE	Ind	M*^	Ind	Ind	Ind		
Palliative Care/Music (Post Exp)	BWR3	3FT deg		X		X	X	X			
Planning Studies/Music	KW43	3FT deg	Mu g	DD-CC	Ind	M*	Ind	Ind	Ind		
Politics/Music	MW13	3FT deg	Mu	DD-AB	Ind	M*^	Ind	Ind	Ind		
Psychology/Music	CW83	3FT deg	Mu g	DD-BBC	Ind	M*^	Ind	Ind	Ind	6	14/16
Publishing/Music	PW53	3FT deg	Mu g	DD-BB	Ind	M/M$3	Ind	Ind	Ind	4	
Rehabilitation/Music (Post Exp)	BWT3	3FT deg		X		X	X	X			
Retail Management/Music	NW53	3FT deg	Mu g	DD-CCD	Ind		Ind	Ind	Ind		
Sociology/Music	LW33	3FT deg	Mu	DD-BCC	Ind	M*^	Ind	Ind	Ind		
Software Engineering/Music	GW73	3FT deg	Mu g	DD-BC	Ind	M*	Ind	Ind	Ind		
Statistics/Music	GW43	3FT deg	Mu g	DD	Ind	M*	Ind	Ind	Ind		
Telecommunications/Music	HWP3	3FT deg									
Tourism/Music	PW73	3FT deg	Mu g	DD-BC	Ind	M*/M*3	Ind	Ind	Ind	2	
Transport Planning/Music	NW93	3FT deg	Mu	DD-CC	Ind	M*	Ind	Ind	Ind		
Water Resources/Music	HWF3	3FT deg									

Univ of PLYMOUTH

TITLE	CODE	COURSE	SUBJECTS	A/AS	ND/C	AGNVQ	IB	SQA(H)	SQA	RATIO	A/AS
Art History with Music	V4W3	3FT deg	Ap g	CCD	MO+3D	D$^	Ind	Ind	Ind		
Cultural Interpretation and Practice with Music	Y3W3	3FT deg	Ap g	CCD	MO+3D	D$^	Ind	Ind	Ind		
English with Music	Q3W3	3FT deg	Ap g	BBC	MO+3D	D$^	Ind	Ind	Ind	2	
Heritage and Landscape with Music	W2WH	3FT deg	Ap g	CCD	MO+3D	D$^	Ind	Ind	Ind		
History with Music	V1W3	3FT deg	Ap g	CCD	MO+3D	D$^	Ind	Ind	Ind		
Media Arts with Music	W2W3	3FT deg	Ap g	CCD	MO+3D	D$^	Ind	Ind	Ind		
Theatre and Performance Studies with Music	WW4H	3FT deg	Ap g	CCD	MO+3D	D$^	Ind	Ind	Ind		
Visual Arts with Music	W2WJ	3FT deg	Ap g	CCD	MO+3D	D$^	Ind	Ind	Ind		

QUEEN'S Univ Belfast

TITLE	CODE	COURSE	SUBJECTS	A/AS	ND/C	AGNVQ	IB	SQA(H)	SQA	RATIO	A/AS
Ethnomusicology	W341	3FT deg	* g	BCC	3M+4D	D*6/^ go	29$	ABBB	Ind	14	
Music (BMus)	W302	3FT deg	Mu g	CCC-CCD	X	D*^ go	28$	ABBB	X	6	15/30
Music/Biblical Studies	VW83	3FT deg	* g	BCC	3M+4D	D*6/^ go	29$	ABBB	Ind		
Music/Celtic	QW53	3FT/4FT deg	* g	BCC	3M+4D	D*6/^ go	29$	ABBB	Ind		
Music/Computer Science	GW53	3FT deg	M/Cs g	BCC	X	D*^ go	29$	X	Ind	6	
Music/English	QW33	3FT deg	E g	BCC	X	D*^ go	29$	ABBB	X	11	
Music/Ethnomusicology	W340	3FT deg	* g	BCC	3M+4D	D*6/^ go	29$	ABBB	Ind	12	
Music/French (4 years)	RW13	4FT deg	F g	BCC	X	D*^ go	29$	ABBB	X		
Music/German (4 years)	RW23	4FT deg	* g	BCC	3M+4D	D*6/^ go	29$	ABBB	Ind		
Music/Italian (4 years)	RW33	4FT deg	* g	BCC	3M+4D	D*6/^ go	29$	ABBB	Ind		
Philosophy/Music	WV37	3FT deg	* g	BCC	3M+4D	D*6/^ go	29$	ABBB	Ind		
Politics/Ethnomusicology	WM3C	3FT deg	* g	BCC	3M+4D	D*6/^ go	29$	ABBB	Ind		
Politics/Music	WM31	3FT deg	* g	BCC	3M+4D	D*6/^ go	29$	ABBB	Ind	7	
Psychology/Music	CW83	3FT deg	* g	BCC	3M+4D	D*6/^ go	29$	ABBB	Ind		
Scholastic Philosophy/Music	VW73	3FT deg	* g	BCC	3M+4D	D*6/^ go	29$	ABBB	Ind		
Social Anthropology/Ethnomusicology	WL3P	3FT deg	* g	BCC	3M+4D	D*6/^ go	29$	ABBB	Ind	3	
Social Anthropology/Music	WL36	3FT deg	* g	BCC	3M+4D	D*6/^ go	29$	ABBB	Ind		
Spanish/Music (4 years)	WR34	4FT deg	* g	BCC	3M+4D	D*6/^ go	29$	ABBB	Ind		

TITLE	CODE	COURSE	SUBJECTS	A/AS	NO/C	RGNVQ	IB	SQA(H)	SQA	RATIO A/AS	

Univ of READING

TITLE	CODE	COURSE	SUBJECTS	A/AS	NO/C	RGNVQ	IB	SQA(H)	SQA	RATIO	A/AS
Music	W300	3FT deg	Mu	BCC	X	M*^	30$	BBBB$	Ind	6	10/26
Music and English Literature	QW33	3FT deg	Mu+El	BBC	X	D*^	31$	BBBB$	Ind	8	
Music and French	RW13	4FT deg	Mu+F	BBC	X	D*^	31$	BBBB$	Ind	14	
Music and German	RW23	4FT deg	Mu g	BCC	X	D*^ go	30$	BBBB$	Ind	8	
Music and History of Art	VW43	3FT deg	Mu	BBD	X	D*^	30$	BBBB$	Ind	5	
Music and Italian	RW33	4FT deg	Mu g	BCC	X	D*^ go	30$	BBBB$	Ind		
Physics and Music	FW33	3FT deg	M+P+Mu	BCC	X		30$	BBBB$	Ind		

Univ College of RIPON & YORK ST JOHN

TITLE	CODE	COURSE	SUBJECTS	A/AS	NO/C	RGNVQ	IB	SQA(H)	SQA	RATIO	A/AS
Music: Performance and Communication Arts	PW33	3FT deg		CC	M	M$	27	BBBC			

ROEHAMPTON INST

TITLE	CODE	COURSE	SUBJECTS	A/AS	NO/C	RGNVQ	IB	SQA(H)	SQA	RATIO	A/AS
Music	W302▼	3FT deg	Mu	CC	4M $	P^	26	BCC	N$		
Music and Applied Consumer Studies	NW93▼	3FT deg	Mu g	12	4M $	P^	26	BCC	N$		
Music and Art for Community	WW13▼	3FT deg	Mu	DD	4M $	P^	26	BCC	N$	4	
Music and Biology	CW13▼	3FT deg	B+Mu	12	4M $	P^ go	26	BCC	N$		
Music and Business Computing	GW73▼	3FT deg	Mu g	12	3D	M^ go	26	BCC	N$		
Music and Business Studies	NW13▼	3FT deg	Mu g	DD	3D $	M^ go	26	BCC	N$	17	
Music and Dance Studies	WW43▼	3FT deg	Mu	CC	2M+2D$	M^	30	BBC	Ind	14	
Music and Drama & Theatre Studies	WWL3▼	3FT deg	Mu+T/E	16	3D $	M^	30	BBC	Ind	28	
Music and Education	XW93▼	3FT deg	Mu	DD	4M $	P^	26	BCC	N$	1	6/10
Music and English Language & Linguistics	QW3H▼	3FT deg	Mu+E/L	CC	2M+2D$	M^	30	BBC	Ind		
Music and English Literature	QW33▼	3FT deg	Mu+E	CC	2M+2D$	M^	28	BBC	Ind	3	
Music and Environmental Studies	FW93▼	3FT deg	Mu+B/Gy	DD	4M $	M^ go	26	BCC	N$	1	
Music and Film & Television Studies	PW43▼	3FT deg	Mu	16	2M+2D$	M^	30	BBC	N$		
Music and French	RW13▼	4FT deg	Mu+F	12	4M $	P^	26	BCC	N$	3	
Music and Geography	LW83▼	3FT deg	Mu+Gy	DD	4M $	P^ go	26	BCC	N$		
Music and Health Studies	BW93▼	3FT deg	Mu+B	12	4M $	P^ go	26	BCC	N$		
Music and History	VW13▼	3FT deg	Mu+H	DD	4M $	P^	26	BCC	N$	4	
Music and Human & Social Biology	CWC3▼	3FT deg	B+Mu	12	4M $	P^ go	26	BCC	N$		
Natural Resource Studies and Music	DW23▼	3FT deg	Mu g	DD	3M	P^ go	24	CCC	N$		
Psychology and Music	WL37▼	3FT deg	Mu g	CC	3D $	M^ go	30	BBC	Ind	10	
Social Policy & Administration and Music	WL34▼	3FT deg	Mu g	DD	4M $	P^	26	BCC	N$		
Sociology and Music	WL33▼	3FT deg	Mu g	DD	4M $	P^ go	26	BCC	N$		
Spanish and Music	RW43▼	4FT deg	Sp+Mu	12	2M+2D$	P^	28	BBC	N$	2	
Sport Studies and Music	WB36▼	3FT deg	Mu g	12	3D $	M^ go	30	BBC	N$		
Theology & Religious Studies and Music	WV38▼	3FT deg	Mu	DD	4M $	P^	26	BCC	N$		
Women's Studies and Music	MW93▼	3FT deg	Mu	DD	4M $	P^	26	BCC	N$		

ROSE BRUFORD COLL

TITLE	CODE	COURSE	SUBJECTS	A/AS	NO/C	RGNVQ	IB	SQA(H)	SQA	RATIO	A/AS
Actor Musician	W4W3	3FT deg	*							10	16/23
Music Technology	W350	3FT deg	*							12	8/18

ROYAL HOLLOWAY, Univ of London

TITLE	CODE	COURSE	SUBJECTS	A/AS	NO/C	RGNVQ	IB	SQA(H)	SQA	RATIO	A/AS
Drama and Music	WW43	3FT deg	Mu+E/T g	BBC	Ind		30$	CSYS		17	
Economics with Music	L1W3	3FT deg	Mu	BBC-BBB	Ind		32	Ind			
French and Music	RW13	4FT deg	F+Mu	BBC-ABC			Ind	Ind		7	
French with Music	R1W3	4FT deg	F+Mu	BBC-ABC			28$	Ind			
German and Music	RW23	4FT deg	G+Mu	BBC			Ind	Ind		4	
German with Music	R2W3	4FT deg	G+Mu	BCC			28$	BBBBC$		1	
Italian and Music	RW33	4FT deg	Mu+L/Ln	BBC			Ind	Ind			
Italian with Music	R3W3	4FT deg	L/Ln+Mu	BBC			30	BBCCC$			
Mathematics and Music	GW13	3FT deg	M+Mu	BCC-BBC	Ind	D^	Ind	Ind		20	

			98 expected requirements							**96 entry stats**	
course details											
TITLE	CODE	COURSE	SUBJECTS	A/AS	ND/C	AGNVQ	IB	SQA(H)	SQA	RATIO	A/AS
Mathematics with Music	G1W3	3FT deg	M+Mu	BCC-BBC	Ind	D^	Ind	Ind			
Music (BMus)	W302	3FT deg	Mu	BCC-BBC			Ind	ABBCC$		11	18/26
Music and Psychology	WC38	3FT deg	Mu g	BBC-BBB	Ind		Ind	Ind			
Music with French	W3R1	3FT deg	F+Mu	BCC-BBC			Ind	ABBCC$			
Music with German	W3R2	3FT deg	G+Mu	BCC-BBC			Ind	ABBCC$			
Music with Italian	W3R3	3FT deg	Mu+L/Ln	BCC-BBC			Ind	ABBCC$			
Music with Japanese Studies	W3T4	3FT deg	L+Mu g	BCC-BBC			Ind	ABBCC$		2	
Music with Management Studies	W3N1	3FT deg	Mu	BCC-BBC			Ind	ABBCC$		4	
Music with Mathematics	W3G1	3FT deg	M+Mu	BCC-BBC			Ind	ABBCC$			
Music with Political Studies	W3MC	3FT deg	Mu	BCC-BBC			Ind	ABBCC$			
Music with Social Policy	W3L4	3FT deg	Mu	BCC-BBC			Ind	ABBCC$			
Music with Spanish	W3R4	3FT deg	L+Mu	BCC-BBC			Ind	ABBCC$			
Physics with Music	F3W3	3FT deg	M+Mu+P	BCC-BBC	5M	DS^	30$	BBBCC$			
Sociology with Music	L3W3	3FT deg	Mu	BCC-BBC	Ind	D^	Ind	Ind			
Foundation Programme Music	Y408	4FT deg									
Univ of SALFORD											
Band Musicianship (3 or 4 Yrs)	W304	3FT/4FT deg	Mu	8	3M	M	Ind	CCCC	Ind	11	6/22
Music Acoustics and Recording	W331	3FT deg	2(M/P/Mu) g	12	5D	M	28	BBBB	Ind	29	22/26
Popular Music and Recording	W350	3FT deg	Mu	12	5D	M	28	ABBB	Ind	18	10/26
SOAS:Sch of Oriental & African St (U of London)											
Music Studies	W300	3FT deg	Mu	20	Ind		30	BBBCC	Ind	7	
Music and African Studies	WT37	3FT deg		20	Ind		30	BBBCC	Ind	1	
Music and Amharic	TW73	4FT deg		20	Ind		30	BBBCC	Ind	1	
Music and Arabic	TW63	4FT deg		22	Ind		31	BBBBC	Ind		
Music and Bengali	TW53	3FT deg		20	Ind		30	BBBCC	Ind		
Music and Burmese	TWM3	4FT deg		20	Ind		30	BBBCC	Ind		
Music and Chinese	TW33	4FT deg		24	Ind		32	BBBBB	Ind	1	
Music and Development Studies	MW93	3FT deg		22	Ind		31	BBBBC	Ind		
Music and Geography	LW83	3FT deg		20	Ind		30	BBBCC	Ind		
Music and Georgian	TW93	3FT deg		22	Ind		31	BBBBC	Ind		
Music and Gujarati	TW5H	3FT deg		20	Ind		30	BBBCC	Ind		
Music and Hausa	TWR3	4FT deg		20	Ind		30	BBBCC	Ind		
Music and Hebrew	QW93	4FT deg		22	Ind		31	BBBBC	Ind		
Music and Hindi	TWN3	3FT deg		20	Ind		30	BBBCC	Ind	4	
Music and History	VW13	3FT deg		20	Ind		30	BBBCC	Ind	2	
Music and History of Art/Archaeology	VWP3	3FT deg		20	Ind		30	BBBCC	Ind	1	
Music and Indonesian	TWMH	3FT/4FT deg		20	Ind		30	BBBCC	Ind		
Music and Japanese	TW43	4FT deg		24	Ind		32	BBBBB	Ind		
Music and Korean	TWNH	4FT deg		16	Ind		28	BBCCC	Ind		
Music and Linguistics	QW33	3FT deg									
Nepali and Music	TW5J	3FT deg		20	Ind		30	BBBCC	Ind		
Persian and Music	TWQ3	3FT deg		22	Ind		31	BBBBC	Ind		
Sanskrit and Music	QWX3	3FT deg		20	Ind		30	BBBCC	Ind		
Sinhalese and Music	TWMJ	3FT deg		20	Ind		30	BBBCC	Ind		
Social Anthropology and Music	LW63	3FT deg		22	Ind		31	BBBBC	Ind		
South Asian Studies and Music	WTH5	3FT deg									
Study of Religions and Music	VW83	3FT deg		20	Ind		30	BBBCC	Ind	4	
Swahili and Music	TWT3	4FT deg		20	Ind		30	BBBCC	Ind		
Tamil and Music	TWNJ	3FT deg		20	Ind		30	BBBCC	Ind		
Thai and Music	WT35	3FT/4FT deg		20	Ind		30	BBBCC	Ind		
Turkish and Music	TWP3	4FT deg		22	Ind		31	BBBBC	Ind		

course details			98 expected requirements							96 entry stats	
TITLE	CODE	COURSE	SUBJECTS	A/AS	ND/C	AGNVQ	IB	SQA(H)	SQA	RATIO A/AS	
Urdu and Music	WT3M	3FT deg		20	Ind		30	BBBCC	Ind		
Vietnamese and Music	WT3N	4FT deg		20	Ind		30	BBBCC	Ind		
Univ College SCARBOROUGH											
Music	W300	3FT deg	Mu g	DD	Ind		27$	Ind	Ind		
Music with Arts	W3Y3	3FT deg	Mu g	EE	Ind		27$	Ind	Ind		
Music with Social Sciences	W3Y2	3FT deg	Mu g	EE	Ind		27$	Ind	Ind		
Univ of SHEFFIELD											
Biblical Studies and Music	VW83	3FT deg	Mu g	BBC-BCC	X	X	30$	ABBB$	Ind		
English and Music	QW33	3FT deg	El+Mu g	BBB	X	X	32$	AABB$	Ind	35	
French and Music	RW13	4FT deg	F+Mu g	BBC	X	X	30$	ABBB$	Ind	7	26/28
German and Music	RW23	4FT deg	G+Mu g	BBC	X	X	30$	ABBB$	Ind	15	
Music	W302	3FT deg	Mu g	BBC-BCC	X	X	30$	ABBB$	Ind	12	20/30
Music and Hispanic Studies	RW43	4FT deg	Mu+Sp g	BBC	X	X	30$	ABBB$	Ind		
Music and Philosophy	VW73	3FT deg	Mu g	BBB	X	X	32$	AABB$	Ind		
Univ College of St MARTIN, LANCASTER AND CUMBRIA											
Performing Arts (Drama, Dance or Music)	WW43	3FT deg	*	CC-CDE	3M+2D$	MQ	28$	BBCC	Ind	7	6/22
Univ of SOUTHAMPTON											
Acoustics and Music	HW73	3FT deg	M+P+Mu	20	Ind $	D^	30$	CSYS	Ind	42	
English and Music	QW33	3FT deg	E+Mu	22	X	Ind	Ind	Ind	X	14	
French and Music	RW13	4FT deg	F+Mu	22	1M+4D	Ind	30$	Ind	Ind		
German and Music	RW23	4FT deg	Mu+G	22	1M+4D	Ind	30$	Ind	Ind	8	
Mathematics and Music	GW13	3FT deg	M+Mu	BBC	Ind	Ind	30	ABBBB	Ind	6	
Music	W300	3FT deg	Mu	22	Ind		Ind	Ind	Ind	4	12/26
ST HELENS COLL											
Music Technology	053W	2FT HND	*	2	N	M*	Ind	Ind	Ind		
Performance and Theatre Arts	043W	2FT HND	*	2	N	P*	Ind	Ind	Ind		
STAFFORDSHIRE Univ											
Music Technology	W350	3FT deg	g	8	3M	M$					
Music Technology	W359	4EXT deg	g	EE	P $	P$	Ind	Ind	Ind		
Univ of STRATHCLYDE											
Applied Music	W300	3FT/4FT deg	g	CC	Ind		Ind	BCC$	Ind		
Univ of SUNDERLAND											
Creative Arts Studies	W341	3FT deg	* g	12	MO		24	CCCCC	N	1	6/14
Politics with Music	M1W3	3FT deg	* g	12	3M	M	24	BCCC	N		
Univ of SURREY											
Music	W300	3FT deg	Mu	BC-BCC	X		32$	ABBB	X	8	14/24
Music and Sound Recording (Tonmeister)	W350	4SW deg	Mu+P+M	ABB-BBC	X		$	AABBB$	X		
Univ of SUSSEX											
Music and Media Studies	WP34	3FT deg	Mu	BBC	MO $	M*^	$	Ind	Ind		
Music in Cultural and Community Studies	W3Y2	3FT deg	Mu	BBC	MO $	M*^	$	Ind	Ind		
Music in English and American Studies	W3Q4	3FT deg	Mu	BBC	MO $	M*^	$	Ind	Ind		
Twentieth Cent Music St in Cultural & Comm St	W3YF	3FT deg	Mu	BBC	MO $	M*^	$	Ind	Ind		
Twentieth Cent Music St in English & Amer St	W3QK	3FT deg	Mu	BBC	MO $	M*^	$	Ind	Ind		
THAMES VALLEY Univ											
American Studies with Music	Q4W3	3FT deg		8-12	MO	M	26	CCC			
Digital Arts with Sound and Music Recording	W9W3	3FT deg		8-12	MO	M		CCC			
English with Music	Q3W3	3FT deg		8-12	MO	M	26	CCC			

Music

course details			98 expected requirements							96 entry stats
TITLE	CODE	COURSE	SUBJECTS	A/AS	ND/C	AGNVQ	IB	SQA(H)	SQA	RATIO A/AS
French with Music	R1W3	3FT deg		8-12	MO	M	26	CCC		
German with Music	R2W3	3FT deg		8-12	MO	M	26	CCC		
History with Music	V1W3	3FT deg		8-12	MO	M	26	CCC		
Information Mgt with Sound and Music Recording	P2WH	3FT deg		8-12	MO	M	26	CCC		
Media Arts with Music	W9WH	3FT deg		8-12	MO	M	26	CCC		
Media Arts with Sound and Music Recording	W9WJ	3FT deg								
Multi-Media Comp with Sound and Music Recording	G5WH	3FT deg		8-12	MO	M	26	CCC		
Music (Perf plus grade 8 and 6 in 2 instruments)	W303▼	3FT Dip		2-4	N	P	24	CC		
Music Technology (Relevant Experience Req)	W350	2FT Dip		2-4	N	P	24	CC		
Pop Mus Perf(Bass/Guitar,Drum,Keybrd,Voc) ex req	W302	2FT Dip		2-4	N	P	24	CC		
Spanish with Music	R4W3	3FT deg		8-12	MO	M	26	CCC		
World Musics	W340	2FT Dip		2-4	N	P	24	CC		
Univ of ULSTER										
Music (3 Yr)	W302▼	3FT deg	Mu	CCC	MO+3D	D*^ gi	28	BBBC	Ind	10 14/24
WELSH COLL of Music and Drama										
Music BA	W300	3FT deg	Mu	12-20	HN	X	Ind	Ind	HN	5 8/26
Performers Diploma (Music)	W301	3FT Dip	Mu	4-8	Ind	X	Ind	Ind	Ind	2 7/18
Performing Arts (Popular Music)	013W	2 HND								
WESTHILL COLL										
Humanities - Creative Arts Music	Y4W9	3FT deg	* g	CC	4M+2D	M^	Ind	Ind	Ind	
Univ of WESTMINSTER										
Commercial Music	W304▼	3FT deg								10 8/28
WIGAN and LEIGH COLL										
Popular Music	113W▼	2FT HND	Mu	D	N	Q	Dip	Ind	Ind	
Univ of WOLVERHAMPTON										
Music (Specialist Route)	W300	3FT deg	Mu	10	4M	M	24	BBBB	Ind	7 8/16
Combined Degrees Music	Y401	3FT deg	Mu	10	4M	M	24	BBBB	Ind	
Combined Degrees Music Popular	Y401	3FT deg		10	4M	M	24	BBBB	Ind	
Univ of YORK										
Music	W300	3FT deg	Mu	BBC	Ind	D$^	28$	BBBC$	Ind	20/30
Music Technology	HW63	3FT/4FT deg	Mu+M g	BBC	Ind	D$^	28$	CSYS$	Ind	20/28
Music/Education	W3X9	3FT deg	Mu	BBC	Ind	D$^	28$	BBBC$	Ind	

course details			98 expected requirements							96 entry stats	
TITLE	CODE	COURSE	SUBJECTS	A/AS	ND/C	AGNVQ	IB	SQA(H)	SQA	RATIO	A/AS
Univ of ABERTAY DUNDEE											
Nursing (pre-registration)	B700	4FT deg	B/C/P	CC	Ind	Ind	Ind	BBCC	Ind		
ANGLIA Poly Univ											
Midwifery	B710▼	3FT deg	* g	12	4M	M go	Dip	BCCC			
Nursing	B700▼	3FT deg	* g	CC	4M	M go	Dip	BCCC	Ind	7	6/18
Nursing and Social Work (Learn Disab) RN/DipSW	BL75▼	3FT deg	* g	CC	4M	M go	Dip	BCCC			
Registered Nurse	B701▼	2FT dip	g	12	4M	M go	Dip	BCCC			
Univ of Wales, BANGOR											
Bachelor of Nursing	B700	3FT deg	S g	12	Ind	D$^ go	26$	CCCC$	Ind	20	
Univ of BIRMINGHAM											
Nursing (BNurs)	B700	4FT deg	* g	CCC	DO$	DG^ go	28$	ABBC	Ind	14	18/26
BOURNEMOUTH Univ											
Clinical Nursing (Adult and Child Health)	B700	3FT deg	2(S/B/So/Ps) g	12-14	MO	M$ go	Ind	CCCC	Ind	7	9/22
Midwifery	B710	3FT deg	B g	12-14	MO	M$ go	Ind	CCCC	Ind	17	
Univ of BRIGHTON											
European Nursing Studies	B740	4FT deg	* g	16	Ind	M$ go	Dip	BBBC	Ind		
Nursing	B700	3FT deg	* g	16	DO $	M$	Dip$	BBBC$	Ind		
BRISTOL, Univ of the W of England											
Community Health Care Nursing(Post Dip,Post Exp)	B705	1FT deg	g	X	X	X	X	X	X		
Nursing/RGN	B700	4FT deg	B/So/Ps g	CC	MO $	M6 go	24$	BCC$	Ind		
BUCKINGHAMSHIRE COLLEGE											
Nursing	B701	3FT deg		12	2D	M	27	CCCC	Ind	3	6/14
Nursing (Dip HE Conversion)	B702	1FT deg			HN						
CANTERBURY CHRIST CHURCH COLL of HE											
Midwifery	B710	4FT deg	* g	CC	MO	M	24	Ind	Ind		
Nursing	B700	4FT deg	* g	CC	MO	M	24	Ind	Ind		
Univ of CENTRAL ENGLAND											
Midwifery	B710	3FT deg	E/S	CC	M+D	MG	Ind	CCCCC	Ind	7	10/24
Nursing (RN)	B700	3FT deg	* g	16	4M $	MG gi	Ind	CCCCC	Ind	10	6/18
Univ of CENTRAL LANCASHIRE											
Midwifery	B710	4FT deg	S	CC	MO+2D$	D$6/^	26$	BBCC	$	9	10/18
Midwifery (18 mth short course-qual nurses only)	B711	2FT deg									
Nursing Studies Pre-Registration	B740	3FT deg	* g	16	DO $	D$6/^	$	BBBB	Ind		10/18
CITY Univ											
Nursing	B700	3FT deg	* g	16-24	4D	DG/S go	Ind	Ind	Ind	23	14/20
DE MONTFORT Univ											
Midwifery	B710▼	4FT deg	* g	16	MO		Ind	Ind	Ind	19	
Nursing (Adult Nursing)	B700▼	3FT deg	S	16	MO	M	X	Ind	Ind	21	16/16
Nursing (Child Health)	B702▼	3FT deg	S	16	MO	M	X	Ind	Ind	17	
Nursing (Mental Health)	B701▼	3FT deg	S	16	MO	M	X	Ind	Ind	4	
Univ of EAST ANGLIA											
Nursing (Adult)	B701	3FT deg	S g								
Nursing (Child)	B704	2FT dip	S g								
Nursing (Learning Disabilities)	B703	3FT deg	S g								
Nursing (Mental Health)	B702	3FT deg	S g								

Nursing 57

TITLE	CODE	COURSE	SUBJECTS	A/AS	ND/C	RGNVQ	IB	SQA(H)	SQA	RATIO	A/AS
course details			*98 expected requirements*							*96 entry stats*	
Univ of EAST LONDON											
Community Health Nursing	B705	1FT deg	* g	12	MO	MG				1	
Nursing Studies (1 year)	B740	1FT deg	* g	12	Ind	Ind	Ind	Ind	Ind	1	
Specialist Community Nursing Practice	B706	1FT deg	* g	12	MO	M				2	
Univ of EDINBURGH											
Nursing (General) (BSc)	B702	4FT deg	g	BBC	Ind		32$	ABBB	Ind	27	
Nursing Honours (BSc)	B703	4FT deg	g	BBC	Ind		32$	ABBB	Ind	9	
Univ of GLAMORGAN											
Nursing (Adult)	B701	3FT deg	* g	CCC	Ind	Ind	Ind	Ind	Ind		
Nursing (Child)	B702	3FT deg	* g	CCC	Ind	Ind	Ind	Ind	Ind		
Nursing (Mental Handicap)	B703	3FT deg	* g	CCC	Ind	Ind	Ind	Ind	Ind		
Nursing (Mental Health)	B704	3FT deg	* g	CCC	Ind	Ind	Ind	Ind	Ind		
Univ of GLASGOW											
Nursing (BN)	B700	4FT deg	C/M/P g	CCC	Ind		28$	BBBC$	X	10	
GLASGOW CALEDONIAN Univ											
Nursing Studies	B700	4SW/5SW deg	S+E	CC	Ind		Ind	BBBC$	Ind	5	12/18
Univ of GREENWICH											
Health and Learning Disabilities	BB97	3FT deg	*	12	N	M$	22	Ind	Ind		
Health with Learning Disabilities	B9B7	3FT deg	*	12	N	M$	22	Ind	Ind		
Midwifery (Pre-Registration)	B710	3FT deg	* g	12-20	M+D	MG go	24	CCC	Ind		
Nursing (Adult Branch Registration)	B730	3FT deg	* g	12-20	1M+1D	MG go	24	CCC	Ind		
Nursing (Child Branch Registration)	B720	3FT deg	* g	12-20	1M+1D	MG go	24	CCC	Ind		
Nursing (Mental Health Registration)	B760	3FT deg	* g	12-20	1M+1D	MG go	24	CCC	Ind		
Care: (Disability)	197B▼	2FT HND	* g	E	N	Ind	Ind	Ind	Ind		
Care: (Older People)	097B▼	2FT HND	* g	E	N	Ind	Ind	Ind	Ind		
Univ of HERTFORDSHIRE											
Nursing & Soc Wrk Sts (Learn Dis) with RN/DipSW	BL75	3FT deg	* g	12-16	4M+3D	D	Ind	Ind	Ind	1	
Nursing with Registration	B700	3FT deg	* g	12-16	4M+3D	D$	26	Ind	Ind	7	10/24
Univ of HUDDERSFIELD											
Midwifery	B710	3FT deg	S g	18	MO+4D$	M$6/^ go	28$	BBBBC$	Ind		
Nursing	B700	3FT deg	S g	CC	Ind	M$6/^ go	Ind	Ind	Ind		
Univ of HULL											
BSc Nursing Sciences (Hons Degree with RGN/RMNH)	B700	4FT deg	g	CCC	MO	M$^ go	26$	BBCCC	Ind	6	16/28
KING'S COLL LONDON (Univ of London)											
Midwifery	B711	2FT deg		X	X	X	X	X	X		
Nursing Studies (4 Yrs)	B700	4FT deg	S g	CCC		DS/G^	Ind	BBCCC	Ind	11	16/22
LANCASTER Univ											
Biochemistry with Biomedicine	BC79	3FT deg									
Univ of LEEDS											
Midwifery	B710	3FT deg	S g	BCC	Ind	Ind	Ind	Ind	Ind		10/20
LEEDS METROPOLITAN Univ											
Midwifery	B710	4FT deg	* g	BB-CCC	4M+2D$	M$6/^ go	28$	BBBBC$	Ind	16	10/20
Nursing (Adult Health)	B700	4FT deg	* g	BB-CCC	4M+2D$	M$6/^ go	28$	BBBBC$	Ind	17	10/20
Nursing (Mental Health)	B701	4FT deg	* g	BB-CCC	4M+2D$	M$6/^ go	28$	BBBBC$	Ind	9	

course details			98 expected requirements							96 entry stats	
TITLE	CODE	COURSE	SUBJECTS	A/AS	NO/C	RGNVQ	IB	SQA(H)	SQA	RATIO	A/AS
Univ of LIVERPOOL											
Nursing (BN with Honours)	B700	4FT deg	B/C/P/M g	BCC	DO	D$+^	Ind	BBBCC	Ind	8	18/30
LIVERPOOL JOHN MOORES Univ											
Midwifery	B710	4FT deg	B	14	5M	D/M6^				26	
Nursing	B700	3FT deg	B	18	5M	D/M6^				13	12/18
LUTON Univ											
Midwifery	B711	3FT deg		12-16	MO/DO	M/D	32	BBCC	Ind		
Univ of MANCHESTER											
Nursing	B700	4FT deg	g	BCC	MO+D	D^	30	BBBBC$	X	12	16/24
MIDDLESEX Univ											
Midwifery (RGN top-up)	B715▼	1/2 FT deg									
Nursing	B700▼	4SW deg	* g	12-16	5M	MG go	28	BBCC	Ind		
NENE COLLEGE											
Midwifery Studies	B710	3FT deg									
Nursing Studies (Adult)	B700	3FT deg									
Nursing Studies (Mental Health)	B705	3FT deg									
Univ of NORTHUMBRIA											
Midwifery Studies, Registered Midwife	B710	3FT deg	g	CCC	Ind	D	26	BBBCC	Ind	9	18/22
Nursing Studies, Registered Nurse (Adult)	B700	3FT deg	g	CCC	4M+4D	D	26	BBBCC	Ind	10	16/24
Nursing Studies, Registered Nurse (Child)	B701	3FT deg	g	CCC	4M+4D	D	26	BBBCC	Ind	1	
Nursing Studies,Registered Nurse,(Mental Health)	B740	3FT deg	g	CCC	4M+4D	D	26	BBBCC	Ind	7	
NORWICH: City COLL											
Environmental Health (Integrated) (4 years)	B701	4FT deg	S g	6	5M	PS go	Ind	Ind	Ind		
Univ of NOTTINGHAM											
Nursing	B700	4FT deg	B g	CCC	MO+D		30$	CCCCC	HN	14	19/26
OXFORD BROOKES Univ											
Accident & Emergency Nursing (Post Exp)	B720	3FT deg		X		X	X	X			
Cancer Care Nursing (Post Exp)	B742	3FT deg		X		X	X	X			
Cardiac Nursing (Post Exp)	B721	3FT deg		X		X	X	X			
Cardio-Thoracic Nursing (Post Exp)	B722	3FT deg		X		X	X	X			
Children's Nursing (Post Exp)	B741	3FT deg		X		X	X	X			
Community District Nursing (Post Exp)	B711	3FT deg		X		X	X	X			
Community Learning Disability (Post Exp)	B712	4FT deg		X		X	X	X			
Community Psychiatric Nursing (Post Exp)	B713	3FT deg		X		X	X	X			
Coronary Care Nursing (Post Exp)	B723	3FT deg		X		X	X	X			
Geography and the Phys Env/Health Care(Post Exp)	BF7V	3FT deg		X		X	X	X			
Geography and the Phys Env/Palliative Care	BFRV	3FT deg		X		X	X	X			
Geratology (Post Experience)	B730	2FT dip		X		X	X	X			
Health Care Studies (Post Exp)	B740	3FT deg		X		X	X	X			
Health Care/Accounting and Finance (Post Exp)	BN74	3FT deg		X		X	X	X			
Health Care/Anthropology (Post Exp)	BL76	3FT deg		X		X	X	X			
Health Care/Biological Chemistry (Post Exp)	BC77	3FT deg		X		X	X	X			
Health Care/Biology (Post Exp)	BC71	3FT deg		X		X	X	X			
Health Care/Business Admin & Mgt (Post Exp)	BN71	3FT deg		X		X	X	X			
Health Care/Cartography (Post Exp)	BF78	3FT deg		X		X	X	X			
Health Care/Cell Biology (Post Exp)	BC7C	3FT deg		X		X	X	X			
Health Care/Combined Studies (Post Exp)	BY74	3FT deg		X		X	X	X			
Health Care/Computer Systems (Post Exp)	BG76	3FT deg		X		X	X	X			

course details

98 expected requirements

96 entry stats

TITLE	CODE	COURSE	SUBJECTS	A/AS	ND/C	AGNVQ	IB	SQA(H)	SQA	RATIO A/AS
Health Care/Computing (Post Exp)	BG75	3FT deg		X		X	X	X		
Health Care/Computing Mathematics (Post Exp)	BG79	3FT deg		X		X	X	X		
Health Care/Ecology (Post Exp)	BC79	3FT deg		X		X	X	X		
Health Care/Economics (Post Exp)	BL71	3FT deg		X		X	X	X		
Health Care/Educational Studies	BX79	3FT deg		X		X	X	X		
Health Care/Electronics (Post Exp)	BH76	3FT deg		X		X	X	X		
Health Care/English Studies (Post Exp)	BQ73	3FT deg		X		X	X	X		
Health Care/Environmental Chemistry (Post Exp)	BF71	3FT deg		X		X	X	X		
Health Care/Environmental Policy (Post Exp)	BK73	3FT deg		X		X	X	X		
Health Care/Environmental Sciences (Post Exp)	BF7X	3FT deg		X		X	X	X		
Health Care/Exercise and Health (Post Exp)	BB67	3FT deg		X		X	X	X		
Health Care/Fine Art (Post Exp)	BW71	3FT deg		X		X	X	X		
Health Care/Food Science and Nutrition(Post Exp)	BD74	3FT deg		X		X	X	X		
Health Care/French Lang and Contemp St(Post Exp)	BR7C	3FT deg		X		X	X	X		
Health Care/French Lang and Literture (Post Exp)	BR71	3FT deg		X		X	X	X		
Health Care/Geography (Post Exp)	BL78	3FT deg		X		X	X	X		
Health Care/Geology (Post Exp)	BF76	3FT deg		X		X	X	X		
Health Care/Geotechnics (Post Exp)	BH72	3FT deg		X		X	X	X		
Health Care/German Language and Contemp Stud	BR7F	3FT deg		X		X	X	X		
Health Care/German Language and Literature	BR72	3FT deg		X		X	X	X		
Health Care/German Studies (Post Exp)	BR7G	3FT deg		X		X	X	X		
Health Visiting (Post Exp)	B714	3FT deg		X		X	X	X		
History of Art/Health Care (Post Exp)	BV74	3FT deg		X		X	X	X		
History/Health Care (Post Exp)	BV71	3FT deg		X		X	X	X		
Hospitality Management St/Health Care (Post Exp)	BN77	3FT deg		X		X	X	X		
Human Biology/Health Care (Post Exp)	BB17	3FT deg		X		X	X	X		
Information Systems/Health Care (Post Exp)	BG7M	3FT deg		X		X	X	X		
Intelligent Systems/Health Care (Post Exp)	BG78	3FT deg		X		X	X	X		
Intensive Care Nursing (Post Exp)	B724	3FT deg		X		X	X	X		
Law/Health Care (Post Exp)	BM73	3FT deg		X		X	X	X		
Leisure Planning/Health Care (Post Exp)	BK7H	3FT deg		X		X	X	X		
Marketing Management/Health Care (Post Exp)	BN7N	3FT deg		X		X	X	X		
Mathematics/Health Care (Post Exp)	BG71	3FT deg		X		X	X	X		
Midwifery	B710	4FT deg	* g	CD	Ind	MG	Ind	Ind	Ind	22 14/28
Music/Health Care (Post Exp)	BW73	3FT deg		X		X	X	X		
Neonatal Nursing	B725	3FT deg								
Neurosciences	B726	3FT deg								
Nursing (Adult)	B701	4FT deg	* g	CD	Ind	MG	Ind	Ind	Ind	4 9/20
Nursing (Children's)	B704	4FT deg	* g	CD	Ind	MG	Ind	Ind	Ind	19 12/24
Nursing (Learning Disabilities)	B703	4FT deg	* g	CD	Ind	MG	Ind	Ind	Ind	2 12/18
Nursing (Mental Health)	B702	4FT deg	* g	CD	Ind	MG	Ind	Ind	Ind	3 4/18
Occupational Health Nursing (Post Exp)	B715	3FT deg		X		X	X	X		
Ophthalmic Nursing (Post Exp)	B727	3FT deg		X		X	X	X		
Orthopaedic & Trauma Care (Post Exp)	B731	2FT dip		X		X	X	X		
Paediatric Community Nursing (Post Exp)	B717	3FT deg		X		X	X	X		
Palliative Care (Post Exp)	B732	2FT dip		X		X	X	X		
Palliative Care/Accounting and Finance(Post Exp)	BNR4	3FT deg		X		X	X	X		
Palliative Care/Anthropology (Post Exp)	BLR6	3FT deg		X		X	X	X		
Palliative Care/Biological Chemistry (Post Exp)	BCR7	3FT deg		X		X	X	X		
Palliative Care/Biology (Post Exp)	BCR1	3FT deg		X		X	X	X		
Palliative Care/Business Admin and Mgt(Post Exp)	BNR1	3FT deg		X		X	X	X		
Palliative Care/Cartography (Post Exp)	BFR8	3FT deg		X		X	X	X		

course details			98 expected requirements							96 entry stats

TITLE	CODE	COURSE	SUBJECTS	A/AS	NO/C	AGNVQ	IB	SQA(H)	SQA	RATIO A/AS
Palliative Care/Cell Biology (Post Exp)	BCRC	3FT deg		X		X	X	X		
Palliative Care/Combined Studies (Post Exp)	BYR4	3FT deg		X		X	X	X		
Palliative Care/Computer Systems (Post Exp)	BGR6	3FT deg		X		X	X	X		
Palliative Care/Computing (Post Exp)	BGR5	3FT deg		X		X	X	X		
Palliative Care/Computing Mathematics (Post Exp)	BGR9	3FT deg		X		X	X	X		
Palliative Care/Ecology (Post Exp)	BCR9	3FT deg		X		X	X	X		
Palliative Care/Economics (Post Exp)	BLR1	3FT deg		X		X	X	X		
Palliative Care/Educational Studies (Post Exp)	BXR9	3FT deg		X		X	X	X		
Palliative Care/Electronics (Post Exp)	BHR6	3FT deg		X		X	X	X		
Palliative Care/English Studies (Post Exp)	BQR3	3FT deg		X		X	X	X		
Palliative Care/Environmental Chem (Post Exp)	BFR1	3FT deg		X		X	X	X		
Palliative Care/Environmental Policy (Post Exp)	BKR3	3FT deg		X		X	X	X		
Palliative Care/Environmental Sciences(Post Exp)	BFRX	3FT deg		X		X	X	X		
Palliative Care/Exercise and Health (Post Exp)	BBR6	3FT deg		X		X	X	X		
Palliative Care/Fine Art (Post Exp)	BWR1	3FT deg		X		X	X	X		
Palliative Care/Food Sci and Nutrition(Post Exp)	BDR4	3FT deg		X		X	X	X		
Palliative Care/French Lang & Cont St (Post Exp)	BRRC	3FT deg		X		X	X	X		
Palliative Care/French Lang and Lit (Post Exp)	BRR1	3FT deg		X		X	X	X		
Palliative Care/Geography (Post Exp)	BLR8	3FT deg		X		X	X	X		
Palliative Care/Geology (Post Exp)	BFR6	3FT deg		X		X	X	X		
Palliative Care/Geotechnics (Post Exp)	BHR2	3FT deg		X		X	X	X		
Palliative Care/Ger Lang & Contemp St (Post Exp)	BRRF	3FT deg		X		X	X	X		
Palliative Care/German Lang and Lit (Post Exp)	BRR2	3FT deg		X		X	X	X		
Palliative Care/German Studies (Post Exp)	BRRG	3FT deg		X		X	X	X		
Palliative Care/Health Care (Post Exp)	B750	3FT deg		X		X	X	X		
Palliative Care/History	BVR1	3FT deg		X		X	X	X		
Palliative Care/History of Art (Post Exp)	BVR4	3FT deg		X		X	X	X		
Palliative Care/Hospitality Mgt St (Post Exp)	BNR7	3FT deg		X		X	X	X		
Palliative Care/Human Biology (Post Exp)	BB1R	3FT deg		X		X	X	X		
Palliative Care/Information Systems (Post Exp)	BGRM	3FT deg		X		X	X	X		
Palliative Care/Intelligent Systems (Post Exp)	BGR8	3FT deg		X		X	X	X		
Palliative Care/Law (Post Exp)	BMR3	3FT deg		X		X	X	X		
Palliative Care/Leisure Planning & Mgt(Post Exp)	BKRH	3FT deg		X		X	X	X		
Palliative Care/Marketing Management (Post Exp)	BNRN	3FT deg		X		X	X	X		
Palliative Care/Mathematics (Post Exp)	BGR1	3FT deg		X		X	X	X		
Palliative Care/Music (Post Exp)	BWR3	3FT deg		X		X	X	X		
Peri-Operative Nursing (Post Exp)	B728	3FT deg		X		X	X	X		
Planning Studies/Health Care (Post Exp)	BK74	3FT deg		X		X	X	X		
Planning Studies/Palliative Care (Post Exp)	BKR4	3FT deg		X		X	X	X		
Politics/Health Care (Post Exp)	BM71	3FT deg		X		X	X	X		
Politics/Palliative Care (Post Exp)	BMR1	3FT deg		X		X	X	X		
Practice Nursing (Post Exp)	B718	3FT deg		X		X	X	X		
Psychology/Health Care (Post Exp)	BC78	3FT deg		X		X	X	X		
Psychology/Palliative Care (Post Exp)	BCR8	3FT deg		X		X	X	X		
Publishing/Health Care (Post Exp)	BP75	3FT deg		X		X	X	X		
Publishing/Palliative Care (Post Exp)	BPR5	3FT deg		X		X	X	X		
Rehabilitation Nursing (Post Exp)	B743	3FT deg		X		X	X	X		
Rehabilitation/Accounting and Finance (Post Exp)	BNT4	3FT deg		X		X	X	X		
Rehabilitation/Anthropology (Post Exp)	BLT6	3FT deg		X		X	X	X		
Rehabilitation/Biological Chemistry (Post Exp)	BCT7	3FT deg		X		X	X	X		
Rehabilitation/Biology (Post Exp)	BCT1	3FT deg		X		X	X	X		
Rehabilitation/Business Admin and Mgt (Post Exp)	BNT1	3FT deg		X		X	X	X		

course details			**98 expected requirements**							**96 entry stats**
TITLE	CODE	COURSE	SUBJECTS	A/AS	ND/C	AGNVQ	IB	SQA(H)	SQA	RATIO A/AS
Rehabilitation/Cartography (Post Exp)	BFT8	3FT deg		X		X	X	X	
Rehabilitation/Cell Biology (Post Exp)	BCTC	3FT deg		X		X	X	X	
Rehabilitation/Combined Studies (Post Exp)	BYT4	3FT deg		X		X	X	X	
Rehabilitation/Computer Systems (Post Exp)	BGT6	3FT deg		X		X	X	X	
Rehabilitation/Computing (Post Exp)	BGT5	3FT deg		X		X	X	X	
Rehabilitation/Computing Mathematics (Post Exp)	BGT9	3FT deg		X		X	X	X	
Rehabilitation/Ecology (Post Exp)	BCT9	3FT deg		X		X	X	X	
Rehabilitation/Economics (Post Exp)	BLT1	3FT deg		X		X	X	X	
Rehabilitation/Educational Studies (Post Exp)	BXT9	3FT deg		X		X	X	X	
Rehabilitation/Electronics (Post Exp)	BHT6	3FT deg		X		X	X	X	
Rehabilitation/English Studies (Post Exp)	BQT3	3FT deg		X		X	X	X	
Rehabilitation/Environmental Chemistry(Post Exp)	BFT1	3FT deg		X		X	X	X	
Rehabilitation/Environmental Policy (Post Exp)	BKT3	3FT deg		X		X	X	X	
Rehabilitation/Environmental Sciences (Post Exp)	BFTX	3FT deg		X		X	X	X	
Rehabilitation/Exercise and Health (Post Exp)	BB6T	3FT deg		X		X	X	X	
Rehabilitation/Fine Art (Post Exp)	BWT1	3FT deg		X		X	X	X	
Rehabilitation/Food Sci and Nutrition (Post Exp)	BDT4	3FT deg		X		X	X	X	
Rehabilitation/French Lang & Cont St (Post Exp)	BRTC	3FT deg		X		X	X	X	
Rehabilitation/French Lang and Lit (Post Exp)	BRT1	3FT deg		X		X	X	X	
Rehabilitation/Geography (Post Exp)	BLT8	3FT deg		X		X	X	X	
Rehabilitation/Geology (Post Exp)	BFT6	3FT deg		X		X	X	X	
Rehabilitation/Geotechnics (Post Exp)	BHT2	3FT deg		X		X	X	X	
Rehabilitation/Ger Lang & Contemp St (Post Exp)	BRTF	3FT deg		X		X	X	X	
Rehabilitation/German Language and Lit(Post Exp)	BRT2	3FT deg		X		X	X	X	
Rehabilitation/German Studies (Post Exp)	BRTG	3FT deg		X		X	X	X	
Rehabilitation/Health Care (Post Exp)	B751	3FT deg		X		X	X	X	
Rehabilitation/History (Post Exp)	BVT1	3FT deg		X		X	X	X	
Rehabilitation/History of Art (Post Exp)	BVT4	3FT deg		X		X	X	X	
Rehabilitation/Hospitality Mgt St (Post Exp)	BNT7	3FT deg		X		X	X	X	
Rehabilitation/Human Biology (Post Exp)	BB1T	3FT deg		X		X	X	X	
Rehabilitation/Information Systems	BGTM	3FT deg		X		X	X	X	
Rehabilitation/Intelligent Systems (Post Exp)	BGT8	3FT deg		X		X	X	X	
Rehabilitation/Law (Post Exp)	BMT3	3FT deg		X		X	X	X	
Rehabilitation/Leisure Planning & Mgt (Post Exp)	BKTH	3FT deg		X		X	X	X	
Rehabilitation/Marketing Management (Post Exp)	BNTN	3FT deg		X		X	X	X	
Rehabilitation/Mathematics (Post Exp)	BGT1	3FT deg		X		X	X	X	
Rehabilitation/Music (Post Exp)	BWT3	3FT deg		X		X	X	X	
Rehabilitation/Palliative Care (Post Exp)	B752	3FT deg		X		X	X	X	
Rehabilitation/Physical Geography (Post Exp)	BFTV	3FT deg		X		X	X	X	
Rehabilitation/Planning Studies (Post Exp)	BKT4	3FT deg		X		X	X	X	
Rehabilitation/Politics (Post Exp)	BMT1	3FT deg		X		X	X	X	
Rehabilitation/Psychology (Post Exp)	BCT8	3FT deg		X		X	X	X	
Rehabilitation/Publishing (Post Exp)	BPT5	3FT deg		X		X	X	X	
Renal & Urology Nursing (Post Exp)	B729	3FT deg		X		X	X	X	
School Health Nursing (Post Exp)	B719	3FT deg		X		X	X	X	
Sociology/Health Care (Post Exp)	BL73	3FT deg		X		X	X	X	
Sociology/Palliative Care (Post Exp)	BLR3	3FT deg		X		X	X	X	
Sociology/Rehabilitation (Post Exp)	BLT3	3FT deg		X		X	X	X	
Software Engineering/Health Care (Post Exp)	BG77	3FT deg		X		X	X	X	
Software Engineering/Palliative Care (Post Exp)	BGR7	3FT deg		X		X	X	X	
Software Engineering/Rehabilitation (Post Exp)	BGT7	3FT deg		X		X	X	X	
Statistics/Health Care (Post Exp)	BG74	3FT deg		X		X	X	X	

			98 expected requirements							96 entry stats	
TITLE	CODE	COURSE	SUBJECTS	A/AS	ND/C	AGNVQ	IB	SQA(H)	SQA	RATIO	A/AS
Statistics/Palliative Care (Post Exp)	BGR4	3FT deg		X		X	X	X			
Statistics/Rehabilitation (Post Exp)	BGT4	3FT deg		X		X	X	X			
Telecommunications/Health Care (Post Exp)	BH7P	3FT deg		X		X	X	X			
Telecommunications/Palliative Care	BHRP	3FT deg									
Telecommunications/Rehabilitation (Post Exp)	BHTP	3FT deg		X		X	X	X			
Tourism/Health Care (Post Exp)	BP77	3FT deg		X		X	X	X			
Tourism/Palliative Care (Post Exp)	BPR7	3FT deg		X		X	X	X			
Tourism/Rehabilitation (Post Exp)	BPT7	3FT deg		X		X	X	X			
Transport Planning/Health Care (Post Exp)	BN79	3FT deg		X		X	X	X			
Transport Planning/Palliative Care (Post Exp)	BNR9	3FT deg		X		X	X	X			
Transport Planning/Rehabilitation	BNT9	3FT deg		X		X	X	X			
Water Resources/Health Care	BH7F	3FT deg		X		X	X	X			
Water Resources/Palliative Care	BHRF	3FT deg		X		X	X	X			
Water Resources/Rehabilitation	BHTF	3FT deg		X		X	X	X			

Univ of PLYMOUTH

Community Health Care Nursing	B705	1FT deg			Ind	Ind	Ind		Ind		

QUEEN MARGARET COLL

Nursing	B740	4FT deg	B/C g	CDD	M+D	D$^ go	Ind$	BBBC$	Ind$	10	12/18

Univ of READING

Community Health St (UKCC reg+2yrs exp. req)	B705	1FT deg		X	X	Ind	X	X	X		

ROBERT GORDON Univ

Nursing	B700	4FT deg	S g	DE	N	Ind	Ind	BBC$	Ind	13	

Univ of SALFORD

Nursing - Registered Nurse (Adult)	B701	3FT deg									
Nursing-Registered Nurse (Child)	B702	3FT deg									

SHEFFIELD HALLAM Univ

Nursing Studies (Adult Care)	B701	3/4FT deg	g	CC	4M+2D	D	Ind	BBBB	Ind		
Nursing Studies (Child Care)	B702	3/4FT deg	g	CC	4M+2D	D	Ind	BBBB	Ind		
Nursing Studies (Mental Health Care)	B703	3/4FT deg	g	CC	4M+2D	D	Ind	BBBB	Ind		

Univ College of St MARTIN, LANCASTER AND CUMBRIA

Midwifery Studies	B710	3FT deg	* g	BB-CCD	3M+3D	M	28$	BBBB$			
Nursing Studies	B700	4FT deg	* g	BB-CCD	3M+3D$	M^	28$	BBBB$	Ind	5	10/22

Univ of SOUTHAMPTON

Midwifery	B710	4FT deg	* g	BCC	Ind	D^	25$	CSYS	Ind	14	20/26
Nursing: Adult Branch	B730	4FT deg	* g	BCC	Ind	D^	25$	CSYS	Ind	17	19/30
Nursing: Child Branch	B720	4FT deg	* g	BCC	Ind	D^	25$	CSYS	Ind	19	23/28

SOUTH BANK Univ

Nursing (Mental Health)	B701	3FT deg	S g	CC	6M	M go	Ind	Ind	Ind		
Nursing (Adult Health)	B700	3FT deg	S g	CC	6M	M go	Ind	Ind	Ind		
Nursing St and Soc Work St (Learn Difficulties)	BL75	3FT deg	g	CC	6M	M go	Ind	Ind	Ind		
Nursing Studies (Child Care)	B702	3FT deg	S g	CC	6M	M go	Ind	Ind	Ind		

Univ of STIRLING

Midwifery	B711	2FT deg									
Midwifery Studies	B710	1/2FT deg									
Nursing	B701	2FT dip									
Nursing & Midwifery Studies	B741	1/2FT deg									
Nursing Studies	B740	1/2FT deg									

course details			98 expected requirements							96 entry stats	
TITLE	CODE	COURSE	SUBJECTS	A/AS	NQ/C	AGNVQ	IB	SQA(H)	SQA	RATIO	A/AS
UNIVERSITY COLLEGE SUFFOLK											
Nursing	B700	3FT deg	*	DD	N $	P$	Ind	Ind	Ind		
Univ of SUNDERLAND											
Nursing (for Registered Nurses)	B700	2FT deg		X	X	X	X	X	X	4	
Univ of SURREY											
Midwifery Studies (RM)	B710	4SW deg	B+C	CCC	2M+3D		28$	BBBB	HN	7	12/24
Nursing Studies (Adult)	B740	4SW deg	B+C	CCC	2M+3D		28$	BBBB	HN	12	8/22
Nursing Studies (Child)	B742	4SW deg	B+C	CCC	2M+3D		28$	BBBB	HN	9	10/26
Nursing Studies (Mental Health)	B741	4SW deg	B+C	CCC	2M+3D		28$	BBBB	HN		
Univ of Wales SWANSEA											
Nursing	B700	3FT deg	2S g	CCC	2M+4D$	D$^ go	26$	BBBCC$	Ind	8	18/26
THAMES VALLEY Univ											
Child Health Nursing	B706	2FT dip									
Child Health Nursing	B702	3FT deg		8-12	MO	M	26	CCC			
Community Practice	B707	2FT dip									
Community Practice	B705	2FT/3FT Dip/deg		2-12	N/MO	P/M	24	CCC			
Mental Health Nursing	B704	2FT dip									
Mental Health Nursing	B703	3FT deg		8-12	MO	M	26	CCC			
Midwifery	B711	2FT dip									
Midwifery	B710	3FT deg		8-12	MO	M	26	CCC			
Midwifery Professional Studies	B715	3FT deg		8-12	MO	M	26	CCC			
Midwifery Professional Studies	B716	2FT dip									
Nursing	B701	2FT dip									
Nursing	B700	3FT deg		8-12	MO	M	26	CCC			
Professional Studies	B741	2FT dip									
Professional Studies	B740	3FT deg		8-12	MO	M	26	CCC			
Univ of ULSTER											
Nursing (including State Registration 4 Yr)	B700▼	4FT deg	B g	BBC	MO+4D	D*6/^ gi	32	ABBB	Ind	22	20/26
Univ of WALES COLL of MEDICINE											
Nursing (2 Yrs for post Dip with 1 Yr clinical)	B700	2FT/4FT deg	* g	CCC	MO+2D$	D$6/^ go	26	BBCCC	Ind	7	18/26

course details			98 expected requirements							96 entry stats
TITLE	CODE	COURSE	SUBJECTS	A/AS	ND/C	AGNVQ	IB	SQA(H)	SQA	RATIO A/AS
Univ of ABERDEEN										
Biomedical Science (Pharmacology)	B9B2	4FT deg	C+2S/C+M+S g	BBC	Ind	MS go	34$	AABB$	Ind	
Pharmacology	B200	4FT deg	C+M+S/C+2S g	CCD	Ind	MS go	24$	BBBC$	Ind	7
ANGLIA Poly Univ										
Environmental Toxicology	BF29▼	3FT deg	B	10	3M	P	Dip$	BCCC	N	
ASTON Univ										
Pharmacy (MPharm)	B300	4FT deg	C+S/M g	22	HN	X	32$	ABBBB$	Ind	11 22/28
Pharmacy (Year Zero)	B308	5FT deg								
BARNSLEY COLL										
Science Foundation *Neuroscience*	Y100	4EXT deg								
Science Foundation *Pharmacology*	Y100	4EXT deg								
Univ of BATH										
Pharmacology	B200	3FT deg	C+M/B	20	Ind	Ind	30$	Ind	Ind	72
Pharmacology	B201	4SW deg	C+M/B	20	Ind	Ind	30$	Ind	Ind	7 20/28
Pharmacy (MPharm)	B300	4FT deg	C+M/P/B	22	Ind	Ind	30$	Ind	Ind	10 22/30
Univ of BRADFORD										
Chemistry with Pharmaceutical & Foren Sc (MChem)	F1BG	4FT deg	C+S g	BBB			Ind	Ind	Ind	
Chemistry with Pharmaceutical & Forensic Science	F1BF	4SW deg	C+S g	BCC	3M+5D$	DS^	Ind	Ind	Ind	
Chemistry with Pharmaceutical & Forensic Science	F1B2	3FT deg	C+S g	BCC	3M+5D$	DS^	Ind	Ind	Ind	5 12/26
Pharmaceutical Management	B2N1	3FT deg	S g	CCD	5M $	MS4/^	Ind	Ind	Ind	2 12/18
Pharmacology	B200	3FT deg	2S g	BB-CCD	3M $	MS4	Ind	Ind	$	7 10/18
Pharmacy	B300	4FT deg	C+2S g	BB-BCC	Ind	MS^	Ind	Ind	Ind	6 16/26
Pharmacy	B301	5SW deg	C+2S g	BB-BCC	Ind	MS^	Ind	Ind	Ind	6 18/26
Univ of BRIGHTON										
Pharmacy (MPharm)	B300	4FT deg	C+2S g	20-24	DO $	Ind^ go	28$	BBBB$	N$	
Univ of BRISTOL										
Pharmacology	B200	3FT deg	2S g	BCC	Ind	D$^	28$	BBBBB	Ind	12 18/30
BRISTOL, Univ of the W of England										
Applied Physiology and Pharmacology	BB12	4SW deg	B+C g	12	4M $	MS go	24$	BCC$	Ind	
CAMBRIDGE Univ										
Natural Sciences *Pharmacology*	Y160▼	3FT deg	2(S/M)	AAA-AAB	Ind		Ind	CSYS	Ind	
CARDIFF Univ of Wales										
Pharmacology	B200	3FT deg	C g	BCC	5M $		Ind	Ind		7 18/24
Pharmacy (4 Yr)	B301	4FT deg	C+B g	24			Ind	AAABB$		
Preliminary Year *Pharmacology*	Y101	4FT deg	*		Ind		Ind	Ind	Ind	
Preliminary Year *Pharmacy*	Y101	5FT deg	*		Ind		Ind	Ind	Ind	
Univ of CENTRAL LANCASHIRE										
Herbal Medicine	B250	3FT/4SW deg	S g	16	MO+3D	M$6/^	28	BBBC	Ind	
Homeopathic Medicine	B251	3FT/4SW deg	S g	16	MO+3D	M$6/^	28	BBBC	Ind	
Physiology/Pharmacology	BB12	3FT deg	C+S	DDD	MO $	MS6/^	26$	BBCC	$	

Pharmacy and Pharmacology 58

course details			98 expected requirements							96 entry stats
TITLE	CODE	COURSE	SUBJECTS	A/AS	ND/C	AGNVQ	IB	SQA(H)	SQA	RATIO A/AS
COVENTRY Univ										
Pharmaceutical Sciences	B300	3FT deg	B g	10	Ind	Ind	Ind	Ind	Ind	
Pharmaceutical Sciences	B301	3FT deg	B g	10	3M	Ind	Ind	Ind	Ind	
Pharmaceutical Sciences with Study in Europe	B303	3FT deg								
Pharmaceutical Sciences with Study in Europe	B302	3FT deg	B g	10	3M	Ind	Ind	Ind	Ind	
DE MONTFORT Univ										
Pharmaceutical and Cosmetic Sciences	B301▼	4SW deg	C+S/M g	10-12	MO	M$	Ind	BBBB	Ind	4 7/20
Pharmacy	B300▼	4FT deg	C+2(M/B/P) g	18-22	HN $	DS^ go	Ind	CSYS	HN$	10 16/26
Univ of DUNDEE										
Biochemistry and Pharmacology	BC27	4FT deg	C+S/2S g	16	5M $	M$	25$	BBBC$	N$	5
Chemistry and Pharmacology	FB12	4FT deg	C+S/2S g	16	5M $	M$	25$	BBBC$	N$	24
Pharmacology	B200	4FT deg	C+S/2S g	16	5M $	M$	25$	BBBC$	N$	7 12/18
Pharmacology and Physiological Sciences	BB21	4FT deg	C+S/2S g	16	5M $	M$	25$	BBBC$	N$	8
Univ of EAST LONDON										
Pharmacology	B200	4SW deg	* g	12	MO	MS	Ind	Ind	Ind	3 4/14
Extended Science — Pharmacology	Y108	4FT deg	* g	8-10	MO	M	Ind	Ind	Ind	
Univ of EDINBURGH										
Pharmacology	B200	4FT deg	C+2(B/M/P) g	BBC	MO $		Dip$	BBBB$	N$	10 18/30
Univ of GLASGOW										
Pharmacology	B200	4FT deg	C/M+S	BBC-CCC N		M	24$	BBBB$	N	8
Pharmacology (with work placement)	B201	4FT deg	C/M+S	BBC-CCC N		M	24$	BBBB$	N	
Univ of GREENWICH										
Pharmaceutical Sciences	B302	3FT/4SW deg	B+C g	10	3M	MS	Dip	BCC	Ind	
Pharmaceutical Sciences with European Study	B301	4SW deg	C+B g	12	Ind	Ind	Dip	BCC	Ind	
Pharmaceutical Sciences with Law	B3M3	3FT deg	B+C g	12	M+D	M	Dip	Ind	Ind	
Pharmaceutical Sciences	203B▼	2FT HND	S	4	N	S				
Univ of HERTFORDSHIRE										
Pharmaceutical Sci's w.deferred ch.of specialism	B304	4FT/4SW deg	C	8-12	4M $	Ind	Ind	Ind	Ind	
Pharmaceutical Sciences	B301	3FT/4SW deg	C	8-12	4M $	Ind	Ind	Ind	Ind	
Pharmaceutical Sciences (Extended)	B308▼	4FT deg								
Pharmaceutical Sciences with a year in Europe	B302	4FT/4SW deg	C	8-12	4M $	Ind	Ind	Ind	Ind	
Pharmaceutical Sciences with yr in North America	B303	4FT/4SW deg	C	8-12	4M $	Ind	Ind	Ind	Ind	
Pharmacology	C1B2	3FT/4SW deg	2S g	14-16	4M $	Ind	24	BCCC	Ind	7 10/14
Pharmacology with a year in Europe	B201	4FT deg	2S g	14-16	4M $	Ind	24	BCCC	Ind	
Pharmacology with a year in North America	B202	4FT deg	2S g	14-16	4M $	Ind	24	BCCC	Ind	
Applied Biology (Pharmacology)	2B1C	2FT HND	B+C g	4-6	N	Ind	Ind	Ind	N	5
KING'S COLL LONDON (Univ of London)										
Biochemistry and Pharmacology	BC27	3FT deg	C+B/M/P	BBC	5M	M	Ind	BCCCC	Ind	5 18/24
Master of Pharmacy	B300	4FT deg	C	BCC			Ind	BCCCC	Ind	14 17/26
Pharmacology	B200	3FT/4SW deg	C+B/M/P	BCC	Ind	Ind	28$	BCCCC$	Ind	13 16/26
Pharmacology with Management	B2N1	4SW deg	C+B/M/P	ABB	X	X	Ind	AAABB	X	14
Pharmacology with Studies in Europe	B203	4SW deg	C+B/M/P g	BCC-CCC	Ind	Ind	28$	BCCC$	Ind	4
Pharmacology with Toxicology	B220	4SW deg	C+B/M/P	BCC-CCC	Ind	DS4^ go	28$	BCCC$	Ind	7 18/24
Physiology and Pharmacology	BB12	3FT/4SW deg	C+S	BCC	MO+3D	MS^	Ind	BCCCC	Ind	3 16/30

 Letts STUDY GUIDES ❤ THE INDEPENDENT

course details			98 expected requirements							96 entry stats	
TITLE	CODE	COURSE	SUBJECTS	A/AS	NO/C	AGNVQ	IB	SQA(H)	SQA	RATIO	A/AS
KINGSTON Univ											
Pharmaceutical Science	BB23	3FT deg	C/B	8	3M $	M	Ind	CCC	Ind	2	4/ 6
Pharmaceutical Science	BB2H	4SW deg	C/B	8	3M $	M	Ind	CCC	Ind	1	4/16
Pharmaceutical Science	BB2J▼	4EXT/5EXTSW deg	*		Ind		Ind	Ind	Ind	3	
Pharmaceutical Science	32BB	2FT HND									
Univ of LEEDS											
Biochemistry-Pharmacology	CB72	3FT/4FT deg	C+P/M/B g	BCC	1M+5D$	Ind	28$	BBBBC	Ind	7	
Chemistry-Pharmacology	BF21	3FT/4FT deg	C+B/M/P g	BCC	2M+5D$	Ind	28$	BBBBC	Ind	19	
Management Studies-Pharmacology	BN21	3FT deg	2(B/C/M/P) g	BCC	2M+5D	Ind	28$	BBBBC	Ind	3	20/24
Pharmacology	B200	3FT/4FT deg	2(B/C/M/P) g	18	1M+4D$	Ind	26$	BBCCC	Ind	5	16/26
Pharmacology-Physiology	BB12	3FT deg	C+M/P/B	BCC	1M+5D$	Ind	28$	BBBBC	Ind	6	20/22
Univ of LIVERPOOL											
Chemistry with Pharmacology	F1B2	3FT deg	C+S g	20	MO $	Ind	31$	BBBCC$	Ind	6	12/26
Chemistry with Pharmacology (MChem)	F1BF	4FT deg	C+S g	20	MO $	Ind	31$	BBBCC$	Ind	5	
Pharmacology	B200	3FT deg	C+M/P/B g	18	MO $	DS^ go	31$	BBBCC$	Ind	10	14/26
BSc Combined Honours *Pharmacology*	Y100	3FT deg	C	18	MO $	Ind	31$	BBBCC$	Ind		
LIVERPOOL JOHN MOORES Univ											
Pharmacy (MPharm)	B301	4FT deg	C+2S	BCC	DO	D^				15	18/26
LUTON Univ											
Biotechnology with Pharmacology	J8B2	3FT deg	g	12-16	MO/DO	M/D	32	BBCC	Ind		
Health Science with Pharmacology	B9B2	3FT deg	g	12-16	MO/DO	M/D	32	BBCC	Ind		
Health Studies with Pharmacology	B9BF	3FT deg	g	12-16	MO/DO	M/D	32	BBCC	Ind		
Law with Pharmacology	M3B2	3FT deg	g	12-16	MO/DO	M/D	32	BBCC	Ind		
Pharmacology and Biology	BC21	3FT deg		12-16	MO/DO	M/D	32	BBCC			
Pharmacology and Biotechnology	BJ28	3FT deg	g	12-16	MO/DO	M/D	32	BBCC			
Pharmacology and Health Science	BB29	3FT deg	g	12-16	MO/DO	M/D	32	BBCC			
Pharmacology and Health Studies	BB2X	3FT deg	g	12-16	MO/DO	M/D	32	BBCC	Ind		
Pharmacology and Human Biology	BB21	3FT deg									
Pharmacology and Law	BM23	3FT deg	g	12-16	MO/DO	M/D	32	BBCC			
Psychology and Pharmacology	BL27	3FT deg	g	12-16	MO/DO	M/D	32	BBCC			
Psychology with Pharmacology	L7B2	3FT deg	g	12-16	MO/DO	M/D	32	BBCC	Ind		
Univ of MANCHESTER											
Chemistry with Medicinal Chemistry	F1B3	3FT deg	C+B	BCC	3M+2D$		30$	CSYS	Ind	3	12/22
Pharmaceutical Sciences	B301	3FT deg	C+2(M/P/S) g	BBC	HN $	X		CSYS	HN		
Pharmacology	B200	3FT deg	C	BCC	2M+4D$	D^	28$	BBBBC	Ind	32	22/26
Pharmacology and Physiology	BB12	3FT deg	C	BCC	2M+4D$	D^	28$	BBBBC	Ind	19	
Pharmacology and Physiology with Ind Exp	BB1F	4SW deg	C	BCC	2M+4D$	D^	28$	BBBBC	Ind		
Pharmacology with Industrial Experience	B201	4SW deg	C	BCC	2M+4D$	D^	28$	BBBBC	Ind	14	20/28
Pharmacology with a Modern Language	B202	4FT deg	C+L	BCC	2M+4D$	D^	28$	BBBBC	Ind		
Pharmacy	B300	4FT deg	C+2(M/P/S) g	BBC	HN $	X	X	CSYS$	HN	11	20/28
MIDDLESEX Univ											
Herbal Medicine	B250▼	3FT/4SW deg	* g	12-16	5M	M$ go	28	BBCC	Ind		
Traditional Chinese Medicine	BT23	3FT deg	S g	18-24	3D	D$ go	28	Ind	Ind		
NAPIER Univ											
Toxicology	B220	3FT/4FT/5SW deg	B/C	DD				BBC			
Univ of NEWCASTLE											
Pharmacology	B200	3FT deg									

course details			98 expected requirements							96 entry stats
TITLE	CODE	COURSE	SUBJECTS	A/AS	NO/C	RGNVQ	IB	SQA(H)	SQA	RATIO A/AS
NESCOT										
Pharmacology	B200	3FT deg	S	EE	N	M	Dip	Ind	N$	9
Pharmacology	B208	4FT deg	*							2
Univ of NOTTINGHAM										
Pharmacy (MPharm Honours)	B300	4FT deg	C+M/P/B g	ABB	X			32$	CSYS$	X	9	26/30
NOTTINGHAM TRENT Univ										
Physiology and Pharmacology	BB12	4SW deg	S g	DDE	Ind	Ind	Dip	C	$	5	8/16
Univ of PORTSMOUTH										
Pharmacological Sciences	BB23	3FT deg	C+S	12	4M $	M$6/^	Dip	CCCCC	Ind	
Pharmacology	B200	3FT deg	C+S	12	4M $	M$6/^	Dip	CCCCC	Ind	4	7/14
Pharmacology	B208▼	4EXT deg	*	Ind	Ind	Ind	Ind	Ind	Ind	7
Pharmacy (MPharm)	B300	4FT deg	C+B+S g	BCC	3M+2D	DS^ go	30$	CSYS	Ind	8	16/24
QUEEN'S Univ Belfast										
Pharmacy (4 years)	B300	4FT deg	C+2(P/B/M) g	ABB	X	X	32$	X	X	4	24/30
ROBERT GORDON Univ										
Pharmaceutical Sciences	B302	3FT deg	C+2S g	CCC	Ind	Ind	Ind	BBCC$	Ind	
Pharmacy	B301	4FT deg	C+2S g	BBC	Ind	Ind	Ind	BBBB$	Ind	9
Univ of SALFORD										
Complementary Medicine and Health Sciences	B250	3FT deg								
SCHOOL of PHARMACY (Univ of London)										
Pharmacy (MPharm) (4 Yrs)	B300	4FT deg	C+M/B/P g	BBB	HN	X	$	BBBCC	X	14	18/28
Toxicology and Pharmacology (4 Yrs)	B220	4SW deg	C+M/B/P g	BCC	HN	X	$	BBBCC	X	9	20/28
Univ of SHEFFIELD										
Pharmacology	B200	3FT deg	C+S g	BCC	6M $	D^	29$	BBBB$	Ind	9	20/28
Pharmacology Foundation Year (4 Yrs)	B201	4FT deg	g	BCC	6M	D^	29	BBBB	Ind	6
Physiology and Pharmacology	BB12	3FT/4EXT deg	S+C g	20	4M+2D	DS6/^	30$	BBBB$	Ind	6	18/28
Univ of SOUTHAMPTON										
Biochemistry and Pharmacology	CB72	3FT/4SW deg	C+B/P/M/Gy g	BCC	$	M^	$	Ind	Ind	6
Biochemistry and Physiology with Foundation Year	CB7F	4FT deg								
Biochemistry with Pharmacology	C7B2	3FT/4SW deg	C+B/P/M/Gy g	BCC	$	M^	$	Ind	Ind	5
Chemistry with Pharmacology	F1B2	3FT deg	C+S g	18	Ind	Ind	28$	CSYS	Ind	13
Pharmacology	B200	3FT/4SW deg	C+B/P/M/Gy g	BCC	$	M^	$	Ind	Ind	6	16/26
Physiology and Pharmacology	BB12	3FT/4SW deg	C+B/P/M g	BCC	$	M^	$	Ind	Ind	5	18/22
Physiology with Pharmacology	B1B2	3FT/4SW deg	C+B/P/M/Gy g	BCC	$	M^	$	Ind	Ind	4
Univ of ST ANDREWS										
Chemistry with Pharmacology	F1B2	3FT/4FT deg	C g	CCC	Ind	Ind	28$	BBBC$	Ind	21
Univ of STRATHCLYDE										
Biochemistry and Pharmacology	CB72	4FT deg	C+B+M/P g	CCC	HN		Ind	BBC$	HN	
Immunology and Pharmacology	CB92	4FT deg	C+B+M/P g	CCC	Ind		Ind	BBC$	Ind	
Pharmacy	B300	4FT deg	C+M/P/B	BBC	HN		Ind	BBBB$	Ind	
Univ of SUNDERLAND										
Chemical and Pharmaceutical Science	FB13▼	3FT/4SW deg	C g	12	MO $	MS	24$	CCCCC$	N$	3	8/17
Chemical and Pharmaceutical Science (Foundation)	FBC3▼	4EXT/5EXTSW deg	*							3
Pharmacology	B200	3FT/4SW deg	C+S g	CC	5M $	MS	24$	CCCC$	N$	5	6/18
Pharmacology (Foundation)	B208▼	4EXT/5EXTSW deg	*							2
Pharmacology and Biocomputing	BG25	3FT/4SW deg	C+S	8	N $	PS	24$	CCCC$	N$	

Letts STUDY GUIDES
THE INDEPENDENT

course details			98 expected requirements							96 entry stats	
TITLE	CODE	COURSE	SUBJECTS	A/AS	ND/C	AGNVQ	IB	SQA(H)	SQA	RATIO	A/AS
Pharmacology and Business Studies	BN21	3FT/4SW deg	C+S	8	N $	PS	24$	CCCC$	N$		
Pharmacology and Physiology	BB12	3FT/4SW deg	2S	8	N$	PS	24$	CCCC$	N$		
Pharmacy	B300	4FT deg	C+2S g	BBC-BCC	2M+3D$	DS^	32$	BBBB$	Ind$	9	18/26
UNIVERSITY COLL LONDON (Univ of London)											
Pharmacology	B200	3FT deg	C+B/M/P g	BCC	MO+2D$	Ind	32$	Ind	Ind	9	16/28
Physiology and Pharmacology	BB12	3FT deg	C+B/M/P g	BCC	MO+2D$	Ind	32$	Ind	Ind	3	16/26
Univ of WESTMINSTER											
Health Sciences: Complementary Therapies	B255	3FT deg									
Univ of WOLVERHAMPTON											
Biochemistry with Pharmacology	C7B2	3FT/4SW deg	C g	DD	N	M	24	CCCC	Ind		
Applied Sciences *Pharmacology*	Y100	3FT/4SW deg	C g	DD	N	M	24	CCCC	Ind		
Applied Sciences (4 Yr) *Pharmacology*	Y110	4FT deg	*								
Combined Degrees *Pharmacology*	Y401	3FT/4SW deg	C g	DD	N	M	24	CCCC	Ind		
Physiology & Pharmacology	21BB	2FT HND	S g	D	N	M	24	CCCC	Ind	5	2/6

course details			98 expected requirements							96 entry stats	
TITLE	CODE	COURSE	SUBJECTS	A/AS	ND/C	AGNVQ	IB	SQA(H)	SQA	RATIO A/AS	
Univ of ABERDEEN											
Accountancy-Philosophy	NV47	4FT deg	* g	BBC	Ind	M$ go	30$	BBBB$	Ind		
Celtic Civilisation-Philosophy	QV57	4FT deg	* g	BBC	Ind	M$ go	30$	BBBB$	Ind		
Cultural History	V900	4FT deg	* g	BBC	Ind	M$ go	30$	BBBB$	Ind	1	
Cultural History with Film Studies	V9W5	4FT deg	* g	BBC	Ind	M$ go	30$	BBBB$	Ind		
Cultural History with History of Religions	V9V8	4FT deg	* g	BBC	Ind	M$ go	30$	BBBB$	Ind	2	
Cultural History with Sociology	V9L3	4FT deg	* g	BBC	Ind	M$ go	30$	BBBB$	Ind		
Cultural History with Women's Studies	V9M9	4FT deg	* g	BBC	Ind	M$ go	30$	BBBB$	Ind		
Economics-Philosophy	LV17	4FT deg	* g	BBC	Ind	M$ go	30$	BBBB$	Ind	6	
English-Philosophy	QV37	4FT deg	* g	BBC	Ind	M$ go	30$	BBBB$	Ind	4	
French-Philosophy	RV17	4FT/5FT deg	* g	BBC	Ind	M$ go	30$	BBBB$	Ind	8	
French-Philosophy (4 Yrs)	VR71	4FT deg	* g	BBC	Ind	M$ go	30$	BBBB$	Ind		
German-Philosophy	RV27	4FT/5FT deg	* g	BBC	Ind	M$ go	30$	BBBB$	Ind		
German-Philosophy (4 Yrs)	VR72	4FT deg	* g	BBC	Ind	M$ go	30$	BBBB$	Ind		
Hispanic Studies-Philosophy	RV47	5FT deg	* g	BBC	Ind	M$ go	30$	BBBB$	Ind		
Hispanic Studies-Philosophy (4 Yrs)	VR74	4FT deg	* g	BBC	Ind	M$ go	30$	BBBB$	Ind		
History of Art-Philosophy	VV47	4FT deg	* g	BBC	Ind	M$ go	30$	BBBB$	Ind		
History-Philosophy	VV17	4FT deg	* g	BBC	Ind	M$ go	30$	BBBB$	Ind	8	
Mathematics-Philosophy	GV17	4FT deg	M g	BBC	Ind	M$ go	30$	BBBB$	Ind	10	
Mental Philosophy	V700	4FT deg	* g	BBC	Ind	M$ go	30$	BBBB$	Ind	3	
Philosophy with Film Studies	V7W5	4FT deg	* g	BBC	Ind	M$ go	30$	BBBB$	Ind	4	
Philosophy with Women's Studies	V7M9	4FT deg	* g	BBC	Ind	M$ go	30$	BBBB$	Ind		
Philosophy-International Relations	VM7C	4FT deg	* g	BBC	Ind	M$ go	30$	BBBB$	Ind	4	
Philosophy-Jurisprudence	VM7H	4FT deg	* g	BBC	Ind	M$ go	30$	BBBB$	Ind		
Philosophy-Management Studies	VN71	4FT deg	* g	BBC	Ind	M$ go	30$	BBBB$	Ind		
Philosophy-Physics	VF73	4FT deg	* g	BBC	Ind	M$ go	30$	BBBB$	Ind		
Philosophy-Politics	VM71	4FT deg	* g	BBC	Ind	M$ go	30$	BBBB$	Ind	4	
Philosophy-Psychology	VC78	4FT deg	* g	BBC	Ind	M$ go	30$	BBBB$	Ind	9	
Philosophy-Religious Studies	VV78	4FT deg	* g	BBC	Ind	M$ go	30$	BBBB$	Ind		
Philosophy-Social Research	LV37	4FT deg	* g	BBC	Ind	M$ go	30$	BBBB$	Ind		
Philosophy-Sociology	VL73	4FT deg	* g	BBC	Ind	M$ go	30$	BBBB$	Ind	7	
Physics with Philosophy	F3V7	4FT deg	2S+M g	CCD	Ind	MS go	24$	BBBC$	Ind		
Sociology with Cultural History	L3V9	4FT deg	* g	BBC	Ind	M$ go	24$	BBBC$	Ind		
ANGLIA Poly Univ											
Art History and European Philosophy & Literature	VV47▼	3FT deg	*	14	6M	M+/^	Dip	BBCC	Ind	6	
Business and European Philosophy and Literature	NV17▼	3FT deg	* g	12	4M	M+/^ go	Dip	BCCC	Ind		
Communication Studs & European Philosophy & Lit	PV37▼	3FT deg	Ap	14	6M	M+/^	Dip$	BBCC	Ind	2	
English Language Studies and Euro Phil. & Lit.	QV17▼	3FT deg	* g	12	4M	M go	Dip	BCCC			
English and European Philosophy and Literature	QV37▼	3FT deg	* g	12	4M	M+/^	Dip	BCCC	Ind	4	10/16
European Philosophy & Lit and Women's Studies	VM79▼	3FT deg	*	12	4M	M	Dip	BCCC	Ind		
European Philosophy & Lit&Maths or Stats/St Mod.	GV17▼	3FT deg	*	12	4M	M+/^	Dip	BCCC	Ind		
European Philosophy & Literature & Graphic Arts	VW72▼	3FT deg	A	14	6M	M+/^	Dip$	BBCC	Ind		
European Philosophy & Literature & Social Policy	VL74▼	3FT deg	*	12	4M	M+/^	Dip	BCCC	Ind	3	
European Philosophy & Literature and French	RV17▼	4FT deg	* g	12	4M	M+/^ go	Dip	BCCC	Ind	6	
European Philosophy & Literature and Geography	VL78▼	3FT deg	Gy g	12	4M	M+/^ go	Dip$	BCCC	Ind		
European Philosophy & Literature and German	RV27▼	4FT deg	* g	12	4M	M+/^ go	Dip	BCCC	Ind		
European Philosophy & Literature and History	VV17▼	3FT deg	*	12	4M	M+/^	Dip	BCCC	Ind	6	
European Philosophy & Literature and Italian	RV37▼	4FT deg	* g	12	4M	M+/^ go	Dip	BCCC	Ind		
European Philosophy & Literature and Law	MV37▼	3FT deg	*	14	6M	M	Dip	BBCC	Ind	1	
European Philosophy & Literature and Music	VW73▼	3FT deg	Mu	12	4M	M+/^	Dip$	BCCC	Ind	1	
European Philosophy & Literature and Politics	VM71▼	3FT deg	*	14	6M	M+/^	Dip	BBCC	Ind		
European Philosophy & Literature and Sociology	LV37▼	3FT deg	*	12	4M	M+/^	Dip	BCCC	Ind	3	

| | | | 98 expected requirements | | | | | | | 96 entry stats | |
| course details | | | | | | | | | | | |
TITLE	CODE	COURSE	SUBJECTS	A/AS	NO/C	RGNVQ	IB	SQA(H)	SQA	RATIO	A/AS
European Philosophy & Literature and Spanish	RV47▼	4FT deg	* g	12	4M	M+/^ go	Dip	BCCC	Ind	3	
European Philosophy and Literature	V700▼	3FT deg	*	12	4M	M+/^	Dip	BCCC	Ind	2	
European Philosophy and Literature & Psychology	CV87▼	3FT deg	S g	16	8M	D go	Dip$	BBCCC	Ind	2	

Univ of BIRMINGHAM

TITLE	CODE	COURSE	SUBJECTS	A/AS	NO/C	RGNVQ	IB	SQA(H)	SQA	RATIO	A/AS
Ancient History & Archaeology/Philosophy	VV67	3FT deg	*	BBB	Ind	D*^	32	ABBB	Ind		
Artificial Intelligence/Philosophy	GV87	3FT deg	* g	BBB	Ind	D*^	32	ABBB	Ind		
Classical Literature and Civilisation/Philosophy	QV87	3FT deg	*	BBB	Ind	D*^	32	ABBB	Ind		
Computer Studies/Philosophy	GV57	3FT deg	* g	BBB	Ind	D*^	32	ABBB	Ind		
East Mediterranean History/Philosophy	VVD7	3FT deg	* g	BBB	Ind	D*^	32	ABBB	Ind		
English/Philosophy	QV37	3FT deg	*	ABB	Ind	D*^	32	ABBB	Ind	18	24/28
French Studies/Philosophy	RV17	4FT deg	F	BBB	Ind	D*^	32$	ABBB	Ind		
German Studies/Philosophy	RV27	4FT deg	G	BBB	Ind	D*^	32$	ABBB	Ind		
Hispanic Studies/Philosophy	RV47	4FT deg	*	BBB	Ind	D*^	32	ABBB	Ind		
History of Art/Philosophy	VV47	3FT deg	*	BBB	Ind	D*^	32	ABBB	Ind	18	
History/Philosophy	VV17	3FT deg	*	BBB	Ind	D*^	32	ABBB	Ind	7	26/30
Italian/Philosophy	RV37	4FT deg	*	BBB	Ind	D*^	32	ABBB	Ind		
Latin/Philosophy	QV67	3FT deg	Ln	BBB	Ind	D*^	32$	ABBB	Ind		
Mathematics/Philosophy	GV17	3FT deg	M	ABB-ABC	Ind	D*^	32$	ABBB	Ind	12	
Media & Cultural Studies/Philosophy	PV47	3FT deg	*	BBB	Ind	D*^	32	ABBB	Ind	84	
Modern Greek Studies/Philosophy	TV27	4FT deg	* g	BBB	Ind	D*^	32	ABBB	Ind		
Music/Philosophy	VW73	3FT deg	Mu	AAB-ABB	Ind	D*^	32$	ABBB	Ind	7	
Philosophy	V700	3FT deg	*	BBB-BBC	Ind	D*^	32	ABBB	Ind	5	18/28
Philosophy and Political Science	VM71	3FT deg	*	BBC	Ind	D+^	32	ABBBB	Ind	6	22/27
Philosophy and Sociology	VL73	3FT deg	*	BBC	Ind	D+^	32	ABBBB	Ind	19	
Philosophy/Portuguese	RV57	4FT deg	*	BBB	Ind	D*^	32	ABBB	Ind		
Philosophy/Russian	RV87	4FT deg	*	BBB	Ind	D*^	32	ABBB	Ind	4	
Philosophy/Sport & Recreation Studies	VB76	3FT deg	*	BBB	Ind	D*^	32	ABBB	Ind		
Philosophy/Theology	VV78	3FT deg	*	BBB	Ind	D*^	32	ABBB	Ind	21	

BOLTON INST

TITLE	CODE	COURSE	SUBJECTS	A/AS	NO/C	RGNVQ	IB	SQA(H)	SQA	RATIO	A/AS
Accountancy and Philosophy	NV47	3FT deg	* g	CD	MO	M*	24	BBCC	Ind		
Art & Design History and Philosophy	VV74	3FT deg	* g	CD	MO	M*	24	BBCC	Ind		
Biology and Philosophy	CV17	3FT deg	* g	CD	MO	M*	24	BBCC	Ind		
Business Economics and Philosophy	LV17	3FT deg	* g	CD	MO	M*	24	BBCC	Ind		
Business Information Systems and Philosophy	GV5R	3FT deg	* g	CD	MO	M*	24	BBCC	Ind		
Business Studies and Philosophy	NV17	3FT deg	* g	CD	MO	M*	24	BBCC	Ind		
Community Studies and Philosophy	LV57	3FT deg	* g	CD	MO	M*	24	BBCC	Ind		
Computing and Philosophy	GV57	3FT deg	* g	CD	MO	M*	24	BBCC	Ind		
Creative Writing and Philosophy	WV97	3FT deg	* g	CD	MO	M*	24	BBCC	Ind		
Design and Philosophy	VW72	3FT deg	* g	CD	MO	M*	24	BBCC	Ind		
Environmental Studies and Philosophy	FV97	3FT deg	* g	CD	MO	M*	24	BBCC	Ind		
European Cultural Studies and Philosophy	TV27	3FT deg	* g	CD	MO	M*	24	BBCC	Ind		
Film and TV Studies and Philosophy	WV57	3FT deg	Me/T g	CD	Ind	Ind	24	BBCC	Ind		
French and Philosophy	RV17	3FT deg	F g	CD	Ind	Ind	24	BBCC	Ind		
Gender & Women's Studies and Philosophy	MV9R	3FT deg	* g	CD	MO	M*	24	BBCC	Ind		
German and Philosophy	RV27	3FT deg	G g	CD	Ind	Ind	24	BBCC	Ind		
History and Organisations, Management & Work	NVD7	3FT deg	* g	CD	MO	M*	24	BBCC	Ind		
History and Philosophy	VV17	3FT deg	* g	CD	MO	M*	24	BBCC	Ind		
Human Resource Management and Philosophy	NV1R	3FT deg	* g	CD	MO	M*	24	BBCC	Ind		
Language Studies and Philosophy	QV17	3FT deg	* g	CD	MO	M*	24	BBCC	Ind		
Law and Philosophy	MV37	3FT deg	* g	CD	MO	M g	24	BBCC	Ind		
Leisure Studies and Philosophy	LV37	3FT deg	* g	CD	MO	M*	24	BBCC	Ind		

Philosophy 59

TITLE	CODE	COURSE	SUBJECTS	A/AS	NO/C	AGNVQ	IB	SQA(H)	SQA	RATIO	A/AS
Literature and Philosophy	QV27	3FT deg	* g	CD	MO	M g	24	BBCC	Ind		
Marketing and Philosophy	VN75	3FT deg	* g	CD	MO	M	24	BBCC	Ind		
Mathematics and Philosophy	GV17	3FT deg	M g	DD	Ind	Ind	24	BBCC	Ind		
Operations Management and Philosophy	NV27	3FT deg	* g	CD	MO	M*	24	BBCC	Ind		
Organisations, Management & Work and Philosophy	NV77	3FT deg	* g	CD	Ind	Ind	24	BBCC	Ind		
Philosophy	V700	3FT deg	* g	CD	MO	M*	24	BBCC	Ind		
Philosophy and Peace & War Studies	VVC7	3FT deg	* g	CD	MO	M*	24	BBCC	Ind		
Philosophy and Psychology	LV77	3FT deg	* g	12	MO	D*	24	BBCC	Ind		
Philosophy and Sociology	LV3R	3FT deg	* g	CD	MO	M g	24	Ind	Ind		
Philosophy and Theatre Studies	WV47	3FT deg	Me/T g	CD	Ind	Ind	24	BBCC	Ind		
Philosophy and Tourism Studies	PV77	3FT deg	* g	CD	MO	M*	24	BBCC	Ind		
Philosophy and Urban and Cultural Studies	VL73	3FT deg	* g	CD	MO	M*	24	BBCC	Ind		
Visual Arts and Philosophy	VW71	3FT deg	* g	10	MO	M*	24	BBCC	Ind		

Univ of BRADFORD

TITLE	CODE	COURSE	SUBJECTS	A/AS	NO/C	AGNVQ	IB	SQA(H)	SQA	RATIO	A/AS
Philosophy	V700	3FT deg	* g	BB-CCC	4M+3D	D*^	Ind	Ind	Ind	8	
Interdisciplinary Human Studies Philosophy	Y402	3FT deg	* g	BB-CCC	4M+3D	D*^	Ind	Ind	Ind		

Univ of BRIGHTON

TITLE	CODE	COURSE	SUBJECTS	A/AS	NO/C	AGNVQ	IB	SQA(H)	SQA	RATIO	A/AS
Humanities Philosophy	Y300	3FT deg	*	CC	Ind	Ind	Ind	Ind	Ind		

Univ of BRISTOL

TITLE	CODE	COURSE	SUBJECTS	A/AS	NO/C	AGNVQ	IB	SQA(H)	SQA	RATIO	A/AS
English and Philosophy	QV37	3FT deg	El g	AAB-ABB	Ind	D$^	33$	AAABB	Ind	20	20/30
Greek and Philosophy	QV77	3FT deg	L	BBC	Ind	D$^	30$	BBBBB	Ind		
Philosophy	V700	3FT deg	*	AAB-BBC	Ind	D$^	30$	BBBBB	Ind	11	24/30
Philosophy and Economics	VL71	3FT deg	* g	ABC	Ind	D$^	32$	CSYS	Ind	9	26/30
Philosophy and French	RV17	4FT deg	F g	BBB	Ind	D$^	30$	CSYS	Ind	20	
Philosophy and German	RV27	4FT deg	G	BBB	Ind	D$^	30$	BBBBB	Ind	3	
Philosophy and Italian	RV37	4FT deg	I/L	BBC	Ind	D$^	30$	BBBBB	Ind		
Philosophy and Mathematics	VG71	3FT deg	M	ABC	Ind	D$^	32$	CSYS	Ind	6	24/28
Philosophy and Politics	VM71	3FT deg	* g	ABB	Ind	D$^	32$	AAABB	Ind	24	28/30
Philosophy and Psychology	VL77	3FT deg	* g	AAB-BBC	Ind	D$^	30$	AAABB	Ind	50	
Philosophy and Russian	RV87	4FT deg	L	BB	Ind	D$^	30$	ABBBB	Ind		
Philosophy and Spanish	RV47	4FT deg	L	BBB-BBC	Ind	D$^	30$	ABBBB	Ind	15	
Philosophy and Theology	VV78	3FT deg	*	BBC	Ind	D$^	30$	BBBBB	Ind	25	
Physics and Philosophy	FV37	3FT deg	P+M	BCC	Ind	D$^	26$	CSYS	Ind	5	22/30
Physics and Philosophy with Study in Cont Europe	VF73	4FT deg	P+ML g	BBC	Ind	D$^	26$	CSYS	Ind	3	
Sociology and Philosophy	LV37	3FT deg	* g	ABB-BBC	Ind	D$^	30$	BBBBB	Ind	8	

BRUNEL Univ, West London

TITLE	CODE	COURSE	SUBJECTS	A/AS	NO/C	AGNVQ	IB	SQA(H)	SQA	RATIO	A/AS
Politics and Philosophy	MV17	3FT deg	*	BCC	5M	D^	28	BBBCC	Ind		12/17

CAMBRIDGE Univ

TITLE	CODE	COURSE	SUBJECTS	A/AS	NO/C	AGNVQ	IB	SQA(H)	SQA	RATIO	A/AS
Philosophy	V700▼	3FT deg	* g	AAB	Ind		Ind	CSYS	Ind	3	28/30
Natural Sciences History & Philosophy of Science	Y160▼	3FT deg	2(S/M) g	AAA-AAB	Ind		Ind	CSYS	Ind		

CARDIFF Univ of Wales

TITLE	CODE	COURSE	SUBJECTS	A/AS	NO/C	AGNVQ	IB	SQA(H)	SQA	RATIO	A/AS
History of Ideas and Philosophy	VVD7	3FT deg	*	BCC	3M+2D		Ind	AABB		2	16/22
Philosophy	V700	3FT deg	*	BCC	3M+2D		Ind	AABB		4	16/24
Philosophy/Ancient History	VV7C	3FT deg	*	BBC	Ind		Ind	AAABB		5	
Philosophy/Archaeology	VV76	3FT deg	*	BBC	Ind		Ind	AABB	X		
Philosophy/Cultural Criticism	MV97	3FT deg	E	ABC	X		Ind	AAABB	X		
Philosophy/Economics	VL71	3FT deg	*	BBC-BBB	7M+7D		Ind	AAAB	Ind	9	

course details			98 expected requirements							96 entry stats	
TITLE	CODE	COURSE	SUBJECTS	A/AS	ND/C	AGNVQ	IB	SQA(H)	SQA	RATIO	A/AS
Philosophy/Education	VX79	3FT deg	*	BBC	Ind	Ind	Ind	Ind	Ind	1	
Philosophy/English Literature	VQ73	3FT deg	E	ABB	X		Ind	AAABB	X	5	20/28
Philosophy/French	VR71	4FT deg	F	BBC	Ind		Ind	ABBBB	Ind	10	
Philosophy/History	VVCR	3FT deg	H	BCC	X		Ind	AABBB	X		
Philosophy/History of Ideas	VVDT	3FT deg	*	BCC							
Philosophy/Italian	VR73	4FT deg	L	BBC	Ind		Ind	ABBBB	Ind		
Philosophy/Language Studies	QV17	3FT deg	*	BBC	Ind		Ind	ABBBB			
Philosophy/Music	VW73	3FT deg	Mu	BCC	X		Ind	Ind	X		
Politics/Philosophy	MVC7	3FT deg		BBC			Ind	AABBB		8	
Psychology/Philosophy	LV77	3FT deg	*	BBB	M0+6D		Ind	AABBB	N	8	22/30
Pure Mathematics/Philosophy	GV17	3FT deg	M	BCC	3M+2D$	Ind	Ind	AABB	Ind		
Religious Studies/Philosophy	VV87	3FT deg	*	BCC						3	20/30
Social Philosophy & App Ethics/History of Ideas	VV7D	3FT deg	*	BCC							
Social Philosophy and App Ethics/Ancient History	VVR1	3FT deg	*	BBC	Ind		Ind	AAABB			
Social Philosophy and App Ethics/Religious Studs	VV7V	3FT deg	*	BBC							
Social Philosophy and Applied Ethics/Archaeology	VV6R	3FT deg	*	BBC	Ind		Ind	AABB	X		
Social Philosophy and Applied Ethics/Economics	VLR1	3FT deg	*	BBC-BBB	7M+7D		Ind	AAAB	Ind		
Social Philosophy and Applied Ethics/Education	VX7X	3FT deg	*	BBC	Ind	Ind	Ind	Ind	Ind		
Social Philosophy and Applied Ethics/English Lit	VQ7J	3FT deg	E	ABB	X		Ind	AAABB	X		
Social Philosophy and Applied Ethics/French	VR7C	4FT deg	F	BBC	Ind		Ind	ABBBB	Ind		
Social Philosophy and Applied Ethics/History	VVRC	3FT deg	H	BCC	X		Ind	AABBB	X		
Social Philosophy and Applied Ethics/Music	VW7H	3FT deg	Mu	BBC	X		Ind	Ind	X	1	
Social Philosophy and Applied Ethics/Politics	VM71	3FT deg		BBC			Ind	AABBB			
Sociology/Philosophy	LVH7	3FT deg	*	BCC						12	
Sociology/Social Philosophy and Applied Ethics	LV37	3FT deg	*	BCC	3M+2D		Ind			2	
Spanish/Philosophy	RV47	4FT deg	L	BBC							
Spanish/Social Philosophy and Applied Ethics	RV4T	4FT deg	L	BBC						1	
Welsh History/Philosophy	VV1R	3FT deg	H	BCC	X		Ind	AABBB	X		
Welsh History/Social Philosophy and App Ethics	VV1T	3FT deg	H	BCC	X		Ind	AABBB	X		
Welsh/Philosophy	QV57	3FT deg	W	BCC							

Univ of CENTRAL LANCASHIRE

Combined Honours Programme Philosophy	Y400	3FT deg	*	12	Ind	M$6/^	26	BCCC	Ind		

CHICHESTER INSTITUTE OF HIGHER EDUCATION

Theology with Study of Religions	V8V9	3FT deg	*	12	Ind	M$	Ind	Ind	Ind		

CITY Univ

Economics/Philosophy	LV17	3FT deg	* g	BCC	3M+4D	D*^	28$	BBBBC	Ind	12	
Journalism/Philosophy	PV67	3FT/4SW deg	* g	BBC-CCC	Ind	D*^	Ind	Ind	Ind	26	
Philosophy/Economics	LVC7	3FT deg	* g	BCC	3M+4D	D*^	28$	BBBBC	Ind		
Philosophy/Psychology	LVR7	3FT deg	* g	BCC	3M+4D	D*^	28$	BBBBC	Ind	6	14/20
Philosophy/Sociology	LVH7	3FT deg	* g	BCC	3M+4D	D*^	28$	BBBBC	Ind	2	
Psychology/Philosophy	CV87	3FT deg	* g	BCC	3M+4D	D*^	28$	BBBBC	Ind	13	20/22
Sociology/Philosophy	LV37	3FT deg	* g	BCC	3M+4D	D*^	28$	BBBBC	Ind		

Univ of DUNDEE

American Studies and Philosophy	QV47	4FT deg	* g	BCC	Ind	D$	29	BBBC	Ind		
Business Economics and Marketing and Philosophy	Y606	4FT deg	* g	BCC	Ind	D$	29	BBBC	Ind		
Contemporary European Studies and Philosophy	TV27	4FT deg	* g	BCC	Ind	D$	29	BBBC	Ind		
Economics and Philosophy	LV17	4FT deg	* g	BCC	Ind	D$	29	BBBC	Ind		
English and Philosophy	QV37	4FT deg	E g	BCC	Ind	D$^	29$	BBBC$	Ind	5	
Financial Economics and Philosophy	LVC7	4FT deg	* g	BCC	Ind	D$	29	BBBC	Ind		
Geography and Philosophy	LV87	4FT deg	* g	BCC	Ind	D$	29	BBBC	Ind	5	

course details			98 expected requirements							96 entry stats	
TITLE	CODE	COURSE	SUBJECTS	A/AS	NO/C	AGNVQ	IB	SQA(H)	SQA	RATIO	A/AS
Mathematics and Philosophy	GV17	4FT deg	M g	BCC	Ind	D$^	29$	BBBC$	Ind		
Modern History and Philosophy	VV17	4FT deg	* g	BCC	Ind	D$	29	BBBC	Ind	7	
Philosophy	V700	4FT deg	* g	BCC	Ind	D$	29	BBBC	Ind	17	
Philosophy and Political Science	MV17	4FT deg	* g	BCC	Ind	D$	29	BBBC	Ind	11	
Philosophy and Psychology	LV77	4FT deg	* g	BCC	Ind	D$	29	BBBC	Ind	12	
Physics and Philosophy	FV37	4FT deg	M+S g	10	5M $	M$^	25$	BBCC$	N$		
Arts and Social Sciences *Philosophy*	Y400	3FT deg	* g	BCC	Ind	D$	29	BBBC	Ind		
Univ of DURHAM											
Chinese with Philosophy	T3V7	4FT deg	*	BBC	Ind	Ind	31	AABBB	Ind		
Classical Studies and Philosophy	QV87	3FT deg	*	BCC	Ind	Ind	Ind	AAABB	Ind	8	
English Literature and Philosophy	QV37	3FT deg	E g	AAB	Ind	Ind	32	AAABB	Ind	20	26/28
Japanese with Philosophy	T4V7	4FT deg	*	BBC	Ind	Ind	31	AABBB	Ind		
Philosophy	V700	3FT deg	*	BBC	5M	Ind	32	AAABB	Ind	5	20/28
Philosophy and Politics	MV17	3FT deg	*	BBB	Ind	Ind	32	AAABB	Ind	7	26/30
Philosophy and Psychology	CV87	3FT deg	* g	ABB	Ind	Ind	33	AAABB	Ind	11	28/30
Philosophy and Theology	VV78	3FT deg	*	BBC	Ind	Ind	32	AAABB	Ind	4	20/30
Arts Combined *Philosophy*	Y300	3FT deg	*	24	MO	Ind	30	AAABB	Ind		
Natural Sciences *Philosophy*	Y160	3FT deg	2S	ABB	Ind	X	33	CSYS	X		
Social Sciences Combined *Philosophy*	Y220	3FT deg	*	ABC	MO	Ind	32	AAABB	Ind		
Univ of EAST ANGLIA											
Economic and Social History and Philosophy	VV37	3FT deg	*	BBC	3M+3D		30	BBBBB	Ind	12	
Economics and Philosophy	LV17	3FT deg	*	BBC	3M+3D		30	BBBBB	Ind	8	
English Literature and Philosophy	VQ73	3FT deg	E	BBB	3M+3D		30	BBBBB	Ind	6	20/26
European Cultural Studies	VT92	4FT deg		BCC			28$	AABB$	Ind		
European and Social Studies	TV29	3FT/4FT deg		BBC	X		29$	AAABB	X	5	12/22
Linguistics and Philosophy	VQ71	3FT deg	F/G	BBC	4M+2D		30	AAAAB	Ind		
Mathematics with Philosophy	G1V7	3FT deg	M	BCC	Ind		32$	BBBC$	X		
Philosophy	V700	3FT deg	*	BBC	3M+3D		30	BBBBB	Ind	4	14/26
Philosophy and Politics	MV17	3FT deg	*	BBC	3M+3D		30	BBBBB	Ind	5	
Philosophy and Sociology	VL73	3FT deg	*	BBC	3M+3D		30	BBBBB	Ind	2	14/22
Philosophy with a Modern European Lang	V7T2	4FT deg	L/*	BBC	3M+3D		30	BBBBB	Ind	4	
Univ of EDINBURGH											
Archaeology and Scottish Ethnology	VV69	4FT deg	g	BBB	Ind	Ind	34	ABBB	Ind		
French and Philosophy	RV17	4FT deg	E g	BBB	Ind	Ind	Dip$	BBBB$	Ind		
German and Philosophy	RV27	4FT deg	L g	BBB	Ind	Ind	Dip$	BBBB$	Ind		
Law and Philosophy	MV37	4FT deg	g	ABB	X		32	AAABB	X	7	
Linguistics and Scottish Ethnology	QV19	4FT deg	g	BBB	Ind	Ind	Dip$	BBBB	Ind		
Mental Philosophy	V700	4FT deg	g	BBB	Ind	Ind	Dip$	BBBB	Ind		
Philosophy and Economics	VL71	4FT deg	g	BBB	Ind	Ind	Dip$	BBBB	Ind		
Philosophy and English Language	VQ7H	4FT deg	E g	BBB	Ind	Ind	Dip$	BBBB$	Ind		
Philosophy and English Literature	VQ73	4FT deg	E g	AAB	Ind	Ind	Dip$	ABBB$	Ind		
Philosophy and German	VR72	4FT deg	L g	BBB	Ind	Ind	Dip$	BBBB$	Ind		
Philosophy and Greek	QV77	4FT deg	g	BBB	Ind	Ind	Dip$	BBBB	Ind		
Philosophy and Linguistics	VQ71	4FT deg	g	BBB	Ind	Ind	Dip$	BBBB	Ind		
Philosophy and Mathematics	VG71	4FT deg	M g	BBB	Ind	Ind	Dip$	ABBC$	Ind		
Philosophy and Politics	VM71	4FT deg	g	BBB	Ind	Ind	Dip$	BBBB	Ind		
Philosophy and Psychology	VL77	4FT deg	g	BBB	Ind	Ind	Dip$	BBBB	Ind		
Philosophy and Systematic Theology	VV78	4FT deg	g	BBB	Ind	Ind	Dip$	BBBB	Ind		

			98 expected requirements							96 entry stats	

course details — *98 expected requirements* — *96 entry stats*

TITLE	CODE	COURSE	SUBJECTS	A/AS	ND/C	AGNVQ	IB	SQA(H)	SQA	RATIO	A/AS
Scottish Ethnology	V910	4FT deg	g	BBB	Ind	Ind	Dip$	BBBB	Ind		
Scottish Ethnology and Celtic	VQ95	4FT deg	L g	BBB	Ind	Ind	Dip$	BBBB$	Ind		
Scottish Ethnology and English Language	VQ93	4FT deg	g	BBB	Ind	Ind	Dip$	BBBB	Ind		
Scottish Ethnology and English Literature	VQ9H	4FT deg	E g	BBB	Ind	Ind	Dip$	BBBB$	Ind		
Scottish Ethnology and Scandinavian Studies	VR97	4FT deg	L g	BBB	Ind	Ind	Dip$	BBBB$	Ind		
Scottish Ethnology and Scottish Historical Studs	VV91	4FT deg	g	BBB	Ind	Ind	Dip$	BBBB	Ind		
Scottish Ethnology and Scottish Literature	VQ92	4FT deg	E g	BBB	Ind	Ind	Dip$	BBBB$	Ind		

Univ of ESSEX

Linguistics and Philosophy	QV17	3FT deg	*	20	MO+2D	Ind	28	BBBB	Ind		
Philosophy	V700	3FT deg	*	20	MO+2D	Ind	28	BBBB	Ind	4	14/22
Philosophy and Artificial Intelligence	GV87	3FT deg	*	24	MO+2D	Ind	28	BBBB	Ind		
Philosophy and History	VV17	3FT deg	*	20	MO+2D	Ind	28	BBBB	Ind	6	
Philosophy and History of Art	VV74	3FT deg	*	20	MO+2D	Ind	28	BBBB	Ind	6	
Philosophy and Literature	QV27	3FT deg	*	20	MO+2D	Ind	28	BBBB	Ind	5	14/24
Philosophy and Music	VW73	3FT deg	*	20	MO+2D	Ind	28	BBBB	Ind		
Philosophy and Politics	MV17	3FT deg	*	20	MO+2D	Ind	28	BBBB	Ind	5	16/18
Philosophy and Sociology	LV37	3FT deg	*	20	MO+2D	Ind	28	BBBB	Ind	2	18/26

Univ of EXETER

Humanities in Contemporary Society	V9L8	3FT deg	*	BBC	MO	M/D$	34	Ind	Ind		

Univ of GLAMORGAN

English Studies and Philosophy	QV37	3FT deg	* g	12	Ind	Ind	Ind	Ind	Ind		
English Studies with Philosophy	Q3V7	3FT deg	* g	12	Ind	Ind	Ind	Ind	Ind		
Government and Philosophy	MV17	3FT deg	* g	12	Ind	Ind	Ind	Ind	Ind		
History and Philosophy	VV17	3FT deg	* g	12	5M	M	Ind	Ind	Ind		
Humanities (Philosophy)	V700	3FT deg	* g	CC	5M	M$	24	CCCC	HN	4	
Philosophy and Psychology	LV77	3FT deg	* g	CC	Ind	Ind	Ind	Ind	Ind		
Philosophy and Religious Studies	VV78	3FT deg	* g	12	Ind	Ind	Ind	Ind	Ind		
Philosophy and Sociology	LV37	3FT deg	* g	12	Ind	Ind	Ind	Ind	Ind		
Psychology with Philosophy	L7V7	3FT deg	* g	CC	5M	M	Ind	Ind	Ind		
Combined Studies (Honours) *Philosophy*	Y400	3FT deg	* g	8-16	Ind	Ind	Ind	Ind	Ind		
Joint Honours *Philosophy*	Y401	3FT deg	* g	8-16	Ind	Ind	Ind	Ind	Ind		
Major/Minor Honours *Philosophy*	Y402	3FT deg	* g	8-16	Ind	Ind	Ind	Ind	Ind		

Univ of GLASGOW

Archaeology/Philosophy	VV67	4FT deg		BBC	HN	M	30	BBBB	Ind	4	
Celtic Civilisation/Philosophy	QV57	4FT deg		BBC	HN	M	30	BBBB	Ind		
Celtic/Philosophy	QVN7	4FT deg		BBC	HN	M	30	BBBB	Ind		
Classical Civilisation/Philosophy	QV87	4FT deg		BBC	HN	M	30	BBBB	Ind	8	
Classical Hebrew/Philosophy	VV7W	4FT deg		BBC	HN	M	30	BBBB	Ind		
Computing/Philosophy	GV57	4FT deg		BBC	HN	M	30	BBBB	Ind		
Czech/Philosophy	TVC7	5FT deg		BBC	HN	M	30	BBBB	Ind		
Economic and Social History/Philosophy	VVH7	4FT deg		BBC	HN	M	30	BBBB	Ind		
Economic and Social History/Philosophy	VV37	4FT deg		BBC	8M	M	30	BBBB	Ind	1	
English/Philosophy	QV37	4FT deg		BBC	HN	M	30	BBBB	Ind	7	22/30
Film and Television Studies/Philosophy	VW75	4FT deg		BBB	HN	D	32	AABB	HN	9	
French/Philosophy	RV17	5FT deg		BBC	HN	M	30	BBBB	Ind	16	
Geography/Philosophy	LV87	4FT deg		BBC	HN	M	30	BBBB	Ind	10	
German/Philosophy	RV27	5FT deg		BBC	HN	M	30	BBBB	Ind		
Greek/Philosophy	QV77	4FT deg		BBC	HN	M	30	BBBB	Ind		

Philosophy 59

TITLE	CODE	COURSE	SUBJECTS	A/AS	ND/C	RGNVQ	IB	SQA(H)	SQA	RATIO A/AS
Hispanic Studies/Philosophy	RV47	5FT deg		BBC	HN	M	30	BBBB	Ind	
History of Art/Philosophy	VV47	4FT deg		BBC	HN	M	30	BBBB	Ind	14
History/Philosophy	VV1R	4FT deg		BBC	HN	M	30	BBBB	Ind	4
Islamic Studies/Philosophy	TV67	4FT deg		BBC	N	M	30	BBBB	Ind	
Italian/Philosophy	RV37	5FT deg		BBC	HN	M	30	BBBB	Ind	
Latin/Philosophy	QV67	4FT deg		BBC	HN	M	30	BBBB	Ind	
Management Studies/Philosophy	NV17	4FT deg		BBC	8M	M	30	BBBB	Ind	3
Management Studies/Philosophy	NVC7	4FT deg		BBC	HN	M	30	BBBB	Ind	
Mathematics/Philosophy	GV17	4FT deg		BBC	HN	M	30	BBBB	Ind	
Mathematics/Philosophy	GV1R	4FT deg	M+S	BBC-CCC	N	M	24$	BBBB$	N	
Music/Philosophy	VW73	4FT deg		BBC	HN	M	30	BBBB	Ind	7
Philosophy	V700	4FT deg		BBC	8M	M	30	BBBB	Ind	12
Philosophy	V702	4FT deg		BBC	HN	M	30	BBBB	Ind	9
Philosophy with Celtic	V7Q5	4FT deg		BBC	8M	M	30	BBBB	Ind	
Philosophy with Czech	V7T1	4FT deg		BBC	8M	M	30	BBBB	Ind	
Philosophy with French	V7R1	4FT deg		BBC	8M	M	30	BBBB	Ind	
Philosophy with German	V7R2	4FT deg		BBC	8M	M	30	BBBB	Ind	
Philosophy with Hispanic Studies	V7R4	4FT deg		BBC	8M	M	30	BBBB	Ind	
Philosophy with Italian	V7R3	4FT deg		BBC	8M	M	30	BBBB	Ind	
Philosophy with Polish	V7TC	4FT deg		BBC	8M	M	30	BBBB	Ind	
Philosophy with Russian	V7R8	4FT deg		BBC	8M	M	30	BBBB	Ind	
Philosophy/Archaeology	VV76	4FT deg		BBC	8M	M	30	BBBB	Ind	
Philosophy/Classical Civilisation	QV8R	4FT deg		BBC	8M	M	30	BBBB	Ind	2
Philosophy/Computing Science	GVM7	4FT deg		BBC	8M	M	30	BBBB	Ind	
Philosophy/Economics	LV1R	4FT deg		BBC	HN	M	30	BBBB	Ind	
Philosophy/Economics	LVD7	4FT deg		BBC	8M	M	30	BBBB	Ind	2
Philosophy/History	VV17	4FT deg		BBC	8M	M	30	BBBB	Ind	5
Philosophy/Mathematics	VG71	4FT deg		BBC	8M	M	30	BBBB	Ind	
Philosophy/Polish	TV17	5FT deg		BBC	HN	M	30	BBBB	Ind	
Philosophy/Politics	MVC7	4FT deg		BBC	HN	M	30	BBBB	Ind	8
Philosophy/Politics	MV17	4FT deg		BBC	8M	M	30	BBBB	Ind	5
Philosophy/Psychology	CV87	4FT deg		BBC	8M	M	30	BBBB	Ind	11
Philosophy/Psychology	CV8R	4FT deg		BBC	HN	M	30	BBBB	Ind	6 20/24
Philosophy/Russian	RV87	5FT deg		BBC	HN	M	30	BBBB	Ind	
Philosophy/Scottish History	VVCT	4FT deg		BBC	HN	M	30	BBBB	Ind	
Philosophy/Scottish History	VVC7	4FT deg		BBC	8M	M	30	BBBB	Ind	
Philosophy/Scottish Literature	QVG7	4FT deg		BBC	HN	M	30	BBBB	Ind	
Philosophy/Sociology	LV37	4FT deg		BBC	HN	M	30	BBBB	Ind	6
Philosophy/Sociology	LVH7	4FT deg		BBC	8M	M	30	BBBB	Ind	4
Physics/Philosophy	FV37	4FT deg	M+P	BBC	HN	M	30	BBBB	Ind	
Physics/Philosophy	FVH7	4FT deg	M+P	BBC-CCC	N	M	24$	BBB$	N	
Theatre Studies/Philosophy	VW74	4FT deg		BBC	HN	M	30	BBBB	Ind	7
Theology & Religious Studies/Philosophy	VV7V	4FT deg		BBC	HN	M	30	BBBB	Ind	5

Univ of GREENWICH

TITLE	CODE	COURSE	SUBJECTS	A/AS	ND/C	RGNVQ	IB	SQA(H)	SQA	RATIO A/AS
Philosophy	V700	3FT deg	* g	10	MO	M	25	BBB	Ind	
Humanities _Philosophy_	Y301	3FT deg	* g	10	MO	M	25	BBB	Ind	

Univ of HERTFORDSHIRE

TITLE	CODE	COURSE	SUBJECTS	A/AS	ND/C	RGNVQ	IB	SQA(H)	SQA	RATIO A/AS
Applied Geology/Philosophy	F6V7	3FT deg	* g	14	MO $	M$ gi	26$	BCCC$	Ind	
Applied Physics/Philosophy	F3V7	3FT deg	M+P	12	3M	M$ gi	24$	CCCC$	Ind	
Computing/Philosophy	G5V7	3FT deg	*	14	MO	M$ gi	26	BCCC	Ind	2
Electronic Music/Philosophy	W3V7	3FT deg	Mu	14	MO $	M$^ gi	26$	BCCC$	Ind	4

course details			98 expected requirements							96 entry stats	
TITLE	CODE	COURSE	SUBJECTS	A/AS	ND/C	AGNVQ	IB	SQA(H)	SQA	RATIO	A/AS
Environmental Science/Philosophy	F9V7	3FT deg	*	14	MO	M$ gi	26	BCCC	Ind		
Historical Studies/Philosophy	VV17	3FT deg	*	14	M+D	Ind	28	CCCCC	Ind		
Human Biology/Philosophy	B1V7	3FT deg	S g	14	MO $	MS gi	26$	BCCC$	Ind	1	
Linguistics/Philosophy	QV17	3FT deg	*	14	M+D	Ind	28	CCCCC	Ind		
Literature/Philosophy	QV37	3FT deg	*	14	M+D	Ind	28	CCCCC	Ind		
Manufacturing Systems/Philosophy	H7V7	3FT deg	*	14	MO	M$ gi	26	BCCC	Ind		
Mathematics/Philosophy	G1V7	3FT deg	M	14	MO $	M$^ gi	26$	BCCC$	Ind	8	
Operational Research/Philosophy	N2V7	3FT deg	*	14	MO	M$ gi	26	BCCC	Ind		
Philosophy	V700	3FT deg	*	14	M+D	Ind	28	CCCCC	Ind	5	11/16
Philosophy/Applied Geology	V7F6	3FT deg	* g	14	MO $	M$ gi	26$	BCCC$	Ind		
Philosophy/Applied Physics	V7F3	3FT deg	M+P	12	3M $	M$ gi	24	CCCC$	Ind		
Philosophy/Computing	V7G5	3FT deg	*	14	MO	M$ gi	26	BCCC	Ind	4	
Philosophy/Electronic Music	V7W3	3FT deg	Mu	14	MO $	M$^ gi	26$	BCCC$	Ind		
Philosophy/Environmental Science	V7F9	3FT deg	*	14	MO	M$ gi	26	BCCC	Ind	1	
Philosophy/Human Biology	V7B1	3FT deg	S g	14	MO $	MS gi	26$	BCCC$	Ind		
Philosophy/Manufacturing Systems	V7H7	3FT deg	*	14	MO	M$ gi	26	BCCC	Ind		
Philosophy/Mathematics	V7G1	3FT deg	M	14	MO $	M$^ gi	26$	BCCC$	Ind		
Philosophy/Minor	V702	3FT deg	*	14	M+D	Ind	28	CCCCC	Ind		
Philosophy/Minor/Minor	V703	3FT deg	*	14	M+D	Ind	28	CCCCC	Ind		
Philosophy/Operational Research	V7N2	3FT deg	*	14	MO	M$ gi	26	BCCC	Ind		
Philosophy/Psychology	V7C8	3FT deg	*	20	4M+4D	D$ gi	26	BBBC	Ind	23	
Psychology/Philosophy	C8V7	3FT deg	*	20	4M+4D	D$ gi	26	BBBC	Ind	22	
Combined Modular Scheme Philosophy	Y100	3FT deg	*	14	MO	M$ gi	26	BCCC	Ind		

HEYTHROP COLL (Univ of London)

Philosophy	V700	3FT deg	*	20-22	Ind	M	Dip	BCCCC	Ind	2	10/26
Philosophy and Theology	VV78	3FT deg	*	20-22	Ind	M	Dip	BCCCC	Ind	3	10/20

Univ of HULL

English/Philosophy	QV37	3FT deg	E	BBB-BCC	MO+D $	M$^ gi	28$	BBBCC	Ind	12	22/22
French/Philosophy	RV17	4FT deg	F	BCC	Ind	M$^ go	28$	BBBCC	Ind		
Gender Studies and Philosophy	MV97	3FT deg	*	BCC-CCC	MO	M$6/^ go	28	BBBCC	Ind	2	
Humanities (History)	VV19	3FT deg	H	BCC	Ind	M*^ gi	26$	BBBCC	Ind		
Humanities (Philosophy)	VV79	3FT deg	*	BCC	MO	M$ go	26$	BBCCC	Ind	14	
Humanities (Theology)	VV89	3FT deg	*	BBB-BC	MO $	M*^ gi	26$	BBBCC	Ind		
Law with Philosophy	M3V7	3FT deg	*	BBB	DO	D$	28	AABBB	Ind		
Mathematics and Philosophy	GV17	3FT deg	M	BCC-BCD	MO $	M$^ go	28$	BBBCC	Ind	4	
Mathematics and Philosophy (4 Yrs)	GV1R	4FT deg	*	CD	N	P*^ gi	24	BCCCC	Ind		
Philosophy	V702	3FT deg	*	BCC	MO	M$6/^ go	26	BBCCC	Ind	5	
Philosophy	V700	3FT deg	*	BCC	MO	M$6/^ go	26	BBCCC	Ind	5	16/22
Philosophy/Politics	MV17	3FT deg	*	BBC-BCC	MO	M$6/^ go	28	BBBCC	Ind	7	
Philosophy/Sociology	LV37	3FT deg	*	BBC-BCC	MO	M$6/^ go	28	BBBCC	Ind	6	
Philosophy/Spanish	RV47	4FT deg	L	BBB-CCC	Ind	M$^ go	28$	BBBCC	Ind		
Philosophy/Theology	VV78	3FT deg	*	BC-BCC	MO	M$6/^ go	26$	BBCCC	Ind	30	
Psychology with Philosophy	C8V7	3FT deg	* g	BBB-BCC	MO+2D	D$^ go	28	BBBCC	Ind	31	
Politics, Philosophy, Economics Philosophy	Y616	3FT deg	*	BBB	MO+2D	Ind	28	BBBCC	Ind		

KEELE Univ

Human Resource Management and Philosophy	NV67	3FT deg	*	BCC	Ind	Ind	28	CSYS	Ind		
Human Resource Management and Philosophy	VN76	4FT deg	*	BBC-BCC	Ind	Ind	28	BBBB	Ind		
Philosophy and American Studies (4 Yrs)	VQ74	4FT deg	*	BCC	Ind	Ind	28	BBBB	Ind		
Philosophy and Ancient History (4 Yrs)	VVR1	4FT deg	*	BCC	Ind	Ind	28	BBBB	Ind		

course details | 98 expected requirements | 96 entry stats

TITLE	CODE	COURSE	SUBJECTS	A/AS	ND/C	AGNVQ	IB	SQA(H)	SQA	RATIO A/AS
Philosophy and Applied Social Studies	LV57	3FT deg	*	BBC-BCC	Ind	Ind	28	CSYS	Ind	
Philosophy and Applied Social Studies (4 Yrs)	VL75	4FT deg	*	BBC-BCC	Ind	Ind	28	BBBB	Ind	
Philosophy and Astrophysics	FV57	3FT deg	P g	BCC	Ind	D$^	28$	CSYS	Ind	
Philosophy and Astrophysics (4 Yrs)	VF75	4FT deg	*	BCC	Ind	Ind	28	BBBB	Ind	
Philosophy and Biochemistry	CV77	3FT deg	C g	BCC	Ind	D$^	28$	CSYS	Ind	
Philosophy and Biochemistry (4 Yrs)	VC77	4FT deg	*	BCC	Ind	Ind	28	BBBB	Ind	
Philosophy and Biological & Medicinal Chemistry	VF7C	4FT deg		BCC	Ind	Ind	28	BBBB	Ind	
Philosophy and Biological and Medicinal Chem	FVC7	3FT deg	C	BCC	Ind	D$^	28$	CSYS	Ind	
Philosophy and Biology	CV17	3FT deg	S g	BCC	Ind	D$^	28$	CSYS	Ind	
Philosophy and Chemistry	FV17	3FT deg	C	BCC	Ind	D$^	28$	CSYS	Ind	
Philosophy and Chemistry (4 Yrs)	VF71	4FT deg	*	BCC	Ind	Ind	28	BBBB	Ind	
Philosophy and Classical Studies (4 Yrs)	VQ78	4FT deg	*	BCC	Ind	Ind	28	BBBB	Ind	
Philosophy and Computer Science (4 Yrs)	VG75	4FT deg	* g	BCC	Ind	Ind	28	BBBB	Ind	
Philosophy and Criminology	MVH7	3FT deg	*	BBB	Ind	Ind	32	CSYS	Ind	
Philosophy and Criminology (4 Yrs)	VM7H	4FT deg	*	BBB	Ind	Ind	32	ABBB	Ind	
Philosophy and Economics	LV17	3FT deg	* g	BCC	Ind	Ind	28	CSYS	Ind	4
Philosophy and Economics (4 Yrs)	VL71	4FT deg	*	BCC	Ind	Ind	28	BBBB	Ind	
Philosophy and Educational Studies (4 Yrs)	XV97	4FT deg	*	BCC	Ind	Ind	28	BBBB	Ind	
Philosophy and Electronic Music	VW7J	3FT deg	Mu	BCC	Ind	D$^	28$	CSYS	Ind	
Philosophy and English	QV37	3FT deg	E	BBC	Ind	D$^	30$	CSYS	Ind	11 20/24
Philosophy and English (4 Yrs)	VQ73	4FT deg	E	BBC	Ind	Ind	30	BBBB	Ind	10
Philosophy and Environmental Management (4 Yrs)	VF7X	4FT deg	*	BCC	Ind	Ind	28	BBBB	Ind	
Philosophy and Finance (4 Yrs)	VN73	4FT deg	*	BBC-BCC	Ind	Ind	28	BBBB	Ind	
Philosophy and French	RV17	3FT deg	F	BCC	Ind	D$^	28$	CSYS	Ind	1
Philosophy and French (4 Yrs)	VR71	4FT deg	*	BBC-BCC	Ind	Ind	28	BBBB	Ind	
Philosophy and French/German (4 Yrs)	VT79	4FT deg	g	BBC	Ind	Ind	30	BBBB	Ind	
Philosophy and French/Russian (4 Yrs)	VT7X	4FT deg	*	BBC	Ind	Ind	30	BBBB	Ind	
Philosophy and French/Russian or Russian Studies	TVX7	3FT deg	F+R	BBC-BCC	Ind	D$^	28$	CSYS	Ind	
Philosophy and Geography	LV87	3FT deg	Gy	BCC	Ind	D$^	28$	CSYS	Ind	6
Philosophy and Geography (4 Yrs)	VL78	4FT deg	*	BCC	Ind	Ind	28	BBBB	Ind	3
Philosophy and Geology	FV67	3FT deg	S g	BCC	Ind	D$^	28$	CSYS	Ind	
Philosophy and Geology (4 Yrs)	VF76	4FT deg	*	BCC	Ind	Ind	28	BBBB	Ind	
Philosophy and German	VR72	4FT deg	* g	BCC	Ind	Ind	28	BBBB	Ind	
Philosophy and German/Russian or Russ St (4 Yrs)	VT7Y	4FT deg	g	BBC	Ind	Ind	30	BBBB	Ind	
Philosophy and History	VV17	3FT deg	*	BBC	Ind	Ind	30	CSYS	Ind	
Philosophy and International History	VV7C	3FT deg	*	BBC-BCC	Ind	Ind	28	CSYS	Ind	
Philosophy and International History (4 Yrs)	VVC7	4FT deg	*	BBC-BCC	Ind	Ind	28	BBBB	Ind	
Philosophy and International Politics	VM7C	4FT deg	*	BCC	Ind	Ind	28	BBBB	Ind	
Philosophy and International Politics	MVC7	3FT deg	*	BCC	Ind	Ind	28	CSYS	Ind	2
Philosophy and Law	MV37	3FT deg	*	BBB	Ind	Ind	32	CSYS	Ind	6
Philosophy and Law (4 Yrs)	VM73	4FT deg	*	BBB	Ind	Ind	32	BBBB	Ind	
Philosophy and Mathematics	GV17	3FT deg	M	BCC	Ind	D$^	28$	CSYS	Ind	
Philosophy and Mathematics (4 Yrs)	VG71	4FT deg	*	BCC	Ind	Ind	28	BBBB	Ind	
Philosophy and Music	VW73	3FT deg	Mu	BBC-BCC	Ind	D$^	28$	CSYS	Ind	
Physics and Philosophy	FV37	3FT deg	P	BCC	Ind	D$^	28$	CSYS	Ind	
Physics and Philosophy (4 Yrs)	VF73	4FT deg	*	BCC	Ind	Ind	28	BBBB	Ind	8
Politics and Philosophy	MV17	3FT deg	*	BCC	Ind	Ind	28	CSYS	Ind	5
Politics and Philosophy (4 Yrs)	VM71	4FT deg	*	BCC	Ind	Ind	28	BBBB	Ind	
Psychology and Philosophy	CV87	3FT deg	* g	BBB	Ind	Ind	32	CSYS	Ind	25
Psychology and Philosophy (4 Yrs)	VC78	4FT deg	*	BBB	Ind	Ind	32	ABBB	Ind	7
Russian Studies and Philosophy	RVV7	3FT deg	*	BCC	Ind	Ind	28	CSYS	Ind	
Russian Studies and Philosophy (4 Yrs)	VR7V	4FT deg	*	BCC	Ind	Ind	28	BBBB	Ind	

			98 expected requirements							96 entry stats
TITLE	CODE	COURSE	SUBJECTS	A/AS	ND/C	AGNVQ	IB	SQA(H)	SQA	RATIO A/AS
Russian and Philosophy	RV87	3FT deg	R	BCC	Ind	D$^	28$	CSYS	Ind	
Russian and Philosophy (4 Yrs)	VR78	4FT deg	*	BCC	Ind	Ind	28	BBBB	Ind	2
Statistics and Philosophy (4 Yrs)	VG74	4FT deg	*	BCC	Ind	Ind	28	BBBB	Ind	
Visual Arts and Philosophy	VW71	3FT deg	*	BCC	Ind	D$^	28	CSYS	Ind	5
Visual Arts and Philosophy (4 Yrs)	WV17	4FT deg	*	BBC-BCC	Ind	Ind	28	BBBB	Ind	

Univ of KENT

History of Science/English	QV35	3FT deg	E	22	2M+4D	Ind	30	Ind	Ind	8
History of Science/English (Post-Colonial Lits)	QVJ5	3FT deg	E	22	2M+4D	Ind	30	Ind	Ind	
History of Science/French	RV15	4FT deg	F	20	3M+3D	Ind	28	Ind	Ind	
History of Science/German	RV25	4FT deg	G	20	3M+3D	Ind	28	Ind	Ind	
History of Science/History	VV15	3FT deg	*	22	2M+4D	Ind	30	Ind	Ind	3
Italian/History of Science	RV35	4FT deg	*	20	3M+3D	Ind	28	Ind	Ind	
Law and Philosophy	MV37	3FT deg	*	26	6D	D$	33	AAAB	Ind	9
Mathematics and Philosophy	GV17	3FT/4SW deg	M	20	Ind	Ind	28	BBBB$	Ind	
Philosophy	V700	3FT deg	*	22	2M+4D	Ind	30	Ind	Ind	7 15/22
Philosophy and Law	MVH7	3FT deg	*	22	2M+4D	Ind	30	Ind	Ind	6
Philosophy and Politics	MV17	3FT deg	*	22	2M+4D	Ind	30	Ind	Ind	27
Philosophy and Social Anthropology	LVP7	3FT deg	*	22	2M+4D	Ind	30	Ind	Ind	4
Philosophy and Social Behaviour	LV7R	3FT deg	*	22	2M+4D	Ind	30	Ind	Ind	11
Philosophy and Social Policy & Administration	LVK7	3FT deg	*	22	2M+4D	Ind	30	Ind	Ind	
Philosophy and Sociology	LVH7	3FT deg	*	22	2M+4D	Ind	30	Ind	Ind	7
Philosophy/Classical Studies	QV87	3FT deg	*	20	3M+3D	Ind	28	Ind	Ind	4
Philosophy/Comparative Literary Studies	VQ72	3FT deg	*	20	3M+3D	Ind	28	Ind	Ind	
Philosophy/Computing	VG75	3FT deg	*	20	3M+3D	Ind	28	Ind	Ind	3
Philosophy/Drama	VW74	3FT deg	*	22	2M+4D	Ind	30	Ind	Ind	
Philosophy/English	QV37	3FT deg	E	22	2M+4D	Ind	30	Ind	Ind	6 20/26
Philosophy/English (Post-Colonial Literatures)	QVJ7	3FT deg	E	22	2M+4D	Ind	30	Ind	Ind	
Philosophy/English language	VQ73	3FT deg	E	20	3M+3D	Ind	28	Ind	Ind	7
Philosophy/European Studies	TV27	4FT deg	L	20	3M+3D	Ind	28	Ind	Ind	
Philosophy/Film Studies	VW75	3FT deg	*	22	2M+4D	Ind	30	Ind	Ind	4 20/22
Philosophy/French	RV17	4FT deg	F	22	2M+4D	Ind	30	Ind	Ind	
Philosophy/German	RV27	4FT deg	G	20	3M+3D	Ind	28	Ind	Ind	
Philosophy/History	VV17	3FT deg	*	22	2M+4D	Ind	30	Ind	Ind	3
Philosophy/History and Theory of Art	VV47	3FT deg	*	22	4M+2D	Ind	30	Ind	Ind	15
Philosophy/History of Science	VV75	3FT deg	*	20	3M+3D	Ind	28	Ind	Ind	2
Philosophy/Italian	RV37	4FT deg	*	20	3M+3D	Ind	28$	Ind	Ind	
Philosophy/Linguistics	VQ71	3FT deg	*	20	3M+3D	Ind	28	Ind	Ind	9
Politics and Government and Philosophy	MVC7	3FT deg	*	BCC	3M+3D	M$	28	BBBB	Ind	3
Social Anthropology and Philosophy	LV67	3FT deg	*	20	3M+3D	M$	28	BBBB	Ind	8
Social Policy and Administration and Philosophy	LV47	3FT deg	*	20	3M+3D	M$	28	BBBB	Ind	
Sociology and Philosophy	LV37	3FT deg	*	20	3M+3D	M$	28	BBBB	Ind	6
Spanish/History of Science	RV45	4FT deg	*	20	3M+3D	Ind	28	Ind	Ind	
Spanish/Philosophy	RV47	4FT deg	*	20	3M+3D	Ind	28	Ind	Ind	
Theology/History of Science	VV85	3FT deg	*	20	3M+3D	Ind	28	Ind	Ind	
Theology/Philosophy	VV78	3FT deg	*	20	3M+3D	Ind	28	Ind	Ind	23

KING ALFRED'S WINCHESTER

Philosophy and American Studies	QV47	3FT deg	*g	14	6M	M	24	BCC	N	3
Philosophy and Business Studies	NV17	3FT deg	*g	14	6M	M	24	BCC	N	1
Philosophy and Contemporary Cultural Studies	MV97	3FT deg	*g	14	6M	M	24	BCC	N	3
Philosophy and Education Studies	VX79	3FT deg	*g	14	6M	M	24	BCC	N	
Philosophy and English Studies	QV37	3FT deg	E	14	X	X	24$	BCC$	X	13

course details			98 expected requirements							96 entry stats
TITLE	CODE	COURSE	SUBJECTS	A/AS	ND/C	AGNVQ	IB	SQA(H)	SQA	RATIO A/AS
Philosophy and Geography	LV87	3FT deg	Gy g	14	X	X	24$	BCC$	X	
Philosophy and History	VV17	3FT deg	* g	14	6M	M	24	BCC	N	
Psychology and Philosophy	LV77	3FT deg	* g	14	6M	M	24	BCC	N	10
Religious Studies and Philosophy	VV78	3FT deg	* g	14	6M	M	24	BCC	N	5
Visual Studies and Philosophy	VW72	3FT deg								6

KING'S COLL LONDON (Univ of London)

Chemistry and Philosophy	FV17	3FT deg	C+S	BBB	X	Ind	28$	BBBBB	X	
Chemistry with Philosophy of Science	F1V5	3FT deg	C+S	18	4M $	Ind	28$	BBCCC	Ind	6
French and Philosophy	RV17	4FT deg	F	BBC						9
German and Philosophy	RV27	3FT deg	G	BBC						4
Greek and Philosophy	QV77	3FT deg	Gk	BBC-BCC						
Mathematics and Philosophy	GV17	3FT deg	M	24	X		30$	AAABB$	X	10
Mathematics with Philosophy of Mathematics	G1V5	3FT deg	M	20	X		28$	AABBB$	X	4	18/30
Mathematics with Philosophy of Maths (4Yr)(MSci)	G1VM	4FT deg	M	20	X		28$	AABBB$	X	
Philosophy	V700	3FT deg	*	BBB						5	14/28
Philosophy and Hispanic Studies	RV47	4FT deg	Sp	BBC-BCC						3
Philosophy and Theology	VV78	3FT deg	*	BBC-BCC						6	22/26
Philosophy with Greek	V7Q7	3FT deg	*	BBC-BCC						7
Physics and Philosophy	FV37	3FT deg	M+P	BBB	Ind		30$	AAABB	X	18
Physics with Philosophy of Science	F3V5	3FT deg	M+P	18	2M+1D		28$	AABBB	Ind	8
War Studies and Philosophy	MV97	3FT deg	*	BBC						4

KINGSTON Univ

History of Ideas/Economics	VL71	3FT deg	* g	16	MO	Ind^	Ind	BBCCC	HN	3
History of Ideas/English Language	QV37	3FT deg	E g	14	MO	Ind^	Ind	BCCCC	HN	
History of Ideas/English Literature	VQ73	3FT deg	E g	16	MO	Ind^	Ind	BBCCC	HN	1	10/22
History of Ideas/History	VV71	3FT deg	H g	16	MO	Ind^	Ind	BBCCC	HN	2
History of Ideas/History of Art, Arch & Design	VV47	3FT deg	* g	16	MO	Ind^	Ind	BBCCC	HN	
Politics/History of Ideas	MV17	3FT deg	* g	14	MO	Ind^	Ind	BCCCC	HN	8
Psychology/History of Ideas	LV77	3FT deg	* g	18	MO	Ind^	Ind	BBBCC	HN	3	8/14
Sociology/History of Ideas	LV37	3FT deg	* g	14	MO	Ind^	Ind	BCCCC	HN	2	10/12
Women's Studies/History of Ideas	MV97	3FT deg	* g	14	MO	Ind^	Ind	BCCCC	HN	5

Univ of Wales, LAMPETER

Philosophical Studies (3 Yrs)	V760▼	3FT deg	*	16	Ind	Ind	Ind	Ind	Ind	
Philosophical Studies and American Literature	QV47	3FT deg			Ind	Ind	Ind	Ind	Ind	
Philosophical Studies and Ancient History	VV1R	3FT deg	*	16	Ind	Ind	Ind	Ind	Ind	
Philosophical Studies and Anthropology	LV67	3FT deg	*	16	Ind	Ind	Ind	Ind	Ind	
Philosophical Studies and Archaeology	VV67	3FT deg	*	16	Ind	Ind	Ind	Ind	Ind	
Philosophical Studies and Australian Studies	LV6R	3FT deg			Ind	Ind	Ind	Ind	Ind	
Philosophical Studies and Church History	VVCR	3FT deg	*	16	Ind	Ind	Ind	Ind	Ind	
Philosophical Studies and Classical Studies	QV87	3FT deg	*	16	Ind	Ind	Ind	Ind	Ind	
Philosophical Studies and Cultural St in Geog	LVV7	3FT deg	*	16	Ind	Ind	Ind	Ind	Ind	
Philosophical Studies and English Literature	QV37	3FT deg	E	18	Ind	Ind	Ind	Ind	Ind	
Philosophical Studies and French	RV17	4FT deg	F	16	Ind	Ind	Ind	Ind	Ind	
Philosophical Studies and Geography	LV87	3FT deg	Gy	16	Ind	Ind	Ind	Ind	Ind	
Philosophical Studies and German	RV27	4FT deg	G	16	Ind	Ind	Ind	Ind	Ind	
Philosophical Studies and German Studies	RVF7	4FT deg	*	16	Ind	Ind	Ind	Ind	Ind	
Philosophical Studies and Greek	QV77	3FT deg	* g	16	Ind	Ind	Ind	Ind	Ind	
Philosophical Studies and History	VV17	3FT deg	H	16	Ind	Ind	Ind	Ind	Ind	
Philosophical Studies and Informatics	GV57▼	3FT deg	*	16	Ind	Ind	Ind	Ind	Ind	
Philosophical Studies and Islamic Studies	TV67	3FT deg	*	16	Ind	Ind	Ind	Ind	Ind	
Philosophical Studies and Latin	QV67	3FT deg	* g	16	Ind	Ind	Ind	Ind	Ind	

course details			98 expected requirements							96 entry stats
TITLE	CODE	COURSE	SUBJECTS	A/AS	NQ/C	AGNVQ	IB	SQA(H)	SQA	RATIO A/AS
Philosophical Studies and Management Techniques	NV17	3FT deg	*	16	Ind	Ind	Ind	Ind	Ind	
Philosophical Studies and Medieval Studies	VV1T	3FT deg		16	Ind	Ind	Ind	Ind	Ind	
Philosophical Studies and Modern Historical St	VVCT	3FT deg			Ind	Ind	Ind	Ind	Ind	
Philosophy (4 Yrs)	V700▼	4FT deg	*	16	Ind	Ind	Ind	Ind	Ind	
Religious Studies and Philosophical Studies	VVR8	3FT deg	*	16	Ind	Ind	Ind	Ind	Ind	
Theology and Philosophical Studies	VV78	3FT deg	*	16	Ind	Ind	Ind	Ind	Ind	
Victorian Studies and Philosophical Studies	VVC7	3FT deg	*	16	Ind	Ind	Ind	Ind	Ind	
Welsh Studies and Philosophical Studies	QV5R	3FT deg	*	16	Ind	Ind	Ind	Ind	Ind	
Welsh and Philosophical Studies	QV57	3FT/4FT deg	W	16	Ind	Ind	Ind	Ind	Ind	
Women's Studies and Philosophical Studies	MV97	3FT deg	*	16	Ind	Ind	Ind	Ind	Ind	
Combined Honours *Philosophical Studies*	Y400	3FT deg	*	14-16	Ind	Ind	Ind	Ind	Ind	
Religion, Ethics and Society *Ethics*	Y652	3FT deg	*	14	Ind	Ind	Ind	Ind	Ind	

LANCASTER Univ

Economics and Philosophy	LV17	3FT deg	* g	BBC-BCC	Ind		32	ABBBB	Ind	
English and Philosophy	QV37	3FT deg	E g	BBC	Ind $		32$	ABBBB$	Ind	
French Studies and Philosophy	RV17	4SW deg	F	BCC	Ind $		30$	BBBBB$	Ind	
German Studies and Philosophy	RV27	4SW deg	G/L	BCC	Ind $		30$	BBBBB$	Ind	
History and History of Science	VV15	3FT deg	H	BBC	Ind $		30$	ABBBB$	Ind	
History and Philosophy	VV17	3FT deg	H	BBC	Ind $		30$	ABBBB$	Ind	
Independent Studies and Philosophy	VY74	3FT deg	*	BCC	Ind		Ind	Ind	Ind	
Italian Studies and Philosophy	RV37	4SW deg	I/L	BCC	Ind $		30$	BBBBB$	Ind	
Linguistics and Philosophy	QV17	3FT deg	* g	BBC	MO		30$	BBBBB$	Ind	
Mathematics and Philosophy	GV17	3FT deg	M	20	MO $		30$	Ind$	Ind	
Philosophy	V700	3FT deg	*	BCC	Ind		30	BBBBB	Ind	
Philosophy and Politics	VM71	3FT deg	*	BCC	Ind		30	BBBBB	Ind	
Philosophy and Religious Studies	VV87	3FT deg	*	BCC-BCD	Ind		30	BBBBC	Ind	
Spanish Studies and Philosophy	RV47	4SW deg	Sp/L	BCC	Ind $		30$	BBBBB$	Ind	
Women's Studies and Philosophy	VM79	3FT deg	*	BCC	Ind		30	BBBBB	Ind	
History and Philosophy and Politics *Philosophy*	Y650	3FT deg	H	BBC	Ind		30$	ABBBB$	Ind	
Philosophy and Politics and Economics *Philosophy*	Y616	3FT deg	* g	BBC	Ind		32	ABBBB	Ind	

Univ of LEEDS

Artificial Intelligence-Philosophy	GV87	3FT deg	M g	BBC	Ind	Ind	Ind	Ind	Ind	
Biology-History and Philosophy of Science	CV15	3FT/4FT deg	B g	BCC	1M+5D$	Ind	28$	BBBBC	Ind	4	20/26
Chemistry-History and Philosophy of Science	FV15	3FT/4FT deg	C+M/P g	BCC	Ind	Ind	28$	BBBBC	Ind	3
Chemistry-Philosophy	FV17	3FT/4FT deg	C+M/P g	BCC	1M+5D$	Ind	28$	BBBBC	Ind	
Computer Science-Philosophy	GV57	3FT deg	M g	BBC	Ind	Ind	Ind	Ind	Ind	
Economics-Philosophy	VL71	3FT deg	g	BBC	Ind	Ind	30	CSYS	Ind	8	24/26
English-Philosophy	QV37	3FT deg	E g	ABB	Ind	Ind	33$	CSYS	Ind	8	26/30
French-Philosophy	RV17	4FT deg	F g	BBB	Ind	Ind	32$	CSYS	Ind	5	24/30
German-Philosophy	RV27	4FT deg	G g	BBC	Ind	Ind	30$	CSYS	Ind	
History and Philosophy of Science-History of Art	VV45	3FT deg	* g	BBC	Ind	Ind	30	CSYS	Ind	
History and Philosophy of Science-Italian	RV35	4FT deg	I g	BBC	Ind	Ind	Ind	Ind	Ind	
History and Philosophy of Science-Italian B	RVH5	4FT deg	L g	BBC	Ind	Ind	Ind	Ind	Ind	
History and Philosophy of Science-Philosophy	VV57	3FT deg	* g	BBC	Ind	Ind	30	CSYS	Ind	3	20/26
History and Philosophy of Science-Religious St	VV5V	3FT deg	* g	BBC	Ind	Ind	30	CSYS	Ind	
History and Philosophy of Science-Sociology	VL53	3FT deg	g	BBC	Ind	Ind	30	CSYS	Ind	
History and Philosophy of Science-Theology	VV58	3FT deg	* g	BBC	Ind	Ind	30	CSYS	Ind	
History-History and Philosophy of Science	VV15	3FT deg	* g	BBC	Ind	Ind	30	CSYS	Ind	7

			98 expected requirements							96 entry stats

course details | **98 expected requirements** | *96 entry stats*

TITLE	CODE	COURSE	SUBJECTS	A/AS	ND/C	AGNVQ	IB	SQA(H)	SQA	RATIO A/AS
History-Philosophy	VV17	3FT deg	* g	BBC	Ind	Ind	30	CSYS	Ind	13 22/24
Italian-Philosophy	RV37	4FT deg	I g	BBC	Ind	Ind	Ind	Ind	Ind	
Italian-Philosophy B	RVH7	4FT deg	L g	BBC	Ind	Ind	Ind	Ind	Ind	
Management Studies-Philosophy	VN71	3FT deg	g	BBC	Ind	Ind	30	CSYS	Ind	15
Mathematics-History and Philosophy of Science	GV15	3FT/4FT deg	M g	BBB	1M+5D$	Ind	32$	ABBBB	Ind	2
Mathematics-Philosophy	GV17	3FT/4FT deg	M g	BBB	1M+5D$	Ind	32$	ABBBB	Ind	13
Mathematics-Philosophy	VG71	3FT deg	M g	BBC	1M+5D$	Ind	30$	ABBBB	Ind	7
Music-Philosophy	VW73	3FT deg	Mu g	BBC	Ind	Ind	30$	CSYS	Ind	6
Philosophy	V700	3FT/4FT deg	* g	BBB	Ind	Ind	30	ABBBB	Ind	4 20/28
Philosophy-Computing	VG75	3FT deg	g	BBC	Ind	Ind	30$	ABBBB	Ind	5
Philosophy-History of Art	VV47	3FT deg	* g	BBC	Ind	Ind	30	CSYS	Ind	4 26/28
Philosophy-Politics	MV17	3FT deg	* g	BBB	Ind	Ind	32	CSYS	Ind	13 24/28
Philosophy-Religious Studies	VV7V	3FT deg	* g	BBC	Ind	Ind	30	CSYS	Ind	9
Philosophy-Russian	RV87	4FT deg	R g	BBC	Ind	Ind	30$	CSYS	Ind	
Philosophy-Russian B	RVV7	4FT deg	L g	BBC	Ind	Ind	30$	CSYS	Ind	
Philosophy-Social Policy	LV47	3FT deg	* g	BBC	Ind	D$^ go	30	CSYS	Ind	
Philosophy-Sociology	LV37	3FT deg	* g	BBB	Ind	D$^ go	32	CSYS	Ind	43
Philosophy-Theology	VV78	3FT deg	* g	BBC	Ind		30	CSYS	Ind	37
Physics-History and Philosophy of Science	FV35	3FT/4FT deg	M+P g	BBB	Ind	Ind	30$	CSYS	Ind	
Physics-Philosophy	FV37	3FT/4FT deg	M+P g	BBB	Ind	Ind	30$	CSYS		31
Psychology-History and Philosophy of Science	CV85	3FT deg	g	ABB	Ind	Ind	33	CSYS	Ind	
Psychology-Philosophy	CV87	3FT deg	g	ABB	Ind	Ind	33	CSYS	Ind	8 24/30

LEEDS METROPOLITAN Univ

Art and Social Studies	VM99	3FT deg	* g		Ind	Ind go	Ind	Ind	Ind	6/16

Univ of LIVERPOOL

English and Philosophy	QV37	3FT deg	E	BBB	Ind		Ind$	AABBB$	Ind	18 20/30
Mathematics and Philosophy	GV17	3FT deg	M	BCC-BBC	Ind	Ind		BBBBB$	Ind	6
Philosophy	V700	3FT deg	*	BBC	MO	Ind	30	BBBBB	Ind	8 18/26
Philosophy and Politics	MV17	3FT deg	*	BCC-BBC	Ind	Ind			Ind	5 16/26
Arts Combined *Philosophy*	Y401	3FT deg	*	BBC-BBB	Ind	Ind	30$	ABBB	Ind	
BA Combined Honours *Philosophy*	Y200	3FT deg	* g	BBB	Ind	Ind	Ind	Ind	Ind	
BSc Combined Honours *Philosophy*	Y100	3FT deg	*	22	MO	Ind	30	BBBBB	Ind	

LIVERPOOL JOHN MOORES Univ

Philosophy & Applied Psych (Phil Jt Awd only)	CV87	3FT deg		16-18	5M+3D	M$^ go	28$	BBCC		8 12/20
Philosophy and Lit,Life & Thought (Phil Jnt Awd)	QV37	3FT deg	E	16-20	5M+3D	PT^	28$	BBBC		6 18/20
Politics and Philosophy (Phil Joint Award only)	VM71	3FT deg	* g	16-18	5M+3D	P$^	28$	CCCC		5 16/18

LSE: LONDON Sch of Economics (Univ of London)

Philosophy	V701	3FT deg	g	BBB	Ind	X	$	Ind	Ind	
Philosophy	V703	3FT deg	g	BBB	Ind	X	$	Ind	Ind	
Philosophy and Economics	LV17	3FT deg	g	ABB	Ind	X	$	Ind	Ind	12 24/30
Philosophy and Mathematics	GV17	3FT deg	M	BBB	Ind	X	$	Ind	Ind	9
Psychology and Philosophy	LV77	3FT deg	g	BBB	Ind	X	$	Ind	Ind	46 26/30

LUTON Univ

Building Conservation and British Studies	VK92	3FT deg		12-16	MO/DO	M/D	32	BBCC	Ind	
Built Environment and British Studies	VN98	3FT deg		12-16	MO/DO	M/D	32	BBCC	Ind	
Built Environment with British Studies	N8V9	3FT deg		12-16	MO/DO	M/D	32	BBCC	Ind	
Contemporary History and British Studies	VV9C	3FT deg		12-16	MO/DO	M/D	32	BBCC	Ind	
Contemporary History with British Studies	V1V9	3FT deg		12-16	MO/DO	M/D	32	BBCC	Ind	

course details			**98 expected requirements**						**96 entry stats**
TITLE	CODE	COURSE	SUBJECTS	A/AS	ND/C	AGNVQ	IB	SQA(H)	SQA	RATIO A/AS
European Language Studies and British Studies	VT92	3FT deg		12-16	MO/DO	M/D	32	BBCC	Ind	
European Language Studies with British Studies	T2V9	3FT deg		12-16	MO/DO	M/D	32	BBCC	Ind	
Geography and British Studies	VF98	3FT deg		12-16	MO/DO	M/D	32	BBCC	Ind	
Geography with British Studies	F8V9	3FT deg		12-16	MO/DO	M/D	32	BBCC	Ind	
Health Studies and British Studies	VB9X	3FT deg		12-16	MO/DO	M/D	32	BBCC	Ind	
Health Studies with British Studies	B9V9	3FT deg		12-16	MO/DO	M/D	32	BBCC	Ind	
Journalism and British Studies	VP96	3FT deg		12-16	MO/DO	M/D	32	BBCC	Ind	
Law and British Studies	VM93	3FT deg		12-16	MO/DO	M/D	32	BBCC	Ind	
Law with British Studies	M3V9	3FT deg		12-16	MO/DO	M/D	32	BBCC	Ind	
Leisure Studies and British Studies	VN97	3FT deg		12-16	MO/DO	M/D	32	BBCC	Ind	
Leisure Studies with British Studies	N7V9	3FT deg		12-16	MO/DO	M/D	32	BBCC	Ind	
Literary Studies in English and British Studies	VQ92	3FT deg		12-16	MO/DO	M/D	32	BBCC	Ind	
Literary Studies in English with British Studies	Q2V9	3FT deg		12-16	MO/DO	M/D	32	BBCC	Ind	
Modern English Studies and British Studies	VQ93	3FT deg		12-16	MO/DO	M/D	32	BBCC	Ind	
Modern English Studies with British Studies	Q3V9	3FT deg		12-16	MO/DO	M/D	32	BBCC	Ind	
Modern History and British Studies	VV91	3FT deg		12-16	MO/DO	M/D	32	BBCC	Ind	
Modern History with British Studies	V1VX	3FT deg		12-16	MO/DO	M/D	32	BBCC	Ind	
Planning Studies and British Studies	VK94	3FT deg		12-16	MO/DO	M/D	32	BBCC	Ind	
Politics and British Studies	VM91	3FT deg		12-16	MO/DO	M/D	32	BBCC	Ind	
Politics with British Studies	M1V9	3FT deg		12-16	MO/DO	M/D	32	BBCC	Ind	
Psychology and British Studies	VL97	3FT deg		12-16	MO/DO	M/D	32	BBCC	Ind	
Psychology with British Studies	L7V9	3FT deg		12-16	MO/DO	M/D	32	BBCC	Ind	
Public Policy & Management with British Studies	M1VX	3FT deg		12-16	MO/DO	M/D	32	BBCC	Ind	
Public Policy and Management and British Studies	VM9C	3FT deg		12-16	MO/DO	M/D	32	BBCC	Ind	
Regional Planning & Development with British St	K4V9	3FT deg		12-16	MO/DO	M/D	32	BBCC	Ind	
Regional Planning and Development and British St	VK9K	3FT deg		12-16	MO/DO	M/D	32	BBCC	Ind	
Social Policy and British Studies	VL94	3FT deg		12-16	MO/DO	M/D	32	BBCC	Ind	
Social Policy with British Studies	L4V9	3FT deg		12-16	MO/DO	M/D	32	BBCC	Ind	
Social Studies and British Studies	VL93	3FT deg		12-16	MO/DO	M/D	32	BBCC	Ind	
Social Studies with British Studies	L3VX	3FT deg		12-16	MO/DO	M/D	32	BBCC	Ind	
Sociology and British Studies	VL9H	3FT deg		12-16	MO/DO	M/D	32	BBCC	Ind	
Sociology with British Studies	L3V9	3FT deg		12-16	MO/DO	M/D	32	BBCC	Ind	
Travel and Tourism and British Studies	VP97	3FT deg		12-16	MO/DO	M/D	32	BBCC	Ind	
Travel and Tourism with British Studies	P7V9	3FT deg		12-16	MO/DO	M/D	32	BBCC	Ind	
Univ of MANCHESTER										
English and Philosophy	VQ73	3FT deg	E	ABB	Ind		32$	AABBB	Ind	11	26/30
German and Philosophy	VR72	4FT deg	G	BBB	Ind		32$	AABBB$	Ind	3
Linguistics and Philosophy	QV17	3FT deg		BBB	X		32$	AABBB		3
Mathematics and Philosophy	GV17	3FT deg	M	22-24	Ind		30$	CSYS	Ind	13
Philosophy	V700	3FT deg		BBB	Ind		32$	AABBB$	Ind	10	22/30
Philosophy and Comparative Religion	VVR8	3FT deg		BBB	Ind		32$	AABBB	Ind	5	26/30
Philosophy and Politics	VM71	3FT deg		BBB	Ind		32$	AABBB$	Ind	6	22/30
Philosophy and Sociology	VL73	3FT deg		BBB	Ind		32$	AABBB$	Ind	21
Philosophy and Theology	VV78	3FT deg		BBB	Ind		32$	AABBB$	Ind	7	22/24
MANCHESTER METROPOLITAN Univ										
Philosophy/American Studies	QV47	3FT deg	*	CC	M+D	D	28	CCCC	Ind	
Philosophy/Applied Social Studies	LV37	3FT deg	*	CC	M+D	D	28	CCCC	Ind	
Philosophy/Business Studies	NV17	3FT deg	*	CC	M+D	D	28	CCCC	Ind	
Philosophy/Cultural Studies	LVH7	3FT deg	*	CC	M+D	D	28	CCCC	Ind	
Philosophy/Dance	VW74	3FT deg	*	CC	M+D	D	28	CCCC	Ind	
Philosophy/Drama	VW7K	3FT deg	*	CC	M+D	D	28	CCCC	Ind	

course details			98 expected requirements							96 entry stats
TITLE	CODE	COURSE	SUBJECTS	A/AS	ND/C	AGNVQ	IB	SQA(H)	SQA	RATIO A/AS
Philosophy/English	QV37	3FT deg	*	CC	M+D	D	28	CCCC	Ind	
Philosophy/Geography	LV87	3FT deg	*	CC	M+D	D	28	CCCC	Ind	
Philosophy/Health Studies	BV97	3FT deg	*	CC	M+D	D	28	CCCC	Ind	
Philosophy/History	VV17	3FT deg	*	CC	M+D	D	28	CCCC	Ind	
Philosophy/Leisure Studies	LV47	3FT deg	*	CC	M+D	D	28	CCCC	Ind	
Philosophy/Music	VW73	3FT deg	*	CC	M+D	D	28	CCCC	Ind	
Religious Studies/Philosophy	VV78	3FT deg	*	CC	M+D	D	28	CCCC	Ind	
Sport/Philosophy	BV67	3FT deg	S	BC	M+D	DS	28	CCCC	Ind	
Visual Arts/Philosophy	VW71	3FT deg	*	CC	M+D	D	28	CCCC	Ind	
Writing/Philosophy	VW7L	3FT deg	*	CC	M+D	D	28	CCCC	Ind	
Humanities/Social Studies Philosophy	Y400	3FT deg	*	CDD	Ind	Ind	Ind	BBB	Ind	

MIDDLESEX Univ

Philosophy	V700▼	3FT deg	* g	12-16	5M	M$ go	28	Ind	Ind	
Joint Honours Degree Philosophy	Y400	3FT deg	* g	12-16	5M	M$ go	28	BBCC	Ind	

NENE COLLEGE

American Studies with Philosophy	Q4V7	3FT deg		DD	5M	M	24	CCC	Ind	
Art and Design with Philosophy	W2V7	3FT deg		DD	5M	M	24	CCC	Ind	
Economics with Philosophy	L1V7	3FT deg	g	6	5M	M	24	CCC	Ind	
English with Philosophy	Q3V7▼	3FT deg		CC	4M+1D	M	24	CCC	Ind	
French with Philosophy	R1V7	3FT deg	F	DD	5M	Ind	24	CCC	Ind	
History with Philosophy	V1V7▼	3FT deg		CD	5M	M	24	CCC	Ind	
Human Biological Studies with Philosophy	B1V7▼	3FT deg	S	DE	5M	M	24	CCC	Ind	
Information Systems with Philosophy	G5V7	3FT deg		6	5M	M	24	CCC	Ind	
Law with Philosophy	M3V7	3FT deg	g	10	3M+2D	M	24	CCC	Ind	
Mathematics with Philosophy	G1V7	3FT deg	M	DD	Ind	Ind	24	CCC	Ind	
Music with Philosophy	W3V7	3FT deg	Mu	DD	5M	M	24	CCC	Ind	
Politics with Philosophy	M1V7	3FT deg		CD	5M	M	24	CCC	Ind	
Psychology with Philosophy	C8V7▼	3FT deg	g	CC	5M+1D	M	24	CCC	Ind	
Sport Studies with Philosophy	N7V7▼	3FT deg	Ss/Pe	12	M+2D	M	24	BBB	Ind	

Univ of NEWCASTLE

Combined Studies (BA) Cosmos and Philosophical Traditions	Y400	3FT deg	*	ABC-BBB	5D	Ind	35$	AAAB	Ind	
Combined Studies (BA) Greek and Roman Culture	Y400	3FT deg	*	ABC-BBB	5D	Ind	35$	AAAB	Ind	

Univ of NORTH LONDON

Biological Science and Philosophy	CV17	3FT/4SW/4EXT deg	B	CD	Ind	Ind	Ind	Ind	Ind	
Business and Philosophy	NV17	3FT deg	* g	12	MO+4D	D	Ind	Ind	Ind	
Chemistry and Philosophy	FV17	3FT/4SW/4EXT deg	C	12	Ind	Ind	Ind	Ind	Ind	
Health Policy and Philosophy	LV47	3FT deg	*	CC	Ind	Ind	Ind	Ind	Ind	
Health Studies and Philosophy	BV97	3FT deg	* g	CC	MO	D	Ind	Ind	Ind	
Law and Philosophy	MV37	3FT deg	*	CC	Ind	Ind	Ind	Ind	Ind	
Mathematics and Philosophy	GV17	3FT/4SW/4EXT deg	M	CD	X	M*^	Ind	Ind	Ind	
Philosophy	V700	3FT deg	*	CD	Ind	Ind	Ind	Ind	Ind	5 6/14
Philosophy and Economics	LV17	3FT deg	* g	12	Ind	Ind	Ind	Ind	Ind	
Politics and Philosophy	MV1T	3FT deg	*	CC	Ind	Ind	Ind	Ind	Ind	
Psychology (Applied) and Philosophy	LV77	3FT deg	* g	CC	Ind	Ind	Ind	Ind	Ind	
Sociology and Philosophy	LV37	3FT deg	*	CC	Ind	Ind	Ind	Ind	Ind	
Combined Honours Philosophy	Y300	3FT deg	*	CC	Ind	Ind	Ind	Ind	Ind	

TITLE	CODE	COURSE	SUBJECTS	A/AS	NO/C	AGNVQ	IB	SQA(H)	SQA	RATIO	A/AS
Univ of NOTTINGHAM											
American Studies and Philosophy	QV47	3FT deg	E	BBC						9	
Classical Civilisation and Philosophy	QV87	3FT deg		BBC						10	
Economics and Philosophy	LV17	3FT deg	* g	AAB-ABB	X		32	Ind	X	14	28/30
English Studies and Philosophy	QV37	3FT deg	E	ABC						30	28/30
French and Philosophy	RV17	4FT deg	F	ABC							
German and Philosophy	RV27	4FT deg	G	BBC							
Greek and Philosophy	QV77	3FT deg		BBC							
Mathematics and Philosophy	GV17	3FT deg	M	AAB-ABB	Ind	Ind	Ind	Ind	Ind	7	26/30
Philosophy	V700	3FT deg		ABC						11	24/30
Philosophy and Theology	VV78	3FT deg		BBC						18	
Physics and Philosophy	FV37	3FT deg	P+M	BB-BBC	Ind		Ind	CSYS	Ind	9	
Psychology and Philosophy	CV87	3FT deg	* g	BBB	Ind		33	Ind	Ind	99	
OXFORD Univ											
Mathematics and Philosophy (4 Yrs)	GV17	4FT deg	M	AAB	DO		36	AAAAA	Ind	2	30/30
Philosophy and Modern Languages (3 Yrs)	TV97	3FT deg	L	AAB	DO		36	AAAAA	Ind	3	
Philosophy and Modern Languages (4 Yrs)	VT79	4FT deg	L	AAB	DO		36	AAAAA	Ind	2	26/30
Philosophy and Theology	VV78	3FT deg	*	AAB-ABB	DO		36	AAAAA	Ind	3	22/30
Physics and Philosophy (4 Yrs)	VF73	4FT deg	M+P	AAB	DO		36	AAAAA	Ind	2	28/30
Physiology with Philosophy	B1V7	3FT deg	*	AAB	DO		36	AAAAA	Ind		
Psychology with Philosophy	C8V7	3FT deg	*	AAB	DO		36	AAAAA	Ind	5	28/30
Philosophy, Politics and Economics *Philosophy*	Y616	3FT deg	*	AAB	DO		36	AAAAA	Ind		
Psychology, Philosophy and Physiology *Philosophy*	Y620	3FT deg	*	AAB	DO		36	AAAAA	Ind		
OXFORD WESTMINSTER COLLEGE											
Contemporary English Studies with Cultural St	Q3V9	3FT deg	E	CE	MO	M	Ind	CCC	Ind		
Contemporary English Studies with Cultural St	Q3VX	2FT Dip	E	CE	MO	M	Ind	CCC	Ind		
Contemporary French Studies with Cultural St	R1V9	3FT deg	F	CE	MO	M	Ind	CCC	Ind		
Contemporary French Studies with Cultural Studs	R1VX	2FT Dip	F	CE	MO	M	Ind	CCC	Ind		
Contemporary Geography Studies with Cultural St	L8VX	2FT Dip	Gy	CE	MO	M	Ind	CCC	Ind		
Contemporary Geography Studies with Cultural St	L8V9	3FT deg	Gy	CE	MO	M	Ind	CCC	Ind		
Contemporary Historical Studies with Cultural St	V1VX	2FT Dip	H	CE	MO	M	Ind	CCC	Ind		
Contemporary Historical Studies with Cultural St	V1V9	3FT deg	H	CE	MO	M	Ind	CCC	Ind		
QUEEN'S Univ Belfast											
History & Philosophy of Sci/Economic & Soc Hist	VV35	3FT deg	* g	BCC	3M+4D	D*6/^ go	29$	ABBB	Ind		
History & Philosophy of Science/Ancient History	VVC5	3FT deg	* g	BCC	3M+4D	D*6/^ go	29$	ABBB	Ind		
History & Philosophy of Science/Archaeology	VV65	3FT deg	* g	BCC	3M+4D	D*6/^ go	29$	ABBB	Ind		
History & Philosophy of Science/Byzantine Stds	QV85	3FT/4FT deg	* g	BCC	3M+4D	D*6/^ go	29$	ABBB	Ind		
History & Philosophy of Science/Classical Stds	VQ58	3FT deg	* g	BCC	3M+4D	D*6/^ go	29$	ABBB	Ind		
History & Philosophy of Science/Greek	QV75	3FT/4FT deg	* g	BCC	3M+4D	D*6/^ go	29$	ABBB	Ind		
Latin/History & Philosophy of Science	VQ56	3FT/4FT deg	* g	BCC	3M+4D	D*6/^ go	29$	ABBB	Ind		
Philosophy	V700	3FT deg	* g	BCC	3M+4D	D*6/^ go	29$	ABBB	Ind	21	
Philosophy/Ancient History	VVC7	3FT deg	* g	BCC	3M+4D	D*6/^ go	29$	ABBB	Ind	5	
Philosophy/Biblical Studies	VV87	3FT deg	* g	BCC	3M+4D	D*6/^ go	29$	ABBB	Ind		
Philosophy/Byzantine Studies	QV87	3FT/4FT deg	* g	BCC	3M+4D	D*6/^ go	29$	ABBB	Ind		
Philosophy/Celtic	QV57	3FT/4FT deg	* g	BCC	3M+4D	D*6/^ go	29$	ABBB	Ind		
Philosophy/Classical Studies	VQ78	3FT deg	* g	BCC	3M+4D	D*6/^ go	29$	ABBB	Ind	6	
Philosophy/Computer Science	GV57	3FT deg	M/Cs g	BCC	X	D*_ go	29$	X	Ind		
Philosophy/Economic & Social History	VV37	3FT deg	* g	BCC	3M+4D	D*6/^ go	29$	ABBB	Ind	4	
Philosophy/English	QV37	3FT deg	E g	BCC	X	D*_ go	29$	ABBB	X	8	20/26

course details　|　98 expected requirements　|　*96 entry stats*

TITLE	CODE	COURSE	SUBJECTS	A/AS	NO/C	AGNVQ	IB	SQA(H)	SQA	RATIO R/AS
Philosophy/French (4 years)	RV17	4FT deg	E g	BCC	X	D*_^ go	29$	ABBB	X	
Philosophy/German (4 years)	RV27	4FT deg	* g	BCC	3M+4D	D*6/^ go	29$	ABBB	Ind	
Philosophy/Greek	QV77	3FT/4FT deg	* g	BCC	3M+4D	D*6/^ go	29$	ABBB	Ind	1
Philosophy/History & Philosophy of Science	VV57	3FT deg	* g	BCC	3M+4D	D*6/^ go	29$	ABBB	Ind	
Philosophy/Italian (4 years)	RV37	4FT deg	* g	BCC	3M+4D	D*6/^ go	29$	ABBB	Ind	
Philosophy/Latin	QV67	3FT/4FT deg	* g	BCC	3M+4D	D*6/^ go	29$	ABBB	Ind	
Philosophy/Music	WV37	3FT deg	* g	BCC	3M+4D	D*6/^ go	29$	ABBB	Ind	
Politics/History & Philosophy of Science	VM51	3FT deg	* g	BCC	3M+4D	D*6/^ go	29$	ABBB	Ind	
Politics/Philosophy	VM71	3FT deg	* g	BCC	3M+4D	D*6/^ go	29$	ABBB	Ind	15
Psychology/History & Philosophy of Science	CV85	3FT deg	* g	BCC	3M+4D	D*6/^ go	29$	ABBB	Ind	8
Psychology/Philosophy	CV87	3FT deg	* g	BCC	3M+4D	D*6/^ go	29$	ABBB	Ind	18
Scholastic Philosophy	V750	3FT deg	* g	BCC	3M+4D	D*6/^ go	29$	ABBB	Ind	
Scholastic Philosophy/Ancient History	VVCR	3FT deg	* g	BCC	3M+4D	D*6/^ go	29$	ABBB	Ind	
Scholastic Philosophy/Biblical Studies	VV8R	3FT deg	* g	BCC	3M+4D	D*6/^ go	29$	ABBB	Ind	
Scholastic Philosophy/Byzantine Studies	QV8R	3FT/4FT deg	* g	BCC	3M+4D	D*6/^ go	29$	ABBB	Ind	
Scholastic Philosophy/Celtic	QV5R	3FT/4FT deg	* g	BCC	3M+4D	D*6/^ go	29$	ABBB	Ind	
Scholastic Philosophy/Classical Studies	VQR8	3FT deg	* g	BCC	3M+4D	D*6/^ go	29$	ABBB	Ind	
Scholastic Philosophy/Economic & Social History	VV3R	3FT deg	* g	BCC	3M+4D	D*6/^ go	29$	ABBB	Ind	
Scholastic Philosophy/Economics	LV1R	3FT deg								
Scholastic Philosophy/English	QV3R	3FT deg	E g	BCC	X	D*_^ go	29$	ABBB	X	5
Scholastic Philosophy/French (4 years)	RV1R	4FT deg	E g	BCC	X	D*_^ go	29$	ABBB	X	
Scholastic Philosophy/German (4 years)	RV2R	4FT deg	* g	BCC	3M+4D	D*6/^ go	29$	ABBB	Ind	
Scholastic Philosophy/Greek	QV7R	3FT/4FT deg	* g	BCC	3M+4D	D*6/^ go	29$	ABBB	Ind	
Scholastic Philosophy/History & Phil of Science	VV5R	3FT deg	* g	BCC	3M+4D	D*6/^ go	29$	ABBB	Ind	
Scholastic Philosophy/Italian (4 years)	RV3R	4FT deg	* g	BCC	3M+4D	D*6/^ go	29$	ABBB	Ind	
Scholastic Philosophy/Latin	QV6R	3FT/4FT deg	* g	BCC	3M+4D	D*6/^ go	29$	ABBB	Ind	
Scholastic Philosophy/Music	VW73	3FT deg	* g	BCC	3M+4D	D*6/^ go	29$	ABBB	Ind	
Scholastic Philosophy/Philosophy	V754	3FT deg	* g	BCC	3M+4D	D*6/^ go	29$	ABBB	Ind	4
Scholastic Philosophy/Politics	MV1R	3FT deg	* g	BCC	3M+4D	D*6/^ go	29$	ABBB	Ind	5
Scholastic Philosophy/Psychology	CV8R	3FT deg	* g	BCC	3M+4D	D*6/^ go	29$	ABBB	Ind	23
Social Anthropology/History & Philosophy of Sci	VL56	3FT deg	* g	BCC	3M+4D	D*6/^ go	29$	ABBB	Ind	
Social Anthropology/Philosophy	VL76	3FT deg	* g	BCC	3M+4D	D*6/^ go	29$	ABBB	Ind	7
Social Anthropology/Scholastic Philosophy	LV67	3FT deg	* g	BCC	3M+4D	D*6/^ go	29$	ABBB	Ind	
Social Policy/History & Philosophy of Science	VL54	3FT deg	* g	BCC	3M+4D	D*6/^ go	29$	ABBB	Ind	
Social Policy/Philosophy	VL74	3FT deg	* g	BCC	3M+4D	D*6/^ go	29$	ABBB	Ind	
Social Policy/Scholastic Philosophy	LV47	3FT deg	* g	BCC	3M+4D	D*6/^ go	29$	ABBB	Ind	
Sociology/History & Philosophy of Science	VL53	3FT deg	* g	BCC	3M+4D	D*6/^ go	29$	ABBB	Ind	
Sociology/Philosophy	VL73	3FT deg	* g	BCC	3M+4D	D*6/^ go	29$	ABBB	Ind	5
Sociology/Scholastic Philosophy	LV37	3FT deg	* g	BCC	3M+4D	D*6/^ go	29$	ABBB	Ind	
Spanish/Philosophy (4 years)	VR74	4FT deg	* g	BCC	3M+4D	D*6/^ go	29$	ABBB	Ind	
Spanish/Scholastic Philosophy (4 years)	VRR4	4FT deg	* g	BCC	3M+4D	D*6/^ go	29$	ABBB	Ind	
Theology and History and Philosophy of Science	VV58	3FT deg								
Theology and Scholastic Philosophy	VV78	3FT deg								

Univ of READING

Art and Philosophy	VW71	4FT deg	*	BCC	Ind	DA^	30	BBBB	Ind		
Art and Philosophy	EV17	4FT deg	*	BCC	Ind	DA^	30	BBBB	Ind		
Computer Science with Philosophy	G5V7	3FT deg	* g	20	3M+2D	D$^ go	30	BBBB	Ind		
Greek and Philosophy	QV77	3FT deg	* g	BCC	Ind	D*^ go	30	BBBB	Ind		
History and Philosophy	VV17	3FT deg	*	BBC	Ind	D*^	31	BBBB	Ind	7	
Latin and Philosophy	QV67	3FT deg	* g	BCC	Ind	D*^ go	30	BBBB	Ind		
Philosophy	V700	3FT deg	*	BCC	Ind	D*^	30	BBBB	Ind	7	16/28
Philosophy and Classical Studies	QV87	3FT deg	*	BCC	Ind	D*^	30	BBBB	Ind	17	

TITLE	CODE	COURSE	SUBJECTS	A/AS	ND/C	AGNVQ	IB	SQA(H)	SQA	RATIO	A/AS
Philosophy and English Literature	VQ73	3FT deg	El	BBC	Ind	D*^	31$	BBBB$	Ind	15	22/26
Philosophy and French	RV17	4FT deg	F	BBC	Ind	D*^	31$	BBBB$	Ind		
Philosophy and German	RV27	4FT deg	*g	BCC	Ind	D$^ go	30	BBBB	Ind		
Philosophy and International Relations	VM71	3FT deg	*	BCC	Ind	D*^	30	BBBB	Ind	8	
Philosophy and Italian	RV37	4FT deg	*g	BCC	Ind	D$^ go	30	BBBB	Ind		
Philosophy and Linguistics	QV17	3FT deg	*	BCC	Ind	D*^	30	BBBB	Ind	7	
Philosophy and Politics	MV17	3FT deg	*	BCC	Ind	D*^	30	BBBB	Ind	8	20/20
Philosophy and Sociology	LV37	3FT deg	*	BCC	Ind	D$^ go	30	BBBB	Ind	42	
Psychology and Philosophy	CV87	3FT deg	*g	BCC	Ind	D*^ go	30	BBBB	Ind	11	20/28

ROEHAMPTON INST

TITLE	CODE	COURSE	SUBJECTS	A/AS	ND/C	AGNVQ	IB	SQA(H)	SQA	RATIO	A/AS
Humanities (English History Theol & Relig St)	VY93▼	3FT deg	E/H	CC	2M+2D$		30	BBC	Ind	2	6/14

Univ of SHEFFIELD

TITLE	CODE	COURSE	SUBJECTS	A/AS	ND/C	AGNVQ	IB	SQA(H)	SQA	RATIO	A/AS
Biblical Studies and Philosophy	VV78	3FT deg	*g	BBC	X	X	30	ABBB	Ind	22	
Biological Sciences and Philosophy	CV17	3FT deg	B+S g	24	3M+3D$	DS6/^	32$	AABB$	Ind	7	
Economics and Philosophy	LV17	3FT deg	*g	BBB	3M+3D	D^	32	AABB	Ind	9	
English and Philosophy	QV37	3FT deg	El g	ABB	X	X	33$	AAAB$	Ind	12	26/30
French and Philosophy	RV17	4FT deg	F g	BBB	X	X	32$	AABB$	Ind	5	26/28
German and Philosophy	RV27	4FT deg	G g	BBB	X	X	32$	AABB$	Ind		
History and Philosophy	VV17	3FT deg	H g	ABB	X	X	33$	AAAB$	Ind	7	28/28
Linguistics and Philosophy	QV17	3FT deg	Ee g	BBB	X	X	32$	AABB$	Ind		
Mathematics and Philosophy	VG7D	3FT deg	M g	BBB	X	X	32$	AABB$	Ind	4	22/30
Music and Philosophy	VW73	3FT deg	Mu g	BBB	X	X	32$	AABB$	Ind		
Philosophy	V700	3FT deg	*g	BBB	X	X	32	AABB	Ind	4	20/30
Philosophy and Hispanic Studies	RV47	4FT deg	L g	BBB	X	X	32$	AABB$	Ind		
Philosophy and Psychology	CV87	3FT deg	*g	AAB	1M+5D	D^	35	AAAA	Ind	48	
Physics and Philosophy	FV37	3FT deg	P+M g	BBC	4M+2D$	DS^	30$	ABBB$	Ind		
Social and Political Studies *Philosophy*	Y220	3FT deg	*g	BBC	4D		30	ABBB	Ind		

Univ College of St MARTIN, LANCASTER AND CUMBRIA

TITLE	CODE	COURSE	SUBJECTS	A/AS	ND/C	AGNVQ	IB	SQA(H)	SQA	RATIO	A/AS
Applied Community Studies/Social Ethics	LV57	3FT deg	*	CD-DDE	3M+2D	M*	28	BCCC	Ind		
English/Social Ethics	QV3R	3FT deg	E	BC-BDE	X	P^	28$	BBBC$	Ind	3	
Geography/Social Ethics	LV8R	3FT deg	Gy	CD-DDE	X	P^	28$	BCCC$	Ind		
Health Studies/Social Ethics	BV97	3FT deg	*	CD-DDE	3M+2D	M*	28$	BCCC	Ind	1	
History/Social Ethics	VV1R	3FT deg	H	CD-DDE	X	P^	28$	BCCC$	Ind		
Mathematics/Social Ethics	GV17	3FT deg	M	DD-DEE	X	P^	28$	BCCC$	Ind		
Religious Studies/Social Ethics	VV8R	3FT deg	*	CD-DDE	3M+2D	M*	28$	BCCC	Ind	1	6/16
Science, Technology and Society/Social Ethics	VY71	3FT deg	g	CD-DDE	3M+2D	M*	28	BCCC	Ind		
Social Ethics	V760	3FT deg	*	CD-DDE	3M+2D	M*	28	BCCC	Ind	3	4/20
Social Ethics/Applied Community Studies	VL7M	3FT deg	*	CD-DDE	3M+2D	M*	28	BCCC	Ind	2	
Social Ethics/Drama	VW74	3FT deg	*	CD-DDE	3M+2D	M*	28	BCCC	Ind	5	
Social Ethics/English	VQ7H	3FT deg	E	CD-DDE	3M+2D	M^	28$	BCCC$	Ind	2	
Social Ethics/Geography	VL7V	3FT deg	Gy	CD-DDE	3M+2D$	M^	28$	BCCC$	Ind		
Social Ethics/Health Administration	VL74	3FT deg	*	CD-DDE	3M+2D	M*	28	BCCC	Ind		
Social Ethics/Health Studies	VB79	3FT deg	*	CD-DDE	3M+2D	M*	28	BCCC	Ind		
Social Ethics/History	VV7C	3FT deg	H	CD-DDE	3M+2D	M^	28$	BCCC$	Ind		
Social Ethics/Mathematics	VG71	3FT deg	M	CD-DDE	3M+2D$	M^	28$	BCCC$	Ind		
Social Ethics/Religious Studies	VV7V	3FT deg	*	CD-DDE	3M+2D	M*	28	BCCC	Ind	3	
Social Ethics/Science, Technology and Society	VY7C	3FT deg	g	CD-DDE	3M+2D	M*	28	BCCC	Ind		

	course details			98 expected requirements							96 entry stats
TITLE		CODE	COURSE	SUBJECTS	A/AS	NO/C	AGNVQ	IB	SQA(H)	SQA	RATIO A/AS

Univ of SOUTHAMPTON

TITLE	CODE	COURSE	SUBJECTS	A/AS	NO/C	AGNVQ	IB	SQA(H)	SQA	RATIO A/AS
Economics and Philosophy	VL71	3FT deg	* g	BCC	Ind	D$^ go	26	Ind	Ind	
English and Philosophy	QV37	3FT deg	E	BBC	X	Ind	Ind	Ind	X	10 16/28
French and Philosophy	RV17	4FT deg	F	BBC	1M+4D	Ind	30$	Ind	Ind	8
German and Philosophy	RV27	4FT deg	G	BCC	1M+4D	Ind	30$	Ind	Ind	
Mathematics and Philosophy	GV17	3FT deg	M	BBC	Ind	Ind	30	ABBBB	Ind	7
Philosophy	V700	3FT deg	*	BCC	1M+4D	Ind	26	Ind	Ind	4 11/22
Philosophy and Mathematics	VG71	3FT deg	M	BCC-BCD	1M+4D	Ind	26	Ind	Ind	4
Philosophy and Politics	VM71	3FT deg	*	BCC	1M+4D	Ind	26	CSYS	Ind	8 18/26
Philosophy and Sociology	VL73	3FT deg	g	BCC	1M+4D	Ind	26	CSYS	Ind	14

Univ of ST ANDREWS

TITLE	CODE	COURSE	SUBJECTS	A/AS	NO/C	AGNVQ	IB	SQA(H)	SQA	RATIO A/AS
Logic and Philosophy of Science-Computer Science	GV5R	3FT/4FT deg	M g	BBB	Ind	Ind	28$	BBCC$	Ind	
Mathematics-Logic and Philosophy of Science	GV1R	3FT/4FT deg	M g	CCC	Ind	Ind	28$	BBBC$	Ind	6
New Testament-Classical Studies	VQ78	4FT deg	* g	BBB	X	Ind	30$	BBC	Ind	
Philosophy	V700	4FT deg	* g	BBB	X	Ind	30$	BBBB	Ind	11
Philosophy-Ancient History	VV17	4FT deg	* g	BBB	X	Ind	30$	BBBB	Ind	9
Philosophy-Art History	VV47	4FT deg	* g	BBB	X	Ind	30$	BBBB	Ind	10
Philosophy-Biblical Studies	VV7V	4FT deg	* g	BBB	X	Ind	30$	BBBB	Ind	4
Philosophy-Economics	LV17	4FT deg	* g	BBB	X	Ind	30$	BBBB	Ind	12
Philosophy-English	QV37	4FT deg	* g	BBB	X	Ind	30$	BBBB	Ind	5 26/28
Philosophy-French	RV17	4FT deg	F g	BBB	X	Ind	30$	BBBB$	Ind	
Philosophy-French with Year Abroad	RVDR	4FT/5FT deg	F g	BBB	X	Ind	30$	BBBB$	Ind	5
Philosophy-German	RV27	4FT deg	* g	BBB	X	Ind	30$	BBBB	Ind	2
Philosophy-German with Year Abroad	RVG7	4FT/5FT deg	* g	BBB	X	Ind	30$	BBBB	Ind	
Philosophy-Greek	QV77	4FT deg	* g	BBB	X	Ind	30$	BBBB	Ind	
Philosophy-International Relations	MV17	4FT deg	* g	AAB	X	Ind	36$	AAAB	Ind	8
Philosophy-Italian	RV37	4FT deg	* g	BBB	X	Ind	30$	BBBB	Ind	
Philosophy-Italian with Year Abroad	RV3R	4FT/5FT deg	* g	BBB	X	Ind	30$	BBBB	Ind	
Philosophy-Latin	QV67	4FT deg	* g	BBB	X	Ind	30$	BBBB	Ind	
Philosophy-Management	VN71	4FT deg	* g	BBB	X	Ind	30$	BBBB	Ind	4
Philosophy-Mathematics	GV17	4FT deg	M g	BBB	X	Ind	30$	BBBB$	Ind	3
Philosophy-Mediaeval History	VVC7	4FT deg	* g	BBB	X	Ind	30$	BBBB	Ind	4
Philosophy-Modern History	VVD7	4FT deg	* g	BBB	X	Ind	30$	BBBB	Ind	3
Physics-Logic and Philosophy of Science	FV3R	4FT deg	P+M	CCC	Ind	Ind	28$	BBBC$	Ind	6
Psychology-Philosophy	LV77	4FT deg	* g	ABB	X	Ind	32$	ABBB	Ind	8
Russian with Year Abroad-Philosophy	RVV7	4FT/5FT deg	* g	BBB	X	Ind	30$	BBBB	Ind	
Russian-Philosophy	RV87	4FT deg	* g	BBB	X	Ind	30$	BBBB	Ind	
Scottish History-Philosophy	VV7C	4FT deg	* g	BBB	X	Ind	30$	BBBB	Ind	
Social Anthropology-Philosophy	LV67	4FT deg	* g	BBB	X	Ind	30$	BBBB	Ind	9
Spanish with Year Abroad-Philosophy	RVL7	4FT/5FT deg	* g	BBB	X	Ind	30$	BBBB	Ind	
Spanish-Philosophy	RV47	4FT deg	* g	BBB	X	Ind	30$	BBBB	Ind	
Statistics-Logic and Philosophy of Science	GV4R	3FT/4FT deg	M g	CCC	Ind	Ind	28$	BBBC$	Ind	
Statistics-Philosophy	GV47	4FT deg	M g	BBB	X	Ind	30$	BBBB$	Ind	
Theological Studies-Philosophy	VV78	4FT deg	* g	BBB	X	Ind	30$	BBBB	Ind	14
European Integration Studies *Philosophy*	Y602	4FT deg	* g	BBB	X	Ind	30$	BBBB	Ind	
General Degree of BSc *Logic and Philosophy of Science*	Y100	3FT deg	B/C/Gy/M/P g	CCC	Ind	Ind	28$	BBBC$	Ind	
General Degree of MA *Philosophy*	Y450	3FT deg	* g	BBB	X	Ind	30$	BBBB	Ind	

course details | 98 expected requirements | 96 entry stats

TITLE	CODE	COURSE	SUBJECTS	A/AS	ND/C	AGNVQ	IB	SQA(H)	SQA	RATIO A/AS
THE UNIVERSITY COLLEGE OF ST MARK AND ST JOHN										
Theology with Philosophy	V8V7	3FT deg	Re	4	MO	M	Dip	CCCC	Ind	
STAFFORDSHIRE Univ										
European Culture/Philosophy	LVP7	3FT deg	g	CD	MO+2D	M	27	BBC	Ind	
Philisophy/Economic Studies	LVC7	3FT deg	g	12	MO+2D	M	27	BBC		
Philosophy	V700	3FT deg	g	CD	MO+2D	M	27	BBC	Ind	
Philosophy/American Studies	VQ74	3FT deg	g	CD	MO+2D	M	27d	BBC	Ind	4
Philosophy/Cultural Studies	VL76	3FT deg	g	CD	MO+2D	M	27	BBC	Ind	1
Philosophy/Development Studies	VM7Y	3FT deg	g	12	MO+2D	M	27	BBC	Ind	
Philosophy/Film Studies	VW75	3FT deg	g	CD	MO+2D	M	27	BBC	Ind	4
Philosophy/French	VR71	3FT/4SW deg	F	CD	MO+2D	M^	27	BBC	Ind	
Philosophy/Geography	VL78	3FT deg	g	CC	MO+2D	M	27	BBB	Ind	2
Philosophy/German	VR72	3FT/4SW deg	G	CD	MO+2D	M^	27	BBC	Ind	
Philosophy/History	VV71	3FT deg	H g	CD	MO+2D	M	27	BBC	Ind	3	7/8
Philosophy/History of Art and Design	VV74	3FT deg	g	CD	MO+2D	M	27	BBC	Ind	1
Philosophy/Information Systems	VG75	3FT deg	g	12	MO+2D	M	27	BBC	Ind	
Philosophy/Law	VM73	3FT deg	g	CCC	HN	M^	27	BBBB	Ind	4
Philosophy/Legal Studies	VM7H	3FT deg	g	CCC	HN	M^	27	BBBB	Ind	
Philosophy/Literature	VQ73	3FT deg	El g	CD	MO+2D	M	27	BBBC	Ind	3	8/18
Philosophy/Media Studies	PV47	3FT deg	g	CD	MO+2D	M	27	BBC	Ind	6
Politics/Philosophy	MVC7	3FT deg	g	12	MO+2D	M	27	BBC	Ind	4
Psychology/Philosophy	LV77	3FT deg	g	18	3M+3D	Ind	27	BBB	Ind	9
Sociology/Philosophy	LV37	3FT deg	g	12	3M	M	24	BCC	Ind	5	6/12
Spanish/Philosophy	RV47	3FT/4SW deg	g	CD	MO+2D	M^	27	BBC	Ind	
Women's Studies/Philosophy	MV97	3FT deg	g	12	MO+2D	M	27	BBC	Ind	
Univ of STIRLING										
Computing Science/Philosophy	GV57	4FT deg	g	CCC	Ind	Ind	28	BBCC	HN	
Economics/Philosophy	LV17	4FT deg	g	CCC	Ind	Ind	28	BBCC	HN	
English Studies/Philosophy	QV37	4FT deg	g	BBC	Ind	Ind	33	BBBB	HN	
Film & Media Studies/Philosophy	VP74	4FT deg	g	BBC	Ind	Ind	35	ABBB	HN	
French/Philosophy	RV17	4FT deg	g	CCC	Ind	Ind	31	BBBC	HN	
German/Philosophy	RV27	4FT deg	g	CCC	Ind	Ind	31	BBBC	HN	
History/Philosophy	VV17	4FT deg	g	CCC	Ind	Ind	28	BBCC	HN	
Japanese/Philosophy	TV47	4FT deg	g	BCC	Ind	Ind	31	BBBC	HN	
Philosophy	V700	4FT deg	g	CCC	Ind	Ind	28	BBCC	HN	
Philosophy/Politics	MV17	4FT deg	Re	BCC	Ind	Ind	31	BBBC	HN	
Philosophy/Psychology	CV87	4FT deg	g	BBC	Ind	Ind	33	BBBB	HN	
Philosophy/Religious Studies	VV78	4FT deg	g	CCC	Ind	Ind	28	BBCC	HN	
Philosophy/Social Policy	LV47	4FT deg	g	BCC	HN	Ind	31	BBBC	HN	
Philosophy/Sociology	LV37	4FT deg	g	CCC	Ind	Ind	28	BBCC	HN	
Spanish/Philosophy	RV47	4FT deg	g	CCC	Ind	Ind	31	BBBC	HN	
Politics, Philosophy and Economics _Philosophy_	Y616	4FT deg	g	BCC	Ind	Ind	31	BBBC	HN	
Univ of STRATHCLYDE										
Arts and Social Sciences _Scottish Studies_	Y440	3FT/4FT deg	g	CCC	Ind		28	BBBBB$	Ind	
Univ of SUNDERLAND										
Chemistry and Philosophy	FV17	3FT deg	C	8	3M	M	Ind	Ind	Ind	
Chemistry with Philosophy	F1V7	3FT deg	C	8	3M	M	Ind	Ind	Ind	
Economics and Philosophy	LV17	3FT deg	* g	10	Ind	M	24	CCCC	Ind	2
Economics with Philosophy	L1V7	3FT deg	*	8	3M	M	Ind	Ind	Ind	

course details | 98 expected requirements | 96 entry stats

TITLE	CODE	COURSE	SUBJECTS	A/AS	NO/C	AGNVQ	IB	SQA(H)	SQA	RATIO	A/AS
English and Philosophy	QV37▼	3FT deg	El g	12	X	M	24$	BCCC$	X	5	6/14
English with Philosophy	Q3V7	3FT deg	*	10	4M	Ind	Ind	Ind	Ind		
French and Philosophy	RV17▼	4FT deg	F g	10	N $	M	24$	CCCC$	N$	4	
French with Philosophy	R1V7	4FT deg	F	8	3M	M	Ind	Ind	Ind		
Geography and Philosophy	LV87▼	3FT deg	Gy/Gl g	12	3M	M	24$	BCCC	N	4	
Geography with Philosophy	L8V7	3FT deg	*	8	3M	M	Ind	Ind	Ind		
Geology and Philosophy	FV67	3FT deg	*	8	3M	M	Ind	Ind	Ind		
Geology with Philosophy	F6V7	3FT deg	*	8	3M	M	Ind	Ind	Ind		
German and Philosophy	RV27▼	4FT deg	G g	10	N $	M	24$	CCCC$	N$		
German with Philosophy	R2V7	4SW deg	G	8	3M	M	Ind	Ind	Ind		
History and Philosophy	VV17▼	3FT deg	H g	12	Ind	M	24	BCCC	Ind	3	
History with Philosophy	V1V7	3FT deg	*	10	4M	M	Ind	Ind	Ind		
Mathematics and Philosophy	GV17	3FT deg	M	8	3M	M	Ind	Ind			
Mathematics with Philosophy	G1V7	3FT deg	M	8	3M	M	Ind	Ind	Ind		
Media Studies and Philosophy	PV47	3FT deg	*	24	Ind	Ind	Ind	Ind			
Media Studies with Philosophy	P4V7	3FT deg	*	24	Ind	Ind	Ind	Ind	Ind		
Philosophy and Physiology	VB71	3FT deg	*	8	3M	Ind	Ind				
Philosophy and Psychology	VC78	3FT deg	* g	14	MO	M	26$	BBCC$	N	3	6/16
Philosophy and Religious Studies	VV78	3FT deg	* g	12	3M	M	24	BCCC	N	2	
Philosophy and Sociology	VL73▼	3FT deg	* g	12	3M	M	24	BCCC	N	5	
Philosophy with American Studies	V7Q4	3FT deg	*	8	3M	Ind	Ind	Ind	Ind		
Philosophy with Chemistry	V7F1	3FT deg	*	8	3M	Ind	Ind	Ind	Ind		
Philosophy with Comparative Literature	V7Q2	3FT deg	El g	12	X	M	24$	BCCC$	X	1	
Philosophy with Economics	V7L1	3FT deg	*	8	3M	Ind	Ind	Ind	Ind		
Philosophy with English	V7Q3	3FT deg	*	10	4M	Ind	Ind	Ind	Ind		
Philosophy with European Studies	V7T2	3FT deg	* g	12	Ind	M	24	BCCC	Ind	1	
Philosophy with French	V7R1	3FT deg	*	8	3M	Ind	Ind	Ind	Ind		
Philosophy with Geography	V7L8	3FT deg	*	8	3M	Ind	Ind	Ind	Ind		
Philosophy with Geology	V7F6	3FT deg	*	8	3M	Ind	Ind	Ind	Ind		
Philosophy with German	V7R2	3FT deg	*	8	3M	Ind	Ind	Ind	Ind		
Philosophy with History	V7V1	3FT deg	*	10	4M	Ind	Ind	Ind	Ind		
Philosophy with History of Art and Design	V7V4	3FT deg	*	8	3M	Ind	Ind	Ind	Ind		
Philosophy with Mathematics	V7G1	3FT deg	*	8	3M	Ind	Ind	Ind	Ind		
Philosophy with Media Studies	V7P4	3FT deg	*	24	Ind	Ind	Ind	Ind	Ind		
Philosophy with Physiology	V7B1	3FT deg	*	8	3M	M	Ind	Ind	Ind		
Philosophy with Psychology	V7C8	3FT deg	*	10	4M	M^	Ind	Ind	Ind		
Philosophy with Religious Studies	V7V8	3FT deg	*	8	3M	M	Ind	Ind	Ind		
Philosophy with Sociology	V7L3	3FT deg	*	10	4M	M	Ind	Ind	Ind		
Physiology with Philosophy	B1V7	3FT deg	*	8	3M	M	Ind	Ind	Ind		
Psychology with Philosophy	C8V7	3FT deg	*	10	4M	M^	Ind	Ind	Ind		
Religious Studies with Philosophy	V8V7	3FT deg	*	8	3M	M	Ind	Ind	Ind		
Sociology with Philosophy	L3V7	3FT deg	*	10	4M	M	Ind	Ind	Ind		

Univ of SUSSEX

TITLE	CODE	COURSE	SUBJECTS	A/AS	NO/C	AGNVQ	IB	SQA(H)	SQA
Philosophy and English in Cultural & Commun St	VQ73	3FT deg	*	BBB	MO	M*6	$	Ind	Ind
Philosophy and English in English & American St	VQ7H	3FT deg	*	BBB	MO	M*6	$	Ind	Ind
Philosophy and English in European Studies	VQ7J	4FT deg	* g	BBB	MO $	M*6 go	$	Ind	Ind
Philosophy in Cognitive and Computing Studies	V7G5	3FT deg	*	BBB	MO	M*6	$	Ind	Ind
Philosophy in Cultural and Community Studies	V7Y2	3FT deg	*	BBB	MO	M*6	$	Ind	Ind
Philosophy in English and American Studies	V7Q4	3FT deg	*	BBB	MO	M*6	$	Ind	Ind
Philosophy in European Studies	V7T2	4FT deg	* g	BBB	MO $	M*6 go	$	Ind	Ind
Philosophy in Social Sciences	V7M9	3FT deg	*	BBB	MO	M*6	$	Ind	Ind
Philosophy with Politics	V7M1	3FT deg	*	BBB	MO	M*6	$	Ind	Ind
Philosophy with Sociology	V7L3	3FT deg	*	BBB	MO	M*6	$	Ind	Ind

course details			98 expected requirements							96 entry stats	
TITLE	CODE	COURSE	SUBJECTS	A/AS	ND/C	AGNVQ	IB	SQA(H)	SQA	RATIO	A/AS
Univ of Wales SWANSEA											
Anthropology and Philosophy	LV67	3FT deg	*	BBC-BCC	1M+5D	Ind	28	BBBBB	Ind	4	14/24
Philosophy	V700	4FT deg	*	BBC	1M+5D	Ind	30	ABBBB	Ind	4	14/28
Philosophy	V704	4FT deg	*	BBC	1M+5D	Ind	30	ABBBB	Ind	4	
Philosophy and Politics	MV17	3FT deg	*	BBC	1M+5D	Ind	30	ABBBB	Ind	4	
Philosophy and Psychology	LV77	3FT deg	* g	BBB	6D	Ind	32	AABBB	Ind	13	
Philosophy and Sociology	LV37	3FT deg	*	BBC-BCC	1M+5D	Ind	28	BBBBB	Ind	2	16/22
Philosophy/American Studies	VQ74	3FT deg	*	BBC	1M+5D	Ind	30	ABBBB	Ind		
Philosophy/Ancient History and Civilisation	VV1R	3FT deg	*	BBC-BCC	1M+5D	X	28	BBBBB	X	3	
Philosophy/English	QV37	3FT deg	E	BBC	X	X	30$	ABBBB$	X	3	14/26
Philosophy/French	RV17	4FT deg	F	BBC-BCC	1M+5D$	Ind	28$	BBBBB$	Ind	2	
Philosophy/German	RV27	4FT deg	G	BBC-BCC	1M+5D$	Ind	28$	BBBBB$	Ind		
Philosophy/Greek	QV77	3FT deg	Gk	BBC-BCC	X	X	28$	BBBBB$	X		
Philosophy/Greek and Roman Studies	QV87	3FT deg	*	BBC-BCC	1M+5D	X	28	BBBBB	X		
Philosophy/History	VV17	3FT deg	*	BBC	1M+5D	Ind	30	ABBBB	Ind	5	
Philosophy/Italian	RV37	4FT deg	L/*	BBC-BCC	1M+5D$	Ind	28$	BBBBB$	Ind		
Politics/Philosophy	MVC7	3FT deg	*	BBC	1M+5D	Ind	30	ABBBB	Ind		
Social Philosophy	V740	3FT deg	*	BBC-BCC	1M+5D	Ind	28	BBBBB	Ind	3	
Spanish/Philosophy	RV47	4FT deg	L/*	BBC-BCC	1M+5D$	Ind	28	BBBBB	Ind		
Welsh/Philosophy	QV57	3FT/4FT deg	W	BBC-BCC	Ind	X	28$	BBBBB$	X		
Joint Hons with defer choice of specialisation (inc Philosophy)	Y220	3FT deg	*	20-22	1M+5D	Ind	28	BBBBB	Ind		
Univ of TEESSIDE											
Cultural Studies	LV69	3FT deg	*	14-16	Ind	M	Ind	Ind	Ind	3	4/16
Univ of ULSTER											
Philosophy (3 Yr)	V700▼	3FT deg	*	CCC	MO+3D	D*6/^ gi	28	BBBC	Ind	19	
Humanities Combined Philosophy	Y320▼	3FT/4SW deg	*	CCC	MO+3D	D*6/^ gi	28	BBBC	Ind		
UNIVERSITY COLL LONDON (Univ of London)											
French and Philosophy (4 Yrs)	RV17	4FT deg	F g	BBC-BBB	3M	X	32$	BBBBC$	Ind	4	24/26
History and Philosophy of Science	V500	3FT deg	g	BCC	Ind	Ind	28	Ind	Ind	1	16/24
History, Philosophy and Social Studies of Sci	V510	3FT deg	g	BCC	Ind	Ind	28	Ind	Ind		
Philosophy	V700	3FT deg	* g	BBC	3M	X	28	BBBBC	Ind	9	16/30
Philosophy and Economics	VL71	3FT deg	g	BBC	3M	X	30$	BBBBC	Ind	6	22/28
Philosophy and Greek	VQ77	3FT deg	Gk g	BBC	3M	X	30$	BBBBC	Ind		
Philosophy and History of Art	VV74	3FT deg	g	BBC	3M	X	28	BBBBC	Ind	11	
Philosophy and Linguistics	VQ71	3FT deg	* g	BBC	3M	X	28	BBBBC	Ind	21	
Science Communication and Policy	V520	3FT deg	g	BCC	Ind	Ind	28	Ind	Ind		
Univ of WARWICK											
Classical Civilisation with Philosophy	Q8V7	3FT deg	* g	BCC	X	X	30	BBBBC		6	20/24
Mathematics and Philosophy	GV17	3FT deg	M g	AAA-AAB	X	X	36$	CSYS$		7	30/30
Philosophy	V700	3FT deg	* g	BBB	X	X	32	AABBB		13	22/28
Philosophy and Literature	VQ72	3FT deg	E g	BBB	X	X	32$	AABBB$		7	22/30
Philosophy and Politics	VM71	3FT deg	* g	BBB	X	X	32	AABBB		10	24/30
Philosophy with Classical Civilisation	V7Q8	3FT deg	* g	BBB	X	X	32	AABBB		14	
Philosophy with Computer Science	V7G5	3FT deg	M g	BBB	X	X	32$	AABBB$		6	
Philosophy with Education	V7X9	3FT deg	* g	BBB	X	X	32	PAABBB		10	
Psychology and Philosophy	LV77	3FT deg	* g	BBB	X	X	32	AABBB		16	24/30

course details			98 expected requirements							96 entry stats	
TITLE	CODE	COURSE	SUBJECTS	A/AS	ND/C	AGNVQ	IB	SQA(H)	SQA	RATIO	A/AS
Univ of WOLVERHAMPTON											
Philosophy (Specialist Route)	V700	3FT deg		12	4M	M	24	BBBB	Ind	6	8/16
Combined Degrees *Philosophy*	Y401	3FT/4SW deg		12	4M	M	24	BBBB	Ind		
Univ of YORK											
Economics/Philosophy (Equal)	LV17	3FT deg	* g	BBB	Ind	D$^ go	30	BBBBB	Ind		
English/Philosophy	Q3V7	3FT deg	E g	ABB-ABC	HN $	D$^	32$	AABB$	Ind		
English/Philosophy (Equal)	QV37	3FT deg	E g	ABB-ABC	HN $	D$^	32$	AABB$	Ind		
History/Philosophy (Equal)	VV17	3FT deg	H	ABC	Ind	D$6/^	32$	ABBB$	Ind		
Linguistics/Philosophy	Q1V7	3FT/4FT deg	*/L	24	Ind	D$^	28$	BBCC$	Ind		
Mathematics/Philosophy (Equal)	GV17	3FT deg	M	22	HN $	DS^	30$	CSYS$	HN$		
Philosophy	V700	3FT deg	*	BBC	Ind	D$6/^	30	BBBC	Ind		20/28
Philosophy/Education	V7X9	3FT deg	*	BBC	Ind	D$6/^	30	BBBC	Ind		
Philosophy/English	V7Q3	3FT deg	E g	BBC	HN $	D$^	30$	ABBB	Ind		22/24
Philosophy/Linguistics	V7Q1	3FT deg	*	22	Ind	D$6/^	30	BBBC	Ind		
Philosophy/Linguistics (Equal)	VQ71	3FT deg	*	24	Ind	D$^	28$	BBBC	Ind		
Philosophy/Politics (Equal)	VM71	3FT deg	* g	BBB	Ind	D$^ go	30	BBBBB	Ind		
Philosophy/Sociology (Equal)	VL73	3FT deg	*	BBC	Ind	D$6/^	30	BBBB	Ind		
Physics/Philosophy	F3V7	3FT deg	M+P	BCC	Ind	DS^	28$	CSYS$	Ind		
Physics/Philosophy with a year in Europe	F3VR	4FT deg	M+P g	BCC	Ind	DS^	28$	CSYS$	Ind		
Philosophy, Politics and Economics *Philosophy*	Y616	3FT deg	* g	BBB	Ind	D$^ go	32	BBBBB	Ind		

course details			98 expected requirements							96 entry stats
TITLE	CODE	COURSE	SUBJECTS	A/AS	ND/C	AGNVQ	IB	SQA(H)	SQA	RATIO A/AS
Univ of ABERDEEN										
Chemistry with Physics	F1F3	4FT deg	C+2S/C+S+M g	CCD	Ind	MS go	24$	BBBC$	Ind	
Mathematics-Physics	GF13	4FT deg	* g	BBC	Ind	M$ go	30$	BBBB$	Ind	
Mathematics-Physics	FG31	3FT/4FT deg	M+S g	CCD	Ind	MS go	24$	BBBB$	Ind	7
Natural Philosophy	F301	4FT deg	* g	BBC	Ind	M$ go	30$	BBBB$	Ind	
Philosophy-Physics	VF73	4FT deg	* g	BBC	Ind	M$ go	30$	BBBB$	Ind	
Physics	F300	4FT deg	M+2S g	CCD	Ind	MS go	24$	BBBC$	Ind	8
Physics with Chemistry	F3F1	4FT deg	M+2S g	CCD	Ind	MS go	24$	BBBC$	Ind	
Physics with French	F3R1	4FT deg	2S+M g	CCD	Ind	MS go	24$	BBBC$	Ind	
Physics with Gaelic	F3Q5	4FT deg	2S+M g	CCD	Ind	MS go	24$	BBBC$	Ind	
Physics with Geology	F3F6	4FT deg	2S+M g	CCD	Ind	MS go	24$	BBBC$	Ind	
Physics with German	F3R2	4FT deg	2S+M g	CCD	Ind	MS go	24$	BBBC$	Ind	
Physics with Hispanic Studies	F3R4	4FT deg	2S+M g	CCD	Ind	MS go	24$	BBBC$	Ind	
Physics with Philosophy	F3V7	4FT deg	2S+M g	CCD	Ind	MS go	24$	BBBC$	Ind	
Univ of Wales, ABERYSTWYTH										
Computer Science/Physics	FG35	3FT deg	P+M g	20	X	MS6/^ g	30$	BBBCC$	Ind	
Earth, Planetary and Space Science	FF65	3FT deg	P+M g	18	3M+2D$	M^ g	29$	BBBCC$	Ind	
Geography/Physics	FF38	3FT deg	P+Gy+M g	20	3M+2D$	MS^ g	30$	BBBCC$	Ind	
Geology/Physics	FF36	3FT deg	M+P g	18	3M+2D$	MS^ g	29$	BBBCC$	Ind	
Mathematics/Physics	FG31	3FT deg	M+P g	16	1M+5D$	MS^ g	28$	BBCC$	Ind	
Physics	F300	3FT deg	P+M g	14	3M $	MS^ g	27$	BBBCC$	Ind	
Physics (4 Yrs Wide Entry)	F301	4FT deg	* g							
Physics (MPhys)	F303	4FT deg	P+M g	14	3M $	MS^ g	27$	BBBCC$	Ind	
Physics (Ordinary)	F302	3FT deg	P+M g	4	N $	PS g	Dip$	DD$	Ind	
Physics with Atmospheric Physics	F363	3FT deg	P+M g	14	3M $	MS^ g	27$	BBBCC$	Ind	
Physics with Atmospheric Physics (MPhys)	F365	4FT deg	P+M g	14	3M $	MS^ g	27$	BBBCC$	Ind	
Physics with Business Studies	F3N1	3FT deg	P+M g	14	3M $	MS^ g	27$	BBBCC$	Ind	
Physics with Education	F3X9	3FT deg	P+M g	14	3M $	MS^ g	27$	BBBCC$	Ind	
Physics with Planetary and Space Physics	F364	3FT deg	P+M g	14	3M $	MS^ g	27$	BBBCC$	Ind	
Physics with Planetary and Space Physics (MPhys)	F366	4FT deg	P+M g	14	3M $	MS^ g	27$	BBBCC$	Ind	
Information and Library St/an approved Sci Sub *Physics*	PY21	3FT deg	P+M g	14	MO $	M^ g	27$	BBBCC$	Ind	
Univ of Wales, BANGOR										
Applied Physics and Electronics	FH36	3FT deg	M+P/Es/Cs g	CC	3M $	M$^ go	26$	BBCC$	Ind	5
Applied Physics and Sports Science	FB36	3FT deg	M+P/Es/Cs g	BDD	3M+1D$	D$^ go	30$	BBBC$	Ind	
BARNSLEY COLL										
Science Foundation *Physics*	Y100	4EXT deg								
Univ of BATH										
Applied Physics	F311	4SW deg	M+P	CCC	Ind	DS^	30$	Ind	Ind	3
Applied Physics	F310	3FT deg	M+P	CCC	Ind	DS^	30$	Ind	Ind	3 · 26/30
Physics	F300	3FT deg	M+P	CC-CCC	Ind	DS^	30$	Ind	Ind	10 · 12/26
Physics	F301	4SW deg	M+P	CC-CCC	Ind	DS^	30$	Ind	Ind	3 · 10/30
Physics (MPhys)	F303	4FT/4SW deg	M+P	BCC	Ind	DS^	30$	Ind	Ind	4 · 10/28
Physics with Communications Technology	F304	3FT deg	M+P	CC-CCC	Ind	DS^	30$	Ind	Ind	6
Physics with Communications Technology (4 Yr SW)	F305	4SW deg	M+P	CC-CCC	Ind	DS^	30$	Ind	Ind	4
Physics with Computing	F308	3FT deg	M+P	CC-CCC	Ind	DS^	30$	Ind	Ind	5 · 8/18
Physics with Computing (4 Yr SW)	F309	4SW deg	M+P	CC-CCC	Ind	DS^	30$	Ind	Ind	
Physics with Study Abroad	F307	4FT deg	M+P	CC-CCC	Ind	DS^	30$	Ind	Ind	13
Natural Sciences *Physics*	Y161	4SW deg	S/M+S/M	20	Ind	DS	30	Ind	Ind	
Natural Sciences *Physics*	Y160	3FT deg	S/M+S/M	20	Ind	DS	30	Ind	Ind	

course details			98 expected requirements							96 entry stats	
TITLE	CODE	COURSE	SUBJECTS	A/AS	ND/C	AGNVQ	IB	SQA(H)	SQA	RATIO	A/AS
BELL COLLEGE OF TECHNOLOGY											
Optical Technology and Instrumentation	F350	3FT deg	P g	6	Ind	Ind	Ind	CCC	20		
Univ of BIRMINGHAM											
Physics	F300	3FT/4FT deg	P+M	BCC	Ind	Ind	30	Ind	Ind	6	12/30
Physics with Astrophysics	F3F5	3FT/4FT deg	P+M	BCC	Ind	Ind	30	Ind	Ind	5	12/26
Physics with Biomedical Physics	F370	3FT/4FT deg	P+M	BCC	Ind	Ind	30	Ind	Ind	3	12/30
Physics with Business Studies	F3N1	3FT/4FT deg	P+M	BBC	Ind	Ind	30	Ind	Ind		
Physics with Electronics	F340	3FT/4FT deg	P+M	BCC	Ind	Ind	30	Ind	Ind	7	22/28
Physics with Geophysics	F3F6	3FT/4FT deg	P+M	BCC	Ind	Ind	30	Ind	Ind	18	
Physics with Study in Continental Europe	F301	4FT deg	P+M g	BCC	Ind	Ind	30	Ind	Ind	11	
Physics with Theoretical Physics	F320	3FT/4FT deg	P+M	BBC	Ind	Ind	30	Ind	Ind	5	14/28
Theoretical Physics and Applied Mathematics	FG31	3FT/4FT deg	P+M	BBC	Ind	Ind	30	Ind	Ind	7	18/30
BRADFORD & ILKLEY Comm COLL											
Applied Sciences *Physical Science*	001Y	2FT HND	S g	2	N $	P		Ind	Ind		
Univ of BRIGHTON											
Chemistry and Physics	FF13	3FT/4SW deg	C/P g	12	MO $	M$	Dip$	BBCC$	Ind		
Computing and Physics	GF53	3FT/4SW deg	S g	12	MO $	M$	Dip$	BBCC$	Ind		
Energy Studies and Physics	JF93	3FT/4SW deg	P g	12	MO $	M$	Dip$	BBCC$	Ind		
Geography and Physics	FF83	3FT/4SW deg	S g	12	MO $	M$	Dip$	BBCC$	Ind		
Mathematics and Physics	GF13	3FT/4SW deg	M g	12	MO $	M$	Dip$	BBCC$	Ind		
Pharmaceutical and Chemical Sciences	FB31	3FT/4SW deg	C g	12	MO $	MS go	Dip$	CCBB$	Ind		
Physics with Management	F3N1	3FT/4SW deg	M/P/S g	12	5M $	MS/M^	Dip$	BBBC$	Ind		
Univ of BRISTOL											
Chemical Physics	F330	3FT deg	M+P+C	BCC	Ind	D$^	28$	CSYS	HN$	8	20/30
Chemical Physics (MSci)	F331	4FT deg	M+P+C	BCC	Ind	D$^	28$	CSYS	HN$	1	
Mathematics and Physics	GF13	3FT deg	M+P	ABC-BBC	Ind	D$^	32$	CSYS	Ind	20	
Mathematics and Physics (MSci)	GF1H	4FT deg	M+P	ABC-BBC	Ind	D$^	32$	CSYS	Ind	11	
Mathematics and Physics with St in Cont Europe	FG31	4FT deg	M+P	ABC-BBC	Ind	D$^	32$	CSYS	Ind	9	
Physics	F300	3FT deg	M+P	BCC	Ind	D$^	26$	CSYS	Ind	6	16/30
Physics (MSci)	F303	4FT deg	M+P	BCC	Ind	D$^	26$	CSYS	Ind	7	20/30
Physics and Philosophy	FV37	3FT deg	P+M	BCC	Ind	D$^	26$	CSYS	Ind	5	22/30
Physics and Philosophy with Study in Cont Europe	VF73	4FT deg	P+ML g	BBC	Ind	D$^	26$	CSYS	Ind	3	
Physics with Astrophysics	F3F5	3FT deg	M+P	BCC	Ind	D$^	26$	CSYS	Ind	10	20/30
Physics with Astrophysics (MSci)	F3FM	4FT deg	M+P	BCC	Ind	D$^	26$	CSYS	Ind	2	22/30
Physics with Study in Continental Europe	F301	4FT deg	M+P g	BCC	Ind	D$^	26$	CSYS	Ind	7	
Physics with Study in Continental Europe (MSci)	F304	4FT deg	M+P	BCC	Ind	D$^	26$	CSYS	Ind		
Physics with a Preliminary Yr	F308	4FT deg	g			D$^				4	
BRUNEL Univ, West London											
Physics	F302	3FT deg	P+M	CC	3M $	Ind^	26$	CCCCC$	Ind	5	
Physics (4 Yrs Thick SW)	F305	4SW deg	P+M	CC	3M $	Ind^	26$	CCCCC$	Ind		
Physics (4 Yrs Thin SW)	F300	4SW deg	P+M	CC	3M $	Ind^	26$	CCCCC$	Ind	3	
Physics (MPhys)	F307	4FT deg	P+M	AB	MO+2D$	Ind^	29$	AAABB$	Ind	4	4/10
Physics with Adv Instrumentation(4 Yrs Thick SW)	F341	4SW deg	P+M	CC	3M $	Ind^	26$	CCCCC$	Ind		
Physics with Adv Instrumentation(4 Yrs Thin SW)	F342	4SW deg	P+M	CC	3M $	Ind^	26$	CCCCC$	Ind		
Physics with Advanced Instrumentation	F345	3FT deg	P+M	CC	3M $	Ind^	26$	CCCCC$	Ind		
Physics with Computer Science	F3GM	3FT deg	P+M	CC	3M $	Ind^	26$	CCCCC	Ind	12	
Physics with Computer Science (4 Yrs Thick SW)	F3GN	4SW deg	P+M	CC	3M $	Ind^	26$	CCCCC	Ind	3	
Physics with Computer Science (4 Yrs Thin SW)	F3G5	4SW deg	P+M	CC	3M $	Ind^	26$	CCCCC$	Ind	3	
Physics with Management Studies	F3N1	3FT deg	P+M	CC	3M $	Ind^	26$	CCCCC$	Ind	3	

course details			98 expected requirements							96 entry stats	
TITLE	CODE	COURSE	SUBJECTS	A/AS	NO/C	AGNVQ	IB	SQA(H)	SQA	RATIO	A/AS
Physics with Management Studies (4 Yrs Thick SW)	F3ND	4SW deg	P+M	CC	3M $	Ind^	26$	CCCCC$	Ind	2	
Physics with Management Studies (4 Yrs Thin SW)	F3NC	4SW deg	P+M	CC	3M $	Ind^	26$	CCCCC$	Ind		
Physics with a Foundation year	F308	4EXT deg	*	CC-EE	N	Ind	Ind	Ind	Ind	1	

CAMBRIDGE Univ

Natural Sciences *Astrophysics*	Y160▼	3FT deg	2(S/M) g	AAA-AAB	Ind		Ind	CSYS	Ind		
Natural Sciences *Physics and Theoretical Physics*	Y160▼	3FT/4FT deg	2(S/M) g	AAA-AAB	Ind		Ind	CSYS	Ind		

CARDIFF Univ of Wales

Astrophysics	F526	3FT deg	P+M	CCC	Ind		Ind	Ind	Ind	5	12/20
Astrophysics	F523	4FT deg	P+M	CCC	Ind		Ind	Ind	Ind	4	16/30
Chemistry and Physics	FF13	3FT deg	P+C+M	CCC	Ind		Ind	Ind	Ind	8	
Computing and Physics	FG35	3FT deg	P+M	CCC	Ind		Ind	Ind	Ind	5	
Physics	F300	3FT deg	P+M	CCC	Ind		Ind	Ind	Ind	4	12/28
Physics	F303	4FT deg	P+M	CCC	Ind		Ind	Ind	Ind	7	20/30
Physics and Mathematics	FG3D	3FT deg	M+P	CCC	Ind	Ind	Ind	Ind	Ind	3	16/24
Physics and Music	FW33	3FT deg	Mu+P+M	BCC	Ind		Ind	Ind	Ind	2	20/28
Physics with Astronomy	F3F5	3FT deg	P+M	CCC	Ind		Ind	Ind	Ind	7	
Physics with Astronomy	F3FM	4FT deg		CCC							
Physics with Medical Physics	F370	3FT deg	P+M	CCC	Ind		Ind	Ind	Ind	5	
Physics with Solid State Electronics	F348	3FT deg	P+M	CCC	Ind		Ind	Ind	Ind		
Theoretical and Computational Physics	F320	3FT deg	P+M	CCC	Ind		Ind	Ind	Ind	6	
Preliminary Year *Astrophysics*	Y121	4FT/5FT deg	*		Ind		Ind	Ind	Ind		
Preliminary Year *Physics*	Y121	4FT/5FT deg	*		Ind		Ind	Ind	Ind		

Univ of CENTRAL LANCASHIRE

Applied Physics	F312	3FT/4FT deg	M+P	CCD	MO+3D$	DS6/^	28$	BBBC	$		
Astrophysics	F521	3FT/4FT deg	M+P	CCD	MO+3D$	DS6/^	28$	BBBC	$		
Observational Astronomy and Instrumentation	F501	3FT/4FT deg	M+P	CCD	MO+5D$	DS6/^	28$	BBBB	$		
Physics	F303	3FT/4FT deg	M+P	CCD	MO+5D$	DS6/^	28$	BBBB$			
Physics and Astronomy	FF53	3FT/4FT deg	M+P	CCD	MO+5D$	DS6/^	28$	BBBB$			
Combined Honours Programme *Applied Physics*	Y400	3FT deg	P+M	8	3M $	PS	24$	CCC	$		
Combined Honours Programme *Astronomy*	Y400	3FT deg	P+M	8	3M $	PS	24$	CCC	$		
Applied Physics	013F	2FT HND	P/M	E	N $	MS	24$	CCC	$		
Observational Astronomy and Instrumentation	005F	2FT HND									

DE MONTFORT Univ

Physics with Business Studies	F3N1▼	3FT/4SW deg	*	12	Ind	M	24$	BBB	$	8	
Combined Sciences *Physics*	Y100▼	2FT Dip	M/P g	4-6	N	P	Dip	BCC	Ind		
Combined Sciences *Physics*	Y108▼	3FT deg	g	2	N	P	Dip	CC	Ind		
Combined Studies *Physics*	Y400▼	3FT/4SW deg	M/P g	10	MO	M	30	BBB	Ind		

Univ of DUNDEE

Applied Physics	F310	4FT deg	M+S g	10	5M $	M$^	25$	BBCC$	N$		
Chemistry and Physics	FF13	4FT deg	M+S g	10	5M $	M$^	25$	BBCC$	N$	4	
Electronic Engineering and Physics	HF63	3FT/4FT deg	M+P/Ds g	12	5M $	M$^	26$	BBCC$	N$	5	
Electronic Engineering and Physics (MEng)	FH3P	4FT/5FT deg	M+P/Ds g	12	5M $	M$^	26$	BBCC$	N$		
Mathematics and Physics	FG31	4FT deg	M+S g	14	5M $	M$^	25$	BBCC$	N$	5	

course details			**98 expected requirements**							*96 entry stats*
TITLE	CODE	COURSE	SUBJECTS	A/AS	NO/C	RGNVQ	IB	SQA(H)	SQA	RATIO A/AS
Physics	F301	3FT deg	M+S g	6	5M $	M$^	25$	BCC$	N$	
Physics	F300	4FT deg	M+S g	10	5M $	M$^	25$	BBCC$	N$	37
Physics (MSci)	F303	4FT/5FT deg	M+S g	10	5M $	M$^	25$	BBCC$	N$	20
Physics and Applied Computing	FG35	4FT deg	M+S g	14	5M $	M$^	25$	BBBC$	N$	8
Physics and Digital Microelectronics	F346	4FT deg	M+S g	10	5M $	M$^	25$	BBCC$	N$	
Physics and Environmental Science	FF39	4FT deg	M+S g	10	5M $	M$^	25$	BBCC$	N$	
Physics and Philosophy	FV37	4FT deg	M+S g	10	5M $	M$^	25$	BBCC$	N$	
Physics and Psychology	FC38	4FT deg	M+S g	10	5M $	M$^	25$	BBCC$	N$	
Physics with French	F3R1	4FT deg	M+S g	10	5M $	M$^	25$	BBCC$	N$	
Physics with German	F3R2	4FT deg	M+S g	10	5M $	M$^	25$	BBCC$	N$	
Physics with Spanish	F3R4	4FT deg	M+S g	10	5M $	M$^	25$	BBCC$	N$	
Univ of DURHAM										
Applied Physics	F313	4FT deg	P+M	18-22	Ind	X	28$	AAAAA$ X		4
Applied Physics	F310	3FT deg	P+M	18-20	Ind	X	28$	AAABB$ X		11
Mathematics and Physics	FG31	3FT deg	M+P	24	X	X	32$	CSYS$ X		5 26/30
Mathematics and Physics (MSci)	FG3C	4FT deg	M+P	24	X	X	32$	CSYS$ X		
Physics	F303	4FT deg	P+M	18-22	Ind	X	28$	AAAAA$ X		5 22/30
Physics	F300	3FT deg	P+M	18-20	Ind	X	28$	AAABB$ X		5 18/30
Physics and Astronomy	FF35	3FT deg	P+M	18-20	Ind	X	28$	AAABB$ X		6
Physics and Astronomy (4 years)	FF3M	4FT deg	P+M	18-22	Ind	X	28$	AAAAA$ X		8
Theoretical Physics	F320	3FT deg	P+M	18-22	Ind	X	28$	AAAAA$ X		8
Natural Sciences *Applied Physics*	Y160	3FT deg	P+M	ABB	Ind	X	33$	CSYS$ X		
Natural Sciences *Physics*	Y160	3FT deg	P+M	ABB	Ind	X	33$	CSYS$ X		
Univ of EAST ANGLIA										
Chemical Physics	FF31	3FT deg	C+P+M	BCC	MO+3D$ Ind		28$	ABBB$	Ind	9
Chemical Physics with 1 yr in Europe (4 yr)	F336	4FT deg	C+P+M	BCC	MO+3D$ Ind		28$	ABBB$	Ind	
Chemical Physics with 1 yr in USA (3yrs)	F335	3FT deg	C+P+M	CCC	DO $	Ind	31$	AAABB$ Ind		4
Univ of EDINBURGH										
Astrophysics	F520	4FT deg	M+P	CCD	MO $		Dip$	BBBC$	N$	6 20/24
Astrophysics (MPhys)	F360	5FT deg	M+P	CCD	MO $		Dip$	BBBC$	N$	6 20/24
Chemical Physics	F334	4FT deg	M+P+C	CCD	MO $		Dip$	BBBC$	N$	5
Chemical Physics (MChem)	F333	5FT deg	M+C+P	CCD	MO $		Dip$	BBBC$	N$	5
Chemical Physics with Industrial Experience	F336	5FT deg	M+P+C	CCD	MO $		Dip$	BBBC$	N$	
Chemical Physics with Industrial Experience	F335	4SW deg	M+P+C	CCD	MO $		Dip$	BBBC$	N$	3
Computational Physics	F350	4FT deg	M+P	CCD	MO $		Dip$	BBBC$	N$	6
Computational Physics (MPhys)	F355	5FT deg	M+P	CCD	MO $		Dip$	BBBC$	N$	4
Computer Science and Physics	GF53	4FT deg	M+P	CCC	MO $		Dip$	BBBB$	N$	
Electronics and Physics (BEng)	HF63	4FT deg	M+P	CCC	MO $		Dip$	BBBB$	N$	12
Mathematical Physics	F326	4FT deg	M+P	CCC	MO $		Dip$	BBBB$	N$	6
Mathematical Physics (MPhys)	F325	5FT deg	M+P	CCC	MO $		Dip$	BBBB$	N$	5
Mathematics and Physics	GF13	4FT deg	M+P	BCC	MO $		Dip$	ABBC$	N$	10
Physics	F300	4FT deg	M+P	CCD	MO $		Dip$	BBBC$	N$	10 22/30
Physics (MPhys)	F303	5FT deg	M+P	CCD	MO $		Dip$	BBBC$	N$	7 18/30
Physics and Electronics (BEng)	FH36	4FT deg	M+P	CCD	MO $		Dip$	BBBC$	N$	6
Physics with Meteorology	F304	4FT deg	M+P	CCD	MO $		Dip$	BBBC	N$	4
Physics with Music	F305	4FT deg	M+P	CCD	MO $		Dip$	BBBC	N$	4

course details			98 expected requirements							96 entry stats	
TITLE	CODE	COURSE	SUBJECTS	A/AS	ND/C	AGNVQ	IB	SQA(H)	SQA	RATIO	A/AS
Univ of ESSEX											
Physics	F300	3FT deg	P+M	16	MO $	X	26$	BBCC	Ind	6	10/16
Physics (MPhys) (4 Yrs)	F303	4FT deg	P+M	16	MO $	X	26$	BBCC	Ind	4	
Physics with Laser Technology	F366	3FT deg	P+M	16	MO $	X	26$	BBCC	Ind	7	
Physics with Laser Technology (MPhys) (4 Yrs)	F363	4FT deg	P+M	16	MO $	X	26$	BBCC	Ind	7	
Physics with Management Studies	F351	4FT deg	* g	4	N	MS	24	CCCC	Ind		
Physics with Optoelectronics	F310	3FT deg	P+M	16	MO $	X	26$	BBCC	Ind		
Physics with Optoelectronics (MPhys) (4 Yrs)	F313	4FT deg	P+M	16	MO $	X	26$	BBCC	Ind		
Physics with a European Language	F3T2	4FT deg	P+M g	16	MO $	X	26$	BBCC	Ind		
Sports Science with Physics	B6F3	3FT deg	P+S	18	MO	D	28$	BBBC	Ind		
Theoretical Physics	F320	3FT deg	P+M	16	MO $	X	26$	BBCC	Ind	12	
Theoretical Physics (MPhys) (4 Yrs)	F323	4FT deg	P+M	16	MO $	X	26$	BBCC	Ind		
Univ of EXETER											
Mathematics and Physics	FG31	3FT deg	M+P/Es	20	MO	M$^	32$	Ind	Ind	12	
Mathematics and Theoretical Physics	FGH1	3FT deg	M+P	20	MO	M$^	32$	Ind	Ind	12	
Physics	F300	3FT deg	M+P	BC-CC	MO	M$^	28$	Ind	Ind	14	6/22
Physics (MPhys)	F303	4FT deg	M+P	BC-CC	MO	M$^	28$	Ind	Ind	7	14/30
Physics with European Study	F301	4FT deg	M+P g	BC-CC	MO	M$^	28$	Ind	Ind	10	
Physics with Medical Applications	F369	3FT deg	M+P	BC-CC	MO	M$^	28$	Ind	Ind		
Physics with Medical Physics (MPhys)	F371	4FT deg	M+P	BC-CC	MO	M$^	28$	Ind	Ind	17	
Physics with North American Study	F3Q4	4FT deg	M+P	BC-CC	MO	M$^	28$				
Physics with Quantum and Laser Technology	F347	3FT deg	M+P	BC-CCC	MO	M$^	28$	Ind	Ind		
Quantum Science and Lasers	F341	4FT deg	M+P	BC-CCC	MO	M$^	28$	Ind	Ind		
Theoretical Physics	F320	3FT deg	M+P	BC-CC	MO	M$^	28$	Ind	Ind	18	
Theoretical Physics (MPhys)	F323	4FT deg	M+P	BC-CC	MO	M$^	28$	Ind	Ind	9	
Theoretical Physics with European Study	F321	4FT deg	M+P g	BC-CC	MO	M$^	28$	Ind	Ind		
Theoretical Physics with North American Study	F3QK	4FT deg	M+P	BC-CC	MO	M$^	28$				
Univ of GLAMORGAN											
Combined Studies (Honours) _Astronomy_	Y400	3FT deg	M/S g	8-16	Ind	Ind	Ind	Ind	Ind		
Univ of GLASGOW											
Astronomy/Classical Hebrew	FV58	4FT deg		BBC	HN	M	30	BBBB	Ind		
Astronomy/Mathematics (MSci)	FG51	4FT deg	M+P	BBC-CCC	N	M	24$	BBBB$	N	6	
Chemical Physics	F334	4FT deg	M+P+C	BCC-CCC	N		24$	BBBB$	N	8	
Electronic Engineering and Physics	FH36	4FT deg	M+P	CCD	MO	ME	24$	BBBBC$	N$	17	
Electronic Engineering with Optoelectronics	H6F3	4FT deg	M+P	CCD	MO	ME	24$	BBBBC$	N$	13	
Film and Television Studies/Physics	FW35	4FT deg		BBB	HN	D	32	AABB	HN		
Management Studies/Physics	FN31	4FT deg		BBC	HN	M	30	BBBB	Ind		
Mathematics/Physics	FGH1	4FT deg	M+P	BBC-CCC	N	M	24$	BBBB$	N	5	
Music/Physics	FW33	4FT deg		BBC	HN	M	30	BBBB	Ind		
Physics	F300	4FT deg	M+P	BBC-CCC	N	M	24$	BBBB$	N	5	
Physics with Geology	F3F6	4FT deg	M+P	BBC-CCC	N	M	24$	BBBB$	N	13	
Physics/Astronomy	FF35	4FT deg	M+P	BBC-CCC	N	M	24$	BBBB$	N	4	
Physics/Electronic Engineering	FHH6	4FT deg	M+P	BBC-CCC	N	M	24$	BBBB$	N	7	
Physics/Music	FWH3	4FT deg	M+P	BBC-CCC	N	M	24$	BBBB$	N		
Physics/Philosophy	FVH7	4FT deg	M+P	BBC-CCC	N	M	24$	BBB$	N		
Physics/Philosophy	FV37	4FT deg	M+P	BBC	HN	M	30	BBBB	Ind		
Physics/Scottish History	FV3C	4FT deg	M+P	BBC	HN	M	30	BBBB	Ind	2	
Physics/Sociology	FL33	4FT deg	M+P	BBC	HN	M	30	BBBB	Ind	2	

Physical Science 60

			98 expected requirements								96 entry stats
TITLE	**CODE**	**COURSE**	**SUBJECTS**	**A/AS**	**ND/C**	**AGNVQ**	**IB**	**SQA(H)**	**SQA**	**RATIO A/AS**
GLASGOW CALEDONIAN Univ										
Instrumentation with Applied Physics	F340	3FT/4FT deg	2S	DD-DE	Ind		Ind	BCC$	Ind	3
Medical Physics Technology	F371	4FT deg	M+P+S	BBC	Ind		Ind	BBBB$	Ind	
Univ of GREENWICH										
Science Education *Physics*	XY71	3FT deg	* g	12	M+D	Ind	24	BCCC	Ind	
HERIOT-WATT Univ										
Applied Physics	F314	4FT deg	M+P	CC	Ind	M$ go	26	BBBC$	Ind	
Applied Physics (MPhys)	F311	4FT deg	M+P	BC	Ind	M$ go	30	AABB$	Ind	
Applied Physics with Microelectro Manuf (MPhys)	F3H7	4FT deg	P+M	BC		M$ go	30	BBBB	Ind	
Computational Physics	F350	3FT/4FT deg	M+P	CC	Ind	M$ go	26	BBBC	Ind	
Computational Physics (MPhys)	F351	4FT deg	M+P	BC	Ind	M$ go	30	AABB	Ind	
General Physics	F301	3FT/4FT deg	M+P	CC	Ind	M$^ go	26	BBBC	Ind	
Mathematics with Physics	G1F3	4FT deg	M+P	CDE	HN	M$_	28	BBB	HN	
Optoelectronics and Laser Engineering	F368	4FT deg	M+P	CC	Ind	M$ go	26	BBBC	Ind	
Optoelectronics and Laser Engineering (MPhys)	F369	4FT deg	M+P	BC	Ind	M$ go	30	AABB	Ind	
Physics	F300	3FT/4FT deg	M+P	CC	Ind	M$^ go	26	BBBC		
Physics (MPhys)	F302	4FT deg	M+P	BC	Ind	M$ go	30	AABB	Ind	
Physics with Education	F3X9	3FT/4FT deg	M+P	CC	Ind	M$^ go	26	BBBC	Ind	
Physics with Education (MPhys)	F3XX	4FT deg	M+P	BC	Ind	M$ go	30	AABB	Ind	
Physics with Environmental Science	F3F9	3FT/4FT deg	M+P	CC	Ind	M$^ go	26	BBBC	Ind	
Physics with Environmental Science (MPhys)	F3FX	4FT deg	M+P	BC	Ind	M$ go	30	AABB	Ind	
Physics with Laser Science	F367	4FT deg	M+P	CC	Ind	M$^ go	26	BBBC	Ind	
Physics with Laser Science (MPhys)	F366	4FT deg	M+P	BC	Ind	M$ go	30	AABB	Ind	
Combined Studies *Physics*	Y100	4FT deg	M+P	DDE	Ind	M$ go	26	BCCC	Ind	
Univ of HERTFORDSHIRE										
Applied Geology/Applied Physics	F6F3	3FT deg	M+P g	12	3M $	M$ gi	24$	CCCC$	Ind	
Applied Geology/Astronomy	F6F5	3FT deg	M g	12	3M $	M$ gi	24$	CCCC$	Ind	
Applied Physics	F315	3FT/4SW deg	M+P	12	3M $	MS gi	24$	CCCC$	Ind	
Applied Physics (Extended)	F318▼	4EXT deg	* g	2	N	Ind	Dip	Ind	Ind	3
Applied Physics/Applied Geology	F3F6	3FT deg	M+P g	12	3M $	M$ gi	24$	CCCC$	Ind	
Applied Physics/Applied Statistics	F3G4	3FT deg	M+P	12	3M $	M$ gi	24$	CCCC$	Ind	
Applied Physics/Astronomy	F3F5	3FT deg	M+P	12	3M $	M$ gi	24$	CCCC$	Ind	4
Applied Physics/Chemistry	F3F1	3FT deg	M+P+C	12	3M $	M$ gi	24$	CCCC$	Ind	2
Applied Physics/Computing	F3G5	3FT deg	M+P	12	3M $	M$ gi	24$	CCCC$	Ind	7
Applied Physics/Economics	F3L1	3FT deg	M+P	12	3M $	M$ gi	24$	CCCC$	Ind	
Applied Physics/Electronic Music	F3W3	3FT deg	M+P+Mu	12	3M	M$^ gi	24$	CCCC$	Ind	
Applied Physics/Electronics	F3H6	3FT deg	M+P g	12	3M $	M$ gi	24$	CCCC$	Ind	
Applied Physics/Environmental Science	F3F9	3FT deg	M+P	12	3M	M$ gi	24$	cCCC$	Ind	
Applied Physics/European Studies	F3T2	3FT deg	M+P	12	3M	M$ gi	24$	CCCC$	Ind	
Applied Physics/Law	F3M3	3FT deg	M+P	18	4M+4D	D$ gi	26$	BBBC$	Ind	
Applied Physics/Manufacturing Systems	F3H7	3FT deg	M+P	12	3M $	M$ gi	24$	CCCC$	Ind	
Applied Physics/Mathematics	F3G1	3FT deg	M+P	12	3M $	M$^ gi	24$	CCCC$	Ind	
Applied Physics/Operational Research	F3N2	3FT deg	M+P	12	3M $	M$ gi	24$	CCCC$	Ind	
Applied Physics/Philosophy	F3V7	3FT deg	M+P	12	3M	M$ gi	24$	CCCC$	Ind	
Applied Physics/Psychology	F3C8	3FT deg	M+P	18	4M+4D	D$ gi	26$	BBBC$	Ind	
Applied Statistics/Applied Physics	G4F3	3FT deg	M+P	12	3M $	M$ gi	24$	CCCC$	Ind	
Astronomy	F500	3FT deg	M g	12	3M $	Ind	24$	CCCC$	Ind	15
Astronomy	F506	3FT deg	M g	12	3M $	MS gi	24$	CCCC$	Ind	
Astronomy (Extended)	F508▼	4EXT deg	* g	2	N	Ind	Dip	Ind	Ind	6

course details | 98 expected requirements | 96 entry stats

TITLE	CODE	COURSE	SUBJECTS	A/AS	NO/C	AGNVQ	IB	SQA(H)	SQA	RATIO	A/AS
Astronomy with Deferred Choice of Specialism	F505	4FT/4SW deg	M g	12	3M $	Ind	24$	CCCC$	Ind		
Astronomy with a year in Europe	F503	4FT deg	M g	8-12	3M $		24$	CCCC$	Ind	2	
Astronomy with a year in North America	F504	4FT deg	M g	8-12	3M $	Ind	24$	CCCC$	Ind	9	
Astronomy/Applied Geology	F5F6	3FT deg	M+g	12	3M $	M$ gi	24$	CCCC$	Ind	3	
Astronomy/Applied Physics	F5F3	3FT deg	M+P	12	3M $	Ind	24$	CCCC$	Ind	4	
Astronomy/Business	F5N1	3FT deg	M g	16	6M+2D	M$6 gi	26$	BBCC$	Ind		
Astronomy/Computing	F5G5	3FT deg	M g	12	3M $	M$ gi	24$	CCCC$	Ind	3	
Astronomy/Economics	F5L1	3FT deg	M g	12	3M $	M$ gi	24$	CCCC$	Ind		
Astronomy/Electronic Music	F5W3	3FT deg	M+Mu g	12	3M	M$^ gi	24$	CCCC$	Ind		
Astronomy/Environmental Science	F5F9	3FT deg	M g	12	3M	M$ gi	24$	CCCC$	Ind		
Astronomy/Human Biology	F5B1	3FT deg	M+S g	12	3M $	M$ gi	24$	CCCC$	Ind		
Astronomy/Law	F5M3	3FT deg	M g	18	4M+4D	D$ gi	26$	BBBC$	Ind		
Astronomy/Linguistic Science	F5Q1	3FT deg	M g	12	MO $	M$ gi	26$	BCCC$	Ind		
Astronomy/Manufacturing Systems	F5H7	3FT deg	M g	12	3M $	M$ gi	24$	CCCC$	Ind		
Astronomy/Mathematics	F5G1	3FT deg	M g	12	3M $	M$^ gi	24$	CCCC$	Ind		
Astronomy/Operational Research	F5N2	3FT deg	M g	12	3M $	M$ gi	24$	CCCC$	Ind		
Astrophysics	F501	3FT deg	M+P g	8-12	3M $	M$ gi	24$	CCCC$	Ind	5	6/12
Astrophysics (Extended)	F528▼	4EXT deg	* g	2	N	Ind	Dip	Ind	Ind	1	
Astrophysics (MPhys)	F502	4FT deg	M+P	12-16	MO+2D	Ind	26	Ind	Ind	6	
Astrophysics with Deferred Choice of Specialism	F523	4FT deg	M+P	12	3M $	Ind	24$	Ind	Ind	1	
Astrophysics with a year in Europe	F521	4FT deg	M+P	8-12	3M $	Ind	24$	Ind	Ind		
Astrophysics with a year in North America	F522	4FT deg	M+P	8-12	3M $	Ind	24$	Ind	Ind	13	
Business/Astronomy	N1F5	3FT deg	M g	16	6M+2D	M$6 gi	26$	BBCC$	Ind		
Chemistry/Applied Physics	F1F3	3FT deg	C+M+P	12	3M $	MS gi	24$	CCCC$	Ind		
Computing/Applied Physics	G5F3	3FT deg	M+P	12	3M $	M$ gi	24$	CCCC$	Ind		
Computing/Astronomy	G5F5	3FT deg	M g	12	3M $	M$ gi	24$	CCCC$	Ind		
Economics/Applied Physics	L1F3	3FT deg	M+P	12	3M $	M$ gi	24$	CCCC$	Ind		
Economics/Astronomy	L1F5	3FT deg	M g	12	3M $	M$ gi	24$	CCCC$	Ind		
Electronic Music/Applied Physics	W3F3	3FT deg	Mu+M+P	12	3M $	M$^ gi	24$	CCCC$	Ind	2	
Electronic Music/Astronomy	W3F5	3FT deg	Mu+M g	12	3M $	M$^ gi	24$	CCCC$	Ind	6	
Electronics/Applied Physics	H6F3	3FT deg	M+P g	12	3M $	M$ gi	24$	CCCC$	Ind		
Environmental Science/Applied Physics	F9F3	3FT deg	M+P	12	3M	M$ gi	24$	CCCC$	Ind	1	
Environmental Science/Astronomy	F9F5	3FT deg	M g	12	3M	M$ gi	24$	CCCC$	Ind		
European Studies/Applied Physics	T2F3	3FT deg	M+P	12	3M	M$ gi	24$	CCCC$	Ind		
Human Biology/Astronomy	B1F5	3FT deg	M g	12	3M $	MS gi	24$	CCCC$	Ind		
Law/Applied Physics	M3F3	3FT deg	M+P	18	4M+4D	D$ gi	26$	BBBC$	Ind		
Law/Astronomy	M3F5	3FT deg	M g	18	4M+4D	D$ gi	26$	BBBC$	Ind		
Linguistic Science/Astronomy	Q1F5	3FT deg	M g	12	MO $	M$ gi	26$	BCCC$	Ind		
Manufacturing Systems/Applied Physics	H7F3	3FT deg	M+P	12	3M $	M$ gi	24$	CCCC$	Ind		
Manufacturing Systems/Astronomy	H7F5	3FT deg	M g	12	3M $	M$ gi	24$	CCCC$	Ind		
Mathematics/Applied Physics	G1F3	3FT deg	M+P	12	3M $	M$^ gi	24$	CCCC$	Ind		
Mathematics/Astronomy	G1F5	3FT deg	M g	12	3M $	M$^ gi	24$	CCCC$	Ind	9	
Operational Research/Applied Physics	N2F3	3FT deg	M+P	12	3M $	M$ gi	24$	CCCC$	Ind		
Operational Research/Astronomy	N2F5	3FT deg	M g	12	3M $	M$ gi	24$	CCCC$	Ind		
Philosophy/Applied Physics	V7F3	3FT deg	M+P	12	3M $	M$ gi	24	CCCC$	Ind		
Physics	F300	3FT deg	M+P	8-12	3M $	Ind	24$	CCCC$	Ind		
Physics (MPhys)	F301	4FT deg	M+P	12-16	4M+2D	Ind	26$	Ind	Ind		
Physics with a year in Europe	F302	4FT/4SW deg	M+P	12	3M $	Ind	24$	CCCC$	Ind		
Physics with a year in North America	F303	4FT deg	M+P	12	3M $	Ind	24$	CCCC$	Ind		
Physics with deferred choice of specialism	F304	4FT/4SW deg	M+P	12	3M $	Ind	24$	CCCC$	Ind		
Psychology/Applied Physics	C8F3	3FT deg	M+P	18	4M+4D	D$ gi	26$	BBBC$	Ind		
Combined Modular Scheme *Applied Physics*	Y100	3FT deg	M+P	12	3M $	M$ gi	24$	CCCC$	Ind		

Physical Science 60

TITLE	CODE	COURSE	SUBJECTS	A/AS	ND/C	RGNVQ	IB	SQA(H)	SQA	RATIO A/AS
Combined Modular Scheme *Applied Physics (Extended)*	Y108▼	4EXT deg	* g	4	N $	Ind	Dip$	DDDD$	Ind	
Combined Modular Scheme *Astronomy*	Y100	3FT deg	M g	12	3M $	M$ gi	24$	CCCC$	Ind	
Combined Modular Scheme *Astronomy (Extended)*	Y108▼	4EXT deg	* g	4	N $	Ind	Dip$	DDDD$	Ind	

Univ of HULL

TITLE	CODE	COURSE	SUBJECTS	A/AS	ND/C	RGNVQ	IB	SQA(H)	SQA	RATIO A/AS
Applied Physics	F310	3FT deg	P+M	CCD-CDD	MO $	M$_^ gi	26$	BBCCC	Ind	5
Applied Physics (4 Yrs) (MPhys)	F313	4FT deg	P+M	CCD-CDD	MO $	M$_^ gi	26$	BBCCC	Ind	
Applied Physics (Yr 1 Franchised)	F311	4FT deg	*	CD	N	P$ gi	24	BCCCC	Ind	1
Applied Physics with Electronics	F344	3FT deg	P+M	CCD-CDD	MO $	M$_^ gi	26$	BBCCC	Ind	3
Applied Physics with Electronics (4 Yrs) (MPhys)	F340	4FT deg	P+M	CCD-CDD	MO $	M$_^ gi	26$	BBCCC	Ind	
Applied Physics with Laser Tech (4 Yrs) (MPhys)	F363	4FT deg	P+M	CCD-CDD	MO $	M$_^ gi	26$	BBCCC	Ind	4
Applied Physics with Laser Technology	F366	3FT deg	P+M	CCD-CDD	MO $	M$_^ gi	26$	BBCCC	Ind	
Environmental Physics	FF38	3FT deg	M+P	18	MO	M$_^ gi	26$	BBBCC	Ind	
International Applied Physics (MPhys)	F312	4FT deg	P+M	CCD	MO	M$_^ gi	26$	BBCCC	Ind	
International Physics (MPhys)	FQ302	4FT deg	P+M	CCD	MO	M$_^ gi	26$	BBCCC	Ind	
Optoelectronics and Laser Systems Eng (4 Yrs)	F368	4FT deg	P+M	CCD-CDD	MO $	M$_^ gi	26$	BBCCC	Ind	4
Physics	F300	3FT deg	P+M	CCD-CDD	MO $	M$_^ gi	26$	BBCCC	Ind	8
Physics (4 Yrs) (MPhys)	F303	4FT deg	P+M	CCD-CDD	MO $	M$_^ gi | 26$	BBCCC	Ind	3	20/24
Physics with Medical Technology	F370	3FT deg	P+M	CCD-CDD	MO $	M$_^ gi	26$	BBCCC	Ind	
Physics with Medical Technology (4 Yrs) (MPhys)	F373	4FT deg	P+M	CCD-CDD	MO $	M$_^ gi	26$	BBCCC	Ind	2
Physics with Medical Technology(Yr 1 Franchised)	F371	4FT deg	*	CD	N	P*_^ gi	24	BCCCC	Ind	1
Physics with Optoelectronics	F346	3FT deg	P+M	CCD-CDD	MO $	M$_^ gi	26$	BBCCC	Ind	
Physics with Optoelectronics (4 Yrs) (MPhys)	F347	4FT deg	P+M	CCD-CDD	MO $	M$_^ gi	26$	BBCCC	Ind	1

IMPERIAL COLL (Univ of London)

TITLE	CODE	COURSE	SUBJECTS	A/AS	ND/C	RGNVQ	IB	SQA(H)	SQA	RATIO A/AS
Maths with Applied Maths/Mathematical Physics	G1F3	3FT deg	M	BBC-ACC	Ind	X	Ind	Ind	Ind	15
Physics	F300	3FT deg	M+P	BBC-CC	HN	Ind	$	CSYS	Ind	5	18/30
Physics (MSci)	F303	4FT deg	M+P	ABC-BC	HN	Ind	$	CSYS	Ind	5	22/30
Physics with Studies in Musical Performance	F3W3	4FT deg	M+P	BCC-CC	HN	Ind	$	CSYS	Ind	7
Physics with Theoretical Physics	F325	3FT deg	M+P	ABC-BC	HN	Ind	$	CSYS	Ind	5	24/30
Physics with a Year in Europe	F308	4FT deg	M+P	BBC-BCC	HN	Ind	$	CSYS	Ind	14
Physics with a Year in Europe (MSci)	F309	4FT deg	M+P	ABC-BCC	HN	Ind	$	CSYS	Ind	2	26/30

KEELE Univ

TITLE	CODE	COURSE	SUBJECTS	A/AS	ND/C	RGNVQ	IB	SQA(H)	SQA	RATIO A/AS
Astrophysics	F520	3FT deg	P g	BCC-CCC	Ind	M$_^ | 28$	CSYS	Ind	7	12/20
Astrophysics	F521	3FT deg	P+M	BCC-CCC	Ind	M$	28$	CSYS	Ind	
Astrophysics and American Studies	QF45	4FT deg	*	BCC	Ind	Ind	28	BBBB	Ind	
Astrophysics and American Studies	FQ54	3FT deg	P g	BCC	Ind	D$_^	28$	CSYS	Ind	
Astrophysics and Ancient History	FV5D	3FT deg	P g	BCC	Ind	D$_^	28$	CSYS	Ind	
Astrophysics and Applied Social Studies	FL55	3FT deg	P g	BCC	Ind	D$_^	28$	CSYS	Ind	
Astrophysics and Applied Social Studies (4 Yrs)	LF55	4FT deg	*	BCC	Ind	Ind	28	BBBB	Ind	
Biochemistry and Astrophysics	CF75	3FT deg	P+C g	BCC-CCC	Ind	M$_^	26$	CSYS	Ind	2
Biochemistry and Astrophysics (4 Yrs)	FC57	4FT deg	*	BCC-CCC	Ind	Ind	26	BBBB	Ind	
Biol & Medicinal Chem and Astrophysics (4 Yrs)	FFC5	4FT deg	*	BCC-CCC	Ind	Ind	26	BBBB	Ind	
Biological and Medicinal Chemistry and Astrophys	FF5C	3FT deg	P+C g	BCC-CCC	Ind	M$_^	26$	CSYS	Ind	
Biology and Astrophysics	CF15	3FT deg	P g	BCC-CCC	Ind	M$_^	26$	CSYS	Ind	
Biology and Astrophysics (4 Yrs)	FC51	4FT deg	*	BCC-CCC	Ind	Ind	26	BBBB	Ind	
Business Administration and Astrophysics	FN59	3FT deg	P g	BCC	Ind	D$_^	28$	CSYS	Ind	
Business Administration and Astrophysics (4 Yrs)	NF95	4FT deg	*	BCC	Ind	Ind	28	BBBB	Ind	
Chemistry and Astrophysics	FF15	3FT deg	P+C g	BCC-CCC	Ind	M$_^	26$	CSYS	Ind	
Chemistry and Astrophysics (4 Yrs)	FF51	4FT deg	*	BCC-CCC	Ind	Ind	26$	BBBB	Ind	
Chemistry and Astrophysics (MSci)	FF5D	4FT deg	C+P	BCC-CCC	Ind	M$_^	26$	CSYS	Ind	

course details

98 expected requirements

96 entry stats

TITLE	CODE	COURSE	SUBJECTS	A/AS	NQ/C	AGNVQ	IB	SQA(H)	SQA	RATIO A/AS
Classical Studies and Astrophysics	FQ58	3FT deg	P g	BCC	Ind	D$^	28$	CSYS	Ind	
Computer Science and Astrophysics	FG55	3FT deg	P g	BCC-CCC	Ind	M$^	26$	CSYS	Ind	13
Computer Science and Astrophysics (4 Yrs)	GF55	4FT deg	*	BCC-CCC	Ind	Ind	26	BBBB	Ind	2
Criminology and Astrophysics	FM5H	3FT deg	P	BBB-BCC	Ind	D$^	28$	CSYS	Ind	
Criminology and Astrophysics (4 Yrs)	MFH5	4FT deg	*	BBB	Ind	Ind	32	ABBB	Ind	
Economics and Astrophysics	FL51	3FT deg	P g	BCC	Ind	D$^	28$	CSYS	Ind	2
Economics and Astrophysics (4 Yrs)	LF15	4FT deg	*	BCC	Ind	Ind	28	BBBB	Ind	
Educational Studies and Astrophysics	FX59	3FT deg	P g	BCC	Ind	D$^	28$	CSYS	Ind	
Educational Studies and Astrophysics (4 Yrs)	XF95	4FT deg	*	BCC	Ind	Ind	28	BBBB	Ind	
Electronic Music and Astrophysics (4 Yrs)	WFJ5	4FT deg	*	BCC	Ind	Ind	28	BBBB	Ind	
English and Astrophysics	FQ53	3FT deg	E+P g	BCC	Ind	D$^	28$	CSYS	Ind	
English and Astrophysics (4 Yrs)	QF35	4FT deg	*	BCC	Ind	Ind	28	BBBB	Ind	
Environmental Management and Astrophysics(4 Yrs)	FFX5	4FT deg	* g	BCC-CCC	Ind	Ind	26	BBBB	Ind	
Finance and Astrophysics	FN53	3FT deg	P g	BCC	Ind	M$^	28$	CSYS	Ind	
Finance and Physics	FN33	3FT deg	P g	BCC	Ind	M$^	28	CSYS	Ind	
French and Astrophysics	FR51	3FT deg	P+F g	BCC	Ind	D$^	28$	CSYS	Ind	
French and Astrophysics (4 Yrs)	RF15	4FT deg	*	BCC	Ind	Ind	28	BBBB	Ind	
French/German and Astrophysics	FT59	3FT deg	F+G+P g	BBC	Ind	D$^	30$	CSYS	Ind	
Geology and Astrophysics	FF56	3FT deg	P g	BCC-CCC	Ind	M$^	26$	CSYS	Ind	
Geology and Astrophysics (4 Yrs)	FF65	4FT deg	*	BCC-CCC	Ind	Ind	26	BBBB	Ind	4
Geology and Astrophysics (MSci)	FF6M	4FT deg	P	BCC-CCC	Ind	M$^	26$	CSYS	Ind	
Geology and Physics (MSci)	FF6H	4FT deg	P	BCC-CCC	Ind	M$^	26$	CSYS	Ind	
German and Astrophysics	FR52	3FT deg	G+P g	BCC	Ind	D$^	28$	CSYS	Ind	
History and Astrophysics	FV51	3FT deg	P g	BCC	Ind	D$^	28$	CSYS	Ind	
History and Astrophysics (4 Yrs)	VF15	4FT deg	*	BCC	Ind	Ind	28	BBBB	Ind	
Human Resource Management and Astrophysics	FN56	3FT deg	P g	BCC	Ind	D$^	28$	CSYS	Ind	
Human Resource Mgt and Astrophysics (4 Yrs)	NF65	4FT deg	*	BCC	Ind	Ind	28	BBBB	Ind	
International History and Astrophysics	FV5C	3FT deg	P g	BCC	Ind	D$^	28$	CSYS	Ind	
International History and Astrophysics (4 Yrs)	VFC5	4FT deg	*	BCC	Ind	Ind	28	BBBB	Ind	
International Politics and Astrophysics	FM5C	3FT deg	P g	BCC	Ind	D$^	28$	CSYS	Ind	
International Politics and Astrophysics (4 Yrs)	MFC5	4FT deg	*	BCC	Ind	Ind	28	BBBB	Ind	
Latin and Astrophysics	FQ56	3FT deg	Ln+P g	BCC	Ind	D$^	28$	CSYS	Ind	
Latin and Astrophysics (4 Yrs)	QF65	4FT deg	*	BCC	Ind	Ind	28	BBBB	Ind	
Management Science and Astrophysics	FN51	3FT deg	P g	BCC	Ind	D$^	28$	CSYS	Ind	
Management Science and Astrophysics (4 Yrs)	NF15	4FT deg	*	BCC	Ind	Ind	28	BBBB	Ind	
Marketing and Astrophysics	FN55	3FT deg	P g	BCC	Ind	D$^	28$	CSYS	Ind	
Mathematics and Astrophysics	FG51	3FT deg	P+M g	BCC-CCC	Ind	M$^	26$	CSYS	Ind	5
Mathematics and Astrophysics (4 Yrs)	GF15	4FT deg	*	BCC-CCC	Ind	Ind	26	BBBB	Ind	
Mathematics and Astrophysics (MSci)	GF1M	4FT deg	P+M g	BCC-CCC	Ind	M$^	26$	CSYS	Ind	
Music and Astrophysics (4 Yrs)	WF35	4FT deg	* g	BCC	Ind	Ind	28	BBBB	Ind	
Neuroscience and Astrophysics	BF15	3FT deg	P+S	BCC-CCC	Ind	M$^	26$	CSYS	Ind	
Neuroscience and Astrophysics (4 Yrs)	BF1M	4FT deg	*	BCC-CCC	Ind	Ind	26$	BBBB	Ind	
Neuroscience and Physics	BF1H	3FT deg	P+S	BCC-CCC	Ind	M$^	26$	CSYS	Ind	
Philosophy and Astrophysics	FV57	3FT deg	P g	BCC	Ind	D$^	28$	CSYS	Ind	
Philosophy and Astrophysics (4 Yrs)	VF75	4FT deg	*	BCC	Ind	Ind	28	BBBB	Ind	
Physics	F300	3FT deg	P	BCC-CCC	Ind	M$^	26$	CSYS	Ind	
Physics (3 Yrs)	F301	3FT deg	P+M	BCC-CCC	Ind	M$	28$	CSYS	Ind	
Physics and American Studies	FQ34	3FT deg	P g	BCC	Ind	D$^	28$	CSYS	Ind	
Physics and American Studies (4 Yrs)	QF43	4FT deg	*	BCC	Ind	Ind	28	BBBB	Ind	
Physics and Ancient History	FV3D	3FT deg	P	BCC	Ind	D$^	28$	CSYS	Ind	
Physics and Applied Social Studies	FL35	3FT deg	P g	BCC	Ind	D$^	28$	CSYS	Ind	
Physics and Applied Social Studies (4 Yrs)	LF53	4FT deg	*	BCC	Ind	Ind	28	BBBB	Ind	

course details | 98 expected requirements | 96 entry stats

TITLE	CODE	COURSE	SUBJECTS	A/AS	NO/C	AGNVQ	IB	SQA(H)	SQA	RATIO A/AS
Physics and Biochemistry	CF73	3FT deg	P+C g	BCC-CCC	Ind	M$^	26$	CSYS	Ind	1
Physics and Biochemistry (4 Yrs)	FC37	4FT deg	*	BCC-CCC	Ind	Ind	26	BBBB	Ind	
Physics and Biochemistry (MSci)	FC3R	4FT deg	P+C	BCC-CCC	Ind	M$^	26$	CSYS	Ind	
Physics and Biological & Medicinal Chem (4 Yrs)	FFC3	4FT deg	*	BCC-CCC	Ind	Ind	26$	BBBB	Ind	
Physics and Biological and Medicinal Chemistry	FFCH	3FT deg	P+C g	BCC-CCC	Ind	M$^	26$	CSYS	Ind	
Physics and Biology	CF13	3FT deg	P g	BCC-CCC	Ind	M$^	26$	CSYS	Ind	2
Physics and Biology (4 Yrs)	FC31	4FT deg	*	BCC-CCC	Ind	Ind	26	BBBB	Ind	
Physics and Biology (MSci)	FC3C	4FT deg	P	BCC-CCC	Ind	M$^	26$	CSYS	Ind	
Physics and Business Administration	FN39	3FT deg	P g	BCC	Ind	D$^	28$	CSYS	Ind	
Physics and Business Administration (4 Yrs)	NF93	4FT deg	*	BCC	Ind	Ind	28	BBBB	Ind	
Physics and Chemistry	FF13	3FT deg	P+C g	BCC-CCC	Ind	M$^	26$	CSYS	Ind	5
Physics and Chemistry (4 Yrs)	FF31	4FT deg	*	BCC-CCC	Ind	Ind	26	BBBB	Ind	
Physics and Chemistry (MSci)	FF3C	4FT deg	P+C g	BCC-CCC	Ind	M$^	26$	CSYS	Ind	
Physics and Classical Studies	FQ38	3FT deg	P	BCC	Ind	D$^	28$	CSYS	Ind	
Physics and Computer Science	FG35	3FT deg	P g	BCC-CCC	Ind	M$^	26$	CSYS	Ind	4
Physics and Computer Science (4 Yrs)	GF53	4FT deg	*	BCC-CCC	Ind	Ind	26	BBBB	Ind	2
Physics and Computer Science (MSci)	GF5H	4FT deg	P g	BCC-CCC	Ind	M$^	26$	CSYS	Ind	
Physics and Criminology	FM3H	3FT deg	P g	BBB-BCC	Ind	D$^	28$	CSYS	Ind	
Physics and Criminology (4 Yrs)	MFH3	4FT deg	*	BBB-BCC	Ind	Ind	28	ABBB	Ind	
Physics and Economics	FL31	3FT deg	P g	BCC	Ind	D$^	28$	CSYS	Ind	2
Physics and Economics (4 Yrs)	LF13	4FT deg	*	BCC	Ind	Ind	28	BBBB	Ind	
Physics and Educational Studies	FX39	3FT deg	P	BCC	Ind	D$^	28$	CSYS	Ind	
Physics and Educational Studies (4 Yrs)	XF93	4FT deg	*	BCC	Ind	Ind	28	BBBB	Ind	1
Physics and Electronic Music (4 Yrs)	WFJ3	4FT deg	* g	BCC	Ind	Ind	28	BBBB	Ind	
Physics and English	FQ33	3FT deg	P+E	BBC-BCC	Ind	D$^	28$	CSYS	Ind	
Physics and English (4 Yrs)	QF33	4FT deg	*	BBC-BCC	Ind	Ind	28	BBBB	Ind	
Physics and Environmental Management (4 Yrs)	FFX3	4FT deg	* g	BCC	Ind	Ind	28	BBBB	Ind	
Physics and French	FR31	3FT deg	P+F	BCC	Ind	D$^	28$	CSYS	Ind	
Physics and French (4 Yrs)	RF13	4FT deg	*	BCC	Ind	Ind	28	BBBB	Ind	3
Physics and French/German	FT39	3FT deg	F+G+P	BBC	Ind	D$^	30$	CSYS	Ind	
Physics and Geology	FF36	3FT deg	P g	BCC	Ind	M$^	28$	CSYS	Ind	
Physics and Geology (4 Yrs)	FF63	4FT deg	*	BCC	Ind	Ind	28	BBBB	Ind	
Physics and German	FR32	3FT deg	G+P	BCC	Ind	D$^	28$	CSYS	Ind	
Physics and History	FV31	3FT deg	P	BCC	Ind	D$^	28$	CSYS	Ind	
Physics and History (4 Yrs)	VF13	4FT deg	*	BCC	Ind	Ind	28	BBBB	Ind	
Physics and Human Resource Management	FN36	3FT deg	P	BCC	Ind	D$^	28$	CSYS	Ind	
Physics and Human Resource Management (4 Yrs)	NF63	4FT deg	*	BCC	Ind	Ind	28	BBBB	Ind	
Physics and International History	FV3C	3FT deg	P	BCC	Ind	D$^	28$	CSYS	Ind	
Physics and International History (4 Yrs)	VFC3	4FT deg	*	BCC	Ind	Ind	28	BBBB	Ind	
Physics and International Politics	FM3C	3FT deg	P g	BCC	Ind	D$^	28$	CSYS	Ind	
Physics and International Politics (4 Yrs)	MFC3	4FT deg	*	BCC	Ind	Ind	28	BBBB	Ind	
Physics and Latin	FQ36	3FT deg	Ln+P	BCC	Ind	D$^	28$	CSYS	Ind	
Physics and Latin (4 Yrs)	QF63	4FT deg	*	BCC	Ind	Ind	28	BBBB	Ind	
Physics and Management Science	FN31	3FT deg	P g	BCC	Ind	D$^	28$	CSYS	Ind	1
Physics and Management Science (4 Yrs)	NF13	4FT deg	*	BCC	Ind	Ind	28	BBBB	Ind	
Physics and Marketing	FN35	3FT deg	P	BCC	Ind	D$^	28$	CSYS	Ind	
Physics and Mathematics	FG31	3FT deg	M+P	BCC-CCC	Ind	M$^	26$	CSYS	Ind	5
Physics and Mathematics (4 Yrs)	GF13	4FT deg	*	BCC-CCC	Ind	Ind	26	BBBB	Ind	1
Physics and Mathematics (MSci)	GF1H	4FT deg	M+P	BCC-CCC	Ind	M$^	26$	CSYS	Ind	
Physics and Music (4 Yrs)	WF33	4FT deg	* g	BCC	Ind	Ind	28	BBBB	Ind	
Physics and Neurosciences (4 Yrs)	BF13	4FT deg	*	BCC-CCC	Ind	Ind	26	BBBB	Ind	
Physics and Philosophy	FV37	3FT deg	P	BCC	Ind	D$^	28$	CSYS	Ind	

Letts STUDY GUIDES
THE INDEPENDENT

course details   98 expected requirements   96 entry stats

TITLE	CODE	COURSE	SUBJECTS	A/AS	NO/C	AGNVQ	IB	SQA(H)	SQA	RATIO A/AS
Physics and Philosophy (4 Yrs)	VF73	4FT deg	*	BCC	Ind	Ind	28	BBBB	Ind	8
Politics and Astrophysics	FM51	3FT deg	P g	BCC	Ind	D$^	28$	CSYS	Ind	
Politics and Astrophysics (4 Yrs)	MF15	4FT deg	*	BCC	Ind	Ind	28	BBBB	Ind	
Politics and Physics (4 Yrs)	MF13	4FT deg	*	BCC	Ind	Ind	28	BBBB	Ind	
Psychology and Astrophysics	CF85	3FT deg	P g	BBB-BCC	Ind	D$^	28$	CSYS	Ind	
Psychology and Physics	CF83	3FT deg	P g	BBB-BCC	Ind	D$^	28$	CSYS	Ind	
Sociol & Soc Anthrop and Astrophysics (4 Yrs)	LF35	4FT deg	*	BCC	Ind	Ind	28	BBBB	Ind	
Sociol & Social Anthropology and Physics (4 Yrs)	LF33	4FT deg	*	BCC	Ind	Ind	28	BBBB	Ind	
Sociology & Social Anthropology and Astrophysics	FL53	3FT deg	P g	BCC	Ind	D$^	28$	CSYS	Ind	
Sociology & Social Anthropology and Physics	FL33	3FT deg	P g	BCC	Ind	D$^	28$	CSYS	Ind	
Statistics and Astrophysics (4 Yrs)	GF45	4FT deg	* g	BCC-CCC	Ind	Ind	26	BBBB	Ind	
Statistics and Physics (4 Yrs)	GF43	4FT deg	*	BCC-CCC	Ind	Ind	26	BBBB	Ind	
Visual Arts and Physics	FW31	3FT deg	P	BCC	Ind	D$^	28$	CSYS	Ind	

Univ of KENT

TITLE	CODE	COURSE	SUBJECTS	A/AS	NO/C	AGNVQ	IB	SQA(H)	SQA	RATIO A/AS
Chemical Physics	F334	3FT deg	M+P+C	16	MO $	Ind	24$	BBBB$		
Chemical Physics with Studies Abroad	F335	4FT deg	M+P+C	16	MO $	Ind	24$	BBBB$		
Economics and Physics	LF13	3FT deg	M+P	18	Ind	Ind	26$	BBBB$	Ind	
Phys with Optoelectronics with Yr in Eur (MPhys)	F366	4FT deg	M+P	18	5M $	Ind	26$	BBBC$	Ind	
Phys with Space Sci & Syst with Yr in Eur(MPhys)	F368	4FT deg	M+P	18	5M $	Ind	26$	BBBC$	Ind	3
Physics	F300	3FT deg	M+P	18	5M $	Ind	26$	BBBC$	Ind	11
Physics (MPhys)	F303	4FT deg	M+P	18	5M $	Ind	26$	BBBC$	Ind	19
Physics and Business Adminstration	FN31	3FT deg	M+P	20	3M+2D$	Ind	28$	BBBB$	Ind	
Physics with Astrophysics	F3F5	3FT deg	M+P	18	5M $	Ind	26$	BBBC$	Ind	13
Physics with Astrophysics (MPhys)	F3FN	4FT deg	M+P	18	5M $	Ind	26$	BBBC$	Ind	18
Physics with Astrophysics with Yr in Eur (MPhys)	F369	4FT deg	M+P	18	5M $	Ind	26$	BBBC$	Ind	
Physics with Astrophysics with a yr in Europe	F3FM	4FT deg	M+P	18	5M $	Ind	26$	BBBC$	Ind	
Physics with Business Studies	F3ND	3FT deg	M+P	18	5M $	Ind	26$	BBBC$	Ind	
Physics with Computational Phys with Yr in Eur	F352	4FT deg	M+P	18	5M $	Ind	26$	BBBC$	Ind	
Physics with Computational Physics	F351	3FT deg	M+P	18	5M $	Ind	26$	BBBC$	Ind	
Physics with Finance	F3N3	3FT deg	M+P	18	5M $	Ind	26$	BBBC$	Ind	
Physics with Management Science	F3N1	3FT deg	M+P	18	5M $	Ind	26$	BBBC$	Ind	
Physics with Optoelectronics	F361	3FT deg	M+P	18	5M $	Ind	26$	BBBC$	Ind	
Physics with Optoelectronics (MPhys)	F367	4FT deg	M+P	18	5M $	Ind	26$	BBBC$	Ind	3
Physics with Optoelectronics with a Yr in Europe	F362	4FT deg	M+P	18	5M $	Ind	26$	BBBC$	Ind	
Physics with Space Sci and Systs with Yr in Eur	F364	4FT deg	M+P	18	5M $	Ind	26$	BBBC$	Ind	
Physics with Space Science and Systems	F365	3FT deg	M+P	18	5M $	Ind	26$	BBBC$	Ind	16
Physics with Space Science and Systems (MPhys)	F363	4FT deg	M+P	18	5M $	Ind	26$	BBBC$	Ind	6 14/24
Physics with a foundation year	F305	4FT deg	* g	N	Ind	Dip	Ind	Ind	1 6/12	
Physics with a year in Europe	F301	4FT deg	M+P	18	5M $	Ind	26$	BBBC$	Ind	
Physics with a year in Europe (MPhys)	F302	4FT deg	M+P	18	5M $	Ind	26$	BBBC$	Ind	
Physics with a year in USA (MPhys)	F304	4FT deg	M+P	18	5M $	Ind	26$	BBBC$	Ind	
Theoretical Physics (MPhys)	F323	4FT deg	M+P	18	5M $	Ind	26$	BBBC$	Ind	
Theoretical Physics with a Year in Europe	F321	4FT deg	M+P	18	5M $	Ind	26$	BBBC$	Ind	2

KING'S COLL LONDON (Univ of London)

TITLE	CODE	COURSE	SUBJECTS	A/AS	NO/C	AGNVQ	IB	SQA(H)	SQA	RATIO A/AS
Chemistry and Physics	FF13	3FT deg	C+P+M	CCC	3M+1D$	Ind	28$	BBBCC	Ind	11
Chemistry and Physics (4 years) (MSci)	FF1H	4FT deg	C+P+M	CCC	3M+1D$	Ind	28$	BBBCC	Ind	
Mathematics and Physics	FG31	3FT deg	M+P	20	X		28$	AABBB$	X	14
Mathematics and Physics (4 years)	FG3D	4FT deg	M+P	20	X		28$	AABBB$	X	1
Mathematics and Physics with Astrophysics	FG3C	3FT deg	M+P	20	X		28$	AABBB	X	17
Physics	F300	3FT deg	M+P	18	2M+1D		28$	AABBB	Ind	17
Physics MSci (4 Yrs)	F303	4FT deg	M+P	18	2M+1D		28$	AABBB	Ind	6 14/28
Physics and Education (4 Yrs)	FX39	4FT deg	M+P g	8	3M		Ind	BBCCC	Ind	1 8/14

| | | | 98 expected requirements | | | | | | | 96 entry stats |
| course details | | | | | | | | | | |

TITLE	CODE	COURSE	SUBJECTS	R/RS	NO/C	RGNVQ	IB	SQA(H)	SQA	RATIO R/RS
Physics and Philosophy	FV37	3FT deg	M+P	BBB	Ind		30$	AAABB	X	18
Physics with 1 year abroad	F305	4FT deg	M+P g	18	2M+1D		28$	AABBB	Ind	
Physics with Astrophysics	F3F5	3FT deg	M+P	18	2M+1D		28$	AABBB	Ind	15
Physics with Computer Science	F3G5	3FT deg	M+P	18	2M+1D		28$	AABBB	Ind	5
Physics with French	F3R1	3FT deg	M+P g	18	2M+1D		28$	AABBB	Ind	
Physics with Management	F3N1	3FT deg	M+P	18	2M+1D		28$	AABBB	Ind	13
Physics with Medical Applications	F370	3FT deg	M+P	18	2M+1D		28$	AABBB	Ind	11
Physics with Philosophy of Science	F3V5	3FT deg	M+P	18	2M+1D		28$	AABBB	Ind	8
Physics with Theology	F3V8	3FT deg	M+P	18	2M+1D		28$	AABBB	Ind	

KINGSTON Univ

TITLE	CODE	COURSE	SUBJECTS	R/RS	NO/C	RGNVQ	IB	SQA(H)	SQA	RATIO R/RS
Applied Biology & Physics	CF13	3FT deg	2(P/B/C) g	10	3M $	Ind	Ind	CCC	Ind	
Computing & Physics	FG35	3FT deg	P/M g	10	3M $	Ind	Ind	CCC	Ind	
Engineering Physics	F380	3FT deg	P/M	8	N	Ind	Ind	Ind	Ind	
Engineering Physics	F388▼	4EXT deg		Ind	Ind	Ind	Ind	Ind	Ind	
Engineering Physics	F384	4SW deg	P/M	8	Ind	Ind	Ind	Ind	Ind	
Geography & Physics	FL38	3FT deg	Gy/P g	10	Ind	Ind	Ind	BCCC	Ind	4
Geology & Physics	FF63	3FT deg	P g	10	3M $	Ind	Ind	CCC	Ind	
Mathematics & Physics	FG31	3FT deg	P+M g	10	3M $	Ind	Ind	CCC	Ind	2
Physics	F308	4EXT deg		Ind	Ind	Ind	Ind	Ind	Ind	
Physics	F300	3FT deg	M+P	CCC	5M $	DS	Ind	Ind	Ind	
Physics & French	FR31	4FT deg	P/F	10	Ind	Ind	Ind	CCC	Ind	
Physics (MPhys)	F304	4FT deg	M+P	CCC	5M $	DS	Ind	Ind	Ind	
Physics and Chemistry	FF31	3FT deg	P/C g	8	3M $	Ind	Ind	CCC	Ind	3
Physics with Business Management	F3ND	4SW deg	P/M	12	2M $	Ind	Ind	CCC	Ind	
Physics with Business Management	F3N1	3FT deg	P/M	12	2M $	Ind	Ind	CCC	Ind	7
Physics with Business Management	F3NC▼	4EXT/5EXTSW deg	*	Ind			Ind	Ind	Ind	
Physics with Electronics & Computing	F3HP▼	4EXT deg	*	Ind			Ind	Ind	Ind	1
Physics with Electronics and Computing	F3H6	3FT deg	P/M	12	2M $	Ind	Ind	CCC	Ind	5
Instrumentation	543F	2FT HND	P/M	2	N	Ind	Ind	Ind	Ind	
Physics with Electronics and Computing	003F	2FT HND	P/M	2	N	Ind	Ind	DD	Ind	1

LANCASTER Univ

TITLE	CODE	COURSE	SUBJECTS	R/RS	NO/C	RGNVQ	IB	SQA(H)	SQA	RATIO R/RS
Engineering Physics	FH36	3FT/4SW deg	M+P g	CCE	MO $		22$	BBCCC$	Ind	
Physics	F300	3FT deg	M+P	CCE	MO $		24$	BBCCC$	Ind	
Physics (inc a year in USA or Canada)	F302	3FT deg	M+P	BBC	MO+2D		26$	BBBCC$	Ind	
Physics (inc a year in USA or Canada) (MPhys)	F305	4FT deg	M+P	BBC	MO+2D		26$	BBBCC$	Ind	
Physics (with Specialised Studies) (MPhys)	F303	4FT deg	M+P	BCE	MO		24$	BBCCC$	Ind	
Physics Studies	F301	3FT deg	P/C/Es g	CCE	MO $		24$	BBBB	Ind	
Physics with Applied Physics	F313	3FT deg	M+P	CCE	MO $		24$	BBCCC$	Ind	
Physics with Applied Physics (MPhys)	F311	4FT deg	M+P	BCE	MO $		24$	BBCCC	Ind	
Physics with Applied Physics(Ind)(3rd Yr in Ind)	F317	4SW deg	M+P	CCE	MO $		24$	BBCCC	Ind$	
Physics with Computational Physics	F376	3FT deg	M+P	CCE	MO $		24$	BBCCC	Ind	
Physics with Computational Physics (MPhys)	F351	4FT deg	M+P	BCE	MO $		24$	BBBCC$	Ind	
Physics with Cosmology (MPhys)	F3F5	4FT deg	M+P	BCE	MO $		24$	BBCCC$	Ind	
Physics with French Studies	F3R1	4SW deg	F+P+M	BCC	MO $		24$	BBCCC$	Ind	
Physics with German Studies	F3R2	4SW deg	P+M+G/L	BCC	MO $		24$	BBCCC$	Ind	
Physics with Italian Studies	F3R3	4SW deg	P+M+I/L	BCC	MO $		24$	BBCCC$	Ind	
Physics with Spanish Studies	F3R4	4SW deg	(M+P)+Sp/*	BCC	MO $		24$	BBCCC$	Ind	
Physics with Theoretical Physics	F320	3FT deg	P+M	CCE	MO $		24$	BBCCC$	Ind	
Physics with Theoretical Physics (MPhys)	F321	4FT deg	P+M	BCE	MO$		24$	BBCCC$	Ind	
Combined Science _Physics_	Y158	3FT deg	P+M	CCD	MO $		28	BBBB$	Ind	
Combined Science (inc a year in USA or Canada) _Physics_	Y155	3FT deg	P+M	BBB	Ind $		32	ABBBB$	Ind	

course details			98 expected requirements							96 entry stats
TITLE	CODE	COURSE	SUBJECTS	A/AS	ND/C	AGNVQ	IB	SQA(H)	SQA	RATIO A/AS
Univ of LEEDS										
Artificial Intelligence-Physics	FG38	3FT deg	M+P g	BCC	1M+5D$	Ind	28$	BBBBC	Ind	11
Astronomy-Mathematics	FG51	3FT deg	M+P g	BBC	1M+5D$	Ind	30$	ABBBB	Ind	
Chemistry-Physics	FF13	3FT/4FT deg	C+M+P g	BCC	1M+5D$	Ind	28$	BBBBC	Ind	21
Computer Science-Physics	FG35	3FT/4FT deg	M+P g	BCC	1M+5D$	Ind	28$	BBBBC	Ind	
Mathematics-Physics	FG31	3FT/4FT deg	M+P g	BBC	1M+5D$	Ind	30$	ABBBC	Ind	13 20/28
Molecular Science and Technology	FF31	3FT/4FT deg	C+P+M g	CCC	Ind	Ind	26$	BBBCC	Ind	
Physics	F300	3FT/4FT deg	P+M g	CCC	1M+4D$	DS△ go	26$	BBBCC	Ind	5 12/28
Physics with Astrophysics	F3F5	3FT/4FT deg	P+M g	CCC	1M+4D$	DS△ go	26$	BBBCC	Ind	6 14/28
Physics with Elect & Instrumentation	F3H6	3FT/4FT deg	P+M g	CCC	1M+4D$	DS△ go	26$	BBBCC	Ind	5
Physics with foundation year	F301	4FT deg	g	Ind	Ind	Ind	Ind	Ind	Ind	9/16
Physics-French	FR31	4FT deg	M+P+F	BBC	Ind	Ind	30$	CSYS	Ind	
Physics-German	FR32	4FT deg	M+P+G	BBC	Ind	Ind	30$	CSYS	Ind	
Physics-History and Philosophy of Science	FV35	3FT/4FT deg	M+P g	BBB	Ind	Ind	30$	CSYS	Ind	
Physics-Philosophy	FV37	3FT/4FT deg	M+P g	BBB	Ind	Ind	30$	CSYS		31
Theoretical Physics	F320	4FT deg	P+M g	BCC	Ind	DS△ go	30$	CSYS	Ind	10 20/28
Univ of LEICESTER										
Physics	F300	3FT deg	P+M g	CCD	3M+2D$	Ind	28$	BBBBC	Ind	
Physics (MPhys)	F303	4FT deg	P+M g	BCC	3M+2D$	Ind	30$	BBBBB	Ind	
Physics w. Space Science and Technology (MPhys)	F366	4FT deg	P+M g	BCC	3M+2D$	Ind	30$	BBBBB	Ind	20/30
Physics with Astrophysics	F3F5	3FT deg	P+M g	CCD	3M+2D$	Ind	28$	BBBBC	Ind	18/22
Physics with Astrophysics (MPhys)	F3FM	4FT deg	P+M g	BCC	3M+2D$	Ind	30$	BBBBB	Ind	18/30
Physics with Medical Physics	F370	3FT deg	P+M g	CCD	3M+2D$	Ind	28$	BBBBC	Ind	
Physics with Space Science and Technology	F365	3FT deg	P+M g	CCD	3M+2D$	Ind	28$	BBBBC	Ind	14/24
BSc with integrated foundation *Physics*	Y101	4EXT deg	* g		N	*			Ind	
Combined Science *Physics*	Y100	3FT deg	P+M g	CCC	MO $	Ind	28$	BBBCC$	HN	
Mathematics with Astronomy	G1F5	3FT deg	M g	20	Ind	DS△	28$	BBBBC$	Ind	
Mathematics with Astronomy	G1FN	4FT deg	M g	20	Ind	DS△	28$	BBBBS	Ind	
Mathematics with Astronomy (European Union)	G1FM	4FT deg	M g	20	Ind	DS△	28$	BBBBC$	Ind	
Univ of LIVERPOOL										
Chemical Physics	F334	3FT deg	P+C+M g	12	MO $	Ind	31$	BBBCC$	Ind	3
Mathematical Physics	F326	3FT deg	P+M g	12	MO $	DS△ go	31$	BBBCC$	Ind	10
Mathematical Physics (MMath)	FG3C	4FT deg	P+M	20	MO $	Ind	31$	BBBCC$	Ind	9
Mathematical Physics (MPhys)	F325	4FT deg	P+M	20	MO $	Ind	31$	BBBCC$	Ind	3
Mathematical Sciences with Physics	G1F3	4FT deg	* g	12	Ind	Ind	Dip	Ind	Ind	
Physics	F300	3FT deg	P+M g	12	MO $	DS△ go	31$	BBBCC$	Ind	7 9/22
Physics (MPhys)	F303	4FT deg	P+M g	12	MO $	DS△ go	31$	BBBCC$	Ind	5 11/26
Physics and Computer Science	FG35	3FT deg	M+P g	12	MO $	DS△ go	31$	BBBCC$	Ind	6
Physics and Electronic Engineering	F340	3FT deg	P+M g	12	MO $	DS△ go	31$	BBBCC$	Ind	17
Physics and Mathematics	FG31	3FT deg	M+P g	12	MO $	DS△ go	31$	BBBCC$	Ind	11
Physics for New Technology	F352	3FT deg	P+M g	12	MO $	DS△ go	31$	BBBCC$	Ind	6
Physics with Materials Science	FF23	3FT deg	P+M g	12	MO $	DS△ go	31$	BBBCC$	Ind	12
Physics with a European Language	F3TF	4FT deg	P+M g	12	MO $	Ind	31$	BBBCC$	Ind	
Physics with a European Language (MPhys)	F3T2	4FT deg	P+M g	12	MO $	Ind	31$	BBBCC$	Ind	9
Radiation Physics and Environmental Science	F3F9	3FT deg	P+M g	12	MO $	DS△ go	31$	BBBCC$	Ind	
LIVERPOOL JOHN MOORES Univ										
Applied Physics	F318	4EXTSW/5EXTSW deg		4						1
Applied Physics	F310	3FT/4SW deg	P	8	3M	D$/M$6				8
Applied Physics (MPhys)	F303	4FT deg	P	10	4M	D$/M$6				

			98 expected requirements							96 entry stats	
course details											
TITLE	CODE	COURSE	SUBJECTS	A/AS	ND/C	AGNVQ	IB	SQA(H)	SQA	RATIO A/AS	
Astrophysics	F520	3FT/4SW deg	M+P	DD	3M	D$/M$6				15	
Astrophysics (MPhys)	F521	4FT deg	M+P	10	4M					24	
Optical Science and Technology	F380	3FT/4SW deg	M/P	8	3M	D$/M$6				6	
Physics and German	F3R2	4SW deg		8	3M	D$/M$6					
LOUGHBOROUGH Univ											
Engineering Physics	F380	3FT deg	M+P	BCC	3M+2D	DS6/^ go	28$	Ind	Ind	5	
Engineering Physics (4 Yr SW)	F382	4SW deg	M+P	BCC	3M+2D	DS6/^ go	28$	Ind	Ind	4	
Engineering Physics with a year in Europe	F381	4SW deg	M+P	BCC	3M+2D	DS6/^ go	28$	Ind	Ind		
Physical Education, Sports Science and Physics	FB36	3FT deg	M+P	20			30$	Ind			
Physics	F300	3FT deg	M+P	BCC	3M+2D	DS6/^ go	28$	Ind	Ind	12	14/22
Physics (4 Yr SW)	F301	4SW deg	M+P	BCC	3M+2D	DS6/^ go	28$	Ind	Ind	6	
Physics (4 Yrs MPhys)	F303	4FT deg	M+P	BCC		DS6/^ go	28$	Ind	Ind	9	
Physics and Mathematics	FG31	3FT deg	M+P	BBC			28$	Ind		7	20/22
Physics and Mathematics (4 Yr SW)	GF13	4SW deg	M+P	BBC			28$	Ind		3	
Physics and Mathematics with a year in Europe	FG3C	4SW deg	M+P	BBC	3M+2D		28$	Ind			
Physics with Computing	F3G5	3FT deg	M+P	BCC	3M+2D	DS6/^ go	28$	Ind	Ind		
Physics with Computing (4 Yr SW)	F3GM	4SW deg	M+P	BCC	3M+2D	DS6/^ go	28$	Ind	Ind		
Physics with Computing and a year in Europe	F3GN	4FT deg	M+P	BCC	3M+2D	DS6/^ go	28$	Ind	Ind		
Physics with Environmental Sci & a yr in Europe	F3FY	4FT deg	M+P	BCC	3M+2D	DS6/^ go	28$	Ind	Ind		
Physics with Environmental Science	F3F9	3FT deg	M+P	BCC	3M+2D	DS6/^ go	28$	Ind	Ind		
Physics with Environmental Science (4 Yr SW)	F3FX	4SW deg	M+P	BCC	3M+2D	DS6/^ go	28$	Ind	Ind		
Physics with Management	F3N1	3FT deg	M+P	BCC	3M+2D	DS6/^ go	28$	Ind	Ind		
Physics with Management (4 Yr SW)	F3NC	4SW deg	M+P	BCC	3M+2D	DS6/^ go	28$	Ind	Ind		
Physics with Management and a year in Europe	F3ND	4SW deg	M+P	BCC	3M+2D	DS6/^ go	28$	Ind	Ind		
Physics with a year in Europe	F302	4SW deg	M+P	BCC	3M+2D	DS6/^ go	28$	Ind	Ind		
Univ of MANCHESTER											
Chemical Physics	F334	3FT deg	C+P+M	BCC	4M+2D$		30$	CSYS	Ind		
Chemistry and Physics	FF13	3FT deg	C+P+M	CCC	4M+2D$		30$	CSYS	Ind	5	
Mathematics and Physics (BSc/MMath & Phys)	FG3C	3FT/4FT deg	M+P	BBC	4M+2D$ D^		30$	CSYS	Ind	20	
Physics (BSc/MPhys)	F300	3FT/4FT deg	M+P	BCC-BBC	4M+2D$ D^		30$	CSYS	Ind	4	16/30
Physics with Astrophysics (BSc/Mphys)	F364	3FT/4FT deg	M+P	BCC-BBC	4M+2D$ D^		30$	CSYS	Ind	5	18/30
Physics with Business and Management (BSc/MPhys)	F3N1	3FT/4FT deg	M+P	BCC-BBC	4M+2D$ D^		30$	CSYS	Ind	4	20/20
Physics with Study in Europe (MPhys)	F301	4FT deg	M+P	BCC-BBC	4M+2D$ D^		30$	CSYS	Ind	4	18/28
Physics with Technological Physics (BSc/Mphys)	F351	3FT/4FT deg	M+P	BBC	4M+2D$ D^		30$	CSYS	Ind	3	21/28
Physics with Theoretical Physics (BSc/MPhys)	F325	3FT/4FT deg	M+P	BBC	4M+2D$ D^		30$	CSYS	Ind	5	22/30
UMIST (Manchester)											
Mathematical Physics	F3G1	3FT deg	M+P g	BBD	Ind	Ind	30$	CSYS	Ind		
Mathematical Physics (MPhys)	F3GC	4FT deg	M+P g	BBD	Ind	Ind	30$	CSYS	Ind		
Mathematics with Astrophysics	G1F5	3FT deg	M g	BBC	Ind	Ind	30$	CSYS	Ind	8	22/28
Physics	F300	3FT deg	M+P g	BCD	4M+1D$	Ind	28$	CSYS	Ind	14	18/22
Physics (MPhys)	F303	4FT deg	M+P g	BCD	4M+1D$	Ind	28$	CSYS	Ind	7	16/30
Physics with Astrophysics	F3F5	3FT deg	M+P g	BCD	4M+1D$	Ind	28$	CSYS	Ind		
Physics with Astrophysics (MPhys)	F3FM	4FT deg	M+P g	BCD	4M+1D$	Ind	28$	CSYS	Ind		
Physics with Computational Physics	F376	3FT deg	M+P g	BCD	4M+1D$	Ind	28$	CSYS	Ind	4	
Physics with Computational Physics (MPhys)	F350	4FT deg	M+P g	BCD	4M+1D$	Ind	28$	CSYS	Ind		
Physics with Environmental Science	F3F9	3FT deg	M+P g	BCD	4M+1D$	Ind	28$	CSYS	Ind	15	
Physics with Environmental Science (MPhys)	F3FY	4FT deg	M+P g	BCD	4M+1D$	Ind	28$	CSYS	Ind	4	
Physics with French (MPhys)	F3R1	4FT deg	M+P g	BCD	4M+1D$	Ind	28$	CSYS	Ind	12	
Physics with German (MPhys)	F3R2	4FT deg	M+P g	BCD	4M+1D$	Ind	28$	CSYS	Ind	3	
Physics with Optoelectronics	F368	3FT deg	M+P g	BCD	4M+1D$	Ind	28$	CSYS	Ind	5	
Physics with Optoelectronics (MPhys)	F369	4FT deg	M+P g	BCD	4M+1D$	Ind	28$	CSYS	Ind	3	

course details			98 expected requirements							96 entry stats
TITLE	CODE	COURSE	SUBJECTS	A/AS	ND/C	RGNVQ	IB	SQR(H)	SQR	RATIO A/AS
MANCHESTER METROPOLITAN Univ										
Applied Physics	F310	3FT deg	M+P g	12-18	1M+3D$	M$	28$	BBBCC$	Ind	
Applied Physics (Foundation)	F308▼	4FT deg	M/P	E	2M $	P$	$	$	Ind	
Applied Physics/Applicable Mathematics	FG31	3FT deg	M+P g	12	5M $	M$	27$	BCCCC$	Ind	
Business Mathematics/Applied Physics	FG3C	3FT deg	M+P g	12	5M $	M$	27$	BCCCC$	C	
Chemistry/Applied Physics	FF13	3FT deg	C+P/M g	12	4M $	M$	26$	CCCCC$	Ind	
Computer Technology/Applied Physics	FG3M	3FT deg	M+P g	12	5M $	M$	27$	BCCCC$	Ind	
Computing Science/Applied Physics	FG35	3FT deg	M+P g	12	5M $	M$	27$	BCCCC$	Ind	
Electronics/Applied Physics	FH3P	3FT deg	M+P g	12	5M $	M$	27$	BCCCC$	Ind	
Engineering Physics	F380	3FT/4SW deg	P+M	12	2M $		Ind	BBCC$	Ind	
Engineering Physics (Foundation)	F388▼	4FT deg	M/P	E	2M $	P$	$	$	Ind	
European Studies/Applied Physics	FT32	3FT deg	M+P g	12	5M $	M$	27$	BCCCC$	Ind	
Geography/Applied Physics	FL38	3FT deg	M+P g	14	MO $	M$	28$	BBCCC$	Ind	
Languages/Applied Physics	FT39	3FT deg	M+P g	14	MO $	M$	28$	BBCCC$	Ind	
Manufacturing/Applied Physics	FH37	3FT deg	M+P g	12	5M $	M$	27$	BCCCC$	Ind	
Materials Science/Applied Physics	FF23	3FT deg	M g	12	5M $	M$	27$	BCCCC$	Ind	
Physics Studies/Applicable Mathematics	FGH1	3FT deg	M g	12	5M $	M$	27$	BCCCC$	Ind	
Physics Studies/Business Mathematics	FGHC	3FT deg	P/M/Ec g	12	5M $	M$	27$	BCCCC$	Ind	
Physics Studies/Chemistry	FF31	3FT deg	C+P/M g	12	4M $	M$	26$	CCCCC$	Ind	
Physics Studies/Computer Technology	FGHM	3FT deg	P/M g	12	5M $	M$	27$	BCCCC$	Ind	
Physics Studies/Computing Science	FGH5	3FT deg	P/M g	12	5M $	M$	27$	BCCCC$	Ind	
Physics Studies/Electronics	FHHP	3FT deg	M+P g	12	5M $	M$	27$	BCCCC$	Ind	
Physics Studies/Environmental Studies	FF39	3FT deg	M/P g	16	1M+3D$	M$	28$	BBBCC$	Ind	
Physics Studies/European Studies	TF23	3FT deg	M/P g	12	5M $		27$	BCCCC$	Ind	
Physics Studies/Geography	LF83	3FT deg	M/P g	14	MO $		28$	BBCCC$	Ind	
Physics Studies/Languages	FTH9	3FT deg	P/M g	14	MO $		28$	BBCCC$	Ind	
Physics Studies/Manufacturing	FHH7	3FT deg	M+P g	12	5M $		27$	BCCCC$	Ind	
Physics Studies/Materials Science	FF32	3FT deg	M/P/C g	12	5M $		27$	BCCCC$	Ind	
Polymer Science/Applied Physics	FJ34	3FT deg	C+P/M g	12	5M $	M$	27$	BCCCC$	Ind	
Polymer Science/Physics Studies	FJH4	3FT deg	C g	12	5M $	M$	27$	BCCCC$	Ind	
Psychology/Applied Physics	FL37	3FT deg	M+P g	18	1M+3D$	D$	28$	BBBCC$	Ind	
Psychology/Physics Studies	LF73	3FT deg	M/P g	18	1M+3D$	D$	28$	BBBCC$	Ind	
Scientific Instrumentation/Applied Physics	FH36	3FT deg	M+P g	12	5M $	M$	27$	BCCCC$	Ind	
Scientific Instrumentation/Physics Studies	HF63	3FT deg	M/P g	12	5M $	M$	27$	BCCCC$	Ind	
Combined Studies (Foundation) *Applied Physics*	Y108	4FT deg	M/P	E	2M $	P$	$	$	Ind	
Combined Studies (Foundation) *Physics Studies*	Y108▼	4FT deg	M/P	E	2M $	P$	$	$	Ind	
NAPIER Univ										
Applied Physics with Computing	F3G5	4FT deg	2(M/P/C/B)	DD	Ind	Ind	Ind	BCC	Ind	
Environmental Physical Science	F374	4FT deg	2(M/P/C/B)	DD	Ind	Ind	Ind	BCC	Ind	
Univ of NEWCASTLE										
Astronomy and Astrophysics	F520	3FT deg	M+P	BCC	Ind		Ind	CSYS	Ind	12
Astronomy and Astrophysics	F521	4FT deg	*	CCC	Ind		Ind	BBBB	Ind	12
Astronomy and Astrophysics (MPhys)	F523	4FT deg	M+P	BCC	Ind		Ind	CSYS	Ind	12
Chemical Physics	F330	3FT deg								
Chemical Physics (4 years)	F331	4								
Chemistry and Physics	FF13	3FT deg	C+P+M	18	4M	Ind	28$	AABBB	Ind	
Computing Science and Physics	FG35	3FT deg	M+P	18	4M	Ind	28$	AABBB	Ind	
Mathematics and Physics	FG31	3FT deg	M+P	18	4M	Ind	28$	AABBB	Ind	8
Physics	F300	3FT deg	M+P	CCC	Ind		Ind	CSYS	Ind	9 10/24
Physics	F301	4FT deg	*	CCC	Ind		Ind	BBBB	Ind	3

	course details			98 expected requirements						96 entry stats	
TITLE	CODE	COURSE	SUBJECTS	A/AS	ND/C	RGNVQ	IB	SQA(H)	SQA	RATIO	A/AS
Physics (MPhys)	F303	4FT deg	M+P	BCC	Ind		Ind	CSYS	Ind	7	18/30
Physics with Medical Applications	F370	3FT deg	M+P	CCC	Ind		Ind	CSYS	Ind	11	
Physics with Medical Applications	F371	4FT deg	*	CCC	Ind		Ind	BBBB	Ind	2	
Theoretical Physics	F321	4FT deg	*	CCC	Ind		Ind	BBBB	Ind	2	
Theoretical Physics	F320	3FT deg	M+P	BCC	Ind		Ind	CSYS	Ind	8	
Theoretical Physics (MPhys)	F323	4FT deg	M+P	BCC	Ind		Ind	CSYS	Ind	4	24/30
Combined Studies _Astronomy and Astrophysics_	Y100	3FT deg	M+P	18	4M	Ind	28$	AAABB	Ind		
Combined Studies (BSc) _Physics_	Y100	3FT deg	M+P	18	4M	Ind	28$	AABBB	Ind		

Univ of NORTH LONDON

Combined Honours _Physics_	Y100	3FT/4SW/4EXT deg	P+M	CC	3M $	MS^	$	Ind	Ind		

Univ of NORTHUMBRIA

Applied Physics	F310	3FT/4SW deg	M/P g	8	3M $	ME	24$	CCC$	Ind	6	
Applied Physics	F318	5EXT deg	* g	2-4	N	P	24	CCC	Ind	2	

Univ of NOTTINGHAM

Chemistry and Molecular Physics	FF31	3FT deg	C+P+M	BBB-BBC	Ind	Ind	32$	Ind	Ind		
Chemistry and Molecular Physics (MSci)(4 Yrs)	FFH1	4FT deg	C+P+M	BBB-BBC	Ind	Ind	32$	Ind	Ind	5	24/30
Mathematical Physics (BSc) (3 Yrs)	F326	3FT deg	P+M	AAA-AAB	Ind	Ind	Ind	Ind	Ind	7	26/30
Mathematical Physics (MSci)(4 Yrs)	F325	4FT deg	P+M	AAA-AAB	Ind	Ind	Ind	Ind	Ind	5	28/30
Physics	F300	3FT deg	P+M	BB-BBC	Ind		Ind	CSYS	Ind	12	20/30
Physics (MSci) (4 Yrs)	F303	4FT deg	P+M	BB-BBC	Ind		Ind	CSYS	Ind	6	22/30
Physics and Philosophy	FV37	3FT deg	P+M	BB-BBC	Ind		Ind	CSYS	Ind	9	
Physics with Applied Physics	F310	3FT deg	P+M	BB-BBC	Ind		Ind	CSYS	Ind	9	
Physics with European Language (4 Yrs)	F3T2	4FT deg	P+M g	BBB-BBC	Ind		Ind	Ind	Ind	9	
Physics with European Language (4 Yrs)	F3TF	4FT deg	P+M g	BB-BBC	Ind		Ind	CSYS	Ind		
Physics with Medical Physics	F370	3FT deg	P+M	BB-BBC	Ind		Ind	CSYS	Ind	16	
Physics with Medical Physics (MSci)	F371	4FT deg	P+M	BBB-BBC	Ind		Ind	Ind	Ind		

NOTTINGHAM TRENT Univ

Applied Physics	F310	3FT deg	M/P g	CD	2M	Ind	Dip	Ind	Ind	6	8/10
Applied Physics (Extended)	F318	4EXT/5EXTSW deg	* g		Ind	Ind	Ind	Ind	Ind		
Applied Physics (MPhys)	F311	4FT deg	M/P g	CD	2M	Ind	Dip	Ind	Ind		
Biology and Physics	CF13	3FT deg	B+M/P g	10	Ind	Ind	Dip	C	Ind	4	
Chemistry and Physics	FF13	3FT deg	C+M/P g	10	Ind	Ind	Dip	C	Ind		
Computing and Physics	FG35	3FT deg	M/P	10	Ind	Ind	Dip	C	Ind	4	10/14
Env Systems & Monitoring & Physics (Env Physics)	FF39	3FT deg	M/P g	10	Ind	Ind	Dip	C	Ind	4	
Information Technology for Sciences and Physics	GF53	3FT deg	M/P g	10	Ind	Ind	Dip	C	Ind		
Mathematics and Physics	FG31	3FT deg	M/P g	10	Ind	Ind	Dip	C	Ind	5	
Physics	F300	3FT deg	M/P g	CC	3M	Ind	Dip	Ind	Ind	2	
Physics in Europe	F301	4FT deg	M/P g	12-14	4M	Ind	Dip	Ind	Ind		
Sport & Exercise Science and Physics	BF63	3FT deg	M/P+B/Pe/Ss g	16	Ind	Ind	Dip	B	Ind		

OXFORD Univ

Physics (3 Yrs)	F300	3FT deg	M+P	AAB	DO		36	AAAAA	Ind	4	28/30
Physics (4 Yrs)	F303	4FT deg	M+P	AAB	DO		36	AAAAA	Ind	2	28/30
Physics and Philosophy (4 Yrs)	VF73	4FT deg	M+P	AAB	DO		36	AAAAA	Ind	2	28/30

Univ of PAISLEY

Physical Science for Microelectronics	F340	3FT/4FT/5SW deg	M+C/P g	CCC-EE	Ind	Ind	Ind	BCC$	Ind	4	
Physics	F300	3FT/4FT/5SW deg	M+P g	CCC-EE	Ind	Ind	Ind	BCC$	Ind	6	
Physics with European Language	F3T2	3FT/4FT/5SW deg	M+P g	CCC-EE	Ind	Ind	Ind	BCC$	Ind		

course details			98 expected requirements							96 entry stats	
TITLE	CODE	COURSE	SUBJECTS	A/AS	ND/C	AGNVQ	IB	SQA(H)	SQA	RATIO A/AS	
Physics with Finance	F3N3	3FT/4FT/5SW deg	M+P g	CCC-EE	Ind	Ind	Ind	BCC$	Ind		
Physics with Management	F3N1	3FT/4FT/5SW deg	M+P g	CCC-EE	Ind	Ind	Ind	BCC$	Ind	10	
Physics with Scientific Computing	F3G5	3FT/4FT/5SW deg	M+P g	CCC-EE	Ind	Ind	Ind	BCC$	Ind	3	
Technological Physics (MSci)	F350	5SW deg	P+M g	DD	Ind	Ind	Ind	BBC$	Ind		

Univ of PLYMOUTH

TITLE	CODE	COURSE	SUBJECTS	A/AS	ND/C	AGNVQ	IB	SQA(H)	SQA	RATIO A/AS	
Chemistry with Astronomy	F1F5	3FT deg	C g	CC	3M	MS^	Ind	CCCC	Ind	5	
Fisheries Studies with Astronomy	J6FM	3FT deg	Ap g	14	5M $	M$	Ind	CCCC	Ind		
Geography with Astronomy	F8FM	3FT deg	Gy g	16-18	X	M$^	Ind	ABBB	Ind	8	
Geology with Astronomy	F6F5	3FT deg	S g	12	4M	MS	Ind	CCC	Ind	16	
Hydrography with Astronomy	F8F5	3FT deg	2(M/P/C/Ap) g	14	5M $	M$	Ind	CCCC	Ind		
Marine Navigation with Astronomy	J9FM	3FT deg	2(M/P/C) g	14	5M $	M$	Ind	CCCC	Ind		
Marine Technology with Astronomy	J6F5	3FT deg	2(M/P/C) g	14	5M $	M$	Ind	CCCC	Ind		
Maritime Business with Astronomy	N1F5	3FT deg	* g	18	5M	M$	Ind	CCCC	Ind		
Mathematics with Astronomy	G1F5	3FT deg	M g	10-15	MO $	M$^	Ind	Ind	Ind	8	
Ocean Science with Astronomy	F7F5	3FT deg	S g	14-16	5M $	M$	Ind	CCCC	Ind	7	
Underwater Studies with Astronomy	F9FM	3FT deg	Ap g	14-16	5M $	M$	Ind	CCCC	Ind		

Univ of PORTSMOUTH

TITLE	CODE	COURSE	SUBJECTS	A/AS	ND/C	AGNVQ	IB	SQA(H)	SQA	RATIO A/AS	
Applied Physics	F310	4SW deg	M+P	6	1M $	MS	Dip	CCCC	Ind		
Applied Physics	F318▼	4FT deg	*		Ind	P*	Ind	Ind	Ind		
Applied Physics (MPhys)	F313	4SW deg	M+P	6	1M $	MS6/^	Dip	CCCC	Ind	2	
Chemistry and Physics	FF13	3FT deg	C+P	10	N $	MS6/^	Dip	Ind	Ind		
Chemistry and Physics	FF1J▼	4FT deg	*		Ind	Ind	Ind	Ind	Ind		
Geographical Science and Physics (Extended)	FF3V▼	4FT deg	*		Ind	Ind	Ind	Ind	Ind		
Mathematics with Astronomy	G1F5	3FT deg	M	10	4M $	M$6/^	Dip$	BCCC			
Physical Electronics and Computing	FG35	3FT deg	P+M	8	N $	MS6/^	Dip	Ind	Ind		
Physics	F300	3FT deg	M+P	4	1M $	MS6/^	Dip	CCC	Ind	20	
Physics	F308▼	4EXT deg	*		Ind	P*	Ind	Ind	Ind	3	
Physics (MPhys)	F303	4FT deg	M+P	4	1M $	MS6/^	Dip	CCC	Ind	2	6/ 8
Physics and Geographical Science	FF38	3FT deg	Gy+P	16	4M	MS6/^	26$	BBBB	Ind	3	
Physics and Mathematics	FG31	3FT deg	M+P	8	1M $	MS6/^	Dip$	BCCC	Ind	9	
Physics and Statistics	FG34	3FT deg	M+P	8	1M $	MS6/^	Dip$	BCCC	Ind		
Science (Physics)	003F	2FT HND	M+P	2	N	PS	Dip	CC	Ind	1	2/10

QUEEN MARY & WESTFIELD COLL (Univ of London)

TITLE	CODE	COURSE	SUBJECTS	A/AS	ND/C	AGNVQ	IB	SQA(H)	SQA	RATIO A/AS	
Astronomy	F500	3FT deg	M+P	24		MS^					
Astronomy (MSci)	F503	4FT deg	M+P	24		MS^					
Astronomy and Mathematics	FG51	3FT deg	M+P	24		MS^					
Astrophysics	F526	3FT deg	M+P	24		MS^					
Astrophysics (MSci)	F523	4FT deg	M+P	24		MS^					
Chemical Physics	F334	3FT deg	C+P	CCC	5M $	MS^	26$	BBBCC			
Chemistry and Physics	FF13	3FT deg	C+P	CCC	5M $	DS	26$	BBBCC			
Instrumentation Physics (MSci)	F345	4FT deg	M+P	24		MS^					
Mathematics and Astrophysics	GF15	3FT deg	M+P	CCC		M$^					
Mathematics and Physics	FG31	3FT deg	M+P	CCC		M$^					
Mathematics with Astrophysics (MSci)	G1FM	4FT deg	M+P	BCC		M$^					
Physics	F300	3FT deg	M+P	24		MS^					
Physics (MSci)	F303	4FT deg	M+P	24		MS^					
Physics and Computer Science	FG35	3FT deg	M+P	24	3M+2D	MS^	28$				
Physics and Economics	FL31	3FT deg	M+P	24		MS^	30$	BBBBB			
Physics and Electronics	FH36	3FT deg	M+P	24		MS^					
Physics and Electronics (MSci)	FH3P	3FT deg	M+P	24		MS^					
Physics and Materials Science	FF23	3FT deg	M+P	24		MS^					

Physical Science 60

	course details			98 expected requirements						96 entry stats
TITLE	CODE	COURSE	SUBJECTS	A/AS	NO/C	AGNVQ	IB	SQA(H)	SQA	RATIO A/AS
Physics and the Environment	F374	3FT deg	M+P	24		MS^				
Physics with Business Studies	F3N1	3FT deg	M+P	24		MS^				
Physics with Computing	F3G5	3FT deg	M+P	24		MS^				
Physics with Medical Physics (MSci)	F370	4FT deg	M+P	24		MS^				
Theoretical Physics	F320	3FT deg	M+P	24		M$^				
Theoretical Physics (MSci)	F323	4FT deg	M+P	24		M$^				
Science and Engineering (4 yrs with Foundation) *Physics*	Y157	4EXT deg		E	N	P				

QUEEN'S Univ Belfast

Applied Mathematics and Physics	GF13	3FT/4FT deg	M+P g	CCC	Ind	Ind	28$	BBBC	Ind	5 18/28
Applied Mathematics and Physics (MSci)	GF1H	4FT deg	M+P g	CCC	X	X	28$	X	Ind	6
Applied Physics	F310	3FT/4FT deg	M+P g	CCC	Ind	Ind	28$	BBBC	Ind	
Applied Physics (MSci)	F312	4FT deg	M+P g	CCC	X	X	28$	X	Ind	3
Computer Science and Physics	GF53	3FT/4FT deg	P+M g	CCC	Ind	Ind	28$	BBBC	Ind	14
Physics	F300	3FT/4FT deg	M+P g	CCC	Ind	Ind	28$	BBBC	Ind	7 16/30
Physics (MSci)	F303	4FT deg	M+P g	CCC	X	X	28$	X	Ind	5 26/30
Physics with Astrophysics	F3F5	3FT/4FT deg	M+P g	CCC	Ind	Ind	28$	BBBC	Ind	10
Physics with Astrophysics (MSci)	F3FN	4FT deg	M+P g	CCC	X	X	28$	X	Ind	4
Physics with Extended Studies in Europe	F308	4FT deg	M+P g	CCC	X	X	28$	X	Ind	7
Physics with Extended Studies in Europe (MSci)	F309	5FT deg	M+P g	CCC	X	X	28$	X	Ind	
Physics with Geology	F3F6	3FT/4FT deg	P+M g	CCC	Ind	Ind	28$	BBBC	Ind	6
Physics with Materials Science	F3J5	3FT/4FT deg	M+P g	CCC	Ind	Ind	28$	BBBC	Ind	
Physics with Materials Science	F3F2	3FT deg								
Theoretical Physics	F320	3FT/4FT deg	M+P g	CCC	Ind	Ind	28$	BBBC	Ind	7
Theoretical Physics (MSci)	F322	4FT deg	M+P g	CCC	X	X	28$	X	Ind	4

Univ of READING

Electronic and Optical Engineering	HF63	3FT deg	M+P g	CCC	4M+1D$ DE^ go		29$	BBBC$	Ind	
Mathematics and Physics	GF13	3FT deg	M+P	BCC	3M+2D$ D$^		30$	BBBB$	Ind	31
Physics	F300	3FT deg	M+P	CCC	4M+1D$ DS^		29$	BBBC$	Ind	8 13/24
Physics & Electronics	F340	3FT deg	M+P	CCC	4M+1D$ DS^		29$	BBBC$	Ind	6
Physics & Electronics with a year in Europe	F341	4FT deg	M+P	CCC	4M+1D$ DS^		29$	BBBC$	Ind	
Physics & Optical Science	F369	3FT deg	M+P	CCC	4M+1D$ DS^		29$	BBBC$	Ind	4
Physics (MPhys)	F303	4FT deg	M+P	BCC	3M+2D$ DS^		30$	BBBB$	Ind	8 19/28
Physics and Mathematics (MPhys/MMath)	FG31	4FT deg	M+P	BCC	3M+2D$ DS^		30$	BBBB$	Ind	
Physics and Meteorology	FF39	3FT deg	M+P	BCD	4M+1D$ DS^		29$	BBBC$	Ind	6
Physics and Music	FW33	3FT deg	M+P+Mu	BCC	X		30$	BBBB$	Ind	
Physics and the Universe	F3F5	3FT deg	M+P	CCC	4M+1D$ DS^		29$	BBBC$	Ind	
Physics and the Universe (MPhys)	F3FM	4FT deg	M+P	BCC	3M+2D$ DS^		30$	BBBB$	Ind	
Physics with Computer Science	F3G5	3FT deg	M+P	CCC	5M $ DS^		29$	BBBC$	Ind	
Physics with Foundation Year	F304	4EXT deg	* g	DDD	3M M*6/^ go		26	BCCC	Ind	2
Physics with a year in Europe	F301	4FT deg	M+P g	CCC	5M$ DS^ go		29$	BBBC$	Ind	
Physics with a year in Europe (MPhys)	F306	4FT deg	M+P g	BCC	3M+2D$ D$^ go		30$	BBBB$	Ind	
Theoretical Physics	F320	3FT deg	M+P	CCC	4M+1D$ DS^		29$	BBBC$	Ind	
Theoretical Physics (MPhys)	F323	4FT deg	M+P	BCC	3M+2D$ DS^		30$	BBBB$	Ind	

ROBERT GORDON Univ

Applied Physics	F310	3FT/4FT deg	P+S g	EE	N	Ind	Ind	CCC$	Ind	5
Applied Science (Applied Physics)	013F	2FT HND	S g	E	N	Ind	Ind	CC$	Ind	6

ROYAL HOLLOWAY, Univ of London

Applied Physics (MSci)	F313	4FT deg	M+P	BBC-BCC	M+D	DS^	30$	BBBCC$		
Applied Physics and Electronics	FH36	3FT deg	M+P	BBC-BCC	MO+2D	DS^	30$	BBBCC$		
Astrophysics (MSci)	F520	4FT deg	M+P	BBC-BCC	M+D	DS^	30$	BBBCC$		38

TITLE	CODE	COURSE	SUBJECTS	A/AS	ND/C	AGNVQ	IB	SQA(H)	SQA	RATIO	A/AS
course details			**98 expected requirements**							**96 entry stats**	
Computer Science and Physics	GF53	3FT/4SW deg	M+P	BCC-BBC	Ind	D^	30$	BBBCC$			
Geology and Astrophysics	FF65	3FT deg	M+P	CCC-BCC	Ind	D^	Ind	Ind		6	
Mathematics and Physics	GF13	3FT deg	M+P	BCC	Ind	D^	Ind	Ind		9	
Physics	F300	3FT deg	M+P	BCC-BBC	5M	DS^	30$	BBBCC$		5	16/22
Physics (MSci)	F303	4FT deg	M+P	BCC-BBC	5M	DS^	30$	BBBCC$		5	16/22
Physics for Management	F3NC	3FT deg	M+P	BCC-BBC	5M	DS^	30$	BBBCC$		5	
Physics with Astrophysics	F3F5	3FT deg	M+P	BCC-BBC	5M	DS^	30$	BBBCC$		22	
Physics with Environmental Studies	F3F9	3FT deg	M+P	BCC-BBC	5M	DS^	30$	BBBCC$		5	
Physics with German	F3R2	3FT deg	P+M+G	BCC-BBC	5M	DS^	30$	BBBCC$			
Physics with Music	F3W3	3FT deg	M+Mu+P	BCC-BBC	5M	DS^	30$	BBBCC$			
Physics with a year in Europe	F307	4FT deg	M+P	BCC-BBC	5M	DS^	30$	BBBCC$			
Theoretical Physics	F320	3FT deg	M+P	BCC-BBC	5M	DS^	30$	BBBCC$			
Theoretical Physics (MSci)	F321	4FT deg	M+P	BCC-BBC	5M	DS^	30$	BBBCC$		10	
Foundation Programme *Physics*	Y408	4FT deg									
Science Foundation Year *Applied Physics*	Y100	4FT deg	*		Ind	Ind	Ind	Ind			
Science Foundation Year *Physics*	Y100	4FT deg	*		Ind	Ind	Ind	Ind			

Univ of SALFORD

TITLE	CODE	COURSE	SUBJECTS	A/AS	ND/C	AGNVQ	IB	SQA(H)	SQA	RATIO	A/AS
Applied Physics (3/4 Yrs)	F314	3FT/4SW deg	M+P	4	Ind	Ind	Ind	Ind	Ind		
Applied Physics (4 Yrs)(M Phys)	F343	4FT/5SW deg	M+P	4	Ind	Ind	Ind	Ind	Ind		
Biochemistry and Physics (3 or 4 Yrs)	FC37	3FT/4SW deg	C+P	BCC-CCD	3M	M	Ind	Ind	Ind	1	
Chemistry and Physics (3 or 4 Yrs)	FF13	3FT/4SW deg	C+P	BCC-CCD	3M	M	Ind	Ind	Ind		
Geography and Physics (3 or 4 Yrs)	FF83	3FT/4SW deg	Gy+P	BCC-BCD	3M	M	Ind	Ind	Ind		
Physics (3 or 4 Yrs)	F300	3FT/4SW deg	M+P	4	Ind	Ind	Ind	CSYS	Ind	5	12/20
Physics (4 Yrs)(M Phys)	F303	4FT deg	M+P	4	Ind	Ind	Ind	CSYS	Ind	6	
Physics and Information Technology	FG35	3FT/4SW deg		BCC-CDD	3M	M	Ind	Ind	Ind		
Physics w. Addit Stud in France (4 Yrs)(M Phys)	F3RC	4FT deg	M+P g	4	Ind	Ind	Ind	CSYS	Ind		
Physics w. Addit Stud in Germany(4 Yrs)(M Phys)	F3RF	4FT deg	M+P g	4	Ind	Ind	Ind	CSYS	Ind	3	
Physics w. Additional Studies in France (4 Yrs)	F3R1	4SW deg	M+P g	4	Ind	Ind	Ind	CSYS	Ind		
Physics w. Additional Studies in Germany (4 Yrs)	F3R2	4SW deg	M+P g	4	Ind	Ind	Ind	CSYS	Ind		
Physics w. Environmental Physics (4 Yrs)(M Phys)	F373	4FT deg	M+P	4	Ind	Ind	Ind	CSYS	Ind		
Physics with Acoustics (3/4 Yrs)	F384	3FT/4SW deg	M+P	4	Ind	Ind	Ind	CSYS	Ind		
Physics with Acoustics (4 Yrs) (MPhys)	F385	4FT deg	M+P	4	Ind	Ind	Ind	CSYS	Ind		
Physics with Computing (3/4 Yrs)	F350	3FT/4SW deg	M+P	4	Ind	Ind	Ind	CSYS	Ind	5	
Physics with Computing (4 Yrs)(M Phys)	F351	4FT deg	M+P	4	Ind	Ind	30$	CSYS	Ind		
Physics with Environmental Physics (3/4 Yrs)	F374	3FT/4SW deg	M+P	4	Ind	Ind	Ind	CSYS	Ind	10	
Physics with Laser Applications (3 or 4 Yrs)	F368	3FT/4SW deg	M+P	4	Ind	Ind	Ind	CSYS	Ind	3	
Physics with Laser Applications (4 Yrs)(M Phys)	F367	4FT deg	M+P	4	Ind	Ind	Ind	CSYS	Ind	3	
Physics with Medical Physics (3/4 Yrs)	F370	3FT/4SW deg	M+P	4	Ind	Ind	Ind	CSYS	Ind	5	
Physics with Medical Physics (4 Yrs)	F371	4FT deg	M+P	4	Ind	Ind	Ind	CSYS	Ind	3	
Physics with Optoelectronics (3 or 4 Yrs)	F355	3FT/4SW deg	M+P	4	Ind	Ind	Ind	CSYS	Ind		
Physics with Optoelectronics (4 Yrs)(M Phys)	F354	4FT deg	M+P	4	Ind	Ind	Ind	CSYS	Ind	4	
Physics with Space Technology (3/4 Yrs)	F360	3FT/4SW deg	M+P	4	Ind	Ind	Ind	CSYS	Ind	4	
Physics with Space Technology (4 Yrs)	F361	4FT deg	M+P	4	Ind	Ind	Ind	CSYS		5	16/22
Physics with a Foundation Year (4 Yrs)	F305	4FT deg	*		Ind	M	Ind	Ind	Ind	1	5/14
Physics with a Year in North America	F304	4FT deg	M+P	4	Ind	Ind	Ind	CSYS	Ind		
Physiology and Physics (3 or 4 yr SW)	CF93	3FT/4SW deg	P+B/C	BCC-CCD	3M	M	Ind	Ind	Ind		

Univ of SHEFFIELD

TITLE	CODE	COURSE	SUBJECTS	A/AS	ND/C	AGNVQ	IB	SQA(H)	SQA	RATIO	A/AS
Chemical Physics	F334	3FT deg	P+M+C g	BCC	5M+1D$ X		29$	BBBB$	Ind	8	
Chemical Physics (MPhys)	F335	4FT deg	P+M+C g	BCC	5M+1D$ X		29$	BBBB$	Ind	21	

			98 expected requirements							96 entry stats

course details — 98 expected requirements — *96 entry stats*

TITLE	CODE	COURSE	SUBJECTS	A/AS	ND/C	AGNVQ	IB	SQA(H)	SQA	RATIO A/AS
Chemistry and Astronomy	FF15	3FT deg	C+M g	BBB	3M+3D$	X	32$	AABB$	Ind	10
Materials Science and Physics	JF53	3FT/4EXT deg	P+M g	BCD	6M $	D$^	28$	BBBC$	Ind	
Mathematics and Astronomy	GF15	3FT deg	M+P g	BBC	4M+2D$	D^	30$	AABC$	Ind	8
Mathematics and Physics	GF13	3FT/4EXT deg	M+P g	24	4M+2D$	D^	28$	ABBC$	Ind	9 22/26
Physics	F300	3FT deg	P+M g	BCC-BBC	6M $	DS^	29$	BBBB$	Ind	11 16/28
Physics (MPhys)	F301	4FT deg	P+M g	BCC-BBC	6M $	DS^	29$	BBBB$	Ind	10 18/30
Physics Foundation Year (4 or 5 Yrs)	F309	4FT/5FT deg	g	BCC-BBC	6M	D^	29	BBBB	Ind	
Physics and Astronomy	FF35	3FT deg	P+M g	BCC-BBC	6M $	DS^	29$	BBBB$	Ind	9 20/26
Physics and Electronics	FFH3	3FT deg	P+M g	BCC-BBC	6M $	DS^	29$	BBBB$	Ind	15
Physics and Medical Physics	F370	3FT deg	P+M g	BCC-BBC	6M $	DS^	29$	BBBB$	Ind	7 24/28
Physics and Philosophy	FV37	3FT deg	P+M g	BBC	4M+2D$	DS^	30$	ABBB$	Ind	
Physics with Astronomy (MPhys)	F3F5	4FT deg	P+M g	BCC-BBC	6M $	DS^	29$	BBBB$	Ind	6 20/30
Physics with Electronics (MPhys)	F340	4FT deg	P+M g	BCC-BBC	6M $	DS^	29$	BBBB$	Ind	4
Physics with Materials Science (4Yrs)	F3J5	4FT/5EXT deg	P+S g	BCD	6M $	DS^	28$	BBBC$	Ind	
Physics with Mathematics (MPhys)	F3G1	4FT/5EXT deg	M+P g	BBC	4M+2D$	DS^	28$	ABBC$	Ind	9
Physics with Medical Physics (MPhys)	F371	4FT deg	P+M g	BCC-BBC	6M $	DS^	29$	BBBB$	Ind	4 18/20
Physics with Study in Europe	F302	3FT deg	P+M g	BCC-BBC	6M $	DS^	29$	BBBB$	Ind	
Physics with study in Europe (MPhys)	F303	4FT deg	P+M g	BCC-BBC	6M $	D^	29$	BBBB$	Ind	
Theoretical Physics	F320	3FT deg	P+M g	BCC-BBC	6M $	DS^	29$	BBBB$	Ind	6 26/30
Theoretical Physics (MPhys) (4 Yrs)	F321	4FT deg	P+M g	BBC-BCC	6M $	DS^	29$	BBBB$		

SHEFFIELD HALLAM Univ

Engineering Physics	F380	4SW deg	P/S/Ph/M g	DD	3M $	P$	Ind	Ind	Ind	
Instrumentation and Measurement (1 Year)	F341	1FT deg		X	HN	X	X	X	X	
Physics and Instrumentation (SW)	F342	4SW deg	P/S/M/Ph	DD	MO $	P$	Ind	Ind	Ind	
Science and Technology	Y100	4SW deg	g	EE	3M	P	Ind	CCCC	Ind	
Combined Studies *Physics*	Y400	3FT deg	S	8	2M	M	Ind	Ind	Ind	
Applied Physics	013F	2FT HND	M/P/Cs/Ph	E	N	P	Ind	Ind	Ind	
Optoelectronics	863F	3SW HND	M/P/Cs/Ph	E	N	P	Ind	Ind	Ind	
Science and Technology	001Y	2FT HND	*	E	N	P	Ind	Ind	Ind	

Univ of SOUTHAMPTON

Chemistry with Physics	F1F3	3FT deg	C+P+M	CCC	Ind	Ind	28$	CSYS	Ind	
Mathematics with Physics	G1F3	3FT deg	M+P	BBC	Ind	Ind	30	ABBBB	Ind	7
Oceanography with Physics	F7F3	3FT deg	P+S/M g	CCC	Ind	Ind	30$	BBBCC	Ind	6
Physics	F300	3FT deg	M+P	BC	Ind	Ind	28$	AAABB	Ind	7 8/30
Physics (4 years) (MPhys)	F303	4FT deg	M+P	BC	Ind	Ind	28$	AAABB	Ind	14 10/24
Physics and Mathematics (4 Yrs)	FG31	4FT deg	M+P	BC	Ind	Ind	28$	AAABB	Ind	8
Physics with Astronomy	F3F5	3FT deg	M+P	BC	Ind	Ind	28$	AAABB	Ind	13
Physics with Astronomy (4 Yrs) (MPhys)	F3FM	4FT deg	M+P	BC	Ind	Ind	28$	AAABB	Ind	8
Physics with Chemistry	F3F1	3FT deg	M+P+C g	BCE	Ind	Ind	28$	AAABB	Ind	
Physics with Computer Science	F3G5	3FT deg	M+P	BC	Ind	Ind	28$	AAABB	Ind	5 18/24
Physics with Electronics	F340	3FT deg	M+P	BC	Ind	Ind	28$	AAABB	Ind	5
Physics with Foundation Year	F301	4FT deg	*		Ind	Ind	Ind	Ind	Ind	6
Physics with Laser Science	F368	3FT deg	M+P	BC	Ind	Ind	28$	AAABB	Ind	7
Physics with Laser Science (4 Yrs) (MPhys)	F369	4FT deg	M+P	BC	Ind	Ind	28$	AAABB	Ind	4
Physics with Mathematics	F3G1	3FT deg	M+P	BC	Ind	Ind	28$	AAABB	Ind	3
Physics with Oceanography	F3F7	3FT deg	M+P g	BC	Ind	Ind	28$	AAABB	Ind	6
Physics with Space Science	F3F9	3FT deg	M+P	BC	Ind	Ind	28$	AAABB	Ind	12
Physics with Space Science (4 Yrs) (MPhys)	F3FX	4FT deg	M+P	BC	Ind	Ind	28$	AAABB	Ind	7 14/26

			98 expected requirements							96 entry stats	
course details											
TITLE	CODE	COURSE	SUBJECTS	A/AS	NO/C	AGNVQ	IB	SQA(H)	SQA	RATIO	A/AS
Univ of ST ANDREWS											
Astrophysics (MSci)	F520	4FT deg	M+P g	CCC	Ind	Ind	28$	BBBC$	Ind	6	16/26
Laser Physics and Optoelectronics (MSci)	FH3P	4FT deg	M+P	CCC	Ind	Ind	28$	BBBC$	Ind	11	
Mathematics-Theoretical Physics	FG3D	4FT deg	M+P g	CCC	X	Ind	28$	BBCC	Ind		
Physics (BSc/MSci)	F300	4FT deg	M+P	CCC	Ind	Ind	28$	BBBC$	Ind	5	20/30
Physics-Chemistry	FF13	3FT/4FT deg	C+P+M	CCC	Ind	Ind	28$	BBBC$	Ind	10	
Physics-Computer Science	GF53	4FT deg	M+P	CCC	Ind	Ind	28$	BBBC$	Ind	4	
Physics-Logic and Philosophy of Science	FV3R	4FT deg	P+M	CCC	Ind	Ind	28$	BBBC$	Ind	6	
Physics-Mathematics	FG3C	4FT deg	M+P g	CCC	X	Ind	28$	BBCC	Ind		
Theoretical Physics (MSci)	F320	4FT deg	M+P	CCC	Ind	Ind	28$	BBBC	Ind	8	
General Degree of BSc _Astrophysics_	Y100	3FT deg	M+P	CCC	Ind	Ind	28$	BBBC$	Ind		
General Degree of BSc _Physics_	Y100	3FT deg	M+P	CCC	Ind	Ind	28$	BBBC$	Ind		
General Degree of BSc _Physics and Electronics_	Y100	3FT deg	M+P	CCC	Ind	Ind	28$	BBBC$	Ind		
General Degree of BSc _Theoretical Physics_	Y100	3FT deg	M+P	CCC	Ind	Ind	28$	BBBC$	Ind		
STAFFORDSHIRE Univ											
Applied Physics	F310	3FT deg	M+P	12	4M	M^	24	BCC	Ind	10	
Applied Physics (MPhys)	F311	4FT deg	M+P	12	4M	M^	24	BCC	Ind		
Electronics and Applied Physics	HF6H	4FT deg									
Electronics and Applied Physics	FHH6	3FT deg	S g	8	3M	M	24	BCC	Ind		
Extended Applied Physics (4 yr)	F319	4EXT deg	g	4	1M	M	24	CCC	Ind		
Extended Physics (4 yr)	F309	4EXT deg	P g	4	N	M	24	CCC	Ind		
Foundation Applied Physics	F318▼	4EXT deg	*	4	N	P	24	CCC	Ind		
Foundation Biology and Physics	CF1H▼	4EXT deg	*	4	N	P	24	CCC	Ind		
Foundation Chemistry and Physics	FF1H▼	4EXT deg	*	4	N	P	24	CCC	Ind		
Foundation Electronics and Applied Physics	HF6J	4EXT deg	*	4	N	P	24	CCC			
Foundation Geology and Physics	FF3P	4EXT deg	*	4	N	P	24	CCC			
Foundation Physics and Computing	FG3N▼	4EXT deg	*	4	N	P	24	CCC	Ind		
Foundation Physics and Electronics	FH3P▼	4EXT deg	*	4	N	P	24	CCC	Ind		
Physics	F300	3FT deg	M+P	12	4M	M	24	BCC	Ind	11	
Physics (MPhys)	F301	4FT deg	M+P	12	4M	M	24	BCC	Ind		
Physics and Electronics	FH3Q	4EXT deg	g	4	M	N	24	CCC	Ind		
Physics/Applied Statistics	FG34	3FT deg	S	8	3M	M	24	BCC	Ind		
Physics/Biochemistry	CF73	3FT deg									
Physics/Biology	CF13	3FT deg	S g	8	3M	M	24	BCC	Ind		
Physics/Business Studies	FN31	3FT deg	S g	12	4M	M	24	BCC	Ind		
Physics/Ceramic Science	FJ33	3FT deg	S g	8	3M	M	24	BCC	Ind		
Physics/Chemistry	FF13	3FT deg	P+C	8	3M	M	24	BCC	Ind		
Physics/Computing	FG35	3FT deg	S	8	3M	M	24	BCC	Ind		
Physics/Electronics	FH36	3FT deg	S	8	3M	M	24	BCC	Ind		
Physics/Geography	FL38	3FT deg	S g	8	3M	M	24	BCC	Ind		
Physics/Geology	FF63	3FT deg	S	8	3M	M	24	BCC	Ind		
Psychology/Physics	LF73	3FT deg	S	8-18	4M	D	24	BCC	Ind		
Sport Sciences and Physics	BF63	3FT deg	S	14	Ind	D	Ind	BBCC	Ind		
Physics	003F	2FT HND	M/P	2	N	P	24	CCC	Ind		
Univ of STRATHCLYDE											
Applied Physics	F310	4FT deg	M+P	CD	HN		24$	BBB$	HN		
Laser Physics and Optoelectronics	F368	4FT deg	M+P	CD	HN		24$	BBB$	HN		
Mathematics and Physics	GF13	4FT deg	M+P g	CD	Ind		30$	BBCC$	Ind		

course details			98 expected requirements							96 entry stats	
TITLE	CODE	COURSE	SUBJECTS	A/AS	ND/C	AGNVQ	IB	SQA(H)	SQA	RATIO A/AS	
Physics	F300	4FT deg	M+P	CD	HN		24$	BBB$	HN		
Physics (MSci)	F303	5FT deg	M+P	BBC	X		24$	ABBB$	X		
Physics and Mathematical Finance	FN33	5FT deg	M+P	BBB	Ind	Ind		AABB$	Ind		
Science Studies (Pass Degree)	Y100	3FT deg	M+P	DD	Ind		Ind	CCC$	Ind		
Physics											

Univ of SURREY

Computer Modelling for Physical Sciences	F3G5	3FT/4SW deg	M+P	BBB-CC	M $	MS^	$	Ind	Ind		
Physics	F300	3FT/4SW deg	M+P	BBB-CC	M $	MS^	$	Ind	Ind	4	6/28
Physics (MPhys)	F303	4FT/4SW deg	M+P	BBB-BC	X	X	Ind	Ind	X	6	24/26
Physics with Management Studies	F3N1	3FT/4SW deg	M+P	BBB-CC	M $	MS^	$	Ind	Ind	7	
Physics with Medical Physics	F370	3FT/4SW deg	M+P	BBB-CC	M $	MS^	$	Ind	Ind	4	
Physics with Medical Physics (MPhys)	F371	4FT/4SW deg	M+P	BBB-BC	X	X	$	Ind	X		
Physics with Nuclear Astrophysics	F3F5	3FT/4SW deg	M+P	BBB-CC	M $	MS^	$	Ind	Ind	4	
Physics with Nuclear Astrophysics (MPhys)	F3FM	4FT/4SW deg	M+P	BBB-BC	X	X	$	Ind	X		
Physics with a Foundation Year	F305	4FT/5SW deg	*	12	Ind	Ind	Ind	Ind	Ind	4	

Univ of SUSSEX

Chemical Physics (MChem)	F337	4FT deg	C/P/Ph+M g	CCC	MO $	MS^	$	Ind	Ind		
Chemical Physics with Eur St (French) (MChem)	F3RD	4FT deg	C/P/Ph+M g	CCC	MO $	MS^ go	$	Ind	Ind		
Chemical Physics with Eur St (German) (MChem)	F3RG	4FT deg	C/P/Ph+M g	CCC	MO $	MS^ go	$	Ind	Ind		
Chemical Physics with Eur St (Spanish) (MChem)	F3RL	4FT deg	C/P/Ph+M g	CCC	MO $	MS^ go	$	Ind	Ind		
Chemical Physics with N. American Studs (MChem)	F3QL	4FT deg	C/P/Ph+M g	BCC	MO $	MS^ go	$	Ind	Ind		
Mathematical Physics	F324	3FT deg	M+P	BCC	MO $	MS^	$	Ind	Ind		
Mathematical Physics (MMath)	F323	4FT deg	M+P	BCC	MO $	MS^	$	Ind	Ind		
Mathematical Physics (MPhys)	F327	4FT deg	M+P	CCC	MO $	MS^	$	Ind	Ind		
Mathematics and Statistics with Physics	G4F3	3FT deg	M+P	BCC	MO $	MS^	$	Ind	Ind		
Mathematics and Statistics with Physics (MMath)	G4FH	4FT deg	M+P	BCC	MO $	MS^	$	Ind	Ind		
Mathematics with Physics	G1F3	3FT deg	M+P	BCC	MO $	MS^	$	Ind	Ind		
Mathematics with Physics (MMath)	G1FH	4FT deg	M+P	BCC	MO $	MS^	$	Ind	Ind		
Physical Science	F315	4FT deg					$	Ind	Ind		
Physics	F300	3FT deg	M+P	CCC	MO $	MS^	$	Ind	Ind		
Physics (4 Yrs) (MPhys)	F303	4FT deg	M+P	CCC	MO $	MS^	$	Ind	Ind		
Physics and Mathematics	FG31	3FT deg	M+P	CCC	MO $	MS^	$	Ind	Ind		
Physics and Mathematics	FG3C	4FT deg	M+P	CCC	MO $	MS^	$	Ind	Ind		
Physics with Astrophysics	FF35	3FT deg	M+P	CCC	MO $	MS^	$	Ind	Ind		
Physics with Astrophysics (MPhys)	FF3M	4FT deg	M+P	CCC	MO $	MS^	$	Ind	Ind		
Physics with Computational Physics	F350	3FT deg	M+P	CCC	MO $	MS^	$	Ind	Ind		
Physics with Computational Physics (MPhys)	F353	4FT deg	M+P	CCC	MO $	MS^	$	Ind	Ind		
Physics with Elect & Optoelectronics (MPhys)	F3HP	4FT deg	M+P	CCC	MO $	MS^	$	Ind	Ind		
Physics with Electronics and Optoelectronics	F3HQ	3FT deg	M+P	CCC	MO $	MS^	$	Ind	Ind		
Physics with Environmental Science	F3F9	3FT deg	M+P+C	CCC	MO $	MS^	$	Ind	Ind		
Physics with Environmental Science (MPhys)	F3FX	4FT deg	M+P+C	CCC	MO $	MS^	$	Ind	Ind		
Physics with European Studies (French)	F3R1	4FT deg	M+P g	CCC	MO $	MS^ go	$	Ind	Ind		
Physics with European Studies (French) (MPhys)	F3RC	4FT deg	M+P g	CCC	MO $	MS^ go	$	Ind	Ind		
Physics with European Studies (German)	F3R2	4FT deg	M+P g	CCC	MO $	MS^ go	$	Ind	Ind		
Physics with European Studies (German)(MPhys)	F3RF	4FT deg	M+P g	CCC	MO $	MS^ go	$	Ind	Ind		
Physics with European Studies (Italian)	F3R3	4FT deg	M+P g	CCC	MO $	MS^ go	$	Ind	Ind		
Physics with European Studies (Russian)	F3R8	4FT deg	M+P g	CCC	MO $	MS^ go	$	Ind	Ind		
Physics with European Studies (Spanish)	F3R4	4FT deg	M+P g	CCC	MO $	MS^ go	$	Ind	Ind		
Physics with European Studies (Spanish) (MPhys)	F3RK	4FT deg	M+P g	CCC	MO $	MS^ go	$	Ind	Ind		
Physics with Management Studies	F3N1	3FT deg	M+P	CCC	MO $	MS^	$	Ind	Ind		
Physics with Management Studies (MPhys)	F3NC	4FT deg	M+P	CCC	MO $	MS^	$	Ind	Ind		
Physics with Mathematics	F3G1	3FT deg	M+P	CCC	MO $	MS^	$	Ind	Ind		
Physics with North American Studies	F3Q4	4FT deg	M+P	CCC	MO $	MS^	$	Ind	Ind		

course details			98 expected requirements							96 entry stats	
TITLE	CODE	COURSE	SUBJECTS	A/AS	ND/C	AGNVQ	IB	SQA(H)	SQA	RATIO	A/AS
Physics with North American Studies (MPhys)	F3QK	4FT deg	M+P	CCC	MO $	MS^	$	Ind	Ind		
Physics with Theoretical Physics	F330	3FT deg	M+P	CCC	MO $	MS^	$	Ind	Ind		
Physics with Theoretical Physics (MPhys)	F333	4FT deg	M+P	CCC	MO $	MS^	$	Ind	Ind		
Theoretical Physics	F325	3FT deg	M+P	CCC	MO $	MS^	$	Ind	Ind		
Theoretical Physics (MPhys)	F328	4FT deg	M+P	CCC	MO $	MS^	$	Ind	Ind		

Univ of Wales SWANSEA

Mathematics and Physics	FG31	3FT deg	M+P	BCC	Ind	Ind	28$	BBBBC$	Ind	14	
Phys with Particle Phys and the Found of Cosmol	F3F5	3FT deg	M+P	CCC	Ind	Ind	26$	Ind	Ind		
Physics	F300	3FT deg	M+P	CCC	Ind	Ind	26$	Ind	Ind	8	
Physics (Integrated Course)	F301	4FT deg	*		Ind	Ind	Ind	Ind	Ind	1	6/15
Physics (MPhys)	F303	4FT deg	M+P	CCC	Ind	Ind	26$	Ind	Ind	3	22/28
Physics with Laser Physics	F368	3FT deg	M+P	CCC	Ind	Ind	26$	Ind	Ind	6	
Physics with Medical Physics	F370	3FT deg	M+P	CCC	Ind	Ind	26$	Ind	Ind		
Physics with a year Abroad	F302	4FT deg	M+P	CCC	Ind	Ind	26$	Ind	Ind		

UNIVERSITY COLL LONDON (Univ of London)

Astronomy	F500	3FT deg	M+P g	BCC-BBC	MO+2D$	Ind	32$	BBBCC$	N$		
Astronomy (MSci)	F502	4FT deg	M+P g	BCC-BBC	MO+2D$	Ind	32$	BBBCC$	N$	3	
Astronomy and Physics	FF53	3FT deg	M+P g	BCC-BBC	MO+2D$	Ind	32$	BBBCC$	N$		
Astronomy and Physics (MSci)	FF5H	4FT deg	M+P g	BCC-BBC	MO+2D$	Ind	32$	BBBCC$	N$	4	28/30
Astrophysics	F520	3FT deg	M+P g	BCC-BBC	MO+2D$	Ind	32$	BBBCC$	N$	37	
Astrophysics (MSci)	F527	4FT deg	M+P g	BCC-BBC	MO+2D$	Ind	32$	BBBCC$	N$	2	20/30
Earth and Space Science	FF65	3FT deg	M+P g	BCC	MO $	Ind	30$	BBCCC$	N$		
Earth and Space Science (MSci)	FF6M	4FT deg	M+P g	BCC	MO $	Ind	30$	BBCCC$	N$		
Mathematics and Astronomy	GF15	3FT deg	M+P g	ABC-ABB	MO $	Ind	30$	AAABB$	N$		
Mathematics and Astronomy (MSci)	GF1M	4FT deg	M+P g	ABC-ABB	MO $	Ind	30$	AAABB$	N$	3	
Mathematics and Physics	GF13	3FT deg	M+P g	ABC-ABB	MO $	Ind	30$	AAABB$	N$		
Mathematics and Physics (MSci)	GF1H	4FT deg	M+P g	ABC-ABB	MO $	Ind	30$	AAABB$	N$	9	
Mathematics with Theoretical Physics	G1F3	3FT deg	M+P g	ABC-ABB	MO $	Ind	30$	AAABB$	N$	14	
Mathematics with Theoretical Physics (MSci)	G1FH	4FT deg	M+P g	ABC-ABB	MO $	Ind	30$	AAABB$	N$	2	26/30
Medical Physics (MSci)	F371	4FT deg	M+P g	BCC-BBC	MO+2D$	Ind	32$	BBBCC$	N$	4	
Physics	F300	3FT deg	M+P g	BCC-BBC	MO+2D$	Ind	32$	BBBCC$	N$	12	22/28
Physics (Applied)	F310	3FT deg	M+P g	BCC-BBC	MO+2D$	Ind	32$	BBBCC$	N$		
Physics (Applied) (MSci)	F313	4FT deg	M+P g	BCC-BBC	MO+2D$	Ind	32$	BBBCC$	N$	6	
Physics (MSci)	F303	4FT deg	M+P g	BCC-BBC	MO+2D$	Ind	32$	BBBCC$	N$	5	20/30
Physics for Advanced Technologies	F3H6	3FT deg	M+P g	BCC-BBC	MO+2D$	Ind	32$	BBBCC$	N$		
Physics for Advanced Technologies (MSci)	F3HP	4FT deg	M+P g	BCC-BBC	MO+2D$	Ind	32$	BBBCC$	N$		
Physics with Climate Science	F374	3FT deg	M+P g	BCC-BBC	MO+2D$	Ind	32$	BBBCC$	N$		
Physics with Climate Science (MSci)	F375	4FT deg	M+P g	BCC-BBC	MO+2D$	Ind	32$	BBBCC$	N$	1	
Physics with Medical Physics	F370	3FT deg	M+P g	BCC-BBC	MO+2D$	Ind	32$	BBBCC$	N$		
Physics with Space Science	F360	3FT deg	M+P g	BCC-BBC	MO+2D$	Ind	32$	BBBCC$	N$	32	
Physics with Space Science (MSci)	F366	4FT deg	M+P g	BCC-BBC	MO+2D$	Ind	32$	BBBCC$	N$	6	24/30
Physical Sciences \ Astronomy	Y100	3FT deg	S g	CCC-BCC	$	Ind	28$	BCCCC$	N$		
Physical Sciences \ Physics	Y100	3FT deg	S g	CCC-BCC	$	Ind	28$	BCCCC$	N$		

Univ of WARWICK

Mathematics and Physics	GF13	3FT deg	M+P g	ABB	X	X	32$	AAABB$		6	24/30
Mathematics and Physics (MPhys)	FG31	4FT deg	M+P g	ABB	X	X	32$	AAABB$		3	24/30
Physics	F300	3FT deg	P+M g	BBC	3M+2D$	DS^	30$	ABBBB$		11	20/30
Physics (MPhys)	F303	4FT deg	P+M g	BBC	3M+2D$	DS^	30	ABBBB$		8	22/30
Physics and Business Studies	FN31	3FT deg	P+M g	BBC	3M+2D$	DS^	30$	ABBBB$		5	
Physics with Computing	F3G5	3FT deg	P+M g	BBC	3M+2D$	DS^	30$	ABBBB$		7	20/28

			98 expected requirements							96 entry stats

TITLE	CODE	COURSE	SUBJECTS	A/AS	NO/C	AGNVQ	IB	SQA(H)	SQA	RATIO A/AS
WESTHILL COLL										
Humanities - Mathematics, Science and Psychology *Science*	Y601	3FT deg	M g	CC	4M+2D	M^	Ind	Ind	Ind	
Univ of YORK										
Computational Physics	F357	4SW deg	M+P	BCC	Ind	DS^	28$	CSYS$	Ind	
Computational Physics (BSc/MPhys)	F350	3FT/4FT deg	M+P	BCC	Ind	DS^	28$	CSYS$	Ind	
Computational Physics (Europe) (BSc/MPhys)	F351	4FT deg	M+P g	BCC	Ind	DS^	28$	CSYS$	Ind	
Mathematics/Physics	G1F3	3FT deg	M+P	20-22	HN $	DS^	30$	CSYS$	HN$	
Mathematics/Physics (Equal)	GF13	3FT deg	M+P	20-22	HN $	DS^	30$	CSYS$	HN$	
Mathematics/Physics (Equal) (MMath)	GF1H	4FT deg	M+P	20-22	HN $	DS^	30$	CSYS$	HN$	
Mathematics/Physics (Equal) with a yr in Europe	GF1J	4FT deg	M+P	20-22	HN $	DS^	30$	CSYS$	HN $	
Mathematics/Physics (MMath)	G1FH	4FT deg	M+P	20-22	HN $	DS^	30$	CSYS$	HN$	
Mathematics/Physics with a year in Europe	G1FJ	4FT deg	M+P	20-22	HN $	DS^	30$	CSYS$	HN $	
Physics (BSc/MPhys)	F300	3FT/4FT deg	M+P	BCC	Ind	DS^	28$	CSYS$	Ind	
Physics with Astrophysics (BSc/MPhys)	F3F5	3FT/4FT deg	M+P	BCC	Ind	DS^	28$	CSYS$	Ind	16/28
Physics with Astrophysics (Europe) (BSc/MPhys)	F3FM	4FT deg	M+P g	BCC	Ind	DS^	28$	CSYS$	Ind	
Physics with Business Management	F3N1	3FT/4FT deg	M+P	BCC	Ind	DS^	28$	CSYS$	Ind	
Physics with Business Management (Europe)	F3NC	4FT deg	M+P g	BCC	Ind	DS^	28$	CSYS$	Ind	
Physics with a Foundation Year	F304	4FT/5FT deg	* g	Ind	Ind	Ind	Ind	Ind	Ind	
Physics with a year in Europe (BSc/MPhys)	F308	4FT deg	M+P g	BCC	Ind	DS^	28$	CSYS$	Ind	
Physics/Education	F3X9	3FT deg	M+P	BCC	Ind	DS^	28$	CSYS$	Ind	
Physics/Education with a year in Europe	F3XX	4FT deg	M+P g	BCC	Ind	DS^	28$	CSYS$	Ind	
Physics/Philosophy	F3V7	3FT deg	M+P	BCC	Ind	DS^	28$	CSYS$	Ind	
Physics/Philosophy with a year in Europe	F3VR	4FT deg	M+P g	BCC	Ind	DS^	28$	CSYS$	Ind	
Theoretical Physics (BSc/MPhys)	F320	3FT/4FT deg	M+P	BCC	Ind	DS^	28$	CSYS$	Ind	
Theoretical Physics (Europe) (BSc/MPhys)	F322	4FT deg	M+P g	BCC	Ind	DS^	28$	CSYS$	Ind	

course details			98 expected requirements							96 entry stats

TITLE	CODE	COURSE	SUBJECTS	A/AS	ND/C	AGNVQ	IB	SQA(H)	SQA	RATIO A/AS
Univ of ABERDEEN										
Land Economy (Planning)	K433	4FT deg	* g	CCD	Ind	M$ go	26$	BBCC	Ind	
Land Economy (Rural Surveying and Planning)	K435	4FT deg	* g	CCD	Ind	M$ go	26$	BBCC	Ind	
Land Economy (Rural Surveying)	K432	4FT deg	* g	CCD	Ind	M$ go	26$	BBCC	Ind	
Land Economy (Urban Surveying and Planning)	K434	4FT deg	* g	CCD	Ind	M$ go	26$	BBCC	Ind	
Land Economy (Urban Surveying)	K431	4FT deg	* g	CCD	Ind	M$ go	26$	BBCC	Ind	
Univ of ABERTAY DUNDEE										
Housing Economy and Society	K4L4	4FT deg			Ind	Ind	Ind		Ind	
ANGLIA Poly Univ										
Housing	K470▼	3FT deg	*	8	2M	P	Dip	CCCC	Ind	
Housing and Law	KM43▼	3FT deg	* g	8	2M	P	Dip	CCCC	Ind	
Law and Property Management	MK34▼	3FT deg								
Planning and Development Surveying	K450▼	3FT deg	* g	8	2M	P go	Dip	CCCC		
Property Management	K472▼	3FT deg	* g	8	2M	P go	Dip	CCCC		
Univ of Wales, BANGOR										
Environmental Planning and Management Management	Y401	3FT deg	* g	10	4M	M$ go	Ind	Ind	Ind	
BELL COLLEGE OF TECHNOLOGY										
Building Control	044K	2FT HND	* g	D	N $	PC	Ind	CC$	Ind	
Univ of BIRMINGHAM										
Geography and Planning	LK84	3FT deg	Gy	BCC	DO $	D+^	30	BBBBB	Ind	5 18/26
Planning and Economics	KL41	3FT deg	*	BBC	Ind	D+^	32	ABBBB	Ind	5
Planning and Public Policy Making and Admin	KL44	3FT deg	*	BCC	Ind	D+^	30	BBBBB	Ind	3
Planning and Social Policy	KL4K	3FT deg	*	BCC	Ind	D+^	30	BBBBB	Ind	5
BOLTON INST										
Accountancy and Urban and Cultural Studies	KN44	3FT deg	* g	CD	MO	M*	24	BBCC	Ind	
Biology and Urban and Cultural Studies	CK14	3FT deg	* g	CD	MO	M*	24	BBCC	Ind	
Business Studies and Urban and Cultural Studies	KN41	3FT deg	* g	CD	MO	M*	24	BBCC	Ind	
Mathematics and Urban and Cultural Studies	GK14	3FT deg	M g	CD	Ind	Ind	24	BBCC	Ind	
Visual Arts and Urban & Cultural Studies	KW41	3FT deg	* g	CD	MO	M*	24	BBCC	Ind	
Univ of BRADFORD										
Planning and Environmental Management	KF49	3FT deg	S g	BCC-CCC	3M $	MS4/^	Ind	Ind	Ind	
Planning and Environmental Management (4 Yrs)	KF4X	4SW deg	S g	BCC-CCC	3M $	MS4/^	Ind	Ind	Ind	
BRISTOL, Univ of the W of England										
Architecture and Planning	KK14	4FT deg	* g	16-18	4M+2D	M*3/^ go	24	BBCC	Ind	
Housing and Development	K472	3/4FT deg	* g	6-8	3M	P*1/^ go	24	CC	Ind	
Real Estate (Valuation and Management)	K460	3FT deg	* g	6-8	3M	P*1/^ go	24	CC	Ind	
Town Planning (Post Graduate)	K402	1FT deg	g	X	X	X	X	X	X	
Town and Country Planning	K401	3FT deg	* g	12-14	MO	M*1/^ go	24	BCC	Ind	
Urban Development and Policy	K464	3FT deg	* g	10-12	5M	P*3/^ go	24	BC	Ind	
Valuation and Estate Management	K461	3FT deg	* g	14-16	5M+1D	M*2/^ go	24	BCC	Ind	
CAMBRIDGE Univ										
Land Economy	KL41▼	3FT deg	* g	AAB	Ind		Ind	CSYS	Ind	2 26/30
CARDIFF Univ of Wales										
City and Regional Planning	K446	5SW deg	*	BCC	Ind	Ind	Ind	Ind	Ind	3 14/24
Univ of Wales INST, CARDIFF										
Housing Studies	K472	3FT deg	* g	8-10	N	P$ go	Ind	CCCC	Ind	2

course details			98 expected requirements							96 entry stats	
TITLE	CODE	COURSE	SUBJECTS	A/AS	NO/C	RGNVQ	IB	SQA(H)	SQA	RATIO	A/AS
Univ of CENTRAL ENGLAND											
Business Studies for Property	NK14	3FT deg		8	2M	M					4/8
Environmental Planning	K440	3FT deg	*	8	2M	M	24	BBCC	Ind	4	6/22
Environmental Planning (Natural Resource Mgt)	K4K3	3FT deg		8	2M	M	24	BBCC		12	
Environmental Planning (Transport & Commun)	K443	3FT deg	*	8	2M	M	24	BBCC	Ind		
Environmental Planning (Urban Design & Cons)	K444	3FT deg	*	8	2M	M	24	BBCC	Ind		
Environmental Planning (Urban Regeneration)	K445	3FT deg	*	8	2M	M	24	BBCC	Ind	5	
Housing	K472	3FT deg	*	8	2M	M	Ind	Ind	Ind	1	4/8
Urban Design	K442	3FT deg	Pf	8	2M	P			Ind		
COVENTRY Univ											
Planning and Economics	LK14	3FT deg	* g	12-16	M+2D	M	Ind	CCC	Ind		
Planning and Geography	LK84	3FT/4SW deg	Gv g	12	Ind	M	Ind	Ind	Ind	7	8/22
Urban & Regional Planning w. Local Economic Dev	K441	3FT/4SW deg	* g	12	3M	M	Ind	Ind	Ind	1	
Urban and Regional Planning	K440	3FT/4SW deg	* g	12	3M	M	Ind	Ind	Ind	1	
Urban and Regional Planning with Recreation	K442	3FT/4SW deg	* g	12	3M	M	Ind	Ind	Ind	1	
DE MONTFORT Univ											
Architecture & Urban Studies	KK14▼	3FT deg	* g	16	4M+2D	M$ go	30	BBBB	Ind	5	
Univ of DUNDEE											
Town and Regional Planning	K420	4FT deg	* g	CDD	Ind	M$	27	BBBC	HN	4	8/22
Univ of DURHAM											
Urban Studies	K460▼	3FT deg	*	CD	Ind	Ind	Dip	BCCCC	Ind		
Urban Studies and European Studies	KT42▼	3FT deg	*	CD	Ind	Ind	Dip	BCCCC	Ind		
Urban Studies with European Studies	K4T2▼	3FT deg	*	CD	Ind	Ind	Dip	BCCCC	Ind		
Urban Studies with French	K4R1▼	3FT deg	*	CD	Ind	Ind	Dip	BCCCC	Ind		
Urban Studies with German	K4R2▼	3FT deg	*	CD	Ind	Ind	Dip	BCCCC	Ind		
Urban Studies with Spanish	K4R4▼	3FT deg	*	CD	Ind	Ind	Dip	BCCCC	Ind		
EDGE HILL Univ COLLEGE											
Urban Management Studies	K460	3FT deg	Gv g	DD	X	P*^	Dip	BBCC$	X	1	
Univ of GLAMORGAN											
Building Control Surveying	K440	2FT deg			Ind	Ind	Ind	Ind	Ind		
Planning and Development Surveying	K450	3FT deg	* g	CD	Ind	Ind	Ind	Ind	Ind		
Urban Studies and Geography	KL48	3FT deg	* g	12	Ind	Ind	Ind	Ind	Ind		
Combined Studies *Urban Studies*	Y400	3FT deg	* g	8-16	Ind	Ind	Ind	Ind	Ind		
Combined Studies (Honours) *Real Estate Management*	Y400	3FT deg	* g	8-16	Ind	Ind	Ind	Ind	Ind		
Joint Honours *Real Estate Management*	Y401	3FT deg	* g	8-16	Ind	Ind	Ind	Ind	Ind		
Joint Honours *Urban Studies*	Y401	3FT deg	* g	8-16	Ind	Ind	Ind	Ind	Ind		
Univ of GREENWICH											
Housing Studies	K472	3FT/4SW deg	* g	16	5M	M	24	CCC	Ind		
HERIOT-WATT Univ											
Town Planning	K440▼	4FT deg	* g	CDD	5M	MC go	28	BBCC	Ind		
Univ of KENT											
Urban Studies (Economics)	KL41	3FT deg	* g	20	3M+3D	M$ go	28	BBBB	Ind	3	
Urban Studies (Social Policy and Administration)	KL44	3FT deg	* g	20	3M+3D	M$ go	28	BBBB	Ind	10	
Urban Studies (Sociology)	KL43	3FT deg	* g	20	3M+3D	M$ go	28	BBBB	Ind	9	

course details			98 expected requirements							96 entry stats
TITLE	CODE	COURSE	SUBJECTS	A/AS	NO/C	AGNVQ	IB	SQA(H)	SQA	RATIO A/AS
KINGSTON Univ										
Property Planning and Development	K450	4SW deg	*	12	N	M$	24	Ind	Ind	10
LEEDS METROPOLITAN Univ										
Urban and Regional Planning	K440	3FT deg								
Univ of LIVERPOOL										
Environment and Planning	K4L8	3FT deg		CCC	Ind	Ind	Ind	Ind	Ind	
Planning	K400	4FT deg		CCC	Ind	Ind	Ind	Ind	Ind	
BA Combined Honours Town and Regional Planning	Y200	3FT deg	* g	BBB	Ind	Ind	Ind	Ind	Ind	
BA Combined Honours Urban Studies	Y200	3FT deg	* g	BBB	Ind	Ind	Ind	Ind	Ind	
LIVERPOOL JOHN MOORES Univ										
Housing Studies	K410	3FT deg		12	5M	M				6
Urban Planning	K460	3FT deg	Gy/E	16	5M	M				9 6/18
Urban Studies and Human Geography	KL48	3FT deg	Gy	12	5M+3D	P$	28$	BBCC		9 12/18
LUTON Univ										
Biochemistry with Regional Planning and Dev	C7K4	3FT deg	g	12-16	MO/DO	M/D	32	BBCC	Ind	
Biotechnology with Regional Planning & Dev	J8K4	3FT deg	g	12-16	MO/DO	M/D	32	BBCC	Ind	
Built Environment with Regional Planning and Dev	N8K4	3FT deg	g	12-16	MO/DO	M/D	32	BBCC	Ind	
Business Systems with Regional Planning and Dev	N1KK	3FT deg	g	12-16	MO/DO	M/D	32	BBCC	Ind	
Business with Regional Planning and Development	N1K4	3FT deg	g	12-16	MO/DO	M/D	32	BBCC	Ind	
Contemp Br & Euro Hist with Regional Plan & Dev	V1K4	3FT deg	g	12-16	MO/DO	M/D	32	BBCC	Ind	
Ecology (Eco Tech) with Regional Planning & Dev	C9K4	3FT deg	g	12-16	MO/DO	M/D	32	BBCC	Ind	
Environmental Sci with Regional Planning & Dev	F9K4	3FT deg	g	12-16	MO/DO	M/D	32	BBCC	Ind	
Environmental St with Regional Planning & Dev	F9KK	3FT deg		12-16	MO/DO	M/D	32	BBCC	Ind	
European Lang St with Regional Planning & Dev	T2K4	3FT deg	L g	12-16	MO/DO	M/D	32	BBCC	Ind	
European Regional Planning and Development	K421	3FT deg	g	12-16	MO/DO	M/D	32	BBCC	Ind	
Health Science with Regional Planning and Dev	B9K4	3FT deg	g	12-16	MO/DO	M/D	32	BBCC	Ind	
Health Studies with Regional Planning and Dev	B9KK	3FT deg	g	12-16	MO/DO	M/D	32	BBCC	Ind	
Housing	K411	3FT deg		12-16	MO/DO	M/D	32	BBCC	Ind	
Housing Studies and Accounting	KN44	3FT deg	g	12-16	MO/DO	M/D	32	BBCC	Ind	
Housing Studies and Building Conservation	KK42	3FT deg	g	12-16	MO/DO	M/D	32	BBCC	Ind	
Housing Studies and Business	NK1K	3FT deg	g	12-16	MO/DO	M/D	32	BBCC	Ind	
Law and Housing Studies	KM4H	3FT deg	g	12-16	MO/DO	M/D	32	BBCC	Ind	
Law with Regional Planning & Development	M3K4	3FT deg	g	12-16	MO/DO	M/D	32	BBCC	Ind	
Leisure Studies with Regional Planning and Dev	N7K4	3FT deg	g	12-16	MO/DO	M/D	32	BBCC	Ind	
Mapping Science with Regional Planning and Dev	F8K4	3FT deg	g	12-16	MO/DO	M/D	32	BBCC	Ind	
Marketing with Regional Planning and Development	N5K4	3FT deg	g	12-16	MO/DO	M/D	32	BBCC	Ind	
Media Practices with Regional Planning and Dev	P4K4	3FT deg	g	12-16	MO/DO	M/D	32	BBCC	Ind	
Modern History with Regional Planning and Dev	V1KK	3FT deg	g	12-16	MO/DO	M/D	32	BBCC	Ind	
Physical Geography with Regional Plann and Dev	F8KK	3FT deg	g	12-16	MO/DO	M/D	32	BBCC	Ind	
Planning St and History of Design & Architecture	VK44	3FT deg		12-16	MO/DO	M/D	32	BBCC	Ind	
Planning Studies and Accounting	KN4K	3FT deg	g	12-16	MO/DO	M/D	32	BBCC	Ind	
Planning Studies and British Studies	VK94	3FT deg		12-16	MO/DO	M/D	32	BBCC	Ind	
Planning Studies and Building Conservation	KK4F	3FT deg	g	12-16	MO/DO	M/D	32	BBCC	Ind	
Planning Studies and Built Environment	KN48	3FT deg	g	12-16	MO/DO	M/D	32	BBCC	Ind	
Planning Studies and Business	KN41	3FT deg	g	12-16	MO/DO	M/D	32	BBCC	Ind	
Planning Studies and Business Systems	KN4D	3FT deg	g	12-16	MO/DO	M/D	32	BBCC	Ind	
Planning Studies and Environmental Science	KF49	3FT deg	g	12-16	MO/DO	M/D	32	BBCC	Ind	
Planning Studies and Geography	KF48	3FT deg	g	12-16	MO/DO	M/D	32	BBCC	Ind	
Planning Studies and Geology	KF46	3FT deg	g	12-16	MO/DO	M/D	32	BBCC	Ind	

course details

TITLE	CODE	COURSE	SUBJECTS	A/AS	NO/C	AGNVQ	IB	SQA(H)	SQA	RATIO A/AS
Planning Studies and Health Studies	KB49	3FT deg	g	12-16	MO/DO	M/D	32	BBCC	Ind	
Planning Studies and Housing Studies	K440	3FT deg	g	12-16	MO/DO	M/D	32	BBCC	Ind	
Planning Studies and Journalism	PK64	3FT deg		12-16	MO/DO	M/D	32	BBCC	Ind	
Planning Studies and Law	KM43	3FT deg	g	12-16	MO/DO	M/D	32	BBCC	Ind	
Planning Studies and Leisure Studies	KN47	3FT deg	G	12-16	MO/DO	M/D	32	BBCC	Ind	
Planning Studies and Physical Geography	KF4V	3FT deg	g	12-16	MO/DO	M/D	32	BBCC	Ind	
Planning Studies and Politics	KM41	3FT deg	g	12-16	MO/DO	M/D	32	BBCC	Ind	
Planning Studies and Public Policy & Management	KM4C	3FT deg	g	12-16	MO/DO	M/D	32	BBCC	Ind	
Planning Studies and Regional Planning and Devel	K430	3FT deg	g	12-16	MO/DO	M/D	32	BBCC	Ind	
Plant Biology with Regional Planning and Dev	C2K4	3FT deg	g	12-16	MO/DO	M/D	32	BBCC	Ind	
Politics with Regional Planning and Development	M1K4	3FT deg	g	12-16	MO/DO	M/D	32	BBCC	Ind	
Property Studies and Housing Studies	KK2K	3FT deg	g	12-16	MO/DO	M/D	32	BBCC	Ind	
Property Studies and Planning Studies	KK4G	3FT deg	g	12-16	MO/DO	M/D	32	BBCC	Ind	
Psychology with Regional Planning and Develop	L7KK	3FT deg	g	12-16	MO/DO	M/D	32	BBCC	Ind	
Public Policy & Management and Housing Studies	MK1L	3FT deg	g	12-16	MO/DO	M/D	32	BBCC	Ind	
Public Policy & Mgt with Reg Planning and Dev	M1KK	3FT deg	g	12-16	MO/DO	M/D	32	BBCC	Ind	
Regional Plan & Dev & Lang & Stylistics in Engl	QKG4	3FT deg	g	12-16	MO/DO	M/D	32	BBCC	Ind	
Regional Plan & Dev and Building Conservation	KK24	3FT deg	g	12-16	MO/DO	M/D	32	BBCC	Ind	
Regional Plan and Dev and Ecology & Biodiversity	CK94	3FT deg	g	12-16	MO/DO	M/D	32	BBCC	Ind	
Regional Plan and Dev and Environmental Science	FK94	3FT deg		12-16	MO/DO	M/D	32	BBCC	Ind	
Regional Planning & Dev & Organisat Behaviour	LK74	3FT deg	g	12-16	MO/DO	M/D	32	BBCC	Ind	
Regional Planning & Dev and Contemporary History	VK14	3FT deg	g	12-16	MO/DO	M/D	32	BBCC	Ind	
Regional Planning & Dev and Environmental Sci	FK9K	3FT deg	g	12-16	MO/DO	M/D	32	BBCC	Ind	
Regional Planning & Dev and Public Policy & Mgt	MKC4	3FT deg	g	12-16	MO/DO	M/D	32	BBCC	Ind	
Regional Planning & Dev with Eco & Biodiversity	K4C9	3FT deg	g	12-16	MO/DO	M/D	32	BBCC	Ind	
Regional Planning & Dev with Geog Info Systems	K422	3FT deg	g	12-16	MO/DO	M/D	32	BBCC	Ind	
Regional Planning & Dev with Human Biology	K4B1	3FT deg	g	12-16	MO/DO	M/D	32	BBCC	Ind	
Regional Planning & Dev with Land Reclamation	K4K3	3FT deg	g	12-16	MO/DO	M/D	32	BBCC	Ind	
Regional Planning & Dev with Org Behaviour	K4L7	3FT deg	g	12-16	MO/DO	M/D	32	BBCC	Ind	
Regional Planning & Dev with Pollution Studies	KF4X	3FT deg	g	12-16	MO/DO	M/D	32	BBCC	Ind	
Regional Planning & Dev with Public Policy & Mgt	K4MC	3FT deg	g	12-16	MO/DO	M/D	32	BBCC	Ind	
Regional Planning & Develop with Biochemistry	K4C7	3FT deg	g	12-16	MO/DO	M/D	32	BBCC	Ind	
Regional Planning & Develop with Biotechnology	K4J8	3FT deg	g	12-16	MO/DO	M/D	32	BBCC	Ind	
Regional Planning & Develop with Plant Biology	K4C2	3FT deg	g	12-16	MO/DO	M/D	32	BBCC	Ind	
Regional Planning & Development	K420	3FT deg	g	12-16	MO/DO	M/D	32	BBCC	Ind	
Regional Planning & Development & Built Environ	NK84	3FT deg	g	12-16	MO/DO	M/D	32	BBCC	Ind	
Regional Planning & Development & Business Systs	NKC4	3FT deg	g	12-16	MO/DO	M/D	32	BBCC	Ind	
Regional Planning & Development & Computer Sci	GK54	3FT deg	g	12-16	MO/DO	M/D	32	BBCC	Ind	
Regional Planning & Development & Human Biology	BK14	3FT deg	g	12-16	MO/DO	M/D	32	BBCC	Ind	
Regional Planning & Development & Mapping Sci	FK84	3FT deg	g	12-16	MO/DO	M/D	32	BBCC	Ind	4
Regional Planning & Development & Plant Biology	CK24	3FT deg	g	12-16	MO/DO	M/D	32	BBCC	Ind	
Regional Planning & Development and Health Sci	BK94	3FT deg	g	12-16	MO/DO	M/D	32	BBCC	Ind	
Regional Planning & Development and Health St	BKX4	3FT deg	g	12-16	MO/DO	M/D	32	BBCC	Ind	
Regional Planning & Development and Housing St	K410	3FT deg	g	12-16	MO/DO	M/D	32	BBCC	Ind	
Regional Planning & Development and Property St	KK2L	3FT deg	g	12-16	MO/DO	M/D	32	BBCC	Ind	
Regional Planning & Development with British St	K4V9	3FT deg		12-16	MO/DO	M/D	32	BBCC	Ind	
Regional Planning & Development with Chinese	K4T3	3FT deg		12-16	MO/DO	M/D	32	BBCC	Ind	
Regional Planning & Development with French	K4R1	3FT deg	F g	12-16	MO/DO	M/D	32	BBCC	Ind	
Regional Planning & Development with German	K4R2	3FT deg	G g	12-16	MO/DO	M/D	32	BBCC	Ind	
Regional Planning & Development with Health Sci	K4B9	3FT deg	g	12-16	MO/DO	M/D	32	BBCC	Ind	
Regional Planning & Development with Health St	K4BX	3FT deg		12-16	MO/DO	M/D	32	BBCC	Ind	
Regional Planning & Development with Italian	K4R3	3FT deg	I g	12-16	MO/DO	M/D	32	BBCC	Ind	

course details | 98 expected requirements | 96 entry stats

TITLE	CODE	COURSE	SUBJECTS	A/AS	NQ/C	AGNVQ	IB	SQA(H)	SQA	RATIO A/AS
Regional Planning & Development with Japanese	K4T4	3FT deg	L g	12-16	MO/DO	M/D	32	BBCC	Ind	
Regional Planning & Development with Journalism	K4P6	3FT deg	g	12-16	MO/DO	M/D	32	BBCC	Ind	
Regional Planning & Development with Management	KN4C	3FT deg	g	12-16	MO/DO	M/D	32	BBCC	Ind	
Regional Planning & Development with Photography	K4W5	3FT deg	g	12-16	MO/DO	M/D	32	BBCC	Ind	
Regional Planning & Development with Spanish	K4R4	3FT deg	Sp g	12-16	MO/DO	M/D	32	BBCC	Ind	
Regional Planning and Dev and European Lang St	TK24	3FT deg	g	12-16	MO/DO	M/D	32	BBCC	Ind	
Regional Planning and Dev and Physical Geography	FKV4	3FT deg	g	12-16	MO/DO	M/D	32	BBCC	Ind	
Regional Planning and Dev with Business Systems	K4NC	3FT deg	g	12-16	MO/DO	M/D	32	BBCC	Ind	
Regional Planning and Dev with Contemp History	K4V1	3FT deg	g	12-16	MO/DO	M/D	32	BBCC	Ind	
Regional Planning and Dev with Environmental Sci	K4F9	3FT deg	g	12-16	MO/DO	M/D	32	BBCC	Ind	
Regional Planning and Dev with Modern History	K4VC	3FT deg	g	12-16	MO/DO	M/D	32	BBCC	Ind	
Regional Planning and Dev with Physical Geog	K4FV	3FT deg	g	12-16	MO/DO	M/D	32	BBCC	Ind	
Regional Planning and Dev with Travel & Tourism	K4P7	3FT deg	g	12-16	MO/DO	M/D	32	BBCC	Ind	
Regional Planning and Develop and Biotechnology	JK84	3FT deg	g	12-16	MO/DO	M/D	32	BBCC	Ind	
Regional Planning and Develop with Leisure St	K4N7	3FT deg	g	12-16	MO/DO	M/D	32	BBCC	Ind	
Regional Planning and Develop with Mapping Sci	K4F8	3FT deg	g	12-16	MO/DO	M/D	32	BBCC	Ind	
Regional Planning and Develop with Multimedia	K4PK	3FT deg	g	12-16	MO/DO	M/D	32	BBCC	Ind	
Regional Planning and Develop with Psychology	K4LR	3FT deg	g	12-16	MO/DO	M/D	32	BBCC	Ind	
Regional Planning and Development & Biochemistry	CK74	3FT deg	g	12-16	MO/DO	M/D	32	BBCC	Ind	
Regional Planning and Development & Leisure St	NK74	3FT deg	g	12-16	MO/DO	M/D	32	BBCC	Ind	
Regional Planning and Development & Modern Hist	VKC4	3FT deg	g	12-16	MO/DO	M/D	32	BBCC	Ind	
Regional Planning and Development and British St	VK9K	3FT deg		12-16	MO/DO	M/D	32	BBCC	Ind	
Regional Planning and Development and Business	NK14	3FT deg	g	12-16	MO/DO	M/D	32	BBCC	Ind	
Regional Planning and Development and Law	MK34	3FT deg	g	12-16	MO/DO	M/D	32	BBCC	Ind	
Regional Planning and Development and Marketing	NK54	3FT deg	g	12-16	MO/DO	M/D	32	BBCC	Ind	
Regional Planning and Development and Politics	MK14	3FT deg	g	12-16	MO/DO	M/D	32	BBCC	Ind	
Regional Planning and Development and Psychology	LKR4	3FT deg	g	12-16	MO/DO	M/D	32	BBCC	Ind	
Regional Planning and Development with Built Env	K4N8	3FT deg	g	12-16	MO/DO	M/D	32	BBCC	Ind	
Regional Planning and Development with Business	K4N1	3FT deg	g	12-16	MO/DO	M/D	32	BBCC	Ind	
Regional Planning and Development with Marketing	K4N5	3FT deg	g	12-16	MO/DO	M/D	32	BBCC	Ind	
Regional Planning and Development with Politics	K4M1	3FT deg	g	12-16	MO/DO	M/D	32	BBCC	Ind	
Sociology and Planning Studies	LKH4	3FT deg		12-16	MO/DO	M/D	32	BBCC	Ind	
Travel and Tourism and Planning Studies	KP4R	3FT deg	g	12-16	MO/DO	M/D	32	BBCC	Ind	
Travel and Tourism and Regional Planning & Dev	KP47	3FT deg	g	12-16	MO/DO	M/D	32	BBCC	Ind	
Travel and Tourism with Regional Plan and Dev	P7K4	3FT deg	g	12-16	MO/DO	M/D	32	BBCC	Ind	
Univ of MANCHESTER										
Landscape Planning and Management	K401	4SW deg	*	BCD	7M	D^	28	BBBCC	Ind	5	18/22
Landscape Planning and Management	K403	4SW deg	*	BCD	7M	D^	28	BBBCC	Ind	
Town and Country Planning	K402	4FT deg	*	BCD	7M		28	BBBCC	Ind	
Town and Country Planning	K400	4FT deg	*	BCD	7M		28	BBBCC	Ind	4	14/24
MIDDLESEX Univ										
Facilities Management	K471▼	3FT deg	* g	12	5M	M$ go	24	Ind	Ind	
Housing Studies	KN48▼	3FT deg	* g	12	5M	M$ go	24	Ind	Ind	
Urban and Rural Development	LK84▼	3FT deg	Gy g	12	5M	M$ go	24	Ind	Ind	
Facilities Management	174K▼	2FT HND	* g	E	N	P$ go	24	Ind	Ind	
Housing Studies	84NK▼	2FT HND	* g	E	N	P$ go				
NAPIER Univ										
Building Control	K440	3FT/4FT deg	*	CCC	MO	M$	Ind	BBCC	Ind	7
Planning and Development Surveying	K450	3FT/4FT deg	*	CCC	MO	M$	Ind	BBCC	Ind	40

TITLE	CODE	COURSE	SUBJECTS	A/AS	ND/C	RGNVQ	IB	SQA(H)	SQA	RATIO A/AS
Univ of NEWCASTLE										
Town Planning (including professional diploma)	K400	5SW deg	* g	BCC	4M	M/6	30	BBB	Ind	4	12/22
NORTH EAST WALES INST of HE										
Geography, Planning and Development	FK84	3FT deg		6-12	3M	M$	Ind	CCC	N$	
Univ of NORTH LONDON										
Leisure Studies and Urban Policy	KN47	3FT deg	* g	12	MO+4D	Ind	Ind	Ind	Ind	
Urban Policy	K460▼	3FT deg	*	CE	MO	M	Dip	CCCCC	Ind	
Combined Honours *Urban Policy*	Y301	3FT deg	*	CC	MO	M	Dip	CCCCC	Ind	
Univ of NORTHUMBRIA										
Architectural and Urban Conservation	KK14	3FT deg	* g	14	5M+1D	M gi	24	BCCC	Ind	
Housing Development	K470	3FT/4SW deg	* g	14	5M+1D	M gi	24	BCCC	Ind	2	8/10
Housing Studies	K410	3FT deg		CDD	5M	Ind	24	BCCC	Ind	
Planning and Development Surveying	KK24	3FT/4SW deg	* g	14	5M+1D	M gi	24	BCCC	Ind	2	6/14
Urban Property Surveying	K460	3FT/4SW deg	* g	14	5M+1D	M gi	24	BCCC	Ind	3	6/20
Urban Property Surveying	064K	2FT HND	* g	6	3M	P gi	24	CCC	Ind	1	2/6
Univ of NOTTINGHAM										
Urban Planning and Management	K440	3FT deg	* g	BCC	Ind	Ind	30	Ind	Ind	7	16/26
NOTTINGHAM TRENT Univ										
Business Administration & Urban Studies	NK14▼	3FT deg	* g	12	Ind	M$ go	Ind	Ind	Ind	3	8/14
English and Urban Studies	QK34	3FT deg	E g	12	Ind	M$ go	Ind	Ind	Ind	2	10/16
Estate Surveying (Extended)	K468▼	4EXT/5EXTSW deg	* g		Ind	Ind	Ind	Ind	Ind	12	
Planning and Development	K450	3FT/4SW deg	* g	12	3M	M$	Ind	Ind	Ind	
OXFORD BROOKES Univ										
Planning Studies	K450	3FT deg	* g	DDD-CC	Ind	M*	Ind	Ind	Ind	4	10/18
Planning Studies/Accounting and Finance	KN44	3FT deg	* g	DDD-BCC	Ind	M*/D*3	Ind	Ind	Ind	
Planning Studies/Anthropology	KL46	3FT deg	* g	DDD-BCC	Ind	M*^	Ind	Ind	Ind	4
Planning Studies/Biological Chemistry	CK74	3FT deg								
Planning Studies/Biology	CK14	3FT deg	S g	CC-DD	Ind	MS	Ind	Ind	Ind	
Planning Studies/Business Administration & Mgt	KN41	3FT deg	* g	DDD-BBC	Ind	M*/MB4	Ind	Ind	Ind	5
Planning Studies/Cartography	FK84	3FT deg	* g	CC-DDD	Ind	M*	Ind	Ind	Ind	3
Planning Studies/Cell Biology	CKC4	3FT deg								
Planning Studies/Combined Studies	KY44	3FT deg		X		X	X	X	
Planning Studies/Computer Systems	GK64	3FT deg	* g	DDD-BC	Ind	M*	Ind	Ind	Ind	
Planning Studies/Computing	GK54	3FT deg	* g	DDD-BC	Ind	M*	Ind	Ind	Ind	
Planning Studies/Computing Mathematics	GK94	3FT deg	* g	BC-DDD	Ind	M*	Ind	Ind	Ind	
Planning Studies/Ecology	CK94	3FT deg	* g	CD-CC	Ind	MS	Ind	Ind	Ind	
Planning Studies/Educational Studies	KX49	3FT deg	* g	CC-DDD	Ind	M*/M*3	Ind	Ind	Ind	
Planning Studies/English Studies	KQ43	3FT deg	* g	DDD-AB	Ind	M*^	Ind	Ind	Ind	
Planning Studies/Environmental Chemistry	FK14	3FT deg								
Planning Studies/Environmental Policy	KK34	3FT deg								
Planning Studies/Environmental Sciences	FKX4	3FT deg	S g	CD-DDD	Ind	M*/DS	Ind	Ind	Ind	5
Planning Studies/Exercise and Health	KB46	3FT deg	S g	DD-CC	Ind	MS	Ind	Ind	Ind	
Planning Studies/Fine Art	KW41	3FT deg	Pf+A g	DDD-BC	Ind	MA^	Ind	Ind	Ind	
Planning Studies/Food Science and Nutrition	DK44	3FT deg	S g	DD-CC	Ind	MS	Ind	Ind	Ind	
Planning Studies/French Language and Contemp St	KR4C	4SW deg	F g	CDD-DDD	Ind	M*^	Ind	Ind	Ind	
Planning Studies/French Language and Literature	KR41	4SW deg	F g	CDD-DDD	Ind	M*^	Ind	Ind	Ind	
Planning Studies/Geography	KL48	3FT deg	* g	DDD-BB	Ind	M*	Ind	Ind	Ind	4	8/20
Planning Studies/Geology	FK64	3FT deg	S/M g	DD-CC	Ind	PS/M	Ind	Ind	Ind	

TITLE	CODE	COURSE	SUBJECTS	A/AS	ND/C	RGNVQ	IB	SQA(H)	SQA	RATIO A/AS

course details | | | **98 expected requirements** | | | | | | | **96 entry stats**

TITLE	CODE	COURSE	SUBJECTS	A/AS	ND/C	RGNVQ	IB	SQA(H)	SQA	RATIO A/AS
Planning Studies/Geotechnics	HK24	3FT deg	S/M/Ds/Es	DD-DDD	Ind	M$	Ind	Ind	Ind	
Planning Studies/German Language and Contemp St	KR4F	4SW deg	G g	CD-DDD	Ind	M*_^	Ind	Ind	Ind	
Planning Studies/German Language and Literature	KR42	4SW deg	G g	CD-DDD	Ind	M*_^	Ind	Ind	Ind	
Planning Studies/German Studies	KR4G	4SW deg	G g	DD-DDD	Ind	M*_^	Ind	Ind	Ind	
Planning Studies/Health Care (Post Exp)	BK74	3FT deg	X		X		X	X		
Planning Studies/History	KV41	3FT deg	* g	DDD-BB	Ind	M*^	Ind	Ind	Ind	
Planning Studies/History of Art	KV44	3FT deg	* g	DDD-BCC	Ind	M*^	Ind	Ind	Ind	
Planning Studies/Hospitality Management Studies	KN47	3FT deg	* g	CC-DDD	Ind	M*/M*3	Ind	Ind		
Planning Studies/Human Biology	BK14	3FT deg								
Planning Studies/Information Systems	GKM4	3FT deg	* g	DDD-BC	Ind	M*	Ind	Ind	Ind	
Planning Studies/Intelligent Systems	GK84	3FT deg	* g	DDD-BC	Ind	M*	Ind	Ind	Ind	
Planning Studies/Law	KM43	3FT deg	* g	DDD-BBB	Ind	M*/D*3	Ind	Ind	Ind	
Planning Studies/Leisure Planning and Management	KKH4	3FT deg								
Planning Studies/Marketing Management	KN4N	3FT deg	* g	DDD-BCC	Ind	M*/D*3	Ind	Ind	Ind	
Planning Studies/Mathematics	GK14	3FT deg	M	DD-CC	Ind	M*_^	Ind	Ind	Ind	
Planning Studies/Music	KW43	3FT deg	Mu g	DD-CC	Ind	M*	Ind	Ind	Ind	
Planning Studies/Palliative Care (Post Exp)	BKR4	3FT deg	X		X		X	X		
Planning Studies/Physical Geography	FKV4	3FT deg								
Politics/Planning Studies	MK14	3FT deg	* g	DDD-AB	Ind	M*^	Ind	Ind	Ind	3
Psychology/Planning Studies	CK84	3FT deg	* g	DD-BBC	Ind	M*^	Ind	Ind	Ind	
Publishing/Planning Studies	KP45	3FT deg	* g	DDD-BB	Ind	M*/M$3	Ind	Ind	Ind	1
Rehabilitation/Planning Studies (Post Exp)	BKT4	3FT deg	X		X		X	X		
Retail Management/Planning Studies	KN45	3FT deg	* g	DD-CCD	Ind		Ind	Ind	Ind	3
Sociology/Planning Studies	KL43	3FT deg	* g	DD-BCC	Ind	M*^	Ind	Ind	Ind	
Software Engineering/Planning Studies	GK74	3FT deg	* g	CD-CC	Ind	M*	Ind	Ind	Ind	
Statistics/Planning Studies	GK44	3FT deg	* g	DD-CC	Ind	M*	Ind	Ind	Ind	
Telecommunications/Planning Studies	HKP4	3FT deg								
Tourism/Planning Studies	KP47	3FT deg	* g	DDD-BC	Ind	M*/M*3	Ind	Ind	Ind	5
Transport Planning/Planning Studies	KN49	3FT deg	* g	DD-DDD	Ind	M*	Ind	Ind	Ind	
Water Resources/Planning Studies	HKF4	3FT deg								

QUEEN'S Univ Belfast

Environmental Planning	K450	3FT deg	* g	BCC	Ind	Ind	28$	BBBB	Ind	11 14/26

Univ of READING

Land Management with Diploma in Planning	K400	4FT deg	* g	22	6M+2D	D$6/^ gi	30	BBBB	Ind	4

Univ of SALFORD

Housing Studies	K470	3FT deg		10	M	M	Ind	Ind	Ind	
Property Management and Investment	K4N3	3FT/4SW deg		BCC-CCC	4M+1D	M	Ind	Ind	Ind	

Univ of SHEFFIELD

Landscape with Planning	K3K4	3FT deg	g	CCC	6M	D^	28$	BBBC$	Ind	4 14/30
Urban Studies and Planning (Grad Dip opt)	K400	3FT/4FT deg	* g	BCC	5M+1D	DC^	29	BBBB	Ind	5 18/26

SHEFFIELD HALLAM Univ

Environmental Planning	K421	3FT deg	*	14	3M	M	Ind	Ind	Ind	
Housing Studies	K472	4SW deg	*	14	3M	M	Ind	Ind	Ind	
Housing and Society	K471	3FT deg	*	14	3M	M	Ind	Ind	Ind	
Planning Studies/Town Planning	K450	4FT deg	*	18	5M	M	Ind	Ind	Ind	
Urban Studies	K460	3FT deg	*	14	3M	M	Ind	Ind	Ind	
Urban and Regional Geography	LK84	3FT deg	*	16	4M	M	Ind	Ind	Ind	
Combined Studies *Town and Country Planning*	Y400	3FT deg	*	16	2M	M	Ind	Ind	Ind	
Combined Studies *Transport Planning*	Y400	3FT deg	*	14	2M	M	Ind	Ind	Ind	

Planning (Town and Country)   61

course details			98 expected requirements							96 entry stats
TITLE	CODE	COURSE	SUBJECTS	A/AS	NO/C	AGNVQ	IB	SQA(H)	SQA	RATIO A/AS
Combined Studies *Urban and Regional Geography*	Y400	3FT deg	*	16	2M	M	Ind	Ind	Ind	
Combined Studies *Urban and Regional Policy*	Y400	3FT deg	*	14	2M	M	Ind	Ind	Ind	
Housing Management	074K	2FT HND	*	4	1M	P	Ind	Ind	Ind	
Planning and Development	054K	2FT HND	*	4	1M	P	Ind	Ind	Ind	

SOUTH BANK Univ

Foundation Town Planning	K448	4EXT deg					Ind	Ind	Ind	
Housing and Accounting	KN4K	3FT deg	Ac/Ec g	14-18	2M+4D	M go	Ind	Ind	Ind	
Housing and Business Information Technology	GK7L	3FT deg	M g	14-18	2M+4D	M go	Ind	Ind	Ind	
Housing and Computing	GK5L	3FT deg	M g	14-18	2M+4D	M go	Ind	Ind	Ind	
Housing and Economics	KL4C	3FT deg	Ec/Bu g	14-18	2M+4D	M go	Ind	Ind	Ind	
Housing and English Studies	KQ4J	3FT deg	E g	14-18	X	M^ go	Ind	Ind	Ind	
Housing and Environmental Policy	FK9K	3FT deg	* g	14-18	2M+4D	M go	Ind	Ind	Ind	
Housing and European Studies	KT42	3FT deg	* g	14-18	2M+4D	M go	Ind	Ind	Ind	
Housing and Food Policy	DK4K	3FT deg	S g	14-18	2M+4D	M go	Ind	Ind	Ind	
Housing and French	KR4C	3FT deg	F g	14-18	2M+4D	M go	Ind	Ind	Ind	
Housing and German	KR4F	3FT deg	G g	14-18	2M+4D	M go	Ind	Ind	Ind	
Housing and German - ab initio	KR4G	3FT deg	* g	14-18	2M+4D	M go	Ind	Ind	Ind	
Housing and Health Studies	LK4K	3FT deg	S g	14-18	2M+4D	M go	Ind	Ind	Ind	
Housing and History	KV4D	3FT deg	H g	14-18	2M+4D	M go	Ind	Ind	Ind	
Human Biology and Housing	BK1K	3FT deg	S g	14-18	2M+4D	M go	Ind	Ind	Ind	
Human Geography and Housing	KL4V	3FT deg	Gy g	14-18	2M+4D	M^ go	Ind	Ind	Ind	
Human Resource Management and Housing	KN46	3FT deg	* g	14-18	2M+4D	M go	Ind	Ind	Ind	
Law and Housing	KM4H	3FT deg	* g	14-18	2M+4D	D^ go	Ind	Ind	Ind	
Management and Housing	KN4C	3FT deg	* g	14-18	2M+4D	M go	Ind	Ind	Ind	
Marketing and Housing	KN45	3FT deg	* g	14-18	2M+4D	M go	Ind	Ind	Ind	
Media Studies and Housing	KP4K	3FT deg	E g	14-18	2M+4D	D go	Ind	Ind	Ind	
Nutrition and Housing	BK4K	3FT deg	S g	14-18	2M+4D	M go	Ind	Ind	Ind	
Planning and Computing	GK54	3FT deg	M g	14-18	2M+4D	M go	Ind	Ind	Ind	
Planning and Environmental Policy	FK94	3FT deg	* g	14-18	2M+4D	M go	Ind	Ind	Ind	
Planning and European Studies	KT4F	3FT deg	* g	14-18	2M+4D	M go	Ind	Ind	Ind	
Planning and Housing	KV4C	3FT deg	* g	14-18	2M+4D	M go	Ind	Ind	Ind	
Planning and Human Geography	KL48	3FT deg	Gy g	14-18	2M+4D	M go	Ind	Ind	Ind	
Planning and Human Resource Management	KN4Q	3FT deg	* g	14-18	2M+4D	M go	Ind	Ind	Ind	
Planning and Management	KN41	3FT deg	* g	14-18	2M+4D	M go	Ind	Ind	Ind	
Planning and Marketing	KN4M	3FT deg	* g	14-18	2M+4D	M go	Ind	Ind	Ind	
Politics and Housing	MK34	3FT deg	* g	14-18	2M+4D	M go	Ind	Ind	Ind	
Politics and Planning	KM41	3FT deg	* g	14-18	4M+2D	M go	Ind	Ind	Ind	
Product Design and Housing	HK7K	3FT deg	Ad g	14-18	2M+4D	M go	Ind	Ind	Ind	
Psychology and Housing	CK8K	3FT deg	S g	14-18	2M+4D	M go	Ind	Ind	Ind	
Social Policy and Housing	LK44	3FT deg	* g	14-18	2M+4D	M go	Ind	Ind	Ind	
Sociology and Housing	KL4H	3FT deg	* g	14-18	4M+2D	M go	Ind	Ind	Ind	
Spanish - ab initio and Housing	RK4K	3FT deg	* g	14-18	2M+4D	M go	Ind	Ind	Ind	
Spanish and Housing	KR4L	3FT deg	Sp g	14-18	2M+4D	M^ go	Ind	Ind	Ind	
Sports Science and Housing	BK6K	3FT deg	S g	14-18	2M+4D	M go	Ind	Ind	Ind	
Technology and Housing	JK9K	3FT deg	* g	14-18	2M+4D	M go	Ind	Ind	Ind	
Technology and Planning	JK94	3FT deg	* g	12-16	4M+2D	M go	Ind	Ind	Ind	
Tourism and Housing	KP4R	3FT deg	L g	14-18	2M+4D	M^ go	Ind	Ind	Ind	
Tourism and Planning	KP47	3FT deg	L g	14-18	4M+2D	M go	Ind	Ind	Ind	
Town Planning	K440	3FT/4SW deg	* g	CC	3M	M go	Ind	Ind	Ind	
Urban Studies and Accounting	KN4L	3FT deg	Ec/Bu g	14-18	2M+4D	M go	Ind	Ind	Ind	

course details | 98 expected requirements | 96 entry stats

TITLE	CODE	COURSE	SUBJECTS	A/AS	ND/C	AGNVQ	IB	SQA(H)	SQA	RATIO A/AS
Urban Studies and Business Information Tech	GK7K	3FT deg	M g	14-18	2M+4D	M go	Ind	Ind	Ind	
Urban Studies and Computing	GK5K	3FT deg	M g	14-18	2M+4D	M go	Ind	Ind	Ind	
Urban Studies and Economics	LK14	3FT deg	Ec/Bu g	14-18	2M+4D	M go	Ind	Ind	Ind	
Urban Studies and English Studies	KQ4H	3FT deg	E g	14-18	X	M go	Ind	Ind	Ind	
Urban Studies and Environmental Policy	FK9L	3FT deg	* g	14-18	2M+4D	M go	Ind	Ind	Ind	
Urban Studies and European Studies	KT4G	3FT deg	* g	14-18	2M+4D	M go	Ind	Ind	Ind	
Urban Studies and Food Policy	DK4L	3FT deg	S g	14-18	2M+4D	M go	Ind	Ind	Ind	
Urban Studies and French	RK14	3FT deg	F g	14-18	2M+4D	M go	Ind	Ind	Ind	
Urban Studies and German	RK24	3FT deg	G g	14-18	2M+4D	M go	Ind	Ind	Ind	
Urban Studies and German - ab initio	RK2K	3FT deg	* g	14-18	2M+4D	M go	Ind	Ind	Ind	
Urban Studies and Health Studies	LK4L	3FT deg	S g	14-18	2M+4D	M go	Ind	Ind	Ind	
Urban Studies and History	VK14	3FT deg	H g	14-18	2M+4D	M go	Ind	Ind	Ind	
Urban Studies and Housing	K410	3FT deg	* g	14-18	2M+4D	M go	Ind	Ind	Ind	
Urban Studies and Human Biology	BK1L	3FT deg	S g	14-18	2M+4D	M go	Ind	Ind	Ind	
Urban Studies and Human Resource Management	KN4P	3FT deg	* g	14-18	2M+4D	M go	Ind	Ind	Ind	
Urban Studies and Law	KM4J	3FT deg	* g	14-18	2M+4D	D go	Ind	Ind	Ind	
Urban Studies and Management	KN4D	3FT deg	* g	14-18	2M+4D	M go	Ind	Ind	Ind	
Urban Studies and Marketing	KN4N	3FT deg	* g	14-18	2M+4D	M go	Ind	Ind	Ind	
Urban Studies and Media Studies	KP4L	3FT deg	E g	14-18	2M+4D	D go	Ind	Ind	Ind	
Urban Studies and Nutrition	BK4L	3FT deg	S g	14-18	2M+4D	M go	Ind	Ind	Ind	
Urban Studies and Planning	K411	3FT deg	* g	14-18	2M+4D	M go	Ind	Ind	Ind	
Urban Studies and Politics	MK14	3FT deg	* g	14-18	2M+4D	M go	Ind	Ind	Ind	
Urban Studies and Product Design	KH47	3FT deg	Ad g	14-18	2M+4D	M go	Ind	Ind	Ind	
Urban Studies and Psychology	KC48	3FT deg	S g	14-18	2M+4D	M go	Ind	Ind	Ind	
Urban Studies and Social Policy	KL4L	3FT deg	* g	14-18	2M+4D	M go	Ind	Ind	Ind	
Urban Studies and Sociology	LK34	3FT deg	* g	14-18	2M+4D	M go	Ind	Ind	Ind	
Urban Studies and Spanish	RK44	3FT deg	S g	14-18	2M+4D	M go	Ind	Ind	Ind	
Urban Studies and Spanish - ab initio	RK4L	3FT deg	* g	14-18	2M+4D	M go	Ind	Ind	Ind	
Urban Studies and Sports Science	KB46	3FT deg	S g	14-18	2M+4D	M go	Ind	Ind	Ind	
Urban Studies and Tourism	PK74	3FT deg	L g	14-18	2M+4D	M go	Ind	Ind	Ind	
Urban Studies and World Theatre	WK44	3FT deg	* g	14-18	2M+4D	M go	Ind	Ind	Ind	
World Theatre and Housing	KW44	3FT deg	* g	14-18	2M+4D	M go	Ind	Ind	Ind	
World Theatre and Planning	KW4L	3FT deg	* g	14-18	2M+4D	M go	Ind	Ind	Ind	

Univ of STRATHCLYDE

TITLE	CODE	COURSE	SUBJECTS	A/AS	ND/C	AGNVQ	IB	SQA(H)	SQA	RATIO A/AS
Environmental Planning	K450	4FT deg	g	CCD	Ind		30	BBBC	HN	
Geography and Planning	KL48	3FT/4FT deg	g	CCC	Ind		28	BBBBB$	Ind	
Arts and Social Sciences _Environmental Planning_	Y440	3FT deg	g	CCC	Ind		28	BBBBB$	Ind	

Univ of ULSTER

TITLE	CODE	COURSE	SUBJECTS	A/AS	ND/C	AGNVQ	IB	SQA(H)	SQA	RATIO A/AS
Housing (4 Yr SW inc DIS & professional recog)	K472▼	4SW deg	* g	CCC	MO+3D	D*6/^ gi	28	BBBC	Ind	10 14/20

UNIVERSITY COLL LONDON (Univ of London)

TITLE	CODE	COURSE	SUBJECTS	A/AS	ND/C	AGNVQ	IB	SQA(H)	SQA	RATIO A/AS
Town and Country Planning	K400	3FT deg	* g	CDD-BCC	3M	Ind	26	BCCCC	Ind	8 12/24

Univ of WESTMINSTER

TITLE	CODE	COURSE	SUBJECTS	A/AS	ND/C	AGNVQ	IB	SQA(H)	SQA	RATIO A/AS
Housing Management & Developmt (with foundation)	K478	4EXT deg	*	D	N					8
Housing Management and Development (Sandwich)	K472	4SW deg	*	DD	3M	M	Ind	BBC	Ind	2
Tourism and Planning	PK74	3FT deg	*	CC	5M	D	Ind	BBB		6 6/14
Tourism and Planning (with foundation)	PK7K	4FT deg	*	D	Ind	P	Ind	Ind	Ind	3
Town Planning	K460	3FT deg	*	12	3M	M	Ind	Ind		5 6/18
Town Planning (with foundation)	K468	4EXT deg	*	D	N	P	Ind	Ind		2
Urban Design	K461	3FT deg	*	CC	5M	M	Ind	BBB		
Urban Design (with foundation)	K469	4EXT deg	*	CC	5M	M	Ind	Ind		

			98 expected requirements							96 entry stats

course details / *98 expected requirements* / *96 entry stats*

TITLE	CODE	COURSE	SUBJECTS	A/AS	ND/C	AGNVQ	IB	SQA(H)	SQA	RATIO A/AS
Univ of ABERDEEN										
Church History-Politics	MV11	4FT deg	* g	BBC	Ind	M$ go	30$	BBBB$	Ind	
Economic History-International Relations	VM3C	4FT deg	* g	BBC	Ind	M$ go	30$	BBBB$	Ind	
Economic History-Politics	VM31	4FT deg	* g	BBC	Ind	M$ go	30$	BBBB$	Ind	
Economics-International Relations	LM1C	4FT deg	* g	BBC	Ind	M$ go	30$	BBBB$	Ind	12
Economics-Politics	LM11	4FT deg	* g	BBC	Ind	M$ go	30$	BBBB$	Ind	7
English-International Relations	QM3C	4FT deg	* g	BBC	Ind	M$ go	30$	BBBB$	Ind	3
French-International Relations	RM1C	4FT/5FT deg	* g	BBC	Ind	M$ go	30$	BBBB$	Ind	7
French-International Relations (4 Yrs)	MRC1	4FT deg	* g	BBC	Ind	M$ go	30$	BBBB$	Ind	
French-Politics	RM11	4FT/5FT deg	* g	BBC	Ind	M$ go	30$	BBBB$	Ind	5
French-Politics (4 Yrs)	MR11	4FT deg	* g	BBC	Ind	M$ go	30$	BBBB$	Ind	
Geography-International Relations	LM81	4FT deg	* g	BBC	Ind	M$ go	30$	BBBB$	Ind	5
German-International Relations	RM2C	4FT/5FT deg	* g	BBC	Ind	M$ go	30$	BBBB$	Ind	
German-International Relations (4 Yrs)	MRC2	4FT deg	* g	BBC	Ind	M$ go	30$	BBBB$	Ind	
German-Politics	RM21	4FT/5FT deg	* g	BBC	Ind	M$ go	30$	BBBB$	Ind	
German-Politics (4 Yrs)	MR12	4FT deg	* g	BBC	Ind	M$ go	30$	BBBB$	Ind	
Hispanic Studies-International Relations	RM4C	4FT/5FT deg	* g	BBC	Ind	M$ go	30$	BBBB$	Ind	
Hispanic Studies-International Relations (4 Yrs)	MRC4	4FT deg	* g	BBC	Ind	M$ go	30$	BBBB$	Ind	
Hispanic Studies-Politics	RM41	4FT/5FT deg	* g	BBC	Ind	M$ go	30$	BBBB$	Ind	
Hispanic Studies-Politics (4 Yrs)	MR14	4FT deg	* g	BBC	Ind	M$ go	30$	BBBB$	Ind	
History-International Relations	VM1C	4FT deg	* g	BBC	Ind	M$ go	30$	BBBB$	Ind	7
History-Politics	VM11	4FT deg	* g	BBC	Ind	M$ go	30$	BBBB$	Ind	7
International Relations-Management Studies	MN1C	4FT deg	* g	BBC	Ind	M$ go	30$	BBBB$	Ind	6
International Relations-Religious Studies	VM81	4FT deg	* g	BBC	Ind	M$ go	30$	BBBB$	Ind	1
Jurisprudence-International Relations	MMHC	4FT deg	* g	BBC	Ind	M$ go	30$	BBBB$	Ind	
Jurisprudence-Politics	MMH1	4FT deg	* g	BBC	Ind	M$ go	30$	BBBB$	Ind	3
Philosophy-International Relations	VM7C	4FT deg	* g	BBC	Ind	M$ go	30$	BBBB$	Ind	4
Philosophy-Politics	VM71	4FT deg	* g	BBC	Ind	M$ go	30$	BBBB$	Ind	4
Political Studies	M100	4FT deg	* g	BBC	Ind	M$ go	30$	BBBB$	Ind	4
Politics-Management Studies	MN11	4FT deg	* g	BBC	Ind	M$ go	30$	BBBB$	Ind	5
Politics-Religious Studies	MV18	4FT deg	* g	BBC	Ind	M$ go	30$	BBBB$	Ind	
Politics-Social Research	LM31	4FT deg	* g	BBC	Ind	M$ go	30$	BBBB$	Ind	8
Politics-Sociology	ML13	4FT deg	* g	BBC	Ind	M$ go	30$	BBBB$	Ind	5
Univ of Wales, ABERYSTWYTH										
European Community and Integration Studies	M165	3FT deg	* g	20	1M+5D	M6 g	30	BBBCC	Ind	
Information and Library Studies/Int Politics	PM11	3FT deg	* g	20	1M+5D	M6 g	30	BBBCC	Ind	
Information and Library Studies/Politics	PM1C	3FT deg	* g	20	1M+5D	M6 g	30	BBBCC	Ind	
International Politics (Major)	M150	3FT deg	* g	20	1M+5D	M6 g	30	BBBCC	Ind	
International Politics (Minor)	M151	3FT deg	* g	20	1M+5D	M6 g	30	BBBCC	Ind	
International Politics and Area Studies	M152	3FT deg	* g	20	1M+5D	M6 g	30	BBBCC	Ind	
International Politics and International History	M160	3FT deg	* g	20	1M+5D	M6 g	30	BBBCC	Ind	
International Politics and Strategic Studies	M164	3FT deg	* g	20	1M+5D	M6 g	30	BBBCC	Ind	
International Politics and The Americas	MQ14	3FT deg	* g	20	1M+5D	M6 g	30	BBBCC	Ind	
International Politics and the Third World	MM19	3FT deg	* g	20	1M+5D	M6 g	30	BBBCC	Ind	
International Politics/Economic and Soc Hist	MVC3	3FT deg	* g	20	1M+5D	M6 g	30	BBBCC	Ind	
International Politics/English	MQ1H	3FT deg	El	20	1M+5D$	M^ g	30$	BBBBC$	Ind	
International Politics/French	MRD1	4FT deg	F g	20	1M+5D$	M^ g	30$	BBBBC$	Ind	
International Politics/Geography	LMW1	3FT deg	Gy g	20-22	3M+2D$	M^ g	31$	BBBBC$	Ind	
International Politics/German	MRD2	4FT deg	G g	20	1M+5D$	M^ g	30$	BBBBC$	Ind	
International Politics/History	MVDD	3FT deg	* g	20	1M+5D	M6 g	30	BBBCC	Ind	
International Relations	M154	3FT deg	* g	20	1M+5D	M6 g	30	BBBCC	Ind	
Italian/International Politics	MRC3	4FT deg	L g	20	1M+5D$	M^ g	30$	BBBBC$	Ind	

			98 expected requirements							*96 entry stats*
course details			SUBJECTS	A/AS	NO/C	AGNVQ	IB	SQA(H)	SQA	RATIO A/AS
TITLE	CODE	COURSE								
Political Studies	M100	3FT deg	* g	20	1M+5D	M6 g	30	BBBCC	Ind	
Political Studies (Major)	M102	3FT deg	* g	20	1M+5D	M6 g	30	BBBCC	Ind	
Political Studies (Minor)	M103	3FT deg	* g	20	1M+5D	M6 g	30	BBBCC	Ind	
Political Studies/Law	MM13	3FT deg	* g	BBB	DO	D g	32	BBBBCC	Ind	
Politics/Economic and Social History	MV13	3FT deg	* g	20	1M+5D	M6 g	30	BBBCC	Ind	
Politics/English	MQ13	3FT deg	El	20	1M+5D$	M^ g	30$	BBBBC$	Ind	
Politics/French	MR11	4FT deg	E g	20	1M+5D$	M^ g	30$	BBBBC$	Ind	
Politics/Geography	LMV1	3FT deg	Gv g	20-22	3M+2D$	M^ g	31$	BBBBC$	Ind	
Politics/German	MR12	4FT deg	G g	20	1M+5D$	M^ g	30$	BBBBC$	Ind	
Politics/History	MV1D	3FT deg	* g	20	1M+5D	M6 g	30	BBBCC	Ind	
Politics/Italian	MR13	4FT deg	L g	20	1M+5D$	M^ g	30$	BBBBC$	Ind	
Spanish/International Politics	MRC4	4FT deg	L g	20	1M+5D$	M^ g	30$	BBBBC$	Ind	
Spanish/Politics	MR14	4FT deg	L g	20	1M+5D$	M^ g	30$	BBBBC$	Ind	
Welsh History/International Politics	MV1C	3FT deg	* g	20	1M+5D	M^ g	30	BBBCC	Ind	
Welsh History/Politics	MVCC	3FT deg	* g	20	1M+5D	M^ g	30	BBBCC	Ind	
Welsh/International Politics	MQ1M	3FT deg	W g	20	1M+5D$	M^ g	30$	BBBBC$	Ind	
Welsh/Politics	MQ15	3FT deg	W g	20	1M+5D$	M^ g	30$	BBBBC$	Ind	

ANGLIA Poly Univ

Art History and Politics	MV14▼	3FT deg	*	14	6M	M+/^	Dip	BBCC	Ind	
Business and Politics	NM11▼	3FT deg	* g	14	6M	M go	Dip	BBCC	Ind	5
Communication Studies and Politics	PM31▼	3FT deg	Ap	14	6M	M+/^	Dip$	BBCC	Ind	
Economics and Politics	LM11▼	3FT deg	* g	14	6M	M+/^	Dip$	BBCC	Ind	22
English Language Studies and Politics	QM11▼	3FT deg	* g	14	4M	M go	Dip	BCCC		
English and Politics	QM31▼	3FT deg	E	14	6M	M+/^	Dip$	BBCC	Ind	10
European Philosophy & Literature and Politics	VM71▼	3FT deg	*	14	6M	M+/^	Dip	BBCC	Ind	
French and Politics	RM11▼	4FT deg	* g	14	6M	M go	Dip	BBCC	Ind	
Geography and Politics	LM81▼	3FT deg	Gv g	14	6M	M+/^	Dip$	BBCC	Ind	
German and Politics	RM21▼	4FT deg	* g	14	6M	M+/^ go	Dip	BBCC	Ind	
History and Politics	VM11▼	3FT deg	*	14	6M	M	Dip$	BBCC	Ind	6
Italian and Politics	RM31▼	4FT deg	* g	14	6M	M+/^ go	Dip	BBCC	Ind	1
Law and Politics	MM31▼	3FT deg	*	14	6M	M	Dip	BBCC	Ind	12
Mathematics or Stats/Stat Mod. and Politics	GM11▼	3FT deg	* g	14	6M	M go	Dip	BBCC	Ind	
Politics and Social Policy	ML14▼	3FT deg	*	14	6M	M	Dip	BBCC	Ind	20
Politics and Sociology	ML13▼	3FT deg	*	14	6M	M+/^	Dip	BBCC	Ind	7
Politics and Spanish	MR14▼	4FT deg	* g	14	6M	M+/^ go	Dip$	BBCC	Ind	
Politics and Women's Studies	MM19▼	3FT deg	*	14	6M	M+/^	Dip	BBCC	Ind	

ASTON Univ

Public Policy & Management/Business Admin	MN1C	3FT/4SW deg	* g	20	3M+7D	D$6/^ go	30	BBBBB	Ind	3 18/22
Public Policy & Management/Chemistry	MF11	3FT/4SW deg	C g	20	3M+7D$	D$^ go		30$	BBBBB$ Ind	
Public Policy & Management/Chemistry (Year Zero)	MF1D	4FT/5SW deg								
Public Policy & Management/Computer Science	GM5C	4FT/5SW deg								
Public Policy & Management/Computer Science	GM51	3FT/4SW deg	* g	20	5M+5D	D$6/^ go	30	BBBBB	Ind	
Public Policy & Management/Electronics	HM61	3FT/4SW deg	M/P g	20	5M+5D$	D$6/^ go	30$	BBBBB$	Ind	
Public Policy & Management/Ergonomics	JMX1	3FT/4SW deg	* g	20	5M+5D	D$6/^ go	30	BBBBB	Ind	
Public Policy & Management/European Studies	MT12	3FT/4SW deg	* g	20	5M+5D	D$6/^ go	30	BBBBB	Ind	
Public Policy & Management/Health & Safety Mgt	JM91	3FT/4SW deg	* g	20	5M+5D	D$6/^ go	30	BBBBB	Ind	2
Public Policy & Management/Human Psychology	LM7C	3FT/4SW deg	* g	22	3M+7D	D$6/^ go	30	BBBBB	Ind	8
Public Policy & Management/Mathematics	GM1C	3FT/4SW deg	M g	20	X	D$^ go		30$	BBBBB$ Ind	5
Public Policy & Management/Medicinal Chem (YrZ)	FM11	4FT/5SW deg								
Public Policy & Management/Medicinal Chemistry	MF1C	3FT/4SW deg	C g	20	5M+5D$	D$^ go		30$	BBBBB$ Ind	
Public Policy & Mgt/Environ Sci & Tech (Yr Zero)	FM9C	4FT/5SW deg								

TITLE	CODE	COURSE	SUBJECTS	A/AS	NO/C	RGNVQ	IB	SQA(H)	SQA	RATIO A/AS
course details			**98 expected requirements**							**96 entry stats**
Public Policy & Mgt/Environmental Science & Tech	FM91	3FT/4SW deg	S g	20	5M+5D$	D$6/^ go	30$	BBBBB$	Ind	
Public Policy & Mgt/Health & Safety Mgt (Yr Z)	JM9C	4FT/5SW deg								
Public Policy & Mgt/Human Psychology (Year Zero)	LM7D	4FT/5SW deg								
Public Policy & Mgt/Product Design (Engineering)	HM71	3FT/4SW deg	S g	20	5M+5D	D$^ go	30$	BBBBB$	Ind	
Social Studies/Public Policy & Management	ML14	3FT/4SW deg	* g	20	3M+7D	D$6/^ go	30	BBBBB	Ind	2 16/26

BARNSLEY COLL

TITLE	CODE	COURSE	SUBJECTS	A/AS	NO/C	RGNVQ	IB	SQA(H)	SQA	RATIO A/AS
Humanities *Geographical St and Politics with Internat Rels*	Y301	3FT deg	H/Gy/Po/E g	EE	4M	MB	Ind	Ind	Ind	
Humanities *Geographical St and Politics with Internat Rels*	Y302	4EXT deg								
Humanities *History and Politics with Internat Relations*	Y302	4EXT deg								
Humanities *History and Politics with Internat Relations*	Y301	3FT deg	H/Gy/Po/E g	EE	4M	MB	Ind	Ind	Ind	
Humanities *Literature and Politics with Internat Relations*	Y301	3FT deg								
Humanities *Literature and Politics with Internat Relations*	Y302	3FT deg								

Univ of BATH

TITLE	CODE	COURSE	SUBJECTS	A/AS	NO/C	RGNVQ	IB	SQA(H)	SQA	RATIO A/AS
Economics and Politics	LM11	3FT deg	g	22	Ind	D^	30	Ind	Ind	9 20/26
Economics and Politics	LMC1	4SW deg	g	22	Ind	D^	30	Ind	Ind	5 22/28
Politics with Economics (3 Yrs)	M1L1	3FT deg	g	22	Ind	D^	30	Ind	Ind	7 22/26
Politics with Economics (4 Yr SW)	M1LC	4SW deg	g	22	Ind	D^	30	Ind	Ind	3 22/30
Russian and Politics (4 Yr SW)	RM81	4SW deg	R	22	Ind	Ind	30	Ind	Ind	3

Univ of BIRMINGHAM

TITLE	CODE	COURSE	SUBJECTS	A/AS	NO/C	RGNVQ	IB	SQA(H)	SQA	RATIO A/AS
Economic History and Political Science	MV13	3FT deg	*	BBC	Ind	D+^	32	ABBBB	Ind	
Economics and Political Science	LM11	3FT deg	*	BBB	Ind	D+^	32	ABBBB	Ind	8 24/28
French Studies/Political Science	MR11	4FT deg	F	BBB	Ind	D*^	32$	ABBB	Ind	27
German Studies/Political Science	MR12	4FT deg	G	BBB	Ind	D*^	32$	ABBB	Ind	
Hispanic Studies/Political Science	MR14	4FT deg	*	BBB	Ind	D*^	32	ABBB	Ind	
History (Modern)/Political Science	MV11	3FT deg	*	BBB	Ind	D*^	32	ABBB	Ind	15 26/26
International Studies with Economics	ML11	3FT deg	*	BBB	Ind	D+^	32	ABBBB	Ind	20
International Studies with French	M1R1	4FT deg	F	BBC	Ind	D+^	32	ABBBB	Ind	7 22/30
International Studies with German	M1R2	4FT deg	G	BBC	Ind	D+^	32	ABBBB	Ind	6
International Studies with Greek	M1Q7	3FT deg	*	BBC	Ind	D+^	32	ABBBB	Ind	
International Studies with Political Science	M156	3FT deg	*	BBB	Ind	D+^	32	ABBBB	Ind	6 22/30
International Studies with Russian	M1R8	3FT deg	R	BBC	Ind	D+^	32	ABBBB	Ind	3
International Studies with Spanish	M1R4	4FT deg	L	BBC	Ind	D+^	32	ABBBB	Ind	10 22/24
Italian/Political Science	MR13	4FT deg	*	BBB	Ind	D*^	32	ABBB	Ind	
Law and Politics	MM31	3FT deg		AAB	DO	D$^ go	34$	CSYS	Ind	13 28/30
Modern Greek Studies/Political Science	MT12	4FT deg	* g	BBB	Ind	D*^	32	ABBB	Ind	
Philosophy and Political Science	VM71	3FT deg	*	BBC	Ind	D+^	32	ABBBB	Ind	6 22/27
Political Science	M100	3FT deg	*	BBB	Ind	D+^	32	ABBBB	Ind	8 22/30
Political Science/Portuguese	MR15	4FT deg	*	BBB	Ind	D*^	32	ABBB	Ind	
Political Science/Russian	MR18	4FT deg	*	BBB	Ind	D*^	32	ABBB	Ind	4
Public Policy, Government and Management	M148	3FT deg	*	BCC	Ind	D+^	30	BBBBB	Ind	3 18/26
Russian & E Eur Studs and Politics & Internat St	R8M1	3FT/4FT deg	R/*	BBC	Ind	D+^		ABBBB	Ind	7
Social Policy and Political Science	LM41	3FT deg	*	BBC	Ind	D+^	32	ABBBB	Ind	13
Sociology and Political Science	LM31	3FT deg	*	BBC	Ind	D+^	32	ABBBB	Ind	16

course details			98 expected requirements							96 entry stats	
TITLE	CODE	COURSE	SUBJECTS	A/AS	ND/C	AGNVQ	IB	SQA(H)	SQA	RATIO	A/AS
Univ of BRADFORD											
Economics/Politics	LM11	3FT deg	*	BB-CCC	Ind	M*4	Ind	Ind	Ind		
International Relations	M155	3FT deg	*	BBB	6D	D*^	Ind	Ind	Ind	3	14/17
Politics	M100	3FT deg	*	BB-CCC	Ind	M*4					
Politics and Society	ML13	3FT deg	*	BBB	6D	D*^	Ind	Ind	Ind	3	18/24
Politics with a Modern Language	TM21	4SW deg	L g	BBB-BCC	Ind	M$^	Ind	Ind	Ind		
Politics/History	MV11	3FT deg	*	BB-CCC	Ind	M*4	Ind	Ind	Ind	3	8/22
Univ of BRIGHTON											
Public Policy & Administration	M140	3FT deg	*	14-16	M0+1D	M$	Ind	BBCC	Ind		
Humanities	Y300	3FT deg	*	CC	Ind	Ind	Ind	Ind	Ind		
Politics											
Univ of BRISTOL											
Economics and Politics	LM11	3FT deg	* g	ABC	Ind	D$^	32$	CSYS	Ind	11	26/30
Philosophy and Politics	VM71	3FT deg	* g	ABB	Ind	D$^	32$	AABBB	Ind	24	28/30
Politics	M100	3FT deg	* g	AAB-ABB	Ind	D$^	34$	AAAAB	Ind	12	24/30
Politics and French	RM11	4FT deg	F	ABB	Ind	D$^	33$	ABBBB	Ind	10	26/30
Politics and German	RM21	4FT deg	G	BBB	Ind	D$^	32$	BBBBB	Ind	12	
Politics and Italian	RM31	4FT deg		BBB	Ind	D$^	32$	BBBBB	Ind	2	
Politics and Russian	RM81	4FT deg		BBB	Ind	D$^	32$	AABBB	Ind		
Politics and Sociology	ML13	3FT deg	* g	ABC	Ind	D$^	32$	ABBBB	Ind	11	28/30
Politics and Spanish	RM41	4FT deg		BBB-BBC	Ind	D$^	32$	ABBBB	Ind	10	
Social Policy and Politics	LM41	3FT deg	* g	BBC	Ind	D$^	26$	CSYS	Ind	36	
Theology and Politics	VM81	3FT deg	*	BBC	Ind	D$^	30$	BBBBB	Ind	11	
BRISTOL, Univ of the W of England											
Politics	M100▼	3FT deg	* g	14-16	5M-6M	M* go	24	BCCC	Ind		
BRUNEL Univ, West London											
European Politics	M146	3FT deg	F/G	BCC	5M	D^	28$	BBBCC$	Ind		
Politics and Contemporary Hist (4 Yrs Thick SW)	MV1D	4SW deg	*	BCC	5M	M^	28	BBBCC	Ind		
Politics and Contemporary History	MV1C	3FT deg	*	BCC	5M	M^	28	BBBCC	Ind	3	10/24
Politics and Contemporary History (4 Yr Thin SW)	MV11	4SW deg	*	BCC	5M	D^	28	BBBCC	Ind	3	8/26
Politics and Economics	LMCD	3FT deg	* g	BCC	5M	D^	28$	BBBCC	Ind	6	
Politics and Economics (4 Yrs Thick SW)	LM11	4SW deg	* g	BCC	5M	D^	28$	BBBCC	Ind		
Politics and Economics (4 Yrs Thin SW)	LM1C	4SW deg	* g	BCC	5M	D^	28$	BBBCC	Ind	6	
Politics and Philosophy	MV17	3FT deg	*	BCC	5M	D^	28	BBBCC	Ind		12/17
Politics and Social Policy	ML14	3FT deg	*	BCC	5M	D^	28	BBBCC	Ind	4	
Politics and Social Policy (4 Yrs Thick SW)	MLD4	4SW deg	*	BCC	5M	D^	28	BBBCC	Ind		
Politics and Social Policy (4 Yrs Thin SW)	MLC4	4SW deg	*	BCC	5M	D^	28	BBBCC	Ind	1	
Politics and Sociology	LM3C	3FT deg	*	BCC	5M	D^ go	28	BBBCC	Ind		
Politics and Sociology (4 Yrs Thin SW)	LM31	4SW deg	*	BCC	5M	D^ go	28	BBBCC	Ind	4	
Univ of BUCKINGHAM											
Economics with Politics	L1M1	2FT deg	M g	14	3M+2D	M	26	BCCC	Ind		
Law and Politics	MM13	2FT deg	*	16	3M+2D	M	26	CCCC	Ind		
Politics and History	MV11	2FT deg	* g	12	5M	M	24	CCCC	Ind		
Politics with Economics	M1L1	2FT deg	* g	14	3M+2D	M	26	BCCC	Ind		
Politics with French	M1R1	2FT deg	F	12	3M+2D	M	26	BCCC	Ind		
Politics with Spanish	M1R4	2FT deg	Sp	12	3M+2D	M	26	BCCC	Ind		
Politics, Economics and Law	Y618	2FT deg	* g	12	5M	M	24	CCCC	Ind		
Politics											

TITLE	CODE	COURSE	SUBJECTS	A/AS	ND/C	RGNVQ	IB	SQA(H)	SQA	RATIO	A/AS
course details			**98 expected requirements**							**96 entry stats**	
CAMBRIDGE Univ											
Social and Political Sciences	LM31▼	3FT deg	* g	AAA-AAB Ind			Ind	CSYS	Ind	4	28/30
CARDIFF Univ of Wales											
Law and Politics	MM31	3FT deg	*	BBB	Ind	Ind	Ind	Ind	Ind	11	22/28
Politics	M100	3FT deg		BBB-BCC			Ind	AABBB		5	20/30
Politics and Economics	LM11	3FT deg	*	BBC-BBB	7M+7D		Ind	AAAB	Ind	11	
Politics and Modern History	MV11	3FT deg	H	BBB-BCC	X		Ind	AABBB	X	7	20/24
Politics and Sociology	LM31	3FT deg	*	BCC						10	
Politics/Education	MX19	3FT deg	*	BBC	Ind	Ind	Ind	ABBBB	Ind	2	
Politics/French	MR11	4FT deg	F	BBC	Ind		Ind	ABBBB	Ind	15	
Politics/German	MR12	4FT deg	G	BCC	Ind		Ind	AABBB	X		
Politics/History of Ideas	MV1D	3FT deg		BBC			Ind	AABBB			
Politics/Italian	MR13	4FT deg	L	BCC	X		Ind	Ind	X		
Politics/Philosophy	MVC7	3FT deg		BBC			Ind	AABBB		8	
Portuguese/Politics	MR15	4FT deg	L	BBC-BCC	X		Ind	Ind	X		
Religious Studies/Politics	VM81	3FT deg		BBC							
Social Philosophy and Applied Ethics/Politics	VM71	3FT deg		BBC			Ind	AABBB			
Spanish/Politics	MR14	4FT deg	L	BBC-BCC	X		Ind	Ind	X		
Welsh/Politics	QM51	3FT deg	W	BBC							
Univ of CENTRAL ENGLAND											
Law with Politics	M3M1	3FT deg	*	CCC	M+5D	M	30	BBCC	Ind	2	10/18
Politics and Contemporary Governance	M142	3FT deg	*	14	MO	M	24	CCCC	Ind	3	10/16
Politics with Law	M1M3	3FT deg	*	14	MO	M	24	CCCC	Ind	4	8/14
Univ of CENTRAL LANCASHIRE											
European Politics and Culture	MT12	3FT deg									
European Studies	M1T2	3FT deg	*	12	MO	M$6/^	24	CCC	Ind		
International Accounting	M155	3FT deg	* g	14	MO+2D	M$6/^	26	BBCC	Ind		
Politics and Government	M140	3FT deg	*	12	Ind	M$6/^	26	BBCC	Ind		
Public Sector Management	M141	3FT deg	*	12	MO	M	26	BCCC	Ind		
Combined Honours Programme Politics	Y400	3FT deg	*	12	MO+3D	M$6/^	26	BCCC	Ind		
Public Administration	041M	2FT HND	*	DD	N	P$6	24	CCC	Ind		
COVENTRY Univ											
History and International Relations	MV11	3FT deg	*	CD	M	M	Ind	CCCC	Ind		
History and Politics	MV1C	3FT deg	*	CD	M	M	Ind	CCCC	Ind		
International Relations and Politics	MM11	3FT deg	*	CD	M	M	Ind	CCCC	Ind	1	
Politics and Geography	LM81	3FT/4SW deg	Po/Gy g	12	Ind	M	Ind	Ind	Ind	4	10/14
Social Policy and International Relations	LM41	3FT deg	*	CD	M	M	Ind	CCCC	Ind		
Social Policy and Politics	LM31	3FT deg	*	CD	M	M	Ind	CCCC	Ind		
Sociology and International Relations	LM3C	3FT deg	* g	CC-CD	3M+3D	M go	Ind	BBB	Ind		
Sociology and Politics	LM3D	3FT deg									
DE MONTFORT Univ											
Economics and Politics (Modular Scheme)	LM11▼	3FT deg	*	16	DO	D	Ind	Ind	Ind		
Politics	M100▼	3FT deg	* g	CCD	MO	M$	28$	ABBB	Ind	8	8/18
Politics and Psychology	LM71▼	3FT deg	*	16	DO	D	Ind	Ind	Ind		
Politics and Sociology	LM31▼	3FT deg	*	16	DO	D	Ind	Ind	Ind		
Public Administration and Managerial Studies	M140▼	4SW deg	* g	14	MO	M	26	CSYS	Ind	3	4/16
Public Policy and Management	M148▼	3FT deg	* g	8	3M	M	Dip	BBB	Ind	5	
Humanities Combined Honours International Relations	Y300▼	3FT deg	* g	CCD	MO	M^	30$	ABBB	Ind		

course details | 98 expected requirements | 96 entry stats

TITLE	CODE	COURSE	SUBJECTS	A/AS	NO/C	AGNVQ	IB	SQA(H)	SQA	RATIO	A/AS
Humanities Combined Honours *Politics*	Y300▼	3FT deg	* g	CCD	MO	M$^	26$	ABBB	Ind		
Humanities Joint Honours *International Relations*	Y301▼	3FT deg	* g	CCD	MO	M$^	28$	ABBB	Ind		
Humanities Joint Honours *Politics*	Y301▼	3FT deg	* g	CCD	MO	M$^	26$	ABBB	Ind		
Public Administration	041M▼	2FT HND	* g	4-6	3M	P	Dip	BBB	Ind	2	2/6

Univ of DUNDEE

TITLE	CODE	COURSE	SUBJECTS	A/AS	NO/C	AGNVQ	IB	SQA(H)	SQA	RATIO	A/AS
American Studies and Political Science	MQ14	4FT deg	* g	BCC	Ind	D$	29	BBBC	Ind	13	
Business Economics and Marketing & Political Sci	Y607	4FT deg	* g	BCC	Ind	D$	29	BBBC	Ind		
Contemporary European St and Political Science	MT12	4FT deg	* g	BCC	Ind	D$	29	BBBC	Ind	9	
Economics and Political Science	LM11	4FT deg	* g	BCC	Ind	D$	29	BBBC	Ind		
English and Political Science	MQ13	4FT deg	E g	BCC	Ind	D$^	29$	BBBC$	Ind	6	
Environmental Science and Political Science	FM91	4FT deg	* g	BCC	Ind	D$	29	BBBC	Ind	4	
Financial Economics and Political Science	LMC1	4FT deg	* g	BCC	Ind	D$	29	BBBC	Ind		
Geography and Political Science	LM81	4FT deg	* g	BCC	Ind	D$	29	BBBC	Ind	4	
Modern History and Political Science	MV11	4FT deg	* g	BCC	Ind	D$	29	BBBC	Ind	3	
Philosophy and Political Science	MV17	4FT deg	* g	BCC	Ind	D$	29	BBBC	Ind	11	
Political Science	M100	4FT deg	* g	BCC	Ind	D$	29	BBBC	Ind	8	
Political Science and Psychology	LM71	4FT deg	* g	BCC	Ind	D$	29	BBBC	Ind	5	
Arts and Social Sciences *Political Science*	Y400	3FT deg	* g	BCC	Ind	D$	29	BBBC	Ind		

Univ of DURHAM

TITLE	CODE	COURSE	SUBJECTS	A/AS	NO/C	AGNVQ	IB	SQA(H)	SQA	RATIO	A/AS
Arabic with Politics	T6M1	4FT deg	*	BBB	Ind	Ind	28	Ind	Ind	8	
Chinese with Politics	T3M1	4FT deg	*	BBC	Ind	Ind	31	AABBB	Ind	4	
Economics and Politics	LM11	3FT deg	* g	ABC	Ind	X	32$	AAABB	Ind	10	26/30
Japanese with Politics	T4M1	4FT deg	*	BBC	Ind	Ind	31	AABBB	Ind	4	
Law and Politics	MM13	3FT deg	*	ABB	DO	Ind	32	AAABB	HN	11	
Law with Politics	M3M1	3FT deg	*	AAB	DO	Ind	32	AAABB	HN	34	
Philosophy and Politics	MV17	3FT deg	*	BBB	Ind	Ind	32	AAABB	Ind	7	26/30
Politics	M100	3FT deg	*	BBB	Ind	Ind	Ind	Ind	Ind	11	22/30
Politics (European Studies)	M176	4FT deg	*	BBB	Ind	Ind	Ind	Ind	Ind	11	24/30
Politics and History	MV11	3FT deg	*	ABC	Ind	Ind	Ind	Ind	Ind	27	28/30
Politics and History of Middle East with Arabic	M1T6	3FT deg		BBC	Ind	Ind	28	Ind	Ind		
Politics and History of Middle East with Persian	M1TP	3FT deg		BBC	Ind	Ind	28	Ind	Ind		
Politics and History of Middle East with Turkish	M1TQ	3FT deg		BBC	Ind	Ind	28	Ind	Ind		
Politics and Sociology	LM31	3FT deg	*	BBB	Ind	Ind	Ind	Ind	Ind	8	26/30
Politics with Law	M1M3	3FT deg	*	BBB	Ind	Ind	Ind	Ind	Ind		
Russian and Politics	MR18	4FT deg	*	24	Ind	Ind	33	AAABB	Ind	4	
Social Sciences Combined *Politics*	Y220	3FT deg	*	ABC	MO	Ind	32	AAABB	Ind		

Univ of EAST ANGLIA

TITLE	CODE	COURSE	SUBJECTS	A/AS	NO/C	AGNVQ	IB	SQA(H)	SQA	RATIO	A/AS
Economic and Social History and Politics	MV13	3FT deg	*	BBC	3M+3D		30	BBBBB	Ind	3	
History and Politics	MV11	3FT deg	H	BBB-BCC	X		30	BBBBB	X	11	18/24
History, American with Politics	V1M1	4FT deg	H	BBC-BCC	X		30	ABBBB	Ind	5	
Philosophy and Politics	MV17	3FT deg	*	BBC	3M+3D		30	BBBBB	Ind	5	
Politics	M100	3FT deg	*	BBC	3M+3D		30	BBBBB	Ind	3	14/26
Politics and Economics	LM11	3FT deg	*	BBC	3M+3D		30	BBBBB	Ind	5	20/28
Politics and Sociology	ML13	3FT deg	*	BBC	3M+3D		30	BBBBB	Ind	6	
Politics with a Modern European Language	M1T2	4FT deg	L/*	BBC	3M+3D		30	BBBBB	Ind	15	

Politics
62

TITLE	CODE	COURSE	SUBJECTS	A/AS	ND/C	AGNVQ	IB	SQA(H)	SQA	RATIO A/AS
Univ of EAST LONDON										
Economics and Politics	LM11	3FT deg	* g	12	MO	M	Ind	Ind	Ind	6
Economics with Politics	L1M1	3FT deg	* g	12	MO	M	Ind			
French and Politics	MR11	3FT deg	* g	12	MO	M	Ind	Ind	Ind	
French with Politics	R1M1	3FT deg	* g	12	MO	M				
German and Politics	MR12	3FT deg	* g	12	MO	M	Ind	Ind	Ind	
German with Politics	R2M1	3FT deg	* g	12	MO	M	Ind			
Health Studies and Politics	LM4D	3FT deg	* g	12	MO	M				
Health Studies with Politics	L4M1	3FT deg	* g	12	MO	M				
History and Politics	MV11	3FT deg	* g	12	MO	M	Ind	Ind	Ind	26
History with Politics	V1M1	3FT deg	* g	12	MO	M	Ind	Ind		
Information Technology and Politics	MG15	3FT deg	* g	12	MO	M	Ind	Ind	Ind	
Information Technology with Politics	G5M1	3FT deg	* g	12	MO	M	Ind	Ind	Ind	
Literature and Politics	MQ13	3FT deg	* g	12	N	M	Ind	Ind	Ind	6
Literature with Politics	Q3MC	3FT deg	* g	12	MO	M	Ind			
Political Economy	M100	3FT deg	* g	12	MO	M	Ind	Ind	Ind	2
Politics	M101	3FT deg	* g	12	MO	M	Ind	Ind	Ind	9 8/10
Politics and Social Policy Research	LM41	3FT deg	* g	12	N	M	Ind	Ind	Ind	4
Politics and Social Sciences	LMH1	3FT deg	* g	12	MO	MB	Ind	Ind	Ind	
Politics and Sociology	LM31	3FT deg	* g	12	MO	M$	Ind	Ind	Ind	19
Politics and Spanish	MR14	3FT deg	* g	12	MO	M^	Ind	Ind	Ind	
Politics and Third World & Development Studies	MM91	3FT deg	* g	12	MO	M	Ind			
Politics with Business Studies	M1N1	3FT deg	* g	12	MO	M	Ind			
Politics with Economics	M1L1	3FT deg	* g	12	MO	M	Ind			
Politics with French	M1R1	3FT deg	* g	12	MO	M	Ind			
Politics with German	M1R2	3FT deg	* g	12	MO	M	Ind			
Politics with Health Studies	M1LK	3FT deg	* g	12	MO	M				
Politics with History	M1V1	3FT deg	* g	12	MO	M	Ind			
Politics with Information Technology	M1G5	3FT deg	* g	12	MO	M	Ind			
Politics with Italian	M1R3	3FT deg	* g	12	MO	M	Ind			
Politics with Literature	M1Q3	3FT deg	* g	12	MO	M	Ind			
Politics with Social Policy Research	M1L4	3FT deg	* g	12	MO	M	Ind			
Politics with Social Sciences	M1L3	3FT deg	* g	12	MO	M	Ind			
Politics with Sociology	M1LH	3FT deg	* g	12	MO	M	Ind			
Politics with Spanish	M1R4	3FT deg	* g	12	MO	M	Ind			
Politics with Third World & Development Studies	M1M9	3FT deg	* g	12	MO	M	Ind			
Politics/Business Studies	MN11	3FT deg	* g	12	MO	M	Ind	Ind	Ind	
Social Sciences with Politics	L3M1	3FT deg	* g	12	MO	M	Ind	Ind	Ind	
Sociology with Politics	L3MC	3FT deg	* g	12	MO	M	Ind	Ind	Ind	
Spanish with Politics	R4M1	3FT deg	* g	12	MO	M	Ind			
Three-Subject Degree _Politics_	Y600	3FT dcg	* g	12	MO	M	Ind	Ind	Ind	
EDGE HILL Univ COLLEGE										
Politics	M104	3FT deg	*	CC	3M+3D	M* / P*^	Dip	BBCC	Ind	2 4/14
Urban Policy Studies	LM3C	3FT deg	*	DD	X	P*_		BBCC	X	
Urban Policy Studies	LM31	3FT deg	*	DD	X	P*_	Dip	BBCC	X	
Univ of EDINBURGH										
Arabic and Politics	TM61	4FT deg	g	BBB	Ind	Ind	Dip$	BBBB	Ind	
Economics and Politics	LM11	4FT deg	g	ABB	Ind		36$	AABB	Ind	7
French and Politics	RM11	4FT deg	E g	BBB	Ind	Ind	Dip$	BBBB$	Ind	
Geography and Politics	LM81	4FT deg	*	ABB	Ind		36$	AABB	Ind	8

TITLE	CODE	COURSE	SUBJECTS	A/AS	ND/C	AGNVQ	IB	SQA(H)	SQA	RATIO A/AS
course details				*98 expected requirements*						*96 entry stats*
German and Politics	RM21	4FT deg	L g	BBB	Ind	Ind	Dip$	BBBB$	Ind	
Law and Politics	MM31	4FT deg	g	ABB	X		32	AAABB	X	8
Modern European Languages and Euro Union Studies	TM21	4FT deg	L g	BBB	Ind	Ind	Dip$	BBBB$	Ind	
Persian and Politics	MT16	4FT deg	g	BBB	Ind	Ind	Dip$	BBBB$	Ind	
Philosophy and Politics	VM71	4FT deg	g	BBB	Ind	Ind	Dip$	BBBB	Ind	
Politics	M100	4FT deg	*	ABB	Ind		36$	AABB	Ind	7
Politics and Economic and Social History	MV13	4FT deg	*	ABB	Ind		36$	AABB	Ind	5
Politics and Modern History	MV11	4FT deg	g	BBB	Ind	Ind	Dip$	BBBB	Ind	
Politics with Environmental Studies	M1F9	4FT deg		ABB			36	AABB		
Politics with Gender Studies	M1M9	4FT deg		ABB			36	AABB		
Scandinavian Studies and Politics	RM71	4FT deg	L g	BBC	Ind	Ind	Dip$	BBBC$	Ind	
Social Policy and Politics	LM41	4FT deg	*	ABB	Ind		36$	AABB	Ind	8
Sociology and Politics	LM31	4FT deg	*	ABB	Ind		36$	AABB	Ind	12
Spanish and Politics	RM41	4FT deg	L g	BBB	Ind	Ind	Dip$	BBBB$	Ind	
Spanish and Portuguese with European Union Studs	RM61	4FT deg	L g	BBB	Ind	Ind	Dip$	BBBB$	Ind	
Social Science *Politics*	Y200	3FT deg	*	ABB	Ind		36$	AABB	Ind	

Univ of ESSEX

TITLE	CODE	COURSE	SUBJECTS	A/AS	ND/C	AGNVQ	IB	SQA(H)	SQA	RATIO A/AS
Economics and Politics	LM11	3FT deg	* g	22	MO+2D	D	28	BBBB	Ind	16
History and Politics	MV11	3FT deg	*	20	MO+2D	Ind	28	BBBB	Ind	9 16/20
Philosophy and Politics	MV17	3FT deg	*	20	MO+2D	Ind	28	BBBB	Ind	5 16/18
Politics	M100	3FT deg	*	22	MO+2D	Ind	28	BBBB	Ind	7 16/28
Politics and Sociology	LM31	3FT deg	*	22	MO+2D	Ind	28	BBBB	Ind	5 16/28

Univ of EXETER

TITLE	CODE	COURSE	SUBJECTS	A/AS	ND/C	AGNVQ	IB	SQA(H)	SQA	RATIO A/AS
Economic & Political Development	LMD1	3FT deg	* g	BBB-CCC	2M+3D	M/D$	30	Ind	Ind	4 18/28
Economic & Political Development with Euro Study	LMDC	4FT deg	g	BBB-CCC	2M+3D	M/D$	30	Ind	Ind	3
Economics and Politics	LM11	3FT deg	* g	ABC	2M+3D	D$	36	Ind	Ind	5 16/28
Economics and Politics with European Study	LM1C	4FT deg	L g	ABC	2M+3D	D$	36	Ind	Ind	8
History and Politics	MV11	3FT deg	*	ABB-BBC	MO	M/D$	34	Ind	Ind	8 22/30
History and Politics with European Study	VM11	4FT deg	L	ABB-BBC	MO	M/D$	34$	Ind	Ind	5
Italian and Politics	MR13	4FT deg	L g	20-22	MO	M$	32	Ind	Ind	
Politics	M100	3FT deg	*	ABB-BBC	MO	D$	34	Ind	Ind	5 16/30
Politics and Society	LM31	3FT deg	*	ABB-BBC	MO	D$	34	Ind	Ind	13 16/22
Politics with European Study	M101	4FT deg	*	ABB-BBC	MO	D$	34	Ind	Ind	20

Univ of GLAMORGAN

TITLE	CODE	COURSE	SUBJECTS	A/AS	ND/C	AGNVQ	IB	SQA(H)	SQA	RATIO A/AS
Economics and Politics	LM1D	3FT deg								
Economics and Public Policy	LM1C	3FT deg								
Government and Economics	ML11	3FT deg	* g	12	MO+1D	M	Ind	Ind	Ind	
Government and History	MV11	3FT deg	* g	12	Ind	Ind	Ind	Ind	Ind	
Government and Law	MM13	3FT deg	* g	18	MO+3D	D	Ind	Ind	Ind	
Government and Philosophy	MV17	3FT deg	* g	12	Ind	Ind	Ind	Ind	Ind	
Government and Politics	M142	3FT deg	* g	12	MO+1D	M	Ind	Ind	Ind	
Government with American Business	M1NC	3FT deg	* g	12-14	MO+3D	M	Ind	Ind	Ind	
Government with American Studies	M1Q4	3FT deg	* g	12	Ind	Ind	Ind	Ind	Ind	
Government with European & International Bus	M1ND	3FT deg	* g	12-14	MO+3D$	M$	Ind	Ind	Ind	
Government with Leisure and Tourism	M1P7	3FT deg	* g	12-14	MO+3D$	M$	Ind	Ind	Ind	
Politics and Public Policy	M143	3FT deg								
Public Management and Statistics	GM4D	3FT deg								
Public Policy and Statistics	GM4C	3FT deg								
Combined Studies (Honours) *Government and Politics*	Y400	3FT deg	* g	8-16	Ind	Ind	Ind	Ind	Ind	

Politics 62

course details | 98 expected requirements | 96 entry stats

TITLE	CODE	COURSE	SUBJECTS	A/AS	ND/C	AGNVQ	IB	SQA(H)	SQA	RATIO A/AS
Joint Honours *Government and Politics*	Y401	3FT deg	* g	8-16	Ind	Ind	Ind	Ind	Ind	
Major/Minor Honours *Government and Politics*	Y402	3FT deg	* g	8-16	Ind	Ind	Ind	Ind	Ind	

Univ of GLASGOW

TITLE	CODE	COURSE	SUBJECTS	A/AS	ND/C	AGNVQ	IB	SQA(H)	SQA	RATIO A/AS
Archaeology/Politics	MV16	4FT deg		BBC	HN	M	30	BBBB	Ind	
Business Economics/Politics	LMC1	4FT deg		BBC	N	M	30	BBBB	N	
Celtic/Politics	MQ15	4FT deg		BBC	HN	M	30	BBBB	Ind	
Classical Civilisation/Politics	MQ18	4FT deg		BBC	HN	M	30	BBBB	Ind	
Classical Hebrew/Politics	MV1W	4FT deg		BBC	HN	M	30	BBBB	Ind	
Computing/Politics	GM51	4FT deg		BBC	HN	M	30	BBBB	Ind	4
Czech/Politics	MT11	5FT deg		BBC	HN	M	30	BBBB	Ind	
Economic and Social History/Politics	MV13	4FT deg		BBC	8M	M	30	BBBB	Ind	6
Economics/Politics	LM11	4FT deg		BBC	8M	M	30	BBBB	Ind	4
English/Politics	MQ13	4FT deg		BBC	HN	M	30	BBBB	Ind	6
Film and Television Studies/Politics	MW15	4FT deg		BBB	HN	D	32	AABB	HN	12
French/Politics	MR11	5FT deg		BBC	HN	M	30	BBBB	Ind	3
Geography/Politics	LM81	4FT deg		BBC	8M	M	30	BBBB	Ind	5
German/Politics	MR12	5FT deg		BBC	HN	M	30	BBBB	Ind	
Greek/Politics	MQ17	4FT deg		BBC	HN	M	30	BBBB	Ind	
Hispanic Studies/Politics	MR14	5FT deg		BBC	HN	M	30	BBBB	Ind	4
History of Art/Politics	MV14	4FT deg		BBC	HN	M	30	BBBB	Ind	
History/Politics	MVC1	4FT deg		BBC	HN	M	30	BBBB	Ind	9 22/26
Islamic Studies/Politics	TM61	4FT deg		BBC	N	M	30	BBBB	Ind	
Italian/Politics	MR13	5FT deg		BBC	HN	M	30	BBBB	Ind	
Latin/Politics	MQ16	4FT deg		BBC	HN	M	30	BBBB	Ind	
Management Studies/Politics	MN11	4FT deg		BBC	8M	M	30	BBBB	Ind	6
Mathematics/Politics	GM11	4FT deg		BBC	HN	M	30	BBBB	Ind	
Music/Politics	MW13	4FT deg		BBC	HN	M	30	BBBB	Ind	
Philosophy/Politics	MVC7	4FT deg		BBC	HN	M	30	BBBB	Ind	8
Philosophy/Politics	MV17	4FT deg		BBC	8M	M	30	BBBB	Ind	5
Polish/Politics	MTC1	5FT deg		BBC	HN	M	30	BBBB	Ind	
Politics	M102	4FT deg		BBC	8M	M	30	BBBB	Ind	7
Politics	M100	4FT deg		BBC	HN	M	30	BBBB	Ind	6
Politics with Celtic	M1Q5	4FT deg		BBC	8M	M	30	BBBB	Ind	
Politics with Czech	M1T1	4FT deg		BBC	8M	M	30	BBBB	Ind	
Politics with French	M1R1	4FT deg		BBC	8M	M	30	BBBB	Ind	7
Politics with German	M1R2	4FT deg		BBC	8M	M	30	BBBB	Ind	
Politics with Hispanic Studies	M1R4	4FT deg		BBC	8M	M	30	BBBB	Ind	
Politics with Italian	M1R3	4FT deg		BBC	8M	M	30	BBBB	Ind	
Politics with Polish	M1TC	4FT deg		BBC	8M	M	30	BBBB	Ind	
Politics with Russian	M1R8	4FT deg		BBC	8M	M	30	BBBB	Ind	
Politics/Archaeology	VM61	4FT deg		BBC	8M	M	30	BBBB	Ind	
Politics/Classical Civilisation	MQ1V	4FT deg		BBC	8M	M	30	BBBB	Ind	
Politics/Computing Science	MG15	4FT deg		BBC	8M	M	30	BBBB	Ind	
Politics/History	MV1D	4FT deg		BBC	8M	M	30	BBBB	Ind	5
Politics/Mathematics	MG11	4FT deg		BBC	8M	M	30	BBBB	Ind	1
Politics/Psychology	CM8C	4FT deg		BBC	HN	M	30	BBBB	Ind	16
Politics/Psychology	CM81	4FT deg		BBC	8M	M	30	BBBB	Ind	4
Politics/Russian	MR18	5FT deg		BBC	HN	M	30	BBBB	Ind	
Politics/Scottish History	MVCC	4FT deg		BBC	8M	M	30	BBBB	Ind	2
Politics/Scottish History	MV1C	4FT deg		BBC	HN	M	30	BBBB	Ind	5

TITLE	CODE	COURSE	SUBJECTS	A/AS	ND/C	AGNVQ	IB	SQA(H)	SQA	RATIO	A/AS
Politics/Scottish Literature	MQ12	4FT deg		BBC	HN	M	30	BBBB	Ind		
Politics/Social and Urban Policy	LM41	4FT deg		BBC	8M	M	30	BBBB	Ind	3	
Politics/Sociology	LM31	4FT deg		BBC	8M	M	30	BBBB	Ind	3	20/28
Theatre Studies/Politics	MW14	4FT deg		BBC	HN	M	30	BBBB	Ind	7	
Theology & Religious Studies/Politics	MV1V	4FT deg		BBC	HN	M	30	BBBB	Ind	6	

GLASGOW CALEDONIAN Univ

TITLE	CODE	COURSE	SUBJECTS	A/AS	ND/C	AGNVQ	IB	SQA(H)	SQA	RATIO	A/AS
Public Administration and Management	MN11	3FT/4FT deg	E+Po	CC	Ind		Ind	BBB$	Ind	3	

GOLDSMITHS COLL (Univ of London)

TITLE	CODE	COURSE	SUBJECTS	A/AS	ND/C	AGNVQ	IB	SQA(H)	SQA	RATIO	A/AS
Economics, Politics and Public Policy	LM11	3FT deg		BCD	MO	M	Dip	BCCCC	N	4	4/20
Politics with Economics	M1L1	3FT deg		BCD	MO	M	Dip	BBBBC	N	2	8/22
Social Policy with Politics	L4M1	3FT deg		BCD	MO	M	Dip	BBBBC	N		

Univ of GREENWICH

TITLE	CODE	COURSE	SUBJECTS	A/AS	ND/C	AGNVQ	IB	SQA(H)	SQA	RATIO	A/AS
Politics	M100	3FT deg	*g	10	MO	M	25	BBB	Ind		
Humanities	Y301	3FT deg	*g	10	MO	M	25	BBB	Ind		
Politics											

Univ of HERTFORDSHIRE

TITLE	CODE	COURSE	SUBJECTS	A/AS	ND/C	AGNVQ	IB	SQA(H)	SQA	RATIO	A/AS
Politics/Economics	M1L1	3FT deg	*g	14	M+D	Ind	26	BBCC			
Politics/Social Policy	M1L4	3FT deg	*g	14	M+D	Ind	26	BBCC	Ind		
Politics/Sociology	M1L3	3FT deg	*g	14	M+D	Ind	26	BBCC	Ind		
Social Policy/Politics	L4M1	3FT deg	*g	14	M+D	Ind	26	BBCC	Ind		
Sociology/Politics	L3MC	3FT deg	*g	14	M+D	Ind	26	BBCC	Ind		

Univ of HUDDERSFIELD

TITLE	CODE	COURSE	SUBJECTS	A/AS	ND/C	AGNVQ	IB	SQA(H)	SQA	RATIO	A/AS
German with Politics	R2M1	4FT deg	G	CCE	Ind	Ind	Ind	BBBC	Ind		
Politics	M100	3FT deg	*	14	MO+3D	M6/^	Ind	BBBC	Ind		
Politics and Economics	ML11	3FT deg	*	14	MO+3D	M6/^	Ind	BBBC	Ind		
Politics with Contemporary History	M1V1	3FT deg	*	14	MO+3D	M6/^	Ind	BBBC	Ind		
Politics with Media Studies	M1P4	3FT deg	*	14	MO+3D	M6/^	Ind	BBBC	Ind		
Politics with Sociology	M1L3	3FT deg	*	14	MO+3D	M6/^	Ind	BBBC	Ind		
Spanish with Politics	R4M1	4FT deg	Sp	CCE	Ind	Ind	Ind	BBBC	Ind	•	

Univ of HULL

TITLE	CODE	COURSE	SUBJECTS	A/AS	ND/C	AGNVQ	IB	SQA(H)	SQA	RATIO	A/AS
British Politics and Legislative Studies (4 Yrs)	M140	4FT deg	*	BBB-BCC	Ind	Ind	28	BBBCC	Ind	2	20/30
European Politics and Legislative Studs (4 Yrs)	M170	4FT deg	F	BBB-BCC	Ind $	Ind	28$	BBBCC	Ind	4	
French/Politics	RM11	4FT deg	F	BBB-BCC	Ind	Ind	28$	BBBCC	Ind	12	
History/Politics	MV11	3FT deg	H	BBC-BCC	Ind	Ind	28	BBBCC	Ind	14	22/26
Law and Politics	MM13	3FT deg	*	BBB	MO	D$^ gi	28$	ABBBB	Ind	4	22/28
Philosophy/Politics	MV17	3FT deg	*	BBC-BCC	MO	M$6/^ go	28	BBBCC	Ind	7	
Politics	M100	3FT deg	*	BBB-BCC	Ind	Ind	28	BBCCC	Ind	4	16/28
Politics and International Relations	M154	3FT deg	*	BBB-BCC	Ind	Ind	28	BBCCC	Ind	4	18/26
Politics with Management	M1N1	3FT deg	*g	BBC-BCC	MO $	M*6/^ go	28$	BBCCC	Ind		
Politics/Social Policy	LM41	3FT deg	*	BBB-BCC	Ind	Ind	28$	BBCCC	Ind	7	
Politics/Sociology	LM31	3FT deg	*	BBC-BCC	Ind	Ind	28$	BBCCC	Ind	20	
Politics, Philosophy, Economics	Y616	3FT deg	*	BBB	MO+2D	Ind	28	BBBCC	Ind		
Politics											

KEELE Univ

TITLE	CODE	COURSE	SUBJECTS	A/AS	ND/C	AGNVQ	IB	SQA(H)	SQA	RATIO	A/AS
Int Pol and German/Russian or Russian St (4 Yrs)	TMYC	4FT deg	G	BCC	Ind	Ind	30$	BBBB	Ind		
Int Politics and Classical Studies (4 Yrs)	QM8C	4FT deg	*	BCC	Ind	Ind	28	BBBB	Ind		
Int Politics and French/Russian or Russian Studs	MTCX	3FT deg	F+R	BBC	Ind	D$^	30$	CSYS	Ind		
Int Politics and German/Russian or Russian Studs	MTCY	3FT deg	G+R	BBC	Ind	D$^	30$	CSYS	Ind		
International Politics and American Studies	MQC4	3FT deg	*	BCC	Ind	Ind	28	CSYS	Ind	5	

Politics 62

		course details		98 expected requirements						96 entry stats	
TITLE	CODE	COURSE	SUBJECTS	A/AS	NO/C	RGNVQ	IB	SQA(H)	SQA	RATIO A/AS	
International Politics and Ancient Hist (4 Yrs)	VMDC	4FT deg	*	BCC	Ind	Ind	28	BBBB	Ind		
International Politics and Ancient History	MVCD	3FT deg	*	BCC	Ind	Ind	28	CSYS	Ind		
International Politics and Astrophysics	FM5C	3FT deg	P g	BCC	Ind	D$^	28$	CSYS	Ind		
International Politics and Astrophysics (4 Yrs)	MFC5	4FT deg	*	BCC	Ind	Ind	28	BBBB	Ind		
International Politics and Biochemistry	CM7C	3FT deg	C	BCC	Ind	D$^	28$	CSYS	Ind		
International Politics and Biochemistry (4 Yrs)	MCC7	4FT deg	*	BCC	Ind	Ind	28	BBBB	Ind		
International Politics and Biology	CM1C	3FT deg	S g	BCC	Ind	D$^	28$	CSYS	Ind		
International Politics and Biology (4 Yrs)	MCC1	4FT deg	*	BCC	Ind	Ind	28	BBBB	Ind		
International Politics and Business Admin(4 Yrs)	NM9C	4FT deg	*	BCC	Ind	Ind	28	BBBB	Ind		
International Politics and Classical Studies	MQC8	3FT deg	*	BCC	Ind	Ind	28	CSYS	Ind		
International Politics and Computer Science	GM5C	3FT deg	* g	BCC	Ind	Ind	28	CSYS	Ind		
International Politics and Criminology	MMHC	3FT deg	*	BBB	Ind	Ind	32	CSYS	Ind		
International Politics and Criminology (4 Yrs)	MMCH	4FT deg	*	BBB	Ind	Ind	32	BBBB	Ind		
International Politics and Economics	LM1C	3FT deg	* g	BCC	Ind	Ind	28	CSYS	Ind	3	
International Politics and Educational Studies	MXC9	3FT deg	*	BCC	Ind	Ind	28	CSYS	Ind		
International Politics and Elect Music (4 Yrs)	WMJC	4FT deg	*	BCC	Ind	Ind	28	BBBB	Ind	2	
International Politics and Electronic Music	MWCJ	3FT deg	Mu	BCC	Ind	D$^	28$	CSYS	Ind		
International Politics and English	QM3C	4FT deg	*	BBC	Ind	D$^	30	BBBB	Ind		
International Politics and English	MQC3	3FT deg	E	BBC	Ind	D$^	30$	CSYS	Ind		
International Politics and Finance	MNC3	3FT deg	* g	BCC	Ind	Ind	28	CSYS	Ind		
International Politics and Finance (4 Yrs)	NM3C	4FT deg	*	BCC	Ind	Ind	28	BBBB	Ind		
International Politics and French/German	MTC9	3FT deg	F+G	BBC	Ind	D$^	30$	CSYS	Ind		
International Politics and Geography	LM8C	3FT deg	Gy	BCC	Ind	D$^	28$	CSYS	Ind	2	16/22
International Politics and Geography (4 Yrs)	MLC8	4FT deg	*	BCC	Ind	Ind	28	BBBB	Ind		
International Politics and Geology	MFC6	4FT deg	*	BCC	Ind	Ind	28	BBBB	Ind		
International Politics and Geology	FM6C	3FT deg	S	BCC	Ind	D$^	28$	CSYS	Ind		
International Politics and German	MRC2	3FT deg	G	BCC	Ind	D$^	28$	CSYS	Ind		
International Politics and German (4 Yrs)	RM2C	4FT deg	G	BCC	Ind	Ind	28$	BBBB	Ind		
International Politics and History	MVC1	3FT deg	*	BCC	Ind	Ind	28	CSYS	Ind	6	18/24
International Politics and History (4 Yrs)	VM1C	4FT deg	*	BCC	Ind	Ind	28	BBBB	Ind	5	
International Politics and Human Resource Mgt	NM6C	4FT deg	*	BBC-BCC	Ind	Ind	28	BBBB	Ind	3	
International Politics and Human Resource Mgt	MNC6	3FT deg	*	BCC	Ind	Ind	28	CSYS	Ind		
International Politics and International History	MVCC	3FT deg	*	BCC	Ind	Ind	28	CSYS	Ind		
International Politics and International History	VMCC	4FT deg	*	BCC	Ind	Ind	28	BBBB	Ind	7	
International Politics and Latin (4 Yrs)	QM6C	4FT deg	*	BCC	Ind	Ind	28	BBBB	Ind		
International Politics and Mathematics	GM1C	3FT deg	M	BCC	Ind	D$^	28$	CSYS	Ind		
International Politics and Statistics	GM4C	3FT deg	M	BCC	Ind	D$^	28$	CSYS	Ind		
International Relations	M154	3FT deg	*	BCC	Ind	Ind	28	CSYS	Ind	5	16/22
International Relations (4 Yrs)	M155	4FT deg	*	BCC	Ind	Ind	28	BBBB	Ind	6	
Latin and International Politics	MQC6	3FT deg	Ln	BCC	Ind	D$^	28$	CSYS	Ind		
Law and International Politics	MMC3	3FT deg	*	BBB	Ind	Ind	32	BBBB	Ind	3	
Law and International Politics (4 Yrs)	MM3C	4FT deg	*	BBB	Ind	Ind	32	CSYS	Ind		
Mathematics and International Politics	MGC1	4FT deg	*	BCC	Ind	Ind	28	BBBB	Ind		
Music and International Politics	MWC3	3FT deg	Mu	BCC	Ind	D$^	28$	CSYS	Ind		
Music and International Politics (4 Yrs)	WM3C	4FT deg	*	BCC	Ind	Ind	28	BBBB	Ind		
Philosophy and International Politics	VM7C	4FT deg	*	BCC	Ind	Ind	28	BBBB	Ind		
Philosophy and International Politics	MVC7	3FT deg	*	BCC	Ind	Ind	28	CSYS	Ind	2	
Physics and International Politics	FM3C	3FT deg	P g	BCC	Ind	D$^	28$	CSYS	Ind		
Physics and International Politics (4 Yrs)	MFC3	4FT deg	*	BCC	Ind	Ind	28	BBBB	Ind		
Politics and American Studies	MQ14	3FT deg	*	BBC-BCC	Ind	Ind	30	CSYS	Ind	3	18/20
Politics and American Studies (4 Yrs)	QM41	4FT deg	*	BBC-BCC	Ind	Ind	30	BBBB	Ind	14	
Politics and Ancient History	MV1D	3FT deg	*	BCC	Ind	Ind	28	CSYS	Ind	4	

course details

TITLE	CODE	COURSE	SUBJECTS	A/AS	NQ/C	AGNVQ	IB	SQA(H)	SQA	RATIO A/AS
Politics and Ancient History (4 Yrs)	VMD1	4FT deg	*	BCC	Ind	Ind	28	BBBB	Ind	
Politics and Applied Social Studies	LM51	3FT deg	*	BBC	Ind	Ind	30	CSYS	Ind	2
Politics and Applied Social Studies (4 Yrs)	ML15	4FT deg	*	BBC-BCC	Ind	Ind	28	BBBB	Ind	
Politics and Astrophysics	FM51	3FT deg	P g	BCC	Ind	D$^	28$	CSYS	Ind	
Politics and Astrophysics (4 Yrs)	MF15	4FT deg	*	BCC	Ind	Ind	28	BBBB	Ind	
Politics and Biological & Medicinal Chem (4 Yrs)	MF1C	4FT deg	*	BCC	Ind	Ind	28	BBBB	Ind	
Politics and Biological and Medicinal Chemistry	FMC1	3FT deg	C g	BCC	Ind	D$^	28$	CSYS	Ind	
Politics and Biology (4 Yrs)	MC11	4FT deg	* g	BCC	Ind	Ind	28	BBBB	Ind	
Politics and Business Administration	MN19	3FT deg	*	BCC	Ind	Ind	28	CSYS	Ind	18
Politics and Business Administration (4 Yrs)	NM91	4FT deg	*	BCC	Ind	Ind	28	BBBB	Ind	4
Politics and Chemistry	FM11	3FT deg	C g	BCC	Ind	D$^	28$	CSYS	Ind	
Politics and Chemistry (4 Yrs)	MF11	4FT deg	*	BCC	Ind	Ind	28	BBBB	Ind	
Politics and Classical Studies	MQ18	3FT deg	*	BCC	Ind	Ind	28	CSYS	Ind	2
Politics and Classical Studies (4 Yrs)	QM81	4FT deg	*	BCC	Ind	Ind	28	BBBB	Ind	
Politics and Computer Science	GM51	3FT deg	* g	BCC	Ind	D$^	28	CSYS	Ind	
Politics and Computer Science (4 Yrs)	MG15	4FT deg	*	BCC	Ind	Ind	28	BBBB	Ind	
Politics and Economics	LM11	3FT deg	* g	BCC	Ind	D$^	28	CSYS	Ind	4 17/22
Politics and Economics (4 Yrs)	ML11	4FT deg	*	BCC	Ind	Ind	28	BBBB	Ind	
Politics and Educational Studies	MX19	3FT deg	*	BCC	Ind	Ind	28	CSYS	Ind	
Politics and Educational Studies (4 Yrs)	XM91	4FT deg	*	BCC	Ind	Ind	28	BBBB	Ind	
Politics and Electronic Music	MW1J	3FT deg	Mu	BCC	Ind	D$^	28$	CSYS	Ind	
Politics and Electronic Music (4 Yrs)	WMJ1	4FT deg	*	BCC	Ind	Ind	28	BBBB	Ind	
Politics and Environmental Management	FMX1	3FT deg	* g	BCC	Ind	D$^	28	CSYS	Ind	4
Politics and Environmental Management (4 Yrs)	MF1X	4FT deg	*	BCC	Ind	Ind	28	BBBB	Ind	
Politics and Finance	MN13	3FT deg	* g	BCC	Ind	Ind	28	CSYS	Ind	
Politics and Finance (4 Yrs)	NM31	4FT deg	*	BCC	Ind	Ind	28	BBBB	Ind	
Politics and French	MR11	3FT deg	F	BCC	Ind	D$^	28$	CSYS	Ind	4
Politics and French (4 Yrs)	RM11	4FT deg	*	BCC	Ind	Ind	28	BBBB	Ind	
Politics and French/German	MT19	3FT deg	F+G	BBC	Ind	D$^	30$	CSYS	Ind	
Politics and French/German (4 Yrs)	TM91	4FT deg	G g	BCC	Ind	Ind	28$	BBBB	Ind	
Politics and French/Russian or Russ St (4 Yrs)	TMX1	4FT deg	*	BCC	Ind	Ind	28	BBBB	Ind	
Politics and French/Russian or Russian Studies	MT1X	3FT deg	F+R	BBC	Ind	D$^	30$	CSYS	Ind	
Politics and Geography	LM81	3FT deg	Gy	BCC	Ind	D$^	28$	CSYS	Ind	6
Politics and Geography (4 Yrs)	ML18	4FT deg	*	BCC	Ind	Ind	28	BBBB	Ind	
Politics and German	MR12	3FT deg	G	BCC	Ind	D$^	28$	CSYS	Ind	
Politics and German (4 Yrs)	RM21	4FT deg	G	BCC	Ind	Ind	28$	BBBB	Ind	
Politics and German/Russian or Russian Studies	TMY1	4FT deg	G g	BCC	Ind	Ind	28$	BBBB	Ind	
Politics and German/Russian or Russian Studies	MT1Y	3FT deg	G+R	BBC	Ind	D$^	30$	CSYS	Ind	
Politics and History	MV11	3FT deg	*	BBC-BCC	Ind	Ind	28	CSYS	Ind	4 18/24
Politics and History (4 Yrs)	VM11	4FT deg	*	BBC-BCC	Ind	Ind	28	BBBB	Ind	9
Politics and International Politics	M151	3FT deg	*	BCC	Ind	Ind	28	CSYS	Ind	
Politics and International Politics (4 Yrs)	M150	4FT deg	*	BCC	Ind	Ind	28	BBBB	Ind	14
Politics and Latin	MQ16	3FT deg	Ln	BCC	Ind	D$^	28$	CSYS	Ind	
Politics and Latin (4 Yrs)	QM61	4FT deg	*	BCC	Ind	Ind	28	BBBB	Ind	
Politics and Law	MM13	3FT deg	*	BBB	Ind	Ind	32	CSYS	Ind	21
Politics and Law (4 Yrs)	MM31	4FT deg	*	BBB	Ind	Ind	32	ABBB	Ind	
Politics and Marketing	MN15	3FT deg	*	BCC	Ind	Ind	28	CSYS	Ind	
Politics and Music (4 Yrs)	WM31	4FT deg	*	BCC	Ind	Ind	28	BBBB	Ind	
Politics and Philosophy	MV17	3FT deg	*	BCC	Ind	Ind	28	CSYS	Ind	5
Politics and Philosophy (4 Yrs)	VM71	4FT deg	*	BCC	Ind	Ind	28	BBBB	Ind	
Politics and Physics (4 Yrs)	MF13	4FT deg	*	BCC	Ind	Ind	28	BBBB	Ind	
Psychology and International Politics (4 Yrs)	MCC8	4FT deg	*	BBB	Ind	Ind	32	BBBB	Ind	

Politics

62

				98 expected requirements						96 entry stats	
course details											
TITLE	CODE	COURSE	SUBJECTS	A/AS	ND/C	GNVQ	IB	SQA(H)	SQA	RATIO A/AS	
Psychology and Politics	CM81	3FT deg	* g	BBB	Ind	Ind	32	CSYS	Ind		
Psychology and Politics (4 Yrs)	MC18	4FT deg	*	BBB	Ind	Ind	32	ABBB	Ind		
Russian Studies and International Pol (4 Yrs)	RMVC	4FT deg	*	BCC	Ind	Ind	28	BBBB	Ind		
Russian Studies and International Politics	MRCV	3FT deg	*	BCC	Ind	Ind	28	CSYS	Ind		
Russian Studies and Politics	MRC8	3FT deg	*	BCC	Ind	Ind	28	CSYS	Ind		
Russian Studies and Politics (4 Yrs)	RM8C	4FT deg	*	BCC	Ind	Ind	28	BBBB	Ind		
Russian and International Politics	MRDV	3FT deg	R	BCC	Ind	D$^	28$	CSYS	Ind		
Russian and International Politics (4 Yrs)	RMWC	4FT deg	*	BCC	Ind	Ind	28	BBBB	Ind		
Russian and Politics	MR18	3FT deg	R	BCC	Ind	D$^	28$	CSYS	Ind		
Russian and Politics (4 Yrs)	RM81	4FT deg	*	BCC	Ind	Ind	28	BBBB	Ind		
Sociol & Soc Anthrop and International Politics	LM3C	3FT deg	*	BCC	Ind	Ind	28	CSYS	Ind	5	
Sociol & Soc Anthropology and Politics (4 Yrs)	ML13	4FT deg	*	BCC	Ind	Ind	28	BBBB	Ind	2	
Sociology & Soc Anthrop and Int Politics (4 Yrs)	MLC3	4FT deg	*	BCC	Ind	Ind	28	BBBB	Ind		
Sociology & Social Anthropology and Politics	LM31	3FT deg	*	BCC	Ind	Ind	28	CSYS	Ind	6	
Statistics and International Politics	MGC4	4FT deg	*	BCC	Ind	Ind	28	BBBB	Ind		
Visual Arts and International Politics (4 Yrs)	WM1C	4FT deg	*	BCC	Ind	Ind	28	BBBB	Ind		
Visual Arts and Politics	MW11	3FT deg	*	BCC	Ind	D$^	28	CSYS	Ind		
Visual Arts and Politics	WM11	4FT deg	*	BCC	Ind	Ind	28	BBBB	Ind		

Univ of KENT

TITLE	CODE	COURSE	SUBJECTS	A/AS	ND/C	GNVQ	IB	SQA(H)	SQA	RATIO A/AS	
Business Administration & Politics & Government	MN11	3FT deg	* g	24	1M+5D	D$ go	32	AABB	Ind		
European Politics	M145	3FT deg	*	20	3M+3D	M$	28	BBBB	Ind		
European Politics (French) (4 Yrs)	M174	4FT deg	F	18	Ind	Ind	26$	BBBB$	Ind		
European Politics (German) (4 Yrs)	M175	4FT deg	* g	18	Ind	Ind	26	BBBB	Ind		
European Politics (Italian) (4 Yrs)	M176	4FT deg	* g	18	Ind	Ind	26	BBBB	Ind		
European Politics with a Yr in Finland (4 Yrs)	M177	4FT deg	*	20	3M+3D	M$	28	BBBB	Ind		
European Studies (Politics & Government) (4 Yrs)	MTC2	4FT deg	L	20	Ind	Ind	28$	BBBB$	Ind		
History and Politics	MV11	3FT deg	*	22	2M+4D	Ind	30	Ind	Ind	6	18/26
Ind Relations & Human Resource Mgt (Pol & Gov)	MN16	3FT deg	* g	BCC	3M+3D	M$ go	28	BBBB	Ind	4	
International Relations with French (4 Yrs)	M170	4FT deg	F	20	Ind	Ind	28$	BBBB$	Ind	6	
International Relations with German (4 Yrs)	M171	4FT deg	G	20	Ind	Ind	28$	BBBB$	Ind		
International Relations with Italian (4 Yrs)	M173	4FT deg	* g	20	3M+3D	Ind	28$	BBBB$	Ind	15	
Philosophy and Politics	MV17	3FT deg	*	22	2M+4D	Ind	30	Ind	Ind	27	
Pol & Int Relations with a Yr in Finland (4 Yrs)	M159	4FT deg	*	22	2M+4D	D$	30	ABBB	Ind	9	
Politics & Government/Accounting and Finance	MN14	3FT deg	* g	BCC	3M+3D	M$ go	28	BBBB	Ind		
Politics & Government/Economics	LM11	3FT deg	* g	BCC	3M+3D	M$ go	28	BBBB	Ind	16	
Politics & Government/Law	MM13	3FT deg	*	26	6D	D$	33	AAAB	Ind	15	
Politics and Government	M142	3FT deg	*	BCC	3M+3D	M$	28	BBBB	Ind	6	20/26
Politics and Government and History	MVC1	3FT deg	*	BCC	3M+3D	M$	28	BBBB	Ind	23	
Politics and Government and Philosophy	MVC7	3FT deg	*	BCC	3M+3D	M$	28	BBBB	Ind	3	
Politics and Government with French (4 Yrs)	MRC1	4FT deg	F	18	Ind	Ind	26$	BBBB$	Ind		
Politics and Government with German (4 Yrs)	MRC2	4FT deg	G	18	Ind	Ind	26$	BBBB$	Ind		
Politics and Government with Italian (4 Yrs)	M1R3	4FT deg	* g	18	4M+2D	Ind	26	BBBB	Ind		
Politics and Govt. with Yr in Finland (4 Yrs)	M143	4FT deg	*	20	3M+3D	M$	28	BBBB	Ind	8	
Politics and International Relations	M158	3FT deg	*	BBC	2M+4D	D$	30	ABBB	Ind	9	18/26
Social Anthropology/Politics & Government	LM61	3FT deg	*	BCC	3M+3D	M$	28	BBBB	Ind		
Social Policy & Admin/Politics & Government	LM41	3FT deg	*	BCC	3M+3D	M$	28	BBBB	Ind		
Sociology/Politics & Government	LMJ1	3FT deg	*	BCC	3M+3D	M$	28	BBBB	Ind	17	

KINGSTON Univ

TITLE	CODE	COURSE	SUBJECTS	A/AS	ND/C	GNVQ	IB	SQA(H)	SQA	RATIO A/AS	
Politics	M100	3FT deg	* g	14	MO	Ind^	Ind	BCCCC	HN	6	8/18
Politics/Economics	ML11	3FT deg	* g	14	MO	Ind^	Ind	BCCCC	HN	2	6/17
Politics/English Language	QM31	3FT deg	E g	14	MO	Ind^	Ind	BCCCC	HN		6/14

course details			98 expected requirements							96 entry stats	
TITLE	CODE	COURSE	SUBJECTS	A/AS	NO/C	RGNVQ	IB	SQA(H)	SQA	RATIO	A/AS
Politics/English Literature	MQ13	3FT deg	E g	16-18	MO	Ind^	Ind	BBCCC	HN	2	12/20
Politics/French	MR11	4FT deg	F g	14	MO	Ind^	Ind	BCCCC	HN	2	
Politics/German	MR12	4FT deg	G g	12-14	MO	Ind^	Ind	BCCCC	HN	7	
Politics/History	MV11	3FT deg	H g	16	MO	Ind^	Ind	BBCCC	HN	9	14/18
Politics/History of Ideas	MV17	3FT deg	* g	14	MO	Ind^	Ind	BCCCC	HN	8	
Psychology/Politics	LM71	3FT deg	* g	18	MO	Ind^	Ind	BBBCC	HN	2	6/16
Social and Economic History/Politics	MV13	3FT deg	* g	14	MO	Ind^	Ind	BCCCC	HN	1	
Sociology/Politics	LM31	3FT deg	* g	14	MO	Ind^	Ind	BCCCC	HN	3	14/18
Spanish/Politics	MR14	4FT deg	Sp g	12-14	MO	Ind^	Ind	BCCCC	HN	1	
Women's Studies/Politics	MM91	3FT deg	* g	14	MO	Ind^	Ind	BCCCC	HN	5	

LANCASTER Univ

Economics and International Relations	LM1C	3FT deg	* g		BBC	MO+4D		32	ABBBB	Ind	
Economics and Politics	ML11	3FT deg	* g		BBC	MO+4D		32	ABBBB	Ind	
French Studies and Politics	RM11	4SW deg	F		BCC	Ind $		30$	BBBBB$	Ind	
German Studies and Politics	RM21	4SW deg	G/L		BCC	Ind $		30$	BBBBB$	Ind	
History and International Relations	VM1C	3FT deg	H		BBC	Ind $		30$	ABBBB$	Ind	
History and Politics	MV11	3FT deg	H		BBC	Ind $		30$	AABBB$	Ind	
Independent Studies and Politics	YM41	3FT deg	*		BCC	Ind		Ind	Ind	Ind	
International Relations and Strategic Studies	M164	3FT deg	*		BCC	Ind		30	BBBBB	Ind	
Italian Studies and Politics	RM31	4SW deg	I/L		BCC	Ind $		30$	BBBBB$	Ind	
Peace Studies and International Relations	MM91	3FT deg	*		BCC-CCC	M+D		30	BBBBB	Ind	
Philosophy and Politics	VM71	3FT deg	*		BCC	Ind		30	BBBBB	Ind	
Political Sociology	ML13	3FT deg	*		BCC	Ind		30	BBBBB	Ind	
Political and Religious Thought	VM81	3FT deg	*		BCC	Ind		30	BBBBB	Ind	
Politics	M100	3FT deg	*		BCC-CCC	Ind		30	BBBBB	Ind	
Politics with International Relations	M155	3FT deg	*		BCC-CCC	Ind		30	BBBBB	Ind	
Spanish Studies and Politics	RM41	4SW deg	Sp/L		BCC	Ind $		30$	BBBBB$	Ind	
History and Philosophy and Politics *Politics*	Y650	3FT deg	H		BBC	Ind $		30$	ABBBB$	Ind	
Philosophy and Politics and Economics *Politics*	Y616	3FT deg	* g		BBC	Ind		32	ABBBB	Ind	

Univ of LEEDS

Arabic-Politics	TM61	4FT deg	Cl/L g		BBC	Ind	Ind	30$	CSYS	Ind	
Chinese-Politics	MT13	4FT deg	L g		BBC	Ind	Ind	30$	CSYS	Ind	
Economic and Social History-Politics	MV13	3FT deg	* g		BBB	Ind	Ind	32	CSYS	Ind	12
Economics-Politics	LM11	3FT deg	g		BBB	Ind	Ind	32	CSYS	Ind	11	24/28
Economics-Politics with North American Studies	LM1C	4FT deg	g		BBB	Ind	Ind	32	CSYS	Ind	5	22/28
European Union Studies	MT12	3FT deg	g		BBC	Ind	Ind	30	Ind	Ind		18/26
French-Politics	RM11	4FT deg	F g		BBC	Ind	Ind	30$	CSYS	Ind	10	24/30
French-Politics and European Parliamentary St	RM1C	4FT deg	E g		BBB	Ind	Ind	Ind	Ind	Ind	
Gender Studies - Politics	MM19	3FT deg	* g		BCC	Ind	Ind	28$	CSYS	Ind	
Geography-Politics	LM81	3FT deg	Gy g		BBB	Ind	Ind	32$	CSYS	Ind	11
International Studies	M154	3FT deg	* g		BBB	Ind	D$^ go | 32$	CSYS	Ind	6	20/30
Italian-Politics A	MR13	4FT deg	I g		BBC	Ind	Ind	Ind	Ind	Ind	
Italian-Politics B	MR1H	4FT deg	L g		BBC	Ind	Ind	Ind	Ind	Ind	
Philosophy-Politics	MV17	3FT deg	* g		BBB	Ind	Ind	32	CSYS	Ind	13	24/28
Political Studies	M100	3FT deg	* g		BBB	Ind	Ind	32	CSYS	Ind	7	22/30
Politics and European Parliamentary Studies	M143	4FT deg	g		BBB	Ind	Ind	Ind	Ind	Ind	
Politics and Parliamentary Studies	M142	4FT deg	* g		BBB	Ind	Ind	32	CSYS	Ind	38	24/30
Politics and Parliamentary Studies-Portuguese	MR15	4FT deg									
Politics and Parliamentary Studies-Russian St	MR18	4FT deg									
Politics-Religious Studies	MV1V	3FT deg	* g		BBB	Ind	Ind	32	CSYS	Ind	

course details			98 expected requirements							96 entry stats
TITLE	CODE	COURSE	SUBJECTS	A/AS	ND/C	RGNVQ	IB	SQA(H)	SQA	RATIO A/AS
Politics-Russian Studies	RM81	4FT deg	R g	BBC	Ind	Ind	30$	CSYS	Ind	
Politics-Social Policy	LM41	3FT deg	* g	BBB	Ind	Ind	32	CSYS	Ind	
Politics-Sociology	LM31	3FT deg	* g	BBB	Ind	Ind	32	CSYS	Ind	10 24/28
Politics-Spanish	RM41	4FT deg	Sp g	BBC	Ind	Ind	30$	CSYS	Ind	8
Politics-Theology	MV18	3FT deg	* g	BBB	Ind	Ind	32	CSYS	Ind	7

LEEDS METROPOLITAN Univ

History and Politics	VM11	3FT deg	* g		Ind	Ind go	Ind	Ind	Ind	6/18
Social Sciences - Politics	M100	3FT deg								

Univ of LEICESTER

French and Politics	RM11	4FT deg	F g	BCD	X	D$^	28$	BBBB$	X	16/20
History and Politics	VM11	3FT deg	H g	BCC	Ind	D$^	28	BBBB$	Ind	20/28
Politics	M100	3FT deg	* g	20	1M+5D	D$^	28	BBBCC	Ind	16/24
Politics and Economic and Social History	MV13	3FT deg	* g	BCC	2M+3D	D$^	28	BBBBC	Ind	16/22
Combined Arts *Politics*	Y300	3FT deg	* g	BCC	DO	D$^	30$	Ind	Ind	
Combined Science *Politics*	Y100	3FT deg	* g	CCC	MO $	D$^	28$	BBBCC	HN	

Univ of LINCOLNSHIRE and HUMBERSIDE

Communications and International Relations	MP13▼	3FT deg	* g	16	1M+3D	D	24	BBCCC	Ind	
Communications and Politics	MP1H▼	3FT deg	* g	16	1M+3D	D	24	BBCCC	Ind	
Criminology and International Relations	MM1H▼	3FT deg	* g	16	1M+3D	D	24	BBCCC	Ind	
Criminology and Politics	MM1J▼	3FT deg	* g	16	1M+3D	D	24	BBCCC	Ind	
Economics and International Relations	LM11▼	3FT deg	* g	16	1M+3D	D	24	BBCCC	Ind	
Economics and Politics	LM1C▼	3FT deg	* g	16	1M+3D	D	24	BBCCC	Ind	
Health Studies and International Relations	LMK1▼	3FT deg	* g	16	1M+3D	P	24	BBCCC	Ind	
Health Studies and Politics	LM4C▼	3FT deg	* g	16	1M+3D	D	24	BBCCC	Ind	
International Relations	M155▼	3FT deg	* g	16	1M+3D	D	24	BBCCC	Ind	
International Relations and Journalism	MP1P▼	3FT deg	* g	18	1M+4D	D	26	BBBCC	Ind	
International Relations and Law	MM13▼	3FT deg	* g	16	1M+3D	D	24	BBCCC	Ind	
International Relations and Management	MN11▼	3FT deg	* g	16	1M+3D	D	24	BBCCC	Ind	
International Relations and Media	MP14▼	3FT deg	* g	18	1M+4D	D	26	BBBCC	Ind	
International Relations and Politics	M145▼	3FT deg	* g	16	1M+3D	D	24	BBCCC	Ind	
International Relations and Social Policy	LML1▼	3FT deg	* g	16	1M+3D	D	24	BBCCC	Ind	
International Relations and Tourism	MP17▼	3FT deg	* g	16	1M+3D	D	24	BBCCC	Ind	
Internationl Relations and Psychology	CM81▼	3FT deg	* g	18	1M+4D	D	26	BBBCC	Ind	
Journalism and Politics	MP16▼	3FT deg	g	18	1M+4D	D	26	BBBCC	Ind	
Law and Politics	MM31▼	3FT deg	* g	16	1M+3D	D	24	BBCCC	Ind	
Management and Politics	MN1C▼	3FT deg	* g	16	1M+3D	D	24	BBCCC	Ind	
Media and Politics	MP1K▼	3FT deg	* g	18	1M+4D	D	26	BBBCC	Ind	
Politics	M100	3FT deg	g	16	1M+3D	D	24	BBCCC	Ind	
Politics and Psychology	CM8C▼	3FT deg	* g	18	1M+4D	D	26	BBBCC	Ind	
Politics and Social Policy	LMLC▼	3FT deg	* g	16	1M+3D	D	24	BBCCC	Ind	
Politics and Tourism	MP1R▼	3FT deg	* g	16	1M+3D	D	24	BBCCC	Ind	

Univ of LIVERPOOL

Modern History and Politics	MV11	3FT deg	H	BBC	Ind			BBBBB$	Ind	8 22/28
Philosophy and Politics	MV17	3FT deg	*	BCC-BBC	Ind	Ind			Ind	5 16/26
Politics	M104	3FT deg	*	BCC	Ind	Ind	Ind	Ind	Ind	6 18/26
Politics and Communication Studies	MP13	3FT deg	*	ABB	Ind	Ind	Ind	Ind	Ind	5 26/30
Arts Combined *Politics*	Y401	3FT deg	*	BBC-BBB	Ind	Ind	30$	ABBB	Ind	
BA Combined Honours *Politics*	Y200	3FT deg	* g	BBB	Ind	Ind	Ind	Ind	Ind	

Letts STUDY GUIDES
THE INDEPENDENT

course details			98 expected requirements							96 entry stats	
TITLE	CODE	COURSE	SUBJECTS	A/AS	ND/C	RGNVQ	IB	SQA(H)	SQA	RATIO	A/AS
LIVERPOOL JOHN MOORES Univ											
Politics and Criminal Justice	MM13	3FT deg		16	5M+3D	X	28$	BCCC		11	14/20
Politics and Economics	LM11	3FT deg		12-14	5M+2D	PB^	28$	CCCC		6	12/18
Politics and European Studies	MTC2	3FT deg		14	5M+2D	P$^	28$	BCCC		2	12/14
Politics and History	MV1C▼	3FT deg		12-14	5M+2D	P$^	28$	CCCC		13	12/20
Politics and Human Geography	LM81	3FT deg	Gv	12-14	5M+3D	P$^	28$	BBCC		3	
Politics and Philosophy (Phil Joint Award only)	VM71	3FT deg	* g	16-18	5M+3D	P$^	28$	CCCC		5	16/18
Sociology and Politics	LM31▼	3FT deg		12-14	M0+2D	D$/M$6^	28$	BCCC		7	12/18
Women's Studies and Politics	MMX1	3FT deg		14	5M+2D	P$^	28$	BCCC		2	13/14
LONDON GUILDHALL Univ											
3D/Spatial Design and International Relations	MWCF	3FT deg	Pf g	DD	M0	M$ go	24	Ind	Ind		
3D/Spatial Design and Politics	MW1F	3FT deg	Pf g	DD	M0	M$ go	24	Ind	Ind		
Int Relations and Commun & Audio Visual Prod St	MPC4	3FT deg	* g	CD-DDD	M0+2D	M$ go	26	Ind	Ind		
International Relations and Accounting	MNC4	3FT deg	* g	DD	M0	M$ go	24	Ind	Ind		
International Relations and Business	MNC1	3FT deg	* g	CD-DDD	M0+2D	M$ go	26	Ind	Ind		
International Relations and Business Economics	LMCC	3FT deg	* g	DD	M0	M$ go	24	Ind	Ind		
International Relations and Business IT	GM7C	3FT deg	* g	DD	M0	M$ go	24	Ind	Ind		
International Relations and Computing	GM5C	3FT deg	* g	DD	M0	M$ go	24	Ind	Ind		
International Relations and Design Studies	MWC2	3FT deg	* g	CD-DDD	M0+2D	M$ go	26	Ind	Ind		
International Relations and Development Studies	MM9C	3FT deg	* g	DD	M0	M$ go	24	Ind	Ind		
International Relations and Economics	LM1C	3FT deg	* g	DD	M0	M$ go	24	Ind	Ind		
International Relations and English	MQC3	3FT deg	* g	CD-DDD	M0+2D	M$ go	26	Ind	Ind		
International Relations and European Studies	MTC2	3FT deg	* g	DD	M0	M$ go	24	Ind	Ind		
International Relations and Financial Services	MNC3	3FT deg	* g	DD	M0	M$ go	24	Ind	Ind		
International Relations and Fine Art	MWC1	3FT deg	* g	CC-CDD	M0+2D	M$ go	26	Ind	Ind		
International Relations and French	MRC1	4FT deg	* g	DD	M0	M$ go	24	Ind	Ind		
International Relations and German	MRC2	4FT deg	* g	DD	M0	M$ go	24	Ind	Ind		
Law and International Relations	MM3C	3FT deg	* g	CC-CDD	M0+2D	M$ go	26	Ind	Ind		
Marketing and International Relations	MNC5	3FT deg	* g	CD-DDD	M0+2D	M$ go	26	Ind	Ind		
Mathematics and International Relations	GM1C	3FT deg	* g	DD	M0	M$ go	24	Ind	Ind		
Modern History and International Relations	MVC1	3FT deg	* g	DD	M0	M$ go	24	Ind	Ind		
Multimedia Systems and International Relations	GMMC	3FT deg	* g	DD	M0	M$ go	24	Ind	Ind		
Politics	M142	3FT deg	* g	DDD-CD	M0	M$ go	24	Ind	Ind		
Politics and Accounting	MN14	3FT deg	* g	DD	M0	M$ go	24	Ind	Ind		
Politics and Business	MN11	3FT deg	* g	CD-DDD	M0+2D	M$ go	24	Ind	Ind		
Politics and Business Economics	LMC1	3FT deg	* g	DD	M0	M$ go	24	Ind	Ind		
Politics and Business Information Technology	GM71	3FT deg	* g	DD	M0	M$ go	24	Ind	Ind		
Politics and Communications & Audio Vis Prod St	MP14	3FT deg	* g	CC-CDD	M0+2D	M$ go	26	Ind	Ind		
Politics and Computing	GM51	3FT deg	* g	DD	M0	M$ go	24	Ind	Ind		
Politics and Design Studies	MW12	3FT deg	* g	CD-DDD	M0+2D	M$ go	24	Ind	Ind		
Politics and Development Studies	MM19	3FT deg	* g	DD	M0	M$ go	24	Ind	Ind		
Politics and Economics	LM11	3FT deg	* g	DD	M0	M$ go	24	Ind	Ind		
Politics and English	MQ13	3FT deg	* g	CD-DDD	M0+2D	M$ go	26	Ind	Ind		
Politics and European Studies	MT12	3FT deg	* g	DD	M0	M$ go	24	Ind	Ind		
Politics and Financial Services	MN13	3FT deg	* g	DD	M0	M$ go	24	Ind	Ind		
Politics and Fine Art	MW11	3FT deg	* g	CC-CDD	M0+2D	M$ go	26	Ind	Ind		
Politics and French	MR11	4FT deg	* g	DD	M0	M$ go	24	Ind	Ind		
Politics and German	MR12	4FT deg	* g	DD	M0	M$ go	24	Ind	Ind		
Politics and International Relations	MM1C	3FT deg	* g	DD	M0	M$ go	24	Ind	Ind		
Politics and Law	MM13	3FT deg	* g	CC-CDD	M0+4D	M$ go	26	Ind	Ind		
Politics and Marketing	MN15	3FT deg	* g	CD-DDD	M0+2D	M$ go	24	Ind	Ind		
Politics and Mathematics	GM11	3FT deg	* g	DD	M0	M$ go	24	Ind	Ind		

course details			98 expected requirements							96 entry stats	
TITLE	CODE	COURSE	SUBJECTS	A/AS	ND/C	AGNVQ	IB	SQA(H)	SQA	RATIO	A/AS
Politics and Modern History	MV11	3FT deg	* g	DD	MO	M$ go	24	Ind	Ind		
Politics and Multimedia Systems	GMM1	3FT deg	* g	DD	MO	M$ go	24	Ind	Ind		
Product Development & Manuf & Internat Relations	JM4C	3FT deg	* g	DD	MO	M$ go	24	Ind	Ind		
Product Development & Manufacture and Politics	JM41	3FT deg	* g	DD	MO	M$ go	24	Ind	Ind		
Psychology and International Relations	CM8C	3FT deg	* g	CD-DDD	MO+2D	M$ go	26	Ind	Ind		
Psychology and Politics	CM81	3FT deg	* g	CD-DDD	MO+2D	M$ go	26	Ind	Ind		
Social Policy & Management and Politics	LM41	3FT deg	* g	CD-DDD	MO	M$ go	24	Ind	Ind		
Social Policy & Mgt and International Relations	LM4C	3FT deg	* g	CD-DDD	MO	M$ go	24	Ind	Ind		
Sociology and International Relations	LM3C	3FT deg	* g	CD-DDD	MO	M$ go	24	Ind	Ind		
Sociology and Politics	LM31	3FT deg	* g	CD-DDD	MO	M$ go	24	Ind	Ind		
Spanish and International Relations	MRC4	4FT deg	* g	DD	MO	M$ go	24	Ind	Ind		
Spanish and Politics	MR14	4FT deg	* g	DD	MO	M$ go	24	Ind	Ind		
Taxation and International Relations	MNCH	3FT deg	* g	DD	MO	M$ go	24	Ind	Ind		
Taxation and Politics	MN1H	3FT deg	* g	DD	MO	M$ go	24	Ind	Ind		
Textile Furnishing Des & International Relations	MWCG	3FT deg	Pf g	DD	MO	M$ go	24	Ind	Ind		
Textile Furnishing Design and Politics	MW1G	3FT deg	Pf g	DD	MO	M$ go	24	Ind	Ind		
Modular Programme *International Relations*	Y400	3FT deg	* g	CC-DD	MO	M$ go	24	Ind	Ind		
Modular Programme *Politics*	Y400	3FT deg	* g	CC-DD	MO	M$ go	24	Ind	Ind		
Modular Programme *Politics*	Y420▼	3FT deg	* g	EE	MO	P	24	Ind	Ind		

LSE: LONDON Sch of Economics (Univ of London)

Government	M140	3FT deg	g	ABB	Ind	X	$	Ind	Ind	15	26/30
Government and Economics	LM11	3FT deg	g	ABB	Ind	X	$	Ind	Ind	46	28/30
Government and History	MV11	3FT deg	g	ABB	Ind	X	$	Ind	Ind	22	
International Relations	M155	3FT deg	g	ABB	Ind	X	$	Ind	Ind	21	26/30
International Relations and History	VM11	3FT deg	g	ABB	Ind	X	$	Ind	Ind		
Russian Joint Studies	MR18	3FT deg	L g	BBB	X	X	$	X	X	8	
Social Policy and Government	LM41	3FT deg	g	BBB	Ind	X	$	Ind	Ind	9	20/28

LOUGHBOROUGH Univ

Economics with Politics	L1M1	3FT deg	* g	20	3D	D*6/^ go	30	Ind	Ind	9	18/18
French and Politics	MR11	3FT deg	F	20			28$	Ind			
German and Politics	MR12	3FT deg	G g	20			28$	Ind			
Politics with Communication and Media Studies	M1P4	3FT deg	* g	20	2M+3D	D*6/^ go	28	Ind	Ind		14/20
Politics with Computing	M1G5	3FT deg	* g	20	2M+3D	D*6/^ go	28	Ind	Ind		
Politics with Economics	M1L1	3FT deg	* g	20	2M+3D	D*6/^ go	28	Ind	Ind		12/20
Politics with English	M1Q3	3FT deg	* g	20	2M+3D	D*6/^ go	28	Ind	Ind		16/22
Politics with French	M1R1	3FT deg	F	20			28$	Ind			
Politics with Geography	M1L8	3FT deg	* g	20	2M+3D	D*6/^ go	28	Ind	Ind		14/20
Politics with German	M1R2	3FT deg	G	20			28$	Ind			
Politics with Social Policy	M1L4	3FT deg	* g	20	2M+3D	D*6/^ go	28	Ind	Ind		16/22
Politics with Social Psychology	M1L7	3FT deg	* g	20	2M+3D	D*6/^ go	28	Ind	Ind		16/20
Politics with Sociology	M1L3	3FT deg	* g	20	2M+3D	D*6/^ go	28	Ind	Ind		14/22
Politics with Spanish	M1R4	3FT deg	Sp	20			28$	Ind			
Spanish and Politics	RM41	3FT deg	Sp	20			28$	Ind			

LSU COLL of HE

English with Politics	Q3M1	3FT deg	E	CD	Ind		Ind	Ind	Ind	18	
Environment and Society with Politics	FM91	3FT deg									
Geography with Politics	L8M1	3FT deg									
Historical and Political Studies	V1M1	3FT deg	H	CDD	Ind		Ind	Ind	Ind	3	6/14
Politics (Combined)	M100	3FT deg									

course details			98 expected requirements							96 entry stats
TITLE	CODE	COURSE	SUBJECTS	A/AS	ND/C	AGNVQ	IB	SQA(H)	SQA	RATIO A/AS
Politics and Ecology	DM21	3FT deg								
Politics and English	QM31	3FT deg								
Politics and Geography	LM81	3FT deg								
Politics and History	VM11	3FT deg								
Politics with Ecology	M1D2	3FT deg	S	DD	Ind		Ind	Ind	Ind	
Politics with English	M1Q3	3FT deg								
Politics with Geography	M1L8	3FT deg								
Politics with Sociology	M1L3	3FT deg	*	DD	Ind		Ind	Ind	Ind	7
Politics with Theology	M1V8	3FT deg	*	DD	Ind		Ind	Ind	Ind	
Sociology and Politics	ML13	3FT deg								
Sociology with Politics	L3M1	3FT deg								
Sport and Health Sciences with Politics	BM61	3FT deg								
Theology and Politics	MV18	3FT deg								
Theology with Politics	V8M1	3FT deg								

LUTON Univ

Accounting with Politics	N4MD	3FT deg	g	12-16	MO/DO	M/D	32	BBCC	Ind	
Accounting with Public Policy & Management	NM4D	3FT deg	g	12-16	MO/DO	M/D	32	BBCC	Ind	
Biochemistry with Public Policy and Management	C7M1	3FT deg	g	12-16	MO/DO	M/D	32	BBCC	Ind	
Biology with Politics	C1M1	3FT deg	g	12-16	MO/DO	M/D	32	BBCC	Ind	
Biotechnology with Public Policy & Management	J8M1	3FT deg	g	12-16	MO/DO	M/D	32	BBCC	Ind	
Built Environment with Politics	N8M1	3FT deg	g	12-16	MO/DO	M/D	32	BBCC	Ind	
Built Environment with Public Policy and Mgt	N8MC	3FT deg	g	12-16	MO/DO	M/D	32	BBCC	Ind	
Business Systems with Politics	N1MD	3FT deg	g	12-16	MO/DO	M/D	32	BBCC		
Business with Politics	N1M1	3FT deg	g	12-16	MO/DO	M/D	32	BBCC	Ind	3
Business with Public Policy and Management	N1MC	3FT deg	g	12-16	MO/DO	M/D	32	BBCC	Ind	
Contemp Br & Euro Hist with Public Policy & Mgt	V1MC	3FT deg	g	12-16	MO/DO	M/D	32	BBCC	Ind	
Contemp British & Euro History with Politics	V1M1	3FT deg	g	12-16	MO/DO	M/D	32	BBCC	Ind	5
Digital Systems Design with Politics	H6MD	3FT deg	g	12-16	MO/DO	M/D	32	BBCC	Ind	
Ecology (Eco Tech) with Politics	C9M1	3FT deg	g	12-16	MO/DO	M/D	32	BBCC	Ind	
Ecology (Eco Tech) with Public Policy & Mgt	C9MC	3FT deg	g	12-16	MO/DO	M/D	32	BBCC	Ind	
European Language St with Public Policy and Mgt	T2MC	3FT deg	L g	12-16	MO/DO	M/D	32	BBCC	Ind	
European Language Studies with Politics	T2M1	4FT deg	L g	12-16	MO/DO	M/D	32	BBCC	Ind	
Geography with Politics	F8MD	3FT deg	g	12-16	MO/DO	M/D	32	BBCC	Ind	
Geography with Public Policy & Management	FMWC	3FT deg	g	12-16	MO/DO	M/D	32	BBCC	Ind	
Geology with Politics	F6M1	3FT deg	g	12-16	MO/DO	M/D	32	BBCC	Ind	
Geology with Public Policy and Management	F6MC	3FT deg	g	12-16	MO/DO	M/D	32	BBCC	Ind	
Health Science with Politics	B9M1	3FT deg	g	12-16	MO/DO	M/D	32	BBCC	Ind	
Health Science with Public Policy and Management	B9MC	3FT deg	g	12-16	MO/DO	M/D	32	BBCC	Ind	
Health Studies with Politics	B9MD	3FT deg	g	12-16	MO/DO	M/D	32	BBCC	Ind	
Integrated Engineering with Politics	H1M1	3FT deg	g	12-16	MO/DO	M/D	32	BBCC	Ind	
Integrated Engineering with Public Policy & Mgt	H1MC	3FT deg	g	12-16	MO/DO	M/D	32	BBCC	Ind	
Law with Politics	M3M1	3FT deg		12-16	MO/DO	M/D	32	BBCC	Ind	
Law with Public Policy & Management	M3MC	3FT deg	g	12-16	MO/DO	M/D	32	BBCC	Ind	
Linguistics with Politics	Q1M1	3FT deg	g	12-16	MO/DO	M/D	32	BBCC	Ind	
Linguistics with Public Policy and Management	Q1MC	3FT deg	g	12-16	MO/DO	M/D	32	BBCC	Ind	
Literary St in English with Public Policy & Mgt	Q2MC	3FT deg		12-16	MO/DO	M/D	32	BBCC	Ind	
Literary Studies in English with Politics	Q2M1	3FT deg		12-16	MO/DO	M/D	32	BBCC	Ind	
Mapping Science with Politics	F8M1	3FT deg	g	12-16	MO/DO	M/D	32	BBCC	Ind	
Mapping Science with Public Policy and Mgt	F8MC	3FT deg	g	12-16	MO/DO	M/D	32	BBCC	Ind	
Marketing with Politics	N5M1	3FT deg	g	12-16	MO/DO	M/D	32	BBCC	Ind	
Marketing with Public Policy and Management	N5MC	3FT deg	g	12-16	MO/DO	M/D	32	BBCC	Ind	
Mathematical Sciences with Public Policy & Mgt	G1M1	3FT deg	g	12-16	MO/DO	M/D	32	BBCC	Ind	

Politics 62

TITLE	CODE	COURSE	SUBJECTS	A/AS	ND/C	RGNVQ	IB	SQA(H)	SQA	RATIO A/AS
			98 expected requirements							**96 entry stats**
Media Practices with Politics	P4M1	3FT deg	g	12-16	MO/DO	M/D	32	BBCC	Ind	
Media Practices with Public Policy & Management	P4MC	3FT deg	g	12-16	MO/DO	M/D	32	BBCC	Ind	
Modern English Stud with Public Policy and Mgt	Q3MC	3FT deg	g	12-16	MO/DO	M/D	32	BBCC	Ind	
Modern English Studies with Politics	Q3M1	3FT deg	g	12-16	MO/DO	M/D	32	BBCC	Ind	
Modern History with Public Policy & Management	V1MD	3FT deg		12-16	MO/DO	M/D	32	BBCC	Ind	
Planning Studies and Politics	KM41	3FT deg	g	12-16	MO/DO	M/D	32	BBCC	Ind	
Planning Studies and Public Policy & Management	KM4C	3FT deg	g	12-16	MO/DO	M/D	32	BBCC	Ind	
Plant Biology with Public Policy & Management	C2M1	3FT deg	g	12-16	MO/DO	M/D	32	BBCC	Ind	
Politics	M100	3FT deg	g	12-16	MO/DO	M/D	32	BBCC	Ind	9 8/14
Politics and Accounting	NMK1	3FT deg	g	12-16	MO/DO	M/D	32	BBCC	Ind	
Politics and Biology	CM11	3FT deg	g	12-16	MO/DO	M/D	32	BBCC	Ind	
Politics and British Studies	VM91	3FT deg		12-16	MO/DO	M/D	32	BBCC	Ind	
Politics and Built Environment	NM81	3FT deg	g	12-16	MO/DO	M/D	32	BBCC	Ind	
Politics and Business	NM11	3FT deg	g	12-16	MO/DO	M/D	32	BBCC	Ind	12
Politics and Business Systems	NMC1	3FT deg	g	12-16	MO/DO	M/D	32	BBCC	Ind	
Politics and Contemporary History	VM11	3FT deg	g	12-16	MO/DO	M/D	32	BBCC	Ind	14
Politics and Ecology & Biodiversity	CM91	3FT deg	g	12-16	MO/DO	M/D	32	BBCC	Ind	
Politics and Environmental Science	FM91	3FT deg	g	12-16	MO/DO	M/D	32	BBCC	Ind	
Politics and European Language Studies	TM21	3FT deg	L g	12-16	MO/DO	M/D	32	BBCC	Ind	
Politics and Geography	FM8D	3FT deg	g	12-16	MO/DO	M/D	32	BBCC	Ind	
Politics and Geology	FM61	3FT deg	g	12-16	MO/DO	M/D	32	BBCC	Ind	
Politics and Health Science	BM91	3FT deg	g	12-16	MO/DO	M/D	32	BBCC	Ind	
Politics and Health Studies	BMX1	3FT deg	g	12-16	MO/DO	M/D	32	BBCC	Ind	
Politics and Language & Stylistics in English	QMG1	3FT deg	g	12-16	MO/DO	M/D	32	BBCC	Ind	
Politics and Law	MM31	3FT deg	g	12-16	MO/DO	M/D	32	BBCC	Ind	19
Politics and Literary Studies in English	QM21	3FT deg	g	12-16	MO/DO	M/D	32	BBCC	Ind	
Politics and Mapping Science	FM81	3FT deg	g	12-16	MO/DO	M/D	32	BBCC	Ind	
Politics and Marketing	NM51	3FT deg	g	12-16	MO/DO	M/D	32	BBCC	Ind	
Politics and Modern English Studies	QM31	3FT deg	g	12-16	MO/DO	M/D	32	BBCC	Ind	
Politics and Modern History	VMC1	3FT deg	g	12-16	MO/DO	M/D	32	BBCC	Ind	
Politics and Organisational Behaviour	LM71	3FT deg	g	12-16	MO/DO	M/D	32	BBCC	Ind	
Politics and Physical Geography	FMV1	3FT deg	g	12-16	MO/DO	M/D	32	BBCC	Ind	
Politics with Accounting	M1NL	3FT deg	g	12-16	MO/DO	M/D	32	BBCC	Ind	
Politics with Biology	M1C1	3FT deg	g	12-16	MO/DO	M/D	32	BBCC	Ind	
Politics with British Studies	M1V9	3FT deg		12-16	MO/DO	M/D	32	BBCC	Ind	
Politics with Built Environment	M1N8	3FT deg	g	12-16	MO/DO	M/D	32	BBCC	Ind	
Politics with Business	M1N1	3FT deg	g	12-16	MO/DO	M/D	32	BBCC	Ind	
Politics with Business Systems	M1NC	3FT deg	g	12-16	MO/DO	M/D	32	BBCC	Ind	
Politics with Chinese	M1T3	3FT deg		12-16	MO/DO	M/D	32	BBCC	Ind	
Politics with Comparative Literature	M1QF	3FT deg	g	12-16	MO/DO	M/D	32	BBCC	Ind	
Politics with Contemporary History	M1V1	3FT deg	g	12-16	MU/DO	M/D	32	BBCC	Ind	
Politics with Ecology & Biodiversity	M1C9	3FT deg	g	12-16	MO/DO	M/D	32	BBCC	Ind	
Politics with Environmental Science	M1F9	3FT deg	g	12-16	MO/DO	M/D	32	BBCC	Ind	
Politics with Film Studies	M1W5	3FT deg	g	12-16	MO/DO	M/D	32	BBCC	Ind	
Politics with Geographical Information Systems	M101	3FT deg	g	12-16	MO/DO	M/D	32	BBCC	Ind	
Politics with Geography	M1FW	3FT deg	g	12-16	MO/DO	M/D	32	BBCC	Ind	
Politics with Geology	M1F6	3FT deg	g	12-16	MO/DO	M/D	32	BBCC	Ind	
Politics with Health Science	M1B9	3FT deg	g	12-16	MO/DO	M/D	32	BBCC	Ind	
Politics with Japanese	M1T4	3FT deg	L g	12-16	MO/DO	M/D	32	BBCC	Ind	
Politics with Language & Stylistics in English	M1QG	3FT deg	g	12-16	MO/DO	M/D	32	BBCC	Ind	
Politics with Literary Studies in English	M1Q2	3FT deg	g	12-16	MO/DO	M/D	32	BBCC	Ind	
Politics with Management	MN1D	3FT deg	g	12-16	MO/DO	M/D	32	BBCC	Ind	

course details | 98 expected requirements | 96 entry stats

TITLE	CODE	COURSE	SUBJECTS	A/AS	ND/C	AGNVQ	IB	SQA(H)	SQA	RATIO A/AS
Politics with Mapping Science	M1F8	3FT deg	g	12-16	MO/DO	M/D	32	BBCC	Ind	
Politics with Marketing	M1N5	3FT deg	g	12-16	MO/DO	M/D	32	BBCC	Ind	
Politics with Modern English Studies	M1Q3	3FT deg	g	12-16	MO/DO	M/D	32	BBCC	Ind	
Politics with Modern History	M1VC	3FT deg	g	12-16	MO/DO	M/D	32	BBCC	Ind	
Politics with Organisational Behaviour	M1L7	3FT deg	g	12-16	MO/DO	M/D	32	BBCC	Ind	
Politics with Physical Geography	M1FV	3FT deg	g	12-16	MO/DO	M/D	32	BBCC	Ind	
Politics with Psychology	M1LR	3FT deg	g	12-16	MO/DO	M/D	32	BBCC	Ind	
Politics with Publishing	M1P5	3FT deg	g	12-16	MO/DO	M/D	32	BBCC	Ind	
Politics with Regional Planning and Development	M1K4	3FT deg	g	12-16	MO/DO	M/D	32	BBCC	Ind	
Politics with Social Studies	M1L3	3FT deg	g	12-16	MO/DO	M/D	32	BBCC	Ind	
Politics with TV Studies	M1WM	3FT deg	g	12-16	MO/DO	M/D	32	BBCC	Ind	
Politics with Travel and Tourism	M1P7	3FT deg	g	12-16	MO/DO	M/D	32	BBCC	Ind	
Psychology and Politics	ML1R	3FT deg	g	12-16	MO/DO	M/D	32	BBCC	Ind	4
Psychology with Politics	L7MC	3FT deg	g	12-16	MO/DO	M/D	32	BBCC	Ind	1
Psychology with Public Policy and Management	L7MD	3FT deg	g	12-16	MO/DO	M/D	32	BBCC	Ind	
Public Policy & Management and Business Systems	NMCC	3FT deg	g	12-16	MO/DO	M/D	32	BBCC	Ind	
Public Policy & Management and Contemporary Hist	VM1C	3FT deg	g	12-16	MO/DO	M/D	32	BBCC	Ind	
Public Policy & Management and Geography	MF18	3FT deg	g	12-16	MO/DO	M/D	32	BBCC	Ind	
Public Policy & Management and Housing Studies	MK1L	3FT deg	g	12-16	MO/DO	M/D	32	BBCC	Ind	
Public Policy & Management and Human Biology	BM1C	3FT deg	g	12-16	MO/DO	M/D	32	BBCC	Ind	
Public Policy & Management and Mathematics	MG11	3FT deg	g	12-16	MO/DO	M/D	32	BBCC	Ind	
Public Policy & Management with Accounting	MN14	3FT deg	g	12-16	MO/DO	M/D	32	BBCC	Ind	
Public Policy & Management with Biochemistry	M1C7	3FT deg	g	12-16	MO/DO	M/D	32	BBCC	Ind	
Public Policy & Management with Biotechnology	M1J8	3FT deg	g	12-16	MO/DO	M/D	32	BBCC	Ind	
Public Policy & Management with British Studies	M1VX	3FT deg		12-16	MO/DO	M/D	32	BBCC	Ind	
Public Policy & Management with Built Environ	M1NV	3FT deg	g	12-16	MO/DO	M/D	32	BBCC	Ind	
Public Policy & Management with Business Systs	M142	3FT deg	g	12-16	MO/DO	M/D	32	BBCC	Ind	
Public Policy & Management with Chinese	M1TH	3FT deg		12-16	MO/DO	M/D	32	BBCC	Ind	
Public Policy & Management with Environ Science	M147	3FT deg	g	12-16	MO/DO	M/D	32	BBCC	Ind	
Public Policy & Management with Geography	MF1V	3FT deg	g	12-16	MO/DO	M/D	32	BBCC	Ind	
Public Policy & Management with Health Studies	M1BX	3FT deg		12-16	MO/DO	M/D	32	BBCC	Ind	
Public Policy & Management with Human Biology	M1B1	3FT deg	g	12-16	MO/DO	M/D	32	BBCC	Ind	
Public Policy & Management with Japanese	M1TK	3FT deg	L g	12-16	MO/DO	M/D	32	BBCC	Ind	
Public Policy & Management with Land Reclamation	M1K3	3FT deg	g	12-16	MO/DO	M/D	32	BBCC	Ind	
Public Policy & Management with Linguistics	M1QC	3FT deg	g	12-16	MO/DO	M/D	32	BBCC	Ind	
Public Policy & Management with Mathematical Sci	M1GD	3FT deg	g	12-16	MO/DO	M/D	32	BBCC	Ind	
Public Policy & Management with Mathematics	MG1C	3FT deg	g	12-16	MO/DO	M/D	32	BBCC	Ind	
Public Policy & Management with Physical Geog	M152	3FT deg	g	12-16	MO/DO	M/D	32	BBCC	Ind	
Public Policy & Management with Plant Biology	M1C2	3FT deg	g	12-16	MO/DO	M/D	32	BBCC	Ind	
Public Policy & Management with Pollution Studs	M1FY	3FT deg	g	12-16	MO/DO	M/D	32	BBCC	Ind	
Public Policy & Management with Publishing	M1PM	3FT deg	g	12-16	MO/DO	M/D	32	BBCC	Ind	
Public Policy & Mgt & Organisational Behaviour	LM7C	3FT deg	g	12-16	MO/DO	M/D	32	BBCC	Ind	
Public Policy & Mgt and Building Conservation	KM21	3FT deg	g	12-16	MO/DO	M/D	32	BBCC	Ind	
Public Policy & Mgt and Literary St in English	QM2C	3FT deg	g	12-16	MO/DO	M/D	32	BBCC	Ind	
Public Policy & Mgt and Mathematical Sciences	GM11	3FT deg	g	12-16	MO/DO	M/D	32	BBCC	Ind	
Public Policy & Mgt with Applied Statistics	M1G4	3FT deg	g	12-16	MO/DO	M/D	32	BBCC	Ind	
Public Policy & Mgt with Ecology & Biodiversity	M1CX	3FT deg	g	12-16	MO/DO	M/D	32	BBCC	Ind	
Public Policy & Mgt with Geographical Info Systs	M141	3FT deg	g	12-16	MO/DO	M/D	32	BBCC	Ind	
Public Policy & Mgt with Lang & Stylist in Engl	M144	3FT deg	g	12-16	MO/DO	M/D	32	BBCC	Ind	
Public Policy & Mgt with Organisational Behav	M1LT	3FT deg	g	12-16	MO/DO	M/D	32	BBCC	Ind	
Public Policy & Mgt with Reg Planning and Dev	M1KK	3FT deg	g	12-16	MO/DO	M/D	32	BBCC	Ind	
Public Policy and Management	M140	3FT deg	g	12-16	MO/DO	M/D	32	BBCC	Ind	6

			98 expected requirements						96 entry stats	
TITLE	CODE	COURSE	SUBJECTS	A/AS	NO/C	AGNVQ	IB	SQA(H)	SQA	RATIO A/AS
Public Policy and Management and Accounting	NMKC	3FT deg	g	12-16	MO/DO	M/D	32	BBCC	Ind	
Public Policy and Management and Biochemistry	CM7C	3FT deg	g	12-16	MO/DO	M/D	32	BBCC	Ind	
Public Policy and Management and Biology	CM1C	3FT deg	g	12-16	MO/DO	M/D	32	BBCC	Ind	
Public Policy and Management and Biotechnology	JM8C	3FT deg	g	12-16	MO/DO	M/D	32	BBCC	Ind	
Public Policy and Management and British Studies	VM9C	3FT deg		12-16	MO/DO	M/D	32	BBCC	Ind	
Public Policy and Management and Built Environ	NM8C	3FT deg	g	12-16	MO/DO	M/D	32	BBCC	Ind	
Public Policy and Management and Business	NM1C	3FT deg	g	12-16	MO/DO	M/D	32	BBCC	Ind	2
Public Policy and Management and Euro Lang Studs	TM2C	3FT deg	g	12-16	MO/DO	M/D	32	BBCC	Ind	
Public Policy and Management and Geology	FM6C	3FT deg	g	12-16	MO/DO	M/D	32	BBCC	Ind	
Public Policy and Management and Health Science	BM9C	3FT deg		12-16	MO/DO	M/D	32	BBCC	Ind	
Public Policy and Management and Health Studies	BMXC	3FT deg	g	12-16	MO/DO	M/D	32	BBCC	Ind	
Public Policy and Management and Law	MM3C	3FT deg	g	12-16	MO/DO	M/D	32	BBCC	Ind	
Public Policy and Management and Linguistics	QM1C	3FT deg	g	12-16	MO/DO	M/D	32	BBCC	Ind	
Public Policy and Management and Mapping Science	FM8C	3FT deg	g	12-16	MO/DO	M/D	32	BBCC	Ind	
Public Policy and Management and Marketing	NM5C	3FT deg	g	12-16	MO/DO	M/D	32	BBCC	Ind	
Public Policy and Management and Media Practices	PM4C	3FT deg	g	12-16	MO/DO	M/D	32	BBCC	Ind	
Public Policy and Management and Modern Engl St	QM3C	3FT deg	g	12-16	MO/DO	M/D	32	BBCC	Ind	
Public Policy and Management and Modern History	VMCC	3FT deg	g	12-16	MO/DO	M/D	32	BBCC	Ind	
Public Policy and Management and Plant Biology	CM21	3FT deg	g	12-16	MO/DO	M/D	32	BBCC	Ind	
Public Policy and Management and Politics	M157	3FT deg	g	12-16	MO/DO	M/D	32	BBCC	Ind	
Public Policy and Management and Property Studs	KM2C	3FT deg	g	12-16	MO/DO	M/D	32	BBCC	Ind	
Public Policy and Management and Psychology	LMRC	3FT deg	g	12-16	MO/DO	M/D	32	BBCC	Ind	
Public Policy and Management with Biology	M1CC	3FT deg	g	12-16	MO/DO	M/D	32	BBCC	Ind	
Public Policy and Management with Business	M159	3FT deg	g	12-16	MO/DO	M/D	32	BBCC	Ind	
Public Policy and Management with Geology	M1FP	3FT deg	g	12-16	MO/DO	M/D	32	BBCC	Ind	
Public Policy and Management with Mapping Sci	M155	3FT deg	g	12-16	MO/DO	M/D	32	BBCC	Ind	
Public Policy and Management with Marketing	M1NM	3FT deg	g	12-16	MO/DO	M/D	32	BBCC	Ind	
Public Policy and Management with Modern History	M153	3FT deg	g	12-16	MO/DO	M/D	32	BBCC	Ind	
Public Policy and Management with Politics	M150	3FT deg	g	12-16	MO/DO	M/D	32	BBCC	Ind	
Public Policy and Management with Psychology	M151	3FT deg	g	12-16	MO/DO	M/D	32	BBCC	Ind	
Public Policy and Management with Social Studs	M1LH	3FT deg	g	12-16	MO/DO	M/D	32	BBCC	Ind	
Public Policy and Mgt and Applied Statistics	GM4C	3FT deg	g	12-16	MO/DO	M/D	32	BBCC	Ind	
Public Policy and Mgt and Ecology & Biodiversity	CM9C	3FT deg	g	12-16	MO/DO	M/D	32	BBCC	Ind	
Public Policy and Mgt and Environmental Science	FM9C	3FT deg	g	12-16	MO/DO	M/D	32	BBCC	Ind	
Public Policy and Mgt with Comparative Lit	M143	3FT deg	g	12-16	MO/DO	M/D	32	BBCC	Ind	
Public Policy and Mgt with Contemporary History	M1VD	3FT deg	g	12-16	MO/DO	M/D	32	BBCC	Ind	
Public Policy and Mgt with Literary St in Engl	M156	3FT deg	g	12-16	MO/DO	M/D	32	BBCC	Ind	
Public Policy and Mgt with Media Practices	M1PL	3FT deg	g	12-16	MO/DO	M/D	32	BBCC	Ind	
Public Policy and Mgt with Modern English Studs	M1QH	3FT deg	g	12-16	MO/DO	M/D	32	BBCC	Ind	
Public Policy and Mgt with Travel & Tourism	M1PR	3FT deg	g	12-16	MO/DO	M/D	32	BBCC	Ind	
Regional Planning & Dev and Public Policy & Mgt	MKC4	3FT dog	g	12-16	MO/DO	M/D	32	BBCC	Ind	
Regional Planning & Dev with Public Policy & Mgt	K4MC	3FT deg	g	12-16	MO/DO	M/D	32	BBCC	Ind	
Regional Planning and Development and Politics	MK14	3FT deg	g	12-16	MO/DO	M/D	32	BBCC	Ind	
Regional Planning and Development with Politics	K4M1	3FT deg	g	12-16	MO/DO	M/D	32	BBCC	Ind	
Social Policy and Politics	LM41	3FT deg		12-16	MO/DO	M/D	32	BBCC	Ind	
Social Policy and Public Policy and Management	LM4C	3FT deg		12-16	MO/DO	M/D	32	BBCC	Ind	
Social Policy with Politics	L4M1	3FT deg		12-16	MO/DO	M/D	32	BBCC	Ind	
Social Policy with Public Policy & Management	L4MC	3FT deg		12-16	MO/DO	M/D	32	BBCC	Ind	
Social Studies and Politics	ML13	3FT deg	g	12-16	MO/DO	M/D	32	BBCC	Ind	
Social Studies and Public Policy & Management	MLC3	3FT deg	g	12-16	MO/DO	M/D	32	BBCC	Ind	3
Social Studies with Politics	L3M1	3FT deg	g	12-16	MO/DO	M/D	32	BBCC	Ind	
Social Studies with Public Policy and Management	L3MC	3FT deg	g	12-16	MO/DO	M/D	32	BBCC	Ind	

	course details			98 expected requirements						96 entry stats	
TITLE	CODE	COURSE	SUBJECTS	A/AS	NO/C	AGNVQ	IB	SQA(H)	SQA	RATIO	A/AS
Travel and Tourism and Politics	MP17	3FT deg	g	12-16	MO/DO	M/D	32	BBCC	Ind		
Travel and Tourism and Public Policy & Mgt	MPC7	3FT deg	g	12-16	MO/DO	M/D	32	BBCC	Ind		
Travel and Tourism with Politics	P7M1	3FT deg	g	12-16	MO/DO	M/D	32	BBCC	Ind		
Travel and Tourism with Public Policy & Mgt	P7MC	3FT deg	g	12-16	MO/DO	M/D	32	BBCC	Ind	1	
Women's Studies and Politics	MM91	3FT deg		12-16	MO/DO	M/D	32	BBCC	Ind		
Women's Studies and Public Policy & Management	MM9C	3FT deg		12-16	MO/DO	M/D	32	BBCC	Ind		
Women's Studies with Politics	M9M1	3FT deg		12-16	MO/DO	M/D	32	BBCC	Ind		
Women's Studies with Public Policy & Management	M9MC	3FT deg		12-16	MO/DO	M/D	32	BBCC	Ind		
Public Administration (Legal Studies)	3M1M	2FT HND	g	4-8	N/MO	P/M	26	CCDD	Ind	1	2/ 6
Public Administration (Social Studies)	4L1M	2FT HND	g	4-8	N/MO	P/M	26	CCDD	Ind	1	2/ 6

Univ of MANCHESTER

Government and Law	MM13	3FT deg		ABB	Ind	D^	32$	CSYS	Ind	9	24/30
Government and Political Theory	M144	3FT deg	* g	BBC	M+6D	D^	32	AABBB	Ind	5	22/28
Philosophy and Politics	VM71	3FT deg		BBB	Ind		32$	AABBB$	Ind	6	22/30
Politics	M100	3FT deg		BBB	6D	D^	32	AABBB	Ind	11	24/30
Politics and Modern History	VM11	3FT deg		BBC-BBB	Ind		Dip	Ind	Ind	5	20/28
Politics and Religion	VM81	3FT deg	*	20-24	Ind		28	BBBBC	Ind	3	18/20

MANCHESTER METROPOLITAN Univ

Public Policy and Administration	M140	4SW deg	* g	12	N	Ind	Ind	BCCC	Ind		8/16
Humanities/Social Studies *Politics*	Y400	3FT deg	*	CDD	Ind	Ind	Ind	BBB	Ind		

MIDDLESEX Univ

Green Politics	M925▼	3FT deg	* g	12	5M	M$ go					
Politics and International Studies	M150▼	3FT deg	* g	12-16	5M	M$ go	28	Ind	Ind		
Joint Honours Degree *Politics and International Studies*	Y400	3FT deg	* g	12-16	5M	M$ go	28	BBCC	Ind		

NENE COLLEGE

Business Administration with Politics	N1M1	3FT deg	g	10	M+1D	M	24	BCC	Ind		
Drama with Politics	W4M1	3FT deg		10	5M+1D	M	24	CCC	Ind		
Education with Politics	X9M1	3FT deg		DD	5M	M	24	CCC	Ind		
French with Politics	R1M1	3FT deg	F	DD	5M	Ind	24	CCC	Ind		
History with Politics	V1M1	3FT deg		CD	5M	M	24	CCC	Ind		
Law with Politics	M3M1	3FT deg	g	10	3M+2D	M	24	CCC	Ind		
Politics with Business Administration	M1N1	3FT deg	g	DD	5M	M	24	CCC	Ind		
Politics with European Union Studies	M1T2	3FT deg									
Politics with French	M1R1	3FT deg	F	DD	5M	M	24	CCC	Ind		
Politics with Geography	M1F8	3FT deg		CD	5M	M	24	CCC	Ind		
Politics with History	M1V1	3FT deg		CD	5M	M	24	CCC	Ind		
Politics with Industry and Enterprise	M1H1	3FT deg	g	CD	5M	M	24	CCC	Ind		
Politics with Law	M1M3	3FT deg	g	CD	5M	M	24	CCC	Ind		
Politics with Media and Popular Culture	M1P4	3FT deg		CD	5M	M	24	CCC	Ind		4/ 8
Politics with Personal Organisational Develop	M1N6	3FT deg		CD	5M	M	24	CCC	Ind		
Politics with Philosophy	M1V7	3FT deg		CD	5M	M	24	CCC	Ind		
Politics with Sociology	M1L3	3FT deg		CD	5M	M	24	CCC	Ind		
Politics with Sport Studies	M1N7	3FT deg		CD	5M	M	24	CCC	Ind		
Politics with Wastes Management & the Environ	M1FX	3FT deg		CD	5M	M	24	CCC	Ind		
Sociology with Politics	L3M1	3FT deg		10	5M	M	24	CCC	Ind		

			98 expected requirements							96 entry stats	
course details											
TITLE	CODE	COURSE	SUBJECTS	A/AS	NO/C	RGNVQ	IB	SQA(H)	SQA	RATIO	A/AS
Univ of NEWCASTLE											
French with Politics	R1M1	4FT deg	F	BBC			$	AABBB$		8	
German with Politics	R2M1	4FT deg	G	20			$	ABBBB$			
Government and European Union Studies	M146	4FT deg	*g	BBC	Ind		30$	AABB	Ind	5	22/28
Politics	M100	3FT deg	*	BBC	Ind		Ind	AABB	Ind	8	22/28
Politics (East Asia)	M160	3FT deg									
Politics and East Asian Studies	MTCM	4FT deg	*	BBC	Ind		Ind	AABB	Ind	2	
Politics and Economics	ML11	3FT deg	*g	BBB-BBC	Ind		Ind	AABB	Ind	9	22/28
Politics and History	VM11	3FT deg	H	BBB	Ind		30$	AABB	Ind	8	24/30
Politics and Social Policy	LM41	3FT deg	*	BBC	Ind		30	AABB	HN	6	18/24
Spanish with Politics	R4M1	4FT deg	Sp	BCC			$	ABBBB$			
Combined Studies (BA) Politics	Y400	3FT deg	*	ABC-BBB	5D	Ind	35$	AAAB	Ind		
Univ of NORTH LONDON											
Business and Politics	NM11	3FT deg	*g	CC	MO+4D	D	Ind	CCCCC	Ind		
Education Studies and Politics	MX19	3FT deg	*	12	Ind	Ind	Ind	Ind	Ind		
European Studies and Politics	MT12	3FT deg	*	CC	Ind	Ind	Ind	Ind	Ind		
History and Politics	VM11	3FT deg	*	CC	MO	M	Ind	Ind	Ind	9	
International Business and Politics	NMC1	3FT deg	*g	CC	MO+4D	D	Ind	Ind	Ind		
Irish Studies and Politics	QM51	3FT deg	*	CC	MO	M	Ind	Ind	Ind	9	
Politics	M100▼	3FT deg	*	CC	MO	M	$	CCCCC	Ind	8	6/10
Politics and Economics	LM1C	3FT deg	*g	CC	Ind	Ind	Ind	Ind	Ind		
Politics and Philosophy	MV1T	3FT deg	*	CC	Ind	Ind	Ind	Ind	Ind		
Combined Honours Politics	Y301	3FT deg	*	CC	MO	M	Dip	CCCCC	Ind		
Univ of NORTHUMBRIA											
French and Politics	MR11	3FT deg			2M+2D	M^	24	BBCCC	Ind		
German and Politics	MR12	3FT deg		CC	2M+2D	M^	24	BBCCC	Ind		
Government and Public Policy	M142	3FT deg	g	14	MO		24	BCCC	Ind	3	8/22
Political Economy	M105	3FT deg	Ec g	8	3M	Ind	24	CCCC	Ind		
Politics	M100	3FT deg	g	14	MO	M$	24	BCCC	Ind		
Politics and Economics	LM11	3FT deg	g	14	Ind		24	BCCC	Ind	4	9/16
Politics and Sociology	LM31	3FT deg	So g	16	3M		24	BBCCC	Ind	3	10/18
Russian and Politics	MR18	3FT deg		CC	2M+2D	M^	24	BBCCC	Ind		
Spanish and Politics	MR14	3FT deg		CC	2M+2D	M^	24	BBCCC	Ind		
Univ of NOTTINGHAM											
Law and Politics	MM13	3FT deg	*	ABB	Ind		34	Ind	Ind	17	24/30
Politics (Hist/Pol or Fren/Pol or Ger/Pol)	M100	3FT deg	*	ABB-BBB	Ind		32	Ind	Ind	13	26/30
Politics with East European Studies	M1T1	3FT deg	*	BBB	Ind		32	Ind	Ind		
NOTTINGHAM TRENT Univ											
International Relations	M158	3FT deg	*g	18	M+D	Ind	28	CCCC	Ind	4	10/20
Policy and Politics	LM41	3FT deg	*g	18	Ind	Ind	Ind	Ind	Ind		14/20
Politics	M100	3FT deg	*g	18	Ind	Ind	Ind	Ind	Ind		10/18
OXFORD Univ											
Philosophy, Politics and Economics Politics	Y616	3FT deg	*	AAB	DO		36	AAAAA	Ind		
OXFORD WESTMINSTER COLLEGE											
Contemporary English Studies with World Studies	Q3M1	3FT deg	E	CE	MO	M	Ind	CCC	Ind		
Contemporary English Studies with World Studies	Q3MC	2FT Dip	E	CE	MO	M	Ind	CCC	Ind		
Contemporary French Studies with World Studies	R1MC	2FT Dip	F	CE	MO	M	Ind	CCC	Ind		

TITLE	CODE	COURSE	SUBJECTS	A/AS	NO/C	AGNVQ	IB	SQA(H)	SQA	RATIO A/AS
course details			**98 expected requirements**							**96 entry stats**
Contemporary French Studies with World Studies	R1M1	3FT deg	F	CE	MO	M	Ind	CCC	Ind	
Contemporary Geography Studies with World Studs	L8M1	3FT deg	Gy	CE	MO	M	Ind	CCC	Ind	
Contemporary Geography Studies with World Studs	L8MC	2FT Dip	Gy	CE	MO	M	Ind	CCC	Ind	
Contemporary Historical Studies with World St	V1M1	3FT deg	H	CE	MO	M	Ind	CCC	Ind	
Contemporary Historical Studies with World St	V1MC	2FT Dip	H	CE	MO	M	Ind	CCC	Ind	

OXFORD BROOKES Univ

TITLE	CODE	COURSE	SUBJECTS	A/AS	NO/C	AGNVQ	IB	SQA(H)	SQA	RATIO A/AS
Politics/Accounting and Finance	MN14	3FT deg	* g	AB-BCC	Ind	M^/D*3	Ind	Ind	Ind	4
Politics/Anthropology	LM61	3FT deg	*	AB-CCC	Ind	M*^	Ind	Ind	Ind	6
Politics/Biological Chemistry	CM71	3FT deg								
Politics/Business Administration and Management	MN11	3FT deg	* g	AB-CCC	Ind	M^/MB3	Ind	Ind	Ind	
Politics/Cartography	FM81	3FT deg	* g	DDD-AB	Ind	M*^	Ind	Ind	Ind	
Politics/Cell Biology	CMC1	3FT deg								
Politics/Combined Studies	MY14	3FT deg		X		X	X	X		
Politics/Computer Systems	GM61	3FT deg	* g	BC-AB	Ind	M*^	Ind	Ind	Ind	
Politics/Computing	GM51	3FT deg	* g	CDD-AB	Ind	M*^	Ind	Ind	Ind	2
Politics/Computing Mathematics	GM91	3FT deg	* g	CD-AB	Ind	M*^	Ind	Ind	Ind	
Politics/Economics	LM11	3FT deg	* g	CCD-AB	Ind	M^/M*3	Ind	Ind	Ind	9 10/20
Politics/Educational Studies	MX19	3FT deg	*	CC-AB	Ind	M^/M*3	Ind	Ind	Ind	2
Politics/Electronics	MH16	3FT deg	S/M	CC-AB	Ind	M$	Ind	Ind	Ind	
Politics/English Studies	MQ13	3FT deg	*	AB-CCC	Ind	M*^	Ind	Ind	Ind	6 16/18
Politics/Environmental Chemistry	MF11	3FT deg								
Politics/Environmental Policy	KM31	3FT deg								
Politics/Environmental Sciences	FMX1	3FT deg	S g	CD-AB	Ind	M^/DS	Ind	Ind	Ind	
Politics/Exercise and Health	MB16	3FT deg	S g	DD-AB	Ind	MS^	Ind	Ind	Ind	
Politics/Fine Art	MW11	3FT deg	Pf+A	BC-AB	Ind	MA^	Ind	Ind	Ind	
Politics/Food Science and Nutrition	DM41	3FT deg	S g	DD-AB	Ind	MS^	Ind	Ind	Ind	
Politics/French Language and Contemp Studies	MR1C	4SW deg	F	CDD-AB	Ind	M*_^_	Ind	Ind	Ind	
Politics/French Language and Literature	MR11	4SW deg	F	CDD-AB	Ind	M*_^_	Ind	Ind	Ind	4
Politics/Geography	LM81	3FT deg	*	CCD-AB	Ind	M*^	Ind	Ind	Ind	14
Politics/Geology	FM61	3FT deg	S/M g	DD-AB	Ind	PS/M*^	Ind	Ind	Ind	
Politics/Geotechnics	HM21	3FT deg	S/M/Ds/Es	DD-AB	Ind	M$^	Ind	Ind	Ind	
Politics/German Language and Contemp Stud	MR1F	4SW deg	G	DDD-AB	Ind	M*_^_	Ind	Ind	Ind	1
Politics/German Language and Literature	MR12	4SW deg	G	DDD-AB	Ind	M*_^_	Ind	Ind	Ind	1
Politics/German Studies	MR1G	4SW deg	G	DDD-AB	Ind	M*_^_	Ind	Ind	Ind	
Politics/Health Care (Post Exp)	BM71	3FT deg		X		X	X	X		
Politics/History	MV11	3FT deg	*	CCD-AB	Ind	M^	Ind	Ind	Ind	9 12/18
Politics/Hospitality Management Studies	MN17	3FT deg	*	DDD-AB	Ind	M^/M*3	Ind	Ind	Ind	
Politics/Human Biology	BM11	3FT deg								
Politics/Information Systems	GMM1	3FT deg	* g	CDD-AB	Ind	M*^	Ind	Ind	Ind	
Politics/Intelligent Systems	MG18	3FR deg	* g	CD-AB	Ind	M*^	Ind	Ind	Ind	
Politics/Law	MM31	3FT deg	*	CCC-AB	Ind	M^/D*3	Ind	Ind	Ind	31
Politics/Leisure Planning and Management	KMH1	3FT deg								
Politics/Marketing Management	NMN1	3FT deg	* g	CCC-AB	Ind	M^/D*3	Ind	Ind	Ind	6
Politics/Mathematics	MG11	3FT deg	M	DD-AB	Ind	M*^	Ind	Ind	Ind	
Politics/Music	MW13	3FT deg	Mu	DD-AB	Ind	M*^	Ind	Ind	Ind	
Politics/Palliative Care (Post Exp)	BMR1	3FT deg		X		X	X	X		
Politics/Physical Geography	FMV1	3FT deg								
Politics/Planning Studies	MK14	3FT deg	* g	DDD-AB	Ind	M*^	Ind	Ind	Ind	3
Psychology/Politics	CM81	3FT deg	* g	AB-CCC	Ind	M*^	Ind	Ind	Ind	26
Publishing/Politics	MP15	3FT deg	* g	CCD-AB	Ind	M^/M$3	Ind	Ind	Ind	3
Rehabilitation/Politics (Post Exp)	BMT1	3FT deg		X		X	X	X		
Sociology/Politics	LM31	3FT deg	*	AB-CCC	Ind	M*^	Ind	Ind	Ind	25

course details | 98 expected requirements | 96 entry stats

TITLE	CODE	COURSE	SUBJECTS	A/AS	ND/C	AGNVQ	IB	SQA(H)	SQA	RATIO A/AS
Software Engineering/Politics	GM71	3FT deg	* g	CD-AB	Ind	M*^	Ind	Ind	Ind	
Statistics/Politics	GM41	3FT deg	* g	DD-AB	Ind	M*^	Ind	Ind	Ind	
Telecommunications/Politics	MH1P	3FT deg								
Tourism/Politics	MP17	3FT deg	* g	CCD-AB	Ind	M^/M*3	Ind	Ind	Ind	9
Water Resources/Politics	HMF1	3FT deg								

Univ of PLYMOUTH

TITLE	CODE	COURSE	SUBJECTS	A/AS	ND/C	AGNVQ	IB	SQA(H)	SQA	RATIO A/AS
Applied Economics with International Relations	LMCC	3FT deg	* g	CDD-CCD MO		M$^	Ind	BCCC	Ind	
Applied Economics with Politics	L1M1	3FT deg	* g	CCD-CDD MO		M$^	Ind	BCCC	Ind	12
Business Economics with Politics	L1MC	3FT deg	* g	CDD-CCD MO		M$^	Ind	BCCC	Ind	
European Economics with Politics	L1MD	3FT deg	* g	CDD-CCD MO		M$^	Ind	BCCC	Ind	
Geography with International Relations	F8MC	3FT deg	Gy g	16-18	X	M$^	Ind	ABBB	Ind	
Geography with Politics	F8M1	3FT deg	Gy g	16-18	X	M$^	Ind	ABBB	Ind	8
Law with International Relations	M3MC	3FT deg	Ap g	BCC-BBC	DO	D12^	Ind	BBBB$	Ind	
Law with Politics	M3M1	3FT deg	Ap g	BCC-BBC	DO	D12^	Ind	BBBB$	Ind	31
Modern Languages with Politics	T9M1	3FT/4SW deg	L g	C	Ind	Ind	Ind	Ind	Ind	
Political Economy with Politics	LM1D	3FT deg	Ap g	CDD-CCD MO $		M$^	Ind	BCCC	Ind	
Politics	M100	3FT deg	* g	14	3M	M$	Ind	BBBB$	Ind	5 8/22
Politics with Applied Economics	M1L1	3FT deg	* g	14	Ind	M$	Ind	BBBC$	Ind	
Politics with Computing	M1G5	3FT deg	* g	14	Ind	M$	Ind	BBBC$	Ind	
Politics with Criminal Justice	M1MJ	3FT deg	* g	16	3M	M$	Ind	BBBC$	Ind	4 10/20
Politics with French	M1R1	3FT deg	F g	14	Ind	M$^	Ind	BBBC$	Ind	
Politics with Geography	M1F8	3FT deg	Gy g	16	5M $	M$	Ind	BBBC$	Ind	
Politics with German	M1R2	3FT deg	G g	14	Ind	M$^	Ind	BBBC$	Ind	
Politics with International Relations	M156	3FT deg	* g	14	3M $	M$	Ind	BBBC$	Ind	1
Politics with Italian	M1R3	3FT deg	* g	14	3M $	M$	Ind	BBBC$	Ind	
Politics with Languages	M1T9	3FT deg	L g	14	Ind	M$^	Ind	BBBC$	Ind	
Politics with Law	M1M3	3FT deg	* g	BCC	Ind	D12^	Ind	BBBC$	Ind	9
Politics with Psychology	M1C8	3FT deg	* g	BCC	MO+3D	D12^	Ind	BBBC$	Ind	7
Politics with Resources, Manuf and the Environ	M1F9	3FT deg	* g	14	3M	M$	Ind	BBBC$	Ind	
Politics with Social Policy	M1L4	3FT deg	* g	14	3M	M$	Ind	BBBC$	Ind	3
Politics with Social Research	M1LJ	3FT deg	* g	14	3M	M$	Ind	BBBC$	Ind	
Politics with Sociology	M1L3	3FT deg	* g	14	3M	M$	Ind	BBBC$	Ind	8
Politics with Spanish	M1R4	3FT deg	Sp g	14	Ind	M$^	Ind	BBBC$	Ind	
Politics with Statistics	M1G4	3FT deg	* g	14	Ind	M$	Ind	BBBC$	Ind	
Politics with Transport	M1N9	3FT deg	* g	14	4M	M$	Ind	BBBC$	Ind	
Psychology with Politics	C8M1	3FT/4SW deg	Ap g	BBC	MO+3D	M12^	Ind	BBBC$	Ind	4
Social Policy with International Relations	L4M1	3FT deg	* g	14	3M	M$	Ind	BBBC$	Ind	
Social Policy with Politics	L4MC	3FT deg	* g	14	3M	M$	Ind	BBBC$	Ind	5
Sociology with International Relations	L3MC	3FT deg	* g	14	3M	M$	Ind	BBBC$	Ind	
Sociology with Politics	L3M1	3FT deg	* g	14	3M	M$	Ind	BBBC$	Ind	7

Univ of PORTSMOUTH

TITLE	CODE	COURSE	SUBJECTS	A/AS	ND/C	AGNVQ	IB	SQA(H)	SQA	RATIO A/AS
International Relations and Politics	M155	3FT deg	*	14	Ind	D*6^	Dip	BBBC	Ind	6/16
Politics	M100	3FT deg	*	14	Ind	D*6/^	Dip	BBBC	Ind	4 8/18

QUEEN MARY & WESTFIELD COLL (Univ of London)

TITLE	CODE	COURSE	SUBJECTS	A/AS	ND/C	AGNVQ	IB	SQA(H)	SQA	RATIO A/AS
Economics and Politics	LM11	3FT deg	g	BBC		M	30$	BBBBB		
French and Politics	MR11	4FT deg	F	BCC		M^	30$			
Geography and Politics	LM81	3FT deg	Gy	BCC		M$^	30$			
German and Politics	MR1F	4FT deg	G	BCC		M^	30$			
Hispanic Studies and Politics	MR14	4FT deg		BCC		M^				
History and Politics	MV11	3FT deg	H	BCC		M^	30$			
Law and Politics	MM13	3FT deg		ABB	DO	D^	32$	AABBB		

course details			98 expected requirements							96 entry stats	
TITLE	CODE	COURSE	SUBJECTS	A/AS	NO/C	AGNVQ	IB	SQA(H)	SQA	RATIO	A/AS
Politics	M102	3FT deg		BCC		D$					
Politics and German Language	MR1G	4FT deg	G	BCC		M	30$				
Russian and Politics	MR18	4FT deg		BCC		M^					

QUEEN'S Univ Belfast

European Area Studies	M1T2	3FT deg	L/* g	BCC	3M+4D	D*6/^ go	29$	ABBB	Ind		
Law with Politics	M3M1	3FT deg	* g	ABB	7D	D*^ go	34$	AAABB	Ind	7	26/30
Politics	M100	3FT deg	* g	BCC	3M+4D	D*6/^ go	29$	ABBB	Ind	4	18/24
Politics/Ancient History	VMC1	3FT deg	* g	BCC	3M+4D	D*6/^ go	29$	ABBB	Ind		
Politics/Byzantine Studies	QM81	3FT/4FT deg	* g	BCC	3M+4D	D*6/^ go	29$	ABBB	Ind		
Politics/Celtic	QM51	3FT/4FT deg	* g	BCC	3M+4D	D*6/^ go	29$	ABBB	Ind	6	
Politics/Classical Studies	MQ18	3FT deg	* g	BCC	3M+4D	D*6/^ go	29$	ABBB	Ind		
Politics/Economic & Social History	VM31	3FT deg	* g	BCC	3M+4D	D*6/^ go	29$	ABBB	Ind		
Politics/Economics	LM11	3FT deg									
Politics/English	QM31	3FT deg	E g	BCC	X	D*^ go	29$	ABBB	X	10	22/26
Politics/Ethnomusicology	WM3C	3FT deg	* g	BCC	3M+4D	D*6/^ go	29$	ABBB	Ind		
Politics/European Area Studies	MT1F	3FT deg	L/* g	BCC	3M+4D	D*6/^ go	29$	ABBB	Ind		
Politics/French (4 years)	RM11	4FT deg	E g	BCC	X	D*^ go	29$	ABBB	X		
Politics/German (4 years)	RM21	4FT deg	* g	BCC	3M+4D	D*6/^ go	29$	ABBB	Ind		
Politics/Greek	QM71	3FT/4FT deg	* g	BCC	3M+4D	D*6/^ go	29$	ABBB	Ind		
Politics/History & Philosophy of Science	VM51	3FT deg	* g	BCC	3M+4D	D*6/^ go	29$	ABBB	Ind		
Politics/Human Geography	LM8C	3FT deg	* g	BCC	3M+4D	D*6/^ go	29$	ABBB	Ind		
Politics/Italian (4 years)	RM31	4FT deg	* g	BCC	3M+4D	D*6/^ go	29$	ABBB	Ind		
Politics/Latin	QM61	3FT/4FT deg	* g	BCC	3M+4D	D*6/^ go	29$	ABBB	Ind		
Politics/Modern History	VM11	3FT deg	* g	BCC	3M+4D	D*6/^ go	29$	ABBB	Ind	5	20/26
Politics/Music	WM31	3FT deg	* g	BCC	3M+4D	D*6/^ go	29$	ABBB	Ind	7	
Politics/Philosophy	VM71	3FT deg	* g	BCC	3M+4D	D*6/^ go	29$	ABBB	Ind	15	
Psychology/Politics	CM8C	3FT deg	* g	BCC	3M+4D	D*6/^ go	29$	ABBB	Ind		
Scholastic Philosophy/Politics	MV1R	3FT deg	* g	BCC	3M+4D	D*6/^ go	29$	ABBB	Ind	5	
Social Anthropology/Politics	ML16	3FT deg	* g	BCC	3M+4D	D*6/^ go	29$	ABBB	Ind	23	
Social Policy/Politics	ML14	3FT deg	* g	BCC	3M+4D	D*6/^ go	29$	ABBB	Ind		
Sociology/Politics	ML13	3FT deg	* g	BCC	3M+4D	D*6/^ go	29$	ABBB	Ind	9	20/26
Spanish/Politics (4 years)	MR14	4FT deg	* g	BCC	3M+4D	D*6/^ go	29$	ABBB	Ind		
Women's Studies/Politics	MM19	3FT deg	* g	BCC	3M+4D	D*6/^ go	29$	ABBB	Ind		

Univ of READING

Classical Studies and Politics	QM81	3FT deg	*	BCC	Ind	D*6/^	30	BBBB	Ind	6	
French and International Relations	RM11	4FT deg	F	BBC	Ind	D*^	31$	BBBB$	Ind		
French and Politics	MR11	4FT deg	F	BBC	Ind	D*^	31$	BBBB$	Ind	7	
German and International Relations	RM21	4FT deg	* g	BCC	Ind	D$^	30	BBBB	Ind		
German and Politics	MR12	4FT deg	* g	BCC	Ind	D$^	30	BBBB	Ind		
International Relations and Economics	ML11	3FT deg	* g	BBC	Ind	D$6/^ go	31	BBBB	Ind	12	
Italian and International Relations	RM31	4FT deg	* g	BCC	Ind	D$6/^ go	30	BBBB	Ind	5	
Italian and Politics	MR13	4FT deg	* g	BCC	Ind	D$6/^ go	30	BBBB	Ind		
Modern History and International Relations	VM11	3FT deg	*	BBC	Ind	D*6/^	31	BBBB	Ind	9	
Modern History and Politics	MV11	3FT deg	*	BBC	Ind	D*6/^	31	BBBB	Ind	10	18/24
Philosophy and International Relations	VM71	3FT deg	*	BCC	Ind	D*^	30	BBBB	Ind	8	
Philosophy and Politics	MV17	3FT deg	*	BCC	Ind	D*^	30	BBBB	Ind	8	20/20
Politics and Economics	LM11	3FT deg	* g	BBC	Ind	D$6/^ go	31	BBBB	Ind	10	18/20
Politics and International Relations	M158	3FT deg	*	22	Ind	D*6/^	31	BBBB	Ind	9	18/24
Sociology and International Relations	ML13	3FT deg	*	BCC	Ind	D$^ go	30	BBBB	Ind	17	
Sociology and Politics	LM31	3FT deg	*	BCC	Ind	D$^ go	30	BBBB	Ind	29	

TITLE	CODE	COURSE	SUBJECTS	A/AS	ND/C	RGNVQ	IB	SQA(H)	SQA	RATIO A/AS
ROBERT GORDON Univ										
Public Policy and Management	M148	3FT/4FT deg	* g	DE	N	Ind	Ind	BBC$	Ind	3
ROYAL HOLLOWAY, Univ of London										
Economics and Public Administration	LM11	3FT deg	*	BCC-BBB	Ind		Ind	Ind		
Economics with Political Studies	L1M1	3FT deg	*	BBC-BBB	Ind		32	Ind		7
French with Political Studies	R1MC	4FT deg	F	BBC-ABC			28$	Ind		1
German with Political Studies	R2MC	4FT deg	G	BCC			28$	BBBBC$		
Italian with Political Studies	R3MC	4FT deg	L/Ln	BBC			30	BBCCC$		
Mathematics with Political Studies	G1MC	3FT deg	M	BCC-BBC	Ind	D^	Ind	Ind		
Music with Political Studies	W3MC	3FT deg	Mu	BCC-BBC			Ind	ABBCC$		
Social Policy and Politics	LM41	3FT deg	*	BCC-BBC	Ind	D^	Ind	Ind		4
Social Policy with Political Studies	L4MC	3FT deg	*	BCC-BBC	Ind	D^	Ind	Ind		5
Sociology and Politics	LM31	3FT deg	*	BCC-BBC	Ind	D^	Ind	Ind		8
Sociology with Political Studies	L3M1	3FT deg	*	BCC-BBC	Ind	D^	Ind	Ind		4
Univ of SALFORD										
Politics and Contemporary History	MV11	3FT deg	g	CCC	M0+4D	M	Ind	Ind	Ind	4 12/22
Politics and Sociology	LM31	3FT deg	* g	CCC	Ind	Ind	Ind	Ind	Ind	5 12/22
SOAS:Sch of Oriental & African St (U of London)										
Politics	M102	3FT deg		20	Ind		30	BBBCC	Ind	4 12/26
Politics and African Studies	TM71	3FT deg		20	Ind		30	BBBCC	Ind	
Politics and Amharic	MT17	4FT deg		20	Ind		30	BBBCC	Ind	
Politics and Arabic	MT16	4FT deg		22	Ind		31	BBBBC	Ind	5
Politics and Bengali	MT15	3FT deg		20	Ind		30	BBBCC	Ind	
Politics and Burmese	MT1M	4FT deg	g	20	Ind		30	BBBCC	Ind	
Politics and Chinese	MT13	4FT deg		24	Ind		32	BBBBB	Ind	
Politics and Development Studies	MM91	3FT deg		22	Ind		31	BBBBC	Ind	8
Politics and Economics	LM11	3FT deg	g	22	Ind		31	BBBBC	Ind	3 18/26
Politics and Geography	LM81	3FT deg		20	Ind		30	BBBCC	Ind	
Politics and Georgian	MT19	3FT deg		22	Ind		31	BBBBC	Ind	
Politics and Gujarati	MTC5	3FT deg		20	Ind		30	BBBCC	Ind	
Politics and Hausa	MT1R	4FT deg		20	Ind		30	BBBCC	Ind	
Politics and Hebrew	MQ19	4FT deg		22	Ind		31	BBBBC	Ind	
Politics and Hindi	MT1N	3FT/4FT deg		20	Ind		30	BBBCC	Ind	
Politics and History	MV11	3FT deg		20	Ind		30	BBBCC	Ind	5
Politics and Indonesian	MTCM	3FT/4FT deg		20	Ind		30	BBBCC	Ind	
Politics and Japanese	MT14	4FT deg		24	Ind		32	BBBBB	Ind	4
Politics and Korean	MTCN	4FT deg		20	Ind		30	BBBCC	Ind	
Politics and Law	MM13	3FT deg		24	Ind		32	BBBBB	Ind	5
Politics and Linguistics	MQ13	3FT deg								
Politics and Nepali	MTDM	3FT deg		20	Ind		30	BBBCC	Ind	
Politics and Persian	MT1Q	3FT deg		22	Ind		31	BBBBC	Ind	
Sanskrit and Politics	MQ1X	3FT deg		20	Ind		30	BBBCC	Ind	
Sinhalese and Politics	MTDN	3FT deg		20	Ind		30	BBBCC	Ind	
Social Anthropology and Politics	LM61	3FT deg		22	Ind		31	BBBBC	Ind	
South Asian Studies and Politics	TMM1	3FT deg								
Study of Religions and Politics	MV18	3FT deg		20	Ind		30	BBBCC	Ind	
Swahili and Politics	MT1T	4FT deg		20	Ind		30	BBBCC	Ind	
Tamil and Politics	MTD5	3FT deg		20	Ind		30	BBBCC	Ind	
Thai and Politics	TM51	3FT/4FT deg		20	Ind		30	BBBCC	Ind	
Turkish and Politics	MT1P	3FT deg		22	Ind		31	BBBBC	Ind	
Urdu and Politics	TM5C	3FT deg		20	Ind		30	BBBCC	Ind	
Vietnamese and Politics	TM5D	4FT deg		20	Ind		30	BBBCC	Ind	1

course details   **98 expected requirements**   *96 entry stats*

				98 expected requirements						96 entry stats	
TITLE	CODE	COURSE	SUBJECTS	A/AS	ND/C	RGNVQ	IB	SQA(H)	SQA	RATIO	A/AS
SSEES:Sch of Slavonic & E European St(U of London)											
Politics with East European Studies	M1T1	3FT deg		BCC		Ind	28	BBBBB			·
Univ of SHEFFIELD											
Economics and Politics	LM11	3FT deg	* g	BBB	3M+3D	D^	32	AABB	Ind	11	24/30
French and Politics	RM11	4FT deg	F g	BBB	X	X	32$	AABB$	Ind	13	
Geography and Politics	LM8C	3FT deg	Gy g	BBB	3M+3D$	D^	32$	AABB$	Ind	9	
German and Politics	RM21	4FT deg	G g	BBC	X	X	30$	ABBB$	Ind	4	
Hispanic Studies and Politics	RM41	4FT deg	Sp g	BBC	X	X	30$	ABBB$	Ind	6	
Japanese Studies and Politics	TM41	4FT deg	* g	BBB	3M+3D	D^	32	AABB	Ind	7	
Modern History and Politics	VM11	3FT deg	H+Po g	BBB	3M+3D$	D^	32$	AABB$	Ind	11	22/30
Politics	M104	3FT deg	* g	BBB	3M+3D	D^	32	AABB	Ind	7	24/30
Russian and Politics	RM81	4FT deg	L g	BBC	X	X	30$	ABBB$	Ind	6	
Social and Political Studies *Politics*	Y220	3FT deg	* g	BBC	4D	D^	30	ABBB	Ind		
SHEFFIELD HALLAM Univ											
Public Policy and Management (1 Year top-up)	M141	1FT deg		X	HN	X	X	X	X		
Public Policy and Management (Full-Time)	M140	3FT deg	g	14	M+D	M4/^	Ind	Ind	Ind		
Public Policy and Management (Sandwich)	NM11	4SW deg	g	14	M+D	M4/^	Ind	Ind	Ind		
Combined Studies *Public Policy and Management*	Y400	3FT deg	* g	14	2M	M	Ind	Ind	Ind		
Public Policy and Management	041M	2FT HND	*	8	M0	M2/^	Ind	Ind	Ind		
Univ of SOUTHAMPTON											
Economics and Politics	LM11	3FT deg	* g	22	Ind	D$^ go	30	ABBBB	Ind	8	18/26
Mod Hist&Pol with Econ/Phil/Quantitative Methods	VM11	3FT deg	H g	22	X	Ind	30$	ABBBB	X	8	20/30
Philosophy and Politics	VM71	3FT deg	*	BCC	1M+4D	Ind	26	CSYS	Ind	8	18/26
Pol & Spanish(or Portuguese)& Latin American St	RM4C	4FT deg	Sp/Pt g	BBC	1M+4D	Ind	30$	Ind	Ind	3	16/24
Politics	M100	3FT deg	* g	22	Ind	D$^ go	30	ABBBB	Ind	8	18/24
Politics and Economic History	MV13	3FT deg	* g	20	Ind	D$^ go	28	BBBBC	Ind	5	20/22
Politics and International Studies	M160	3FT deg	* g	22	Ind	D$^ go	30	ABBBB	Ind	9	20/26
Politics and Law	MM13	3FT deg	* g	24	Ind	D$^ go	32	AABBB	Ind	13	20/28
Politics and Sociology	LM31	3FT deg	* g	20	Ind	D$^ go	28	BBBBC	Ind	11	20/22
Public and Social Administration	LMK1	3FT deg	* g	20	Ind	D$^ go	28	BBBBC	Ind		
SOUTHAMPTON INST											
Political Studies	M101	3FT deg	*	8	M0	M$	Dip	CCCC	N	1	8/16
Public Administration	041M	2FT HND	*	2	N	P$	Dip	CCCC	N	1	2/6
SOUTH BANK Univ											
Politics	M100	3FT deg	* g	CC	3M+4D	M go	Ind	Ind	Ind		
Politics and Business Information Technology	GM71	3FT deg	M g	12-16	4M+2D	M go	Ind	Ind	Ind		
Politics and Economics	LM11	3FT deg	Bu/Ec g	14-18	2M+4D	M go	Ind	Ind	Ind		
Politics and English Studies	MQ13	3FT deg	E g	14-18	X	M^ go	Ind	Ind	Ind		
Politics and Food Policy	DM41	3FT deg	S g	12-16	4M+2D	M go	Ind	Ind	Ind		
Politics and Health Studies	LM41	3FT deg	S g	12-16	4M+2D	M go	Ind	Ind	Ind		
Politics and History	MV11	3FT deg	H g	12-16	4M+2D	M^ go	Ind	Ind	Ind		
Politics and Human Biology	BM11	3FT deg	S g	12-16	4M+2D	M go	Ind	Ind	Ind		
Politics and Human Resource Management	MN1P	3FT deg	* g	14-18	2M+4D	M go	Ind	Ind	Ind		
Politics and Law	MM31	3FT deg	g	14-18	2M+4D	D go	Ind	Ind	Ind		
Politics and Management	MN11	3FT deg	g	12-16	4M+2D	M go	Ind	Ind	Ind		
Politics and Marketing	MN15	3FT deg	* g	14-18	2M+4D	M go	Ind	Ind	Ind		
Politics and Media Studies	MP14	3FT deg	E g	14-18	2M+4D	D go	Ind	Ind	Ind		
Politics and Nutrition	BM41	3FT deg	S g	12-16	4M+2D	M go	Ind	Ind	Ind		

TITLE	CODE	COURSE	SUBJECTS	A/AS	ND/C	RGNVQ	IB	SQA(H)	SQA	RATIO A/AS
			98 expected requirements							96 entry stats
Politics and Planning	KM41	3FT deg	* g	14-18	4M+2D	M go	Ind	Ind	Ind	
Social Policy and Politics	LM4C	3FT deg	g	12-16	4M+2D	M go	Ind	Ind	Ind	
Sociology and Politics	LM31	3FT deg	* g	12-16	4M+2D	M go	Ind	Ind	Ind	
Sports Science and Politics	BM61	3FT deg	S g	14-18	2M+4D	M go	Ind	Ind	Ind	
Tourism and Politics	MP17	3FT deg	L g	12-16	4M+2D	M go	Ind	Ind	Ind	
Urban Studies and Politics	MK14	3FT deg	* g	14-18	2M+4D	M go	Ind	Ind	Ind	
World Theatre and Politics	MW14	3FT deg	* g	14-18	2M+4D	M go	Ind	Ind	Ind	

Univ of ST ANDREWS

TITLE	CODE	COURSE	SUBJECTS	A/AS	ND/C	RGNVQ	IB	SQA(H)	SQA	RATIO A/AS
International Relations-Arabic	MT16	4FT deg	* g	AAB	X	Ind	36$	AAAB	Ind	6
International Relations-Art History	MV14	4FT deg	* g	AAB	X	Ind	36$	AAAB	Ind	
International Relations-Classical Studies	MQ18	4FT deg	* g	AAB	X	Ind	36$	AAAB	Ind	
International Relations-Economics	LM11	4FT deg	* g	AAB	X	Ind	36$	AAAB	Ind	17
International Relations-French	MR11	4FT deg	F g	AAB	X	Ind	36$	AAAB$	Ind	6
International Relations-French with Year Abroad	MR1C	4FT/5FT deg	F g	AAB	X	Ind	36$	AAAB$	Ind	9
International Relations-Geography	LM81	4FT deg	* g	AAB	X	Ind	36$	AAAB	Ind	19
International Relations-German	MR12	4FT deg	* g	AAB	X	Ind	36$	AAAB	Ind	
International Relations-German with Year Abroad	MR1F	4FT/5FT deg	* g	AAB	X	Ind	36$	AAAB	Ind	
Italian with Year Abroad-International Relations	MR1H	4FT/5FT deg	* g	AAB	X	Ind	36$	AAAB	Ind	
Italian-International Relations	MR13	4FT deg	* g	AAB	X	Ind	36$	AAAB	Ind	
Management-International Relations (Arts)	MN11	4FT deg	* g	AAB	X	Ind	36$	AAAB	Ind	7
Mediaeval History-International Relations	MV11	4FT deg	* g	AAB	X	Ind	36$	AAAB	Ind	
Modern History-International Relations	VM11	4FT deg	* g	AAB	X	Ind	36$	AAAB	Ind	4
Modern Langs with Int Rels (with Int Yr Abroad)	T9M1	4FT/5FT deg	* g	AAB	X	Ind	36$	AAAB	Ind	4
Modern Languages with International Relations	T9MC	4FT deg	* g	AAB	X	Ind	36$	AAAB	Ind	
Philosophy-International Relations	MV17	4FT deg	* g	AAB	X	Ind	36$	AAAB	Ind	8
Psychology-International Relations	LM71	4FT deg	* g	AAB*	X	Ind	36$	AAAB	Ind	5
Russian with Year Abroad-International Relations	MRC8	4FT/5FT deg	* g	AAB	X	Ind	36$	AAAB	Ind	
Russian-International Relations	MR18	4FT deg	* g	AAB	X	Ind	36$	AAAB	Ind	2
Scottish History-International Relations	MV1C	4FT deg	* g	AAB	X	Ind	36$	AAAB	Ind	
Social Anthropology-International Relations	LM61	4FT deg	* g	AAB	X	Ind	36$	AAAB	Ind	15
Spanish with Year Abroad-International Relations	MRC4	4FT/5FT deg	* g	AAB	X	Ind	36$	AAAB	Ind	6
Spanish-International Relations	MR14	4FT deg	* g	AAB	X	Ind	36$	AAAB	Ind	4
Theological Studies-International Relations	MV18	4FT deg	* g	AAB	X	Ind	36$	AAAB	Ind	
European Integration Studies International Relations	Y602	4FT deg	* g	BBB	X	Ind	36$	BBBB	Ind	
General Degree of MA International Relations	Y450	3FT deg	* g	AAB	X	Ind	30$	AABB	Ind	

The Modern History-International Relations row also shows "30/30" in the far right.

STAFFORDSHIRE Univ

TITLE	CODE	COURSE	SUBJECTS	A/AS	ND/C	RGNVQ	IB	SQA(H)	SQA	RATIO A/AS
European Culture and International Relations	LMPC	3FT deg	g	12	MO+2D	M	27	BBC	Ind	
International Relations	M150	3FT deg	g	12	3M	M	24	BCC	Ind	5
International Relations/American Studies	MQ1K	3FT deg	g	12	MO+2D	M	27	BBC	Ind	2
International Relations/Cultural Studies	ML1P	3FT deg	g	12	MO+2D	M	27	BBC	Ind	
International Relations/Development Studies	MMDY	3FT deg	g	12	3M	M	24d	BCC	Ind	3
International Relations/Economic Studies	LM11	3FT deg								
International Relations/Film Studies	MWC5	3FT deg	g	12	MO+2D	M	27	BBC	Ind	2
International Relations/French	MR1C	3FT/4SW deg	F g	12	4M+2D	M^	26	BCC	Ind	4
International Relations/Geography	ML1V	3FT deg	g	14	4M+1D	M	26	ABB	Ind	3
International Relations/German	MR1F	3FT/4SW deg	G g	12	4M+2D	M^	26	BCC	Ind	
International Relations/History	MV11	3FT deg	H g	12	MO+2D	M	27	BBC	Ind	5
International Relations/History of Art & Design	MV1K	3FT deg	g	12	MO+2D	M	27	BBC	Ind	
International Relations/Information Systems	MG1M	3FT deg	g	12	3M	M	24	BCC	Ind	
Law/International Relations	MM3C	3FT deg	g	18	HN	M^	26	BBBB	Ind	6

The International Relations row also shows "6/14", and International Relations/American Studies shows "8/18" in the far right.

	course details			98 expected requirements							96 entry stats	
TITLE		CODE	COURSE	SUBJECTS	A/AS	NO/C	RGNVQ	IB	SQA(H)	SQA	RATIO	A/AS
Legal Studies/International Relations		MM3D	3FT deg	g	18	HN	M^	26	BBBB	Ind		
Literature/International Relations		QM3C	3FT deg	El g	12	MO+2D	M	27	BBC	Ind	1	
Media Studies/International Relations		MPC4	3FT deg	g	12	MO+2D	M	27	BBC	Ind	9	
Politics		M100	3FT deg	g	12	3M	M	24	BCC	Ind	5	7/22
Politics/American Studies		MQC4	3FT deg	g	12	MO+2D	M	27	BBC	Ind	6	
Politics/Business Studies		MNC1	3FT deg	g	16	MO+2D	M$	24	BBB	Ind	6	
Politics/Cultural Studies		MLC6	3FT deg	g	12	MO+2D	D	27	BBC	Ind		
Politics/Development Studies		MMDX	3FT deg	g	12	3M	M	24	BCC	Ind		
Politics/Economic Studies		LM1D	3FT deg	g	12	4M	M	24	BBC			
Politics/Environmental Studies		MFC9	3FT deg	g	14	4M+1D	M	26	BBB	Ind		
Politics/European Culture		LMP1	3FT deg	g	12	MO+2D	M	27	BBC	Ind		
Politics/Film Studies		MWCM	3FT deg	g	12	MO+2D	M	27	BBC	Ind		
Politics/French		MRC1	3FT/4SW deg	E g	12	4M+2D	M^	26	BCC	Ind		
Politics/German		MRC2	3FT/4SW deg	G g	12	4M+2D	M^	26	BCC	Ind		
Politics/History		MVC1	3FT deg	H g	12	MO+2D	M	27	BBC	Ind	8	10/14
Politics/History of Art and Design		MVC4	3FT deg	g	12	MO+2D	M	27	BBC	Ind		
Politics/Information Systems		MGC5	3FT deg	g	12	3M	M	24	BCC	Ind	1	
Politics/International Relations		M156	3FT deg	g	12	3M	M	24	BCC	Ind	4	
Politics/Law		MMC3	3FT deg	g	18	HN	M^	26	BBBB	Ind	3	12/20
Politics/Legal Studies		MMCH	3FT deg	g	18	HN	M^	26d	BBBB	Ind		
Politics/Media Studies		MPCK	3FT deg	g	12	MO+2D	D	27	BBC	Ind	25	
Politics/Philosophy		MVC7	3FT deg	g	12	MO+2D	M	27	BBC	Ind	4	
Psychology/International Relations		LM7C	3FT deg	g	18	3M+3D	Ind	27	BBB	Ind	1	
Psychology/Politics		LMR1	3FT deg	g	18	3M+3D	Ind	27	BBB	Ind		
Sociology/International Relations		LM3C	3FT deg	g	12	3M	M	24	BCC	Ind		
Sociology/Politics		LMH1	3FT deg	g	12	3M	M	24	BCC	Ind	4	
Spanish/International Relations		RM4C	3FT/4SW deg	g	12	3M	M^	26	BCC	Ind	7	
Spanish/Politics		RMK1	3FT/4SW deg	g	12	3M	M^	26	BCC	Ind		
Women's Studies/Computing		GM51	3FT deg	g	12	Ind	M	Ind	BBB	Ind		
Women's Studies/International Relations		MM9C	3FT deg	g	12	3M	M	24	BCC	Ind		
Women's Studies/Politics		MMX1	3FT deg	g	12	3M	M	24	BCC	Ind		

Univ of STIRLING

Business Studies/Politics		MN11	4FT deg	g	BBC	Ind	Ind	33	BBBB	HN		
Economics/Politics		LM11	4FT deg	g	CCC	Ind	Ind	28	BBCC	HN		
English Studies/Politics		QM31	4FT deg	g	BBC	Ind	Ind	33	BBBB	HN		
Film & Media Studies/Politics		PM41	4FT deg	g	BBC	Ind	Ind	35	ABBB	HN		
French/Politics		QR11	4FT deg	El g	CCC	Ind	Ind	31	BBBC	HN		
German/Politics		MR12	4FT deg	g	CCC	Ind	Ind	31	BBBC	HN		
History/Politics		MV11	4FT deg	g	BCC	Ind	Ind	31	BBBC	HN		
Human Resources Management/Politics		MN1C	4FT deg	g	BBC	Ind	Ind	33	BBBB	HN		
Japanese/Politics		MT14	4FT deg	g	BCC	Ind	Ind	31	BBBC	HN		
Philosophy/Politics		MV17	4FT deg	g	BCC	Ind	Ind	31	BBBC	HN		
Politics		M100	4FT deg	g	BCC	Ind	Ind	31	BBBC	HN		
Politics/Business Law		MM13	4FT deg	g	BCC	HN	Ind	33	BBBB	HN		
Politics/Religious Studies		MV18	4FT deg	g	BCC	Ind	Ind	31	BBBC	HN		
Politics/Social Policy		ML14	4FT deg	g	BCC	Ind	Ind	31	BBBC	HN		
Politics/Sociology		ML13	4FT deg	g	BCC	Ind	Ind	31	BBBC	HN		
Spanish/Politics		MR14	4FT deg	El g	CCC	Ind	Ind	31	BBBC	HN		
Politics, Philosophy and Economics _Politics_		Y616	4FT deg	g	BCC	Ind	Ind	31	BBBC	HN		

Politics 62

course details			98 expected requirements							96 entry stats
TITLE	CODE	COURSE	SUBJECTS	A/AS	NO/C	AGNVQ	IB	SQA(H)	SQA	RATIO A/AS
Univ of STRATHCLYDE										
Arts and Social Sciences	Y440	3FT/4FT deg	g	CCC	Ind		28	BBBBB$	Ind	
Politics										
Univ of SUNDERLAND										
Chemistry and Politics	FM11	3FT deg	<u>C</u>	8	3M	M	Ind	Ind	Ind	
Chemistry with Politics	F1M1	3FT deg	<u>C</u>	8	3M	M	Ind	Ind	Ind	
Economics and Politics	LM11	3FT deg	* g	10	N	M	24	CCCC	N	
Economics with Politics	L1M1	3FT deg	*	8	3M	M	Ind	Ind	Ind	
English and Politics	QM31▼	3FT deg	<u>El</u> g	12	Ind	M	24$	BCCC$	Ind	4
English with Politics	Q3M1	3FT deg	*	10	4M	M	Ind	Ind	Ind	
French and Politics	RM11▼	4FT deg	<u>F</u> g	10	N $	M	24$	CCCC$	N$	
French with Politics	R1M1	4FT deg	F	8	3M	M	Ind	Ind	Ind	
Geography and Politics	LM81▼	3FT deg	<u>Gy/Gl</u> g	12	Ind	M	24$	BCCC	Ind	
Geography with Politics	L8M1	3FT deg	*	8	3M	M	Ind	Ind	Ind	
Geology and Politics	FM61	3FT deg	*	8	3M	M	Ind	Ind		
Geology with Politics	F6M1	3FT deg	*	8	3M	M	Ind	Ind	Ind	
German and Politics	RM21▼	4FT deg	G g	10	N $	M	24$	CCCC$	N$	
German with Politics	R2M1	4SW deg	<u>G</u>	8	3M	M	Ind	Ind	Ind	
History and Politics	VM11▼	3FT deg	<u>H</u> g	12	Ind	M	24	BCCC	Ind	3 4/24
History with Politics	V1M1	3FT deg	*	10	4M	M	Ind	Ind	Ind	
Mathematics and Politics	GM11	3FT deg	<u>M</u>	8	3M	M	Ind	Ind		
Mathematics with Politics	G1M1	3FT deg	<u>M</u>	8	3M	M	Ind	Ind	Ind	
Media Studies and Politics	PM41	3FT deg	* g	12	3M	M	24	BCCC	N	
Media Studies with Politics	P4M1	3FT deg	*	24	Ind	Ind	Ind	Ind	Ind	
Physiology and Politics	BM11	3FT deg	*	8	3M	M	Ind	Ind		
Physiology with Politics	B1M1	3FT deg	*	8	3M	M	Ind	Ind	Ind	
Politics and Psychology	MC18	3FT deg	* g	14	MO	M	26$	BBCC$	N	4
Politics and Religious Studies	MV18▼	3FT deg	* g	12	3M	M	24	BCCC	N	2
Politics and Sociology	ML13▼	3FT deg	* g	12	3M	M	24	BCCC	N	4
Politics with American Studies	M1Q4	3FT deg	* g	12	3M	M	24	BCCC	N	4
Politics with Chemistry	M1F1	3FT deg	*	8	3M	M	Ind	Ind	Ind	
Politics with Comparative Literature	M1Q2	3FT deg	*	8	3M	M	Ind	Ind	Ind	
Politics with Economics	M1L1	3FT deg	*	8	3M	M	Ind	Ind	Ind	
Politics with English	M1Q3	3FT deg	*	10	4M	M	Ind	Ind	Ind	
Politics with European Studies	M1T2	3FT deg	* g	12	3M	M	24	BCCC	N	8
Politics with French	M1R1	3FT deg	*	8	3M	M	Ind	Ind	Ind	
Politics with Gender Studies	M1M9	3FT deg	* g	12	3M	M	24	BCCC	N	2
Politics with Geography	M1L8	3FT deg	*	8	3M	M	Ind	Ind	Ind	
Politics with Geology	M1F6	3FT deg	*	8	3M	M	Ind	Ind	Ind	
Politics with German	M1R2	3FT deg	*	8	3M	M	Ind	Ind	Ind	
Politics with History	M1V1	3FT deg	*	10	4M	M	Ind	Ind	Ind	
Politics with History of Art and Design	M1V4	3FT deg	*	8	3M	M	Ind	Ind	Ind	
Politics with Mathematics	M1G1	3FT deg	*	8	3M	M	Ind	Ind	Ind	
Politics with Media Studies	M1P4	3FT deg	*	24	Ind	Ind	Ind	Ind	Ind	
Politics with Music	M1W3	3FT deg	* g	12	3M	M	24	BCCC	N	
Politics with Physiology	M1B1	3FT deg	*	8	3M	M	Ind	Ind	Ind	
Politics with Psychology	M1C8	3FT deg	*	10	4M	M^	Ind	Ind	Ind	
Politics with Religious Studies	M1V8	3FT deg	*	8	3M	M	Ind	Ind	Ind	
Politics with Sociology	M1L3	3FT deg	*	10	4M	M	Ind	Ind	Ind	
Psychology with Politics	C8M1	3FT deg	*	10	4M	M^	Ind	Ind	Ind	
Religious Studies with Politics	V8M1	3FT deg	*	8	3M	M	Ind	Ind	Ind	
Sociology with Politics	L3M1	3FT deg	*	10	4M	M	Ind	Ind	Ind	

course details			98 expected requirements							96 entry stats	
TITLE	CODE	COURSE	SUBJECTS	A/AS	ND/C	AGNVQ	IB	SQA(H)	SQA	RATIO A/AS	

Univ of SUSSEX

International Relations in African & Asian St	M1TM	3FT deg	*	BBC	MO	M*6	$	Ind	Ind		
International Relations in Eng and American St	M1QK	3FT deg	*	BBC	MO	M*6	$	Ind	Ind		
International Relations in European Studies	M1TF	4FT deg	* g	BBC	MO $	M*6 go	$	Ind	Ind		
International Relations in Social Sciences	M1MX	3FT deg	*	BBC	MO	M*6	$	Ind	Ind		
International Relations with Development Studs	MM1Y	3FT deg	*	BBC	MO	M*6	$	Ind	Ind		
Philosophy with Politics	V7M1	3FT deg	*	BBB	MO	M*6	$	Ind	Ind		
Politics in African and Asian Studies	M1T5	3FT deg	*	BBC	MO	M*6	$	Ind	Ind		
Politics in English and American Studies	M1QL	3FT deg	*	BBC	MO	M*6	$	Ind	Ind		
Politics in European Studies	M1TG	4FT deg	* g	BBC	MO $	M*6 go	$	Ind	Ind		
Politics in Social Sciences	M1M9	3FT deg	*	BBC	MO	M*6	$	Ind	Ind		
Politics with Development Studies	M1MY	3FT deg	*	BBC	MO	M*6	$	Ind	Ind		
Politics with North American Studies	M1Q4	4FT deg	*	BBC	MO	M*6	$	Ind	Ind		

Univ of Wales SWANSEA

American Studies and Politics	MQ14	3FT deg	*	BBC	1M+5D	Ind	30	ABBBB	Ind	6	
Anthropology and Politics	ML16	3FT deg	*	BBC	1M+5D	Ind	30	ABBBB	Ind		
Development Studies and International Relations	MM91	3FT deg	*	BBC	1M+5D	Ind	30	ABBBB	Ind		
Development Studies and Politics	MM19	3FT deg	*	BBC	1M+5D	Ind	30	ABBBB	Ind		
Economics and Politics	LM11	3FT deg	* g	BBC	1M+5D	Ind	30	ABBBB	Ind	2	14/22
European Politics	M170	4FT deg	*	BBC	1M+5D	Ind	30	ABBBB	Ind		
French/European Politics	RM11	4FT deg	F	BBC	1M+5D$	Ind	30$	ABBBB$	Ind	4	
German/European Politics	RM21	4FT deg	G	BBC	1M+5D$	Ind	30$	ABBBB$	Ind		
Italian/European Politics	MR1H	4FT deg	L/*	BBC	1M+5D$	Ind	30$	ABBBB$	Ind		
Law and Politics	MM13	3FT deg	*	BBB-BBC	1M+5D	Ind	30	ABBBB	Ind	4	14/24
Philosophy and Politics	MV17	3FT deg	*	BBC	1M+5D	Ind	30	ABBBB	Ind	4	
Politics	M100	3FT deg	*	BBC	1M+5D	Ind	30	ABBBB	Ind	3	12/24
Politics	M102	3FT deg	*	BBC	1M+5D	Ind	30	ABBBB	Ind	9	
Politics and Social History	VM31	3FT deg	*	BBC	1M+5D	Ind	30	ABBBB	Ind		
Politics and Social Policy	LM41	3FT deg	*	BBC-BCC	1M+5D	Ind	28	BBBBB	Ind	4	
Politics and Sociology	LM31	3FT deg	*	BBC	1M+5D	Ind	30	ABBBB	Ind	4	
Politics with International Relations	M155	3FT deg	*	BBC	1M+5D	Ind	30	ABBBB	Ind	10	
Politics with International Relations	M154	3FT deg	*	BBC	1M+5D	Ind	30	ABBBB	Ind	12	
Politics/Ancient History and Civilisation	VMC1	3FT deg	*	BBC	1M+5D	X	30	ABBBB	X		
Politics/English	MQ13	3FT deg	E	BBB	X	X	32$	AABBB$	X	5	18/26
Politics/French	MR11	4FT deg	F	BBC-BCC	1M+5D$	Ind	28$	BBBBB$	Ind	4	
Politics/German	MR12	4FT deg	G	BBC-BCC	1M+5D$	Ind	28$	BBBBB$	Ind		
Politics/History	MV11	3FT deg	*	BBC	1M+5D	Ind	30	ABBBB	Ind	3	14/20
Politics/Italian	MR13	4FT deg	L/*	BBC-BCC	1M+5D	Ind	28	BBBBB	Ind		
Politics/Philosophy	MVC7	3FT deg	*	BBC	1M+5D	Ind	30	ABBBB	Ind		
Russian Studies/Politics	MRC8	3FT deg	*	BBC	1M+5D	Ind	30	ABBBB	Ind		
Russian/European Politics	MR1V	4FT deg	L/*	BBC-BCD	1M+5D	Ind	28$	BBBBC$	Ind		
Russian/Politics	MR18	4FT deg	L/*	BBC-BCC	1M+5D	Ind	28$	BBBBB$	Ind	2	
Spanish/European Politics	MR1K	4FT deg	L/*	BBC	1M+5D$	Ind	30$	ABBBB$	Ind		
Spanish/Politics	MR14	4FT deg	L/*	BBC-BCC	1M+5D	Ind	28	BBBBB	Ind	5	
Welsh/European Politics	MQ15	3FT/4FT deg	W	BBC-BCC	1M+5D$	X	28$	BBBBB$	X		
Welsh/Politics	MQC5	3FT/4FT deg	W	BBC-BCC	1M+5D$	X	28$	BBBBB$	X		
Joint Hons with defer choice of specialisation (inc Politics)	Y220	3FT deg	*	20-22	1M+5D	Ind	28	BBBBB	Ind		

1390

	course details			98 expected requirements							96 entry stats	
TITLE	CODE	COURSE	SUBJECTS	A/AS	ND/C	AGNVQ	IB	SQA(H)	SQA	RATIO A/AS	
Univ of TEESSIDE											
History and Politics	MV1C	3FT deg	*	14	Ind		Ind	Ind	Ind		
Law and Politics	MM31	3FT deg	*	18	DO	D	Ind	Ind	Ind		
Politics (Jt Hons available)	M100	3FT deg	*	12-14	Ind		Ind	Ind	Ind	4	4/22
Politics and English	MQ1J	3FT deg	*	12-14	Ind		Ind	Ind	Ind		
Politics and History	MV1D	3FT deg	*	12-14	Ind		Ind	Ind	Ind		
Public Administration (Jt Hons available)	M140	3FT deg	* g	10-12	Ind		Ind	Ind	Ind	3	8/12
Modular Degree Scheme 　Politics	Y401	3FT deg									
Modular Degree Scheme 　Public Administration	Y401	3FT deg									
Public Administration	041M▼	2FT HND	*	2	Ind		Ind	Ind	Ind	1	2/6
THAMES VALLEY Univ											
American Studies with Politics & Int Relations	Q4M1	3FT deg		8-12	MO	M	26	CCC			
Business Studies with Politics & Int Rels (Dip)	N1M1	3FT/4SW deg		8-12	MO	M	26	CCC			
Economics with Politics and International Rels	L1M1	3FT deg		8-12	MO	M	26	CCC			
English Lang & Communs with Politics & Int Rels	Q1M1	3FT deg		8-12	MO	M	24	CCC			
English with Politics & International Relations	Q3M1	3FT deg		8-12	MO	M	26	CCC			
Envir Policy & Mgt with Politics & Int Relations	F9M1	3FT deg		8-12	MO	M	26	CCC			
European St with Politics and Int Relations	T2M1	3FT deg		8-12	MO	M	26	CCC			
French with Politics and International Relations	R1M1	3FT deg		8-12	MO	M	26	CCC			
German with International Studies	R2MD	3FT deg		8-12	MO	M	26	CCC			
German with Politics and International Relations	R2M1	3FT deg		8-12	MO	M	26	CCC			
History with Politics & International Relations	V1M1	3FT deg		8-12	MO	M	26	CCC			
International St with Politics & Int Relations	M9M1	3FT deg		8-12	MO	M	26	CCC			
Politics & Int Relations with Business Economics	M1LC	3FT deg		8-12	MO	M	26	CCC			
Politics & Int Rels with Environ Policy & Mgt	M1F9	3FT deg		8-12	MO	M	26	CCC			
Politics & International Relations with Business	M1N1	3FT deg		8-12	MO	M	26	CCC			
Politics & International Relations with Int St	M1MX	3FT deg		8-12	MO	M	26	CCC			
Politics & International Relations with Spanish	M1R4	3FT deg		8-12	MO	M	26	CCC			
Politics and Int Relations with American Studies	M1Q4	3FT deg		8-12	MO	M	26	CCC			
Politics and Int Relations with English Lang St	M1Q1	3FT deg		8-12	MO	M	26	CCC			
Politics and Int Relations with European Studies	M1T2	3FT deg		8-12	MO	M	26	CCC			
Politics and International Relations with Econ	M1L1	3FT deg		8-12	MO	M	26	CCC			
Politics and International Relations with French	M1R1	3FT deg		8-12	MO	M	26	CCC			
Politics and International Relations with German	M1R2	3FT deg		8-12	MO	M	26	CCC			
Politics and International Relations with Hist	M1V1	3FT deg		8-12	MO	M	26	CCC			
Politics and International Relations with Law	M1M3	3FT deg		8-12	MO	M	26	CCC			
Sociology with Politics and Int Relations	L3M1	3FT deg		8-12	MO	M	26	CCC			
Spanish with Politics & International Relations	R4M1	3FT deg		8-12	MO	M	26	CCC			
Univ of ULSTER											
Economics and Government (3 Yr Hons)	LM11▼	3FT deg	* g	CCC	MO+3D	D*6/^ gi	28	BBBB	Ind	14	18/18
Government and Law	MM13▼	3FT deg	* g	BBC	MO+4D	D*6/^ gi	32	ABBB	Ind	15	22/26
International Studies	M150▼	3FT deg	*	CCC	MO+3D	D*6/^ gi	28	BBBC	Ind	8	14/20
Modern Studies in the Humanities 　The Modern State	Y321▼	3FT deg	*	CCC	MO+3D	D*6/^ gi	28	BBBC	Ind		
Univ of WARWICK											
Economics and International Studies	LM1C	3FT deg	g	AAB	DO $	Ind	34	AAAAB		13	26/30
Economics and Politics	LM11	3FT deg	g	AAB	DO $	Ind	34	AAAAB		13	26/30
French with International St (4 Yrs inc yr abrd)	R1M1	4FT deg	E g	BBC	X	X	32$	AABBB$		7	20/30
German and Politics (4 Yrs inc yr abroad)	RM21	4FT deg	G g	BBC-BCC	X	X	29$	ABBBB$		8	

| | | | 98 expected requirements | | | | | | | 96 entry stats | |
| **course details** | | | | | | | | | | | |
TITLE	CODE	COURSE	SUBJECTS	A/AS	NQ/C	AGNVQ	IB	SQA(H)	SQA	RATIO	A/AS
German with Int Studies (4 Yrs inc yr abroad)	R2M1	4FT deg	G g	BCC	X	X	28$	ABBBB$		7	20/26
History and Politics	VM11	3FT deg	* g	ABB	X	X	32$	AAABB		9	24/30
Italian with Int Studies (4 Yrs inc yr abroad)	R3M1	4FT deg	E/L g	BCC	X	X	29$	ABBCC$		32	
Philosophy and Politics	VM71	3FT deg	* g	BBB	X	X	32	AABBB		10	24/30
Politics	M100	3FT deg	* g	ABB-BBB	Ind	Ind	32	AAABB		8	24/30
Politics and Sociology	ML13	3FT deg	* g	ABB	Ind	Ind	32	AAABB		13	
Politics with French (4 Yrs inc year abroad)	M1R1	4FT deg	F g	ABB-BBB	X	X	32$	AAABB$		17	
Politics with International Studies	M160	3FT deg	* g	ABB-BBB	Ind	Ind	32	AAABB		10	24/30

Univ of WESTMINSTER

Politics	M100	3FT deg	*	BC	MO+3D	D	26	BBB			

Univ of WOLVERHAMPTON

Politics (Specialist Route)	M100	3FT deg		12	4M	M	24	BBBB	Ind	8	8/14
Combined Degrees *Politics*	Y401	3FT/4SW deg		12	4M	M	24	BBBB	Ind		

Univ of YORK

Economics/Politics (Equal)	LM11	3FT deg	* g	BBB	Ind	D$^ go	30	BBBBB	Ind		22/30
English/Politics	Q3M1	3FT deg	E g	ABB-ABC	HN $	D$^	32$	AABB$	Ind		
History/Politics (Equal)	VM11	3FT deg	H	ABC	Ind	D$6/^	32$	ABBB$	Ind		24/28
Philosophy/Politics (Equal)	VM71	3FT deg	* g	BBB	Ind	D$^ go	30	BBBBB	Ind		
Politics	M100	3FT deg	*	BBB	Ind	D*^	30	BBBBB	Ind		20/30
Politics/Economic and Social History (Equal)	MV13	3FT deg	* g	BCC	DO	D*^	28	BBBC	Ind		
Politics/Education	M1X9	3FT deg	*	BBC	Ind	D*^	28	BBBB	Ind		
Politics/English	M1Q3	3FT deg	E g	BBC	HN $	D$^	30$	ABBB	Ind		20/24
Politics/Sociology (Equal)	ML13	3FT deg	*	BBC	Ind	D$6/^	28	BBBB	Ind		26/30
Philosophy, Politics and Economics *Politics*	Y616	3FT deg	* g	BBB	Ind	D$^ go	32	BBBBB	Ind		

TITLE	CODE	COURSE	SUBJECTS	A/AS	ND/C	AGNVQ	IB	SQA(H)	SQA	RATIO A/AS
Univ of ABERDEEN										
Computing Science-Psychology	GC58	4FT deg	M+2S g	CCD	Ind	MS go	24$	BBBC$	Ind	6
Philosophy-Psychology	VC78	4FT deg	* g	BBC	Ind	M$ go	30$	BBBB$	Ind	9
Psychology	C800	4FT deg	3S/2S+M g	CCD	Ind	MS go	24$	BBBC$	Ind	7
Psychology (MA)	C802	4FT deg	* g	BBC	Ind	M$ go	30$	BBBB$	Ind	5
Psychology with French	C8R1	4FT deg	3S/2S+M g	CCD	Ind	MS go	24$	BBBC$	Ind	
Psychology with French (MA)	C8RC	4FT deg	* g	BBC	Ind	M$ go	30$	BBBB$	Ind	
Psychology with Gaelic	C8Q5	4FT deg	3S/2S+M g	CCD	Ind	MS go	24$	BBBC$	Ind	
Psychology with Gaelic (MA)	C8QM	4FT deg	* g	BBC	Ind	MS go	30$	BBBB$	Ind	
Psychology with German	C8R2	4FT deg	3S/2S+M g	CCD	Ind	MS go	24$	BBBC$	Ind	
Psychology with German (MA)	C8RF	4FT deg	* g	BBC	Ind	MS go	30$	BBBB$	Ind	
Psychology with Spanish	C8R4	4FT deg	3S/2S+M g	CCD	Ind	MS go	24$	BBBC$	Ind	
Psychology with Spanish (MA)	C8RK	4FT deg	* g	BBC	Ind	MS go	30$	BBBB$	Ind	
Psychology-Statistics	CG84	4FT deg	3S/2S+M g	CCD	Ind	M$ go	24$	BBBC$	Ind	
Psychology-Statistics (MA)	CG8K	4FT deg	* g	BBC	Ind	M$ go	30$	BBBB$	Ind	
Univ of ABERTAY DUNDEE										
Behavioural Science	L730	4FT deg	E	CC	Ind	Ind	Ind	BBCC	Ind	
Psychology with Biology	CC81	4FT/5SW deg	E	CD	Ind	Ind	Ind	BBC	Ind	
Psychology with Mathematics	CG81	4FT/5SW deg	E	CD	Ind	Ind	Ind	BBC	Ind	
ANGLIA Poly Univ										
Animal Behaviour and Psychology	CC1V▼	3FT deg	S g	16	8M	M go	Dip	BBCCC	N	5
Biology and Psychology	CC18▼	3FT deg	B	16	8M	D go	Dip$	BBCCC	N	10
Biomedical Science and Psychology	BC98▼	3FT deg	B	16	8M	D go	Dip$	BBCCC	N	
Business and Psychology	CN81▼	3FT deg	* g	16	8M	D go	Dip	BBCCC	Ind	7
Chemistry and Psychology	CF81▼	3FT deg	S g	16	8M	M go	Dip$	BBCCC	N	
Computer Science and Psychology	CG85▼	3FT deg	S g	16	8M	D go	Dip$	BBCC	N	3
Criminology and Psychology	CM8H▼	3FT deg	g	16	8M	D go	Dip	BBCCC	Ind	
Ecology and Conservation and Psychology	CD82▼	3FT deg	S g	16	3M	M go	Dip$	BBCCC	N	
European Philosophy and Literature & Psychology	CV87▼	3FT deg	S g	16	8M	D go	Dip$	BBCCC	Ind	2
Forensic Science and Psychology	BC18▼	3FT deg	g	16	8M	D go	Dip	BBCC		
French and Psychology	CR81▼	3FT deg	S g	16	8M	D go	Dip$	BBCC	Ind	
Geography and Psychology	CF88▼	3FT deg	Gy g	16	8M	D go	Dip$	BBCCC	N	
Geology and Psychology	CF86▼	3FT deg	S g	16	8M	D go	Dip$	BBCCC	N	2
German and Psychology	CR82▼	3FT deg	S g	16	8M	D go	Dip$	BBCCC	N	
Imaging Science and Psychology	CW85▼	3FT deg	S g	16	8M	D go	Dip$	BBCCC	Ind	
Instrumentation Electronics and Psychology	CH86▼	3FT deg	S g	16	8M	D go	Dip$	BBCCC	N	
Italian and Psychology	CR83▼	3FT deg	S g	16	8M	D go	Dip$	BBCCC		4
Law and Psychology	CM83▼	3FT deg	S g	16	8M	D go	Dip$	BBCCC	Ind	9 10/18
Mathematics or Stats/Stat Mod. and Psychology	CG81▼	3FT deg	S g	16	8M	D go	Dip$	BBCCC	N	5
Music and Psychology	CW83▼	3FT deg	Mu g	16	8M	D	Dip	BB	Ind	5
Ophthalmic Dispensing and Psychology	BC58▼	3FT deg	S g	16	8M	D go	Dip$	BBCCC	N	
Psychology	C800▼	3FT deg	S g	16	8M	D go	Dip$	BBCCC		
Psychology and Real Time Computer Systems	CG8M▼	3FT deg	S g	16	8M	D	Dip$	BBCCC	N	
Psychology and Social Policy	CL84▼	3FT deg	S g	16	8M	D go	Dip$	BBCCC	Ind	10
Psychology and Sociology	CL83▼	3FT deg	S g	16	8M	D go	Dip$	BBCCC	N	5 8/18
Psychology and Spanish	CR84▼	4FT deg	S g	16	8M	D go	Dip$	BBCCC	N	
Psychology and Women's Studies	CM89▼	3FT deg	S g	16	8M	D go	Dip$	BBCCC	N	5
ASTON Univ										
Human Psychology	L700	3FT deg	* g	22-24	3M+7D	D$6/^ go	32	ABBBB	Ind	7 18/26
Human Psychology	L701	4SW deg	* g	22-24	3M+7D	D$6/^ go	32	ABBBB	Ind	6 20/26
Human Psychology (Year Zero)	L705	4FT deg								
Human Psychology (Year Zero)	L708	5SW deg								

Letts STUDY GUIDES
THE INDEPENDENT

TITLE	CODE	COURSE	SUBJECTS	A/AS	ND/C	AGNVQ	IB	SQA(H)	SQA	RATIO	A/AS
		course details			98 expected requirements					96 entry stats	
Human Psychology/Biology	CL17	3FT/4SW deg	B g	20	3M+7D$	D$_^ go	30$	BBBBB$	Ind	4	20/26
Human Psychology/Biology (Year Zero)	CL1R	4FT/5SW deg									
Human Psychology/Business Admin (Year Zero)	NL17	4FT/5SW deg									
Human Psychology/Business Administration	LN71	3FT/4SW deg	* g	22	3M+7D	D$6/^ go	31	ABBBB	Ind	6	20/28
Human Psychology/Chemistry	FL17	3FT/4SW deg	C g	20	3M+7D$	D$_^ go	30$	BBBBB$	Ind	14	
Human Psychology/Chemistry (Year Zero)	FL1R	4FT/5SW deg									
Human Psychology/Computer Science	LG75	3FT/4SW deg	* g	20	3M+7D	D$6/^ go	30	BBBBB	Ind	14	
Human Psychology/Computer Science (Year Zero)	LG7M	4FT/5SW deg									
Human Psychology/Engineering Management	LH7R	3FT/4SW deg	S g	20	5M+5D$	D$_ go	30$	BBBBB$			
Human Psychology/French	LR71	4SW deg	F g	20	X	D$_ go	30$	BBBBB$	Ind	4	20/24
Human Psychology/German	LR72	4SW deg	G g	20	X	D$_ go	30$	BBBBB$	Ind		
Human Psychology/German (Year Zero)	LR7F	5SW deg									
Human Psychology/Health & Safety Management	JL97	3FT/4SW deg	* g	20	5M+5D	D$6/^ go	30	BBBBB	Ind		
Human Psychology/Health & Safety Mgt (Year Zero)	JL9R	4FT/5SW deg									
Product Design (Engineering)/Human Psychology	LH77	3FT/4SW deg	S g	20	5M+5D$	D$_ go	30$	BBBBB$	Ind		
Psychology & Management (Year Zero)	LN7D	4FT/5SW deg									
Psychology and Management	LN7C	3FT/4SW deg	* g	BBC	3M+7D	D$6/^ go	32	ABBBB	Ind	7	18/26
Public Policy & Management/Human Psychology	LM7C	3FT/4SW deg	* g	22	3M+7D	D$6/^ go	30	BBBBB	Ind	8	
Public Policy & Mgt/Human Psychology (Year Zero)	LM7D	4FT/5SW deg									
Social Studies/Human Psychology	LL74	3FT/4SW deg	* g	22	3M+7D	D$6/^ go	31	ABBBB	Ind	12	20/26
Social Studies/Human Psychology (Year Zero)	LL7K	4FT/5SW deg									

Univ of Wales, BANGOR

TITLE	CODE	COURSE	SUBJECTS	A/AS	ND/C	AGNVQ	IB	SQA(H)	SQA	RATIO	A/AS
Computer Systems with Psychology	H6C8	3FT deg	* g	CC	3M	M$6/^ go	26$	BBCC	Ind		
Criminology and Psychology	MC38	3FT deg	* g	BBB	M0	D*^ go	30$	BBBB$	Ind		
Mathematics and Psychology	CG81	3FT deg	M g	18	M0	D$_ go	28$	BBBC$	Ind	12	
Psychology	C800	3FT deg	* g	BCC	M0	D$6/^ go	30	BBBB	Ind	4	14/24
Psychology	C802	3FT deg	* g	BCC	M0	D$6/^ go	30	BBBB	Ind	4	14/26
Psychology with Health Psychology	C840	3FT deg	* g	BCC	M0	D$6/^ go	30	BBBB	Ind	6	14/20
Psychology with Health Psychology	C842	3FT deg	* g	BCC	M0	D$6/^ go	30	BBBB	Ind	5	16/20
Psychology/Education (Taught in Welsh)	CX89	3FT deg	* g	BCC	Ind	D$6/^ go	Ind	X	X	4	
Psychology/Linguistics	CQ81	3FT deg	* g	BCC	M0	D$6/^ go	30	BBBB	Ind	13	
Psychology/Mathematics	CGV1	3FT deg	M g	18	M0	D$6/^ go	28$	BBBC$	Ind		
Psychology/Physical Education	CB86	3FT deg	* g	BCC	2M+3D	D$6/^ go	30	BBBB	Ind		
Social Policy/Psychology	CL84	3FT deg	* g	BCC	M0	D$6/^ go	30	BBBB	Ind		
Sociology/Psychology	CL83	3FT deg	* g	BCC	M0	D*6/^ go	30	BBBB	Ind	9	20/24
Sports Science/Psychology	BC68	3FT deg	* g	20	5D	D*6/^ go	30	BBBB	Ind		

BARNSLEY COLL

TITLE	CODE	COURSE	SUBJECTS	A/AS	ND/C	AGNVQ	IB	SQA(H)	SQA	RATIO	A/AS
Combined Studies Social Science	Y400	3FT deg	* g	EE	4M	M*	Ind	Ind	Ind		

Univ of BATH

TITLE	CODE	COURSE	SUBJECTS	A/AS	ND/C	AGNVQ	IB	SQA(H)	SQA	RATIO	A/AS
Psychology with Sociology (4 Yr SW)	C8L3	4SW deg	g	24	6D	D^	30	AABBB	Ind		

BATH COLL of HE

TITLE	CODE	COURSE	SUBJECTS	A/AS	ND/C	AGNVQ	IB	SQA(H)	SQA	RATIO	A/AS
Combined Awards Psychology	Y400	3FT deg	*		N		Ind	$	$		
Modular Programme (DipHE) Psychology	Y460	2FT Dip	*		N		Ind	$	$		

Univ of BIRMINGHAM

TITLE	CODE	COURSE	SUBJECTS	A/AS	ND/C	AGNVQ	IB	SQA(H)	SQA	RATIO	A/AS
Mathematics and Psychology	CG81	3FT deg	M	ABC	Ind	Ind	30	Ind	Ind	5	22/30
Psychology	C800	3FT deg	Ps/M/P/C/B	BBB	Ind	Ind	33	Ind	Ind	9	24/30
Psychology and Artificial Intelligence	CG85	3FT deg	* g	BBB	Ind	Ind	33	Ind	Ind	19	24/28
Psychology and Sports Science	CC87	3FT deg	S g	BBB	Ind	Ind	33	Ind	Ind	17	22/28

Psychology 63

TITLE	CODE	COURSE	SUBJECTS	A/AS	ND/C	AGNVQ	IB	SQA(H)	SQA	RATIO A/AS
BOLTON INST										
Accountancy and Psychology	NL47	3FT deg	* g	12	MO	D*	24	BBCC	Ind	
Art & Design History and Psychology	VL47	3FT deg	* g	12	MO	D*	24	BBCC	Ind	
Biology and Psychology	CL17	3FT deg	* g	12	MO	D*	24	BBCC	Ind	
Business Economics and Psychology	LL17	3FT deg	* g	12	MO	D*	24	BBCC	Ind	
Business Information Systems and Psychology	GL5R	3FT deg	* g	12	MO	D*	24	BBCC	Ind	
Business Studies and Psychology	LN71	3FT deg	* g	12	MO	D*	24	BBCC	Ind	
Community Studies and Psychology	LL57	3FT deg	* g	12	MO	D*	24	BBCC	Ind	
Computing and Psychology	GL57	3FT deg	* g	12	MO	D*	24	BBCC	Ind	
Creative Writing and Psychology	LW7X	3FT deg	* g	12	MO	D*	24	BBCC	Ind	
Design and Psychology	LW72	3FT deg	* g	12	MO	D*	24	BBCC	Ind	
Environmental Studies and Psychology	FL97	3FT deg	* g	12	MO	D*	24	BBCC	Ind	
European Cultural Studies and Psychology	TL27	3FT deg	* g	12	MO	D*	24	BBCC	Ind	
Film & TV Studies and Psychology	LW75	3FT deg	Me/T g	12	Ind	Ind	24	BBCC	Ind	
French and Psychology	RL17	3FT deg	F g	12	Ind	Ind	24	BBCC	Ind	
Gender & Women's Studies and Psychology	ML97	3FT deg	* g	12	MO	D*	24	BBCC	Ind	
German and Psychology	RL27	3FT deg	G g	14	Ind	Ind	24	BBCC	Ind	
History and Psychology	LV71	3FT deg	* g	12	MO	D*	24	BBCC	Ind	
Human Resource Management and Psychology	LN7C	3FT deg	* g	12	MO	D*	24	BBCC	Ind	
Law and Psychology	ML37	3FT deg	* g	12	MO	D*	24	BBCC	Ind	
Leisure Studies and Psychology	LL7H	3FT deg	* g	12	MO	D*	24	BBCC	Ind	
Literature and Psychology	QL27	3FT deg	* g	12	MO	D*	24	BBCC	Ind	
Mathematics and Psychology	GL17	3FT deg	M g	DD	Ind	Ind	24	BBCC	Ind	
Operations Management and Psychology	LN72	3FT deg	* g	12	MO	D*	24	BBCC	Ind	
Organisations, Management & Work and Psychology	NL77	3FT deg	* g	12	MO	D*	24	BBCC	Ind	
Peace & War Studies and Psychology	LV7C	3FT deg	* g	12	MO	D*	24	BBCC	Ind	
Philosophy and Psychology	LV77	3FT deg	* g	12	MO	D*	24	BBCC	Ind	
Psychology	C801	3FT deg	* g	12	MO	D*	24	BBBC	Ind	
Psychology and Sociology	LL3R	3FT deg	* g	12	MO	M	24	Ind	Ind	
Psychology and Statistics	GL47	3FT deg	* g	12	MO	M	24	Ind	Ind	
Psychology and Urban and Cultural Studies	LL37	3FT deg	* g	12	MO	D*	24	BBCC	Ind	
Social Psychology	C840	3FT deg	* g	12	MO	D*				
Theatre Studies and Psychology	WL47	3FT deg	Me/T g	12	Ind	Ind	24	BBCC	Ind	
Visual Arts and Psychology	LW71	3FT deg	* g	12	MO	D*	24	BBCC	Ind	
BOURNEMOUTH Univ										
Applied Psychology and Computing	C878	3FT deg	S g	14-16	MO+3D	M$ go	Ind	CCCCC	Ind	1 8/18
Applied Psychology and Computing	C879▼	4EXT deg	* g	14-16	MO+3D	M$ go	Ind	CCCCC	Ind	1
Univ of BRADFORD										
Psychology	L700	3FT deg	* g	BB-CCC	4M+3D	D*^	Ind	Ind	Ind	12 10/20
Sociology/Social Psychology	LL37	3FT deg	*	BB-CCC	Ind	M*4	Ind	Ind	Ind	3 8/20
Interdisciplinary Human Studies *Psychology*	Y402	3FT deg	* g	BB-CCC	4M+3D	D*^	Ind	Ind	Ind	
Univ of BRISTOL										
Philosophy and Psychology	VL77	3FT deg	* g	AAB-BBC	Ind	D$^	30$	AABBB	Ind	50
Psychology	L700	3FT deg	* g	BBB	Ind	D$^	32$	AABBB	Ind	45 22/28
Psychology	C800	3FT deg	2S g	BBB	Ind	D$^	32$	AABBB	Ind	11 22/30
Psychology and Zoology	CC83	3FT deg	B+S g	BBB	Ind	D$^	32$	CSYS	Ind	17 26/28
BRISTOL, Univ of the W of England										
Biology and Psychology	CC18	3FT/4SW deg	B+C g	8	3M $	PS go	24$	CCC$	Ind	
Chemistry and Psychology	FC18	3FT/4SW deg	C g	6	N $	PS go	24$	CC$	N$	
Psychology	C800	3FT deg	* g	20	4M+2D$	M$6/^ go	28	BBBB	Ind	

TITLE	CODE	COURSE	SUBJECTS	A/AS	NO/C	AGNVQ	IB	SQA(H)	SQA	RATIO A/AS

TITLE	CODE	COURSE	SUBJECTS	A/AS	NO/C	AGNVQ	IB	SQA(H)	SQA	RATIO A/AS
Psychology and Health Science	C8B9	3FT deg	* g	20	4M+2D$	M$6/^ go	28	BBBB	Ind	
Psychology and Information Technology in Science	CG85	3FT/4SW deg	S g	6	N $	PS go	24$	CC$	Ind	
Joint Honours Programme *Psychology and Linguistics*	Y401	3FT deg	* g	14-16	5M	M$ go	24	BCCC	Ind	
Joint Honours Programme *Psychology and Sociology*	Y401	3FT deg	* g	14-16	5M	M$ go	24	BCCC	Ind	
BRUNEL Univ, West London										
Psychology (4 Yrs Thin SW)	C800	4SW deg	* g	BBB-BCC	3M+2D	M*^ go	28$	BBBCC	Ind	13 20/26
Psychology and Social Anthropol (4 Yrs Thin SW)	CL86	4SW deg	* g	BBB-BCC	3M+2D	M*^ go	28$	BBBCC	Ind	8
Psychology and Sociology (4 Yrs Thin SW)	CL83	4SW deg	* g	BBB-BCC	3M+2D	M*^ go	28$	BBBCC	Ind	13 20/24
Univ of BUCKINGHAM										
Psychology with Business Studies	C8N1	2FT deg	* g	14	5M	M	26	BCCC	Ind	
Psychology with English Language Studies (EFL)	C8Q3	3FT deg	*	14	5M	M	26	BCCC	Ind	
Psychology with French	C8R1	2FT deg	*	14	5M	M	26	BCCC	Ind	
Psychology with Information Systems	C8G5	2FT deg	* g	14	5M	M	24	CCCC	Ind	
Psychology with Spanish	C8R4	2FT deg	*	14	5M	M	26	BCCC	Ind	
BUCKINGHAMSHIRE COLLEGE										
Business Administration with Leisure Management	N1L7	3FT deg								
Psychology	L700	3FT deg	g	14	2D	M	27	CCCC	Ind	5 8/14
Psychology and Criminology	LM73	3FT deg		14	2D	M	27	CCCC	Ind	11 9/22
Sociology and Psychology	LL37	3FT deg		12	2D	M	27	CCCC	Ind	3 8/18
CAMBRIDGE Univ										
Natural Sciences *Psychology*	Y160▼	3FT deg	2(S/M) g	AAA-AAB	Ind		Ind	CSYS	Ind	
CANTERBURY CHRIST CHURCH COLL of HE										
American Studies with Psychology	Q4L7	4FT deg	Ps g	CC	MO	M	24	Ind	Ind	9
Art with Psychology	W1L7	3FT deg	A+Ps g	CC	MO	M	24	Ind	Ind	31
Business Studies with Psychology	N1L7	3FT deg	Ps g	CC	MO	M	24	Ind	Ind	27
Early Childhood Studies with Psychology	X9L7	3FT deg	Ps g	CC	MO	M	24	Ind	Ind	33
English with Psychology	Q3L7	3FT deg	E+Ps	CC	MO	M	24	Ind	Ind	
Geography with Psychology	L8L7	3FT deg	Gy+Ps g	CC	MO	M	24	Ind	Ind	1
History with Psychology	V1L7	3FT deg	H+Ps g	CC	MO	M	24	Ind	Ind	6
Marketing with Psychology	N5L7	3FT deg	Ps g	CC	MO	M	24	Ind	Ind	
Mathematics with Psychology	G1L7	3FT deg	M+Ps g	DD	Ind	Ind	24	Ind	Ind	
Media Studies with Psychology	P4L7	3FT deg	Ps g	CC	MO	M	24	Ind	Ind	
Music with Psychology	W3L7	3FT deg	Mu+Ps g	CC	MO	M	24	Ind	Ind	
Psychology and American Studies	LQ74	3FT deg	Ps g	CC	MO	M	24	Ind	Ind	5
Psychology and Art	LW71	3FT deg	Ps+A g	CC	MO	M	24	Ind	Ind	
Psychology and Business Studies	NL17	3FT deg	Ps g	CC	MO	M	24	Ind	Ind	
Psychology and Early Childhood Studies	XL97	3FT deg	Ps g	CC	MO	M	24	Ind	Ind	23
Psychology and English	LQ73	3FT deg	Ps+E g	CC	MO	M	24	Ind	Ind	
Psychology and French	LR71	3FT deg	Ps+F g	CC	MO	M	24	Ind	Ind	
Psychology and Geography	LL87	3FT deg	Ps+Gy g	CC	MO	M	24	Ind	Ind	
Psychology and History	LV71	3FT deg	Ps+H g	CC	MO	M	24	Ind	Ind	
Psychology and Marketing	NL57	3FT deg	Ps g	CC	MO	M	24	Ind	Ind	
Psychology and Mathematics	LG71	3FT deg	Ps+M g	DD	Ind	Ind	24	Ind	Ind	
Psychology and Media Studies	LP74	3FT deg	Ps g	CC	MO	M	24	Ind	Ind	
Psychology and Music	LW73	3FT deg	Ps+Mu g	CC	MO	M	24	Ind	Ind	
Psychology and Social Science	LL37	3FT deg	Ps g	CC	MO	M	24	Ind	Ind	7
Psychology with American Studies	L7Q4	3FT deg	Ps g	CC	MO	M	24	Ind	Ind	
Psychology with Art	L7W1	3FT deg	Ps+A g	CC	MO	M	24	Ind	Ind	10

TITLE	CODE	COURSE	SUBJECTS	A/AS	NO/C	RGNVQ	IB	SQA(H)	SQA	RATIO A/AS
					98 expected requirements					**96 entry stats**
Psychology with Business Studies	L7N1	3FT deg	Ps g	CC	MO	M	24	Ind	Ind	11
Psychology with Early Childhood Studies	L7X9	3FT deg	Ps g	CC	MO	M	24	Ind	Ind	
Psychology with English	L7Q3	3FT deg	Ps+E g	CC	MO	M	24	Ind	Ind	
Psychology with French	L7R1	3FT deg	Ps+F g	CC	MO	M	24	Ind	Ind	
Psychology with Geography	L7L8	3FT deg	Ps+Gy g	CC	MO	M	24	Ind	Ind	
Psychology with History	L7V1	3FT deg	Ps+H g	CC	MO	M	24	Ind	Ind	
Psychology with Marketing	L7N5	3FT deg	Ps g	CC	MO	M	24	Ind	Ind	
Psychology with Mathematics	L7G1	3FT deg	Ps+M g	DD	Ind	Ind	24	Ind	Ind	
Psychology with Media Studies	L7P4	3FT deg	Ps g	CC	MO	M	24	Ind	Ind	
Psychology with Music	L7W3	3FT deg	Ps+Mu g	CC	MO	M	24	Ind	Ind	
Psychology with Religious Studies	L7V8	3FT deg	Ps g	CC	MO	M	24	Ind	Ind	
Psychology with Science	L7Y1	3FT deg	Ps+S g	DD	Ind	Ind	24	Ind	Ind	
Psychology with Social Science	L7L3	3FT deg	Ps g	CC	MO	M	24	Ind	Ind	4
Psychology with Statistics	L7G4	3FT deg	Ps+M g	DD	Ind	Ind	24	Ind	Ind	
Psychology with Tourism Studies	L7P7	3FT deg	Ps g	CC	MO	M	24	Ind	Ind	
Religious Studies and Psychology	LV78	3FT deg	Ps g	CC	MO	M	24	Ind	Ind	
Religious Studies with Psychology	V8L7	3FT deg	Ps g	CC	MO	M	24	Ind	Ind	
Science and Psychology	LY71	3FT deg	S+Ps g	DD	Ind	Ind	24	Ind	Ind	
Science with Psychology	Y1L7	3FT deg	S+Ps g	DD	Ind	Ind	24	Ind	Ind	
Social Science with Psychology	L3L7	3FT deg	Ps g	CC	MO	M	24	Ind	Ind	5 10/13
Statistics and Psychology	GL47	3FT deg	M+Ps g	DD	Ind	Ind	24	Ind	Ind	
Statistics with Psychology	G4L7	3FT deg	M+Ps g	DD	Ind	Ind	24	Ind	Ind	
Tourism Studies and Psychology	PL77	3FT deg	Ps g	CC	MO	M	24	Ind	Ind	1
Tourism Studies with Psychology	P7L7	3FT deg	Ps g	CC	MO	M	24	Ind	Ind	

CARDIFF Univ of Wales

TITLE	CODE	COURSE	SUBJECTS	A/AS	NO/C	RGNVQ	IB	SQA(H)	SQA	RATIO A/AS
Applied Psychology	C813	4SW deg	*	BBB	MO+6D$	D*^ go	31	AABBB	N	5 22/30
Applied Psychology	C812	4SW deg	*	BBB	MO+6D$	D*^ go	31	AABBB	N	5 22/30
Physiology and Psychology	BC18	3FT deg	B/C+M/P g	BCC	MO+3D$	DS^ go	Ind	BBBB$	Ind	14
Psychology	C802	3FT deg	*	BBB	MO+6D	D*^ go	31	AABBB	N	6 22/30
Psychology	C800	3FT deg	*	BBB	MO+6D	D*^ go	31	AABBB	N	7 24/28
Psychology/Education	LX79	3FT deg	*	BBB	MO+6D		Ind	AABBB	N	13 26/28
Psychology/English Literature	LQ73	3FT deg	E g	ABB	MO+6D		Ind	AABBB	N	6 24/30
Psychology/Philosophy	LV77	3FT deg	*	BBB	MO+6D		Ind	AABBB	N	8 22/30
Sociology and Psychology	LL37	3FT deg	*	BBB	MO+6D$		Ind	AABBB	N	63

Univ of Wales INST, CARDIFF

TITLE	CODE	COURSE	SUBJECTS	A/AS	NO/C	RGNVQ	IB	SQA(H)	SQA	RATIO A/AS
Psychology and Communication	L720	3FT deg	* g	16-18	4M+2D	D$ go	Ind	BBCC	Ind	7 12/22

Univ of CENTRAL LANCASHIRE

TITLE	CODE	COURSE	SUBJECTS	A/AS	NO/C	RGNVQ	IB	SQA(H)	SQA	RATIO A/AS
Psychology/Applied Psychology	C800	3FT deg	* g	18	MO+5D$	D$6/^	28$	BBBB$	$	
Combined Honours Programme Psychology	Y400	3FT deg	* g	16	MO+4D	D$6/^	28	BBBC	Ind	

CHELTENHAM & GLOUCESTER COLL of HE

TITLE	CODE	COURSE	SUBJECTS	A/AS	NO/C	RGNVQ	IB	SQA(H)	SQA	RATIO A/AS
Business Management and Psychology	NL17	3FT deg	g	12-16	4M+3D	MB3	26	CCCC	Ind	
Business Management with Psychology	N1L7	4SW deg	g	12-16	4M+3D	MB3	26	CCCC	Ind	
English Studies and Psychology	LQ73	3FT deg	E g	12-16	4M+3D	M^	26	CCCC	Ind	
English Studies with Psychology	Q3L7	3FT deg	E+M g	12-16	4M+3D	M^	26	CCCC	Ind	
Financial Management and Psychology	NL37	3FT deg	g	10-14	5M+2D	M3	26	CCCC	Ind	
Financial Management with Psychology	N3L7	4SW deg	g	10-14	5M+2D	M3	26	CCCC	Ind	
Financial Services Mgt and Psychology	LN73	3FT deg	g	10-14	5M+2D	M3	26	CCCC	Ind	
Financial Services Mgt with Psychology	N3LR	4SW deg	g	8-12	5M+2D	M3	26	CCCC	Ind	
Geography and Psychology	LL87	3FT deg	*	12-14	MO	M3^	26	CCCC	Ind	
Geography with Psychology	L8LR	3FT deg	M g	12-14	MO	M3^	26	CCCC	Ind	

TITLE	CODE	COURSE	SUBJECTS	A/AS	ND/C	RGNVQ	IB	SQA(H)	SQA	RATIO A/AS
History and Psychology	LV71	3FT deg	H g	12-16	4M+3D	M3^	26	CCCC	Ind	
History with Psychology	V1L7	3FT deg	H g	12-16	4M+3D	M3^	26	CCCC	Ind	
Human Geography and Psychology	LL78	3FT deg	M g	12-16	4M+3D	M3	26	CCCC	Ind	
Human Geography with Psychology	L8L7	3FT deg	g	12-16	4M+3D	M3	26	CCCC	Ind	
Human Resource Management and Psychology	NLC7	3FT deg	g	12-16	5M+2D	MB3	26	CCCC	Ind	
Human Resource Mgt with Psychology	N1LR	4SW deg	g	12	5M+2D	MB3	26	CCCC	Ind	
Marketing Management and Psychology	NL57	3FT deg	g	12	5M+2D	MB3	26	CCCC	Ind	
Marketing Management with Psychology	N5L7	4SW deg	g	12	5M+2D	MB3	26	CCCC	Ind	
Multimedia and Psychology	GL57	3FT deg	g	12	5M+2D	MI3	26	CCCC	Ind	
Multimedia with Psychology	G5L7	3FT deg	g	8-12	M0	MI3	26	CCCC	Ind	
Multimedia with Psychology	G5LR	4SW deg	M g	8-12	M0	MI3	24	CCCC	Ind	
Psychology and Religious Studies	LV78	3FT deg	g	12	M0	M3^	26	CCCC	Ind	
Psychology and Sociological Studies	LL37	3FT deg	g	12-16	4M+3D	M3^	26	CCCC	Ind	
Psychology and Sport and Exercise Sciences	BL67	3FT deg	S g	12-16	4M+3D	ML3/^	26	CCCC	Ind	
Psychology and Women's Studies	LM79	3FT deg	g	12-16	5M+2D	M3^	26	CCCC	Ind	
Psychology with Business Management	L7N1	3FT deg	g	12-16	4M+3D	M3^	26	CCCC	Ind	
Psychology with Combined Arts	L7Y3	3FT deg	g	12-16	M0	M3^	26	CCCC	Ind	
Psychology with English Studies	L7Q3	3FT deg	g	12-16	4M+3D	M3^	26	CCCC	Ind	
Psychology with Financial Management	L7N3	3FT deg	g	12-16	5M+2D	M3^	26	CCCC	Ind	
Psychology with Financial Services Management	L7NH	3FT deg	g	12-16	5M+2D	M3^	26	CCCC	Ind	
Psychology with Geography	L7LV	3FT deg	g	12-16	M0	M3^	26	CCCC	Ind	
Psychology with History	L7V1	3FT deg	g	12-16	4M+3D	M3^	26	CCCC	Ind	
Psychology with Human Geography	L7L8	3FT deg	g	12-16	4M+3D	M3^	26	CCCC	Ind	
Psychology with Human Resource Management	L7NC	3FT deg	g	12-16	5M+2D	M3^	26	CCCC	Ind	
Psychology with Information Technology	L7G5	3FT deg	g	12-16	M0	M3^	26	CCCC	Ind	
Psychology with Marketing Management	L7N5	3FT deg	g	12-16	5M+2D	M3^	26	CCCC	Ind	
Psychology with Media Communications	L7P4	3FT deg	g	12-16	M0	M3^	26	CCCC	Ind	
Psychology with Multimedia	GLM7	3FT deg	g	12	5M+2D	M3^	26	CCCC	Ind	
Psychology with Religious Studies	L7V8	3FT deg	g	12	4M+3D	M3^	26	CCCC	Ind	
Psychology with Sociological Studies	L7L3	3FT deg	g	12-16	4M+3D	M3^	26	CCCC	Ind	
Psychology with Sport and Exercise Sciences	L7B6	3FT deg	g	12-16	4M+3D	M3^	26	CCCC	Ind	
Psychology with Visual Arts	L7W1	3FT deg	* g	12-16	4M+3D	M3	26	CCCC	Ind	
Psychology with Women's Studies	L7M9	3FT deg	g	12	4M+3D	M3^	26	CCCC	Ind	
Religious Studies with Psychology	V8L7	3FT deg	*	8-12	M0	M3^	26	CCCC	Ind	
Sociological Studies with Psychology	L3L7	3FT deg	*	12-16	4M+3D	MG3	26	CCCC	Ind	
Sport & Exercise Sciences with Psychology	B6L7	3FT deg	S	12-16	4M+3D	ML3	26	CCCC	Ind	
Visual Arts with Psychology	W1L7	3FT deg	A	10-14	5M+2D	MA3	26	CCCC	Ind	
Women's Studies with Psychology	M9L7	3FT deg	*	12	M0	M3	26	CCCC	Ind	

UNIVERSITY COLLEGE CHESTER

TITLE	CODE	COURSE	SUBJECTS	A/AS	ND/C	RGNVQ	IB	SQA(H)	SQA	RATIO A/AS
Art and Psychology	WL97	3FT deg	g	12	M	P^	Ind	CCCC	$	10	14/20
Art with Psychology	W9L7	3FT deg	g	12	M	P^	Ind	CCCC	$	6	
Biology and Psychology	CL17	3FT deg	B g	10	M	P^	Ind	CCCC	$	4	8/13
Biology with Psychology	C1L7	3FT deg	B g	10	M	P^	Ind	CCCC	$		
Computer Science/IT with Psychology	G5L7	3FT deg	g	10	M	M	Ind	CCCC	$	7	
Computer Studies/IT and Psychology	GL57	3FT deg	g	10	M	M	Ind	CCCC	$	7	
Drama and Theatre Studies and Psychology	WL47	3FT deg	g	12	M	P	Ind	CCCC	$	24	
Drama and Theatre Studies with Psychology	W4L7	3FT deg	g	12	M	M	Ind	CCCC	$	21	
English Literature and Psychology	QL37	3FT deg	E g	12	M	P^	Ind	CCCC	$	18	14/16
English with Psychology	Q3L7	3FT deg	E g	12	M	P^	Ind	CCCC	$	15	12/16
Geography and Psychology	FL87	3FT deg	Gy/Gl g	12	M	P^	Ind	CCCC	$	7	
Geography with Psychology	F8L7	3FT deg	Gy/Gl g	10	M	P^	Ind	CCCC	$	12	
History and Psychology	VL17	3FT deg	H/Ec/So g	12	M	P^	Ind	CCCC	$	11	

course details			98 expected requirements							96 entry stats
TITLE	CODE	COURSE	SUBJECTS	A/AS	NO/C	AGNVQ	IB	SQA(H)	SQA	RATIO A/AS
History with Psychology	V1L7	3FT deg	H/Ec/So g	12	M	M	Ind	CCCC	$	5
Mathematics and Psychology	GL17	3FT deg	M g	10	M	P^	Ind	CCCC	$	6
Mathematics with Psychology	G1L7	3FT deg	M	10	M	P^	Ind	CCCC	$	5
PE/Sports Science with Psychology	B6L7	3FT deg	g	10	M	P^	Ind	CCCC	$	
Physical Education/Sports Science and Psychology	BL67	3FT deg	g	10	M	P^	Ind	CCCC	$	
Psychology and Theology and Religious Studies	LV78	3FT deg	g	12	M	P^	Ind	CCCC	$	14
Psychology with Art	L7W9	3FT deg	g	12	M	M	Ind	CCCC	$	32
Psychology with Biology	L7C1	3FT deg	B g	10	M	P^	Ind	CCCC	$	7
Psychology with Computer Science/IT	L7G5	3FT deg	g	10	M	M	Ind	CCCC	$	4 10/18
Psychology with Drama and Theatre Studies	L7W4	3FT deg	g	12	M	P^	Ind	CCCC	$	10
Psychology with English Literature	L7Q3	3FT deg	E g	12	M	P^	Ind	CCCC	$	37
Psychology with French	L7R1	3FT deg	g	12	M	M	Ind	CCCC	$	4 12/16
Psychology with Geography	L7F8	3FT deg	Gy/Gl g	10	M	P^	Ind	CCCC	$	19
Psychology with German	L7R2	3FT deg	g	12	M	M	Ind	CCCC	$	7
Psychology with History	L7V1	3FT deg	H/Ec/So g	12	M	M	Ind	CCCC$	$	10
Psychology with Mathematics	L7G1	3FT deg	M	10	M	P^	Ind	CCCC	$	
Psychology with PE/Sports Science	L7B6	3FT deg	g	10	M	P^	Ind	CCCC	$	
Psychology with Social Science	L7L3	3FT deg	g	10	M	P^	Ind	CCCC	$	
Psychology with Theology and Religious Studies	L7V8	3FT deg	g	12	M	M	Ind	CCCC	$	11
Theology and Religious Studies with Psychology	V8L7	3FT deg	g	12	M	M	Ind	CCCC	$	10

CITY Univ

Economics/Psychology	LL17	3FT deg	* g	BCC	3M+4D	D*^	28$	BBBBC	Ind	9
Journalism/Psychology	LP76	3FT/4SW deg	* g	BBC-CCC Ind	Ind	D*_	Ind	Ind	Ind	26 18/22
Philosophy/Psychology	LVR7	3FT deg	* g	BCC	3M+4D	D*^	28$	BBBBC	Ind	6 14/20
Psychology	C800	3FT deg	* g	BCC	3M+4D	D*^	28$	BBBBC	Ind	22 18/24
Psychology and Health	BC98	3FT deg	* g	BCC	3M+4D	D*^	28$	BBBBC	Ind	22
Psychology/Economics	CL81	3FT deg	* g	BCC	3M+4D	D*^	28$	BBBBC	Ind	
Psychology/Philosophy	CV87	3FT deg	* g	BCC	3M+4D	D*^	28$	BBBBC	Ind	13 20/22
Psychology/Sociology	LC38	3FT deg	* g	BCC	3M+4D	D*^	28$	BBBBC	Ind	17 20/22
Psychology/Systems Science	C8M9	3FT deg	* g	BCC	3M+4D	D*^	28$	BBBBC	Ind	11
Sociology/Psychology	LLH7	3FT deg	* g	BCC	3M+4D	D*^	28$	BBBBC	Ind	17

COVENTRY Univ

Psychology	C800	3FT deg	* g	CC	2M+4D	D g	Ind	BBBB	Ind	8 8/18
Psychology and Biological Sciences	CC18	3FT/4SW deg	* g	CC	3M+3D	M^ go	Ind	BBB	Ind	1 9/12
Psychology and Computing	CG85	3FT/4SW deg	* g	CC	3M+3D	M go	Ind	BBB	Ind	5
Psychology and French	RC18	4FT deg	F	CD	M	M	Ind	CCCC$	Ind	
Psychology and German	RC28	4FT deg	*	CD	M	M	Ind	CCCC	Ind	
Psychology and History	CV81	3FT deg	*	CD	M	M	Ind	CCCC	Ind	
Psychology and Italian	RC38	4FT deg	*	CD	M	M	Ind	CCCC	Ind	
Russian and Psychology	RC88	4FT deg	*	CD	M	M	Ind	CCCC	Ind	
Sociology and Psychology	LL37	3FT deg	* g	CC-CD	3M+3D	M go	Ind	BBB	Ind	2 8/16
Spanish and Psychology	RC48	4FT deg	*	CD	M	M	Ind	CCCC	Ind	
Statistics and Psychology	CG84	3FT/4SW deg	* g	CC	3M+3D	M^ go	Ind	BBB	Ind	3

DE MONTFORT Univ

Economics and Psychology (Modular Scheme)	LL17▼	3FT deg	*	16	DO	D	Ind	Ind	Ind	
Human Psychology	L703▼	3FT deg	* g	20	2M+4D		Ind	Ind	Ind	15 12/20
Politics and Psychology	LM71▼	3FT deg	*	16	DO	D	Ind	Ind	Ind	
Psychology and Sociology	LL37▼	3FT deg	*	16	DO	D	Ind	Ind	Ind	1
Social Psychology	L740▼	3FT deg	* g	16	D	D	32	BBB	Ind	

TITLE	CODE	COURSE	SUBJECTS	A/AS	ND/C	RGNVQ	IB	SQA(H)	SQA	RATIO	A/AS
Univ of DERBY											
Psychology	C820	3FT deg	*	18-20	3M+3D	D$	30	BBBCC	Ind	13	14/26
Credit Accumulation Modular Scheme *Business Psychology*	Y600	3FT deg	*	12	MO	M	Ind	CCCC	Ind		
Credit Accumulation Modular Scheme *Psychology*	Y600	3FT deg	*	14	MO	M	28	BBCC	Ind		
Univ of DUNDEE											
American Studies and Psychology	LQ74	4FT deg	* g	BCC	Ind	D$	29	BBBC	Ind	9	
Business Economics and Marketing and Psychology	Y608	4FT deg	* g	BCC	Ind	D$	29	BBBC	Ind		
Computing and Cognitive Science	CG85	4FT deg	S g	14	5M $	M$	25$	BBBC$	N$		
Contemporary European Studies and Psychology	LT72	4FT deg	* g	BCC	Ind	D$	29	BBBC	Ind	6	
Economics and Psychology	LL17	4FT deg	* g	BCC	Ind	D$	29	BBBC	Ind	5	
English and Psychology	LQ73	4FT deg	E g	BCC	Ind	D$^	29$	BBBC$	Ind	5	
Financial Economics and Psychology	LLC7	4FT deg	* g	BCC	Ind	D$	29	BBBC	Ind		
Geography and Psychology	LL78	4FT deg	* g	BCC	Ind	D$	29	BBBC	Ind	4	
Mathematics and Psychology	GL17	4FT deg	M g	BCC	Ind	D$^	29$	BBBC$	Ind	10	
Mathematics and Psychology	LG71	4FT deg	M g	14	5M $	M$^	25$	BBCC$	N$		
Modern History and Psychology	LV71	4FT deg	* g	BCC	Ind	D$	29	BBBC	Ind	5	
Philosophy and Psychology	LV77	4FT deg	* g	BCC	Ind	D$	29	BBBC	Ind	12	
Physics and Psychology	FC38	4FT deg	M+S g	10	5M $	M$^	25$	BBCC$	N$		
Political Science and Psychology	LM71	4FT deg	* g	BCC	Ind	D$	29	BBBC	Ind	5	
Psychology	L700	4FT deg	* g	BCC	Ind	D$	29	BBBC	Ind	5	18/22
Psychology	C800	4FT deg	2S g	14	5M $	M$	25$	BBCC$	N$	7	12/24
Psychology and Applied Computing	LG75	4FT deg	S g	14	5M $	M$	25$	BBBC$	N$	3	
Psychology and Statistics	LG74	4FT deg	M g	14	5M $	M$^	25$	BBBC$	N$		
Arts and Social Sciences *Psychology*	Y400	3FT deg	* g	BCC	Ind	D$	29	BBBC	Ind		
Univ of DURHAM											
Anthropology and Psychology	LC68	3FT deg	* g	ABB-BBB	Ind	Ind	33	AAABB	Ind	27	
Applied Psychology	L710	3FT deg									
Philosophy and Psychology	CV87	3FT deg	* g	ABB	Ind	Ind	33	AAABB	Ind	11	28/30
Psychology	C800	3FT deg	2S g	ABB-BBB	Ind	Ind	33$	AAABB	Ind	15	24/30
Psychology	C802	3FT deg	* g	ABB-BBB	Ind	Ind	33	AAABB	Ind	14	24/30
Psychology and Sociology	LC38	3FT deg	* g	ABB-BBB	Ind	Ind	33	AAABB	Ind	16	
Natural Sciences *Psychology*	Y160	3FT deg	2S	ABB	Ind	X	33	CSYS	Ind		
Social Sciences Combined *Psychology*	Y220	3FT deg	* g	ABC	MO	Ind	32	AAABB	Ind		
Univ of EAST ANGLIA											
Psychosocial Studies	C840	3FT deg		BBC-BCC	MO+3D$	Ind	28$	BBBB	Ind		
Univ of EAST LONDON											
Anthropology and Psychosocial Studies	LL67	3FT deg	* g	12	MO	MG	Ind	Ind	Ind	8	
Anthropology with Psychosocial Studies	L6L7	3FT deg	* g	12	MO	M	Ind	Ind	Ind		
Biology and Psychosocial Studies	CL17	3FT deg	* g	12	MO	M$	Ind	Ind	Ind		
Biology with Psychology	CC18	3FT deg	* g	12	MO	D^	Ind	Ind	Ind		
Biology with Psychosocial Studies	C1L7	3FT deg	* g	12	MO	M	Ind	Ind	Ind		
Communication Studies and Psychosocial Studies	LP73	3FT deg	* g	12	MO	MG	Ind	Ind	Ind	3	
Communication Studies with Psychosocial Studies	P3L7	3FT deg	* g	12	MO	M	Ind	Ind	Ind		
Economics and Psychosocial Studies	LL17	3FT deg	* g	12	MO	M$	Ind	Ind	Ind		
Economics with Psychosocial Studies	L1L7	3FT deg	* g	12	MO	M	Ind				
Education & Community St & Psychosocial Studies	LX79	3FT deg	* g	12	MO	M$	Ind	Ind	Ind	3	

Psychology 63

course details   98 expected requirements   96 entry stats

TITLE	CODE	COURSE	SUBJECTS	R/AS	NO/C	AGNVQ	IB	SQA(H)	SQA	RATIO R/AS
Education & Community St with Psychosocial St	X9L7	3FT deg	*g	12	MO	M				
French and Psychosocial Studies	LR71	3FT deg	*g	12	MO	M$	Ind	Ind	Ind	
German and Psychosocial Studies	LR72	3FT deg	*g	12	MO	M$	Ind	Ind	Ind	
Health Studies and Psychosocial Studies	BL97	3FT deg	*g	12	MO	M	Ind	Ind	Ind	
Health Studies with Psychosocial Studies	B9L7	3FT deg	*g	12	MO	M	Ind	Ind	Ind	
History and Psychosocial Studies	LV71	3FT deg	*g	12	MO	M$	Ind	Ind	Ind	2
History of Art Design & Film and Psychosocial St	LV74	3FT deg	*g	12	MO	M$	Ind	Ind	Ind	
History of Art Design & Film w. Psychosocial St	V4L7	3FT deg	*g	12	MO	M	Ind	Ind		
Information Technology with Psychosocial Studies	G5L7	3FT deg	*g	12	MO	M	Ind	Ind	Ind	
Law and Psychosocial Studies	LM73	3FT deg	*g	14	MO	M$	Ind	Ind	Ind	7
Law with Psychosocial Studies	M3L7	3FT deg	*g	14	MO	M				
Maths, Stats & Computing with Psychology	G9L7	3FT deg	*g	12	MO	M				
Psychology	C800	3FT deg	*g	16	DO	D^	Ind	Ind	Ind	5 10/20
Psychology with Archaeological Sciences	L7F4	3FT deg	*g	12	MO	M				
Psychology with Biology	L7B1	3FT deg	*g	12	MO	M				
Psychology with Health Studies	L7LK	3FT deg	*g	12	MO	M				
Psychology with Maths, Stats & Computing	L7G9	3FT deg	*g	12	MO	M				
Psychosocial Sciences and Social Policy Research	LL74	3FT deg	*g	12	MO	M	Ind	Ind	Ind	
Psychosocial Studies	L741	3FT deg	*g	12	MO	MG	Ind	Ind	Ind	3 4/20
Psychosocial Studies and Social Sciences	LY72	3FT deg	*g	12	MO	M				
Psychosocial Studies and Sociology	LL73	3FT deg	*g	12	MO	M$	Ind	Ind	Ind	4
Psychosocial Studies and Spanish	LR74	3FT deg	*g	12	MO	M^	Ind	Ind	Ind	
Psychosocial Studies and Women's Studies	LM79	3FT deg	*g	12	MO	M	Ind	Ind	Ind	
Psychosocial Studies with Anthropology	L7L6	3FT deg	*g	12	MO	M	Ind	Ind	Ind	
Psychosocial Studies with Biology	L7C1	3FT deg	*g	12	MO	M	Ind	Ind	Ind	
Psychosocial Studies with Communication Studies	L7P3	3FT deg	*g	12	MO	M	Ind	Ind	Ind	
Psychosocial Studies with Economics	L7L1	3FT deg	*g	12	MO	M	Ind	Ind	Ind	
Psychosocial Studies with Ed & Community Studies	L7X9	3FT deg	*g	12	MO	M	Ind	Ind	Ind	
Psychosocial Studies with French	L7R1	3FT deg	*g	12	MO	M	Ind	Ind	Ind	
Psychosocial Studies with German	L7R2	3FT deg	*g	12	MO	M	Ind	Ind	Ind	
Psychosocial Studies with Health Studies	L7B9	3FT deg	*g	12	MO	M	Ind	Ind	Ind	
Psychosocial Studies with Hist of Art Des & Film	L7V4	3FT deg	*g	12	MO	M	Ind	Ind	Ind	
Psychosocial Studies with History	L7V1	3FT deg	*g	12	MO	M	Ind	Ind	Ind	
Psychosocial Studies with Information Technology	L7G5	3FT deg	*g	12	MO	M	Ind	Ind	Ind	
Psychosocial Studies with Italian	L7R3	3FT deg	*g	12	MO	M	Ind	Ind	Ind	
Psychosocial Studies with Law	L7M3	3FT deg	*g	12	MO	M	Ind	Ind	Ind	
Psychosocial Studies with Professional Studies	L742	3FT deg	*g	12	MO	MG	Ind	Ind	Ind	2 6/12
Psychosocial Studies with Social Policy Research	L7L4	3FT deg	*g	12	MO	M	Ind	Ind	Ind	
Psychosocial Studies with Social Sciences	L7L3	3FT deg	*g	12	MO	M	Ind	Ind	Ind	
Psychosocial Studies with Sociology	L7LH	3FT deg	*g	12	MO	M	Ind	Ind	Ind	
Psychosocial Studies with Spanish	L7R4	3FT deg	*g	12	MO	M	Ind	Ind	Ind	
Psychosocial Studies with Women's Studies	L7M9	3FT deg	*g	12	MO	M	Ind	Ind	Ind	
Social Policy Research with Psychosocial Studies	L4L7	3FT deg	*g	12	MO	M	Ind	Ind	Ind	
Social Sciences with Psychosocial Studies	L3L7	3FT deg	*g	12	MO	M	Ind	Ind	Ind	
Sociology with Psychosocial Studies	L3LR	3FT deg	*g	12	MO	M	Ind	Ind	Ind	
Women's Studies with Psychosocial Studies	M9LR	3FT deg	*g	12	MO	M	Ind			
Three-Subject Degree Psychosocial Studies	Y600	3FT deg	*g	12	MO	M	Ind	Ind	Ind	

EDGE HILL Univ COLLEGE

TITLE	CODE	COURSE	SUBJECTS	R/AS	NO/C	AGNVQ	IB	SQA(H)	SQA	RATIO R/AS
Psychology	L700	3FT deg	Ps	CC	3M+3D	M* / P*^	Dip	BBCC	Ind	

course details			98 expected requirements							96 entry stats	
TITLE	CODE	COURSE	SUBJECTS	A/AS	ND/C	AGNVQ	IB	SQA(H)	SQA	RATIO	A/AS
Univ of EDINBURGH											
Artificial Intelligence and Psychology	GL87	4FT deg	2S g	BBC	MO $		Dip$	BBBB$	N$		
Philosophy and Psychology	VL77	4FT deg	g	BBB	Ind	Ind	Dip$	BBBB	Ind		
Psychology	C800	4FT deg	C+B/M/P g	ABB	MO $		Dip$	ABBB	N$	9	24/28
Psychology	L700	4FT deg	g	AAB	Ind		38$	AABB	Ind	6	
Psychology and Business Studies	LN71	4FT deg	g	AAB	Ind		38	AABB	Ind	9	
Psychology and Linguistics	LQ71	4FT deg	g	AAB	Ind		38	AABB	Ind	11	
Sociology and Psychology	LL37	4FT deg		AAB			38	AABB			
Social Science *Psychology*	Y200	3FT deg	g	AAB	Ind		38$	AABB	Ind		
Univ of ESSEX											
Biochemistry and Psychology	CC78	3FT deg	C+S/M g	20	MO $	D	28$	BBBC	Ind	1	14/18
Cognitive Science	C8G5	3FT deg	* g	22	MO+2D	D	28	BBBB	Ind		
Psychology	C802	3FT deg	* g	22	MO+3D	Ind	28	AABBB	Ind	6	18/26
Psychology	C800	3FT deg	* g	22	MO+3D	Ind	28	AABBB	Ind	7	10/22
Univ of EXETER											
Cognitive Science	CGV5	3FT deg	M g	20	MO	M$^	32$	Ind	Ind	3	18/22
Psychology (BA)	L700	3FT deg	* g	AAB-BBB	MO	D$	36	Ind	Ind	17	26/30
Psychology (BSc)	C800	3FT deg	S/Gy/PS g	ABB-BBB	MO	D$^	36$	Ind	Ind	8	20/30
Psychology with European Study	L701	4FT deg	L g	AAB-BBB	MO	D$^	36$	Ind	Ind	9	20/30
Univ of GLAMORGAN											
English Studies and Psychology	LQ73	3FT deg	* g	CC	Ind	Ind	Ind	Ind	Ind		
English Studies with Psychology	Q3L7	3FT deg	* g	CC	Ind	Ind	Ind	Ind	Ind		
Geography and Psychology	LL87	3FT deg	* g	CC	Ind	Ind	Ind	Ind	Ind		
History and Psychology	LV71	3FT deg	* g	CC	Ind	Ind	Ind	Ind	Ind		
Humanities (Psychology)	L703	3FT deg	* g	CC	5M	M$	24	CCCC	HN	4	6/18
Mathematics and Psychology	GL17	3FT deg	M g	CC	5M $	M$	Ind	Ind	Ind		
Mathematics with Psychology	G1L7	3FT deg	M g	12	Ind	Ind	Ind	Ind	Ind		
Media Studies and Psychology	PL47	3FT deg	Me/T/E g	14	Ind	Ind	Ind	Ind	Ind		
Media Studies with Psychology	P4L7	3FT deg	Me/T/E g	14	Ind	Ind	Ind	Ind	Ind		
Philosophy and Psychology	LV77	3FT deg	* g	CC	Ind	Ind	Ind	Ind	Ind		
Psychology	L700	3FT deg	* g	CC	5M	M	Ind	Ind	Ind		
Psychology and Religious Studies	LV78	3FT deg	* g	CC	Ind	Ind	Ind	Ind	Ind		
Psychology and Sociology	LL37	3FT deg	* g	CC	Ind	Ind	Ind	Ind	Ind		
Psychology and Theatre & Media Drama	LW74	3FT deg	T/E g	14	Ind	Ind	Ind	Ind	Ind		
Psychology and Visual Arts	LW71	3FT deg	A g	CC	Ind	Ind	Ind	Ind	Ind		
Psychology with Anthropology	L7L6	3FT deg	* g	CC	5M	M	Ind	Ind	Ind		
Psychology with Criminal Justice	L7M3	3FT deg	Lw/Ps/So g	14	Ind	Ind	Ind	Ind	Ind		
Psychology with Criminology	L7MH	3FT deg	Lw/Ps/So g	14	Ind	Ind	Ind	Ind	Ind		
Psychology with Philosophy	L7V7	3FT deg	* g	CC	5M	M	Ind	Ind	Ind		
Psychology with Sociology	L7L3	3 deg	* g	CC	5M	M	Ind	Ind	Ind		
Psychology with Statistics	L7G4	3FT deg									
Psychology with Visual Arts	L7W1	3FT deg	A g	CC	5M	M	Ind	Ind	Ind		
Psychology with Women's Studies	L7M9	3FT deg	* g	CC	5M	M	Ind	Ind	Ind		
Sociology with Psychology	L3L7	3FT deg	* g	CC	5M	M	Ind	Ind	Ind		
Statistics with Psychology	G4L7	3FT deg	M g	CC	Ind	Ind	Ind	Ind	Ind		
Combined Studies (Honours) *Psychology*	Y400	3FT deg	* g	8-16	Ind	Ind	Ind	Ind	Ind		
Joint Honours *Psychology*	Y401	3FT deg	* g	8-16	Ind	Ind	Ind	Ind	Ind		
Major/Minor Honours *Psychology*	Y402	3FT deg	* g	8-16	Ind	Ind	Ind	Ind	Ind		

Psychology   63

				98 expected requirements							96 entry stats	
course details												
TITLE	CODE	COURSE	SUBJECTS	A/AS	NQ/C	RGNVQ	IB	SQA(H)	SQA	RATIO	A/AS
Univ of GLASGOW												
Anthropology/Psychology	LC68	4FT deg		BBC	N	M	30	BBBB	Ind		
Archaeology/Psychology	CV86	4FT deg		BBC	HN	M	30	BBBB	Ind	9	
Business Economics/Psychology	LCC8	4FT deg		BBC	N	M	30	BBBB	N		
Celtic Civilisation/Psychology	CQ8M	4FT deg		BBC	HN	M	30	BBBB	Ind		
Celtic/Psychology	CQ85	4FT deg		BBC	HN	M	30	BBBB	Ind	1	
Classical Civilisation/Psychology	CQ88	4FT deg		BBC	HN	M	30	BBBB	Ind	3	
Classical Hebrew/Psychology	CV8W	4FT deg		BBC	HN	M	30	BBBB	Ind		
Computing Science/Psychology	CG85	4FT deg	M+S	BBC-CCC	N	M	24$	BBBB$	N	3	
Computing/Psychology	GC58	4FT deg		BBC	HN	M	30	BBBB	Ind	12	
Czech/Psychology	CT81	5FT deg		BBC	HN	M	30	BBBB	Ind		
Economic and Social History/Psychology	CV83	4FT deg		BBC	8M	M	30	BBBB	Ind	2	
Economic and Social History/Psychology	CV8H	4FT deg		BBC	HN	M	30	BBBB	Ind	7	
Economics/Psychology	LC18	4FT deg		BBC	HN	M	30	BBBB	Ind	6	
Economics/Psychology	CL81	4FT deg		BBC	8M	M	30	BBBB	Ind	4	
English/Psychology	CQ83	4FT deg		BBC	HN	M	30	BBBB	Ind	5	24/26
French/Psychology	CR81	5FT deg		BBC	HN	M	30	BBBB	Ind	7	
German/Psychology	CR82	5FT deg		BBC	HN	M	30	BBBB	Ind	4	
Hispanic Studies/Psychology	CR84	5FT deg		BBC	HN	M	30	BBBB	Ind	8	
History of Art/Psychology	CV84	4FT deg		BBC	HN	M	30	BBBB	Ind	4	
History/Psychology	CV8C	4FT deg		BBC	HN	M	30	BBBB	Ind	13	
Islamic Studies/Psychology	TC68	4FT deg		BBC	N	M	30	BBBB	Ind		
Italian/Psychology	CR83	5FT deg		BBC	HN	M	30	BBBB	Ind	4	
Management Studies/Psychology	CN8C	4FT deg		BBC	HN	M	30	BBBB	Ind	14	
Management Studies/Psychology	CN81	4FT deg		BBC	8M	M	30	BBBB	Ind	10	
Music/Psychology	CW83	4FT deg		BBC	HN	M	30	BBBB	Ind	17	
Philosophy/Psychology	CV8R	4FT deg		BBC	HN	M	30	BBBB	Ind	6	20/24
Philosophy/Psychology	CV87	4FT deg		BBC	8M	M	30	BBBB	Ind	11	
Physiology/Psychology	BC18	4FT deg	C/M+S	BBC-CCC	N	M	24$	BBBB$	N	5	
Politics/Psychology	CM81	4FT deg		BBC	8M	M	30	BBBB	Ind	4	
Politics/Psychology	CM8C	4FT deg		BBC	HN	M	30	BBBB	Ind	16	
Psychology	C801	4FT deg		BBC	HN	M	30	BBBB	Ind	8	22/26
Psychology	C800	4FT deg	2S	BBC-CCC	N	M	24$	BBBB$	N	7	18/26
Psychology	C802	4FT deg		BBC	8M	M	30	BBBB	Ind	6	20/24
Psychology with Celtic	C8Q5	4FT deg		BBC	8M	M	30	BBBB	Ind	5	
Psychology with Czech	C8T1	4FT deg		BBC	8M	M	30	BBBB	Ind		
Psychology with French	C8R1	4FT deg		BBC	8M	M	30	BBBB	Ind	6	
Psychology with German	C8R2	4FT deg		BBC	8M	M	30	BBBB	Ind		
Psychology with Hispanic Studies	C8R4	4FT deg		BBC	8M	M	30	BBBB	Ind	9	
Psychology with Italian	C8R3	4FT deg		BBC	8M	M	30	BBBB	Ind		
Psychology with Polish	C8TC	4FT deg		BBC	8M	M	30	BBBB	Ind		
Psychology with Russian	C8R8	4FT deg		BBC	8M	M	30	BBBB	Ind		
Psychology/Archaeology	VC68	4FT deg		BBC	8M	M	30	BBBB	Ind	4	
Psychology/Computing Science	CG8M	4FT deg		BBC	8M	M	30	BBBB	Ind	8	
Psychology/History	CV81	4FT deg		BBC	8M	M	30	BBBB	Ind	6	
Psychology/Russian	CR88	5FT deg		BBC	8M	M	30	BBBB	Ind		
Psychology/Scottish History	CVV1	4FT deg		BBC	HN	M	30	BBBB	Ind	6	
Psychology/Scottish History	CVVC	4FT deg		BBC	8M	M	30	BBBB	Ind	5	
Psychology/Scottish Literature	CQ82	4FT deg		BBC	HN	M	30	BBBB	Ind		
Psychology/Social and Urban Policy	LC48	4FT deg		BBC	8M	M	30	BBBB	Ind	4	
Psychology/Sociology	LC3V	4FT deg		BBC	8M	M	30	BBBB	Ind	6	
Psychology/Sociology	LC38	4FT deg		BBC	HN	M	30	BBBB	Ind	8	

TITLE	CODE	COURSE	SUBJECTS	A/AS	ND/C	RGNVQ	IB	SQA(H)	SQA	RATIO	A/AS
Social and Urban Policy/Psychology	LL4R	4FT deg		BBC	HN	M	30	BBBB	Ind	15	
Theatre Studies/Psychology	CW84	4FT deg		BBC	HN	M	30	BBBB	Ind	9	
Theology & Religious Studies/Psychology	CV8V	4FT deg		BBC	HN	M	30	BBBB	Ind	3	

GLASGOW CALEDONIAN Univ

TITLE	CODE	COURSE	SUBJECTS	A/AS	ND/C	RGNVQ	IB	SQA(H)	SQA	RATIO	A/AS
Psychology	L700	3FT/4FT deg	S/M+Gy	CCD	Ind		Ind	BBBCC$	Ind	8	14/18

GOLDSMITHS COLL (Univ of London)

TITLE	CODE	COURSE	SUBJECTS	A/AS	ND/C	RGNVQ	IB	SQA(H)	SQA	RATIO	A/AS
Mathematics and Psychology	CG81	3FT deg	M	CCC	MO	M	Dip	BBBCC	N		
Psychology	C800	3FT deg		BBC	MO	M	Dip	ABBBB	N	9	16/24
Psychology with Computer Science	C8G5	3FT deg		BBC	MO	M	Dip	ABBBB	N	9	
Psychology with a European Language (4 Yrs)	C8T9	4FT deg	L	BBC	MO	M	Dip	ABBBB	N	10	

Univ of GREENWICH

TITLE	CODE	COURSE	SUBJECTS	A/AS	ND/C	RGNVQ	IB	SQA(H)	SQA	RATIO	A/AS
Economics and Psychology	LL17	3FT deg	* g	16	3M	Ind	Ind	ABC	Ind		
Economics with Psychology	L1L7	3FT deg	* g	16	3M	Ind	Ind	ABC	Ind		
Health and Psychology	BC98	3FT deg	* g	16	N	M$	22	Ind	Ind		
Health with Psychology	B9C8	3FT deg	* g	12	N	M$	22	Ind	Ind		
Psychology (FT and SW modes)	C800	3FT/4SW deg	* g	16	1M+1D	Ind	Ind	Ind	Ind		
Psychology with Statistics	C8G4	3FT/4SW deg	M g	16	1M+1D	Ind	24	Ind	Ind		
Sociology with Psychology	L3L7	3FT deg	* g	14	3M	Ind	Ind	Ind	Ind		

HERIOT-WATT Univ

TITLE	CODE	COURSE	SUBJECTS	A/AS	ND/C	RGNVQ	IB	SQA(H)	SQA	RATIO	A/AS
Applied Psychology	L700	4FT deg	*	CCC	HN	M$ go	28	BBBC	HN		
Applied Psychology and Computer Science	GL57	4FT deg	M	CCC	HN	M$ go	30	BBBC$	Ind		
Applied Psychology with Biology	L7C1	4FT deg	*	CCC	HN	M$ go	30	BBBC	Ind		

Univ of HERTFORDSHIRE

TITLE	CODE	COURSE	SUBJECTS	A/AS	ND/C	RGNVQ	IB	SQA(H)	SQA	RATIO	A/AS
Applied Physics/Psychology	F3C8	3FT deg	M+P	18	4M+4D	D$ gi	26$	BBBC$	Ind		
Business/Psychology	N1C8	3FT deg	*	20	4M+4D	D$ gi	26	BBBC	Ind	10	18/20
Cognitive Science	C801	3FT deg	* g	14-18	Ind	Ind	Ind	Ind	Ind	2	8/20
Computing/Psychology	G5C8	3FT deg	*	20	4M+4D	D$ gi	26	BBBC	Ind		
Economics/Psychology	L1C8	3FT deg	*	20	4M+4D	D$ gi	26	BBBC	Ind		
Environmental Science/Psychology	F9C8	3FT deg	*	20	4M+4D	D$ gi	26	BBBC	Ind		
Human Biology/Psychology	B1C8	3FT deg	S g	20	4M+4D	DS gi	26$	BBBC$	Ind	8	
Linguistic Science/Psychology	Q1C8	3FT deg	*	20	4M+4D	D$ gi	28	BBBC	Ind		
Operational Research/Psychology	N2C8	3FT deg	*	20	4M+4D	D$ gi	26	BBBC	Ind		
Philosophy/Psychology	V7C8	3FT deg	*	20	4M+4D	D$ gi	26	BBBC	Ind	23	
Psychology	C800	3FT deg	* g	22	DO	D$ go	32	ABBBB	Ind	5	12/22
Psychology/Applied Physics	C8F3	3FT deg	M+P	18	4M+4D	D$ gi	26$	BBBC$	Ind		
Psychology/Business	C8N1	3FT deg	*	20	4M+4D	D$ gi	26	BBBC	Ind	14	
Psychology/Computing	C8G5	3FT deg	*	20	4M+4D	D$ gi	26	BBBC	Ind	19	
Psychology/Economics	C8L1	3FT deg	*	20	4M+4D	D$ gi	26	BBBC	Ind	5	
Psychology/Environmental Science	C8F9	3FT deg	*	20	4M+4D	D$ gi	26	BBBC	Ind	6	
Psychology/Human Biology	C8B1	3FT deg	S g	20	4M+4D	D$ gi	26$	BBBC$	Ind	7	16/20
Psychology/Linguistic Science	C8Q1	3FT deg	*	20	4M+4D	D$ gi	28	BBBC	Ind		
Psychology/Operational Research	C8N2	3FT deg	*	20	4M+4D	D$ gi	26	BBBC	Ind	6	
Psychology/Philosophy	C8V7	3FT deg	*	20	4M+4D	D$ gi	26	BBBC	Ind	22	
Combined Modular Scheme Psychology	Y100	3FT deg	*	20	4M+4D	D$ gi	26	BBBC	Ind		
Combined Modular Scheme Psychology (Extended)	Y109▼	4EXT deg	*	4	N	P$ gi	Dip	DDDD	Ind		

Univ of HUDDERSFIELD

TITLE	CODE	COURSE	SUBJECTS	A/AS	ND/C	RGNVQ	IB	SQA(H)	SQA	RATIO	A/AS
Behavioural Sciences	L730	3FT deg	* g	14	MO+2D	M gi	Ind	BBBC	Ind		
Computing and Psychology	GL57	3FT deg	* g	14-16	MO	M go	Ind	BBB	Ind		
Psychology	L700	3FT deg	* g	18	MO+5D	M6/^ gi	Ind	BBBB	Ind		

Psychology 63

course details			98 expected requirements							96 entry stats	
TITLE	CODE	COURSE	SUBJECTS	A/AS	ND/C	RGNVQ	IB	SQA(H)	SQA	RATIO	A/AS
Univ of HULL											
Psychology	C800	3FT deg	* g	BBC	2M+2D	D$^ go	28	BBBCC	Ind	8	20/26
Psychology with Anthropology	C8L6	3FT deg	* g	BBB-BCC	2M+2D	D$^ go	28	BBBCC	Ind	22	
Psychology with Counselling	C822	3FT deg	* g	BBB	DO	D$+	28	ABBBB	Ind		
Psychology with Occupational Psychology (4 Yrs)	C823	4FT deg	* g	BBC	2M+2D	D$^ go	28	BBBCC	Ind	9	22/24
Psychology with Philosophy	C8V7	3FT deg	* g	BBB-BCC	MO+2D	D$^ go	28	BBBCC	Ind	31	
Psychology with Sociology	C8L3	3FT deg	* g	BBB-BCC	2M+2D	D$^ go	28	BBBCC	Ind	68	
KEELE Univ											
Finance and Psychology	CN83	3FT deg	* g	BBB	Ind	Ind	32	CSYS	Ind		
Geography and Psychology	CL88	3FT deg	Gy g	BBB	Ind	D$^	32$	CSYS	Ind	11	
International History and Psychology	CV8C	3FT deg	* g	BBB	Ind	Ind	32	CSYS	Ind		
Neuroscience and Psychology	BC18	3FT deg	2S	BBB-BBC	Ind	D$^	30$	CSYS	Ind	1	18/26
Psychology and American Studies	CQ84	3FT deg	* g	BBB	Ind	Ind	32	CSYS	Ind	6	
Psychology and American Studies (4 Yrs)	QC48	4FT deg	*	BBB	Ind	Ind	32	ABBB	Ind	5	
Psychology and Ancient History	CV8D	3FT deg	* g	BBB	Ind	Ind	32	CSYS	Ind		
Psychology and Applied Social Studies (4 Yrs)	LC58	4FT deg	* g	BBB	Ind	Ind	32	ABBB	Ind		
Psychology and Astrophysics	CF85	3FT deg	P g	BBB-BCC	Ind	D$^	28$	CSYS	Ind		
Psychology and Biochemistry	CC87	3FT deg	C g	BBB-BCC	Ind	D$^	28$	CSYS	Ind		
Psychology and Biochemistry (4 yrs)	CC78	4FT deg	*	BBB-BCC	Ind	Ind	32	ABBB	Ind	2	
Psychology and Biological & Medicinal Chemistry	FCC8	4FT deg	*	BBB-BCC	Ind	Ind	28	ABBB	Ind		
Psychology and Biology	CC81	3FT deg	S g	BBB-BCC	Ind	D$^	28$	CSYS	Ind	7	
Psychology and Biology (4 Yrs)	CC18	4FT deg	*	BBB	Ind	Ind	32	ABBB	Ind		
Psychology and Business Administration (4 Yrs)	NC98	4FT deg	*	BBB	Ind	Ind	32	ABBB	Ind		
Psychology and Chemistry (4 Yrs)	FC18	4FT deg	*	BBB-BCC	Ind	Ind	28	BBBB	Ind		
Psychology and Classical Studies	CQ88	3FT deg	* g	BBB	Ind	Ind	32	CSYS	Ind		
Psychology and Computer Science	CG85	3FT deg	* g	BBB	Ind	Ind	32	CSYS	Ind		
Psychology and Computer Science (4 Yrs)	GC58	4FT deg	*	BBB	Ind	Ind	32	ABBB	Ind	6	
Psychology and Criminology	CM8H	3FT deg	* g	ABB	Ind	Ind	32	CSYS	Ind	14	24/28
Psychology and Criminology (4 Yrs)	MCH8	4FT deg	*	ABB	Ind	Ind	32	ABBB	Ind	4	14/30
Psychology and Economics	CL81	3FT deg	* g	BBB	Ind	Ind	32	CSYS	Ind		
Psychology and Economics (4 Yrs)	LC18	4FT deg	*	BBB	Ind	Ind	32	ABBB	Ind		
Psychology and Educational Studies	CX89	3FT deg	* g	BBB	Ind	Ind	32	CSYS	Ind	11	
Psychology and Educational Studies (4 Yrs)	XC98	4FT deg	*	BBB	Ind	Ind	32	ABBB	Ind	8	
Psychology and Electronic Music	CW8J	3FT deg	Mu g	BBB	Ind	D$^	32$	CSYS	Ind	2	
Psychology and Electronic Music (4 Yrs)	WCJ8	4FT deg	*	BBB	Ind	Ind	32	ABBB	Ind		
Psychology and English	CQ83	3FT deg	E g	BBB	Ind	D$^	32$	CSYS	Ind	8	20/30
Psychology and English (4 Yrs)	QC38	4FT deg	*	BBB	Ind	Ind	32	ABBB	Ind	9	
Psychology and Environmental Management	CF8X	3FT deg	* g	BBB	Ind	Ind	32$	CSYS	Ind		
Psychology and Environmental Management (4 Yrs)	FCX8	4FT deg	*	BBB	Ind	Ind	32	ABBB	Ind		
Psychology and French (4 Yrs)	RC18	4FT deg	* g	BBB	Ind	Ind	32	ABBB	Ind		
Psychology and Geology	CF86	3FT deg	S g	BBB-BCC	Ind	D$^	28$	CSYS	Ind		
Psychology and Geology (4 Yrs)	FC68	4FT deg	*	BBB	Ind	Ind	32	ABBB	Ind		
Psychology and German	CR82	3FT deg	G g	BBB	Ind	D$^	32$	CSYS	Ind		
Psychology and German/Russian or Russian Studies	CT8Y	3FT deg	G+R	BBB	Ind	D$^	32$	CSYS	Ind		
Psychology and History	CV81	3FT deg	* g	BBB	Ind	Ind	32	CSYS	Ind	30	
Psychology and History (4 Yrs)	VC18	4FT deg	*	BBB	Ind	Ind	32	ABBB	Ind	5	
Psychology and Human Resource Management	CN86	3FT deg	* g	BBB	Ind	Ind	32	CSYS	Ind	20	
Psychology and Human Resource Management (4 Yrs)	NC68	4FT deg	*	BBB	Ind	Ind	32	ABBB	Ind		
Psychology and International History (4 Yrs)	VCC8	4FT deg	*	BBB	Ind	Ind	32	ABBB	Ind		
Psychology and International Politics (4 Yrs)	MCC8	4FT deg	*	BBB	Ind	Ind	32	BBBB	Ind		
Psychology and Latin	CQ86	3FT deg	Ln g	BBB	Ind	D$^	32$	CSYS	Ind		
Psychology and Latin (4 Yrs)	QC68	4FT deg	*	BBB	Ind	Ind	32	ABBB	Ind		

| | | | 98 expected requirements | | | | | | 96 entry stats | |
| course details | | | | | | | | | | |
TITLE	CODE	COURSE	SUBJECTS	A/AS	ND/C	AGNVQ	IB	SQA(H)	SQA	RATIO	A/AS
Psychology and Law	CM83	3FT deg	*	BBB	Ind	Ind	32	CSYS	Ind	14	24/28
Psychology and Mathematics	CG81	3FT deg	M g	BBB	Ind	D$^	32$	CSYS	Ind	16	
Psychology and Mathematics (4 Yrs)	GC18	4FT deg	*	BBB	Ind	Ind	32	ABBB	Ind		
Psychology and Music	CW83	3FT deg	Mu g	BBB	Ind	D$^	32$	CSYS	Ind	14	
Psychology and Music (4 Yrs)	WC38	4FT deg	*	BBB	Ind	Ind	32	ABBB	Ind	3	
Psychology and Neurosciences (4 Yrs)	BC1V	4FT deg	*	BBB-BBC	Ind	Ind	30	BBBB	Ind		
Psychology and Philosophy	CV87	3FT deg	* g	BBB	Ind	Ind	32	CSYS	Ind	25	
Psychology and Philosophy (4 Yrs)	VC78	4FT deg	*	BBB	Ind	Ind	32	ABBB	Ind	7	
Psychology and Physics	CF83	3FT deg	P g	BBB-BCC	Ind	D$^	28$	CSYS	Ind		
Psychology and Politics	CM81	3FT deg	* g	BBB	Ind	Ind	32	CSYS	Ind		
Psychology and Politics (4 Yrs)	MC18	4FT deg	*	BBB	Ind	Ind	32	ABBB	Ind		
Psychology and Sociology and Social Anthropology	CL83	3FT deg	* g	BBB	Ind	Ind	32	CSYS	Ind	12	20/24
Russian Studies and Psychology	CR8V	3FT deg	* g	BBB	Ind	Ind	32	CSYS	Ind		
Russian and Psychology	CR88	3FT deg	R g	BBB	Ind	D$^	32$	CSYS	Ind		
Sociol & Soc Anthropology and Psychology (4 Yrs)	LC38	4FT deg	*	BBB	Ind	Ind	32	ABBB	Ind	4	
Statistics and Psychology	CG84	3FT deg	M g	BBB	Ind	D$^	32$	CSYS	Ind		
Statistics and Psychology (4 Yrs)	GC48	4FT deg	*	BBB	Ind	Ind	32	ABBB	Ind		
Visual Arts and Psychology	CW81	3FT deg	* g	BBB	Ind	D$^	32	CSYS	Ind	10	

Univ of KENT

App Soc Psychology with Clinical Psych (4 Yr SW)	C821	4SW deg	* g	26	6D	D$ go	33	AAAB	Ind	12	
Applied Psychology (4Yr SW)	C878	4SW deg	* g	BBB	1M+5D	D$ go	32	AABB	Ind	19	
Applied Psychology with Clinical Psych (4Yr SW)	C823	4SW deg	* g	26	6D	D$ go	33	AAAB	Ind	14	
Applied Social Psychology (4Yr SW)	C841	4SW deg	* g	BBB	1M+5D	D$ go	32	AABB	Ind	52	
Computing and Social Psychology	GL57	3FT deg	* g	26	6D	D$ go	33	AAAB	Ind		
Computing and Social Psychology	CG85	3FT deg	* g	26	6D+5D	D$ go	33	AAAB	Ind		
European Social Psychology (4 Yrs)	L771	4FT deg	L g	22	Ind	Ind	30$	ABBB$	Ind	7	
European Social Psychology (4 Yrs)	C845	4FT deg	L g	22	Ind	Ind	30$	ABBB$	Ind	3	
Ind Relations & Human Resource Mgt (Soc Psychol)	LN76	3FT deg	* g	26	6D	D$ go	33	AAAB	Ind		
Philosophy and Social Behaviour	LV7R	3FT deg	*	22	2M+4D	Ind	30	Ind	Ind	11	
Psychology	C800	3FT deg	* g	BBB	1M+5D	D$ go	32	AABB	Ind	7	19/28
Psychology and Social Anthropology	CL86	3FT deg	* g	26	6D	D$ go	33	AAAB	Ind	23	
Psychology and Sociology	CL83	3FT deg	* g	26	6D	D$ go	33	AAAB	Ind	30	
Psychology with Clinical Psychology	C822	3FT deg	* g	26	6D	D$ go	33	AAAB	Ind	13	22/28
Psychology with a year in Europe (4 Yrs)	C880	4FT deg	L g	22	Ind	Ind	30$	ABBB$	Ind	14	
Social Psychology	C840	3FT deg	* g	BBB	1M+5D	D$ go	32	AABB	Ind	6	10/22
Social Psychology with Clinical Psychology	C820	3FT deg	* g	26	6D	D$ go	33	AAAB	Ind	12	
Social Psychology with Computing	C8G5	3FT deg	* g	BBB	1M+5D	D$ go	32	AABB	Ind		
Social Psychology/Social Anthropology	LL67	3FT deg	* g	26	6D	D$ go	33	AAAB	Ind		
Sociology/Social Psychology	LL37	3FT deg	* g	26	6D	D$ go	33	AAAB	Ind		

KING ALFRED'S WINCHESTER

Psychology	L700	3FT deg	* g	14	6M	M	24	BCC	N		
Psychology and Business Studies	LN71	3FT deg	* g	14	6M	M	24	BCC	N	8	
Psychology and Computing	GL57	3FT deg	* g	14	6M	M	24	BCC	N	1	
Psychology and Contemporary Cultural Studies	LM79	3FT deg	* g	14	6M	M	24	BCC	N	2	
Psychology and Dance Studies	LW7K	3FT deg	* g	14	6M	M	24	BCC	N	7	
Psychology and Drama Studies	LW74	3FT deg	* g	14	6M	M	24	BCC	N	3	8/20
Psychology and Education Studies	LX79	3FT deg	* g	14	6M	M	24	BCC	N	5	12/16
Psychology and English Studies	LQ73	3FT deg	E	14	X	X	24$	BCC$	X	9	
Psychology and History	LV71	3FT deg	* g	14	6M	M	24	BCC	N	3	
Psychology and Japanese Language	LT74	3FT deg	L g	14	X	X	24$	BCC$	X		
Psychology and Media & Film Studies	LP74	3FT deg	* g	14	6M	M	24	BCC	N	10	10/12

course details			98 expected requirements							96 entry stats	
TITLE	CODE	COURSE	SUBJECTS	A/AS	ND/C	RGNVQ	IB	SQA(H)	SQA	RATIO	A/AS
Psychology and Music (World)	LW73	3FT deg	* g	14	6M	M	24	BCC	N	2	
Psychology and Philosophy	LV77	3FT deg	* g	14	6M	M	24	BCC	N	10	
Religious Studies and Psychology	LV78	3FT deg	* g	14	6M	M	24	BCC	N	3	
Social Biology and Psychology	CL17	3FT deg	B g	14	6M $	M	24$	BCC$	N$	5	
Sports Studies and Psychology	LL7H	3FT deg	* g	14	6M	M	24	BCC	N		
Visual Studies and Psychology	LW72	3FT deg	A/Ad g	14	6M $	M	24$	BCC$	N$	4	14/24
KINGSTON Univ											
Psychology/French	LR71	4FT deg	F g	16	MO	Ind^	Ind	BBCCC	HN	3	8/18
Psychology/German	LR72	4FT deg	G g	16	MO	Ind^	Ind	BBCCC	HN	5	
Psychology/History	LV71	3FT deg	H g	18	MO	Ind^	Ind	BBBCC	HN	9	
Psychology/History of Ideas	LV77	3FT deg	* g	18	MO	Ind^	Ind	BBBCC	HN	3	8/14
Psychology/Politics	LM71	3FT deg	* g	18	MO	Ind^	Ind	BBBCC	HN	2	6/16
Sociology/Psychology	LL37	3FT deg	* g	18	DO	Ind^	Ind	BBBCC	HN	6	10/22
Spanish/Psychology	LR74	4FT deg	Sp g	16	MO	Ind^	Ind	BBCCC	HN	17	
LANCASTER Univ											
Educational Studies and Psychology	XC98	3FT deg	* g	BCC	DO		30	ABBBB	Ind		
French Studies and Psychology	CR81	4SW deg	F g	BBC	DO $		32$	ABBBB$	Ind		
German Studies and Psychology	CR82	4SW deg	G/L g	BBC	DO $		32$	ABBBB$	Ind		
Italian Studies and Psychology	CR83	4SW deg	I/L g	BBC	DO $		32$	ABBBB$	Ind		
Linguistics and Psychology	CQ81	3FT deg	* g	BBC	DO		32	ABBBB	Ind		
Organisation Studies and Psychology	CN81	3FT deg	* g	BBC	DO		32	ABBBB	Ind		
Psychology	C800	3FT deg	* g	BBC	DO		32	ABBBB	Ind		
Psychology	C802	3FT deg	* g	BBC	DO		32	ABBBB	Ind		
Spanish Studies and Psychology	CR84	4SW deg	Sp/L g	BBC	DO $		32$	ABBBB$	Ind		
Women's Studies and Psychology	CM89	3FT deg	* g	BBC	DO		32	ABBBB	Ind		
Combined Science *Psychology*	Y158	3FT deg	* g	CCD	MO		28	BBBB	Ind		
Combined Science (inc a year in USA or Canada) *Psychology*	Y155	3FT deg	* g	BBB	Ind		32	AABBB	Ind		
Univ of LEEDS											
Cognitive Science	CG8N	3FT deg	g	BBC	1M+5D$	Ind	30$	ABBBB	Ind	5	20/24
Management Studies-Psychology	NC18	3FT deg	g	ABB	Ind	Ind	33	CSYS	Ind	12	26/30
Psychology	C800	3FT deg	g	ABB	Ind	Ind	33	CSYS	Ind	8	24/30
Psychology-History and Philosophy of Science	CV85	3FT deg	g	ABB	Ind	Ind	33	CSYS	Ind		
Psychology-Philosophy	CV87	3FT deg	g	ABB	Ind	Ind	33	CSYS	Ind	8	24/30
Psychology-Sociology	LC38	3FT deg	g	ABB	Ind	D$^ go	33	CSYS	Ind	14	18/28
LEEDS, TRINITY & ALL SAINTS Univ COLL											
Psychology-Management	LN71	3FT deg	* g	BCC-BD	MO	X	24	BBCCC	Ind	7	8/20
Psychology-Media	LP74	3FT deg	* g	BBC-BD	MO	X	24	BBCCC	Ind	15	8/22
LEEDS METROPOLITAN Univ											
Social Sciences - Psychology	L700	3FT deg									
Univ of LEICESTER											
Psychology	C800	3FT deg	* g	BBB	6D	D$^ gi	32	AABBB	Ind		20/28
Psychology with Sociology	C8L3	3FT deg	* g	BBB	DO	DS^ gi	32	AABBB	Ind		14/30
Combined Arts *Psychology*	Y300	3FT deg	g	BCC	DO	D$^ gi	30$	Ind	Ind		
Combined Science *Psychology*	Y100	3FT deg	g	CCC	MO $	D$^ gi	28$	BBBCC$	HN		

course details | 98 expected requirements | 96 entry stats

TITLE	CODE	COURSE	SUBJECTS	A/AS	NO/C	RGNVQ	IB	SQA(H)	SQA	RATIO A/AS
Univ of LINCOLNSHIRE and HUMBERSIDE										
Communications and Psychology	CP83▼	3FT deg	* g	18	1M+4D	D	26	BBBCC	Ind	
Criminology and Psychology	CM83▼	3FT deg	* g	18	1M+4D	D	26	BBBCC	Ind	
Economics and Psychology	CL81▼	3FT deg	* g	18	1M+4D	D	26	BBBCC	Ind	
Health Studies and Psychology	CL8K▼	3FT deg	* g	18	1M+4D	D	26	BBBCC	Ind	
Internationl Relations and Psychology	CM81▼	3FT deg	* g	18	1M+4D	D	26	BBBCC	Ind	
Journalism and Psychology	CP86▼	3FT deg	* g	18	1M+4D	D	26	BBBCC	Ind	
Management and Psychology	CN81▼	3FT deg	* g	18	1M+4D	D	26	BBBCC	Ind	
Media and Psychology	CP84▼	3FT deg	* g	18	1M+4D	D	26	BBBCC	Ind	
Politics and Psychology	CM8C▼	3FT deg	* g	18	1M+4D	D	26	BBBCC	Ind	
Psychology	C800▼	3FT deg	g	18	1M+4D	D	26	BBBCC	Ind	
Psychology and Social Policy	CL84▼	3FT deg	* g	18	1M+4D	D	26	BBBCC	Ind	
Psychology and Tourism	CP87▼	3FT deg	* g	18	1M+4D	D	26	BBBCC	Ind	
Univ of LIVERPOOL										
Psychology	C800	3FT deg	* g	22-24	Ind	Ind	31$	BBBBB$	Ind	11 22/30
Psychology (2x2, Wirral, mature applicants only)	C801	4FT deg	*	20	Ind	Ind	Ind	Ind	Ind	
Arts Combined *Psychology*	Y401	3FT deg	*	BBB	Ind	Ind	30$	ABBB	Ind	
BA Combined Honours *Psychology*	Y200	3FT deg	* g	BBB	Ind	Ind	Ind	Ind	Ind	
BSc Combined Honours *Psychology*	Y100	3FT deg	2S	22	Ind	Ind	31$	BBBBB$	Ind	
LIVERPOOL HOPE Univ COLL										
Psychology/American Studies	QC48	3FT deg	g	12	8M	M$ go	Ind	Ind	Ind	10
Psychology/Art	WC98	3FT deg	A/Fa g	12	8M	MA /P*^ go	Ind	Ind	Ind	6 10/22
Psychology/Drama & Theatre Studies	WC48	3FT deg	g	12	8M	M* go	Ind	Ind	Ind	13
Psychology/English	QC38	3FT deg	El g	12	8M	P*^ go	Ind	Ind	Ind	5 10/21
Psychology/Environmental Studies	FC98	3FT deg	B/Gy/En g	10	6M	M$ go	Ind	Ind	Ind	6
Psychology/European Studies	TC28	3FT deg	* g	12	8M	M* go	Ind	Ind	Ind	
Psychology/French	RC18	3FT deg	F g	12	8M	P*^ go	Ind	Ind	Ind	6
Psychology/Human & Applied Biology	CC18	3FT deg	B g	10	6M	MS /P*^ go	Ind	Ind	Ind	11 12/14
Psychology/Information Technology	GC58	3FT deg	g	10	6M	M* go	Ind	Ind	Ind	4 8/18
Psychology/Mathematics	GC18	3FT deg	M	10	6M	P*^	Ind	Ind	Ind	17
Sociology/Psychology	CL83	3FT deg	g	12	8M	M* go	Ind	Ind	Ind	5 8/16
Sport, Recreation & Physical Educ/Psychology	CB86	3FT deg	g	10	6M	M* go	Ind	Ind	SQA	
Theology & Religious Studies/Psychology	CV88	3FT deg	g	12	8M	M* go	Ind	Ind	Ind	6
LIVERPOOL JOHN MOORES Univ										
Applied Psychology	C870	3FT deg	* g	16	5M+3D	M$^ go	28$	BBCC		24 12/26
Applied Psychology and Applied Community Studies	LC58	3FT deg	* g	16	5M+3D	M$^ go		BBCC		3 14/18
Criminal Justice and Applied Psychology	CM83	3FT deg	* g	16	5M+3D	X	28$	BBCC		30 14/26
Health and Applied Psychology	BC98	3FT deg	* g	16	5M+3D	M$^ go	28$	BBCC		5 14/18
Literature,Life & Thought & Applied Psychology	CQ83	3FT deg	E	16-20	5M+3D		28$	BBBC		5 18/22
Media and Cultural Studs and Applied Psychology	CP84	3FT deg	* g	16-18	5M+3D	X	28$	BBBC		7 18/22
Philosophy & Applied Psych (Phil Jt Awd only)	CV87	3FT deg		16-18	5M+3D	M$^ go	28$	BBCC		8 12/20
Psychology and Biology	CC18	3FT deg		10-12	5M	M go				
Sociology and Applied Psychology	CL83	3FT deg	* g	16	MO+3D	M$^ go	28$	BBCC		38 14/18
Sports Science and Applied Psychology	CB86	3FT deg	S g	CCC	5M+3D	DS/MS6 go	28$	BBBB		13 18/22
LONDON GUILDHALL Univ										
3D/Spatial Design and Psychology	CW8F	3FT deg	Pf g	CC-CDD	MO+5D	D$ go	26	Ind	Ind	
Computing with Human Factors	G5C8	3FT deg	* g	CD	MO $	M$ go	$	Ind	Ind	
Psychology	C830	3FT deg	* g	BC-CC	8M+4D	D$ go	26	Ind	Ind	

Psychology 63

TITLE	CODE	COURSE	SUBJECTS	A/AS	NO/C	RGNVQ	IB	SQA(H)	SQA	RATIO A/AS
Psychology & Communications & Audio Vis Prod St	CP84	3FT deg	* g	CC	MO+4D	M$ go	26	Ind	Ind	
Psychology and Accounting	CN84	3FT deg	* g	CD-DDD	MO+2D	M$ go	24	Ind	Ind	
Psychology and Business	CN81	3FT deg	* g	CC-CDD	MO+4D	M$ go	26	Ind	Ind	
Psychology and Business Economics	CL8C	3FT deg	* g	CD-DDD	MO+2D	M$ go	26	Ind	Ind	
Psychology and Business Information Technology	CG87	3FT deg	* g	CD-DDD	MO+2D	M$ go	26	Ind	Ind	
Psychology and Computing	CG85	3FT deg	* g	CD-DDD	MO+2D	M$ go	26	Ind	Ind	
Psychology and Design Studies	CW82	3FT deg	* g	CC-CDD	MO+3D	M$ go	26	Ind	Ind	
Psychology and Development Studies	CM89	3FT deg	* g	CD-DDD	MO+2D	M$ go	26	Ind	Ind	
Psychology and Economics	CL81	3FT deg	* g	CD-DDD	MO+2D	M$ go	26	Ind	Ind	
Psychology and English	CQ83	3FT deg	* g	CC-CDD	MO+4D	M$ go	26	Ind	Ind	
Psychology and European Studies	CT82	3FT deg	* g	CD-DDD	MO+2D	M$ go	26	Ind	Ind	
Psychology and Financial Services	CN83	3FT deg	* g	CD-DDD	MO+2D	M$ go	26	Ind	Ind	
Psychology and Fine Art	CW81	3FT deg	* g	CC	MO+4D	M$ go	26	Ind	Ind	
Psychology and French	CR81	4FT deg	* g	CD-DDD	MO+2D	M$ go	26	Ind	Ind	
Psychology and German	CR82	4FT deg	* g	CD-DDD	MO+2D	M$ go	26	Ind	Ind	
Psychology and International Relations	CM8C	3FT deg	* g	CD-DDD	MO+2D	M$ go	26	Ind	Ind	
Psychology and Law	CM83	3FT deg	* g	CC	MO+3D	M$ go	26	Ind	Ind	
Psychology and Marketing	CN85	3FT deg	* g	CC-CDD	MO+2D	M$ go	26	Ind	Ind	
Psychology and Mathematics	CG81	3FT deg	* g	CD-DDD	MO+2D	M$ go	26	Ind	Ind	
Psychology and Modern History	CV81	3FT deg	* g	CD-DDD	MO+2D	M$ go	26	Ind	Ind	
Psychology and Multimedia Systems	CG8M	3FT deg	* g	CD-DDD	MO+2D	M$ go	26	Ind	Ind	
Psychology and Politics	CM81	3FT deg	* g	CD-DDD	MO+2D	M$ go	26	Ind	Ind	
Psychology and Product Development & Manufacture	CJ84	3FT deg	* g	CD-DDD	MO+2D	M$ go	26	Ind	Ind	
Social Policy & Management and Psychology	CL84	3FT deg	* g	CC-CDD	MO+2D	M$ go	26	Ind	Ind	
Sociology and Psychology	CL83	3FT deg	* g	CC-CDD	MO+2D	M$ go	26	Ind	Ind	
Spanish and Psychology	CR84	4FT deg	* g	CD-DDD	MO+2D	M$ go	26	Ind	Ind	
Taxation and Psychology	CN8H	3FT deg	* g	CD-DDD	MO	M$ go	24	Ind	Ind	
Textile Furnishing Design and Psychology	CW8G	3FT deg	Pf g	CD-DDD	MO+2D	M$ go	24	Ind	Ind	
Modular Programme *Psychology*	Y400	3FT deg	* g	BC-CC	MO+2D	M$ go	24	Ind	Ind	

LSE: LONDON Sch of Economics (Univ of London)

TITLE	CODE	COURSE	SUBJECTS	A/AS	NO/C	RGNVQ	IB	SQA(H)	SQA	RATIO A/AS
Psychology and Philosophy	LV77	3FT deg	g	BBB	Ind	X	$	Ind	Ind	46 26/30
Social Policy with Social Psychology	L4L7	3FT deg	g	BBB	Ind		$	Ind	Ind	16

LOUGHBOROUGH Univ

TITLE	CODE	COURSE	SUBJECTS	A/AS	NO/C	RGNVQ	IB	SQA(H)	SQA	RATIO A/AS
Politics with Social Psychology	M1L7	3FT deg	* g	20	2M+3D	D*6/^ go	28	Ind	Ind	16/20
Psychology	C800	3FT deg	* g	BBC		DS6/^ go	30	Ind		9 20/26
Psychology (4 Yr SW)	C801	4SW deg	* g	BBC		DS6/^ go	30	Ind		13
Psychology with Ergonomics	C8J9	3FT deg	* g	BBC		DS6/^ go	30	Ind		9
Psychology with Ergonomics (4 Yr SW)	C8JY	4SW deg	* g	BBC		DS6/^ go	30	Ind		3
Social Psychology	L740	3FT deg	*	22	2M+3D	D*6/^ go	30	Ind		5 20/26

LSU COLL of HE

TITLE	CODE	COURSE	SUBJECTS	A/AS	NO/C	RGNVQ	IB	SQA(H)	SQA	RATIO A/AS
Art and Psychology	EL17	3FT deg								
Art with Psychology	E1L7	3FT deg	A	DD	Ind		Ind	Ind	Ind	
Art with Psychology	W1L7	3FT deg	A	DD	Ind		Ind	Ind	Ind	5 10/20
English with Psychology	Q3L7	3FT deg	E	CD	Ind		Ind	Ind	Ind	5 6/14
Environment and Society with Psychology	FL97	3FT deg								
History with Psychology	V1L7	3FT deg	H	CD	Ind		Ind	Ind	Ind	9
Psychology and Art	WL17	3FT deg								
Psychology and English	QL37	3FT deg								
Psychology and History	VL17	3FT deg								
Psychology and Life Sciences	CL97	3FT deg								

course details			98 expected requirements							96 entry stats
TITLE	CODE	COURSE	SUBJECTS	A/AS	NO/C	AGNVQ	IB	SQA(H)	SQA	RATIO A/AS
Sociology and Psychology	LL73	3FT deg								
Sport and Health Sciences with Psychology	BL6R	3FT deg								
Sports Science and Psychology	BL67	3FT deg								
Theology with Psychology	V8L7	3FT deg								

LUTON Univ

Accounting with Organisational Behaviour	N4LT	3FT deg	g	12-16	MO/DO	M/D	32	BBCC	Ind	
Accounting with Psychology	NL4T	3FT deg	g	12-16	MO/DO	M/D	32	BBCC	Ind	
Biochemistry with Psychology	C7L7	3FT deg	g	12-16	MO/DO	M/D	32	BBCC	Ind	
Biology with Organisational Behaviour	C1L7	3FT deg	g	12-16	MO/DO	M/D	32	BBCC	Ind	
Biology with Psychology	C1LR	3FT deg	g	12-16	MO/DO	M/D	32	BBCC	Ind	
Biotechnology with Psychology	J8L7	3FT deg	g	12-16	MO/DO	M/D	32	BBCC	Ind	
Broadcasting & Media Technology with Psychology	H6L7	3FT deg		12-16	MO/DO	M/D	32	BBCC	Ind	
Built Environment with Organisational Behaviour	N8L7	3FT deg	g	12-16	MO/DO	M/D	32	BBCC	Ind	
Business Systems with Organisational Behaviour	N1L7	3FT deg	g	12-16	MO/DO	M/D	32	BBCC	Ind	
Business Systems with Psychology	N1LT	3FT deg	g	12-16	MO/DO	M/D	32	BBCC	Ind	
Business with Psychology	N1LR	3FT deg	g	12-16	MO/DO	M/D	32	BBCC	Ind	
Contemp Br & Euro Hist with Organisational Behav	V1L7	3FT deg	g	12-16	MO/DO	M/D	32	BBCC	Ind	
Contemp British & Euro History with Psychology	V1LR	3FT deg	g	12-16	MO/DO	M/D	32	BBCC	Ind	
Digital Systems Design with Organisational Behav	H6LT	3FT deg	g	12-16	MO/DO	M/D	32	BBCC	Ind	
Ecology (Eco Tech) with Organis Behaviour	C9L7	3FT deg	g	12-16	MO/DO	M/D	32	BBCC	Ind	
Electronic System Design with Organis Behaviour	HL67	3FT deg	g	12-16	MO/DO	M/D	32	BBCC	Ind	
Environmental Sci with Organisational Behaviour	F9L7	3FT deg	g	12-16	MO/DO	M/D	32	BBCC	Ind	
Environmental Science with Psychology	F9LR	3FT deg	g	12-16	MO/DO	M/D	32	BBCC	Ind	
Environmental Studies with Psychology	F9LT	3FT deg		12-16	MO/DO	M/D	32	BBCC	Ind	
European Language St with Organisational Behav	T2L7	3FT deg	L g	12-16	MO/DO	M/D	32	BBCC	Ind	
Geography with Psycology	F8LR	3FT deg	g	12-16	MO/DO	M/D	32	BBCC	Ind	
Geology with Organisational Behaviour	F6L7	3FT deg	g	12-16	MO/DO	M/D	32	BBCC	Ind	
Geology with Psychology	F6LR	3FT deg	g	12-16	MO/DO	M/D	32	BBCC	Ind	
Health Science with Psychology	B9LR	3FT deg	g	12-16	MO/DO	M/D	32	BBCC	Ind	
Health Studies with Organisational Behaviour	B9L7	3FT deg	g	12-16	MO/DO	M/D	32	BBCC	Ind	
Health Studies with Psychology	B9LT	3FT deg	g	12-16	MO/DO	M/D	32	BBCC	Ind	
Integrated Engineering with Org Behaviour	H1L7	3FT deg	g	12-16	MO/DO	M/D	32	BBCC	Ind	
Integrated Engineering with Psychology	H1LR	3FT deg	g	12-16	MO/DO	M/D	32	BBCC	Ind	
Law with Organisational Behaviour	M3L7	3FT deg	g	12-16	MO/DO	M/D	32	BBCC	Ind	
Leisure Studies with Organisational Behaviour	N7L7	3FT deg	g	12-16	MO/DO	M/D	32	BBCC	Ind	
Leisure Studies with Psychology	N7LR	3FT deg	g	12-16	MO/DO	M/D	32	BBCC	Ind	
Linguistics with Organisational Behaviour	Q1L7	3FT deg	g	12-16	MO/DO	M/D	32	BBCC	Ind	
Literary Studies in English with Org Behaviour	Q2LT	3FT deg		12-16	MO/DO	M/D	32	BBCC	Ind	
Literary Studies in English with Psychology	Q2L7	3FT deg		12-16	MO/DO	M/D	32	BBCC	Ind	
Marketing with Psychology	N5LR	3FT deg	g	12-16	MO/DO	M/D	32	BBCC	Ind	3
Mathematical Sciences with Org Behaviour	G1L7	3FT deg	g	12-16	MO/DO	M/D	32	BBCC	Ind	
Media Practices with Psychology	P4LR	3FT deg		12-16	MO/DO	M/D	32	BBCC	Ind	3
Media Production with Organisational Behaviour	P4L7	3FT deg	g	12-16	MO/DO	M/D	32	BBCC	Ind	
Media Production with Psychology	P4LT	3FT deg	g	12-16	MO/DO	M/D	32	BBCC	Ind	
Modern English St with Organisational Behaviour	Q3L7	3FT deg		12-16	MO/DO	M/D	32	BBCC	Ind	
Modern English Studies with Psychology	Q3LR	3FT deg	g	12-16	MO/DO	M/D	32	BBCC	Ind	
Modern History with Organisational Behaviour	V1LT	3FT deg	g	12-16	MO/DO	M/D	32	BBCC	Ind	
Org Behaviour and Language & Stylistics in Engl	QLG7	3FT deg	g	12-16	MO/DO	M/D	32	BBCC	Ind	
Organisational Behav & Integrated Engineering	HL17	3FT deg	g	12-16	MO/DO	M/D	32	BBCC	Ind	
Organisational Behaviour & Literary St in Engl	QL27	3FT deg	g	12-16	MO/DO	M/D	32	BBCC	Ind	
Organisational Behaviour & Mathematical Sciences	GL17	3FT deg	g	12-16	MO/DO	M/D	32	BBCC	Ind	
Organisational Behaviour and Accounting	NLK7	3FT deg	g	12-16	MO/DO	M/D	32	BBCC	Ind	

Psychology 63

			98 expected requirements							96 entry stats	

TITLE	CODE	COURSE	SUBJECTS	A/AS	NQ/C	AGNVQ	IB	SQA(H)	SQA	RATIO A/AS	
Organisational Behaviour and Applied Statistics	GL47	3FT deg	g	12-16	MO/DO	M/D	32	BBCC	Ind		
Organisational Behaviour and Biology	CL17	3FT deg	g	12-16	MO/DO	M/D	32	BBCC	Ind		
Organisational Behaviour and Built Environment	NL87	3FT deg	g	12-16	MO/DO	M/D	32	BBCC	Ind		
Organisational Behaviour and Business Systems	NLC7	3FT deg	g	12-16	MO/DO	M/D	32	BBCC	Ind	2	
Organisational Behaviour and Computer Science	GL57	3FT deg	g	12-16	MO/DO	M/D	32	BBCC	Ind		
Organisational Behaviour and Contemporary Hist	VL17	3FT deg	g	12-16	MO/DO	M/D	32	BBCC	Ind		
Organisational Behaviour and Digital Systs Des	HLP7	3FT deg	g	12-16	MO/DO	M/D	32	BBCC	Ind		
Organisational Behaviour and Ecol & Biodiversity	CL97	3FT deg	g	12-16	MO/DO	M/D	32	BBCC	Ind		
Organisational Behaviour and Environmental Sci	FL97	3FT deg	g	12-16	MO/DO	M/D	32	BBCC	Ind		
Organisational Behaviour and Euro Language Studs	TL27	3FT deg	L g	12-16	MO/DO	M/D	32	BBCC	Ind		
Organisational Behaviour and Geology	FL67	3FT deg	g	12-16	MO/DO	M/D	32	BBCC	Ind		
Organisational Behaviour and Health Studies	BLX7	3FT deg	g	12-16	MO/DO	M/D	32	BBCC	Ind		
Organisational Behaviour and Law	ML37	3FT deg	g	12-16	MO/DO	M/D	32	BBCC	Ind		
Organisational Behaviour and Leisure Studies	NL77	3FT deg	g	12-16	MO/DO	M/D	32	BBCC	Ind		
Organisational Behaviour and Linguistics	QL17	3FT deg	g	12-16	MO/DO	M/D	32	BBCC	Ind		
Organisational Behaviour and Mathematics	LG71	3FT deg	g	12-16	MO/DO	M/D	32	BBCC	Ind		
Organisational Behaviour and Media Production	PLL7	3FT deg	g	12-16	MO/DO	M/D	32	BBCC	Ind		
Organisational Behaviour and Modern English St	QL37	3FT deg	g	12-16	MO/DO	M/D	32	BBCC	Ind		
Physical Geography and Organisational Behaviour	LF7V	3FT deg		12-16	MO/DO	M/D	32	BBCC	Ind		
Physical Geography with Organisational Behaviour	F8L7	3FT deg	g	12-16	MO/DO	M/D	32	BBCC	Ind		
Physical Geography with Psychology	F8LT	3FT deg	g	12-16	MO/DO	M/D	32	BBCC	Ind		
Plant Biology with Psychology	C2L7	3FT deg	g	12-16	MO/DO	M/D	32	BBCC	Ind		
Politics and Organisational Behaviour	LM71	3FT deg	g	12-16	MO/DO	M/D	32	BBCC	Ind		
Politics with Organisational Behaviour	M1L7	3FT deg	g	12-16	MO/DO	M/D	32	BBCC	Ind		
Politics with Psychology	M1LR	3FT deg	g	12-16	MO/DO	M/D	32	BBCC	Ind		
Psychology	L700	3FT deg	g	12-16	MO/DO	M/D	32	BBCC	Ind	4	6/16
Psychology and Accounting	NLKR	3FT deg	g	12-16	MO/DO	M/D	32	BBCC	Ind		
Psychology and Artificial Intelligence	GL87	3FT deg		12-16	MO/DO	M/D	32	BBCC	Ind		
Psychology and Biochemistry	CL77	3FT deg	g	12-16	MO/DO	M/D	32	BBCC	Ind		
Psychology and Biology	CL1R	3FT deg	g	12-16	MO/DO	M/D	32	BBCC	Ind	9	
Psychology and British Studies	VL97	3FT deg		12-16	MO/DO	M/D	32	BBCC	Ind		
Psychology and Business	NL1R	3FT deg	g	12-16	MO/DO	M/D	32	BBCC	Ind	52	
Psychology and Business Systems	NLCR	3FT deg	g	12-16	MO/DO	M/D	32	BBCC	Ind		
Psychology and Computer Science	GL5R	3FT deg	g	12-16	MO/DO	M/D	32	BBCC	Ind	12	
Psychology and Contemporary History	VL1R	3FT deg	g	12-16	MO/DO	M/D	32	BBCC	Ind	6	
Psychology and Geography	FL87	3FT deg	g	12-16	MO/DO	M/D	32	BBCC	Ind		
Psychology and Geology	FL6R	3FT deg	g	12-16	MO/DO	M/D	32	BBCC	Ind		
Psychology and Health Science	BL9R	3FT deg	g	12-16	MO/DO	M/D	32	BBCC	Ind	12	
Psychology and Health Studies	BLXR	3FT deg	g	12-16	MO/DO	M/D	32	BBCC	Ind	6	
Psychology and Human Biology	BL17	3FT deg	g	12-16	MO/DO	M/D	32	BBCC	Ind		
Psychology and Journalism	PL67	3FT deg		12-16	MO/DO	M/D	32	BBCC	Ind		
Psychology and Language & Stylistics in English	QLGR	3FT deg	g	12-16	MO/DO	M/D	32	BBCC	Ind	2	
Psychology and Law	ML3R	3FT deg		12-16	MO/DO	M/D	32	BBCC	Ind		
Psychology and Leisure Studies	NL7R	3FT deg	g	12-16	MO/DO	M/D	32	BBCC	Ind		
Psychology and Literary Studies in English	QL2T	3FT deg		12-16	MO/DO	M/D	32	BBCC	Ind		
Psychology and Mapping Science	FL8R	3FT deg		12-16	MO/DO	M/D	32	BBCC	Ind		
Psychology and Marketing	NL5R	3FT deg	g	12-16	MO/DO	M/D	32	BBCC	Ind	13	
Psychology and Media Practices	PL4R	3FT deg	g	12-16	MO/DO	M/D	32	BBCC	Ind		
Psychology and Media Production	PLLR	3FT deg	g	12-16	MO/DO	M/D	32	BBCC	Ind		
Psychology and Modern English Studies	QL3R	3FT deg	g	12-16	MO/DO	M/D	32	BBCC	Ind	7	
Psychology and Pharmacology	BL27	3FT deg	g	12-16	MO/DO	M/D	32	BBCC	Ind		
Psychology and Plant Biology	CL27	3FT deg	g	12-16	MO/DO	M/D	32	BBCC	Ind		

course details | 98 expected requirements | 96 entry stats

TITLE	CODE	COURSE	SUBJECTS	A/AS	NO/C	RGNVQ	IB	SQA(H)	SQA	RATIO A/AS
Psychology and Politics	ML1R	3FT deg	g	12-16	MO/DO	M/D	32	BBCC	Ind	4
Psychology with Accounting	L7NL	3FT deg	g	12-16	MO/DO	M/D	32	BBCC	Ind	
Psychology with Animation	L7WG	3FT deg	g	12-16	MO/DO	M/D	32	BBCC	Ind	
Psychology with Biochemistry	L7C7	3FT deg	g	12-16	MO/DO	M/D	32	BBCC	Ind	
Psychology with Biology	L7CC	3FT deg	g	12-16	MO/DO	M/D	32	BBCC	Ind	10
Psychology with Biotechnology	L758	3FT deg		12-16	MO/DO	M/D	32	BBCC	Ind	
Psychology with British Studies	L7V9	3FT deg		12-16	MO/DO	M/D	32	BBCC	Ind	
Psychology with Business	L739	3FT deg	g	12-16	MO/DO	M/D	32	BBCC	Ind	13
Psychology with Business Systems	L7N1	3FT deg	g	12-16	MO/DO	M/D	32	BBCC	Ind	
Psychology with Chinese	L7T3	3FT deg		12-16	MO/DO	M/D	32	BBCC	Ind	
Psychology with Comparative Literature	L7QF	3FT deg	g	12-16	MO/DO	M/D	32	BBCC	Ind	
Psychology with Contemporary History	L7VD	3FT deg	g	12-16	MO/DO	M/D	32	BBCC	Ind	
Psychology with Film Studies	L7W5	3FT deg		12-16	MO/DO	M/D	32	BBCC	Ind	
Psychology with French	L7R1	3FT deg	F g	12-16	MO/DO	M/D	32	BBCC	Ind	
Psychology with Geographical Information Systs	L701	3FT deg		12-16	MO/DO	M/D	32	BBCC	Ind	
Psychology with Geography	L7FW	3FT deg		12-16	MO/DO	M/D	32	BBCC	Ind	
Psychology with Geology	L7FP	3FT deg	g	12-16	MO/DO	M/D	32	BBCC	Ind	
Psychology with German	L7R2	3FT deg	G g	12-16	MO/DO	M/D	32	BBCC	Ind	4
Psychology with Health Science	L7B9	3FT deg	g	12-16	MO/DO	M/D	32	BBCC	Ind	3
Psychology with Health Studies	L7BX	3FT deg		12-16	MO/DO	M/D	32	BBCC	Ind	
Psychology with Human Biology	L7B1	3FT deg	g	12-16	MO/DO	M/D	32	BBCC	Ind	
Psychology with Japanese	L7T4	3FT deg	L g	12-16	MO/DO	M/D	32	BBCC	Ind	
Psychology with Journalism	L7PP	3FT deg	g	12-16	MO/DO	M/D	32	BBCC	Ind	
Psychology with Language & Stylistics in English	L732	3FT deg	g	12-16	MO/DO	M/D	32	BBCC	Ind	
Psychology with Leisure Studies	L7NR	3FT deg	g	12-16	MO/DO	M/D	32	BBCC	Ind	
Psychology with Management	LN71	3FT deg	g	12-16	MO/DO	M/D	32	BBCC	Ind	
Psychology with Mapping Science	L741	3FT deg	g	12-16	MO/DO	M/D	32	BBCC	Ind	
Psychology with Marketing	L7N5	3FT deg	g	12-16	MO/DO	M/D	32	BBCC	Ind	9
Psychology with Media Practices	L7P4	3FT deg	g	12-16	MO/DO	M/D	32	BBCC	Ind	
Psychology with Media Production	L736	3FT deg	g	12-16	MO/DO	M/D	32	BBCC	Ind	
Psychology with Modern English Studies	L7QH	3FT deg	g	12-16	MO/DO	M/D	32	BBCC	Ind	2
Psychology with Multimedia	L737	3FT deg	g	12-16	MO/DO	M/D	32	BBCC	Ind	
Psychology with Pharmacology	L7B2	3FT deg	g	12-16	MO/DO	M/D	32	BBCC	Ind	
Psychology with Photography	L7WN	3FT deg	g	12-16	MO/DO	M/D	32	BBCC	Ind	
Psychology with Physical Geography	L735	3FT deg	g	12-16	MO/DO	M/D	32	BBCC	Ind	5
Psychology with Plant Biology	L7C2	3FT deg	g	12-16	MO/DO	M/D	32	BBCC	Ind	
Psychology with Politics	L7MC	3FT deg	g	12-16	MO/DO	M/D	32	BBCC	Ind	1
Psychology with Public Policy and Management	L7MD	3FT deg	g	12-16	MO/DO	M/D	32	BBCC	Ind	
Psychology with Publishing	L7P5	3FT deg	g	12-16	MO/DO	M/D	32	BBCC	Ind	
Psychology with Regional Planning and Develop	L7KK	3FT deg	g	12-16	MO/DO	M/D	32	BBCC	Ind	
Psychology with Social Studies	L7LH	3FT deg	g	12-16	MO/DO	M/D	32	BBCC	Ind	2 6/16
Psychology with Spanish	L7R4	3FT deg	Sp g	12-16	MO/DO	M/D	32	BBCC	Ind	2
Psychology with TV Studies	LW75	3FT deg		12-16	MO/DO	M/D	32	BBCC	Ind	
Psychology with Video Production	L7WM	3FT deg	g	12-16	MO/DO	M/D	32	BBCC	Ind	
Public Policy & Mgt & Organisational Behaviour	LM7C	3FT deg	g	12-16	MO/DO	M/D	32	BBCC	Ind	
Public Policy & Mgt with Organisational Behav	M1LT	3FT deg	g	12-16	MO/DO	M/D	32	BBCC	Ind	
Public Policy and Management and Psychology	LMRC	3FT deg	g	12-16	MO/DO	M/D	32	BBCC	Ind	
Regional Planning & Dev & Organisat Behaviour	LK74	3FT deg	g	12-16	MO/DO	M/D	32	BBCC	Ind	
Regional Planning & Dev with Org Behaviour	K4L7	3FT deg	g	12-16	MO/DO	M/D	32	BBCC	Ind	
Regional Planning and Develop with Psychology	K4LR	3FT deg	g	12-16	MO/DO	M/D	32	BBCC	Ind	
Regional Planning and Development and Psychology	LKR4	3FT deg	g	12-16	MO/DO	M/D	32	BBCC	Ind	
Social Studies and Organisational Behaviour	LL73	3FT deg	g	12-16	MO/DO	M/D	32	BBCC	Ind	

Psychology

			98 expected requirements							96 entry stats
TITLE	**CODE**	**COURSE**	**SUBJECTS**	**A/AS**	**ND/C**	**RGNVQ**	**IB**	**SQA(H)**	**SQA**	**RATIO A/AS**
Social Studies and Psychology	LLR3	3FT deg	g	12-16	MO/DO	M/D	32	BBCC	Ind	10
Social Studies with Organisational Behaviour	L3L7	3FT deg	g	12-16	MO/DO	M/D	32	BBCC	Ind	
Social Studies with Psychology	L3LR	3FT deg	g	12-16	MO/DO	M/D	32	BBCC	Ind	3
Sociology and Organisational Behaviour	LLHR	3FT deg		12-16	MO/DO	M/D	32	BBCC	Ind	
Sociology and Psychology	LLH7	3FT deg		12-16	MO/DO	M/D	32	BBCC	Ind	
Sociology with Psychology	L3LT	3FT deg		12-16	MO/DO	M/D	32	BBCC	Ind	
Travel and Tourism and Organisational Behaviour	LP77	3FT deg	g	12-16	MO/DO	M/D	32	BBCC	Ind	
Travel and Tourism with Organisational Behaviour	P7L7	3FT deg	g	12-16	MO/DO	M/D	32	BBCC	Ind	
Women's Studies and Psychology	ML97	3FT deg		12-16	MO/DO	M/D	32	BBCC	Ind	
Women's Studies with Psychology	M9LR	3FT deg		12-16	MO/DO	M/D	32	BBCC	Ind	

Univ of MANCHESTER

TITLE	CODE	COURSE	SUBJECTS	A/AS	ND/C	RGNVQ	IB	SQA(H)	SQA	RATIO A/AS
Psychology	C802	3FT deg	g	ABB	6D	X	32$	ABBBB$	Ind	33	24/30
Psychology	C800	3FT deg	g	ABB	6D	X	32$	ABBBB$	Ind	11	22/30
Psychology (European Programme)	C801	4FT deg	F g	ABB	6D	X	32$	ABBBB$	Ind	8	24/30
Psychology and Neuroscience	BC18	3FT deg	B	BBC	1M+5D$	D^	30$	ABBBC$	Ind	21	20/28
Psychology and Neuroscience with Ind Exp	BC1V	4SW deg	B	BBC	1M+5D$	D^	30$	ABBBB$	Ind	9	24/28

MANCHESTER METROPOLITAN Univ

TITLE	CODE	COURSE	SUBJECTS	A/AS	ND/C	RGNVQ	IB	SQA(H)	SQA	RATIO A/AS
Psychology	L700	3FT deg	* g	CCC	Ind	D$	Ind	BBBC	Ind	14/24
Psychology and Speech Pathology	BL97	4FT deg	* g	BCC	Ind	Ind	Ind	BBBB	Ind	20/22
Psychology/Applied Physics	FL37	3FT deg	M+P g	18	1M+3D$	D$	28$	BBBCC$	Ind	
Psychology/Biology	CL17	3FT deg	* g	18	MO	D$	28	BBCCC	Ind	12/20
Psychology/Business Mathematics	GLC7	3FT deg	M/P/Ec g	18	2M+4D$	D$	29$	BBBBC$	Ind	
Psychology/Chemistry	FL17	3FT deg	C g	18	MO $	D$	28$	BBCCC$	Ind	
Psychology/Computer Technology	GLM7	3FT deg	* g	18	1M+3D	D$	28	BBBCC	Ind	
Psychology/Computing Science	GL57	3FT deg	* g	18	2M+4D	D$	29	BBBBC	Ind	
Psychology/Economics	LL17	3FT deg	* g	CCC	2M+4D	D$	29	BBBBC	Ind	
Psychology/Geography	LL78	3FT deg	* g	CCC	2M+4D	D$	29	BBBBC	Ind	14/18
Psychology/Languages	LT79	3FT deg	* g	CCC	2M+4D	D$	29	BBBBC	Ind	
Psychology/Manufacturing	HL77	3FT deg	* g	18	1M+3D	D$	28	BBBCC	Ind	
Psychology/Physics Studies	LF73	3FT deg	M/P g	18	1M+3D$	D$	28$	BBBCC$	Ind	
Scientific Instrumentation/Psychology	HL67	3FT deg	M/P g	18	1M+3D$	M$	28$	BBBCC$	Ind	
Social Studies of Technology/Psychology	LL37	3FT deg	* g	18	2M+4D	D$	29	BBBBC	Ind	
Speech Pathology and Therapy	B950	3FT deg	* g	CCC	Ind	D	Ind	BBBC	Ind	16/24

MIDDLESEX Univ

TITLE	CODE	COURSE	SUBJECTS	A/AS	ND/C	RGNVQ	IB	SQA(H)	SQA	RATIO A/AS
Cognitive Science	C878▼	3FT deg	* g	14-18	MO	M$ go	28	BCCCC	Ind	
Psychology	C800▼	4SW deg	* g	14-18	MO	M$ go	28	BCCCC	Ind	
Joint Honours Degree *Cognitive Science*	Y400	3FT/4SW deg	* g	12-16	5M	M$ go	28	Ind	Ind	
Joint Honours Degree *Psychology*	Y400	3FT deg	* g	14-18	MO	M$ go	28	BCCCC	Ind	

NAPIER Univ

TITLE	CODE	COURSE	SUBJECTS	A/AS	ND/C	RGNVQ	IB	SQA(H)	SQA	RATIO A/AS
Social Sciences	LL37	3FT/4FT deg	g	CD	Ind	Ind	Ind	BCCC	Ind	10/10

NENE COLLEGE

TITLE	CODE	COURSE	SUBJECTS	A/AS	ND/C	RGNVQ	IB	SQA(H)	SQA	RATIO A/AS
Art and Design with Psychology	W2C8	3FT deg	g	DD	5M	M	24	CCC	Ind	8/20
Behavioural Sciences	CL83	3FT deg	g	14	5M+1D	M	24	CCC	Ind	10/20
Business Administration with Psychology	N1C8	3FT deg	g	10	M+1D	M	24	BCC	Ind	6/14
Drama with Psychology	W4C8	3FT deg	g	10	5M+1D	M	24	CCC	Ind	6/16
Education with Psychology	X9C8	3FT deg	g	DD	5M	M	24	CCC	Ind	8/14
English with Psychology	Q3C8▼	3FT deg	g	CC	4M+1D	M	24	CCC	Ind	8/22
French with Psychology	R1C8	3FT deg	F g	DD	5M	Ind	24	CCC	Ind	

TITLE	CODE	COURSE	SUBJECTS	A/AS	NO/C	AGNVQ	IB	SQA(H)	SQA	RATIO A/AS
course details			*98 expected requirements*							*96 entry stats*
History with Psychology	V1C8 ▼	3FT deg	g	CD	5M	M	24	CCC	Ind	
Human Biological Studies with Psychology	B1C8 ▼	3FT deg	S g	DE	5M	M	24	CCC	Ind	4/12
Industry and Enterprise with Psychology	H1C8	3FT deg	g	EE	3M	P	24	CCC	Ind	
Law with Psychology	M3C8	3FT deg	g	10	3M+2D	M	24	CCC	Ind	7/12
Management Science with Psychology	G4C8	3FT deg	g	DD	5M	M	24	CCC	Ind	
Mathematics with Psychology	G1C8	3FT deg	M	DD	Ind	Ind	24	CCC	Ind	
Psychology	C800	3FT deg	g	14	5M+D	M	24	CCC	Ind	10/20
Psychology with Art and Design	C8W2	3FT deg	g	CC	5M+1D	M	24	CCC	Ind	
Psychology with Business Administration	C8N1	3FT deg	g	CC	5M+1D	M	24	CCC	Ind	
Psychology with Drama	C8W4	3FT deg	g	CC	5M+1D	M	24	CCC	Ind	
Psychology with Education	C8X9	3FT deg	g	CC	5M+1D	M	24	CCC	Ind	12/18
Psychology with English	C8Q3 ▼	3FT deg	g	CC	5M+1D	M	24	CCC	Ind	6/20
Psychology with History	C8V1 ▼	3FT deg	g	CC	5M+1D	M	24	CCC	Ind	
Psychology with Human Biological Studies	C8B1 ▼	3FT deg	g	CC	5M+1D	M	24	CCC	Ind	12/16
Psychology with Law	C8M3	3FT deg	g	CC	5M+1D	M	24	CCC	Ind	12/22
Psychology with Management Science	C8G4	3FT deg	g	CC	5M+1D	M	24	CCC	Ind	
Psychology with Mathematics	C8G1	3FT deg	M	CC	5M+1D	M	24	CCC	Ind	
Psychology with Media and Popular Culture	C8P4 ▼	3FT deg	g	CC	5M+1D	M	24	CCC	Ind	10/16
Psychology with Personal & Organisational Devel	C8N6 ▼	3FT deg	g	CC	5M+D	M	24	CCC	Ind	
Psychology with Philosophy	C8V7 ▼	3FT deg	g	CC	5M+1D	M	24	CCC	Ind	
Psychology with Sociology	C8L3 ▼	3FT deg	g	CC	5M+1D	M	24	CCC	Ind	10/18
Psychology with Sport Studies	C8N7 ▼	3FT deg	g	CC	5M+1D	M	24	CCC	Ind	
Sociology with Psychology	L3C8 ▼	3FT deg	g	10	5M	M	24	CCC	Ind	6/14
Sport Studies with Psychology	N7C8 ▼	3FT deg	Ss/Pe g	12	M+2D	M	24	BBB	Ind	

Univ of NEWCASTLE

TITLE	CODE	COURSE	SUBJECTS	A/AS	NO/C	AGNVQ	IB	SQA(H)	SQA	RATIO A/AS
Computing Science and Psychology	CG85	3FT deg	M	24	Ind	Ind	30$	AAABB	Ind	
Mathematics and Psychology	CG81	3FT deg	M	24	Ind	Ind	30$	AAABB	Ind	5 20/26
Psychology	C800	3FT deg	* g	BBB	DO		32	AAABB	Ind	13 24/28
Psychology	C802	3FT deg	* g	BBB	DO		32	AAABB	Ind	1 22/28
Psychology and Statistics	CG84	3FT deg	M	24	Ind	Ind	30$	AAABB	Ind	
Combined Studies (BA) *Psychology*	Y400	3FT deg	*	ABC-BBB	5D	Ind	35$	AAAB	Ind	
Combined Studies (BSc) *Psychology*	Y100	3FT deg	2S	22	4M+1D	Ind	30$	AABBB	Ind	

NEWMAN COLLEGE OF HIGHER EDUCATION

TITLE	CODE	COURSE	SUBJECTS	A/AS	NO/C	AGNVQ	IB	SQA(H)	SQA	RATIO A/AS
Biological Science and Social & Applied Psychol.	CL17	3FT deg	*	CC	3M	M*	Dip	CCC	Ind	
Expressive English & Social & Applied Psychology	LW74	3FT deg	*	CC	3M	M*	Dip	CCC	Ind	
Geography and Social and Applied Psychology	LF78	3FT deg	*	CC	3M	M*	Dip	CCC	Ind	
PE & Sports Stds & Social & Applied Psychology	LX79	3FT deg	*	CC	3M	M*	Dip	CCC	Ind	

Univ of Wales COLLEGE, NEWPORT

TITLE	CODE	COURSE	SUBJECTS	A/AS	NO/C	AGNVQ	IB	SQA(H)	SQA	RATIO A/AS
Social Welfare and Human Behaviour	LL47	3FT deg		8	M	M				

NORTH EAST WALES INST of HE

TITLE	CODE	COURSE	SUBJECTS	A/AS	NO/C	AGNVQ	IB	SQA(H)	SQA	RATIO A/AS
English with Psychology	Q3C8	3FT deg		6-12	4M	M$	Ind	BBB	N$	
English/Psychology	QC38	3FT deg		4-12	3M	M$	Ind	BBB	N$	
History with Psychology	V1C8	3FT deg		6-12	4M	M$	Ind	BBB	N$	
History/Psychology	VC18	3FT deg		6-12	4M	M$	Ind	BBB	N$	
Media Studies/Psychology	PC48	3FT deg		6-12	4M	M$	Ind	BBB	N$	

Psychology 63

			98 expected requirements							96 entry stats

course details · **98 expected requirements** · *96 entry stats*

TITLE	CODE	COURSE	SUBJECTS	A/AS	ND/C	AGNVQ	IB	SQA(H)	SQA	RATIO A/AS
Univ of NORTH LONDON										
Business and Applied Psychology	NL17	3FT deg	* g	CC	MO+4D	D	Ind	CCCCC	Ind	
Psychology (Applied)	L710	3FT deg	*	CC	MO	M	$	CCCCC	Ind	11 8/16
Psychology (Applied) and Education Studies	LX79	3FT deg	* g	CC	Ind	Ind	Ind	Ind	Ind	
Psychology (Applied) and Human Resource Studies	LN71	3FT deg	* g	CC	Ind	Ind	Ind	Ind	Ind	
Psychology (Applied) and Philosophy	LV77	3FT deg	* g	CC	Ind	Ind	Ind	Ind	Ind	
Psychology (Applied) and Women's Studies	LM79	3FT deg	* g	CC	Ind	Ind	Ind	Ind	Ind	
Combined Honours *Psychology*	Y100	3FT/4SW/4EXT deg	* g	12	4M $	M* go	$	Ind	Ind	
Combined Honours *Psychology (Applied)*	Y301	3FT deg	*	CC	MO	M	$	CCCCC	Ind	
Univ of NORTHUMBRIA										
Computing with Cognitive Psychology	G5C8	4SW deg	* g	14	5M	M gi	24	BBBC	Ind	
Psychology	C800	3FT deg	g	CCC	1M+4D	M^	26	BBBCC	Ind	8 16/24
Psychology with Computing	C8G5	3FT deg	g	CCC	1M+4D	M^	26	BBBCC	Ind	
Combined Honours *Psychology*	Y400▼	3FT deg	g	12-20	MO+3D	DG	26	BBCCC	Ind	
NORWICH: City COLL										
Human Life Sciences and Psychology	CL97	3FT/4FT deg	2S	10	5M	P$ go	Ind	Ind	Ind	
Human Life Sciences with Psychology	C9L7	3FT/4FT deg	2S	10	5M	P$ go	Ind	Ind	Ind	
Psychology with English	L7Q3	3FT deg	* g	12		X	Ind	Ind	Ind	
Psychology with History	L7V1	3FT deg	* g	12		X	Ind	Ind	Ind	
Psychology with Human Life Sciences	L7C9	3FT deg	S	12	5M	P	Ind	Ind	Ind	
Psychology with Sociology	L7L3	3FT deg	* g	12	5M	P	Ind	Ind	Ind	
Combined Arts *Psychology*	Y300	3FT deg	* g	12	Ind		Ind	Ind	Ind	
Combined Science *Neuropsychology*	Y100	3FT/4FT deg	2S	10	5M		Ind	Ind	Ind	
Univ of NOTTINGHAM										
Artificial Intelligence and Psychology	C878	3FT deg	M+P/B/C g	BBC	Ind		Ind	Ind	Ind	11 26/28
Behavioural Science	CCH8	3FT deg	B+M/C/P g	BBB	Ind	Ind	Ind	Ind	Ind	12 26/30
Computer Sci, Artificial Intelligence & Psych	CG85	3FT deg	M	BBB-BBC	Ind		Ind	Ind	Ind	10 22/30
Psychology	C802	3FT deg	* g	ABC	Ind		33	Ind	Ind	40 22/30
Psychology	C800	3FT deg	M/P/B g	ABB	Ind		Ind	Ind	Ind	31 24/30
Psychology and Philosophy	CV87	3FT deg	* g	BBB	Ind		33	Ind	Ind	99
Psychology and Sociology	CL83	3FT deg	* g	BBB	Ind	Ind	32	Ind	Ind	30 6/28
NOTTINGHAM TRENT Univ										
Environment and Psychology	CF89	3FT deg	* g	12	Ind	Ind	Ind	Ind	Ind	10/16
Industrial Management and Psychology	CN86	3FT deg	* g	12	Ind	Ind	Ind	Ind	Ind	10/14
Mathematics & Statistics and Psychology	CG81	3FT deg	M/Ps	12	Ind	M go	Ind	Ind	Ind	
Psychology	C000	3FT deg	* g	18-20	Ind	Ind	Ind	BBBC	Ind	27 20/28
Humanities *Psychology and Sociology*	Y301	3FT/4SW deg								
OXFORD Univ										
Experimental Psychology	C830	3FT deg	*	AAB	DO		36	AAAAA	Ind	4 26/30
Physiology with Psychology	B1C8	3FT deg	*	AAB	DO		36	AAAAA	Ind	2 28/30
Psychology with Philosophy	C8V7	3FT deg	*	AAB	DO		36	AAAAA	Ind	5 28/30
Psychology, Philosophy and Physiology *Psychology*	Y620	3FT deg	*	AAB	DO		36	AAAAA	Ind	

TITLE	CODE	COURSE	SUBJECTS	A/AS	NQ/C	AGNVQ	IB	SQA(H)	SQA	RATIO	A/AS
OXFORD BROOKES Univ											
Environmental Chemistry/Anthropology	LF71	3FT deg									
Psychology/Accounting and Finance	CN84	3FT deg	* g	BCC-BBC	Ind	M^/D*3	Ind	Ind	Ind		
Psychology/Anthropology	CL86	3FT deg	* g	BCC-BBC	Ind	M*^	Ind	Ind	Ind	45	
Psychology/Biological Chemistry	CC78	3FT deg									
Psychology/Biology	CC18	3FT deg	S g	DD-BBC	Ind	MS/M*^	Ind	Ind	Ind	14	16/18
Psychology/Business Administration & Management	CN81	3FT deg	* g	BBC-BBC	Ind	M^/MB4	Ind	Ind	Ind	79	
Psychology/Cartography	CF88	3FT deg	* g	DDD-BBC	Ind	M*^	Ind	Ind	Ind		
Psychology/Cell Biology	CCC8	3FT deg									
Psychology/Combined Studies	CY84	3FT deg		X		X	X	X			
Psychology/Computer Systems	CG86	3FT deg	* g	CDD-BBC	Ind	M*^	Ind	Ind	Ind		
Psychology/Computing	CG85	3FT deg	* g	CDD-BBC	Ind	M*^	Ind	Ind	Ind	16	
Psychology/Computing Mathematics	CG89	3FT deg	* g	CD-BBC	Ind	M*^	Ind	Ind	Ind	3	
Psychology/Ecology	CC89	3FT deg	* g	CD-BBC	Ind	MS/M*^	Ind	Ind	Ind		
Psychology/Economics	CL81	3FT deg	* g	CCD-BBC	Ind	M^/M*3	Ind	Ind	Ind	6	
Psychology/Educational Studies	CX89	3FT deg	* g	CC-BBC	Ind	M^/M*3	Ind	Ind	Ind	31	
Psychology/Electronics	CH86	3FT deg	S/M g	CC-BBC	Ind	MS/M*^	Ind	Ind	Ind		
Psychology/English Studies	CQ83	3FT deg	* g	AB-BCC	Ind	M*^	Ind	Ind	Ind	28	
Psychology/Environmental Chemistry	FC18	3FT deg									
Psychology/Environmental Policy	CK83	3FT deg									
Psychology/Environmental Sciences	CF8X	3FT deg	S g	CD-BBC	Ind	M^/DS	Ind	Ind	Ind	4	
Psychology/Exercise and Health	CB86	3FT deg	S g	DD-BBC	Ind	MS/M*^	Ind	Ind	Ind		
Psychology/Fine Art	CW81	3FT deg	A+Pf g	BC-BBC	Ind	MA^	Ind	Ind	Ind	13	
Psychology/Food Science and Nutrition	CD84	3FT deg	S g	DD-BBC	Ind	MS/M*^	Ind	Ind	Ind		
Psychology/French Language and Contemp Studies	CR8C	4SW deg	F g	CDD-BBC	Ind	M*_	Ind	Ind	Ind	11	
Psychology/French Language and Literature	CR81	4SW deg	F g	CDD-BBC	Ind	M*_	Ind	Ind	Ind	11	
Psychology/Geography	CL88	3FT deg	* g	CCD-BBC	Ind	M*^	Ind	Ind	Ind		
Psychology/Geology	CF86	3FT deg	S/M g	DD-BBC	Ind	PS/M*^	Ind	Ind	Ind		
Psychology/Geotechnics	CH82	3FT deg	S/M/Ds/Es g	DD-BBC	Ind	MS/M*^	Ind	Ind	Ind		
Psychology/German Language and Contemp Stud	CR8F	4SW deg	G g	DDD-BBC	Ind	M*_	Ind	Ind	Ind		
Psychology/German Language and Literature	CR82	4SW deg	G g	DDD-BBC	Ind	M*_	Ind	Ind	Ind		
Psychology/German Studies	CR8G	4SW deg		DDD-BBC	Ind	M*_	Ind	Ind	Ind		
Psychology/Health Care (Post Exp)	BC78	3FT deg		X		X	X	X			
Psychology/History	CV81	3FT deg	* g	CCD-BBC	Ind	M*^	Ind	Ind	Ind		
Psychology/History of Art	CV84	3FT deg	* g	BCC-BBC	Ind	M*^	Ind	Ind	Ind	6	
Psychology/Hospitality Management Studies	CN87	3FT deg	* g	DDD-BBC	Ind	M^/M*3	Ind	Ind	Ind	12	
Psychology/Human Biology	BC18	3FT deg									
Psychology/Information Systems	CG8M	3FT deg		CD-BBC	Ind	M*^	Ind	Ind	Ind		
Psychology/Intelligent Systems	CG88	3FT deg	* g	CD-BBC	Ind	M*^	Ind	Ind	Ind		
Psychology/Law	CM83	3FT deg	* g	BBB-BBC	Ind	M^/D*3	Ind	Ind	Ind	37	
Psychology/Leisure Planning and Management	CK8H	3FT deg									
Psychology/Marketing Management	CN8N	3FT deg	* g	BCC-BBC	Ind	M^/D*3	Ind	Ind	Ind	74	
Psychology/Mathematics	CG81	3FT deg	M g	DD-BBC	Ind	M*^	Ind	Ind	Ind	4	14/20
Psychology/Music	CW83	3FT deg	Mu g	DD-BBC	Ind	M*^	Ind	Ind	Ind	6	14/16
Psychology/Palliative Care (Post Exp)	BCR8	3FT deg		X		X	X	X			
Psychology/Physical Geography	CF8V	3FT deg									
Psychology/Planning Studies	CK84	3FT deg	* g	DD-BBC	Ind	M*^	Ind	Ind	Ind		
Psychology/Politics	CM81	3FT deg	* g	AB-CCC	Ind	M*^	Ind	Ind	Ind	26	
Publishing/Psychology	CP85	3FT deg	* g	CCD-BBC	Ind	M^/M$3	Ind	Ind	Ind	12	
Rehabilitation/Psychology (Post Exp)	BCT8	3FT deg		X		X	X	X			
Sociology/Psychology	CL83	3FT deg	* g	BCC-BBC	Ind	M*^	Ind	Ind	Ind	28	
Software Engineering/Psychology	CG87	3FT deg	* g	CC-BC	Ind	M*^	Ind	Ind	Ind		

			98 expected requirements							96 entry stats

TITLE	CODE	COURSE	SUBJECTS	A/AS	NO/C	RGNVQ	IB	SQA(H)	SQA	RATIO A/AS
Statistics/Psychology	CG84	3FT deg	* g	DD-BBC	Ind	M*^	Ind	Ind	Ind	14
Telecommunications/Psychology	CH8P	3FT deg								
Tourism/Psychology	CP87	3FT deg	* g	CCD-BBC	Ind	M^/M*3	Ind	Ind	Ind	
Transport Planning/Psychology	CN89	3FT deg	* g	BBC-DDD	Ind	M*^	Ind	Ind	Ind	
Water Resources/Psychology	CH8F	3FT deg								

Univ of PAISLEY

TITLE	CODE	COURSE	SUBJECTS	A/AS	NO/C	RGNVQ	IB	SQA(H)	SQA	RATIO A/AS
Psychology and Biology	CC81	3FT/4FT deg	* g	CC	Ind	Ind	Ind	BCCC$	Ind	
Psychology and Chemistry	CF81	3FT/4FT deg	* g	CC	Ind	Ind	Ind	BCCC$	Ind	

Univ of PLYMOUTH

TITLE	CODE	COURSE	SUBJECTS	A/AS	NO/C	RGNVQ	IB	SQA(H)	SQA	RATIO A/AS
Applied Economics with Psychology	L1C8	3FT deg	* g	BBC	MO	M$^	Ind	Ind	Ind	
Business Economics with Psychology	L1CV	3FT deg	* g	BBC	MO	M$^	Ind	Ind	Ind	
European Economics with Psychology	L1CW	3FT deg	* g	BBC	MO	M$^	Ind	Ind	Ind	
Human Biology with Psychology	C9C8	3FT/4SW deg	B g	14-18	4M $	Ind	Ind	BBBB	Ind	9 16/16
Law with Psychology	M3C8	3FT deg	Ap g	BCC-BBC	DO	D12^	Ind	BBBB$	Ind	31
Modern Languages with Psychology	T9C8	3FT/4SW deg	L g	C	Ind	Ind	Ind	Ind	Ind	
Political Economy with Psychology	LC1V	3FT deg	Ap g	BBC	MO $	M$^	Ind	Ind	Ind	
Politics with Psychology	M1C8	3FT deg	* g	BCC	MO+3D	D12^	Ind	BBBC$	Ind	7
Psychology	C800	3FT/4SW deg	Ap g	BBC	MO+3D	Ind	Ind	BBBC$	Ind	5 14/24
Psychology with Applied Economics	C8L1	3FT/4SW deg	Ap g	BBC	MO+3D	M12^	Ind	BBBC$	Ind	8
Psychology with Computing	C8G5	3FT/4SW deg	Ap g	BBC	MO+3D	M12^	Ind	BBBC$	Ind	
Psychology with Criminal Justice	C8MH	3FT/4SW deg	Ap g	BBB	4D	M12^	Ind	BBBC$	Ind	25 12/20
Psychology with French	C8R1	3FT/4SW deg	E g	BBC	MO+3D	M12^	Ind	BBBC$	Ind	
Psychology with German	C8R2	3FT/4SW deg	G g	BBC	MO+3D	M12^	Ind	BBBC$	Ind	
Psychology with Human Biology	C8C9	3FT/4SW deg	B g	BBC	MO+3D	M12^	Ind	BBBC$	Ind	7 16/26
Psychology with Italian	C8R3	3FT/4SW deg	Ap g	BBC	MO+3D	M12^	Ind	BBBC$	Ind	
Psychology with Languages	C8T9	3FT/4SW deg	L g	BBC	MO+3D	M12^	Ind	BBBC$	Ind	6 18/20
Psychology with Law	C8M3	3FT/4SW deg	Ap g	BBC	MO+3D	M12^	Ind	BBBC$	Ind	7 20/26
Psychology with Politics	C8M1	3FT/4SW deg	Ap g	BBC	MO+3D	M12^	Ind	BBBC$	Ind	4
Psychology with Resources, Manuf and the Environ	C8F9	3FT/4SW deg	Ap g	BBC	MO+3D	M12^	Ind	BBBC$	Ind	
Psychology with Social Policy	C8L4	3FT/4SW deg	Ap g	BBC	MO 3D	M12^	Ind	BBBC$	Ind	11
Psychology with Sociology	C8L3	3FT/4SW deg	Ap g	BBC	MO+3D	M12^	Ind	BBBC$	Ind	9 16/26
Psychology with Spanish	C8R4	3FT/4SW deg	Sp g	BBC	MO+3D	M12^	Ind	BBBC$	Ind	
Psychology with Statistics	C8G4	3FT/4SW deg	Ap g	BCC	MO+3D	M12^	Ind	BBBC$	Ind	6
Social Policy with Psychology	L4C8	3FT deg	* g	BCC	2M+3D	D12^	Ind	BBBC$	Ind	8
Sociology with Psychology	L3C8	3FT deg	* g	BCC	2M+3D	D12^	Ind	BBBC$	Ind	10 16/18
Statistics(App) with Psychology	G4C8	3FT deg	M/St g	10	MO $	M$	Ind	BBCC	Ind	6

Univ of PORTSMOUTH

TITLE	CODE	COURSE	SUBJECTS	A/AS	NO/C	RGNVQ	IB	SQA(H)	SQA	RATIO A/AS
Psychology	C800	3FT deg	S g	20	Ind	D$6/^ go	30$	Ind	Ind	5 12/22

QUEEN MARGARET COLL

TITLE	CODE	COURSE	SUBJECTS	A/AS	NO/C	RGNVQ	IB	SQA(H)	SQA	RATIO A/AS
Combined Studies Psychology	Y600	3FT/4FT deg	*	BC	M+D	M/D$^ go	Ind	BBBC	Ind	

QUEEN'S Univ Belfast

TITLE	CODE	COURSE	SUBJECTS	A/AS	NO/C	RGNVQ	IB	SQA(H)	SQA	RATIO A/AS
Psychology (not minor)	C800	3FT deg	* g	BCC	3M+4D	D*6/^ go	29$	ABBB	Ind	10 20/28
Psychology/Byzantine Studies	CQ88	3FT/4FT deg	* g	BCC	3M+4D	D*6/^ go	29$	ABBB	Ind	
Psychology/Economic & Social History	CV83	3FT deg	* g	BCC	3M+4D	D*6/^ go	29$	ABBB	Ind	
Psychology/English	CQ83	3FT deg	E g	BCC	X	D*^ go	29$	ABBB	X	8 20/28
Psychology/Greek	CQ87	3FT/4FT deg	* g	BCC	3M+4D	D*6/^ go	29$	ABBB	Ind	
Psychology/History & Philosophy of Science	CV85	3FT deg	* g	BCC	3M+4D	D*6/^ go	29$	ABBB	Ind	8
Psychology/Latin	CQ86	3FT/4FT deg	* g	BCC	3M+4D	D*6/^ go	29$	ABBB	Ind	
Psychology/Music	CW83	3FT deg	* g	BCC	3M+4D	D*6/^ go	29$	ABBB	Ind	

TITLE	CODE	COURSE	SUBJECTS	A/AS	NO/C	RGNVQ	IB	SQA(H)	SQA	RATIO A/AS
course details			**98 expected requirements**							**96 entry stats**
Psychology/Philosophy	CV87	3FT deg	* g	BCC	3M+4D	D*6/^ go	29$	ABBB	Ind	18
Psychology/Politics	CM8C	3FT deg	* g	BCC	3M+4D	D*6/^ go	29$	ABBB	Ind	
Scholastic Philosophy/Psychology	CV8R	3FT deg	* g	BCC	3M+4D	D*6/^ go	29$	ABBB	Ind	23
Social Anthropology/Psychology	CL86	3FT deg	* g	BCC	3M+4D	D*6/^ go	29$	ABBB	Ind	12 20/26
Social Policy/Psychology	CL84	3FT deg	* g	BCC	3M+4D	D*6/^ go	29$	ABBB	Ind	
Sociology/Psychology	CL83	3FT deg	* g	BCC	3M+4D	D*6/^ go	29$	ABBB	Ind	23 20/26

Univ of READING

TITLE	CODE	COURSE	SUBJECTS	A/AS	NO/C	RGNVQ	IB	SQA(H)	SQA	RATIO A/AS
Art and Psychology	CW81	4FT deg	* g	BCC	Ind	DA^ go	30	BBBB	Ind	18 18/26
Art and Psychology	EC18	4FT deg	* g	BCC	Ind	DA^ go	30	BBBB	Ind	
Intelligent Systems	GC88	3FT deg	B/C/M/P g	20	3M+2D$	D$^ go	30$	BBBB$	Ind	23
Mathematics and Psychology	GC18	3FT deg	M	BCC	3M+2D$	D$^	30$	BBBB$	Ind	10 24/24
Psychology	C802	3FT deg	* g	BCC	Ind	D*6/^ go	30	BBBB	Ind	13 20/26
Psychology (BSc)	C800	3FT deg	S g	BCC	3M+2D	DS^ go	30	BBBB$	Ind	20 18/24
Psychology and Linguistics	CQ81	3FT deg	* g	BCC	Ind	D*6/^ go	30	BBBB	Ind	11
Psychology and Philosophy	CV87	3FT deg	* g	BCC	Ind	D*^ go	30	BBBB	Ind	11 20/28
Psychology and Physiology	CB81	3FT deg	C g	BCC	3M+2D$	DS^ go	30$	BBBB$	Ind	22
Psychology and Sociology	CL83	3FT deg	* g	BCC	Ind	D$^ go	30	BBBB	Ind	22 20/28
Psychology and Statistics	CG84	3FT deg	* g	BCC	3M+2D	D$^ go	30	BBBB$	Ind	3 18/22
Psychology and Zoology	CC38	3FT deg	B/C/M g	BCC	3M+2D$	DS^ go	30$	BBBB$	Ind	8 17/28

Univ College of RIPON & YORK ST JOHN

TITLE	CODE	COURSE	SUBJECTS	A/AS	NO/C	RGNVQ	IB	SQA(H)	SQA	RATIO A/AS
Applied Social Sciences/Psychology	L3L7	3FT deg	g	CC	M	M*	27	BBBC		
Language Studies (English)/Psychology	Q1L7	3FT deg	g	16	M	M*^	30	BBBB		
Physical Education/Psychology	B6L7	3FT deg	g	BB-CCC	MO+3D	D$6/^	30	ABBB		
Psychology/Applied Social Sciences	L7L3	3FT deg	g	16	M	M	30	BBBB		
Psychology/Language Studies (English)	L7Q1	3FT deg	g	16	M	M	30	BBBB		
Psychology/Physical Education	L7B6	3FT deg	g	16	M	M	30	BBBB		
Psychology/Theology	L7V8	3FT deg	g	16	M	M	30	BBBB		
Psychology/Women's Studies	L7M9	3FT deg	g	16	M	M	30	BBBB		
Theology/Psychology	V8L7	3FT deg	g	12	M	M*	27	BBBC		

ROEHAMPTON INST

TITLE	CODE	COURSE	SUBJECTS	A/AS	NO/C	RGNVQ	IB	SQA(H)	SQA	RATIO A/AS
Psychology	L700▼	3FT deg	g	CC	3D	M$ go	30	BBC	Ind	
Psychology & Counselling	L745▼	3FT deg	g	CC	3D	M$ go	30	BBC	Ind	16 10/24
Psychology and Applied Consumer Studies	LN79▼	3FT deg	g	CC	3D	M$ go	30	BBC	N$	
Psychology and Art for Community	WL17▼	3FT deg	g	CC	3D	M$ go	30	BBC	Ind	6
Psychology and Biology	CL17▼	3FT deg	B g	CC	3D $	M$ go	30	BBC	N$	10
Psychology and Business Computing	GL77▼	3FT deg	g	CC	3D	M^ go	30	BBC	N$	
Psychology and Business Studies	NL17▼	3FT deg	g	CC	3D	M$ go	30	BBC	N$	14
Psychology and Dance Studies	WL47▼	3FT deg	g	CC	3D	M$^ go	30	BBC	Ind	9
Psychology and Drama & Theatre Studies	WLL7▼	3FT deg	T/E g	16	3D	MS^ go	30	BBC	Ind	7
Psychology and Education	XL97▼	3FT deg	g	CC	3D	M$ go	30	BBC	Ind	16
Psychology and English Language & Linguistics	QLH7▼	3FT deg	E/L g	CC	3D $	M$^ go	30	BBC	Ind	5
Psychology and English Literature	QL37▼	3FT deg	E g	CC	3D $	M^ go	30	BBC	Ind	6 16/20
Psychology and Environmental Studies	FL97▼	3FT deg	B/Gy g	CC	3D $	M$ go	30	BBC	Ind	11
Psychology and Film & Television Studies	LP74▼	3FT deg	g	16	3D	M$^ go	30	BBC	N$	35
Psychology and French	LR71▼	4FT deg	E g	CC	3D $	M^ go	30	BBC	Ind	21
Psychology and Geography	LL87▼	3FT deg	Gy g	CC	3D $	M$ go	30	BBC	Ind	
Psychology and Health Studies	BL97▼	3FT deg	B g	CC	3D $	M$ go	30	BBC	N$	3
Psychology and History	VL17▼	3FT deg	H g	CC	3D $	M^ go	30	BBC	Ind	
Psychology and Human & Social Biology	LC7C▼	3FT deg	B g	CC	3D	M$ go	30	BBC	Ind	3
Psychology and Music	WL37▼	3FT deg	Mu g	CC	3D $	M^ go	30	BBC	Ind	10
Psychology and Natural Resource Studies	DL27▼	3FT deg	g	CC	3D	M$ go	30	BBC	N$	

Psychology 63

TITLE	CODE	COURSE	SUBJECTS	A/AS	NQ/C	RGNVQ	IB	SQA(H)	SQA	RATIO A/AS
Social Policy & Administration and Psychology	LL74▼	3FT deg	g	CC	3D	M$ go	30	BBC	Ind	16
Sociology and Psychology	LL73▼	3FT deg	g	CC	3D	M$ go	30	BBC	Ind	9 10/24
Spanish and Psychology	LR74▼	4FT deg	Sp g	CC	3D	M$ go	30	BBC	N$	
Sport Studies and Psychology	LB76▼	3FT deg	S g	CC	3D	MS go	30	BBC	Ind	
Theology & Religious Studies and Psychology	LV78▼	3FT deg	g	CC	3D $	M$ go	30	BBC	Ind	4
Women's Studies and Psychology	LM79▼	3FT deg	g	CC	3D	M$ go	30	BBC	Ind	4
ROYAL HOLLOWAY, Univ of London										
Biochemistry with Psychology	C7C8	3FT deg	C+B/M/P g	BCC	3M+2D	DS^	28$	BBBCC$		
Cognitive Science	CG85	3FT deg	M	BBC	Ind	D^	30$	Ind		
Mathematics and Psychology	GC18	3FT deg	M	BBC	Ind	D^	Ind	Ind		8
Music and Psychology	WC38	3FT deg	Mu g	BBC-BBB	Ind		Ind	Ind		
Psychology	C800	3FT deg	g	BBB	5M		32	BBBBB$		7 18/28
Foundation Programme Psychology	Y408	4FT deg								
Univ of SHEFFIELD										
Cognitive Science	C878	3FT deg	g	BBB	3M+3D	D6/^	32$	ABBB	Ind	6 22/30
Philosophy and Psychology	CV87	3FT deg	* g	AAB	1M+5D	D^	35	AAAA	Ind	48
Psychology	C802	3FT deg	* g	ABB	2M+4D	D^	33	AAAB	Ind	12 26/30
Psychology	C800	3FT deg	2S g	ABB	2M+4D	D6/^	33$	AAAB$	Ind	18 26/30
Psychology and Sociology	CL83	3FT deg	* g	AAB	1M+5D	D^	35	AAAA	Ind	33
SHEFFIELD HALLAM Univ										
Psychology	L700	3FT deg	*	BCC	5D	DG	Ind	Ind	Ind	
Combined Studies Psychology	Y400	3FT deg	*	18	2M	M	Ind	Ind	Ind	
Univ College of St MARTIN, LANCASTER AND CUMBRIA										
Psychology	L700▼	3FT deg	*	BC		M^	28$	BBBB$		
Univ of SOUTHAMPTON										
Physiology with Psychology	B1C8	3FT deg	C+B/P/M/Gy g	BCC	$	M^	$	Ind	Ind	6
Psychology	C800	3FT deg	* g	22-24	Ind	D$^ go	32	AABBB	Ind	
Psychology with Physiology	C8B1	3FT deg	B g	22	Ind	D$^ go	30$	ABBBB$	Ind	29
SOUTHAMPTON INST										
Psychology	C800	3FT deg	*	16	MO	M$	Dip	BBBB	N	
SOUTH BANK Univ										
Psychology	C800	3FT deg	S g	BCC	MO	M go	Ind	Ind	Ind	
Psychology and Business Information Technology	CG87	3FT deg	S g	14-18	2M+4D	M go	Ind	Ind	Ind	
Psychology and Computing	CG85	3FT deg	S+M g	14-18	4M+2D	M go	Ind	Ind	Ind	
Psychology and Economics	CL81	3FT deg	Bu/Ec+S g	14-18	4M+2D	M go	Ind	Ind	Ind	
Psychology and English Studies	CQ83	3FT deg	E+S g	14-18	X	M^ go	Ind	Ind	Ind	
Psychology and European Studies	CT82	3FT deg	S g	14-18	2M+4D	M go	Ind	Ind	Ind	
Psychology and Food Policy	CD84	3FT deg	S g	14-18	2M+4D	M go	Ind	Ind	Ind	
Psychology and French	CR81	3FT deg	F+S g	14-18	2M+4D	M go	Ind	Ind	Ind	
Psychology and Health Studies	CL84	3FT deg	S g	14-18	2M+4D	M go	Ind	Ind	Ind	
Psychology and History	CV81	3FT deg	S+H g	14-18	2M+4D	M^ go	Ind	Ind	Ind	
Psychology and Housing	CK8K	3FT deg	S g	14-18	2M+4D	M go	Ind	Ind	Ind	
Psychology and Human Biology	BC18	3FT deg	S g	14-18	2M+4D	M go	Ind	Ind	Ind	
Psychology and Human Resource Management	CN86	3FT deg	S g	14-18	2M+4D	M go	Ind	Ind	Ind	
Psychology and Law	CM83	3FT deg	S g	14-18	2M+4D	M go	Ind	Ind	Ind	
Psychology and Management	CN81	3FT deg	S g	14-18	2M+4D	M go	Ind	Ind	Ind	
Psychology and Marketing	CN85	3FT deg	S g	14-18	2M+4D	M go	Ind	Ind	Ind	

			98 expected requirements							96 entry stats	
TITLE	CODE	COURSE	SUBJECTS	A/AS	NO/C	AGNVQ	IB	SQA(H)	SQA	RATIO	A/AS
Psychology and Media Studies	CP84	3FT deg	E+S g	14-18	2M+4D	M go	Ind	Ind	Ind		
Psychology and Nutrition	BC48	3FT deg	S g	14-18	4M+2D	M go	Ind	Ind	Ind		
Psychology and Product Design	CH87	3FT deg	Ad+S g	14-18	4M+2D	M go	Ind	Ind	Ind		
Social Policy and Psychology	CL8K	3FT deg	S g	14-18	4M+2D	M go	Ind	Ind	Ind		
Sociology and Psychology	CL83	3FT deg	S g	14-18	4M+2D	M go	Ind	Ind	Ind		
Spanish - ab initio and Psychology	CR84	3FT deg	S g	14-18	2M+4D	M go	Ind	Ind	Ind		
Sports Science and Psychology	BC68	3FT deg	S g	14-18	2M+4D	M go	Ind	Ind	Ind		
Tourism and Psychology	CP87	3FT deg	S g	14-18	2M+4D	M go	Ind	Ind	Ind		
Urban Studies and Psychology	KC48	3FT deg	S g	14-18	2M+4D	M go	Ind	Ind	Ind		
World Theatre and Psychology	CW84	3FT deg	S g	14-18	2M+4D	M go	Ind	Ind	Ind		

Univ of ST ANDREWS

TITLE	CODE	COURSE	SUBJECTS	A/AS	NO/C	AGNVQ	IB	SQA(H)	SQA	RATIO	A/AS
Psychology (Arts)	C802	4FT deg	* g	ABB	X	Ind	32$	ABBB	X	9	22/26
Psychology (Science)	C800	3FT/4FT deg	B/C/Gy/M/P g	ABB	Ind	Ind	32$	ABBB$	Ind	12	
Psychology with French	C8R1	4FT deg	F g	ABB	X	Ind	32$	ABBB$	Ind		
Psychology with French (with Integ Year Abroad)	C8RC	4FT/5FT deg	F g	ABB	X	Ind	32$	ABBB$	Ind		
Psychology-Art History	LV74	4FT deg	* g	ABB	X	Ind	32$	BBBBB	Ind		
Psychology-Economics (Arts)	LL71	4FT deg	* g	ABB	X	Ind	32$	BBBBB	Ind	4	
Psychology-Economics (Science)	CLV1	4FT deg	* g	ABB	X	Ind	32$	BBBBB	Ind		
Psychology-English	LQ73	4FT deg	* g	ABB	X	Ind	32$	BBBBB	Ind	8	
Psychology-French	LR71	4FT deg	F g	ABB	X	Ind	32$	BBBBB$	Ind	4	
Psychology-French with Year Abroad	LR7C	4FT/5FT deg	F g	ABB	X	Ind	32$	BBBBB$	Ind	5	
Psychology-Geography	CL88	4FT deg	* g	ABB	X	Ind	32$	ABBB	Ind		
Psychology-German	LR72	4FT deg	* g	ABB	X	Ind	32$	ABBB	Ind		
Psychology-German with Year Abroad	LR7F	4FT/5FT deg	* g	ABB	X	Ind	32$	ABBB	Ind	7	
Psychology-International Relations	LM71	4FT deg	* g	AAB	X	Ind	36$	AAAB	Ind	5	
Psychology-Management (Arts)	LN71	4FT deg	* g	ABB	X	Ind	32$	BBBBB	Ind	7	
Psychology-Mathematics (Arts)	LG71	4FT deg	M g	ABB	X	Ind	32$	ABBB$	Ind		
Psychology-Mathematics (Science)	GC18	3FT/4FT deg	M g	ABB	Ind	Ind	34$	ABBB$	Ind	6	
Psychology-Mediaeval History	LV71	4FT deg	* g	ABB	X	Ind	32$	ABBB	Ind		
Psychology-Modern History	LV7C	4FT deg	g	ABB	X	Ind	32$	ABBB$	Ind		
Psychology-Philosophy	LV77	4FT deg	* g	ABB	X	Ind	32$	ABBB	Ind	8	
Social Anthropology-Psychology	LL76	4FT deg	* g	ABB	X	Ind	32$	ABBB	Ind	15	
Statistics-Psychology (Science)	CG84	3FT/4FT deg	M g	ABB	Ind	Ind	32$	ABBB$	Ind		
General Degree of BSc Psychology	Y100	3FT deg	B/C/Gy/M/P g	CCC	Ind	Ind	28$	BBBC$	Ind		
General Degree of MA Psychology	Y450	3FT deg	* g	BBB	X	Ind	30$	BBBB	Ind		

STAFFORDSHIRE Univ

TITLE	CODE	COURSE	SUBJECTS	A/AS	NO/C	AGNVQ	IB	SQA(H)	SQA	RATIO	A/AS
Psychology	C800	3FT deg	*	18	3M+3D	D	Ind	BBB	Ind	6	12/24
Psychology and Criminology	CM83	3FT deg									
Psychology/Applied Statistics	GL47	3FT deg	g	18	3M+3D	D/M^	27	BBB	Ind		
Psychology/Biology	CL17	3FT deg	g	18	3M+3D	D/M^	27	BBB	Ind	12	14/18
Psychology/Computing	LG75	3FT deg	g	18	3M+3D	Ind	27	BBB	Ind		
Psychology/Cultural Studies	LL76	3FT deg	g	18	3M+3D	Ind	27	BBB	Ind		
Psychology/Development Studies	LM7Y	3FT deg	g	18	3M+3D	Ind	27	BBB	Ind	6	
Psychology/Electronics	LH76	3FT deg	S	8-18	4M	D	24	BBB	Ind	3	
Psychology/Environmental Studies	LF79	3FT deg	*	18	3M+3D	D	Ind	BBB	Ind		
Psychology/Film Studies	LW75	3FT deg	g	18	3M+3D	Ind	27	BBB	Ind	23	
Psychology/French	LR71	3FT/4SW deg	F g	18	3M+3D	Ind	27	BBB	Ind	10	
Psychology/Geography	LL78	3FT deg	g	18	3M+3D	Ind	30	AAA	Ind	9	
Psychology/German	LR72	3FT/4SW deg	G g	18	3M+3D	Ind	27	BBB	Ind	4	
Psychology/History	LV71	3FT deg	H g	18	3M+3D	Ind	27	BBB	Ind	4	12/24

Psychology 63

	course details			98 expected requirements							96 entry stats	
TITLE	CODE	COURSE	SUBJECTS	R/AS	NO/C	AGNVQ	IB	SQA(H)	SQA	RATIO	R/AS
Psychology/History of Art and Design	LV74	3FT deg	g	18	3M+3D	Ind	27	BBB	Ind		
Psychology/International Relations	LM7C	3FT deg	g	18	3M+3D	Ind	27	BBB	Ind	1	
Psychology/Law	LM73	3FT deg	g	18	3D	M^	26	BBBB	Ind	5	12/18
Psychology/Legal Studies	LM7H	3FT deg	g	18	3D	M^	26	BBBB	Ind	18	
Psychology/Literature	LQ73	3FT deg	g	18	3M+3D	Ind	27	BBB	Ind	5	12/20
Psychology/Media Studies	LP74	3FT deg	g	18	3M+3D	Ind	27	BBB	Ind	17	
Psychology/Philosophy	LV77	3FT deg	g	18	3M+3D	Ind	27	BBB	Ind	9	
Psychology/Physics	LF73	3FT deg	S	8-18	4M	D	24	BCC	Ind		
Psychology/Physiology	BL17	3FT deg									
Psychology/Politics	LMR1	3FT deg	g	18	3M+3D	Ind	27	BBB	Ind		
Sociology/Psychology	LL37	3FT deg	g	18	3M+3D	Ind	27	BBB	Ind	5	10/26
Spanish/Psychology	RL47	3FT/4SW deg	g	18	3M+3D	Ind	27	BBB	Ind		
Sport Sciences and Psychology	BC68	3FT deg									
Women's Studies/Psychology	ML97	3FT deg	g	18	3M	Ind	27	BBB	Ind	12	

Univ of STIRLING

TITLE	CODE	COURSE	SUBJECTS	R/AS	NO/C	AGNVQ	IB	SQA(H)	SQA	RATIO	R/AS
Biology/Psychology	CC18	4FT deg	S g	CCD	Ind	Ind	28	BBCC	HN		
Business Studies/Psychology	CN81	4FT deg	g	BBC	Ind	Ind	33	BBBB	HN		
Computing Science/Psychology	CG85	4FT deg	g	CCC	Ind	Ind	28	BBCC	HN		
Film & Media Studies/Psychology	CP84	4FT deg	g	BBC	Ind	Ind	35	ABBB	HN		
French/Psychology	RC18	4FT deg	g	CCC	Ind	Ind	31	BBBC	HN		
Human Resources Management/Psychology	NL17	4FT deg	g	BBC	Ind	Ind	33	BBBB	HN		
Management Science/Psychology	CNV1	4FT deg	g	BBC	Ind	Ind	33	BBBB	HN		
Marketing/Psychology	CN85	4FT deg	g	BBC	Ind	Ind	33	BBBB	HN		
Mathematics/Psychology	CG81	4FT deg	M g	CCC	Ind	Ind	28	BBCC	HN		
Philosophy/Psychology	CV87	4FT deg	g	BBC	Ind	Ind	33	BBBB	HN		
Psychology	C800	4FT deg	g	BBC	Ind	Ind	33	BBBB	HN		
Psychology/Social Policy	CL84	4FT deg	g	BCC	Ind	Ind	31	BBBC	HN		
Psychology/Sociology	CL83	4FT deg	g	BCC	Ind	Ind	31	BBBC	HN		

Univ of STRATHCLYDE

TITLE	CODE	COURSE	SUBJECTS	R/AS	NO/C	AGNVQ	IB	SQA(H)	SQA	RATIO	R/AS
Arts and Social Sciences *Psychology*	Y440	3FT/4FT deg	g	CCC	Ind		28	BBBBB$	Ind		

UNIVERSITY COLLEGE SUFFOLK

TITLE	CODE	COURSE	SUBJECTS	R/AS	NO/C	AGNVQ	IB	SQA(H)	SQA	RATIO	R/AS
Art & Design and Behavioural Studies	LW72	3FT deg	Pf	EE	N $	P$	Ind	Ind	Ind		
Art & Design and Behavioural Studies	EW7F	3FT deg	Pf	EE	N $	P$	Ind	Ind	Ind		
Behavioural Studies and Business Studies	LN7C	3FT deg	*	DE	N $	P$	Ind	Ind	Ind		
Behavioural Studies and Cultural Studies	LY73	3FT deg	*	DC	N $	P$	Ind	Ind	Ind		
Behavioural Studies and Early Childhood Studies	LX79	3FT deg	*	DD	N $	P$	Ind	Ind	Ind		
Behavioural Studies and Environmental Studies	FL97	3FT deg	S/Gy	DE	N $	P$	Ind	Ind	Ind		
Behavioural Studies and Information Technology	GL57	3FT deg	*	DE	N $	P$	Ind	Ind	Ind		
Behavioural Studies and Literary Studies	LQ72	3FT deg	E	DC	N $	P$	Ind	Ind	Ind		
Behavioural Studies and Management	LN71	3FT deg	*	DE	N $	P$	Ind	Ind	Ind		
Behavioural Studies and Media Studies	LP74	3FT deg	*	DC	N $	P$	Ind	Ind	Ind		
Behavioural Studies and Product Design and Manuf	LH77	3FT deg	*	DE	N $	P$	Ind	Ind	Ind		
Behavioural Studies with Applied Biological Sci	L7C1	3FT deg	S	DD	N $	P$	Ind	Ind	Ind		
Behavioural Studies with Art & Design	L7W2	3FT deg	Pf	DD	N $	P$	Ind	Ind	Ind		
Behavioural Studies with Business Studies	L7N1	3FT deg	*	DD	N $	P$	Ind	Ind	Ind		
Behavioural Studies with Cultural Studies	L7Y3	3FT deg	*	DD	N $	P$	Ind	Ind	Ind		
Behavioural Studies with Early Childhood Studies	L7X9	3FT deg	*	DD	N $	P$	Ind	Ind	Ind		
Behavioural Studies with Human Science	L7B1	3FT deg	S	DD	N $	P$	Ind	Ind	Ind		
Behavioural Studies with Information Technology	L7G5	3FT deg	*	DD	N $	P$	Ind	Ind	Ind		
Behavioural Studies with Literary Studies	L7Q2	3FT deg	E	DD	N $	P$	Ind	Ind	Ind		

TITLE	CODE	COURSE	SUBJECTS	A/AS	NO/C	AGNVQ	IB	SQA(H)	SQA	RATIO A/AS
Behavioural Studies with Management	L7NC	3FT deg	*	DD	N $	P$	Ind	Ind	Ind	
Behavioural Studies with Media Studies	L7P4	3FT deg	*	DD	N $	P$	Ind	Ind	Ind	
Behavioural Studies with Product Design & Manuf	L7H7	3FT deg	*	DD	N $	P$	Ind	Ind	Ind	
Behavioural Studies with Social Policy	L7L4	3FT deg	S	DD	Ind		Ind	Ind	Ind	

Univ of SUNDERLAND

TITLE	CODE	COURSE	SUBJECTS	A/AS	NO/C	AGNVQ	IB	SQA(H)	SQA	RATIO A/AS
Biology and Psychology	CC18	3FT deg	g	12	MO	M	24$	BCCC$	N	5 10/16
Biology with Psychology	C1C8	3FT deg	B/C	10	4M	M^	Ind	Ind	Ind	
Business Studies and Psychology	NC18	3FT deg	g	14	MO	M	26$	BBCC$	N	8 8/12
Business Studies with Psychology	N1C8	3FT/4SW deg	*	10	4M	M^	Ind	Ind	Ind	
Chemistry and Psychology	FC18	3FT deg	C	10	4M	M	Ind	Ind	Ind	
Chemistry with Psychology	F1C8	3FT deg	C	10	4M	M^	Ind	Ind	Ind	
Computer Studies and Psychology	GC58	3FT deg	* g	12	MO	M	24$	BCCC$	N	3
Computer Studies with Psychology	G5C8	3FT/4SW deg	*	10	4M	M^	Ind	Ind	Ind	
Economics and Psychology	LC18	3FT deg	* g	10	N	M	24$	CCCC$	N	
Economics with Psychology	L1C8	3FT deg	*	10	4M	M^	Ind	Ind	Ind	
English with Psychology	Q3C8	3FT deg	*	12	3M+1D	M^	Ind	Ind	Ind	
French and Psychology	RC18	4FT deg	F g	12	3M $	M	24$	BCCC$	N$	6
French with Psychology	R1C8	4FT deg	F	10	4M	M^	Ind	Ind	Ind	
Geography and Psychology	LC88	3FT deg	Gy/Gl g	14	Ind	M	26$	BBCC$	Ind	6
Geography with Psychology	L8C8	3FT deg	*	10	4M	M^	Ind	Ind	Ind	
Geology and Psychology	FC68	3FT deg	Gy/Gl g	12	3M $	M	24$	BCCC$	N$	1
German and Psychology	RC28	4FT deg	G g	12	3M $	M	24$	BCCC$	N$	2
German with Psychology	R2C8	4SW deg	G	10	4M	M^	Ind	Ind	Ind	
History and Psychology	VC18	3FT deg	H g	14	Ind	M	26$	BBCC$	Ind	4
History with Psychology	V1C8	3FT deg	*	12	3M+1D	M^	Ind	Ind	Ind	
Mathematics and Psychology	GC18	3FT deg	M g	12	3M $	M	24$	BCCC$	N$	2
Mathematics with Psychology	G1C8	3FT deg	M	10	4M	M^	Ind	Ind	Ind	
Media Studies and Psychology	PC48	3FT deg	* g	14	MO	M	26$	BBCC$	N	5 13/18
Media Studies with Psychology	P4C8	3FT deg	*	26	Ind	Ind	Ind	Ind	Ind	
Philosophy and Psychology	VC78	3FT deg	* g	14	MO	M	26$	BBCC$	N	3 6/16
Philosophy with Psychology	V7C8	3FT deg	*	10	4M	M^	Ind	Ind	Ind	
Physiology and Psychology	BC18	3FT deg	B/C g	12	3M $	M	26$	BCCC$	N$	9
Physiology with Psychology	B1C8	3FT deg	*	10	4M	M^	Ind	Ind	Ind	
Politics and Psychology	MC18	3FT deg	* g	14	MO	M	26$	BBCC$	N	4
Politics with Psychology	M1C8	3FT deg	*	10	4M	M^	Ind	Ind	Ind	
Psychology	L700	3FT deg	* g	CCC	X	D$^	28	BBBC	Ind	4 6/20
Psychology and Religious Studies	CV88	3FT deg	* g	14	MO $	M	26$	BBCC$	N	6
Psychology and Sociology	CL83	3FT deg	* g	14	MO	M	26$	BBCC$	N	3 4/16
Psychology with American Studies	C8Q4	3FT deg	* g	14	MO	M	26$	BBCC$	N	3 8/22
Psychology with Biology	C8C1	3FT deg	*	10	4M	M^	Ind	Ind	Ind	
Psychology with Business Studies	C8N1	3FT deg	*	10	4M	M^	Ind	Ind	Ind	
Psychology with Chemistry	C8F1	3FT deg	*	10	4M	M^	Ind	Ind	Ind	
Psychology with Comparative Literature	C8Q2	3FT deg	*	10	4M	M^	Ind	Ind	Ind	
Psychology with Computer Studies	C8G5	3FT deg	*	10	4M	M^	Ind	Ind	Ind	
Psychology with Economics	C8L1	3FT deg	*	10	4M	M^	Ind	Ind	Ind	
Psychology with European Studies	C8T2	3FT deg	* g	14	MO	M	26$	BBCC$	N	
Psychology with French	C8R1	3FT deg	*	10	4M	M^	Ind	Ind	Ind	
Psychology with Gender Studies	C8M9	3FT deg	* g	14	MO	M	26$	BBCC$	N	2
Psychology with Geography	C8L8	3FT deg	*	10	4M	M^	Ind	Ind	Ind	
Psychology with German	C8R2	3FT deg	*	10	4M	M^	Ind	Ind	Ind	
Psychology with History	C8V1	3FT deg	*	12	3M+1D	M^	Ind	Ind	Ind	
Psychology with History of Art and Design	C8V4	3FT deg	*	10	4M	M^	Ind	Ind	Ind	

Psychology 63

			98 expected requirements							96 entry stats

TITLE	CODE	COURSE	SUBJECTS	A/AS	ND/C	RGNVQ	IB	SQA(H)	SQA	RATIO A/AS
Psychology with Mathematics	C8G1	3FT deg	*	10	4M	M^	Ind	Ind	Ind	
Psychology with Media Studies	C8P4	3FT deg	*	26	Ind	Ind	Ind	Ind	Ind	
Psychology with Philosophy	C8V7	3FT deg	*	10	4M	M^	Ind	Ind	Ind	
Psychology with Physiology	C8B1	3FT deg	*	10	4M	M^	Ind	Ind	Ind	
Psychology with Politics	C8M1	3FT deg	*	10	4M	M^	Ind	Ind	Ind	
Psychology with Religious Studies	C8V8	3FT deg	*	10	4M	M^	Ind	Ind	Ind	
Psychology with Sociology	C8L3	3FT deg	*	12	3M+1D	M^	Ind	Ind	Ind	
Psychology with Spanish	C8R4	3FT deg	*	10	4M	M^	Ind	Ind	Ind	
Religious Studies with Psychology	V8C8	3FT deg	*	10	4M	M^	Ind	Ind	Ind	
Sociology with Psychology	L3C8	3FT deg	*	12	3M+1D	M^	Ind	Ind	Ind	
Univ of SURREY										
Applied Psychology/Sociology	CL83	4SW deg	* g	BBC	Ind	M$ go	Ind	Ind	Ind	7 16/22
Psychology	C800	4SW deg	* g	BBC	Ind	Ind	Ind	Ind	Ind	10 18/26
Univ of SUSSEX										
Applied Psychology	C8Y2	3FT deg	* g	BBB	MO	M*6 go	$	Ind	Ind	
Developmental Psychology	C8YF	3FT deg	* g	BBB	MO $	M*6 go	$	Ind	Ind	
Psychology	C800	3FT deg	* g	BBB	MO $	M*6 go	$	Ind	Ind	
Psychology	C8GM	3FT deg	* g	BBB	MO $	M*6 go	$	Ind	Ind	
Psychology with North American Studies	C8Q4	4FT deg	* g	BBB	MO $	M*6 go	$	Ind	Ind	
Social Psychology	L7M9	3FT deg	* g	BBB	MO $	M*6 go	$	Ind	Ind	
Univ of Wales SWANSEA										
Anthropology and Psychology	LL67	3FT deg	* g	BBB-BBC	1M+5D	Ind	30	ABBBB	Ind	7 18/22
Biological Sciences and Psychology	CC18	3FT deg	B g	BBC	1M+5D$	Ind	30$	ABBBB$	Ind	7 18/26
Computer Science and Psychology	CG85	3FT deg	* g	BBC-BCC	1M+5D	Ind	30	BBBBB	Ind	4
Economics and Psychology	LL17	3FT deg	* g	BBB-BBC	1M+5D	Ind	30	ABBBB	Ind	8
Law and Psychology	LM73	3FT deg	* g	BBB-BCC	1M+5D	Ind	30$	ABBBB$	Ind	
Philosophy and Psychology	LV77	3FT deg	* g	BBB	6D	Ind	32	AABBB	Ind	13
Psychology	L700	3FT deg	* g	BBB	6D	Ind	32	AABBB	Ind	4 16/26
Psychology	C800	3FT deg	* g	BBC	1M+5D	Ind	30	ABBBB	Ind	5 16/26
Psychology and French	LR71	3FT deg	E g	BBC	1M+5D$	Ind	30$	ABBBB$	Ind	
Psychology and German	LR72	4FT deg	G g	BBC	1M+5D$	Ind	30$	ABBBB$	Ind	
Psychology and Italian	LR73	4FT deg	L/*	BBC	1M+5D$	Ind	30$	ABBBB$	Ind	
Psychology and Law	LM7H	3FT deg	* g	BBC	1M+5D	Ind	30$	ABBBB$	Ind	
Psychology and Sociology	LL37	3FT deg	* g	BBB-BBC	1M+5D	Ind	30	ABBBB	Ind	8 16/26
Russian and Psychology	LR78	4FT deg	L g							
Spanish and Psychology	LR74	4FT deg	L/* g	BBC	1M+5D$	Ind	30$	ABBBB$	Ind	
Welsh and Psychology	LQ75	4FT deg	L/*	BBC	1M+5D$	Ind	30$	ABBBB$	Ind	
Joint Hons with defer choice of specialisation (inc Psychology)	Y220	3FT deg	* g	20-22	1M+5D	Ind	28	BBBBB	Ind	
Univ of TEESSIDE										
Cognitive Sciences	C870	3FT deg	S	14-16	Ind	Ind	Ind	BBCCC	Ind	
Psychology (Jt Hons available)	L700	3FT deg	S	14-16	Ind	Ind	Ind	BBCCC	Ind	4 10/20
Psychology and Sociology	LL73	3FT deg	S	14-16	Ind	Ind	Ind	BBCCC	Ind	4 8/16
Modular Degree Scheme *Psychology*	Y401	3FT deg								
THAMES VALLEY Univ										
American Studies with Psychology	Q4C8	3FT deg		8-12	MO	M	26	CCC		
English Lang and Communications with Psychology	Q1C8	3FT deg		8-12	MO	M	26	CCC		
English with Psychology	Q3C8	3FT deg		8-12	MO	M	26	CCC		
Health Studies with Psychology	L4C8	3FT deg		8-12	MO	M	26	CCC		

course details			98 expected requirements							96 entry stats

TITLE	CODE	COURSE	SUBJECTS	A/AS	NO/C	AGNVQ	IB	SQA(H)	SQA	RATIO A/AS
Health and Community Psychology	L745	3FT deg		8-12	MO	M	26	CCC		
History with Psychology	V1C8	3FT deg		8-12	MO	M	26	CCC		
Human Resource Management with Psychology	N6C8	3FT deg		8-12	MO	M	26	CCC		
Marketing with Psychology	N5C8	3FT deg		8-12	MO	M	26	CCC		
Psychology	C800▼	3FT deg	* g	8-12	MO	M	26	CCC		
Psychology with Advertising	C8P3	3FT deg		8-12	MO	M	26	CCC		
Psychology with Business	C8N1	3FT deg		8-12	MO	M	26	CCC		
Psychology with Community Law	C8MH	3FT deg		8-12	MO	M	26	CCC		
Psychology with Criminal Justice	C8MJ	3FT deg		8-12	MO	M	26	CCC		
Psychology with English	C8Q3	3FT deg		8-12	MO	M	26	CCC		
Psychology with English Language Studies	C8Q1	3FT deg		8-12	MO	M	26	CCC		
Psychology with French	C8R1	3FT deg		8-12	MO	M	26	CCC		
Psychology with German	C8R2	3FT deg		8-12	MO	M	26	CCC		
Psychology with Health Studies	C8L4	3FT deg		8-12	MO	M	26	CCC		
Psychology with Human Resource Management	C8N6	3FT deg		8-12	MO	M	26	CCC		
Psychology with Information Management	C8P2	3FT deg		8-12	MO	M	26	CCC		
Psychology with Language and Communication	C8PH	3FT deg		8-12	MO	M	26	CCC		
Psychology with Marketing	C8N5	3FT deg		8-12	MO	M	26	CCC		
Psychology with Media Studies	C8W9	3FT deg		8-12	MO	M	26	CCC		
Psychology with Sociology	C8L3	3FT deg		8-12	MO	M	26	CCC		
Psychology with Spanish	C8R4	3FT deg		8-12	MO	M	26	CCC		
Psychology with Women's Studies	C8M9	3FT deg		8-12	MO	M	26	CCC		
Sociology with Psychology	L3C8	3FT deg		8-12	MO	M	26	CCC		

Univ of ULSTER

TITLE	CODE	COURSE	SUBJECTS	A/AS	NO/C	AGNVQ	IB	SQA(H)	SQA	RATIO A/AS
Applied Psychology (4 Yrs)	C810▼	4FT deg	* g	BBC	MO+4D	D*6/^ gi	32	ABBB	Ind	29	18/24
Psychology with Organisational Science	C8N2▼	3FT deg	g	CCC	MO+3D	D*6/^ gi	28	BBBC	Ind	6	10/20
Social Psychology (inc DIS)	C840▼	3FT/4SW deg	* g	CCC	MO+3D	D*6/^ gi	28	BBBC	Ind	21	12/24
Social Psychology and Sociology (inc DIS)	C8L3▼	3FT/4SW deg	* g	CCC	MO+3D	D*6/^ gi	28	BBBC	Ind	23	14/20

UNIVERSITY COLL LONDON (Univ of London)

TITLE	CODE	COURSE	SUBJECTS	A/AS	NO/C	AGNVQ	IB	SQA(H)	SQA	RATIO A/AS
Computer Science with Cognitive Science	G5C8	3FT deg	M g	BBB	MO $	Ind	32$	ABBBB$	Ind	8	
Computer Science with Cognitive Science (MSci)	G5CV	4FT deg	M g	BBB	MO $	Ind	32$	ABBBB$	Ind		
Linguistics with Cognitive Science	Q1C8	3FT deg	* g	BBC	3M	Ind	28	BBBCC	Ind	8	
Psychology	C800	3FT deg	* g	ABB	MO+4D	Ind	34$	Ind	Ind	13	24/30
Psychology with Cognitive Science	C808	3FT deg	M g	ABB	MO+4D	Ind	34$	Ind	Ind	32	

Univ of WARWICK

TITLE	CODE	COURSE	SUBJECTS	A/AS	NO/C	AGNVQ	IB	SQA(H)	SQA	RATIO A/AS
Chemistry with Psychology	F1C8	3FT deg	C+S/M g	BCC	M+D $	DS^	28$	BBBBB$		5	16/20
Education and Psychology	XL97	3FT deg	* g	BBB	X	X	32	AABBB		9	24/30
Psychology	C800	3FT deg	* g	BBB-BBC	Ind	Ind	32	AABBB		12	22/30
Psychology and Philosophy	LV77	3FT deg	* g	BBB	X	X	32	AABBB		16	24/30

WESTHILL COLL

TITLE	CODE	COURSE	SUBJECTS	A/AS	NO/C	AGNVQ	IB	SQA(H)	SQA	RATIO A/AS
Humanities - Mathematics, Science and Psychology *Psychology*	Y601	3FT deg	M g	CC	4M+2D	M^	Ind	Ind	Ind		

Univ of WESTMINSTER

TITLE	CODE	COURSE	SUBJECTS	A/AS	NO/C	AGNVQ	IB	SQA(H)	SQA	RATIO A/AS
Cognitive Science	C878	3FT deg	*	CC	3M	M	Ind	Ind	Ind	1	4/14
Psychological Sciences	C800	3FT deg	B	CC	4M	M	Ind	Ind		3	8/18
Psychology	C801	3FT deg	*	BC	MO+3D		Ind	BBB		10	12/22

WIRRAL METROPOLITAN COLLEGE

TITLE	CODE	COURSE	SUBJECTS	A/AS	NO/C	AGNVQ	IB	SQA(H)	SQA	RATIO A/AS
Psychology	C801	4FT deg		Ind	Ind	Ind	Ind	Ind	Ind		

---

course details | 98 expected requirements | 96 entry stats

TITLE	CODE	COURSE	SUBJECTS	A/AS	ND/C	AGNVQ	IB	SQA(H)	SQA	RATIO	A/AS
Univ of WOLVERHAMPTON											
Psychology	C800	3FT/4SW deg	* g	18	4D	D	28	BBBB	Ind	6	14/22
Applied Sciences — Psychology	Y100	3FT/4SW deg	S g	16	4M	D	24	BBBB	Ind		
Combined Degrees — Psychology	Y401	3FT/4SW deg	g	18	4D	D	28	BBBB	Ind		
WORCESTER COLL of HE											
Psychology	L700	3FT deg	g	CC	Ind	M	Ind	Ind	Ind	5	8/18
Psychology/Art & Design	WL97	3FT deg	A g	CC	Ind	M	Ind	Ind	Ind	5	10/18
Psychology/Biological Science	CL17	3FT deg	S g	CC	Ind	M	Ind	Ind	Ind	4	
Psychology/Business Management	NL17	3FT deg	g	CC	Ind	M	Ind	Ind	Ind	12	
Psychology/Drama	WL47	3FT deg	g	CC	Ind	M	Ind	Ind	Ind	7	
Psychology/Economy and Society	LL17	3FT deg	g	CC	Ind	M	Ind	Ind	Ind		
Psychology/Education Studies	XL97	3FT deg	g	CC	Ind	M	Ind	Ind	Ind	7	
Psychology/English and Literary Studies	QL37	3FT deg	g	CC	Ind	M	Ind	Ind	Ind	5	12/18
Psychology/Environmental Science	FL97	3FT deg	g	CC	Ind	M	Ind	Ind	Ind		
Psychology/Geography	LL87	3FT deg	g	CC	Ind	M	Ind	Ind	Ind		
Psychology/Health Studies	BL97	3FT deg	g	CC	Ind	M	Ind	Ind	Ind	7	
Psychology/Information Technology	GL57	3FT deg	g	CC	Ind	M	Ind	Ind	Ind	5	
Sociology/Psychology	LL73	3FT deg	g	CC	Ind	M	Ind	Ind	Ind	5	8/22
Urban Studies/Psychology	LL7V	3FT deg	g	CC	Ind	M	Ind	Ind	Ind	4	
Women's Studies/Psychology	LM79	3FT deg	g	CC	Ind	M	Ind	Ind	Ind	4	
Univ of YORK											
Psychology	C800	3FT deg	* g	BBB	Ind	D$^ go	32	AABBB	Ind		24/28

course details | 98 expected requirements | 96 entry stats

TITLE	CODE	COURSE	SUBJECTS	A/AS	ND/C	AGNVQ	IB	SQA(H)	SQA	RATIO A/AS
Univ of ABERDEEN										
Accountancy-Social Research	LN34	4FT deg	* g	BBC	Ind	M$ go	30$	BBBB$	Ind	
Accountancy-Sociology	NL43	4FT deg	* g	BBC	Ind	M$ go	30$	BBBB$	Ind	
Celtic Civilisation-Social Research	LQ3M	4FT deg	* g	BBC	Ind	M$ go	30$	BBBB$	Ind	
Celtic Civilisation-Sociology	LQ35	4FT deg	* g	BBC	Ind	M$ go	30$	BBBB$	Ind	
Celtic-Social Research	LQ3N	4FT deg	* g	BBC	Ind	M$ go	30$	BBBB$	Ind	
Celtic-Sociology	QL53	4FT deg	* g	BBC	Ind	M$ go	30$	BBBB$	Ind	2
Cultural History with Sociology	V9L3	4FT deg	* g	BBC	Ind	M$ go	30$	BBBB$	Ind	
Cultural History with Women's Studies	V9M9	4FT deg	* g	BBC	Ind	M$ go	30$	BBBB$	Ind	
Economic History-Social Research	LV33	4FT deg	* g	BBC	Ind	M$ go	30$	BBBB$	Ind	
Economic History-Sociology	VL33	4FT deg	* g	BBC	Ind	M$ go	30$	BBBB$	Ind	
Economics-Sociology	LL13	4FT deg	* g	BBC	Ind	M$ go	30$	BBBB$	Ind	
English with Womens Studies	Q3M9	4FT deg	* g	BBC	Ind	M$ go	30$	BBBB$	Ind	
English-Social Research	LQ33	4FT deg	* g	BBC	Ind	M$ go	30$	BBBB$	Ind	7
English-Sociology	QL33	4FT deg	* g	BBC	Ind	M$ go	30$	BBBB$	Ind	6
Entrepreneurship-Social Research	NLC3	4FT deg	* g	BBC	Ind	M$ go	30$	BBBB$	Ind	
Entrepreneurship-Sociology	LNHC	4FT deg	* g	BBC	Ind	M$ go	30$	BBBB$	Ind	
French with Women's Studies	R1M9	5FT deg	* g	BBC	Ind	M$ go	30$	BBBB$	Ind	
French with Women's Studies (4 Yrs)	R1MX	4FT deg	* g	BBC	Ind	M$ go	30$	BBBB$	Ind	
French-Social Research	LR31	4FT/5FT deg	* g	BBC	Ind	M$ go	30$	BBBB$	Ind	
French-Social Research (4 Yrs)	LR3C	4FT deg	* g	BBC	Ind	M$ go	30$	BBBB$	Ind	
French-Sociology	RL13	4FT/5FT deg	* g	BBC	Ind	M$ go	30$	BBBB$	Ind	
French-Sociology (4 Yrs)	RL1H	4FT deg	* g	BBC	Ind	M$ go	30$	BBBB$	Ind	
Geography-Social Research	LL38	4FT deg	* g	BBC	Ind	M$ go	30$	BBBB$	Ind	
Geography-Sociology	LL83	4FT deg	* g	BBC	Ind	M$ go	30$	BBBB$	Ind	6
German with Women's Studies	R2M9	5FT deg	* g	BBC	Ind	M$ go	30$	BBBB$	Ind	
German with Women's Studies (4 Yrs)	R2MX	4FT deg	* g	BBC	Ind	M$ go	30$	BBBB$	Ind	
German-Social Research	LR32	4FT/5FT deg	* g	BBC	Ind	M$ go	30$	BBBB$	Ind	
German-Social Research (4 Yrs)	LR3F	4FT deg	* g	BBC	Ind	M$ go	30$	BBBB$	Ind	
German-Sociology	RL23	4FT/5FT deg	* g	BBC	Ind	M$ go	30$	BBBB$	Ind	
German-Sociology (4 Yrs)	RL2H	4FT deg	* g	BBC	Ind	M$ go	30$	BBBB$	Ind	
Hispanic Studies with Women's Studies	R4M9	5FT deg	* g	BBC	Ind	M$ go	30$	BBBB$	Ind	
Hispanic Studies with Women's Studies (4 Yrs)	R4MX	4FT deg	* g	BBC	Ind	M$ go	30$	BBBB$	Ind	
Hispanic Studies-Social Research	LR34	4FT/5FT deg	* g	BBC	Ind	M$ go	30$	BBBB$	Ind	
Hispanic Studies-Social Research (4 Yrs)	LR3K	4FT deg	* g	BBC	Ind	M$ go	30$	BBBB$	Ind	
Hispanic Studies-Sociology	RL43	4FT/5FT deg	* g	BBC	Ind	M$ go	30$	BBBB$	Ind	
Hispanic Studies-Sociology (4 Yrs)	RL4H	4FT deg	* g	BBC	Ind	M$ go	30$	BBBB$	Ind	
History of Art with Women's Studies	V4M9	4FT deg	* g	BBC	Ind	M$ go	30$	BBBB$	Ind	
History with Women's Studies	V1M9	4FT deg	* g	BBC	Ind	M$ go	30$	BBBB$	Ind	
History-Social Research	LV31	4FT deg	* g	BBC	Ind	M$ go	30$	BBBB$	Ind	
History-Sociology	VL13	4FT deg	* g	BBC	Ind	M$ go	30$	BBBB$	Ind	4
Jurisprudence-Social Research	LM33	4FT deg	* g	BBC	Ind	M$ go	30$	BBBB$	Ind	
Jurisprudence-Sociology	MLH3	4FT deg	* g	BBC	Ind	M$ go	30$	BBBB$	Ind	
Philosophy with Women's Studies	V7M9	4FT deg	* g	BBC	Ind	M$ go	30$	BBBB$	Ind	
Philosophy-Social Research	LV37	4FT deg	* g	BBC	Ind	M$ go	30$	BBBB$	Ind	
Philosophy-Sociology	VL73	4FT deg	* g	BBC	Ind	M$ go	30$	BBBB$	Ind	7
Politics-Social Research	LM31	4FT deg	* g	BBC	Ind	M$ go	30$	BBBB$	Ind	8
Politics-Sociology	ML13	4FT deg	* g	BBC	Ind	M$ go	30$	BBBB$	Ind	5
Religious Studies with Women's Studies	V8M9	4FT deg	* g	BBC	Ind	M$ go	30$	BBBB$	Ind	
Social Research-Management Studies	LN3C	4FT deg	* g	BBC	Ind	M$ go	30$	BBBB$	Ind	6
Sociology	L300	4FT deg	* g	BBC	Ind	M$ go	30$	BBBB$	Ind	3
Sociology with Cultural History	L3V9	4FT deg	* g	BBC	Ind	M$ go	24$	BBBC$	Ind	

Sociology and Anthropology 64

course details			98 expected requirements							96 entry stats	
TITLE	CODE	COURSE	SUBJECTS	A/AS	ND/C	AGNVQ	IB	SQA(H)	SQA	RATIO A/AS	
Sociology-Management Studies	LN31	4FT deg	* g	BBC	Ind	M$ go	30$	BBBB$	Ind	4	
Sociology-Religious Studies	LV38	4FT deg	* g	BBC	Ind	M$ go	30$	BBBB$	Ind	12	
Univ of ABERTAY DUNDEE											
Social Science	L300	4FT deg	*	CD	Ind	Ind	Ind	BBC	Ind		
Univ of Wales, ABERYSTWYTH											
International Politics and the Third World	MM19	3FT deg	* g	20	1M+5D	M6 g	30	BBBCC	Ind		
ANGLIA Poly Univ											
Art History and Sociology	LV34▼	3FT deg	*	14	6M	M+/^	Dip	BBCC	Ind		
Art History and Women's Studies	VM49▼	3FT deg	*	14	6M	M+/^	Dip	BBCC	Ind	3	
Business Studies and Leisure Planning & Develop	NL1H▼	3FT deg	* g	14	6M	M go	Dip	BBCC	Ind		
Business and Sociology	NL13▼	3FT deg	* g	12	4M	M go	Dip	BCCC	Ind	8	12/16
Business and Women's Studies	NM19▼	3FT deg	* g	10	3M	P go	Dip	BCCC	Ind	1	
Communication Studies and Sociology	PL33▼	3FT deg	Ap	14	6M	M+/^	Dip$	BBCC	Ind	6	14/16
Communication Studies and Women's Studies	PM39▼	3FT deg	Ap	14	6M	M+/^	Dip$	BBCC	Ind	4	
Criminology and Sociology	ML33▼	3FT deg	g	12	4M	M go	Dip	BCCC	Ind		
Economics and Sociology	LL13▼	3FT deg	* g	12	4M	M go	Dip	BCCC	Ind		
Economics and Women's Studies	LM19▼	3FT deg	* g	12	4M	M go	Dip	BCCC	Ind		
English Language Studies and Intercultural St	QL36▼	3FT deg	* g	12	4M	M go	Dip	BCCC			
English Language Studies and Sociology	QL13▼	3FT deg	* g	12	4M	M go	Dip	BCCC			
English Language Studies and Women's Studies	QM19▼	3FT deg	* g	12	4M	M go	Dip	BCCC			
English and Sociology	QL33▼	3FT deg	E	12	4M	M+/^	Dip$	BCCC	Ind	6	10/20
English and Women's Studies	QM39▼	3FT deg	E	12	4M	M+/^	Dip$	BCCC	Ind	4	
European Philosophy & Lit and Women's Studies	VM79▼	3FT deg	*	12	4M	M	Dip	BCCC			
European Philosophy & Literature and Sociology	LV37▼	3FT deg	*	12	4M	M+/^	Dip	BCCC	Ind	3	
French and Intercultural Studies	RL16▼	4FT deg	* g	12	4M	M go		BCCC			
French and Sociology	LR31▼	4FT deg	* g	12	4M	M go	Dip	BCCC	Ind	8	
French and Women's Studies	RM19▼	4FT deg	* g	12	4M	M go	Dip	BCCC	Ind	2	
Geography and Sociology	LL83▼	3FT deg	Gv g	12	4M	M+/^ go	Dip$	BCCC	Ind		
German and Intercultural Studies	RL26▼	4FT deg	* g	12	4M	M go	Dip	BCCC			
German and Sociology	LR32▼	4FT deg	* g	12	4M	M+/^ go	Dip	BCCC	Ind		
German and Women's Studies	RM29▼	4FT deg	* g	12	4M	M+/^ go	Dip	BCCC	Ind		
Graphic Arts and Sociology	LW32▼	3FT deg	A	14	6M	M+/^	Dip$	BBCC	Ind	2	
Graphic Arts and Women's Studies	WM29▼	3FT deg	A	14	6M	M+/^	Dip$	BBCC	Ind		
History and Sociology	LV31▼	3FT deg	Ap	12	4M	M+/^	Dip$	BCCC	Ind	4	14/16
History and Women's Studies	VM19▼	3FT deg	Ap	12	4M	M+/^	Dip$	BCCC	Ind	7	
Italian and Intercultural Studies	RL36▼	4FT deg	* g	12	4M	M go	Dip	BCCC			
Italian and Sociology	RL33▼	4FT deg	* g	12	4M	M+/^ go	Dip	BCCC	Ind		
Italian and Women's Studies	RM39▼	4FT deg	* g	12	4M	M go	Dip	BCCC	Ind	1	
Law and Sociology	LM33▼	3FT deg	*	14	6M	M	Dip	BBCC	Ind	8	14/16
Law and Women's Studies	MM39▼	3FT deg	*	14	6M	M	Dip	BBCC	Ind	12	
Multimedia and Leisure Planning and Development	GL53▼	3FT deg	g	8	N	Ind go	Dip	CCCC	Ind		
Politics and Sociology	ML13▼	3FT deg	*	14	6M	M+/^	Dip	BBCC	Ind	7	
Politics and Women's Studies	MM19▼	3FT deg	*	14	6M	M+/^	Dip	BBCC	Ind		
Psychology and Sociology	CL83▼	3FT deg	S g	16	8M	D go	Dip$	BBCCC	N	5	8/18
Psychology and Women's Studies	CM89▼	3FT deg	S g	16	8M	D go	Dip$	BBCCC	N	5	
Social Policy and Sociology	LL43▼	3FT deg	*	12	4M $	M	Dip	BCCC	Ind	8	
Social Policy and Women's Studies	LM49▼	3FT deg	*	12	4M	M go	Dip	BCCC	Ind	3	
Sociology	L300▼	3FT deg	*	12	4M	M	Dip	BCCC	Ind	6	12/20
Sociology and Spanish	LR34▼	4FT deg	* g	12	4M	M go	Dip	BCCC			
Sociology and Women's Studies	LM39▼	3FT deg	*	12	4M	M	Dip	BCCC	Ind	10	
Spanish and Intercultural Studies	RL46▼	4FT deg	* g	12	4M	M go	Dip	BCCC			
Spanish and Women's Studies	RM49▼	4FT deg	* g	12	4M	M go	Dip	BCCC	Ind	2	

TITLE	CODE	COURSE	SUBJECTS	A/AS	NO/C	AGNVQ	IB	SQA(H)	SQA	RATIO	A/AS
course details			*98 expected requirements*							*96 entry stats*	
Univ of Wales, BANGOR											
French (Syllabus A) and Women's Studies	MR91	4FT deg	E g	18	X	D*^ go	28$	BBBC$	X		
French (Syllabus B) and Women's Studies	MR9C	4FT deg	E g	18	X	D*^ go	28$	BBBC$	X		
German and Women's Studies	MR92	4FT deg	* g	18	X	D*^ go	28	BBBC	X		
Russian and Women's Studies	MR98	4FT deg	* g	18	X	D*^ go	28	BBBC	X		
Sociology	L300	3FT deg	* g	18	5M	D*6/^ go	28	BBBC	Ind	4	14/24
Sociology with Social Policy	L3L4	3FT deg	* g	18	5M	D*6/^ go	28	BBBC	Ind	5	14/18
Sociology/Criminology	LM33	3FT deg	* g	18	5M	D*6/^ go	28	BBBC	Ind	5	12/22
Sociology/Economics	LL13	3FT deg	* g	18	3M+2D	D$6/^ go	28	BBBC	Ind	3	
Sociology/English	LQ33	3FT deg	E g	CCC	X	D*^ go	28$	BBBC$	X	5	18/20
Sociology/History	LV31	3FT deg	H g	CCC	Ind	D*^ go	28$	BBBC$	Ind	11	
Sociology/Linguistics	LQ31	3FT deg	* g	CCD	5M	D*6/^ go	28	BBBC	Ind	7	
Sociology/Physical Education	LB36	3FT deg	* g	CCC	5D	D*6/^ go	28	BBBC	Ind		
Sociology/Psychology	CL83	3FT deg	* g	BCC	MO	D*6/^ go	30	BBBB	Ind	9	20/24
Sociology/Religious Studies	LV38	3FT deg	* g	CCD	5M	D*6/^ go	28	BBBC	Ind	12	
Sports Science/Sociology	BL63	3FT deg	* g	20	5D	D*6/^ go	30	BBBC	Ind		
Welsh History/Sociology	LV3C	3FT deg	H g	CCD	Ind	D*^ go	28$	BBBC$	Ind		
Welsh/Sociology	LQ35	3FT/4FT deg	W g	CCD	Ind	D*^ go	Ind	X	X	4	
Women's Studies and Criminology	MM39	3FT deg	* g	18	5M	D*6/^ go	28	BBBC	Ind		
Women's Studies and English	MQ93	3FT deg	E g	18	X	D*6/^ go	28$	BBBC$	X		
Women's Studies and History	MV91	3FT deg	H g	18	Ind	D*6/^ go	28$	BBBC$	Ind		
Women's Studies and Linguistics	MQ91	3FT deg	* g	18	Ind	D*6/^ go	28	BBBC	Ind		
Women's Studies and Religious Studies	MV98	3FT deg	* g	18	5M	D*6/^ go	28	BBBC	Ind		
Women's Studies and Social Policy	LM49	3FT deg	* g	18	5M	D*6/^ go	28	BBBC	Ind		
Women's Studies and Sociology	LM39	3FT deg	* g	18	5M	D*6/^ go	28	BBBC	Ind		
BARNSLEY COLL											
Combined Studies Social Science	Y400	3FT deg	* g	EE	4M	M*	Ind	Ind	Ind		
Univ of BATH											
Psychology with Sociology (4 Yr SW)	C8L3	4SW deg	g	24	6D	D^	30	AABBB	Ind		
Sociology	L300	3FT deg	*	22	1M+5D$	Ind	30	ABBBB	Ind	8	12/28
Sociology (4 Yr SW)	L304	4SW deg	*	22	1M+5D$	Ind	30	ABBBB	Ind		
Sociology with Industrial Relations (4 Yr SW)	L3N6	4SW deg	*	22	1M+5D$	Ind	30	ABBBB	Ind	7	
BATH COLL of HE											
Social Sciences	L340	3FT deg		CC	N		Ind	$	$	3	6/15
Sociology	L300	3FT deg		CC	N		Ind	$	$	18	
Combined Awards Sociology	Y400	3FT deg	*		N		Ind	$	$		
Modular Programme (DipHE) Sociology	Y460	2FT Dip	*		N		Ind	$	$		
BELL COLLEGE OF TECHNOLOGY											
Social Science	043L	2FT HND	Ap g	DD-D	N $	P$	Ind	CC$	12$		
Univ of BIRMINGHAM											
History and Social Science	VL13	3FT deg	*	BCC	DO		30	BBBBB	Ind	4	20/26
Philosophy and Sociology	VL73	3FT deg	*	BBC	Ind	D+^	32	ABBBB	Ind	19	
Russian and East European Studies and Sociology	R8L3	3FT/4FT deg	R/*	BBC	Ind	D+^		ABBBB	Ind		
Social Policy and Sociology	LL43	3FT deg	*	BBC	Ind	D+^	32	ABBBB	Ind	15	20/24
Sociology and Economic History	LV33	3FT deg	*	BBC	Ind	D+^	32	ABBBB	Ind	14	
Sociology and Political Science	LM31	3FT deg	*	BBC	Ind	D+^	32	ABBBB	Ind	16	

Sociology and Anthropology 64

			98 expected requirements							96 entry stats
TITLE	CODE	COURSE	SUBJECTS	A/AS	ND/C	AGNVQ	IB	SQA(H)	SQA	RATIO A/AS
BLACKBURN COLL										
Leisure Studies (HND Top-up)	L350	2FT deg		X	HN $					
Leisure Studies	053L	2FT HND		2	N	P				
BOLTON INST										
Accountancy and Gender and Women's Studies	MN94	3FT deg	* g	CD	MO	M*	24	BBCC	Ind	
Accountancy and Leisure Studies	NL4H	3FT deg	* g	CD	MO	M*	24	BBCC	Ind	
Accountancy and Sociology	LN34	3FT deg	* g	CD	MO	M	24	Ind	Ind	
Art & Design History and Leisure Studies	VL4H	3FT deg	* g	CD	MO	M*	24	BBCC	Ind	
Art & Design History and Sociology	LV3K	3FT deg	* g	CD	MO	M	24	Ind	Ind	
Art & Design History and Urban & Cultural Studs	LV34	3FT deg	* g	CD	MO	M*	24	BBCC	Ind	
Art and Design History and Gender and Women's St	VM49	3FT deg	* g	CD	MO	M*	24	BBCC	Ind	
Biology and Gender & Women's Studies	MC91	3FT deg	* g	CD	MO	M*	24	BBCC	Ind	
Biology and Leisure Studies	CL1H	3FT deg	* g	CD	MO	M*	24	BBCC	Ind	
Business Economics and Gender and Women's Studs	LM19	3FT deg	* g	CD	MO	M*	24	BBCC	Ind	
Business Economics and Leisure Studies	LL13	3FT deg	* g	CD	MO	M*	24	BBCC	Ind	
Business Economics and Sociology	LL1J	3FT deg	* g	CD	MO	M	24	Ind	Ind	
Business Economics and Urban and Cultural Studs	LL1H	3FT deg	* g	CD	MO	M*	24	BBCC	Ind	
Business Info Systems and Gender & Women's Studs	GM59	3FT deg	* g	CD	MO	M*	24	BBCC	Ind	
Business Info Systems and Urban & Cultural St	GL5J	3FT deg	* g	CD	MO	M*	24	BBCC	Ind	
Business Information Systems and Leisure Studies	GLMH	3FT deg	* g	CD	MO	M*	24	BBCC	Ind	
Business Information Systems and Sociology	LG35	3FT deg	* g	CD	MO	M	24	Ind	Ind	
Business Studies and Gender & Women's Studies	MN9C	3FT deg	* g	CD	MO	M*	24	BBCC	Ind	
Business Studies and Leisure Studies	NL1H	3FT deg	* g	CD	MO	M*	24	BBCC	Ind	
Business Studies and Peace and War Studies	NM19	3FT deg	* g	CD	MO	M*	24	BBCC	Ind	
Business Studies and Sociology	LN3C	3FT deg	* g	CD	MO	M	24	Ind	Ind	
Community Studies	L340	3FT deg	* g	CD	MO	M*	24	BBCC	Ind	
Community Studies and Gender and Women's Studies	LM59	3FT deg	* g	CD	MO	M*	24	BBCC	Ind	
Community Studies and Leisure Studies	LL5H	3FT deg	* g	CD	MO	M*	24	BBCC	Ind	
Community Studies and Sociology	L341	3FT deg	* g	CD	MO	M	24	Ind	Ind	
Community Studies and Urban and Cultural Studies	LL53	3FT deg	* g	CD	MO	M*	24	BBCC	Ind	
Computing and European Cultural Studies	GLM3	3FT deg	* g	CD	MO	M*	24	BBCC	Ind	
Computing and Gender & Women's Studies	LG65	3FT deg	* g	CD	MO	M*	24	BBCC	Ind	
Computing and Leisure Studies	GL5H	3FT deg	* g	CD	MO	M*	24	BBCC	Ind	
Computing and Sociology	LG3M	3FT deg	* g	CD	MO	M	24	Ind	Ind	
Computing and Urban and Cultural Studies	GL53	3FT deg	* g	CD	MO	M*	24	BBCC	Ind	
Creative Writing and Gender and Women's Studies	WM99	3FT deg	* g	CD	MO	M*	24	BBCC	Ind	
Creative Writing and Leisure Studies	LWH9	3FT deg	* g	CD	MO	M*	24	BBCC	Ind	
Creative Writing and Sociology	LW3X	3FT deg	* g	CD	MO	M	24	Ind	Ind	
Creative Writing and Urban and Cultural Studies	WL93	3FT deg	* g	CD	MO	M*	24	BBCC	Ind	
Design and Gender & Women's Studies	MW92	3FT deg	* g	CD	MO	M*	24	BBCC	Ind	
Design and Leisure Studies	LWH2	3FT dcg	* g	CD	MO	M*	24	BBCC	Ind	
Design and Urban & Cultural Studies	LW32	3FT deg	* g	CD	MO	M*	24	BBCC	Ind	
Environmental Studies and European Cultural St	FL96	3FT deg	* g	CD	MO	M*	24	BBCC	Ind	
Environmental Studies and Gender & Women's Studs	FM99	3FT deg	* g	CD	MO	M*	24	BBCC	Ind	
Environmental Studies and Leisure Studies	FL9H	3FT deg	* g	CD	MO	M*	24	BBCC	Ind	
Environmental Studies and Sociology	FL9J	3FT deg	* g	CD	MO	M	24	Ind	Ind	
Environmental Studies and Urban & Cultural Studs	FL93	3FT deg	* g	CD	MO	M*	24	BBCC	Ind	
European Cult St & Gender & Women's Studies	TM29	3FT deg	* g	CD	MO	M*	24	BBCC	Ind	
European Cult St & Urban & Cultural Studies	TL23	3FT deg	* g	CD	MO	M*	24	BBCC	Ind	
European Cultural & Social Studies and Sociology	LT32	3FT deg	* g	CD	MO	M	24	Ind	Ind	
European Cultural Studies and Leisure Studies	LL63	3FT deg	* g	CD	MO	M*	24	BBCC	Ind	
Film & TV Studies and Urban & Cultural Studies	WL53	3FT deg	Me/T g	CD	Ind	Ind	24	BBCC	Ind	

course details

98 expected requirements

96 entry stats

TITLE	CODE	COURSE	SUBJECTS	A/AS	ND/C	RGNVQ	IB	SQA(H)	SQA	RATIO A/AS
Film and TV Studies and Sociology	LW35	3FT deg	Me/T g	CD	MO	M	24	Ind	Ind	
French and Gender and Women's Studies	RM19	3FT deg	F g	CD	Ind	Ind	24	BBCC	Ind	
French and Leisure Studies	RL1H	3FT deg	F g	CD	Ind	Ind	24	BBCC	Ind	
French and Sociology	LR31	3FT deg	F g	CD	Ind	Ind	24	Ind	Ind	
French and Urban and Cultural Studies	RL13	3FT deg	F g	CD	Ind	Ind	24	BBCC	Ind	
Gender & Women's St & Organisations, Mgt & Work	MN97	3FT deg	* g	CD	MO	M*	24	BBCC	Ind	
Gender & Women's Studies & Urban & Cultural St	ML9J	3FT deg	* g	CD	MO	M*	24	BBCC	Ind	
Gender & Women's Studies and History	MV9D	3FT deg	* g	CD	MO	M*	24	BBCC	Ind	
Gender & Women's Studies and Literature	MQ92	3FT deg	* g	CD	10-12M	M*	24	BBCC	Ind	
Gender & Women's Studies and Peace & War Studies	MVXC	3FT deg	* g	CD	MO	M*	24	BBCC	Ind	
Gender & Women's Studies and Philosophy	MV9R	3FT deg	* g	CD	MO	M*	24	BBCC	Ind	
Gender & Women's Studies and Psychology	ML97	3FT deg	* g	12	MO	D*	24	BBCC	Ind	
Gender & Women's Studies and Sociology	LW3Y	3FT deg	* g	CD	MO	M	24	Ind	Ind	
Gender & Women's Studies and Theatre Studies	WM49	3FT deg	Me/T g	CD	Ind	Ind	24	BBCC	Ind	
Gender & Women's Studies and Tourism Studies	MP97	3FT deg	* g	CD	MO	M*	24	BBCC	Ind	
Gender and Women's Studies and Film and TV Studs	MW95	3FT deg	Me/T g	CD	Ind	Ind	24	BBCC	Ind	
Gender and Women's Studies and German	RM29	3FT deg	G g	CD	Ind	Ind	24	BBCC	Ind	
Gender and Women's Studies and Law	MM39	3FT deg	* g	CD	MO	M*	24	BBCC	Ind	
Gender and Women's Studies and Leisure Studies	ML9H	3FT deg	* g	CD	MO	M*	24	BBCC	Ind	
Gender and Women's Studies and Marketing	MN95	3FT deg	* g	CD	MO	M*	24	BBCC	Ind	
Gender and Women's Studies and Mathematics	MG91	3FT deg	M g	CD	Ind	Ind	24	BBCC	Ind	
Gender and Women's Studies and Operations Mgt	MN92	3FT deg	* g	CD	MO	M*	24	BBCC	Ind	
Gender and Women's Studs and Human Resource Mgt	MN91	3FT deg	* g	CD	MO	M*	24	BBCC	Ind	
German and Leisure Studies	RL2H	3FT deg	G g	CD	Ind	Ind	24	BBCC	Ind	
German and Sociology	LR32	3FT deg	G g	CD	Ind	Ind	24	Ind	Ind	
German and Urban and Cultural Studies	RL23	3FT deg	G g	CD	Ind	Ind	24	BBCC	Ind	
History and Leisure Studies	LV31	3FT deg	* g	CD	MO	M*	24	BBCC	Ind	
History and Sociology	LV3D	3FT deg	* g	CD	MO	M	24	Ind	Ind	
History and Urban & Cultural Studies	VL13	3FT deg	* g	CD	MO	M*	24	BBCC	Ind	
Human Resource Management and Leisure Studies	LNH1	3FT deg	* g	CD	MO	M*	24	BBCC	Ind	
Human Resource Management and Sociology	LN3D	3FT deg	* g	CD	MO	M	24	Ind	Ind	
Human Resource Mgt and Urban and Cultural Studs	LN31	3FT deg	* g	CD	MO	M*	24	BBCC	Ind	
Law and Sociology	LM3H	3FT deg	* g	CD	MO	M	24	Ind	Ind	
Law and Urban and Cultural Studies	LM33	3FT deg	* g	CD	MO	M*	24	BBCC	Ind	
Leisure Studies and Film & TV Studies	LWH5	3FT deg	Me/T g	CD	Ind	Ind	24	BBCC	Ind	
Leisure Studies and Literature	LQ31	3FT deg	* g	CD	MO	M*	24	BBCC	Ind	
Leisure Studies and Marketing	LNH5	3FT deg	* g	CD	MO	M*	24	BBCC	Ind	
Leisure Studies and Mathematics	GL13	3FT deg	M g	CD	Ind	Ind	24	BBCC	Ind	
Leisure Studies and Operations Management	LN32	3FT deg	* g	CD	MO	M*	24	BBCC	Ind	
Leisure Studies and Organisations, Mgt & Work	LN37	3FT deg	* g	CD	MO	M*	24	BBCC	Ind	
Leisure Studies and Peace & War Studies	LV3C	3FT deg	* g	CD	MO	M*	24	BBCC	Ind	
Leisure Studies and Philosophy	LV37	3FT deg	* g	CD	MO	M*	24	BBCC	Ind	
Leisure Studies and Psychology	LL7H	3FT deg	* g	12	MO	D*	24	BBCC	Ind	
Leisure Studies and Sociology	L381	3FT deg	* g	CD	MO	M	24	Ind	Ind	
Leisure Studies and Statistics	GL4H	3FT deg	* g	CD	MO	M	24	Ind	Ind	
Leisure Studies and Theatre Studies	WL4H	3FT deg	Me/T g	CD	Ind	Ind	24	BBCC	Ind	
Leisure Studies and Tourism Studies	PL7H	3FT deg	* g	CD	MO	M*	24	BBCC	Ind	
Leisure Studies and Urban and Cultural Studies	L380	3FT deg	* g	CD	MO	M*	24	BBCC	Ind	
Literature and Sociology	LQ32	3FT deg	* g	CD	MO	M	24	Ind	Ind	
Literature and Urban & Cultural Studies	QL23	3FT deg	* g	CD	MO	M*	24	BBCC	Ind	
Marketing and Sociology	LN3M	3FT deg	* g	CD	MO	M	24	Ind	Ind	
Marketing and Urban & Cultural Studies	LN35	3FT deg	* g	CD	MO	M*	24	BBCC	Ind	

TITLE	CODE	COURSE	SUBJECTS	A/AS	NO/C	AGNVQ	IB	SQA(H)	SQA	RATIO A/AS
course details			98 expected requirements							96 entry stats
Mathematics and Sociology	GL1H	3FT deg	M g	CD	MO	Ind	24	Ind	Ind	
Operations Management & Sociology	LN3G	3FT deg	* g	CD	MO	M	24	Ind	Ind	
Operations Management and Urban and Cultural St	LN3F	3FT deg	* g	CD	Ind	Ind	24	BBCC	Ind	
Organisations, Management & Work and Sociology	LN3T	3FT deg	* g	CD	MO	M	24	Ind	Ind	
Organisations, Mgt & Work and Urban & Culture St	LN3R	3FT deg	* g	CD	MO	M*	24	BBCC	Ind	
Peace & War Studies and Sociology	VL1H	3FT deg	* g	CD	MO	M	24	Ind	Ind	
Peace & War Studies and Urban & Cultural Studies	VLC3	3FT deg	* g	CD	MO	M*	24	BBCC	Ind	
Philosophy and Sociology	LV3R	3FT deg	* g	CD	MO	M	24	Ind	Ind	
Philosophy and Urban and Cultural Studies	VL73	3FT deg	* g	CD	MO	M*	24	BBCC	Ind	
Psychology and Sociology	LL3R	3FT deg	* g	12	MO	M	24	Ind	Ind	
Psychology and Urban and Cultural Studies	LL37	3FT deg	* g	12	MO	D*	24	BBCC	Ind	
Sociology and Theatre Studies	LV3L	3FT deg	Me/T g	CD	MO	M	24	Ind	Ind	
Sociology and Tourism Studies	LP3R	3FT deg	* g	CD	MO	M	24	Ind	Ind	
Sociology and Urban & Cultural Studies	L342	3FT deg	* g	CD	MO	M	24	Ind	Ind	
Theatre Studies and Urban & Cultural Studies	WL43	3FT deg	Me/T g	CD	Ind	Ind	24	BBCC	Ind	
Tourism Studies and Urban and Cultural Studies	LP37	3FT deg	* g	CD	MO	M*	24	BBCC	Ind	
Visual Arts and Gender & Women's Studies	MW91	3FT deg	* g	CD	MO	M*	24	BBCC	Ind	
Visual Arts and Gender & Women's Studies	MW9X	3FT deg	* g	CD	MO	M*	24	BBCC	Ind	
Visual Arts and Leisure Studies	LW31	3FT deg	* g	CD	MO	M*	24	BBCC	Ind	

Univ of BRADFORD

TITLE	CODE	COURSE	SUBJECTS	A/AS	NO/C	AGNVQ	IB	SQA(H)	SQA	RATIO A/AS
Conflict Resolution	M931	3FT deg	*	BBB	6D	D*^	Ind	Ind	Ind	3
Defence and Security Studies	M932	3FT deg	*	BBB	D6	D*^	Ind	Ind	Ind	15
Development Studies	M920	3FT deg	*	BBB	6D	D*^	Ind	Ind	Ind	6
Economics/Sociology	LL13	3FT deg	*	BB-CCC	Ind	M*4	Ind	Ind	Ind	
Peace Studies	M930	3FT deg	*	BBB	6D	D*^	Ind	Ind	Ind	2 6/22
Politics and Society	ML13	3FT deg	*	BBB	6D	D*^	Ind	Ind	Ind	3 18/24
Sociology	L300	3FT deg	* g	BB-CCC	4M+3D	D*^	Ind	Ind	Ind	7 14/20
Sociology/Social Psychology	LL37	3FT deg	*	BB-CCC	Ind	M*4	Ind	Ind	Ind	3 8/20
Women's Studies and Social Policy	LM49	3FT deg	*	CCC	Ind	M$4	Ind	Ind	Ind	3 6/14
Interdisciplinary Human Studies Sociology	Y402	3FT deg	* g	BB-CCC	4M+3D	D*^	Ind	Ind	Ind	

BRADFORD & ILKLEY Comm COLL

TITLE	CODE	COURSE	SUBJECTS	A/AS	NO/C	AGNVQ	IB	SQA(H)	SQA	RATIO A/AS
Leisure, Recreation & Community	L350	3FT deg	*	8	MO	M	Dip	CCC	Ind	
Women's Studies and Community Studies	LM59	3FT deg	*	8	MO	M	Dip	CCC	Ind	

BRETTON HALL

TITLE	CODE	COURSE	SUBJECTS	A/AS	NO/C	AGNVQ	IB	SQA(H)	SQA	RATIO A/AS
Child and Family Studies	LX39	3FT deg								4/16
Culture and Society	M900	3FT deg	So	CD-CC	MO		Ind	CCC	Ind	3 8/16

Univ of BRIGHTON

TITLE	CODE	COURSE	SUBJECTS	A/AS	NO/C	AGNVQ	IB	SQA(H)	SQA	RATIO A/AS
Cultural and Historical Studies	LV61	3FT deg	*	CC	Ind	Ind	Ind	Ind	Ind	

Univ of BRISTOL

TITLE	CODE	COURSE	SUBJECTS	A/AS	NO/C	AGNVQ	IB	SQA(H)	SQA	RATIO A/AS
Economics and Sociology	LL13	3FT deg	* g	ABC	Ind	D$^	32$	CSYS	Ind	12
Politics and Sociology	ML13	3FT deg	* g	ABC	Ind	D$^	32$	ABBBB	Ind	11 28/30
Social Policy and Sociology	LL43	3FT deg	* g	BBC	Ind	D$^	26$	CSYS	Ind	8 20/28
Sociology	L300	3FT deg	* g	BCC	Ind	D$^	26$	BBBBC	Ind	9 20/30
Sociology and Philosophy	LV37	3FT deg	* g	ABB-BBC	Ind	D$^	30$	BBBBB	Ind	8
Sociology with Study in Continental Europe	L301	4FT deg	L g	BCC	Ind	D$^	26$	BBBBC	Ind	6
Theology and Sociology	VL83	3FT deg	* g	BBC	Ind	D$^	30$	BBBBB	Ind	12

BRISTOL, Univ of the W of England

TITLE	CODE	COURSE	SUBJECTS	A/AS	NO/C	AGNVQ	IB	SQA(H)	SQA	RATIO A/AS
Cultural & Media Studies	L6P3	3FT deg	* g	BBC	3M+3D	M$^ go	30	ABBB	Ind	
Cultural & Media Studies and History	LV61	3FT deg	* g	CCC	2D+4M	M$^ go	26	BBBC	Ind	

course details			98 expected requirements							96 entry stats	
TITLE	CODE	COURSE	SUBJECTS	A/AS	ND/C	AGNVQ	IB	SQA(H)	SQA	RATIO A/AS	
Drama and Cultural & Media Studies	WL46	3FT deg	Ap g	BBC	3M+3D	M$^ go	30	ABBB	Ind		
Information Systems and Social Science	G5L3	3FT deg	* g	14-16	5M-6M	M* go	24	BCCC	Ind		
Science, Society and the Media	F9P4	3FT deg	* g	12	4M	M* go	24	BCC	Ind		
Social Sciences	L340▼	3FT deg	* g	14-16	5M-6M	M* go	24	BCCC	Ind		
Sociology	L300▼	3FT deg	* g	14-16	5M-6M	M* go	24	BCCC	Ind		
Joint Honours Programme *Psychology and Sociology*	Y401	3FT deg	* g	14-16	5M	M$ go	24	BCCC	Ind		
Joint Honours Programme *Sociology and Linguistics*	Y401	3FT deg	* g	14-16	5M	M$ go	24	BCCC	Ind		
Science Foundation Year *Science, Society and the Media*	Y120	4EXT deg	M/S g	E	N	PS go	24$	Ind	N $		

BRUNEL Univ, West London

History and Anthropology	LV61	3FT deg									
History and Sociology	LV31	3FT deg	* g	BCC	5M	D^ go	28$	BBBCC	Ind		
Politics and Sociology	LM3C	3FT deg	*	BCC	5M	D^ go	28	BBBCC	Ind		
Politics and Sociology (4 Yrs Thin SW)	LM31	4SW deg	*	BCC	5M	D^ go	28	BBBCC	Ind	4	
Psychology and Social Anthropol (4 Yrs Thin SW)	CL86	4SW deg	* g	BBB-BCC	3M+2D	M*^ go	28$	BBBCC	Ind	8	
Psychology and Sociology (4 Yrs Thin SW)	CL83	4SW deg	* g	BBB-BCC	3M+2D	M*^ go	28$	BBBCC	Ind	13	20/24
Soc Anthrop and Communications (4 Yrs Thin SW)	LP63	4SW deg	* g	BCC	5M	D^ go	28	BBBCC	Ind	9	
Social Anthropology and Sociology(4 Yrs Thin SW)	LL36	4SW deg	* g	BCC	5M	D^ go	28	BBBCC	Ind	8	10/18
Sociology (4 Yrs Thin SW)	L300	4SW deg	* g	BCC	5M	D^ go	28	BBBCC	Ind	8	18/20
Sociology and Communication (4 Yrs Thin SW)	LP33	4SW deg	* g	BCC	5M	D^ go	28	BBBCC	Ind	9	12/14

BUCKINGHAMSHIRE COLLEGE

Social Work Studies with Gender Studies	L5M9	3FT deg									
Sociology	L300	3FT deg		10	2D	M	27	CCCC	Ind	5	4/17
Sociology and Criminology	LM33	3FT deg		12	2D	M	27	CCCC	Ind	5	6/16
Sociology and Psychology	LL37	3FT deg		12	2D	M	27	CCCC	Ind	3	8/18
Sociology with Gender Studies	L3M9	3FT deg		10-12	2D	M	27	CCCC	Ind		
Sociology with Social Policy	L3L4	3FT deg		12	2D	M	27	CCCC	Ind		

CAMBRIDGE Univ

Archaeology and Anthropology	LV66▼	3FT deg	* g	AAB	Ind		Ind	CSYS	Ind	2	28/30
Social and Political Sciences	LM31▼	3FT deg	* g	AAA-AAB	Ind		Ind	CSYS	Ind	4	28/30

CANTERBURY CHRIST CHURCH COLL of HE

American Studies with Social Science	Q4L3	4FT deg	* g	CC	MO	M	24	Ind	Ind	2	8/14
Applied Social Sciences	L310	3FT deg	* g	CC	MO	M	24	Ind	Ind	51	
Art and Social Science	LW31	3FT deg	A g	CC	MO	M	24	Ind	Ind	4	
Art with Social Science	W1L3	3FT deg	A g	CC	MO	M	24	Ind	Ind	2	
Business Studies and Social Science	NL13	3FT deg	* g	CC	MO	M	24	Ind	Ind	4	
Business Studies with Social Science	N1L3	3FT deg	* g	CC	MO	M	24	Ind	Ind	3	
Early Childhood Studies and Social Science	LX39	3FT deg	* g	CC	MO	M	24	Ind	Ind	1	
Early Childhood Studies with Social Sciences	X9L3	3FT deg	* g	CC	MO	M	24	Ind	Ind	1	10/18
English and Social Science	LQ33	3FT deg	E	CC	MO	M	24	Ind	Ind	7	
English with Social Science	Q3L3	3FT deg	E	CC	MO	M	24	Ind	Ind	2	6/24
French and Social Science	LR31	3FT deg	F g	CC	MO	M	24	Ind	Ind		
Geography and Social Science	LL83	3FT deg	G g	CC	MO	M	24	Ind	Ind	1	
Geography with Social Science	L8L3	3FT deg	G g	CC	MO	M	24	Ind	Ind	2	
History and Social Science	LV31	3FT deg	H g	CC	MO	M	24	Ind	Ind	5	
History with Social Science	V1L3	3FT deg	H g	CC	MO	M	24	Ind	Ind	3	10/14
Information Technology and Social Science	GL53	3FT deg	* g	CC	MO	M	24	Ind	Ind		
Information Technology with Social Science	G5L3	3FT deg	* g	CC	MO	M	24	Ind	Ind		
Marketing and Social Science	NL53	3FT deg	* g	CC	MO	M	24	Ind	Ind	1	

course details

98 expected requirements

96 entry stats

TITLE	CODE	COURSE	SUBJECTS	A/AS	ND/C	AGNVQ	IB	SQA(H)	SQA	RATIO	A/AS
Marketing with Social Science	N5L3	3FT deg	* g	CC	MO	M	24	Ind	Ind		6/18
Mathematics and Social Science	GL13	3FT deg	M g	DD	Ind	Ind	24	Ind	Ind		
Mathematics with Social Science	G1L3	3FT deg	M g	DD	Ind	Ind	24	Ind	Ind	2	
Media Studies and Social Science	LP34	3FT deg	* g	CC	MO	M	24	Ind	Ind		
Media Studies with Social Science	P4L3	3FT deg	* g	CC	MO	M	24	Ind	Ind		
Music and Social Science	LW33	3FT deg	Mu g	CC	MO	M	24	Ind	Ind	1	
Music with Social Science	W3L3	3FT deg	Mu g	CC	MO	M	24	Ind	Ind	1	14/26
Psychology and Social Science	LL37	3FT deg	Ps g	CC	MO	M	24	Ind	Ind	7	
Psychology with Social Science	L7L3	3FT deg	Ps g	CC	MO	M	24	Ind	Ind	4	
Radio, Film and Television St and Social Science	WL53	3FT deg	* g	CC	MO	M	24	Ind	Ind	2	
Radio, Film and Television Studs with Social St	W5L3	3FT deg	* g	CC	MO	M	24	Ind	Ind	3	
Religious Studies and Social Science	VL83	3FT deg	* g	CC	MO	M	24	Ind	Ind	1	6/8
Religious Studies with Social Science	V8L3	3FT deg	* g	CC	MO	M	24	Ind	Ind	4	
Science and Social Science	LY31	3FT deg	S g	DD	Ind	Ind	24	Ind	Ind	2	
Science with Social Science	Y1L3	3FT deg	S g	DD	Ind	Ind	24	Ind	Ind		
Social Science and American Studies	QL43	3FT deg	* g	CC	MO	M	24	Ind	Ind	1	
Social Science with American Studies	L3Q4	3FT deg	* g	CC	MO	M	24	Ind	Ind	5	
Social Science with Art	L3W1	3FT deg	A g	CC	MO	M	24	Ind	Ind	2	
Social Science with Business Studies	L3N1	3FT deg	* g	CC	MO	M	24	Ind	Ind	7	
Social Science with Early Childhood Studies	L3X9	3FT deg	* g	CC	MO	M	24	Ind	Ind	1	
Social Science with English	L3Q3	3FT deg	E g	CC	MO	M	24	Ind	Ind	2	10/20
Social Science with French	L3R1	3FT deg	F g	CC	MO	M	24	Ind	Ind		
Social Science with Geography	L3L8	3FT deg	Gy g	CC	MO	M	24	Ind	Ind	1	
Social Science with History	L3V1	3FT deg	H g	CC	MO	M	24	Ind	Ind	6	
Social Science with Information Technology	L3G5	3FT deg	* g	CC	MO	M	24	Ind	Ind	1	
Social Science with Marketing	L3N5	3FT deg	* g	CC	MO	M	24	Ind	Ind		
Social Science with Mathematics	L3G1	3FT deg	M g	DD	Ind	Ind	24	Ind	Ind		
Social Science with Media Studies	L3P4	3FT deg	* g	CC	MO	M	24	Ind	Ind		
Social Science with Music	L3W3	3FT deg	Mu g	CC	MO	M	24	Ind	Ind		
Social Science with Psychology	L3L7	3FT deg	Ps g	CC	MO	M	24	Ind	Ind	5	10/13
Social Science with Radio Film and Television St	L3W5	3FT deg	* g	CC	MO	M	24	Ind	Ind		
Social Science with Religious Studies	L3V8	3FT deg	* g	CC	MO	M	24	Ind	Ind	3	
Social Science with Sport Science	L3B6	3FT deg	* g	CC	MO	M	24	Ind	Ind		
Social Science with Statistics	L3G4	3FT deg	M g	DD	Ind	Ind	24	Ind	Ind		
Social Science with Tourism Studies	L3P7	3FT deg	* g	CC	MO	M	24	Ind	Ind	4	
Sport Science and Social Science	BL63	3FT deg	* g	CC	MO	M	24	Ind	Ind		
Sport Science with Social Science	B6L3	3FT deg	* g	CC	MO	M	24	Ind	Ind		
Statistics and Social Science	GL43	3FT deg	M g	DD	Ind	Ind	24	Ind	Ind		
Statistics with Social Science	G4L3	3FT deg	M g	DD	Ind	Ind	24	Ind	Ind		
Tourism Studies and Social Science	LP37	3FT deg	* g	CC	MO	M	24	Ind	Ind		
Tourism Studies with Social Science	P7L3	3FT deg	* g	CC	MO	M	24	Ind	Ind	2	

CARDIFF Univ of Wales

TITLE	CODE	COURSE	SUBJECTS	A/AS	ND/C	AGNVQ	IB	SQA(H)	SQA	RATIO	A/AS
Cultural Criticism/Ancient History	MV91	3FT deg	E	ABC	Ind	Ind	Ind	Ind	Ind		
Cultural Criticism/Archaeology	MV96	3FT deg	E	ABC	X		Ind	AAABB	X		
English Literature/Cultural Criticism	MQ9H	3FT deg	E	ABB	X		Ind	AAABB	X		18/24
French/Cultural Criticism	MR91	4FT deg	E	ABC	Ind	Ind	Ind	Ind	Ind		
German/Cultural Criticism	MR92	4FT deg	E	ABC	Ind	Ind	Ind	Ind	Ind		
History of Ideas/Cultural Criticism	MV9D	3FT deg	E	ABC	X		Ind	AAABB	X		
Italian/Cultural Criticism	MR93	4FT deg	E	ABC	Ind	Ind	Ind	Ind	Ind		
Language Studies/Cultural Criticism	MQ91	3FT deg	E	ABC	X		Ind	AAABB	X		
Law and Sociology	ML33	3FT deg	*	BBB	Ind	Ind	Ind	Ind	Ind	8	20/30
Music/Cultural Criticism	MW93	3FT deg	Mu+E	ABC	X		Ind	AAABB	X		

Letts STUDY GUIDES
THE INDEPENDENT

			98 expected requirements							96 entry stats

course details / *98 expected requirements* / *96 entry stats*

TITLE	CODE	COURSE	SUBJECTS	A/AS	ND/C	AGNVQ	IB	SQA(H)	SQA	RATIO A/AS
Philosophy/Cultural Criticism	MV97	3FT deg	E	ABC	X		Ind	AAABB	X	
Politics and Sociology	LM31	3FT deg	*	BCC						10
Portuguese/Cultural Criticism	MR95	4FT deg	E	ABC	Ind	Ind	Ind	Ind	Ind	
Religious Studies/Cultural Criticism	MV98	3FT deg	E	ABC	Ind	Ind	Ind	Ind	Ind	
Sociology	L300	3FT deg	*	CCC	Ind	Ind	Ind	Ind	Ind	4 14/24
Sociology and Economics	LL13	3FT deg	*	BBC-BBB	7M+7D		Ind	AAAB	Ind	9
Sociology and Education	LX39	3FT deg	*	BCC	3M+2D	Ind	Ind	Ind	Ind	5 16/20
Sociology and Industrial Relations	LN36	3FT deg	*	BBC-BBB	7M+7D		Ind	AABBB	Ind	7
Sociology and Psychology	LL37	3FT deg	*	BBB	MO+6D$		Ind	AABBB	N	63
Sociology and Social Policy	LL34	3FT deg	*	CCC	Ind	Ind	Ind	Ind	Ind	8 12/20
Sociology/Ancient History	LV3C	3FT deg	*	BCC	3M+2D		Ind	Ind		
Sociology/Archaeology	LV36	3FT deg	*	BCC	3M+2D		Ind	Ind	X	
Sociology/Cultural Criticism	ML93	3FT deg	E	ABC	X		Ind	AAABB	X	7
Sociology/French	LR31	4FT deg	F	BBC	Ind		Ind	ABBBB	Ind	12
Sociology/German	LR32	4FT deg	G	BCC	3M+2D		Ind	Ind	X	
Sociology/History	LV31	3FT deg	H	BBC-BCC	X		Ind	ABBBB	X	12
Sociology/History of Ideas	LV3D	3FT deg	*	BCC			Ind			
Sociology/Italian	LR33	4FT deg	L	BCC	Ind		Ind	Ind	Ind	3
Sociology/Journalism, Film and Broadcasting	LP33	3FT deg	*	BBC	Ind	Ind	30	ABBBB	Ind	
Sociology/Music	LW33	3FT deg	Mu	BBC						
Sociology/Philosophy	LVH7	3FT deg	*	BCC						12
Sociology/Portuguese	LR35	4FT deg	L	BBC-BCC						
Sociology/Religious Studies	LV38	3FT deg	*	BCC	3M+2D					13
Sociology/Social Philosophy and Applied Ethics	LV37	3FT deg	*	BCC	3M+2D		Ind			2
Spanish/Cultural Criticism	MR94	4FT deg	E	ABC	Ind	Ind	Ind	Ind	Ind	
Spanish/Sociology	LR34	4FT deg	L	BBC-BCC	3M+2D		Ind	Ind	Ind	
Welsh History/Cultural Criticism	MV9C	3FT deg	E	ABC	Ind	Ind	Ind	Ind	Ind	
Welsh History/Sociology	VLC3	3FT deg	H	BBC-BCC	X		Ind	ABBBB	X	
Welsh/Cultural Criticism	MQ95	3FT deg	E	ABC	X		Ind	AAABB	X	
Welsh/Sociology	QL53	3FT deg	W	BCC						3

Univ of CENTRAL ENGLAND

Sociology	L300	3FT deg	* g	CC	4M	M$	Ind	CCCCC	Ind	5 10/16

Univ of CENTRAL LANCASHIRE

Social Work and Welfare Studies	LL35	3FT deg	*	12	MO+2D$	M$6/^	26$	BBCC	$	
Social Work, Health and Welfare Studies (Year 0)	LL3M	1FT deg	*							
Sociology	L300	3FT deg	*	16	MO+5D	D$6/^	28$	BBCC	Ind	
Women's Studies	M903	3FT deg	*	12	Ind	M$6/^	26	BCCC	Ind	
Combined Honours Programme Race & Ethnic Studies	Y400	3FT deg	*	12	MO+2D	M$6/^	26	BCCC	Ind	
Combined Honours Programme Sociology	Y400	3FT deg	*	16	MO+4D	D$6/^	28	BBBC	Ind	
Combined Honours Programme Womens Studies	Y400	3FT deg	*	12	MO+2D	M$6/^	26	BCCC	Ind	
Health, Childhood and Social Studies	43LL▼	2FT HND	* g	E	PO+2M	P$	24$	CCC	Ind	

CHELTENHAM & GLOUCESTER COLL of HE

Business Computer Systems and Women's Studies	GM5X	3FT deg	*	8-12	MO	M	24	CCCC	Ind	
Business Computer Systems with Women's Studies	G5MX	3FT deg	*	8-12	MO	M	24	CCCC	Ind	
Business Management and Sociological Studies	NL13	3FT deg	*	12-16	4M+3D	MB3	26	CCCC	Ind	
Business Management and Women's Studies	NM19	3FT deg	*	12	5M+2D	MB3	26	CCCC	Ind	
Business Management with Sociological Studies	N1L3	4SW deg	*	12-16	4M+3D	MB3	26	CCCC	Ind	
Business Management with Women's Studies	N1M9	4SW deg	*	12	4M+3D	MB3	26	CCCC	Ind	
Computing and Women's Studies	GM5Y	3FT deg	*	8-12	MO	M	24	CCCC	Ind	

Sociology and Anthropology 64

course details

TITLE	CODE	COURSE	SUBJECTS	A/AS	ND/C	AGNVQ	IB	SQA(H)	SQA	RATIO A/AS
Computing with Women's Studies	G5MY	3FT deg	*	8-12	MO	M	24	CCCC	Ind	
English Studies and Sociological Studies	LQ33	3FT deg	E	12-16	4M+3D	M^	26	CCCC	Ind	
English Studies and Women's Studies	MQ93	3FT deg	E	12	5M+2D	M^	26	CCCC	Ind	
English Studies with Sociological Studies	Q3L3	3FT deg	E	12-16	4M+3D	M^	26	CCCC	Ind	
English Studies with Women's Studies	Q3M9	3FT deg	E	12-14	4M+3D	M^	26	CCCC	Ind	
Environmental Policy and Sociological Studies	FL93	3FT deg	*	10-14	5M+2D	M3	26	CCCC	Ind	
Environmental Policy with Sociological Studies	F9L3	3FT deg	*	12-16	5M+2D	M3	26	CCCC	Ind	
Fashion and Women's Studies	WM29	3FT deg	*	10-14	MO	M3	26	CCCC	Ind	
Fashion with Women's Studies	W2M9	3FT deg	*	10-14	MO	M3	26	CCCC	Ind	
Financial Management and Sociological Studies	NL33	3FT deg	*	10-14	5M+2D	M3	26	CCCC	Ind	
Financial Management and Women's Studies	MN93	3FT deg	*	8-12	5M+2D	M3	26	CCCC	Ind	
Financial Management with Sociological Studies	N3L3	4SW deg	*	10-14	5M+2D	M3	26	CCCC	Ind	
Financial Management with Women's Studies	N3M9	4SW deg	*	10	5M+2D	M3	26	CCCC	Ind	
Geography and Sociological Studies	LLH8	3FT deg	*	12	MO	M3^	26	CCCC	Ind	
Geography and Women's Studies	LM8X	3FT deg	*	12	MO	M3^	26	CCCC	Ind	
Geography with Sociological Studies	L8LH	3FT deg	*	12	MO	M3^	26	CCCC	Ind	
Geography with Women's Studies	L8MX	3FT deg	*	12	MO	M3^	26	CCCC	Ind	
History and Sociological Studies	LV31	3FT deg	H	12-16	4M+3D	M3^	26	CCCC	Ind	
History and Women's Studies	MV91	3FT deg	H	12	5M+2D	M3^	26	CCCC	Ind	
History with Sociological Studies	V1L3	3FT deg	H	10-14	4M+3D	M3^	26	CCCC	Ind	
History with Women's Studies	V1M9	3FT deg	H	12	4M+3D	M3^	26	CCCC	Ind	
Human Geography and Sociological Studies	LL38	3FT deg	*	12-16	4M+3D	M3	26	CCCC	Ind	
Human Geography and Women's Studies	LM89	3FT deg	*	12	5M+2D	M3	26	CCCC	Ind	
Human Geography with Sociological Studies	L8L3	3FT deg	*	12	4M+3D	M3	26	CCCC	Ind	
Human Geography with Women's Studies	L8M9	3FT deg	*	10-14	4M+3D	M3	26	CCCC	Ind	
Human Resource Management and Sociological Studs	NLC3	3FT deg	*	12	5M+2D	MB3	26	CCCC	Ind	
Human Resource Management and Women's Studies	MN91	3FT deg	*	8-12	MO	MB3	26	CCCC	Ind	
Human Resource Mgt with Sociological Studies	N1LH	4SW deg	*	12	5M+2D	MB3	26	CCCC	Ind	
Human Resource Mgt with Women's Studies	N1MX	4SW deg	*	10	5M+2D	MB3	26	CCCC	Ind	
Information Technology and Women's Studies	GM59	3FT/4SW deg	*	8	MO	M	24	CCCC	Ind	
Information Technology with Women's Studies	G5M9	3FT deg	*	8-12	MO	M3	24	CCCC	Ind	
Marketing Management and Sociological Studies	NL53	3FT deg	*	12	5M+2D	MB3	26	CCCC	Ind	
Marketing Management and Women's Studies	MN95	3FT deg	*	8-12	MO	MB3	26	CCCC	Ind	
Marketing Management with Sociological Studies	N5L3	4SW deg	*	12	5M+2D	MB3	26	CCCC	Ind	
Marketing Management with Women's Studies	N5M9	4SW deg	*	8-12	MO	MB3	26	CCCC	Ind	
Media Communications and Women's Studies	MP94	3FT deg	*	10-14	5M+2D	MP3	26	CCCC	Ind	
Media Communications with Women's Studies	P4M9	3FT deg	*	12	4M+3D	MP3	26	CCCC	Ind	
Multimedia and Sociological Studies	GL53	3FT deg	*	12	5M+2D	MI3	26	CCCC	Ind	
Multimedia and Women's Studies	GMM9	3FT deg	*	8-12	MO	MI3	26	CCCC	Ind	
Multimedia with Sociological Studies	G5L3	3FT deg	*	8-12	MO	MI3	26	CCCC	Ind	
Multimedia with Sociological Studies	G5LH	4SW deg	*	8-12	MO	MI3	24	CCCC	Ind	
Multimedia with Women's Studies	GMMY	4SW deg	*	8-12	MO	MI3	24	CCCC	Ind	
Multimedia with Women's Studies	GMMX	3FT deg	*	8-12	MO	MI3	26	CCCC	Ind	
Performance Arts and Women's Studies	WM49	3FT deg	*	8-12	5M+2D	M3	26	CCCC	Ind	
Performance Arts with Women's Studies	W4M9	3FT deg	*	8-12	5M+2D	M3	26	CCCC	Ind	
Physical Geography and Sociological Studies	FL83	3FT deg	*	12	5M+2D	M3^	26	CCCC	Ind	
Physical Geography with Sociological Studies	F8L3	3FT deg	*	12	5M+2D	M3^	26	CCCC	Ind	
Psychology and Sociological Studies	LL37	3FT deg	g	12-16	4M+3D	M3^	26	CCCC	Ind	
Psychology and Women's Studies	LM79	3FT deg	g	12-16	5M+2D	M3^	26	CCCC	Ind	
Psychology with Sociological Studies	L7L3	3FT deg	g	12-16	4M+3D	M3^	26	CCCC	Ind	
Psychology with Women's Studies	L7M9	3FT deg	g	12	4M+3D	M3^	26	CCCC	Ind	
Religious Studies and Sociological Studies	LV38	3FT deg	*	8-12	MO	M3^	26	CCCC	Ind	

course details | 98 expected requirements | 96 entry stats

TITLE	CODE	COURSE	SUBJECTS	A/AS	ND/C	AGNVQ	IB	SQA(H)	SQA	RATIO A/AS
Religious Studies and Women's Studies	MV98	3FT deg	*	8-12	M0	M3^	26	CCCC	Ind	
Religious Studies with Sociological Studies	V8L3	3FT deg	*	8-12	M0	M3^	26	CCCC	Ind	
Religious Studies with Women's Studies	V8M9	3FT deg	*	8-12	M0	M3^	26	CCCC	Ind	
Sociological Studies & Sport & Exercise Sciences	LB36	3FT deg	S	12-16	4M+3D	MG3	26	CCCC	Ind	
Sociological Studies and Women's Studies	LM39	3FT deg	*	12	5M+2D	MG3	26	CCCC	Ind	
Sociological Studies with Business Management	L3N1	3FT deg	*	12	4M+3D	MG3	26	CCCC	Ind	
Sociological Studies with Combined Arts	L3Y3	3FT deg	*	12	M0	M3^	26	CCCC	Ind	
Sociological Studies with English Studies	L3Q3	3FT deg	*	12-16	4M+3D	MG3	26	CCCC	Ind	
Sociological Studies with Environmental Policy	L3F9	3FT deg	*	12	4M+3D	MG3	26	CCCC	Ind	
Sociological Studies with Financial Management	L3N3	3FT deg	*	12	M0	MG3	26	CCCC	Ind	
Sociological Studies with Geography	L3LV	3FT deg	*	12	M0	M3^	26	CCCC	Ind	
Sociological Studies with History	L3V1	3FT deg	*	12-14	4M+3D	MG3	26	CCCC	Ind	
Sociological Studies with Human Geography	L3L8	3FT deg	*	12	4M+3D	MG3	26	CCCC	Ind	
Sociological Studies with Human Resource Mgt	L3NC	3FT deg	*	12	M0	MG3	26	CCCC	Ind	
Sociological Studies with Marketing Management	L3N5	3FT deg	*	12	M0	MG3	26	CCCC	Ind	
Sociological Studies with Multimedia	GLM3	3FT deg	*	12	M0	MG3	26	CCCC	Ind	
Sociological Studies with Physical Geography	L3F8	3FT deg	*	12	4M+3D	MG3	26	CCCC	Ind	
Sociological Studies with Psychology	L3L7	3FT deg	*	12-16	4M+3D	MG3	26	CCCC	Ind	
Sociological Studies with Religious Studies	L3V8	3FT deg	*	12	5M+2D	MG3	26	CCCC	Ind	
Sociological Studies with Sport and Exercise Sci	L3B6	3FT deg	*	12-16	4M+3D	M$3	26	CCCC	Ind	
Sociological Studies with Women's Studies	L3M9	3FT deg	*	12-16	5M+2D	MG3	26	CCCC	Ind	
Sport & Exercise Sciences and Women's Studies	BM69	3FT deg	*	12-16	5M+2D	ML3	26	CCCC	Ind	
Sport & Exercise Sciences with Sociological St	B6L3	3FT deg	S	12-16	4M+3D	ML3	26	CCCC	Ind	
Sport & Exercise Sciences with Women's Studies	B6M9	3FT deg	*	12-16	4M+3D	ML3	26	CCCC	Ind	
Tourism Management and Women's Studies	PM79	3FT deg	*	12-16	5M+2D	ML3	26	CCCC	Ind	
Tourism Management with Women's Studies	P7M9	4SW deg	*	12	M0	ML3	26	CCCC	Ind	
Visual Arts and Women's Studies	WM19	3FT deg	A	8-12	5M+2D	MA3	26	CCCC	Ind	
Visual Arts with Women's Studies	W1M9	3FT deg	A	10-12	5M+2D	MA3	26	CCCC	Ind	
Women's Studies with Business Computer Systems	M9GM	3FT deg	*	8-12	M0	M3	26	CCCC	Ind	
Women's Studies with Business Management	M9N1	3FT deg	*	12	M0	M3	26	CCCC	Ind	
Women's Studies with Combined Arts	M9Y3	3FT deg	*	8-12	M0	M3^	26	CCCC	Ind	
Women's Studies with Computing	M9GN	3FT deg	*	8-12	M0	M3	26	CCCC	Ind	
Women's Studies with English Studies	M9Q3	3FT deg	*	8-14	M0	M3	26	CCCC	Ind	
Women's Studies with Fashion	M9W2	3SW deg	*	8-12	M0	M3	26	CCCC	Ind	
Women's Studies with Financial Management	M9N3	3FT deg	*	8-12	M0	M3	26	CCCC	Ind	
Women's Studies with Geography	M9LV	3FT deg	*	8-12	M0	M3^	26	CCCC	Ind	
Women's Studies with History	M9V1	3FT deg	*	8-12	M0	M3	26	CCCC	Ind	
Women's Studies with Human Geography	M9L8	3FT deg	*	8-12	M0	M3	26	CCCC	Ind	
Women's Studies with Human Resource Management	M9NC	3FT deg	*	8-12	M0	M3	26	CCCC	Ind	
Women's Studies with Information Technology	M9G5	3FT deg	*	8-12	M0	M3	26	CCCC	Ind	
Women's Studies with Marketing Management	M9N5	3FT deg	*	8-12	M0	M3	26	CCCC	Ind	
Women's Studies with Media Communications	M9P4	3FT deg	*	8-12	M0	M3	26	CCCC	Ind	
Women's Studies with Modern Languages (French)	M9R1	3FT deg	g	8-12	M0	M3	26	CCCC	Ind	
Women's Studies with Multimedia	GMN9	3FT deg	*	8	M0	M3	26	CCCC	Ind	
Women's Studies with Performance Arts	M9W4	3FT deg	*	10-12	5M+2D	M3	26	CCCC	Ind	
Women's Studies with Psychology	M9L7	3FT deg	*	12	M0	M3	26	CCCC	Ind	
Women's Studies with Religious Studies	M9V8	3FT deg	*	8-12	M0	M3	26	CCCC	Ind	
Women's Studies with Sociological Studies	M9L3	3FT deg	*	8-12	M0	M3	26	CCCC	Ind	
Women's Studies with Sport & Exercise Sciences	M9B6	3FT deg	S	8-12	M0	M3	26	CCCC	Ind	
Women's Studies with Tourism Management	M9P7	3FT deg	*	8-12	M0	M3	26	CCCC	Ind	
Women's Studies with Visual Arts	M9W1	3FT deg	*	10-12	5M+2D	M3	26	CCCC	Ind	

Sociology and Anthropology 64

TITLE	CODE	COURSE	SUBJECTS	A/AS	ND/C	AGNVQ	IB	SQA(H)	SQA	RATIO A/AS
UNIVERSITY COLLEGE CHESTER										
Biology with Social Science	C1L3	3FT deg	B g	10	M	P^	Ind	CCCC	$	
Computer Science/IT with Social Science	G5L3	3FT deg	g	10	M	M	Ind	CCCC	$	
Geography with Social Science	F8L3	3FT deg	C g	10	M	P^	Ind	CCCC	$	
Mathematics with Social Science	G1L3	3FT deg	M g	10	M	P^	Ind	CCCC	$	
Physical Education/Sports Science with Soc Sci	B6L3	3FT deg	g	10	M	P^	Ind	CCCC	$	
Psychology with Social Science	L7L3	3FT deg	g	10	M	P^	Ind	CCCC	$	
Combined Subjects (4 Yrs) Franchised	Y400	4FT deg	*		Ind	Ind	Ind	Ind		
Cultural Studies										
CHICHESTER INSTITUTE OF HIGHER EDUCATION										
English Language Teaching (EFL) and Women's St	QM19	3FT deg	E	12	Ind	M_^	Ind	Ind	Ind	
English with Women's Studies	Q3M9	3FT deg	E	12	Ind	M^	Ind	Ind	Ind	2 10/10
Environmental Science and Women's Studies	FM99	3FT deg	*	12	Ind	M$	Ind	Ind	Ind	
History with Women's Studies	V1M9	3FT deg	H	12	Ind	M$	Ind	Ind	Ind	1
Social Studies	L340	3FT deg	*	12	Ind	M$	Ind	Ind	Ind	1 4/8
Study of Religions with Women's Studies	V8M9	3FT deg	Re	12	Ind	M$	Ind	Ind	Ind	
Theology and Women's Studies	VM89	3FT deg	*	12	Ind	M$	Ind	Ind	Ind	
Theology with Women's Studies	V8MX	3FT deg	*	12	Ind	M$	Ind	Ind	Ind	
Women's Studies and English	MQ93	3FT deg	E	12	Ind	M$^	Ind	Ind	Ind	
Women's Studies and History	MV91	3FT deg	H	12	Ind	M$	Ind	Ind	Ind	
Women's Studies and Media Studies	MP94	3FT deg	*	12	Ind	M$	Ind	Ind	Ind	
Women's Studies and Related Arts	MW99	3FT deg	*	12	Ind	M$	Ind	Ind	Ind	
Women's Studies and Study of Religions	MV98	3FT deg	*	12	Ind	M$	Ind	Ind	Ind	
Women's Studies and Theology	MV9V	3FT deg	*	12	Ind	M$	Ind	Ind	Ind	
CITY Univ										
Economics/Sociology	LL13	3FT deg	* g	BCC	3M+4D	D*^	28$	BBBBC	Ind	7
Journalism/Sociology	LP36	3FT/4SW deg	* g	BBC-CCC	Ind	D*_^_	Ind	Ind	Ind	22 18/28
Philosophy/Sociology	LVH7	3FT deg	* g	BCC	3M+4D	D*^	28$	BBBBC	Ind	2
Psychology/Sociology	LC38	3FT deg	* g	BCC	3M+4D	D*^	28$	BBBBC	Ind	17 20/22
Psychology/Systems Science	C8M9	3FT deg	* g	BCC	3M+4D	D*^	28$	BBBBC	Ind	11
Social Sciences	L340	3FT deg	* g	BCC	3M+4D	D*^	28$	BBBBC	Ind	22 16/18
Sociology	L300	3FT deg	* g	BCC	3M+4D	D*^	28$	BBBBC	Ind	7 16/22
Sociology/Economics	LLC3	3FT deg	* g	BCC	3M+4D	D*^	28$	BBBBC	Ind	4
Sociology/Media Studies	PL43	3FT deg	* g	BCC	3M+4D	D*^	28$	BBBBC	Ind	13 16/24
Sociology/Philosophy	LV37	3FT deg	* g	BCC	3M+4D	D*^	28$	BBBBC	Ind	
Sociology/Psychology	LLH7	3FT deg	* g	BCC	3M+4D	D*^	28$	BBBBC	Ind	17
CITY of LIVERPOOL Comm COLL										
Leisure Studies	053L	2FT HND								
COLCHESTER INST										
Communications & Media Studies/Sociology	PL33	3FT deg		CC	Ind	Ind	Ind	Ind	Ind	6
English/Sociology	QL33	3FT deg		CC	Ind	Ind	Ind	Ind	Ind	6
History/Sociology	VL13	3FT deg		CC	Ind	Ind	Ind	Ind	Ind	7
COVENTRY Univ										
Sikh Studies	M915	3FT deg								
Social Policy and Politics	LM31	3FT deg	*	CD	M	M	Ind	CCCC	Ind	
Sociology	L300	3FT deg	* g	CC-CD	3M+3D	M go	Ind	BBB	Ind	1 6/16
Sociology and French	RL13	3FT deg								
Sociology and German	RL23	3FT deg								
Sociology and History	LV31	3FT deg	* g	CC-CD	3M+3D	M go	Ind	BBB	Ind	
Sociology and International Relations	LM3C	3FT deg	* g	CC-CD	3M+3D	M go	Ind	BBB	Ind	

TITLE	CODE	COURSE	SUBJECTS	A/AS	ND/C	AGNVQ	IB	SQA(H)	SQA	RATIO	A/AS
course details			| *98 expected requirements*							| *96 entry stats*	
Sociology and Italian	RL33	3FT deg									
Sociology and Politics	LM3D	3FT deg									
Sociology and Psychology	LL37	3FT deg	* g	CC-CD	3M+3D	M go	Ind	BBB	Ind	2	8/16
Sociology and Russian	RL83	3FT deg									
Sociology and Social Policy	LL34	3FT deg	* g	CC-CD	3M+3D	M go	Ind	BBB	Ind	2	8/12
Spanish and Sociology	RL43	3FT deg									
Third World Development Studies	L8M9	3FT deg	* g	12-14	Ind	M	Ind	Ind	Ind	8	8/16
Women's Studies and Social Science	ML93	3FT deg	* g	CC-CD	3M+3D	M	Ind	BBB	Ind	5	

DE MONTFORT Univ

TITLE	CODE	COURSE	SUBJECTS	A/AS	ND/C	AGNVQ	IB	SQA(H)	SQA	RATIO	A/AS
Economics and Sociology (Modular Scheme)	LL13▼	3FT deg	*	16	DO	D	Ind	Ind	Ind		
Film & Popular Culture	PL43▼	3FT deg	g	12	10M+2D	M	Ind	BCCC	Ind		
Leisure and Recreation Studies	LN37▼	3FT deg	g	12-14	9M+3D	M	Ind	BBCCC	Ind	5	6/18
Politics and Sociology	LM31▼	3FT deg	*	16	DO	D	Ind	Ind	Ind		
Psychology and Sociology	LL37▼	3FT deg	*	16	DO	D	Ind	Ind	Ind	1	
Sociology	L300▼	3FT deg	So g	12	10M+2D	M	Ind	BCCC	Ind	6	6/22
Sports Studies/Science	BL63▼	3FT deg	S g	14	7M+5D	M^	Ind	BBBCC	Ind	6	10/18
Humanities Combined Honours *South Asian Studies*	Y300▼	3FT deg	* g	CCD	MO	M$^	26$	ABBB	Ind		
Humanities Combined Honours *Women's Studies*	Y300▼	3FT deg	* g	CCD	MO	M$^	26$	ABBB	Ind		

Univ of DERBY

TITLE	CODE	COURSE	SUBJECTS	A/AS	ND/C	AGNVQ	IB	SQA(H)	SQA	RATIO	A/AS
Development Studies	M9L3	3FT deg		12	N $	M$	26$	CCCC	Ind		
Social Cultural and Religious Studies	LV38	3FT deg		12	3M+2D	M$	27	CCCC	Ind		
Social and Cultural Studies	L340	3FT deg	So	12	3M+2D	M$	27	CCCC	Ind	5	6/18
Sociology	L300	3FT deg		12	3M+2D	M$	27	CCCC	Ind		7/16
Credit Accumulation Modular Scheme *Applied Studies (Yr 2 entry only)*	Y600	3FT deg		X	X	X	X	X	X		
Credit Accumulation Modular Scheme *Sociology*	Y600	3FT deg	*	12	MO	M	Ind	CCCC	Ind		

DONCASTER COLL

TITLE	CODE	COURSE	SUBJECTS	A/AS	ND/C	AGNVQ	IB	SQA(H)	SQA	RATIO	A/AS
Combined Studies *Social & Employment Studies*	Y300	3FT deg		EE	N	Ind	Ind	Ind	Ind		

Univ of DURHAM

TITLE	CODE	COURSE	SUBJECTS	A/AS	ND/C	AGNVQ	IB	SQA(H)	SQA	RATIO	A/AS
Anthropology	L602	3FT deg	*	BBC	Ind	Ind	32	AABBC	Ind	6	18/28
Anthropology and Archaeology	LF64	3FT deg	*	BBC	MO	Ind	28	AAABB	Ind	10	20/28
Anthropology and Psychology	LC68	3FT deg	* g	ABB-BBB	Ind	Ind	33	AAABB	Ind	27	
Anthropology and Sociology	LL36	3FT deg	*	BBC	Ind	Ind	33	AABCC	Ind	8	
Arabic with Anthropology	T6L6	4FT deg	*	BBC	Ind	Ind	28	Ind	Ind		
Arabic with Mid-East and Islamic Studies	TM69	4FT deg	*	BBC	Ind	Ind	28	Ind	Ind	4	14/24
Arabic with Sociology and Social Policy	T6L3	4FT deg	*	BBC	Ind	Ind	28	Ind	Ind	4	
Economics and Sociology	LL13	3FT deg	* g	ABC	Ind	X	32$	AAABB	Ind		
Human Sciences	L600▼	3FT deg	*	12	Ind	Ind	Dip	CCCCC	Ind	1	
Law and Sociology	LM33	3FT deg	*	ABB	DO	Ind	32	AAABB	HN		
Law with Sociology	M3L3	3FT deg	*	AAB	DO	Ind	32	AAABB	HN		
Politics and Sociology	LM31	3FT deg	*	BBB	Ind	Ind	Ind	Ind	Ind	8	26/30
Psychology and Sociology	LC38	3FT deg	* g	ABB-BBB	Ind	Ind	33	AAABB	Ind	16	
Sociology	L300	3FT deg	*	BCC	Ind	Ind	30	Ind	Ind	5	16/26
Sociology and History	LV31	3FT deg	*	ABC	Ind	Ind	Ind	Ind	Ind		
Sociology and Social Policy	LL34	3FT deg	*	BCC	Ind	Ind	30	Ind	Ind	5	18/22
Sociology with Law	L3M3	3FT deg	*	BCC	Ind	Ind	30	Ind	Ind	11	
Natural Sciences *Anthropology*	Y160	3FT deg	2S	ABB	Ind	X	33	CSYS	X		

TITLE	CODE	COURSE	SUBJECTS	A/AS	NQ/C	RGNVQ	IB	SQA(H)	SQA	RATIO A/AS
Social Sciences Combined *Anthropology*	Y220	3FT deg	*	ABC	MO	Ind	32	AAABB	Ind	
Social Sciences Combined *Sociology*	Y220	3FT deg	*	ABC	MO	Ind	32	AAABB	Ind	

Univ of EAST ANGLIA

TITLE	CODE	COURSE	SUBJECTS	A/AS	NQ/C	RGNVQ	IB	SQA(H)	SQA	RATIO A/AS
Development Studies with a Language	M9T9	3FT deg	*	BBC			Ind	Ind	Ind	
Development Studies(Econ, Politics & Soc Policy)	M921	3FT deg	* g	CCC	3M		Ind	Ind	Ind	3 14/24
Development Studs w def choice of spec (BA/BSc)	M920	3FT deg	* g	CCC	3M		Ind	Ind	Ind	2 14/28
Philosophy and Sociology	VL73	3FT deg	*	BBC	3M+3D		30	BBBBB	Ind	2 14/22
Politics and Sociology	ML13	3FT deg	*	BBC	3M+3D		30	BBBBB	Ind	6
Sociology	L300	3FT deg	*	BBC	3M+3D		30	BBBBB	Ind	4 12/22
Sociology and Economic and Social History	LV33	3FT deg	*	BBC	3M+3D		30	BBBBB	Ind	2
Sociology and Economics	LL31	3FT deg	*	BBC	3M+3D		30	BBBBB	Ind	9
Sociology with a Modern European Language	L3T2	4FT deg	L/*	BBC	3M+3D		30	BBBBB	Ind	12
Anthropology, Archaeology and Art History *Anthropology*	Y400	3FT deg	*	BBC	Ind		Ind	BBBBB	Ind	
Economic and Social Studies (4Yrs) *Social Studies*	Y200	4FT deg	*						Ind	

Univ of EAST LONDON

TITLE	CODE	COURSE	SUBJECTS	A/AS	NQ/C	RGNVQ	IB	SQA(H)	SQA	RATIO A/AS
Anthropology	L602	3FT deg	* g	12	MO	M	Ind	Ind	Ind	2 6/18
Anthropology and Archaeological Sciences	FL46	3FT deg	* g	12	MO	M	Ind	Ind	Ind	2 8/14
Anthropology and Biology	LC61	3FT deg	* g	12	MO	M	Ind	Ind	Ind	
Anthropology and Environmental Sciences	FL96	3FT deg	* g	12	MO	M	Ind			
Anthropology and French	LR61	3FT deg	*	12	MO	M^	Ind			
Anthropology and German	LR62	3FT deg	* g	12	MO	M^				
Anthropology and Linguistics	LQ6C	3FT deg	* g	12	MO	X	Ind	Ind	Ind	4
Anthropology and Psychosocial Studies	LL67	3FT deg	* g	12	MO	MG	Ind	Ind	Ind	8
Anthropology and Social Policy Research	LL64	3FT deg	* g	12	MO	M	Ind	Ind	Ind	
Anthropology and Spanish	LR64	3FT deg	* g	12	MO	M^	Ind	Ind	Ind	
Anthropology and Third World & Development St	MLY6	3FT deg	* g	12	MO	M	Ind	Ind	Ind	10
Anthropology and Women's Studies	ML96	3FT deg	* g	12	MO	M	Ind	Ind	Ind	2
Anthropology with Archaeological Sciences	L6F4	3FT deg	* g	12	MO	M	Ind	Ind	Ind	
Anthropology with Biology	L6C1	3FT deg	* g	12	MO	M	Ind	Ind	Ind	
Anthropology with Environmental Sciences	L6F9	3FT deg	* g	12	MO	M	Ind	Ind	Ind	
Anthropology with French	L6R1	3FT deg	* g	12	MO	M	Ind	Ind	Ind	
Anthropology with German	L6R2	3FT deg	* g	12	MO	M^	Ind	Ind	Ind	
Anthropology with Health Studies	L6B9	3FT deg	* g	12	MO	M	Ind	Ind	Ind	
Anthropology with Italian	LR63	3FT deg	* g	12	MO	M^	Ind	Ind	Ind	
Anthropology with Linguistics	L6Q1	3FT deg	* g	12	MO	M	Ind	Ind	Ind	
Anthropology with Psychosocial Studies	L6L7	3FT deg	* g	12	MO	M	Ind	Ind	Ind	
Anthropology with Social Policy Research	L6L4	3FT deg	* g	12	MO	M	Ind	Ind	Ind	
Anthropology with Sociology	L6L3	3FT deg	* g	12	MO	M	Ind	Ind	Ind	
Anthropology with Spanish	L6R4	3FT deg	* g	12	MO	M	Ind	Ind	Ind	
Anthropology with Third World & Development St	L6M9	3FT deg	* g	12	MO	M	Ind	Ind	Ind	
Anthropology with Women's Studies	L6MY	3FT deg	* g	12	MO	M	Ind	Ind	Ind	
Archaeological Sciences and Sociology	FL43	3FT deg	* g	12	MO	M$	Ind	Ind	Ind	
Biology with Anthropology	C1L6	3FT deg	* g	12	MO	M	Ind	Ind	Ind	
Business Studies and Cultural Studies	LNP1	3FT deg	* g	14	MO	M				
Business Studies and Women's Studies	NM1X	3FT deg	* g	14	MO	MB				
Business Studies with Cultural Studies	N1L6	3FT deg	* g	14	MO	MB				
Business Studies with Sociology	N1L3	3FT deg	* g	14	MO	MB				
Business Studies with Women's Studies	N1M9	3FT deg	* g	14	MO	MB				

course details

TITLE	CODE	COURSE	SUBJECTS	A/AS	NO/C	AGNVQ	IB	SQA(H)	SQA	RATIO A/AS
Communication Studies and Sociology	LP33	3FT deg	*g	12	MO	M$	Ind	Ind	Ind	5
Communication Studies and Third World & Dev St	MPY3	3FT deg	*g	12	MO	M	Ind	Ind	Ind	
Communication Studies and Women's Studies	MP93	3FT deg	*g	12	MO	M	Ind	Ind	Ind	2
Communication Studies with Sociology	P3L3	3FT deg	*g	12	MO	M	Ind	Ind		
Communication Studies with Third World & Dev St	P3M9	3FT deg	*g	12	MO	M	Ind	Ind		
Communication Studies with Women's Studies	P3MX	3FT deg	*g	12	MO	M	Ind	Ind		
Cultural Studies	L610	3FT deg	*g	14	N	M$	Ind	Ind	Ind	2 10/18
Cultural Studies and Business Studies	LN61	3FT deg	*g	14	MO	M				
Cultural Studies and French	LRP1	3FT deg	*g	14	N	M^				
Cultural Studies and German	LRP2	3FT deg	*g	14	N	M^				
Cultural Studies and Hist of Art Design & Film	LVP4	3FT deg	*g	14	MO	M				3
Cultural Studies and History	LVP1	3FT deg	*g	14	N	M	Ind	Ind	Ind	6
Cultural Studies and Information Technology	GL5P	3FT deg	*g	14	MO	M .				
Cultural Studies and Linguistics	LQ61	3FT deg	*g	12	MO	M				
Cultural Studies and Literature	LQP3	3FT deg	*g	14	N	X	Ind	Ind	Ind	3
Cultural Studies and Media Studies	LPP4	3FT deg	*g	14	N	D	Ind	Ind	Ind	14
Cultural Studies and Spanish	LRP4	3FT deg	*g	14	N	M^				
Cultural Studies and Third World & Dev Studies	LMPY	3FT deg	*g	14	N	M	Ind	Ind	Ind	6
Cultural Studies and Women's Studies	LMPX	3FT deg	*g	14	N	M	Ind	Ind	Ind	
Cultural Studies with Business Studies	L6N1	3FT deg	*g	14	MO	M	Ind	Ind	Ind	
Cultural Studies with Hist of Art Design & Film	L6V4	3FT deg	*g	12	MO	M	Ind	Ind	Ind	
Cultural Studies with History	L6V1	3FT deg	*g	14	MO	M	Ind	Ind	Ind	
Cultural Studies with Information Technology	L6G5	3FT deg	*g	14	MO	M	Ind	Ind	Ind	
Cultural Studies with Linguistics	L6QC	3FT deg	*g	12	MO	M				
Cultural Studies with Literature	L6Q3	3FT deg	*g	14	MO	M	Ind	Ind	Ind	
Cultural Studies with Media Studies	L3P4	3FT deg	*g	14	MO	M	Ind	Ind	Ind	
Cultural Studies with Third World & Dev Studies	L6MX	3FT deg	*g	14	MO	M	Ind	Ind	Ind	
Cultural Studies with Women's Studies	LM6X	3FT deg	*g	16	MO	M	Ind	Ind	Ind	
Development Studies	M920	3FT deg	*g	12	MO	M	Ind	Ind	Ind	3
Economics and Social Sciences	LL1H	3FT deg	*g	12	MO	MB	Ind	Ind	Ind	
Economics and Third World & Development Studies	LM1Y	3FT deg	*g	12	MO	M	Ind	Ind	Ind	
Economics with Third World & Development Studies	L1M9	3FT deg	*g	12	MO	M	Ind			
Education & Commun St w. Third World & Devel St	X9M9	3FT deg	*g	12	MO	M	Ind			
Education & Community St & Third World & Dev St	MXY9	3FT deg	*g	12	MO	M	Ind	Ind	Ind	
Education & Community Studies and Sociology	LX39	3FT deg	*g	12	MO	M$	Ind	Ind	Ind	3
Education & Community Studies and Women's St	MX99	3FT deg	*g	12	MO	M	Ind	Ind	Ind	
Education & Community Studies with Sociology	X9L3	3FT deg	*g	12	MO	M				
Education & Community Studies with Women's St	X9MX	3FT deg	*g	12	MO	M				
Environmental Sciences and Sociology	FL9H	3FT deg	*g	12	MO	M				
Environmental Sciences and Third World & Dev St	FM9Y	3FT deg	*g	12	MO	M	Ind	Ind	Ind	8
Environmental Sciences with Anthropology	F9L6	3FT deg	*g	12	MO	M	Ind	Ind		
Environmental Sciences with Sociology	F9L3	3FT deg	*g	12	MO	M	Ind	Ind		
Environmental Sciences with Third World & Dev St	F9M9	3FT deg	*g	12	MO	M	Ind	Ind		
European Studies and Third World & Dev Studies	MTY2	3FT deg	*g	12	MO	M	Ind	Ind	Ind	
European Studies with Anthropology	T2L6	3FT deg	*g	12	MO	M	Ind	Ind		
European Studies with Sociology	T2L3	3FT deg	*g	12	MO	M	Ind	Ind		
European Studies with Third World & Dev Studies	T2MX	3FT deg	*g	12	MO	M	Ind	Ind		
French and Sociology	LR31	3FT deg	*g	12	MO	M$	Ind	Ind	Ind	
French and Third World & Development Studies	MR91	3FT deg	*g	12	MO	M	Ind	Ind	Ind	
French and Women's Studies	MRX1	3FT deg	*g	12	MO	M	Ind	Ind	Ind	
French with Anthropology	R1L6	3FT deg	*g	12	MO	M	Ind			
French with Cultural Studies	R1LP	3FT deg	*g	12	MO	M	Ind			

Sociology and Anthropology — 64

course details | 98 expected requirements | 96 entry stats

TITLE	CODE	COURSE	SUBJECTS	A/AS	NO/C	AGNVQ	IB	SQA(H)	SQA	RATIO A/AS
French with Sociology	R1L3	3FT deg	*g	12	MO	M				
French with Women's Studies	R1M9	3FT deg	*g	12	MO	M				
German and Sociology	LR32	3FT deg	*g	12	MO	M$	Ind	Ind	Ind	
German and Third World & Development Studies	MR92	3FT deg	*g	12	MO	M	Ind	Ind	Ind	
German and Women's Studies	MRX2	3FT deg	*g	12	MO	M	Ind	Ind	Ind	
German with Anthropology	R2L6	3FT deg	*g	12	MO	M				
German with Cultural Studies	R2LP	3FT deg	*g	12	MO	M	Ind			
German with Sociology	R2L3	3FT deg	*g	12	MO	M	Ind			
German with Women's Studies	R2M9	3FT deg	*g	12	MO	M	Ind			
Health Studies and Sociology	BL93	3FT deg	*g	12	MO	M	Ind	Ind	Ind	
Health Studies and Third World & Dev Studies	BM9Y	3FT deg	*g	12	MO	M	Ind	Ind	Ind	
Health Studies and Women's Studies	BM99	3FT deg	*g	14	MO	M	Ind	Ind	Ind	
Health Studies with Anthropology	B9L6	3FT deg	*g	12	MO	M	Ind	Ind	Ind	
Health Studies with Sociology	B9L3	3FT deg	*g	12	MO	M	Ind	Ind	Ind	
Health Studies with Third World & Dev Studies	B9M9	3FT deg	*g	12	MO	M	Ind	Ind	Ind	
Health Studies with Women's Studies	B9MX	3FT deg	*g	12	MO	M	Ind	Ind	Ind	
History and Sociology	LV31	3FT deg	*g	12	MO	M$	Ind	Ind	Ind	4
History and Third World & Development Studies	MVY1	3FT deg	*g	12	MO	M	Ind	Ind	Ind	2
History and Women's Studies	MV91	3FT deg	*g	12	MO	M	Ind	Ind	Ind	
History of Art Design & Film and Women's Studies	MV94	3FT deg	*g	12	MO	M	Ind	Ind	Ind	
History of Art Design & Film with Cultural St	V4L6	3FT deg	*g	12	MO	M	Ind	Ind		
History of Art Design & Film with Women's St	V4M9	3FT deg	*g	12	MO	M	Ind	Ind		
History with Cultural Studies	V1L6	3FT deg	*g	12	MO	M				
History with Sociology	V1L3	3FT deg	*g	12	MO	M	Ind	Ind		
History with Women's Studies	V1M9	3FT deg	*g	12	MO	M	Ind	Ind		
Information Technology & Third World & Devel St	GM5Y	3FT deg	*g	12	MO	M	Ind	Ind	Ind	3
Information Technology and Social Sciences	GL5H	3FT deg	*g	12	MO	MB	Ind	Ind	Ind	3
Information Technology and Women's Studies	GM59	3FT deg	*g	12	MO	M	Ind	Ind	Ind	
Information Technology with Anthropology	G5L6	3FT deg	*g	12	MO	M	Ind	Ind	Ind	
Information Technology with Cultural Studies	GL5Q	3FT deg	*g	12	MO	M	Ind	Ind	Ind	
Information Technology with Social Sciences	G5L3	3FT deg	*g	12	MO	M	Ind	Ind	Ind	
Information Technology with Third World & Dev St	G5M9	3FT deg	*g	12	MO	M	Ind	Ind	Ind	
Information Technology with Women's Studies	G5MX	3FT deg	*g	12	MO	M	Ind	Ind	Ind	
Law and Social Sciences	LMH3	3FT deg	*g	14	MO	MB	Ind	Ind	Ind	4
Law and Sociology	LM33	3FT deg	*g	14	MO	M$	Ind	Ind	Ind	15
Law and Third World & Development Studies	MM93	3FT deg	*g	14	MO	M				
Law with Social Sciences	M3L3	3FT deg	*g	14	MO	M				
Law with Third World & Development Studies	M3M9	3FT deg	*g	14	MO	M				
Law, Culture and Society	LM3H	3FT deg	*g	14	MO	M				
Linguistics and Sociology	LQ31	3FT deg	*g	14	MO	M$	Ind	Ind	Ind	3
Linguistics with Anthropology	Q1L6	3FT deg	*g	12	MO	M				
Linguistics with Cultural Studies	Q1LP	3FT deg	*g	12	MO	M				
Linguistics with Sociology	Q1L3	3FT deg	*g	12	MO	M				
Literature and Third World & Development Studies	MQY3	3FT deg	*g	12	N	M	Ind	Ind	Ind	1
Literature and Women's Studies	QM39	3FT deg	*g	12	MO	M	Ind			
Literature with Cultural Studies	Q3L6	3FT deg	*g	12	MO	M	Ind			
Literature with Third World & Development St	Q3M9	3FT deg	*g	12	MO	M	Ind			
Literature with Women's Studies	Q3MX	3FT deg	*g	12	MO	M	Ind			
Media Studies and Women's Studies	P4MX	3FT deg	*g	14	MO	M				
Media Studies with Cultural Studies	P4L6	3FT deg	*g	14	MO	M				
Media Studies with Women's Studies	P4M9	3FT deg	*g	14	MO	M				
Politics and Social Sciences	LMH1	3FT deg	*g	12	MO	MB	Ind	Ind	Ind	

			98 expected requirements							96 entry stats	
TITLE	CODE	COURSE	SUBJECTS	A/AS	NO/C	AGNVQ	IB	SQA(H)	SQA	RATIO A/AS	
Politics and Sociology	LM31	3FT deg	*g	12	M0	M$	Ind	Ind	Ind	19	
Politics and Third World & Development Studies	MM91	3FT deg	*g	12	M0	M	Ind				
Politics with Social Sciences	M1L3	3FT deg	*g	12	M0	M	Ind				
Politics with Sociology	M1LH	3FT deg	*g	12	M0	M	Ind				
Politics with Third World & Development Studies	M1M9	3FT deg	*g	12	M0	M	Ind				
Psychosocial Studies and Sociology	LL73	3FT deg	*g	12	M0	M$	Ind	Ind	Ind	4	
Psychosocial Studies and Women's Studies	LM79	3FT deg	*g	12	M0	M	Ind	Ind	Ind		
Psychosocial Studies with Anthropology	L7L6	3FT deg	*g	12	M0	M	Ind	Ind	Ind		
Psychosocial Studies with Social Sciences	L7L3	3FT deg	*g	12	M0	M	Ind	Ind	Ind		
Psychosocial Studies with Sociology	L7LH	3FT deg	*g	12	M0	M	Ind	Ind	Ind		
Psychosocial Studies with Women's Studies	L7M9	3FT deg	*g	12	M0	M	Ind	Ind	Ind		
Social Policy Research and Social Sciences	LL4H	3FT deg	*g	12	M0	MB	Ind	Ind	Ind		
Social Policy Research and Sociology	LL34	3FT deg	*g	12	M0	M	Ind	Ind	Ind		
Social Policy Research and Third World & Dev St	LMKY	3FT deg	*g	12	M0	M	Ind	Ind	Ind		
Social Policy Research and Women's Studies	LM49	3FT deg	*g	12	M0	M	Ind	Ind	Ind		
Social Policy Research with Anthropology	L4L6	3FT deg	*g	12	M0	M					
Social Policy Research with Social Sciences	L4L3	3FT deg	*g	12	M0	M	Ind	Ind	Ind		
Social Policy Research with Sociology	L4LH	3FT deg	*g	12	M0	M	Ind	Ind	Ind		
Social Policy Research with Third World & Dev St	L4MX	3FT deg	*g	12	M0	M					
Social Policy Research with Women's Studies	L4M9	3FT deg	*g	12	M0	M					
Social Sciences	L322	3FT deg	*g	12	M0	MB	Ind	Ind	Ind	5	6/20
Social Sciences and Sociology	L340	3FT deg	*g	12	M0	M$	Ind	Ind	Ind		
Social Sciences and Third World & Development St	LMHY	3FT deg	*g	12	M0	M	Ind	Ind	Ind		
Social Sciences with Economics	L3L1	3FT deg	*g	12	M0	M	Ind	Ind	Ind		
Social Sciences with European Studies	L3T2	3FT deg	*g	12	M0	M	Ind	Ind	Ind		
Social Sciences with Information Technology	L3G5	3FT deg	*g	12	M0	M	Ind	Ind	Ind		
Social Sciences with Law	L3M3	3FT deg	*g	12	M0	M	Ind	Ind	Ind		
Social Sciences with Politics	L3M1	3FT deg	*g	12	M0	M	Ind	Ind	Ind		
Social Sciences with Psychosocial Studies	L3L7	3FT deg	*g	12	M0	M	Ind	Ind	Ind		
Social Sciences with Social Policy Research	L3L4	3FT deg	*g	12	M0	M	Ind	Ind	Ind		
Sociology	L300	3FT deg	*g	12	M0	M$	Ind	Ind	Ind	4	4/14
Sociology and Spanish	LR34	3FT deg	*g	12	M0	M^	Ind	Ind	Ind	3	
Sociology and Third World & Development Studies	LM3Y	3FT deg	*g	12	M0	M	Ind	Ind	Ind	6	
Sociology and Women's Studies	LM3X	3FT deg	*g	12	M0	M	Ind	Ind	Ind		
Sociology with Anthropology	L3L6	3FT deg	*g	12	M0	M	Ind	Ind	Ind		
Sociology with Archaeological Sciences	L3F4	3FT deg	*g	12	M0	M	Ind	Ind	Ind		
Sociology with Business Studies	L3N1	3FT deg	*g	12	M0	M	Ind	Ind	Ind		
Sociology with Communication Studies	L3P3	3FT deg	*g	12	M0	M	Ind	Ind	Ind		
Sociology with Education & Community Studies	L3X9	3FT deg	*g	12	M0	M	Ind	Ind	Ind		
Sociology with Environmental Sciences	L3F9	3FT deg	*g	12	M0	M	Ind	Ind	Ind		
Sociology with European Studies	L3TF	3FT deg	*g	12	M0	M	Ind	Ind	Ind		
Sociology with French	L3R1	3FT deg	*g	12	M0	M	Ind	Ind	Ind		
Sociology with German	L3R2	3FT deg	*g	12	M0	M	Ind	Ind	Ind		
Sociology with Health Studies	L3B9	3FT deg	*g	12	M0	M	Ind	Ind	Ind		
Sociology with History	L3V1	3FT deg	*g	12	M0	M	Ind	Ind	Ind		
Sociology with Italian	L3R3	3FT deg	*g	12	M0	M	Ind	Ind	Ind		
Sociology with Law	L3MH	3FT deg	*g	12	M0	M	Ind	Ind	Ind		
Sociology with Linguistics	L3Q1	3FT deg	*g	12	M0	M	Ind	Ind	Ind		
Sociology with Politics	L3MC	3FT deg	*g	12	M0	M	Ind	Ind	Ind		
Sociology with Psychosocial Studies	L3LR	3FT deg	*g	12	M0	M	Ind	Ind	Ind		
Sociology with Social Policy Research	L3LK	3FT deg	*g	12	M0	M	Ind	Ind	Ind		
Sociology with Social Sciences	L342	3FT deg	*g	12	M0	M	Ind	Ind	Ind		

Sociology and Anthropology 64

TITLE	CODE	COURSE	SUBJECTS	A/AS	NO/C	AGNVQ	IB	SQA(H)	SQA	RATIO A/AS
Sociology with Spanish	L3R4	3FT deg	* g	12	MO	M	Ind	Ind	Ind	
Sociology with Third World & Development Studies	L3MX	3FT deg	* g	12	MO	M	Ind	Ind	Ind	
Sociology with Women's Studies	L3MY	3FT deg	* g	12	MO	M	Ind	Ind	Ind	
Spanish and Third World & Development Studies	RM49	3FT deg	* g	12	MO	M	Ind			
Spanish and Women's Studies	RM4X	3FT deg	* g	12	MO	M	Ind			
Spanish with Anthropology	R4L6	3FT deg	* g	12	MO	M	Ind			
Spanish with Cultural Studies	R4LP	3FT deg	* g	12	MO	M	Ind			
Spanish with Sociology	R4L3	3FT deg	* g	12	MO	M	Ind			
Third World & Development St with Anthropology	M9L6	3FT deg	* g	12	MO	M	Ind	Ind		
Third World & Development St with Environ Sci	M9F9	3FT deg	* g	12	MO	M	Ind	Ind		
Third World & Development St with Women's St	M901	3FT deg	* g	12	MO	M	Ind	Ind		
Third World & Development Stds with Cultural St	M9LP	3FT deg	* g	12	MO	M	Ind	Ind		
Third World & Development Stds with Ed & Comm St	M9X9	3FT deg	* g	12	MO	M	Ind	Ind		
Third World & Development Stds with Soc Pol Res	M9L4	3FT deg	* g	12	MO	M	Ind	Ind		
Third World & Development Stds with Social Sci	M9L3	3FT deg	* g	12	MO	M	Ind	Ind		
Third World & Development Studies and Women's St	M902	3FT deg	* g	12	MO	M	Ind	Ind		
Third World & Development Studies with Bus Stds	M9N1	3FT deg								
Third World & Development Studies with Economics	M9L1	3FT deg	* g	12	MO	M	Ind	Ind		
Third World & Development Studies with French	M9R1	3FT deg	* g	12	MO	M	Ind	Ind		
Third World & Development Studies with German	M9R2	3FT deg	* g	12	MO	M	Ind	Ind		
Third World & Development Studies with Health St	M9B9	3FT deg	* g	12	MO	M	Ind	Ind		
Third World & Development Studies with History	M9V1	3FT deg	* g	12	MO	M	Ind	Ind		
Third World & Development Studies with IT	M9G5	3FT deg	* g	12	MO	M	Ind	Ind		
Third World & Development Studies with Italian	M9R3	3FT deg	* g	12	MO	M	Ind	Ind		
Third World & Development Studies with Law	M9M3	3FT deg	* g	12	MO	M				
Third World & Development Studies with Sociology	M9LH	3FT deg	* g	12	MO	M	Ind	Ind		
Third World & Development Studies with Spanish	M9R4	3FT deg	* g	12	MO	M	Ind	Ind		
Women and New Technology	MJ99	3FT deg	* g	12	MO	M	Ind	Ind	Ind	3
Women's Studies	M903	3FT deg	* g	12	MO	D	Ind	Ind	Ind	3
Women's Studies with Anthropology	M9LQ	3FT deg	* g	12	MO	M	Ind			
Women's Studies with Business Studies	M9NC	3FT deg	* g	12	MO	M	Ind			
Women's Studies with Communication Studies	M9PH	3FT deg	* g	12	MO	M	Ind			
Women's Studies with Cultural Studies	MLXQ	3FT deg	* g	12	MO	M	Ind			
Women's Studies with Education & Community St	M9XX	3FT deg	* g	12	MO	M	Ind			
Women's Studies with French	M9RC	3FT deg	* g	12	MO	M	Ind			
Women's Studies with German	M9RF	3FT deg	* g	12	MO	M	Ind			
Women's Studies with Health Studies	M9BX	3FT deg	* g	12	MO	M	Ind			
Women's Studies with History	M9VC	3FT deg	* g	12	MO	M	Ind			
Women's Studies with History of Art Des & Film	M9VK	3FT deg	* g	12	MO	M	Ind			
Women's Studies with Information Technology	M9GM	3FT deg	* g	12	MO	M	Ind			
Women's Studies with Italian	M9RH	3FT deg	* g	12	MO	M	Ind			
Women's Studies with Literature	M9QH	3FT deg	* g	12	MO	M	Ind			
Women's Studies with Media Studies	M9PK	3FT deg	* g	12	MO	M	Ind			
Women's Studies with Psychosocial Studies	M9LR	3FT deg	* g	12	MO	M	Ind			
Women's Studies with Social Policy Research	M9LK	3FT deg	* g	12	MO	M	Ind			
Women's Studies with Sociology	M9LJ	3FT deg	* g	12	MO	M	Ind			
Women's Studies with Spanish	M9RK	3FT deg	* g	12	MO	M	Ind			
Women's Studies with Third World&Development St	M904	3FT deg	* g	12	MO	M	Ind			
Three-Subject Degree *Anthropology*	Y600	3FT deg	* g	12	MO	M	Ind	Ind	Ind	
Three-Subject Degree *Cultural Studies*	Y600	3FT deg	* g	12	MO	M	Ind	Ind	Ind	

course details			98 expected requirements							96 entry stats	
TITLE	CODE	COURSE	SUBJECTS	A/AS	ND/C	RGNVQ	IB	SQA(H)	SQA	RATIO A/AS	
Three-Subject Degree *Sociology*	Y600	3FT deg	*g	12	MO	M	Ind	Ind	Ind		
Three-Subject Degree *Third World Studies*	Y600	3FT deg	*g	12	MO	M	Ind	Ind	Ind		
Three-Subject Degree *Women & Socio-Historic Processes*	Y600	3FT deg	*g	12	MO	M	Ind	Ind	Ind		
Three-Subject Degree *Women & Technology*	Y600	3FT deg	*g	12	MO	M	Ind	Ind	Ind		
Three-Subject Degree *Women & the Arts*	Y600	3FT deg	*g	12	MO	M	Ind	Ind	Ind		

EDGE HILL Univ COLLEGE

TITLE	CODE	COURSE	SUBJECTS	A/AS	ND/C	RGNVQ	IB	SQA(H)	SQA	RATIO	A/AS
Applied Social Sciences	L311	3FT deg	*	CC	3M+3D	M* / P*^	Dip	BBCC	Ind		
Applied Social Sciences	L310	3FT deg	*	CC	3M+3D	M* / P*^	Dip	BBCC	Ind	3	8/18
Applied Social Sciences and Sports Studies	BL63	3FT deg	*	CC	3M+3D	M* / P*^	Dip	BBCC	Ind		
Applied Social Sciences and Urban Policy Studies	LM3Y	3FT deg	*	CD	3M+3D	M* / P*^	Dip	BBCC	Ind	6	
Commun & Race Rels & Contemp Religion & Beliefs	VM89	3FT deg	*	DD	3M+3D	M* / P*^	Dip	BBCC	Ind		
Communication Studies & Applied Social Sciences	LP33	3FT deg		CC	3M+3D	M* / P*^_	Dip	BBCC	Ind		
Community & Race Relations & Applied Social Sci	LM3X	3FT deg	*	CD	3M+3D	M* / P*^	Dip	BBCC	Ind	6	
Critical Criminology & Disability & Community St	MM9H	3FT deg	*g	CD	3M+3D	M*/ P*^ go	Dip	BBCC$			
Critical Criminology and Applied Social Sciences	LM33	3FT deg	*	CC	3M+3D	M* / P*^_	Dip	BBCC			
Critical Criminology and Community & Race Rel	MM39	3FT deg	*	CD	3M+3D	M* / P*^_	Dip	BBCC			
Critical Criminology and Urban Policy Studies	MM93	3FT deg	*	CD	3M+3D	M* / P*^_	Dip	BBCC			
Critical Criminology and Women's Studies	MM3X	3FT deg	*	CD	3M+3D	M* / P*^_	Dip	BBCC			
Disability & Comm Studies & Applied Social Sci	LL35	3FT deg	*	CD	3M+3D	M* / P*^	Dip	BBCC	Ind	. 3	4/12
Disability & Community Studies & Urban Pol St	LM59	3FT deg	*	DD	4M+2D	M* / P*^	Dip	BBCC	Ind	6	
Drama and Applied Social Sciences	LW34	3FT deg	*	CC	3M+3D	M* / P*^	Dip	BBCC	Ind		
English and Applied Social Sciences	LQ33	3FT deg	E	CC	X	P*^	Dip	BBCC$	X		
Geography and Applied Social Sciences	LL83	3FT deg	Gy g	CD	X	X	Dip	BBCC$	X		
Geography and Urban Policy Studies	LM8Y	3FT deg	Gy g	DD	X	P*^	Dip	BBCC$	X	20	
Geography and Women's Studies	LM89	3FT deg	Gy g	CD	X	P*^	Dip	BBCC$	X		
History and Applied Social Sciences	LV31	3FT deg	H	CC	3M+3D	P*^	Dip	BBCC$	X		
History and Urban Policy Studies	MVY1	3FT deg	H	DD	X	P*^	Dip	BBCC$	X		
Modern European Studies and Urban Policy Studies	MTY2	3FT deg	*	DD	3M+3D	M* / P*^	Dip	BBCC	Ind		
Race and the City	M900	3FT deg	*	DD	4M+2D	M* / P*^	Dip	BBCC	Ind	2	6/14
Sport and the City	BM69	3FT deg	*	CD	3M+3D	M* / P*^	Dip	BBCC	Ind		
Urban Policy Studies	LM3C	3FT deg	*	DD	X	P*^		BBCC	X		
Urban Policy Studies	LM31	3FT deg	*	DD	X	P*^	Dip	BBCC	X		
Women's Studies and Applied Social Sciences	LM39	3FT deg	*	CC	3M+3D	M* / P*^	Dip	BBCC	Ind	4	4/12
Women's Studies and Communication Studies	MP93	3FT deg	*	CC	3M+3D	M* / P*^	Dip	BBCC	Ind	5	
Women's Studies and Community & Race Relations	M910	3FT deg	*	CD	3M+3D	M* / P*^	Dip	BBCC	Ind	7	
Women's Studies and English	MQ93	3FT deg	E	CC	X	P*^_	Dip	BBCC$	X	2	6/14
Women's Studies and History	MV91	3FT deg	H	CD	X	P*^_	Dip	BBCC$	X	2	10/14

Univ of EDINBURGH

TITLE	CODE	COURSE	SUBJECTS	A/AS	ND/C	RGNVQ	IB	SQA(H)	SQA	RATIO	A/AS
Arabic and Social Anthropology	LT66	4FT deg	g	BBB	Ind	Ind	Dip$	BBBB	Ind		
Archaeology and Social Anthropology	VL66	4FT deg	*	AAB	Ind		38$	ABBB	Ind	8	
Economics and Sociology	LL13	4FT deg	g	BBB	Ind		34$	ABBB	Ind	4	
Geography and Social Anthropology	LL86	4FT deg	*	AAB	Ind		38$	AABB	Ind	7	
Geography and Sociology	LL83	4FT deg	*	ABB	Ind		36$	AABB	Ind	7	
Geography with Gender Studies	L8M9	4FT deg	*	ABB	Ind		36$	AABB	Ind		
History and Sociology	VL13	4FT deg	g	BBB	Ind	Ind	Dip$	BBBB	Ind		
Law and Sociology	ML33	4FT deg	g	ABB	X		32	AAABB	X	17	
Linguistics and Social Anthropology	QL16	4FT deg	g	BBB	Ind	Ind	Dip$	BBBB	Ind		
Politics with Gender Studies	M1M9	4FT deg		ABB			36	AABB			

Sociology and Anthropology

course details			98 expected requirements							96 entry stats	
TITLE	CODE	COURSE	SUBJECTS	A/AS	NO/C	RGNVQ	IB	SQA(H)	SQA	RATIO	A/AS
Social Anthropology	L600	4FT deg	*	AAB	Ind		38$	AABB	Ind	5	
Social Anthropology and Linguistics	LQ61	4FT deg	*	AAB	Ind		38$	ABBB	Ind	20	
Social Anthropology and Social History	LV63	4FT deg	*	AAB	Ind		38$	ABBB	Ind	10	
Social Anthropology and Social Policy	LL64	4FT deg	*	AAB	Ind		38$	ABBB	Ind	11	
Social Anthropology and Sociology	LL63	4FT deg	*	AAB	Ind		38$	ABBB	Ind	10	
Social Anthropology with Development	LM69	4FT deg	*	AAB	Ind		38$	ABBB	Ind	18	
Social Anthropology with Environmental Studies	L6F9	4FT deg		AAB			38	ABBB			
Social Anthropology with Gender Studies	L6M9	4FT deg	*	AAB	Ind		38$	ABBB	Ind	12	
Social Anthropology with South Asian Studies	L6T5	4FT deg	*	AAB	Ind		38$	ABBB	Ind		
Social Policy and Sociology	LL43	4FT deg	*	BBB	Ind		34$	ABBB	Ind	7	
Social Policy with Gender Studies	L4M9	4FT deg	*	BBB	Ind		34$	ABBB	Ind		
Sociology	L300	4FT deg	*	BBB	Ind		34$	ABBB	Ind	8	
Sociology and Politics	LM31	4FT deg	*	ABB	Ind		36$	AABB	Ind	12	
Sociology and Psychology	LL37	4FT deg		AAB			38	AABB			
Sociology and Social Anthropology	LL36	4FT deg	*	AAB	Ind		38$	ABBB	Ind	19	
Sociology and Social and Economic History	LV33	4FT deg	*	BBB	Ind		34$	ABBB	Ind	12	
Sociology with Environmental Studies	L3F9	4FT deg		BBB			34	ABBB			
Sociology with Gender Studies	L3M9	4FT deg	*	BBB	Ind		34$	ABBB	Ind		
Sociology with Scottish Society	L375	4FT deg	*	BBB	Ind		34$	ABBB	Ind		
Sociology with South Asian Studies	L3T5	4FT deg	*	BBB	Ind		34$	ABBB	Ind	4	
Social Science *Social Anthropology*	Y200	3FT deg	*	AAB	Ind		38$	ABBB	Ind		
Social Science *Sociology*	Y200	3FT deg	*	BBB	Ind		34$	ABBB	Ind		
Univ of ESSEX											
Accounting and Sociology	NL43	3FT deg	*g	20	MO+3D	D	28	BBBB	Ind		
English Language and British Studies	QV19	3FT deg	*	20			28	BBBB			
History and Sociology	LV31	3FT deg	*	20	MO+2D	Ind	28	BBBB	Ind	7	
Literature and Sociology	LQ32	3FT deg	*	20	MO+2D	Ind	28	BBBB	Ind	10	
Philosophy and Sociology	LV37	3FT deg	*	20	MO+2D	Ind	28	BBBB	Ind	2	18/26
Politics and Sociology	LM31	3FT deg	*	22	MO+2D	Ind	28	BBBB	Ind	5	16/28
Sociology	L300	3FT deg	*	22	MO+2D	D	28	BBBB	Ind	5	12/28
Sociology and History of Art	LV34	3FT deg	*	20	MO+2D	Ind	28	BBBB	Ind		
Sociology and Music	LW33	3FT deg	*	20	MO+2D	Ind	28	BBBB	Ind		
Sociology and Social Policy	LL34	3FT deg	*	22	MO+2D	D	28	BBBB	Ind	6	
Univ of EXETER											
History and Society	LV33	3FT deg	*	BBB-CCC	MO	M/D$	35	Ind	Ind	5	16/24
Law and Society	LM33	3FT deg	*	BBC	MO	M/D$^	34$	Ind	Ind	14	22/26
Politics and Society	LM31	3FT deg	*	ABB-BBC	MO	D$	34	Ind	Ind	13	16/22
Sociology	L300	3FT deg	*g	BBC-CCC	MO	D$	30	Ind	Ind	10	16/26
Sociology with European Study	LT32	4FT deg	*g	BBB-CCC	MO	M/D$	30				
Univ of GLAMORGAN											
Biological Science and Sociology	CL13	3FT deg	M/S g	12	Ind	Ind	Ind	Ind	Ind		
Criminology	L350	3FT deg	Lw/Ps/So g	18	Ind	Ind	Ind	Ind	Ind		
English Studies and Sociology	LQ33	3FT deg	*g	12	Ind	Ind	Ind	Ind	Ind		
English Studies with Sociology	Q3L3	3FT deg	*g	12	Ind	Ind	Ind	Ind	Ind		
Environment and Social Values	FL93	3FT deg	*g	CD	3M $	M$	Ind	Ind	Ind	2	6/20
Geography and Sociology	LL38	3FT deg	*g	12	Ind	Ind	Ind	Ind	Ind		
History and Sociology	LV31	3FT deg	*g	12	5M	M	Ind	Ind	Ind		
History with Anthropology	V1L6	3FT deg	*g	12	5M	M	Ind	Ind	Ind		
Humanities (Sociology)	L300	3FT deg	*g	CC	5M	M$	24	CCCC	HN	6	6/12

course details   **98 expected requirements**   *96 entry stats*

TITLE	CODE	COURSE	SUBJECTS	A/AS	ND/C	AGNVQ	IB	SQA(H)	SQA	RATIO A/AS
Humanities (Women's Studies)	M904	3FT deg	* g	CC	5M	M$	24	CCCC	HN	
Media Studies and Sociology	LP34	3FT deg	Me/T/E g	14	Ind	Ind	Ind	Ind	Ind	
Media Studies with Sociology	P4L3	3FT deg	Me/T/E g	14	Ind	Ind	Ind	Ind	Ind	
Philosophy and Sociology	LV37	3FT deg	* g	12	Ind	Ind	Ind	Ind	Ind	
Psychology and Sociology	LL37	3FT deg	* g	CC	Ind	Ind	Ind	Ind	Ind	
Psychology with Anthropology	L7L6	3FT deg	* g	CC	5M	M	Ind	Ind	Ind	
Psychology with Sociology	L7L3	3 deg	* g	CC	5M	M	Ind	Ind	Ind	
Psychology with Women's Studies	L7M9	3FT deg	* g	CC	5M	M	Ind	Ind	Ind	
Religious Studies and Sociology	LV38	3FT deg	* g	12	Ind	Ind	Ind	Ind	Ind	
Religious Studies with Anthropology	V8L6	3FT deg	* g	12	5M	M	Ind	Ind	Ind	
Sociology	L301	3FT deg	* g	CC	Ind	Ind	Ind	Ind	Ind	
Sociology and Women's Studies	LM39	3FT deg	* g	12	Ind	Ind	Ind	Ind	Ind	
Sociology with Anthropology	L3L6	3FT deg	* g	12	5M	M	Ind	Ind	Ind	
Sociology with Criminal Justice	L3M3	3FT deg	Lw/Ps/So g	14	Ind	Ind	Ind	Ind	Ind	
Sociology with Criminology	L3MH	3FT deg	Lw/Ps/So g	14	Ind	Ind	Ind	Ind	Ind	
Sociology with Psychology	L3L7	3FT deg	* g	CC	5M	M	Ind	Ind	Ind	
Combined Studies (Honours) *Cultural Studies*	Y400	3FT deg	* g	8-16	Ind	Ind	Ind	Ind	Ind	
Combined Studies (Honours) *Sociology*	Y400	3FT deg	* g	8-16	Ind	Ind	Ind	Ind	Ind	
Combined Studies (Honours) *Women's Studies*	Y400	3FT deg	* g	8-16	Ind	Ind	Ind	Ind	Ind	
Joint Honours *Sociology*	Y401	3FT/4SW deg	* g	8-16	Ind	Ind	Ind	Ind	Ind	
Joint Honours *Women's Studies*	Y401	3FT deg	* g	8-16	Ind	Ind	Ind	Ind	Ind	
Major/Minor Honours *Sociology*	Y402	3FT deg	* g	8-16	Ind	Ind	Ind	Ind	Ind	
Major/Minor Honours *Women's Studies*	Y402	3FT deg	* g	8-16	Ind	Ind	Ind	Ind	Ind	

Univ of GLASGOW

TITLE	CODE	COURSE	SUBJECTS	A/AS	ND/C	AGNVQ	IB	SQA(H)	SQA	RATIO A/AS
Anthropology with Celtic	LQ65	4FT deg		BBC	N	M	30	BBBB	Ind	
Anthropology with French	LR61	4FT deg		BBC	N	M	30	BBBB	Ind	
Anthropology with German	LR62	4FT deg		BBC	N	M	30	BBBB	Ind	
Anthropology with Hispanic Studies	LR64	4FT deg		BBC	N	M	30	BBBB	Ind	
Anthropology with Italian	LR63	4FT deg		BBC	N	M	30	BBBB	Ind	
Anthropology with Polish	LT61	4FT deg		BBC	N	M	30	BBBB	Ind	
Anthropology with Russian	LR68	4FT deg		BBC	N	M$	30	BBBB	HN	
Anthropology/Archaeology	LV66	4FT deg		BBC	N	M	30	BBBB	Ind	
Anthropology/Computing Science	LG65	4FT deg		BBC	N	M	30	BBBB	Ind	
Anthropology/History	LV61	4FT deg		BBC	N	M	30	BBBB	Ind	
Anthropology/Psychology	LC68	4FT deg		BBC	N	M	30	BBBB	Ind	
Anthropology/Scottish History	LV6C	4FT deg		BBC	N	M	30	BBBB	Ind	
Anthropology/Sociology	LV63	4FT deg		BBC	N	M	30	BBBB	Ind	
Archaeology/Sociology	LV36	4FT deg		BBC	HN	M	30	BBBB	Ind	
Business Economics/Sociology	LLC3	4FT deg		BBC	N	M	30	BBBB	N	
Classical Civilisation/Sociology	LQ38	4FT deg		BBC	HN	M	30	BBBB	Ind	
Classical Hebrew/Sociology	LV3W	4FT deg		BBC	HN	M	30	BBBB	Ind	
Computing/Sociology	GL53	4FT deg		BBC	HN	M	30	BBBB	Ind	
Czech/Sociology	LT31	5FT deg		BBC	HN	M	30	BBBB	Ind	
Economic and Social History/Sociology	LV33	4FT deg		BBC	8M	M	30	BBBB	Ind	7
Economics/Sociology	LLD3	4FT deg		BBC	8M	M	30	BBBB	Ind	3
English/Sociology	LQ33	4FT deg		BBC	HN	M	30	BBBB	Ind	6 22/24
Film and Television Studies/Sociology	LW35	4FT deg		BBB	HN	D	32	AABB	HN	9

Sociology and Anthropology 64

				98 expected requirements						96 entry stats	
TITLE	CODE	COURSE	SUBJECTS	A/AS	ND/C	AGNVQ	IB	SQA(H)	SQA	RATIO	A/AS
French/Sociology	LR31	5FT deg		BBC	HN	M	30	BBBB	Ind	8	
Geography/Sociology	LL38	4FT deg		BBC	8M	M	30	BBBB	Ind	4	
German/Sociology	LR32	5FT deg		BBC	HN	M	30	BBBB	Ind		
Greek/Sociology	LQ37	4FT deg		BBC	HN	M	30	BBBB	Ind		
Hispanic Studies/Sociology	LR34	5FT deg		BBC	HN	M	30	BBBB	Ind		
History of Art/Sociology	LV34	4FT deg		BBC	HN	M	30	BBBB	Ind		
History/Sociology	LVH1	4FT deg		BBC	HN	M	30	BBBB	Ind	17	
Islamic Studies/Sociology	TL63	4FT deg		BBC	N	M	30	BBBB	Ind		
Italian/Sociology	LR33	5FT deg		BBC	HN	M	30	BBBB	Ind		
Latin/Sociology	LQ36	4FT deg		BBC	HN	M	30	BBBB	Ind		
Management Studies/Sociology	LN31	4FT deg		BBC	8M	M	30	BBBB	Ind	6	
Music/Sociology	LW33	4FT deg		BBC	HN	M	30	BBBB	Ind		
Philosophy/Sociology	LV37	4FT deg		BBC	HN	M	30	BBBB	Ind	6	
Philosophy/Sociology	LVH7	4FT deg		BBC	8M	·M	30	BBBB	Ind	4	
Physics/Sociology	FL33	4FT deg	M+P	BBC	HN	M	30	BBBB	Ind	2	
Politics/Sociology	LM31	4FT deg		BBC	8M	M	30	BBBB	Ind	3	20/28
Psychology/Sociology	LC3V	4FT deg		BBC	8M	M	30	BBBB	Ind	6	
Psychology/Sociology	LC38	4FT deg		BBC	HN	M	30	BBBB	Ind	8	
Russian/Sociology	LR38	5FT deg		BBC	HN	M	30	BBBB	Ind		
Scottish History/Sociology	LV3C	4FT deg		BBC	HN	M	30	BBBB	Ind	8	
Scottish Literature/Sociology	LQH2	4FT deg		BBC	HN	M	30	BBBB	Ind		
Social and Urban Policy/Sociology	LLH4	4FT deg		BBC	8M	M	30	BBBB	Ind	5	
Sociology	L300	4FT deg		BBC	8M	M	30	BBBB	Ind	8	20/22
Sociology with Celtic	L3Q5	4FT deg		BBC	8M	M	30	BBBB	Ind		
Sociology with Czech	L3T1	4FT deg		BBC	8M	M	30	BBBB	Ind		
Sociology with French	L3R1	4FT deg		BBC	8M	M	30	BBBB	Ind	1	
Sociology with German	L3R2	4FT deg		BBC	8M	M	30	BBBB	Ind		
Sociology with Hispanic Studies	L3R4	4FT deg		BBC	8M	M	30	BBBB	Ind		
Sociology with Italian	L3R3	4FT deg		BBC	8M	M	30	BBBB	Ind		
Sociology with Polish	L3TC	4FT deg		BBC	8M	M	30	BBBB	Ind		
Sociology with Russian	L3R8	4FT deg		BBC	8M	M	30	BBBB	Ind		
Sociology/Archaeology	VL63	4FT deg		BBC	8M	M	30	BBBB	Ind		
Sociology/Computing Science	LG35	4FT deg		BBC	8M	M	30	BBBB	Ind		
Sociology/History	LV31	4FT deg		BBC	8M	M	30	BBBB	Ind	7	
Sociology/Scottish History	LVJC	4FT deg		BBC	8M	M	30	BBBB	Ind	2	
Theatre Studies/Sociology	LW34	4FT deg		BBC	HN	M	30	BBBB	Ind	5	
Theology & Religious Studies/Sociology	LV3V	4FT deg		BBC	HN	M	30	BBBB	Ind		

GLASGOW CALEDONIAN Univ

Leisure Management	N7L3	4SW deg	E+M	CC	Ind		Ind	BBCC$	Ind		
Social Sciences	L340	3FT/4FT deg	E	CCD	Ind		Ind	BBBC$	Ind	4	14/18

GOLDSMITHS COLL (Univ of London)

Anthropology	L600	3FT deg		BBC	DO	D	Dip	BBBCC	N	4	8/24
Anthropology and Communication Studies	LW69	3FT deg		BBC	DO	D	Dip	BBBCC	N		12/24
Anthropology and Sociology	LL36	3FT deg		BBC	MO	M	Dip	BBBCC	N	7	18/20
Communication Studies and Sociology	LW39	3FT deg		BBC	DO	D	Dip	ABBBB	N	7	16/28
History and Sociology	LV31	3FT deg		BCC	MO	M	Dip	BBBCC	N	6	16/20
Sociology	L300	3FT deg		BCC	MO	M	Dip	BBBBC	N	3	10/22

Univ of GREENWICH

Applied Statistics with Social Science	G4M9	3FT/4SW deg	*g	CE	Ind	Ind	Ind	Ind	Ind		
Economics with Sociology	L1L3	3FT deg	*g	14	3M	Ind	25	ABC	Ind		
Health and Sociology	BL93	3FT deg	*g	12	N	M$	22	Ind	Ind		

course details			98 expected requirements							96 entry stats
TITLE	CODE	COURSE	SUBJECTS	A/AS	ND/C	AGNVQ	IB	SQA(H)	SQA	RATIO A/AS
Health with Sociology	B9L3	3FT deg	* g	12	N	M$	22	Ind	Ind	
Law with Sociology	M3L3	3FT deg	* g	18	DO	Ind	28	BBBBC	Ind	
Media and Society	LP34	3FT deg	* g	10	MO	M	25	BBB	Ind	
Sociology	L300	3FT deg	* g	14	3M	Ind	Ind	Ind	Ind	
Sociology & Economics	LL31	3FT deg	* g	14	3M	Ind	Ind	Ind	Ind	
Sociology with Economics	L3L1	3FT deg	* g	14	3M	Ind	Ind	Ind	Ind	
Sociology with Psychology	L3L7	3FT deg	* g	14	3M	Ind	Ind	Ind	Ind	
Humanities Society, Culture	Y301	3FT deg	* g	12	MO	M	25	BBB	Ind	

GYOSEI International COLL

Business with Culture Studies	N1L3	3FT/4FT deg	*	BCC	Ind		Ind	Ind	Ind	

Univ of HERTFORDSHIRE

Economics with options	L3L1	3FT deg	* g	14	M+D	Ind	26	BBCC	Ind	
European Studies	L3T2	3FT deg	* g	14	M+D	Ind	26	BBCC	Ind	
Politics/Sociology	M1L3	3FT deg	* g	14	M+D	Ind	26	BBCC	Ind	
Social Policy/Sociology	L4L3	3FT deg	* g	14	M+D	Ind	26	BBCC	Ind	
Social Sciences	L322	3FT deg	* g	14	M+D	Ind	26	BBCC	Ind	3 6/18
Sociology/Economics	L3LC	3FT deg	* g	14	M+D	Ind	26	BBCC	Ind	
Sociology/Politics	L3MC	3FT deg	* g	14	M+D	Ind	26	BBCC	Ind	
Sociology/Social Policy	L3LK	3FT deg	* g	14	M+D	Ind	26	BBCC	Ind	

HEYTHROP COLL (Univ of London)

Theology and Society	V8L3	3FT deg	*	18-20	Ind	M	Dip	BCCCC	Ind	8

Univ of HUDDERSFIELD

History with Sociology	V1L3	3FT deg	H	14-16	Ind	Ind	Ind	Ind	Ind	
Politics with Sociology	M1L3	3FT deg	*	14	MO+3D	M6/^	Ind	BBBC	Ind	
Sociology	L300	3FT deg	* g	12	MO	M gi	Ind	BBCC	Ind	

Univ of HULL

Economic and Social History/Sociology	LV33	3FT deg	*	BBC-BCC	MO	M$6/^ go	28	BBCCC	Ind	2 16/22
Gender Studies and American Studies	MQ94	3FT deg	*	BBB-BCC	Ind	M$6/^ go	26	BBCCC	Ind	
Gender Studies and Dutch	MT92	4FT deg	* g	BBC-CCD	MO	M$6/^ go	26	BBCCC	Ind	
Gender Studies and English	MQ93	3FT deg	E	BBB-BCC	Ind	M$6/^ go	28	BBBCC	Ind	4
Gender Studies and French	MR91	4FT deg	F	BCC	Ind	M$6/^ go	28$	BBBCC	Ind	3
Gender Studies and German	MR92	4FT deg	G	BCC-CCC	Ind	M$6/^ go	28$	BBBCC	Ind	2
Gender Studies and Italian	MR93	4FT deg	L	BCC-CCC	Ind	M$6/^ go	28$	BBBCC	Ind	
Gender Studies and Philosophy	MV97	3FT deg	*	BCC-CCC	MO	M$6/^ go	28	BBBCC	Ind	2
Gender Studies and Scandinavian Studies	MR97	4FT deg	*	BCC-CCC	MO	M$6/^ go	28$	BBCCC	Ind	
Gender Studies and Social Policy	ML94	3FT deg	* g	BBC-BCC	M+D $	M$6/^ go	28	BBBCC	Ind	
Gender Studies and Sociology and Anthropology	ML93	3FT deg	*	BBC-BCC	MO	M$6/^ go	28	BBCCC	Ind	3 12/24
Gender Studies and Spanish	MR94	4FT deg	L	BCC-CCC	MO $	M$6/^ go	28$	BBCCC	Ind	2
Geography/Sociology	LL38	3FT deg	Gv	BBC-BCC	Ind	D$^ go	28$	BBBCC	Ind	10 24/24
Law and Sociology	LM33	3FT deg	*	22	MO	D$^ gi	28$	ABBBB	Ind	25
Management/Sociological Systems	LN31	3FT deg	* g	BBC	MO+3D	D$^/6 go	28$	BBBBC	Ind	
Philosophy/Sociology	LV37	3FT deg	*	BBC-BCC	MO	M$6/^ go	28	BBBCC	Ind	6
Politics/Sociology	LM31	3FT deg	*	BBC-BCC	Ind	Ind	28$	BBCCC	Ind	20
Psychology with Anthropology	C8L6	3FT deg	* g	BBB-BCC	2M+2D	D$^ go	28	BBBCC	Ind	22
Psychology with Sociology	C8L3	3FT deg	* g	BBB-BCC	2M+2D	D$^ go	28	BBBCC	Ind	68
Social Policy/Sociology	LL34	3FT deg	*	BBB-BCC	Ind	DG^ gi	28$	BBCCC	Ind	26
Sociology	L300	3FT deg	*	BBC	4M+2D	M$^ gi	26	BBCCC	Ind	5 14/22
Sociology and Soc Anthropology with Develop St	L3M9	3FT deg	*	BBC	4M+2D	M$^ gi	28	BBCCC	Ind	5 17/22
Sociology and Social Anthropology	LL36	3FT deg	*	BBC	4M+2D	M$^ gi	28	BBCCC	Ind	4 14/22
Sociology/Theology	LV38	3FT deg	*	BBC-CCD	MO	M$^ gi	28	BBCCC	Ind	3

Sociology and Anthropology 64

KEELE Univ

TITLE	CODE	COURSE	SUBJECTS	A/AS	ND/C	RGNVQ	IB	SQA(H)	SQA	RATIO	A/AS
Psychology and Sociology and Social Anthropology	CL83	3FT deg	* g	BBB	Ind	Ind	32	CSYS	Ind	12	20/24
Russian Studies and Sociology & Soc Anthropology	LR3V	3FT deg	*	BCC	Ind	Ind	28	CSYS	Ind		
Sociol & Soc Anthrop & French/Russian or Russ St	LT3X	3FT deg	F+R	BBC	Ind	D$^	30$	CSYS	Ind		
Sociol & Soc Anthrop & French/Russian or Russ St	TLX3	4FT deg	*	BCC	Ind	Ind	28	BBBB	Ind		
Sociol & Soc Anthrop and Applied Social St(4Yrs)	LL53	4FT deg	*	BBC	Ind	Ind	30	BBBB	Ind	6	
Sociol & Soc Anthrop and Astrophysics (4 Yrs)	LF35	4FT deg	*	BCC	Ind	Ind	28	BBBB	Ind		
Sociol & Soc Anthrop and Biochemistry (4 Yrs)	LC37	4FT deg	*	BCC	Ind	Ind	28	BBBB	Ind		
Sociol & Soc Anthrop and Biological & Med Chem	FLC3	3FT deg	C g	BCC	Ind	D$^	28$	CSYS	Ind		
Sociol & Soc Anthrop and Biological & Med Chem	LF3C	4FT deg	*	BCC	Ind	Ind	28	BBBB	Ind		
Sociol & Soc Anthrop and Criminology (4 Yrs)	ML3J	4FT deg	*	BBB	Ind	Ind	32	ABBB	Ind	4	
Sociol & Soc Anthrop and Environment Mgt (4 Yrs)	LF3X	4FT deg	*	BCC	Ind	Ind	28	BBBB	Ind		
Sociol & Soc Anthrop and Human Resource Mgt(4Yr)	NLP3	4FT deg	*	BCC	Ind	Ind	28	BBBB	Ind	1	
Sociol & Soc Anthrop and Internat Hist (4 Yrs)	VLC3	4FT deg	*	BCC	Ind	Ind	28	BBBB	Ind		
Sociol & Soc Anthrop and International History	LV3C	3FT deg	*	BCC	Ind	Ind	28	CSYS	Ind	5	
Sociol & Soc Anthrop and International Politics	LM3C	3FT deg	*	BCC	Ind	Ind	28	CSYS	Ind	5	
Sociol & Soc Anthropology and Chemistry (4 Yrs)	LF31	4FT deg	*	BCC	Ind	Ind	28	BBBB	Ind		
Sociol & Soc Anthropology and Economics (4 Yrs)	LL31	4FT deg	*	BCC	Ind	Ind	28	BBBB	Ind		
Sociol & Soc Anthropology and Environmental Mgt	FLX3	3FT deg	* g	BCC	Ind	Ind	28	CSYS	Ind	5	
Sociol & Soc Anthropology and Geography (4 Yrs)	LL83	4FT deg	*	BCC	Ind	Ind	28	BBBB	Ind	10	
Sociol & Soc Anthropology and Maths (4 Yrs)	LG31	4FT deg	*	BCC	Ind	Ind	28	BBBB	Ind		
Sociol & Soc Anthropology and Politics (4 Yrs)	ML13	4FT deg	*	BCC	Ind	Ind	28	BBBB	Ind	2	
Sociol & Soc Anthropology and Psychology (4 Yrs)	LC38	4FT deg	*	BBB	Ind	Ind	32	ABBB	Ind	4	
Sociol & Soc Anthropology and Russian St (4 Yrs)	RLV3	4FT deg	*	BCC	Ind	Ind	28	BBBB	Ind		
Sociol & Social Anthrop and Human Resource Mgt	LN3P	3FT deg	*	BCC	Ind	Ind	28	CSYS	Ind	4	
Sociol & Social Anthropology and Business Admin	LN39	3FT deg	*	BCC	Ind	Ind	28	CSYS	Ind	6	18/28
Sociol & Social Anthropology and French (4 Yrs)	RL13	4FT deg	*	BCC	Ind	Ind	28	BBBB	Ind		
Sociol & Social Anthropology and Geology (4 Yrs)	LF36	4FT deg	*	BCC	Ind	Ind	28	BBBB	Ind		
Sociol & Social Anthropology and Physics (4 Yrs)	LF33	4FT deg	*	BCC	Ind	Ind	28	BBBB	Ind		
Sociol & Social Anthropology and Russian (4 Yrs)	RL83	4FT deg	*	BCC	Ind	Ind	28	BBBB	Ind		
Sociology & Soc Anthrop & Computer Sci (4 Yrs)	LG35	4FT deg	* g	BCC	Ind	Ind	28	BBBB	Ind		
Sociology & Soc Anthrop and Applied Social Studs	LL35	3FT deg	*	BBC-BCC	Ind	Ind	28	CSYS	Ind	5	16/22
Sociology & Soc Anthrop and Educational St(4Yrs)	XL93	4FT deg	*	BBC-BCC	Ind	Ind	28	BBBB	Ind		
Sociology & Soc Anthrop and Int Politics (4 Yrs)	MLC3	4FT deg	*	BCC	Ind	Ind	28	BBBB	Ind		
Sociology & Soc Anthropology and English (4 Yrs)	QL33	4FT deg	*	BBC	Ind	Ind	30	BBBB	Ind	8	
Sociology & Social Anthrop & American St (4 Yrs)	QL43	4FT deg	*	BBC-BCC	Ind	Ind	28	BBBB	Ind		
Sociology & Social Anthrop & Ancient Hist(4 Yrs)	VLD3	4FT deg	*	BCC	Ind	Ind	28	BBBB	Ind		
Sociology & Social Anthroplgy and Biochemistry	CL73	3FT deg	C g	BCC	Ind	D$^	28$	CSYS	Ind		
Sociology & Social Anthropol and German (4 Yrs)	RL23	4FT deg	g	BCC	Ind	Ind	28	BBBB	Ind		
Sociology & Social Anthropology & Finance(4 Yrs)	NL33	4FT deg	* g	BBC-BCC	Ind	Ind	28	BBBB	Ind		
Sociology & Social Anthropology and Astrophysics	FL53	3FT deg	P g	BCC	Ind	D$^	28$	CSYS	Ind		
Sociology & Social Anthropology and Biology	CL13	3FT deg	S g	BCC	Ind	D$^	28$	CSYS	Ind	5	
Sociology & Social Anthropology and Chemistry	FL13	3FT deg	C g	BCC	Ind	D$^	28$	CSYS	Ind		
Sociology & Social Anthropology and Criminology	LM3J	3FT deg	*	BBB	Ind	Ind	32	CSYS	Ind	23	26/26
Sociology & Social Anthropology and Economics	LL13	3FT deg	* g	BCC	Ind	Ind	28	CSYS	Ind	2	
Sociology & Social Anthropology and Elect Music	LW3J	3FT deg	Mu	BCC	Ind	D$^	28$	CSYS	Ind		
Sociology & Social Anthropology and English	LQ33	3FT deg	E	BBC	Ind	D$^	30$	CSYS	Ind	7	20/24
Sociology & Social Anthropology and French	LR31	3FT deg	F	BCC	Ind	D$^	28$	CSYS	Ind		
Sociology & Social Anthropology and Geography	LL38	3FT deg	Gy	BCC	Ind	D$^	28$	CSYS	Ind	7	18/26
Sociology & Social Anthropology and Geology	FL63	3FT deg	S g	BCC	Ind	D$^	28$	CSYS	Ind		
Sociology & Social Anthropology and History	LV31	3FT deg	*	BCC	Ind	Ind	28	CSYS	Ind	7	
Sociology & Social Anthropology and Law	LM33	3FT deg	*	BBB	Ind	Ind	32	CSYS	Ind	20	

course details

TITLE	CODE	COURSE	SUBJECTS	A/AS	NO/C	AGNVQ	IB	SQA(H)	SQA	RATIO A/AS
Sociology & Social Anthropology and Law (4 Yrs)	ML33	4FT deg	*	BBB	Ind	Ind	32	BBBB	Ind	
Sociology & Social Anthropology and Marketing	LN35	3FT deg	*	BCC	Ind	Ind	28	CSYS	Ind	9
Sociology & Social Anthropology and Mathematics	GL13	3FT deg	M	BCC	Ind	D$^	28$	CSYS	Ind	
Sociology & Social Anthropology and Music	LW33	3FT deg	Mu	BBC-BCC	Ind	D$^	28$	CSYS	Ind	
Sociology & Social Anthropology and Physics	FL33	3FT deg	P g	BCC	Ind	D$^	28$	CSYS	Ind	
Sociology & Social Anthropology and Politics	LM31	3FT deg	*	BCC	Ind	Ind	28	CSYS	Ind	6
Sociology & Social Anthropology and Russian	LR38	3FT deg	R	BCC	Ind	D$^	28$	CSYS	Ind	
Sociology and Soc Anthrop & Classical St (4 Yrs)	QL83	4FT deg	*	BCC	Ind	Ind	28	BBBB	Ind	
Statistics and Sociol & Soc Anthropology (4 Yrs)	LG34	4FT deg	*	BCC	Ind	Ind	28	BBBB	Ind	
Statistics and Sociology & Social Anthropology	GL43	3FT deg	M	BCC	Ind	D$^	28$	CSYS	Ind	
Visual Arts and Sociology & Social Anthropology	LW31	3FT deg	*	BBC-BCC	Ind	D$^	28	CSYS	Ind	
Visual Arts and Sociology & Social Anthropology	WL13	4FT deg	*	BBC	Ind	Ind	30	BBBB	Ind	

Univ of KENT

TITLE	CODE	COURSE	SUBJECTS	A/AS	NO/C	AGNVQ	IB	SQA(H)	SQA	RATIO A/AS
Anthropology	L601	3FT deg	* g	20	3M+3D	M$ go	28	BBBB	Ind	
English and Sociology	LQ33	3FT deg	E	22	2M+4D	Ind	30	Ind	Ind	8 22/24
European Studies (Sociology) (4 Yrs)	LT32	4FT deg	L	20	Ind	Ind	28$	BBBB$	Ind	
History and Social Anthropology	LVP1	3FT deg	*	22	2M+4D	Ind	30	Ind	Ind	21
Ind Relations & Human Resource Mgt (Sociology)	LN36	3FT deg	* g	20	3M+3D	M$ go	28	BBBB	Ind	9
Philosophy and Social Anthropology	LVP7	3FT deg	*	22	2M+4D	Ind	30	Ind	Ind	4
Philosophy and Sociology	LVH7	3FT deg	*	22	2M+4D	Ind	30	Ind	Ind	7
Psychology and Social Anthropology	CL86	3FT deg	* g	26	6D	D$ go	33	AAAB	Ind	23
Psychology and Sociology	CL83	3FT deg	* g	26	6D	D$ go	33	AAAB	Ind	30
Social Anthroplgy with German (4 Yrs)	L676	4FT deg	G	18	Ind	Ind	26$	BBBB$	Ind	
Social Anthropology	L600	3FT deg	*	20	3M+3D	M$	28	BBBB	Ind	6 16/24
Social Anthropology and History	LV61	3FT deg	*	20	3M+3D	M$	28	BBBB	Ind	9
Social Anthropology and Philosophy	LV67	3FT deg	*	20	3M+3D	M$	28	BBBB	Ind	8
Social Anthropology with French (4 Yrs)	L675	4FT deg	F	18	Ind	Ind	26$	BBBB$	Ind	16
Social Anthropology with Italian (4 Yrs)	L673	4FT deg	* g	18	4M+2D	M$ go	26	BBBB	Ind	2
Social Anthropology with Spanish (4 Yrs)	L674	4FT deg	* g	20	3M+3D	M$ go	28	BBBB	Ind	4
Social Anthropology with a Yr in Finland (4 Yrs)	L677	4FT deg	*	20	3M+3D	M$	28	BBBB	Ind	
Social Anthropology with a Yr in Holland (4 Yrs)	L672	4FT deg	*	18	4M+2D	M$	26	BBBB	Ind	
Social Anthropology/Accounting and Finance	LN64	3FT deg	* g	20	3M+3D	M$ go	28	BBBB	Ind	
Social Anthropology/Economics	LL16	3FT deg	* g	20	3M+3D	M$ go	28	BBBB	Ind	
Social Anthropology/Law	LM63	3FT deg	*	26	6D	D$	33	AAAB	Ind	
Social Anthropology/Politics & Government	LM61	3FT deg	*	BCC	3M+3D	M$	28	BBBB	Ind	
Social Policy & Admin/Social Anthropology	LL46	3FT deg	*	20	3M+3D	M$	28	BBBB	Ind	
Social Psychology/Social Anthropology	LL67	3FT deg	* g	26	6D	D$ go	33	AAAB	Ind	
Social Sciences	L340▼	3FT deg			Ind	Ind	Ind	Ind	Ind	5
Sociol & Soc Anthrop with yr in Finland (4 Yrs)	LL3P	4FT deg	*	20	3M+3D	M$	28	BBBB	Ind	
Sociology	L300	3FT deg	*	20	3M+3D	M$	28	BBBB	Ind	5 14/22
Sociology and English	LQH3	3FT deg	E	20	Ind	Ind	28$	BBBB$	Ind	7 18/24
Sociology and Philosophy	LV37	3FT deg	*	20	3M+3D	M$	28	BBBB	Ind	6
Sociology with Italian (4 Yrs)	L373	4FT deg	* g	18	4M+2D	M$ go	26	BBBB	Ind	6
Sociology with a year in Finland (4 Yrs)	L301	4FT deg	*	20	3M+3D	M$	28	BBBB	Ind	
Sociology/Accounting and Finance	NL43	3FT deg	* g	20	3M+3D	M$ go	28	BBBB	Ind	
Sociology/Economics	LL13	3FT deg	* g	20	3M+3D	M$ go	28	BBBB	Ind	3
Sociology/Law	LM33	3FT deg	*	26	6D	D$	33	AAAB	Ind	24
Sociology/Politics & Government	LMJ1	3FT deg	*	BCC	3M+3D	M$	28	BBBB	Ind	17
Sociology/Social Anthropology	LL36	3FT deg	*	20	3M+3D	M$	28	BBBB	Ind	8
Sociology/Social Policy & Administration	LL34	3FT deg	*	20	3M+3D	M$	28	BBBB	Ind	5
Sociology/Social Psychology	LL37	3FT deg	* g	26	6D	D$ go	33	AAAB	Ind	
Urban Studies (Sociology)	KL43	3FT deg	* g	20	3M+3D	M$ go	28	BBBB	Ind	9

course details			98 expected requirements							96 entry stats	
TITLE	CODE	COURSE	SUBJECTS	A/AS	ND/C	AGNVQ	IB	SQA(H)	SQA	RATIO	A/AS
KING ALFRED'S WINCHESTER											
Contemporary Cultural Studies and American Studs	MQ94	3FT deg	* g	14	6M	M	24	BCC	N	3	
Dance Studies and Contemporary Cultural Studies	MW9K	3FT deg	* g	14	6M	M	24	BCC	N	4	
Drama Studies and Contemporary Cultural Studies	MW94	3FT deg	* g	14	6M	M	24	BCC	N	3	
Education Studies & Contemporary Cultural Studs	MX99	3FT deg	* g	14	6M	M	24	BCC	N		
English Studies and Contemporary Cultural Studs	MQ93	3FT deg	E	14	X	X	24$	BCC$	X	5	
Geography and Contemporary Cultural Studies	LM89	3FT deg	Gy g	14	X	X	24$	BCC$	X		
History and Contemporary Cultural Studies	MV91	3FT deg	H g	14	X	X	24$	BCC$	X		
Japanese Language and Contemporary Cultural St	MT94	3FT deg	L g	14	X	X	24$	BCC$	X		
Media & Film Studies & Contemporary Cultural St	MP94	3FT deg	* g	14	6M	M	24	BCC	N	7	8/20
Philosophy and Contemporary Cultural Studies	MV97	3FT deg	* g	14	6M	M	24	BCC	N	3	
Psychology and Contemporary Cultural Studies	LM79	3FT deg	* g	14	6M	M	24	BCC	N	2	
Social and Professional St (Learning Disabils)	L340	3FT deg	* g	8	6M	M	24	CCC	N	3	6/14
Sports Studies and Dance Studies	WLKH	3FT deg	* g	14	6M	M	24	BCC	N		
Sports Studies and Geography	LL8H	3FT deg	Gy g	14	X	X	24$	BCC$	X		
Visual Studies and Contemporary Culture Studies	MW92	3FT deg									
KING'S COLL LONDON (Univ of London)											
War Studies	M940	3FT deg	*	BBC						6	22/30
War Studies and Classical Studies	MQ98	3FT deg		BBC							
War Studies and French	MR91	4FT deg	F	BBC						3	
War Studies and Geography	ML98	3FT deg	Gy	BCC						23	
War Studies and German	MR92	4FT deg	G	BCC						3	
War Studies and History	MV91	3FT deg	H	ABB-BBC						13	24/28
War Studies and Modern Greek	MT92	3FT deg	*	BBC							
War Studies and Philosophy	MV97	3FT deg	*	BBC						4	
War Studies and Portuguese	MR95	3FT deg		BBC							
War Studies and Theology	MV98	3FT deg	*	BBC							
War Studies with Applied Computing	M9G5	3FT deg	*	BBC							
KINGSTON Univ											
Sociology	L300	3FT deg	* g	14-16	MO	Ind^	Ind	BCCCC	HN	5	8/20
Sociology/Economics	LL31	3FT deg	* g	14	MO	Ind^	Ind	BCCCC	HN	8	
Sociology/English Literature	LQ33	3FT deg	E g	18	MO	Ind^	Ind	BBBCC	HN	6	16/22
Sociology/History	LV31	3FT deg	H g	14	MO	Ind^	Ind	BCCCC	HN	4	
Sociology/History of Art, Architecture & Design	VL43	3FT deg	* g	16	MO	Ind^	Ind	BBCCC	HN		
Sociology/History of Ideas	LV37	3FT deg	* g	14	MO	Ind^	Ind	BCCCC	HN	2	10/12
Sociology/Politics	LM31	3FT deg	* g	14	MO	Ind^	Ind	BCCCC	HN	3	14/18
Sociology/Psychology	LL37	3FT deg	* g	18	DO	Ind^	Ind	BBBCC	HN	6	10/22
Sociology/Social and Economic History	LV33	3FT deg	* g	14	MO	Ind^	Ind	BCCCC	HN	2	
Women's Studies/English Literature	MQ93	3FT deg	E g	16-18	MO	Ind^	Ind	BBCCC	HN	5	
Women's Studies/French	RM19	4FT deg	F g	14	MO	Ind^	Ind	BCCCC	HN	2	
Women's Studies/History of Art, Arch & Design	MV94	3FT deg	* g	16	MU	Ind^	Ind	BBCCC	HN		
Women's Studies/History of Ideas	MV97	3FT deg	* g	14	MO	Ind^	Ind	BCCCC	HN	5	
Women's Studies/Politics	MM91	3FT deg	* g	14	MO	Ind^	Ind	BCCCC	HN	5	
Women's Studies/Social and Economic History	MV93	3FT deg	* g	14	MO	Ind^	Ind	BCCC	HN	1	
Women's Studies/Sociology	ML93	3FT deg	* g	14	MO	Ind^	Ind	BCCCC	HN	8	
Univ of Wales, LAMPETER											
Anthropology	L600	3FT deg	*	16	Ind	Ind	Ind	Ind	Ind		
Anthropology and American Literature	LQ64	3FT deg			Ind	Ind	Ind	Ind	Ind		
Anthropology and Ancient History	LV61	3FT deg	*	16	Ind	Ind	Ind	Ind	Ind		
Anthropology and Religion	VL86	3FT deg	*	16-18	Ind	Ind	Ind	Ind	Ind		
Archaeology and Anthropology	LV6P	3FT deg	*	16-18	Ind	Ind	Ind	Ind	Ind		

course details

TITLE	CODE	COURSE	SUBJECTS	A/AS	NO/C	AGNVQ	IB	SQA(H)	SQA	RATIO A/AS
Archaeology and Anthropology	LV66	3FT deg	*	16	Ind	Ind	Ind	Ind	Ind	
Australian Studies	L601	3FT deg			Ind	Ind	Ind	Ind	Ind	
Australian Studies and American Literature	LQ6K	3FT deg			Ind	Ind	Ind	Ind	Ind	
Australian Studies and Ancient History	LVPC	3FT deg			Ind	Ind	Ind	Ind	Ind	
Australian Studies and Anthropology	L610	3FT deg			Ind	Ind	Ind	Ind	Ind	
Australian Studies and Archaeology	LV6Q	3FT deg			Ind	Ind	Ind	Ind	Ind	
Church History and Anthropology	LV6C	3FT deg	*	16	Ind	Ind	Ind	Ind	Ind	
Church History and Australian Studies	VLC6	3FT deg			Ind	Ind	Ind	Ind	Ind	
Classical Studies and Anthropology	LQ68	3FT deg	*	16	Ind	Ind	Ind	Ind	Ind	
Classical Studies and Australian Studies	LQP8	3FT deg			Ind	Ind	Ind	Ind	Ind	
Cultural Studies in Geography and Anthropology	LL6V	3FT deg	Gy	14	Ind	Ind	Ind	Ind	Ind	
Cultural Studies in Geography and Australian St	LL8P	3FT deg			Ind	Ind	Ind	Ind	Ind	
English Literature and Anthropology	LQ63	3FT deg	E	16-18	Ind	Ind	Ind	Ind	Ind	
English Literature and Australian Studies	QL36	3FT deg			Ind	Ind	Ind	Ind	Ind	
French and Anthropology	LR61	4FT deg	F	16	Ind	Ind	Ind	Ind	Ind	
French and Australian Studies	LR6C	3FT deg	F		Ind	Ind	Ind	Ind	Ind	
Geography and Anthropology	LL68	3FT deg	Gy	16	Ind	Ind	Ind	Ind	Ind	
Geography and Australian Studies	LL86	3FT deg	Gy		Ind	Ind	Ind	Ind	Ind	
German Studies and Anthropology	LR6F	4FT deg	*	16	Ind	Ind	Ind	Ind	Ind	
German Studies and Australian Studies	LRP2	3FT deg			Ind	Ind	Ind	Ind	Ind	
German and Anthropology	LR62	4FT deg	G	16	Ind	Ind	Ind	Ind	Ind	
German and Australian Studies	LR6G	3FT deg	G		Ind	Ind	Ind	Ind	Ind	
Greek and Anthropology	LQ67	3FT deg	* g	16	Ind	Ind	Ind	Ind	Ind	
Greek and Australian Studies	LQ6R	3FT deg	* g		Ind	Ind	Ind	Ind	Ind	
History and Anthropology	LVP1	3FT deg	H	16	Ind	Ind	Ind	Ind	Ind	
History and Australian Studies	VLCP	3FT deg	H		Ind	Ind	Ind	Ind	Ind	
Informatics and Anthropology	GL56	3FT deg	*	14-16	Ind	Ind	Ind	Ind	Ind	
Informatics and Australian Studies	GL5P	3FT deg			Ind	Ind	Ind	Ind	Ind	
Islamic Studies and Anthropology	LT66	3FT deg	*	14	Ind	Ind	Ind	Ind	Ind	
Islamic Studies and Australian Studies	TL66	3FT deg			Ind	Ind	Ind	Ind	Ind	
Latin and Anthropology	LQ66	3FT deg	* g	16	Ind	Ind	Ind	Ind	Ind	
Latin and Australian Studies	QL66	3FT deg			Ind	Ind	Ind	Ind	Ind	
Management Techniques and Anthropology	NL16	3FT deg	*	16	Ind	Ind	Ind	Ind	Ind	
Management Techniques and Australian Studies	LN61	3FT deg			Ind	Ind	Ind	Ind	Ind	
Medieval Studies and Anthropology	VL16	3FT deg	*	16	NO/C	Ind	Ind	Ind	Ind	
Medieval Studies and Australian Studies	VLD6	3FT deg			Ind	Ind	Ind	Ind	Ind	
Modern Historical Studies and Anthropology	VL1P	3FT deg			Ind	Ind	Ind	Ind	Ind	
Modern Historical Studies and Australian Studies	VLCQ	3FT deg			Ind	Ind	Ind	Ind	Ind	
Philosophical Studies and Anthropology	LV67	3FT deg	*	16	Ind	Ind	Ind	Ind	Ind	
Philosophical Studies and Australian Studies	LV6R	3FT deg			Ind	Ind	Ind	Ind	Ind	
Religious Studies and Anthropology	LV68	3FT deg	*	14	Ind	Ind	Ind	Ind	Ind	
Religious Studies and Australian Studies	LV6V	3FT deg			Ind	Ind	Ind	Ind	Ind	
Theology and Anthropology	LV6W	3FT deg	*	16	Ind	Ind	Ind	Ind	Ind	
Theology and Australian Studies	LVP8	3FT deg			Ind	Ind	Ind	Ind	Ind	
Victorian Studies and Anthropology	LV6D	3FT deg	*	16	Ind	Ind	Ind	Ind	Ind	
Victorian Studies and Australian Studies	VLDP	3FT deg			Ind	Ind	Ind	Ind	Ind	
Welsh Studies and Anthropology	LQ6M	3FT deg	*	16	Ind	Ind	Ind	Ind	Ind	
Welsh Studies and Australian Studies	LQP5	3FT deg			Ind	Ind	Ind	Ind	Ind	
Welsh and Anthropology	LQ65	3FT/4FT deg	W	16	Ind	Ind	Ind	Ind	Ind	
Welsh and Australian Studies	LQ6N	3FT deg			Ind	Ind	Ind	Ind	Ind	
Women's Studies and American Literature	MQ94	3FT deg			Ind	Ind	Ind	Ind	Ind	
Women's Studies and Ancient History	MV91	3FT deg	*	16	Ind	Ind	Ind	Ind	Ind	

course details | 98 expected requirements | 96 entry stats

TITLE	CODE	COURSE	SUBJECTS	A/AS	ND/C	AGNVQ	IB	SQA(H)	SQA	RATIO A/AS
Women's Studies and Anthropology	LM69	3FT deg	*	16	Ind	Ind	Ind	Ind	Ind	
Women's Studies and Archaeology	MV96	3FT deg	*	18	Ind	Ind	Ind	Ind	Ind	
Women's Studies and Australian Studies	ML96	3FT deg			Ind	Ind	Ind	Ind	Ind	
Women's Studies and Church History	MV9C	3FT deg	*	14	Ind	Ind	Ind	Ind	Ind	
Women's Studies and Classical Studies	MQ98	3FT deg	*	16	Ind	Ind	Ind	Ind	Ind	
Women's Studies and Cultural Studs in Geography	LM8X	3FT deg	*	16	Ind	Ind	Ind	Ind	Ind	
Women's Studies and English Literature	MQ93	3FT deg	E	18	Ind	Ind	Ind	Ind	Ind	
Women's Studies and French	MR91	4FT deg	F	16	Ind	Ind	Ind	Ind	Ind	
Women's Studies and Geography	LM89	3FT deg	Gy	16	Ind	Ind	Ind	Ind	Ind	
Women's Studies and German	MR92	4FT deg	G	16	Ind	Ind	Ind	Ind	Ind	
Women's Studies and German Studies	RM29	4FT deg	*	16	Ind	Ind	Ind	Ind	Ind	
Women's Studies and Greek	MQ97	3FT deg	g	16	Ind	Ind	Ind	Ind	Ind	
Women's Studies and History	MV9D ▼	3FT deg	H	16	Ind	Ind	Ind	Ind	Ind	
Women's Studies and Informatics	GM59	3FT deg	*	14	Ind	Ind	Ind	Ind	Ind	
Women's Studies and Islamic Studies	MT96	3FT deg	*	14	Ind	Ind	Ind	Ind	Ind	
Women's Studies and Latin	MQ96	3FT deg	g	16	Ind	Ind	Ind	Ind	Ind	
Women's Studies and Management Techniques	MN91	3FT deg	*	14	Ind	Ind	Ind	Ind	Ind	
Women's Studies and Medieval Studies	VM19	3FT deg	*	16	Ind	Ind	Ind	Ind	Ind	
Women's Studies and Modern Historical Studies	VM1X	3FT deg			Ind	Ind	Ind	Ind	Ind	
Women's Studies and Philosophical Studies	MV97	3FT deg	*	16	Ind	Ind	Ind	Ind	Ind	
Women's Studies and Religious Studies	MV98	3FT deg	*	14	Ind	Ind	Ind	Ind	Ind	
Women's Studies and Theology	MV9V	3FT deg	*	14	Ind	Ind	Ind	Ind	Ind	
Women's Studies and Victorian Studies	VMC9	3FT deg	*	14	Ind	Ind	Ind	Ind	Ind	
Women's Studies and Welsh	MQ95	3FT deg	W	16	Ind	Ind	Ind	Ind	Ind	
Women's Studies and Welsh Studies	MQ9M	3FT deg	*	16	Ind	Ind	Ind	Ind	Ind	
Combined Honours *Anthropology*	Y400	3FT deg	*	14-16	Ind	Ind	Ind	Ind	Ind	
Combined Honours *Women's Studies*	Y400	3FT deg	*	14-16	Ind	Ind	Ind	Ind	Ind	

LANCASTER Univ

TITLE	CODE	COURSE	SUBJECTS	A/AS	ND/C	AGNVQ	IB	SQA(H)	SQA	RATIO A/AS
American Studies and Women's Studies	QM49	3FT deg	E/H	BBC	Ind		32	ABBBB	Ind	
Criminology and Women's Studies	MM39	3FT deg	*	CCC	M+D		30	ABBBB	Ind	
Economics and Sociology	LL31	3FT deg	*g	22	MO+4D		32	ABBBB	Ind	
Educational Studies and Sociology	XL93	3FT deg	*	BCC-CCC	Ind		30	BBBBB	Ind	
Independent Studies and Sociology	LY34	3FT deg	*	20	Ind		Ind	Ind	Ind	
Organisational Studies and Sociology	NL13	3FT deg	*	BCC	MO+2D		30	BBBBB	Ind	
Peace Studies and International Relations	MM91	3FT deg	*	BCC-CCC	M+D		30	BBBBB	Ind	
Political Sociology	ML13	3FT deg	*	BCC	Ind		30	BBBBB	Ind	
Religious Studies and Sociology	VL83	3FT deg	*	BCD	Ind		28	BBBB	Ind	
Sociology	L300	3FT deg	*	20	MO		30	BBBBB	Ind	
Women's Studies	M900	3FT deg	*	CCC	Ind		32	BBBBB	Ind	
Women's Studies and Applied Social Science	LM49	3FT deg	*	CCC	MO		30	BBBBB	Ind	
Women's Studies and Educational Studies	XM99	3FT deg	*	CCC	MO		30	ABBB	Ind	
Women's Studies and English	QM39	3FT deg	E g	BBB	DO $		32$	ABBBB$	Ind	
Women's Studies and History	VM19	3FT deg	H	BBC	Ind $		30$	ABBBB$	Ind	
Women's Studies and Philosophy	VM79	3FT deg	*	BCC	Ind		30	BBBBB	Ind	
Women's Studies and Psychology	CM89	3FT deg	*g	BBC	DO		32	ABBBB	Ind	
Women's Studies and Religious Studies	VM89	3FT deg	*	18	Ind		28	BBBB	Ind	
Women's Studies and Sociology	LM39	3FT deg	*	20	MO		30	BBBBB	Ind	
Culture, Media and Communication *Cultural Anthropology*	Y400	3FT deg	*	BBB-BBC	M+D		30	ABBBB	Ind	
Culture, Media and Communication *Sociology & Psychology of Communication*	Y400	3FT deg	*	BBB-BBC	M+D		30	ABBBB	Ind	

			98 expected requirements							96 entry stats	
TITLE	CODE	COURSE	SUBJECTS	A/AS	ND/C	AGNVQ	IB	SQA(H)	SQA	RATIO	A/AS

Univ of LEEDS

TITLE	CODE	COURSE	SUBJECTS	A/AS	ND/C	AGNVQ	IB	SQA(H)	SQA	RATIO	A/AS
Chinese-Sociology	LT33	4FT deg	L g	BBC	Ind	Ind	30$	CSYS	Ind		
Development Studies	M920	3FT deg	* g	BBC	Ind	Ind	30$	CSYS	Ind	5	20/28
Economic and Social History-Gender Studies	MV93	3FT deg	* g	BCC	Ind	Ind	28$	CSYS	Ind		
Economic and Social History-Sociology	LV33	3FT deg	* g	BBC	Ind	Ind	30	CSYS	Ind		
Economics-Sociology	LL13	3FT deg	g	BBB	Ind	Ind	32	CSYS	Ind	12	
English-Sociology	QL33	3FT deg	E g	BBB	Ind	Ind	32$	CSYS	Ind	16	24/28
Gender Studies	M900	3FT deg	* g	BCC	Ind	Ind	28$	CSYS	Ind	2	18/24
Gender Studies - Industrial Studies	MN96	3FT deg	* g	BCC	Ind	Ind	28$	CSYS	Ind		
Gender Studies - Politics	MM19	3FT deg	* g	BCC	Ind	Ind	28$	CSYS	Ind		
Gender Studies - Social Policy	LM49	3FT deg	* g	BCC	Ind	Ind	28$	CSYS	Ind		
Gender Studies - Sociology	LM39	3FT deg	* g	BCC	Ind	Ind	28$	CSYS	Ind		
Geography-Sociology	LL38	3FT deg	Gv g	BBB	Ind	D$^ go	32$	CSYS	Ind	18	
History and Philosophy of Science-Sociology	VL53	3FT deg	g	BBC	Ind	Ind	30	CSYS	Ind		
History of Art-Sociology	VL43	3FT deg	g	BBC	Ind	Ind	30	CSYS	Ind		
History-Sociology	VL13	3FT deg	g	BBC	Ind	Ind	30	CSYS	Ind	12	22/26
Philosophy-Sociology	LV37	3FT deg	* g	BBB	Ind	D$^ go	32	CSYS	Ind	43	
Politics-Sociology	LM31	3FT deg	* g	BBB	Ind	Ind	32	CSYS	Ind	10	24/28
Psychology-Sociology	LC38	3FT deg	g	ABB	Ind	D$^ go	33	CSYS	Ind	14	18/28
Religious Studies-Sociology	LV3V	3FT deg	* g	BBC	Ind	D$^ go	30$	CSYS	Ind	25	
Russian-Sociology	RL83	4FT deg	R g	BBC	Ind	Ind	30$	CSYS	Ind		
Russian-Sociology B	RLV3	4FT deg	L g	BBC	Ind	Ind	30$	CSYS	Ind		
Social Policy-Sociology	LL34	3FT deg	* g	BBC	Ind	D$^ go	30	CSYS	Ind	6	20/28
Sociology	L300	3FT deg	* g	BBC	Ind	D$^ go	30	CSYS	Ind	7	20/26
Sociology-Theology	LV38	3FT deg	* g	BBC	Ind	D$^ go	30	CSYS	Ind	13	

LEEDS, TRINITY & ALL SAINTS Univ COLL

TITLE	CODE	COURSE	SUBJECTS	A/AS	ND/C	AGNVQ	IB	SQA(H)	SQA	RATIO	A/AS
Sociology-Management	LN31	3FT deg	* g	BCC-CCD	MO	X	24	BBCCC	Ind	3	10/20
Sociology-Media	LP34	3FT deg	* g	BCC-CCD	MO	X	24	BBCCC	Ind	6	8/24

LEEDS METROPOLITAN Univ

TITLE	CODE	COURSE	SUBJECTS	A/AS	ND/C	AGNVQ	IB	SQA(H)	SQA	RATIO	A/AS
Art and Social Studies	VM99	3FT deg	* g		Ind	Ind go	Ind	Ind	Ind		6/16
Leisure Studies	L380	3FT deg	* g	18	2M+4D	DL go	26	BBBB	Ind	9	12/22
Media and Popular Culture	L670	3FT deg									
Social Sciences - Generic Award	L340	3FT deg	* g	BCC	3M+4D	M$6/^ go	28	BBBBB	Ind	11	14/24
Social Sciences - Sociology	L300	3FT deg									

Univ of LEICESTER

TITLE	CODE	COURSE	SUBJECTS	A/AS	ND/C	AGNVQ	IB	SQA(H)	SQA	RATIO	A/AS
Archaeology and Sociology	LV36	3FT deg	*	18-20	MO	D$^	28	BBBBB	Ind		8/18
European Studies	TM29	4FT deg	F g	BBC-BCC	2M+4D	D$^ gi	30$	ABBBB$	Ind		14/26
Psychology with Sociology	C8L3	3FT deg	* g	BBB	DO	DS^ gi	32	AABBB	Ind		14/30
Sociology	L302	3FT deg	* g	BCC	MO	D$^	28	BBBBC	Ind		14/26
Sociology	L300	3FT deg	* g	BCC	MO	D$^	28	BBBBC	Ind		16/24
Combined Arts Sociology	Y300	3FT deg	* g	BCC	DO	D$^	30$	Ind	Ind		
Combined Science Sociology	Y100	3FT deg	* g	CCC	MO $	D$^	28$	BBBCC$	HN		

Univ of LINCOLNSHIRE and HUMBERSIDE

TITLE	CODE	COURSE	SUBJECTS	A/AS	ND/C	AGNVQ	IB	SQA(H)	SQA	RATIO	A/AS
Applied Social Science	L322▼	3FT deg	* g	12	3M+1D	M	24	CCCC	Ind		
Applied Social Science and Business	LN3C	3FT deg	* g	12	3M+1D	M	24	CCCC	Ind		

Univ of LIVERPOOL

TITLE	CODE	COURSE	SUBJECTS	A/AS	ND/C	AGNVQ	IB	SQA(H)	SQA	RATIO	A/AS
Sociology	L302	3FT deg	*	BCC	Ind	Ind	Ind	Ind	Ind	8	18/26
Sociology and Social Policy	LL34	3FT deg	*	BCC	Ind	Ind	Ind	Ind	Ind	13	16/24

course details   98 expected requirements   96 entry stats

TITLE	CODE	COURSE	SUBJECTS	A/AS	ND/C	AGNVQ	IB	SQA(H)	SQA	RATIO A/AS
Arts Combined *Sociology*	Y401	3FT deg	*	BBC-BBB	Ind	Ind	30$	ABBB	Ind	
Arts Combined *Women's Studies*	Y401	3FT deg	*	BBC-BBB	Ind	Ind	30$	ABBB	Ind	
BA Combined Honours *Sociology*	Y200	3FT deg	* g	BBB	Ind	Ind	Ind	Ind	Ind	
BA Combined Honours *Third World Studies*	Y200	3FT deg	* g	BBB	Ind	Ind	Ind	Ind	Ind	

LIVERPOOL HOPE Univ COLL

TITLE	CODE	COURSE	SUBJECTS	A/AS	ND/C	AGNVQ	IB	SQA(H)	SQA	RATIO A/AS
Sociology/American Studies	QL43	3FT deg	*	12	8M	M$	Ind	Ind	Ind	13
Sociology/Art	WL93	3FT deg	A/Fa	12	8M	MA /P*^	Ind	Ind	Ind	12
Sociology/English	QL33	3FT deg	El	12	8M	P*^	Ind	Ind	Ind	4 8/18
Sociology/European Studies	TL23	3FT deg	*	12	8M	M*	Ind	Ind	Ind	
Sociology/Geography	FL83	3FT deg	Gy	12	8M	M$ /P*^	Ind	Ind	Ind	5 6/10
Sociology/History	VL13	3FT deg	H	12	8M	P*^	Ind	Ind	Ind	4 8/16
Sociology/Human & Applied Biology	CL13	3FT deg	B g	12	8M	M$ go	Ind	Ind	Ind	
Sociology/Information Technology	GL53	3FT deg	*	12	8M	M*	Ind	Ind	Ind	4
Sociology/Mathematics	GL13	3FT deg	M	12	8M	P*^	Ind	Ind	Ind	5
Sociology/Music	WL33	3FT deg	Mu	12	8M	P*^	Ind	Ind	Ind	3
Sociology/Psychology	CL83	3FT deg	g	12	8M	M* go	Ind	Ind	Ind	5 8/16
Sport, Recreation & Physical Education/Sociology	LB36	3FT deg	*	12	8M	M*	Ind	Ind	Ind	
Theology & Religious Studies/Sociology	LV38	3FT deg	*	12	8M	M*	Ind	Ind	Ind	7

LIVERPOOL JOHN MOORES Univ

TITLE	CODE	COURSE	SUBJECTS	A/AS	ND/C	AGNVQ	IB	SQA(H)	SQA	RATIO A/AS
Media and Cultural Studies	LP64	3FT deg		14-18	5M+3D	X	28$	BBBC		28 14/24
Sociology and Applied Community Studies	LL5H	3FT deg	* g	12-14	M0	D$/M$6	28$	BCCC		8 14/16
Sociology and Applied Psychology	CL83	3FT deg	* g	16	M0+3D	M$^ go	28$	BBCC		38 14/18
Sociology and Criminal Justice	LM3H	3FT deg		16	M0+3D	X	28$	BCCC		21 14/20
Sociology and History	LV31▼	3FT deg		12-14	M0+2D	D$/M$6	28$	BCCC		5 12/20
Sociology and Media and Cultural Studies	LP34▼	3FT deg		14-18	M0+3D	X	28$	BBBB		10 14/24
Sociology and Politics	LM31▼	3FT deg		12-14	M0+2D	D$/M$6^	28$	BCCC		7 12/18
Women's Studies and Criminal Justice	MM3Y	3FT deg		16	5M+3D	X	28$	BCCC		5
Women's Studies and Politics	MMX1	3FT deg		14	5M+2D	P$^	28$	BCCC		2 13/14
Women's Studies and Sociology	LM39	3FT deg		14	M0+2D	D$/M$6	28$	BCCC		6 12/16
Womens Studies and Literature, Life and Thought	MQ93▼	3FT deg	E	14-20	5M+3D	PT^	28$	BBBC		1 12/14
International Students Foundation Year *Brit Culture for Int Studs*	Y600	1FT deg								

LONDON GUILDHALL Univ

TITLE	CODE	COURSE	SUBJECTS	A/AS	ND/C	AGNVQ	IB	SQA(H)	SQA	RATIO A/AS
3D/Spatial Design and Development Studies	MW9F	3FT deg	Pf g	DD	M0	M$ go	24	Ind	Ind	
3D/Spatial Design and Sociology	LW3F	3FT deg	Pf g	DD	M0	M$ go	24	Ind	Ind	
Development St & Business Information Technology	GM79	3FT deg	* g	DD	M0	M$ go	24	Ind	Ind	
Development St & Commun & Audio Visual Prod St	MP94	3FT deg	* g	CC-CDD	M0+4D	M$ go	26	Ind	Ind	
Development Studies and Accounting	MN94	3FT deg	* g	DD	M0	M$ go	24	Ind	Ind	
Development Studies and Business	MN91	3FT deg	* g	CD-DDD	M0+2D	M$ go	24	Ind	Ind	
Development Studies and Business Economics	LMC9	3FT deg	* g	DD	M0	M$ go	24	Ind	Ind	
Development Studies and Computing	GM59	3FT deg	* g	DD	M0	M$ go	24	Ind	Ind	
Development Studies and Design Studies	MW92	3FT deg	* g	CD-DDD	M0+2D	M$ go	24	Ind	Ind	
Economics and Development Studies	LM19	3FT deg	* g	DD	M0	M$ go	24	Ind	Ind	
English and Development Studies	MQ93	3FT deg	* g	CD-DDD	M0+2D	M$ go	24	Ind	Ind	
European Studies and Development Studies	MT92	3FT deg	* g	DD	M0	M$ go	24	Ind	Ind	
Financial Services and Development Studies	MN93	3FT deg	* g	DD	M0	M$ go	24	Ind	Ind	
Fine Art and Development Studies	MW91	3FT deg	Pf g	CC-CDD	M0+2D	M$ go	26	Ind	Ind	
French and Development Studies	MR91	4FT deg	* g	DD	M0	M$ go	24	Ind	Ind	

course details

TITLE	CODE	COURSE	SUBJECTS	A/AS	ND/C	AGNVQ	IB	SQA(H)	SQA	RATIO A/AS
German and Development Studies	MR92	4FT deg	* g	DD	MO	M$ go	24	Ind	Ind	
International Relations and Development Studies	MM9C	3FT deg	* g	DD	MO	M$ go	24	Ind	Ind	
Law and Development Studies	MM39	3FT deg	* g	CC-CDD	MO+2D	M$ go	26	Ind	Ind	
Marketing and Development Studies	MN95	3FT deg	* g	CD-DDD	MO+2D	M$ go	26	Ind	Ind	
Mathematics and Development Studies	GM19	3FT deg	* g	DD	MO	M$ go	24	Ind	Ind	
Modern History and Development Studies	MV91	3FT deg	* g	DD	MO	M$ go	24	Ind	Ind	
Multimedia Systems and Development Studies	GMM9	3FT deg	* g	DD	MO	M$ go	24	Ind	Ind	
Politics and Development Studies	MM19	3FT deg	* g	DD	MO	M$ go	24	Ind	Ind	
Product Development & Manuf & Development Studs	JM49	3FT deg	* g	DD	MO	M$ go	24	Ind	Ind	
Psychology and Development Studies	CM89	3FT deg	* g	CD-DDD	MO+2D	M$ go	26	Ind	Ind	
Social Policy & Management and Development Studs	LM49	3FT deg	* g	CD-DDD	MO	M$ go	24	Ind	Ind	
Sociology	L300	3FT deg	* g	12-14	MO	M$ go	24	Ind	Ind	
Sociology & Communications & Audio Vis Prod St	LP34	3FT deg	* g	CC	MO+4D	M$ go	26	Ind	Ind	
Sociology and Accounting	LN34	3FT deg	* g	CD-DDD	MO	M$ go	24	Ind	Ind	
Sociology and Business	LN31	3FT deg	* g	CC-CDD	MO+2D	M$ go	26	Ind	Ind	
Sociology and Business Economics	LL3C	3FT deg	* g	CD-DDD	MO	M$ go	24	Ind	Ind	
Sociology and Business Information Technology	GL73	3FT deg	* g	CD-DDD	MO	M$ go	24	Ind	Ind	
Sociology and Computing	GL53	3FT deg	* g	CD-DDD	MO	M$ go	24	Ind	Ind	
Sociology and Design Studies	LW32	3FT deg	* g	CC-CDD	MO+2D	M$ go	26	Ind	Ind	
Sociology and Development Studies	LM39	3FT deg	* g	CD-DDD	MO	M$ go	24	Ind	Ind	
Sociology and Economics	LL13	3FT deg	* g	CD-DDD	MO	M$ go	24	Ind	Ind	
Sociology and English	LQ33	3FT deg	* g	CC-CDD	MO+2D	M$ go	26	Ind	Ind	
Sociology and European Studies	LT32	3FT deg	* g	CD-DDD	MO	M$ go	24	Ind	Ind	
Sociology and Financial Services	LN33	3FT deg	* g	CD-DDD	MO	M$ go	24	Ind	Ind	
Sociology and Fine Art	LW31	3FT deg	* g	CC	MO+4D	M$ go	26	Ind	Ind	
Sociology and French	LR31	4FT deg	* g	CD-DDD	MO	M$ go	24	Ind	Ind	
Sociology and German	LR32	4FT deg	* g	CD-DDD	MO	M$ go	24	Ind	Ind	
Sociology and International Relations	LM3C	3FT deg	* g	CD-DDD	MO	M$ go	24	Ind	Ind	
Sociology and Law	LM33	3FT deg	* g	CC	MO+4D	M$ go	26	Ind	Ind	
Sociology and Marketing	LN35	3FT deg	* g	CC-CDD	MO+2D	M$ go	26	Ind	Ind	
Sociology and Mathematics	GL13	3FT deg	* g	CD-DDD	MO	M$ go	24	Ind	Ind	
Sociology and Modern History	LV31	3FT deg	* g	CD-DDD	MO	M$ go	24	Ind	Ind	
Sociology and Multimedia Systems	GLM3	3FT deg	* g	CD-DDD	MO	M$ go	24	Ind	Ind	
Sociology and Politics	LM31	3FT deg	* g	CD-DDD	MO	M$ go	24	Ind	Ind	
Sociology and Product Development & Manufacture	JL43	3FT deg	* g	CD-DDD	MO	M$ go	24	Ind	Ind	
Sociology and Psychology	CL83	3FT deg	* g	CC-CDD	MO+2D	M$ go	26	Ind	Ind	
Spanish and Development Studies	MR94	4FT deg	* g	DD	MO	M$ go	24	Ind	Ind	
Spanish and Sociology	LR34	4FT deg	* g	CD-DDD	MO	M$ go	24	Ind	Ind	
Taxation and Development Studies	MN9H	3FT deg	* g	DD	MO	M$ go	24	Ind	Ind	
Taxation and Sociology	LN3H	3FT deg	* g	CD-DDD	MO	M$ go	24	Ind	Ind	
Textile Furnishing Design and Development Studs	MW9G	3FT deg	Pf g	DD	MO	M$ go	24	Ind	Ind	
Textile Furnishing Design and Sociology	LW3G	3FT deg	Pf g	CD-DDD	MO+2D	M$ go	24	Ind	Ind	
Modular Programme *Development Studies*	Y400	3FT deg	* g	CC-DD	MO	M$ go	24	Ind	Ind	
Modular Programme *Sociology*	Y400	3FT deg	* g	CC-DD	MO	M$ go	24	Ind	Ind	

LSE: LONDON Sch of Economics (Univ of London)

TITLE	CODE	COURSE	SUBJECTS	A/AS	ND/C	AGNVQ	IB	SQA(H)	SQA	RATIO A/AS
Anthropology	L601	3FT deg		BBB	Ind	X	$	Ind	Ind	
Anthropology	L603	3FT deg		BBB	Ind	X	$	Ind	Ind	
Anthropology and Law	ML36	3FT deg		BBB	Ind	X	$	Ind	Ind	
Social Policy and Sociology	LL34	3FT deg	g	BBB	Ind	X	$	Ind	Ind	43
Sociology	L301	3FT deg	g	BBB	Ind	X	$	Ind	Ind	

Sociology and Anthropology

			98 expected requirements							96 entry stats	
TITLE	CODE	COURSE	SUBJECTS	A/AS	ND/C	AGNVQ	IB	SQA(H)	SQA	RATIO	A/AS
LOUGHBOROUGH Univ											
Economics with Sociology	L1L3	3FT deg	* g	20	3D	D*6/^ go	30	Ind	Ind	6	
Physical Education and Sports Sci and Soc Sci	BL63	3FT deg	* g	24	4D		30	Ind	Ind		
Politics with Sociology	M1L3	3FT deg	* g	20	2M+3D	D*6/^ go	28	Ind	Ind		14/22
Sociology	L300	3FT deg	*	20	2M+3D	D*6/^ go	30	Ind		5	16/26
LSU COLL of HE											
English with Sociology	Q3L3	3FT deg	E	CD	Ind		Ind	Ind	Ind	5	6/20
European Studies with Sociology	T2L3	3FT deg	Gy/H/Po	DD	Ind		Ind	Ind	Ind	11	
History with Sociology	V1L3	3FT deg	H	CD	Ind		Ind	Ind	Ind	4	8/16
Politics with Sociology	M1L3	3FT deg	*	DD	Ind		Ind	Ind	Ind	7	
Sociology (Combined)	L300	3FT deg									
Sociology and English	QL33	3FT deg									
Sociology and European Studies	TL23	3FT deg									
Sociology and Geography	LL83	3FT deg									
Sociology and History	VL13	3FT deg									
Sociology and Politics	ML13	3FT deg									
Sociology and Psychology	LL73	3FT deg									
Sociology with English	L3Q3	3FT deg									
Sociology with European Studies	L3T2	3FT deg									
Sociology with Geography	L3L8	3FT deg									
Sociology with History	L3V1	3FT deg									
Sociology with Politics	L3M1	3FT deg									
Sociology with Theology	L3V8	3FT deg	*	DD	Ind		Ind	Ind	Ind	7	
Sport Studies	LN37	3FT deg	S/Ss/Pe	CC							
Sport and Health Sciences with Sociology	BL6H	3FT deg									
Sports Science and Sociology	LB36	3FT deg									
Theology and Sociology	LV38	3FT deg									
Theology with Sociology	V8L3	3FT deg									
LUTON Univ											
Built Environment with Social Studies	N8L3	3FT deg	g	12-16	MO/DO	M/D	32	BBCC	Ind		
Business Systems with Social Studies	N1LH	3FT deg	g	12-16	MO/DO	M/D	32	BBCC	Ind		
Business with Social Studies	N1L3	3FT deg	g	12-16	MO/DO	M/D	32	BBCC	Ind	3	
Contemp Br & Euro History with Social Studies	V1L3	3FT deg	g	12-16	MO/DO	M/D	32	BBCC	Ind		
Digital Systems Design with Social Studies	H6LH	3FT deg	g	12-16	MO/DO	M/D	32	BBCC	Ind		
Environmental Science with Social Studies	F9L3	3FT deg	g	12-16	MO/DO	M/D	32	BBCC	Ind		
Environmental Studies with Social Studies	F9LH	3FT deg		12-16	MO/DO	M/D	32	BBCC	Ind		
European Language Studies with Social Studies	T2L3	4FT deg	L g	12-16	MO/DO	M/D	32	BBCC	Ind		
Geography with Social Studies	F8LJ	3FT deg	g	12-16	MO/DO	M/D	32	BBCC	Ind		
Health & Social Studies	BLY3	1FT deg	*		Ind	Ind	Ind	Ind	Ind	1	
Health Science with Social Studies	B9L3	3FT deg	g	12-16	MO/DO	M/D	32	BBCC	Ind		
Health Studies with Social Studies	B9LH	3FT deg	g	12-16	MO/DO	M/D	32	BBCC	Ind		
Law with Social Studies	M3L3	3FT deg	g	12-16	MO/DO	M/D	32	BBCC	Ind		
Leisure Studies with Social Studies	N7L3	3FT deg	g	12-16	MO/DO	M/D	32	BBCC	Ind		
Linguistics with Social Studies	Q1L3	3FT deg	g	12-16	MO/DO	M/D	32	BBCC	Ind		
Mapping Science with Social Studies	F8L3	3FT deg	g	12-16	MO/DO	M/D	32	BBCC	Ind		
Marketing with Social Studies	N5L3	3FT deg	g	12-16	MO/DO	M/D	32	BBCC	Ind		
Mathematical Sciences with Social Studies	G1L3	3FT deg	g	12-16	MO/DO	M/D	32	BBCC	Ind		
Mathematics with Social Studies	G1LH	3FT deg	g	12-16	MO/DO	M/D	32	BBCC	Ind		
Media Practices with Social Studies	P4L3	3FT deg	g	12-16	MO/DO	M/D	32	BBCC	Ind		
Media Production with Social Studies	P4LH	3FT deg	g	12-16	MO/DO	M/D	32	BBCC	Ind		
Modern History with Social Studies	V1LH	3FT deg	g	12-16	MO/DO	M/D	32	BBCC	Ind		

course details   98 expected requirements   96 entry stats

TITLE	CODE	COURSE	SUBJECTS	A/AS	NO/C	AGNVQ	IB	SQA(H)	SQA	RATIO	A/AS
Physical Geography with Social Studies	F8LH	3FT deg	g	12-16	MO/DO	M/D	32	BBCC	Ind		
Politics with Social Studies	M1L3	3FT deg	g	12-16	MO/DO	M/D	32	BBCC	Ind		
Psychology with Social Studies	L7LH	3FT deg	g	12-16	MO/DO	M/D	32	BBCC	Ind	2	6/16
Public Policy and Management with Social Studs	M1LH	3FT deg	g	12-16	MO/DO	M/D	32	BBCC	Ind		
Social Policy with Sociology	L4L3	3FT deg		12-16	MO/DO	M/D	32	BBCC	Ind		
Social Studies	L340	3FT deg	g	12-16	MO/DO	M/D	32	BBCC	Ind		4/16
Social Studies & Language & Stylistics in Engl	QLG3	3FT deg	g	12-16	MO/DO	M/D	32	BBCC	Ind		
Social Studies and Applied Statistics	GL43	3FT deg	g	12-16	MO/DO	M/D	32	BBCC	Ind		
Social Studies and British Studies	VL93	3FT deg		12-16	MO/DO	M/D	32	BBCC	Ind		
Social Studies and Business	NL13	3FT deg	g	12-16	MO/DO	M/D	32	BBCC	Ind		
Social Studies and Business Systems	NLC3	3FT deg	g	12-16	MO/DO	M/D	32	BBCC	Ind		
Social Studies and Computer Science	GL53	3FT deg	g	12-16	MO/DO	M/D	32	BBCC	Ind		
Social Studies and Contemporary History	VL13	3FT deg	g	12-16	MO/DO	M/D	32	BBCC	Ind	3	
Social Studies and Environmental Science	FL93	3FT deg	g	12-16	MO/DO	M/D	32	BBCC	Ind		
Social Studies and European Language Studies	TL23	3FT deg	L g	12-16	MO/DO	M/D	32	BBCC	Ind		
Social Studies and Geography	LF38	3FT deg	g	12-16	MO/DO	M/D	32	BBCC	Ind		
Social Studies and Health Science	BL93	3FT deg	g	12-16	MO/DO	M/D	32	BBCC	Ind		
Social Studies and Health Studies	BLX3	3FT deg	g	12-16	MO/DO	M/D	32	BBCC	Ind	2	
Social Studies and Journalism	PL63	3FT deg		12-16	MO/DO	M/D	32	BBCC	Ind		
Social Studies and Law	ML33	3FT deg	g	12-16	MO/DO	M/D	32	BBCC	Ind	25	
Social Studies and Leisure Studies	NL73	3FT deg	g	12-16	MO/DO	M/D	32	BBCC	Ind		
Social Studies and Linguistics	QL13	3FT deg	g	12-16	MO/DO	M/D	32	BBCC	Ind		
Social Studies and Mapping Science	FL83	3FT deg	g	12-16	MO/DO	M/D	32	BBCC	Ind		
Social Studies and Marketing	NL53	3FT deg	g	12-16	MO/DO	M/D	32	BBCC	Ind		
Social Studies and Mathematical Sciences	GL13	3FT deg	g	12-16	MO/DO	M/D	32	BBCC	Ind		
Social Studies and Mathematics	LG31	3FT deg	g	12-16	MO/DO	M/D	32	BBCC	Ind		
Social Studies and Modern English Studies	QL33	3FT deg	g	12-16	MO/DO	M/D	32	BBCC	Ind	6	
Social Studies and Modern History	VLC3	3FT deg	g	12-16	MO/DO	M/D	32	BBCC	Ind		
Social Studies and Organisational Behaviour	LL73	3FT deg	g	12-16	MO/DO	M/D	32	BBCC	Ind		
Social Studies and Physical Geography	FLV3	3FT deg	g	12-16	MO/DO	M/D	32	BBCC	Ind		
Social Studies and Politics	ML13	3FT deg	g	12-16	MO/DO	M/D	32	BBCC	Ind		
Social Studies and Psychology	LLR3	3FT deg	g	12-16	MO/DO	M/D	32	BBCC	Ind	10	
Social Studies and Public Policy & Management	MLC3	3FT deg	g	12-16	MO/DO	M/D	32	BBCC	Ind	3	
Social Studies with Animation	L3WF	3FT deg	g	12-16	MO/DO	M/D	32	BBCC	Ind		
Social Studies with Applied Statistics	L3G4	3FT deg	g	12-16	MO/DO	M/D	32	BBCC	Ind		
Social Studies with British Studies	L3VX	3FT deg		12-16	MO/DO	M/D	32	BBCC	Ind		
Social Studies with Business	L3N1	3FT deg	g	12-16	MO/DO	M/D	32	BBCC	Ind		
Social Studies with Business Systems	L3NC	3FT deg	g	12-16	MO/DO	M/D	32	BBCC	Ind		
Social Studies with Chinese	L3TH	3FT deg		12-16	MO/DO	M/D	32	BBCC	Ind		
Social Studies with Comparative Literature	L3QF	3FT deg	g	12-16	MO/DO	M/D	32	BBCC	Ind		
Social Studies with Contemporary History	L3V1	3FT deg	g	12-16	MO/DO	M/D	32	BBCC	Ind		
Social Studies with Environmental Science	L3F9	3FT deg	g	12-16	MO/DO	M/D	32	BBCC	Ind		
Social Studies with Film Studies	L3WM	3FT deg	g	12-16	MO/DO	M/D	32	BBCC	Ind		
Social Studies with Geographical Info Systems	L342	3FT deg	g	12-16	MO/DO	M/D	32	BBCC	Ind		
Social Studies with Geography	L3FW	3FT deg	g	12-16	MO/DO	M/D	32	BBCC	Ind		
Social Studies with Health Science	L3B9	3FT deg	g	12-16	MO/DO	M/D	32	BBCC	Ind		
Social Studies with Japanese	L3T4	3FT deg	L g	12-16	MO/DO	M/D	32	BBCC	Ind		
Social Studies with Journalism	L3P6	3FT deg	g	12-16	MO/DO	M/D	32	BBCC	Ind		
Social Studies with Land Reclamation	L3K3	3FT deg	64	12-16	MO/DO	M/D	32	BBCC	Ind		
Social Studies with Lang & Stylistics in English	L3QG	3FT deg	g	12-16	MO/DO	M/D	32	BBCC	Ind		
Social Studies with Leisure Studies	L3N7	3FT deg	g	12-16	MO/DO	M/D	32	BBCC	Ind		
Social Studies with Linguistics	L3Q1	3FT deg	g	12-16	MO/DO	M/D	32	BBCC	Ind		

Sociology and Anthropology

course details			98 expected requirements							96 entry stats
TITLE	CODE	COURSE	SUBJECTS	A/AS	NO/C	AGNVQ	IB	SQA(H)	SQA	RATIO A/AS
Social Studies with Mapping Science	L3F8	3FT deg	g	12-16	MO/DO	M/D	32	BBCC	Ind	
Social Studies with Marketing	L3N5	3FT deg	g	12-16	MO/DO	M/D	32	BBCC	Ind	
Social Studies with Mathematical Sciences	L3GC	3FT deg	g	12-16	MO/DO	M/D	32	BBCC	Ind	
Social Studies with Mathematics	L3GD	3FT deg	g	12-16	MO/DO	M/D	32	BBCC	Ind	
Social Studies with Modern English Studies	L3Q3	3FT deg	g	12-16	MO/DO	M/D	32	BBCC	Ind	4
Social Studies with Modern History	L3VC	3FT deg	g	12-16	MO/DO	M/D	32	BBCC	Ind	
Social Studies with Multimedia	L3PK	3FT deg	g	12-16	MO/DO	M/D	32	BBCC	Ind	
Social Studies with Organisational Behaviour	L3L7	3FT deg	g	12-16	MO/DO	M/D	32	BBCC	Ind	
Social Studies with Physical Geography	L3FV	3FT deg	g	12-16	MO/DO	M/D	32	BBCC	Ind	
Social Studies with Politics	L3M1	3FT deg	g	12-16	MO/DO	M/D	32	BBCC	Ind	
Social Studies with Psychology	L3LR	3FT deg	g	12-16	MO/DO	M/D	32	BBCC	Ind	3
Social Studies with Public Policy and Management	L3MC	3FT deg	g	12-16	MO/DO	M/D	32	BBCC	Ind	
Social Studies with Publishing	L3P5	3FT deg	g	12-16	MO/DO	M/D	32	BBCC	Ind	
Social Studies with TV Studies	L3WN	3FT deg	g	12-16	MO/DO	M/D	32	BBCC	Ind	
Social Studies with Travel and Tourism	L3P7	3FT deg	g	12-16	MO/DO	M/D	32	BBCC	Ind	
Social Studies with Video Production	L3W5	3FT deg	g	12-16	MO/DO	M/D	32	BBCC	Ind	
Sociology	L300	3FT deg		12-16	MO/DO	M/D	32	BBCC	Ind	
Sociology and British Studies	VL9H	3FT deg		12-16	MO/DO	M/D	32	BBCC	Ind	
Sociology and Built Environment	LNH8	3FT deg		12-16	MO/DO	M/D	32	BBCC	Ind	
Sociology and Business	LNH1	3FT deg		12-16	MO/DO	M/D	32	BBCC	Ind	
Sociology and Contemporary History	LVHC	3FT deg		12-16	MO/DO	M/D	32	BBCC	Ind	
Sociology and European Language Studies	LTH2	3FT deg		12-16	MO/DO	M/D	32	BBCC	Ind	
Sociology and Geography	LFH8	3FT deg		12-16	MO/DO	M/D	32	BBCC	Ind	
Sociology and Health Science	LBH9	3FT deg		12-16	MO/DO	M/D	32	BBCC	Ind	
Sociology and Health Studies	LBHX	3FT deg		12-16	MO/DO	M/D	32	BBCC	Ind	
Sociology and Law	LMH3	3FT deg		12-16	MO/DO	M/D	32	BBCC	Ind	
Sociology and Linguistics	LQH1	3FT deg		12-16	MO/DO	M/D	32	BBCC	Ind	
Sociology and Literary Studies in English	LQH2	3FT deg		12-16	MO/DO	M/D	32	BBCC	Ind	
Sociology and Marketing	LNH5	3FT deg		12-16	MO/DO	M/D	32	BBCC	Ind	
Sociology and Media Practices	LPH4	3FT deg		12-16	MO/DO	M/D	32	BBCC	Ind	
Sociology and Modern English Studies	LQH3	3FT deg		12-16	MO/DO	M/D	32	BBCC	Ind	
Sociology and Organisational Behaviour	LLHR	3FT deg		12-16	MO/DO	M/D	32	BBCC	Ind	
Sociology and Planning Studies	LKH4	3FT deg		12-16	MO/DO	M/D	32	BBCC	Ind	
Sociology and Psychology	LLH7	3FT deg		12-16	MO/DO	M/D	32	BBCC	Ind	
Sociology with British Studies	L3V9	3FT deg		12-16	MO/DO	M/D	32	BBCC	Ind	
Sociology with Built Environment	L3K2	3FT deg		12-16	MO/DO	M/D	32	BBCC	Ind	
Sociology with Business	L3NX	3FT deg		12-16	MO/DO	M/D	32	BBCC	Ind	
Sociology with Chinese	L3T3	3FT deg		12-16	MO/DO	M/D	32	BBCC	Ind	
Sociology with Contemporary History	L3VD	3FT deg		12-16	MO/DO	M/D	32	BBCC	Ind	
Sociology with Geography	L306	3FT deg		12-16	MO/DO	M/D	32	BBCC	Ind	
Sociology with Health Science	L3BY	3FT deg		12-16	MO/DO	M/D	32	BBCC	Ind	
Sociology with Health Studies	L3BX	3FT deg		12-16	MO/DO	M/D	32	BBCC	Ind	
Sociology with Linguistics	L3QC	3FT deg		12-16	MO/DO	M/D	32	BBCC	Ind	
Sociology with Literary Studies in English	L3Q2	3FT deg		12-16	MO/DO	M/D	32	BBCC	Ind	
Sociology with Marketing	L3NM	3FT deg		12-16	MO/DO	M/D	32	BBCC	Ind	
Sociology with Media Practices	L3P4	3FT deg		12-16	MO/DO	M/D	32	BBCC	Ind	
Sociology with Modern English Studies	L3QH	3FT deg		12-16	MO/DO	M/D	32	BBCC	Ind	
Sociology with Organisational Behaviour	L307	3FT deg		12-16	MO/DO	M/D	32	BBCC	Ind	
Sociology with Psychology	L3LT	3FT deg		12-16	MO/DO	M/D	32	BBCC	Ind	
Sociology with Social Policy	L3L4	3FT deg		12-16	MO/DO	M/D	32	BBCC	Ind	
Sociology with Travel and Tourism	L3PR	3FT deg		12-16	MO/DO	M/D	32	BBCC	Ind	
Travel and Tourism and Social Studies	LP37	3FT deg	g	12-16	MO/DO	M/D	32	BBCC	Ind	

TITLE	CODE	COURSE	SUBJECTS	A/AS	ND/C	RGNVQ	IB	SQA(H)	SQA	RATIO A/AS
Travel and Tourism and Sociology	LPH7	3FT deg		12-16	MO/DO	M/D	32	BBCC	Ind	
Travel and Tourism with Social Studies	P7L3	3FT deg	g	12-16	MO/DO	M/D	32	BBCC	Ind	
Women's Studies	M900	3FT deg	g	12-16	MO/DO	M/D	32	BBCC	Ind	5
Women's Studies and Accounting	MN94	3FT deg		12-16	MO/DO	M/D	32	BBCC	Ind	
Women's Studies and Biology	MC91	3FT deg		12-16	MO/DO	M/D	32	BBCC	Ind	
Women's Studies and Built Environment	MN98	3FT deg		12-16	MO/DO	M/D	32	BBCC	Ind	
Women's Studies and Business Systems	MN9C	3FT deg		12-16	MO/DO	M/D	32	BBCC	Ind	
Women's Studies and Contemporary History	MV9C	3FT deg		12-16	MO/DO	M/D	32	BBCC	Ind	
Women's Studies and Environmental Science	MF99	3FT deg		12-16	MO/DO	M/D	32	BBCC	Ind	
Women's Studies and Geology	MF96	3FT deg		12-16	MO/DO	M/D	32	BBCC	Ind	
Women's Studies and Health Studies	MB9X	3FT deg		12-16	MO/DO	M/D	32	BBCC	Ind	
Women's Studies and Journalism	PM69	3FT deg		12-16	MO/DO	M/D	32	BBCC	Ind	
Women's Studies and Leisure Studies	MN97	3FT deg		12-16	MO/DO	M/D	32	BBCC	Ind	
Women's Studies and Modern English Studies	MQ93	3FT deg		12-16	MO/DO	M/D	32	BBCC	Ind	
Women's Studies and Politics	MM91	3FT deg		12-16	MO/DO	M/D	32	BBCC	Ind	
Women's Studies and Psychology	ML97	3FT deg		12-16	MO/DO	M/D	32	BBCC	Ind	
Women's Studies and Public Policy & Management	MM9C	3FT deg		12-16	MO/DO	M/D	32	BBCC	Ind	
Women's Studies and Social Policy	LM49	3FT deg		12-16	MO/DO	M/D	32	BBCC	Ind	
Women's Studies and Sociology	LMH9	3FT deg		12-16	MO/DO	M/D	32	BBCC	Ind	
Women's Studies and Travel and Tourism	MP97	3FT deg		12-16	MO/DO	M/D	32	BBCC	Ind	
Women's Studies with Accounting	M9N4	3FT deg		12-16	MO/DO	M/D	32	BBCC	Ind	
Women's Studies with Biology	M9C1	3FT deg		12-16	MO/DO	M/D	32	BBCC	Ind	
Women's Studies with Built Environment	M9N8	3FT deg		12-16	MO/DO	M/D	32	BBCC	Ind	
Women's Studies with Business Systems	M9NC	3FT deg		12-16	MO/DO	M/D	32	BBCC	Ind	
Women's Studies with Contemporary History	M9V1	3FT deg		12-16	MO/DO	M/D	32	BBCC	Ind	
Women's Studies with Environmental Science	M9F9	3FT deg		12-16	MO/DO	M/D	32	BBCC	Ind	
Women's Studies with Geology	M9F6	3FT deg		12-16	MO/DO	M/D	32	BBCC	Ind	
Women's Studies with Health Studies	M9BX	3FT deg		12-16	MO/DO	M/D	32	BBCC	Ind	
Women's Studies with Leisure Studies	M9N7	3FT deg		12-16	MO/DO	M/D	32	BBCC	Ind	
Women's Studies with Modern English Studies	M9Q3	3FT deg		12-16	MO/DO	M/D	32	BBCC	Ind	
Women's Studies with Politics	M9M1	3FT deg		12-16	MO/DO	M/D	32	BBCC	Ind	
Women's Studies with Psychology	M9LR	3FT deg		12-16	MO/DO	M/D	32	BBCC	Ind	
Women's Studies with Public Policy & Management	M9MC	3FT deg		12-16	MO/DO	M/D	32	BBCC	Ind	
Women's Studies with Travel and Tourism	M9P7	3FT deg		12-16	MO/DO	M/D	32	BBCC	Ind	

Univ of MANCHESTER

TITLE	CODE	COURSE	SUBJECTS	A/AS	ND/C	RGNVQ	IB	SQA(H)	SQA	RATIO A/AS
Comparative Religion and Social Anthropology	VL86	3FT deg		20-24	Ind		X	BBBBC	Ind	6 · 26/28
Comparative Religion and Sociology	VL83	3FT deg		20-24	Ind		X	BBBBC	Ind	4 · 18/26
History and Sociology	VL13	3FT deg	*	BBC-BBB			30	CSYS$	Ind	5 · 18/26
Leisure Management	LN37	3FT deg	*	20-24	MO+5D	D^	28	ABBBB	Ind	
Linguistics and Social Anthropology	QL16	3FT deg		BBB	X		32$	AABBB		3 · 22/24
Linguistics and Sociology	QL13	3FT deg		BBB	X		32$	AABBB		15
Philosophy and Sociology	VL73	3FT deg		BBB	Ind		32$	AABBB$	Ind	21
Social Anthropology	L602	3FT deg	g	BBC	M+6D	D^	32	AABBB	Ind	9 · 20/26
Social Anthropology	L600	3FT deg		ABB-BBB	6D	D^	34	AAABB	Ind	7 · 22/30
Sociology	L300	3FT deg		BBC	1M+5D	D^	30	BBBCC	Ind	11 · 18/28
Sociology	L302	3FT deg	g	BBC	M+6D	D^	32	AABBB	Ind	30

MANCHESTER METROPOLITAN Univ

TITLE	CODE	COURSE	SUBJECTS	A/AS	ND/C	RGNVQ	IB	SQA(H)	SQA	RATIO A/AS
Applied Social Studies	L340	3FT deg	*	EE	Ind	M$	Ind	Ind	Ind	
Applied Social Studies/American Studies	LQ34	3FT deg	*	CC	M	D	28	CCCC	Ind	
Business Studies/Applied Social Studies	LN31	3FT deg	*	CC	M	D	28	BBB	Ind	
Cultural Studies/American Studies	LQ3H	3FT deg	*	CC	M+D	D	28	CCCC	Ind	

course details			**98 expected requirements**						**96 entry stats**
TITLE	CODE	COURSE	SUBJECTS	A/AS	NO/C	AGNVQ	IB	SQA(H)	SQA	RATIO A/AS
Cultural Studies/Applied Social Studies	LL3H	3FT deg	*	CC	M+D	D	28	CCCC	Ind	
Cultural Studies/Business Studies	LNH1	3FT deg	*	CC	M+D	D	28	CCCC	Ind	
Dance/Applied Social Studies	LW34	3FT deg	*	CC	M+D	D	28	CCCC	Ind	
Dance/Cultural Studies	LWH4	3FT deg	*	CC	M+D	D	28	CCCC	Ind	
Drama/Applied Social Studies	LW3K	3FT deg	*	CC	M+D	D	28	CCCC	Ind	
Drama/Cultural Studies	LWHK	3FT deg	*	CC	M+D	D	28	CCCC	Ind	
English/Applied Social Studies	LQ33	3FT deg	*	CC	M+D	D	28	CCCC	Ind	
English/Cultural Studies	LQH3	3FT deg	*	CC	M+D	D	28	CCCC	Ind	
Geography/Applied Social Studies	LL83	3FT deg	*	CC	M+D	D	28	CCCC	Ind	
Geography/Cultural Studies	LL8H	3FT deg	*	CC	M+D	D	28	CCCC	Ind	
Health Studies/Applied Social Studies	BL93	3FT deg	*	CC	M+D	D	28	CCCC	Ind	
Health Studies/Cultural Studies	BL9H	3FT deg	*	CC	M+D	D	28	CCCC	Ind	
History/Applied Social Studies	LV31	3FT deg	*	CC	M+D	D	28	CCCC	Ind	
History/Cultural Studies	LVH1	3FT deg	*	CC	M+D	D	28	CCCC	Ind	
Internat Studs in Soc Sci/Maitrise de Sci et Tec	L341	4FT deg	F g	CC	Ind	Ind	Ind	Ind	Ind	
Leisure Studies/Applied Social Studies	LL43	3FT deg	*	CC	M+D	D	28	CCCC	Ind	
Leisure Studies/Cultural Studies	LL4H	3FT deg	*	CC	M+D	D	28	CCCC	Ind	
Music/Applied Social Studies	LW33	3FT deg	*	CC	M+D	D	28	CCCC	Ind	
Music/Cultural Studies	LWH3	3FT deg	*	CC	M+D	D	28	CCCC	Ind	
Philosophy/Applied Social Studies	LV37	3FT deg	*	CC	M+D	D	28	CCCC	Ind	
Philosophy/Cultural Studies	LVH7	3FT deg	*	CC	M+D	D	28	CCCC	Ind	
Religious Studies/Applied Social Studies	LV38	3FT deg	*	CC	M+D	D	28	CCCC	Ind	
Religious Studies/Cultural Studies	LVH8	3FT deg	*	CC	M+D	D	28	CCCC	Ind	
Social Science	L322	3FT deg	* g	CC	1M+4D	Ind	Ind	BBCC	Ind	7/16
Social St of Technol/Scientific Instrumentation	HL63	3FT deg	M/P g	12	5M $	M$	27$	BCCCC$	Ind	
Social Studies of Technology/Applicable Maths	GL13	3FT deg	M g	12	5M $	M$	27$	BCCCC$	Ind	
Social Studies of Technology/Biology	CL13	3FT deg	* g	12	5M	M$	27	BCCCC	Ind	
Social Studies of Technology/Chemistry	FL13	3FT deg	C g	12	5M $	M$	27$	BCCCC$	Ind	
Social Studies of Technology/Computer Technology	GLM3	3FT deg	* g	12	5M	M$	27	BCCCC	Ind	
Social Studies of Technology/Computing Science	GL53	3FT deg	* g	16	1M+3D	M$	28	BBBCC	Ind	
Social Studies of Technology/Electronics	HLP3	3FT deg	* g	12	5M	M$	27	BCCCC	Ind	
Social Studies of Technology/Environmental Studs	FL93	3FT deg	* g	16	1M+3D	M$	28	BBBCC	Ind	
Social Studies of Technology/European Studies	LT32	3FT deg	* g	16	1M+3D	M$	28	BBBCC	Ind	
Social Studies of Technology/Geography	LL38	3FT deg	* g	18	2M+4D	M$	29	BBBBC	Ind	
Social Studies of Technology/Languages	LT39	3FT deg	* g	18	2M+4D	M$	29	BBBBC	Ind	
Social Studies of Technology/Manufacturing	HL73	3FT deg	* g	12	5M	M$	27	BCCCC	Ind	
Social Studies of Technology/Materials Science	FL23	3FT deg	M/P/C g	12	5M $	M$	27$	BCCCC$	Ind	
Social Studies of Technology/Polymer Science	JL43	3FT deg	C g	12	5M $	M$	27$	BCCCC$	Ind	
Social Studies of Technology/Psychology	LL37	3FT deg	* g	18	2M+4D	D$	29	BBBBC	Ind	
Social Studs of Technology/Business Mathematics	GLC3	3FT deg	M/P/Ec g	12	5M $	M$	27$	BCCCC$	Ind	
Social Work Studies (1 year top-up)	L342	1FT deg		X	X	X				
Sociology	L300	3FT deg	So g	CC	1M+4D	Ind	Ind	BBCC	Ind	
Sport/Applied Social Studies	BL63	3FT deg	S	BC	M+D	DS	28	CCCC	Ind	
Sport/Cultural Studies	BL6H	3FT deg	S	BC	M+D	DS	28	CCCC	Ind	
Visual Arts/Applied Social Studies	LW31	3FT deg	*	CC	M+D	D	28	CCCC	Ind	
Visual Arts/Cultural Studies	LWH1	3FT deg	*	CC	M+D	D	28	CCCC	Ind	
Writing/Applied Social Studies	LW3L	3FT deg	*	CC	M+D	D	28	CCCC	Ind	
Writing/Cultural Studies	LWHL	3FT deg	*	CC	M+D	D	28	CCCC	Ind	
Humanities/Social Studies	Y400	3FT deg	*	CDD	Ind	Ind	Ind	BBB	Ind	
Sociology										

course details			98 expected requirements							96 entry stats
TITLE	CODE	COURSE	SUBJECTS	A/AS	NVQ/C	RGNVQ	IB	SQA(H)	SQA	RATIO A/AS
MIDDLESEX Univ										
Criminology	L350▼	3FT deg	* g	12-16	5M	M$ go	28	BCCCC	Ind	
Media and Cultural Studies	LP64▼	3FT deg	* g	12-16	5M	M$ go	28	Ind	Ind	
Race and Culture	LM69▼	3FT deg	* g	12-16	5M	M$ go	28	Ind	Ind	
Social Science (DipSW top-up)	LL35▼	1FT deg	X	X	X	X	X	X	X	
Social Science (Social Work)	L3L5▼	3FT/4SW deg	* g	12-16	5M	M$ go	28	BBCC	Ind	
Sociology	L300▼	3FT/4SW deg	* g	12-16	5M	M$ go	28	BBCC	Ind	
Third World Studies	M920▼	3FT deg	* g	12-16	5M	M$ go	28	Ind	Ind	
Women's Studies	M900▼	3FT deg	* g	12-16	5M	M$ go	28	Ind	Ind	
Joint Honours Degree Criminology	Y400	3FT deg	* g	12-16	5M	M$ go	28	BBCC	Ind	
Joint Honours Degree Race & Culture	Y400	3FT deg	* g	12-16	5M	M$ go	28	CCCC	Ind	
Joint Honours Degree Sociology	Y400	3FT deg	* g	12-16	5M	M$ go	28	BBCC	Ind	
Joint Honours Degree Third World Studies	Y400	3FT deg	* g	16	5M	M$ go	28	BBCC	Ind	
Joint Honours Degree Women's Studies	Y400	3FT deg	*	12-16	5M	M$ go	28	BBCC	Ind	
NAPIER Univ										
Social Sciences	LL37	3FT/4FT deg	g	CD	Ind	Ind	Ind	BCCC	Ind	10/10
Social and Management Sciences	LN31	3FT/4FT deg	g	CD	Ind	Ind	Ind	BCCC	Ind	3 10/12
NENE COLLEGE										
American Studies with Sociology	Q4L3	3FT deg		DD	5M	M	24	CCC	Ind	
American Studies with Third World Development	Q4M9	3FT deg		DD	5M	M	24	CCC	Ind	
Art and Design with Sociology	W2L3	3FT deg		DD	5M	M	24	CCC	Ind	
Behavioural Sciences	CL83	3FT deg	g	14	5M+1D	M	24	CCC	Ind	10/20
Business Admin with Third World Development	N1M9	3FT deg	g	10	M+1D	M	24	BCC	Ind	
Earth Science with Third World Development	F9M9	3FT deg		DD	5M	M	24	CCC	Ind	
Economics with Sociology	L1L3	3FT deg	g	6	5M	M	24	CCC	Ind	
Economics with Third World Development	L1M9	3FT deg	g	6	5M	M	24	CCC	Ind	
English with Sociology	Q3L3▼	3FT deg		CC	4M+1D	M	24	CCC	Ind	
French with Sociology	R1L3	3FT deg	F	DD	5M	Ind	24	CCC	Ind	
Geography with Sociology	F8L3	3FT deg	Gy	8	5M	M	24	CCC	Ind	
Geography with Third World Development	F8M9	3FT deg	Gy	8	5M	M	24	CCC	Ind	
History with Sociology	V1L3▼	3FT deg		CD	5M	M	24	CCC	Ind	
Human Biological Studies with Sociology	B1L3▼	3FT deg	S	DE	5M	M	24	CCC	Ind	6/ 8
Information Systems with Sociology	G5L3	3FT deg		6	5M	M	24	CCC	Ind	
Law with Sociology	M3L3	3FT deg	g	10	3M+2D	M	24	CCC	Ind	6/18
Management Science with Sociology	G4L3	3FT deg	g	DD	5M	M	24	CCC	Ind	
Music with Sociology	W3L3	3FT deg	Mu	DD	5M	M	24	CCC	Ind	
Politics with Sociology	M1L3	3FT deg		CD	5M	M	24	CCC	Ind	
Psychology with Sociology	C8L3▼	3FT deg	g	CC	5M+1D	M	24	CCC	Ind	10/18
Sociology	L300	3FT deg		12	5M	M	24	CCC	Ind	
Sociology with American Studies	L3Q4	3FT deg		10	5M	M	24	CCC	Ind	
Sociology with Art and Design	L3W2	3FT deg		10	5M	M	24	CCC	Ind	
Sociology with Economics	L3L1	3FT deg	g	10	5M	M	24	CCC	Ind	
Sociology with English	L3Q3▼	3FT deg	g	10	5M	M	24	CCC	Ind	6/14
Sociology with French	L3R1	3FT deg	F	10	5M	M	24	CCC	Ind	
Sociology with Geography	L3F8	3FT deg		10	5M	M	24	CCC	Ind	
Sociology with Health Studies	L3L5▼	3FT deg		10	5M	M	24	CCC	Ind	
Sociology with History	L3V1▼	3FT deg		10	5M	M	24	CCC	Ind	

course details				98 expected requirements							96 entry stats	
TITLE	CODE	COURSE	SUBJECTS	A/AS	NO/C	AGNVQ	IB	SQA(H)	SQA	RATIO A/AS	
Sociology with Human Biological Studies	L3B1▼	3FT deg		10	5M	M	24	CCC	Ind		
Sociology with Information Systems	L3G5	3FT deg		10	5M	M	24	CCC	Ind		
Sociology with Law	L3M3	3FT deg	g	10	5M	M	24	CCC	Ind		
Sociology with Marketing Communications	L3N5▼	3FT deg		10	5M	M	24	CCC	Ind		
Sociology with Media and Popular Culture	L3P4▼	3FT deg		10	5M	M	24	CCC	Ind	10/12	
Sociology with Personal & Organisational Develop	L3N6▼	3FT deg		10	5M	M	24	CCC	Ind		
Sociology with Politics	L3M1	3FT deg		10	5M	M	24	CCC	Ind		
Sociology with Property Management	L3N8	3FT deg		10	5M	M	24	CCC	Ind		
Sociology with Psychology	L3C8▼	3FT deg	g	10	5M	M	24	CCC	Ind	6/14	
Sociology with Third World Development	L3M9▼	3FT deg		10	5M	M	24	CCC	Ind		

Univ of NEWCASTLE

Social Studies	L340	3FT deg	*	BCC	Ind		30	BBBBB	HN	8	20/26
Combined Studies (BA) Social Studies	Y400	3FT deg	*	ABC-BBB	5D	Ind	35$	AAAB	Ind		

NORTHBROOK COLLEGE Sussex

Photography, Media and Society	E5L3	3FT deg	Fa/Me/Py/Ar	2	N		Ind	Ind	Ind		
Photography, Media and Society	W5L3	3FT deg	Fa/Me/Py/Ar	2	N		Ind	Ind	Ind		

NORTH EAST WALES INST of HE

Applied Social Studies/Sociology	L340	3FT deg									
English with Sociology	Q3L3	3FT deg		6-12	4M	M$	Ind	BBB	N$		
English/Sociology	QL33	3FT deg		6-12	3M	M$	Ind	CCC	N$		
History with Sociology	V1L3	3FT deg		6-12	4M	M$	Ind	BBB	N$		
History/Sociology	VL13	3FT deg		6-12	4M	M$	Ind	BBB	N$		
Media Studies/Sociology	PL43	3FT deg		6-12	3M	M$	Ind	CCC	N$		
Sociology/Welsh Studies	LQ35	3FT deg		6-12	4M	M$	Ind	BBB	N$		

NORTH EAST WORCESTERSHIRE COLL

Leadership Studies (Public Service)	059M	2FT HND									

Univ of NORTH LONDON

Business and Sociology	LN31	3FT deg	*	CC	Ind	Ind	Ind	Ind	Ind		
Comm & Cultural Studies & Business	LNP1	3FT deg	Me/Cm/E/So g	CC	Ind	Ind	Ind	Ind	Ind		
Communication & Cultural Studies & Arts Mgt	LN61	3FT deg	Cm/Me/E/So g	CC	MO	M	Ind	Ind	Ind	8	
Communication & Cultural Studies & Theatre Studs	LW64	3FT deg	Me/Cm/E/So	CC	MO	M	Ind	Ind	Ind	9	
Communication & Cultural Studies and Film Studs	LW65	3FT deg	E/So/Me/Cm	BC	Ind	M	Ind	Ind	Ind	6	10/20
Communication and Cultural Studies	LP63▼	3FT deg	*	CC	MO	M	$	CCCCC	Ind	6	8/20
Critical Theory and Communication & Cultural St	LP6H	3FT deg	Me/Cm/E/So	CC	Ind	Ind	Ind	Ind	Ind		
Economics and Sociology	LL13	3FT deg	* g	CC	MO+4D	Ind	Ind	Ind	Ind		
Education Studies and Sociology	LX3X	3FT deg	*	CC	Ind	Ind	Ind	Ind	Ind		
European Studies and Sociology	LT32	3FT deg	*	CC	Ind	Ind	Ind	Ind	Ind		
Health Policy and Women's Studies	LM4X	3FT deg	*	CC	Ind	Ind	Ind	Ind	Ind		
Health Studies and Women's Studies	BM99	3FT deg	* g	CC	MO	D	Ind	Ind	Ind		
Human Resource Studies and Women's Studies	NM19	3FT deg	* g	CC	MO+4D	D	Ind	Ind	Ind		
Leisure Studies and Social Research	LN37	3FT deg	* g	CC	MO+4D	Ind	Ind	Ind	Ind		
Leisure Studies and Sociology	LN3R	3FT deg	* g	12-14	MO+4D	Ind	Ind	Ind	Ind		
Marketing and Communication & Cultural Studies	LN65	3FT deg	Cm/Me/E/So g	CC	Ind	Ind	Ind	Ind	Ind		
Marketing and Social Research	LN35	3FT deg	* g	CC	MO+4D	Ind	Ind	Ind	Ind		
Psychology (Applied) and Women's Studies	LM79	3FT deg	* g	CC	Ind	Ind	Ind	Ind	Ind		
Social Research	L310▼	3FT deg	*	CC	MO	M	$	CCCCC	Ind	6	
Social Research and Caribbean Studies	LT37	3FT deg	* g	CC	MO	M	Ind	Ind	Ind	5	
Social Research and Education	LX39	3FT deg	* g	CC	Ind	Ind	Ind	Ind	Ind		
Social Research and Irish Studies	LQ35	3FT deg	* g	CC	MO	M	Ind	Ind	Ind		

course details			98 expected requirements							96 entry stats	
TITLE	CODE	COURSE	SUBJECTS	A/AS	ND/C	AGNVQ	IB	SQA(H)	SQA	RATIO	A/AS
Social Research and South Asian Studies	LT35	3FT deg	* g	CC	MO	M	Ind	Ind	Ind		
Social Research and Statistics	LG34	3FT deg	* g	CD	4M $	M	Ind	Ind	Ind	3	
Sociology and History	LV31	3FT deg	*	CC	Ind	Ind	Ind	Ind	Ind		
Sociology and Irish Studies	LQ3M	3FT deg	*	CC	Ind	Ind	Ind	Ind	Ind		
Sociology and Marketing	LN3M	3FT deg	* g	CC	Ind	Ind	Ind	Ind	Ind		
Sociology and Philosophy	LV37	3FT deg	*	CC	Ind	Ind	Ind	Ind	Ind		
Sociology and South Asian Studies	LT3M	3FT deg	*	CC	Ind	Ind	Ind	Ind	Ind		
Sociology and Women's Studies	LM39	3FT deg	*	CC	Ind	Ind	Ind	Ind	Ind		
Women's Studies and Law	MM39	3FT deg	*	CC	Ind	Ind	Ind	Ind	Ind		
Women's Studies and Social Policy	LM49	3FT deg	*	CC	Ind	Ind	Ind	Ind	Ind		
Combined Honours *Sociology*	Y301	3FT deg	*	CC	MO	M	Ind	CCCCC	Ind		
Combined Honours *Women's Studies*	Y300	3FT deg	*	CC	Ind	Ind	Ind	Ind	Ind		

Univ of NORTHUMBRIA

Criminology And Sociology	LM33	3FT deg	So g	BC	2M+2D	M	24	BCCC	Ind		
English and Women's Cultures	QM39	3FT deg	E	BCC	MO+4D		26	BBBCC	Ind	4	
History and Sociology	LV31	3FT deg	H+So	18	MO+4D		26	Ind	Ind	18	
Human Organisations	L310	3FT deg		16	4M	M	24	CSYS	Ind	3	
Politics and Sociology	LM31	3FT deg	So g	16	3M		24	BBCCC	Ind	3	10/18
Sociology	L300	3FT deg	So g	BC	2M+2D		24	BCCC	Ind	6	10/22
Sociology and Social Research	L301	4FT deg	So g	BC	2M+2D		24	BCCC	Ind	8	
Combined Honours *Sociology*	Y400▼	3FT deg	g	12-20	MO+3D	DG	26	BBCCC	Ind		

NORWICH: City COLL

Psychology with Sociology	L7L3	3FT deg	* g	12	5M	P	Ind	Ind	Ind		
Combined Arts *Sociology*	Y300	3FT deg	* g	12	Ind		Ind	Ind	Ind		

Univ of NOTTINGHAM

Social and Cultural Studies	L372	3FT deg	*	BBC	Ind	Ind	30	Ind	Ind	13	21/30
Sociology	L300	3FT deg	*	BBC	Ind	Ind	30	Ind	Ind	26	19/30
Sociology with East European Studies	L3T1	3FT deg	*	BBC	Ind	Ind	30	Ind	Ind		

NOTTINGHAM TRENT Univ

Criminology	L330	3FT deg	H/So/Ps/Lw	18-20	5D	Ind	Ind	BBBC	Ind	14	14/24
Environment and Human Sciences	YL43	3FT deg	* g	12	Ind	M$ go	Ind	Ind	Ind		8/18
Media and Cultural Studies	LP64	3FT deg	* g	16-18	M+D	Ind	28	CCCC	Ind	1	14/22
Social Sciences	L322▼	3FT deg	* g	BB-CCC	1M+4D		Ind	BBBC	Ind	4	12/22
Humanities *Individual and Society*	Y301	3FT/4SW deg	* g	14-16	M+D	Ind	28	CCCC	Ind		
Humanities *Media and Cultural Studies*	Y301	3FT/4SW deg	* g	14-16	M+D	Ind	28	CCCC	Ind		

OXFORD Univ

Archaeology and Anthropology	LV66	3FT deg	*	AAB-ABB	DO		36	AAAAA	Ind	3	22/30
Human Sciences *Social Anthropology*	Y400	3FT deg	*	AAB-ABB	DO		36	AAAAA	Ind		
Human Sciences *Sociology*	Y400	3FT deg	*	AAB-ABB	DO		36	AAAAA	Ind		

OXFORD WESTMINSTER COLLEGE

Contemporary English Studies with Development St	Q3LH	2FT Dip	E	CE	MO	M	Ind	CCC	Ind		
Contemporary English Studies with Development St	Q3L3	3FT deg	E	CE	MO	M	Ind	CCC	Ind		

			98 expected requirements							96 entry stats	

course details ・ *98 expected requirements* ・ *96 entry stats*

TITLE	CODE	COURSE	SUBJECTS	A/AS	ND/C	AGNVQ	IB	SQA(H)	SQA	RATIO	A/AS
Contemporary French Studies with Development St	R1L3	3FT deg	F	CE	MO	M	Ind	CCC	Ind		
Contemporary French Studies with Development St	R1LH	2FT Dip	F	CE	MO	M	Ind	CCC	Ind		
Contemporary Geography Studs with Development St	L8L3	3FT deg	Gy	CE	MO	M	Ind	CCC	Ind		
Contemporary Geography Studs with Development St	L8LH	2FT Dip	Gy	CE	MO	M	Ind	CCC	Ind		
Contemporary Historical Studies with Dev Studies	V1L3	3FT deg	H	CE	MO	M	Ind	CCC	Ind		
Contemporary Historical Studs w. Development St	V1LH	2FT Dip	H	CE	MO	M	Ind	CCC	Ind		

OXFORD BROOKES Univ

TITLE	CODE	COURSE	SUBJECTS	A/AS	ND/C	AGNVQ	IB	SQA(H)	SQA	RATIO	A/AS
Anthropology/Accounting and Finance	LN64	3FT deg	* g	BCC	Ind	D*3/M*^	Ind	Ind	Ind		
Biological Chemistry/Anthropology	CL76	3FT deg	S g	DD-BCC	Ind		Ind	Ind	Ind		
Biology/Anthropology	CL16	3FT deg	S g	DD-BCC	Ind	MS^	Ind	Ind	Ind	2	14/20
Business Administration and Mgt/Anthropology	LN61	3FT deg	* g	BCC-BBC	Ind	MB4/^4	Ind	Ind	Ind		
Cartography/Anthropology	FL86	3FT deg	* g	DDD-BCC	Ind	M*^	Ind	Ind	Ind		
Cell Biology/Anthropology	CLC6	3FT deg									
Combined Studies/Anthropology	LY64	3FT deg		X		X	X	X			
Computer Systems/Anthropology	GL66	3FT deg	* g	BC-BCC	Ind	M*^	Ind	Ind	Ind		
Computing Mathematics/Anthropology	GL96	3FT deg	* g	CD-BCC	Ind	M*^	Ind	Ind	Ind		
Computing/Anthropology	GL56	3FT deg	* g	CDD-BCC	Ind	M*^	Ind	Ind	Ind		
Ecology/Anthropology	CL96	3FT deg	* g	CD-BCC	Ind	MS/M*^	Ind	Ind	Ind	2	
Economics/Anthropology	LL16	3FT deg	* g	BB-CCD	Ind	M*^/3	Ind	Ind	Ind		
Educational Studies/Anthropology	LX69	3FT deg	*	CC-BCC	Ind	M*^/3	Ind	Ind	Ind	4	
Electronics/Anthropology	HL66	3FT deg	S/M	CC-BCC	Ind	M$/M*^	Ind	Ind	Ind		
English Studies/Anthropology	LQ63	3FT deg	*	AB-BCC	Ind	M*^	Ind	Ind	Ind	9	
Environmental Policy/Anthropology	KL36	3FT deg									
Environmental Sciences/Anthropology	FLX6	3FT deg	S g	CD-BCC	Ind	M*^/DS	Ind	Ind	Ind	3	
Exercise and Health/Anthropology	LB66	3FT deg	S	DD-BCC	Ind	MS^	Ind	Ind	Ind		
Fine Art/Anthropology	LW61	3FT deg	Pf+A	BC-BCC	Ind	MA^	Ind	Ind	Ind		
Food Science and Nutrition/Anthropology	DL46	3FT deg	S g	DD-BCC	Ind	MS^	Ind	Ind	Ind	3	
French Language and Contemp Studies/Anthropology	LR6C	4SW deg	F	CDD-BCC	Ind	M*^	Ind	Ind	Ind		
French Language and Literature/Anthropology	LR61	4SW deg	F	CDD-BCC	Ind	M*^	Ind	Ind	Ind	1	
Geography and the Phys Env/Anthropology	FLV6	3FT deg									
Geography/Anthropology	LL68	3FT deg	*	BB-CCD	Ind	M*^	Ind	Ind	Ind	26	
Geotechnics/Anthropology	HL26	3FT deg	S/M/Ds/Es	DD-BCC	Ind	M$^	Ind	Ind	Ind		
German Language and Contemp Stud/Anthropology	LR6F	4SW deg	G	DDD-BCC	Ind	M*^	Ind	Ind	Ind		
German Studies/Anthropology	LR6G	4SW deg			Ind		Ind	Ind	Ind		
Health Care/Anthropology (Post Exp)	BL76	3FT deg		X		X	X	X			
History of Art/Anthropology	LV64	3FT deg	*	BCC	Ind	M*^	Ind	Ind	Ind	7	16/20
History/Anthropology	LV61	3FT deg	*	BB-CCD	Ind	M*^	Ind	Ind	Ind	44	
Hospitality Management Studies/Anthropology	LN67	3FT deg	*	DDD-BCC	Ind	M*^/M*3	Ind	Ind	Ind	1	
Human Biology/Anthropology	BL16	3FT deg			Ind		Ind	Ind	Ind		
Information Systems/Anthropology	GLM6	3FT deg	* g	CDD-BCC	Ind	M*^	Ind	Ind	Ind	1	
Intelligent Systems/Anthropology	GL86	3FT deg	* g	CD-BCC	Ind	M*/D*3	Ind	Ind	Ind		
Law/Anthropology	LM63	3FT deg	*	BCC-BBB	Ind	M*^/D*	Ind	Ind	Ind		
Leisure Planning/Anthropology	KLH6	3FT deg									
Marketing Management/Anthropology	LN6N	3FT deg	* g	BCC	Ind	M*^/D*3	Ind	Ind	Ind		
Music/Anthropology	LW63	3FT deg	Mu	DD-BCC	Ind	M/M*^	Ind	Ind	Ind	3	
Palliative Care/Anthropology (Post Exp)	BLR6	3FT deg		X		X	X	X			
Planning Studies/Anthropology	KL46	3FT deg	* g	DDD-BCC	Ind	M*^	Ind	Ind	Ind	4	
Politics/Anthropology	LM61	3FT deg	*	AB-CCC	Ind	M*^	Ind	Ind	Ind	6	
Psychology/Anthropology	CL86	3FT deg	* g	BCC-BBC	Ind	M*^	Ind	Ind	Ind	45	
Publishing/Anthropology	LP65	3FT deg	* g	BB-CCD	Ind	M*^/M$	Ind	Ind	Ind	3	
Rehabilitation/Anthropology (Post Exp)	BLT6	3FT deg		X		X	X	X			
Sociology/Accounting and Finance	LN34	3FT deg	* g	BCC	Ind	M*^/D*3	Ind	Ind	Ind		

course details | 98 expected requirements | 96 entry stats

TITLE	CODE	COURSE	SUBJECTS	A/AS	ND/C	AGNVQ	IB	SQA(H)	SQA	RATIO A/AS
Sociology/Anthropology	LL36	3FT deg	*	BCC	Ind	M*^	Ind	Ind	Ind	12
Sociology/Biological Chemistry	CL73	3FT deg								
Sociology/Biology	CL13	3FT deg	S/M g	DD-BCC	Ind	MS/M*^	Ind	Ind	Ind	
Sociology/Business Administration & Management	LN31	3FT deg	* g	BCC-BBC	Ind	M*^/MB4	Ind	Ind	Ind	17
Sociology/Cartography	FL83	3FT deg	* g	DDD-BCC	Ind	M*^	Ind	Ind	Ind	
Sociology/Cell Biology	CLC3	3FT deg								
Sociology/Combined Studies	LY34	3FT deg		X		X	X	X		
Sociology/Computer Systems	GL63	3FT deg	* g	CDD-BCC	Ind	M*^	Ind	Ind	Ind	
Sociology/Computing Mathematics	GL93	3FT deg	* g	CD-BCC	Ind	M*^	Ind	Ind	Ind	
Sociology/Ecology	CL93	3FT deg	* g	CD-BCC	Ind	MS/M*^	Ind	Ind	Ind	
Sociology/Economics	LL13	3FT deg	* g	BB-CCD	Ind	M*^/M*3	Ind	Ind	Ind	
Sociology/Educational Studies	LX39	3FT deg	*	CC-BCC	Ind	M*^/M*3	Ind	Ind	Ind	7
Sociology/Electronics	HL63	3FT deg	S/M	CC-BCC	Ind	M$/M*^	Ind	Ind	Ind	
Sociology/English Studies	LQ33	3FT deg	*	AB-BCC	Ind	M*^	Ind	Ind	Ind	15
Sociology/Environmental Chemistry	LF31	3FT deg								
Sociology/Environmental Policy	KL33	3FT deg								
Sociology/Environmental Sciences	FLX3	3FT deg	S g	CD-BCC	Ind	M*^/DS	Ind	Ind	Ind	4
Sociology/Exercise and Health	LB36	3FT deg	S g	DD-BCC	Ind	MS/M*^	Ind	Ind	Ind	
Sociology/Fine Art	LW31	3FT deg	Pf+A g	BC-BCC	Ind	MA^	Ind	Ind	Ind	
Sociology/Food Science and Nutrition	DL43	3FT deg	S g	DD-BCC	Ind	MS/M*^	Ind	Ind	Ind	
Sociology/French Language and Contemp Studies	LR3C	4SW deg	F	CDD-BCC	Ind	M*_	Ind	Ind	Ind	16
Sociology/French Language and Literature	LR31	4SW deg	F	CDD-BCC	Ind	M*_	Ind	Ind	Ind	5
Sociology/Geography	LL38	3FT deg	*	BB-CCD	Ind	M*^	Ind	Ind	Ind	34
Sociology/Geology	FL63	3FT deg	S/M g	DD-BCC	Ind	PS/M*^	Ind	Ind	Ind	
Sociology/Geotechnics	HL23	3FT deg	S/M/Ds/Es	DD-BCC	Ind	M$/M*^	Ind	Ind	Ind	
Sociology/German Language and Contemp Stud	LR3F	4SW deg	G	DDD-BCC	Ind	M*_	Ind	Ind	Ind	
Sociology/German Language and Literature	LR32	4SW deg	G	DDD-BCC	Ind	M*_	Ind	Ind	Ind	
Sociology/German Studies	LR3G	4SW deg	G	DDD-BCC	Ind	M*_	Ind	Ind	Ind	
Sociology/Health Care (Post Exp)	BL73	3FT deg		X		X	X	X		
Sociology/History	LV31	3FT deg	*	BB-CCD	Ind	M*^	Ind	Ind	Ind	18
Sociology/History of Art	LV34	3FT deg	*	BCC	Ind	M*^	Ind	Ind	Ind	2 · 18/20
Sociology/Hospitality Management Studies	LN37	3FT deg	* g	BCC	Ind	M*^/M*3	Ind	Ind	Ind	
Sociology/Human Biology	BL13	3FT deg								
Sociology/Information Systems	GLM3	3FT deg		CDD-BCC	Ind	M*^	Ind	Ind	Ind	
Sociology/Intelligent Systems	GL83	3FT deg	* g	CDD-BCC	Ind	M*^	Ind	Ind	Ind	2
Sociology/Law	LM33	3FT deg	*	BCC-BBB	Ind	M*^/D*3	Ind	Ind	Ind	20
Sociology/Leisure Planning and Management	KLH3	3FT deg								
Sociology/Marketing Management	LN3N	3FT deg	* g	BCC	Ind	M*^/D*3	Ind	Ind	Ind	22
Sociology/Mathematics	GL13	3FT deg	M	DD-BCC	Ind	M*^	Ind	Ind	Ind	
Sociology/Music	LW33	3FT deg	Mu	DD-BCC	Ind	M*^	Ind	Ind	Ind	
Sociology/Palliative Care (Post Exp)	BLR3	3FT deg		X		X	X	X		
Sociology/Physical Geography	FLV3	3FT deg								
Sociology/Planning Studies	KL43	3FT deg	* g	DD-BCC	Ind	M*^	Ind	Ind	Ind	
Sociology/Politics	LM31	3FT deg	*	AB-CCC	Ind	M*^	Ind	Ind	Ind	25
Sociology/Psychology	CL83	3FT deg	* g	BCC-BBC	Ind	M*^	Ind	Ind	Ind	28
Sociology/Publishing	LP35	3FT deg	* g	BB-CCD	Ind	M*^/M$3	Ind	Ind	Ind	3
Sociology/Rehabilitation (Post Exp)	BLT3	3FT deg		X		X	X	X		
Sociology/Retail Management	LN35	3FT deg	* g	CCD-BCC	Ind		Ind	Ind	Ind	
Software Engineering/Anthropology	GL76	3FT deg	* g	CDD-BCC	Ind	M*^	Ind	Ind	Ind	
Software Engineering/Sociology	GL73	3FT deg	* g	CDD-BCC	Ind	M*^	Ind	Ind	Ind	
Statistics/Anthropology	GL46	3FT deg	* g	DD-BCC	Ind	M*^	Ind	Ind	Ind	
Statistics/Sociology	GL43	3FT deg	* g	DD-BCC	Ind	M*^	Ind	Ind	Ind	

| | | | 98 expected requirements | | | | | | | 96 entry stats |
| | | | | | | | | | | |

course details										

TITLE	CODE	COURSE	SUBJECTS	A/AS	NO/C	AGNVQ	IB	SQA(H)	SQA	RATIO A/AS
Telecommunications/Anthropology	HLP6	3FT deg								
Telecommunications/Sociology	HLP3	3FT deg								
Tourism/Anthropology	LP67	3FT deg	* g	BCC-CCD	Ind	M*^/M*3	Ind	Ind	Ind	15
Tourism/Sociology	LP37	3FT deg	* g	BCC-CCD	Ind	M*^/M*3	Ind	Ind	Ind	
Transport Planning/Anthropology	LN69	3FT deg	* g	BCC-DDD	Ind	M*^	Ind	Ind	Ind	
Transport Planning/Sociology	LN39	3FT deg	* g	BCC-DDD	Ind	M*^	Ind	Ind	Ind	
Water Resources/Anthropology	HLF6	3FT deg								
Water Resources/Sociology	HLF3	3FT deg								

Univ of PAISLEY

Applied Social Studies	L310	3FT/4FT deg	* g	CC	Ind	Ind	Ind	BBB$	Ind	4	6/18

Univ of PLYMOUTH

Applied Economics with Sociology	L1L3	3FT deg	Ap g	CCD-CDD	MO	M$^	Ind	BCCC	Ind	
Business Economics with Sociology	L1LH	3FT deg	Ap g	CDD-CCD	MO	M$^	Ind	BCCC	Ind	
European Economics with Sociology	L1LJ	3FT deg	Ap g	CDD-CCD	MO	M$^	Ind	BCCC	Ind	
Geography with Social Research	F8LH	3FT deg	Gy g	16-18	X	M$^	Ind	Ind	Ind	
Geography with Sociology	F8L3	3FT deg	Gy g	16-18	X	M$^	Ind	Ind	Ind	22
Law with Sociology	M3L3	3FT deg	Ap g	BCC-BBC	DO	D12^	Ind	BBBB$	Ind	46
Modern Languages with Sociology	T9L3	3FT/4SW deg	L g	C	Ind	Ind	Ind	Ind	Ind	
Political Economy with Sociology	LL1H	3FT deg	Ap g	CDD-CCD	MO $	M$^	Ind	BCCC	Ind	
Politics with Social Research	M1LJ	3FT deg	* g	14	3M	M$	Ind	BBBC$	Ind	
Politics with Sociology	M1L3	3FT deg	* g	14	3M	M$	Ind	BBBC$	Ind	8
Psychology with Sociology	C8L3	3FT/4SW deg	Ap g	BBC	MO+3D	M12^	Ind	BBBC$	Ind	9	16/26
Social Policy with Social Research	L4LH	3FT deg	* g	14	3M	M$	Ind	BBBC$	Ind	
Social Policy with Sociology	L4L3	3FT deg	* g	14	3M	M$	Ind	BBBC$	Ind	3	8/16
Sociology	L300	3FT deg	* g	14	3M	M$	Ind	BBBC$	Ind	7	8/18
Sociology with Applied Economics	L3L1	3FT deg	* g	14	3M	M$	Ind	BBBC$	Ind	
Sociology with Computing	L3G5	3FT deg	* g	14	Ind	M$	Ind	BBBC$	Ind	8
Sociology with Criminal Justice	L3M3	3FT deg	* g	16	3M	M$	Ind	BBBC$	Ind	5	8/18
Sociology with French	L3R1	3FT deg	F g	14	Ind	M$^	Ind	BBBC$	Ind	
Sociology with Geography	L3F8	3FT deg	Gy g	16	5M $	M$^	Ind	BBBC$	Ind	9
Sociology with German	L3R2	3FT deg	G g	14	Ind	M$^	Ind	BBBC$	Ind	
Sociology with Human Biology	L3C9	3FT deg	B g	BBC	2M+3D$	M$^	Ind	BBBC$	Ind	6
Sociology with International Relations	L3MC	3FT deg	* g	14	3M	M$	Ind	BBBC$	Ind	
Sociology with Italian	L3R3	3FT deg	* g	14	3M $	M$	Ind	BBBC$	Ind	
Sociology with Languages	L3T9	3FT deg	L g	14	3M	M$^	Ind	BBBC$	Ind	10
Sociology with Law	L3MH	3FT deg	* g	BCC	Ind	D12^	Ind	BBBC$	Ind	28
Sociology with Politics	L3M1	3FT deg	* g	14	3M	M$	Ind	BBBC$	Ind	7
Sociology with Psychology	L3C8	3FT deg	* g	BCC	2M+3D	D12^	Ind	BBBC$	Ind	10	16/18
Sociology with Social Policy	L3L4	3FT deg	* g	14	3M	M$	Ind	BBBC$	Ind	4	8/22
Sociology with Social Research	L310	3FT deg	* g	14	3M	M$	Ind	BBBC$	Ind	
Sociology with Spanish	L3R4	3FT deg	Sp g	14	Ind	M$^	Ind	BBBC$	Ind	
Sociology with Statistics	L3G4	3FT deg	* g	14	Ind	M$^	Ind	BBBC$	Ind	

Univ of PORTSMOUTH

Cultural Studies and Sociology	L375	3FT deg	E/So	12	Ind	M$6/^	26	BCCC	Ind	
Cultural and Historical Studies	LV31	3FT deg	E/H	12	Ind	M$6/^	26	BCCC	Ind	
Economic History and Historical Geography	LV38	3FT deg	Gy	12	4M $	M*	Dip	BBCC	Ind	
Information Technology and Society	GL53	4SW deg	*	14	6M	M* go	28	CCCC	Ind	2	6/16
Sociology	L300	3FT deg	*	12	Ind	D$6/^	26	Ind	Ind	5	7/18

QUEEN MARGARET COLL

Social Sciences and Health	BL93	3FT/4FT deg	*	CC	M+D	D$ go	Ind	BBB	Ind	4	12/16

course details | 98 expected requirements | 96 entry stats

TITLE	CODE	COURSE	SUBJECTS	A/AS	NO/C	RGNVQ	IB	SQA(H)	SQA	RATIO A/AS
QUEEN'S Univ Belfast										
Management with Sociology	N1L3	3FT deg	* g	BBB	2M+5D	D*^ go	32$	AABBB	Ind	
Social Anthropology	L600	3FT deg	* g	BCC	3M+4D	D*6/^ go	29$	ABBB	Ind	11 16/22
Social Anthropology/Ancient History	VLC6	3FT deg	* g	BCC	3M+4D	D*6/^ go	29$	ABBB	Ind	7
Social Anthropology/Archaeology	VL66	3FT deg	* g	BCC	3M+4D	D*6/^ go	29$	ABBB	Ind	10
Social Anthropology/Biblical Studies	VL86	3FT deg	* g	BCC	3M+4D	D*6/^ go	29$	ABBB	Ind	
Social Anthropology/Byzantine Studies	QL86	3FT/4FT deg	* g	BCC	3M+4D	D*6/^ go	29$	ABBB	Ind	
Social Anthropology/Celtic	QL56	3FT/4FT deg	* g	BCC	3M+4D	D*6/^ go	29$	ABBB	Ind	7
Social Anthropology/Classical Studies	LQ68	3FT deg	* g	BCC	3M+4D	D*6/^ go	29$	ABBB	Ind	
Social Anthropology/Economic & Social History	VL36	3FT deg	* g	BCC	3M+4D	D*6/^ go	29$	ABBB	Ind	
Social Anthropology/English	QL36	3FT deg	E g	BCC	X	D*^ go	29$	ABBB	X	11
Social Anthropology/Ethnomusicology	WL3P	3FT deg	* g	BCC	3M+4D	D*6/^ go	29$	ABBB	Ind	3
Social Anthropology/French (4 years)	RL16	4FT deg	F g	BCC	X	D*^ go	29$	ABBB	X	4
Social Anthropology/Geography	LL86	3FT deg	Gy g	BCC	X	D*^ go	29$	X	X	7 20/20
Social Anthropology/German (4 years)	RL26	4FT deg	* g	BCC	3M+4D	D*6/^ go	29$	ABBB	Ind	
Social Anthropology/Greek	QL76	3FT/4FT deg	* g	BCC	3M+4D	D*6/^ go	29$	ABBB	Ind	
Social Anthropology/History & Philosophy of Sci	VL56	3FT deg	* g	BCC	3M+4D	D*6/^ go	29$	ABBB	Ind	
Social Anthropology/Italian (4 years)	RL36	4FT deg	* g	BCC	3M+4D	D*6/^ go	29$	ABBB	Ind	
Social Anthropology/Latin	QL66	3FT/4FT deg	* g	BCC	3M+4D	D*6/^ go	29$	ABBB	Ind	
Social Anthropology/Modern History	VL16	3FT deg	* g	BCC	3M+4D	D*6/^ go	29$	ABBB	Ind	8 22/26
Social Anthropology/Music	WL36	3FT deg	* g	BCC	3M+4D	D*6/^ go	29$	ABBB	Ind	
Social Anthropology/Philosophy	VL76	3FT deg	* g	BCC	3M+4D	D*6/^ go	29$	ABBB	Ind	7
Social Anthropology/Politics	ML16	3FT deg	* g	BCC	3M+4D	D*6/^ go	29$	ABBB	Ind	23
Social Anthropology/Psychology	CL86	3FT deg	* g	BCC	3M+4D	D*6/^ go	29$	ABBB	Ind	12 20/26
Social Anthropology/Scholastic Philosophy	LV67	3FT deg	* g	BCC	3M+4D	D*6/^ go	29$	ABBB	Ind	
Social Policy/Social Anthropology	LL64	3FT deg	* g	BCC	3M+4D	D*6/^ go	29$	ABBB	Ind	
Sociology	L300	3FT deg	* g	BCC	3M+4D	D*6/^ go	29$	ABBB	Ind	7 18/26
Sociology/Byzantine Studies	QL83	3FT/4FT deg	* g	BCC	3M+4D	D*6/^ go	29$	ABBB	Ind	
Sociology/Economic & Social History	VL33	3FT deg	* g	BCC	3M+4D	D*6/^ go	29$	ABBB	Ind	
Sociology/English	QL33	3FT deg	E g	BCC	X	D*^ go	29$	ABBB	X	10 20/28
Sociology/Greek	QL73	3FT/4FT deg	* g	BCC	3M+4D	D*6/^ go	29$	ABBB	Ind	
Sociology/History & Philosophy of Science	VL53	3FT deg	* g	BCC	3M+4D	D*6/^ go	29$	ABBB	Ind	
Sociology/Human Geography	LL3V	3FT deg	* g	BCC	3M+4D	D*6/^ go	29$	ABBB	Ind	
Sociology/Latin	QL63	3FT/4FT deg	* g	BCC	3M+4D	D*6/^ go	29$	ABBB	Ind	
Sociology/Modern History	VL13	3FT deg	* g	BCC	3M+4D	D*6/^ go	29$	ABBB	Ind	
Sociology/Philosophy	VL73	3FT deg	* g	BCC	3M+4D	D*6/^ go	29$	ABBB	Ind	5
Sociology/Politics	ML13	3FT deg	* g	BCC	3M+4D	D*6/^ go	29$	ABBB	Ind	9 20/26
Sociology/Psychology	CL83	3FT deg	* g	BCC	3M+4D	D*6/^ go	32$	ABBB	Ind	23 20/26
Sociology/Scholastic Philosophy	LV37	3FT deg	* g	BCC	3M+4D	D*6/^ go	29$	ABBB	Ind	
Sociology/Social Anthropology	LL63	3FT deg	* g	BCC	3M+4D	D*6/^ go	29$	ABBB	Ind	6 18/20
Sociology/Social Policy	LL43	3FT deg	* g	BCC	3M+4D	D*6/^ go	29$	ABBB	Ind	
Spanish/Social Anthropology (4 years)	LR64	4FT deg	* g	BCC	3M+4D	D*6/^ go	29$	ABBB	Ind	6
Women's Studies	M900	3FT deg	* g	BCC	3M+4D	D*6/^ go	29$	ABBB	Ind	6
Women's Studies/Economic & Social History	MV9H	3FT deg	* g	BCC	3M+4D	D*6/^ go	29$	ABBB	Ind	
Women's Studies/English	QM39	3FT deg	E g	BCC	X	D*^ go	29$	ABBB	X	
Women's Studies/Politics	MM19	3FT deg	* g	BCC	3M+4D	D*6/^ go	29$	ABBB	Ind	
Women's Studies/Social Anthropology	LM69	3FT deg	* g	BCC	3M+4D	D*6/^ go	29$	ABBB	Ind	
Women's Studies/Social Policy	LM49	3FT deg	* g	BCC	3M+4D	D*6/^ go	29$	ABBB	Ind	
Women's Studies/Sociology	LM39	3FT deg								

course details			98 expected requirements							96 entry stats	
TITLE	CODE	COURSE	SUBJECTS	A/AS	ND/C	AGNVQ	IB	SQA(H)	SQA	RATIO	A/AS
Univ of READING											
Ancient History and Sociology	VL13	3FT deg	*	BCC	Ind	D$^ go	30	BBBB	Ind	6	
Classical Studies and Sociology	QL83	3FT deg	*	BCC	Ind	D$^ go	30	BBBB	Ind		
Economics and Sociology	LL13	3FT deg	* g	BCC	Ind	D$^ go	30	BBBB	Ind	13	
English Literature and Sociology	LQ33	3FT deg	El	BBC	Ind	D$^	31$	BBBB$	Ind	19	22/26
French and Sociology	LR31	4FT deg	F	BBC	Ind	D$^ go	31$	BBBB$	Ind	3	22/28
German and Sociology	LR32	4FT deg	* g	BCC	Ind	D$^ go	30	BBBB	Ind	3	
History and Sociology	LV31	3FT deg	*	BBC	Ind	D$^ go	31	BBBB	Ind	33	
Philosophy and Sociology	LV37	3FT deg	*	BCC	Ind	D$^ go	30	BBBB	Ind	42	
Psychology and Sociology	CL83	3FT deg	* g	BCC	Ind	D$^ go	30	BBBB	Ind	22	20/28
Sociology	L300	3FT deg	*	BCC	Ind	D$^ go	30	BBBB	Ind	12	18/26
Sociology and International Relations	ML13	3FT deg	*	BCC	Ind	D$^ go	30	BBBB	Ind	17	
Sociology and Politics	LM31	3FT deg	*	BCC	Ind	D$^ go	30	BBBB	Ind	29	
Univ College of RIPON & YORK ST JOHN											
Applied Social Sciences/Design & Technology	L3W2	3FT deg		CC	M	MA	27	BBBC			
Applied Social Sciences/Environmental Science	L3F9	3FT deg	g	CC	M	M*	27	BBBC			
Applied Social Sciences/Geography	L3L8	3FT deg	Gy	CC	X	M*^	27	BBBC		5	
Applied Social Sciences/History	L3V1	3FT deg	H	CC	M	M*^	27	BBBC			
Applied Social Sciences/Language Studs (English)	L3Q1	3FT deg		CC	M	M	27	BBBC		3	10/20
Applied Social Sciences/Physical Education	L3B6	3FT deg		CC	MO	M*	27	BBBC			
Applied Social Sciences/Psychology	L3L7	3FT deg	g	CC	M	M*	27	BBBC			
Applied Social Sciences/Theology	L3V8	3FT deg		CC	M	M	27	BBBC		4	14/18
Applied Social Sciences/Women's Studies	L3M9	3FT deg		CC	M	M	27	BBBC		3	10/18
Cultural Studies	L610	3FT deg		12	M	M*	27	BBBC			
Cultural Studies with Education	L6X9	3FT deg		12	M	M*	27	BBBC			
Cultural Studies with English	L6Q3	3FT deg		12	M	M*	27	BBBC			
Cultural Studies with European Studies	L6T2	3FT deg		12	M	M*	27	BBBC			
Design and Technology/Applied Social Sciences	W2L3	3FT deg	Pf	CD	M	MA	27	BBBC			
Design and Technology/Applied Social Sciences	E2L3	3FT deg	Pf	CD	MO	MA	27	BBBC			
English Studies with Cultural Studies	Q3L6	3FT deg	E	16	Ind	M*^	30	BBBB			
English/Women's Studies	Q3M9	3FT deg	E	16	Ind	M*^	30	BBBB		5	14/22
Environmental Science/Applied Social Sciences	F9L3	3FT deg	g	DD	M	M*	27	BBCC			
Geography/Applied Social Sciences	L8L3	3FT deg	Gy	CCD	X	M*^	30	BBBB		4	18/20
History/Applied Social Sciences	V1L3	3FT deg	H	14	X	M*^	30	BBBB			
History/Women's Studies	V1M9	3FT deg	H	14	X	M*^	30	BBBB		3	
Language Studies (English)/Women's Studies	Q1M9	3FT deg		16	M	M*^	30	BBBB			
Language Studs (Engl)/Applied Social Sciences	Q1L3	3FT deg		16	M	M*^	30	BBBB		2	8/22
Physical Education/Applied Social Sciences	B6L3	3FT deg		BB-CCC	MO+3D	D$6/^	30	ABBB			
Psychology/Applied Social Sciences	L7L3	3FT deg	g	16	M	M	30	BBBB			
Psychology/Women's Studies	L7M9	3FT deg	g	16	M	M	30	BBBB			
Theology/Applied Social Sciences	V8L3	3FT deg		12	M	M*	27	BBBC		1	6/18
Theology/Women's Studies	V8M9	3FT deg		12	M	M*	27	BBBC		1	8/12
ROBERT GORDON Univ											
Applied Social Studies with Diploma in Soc Work	L340	4FT deg	E g	DE	N	Ind	Ind	BCC$	Ind	8	
ROEHAMPTON INST											
Anthropology	L600▼	3FT deg	g	12	4M	M$	28	BCC	N		
Sociology	L300▼	3FT deg	g	DD	4M	P$ go	26	BCC	N	6	4/18
Sociology and Applied Consumer Studies	LN39▼	3FT deg	g	12	4M	P$ go	26	BCC	N		
Sociology and Art for Community	WL13▼	3FT deg	g	DD	3M	P$ go	24	CCC	N	1	
Sociology and Biology	CL13▼	3FT deg	B g	12	4M $	P$ go	26	BCC	N$		
Sociology and Business Computing	GL73▼	3FT deg	g	12	3D	M$ go	26	BCC	N$		

			98 expected requirements							96 entry stats	
TITLE	CODE	COURSE	SUBJECTS	A/AS	NO/C	AGNVQ	IB	SQA(H)	SQA	RATIO	A/AS
Sociology and Business Studies	NL13▼	3FT deg	g	DD	3D	M$ go	26	BCC	N$	3	8/12
Sociology and Dance Studies	WL43▼	3FT deg	g	CC	2M+2D	M$^ go	30	BBC	Ind		
Sociology and Drama & Theatre Studies	WLL3▼	3FT deg	E/T g	16	3D	M$^ go	30	BBC	Ind	4	
Sociology and Education	XL93▼	3FT deg	g	DD	3M	P$ go	24	CCC	N	5	
Sociology and English Language & Linguistics	QL3H▼	3FT deg	E/L g	CC	2M+2D$	M$^ go	30	BBC	Ind	7	
Sociology and English Literature	QL33▼	3FT deg	E g	CC	2M+2D$	M^ go	28	BBC	Ind	8	12/14
Sociology and Environmental Studies	FL93▼	3FT deg	B/Gy g	DD	4M $	P$ go	26	BCC	N$		
Sociology and Film & Television Studies	LP34▼	3FT deg	g	16	2M+2D$	M$^ go	30	BBC	N$	17	
Sociology and French	RL13▼	4FT deg	F g	12	4M $	P^ go	26	BCC	N$		
Sociology and Geography	LL83▼	3FT deg	Gy g	DD	4M $	P$ go	26	BCC	N$	11	
Sociology and Health Studies	LB39▼	3FT deg	B g	12	4M	P$ go	26	BCC	N$	5	
Sociology and History	VL13▼	3FT deg	H g	DD	4M $	P^ go	26	BCC	N$	9	
Sociology and Human & Social Biology	CLC3▼	3FT deg	B g	12	3M	P$ go	24	CCC	N$	3	
Sociology and Music	WL33▼	3FT deg	Mu g	DD	4M $	P^ go	26	BCC	N$		
Sociology and Natural Resource Studies	DL23▼	3FT deg	g	DD	3M	P$ go	24	CCC	N$		
Sociology and Psychology	LL73▼	3FT deg	g	CC	3D	M$ go	30	BBC	Ind	9	10/24
Sociology and Social Policy & Administration	LL43▼	3FT deg	g	DD	3M	P$ go	24	CCC	N	4	4/ 8
Spanish and Sociology	LR34▼	4FT deg	Sp g	12	2M+2D$	P$ go	28	BBC	N$		
Sport Studies	B6L3▼	3FT deg	S g	14	3D		30	BBC	N		
Sport Studies and Sociology	LB36▼	3FT deg	S g	12	3D	MS go	30	BBC	N$		
Theology & Religious Studies and Sociology	LV38▼	3FT deg	g	DD	3M	P$ go	24	CCC	N	4	
Women's Studies	M903▼	3FT deg	*	DD	3M	P$	24	CCC	N	4	
Women's Studies and Applied Consumer Studies	NM99▼	3FT deg	g	12	4M	P$ go	26	BCC	N		
Women's Studies and Art for Community	WM19▼	3FT deg	*	DD	3M	P$	24	CCC	N		
Women's Studies and Biology	CM19▼	3FT deg	B	12	3M $	P$ go	24	CCC	N$		
Women's Studies and Business Computing	GM79▼	3FT deg	g	12	3D	M$ go	26	BCC	N$		
Women's Studies and Business Studies	NM19▼	3FT deg	g	DD	3D	M$ go	26	BCC	N$		
Women's Studies and Dance Studies	MW9K▼	3FT deg	*	CC	2M+2D	M$^	30	BBC	N$		
Women's Studies and Drama & Theatre Studies	WM49▼	3FT deg	T/E	16	3D	M$^	30	BBC	Ind		
Women's Studies and Education	XM99▼	3FT deg	*	DD	3M	P$	24	CCC	N	6	
Women's Studies and English Lang & Linguistics	QM3Y▼	3FT deg	E/L	CC	2M+2D	M$^	30	BBC	Ind		
Women's Studies and English Literature	QM39▼	3FT deg	E	CC	2M+2D$	M^	28	BBC	Ind	6	
Women's Studies and Environmental Studies	FM99▼	3FT deg	B/Gy	DD	4M $	P$ go	26	BCC	N$		
Women's Studies and Film & Television Studies	MP94▼	3FT deg	*	16	2M+2D$	M$^	30	BBC	N$	18	
Women's Studies and French	RM19▼	4FT deg	F	12	4M $	P^	26	BCC	N$		
Women's Studies and Geography	LM89▼	3FT deg	Gy	DD	4M $	P$ go	26	BCC	N$		
Women's Studies and Health Studies	BM99▼	3FT deg	B	12	4M $	P$ go	26	BCC	N$	5	
Women's Studies and History	VM19▼	3FT deg	H	DD	4M $	P^	26	BCC	N$	3	
Women's Studies and Human & Social Biology	CM1X▼	3FT deg	B	12	3M	P$ go	24	CCC	N$		
Women's Studies and Music	MW93▼	3FT deg	Mu	DD	4M $	P^	26	BCC	N$		
Women's Studies and Natural Resource Studies	DM29▼	3FT deg	g	DD	3M	P$ go	24	CCC	N$		
Women's Studies and Psychology	LM79▼	3FT deg	g	CC	3D	M$ go	30	BBC	Ind	4	
Women's Studies and Social Policy & Admin	LM49▼	3FT deg	g	DD	3M	P$ go	24	CCC	N	5	
Women's Studies and Sociology	LM39▼	3FT deg	g	DD	3M	P$ go	24	CCC	N	2	8/11
Women's Studies and Spanish	RM49▼	4FT deg	Sp	12	2M+2D$	P$ go	28	BBC	N$		
Women's Studies and Sport Studies	BM69▼	3FT deg	S g	12	3D	MS go	30	BBC	N$		
Women's Studies and Theology & Religious Studies	VM89▼	3FT deg	*	DD	3M	P$ go	24	CCC	N	5	

ROYAL HOLLOWAY, Univ of London

Economics with Sociology	L1L3	3FT deg	*	BBC-BBB	Ind		32	Ind			
French with Sociology	R1L3	4FT deg	F	BBC-ABC			28$	Ind		6	
German with Sociology	R2L3	4FT deg	G	BCC			28$	BBBBC$			
Italian with Sociology	R3L3	4FT deg	L/Ln	BBC			30	BBCCC$		1	

Sociology and Anthropology 64

course details | 98 expected requirements | 96 entry stats

TITLE	CODE	COURSE	SUBJECTS	A/AS	ND/C	AGNVQ	IB	SQA(H)	SQA	RATIO	A/AS
Social Policy with Sociology	L4L3	3FT deg	*	BCC-BBC	Ind	D^	Ind	Ind			
Sociology and Economics	LL13	3FT deg	*	BCC-BBB	Ind	D^	Ind	Ind			
Sociology and Politics	LM31	3FT deg	*	BCC-BBC	Ind	D^	Ind	Ind		8	
Sociology and Social Policy	LL34	3FT deg	*	BBC-BCC	Ind	D^	Ind	Ind		7	14/24
Sociology with Economics	L3L1	3FT deg	*	BCC-BBC	Ind	D^	Ind	Ind		1	
Sociology with French	L3R1	3FT deg	F	BCC-BBC	Ind	D^	Ind	Ind			
Sociology with German	L3R2	3FT deg	G	BCC-BBC	Ind	D^	Ind	Ind		2	
Sociology with Italian	L3R3	3FT deg	L/Ln	BCC-BBC	Ind	D^	Ind	Ind			
Sociology with Japanese Studies	L3T4	3FT deg	L g	BCC-BBC	Ind	D^	Ind	Ind			
Sociology with Management Studies	L3N1	3FT deg	*	BCC-BBC	Ind	D^	Ind	Ind		6	
Sociology with Mathematics	L3G1	3FT deg	M	BCC-BBC	Ind	D^	Ind	Ind			
Sociology with Music	L3W3	3FT deg	Mu	BCC-BBC	Ind	D^	Ind	Ind			
Sociology with Political Studies	L3M1	3FT deg	*	BCC-BBC	Ind	D^	Ind	Ind		4	
Sociology with Social Policy	L3L4	3FT deg	*	BCC-BBC	Ind	D^	Ind	Ind			
Sociology with Spanish	L3R4	3FT deg	L	BCC-BBC	Ind	D^	Ind	Ind			
Foundation Programme Sociology	Y408	4FT deg									

Univ of SALFORD

TITLE	CODE	COURSE	SUBJECTS	A/AS	ND/C	AGNVQ	IB	SQA(H)	SQA	RATIO	A/AS
Applied Social Studies	L340	3FT deg									
Politics and Sociology	LM31	3FT deg	* g	CCC	Ind	Ind	Ind	Ind	Ind	5	12/22
Sociology	L300	3FT deg	* g	BCC-CCD	Ind	Ind	Ind	Ind	Ind	5	8/20
Sociology and Cultural Studies	L3Y6	3FT deg	* g	BCC-CCD	Ind	Ind	Ind	Ind	Ind	6	14/22

SOAS:Sch of Oriental & African St (U of London)

TITLE	CODE	COURSE	SUBJECTS	A/AS	ND/C	AGNVQ	IB	SQA(H)	SQA	RATIO	A/AS
Development Studies and African Studies	TM79	3FT deg		22	Ind		31	BBBBC	Ind		
Development Studies and Amharic	MT97	4FT deg		22	Ind		31	BBBBC	Ind		
Development Studies and Arabic	MT96	4FT deg		22	Ind		31	BBBBC	Ind	2	
Development Studies and Bengali	MT95	3FT deg		22	Ind		31	BBBBC	Ind		
Development Studies and Burmese	TMM9	4FT deg		22	Ind		31	BBBBC	Ind		
Development Studies and Chinese	MT93	4FT deg		24	Ind		32	BBBBB	Ind		
Economics and Development Studies	ML91	3FT deg	g	22	Ind		31	BBBBC	Ind	5	
Geography and Development Studies	ML98	3FT deg		22	Ind		31	BBBBC	Ind	1	16/24
Georgian and Development Studies	MT99	3FT deg		22	Ind		31	BBBBC	Ind		
Gujarati and Development Studies	TM59	3FT deg		22	Ind		31	BBBBC	Ind		
Hausa and Development Studies	MT9R	4FT deg		22	Ind		31	BBBBC	Ind		
Hindi and Development Studies	MT9M	3FT/4FT deg		22	Ind		31	BBBBC	Ind	3	
History and Development Studies	MV9C	3FT deg		22	Ind		31	BBBBC	Ind	5	
Indonesian and Development Studies	MT9N	3FT/4FT deg		22	Ind		31	BBBBC	Ind		
Korean and Development Studies	TM5Y	4FT deg		22	Ind		31	BBBBC	Ind		
Law and Development Studies	MM93	3FT deg		24	Ind		32	BBBBB	Ind	2	
Linguistics and Development Studies	MQ93	3FT deg									
Music and Development Studies	MW93	3FT deg		22	Ind		31	BBBBC	Ind		
Nepali and Development Studies	MTXN	3FT deg		22	Ind		31	BBBBC	Ind		
Persian and Development Studies	MT9Q	3FT deg		22	Ind		31	BBBBC	Ind		
Politics and Development Studies	MM91	3FT deg		22	Ind		31	BBBBC	Ind	8	
Sinhalese and Development Studies	MTXM	3FT deg		22	Ind		31	BBBBC	Ind		
Social Anthropology	L600	3FT deg		22	Ind		31	BBBBC	Ind	12	24/28
Social Anthropology and African Studies	TL76	3FT deg		22	Ind		31	BBBBC	Ind	10	
Social Anthropology and Amharic	LT67	4FT deg		22	Ind		31	BBBBC	Ind		
Social Anthropology and Arabic	LT66	4FT deg		22	Ind		31	BBBBC	Ind		
Social Anthropology and Bengali	LT65	3FT deg		22	Ind		31	BBBBC	Ind		
Social Anthropology and Burmese	LT6M	4FT deg		22	Ind		31	BBBBC	Ind		
Social Anthropology and Chinese	LT63	4FT deg		24	Ind		32	BBBBB	Ind	10	

course details

TITLE	CODE	COURSE	SUBJECTS	A/AS	NO/C	AGNVQ	IB	SQA(H)	SQA	RATIO A/AS
Social Anthropology and Development Studies	ML96	3FT deg		22	Ind		31	BBBBC	Ind	6 20/26
Social Anthropology and Economics	LL16	3FT deg	g	22	Ind		31	BBBBC	Ind	
Social Anthropology and Geography	LL86	3FT deg		22	Ind		31	BBBBC	Ind	
Social Anthropology and Georgian	LT69	3FT deg		22	Ind		31	BBBBC	Ind	
Social Anthropology and Gujarati	LTP5	3FT deg		22	Ind		31	BBBBC	Ind	
Social Anthropology and Hausa	LT6R	4FT deg		22	Ind		31	BBBBC	Ind	
Social Anthropology and Hebrew	LQ69	4FT deg		22	Ind		31	BBBBC	Ind	
Social Anthropology and Hindi	LT6N	3FT/4FT deg		22	Ind		31	BBBBC	Ind	
Social Anthropology and History	LV61	3FT deg		22	Ind		31	BBBBC	Ind	6
Social Anthropology and History of Art/Archaeolo	LV66	3FT deg		22	Ind		31	BBBBC	Ind	12
Social Anthropology and Indonesian	LTPM	3FT/4FT deg		22	Ind		31	BBBBC	Ind	9
Social Anthropology and Japanese	LT64	4FT deg		24	Ind		32	BBBBB	Ind	
Social Anthropology and Korean	LTPN	4FT deg		22	Ind		31	BBBBC	Ind	1
Social Anthropology and Law	LM63	3FT deg		24	Ind		32	BBBBB	Ind	
Social Anthropology and Linguistics	LQ61	3FT deg		22	Ind		31	BBBBC	Ind	4
Social Anthropology and Music	LW63	3FT deg		22	Ind		31	BBBBC	Ind	
Social Anthropology and Nepali	LTQM	3FT deg		22	Ind		31	BBBCC	Ind	
Social Anthropology and Persian	LT6Q	3FT deg		22	Ind		31	BBBBC	Ind	
Social Anthropology and Politics	LM61	3FT deg		22	Ind		31	BBBBC	Ind	
Social Anthropology and Sanskrit	LQ6X	3FT deg		22	Ind		31	BBBBC	Ind	
Social Anthropology and Sinhalese	TLM6	3FT deg		22	Ind		31	BBBBC	Ind	
South Asian Studies and Development Studies	TMMX	3FT deg								
South Asian Studies and Social Anthropology	TL5Q	3FT deg								
Study of Religions and Social Anthropology	LV68	3FT deg		22	Ind		31	BBBBC	Ind	6
Swahili and Development Studies	MT9T	4FT deg		22	Ind		31	BBBBC	Ind	
Swahili and Social Anthropology	LT6T	4FT deg		22	Ind		31	BBBBC	Ind	
Tamil and Development Studies	MTY5	3FT deg		22	Ind		31	BBBBC	Ind	
Tamil and Social Anthropology	LTQ5	3FT deg		22	Ind		31	BBBBC	Ind	
Thai and Development Studies	MTYM	3FT/4FT deg		22	Ind		31	BBBBC	Ind	
Thai and Social Anthropology	LTQN	3FT/4FT deg		22	Ind		31	BBBBC	Ind	
Tibetan and Development Studies	MTYN	3FT deg		22	Ind		31	BBBBC	Ind	
Turkish and Development Studies	MT9P	4FT deg		22	Ind		31	BBBBC	Ind	
Turkish and Social Anthropology	LT6P	4FT deg		22	Ind		31	BBBBC	Ind	
Urdu and Development Studies	MTX5	3FT deg		22	Ind		31	BBBBC	Ind	
Urdu and Social Anthropology	TL56	3FT deg		22	Ind		31	BBBBC	Ind	
Vietnamese and Development Studies	TM5X	4FT deg		20	Ind		30	BBBCC	Ind	
Vietnamese and Social Anthropology	TL5P	4FT deg		22	Ind		31	BBBBC	Ind	1

Univ College SCARBOROUGH

Social and Cultural Studies with Arts	L3Y3	3FT deg	* g	DE	Ind	P	27$	Ind	Ind	
Social and Cultural Studies with Sciences	L3Y1	3FT deg	* g	DE	Ind	P	27$	Ind	Ind	
Social and Cultural Studies with Social Sciences	L3Y2	3FT deg	* g	DE	Ind	P	27$	Ind	Ind	

Univ of SHEFFIELD

Economics and Sociology	LL13	3FT deg	* g	BBC	4D	D^	30	ABBB	Ind	19
English Language and Sociology	QL33	3FT deg	E g	BBC	2M+4D$	D^	29$	BBBB$	Ind	36
Geography and Sociology	LL83	3FT deg	Gy g	BBC	4D $	D^	30$	ABBB$	Ind	9 22/30
Japanese Studies and Sociology	TL43	4FT deg	* g	BBC	4D	D^	30	ABBB	Ind	4
Psychology and Sociology	CL83	3FT deg	* g	AAB	1M+5D	D^	35	AAAA	Ind	33
Social Policy and Sociology	LL43	3FT deg	* g	BBC	4D	D^	30	ABBB	Ind	7 20/30
Sociology	L300	3FT deg	* g	BBC	4D	D^	30	ABBB	Ind	9 20/28
Social and Political Studies	Y220	3FT deg	* g	BBC	4D	D^	30	ABBB	Ind	
Sociological Studies										

			98 expected requirements							96 entry stats	
course details										*96 entry stats*	
TITLE	CODE	COURSE	SUBJECTS	A/AS	NO/C	AGNVQ	IB	SQA(H)	SQA	RATIO	A/AS
SHEFFIELD HALLAM Univ											
Applied Social Studies (Applied Option)	L310	3FT deg	*	CCC	7D	D	Ind	Ind	Ind		
Mathematics with Women's Studies	G1M9	3FT/4SW deg	M/St	EE	3M	P	Ind	Ind	Ind		
Sociology	L300	3FT deg	*	CCC	7D	D	Ind	Ind	Ind		
Combined Studies *Urban and Regional Policy*	Y400	3FT deg	*	14	2M	M	Ind	Ind	Ind		
SOLIHULL COLL											
Cultural Studies	LQ33	3FT deg	*	EE	MO	M	Dip	Ind	Ind		
Univ of SOUTHAMPTON											
History and Sociology	VL13	3FT deg	H g	22	X	Ind	30$	ABBBB	X	21	
Philosophy and Sociology	VL73	3FT deg	g	BCC	1M+4D	Ind	26	CSYS	Ind	14	
Politics and Sociology	LM31	3FT deg	* g	20	Ind	D$^ go	28	BBBBC	Ind	11	20/22
Sociology	L300	3FT deg	* g	18-20	Ind	D$^ go	28	BBBBC	Ind	11	16/24
Sociology & Social Policy(with Social Work Stud)	LL3K	4FT deg	* g	18-20	Ind	D$^ go	28	BBBBC	Ind	12	8/28
Sociology and Social Policy	LL34	3FT deg	* g	18-20	Ind	D$^ go	28	BBBBC	Ind	8	16/24
SOUTHAMPTON INST											
Social Science	L322	3FT deg	*	10	MO	M$	Dip	CCCC	N	2	8/16
SOUTH BANK Univ											
Media and Society	PL43	3FT deg	El/Ee	BCC	4D	D go	Ind	Ind	Ind		
Social Sciences	L322	3FT deg	* g	CC	DO	M go	Ind	Ind	Ind		
Sociology and Accounting	LN34	3FT deg	Ac/Ec g	12-16	4M+2D	M go	Ind	Ind	Ind		
Sociology and English Studies	LQ3H	3FT deg	E g	14-18	X	M^ go	Ind	Ind	Ind		
Sociology and Environmental Policy	FL93	3FT deg	* g	14-18	2M+4D	M go	Ind	Ind	Ind		
Sociology and European Studies	LT32	3FT deg	* g	14-18	2M+4D	M go	Ind	Ind	Ind		
Sociology and French	LR31	3FT deg	F g	12-16	4M+2D	M go	Ind	Ind	Ind		
Sociology and German	LR3F	3FT deg	G g	14-18	2M+4D	M go	Ind	Ind	Ind		
Sociology and German - ab initio	LR32	3FT deg	G g	12-16	4M+2D	M go	Ind	Ind	Ind		
Sociology and Health Studies	LL43	3FT deg	S g	12-16	4M+2D	M go	Ind	Ind	Ind		
Sociology and Housing	KL4H	3FT deg	* g	14-18	4M+2D	M go	Ind	Ind	Ind		
Sociology and Human Geography	LL83	3FT deg	Gy g	12-16	4M+2D	M go	Ind	Ind	Ind		
Sociology and Human Resource Management	LN36	3FT deg	* g	14-18	2M+4D	M go	Ind	Ind	Ind		
Sociology and Law	LM33	3FT deg	* g	14-18	2M+4D	D go	Ind	Ind	Ind		
Sociology and Management	LN31	3FT deg	* g	12-16	4M+2D	M go	Ind	Ind	Ind		
Sociology and Marketing	LN35	3FT deg	* g	14-18	2M+4D	M go	Ind	Ind	Ind		
Sociology and Media Studies	LP34	3FT deg	E g	14-18	2M+4D	D go	Ind	Ind	Ind		
Sociology and Politics	LM31	3FT deg	* g	12-16	4M+2D	M go	Ind	Ind	Ind		
Sociology and Psychology	CL83	3FT deg	S g	14-18	4M+2D	M go	Ind	Ind	Ind		
Spanish - ab initio and Sociology	LR34	3FT deg	* g	12-16	4M+2D	M go	Ind	Ind	Ind		
Spanish and Sociology	LR3K	3FT deg	Sp g	14-18	2M+4D	M^ go	Ind	Ind	Ind		
Technology and Sociology	JL93	3FT deg	* g	12-16	4M+2D	M go	Ind	Ind	Ind		
Tourism and Sociology	LP37	3FT deg	L g	12-16	4M+2D	M go	Ind	Ind	Ind		
Urban Studies and Sociology	LK34	3FT deg	* g	14-18	2M+4D	M go	Ind	Ind	Ind		
World Theatre and Sociology	LW34	3FT deg	* g	14-18	2M+4D	M go	Ind	Ind	Ind		
Univ of ST ANDREWS											
Social Anthropology	L600	4FT deg	* g	BBB	X	Ind	30$	BBBB	Ind	12	
Social Anthropology with Geography	L6L8	4FT deg	* g	BBB	X	Ind	30$	BBBB	Ind		
Social Anthropology-Arabic	LT66	4FT deg	* g	BBB	X	Ind	30$	BBBB	Ind		
Social Anthropology-Art History	LV64	4FT deg	* g	BBB	X	Ind	30$	BBBB	Ind	5	
Social Anthropology-Classical Studies	LQ68	4FT deg	* g	BBB	X	Ind	30$	BBBB	Ind		
Social Anthropology-Economics	LL16	4FT deg	* g	BBB	X	Ind	32$	BBBB	Ind	2	

TITLE	CODE	COURSE	SUBJECTS	A/AS	ND/C	RGNVQ	IB	SQA(H)	SQA	RATIO A/AS
course details			**98 expected requirements**							**96 entry stats**
Social Anthropology-English	QL36	4FT deg	* g	BBB	X	Ind	30$	BBBB	Ind	6
Social Anthropology-French	LR61	4FT deg	E g	BBB	X	Ind	30$	BBBB$	Ind	
Social Anthropology-French with Year Abroad	LR6C	4FT/5FT deg	E g	BBB	X	Ind	30$	BBBB$	Ind	6
Social Anthropology-Geography	LL68	4FT deg	* g	BBB	X	Ind	30$	BBBB	Ind	6
Social Anthropology-International Relations	LM61	4FT deg	* g	AAB	X	Ind	36$	AAAB	Ind	15
Social Anthropology-Italian	LR63	4FT deg	* g	BBB	X	Ind	30$	BBBB	Ind	
Social Anthropology-Italian with Year Abroad	RL36	4FT/5FT deg	* g	BBB	X	Ind	30$	BBBB	Ind	
Social Anthropology-Mediaeval History	LV61	4FT deg	* g	BBB	X	Ind	30$	BBBB	Ind	11
Social Anthropology-Modern History	LV6D	4FT deg	* g	BBB	X	Ind	30$	BBBB	Ind	
Social Anthropology-Philosophy	LV67	4FT deg	* g	BBB	X	Ind	30$	BBBB	Ind	9
Social Anthropology-Psychology	LL76	4FT deg	* g	ABB	X	Ind	32$	ABBB$	Ind	15
Social Anthropology-Russian	LR68	4FT deg	* g	BBB	X	Ind	30$	BBBB	Ind	
Social Anthropology-Russian with Year Abroad	LR6V	4FT/5FT deg	* g	BBB	X	Ind	30$	BBBB	Ind	
Social Anthropology-Scottish History	LV6C	4FT deg	* g	BBB	X	Ind	30$	BBBB	Ind	7
Spanish with Year Abroad-Social Anthropology	LR6K	4FT/5FT deg	* g	BBB	X	Ind	30$	BBBB	Ind	
Spanish-Social Anthropology	LR64	4FT deg	* g	BBB	X	Ind	32$	BBBB	Ind	
Theological Studies-Social Anthropology	LV68	4FT deg	* g	BBB	X	Ind	30$	BBBB	Ind	5
General Degree of MA *Social Anthropology*	Y450	3FT deg	* g	BBB	X	Ind	30$	BBBB	Ind	

THE UNIVERSITY COLLEGE OF ST MARK AND ST JOHN

TITLE	CODE	COURSE	SUBJECTS	A/AS	ND/C	RGNVQ	IB	SQA(H)	SQA	RATIO A/AS
Community Studies/Development Studies	L5M9	3FT deg		10	MO	M	Dip	Ind	Ind	
Development Studies/Community Studies	M9L5	3FT deg		8-10	MO	M	Ind	Ind	Ind	
Development Studies/Geography	M9L8	3FT deg		8-10	MO	M	Ind	Ind	Ind	
Development Studies/History	M9V1	3FT deg		8-10	MO	M	Ind	Ind	Ind	
Development Studies/Public Relations	M9P3	3FT deg		8-10	MO	M	Ind	Ind	Ind	
Development Studies/Sociology	M9L3	3FT deg		8-10	MO	M	Ind	Ind	Ind	
English (Literary Studies)/Sociology	Q3L3	3FT deg	El	12-16	Ind	M	Ind	Ind	Ind	
English Language Studies/Sociology	Q1L3	3FT deg		12	MO	M	Ind	Ind	Ind	
Geography/Development Studies	L8M9	3FT deg	Gy	8-10	MO	M	Ind	Ind	Ind	
Geography/Sociology	L8L3	3FT deg	Gy	8-10	MO	M	Ind	Ind	Ind	
History/Development Studies	V1M9	3FT deg	H	12	MO	M	Ind	Ind	Ind	
History/Sociology	V1L3	3FT deg	H	12	MO	M	Ind	Ind	Ind	
Media Studies/Sociology	P4L3	3FT deg		16	MO	M	Ind	Ind	Ind	
Public Relations/Development Studies	P3M9	3FT deg		16	MO	M	Ind	Ind	Ind	
Sociology/Development Studies	L3M9	3FT deg	So	8	MO	M	Ind	Ind	Ind	
Sociology/English (Literary Studies)	L3Q3	3FT deg	So	8	MO	M	Ind	Ind	Ind	
Sociology/English Language Studies	L3Q1	3FT deg	So	8	MO	M	Ind	Ind	Ind	
Sociology/Geography	L3L8	3FT deg	So	8	MO	M	Ind	Ind	Ind	
Sociology/History	L3V1	3FT deg	So	8	MO	M	Ind	Ind	Ind	
Sociology/Media Studies	L3P4	3FT deg	So	8	MO	M	Ind	Ind	Ind	
Sociology/Theology	L3V8	3FT deg	So	8	MO	M	Ind	Ind	Ind	
Sociology/Theology & Philosophy	L3VV	3FT deg	So	8	MO	M	Ind	Ind	Ind	
Theology & Philosophy/Sociology	V8L3	3FT deg	Re	4	MO	M	Dip	CCCC	Ind	
Theology/Sociology	V8LH	3FT deg	Re	4	MO	M	Dip	CCCC	Ind	

ST MARY'S Univ COLL

TITLE	CODE	COURSE	SUBJECTS	A/AS	ND/C	RGNVQ	IB	SQA(H)	SQA	RATIO A/AS
Gender Studies and Biology	CM19	3FT deg	B/C	4-8	Ind	Ind	Ind	BBBB$	Ind	
Gender Studies and Classical Studies	MQ98	3FT deg	*	4-8	Ind	Ind	Ind	BBBB	Ind	
Gender Studies and Drama	MW94	3FT deg	*	8-12	Ind	Ind	Ind	BBBB	Ind	
Gender Studies and Education Studies	MX99	3FT deg	*	4-8	Ind	Ind	Ind	BBBB	Ind	
Geography and Gender Studies	FM89	3FT deg	Gy	4-8	Ind	Ind	Ind	BBBB$	Ind	
Heritage Management and Gender Studies	MN99	3FT deg	*	4-8	Ind	Ind	Ind	BBBB	Ind	
History and Gender Studies	MV91	3FT deg	H	4-8	Ind	Ind	Ind	BBBB$	Ind	

Sociology and Anthropology 64

TITLE	CODE	COURSE	SUBJECTS	A/AS	ND/C	AGNVQ	IB	SQA(H)	SQA	RATIO A/AS
Management Studies and Gender Studies	MN91	3FT deg	* g	4-8	Ind	Ind	Ind	BBBB	Ind	
Media Arts and Gender Studies	MP94	3FT deg	*	4-8	Ind	Ind	Ind	BBBB	Ind	
Sociology	L300	3FT deg	*	8-12	Ind	Ind	Ind	BBBB	Ind	
Sociology and Biology	CL13	3FT deg	B/C	4-8	Ind	Ind	Ind	BBBB$	Ind	
Sociology and Drama	WLL3	3FT deg	*	8-12	Ind	Ind	Ind	BBBB	Ind	
Sociology and English	QL33	3FT deg	E	8-12	X	X	Ind	BBBB$	X	
Sociology and Environmental Investigation St	FL93	3FT deg	S/2S	4-8	Ind	Ind	Ind	BBBB	Ind	
Sociology and Environmental Studies	FLX3	3FT deg	*	4-8	Ind	Ind	Ind	BBBB	Ind	
Sociology and Gender Studies	LM39	3FT deg	*	4-8	Ind	Ind	Ind	BBBB	Ind	
Sociology and Geography	FL83	3FT deg	Gy	4-8	Ind	Ind	Ind	BBBB$	Ind	
Sociology and Heritage Management	LN39	3FT deg	*	4-8	Ind	Ind	Ind	BBBB	Ind	
Sociology and History	VL13	3FT deg	H	4-8	Ind	Ind	Ind	BBBB$	Ind	
Sociology and Integrated Scientific Studies	LY31	3FT deg	S/2S	4-8	Ind	Ind	Ind	BBBB$	Ind	
Sociology and Irish Studies	LQ35	3FT deg	*	4-8	Ind	Ind	Ind	BBBB	Ind	
Sociology and Media Arts	LP34	3FT deg	*	4-8	Ind	Ind	Ind	BBBB	Ind	
Sport Rehabilitation and Gender Studies	BM99	3FT deg	B g	12-14	X	X	Ind	BBBB$	X	
Sport Rehabilitation and Sociology	BL93	3FT deg	B g	12-14	X	X	Ind	BBBB$	X	
Sport Science and Gender Studies	BM69	3FT deg	S g	8-12	Ind	Ind	Ind	BBBB$	Ind	
Theology and Religious Studies and Gender St	MV98	3FT deg	*	4-8	Ind	Ind	Ind	BBBB	Ind	
Theology and Religious Studies and Sociology	VL83	3FT deg	*	4-8	Ind	Ind	Ind	BBBB	Ind	

STAFFORDSHIRE Univ

TITLE	CODE	COURSE	SUBJECTS	A/AS	ND/C	AGNVQ	IB	SQA(H)	SQA	RATIO A/AS
Cultural Studies	L674	3FT deg	g	CD	MO+2D	M	27	BBC	Ind	3 6/16
Cultural Studies/American Studies	LQ64	3FT deg	g	CD	MO+2D	M	27	BBC	Ind	9
Development Studies/American Studies	MQY4	3FT deg	g	12	MO+2D	M	27	BBC	Ind	
Development Studies/Computing	GMMY	3FT deg	g	12	3M	M	Ind	BBB	Ind	
Economic Studies/Development Studies	LM19	3FT deg	g	12	4M	M	24	BBC		
Environmental Studies/Cultural Studies	FL96	3FT deg	* g	CC	MO+2D	M	Ind	BBB	Ind	
Environmental Studies/Development Studies	FM9Y	3FT deg	* g	14	4M+1D	M	Ind	BBB	Ind	5
European Culture and International Relations	LMPC	3FT deg	g	12	MO+2D	M	27	BBC	Ind	
European Culture/Cultural Studies	L675	3FT deg	g	CD	MO+2D	M	27	BBC	Ind	
European Culture/Development Studies	LMPY	3FT deg	g	12	MO+2D	M	27	BBC	Ind	
European Culture/French	LRP1	3FT deg	F g	CD	MO+2D	M^	27	BBC	Ind	
European Culture/German	LRP2	3FT deg	G g	CD	MO+2D	M^	27	BBC	Ind	
European Culture/History	LVP1	3FT deg	H g	CD	MO+2D	M	27	BBC	Ind	
European Culture/History of Art and Design	LVP4	3FT deg	g	CD	MO+2D	M	27	BBC	Ind	
European Culture/Literature	LQP3	3FT deg	g	CD	MO+2D	M	27	BBC	Ind	
European Culture/Media Studies	LPP4	3FT deg	g	CD	MO+2D	M	27	BBC	Ind	
European Culture/Philosophy	LVP7	3FT deg	g	CD	MO+2D	M	27	BBC	Ind	
European Culture/Spanish	LRP4	3FT deg	g	CD	MO+2D	M	27	BBC	Ind	1
European Media, Culture and Politics	PL43	3FT deg	g	CD	MO+2D	M	27	BBC		
Film Studies/Cultural Studies	LW65	3FT deg	g	CD	MO+2D	M	27	BBC	Ind	2 12/18
Film Studies/Development Studies	MWY5	3FT deg	g	12	MO+2D	M	27	BBC	Ind	
Film Studies/European Culture	LWP5	3FT deg	g	CD	MO+2D	M	27	BBC	Ind	
French/Cultural Studies	RL16	3FT/4SW deg	F g	CD	MO+2D	M^	26	BBC	Ind	8
French/Development Studies	RM1Y	3FT/4SW deg	F g	12	4M+2D	M^	26	BCC	Ind	
Geography/Cultural Studies	LL86	3FT deg	g	CC	MO+2D	M	27	BBB	Ind	2
Geography/Development Studies	LM8Y	3FT deg	g	14	4M+1D	M	26	ABB	Ind	6 8/14
History of Art and Design/Cultural Studies	VL46	3FT deg	g	CD	MO+2D	M	27	BBC	Ind	4
History of Art and Design/Development Studies	VM4Y	3FT deg	g	12	MO+2D	M	27	BBC	Ind	
History/Cultural Studies	VL16	3FT deg	H g	CD	MO+2D	M	27	BBC	Ind	4
History/Development Studies	VM1Y	3FT deg	H g	12	MO+2D	M	27	BBC	Ind	4
Information Systems/Cultural Studies	GL56	3FT deg	g	12	Ind	M	27	BBC	Ind	

course details			*98 expected requirements*							*96 entry stats*
TITLE	CODE	COURSE	SUBJECTS	A/AS	NO/C	AGNVQ	IB	SQA(H)	SQA	RATIO A/AS
Information Systems/Development Studies	GM5Y	3FT deg	g	12	3M	M	Ind	BBB	Ind	
International Relations/Cultural Studies	ML1P	3FT deg	g	12	MO+2D	M	27	BBC	Ind	
International Relations/Development Studies	MMDY	3FT deg	g	12	3M	M	24d	BCC	Ind	3
Literature/Cultural Studies	QL36	3FT deg	El g	CD	MO+2D	M	27	BBC	Ind	2 8/16
Literature/Development Studies	QM3Y	3FT deg	El g	12	MO+2D	M	27	BBC	Ind	
Media Studies/Cultural Studies	PL46	3FT deg	g	CD	MO+2D	M	27	BBC	Ind	5 6/16
Media Studies/Development Studies	MPY4	3FT deg	g	12	MO+2D	M	27	BBC	Ind	
Philosophy/Cultural Studies	VL76	3FT deg	g	CD	MO+2D	M	27	BBC	Ind	1
Philosophy/Development Studies	VM7Y	3FT deg	g	12	MO+2D	M	27	BBC	Ind	
Politics/Cultural Studies	MLC6	3FT deg	g	12	MO+2D	D	27	BBC	Ind	
Politics/Development Studies	MMDX	3FT deg	g	12	3M	M	24	BCC	Ind	
Politics/European Culture	LMP1	3FT deg	g	12	MO+2D	M	27	BBC	Ind	
Psychology/Cultural Studies	LL76	3FT deg	g	18	3M+3D	Ind	27	BBB	Ind	
Psychology/Development Studies	LM7Y	3FT deg	g	18	3M+3D	Ind	27	BBB	Ind	6
Sociology	L300	3FT deg	g	12	3M	M	24	BCC	Ind	4 6/16
Sociology/American Studies	LQ34	3FT deg	g	12	MO+2D	M	27	BBC	Ind	6
Sociology/Applied Statistics	GL43	3FT deg	g	12	3M	M	24	BCC	Ind	
Sociology/Business Studies	LN31	3FT deg	g	CCD	MO+2D	M$	24	BBB	Ind	4 12/12
Sociology/Computing	LG35	3FT deg	g	12	3M	M	24	BBB	Ind	
Sociology/Cultural Studies	LL36	3FT deg	g	12	MO+2D	M	Ind	BBB	Ind	8
Sociology/Development Studies	LM3Y	3FT deg	g	12	3M	M	24	BCC	Ind	2
Sociology/Economic Studies	LL13	3FT deg								
Sociology/Environmental Studies	LF39	3FT deg	*	12-14	4M+1D	M	Ind	BBB	Ind	5
Sociology/Geography	LL38	3FT deg	g	CC	3M+1D	M	24	BBB	Ind	9
Sociology/German	LR32	3FT/4SW deg	G g	12	4M+2D	M^	26	BCC	Ind	
Sociology/History	LV31	3FT deg	H g	12	MO+2D	M	27	BBC	Ind	6 12/20
Sociology/Information Systems	LG3M	3FT deg	g	12	3M	M	24	BBB	Ind	4
Sociology/International Relations	LM3C	3FT deg	g	12	3M	M	24	BCC	Ind	
Sociology/Law	LM33	3FT deg	g	18	3D	M^	26	BBBB	Ind	5 10/20
Sociology/Legal Studies	LM3H	3FT deg	g	18	3D	M^	26	BBBB	Ind	4
Sociology/Literature	LQ33	3FT deg	g	12	3M	M	24	BCC	Ind	3 8/18
Sociology/Media Studies	LP34	3FT deg	g	12	MO+2D	M	27	BBC	Ind	12
Sociology/Philosophy	LV37	3FT deg	g	12	3M	M	24	BCC	Ind	5 6/12
Sociology/Politics	LMH1	3FT deg	g	12	3M	M	24	BCC	Ind	4
Sociology/Psychology	LL37	3FT deg	g	18	3M+3D	Ind	27	BBB	Ind	5 10/26
Spanish/Cultural Studies	RL46	3FT/4SW deg	g	CD	MO+2D	M^	27	BBC	Ind	7
Spanish/Development Studies	RM4Y	3FT/4SW deg	g	12	3M	M^	26	BCC	Ind	
Spanish/Sociology	RL43	3FT/4SW deg	g	12	3M	M^	26	BCC	Ind	
Sport and Leisure Studies	BL63	3FT deg	*	16	2M+4D	D	Ind	BBCC		
Women's Studies/American Studies	MQ9K	3FT deg	g	12	MO+2D	M	27	BBC	Ind	1
Women's Studies/Cultural Studies	ML9P	3FT deg	g	12	MO+2D	M	27	BBC	Ind	
Women's Studies/Development Studies	M902	3FT deg	g	12	3M	M	24	BCC	Ind	1
Women's Studies/Environmental Studies	MF99	3FT deg	g	CC	3M+1D	M	24	BBB	Ind	
Women's Studies/Film Studies	MW95	3FT deg	g	12	MO+2D	M	27	BBC	Ind	
Women's Studies/French	MR91	3FT/4SW deg	F g	12	4M+2D	M^	26	BCC	Ind	
Women's Studies/Geography	ML98	3FT deg	g	CC	3M+1D	M	24	BBB	Ind	
Women's Studies/German	MR92	3FT/4SW deg	G g	12	4M+2D	M^	26	BCC	Ind	
Women's Studies/History of Art & Design	MV94	3FT deg	g	12	MO+2D	M	27	BBC	Ind	
Women's Studies/Information Systems	MG95	3FT deg	g	12	3M	M	24	BCC	Ind	
Women's Studies/International Relations	MM9C	3FT deg	g	12	3M	M	24	BCC	Ind	
Women's Studies/Law	MM93	3FT deg	g	18	HN	M^	26d	BBBB	Ind	7
Women's Studies/Legal Studies	MM9H	3FT deg	g	18	HN	M^	26	BBBB	Ind	

course details				**98 expected requirements**						**96 entry stats**
TITLE	CODE	COURSE	SUBJECTS	A/AS	ND/C	AGNVQ	IB	SQA(H)	SQA	RATIO A/AS
Women's Studies/Literature	MQ93	3FT deg	El g	12	MO+2D	M	27	BBC	Ind	4
Women's Studies/Philosophy	MV97	3FT deg	g	12	MO+2D	M	27	BBC	Ind	
Women's Studies/Politics	MMX1	3FT deg	g	12	3M	M	24	BCC	Ind	
Women's Studies/Psychology	ML97	3FT deg	g	18	3M	Ind	27	BBB	Ind	12
Women's Studies/Sociology	ML93	3FT deg	g	12	3M	M	24	BCC	Ind	3 6/14
Univ of STIRLING										
Business Studies/Sociology	NL13	4FT deg	g	BBC	Ind	Ind	33	BBBB	HN	
Computing Science/Sociology	GL53	4FT deg	g	CCC	Ind	Ind	28	BBCC	HN	
Economics/Sociology	LL13	4FT deg	g	BCC	Ind	Ind	31	BBBC	HN	
English Studies/Sociology	LQ33	4FT deg	g	BBC	Ind	Ind	33	BBBB	HN	
French/Sociology	LR31	4FT deg	g	CCC	Ind	Ind	31	BBBC	HN	
German/Sociology	LR32	4FT deg	g	CCC	Ind	Ind	31	BBBC	HN	
History/Sociology	LV31	4FT deg	g	BCC	Ind	Ind	31	BBBC	HN	
Human Resources Management/Sociology	NL1H	4FT deg	g	BBC	Ind	Ind	33	BBBB	HN	
Japanese/Sociology	LT34	4FT deg	g	BCC	Ind	Ind	31	BBBC	HN	
Marketing/Sociology	LN35	4FT deg	g	BBC	Ind	Ind	33	BBBB	HN	
Mathematics/Sociology	GL13	4FT deg	M g	CCC	Ind	Ind	28	BBCC	HN	
Philosophy/Sociology	LV37	4FT deg	g	CCC	Ind	Ind	28	BBCC	HN	
Politics/Sociology	ML13	4FT deg	g	BCC	Ind	Ind	31	BBBC	HN	
Psychology/Sociology	CL83	4FT deg	g	BCC	Ind	Ind	31	BBBC	HN	
Religious Studies/Sociology	LV38	4FT deg	g	CCC	Ind	Ind	28	BBCC	HN	
Sociology	L300	4FT deg	g	BCC			31	BBBC		
Sociology/Film & Media Studies	LP34	4FT deg	g	BBC	Ind	Ind	35	ABBB	HN	
Sociology/Management Science	LN31	4FT deg	g	BCC	Ind	Ind	31	BBBC	HN	
Sociology/Social Policy	L430	4FT deg	g	BCC	Ind	Ind	31	BBBC	HN	
Spanish/Sociology	LR34	4FT deg	g	CCC	Ind	Ind	31	BBBC	HN	
Univ of STRATHCLYDE										
Arts and Social Sciences Sociology	Y440	3FT/4FT deg	g	CCC	Ind		28	BBBBB$	Ind	
UNIVERSITY COLLEGE SUFFOLK										
Applied Biological Science with Behavioural St	C1L3	3FT deg	S	EE	N $	PS	Ind	Ind	Ind	
Art & Design with Behavioural Studies	W2L3	3FT deg	Pf	EE	N $	P$	Ind	Ind	Ind	
Art & Design with Behavioural Studies	E2L3	3FT deg	Pf	EE	N $	P$	Ind	Ind	Ind	
Business Studies with Behavioural Studies	N1L3	3FT deg	*	EE	N $	P$	Ind	Ind	Ind	
Business Studies with Leisure Studies	N1LH	3FT deg	*	EE	N $	P$	Ind	Ind	Ind	
Early Childhood Studies with Behavioural Studies	X9LH	3FT deg	*	DD	N $	P$	Ind	Ind	Ind	
Environmental Studies with Leisure Studies	F9LH	3FT deg	S	EE	N $	P$	Ind	Ind	Ind	
Information Technology with Behavioural Studies	G5L3	3FT deg	*	EE	N $	P$	Ind	Ind	Ind	
Media Studies with Behavioural Studies	P4L3	3FT deg	*	CE	N $	P$	Ind	Ind	Ind	
Media Studies with Leisure Studies	P4LI1	3FT deg	*	CE	N $	P$	Ind	Ind	Ind	
Product Design & Manufacture with Behavioural St	H7L3	3FT deg	*	DE	N $	P$	Ind	Ind	Ind	
Univ of SUNDERLAND										
Biology and Sociology	CL13	3FT deg	B/C	10	4M	M	Ind	Ind	Ind	
Biology with Sociology	C1L3	3FT deg	B/C	10	4M	M	Ind	Ind	Ind	
Business Studies with Sociology	N1L3	3FT/4SW deg	*	10	4M	M	Ind	Ind	Ind	
Chemistry and Sociology	FL13	3FT deg	C	10	4M	M	Ind	Ind	Ind	
Chemistry with Sociology	F1L3	3FT deg	C	10	4M	M	Ind	Ind	Ind	
Computer Studies and Sociology	GL53	3FT deg	* g	10	N	M	24	CCCC	N	
Computer Studies with Sociology	G5L3	3FT/4SW deg	*	10	4M	M	Ind	Ind	Ind	
Economics with Sociology	L1L3	3FT deg	*	8	3M	M	Ind	Ind	Ind	
English and Sociology	QL33▼	3FT deg	El g	12	Ind	M	24$	BCCC$	Ind	3 6/12

course details | 98 expected requirements | 96 entry stats

TITLE	CODE	COURSE	SUBJECTS	A/AS	ND/C	AGNVQ	IB	SQA(H)	SQA	RATIO A/AS
English with Gender Studies	Q3M9	3FT deg	El g	12	Ind	M	24$	BCCC$	Ind	2
English with Sociology	Q3L3	3FT deg	*	12	3M+1D	M	Ind	Ind	Ind	
French and Sociology	RL13▼	4FT deg	F g	10	N $	M	24$	CCCC$	N$	
French with Gender Studies	R1M9	4FT deg	F g	10	N $	M	24$	CCCC$	N$	
French with Sociology	R1L3	4FT deg	F	10	4M	M	Ind	Ind	Ind	
Geography and Sociology	LL83▼	3FT deg	Gy/Gl g	12	Ind	M	24	BCCC	Ind	
Geography with Gender Studies	L8M9	3FT deg	*	8	3M	M	Ind	Ind	Ind	
Geography with Sociology	L8L3	3FT deg	*	10	4M	M	Ind	Ind	Ind	
Geology and Sociology	FL63	3FT deg	*	10	4M	M	Ind	Ind		
Geology with Sociology	F6L3	3FT deg	*	10	4M	M	Ind	Ind	Ind	
History and Sociology	VL13▼	3FT deg	H g	12	Ind	M	24	BCCC	Ind	3 6/12
History with Gender Studies	V1M9	3FT deg	H g	12	Ind	M	24$	BCCC	Ind	
History with Sociology	V1L3	3FT deg	*	12	3M+1D	M	Ind	Ind	Ind	
Mathematics and Sociology	GL13	3FT deg	M	10	4M	M	Ind	Ind		
Mathematics with Sociology	G1L3	3FT deg	M	10	4M	M	Ind	Ind	Ind	
Media Studies and Sociology	PL43	3FT deg	* g	12	3M	M	24$	BCCC$	N	18
Media Studies with Gender Studies	P4M9	3FT deg	* g	12	Ind	M	24	BCCC	Ind	11
Media Studies with Sociology	P4L3	3FT deg	*	26	Ind	Ind	Ind	Ind	Ind	
Philosophy and Sociology	VL73▼	3FT deg	* g	12	3M	M	24	BCCC	N	5
Philosophy with Sociology	V7L3	3FT deg	*	10	4M	M	Ind	Ind	Ind	
Physiology and Sociology	BL13	3FT deg	*	10	4M	M	Ind	Ind		
Physiology with Gender Studies	B1M9	3FT deg	*	8	3M	M	Ind	Ind	Ind	
Physiology with Sociology	B1L3	3FT deg	*	10	4M	M	Ind	Ind	Ind	
Politics and Sociology	ML13▼	3FT deg	* g	12	3M	M	24	BCCC	N	4
Politics with Gender Studies	M1M9	3FT deg	* g	12	3M	M	24	BCCC	N	2
Politics with Sociology	M1L3	3FT deg	*	10	4M	M	Ind	Ind	Ind	
Psychology and Sociology	CL83	3FT deg	* g	14	MO	M	26$	BBCC$	N	3 4/16
Psychology with Gender Studies	C8M9	3FT deg	* g	14	MO	M	26$	BBCC$	N	2
Psychology with Sociology	C8L3	3FT deg	*	12	3M+1D	M^	Ind	Ind	Ind	
Religious Studies with Gender Studies	V8M9	3FT deg	* g	12	3M	M	24	BCCC	N	3
Religious Studies with Sociology	V8L3	3FT deg	*	10	4M	M	Ind	Ind	Ind	
Social Science	L322	3FT deg	g	CD	2M+1D	Ind	24	CCCCC	N	4 6/16
Social Science (Applied)	L310	3FT deg	g	CD	2M+1D	Ind	24	CCCCC	N	3 6/14
Sociology	L300	3FT deg	* g	CC	2M+1D	Ind	24	CCCCC	N	7 6/16
Sociology and Religious Studies	VL83▼	3FT deg	* g	12	3M	M	24	BCCC	N	
Sociology with American Studies	L3Q4	3FT deg	* g	12	3M	M	24	BCCC	N	3 6/ 8
Sociology with Biology	L3C1	3FT deg	*	10	4M	M	Ind	Ind	Ind	
Sociology with Business Studies	L3N1	3FT deg	*	10	4M	M	Ind	Ind	Ind	
Sociology with Chemistry	L3F1	3FT deg	*	10	4M	M	Ind	Ind	Ind	
Sociology with Comparative Literature	L3Q2	3FT deg	El g	12	Ind	M	24$	BCCC$	Ind	1
Sociology with Computer Studies	L3G5	3FT deg	*	10	4M	M	Ind	Ind	Ind	
Sociology with English	L3Q3	3FT deg	*	12	3M+1D	M	Ind	Ind	Ind	
Sociology with European Studies	L3T2	3FT deg	* g	12	3M	M	24	BCCC	N	
Sociology with French	L3R1	3FT deg	*	10	4M	M	Ind	Ind	Ind	
Sociology with Gender Studies	L3M9	3FT deg	* g	12	3M	M	24	BCCC	N	7
Sociology with Geography	L3L8	3FT deg	*	10	4M	M	Ind	Ind	Ind	
Sociology with Geology	L3F6	3FT deg	*	10	4M	M	Ind	Ind	Ind	
Sociology with History	L3V1	3FT deg	*	12	3M+1D	M	Ind	Ind	Ind	
Sociology with Mathematics	L3G1	3FT deg	*	10	4M	M	Ind	Ind	Ind	
Sociology with Media Studies	L3P4	3FT deg	*	26	Ind	Ind	Ind	Ind	Ind	
Sociology with Philosophy	L3V7	3FT deg	*	10	4M	M	Ind	Ind	Ind	
Sociology with Politics	L3M1	3FT deg	*	10	4M	M	Ind	Ind	Ind	

Sociology and Anthropology   64

	course details		98 expected requirements							96 entry stats
TITLE	CODE	COURSE	SUBJECTS	A/AS	ND/C	AGNVQ	IB	SQA(H)	SQA	RATIO A/AS
Sociology with Psychology	L3C8	3FT deg	*	12	3M+1D	M^	Ind	Ind	Ind	
Sociology with Religious Studies	L3V8	3FT deg	*	10	4M	M	Ind	Ind	Ind	
Sociology with Spanish	L3R4▼	3FT deg	*	10	4M	M	Ind	Ind	Ind	2

Univ of SURREY

Applied Psychology/Sociology	CL83	4SW deg	* g	BBC	Ind	M$ go	Ind	Ind	Ind	7	16/22
Economics and Sociology	LLCH	3FT/4SW deg	M+E g	BCC	Ind	M$^ go	32$	BBBB	Ind	2	12/22
Linguistic and International Studies	MT92	4SW deg	F/G/R	BBC-CCC	3M+3D$		30$	ABBCC	Ind		
Sociology	L300	3FT deg	M+E g	CCC	Ind	M$ go	32$	BBBB	Ind	7	14/22
Sociology	L301	4SW deg	M+E g	CCC	Ind	M$ go	32$	BBBB	Ind	4	14/24

Univ of SUSSEX

American Studies (Social Studies)	Q4M9	4FT deg	*	BBB	MO	M*6	$	Ind	Ind	
Contemporary History in Social Sciences	V1MX	3FT deg	*	BBB	MO	M*6	$	Ind	Ind	
Economics in Social Sciences	L1M9	3FT deg	* g	BBB	MO $	M*6 go	$	Ind	Ind	
Economics with Development Studies	L1MY	3FT deg	* g	BBB	MO $	M*6 go	$	Ind	Ind	
English with Development Studies	Q3MY	3FT deg	*	BBB	MO	M*6	$	Ind	Ind	
Environmental Science with Development Studies	F9M9	3FT deg	2(C/P/M) g	CCC	MO $	MS go	$	Ind	Ind	
French with Development Studies	R1MY	4FT deg	F	BCC	MO $	M*_^_	$	Ind	Ind	
Geography in Social Sciences	L8M9	3FT deg	*	BBC	MO	M*6	$	Ind	Ind	
Geography with Development Studies	L8MY	3FT deg	*	BBC	MO	M*6	$	Ind	Ind	
History with Development Studies	V1MY	3FT deg	*	BBB	MO	M*6	$	Ind	Ind	
International Relations in Social Sciences	M1MX	3FT deg	*	BBC	MO	M*6	$	Ind	Ind	
International Relations with Development Studs	MM1Y	3FT deg	*	BBC	MO	M*6	$	Ind	Ind	
Philosophy in Social Sciences	V7M9	3FT deg	*	BBB	MO	M*6	$	Ind	Ind	
Philosophy with Sociology	V7L3	3FT deg	*	BBB	MO	M*6	$	Ind	Ind	
Politics in Social Sciences	M1M9	3FT deg	*	BBC	MO	M*6	$	Ind	Ind	
Politics with Development Studies	M1MY	3FT deg	*	BBC	MO	M*6	$	Ind	Ind	
Social Anthropology in African & Asian Studies	L6T5	3FT deg	*	BBC	MO	M*6	$	Ind	Ind	
Social Anthropology in Cultural & Community St	L6Y2	3FT deg	*	BBC	MO	M*6	$	Ind	Ind	
Social Anthropology in European Studies	L6T2	4FT deg	* g	BBC	MO $	M*6 go	$	Ind	Ind	
Social Anthropology with Development Studies	L6MY	3FT deg	*	BBC	MO	M*6	$	Ind	Ind	
Social Psychology	L7M9	3FT deg	* g	BBB	MO $	M*6 go	$	Ind	Ind	
Sociology in African and Asian Studies	L3T5	3FT deg	*	BBB	MO	M*6	$	Ind	Ind	
Sociology in Cultural & Community Studies	L3Y2	3FT deg	*	BBB	MO	M*6	$	Ind	Ind	
Sociology in Social Sciences	L3M9	3FT deg	*	BBB	MO	M*6	$	Ind	Ind	
Sociology with Development Studies	L3MY	3FT deg	*	BBB	MO	M*6	$	Ind	Ind	

Univ of Wales SWANSEA

American Studies and Anthropology	LQ64	3FT deg	*	BBC	Ind	Ind	30	ABBBB	Ind	4	
American Studies and Sociology	LQ34	3FT deg	*	BBC	Ind	Ind	30	ABBBB	Ind	11	
Anthropology	L600	3FT deg	*	BBC-BCC	1M+5D	Ind	30	ABBBB	Ind	6	16/22
Anthropology and Development Studies	LM69	3FT deg	*	BBC	1M+5D	Ind	30	ABBBB	Ind	6	16/20
Anthropology and Geography	LL68	3FT deg	Gy	BBC	1M+5D$	Ind	30$	ABBBB$	Ind	4	
Anthropology and Philosophy	LV67	3FT deg	*	BBC-BCC	1M+5D	Ind	28	BBBBB	Ind	4	14/24
Anthropology and Politics	ML16	3FT deg	*	BBC	1M+5D	Ind	30	ABBBB	Ind	4	
Anthropology and Psychology	LL67	3FT deg	* g	BBB-BBC	1M+5D	Ind	30	ABBBB	Ind	7	18/22
Anthropology and Social History	LV63	3FT deg	*	BBC	Ind	Ind	30	ABBBB	Ind	4	
Anthropology and Social Policy	LL46	3FT deg	*	BBC-BCC	1M+5D	Ind	28	BBBBB	Ind	8	
Anthropology and Sociology	LL36	3FT deg	*	BBC	1M+5D	Ind	30	ABBBB	Ind	4	14/24
Anthropology/Ancient History & Civilisation	LV61	3FT deg	*	BBC-BCC	Ind	Ind	28	BBBBB	X	8	
Development Studies	M920	3FT deg	*	BB-BBC	1M+5D	Ind	30	ABBBB	Ind	4	14/24
Development Studies and Economics	LM19	3FT deg	* g	BB-BBC	Ind	Ind	30	ABBBB	Ind		
Development Studies and Geography	LM89	3FT deg	Gy	BBC	1M+5D$	Ind	30$	ABBBB$	Ind	7	12/18

TITLE	CODE	COURSE	SUBJECTS	A/AS	ND/C	AGNVQ	IB	SQA(H)	SQA	RATIO	A/AS
course details			**98 expected requirements**							**96 entry stats**	
Development Studies and International Relations	MM91	3FT deg	*	BBC	1M+5D	Ind	30	ABBBB	Ind		
Development Studies and Politics	MM19	3FT deg	*	BBC	1M+5D	Ind	30	ABBBB	Ind		
Development Studies and Social Policy	LM49	3FT deg	*	BBC-BCC	1M+5D	Ind	28	BBBBB	Ind	3	
Development Studies and Sociology	LM39	3FT deg	*	BBC	1M+5D	Ind	30	ABBBB	Ind	11	
Development Studies and Spanish	MR94	4FT deg	L/*	BBC	1M+5D$	Ind	30$	ABBBB$	Ind	1	
English/Anthropology	LQ63	3FT deg	E	BBC	X	X	30$	ABBBB$	X	3	20/22
French/Anthropology	LR61	4FT deg	F	BBC	1M+5D$	Ind	30$	ABBBB$	Ind		
Geography and Sociology	LL38	3FT deg	Gy	BBC	1M+5D$	Ind	30$	ABBBB$	Ind	7	
German/Anthropology	LR62	4FT deg	G	BBC	1M+5D$	Ind	30$	ABBBB$	Ind		
History/Anthropology	VL16	3FT deg	*	BBC	Ind	Ind	30	ABBBB	Ind	7	
Italian/Anthropology	LR63	4FT deg	L/*	BBC	1M+5D$	Ind	30$	ABBBB$	Ind		
Medieval Studies/Anthropology	LVP1	3FT deg	H	BBC	X	Ind	Ind	Ind	X		
Philosophy and Sociology	LV37	3FT deg	*	BBC-BCC	1M+5D	Ind	28	BBBBB	Ind	2	16/22
Politics and Sociology	LM31	3FT deg	*	BBC	1M+5D	Ind	30	ABBBB	Ind	4	
Psychology and Sociology	LL37	3FT deg	* g	BBB-BBC	1M+5D	Ind	30	ABBBB	Ind	8	16/26
Russian/Anthropology	RL86	4FT deg	L/*	BCC	1M+5D$	Ind	28$	BBBBC$	Ind		
Social History and Sociology	LV33	3FT deg	*	BBC	1M+5D	Ind	30	ABBBB	Ind		
Social Policy and Sociology	LL43	3FT deg	*	BBC-BCC	1M+5D	Ind	28	BBBBB	Ind	5	12/18
Sociology	L300	3FT deg	*	BBC-BCC	1M+5D	Ind	30	ABBBB	Ind	5	14/22
Sociology/English	LQ33	3FT deg	E	BBC	X	X	30$	ABBBB$	X	5	20/24
Sociology/French	LR31	4FT deg	F	BBC	1M+5D$	Ind	30$	ABBBB$	Ind	8	
Sociology/German	LR32	4FT deg	G	BBC	1M+5D$	Ind	30$	ABBBB$	Ind	2	
Sociology/History	LV31	3FT deg	*	BBC	Ind	Ind	30	ABBBB	Ind	3	20/26
Sociology/Italian	LR33	4FT deg	L/*	BBC	1M+5D$	Ind	30$	ABBBB$	Ind		
Sociology/Medieval Studies	VL13	3FT deg	H	BBC	X	Ind	Ind	Ind	X		
Sociology/Russian	RL83	4FT deg	L/*	BCC	1M+5D$	Ind	28$	BBBBC$	Ind		
Spanish/Anthropology	RL46	4FT deg	L/*	BBC	1M+5D$	Ind	30$	ABBBB$	Ind	3	
Spanish/Sociology	LR34	4FT deg	L/*	BBC	1M+5D$	Ind	30$	ABBBB$	Ind		
Welsh/Anthropology	LQ65	3FT/4FT deg	W	BCC	1M+5D$	X	28$	BBBBB$	Ind		
Welsh/Sociology	LQ35	3FT/4FT deg	W	BCC	1M+5D$	X	28	BBBBB$	Ind	6	
Joint Hons with defer choice of specialisation (inc Social Anthropology)	Y220	3FT deg	*	20-22	1M+5D	Ind	28	BBBBB	Ind		
Joint Hons with defer choice of specialisation (inc Sociology)	Y220	3FT deg	*	20-22	1M+5D	Ind	28	BBBBB	Ind		

SWANSEA INST of HE

TITLE	CODE	COURSE	SUBJECTS	A/AS	ND/C	AGNVQ	IB	SQA(H)	SQA	RATIO	A/AS
Sports Studies	LN37	3FT deg	Pe+Ss	10	4M	M	Ind	Ind	Ind		
Leisure Studies	083L	2FT HND		2-6	5M+1D		Ind	Ind	Ind		

Univ of TEESSIDE

TITLE	CODE	COURSE	SUBJECTS	A/AS	ND/C	AGNVQ	IB	SQA(H)	SQA	RATIO	A/AS
Criminology (Jt Hons available)	L3M3	3FT deg	*	16-18	MO	M	Ind	BBCCC	Ind	7	10/18
Cultural Studies	LV69	3FT deg	*	14-16	Ind	M	Ind	Ind	Ind	3	4/16
Cultural Studies and English	LQ33	3FT deg	*	14-16	Ind	M	Ind	Ind	Ind		
Psychology and Criminology	LM3J	3FT deg	S	14-16	Ind	Ind	Ind	BBCCC	Ind		
Psychology and Sociology	LL73	3FT deg	S	14-16	Ind	Ind	Ind	BBCCC	Ind	4	8/16
Social Science and Information Technology	GL53	3FT deg	* g	14	Ind	Ind	Ind	BCCCC	Ind		
Sociology (Jt Hons available)	L300	3FT deg	*	12-14	Ind		Ind	Ind	Ind	4	4/18
Modular Degree Scheme *Cultural Studies*	Y401	3FT deg									
Modular Degree Scheme *Social Sciences*	Y401	3FT deg									
Modular Degree Scheme *Sociology*	Y401	3FT deg									

Sociology and Anthropology   64

course details			**98 expected requirements**							**96 entry stats**
TITLE	CODE	COURSE	SUBJECTS	A/AS	NO/C	AGNVQ	IB	SQA(H)	SQA	RATIO A/AS
THAMES VALLEY Univ										
American Studies with International Studies	Q4MX	3FT deg		8-12	MO	M	26	CCC		
American Studies with Sociology	Q4L3	3FT deg		8-12	MO	M	26	CCC		
American Studies with Women's Studies	Q4M9	3FT deg		8-12	MO	M	26	CCC		
Economics with International Studies	L1MX	3FT deg		8-12	MO	M	26	CCC		
Economics with Sociology	LL13	3FT deg		8-12	MO	M	26	CCC		
Economics with Women's Studies	L1M9	3FT deg		8-12	MO	M	24	CCC		
English Lang and Communications with Sociology	Q1L3	3FT deg		8-12	MO	M	26	CCC		
English Language and Communications with Int St	Q1MX	3FT deg		8-12	MO	M	26	CCC		
English with Sociology	Q3L3	3FT deg		8-12	MO	M	26	CCC		
English with Women's Studies	Q3M9	3FT deg		8-12	MO	M	26	CCC		
Environmental Policy and Mgt with Int Studies	F9MX	3FT deg		8-12	MO	M	26	CCC		
Environmental Policy and Mgt with Sociology	F9L3	3FT deg		8-12	MO	M	26	CCC		
European Studies with International Studies	T2MX	3FT deg		8-12	MO	M	26	CCC		
European Studies with Sociology	T2L3	3FT deg		8-12	MO	M	26	CCC		
French with International Studies	R1MX	3FT deg		8-12	MO	M	26	CCC		
Health Studies with Sociology	L4L3	3FT deg		8-12	MO	M	26	CCC		
Health Studies with Women's Studies	L4M9	3FT deg		8-12	MO	M	26	CCC		
History with International Studies	V1MX	3FT deg		8-12	MO	M	26	CCC		
History with Sociology	V1L3	3FT deg		8-12	MO	M	26	CCC		
History with Women's Studies	V1M9	3FT deg		8-12	MO	M	26	CCC		
International St with Environmental Policy & Mgt	M9F9	3FT deg		8-12	MO	M	26	CCC		
International St with Politics & Int Relations	M9M1	3FT deg		8-12	MO	M	26	CCC		
International Studies with American Studies	M9Q4	3FT deg		8-12	MO	M	26	CCC		
International Studies with Business	M9N1	3FT deg		8-12	MO	M	26	CCC		
International Studies with Economics	M9L1	3FT deg		8-12	MO	M	26	CCC		
International Studies with English Language St	M9Q1	3FT deg		8-12	MO	M	26	CCC		
International Studies with European Studies	M9T2	3FT deg		8-12	MO	M	26	CCC		
International Studies with French	M9R1	3FT deg		8-12	MO	M	26	CCC		
International Studies with German	M9R2	3FT deg		8-12	MO	M	26	CCC		
International Studies with History	M9V1	3FT deg		8-12	MO	M	26	CCC		
International Studies with Marketing	M9N5	3FT deg		8-12	MO	M	26	CCC		
International Studies with Sociology	M9L3	3FT deg		8-12	MO	M	26	CCC		
International Studies with Spanish	M9R4	3FT deg		8-12	MO	M	26	CCC		
Media Arts with Sociology	W9L3	3FT deg								
Media Arts with Women's Studies	W9M9	3FT deg		8-12	MO	M	26	CCC		
Multi-Media Computing with Sociology	G5L3	3FT deg		8-12	MO	M	26	CCC		
Politics & International Relations with Int St	M1MX	3FT deg		8-12	MO	M	26	CCC		
Psychology with Sociology	C8L3	3FT deg		8-12	MO	M	26	CCC		
Psychology with Women's Studies	C8M9	3FT deg		8-12	MO	M	26	CCC		
Sociology with Advertising	L3P3	3FT deg		8-12	MO	M	26	CCC		
Sociology with American Studies	L3Q4	3FT deg		8-12	MO	M	26	CCC		
Sociology with Business	L3N1	3FT deg		8-12	MO	M	26	CCC		
Sociology with Community Law	L3MH	3FT deg		8-12	MO	M	26	CCC		
Sociology with Criminal Justice	L3MJ	3FT deg		8-12	MO	M	26	CCC		
Sociology with Economics	L3L1	3FT deg		8-12	MO	M	26	CCC		
Sociology with English	L3Q3	3FT deg		8-12	MO	M	26	CCC		
Sociology with English Language Studies	L3Q1	3FT deg		8-12	MO	M	26	CCC		
Sociology with Environmental Policy and Mgt	L3F9	3FT deg		8-12	MO	M	26	CCC		
Sociology with European Studies	L3T2	3FT deg		8-12	MO	M	26	CCC		
Sociology with French	L3R1	3FT deg		8-12	MO	M	26	CCC		
Sociology with German	L3R2	3FT deg		8-12	MO	M	26	CCC		
Sociology with Health Studies	L3L4	3FT deg		8-12	MO	M	26	CCC		

course details | 98 expected requirements | 96 entry stats

TITLE	CODE	COURSE	SUBJECTS	A/AS	ND/C	AGNVQ	IB	SQA(H)	SQA	RATIO	A/AS
Sociology with History	L3V1	3FT deg		8-12	MO	M	26	CCC			
Sociology with International Studies	L3MX	3FT deg		8-12	MO	M	26	CCC			
Sociology with Law	L3M3	3FT deg		8-12	MO	M	26	CCC			
Sociology with Marketing	L3N5	3FT deg		8-12	MO	M	26	CCC			
Sociology with Media Studies	L3W9	3FT deg		8-12	MO	M	26	CCC			
Sociology with Politics and Int Relations	L3M1	3FT deg		8-12	MO	M	26	CCC			
Sociology with Psychology	L3C8	3FT deg		8-12	MO	M	26	CCC			
Sociology with Radio Broadcasting	L3H6	3FT deg		8-12	MO	M	26	CCC			
Sociology with Spanish	L3R4	3FT deg		8-12	MO	M	26	CCC			
Sociology with Visual Cultures	L3W1	3FT deg		8-12	MO	M	26	CCC			
Sociology with Women's Studies	L3M9	3FT deg		8-12	MO	M	26	CCC			
Spanish with International Studies	R4MX	3FT deg		8-12	MO	M	26	CCC			
Tourism with International Studies	P7MX	3FT deg		8-12	MO	M	26	CCC			
Leisure Studies	083L▼	2FT HND		2-4	N	P	24	CC			

Univ of ULSTER

TITLE	CODE	COURSE	SUBJECTS	A/AS	ND/C	AGNVQ	IB	SQA(H)	SQA	RATIO	A/AS
Peace and Conflict Studies (3 Yr)	M930▼	3FT deg	*	CCC	MO+3D	D*6/^ gi	28	BBBC	Ind	10	12/18
Social Psychology and Sociology (inc DIS)	C8L3▼	3FT/4SW deg	* g	CCC	MO+3D	D*6/^ gi	28	BBBC	Ind	23	14/20
Sociology (3 Yrs)	L300▼	3FT/4SW deg	* g	BBC	MO+4D	D*6/^ gi	32	ABBB	Ind	34	14/20
Modern Studies in the Humanities — Individual and Society	Y321▼	3FT deg	*	CCC	MO+3D	D*6/^ gi	28	BBBC	Ind		

UNIVERSITY COLL LONDON (Univ of London)

TITLE	CODE	COURSE	SUBJECTS	A/AS	ND/C	AGNVQ	IB	SQA(H)	SQA	RATIO	A/AS
Ancient History and Social Anthropology	VL16	3FT deg	* g	BCC-BBB	3M	Ind	30$	BBBCC	Ind	13	20/24
Anthropology	L602	3FT deg	* g	BBC-BBB	3M $	Ind	34$	Ind	Ind	8	18/28
Anthropology and Geography BA	LL68	3FT deg	g	BBC	3M $	Ind	30$	BBBCC	Ind	6	20/26
Anthropology and Geography BSc	LF68	3FT deg	g	BBC	3M $	Ind	30$	Ind	Ind	3	
Anthropology and Linguistics	LQ61	3FT deg	* g	BBC	3M	D$^ go	34$	BBBCC	Ind	9	26/28

Univ Col WARRINGTON

TITLE	CODE	COURSE	SUBJECTS	A/AS	ND/C	AGNVQ	IB	SQA(H)	SQA	RATIO	A/AS
Leisure Studies	73NL	2FT HND	* g	8	Ind	Ind	Ind	Ind	Ind		

Univ of WARWICK

TITLE	CODE	COURSE	SUBJECTS	A/AS	ND/C	AGNVQ	IB	SQA(H)	SQA	RATIO	A/AS
History and Sociology	VL13	3FT deg	* g	BBB-BBC	X	X	29$	AABBB		14	22/30
Law and Sociology (4 Yrs)	ML33	4FT deg	* g	ABB-BBB	X	Ind	34	AAABB		9	24/30
Politics and Sociology	ML13	3FT deg	* g	ABB	Ind	Ind	32	AAABB		13	
Sociology	L300	3FT deg	* g	BBC-BCC	Ind	Ind	30	ABBCC		13	10/30
Sociology and Education	LX39	3FT deg	* g	BCC	Ind	Ind	30	ABBBC		26	
Sociology with Social Policy	LL34	3FT deg	* g	BCC	Ind	Ind	30	ABBCC		10	6/26

WESTHILL COLL

TITLE	CODE	COURSE	SUBJECTS	A/AS	ND/C	AGNVQ	IB	SQA(H)	SQA	RATIO	A/AS
Humanities - Race and Ethnic Studies	ML93	3FT deg	* g	CC	4M+2D	M^	Ind	Ind	Ind		

Univ of WESTMINSTER

TITLE	CODE	COURSE	SUBJECTS	A/AS	ND/C	AGNVQ	IB	SQA(H)	SQA	RATIO	A/AS
Social Science	L322	3FT deg	*	BC	MO+3D	M	Ind	BBB		4	8/18
Sociology	L300	3FT deg	*	BC	MO+3D	D	26	BBB			

Univ of WOLVERHAMPTON

TITLE	CODE	COURSE	SUBJECTS	A/AS	ND/C	AGNVQ	IB	SQA(H)	SQA	RATIO	A/AS
Media and Cultural Studies (Specialist Route)	PL46	3FT deg		12-14	4M	D	24	BBBB	Ind		
Sociology (Specialist Route)	L300	3FT deg		16	4M	M	24	BBBB	Ind	9	6/22
Women's Studies (Specialist Route)	M900	3FT deg		12	4M	M	24	BBBB	Ind	3	
Combined Degrees — Sociology	Y401	3FT/4SW deg		14	4M	M	24	BBBB	Ind		
Combined Degrees — War Studies	Y401	3FT/4SW deg		12	4M	M	24	BBBB	Ind		
Combined Degrees — Women's Studies	Y401	3FT/4SW deg		12	4M	M	24	BBBB	Ind		

course details			98 expected requirements							96 entry stats	
TITLE	CODE	COURSE	SUBJECTS	A/AS	ND/C	AGNVQ	IB	SQA(H)	SQA	RATIO	A/AS
WORCESTER COLL of HE											
Sociology	L300	3FT deg		DD	Ind	M	Ind	Ind	Ind	9	8/20
Sociology/Art & Design	WL93	3FT deg	A	DD	Ind	M	Ind	Ind	Ind	2	
Sociology/Biological Science	CL13	3FT deg	S	DD	Ind	M	Ind	Ind	Ind		
Sociology/Business Management	NL13	3FT deg		DD	Ind	M	Ind	Ind	Ind	25	
Sociology/Drama	WL43	3FT deg		DD	Ind	M	Ind	Ind	Ind	4	
Sociology/Economy and Society	LL13	3FT deg		DD	Ind	M	Ind	Ind	Ind	9	
Sociology/Education Studies	XL93	3FT deg		DD	Ind	M	Ind	Ind	Ind	3	
Sociology/English and Literary Studies	QL33	3FT deg		CC	Ind	M	Ind	Ind	Ind	4	12/18
Sociology/Environmental Science	FL93	3FT deg		DD	Ind	M	Ind	Ind	Ind		
Sociology/Geography	LL83	3FT deg		DD	Ind	M	Ind	Ind	Ind	5	
Sociology/Health Studies	BL93	3FT deg	g	DD	Ind	M	Ind	Ind	Ind	4	
Sociology/History	VL13	3FT deg		DD	Ind	M	Ind	Ind	Ind	3	
Sociology/Information Technology	GL53	3FT deg		DD	Ind	M	Ind	Ind	Ind		
Sociology/Psychology	LL73	3FT deg	g	CC	Ind	M	Ind	Ind	Ind	5	8/22
Sports Studies/Sociology	LB36	3FT deg		CC	Ind	M	Ind	Ind	Ind		
Urban Studies/Sociology	LL3V	3FT deg		DD	Ind	M	Ind	Ind	Ind	3	
Women's Studies/Art and Design	WM99	3FT deg	A	DD	Ind	M	Ind	Ind	Ind		
Women's Studies/Business Management	NM19	3FT deg		DD	Ind	M	Ind	Ind	Ind		
Women's Studies/Drama	WM49	3FT deg		DD	Ind	M	Ind	Ind	Ind		
Women's Studies/Economy and Society	LM19	3FT deg		DD	Ind	M	Ind	Ind	Ind		
Women's Studies/Education Studies	XM99	3FT deg		DD	Ind	M	Ind	Ind	Ind		
Women's Studies/English and Literary Studies	QM39	3FT deg		CC	Ind	M	Ind	Ind	Ind	3	
Women's Studies/Environmental Science	FM99	3FT deg		DD	Ind	M	Ind	Ind	Ind		
Women's Studies/Geography	LM89	3FT deg		DD	Ind	M	Ind	Ind	Ind	2	
Women's Studies/Health Studies	BM99	3FT deg	g	DD	Ind	M	Ind	Ind	Ind		
Women's Studies/History	VM19	3FT deg		DD	Ind	M	Ind	Ind	Ind	8	
Women's Studies/Information Technology	MG95	3FT deg		DD	Ind	M	Ind	Ind	Ind		
Women's Studies/Psychology	LM79	3FT deg	g	CC	Ind	M	Ind	Ind	Ind	4	
Women's Studies/Sociology	LM39	3FT deg		DD	Ind	M	Ind	Ind	Ind	3	
Women's Studies/Urban Studies	LMV9	3FT deg		DD	Ind	M	Ind	Ind	Ind		
WORCESTER COLLEGE of Technology											
Leisure Studies	053L	2FT HND	*		2	N	P				
Univ of YORK											
Economics/Sociology (Equal)	LL13	3FT deg	* g	BBC	DO	D$^	30	BBBB	Ind		
History/Sociology	V1L3	3FT deg	H	ABC	Ind	D$6/^	32$	ABBB$	Ind		
Philosophy/Sociology (Equal)	VL73	3FT deg	*	BBC	Ind	D$6/^	30	BBBB	Ind		
Politics/Sociology (Equal)	ML13	3FT deg	*	BBC	Ind	D$6/^	28	BBBB	Ind	26/30	
Sociology	L300	3FT deg	*	BCC	Ind	D$6/^	28	BBBB	Ind	20/26	
Sociology/Economic and Social History (Equal)	LV33	3FT deg	* g	BCC-CCC	Ind	D$^	28	BBBC	Ind		
Sociology/Education	L3X9	3FT deg	*	BCC	Ind	D$6/^	28	BBBB	Ind	18/24	
Sociology/Social Policy (Equal)	LL34	3FT deg	*	BCC	Ind	D$6/^	28	BBCC	Ind	18/30	

TITLE	CODE	COURSE	SUBJECTS	A/AS	ND/C	RGNVQ	IB	SQA(H)	SQA	RATIO A/AS
Univ of ABERTAY DUNDEE										
Housing Economy and Society	K4L4	4FT deg			Ind	Ind	Ind		Ind	
ANGLIA Poly Univ										
Business and Social Policy	NL14▼	3FT deg	* g	12	4M	M go	Dip	BCCC	Ind	2
Communication Studies and Social Policy	PL34▼	3FT deg	Ap	14	6M	M+/^	Dip$	BBCC	Ind	
Community Specialist Practice	L520▼	3FT deg		12	4M	M	Dip	BCCC	Ind	
Criminology and Social Policy	LM43▼	3FT deg	g	12	4M	M go	Dip	BCCC	Ind	
Economics and Social Policy	LL14▼	3FT deg	* g	12	4M	M go	Dip	BCCC	Ind	
English Language Studies and Social Policy	LQ41▼	3FT deg	* g	12	4M	M go	Dip	BCCC		
English and Social Policy	QL34▼	3FT deg	E	12	4M	M+/^	Dip$	BCCC	Ind	1
European Philosophy & Literature & Social Policy	VL74▼	3FT deg	*	12	4M	M+/^	Dip	BCCC	Ind	3
French and Social Policy	RL14▼	4FT deg	* g	12	4M	M	Dip	BCCC	Ind	
Geography and Social Policy	LL84▼	3FT deg	Gy g	12	4M $	M+/^ go	Dip$	BCCC	Ind	
German and Social Policy	RL24▼	4FT deg	* g	12	4M $	M+/^ go	Dip	BCCC	Ind	
Health & Welfare (European Social Policy)	L403▼	3FT deg	*	10	3M	P	Dip	BCCC	Ind	1
Health, Welfare & Social Policy	L402▼	3FT deg	*	10	3M	P	Dip	BCCC	Ind	2	8/18
History and Social Policy	VL14▼	3FT deg	Ap	12	4M $	M+/^	Dip$	BCCC	Ind	3
Italian and Social Policy	RL34▼	4FT deg	* g	12	4M $	M+/^ go	Dip	BCCC	Ind	
Law and Social Policy	ML34▼	3FT deg	*	14	6M	M	Dip	BBCC	Ind	9
Mathematics or Stats/Stat Mod. and Social Policy	GL14▼	3FT deg	* g	12	4M	M go	Dip	BCCC	N	
Nursing and Social Work (Learn Disab) RN/DipSW	BL75▼	3FT deg	* g	CC	4M	M go	Dip	BCCC		
Politics and Social Policy	ML14▼	3FT deg	*	14	6M	M	Dip	BBCC	Ind	20
Psychology and Social Policy	CL84▼	3FT deg	S g	16	8M	D go	Dip$	BBCCC	Ind	10
Social Policy and Sociology	LL43▼	3FT deg	*	12	4M $	M	Dip	BCCC	Ind	8
Social Policy and Spanish	LR44▼	4FT deg	* g	12	4M	M go	Dip	BCCC	Ind	
Social Policy and Women's Studies	LM49▼	3FT deg	*	12	4M	M go	Dip	BCCC	Ind	3
ASTON Univ										
Social Studies/Biology	CL14	3FT/4SW deg	B g	18	5M+5D$	D$^ go	29$	BBBBC$	Ind	2
Social Studies/Biology (Year Zero)	CL1K	4FT/5SW deg								
Social Studies/Business Administration	LN41	3FT/4SW deg	* g	20	3M+7D	D$6/^ go	30	BBBBB	Ind	3	16/24
Social Studies/Electronics	HL64	3FT/4SW deg	M/P g	18	5M+5D$	D$6/^ go	29$	BBBBC$	Ind	
Social Studies/Engineering Management	HL74	3FT/4SW deg	S g	18	5M+5D$	D$^ go	29$	BBBBC$	Ind	
Social Studies/Environmental Sci & Tech (Yr Z)	FL9K	4FT/5SW deg								
Social Studies/Environmental Sci & Technology	FL94	3FT/4SW deg	S g	18	5M+5D$	D$6/^ go	29$	BBBBC$	Ind	
Social Studies/Ergonomics	JLX4	3FT/4SW deg	* g	20	5M+5D	D$6/^ go	30	BBBBB	Ind	
Social Studies/European Studies	LT42	3FT/4SWdeg	* g	18	5M+5D	D$6/^ go	29	BBBBC	Ind	
Social Studies/French	LR41	4SW deg	F g	20	X	D$^ go	30$	BBBBB$	Ind	4
Social Studies/German	LR42	4SW deg	G g	18	X	D$^ go	29$	BBBBC$	Ind	2
Social Studies/Health & Safety Management	JL94	3FT/4SW deg	* g	18	5M+5D	D$6/^ go	29	BBBBC	Ind	1
Social Studies/Health & Safety Mgt (Year Zero)	JL9K	4FT/5SW deg								
Social Studies/Human Psychology	LL74	3FT/4SW deg	* g	22	3M+7D	D$6/^ go	31	ABBBB	Ind	12	20/26
Social Studies/Human Psychology (Year Zero)	LL7K	4FT/5SW deg								
Social Studies/Mathematics	GL14	3FT/4SW deg	M g	22	X	D$6/^ go	31$	ABBBB$	Ind	4
Social Studies/Medicinal Chemistry	LF41	3FT/4SW deg	C g	20	5M+5D$	D$^ go	30$	BBBBB$	Ind	
Social Studies/Medicinal Chemistry (Year Zero)	LF4C	4FT/5SW deg								
Social Studies/Public Policy & Management	ML14	3FT/4SW deg	* g	20	3M+7D	D$6/^ go	30	BBBBB	Ind	2	16/26
Univ of Wales, BANGOR										
Business and Social Administration	L4N1	3FT deg	* g	12	4M	M$ go	Ind	Ind	Ind	
Social Policy/Criminology	LM43	3FT deg	* g	18	5M	D*6/^ go	28	BBBC	Ind	8	16/18
Social Policy/Economics	LL14	3FT deg	* g	18	3M+2D	D$6/^ go	28	BBBC	Ind	
Social Policy/Education (Taught in Welsh)	LX49	3FT deg	* g	16	Ind	D*6/^ go	Ind	X	X	

Social Policy, Social Work and Administration 65

TITLE	CODE	COURSE	SUBJECTS	A/AS	ND/C	AGNVQ	IB	SQA(H)	SQA	RATIO A/AS
Social Policy/English	LQ43	3FT deg	E g	CCC	X	D*_^ go	28$	BBBC$	X	
Social Policy/History	LV41	3FT deg	H g	18	Ind	D*_^ go	28$	BBBC$	Ind	
Social Policy/Psychology	CL84	3FT deg	* g	BCC	MO	D$6/^ go	30	BBBB	Ind	
Social Policy/Religious Studies	LV48	3FT deg	* g	CCD	Ind	D*6/^ go	28	BBBC	Ind	3
Sociology with Social Policy	L3L4	3FT deg	* g	18	5M	D*6/^ go	28	BBBC	Ind	5	14/18
Sports Science and Social Policy	BL64	3FT deg	* g	20	5D	D*6/^ go	30	BBBB	Ind	
Welsh History/Social Policy	LV4C	3FT deg	H g	CCD	Ind	D*_^ go	28$	BBBC$	Ind	
Welsh/Social Policy	LQ45	3FT/4FT deg	W g	CCD	Ind	D*_^ go	Ind	X	X	
Women's Studies and Social Policy	LM49	3FT deg	* g	18	5M	D*6/^ go	28	BBBC	Ind	

BARNSLEY COLL
Combined Studies / Social Science	Y400	3FT deg	* g	EE	4M	M*	Ind	Ind	Ind	

Univ of BATH
Social Policy and Administration	L404	3FT deg	*	20	Ind	D*^	30	ABBBB	Ind	19
Social Policy and Administration	L405	4SW deg	*	20	Ind	D*^	30	ABBBB	Ind	4	22/26
Sociology and Social Studies	L501	4SW deg	*	BCC	Ind	D*	28	CSYS	Ind	9	18/22

BATH COLL of HE
| Combined Awards / Health Studies | Y400 | 3FT deg | * | | N | | X | $ | $ | |
| Modular Programme (DipHE) / Health Studies | Y460 | 2FT Dip | * | | N | | X | $ | $ | |

Univ of BIRMINGHAM
Planning and Public Policy Making and Admin	KL44	3FT deg	*	BCC	Ind	D+^	30	BBBBB	Ind	3
Planning and Social Policy	KL4K	3FT deg	*	BCC	Ind	D+^	30	BBBBB	Ind	5
Public and Social Policy Management	L460	3FT deg	*	BCC	Ind	D+^	30	BBBBB	Ind	5	20/24
Russian & East European Studies & Social Policy	RL84	3FT/4FT deg	R/*	BBC	Ind	D+^		ABBBB	Ind	
Social Policy	L400	3FT deg	*	BCC	Ind	D+^	30	BBBBB	Ind	8	16/28
Social Policy and Political Science	LM41	3FT deg	*	BBC	Ind	D+^	32	ABBBB	Ind	13
Social Policy and Sociology	LL43	3FT deg	*	BBC	Ind	D+^	32	ABBBB	Ind	15	20/24

BLACKBURN COLL
| Public Administration | 004L | 2FT HND | | 2 | N | P | | | | |

BOLTON INST
Accountancy and Community Studies	LN54	3FT deg	* g	CD	MO	M*	24	BBCC	Ind	
Art & Design History and Community Studies	LV54	3FT deg	* g	CD	MO	M*	24	BBCC	Ind	
Biology and Community Studies	LC51	3FT deg	* g	CD	MO	M*	24	BBCC	Ind	
Business Economics and Community Studies	LL15	3FT deg	* g	CD	MO	M*	24	BBCC	Ind	
Business Information Systems and Community Studs	GL75	3FT deg	* g	CD	MO	M*	24	BBCC	Ind	
Business Studies and Community Studies	LN5C	3FT deg	* g	CD	MO	M*	24	BBCC	Ind	
Community Studies and Computing	LG55	3FT deg	* g	CD	MO	M*	24	BBCC	Ind	
Community Studies and Creative Writing	LW5X	3FT deg	* g	CD	MO	M*	24	BBCC	Ind	
Community Studies and Environmental Studies	FL95	3FT deg	* g	CD	MO	M*	24	BBCC	Ind	
Community Studies and European Cultural Studies	LT52	3FT deg	* g	CD	MO	M*	24	BBCC	Ind	
Community Studies and Film & TV Studies	LW55	3FT deg	Me/T g	CD	Ind	Ind	24	BBCC	Ind	
Community Studies and French	LR51	3FT deg	F g	CD	Ind	Ind	24	BBCC	Ind	
Community Studies and Gender and Women's Studies	LM59	3FT deg	* g	CD	MO	M*	24	BBCC	Ind	
Community Studies and German	RL25	3FT deg	G g	CD	Ind	Ind	24	BBCC	Ind	
Community Studies and History	LV51	3FT deg	* g	CD	MO	M*	24	BBCC	Ind	
Community Studies and Human Resource Management	LN51	3FT deg	* g	CD	MO	M*	24	BBCC	Ind	
Community Studies and Law	LM53	3FT deg	* g	CD	MO	M*	24	BBCC	Ind	
Community Studies and Leisure Studies	LL5H	3FT deg	* g	CD	MO	M*	24	BBCC	Ind	

course details | 98 expected requirements | 96 entry stats

TITLE	CODE	COURSE	SUBJECTS	A/AS	ND/C	AGNVQ	IB	SQA(H)	SQA	RATIO A/AS
Community Studies and Literature	LQ52	3FT deg	* g	CD	MO	M*	24	BBCC	Ind	
Community Studies and Marketing	LN55	3FT deg	* g	CD	MO	M*	24	BBCC	Ind	
Community Studies and Mathematics	GL15	3FT deg	M g	DD	Ind	Ind	24	BBCC	Ind	
Community Studies and Operations Management	LN52	3FT deg	* g	CD	MO	M*	24	BBCC	Ind	
Community Studies and Organisations, Mgt & Work	LN57	3FT deg	* g	CD	MO	M*	24	BBCC	Ind	
Community Studies and Peace & War Studies	LV5C	3FT deg	* g	CD	MO	M*	24	BBCC	Ind	
Community Studies and Philosophy	LV57	3FT deg	* g	CD	MO	M*	24	BBCC	Ind	
Community Studies and Psychology	LL57	3FT deg	* g	12	MO	D*	24	BBCC	Ind	
Community Studies and Theatre Studies	LW54	3FT deg	Me/T g	CD	Ind	Ind	24	BBCC	Ind	
Community Studies and Tourism Studies	LP57	3FT deg	* g	CD	MO	M*	24	BBCC	Ind	
Community Studies and Urban and Cultural Studies	LL53	3FT deg	* g	CD	MO	M*	24	BBCC	Ind	
Design and Community Studies	LW52	3FT deg	* g	CD	MO	M*	24	BBCC	Ind	
Visual Arts and Community Studies	LW51	3FT deg	* g	CD	MO	M*	24	BBCC	Ind	

Univ of BRADFORD

TITLE	CODE	COURSE	SUBJECTS	A/AS	ND/C	AGNVQ	IB	SQA(H)	SQA	RATIO A/AS
Applied Social Studies (with Dip SW)	L500	4SW deg	*	AA-BCC	MO+8D	DG4/^	Ind	Ind	Ind	11	14/26
Social Policy Studies	L400	3FT deg	*	CCC	Ind	M*4	Ind	Ind	Ind	4	10/18
Women's Studies and Social Policy	LM49	3FT deg	*	CCC	Ind	M$4	Ind	Ind	Ind	3	6/14

BRADFORD & ILKLEY Comm COLL

TITLE	CODE	COURSE	SUBJECTS	A/AS	ND/C	AGNVQ	IB	SQA(H)	SQA	RATIO A/AS
Applied Social Policy and Community Studies	LL45	3FT deg	*	8	MO	M	Dip	CCC	Ind	
Care Management	L450	2FT Dip	*	4	MO	P	Ind	Ind	Ind	
Community Studies	L521	3FT deg	*	8	MO	M	Dip	CCC	Ind	
Consumer, Health & Community St (Health St)	L530	3FT deg	*	8	MO	M	Dip	CCC	Ind	
Education and Community Studies	LX59	3FT deg	*	8	MO	M	Dip	CCC	Ind	
Social Work (incorp prof qualification) (20+)	L501	2FT Dip	*	8	MO	M	Ind	CCC	Ind	
Social and Community Care	L540	3FT deg	*	8	MO	M	Dip	CCC	Ind	
Women's Studies and Community Studies	LM59	3FT deg	*	8	MO	M	Dip	CCC	Ind	
Youth and Community Development (inc prof qual)	L522	3FT deg	*	8	MO	M	Dip	CCC	Ind	
Youth and Community Development (inc prof qual)	L525	2FT Dip	*	8	MO	M	Dip	CCC	Ind	

Univ of BRIGHTON

TITLE	CODE	COURSE	SUBJECTS	A/AS	ND/C	AGNVQ	IB	SQA(H)	SQA	RATIO A/AS
Social Policy and Administration	L400	3FT deg	*	14-16	MO+1D	M$	Ind	BBCC	Ind	

Univ of BRISTOL

TITLE	CODE	COURSE	SUBJECTS	A/AS	ND/C	AGNVQ	IB	SQA(H)	SQA	RATIO A/AS
Early Childhood Studies	L5X9	3FT deg	* g	BCC	Ind	D$^ | 28$	CSYS	Ind	10	20/26
Social Policy and Planning	L400	3FT deg	* g	CCC	Ind	D$^ | 26$	BBBCC	Ind	4	16/20
Social Policy and Politics	LM41	3FT deg	* g	BBC	Ind	D$^ | 26$	CSYS	Ind	36	
Social Policy and Sociology	LL43	3FT deg	* g	BBC	Ind	D$^ | 26$	CSYS	Ind	8	20/28
Social Work with Social Welfare	L5L4	3FT deg	* g	BBC	Ind	D*^	26$	BBBCC	Ind	

BRISTOL, Univ of the W of England

TITLE	CODE	COURSE	SUBJECTS	A/AS	ND/C	AGNVQ	IB	SQA(H)	SQA	RATIO A/AS
Community and Yth Work(1 Yr FT RELEVANT exp req)	L520	2FT Dip	* g	EE	N	P$ go	24	CC	N	
Health & Community Studies(1 Yr top up post Dip)	L530	1FT deg	g	X	X	X	X	X	X	

BRUNEL Univ, West London

TITLE	CODE	COURSE	SUBJECTS	A/AS	ND/C	AGNVQ	IB	SQA(H)	SQA	RATIO A/AS
Ethico Legal Issues in Health Care	L4M3	3FT deg	B	12-20	Ind	MG	Ind	Ind	Ind	
Health Information Science	L4G5	3FT deg	B	12-20	Ind	MG	Ind	Ind	Ind	
Health Promotion	L451	3FT deg	B	12-20	Ind	MG	Ind	Ind	Ind	
Health Service Administration	LN41	3FT deg	B	12-20	Ind	MG	Ind	Ind	Ind	
Health Studies	L450	3FT deg	B	12-20	Ind	MG	Ind	Ind	Ind	
Occupational Health and Safety	L531	3FT deg	B	12-20	Ind	MG	Ind	Ind	Ind	
Overseas Community Health Development	L530	3FT deg	B	12-20	Ind	MG	Ind	Ind	Ind	
Politics and Social Policy	ML14	3FT deg	*	BCC	5M	D^	28	BBBCC	Ind	4
Politics and Social Policy (4 Yrs Thick SW)	MLD4	4SW deg	*	BCC	5M	D^	28	BBBCC	Ind	
Politics and Social Policy (4 Yrs Thin SW)	MLC4	4SW deg	*	BCC	5M	D^	28	BBBCC	Ind	1

Social Policy, Social Work and Administration   65

course details			98 expected requirements							96 entry stats	
TITLE	CODE	COURSE	SUBJECTS	A/AS	NO/C	RGNVQ	IB	SQA(H)	SQA	RATIO	A/AS
Univ of BUCKINGHAM											
Policy Studies	L420	2FT deg	*	14	5M	M	24	CCCC	Ind		
BUCKINGHAMSHIRE COLLEGE											
Criminology with Social Policy	M3L4	3FT deg		12	2D	M	27	CCCC	Ind		
Social Work St with Dip in Soc Wk (Min 20 yrs)	L501	3FT deg		X						15	
Social Work St with Dip in Soc Wk (Min 20 yrs)	L503	2FT Dip		X						35	
Social Work Studies (Post CQSW/DipSW)	L502	1FT deg		X						13	
Social Work Studies with Gender Studies	L5M9	3FT deg									
Social Work Studies with Social Policy	L5L4	3FT deg									
Sociology with Research Methods	L510	3FT deg									
Sociology with Social Policy	L3L4	3FT deg		12	2D	M	27	CCCC	Ind		
CARDIFF Univ of Wales											
Social Policy	L402	3FT deg	*	CCC	Ind	Ind	Ind	Ind	Ind	4	12/26
Social Policy/Journalism, Film and Broadcasting	LP43	3FT deg	*	BBC	Ind	Ind	30	ABBBB	Ind		
Sociology and Social Policy	LL34	3FT deg	*	CCC	Ind	Ind	Ind	Ind	Ind	8	12/20
Univ of Wales INST, CARDIFF											
Community Studies (Learning Disabilities)	L501	3FT deg	* g	X			Ind	CCCC	Ind	9	
Community Studies (Social Work)	L500	3FT deg	* g	X			Ind	CCCC	Ind	17	
Social Work	L502	2FT Dip	* g	X			Ind	CCCC	Ind	17	
Univ of CENTRAL ENGLAND											
Combined Health Studies	BL94	3FT deg	* g	8-12	4M	M$ gi	Ind	CCCCC	Ind	6	8/22
Social Work (>19 Years)	L501	3FT deg	g	CC	4M	M$	Ind	Ind	Ind	20	14/15
Univ of CENTRAL LANCASHIRE											
Health St (Health Policy and Mgt (year 2 entry)	L452	2FT deg									
Health Studies	LB49	3FT deg	*	12	MO	M$	24$	CCC	Ind		
Health Studies (Community Health) (year 2 entry)	L532	2FT deg									
Health Studies (Health Promotion) (year 2 entry)	L451	2FT deg									
Social Policy and Administration	L400	3FT deg	*	12	MO	M$6/^	26$	BCCC	Ind		
Social Work and Community Studies (Top up Year)	L521	1FT Deg		X	X	X	X	X	X		
Social Work and Community Studies (with DSW)	L522	3FT deg	*	CC	MO+2D$	M$6/^	26$	BBCC	$		
Social Work and Welfare Studies	LL35	3FT deg	*	12	MO+2D$	M$6/^	26$	BBCC	$		
Social Work, Health and Welfare Studies (Year 0)	LL3M	1FT deg	*								
Combined Honours Programme Health Studies	Y400	3FT deg	*	12	MO+2D	M$6/^	26	BCCC	Ind		
Combined Honours Programme Social Policy	Y400	3FT deg	*	14	MO+3D	M$6/^	26	BBCC	Ind		
Health and Welfare Studies	054L▼	2FT HND	* g	EE	N $	P$	24$	CCC	Ind		
Health, Childhood and Social Studies	43LL▼	2FT HND	* g	E	PO+2M	P$	24$	CCC	Ind		
CHELTENHAM & GLOUCESTER COLL of HE											
Social Work	L501	2FT Dip			Ind	Ind	Ind	Ind	Ind		
UNIVERSITY COLLEGE CHESTER											
Health and Community Studies	L530	3FT deg	g	6	Ind	M	Ind	CCC	$	3	6/16
Health and Community Studies	L531	3FT deg	g	6	Ind	M	Ind	CCC	$	4	6/14
CHICHESTER INSTITUTE OF HIGHER EDUCATION											
Health Studies	L450	3FT deg	* g	12	Ind	M$	Ind	Ind	Ind		
COLCHESTER INST											
Health and Social Care	035L	2FT HND	g	EE	N	P$	Ind	Ind	Ind		

course details			98 expected requirements							96 entry stats	
TITLE	CODE	COURSE	SUBJECTS	A/AS	ND/C	RGNVQ	IB	SQA(H)	SQA	RATIO	A/AS
CORNWALL COLLEGE WITH DUCHY COLLEGE											
Social Work	L500	2FT Dip	*	CD	N	P	Ind	Ind	N		
COVENTRY Univ											
Development and Health in Disaster Management	LJ49	3FT deg	* g	14	5M	M	Ind	Ind	Ind		6/12
Law and Social Policy	LM43	3FT deg	*	CCC	D	D	Ind	BBBB	Ind		
Social Policy and International Relations	LM41	3FT deg	*	CD	M	M	Ind	CCCC	Ind		
Social Policy and Italian	RL34	3FT deg									
Social Policy and Russian	RL84	3FT deg									
Social Welfare	L501	3FT deg	* g	CC	2M+2D	MG go	Ind	Ind	Ind	1	
Social Work	L500	3FT deg	* g	CC	2M+2D	MG go	Ind	Ind	Ind	20	8/16
Sociology and Social Policy	LL34	3FT deg	* g	CC-CD	3M+3D	M go	Ind	BBB	Ind	2	8/12
Sport Science and Health Science	B6L4▼	3FT deg	S g	8	5M	Ind	Ind	Ind	Ind		
DE MONTFORT Univ											
Law and Public Policy	M3L4▼	3FT deg	* g	BBC	6D	M^	30	BBBBB	X		
Marketing/Business Economics	LN51▼	3FT deg	* g	18	3M+3D	M	32	AABB	X		
Public Policy/Accounting	LN44▼	3FT deg	* g	18	3M+3D	M	32	AABB	X		
Public Policy/Business	LN41▼	3FT deg	* g	18	3M+3D	M	32	AABB	X		
Public Policy/Business Economics	LL41▼	3FT deg	* g	18	3M+3D	M	32	AABB	X		
Public Policy/Finance	LN43▼	3FT deg	* g	18	3M+3D	M	32	AABB	X		
Public Policy/Human Resource Management	LN46▼	3FT deg	* g	18	3M+3D	M	32	AABB	X		
Public Policy/Management	LN4C▼	3FT deg	* g	18	3M+3D	M	32	AABB	X		
Public Policy/Marketing	LN45▼	3FT deg	* g	18	3M+3D	M	32	AABB	X		
Youth and Community Development	L520▼	2FT Dip	Pf g		Ind		Ind	Ind	Ind	5	
Univ of DERBY											
Applied Community and Youth Studies	L520	3FT deg		8	N $	M$	Ind	CDDD	Ind	6	
Applied Social Work (Incorp Dip in Soc Work)	L510	3FT deg			Ind	Ind	Ind	Ind	Ind	139	
DEWSBURY COLL											
Social Care	004L	2FT HND		E	3M	P	Ind	Ind	Ind		
Univ of DUNDEE											
Social Work	L500	4FT deg	* g	BCC	Ind	D$	29	BBBC	Ind	9	
Univ of DURHAM											
Community and Youth Work	L525	2FT Dip	*	X	Ind	Ind	Ind	Ind	Ind	10	
Community and Youth Work Studies	L520	3FT deg	*	X	Ind	Ind	Ind	Ind	Ind	6	
Sociology and Social Policy	LL34	3FT deg	*	BCC	Ind	Ind	30	Ind	Ind	5	18/22
Social Sciences Combined *Social Policy*	Y220	3FT deg	*	ABC	MO	Ind	32	AAABB	Ind		
Univ of EAST LONDON											
Anthropology and Social Policy Research	LL64	3FT deg	* g	12	MO	M	Ind	Ind	Ind		
Anthropology with Social Policy Research	L6L4	3FT deg	* g	12	MO	M	Ind	Ind	Ind		
Archaeological Sciences and Health Studies	FL4K	3FT deg	* g	12	MO	M					
Communication Studies and Health Studies	PL34	3FT deg	* g	12	MO	M					
Communication Studies with Health Studies	P3L4	3FT deg	* g	12	MO	M					
Economics and Social Policy Research	LL1K	3FT deg	* g	12	MO						
Economics with Social Policy Research	L1L4	3FT deg	* g	12	MO	M	Ind				
Education & Community Studies and Soc Pol Res	LX49	3FT deg	* g	12	MO	M					
Education & Community Studies with Soc Pol Res	X9L4	3FT deg	* g	12	MO	M					
Education and Community Studies	XL95	3FT deg	* g	12	MO	M	Ind	Ind	Ind	6	
European Studies with Social Policy Research	T2L4	3FT deg	* g	12	MO	M	Ind	Ind			
French and Social Policy Research	LR41	3FT deg	* g	12	MO	M	Ind	Ind	Ind		

Social Policy, Social Work and Administration   65

| | | | course details | | | | 98 expected requirements | | | | | | 96 entry stats |

TITLE	CODE	COURSE	SUBJECTS	A/AS	ND/C	AGNVQ	IB	SQA(H)	SQA	RATIO A/AS
French with Social Policy Research	R1L4	3FT deg	* g	12	MO	M				
German with Social Policy Research	R2L4	3FT deg	* g	12	MO	M	Ind			
Health Studies and Maths, Stats & Computing	LG49	3FT deg	* g	12	MO	M				
Health Studies and Politics	LM4D	3FT deg	* g	12	MO	M				
Health Studies and Social Policy Research	BL94	3FT deg	* g	12	MO	M	Ind	Ind	Ind	
Health Studies and Social Sciences	LY42	3FT deg	* g	12	MO	M				
Health Studies with Accounting & Finance	L4N4	3FT deg	* g	12	MO	M	Ind	Ind	Ind	
Health Studies with Communication Studies	L4P3	3FT deg	* g	12	MO	M				
Health Studies with Maths, Stats & Computing	L4G9	3FT deg	* g	12	MO	M				
Health Studies with Politics	L4M1	3FT deg	* g	12	MO	M				
Health Studies with Social Policy Research	B9L4	3FT deg	* g	12	MO	M	Ind	Ind	Ind	
Health Studies with Social Sciences	L4Y2	3FT deg	* g	12	MO	M				
Human Services and Social Welfare	L540	3FT deg	* g	12	MO	M				
Human Welfare and Social Welfare (with Dip SW)	L541	3FT deg	* g	12	MO	M				
Information Technology & Social Policy Research	GL54	3FT deg	* g	12	MO	M	Ind	Ind	Ind	
Information Technology with Social Pol Research	G5L4	3FT deg	* g	12	MO	M	Ind	Ind	Ind	
International Human Services	L545	4SW deg	* g	12	MO	M	Ind	Ind	Ind	
International Human Services (including Dip SW)	L546	3FT deg	* g	12	MO	M				
International Social Work Studies	L515	1FT deg	* g	12	MO	M	Ind	Ind	Ind	
Maths, Stats & Computing with Health Studies	G9L4	3FT deg	* g	12	MO	M				
Playwork	L530▼	2FT Dip	* g	12	MO	M	Ind	Ind	Ind	2
Politics and Social Policy Research	LM41	3FT deg	* g	12	N	M	Ind	Ind	Ind	4
Politics with Health Studies	M1LK	3FT deg	* g	12	MO	M				
Politics with Social Policy Research	M1L4	3FT deg	* g	12	MO	M	Ind			
Psychology with Health Studies	L7LK	3FT deg	* g	12	MO	M				
Psychosocial Sciences and Social Policy Research	LL74	3FT deg	* g	12	MO	M	Ind	Ind	Ind	
Psychosocial Studies with Social Policy Research	L7L4	3FT deg	* g	12	MO	M	Ind	Ind	Ind	
Social Policy Research	L460	3FT deg	* g	12	MO	M	Ind	Ind	Ind	6
Social Policy Research (Health)	L402	3FT deg	* g	12	MO	M	Ind	Ind	Ind	7
Social Policy Research and Social Sciences	LL4H	3FT deg	* g	12	MO	MB	Ind	Ind	Ind	
Social Policy Research and Sociology	LL34	3FT deg	* g	12	MO	M	Ind	Ind	Ind	
Social Policy Research and Spanish	LR44	3FT deg	* g	12	MO	M^	Ind	Ind	Ind	
Social Policy Research and Third World & Dev St	LMKY	3FT deg	* g	12	MO	M	Ind	Ind	Ind	
Social Policy Research and Women's Studies	LM49	3FT deg	* g	12	MO	M	Ind	Ind	Ind	
Social Policy Research with Anthropology	L4L6	3FT deg	* g	12	MO	M				
Social Policy Research with Business Studies	L4N1	3FT deg	* g	12	MO	M	Ind	Ind	Ind	
Social Policy Research with Economics	L4L1	3FT deg	* g	12	MO	M	Ind	Ind	Ind	
Social Policy Research with Educ & Community St	L4X9	3FT deg	* g	12	MO	M	Ind	Ind	Ind	
Social Policy Research with French	L4R1	3FT deg	* g	12	MO	M	Ind	Ind	Ind	
Social Policy Research with German	L4R2	3FT deg	* g	12	MO	M	Ind	Ind	Ind	
Social Policy Research with Health Studies	L4B9	3FT deg	* g	12	MO	M	Ind	Ind	Ind	
Social Policy Research with IT	L4G5	3FT deg	* g	12	MO	M	Ind	Ind	Ind	
Social Policy Research with Italian	L4R3	3FT deg	* g	12	MO	M	Ind	Ind	Ind	
Social Policy Research with Psychosocial Studies	L4L7	3FT deg	* g	12	MO	M	Ind	Ind	Ind	
Social Policy Research with Social Sciences	L4L3	3FT deg	* g	12	MO	M	Ind	Ind	Ind	
Social Policy Research with Sociology	L4LH	3FT deg	* g	12	MO	M	Ind	Ind	Ind	
Social Policy Research with Spanish	L4R4	3FT deg	* g	12	MO	M	Ind	Ind	Ind	
Social Policy Research with Third World & Dev St	L4MX	3FT deg	* g	12	MO	M				
Social Policy Research with Women's Studies	L4M9	3FT deg	* g	12	MO	M				
Social Sciences with Health Studies	Y2L4	3FT deg	* g	12	MO	M				
Social Sciences with Social Policy Research	L3L4	3FT deg	* g	12	MO	M	Ind	Ind	Ind	
Social Work Studies	L500	3FT deg	* g	12	MO	M	Ind	Ind	Ind	

TITLE	CODE	COURSE	SUBJECTS	A/AS	ND/C	AGNVQ	IB	SQA(H)	SQA	RATIO A/AS
			98 expected requirements							**96 entry stats**
Sociology with Social Policy Research	L3LK	3FT deg	* g	12	MO	M	Ind	Ind	Ind	
Spanish with Social Policy Research	R4L4	3FT deg	* g	12	MO	M	Ind			
Third World & Development Stds with Soc Pol Res	M9L4	3FT deg	* g	12	MO	M	Ind	Ind		
Women's Studies with Social Policy Research	M9LK	3FT deg	* g	12	MO	M	Ind			
Three-Subject Degree *Health Studies*	Y600	3FT deg	* g	12	MO	M	Ind	Ind	Ind	
Three-Subject Degree *Social Policy Research*	Y600	3FT deg	* g	12	MO	M	Ind	Ind	Ind	

EDGE HILL Univ COLLEGE

TITLE	CODE	COURSE	SUBJECTS	A/AS	ND/C	AGNVQ	IB	SQA(H)	SQA	RATIO A/AS
Disability & Comm Studies & Applied Social Sci	LL35	3FT deg	*	CD	3M+3D	M* / P*^	Dip	BBCC	Ind	3 4/12
Disability & Community Studies & Urban Pol St	LM59	3FT deg	*	DD	4M+2D	M* / P*^	Dip	BBCC	Ind	6

Univ of EDINBURGH

TITLE	CODE	COURSE	SUBJECTS	A/AS	ND/C	AGNVQ	IB	SQA(H)	SQA	RATIO A/AS
Geography and Social Policy	LL84	4FT deg	*	ABB	Ind		36$	AABB	Ind	6
Law and Social Policy	ML34	4FT deg	g	ABB	X		32	AAABB	X	
Scandinavian Studies and Social Policy	RL74	4FT deg	L g	BBC	Ind	Ind	Dip$	BBBC$	Ind	
Social Anthropology and Social Policy	LL64	4FT deg	*	AAB	Ind		38$	ABBB	Ind	11
Social Policy	L420	4FT deg	*	BBB	Ind		34	ABBB	Ind	6
Social Policy and Economics	LL41	4FT deg	*	BBB	Ind		34$	ABBB	Ind	
Social Policy and Politics	LM41	4FT deg	*	ABB	Ind		36$	AABB	Ind	8
Social Policy and Social and Economic History	LV43	4FT deg	*	BBB	Ind		34	ABBB	Ind	6
Social Policy and Sociology	LL43	4FT deg	*	BBB	Ind		34$	ABBB	Ind	7
Social Policy with Environmental Studies	L4F9	4FT deg		BBB			34	ABBB		
Social Policy with Gender Studies	L4M9	4FT deg	*	BBB	Ind		34$	ABBB	Ind	
Social Science *Social Policy*	Y200	3FT deg	*	BBC	Ind		34$	BBBB	Ind	

Univ of ESSEX

TITLE	CODE	COURSE	SUBJECTS	A/AS	ND/C	AGNVQ	IB	SQA(H)	SQA	RATIO A/AS
Sociology and Social Policy	LL34	3FT deg	*	22	MO+2D	D	28	BBBB	Ind	6

Univ of EXETER

TITLE	CODE	COURSE	SUBJECTS	A/AS	ND/C	AGNVQ	IB	SQA(H)	SQA	RATIO A/AS
Society, Economy and Social Policy	L429	3FT deg	* g	BBB-CCC	MO	D$	30	Ind	Ind	7 18/26

Univ of GLASGOW

TITLE	CODE	COURSE	SUBJECTS	A/AS	ND/C	AGNVQ	IB	SQA(H)	SQA	RATIO A/AS
Business Economics/Social and Urban Policy	LLC4	4FT deg		BBC	N	M	30	BBBB	N	
Celtic Civilisation/Social and Urban Policy	LQLM	4FT deg		BBC	HN	M	30	BBBB	Ind	
Computing/Social and Urban Policy	GL5K	4FT deg		BBC	8M	M	30	BBBB	Ind	
Economic and Social Hist/Social & Urban Policy	LV43	4FT deg		BBC	8M	M	30	BBBB	Ind	
Economics/Social and Urban Policy	LL14	4FT deg		BBC	8M	M	30	BBBB	Ind	
Film and Television St/Social and Urban Policy	LW45	4FT deg		BBB	HN	D	32	AABB	HN	
Geography/Social and Urban Policy	LL48	4FT deg		BBC	8M	M	30	BBBB	Ind	7
Management Studies/Social and Urban Policy	LN41	4FT deg		BBC	8M	M	30	BBBB	Ind	
Politics/Social and Urban Policy	LM41	4FT deg		BBC	8M	M	30	BBBB	Ind	3
Psychology/Social and Urban Policy	LC48	4FT deg		BBC	8M	M	30	BBBB	Ind	4
Social and Urban Policy with Celtic	L4Q5	4FT deg		BBC	8M	M	30	BBBB	Ind	
Social and Urban Policy with Czech	L4T1	4FT deg		BBC	8M	M	30	BBBB	Ind	
Social and Urban Policy with German	L4R2	4FT deg		BBC	8M	M	30	BBBB	Ind	
Social and Urban Policy with Hispanic Studies	L4R4	4FT deg		BBC	8M	M	30	BBBB	Ind	
Social and Urban Policy with Italian	L4R3	4FT deg		BBC	8M	M	30	BBBB	Ind	
Social and Urban Policy with Russian	L4R8	4FT deg		BBC	8M	M	30	BBBB	Ind	
Social and Urban Policy/Celtic	LQ45	4FT deg		BBC	HN	M	30	BBBB	Ind	
Social and Urban Policy/Classical Civilisation	LQ48	4FT deg		BBC	HN	M	30	BBBB	Ind	
Social and Urban Policy/Classical Civilisation	LQ4V	4FT deg		BBC	8M	M	30	BBBB	Ind	
Social and Urban Policy/Classical Hebrew	LQ49	4FT deg		BBC	HN	M	30	BBBB	Ind	
Social and Urban Policy/Computing Science	GL54	4FT deg		BBC	8M	M	30	BBBB	Ind	

Social Policy, Social Work and Administration   65

| course details | | | 98 expected requirements | | | | | | | 96 entry stats |

TITLE	CODE	COURSE	SUBJECTS	A/AS	NO/C	AGNVQ	IB	SQA(H)	SQA	RATIO A/AS
Social and Urban Policy/Czech	LT41	5FT deg		BBC	HN	M	30	BBBB	Ind	
Social and Urban Policy/English	LQ43	4FT deg		BBC	HN	M	30	BBBB	Ind	
Social and Urban Policy/Greek	LQ47	4FT deg		BBC	HN	M	30	BBBB	Ind	
Social and Urban Policy/Hispanic Studies	LR44	5FT deg		BBC	HN	M	30	BBBB	Ind	
Social and Urban Policy/History	LV41	4FT deg		BBC	8M	M	30	BBBB	Ind	4
Social and Urban Policy/History of Art	LV44	4FT deg		BBC	HN	M	30	BBBB	Ind	
Social and Urban Policy/Latin	LQ46	4FT deg		BBC	HN	M	30	BBBB	Ind	
Social and Urban Policy/Music	LW43	4FT deg		BBC	HN	M	30	BBBB	Ind	
Social and Urban Policy/Polish	LT4C	5FT deg		BBC	HN	M	30	BBBB	Ind	
Social and Urban Policy/Psychology	LL4R	4FT deg		BBC	HN	M	30	BBBB	Ind	15
Social and Urban Policy/Russian	LR48	5FT deg		BBC	HN	M	30	BBBB	Ind	
Social and Urban Policy/Sociology	LLH4	4FT deg		BBC	8M	M	30	BBBB	Ind	5
Social and Urban Policy/Theatre Studies	LW44	4FT deg		BBC	HN	M	30	BBBB	Ind	

GLASGOW CALEDONIAN Univ

TITLE	CODE	COURSE	SUBJECTS	A/AS	NO/C	AGNVQ	IB	SQA(H)	SQA	RATIO A/AS
Social Work	L500	3FT deg		X	Ind		Ind	X	Ind	

GOLDSMITHS COLL (Univ of London)

TITLE	CODE	COURSE	SUBJECTS	A/AS	NO/C	AGNVQ	IB	SQA(H)	SQA	RATIO A/AS
Community and Youth Work (Post Experience)	L520	2FT Dip				M				5
Social Policy	L402	3FT deg		BCD	MO	M	Dip	BBBBC	N	5 6/20
Social Policy with Economics	L4L1	3FT deg		BCD	MO	M	Dip	BBBBC	N	
Social Policy with Politics	L4M1	3FT deg		BCD	MO	M	Dip	BBBBC	N	

Univ of GREENWICH

TITLE	CODE	COURSE	SUBJECTS	A/AS	NO/C	AGNVQ	IB	SQA(H)	SQA	RATIO A/AS
Care: (Early Years)	115L▼	2FT HND	* g	EE	N	Ind	Ind	Ind	Ind	

Univ of HERTFORDSHIRE

TITLE	CODE	COURSE	SUBJECTS	A/AS	NO/C	AGNVQ	IB	SQA(H)	SQA	RATIO A/AS
Nursing & Soc Wrk Sts (Learn Dis) with RN/DipSW	BL75	3FT deg	* g	12-16	4M+3D	D	Ind	Ind	Ind	1
Politics/Social Policy	M1L4	3FT deg	* g	14	M+D	Ind	26	BBCC	Ind	
Social Policy/Economics	L4L1	3FT deg	* g	14	M+D	Ind	26	BBCC	Ind	
Social Policy/Politics	L4M1	3FT deg	* g	14	M+D	Ind	26	BBCC	Ind	
Social Policy/Sociology	L4L3	3FT deg	* g	14	M+D	Ind	26	BBCC	Ind	
Social Work with Diploma in Social Work	L500	3FT deg		12	3M+3D	Ind	26	Ind	Ind	11 8/18
Sociology/Social Policy	L3LK	3FT deg	* g	14	M+D	Ind	26	BBCC	Ind	

Univ of HUDDERSFIELD

TITLE	CODE	COURSE	SUBJECTS	A/AS	NO/C	AGNVQ	IB	SQA(H)	SQA	RATIO A/AS
Applied Social Studies	L4L5	3FT deg	* g	10-14	MO	M go	Ind	Ind	Ind	
Health with Community Studies	L530	3FT deg	* g	10-14	MO	M go	Ind	Ind	Ind	
Health with Sports Studies	BL65	3FT deg	* g	14-18	6M $	D$ gi	Ind	BBBC	Ind	
Social Work (Including DipSW. minimum age 19)	L500	3FT deg	* g	EE	3M	M go	Ind	Ind	Ind	
Science (Extended) *Health with Sports Studies*	Y108	4FT deg	* g	EE	N	P$ gi	Ind	Ind	Ind	

Univ of HULL

TITLE	CODE	COURSE	SUBJECTS	A/AS	NO/C	AGNVQ	IB	SQA(H)	SQA	RATIO A/AS
Gender Studies and Social Policy	ML94	3FT deg	* g	BBC-BCC	M+D $	M$6/^ go	28	BBBCC	Ind	
Politics/Social Policy	LM41	3FT deg	*	BBB-BCC	Ind	Ind	28$	BBCCC	Ind	7
Social Policy and Administration	L400	3FT deg	*	20-24	MO+4D	DG^ gi	26	BBCCC	Ind	2 10/26
Social Policy and Criminology	L460	3FT deg	*	20-24	MO+4D	DG^ gi	28	BBCCC	Ind	7 16/26
Social Policy and Health	L453	3FT deg	*	20-24	MO+4D	DG^ gi	26	BBCCC	Ind	6
Social Policy/Sociology	LL34	3FT deg	*	BBB-BCC	Ind	DG^ gi	28$	BBCCC	Ind	26
Social Work and Social Policy (incl Diploma)	LL45	3FT deg	*	20-24	MO+4D	DG^ gi	28	ABBCC	Ind	13 16/28

KEELE Univ

TITLE	CODE	COURSE	SUBJECTS	A/AS	NO/C	AGNVQ	IB	SQA(H)	SQA	RATIO A/AS
Applied Social Studies and American Studies	LQ54	3FT deg	*	BBC-BCC	Ind	Ind	30	CSYS	Ind	
Applied Social Studies and Ancient History	LV5D	3FT deg	*	BBC-BCC	Ind	Ind	28	CSYS	Ind	4
Applied Social Studs and Ancient History (4 Yrs)	VLD5	4FT deg	*	BBC-BCC	Ind	Ind	28	BBBB	Ind	

Letts STUDY GUIDES
THE INDEPENDENT

course details			*98 expected requirements*							*96 entry stats*	
TITLE	CODE	COURSE	SUBJECTS	A/AS	NO/C	AGNVQ	IB	SQA(H)	SQA	RATIO	A/AS
Astrophysics and Applied Social Studies	FL55	3FT deg	P g	BCC	Ind	D$^	28$	CSYS	Ind		
Astrophysics and Applied Social Studies (4 Yrs)	LF55	4FT deg	*	BCC	Ind	Ind	28	BBBB	Ind		
Biochemistry and Applied Social Studies	CL75	3FT deg	C g	BCC	Ind	D$^	28$	CSYS	Ind		
Biochemistry and Applied Social Studies (4 Yrs)	LC57	4FT deg	*	BCC	Ind	Ind	28	BBBB	Ind		
Biology and Applied Social Studies	CL15	3FT deg	S g	BCC	Ind	D$^	28$	CSYS	Ind	2	
Biology and Applied Social Studies (4 Yrs)	LC51	4FT deg	*	BCC	Ind	Ind	28	BBBB	Ind		
Business Admin and Applied Social Studs (4 Yrs)	NL95	4FT deg	*	BBC	Ind	Ind	30	BBBB	Ind		
Business Administration and Applied Social Studs	LN59	3FT deg	*	BBC	Ind	Ind	30	CSYS	Ind	5	
Classical Studies and Applied Social St (4 Yrs)	QL85	4FT deg	*	BBC-BCC	Ind	Ind	28	BBBB	Ind		
Classical Studies and Applied Social Studies	LQ58	3FT deg	*	BCC	Ind	Ind	28	CSYS	Ind		
Computer Science and Applied Social Studies	GL55	3FT deg	*	BCC	Ind	D$^	28	CSYS	Ind		
Criminology and Applied Social Studies	LM5H	3FT deg	*	BBB	Ind	Ind	32	CSYS	Ind	7	22/26
Criminology and Applied Social Studies (4 Yrs)	MLH5	4FT deg	*	BBB	Ind	Ind	32	ABBB	Ind	5	
Economics and Applied Social Studies	LL15	3FT deg	* g	BCC	Ind	Ind	28	CSYS	Ind		
Educational Studies and Applied Social Studies	LX59	3FT deg	*	BBC-BCC	Ind	Ind	28	CSYS	Ind		
Electronic Music & Applied Social Studs (4 Yrs)	WLJ5	4FT deg	*	BBC-BCC	Ind	Ind	28	BBBB	Ind		
Electronic Music and Applied Social Studies	LW5J	3FT deg	Mu	BCC	Ind	D$^	28$	CSYS	Ind		
English and Applied Social Studies	LQ53	3FT deg	E	BBB-BBC	Ind	D$^	30$	CSYS	Ind	5	
English and Applied Social Studies (4 Yrs)	QL35	4FT deg	*	BBB-BBC	Ind	Ind	30	BBBB	Ind		
Environmental Management and App Social Studies	FLX5	3FT deg	g	BBC-BCC	Ind	Ind	28	CSYS	Ind		
Finance and Applied Social Studies	LN53	3FT deg	* g	BBB-BBC	Ind	Ind	30	CSYS	Ind		
Finance and Applied Social Studies (4 Yrs)	NL35	4FT deg	*	BBC	Ind	Ind	30	BBBB	Ind		
Geography and Applied Social Studies	LL58	3FT deg	Gy	BCC	Ind	D$^	28$	CSYS	Ind		
Geography and Applied Social Studies (4 Yrs)	LL85	4FT deg	*	BCC	Ind	Ind	28	BBBB	Ind		
Geology and Applied Social Studies	FL65	3FT deg	S g	BCC	Ind	D$^	28$	CSYS	Ind		
Geology and Applied Social Studies (4 Yrs)	LF56	4FT deg	*	BCC	Ind	Ind	28	BBBB	Ind		
German and Applied Social Studies	LR52	3FT deg	G	BCC-BBC	Ind	D$^	28$	CSYS	Ind		
German and Applied Social Studies (4 Yrs)	RL25	4FT deg	G	BCC	Ind	Ind	28$	BBBB	Ind		
German/Russian or Rus St & Applied Soc St (4Yrs)	TLY5	4FT deg	G	BBC-BCC	Ind	Ind	28$	BBBB	Ind		
German/Russian or Russ St and Applied Social St	LT5Y	3FT deg	G+R g	BBC	Ind	D$^	30$	CSYS	Ind		
History and Applied Social Studies	LV51	3FT deg	*	BBC	Ind	Ind	30	CSYS	Ind	3	
History and Applied Social Studies (4 Yrs)	VL15	4FT deg	*	BBC	Ind	Ind	30	BBBB	Ind		
Human Resource Management and Applied Social St	LN56	3FT deg	*	BBC	Ind	Ind	30	CSYS	Ind	4	
Human Resource Mgt and App Social St (4 Yrs)	NL65	4FT deg	*	BBC	Ind	Ind	30	BBBB	Ind	3	
International History and Applied Social St	VLC5	4FT deg	*	BBC-BCC	Ind	Ind	28	BBBB	Ind	2	
International History and Applied Social Studies	LV5C	3FT deg	*	BBC-BCC	Ind	Ind	28	CSYS	Ind	4	
Latin and Applied Social Studies	LQ56	3FT deg	Ln	BCC	Ind	D$^	28$	CSYS	Ind		
Latin and Applied Social Studies (4 Yrs)	QL65	4FT deg	*	BCC	Ind	Ind	28	BBBB	Ind		
Law and Applied Social Studies	LM53	3FT deg	*	BBB	Ind	Ind	32	CSYS	Ind		
Law and Applied Social Studies (4 Yrs)	ML35	4FT deg	*	BBB	Ind	Ind	32	BBBB	Ind		
Mathematics and Applied Social Studies	GL15	3FT deg	M	BCC	Ind	D$^	28$	CSYS	Ind	1	
Mathematics and Applied Social Studies (4 Yrs)	LG51	4FT deg	*	BCC	Ind	Ind	28	BBBB	Ind		
Music and Applied Social Studies	LW53	3FT deg	Mu	BBC	Ind	D$^	30$	CSYS	Ind		
Music and Applied Social Studies (4 Yrs)	WL35	4FT deg	*	BBC	Ind	Ind	30	BBBB	Ind		
Philosophy and Applied Social Studies	LV57	3FT deg	*	BBC-BCC	Ind	Ind	28	CSYS	Ind		
Philosophy and Applied Social Studies (4 Yrs)	VL75	4FT deg	*	BBC-BCC	Ind	Ind	28	BBBB	Ind		
Physics and Applied Social Studies	FL35	3FT deg	P g	BCC	Ind	D$^	28$	CSYS	Ind		
Physics and Applied Social Studies (4 Yrs)	LF53	4FT deg	*	BCC	Ind	Ind	28	BBBB	Ind		
Politics and Applied Social Studies	LM51	3FT deg	*	BBC	Ind	Ind	30	CSYS	Ind	2	
Politics and Applied Social Studies (4 Yrs)	ML15	4FT deg	*	BBC-BCC	Ind	Ind	28	BBBB	Ind		
Psychology and Applied Social Studies (4 Yrs)	LC58	4FT deg	* g	BBB	Ind	Ind	32	ABBB	Ind		
Russian Studies and Applied Social Studies	LR5V	3FT deg	*	BCC	Ind	Ind	28	CSYS	Ind		

TITLE	CODE	COURSE	SUBJECTS	A/AS	ND/C	AGNVQ	IB	SQA(H)	SQA	RATIO A/AS
course details			*98 expected requirements*							*96 entry stats*
Russian Studies and Applied Social Studs (4 Yrs)	RLV5	4FT deg	*	BCC	Ind	Ind	28	BBBB	Ind	
Russian and Applied Social Studies	LR58	3FT deg	R	BCC	Ind	D$^	28$	CSYS	Ind	
Russian and Applied Social Studies (4 Yrs)	RL85	4FT deg	*	BCC	Ind	Ind	28	BBBB	Ind	
Sociol & Soc Anthrop and Applied Social St(4Yrs)	LL53	4FT deg	*	BBC	Ind	Ind	30	BBBB	Ind	6
Sociology & Soc Anthrop and Applied Social Studs	LL35	3FT deg	*	BBC-BCC	Ind	Ind	28	CSYS	Ind	5 16/22
Statistics and Applied Social Studies	GL45	3FT deg	M	BCC	Ind	D$^	28$	CSYS	Ind	
Statistics and Applied Social Studies (4 Yrs)	LG54	4FT deg	*	BCC	Ind	Ind	28	BBBB	Ind	
Visual Arts and Applied Social Studies (4 Yrs)	WL15	4FT deg	*	BBC-BCC	Ind	Ind	28	BBBB	Ind	

Univ of KENT

TITLE	CODE	COURSE	SUBJECTS	A/AS	ND/C	AGNVQ	IB	SQA(H)	SQA	RATIO A/AS
British and American Policy Studies (4 Yrs)	L441	4FT deg	* g	20	3M+3D	M$ go	28	BBBB	Ind	3
European Studies (Social Pol and Admin) (4 Yrs)	LTK2	4FT deg	L	20	Ind	Ind	28$	BBBB$	Ind	
Ind Relations & Human Res Mgt (Soc Pol & Admin)	NL64	3FT deg	* g	20	3M+3D	M$ go	28	BBBB	Ind	5
Law and Welfare	LM43	3FT deg	*	22	2M+4D	D$	30	ABBB	Ind	6
Philosophy and Social Policy & Administration	LVK7	3FT deg	*	22	2M+4D	Ind	30	Ind	Ind	
Social Policy & Admin/Accounting and Finance	LN44	3FT deg	* g	20	3M+3D	M$ go	28	BBBB	Ind	
Social Policy & Admin/Politics & Government	LM41	3FT deg	*	BCC	3M+3D	M$	28	BBBB	Ind	
Social Policy & Admin/Social Anthropology	LL46	3FT deg	*	20	3M+3D	M$	28	BBBB	Ind	
Social Policy & Administration/Economics	LL14	3FT deg	* g	20	3M+3D	M$ go	28	BBBB	Ind	
Social Policy and Administration	L430	3FT deg	*	20	3M+3D	M$	28	BBBB	Ind	3 16/26
Social Policy and Administration and Philosophy	LV47	3FT deg	*	20	3M+3D	M$	28	BBBB	Ind	
Social Policy and Administration with Computing	L4G5	3FT deg	* g	20	3M+3D	M$ go	28	BBBB	Ind	3
Social Policy and Public Management	LN41	3FT deg	* g	18	4M+2D	M$ go	26	BBBB	Ind	
Sociology/Social Policy & Administration	LL34	3FT deg	*	20	3M+3D	M$	28	BBBB	Ind	5
Urban Studies (Social Policy and Administration)	KL44	3FT deg	* g	20	3M+3D	M$ go	28	BBBB	Ind	10

KINGSTON Univ

TITLE	CODE	COURSE	SUBJECTS	A/AS	ND/C	AGNVQ	IB	SQA(H)	SQA	RATIO A/AS
Applied Social Science	L510	3FT deg	* g	14-16	MO	Ind^	Ind	BBCCC	HN	3 6/18
Community Care Management	L530	3FT deg				Ind				
Family and Childcare Studies	L540	3FT deg				Ind				

LANCASTER Univ

TITLE	CODE	COURSE	SUBJECTS	A/AS	ND/C	AGNVQ	IB	SQA(H)	SQA	RATIO A/AS
Applied Social Science	L430	3FT deg	*	CCC	M+D		30	ABBBB	Ind	
Criminology and Applied Social Science	LM43	3FT deg	*	CCC	M+D		30	ABBBB	Ind	
Educational Studies and Applied Social Science	LX49	3FT deg	*	CCC	Ind		30	BBBBB	Ind	
Independent Studies and Applied Social Science	YL44	3FT deg	*	CCC	Ind		Ind	Ind	Ind	
Social Work (including DipSW)	L500	3FT deg	*	BCC	M+D		32	ABBBB	Ind	
Women's Studies and Applied Social Science	LM49	3FT deg	*	CCC	MO		30	BBBBB	Ind	

Univ of LEEDS

TITLE	CODE	COURSE	SUBJECTS	A/AS	ND/C	AGNVQ	IB	SQA(H)	SQA	RATIO A/AS
Economic and Social History-Social Policy	LV43	3FT deg	* g	BBC	Ind	Ind	30	CSYS	Ind	
Economics-Social Policy	LL14	3FT deg	g	BBC	Ind	Ind	30	CSYS	Ind	15
English-Social Policy	QL34	3FT deg	E q	BBC	Ind	Ind	30$	CSYS	Ind	6 22/28
Gender Studies - Social Policy	LM49	3FT deg	* g	BCC	Ind	Ind	28$	CSYS	Ind	
Geography-Social Policy	LL48	3FT deg	Gy g	BBC	Ind	D$^ go	30$	CSYS	Ind	4
History-Social Policy	VL14	3FT deg	* g	BBC	Ind	Ind	30	CSYS	Ind	6
Philosophy-Social Policy	LV47	3FT deg	* g	BBC	Ind	D$^ go	30	CSYS	Ind	
Politics-Social Policy	LM41	3FT deg	* g	BBB	Ind	Ind	32	CSYS	Ind	
Religious Studies-Social Policy	LV48	3FT deg	* g	BBC	Ind	D$^ go	30	CSYS	Ind	
Social Policy and Administration	L430	3FT deg	* g	BCC	Ind	D$^ go	28	CSYS	Ind	7 18/26
Social Policy-Sociology	LL34	3FT deg	* g	BBC	Ind	D$^ go	30	CSYS	Ind	6 20/28
Social Policy-Theology	LV4V	3FT deg	* g	BBC	Ind	D$^ go	30	CSYS	Ind	2

TITLE	CODE	COURSE	SUBJECTS	A/AS	ND/C	AGNVQ	IB	SQA(H)	SQA	RATIO	A/AS
LEEDS METROPOLITAN Univ											
Community and Youth Studies	L520	3FT deg								4	
Health Studies	L450	3FT deg	* g	CC	3M+2D	MG/PG^ go	26	BBCC	Ind	6	8/20
Health Studies with Communications	L4P3	3FT deg									
Playwork (Post-Experience)	L530▼	2FT Dip	* g	X	X	X	X	X	Ind	2	6/10
Professional Studies (Playwork)	L531	1FT deg									
Professional Studies (Social Work)	L511	1FT deg									
Professional Studies (Youth and Community Work)	L521	1FT deg									
Social Sciences - Social Policy and Admin	L402	3FT deg	* g	BC-CCD	3M+2D	D$ go	27	BBBC	Ind	5	8/18
Univ of LINCOLNSHIRE and HUMBERSIDE											
Business and Social Work	NL15	3FT deg	* g	14	2M+2D		24	BCCC	Ind		
Communications and Health Studies	LP43▼	3FT deg	* g	16	1M+3D	D	24	BBCCC	Ind		
Communications and Social Policy	LP4H▼	3FT deg	* g	14	2M+2D	M	24	BCCC	Ind		
Criminology and Health Studies	LMKH▼	3FT deg	* g	16	1M+3D	D	24	BBCCC	Ind		
Criminology and Social Policy	LM43▼	3FT deg	* g	16	1M+3D	D	24	BBCCC	Ind		
Economics and Health Studies	LL1K▼	3FT deg	* g	16	1M+3D	D	24	BBCCC	Ind		
Economics and Social Policy	LL14▼	3FT deg	* g	16	1M+3D	D	24	BBCCC	Ind		
Health Studies	L450▼	3FT deg	g	16	1M+3D	D	24	BBCCC	Ind		
Health Studies and International Relations	LMK1▼	3FT deg	* g	16	1M+3D	P	24	BBCCC	Ind		
Health Studies and Journalism	LP46▼	3FT deg	* g	18	1M+4D	D	26	BBBCC	Ind		
Health Studies and Law	LMK3▼	3FT deg	* g	16	1M+3D	D	24	BBCCC	Ind		
Health Studies and Management	LN41▼	3FT deg	* g	16	1M+3D	D	24	BBCCC	Ind		
Health Studies and Media	LPK4▼	3FT deg	* g	18	1M+4D	D	26	BBBCC	Ind		
Health Studies and Politics	LM4C▼	3FT deg	* g	16	1M+3D	D	24	BBCCC	Ind		
Health Studies and Psychology	CL8K▼	3FT deg	* g	18	1M+4D	D	26	BBBCC	Ind		
Health Studies and Social Policy	L451▼	3FT deg	* g	16	1M+3D	D	24	BBCCC	Ind		
Health Studies and Tourism	LPK7▼	3FT deg	* g	16	1M+3D	D	24	BBCCC	Ind		
International Relations and Social Policy	LML1▼	3FT deg	* g	16	1M+3D	D	24	BBCCC	Ind		
Journalism and Social Policy	LP4P▼	3FT deg	* g	18	1M+4D	D	26	BBBCC	Ind		
Law and Social Policy	LM4H▼	3FT deg	* g	16	1M+3D	D	24	BBCCC	Ind		
Management and Social Policy	LN4C▼	3FT deg	* g	14	2M+2D	M	24	BCCC	Ind		
Media and Social Policy	LP44▼	3FT deg	* g	18	1M+4D	D	26	BBBCC	Ind		
Politics and Social Policy	LMLC▼	3FT deg	* g	16	1M+3D	D	24	BBCCC	Ind		
Psychology and Social Policy	CL84▼	3FT deg	* g	18	1M+4D	D	26	BBBCC	Ind		
Social Policy	L400▼	3FT deg	* g	14	2M+2D	M	24	BCCC	Ind		
Social Policy and Tourism	LP47▼	3FT deg	* g	14	2M+2D	M	24	BCCC	Ind		
Social Work	L500	3FT deg	g	14	Ind	Ind	Ind	BCCC	Ind		
Social Work and Administration	LN5C	3FT deg	g	14	Ind	Ind	Ind	BCCC	Ind		
Health Studies	054L▼	2FT HND	g								
Univ of LIVERPOOL											
Sociology and Social Policy	LL34	3FT deg	*	BCC	Ind	Ind	Ind	Ind	Ind	13	16/24
LIVERPOOL JOHN MOORES Univ											
Applied Community Studies	L520	3FT deg		CC	5M	M		CCCC		7	8/12
Applied Psychology and Applied Community Studies	LC58	3FT deg	* g	16	5M+3D	M$^ go		BBCC		3	14/18
Sociology and Applied Community Studies	LL5H	3FT deg	* g	12-14	MO	D$/M$6	28$	BCCC		8	14/16
LONDON GUILDHALL Univ											
3D/Spatial Design and Social Policy & Management	LW4F	3FT deg	Pf g	DD	MO	M$ go	24	Ind	Ind		
Social Policy & Management & Business Economics	LL4C	3FT deg	* g	CD-DDD	MO	M$ go	24	Ind	Ind		
Social Policy & Management & Financial Services	LN43	3FT deg	* g	CD-DDD	MO	M$ go	24	Ind	Ind		
Social Policy & Management and Accounting	LN44	3FT deg	* g	CD-DDD	MO	M$ go	24	Ind	Ind		

Social Policy, Social Work and Administration 65

			course details				98 expected requirements							96 entry stats	
TITLE	CODE	COURSE		SUBJECTS	A/AS	ND/C	AGNVQ	IB	SQA(H)	SQA	RATIO	A/AS
Social Policy & Management and Business	LN41	3FT deg		* g	CD-DDD	MO	M$ go	24	Ind	Ind		
Social Policy & Management and Business IT	GL74	3FT deg		* g	CD-DDD	MO	M$ go	24	Ind	Ind		
Social Policy & Management and Computing	GL54	3FT deg		* g	CD-DDD	MO	M$ go	24	Ind	Ind		
Social Policy & Management and Design Studies	LW42	3FT deg		* g	CD-DDD	MO	M$ go	24	Ind	Ind		
Social Policy & Management and Development Studs	LM49	3FT deg		* g	CD-DDD	MO	M$ go	24	Ind	Ind		
Social Policy & Management and Economics	LL14	3FT deg		* g	CD-DDD	MO	M$ go	24	Ind	Ind		
Social Policy & Management and English	LQ43	3FT deg		* g	CC-CDD	MO+2D	M$ go	26	Ind	Ind		
Social Policy & Management and European Studies	LT42	3FT deg		* g	CD-DDD	MO	M$ go	24	Ind	Ind		
Social Policy & Management and Fine Art	LW41	3FT deg		* g	CC-CDD	MO+2D	M$ go	26	Ind	Ind		
Social Policy & Management and French	LR41	4FT deg		* g	CD-DDD	MO	M$ go	24	Ind	Ind		
Social Policy & Management and German	LR42	4FT deg		* g	CD-DDD	MO	M$ go	24	Ind	Ind		
Social Policy & Management and Law	LM43	3FT deg		* g	CC-CDD	MO+2D	M$ go	26	Ind	Ind		
Social Policy & Management and Marketing	LN45	3FT deg		* g	CD-DDD	MO	M$ go	24	Ind	Ind		
Social Policy & Management and Mathematics	GL14	3FT deg		* g	CD-DDD	MO	M$ go	24	Ind	Ind		
Social Policy & Management and Modern History	LV41	3FT deg		* g	CD-DDD	MO	M$ go	24	Ind	Ind		
Social Policy & Management and Multimedia Systs	GLM4	3FT deg		* g	CD-DDD	MO	M$ go	24	Ind	Ind		
Social Policy & Management and Politics	LM41	3FT deg		* g	CD-DDD	MO	M$ go	24	Ind	Ind		
Social Policy & Management and Psychology	CL84	3FT deg		* g	CC-CDD	MO+2D	M$ go	26	Ind	Ind		
Social Policy & Mgt & Commun & Audio Vis Prod St	LP44	3FT deg		* g	CC	MO+3D	M$ go	26	Ind	Ind		
Social Policy & Mgt and International Relations	LM4C	3FT deg		* g	CD-DDD	MO	M$ go	24	Ind	Ind		
Social Policy & Mgt and Product Develop & Manuf	JL44	3FT deg		* g	CD-DDD	MO	M$ go	24	Ind	Ind		
Social Policy and Management	L460	3FT deg		* g	12-14	MO	M$ go	24	Ind	Ind		
Spanish and Social Policy & Management	LR44	4FT deg		* g	CD-DDD	MO	M$ go	24	Ind	Ind		
Taxation and Social Policy & Management	LN4H	3FT deg		* g	CD-DDD	MO	M$ go	24	Ind	Ind		
Textile Furnishing Design & Social Policy & Mgt	LW4G	3FT deg		Pf g	DD	MO	M$ go	24	Ind	Ind		
Modular Programme 　*Social Policy and Management*	Y400	3FT deg		* g	CC-DD	MO	M$ go	24	Ind	Ind		
LSE: LONDON Sch of Economics (Univ of London)												
Social Policy & Administration	L400	3FT deg		g	BBB	Ind	X	$	Ind	Ind	5	22/26
Social Policy and Government	LM41	3FT deg		g	BBB	Ind	X	$	Ind	Ind	9	20/28
Social Policy and Population Studies	LL41	3FT deg		g	BBB	Ind	X	$	Ind	Ind		
Social Policy and Sociology	LL34	3FT deg		g	BBB	Ind	X	$	Ind	Ind	43	
Social Policy with Social Psychology	L4L7	3FT deg		g	BBB	Ind		$	Ind	Ind	16	
LOUGHBOROUGH Univ												
Economics with Social Policy	L1L4	3FT deg		* g	20	3D	D*6/^ go	30	Ind	Ind	4	
Politics with Social Policy	M1L4	3FT deg		* g	20	2M+3D	D*6/^ go	28	Ind	Ind		16/22
Social Policy	L400	3FT deg		*	18	2M+3D	DG6/^ go	30	Ind		3	14/22
LUTON Univ												
Community Management	L521	3FT deg		g	12-16	MO/DO	M/D	32	BBCC	Ind	2	6/10
Health Science	L451	3FT deg		g	12-16	MO/DO	M/D	32	BBCC	Ind		
Health Studies	L450	3FT deg		g	12-16	MO/DO	M/D	32	BBCC	Ind	51	
Social Policy	L400	3FT deg		g	12-16	MO/DO	M/D	32	BBCC	Ind	8	4/14
Social Policy and Applied Statistics	LG44	3FT deg			12-16	MO/DO	M/D	32	BBCC	Ind		
Social Policy and British Studies	VL94	3FT deg			12-16	MO/DO	M/D	32	BBCC	Ind		
Social Policy and Built Environment	LN48	3FT deg			12-16	MO/DO	M/D	32	BBCC	Ind		
Social Policy and Business	LN41	3FT deg			12-16	MO/DO	M/D	32	BBCC	Ind		
Social Policy and Contemporary History	LV4C	3FT deg			12-16	MO/DO	M/D	32	BBCC	Ind		
Social Policy and Health Studies	LB4X	3FT deg			12-16	MO/DO	M/D	32	BBCC	Ind		
Social Policy and Journalism	PL64	3FT deg			12-16	MO/DO	M/D	32	BBCC	Ind		
Social Policy and Law	LM43	3FT deg			12-16	MO/DO	M/D	32	BBCC	Ind		
Social Policy and Leisure Studies	LN47	3FT deg			12-16	MO/DO	M/D	32	BBCC	Ind		

course details | 98 expected requirements | 96 entry stats

TITLE	CODE	COURSE	SUBJECTS	A/AS	ND/C	RGNVQ	IB	SQA(H)	SQA	RATIO A/AS
Social Policy and Linguistics	LQ41	3FT deg		12-16	MO/DO	M/D	32	BBCC	Ind	
Social Policy and Modern History	LV41	3FT deg		12-16	MO/DO	M/D	32	BBCC	Ind	
Social Policy and Politics	LM41	3FT deg		12-16	MO/DO	M/D	32	BBCC	Ind	
Social Policy and Public Policy and Management	LM4C	3FT deg		12-16	MO/DO	M/D	32	BBCC	Ind	
Social Policy with Applied Statistics	L4G4	3FT deg		12-16	MO/DO	M/D	32	BBCC	Ind	
Social Policy with British Studies	L4V9	3FT deg		12-16	MO/DO	M/D	32	BBCC	Ind	
Social Policy with Built Environment	L4N8	3FT deg		12-16	MO/DO	M/D	32	BBCC	Ind	
Social Policy with Business	L4N1	3FT deg		12-16	MO/DO	M/D	32	BBCC	Ind	
Social Policy with Chinese	L4T3	3FT deg		12-16	MO/DO	M/D	32	BBCC	Ind	
Social Policy with Contemporary History	L4VC	3FT deg		12-16	MO/DO	M/D	32	BBCC	Ind	
Social Policy with Environmental Science	L4F9	3FT deg		12-16	MO/DO	M/D	32	BBCC	Ind	
Social Policy with Health Studies	L4BX	3FT deg		12-16	MO/DO	M/D	32	BBCC	Ind	
Social Policy with Journalism	L4P6	3FT deg		12-16	MO/DO	M/D	32	BBCC	Ind	
Social Policy with Leisure Studies	L4N7	3FT deg		12-16	MO/DO	M/D	32	BBCC	Ind	
Social Policy with Linguistics	L4Q1	3FT deg		12-16	MO/DO	M/D	32	BBCC	Ind	
Social Policy with Modern History	L4V1	3FT deg		12-16	MO/DO	M/D	32	BBCC	Ind	
Social Policy with Politics	L4M1	3FT deg		12-16	MO/DO	M/D	32	BBCC	Ind	
Social Policy with Public Policy & Management	L4MC	3FT deg		12-16	MO/DO	M/D	32	BBCC	Ind	
Social Policy with Sociology	L4L3	3FT deg		12-16	MO/DO	M/D	32	BBCC	Ind	
Social Policy with Travel and Tourism	L4P7	3FT deg		12-16	MO/DO	M/D	32	BBCC	Ind	
Social Work (CCETSW)	L500	2FT Dip	g		Ind	Ind	Ind	Ind	Ind	29
Sociology and Social Policy	LM4H	3FT deg		12-16	MO/DO	M/D	32	BBCC	Ind	
Sociology with Social Policy	L3L4	3FT deg		12-16	MO/DO	M/D	32	BBCC	Ind	
Travel and Tourism and Social Policy	LP47	3FT deg		12-16	MO/DO	M/D	32	BBCC	Ind	
Women's Studies and Social Policy	LM49	3FT deg		12-16	MO/DO	M/D	32	BBCC	Ind	
Public Administration (Social Studies)	4L1M	2FT HND	g	4-8	N/MO	P/M	26	CCDD	Ind	1	2/6

Univ of MANCHESTER

| Social Policy | L402 | 3FT deg | g | BBC | M+6D | D^ | 32 | AABBB | Ind | 23 | |
| Social Policy | L420 | 3FT deg | * | BCC | M+4D | D^ | 28 | ABBBB | Ind | 6 | 18/26 |

MANCHESTER METROPOLITAN Univ

Applied Community Studies	L521	3FT deg	* g	DD	5M	M$	Ind	Ind	Ind	6/16
Applied Social Studies (by Independent Study)	L510	3FT deg	* g	CDD	4M		28	BCC	Ind	4/16
Health Studies	L450	3FT deg	* g	CC	M+D	M$	Ind	BBBBB	Ind	8/16
Leisure Studies/American Studies	LQ44	3FT deg	*	CC	M+D	D	28	CCCC	Ind	
Leisure Studies/Applied Social Studies	LL43	3FT deg	*	CC	M+D	D	28	CCCC	Ind	
Leisure Studies/Business Studies	LN41	3FT deg	*	CC	M+D	D	28	CCCC	Ind	
Leisure Studies/Cultural Studies	LL4H	3FT deg	*	CC	M+D	D	28	CCCC	Ind	
Leisure Studies/Dance	LW44	3FT deg	*	CC	M+D	D	28	CCCC	Ind	
Leisure Studies/Design & Technology	LW42	3FT deg	*	CC	M+D	D	28	CCCC	Ind	
Leisure Studies/Drama	LW4K	3FT deg	*	CC	M+D	D	28	CCCC	Ind	
Leisure Studies/English	LQ43	3FT deg	*	CC	M+D	D	28	CCCC	Ind	
Leisure Studies/Environmental Science	FL94	3FT deg	* g	DD	M+D	D	28	CCCC	Ind	
Leisure Studies/Geography	LL84	3FT deg	* g	DD	M+D	D	28	CCCC	Ind	
Leisure Studies/Health Studies	BL94	3FT deg	*	CC	M+D	D	28	CCCC	Ind	
Leisure Studies/History	LV41	3FT deg	*	CC	M+D	D	28	CCCC	Ind	
Life Science/Leisure Studies	CL14	3FT deg	* g	DD	M+D	D	28	CCCC	Ind	
Music/Leisure Studies	LW43	3FT deg	*	CC	M+D	D	28	CCCC	Ind	
Philosophy/Leisure Studies	LV47	3FT deg	*	CC	M+D	D	28	CCCC	Ind	
Religious Studies/Leisure Studies	LV48	3FT deg	*	CC	M+D	D	28	CCCC	Ind	
Social Work/Diploma in Social Work (21 years)	L500	3FT deg	*		Ind	MG	Ind	Ind	Ind	
Sport/Leisure Studies	BL64	3FT deg	S	BC	M+D	DS	28	CCCC	Ind	

TITLE	CODE	COURSE	SUBJECTS	A/AS	ND/C	AGNVQ	IB	SQA(H)	SQA	RATIO A/AS
Visual Arts/Leisure Studies	LW41	3FT deg	*	CC	M+D	D	28	CCCC	Ind	
Writing/Leisure Studies	LW4L	3FT deg	*	CC	M+D	D	28	CCCC	Ind	
Youth and Community Work	L523	3FT deg	*	X		P				
Youth and Community Work	L520	2FT Dip	*		Ind		Ind	Ind	Ind	
Youth and Community Work Studies (1 year top-up)	L522	1FT deg		X	HN	X				

MIDDLESEX Univ

TITLE	CODE	COURSE	SUBJECTS	A/AS	ND/C	AGNVQ	IB	SQA(H)	SQA	RATIO A/AS
Health Sciences	L450▼	3FT deg	*g	12-16	5M	M$ go	28	BBCC	Ind	
Social Policy	L402▼	4SW deg	*g	12-16	5M	M$ go	28	BBCC	Ind	
Social Science (DipSW top-up)	LL35▼	1FT deg	X	X	X	X	X	X	X	
Social Science (Social Work)	L3L5▼	3FT/4SW deg	*g	12-16	5M	M$ go	28	BBCC	Ind	
Social Work (For Mature Students) (2yrs)	L500▼	2FT deg	X	X	X	X	X	X	X	
Joint Honours Degree *Health Studies*	Y400	3FT deg	*g	12-16	5M	MG go	28	BBCC	Ind	
Joint Honours Degree *Social Policy*	Y400	3FT deg	*g	12-16	5M	M$ go	28	BBCC	Ind	
Joint Honours Degree *Social Research Methods*	Y400	3FT deg	*g	12-16	5M	M$ go	28	BBCC	Ind	

MORAY HOUSE Inst of Ed

TITLE	CODE	COURSE	SUBJECTS	A/AS	ND/C	AGNVQ	IB	SQA(H)	SQA	RATIO A/AS
Social Work	L500	3FT deg			Ind	Ind			Ind	

NAPIER Univ

TITLE	CODE	COURSE	SUBJECTS	A/AS	ND/C	AGNVQ	IB	SQA(H)	SQA	RATIO A/AS
Health Studies	L450	4FT/5SW deg		DD	Ind	Ind	Ind	BBC	Ind	

NENE COLLEGE

TITLE	CODE	COURSE	SUBJECTS	A/AS	ND/C	AGNVQ	IB	SQA(H)	SQA	RATIO A/AS
Business Administration with Health Studies	N1L5	3FT deg	g	10	M+1D	M	24	BCC	Ind	
Education with Health Studies	X9L5	3FT deg		D	5M	M	24	CCC	Ind	
Geography with Health Studies	F8L5	3FT deg	Gy	8	5M	M	24	CCC	Ind	
History with Health Studies	V1L5▼	3FT deg		CD	5M	M	24	CCC	Ind	
Human Biological Studies with Health Studies	B1L5▼	3FT deg	S	DE	5M	M	24	CCC	Ind	
Sociology with Health Studies	L3L5▼	3FT deg		10	5M	M	24	CCC	Ind	
Sport Studies with Health Studies	N7L5▼	3FT deg	Ss/Pe	12	M+2D	M	24	BBB	Ind	

Univ of NEWCASTLE

TITLE	CODE	COURSE	SUBJECTS	A/AS	ND/C	AGNVQ	IB	SQA(H)	SQA	RATIO A/AS
Economics and Social Policy	LL14	3FT deg	*g	BCC	Ind		30	ABBB	HN	5 20/28
Politics and Social Policy	LM41	3FT deg	*	BBC	Ind		30	AABB	HN	6 18/24
Social Policy	L400	3FT deg	*	BCC	Ind		30	BBBBB	HN	8 16/26
Combined Studies (BA) *Social Policy*	Y400	3FT deg	*	ABC-BBB	5D	Ind	35$	AAAB	Ind	

Univ of Wales COLLEGE, NEWPORT

TITLE	CODE	COURSE	SUBJECTS	A/AS	ND/C	AGNVQ	IB	SQA(H)	SQA	RATIO A/AS
Health and Social Care	L450	3FT deg		8	M+D	M$	Ind	Ind	Ind	
Social Welfare and Human Behaviour	LL47	3FT deg		8	M	M				
Social Welfare and Legal Studies	LM43	3FT deg		8	M	M				
Social Welfare and Organisations	LN41	3FT deg		8	MO	M				
Health and Social Care Management	054L	2FT HND		4	N	P$	Ind	Ind	Ind	
Technology in Caring Contexts	59LJ▼	2FT HND								

NORTH EAST WORCESTERSHIRE COLL

TITLE	CODE	COURSE
Caring Services (Social Care)	045L	2FT HND

NORTHERN COLL

TITLE	CODE	COURSE
Social Work (entry according to qualifications)	L500▼	1FT/2FT/3FTDip/deg

course details			98 expected requirements							96 entry stats	
TITLE	CODE	COURSE	SUBJECTS	A/AS	NO/C	RGNVQ	IB	SQA(H)	SQA	RATIO	A/AS
Univ of NORTH LONDON											
European Social Work	L500	3FT deg	*	CC	MP	M	$	CCCCC	Ind		
European Studies and Public Administration	LT42	3FT deg	*	CC	Ind	Ind	Ind	Ind	Ind		
Health Policy	L460	3FT deg	*	CC	MO	M	$	CCCCC	Ind		
Health Policy and Philosophy	LV47	3FT deg	*	CC	Ind	Ind	Ind	Ind	Ind		
Health Policy and Sports Management	LN47	3FT deg	* g	CC	MO+4D	Ind	Ind	Ind	Ind		
Health Policy and Women's Studies	LM4X	3FT deg	*	CC	Ind	Ind	Ind	Ind	Ind		
Health Studies	BL94▼	3FT deg	*	CC	MO	M	$	CCCCC	Ind	10	
Human Resource Studies and Public Administration	NL14	3FT deg	* g	CC	MO+4D	M	Ind	Ind	Ind	4	
Public Administration and Education Studies	LX49	3FT deg	*	CC	Ind	Ind	Ind	Ind	Ind		
Public Administration and Social Policy	L400▼	3FT deg	*	CC	MO	M	Dip	CCCCC	Ind		
Social Work/DipSW	L510	3FT deg	*	CC	MO	M	$	CCCCC	Ind	45	
Women's Studies and Social Policy	LM49	3FT deg	*	CC	Ind	Ind	Ind	Ind	Ind		
Combined Honours *Health Studies*	Y301	3FT deg	*	CC	MO	M	Dip	CCCCC	Ind		
Combined Honours *Social Research*	Y301	3FT deg	*	CC	MO	M	Dip	CCCCC	Ind		
Univ of NORTHUMBRIA											
Community Health Care Studies	L532	1FT deg		X	X	X	X	X	X		
Criminology And Social Research	LM43	4FT deg	So g	BC	2M+2D	M	24	BCCC	Ind		
Disability Studies and Professional Practice St	L540	3FT deg	g	10	4M	M	24	CCC	Ind		
Playwork	L530	2FT Dip	g	12	3M+1D	M	24	CCCC	Ind	7	
Social Work	L501	2FT Dip		X	X	X	X	X	X	15	
Social Work Studies	L500	3FT deg		X	X	X	X	X	X	18	
Univ of NOTTINGHAM											
Social Policy and Administration	L400	3FT deg	*	BBC	Ind	Ind	30	Ind	Ind	14	20/30
Social Policy with East European Studies	L4T1	3FT deg	*	BBC	Ind	Ind	30	Ind	Ind		
NOTTINGHAM TRENT Univ											
Policy and Politics	LM41	3FT deg	* g	18	Ind	Ind	Ind	Ind	Ind		14/20
OXFORD BROOKES Univ											
Applied Social Studies	L501	3FT deg			Ind		Ind	Ind	Ind		
Social Work (Diploma)	L500	2FT Dip	*		Ind		Ind	Ind	Ind	63	
Univ of PAISLEY											
European Policy Studies	L461	3FT/4FT deg	* g	CC	Ind	Ind	Ind	BBB$	Ind		
Univ of PLYMOUTH											
Applied Economics with Social Policy	L1L4	3FT deg	Ap g	CCD-CDD	MO	M$^	Ind	BCCC	Ind	7	
Business Economics with Social Policy	L1LK	3FT deg	Ap g	CDD-CCD	MO	M$^	Ind	BCCC	Ind		
Community Work with Social Policy	L5L4	4SW deg	* g	14	3M	M$	Ind	BBBC$	Ind	8	10/20
European Economics with Social Policy	L1LL	3FT deg	Ap g	CDD-CCD	MO	M$^	Ind	BCCC	Ind		
Geography with Social Policy	F8L4	3FT deg	Gy g	16-18	X	M$^	Ind	ABBB	Ind	15	
Law with Social Policy	M3L4	3FT deg	Ap g	BCC-BBC	DO	D12^	Ind	BBBB$	Ind		
Modern Languages with Social Policy	T9L4	3FT/4SW deg	L g	C	Ind	Ind	Ind	Ind	Ind		
Political Economy with Social Policy	LL1K	3FT deg	Ap g	CDD-CCD	MO $	M$^	Ind	BCCC	Ind		
Politics with Social Policy	M1L4	3FT deg	* g	14	3M	M$	Ind	BBBC$	Ind	3	
Psychology with Social Policy	C8L4	3FT/4SW deg	Ap g	BBC	MO 3D	M12^	Ind	BBBC$	Ind	11	
Social Policy	L400	3FT deg	* g	14	3M	M$	Ind	BBBC$	Ind	7	10/16
Social Policy and Administration	L404	3FT deg	* g	14	3M	M$	Ind	BBBC$	Ind	6	
Social Policy with Applied Economics	L4L1	3FT deg	* g	14	3M	M$	Ind	BBBC$	Ind	2	
Social Policy with Criminal Justice	L4MH	3FT deg	* g	16	3M	M$	Ind	BBBC$	Ind	5	6/18
Social Policy with French	L4R1	3FT deg	F g	14	Ind	M$^	Ind	BBBC$	Ind		

| | | | 98 expected requirements | | | | | | | 96 entry stats | |
| course details | | | | | | | | | | | |
TITLE	CODE	COURSE	SUBJECTS	A/AS	ND/C	AGNVQ	IB	SQA(H)	SQA	RATIO	A/AS
Social Policy with Geography	L4F8	3FT deg	Gy g	16	5M $	M$^	Ind	BBBC$	Ind		
Social Policy with German	L4R2	3FT deg	G g	14	Ind	M$^	Ind	BBBC$	Ind		
Social Policy with International Relations	L4M1	3FT deg	* g	14	3M	M$	Ind	BBBC$	Ind		
Social Policy with Italian	L4R3	3FT deg	* g	14	3M $	M$	Ind	BBBC$	Ind		
Social Policy with Languages	L4T9	3FT deg	L g	14	Ind	M$^	Ind	BBBC$	Ind	3	
Social Policy with Law	L4M3	3FT deg	* g	BCC	Ind	D12^	Ind	BBBC$	Ind		
Social Policy with Politics	L4MC	3FT deg	* g	14	3M	M$	Ind	BBBC$	Ind	5	
Social Policy with Psychology	L4C8	3FT deg	* g	BCC	2M+3D	D12^	Ind	BBBC$	Ind	8	
Social Policy with Social Research	L4LH	3FT deg	* g	14	3M	M$	Ind	BBBC$	Ind		
Social Policy with Sociology	L4L3	3FT deg	* g	14	3M	M$	Ind	BBBC$	Ind	3	8/16
Social Policy with Spanish	L4R4	3FT deg	Sp g	14	Ind	M$^	Ind	BBBC$	Ind		
Social Policy with Statistics	L4G4	3FT deg	* g	14	Ind	M$	Ind	BBBC$	Ind		
Sociology with Social Policy	L3L4	3FT deg	* g	14	3M	M$	Ind	BBBC$	Ind	4	8/22
Caring Services(Including Management)(Somerset)	345L	2FT HND	*	C-E	M	MG	Ind	Ind	Ind	3	

Univ of PORTSMOUTH

European Public Policy	L460	3FT deg	*	12	Ind	M$6/^	26	Ind	Ind	4	8/15
Health and Social Care Studies (Post experience)	L450	3FT deg	*	X	X	X	X	X	X		
Social Policy and Administration	L402	3FT deg	*	12	Ind	M$6/^	26	Ind	Ind	3	6/18

QUEEN MARGARET COLL

Combined Studies Applied Sociology & Social Policy	Y600	3FT/4FT deg	*	BC	M+D	M/D$^ go	Ind	BBBC	Ind		

QUEEN'S Univ Belfast

Management with Social Policy	N1L4	3FT deg	* g	BBB	2M+5D	D*^ go	32$	AABBB	Ind		
Social Policy/Byzantine Studies	QL84	3FT/4FT deg	* g	BCC	3M+4D	D*6/^ go	29$	ABBB	Ind		
Social Policy/Economic & Social History	VL34	3FT deg	* g	BCC	3M+4D	D*6/^ go	29$	ABBB	Ind		
Social Policy/English	QL34	3FT deg	E g	BCC	X	D*^ go	29$	ABBB	X		
Social Policy/Greek	QL74	3FT/4FT deg	* g	BCC	3M+4D	D*6/^ go	29$	ABBB	Ind		
Social Policy/History & Philosophy of Science	VL54	3FT deg	* g	BCC	3M+4D	D*6/^ go	29$	ABBB	Ind		
Social Policy/Human Geography	LL4V	3FT deg	* g	BCC	3M+4D	D*6/^ go	29$	ABBB	Ind		
Social Policy/Latin	QL64	3FT/4FT deg	* g	BCC	3M+4D	D*6/^ go	29$	ABBB	Ind		
Social Policy/Modern History	VL14	3FT deg	* g	BCC	3M+4D	D*6/^ go	29$	ABBB	Ind		
Social Policy/Philosophy	VL74	3FT deg	* g	BCC	3M+4D	D*6/^ go	29$	ABBB	Ind		
Social Policy/Politics	ML14	3FT deg	* g	BCC	3M+4D	D*6/^ go	29$	ABBB	Ind		
Social Policy/Psychology	CL84	3FT deg	* g	BCC	3M+4D	D*6/^ go	29$	ABBB	Ind		
Social Policy/Scholastic Philosophy	LV47	3FT deg	* g	BCC	3M+4D	D*6/^ go	29$	ABBB	Ind		
Social Policy/Social Anthropology	LL64	3FT deg	* g	BCC	3M+4D	D*6/^ go	29$	ABBB	Ind		
Sociology/Social Policy	LL43	3FT deg	* g	BCC	3M+4D	D*6/^ go	29$	ABBB	Ind		
Women's Studies/Social Policy	LM49	3FT deg	* g	BCC	3M+4D	D*6/^ go	29$	ABBB	Ind		

Univ of READING

Community and Youth St (Post-Experience)	L520	3FT deg		X	X	Ind	X	X	X		
Community and Youth Studies (Post-experience)	L521	2FT Dip		X	X	Ind	X	X	X		

ROEHAMPTON INST

Social Policy & Admin & Applied Consumer Studs	LN49▼	3FT deg	g	12	4M	P$ go	26	BCC	N	2	
Social Policy & Admin & Natural Resource Studs	DL24▼	3FT deg	g	DD	3M	P$ go	24	CCC	N$		
Social Policy & Admin and Art for Community	WL14▼	3FT deg	g	DD	3M	P$ go	24	CCC	N	3	
Social Policy & Admin and Business Computing	GL74▼	3FT deg	g	12	3D	M$ go	26	BCC	N$		
Social Policy & Admin and Business Studies	NL14▼	3FT deg	g	DD	3D	M$ go	26	BCC	N$	4	
Social Policy & Admin and Drama & Theatre Studs	LW4L▼	3FT deg	E/T	16	2M+2D$	M$^	30	BBC	N$	3	
Social Policy & Admin and Eng Lang & Linguistics	QLH4▼	3FT deg	E/L g	CC	2M+2D$	M$^	30	BBC	Ind		
Social Policy & Admin and Film & Television St	LP44▼	3FT deg	*	16	2M+2D$	M$^	30	BBC	N$	5	

course details | 98 expected requirements | 96 entry stats

TITLE	CODE	COURSE	SUBJECTS	A/AS	ND/C	AGNVQ	IB	SQA(H)	SQA	RATIO	A/AS
Social Policy & Admin and Human & Social Biology	LC4C▼	3FT deg	B g	12	3M	P$	24	CCC	N$		
Social Policy & Administration	L400▼	3FT deg	g	DD	4M	P$	26	BCC	N	5	4/14
Social Policy & Administration & English Lit	QL34▼	3FT deg	E g	CC	2M+2D$	M^	28	BBC	Ind	6	
Social Policy & Administration & Enviro Studies	FL94▼	3FT deg	B/Gy g	DD	4M $	P$ go	26	BCC	N$		
Social Policy & Administration & Health Studies	BL9L▼	3FT deg	B g	12	4M	P$ go	26	BCC	N$	5	
Social Policy & Administration and Biology	CL14▼	3FT deg	B	12	4M $	P$ go	26	BCC	N$		
Social Policy & Administration and Dance Studies	WL44▼	3FT deg	g	CC	2M+2D	M$^	30	BBC	Ind		
Social Policy & Administration and Education	XL94▼	3FT deg	g	DD	3M	P$	24	CCC	N	3	
Social Policy & Administration and French	RL14▼	4FT deg	F g	12	4M $	P^	26	BCC	N$		
Social Policy & Administration and Geography	LL84▼	3FT deg	Gy g	DD	4M $	P$ go	26	BCC	N$	2	
Social Policy & Administration and History	VL14▼	3FT deg	H g	DD	4M $	P^	26	BCC	N$	2	
Social Policy & Administration and Music	WL34▼	3FT deg	Mu g	DD	4M $	P^	26	BCC	N$		
Social Policy & Administration and Psychology	LL74▼	3FT deg	g	CC	3D	M$ go	30	BBC	Ind	16	
Sociology and Social Policy & Administration	LL43▼	3FT deg	g	DD	3M	P$ go	24	CCC	N	4	4/8
Spanish and Social Policy & Administration	LR44▼	4FT deg	Sp	12	2M+2D$	P$ go	28	BBC	N$		
Sport Studies and Social Policy & Administration	LB46▼	3FT deg	S g	12	3D	MS go	30	BBC	N$		
Theology & Religious St and Soc Policy & Admin	LV48▼	3FT deg	g	DD	3M	P$	24	CCC	N		
Women's Studies and Social Policy & Admin	LM49▼	3FT deg	g	DD	3M	P$ go	24	CCC	N	5	

ROYAL HOLLOWAY, Univ of London

TITLE	CODE	COURSE	SUBJECTS	A/AS	ND/C	AGNVQ	IB	SQA(H)	SQA	RATIO	A/AS
Economics and Social Policy	LL14	3FT deg	*	BCC-BBB	Ind		Ind	Ind		9	
Economics with Social Policy	L1L4	3FT deg	*	BBC-BBB	Ind		32	Ind			
French with Social Policy	R1L4	4FT deg	F	BBC-ABC			28$	Ind			
German with Social Policy	R2L4	4FT deg	G	BCC			28$	BBBBC$			
Italian with Social Policy	R3L4	4FT deg	L/Ln	BBC			30	BBCCC$			
Management Studies with Social Policy	N1L4	3FT deg	*	BBC-BBB	2M+3D	D^	30	Ind		6	
Mathematics with Social Policy	G1L4	3FT deg	M	BCC-BBC	Ind	D^	Ind	Ind			
Music with Social Policy	W3L4	3FT deg	Mu	BCC-BBC			Ind	ABBCC$			
Social Policy	L420	3FT deg	*	BCC-BBC	Ind	D^	Ind	Ind		4	18/24
Social Policy and Politics	LM41	3FT deg	*	BCC-BBC	Ind	D^	Ind	Ind		4	
Social Policy with Economics	L4L1	3FT deg	*	BCC-BBC	Ind	D^	Ind	Ind			
Social Policy with Environmental Studies	L4F9	3FT deg	*	BCC-BBC	Ind	D^	Ind	Ind		6	
Social Policy with Japanese Studies	L4T4	3FT deg	L g	BCC-BBC	Ind	D^	Ind	Ind			
Social Policy with Management Studies	L4N1	3FT deg	*	BCC-BCC	Ind	D^	Ind	Ind			
Social Policy with Mathematics	L4G1	3FT deg	M	BCC-BBC	Ind	D^	Ind	Ind			
Social Policy with Political Studies	L4MC	3FT deg	*	BCC-BBC	Ind	D^	Ind	Ind		5	
Social Policy with Sociology	L4L3	3FT deg	*	BCC-BBC	Ind	D^	Ind	Ind			
Social Policy with Spanish	L4R4	3FT deg	L	BCC-BBC	Ind	D^	Ind	Ind			
Sociology and Social Policy	LL34	3FT deg	*	BBC-BCC	Ind	D^	Ind	Ind		7	14/24
Sociology with Social Policy	L3L4	3FT deg	*	BCC-BBC	Ind	D^	Ind	Ind			
Foundation Programme _Social Policy_	Y408	4FT deg									

Univ of SALFORD

TITLE	CODE	COURSE	SUBJECTS	A/AS	ND/C	AGNVQ	IB	SQA(H)	SQA	RATIO	A/AS
Health Science and Social Policy	BL94	3FT deg	g	12	6M	M					
Social Policy	L400	3FT deg									
Social Work	L501	3FT Dip	* g	12	Ind	Ind	Ind	CCCC	Ind	99	
Social Work Studies	L500	4FT deg	* g	12	Ind	Ind	Ind	CCCC	Ind	32	

Univ of SHEFFIELD

TITLE	CODE	COURSE	SUBJECTS	A/AS	ND/C	AGNVQ	IB	SQA(H)	SQA	RATIO	A/AS
Economics and Social Policy	LL14	3FT deg	* g	BBC	4D	D^	30	ABBB	Ind	18	
Social Policy and Sociology	LL43	3FT deg	* g	BBC	4D	D^	30	ABBB	Ind	7	20/30

Social Policy, Social Work and Administration   65

TITLE	CODE	COURSE	SUBJECTS	A/AS	ND/C	AGNVQ	IB	SQA(H)	SQA	RATIO A/AS
SHEFFIELD HALLAM Univ										
Social Policy	L402	3FT deg	*	CCC	7D	M	Ind	Ind	Ind	
Social Work Studies	L500	3FT deg	*	CC	N	M	Ind	Ind	Ind	
Combined Studies *Social Policy*	Y400	3FT deg	*	14	2M	M	Ind	Ind	Ind	
SHEFFIELD COLL										
Caring Services (Social Care)	045L	2FT HND	*	X	4M+2D	Ind	Ind	Ind	Ind	
Univ College of St MARTIN, LANCASTER AND CUMBRIA										
Applied Community Studies/Art and Design	LW51	3FT deg	A	CD-DDE	3M+2D$	MA	28$	BCCC$	Ind	2
Applied Community Studies/Business Mgt Studies	LN51	3FT deg	*	CD-DDE	3M+2D	M	28	BCCC		
Applied Community Studies/Drama	LW54	3FT deg	*	CD-DDE	3M+2D	M*	28$	BCCC	Ind	8
Applied Community Studies/Education Studies	LX59	3FT deg	*	CD-DDE	3M+2D	M*	28$	BCCC	Ind	2
Applied Community Studies/Geography	LL58	3FT deg	Gy	CD-DDE	3M+2D	M^	28$	BCCC$	Ind	
Applied Community Studies/Health Administration	LL54	3FT deg	*	CD-DDE	3M+2D	M*	28$	BCCC	Ind	1
Applied Community Studies/Health Studies	LB59	3FT deg	*	CD-DDE	3M+2D	M*	28$	BCCC	Ind	2
Applied Community Studies/History	LV51	3FT deg	H	CD-DDE	3M+2D$	M^	28$	BCCC		
Applied Community Studies/Physical Ed & Spts Std	LX5X	3FT deg	*	CD-DDE	3M+2D	M*	28	BCCC		
Applied Community Studies/Religious Studies	LV58	3FT deg	*	CD-DDE	3M+2D	M*	28	BCCC	Ind	1
Applied Community Studies/Science, Tech & Soc	LY51	3FT deg	g	CD-DDE	3M+2D	M*	28	BCCC		
Applied Community Studies/Social Ethics	LV57	3FT deg	*	CD-DDE	3M+2D	M*	28	BCCC	Ind	
Art and Design/Applied Community Studies	WL1M	3FT deg	A	CC-CDE	3M+2D$	MA	28$	BBCC$	Ind	1
Art and Design/Health Administration	WL1K	3FT deg	A	CC-CDE	3M+2D$	MA	28$	BBCC$	Ind	
Business Management Studies/Applied Community St	NL1M	3FT deg	*	CD-CEE	3M+2D	M*	28	BCCC		
Business Management Studies/Health Admin	NL14	3FT deg	*	CD-CEE	3M+2D	M	28	BCCC		
Community and Youth Studies	L520	3FT deg	*	EE	3M+2D$	P*	28$	BCCC	Ind	4	4/20
English/Health Administration	QL34	3FT deg	E	BC-BDE	X	P^	28$	BBBC$	Ind	
Geography/Applied Community Studies	LL8M	3FT deg	Gy	CD-DDE	X	P^	28$	BCCC$	Ind	
Health Studies/Applied Community Studies	BL95	3FT deg	*	CD-DDE	3M+2D	M*	28	BCCC	Ind	8
Health Studies/Health Administration	BL94	3FT deg	*	CD-DDE	3M+2D	M*	28	BCCC	Ind	5
History/Applied Community Studies	VL15	3FT deg	H	CD-DDE	X	P^	28$	BCCC$		
History/Health Administration	VL14	3FT deg	H	CD-DDE	X	P^	28$	BCCC$	Ind	
Mathematics/Health Administration	GL14	3FT deg	M	DD-DEE	X	P^	28$	BCCC$	Ind	
Religious Studies/Applied Community Studies	VL8M	3FT deg	*	CD-DDE	3M+2D	M*	28$	BCCC	Ind	
Science, Technology & Society/Applied Commun St	YL15	3FT deg	g	CD-DDE	3M+2D	M*	28	BCCC		
Science,Technology & Society/Health Admin	LY41	3FT deg	g	CD-DDE	3M+2D	M*	28$	BCCC	Ind	
Social Ethics/Applied Community Studies	VL7M	3FT deg	*	CD-DDE	3M+2D	M*	28	BCCC	Ind	2
Social Ethics/Health Administration	VL74	3FT deg	*	CD-DDE	3M+2D	M*	28	BCCC	Ind	
Univ of SOUTHAMPTON										
Public and Social Administration	LMK1	3FT deg	* g	20	Ind	D$^ go	28	BBBBC	Ind	
Social Policy and Administration	L4UU	3H deg	* g	18-20	Ind	D$^ go	28	BBBBC	Ind	36
Sociology & Social Policy(with Social Work Stud)	LL3K	4FT deg	* g	18-20	Ind	D$^ go	28	BBBBC	Ind	12	8/28
Sociology and Social Policy	LL34	3FT deg	* g	18-20	Ind	D$^ go	28	BBBBC	Ind	8	16/24
SOUTH BANK Univ										
Environmental Policy	F9L4	3 deg	* g	14-18	2M+4D	M go	Ind	Ind	Ind	
Health Informatics	GL5L	3FT deg	M g	CC	4M+2D	M go	Ind	Ind	Ind	
Health Studies & Business Information Technology	GL74	3FT deg	M+S g	12-16	4M+2D	M go	Ind	Ind	Ind	
Health Studies and Computing	GL54	3FT deg	M+S g	12-16	4M+2D	M go	Ind	Ind	Ind	
Health Studies and Economics	LL14	3FT deg	Ec/Bu g	12-16	4M+2D	M go	Ind	Ind	Ind	
Health Studies and English Studies	LQ43	3FT deg	E+S g	14-18	X	M^ go	Ind	Ind	Ind	
Health Studies and European Studies	LT4F	3FT deg	S g	14-18	2M+4D	M go	Ind	Ind	Ind	

course details — *98 expected requirements* — *96 entry stats*

Letts STUDY GUIDES
THE INDEPENDENT

course details			98 expected requirements							96 entry stats
TITLE	CODE	COURSE	SUBJECTS	A/AS	NO/C	AGNVQ	IB	SQA(H)	SQA	RATIO A/AS
Health Studies and Food Policy	DL44	3FT deg	S g	12-16	4M+2D	M go	Ind	Ind	Ind	
Health Studies and French	LR41	3FT deg	F+S g	12-16	4M+2D	M go	Ind	Ind	Ind	
Health Studies and German	RL24	3FT deg	S+G g	14-18	2M+4D	M go	Ind	Ind	Ind	
Health Studies and German - ab initio	LR42	3FT deg	S g	12-16	4M+2D	M go	Ind	Ind	Ind	
Housing and Health Studies	LK4K	3FT deg	S g	14-18	2M+4D	M go	Ind	Ind	Ind	
Human Biology and Health Studies	BL14	3FT deg	S g	12-16	4M+2D	M go	Ind	Ind	Ind	
Human Resource Management and Health Studies	NL64	3FT deg	S g	14-18	2M+4D	M go	Ind	Ind	Ind	
Management and Health Studies	LN41	3FT deg	S g	12-16	4M+2D	M go	Ind	Ind	Ind	
Marketing and Health Studies	LN45	3FT deg	S g	14-18	2M+4D	M go	Ind	Ind	Ind	
Nursing St and Soc Work St (Learn Difficulties)	BL75	3FT deg	g	CC	6M	M go	Ind	Ind	Ind	
Nutrition and Health Studies	BL44	3FT deg	S g	12-16	4M+2D	M go	Ind	Ind	Ind	
Politics and Health Studies	LM41	3FT deg	S g	12-16	4M+2D	M go	Ind	Ind	Ind	
Psychology and Health Studies	CL84	3FT deg	S g	14-18	2M+4D	M go	Ind	Ind	Ind	
Social Policy and Accounting	LN4K	3FT deg	Ac/Ec g	12-16	4M+2D	M go	Ind	Ind	Ind	
Social Policy and English Studies	QL34	3FT deg	E g	14-18	X	M^ go	Ind	Ind	Ind	
Social Policy and Environmental Policy	FL9K	3FT deg	* g	14-18	2M+4D	M go	Ind	Ind	Ind	
Social Policy and European Studies	LT42	3FT deg	* g	14-18	2M+4D	M go	Ind	Ind	Ind	
Social Policy and French	LR4C	3FT deg	F g	12-16	4M+2D	M go	Ind	Ind	Ind	
Social Policy and German	LR4G	3FT deg	G g	14-18	2M+4D	M go	Ind	Ind	Ind	
Social Policy and German - ab initio	LR4F	3FT deg	g	12-16	4M+2D	M go	Ind	Ind	Ind	
Social Policy and Health Studies	LL41	3FT deg	S g	12-16	4M+2D	M go	Ind	Ind	Ind	
Social Policy and Housing	LK44	3FT deg	* g	14-18	2M+4D	M go	Ind	Ind	Ind	
Social Policy and Human Geography	LL84	3FT deg	Gy g	12-16	4M+2D	M go	Ind	Ind	Ind	
Social Policy and Human Resource Management	LN46	3FT deg	* g	14-18	2M+4D	M go	Ind	Ind	Ind	
Social Policy and Law	LM4H	3FT deg	* g	14-18	2M+4D	D go	Ind	Ind	Ind	
Social Policy and Management	LN4C	3FT deg	* g	12-16	4M+2D	M go	Ind	Ind	Ind	
Social Policy and Marketing	LN4M	3FT deg	* g	14-18	4M+2D	M go	Ind	Ind	Ind	
Social Policy and Media Studies	LP4K	3FT deg	E g	14-18	2M+4D	D go	Ind	Ind	Ind	
Social Policy and Politics	LM4C	3FT deg	g	12-16	4M+2D	M go	Ind	Ind	Ind	
Social Policy and Psychology	CL8K	3FT deg	S g	14-18	4M+2D	M go	Ind	Ind	Ind	
Sociology and Health Studies	LL43	3FT deg	S g	12-16	4M+2D	M go	Ind	Ind	Ind	
Spanish - ab initio and Health Studies	LR44	3FT deg	S g	12-16	4M+2D	M go	Ind	Ind	Ind	
Spanish - ab initio and Social Policy	LR4K	3FT deg	* g	12-16	4M+2D	M go	Ind	Ind	Ind	
Spanish and Health Studies	RL44	3FT deg	Sp+S g	14-18	2M+4D	M^ go	Ind	Ind	Ind	
Spanish and Social Policy	LR4L	3FT deg	Sp g	14-18	2M+4D	M^ go	Ind	Ind	Ind	
Sports Science and Health Studies	BL64	3FT deg	S g	12-16	4M+2D	M go	Ind	Ind	Ind	
Technology and Health Studies	JL94	3FT deg	S g	12-16	4M+2D	M go	Ind	Ind	Ind	
Technology and Social Policy	JL9K	3FT deg	* g	12-16	4M+2D	M go	Ind	Ind	Ind	
Tourism and Health Studies	LP47	3FT deg	S+L g	12-16	4M+2D	M go	Ind	Ind	Ind	
Tourism and Social Policy	LP4R	3FT deg	L g	12-16	4M+2D	M go	Ind	Ind	Ind	
Urban Studies and Health Studies	LK4L	3FT deg	S g	14-18	2M+4D	M go	Ind	Ind	Ind	
Urban Studies and Social Policy	KL4L	3FT deg	* g	14-18	2M+4D	M go	Ind	Ind	Ind	
World Theatre and Health Studies	LW44	3FT deg	S g	14-18	2M+4D	M go	Ind	Ind	Ind	
World Theatre and Social Policy	LW4K	3FT deg	* g	14-18	2M+4D	M go	Ind	Ind	Ind	

ST HELENS COLL

Caring Services (Social Care)	045L	2FT HND	*	2	N	P*	Dip	Ind	Ind	
Public and Uniformed Services	064L	2FT HND	*	2	N	P*	Dip	Ind	N	

THE UNIVERSITY COLLEGE OF ST MARK AND ST JOHN

Art & Design/Community Studies	W1L5	3FT deg		4	MO	M	Dip	CCCC	Ind	
Community Studies & Youth Studies	L520	3FT deg		10	MO	M	Dip	Ind	Ind	
Community Studies/Art & Design	L5W1	3FT deg		4	MO	M	Dip	CCCC	Ind	

			98 expected requirements							96 entry stats

TITLE	CODE	COURSE	SUBJECTS	A/AS	ND/C	AGNVQ	IB	SQA(H)	SQA	RATIO A/AS
Community Studies/Development Studies	L5M9	3FT deg		10	MO	M	Dip	Ind	Ind	
Community Studies/Physical Recreation Progs	L5N7	3FT deg		10	MO	M	Dip	Ind	Ind	
Community Studies/Public Relations	L5P3	3FT deg		10	MO	M	Dip	CCCC	Ind	
Community Studies/Sports Science	L5B6	3FT deg		10	MO	M	Dip	Ind	Ind	
Development Studies/Community Studies	M9L5	3FT deg		8-10	MO	M	Ind	Ind	Ind	
Physical Recreation Programmes/Community St	N7LM	3FT deg		10	MO	M	Ind	Ind	Ind	
Public Relations/Community Studies	P3L5	3FT deg		16	MO	M	Ind	Ind	Ind	
Sports Science/Community Studies	B6L5	3FT deg		8	MO	M	Ind	Ind	Ind	

STAFFORDSHIRE Univ

TITLE	CODE	COURSE	SUBJECTS	A/AS	ND/C	AGNVQ	IB	SQA(H)	SQA	RATIO A/AS
Applied Social Studies	L510	3FT deg	*		Ind	Ind	Ind	Ind	Ind	
Applied Social Studies (20+/Post Exp)/(CCETSW)	L511	2FT Dip	*		Ind		Ind	Ind	Ind	8
Health Studies	L450	3FT deg	g	12	4M	M	24	BBB		
Occupational Health and Environment Technology	LJ59	3FT deg								

Univ of STIRLING

TITLE	CODE	COURSE	SUBJECTS	A/AS	ND/C	AGNVQ	IB	SQA(H)	SQA	RATIO A/AS
Business Studies/Social Policy	NL14	4FT deg	g	BBC	Ind	Ind	33	BBBB	HN	
Economics/Social Policy	L422	4FT deg	g	BCC	Ind	Ind	31	BBBC	HN	
Film & Media Studies/Social Policy	PL44	4FT deg	g	BBC	Ind	Ind	35	ABBB	HN	
History/Social Policy	LV4C	4FT deg	g	BCC	Ind	Ind	31	BBBC	HN	
Human Resources Management/Social Policy	NL1K	4FT deg	g	BBC	Ind	Ind	33	BBBB	HN	
Marketing/Social Policy	LN45	4FT deg	g	BBC	Ind	Ind	33	BBBB	HN	
Mathematics/Social Policy	GL14	4FT deg	M g	CCC	Ind	Ind	28	BBCC	HN	
Philosophy/Social Policy	LV47	4FT deg	g	BCC	HN	Ind	31	BBBC	HN	
Politics/Social Policy	ML14	4FT deg	g	BCC	Ind	Ind	31	BBBC	HN	
Psychology/Social Policy	CL84	4FT deg	g	BCC	Ind	Ind	31	BBBC	HN	
Religious Studies/Social Policy	LV48	4FT deg	g	CCC	Ind	Ind	28	BBCC	HN	
Social Policy	L400	4FT deg	g	BCC	Ind	Ind	31	BBBC	HN	
Social Policy/Management Science	LN41	4FT deg	g	BCC	Ind	Ind	31	BBBC	HN	
Social Work(inc Dip in Soc Wk CCETSW (Hons Only)	L500	4FT deg	g	BCC	Ind	Ind	31	BBBC	HN	
Sociology/Social Policy	L430	4FT deg	g	BCC	Ind	Ind	31	BBBC	HN	

STOCKPORT COLL of F and HE

TITLE	CODE	COURSE	SUBJECTS	A/AS	ND/C	AGNVQ	IB	SQA(H)	SQA	RATIO A/AS
Professional Studies (Social Care)	L510	4FT deg	g	4	N	PG	Ind	Ind	Ind	
Caring Services	035L	2FT HND	* g	4	N	PG	Ind	Ind	Ind	

Univ of STRATHCLYDE

TITLE	CODE	COURSE	SUBJECTS	A/AS	ND/C	AGNVQ	IB	SQA(H)	SQA	RATIO A/AS
Social Work	L500	3FT deg	g	DD	Ind		Ind	CCC$	HN	

UNIVERSITY COLLEGE SUFFOLK

TITLE	CODE	COURSE	SUBJECTS	A/AS	ND/C	AGNVQ	IB	SQA(H)	SQA	RATIO A/AS
Applied Biological Science with Social Policy	C1L4	3FT deg	S	EE	N $	PS	Ind	Ind	Ind	
Art & Design with Social Policy	W2L4	3FT deg	Pf	EE	N $	P$	Ind	Ind	Ind	
Art & Design with Social Policy	E2L4	3FT deg	Pf	EE	N $	P$	Ind	Ind	Ind	
Behavioural Studies with Social Policy	L7L4	3FT deg	S	DD	Ind		Ind	Ind	Ind	
Business Studies with Social Policy	N1L4	3FT deg	*	EE	N $	P$	Ind	Ind	Ind	
Early Childhood Studies with Social Policy	X9L4	3FT deg	*	DD	N $	P$	Ind	Ind	Ind	
Environmental Studies with Social Policy	F9L4	3FT deg	S	EE	N $	P$	Ind	Ind	Ind	
Information Technology with Social Policy	G5L4	3FT deg	*	EE	N $	P$	Ind	Ind	Ind	
Media Studies with Social Policy	P4L4	3FT deg	*	CE	N $	P$	Ind	Ind	Ind	
Product Design & Manufacture with Social Policy	H7L4	3FT deg	*	EE	N $	P$	Ind	Ind	Ind	
Social Work	L500	2FT Dip	* g	X	Ind		Ind	CCC	Ind	

TITLE	CODE	COURSE	SUBJECTS	A/AS	NO/C	AGNVQ	IB	SQA(H)	SQA	RATIO A/AS	

Univ of SUNDERLAND

TITLE	CODE	COURSE	SUBJECTS	A/AS	NO/C	AGNVQ	IB	SQA(H)	SQA	RATIO	A/AS
Community & Youth Wk St (21 Yrs + prev exp pref)	L521	2FT Dip	* g	X	Ind		Ind	Ind	Ind	9	
Community & Youth Work St(21 Yrs + prev exp req)	L520	3FT deg	* g	X	Ind		Ind	Ind	Ind	7	
Health Studies	BL94▼	3FT deg	* g	12	MO$	M$	24$	BCCC$	N$	2	6/14
Health Studies (Foundation)	BL9K▼	4EXT deg	*							2	

Univ of SUSSEX

TITLE	CODE	COURSE	SUBJECTS	A/AS	NO/C	AGNVQ	IB	SQA(H)	SQA	RATIO	A/AS
Social Policy	L4Y2	3FT deg	*	BBC	MO	M*6	$	Ind	Ind		

Univ of Wales SWANSEA

TITLE	CODE	COURSE	SUBJECTS	A/AS	NO/C	AGNVQ	IB	SQA(H)	SQA	RATIO	A/AS
Anthropology and Social Policy	LL46	3FT deg	*	BBC-BCC	1M+5D	Ind	28	BBBBB	Ind	8	
Development Studies and Social Policy	LM49	3FT deg	*	BBC-BCC	1M+5D	Ind	28	BBBBB	Ind	3	
Early Childhood Studies	L5X9	3FT deg	*	BCC	1M+4D$	Ind	28	BBBBC	Ind		
Economics and Social Policy	LL41	3FT deg	* g	BBC-BCC	1M+5D	Ind	28	BBBBB	Ind		
Geography and Social Policy	LL48	3FT deg	Gy	BBC-BCC	1M+5D$	Ind	30$	BBBBB$	Ind	3	
Politics and Social Policy	LM41	3FT deg	*	BBC-BCC	1M+5D	Ind	28	BBBBB	Ind	4	
Social History and Social Policy	LV43	3FT deg	*	BBC-BCC	1M+5D	Ind	28	BBBBB	Ind	5	
Social Policy	L400	3FT deg	*	BCC	1M+5D	Ind	28	BBBBB	Ind		
Social Policy and Sociology	LL43	3FT deg	*	BBC-BCC	1M+5D	Ind	28	BBBBB	Ind	5	12/18
Joint Hons with defer choice of specialisation (inc Social Policy)	Y220	3FT deg	*	20-22	1M+5D	Ind	28	BBBBB	Ind		

Univ of TEESSIDE

TITLE	CODE	COURSE	SUBJECTS	A/AS	NO/C	AGNVQ	IB	SQA(H)	SQA	RATIO	A/AS
Social Policy	L402	3FT deg	*	12-14	Ind		Ind	Ind	Ind	2	6/16
Social Work/DipHE Social Work	L500	3FT deg									
Modular Degree Scheme Social Policy	Y401	3FT deg									

THAMES VALLEY Univ

TITLE	CODE	COURSE	SUBJECTS	A/AS	NO/C	AGNVQ	IB	SQA(H)	SQA	RATIO	A/AS
Business Administration with Health Studies	N1LK	3FT deg		8-12	MO	M	26	CCC			
Food and Drink Consumer Studies with Health St	D4L4	3FT deg		8-12	MO	M	26	CCC			
Health Studies	L451	2FT Dip		2-4	N	P	24	CC			
Health Studies	L450	3FT deg		8-12	MO	M	26	CCC			
Health Studies with Business	L4N1	3FT deg		8-12	MO	M	26	CCC			
Health Studies with Community Law	L4M3	3FT deg		8-12	MO	M	26	CCC			
Health Studies with English Language Studies	L4Q1	3FT deg		8-12	MO	M	26	CCC			
Health Studies with Environmental Policy and Mgt	L4F9	3FT deg		8-12	MO	M	26	CCC			
Health Studies with Psychology	L4C8	3FT deg		8-12	MO	M	26	CCC			
Health Studies with Sociology	L4L3	3FT deg		8-12	MO	M	26	CCC			
Health Studies with Women's Studies	L4M9	3FT deg		8-12	MO	M	26	CCC			
Leisure Management with Health Studies	N7LK	3FT deg		8-12	MO	M	26	CCC			
Psychology with Health Studies	C8L4	3FT deg		8-12	MO	M$	26	CCC			
Sociology with Health Studies	L3L4	3FT deg		8-12	MO	M	26	CCC			

Univ of ULSTER

TITLE	CODE	COURSE	SUBJECTS	A/AS	NO/C	AGNVQ	IB	SQA(H)	SQA	RATIO	A/AS
Combined Social Policy	L401▼	2FT deg	* g	CCC	MO+3D	D*6/^ gi	28	BBBC			
Community Youth Work incl prof recog (2 Yrs)	L521▼	2FT Dip	*	CCD	MO+2D	D* gi	27	BBCC	Ind	26	
Social Administration and Policy	L400▼	3FT deg	* g	CCC	MO+3D	D*6/^ gi	28	BBBC	Ind	22	
Social Work (inc Dip in Soc Wk CCETSW DIS)	L500▼	3FT/4SW deg	* g	BBC	MO+4D	D*6/^ gi	32	ABBB	Ind	30	10/26

Univ of WARWICK

TITLE	CODE	COURSE	SUBJECTS	A/AS	NO/C	AGNVQ	IB	SQA(H)	SQA	RATIO	A/AS
Sociology with Social Policy	LL34	3FT deg	* g	BCC	Ind	Ind	30	ABBCC		10	6/26

WARWICKSHIRE COLLEGE, ROYAL LEAMINGTON SPA

TITLE	CODE	COURSE	SUBJECTS	A/AS	NO/C	AGNVQ	IB	SQA(H)	SQA	RATIO	A/AS
Caring Services	045L	2FT HND									

course details			98 expected requirements							96 entry stats	
TITLE	CODE	COURSE	SUBJECTS	A/AS	ND/C	AGNVQ	IB	SQA(H)	SQA	RATIO	A/AS
WEST HERTS COLL											
Social Care	035L	2FT HND	*	4						2	2/8
WESTHILL COLL											
Community & Youth Studies	L525	2FT Dip	* g	CC	4M+2D	M^	Ind	Ind	Ind	14	
Community and Youth Studies	L500	3FT deg	* g	CC	4M+2D	M^	Ind	Ind	Ind	3	
Humanities - Race and Ethnic Studies	ML93	3FT deg	* g	CC	4M+2D	M^	Ind	Ind	Ind		
Humanities - Sport, PE and Community Studies	B6L4	3FT deg	* g	CC	4M+2D	M^	Ind	Ind	Ind		
WIGAN and LEIGH COLL											
Caring Services (Social Care)	045L▼	2FT HND		6	N	Ind	Dip		N		
Univ of WOLVERHAMPTON											
Combined Degrees Social Policy	Y401	3FT/4SW deg		14	4M	M	24	BBBB	Ind		
WORCESTER COLL of HE											
Early Childhood Studies	L500	1FT deg									
Health Studies	L450	3FT deg	g	DD	Ind	M	Ind	Ind	Ind	4	
Early Childhood Studies	005L	2FT HND		E	N	Ind	Ind	Ind	Ind	3	4/14
WORCESTER COLLEGE of Technology											
Caring Services (Social Care)	045L	2FT HND		2	N						
Univ of YORK											
Social Policy	L430	3FT deg	*	BCC	Ind	D$6/^	28	BBCC	Ind		12/20
Sociology/Social Policy (Equal)	LL34	3FT deg	*	BCC	Ind	D$6/^	28	BBCC	Ind		18/30
YORKSHIRE COAST COLLEGE of F and HE											
Social Care	045L	2FT HND	*	6	MO	M	Ind	Ind	Ind		

course details			98 expected requirements							96 entry stats
TITLE	CODE	COURSE	SUBJECTS	A/AS	NO/C	AGNVQ	IB	SQA(H)	SQA	RATIO A/AS
Univ of ABERDEEN										
Sports and Exercise Science	B600	4FT deg	3S/2S+M g	CCD	Ind	MS go	24$	BBBC$	Ind	
ANGLIA Poly Univ										
Sports Science	B601▼	2FT deg	S	10	3M	M go	Dip$	BCCC		
Sports Science	B600▼	3FT deg	S	10	3M	P go	Dip$	BCCC	Ind	
Sports Science	006B▼	2FT HND	* g	4	N	P go	Dip	CCC	Ind	
Univ of Wales, BANGOR										
Applied Physics and Sports Science	FB36	3FT deg	M+P/Es/Cs g	BDD	3M+1D$	D$^_ go	30$	BBBC$	Ind	
Chemistry and Physical Education	FB16	3FT deg	C g	14	3M $	MS3 go	26$	BBCC$	Ind	
Chemistry and Sports Science	BF61	3FT deg	C g	14	3M $	MS3 go	26$	BBCC$	Ind	
Computer Systems and Sports Science	BH66	3FT deg	M+P/Es/Cs g	BDD	3M+1D$	D$6/^ go	30$	BBBC$	Ind	
Education & Sports Science (Taught in Welsh)	BX6X	3FT deg	* g	BCC	5D $	D*^ go	30$	X	X	
Electronic Engineering & Sports Science	HB66	3FT deg	M+P/Es/Cs g	BDD	3M+1D$	D$6/^ go	30$	BBBC$	Ind	
Mathematics and Physical Education	GBC6	3FT deg	M g	CCC	2M+2D$	D$^_ go	30$	BBBC$	Ind	
Mathematics and Sports Science	BG6C	3FT deg	M g	CCC	2M+2D$	D$^_ go	30$	BBBC$	Ind	
Physical Education/Education (Taught in Welsh)	XB96	3FT deg	* g	CCC	Ind	D*^ go	Ind	X	X	
Physical Education/French (Syllabus A)	RB16	4FT deg	F g	20	X	D*_ go	30$	BBBB$	X	
Physical Education/French (Syllabus B)	RBC6	4FT deg	F g	20	X	D*_ go	30$	BBBB$	X	
Physical Education/German	RB26	4FT deg	* g	20	X	D*_ go	30$	BBBB$	X	
Physical Education/Linguistics	QB16	3FT deg	* g	20	5D	D*^ go	28	BBBC	Ind	
Psychology/Physical Education	CB86	3FT deg	* g	BCC	2M+3D	D$6/^ go	30	BBBB	Ind	
Religious Studies/Physical Education	VB86	3FT deg	* g	CCC	Ind	D*6/^ go	28	BBBC	Ind	
Russian/Physical Education	RB86	4FT deg	* g	CCC	5D	D*6/^ go	28	BBBC	Ind	
Sociology/Physical Education	LB36	3FT deg	* g	CCC	5D	D*6/^ go	28	BBBC	Ind	
Sport,Health and Physical Education	B650	3FT deg	* g	20	5D	D*6/^ go	30	BBBB		
Sports Science	B600	3FT deg	* g	20	5D	D*6/^ go	30	BBBB	Ind	
Sports Science and Social Policy	BL64	3FT deg	* g	20	5D	D*6/^ go	30	BBBB	Ind	
Sports Science/Education (Taught in Welsh)	BX69	3FT deg	* g	20	5D	D*6/^ go	30	X	X	
Sports Science/French (Syllabus A)	BR61	4FT deg	F g	20	X	D*_ go	30$	BBBB$	X	
Sports Science/French (Syllabus B)	BR6C	4FT deg	F g	20	X	D*_ go	30$	BBBB$	X	
Sports Science/German	BR62	4FT deg	* g	20	X	D*6/^ go	30	BBBB	X	
Sports Science/Linguistics	BQ61	3FT deg	* g	20	5D	D*6/^ go	30	BBBC	Ind	
Sports Science/Psychology	BC68	3FT deg	* g	20	5D	D*6/^ go	30	BBBB	Ind	
Sports Science/Religious Studies	BV68	3FT deg	* g	20	5D	D*6/^ go	30	BBBC	Ind	
Sports Science/Russian	BR68	4FT deg	* g	20	5D	D*6/^ go	30	BBBC	Ind	
Sports Science/Sociology	BL63	3FT deg	* g	20	5D	D*6/^ go	30	BBBC	Ind	
Welsh/Physical Education	QB56	3FT/4FT deg	W g	CCC	Ind	D*_ go	Ind	X	X	
Welsh/Sports Science	BQ65	3FT/4FT deg	W g	CCC	Ind	D*_ go	Ind	X	X	
BARNSLEY COLL										
Leisure Studies	087N	2FT HND	*	4	4M	M*	Ind	Ind	Ind	
BASINGSTOKE COLLEGE of Technology										
Sports Science	006B	2FT HND								
BELL COLLEGE OF TECHNOLOGY										
Sports Coaching with Sports Development	6B9X	2FT HND	Ap g	DD-D	N $	P$	Ind	CC$	12$	
Univ of BIRMINGHAM										
Ancient History & Archaeology/Sport & Recr Studs	VB66	3FT deg	*	BBB	Ind	D*^	32	ABBB	Ind	
Dance/Sport & Recreation Studies	WB4P	3FT deg	*	BBB	Ind	D*^	32	ABBB	Ind	
Drama/Sport & Recreation Studies	WB46	3FT deg	*	BBB	Ind	D*^	32	ABBB	Ind	
East Mediterranean History/Sport & Recr Studies	VBD6	3FT deg	* g	BBB	Ind	D*^	32	ABBB	Ind	

TITLE	CODE	COURSE	SUBJECTS	A/AS	ND/C	AGNVQ	IB	SQA(H)	SQA	RATIO A/AS
English/Sport & Recreation Studies	QB36	3FT deg	*	BBB	Ind	D*^	32	ABBB	Ind	
French Studies/Sport & Recreation Studies	RB16	4FT deg	F	BBB	Ind	D*⌐	32$	ABBB	Ind	
Geography and Sports Science	BF68	3FT deg								
German Studies/Sport & Recreation Studies	RB26	4FT deg	G	BBB	Ind	D*⌐	32$	ABBB	Ind	
Hispanic Studies/Sport & Recreation Studies	RB46	4FT deg	*	BBB	Ind	D*^	32	ABBB	Ind	
History/Sport & Recreation Studies	VB16	3FT deg	*	BBB	Ind	D*^	32	ABBB	Ind	
Italian/Sport & Recreation Studies	RB36	4FT deg	*	BBB	Ind	D*^	32	ABBB	Ind	
Latin/Sport & Recreation Studies	QB66	3FT deg	Ln	BBB	Ind	D*⌐	32$	ABBB	Ind	
Modern Greek Studies/Sport & Recreation Studies	TB26	4FT deg	* g	BBB	Ind	D*^	32	ABBB	Ind	
Music/Sport & Recreation Studies	WB36	3FT deg	Mu	AAB-ABB	Ind	D*⌐	32$	ABBB	Ind	
Philosophy/Sport & Recreation Studies	VB76	3FT deg	*	BBB	Ind	D*^	32	ABBB	Ind	
Portuguese/Sport & Recreation Studies	RB56	4FT deg	*	BBB	Ind	D*^	32	ABBB	Ind	
Russian/Sport & Recreation Studies	RB86	4FT deg	*	BBB	Ind	D*^	32	ABBB	Ind	
Sport & Recreation Studies/Theology	VB86	3FT deg	*	BBB	Ind	D*^	32	ABBB	Ind	
Sport and Recreation Studies	B600	3FT deg	*	BBC	Ind		32	Ind	Ind	

BOLTON INST

Sports Development & Exercise Science	B600	3FT deg	* g	CD	MO	M	24	Ind	Ind	

Univ of BRIGHTON

Leisure and Sport Management	LN3R	3FT deg	* g	BC	3M+3D	M^ go/D go	26	BBBCC	Ind	
Leisure and Sport Studies	LN37	3FT deg	* g	BC	3M+3D	M^ go/D go	26	BBBCC	Ind	
Sport and Exercise Science	B600	3FT deg	* g	18	2M+5D	D/M6/^	28	BBBCC	Ind	

BRUNEL Univ, West London

Sport Sciences	B600	3FT deg	* g	18	1M+3D	D	29	BBCCC	N	
Sport Sciences/Accounting	B6NK	3FT deg	* g	18	1M+3D	D	29	BBCC	Ind	
Sport Sciences/Business Studies	B6NC	3FT deg	Ec g	18	1M+3D	D	29	BBCC	Ind	
Sport Sciences/Computer Studies	B6GM	3FT deg	* g	18	1M+3D	D	29	BBCC	Ind	
Sports Sciences/Leisure Management	BN67	3FT deg	* g	18	1M+3D	D	29	BBCC	Ind	

BUCKINGHAMSHIRE COLLEGE

Leisure Management and Sports Studies	BN67	3FT deg		8-10	1D	M	27	CCCC	Ind	

CANTERBURY CHRIST CHURCH COLL of HE

American Studies with Sport Science	Q4B6	4FT deg	* g	CC	MO	M	24	Ind	Ind	
Art with Sport Science	W1B6	3FT deg	A g	CC	MO	M	24	Ind	Ind	
Business Studies with Sport Science	N1B6	3FT deg	* g	CC	MO	M	24	Ind	Ind	
Early Childhood Studies with Sport Science	X9B6	3FT deg	* g	CC	MO	M	24	Ind	Ind	
English with Sport Science	Q3B6	3FT deg	E	CC	MO	M	24	Ind	Ind	
Geography with Sport Science	L8B6	3FT deg	Gy g	CC	MO	M	24	Ind	Ind	
History with Sport Science	V1B6	3FT deg	H g	CC	MO	M	24	Ind	Ind	
Marketing with Sport Science	N5B6	3FT deg	* g	CC	MO	M	24	Ind	Ind	
Mathematics with Sport Science	G1B6	3FT deg	M g	DD	Ind	Ind	24	Ind	Ind	
Media Studies with Sport Science	P4B6	3FT deg	* g	CC	MO	M	24	Ind	Ind	
Music with Sport Science	W3B6	3FT deg	Mu g	CC	MO	M	24	Ind	Ind	
Religious Studies with Sport Science	V8B6	3FT deg	* g	CC	MO	M	24	Ind	Ind	
Science with Sport Science	Y1B6	3FT deg	S g	DD	Ind	Ind	24	Ind	Ind	
Social Science with Sport Science	L3B6	3FT deg	* g	CC	MO	M	24	Ind	Ind	
Sport Science and American Studies	BQ64	3FT deg	* g	CC	MO	M	24	Ind	Ind	
Sport Science and Art	WB16	3FT deg	A g	CC	MO	M	24	Ind	Ind	
Sport Science and Business Studies	NB16	3FT deg	* g	CC	MO	M	24	Ind	Ind	
Sport Science and Early Childhood Studies	BX69	3FT deg	* g	CC	MO	M	24	Ind	Ind	
Sport Science and English	BQ63	3FT deg	E	CC	MO	M	24	Ind	Ind	
Sport Science and French	BR61	3FT deg	F g	CC	MO	M	24	Ind	Ind	

			98 expected requirements							96 entry stats	
TITLE	CODE	COURSE	SUBJECTS	A/AS	ND/C	RGNVQ	IB	SQA(H)	SQA	RATIO	A/AS
Sport Science and Geography	LB86	3FT deg	Gy g	CC	MO	M	24	Ind	Ind		
Sport Science and History	BV61	3FT deg	H g	CC	MO	M	24	Ind	Ind		
Sport Science and Marketing	BN65	3FT deg	* g	CC	MO	M	24	Ind	Ind		
Sport Science and Mathematics	GB16	3FT deg	M g	DD	Ind	Ind	24	Ind	Ind		
Sport Science and Media Studies	BP64	3FT deg	* g	CC	MO	M	24	Ind	Ind		
Sport Science and Music	BW63	3FT deg	Mu g	CC	MO	M	24	Ind	Ind		
Sport Science and Religious Studies	BV68	3FT deg	* g	CC	MO	M	24	Ind	Ind		
Sport Science and Science	BY61	3FT deg	S g	DD	Ind	Ind	24	Ind	Ind		
Sport Science and Social Science	BL63	3FT deg	* g	CC	MO	M	24	Ind	Ind		
Sport Science with American Studies	B6Q4	3FT deg	* g	CC	MO	M	24	Ind	Ind		
Sport Science with Art	B6W1	3FT deg	A g	CC	MO	M	24	Ind	Ind		
Sport Science with Business Studies	B6N1	3FT deg	* g	CC	MO	M	24	Ind	Ind		
Sport Science with Early Childhood Studies	B6X9	3FT deg	* g	CC	MO	M	24	Ind	Ind		
Sport Science with English	B6Q3	3FT deg	E g	CC	MO	M	24	Ind	Ind		
Sport Science with French	B6R1	3FT deg	F g	CC	MO	M	24	Ind	Ind		
Sport Science with Geography	B6L8	3FT deg	Gy g	CC	MO	M	24	Ind	Ind		
Sport Science with History	B6V1	3FT deg	H g	CC	MO	M	24	Ind	Ind	2	
Sport Science with Marketing	B6N5	3FT deg	* g	CC	MO	M	24	Ind	Ind		
Sport Science with Mathematics	B6G1	3FT deg	M g	DD	Ind	Ind	24	Ind	Ind		
Sport Science with Media Studies	B6P4	3FT deg	* g	CC	MO	M	24	Ind	Ind		
Sport Science with Music	B6W3	3FT deg	Mu g	CC	MO	M	24	Ind	Ind		
Sport Science with Religious Studies	B6V8	3FT deg	* g	CC	MO	M	24	Ind	Ind		
Sport Science with Science	B6Y1	3FT deg	S g	DD	Ind	Ind	24	Ind	Ind		
Sport Science with Social Science	B6L3	3FT deg	* g	CC	MO	M	24	Ind	Ind		
Sport Science with Statistics	B6G4	3FT deg	M g	DD	Ind	Ind	24	Ind	Ind		
Sport Science with Tourism Studies	B6P7	3FT deg	* g	CC	MO	M	24	Ind	Ind		
Statistics and Sport Science	BG64	3FT deg	M g	DD	Ind	Ind	24	Ind	Ind		
Statistics with Sport Science	G4B6	3FT deg	M g	DD	Ind	Ind	24	Ind	Ind		
Tourism Studies and Sport Science	PB76	3FT deg	* g	CC	MO	M	24	Ind	Ind		
Tourism Studies with Sport Science	P7B6	3FT deg	* g	CC	MO	M	24	Ind	Ind		

Univ of Wales INST, CARDIFF

Sport and Exercise Sciences	B600	3FT deg	* g	BB	4D	D*^ go	Ind	CCCC	Ind	21	16/24
Sport and Human Movement Studies	B601	3FT deg	* g	BB	4D	D$^ go	Ind	CCCC	Ind	4	12/22

Univ of CENTRAL LANCASHIRE

Sports Science	B600	3FT deg	S g	18	MO+5D	D$6/^	28$	BBBB	Ind		
Sports Studies	006B▼	2FT HND	* g	DD	MO	P$	24$	CCC	Ind		

CHELTENHAM & GLOUCESTER COLL of HE

Business Management and Sport & Exercise Sci	NB16	3FT deg	S	12-16	4M+3D	MB3	26	CCCC	Ind		
Business Management with Sport and Exercise Sci	N1B6	4SW deg	S	12-16	4M+3D	MB3	26	CCCC	Ind		
Catering Management and Sport and Exercise Sci	NB76	3FT deg	S	8-12	5M+3D	MH3	26	CCCC	Ind		
Catering Management with Sport and Exercise Sci	N7B6	4SW deg	S	8-12	5M+2D	MH3	24	CCCC	Ind		
Countryside Planning and Sport and Exercise Sci	DBF6	3FT deg	S	8-14	5M+2D	MK/DL	26	CCCC	Ind		
Countryside Planning with Sport and Exercise Sci	D2B6	3FT deg	S	8-14	5M+2D	MK	26	CCCC	Ind		
English Studies and Sport and Exercise Sciences	QB36	3FT deg	S+E	12-16	4M+3D	M^	26	CCCC	Ind		
English Studies with Sport and Exercise Sciences	Q3B6	3FT deg	E+S g	12-16	4M+3D	M^	26	CCCC	Ind		
Environmental Policy and Sport and Exercise Sci	FB96	3FT deg	S	8-14	MO	M3	26	CCCC	Ind		
Environmental Policy with Sport and Exercise Sci	F9BP	3FT deg	S g	10-14	5M+2D	M3	26	CCCC	Ind		
Financial Management and Sport and Exercise Sci	BN63	3FT deg	S	10-14	5M+2D	ML3	26	CCCC	Ind		
Financial Management with Sport & Exercise Sci	N3B6	4SW deg	*	10-14	5M+2D	M3	26	CCCC	Ind		
Financial Services Mgt and Sport & Exercise Sci	NB36	3FT deg	S	10-14	5M+2D	M3	26	CCCC	Ind		
Financial Services Mgt with Sport & Exercise Sci	N3BP	4SW deg	g	10-12	5M+2D	M3	26	CCCC	Ind		

	course details			*98 expected requirements*						*96 entry stats*
TITLE	CODE	COURSE	SUBJECTS	A/AS	ND/C	RGNVQ	IB	SQA(H)	SQA	RATIO A/AS
Geography and Sport and Exercise Sciences	BL68	3FT deg	*	12-16	M0	ML3	26	CCCC	Ind	
Geography with Sport and Exercise Sciences	L8BP	3FT deg	*	12-16	M0	ML3	26	CCCC	Ind	
Geology and Sport and Exercise Sciences	BF66	3FT deg	S	12-16	M0	ML3	24	CCCC	Ind	
Geology with Sport and Exercise Sciences	F6B6	3FT deg	S	8-12	M0	M3	26	CCCC	Ind	
History and Sport & Exercise Sciences	VB16	3FT deg	H+S	12-16	5M+2D	M3^	26	CCCC	Ind	
History with Sport & Exercise Sciences	V1B6	3FT deg	H+S g	12-16	4M+3D	M3^	26	CCCC	Ind	
Hotel Management and Sport and Exercise Sciences	NBR6	3FT deg	S	12	4M+3D	M$3	26	CCCC	Ind	
Hotel Management with Sport and Exercise Sci	N7BQ	4SW deg	g	12	5M+2D	MH3	26	CCCC	Ind	
Human Geography and Sport and Exercise Sciences	LB86	3FT deg	S	12-16	4M+3D	ML3	26	CCCC	Ind	
Human Geography with Sport and Exercise Sciences	L8B6	3FT deg	S	12-16	4M+3D	M3	26	CCCC	Ind	
Human Resource Management and Sport & Exer Sci	BN61	3FT deg	S	12	5M+2D	M$3	26	CCCC	Ind	
Human Resource Mgt with Sport and Exercise Sci	NBC6	4SW deg	*	12	5M+2D	MB3	26	CCCC	Ind	
Leisure Management & Sport and Exercise Sciences	BN67	3FT deg	S	12-16	4M+3D	ML3	26	CCCC	Ind	
Leisure Management with Sport and Exercise Sci	N7BP	4SW deg	*	12-16	4M+3D	ML3	26	CCCC	Ind	
Marketing Management and Sport and Exercise Sci	BN65	3FT deg	S	12-16	5M+2D	M$3	26	CCCC	Ind	
Marketing Management with Sport and Exercise Sci	N5B6	4SW deg	S	12	5M+2D	MB3	26	CCCC	Ind	
Natural Resource Mgt and Sport and Exercise Sci	FBX6	3FT deg	S	8-12	5M+2D	ML3	26	CCCC	Ind	
Natural Resource Mgt with Sport and Exercise Sci	F9B6	3FT deg	S	8-12	5M+2D	M3	26	CCCC	Ind	
Performance Arts and Sport & Exercise Sciences	WB46	3FT deg	*	12-16	4M+3D	M3	26	CCCC	Ind	
Performance Arts with Sport & Exercise Sciences	W4B6	3FT deg	*	10-14	5M+2D	M3	26	CCCC	Ind	
Physical Geography and Sport and Exercise Sci	FB86	3FT deg	S	12-16	5M+2D	ML3	26	CCCC	Ind	
Physical Geography with Sport and Exercise Sci	F8B6	3FT deg	*	12	5M+2D	M3^	26	CCCC	Ind	
Psychology and Sport and Exercise Sciences	BL67	3FT deg	S g	12-16	4M+3D	ML3/^	26	CCCC	Ind	
Psychology with Sport and Exercise Sciences	L7B6	3FT deg	g	12-16	4M+3D	M3^	26	CCCC	Ind	
Religious Studies and Sport & Exercise Sciences	BV68	3FT deg	S	8-12	M0	M3^	26	CCCC	Ind	
Religious Studies with Sport & Exercise Sciences	V8B6	3FT deg	*	8-12	M0	M3^	26	CCCC	Ind	
Sociological Studies & Sport & Exercise Sciences	LB36	3FT deg	S	12-16	4M+3D	MG3	26	CCCC	Ind	
Sociological Studies with Sport and Exercise Sci	L3B6	3FT deg	*	12-16	4M+3D	M$3	26	CCCC	Ind	
Sport & Exercise Sciences and Tourism Management	BP67	3FT deg	S	12-16	4M+3D	ML3	26	CCCC	Ind	
Sport & Exercise Sciences and Visual Arts	BW61	3FT deg	A	12-16	4M+3D	MA3	26	CCCC	Ind	
Sport & Exercise Sciences and Women's Studies	BM69	3FT deg	*	12-16	5M+2D	ML3	26	CCCC	Ind	
Sport & Exercise Sciences with Business Mgt	B6N1	3FT deg	S	12-16	4M+3D	ML3	26	CCCC	Ind	
Sport & Exercise Sciences with Catering Mgt	B6N7	3FT deg	S	12-16	4M+3D	ML3	26	CCCC	Ind	
Sport & Exercise Sciences with Countryside Plan	B6DF	3FT deg	*	12-16	4M+3D	ML3	26	CCCC	Ind	
Sport & Exercise Sciences with English Studies	B6Q3	3FT deg	*	12-16	4M+3D	ML3	26	CCCC	Ind	
Sport & Exercise Sciences with Enviro Policy	B6FX	3FT deg	*	12-16	4M+3D	ML3	26	CCCC	Ind	
Sport & Exercise Sciences with Financial Mgt	B6NH	3FT deg	S	12-16	M0	ML3	26	CCCC	Ind	
Sport & Exercise Sciences with Financial Ser Mgt	B6N3	3FT deg	S	12-16	4M+3D	ML3	26	CCCC	Ind	
Sport & Exercise Sciences with Geography	B6LV	3FT deg	*	12-16	M0	M3^	26	CCCC	Ind	
Sport & Exercise Sciences with Geology	B6F6	3FT deg	*	12-16	M0	M3^	26	CCCC	Ind	
Sport & Exercise Sciences with History	B6V1	3FT deg	S	12-16	4M+3D	ML3	26	CCCC	Ind	
Sport & Exercise Sciences with Hotel Management	B6NT	3FT deg	S	12-16	4M+3D	ML3	26	CCCC	Ind	
Sport & Exercise Sciences with Human Geography	B6L8	3FT deg	*	12-16	4M+3D	ML3	26	CCCC	Ind	
Sport & Exercise Sciences with Human Res Mgt	B6NC	3FT deg	S	12-16	M0	ML3	26	CCCC	Ind	
Sport & Exercise Sciences with Leisure Mgt	B6NR	3FT deg	S	12-16	4M+3D	ML3	26	CCCC	Ind	
Sport & Exercise Sciences with Marketing Mgt	B6NM	3FT deg	S	12-16	M0	ML3	26	CCCC	Ind	
Sport & Exercise Sciences with Mod Lang (French)	B6RD	3FT deg	F g	12-16	4M+3D	ML3	26	CCCC	Ind	
Sport & Exercise Sciences with Natural Res Mgt	B6F9	3FT deg	*	12-16	4M+3D	ML3	26	CCCC	Ind	
Sport & Exercise Sciences with Performance Arts	B6W4	3FT deg	*	14	4M+3D	M3	26	CCCC	Ind	
Sport & Exercise Sciences with Physical Geog	B6F8	3FT deg	*	12-16	4M+3D	ML3	26	CCCC	Ind	
Sport & Exercise Sciences with Psychology	B6L7	3FT deg	S	12-16	4M+3D	ML3	26	CCCC	Ind	
Sport & Exercise Sciences with Religious Studies	B6V8	3FT deg	*	12-16	4M+3D	ML3	26	CCCC	Ind	
Sport & Exercise Sciences with Sociological St	B6L3	3FT deg	S	12-16	4M+3D	ML3	26	CCCC	Ind	

TITLE	CODE	COURSE	SUBJECTS	A/AS	NO/C	AGNVQ	IB	SQA(H)	SQA	RATIO A/AS
			98 expected requirements							*96 entry stats*
Sport & Exercise Sciences with Tourism Mgt	B6PT	3FT deg	S	12-16	4M+3D	ML3	26	CCCC	Ind	
Sport & Exercise Sciences with Women's Studies	B6M9	3FT deg	*	12-16	4M+3D	ML3	26	CCCC	Ind	
Sport and Exercise Sciences	B600	3FT deg	*	14-18	4M+3D	D	26	CCCC	Ind	
Sport and Exercise Sciences with Visual Arts	B6W1	3FT deg	*	14	4M+3D	MA3	26	CCCC	Ind	
Tourism Management with Sport and Exercise Sci	P7B6	4SW deg	*	12-16	4M+3D	ML3	26	CCCC	Ind	
Visual Arts with Sport & Exercise Sciences	W1B6	3FT deg	A	10-14	5M+2D	MA3	26	CCCC	Ind	
Women's Studies with Sport & Exercise Sciences	M9B6	3FT deg	S	8-12	MO	M3	26	CCCC	Ind	

UNIVERSITY COLLEGE CHESTER

TITLE	CODE	COURSE	SUBJECTS	A/AS	NO/C	AGNVQ	IB	SQA(H)	SQA	RATIO A/AS
Art and Physical Education/Sports Science	WB96	3FT deg	*	12	M	P^	Ind	CCCC	$	
Art with Physical Education/Sports Science	W9B6	3FT deg	*	12	M	P^	Ind	CCCC	$	
Biology and Physical Education/Sports Science	CB16	3FT deg	B	10	M	P^	Ind	CCCC	$	
Biology with Physical Education/Sports Science	C1B6	3FT deg	B	10	M	P^	Ind	CCCC	$	
Computer Science/IT with PE/Sports Science	G5B6	3FT deg	g	10	M	P^	Ind	CCCC	$	
Computer Studies/IT and PE/Sports Science	GB56	3FT deg	g	10	M	P^	Ind	CCCC	$	
Drama and Theatre Studies and PE/Sports Science	WB46	3FT deg	*	CC	M	P^	Ind	CCCC	$	
Drama and Theatre Studies with PE/Sports Science	W4B6	3FT deg	*	12	M	P^	Ind	CCCC	$	
English Literature and PE/Sports Science	QB36	3FT deg	E	CC	M	P^	Ind	CCCC	$	
English with Physical Education/Sports Science	Q3B6	3FT deg	E	CC	M	P^	Ind	CCCC	$	
Geography and Physical Education/Sports Science	FB86	3FT deg	Gy/Gl	CC	M	P^	Ind	CCCC	$	
Geography with Physical Education/Sports Science	F8B6	3FT deg	Gy/Gl	CC	M	P^	Ind	CCCC	$	
History and Physical Education/Sports Science	VB16	3FT deg	H/Ec/So	CC	M	P^	Ind	CCCC	$	
History with Physical Education/Sports Science	V1B6	3FT deg	H/Ec/So	CC	M	P^	Ind	CCCC	$	
Mathematics and PE/Sports Science	GB16	3FT deg	M	10	M	P^	Ind	CCCC	$	
Mathematics with PE/Sports Science	G1B6	3FT deg	M	10	M	P^	Ind	CCCC	$	
PE/Sports Science and Theology & Religious Studs	BV68	3FT deg	*	12	M	P^	Ind	CCCC	$	
PE/Sports Science with Biology	B6C1	3FT deg	B	10	M	P^	Ind	CCCC	$	
PE/Sports Science with Computer Science/IT	B6G5	3FT deg	g	10	M	P^	Ind	CCCC	$	
PE/Sports Science with Drama and Theatre Studies	B6W4	3FT deg	*	12	M	P^	Ind	CCCC	$	
PE/Sports Science with English Literature	B6Q3	3FT deg	E	CC	M	P^	Ind	CCCC	$	
PE/Sports Science with Geography	B6F8	3FT deg	Gy/Gl	CC	M	P^	Ind	CCCC	$	
PE/Sports Science with History	B6V1	3FT deg	H/Ec/So	CC	M	P^	Ind	CCCC	$	
PE/Sports Science with Mathematics	B6G1	3FT deg	M	10	M	P^	Ind	CCCC	$	
PE/Sports Science with Psychology	B6L7	3FT deg	g	10	M	P^	Ind	CCCC	$	
PE/Sports Science with Theology and Religious St	B6V8	3FT deg	*	12	M	P^	Ind	CCCC	$	
Physical Education/Sports Science and Psychology	BL67	3FT deg	g	10	M	P^	Ind	CCCC	$	
Physical Education/Sports Science with Art	B6W9	3FT deg	*	CC	M	P^	Ind	CCCC	$	
Physical Education/Sports Science with French	B6R1	3FT deg	g	12	M	P^	Ind	CCCC	$	
Physical Education/Sports Science with German	B6R2	3FT deg	g	12	M	P^	Ind	CCCC	$	
Physical Education/Sports Science with Soc Sci	B6L3	3FT deg	g	10	M	P^	Ind	CCCC	$	
Psychology with PE/Sports Science	L7B6	3FT deg	g	10	M	P^	Ind	CCCC	$	
Theology and Religious St with PE/Sports Science	V8B6	3FT deg	*	12	M	P^	Ind	CCCC	$	

CHICHESTER INSTITUTE OF HIGHER EDUCATION

TITLE	CODE	COURSE	SUBJECTS	A/AS	NO/C	AGNVQ	IB	SQA(H)	SQA	RATIO A/AS
Sports Science	B600	3FT deg	* g	14	Ind	M$^	Ind	Ind	Ind	

COVENTRY Univ

TITLE	CODE	COURSE	SUBJECTS	A/AS	NO/C	AGNVQ	IB	SQA(H)	SQA	RATIO A/AS
Equine and Sport Sciences	BD62	3FT deg								
Materials Technology with Sports Science	J5BP	3FT deg	S g	12	Ind	Ind	Ind	Ind	Ind	
Materials Technology with Sports Science	J5B6	3FT deg	S g	12	Ind	Ind	Ind	Ind	Ind	
Mathematical Studies & Sports Science	GB96	3FT/4SW deg	M+B	14-18	Ind	Ind	Ind	Ind	Ind	
Sport Science	B600	3FT deg	S g	12	5M	Ind	Ind	Ind	Ind	
Sport Science and Health Science	B6L4▼	3FT deg	S g	8	5M	Ind	Ind	Ind	Ind	
Sport Science with Human Resource Management	BN67▼	3FT deg	S g	8	5M	Ind	Ind	Ind	Ind	6/14

course details			98 expected requirements							96 entry stats	
TITLE	CODE	COURSE	SUBJECTS	A/AS	ND/C	AGNVQ	IB	SQA(H)	SQA	RATIO	A/AS
DE MONTFORT Univ											
Equine Sports Science	BD62▼	3FT deg	S g	CD	MO	M	Ind	BBBB	Ind		
Sports Engineering	H3B6▼	3FT/4SW deg	M+P g	16	4M	M^	26$	BBBB	Ind		
Sports Studies/Science	BL63▼	3FT deg	S g	14	7M+5D	M^	Ind	BBBCC	Ind	6	10/18
Sports Studies	006B▼	2FT HND	g	6	M	P	Dip	BB	Ind		
Univ of DURHAM											
Sport in the Community	BX69	3FT deg	Pe/B	BBC	Ind	Ind	32$	AABBB$	Ind		14/20
Sports Science	B600	3FT deg	B+C	12-18	Ind	Ind	Dip	BBBB	Ind		
Univ of EAST LONDON											
Three-Subject Degree *Fitness & Health*	Y600	3FT deg	* g	12	MO	M	Ind	Ind	Ind		
EDGE HILL Univ COLLEGE											
Applied Social Sciences and Sports Studies	BL63	3FT deg	*	CC	3M+3D	M* / P*^	Dip	BBCC	Ind		
Biology and Sports Studies	BC61	3FT deg	S g	CD	3M+3D	PS^ go	Dip	BBCC$	Ind		
Environmental Management and Sports Studies	BF69	3FT deg	2(B/C/En/P) g	CD	3M+3D	MS / P*	Dip	BBCC	Ind		
Geography and Sports Studies	BL68	3FT deg	Gy g	CC	X	P*^	Dip	BBCC$	X		
History and Sports Studies	BV61	3FT deg	H	CC	X	P*^	Dip	BBCC$	X		
Science and Sports Studies	BY61	3FT deg	2(B/C/En/P) g	CD	3M+3D	MS / P*^	Dip	BBCC$	Ind		
Sport and the City	BM69	3FT deg	*	CD	3M+3D	M* / P*^	Dip	BBCC	Ind		
Sports Studies	B600	3FT deg	*	CC	3M+3D	M* / P*^	Dip	BBCC	Ind		
Sports Studies and Information Systems	BG65	3FT deg	* g	CC	3M+3D	M* / P*^	Dip	BBCC	Ind		
Sports Studies and Mathematics	BG61	3FT deg	* g	CD	3M+3D	M* / P*^	Dip	BBCC	Ind		
Univ of ESSEX											
Sports Science with Biochemistry	B6C7	3FT deg	C+S	18	MO	D	28$	BBBC	Ind		
Sports Science with Biology	B6C1	3FT deg	2S	18	MO	D	28	BBBC	Ind		
Sports Science with Physics	B6F3	3FT deg	P+S	18	MO	D	28$	BBBC	Ind		
Univ of EXETER											
Exercise and Sport Sciences	B600	3FT deg	* g	BBC-BCC	MO	M/D$	32	Ind	Ind		16/26
FARNBOROUGH COLL of Technology											
Science and Management of Exercise and Health	BN67	3FT deg	g	10	Ind	M*	Ind	Ind	Ind	3	8/13
Science and Management of Health and Fitness	67BN	2FT HND	g	4	Ind	P*	Ind	Ind	Ind	2	2/12
Univ of GLAMORGAN											
Applied Sports Science	B600	3FT deg	M/S g	12	5M $	M$	Ind	Ind	Ind		
Biological Science and Sports Science	BC61	3FT deg	M/S g	DD	5M $	M$	Ind	Ind	Ind		
Biological Science with Sports Science	C1B6	3FT deg	M/S g	DD	5M $	M$	Ind	Ind	Ind		
Chemical Science and Sports Science	BF61	3FT deg	M/S g	DD	5M $	M$	Ind	Ind	Ind		
Chemical Science with Sports Science	F1B6	3FT deg	M/S g	DD	5M $	M$	Ind	Ind	Ind		
Environmental Pollution Science and Sports Sci	BF69	3FT deg	M/S g	DD	5M $	M$	Ind	Ind	Ind		
Environmental Pollution Science with Sports Sci	F9B6	3FT deg	M/S g	DD	5M $	M$	Ind	Ind	Ind		
Geological Science and Sports Science	BF66	3FT deg	M/S g	DD	5M $	M$	Ind	Ind	Ind		
Geological Science with Sports Science	F6B6	3FT deg	M/S g	DD	5M $	M$	Ind	Ind	Ind		
Mathematics and Sports Science	BG61	3FT deg	M/S g	12	Ind	Ind	Ind	Ind	Ind		
Mathematics with Sports Science	G1B6	3FT deg	M/S g	12	Ind	Ind	Ind	Ind	Ind		
Minerals Surveying and Sports Science	JB16	3FT deg	M/S g	DD	5M $	M$	Ind	Ind	Ind		
Minerals Surveying with Sports Science	J1B6	3FT deg	M/S g	DD	5M $	M$	Ind	Ind	Ind		
Sports Equipment Design	H3B6	3FT deg									
Sports Psychology	B601	3FT deg	S g	12	Ind	Ind	Ind	Ind	Ind		6/14
Sports Science with Biological Science	B6C1	3FT deg	M/S g	DD	5M $	M$	Ind	Ind	Ind		
Sports Science with Chemical Science	B6F1	3FT deg	M/S g	DD	5M $	M$	Ind	Ind	Ind		
Sports Science with Environmental Pollution Sci	B6F9	3FT deg	M/S g	12	5M $	M$	Ind	Ind	Ind		

course details			98 expected requirements							96 entry stats	
TITLE	CODE	COURSE	SUBJECTS	A/AS	NO/C	AGNVQ	IB	SQA(H)	SQA	RATIO	A/AS
Sports Science with Geography	B6L8	3FT deg	M/S g	12	Ind	Ind	Ind	Ind	Ind		
Sports Science with Geological Science	B6F6	3FT deg	M/S g	DD	5M $	M$	Ind	Ind	Ind		
Sports Science with Minerals Surveying Science	B6J1	3FT deg	M/S g	DD	5M $	M$	Ind	Ind	Ind		
Combined Studies (Honours) *Sports Science*	Y400	3FT deg	S g	8-16	Ind	Ind	Ind	Ind	Ind		
Major/Minor Honours *Sports Science*	Y402	3FT deg	M/S g	8-16	Ind	Ind	Ind	Ind	Ind		
Applied Sports Science	006B▼	2FT HND	M/S g	6	N $	P$	Ind	Ind	Ind		
Sports Sci (Outdoor Activities)-(Pembrokeshire)	76NB▼	2FT HND	S g	6	Ind	Ind	Ind	Ind	Ind		
Sports Science (Exercise Analysis)	206B▼	2FT HND	S g	6	Ind	Ind	Ind	Ind	Ind	1	
Sports Science (Health and Exercise)	506B▼	2FT deg	S g	6	Ind	Ind	Ind	Ind	Ind		
Sports Science (Human Movement)	106B▼	2FT HND	S g	6	Ind	Ind	Ind	Ind	Ind		
Sports Science (Marine Pursuits)	406B▼	2FT HND	S g	6	Ind	Ind	Ind	Ind	Ind		

Univ of GLASGOW

Physical Activity, Sports Science and Nutrition	BB46	4FT deg	C/M+S	BBC-CCC	N	M	24$	BBBB$	N		
Physiology with Sports Science	B1B6	4FT deg	C/M+S	BBC-CCC	N	M	24$	BBBB$	N		
Sports Medicine	BB69	4FT deg	C/M+S	BBC-CCC	N	M	24$	BBBB$	N		

Univ of GREENWICH

Fitness Science	B601	3FT deg	B	12	4M	MS	Dip	BBC	Ind		
Sports Science	B600	3FT deg	B/C	16	3M	DS	Dip	BBB	Ind		

Univ of HUDDERSFIELD

Health with Sports Studies	BL65	3FT deg	* g	14-18	6M $	D$ gi	Ind	BBBC	Ind		
Science (Extended) *Health with Sports Studies*	Y108	4FT deg	* g	EE	N	P$ gi	Ind	Ind	Ind		

Univ of HULL

Chemistry with Sports Science	F1B6	3FT deg									
Physical Education and Sports Sci with Biology	B601	3FT deg	B	18-20	MO $	M$^/6	28$	BBBCC	Ind		
Physical Education and Sports Science with Biol	B6C1	3FT deg	B	18-20	MO $	M$^/6	28$	BBBCC	Ind		
Physical Education and Sports Science with Chem	B6F1	3FT deg	C	18-20	MO $	M$6	26$	BBBCC			
Physical Education and Sports Science with Maths	B6G1	3FT deg	M	18-20	3M $	M$^ gi	25$	BBBCC	Ind		
Physical Education and Sports Science with Mgt	B6N1	3FT deg	*	18-20	3M	M$6 gi	25$	BBBCC	Ind		

KING ALFRED'S WINCHESTER

Sports Studies and Business Studies	NL1H	3FT deg	* g	14	6M	M	24	BCC	N		
Sports Studies and Computing	GL5H	3FT deg	* g	14	6M	M	24	BCC	N		
Sports Studies and Education Studies	LXH9	3FT deg	* g	14	6M	M	24	BCC	N		
Sports Studies and History	VL1H	3FT deg	* g	14	6M	M	24	BCC	N		
Sports Studies and Media & Film Studies	PL4H	3FT deg	* g	14	6M	M	24	BCC	N		
Sports Studies and Psychology	LL7H	3FT deg	* g	14	6M	M	24	BCC	N		
Sports Studies and Social Biology	CL1H	3FT deg	B g	14	6M $	M	24$	BCC$	N$		

KINGSTON Univ

Sports Science	B600	3FT deg	B g	18	$	Ind	Ind	Ind	Ind	16	8/26
Sports Science	B608▼	4EXT deg	*		Ind		Ind	Ind	Ind	12	

Univ of LEEDS

Sports Science (Outdoor Activities)	B600	3FT deg	B/C/M/P g	BBC	Ind	Ind	Ind	Ind	Ind		14/24
Sports Science and Physiology	BB16	3FT deg	B/C/M/P g	BBC	1M+5D$	Ind	30$	ABBBB	Ind		

LEEDS, TRINITY & ALL SAINTS Univ COLL

Sport, Health and Leisure-Management	BN61	3FT deg	* g	BBB-CCC	MO+3D	Ind	26	AABBB	Ind		
Sport, Health and Leisure-Media	BP64	3FT deg	* g	BBB-CCC	MO+3D	Ind	26	AABBB	Ind		
Sport, Health, Exercise and Nutrition	B600	3FT deg	* g	BBB-CCD	MO+3D	Ind	26	AABBB	Ind		

course details | 98 expected requirements | 96 entry stats

TITLE	CODE	COURSE	SUBJECTS	A/AS	NO/C	AGNVQ	IB	SQA(H)	SQA	RATIO	A/AS
LEEDS METROPOLITAN Univ											
Sport and Exercise Science	B600	3FT deg	* g	20	2M+5D	DS go	28	BBBBB	Ind	14	16/24
Sport and Recreation Development	B6N7	3FT deg	* g	20	2M+5D	D$ go	28	BBBBB	Ind	24	16/26
Univ of LIVERPOOL											
Human Movement Science	B600	3FT deg	2S g	18	MO $	Ind	31$	BBBCC$	Ind		
BSc Combined Honours _Human Movement Science_	Y100	3FT deg	B	18	MO $	Ind	31$	BBBCC$	Ind		
LIVERPOOL HOPE Univ COLL											
Health & Physical Recreation	BB96	3FT deg	* g	12	8M	M$ go	Ind	Ind	Ind		
Sport, Recreation & P.E./Drama & Theatre Studies	WB46	3FT deg	g	12	8M	M* go	Ind	Ind	Ind		
Sport, Recreation & P.E./Environmental Studies	FB96	3FT deg	B/Gy/En g	10	6M	M$ go	Ind	Ind	Ind		
Sport, Recreation & P.E./Human & Applied Biology	CB16	3FT deg	B g	10	6M	M$ /P*^ go	Ind	Ind	Ind		
Sport, Recreation & Physical Educ/Mathematics	GB16	3FT deg	M	10	6M	P*^	Ind	Ind	Ind		
Sport, Recreation & Physical Educ/Psychology	CB86	3FT deg	g	10	6M	M* go	Ind	Ind	Ind		
Sport, Recreation & Physical Education/English	QB36	3FT deg	El	12	8M	P*^	Ind	Ind	Ind		
Sport, Recreation & Physical Education/French	RB16	3FT deg	F	12	8M	P*^	Ind	Ind	Ind		
Sport, Recreation & Physical Education/Geography	FB86	3FT deg	Gy g	10	6M	M$ go	Ind	Ind	Ind		
Sport, Recreation & Physical Education/History	VB16	3FT deg	H	12	8M	P*^	Ind	Ind	Ind		
Sport, Recreation & Physical Education/Music	WB36	3FT deg	Mu	12	8M	P*^	Ind	Ind	Ind		
Sport, Recreation & Physical Education/Sociology	LB36	3FT deg	*	12	8M	M*	Ind	Ind	Ind		
Sport,Recreation & P.E./European Studies	TB26	3FT deg	*	12	8M	M*	Ind	Ind	Ind		
LIVERPOOL JOHN MOORES Univ											
Coaching Science	BX69	3FT deg		BCC	MO+5D	MS^	Ind	BBBC		16	
Sports Science	B600	3FT deg		BBC-BCC	MO+5D	MS^	Ind	BBBC		25	16/24
Sports Science and Applied Psychology	CB86	3FT deg	S g	CCC	5M+3D	DS/MS6 go	28$	BBBB		13	18/22
LOUGHBOROUGH Univ											
Chemistry and Physical Education and Sports Sci	FB16	3FT deg	C	20	3M+2D		30$	Ind	Ind		
English and Physical Education and Sports Sci	QB36	3FT deg	E	24			30	Ind			
Geography & Physical Education and Sports Sci	FB86	3FT deg	Gy	24			30$	Ind			
Physical Education and Sports Sci and Soc Sci	BL63	3FT deg	* g	24	4D		30	Ind	Ind		
Physical Education and Sports Science	BX69	3FT deg	* g	26	4D	DS6/^ go	30	Ind	Ind		
Physical Education and Sports Science and Maths	BG61	3FT deg	M	24			30$	Ind			
Physical Education, Sports Science and Physics	FB36	3FT deg	M+P	20			30$	Ind			
Physical Education, Sports Science and Recr Mgt	BN67	3FT deg	* g	26	4D	DL6/^ go	30	Ind	Ind		
LSU COLL of HE											
Environment and Society with Sports Science	BF69	3FT deg									
Sport and Health Sciences (Combined)	B600	3FT deg									
Sport and Health Sciences with Ecology	BF66	3FT deg									
Sport and Health Sciences with Geography	BL6V	3FT deg									
Sport and Health Sciences with Politics	BM61	3FT deg									
Sport and Health Sciences with Psychology	BL6R	3FT deg									
Sport and Health Sciences with Sociology	BL6H	3FT deg									
Sports Science and Ecology	DB26	3FT deg									
Sports Science and Geography	BL68	3FT deg									
Sports Science and Life Sciences	CB96	3FT deg									
Sports Science and Psychology	BL67	3FT deg									
Sports Science and Sociology	LB36	3FT deg									

TITLE	CODE	COURSE	SUBJECTS	A/AS	NO/C	RGNVQ	IB	SQA(H)	SQA	RATIO A/AS
LUTON Univ										
Sport and Fitness Studies	BN67	3FT deg	g	12-16	MO/DO	M/D	32	BBCC	Ind	
Sports and Fitness Science	B6N7	3FT deg	g	12-16	MO/DO	M/D	32	BBCC	Ind	1
Sport and Health Science	96BB	2FT HND	g	12-16	MO/DO	M/D	32	BBCC	Ind	
MANCHESTER METROPOLITAN Univ										
Health Studies with French	B6R1	4FT deg	F		M+D	M$	Ind	Ind	Ind	
Sport and Exercise Science	B600	3FT deg	S g	BCC	4M+1D	D	28	BBB$	Ind	12/24
Sport/American Studies	BQ64	3FT deg	S	BC	M+D	DS	28	CCCC	Ind	
Sport/Applied Social Studies	BL63	3FT deg	S	BC	M+D	DS	28	CCCC	Ind	
Sport/Business Studies	BN61	3FT deg	S	BC	M+D	DS	28	CCCC	N$	
Sport/Cultural Studies	BL6H	3FT deg	S	BC	M+D	DS	28	CCCC	Ind	
Sport/Dance	BW64	3FT deg	S	BC	M+D	DS	28	CCCC	Ind	
Sport/Design & Technology	BW62	3FT deg	S	BC	M+D	DS	28	CCCC	Ind	
Sport/Drama	BW6K	3FT deg	S	BC	M+D	DS	28	CCCC	Ind	
Sport/English	BQ63	3FT deg	S	BC	M+D	DS	28	CCCC	Ind	
Sport/Environmental Science	BF69	3FT deg	S	BC	M+D	DS	28	CCCC	Ind	
Sport/Geography	BL68	3FT deg	S	BC	M+D	DS	28	CCCC	Ind	
Sport/Health Studies	BB69	3FT deg	S	BC	M+D	DS	28	CCCC	Ind	
Sport/History	BV61	3FT deg	S	BC	M+D	DS	28	CCCC	Ind	
Sport/Leisure Studies	BL64	3FT deg	S	BC	M+D	DS	28	CCCC	Ind	
Sport/Life Science	BC61	3FT deg	S	BC	M+D	DS	28	CCCC	Ind	
Sport/Music	BW63	3FT deg	S	BC	M+D	DS	28	CCCC	Ind	
Sport/Philosophy	BV67	3FT deg	S	BC	M+D	DS	28	CCCC	Ind	
Sport/Religious Studies	BV68	3FT deg	S	BC	M+D	DS	28	CCCC	Ind	
Visual Arts/Sport	BW61	3FT deg	*	CC	M+D	D	28	CCCC	Visual	
Writing/Sport	BW6L	3FT deg	*	CC	M+D	D	28	CCCC	Ind	
MIDDLESEX Univ										
Sports Performance Therapy	B610▼	3FT/4FT deg		12-16	5M	M$ go	28	Ind	Ind	
Health, Fitness and Beauty Therapies	86WB▼	2FT HND	* g	DD	N	P$ go	Dip	Ind	Ind	
MORAY HOUSE Inst of Ed										
Applied Sport Sciences	B610	3FT/4FT deg	g	BC-CCD	Ind	Ind		BBBC	Ind	12 14/20
NEWCASTLE COLL										
Science (Sports Studies)	087N▼	2FT HND								
Univ of Wales COLLEGE, NEWPORT										
Sports Studies and Archaeology	BV66	3FT deg		10	M+D	D$	Ind	Ind	Ind	
Sports Studies and English	BQ63	3FT deg		10	M+D	D$	Ind	Ind	Ind	
Sports Studies and Environmental Studies	BF69	3FT deg		10	M+D	D$	Ind	Ind	Ind	
Sports Studies and Geography	BL68	3FT deg		10	M+D	D$	Ind	Ind	Ind	
Sports Studies and History	BV61	3FT deg		10	M+D	D$	Ind	Ind	Ind	
Sports Studies and Information Technology	BG65	3FT deg		10	M+D	D$	Ind	Ind	Ind	
Sports Studies and Religious Studies	BV68	3FT deg		10	M+D	D$	Ind	Ind	Ind	
NORTH EAST WALES INST of HE										
Sports Science	B600	3FT deg		8-12	3M	M$	Ind	BBB	N$	
Univ of NORTH LONDON										
Health Studies and Sports Management	BB96	3FT deg	* g	CC	Ind	Ind	Ind	Ind	Ind	
Human Nutrition and Sports Management	BB4P	3FT/4SW/4EXT deg	B/C g	12	MO+4D	DS	Ind	Ind	Ind	
Sports Science	B600	3FT/4SW/4EXT deg	B/(Ss+S)	12	4M $	MS	$	Ind	Ind	8/14
Sports Science & Fitness Evaluation (2 Yrs)	B601	2FT Dip	g	8-12	3M $	MS go	Ind	Ind	Ind	
Sports Science and Human Nutrition	BB46	3FT/4SW/4EXT deg	B/Ss	12	4M $	MS	$	Ind	Ind	

course details			98 expected requirements							96 entry stats	
TITLE	CODE	COURSE	SUBJECTS	A/AS	ND/C	RGNVQ	IB	SQA(H)	SQA	RATIO	A/AS
Sports Science and Sports Therapy	BW68	3FT/4SW/4EXT deg	B/(Ss+S)	18	5M $	MS	$	Ind	Ind		12/16
Sports and Biological Sciences	CB16	3FT/4SW/4EXT deg	B/(Ss+S)	12	4M $	MS	$	Ind	Ind		
Combined Honours Arts Management	Y400	3FT deg	* g	14	MO+4D	Ind	Ind	CCCC	Ind		
Combined Honours Sports Management	Y400	3FT deg	* g	14	MO+4D	Ind	Ind	CCCC	Ind		
Combined Honours Sports Science	Y100	3FT/4SW/4EXT deg	B/Ss	12	4M $	MS	Ind	Ind	Ind		

Univ of NORTHUMBRIA

Geography and Sport Studies	LB86	3FT deg	g	BCC	1M+5D	D+/^	28	BBBBC	Ind		
Sport Studies	B6N7	3FT deg	g	BCC	1M+5D	D+/^	28	BBBBC	Ind	17	14/26

NOTTINGHAM TRENT Univ

Sport & Exercise Science & IT for Science	BG6M	3FT deg	B+Pe/Ss g	16	Ind	Ind	Dip	B	Ind		
Sport & Exercise Science and Biology	BC61	3FT deg	B g	18	Ind	Ind	Dip	B	Ind		
Sport & Exercise Science and Chemistry	BF61	3FT deg	C+B/Pe/Ss g	16	Ind	Ind	Dip	B	Ind		
Sport & Exercise Science and Computing	BG65	3FT deg	B+Pe/Ss g	16	Ind	Ind	Dip	B	Ind		
Sport & Exercise Science and Mathematics	BG61	3FT deg	M+B/Pe/Ss g	16	Ind	Ind	Dip	B	Ind		
Sport & Exercise Science and Physics	BF63	3FT deg	M/P+B/Pe/Ss g	16	Ind	Ind	Dip	B	Ind		
Sport (Administration & Science)	BN67	3FT deg	S/M g	BB	Ind	Ind	Dip	BBC	$		
Sport Science (Administration and Coaching)	B6N7▼	3FT deg	S g	CC	Ind	Ind	Dip	BB	$		
Sports Science and Sports Injuries	BB69▼	3FT deg	S/Pe/Ss g	CCC	Ind	Ind	Dip	BB	Ind		
Sport (Coaching, Business and Exercise Science)	9X6B▼	2FT HND	* g	DD	N	Ind	Dip	C	$		
Sport (Science and Recreation Management)	76NB▼	2FT HND	S/Pe/Ss g	6	MO	Ind	Dip	C	$		2/ 8
Sport Science (Administration & Coaching)	7N6B▼	2FT HND	S g	DD	Ind	Ind	Dip	C	$		
Sport Science with Sports Injuries	9B6B▼	2FT HND	S/Pe/Ss g	DD	Ind	Ind	Dip	C	Ind		

OXFORD BROOKES Univ

Exercise & Health/Cartography	FB86	3FT deg	S	DD-CC	Ind	MS	Ind	Ind	Ind		
Exercise & Health/English Studies	QB36	3FT deg	S g	DD-AB	Ind	MS/M*^	Ind	Ind	Ind		
Exercise & Health/Environmental Sciences	FBX6	3FT deg	S g	DD-CD	Ind	MS/DS	Ind	Ind	Ind		
Exercise and Health/Accounting and Finance	NB46	3FT deg	S	DD-BCC	Ind	MS/D*3	Ind	Ind	Ind		
Exercise and Health/Anthropology	LB66	3FT deg	S	DD-BCC	Ind	MS^	Ind	Ind	Ind		
Exercise and Health/Biological Chemistry	CB76	3FT deg									
Exercise and Health/Biology	CB16	3FT deg	S g	DD	Ind	MS	Ind	Ind	Ind		
Exercise and Health/Business Admin & Management	NB16	3FT deg	S	DD-BBC	Ind	MS/MB4	Ind	Ind	Ind		
Exercise and Health/Cell Biology	BC6C	3FT deg									
Exercise and Health/Combined Studies	BY64	3FT deg		X		X	X	X			
Exercise and Health/Computer Systems	GB66	3FT deg	S g	DD-BC	Ind	MS	Ind	Ind	Ind		
Exercise and Health/Computing	GB56	3FT deg	S g	DD-BC	Ind	MS	Ind	Ind	Ind		
Exercise and Health/Computing Mathematics	GB96	3FT deg	S g	DD-CD	Ind	MS	Ind	Ind	Ind		
Exercise and Health/Ecology	CB96	3FT deg	S g	DD-CD	Ind	MS	Ind	Ind	Ind		
Exercise and Health/Economics	LB16	3FT deg	S g	DD-BB	Ind	MS/M*3	Ind	Ind	Ind		
Exercise and Health/Educational Studies	XB96	3FT deg	S g	CD-CC	Ind	MS/M*3	Ind	Ind	Ind		
Exercise and Health/Electronics	HB66	3FT deg	S/M	DD-CC	Ind	MS	Ind	Ind	Ind		
Exercise and Health/Environmental Chemistry	BF61	3FT deg									
Exercise and Health/Environmental Policy	KB36	3FT deg									
Fine Art/Exercise and Health	WB16	3FT deg	Pf+A+S	DD-BC	Ind	MA^/MS	Ind	Ind	Ind		
Food Science and Nutrition/Exercise and Health	DB46	3FT deg	S g	DD	Ind	MS	Ind	Ind	Ind		
French Language and Contemp St/Exercise & Health	RBC6	4SW deg	F+S	DD-CC	Ind	MS	Ind	Ind	Ind		
French Language and Literature/Exercise & Health	RB16	4SW deg	F+S	DD-CC	Ind	MS^	Ind	Ind	Ind		
Geography and the Phys Env/Exercise and Health	BF6V	3FT deg									
Geography/Exercise and Health	LB86	3FT deg	S	DD-BB	Ind	MS	Ind	Ind	Ind		
Geology/Exercise and Health	FB66	3FT deg	S/M g	DD	Ind	PS/MS	Ind	Ind	Ind		

	course details		98 expected requirements							96 entry stats

TITLE	CODE	COURSE	SUBJECTS	A/AS	NO/C	AGNVQ	IB	SQA(H)	SQA	RATIO A/AS
Geotechnics/Exercise and Health	HB26	3FT deg	S/M/Ds/Es	DD-CC	Ind	M$	Ind	Ind	Ind	
German Language & Literature/Exercise & Health	RB26	4SW deg	G+S/M	DD-DDD	Ind		Ind	Ind	Ind	
German Language and Contemp St/Exercise & Health	RBF6	4SW deg	G+S g	DD-DDD	Ind	MS^	Ind	Ind	Ind	
German Studies/Exercise and Health	BR6G	3FT deg								
Health Care/Exercise and Health (Post Exp)	BB67	3FT deg		X		X	X	X		
History of Art/Exercise and Health	VB46	3FT deg	S g	DD-BCC	Ind	MS/M*^	Ind	Ind	Ind	
History/Exercise and Health	VB16	3FT deg	S g	DD-BB	Ind	MS^	Ind	Ind	Ind	
Hospitality Management Studies/Exercise & Health	NB76	3FT deg	S/M	DD-CC	Ind	MS/M*3	Ind	Ind	Ind	
Human Biology/Exercise and Health	BB16	3FT deg								
Information Systems/Exercise and Health	GBM6	3FT deg	S g	DD-BC	Ind	MS	Ind	Ind	Ind	
Intelligent Systems/Exercise and Health	GB86	3FT deg	S g	DD-CD	Ind	MS	Ind	Ind	Ind	
Law/Exercise and Health	MB36	3FT deg	S g	DD-BBB	Ind	MS/D*3	Ind	Ind	Ind	
Leisure Planning/Exercise and Health	KBH6	3FT deg								
Marketing Management/Exercise and Health	NBN6	3FT deg	S g	DD-BCC	Ind	MS/D*3	Ind	Ind	Ind	
Mathematics/Exercise and Health	GB16	3FT deg	M g	DD-DDE	Ind	MS/M^	Ind	Ind	Ind	
Music/Exercise and Health	WB36	3FT deg	Mu+S g	DD	Ind	MS	Ind	Ind	Ind	
Palliative Care/Exercise and Health (Post Exp)	BBR6	3FT deg		X		X	X	X		
Planning Studies/Exercise and Health	KB46	3FT deg	S g	DD-CC	Ind	MS	Ind	Ind	Ind	
Politics/Exercise and Health	MB16	3FT deg	S g	DD-AB	Ind	MS^	Ind	Ind	Ind	
Psychology/Exercise and Health	CB86	3FT deg	S g	DD-BBC	Ind	MS/M*^	Ind	Ind	Ind	
Publishing/Exercise and Health	PB56	3FT deg	S g	DD-BB	Ind	MS/M$3	Ind	Ind	Ind	
Rehabilitation/Exercise and Health (Post Exp)	BB6T	3FT deg		X		X	X	X		
Retail Management/Exercise & Health	NB56	3FT deg	S/M g	DD-CCD	Ind		Ind	Ind	Ind	
Sociology/Exercise and Health	LB36	3FT deg	S g	DD-BCC	Ind	MS/M*^	Ind	Ind	Ind	
Software Engineering/Exercise and Health	GB76	3FT deg	S g	DD-BC	Ind	MS	Ind	Ind	Ind	
Statistics/Exercise and Health	GB46	3FT deg	S g	DD	Ind	MS	Ind	Ind	Ind	
Telecommunications/Exercise and Health	HBP6	3FT deg								
Tourism/Exercise and Health	PB76	3FT deg	S g	DD-BC	Ind	MS/M*3	Ind	Ind	Ind	
Transport Planning/Exercise and Health	NB96	3FT deg	S g	DD-CC	Ind	MS	Ind	Ind	Ind	
Water Resources/Exercise and Health	BH6F	3FT deg								

Univ of PORTSMOUTH

TITLE	CODE	COURSE	SUBJECTS	A/AS	NO/C	AGNVQ	IB	SQA(H)	SQA	RATIO A/AS
Exercise and Health Science	BB69	3FT deg	S	16	MO	D$6/^	26	BBBB	Ind	
Sports Science	B600	3FT deg	S	18	MO	D$6/^	26	BBBB	Ind	
Sports Science (Foundation)	B608	3FT deg	*	Ind	Ind	Ind	Ind	Ind	Ind	4/14
Sports Technology	B650	3FT deg	S	16	MO	D$6/^	26	BBBB	Ind	

Univ College of RIPON & YORK ST JOHN

TITLE	CODE	COURSE	SUBJECTS	A/AS	NO/C	AGNVQ	IB	SQA(H)	SQA	RATIO A/AS
Applied Social Sciences/Physical Education	L3B6	3FT deg		CC	MO	M*	27	BBBC		
Geography/Physical Education	L8B6	3FT deg	Gy	CCD	X	M*^	30	BBBB		
Physical Education/Applied Social Sciences	B6L3	3FT deg		BB-CCC	MO+3D	D$6/^	30	ABBB		
Physical Education/Geography	B6L8	3FT deg	Gy	BB-CCC	X	D$^	30	ABBB		
Physical Education/Management Studies	B6N1	3FT deg	g	BB-CCC	MO+3D	D$6/^ g	30	ABBB		
Physical Education/Psychology	B6L7	3FT deg	g	BB-CCC	MO+3D	D$6/^	30	ABBB		
Psychology/Physical Education	L7B6	3FT deg	g	16	M	M	30	BBBB		

ROEHAMPTON INST

TITLE	CODE	COURSE	SUBJECTS	A/AS	NO/C	AGNVQ	IB	SQA(H)	SQA	RATIO A/AS
Leisure Managment Studies and Sports Studies	BN67	3FT deg								
Sport Studies	B6L3▼	3FT deg	S g	14	3D		30	BBC	N	
Sport Studies and Applied Consumer Studies	NB96▼	3FT deg	S g	12	3D	MS go	30	BBC	N$	
Sport Studies and Art for Commmunity	BW61▼	3FT deg	S g	12	3D	MS go	30	BBC	N$	
Sport Studies and Biology	CB16▼	3FT deg	B g	12	3D $	MS go	30	BBC	N$	
Sport Studies and Business Computing	GB76▼	3FT deg	S g	12	2M+2D	M$ go	28	BCC	N$	
Sport Studies and Business Studies	NB16▼	3FT deg	S g	12	3D	MS go	30	BBC	Ind	

			98 expected requirements							96 entry stats
TITLE	CODE	COURSE	SUBJECTS	A/AS	ND/C	RGNVQ	IB	SQA(H)	SQA	RATIO A/AS
Sport Studies and Dance Studies	WB46▼	3FT deg	S g	CC	3D	MS^ go	30	BBC	Ind	
Sport Studies and Drama & Theatre Studies	BW6L▼	3FT deg	E/T g	16	2M+2D$	MS^ go	30	BBC	Ind	
Sport Studies and Education	XB96▼	3FT deg	S g	12	3D	MS go	30	BBC	N$	
Sport Studies and English Language & Linguistics	QBH6▼	3FT deg	S+E/L g	CC	3D $	MS go	30	BBC	Ind	
Sport Studies and English Literature	QB36▼	3FT deg	S+E g	CC	3D $	MS^ go	30	BBC	Ind	
Sport Studies and Environmental Studies	FB96▼	3FT deg	B/Gy g	12	3D $	MS go	30	BBC	N$	
Sport Studies and Film & Television Studies	PB46▼	3FT deg	S g	16	3D	MS^ go	30	BBC	N$	
Sport Studies and French	RB16▼	4FT deg	F+S g	12	3D	M^ go	30	BBC	N$	
Sport Studies and Geography	LB86▼	3FT deg	Gy g	12	3D $	MS go	30	BBC	N$	
Sport Studies and Health Studies	BB69▼	3FT deg	B g	12	3D	MS go	30	BBC	N$	
Sport Studies and History	VB16▼	3FT deg	H g	12	3D $	M^ go	30	BBC	N$	
Sport Studies and Human & Social Biology	CBC6▼	3FT deg	B g	12	3D $	MS go	30	BBC	N$	
Sport Studies and Music	WB36▼	3FT deg	Mu g	12	3D $	M^ go	30	BBC	N$	
Sport Studies and Natural Resource Studies	DB26▼	3FT deg	g	12	2M+2D	M$ go	28	BCC	N$	
Sport Studies and Psychology	LB76▼	3FT deg	S g	CC	3D	MS go	30	BBC	Ind	
Sport Studies and Social Policy & Administration	LB46▼	3FT deg	S g	12	3D	MS go	30	BBC	N$	
Sport Studies and Sociology	LB36▼	3FT deg	S g	12	3D	MS go	30	BBC	N$	
Sport Studies and Spanish	RB46▼	4FT deg	Sp+S g	12	3D	MS go	30	BBC	N$	
Theology & Religious Studies and Sport Studies	BV68▼	3FT deg	S g	12	3D	MS go	30	BBC	N$	
Women's Studies and Sport Studies	BM69▼	3FT deg	S g	12	3D	MS go	30	BBC	N$	

Univ of SALFORD

Exercise and Health Sciences	BB69	3FT deg								
Sports Rehabilitation	BB96	3FT deg								16/22

SHEFFIELD HALLAM Univ

Sport and Exercise Science	B600	3FT deg	S g	16	6M+4D	D	Ind	Ind	Ind	
Combined Studies *Sports Science*	Y400	3FT deg	*	14	2M	M	Ind	Ind	Ind	

Univ College of St MARTIN, LANCASTER AND CUMBRIA

Applied Community Studies/Physical Ed & Spts Std	LX5X	3FT deg	*	CD-DDE	3M+2D	M*	28	BCCC		
English/Physical Education & Sports Studies	QX3X	3FT deg	E	BC-BDE	X	P^	28$	BBBC$		
Geography/Physical Education & Sports Studies	LX8X	3FT deg	Gy	CD-DDE	X	P^	28$	BCCC$		
Health Studies/Physical Education & Sports Stds	BX9X	3FT deg	*	CD-DDE	3M+2D	M	28	BCCC		
History/Physical Education & Sports Studies	VX1X	3FT deg	H	CD-DDE	X	P^	28$	BCCC$		
Mathematics/Physical Education & Sports Studies	GX1X	3FT deg	M	DD-DEE	X	P^	28$	BCCC$		
Outdoor Studies	X900▼	3FT deg	g	BC-CDD	3M+3D	M	28$	BBBC$		
Religious Studies/Physical Education & Sports St	VX8X	3FT deg	*	CD-DDE	3M+2D	M*	28	BCCC		
Science, Technology & Society/PE & Sport Studies	XYX1	3FT deg	g	CD-DDE	3M+2D	M	28	BCCC		
Sports Science	B600	3FT deg	* g	BB-CCD	3M+3D	M^	28	BBBB	Ind	

SOLIHULL COLL

Sports Science	006B	2FT HND	*	E	N	P	Ind	Ind	Ind	

SOUTH BANK Univ

Sport and Exercise Science	B600	3FT deg	S g	DD	N	M go	Ind	Ind	Ind	
Sports Product Design	H7B6	3FT deg	S+Ad/A g	14-18	2M+4D	M go	Ind	Ind	Ind	
Sports Science and Accounting	BN64	3FT deg	S+Ec/Ac g	12-16	4M+2D	M go	Ind	Ind	Ind	
Sports Science and Computing	BG65	3FT deg	S+M g	12-16	4M+2D	M go	Ind	Ind	Ind	
Sports Science and English Studies	BQ63	3FT deg	E+S g	14-18	X	M^ go	Ind	Ind	Ind	
Sports Science and Environmental Policy	BF69	3FT deg	S g	14-18	4M+2D	M go	Ind	Ind	Ind	
Sports Science and European Studies	BT62	3FT deg	S g	14-18	2M+4D	M go	Ind	Ind	Ind	
Sports Science and German	BR6F	3FT deg	S+G g	14-18	2M+4D	M^ go	Ind	Ind	Ind	

course details

98 expected requirements

96 entry stats

TITLE	CODE	COURSE	SUBJECTS	A/AS	NO/C	AGNVQ	IB	SQA(H)	SQA	RATIO A/AS
Sports Science and Health Studies	BL64	3FT deg	S g	12-16	4M+2D	M go	Ind	Ind	Ind	
Sports Science and Housing	BK6K	3FT deg	S g	14-18	2M+4D	M go	Ind	Ind	Ind	
Sports Science and Human Geography	BL68	3FT deg	Gy+S g	12-16	4M+2D	M go	Ind	Ind	Ind	
Sports Science and Human Resource Management	BN66	3FT deg	S g	14-18	2M+4D	M go	Ind	Ind	Ind	
Sports Science and Law	BM63	3FT deg	S g	14-18	2M+4D	M go	Ind	Ind	Ind	
Sports Science and Management	BN61	3FT deg	S g	12-16	4M+2D	M go	Ind	Ind	Ind	
Sports Science and Marketing	BN65	3FT deg	S g	14-18	2M+4D	M go	Ind	Ind	Ind	
Sports Science and Media Studies	BP64	3FT deg	E+S g	14-18	2M+4D	M go	Ind	Ind	Ind	
Sports Science and Politics	BM61	3FT deg	S g	14-18	2M+4D	M go	Ind	Ind	Ind	
Sports Science and Psychology	BC68	3FT deg	S g	14-18	2M+4D	M go	Ind	Ind	Ind	
Technology and Sports Science	BJ69	3FT deg	S g	12-16	4M+2D	M go	Ind	Ind	Ind	
Tourism and Sports Science	BP67	3FT deg	S+L g	12-16	4M+2D	M go	Ind	Ind	Ind	
Urban Studies and Sports Science	KB46	3FT deg	S g	14-18	2M+4D	M go	Ind	Ind	Ind	
World Theatre and Sports Science	BW64	3FT deg	S g	14-18	2M+4D	M go	Ind	Ind	Ind	

SOUTHWARK COLL

TITLE	CODE	COURSE	SUBJECTS	A/AS	NO/C	AGNVQ	IB	SQA(H)	SQA	RATIO A/AS
Sports Coaching and Management	76NB	2FT HND	Bu/S/Ss/Pe/Ph	E	Ind	Ind	Ind	Ind	Ind	

ST HELENS COLL

TITLE	CODE	COURSE	SUBJECTS	A/AS	NO/C	AGNVQ	IB	SQA(H)	SQA	RATIO A/AS
Sports Studies	006B	2FT HND	B/Pe/Ss	2	N$	P$	Ind	Ind	Ind	

THE UNIVERSITY COLLEGE OF ST MARK AND ST JOHN

TITLE	CODE	COURSE	SUBJECTS	A/AS	NO/C	AGNVQ	IB	SQA(H)	SQA	RATIO A/AS
Community Studies/Sports Science	L5B6	3FT deg		10	MO	M	Dip	Ind	Ind	
Geography/Sports Science	L8B6	3FT deg	Gy	8-10	MO	M	Ind	Indd	Ind	
Information Technology/Sports Science	G5B6	3FT deg		4	MO	M	Dip	CCCC	Ind	
Leisure & Tourism Studies/Sports Science	P7B6	3FT deg		8	MO	M	Ind	Ind	Ind	
Public Relations/Sports Science	P3B6	3FT deg		16	MO	M	Ind	Ind	Ind	
Sports Science/Community Studies	B6L5	3FT deg		8	MO	M	Ind	Ind	Ind	
Sports Science/Geography	B6L8	3FT deg		8	SPO	M	Ind	Ind	Ind	
Sports Science/Information Technology	B6G5	3FT deg		8	MO	M	Ind	Ind	Ind	
Sports Science/Leisure & Tourism Studies	B6P7	3FT deg		8	MO	M	Ind	Ind	Ind	
Sports Science/Public Relations	B6P3	3FT deg		8	MO	M	Ind	Ind	Ind	

ST MARY'S Univ COLL

TITLE	CODE	COURSE	SUBJECTS	A/AS	NO/C	AGNVQ	IB	SQA(H)	SQA	RATIO A/AS
Sport Rehabilitation and Sport Science	BB96	3FT deg	B g	12-14	X	X	Ind	BBBB$	X	
Sport Science and Biology	CB16	3FT deg	B/C g	8-12	Ind	Ind	Ind	BBBB$	Ind	
Sport Science and Drama	WBL6	3FT deg	S g	12-14	Ind	Ind	Ind	BBBB$	Ind	
Sport Science and English	QB36	3FT deg	E+S g	12-14	X	X	Ind	BBBB$	X	
Sport Science and Environmental Investigation St	BF69	3FT deg	S/2S g	8-12	Ind	Ind	Ind	BBBB	Ind	
Sport Science and Environmental Studies	BF6X	3FT deg	S g	8-12	Ind	Ind	Ind	BBBB	Ind	
Sport Science and Gender Studies	BM69	3FT deg	S g	8-12	Ind	Ind	Ind	BBBB$	Ind	
Sport Science and Geography	FB86	3FT deg	Gy+S g	8-12	Ind	Ind	Ind	BBBB$	Ind	
Sport Science and Heritage Management	BN69	3FT deg	S g	8-12	Ind	Ind	Ind	BBBB$	Ind	
Sport Science and History	VB16	3FT deg	H+S g	8-12	Ind	Ind	Ind	BBBB$	Ind	
Sport Science and Integrated Scientific Studies	BY61	3FT deg	S/2S g	8-12	Ind	Ind	Ind	BBBB$	Ind	
Sport Science and Irish Studies	QB56	3FT deg	S g	8-12	Ind	Ind	Ind	BBBB$	Ind	
Sport Science and Media Arts	BP64	3FT deg	S g	8-12	Ind	Ind	Ind	BBBB$	Ind	
Theology and Religious Studies and Sport Science	VB86	3FT deg	S g	8-12	Ind	Ind	Ind	BBBB$	Ind	

STAFFORDSHIRE Univ

TITLE	CODE	COURSE	SUBJECTS	A/AS	NO/C	AGNVQ	IB	SQA(H)	SQA	RATIO A/AS
Sport Sciences and Biology	BC61	3FT deg	S	14	Ind	D	Ind	BBCC	Ind	
Sport Sciences and Chemistry	BF61	3FT deg	S	14	Ind	D	Ind	BBCC	Ind	
Sport Sciences and Electronics	BH66	3FT deg	S	14	Ind	D	Ind	BBCC	Ind	
Sport Sciences and Geography	BF68	3FT deg	S	14	Ind	D	Ind	BBCC	Ind	
Sport Sciences and Geology	BF66	3FT deg	S	14	Ind	D	Ind	BBCC	Ind	
Sport Sciences and Information Systems	BG65	3FT deg	S	14	Ind	D	Ind	BBCC	Ind	

course details				98 expected requirements						96 entry stats
TITLE	CODE	COURSE	SUBJECTS	A/AS	ND/C	AGNVQ	IB	SQA(H)	SQA	RATIO A/AS
Sport Sciences and Physics	BF63	3FT deg	S	14	Ind	D	Ind	BBCC	Ind	
Sport Sciences and Psychology	BC68	3FT deg								
Sport and Leisure Management	BN67	3FT deg	*	16	2M+4D	D	Ind	BBCC	Ind	
Sport and Leisure Studies	BL63	3FT deg	*	16	2M+4D	D	Ind	BBCC	Ind	
Sport, Recreation and Tourism	PB76	3FT deg	*	16	2M+4D	DL	28	BBCC	Ind	
Sports Equipment Technology	H3B6	4EXT deg	g	EE	P $	P$	Ind	Ind	Ind	
Sports Studies	B600	3FT deg	*	16	2M+4D	D	Ind	BBCC	Ind	
Sports and Exercise Sciences	B601	3FT deg	S	14	Ind	D	Ind	BBCC	Ind	

Univ of STIRLING

Accountancy/Sports Studies	NB46	4FT deg	g	BCC	HN	Ind	33	BBBB	HN	
Business Studies/Sports Studies	NB16	4FT deg	g	BBC	Ind	Ind	33	BBBB	HN	
Economics/Sports Studies	LB16	4FT deg	g	CCC	Ind	Ind	28	BBCC	HN	
Financial Studies/Sports Studies	NB36	4FT deg	g	BCC	Ind	Ind	31	BBBC	HN	
Human Resources Management/Sports Studies	NBC6	4FT deg	g	BBC	Ind	Ind	33	BBBB	HN	
Management Science/Sports Studies	NBD6	4FT deg	g	BCC	Ind	Ind	31	BBBC	HN	
Marketing/Sports Studies	NB56	4FT deg	g	BBC	Ind	Ind	33	BBBB	HN	

Univ of STRATHCLYDE

Sport and Exercise Science	B600	4FT deg	M+S g	BB	Ind		Ind	AAB$	Ind	
Sport in the Community	BX69	3FT/4FT deg	E g	CC	Ind		Ind	BBC$	Ind	

Univ of SUNDERLAND

Sport, Physical Activity and Health	BB69	3FT/4SW deg	S g	18	3M+2D$ MS^		28	BBCCC	Ind	
Sports Science	B600	3FT/4SW deg	S g	18	3M+2D$ MS^		28	BBCCC	Ind	
Sports Science (Foundation)	B608▼	4EXT/5EXTSW deg	*							

Univ of Wales SWANSEA

Sports Science	B600	3FT deg	S g	BCC-BBB	1M+5D$	Ind	28$	BBBBB$	X	

Univ of TEESSIDE

Sport Science	B600	3FT deg	*	16	Ind		Ind	Ind	Ind	
Sport Science and Mathematics	BG61	3FT/4SW deg	*	16	Ind		Ind	Ind	Ind	
Sports Science and Mathematics	GB16	3FT deg								
Modular Degree Scheme *Sport Science*	Y401	3FT deg								

Univ of ULSTER

Sport and Leisure St (3 Yr or 4 Yr SW inc DIS)	BN67▼	3FT/4SW deg	* g	BBC	MO+4D	D*6/^ gi	32	ABBB	Ind	22 20/26

Univ Col WARRINGTON

Sports Studies with Business Management and IT	BN61	3FT deg	* g	12-14	Ind	Ind	Ind	Ind	Ind	

WESTHILL COLL

Humanities - Sport, PE and Community Studies	B6L4	3FT deg	* g	CC	4M+2D	M^	Ind	Ind	Ind	

WIGAN and LEIGH COLL

Sports Science (Sports Studies)	006B▼	2FT HND		6	N	Ind	Dip		N	

Univ of WOLVERHAMPTON

Sports Studies (Specialist Route)	BN67	3FT deg		14	4M	M	24	BBBB	Ind	
Applied Sciences *Exercise Science*	Y100	3FT/4SW deg	g	DD	N	M	24	CCCC	Ind	
Applied Sciences (4 yrs) *Exercise Science*	Y110	4FT deg	*							
Combined Degrees *Exercise Science*	Y401	3FT/4SW deg	g	DD	N	M	24	CCCC	Ind	
Combined Degrees *Sports Studies*	Y401	3FT deg		14	4M	M	24	BBBB	Ind	

course details			98 expected requirements							96 entry stats
TITLE	CODE	COURSE	SUBJECTS	A/AS	ND/C	AGNVQ	IB	SQA(H)	SQA	RATIO A/AS
WORCESTER COLL of HE										
Sports Studies	B6X9	3FT deg		CC	Ind	M	Ind	Ind	Ind	
Sports Studies/Biological Science	CB16	3FT deg	S	CC	Ind	M	Ind	Ind	Ind	
Sports Studies/Business Management	NB16	3FT deg		CC	Ind	M	Ind	Ind	Ind	
Sports Studies/Education Studies	XB96	3FT deg		CC	Ind	M	Ind	Ind	Ind	
Sports Studies/English and Literary Studies	QB36	3FT deg		CC	Ind	M	Ind	Ind	Ind	
Sports Studies/Geography	LB86	3FT deg		CC	Ind	M	Ind	Ind	Ind	
Sports Studies/Health Studies	BB96	3FT deg	g	CC	Ind	M	Ind	Ind	Ind	
Sports Studies/History	VB16	3FT deg		CC	Ind	M	Ind	Ind	Ind	
Sports Studies/Information Technology	GB56	3FT deg		CC	Ind	M	Ind	Ind	Ind	
Sports Studies/Sociology	LB36	3FT deg		CC	Ind	M	Ind	Ind	Ind	
YORKSHIRE COAST COLLEGE of F and HE										
Science (Sports Studies)	006B	2FT HND	*	6	4M	M	Ind	Ind	Ind	

				98 expected requirements						96 entry stats	
TITLE	CODE	COURSE	SUBJECTS	A/AS	NO/C	AGNVQ	IB	SQA(H)	SQA	RATIO A/AS	

ANGLIA Poly Univ

Art	XW71▼	3FT deg	A g	12	4M	M	Dip$	BCCC	Ind		
Modern Languages (French)	XR71▼	2FT deg	* g							3	
Primary	X500▼	3FT deg	* g	12	4M	M^ go	Dip	BCCC	N	6	8/22
Science	XY71▼	2FT deg	S g	12	4M	M go	Dip$	BCCC	Ind	2	

Univ of Wales, BANGOR

Art and Craft and Design	X5W9	3FT deg	Ad g	10	4M	M$ go	Ind	Ind	Ind		
Design & Technology	X7W2	3FT deg	Ds g	10	4M	M$ go	Ind	Ind	Ind		
Design and Technology	X5W2	3FT deg	Ds g	10	4M	M$ go	Ind	Ind	Ind		
English Literature	X5Q3	3FT deg	E g	12	4M	M$ go	Ind	Ind	Ind		
Geography	X5L8	3FT deg	Gy g	10	4M	M$ go	Ind	Ind	Ind		
History	X5V1	3FT deg	H g	10	4M	M$ go	Ind	Ind	Ind		
Mathematics	X5G1	3FT deg	M g	8	4M	M$ go	Ind	Ind	Ind		
Music	X5W3	3FT deg	Mu g	10	4M	M$ go	Ind	Ind	Ind		
Physical Education	X5X8	3FT deg	* g	12	4M	M$ go	Ind	Ind	Ind		
Religious Studies	X5V8	3FT deg	* g	10	4M	M$ go	Ind	Ind	Ind		
Science	X5Y1	3FT deg	S g	8	4M	M$ go	Ind	Ind	Ind		
Welsh (1st or 2nd Language)	X5Q5	3FT deg	* g	8	4M	M$ go	Ind	Ind	Ind		

Univ of BATH

Biology with Education (4 Yrs with QTS)	C1X7	4FT deg	B+S	20	Ind	Ind	28$	Ind	Ind		
Chemistry with Education (4 Yrs with QTS)	F1X7	4FT deg	C g	18	Ind	D^	28	Ind	Ind		
Physics with Education (4 Yrs with QTS)	F3X7	4FT deg	M+P	CCC	Ind	DS^	30	Ind	Ind		

BATH COLL of HE

Primary	X500	4FT deg	g	CD	$	$	Ind	Ind	Ind	9	8/22

BISHOP GROSSETESTE COLL

Art (Inc Art/Design) (nlp) (4 Yrs)	X2W1	4FT deg	A g	DD	9M	MA go	Ind	Ind	Ind		
Art (Inc Art/Design) (upr) (4 Yrs)	X4W1	4FT deg	A g	DD	9M	MA go	Ind	Ind	Ind		
Drama (nlp) (4 Yrs)	X2W4	4FT deg	* g	DD	9M	M*^ go	Ind	Ind	Ind		
Drama (upr) (4 Yrs)	X4W4	4FT deg	* g	DD	9M	M*^ go	Ind	Ind	Ind		
English (nlp) (4 Yrs)	X2Q3	4FT deg	E g	CD	9M	M*^ go	Ind	Ind	Ind		
English (upr) (4 Yrs)	X4Q3	4FT deg	E g	CD	9M	M*^ go	Ind	Ind	Ind		
Geography (nlp) (4 Yrs)	X2L8	4FT deg	Gy g	DD	9M	M*^ go	Ind	Ind	Ind		
Geography (upr) (4 Yrs)	X4L8	4FT deg	Gy g	DD	9M	M*^ go	Ind	Ind	Ind		
History (nlp) (4 Yrs)	X2V1	4FT deg	* g	DD	9M	M*^ go	Ind	Ind	Ind		
History (upr) (4 Yrs)	X4V1	4FT deg	* g	DD	9M	M*^ go	Ind	Ind	Ind		
Mathematics with Technology (nlp) (4 Yrs)	X2G1	4FT deg	M g	DD	9M	M*^ go	Dip$	Ind	Ind		
Mathematics with Technology (upr) (4 Yrs)	X4G1	4FT deg	M g	DD	9M	M*^ go	Ind	Ind	Ind		
Music (nlp) (4 Yrs)	X2W3	4FT deg	Mu g	DD	9M	M*^ go	Ind	Ind	Ind		
Music (upr) (4 Yrs)	X4W3	4FT deg	Mu g	DD	9M	M*^ go	Ind	Ind	Ind		
Primary Range (3 Yrs)	X500	3FT deg	M/E g	DC	X	X	Ind	Ind	Ind		
Religious Studies (nlp) (4 Yrs)	X2V8	4FT deg	* g	DD	9M	MG go	Ind	Ind	Ind		
Religious Studies (upr) (4 Yrs)	X4V8	4FT deg	* g	DD	9M	MG go	Ind	Ind	Ind		
Science (nlp) (4 Yrs)	X2Y1	4FT deg	B/C/P g	DD	9M	M*^ go	Ind	Ind	Ind		
Science (upr) (4 Yrs)	X4Y1	4FT deg	B/C/P g	DD	9M	M*^ go	Ind	Ind	Ind		

BOLTON INST

Law and Leisure Studies	MX38	3FT deg	* g	CD	MO	M g	24	BBCC	Ind		

BRADFORD & ILKLEY Comm COLL

Creative Arts, Art, Music and Drama	X501	3FT/4FT deg	g	8	MO	M	Dip	CCC	Ind		
Humanities, History, Geography and Religious St	X502	3FT/4FT deg	g	8	MO	M	Dip	CCC	Ind		

| | | | 98 expected requirements | | | | | | | 96 entry stats | |
| course details | | | | | | | | | | | |
TITLE	CODE	COURSE	SUBJECTS	A/AS	ND/C	AGNVQ	IB	SQA(H)	SQA	RATIO	A/AS
Primary Education with QTS - Language and Lit	X5T9	3FT/4FT deg	g	8	MO	M	Dip	CCC	Ind	9	6/20
Primary Education with QTS - Mathematics	X5G1	3FT/4FT deg	g	8	MO	M	Dip	CCC	Ind	6	
Primary Education with QTS - Science	X5Y1	3FT/4FT deg	g	8	MO	M	Dip	CCC	Ind	6	10/10
BRETTON HALL											
Art-Early Years Education (4 Yrs)	XW29	4FT deg	A	CD-CC	MO			Ind	CCC	Ind	5	8/18
Art-Primary Education (4 Yrs)	XW59	4FT deg	A	CD-CC	MO		Ind	CCC	Ind	4	8/20
English-Early Years Education (4 Yrs)	XQ23	4FT deg	E	CD-CC	MO		Ind	CCC	Ind	9	10/20
English-Primary Education (4 Yrs)	XQ53	4FT deg	E	CD-CC	MO		Ind	CCC	Ind	10	8/20
Environmental Science-Early Years Educ (4 Yrs)	XF29	4FT deg	S	CD-CC	MO		Ind	CCC	Ind	5	6/12
Environmental Science-Primary Education (4 Yrs)	XF59	4FT deg	S	CD-CC	MO		Ind	CCC	Ind	3	6/14
Music-Primary Education (4 Yrs)	XW53	4FT deg	Mu	CD-CC	MO		Ind	CCC	Ind	8	6/14
Secondary Technology	XJ79	2FT deg									
Univ of BRIGHTON											
Business Educ with Information Tech with QTS	X7N1	4FT deg	Ap g	12	3M $	MB go	Ind	BBCC$	Ind		
Business Education with QTS	X7NC	2FT deg	g	X	HN $	X	X	X	X		
Design and Technology Education with QTS	X7W2	2FT deg	* g	X	HN	X	Ind	Ind	Ind		
Design and Technology Education with QTS	X7WF	4FT deg	Ds g	12	Ind	M$ go	Ind	Ind	Ind		
Educ Upr Prim/Lwr Sec (7-14) QTS (Design & Tech)	XW62	4FT deg	DS g	12	Ind	M$ go	Ind	Ind	Ind		
Educ Upr Prim/Lwr Sec (7-14) QTS (English)	XQ63	4FT deg	E g	12	Ind	M$ go	Ind	Ind	Ind		
Educ Upr Prim/Lwr Sec (7-14) QTS (Mathematics)	XG61	4FT deg	M g	12	Ind	M$ go	Ind	Ind	Ind		
Educ Upr Prim/Lwr Sec (7-14) QTS (Physical Educa	XX68	3 deg									
Educ Upr Prim/Lwr Sec (7-14) QTS (Religious St)	XV68	4FT deg	Re g	12	Ind	M$ go	Ind	Ind	Ind		
Educ Upr Prim/Lwr Sec (7-14) QTS (Science)	XY61	4FT deg	S g	12	Ind	M$ go	Ind	Ind	Ind		
Educ Upr Prim/Lwr Sec (7-14) QTS Modern Language	XT62	3FT deg									
Information Technology Education with QTS	X7G5	2FT deg	g	X	HN	X	Ind	Ind	Ind		
Maths Education with QTS	XG71	2FT deg	g	X	HN $	X	X	X	X		
Modern Languages with QTS	X7T2	2FT deg	g	X	HN $	X	X	X	X		
Physical Education with QTS	X7X8	4FT deg	* g	BC	3M+3D	D/M^/M6 go	26	BBBB	Ind		
Primary Education-Early Yrs (3-8) with QTS	X200	4FT deg	* g	12	DO	M go	Ind	Ind	Ind		
Primary Education-Later Yrs (7-12) with QTS	X400	4FT deg	* g	12	DO	M go	Ind	Ind	Ind		
Science Education with QTS	XF79	2FT deg	g	X	HN $	X	X	X	X		
BRISTOL, Univ of the W of England											
Art (QTS)	X3W9	4FT deg	A g	10	3M $	P$^ go	24$	CCC$	Ind		
Art (QTS)	X4W9	4FT deg	A g	10	3M $	P$^ go	24$	CCC$	Ind		
Biological Science (QTS)	X3C1	4FT deg	B g	10	3M $	P$^ go	24$	CCC$	Ind		
Biological Science (QTS)	X4C1	4FT deg	B g	10	3M $	P$^ go	24$	CCC$	Ind		
Business Education (QTS)	XN71	4FT deg	Bu/Ec g	EE	3M $	P$^ go	24$	CC$	Ind		
Design and Technology (QTS 7-14)	X6W2	4FT deg	Ap g	10	X	P$^ go	24$	CCC$	Ind		
Design and Technology (QTS)	XW72	4FT deg	Ds g	EE	3M $	P$^ go	24$	CC$	Ind		
English (QTS)	X4Q3	4FT deg	El g	10	X	P$^ go	24$	CCC$	Ind		
English (QTS)	X3Q3	4FT deg	El g	10	X	P$^ go	24$	CCC$	Ind		
Geography (QTS)	X3L8	4FT deg	Gy g	10	X	P$^ go	24$	CCC$	Ind		
Geography (QTS)	X4L8	4FT deg	Gy g	10	X	P$^ go	24$	CCC$	Ind		
History (QTS)	X4V1	4FT deg	H g	10	X	P$^ go	24$	CCC$	Ind		
History (QTS)	X3V1	4FT deg	H g	10	X	P$^ go	24$	CCC$	Ind		
Mathematics (QTS)	X3G1	4FT deg	M g	10	X	P$^ go	24$	CCC$	Ind		
Mathematics (QTS)	X4G1	4FT deg	M g	10	X	P$^ go	24$	CCC$	Ind		
Mathematics (QTS)	XG71	4FT deg	M g	EE	X	P$^ go	24$	CC$	Trind		
Secondary Business Education (QTS)	X7N1	2FT deg	g	X	HN $	X	X	X	Ind		
Secondary Design and Technology (QTS)	X7W2	2FT deg	g	X	HN $	X	X	X	Ind		
Secondary Mathematics (QTS)	X7G1	2FT deg	g	X	HN $	X	X	X	X		

			98 expected requirements							96 entry stats	
TITLE	CODE	COURSE	SUBJECTS	A/AS	NO/C	AGNVQ	IB	SQA(H)	SQA	RATIO	A/AS
BRUNEL Univ, West London											
Education Primary (BA/QTS)	X500	3FT deg	* g	14-16	MO $	M* go	20$	BCCC$	Ind		
Secondary Edu & Phys Ed with English (BA/QTS)	X7X8	4FT deg	E g	16	MO	M+ go	26$	BCCC$	Ind		
Secondary Edu & Phys Ed with Geography (BSc/QTS)	X7XV	4FT deg	Gy/Gl g	16	MO	M+ go	26$	BCCC$	Ind		
Secondary Edu & Phys Ed with Relig Studs (BA/QTS)	X701	4FT deg	* g	16	MO	M+ go	26$	BCCC$	Ind		
Secondary Educ & Phys Ed with Bus IT (BSc/QTS)	X7XW	4FT deg	* g	16	MO	M+ go	26$	BCCC$	Ind		
CAMBRIDGE Univ											
Biological Sciences with Education (4 years QTS)	XC51▼	4FT deg	B g	BCC	Ind		30$		Ind	4	18/26
Drama with Education (4 years QTS)	XW54▼	4FT deg	* g	BCC	Ind		30$		Ind	4	18/26
English with Education (4 years QTS)	XQ53▼	4FT deg	* g	BBC	Ind		30$		Ind	4	18/28
Geography with Education (4 years QTS)	XL58▼	4FT deg	* g	BCC	Ind		30$		Ind	4	18/28
History with Education (4 years QTS)	XV51▼	4FT deg	* g	BCC	Ind		30$		Ind	3	20/24
Mathematics with Education (4 years QTS)	XG51▼	4FT deg	M g	BCC	Ind		30$		Ind	3	16/28
Music with Education (4 years QTS)	XW53▼	4FT deg	Mu g	BCC	Ind		30$		Ind	2	16/24
Religious Studies with Education (4 years QTS)	XV58▼	4FT deg	* g	BCC	Ind		30$		Ind	2	16/24
CANTERBURY CHRIST CHURCH COLL of HE											
Art QTS (lpr)	XW31	4FT deg	A g	CC	MO	M	24	Ind	Ind	12	
Art QTS (upr)	XW41	4FT deg	A g	CC	MO	M	24	Ind	Ind	14	
Early Years Education (nursery/lower primary)	X200	4FT deg	* g	CC	MO	M	24	Ind	Ind		
English QTS (lpr)	XQ33	4FT deg	E g	CC	MO	M	24	Ind	Ind	7	12/24
English QTS (upr)	XQ43	4FT deg	E g	CC	MO	M	24	Ind	Ind	7	11/16
Geography QTS (lpr)	XL38	4FT deg	Gy g	CC	MO	M	24	Ind	Ind	9	
Geography QTS (upr)	XL48	4FT deg	Gy g	CC	MO	M	24	Ind	Ind	9	18/22
History QTS (lpr)	XV31	4FT deg	H g	CC	MO	M	24	Ind	Ind	7	
History QTS (upr)	XV41	4FT deg	H g	CC	MO	M	24	Ind	Ind	11	
Lower Primary QTS (4-8 years)	X300	4FT deg	* g	CC	MO	M	24	Ind	Ind		
Mathematics QTS (lpr)	XG31	4FT deg	M g	CC	MO	M	24	Ind	Ind	5	
Mathematics QTS (upr)	XG41	4FT deg	M g	CC	MO	M	24	Ind	Ind	13	
Music QTS (lpr)	XW33	4FT deg	Mu g	CC	MO	M	24	Ind	Ind	18	
Music QTS (upr)	XW43	4FT deg	Mu g	CC	MO	M	24	Ind	Ind		
Religious Studies QTS (lpr)	XV38	4FT deg	* g	CC	MO	M	24	Ind	Ind	5	
Religious Studies QTS (upr)	XV48	4FT deg	* g	CC	MO	M	24	Ind	Ind	10	
Science QTS (lpr)	XY31	4FT deg	S g	CC	MO	M	24	Ind	Ind	5	
Science QTS (upr)	XY41	4FT deg	S g	CC	MO	M	24	Ind	Ind	11	
Special Educational Needs	XX59	4FT deg	* g	CC	MO	M	24	Ind	Ind		
Sport Science QTS (lpr)	XB36	4FT deg	* g	CC	MO	M	24	Ind	Ind		
Sport Science QTS (upr)	XB46	4FT deg	* g	CC	MO	M	24	Ind	Ind		
Upper Primary QTS (7-12 years)	X400	4FT deg	* g	CC	MO	M	24	Ind	Ind		
Univ of Wales INST, CARDIFF											
Drama (Secondary)	X7WX	3FT/4FT deg	* g	12	3M+3D	M$6/△ go	Ind	Ind	Ind	5	6/22
Music (BA See Prospectus)	X7W3	2FT deg	g	X		M$△ go				1	
Primary Education with QTS	X500	3FT deg	*	12	3M+3D	M$6/△ go	Ind	CCCC	Ind		
Welsh (BA See Prospectus)	X7Q5	2FT deg	* g	X	Ind	M$△ go				1	
Univ of CENTRAL ENGLAND											
Music (age 21+) (Secondary with QTS)	XW73	2FT deg	* g		Ind	Ind	Ind	Ind	Ind	2	
Primary Education (Options)	X500	4FT deg	g	4-20	Ind	Ind	$	$	Ind	10	6/20
CHELTENHAM & GLOUCESTER COLL of HE											
Early Years (2 Yr BEd)	X300	2FT deg		Ind	Ind	Ind	Ind	Ind	Ind		
Later Years (2 Yr BEd)	X400	2FT deg		Ind	Ind	Ind	Ind	Ind	Ind		
Primary Education: Early Years	X301	3FT deg	E/M/S g	12	MO	Ind	26	CCCC	Ind		
Primary Education: Later Years	X401	3FT deg	E/M/S g	12	MO	Ind	26	CCCC	Ind		

course details			98 expected requirements							96 entry stats	
TITLE	CODE	COURSE	SUBJECTS	A/AS	ND/C	AGNVQ	IB	SQA(H)	SQA	RATIO	A/AS
UNIVERSITY COLLEGE CHESTER											
Art (lpr)	X3W1	4FT deg	g	12	$	P^	Ind	CCCC	$	17	15/20
Art (upr)	X4W1	4FT deg	g	12	$	P^	Ind	CCCC	$	27	
Biology (lpr) (4 Yrs)	X3C1	4FT deg	B g	12	$	P^	Ind	CCCC	$	12	12/24
Biology (upr) (4 Yrs)	X4C1	4FT deg	B g	12	$	P^	Ind	CCCC	$	23	
Drama and Theatre Studies (lpr)	X3W4	4FT deg	g	12	$	M	Ind	CCCC	$	19	10/20
Drama and Theatre Studies (upr)	X4W4	4FT deg	g	12	$	M	Ind	CCCC	$	18	14/18
English Literature (lpr)	X3Q3	4FT deg	E g	12	$	P^	Ind	CCCC	$	34	10/22
English Literature (upr)	X4Q3	4FT deg	E g	12	$	P^	Ind	CCCC	$	23	12/22
Geography (lpr)	X3L8	4FT deg	Gy/Gl g	12	M	P^	Ind	CCCC	$	20	12/16
Geography (upr)	X4L8	4FT deg	Gy/Gl g	12	M	P^	Ind	CCCC	$	18	16/20
History (lpr)	X3V1	4FT deg	H/Ec/So g	12	$	P^	Ind	CCCC	$	14	12/20
History (upr)	X4V1	4FT deg	H/Ec/So g	12	$	P^	Ind	CCCC	$	16	12/18
Mathematical Studies (lpr)	X3G9	4FT deg	g	12	M	P^	Ind	CCCC	$		
Mathematical Studies (upr)	X4G9	4FT deg	g	12	M	P^	Ind	CCCC	$		
Mathematics (lpr)	X3G1	4FT deg	g	12	M	P^	Ind	CCCC	$	8	12/30
Mathematics (upr)	X4G1	4FT deg	g	12	M	P^	Ind	CCCC	$	9	11/22
Physical Education (lpr)	X3X8	4FT deg	g	12	M	P^	Ind	CCCC	$	24	
Physical Education (upr)	X4X8	4FT deg	g	12	M	P^	Ind	CCCC	$	46	10/14
Theology and Religious Studies (lpr)	X3V8	4FT deg	g	12	$	M	Ind	CCCC	$	24	
Theology and Religious Studies (upr)	X4V8	4FT deg	g	12	$	M	Ind	CCCC	$	23	
CHICHESTER INSTITUTE OF HIGHER EDUCATION											
Mathematics (QTS)	XG7C	2FT deg	M g	12	Ind	M^	Ind	Ind	Ind	3	
Mathematics (QTS)(sec)	XG71	4FT deg	M g	12	Ind	M^	Ind	Ind	Ind	4	
Physical Education (QTS)(sec)	XX78	4FT deg	* g	12	Ind	M$+ go	Ind	Ind	Ind	10	6/18
Primary Early Years (4 years)	XY34	4FT deg	* g	12	Ind	M$ go	Ind	Ind	Ind		
Sports Studies	X206	3FT deg	* g	14	Ind	M$^	Ind	Ind	Ind		
DE MONTFORT Univ											
Biomedical Sciences and Chemistry with QTS	X7BX▼	4FT deg	B+C g	10	4M $	M	24$	BBB	$		
Biomedical Sciences with QTS	X7B9▼	4FT deg	B+C g	12-14	6M $	MS6 gi	28$	BBBB$	X		
Chemistry Options with QTS	FX1T▼	3FT deg	C	12	3M $		24$	BBB			
Chemistry with Business Studies with QTS	X7FC▼	4FT deg	*	12	3M $	M	24$	BBB			
Chemistry with QTS	FX17▼	3FT deg	*	12	3M $	M	24$	BBB			
Chemistry, Applied with QTS	X7F1▼	4FT deg	C g	8	3M $	M	24$	BBB			
Modular Scheme (Primary Education)	X500▼	4FT deg	* g	12-14	5D	M* go	Ind	BBCC	Ind	7	8/22
Physical Education Secondary	XX78▼	4FT deg	A/S/E/Gy/H/M g	12	3D	M	Ind	BBCC	Ind	7	10/20
Physics with Business Studies and QTS	X7F3▼	4FT deg	*	12	Ind	M	24$	BBB	$		
Univ of DERBY											
Primary	X500	3FT deg	g	CC	4M+1D	M$	27$	CCCC$	Ind	13	8/18
Univ of DURHAM											
Education (BA Honours)	X6Y4	3FT deg	* g	BCC-BCD	Ind	Ind	X	BBBCC	X	10	16/24
Primary Teaching (Science)	X5Y1▼	2FT deg		X		X	X	X		3	
EDGE HILL Univ COLLEGE											
Art and Design (nlp)	XW22	4FT deg	A g	CC	3M+3D	MA/ P*^ go	Dip	BBCC$	Ind	11	10/22
Art and Design (upr)	XW42	4FT deg	A g	CC	3M+3D	MA/ P*^ go	Dip	BBCC$	Ind	11	12/26
Business Education (QTS)	X7N1	2FT deg	g		HN $	X	X	X	HN$	4	
Design & Technology (upr)	XW4F	4FT deg	Ds g	DD	4M+2D	MN/ P*^ go	Dip	BBCC$	Ind		
Design and Technology (QTS)	X7W2	2FT deg	g		HN $	X			HN$	2	
Design and Technology (nlp)	XW2F	4FT deg	Ds g	DD	4M+2D	MN/ P*^ go	Dip	BBCC$	Ind		
English (nlp)	XQ23	4FT deg	E g	CC	X	P*^ go	Dip	BBCC$	X	17	14/26

course details			98 expected requirements							96 entry stats	
TITLE	CODE	COURSE	SUBJECTS	A/AS	NO/C	AGNVQ	IB	SQA(H)	SQA	RATIO	A/AS
English (upr)	XQ43	4FT deg	E g	CC	X	P*^ go	Dip	BBCC$	X	14	10/26
Geography (nlp)	XL28	4FT deg	Gy g	CC	X	P*^ go	Dip	BBCC$	X	7	16/20
Geography (upr)	XL48	4FT deg	Gy g	CC	X	P*^ go	Dip	BBCC$	X	12	16/20
History (nlp)	XV21	4FT deg	H g	CC	3M+3D	P*^ go	Dip	BBCC$	X	10	14/20
History (upr)	XV41	4FT deg	H g	CC	3M+3D	P*^ go	Dip	BBCC$	X	12	14/26
Mathematical Studies (nlp) (4 Yrs QTS)	XG21	4FT deg	* g	DD	3M+3D	M* / P*^ go	Dip	BBCC	Ind	3	7/18
Mathematical Studies (upr) (4 Yrs QTS)	XG41	4FT deg	* g	DD	3M+3D	M* / P*^ go	Dip	BBCC	Ind	5	8/14
Mathematics (QTS)	X7G1	2FT deg	g		HN $	X			HN$	2	
Music (nlp)	XW23	4FT deg	* g	DD	3M+3D	M* / P*^ go	Dip	BBCC	Ind	6	8/16
Music (upr)	XW43	4FT deg	* g	DD	3M+3D	M* / P*^ go	Dip	BBCC	Ind	12	
Natural Sciences (nlp)	XC21	4FT deg	B g	CD	3M+3D	MS/ P*^ go	Dip	BBCC$	Ind	6	14/18
Natural Sciences (upr)	XC41	4FT deg	B g	CD	3M+3D	MS/ P*^ go	Dip	BBCC$	Ind	7	10/16
Physical Education (nlp)	XX28	4FT deg	* g	CC	3M+3D	M* / P*^ go	Dip	BBCC	Ind	15	
Physical Education (upr)	XX48	4FT deg	* g	CC	3M+3D	M* / P*^ go	Dip	BBCC	Ind	22	10/16
Religious Studies (nlp)	XV28	4FT deg	Re g	CC	3M+3D	M* / P*^ go	Dip	BBCC$	X	22	
Religious Studies (upr)	XV48	4FT deg	Re g	CC	3M+3D	M* / P*^ go	Dip	BBCC$	X	12	
Science (QTS)	X7Y1	2FT deg	g		HN $	X			HN$	1	

Univ of EXETER

Educational Studies (Prim) and Biology/Sci Ed	XC41	4FT deg	S g	CCC-DD	MO+2D	M$^	30$	Ind	Ind	6	10/22
Educational Studies (Prim) and Chemistry/Sci Ed	XF41	4FT deg	S g	CCC-DD	MO+2D	M$^	28$	Ind	Ind		
Educational Studies (Prim) and Mathematics	XG41	4FT deg	M	CCC-DD	MO+2D	M$^	28$	Ind	Ind	6	10/22
Educational Studies (Prim) and Physics/Sci Ed	XF43	4FT deg	S g	CCC-DD	MO+2D	M$^	28$	Ind	Ind	4	
Educational Studies (Prim) and Sci/Sci Ed	XF49	4FT deg	S g	CCC-DD	MO+2D	M$^	28$	Ind	Ind	10	
Educational Studies (Sec) and Biology/Sci Ed	XC71	4FT deg	S g	CCC-DD	MO+2D	M$^	28$	Ind	Ind	8	
Educational Studies (Sec) and Chemistry/Sci Ed	XF71	4FT deg	S g	CCC-DD	MO+2D	M$^	28$	Ind	Ind	4	
Educational Studies (Sec) and Mathematics	XG71	4FT deg	M	CCC-DD	MO+2D	M$^	28$	Ind	Ind	2	8/20
Educational Studies (Sec) and Physics/Sci Ed	XF73	4FT deg	S g	CCC-DD	MO+2D	M$^	28$	Ind	Ind	3	
Educational Studies (Sec) and Sci/Sci Ed	XF79	4FT deg	S g	CCC-DD	MO+2D	M$^	28$	Ind	Ind	1	10/18

GOLDSMITHS COLL (Univ of London)

Education (Primary-Early Years)	X300	3FT deg	g	CC	MO		Dip	BCCC	N	9	6/22
Education (Primary-Junior)	X400	3FT deg	g	CC	MO		Dip	BCCC	N	10	8/26
Education with Design & Technology	X7WF	4FT deg	g	CD	MO	M	Dip	BCCC	N	5	

Univ of GREENWICH

Business Studies with Information Tech Education	XN71	2FT deg	* g	12	M+D		24	BCCC	Ind		
Business Studies with Information Tech Education	XN7D	3FT deg	* g	12	1M+1D	M$+	24	BCCC	Ind		
Business Studies with Information Technology Ed	XN7C	3FT deg									
Design and Technology Education	XW7F	2FT deg	* g	12	M+D		24	BCCC	Ind		
Design and Technology Education	XW72	3FT deg	* g	10	M+D	M$+	24	BCCC	Ind		
Mathematics Education	XG71	2FT deg	* g	12	HN	Ind	X	X	HN		
Physical Education	XX78	3FT deg	* g	10	1M+1D	M$+	24	BCCC	Ind		
Primary Teaching Studies	X501	3FT deg	g	12	1M+1D	M$+	24	BCCC			
Primary Teaching Studies (English)	XQ53	4FT deg	E g	12	1M+1D	M$+	24	BCCC			
Primary Teaching Studies (Maths)	XG51	4FT deg	M g	12	1M+1D	M$+	24	BCCC			
Primary Teaching Studies (Science)	XY51	4FT deg	S g	12	1M+1D	M$+	24	BCCC			
Primary/Secondary Teaching St (Des & Tech)w. QTS	XW62	4FT deg	* g	12	1M+1D	M$+	24	BCCC	Ind		
Primary/Secondary Teaching St (Mathematics)w.QTS	XG61	4FT deg	* g	12	1M+1D	M$+	24	BCCC	Ind		
Primary/Secondary Teaching St (Science) w. QTS	XY61	4FT deg	* g	12	1M+1D	M$+	24	BCCC	Ind		
Science Education	XY71	2FT deg	g	X	HN		X	X	HN		

course details | 98 expected requirements | 96 entry stats

TITLE	CODE	COURSE	SUBJECTS	A/AS	ND/C	AGNVQ	IB	SQA(H)	SQA	RATIO	A/AS
Univ of HERTFORDSHIRE											
Mathematics with Qualified Teacher Status	G1X7	4FT deg	* g	12	MO	M*+	26	Ind	Ind		
Overseas Educational Studies	X502	1FT deg									
Primary Education with Art	XW51	4FT deg	A/Ad g	12	M+D	DA	Ind	Ind	Ind		8/20
Primary Education with English Lit and Lang	XQ53	4FT deg	Ee/E g	18			Ind	Ind	Ind		10/20
Primary Education with Geog & Environmental St	XF58	4FT deg	* g	12			Ind	Ind	Ind		
Primary Education with Mathematics	XG51	4FT deg	*	10			Ind	Ind	Ind		
Primary Education with Religious Studies	XV58	4FT deg	*	12			Ind	Ind	Ind		
Primary Education with Science	XY51	4FT deg	S g	10	M+D	DS	Ind	Ind	Ind		8/18
Primary QTS for Students with Overseas Quals	X501	2FT deg									
Univ of HUDDERSFIELD											
Business Studies (2 Yrs)	XN71	2ACC deg	g	X	HN	X	X	X	HN		
Design & Technology (2 Yrs)	XW72	2ACC deg	g	X	HN	X	X	X	HN		
Information Technology (2 Yrs)	XG75	2ACC deg	g	X	HN	X	X	X	HN		
Mathematics (2 Yr BEd)	XG71	2ACC deg	g	X	HN	X	X	X	HN		
Music (2 Yr BEd)	XW73	2ACC deg	g	X	HN	X	X	X	HN		
Science (2 Yr BEd)	XY71	2ACC deg	g	X	HN	X	X	X	HN		
Univ of HULL											
Biology with Education (QTS)	C1X7	4FT deg	2S g	BCC-CCD	MO $	M$^ go	25$	BBCCC	Ind	2	12/14
Chemistry with Education (QTS)	F1X7	4FT deg	C g	CCD	MO $	M$^ go	26$	BCCCC	Ind	3	
Mathematics with Education (QTS)	G1X7	4FT deg	M g	BCD	MO $	M$^ go	26$	BCCCC	Ind	8	
KEELE Univ											
Psychology and Conductive Education	CX85	4FT deg	* g	BBB	Ind	Ind	32	BBBB	Ind		14/22
KING ALFRED'S WINCHESTER											
Art (lpr) (4 Yrs QTS)	XW31	4FT deg	A/Ad g	12	6M $	M	24$	BCC$	N$	11	13/16
Art (upr) (4 Yrs QTS)	XW41	4FT deg	A/Ad g	12	6M $	M	24$	BCC$	N$	8	10/18
Design & Technology (lpr) (4 Yrs QTS)	XJ39	4FT deg	Ds/Ad g	12	6M $	M	24$	BCC$	N$	3	12/13
Design & Technology (upr) (4 Yrs QTS)	XJ49	4FT deg	Ds/Ad g	12	6M $	M	24$	BCC$	N$	5	10/20
Design and Technology	X7W2	2FT deg	g	X	HN	X	X	X	HN	1	
Design and Technology (3 Yrs QTS)	XW72	3FT deg	Ds/Ad g	10	6M $	M	24$	CCC$	N$	3	
Design and Technology (pr/sec QTS)	XJ79	4FT deg	Ds/Ad g	12	6M $	M	24$	BCC$	N$		
Drama (lpr) (4 Yrs QTS)	XW34	4FT deg	T/E g	12	6M $	M	24$	BCC$	N$	8	6/16
Drama (upr) (4 Yrs QTS)	XW44	4FT deg	T/E g	12	6M $	M	24$	BCC$	N$	12	6/16
Early Years (1pr) QTS	X3X9	4FT deg	* g	12	6M	M	24	BCC	N		
English (lpr) (4 Yrs QTS)	XQ33	4FT deg	E g	12	X	X	24$	BCC$	X	10	8/22
English (upr) (4 Yrs QTS)	XQ43	4FT deg	E g	12	X	X	24$	BCC$	X	10	10/20
Geography (lpr) (4 Yrs QTS)	XF38	4FT deg	Gy/En g	12	X	X	24$	BCC$	X	11	6/18
Geography (upr) (4 Yrs QTS)	XF48	4FT deg	Gy/En g	12	X	X	24$	BCC$	X	7	6/24
History (lpr) (4 Yrs QTS)	XV31	4FT deg	H g	12	X	X	24$	BCC$	X	7	8/14
History (upr) (4 Yrs QTS)	XV41	4FT deg	H g	12	X	X	24$	BCC$	X	15	
Human Movement Studies (lpr) (4 Yrs QTS)	XX38	4FT deg	B/Ss/So/Ps g	12	6M $	M	24$	BCC$	N$	5	10/16
Human Movement Studies (upr) (4 Yrs QTS)	XX48	4FT deg	B/Ss/So/Ps g	12	6M $	M	24$	BCC$	N$	6	6/16
Music (lpr) (4 Yrs QTS)	XW33	4FT deg	Mu g	12	X	X	24$	BCC$	X	7	10/16
Music (upr) (4 Yrs QTS)	XW43	4FT deg	Mu g	12	X	X	24$	BCC$	X	7	10/12
Religious Studies (lpr) (4 Yrs QTS)	XV38	4FT deg	Re/So/Ps g	12	X	X	24$	BCC$	X	4	6/24
Religious Studies (upr) (4 Yrs QTS)	XV48	4FT deg	Re/So/Ps g	12	X	X	24$	BCC$	X	8	8/16
Science (pr/sec) QTS	XY71	4FT deg	S g	12	6M $	M	24$	BCC$	TN$		
Social Biology (1pr) (4 Yrs QTS)	XC31	4FT deg	B/C/Gy/P	12	6M $	M	24$	BCC$	N$		
Social Biology (upr) (4 Yrs QTS)	XC41	4FT deg	B/C/Gy/P	12	6M $	M	24$	BCC$	N$	1	11/14

| | | | 98 expected requirements | | | | | | | 96 entry stats | |
TITLE	CODE	COURSE	SUBJECTS	A/AS	ND/C	AGNVQ	IB	SQA(H)	SQA	RATIO	A/AS
KINGSTON Univ											
Primary English and Drama (3-8 Years)	XQ23	4FT deg	E/T g	CD	Ind	Ind	Ind	Ind	Ind	9	8/18
Primary English and Drama (7-11 Years)	XQ63	4FT deg	E/T g	CD	Ind	Ind	Ind	Ind	Ind	7	8/18
Primary History & Geography (3-8 Years)	XV21	4FT deg	H/Gy g	CD	Ind	Ind	Ind	Ind	Ind	4	8/20
Primary History & Geography (7-11 Years)	XV61	4FT deg	H/Gy g	CD	Ind	Ind	Ind	Ind	Ind	4	10/18
Primary Mathematics & Information Tech (7-11 Yr)	XG69	4FT deg		CD	Ind	Ind	Ind	Ind	Ind		
Primary Mathematics and Information Tech (3-8Yr)	XG29	4FT deg		CD	Ind	Ind	Ind	Ind	Ind		
Primary Music (3-8 Years)	XW23	4FT deg	Mu g	CD	Ind	Ind	Ind	Ind	Ind	3	8/10
Primary Music (7-11 Years)	XW63	4FT deg	Mu g	CD	Ind	Ind	Ind	Ind	Ind	4	8/12
Primary Science (3-8 Years)	XY21	4FT deg	B/C/P g	CD	Ind	Ind	Ind	Ind	Ind	4	8/16
Primary Science (7-11 Years)	XY61	4FT deg	B/C/P g	CD	Ind	Ind	Ind	Ind	Ind	5	12/15
LEEDS, TRINITY & ALL SAINTS Univ COLL											
English-Primary Education (3-8Yrs) (4 Yrs)	XQ23	4FT deg	g	BBB-CDD Ind	X		26$	BBBCC	Ind	58	16/20
English-Primary Education (7-11Yrs) (4 Yrs)	XQ43	4FT deg	g	BBB-CDD Ind	X		26$	BBBCC	Ind	17	8/20
History-Primary Education (3-8Yrs) (4 Yrs)	XV21	4FT deg	H g	BC-CD Ind	X		24$	BBBCC	Ind	17	12/22
History-Primary Education (7-11Yrs) (4 Yrs)	XV41	4FT deg	H g	BC-CD Ind	X		24$	BBBCC	Ind	10	12/22
Mathematics-Primary Educ (3-8Yrs) (4 Yrs)	XG21	4FT deg	M g	DD Ind	X		24$	BBCCC	Ind	21	
Mathematics-Primary Educ (7-11Yrs) (4 Yrs)	XG41	4FT deg	M g	DD Ind	X		24$	BBCCC	Ind	8	6/12
Mathematics-Secondary Educ (4 Yrs)	XG71	4FT deg	M g	DD Ind	X		24$	BBCCC	Ind	5	
Physical Education-Primary Ed (3-8Yrs) (4 Yrs)	XX28	4FT deg	* g	BBB-CCD	4D	Ind	26	BBBCC	Ind	13	10/14
Physical Education-Primary Ed (7-11Yrs) (4 Yrs)	XX48	4FT deg	* g	BBB-CCD	4D	Ind	26	BBBCC	Ind	26	12/22
Science and Technology-Prim Ed (3-8Yrs) (4 Yr)	XY21	4FT deg	B/C/P g	BCC-DD Ind	X		24$	BBCCC	Ind	9	
Science and Technology-Prim Ed (7-11Yrs) (4 Yrs)	XY41	4FT deg	B/C/P g	BCC-DD	MO	X	24$	BBCCC	Ind	3	6/14
Technology (inc Business St)-Secondary Ed (4Yrs)	XJ7X	4FT deg	B/C/P g	CCD-DD Ind	Ind		24	CCCC	Ind	3	
Technology (inc Food St)-Secondary Educ (4 Yrs)	XJ7Y	4FT deg	B/C/P g	CCD-DD Ind	Ind		24	CCCC	Ind	3	
Technology (inc Information Tech)-Sec Ed (4 Yrs)	XJT9	4FT deg	B/C/P g	CCD-DD Ind	Ind		24	CCCC	Ind	3	
Technology-Secondary Education (4 Yrs)	XJ79	4FT deg	B/C/P g	CCD-DD Ind	Ind		24	CCCC	Ind	2	8/10
Theology-Primary Education (3-8Yrs) (4 Yrs)	XV28	4FT deg	* g	CCD-DD	MO	Ind	24	BBCCC	Ind	25	14/16
Theology-Primary Education (7-11Yrs) (4 Yrs)	XV48	4FT deg	* g	CCD-DD	MO	Ind	24	BBCCC	Ind	7	6/18
Theology-Secondary Education (4 Yrs)	XV78	4FT deg	* g	CCD-DD	MO	Ind	24	BBCCC	Ind	2	4/20
LEEDS METROPOLITAN Univ											
Design Technology with English	XW62	3FT deg									6/16
Information Technology with English	XG65	3FT deg									
Mathematics with History	XG6C	3FT deg									
Mathematics with Physical Education	XG61	3FT deg	g	8-10	Ind	Ind go	Ind	BBBB$	Ind		6/18
Primary Education	X500	3FT deg	* g	8-12	6M	Ind go	26	BBC	Ind	27	10/22
Secondary Design Tech (2 Yrs) (Post-Experience)	XW7F	2FT deg	g	X	HN	X	X	X	HN	3	
Secondary Design Technology	XW72	4FT deg	g	8-10	5M	M$ go	Ind	BBBB$	Ind	24	
Secondary Information Technol (2 Yrs) (Post-Exp)	XG75	2FT deg									
Secondary Mathematics	XG7C	3FT deg	M g	8-10	Ind	Ind go	Ind	BBBB$	Ind	5	8/18
Secondary Mathematics (2 Yrs) (Post-Experience)	XG71	2FT deg	g	X	HN	X	X	X	HN	3	
Secondary Physical Education	XX78	4FT deg	g	16	5M	ML^ go	Ind	BBBB$	Ind	24	14/24
LIVERPOOL HOPE Univ COLL											
Art (nlp)	X2W1	4FT deg	A/Fa g	10	6M	MA /P*^ go	Ind	Ind	Ind	10	10/16
Art (upm)	X4W1	4FT deg	A/Fa g	10	6M	MA /P*^ go	Ind	Ind	Ind	45	
English (nlp)	X2Q3	4FT deg	El g	10	6M	P*^ go	Ind	Ind	Ind	12	8/22
English (upm)	X4Q3	4FT deg	El g	10	6M	P*^ go	Ind	Ind	Ind	14	8/18
Geography (nlp)	X2F8	4FT deg	Gy g	10	6M	M$ go	Ind	Ind	Ind	16	
Geography (upm)	X4F8	4FT deg	Gy g	10	6M	M$ go	Ind	Ind	Ind	8	8/12
History (nlp)	X2V1	4FT deg	H g	10	6M	P*^ go	Ind	Ind	Ind	10	10/18
History (upm)	X4V1	4FT deg	H g	10	6M	P*^ go	Ind	Ind	Ind	8	8/18

TITLE	CODE	COURSE	SUBJECTS	A/AS	ND/C	AGNVQ	IB	SQA(H)	SQA	RATIO	A/AS
Human & Applied Biology (nlp)	X2C1	4FT deg	B g	10	6M	MS /P*_^ go	Ind	Ind	Ind	9	10/10
Human & Applied Biology (upm)	X4C1	4FT deg	B g	10	6M	MS /P*_^ go	Ind	Ind	Ind	8	
Information Technology (nlp)	X2G5	4FT deg	g	10	6M	M* go	Ind	Ind	Ind	11	
Information Technology (upm)	X4G5	4FT deg	g	10	6M	M* go	Ind	Ind	Ind	8	
Mathematics (nlp)	X2G1	4FT deg	M	10	6M	P*_^	Ind	Ind	Ind	24	
Mathematics (upm)	X4G1	4FT deg	M	10	6M	P*_^	Ind	Ind	Ind	9	12/16
Music (nlp)	X2W3	4FT deg	Mu g	10	6M	MQ /P*_^ go	Ind	Ind	Ind	12	
Music (upm)	X4W3	4FT deg	Mu g	10	6M	MQ /P*_^ go	Ind	Ind	Ind	9	
Sport, Recreation & Physical Education (nlp)	X2X8	4FT deg	g	10	6M	M* go	Ind	Ind	Ind	28	
Sport, Recreation & Physical Education (upm)	X4X8	4FT deg	g	10	6M	M* go	Ind	Ind	Ind	47	10/18
Theology & Religious Studies (nlp)	X2V8	4FT deg	g	10	6M	M* go	Ind	Ind	Ind	8	8/24
Theology & Religious Studies (upm)	X4V8	4FT deg	g	10	6M	M* go	Ind	Ind	Ind	18	

LIVERPOOL JOHN MOORES Univ

TITLE	CODE	COURSE	SUBJECTS	A/AS	ND/C	AGNVQ	IB	SQA(H)	SQA	RATIO	A/AS
Art and Design and Technology (Primary 7-11)	XW42	4FT deg		16	5M	M$^ go				7	8/18
Biology with Science (2 Yr BEd)	X7C1	2FT deg		X	X		X	X	X	5	
Chemistry with Science (2 Yr BEd)	X7F1	2FT deg		X	X		X	X	X		
Dance	XW74	3FT deg		12	5D	M					
Design and Technology (2 Yrs)(Secondary)	X7W2	2FT deg		X	X		X	X	X	3	
Design and Technology (Secondary)	XW72	4FT deg		EE	5M	D$/M$6				8	8/14
English (Primary 7-11)	XQ43	4FT deg		16	5M	M$^ go				27	12/24
English (Upper Primary/Middle)	XQ63	3FT deg		16	5M	M$^ go					
Mathematics (Primary)	XG41	3FT deg		16	5M	M$^ go					
Mathematics (Upper Primary/Middle)	XG61	3FT deg		16	5M	M$^					
Outdoor and Science Education (Secondary)	XF79	4FT deg	S	16	5M	M$^				4	6/18
Physical Education (Primary 7-11)	XX48	4FT deg		16	5M	M$^				23	8/20
Physical Education (Secondary)	XX78	4FT deg		16	3M+2D	M$^				14	10/22
Physical Education (Upper Primary/Middle)	XX68	3FT deg		16	5M	M$^					
Physics with Science (2 Yr BEd)	X7F3	2FT deg		X	X		X	X	X	8	
Science (Upper Primary/Middle)	XY61	3FT deg		16	5M	M$^					6/10
Science and Environmental Studies (Primary 7-11)	XF49	4FT deg		16	5M	M$^				8	10/18
Technology (Upper Primary/Middle)	XJ69	3FT deg		16	5M	M$^					

LOUGHBOROUGH Univ

TITLE	CODE	COURSE	SUBJECTS	A/AS	ND/C	AGNVQ	IB	SQA(H)	SQA	RATIO	A/AS
Industrial Design and Technology with Ed (4 Yr)	XH77	4FT deg	* g	12	5M		28$	Ind	Ind	2	10/20

LSU COLL of HE

TITLE	CODE	COURSE	SUBJECTS	A/AS	ND/C	AGNVQ	IB	SQA(H)	SQA	RATIO	A/AS
Art and Design (4 Yrs)	X5WC	4FT deg	A g	DE	Ind		Ind	Ind	Ind		
Biological Sciences (upr) (4 Yrs)	X5CC	4FT deg	S g	DE	Ind		Ind	Ind	Ind		
Geography (upr) (4 Yrs)	X5LV	4FT deg	Gy g	DD	Ind		Ind	Ind	Ind		
Mathematics (upr) (4 Yrs)	X5GC	4FT deg	M g	EE	Ind		Ind	Ind	Ind		
Religious Studies (4 Yrs)	X5VV	4FT deg	Re g	DE	Ind		Ind	Ind	Ind		

MANCHESTER METROPOLITAN Univ

TITLE	CODE	COURSE	SUBJECTS	A/AS	ND/C	AGNVQ	IB	SQA(H)	SQA	RATIO	A/AS
Business and Information Technology Education	XN71	2FT deg	* g	X	HN $	X	X	X	X		
Design Technology (2 yrs post A level study req)	XW72	2FT deg	* g	X	HN $	X	X	X	X		
Junior (QTS)	X401	4FT deg	* g	CC	N		Ind	Ind	Ind		6/20
Mathematics	XG71	3FT deg	M g	EE	N $	M$_^	Dip	Ind	Ind		6/18
Mathematics (Subj - 1yr Post A-Level study Req)	XG7D	2FT deg	* g	X	HN $		Ind	X	X		
Mathematics(Subj conv-1yr post A lev study req)	XG7C	2FT deg	M g	X	Ind $	Ind	Ind	X	X		
Nursery/Infant (QTS)	X201	4FT deg	* g	CC	M/D	D	Ind	Ind	Ind		6/20
Primary (Education)	X500	4FT deg	g	CE-EE	3M $	P$2/^	Dip	Ind	Ind		6/22
Secondary (QTS)	X700	4FT deg	* g	CC-DD	N	M	Ind	Ind	Ind		8/20

			98 expected requirements							96 entry stats
course details										
TITLE	CODE	COURSE	SUBJECTS	A/AS	ND/C	AGNVQ	IB	SQA(H)	SQA	RATIO A/AS
MIDDLESEX Univ										
Design and Technology (2 yr)	XW72▼		2FT deg		X	HN	X	X	X	
Primary Education	X500▼	3FT deg	* g	BC	X	X	24	Ind	Ind	
MORAY HOUSE Inst of Ed										
Computer Science and Education	GX57	3FT/4FT deg	g	DD	Ind	Ind		CCC$	Ind	
Physical Education	XX78	4FT deg	g	CCD	Ind	Ind		BBCC$	Ind	13
Primary Education	X500	4FT deg	g	CCD	Ind	Ind		BBCC$	Ind	11 10/14
Technology	JX97	4FT deg	g	DD	Ind	Ind		CCC$	Ind	3
NENE COLLEGE										
Primary (4-7)	X300	3FT deg	g	12	5M	M	24	CCC	Ind	8/20
Primary (7-11)	X400	3FT deg	g	12	5M	M	24	CCC	Ind	8/18
Univ of NEWCASTLE										
Combined Studies (BA) *Physical Education and Sports Studies*	Y400	3FT deg	*	ABC-BBB	5D	Ind	35$	AAAB	Ind	
NEWMAN COLLEGE OF HIGHER EDUCATION										
English (Secondary)	XQ73	3FT/4FT deg	E g	CC	3M	M*^	Dip	CCC	Ind	1 6/20
Information Technology (Key Stage 2/3)	XG65	3FT/4FT deg	* g	CC	3M	M*^	Dip	CCC	Ind	
Primary (4-12 years with subject options)	X503	3FT deg	* g	CC	3M	M*^	Dip	CCC	Ind	
Primary (4-12 years with subject options)	X501	4FT deg	* g	CC	3M	M*^	Dip	CCC	Ind	
Science (Key Stage 2/3)	XY61	3FT/4FT deg	* g	CC	3M	M*^	Dip	CCC	Ind	
Univ of Wales COLLEGE, NEWPORT										
Design and Technology	X7W2	2FT deg	g	X	HN	X	X	X	Ind	
Education Primary with QTS	X500	3FT deg	g	10-12	M+D	D$	Ind	Ind	Ind	
Maths/Science	X7G1	2FT deg	M/S g	X	HN	X	X	X	Ind	
NORTH EAST WALES INST of HE										
Education (Primary) with QTS	X503	3FT deg		8	5M	M$	Ind	Ind	N$	
NORTHERN COLL										
Music (Secondary)	XW73▼	4FT deg	g	CD				CCC$		4
Primary	X500▼	4FT deg	g	BC				BBB$		6
Technology with Education	J9X7▼	4FT deg								
Univ of NORTH LONDON										
Education (Primary)	X500	4FT deg	*	CC	N	Ind	X	Ind	Ind	11 4/14
Education (Secondary Mathematics)	XG71	2FT deg	M	CC	X	X	X	X	X	23
Univ of NORTHUMBRIA										
General Primary	X500	3FT deg	g	14	1M+3D	D	24	BCCC	Ind	16 12/24
Mathematics	XG71	2FT deg	g	X	HN	X	X	X	HN	10
Modern Languages (French)	XR71	2FT deg	g	X	HN	X	X	X	HN	12
Modern Languages (German)	XR72	2FT deg	g	X	HN	X	X	X	HN	
Modern Languages (Spanish)	XR74	2FT deg	g	X	HN	X	X	X	HN	
Physics	XF73	2FT deg	g	X	HN	X	X	X	HN	5
Technology (Design and Technology)	XW72	2FT deg	g	X	HN	X	X	X	HN	3
Technology (Home Economics/Textiles)	XN71	2FT deg	g	X	HN	X	X	X	HN	6
NOTTINGHAM TRENT Univ										
Design and Technology Education (BSc with QTS)	XW62	4FT deg	Ds/Me g	10	Ind	Ind	Ind	Ind	Ind	
Primary Education (BA with QTS)	X501	4FT deg	g	10	4M	Ind	Ind	BBCC	N	19 10/22
Secondary (shortened) Business Education	X7N1	2FT deg	g	X	HN	X		X	HN	3
Secondary (shortened) Design & Technology	X7W2	2FT deg	g	X	HN	X		X	HN	2

course details			98 expected requirements							96 entry stats	
TITLE	CODE	COURSE	SUBJECTS	A/AS	ND/C	AGNVQ	IB	SQA(H)	SQA	RATIO	A/AS
Secondary (shortened) Maths	X7G1	2FT deg	g	X	HN	X		X	HN	2	
Secondary (shortened) Science	X7Y1	2FT deg	g	X	HN	X		X	HN	2	
Secondary Design and Technology	XW72	4FT deg	* g	8	3M $	Ind	Ind$	CCCC	N	4	6/12
OXFORD WESTMINSTER COLLEGE											
English (4 Yrs)	XQ53	4FT deg	E g	CE	MO	M	Ind	CCC	Ind		
French (4 Yrs)	XR51	4FT deg	F g	CE	MO	M	Ind	CCC	Ind		
Mathematics (4 Yrs)	XG51	4FT deg	M g	EE	MO	M	Ind	CCC	Ind		
Religious Studies (4 Yrs)	XV58	4FT deg	Re g	CE	MO	M	Ind	CCC	Ind		
Science in the Environment (4 Yrs)	XF59	4FT deg	S g	EE	MO	M	Ind	CCC	Ind		
OXFORD BROOKES Univ											
Teacher Education	X500	3FT deg	* g	CC-DDD	Ind	M*3	Ind	Ind	Ind	1	10/22
Univ of PAISLEY											
Primary Education	X500▼	4FT deg	* g	CCD-BB	Ind	Ind	Ind	BBBB$	Ind	11	
Univ of PLYMOUTH											
Art & Design and General Primary 3-8 Years	X3W9	4FT deg	Ad g	E	N $	M^	Ind	Ind	Ind	10	8/20
Art & Design and General Primary 7-12 Years	X6W9	4FT deg	Ad g	E	N $	M^	Ind	Ind	Ind	8	8/18
Early Childhood Studies 3-8 yrs	X300	4FT deg	Ap g	2	N $	M$^ go	Ind	Ind	Ind	3	6/12
English and General Primary 3-8 Yrs	X3Q3	4FT deg	E g	2	N $	M^	Ind	Ind	Ind	28	10/16
English and General Primary 7-12 Yrs	X6Q3	4FT deg	E g	2	N $	M^	Ind	Ind	Ind	20	8/18
Geography and General Primary 3-8 Yrs	X3L8	4FT deg	Gy g	2	N $	M$^	Ind	Ind	Ind	12	6/20
Geography and General Primary 7-12 Yrs	X6L8	4FT deg	Gy g	2	N $	M$^	Ind	Ind	Ind	10	12/24
History and General Primary 3-8 Yrs	X3V1	4FT deg	Ap g	E	Ind	M$^	Ind	Ind	Ind	8	8/14
History and General Primary 7-12 Yrs	X6V1	4FT deg	Ap g	E	Ind	M$^	Ind	Ind	Ind	9	14/16
Information Technology (Key Stage 2/3)	X6G5	4FT deg	Ap g	2	N $	M$^	Ind		Ind		
Mathematics (Key Stage 2/3)	X6GC	4FT deg	M g	2	Ind	M$^	Ind		Ind		
Mathematics and General Primary 3-8 Yrs	X3G1	4FT deg	M g	2	N $	M$^	Ind	Ind	Ind	7	12/14
Mathematics and General Primary 7-12 Yrs	X6G1	4FT deg	M g	2	N $	M$^	Ind	Ind	Ind	7	8/12
Music and General Primary 3-8 Years	X3W3	4FT deg	Mu g	2	P $	M$^	Ind	Ind	Ind	5	8/20
Music and General Primary 7-12 Years	X6W3	4FT deg	Mu g	2	P $	M$^	Ind	Ind	Ind	5	4/12
Physical Education and General Primary 3-8 Yrs	X3X8	4FT deg	Pe g	E	N $	M$^	Ind	Ind	Ind	12	8/16
Physical Education and General Primary 7-12 Yrs	X6X8	4FT deg	Pe g	E	N $	M$^	Ind	Ind	Ind	12	6/12
Science (Key Stage 2/3)	X6FX	4FT deg	S g	2	N $	M$^	Ind		Ind		
Science and General Primary 3-8 Years	X3F9	4FT deg	S g	2	N $	M$^	Ind	Ind	Ind	7	6/18
Science and General Primary 7-12 Years	X6F9	4FT deg	S g	2	N $	M$^	Ind	Ind	Ind	8	10/16
Special Edu Needs & General Primary (7-12 years)	X6X9	4FT deg	Ap g	2	N $	M$^	Ind		Ind		
Special Educ Needs & General Primary (3-8 years)	X3X9	4FT deg	Ap g	2	N $	M$^	Ind		Ind		
Theatre & Performance St & Gen Prim 3-8 Yrs	X3W4	4FT deg	T g	E	N $	M$^	Ind$	Ind	Ind	7	8/14
Theatre & Performance St Gen Prim 7-12 Yrs	X6W4	4FT deg	T g	E	N $	M$^	Ind	Ind	Ind	7	6/16
Univ of PORTSMOUTH											
Secondary Science	XY71	2ACC deg	S g	X	HN $	X	X	X	X	1	
Univ of READING											
Educational St (Prim) with Art (4 Yrs)	X5W1	4FT deg	A+Pf g	BC	Ind	Ind	28$	BBBC$	Ind	13	10/24
Educational St (Prim) with English (4 Yrs)	X5Q3	4FT deg	E g	BC	Ind	Ind	28$	BBBC$	Ind	19	14/26
Educational St (Prim) with Geog & Env (4 Yrs)	X5L8	4FT deg	Gy g	BC	Ind	Ind	28$	BBBC$	Ind	10	14/26
Educational St (Prim) with History (4 Yrs)	X5V1	4FT deg	H g	BC	Ind	Ind	28$	BBBC$	Ind	8	8/20
Educational St (Prim) with Mathematics(4 Yrs)	X5G1	4FT deg	M g	BC	Ind	Ind	28$	BBBC$	Ind	5	12/28
Educational St (Prim) with Music (4 Yrs)	X5W3	4FT deg	Mu g	BC	Ind	Ind	28$	BBBC$	Ind	6	12/20
Educational St (Prim) with Physical Ed (4 Yrs)	X5X8	4FT deg	* g	BC	Ind	Ind	28$	BBBC$	Ind	8	10/20
Educational St (Prim) with Science (4 Yrs)	X5C1	4FT deg	S g	BC	Ind	Ind	28$	BBBC$	Ind	8	12/20
Educational St (Prim) with Technology (4 Yrs)	X5J9	4FT deg	* g	BC	Ind	Ind	28$	BBBC$	Ind	4	12/16

course details			98 expected requirements							96 entry stats	
TITLE	CODE	COURSE	SUBJECTS	A/AS	ND/C	AGNVQ	IB	SQA(H)	SQA	RATIO	A/AS
Univ College of RIPON & YORK ST JOHN											
English Studies-Primary Educ (nlp)	XQ23	4FT deg	E g	CCD	X	D*_^_ g	30	BBBB		12	12/24
English Studies-Primary Educ (upr)	XQ43	4FT deg	E g	CCD	X	D+_^_ g	30	BBBB		11	12/26
French Studies-Primary Educ (upr)	XR41	4FT deg	F g	DD	X	M*_^_ g	27	BBBC		3	8/22
Mathematics-Primary Educ (nlp)	XG21	4FT deg	M g	DD	X	M*_^_ g	27	BBCC		4	8/14
Mathematics-Primary Educ (upr)	XG41	4FT deg	M g	DD	X	M*_^_ g	27	BBCC		6	8/20
Music-Primary Educ (upr)	XW43	4FT deg	Mu g	CD	X	M*_^_ g	27	BBBC		5	8/22
Music-Primary Education (nlp)	XW23	4FT deg	Mu g	CD	X	M*_^_ g	27	BBBC		8	14/19
Theology and Rel Studs-Primary Educ (nlp)	XV28	4FT deg	g	CC	MO+2D	M	27	BBCC		6	14/24
Theology and Rel Studs-Primary Educ (upr)	XV48	4FT deg	g	CC	MO+2D	M	27	BBCC		5	14/22
ROBERT GORDON Univ											
Mathematics and Computing with Education	G1X7	4FT deg	M+E g	DD	Ind	Ind	Ind	BCC$	Ind		
ROEHAMPTON INST											
Teaching St with Science & Mathematical St	X4G1▼	4FT deg	g	DD	3M	P$ go	24	CCC	N$		
Teaching Studies with Art for Community	X2W1▼	4FT deg	g	DD	3M	P$ go	24	CCC	N		
Teaching Studies with Art for Community	X3W1▼	4FT deg	g	DD	3M	P$ go	24	CCC	N	4	6/16
Teaching Studies with Art for Community	X4W1▼	4FT deg	g	DD	3M	P$ go	24	CCC	N	21	
Teaching Studies with Design & Technology	X3J9▼	4FT deg	g	DD	3M	P$ go	24	CCC	N$		
Teaching Studies with Design & Technology	X4J9▼	4FT deg	g	DD	3M	P$ go	24	CCC	N$		
Teaching Studies with Design & Technology	X2J9▼	4FT deg	g	DD	3M	P$ go	24	CCC	N$		
Teaching Studies with Drama & Theatre Studies	X2WK▼	4FT deg	T/E g	16	3D	M$_^_ go	30	BBC	Ind		
Teaching Studies with Drama & Theatre Studies	X3WK▼	4FT deg	T/E g	16	3D	M$_^_ go	30	BBC	Ind	14	12/18
Teaching Studies with Drama & Theatre Studies	X4WK▼	4FT deg	T/E g	16	3D	M$_^_ go	30	BBC	Ind	7	8/16
Teaching Studies with English Lang & Linguistics	X3QH▼	4FT deg	E/L g	CC	2M+2D$	M$_^_ go	30	BBC	Ind	4	10/26
Teaching Studies with English Literature	X4Q3▼	4FT deg	E g	CC	2M+2D$	M_^_ go	28	BBC	Ind	9	10/20
Teaching Studies with English Literature	X3Q3▼	4FT deg	E g	CC	2M+2D$	M_^_ go	28	BBC	Ind	8	8/20
Teaching Studies with English Literature	X2Q3▼	4FT deg	E g	CC	2M+2D$	M_^_ go	28	BBC	Ind		
Teaching Studies with Environmental Studies	X2F9▼	4FT deg	B/Gy g	DD	4M $	P$ go	26	BCC	N$		
Teaching Studies with Environmental Studies	X3F9▼	4FT deg	B/Gy g	DD	4M $	P$ go	26	BCC	N$	3	5/10
Teaching Studies with Environmental Studies	X4F9▼	4FT deg	B/Gy g	DD	4M $	P$ go	26	BCC	N$	6	
Teaching Studies with French Studies	X4R1▼	4FT/5SW deg	F g	12	4M $	P_^_ go	26	BCC	N$	4	8/22
Teaching Studies with Geography	X3L8▼	4FT deg	Gy g	DD	4M $	P$ go	6	BCC	N$	3	4/20
Teaching Studies with Geography	X4L8▼	4FT deg	Gy g	DD	4M $	P$ go	26	BCC	N$	5	6/24
Teaching Studies with Geography	X2L8▼	4FT deg	Gy g	DD	4M $	P$ go	26	BCC	N$		
Teaching Studies with History	X2V1▼	4FT deg	H g	DD	4M $	P_^_ go	26	BCC	N$		
Teaching Studies with History	X3V1▼	4FT deg	H g	DD	4M $	P_^_ go	26	BCC	N$	7	10/16
Teaching Studies with History	X4V1▼	4FT deg	H g	DD	4M $	P_^_ go	26	BCC	N$	5	10/20
Teaching Studies with Music	X4W3▼	4FT deg	Mu g	DD	4M $	P_^_ go	26	BCC	N$	5	6/10
Teaching Studies with Music	X3W3▼	4FT deg	Mu g	DD	4M $	P_^_ go	26	BCC	N$	8	16/24
Teaching Studies with Music	X2W3▼	4FT deg	Mu g	DD	4M $	P_^_ go	26	BCC	N$		
Teaching Studies with Physical Education	X2X8▼	3FT deg	g	12	4M	M go	26	BCC	N$		
Teaching Studies with Physical Education	X3X8▼	4FT deg	g	12	4M	M go	26	BCC	N$		
Teaching Studies with Physical Education	X4X8▼	4FT deg	g	12	4M	M go	26	BCC	N$		
Teaching Studies with Science & Mathematical St	X2G1▼	4FT deg	g	DD	3M	P$ go	24	CCC	N$		
Teaching Studies with Science & Mathematical St	X3G1▼	4FT deg	g	DD	3M	P$ go	24	CCC	N$		
Teaching Studies with Sciences	X3Y1▼	4FT deg	B g	6	3M	P$ go	24	CCC	N	8	
Teaching Studies with Sciences	X4Y1▼	4FT deg	B g	12	3M	P$ go	24	CCC	N	6	6/14
Teaching Studies with Sciences	X2Y1▼	4FT deg	B g	12	3M	P$ go	24	CCC	N		
Teaching Studies with Theology & Religious St	X4V8▼	4FT deg	g	DD	3M	P$ go	24	CCC	N	6	8/14
Teaching Studies with Theology & Religious Studs	X3V8▼	4FT deg	g	DD	3M	P$ go	24	CCC	N	6	6/22
Teaching Studies with Theology & Religious Studs	X2V8▼	4FT deg	g	DD	3M	P$ go	24	CCC	N		
Teaching Studs with English Lang & Linguistics	X2QH▼	4FT deg	E/L g	CC	2M+2D$	M$_^_ go	30	BBC	Ind		
Teaching Studs with English Lang & Linguistics	X4QH▼	4FT deg	E/L g	CC	2M+2D$	M$_^_ go	30	BBC	Ind	6	

			98 expected requirements							96 entry stats	
course details											
TITLE	CODE	COURSE	SUBJECTS	A/AS	ND/C	AGNVQ	IB	SQA(H)	SQA	RATIO	A/AS
Univ College SCARBOROUGH											
Art and Design-Primary Education	XW51	3FT deg	A g	DD	Ind		27$	Ind	Ind		
Biological Studies - Primary Education	XC51	3FT deg	B g	DD	Ind	P	27$	Ind	Ind		
Mathematics - Primary Education	XG51	3FT deg	M g	DD	Ind	P	27$	Ind	Ind		
Music - Primary Education	XW53	3FT deg	Mu g	DD	Ind		27$	Ind	Ind		
SHEFFIELD HALLAM Univ											
Design and Technology	XW7F	2FT deg		X	HN	X	X	X	X		
Chemistry	XF71	2FT deg		X	HN	X	X	X	X		
Design and Technology	XW72	3FT deg	2(A/Ad/Ds/P)	EE	N	M$	Ind	Ind	Ind		
Mathematics	XG71	3FT deg	M	DE	N	M^	Ind	Ind	Ind		
Mathematics	XG7C	2FT deg		X	HN	X	X	X	X		
Physical Education	XX78	3FT deg	*	14	MO+4D	D	Ind	Ind	Ind		
Physics	XF73	2FT deg		X	HN	X	X	X	X		
Primary Education (2-year route)	X500	2FT deg									
Primary Education with QTS (English)	XQ53	3FT deg									
Primary Education with QTS (Geography)	XF58	3FT deg									
Primary Education with QTS (History)	XV51	3FT deg									
Primary Education with QTS (Mathematics)	XG51	3FT deg									
Primary Education with QTS (Science)	XY51	3FT deg									
Primary Education with QTS (Technology)	XJ59	3FT deg									
Science	XY71	3FT deg	S	EE	N	M^	Ind	Ind	Ind		
Univ College of St MARTIN, LANCASTER AND CUMBRIA											
Art and Design/Education (nlp) (4 Yrs)	X2W1	4FT deg	A g	CD-CEE	3M+2D$	MA	28$	BBCC$	Ind	3	8/22
Art and Design/Education (upr) (4 Yrs)	X4W1	4FT deg	A g	CD-CEE	3M+2D$	MA	28$	BBCC$	Ind	6	12/20
Biological Studies/Education (nlp) (4 Yrs)	X2C1	4FT deg	B g	CD-CEE	X	MS	28$	BBCC$	Ind	4	10/26
Biological Studies/Education (upr) (4 Yrs)	X4C1	4FT deg	B g	CD-CEE	X	MS	28$	BBCC$	Ind	4	8/20
English/Education (nlp)	X2QH▼	4FT deg	E g	BC-CDD	X	P^	28$	BBBC$			
English/Education (nlp) (4 Yrs)	X2Q3▼	4FT deg	E g	BC-CDD	X	P^	28$	BBBC$	Ind	13	12/24
English/Education (upr)	X4QH▼	4FT deg	E g	BC-CDD	X	P^	28$	BBBC$			
English/Education (upr) (4 Yrs)	X4Q3▼	4FT deg	E g	BC-CDD	X	P^	28$	BBBC$	Ind	8	12/22
Geography/Education (nlp)	X2LV▼	4FT deg	Gy g	CD-CEE	X	P^	28$	BCCC$			
Geography/Education (nlp) (4 Yrs)	X2L8▼	4FT deg	Gy g	CD-CEE	X	P^	28$	BCCC$	Ind	5	10/20
Geography/Education (upr)	X4LV▼	4FT deg	Gy g	CD-CEE	X	P^	28$	BCCC$			
Geography/Education (upr) (4 Yrs)	X4L8▼	4FT deg	Gy g	CD-CEE	X	P^	28$	BCCC$	Ind	5	10/26
History/Education (nlp)	X2VC▼	4FT deg	H g	CD-CEE	X	P^	28$	BCCC$			
History/Education (nlp) (4 Yrs)	X2V1▼	4FT deg	H g	CD-CEE	X	X	28$	BCCC$	Ind	3	12/22
History/Education (upr)	X4VC▼	4FT deg	H g	CD-CEE	X	X	28$	BCCC$			
History/Education (upr) (4 Yrs)	X4V1▼	4FT deg	H g	CD-CEE	X	X	28$	BBCC$	Ind	7	10/24
IT/Professional Studies	X6G5▼	4FT deg									
Mathematics Education (2 Yrs)	X7G1	2FT deg	M g		HN		X	X	Ind	3	
Mathematics/Education (nlp) (4 Yrs)	X2G1	4FT deg	M g	DD-DEE	X	P^	28$	BCCC$	Ind	5	6/24
Mathematics/Education (upr) (4 Yrs)	X4G1	4FT deg	M g	DD-DEE	X	P^	28$	BCCC$	Ind	2	6/28
Modern Languages/Professional Studies	X6T9▼	4FT deg									
Music/Education (nlp) (4 Yrs)	X2W3	4FT deg	Mu g	DD-DEE	X	X	28$	BCCC$	Ind	4	10/20
Music/Education (upr) (4 Yrs)	X4W3	4FT deg	Mu g	DD-DEE	X	X	28$	BCCC$	Ind	8	6/12
Physical Education/Education (nlp)	X2XV▼	4FT deg	g	CD	3M+2D	M$	28$	BCCC$			
Physical Education/Education (upr)	X4XV▼	4FT deg	g	CD	2M+2D	M$	28$	BCCC$			
Physical Science Education	X7Y1	2FT deg	g		HN	X	X	X		5	
Professional Studies for Primary Teaching (nlp)	X201▼	4FT deg	g	CC	3M+2D	M*	28	BBCC		10	14/21
Religious Studies/Education (nlp) (4 Yrs)	X2V8▼	4FT deg	g	CD	3M+2D$	M*	28$	BCCC	Ind	6	14/26
Religious Studies/Education (upr) (4 Yrs)	X4V8▼	4FT deg	g	CD	3M+2D$	M*	28$	BCCC	Ind	8	12/20

TITLE	CODE	COURSE	SUBJECTS	A/AS	NQ/C	AGNVQ	IB	SQA(H)	SQA	RATIO A/AS
SOUTH BANK Univ										
Teaching Studies (Primary)	X500	4FT deg	M+E g	CD	Ind	M go	Ind	Ind	Ind	
Teaching Studies (Shortened Primary)	X502	2FT deg		X	X	X	Ind	Ind	Ind	
ST ANDREW'S COLL Glasgow										
Music - Secondary	WX37	4FT deg	* g	BC				BBC$	$	7
Primary	X500	4FT deg	* g	CCC				BBB$	$	7
Theology-Secondary	VX87	4FT deg	* g	BC-CCD				BBB$	$	3
THE UNIVERSITY COLLEGE OF ST MARK AND ST JOHN										
Design & Technology-Primary Education	X5W2	4FT deg		8	MO	M	Dip	CCCC	Ind	
Design & Technology-Secondary Education	X7W2	4FT deg		4	MO	M	Dip	CCCC	Ind	
English-Primary Education	X5Q3	4FT deg	El	8	Ind	M	Ind	Ind	Ind	
Geography-Primary Education	X5L8	4FT deg	Gy	8	MO	M	Dip	CCCC	Ind	
History-Primary Education	X5V1	4FT deg	H	8	MO	M	Dip	CCCC	Ind	
Mathematics-Primary Education	X5G1	4FT deg	M	4-8	Ind	M	Dip	CCCC	Ind	
Mathematics-Secondary Education	X7G1	4FT deg								
Physical Education-Primary Education	X5X8	4FT deg		8	MO	M	Dip	CCCC	Ind	
Physical Education-Secondary Education	X7X8	4FT deg		8	MO	M	Ind	Ind	Ind	
Religious Studies-Primary Education	X5V8	4FT deg	Re	8	MO	M	Dip	CCCC	Ind	
Science-Primary Education	X5Y1	4FT deg	S	4-8	MO	M	Dip	CCCC	Ind	
ST MARY'S Univ COLL										
Biology (4 Yrs)	X5C1	4FT deg	B/C g	8-12	Ind	Ind	Ind	BBBB$	Ind	
Drama (4 Yrs)	X5W4	4FT deg	* g	12-14	Ind	Ind	Ind	BBBB	Ind	
English (4 Yrs)	X5Q3	4FT deg	E g	12-14	X	X	Ind	BBBB$	X	
Geography (4 Yrs)	X5L8	4FT deg	Gy g	12-14	Ind	Ind	Ind	BBBB$	Ind	
History (4 Yrs)	X5V1	4FT deg	H g	12-14	Ind	Ind	Ind	BBBB$	Ind	
Physical Education (4 Yrs)	X5X8	4FT deg	S g	12-14	Ind	Ind	Ind	BBBB$	Ind	
Physical Education (Sec)	X740	4FT deg	S g	12-14	Ind	Ind	Ind	BBBB$	Ind	
Theology and Religious Studies (4 Yrs)	X5V8	4FT deg	* g	12-14	Ind	Ind	Ind	BBBB	Ind	
Univ of STIRLING										
Biology/Chemistry/Education	YX17	4/5FT deg	C	CCD	HN	Ind	28	BBCC	HN	
Business Studies/Computing Science/Education	NXC7	4/5FT deg		CCC	HN	Ind	28	BBCC	HN	
Business Studies/Education	NX17	4/5FT deg	g	BBC	Ind	Ind	33	BBBB	HN	
Computing Science/Mathematics/Education	GX97	4/5FT deg	M	CCC	HN	Ind	28	BBCC	HN	
Education/Biochemistry	CX77	4/5FT deg	C g	CCD	Ind	Ind	28	BBCC	HN	
Education/Biology	CX17	4/5FT deg	S g	CCD	Ind	Ind	28	BBCC	HN	
Education/Chemistry	FX17	4/5FT deg	C g	CCD	Ind	Ind	28	BBCC	HN	
Education/Computing Science	GX57	4/5FT deg	g	CCC	Ind	Ind	28	BBCC	HN	
Education/English & Commonwealth Literature	QX27	4/5FT deg	g	BBC	HN	Ind	33	BBBB	HN	
Education/English Studies	QX37	4/5FT deg	g	BBC	Ind	Ind	33	BBBB	HN	
Education/Film & Media Studies	PX47	4/5FT deg	g	BBC	Ind	Ind	35	ABBB	HN	
Education/French	RX17	4/5FT deg	g	CCC	Ind	Ind	31	BBBC	HN	
Education/German	RX27	4/5FT deg	g	CCC	Ind	Ind	31	BBBC	HN	
Education/History	VX17	4/5FT deg	g	BCC	Ind	Ind	31	BBBC	HN	
Education/Mathematics	GX17	4/5FT deg	M g	CCC	Ind	Ind	28	BBCC	HN	
Education/Mathematics and its Applications	GXC7	4/5FT deg	M g	CCC	Ind	Ind	28	BBCC	HN	
Education/Religious Studies	VX87	4/5FT deg	g	CCC	Ind	Ind	28	BBCC	HN	
Education/Spanish	RX47	4/5FT deg	g	CCC	Ind	Ind	31	BBBC	HN	
English/History/Education	QXH7	4/5FT deg		BBC	HN	Ind	33	BBBB	HN	
English/Religious Studies/Education	QXJ7	4/5FT deg		BBC	HN	Ind	33	BBBB	HN	
French/German/Education	RXC7	4/5FT deg		CCC	HN	Ind	31	BBBC	HN	

course details			98 expected requirements							96 entry stats	
TITLE	CODE	COURSE	SUBJECTS	A/AS	NO/C	AGNVQ	IB	SQA(H)	SQA	RATIO	A/AS
French/Spanish/Education	RXD7	4/5FT deg		CCC	HN	Ind	31	BBBC	HN		
German/Spanish/Education	RXF7	4/5FT deg		CCC	HN	Ind	31	BBBC	HN		
History/Religious Studies/Education	VXC7	4/5FT deg		CCC	HN	Ind	28	BBCC	HN		

Univ of STRATHCLYDE

Design and Technology	J9X7	4FT deg	M/S g	CC	Ind		Ind	BBC$	HN		
Mathematics with Teaching Qual (Secondary)	G1X7	4FT/5FT deg	M g	CD	Ind		30$	BBBC$	Ind		
Physics with Teaching Qualification (Secondary)	F3X7	4FT deg	M+P g	CC	Ind		24$	BBCC$	Ind		
Primary Education	X500	4FT deg	E g	BC	Ind		Ind	BBBC$	Ind		

Univ of SUNDERLAND

Business Education	XN71	4FT deg	g	8	Ind	P$ go	24	CCCC	N$	3	8/18
Business Education (2 Yrs)	XN7C	2FT deg	g	X	HN $	X	X	X	HN$	4	
Design and Technology (2 years)	X7WF	2FT deg	g	X	HN $	X	X	X	HN$		
Design and Technology (3 years)	X7W2	3FT deg	Ds/Ad g	8	Ind	P$ go	24$	CCC$	Ind		
English Education	XQ73	3FT deg	E/El g	12	3M+2D	M$^ g	24	CCCCC$	N$	4	6/14
Geography Education	XL78	3FT deg	Gy g	12	Ind	M$^ go	24	CCCCC$	N$	2	6/12
Information Technology Education	XG7M	3FT deg	Ap	12	HN $	M$	24$		N$		
Information Technology Education (QTS)	XG75	2FT deg	Ap	12	HN $	X	X	X	HN$	1	
Key Stage 2/3 Education	X600	2FT deg	g	X	HN $	X	X	X	HN$	1	
Mathematics Education	XG7C	3FT deg	M g	12	Ind	P$^	24$	CCCCC$	Ind		
Mathematics Education (2 Yrs)	XG71	2FT deg	g	X	HN $	X	X	X	HN$	5	
Mod Foreign Language Educ(French w.Germ or Span)	XR71	2FT deg	g	X	HN $	X	X	X	HN$	5	
Mod Foreign Language Educ(Germ w.French or Span)	XR72	2FT deg	g	X	HN $	X	X	X	HN$	1	
Mod Foreign Language Educ(Span w.French or Germ)	XR74	2FT deg	g	X	HN $	X	X	X	HN$		
Music Education (College Diploma Req in Music)	XW73	2FT deg	g	X	HN $	X	X	X	HN $	2	
Primary Education	X500	3FT deg	* g	14	3M+2D	M$6/^ go	26	BBCCC	N$	12	10/22
Primary Education	X501	2FT deg	g	X	HN $	X	X	X	HN$	6	
Religious Education	XV78	3FT deg	Re g	12	Ind	M$^ go	24	CCCCC$	N$		7/12
Science Education	XY71	2FT deg	g	X	HN $	X	X	X	HN$	2	
Technology Education	XW72	4FT deg	Ds/Es/Ad g	8	Ind $	P$ go	24$	CCC$	Ind	2	8/ 9
Technology Education (2 Yrs)	XW7F	2FT deg	g	X	HN $	X	X	X	HN$	4	

SWANSEA INST of HE

Business Education (11-18)	XN71	4FT deg	g	10	MO+3D	Ind	Ind	Ind	Ind	2	
Primary Education	X500	3FT/4FT deg		12						6	8/18

TRINITY COLL Carmarthen

Art, Craft and Design	XW59	3FT deg	A/Fa g	DD-CC	Ind		Ind	Ind	Ind	4	8/18
English	XQ53	3FT deg	E g	DD-CC	Ind		Ind	Ind	Ind	6	6/18
Geography	XL58	3FT deg	Gy g	DD-CC	Ind		Ind	Ind	Ind	4	8/12
History	XV51	3FT deg	H g	DD-CC	Ind		Ind	Ind	Ind	14	
Mathematics	XG51	3FT deg	M g	DD-CC	Ind		Ind	Ind	Ind	6	6/10
Music	XW53	3FT deg	g	DD-CC	Ind		Ind	Ind	Ind	3	6/16
Physical Education	XX58	3FT deg	* g	DD-CC	Ind		Ind	Ind	Ind	5	6/16
Religious Studies	XV58	3FT deg	* g	DD-CC	Ind		Ind	Ind	Ind	4	8/18
Science and the Environment	XF59	3FT deg	S g	DD-CC	Ind		Ind	Ind	Ind	4	8/20
Technology	XJ59	3FT deg	* g	DD-CC	Ind		Ind	Ind	Ind	2	8/13
Welsh	XQ55	3FT deg	W g	DD-CC	Ind		Ind	Ind	Ind	5	8/18

Univ of WARWICK

With specialism in Arts (Lower Primary) (QTS)	X3Y3	4FT deg	A/Ad/Mu/Pa/T g	BCC-CCC	X	X	28$	BBBBC$		2	14/24
With specialism in Arts (Upper Primary) (QTS)	X4Y3	4FT deg	A/Ad/Mu/Pa/T g	BCC-CCC	X	X	28$	BBBBC$		1	14/24
With specialism in English (Lower Primary) (QTS)	X3Q3	4FT deg	E g	BBC	X	X	32$	ABBBB$		11	22/28
With specialism in English (Upper Primary) (QTS)	X4Q3	4FT deg	E g	BBC	X	X	32$	ABBBB$		14	20/30

course details			98 expected requirements							96 entry stats	
TITLE	CODE	COURSE	SUBJECTS	A/AS	ND/C	AGNVQ	IB	SQA(H)	SQA	RATIO	A/AS
With specialism in Mathematics (Lr Primary)(QTS)	X3G1	4FT deg	M g	CCC	X	X	28$	BBBBC		4	16/26
With specialism in Mathematics (Upr Prim) (QTS)	X4G1	4FT deg	M g	CCC	X	X	28$	BBBBC		9	18/24
With specialism in Science (Lower Primary)((QTS)	X3Y1	4FT deg	B g	CCC	X	X	28$	BBBBC$		5	14/24
With specialism in Science (Upper Primary) (QTS)	X4Y1	4FT deg	B g	CCC	X	X	28$	BBBBC$		5	16/26
Univ of WOLVERHAMPTON											
Primary	X500	3FT deg	g	B-E			Ind	Ind	Ind	13	6/18
Secondary	X700	3FT deg	g	B-E			Ind	Ind	Ind	2	6/22
Secondary (Two Year Version)	X701	2FT deg	g		HN		X	X	X	3	
WORCESTER COLL of HE											
Art	XW51	4FT deg	A g	12	Ind	Ind	Ind	Ind	Ind	5	8/18
Biological Science	XC51	4FT deg	B g	12	Ind	Ind	Ind	Ind	Ind	8	9/24
English	XQ53	4FT deg	E g	12	Ind	Ind	Ind	Ind	English	13	12/22
Physical Education	XX58	4FT deg	g	12	Ind	Ind	Ind	Ind	Ind	14	8/16
Physical Education (Key Stage 2/3)	XX68	4FT deg									
Primary - Early Years	X300	3FT deg	g	12	Ind	Ind	Ind	Ind	Ind	2	10/20
Primary - Later Years	X400	3FT deg	g	12	Ind	Ind	Ind	Ind	Ind	1	10/20

TITLE	CODE	COURSE	SUBJECTS	A/AS	NO/C	AGNVQ	IB	SQA(H)	SQA	RATIO A/AS
Univ of ABERDEEN										
Biblical Studies	V820	4FT deg	* g	BBC	Ind	M$ go	30$	BBBB$	Ind	4
Cultural History with History of Religions	V9V8	4FT deg	* g	BBC	Ind	M$ go	30$	BBBB$	Ind	2
Divinity (BD)	V800	4FT deg	* g	CC	Ind	M* go	24	BBCC	Ind	3
English with Religious Studies	Q3V8	4FT deg	* g	BBC	Ind	M$ go	30$	BBBB$	Ind	
English-Religious Studies	QV38	4FT deg	* g	BBC	Ind	M$ go	30$	BBBB$	Ind	
History of Art-Religious Studies	VV48	4FT deg	* g	BBC	Ind	M$ go	30$	BBBB$	Ind	
History-Religious Studies	VV18	4FT deg	* g	BBC	Ind	M$ go	30$	BBBB$	Ind	9
International Relations-Religious Studies	VM81	4FT deg	* g	BBC	Ind	M$ go	30$	BBBB$	Ind	1
Licence in Theology	V880	3FT deg	* g	CC	Ind	M* go	24	BBCC	Ind	
Philosophy-Religious Studies	VV78	4FT deg	* g	BBC	Ind	M$ go	30$	BBBB$	Ind	
Politics-Religious Studies	MV18	4FT deg	* g	BBC	Ind	M$ go	30$	BBBB$	Ind	
Religious Studies	V801	3FT/4FT deg	* g	BBC	Ind	M$ go	30$	BBBB$	Ind	
Religious Studies with Film Studies	V8W5	4FT deg	* g	BBC	Ind	M$ go	30$	BBBB$	Ind	
Religious Studies with Women's Studies	V8M9	4FT deg	* g	BBC	Ind	M$ go	30$	BBBB$	Ind	
Religious Studies-Celtic	VQ85	5FT deg	* g	BBC	Ind	M$ go	30$	BBBB$	Ind	
Religious Studies-Celtic (4 Yrs)	QV58	4FT deg	* g	BBC	Ind	M$ go	30$	BBBB$	Ind	
Religious Studies-French	VR81	4FT/5FT deg	* g	BBC	Ind	M$ go	30$	BBBB$	Ind	
Religious Studies-French (4 Yrs)	RV18	4FT deg	* g	BBC	Ind	M$ go	30$	BBBB$	Ind	
Religious Studies-German	VR82	4FT/5FT deg	* g	BBC	Ind	M$ go	30$	BBBB$	Ind	
Religious Studies-German (4 Yrs)	RV28	4FT deg	* g	BBC	Ind	M$ go	30$	BBBB$	Ind	
Religious Studies-Hispanic Studies	VR84	4FT/5FT deg	* g	BBC	Ind	M$ go	30$	BBBB$	Ind	
Religious Studies-Hispanic Studies (4 Yrs)	RV48	4FT deg	* g	BBC	Ind	M$ go	30$	BBBB$	Ind	
Sociology-Religious Studies	LV38	4FT deg	* g	BBC	Ind	M$ go	30$	BBBB$	Ind	12
Theology (B TH)	V802	4FT deg	* g	CC	Ind	M* go	24$	BBCC	Ind	2
Theology with French	V8R1	3FT deg	* g	CC	Ind	M* go	24$	BBCC	Ind	
Theology with Gaelic	V8Q5	3FT deg	* g	CC	Ind	M* go	24$	BBCC	Ind	
Theology with German	V8R2	3FT deg	* g	CC	Ind	M* go	24$	BBCC	Ind	
Theology with Spanish	V8R4	3FT deg	* g	CC	Ind	M* go	24$	BBCC	Ind	
Univ of Wales, BANGOR										
Biblical Studies	V820	3FT deg	* g	CCC	Ind	D*6/^ go	26	BBCC	Ind	
Diploma in Theology	V870	3FT Dip	* g							2
Religious Studies	V840	3FT deg	* g	CCC	Ind	D*6/^ go	26	BBCC	Ind	7
Religious Studies/Education (Taught in Welsh)	VX89	3FT deg	* g	CCD	Ind	D*6/^ go	Ind	X	X	3
Religious Studies/English	QV38	3FT deg	E g	CCC	X	D*_/^ go	28$	BBBC$	X	5
Religious Studies/German	RV28	4FT deg	* g	CCD	X	D*6/^ go	28$	BBBC$	X	
Religious Studies/History	VV18	3FT deg	H g	CCC	Ind	D*_/^ go	28$	BBBC$	Ind	2	16/22
Religious Studies/Physical Education	VB86	3FT deg	* g	CCC	Ind	D*6/^ go	28	BBBC	Ind	
Russian/Religious Studies	RV88	4FT deg	* g	CCD	Ind	D*6/^ go	28	BBBC	Ind	
Social Policy/Religious Studies	LV48	3FT deg	* g	CCD	Ind	D*6/^ go	28	BBBC	Ind	3
Sociology/Religious Studies	LV38	3FT deg	* g	CCD	5M	D*6/^ go	28	BBBC	Ind	12
Sports Science/Religious Studies	BV68	3FT deg	* g	20	5D	D*6/^ go	30	BBBC	Ind	
Theology (B Theol)	V806	3FT deg	* g	CCC	Ind	D*6/^ go	26	BBCC	Ind	1	6/18
Theology (BD)	V800	3FT deg	* g	CCC	Ind	D*6/^ go	26	BBCC	Ind	3
Welsh History/Religious Studies	VVC8	3FT deg	H g	CCD	Ind	D*_/^ go	28$	BBBC$	Ind	
Welsh/Religious Studies	QV58	3FT/4FT deg	W g	CCD	Ind	D*_/^ go	Ind	X	X	4
Women's Studies and Religious Studies	MV98	3FT deg	* g	18	5M	D*6/^ go	28	BBBC	Ind	
BATH COLL of HE										
Study of Religions	V800	3FT deg	*		N		Ind	$	$	9
Combined Awards *Study of Religions*	Y400	3FT deg	*		N		Ind	$	$	
Modular Programme (DipHE) *Study of Religions*	Y460	2FT Dip	*		N		Ind	$	$	

course details			98 expected requirements							96 entry stats
TITLE	CODE	COURSE	SUBJECTS	A/AS	ND/C	AGNVQ	IB	SQA(H)	SQA	RATIO A/AS
Univ of BIRMINGHAM										
African Studies/Theology	TV78	3FT deg	*	BBB	Ind	D*^	32	ABBB	Ind	
Ancient History & Archaeology/Theology	VV68	3FT deg	*	BBB	Ind	D*^	32	ABBB	Ind	8
Artificial Intelligence/Theology	GV88	3FT deg	* g	BBB	Ind	D*^	32	ABBB	Ind	
Classical Literature and Civilisation/Theology	QV88	3FT deg	*	BBB	Ind	D*^	32	ABBB	Ind	
Computer Studies/Theology	GV58	3FT deg	* g	BBB	Ind	D*^	32	ABBB	Ind	
East Mediterranean History/Theology	VVD8	3FT deg	* g	BBB	Ind	D*^	32	ABBB	Ind	2
English/Theology	QV38	3FT deg	*	BBB	Ind	D*^	32	ABBB	Ind	19
French Studies/Theology	RV18	4FT deg	F	BBB	Ind	D*_^	32$	ABBB	Ind	
Geography/Theology	LV88	3FT deg	Gy	BBB	Ind	D*_^	32$	ABBB	Ind	6
German Studies/Theology	RV28	4FT deg	G	BBB	Ind	D*_^	32$	ABBB	Ind	
Hispanic Studies/Theology	RV48	4FT deg	*	BBB	Ind	D*^	32	ABBB	Ind	
History of Art/Theology	VV48	3FT deg	*	BBB	Ind	D*^	32	ABBB	Ind	6
History/Theology	VV18	3FT deg	*	BBB	Ind	D*^	32	ABBB	Ind	8
Italian/Theology	RV38	4FT deg	*	BBB	Ind	D*^	32	ABBB	Ind	
Latin/Theology	QV68	3FT deg	Ln	BBB	Ind	D*_^	32$	ABBB	Ind	
Mathematics/Theology	GV18	3FT deg	M g	ABB-ABC	Ind	D*_^	32$	ABBB	Ind	
Media & Cultural Studies/Theology	PV48	3FT deg	*	BBB	Ind	D*^	32	ABBB	Ind	
Modern Greek Studies/Theology	TV28	4FT deg	* g	BBB	Ind	D*^	32	ABBB	Ind	
Music/Theology	VW83	3FT deg	Mu	AAB-ABB	Ind	D*_^	32$	ABBB	Ind	
Philosophy/Theology	VV78	3FT deg	*	BBB	Ind	D*^	32	ABBB	Ind	21
Portuguese/Theology	RV58	4FT deg	*	BBB	Ind	D*^	32	ABBB	Ind	
Russian/Theology	RV88	4FT deg	*	BBB	Ind	D*^	32	ABBB	Ind	
Sport & Recreation Studies/Theology	VB86	3FT deg	*	BBB	Ind	D*^	32	ABBB	Ind	
Theology	V800	3FT deg	*	BBC	Ind	D*^	32	ABBB	Ind	6 18/28
BISHOP GROSSETESTE COLL										
Religion in Contemporary Society	V860	3FT deg	*	8	9M	MG go	Ind	Ind	Ind	
Univ of BRISTOL										
Philosophy and Theology	VV78	3FT deg	*	BBC	Ind	D$^	30$	BBBBB	Ind	25
Theology and Politics	VM81	3FT deg	*	BBC	Ind	D$^	30$	BBBBB	Ind	11
Theology and Religious Studies	V816	3FT deg	*	BCC	Ind	D$^	28$	BBBBB	Ind	6 14/28
Theology and Sociology	VL83	3FT deg	* g	BBC	Ind	D$^	30$	BBBBB	Ind	12
BRISTOL, Univ of the W of England										
Theological Studies (Wesley College)	V800▼	3FT deg	* g	8	Ind	P*^ go	24	CCC	Ind	
CAMBRIDGE Univ										
Religious Studies with Education Studies (BA)	V8X9▼	3FT deg	* g	AAB	Ind		Ind	CSYS	Ind	
Theology and Religious Studies	V800▼	3FT deg	* g	AAB	Ind		Ind	CSYS	Ind	2 28/30
CANTERBURY CHRIST CHURCH COLL of HE										
American Studies with Religious Studies	Q4V8	4FT deg	* g	CC	MO	M	24	Ind	Ind	
Art with Religious Studies	W1V8	3FT deg	A g	CC	MO	M	24	Ind	Ind	3
Business Studies with Religious Studies	N1V8	3FT deg	* g	CC	MO	M	24	Ind	Ind	
Early Childhood Studies with Religious Studies	X9V8	3FT deg	* g	CC	MO	M	24	Ind	Ind	3
English with Religious Studies	Q3V8	3FT deg	E	CC	MO	M	24	Ind	Ind	3 10/12
Geography with Religious Studies	L8V8	3FT deg	Gy g	CC	MO	M	24	Ind	Ind	2
History with Religious Studies	V1V8	3FT deg	H g	CC	MO	M	24	Ind	Ind	
Information Technology with Religious Studies	G5V8	3FT deg	* g	CC	MO	M	24	Ind	Ind	
Marketing with Religious Studies	N5V8	3FT deg	* g	CC	MO	M	24	Ind	Ind	
Mathematics with Religious Studies	G1V8	3FT deg	M g	DD	Ind	Ind	24	Ind	Ind	3
Media Studies with Religious Studies	P4V8	3FT deg	* g	CC	MO	M	24	Ind	Ind	
Music with Religious Studies	W3V8	3FT deg	Mu g	CC	MO	M	24	Ind	Ind	

| | | | 98 expected requirements | | | | | | 96 entry stats | |
| course details | | | | | | | | | | |

TITLE	CODE	COURSE	SUBJECTS	A/AS	ND/C	AGNVQ	IB	SQA(H)	SQA	RATIO A/AS
Psychology with Religious Studies	L7V8	3FT deg	Ps g	CC	MO	M	24	Ind	Ind	
Radio, Film & Television Studs with Religious St	W5V8	3FT deg	* g	CC	MO	M	24	Ind	Ind	5
Religious Studies	V840	3FT deg	* g	CC	MO	M	24	Ind	Ind	4
Religious Studies and American Studies	QV48	3FT deg	* g	CC	MO	M	24	Ind	Ind	
Religious Studies and Art	VW81	3FT deg	A g	CC	MO	M	24	Ind	Ind	3
Religious Studies and Business Studies	VN81	3FT deg	* g	CC	MO	M	24	Ind	Ind	
Religious Studies and Early Childhood Studies	XV98	3FT deg	* g	CC	MO	M	24	Ind	Ind	
Religious Studies and English	QV38	3FT deg	E g	CC	MO	M	24	Ind	Ind	3
Religious Studies and French	RV18	3FT deg	F g	CC	MO	M	24	Ind	Ind	
Religious Studies and Geography	LV88	3FT deg	Gy g	CC	MO	M	24	Ind	Ind	
Religious Studies and History	VV18	3FT deg	H g	CC	MO	M	24	Ind	Ind	
Religious Studies and Information Technology	GV58	3FT deg	* g	CC	MO	M	24	Ind	Ind	
Religious Studies and Marketing	VN85	3FT deg	* g	CC	MO	M	24	Ind	Ind	
Religious Studies and Mathematics	VG81	3FT deg	M g	DD	Ind	Ind	24	Ind	Ind	
Religious Studies and Media Studies	PV48	3FT deg	* g	CC	MO	M	24	Ind	Ind	
Religious Studies and Music	VW83	3FT deg	Mu g	CC	MO	M	24	Ind	Ind	2
Religious Studies and Psychology	LV78	3FT deg	Ps g	CC	MO	M	24	Ind	Ind	
Religious Studies and Radio, Film and TV Studies	WV58	3FT deg	* g	CC	MO	M	24	Ind	Ind	
Religious Studies and Social Science	VL83	3FT deg	* g	CC	MO	M	24	Ind	Ind	1 6/8
Religious Studies with American Studies	V8Q4	3FT deg	* g	CC	MO	M	24	Ind	Ind	
Religious Studies with Art	V8W1	3FT deg	A g	CC	MO	M	24	Ind	Ind	
Religious Studies with Business Studies	V8N1	3FT deg	* g	CC	MO	M	24	Ind	Ind	
Religious Studies with Early Childhood Studies	V8W9	3FT deg	* g	CC	MO	M	24	Ind	Ind	
Religious Studies with English	V8Q3	3FT deg	E g	CC	MO	M	24	Ind	Ind	
Religious Studies with French	V8R1	3FT deg	F g	CC	MO	M	24	Ind	Ind	
Religious Studies with Geography	V8L8	3FT deg	Gy g	CC	MO	M	24	Ind	Ind	
Religious Studies with History	V8V1	3FT deg	H g	CC	MO	M	24	Ind	Ind	
Religious Studies with Information Technology	V8G5	3FT deg	* g	CC	MO	M	24	Ind	Ind	
Religious Studies with Marketing	V8N5	3FT deg	* g	CC	MO	M	24	Ind	Ind	
Religious Studies with Mathematics	V8G1	3FT deg	M g	DD	Ind	Ind	24	Ind	Ind	
Religious Studies with Media Studies	V8P4	3FT deg	* g	CC	MO	M	24	Ind	Ind	
Religious Studies with Music	V8W3	3FT deg	Mu g	CC	MO	M	24	Ind	Ind	
Religious Studies with Psychology	V8L7	3FT deg	Ps g	CC	MO	M	24	Ind	Ind	
Religious Studies with Science	V8Y1	3FT deg	S g	DD	Ind	Ind	24	Ind	Ind	
Religious Studies with Social Science	V8L3	3FT deg	* g	CC	MO	M	24	Ind	Ind	4
Religious Studies with Sport Science	V8B6	3FT deg	* g	CC	MO	M	24	Ind	Ind	
Religious Studies with Statistics	V8G4	3FT deg	M g	DD	Ind	Ind	24	Ind	Ind	
Religious Studies with Tourism Studies	V8P7	3FT deg	* g	CC	MO	M	24	Ind	Ind	
Religious Studs with Radio, Film and TV Studies	V8W5	3FT deg	* g	CC	MO	M	24	Ind	Ind	
Science and Religious Studies	YV18	3FT deg	S g	DD	Ind	Ind	24	Ind	Ind	
Science with Religious Studies	Y1V8	3FT deg	S g	DD	Ind	Ind	24	Ind	Ind	
Social Science with Religious Studies	L3V8	3FT deg	* g	CC	MO	M	24	Ind	Ind	3
Sport Science and Religious Studies	BV68	3FT deg	* g	CC	MO	M	24	Ind	Ind	
Sport Science with Religious Studies	B6V8	3FT deg	* g	CC	MO	M	24	Ind	Ind	
Statistics and Religious Studies	GV48	3FT deg	M g	DD	Ind	Ind	24	Ind	Ind	
Statistics with Religious Studies	G4V8	3FT deg	M g	DD	Ind	Ind	24	Ind	Ind	
Theology	V800	3FT deg								
Tourism Studies and Religious Studies	VP87	3FT deg	* g	CC	MO	M	24	Ind	Ind	
Tourism Studies with Religious Studies	P7V8	3FT deg	* g	CC	MO	M	24	Ind	Ind	

TITLE	CODE	COURSE	SUBJECTS	A/AS	NO/C	AGNVQ	IB	SQA(H)	SQA	RATIO	A/AS
CARDIFF Univ of Wales											
Religious Studies	V840	3FT deg	*	BCC	3M+2D		Ind	AABBB		3	16/24
Religious Studies/Ancient History	VV8C	3FT deg	*	BCC	Ind		Ind	AAABB			
Religious Studies/Archaeology	VV86	3FT deg	*	BCC	Ind		Ind	AABB	X		
Religious Studies/Cultural Criticism	MV98	3FT deg	E	ABC	Ind	Ind	Ind	Ind	Ind		
Religious Studies/Education	VX89	3FT deg	*	BCC	Ind	Ind	Ind	Ind	Ind	4	18/24
Religious Studies/English Literature	VQ83	3FT deg	E	ABB	X		Ind	AAABB	X	18	
Religious Studies/German	VR82	4FT deg	G	BCC			Ind				
Religious Studies/History	VV81	3FT deg	H	BBC-BCC	X		Ind	ABBBB	X	4	24/30
Religious Studies/History of Ideas	VV8D	3FT deg	*	BCC							
Religious Studies/Italian	VR83	4FT deg	L	BCC	Ind		Ind	Ind	Ind		
Religious Studies/Music	VW83	3FT deg	Mu	BCC	X		Ind	Ind	X		
Religious Studies/Philosophy	VV87	3FT deg	*	BCC						3	20/30
Religious Studies/Politics	VM81	3FT deg		BBC							
Religious Studies/Portuguese	RV58	4FT deg	L	BBC-BCC							
Religious Studies/Pure Mathematics	VG81	3FT deg	M	BCC	Ind	Ind	Ind	BBBBC	Ind		
Social Philosophy and App Ethics/Religious Studs	VV7V	3FT deg	*	BBC							
Sociology/Religious Studies	LV38	3FT deg	*	BCC	3M+2D					13	
Spanish/Religious Studies	RV48	4FT deg	L	BBC-BCC							
Theology (BD)	V800	3FT deg	*	BCC	3M+2D			AABBB		3	14/22
Theology BTh	V830	3FT deg		BCC	Ind			ABBBB		8	
Welsh History/Religious Studies	VVC8	3FT deg	H	BBC-BCC	X		Ind	ABBBB	X		
Welsh/Religious Studies	QV58	3FT deg	W	BCC						3	
CHELTENHAM & GLOUCESTER COLL of HE											
Business Computer Systems and Religious Studies	VG85	3FT deg	*	8	MO	M	24	CCCC	Ind		
Business Computer Systems with Religious Studies	G5V8	3FT deg	*	8	MO	M	24	CCCC	Ind		
English Studies and Religious Studies	QV38	3FT deg	E	8-12	5M+2D	M^	26	CCCC	Ind		
English Studies with Religious Studies	Q3V8	3FT deg	E	12	4M+3D	M^	26	CCCC	Ind		
Environmental Policy and Religious Studies	FV98	3FT deg	*	8-10	MO	M3	26	CCCC	Ind		
Environmental Policy with Religious Studies	F9V8	3FT deg	*	8-10	MO	M3	26	CCCC	Ind		
Geology with Religious Studies	F6V8	3FT deg	*	8	MO	M3	26	CCCC	Ind		
History and Religious Studies	VV18	3FT deg	H	8-12	5M+2D	M3^	26	CCCC	Ind		
History with Religious Studies	V1V8	3FT deg	H	10-14	4M+3D	M3^	26	CCCC	Ind		
Human Geography and Religious Studies	LV88	3FT deg	*	8-12	5M+2D	M3	26	CCCC	Ind		
Information Technology and Religious Studies	GV58	3FT/4SW deg	*	8	MO	M3	24	CCCC	Ind		
Information Technology with Religious Studies	G5VV	3FT deg	*	8	MO	M3	24	CCCC	Ind		
Media Communications and Religious Studies	PV48	3FT deg	*	8-14	MO	MP3	26	CCCC	Ind		
Media Communications with Religious Studies	P4V8	3FT deg	*	12	4M+3D	MP3	26	CCCC	Ind		
Performance Arts and Religious Studies	WV48	3FT deg	*	8-12	5M+2D	M3	26	CCCC	Ind		
Performance Arts with Religious Studies	W4V8	3FT deg	*	10-14	5M+2D	M3	26	CCCC	Ind		
Psychology and Religious Studies	LV78	3FT deg	g	12	MO	M3^	26	CCCC	Ind		
Psychology with Religious Studies	L7V8	3FT deg	g	12	4M+3D	M3^	26	CCCC	Ind		
Religious Studies and Sociological Studies	LV38	3FT deg	*	8-12	MO	M3^	26	CCCC	Ind		
Religious Studies and Sport & Exercise Sciences	BV68	3FT deg	S	8-12	MO	M3^	26	CCCC	Ind		
Religious Studies and Visual Arts	VW81	3FT deg	A	8-12	5M+2D	MA3	26	CCCC	Ind		
Religious Studies and Women's Studies	MV98	3FT deg	*	8-12	MO	M3^	26	CCCC	Ind		
Religious Studies with Business Computer Systems	V8GM	3FT deg	*	8	MO	M3^	26	CCCC	Ind		
Religious Studies with Combined Arts	V8Y3	3FT deg	*	8-12	MO	M3^	26	CCCC	Ind		
Religious Studies with English Studies	V8Q3	3FT deg	*	8-12	MO	M3^	26	CCCC	Ind		
Religious Studies with Environmental Policy	V8F9	3FT deg	*	8-12	MO	M3^	26	CCCC	Ind		
Religious Studies with History	V8V1	3FT deg	*	8-12	MO	M3^	26	CCCC	Ind		
Religious Studies with Human Geography	V8L8	3FT deg	*	8-12	MO	M3^	26	CCCC	Ind		

course details | *98 expected requirements* | *96 entry stats*

			98 expected requirements						96 entry stats

course details   **98 expected requirements**   *96 entry stats*

TITLE	CODE	COURSE	SUBJECTS	A/AS	ND/C	AGNVQ	IB	SQA(H)	SQA	RATIO A/AS
Religious Studies with Information Technology	V8G5	3FT/4SW deg	*	8	MO	M3^	26	CCCC	Ind	
Religious Studies with Media Communications	V8P4	3FT deg	*	8-14	MO	M3^	26	CCCC	Ind	
Religious Studies with Performance Arts	V8W4	3FT deg	*	8-12	5M+2D	M3	26	CCCC	Ind	
Religious Studies with Psychology	V8L7	3FT deg	*	8-12	MO	M3^	26	CCCC	Ind	
Religious Studies with Sociological Studies	V8L3	3FT deg	*	8-12	MO	M3^	26	CCCC	Ind	
Religious Studies with Sport & Exercise Sciences	V8B6	3FT deg	*	8-12	MO	M3^	26	CCCC	Ind	
Religious Studies with Visual Arts	V8W1	3FT deg	*	8-12	5M+2D	MA3	26	CCCC	Ind	
Religious Studies with Women's Studies	V8M9	3FT deg	*	8-12	MO	M3^	26	CCCC	Ind	
Sociological Studies with Religious Studies	L3V8	3FT deg	*	12	5M+2D	MG3	26	CCCC	Ind	
Sport & Exercise Sciences with Religious Studies	B6V8	3FT deg	*	12-16	4M+3D	ML3	26	CCCC	Ind	
Visual Arts with Religious Studies	W1V8	3FT deg	A	10-14	5M+2D	MA3	26	CCCC	Ind	
Women's Studies with Religious Studies	M9V8	3FT deg	*	8-12	MO	M3	26	CCCC	Ind	

UNIVERSITY COLLEGE CHESTER

TITLE	CODE	COURSE	SUBJECTS	A/AS	ND/C	AGNVQ	IB	SQA(H)	SQA	RATIO A/AS
Art and Theology and Religious Studies	WV98	3FT deg	*	12	M	P^	Ind	CCCC	$	5
Art with Theology and Religious Studies	W9V8	3FT deg	*	12	M	P^	Ind	CCCC	$	
Biology and Theology and Religious Studies	CV18	3FT deg	B	12	M	P^	Ind	CCCC	$	1
Biology with Theology and Religious Studies	C1V8	3FT deg	B	12	M	P^	Ind	CCCC	$	
Church and Society	VV38	3FT deg		12	MO	P	Ind	CCCC	$	
Computer Science/IT & Theology and Religious St	GV58	3FT deg	g	12	M	M	Ind	CCCC	$	
Computer Science/IT with Theology and Rel St	G5V8	3FT deg	g	12	M	P^	Ind	CCCC	$	
Drama & Theatre Studies & Theology & Rel St	WV48	3FT deg	*	12	M	M	Ind	CCCC	$	5
Drama and Theatre St with Theology and Rel St	W4V8	3FT deg	*	12	M	M	Ind	CCCC	$	13
English Literature and Theology and Rel St	QV38	3FT deg	E	12	M	P^	Ind	CCCC	$	28
English with Theology and Religious Studies	Q3V8	3FT deg	E	12	M	P^	Ind	CCCC	$	4
Geography and Theology and Religious Studies	FV88	3FT deg	Gy/Gl	12	M	P^	Ind	CCCC	$	5
Geography with Theology and Religious Studies	F8V8	3FT deg	Gy/Gl	12	M	P^	Ind	CCCC	$	
History and Theology and Religious Studies	VV18	3FT deg	H/Ec/So	12	M	M	Ind	CCCC	$	5
History with Theology and Religious Studies	V1V8	3FT deg	H/Ec/So	12	M	M	Ind	CCCC	$	4
Mathematics and Theology and Religious Studies	GV18	3FT deg	M	12	M	P^	Ind	CCCC	$	1
Mathematics with Theology and Religious Studies	G1V8	3FT deg	M	12	M	P^	Ind	CCCC	$	1
PE/Sports Science and Theology & Religious Studs	BV68	3FT deg	*	12	M	P^	Ind	CCCC	$	
PE/Sports Science with Theology and Religious St	B6V8	3FT deg	*	12	M	P^	Ind	CCCC	$	
Psychology and Theology and Religious Studies	LV78	3FT deg	g	12	M	P^	Ind	CCCC	$	14
Psychology with Theology and Religious Studies	L7V8	3FT deg	g	12	M	M	Ind	CCCC	$	11
Theology and Rel St with Drama and Theatre Studs	V8W4	3FT deg	*	12	M	M	Ind	CCCC	$	
Theology and Religious St with Computer Sci/IT	V8G5	3FT deg	g	12	M	M	Ind	CCCC	$	
Theology and Religious St with PE/Sports Science	V8B6	3FT deg	*	12	M	P^	Ind	CCCC	$	
Theology and Religious Studies	V800	3FT deg		12	M	M	Ind	CCCC	$	
Theology and Religious Studies with Art	V8W9	3FT deg	*	12	M	M	Ind	CCCC	$	4
Theology and Religious Studies with Biology	V8C1	3FT deg	B	12	M	P^	Ind	CCCC	$	
Theology and Religious Studies with English Lit	V8Q3	3FT deg	E	12	M	P^	Ind	CCCC	$	4
Theology and Religious Studies with French	V8R1	3FT deg	g	12	M	M	Ind	CCCC	$	6
Theology and Religious Studies with Geography	V8F8	3FT deg	Gy/Gl	12	M	P^	Ind	CCCC	$	
Theology and Religious Studies with German	V8R2	3FT deg	g	12	M	M	Ind	CCCC	$	
Theology and Religious Studies with History	V8V1	3FT deg	H/Ec/So	12	M	M	Ind	CCCC	$	8
Theology and Religious Studies with Mathematics	V8G1	3FT deg	M	12	M	P^	Ind	CCCC	$	
Theology and Religious Studies with Psychology	V8L7	3FT deg	g	12	M	M	Ind	CCCC	$	10

CHICHESTER INSTITUTE OF HIGHER EDUCATION

TITLE	CODE	COURSE	SUBJECTS	A/AS	ND/C	AGNVQ	IB	SQA(H)	SQA	RATIO A/AS
Art and Study of Religions	WV18	3FT deg	A+Pf	12	Ind	M$+^	Ind	Ind	Ind	6
Art and Theology	WV1V	3FT deg	A+Pf	12	Ind	M^+	Ind	Ind	Ind	
Art with Study of Religions	W1V8	3FT deg	A+Pf	12	Ind	M$+^	Ind	Ind	Ind	

Theology 68

			98 expected requirements						96 entry stats
course details									
TITLE	CODE	COURSE	SUBJECTS	A/AS	ND/C	AGNVQ	IB	SQA(H)	SQA	RATIO A/AS
Art with Study of Religions	E1V8	3FT deg	A+Pf g	12	Ind	M$+^	Ind	Ind	Ind	
Art with Theology	W1VV	3FT deg	A+Pf	12	Ind	M$	Ind	Ind	Ind	
Dance and Study of Religions	VW84	3FT deg	Pf	12	Ind	M$+	Ind	Ind	Ind	
Dance and Theology	WV48	3FT deg	Pf	12	Ind	M$+	Ind	Ind	Ind	
Dance with Study of Religions	W4V8	3FT deg	Pf	12	Ind	M$+	Ind	Ind	Ind	
Dance with Theology	W4VV	3FT deg	Pf	12	Ind	M$	Ind	Ind	Ind	
English Lang Teaching (EFL) and St of Religions	QV18	3FT deg	E	12	Ind	M^	Ind	Ind	Ind	
English and Study of Religions	QV38	3FT deg	E	12	Ind	M^	Ind	Ind	Ind	7
English and Theology	QV3V	3FT deg	E	12	Ind	M$	Ind	Ind	Ind	
English with Study of Religions	Q3V8	3FT deg	E	12	Ind	M^	Ind	Ind	Ind	4
English with Theology	Q3VV	3FT deg	E	12	Ind	M$	Ind	Ind	Ind	
Environmental Science and Study of Religions	VF89	3FT deg	* g	12	Ind	M$	Ind	Ind	Ind	
Environmental Science and Theology	FV98	3FT deg	*	12	Ind	M^	Ind	Ind	Ind	
Geography and Study of Religions	LV88	3FT deg	Gy	12	Ind	M$	Ind	Ind	Ind	
Geography and Theology	LV8V	3FT deg	Gy	12	Ind	M$	Ind	Ind	Ind	
Geography with Study of Religions	L8V8	3FT deg	Gy	12	Ind	M$	Ind	Ind	Ind	
Geography with Theology	L8VV	3FT deg	Gy	12	Ind	M$	Ind	Ind	Ind	
History and Study of Religions	VV18	3FT deg	H	12	Ind	M$	Ind	Ind	Ind	
History with Study of Religions	V1V8	3FT deg	H	12	Ind	M$	Ind	Ind	Ind	
History with Theology	V1VV	3FT deg	H	12	Ind	M$	Ind	Ind	Ind	
Mathematics and Study of Religions	GV18	3FT deg	M	12	Ind	M^	Ind	Ind	Ind	
Mathematics and Theology	GV1V	3FT deg	A+Pf	12	Ind	M$	Ind	Ind	Ind	
Mathematics with Study of Religions	G1V8	3FT deg	M	12	Ind	M^	Ind	Ind	Ind	
Mathematics with Theology	G1VV	3FT deg	M	12	Ind	M^	Ind	Ind	Ind	
Media Studies and Study of Religions	PV48	3FT deg	*	12	Ind	M$	Ind	Ind	Ind	7
Media Studies and Theology	PV4V	3FT deg	*	12	Ind	M$	Ind	Ind	Ind	
Media Studies with Study of Religions	P4V8	3FT deg	*	12	Ind	M$	Ind	Ind	Ind	
Media Studies with Theology	P4VV	3FT deg	*	12	Ind	M$	Ind	Ind	Ind	
Music and Study of Religions	VW83	3FT deg	Mu	12	Ind	M$+	Ind	Ind	Ind	1
Music and Theology	WV38	3FT deg	Mu+Pf	12	Ind	M^+	Ind	Ind	Ind	
Music with Study of Religions	W3V8	3FT deg	Mu	12	Ind	M$+	Ind	Ind	Ind	4
Music with Theology	W3VV	3FT deg	Mu+Pf	12	Ind	M^+	Ind	Ind	Ind	
Related Arts and Study of Religions	WV98	3FT deg	*	12	Ind	M$	Ind	Ind	Ind	
Related Arts and Theology	WV9V	3FT deg	Pf	12	Ind	M$	Ind	Ind	Ind	
Study of Religions	V800	3FT deg	*	12	Ind	M$	Ind	Ind	Ind	15
Study of Religions with Art	V8W1	3FT deg	*	12	Ind	M$	Ind	Ind	Ind	2
Study of Religions with Dance	V8W4	3FT deg	*	12	Ind	M$	Ind	Ind	Ind	
Study of Religions with Education Studs(Opt.QTS)	V8X9	3FT/4FT deg	* g	12	Ind	M$ go	Ind	Ind	Ind	3 5/16
Study of Religions with Eng Lang Teaching(EFL)	V8Q1	3FT deg	* g	12	Ind	M$	Ind	Ind	Ind	
Study of Religions with English	V8Q3	3FT deg	*	12	Ind	M$	Ind	Ind	Ind	2
Study of Religions with Environmental Science	V8F9	3FT deg	* g	12	Ind	M$	Ind	Ind	Ind	
Study of Religions with Geography	V8L8	3FT deg	*	12	Ind	M$	Ind	Ind	Ind	
Study of Religions with History	V8V1	3FT deg	*	12	Ind	M$	Ind	Ind	Ind	6
Study of Religions with Mathematics	V8G1	3FT deg	* g	12	Ind	M$	Ind	Ind	Ind	
Study of Religions with Media Studies	V8P4	3FT deg	*	12	Ind	M$	Ind	Ind	Ind	
Study of Religions with Music	V8W3	3FT deg	*	12	Ind	M$	Ind	Ind	Ind	
Study of Religions with Related Arts	V8W9	3FT deg	*	12	Ind	M$	Ind	Ind	Ind	
Study of Religions with Theology	V8VV	3FT deg	*	12	Ind	M$	Ind	Ind	Ind	
Study of Religions with Women's Studies	V8M9	3FT deg	Re	12	Ind	M$	Ind	Ind	Ind	
Theology and English	VQ83	3FT deg	E	12	Ind	M^	Ind	Ind	Ind	
Theology and Geography	VL88	3FT deg	Gy	12	Ind	M^	Ind	Ind	Ind	
Theology and History	VV81	3FT deg	H	12	Ind	M^	Ind	Ind	Ind	

course details			98 expected requirements							96 entry stats
TITLE	CODE	COURSE	SUBJECTS	A/AS	ND/C	AGNVQ	IB	SQA(H)	SQA	RATIO A/AS
Theology and Mathematics	VG81	3FT deg	M	12	Ind	M^	Ind	Ind	Ind	
Theology and Media Studies	VP84	3FT deg	*	12	Ind	M$	Ind	Ind	Ind	
Theology and Study of Religions	VV88	3FT deg	*	12	Ind	M$	Ind	Ind	Ind	
Theology and Women's Studies	VM89	3FT deg	*	12	Ind	M$	Ind	Ind	Ind	
Theology with Art	V8WC	3FT deg	Pf	12	Ind	M$	Ind	Ind	Ind	
Theology with Dance	V8WK	3FT deg	Pf	12	Ind	M$	Ind	Ind	Ind	
Theology with English	V8QH	3FT deg	*	12	Ind	M$	Ind	Ind	Ind	
Theology with Environmental Science	V8FX	3FT deg	*	12	Ind	M$	Ind	Ind	Ind	
Theology with Geography	V8LV	3FT deg	*	12	Ind	M$	Ind	Ind	Ind	
Theology with History	V8VC	3FT deg	*	12	Ind	M$	Ind	Ind	Ind	
Theology with Mathematics	V8GC	3FT deg	* g	12	Ind	M$	Ind	Ind	Ind	
Theology with Media Studies	V8PK	3FT deg	*	12	Ind	M$	Ind	Ind	Ind	
Theology with Music	V8WH	3FT deg	*	12	Ind	M$	Ind	Ind	Ind	
Theology with Related Arts	V8WX	3FT deg	*	12	Ind	M$	Ind	Ind	Ind	
Theology with Study of Religions	V8V9	3FT deg	*	12	Ind	M$	Ind	Ind	Ind	
Theology with Women's Studies	V8MX	3FT deg	*	12	Ind	M$	Ind	Ind	Ind	
Women's Studies and Study of Religions	MV98	3FT deg	*	12	Ind	M$	Ind	Ind	Ind	
Women's Studies and Theology	MV9V	3FT deg	*	12	Ind	M$	Ind	Ind	Ind	

DE MONTFORT Univ

Humanities Combined Honours *Jain Studies*	Y300▼	3FT deg	* g	CCD	MO	M$^	26$	CSYS$	X	

Univ of DERBY

Social Cultural and Religious Studies	LV38	3FT deg		12	3M+2D	M$	27	CCCC	Ind	
Credit Accumulation Modular Scheme *Religions, Culture & Belief*	Y600	3FT deg	*	12	MO	M	Ind	CCCC	Ind	

Univ of DURHAM

Classics and Theology	QV88	3FT deg		Ind	Ind		Ind	Ind	Ind	
Music and Theology	VW83	3FT deg	Mu	BBC	Ind		Ind	Ind	Ind	
Philosophy and Theology	VV78	3FT deg	*	BBC	Ind		32	AAABB	Ind	4 20/30
Theology	V800	3FT deg	*	BBC	Ind		30	AABBB	Ind	4 18/30
Arts Combined *Theology*	Y300	3FT deg	*	24	Ind		30	AABBB	Ind	

EDGE HILL Univ COLLEGE

Commun & Race Rels & Contemp Religion & Beliefs	VM89	3FT deg	*	DD	3M+3D	M* / P*^	Dip	BBCC	Ind	
History and Contemporary Religion & Beliefs	VV81	3FT deg	H	DD	3M+3D	P*^	Dip	BBCC$	Ind	

Univ of EDINBURGH

BA (Divinity)	QV88	3FT deg	L	BCC	Ind		Ind	BCCC	Ind	20
BA (Religious Studies)	V842	3FT deg		BCC	Ind		Ind	BCCC	Ind	4 16/20
BD with or without Honours	V800	3FT/4FT deg		BCC	Ind		Ind	BCCC$	Ind	2 20/28
Certificate in Christian Education	V860	1FT Dip		CC	Ind		Ind	CCC	Ind	
Certificate in Pastoral Studies	V850	2FT Dip		CC	Ind		Ind	CCC	Ind	1
Certificate in Theology	V870	1FT Dip		CC	Ind		Ind	CCC	Ind	2
Licentiate in Theology	V880	3FT Dip		CC	Ind		Ind	CCC	Ind	3
MA (Divinity)	QV8V	4FT deg	L	BCC	Ind		Ind	BCCC$	Ind	13
MA (Religious Studies) Honours	V840	4FT deg		BCC	Ind		Ind	BCCC	Ind	2 16/28
Philosophy and Systematic Theology	VV78	4FT deg	g	BBB	Ind	Ind	Dip$	BBBB	Ind	

Univ of EXETER

Theological Studies	V804	3FT deg	*	BBC-BCC	MO	M/D$	28	Ind	Ind	6 16/28

course details			98 expected requirements							96 entry stats
TITLE	CODE	COURSE	SUBJECTS	A/AS	NO/C	AGNVQ	IB	SQA(H)	SQA	RATIO A/AS
Univ of GLAMORGAN										
English Studies and Religious Studies	QV38	3FT deg	*g	12	Ind	Ind	Ind	Ind	Ind	
History and Religious Studies	VV18	3FT deg	*g	12	5M	M	Ind	Ind	Ind	
Humanities (Religion)	V800	3FT deg	*g	CC	5M	M$	24	CCCC	HN	7
Philosophy and Religious Studies	VV78	3FT deg	*g	12	Ind	Ind	Ind	Ind	Ind	
Psychology and Religious Studies	LV78	3FT deg	*g	CC	Ind	Ind	Ind	Ind	Ind	
Religious Studies and Sociology	LV38	3FT deg	*g	12	Ind	Ind	Ind	Ind	Ind	
Religious Studies and Welsh Studies	QV58	3FT deg	*g	12	5M	M	Ind	Ind	Ind	
Religious Studies with Anthropology	V8L6	3FT deg	*g	12	5M	M	Ind	Ind	Ind	
Combined Studies (Honours) *Religious Studies*	Y400	3FT deg	*g	8-16	Ind	Ind	Ind	Ind	Ind	
Joint Honours *Religious Studies*	Y401	3FT deg	*g	8-16	Ind	Ind	Ind	Ind	Ind	
Major/Minor Honours *Religious Studies*	Y402	3FT deg	*g	8-16	Ind	Ind	Ind	Ind	Ind	
Univ of GLASGOW										
Archaeology/Classical Hebrew	VV86	4FT deg		BBC	HN	M	30	BBBB	Ind	
Celtic Civilisation/Classical Hebrew	QV5V	4FT deg		BBC	HN	M	30	BBBB	Ind	
Celtic Civilisation/Theology and Religious St	QV58	4FT deg		BBC	HN	M	30	BBBB	Ind	
Classical Civilisation/Theology & Religious St	QV8V	4FT deg		BBC	HN	M	30	BBBB	Ind	
Classical Hebrew/Celtic	QV5W	4FT deg		BBC	HN	M	30	BBBB	Ind	
Classical Hebrew/Czech	TV1W	5FT deg		BBC	HN	M	30	BBBB	Ind	
Classical Hebrew/Economic and Social History	VV3W	4FT deg		BBC	HN	M	30	BBBB	Ind	
Classical Hebrew/Economics	LVCW	4FT deg		BBC	HN	M	30	BBBB	Ind	
Classical Hebrew/English	QV3W	4FT deg		BBC	HN	M	30	BBBB	Ind	
Classical Hebrew/Film and Television Studies	VW85	4FT deg		BBB	HN	D	32	AABB	Ind	
Classical Hebrew/Geography	LV8W	4FT deg		BBC	HN	M	30	BBBB	Ind	
Classical Hebrew/Greek	QV7W	4FT deg		BBC	HN	M	30	BBBB	Ind	
Classical Hebrew/History of Art	VV4W	4FT deg		BBC	HN	M	30	BBBB	Ind	
Classical Hebrew/Mathematics	GV1W	4FT deg		BBC	HN	M	30	BBBB	Ind	
Classical Hebrew/Music	VWW3	4FT deg		BBC	HN	M	30	BBBB	Ind	
Classical Hebrew/Philosophy	VV7W	4FT deg		BBC	HN	M	30	BBBB	Ind	
Classical Hebrew/Politics	MV1W	4FT deg		BBC	HN	M	30	BBBB	Ind	
Classical Hebrew/Psychology	CV8W	4FT deg		BBC	HN	M	30	BBBB	Ind	
Classical Hebrew/Scottish History	VVWC	4FT deg		BBC	HN	M	30	BBBB	Ind	
Classical Hebrew/Scottish Literature	QV2W	4FT deg		BBC	HN	M	30	BBBB	Ind	
Classical Hebrew/Sociology	LV3W	4FT deg		BBC	HN	M	30	BBBB	Ind	
Classical Hebrew/Theatre Studies	VWW4	4FT deg		BBC	HN	M	30	BBBB	Ind	
Film and Television St/Theology & Religious St	VWV5	4FT deg		BBB	HN	D	32	AABB	HN	1
History/Theology & Religious Studies	VV1V	4FT deg		BBC	HN	M	30	BBBB	Ind	4
Management Studies/Theology & Religious Studies	NV18	4FT deg		BBC	HN	M	30	BBBB	Ind	
Ministry (General)	V850	4FT deg		CCD	HN		26	BBBC	Ind	
Scottish History/Theology & Religious Studies	VVCV	4FT deg		BBC	HN	M	30	BBBB	Ind	
Theology & Religious Studies/Archaeology	VV6V	4FT deg		BBC	HN	M	30	BBBB	Ind	
Theology & Religious Studies/Celtic	QVM8	4FT deg		BBC	HN	M	30	BBBB	Ind	
Theology & Religious Studies/Classical Hebrew	QV9V	4FT deg		BBC	HN	M	30	BBBB	Ind	
Theology & Religious Studies/Czech	TVD8	5FT deg		BBC	HN	M	30	BBBB	Ind	
Theology & Religious Studies/Economic History	VV83	4FT deg		BBC	8M	M	30	BBBB	Ind	
Theology & Religious Studies/Economics	LV1V	4FT deg		BBC	HN	M	30	BBBB	Ind	
Theology & Religious Studies/English	QV3V	4FT deg		BBC	HN	M	30	BBBB	Ind	
Theology & Religious Studies/French	RV1V	5FT deg		BBC	HN	M	30	BBBB	Ind	
Theology & Religious Studies/Geography	LV8V	4FT deg		BBC	HN	M	30	BBBB	Ind	

				98 expected requirements							96 entry stats	

course details

TITLE	CODE	COURSE	SUBJECTS	A/AS	ND/C	AGNVQ	IB	SQA(H)	SQA	RATIO	A/AS
Theology & Religious Studies/Greek	QV7V	4FT deg		BBC	HN	M	30	BBBB	Ind		
Theology & Religious Studies/Hispanic Studies	RV4V	5FT deg		BBC	HN	M	30	BBBB	Ind		
Theology & Religious Studies/History of Art	VV4V	4FT deg		BBC	HN	M	30	BBBB	Ind		
Theology & Religious Studies/Latin	QV68	4FT deg		BBC	HN	M	30	BBBB	Ind		
Theology & Religious Studies/Mathematics	GV1V	4FT deg		BBC	HN	M	30	BBBB	Ind		
Theology & Religious Studies/Music	VWV3	4FT deg		BBC	HN	M	30	BBBB	Ind		
Theology & Religious Studies/Philosophy	VV7V	4FT deg		BBC	HN	M	30	BBBB	Ind	5	
Theology & Religious Studies/Polish	TVCV	5FT deg		BBC	HN	M	30	BBBB	Ind		
Theology & Religious Studies/Politics	MV1V	4FT deg		BBC	HN	M	30	BBBB	Ind	6	
Theology & Religious Studies/Psychology	CV8V	4FT deg		BBC	HN	M	30	BBBB	Ind	3	
Theology & Religious Studies/Russian	RV88	5FT deg		BBC	HN	M	30	BBBB	Ind		
Theology & Religious Studies/Sociology	LV3V	4FT deg		BBC	HN	M	30	BBBB	Ind		
Theology & Religious Studies/Theatre Studies	VWV4	4FT deg		BBC	HN	M	30	BBBB	Ind		
Theology/Religious Studies	V800	4FT deg		CCD	HN		26	BBBC	Ind	1	14/16
Theology/Religious Studies	V848	4FT deg		CCD	HN		26	BBBC	Ind	6	

Univ of GREENWICH

Theological Studies	V800	3FT deg	* g	10	MO	M	25	BBB	Ind		

Univ of HERTFORDSHIRE

Philosophy/Modern Language	TV98	3FT deg	Ap	14	M+D	Ind	28	CCCC	Ind		

HEYTHROP COLL (Univ of London)

Biblical Studies	V820	3FT deg	*	18-20	Ind	M	Dip	BCCCC	Ind	7	
Philosophy and Theology	VV78	3FT deg	*	20-22	Ind	M	Dip	BCCCC	Ind	3	10/20
Theology	V801	3FT deg	*	18-20	Ind	M	Dip	BCCCC	Ind	5	12/16
Theology (BD Honours)	V800	3FT deg	*	18-20	Ind	M	Dip	BCCCC	Ind	8	
Theology and Society	V8L3	3FT deg	*	18-20	Ind	M	Dip	BCCCC	Ind	8	
Theology for Ministry	V850	3FT deg	*	18-20	Ind	M	Dip	BCCCC	Ind	7	

Univ of HULL

Drama/Theology	VW84	3FT deg		BBB-BCC	Ind	D$^ go	28	BBBCC	Ind		
English/Theology	QV38	3FT deg	E	BBB-BC	MO+D $	M$^ gi	28$	BBBCC	Ind		
Humanities (Theology)	VV89	3FT deg	*	BBB-BC	MO $	M*_ gi	26$	BBBCC	Ind		
Philosophy/Theology	VV78	3FT deg	*	BC-BCC	MO	M$6/^ go	26$	BBCCC	Ind	30	
Sociology/Theology	LV38	3FT deg	*	BBC-CCD	MO	M$^ gi	28	BBCCC	Ind	3	
Theology	V800	3FT deg	*	BC-CCD	MO $	M*^ gi	26$	BBBCC	Ind	11	14/20

Univ of KENT

Theology and Religious Studies	V816	3FT deg	*	20	3M+3D	Ind	28	Ind	Ind	8	20/26
Theology/Classical Studies	QV88	3FT deg	*	20	3M+3D	Ind	28	Ind	Ind		
Theology/Comparative Literary Studies	VQ82	3FT deg	*	20	3M+3D	Ind	28	Ind	Ind	1	
Theology/Computing	VG85	3FT deg	*	20	3M+3D	Ind	28	Ind	Ind		
Theology/Drama	VW84	3FT deg	*	22	2M+4D	Ind	30	Ind	Ind	2	
Theology/English	QV38	3FT deg	E	22	2M+4D	Ind	30	Ind	Ind	10	
Theology/English (Post-Colonial Literatures)	QVJ8	3FT deg	E	22	2M+4D	Ind	30	Ind	Ind		
Theology/English Language	VQ83	3FT deg	E	20	3M+3D	Ind	28	Ind	Ind		
Theology/European Studies	TV28	4FT deg	L	20	3M+3D	Ind	28	Ind	Ind		
Theology/Film Studies	VW85	3FT deg	*	22	2M+4D	Ind	30	Ind	Ind		
Theology/French	RV18	4FT deg	F	20	3M+3D	Ind	28	Ind	Ind	3	
Theology/German	RV28	4FT deg	G	20	3M+3D	Ind	28	Ind	Ind		
Theology/History	VV18	3FT deg	*	22	2M+4D	Ind	30	Ind	Ind	6	
Theology/History and Theory of Art	VV48	3FT deg	*	20	2M+4D	Ind	28	Ind	Ind		
Theology/History of Science	VV85	3FT deg	*	20	3M+3D	Ind	28	Ind	Ind		
Theology/Italian	RV38	4FT deg	*	20	3M+3D	Ind	28	Ind	Ind	1	

Theology 68

course details | 98 expected requirements | 96 entry stats

TITLE	CODE	COURSE	SUBJECTS	A/AS	ND/C	AGNVQ	IB	SQA(H)	SQA	RATIO A/AS
Theology/Linguistics	VQ81	3FT deg	*	20	3M+3D	Ind	28	Ind	Ind	
Theology/Philosophy	VV78	3FT deg	*	20	3M+3D	Ind	28	Ind	Ind	23
Theology/Spanish	RV48	4FT deg	*	20	3M+3D	Ind	28	Ind	Ind	

KING ALFRED'S WINCHESTER

TITLE	CODE	COURSE	SUBJECTS	A/AS	ND/C	AGNVQ	IB	SQA(H)	SQA	RATIO A/AS
Religious Studies and American Studies	QV48	3FT deg	*g	14	6M	M	24	BCC	N	
Religious Studies and Archaeology	FV48	3FT deg	*g	14	6M	M	24	BCC	N	
Religious Studies and Education Studies	VX89	3FT deg	*g	14	6M	M	24	BCC	N	1
Religious Studies and English Studies	QV38	3FT deg	E	14	X	X	24$	BCC$	X	7
Religious Studies and History	VV18	3FT deg	*g	14	6M	M	24	BCC	N	
Religious Studies and Media & Film Studies	PV48	3FT deg	*g	14	6M	M	24	BCC	N	3
Religious Studies and Music (World)	VW83	3FT deg	*g	14	6M	M	24	BCC	N	1
Religious Studies and Philosophy	VV78	3FT deg	*g	14	6M	M	24	BCC	N	5
Religious Studies and Psychology	LV78	3FT deg	*g	14	6M	M	24	BCC	N	3

KING'S COLL LONDON (Univ of London)

TITLE	CODE	COURSE	SUBJECTS	A/AS	ND/C	AGNVQ	IB	SQA(H)	SQA	RATIO A/AS
Biblical Studies	V820	3FT deg	*	20						
Philosophy and Theology	VV78	3FT deg	*	BBC-BCC						6 22/26
Physics with Theology	F3V8	3FT deg	M+P	18	2M+1D		28$	AABBB	Ind	
Religious Studies	V840	3FT deg	*	20						4 12/28
Theology	V800	3FT deg	*	20						5 8/26
War Studies and Theology	MV98	3FT deg	*	BBC						
Afro-Portuguese, Brazilian and Religious Studies *Religious Studies*	Y654	3FT/4FT deg	*	BCC						

Univ of Wales, LAMPETER

TITLE	CODE	COURSE	SUBJECTS	A/AS	ND/C	AGNVQ	IB	SQA(H)	SQA	RATIO A/AS
Anthropology and Religion	VL86	3FT deg	*	16-18	Ind	Ind	Ind	Ind	Ind	
Divinity	V806▼	3FT deg	*	14	Ind	Ind	Ind	Ind	Ind	
Modern Historical Studies and Classical Studies	VVV1	3FT deg			Ind	Ind	Ind	Ind	Ind	
Religious Studies	V840	3FT deg	*	14	Ind	Ind	Ind	Ind	Ind	
Religious Studies and American Literature	QV48	3FT deg			Ind	Ind	Ind	Ind	Ind	
Religious Studies and Ancient History	VVCV	3FT deg	*	16	Ind	Ind	Ind	Ind	Ind	
Religious Studies and Anthropology	LV68	3FT deg	*	14	Ind	Ind	Ind	Ind	Ind	
Religious Studies and Archaeology	VVP8	3FT deg	*	16	Ind	Ind	Ind	Ind	Ind	
Religious Studies and Australian Studies	LV6V	3FT deg			Ind	Ind	Ind	Ind	Ind	
Religious Studies and Church History	VV1W	3FT deg	*	14	Ind	Ind	Ind	Ind	Ind	
Religious Studies and Classical Studies	QVV8	3FT deg	*	16	Ind	Ind	Ind	Ind	Ind	
Religious Studies and Cultural St in Geography	LVVV	3FT deg	*	16	Ind	Ind	Ind	Ind	Ind	
Religious Studies and English Literature	QVH8	3FT deg	E	18	Ind	Ind	Ind	Ind	Ind	
Religious Studies and French	RVC8	4FT deg	F	16	Ind	Ind	Ind	Ind	Ind	
Religious Studies and Geography	LVV8	3FT deg	Gy	16	Ind	Ind	Ind	Ind	Ind	
Religious Studies and German	RVF8	4FT deg	G	16	Ind	Ind	Ind	Ind	Ind	
Religious Studies and German Studies	RVG8	4FT deg	*	16	Ind	Ind	Ind	Ind	Ind	
Religious Studies and Greek	QVR8	3FT deg	*g	16	Ind	Ind	Ind	Ind	Ind	
Religious Studies and History	VVC8	3FT deg	H	16	Ind	Ind	Ind	Ind	Ind	
Religious Studies and Informatics	GV58	3FT deg	*	14	Ind	Ind	Ind	Ind	Ind	
Religious Studies and Islamic Studies	TV68	3FT deg	*	14	Ind	Ind	Ind	Ind	Ind	
Religious Studies and Latin	QVP8	3FT deg	*g	16	Ind	Ind	Ind	Ind	Ind	
Religious Studies and Management Techniques	NV18	3FT deg	*	14	Ind	Ind	Ind	Ind	Ind	
Religious Studies and Medieval Studies	VV81	3FT deg	*	16	Ind	Ind	Ind	Ind	Ind	
Religious Studies and Modern Historical Studies	VVVC	3FT deg			Ind	Ind	Ind	Ind	Ind	
Religious Studies and Philosophical Studies	VVR8	3FT deg	*	16	Ind	Ind	Ind	Ind	Ind	
Theology	V870▼	2FT Dip	*		Ind	Ind	Ind	Ind	Ind	
Theology	V801▼	3FT deg	*	14	Ind	Ind	Ind	Ind	Ind	
Theology	V800	3FT deg	*	14	Ind	Ind	Ind	Ind	Ind	

course details   98 expected requirements   96 entry stats

TITLE	CODE	COURSE	SUBJECTS	A/AS	NO/C	AGNVQ	IB	SQA(H)	SQA	RATIO A/AS
Theology and American Literature	QV4V	3FT deg			Ind	Ind	Ind	Ind	Ind	
Theology and Ancient History	VVDV	3FT deg	*	16	Ind	Ind	Ind	Ind	Ind	
Theology and Anthropology	LV6W	3FT deg	*	16	Ind	Ind	Ind	Ind	Ind	
Theology and Archaeology	VV68	3FT deg	*	18	Ind	Ind	Ind	Ind	Ind	
Theology and Australian Studies	LVP8	3FT deg			Ind	Ind	Ind	Ind	Ind	
Theology and Church History	VV1V	3FT deg	*	14	Ind	Ind	Ind	Ind	Ind	
Theology and Classical Studies	QV88	3FT deg	*	16	Ind	Ind	Ind	Ind	Ind	
Theology and Cultural Studies in Geography	VL88	3FT deg	*	16	Ind	Ind	Ind	Ind	Ind	
Theology and English Literature	QV38	3FT deg	E	18	Ind	Ind	Ind	Ind	Ind	
Theology and French	RV18	4FT deg	F	16	Ind	Ind	Ind	Ind	Ind	
Theology and Geography	LV88	3FT deg	Gy	16	Ind	Ind	Ind	Ind	Ind	
Theology and German	RV28	4FT deg	G	16	Ind	Ind	Ind	Ind	Ind	
Theology and German Studies	RV2V	4FT deg	*	16	Ind	Ind	Ind	Ind	Ind	
Theology and Greek	QV78	3FT deg	* g	16	Ind	Ind	Ind	Ind	Ind	
Theology and History	VV18	3FT deg	H	16	Ind	Ind	Ind	Ind	Ind	
Theology and Informatics	GV5V	3FT deg	*	14	Ind	Ind	Ind	Ind	Ind	
Theology and Islamic Studies	TV6V	3FT deg	*	14	Ind	Ind	Ind	Ind	Ind	
Theology and Latin	QV68	3FT deg	* g	16	Ind	Ind	Ind	Ind	Ind	
Theology and Management Techniques	NV1V	3FT deg	*	14	Ind	Ind	Ind	Ind	Ind	
Theology and Medieval Studies	VV8C	3FT deg	*	16	Ind	Ind	Ind	Ind	Ind	
Theology and Modern Historical Studies	VVVD	3FT deg			Ind	Ind	Ind	Ind	Ind	
Theology and Philosophical Studies	VV78	3FT deg	*	16	Ind	Ind	Ind	Ind	Ind	
Theology and Religious Studies	V816	3FT deg	*	14	Ind	Ind	Ind	Ind	Ind	
Victorian Studies and Religious Studies	VVD8	3FT deg	*	14	Ind	Ind	Ind	Ind	Ind	
Victorian Studies and Theology	VVCW	3FT deg	*	14	Ind	Ind	Ind	Ind	Ind	
Welsh Studies and Religious Studies	QVMV	3FT deg	*	14	Ind	Ind	Ind	Ind	Ind	
Welsh Studies and Theology	QVM8	3FT deg	*	14	Ind	Ind	Ind	Ind	Ind	
Welsh and Religious Studies	QVN8	3FT/4FT deg	W	14	Ind	Ind	Ind	Ind	Ind	
Welsh and Theology	QV58	3FT/4FT deg	W	14	Ind	Ind	Ind	Ind	Ind	
Women's Studies and Religious Studies	MV98	3FT deg	*	14	Ind	Ind	Ind	Ind	Ind	
Women's Studies and Theology	MV9V	3FT deg	*	14	Ind	Ind	Ind	Ind	Ind	
Combined Honours *Religious Studies*	Y400	3FT deg	*	14-16	Ind	Ind	Ind	Ind	Ind	
Combined Honours *Theology*	Y400	3FT deg	*	14-16	Ind	Ind	Ind	Ind	Ind	
Religion, Ethics and Society *Religion*	Y652	3FT deg	*	14	Ind		Ind	Ind	Ind	

LANCASTER Univ

TITLE	CODE	COURSE	SUBJECTS	A/AS	NO/C	AGNVQ	IB	SQA(H)	SQA	RATIO A/AS
Art History and Religious Studies	WV18	3FT deg	*	BCC-BCD	MO		30	BBBBB	Ind	
Educational Studies and Religious Studies	XV98	3FT deg	*	18	MO		30	ABBB	Ind	
English and Religious Studies	QV38	3FT deg	E g	BBC	Ind $		32$	ABBBB$	Ind	
French Studies and Religious Studies	RV18	4SW deg	F	BCC	Ind $		30$	BBBBB$	Ind	
German Studies and Religious Studies	RV28	4SW deg	G/L	BCC	Ind $		30$	BBBBB$	Ind	
History and Religious Studies	VV18	3FT deg	H	BBC	Ind $		30$	ABBBB$	Ind	
Independent Studies and Religious Studies	YV48	3FT deg	*	18	Ind		Ind	Ind	Ind	
Italian Studies and Religious Studies	RV38	4SW deg	I/L	BCC	Ind $		30$	BBBBB$	Ind	
Philosophy and Religious Studies	VV87	3FT deg	*	BCC-BCD	Ind		30	BBBBC	Ind	
Political and Religious Thought	VM81	3FT deg	*	BCC	Ind		30	BBBBB	Ind	
Religious Studies	V840	3FT deg	*	18	Ind		28	BBBB	Ind	
Religious Studies and Sociology	VL83	3FT deg	*	BCD	Ind		28	BBBB	Ind	
Spanish Studies and Religious Studies	RV48	4SW deg	Sp/L	BCC	Ind $		30$	BBBBB$	Ind	
Theatre Studies and Religious Studies	WV48	3FT deg	*	BBC-BCC	Ind		30	BBBBB	Ind	
Women's Studies and Religious Studies	VM89	3FT deg	*	18	Ind		28	BBBB	Ind	

course details			98 expected requirements							96 entry stats
TITLE	CODE	COURSE	SUBJECTS	A/AS	ND/C	AGNVQ	IB	SQA(H)	SQA	RATIO A/AS
Univ of LEEDS										
Arabic and Islamic Studies	TVP8	4FT deg	Cl/L g	BBC	Ind	Ind	30$	CSYS	Ind	15
Arabic-Religious Studies	TV6V	4FT deg	Cl/L g	BBC	Ind	Ind	30	CSYS	Ind	
Arabic-Theology	TV68	4FT deg	Cl/L g	BBC	Ind	Ind	30	CSYS	Ind	
Classical Literature-Religious Studies	QV8V	3FT deg	* g	BBC	Ind	Ind	30	CSYS	Ind	
Classical Literature-Theology	QV88	3FT deg	* g	BBC	Ind	Ind	30	CSYS	Ind	
English-Religious Studies	QV3V	3FT deg	E g	BBC	Ind	Ind	30$	CSYS	Ind	7
English-Theology	QV38	3FT deg	E g	BBC	Ind	Ind	30$	CSYS	Ind	10
French-Religious Studies	RV1V	4FT deg	E g	BBC	Ind	Ind	30$	CSYS	Ind	3
French-Theology	RV18	4FT deg	E g	BBC	Ind	Ind	30$	CSYS	Ind	
German-Religious Studies	RV2V	4FT deg	G g	BBC	Ind	Ind	30$	CSYS	Ind	
German-Theology	RV28	4FT deg	G g	BBC	Ind	Ind	30$	CSYS	Ind	
Greek Civilisation-Religious Studies	QVWV	3FT deg	* g	BBC	Ind	Ind	30	CSYS	Ind	
Greek Civilisation-Theology	QVW8	3FT deg	* g	BBC	Ind	Ind	30	CSYS	Ind	4
History and Philosophy of Science-Religious St	VV5V	3FT deg	* g	BBC	Ind	Ind	30	CSYS	Ind	
History and Philosophy of Science-Theology	VV58	3FT deg	* g	BBC	Ind	Ind	30	CSYS	Ind	
History of Art-Religious Studies	VV4V	3FT deg	* g	BBC	Ind	Ind	30	CSYS	Ind	
History of Art-Theology	VV48	3FT deg	* g	BBC	Ind	Ind	30	CSYS	Ind	7
History-Religious Studies	VV1V	3FT deg	* g	BBC	Ind	Ind	30	CSYS	Ind	
History-Theology	VV18	3FT deg	* g	BBC	Ind	Ind	30	CSYS	Ind	9
Italian-Religious Studies	RV38	4FT deg	I g	BBC	Ind	Ind	Ind	Ind	Ind	
Italian-Religious Studies B	RVH8	4FT deg	L g	BBC	Ind	Ind	Ind	Ind	Ind	
Italian-Theology	RV3V	4FT deg	I g	BBC	Ind	Ind	Ind	Ind	Ind	
Italian-Theology B	RVHV	4FT deg	L g	BBC	Ind	Ind	Ind	Ind	Ind	
Latin-Religious Studies	QV6V	3FT deg	Ln g	BBC	Ind	Ind	30$	CSYS	Ind	
Latin-Theology	QV68	3FT deg	Ln g	BBC	Ind	Ind	30$	CSYS	Ind	
Music-Religious Studies	VWV3	3FT deg	Mu g	BBC	Ind	Ind	30$	CSYS	Ind	
Music-Theology	VW83	3FT deg	Mu g	BBC	Ind	Ind	30$	CSYS	Ind	
Philosophy-Religious Studies	VV7V	3FT deg	* g	BBC	Ind	Ind	30	CSYS	Ind	9
Philosophy-Theology	VV78	3FT deg	* g	BBC	Ind		30	CSYS	Ind	37
Politics-Religious Studies	MV1V	3FT deg	* g	BBB	Ind	Ind	32	CSYS	Ind	
Politics-Theology	MV18	3FT deg	* g	BBB	Ind	Ind	32	CSYS	Ind	7
Religious Studies-Russian	RV8V	4FT deg	R g	BBC	Ind	Ind	30$	CSYS	Ind	
Religious Studies-Russian B	RVVV	4FT deg	L g	BBC	Ind	Ind	30	CSYS	Ind	
Religious Studies-Social Policy	LV48	3FT deg	* g	BBC	Ind	D$^ go	30	CSYS	Ind	
Religious Studies-Sociology	LV3V	3FT deg	* g	BBC	Ind	D$^ go	30$	CSYS	Ind	25
Russian-Theology	RV88	4FT deg	R g	BBC	Ind	Ind	30$	CSYS	Ind	
Russian-Theology B	RVV8	4FT deg	L g	BBC	Ind	Ind	30	CSYS	Ind	
Social Policy-Theology	LV4V	3FT deg	* g	BBC	Ind	D$^ go	30	CSYS	Ind	2
Sociology-Theology	LV38	3FT deg	* g	BBC	Ind	D$^ go	30	CSYS	Ind	13
Theology and Religious Studies	V816	3FT deg	* g	BCD	Ind	D$6/^ go	28	CSYS	Ind	5	14/26
LEEDS, TRINITY & ALL SAINTS Univ COLL										
Theology	V800	3FT deg	* g	BCC-CC	MO	Ind	24	BBCCC	Ind	7	8/19
LIVERPOOL HOPE Univ COLL										
Theology & Religious St/Environmental Studies	FV98	3FT deg	B/Gy/En	12	8M	M$	Ind	Ind	Ind	
Theology & Religious St/Human & Applied Biology	CV18	3FT deg	B g	12	8M	M$ /M*^ go	Ind	Ind	Ind	2
Theology & Religious Studies (Honours)	V816	3FT deg	*	12	8M	M*	Ind	Ind	Ind	4	10/20
Theology & Religious Studies/Drama & Theatre St	WV48	3FT deg	g	12	8M	M* go	Ind	Ind	Ind	8
Theology & Religious Studies/English	QV38	3FT deg	El	12	8M	P*^	Ind	Ind	Ind	3	12/14
Theology & Religious Studies/European Studies	TV28	3FT deg	*	12	8M	M*	Ind	Ind	Ind	
Theology & Religious Studies/French	RV18	3FT deg	F	12	8M	P*^	Ind	Ind	Ind	

TITLE	CODE	COURSE	SUBJECTS	A/AS.	ND/C	AGNVQ	IB	SQA(H)	SQA	RATIO A/AS
course details			*98 expected requirements*							*96 entry stats*
Theology & Religious Studies/Geography	FV88	3FT deg	Gy	12	8M	M$	Ind	Ind	Ind	7
Theology & Religious Studies/History	VV18	3FT deg	H	12	8M	P*^	Ind	Ind	Ind	3
Theology & Religious Studies/Mathematics	GV18	3FT deg	M	12	8M	P*^	Ind	Ind	Ind	3
Theology & Religious Studies/Music	WV38	3FT deg	Mu	12	8M	P*^	Ind	Ind	Ind	2
Theology & Religious Studies/Psychology	CV88	3FT deg	g	12	8M	M* go	Ind	Ind	Ind	6
Theology & Religious Studies/Sociology	LV38	3FT deg	*	12	8M	M*	Ind	Ind	Ind	7

LSU COLL of HE

TITLE	CODE	COURSE	SUBJECTS	A/AS.	ND/C	AGNVQ	IB	SQA(H)	SQA	RATIO A/AS
English with Theology	Q3V8	3FT deg	E	CD	Ind		Ind	Ind	Ind	4
Environment and Society with Theology	FV98	3FT deg								
European Studies with Theology	T2V8	3FT deg								
History with Theology	V1V8	3FT deg	H	CD	Ind		Ind	Ind	Ind	6
Politics with Theology	M1V8	3FT deg	*	DD	Ind		Ind	Ind	Ind	
Sociology with Theology	L3V8	3FT deg	*	DD	Ind		Ind	Ind	Ind	7
Theology (Combined)	V800	3FT deg	*	DD	Ind		Ind	Ind	Ind	4 12/28
Theology and English	QV38	3FT deg								
Theology and History	VV18	3FT deg								
Theology and Politics	MV18	3FT deg								
Theology and Sociology	LV38	3FT deg								
Theology with English	V8Q3	3FT deg								
Theology with European Studies	V8T2	3FT deg								
Theology with History	V8V1	3FT deg								
Theology with Politics	V8M1	3FT deg								
Theology with Psychology	V8L7	3FT deg								
Theology with Sociology	V8L3	3FT deg								

Univ of MANCHESTER

TITLE	CODE	COURSE	SUBJECTS	A/AS.	ND/C	AGNVQ	IB	SQA(H)	SQA	RATIO A/AS
Biblical Studies	V820	3FT deg	*	20-24	Ind		28	BBBBC	Ind	27
Comparative Religion	V840	3FT deg		20-24	Ind			BBBBC	Ind	5 18/26
Comparative Religion and Social Anthropology	VL86	3FT deg		20-24	Ind		X	BBBBC	Ind	6 26/28
Comparative Religion and Sociology	VL83	3FT deg		20-24	Ind		X	BBBBC	Ind	4 18/26
Middle Eastern Langs and Comparative Religion	TV68	3FT/4FT deg	g	BCC-BBC	2M+5D		30	ABBBB	Ind	4
Philosophy and Comparative Religion	VVR8	3FT deg		BBB	Ind		32$	AABBB	Ind	5 26/30
Philosophy and Theology	VV78	3FT deg		BBB	Ind		32$	AABBB$	Ind	7 22/24
Politics and Religion	VM81	3FT deg	*	20-24	Ind		28	BBBBB	Ind	3 18/20
Theology and Religious Studies	V816	3FT deg	*	18-24	Ind		26	BBBCC	Ind	5 14/28

MANCHESTER METROPOLITAN Univ

TITLE	CODE	COURSE	SUBJECTS	A/AS.	ND/C	AGNVQ	IB	SQA(H)	SQA	RATIO A/AS
Religious Studies/American Studies	QV48	3FT deg	*	CC	M+D	D	28	CCCC	Ind	
Religious Studies/Applied Social Studies	LV38	3FT deg	*	CC	M+D	D	28	CCCC	Ind	
Religious Studies/Business Studies	NV18	3FT deg	*	CC	M+D	D	28	CCCC	Ind	
Religious Studies/Cultural Studies	LVH8	3FT deg	*	CC	M+D	D	28	CCCC	Ind	
Religious Studies/Dance	VW84	3FT deg	*	CC	M+D	D	28	CCCC	Ind	
Religious Studies/Drama	VW8K	3FT deg	*	CC	M+D	D	28	CCCC	Ind	
Religious Studies/English	QV38	3FT deg	*	CC	M+D	D	28	CCCC	Ind	
Religious Studies/Geography	LV88	3FT deg	*	CC	M+D	D	28	CCCC	Ind	
Religious Studies/Health Studies	BV98	3FT deg	*	CC	M+D	D	28	CCCC	Ind	
Religious Studies/History	VV18	3FT deg	*	CC	M+D	D	28	CCCC	Ind	
Religious Studies/Leisure Studies	LV48	3FT deg	*	CC	M+D	D	28	CCCC	Ind	
Religious Studies/Music	VW83	3FT deg	*	CC	M+D	D	28	CCCC	Ind	
Religious Studies/Philosophy	VV78	3FT deg	*	CC	M+D	D	28	CCCC	Ind	
Sport/Religious Studies	BV68	3FT deg	S	BC	M+D	DS	28	CCCC	Ind	
Visual Arts/Religious Studies	VW81	3FT deg	*	CC	M+D	D	28	CCCC	Ind	
Writing/Religious Studies	VW8L	3FT deg	*	CC	M+D	D	28	CCCC	Ind	

| | | | | 98 expected requirements | | | | | | 96 entry stats |
| course details | | | | | | | | | | |
TITLE	CODE	COURSE	SUBJECTS	A/AS	ND/C	RGNVQ	IB	SQA(H)	SQA	RATIO A/AS
MIDDLESEX Univ										
Christian Studies	V860▼	3FT deg	* g	12-16	5M	M$ go	28	Ind	Ind	
Pastoral Studies	V851▼	3FT deg	* g	12-16	5M	M$ go	28	Ind	Ind	
Religious Studies	V800▼	3FT deg	* g	12-16	5M	M$ go	28	Ind	Ind	
Theology for Ministry	V850▼	3FT deg								
Joint Honours Degree *Christian Studies*	Y400	3FT deg	* g	12-16	5M	X	28	BBCC	Ind	
Joint Honours Degree *Religious Studies*	Y400	3FT deg	* g	12-16	5M	M$ go	28	BBCC	Ind	
Univ of NEWCASTLE										
Religious Studies	V840	3FT deg	*	BCC	Ind	Ind	Ind	BBBBB	Ind	6 12/26
Combined Studies (BA) *Biblical Studies*	Y400	3FT deg	*	ABC-BBB	5D	Ind	35$	AAAB	Ind	
Combined Studies (BA) *Religious Studies*	Y400	3FT deg	*	ABC-BBB	5D	Ind	35$	AAAB	Ind	
NEWMAN COLLEGE OF HIGHER EDUCATION										
Biological Science and Theology	CV18	3FT deg	*	CC	3M	M*	Dip	CCC	Ind	
History and Theology	VV18	3FT deg	*	CC	3M	M*	Dip	CCC	Ind	
PE and Sports Studies and Theology	VX89	3FT deg	*	CC	3M	M*	Dip	CCC	Ind	
Theology and Expressive English	VW84	3FT deg	*	CC	3M	M*	Dip	CCC	Ind	
Theology and Geography	FV88	3FT deg	*	CC	3M	M*	Dip	CCC	Ind	
Univ of Wales COLLEGE, NEWPORT										
Religious Studies and English	QV38	3FT deg		10	M+D	D$	Ind	Ind	Ind	
Religious Studies and European Studies	TV28	3FT deg		10	M+D	D$	Ind	Ind	Ind	
Religious Studies and Geography	LV88	3FT deg		10	M+D	D$	Ind	Ind	Ind	
Religious Studies and History	VV18	3FT deg		10	M+D	D$	Ind	Ind	Ind	
Sports Studies and Religious Studies	BV68	3FT deg		10	M+D	D$	Ind	Ind	Ind	
Univ of NOTTINGHAM										
Classical Civilisation and Theology	QV88	3FT deg		CCC						
English Studies and Theology	QV38	3FT deg	E	BBC						8 26/30
German and Theology	RV28	4FT deg	G	BBC-BCC						2
Greek and Theology	QV78	3FT deg		BCC						
Latin and Theology	QV68	3FT deg	Ln	BCC						2
Philosophy and Theology	VV78	3FT deg		BBC						18
Theology	V800	3FT deg		BBC						15 20/28
OXFORD Univ										
Philosophy and Theology	VV78	3FT deg	*	AAB-ABB	DO		36	AAAAA	Ind	3 22/30
Theology	V800	3FT deg	*	AAB-ABB	DO		36	AAAAA	Ind	2 26/30
OXFORD WESTMINSTER COLLEGE										
Contemporary English Studies with Interfaith St	Q3VV	2FT Dip	E	CE	MO	M	Ind	CCC	Ind	
Contemporary English Studies with Interfaith St	Q3V8	3FT deg	E	CE	MO	M	Ind	CCC	Ind	
Contemporary French Studies with Interfaith St	R1VV	2FT Dip	F	CE	MO	M	Ind	CCC	Ind	
Contemporary French Studies with Interfaith St	R1V8	3FT deg	F	CE	MO	M	Ind	CCC	Ind	
Contemporary Geography Studs with Interfaith St	L8V8	3FT deg	Gy	CE	MO	M	Ind	CCC	Ind	
Contemporary Geography Studs with Interfaith St	L8VV	2FT Dip	Gy	CE	MO	M	Ind	CCC	Ind	
Contemporary Historical Studies w. Interfaith St	V1V8	3FT deg	H	CE	MO	M	Ind	CCC	Ind	
Contemporary Historical Studs with Interfaith St	V1VV	2FT Dip	H	CE	MO	M	Ind	CCC	Ind	
Theology	V840	4FT deg		CE	MO	M	Ind	CCC	Ind	
Theology (2 Yrs)	V800	2FT Dip		CE	MO	M	Ind	CCC	Ind	

			98 expected requirements							96 entry stats	
TITLE	CODE	COURSE	SUBJECTS	R/RS	ND/C	RGNVQ	IB	SQA(H)	SQA	RATIO R/RS	

Univ of PORTSMOUTH

TITLE	CODE	COURSE	SUBJECTS	R/RS	ND/C	RGNVQ	IB	SQA(H)	SQA	RATIO R/RS
Economic History and Historical Geography	LV38	3FT deg	Gy	12	4M $	M*	Dip	BBCC	Ind	

QUEEN'S Univ Belfast

TITLE	CODE	COURSE	SUBJECTS	R/RS	ND/C	RGNVQ	IB	SQA(H)	SQA	RATIO R/RS
Biblical Studies	V820	3FT deg	* g	BCC	3M+4D	D*6/^ go	29$	ABBB	Ind	19
Biblical Studies/Ancient History	VVC8	3FT deg	* g	BCC	3M+4D	D*6/^ go	29$	ABBB	Ind	
Biblical Studies/Archaeology	VV68	3FT deg	* g	BCC	3M+4D	D*6/^ go	29$	ABBB	Ind	
Byzantine Studies/Biblical Studies	VQ88	3FT/4FT deg	* g	BCC	3M+4D	D*6/^ go	29$	ABBB	Ind	
Celtic/Biblical Studies	VQ85	3FT/4FT deg	* g	BCC	3M+4D	D*6/^ go	29$	ABBB	Ind	
Classical Studies/Biblical Studies	QV88	3FT deg	* g	BCC	3M+4D	D*6/^ go	29$	ABBB	Ind	
Diploma in Theology (2 years)	V870	2FT Dip	* g	CCC	4M+3D	D*6/^ go	28$	ABBB	Ind	5
Divinity (BD)	V800	3FT deg	* g	CCC	4M+3D	D*6/^ go	28$	BBBB	Ind	2
Economic & Social History/Biblical Studies	VV83	3FT deg	* g	BCC	3M+4D	D*6/^ go	29$	ABBB	Ind	
English/Biblical Studies	VQ83	3FT deg	E g	BCC	X	D*^ go	29$	ABBB	X	8
Greek/Biblical Studies	VQ87	3FT/4FT deg	* g	BCC	3M+4D	D*6/^ go	29$	ABBB	Ind	
Latin/Biblical Studies	VQ86	3FT/4FT deg	* g	BCC	3M+4D	D*6/^ go	29$	ABBB	Ind	
Music/Biblical Studies	VW83	3FT deg	* g	BCC	3M+4D	D*6/^ go	29$	ABBB	Ind	
Philosophy/Biblical Studies	VV87	3FT deg	* g	BCC	3M+4D	D*6/^ go	29$	ABBB	Ind	
Scholastic Philosophy/Biblical Studies	VV8R	3FT deg	* g	BCC	3M+4D	D*6/^ go	29$	ABBB	Ind	
Social Anthropology/Biblical Studies	VL86	3FT deg	* g	BCC	3M+4D	D*6/^ go	29$	ABBB	Ind	
Theology (BTh)	V802	3FT deg	* g	CCC	4M+3D	D*6/^ go	28$	ABBB	Ind	4 14/20
Theology and English	QV38	3FT deg								
Theology and History and Philosophy of Science	VV58	3FT deg								
Theology and Scholastic Philosophy	VV78	3FT deg								

Univ College of RIPON & YORK ST JOHN

TITLE	CODE	COURSE	SUBJECTS	R/RS	ND/C	RGNVQ	IB	SQA(H)	SQA	RATIO R/RS
Applied Social Sciences/Theology	L3V8	3FT deg		CC	M	M	27	BBBC		4 14/18
English/Theology	Q3V8	3FT deg	E	16	Ind	M*^	27	BBBB		
History/Theology	V1V8	3FT deg	H	14	X	M*^	30	BBBB		6
Psychology/Theology	L7V8	3FT deg	g	16	M	M	30	BBBB		
Theology/Applied Social Sciences	V8L3	3FT deg		12	M	M*	27	BBBC		1 6/18
Theology/Education	VX89	3FT deg	g	12	M	M	27	BBBC		
Theology/English	V8Q3	3FT deg	E	12	M	M*	27	BBBC		
Theology/History	V8V1	3FT deg	H	12	X	M*^	27	BBBC		2 8/12
Theology/Psychology	V8L7	3FT deg	g	12	M	M*	27	BBBC		
Theology/Women's Studies	V8M9	3FT deg		12	M	M*	27	BBBC		1 8/12

ROEHAMPTON INST

TITLE	CODE	COURSE	SUBJECTS	R/RS	ND/C	RGNVQ	IB	SQA(H)	SQA	RATIO R/RS
Theology & Relig St and English Lang & Linguist	QVH8▼	3FT deg	E/L	CC	2M+2D$	M$^	30	BBC	Ind	3
Theology & Relig Studs & Natural Resource Studs	DV28▼	3FT deg	g	DD	3M	P$ go	24	CCC	N$	
Theology & Religious St and Film & Television St	PV48▼	3FT deg	*	16	2M+2D$	M$^	30	BBC	N$	
Theology & Religious St and Human & Social Biol	CVC8▼	3FT deg	B	DD	3M	P$ go	24	CCC	N$	
Theology & Religious St and Soc Policy & Admin	LV48▼	3FT deg	g	DD	3M	P$	24	CCC	N	
Theology & Religious St/Drama & Theatre Studies	WVL8▼	3FT deg	E/T	16	3D	M$^	30	BBC	Ind	4
Theology & Religious Studies	V800▼	3FT deg	*	DD	3M	P$	24	CCC	N	5 4/12
Theology & Religious Studies and App Consumer St	NV98▼	3FT deg	g	12	4M	P$ go	26	BCC	N	
Theology & Religious Studies and Biology	CV18▼	3FT deg	B	12	4M $	P$ go	26	BCC	N$	
Theology & Religious Studies and Business Comp	GV78▼	3FT deg	g	12	3D	M$ go	26	BCC	N$	
Theology & Religious Studies and Business Studs	NV18▼	3FT deg	g	DD	3D	M$ go	26	BCC	N$	2
Theology & Religious Studies and Dance Studies	WV48▼	3FT deg	*	CC	3D	M$^	30	BBC	Ind	
Theology & Religious Studies and Education	XV98▼	3FT deg	*	DD	3M	P$	24	CCC	N	4/10
Theology & Religious Studies and English Lit	QV38▼	3FT deg	E	CC	2M+2D$	M^	28	BBC	Ind	15
Theology & Religious Studies and French	RV18▼	4FT deg	F	12	4M $	P^	26	BCC	N$	
Theology & Religious Studies and Geography	LV88▼	3FT deg	Gy	DD	4M $	P$ go	26	BCC	N$	

course details | 98 expected requirements | 96 entry stats

TITLE	CODE	COURSE	SUBJECTS	A/AS	ND/C	AGNVQ	IB	SQA(H)	SQA	RATIO A/AS
Theology & Religious Studies and Health Studies	BV98▼	3FT deg	B g	12	4M	P$ go	26	BCC	N$	1
Theology & Religious Studies and History	VV18▼	3FT deg	H	DD	4M $	P^	26	BCC	N$	5
Theology & Religious Studies and Music	WV38▼	3FT deg	Mu	DD	4M $	P^	26	BCC	N$	
Theology & Religious Studies and Psychology	LV78▼	3FT deg	g	CC	3D $	M$ go	30	BBC	Ind	4
Theology & Religious Studies and Sociology	LV38▼	3FT deg	g	DD	3M	P$ go	24	CCC	N	4
Theology & Religious Studies and Spanish	RV48▼	4FT deg	Sp	12	2M+2D$	P$ go	28	BBC	N$	
Theology & Religious Studies and Sport Studies	BV68▼	3FT deg	S g	12	3D	MS go	30	BBC	N$	
Theology & Religious Studs and Art for Community	WV18▼	3FT deg	*	DD	3M	P$	24	CCC	N	1
Theology & Religious Studs and Environmental St	FV98▼	3FT deg	B/Gy	DD	4M $	P$ go	26	BCC	N$	
Women's Studies and Theology & Religious Studies	VM89▼	3FT deg	*	DD	3M	P$ go	24	CCC	N	5
Humanities (English History Theol & Relig St)	VY93▼	3FT deg	E/H	CC	3D $		30	BBC	Ind	
Theology and Religious Studies										

SOAS:Sch of Oriental & African St (U of London)

TITLE	CODE	COURSE	SUBJECTS	A/AS	ND/C	AGNVQ	IB	SQA(H)	SQA	RATIO A/AS
Comparative Religion	V840	3FT deg		20	Ind		30	BBBCC	Ind	3 16/28
South Asian Studies and Study of Religions	VT8N	3FT deg								
Study of Religions and African Studies	VT87	3FT deg		20	Ind		30	BBBCC	Ind	
Study of Religions and Amharic	TV78	4FT deg		20	Ind		30	BBBCC	Ind	
Study of Religions and Arabic	TV68	4FT deg		22	Ind		31	BBBBC	Ind	5
Study of Religions and Bengali	TV58	3FT deg		20	Ind		30	BBBCC	Ind	
Study of Religions and Burmese	TVM8	4FT deg		20	Ind		30	BBBCC	Ind	
Study of Religions and Chinese	TV38	4FT deg		24	Ind		32	BBBBB	Ind	2
Study of Religions and Economics	LV18	3FT deg	g	20	Ind		30	BBBCC	Ind	3
Study of Religions and Geography	LV88	3FT deg		20	Ind		30	BBBCC	Ind	
Study of Religions and Georgian	TV98	3FT deg		22	Ind		31	BBBBC	Ind	
Study of Religions and Gujarati	TV5V	3FT deg		20	Ind		30	BBBCC	Ind	
Study of Religions and Hausa	TVR8	4FT deg		20	Ind		30	BBBCC	Ind	
Study of Religions and Hebrew	QV98	4FT deg		22	Ind		31	BBBBC	Ind	
Study of Religions and Hindi	TVN8	3FT/4FT deg		20	Ind		30	BBBCC	Ind	
Study of Religions and History	VV18	3FT deg		20	Ind		30	BBBCC	Ind	1
Study of Religions and History of Art/Archaeolog	VV68	3FT deg		20	Ind		30	BBBCC	Ind	4
Study of Religions and Indonesian	TV5W	3FT/4FT deg		20	Ind		30	BBBCC	Ind	
Study of Religions and Japanese	TV48	4FT deg		24	Ind		32	BBBBB	Ind	
Study of Religions and Korean	TVNV	4FT deg		20	Ind		30	BBBCC	Ind	
Study of Religions and Law	MV38	3FT deg		24	Ind		32	BBBBB	Ind	2
Study of Religions and Linguistics	QV18	3FT deg		20	Ind		30	BBBCC	Ind	
Study of Religions and Music	VW83	3FT deg		20	Ind		30	BBBCC	Ind	4
Study of Religions and Nepali	TVMV	3FT deg		20	Ind		30	BBBCC	Ind	
Study of Religions and Persian	TVQ8	3FT deg		22	Ind		31	BBBBC	Ind	
Study of Religions and Politics	MV18	3FT deg		20	Ind		30	BBBCC	Ind	
Study of Religions and Sanskrit	QVX8	3FT deg		20	Ind		30	BBBCC	Ind	1
Study of Religions and Sinhalese	TVNW	3FI deg		20	Ind		30	BBBCC	Ind	
Study of Religions and Social Anthropology	LV68	3FT deg		22	Ind		31	BBBBC	Ind	6
Swahili and Study of Religions	TVT8	4FT deg		20	Ind		30	BBBCC	Ind	
Tamil and Study of Religions	VT85	3FT deg		20	Ind		30	BBBCC	Ind	
Thai and Study of Religions	VT8M	3FT/4FT deg		20	Ind		30	BBBCC	Ind	4
Tibetan and Study of Religions	V8TM	3FT deg		20	Ind		30	BBBCC	Ind	
Turkish and Study of Religions	VT8P	4FT deg		22	Ind		31	BBBBC	Ind	
Urdu and Study of Religions	VTV5	3FT deg		20	Ind		30	BBBCC	Ind	
Vietnamese and Study of Religions	VTVM	4FT deg		20	Ind		30	BBBCC	Ind	

SSEES:Sch of Slavonic & E European St(U of London)

TITLE	CODE	COURSE	SUBJECTS	A/AS	ND/C	AGNVQ	IB	SQA(H)	SQA	RATIO A/AS
History (Central & East European) and Jewish St	VV18	4FT deg	H	BCC	3M $	Ind	28	BBBBB		2

TITLE	CODE	COURSE	SUBJECTS	A/AS	ND/C	AGNVQ	IB	SQA(H)	SQA	RATIO	A/AS
course details			**98 expected requirements**							**96 entry stats**	

Univ of SHEFFIELD

TITLE	CODE	COURSE	SUBJECTS	A/AS	ND/C	AGNVQ	IB	SQA(H)	SQA	RATIO	A/AS
Biblical Studies	V820	3FT deg	* g	BBC	X	X	30	ABBB	Ind	3	12/22
Biblical Studies and English	QV38	3FT deg	E g	BBB	X	X	32$	AABB$	Ind		
Biblical Studies and German	RV28	4FT deg	G g	BBC	X	X	30$	ABBB$	Ind		
Biblical Studies and Linguistics	QV18	3FT deg	Ee g	BBC	X	X	30	ABBB	Ind		
Biblical Studies and Music	VW83	3FT deg	Mu g	BBC-BCC	X	X	30$	ABBB$	Ind		
Biblical Studies and Philosophy	VV78	3FT deg	* g	BBC	X	X	30	ABBB	Ind	22	

Univ College of St MARTIN, LANCASTER AND CUMBRIA

TITLE	CODE	COURSE	SUBJECTS	A/AS	ND/C	AGNVQ	IB	SQA(H)	SQA	RATIO	A/AS
Applied Community Studies/Religious Studies	LV58	3FT deg	*	CD-DDE	3M+2D	M*	28	BCCC	Ind	1	
Art and Design/Religious Studies	WV18	3FT deg	A	CC-CDE	3M+2D$	MA	28$	BBCC$	Ind		
Business Management Studies/Religious Studies	NV18	3FT deg	*	CD-CEE	3M+2D	M	28	BCCC			
Christian Ministry	V860	3FT deg	*	CC-CDE	3M+2D$	M*	28$	BBCC	Ind	2	12/24
English/Religious Studies	QV3V	3FT deg	E	BC-BDE	X	P^	28$	BBBC$	Ind	4	
Health Studies/Religious Studies	BV98	3FT deg	*	CD-DDE	3M+2D	M*	28	BCCC	Ind		
History/Religious Studies	VV1V	3FT deg	H	CD-DDE	X	P^	28$	BCCC$	Ind		
Mathematics/Religious Studies	GV18	3FT deg	M	DD-DEE	X	X	28$	BCCC$	Ind		
Religious Studies	V800	3FT deg	*	CD-DDE	3M+2D	M*	28$	BCCC	Ind	3	6/14
Religious Studies/Applied Community Studies	VL8M	3FT deg	*	CD-DDE	3M+2D	M*	28$	BCCC	Ind		
Religious Studies/Art and Design	VW8C	3FT deg	A	CD-DDE	X	M^	28$	BCCC	Ind	3	
Religious Studies/Business Management Studies	VN81	3FT deg	*	CD-DDE	3M+2D	M	28	BCCC			
Religious Studies/Education Studies	VX89	3FT deg	*	CD-DDE	3M+2D$	M*	28$	BCCC	Ind		
Religious Studies/English	VQ8H	3FT deg	E	CD-DDE	X	M^	28$	BCCC$	Ind	3	
Religious Studies/Health Studies	VB89	3FT deg	*	CD-DDE	3M+2D	M*	28$	BCCC	Ind	1	
Religious Studies/History	VV8C	3FT deg	H	CD-DDE	3M+2D$	M^	28$	BCCC$	Ind		
Religious Studies/Mathematics	VG81	3FT deg	M	CD-DDE	3M+2D$	M^	28$	BCCC$	Ind		
Religious Studies/Physical Education & Sports St	VX8X	3FT deg	*	CD-DDE	3M+2D	M*	28	BCCC			
Religious Studies/Science, Technology & Society	VY81	3FT deg	g	CD-DDE	3M+2D	M*	28$	BCCC	Ind		
Religious Studies/Social Ethics	VV8R	3FT deg	*	CD-DDE	3M+2D	M*	28$	BCCC	Ind	1	6/16
Science, Technology and Society/Religious Studs	VY8C	3FT deg	g	CD-DDE	3M+2D	M*	28	BCCC	Ind		
Social Ethics/Religious Studies	VV7V	3FT deg	*	CD-DDE	3M+2D	M*	28	BCCC	Ind	3	

Univ of ST ANDREWS

TITLE	CODE	COURSE	SUBJECTS	A/AS	ND/C	AGNVQ	IB	SQA(H)	SQA	RATIO	A/AS
Biblical Studies	V820	4FT deg	* g	BBC	X	Ind	30$	BBBB	Ind	7	
Biblical Studies-Ancient History	VV18	4FT deg	* g	BBB	X	Ind	30$	BBBB	Ind	4	
Classical Studies-Biblical Studies	VQ88	4FT deg	* g	BBC	X	Ind	30$	BBBB	Ind		
Divinity BD (General and Honours)	V800	3FT/4FT deg	* g	CCC	X	Ind	28$	BBCC	Ind	10	
Economics-Biblical Studies	LV18	4FT deg	* g	BBB	X	Ind	30$	BBBB	Ind		
English-Biblical Studies	QV3W	4FT deg	* g	BBB	X	Ind	30$	BBBB	Ind		
French with Year Abroad-Biblical Studies	RVC8	4FT/5FT deg	E g	BBB	X	Ind	30$	BBBB$	Ind		
French-Biblical Studies	RV18	4FT deg	E g	BBB	X	Ind	30$	BBBB$	Ind		
German with Year Abroad-Biblical Studies	RVFV	4FT/5FT deg	* g	BBC	X	Ind	30$	BBBB	Ind		
German-Biblical Studies	RV28	4FT deg	* g	BBC	X	Ind	30$	BBBB	Ind	1	
Greek-Biblical Studies	QV78	4FT deg	* g	BBC	X	Ind	30$	BBBB	Ind		
Hebrew-Biblical Studies	QV98	4FT deg	* g	BBC	X	Ind	30$	BBBB	Ind		
New Testament - Modern History	VV81	4FT deg	* g	BBB	X	Ind	30$	BBBB	Ind		
New Testament-German	RV2V	4FT deg	* g	BBC	X	Ind	30$	BBBB	Ind		
New Testament-German with Year Abroad	RVFW	4FT/5FT deg	* g	BBC	X	Ind	30$	BBBB	Ind		
New Testament-Greek	QV7W	4FT deg	* g	BBC	X	Ind	30$	BBBB	Ind		
New Testament-Hebrew	QV9V	4FT deg	* g	BBC	X	Ind	30$	BBBB	Ind		
New Testament-Latin	QV6W	4FT deg	* g	BBC	X	Ind	30$	BBBB	Ind		
Philosophy-Biblical Studies	VV7V	4FT deg	* g	BBB	X	Ind	30$	BBBB	Ind	4	
Theological Studies-Classical Studies	QV88	4FT deg	* g	BBC	X	Ind	30$	BBBB	Ind		

Theology 68

course details				98 expected requirements						96 entry stats
TITLE	CODE	COURSE	SUBJECTS	A/AS	NO/C	AGNVQ	IB	SQA(H)	SQA	RATIO A/AS
Theological Studies-English	QV38	4FT deg	* g	BBB	X	Ind	30$	BBBB	Ind	12
Theological Studies-French	VR81	4FT deg	E g	BBB	X	Ind	30$	BBBB$	Ind	
Theological Studies-French with Year Abroad	VR8C	4FT/5FT deg	E g	BBB	X	Ind	30$	BBBB	Ind	
Theological Studies-Geography	LV88	4FT deg								
Theological Studies-German	RV2W	4FT deg	* g	BBC	X	Ind	30$	BBBB	Ind	
Theological Studies-German with Year Abroad	RVF8	4FT/5FT deg	* g	BBC	X	Ind	30$	BBBB	Ind	
Theological Studies-International Relations	MV18	4FT deg	* g	AAB	X	Ind	36$	AAAB	Ind	
Theological Studies-Modern History	VV1V	4FT deg	* g	BBB	X	Ind	30$	BBBB	Ind	
Theological Studies-Philosophy	VV78	4FT deg	* g	BBB	X	Ind	30$	BBBB	Ind	14
Theological Studies-Social Anthropology	LV68	4FT deg	* g	BBB	X	Ind	30$	BBBB	Ind	5
Theology (Licentiate in Theology)	V880	3FT deg	* g	CCC	X	Ind	28$	BBB	Ind	
Theology MTheol (General and Honours)	V808	3FT/4FT deg	* g	CCC	X	Ind	28$	BBB	Ind	2 10/26
General Degree of MA Biblical Studies	Y450	3FT deg	* g	BBB	X	Ind	30$	BBBB	Ind	
General Degree of MA Theology	Y450	3FT deg	* g	BBB	X	Ind	30$	BBBB	Ind	

THE UNIVERSITY COLLEGE OF ST MARK AND ST JOHN

Art and Design/Theology and Philosophy	W1V8	3FT deg		4	MO	M	Dip	CCCC	Ind	
English (Literary Studies)/Theology & Philosophy	Q3V8	3FT deg	El	12-16	Ind	M	Ind	Ind	Ind	
History/Theology	V1VV	3FT deg	H	12	MO	M	Ind	Ind	Ind	
History/Theology & Philosophy	V1V8	3FT deg	H	12	MO	M	Ind	Ind	Ind	
Sociology/Theology	L3V8	3FT deg	So	8	MO	M	Ind	Ind	Ind	
Sociology/Theology & Philosophy	L3VV	3FT deg	So	8	MO	M	Ind	Ind	Ind	
Theology & Philosophy/Art & Design	V8W1	3FT deg	Re	4	MO	M	Dip	CCCC	Ind	
Theology & Philosophy/English (Literary Studies)	V8Q3	3FT deg	Re	4	MO	M	Dip	CCCC	Ind	
Theology & Philosophy/History	V8V1	3FT deg	Re	4	MO	M	Dip	CCCC	Ind	
Theology & Philosophy/Sociology	V8L3	3FT deg	Re	4	MO	M	Dip	CCCC	Ind	
Theology with Philosophy	V8V7	3FT deg	Re	4	MO	M	Dip	CCCC	Ind	
Theology/History	V8VC	3FT deg	Re	4	MO	M	Dip	CCCC	Ind	
Theology/Sociology	V8LH	3FT deg	Re	4	MO	M	Dip	CCCC	Ind	

ST MARY'S Univ COLL

Theology	V801	3FT deg	*	8-12	Ind	Ind	Ind	BBBB	Ind	
Theology and Religious St & Environ Investig St	FV98	3FT deg	S/2S	4-8	Ind	Ind	Ind	BBBB	Ind	
Theology and Religious St and Integrated Sci St	VY81	3FT deg	S/2S	4-8	Ind	Ind	Ind	BBBB$	Ind	
Theology and Religious Studies	V800	3FT deg	*	8-12	Ind	Ind	Ind	BBBB	Ind	
Theology and Religious Studies and Biology	VC81	3FT deg	B/C	4-8	Ind	Ind	Ind	BBBB$	Ind	
Theology and Religious Studies and Classical St	VQ88	3FT deg	*	4-8	Ind	Ind	Ind	BBBB	Ind	
Theology and Religious Studies and Drama	VW84	3FT deg	*	8-12	Ind	Ind	Ind	BBBB	Ind	
Theology and Religious Studies and Education St	VX8X	3FT deg	*	4-8	Ind	Ind	Ind	BBBB	Ind	
Theology and Religious Studies and English	QV38	3FT deg	E	8-12	X	X	Ind	BBBB$	X	
Theology and Religious Studies and Environ St	FVX8	3FT deg	S/2S	4-8	Ind	Ind	Ind	BBBB	Ind	
Theology and Religious Studies and Gender St	MV98	3FT deg	*	4-8	Ind	Ind	Ind	BBBB	Ind	
Theology and Religious Studies and History	VV81	3FT deg	H	4-8	Ind	Ind	Ind	BBBB$	Ind	
Theology and Religious Studies and Irish Studies	QV58	3FT deg	*	4-8	Ind	Ind	Ind	BBBB	Ind	
Theology and Religious Studies and Management St	NV18	3FT deg	* g	4-8	Ind	Ind	Ind	BBBB	Ind	
Theology and Religious Studies and Sociology	VL83	3FT deg	*	4-8	Ind	Ind	Ind	BBBB	Ind	
Theology and Religious Studies and Sport Science	VB86	3FT deg	S g	8-12	Ind	Ind	Ind	BBBB$	Ind	

Univ of STIRLING

English Studies/Religious Studies	QV38	4FT deg	g	BBC	Ind	Ind	33	BBBB	HN	
French/Religious Studies	RV18	4FT deg	g	CCC	Ind	Ind	31	BBBC	HN	
German/Religious Studies	RV28	4FT deg	g	CCC	Ind	Ind	31	BBBC	HN	

Letts STUDY GUIDES
THE INDEPENDENT

course details			**98 expected requirements**							**96 entry stats**
TITLE	CODE	COURSE	SUBJECTS	A/AS	ND/C	AGNVQ	IB	SQA(H)	SQA	RATIO A/AS
History/Religious Studies	VV18	4FT deg	g	CCC	Ind	Ind	28	BBCC	HN	
Philosophy/Religious Studies	VV78	4FT deg	g	CCC	Ind	Ind	28	BBCC	HN	
Politics/Religious Studies	MV18	4FT deg	g	BCC	Ind	Ind	31	BBBC	HN	
Religious Studies	V840	4FT deg	g	CCC	Ind	Ind	28	BBCC	HN	
Religious Studies/Film & Media Studies	VP84	4FT deg	g	BBC	Ind	Ind	35	ABBB	HN	
Religious Studies/Social Policy	LV48	4FT deg	g	CCC	Ind	Ind	28	BBCC	HN	
Religious Studies/Sociology	LV38	4FT deg	g	CCC	Ind	Ind	28	BBCC	HN	
Religious Studies/Spanish	RV48	4FT deg	g	CCC	Ind	Ind	31	BBBC	HN	

Univ of SUNDERLAND

TITLE	CODE	COURSE	SUBJECTS	A/AS	ND/C	AGNVQ	IB	SQA(H)	SQA	RATIO A/AS
Biology and Religious Studies	CV18	3FT deg	B/C	8	3M	M	Ind	Ind	Ind	
Biology with Religious Studies	C1V8	3FT deg	B/C	8	3M	M	Ind	Ind	Ind	
Business Studies and Religious Studies	NV18	3FT/4SW deg	*	8	3M	M	Ind	Ind	Ind	
Business Studies with Religious Studies	N1V8	3FT/4SW deg	*	8	3M	M	Ind	Ind	Ind	
Chemistry and Religious Studies	FV18	3FT deg	C	8	3M	M	Ind	Ind	Ind	
Chemistry with Religious Studies	F1V8	3FT deg	C	8	3M	M	Ind	Ind	Ind	
Computer Studies and Religious Studies	GV58	3FT deg	* g	10	N	M	24	CCCC	N	
Computer Studies with Religious Studies	G5V8	3FT/4SW deg	*	8	3M	M	Ind	Ind	Ind	
Economics and Religious Studies	LV18	3FT deg	*	8	3M	M	Ind	Ind	Ind	
Economics with Religious Studies	L1V8	3FT deg	*	8	3M	M	Ind	Ind	Ind	
English and Religious Studies	QV38▼	3FT deg	El g	12	Ind	M	24$	BCCC$	Ind	4
English with Religious Studies	Q3V8	3FT deg	*	10	4M	M	Ind	Ind	Ind	
French and Religious Studies	RV18▼	4FT deg	F g	10	N $	M	24$	CCCC$	N$	
French with Religious Studies	R1V8	4FT deg	F	8	3M	M	Ind	Ind	Ind	
Geology and Religious Studies	FV68	3FT deg	*	8	3M	M	Ind	Ind		
German and Religious Studies	RV28▼	4FT deg	G g	10	N $	M	24$	CCCC$	N$	
German with Religious Studies	R2V8	4SW deg	G	8	3M	M	Ind	Ind	Ind	
History and Religious Studies	VV18▼	3FT deg	H g	12	Ind	M	24	BCCC	Ind	3
History with Religious Studies	V1V8	3FT deg	*	10	4M	M	Ind	Ind	Ind	
Media Studies and Religious Studies	PV48	3FT deg	*	24	Ind	Ind	Ind	Ind		
Media Studies with Religious Studies	P4V8	3FT deg	*	24	Ind	Ind	Ind	Ind	Ind	
Philosophy and Religious Studies	VV78	3FT deg	* g	12	3M	M	24	BCCC	N	2
Philosophy with Religious Studies	V7V8	3FT deg	*	8	3M	M	Ind	Ind	Ind	
Physiology and Religious Studies	BV18	3FT deg	*	8	3M	M	Ind	Ind		
Physiology with Religious Studies	B1V8	3FT deg	*	8	3M	M	Ind	Ind	Ind	
Politics and Religious Studies	MV18▼	3FT deg	* g	12	3M	M	24	BCCC	N	2
Politics with Religious Studies	M1V8	3FT deg	*	8	3M	M	Ind	Ind	Ind	
Psychology and Religious Studies	CV88	3FT deg	* g	14	MO $	M	26$	BBCC$	N	6
Psychology with Religious Studies	C8V8	3FT deg	*	10	4M	M^	Ind	Ind	Ind	
Religious Studies and Geography	L8V8▼	3FT deg	Gy/Gl g	12	Ind	M	24	BCCC	Ind	
Religious Studies and Spanish	VR84	4SW deg	*	8	3M	M	Ind	Ind		
Religious Studies with Biology	V8C1	3FT deg	*		3M	M	Ind	Ind	Ind	Ind
Religious Studies with Business Studies	V8N1	3FT deg	*	8	3M	M	Ind	Ind	Ind	
Religious Studies with Chemistry	V8F1	3FT deg	*	8	3M	M	Ind	Ind	Ind	
Religious Studies with Comparative Literature	V8Q2	3FT deg	El g	12	Ind	M	24$	BCCC$	Ind	
Religious Studies with Computer Studies	V8G5	3FT deg	*	8	3M	M	Ind	Ind	Ind	
Religious Studies with Economics	V8L1	3FT deg	*	8	3M	M	Ind	Ind	Ind	
Religious Studies with English	V8Q3	3FT deg	*	10	4M	M	Ind	Ind	Ind	
Religious Studies with European Studies	V8T2	3FT deg	* g	12	3M	M	24	BCCC	N	
Religious Studies with French	V8R1	3FT deg	*	8	3M	M	Ind	Ind	Ind	
Religious Studies with Gender Studies	V8M9	3FT deg	* g	12	3M	M	24	BCCC	N	3
Religious Studies with Geology	V8F6	3FT deg	*	8	3M	M	Ind	Ind	Ind	
Religious Studies with German	V8R2	3FT deg	*	8	3M	M	Ind	Ind	Ind	

course details			98 expected requirements							96 entry stats	
TITLE	CODE	COURSE	SUBJECTS	A/AS	ND/C	AGNVQ	IB	SQA(H)	SQA	RATIO	A/AS
Religious Studies with History	V8V1	3FT deg	*	10	4M	M	Ind	Ind	Ind		
Religious Studies with History of Art and Design	V8V4	3FT deg	*	8	3M	M	Ind	Ind	Ind		
Religious Studies with Media Studies	V8P4	3FT deg	*	24	Ind	Ind	Ind	Ind	Ind		
Religious Studies with Philosophy	V8V7	3FT deg	*	8	3M	M	Ind	Ind	Ind		
Religious Studies with Physiology	V8B1	3FT deg	*	8	3M	M	Ind	Ind	Ind		
Religious Studies with Politics	V8M1	3FT deg	*	8	3M	M	Ind	Ind	Ind		
Religious Studies with Psychology	V8C8	3FT deg	*	10	4M	M^	Ind	Ind	Ind		
Religious Studies with Sociology	V8L3	3FT deg	*	10	4M	M	Ind	Ind	Ind		
Religious Studies with Spanish	V8R4	3FT deg	*	8	3M	M	Ind	Ind	Ind		
Sociology and Religious Studies	VL83▼	3FT deg	* g	12	3M	M	24	BCCC	N		
Sociology with Religious Studies	L3V8	3FT deg	*	10	4M	M	Ind	Ind	Ind		
TRINITY COLL Carmarthen											
Astudiaethau Crefydd	V842	3FT deg	g	DD-CC	Ind		Ind	Ind	Ind	7	
Astudiaethau Theatr/Astudiaethau Crefydd	WV48	3FT deg	T+Re g								
Cymraeg/Astudiaethau Crefydd	QV5W	3FT deg	W+Re g	DD-CC	Ind		Ind	Ind	Ind	3	
Hanes/Astudiaethau Crefydd	VV1W	3FT deg	H g	DD-CC	Ind		Ind	Ind	Ind		
Religious Studies	V840	3FT deg	Re g	DD-CC	Ind		Ind	Ind	Ind	4	6/18
Religious Studies/Archaeology	VV68	3FT deg	g	DD-CC	Ind		Ind	Ind	Ind	4	
Religious Studies/English	QV38	3FT deg	Re+E g	DD-CC	Ind		Ind	Ind	Ind	4	
Religious Studies/History	VV18	3FT deg	Re+H g	DD-CC	Ind		Ind	Ind	Ind	4	
Theatre Studies/Religious Studies	VW84	3FT deg	g	DD-CC	Ind		Ind	Ind	Ind		
Welsh Studies/Religious Studies	QV58	3FT deg	Re g	DD-CC	Ind		Ind	Ind	Ind		
Dyniaethau *Astudiaethau Crefydd*	Y321	3FT deg	* g	DD-CC	Ind		Ind	Ind	Ind		
Humanities *Religious Studies*	Y320	3FT deg	* g	DD-CC	Ind		Ind	Ind	Ind		
WESTHILL COLL											
Applied Theological Studies (Christian or Islam)	V800	3FT deg	* g	CC	4M+2D	M^	Ind	Ind	Ind	2	8/18
Humanities - History:Islam & the Christian West	VV18	3FT deg	* g	CC	4M+2D	M^	Ind	Ind	Ind		
Univ of WOLVERHAMPTON											
Religious Studies (Specialist Route)	V800	3FT deg		10	4M	M	24	BBBB	Ind	7	10/14
Combined Degrees *Applied Theology*	Y401	3FT/4SW deg	*	10	4M	M	24	BBBB	Ind		
Combined Degrees *Religious Studies*	Y401	3FT deg		10	4M	M	24	BBBB	Ind		

course details			98 expected requirements							96 entry stats	
TITLE	CODE	COURSE	SUBJECTS	A/AS	ND/C	AGNVQ	IB	SQA(H)	SQA	RATIO	A/AS
Univ of ABERTAY DUNDEE											
Tourism	P700	4FT deg		CC	Ind	Ind	Ind	BBC	HN		
AMERSHAM & WYCOMBE COLL											
Travel and Tourism Management	057P	2FT HND	*		N	P $	Ind	Ind	Ind		
Univ of Wales, BANGOR											
Leisure and Tourism Resource Management	NP77	3FT deg	* g	10	4M	M$ go	Ind	Ind	Ind		
BARNSLEY COLL											
Travel and Tourism Management	007P	2FT HND	*	E	2M	P*	Ind	Ind	Ind		
BELL COLLEGE OF TECHNOLOGY											
Business Administration with Travel and Tourism	7P1N	2FT HND	Ap g	DD-D	N $	P$	Ind	CC$	12$		
BIRMINGHAM COLL of Food, Tourism & Creative St											
Hospitality and Tourism Management	NP77	4SW deg	* g	10	MO	M$ gi	Ind	Ind	Ind		
Tourism Business Management	PN71	3FT deg	* g	12	MO	M$ gi	Ind	Ind	Ind	5	6/16
Tourism Management	P700	3FT deg	* g	18	Ind	D$6/^ gi	Ind	Ind	Ind		
Business (Tourism)	007P	2FT HND	* g	4	4M	P$	Ind	Ind	Ind	2	1/9
BLACKBURN COLL											
Travel and Tourism	007P	2FT HND		2	N	P					
BLACKPOOL & FYLDE COLL											
Hospitality Management (with Tourism)	N7PR	3FT deg	*	10	4M	M$	Ind	Ind	Ind		
Business Studies (Leisure & Tourism)	77NP	2FT HND	*	4	3M	P$	Ind	Ind	Ind		
BOLTON INST											
Accountancy and Tourism Studies	NP47	3FT deg	* g	CD	MO	M*	24	BBCC	Ind		
Art & Design History and Tourism Studies	VP47	3FT deg	* g	CD	MO	M*	24	BBCC	Ind		
Biology and Tourism Studies	CP17	3FT deg	* g	CD	MO	M*	24	BBCC	Ind		
Business Economics and Tourism Studies	LP17	3FT deg	* g	CD	MO	M*	24	BBCC	Ind		
Business Information Systems and Tourism Studies	GP5R	3FT deg	* g	CD	MO	M*	24	BBCC	Ind		
Business Studies and Tourism Studies	NP17	3FT deg	* g	CD	MO	M*	24	BBCC	Ind		
Community Studies and Tourism Studies	LP57	3FT deg	* g	CD	MO	M*	24	BBCC	Ind		
Computing and Tourism Studies	GP57	3FT deg	* g	CD	MO	M*	24	BBCC	Ind		
Creative Writing and Tourism Studies	PW7X	3FT deg	* g	CD	MO	M*	24	BBCC	Ind		
Design and Tourism Studies	PW72	3FT deg	* g	CD	MO	M*	24	BBCC	Ind		
Environmental Studies and Tourism Studies	FP97	3FT deg	* g	CD	MO	M*	24	BBCC	Ind		
European Cultural Studies and Tourism Studies	TP27	3FT deg	* g	CD	10-12M	M*	24	BBCC	Ind		
Film & TV Studies and Tourism Studies	PW75	3FT deg	Me/T g	CD	Ind	Ind	24	BBCC	Ind		
French and Tourism Studies	RP17	3FT deg	F g	CD	Ind	Ind	24	BBCC	Ind		
Gender & Women's Studies and Tourism Studies	MP97	3FT deg	* g	CD	MO	M*	24	BBCC	Ind		
German and Tourism Studies	RP27	3FT deg	G g	CD	Ind	Ind	24	BBCC	Ind		
History and Tourism Studies	PV71	3FT deg	* g	CD	MO	M*	24	BBCC	Ind		
Human Resource Management and Tourism Studies	NP1R	3FT deg	* g	CD	MO	M*	24	BBCC	Ind		
International Tourism (French)	P7R1	3FT deg	* g	CD	MO	M*	24	BBCC	Ind		
International Tourism (German)	P7R2	3FT deg	* g	CD	MO	M*	24	BBCC	Ind		
International Tourism (Spanish)	P7R4	3FT deg	* g	CD	MO	M*	24	BBCC	Ind		
Law and Tourism Studies	MP37	3FT deg	* g	CD	MO	M g	24	BBCC	Ind		
Leisure Studies and Tourism Studies	PL7H	3FT deg	* g	CD	MO	M*	24	BBCC	Ind		
Literature and Tourism Studies	PQ72	3FT deg	* g	CD	MO	M*	24	BBCC	Ind		
Marketing and Tourism Studies	NP5R	3FT deg	* g	CD	MO	M*	24	BBCC	Ind		
Mathematics and Tourism Studies	GP17	3FT deg	M g	CD	Ind	Ind	24	BBCC	Ind		
Operations Management and Tourism Studies	NP27	3FT deg	* g	CD	Ind	Ind	24	BBCC	Ind		

course details			98 expected requirements							96 entry stats	
TITLE	CODE	COURSE	SUBJECTS	A/AS	NO/C	RGNVQ	IB	SQA(H)	SQA	RATIO	R/AS
Organisations, Management & Work and Tourism St	NP77	3FT deg	* g	CD	MO	M*	24	BBCC	Ind		
Peace & War Studies and Tourism Studies	PV7C	3FT deg	* g	CD	MO	M*	24	BBCC	Ind		
Philosophy and Tourism Studies	PV77	3FT deg	* g	CD	MO	M*	24	BBCC	Ind		
Sociology and Tourism Studies	LP3R	3FT deg	* g	CD	MO	M	24	Ind	Ind		
Theatre Studies and Tourism Studies	PW74	3FT deg	Me/T g	CD	Ind	Ind	24	BBCC	Ind		
Tourism Management	P700	3FT deg	* g	CD	MO	M*	24	BBCC	Ind		
Tourism Studies and Statistics	GP47	3FT deg	* g	CD	MO	M	24	Ind	Ind		
Tourism Studies and Transport Studies	PJ79	3FT deg	* g	10	MO	M*	Ind	Ind	Ind		
Tourism Studies and Urban and Cultural Studies	LP37	3FT deg	* g	CD	MO	M*	24	BBCC	Ind		
Visual Arts and Tourism Studies	PW71	3FT deg	* g	CD	MO	M*	24	BBCC	Ind		
BOURNEMOUTH Univ											
Tourism Studies	P700	4SW deg	* g	12-18	DO	D$ go	Ind	CCCCC	Ind	12	16/24
Tourism and Business	71PN▼	2FT HND	* g	4	4M	P$ go	Ind	CCC	Ind	9	4/10
BRADFORD & ILKLEY Comm COLL											
Travel & Tourism Management	007P	2FT HND	*	4	MO	P	Ind	Ind	N		
Univ of BRIGHTON											
International Tourism Management	P700	4SW deg	* g	16	MO+2D	D gi	Dip	BBBB	Ind		
Tourism Management	PN71	3FT/4SW deg	* g	12	MO	M go	Dip	BBCC	Ind		
Travel Management	P701	3FT/4SW deg	* g	12	MO	M go	Dip	BBCC	Ind		
BRISTOL, Univ of the W of England											
European Business Studies with Tourism	N1PR	4FT deg	* g	16	MO+2D	M$6/^ go	24	BBCC	Ind		
Univ of BUCKINGHAM											
Business Studies with Tourism	N1P7	2FT deg	* g	14	3M+2D	M	26	BCCC	Ind	16	
BUCKINGHAMSHIRE COLLEGE											
Business Administration with Tourism	N1P7	3FT deg									
Business Studies with Tourism	N1PR	3FT deg									
Leisure Management with Tourism	N7P7	3FT deg		8-10	1D	M	27	CCCC	Ind		
Tourism	P700	3FT deg		8-10	1D	M	27	CCCC	Ind	5	6/18
Tourism (Top up)	P701	1FT deg			HN					5	
Tourism and Heritage Studies	PV71	3FT deg									
Tourism and Leisure Management	PN77	3FT deg		8-10	1D	M	27	CCCC	Ind		
Tourism with French	P7R1	3FT deg		8-10	1D	M	27	CCCC	Ind		
Tourism with German	P7R2	3FT deg		8-10	1D	M	27	CCCC	Ind		
Tourism with Heritage Studies	P7V1	3FT deg									
Tourism with Italian	P7R3	3FT deg		8-10	1D	M	27	CCCC	Ind		
Tourism with Leisure Management	P7N7	3FT deg									
Tourism with Marketing	P7N5	3FT deg		8-10	1D	M	27	CCCC	Ind		
Tourism with Spanish	P7R4	3FT deg	g	8-10	1D	M	27	CCCC	Ind		
Travel and Tourism Management	NP77	3FT deg		8-10	1D	M	27	CCCC	Ind		
Travel and Tourism Management with French	PR71	3FT deg	F	8-10	1D	M	27	CCCC	Ind		
Travel and Tourism Management with German	PR72	3FT deg	G	8-10	1D	M	27	CCCC	Ind		
Travel and Tourism Management with Italian	PR73	3FT deg	I	8-10	1D	M	27	CCCC	Ind		
Travel and Tourism Management with Spanish	PR74	3FT deg	Sp	8-10	1D	M	27	CCCC	Ind		
Tourism Management	007P	2FT HND		8-10	1D	M	Ind	CCCC	Ind	5	2/8
CANTERBURY CHRIST CHURCH COLL of HE											
Art with Tourism Studies	W1P7	3FT deg	A g	CC	MO	M	24	Ind	Ind	3	
Business Studies with Tourism Studies	N1P7	3FT deg	* g	CC	MO	M	24	Ind	Ind	4	8/14
English with Tourism	Q3P7	3FT deg	E	CC	MO	M	24	Ind	Ind		
Geography with Tourism Studies	L8P7	3FT deg	Gy g	CC	MO	M	24	Ind	Ind	3	

TITLE	CODE	COURSE	SUBJECTS	A/AS	ND/C	AGNVQ	IB	SQA(H)	SQA	RATIO A/AS
course details			*98 expected requirements*							*96 entry stats*
History with Tourism Studies	V1P7	3FT deg	H g	CC	MO	M	24	Ind	Ind	
Information Technology with Tourism Studies	G5P7	3FT deg	* g	CC	MO	M	24	Ind	Ind	2
Mathematics with Tourism	G1P7	3FT deg	M g	DD	Ind	Ind	24	Ind	Ind	
Music with Tourism Studies	W3P7	3FT deg	Mu g	CC	MO	M	24	Ind	Ind	
Psychology with Tourism Studies	L7P7	3FT deg	Ps g	CC	MO	M	24	Ind	Ind	
Radio, Film & Television Studies with Tourism St	W5P7	3FT deg	* g	CC	MO	M	24	Ind	Ind	32
Religious Studies with Tourism Studies	V8P7	3FT deg	* g	CC	MO	M	24	Ind	Ind	
Social Science with Tourism Studies	L3P7	3FT deg	* g	CC	MO	M	24	Ind	Ind	4
Sport Science with Tourism Studies	B6P7	3FT deg	* g	CC	MO	M	24	Ind	Ind	
Statistics with Tourism Studies	G4P7	3FT deg	M g	CC	MO	M	24	Ind	Ind	
Tourism Studies and Art	PW71	3FT deg	A g	CC	MO	M	24	Ind	Ind	
Tourism Studies and Business Studies	PN71	3FT deg	* g	CC	MO	M	24	Ind	Ind	2 6/10
Tourism Studies and French	PR71	3FT deg	F g	CC	MO	M	24	Ind	Ind	
Tourism Studies and History	PV71	3FT deg	H g	CC	MO	M	24	Ind	Ind	8
Tourism Studies and Information Technology	GP57	3FT deg	* g	CC	MO	M	24	Ind	Ind	1
Tourism Studies and Mathematics	GP17	3FT deg	M g	DD	Ind	Ind	24	Ind	Ind	
Tourism Studies and Music	PW73	3FT deg	Mu g	CC	MO	M	24	Ind	Ind	
Tourism Studies and Psychology	PL77	3FT deg	Ps g	CC	MO	M	24	Ind	Ind	1
Tourism Studies and Radio, Film and TV Studies	PW75	3FT deg	* g	CC	MO	M	24	Ind	Ind	20
Tourism Studies and Religious Studies	VP87	3FT deg	* g	CC	MO	M	24	Ind	Ind	
Tourism Studies and Social Science	LP37	3FT deg	* g	CC	MO	M	24	Ind	Ind	
Tourism Studies and Sport Science	PB76	3FT deg	* g	CC	MO	M	24	Ind	Ind	
Tourism Studies and Statistics	GP47	3FT deg	M g	DD	Ind	Ind	24	Ind	Ind	
Tourism Studies with Art	P7W1	3FT deg	A g	CC	MO	M	24	Ind	Ind	5
Tourism Studies with Business Studies	P7N1	3FT deg	* g	CC	MO	M	24	Ind	Ind	2
Tourism Studies with English	P7Q3	3FT deg	E g	CC	MO	M	24	Ind	Ind	
Tourism Studies with French	P7R1	3FT deg	F g	CC	MO	M	24	Ind	Ind	
Tourism Studies with Geography	P7L8	3FT deg	Gy g	CC	MO	M	24	Ind	Ind	1
Tourism Studies with History	P7V1	3FT deg	H g	CC	MO	M	24	Ind	Ind	
Tourism Studies with Information Technology	P7G5	3FT deg	* g	CC	MO	M	24	Ind	Ind	
Tourism Studies with Mathematics	P7G1	3FT deg	M g	DD	Ind	Ind	24	Ind	Ind	
Tourism Studies with Music	P7W3	3FT deg	Mu g	CC	MO	M	24	Ind	Ind	
Tourism Studies with Psychology	P7L7	3FT deg	Ps g	CC	MO	M	24	Ind	Ind	
Tourism Studies with Radio, Film & Television St	P7W5	3FT deg	* g	CC	MO	M	24	Ind	Ind	
Tourism Studies with Religious Studies	P7V8	3FT deg	* g	CC	MO	M	24	Ind	Ind	
Tourism Studies with Science	P7Y1	3FT deg	S g	DD	Ind	Ind	24	Ind	Ind	
Tourism Studies with Social Science	P7L3	3FT deg	* g	CC	MO	M	24	Ind	Ind	2
Tourism Studies with Sport Science	P7B6	3FT deg	* g	CC	MO	M	24	Ind	Ind	
Tourism Studies with Statistics	P7G4	3FT deg	M g	DD	Ind	Ind	24	Ind	Ind	
Tourism and English	QP37	3FT deg	E g	CC	MO	M	24	Ind	Ind	
Tourism and Geography	LP87	3FT deg	Gy g	CC	MO	M	24	Ind	Ind	1
Tourism and Science	PY71	3FT deg	S g	DD	Ind	Ind	24	Ind	Ind	

Univ of Wales INST, CARDIFF

TITLE	CODE	COURSE	SUBJECTS	A/AS	ND/C	AGNVQ	IB	SQA(H)	SQA	RATIO A/AS
Hotel Management with Tourism	N7PT	3FT/4SW deg	* g	12-16	MO	M$ go	Ind	CCCC	Ind	15
Recreation and Leisure with Tourism	N7P7	3FT/4SW deg	* g	12-16	MO	D$^ go	Ind	CCCC	Ind	17
Tourism	P700	3FT/4SW deg	* g	16	MO	DL^ go	Ind	CCC	Ind	7 8/16
Tourism and Hotel Management	NP77	3FT/4SW deg	* g	14-16	MO	D$^ go	Ind	CCCC	Ind	18
Tourism and Recreation and Leisure	PN77	3FT/4SW deg	* g	14-16	MO	DL^ go	Ind	CCCC	Ind	7
Tourism with Catering Management	P7NR	3FT/4SW deg	* g	12-16	MO	D$^ go	Ind	CCCC	Ind	5
Tourism with Hotel Management	P7N7	3FT/4SW deg	* g	12-16	MO	D$^ go	Ind	CCCC	Ind	32
Tourism with Recreation and Leisure	P7NT	3FT/4SW deg	* g	14-16	MO	DL^ go	Ind	CCCC	Ind	8 9/12
Business and Finance: Tourism	007P	2FT HND	* g	6	MO	MB go	Ind	CC	Ind	6 6/10

	course details			98 expected requirements							96 entry stats
TITLE		CODE	COURSE	SUBJECTS	A/AS	NO/C	AGNVQ	IB	SQA(H)	SQA	RATIO A/AS
Univ of CENTRAL ENGLAND											
Hospitality Management with Tourism		N7P7	4SW deg	*g	12	MO	M	24	CCC		
Univ of CENTRAL LANCASHIRE											
International Tourism		P700	4SW deg	*g	16	MO+6D	M$6/^	28	BBBC	Ind	
Languages with Tourism		T9P7	4SW deg	L	14	Ind	M$^	26$	BBCC$	Ind	
Combined Honours Programme *Tourism & Leisure*		Y400	3FT deg	*	12	4M+2D	M$6/^	26	BCCC	Ind	
Business with Tourism and Leisure		7P1N	2FT HND	*g	8	MO	M$	24	CCC	Ind	
Hospitality and Tourism		77PN▼	2FT HND	*g	E	N	P$	24$	CCC	Ind	
Sustainable Tourism		007P▼	2FT HND	*	E	N	P	Ind	CCC	Ind	
Travel and Tourism		107P▼	2FT HND	*g	DD	MO	M$	24$	CCC	Ind	
CHELTENHAM & GLOUCESTER COLL of HE											
Business Info Technology and Tourism Mgt		GP57	3FT/4SW deg	*	8-12	5M+2D	ML3	24	CCCC	Ind	
Business Info Technology with Tourism Management		G5P7	3FT/4SW deg	*	8-12	MO	M	24	CCCC	Ind	
Business Management with Tourism Management		N1PT	4SW deg	*	12-16	4M+3D	MB3	26	CCCC	Ind	
Catering Management and Tourism Management		NP7T	4SW deg	*	8-12	5M+2D	MH3	24	CCCC	Ind	
Catering Management with Tourism Management		N7P7	4SW deg	*	8-12	5M+2D	MH3	24	CCCC	Ind	
Computing and Tourism Management		GPM7	3FT deg	*	8-12	5M+2D	ML3	24	CCCC	Ind	
Computing with Tourism Management		G5PR	3FT deg	*	8-12	MO	M	24	CCCC	Ind	
Countryside Planning and Tourism Management		DP27	3FT deg	*	8-14	4M+2D	M$	26	CCCC	Ind	
Countryside Planning with Tourism Management		D2PT	3FT deg	*	8-14	MO	MK	26$	CCCC	Ind	
English Studies and Tourism Management		PQ73	3FT deg	E	12-16	4M+3D	M^	26	CCCC	Ind	
English Studies with Tourism Management		Q3P7	3FT deg	E	12-16	4M+3D	M^	26	CCCC	Ind	
Environmental Policy and Tourism Management		FP97	3FT deg	*	10-14	4M+3D	M3	26	CCCC	Ind	
Environmental Policy with Tourism Management		F9PT	3FT deg	*	10-14	5M+2D	M3	26	CCCC	Ind	
Financial Management and Tourism Management		NP37	4SW deg	*	10-16	5M+2D	ML3	26	CCCC	Ind	
Financial Management with Tourism Management		N3P7	4SW deg	*	10-14	5M+2D	M3	26	CCCC	Ind	
Financial Services Mgt and Tourism Management		PN73	4SW deg	*	10-14	5M+2D	ML3	26	CCCC	Ind	
Financial Services Mgt with Tourism Management		N3PR	4SW deg	*	10-14	5M+2D	M3	26	CCCC	Ind	
Geography with Tourism Management		L8PR	3FT deg	*	12-16	MO	ML3	26	CCCC	Ind	
History and Tourism Management		PV71	3FT deg	H	12-16	4M+3D	M3^	26	CCCC	Ind	
History with Tourism Management		V1P7	3FT deg	H	10-14	4M+3D	M3^	26	CCCC	Ind	
Hotel Management and Tourism Management		NPR7	4SW deg	*	12-16	4M+3D	M$3	26	CCCC	Ind	
Hotel Management with Tourism Management		N7PT	4SW deg	*	12	4M+3D	MH3	26	CCCC	Ind	
Human Geography and Tourism Management		LP87	3FT deg	*	12-16	4M+3D	ML3	26	CCCC	Ind	
Human Geography with Tourism Management		L8P7	3FT deg	*	12-16	4M+3D	M3	26	CCCC	Ind	
Human Resource Management and Tourism Management		NP17	4SW deg	*	12-16	5M+2D	M$3	26	CCCC	Ind	
Human Resource Mgt with Tourism Management		N1P7	4SW deg	*	12-16	5M+2D	MB3	26	CCCC	Ind	
Leisure Management and Tourism Management		PN77	4SW deg	*	12-16	4M+3D	ML3	26	CCCC	Ind	
Leisure Management with Tourism Management		N7PR	4SW deg	*	12-16	4M+3D	ML3	26	CCCC	Ind	
Marketing Management and Tourism Management		NP57	4SW deg	*	12-16	5M+2D	M$3	26	CCCC	Ind	
Marketing Management with Tourism Management		N5P7	4SW deg	*	12-16	5M+2D	MB3	26	CCCC	Ind	
Multimedia and Tourism Management		GPN7	3FT deg	*	12-16	5M+2D	MI3	26	CCCC	Ind	
Multimedia with Tourism Management		G5PT	3FT deg	*	12	5M+2D	MI3	26	CCCC	Ind	
Multimedia with Tourism Management		GPMR	4SW deg	*	8-12	MO	MI3	24	CCCC	Ind	
Physical Geography and Tourism Management		FP87	3FT deg	*	12	5M+2D	ML3	26	CCCC	Ind	
Physical Geography with Tourism Management		F8P7	3FT deg	*	12	5M+2D	M3^	26	CCCC	Ind	
Sport & Exercise Sciences and Tourism Management		BP67	3FT deg	S	12-16	4M+3D	ML3	26	CCCC	Ind	
Sport & Exercise Sciences with Tourism Mgt		B6PT	3FT deg	S	12-16	4M+3D	ML3	26	CCCC	Ind	
Tourism Management and Women's Studies		PM79	3FT deg	*	12-16	5M+2D	ML3	26	CCCC	Ind	
Tourism Management with Business Info Technology		P7G5	4SW deg	*	12	4M+3D	ML3	26	CCCC	Ind	

course details				**98 expected requirements**							*96 entry stats*
TITLE	CODE	COURSE	SUBJECTS	A/AS	ND/C	AGNVQ	IB	SQA(H)	SQA	RATIO A/AS	
Tourism Management with Business Management	P7N1	4SW deg	*	12-16	4M+3D	ML3	26	CCCC	Ind		
Tourism Management with Catering Management	P7N7	4SW deg	*	12	4M+3D	ML3	26	CCCC	Ind		
Tourism Management with Computing	P7GM	4SW deg	*	12	4M+3D	ML3	26	CCCC	Ind		
Tourism Management with Countryside Planning	P7D2	4SW deg	*	12-16	4M+3D	ML3	26	CCCC	Ind		
Tourism Management with English Studies	P7Q3	4SW deg	*	12-16	4M+3D	ML3	26	CCCC	Ind		
Tourism Management with Environmental Policy	P7FX	4SW deg	*	12-16	4M+3D	ML3	26	CCCC	Ind		
Tourism Management with Financial Management	P7N3	4SW deg	*	12-16	5M+2D	ML3	26	CCCC	Ind		
Tourism Management with Financial Services Mgt	P7NH	4SW deg	*	12-16	5M+2D	ML3	26	CCCC	Ind		
Tourism Management with History	P7V1	4SW deg	*	12-16	5M+2D	ML3	26	CCCC	Ind		
Tourism Management with Hotel Management	P7NR	4SW deg	*	12-16	4M+3D	ML3	26	CCCC	Ind		
Tourism Management with Human Geography	P7L8	4SW deg	*	12-16	4M+3D	ML3	26	CCCC	Ind		
Tourism Management with Human Resource Mgt	P7NC	4SW deg	*	12-16	5M+2D	ML3	26	CCCC	Ind		
Tourism Management with Leisure Management	P7NT	4SW deg	*	12-16	4M+3D	ML3	26	CCCC	Ind		
Tourism Management with Marketing Management	P7N5	4SW deg	*	12-16	5M+2D	ML3	26	CCCC	Ind		
Tourism Management with Modern Languages(French)	P7R1	4SW deg	g	12-16	4M+3D	ML3	26	CCCC	Ind		
Tourism Management with Multimedia	GP5R	4SW deg	*	12	MO	ML3	26	CCCC	Ind		
Tourism Management with Physical Geography	P7F8	4SW deg	*	12	4M+3D	ML3	26	CCCC	Ind		
Tourism Management with Sport and Exercise Sci	P7B6	4SW deg	*	12-16	4M+3D	ML3	26	CCCC	Ind		
Tourism Management with Women's Studies	P7M9	4SW deg	*	12	MO	ML3	26	CCCC	Ind		
Women's Studies with Tourism Management	M9P7	3FT deg	*	8-12	MO	M3	26	CCCC	Ind		

CITY COLLEGE Manchester

Leisure and Tourism Management	77PN	2FT HND									

COVENTRY Univ

Tourism Management	P700	4SW deg	* g	12-16	M+4D	MO	Ind	CCC	Ind		

CUMBRIA COLL of A & D

Heritage Management	P7N9	3FT deg	*	EE	N	M	Ind	BB	Ind	3	
Tourism and Heritage Management	79PN	2FT HND	*	E	N	M	Ind	B	Ind	2	2/4

Univ of DERBY

Tourism	P700	3FT deg	*	14	MO+2D	D$	28	BBCC	Ind	5	10/20
Credit Accumulation Modular Scheme *Tourism*	Y600	3FT deg	*	12	MO	M	Ind	CCCC	Ind		

FARNBOROUGH COLL of Technology

Hotel and Hospitality Management (Tourism)	77PN	2FT HND		6	N		Ind	Ind	Ind	11	
Leisure Studies (Travel and Tourism)	77NP	2FT HND	g	6	Ind	P*	Ind	Ind	Ind	7	

Univ of GLAMORGAN

Government with Leisure and Tourism	M1P7	3FT deg	* g	12-14	MO+3D$	M$	Ind	Ind	Ind		
Leisure and Tourism Management	NP77	3FT deg	* g	14	MO+3D	M$	Ind	Ind	Ind		
Combined Studies (Honours)	Y400	3FT deg	* g	8-16	Ind	Ind	Ind	Ind	Ind		
Leisure & Tourism Management *Joint Honours*	Y401	3FT deg	* g	8-16	Ind	Ind	Ind	Ind	Ind		
Leisure & Tourism Management *Major/Minor Honours*	Y402	3FT deg	* g	8-16	Ind	Ind	Ind	Ind	Ind		
Leisure & Tourism Management											

GLASGOW CALEDONIAN Univ

Tourism Management	P700	4FT/4SW deg	E+M+L	CC	Ind		Ind	BBCC$	Ind	15	

Univ of GREENWICH

Tourism Management/Language	PT79	3FT deg	* g	16	MO+4D	M	24	CCC	Ind		
Tourism Management	77PN▼	2FT HND	* g	6	MO	Ind		CC	Ind		

			98 expected requirements							96 entry stats	
course details			SUBJECTS	A/AS	ND/C	RGNVQ	IB	SQA(H)	SQA		
TITLE	CODE	COURSE								RATIO	A/AS
HEREFORDSHIRE COLLEGE of Technology											
Tourism Management	P700	3FT deg	*	8	Ind	M	Ind	CC	N		
Tourism Management	007P	2FT HND	*	4	Ind	M	Ind	CC	N	10	2/ 6
Univ of HERTFORDSHIRE											
Tourism Management	P700	4SW deg	* g	18	DO	DB/L	28$	BBBB	Ind	10	10/18
Business with Leisure and Tourism	71PN▼	2FT HND	* g	2	MO	Ind	24	CCCD	Ind		
Travel and Tourism Management	007P▼	2FT HND	* g	8	MO	M	Ind	Ind	Ind	16	4/14
Univ of Wales, LAMPETER											
Tourism and Heritage Management	PN79	3FT deg		16-18	Ind	Ind	Ind	Ind	Ind		
LEEDS METROPOLITAN Univ											
International Tourism Management	P702	3FT/4SW deg	L g	20	4M+4D$	D$2/^ go	28$	ABBBC$	Ind		12/14
Tourism Management	P700	3FT/4SW deg	* g	18	4M+4D	D$2/^ go	28	BBBBC	Ind	12	16/26
Tourism Management	007P	2FT/3SW HND	* g	8	MO	M$ go	Dip	BCC	Ind		6/14
Univ of LINCOLNSHIRE and HUMBERSIDE											
Communications and Tourism	PP37▼	3FT deg	* g	14	2M+2D	M		24	BCCC	Ind	
Criminology and Tourism	MPH7▼	3FT deg	* g	16	1M+3D	D		24	BBCCC	Ind	
Economics and Tourism	LP17▼	3FT deg	* g	16	1M+3D	D		24	BBCCC	Ind	
European Tourism	P700▼	3FT deg	* g	14	2M+2D	M		24	BCCC	Ind	
Health Studies and Tourism	LPK7▼	3FT deg	* g	16	1M+3D	D		24	BBCCC	Ind	
International Relations and Tourism	MP17▼	3FT deg	* g	16	1M+3D	D		24	BBCCC	Ind	
International Tourism	P701▼	3FT deg	F/G/Sp g	14	2M+2D	Ind		Ind	BCCC	Ind	
Journalism and Tourism	PP67▼	3FT deg	* g	18	1M+4D	D		26	BBBCC	Ind	
Law and Tourism	MP37▼	3FT deg	* g	16	1M+3D	D		24	BBCCC	Ind	
Management and Tourism	NP1R▼	3FT deg	* g	14	2M+2D	M		24	BCCC	Ind	
Marketing and Tourism Operations	NP5R▼	3FT deg	g	8		M					
Media and Tourism	PP47▼	3FT deg	* g	18	1M+4D	D		26	BBBCC	Ind	
Politics and Tourism	MP1R▼	3FT deg	* g	16	1M+3D	D		24	BBCCC	Ind	
Psychology and Tourism	CP87▼	3FT deg	* g	18	1M+4D	D		26	BBBCC	Ind	
Social Policy and Tourism	LP47▼	3FT deg	* g	14	2M+2D	M		24	BCCC	Ind	
Tourism	P702▼	3FT deg	* g	14	2M+2D	M		24	BCCC	Ind	
Travel and Tourism	007P▼	2FT HND	* g								
LIVERPOOL JOHN MOORES Univ											
Tourism and Leisure with a Modern Foreign Langua	P7T9	3FT deg	L	16	3M+4D						
LONDON INST											
International Travel and Tourism Management	NP77	3FT deg									
LUTON Univ											
Accounting with Travel & Tourism	N4PR	3FT deg	g	12-16	MO/DO	M/D	32	BBCC	Ind		
Biochemistry with Travel & Tourism	C7P7	3FT deg	g	12-16	MO/DO	M/D	32	BBCC	Ind		
Biotechnology with Travel & Tourism	J8P7	3FT deg	g	12-16	MO/DO	M/D	32	BBCC	Ind		
Business Systems with Travel and Tourism	N1P7	3FT deg	g	12-16	MO/DO	M/D	32	BBCC	Ind		
Contemp Br & Euro Hist with Travel and Tourism	V1P7	3FT deg	g	12-16	MO/DO	M/D	32	BBCC	Ind		
Ecology (Eco Tech) with Travel & Tourism	C9P7	3FT deg	g	12-16	MO/DO	M/D	32	BBCC	Ind		
Geography with Travel & Tourism	F8PT	3FT deg	g	12-16	MO/DO	M/D	32	BBCC	Ind		
Geology with Travel and Tourism	F6P7	3FT deg	g	12-16	MO/DO	M/D	32	BBCC	Ind		
Health Science with Travel and Tourism	B9P7	3FT deg	g	12-16	MO/DO	M/D	32	BBCC	Ind		
Health Studies with Travel and Tourism	B9PR	3FT deg	g	12-16	MO/DO	M/D	32	BBCC	Ind		
Leisure Studies with Travel and Tourism	N7P7	3FT deg	g	12-16	MO/DO	M/D	32	BBCC	Ind		
Mapping Science with Travel and Tourism	F8P7	3FT deg	g	12-16	MO/DO	M/D	32	BBCC	Ind		
Marketing with Travel and Tourism	N5P7	3FT deg	g	12-16	MO/DO	M/D	32	BBCC	Ind		

course details

TITLE	CODE	COURSE	SUBJECTS	A/AS	ND/C	AGNVQ	IB	SQA(H)	SQA	RATIO A/AS
Media Practices with Travel and Tourism	P4P7	3FT deg	g	12-16	MO/DO	M/D	32	BBCC	Ind	
Modern English Studies with Travel and Tourism	Q3P7	3FT deg	g	12-16	MO/DO	M/D	32	BBCC	Ind	
Modern History with Travel and Tourism	V1PR	3FT deg	g	12-16	MO/DO	M/D	32	BBCC	Ind	
Physical Geography with Travel and Tourism	F8PR	3FT deg	g	12-16	MO/DO	M/D	32	BBCC	Ind	6
Plant Biology with Travel & Tourism	C2P7	3FT deg	g	12-16	MO/DO	M/D	32	BBCC	Ind	
Politics with Travel and Tourism	M1P7	3FT deg	g	12-16	MO/DO	M/D	32	BBCC	Ind	
Public Policy and Mgt with Travel & Tourism	M1PR	3FT deg	g	12-16	MO/DO	M/D	32	BBCC	Ind	
Regional Planning and Dev with Travel & Tourism	K4P7	3FT deg	g	12-16	MO/DO	M/D	32	BBCC	Ind	
Social Policy with Travel and Tourism	L4P7	3FT deg		12-16	MO/DO	M/D	32	BBCC	Ind	
Social Studies with Travel and Tourism	L3P7	3FT deg	g	12-16	MO/DO	M/D	32	BBCC	Ind	
Sociology with Travel and Tourism	L3PR	3FT deg		12-16	MO/DO	M/D	32	BBCC	Ind	
Travel & Tourism with Accounting	P7NK	3FT deg	g	12-16	MO/DO	M/D	32	BBCC	Ind	
Travel & Tourism with Biochemistry	P7C7	3FT deg	g	12-16	MO/DO	M/D	32	BBCC	Ind	
Travel & Tourism with Biotechnology	P7J8	3FT deg	g	12-16	MO/DO	M/D	32	BBCC	Ind	
Travel & Tourism with Ecology (Ecological Tech)	P7C9	3FT deg	g	12-16	MO/DO	M/D	32	BBCC	Ind	
Travel & Tourism with Geographical Info Systems	P702	3FT deg	g	12-16	MO/DO	M/D	32	BBCC	Ind	
Travel & Tourism with Geography	P7FW	3FT deg	g	12-16	MO/DO	M/D	32	BBCC	Ind	
Travel & Tourism with Human Biology	P7B1	3FT deg	g	12-16	MO/DO	M/D	32	BBCC	Ind	
Travel & Tourism with Japanese	P7T4	3FT deg	L g	12-16	MO/DO	M/D	32	BBCC	Ind	
Travel & Tourism with Lang & Stylistics in Engl	P7QG	3FT deg	g	12-16	MO/DO	M/D	32	BBCC	Ind	
Travel & Tourism with Management	P7N1	3FT deg	g	12-16	MO/DO	M/D	32	BBCC	Ind	
Travel & Tourism with Photography	P7WM	3FT deg	g	12-16	MO/DO	M/D	32	BBCC	Ind	
Travel & Tourism with Plant Biology	P7C2	3FT deg	g	12-16	MO/DO	M/D	32	BBCC	Ind	
Travel and Tourism	P700	3FT deg	g	12-16	MO/DO	M/D	32	BBCC	Ind	7 8/16
Travel and Tourism and Accounting	NPK7	3FT deg	g	12-16	MO/DO	M/D	32	BBCC	Ind	
Travel and Tourism and Biochemistry	CP77	3FT deg	g	12-16	MO/DO	M/D	32	BBCC	Ind	
Travel and Tourism and Biology	CP17	3FT deg	g	12-16	MO/DO	M/D	32	BBCC	Ind	
Travel and Tourism and Biotechnology	JP87	3FT deg	g	12-16	MO/DO	M/D	32	BBCC	Ind	
Travel and Tourism and British Studies	VP97	3FT deg		12-16	MO/DO	M/D	32	BBCC	Ind	
Travel and Tourism and Computer Science	GP57	3FT deg	g	12-16	MO/DO	M/D	32	BBCC	Ind	
Travel and Tourism and Contemporary History	VP17	3FT deg	g	12-16	MO/DO	M/D	32	BBCC	Ind	
Travel and Tourism and Ecology & Biodiversity	CP97	3FT deg	g	12-16	MO/DO	M/D	32	BBCC	Ind	
Travel and Tourism and Environmental Science	FP97	3FT deg	g	12-16	MO/DO	M/D	32	BBCC	Ind	
Travel and Tourism and Geography	FP8R	3FT deg	g	12-16	MO/DO	M/D	32	BBCC	Ind	
Travel and Tourism and Geology	FP67	3FT deg	g	12-16	MO/DO	M/D	32	BBCC	Ind	
Travel and Tourism and Health Science	BP97	3FT deg	g	12-16	MO/DO	M/D	32	BBCC	Ind	
Travel and Tourism and Health Studies	BPX7	3FT deg	g	12-16	MO/DO	M/D	32	BBCC	Ind	
Travel and Tourism and Human Biology	BP17	3FT deg	g	12-16	MO/DO	M/D	32	BBCC	Ind	
Travel and Tourism and Journalism	PP67	3FT deg		12-16	MO/DO	M/D	32	BBCC	Ind	
Travel and Tourism and Lang & Stylistics in Engl	QPG7	3FT deg	g	12-16	MO/DO	M/D	32	BBCC	Ind	
Travel and Tourism and Leisure Studies	NP77	3FT deg	g	12-16	MO/DO	M/D	32	BBCC	Ind	
Travel and Tourism and Mapping Science	FP87	3FT deg	g	12-16	MO/DO	M/D	32	BBCC	Ind	
Travel and Tourism and Marketing	NP57	3FT deg	g	12-16	MO/DO	M/D	32	BBCC	Ind	5
Travel and Tourism and Media Practices	PP47	3FT deg	g	12-16	MO/DO	M/D	32	BBCC	Ind	5
Travel and Tourism and Media Production	PPL7	3FT deg	g	12-16	MO/DO	M/D	32	BBCC	Ind	
Travel and Tourism and Modern English Studies	QP37	3FT deg	g	12-16	MO/DO	M/D	32	BBCC	Ind	7
Travel and Tourism and Organisational Behaviour	LP77	3FT deg	g	12-16	MO/DO	M/D	32	BBCC	Ind	
Travel and Tourism and Physical Geography	FPV7	3FT deg	g	12-16	MO/DO	M/D	32	BBCC	Ind	
Travel and Tourism and Planning Studies	KP4R	3FT deg		12-16	MO/DO	M/D	32	BBCC	Ind	
Travel and Tourism and Plant Biology	CP27	3FT deg	g	12-16	MO/DO	M/D	32	BBCC	Ind	
Travel and Tourism and Politics	MP17	3FT deg	g	12-16	MO/DO	M/D	32	BBCC	Ind	
Travel and Tourism and Public Policy & Mgt	MPC7	3FT deg	g	12-16	MO/DO	M/D	32	BBCC	Ind	

course details			98 expected requirements							96 entry stats
TITLE	CODE	COURSE	SUBJECTS	A/AS	ND/C	AGNVQ	IB	SQA(H)	SQA	RATIO A/AS
Travel and Tourism and Regional Planning & Dev	KP47	3FT deg	g	12-16	MO/DO	M/D	32	BBCC	Ind	
Travel and Tourism and Social Policy	LP47	3FT deg		12-16	MO/DO	M/D	32	BBCC	Ind	
Travel and Tourism and Social Studies	LP37	3FT deg	g	12-16	MO/DO	M/D	32	BBCC	Ind	
Travel and Tourism and Sociology	LPH7	3FT deg		12-16	MO/DO	M/D	32	BBCC	Ind	
Travel and Tourism with Biology	P7C1	3FT deg	g	12-16	MO/DO	M/D	32	BBCC	Ind	
Travel and Tourism with British Studies	P7V9	3FT deg		12-16	MO/DO	M/D	32	BBCC	Ind	
Travel and Tourism with Chinese	P7T3	3FT deg		12-16	MO/DO	M/D	32	BBCC	Ind	
Travel and Tourism with Comparative Literature	P7QF	3FT deg	g	12-16	MO/DO	M/D	32	BBCC	Ind	
Travel and Tourism with Computer Science	P7G5	3FT deg	g	12-16	MO/DO	M/D	32	BBCC	Ind	
Travel and Tourism with Contemp Br & Euro Hist	P7V1	3FT deg	g	12-16	MO/DO	M/D	32	BBCC	Ind	
Travel and Tourism with Environmental Science	P7F9	3FT deg	g	12-16	MO/DO	M/D	32	BBCC	Ind	
Travel and Tourism with French	P7R1	3FT deg	F g	12-16	MO/DO	M/D	32	BBCC	Ind	
Travel and Tourism with Geology	P7F6	3FT deg	g	12-16	MO/DO	M/D	32	BBCC	Ind	
Travel and Tourism with German	P7R2	3FT deg	G g	12-16	MO/DO	M/D	32	BBCC	Ind	12
Travel and Tourism with Health Science	P7B9	3FT deg	g	12-16	MO/DO	M/D	32	BBCC	Ind	
Travel and Tourism with Italian	P7R3	3FT deg	I g	12-16	MO/DO	M/D	32	BBCC	Ind	
Travel and Tourism with Journalism	P7P6	3FT deg	g	12-16	MO/DO	M/D	32	BBCC	Ind	
Travel and Tourism with Leisure Studies	P7N7	3FT deg	g	12-16	MO/DO	M/D	32	BBCC	Ind	
Travel and Tourism with Mapping Science	P7F8	3FT deg	g	12-16	MO/DO	M/D	32	BBCC	Ind	
Travel and Tourism with Marketing	P7N5	3FT deg		12-16	MO/DO	M/D	32	BBCC	Ind	
Travel and Tourism with Media Practices	P7P4	3FT deg	g	12-16	MO/DO	M/D	32	BBCC	Ind	
Travel and Tourism with Media Production	P7PL	3FT deg		12-16	MO/DO	M/D	32	BBCC	Ind	
Travel and Tourism with Modern English Studies	P7Q3	3FT deg	g	12-16	MO/DO	M/D	32	BBCC	Ind	
Travel and Tourism with Multimedia	P7PK	3FT deg	g	12-16	MO/DO	M/D	32	BBCC	Ind	
Travel and Tourism with Organisational Behaviour	P7L7	3FT deg	g	12-16	MO/DO	M/D	32	BBCC	Ind	
Travel and Tourism with Physical Geography	P7FV	3FT deg	g	12-16	MO/DO	M/D	32	BBCC	Ind	
Travel and Tourism with Politics	P7M1	3FT deg	g	12-16	MO/DO	M/D	32	BBCC	Ind	
Travel and Tourism with Public Policy & Mgt	P7MC	3FT deg	g	12-16	MO/DO	M/D	32	BBCC	Ind	1
Travel and Tourism with Regional Plan and Dev	P7K4	3FT deg	g	12-16	MO/DO	M/D	32	BBCC	Ind	
Travel and Tourism with Social Studies	P7L3	3FT deg	g	12-16	MO/DO	M/D	32	BBCC	Ind	
Travel and Tourism with Spanish	P7R4	3FT deg	Sp g	12-16	MO/DO	M/D	32	BBCC	Ind	8
Travel and Tourism with Video Production	P7W5	3FT deg	g	12-16	MO/DO	M/D	32	BBCC	Ind	
Women's Studies and Travel and Tourism	MP97	3FT deg		12-16	MO/DO	M/D	32	BBCC	Ind	
Women's Studies with Travel and Tourism	M9P7	3FT deg		12-16	MO/DO	M/D	32	BBCC	Ind	
MANCHESTER METROPOLITAN Univ										
Hotel Management with Tourism	N7P7	4SW deg	* g	14	Ind	D	28	BBC	Ind	8/18
Hotel Management with Tourism	7P7N	3SW HND	* g	6	Ind	M	24	CCC	Ind	4/ 8
NAPIER Univ										
Hospitality (Tourism Management)	P700	4FT deg	*	CC-DDD	Ind	Ind	Ind	BBCC	Ind	7 8/18
Languages and Tourism	PT79	3FT/4FT deg	*	CCD	Ind	Ind	Ind	BBCC	Ind	
Marketing and Tourism	NP57	3FT/4FT deg	*	CCD	Ind	Ind	Ind	BBCC	Ind	
NEWCASTLE COLL										
Travel and Tourism Management	007P▼	2FT HND								
NORTHBROOK COLLEGE Sussex										
British Tourism	P700	3FT deg		10	4M	M				
Business and Travel and Tourism Management	71PN	2FT HND	*	6-8	3M	Ind	Dip	Ind	Ind	
Travel and Tourism	007P	2FT HND	*	6-8	3M	Ind	Dip	Ind	Ind	
NORTH EAST WALES INST of HE										
Leisure Studies	77NP	2FT HND		2-6	N	P$	Ind	CC	N$	

course details			98 expected requirements							96 entry stats	
TITLE	CODE	COURSE	SUBJECTS	A/AS	NO/C	AGNVQ	IB	SQA(H)	SQA	RATIO A/AS	
NORTH EAST WORCESTERSHIRE COLL											
Travel and Tourism	007P	2FT HND									
Univ of NORTH LONDON											
Education Studies and Tourism	PX79	3FT deg	* g	12	Ind	Ind	Ind	Ind	Ind		
International Leisure & Tourism Management	PN7R	4SW deg	* g	14	MO+4D	Ind	Ind	CCCC	Ind		
Leisure and Tourism Management	PN77	4SW deg	* g	14	4D	Ind	Ind	CCCC	Ind		
Tourism Studies and Caribbean Studies	PT77	3FT deg	* g	CC	MO+4D	D	Ind	Ind	Ind	27	
Tourism Studies and Geography	FP87	3FT deg	* g	12-14	Ind	Ind	Ind	Ind	Ind		
Tourism and South Asian Studies	PT75	3FT deg	* g	CC	MO+4D	D	Ind	Ind	Ind		
Combined Honours _Tourism Studies_	Y400	3FT deg	* g	14	MO+4D	Ind	Ind	CCCC	Ind		
Tourism Management	77PN	2FT HND	* g	6	10M	Ind	Ind	CCC	Ind		
Univ of NORTHUMBRIA											
Travel and Tourism (1 year top-up)	P701	1FT deg	X	X	HN	X	X	X	HN	2	
Travel and Tourism Management	P700	4SW deg	* g	CCC	MO+4D	D4	26	BBBCC	Ind	12	12/22
NORWICH: City COLL											
Travel and Tourism (HND top up)	P700	1FT deg		X	HN	X	Dip				
Travel and Tourism	007P	2FT HND	* g	6	M	MB/H/L go	Ind	Ind	Ind	6	4/13
OXFORD BROOKES Univ											
Tourism/Accounting and Finance	NP47	3FT deg	* g	BCC-CCD	Ind	M*3/D*3	Ind	Ind	Ind	4	
Tourism/Anthropology	LP67	3FT deg	* g	BCC-CCD	Ind	M*^/M*3	Ind	Ind	Ind	15	
Tourism/Biological Chemistry	CP77	3FT deg									
Tourism/Biology	CP17	3FT deg	S g	DD-BC	Ind	MS/M*3	Ind	Ind	Ind		
Tourism/Business Administration & Management	NP17	3FT deg	* g	CCD-BBC	Ind	M*3/MB4	Ind	Ind	Ind	87	
Tourism/Cartography	FP87	3FT deg	* g	DDD-BC	Ind	M*/M*3	Ind	Ind	Ind	2	
Tourism/Cell Biology	CPC7	3FT deg									
Tourism/Combined Studies	PY74	3FT deg		X		X	X	X			
Tourism/Computer Systems	GP67	3FT deg	* g	CDD-BC	Ind	M*/M*3	Ind	Ind	Ind		
Tourism/Computing	GP57	3FT deg	* g	CDD-BC	Ind	M*/M*3	Ind	Ind	Ind	2	
Tourism/Computing Mathematics	GP97	3FT deg	* g	CD-BC	Ind	M*/M*3	Ind	Ind	Ind		
Tourism/Ecology	CP97	3FT deg	* g	CD-BC	Ind	MS/M*3	Ind	Ind	Ind		
Tourism/Economics	LP17	3FT deg	* g	BB-CCD	Ind	M*3	Ind	Ind	Ind	5	
Tourism/Educational Studies	PX79	3FT deg	* g	CC-BC	Ind	M*3	Ind	Ind	Ind		
Tourism/Electronics	HP67	3FT deg	S/M	CC-BC	Ind	MS/M*3	Ind	Ind	Ind		
Tourism/Environmental Chemistry	PF71	3FT deg									
Tourism/Environmental Policy	KP37	3FT deg									
Tourism/Environmental Sciences	FPX7	3FT deg	S g	CD-BC	Ind	M*3/DS	Ind	Ind	Ind		
Tourism/Exercise and Health	PB76	3FT deg	S g	DD-BC	Ind	MS/M*3	Ind	Ind	Ind		
Tourism/Fine Art	PW71	3FT deg	Pf+A g	BC-CCD	Ind	MA^/M*3	Ind	Ind	Ind		
Tourism/Food Science and Nutrition	DP47	3FT deg	S g	DD-BC	Ind	MS/M*3	Ind	Ind	Ind		
Tourism/French Language and Contemp Studies	PR7C	4SW deg	F g	CDD-BC	Ind	M^/M*3	Ind	Ind	Ind		
Tourism/French Language and Literature	PR71	4SW deg	F g	CDD-BC	Ind	M^/M*3	Ind	Ind	Ind	14	
Tourism/Geography	LP87	3FT deg	* g	BB-CCD	Ind	M*/M*3	Ind	Ind	Ind	14	
Tourism/Geotechnics	HP27	3FT deg	S/M/Ds/Es	DD-BC	Ind	MS/M*3	Ind	Ind	Ind		
Tourism/German Language and Contemp Stud	PR7F	4SW deg	G g	DDD-BC	Ind	M^/M*3	Ind	Ind	Ind		
Tourism/German Language and Literature	PR72	4SW deg	G g	DDD-BC	Ind	M^/M*3	Ind	Ind	Ind		
Tourism/German Studies	PR7G	4SW deg	G g	DDD-BB	Ind	M^/M*3	Ind	Ind	Ind		
Tourism/Health Care (Post Exp)	BP77	3FT deg		X		X	X	X			
Tourism/History	PV71	3FT deg	* g	BB-CCD	Ind	M^/M*3	Ind	Ind	Ind	7	
Tourism/History of Art	PV74	3FT deg	* g	BCC-CCD	Ind	M^/M*3	Ind	Ind	Ind	6	

Tourism 69

			98 expected requirements							96 entry stats
course details										
TITLE	CODE	COURSE	SUBJECTS	A/AS	ND/C	AGNVQ	IB	SQA(H)	SQA	RATIO A/AS
Tourism/Hospitality Management Studies	NP77	3FT deg	* g	DDD-BC	Ind	M*3	Ind	Ind	Ind	9
Tourism/Human Biology	BP17	3FT deg								
Tourism/Information Systems	GPM7	3FT deg	* g	CDD-BC	Ind	M*/M*3	Ind	Ind	Ind	6
Tourism/Intelligent Systems	GP87	3FT deg	* g	CD-BC	Ind	M*/M*3	Ind	Ind	Ind	
Tourism/Law	MP37	3FT deg	* g	CCD-BBB	Ind	M*3/D*3	Ind	Ind	Ind	
Tourism/Leisure Planning and Management	KPH7	3FT deg								
Tourism/Marketing Management	PN7N	3FT deg	* g	CCD-BCC	Ind	M*3/D*3	Ind	Ind	Ind	81
Tourism/Music	PW73	3FT deg	Mu g	DD-BC	Ind	M*/M*3	Ind	Ind	Ind	2
Tourism/Palliative Care (Post Exp)	BPR7	3FT deg		X		X	X	X		
Tourism/Physical Geography	FPV7	3FT deg								
Tourism/Planning Studies	KP47	3FT deg	* g	DDD-BC	Ind	M*/M*3	Ind	Ind	Ind	5
Tourism/Politics	MP17	3FT deg	* g	CCD-AB	Ind	M^/M*3	Ind	Ind	Ind	9
Tourism/Psychology	CP87	3FT deg	* g	CCD-BBC	Ind	M^/M*3	Ind	Ind	Ind	
Tourism/Publishing	PP75	3FT deg	* g	CCC-CCD	Ind	M$3	Ind	Ind	Ind	4
Tourism/Rehabilitation (Post Exp)	BPT7	3FT deg		X		X	X	X		
Tourism/Sociology	LP37	3FT deg	* g	BCC-CCD	Ind	M*^/M*3	Ind	Ind	Ind	
Tourism/Software Engineering	GP77	3FT deg	* g	CDD-BC	Ind	M*/M*3	Ind	Ind	Ind	
Tourism/Statistics	GP47	3FT deg	* g	DD-BC	Ind	M*/M*3	Ind	Ind	Ind	
Tourism/Telecommunications	PH7P	3FT deg								
Transport Planning/Tourism	PN79	3FT deg	* g	BB-DDD	Ind	M*/M*3	Ind	Ind	Ind	5
Water Resources/Tourism	HPF7	3FT deg								

Univ of PAISLEY

Tourism	P700▼	3FT/4FT deg	E g	CC	Ind	Ind	Ind	BBC$	Ind	

Univ of PLYMOUTH

Tourism Management	P700	3FT/4SW deg	Ap g	14	MO	M$	Ind	BCCC	Ind	11 8/18
Tourism Management (European)(South Devon)	P702	2/3FT Dip	L g	6	5M	M$	Ind	Ind	Ind	14
Tourism Mgt Stage one degree Modules	P708	3FT/4SW deg	Ap g	14	MO	M$	Ind	BCCC	Ind	
Tourism Management (South Devon)	107P	2FT HND	* g	6	5M	M$	Ind	Ind	Ind	7 4/10

Univ of PORTSMOUTH

Hospitality Management with Tourism	NP77	3FT deg	*	12	5M+1D	M$6/^ go	Dip	CCCCC	Ind	

QUEEN MARGARET COLL

Hospitality and Tourism Management	NP77	3FT/4FT deg	* g	CD	M+D	M$ go	Ind	BBC	Ind	6 10/12
Tourism Management	P700	3FT/4FT deg	* g	CD	M+D	M/D$ go	Ind	BBC	Ind	6 10/14
Combined Studies *Tourism Studies*	Y600	3FT/4FT deg	*	BC	M+D	M/D$^ go	Ind	BBBC	Ind	

Univ College of RIPON & YORK ST JOHN

Heritage St: Environmental, Leis & Heritage Mgt	N7P7	3FT deg		CD	M	M	27	BBBC		

ROBERT GORDON Univ

Tourism and Hospitality Management	PN77	3FT/4FT deg	* g	DE	N	Ind	Ind	BCC$	Ind	

SCOTTISH Agric COLL

Rural Recreation and Tourism	27DP▼	2FT HND	*	D	N $	P$	Ind	CC	Ind	2

Univ College SCARBOROUGH

Leisure and Tourism Management	NP77	3FT deg	* g	DD	Ind	P	27$	Ind	Ind	

SHEFFIELD HALLAM Univ

Hotel and Tourism Management	NP77	3FT/4SW deg	*	16	6M+4D	D	Ind	Ind	Ind	
Tourism Management	PN7R	3FT deg	*	16	8M+2D	M	Ind	Ind	Ind	
Tourism and Recreation Management	PN77	3FT deg	*	16	6M+2D	D	Ind	Ind	Ind	
Combined Studies *Tourism*	Y400	3FT deg	*	14	2M	M	Ind	Ind	Ind	

			98 expected requirements							96 entry stats
TITLE	CODE	COURSE	SUBJECTS	A/AS	ND/C	AGNVQ	IB	SQA(H)	SQA	RATIO A/AS
SOLIHULL COLL										
Travel and Tourism Management	007P	2FT HND	*	E	N	P	Dip	Ind	Ind	
SOUTHAMPTON INST										
Leisure Studies (Tourism)	107P	2FT HND	*	6	MO	M$	Dip	CCCC	N	2/10
SOUTH BANK Univ										
International Hotel and Tourism Management	PN77	3FT deg	L g	CC	6M	M go	Ind	Ind	Ind	
Modern Languages and International Tourism	PT7F	4SW deg	L g	CC	6M	M go	Ind	Ind	Ind	
Tourism Management	P700	4SW deg	L g	CC	6M	M go	Ind	Ind	Ind	
Tourism and Accounting	NP47	3FT deg	L+Ac/Ec g	12-16	4M+2D	M go	Ind	Ind	Ind	
Tourism and Business Information Technology	GP77	3FT deg	M+L g	12-16	4M+2D	M go	Ind	Ind	Ind	
Tourism and Economics	LP17	3FT deg	Ec/Bu+L g	12-16	4M+2D	M go	Ind	Ind	Ind	
Tourism and Environmental Policy	FP97	3FT deg	L g	14-18	4M+2D	M go	Ind	Ind	Ind	
Tourism and European Studies	PT72	3FT deg	L g	14-18	2M+4D	M^ go	Ind	Ind	Ind	
Tourism and Food Policy	DP47	3FT deg	S+L g	12-16	4M+2D	M go	Ind	Ind	Ind	
Tourism and French	PR71	3FT deg	F g	12-16	4M+2D	M go	Ind	Ind	Ind	
Tourism and German	PR7F	3FT deg	G g	12-16	4M+2D	M go	Ind	Ind	Ind	
Tourism and German - ab initio	PR72	3FT deg	g	12-16	4M+2D	M go	Dip	Ind	Ind	
Tourism and Health Studies	LP47	3FT deg	S+L g	12-16	4M+2D	M go	Ind	Ind	Ind	
Tourism and History	PV71	3FT deg	L+H g	12-16	4M+2D	M^ go	Ind	Ind	Ind	
Tourism and Housing	KP4R	3FT deg	L g	14-18	2M+4D	M^ go	Ind	Ind	Ind	
Tourism and Human Biology	BP17	3FT deg	S+L g	12-16	4M+2D	M go	Ind	Ind	Ind	
Tourism and Human Geography	LP87	3FT deg	Gy+L g	12-16	4M+2D	M go	Ind	Ind	Ind	
Tourism and Human Resource Management	NP67	3FT deg	L g	14-18	2M+4D	M^ go	Ind	Ind	Ind	
Tourism and Law	MP37	3FT deg	L g	14-18	2M+4D	D go	Ind	Ind	Ind	
Tourism and Marketing	NP57	3FT deg	L g	14-18	2M+4D	M go	Ind	Ind	Ind	
Tourism and Media Studies	PP47	3FT deg	E+L g	14-18	2M+4D	D go	Ind	Ind	Ind	
Tourism and Nutrition	BP47	3FT deg	S+L g	12-16	4M+2D	M go	Ind	Ind	Ind	
Tourism and Planning	KP47	3FT deg	L g	14-18	4M+2D	M go	Ind	Ind	Ind	
Tourism and Politics	MP17	3FT deg	L g	12-16	4M+2D	M go	Ind	Ind	Ind	
Tourism and Psychology	CP87	3FT deg	S g	14-18	2M+4D	M go	Ind	Ind	Ind	
Tourism and Social Policy	LP4R	3FT deg	L g	12-16	4M+2D	M go	Ind	Ind	Ind	
Tourism and Sociology	LP37	3FT deg	L g	12-16	4M+2D	M go	Ind	Ind	Ind	
Tourism and Spanish	PR7K	3FT deg	Sp g	14-18	2M+4D	M^ go	Ind	Ind	Ind	
Tourism and Spanish - ab initio	PR74	3FT deg	g	12-16	4M+2D	M go	Ind	Ind	Ind	
Tourism and Sports Science	BP67	3FT deg	S+L g	12-16	4M+2D	M go	Ind	Ind	Ind	
Tourism and Technology	JP97	3FT deg	L G	12-16	4M+2D	M go	Ind	Ind	Ind	
Tourism and World Theatre	PW74	3FT deg	* g	14-18	2M+4D	M go	Dip	Ind	Ind	
Urban Studies and Tourism	PK74	3FT deg	L g	14-18	2M+4D	M go	Ind	Ind	Ind	
THE UNIVERSITY COLLEGE OF ST MARK AND ST JOHN										
Art & Design/Leisure & Tourism Studies	W1P7	3FT deg		4	MO	M	Dip	CCCC	Ind	
Geography/Leisure & Tourism Studies	L8P7	3FT deg	Gy	8-10	MO	M	Ind	Ind	Ind	
Leisure & Tourism Studies/Art & Design	P7W1	3FT deg		8	MO	M	Ind	Ind	Ind	
Leisure & Tourism Studies/Geography	P7L8	3FT deg		8	MO	M	Ind	Ind	Ind	
Leisure & Tourism Studies/Physical Recr Prog	P7N7	3FT deg		8	MO	M	Ind	Ind	Ind	
Leisure & Tourism Studies/Public Relations	P7P3	3FT deg		8	MO	M	Ind	Ind	Ind	
Leisure & Tourism Studies/Sports Science	P7B6	3FT deg		8	MO	M	Ind	Ind	Ind	
Physical Recreation Programmes/Leis & Tour St	N7P7	3FT deg		10	MO	M	Ind	Ind	Ind	
Public Relations/Leisure & Tourism Studies	P3P7	3FT deg		16	MO	M	Ind	Ind	Ind	
Sports Science/Leisure & Tourism Studies	B6P7	3FT deg		8	MO	M	Ind	Ind	Ind	

TITLE	CODE	COURSE	SUBJECTS	A/AS	NO/C	AGNVQ	IB	SQA(H)	SQA	RATIO A/AS
STAFFORDSHIRE Univ										
Business Studies with Tourism	N1P7	3FT/4SW deg	g	CCD	MO+2D	M$	24	BBB	Ind	6 8/22
Sport, Recreation and Tourism	PB76	3FT deg	*	16	2M+4D	DL	28	BBCC	Ind	
STOCKPORT COLL of F and HE										
Travel and Tourism Management	007P	2FT HND	M/E g	E	N	P				
UNIVERSITY COLLEGE SUFFOLK										
Business Studies with Tourism Studies	N1P7	3FT deg	*	EE	N $	P$	Ind	Ind	Ind	
Environmental Studies with Tourism Studies	F9P7	3FT deg	S	EE	N $	P$	Ind	Ind	Ind	
Media Studies with Tourism Studies	P4P7	3FT deg	*	CE	N $	P$	Ind	Ind	Ind	
Business (Tourism)	71PN	2FT HND	*	E	N	P*	Ind	Ind	Ind	
Leisure and Tourism Studies	77PN	2FT HND	*	E	N	P*	Ind	Ind	Ind	
Univ of SUNDERLAND										
Tourism Development Studies	P700	3FT deg	* g	8	3M $	M$	24$	CCCC	N$	1 4/12
Tourism Development Studies (Foundation)	P708	4FT/5SW deg			Ind	Ind	Ind	Ind	Ind	
SWANSEA INST of HE										
Tourism Management	P700	3FT deg	*	10		M	Ind	Ind	Ind	
Univ of TEESSIDE										
Business and Countryside Tourism	17NP▼	2FT HND								
Business and Travel and Tourism	71PN▼	2FT HND								
THAMES VALLEY Univ										
Environmental Policy and Management with Tourism	F9P7	3FT deg		8-12	MO	M	26	CCC		
Food and Drink Consumer Studies with Tourism	D4P7	3FT deg		8-12	MO	M	26	CCC		
French with Tourism	R1P7	3FT deg		8-12	MO	M	26	CCC		
Hospitality Management with Tourism	N7P7	3FT deg		8-12	MO	M	26	CCC		
Leisure Management with Tourism	N7PT	3FT deg		8-12	MO	M	26	CCC		
Recreation Management with Tourism	N7PR	3FT deg		8-12	MO	M	26	CCC		
Tourism with Advertising	P7P3	3FT deg		8-12	MO	M	26	CCC		
Tourism with Business	P7N1	3FT deg		8-12	MO	M	26	CCC		
Tourism with English Language Studies	P7Q1	3FT deg		8-12	MO	M	26	CCC		
Tourism with Environmental Policy and Management	P7F9	3FT deg		8-12	MO	M	26	CCC		
Tourism with Food Services Management	P7N9	3FT deg		8-12	MO	M	26	CCC		
Tourism with Food and Drink Consumer Studies	P7D4	3FT deg		8-12	MO	M	26	CCC		
Tourism with French	P7R1	3FT deg		8-12	MO	M	26	CCC		
Tourism with German	P7R2	3FT deg		8-12	MO	M	26	CCC		
Tourism with Hospitality Management	P7N7	3FT deg		8-12	MO	M	26	CCC		
Tourism with Hotel Management	P7ND	3FT deg		8-12	MO	M	26	CCC		
Tourism with Human Resource Management	P7N6	3FT deg		8-12	MO	M	26	CCC		
Tourism with Information Management	P7P2	3FT deg		8-12	MO	M	26	CCC		
Tourism with Information Systems	P7G5	3FT deg		8-12	MO	M	26	CCC		
Tourism with International Studies	P7MX	3FT deg		8-12	MO	M	26	CCC		
Tourism with Leisure Management	P7NT	3FT deg		8-12	MO	M	26	CCC		
Tourism with Marketing	P7N5	3FT deg		8-12	MO	M	26	CCC		
Tourism with Media Studies	P7W9	3FT deg		8-12	MO	M	26	CCC		
Tourism with Recreation Management	P7NR	3FT deg		8-12	MO	M	26	CCC		
Tourism with Retail Management	P7NM	3FT deg		8-12	MO	M	26	CCC		
Tourism with Spanish	P7R4	3FT deg		8-12	MO	M	26	CCC		
Hospitality and Tourism	7P1N▼	3SW HND	*	4	MO	P	24	CC		
Travel and Tourism	007P	2FT HND		2-4	N	P	24	CC		

course details			98 expected requirements							96 entry stats	
TITLE	CODE	COURSE	SUBJECTS	A/AS	ND/C	AGNVQ	IB	SQA(H)	SQA	RATIO	R/AS
Univ of ULSTER											
Hotel and Tourism Mgt (4 Yr SW inc DIS)	NP77▼	4SW deg	* g	BCC	MO+4D	D*6/^ gi	30	BBBB	Ind	19	14/24
WEST HERTS COLL											
Hotel Catering and Leisure Management	77PN	2FT HND	*	2	N					2	2/8
Univ of WESTMINSTER											
Tourism and Planning	PK74	3FT deg	*	CC	5M	D	Ind	BBB		6	6/14
Tourism and Planning (with foundation)	PK7K	4FT deg	*	D	Ind	P	Ind	Ind	Ind	3	
WESTMINSTER COLLEGE											
Travel and Tourism Management	007P	2FT HND	*	2	3M	P$	Ind	Ind	Ind		
WIRRAL METROPOLITAN COLLEGE											
Travel and Tourism Management	007P	2FT HND			Ind	Ind	Ind	Ind	Ind		
Univ of WOLVERHAMPTON											
Tourism (Specialist Route)	P701	3FT deg	g	14	4M	M	24	BBBB	Ind	12	
Combined Degrees *Tourism*	Y401	3FT deg	g	14	4M	M	24	BBBB	Ind		
YORKSHIRE COAST COLLEGE of F and HE											
Travel and Tourism Management	77NP	2FT HND	*	6	4M	M	Ind	Ind	Ind		

course details			98 expected requirements							96 entry stats	
TITLE	CODE	COURSE	SUBJECTS	A/AS	NO/C	AGNVQ	IB	SQA(H)	SQA	RATIO	A/AS
Univ of BRISTOL											
Veterinary Science, BVSc	D100	5FT deg	C+B+S g	AAA	X	X	33$	AAAAB	X	18	28/30
CAMBRIDGE Univ											
Veterinary Medicine	D100▼	6FT deg	C+S/M g	AAA	X		Ind	CSYS	X	7	28/30
Univ of EDINBURGH											
Veterinary Science BVM & S(Rel. Work Exp. Req'd)	D100	5FT deg	C+2(B/M/P)	AAB	X		34$	AAABB$	X	13	28/30
Univ of GLASGOW											
Veterinary Science (BVMS)	D100	5FT deg	C+B+M/P	AAB	X		Ind	AAABB	X	13	28/30
Univ of LIVERPOOL											
Veterinary Science (BVSc)(Relevant work exp req)	D100	5FT deg	C+2(B/M/P/Ap)g	AAA	X	X	$	CSYS	X	19	26/30
ROYAL VETERINARY COLL (Univ of London)											
Veterinary Medicine	D100	5FT deg	B+C	AAA	X	X	$	CSYS	X	7	28/30

TITLE	CODE	COURSE	SUBJECTS	A/AS	ND/C	AGNVQ	IB	SQA(H)	SQA	RATIO A/AS
Univ of ABERDEEN										
Biochemistry (Parasitology)	C7C3	4FT deg	3S/2S+M g	CCD	Ind	MS go	24$	BBBC$	Ind	
Mathematics-Zoology	CG31	4FT deg	M+2S g	CCD	Ind	MS go	24$	BBBC$	Ind	5
Zoology	C300	4FT deg	3S/2S+M g	CCD	Ind	MS go	24$	BBBC$	Ind	5
Zoology (Animal Ecology)	C302	4FT deg	3S/2S+M g	CCD	Ind	MS go	24$	BBBC$	Ind	5
Zoology (Cell Biology and Immunology)	C329	4FT deg	3S/2S+M g	CCD	Ind	MS go	24$	BBBC$	Ind	13
Zoology (Marine and Fisheries Biology)	C320	4FT deg	3S/2S+M g	CCD	Ind	MS go	24$	BBBC$	Ind	6
Zoology (Parasitology)	C340	4FT deg	3S/2S+M g	CCD	Ind	MS go	24$	BBBC$	Ind	6
Univ of Wales, ABERYSTWYTH										
Zoology	C300	3FT deg	B/C g	16-18	3M $	MS6/^ g	29$	BBBCC$	Ind	
Zoology and Microbiology	CC35	3FT deg	B/C g	16-18	3M $	MS6/^ g	29$	BBBCC$	Ind	
Information and Library St/an approved Sci Sub _Zoology_	PY21	3FT deg	B/C g	16-18	3M $	MS6/^ g	29$	BBBCC$	Ind	
Univ of Wales, BANGOR										
Marine Biology and Zoology	CC13	3FT deg	B+2S g	CCC	4M $	DS^ go	28$	BBBC$	Ind	27
Zoology	C300	3FT deg	B+S g	CCC	4M $	D$^ go	28$	BBBC$	Ind	5 12/24
Zoology with Animal Ecology	C3D2	3FT deg	B+S g	BCC	4M $	DS^ go	28$	BBBC$	Ind	5 11/20
Zoology with Marine Zoology	C320	3FT deg	B+S g	BCC	4M $	D$^ go	28$	BBBC$	Ind	6 14/24
BARNSLEY COLL										
Science Foundation _Zoology_	Y100	4EXT deg								
Univ of BIRMINGHAM										
Biological Sciences (Animal Biology)	C300	3FT deg	B+S/M/Gy/Gl/Ps g	BCC	Ind	Ind	30	Ind	Ind	9 16/26
Univ of BRISTOL										
Psychology and Zoology	CC83	3FT deg	B+S g	BBB	Ind	D$^	32$	CSYS	Ind	17 26/28
Zoology	C300	3FT deg	B+S g	BBC	Ind	D$^	32$	CSYS	Ind	10 24/28
CAMBRIDGE Univ										
Natural Sciences _Zoology_	Y160▼	3FT deg	2(S/M) g	AAA-AAB	Ind		Ind	CSYS	Ind	
CARDIFF Univ of Wales										
Zoology	C300	3FT deg	B+M/P/C g	BBB-BCC	MO $	Ind	30$	BBBB$	Ind	6 16/26
Zoology	C301	4SW deg	B+M/P/C g	BBB-BCC	MO $	Ind	30$	BBBB$	Ind	5 18/24
Preliminary Year _Zoology_	Y101	4FT/5SW deg	* g		Ind	Ind	Ind	Ind	Ind	
Univ of DUNDEE										
Zoology	C300	4FT deg	C+S/2S g	16	5M $	M$	25$	BBBC$	N$	8
Univ of DURHAM										
Zoology	C300	3FT deg	B+C	BCC-CCC	3M+2D$	Ind	28	AAABB	Ind	16 20/30
Univ of EAST ANGLIA										
Zoology and Physiology	BC13	3FT deg	C+P/M/B	CCC	3D $		28$	BBBCC$	Ind	9 16/22
Univ of EAST LONDON										
Animal Biology	C300	3FT deg	* g	12	MO	MS	Ind	Ind	Ind	6 6/8
Extended Science _Animal Biology_	Y108	4FT deg	* g	8-10	MO	M				
Univ of EDINBURGH										
Zoology	C300	4FT deg	C+2(B/M/P) g	BBC	MO $		Dip$	BBBB	N$	6 18/30

Zoology 71

TITLE	CODE	COURSE	SUBJECTS	A/AS	ND/C	AGNVQ	IB	SQA(H)	SQA	RATIO A/AS
Univ of GLASGOW										
Parasitology	C340	4FT deg	C/M+S	BBC-CCC	N	M	24$	BBBB$	N	10
Parasitology (with work placement)	C341	4FT deg	C/M+S	BBC-CCC	N	M	24$	BBBB$	N	
Zoology	C300	4FT deg	C/M+S	BBC-CCC	N	M	24$	BBBB$	N	5
Zoology (with work placement)	C301	4FT deg	C/M+S	BBC-CCC	N	M	24$	BBBB$	N	
IMPERIAL COLL (Univ of London)										
Parasitology	C340	3FT deg	B+C/M/P	BCC	MO+2D	Ind	30$	Ind	Ind	
Zoology	C300	3FT deg	B+C/M/P	BCC	MO+2D	Ind	30$	Ind	Ind	12 20/26
Univ of LEEDS										
Applied Zoology	C310	3FT deg	B g	BCC	1M+4D$	Ind	28$	BBBBC	Ind	5 16/20
Biochemistry-Zoology	CC37	3FT/4FT deg	C+B g	BCC	1M+5D$	Ind	28$	BBBBC	Ind	5
Microbiology-Zoology	CC35	3FT/4FT deg	C+B g	BCC	1M+5D$	Ind	28$	BBBBC	Ind	9
Zoology	C300	3FT deg	B g	BBC	1M+5D$	Ind	29$	ABBBC	Ind	6 16/30
Univ of LEICESTER										
Biological Sciences (Zoology)	C300	3FT deg	B+C g	18-20	DO $	D$4/^ gi	28$	BBBCC$	Ind	14/26
Univ of LIVERPOOL										
Zoology	C300	3FT deg	B+S g	18	MO $	DS^ go	31$	BBBCC$	Ind	14 16/26
BSc Combined Honours Zoology	Y100	3FT deg	B	18	MO $	Ind	31$	BBBCC$	Ind	
LIVERPOOL JOHN MOORES Univ										
Applied Zoology	C310	3FT/4SW deg		8	3M	M				4 6/14
Applied Zoology (Foundation)	C318	4FT/5SW deg								5 10/12
Univ of MANCHESTER										
Zoology	C300	3FT deg	B+C g	BCD	3M+3D$	D^	26$	BBBCC	Ind	14 18/28
Zoology with Industrial Experience	C301	4SW deg	B+C g	BCD	3M+3D$	D^	26$	BBBCC	Ind	6 20/26
Zoology with a Modern Language	C303	4FT deg	B+C+L g	BCD	3M+3D$	D^	26$	BBBCC	Ind	10
Univ of NEWCASTLE										
Animal Science	C305	3FT deg	2S g	CCD	Ind	Ind	Ind	AABB	Ind	5 10/28
Entomology and Pest Management	CD32	3FT deg	2S g	CCD	Ind	Ind	Ind	AABB	Ind	
Wildlife Biology	C306	3FT deg	2S g	CCD	Ind	Ind	Ind	AABB	Ind	22
Zoology	C300	3FT deg	B+C	BBC-BCC	HN	Ind	30$	ABBB	Ind	10 18/26
Univ of NOTTINGHAM										
Behavioural Science	CCH8	3FT deg	B+M/C/P g	BBB	Ind	Ind	Ind	Ind	Ind	12 26/30
Zoology	C300	3FT deg	B+C g	BBB-BBC	6M $	D	30$	BBBBC$	Ind	13 24/28
QUEEN MARY & WESTFIELD COLL (Univ of London)										
Zoology	C300	3FT deg	B+C/P/M	16	6M $	MS^/DS	26$	BBBCC		
QUEEN'S Univ Belfast										
Zoology	C300	3FT/4FT deg	B+C	CCC	Ind	Ind	28$	BBBC	Ind	6 16/24
Univ of READING										
Animal Physiology	C305	3FT deg	B/C g	18	4M+1D$	DS^ go	29$	BBBC$	Ind	21
Botany and Zoology	CC23	3FT deg	B g	16	5M $	DS^ go	28$	BBBC$	Ind	5 12/18
Psychology and Zoology	CC38	3FT deg	B/C/M g	BCC	3M+2D$	DS^ go	30$	BBBB$	Ind	8 17/28
Zoology	C300	3FT deg	B g	18	4M+1D$	DS^ go	29$	BBBC$	Ind	9 14/22
ROEHAMPTON INST										
Zoology	C300▼	3FT deg	B g	12	4M	M$ go	28	BCC	N$	

			98 expected requirements							96 entry stats	
course details											
TITLE	CODE	COURSE	SUBJECTS	A/AS	NO/C	AGNVQ	IB	SQA(H)	SQA	RATIO	A/AS
ROYAL HOLLOWAY, Univ of London											
Zoology	C300	3FT deg	B+C/S g	BCC	4M	DS^	28$	BBBCC$		4	12/22
Zoology with Physiology	C3B1	3FT deg	B+C/S g	BCC	4M	DS^	28$	BBBCC$		4	14/20
Science Foundation Year *Zoology*	Y100	4FT deg	*		Ind	Ind	Ind	Ind			
Univ of SHEFFIELD											
Zoology	C300	3FT deg	B+S g	20	6M $	DS6/^	30$	BBBB$	Ind	9	20/28
Zoology and Genetics	CC34	3FT/4EXT deg	C+S g	BCD	6M $	D^	28$	BBBC$	Ind	37	
Univ of SOUTHAMPTON											
Zoology	C300	3FT deg	B g	BCC	5M+1D$	Ind^	28$	BBBBC	Ind	13	18/28
Univ of ST ANDREWS											
Animal Biology	C304	3FT/4FT deg	B/C/Gy/M/P g	BBC	Ind	Ind	28$	BBBB$	Ind	16	
General Degree of BSc *Animal Biology*	Y100	3FT deg	B/C/Gy/M/P g	CCC	Ind	Ind	28$	BBBC$	Ind		
STAFFORDSHIRE Univ											
Animal Biology	C300	3FT deg									
Animal Biology	C301	4EXT deg	g	4	1M	P	24	CCC			
Univ of Wales SWANSEA											
Zoology	C300	3FT deg	B	CCC	2M+3D$	DS^	28$	BBBCC$	Ind	9	14/22
UNIVERSITY COLL LONDON (Univ of London)											
Zoology	C300	3FT deg	C+B/M/P g	BCC-BBB	3M+2D$	Ind	32$	Ind	Ind	7	20/30

Combined Programmes (with Course Descriptions) 72

			98 expected requirements							96 entry stats	

TITLE	CODE	COURSE	SUBJECTS	A/AS	ND/C	AGNVQ	IB	SQA(H)	SQA	RATIO	A/AS
Univ of ABERDEEN											
Combined Studies (MA)	Y450	3FT/4FT deg	* g	BBC	Ind	M$ go	30$	BBBB$	Ind	5	
Science	Y100	3FT/4FT deg	3S/2S+M g	CCD	Ind	MS go	24$	BBBC$	Ind		
Univ of Wales, ABERYSTWYTH											
Information and Library St/an approved Sci Sub	PY21	3FT deg	* g	BCC	Ind	Ind	Ind		Ind		
ANGLIA Poly Univ											
Combined Sciences	Y100▼	3FT deg	2S g	10	3M	P go	Dip$	BCCC	Ind	1	4/8
Negotiated Route	Y600▼	3FT/4FT deg	*	12	4M	M	Dip	BCCC	Ind	4	
Negotiated Route	Y601▼	4FT deg	*	12	4M	M	Dip	BCCC	Ind		
Univ of Wales, BANGOR											
Contemporary Studies: Literature, Hist, Culture	Y300	3FT deg	E+H g	CCC	X	D*^ go	28$	BBBC$	X		
Environmental Planning and Management	Y401	3FT deg	* g	10	4M	M$ go	Ind	Ind	Ind		
French, German and Russian	Y600	4FT deg	F g	BBC	X	D*^ go	30$	AABB$	X		
BARNSLEY COLL											
Combined Studies	Y400	3FT deg	* g	EE	4M	M*	Ind	Ind	Ind		
Combined Studies	Y401	3FT deg	Pf	EE	4M	M*	Ind	Ind	Ind		
Combined Studies	E401	3FT deg	Pf g	EE	4M	M*	Ind	Ind	Ind		
Humanities	Y301	3FT deg	H/Gy/Po/E g	EE	4M	MB	Ind	Ind	Ind		
Humanities	Y302	4EXT deg									
Science Foundation	Y100	4EXT deg									
Univ of BATH											
Foundation Course in Science and Engineering	Y108	1FT EXT deg								20	
Natural Sciences	Y160	3FT deg	S/M+S/M	20	Ind	DS	30	Ind	Ind	6	16/30
Natural Sciences	Y161	4SW deg	S/M+S/M	20	Ind	DS	30	Ind	Ind	5	14/28
BATH COLL of HE											
Combined Awards	Y400	3FT deg			N		Ind	$	$	6	8/22
Modular Programme (DipHE)	Y460	2FT Dip			N		Ind	$	$	2	6/13
Modular Programme (DipHE) Cultural Studies	Y460	2FT Dip									
Univ of BIRMINGHAM											
Mechanical Engineering, Manuf and Management	Y600	4FT deg	M+P	BBB	X	X	33$	CSYS	X	3	26/30
Natural Sciences	Y160	3FT deg	2S g	22	Ind	Ind	30	Ind	Ind		
Natural Sciences with Study in Continental Euro	Y165	4FT deg	2S g	22	Ind	Ind	30	Ind	Ind		
BLACKBURN COLL											
Science (Foundation Year)	Y100	4EXT deg									
BOLTON INST											
Science, Society & Environment	Y100	3FT deg	* g	CD	MO	M	24	Ind	Ind		
Univ of BRADFORD											
Interdisciplinary Human Studies	Y402	3FT deg	* g	BB-CCC	4M+3D	D*^	Ind	Ind	Ind	4	12/22
BRADFORD & ILKLEY Comm COLL											
Combined Studies	Y200	3FT deg	*	8	MO	M	Dip	CCC	Ind		
Univ of BRIGHTON											
Humanities	Y300	3FT deg	*	CC	Ind	Ind	Ind	Ind	Ind		

TITLE	CODE	COURSE	SUBJECTS	A/AS	ND/C	AGNVQ	IB	SQA(H)	SQA	RATIO A/AS
course details			**98 expected requirements**							*96 entry stats*
BRISTOL, Univ of the W of England										
Combined Studies (Swindon College)	Y400▼	2FT Dip	* g	6-10	N	P*	24	CCC	Ind	
Joint Honours Programme	Y401	3FT/4FT deg	Ap g	14-16	5M $	M$ go	24$	BCCC$	Ind	
Science Foundation Year	Y120▼	4EXT/5EXTSW deg	M/S g	E	N $	PS go	24$	Ind	N$	
BRUNEL Univ, West London										
Foundations of Science (1 Yr Conv Prog)	Y100	4FT/5EXTSW deg	*	DD	N	M	24	Ind	Ind	4/12
Humanities	Y300	3FT deg	Ap	12-16	MO $	M* go	26$	BCCC$	Ind	
Natural Sciences	Y160	3FT deg	2S	CD	3M $	Ind^	26$	Ind	Ind	3	4/24
Philosophy, Politics and Economics	Y616	3FT deg	* g	BCC	5M	D^	28	BBBCC	Ind	
Univ of BUCKINGHAM										
Politics, Economics and Law	Y618	2FT deg	* g	12	5M	M	24	CCCC	Ind	
CAMBRIDGE Univ										
Natural Sciences	Y160▼	3FT deg	2(S/M) g	AAA-AAB Ind			Ind	CSYS	Ind	3	30/30
CANTERBURY CHRIST CHURCH COLL of HE										
American Studies with Science	Q4Y1	4FT deg	S g	DD	Ind	Ind	24	Ind	Ind	
Art with Science	W1Y1	3FT deg	A+S g	DD	Ind	Ind	24	Ind	Ind	
Business Studies with Science	N1Y1	3FT deg	S g	DD	Ind	Ind	24	Ind	Ind	
Early Childhood Studies with Science	X9Y1	3FT deg	S g	DD	Ind	Ind	24	Ind	Ind	3
English with Science	Q3Y1	3FT deg	E+S	DD	Ind	Ind	24	Ind	Ind	
Geography with Science	L8Y1	3FT deg	Gy+S g	DD	Ind	Ind	24	Ind	Ind	
History with Science	V1Y1	3FT deg	H+S g	CC	MO	M	24	Ind	Ind	
Information Technology with Science	G5Y1	3FT deg	S g	DD	Ind	Ind	24	Ind	Ind	
Marketing with Science	N5Y1	3FT deg	S g	DD	Ind	Ind	24	Ind	Ind	
Mathematics with Science	G1Y1	3FT deg	M+S g	DD	Ind	Ind	24	Ind	Ind	3
Media Studies with Science	P4Y1	3FT deg	S g	DD	Ind	Ind	24	Ind	Ind	
Music with Science	W3Y1	3FT deg	Mu+S g	DD	Ind	Ind	24	Ind	Ind	
Psychology with Science	L7Y1	3FT deg	Ps+S g	DD	Ind	Ind	24	Ind	Ind	
Radio, Film & Television Studies with Science	W5Y1	3FT deg	S g	CC	MO	M	24	Ind	Ind	
Religious Studies with Science	V8Y1	3FT deg	S g	DD	Ind	Ind	24	Ind	Ind	
Science	Y100	3FT deg	S g	DD	Ind	Ind	24	Ind	Ind	
Science	Y101	2FT Dip	* g	D	Ind	Ind	24	Ind	Ind	
Science and American Studies	QY41	3FT deg	S g	DD	Ind	Ind	24	Ind	Ind	
Science and Art	YW11	3FT deg	A+S g	DD	Ind	Ind	24	Ind	Ind	
Science and Business Studies	YN11	3FT deg	S g	DD	Ind	Ind	24	Ind	Ind	
Science and Early Childhood Studies	XY91	3FT deg	S g	DD	Ind	Ind	24	Ind	Ind	
Science and English	QY31	3FT deg	E+S	DD	Ind	Ind	24	Ind	Ind	
Science and French	RY11	3FT deg	F+S g	DD	Ind	Ind	24	Ind	Ind	
Science and Geography	LY81	3FT deg	Gy+S g	DD	Ind	Ind	24	Ind	Ind	
Science and History	VY11	3FT deg	H+S g	DD	Ind	Ind	24	Ind	Ind	
Science and Information Technology	GY51	3FT deg	S g	DD	Ind	Ind	24	Ind	Ind	
Science and Marketing	NY51	3FT deg	S g	DD	MO	Ind	24	Ind	Ind	
Science and Mathematics	GY11	3FT deg	M+S g	DD	Ind	Ind	24	Ind	Ind	
Science and Media Studies	PY41	3FT deg	S	DD	Ind	Ind	24	Ind	Ind	
Science and Music	WY31	3FT deg	Mu+S g	DD	Ind	Ind	24	Ind	Ind	
Science and Psychology	LY71	3FT deg	S+Ps g	DD	Ind	Ind	24	Ind	Ind	
Science and Radio, Film and Television Studies	WY51	3FT deg	S g	DD	Ind	Ind	24	Ind	Ind	

course details			98 expected requirements							96 entry stats	
TITLE	CODE	COURSE	SUBJECTS	A/AS	ND/C	AGNVQ	IB	SQA(H)	SQA	RATIO A/AS	
Science and Religious Studies	YV18	3FT deg	S g	DD	Ind	Ind	24	Ind	Ind		
Science and Social Science	LY31	3FT deg	S g	DD	Ind	Ind	24	Ind	Ind	2	
Science with Art	Y1W1	3FT deg	A+S g	DD	Ind	Ind	24	Ind	Ind		
Science with Business Studies	Y1N1	3FT deg	S g	DD	Ind	Ind	24	Ind	Ind	1	
Science with English	Y1Q3	3FT deg	S+E	DD	Ind	Ind	24	Ind	Ind		
Science with French	Y1R1	3FT deg	S+F g	DD	Ind	Ind	24	Ind	Ind		
Science with Geography	Y1L8	3FT deg	S+Gy g	DD	Ind	Ind	24	Ind	Ind		
Science with History	Y1V1	3FT deg	S+H g	DD	Ind	Ind	24	Ind	Ind		
Science with Information Technology	Y1G5	3FT deg	S g	DD	Ind	Ind	24	Ind	Ind	6	
Science with Mathematics	Y1G1	3FT deg	M+S g	DD	Ind	Ind	24	Ind	Ind		
Science with Music	Y1W3	3FT deg	Mu+S g	DD	Ind	Ind	24	Ind	Ind		
Science with Psychology	Y1L7	3FT deg	S+Ps g	DD	Ind	Ind	24	Ind	Ind		
Science with Radio, Film & Television Studies	Y1W5	3FT deg	S g	DD	Ind	Ind	24	Ind	Ind		
Science with Religious Studies	Y1V8	3FT deg	S g	DD	Ind	Ind	24	Ind	Ind		
Science with Social Science	Y1L3	3FT deg	S g	DD	Ind	Ind	24	Ind	Ind		
Science with Sport Science	Y1B6	3FT deg	S g	DD	Ind	Ind	24	Ind	Ind		
Science with Statistics	Y1G4	3FT deg	S+M g	DD	Ind	Ind	24	Ind	Ind		
Sport Science and Science	BY61	3FT deg	S g	DD	Ind	Ind	24	Ind	Ind		
Sport Science with Science	B6Y1	3FT deg	S g	DD	Ind	Ind	24	Ind	Ind		
Statistics and Science	GY41	3FT deg	S+M g	DD	Ind	Ind	24	Ind	Ind		
Statistics with Science	G4Y1	3FT deg	M+S g	DD	Ind	Ind	24	Ind	Ind		
Tourism Studies with Science	P7Y1	3FT deg	S g	DD	Ind	Ind	24	Ind	Ind		
Tourism and Science	PY71	3FT deg	S g	DD	Ind	Ind	24	Ind	Ind		
CARDIFF Univ of Wales											
Preliminary Year	Y121	4FT deg								1	7/24
Preliminary year	Y101	4FT deg								4	12/28
Univ of CENTRAL LANCASHIRE											
Combined Honours (Year Zero)	Y408▼	4FT deg	* g								
Combined Honours Programme	Y400	3FT/4SW deg									
Science (Year Zero)	Y108▼	1FT deg									
Combined Honours Programme	Y400	3FT deg	Ar	12	MO+3D	M$6/^	26	BCCC$	Ind		
CHELTENHAM & GLOUCESTER COLL of HE											
English Studies with Combined Arts	Q3Y3	3FT deg	E	12-14	MO	M3^	26	CCCC	Ind		
Fashion with Combined Arts	W2Y3	3FT deg	*	10-14	MO	M3	26	CCCC	Ind		
History with Combined Arts	V1Y3	3FT deg	H	12	MO	M3^	26	CCCC	Ind		
Human Geography with Combined Arts	L8Y3	3FT deg	*	12	MO	M3^	26	CCCC	Ind		
Media Communications with Combined Arts	P4Y3	3FT deg	*	12	MO	M3^	26	CCCC	Ind		
Multimedia with Combined Arts	G5Y3	3FT deg	*	8-12	MO	MI3	24	CCCC	Ind		
Multimedia with Combined Arts	G5YH	4SW deg	*	8-12	MO	MI3	26	CCCC	Ind		
Performance Arts with Combined Arts	W4Y3	3FT deg	*	10-14	5M+2D	M3	26	CCCC	Ind		
Psychology with Combined Arts	L7Y3	3FT deg	g	12-16	MO	M3^	26	CCCC	Ind		
Religious Studies with Combined Arts	V8Y3	3FT deg	*	8-12	MO	M3^	26	CCCC	Ind		
Sociological Studies with Combined Arts	L3Y3	3FT deg	*	12	MO	M3^	26	CCCC	Ind		
Visual Arts with Combined Arts	W1Y3	3FT deg	A	10-14	5M+2D	MA3	26	CCCC	Ind		
Women's Studies with Combined Arts	M9Y3	3FT deg	*	8-12	MO	M3^	26	CCCC	Ind		

course details			98 expected requirements							96 entry stats	
TITLE	CODE	COURSE	SUBJECTS	A/AS	ND/C	AGNVQ	IB	SQA(H)	SQA	RATIO A/AS	
UNIVERSITY COLLEGE CHESTER											
Combined Subjects (4 Yrs) Franchised	Y400	4FT deg	*		Ind	Ind	Ind	Ind			
CORNWALL COLLEGE WITH DUCHY COLLEGE											
Marine Studies	Y409	3FT deg	Cs/Ds/S/M/P	4	N	P	Ind	Ind	Ind		
Marine Studies (Foundation)	Y408	1FT deg	*	X							
Science (Foundation)	Y108	1FT deg	*								
Social Science	Y200	3FT deg	*	14	5M	M	Ind	Ind	Ind		
COVENTRY Univ											
Applied Science	Y101▼	3FT deg									
General Degree (CAT route)	Y600	3FT deg									
DE MONTFORT Univ											
Combined Sciences	Y100▼	2FT Dip	g	4-6	N	P	Dip	BCC	Ind	3	
Combined Sciences (Extended Science)	Y108▼	4FT/5SW deg	g	2	N	P	Dip	CC	Ind	4	
Combined Studies	Y400▼	3FT/4SW deg	g	10-14	2M+4D	D	30	BBB	Ind	4	6/16
Humanities Combined Honours	Y300▼	3FT deg	* g	CCD	MO	M^	30$	ABBB	Ind	4	8/22
Humanities Joint Honours	Y301▼	3FT deg	* g	CCD	MO	M$^	28$	ABBB	Ind	4	10/22
Modular Studies Joint Honours/Combined Honours	Y600▼	3FT deg									
Natural Sciences	Y160▼	3FT deg	S g	10	P $	MO	Ind	Ind	Ind		
Natural Sciences with QTS	Y161▼	3FT deg	S g	10	P $	MO	Ind	Ind	Ind		
Univ of DERBY											
Combined Sciences	Y100	3FT deg	S	10	N $	MS	26$	CCCC	Ind		
Combined Subject Programme (Foundation)	Y608▼	3FT deg	*		Ind	Ind	Ind	Ind	Ind		
Credit Accumulation Modular Scheme	Y600▼	3FT deg	*	8-16	MO	M	Ind	CCCC	Ind	3	6/18
Science (Combined Science)	001Y	2FT HND	S	4	N $	PS	Dip$	DDD$	Ind		2/4
Science (Combined Science/Geology)	16YF	2FT HND	S	4	N	PS	Dip$	DDD$	Ind	1	
DONCASTER COLL											
Combined Studies	Y300	3FT deg		EE	N	Ind	Ind	Ind	Ind	1	
Univ of DUNDEE											
Arts and Social Sciences	Y400	3FT deg	* g	BCC	Ind	D$	29	BBBC	Ind	2	
Science	Y100	3FT deg	2S g	10	5M $	M$	25$	BBCC$	N$		
Univ of DURHAM											
Arts Combined	Y300	3FT deg	*	24	MO	Ind	30	AAABB	Ind	5	22/30
Combined Hons in Lit Studs, History & Philosophy	Y600▼	3FT deg	*	18	Ind	Ind	Dip	BBBB	Ind		
Natural Sciences	Y160	3FT deg	2S	ABB	Ind	X	33	CSYS	X	7	24/30
Science and Childhood in Society	XY91▼	3FT deg	* g	EE	MO	Ind	Dip	CCCC	Ind		8/11
Social Sciences Combined	Y220	3FT deg	*	ABC	MO	Ind	32	AAABB	Ind	5	22/30
Univ of EAST ANGLIA											
Anthropology, Archaeology and Art History	Y400	3FT deg	*	BBC	Ind		Ind	BBBBB	Ind	8	12/22
Economic and Social Studies (4 years)	Y200	4FT deg	*					Ind			
Natural Sciences	Y160	4FT deg	B/C/M/P	CCC	MO+1D$	Ind	27$	BBBB	Ind		
Philosophy, Politics and Economics	Y616	3FT deg	*	BBC	3M+3D		30	BBBBB	Ind	6	20/24

Combined Programmes (with Course Descriptions) 72

course details			98 expected requirements							96 entry stats
TITLE	CODE	COURSE	SUBJECTS	A/AS	NO/C	AGNVQ	IB	SQA(H)	SQA	RATIO A/AS
Univ of EAST LONDON										
Economics with Social Sciences	L1Y2	3FT deg	* g	12	MO	M	Ind			
Extended Science	Y108	4FT deg	* g	8-10	MO	M	Ind	Ind	Ind	
Health Studies and Social Sciences	LY42	3FT deg	* g	12	MO	M				
Health Studies with Social Sciences	L4Y2	3FT deg	* g	12	MO	M				
Negotiated Degree Programme	Y401	3FT deg	* g	12	MO	M	Ind	Ind	Ind	17
Psychosocial Studies and Social Sciences	LY72	3FT deg	* g	12	MO	M				
Social Sciences with Health Studies	Y2L4	3FT deg	* g	12	MO	M				
Three-Subject Degree	Y600	3FT deg	* g	12	MO	M	Ind	Ind	Ind	
EDGE HILL Univ COLLEGE										
Science Studies	Y101	3FT deg								
Science Studies	Y100	3FT deg	S g	DD	3M+3D	M*/ P*△ go	Dip	BBCC$	Ind	
Science and Geography	LY81	3FT deg	S+Gy g	DD	X	PS△ go	Dip	BBCC$	Ind	
Science and Mathematics	GY11	3FT deg	2(B/C/En/P) g	DD	3M+3D	MS / P*△	Dip	BBCC$	Ind	
Science and Sports Studies	BY61	3FT deg	2(B/C/En/P) g	CD	3M+3D	MS / P*△	Dip	BBCC$	Ind	
Univ of EDINBURGH										
MA General	Y400	3FT deg	g	BBB	Ind	Ind	Dip$	BBBB	Ind	
Social Science (BSc)	Y200	3FT deg	*	AAB-BBB	Ind		34	ABBB	Ind	15
Univ of ESSEX										
Comparative Studies	Y400	3FT deg	*	20	MO+2D	Ind	28	BBBB	Ind	10/18
European Studies (4 Yrs)	T9Y4	4FT deg	F/*	20	MO+2D	Ind	28	BBBB	Ind	5	12/20
Social Sciences	Y201	3FT deg	*	20	MO+2D	D	28	BBBB	Ind	2	10/18
Univ of GLAMORGAN										
Combined Studies (Honours)	Y400	3FT deg	g	8-16	Ind	Ind	Ind	Ind	Ind	6	10/20
Humanities	Y301▼	3FT deg	* g	CC	5M	M$	24	CCCC	HN	2	6/16
Joint Honours	Y401	3FT deg	g	8-16	Ind	Ind	Ind	Ind	Ind	9	6/22
Major/Minor Honours	Y402	3FT deg	g	8-16	Ind	Ind	Ind	Ind	Ind	5	8/20
Science Foundation Year	Y120▼	3FT/4SW deg	* g	E	Ind	Ind	Ind	Ind	Ind	6/12
Univ of GLASGOW										
General Science	Y107	3FT deg	2S	BBC-CCC	N	M	24$	BBBB$	N	5
MA (Applied Social Sciences)	Y203	3FT deg		BBC	8M	M	30	BBBB	Ind	7
MA General Humanities	Y400	3FT deg		BBC	HN	M	30	BBBB	Ind	2	20/28
MA Liberal Arts	Y300	3FT deg		BBC	HN	M	30	BBBB	Ind	
MA Liberal Arts	Y301	3FT deg		BBC	HN	M	30	BBBB	N	
GLASGOW CALEDONIAN Univ										
Science	Y100	3FT deg	M+S	DD	Ind		Ind	CCC$	Ind	3
Univ of GREENWICH										
Analytical Science with European Study	Y101	3FT/4SW deg	C+S g	8	3M	MS	Dip	CCC	Ind	
Analytical Sciences	Y120	3FT/4SW deg	C+S g	8	3M	MS	Dip	CCC	Ind	
Humanities	Y301	3FT deg	* g	12	MO	M	25	BBB	Ind	
Humanities, Media and Society	Y401	3FT deg								
Science (Extended)	Y103▼	4FT deg	*	4		Ind		Ind	Ind	
Science and Technology (Extended)	Y1J9	4EXT deg	* g	EE	3M $	Ind	Ind	CCC$	Ind	
HERIOT-WATT Univ										
Combined Studies (BA)	Y300	4FT deg	*	CCC	Ind	M$ go	30	BBBB	Ind	
Combined Studies BSc	Y100	4FT deg	M	DDE	Ind	M$ go	26	BCCC	Ind	

course details			98 expected requirements							96 entry stats	
TITLE	CODE	COURSE	SUBJECTS	A/AS	ND/C	AGNVQ	IB	SQA(H)	SQA	RATIO	A/AS
Univ of HERTFORDSHIRE											
Combined Modular Scheme	Y100	3FT deg		12-20		Ind			Ind	13	12/20
Combined Modular Scheme (Science) (Extended)	Y108▼	4EXT deg	* g	4	N $	Ind	Dip$	DDDD$	Ind	1	
Combined Modular Scheme Ext (Info Sciences)	Y109▼	4EXT deg	*	4	N	P$ gi	Dip	DDDD	Ind		
Contemporary Studies	Y400▼	3FT deg	*	14	Ind	Ind	28	Ind	Ind	4	
Humanities	Y300▼	3FT deg	*	14	M+D	Ind	28	CCCCC	Ind	2	8/24
International Foundation Programme	Y410	1FT deg	*	X	X	X	Ind	X	X		
Univ of HUDDERSFIELD											
Science	Y100	3FT/4SW deg	S g	6-14	N	M$ go	Ind	Ind	Ind		
Science (Extended)	Y108	4FT/5SW deg	* g	EE	N	P$ gi	Ind	Ind	Ind		
Univ of HULL											
Politics, Philosophy, Economics	Y616	3FT deg	*	BBB	MO+2D	Ind	28	BBBCC	Ind	12	18/26
JEWS' COLL (Univ of London)											
Jewish Studies (3 Yrs)	Y400	3FT deg	*	18	Ind		Ind	CSYS	Ind	3	
KEELE Univ											
Philosophy, Politics and Economics	Y616	3FT deg	* g	BCC	Ind	Ind	28	CSYS	Ind	6	14/24
Philosophy, Politics and Economics (4 Yrs)	Y617	4FT deg	*	BCC	Ind	Ind	28	BBBB	Ind	7	
Univ of KENT											
European Arts (Combined Arts)	Y301	3FT deg		26	6D	Ind	34	Ind	Ind		
European Arts (Visual & Performed Arts)	Y311	3FT deg		26	6D	Ind	34	Ind	Ind		
The Visual and Performed Arts	Y310	3FT deg	*	22	2M+4D	Ind	30	Ind	Ind	24	
KING'S COLL LONDON (Univ of London)											
Afro-Portuguese, Brazilian and Rel St (3/4 Yrs)	Y654	3FT/4FT deg	*	BCC						8	
European Studies	T2Y3	4FT deg	L	ABB						7	26/30
KINGSTON Univ											
Joint Honours	Y100▼	4EXT/5EXT deg	*		Ind		Ind	Ind	Ind		
Univ of Wales, LAMPETER											
Combined Honours	Y400	3FT deg	*	14-16	Ind	Ind	Ind	Ind	Ind		
Religion, Ethics and Society	Y652	3FT deg	*	14	Ind	Ind	Ind	Ind	Ind		
LANCASTER Univ											
Combined Science	Y158	3FT deg	* g	CCD	MO $		28$	BBBB$	Ind		
Combined Science (inc a year in USA or Canada)	Y155	3FT deg	* g	BBB	MO $		32$	AABBB$	Ind		
Criminology and Independent Studies	MY34	3FT deg	*	CCC	M+D		30	ABBBB	Ind		
Culture, Media and Communication	Y400	3FT deg	*	BBB-BBC	M+D		30	ABBBB	Ind		
Economics & Mathematics & Operational Research	Y642	3FT deg	M	BCC	MO $		30$	BBBBB$	Ind		
History, Philosophy and Politics	Y650	3FT deg	H	BBC	Ind $		30$	ABBBB$	Ind		
Independent Studies	Y410	3FT deg	*		Ind		Ind	Ind	Ind		
Independent Studies and Applied Social Science	YL44	3FT deg	*	CCC	Ind		Ind	Ind	Ind		
Independent Studies and Educational Studies	YX49	3FT deg	*	CCC	Ind		Ind	Ind	Ind		
Independent Studies and Philosophy	VY74	3FT deg	*	BCC	Ind		Ind	Ind	Ind		
Independent Studies and Politics	YM41	3FT deg	*	BCC	Ind		Ind	Ind	Ind		
Independent Studies and Religious Studies	YV48	3FT deg	*	18	Ind		Ind	Ind	Ind		
Independent Studies and Sociology	LY34	3FT deg	*	20	Ind		Ind	Ind	Ind		
Independent Studies and Theatre Studies	YW44	3FT deg	*	BBC	Ind		Ind	Ind	Ind		
Philosophy and Politics and Economics	Y616	3FT deg	* g	BBC	Ind		32	ABBBB	Ind		

TITLE	CODE	COURSE	SUBJECTS	A/AS	NO/C	AGNVQ	IB	SQA(H)	SQA	RATIO	A/AS
Univ of LEEDS											
Interdisciplinary Science (Foundation)	Y101▼	4FT/5FT deg	*g	Ind	Ind	Ind	Ind	Ind	Ind	1	10/10
LEEDS, TRINITY & ALL SAINTS Univ COLL											
Interdisciplinary Science (Foundation)	Y101	1FT deg		Ind	Ind	Ind	Ind	Ind	Ind		
LEEDS METROPOLITAN Univ											
Social Sciences - Joint Award	Y200	3FT deg									
Univ of LEICESTER											
BSc with integrated foundation	Y101	4EXT deg	*g		N	*			Ind		
Combined Arts	Y300	3FT deg	g	BCC	DO	D$^	30$	Ind	X	6	18/26
Combined Science	Y100	3FT deg	g	CCC	MO $	DS^	28$	BBBCC$	Ind	4	14/24
Univ of LINCOLNSHIRE and HUMBERSIDE											
Combined Studies	Y400▼	3FT deg	*	14	2M+2D	M	24	BCCC			
Humanities	Y300▼	3FT deg	g	16	1M+3D	D	24	BBCCC	Ind		
Univ of LIVERPOOL											
Arts Combined	Y401	3FT/4FT deg	*g	BBB	Ind	Ind	30	ABBB	Ind	13	22/30
BA Combined Honours	Y200	3FT deg	*g	BBB	Ind	Ind	Ind	Ind	Ind	13	18/28
BSc Combined Honours	Y100	3FT deg	*g	18-22	MO $	Ind	31$	BBBCC$	Ind	7	18/28
Modular Science/Eng with Foundation Element	Y108	4EXT/5EXT deg	2(M/P/C)	10	MO $	Ind	24$	CCCDD$	Ind		6/12
LIVERPOOL JOHN MOORES Univ											
International Students Foundation Year	Y600	1FT deg									
Natural Sciences	Y160	3FT deg		8	3M	M					
LONDON GUILDHALL Univ											
Modular Programme	Y400	3FT deg	*g	BB-DD	MO	D/M$ go	24	Ind	Ind		
Modular Programme	Y420▼	3FT deg	*g	EE	MO	P	24	Ind	Ind		
Modular Programme (Sociology/Politics/History)	Y421▼	3FT deg	*g	EE	MO	P	24	Ind	Ind		
Politics, Philosophy and Economy	Y616	3FT deg									
LSE: LONDON Sch of Economics (Univ of London)											
Business Mathematics and Statistics	Y240	3FT deg	M	BBB-AAB	Ind	X	$	Ind	Ind	7	28/30
LUTON Univ											
Combined Studies	Y400	3FT deg	g	12-16	MO/DO	M/D	32	BBCC	Ind	1	6/14
Foundation Science	Y100	1FT deg	*		Ind	Ind	Ind	Ind	Ind	1	
Humanities/Media (Foundation)	YP34	1FT deg			Ind	Ind	Ind	Ind	Ind		
Univ of MANCHESTER											
Combined Studies	Y300	3FT deg	*	BBC-BBB	Ind	D^	32	BBBBC	X	6	20/28
Econ Honours - Any area of Study	Y200	3FT deg	*g	BBC	MO+6D	D^	Ind	AABBB	Ind	5	21/30
MANCHESTER METROPOLITAN Univ											
Combined Studies (Foundation)	Y108▼	4FT deg	M/P	E	2M $	P$	$	$	Ind		
Humanities/Social Studies	Y400	3FT deg	*	CDD	Ind	Ind	Ind	BBB	Ind		10/20
Interdisciplinary Studies (Options)	Y416	2FT Dip	*	DD	N	Ind	Ind	Ind	Ind		6/14
MIDDLESEX Univ											
Joint Honours Degree	Y400	3FT/4FT deg	*g	12-18	5M	M/D$ go	26	BBCC	Ind		
NAPIER Univ											
Combined Studies Programme (CAT)	Y400	3FT/4FT deg	*							8	
Science with Management Studies	Y1N1	4FT/5SW deg	2(M/P/C/B)	DD	Ind	Ind	Ind	BCC	Ind		

			98 expected requirements						96 entry stats	
course details											
TITLE	CODE	COURSE	SUBJECTS	A/AS	ND/C	AGNVQ	IB	SQA(H)	SQA	RATIO	A/AS
Univ of NEWCASTLE											
Combined Studies (BA)	Y400	3FT deg	*	ABC-BBB	5D	Ind	35$	AAAB	Ind	5	20/28
Combined Studies (BSc)	Y101▼	4FT deg	*	18	4M	Ind	28	AABBB	Ind	3	
Combined Studies (BSc)	Y100	3FT deg	2S	18-22	4M	Ind	28	AABBB	Ind	7	18/26
Univ of Wales COLLEGE, NEWPORT											
Humanities	Y308	3FT/4FT HND/deg									
Labour Studies	Y408	3FT/4FT HND/deg									
Science	Y108	3FT/4FT HND/deg									
Social Studies	Y208	3FT/4FT HND/deg									
NORTH EAST WALES INST of HE											
Combined Studies	Y400	3FT deg									
NORTH LINCOLNSHIRE COLLEGE											
Science/Engineering/Computer St Foundation Year	Y100	1FT deg	*	2	N	P*	Ind	Ind	Ind		
Univ of NORTH LONDON											
Combined Honours-Applied Social Science	Y301	3FT deg	*	CC	MO	M	Ind	Ind	Ind	5	6/14
Combined Honours-Business	Y400	3FT deg	* g	14	MO+4D	Ind	Ind	CCCC	Ind	13	8/16
Combined Honours-Humanities	Y300	3FT deg	*	CC	Ind	Ind	Ind	Ind	Ind	4	6/20
Combined Honours-Interfaculty	Y600	3FT deg	*		Ind	Ind	Ind	Ind	Ind	6	7/18
Combined Honours-Science	Y100	3FT/4SW/4EXT deg	*	CC	3M	M$	Dip		Ind	8	10/12
Univ of NORTHUMBRIA											
Combined Honours	Y400▼	3FT deg	g	12-20	MO+3D	D	26	BBCCC	Ind	3	6/20
Social Sciences	Y200	3FT deg		CC	3M+1D	M	24	CCCC	Ind		
NORWICH: City COLL											
Combined Arts	Y300	3FT deg	* g	12	Ind		Ind	Ind	Ind	3	8/18
Combined Science	Y100	3FT/4FT deg	2S	10	5M		Ind	Ind	Ind	5	
NOTTINGHAM TRENT Univ											
Combined Studies in Science (Extended)	Y108▼	4EXT deg	* g		Ind	Ind	Ind	Ind	Ind		6/10
Environment and Human Sciences	YL43	3FT deg	* g	12	Ind	M$ go	Ind	Ind	Ind		8/18
Human Services	Y200	3FT deg	* g	14-18	Ind	Ind	Ind	Ind	Ind		8/14
Humanities	Y301	3FT/4SW deg	* g	14-16	M+D	Ind	28	CCCC	Ind	5	12/22
OXFORD Univ											
Engineering,Economics and Management (4 Yrs)	Y630	4FT deg	M+P	AAB	DO		36	AAAAA	Ind	3	28/30
Human Sciences	Y400	3FT deg	*	AAB-ABB	DO		36	AAAAA	Ind	3	26/30
Materials,Economics and Management (4 Yrs)	Y634	4FT deg	2S	AAB-ABB	DO		36	AAAAA	Ind	2	30/30
Philosophy, Politics and Economics	Y616	3FT deg	*	AAB	DO		36	AAAAA	Ind	3	26/30
Psychology, Philosophy and Physiology	Y620	3FT deg	*	AAB	DO		36	AAAAA	Ind	4	28/30
OXFORD BROOKES Univ											
Combined Studies	Y400	3FT deg		X		X	X	X			
Combined Studies/Accounting and Finance	NY44	3FT deg		X		X	X	X			
Combined Studies/Anthropology	LY64	3FT deg		X		X	X	X			
Combined Studies/Biological Chemistry	CY74	3FT deg		X		X	X	X			
Combined Studies/Biology	CY14	3FT deg		X		X	X	X			
Combined Studies/Business Administration and Mgt	NY14	3FT deg		X		X	X	X			
Combined Studies/Cartography	FY84	3FT deg		X		X	X	X			

Combined Programmes (with Course Descriptions) 72

course details			98 expected requirements							96 entry stats	
TITLE	CODE	COURSE	SUBJECTS	A/AS	ND/C	AGNVQ	IB	SQA(H)	SQA	RATIO	A/AS
Combined Studies/Cell Biology	CYC4	3FT deg		X		X	X	X			
Computer Systems/Combined Studies	GY64	3FT deg		X		X	X	X			
Computing Mathematics/Combined Studies	GY94	3FT deg		X		X	X	X			
Computing/Combined Studies	GY54	3FT deg		X		X	X	X			
Ecology/Combined Studies	CY94	3FT deg		X		X	X	X			
Economics/Combined Studies	LY14	3FT deg		X		X	X	X			
Educational Studies/Combined Studies	XY94	3FT deg		X		X	X	X			
Electronics/Combined Studies	HY64	3FT deg		X		X	X	X			
English Studies/Combined Studies	QY34	3FT deg		X		X	X	X			
Environmental Chemistry/Combined Studies	FY14	3FT deg		X		X	X	X			
Environmental Policy/Combined Studies	KY34	3FT deg		X		X	X	X			
Environmental Sciences/Combined Studies	FYX4	3FT deg		X		X	X	X			
Exercise and Health/Combined Studies	BY64	3FT deg		X		X	X	X			
Extended Science	Y100	4FT deg	*g	EE	Ind	P*	Ind	Ind	Ind	1	6/12
Fine Art/Combined Studies	WY14	3FT deg		X		X	X	X			
Food Science and Nutrition/Combined Studies	DY44	3FT deg		X		X	X	X			
French Language and Contemp Studies/Combined St	RYC4	3FT deg		X		X	X	X			
French Language and Literature/Combined Studies	RY14	3FT deg		X		X	X	X			
Geography and the Phys Env/Combined Studies	FYV4	3FT deg		X		X	X	X			
Geography/Combined Studies	LY84	3FT deg		X		X	X	X			
Geology/Combined Studies	FY64	3FT deg									
Geotechnics/Combined Studies	HY24	3FT deg		X		X	X	X			
German Language and Contemp Stud/Combined St	RYF4	3FT deg		X		X	X	X			
German Language and Literature/Combined Studies	RY24	3FT deg		X		X	X	X			
German Studies/Combined Studies	RYG4	3FT deg		X		X	X	X			
Health Care/Combined Studies (Post Exp)	BY74	3FT deg		X		X	X	X			
History of Art/Combined Studies	VY44	3FT deg		X		X	X	X			
History/Combined Studies	VY14	3FT deg		X		X	X	X			
Hospitality Management Studies/Combined Studies	NY74	3FT deg		X		X	X	X			
Human Biology/Combined Studies	BY14	3FT deg		X		X	X	X	Ind		
Information Systems/Combined Studies	GYM4	3FT deg		X		X	X	X			
Intelligent Systems/Combined Studies	GY84	3FT deg		X		X	X	X			
International Foundation	Y300	1FT deg			Ind		Ind	Ind	Ind		
Law/Combined Studies	MY34	3FT deg		X		X	X	X			
Leisure Planning/Combined Studies	KYH4	3FT deg		X		X	X	X			
Marketing Management/Combined Studies	NYN4	3FT deg		X		X	X	X			
Mathematics/Combined Studies	GY14	3FT deg		X		X	X	X			
Music/Combined Studies	WY34	3FT deg		X		X	X	X			
Palliative Care/Combined Studies (Post Exp)	BYR4	3FT deg		X		X	X	X			
Planning Studies/Combined Studies	KY44	3FT deg		X		X	X	X			
Politics/Combined Studies	MY14	3FT deg		X		X	X	X			
Psychology/Combined Studies	CY84	3FT deg		X		X	X	X			
Publishing/Combined Studies	PY54	3FT deg		X		X	X	X			
Rehabilitation/Combined Studies (Post Exp)	BYT4	3FT deg		X		X	X	X			
Sociology/Combined Studies	LY34	3FT deg		X		X	X	X			
Software Engineering/Combined Studies	GY74	3FT deg		X		X	X	X			
Statistics/Combined Studies	GY44	3FT deg		X		X	X	X			
Telecommunications/Combined Studies	HYP4	3FT deg		X		X	X	X			
Tourism/Combined Studies	PY74	3FT deg		X		X	X	X			
Transport Planning/Combined Studies	NY94	3FT deg		X		X	X	X			
Water Resources/Combined Studies	HYF4	3FT deg		X		X	X	X			

course details			98 expected requirements							96 entry stats	
TITLE	CODE	COURSE	SUBJECTS	A/AS	ND/C	RGNVQ	IB	SQA(H)	SQA	RATIO	A/AS
Univ of PAISLEY											
Combined Studies	Y400▼	3FT/4FT deg	* g	CD	Ind	Ind	Ind	BBCC	Ind	2	
General Science	Y100	3FT deg	* g	CCC-EE	Ind	Ind	Ind	BCC$	Ind	13	
Science and Technology	JY91	2FT Dip	* g	EE	Ind	Ind	Ind	CCC$	Ind		
Science with Geology	Y1F6	5SW deg	M g	CCC-EE	Ind	Ind	Ind	BCC$	Ind		
Univ of PLYMOUTH											
Art Hist with Cultural Interpretation & Practice	V4Y3	3FT deg	Ap g	CCD	MO+3D	D$^	Ind	Ind	Ind		
Arts/Social Sci/Science Stage 1 Degree Modules	Y400▼	1FT deg	Ap g	Ind	Ind	M go	Ind	Ind	Ind	1	8/16
Cult Interpret & Pract with Heritage & Landscape	Y3W2	3FT deg	Ap g	CCD	MO+3D	D$^	Ind	Ind	Ind		
Cult Interpret & Practice with Theatre Perf St	Y3W4	3FT deg	Ap g	CCD	MO+3D	D$^	Ind	Ind	Ind		
Cultural Interpretation & Practice with Media Arts	Y3WF	3FT deg	Ap g	CCD	MO+3D	D$^	Ind	Ind	Ind		
Cultural Interpret and Practice with Visual Arts	Y3WG	3FT deg	Ap g	CCD	MO+3D	D$^	Ind	Ind	Ind		
Cultural Interpretation & Practice with Art Hist	Y3V4	3FT deg	Ap g	CCD	MO+3D	D$^	Ind	Ind	Ind		
Cultural Interpretation & Practice with Educ St	Y3X9	3FT deg	Ap g	CCD	MO+3D	D$^	Ind	Ind	Ind		
Cultural Interpretation & Practice with English	Y3Q3	3FT deg	Ap g	CCD	MO+3D	D$^	Ind	Ind	Ind		
Cultural Interpretation & Practice with History	Y3V1	3FT deg	Ap g	CCD	MO+3D	D$^	Ind	Ind	Ind		
Cultural Interpretation and Practice with Music	Y3W3	3FT deg	Ap g	CCD	MO+3D	D$_^	Ind	Ind	Ind		
English with Cultural Interpretation & Practice	Q3Y3	3FT deg	E g	BBC	MO+3D	D$_^	Ind	Ind	Ind		
Extended Science (Foundation Year)	Y108	1FT/4EXT deg	S	2	Ind	P$	Ind	Ind	Ind	1	4/13
Heritage & Landscape w. Cult Interpret & Pract	W2Y3	3FT deg	Ap g	CCD	MO+3D	D$^	Ind	Ind	Ind		
History with Cultural Interpretation & Practice	V1Y3	3FT deg	Ap g	CCD	MO+3D	D$_^	Ind	Ind	Ind		
Media Arts with Cult Interpretation and Practice	W2YH	3FT deg	Ap g	CCD	MO+3D	D$_^	Ind	Ind	Ind		
Theatre & Perf St with Cult Interpret & Practice	W4Y3	3FT deg	Ap g	CCD	MO+3D	D$_^	Ind	Ind	Ind		
Visual Arts with Cult Interpretation & Practice	W2YJ	3FT deg	Ap g	CCD	MO+3D	D$_^	Ind	Ind	Ind		
QUEEN MARGARET COLL											
Combined Studies	Y600	3FT/4FT deg	*	BC	M+D	M/D$^ go	Ind	BBBC	Ind	9	12/18
QUEEN MARY & WESTFIELD COLL (Univ of London)											
Combined Honours	Y158	3FT deg	2S	BCD		DS	26$				
Science and Engineering (4 yrs with Foundation)	Y157	4EXT deg		E	N	P					
ROEHAMPTON INST											
Human Sciences	Y200▼	3FT deg	B	12	3M $	P$	26	BCC	N$	2	4/12
Humanities (English History Theol & Relig St)	VY93▼	3FT deg	E/H	CC	2M+2D$		30	BBC	Ind	2	6/14
ROYAL HOLLOWAY, Univ of London											
Foundation Programme	Y408	4FT deg									
Science Foundation Year	Y100▼	4FT deg	*		Ind	Ind	Ind	Ind		3	
Science and the Media	Y1P4	3FT deg	S	BBC-CCC	Ind	DS_^	28$	Ind		6	
SCOTTISH Agric COLL											
Rural Business Management	Y400▼	3FT/4FT deg	S/M	CD	Ind	M$	Ind	BBC$	Ind	2	
SCOTTISH COLLEGE of TEXTILES											
Combined Studies	Y100	4FT deg	*	CC	Ind	M$	30	BBC	Ind	2	
Combined Studies	Y300	4FT deg	*	CC	Ind	M$	30	BBC	Ind	4	
Univ of SALFORD											
Independent Studies in Science and Technology	Y100	4FT deg		Ind	Ind	Ind	Ind	Ind			
Science Foundation Year (4 Yrs)	Y120	4FT deg	*	Ind	Ind	Ind	Ind	Ind		1	
Sociology and Cultural Studies	L3Y6	3FT deg	* g	BCC-CCD	Ind	Ind	Ind	Ind	Ind	6	14/22

course details			98 expected requirements							96 entry stats
TITLE	CODE	COURSE	SUBJECTS	A/AS	ND/C	AGNVQ	IB	SQA(H)	SQA	RATIO A/AS
Univ College SCARBOROUGH										
Dance with Arts	W4YH	3FT deg	* g	DD	Ind	P	27$	Ind	Ind	
Dance with Social Sciences	W4YF	3FT deg	* g	DD	Ind	P	27$	Ind	Ind	
English with Arts	Q3Y3	3FT deg	E g	CC	Ind	M	28$	Ind	Ind	
English with Social Sciences	Q3Y2	3FT deg	E g	CC	Ind	M	28$	Ind	Ind	
Environmental Science with Arts	F9Y3	3FT deg	Gy/B g	EE	Ind	P	27$	Ind	Ind	
Environmental Science with Sciences	F9Y1	3FT deg	Gy/B g	EE	Ind	P	27$	Ind	Ind	
Environmental Science with Social Sciences	F9Y2	3FT deg	Gy/B g	EE	Ind	P	27$	Ind	Ind	
Leisure and Tourism with Arts	N7Y3	3FT deg	* g	DD	Ind	P	27$	Ind	Ind	
Leisure and Tourism with Sciences	N7Y1	3FT deg	* g	DD	Ind	P	27$	Ind	Ind	
Leisure and Tourism with Social Sciences	N7Y2	3FT deg	* g	DD	Ind	P	27$	Ind	Ind	
Management with Arts	N1Y3	3FT deg	* g	DD	Ind	P	27$	Ind	Ind	
Management with Sciences	N1Y1	3FT deg	* g	DD	Ind	P	27$	Ind	Ind	
Management with Social Sciences	N1Y2	3FT deg	* g	DD	Ind	P	27$	Ind	Ind	
Marketing with Arts	N5Y3	3FT deg	* g	DD	Ind	P	27$	Ind	Ind	
Marketing with Sciences	N5Y1	3FT deg	* g	DD	Ind	P	27$	Ind	Ind	
Marketing with Social Sciences	N5Y2	3FT deg	* g	DD	Ind	P	27$	Ind	Ind	
Music with Arts	W3Y3	3FT deg	Mu g	EE	Ind		27$	Ind	Ind	
Music with Social Sciences	W3Y2	3FT deg	Mu g	EE	Ind		27$	Ind	Ind	
Social and Cultural Studies with Arts	L3Y3	3FT deg	* g	DE	Ind	P	27$	Ind	Ind	
Social and Cultural Studies with Sciences	L3Y1	3FT deg	* g	DE	Ind	P	27$	Ind	Ind	
Social and Cultural Studies with Social Sciences	L3Y2	3FT deg	* g	DE	Ind	P	27$	Ind	Ind	
Theatre Studies with Arts	W4Y3	3FT deg	T/E g	DD	Ind	P	27$	Ind	Ind	
Theatre Studies with Social Sciences	W4Y2	3FT deg	T/E g	DD	Ind	P	27$	Ind	Ind	
Visual Art with Arts	W1Y3	3FT deg	A g	CD	Ind	M	28$	Ind	Ind	
Visual Art with Arts	E1Y3	3FT deg	A g	CD	Ind	M	28$	Ind	Ind	
Visual Art with Social Sciences	E1Y2	3FT deg	A g	CD	Ind	M	28$	Ind	Ind	
Visual Art with Social Sciences	W1Y2	3FT deg	A g	CD	Ind	M	28$	Ind	Ind	
Univ of SHEFFIELD										
Economics with Mathematics and Statistics	Y620	3FT deg	M g	22	4M+2D$	D^	30$	ABBB$	Ind	
Science Foundation Year (4 or 5 Yrs)	Y100	4FT/5FT deg	* g							6 8/24
Social and Political Studies	Y220	3FT deg	* g	BBC	4D	D^	30	ABBB	Ind	5 20/30
SHEFFIELD HALLAM Univ										
Combined Studies	Y400▼	3FT deg	*	18	2M	M	Ind	Ind	Ind	
Combined Studies (Foundation)	Y408▼	4EXT deg								
Science (Foundation Course)	Y108▼	4EXT/5EXTSW deg	*	E	N	P	Ind	Ind	Ind	
Science and Technology	001Y	2FT HND	*	E	N	P	Ind	Ind	Ind	
Univ College of St MARTIN, LANCASTER AND CUMBRIA										
Applied Community Studies/Science, Tech & Soc	LY51	3FT deg	g	CD-DDE	3M+2D	M*	28	BCCC		
Art and Design/Science,Technology and Society	WY11	3FT deg	A g	CC-CDE	3M+2D	MA	28$	BBCC$	Ind	
Business Management Studies/Sci, Technol & Soc	NY11	3FT deg	g	CD-CEE	3M+2D	M	28	BCCC		
English/Science, Technology and Society	QY31	3FT deg	E g	BC-BDE	X	P^	28$	BBBC$	Ind	
Geography/Science, Technology and Society	LY81	3FT deg	Gy g	CD-DDE	X	P^	28$	BCCC$	Ind	
Mathematics/Science, Technology and Society	GY11	3FT deg	M g	DD-DEE	X	P^	28$	BCCC$	Ind	
Religious Studies/Science, Technology & Society	VY81	3FT deg	g	CD-DDE	3M+2D	M*	28$	BCCC	Ind	
Science, Technology & Society/Applied Commun St	YL15	3FT deg	g	CD-DDE	3M+2D	M*	28	BCCC		

course details | 98 expected requirements | 96 entry stats

TITLE	CODE	COURSE	SUBJECTS	A/AS	ND/C	RGNVQ	IB	SQA(H)	SQA	RATIO A/AS
Science, Technology & Society/PE & Sport Studies	XYX1	3FT deg	g	CD-DDE	3M+2D	M	28	BCCC		
Science, Technology and Society	Y100	3FT deg	g	CD-DDE	3M+2D	M*	28	BCCC	Ind	
Science, Technology and Society/Art and Design	WYC1	3FT deg	A g	CD-DDE	X	M^	28$	BCCC$	Ind	
Science, Technology and Society/Business Mgt St	YN11	3FT deg	g	CD-DDE	3M+2D	M*	28	BCCC		
Science, Technology and Society/Drama	WY41	3FT deg	g	CD-DDE	3M+2D	M*	28	BCCC	Ind	
Science, Technology and Society/Education Studs	XY91	3FT deg	g	CD-DDE	3M+2D	M*	28	BCCC	Ind	
Science, Technology and Society/English	QY3C	3FT deg	E g	CD-DDE	X	M^	28$	BCCC$		
Science, Technology and Society/Geography	LY8C	3FT deg	Gy g	CD-DDE	X	M^	28$	BCCC$		
Science, Technology and Society/Mathematics	GY1C	3FT deg	M g	CD-DDE	X	M^	28$	BCCC$	Ind	
Science, Technology and Society/Religious Studs	VY8C	3FT deg	g	CD-DDE	3M+2D	M*	28	BCCC	Ind	
Science, Technology and Society/Social Ethics	VY71	3FT deg	g	CD-DDE	3M+2D	M*	28	BCCC	Ind	
Science,Technology & Society/Health Admin	LY41	3FT deg	g	CD-DDE	3M+2D	M*	28$	BCCC	Ind	
Social Ethics/Science, Technology and Society	VY7C	3FT deg	g	CD-DDE	3M+2D	M*	28	BCCC	Ind	

Univ of ST ANDREWS

TITLE	CODE	COURSE	SUBJECTS	A/AS	ND/C	RGNVQ	IB	SQA(H)	SQA	RATIO A/AS
European Integration Studies	Y602	4FT deg	* g	BBB	X	Ind	30$	BBBB	Ind	10
European Integration Studies(with Int Yr Abroad)	Y603	4FT/5FT deg	* g	BBB	X	Ind	30$	BBBB	Ind	10
General Degree of BSc	Y100	3FT deg	B/C/Gy/M/P g	CCC	Ind	Ind	28$	BBBC$	Ind	
General Degree of MA	Y450	3FT deg	* g	BBB	X	Ind	30$	BBBB	Ind	10

ST MARY'S Univ COLL

TITLE	CODE	COURSE	SUBJECTS	A/AS	ND/C	RGNVQ	IB	SQA(H)	SQA	RATIO A/AS
Integrated Scientific Studies and Classical St	QY81	3FT deg	S/2S	4-8	Ind	Ind	Ind	BBBB$	Ind	
Integrated Scientific Studies and Drama	WY41	3FT deg	S/2S	8-12	Ind	Ind	Ind	BBBB$	Ind	
Integrated Scientific Studies and Education St	XYX1	3FT deg	S/2S	4-8	Ind	Ind	Ind	BBBB$	Ind	
Integrated Scientific Studies and Heritage Mgt	NY91	3FT deg	S/2S	4-8	Ind	Ind	Ind	BBBB$	Ind	
Integrated Scientific Studies and History	VY11	3FT deg	S/2S+H	4-8	Ind	Ind	Ind	BBBB$	Ind	
Management Studies and Integrated Scientific St	NY11	3FT deg	S/2S g	4-8	Ind	Ind	Ind	BBBB$	Ind	
Media Arts and Integrated Scientific Studies	PY41	3FT deg	S/2S	4-8	Ind	Ind	Ind	BBBB$	Ind	
Sociology and Integrated Scientific Studies	LY31	3FT deg	S/2S	4-8	Ind	Ind	Ind	BBBB$	Ind	
Sport Rehabilitation & Integrated Scientific St	BY91	3FT deg	B g	12-14	X	X	Ind	BBBB$	X	
Sport Science and Integrated Scientific Studies	BY61	3FT deg	S/2S g	8-12	Ind	Ind	Ind	BBBB$	Ind	
Theology and Religious St and Integrated Sci St	VY81	3FT deg	S/2S	4-8	Ind	Ind	Ind	BBBB$	Ind	

STAFFORDSHIRE Univ

TITLE	CODE	COURSE	SUBJECTS	A/AS	ND/C	RGNVQ	IB	SQA(H)	SQA	RATIO A/AS
Combined Studies	Y300	3FT deg	g	10-12	MO+2D	M	27	BBC		
Foundation Business, Computing, Eng, & Health	Y400▼	1FT deg								
Social Science	Y200	3FT deg	g	12	3M	M	24	BCC	Ind	

Univ of STIRLING

TITLE	CODE	COURSE	SUBJECTS	A/AS	ND/C	RGNVQ	IB	SQA(H)	SQA	RATIO A/AS
Politics, Philosophy and Economics	Y616	4FT deg	g	BCC	Ind	Ind	31	BBBC	HN	

STOCKPORT COLL of F and HE

TITLE	CODE	COURSE	SUBJECTS	A/AS	ND/C	RGNVQ	IB	SQA(H)	SQA	RATIO A/AS
Science	001Y	2FT HND	C/B	E	N	PS	Dip	BBCC	N	

Univ of STRATHCLYDE

TITLE	CODE	COURSE	SUBJECTS	A/AS	ND/C	RGNVQ	IB	SQA(H)	SQA	RATIO A/AS
Arts and Social Sciences	Y440	3FT/4FT deg	g	CCC	Ind		28	BBBBB$	Ind	
Science Studies (Pass Degree)	Y100	3FT deg	M+S	DD	Ind		Ind	CCC$	Ind	

Combined Programmes (with Course Descriptions) 72

TITLE	CODE	COURSE	SUBJECTS	A/AS	ND/C	AGNVQ	IB	SQA(H)	SQA	RATIO A/AS
UNIVERSITY COLLEGE SUFFOLK										
Applied Biological Science with Cultural Studies	C1Y3	3FT deg	S	EE	N $	PS	Ind	Ind	Ind	
Art & Design and Cultural Studies	EY23	3FT deg	Pf	EC	N $	P$	Ind	Ind	Ind	
Art & Design and Cultural Studies	WY23	3FT deg	Pf	EC	N $	P$	Ind	Ind	Ind	
Art & Design with Cultural Studies	W2Y3	3FT deg	Pf	EE	N $	P$	Ind	Ind	Ind	
Art & Design with Cultural Studies	E2Y3	3FT deg	Pf	EE	N $	P$	Ind	Ind	Ind	
Behavioural Studies and Cultural Studies	LY73	3FT deg	*	DC	N $	P$	Ind	Ind	Ind	
Behavioural Studies with Cultural Studies	L7Y3	3FT deg	*	DD	N $	P$	Ind	Ind	Ind	
Business Studies and Cultural Studies	NY13	3FT deg	*	CE	N $	P$	Ind	Ind	Ind	
Business Studies with Cultural Studies	N1Y3	3FT deg	*	EE	N $	P$	Ind	Ind	Ind	
Cultural Studies and Applied Biological Science	YC31	3FT deg	S	CE	N $	P$	Ind	Ind	Ind	
Cultural Studies and Early Childhood Studies	YX39	3FT deg	*	CD	N $	P$	Ind	Ind	Ind	
Cultural Studies and Environmental Studies	YF39	3FT deg	*	CE	N $	P$	Ind	Ind	Ind	
Cultural Studies and Information Technology	YG35	3FT deg	*	CE	N $	P$	Ind	Ind	Ind	
Cultural Studies and Literary Studies	YQ32	3FT deg	E	CE	N $	P$	Ind	Ind	Ind	
Cultural Studies and Management	YN31	3FT deg	*	CE	N $	P$	Ind	Ind	Ind	
Cultural Studies and Media Studies	YP34	3FT deg	*	CE	N $	P$	Ind	Ind	Ind	
Early Childhood Studies with Cultural Studies	X9Y3	3FT deg	*	DD	N $	P$	Ind	Ind	Ind	
Environmental Studies with Cultural Studies	F9Y3	3FT deg	S/Gy	EE	N $	P$	Ind	Ind	Ind	
Foundation Science	Y108	4FT deg		EE	N	P*	Ind	Ind	Ind	
Individual Studies	Y400	3FT deg	*	EE	Ind	Ind	Ind	Ind	Ind	
Individual Studies	Y100	3FT deg	*	EE	Ind	Ind	Ind	Ind	Ind	
Media Studies with Cultural Studies	P4Y3	3FT deg	*	CE	N $	P$	Ind	Ind	Ind	
Product Design & Manufacture and Cultural Studs	HY73	3FT deg	*	CE	N $	P$	Ind	Ind	Ind	
Product Design & Manufacture with Cultural Studs	H7Y3	3FT deg	*	EE	N $	P$	Ind	Ind	Ind	
Univ of SUNDERLAND										
Independent Programmes (Modular Credit Scheme)	Y400	3FT deg								
Univ of SUSSEX										
Applied Psychology	C8Y2	3FT deg	* g	BBB	MO	M*6 go	$	Ind	Ind	
Arts, Humanities and Social Sciences	Y200▼	4FT deg								
Developmental Psychology	C8YF	3FT deg	* g	BBB	MO $	M*6 go	$	Ind	Ind	
English in Cultural and Community Studies	Q3Y2	3FT deg	*	BBB	MO	M*6	$	Ind	Ind	
Geography in Cultural and Community Studies	L8Y2	3FT deg	*	BBC	MO	M*6	$	Ind	Ind	
History in Cultural and Community Studies	V1Y2	3FT deg	*	BBB	MO	M*6	$	Ind	Ind	
History of Art in Cultural and Community Studs	V4Y2	3FT deg	*	BBB	MO	M*6	$	Ind	Ind	
Human Sciences (4 Yrs)	Y400	4FT deg	S g	BBB	MO $	MS6 go	$	Ind	Ind	
Media Studies in Cultural and Community Studs	P4Y2	3FT deg	*	BBB	MO	M*6	$	Ind	Ind	
Music in Cultural and Community Studies	W3Y2	3FT deg	Mu	BBC	MO $	M*^	$	Ind	Ind	
Philosophy in Cultural and Community Studies	V7Y2	3FT deg	*	BBB	MO	M*6	$	Ind	Ind	
Social Anthropology in Cultural & Community St	L6Y2	3FT deg	*	BBC	MO	M*6	$	Ind	Ind	
Social Policy	L4Y2	3FT deg	*	BBC	MO	M*6	$	Ind	Ind	
Sociology in Cultural & Community Studies	L3Y2	3FT deg	*	BBB	MO	M*6	$	Ind	Ind	
Twentieth Cent Music St in Cultural & Comm St	W3YF	3FT deg	Mu	BBC	MO $	M*^	$	Ind	Ind	
Univ of Wales SWANSEA										
Economics and Social Studies Foundation Year	Y221	1FT deg	*		X	X	X	X	X	
Foundation Year	Y100	1FT deg	*		Ind	Ind	Ind	Ind	Ind	
Joint Hons with defer choice of specialisation	Y220	3FT deg	*	20-22	1M+5D	Ind	28	BBBBB	Ind	2 13/24

TITLE	CODE	COURSE	SUBJECTS	A/AS	ND/C	AGNVQ	IB	SQA(H)	SQA	RATIO A/AS
course details			*98 expected requirements*							*96 entry stats*
SWANSEA INST of HE										
Joint Honours	Y300	3FT deg		8	N				N	2 4/12
Univ of TEESSIDE										
Combined Studies (Design)	Y400	3FT deg								
Combined Studies (Humanities)	Y301	3FT deg	*	14-16	Ind		Ind	Ind	Ind	2 8/17
Extended Science	Y109	4FT deg								
Modular Degree Scheme	Y401	3FT deg								
Philosophy, Politics and Economics	Y616	3FT deg	*	12-14	Ind		Ind	Ind	Ind	
Science and Technology Combined Honours Scheme	Y108	3FT deg								
Social Sciences	Y200	3FT deg	*	12-14	Ind		Ind	Ind	Ind	
Social Sciences Combined Honours	Y201	3FT deg								
TRINITY COLL Carmarthen										
Dyniaethau (Options)	Y321	3FT deg	g	DD-CC	Ind		Ind	Ind	Ind	1 4/10
Humanities (Options)	Y320	3FT deg	g	DD-CC	Ind		Ind	Ind	Ind	1 4/12
Univ of ULSTER										
Combined Studies	Y200▼	3FT deg	* g	CC	MO+D	D*6/^ gi	22	CCCD	Ind	7 14/16
Humanities Combined	Y320▼	3FT/4FT deg	*	CCC	MO+3D	D*6/^ gi	28	BBBC	Ind	14 16/22
Modern Studies in the Humanities (3/4 Yr)	Y321▼	3FT/4SW deg	*	CCC	MO+3D	D*6/^ gi	28	BBBC	Ind	5 12/18
UNIVERSITY COLL LONDON (Univ of London)										
Human Sciences	Y400	3FT deg	S g	BBC-ABB	MO+3D$	Ind	34$	BBBBB	Ind	5 20/30
Physical Sciences	Y100	3FT deg	S g	CCC-BCC	$	Ind	28$	BCCCC$	N$	2 16/30
Physical Sciences (MSci)	Y101	4FT deg	S g	CCC-BCC	$	Ind	28$	BCCCC$	N$	
Statistics,Computing,Operational Res & Economics	Y624	3FT deg	M g	BCC	MO $	Ind	30$	BBCCC$	N$	47
Statistics,Operational Res & a European Language	Y625	3FT deg	M g	BCC	MO $	Ind	30$	BBCCC$	N$	4
Univ Col WARRINGTON										
Combined Studies (Mature Student Programme)	Y400	3FT deg	*		Ind	Ind	Ind	Ind	Ind	1 8/8
Univ of WARWICK										
Maths-Operational Research-Statistics-Economics	Y602	3FT deg	M g	ABC	X	X	32$	AABBB$		3 24/30
WESTHILL COLL										
Humanities - Childhood Studies	Y600	3FT deg	* g	CC	4M+2D	M^	Ind	Ind	Ind	
Humanities - Creative Arts	Y4W9	3FT deg	* g	CC	4M+2D	M^	Ind	Ind	Ind	
Humanities - Mathematics, Science and Psychology	Y601	3FT deg	M g	CC	4M+2D	M^	Ind	Ind	Ind	
Humanities - Nineteenth and Twentieth Century St	Y602	3FT deg	* g	CC	4M+2D	M^	Ind	Ind	Ind	
Univ of WESTMINSTER										
Combined Honours	Y200	3FT deg	*	14-16	MO+3D	D	26	BBB	Ind	
Interdisciplinary Studies	Y400	3FT deg								
WIRRAL METROPOLITAN COLLEGE										
Combined Studies (Cultural Studies)	Y200	3FT deg			Ind	Ind	Ind	Ind	Ind	
Science	001Y	2FT HND			Ind	Ind	Ind	Ind	Ind	
Univ of WOLVERHAMPTON										
Applied Sciences	Y100	3FT/4SW deg	S g	DD	N	M	24	CCCC	Ind	2 6/16
Applied Sciences (4 Yrs)	Y110▼	3FT/4SW deg	*							
Combined Degrees	Y401	3FT/4SW deg		8-20	4M	M	24	CCCC	Ind	6 8/22
Combined Degrees	E401	3FT/4SW deg		8-20	4M	M	24	CCCC	Ind	

course details			98 expected requirements							96 entry stats
TITLE	CODE	COURSE	SUBJECTS	A/AS	ND/C	AGNVQ	IB	SQA(H)	SQA	RATIO A/AS
WRITTLE COLL										
Agriculture (Science)	D2Y1	3FT/4SW deg	Ap g	14	MO	M	Ind	Ind	Ind	
Univ of YORK										
Philosophy, Politics and Economics	Y616	3FT deg	* g	BBB	Ind	D$^ go	32	BBBBB	Ind	20/30

Table 72
Course Descriptions
1587

Univ of ABERDEEN

BSc Y100

Some 30 subjects/courses are available, offering a wide range of experience in differing fields of study within a very flexible course structure. Four subjects are chosen in the first year out of twelve or so; generally, six further courses are studied in the second and third years for the non-honours degree - either continuing studies in subjects from the first year or moving on to more specialist work in related subjects, in the biological, chemical, physical and mathematical sciences, geography and psychology.

Principal Subjects

Agricultural Biotechnology, Agricultural Economics, Agriculture, Animal Science, Biochemistry, Biological Sciences of Agriculture, Biology, Biotechnology, Chemistry, Computing Science, Countryside and Environmental Management, Crop Science, Crop and Soil Science, Environmental Microbiology, Environmental Science, Forestry, Genetics, Geography, Geology and Petroleum Geology, Human Life Sciences, Mathematics, Neuroscience, Pharmacology, Physiology, Plant Science, Psychology, Soil Science, Statistics, Tropical Environmental Science, Zoology.

MA Y450

The traditional Scottish three-year non-honours degree which combines breadth of study and flexibility of choice in the arts, sciences and social sciences with advanced study in two or more subjects. There is a great range of almost 60 subjects to choose from. Full details are given in the prospectus.

Principal Subjects

Accountancy, Agricultural Economics, Biblical Studies, Celtic, Celtic Civilisation, Church History, Computing Science, Countryside and Environmental Management, Cultural History, Economic History, Economics, English, English and Scottish Literature, European Studies, French, Gaelic, Geography, German, Hispanic Studies (Latin American), Hispanic Studies (Spanish), History of Art, History, Historical Studies, International Relations, Jurisprudence, Management Studies, Mathematics, Philosophy, Politics, Psychology, Sociology, Statistics.

ANGLIA Poly Univ

Combined Sciences Y100

A combination of three science subjects (roughly in equal proportions). Four modules are studied in each subject in each year. It is designed for students needing a broad science education (eg teaching).

Principal Subjects

Animal Behaviour, Audio technology, Biomedical Science, Cell & Molecular Biology, Chemistry, Computer Science, Ecology & Conservation, Environmental Biology, Geology, Instrumentation Electronics, Mathematics, Microbiology, Physics, Statistics, Psychology.

Negotiated Route Y600

The Negotiated Route Scheme is intended to enable students to compose programmes of modules which may be chosen from more than one degree course. The Scheme is particularly suitable for mature students wishing to claim credit for prior learning or experience. Applicants are invited to submit proposals, with advice from the University, detailing this route. Contact the Negotiated Route Coordinator at the Cambridge address, in the first instance.

Negotiated Route Y601

This as a Negotiated Route to enable students to study two or three programmes of modules not normally offered as a combined honours degree course.

BANGOR, Univ of WALES

Environmental Planning and Management Y401

This course is suitable for students with an interest in the environment and associated planning and management strategies. Throughout there is an emphasis on relating theory to practical experience. The main objectives are to study the principal environmental planning systems of Britain and to examine strategies for managing specific environments. Comparative studies will be made of world-wide, and particularly European, examples. The course aims to extend students' understanding of the biosphere and the socio-economic bases of our environmental inheritance.

Principal Subjects

Environmental Planning, Management.

BARNSLEY COLLEGE

Pure Science Foundation Y100

In this foundation year, science subjects are studied by a variety of methods including lectures and practical laboratory sessions. Tutorial support and student centred learning materials are also available. Three subjects are chosen from Biology, Chemistry, Mathematics, Physics, Additional Biology and Additional Mathematics. Assessment is by end of year examinations and continuous assessment of course work. The course can lead to BSc (Hons) Pure Science at Sheffield University in any of Chemistry, Physics, Biochemistry, Ecology, Molecular Biology, Physiology, Computer Science, Anatomy and Cell Biology, Biological Sciences, Genetics, Neuroscience, Plant Sciences, Mathematics, Animal and Plant Biology, Biomedical Science, Microbiology, Pharmacology, Zoology.

Table 72
Course Descriptions

Humanities Y301

In Year 1, students select 5 subjects from History, Literature, Politics and International Relations, Classical Studies and Archaeology, English Language and Communication Studies, Philosophy, Geographical Studies plus Study Skills and Information Technology. In Years 2 and 3, students select 2 from History (with Archaeology option), Literature (with language option), Politics and International Relations, Geographical Studies. Field trips will be an integral part of the course where appropriate. Assessment is by 50% course work, 50% examinations. Mature applicants who do not have the entry qualifications for the 3-year course may apply for the 4-year extended degree.

Extended Degree in Humanities Y302

In Year 0, students select 3 subjects from History, Literature, Politics, Communication Studies, Philosophy, European Studies plus Study Skills. Assessment is by 50% course work, 50% examinations. Successful students proceed to Year 1 of BA Humanities degree.

Combined Studies Y400

This Honours Degree programme is both focused and flexible. Students join one of seven Pathways: Fine Art; Design; Journalism; Media; Performing Arts; Sport, Recreation and Tourism or Social Science. Full-time students follow six modules of study in each of the three years of the course, at least four but no more than five of these from their own Pathway. The remaining one or two modules may be chosen from another Pathway or from among additional units in Computing, Humanities, Music etc.

Univ of BATH

Natural Sciences Y160,Y161

This broadly-based degree is modular in structure drawn from biological sciences, the physical and engineering sciences. The course will be available with management, modern language and sports science options.
Principal Subjects
Biology, Chemistry, Materials Science, Mathematics, Physics.

BATH COLL of HE

Combined Awards Y400

Bath College's Modular Scheme enables you to tailor your studies to your individual needs and interests. The emphasis is on flexibility and student choice. Most subjects and awards offer a variety of modules from which you can choose, and you can adjust your selection of modules as your studies progress. Requests to change the subjects being studied are also considered sympathetically on an individual basis.

Full-time students study six modules per year, three in the Autumn semester and three in the Spring semester. The scheme is also open to part-time students who can take one to four modules a year.

The Scheme includes a variety of awards: Specialised Awards eg BA/BSc (Honours) with Qualified Teacher Status; Single Awards eg BA (Honours) History; and Combined Awards (pairs of subjects in Joint or Major/Minor combinations). Specialised and Single Awards are listed in the prospectus, and have their own UCAS codes. Use Y400 when applying for a Combined Award.

The Combined Awards allow students to study two subjects, either as a Joint Combination or as Major/Minor combinations. The aim of the Combined Awards is to provide a flexible programme of study extending across the arts, humanities, social sciences and environmental sciences. You can choose combinations which complement each other or offer a contrasting experience, eg English and History, or Environmental Biology and Study of Religions. As well as your subject studies, there is a limited number of elective modules. You can use these to take extra modules in the subjects for which you are registered, or, depending on availability, they can be chosen from other subjects, to broaden your interests or meet particular career needs. In the first year, you take two introductory modules in each of the two subjects for which you are registered. The other two modules are electives, which are selected during induction week from a wide range on offer (subject to availability and timetabling). A full list of the available modules is provided in the student handbook, which you receive at registration. In the second and third years, you take a specified minimum number of modules in each of your two subjects, including any compulsory modules. The minimum number will depend upon whether you are registered for a Major/Minor or Joint route. Additionally, you may take up to two elective modules.

Joint and Major/Minor programmes of study lead to either BA Honours or BSc Honours, depending upon the subject combination chosen, eg BA (Honours) English and History, BSc (Honours) Sociology with Geography. Please check in the prospectus that the chosen combination of subjects is available. Some subjects are available as Minor only, or as Minor or Joint only.
Subjects Available
Applicable Mathematics, Business Studies, Creative Studies in English, Cultural Studies, Design & Technology, English Studies, Environmental Biology, Food Studies, Geography, Global Futures, Health Studies, History, International Education, Irish Studies, Mass Communications, Music, Psychology, Remote Sensing & Geographic Information Systems, Sociology, Study of Religions.

Table 72
Course Descriptions

1589

Diploma of Higher Education Y460

As well as its degree programmes, Bath College also provides applicants with the opportunity to follow the DipHE programme (two years full-time or part-time equivalent). Diploma students are registered for two subjects on admission, and follow the same patterns of study as students registered for years one and two of Bath College's Combined Awards degree programmes (see entry for details).

We believe that the DipHE is attractive to students who are seeking only a two year course, or who have no clear degree end point in mind at the time of application. It is particularly attractive to mature students resident in the Bath/Bristol region, and plays a major role in our widening access into higher education. We do recognise that for most students the DipHE is a 'staging post' towards a higher award. On completion of the DipHE, most of our students successfully apply to join one of our degree awards, though some transfer to another HE institution. We should emphasise that transfer is not automatic; it is dependent upon satisfactory academic progress. Some subjects and subject combinations are only available to Diploma level. Students intending to progress further must make sure that their particular route is available to degree level. See the prospectus for further details. Please check in the prospectus that the chosen combination of subjects is available.

Subjects Available

Applicable Mathematics, Art, Business Studies, Creative Studies in English, Cultural Studies, Design & Technology, English Studies, Environmental Biology, Food Studies, Geography, Global Futures, Health Studies, History, International Education, Irish Studies, Mass Communications, Music, Psychology, Remote Sensing & Geographic Information Systems, Sociology, Study of Religions, Textile Design Studies.

Univ of BIRMINGHAM

Mechanical Engineering, Manufacturing and Management Y600

The main aim of this programme is to produce graduates with entrepreneurial ability as well as skills in engineering and executive management.

The programme leads to a Master of Engineering and Management degree, and includes the following subject areas: mechanical engineering, economics, marketing, industrial relations, industrial design, production engineering and an optional language. In the third and fourth years students specialise in Manufacturing, Design or Entrepreneurial Engineering.

Principal Subjects

Management, Manufacturing, Mechanical Engineering.

Univ of BRADFORD

Interdisciplinary Human Studies Y402

Aims to make use of several ways of thinking - philosophical, literary, sociological, psychological - traditionally pursued as separate disciplines to illuminate some of the more important topics in the study of human beings. Built on the assumption that the understanding of people and their affairs is best approached from an interdisciplinary perspective. Thorough grounding in basic component subjects, with opportunity to concentrate on a particular aspect later on - though still from an interdisciplinary perspective. Links rigorous intellectual thought to a wide range of contemporary social and ethical issues. Considerable emphasis on continuous assessment of course work rather than formal examinations.

Principal Subjects

Communications, Literature, Philosophy, Psychology, Sociology.

BRADFORD & ILKLEY Comm COLL

Combined Studies Y200

The Combined Studies programme offers students a range of opportunities at higher education level. It allows you the opportunity to build a programme of studies which meets your own vocational, academic and personal needs. In consultation with College Tutors you design a programme of studies which develops the skills, knowledge and understanding which you need to gain. In this way, it is possible for you to design a course which draws on modules from our established range of higher education courses but combines them together in a way which is particular to your individual needs and interests. The programme operates on both the Bradford and Ilkley Campuses. It is a credit based system; all modules of study included in the programme have been given a credit rating and it is possible for students, by acquiring sufficient credit points, to gain a range of University of Bradford qualifications, eg Certificate of Higher Education, Degree, Honours Degree and College Certificates and Diplomas.

The programme allows for the possibility of giving students credit for their prior learning whether this was gained on other courses, knowledge acquired through 'in-house' company training or areas of expertise developed through a professional context or personal interest. Examples of modules which are available under the programme would include: Art, Business Economics, Business Organisation, Community Studies, Drama, European Business Environment, Historical Studies, Human Studies, Information Technology, Language Studies including European Languages, Leisure and Society, Organisation Studies, Psychology, Sociology, South Asian Studies, Trade Union Studies, Urban Studies, Welfare Rights, Women's Studies. Each study module is normally taught for two hours per week.

In addition to the wide range of taught modules available, students undertake a range of independent studies. Independent study allows you the opportunity to design and follow part of your own programme of study under the supervision of a nominated tutor.

Table 72
Course Descriptions

Univ of BRIGHTON

Humanities Y300

This interdisciplinary degree uses a range of approaches from philosophy, cultural theory, modern history, political theory and economic analysis to investigate social and political issues in Britain and the contemporary world in a framework designed to foster the development of transferable intellectual and communicative skills.

Principal Subjects

Modern History, Philosophy, Politics.

BRISTOL, Univ of the W of England

Science Foundation Year Y120

This programme of study is intended for those who do not have the necessary qualifications for entry to the first year of named degree awards within the Faculty of Applied Sciences. On entry, students are admitted to one of the following named award routes which are extended by one year to include the science foundation year:

Applied Biological Sciences
Applied Chemical Sciences
Biomedical Sciences
Business Studies with Combined Science
Combined Sciences
Environmental Chemistry
Environmental Health
Environmental Science
Science, Society and the Media

Brunel: Univ of W. London

Foundations of Science Y100

Provides a route for students who lack the required science qualifications to undertake any course in the faculty of science after successful completion of a foundation year. Students register for a BSc degree and choose a particular discipline at the end of the foundation year. A compulsory core of mathematics, physics, study skills and project, supplemented by options in biology/biochemistry, chemistry and further project work. The department of mathematics and statistics hosts all students and provides regular tutorial and pastoral support.

Natural Sciences Y160

Broadly-based honours degree course designed for students who do not wish to study a particular field of science in depth (because they have a broad range of interests, or perhaps because they wish to keep open a wide spectrum of career options) or for whom the additional experience and maturity gained from a four-year thin sandwich course may be inappropriate. In the first two years of the course four subjects are studied from biology, biochemistry, chemistry, physics, mathematics, and computer science, and in their final year students will specialise in two subjects.

Univ of BUCKINGHAM

Politics, Economics and Law Y618

This offers courses in political institutions, political theory (both historical and analytical) and European politics, the principles of economics and the history of economic thought and public law. In addition, students can choose options from a wide range of economics courses (including money and banking and the economics of Europe) and law courses (including contract, tort, crime, and labour law)

Principal Subjects

Economics, Law, Politics.

Modern History, Politics and English Literature Y651

This course offers an honours degree in the combined disciplines of Modern History, English Literature and Politics. Links are fostered between these subjects, the emphasis in English Literature being on the historical context rather than literary theory. The department's strength is British History and Literature of the 19th century. The politics element of the course is designed to complement the previous disciplines and equip students with a thorough knowledge of modern political institutions and political theories, both historical and analytical.

Principal Subjects

English Literature, Modern History, Politics.

Table 72
Course Descriptions

1591

CAMBRIDGE Univ

Natural Sciences Y160
A broadly based course, in which 3 experimental sciences are studied in the first year, plus one of two Mathematics courses. Specialisation in a single subject is only possible in the third year.
Principal Subjects
Anatomy, Animal Biology, Astrophysics, Biochemistry, Biochemistry and Molecular Biology, Biology of Cells, Biology of Organisms, Chemical Engineering, Chemistry, Crystalline State, Ecology, Fluid Mechanics, Genetics, Geological Sciences, History & Philosophy of Science, Materials and Mineral Sciences, Materials Science & Metallurgy, Mineralogy and Petrology, Molecular Cell Biology, Neuroscience, Pathology, Pharmacology, Physics, Physiology, Plant Sciences, Psychology, Quantitative Biology, Zoology.

Univ of CENTRAL LANCASHIRE

Combined Honours Programme Y400
A modular programme which allows students to combine subjects across all disciplines. Students study three subjects in the first year before choosing two subjects for their eventual named major/minor or joint honours award. Applicants must refer to the prospectus for details of the timetable system for subject combinations and for information on specific subject entry requirements.
Principal Subjects
Accounting, American Literature, American Studies, Applied Microbiology, Applied Physics, Astronomy, Audio Visual Med Stud, Biochemistry, Business, Business Information Systems, Chemistry, Computing, Creative Design for Fashion, Cultural Studies, Deaf Studies, Design History, Design Studies, Development Studies, Economics, Education Studies, Electronics, English, Environmental Management, European Studies, Fashion Promotion and Media, French/Bus French, Geography, German/Bus German, Health Studies, History, Italian, Japanese, Journalism, Law, Linguistics, Management, Manufacturing, Marketing, Mathematics, Media Technology, Organisation Studies, Philosophy, Physiology/Pharmacology, Politics, Psychology, Public Relations, Race & Ethnic Studies, Social Policy, Sociology, Spanish/Bus Spanish, Statistics, Tourism & Leisure, Visual Studies, Women's Studies.

CHESTER COLL

BA/BSc Combined Subjects (4 Year) Franchised Y400
This four-year programme is designed for mature applicants who would like to study for a degree but may lack the formal qualifications for direct entry to higher education. The first year is spent at the Welsh College of Horticulture where students choose one of two pathways into years two, three and four of their combined honours degree at Chester College. The Environmental Studies Route entails the study of plant and animal biology and their relationship to our physical environment. The Humanities and Design Route consists of language and literature studies, the examination of historical developments in culture and the use of land, and the use of natural forms in the design of gardens, landscapes and works of art. Information Technology is an integral part of both routes. During the second, third and fourth years, students will choose from a list of suitable subjects leading to a combined honours BA or BSc degree.
Principal Subjects
Cultural Studies, Environmental Science, Plant & Animal Biology.

DE MONTFORT Univ

Combined Sciences Y100
This course is offered jointly by Boston College and De Montfort University. In addition to school and college leavers, this course is particularly suitable for mature students who wish to return to study, for whom special provision is made to gain entry and specific tutorial support is provided.
In the first year of the course three options are studied from the following: Psychology, Biology, Chemistry or Physics. In addition to the main study options students will undertake compulsory modules in Professional Skills which are designed to complement the subjects studied, and to develop certain general skills. In the second year, two of the main subject options will be carried forward from year one and studied in greater depth.
Principal Subjects
Biology, Chemistry, Physics, Human Psychology.

Combined Arts-Humanities (FP) Y300
Students qualify for a degree named by the subjects in which they chose to specialise. Each of the 17 subject areas offers a number of courses from which students select a programme of study to suit individual needs. The extent to which specialisation occurs depends on the pattern of study selected. The academic year is divided into two semesters and full time students are normally required to undertake four courses each semester. Each course has been designed to require 120 hours of student learning time per semester and the amount of time students need to devote to attending lectures and workshops is determined by the nature of the subject or the courses chosen. Courses in the scheme are offered at two levels. Level 1, the introductory level, is normally completed by full-time students in two semesters (one academic year). Level 3 is normally completed in a further four semesters (two academic years). The scheme is designed to lead to the award of BA honours degree after three years of full-time study. For students wishing to pause in their studies, or terminate them, Certificate and Diploma of Higher Education awards are also available, after the acquisition of 8 Level 1 and 8 Level 3 Credits respectively.

Table 72
Course Descriptions

Students register on the Combined Honours programme and nominate subjects. The scheme is designed to allow students to take a broad-based set of courses at Level 1, perhaps sampling subjects of which they had little or no previous experience. If, as a result of gaining some understanding of a range of subjects, students wish to change their initial subject registration, they are able to do so provided a sound case can be advanced, and the subject areas into which transfer is proposed are not already oversubscribed. Every course produces an outline which spells out the way the course will be delivered, books which need to be bought and read, tools or equipment required, and how and when students will be assessed.

In order to help students acquire skills which will be invaluable in both the academic world and the world of work, all students take a course in Communication and Professional Studies at Level 1. CPST develops team skills and covers research and planning, word-processing use of audio-visual aids and report-writing. Oral communication is practised through practical presentations, while group work includes problem-solving and working to deadlines.

Principal Subjects

American Studies, Arts Management, South Asian Studies, Education, English, French Studies, German Studies, Hispanic Studies, History, History of Art and Design, Jain Studies, International Relations, Media Studies, Performing Arts, Politics, Fine Art, Women's Studies.

Joint Arts-Humanities (FP) Y301

Students qualify for a degree named by the subjects in which they chose to specialise. Each of the 14 subject areas offers a number of courses from which students select a programme of study to suit individual needs. The extent to which specialisation occurs depends on the pattern of study selected. The academic year is divided into two semesters and full time students are normally required to undertake four courses each semester. Each course has been designed to require 120 hours of student learning time per semester and the amount of time students need to devote to attending lectures and workshops is determined by the nature of the subject and the approach of the courses chosen. Courses in the scheme are offered at two levels. Level 1, the introductory level, is normally completed by full-time students in two semesters (one academic year). Level 3 is normally completed in a further four semesters (two academic years). The programme is designed to lead to the award of BA honours degree after three years of full-time study. For students wishing to pause in their studies, or terminate them, Certificate and Diploma of Higher Education awards are also available, after the acquisition of 8 Level 1 and 8 Level 3 Credits respectively.

Students register on the Joint Honours programme in two subjects. However, the scheme is designed to allow students to take a broad-based set of courses at Level 1, perhaps sampling subjects of which they had little or no previous experience. If, as a result of gaining some understanding of a range of subjects, students wish to change their initial subject registration, they are able to do so provided a sound case can be advanced, and the subject areas into which transfer is proposed are not already oversubscribed. Every course produces an outline which spells out the way the course will be delivered, books which need to be bought and read, tools or equipment required, and how and when students will be assessed. In order to help students acquire skills which will be invaluable in both the academic world and the world of work, all students take a course in Communication and Professional Studies at Level 1. CPST develops team skills and covers research and planning, word-processing, use of audio-visual aids and report-writing. Oral communication is practised through practical presentations, while group work includes problem-solving and working to deadlines.

Principal Subjects

American Studies, Arts Management, English, French Studies, German Studies, Hispanic Studies, History, History of Art and Design, Media Studies, International Relations, Performing Arts, Politics, South Asian Studies, Fine Art.

Combined Studies (FP) Y400

Students normally study three subjects along with professional skills in the first year, some of which require no previous knowledge. Two of these subjects are carried on to the second and final years, one becoming the major subject in the final year. The course, through its modular structure, has routes leading to a unique range of exemptions from membership requirements of professional bodies (see subject descriptions for further details). The Combined Studies course offers a wide range of subjects. Offers of a place will normally be made on the basis of the student's expressed interests. However, all applicants can be counselled regarding their subject choice before an offer is made, if they wish. In addition to study facilities on the University campus, special arrangements have been made to offer the first year in the most popular subjects at selected colleges listed above. These different locations enable mature students to complete the first year of their degree successfully before relocating to Leicester. The course has a modular credit structure and all applicants to whom an offer is made will receive a course handbook explaining that structure. Students are carefully counselled to help them in their final selection of subjects before the second year. All permitted subject combinations have strong contemporary vocational relevance.

Principal Subjects

Accounting, Biology, Chemistry, Computing, Computing - Enhanced Route, Human Resource Management, Language Studies - French, Language Studies - German, Law, Law - Qualifying route, Management Science, Marketing, Mathematical Science, Physics, Psychology of Human Communication, Human Psychology.

Combined Studies (Extended Sciences) Y108

This course is offered jointly by Boston College and De Montfort University. In addition to school leavers, this course is particularly suitable for mature students who wish to return to study. This degree is an extended form, where an additional foundation year is built into the course. The foundation year enables candidates who do not have the usual A level entry requirements to gain the necessary background in Biology, Chemistry, Physics and Mathematics. On successful completion of the foundation year students may elect to study a Combined Studies degree or the DipHE (Combined Sciences). In the degree course the level one students study Professional Skills and three subject options. Two of these subjects are carried on to levels 2 and 3, one becoming the major subject in the final year. The degree route includes the subject option of Computing, whilst the DipHE route includes the subject option of Psychology. Not every subject combination is possible, therefore applicants should consult the University Prospectus or Programme booklet for details.

Principal Subjects

Biology, Chemistry, Computing, Mathematics, Physics.

Letts STUDY GUIDES
THE INDEPENDENT

Table 72
Course Descriptions

1593

BA/BSc Modular Studies Joint Honours & Combined Honours Y600
Students select TWO subjects (Joint Honours) or THREE subjects (Combined Honours) from the following: Accounting, American Studies, Arts Management, Computing, Education, English, English for Specific Purposes, European Studies, Fine Art, History, History of Art & Design, Human Resource Management, International Relations, French Studies, German Studies, Hispanic Studies, Law, Management Science, Marketing, Mathematical Sciences, Media Studies, Performing Arts, Politics, Psychology of Human Communication, South Asian Studies, Women's Studies.

Univ of DERBY

Combined Subject Programme (CAMS) Y600
This highly flexible Modular Scheme offering over 50 subjects enables you to be the architect of your Combined Subject Programme. In Stage 1 you choose three subjects. The selection of additional modules allows you to shape the programme to your particular needs. In Stages 2 and 3 you can specialise in two subjects in a Major Subject Pathway (Major/Minor), or in a Joint Subject Pathway (Joint/Joint), or you can continue with all three for a Minor Subject Pathway (Minor/Minor/Minor). A system of timetable zones enables you to confirm that your chosen subject combination is available.
Principal Subjects
Accounting, American Studies, Applicable Mathematics, Applied Studies, Architectural Design, The Healing Arts, Biology, Business Administration, Business Psychology, Computer Studies, Dance, Eco Design, Economics, Education, Environmental Monitoring and Management, Environmental Studies, European Studies, Experience of Writing, Fine Art, Film and Television, French, Geography, Geology, German, Heritage and History, Heritage Conservation, History of Art and Photography, History of Design, History, Human Resource Management, Information Systems, Law, Literature, Local History, Management, Marketing, Music, Music Technology, Photography and Time Based Media, Product Design, Psychology, Religions, Culture & Belief, Russian, Sociology, Spanish, Statistics, Technology Management, Theatre Studies, Tourism, Visual Communications.

DONCASTER COLL

Combined Studies Y300
See prospectus for further details.
Principal Subjects
Combined Studies, Social and Employment Studies, Social and Literary Studies, Social and Urban Studies.

Univ of DUNDEE

Science Y100
The degree provides a flexible balance between breadth and depth of study. Courses are available at three levels: first, second and third science. Seven courses are taken over the three years of study and of these at least two must be at second science level. Within this structure the student has considerable scope for determining the content of his/her programme of study.
Principal Subjects
Accountancy, Anatomical Sciences, Biochemistry, Biology, Botany, Economics, Electronics, Environmental Science, Microbiology, Molecular Biology, Pharmacology, Physiological Sciences, Psychology, Zoology.

MA Combined Honours Y300
The course offers combinations of three subjects from those available for Joint Honours in the Faculty of Arts and Social Sciences. The choice of Combined Honours subjects is made by students, subject only to any timetabling constraints. Practical French, German or Spanish may be included within a Combined Honours degree.
Principal Subjects
American Studies, Business Economics and Marketing, Contemporary European Studies, Economics, Education, English, Environmental Science, Financial Economics, Geography, Mathematics, Modern History, Philosophy, Political Science, Psychology, Social Work.

MA Arts and Social Sciences Y400
The degree is designed to achieve maximum flexibility to meet the differing needs of individual students. Courses are available at three levels: general, intermediate and advanced. In order to obtain the degree, ten credits must be accumulated. Each general or intermediate course counts as one credit and an advanced course gains two credits. Each student must take at least one course to advanced level and must include courses in three different subjects during the three years of study. In addition to the Principal Subjects which can be studied throughout, the following subjects are available for part of the course: Practical French, Business Law, Information Processing, Information Technology, or a Science subject.
Principal Subjects
American Studies, Business Economics and Marketing, Contemporary European Studies, Economics, Education, English, Environmental Science, Financial Economics, Geography, Mathematics, Modern History, Philosophy, Political Science, Psychology, Social Work.

Table 72
Course Descriptions

Univ of DURHAM

Natural Sciences Y160

An honours course designed primarily for students who wish to pursue a broad-based, but in-depth science course which allows various degrees of specialisation. Students commonly study 3-5 subjects during the three years of the course, including subjects taken for the first time in the second year. The degree also caters for the requirements of many applicants who might be considering a joint honours course, in that combinations of two subjects may be taken throughout the course leading to a named Joint degree in those two subjects. Certain course combinations may not be compatible due to timetable constraints. It is possible to include subjects from other faculties, up to a maximum of one third of a degree and subject to timetable constraints.

Principal Subjects

Anthropology, Applied Physics, Archaeology, Biology, Chemistry, Computer Science, Electronic Engineering, Geography, Geology, Mathematics, Philosophy, Physics, Psychology.

Social Sciences Combined Y220

This combined studies course is intended for those who wish to pursue a broad-based course covering several social science disciplines or for those who wish to pursue a theme of study such as business, which embraces a number of diverse subjects. To maintain continuation of study, students are expected to take courses from three subjects throughout all three years. Some subject combinations may be incompatible - consult prospectus.

Principal Subjects

Anthropology, Archaeology, Economics, Geography, History, Islamic Studies, Management Studies, Philosophy, Politics, Psychology, Social Policy, Sociology.

Arts Combined Y300

This combined studies course offers applicants the opportunity to follow a broad-based degree pattern, in which three subjects are studied over three years. Students have the chance to continue with subjects with which they are familiar at A level and develop interests in areas new to them. In the majority of cases, Combined Honours students take in each subject a proportion of the course followed by specialist students and work to the same level, thereby achieving a high standard of attainment across a broad range. Some subject combinations may not be possible: Please see prospectus. Applicants wishing to study three modern languages should apply for Modern Languages (T900).

Principal Subjects

Ancient History, East Asian History, English, French, German, Greek, Greek and Roman Civilisation, Italian, Latin, Linguistics, Mathematics (Applied), Mathematics (Pure), Middle Eastern and Islamic Studies, Music, Philosophy, Russian, Russian Studies, Spanish, Theology.

Univ of EAST ANGLIA

Economic and Social Studies (4 years) Y200

A four year degree designed for students who do not have the traditional qualifications to take a degree. First year: a foundation year consisting of equal study of Economics, History, Sociology and Politics. Second year: progression on to one of the degree courses offered by the School of Economic and Social Studies.

Principal Subjects

Economics, Social Studies.

Anthropology, Archaeology and Art History Y400

A three year degree looking at human visual culture from the standpoints of the three disciplines which explore art, architecture and display.

First year: units in the methods of the history and anthropology of art taught alongside a modern foreign language. Second year: three units in archaeology of landscape, architecture and the urban environment, three units in art history and anthropology of art. Third year: units in two of the three disciplines plus a dissertation combining all three.

Principal Subjects

Art History, Archaeology, Anthropology.

Philosophy, Politics and Economics Y616

A programme combining study of philosophy, politics and economics. Understanding how human aspirations, political institutions and economic forces relate to one another. Questions of theory, practice and ethics are treated together in two interdisciplinary modules available only to P.P.E. students: public choice and aspects of explanation.

Principal Subjects

Philosophy, Economics, Politics, Natural Sciences

Course Code Y160

A four-year programme leading to a BSc Honours degree suitable for mature students without standard university entrance qualifications or students with A levels in non-science subjects. Year 1 foundation year: biology, chemistry, mathematics and physics studied. From year 2, a main subject and two subsidiary subjects chosen from: biological sciences, chemical sciences, environmental sciences, mathematics and physics. Students may specialise further as course proceeds. Direct entry to year 2 possible with suitable science/mathematics A levels. Transfer to other science or mathematics courses possible at end of foundation year in appropriate cases.

Table 72 1595
Course Descriptions

Univ of EAST LONDON

Three-Subject Degree Y600

This course is suitable for both those who wish to construct broad-ranging programmes of study and those who have not yet finalised their choice of subjects. Students select three subject areas from the thirty seven on offer from across the University and study these in equal proportions over their first full-time year (or part-time equivalent). There are no restrictions on subject combinations though there are some timetabling constraints (contact the University for further details). At the end of the first full-time year, students may continue with all three subjects or may drop one so as to continue with two in approximately equal proportions.

Negotiated Degree Programme Y401

This provision is aimed at students who wish to construct an individualised programme of study which matches their past experience and interests and which they may study at their own pace. Each component of study, which may be drawn from any of the University's courses, from workplace projects, from independent study etc is credit-rated and students must accumulate 360 credits for an honours degree or lower amounts for other awards within the scheme. In every case the proposed programme must demonstrate coherence and be agreed. Credit for prior learning, whether by means of study on a course or from experience, may be obtained.

Extended Science Y108

Upon completion of this course, students will proceed to the appropriate BSc and BSc Hons course. The choice of final course may be determined after commencement of study.

Univ of EDINBURGH

BSc (Social Science) Y200

See prospectus for further details.
Principal Subjects
Archaeology, Architectural History, Business Studies, Canadian Studies, Economic & Social History, Economics, Geography, Politics, Psychology, Social Anthropology, Social Policy, Sociology.

MA General Y400

See prospectus for further details.
Principal Subjects
Ancient History, Arabic, Celtic, Chinese, Classical Archaeology, English Language, English Literature, French, German, Greek, History, History of Art, Italian, Japanese, Latin, Linguistics, Mathematics, Medieval History, Persian, Philosophy, Russian, Sanskrit, Scandinavian Studies, Scottish Ethnology, Scottish Historical Studies, Scottish Literature, Spanish.

Univ of Essex

European Studies T9Y4

Up to half the degree consists of courses in either one or two European languages. French is available only post A level but German, Russian or Spanish can be taken from beginners' or other appropriate level. Two "themes" are offered within the degree: in the Comparative Studies theme, a course in the European Enlightenment is taken with courses in art history, history, literature, philosophy, politics or sociology. In the Social Science variant there are courses in economics, history, law, politics and sociology. In both themes the emphasis is on the study of modern Europe, East and West. There are bridging seminars in the second and final years and the third year is spent in Europe.

Comparative Studies: Choice of Specialist Scheme Deferred Y400

If you are interested in a degree based on arts or humanities subjects but are not sure what subject or combination of subjects you wish to study, you can be admitted to the multidisciplinary First Year of the School of Comparative Studies under the Choice Deferred course code. You will have the opportunity to study four courses, one of which will be the European Enlightenment (the other available courses are listed below) and your final choice of degree can be made at the end of the First Year. History of Art in the Eighteenth Century, the Making of Early Modern Europe 1500-1770, Introduction to Linguistics, Literature, Introduction to Politics, Sociological Analysis I, a Modern Language, Introduction to Latin American, Introduction to Russia, Introduction to the United States.

Choice of Specialist Scheme Deferred (Social Sciences) Y201

If you are interested in a degree in the Social Sciences but are not sure what subject or combination of subjects you wish to study, you can be admitted to the multidisciplinary First Year in the School of Social Sciences under the Choice Deferred course code. You will have the opportunity to study four courses, most of which are listed below, and your final choice of degree can be made at the end of the First Year.
Introduction to Accountancy, Economic Theory and Policy, the Making of Early Modern Europe, Introduction to Linguistics, Introduction to Philosophy, Introduction to Politics, Introduction to Psychology, Sociological Analysis I, Computer Applications, Logic and Scientific Method, Mathematics, a modern language.

Table 72
Course Descriptions

Combined Studies (Honours) Y400

The Combined Studies degree scheme enables students to design their own study programme from Modules drawn from the University's full range of courses, subject to availability. Applicants can select from three to five subject areas, but should ensure that the group of subjects chosen does not already exist within a named award.

Principal Subjects

Accounting & Finance, American Studies, Astronomy, Art, Art History, Biological Science, Biotechnology, Building Management, Building Surveying, Business Studies, Chemical Engineering, Chemical Science, Civil Engineering, Computer Studies, Construction, Criminal Justice, Criminology, Design, Electronics, Energy & Environmental Technology, Energy Management, English Studies, English as a Foreign Language, Environment and Social Values (Green Studies), Environmental Pollution Science, Environmental Technology, Estate Management Surveying, Forensic Measurement, French, Geography, Geological Science, German, History, Image Processing, Information Systems, Information Technology, Instrumentation, Italian, Language/Linguistics, Law, Leisure & Tourism Management, Manufacturing, Marketing, Mathematics, Media Electronics, Media Studies, Medical Electronics, Minerals Surveying, Philosophy, Police Studies, Psychology, Public Management, Public Policy, Quantity Surveying, Recreation Management, Religious Studies, Signal Processing, Sociology, Software Engineering, Spanish, Sports Science, Statistics, Theatre & Media Drama, Welsh, Welsh Studies, Women's Studies, Economics, European Law.

GLASGOW Univ

MA Ordinary Y400

The core curriculum is built round the MA subjects listed in the UCAS Handbook but students can include: Anthropology, Education, Environmental Science, Exploring the Cosmos, Latin American Studies, Religion, Civil Law, Jurisprudence or MA (Social Sciences) or BSc courses in their curriculum. Please see prospectus for details.

Principal Subjects

Archaeology, Astronomy, Biblical Studies, Celtic Civilisation, Civil Law, Classical Civilisation, Computing Science, Czech, Economic & Social History, English Language, English Literature, Film & Television Studies, French Language & Literature, Gaelic, Geography, German, Greek, Hebrew (Classical), Hispanic Studies, History, History of Art, Humanities Computing, Italian, Latin (Humanity), Latin American Studies, Management Studies, Mathematics, Music, Philosophy, Physics, Polish, Political Economy, Politics, Psychology, Russian, Scottish History, Scottish Literature, Social Policy,Sociology, Statistics, Theatre Studies, Theology & Church History.

MA (Applied Social Sciences) Y203

At least half of the curriculum is formed from MA (Social Sciences) subjects listed in the UCAS Handbook. The core also involves a compulsory interdisciplinary Applied Social Sciences project in third year. Students can also study: Anthropology, Cities and Change, Housing, Economy and Society, Industrial Relations, Latin American Studies, Statistics, Accountancy, Civil Law, Jurisprudence, and MA (Arts) and BSc subjects listed in the UCAS Handbook.

Core Subjects

Economic and Social History, Geography, Management Studies, Philosophy, Political Economy (Economics), Politics, Psychology, Social Policy, Sociology.

GLASGOW CALEDONIAN Univ

BSC Science Y100

This programme has been designed to provide a broad based Science Education. Applicants who have at least one Science Higher and standard Grades in appropriate science subjects are eligible for entry to this programme. If after first year a student finds a particular subject interesting, transfer to a specialist science programme may be possible. The subjects studied are Biology, Chemistry, Psychology, Physics, Mathematics and Information Technology.

Univ of GREENWICH

Analytical Science with European Study Y101
See prospectus for further details.
Principal Subjects
Chemistry.

Humanities Y301
See prospectus for further details.
Principal Subjects
Literary Studies, Modern History, Philosophy, Politics, Society, Culture.

Table 72
Course Descriptions

1597

HERIOT-WATT Univ, EDINBURGH

BSc Combined Studies Ordinary and Honours Y100

This Honours or Ordinary degree programme is designed to provide increased flexibility in a student's choice of subject(s) and in particular to facilitate access to science and engineering for applicants without the standard qualifications for those subjects. The programme is based on the principle of credit accumulation and credit may be given for a wide range of prior studies. Students choose an agreed programme of study each year and are required to aggregate credits from at least three departments over the first and second years and from at least two departments in the third and fourth (Honours) years.

Principal Subjects

Actuarial Mathematics & Statistics, Biological Science, Building, Chemical Engineering, Chemistry, Civil Engineering, Computer Science, Electrical & Electronic Engineering, Mathematics, Mechanical Engineering, Physics.

BA Combined Studies Ordinary and Honours Y300

This Honours or Ordinary degree programme is designed to provide increased flexibility in a student's choice of subject(s). The programme is based on the principle of credit accumulation and credit may be given for a wide range of prior studies. Students choose an agreed programme of study each year and are required to aggregate credits from at least three departments over the first and second years, and from at least two departments in the third and fourth (Honours) years.

Principal Subjects

Accountancy, Business Organisation, Economics, Languages.

Univ of HERTFORDSHIRE

Combined Modular Scheme Y100/Y108/Y109

Applicants list two subjects on their application forms. A third Year 1 subject is chosen after induction week. Two or three subjects are continued in Year 2, with two subjects continued in Year 3. There is a wide choice of subjects but not every subject combination is possible. Applicants should consult the UCAS Handbook, University Prospectus, or Scheme Booklet for details. The title of the degree award is determined by the subject balance of the final year - eg BSc Astrophysics, BSc Environmental Studies with Business, BSc Computing and Psychology.

Principal Subjects

Applied Geology, Applied Physics, Applied Statistics, Astronomy, Business, Chemistry, Computing, Economics, Electronic Music, Electronics, Environmental Science, European Studies, Human Biology, Law, Manufacturing Systems, Mathematics, Operational Research, Philosophy, Psychology.

Univ of HUDDERSFIELD

Science (Extended) Y108

The BSc Science Foundation year is a conversion course which prepares students for entry to the following degree courses: BSc Chemistry (all pathways); BSc Catering and Food Management; BSc Environmental Analysis; BSc Food and Nutrition; BSc Human Ecology; BSc Molecular and Cellular Biology, BSc Podiatry. It prepares students whose GCE A level qualifications are in other disciplines, or who have qualifications of a vocational kind, for subsequent years of the above courses.

Principal Subjects

Catering & Food Management, Chemistry (all pathways), Environmental Analysis, Food and Nutrition, Human Ecology, Molecular and Cellular Biology, Podiatry.

Univ of HULL

Politics, Philosophy, Economics Y616

This degree encourages the study of a wider range of related courses while specialising, as far as you wish, in one of them. The syllabus emphasises points of contact between disciplines.

Principal Subjects

Economics, Philosophy, Politics.

JEWS' COLL (Univ of London)

Jewish Studies (3 Yrs) Y400

In year 1, students are enrolled for seven compulsory courses, generally two in Talmud and Jewish Law, three in Biblical studies, one in Contextual Studies and one in either Jewish history or Hebrew Grammar. In year 2, there is a measure of specialisation. Although the two courses in Biblical Studies and the two courses in Rabbinical Literature are compulsory, the remaining two courses can be selected from available courses. In year 3, the student is able to offer any five course units. One must be a research project.

Principal Subjects

Biblical Studies (Hebrew texts), Rabbinical Literature.

Table 72
Course Descriptions

KEELE Univ

Philosophy, Politics & Economics Y616
This honours degree course is taught jointly by the departments of Politics, Philosophy and Economics. Students study the three subjects equally throughout the three-year programme. The core courses in Philosophy cover the following areas: Principles of Philosophy, Moral and Political Philosophy. Politics introduces students to three main areas of study: Comparative Politics; Political Thought and Political Sociology. The Economics core courses cover Microeconomics, Macroeconomics and Quantitative and Theoretical and Applied Economics. In addition to the core courses students are able to choose special subjects from a wide range of options.
Principal Subjects
Economics, Philosophy, Politics.

Philosophy, Politics & Economics (4 Yrs) Y617
A four year honours degree programme, the first year of which is the Keele Foundation Year. The following three years are spent studying Politics, Philosophy and Economics equally. The core courses in Philosophy cover the following areas: Principles of Philosophy; Moral and Political Philosophy. Politics introduces students to three main areas of study: Comparative Politics, Political Thought and Political Sociology. The Economics core courses cover Microeconomics, Macroeconomics and Quantitative Methods and Theoretical and Applied Economics. In addition to the core courses students are able to choose special subjects from a wide range of options.
Principal Subjects
Economics, Philosophy, Politics.

Univ of KENT

The Visual and Performed Arts Y310
See prospectus for further details.

KING'S COLL LONDON (Univ of London)

European Studies T2Y3
See prospectus for further details.
Principal Subjects
French, German.

Afro-Portuguese, Brazilian and Religious Studies Y654
See prospectus for further details.
Principal Subjects
Afro-Portuguese, Brazilian Studies, Religious Studies.

KINGSTON Univ

Joint Honours Y100
The Science Foundation course feeds into a number of our Science courses listed within the main tables.

Univ of Wales, LAMPETER

Religion, Ethics and Society Y652
An interdisciplinary degree scheme drawing on the departments of English, History, Philosophy, and Theology and Religious Studies. The course involves a study of civilizations within the context of two of their most important determinants: religion and ethics. While these forces, and the connection between them, are central to the degree scheme, the course is very different from a traditional degree in Theology in that it is more philosophical, more broadly based, and, in its study of religion, by no means solely concerned with Christianity.
Principal Subjects
Ethics, Religion, Society.

Combined Honours Y400
Applicants will have a choice of three subjects.
Principal Subjects
Ancient History, Anthropology, Arabic, Archaeology, Cultural Studies in Geography, Church History, Classical Studies, English Literature, Greek, Geography Physical, History, Informatics, Islamic Studies, Latin, Management, Philosophical Studies, Religious Studies, Theology, Victorian Studies, Welsh, Welsh Studies.

Table 72
Course Descriptions

1599

LANCASTER Univ

Culture, Media & Communication Y400

Investigates current concepts of culture, and examines the effects of various media and social institutions in shaping our perceptions of ourselves and the world in which we live; also the cultural impact of social institutions such as the mass media. In the second and third years, students take a workshop-based course developing analytical and practical skills, including audio and video production.

Principal Subjects

Cultural Anthropology, Language & Social Life, Marketing, Media, Sociology & Psychology of Communication, Visual representation, Contemporary Culture.

History-Philosophy-Politics Y650

Students take equally proportioned courses in all three subjects throughout the degree. Students are encouraged to select their own courses to complement their interests in each of the subjects.

Principal Subjects

History, Philosophy, Politics.

Independent Studies Y410

This degree course offers the opportunity to construct an individual programme of study, based partly on orthodox courses taught by departments across the University, including Science and Management as well as Social Sciences and Humanities and partly on individual project or dissertation work. See prospectus for recent topics studied by students. There are no principal subjects in this degree course. Students will take subjects relevant to their proposed project, and the subjects can be chosen from any offered by the University (provided that any prior knowledge of a subject, if required, can be demonstrated).

Philosophy, Politics & Economics Y616

Students take equally proportioned courses in all three subjects throughout the degree. Students are encouraged to select their own courses to complement their interests in each of the subjects.

Principal Subjects

Philosophy, Politics, Economics.

Univ of LEICESTER

Combined Science Y100

An honours degree offering an unusually flexible scheme of study, with 26 subjects available from Science, Arts and Social Sciences. You can take as few as two subjects or as many as five. Many subjects have links with European institutions under the ERASMUS scheme so you may be able to spend some time in Europe. Please see Leicester University's prospectus for full details.

Principal Subjects

Applied Mathematics, Archaeology, Biological Sciences, Chemistry, Computer Science, Economics, Geography, Geology, History of Science, Physics, Psychology, Pure Mathematics.

Combined Arts Y300

This honours degree offers you the opportunity to study new subjects in combinations which are not normally available in other degrees, to give you a balanced combination of breadth and depth. You choose from a range of arts, social science, and science subjects, taking two subjects in all three years and a third subject in the first two years only. Many subjects have links with European institutions under the ERASMUS scheme so you may be able to spend some time in Europe. Please see Leicester University's prospectus for full details.

Principal Subjects

Ancient History, Archaeology, Economic & Social History, Economics, English, French, Geography, German, History, History of Art, Italian, Politics, Psychology, Pure Mathematics, Sociology. The following languages are available as ab initio one year courses: German, Italian, Latin, Spanish.

Sciences Foundation Course Y101

This one-year full-time course is designed mainly for mature students (over 21) or international students from outside the EU wishing to achieve a university science degree but currently not possessing the normal educational qualifications or background. Applications are also welcomed from those holding qualifications not appropriate to the chosen degree and from those with overseas qualifications.

The course leads directly into 3 and 4 year honours degrees in the Science Faculty in Biological Sciences, Chemistry, Combined Science, Computer Science, Geology, Mathematics and Physics. Core modules are: Information Technology and Study Skills. Three subjects from Biology, Chemistry, Mathematics, Further Mathematics, Physics, Computing, Economics, Geography and Statistics are also taken.

Table 72
Course Descriptions

Univ of LIVERPOOL

BA Combined Honours Y200

Several departments (mainly but not exclusively Architecture and Building Engineering, Civic Design, Economics and Accounting, Economic and Social History, English, Geography, History, Irish Studies, Law, Modern Languages, Politics and Communication Studies, Psychology and Sociology) cooperate to provide the taught content of this degree, which may be studied in one of three ways:

Mode 1: a 'two subject degree'
Mode 2: a degree combining several disciplines of demonstrable interrelationship;
Mode 3: a 'pathway' degree following a specific interdisciplinary route.

Principal Subjects

Archaeology, Biology, Classics, Communication Studies, Computer Science, Economic and Social History, Economics and Accounting, Egyptology, English Language and Literature, French, Geography, German, Hispanic Studies, History, History of Art, Irish Studies, Law, Mathematics, Philosophy, Politics, Psychology, Sociology, Third World Studies, Urban Studies, Women's Studies.

BA Combined Honours Y401

A multi-disciplinary, full-time undergraduate degree course leading to award of BA Honours. The study programme extends over three years, or four where a Modern Foreign Language is included. Three subjects are studied in the first year, two of which are then continued.

Principal Subjects

Ancient History, Archaeology, Biology, Catalan, Classics and Classical Studies, Computer Science, Earth Sciences, Economic and Social History, Economics, Egyptology, English, French, Geography, German, Hebrew (Classical), History, History of Art and Architecture, Irish Studies, Latin American Studies, Mathematics, Music, Philosophy, Politics, Popular Music, Portuguese, Psychology, Pure Mathematics, Russian and Soviet Studies, Sociology, Spanish, Women's Studies.

BSc Combined Honours Y100

The aim of this proposed new course is to cater for science-based students who for reasons of basic interest, or vocation, wish to study a combination of two disciplines in depth over a period of three years. Students may choose two subjects from those listed, although certain combinations may not be available. The two subjects may not take up all of the eight units studied in each year, so it may be possible to study one or two units in another subject area and so develop a third theme.

Principal Subjects

Archaeology, Biochemistry*, Computer Studies, Earth Science, Genetics*, Geography, Human Movement Science, Management, Materials Science, Mathematics, Microbiology*, Philosophy, Pharmacology, Physiology, Plant Science, Psychology, Zoology.

* Grouped subjects, only one of which may be chosen.

LIVERPOOL JOHN MOORES Univ

International Students Foundation Year Y600

The course provides a firm understanding of written and spoken English, mathematics and information technology, in order to enable international students to qualify for entry to a degree or diploma course at the University.

Principal Subjects

British Culture for International Students, English for International Students.

LONDON GUILDHALL Univ

Modular Programme Y400

The Modular Programme at London Guildhall University gives students the opportunity to study two or three subjects during Level 1 before committing themselves to a named degree programme. (Full-time students will normally take one year to complete Level 1, whilst part-time students will normally take between one and a half and two years.) Depending on the choices made on application, together with decisions made at the end of Level 1, students will be awarded single subject, joint or combined studies honours degrees upon successful completion of the course. Three types of course are available within the Modular Programme:

Single Honours - Deferred Specialist Degree: Students may select two Single Honours Deferred Specialist Degree subjects on application and decide at the end of Level 1 whether to specialise in one of these or continue to study both as a joint degree. Alternatively, one Single Honours Deferred Specialist degree subject may be chosen on application and combined with a joint and a minor subject. This can lead to a single subject, joint or combined honours degree.

Joint Honours Degrees: Any two subjects offered can be combined, subject to timetabling constraints and the limitations listed below. Students may defer their final choice of joint degree until the end of Level 1 by studying three joint degree subjects during Level 1, and dropping one of these at the end of that level. Alternatively, students may continue to study three subjects to gain a combined studies honours degree.

Letts STUDY GUIDES
THE INDEPENDENT

Table 72
Course Descriptions

1601

Minor Subjects: A minor may be studied to complement a single honours degree or as part of a combined studies degree. It represents around 25% of a degree content and is recorded on the degree certificate, eg BA(Hons) Geography with Economics. Limitations. Almost any combination of subject areas is possible, subject only to timetabling constraints. However, it is not possible to study the following combinations:

Sociology and Social Policy & Management (as Single Honours Deferred Specialist Degree subjects); -More than two languages (of these, only one not studied previously may be included)

For full details of the Modular Programme together with important information on how to apply, please refer to the undergraduate prospectus.

Principal Subjects

Accounting Studies, Business, Business Economics, Business Information Technology, Communications and Audio Visual Production Studies, Computing, Design Studies, Development Studies, Economics, English, Environmental Studies, European Studies, Financial Services, Fine Art, French, Furnishings, Furniture Design, Geography, German, Human Resource Management, Insurance, Interior Design, International Relations, Law, Marketing, Mathematics, Modern History, Multimedia Systems, Politics, Psychology, Social Policy and Management, Sociology, Spanish, Taxation.

Modular Programme Y420

Y420 courses involve study of Levels 1 and 2 at South Thames College. For Level 3, students transfer to London Guildhall University to gain a university degree. Alternatively, students may leave the College after Level 2 to gain a Diploma of Higher Education.

Principal Subjects

Accountancy, Business Information Technology, Computing, Economics, Politics.

Modular Programme Y421

Y421 courses involve study at Level 1 at Southwark College. For Levels 2+3 students transfer to London Guildhall University to gain a university degree. Alternatively students may leave the College after Level 1 to gain a Certificate of Higher Education.

Principal Subjects

Politics, Sociology, Modern History.

LSE: LONDON School of Economics (Univ of London)

Business Mathematics and Statistics Y240

This degree enables students who have enjoyed mathematics at A level to develop their skills in the areas of mathematics and statistics and at the same time apply them in areas relevant to Business by following courses available in more than one department at the School.

All students follow the common first year but in their second and third years they may choose options which will concentrate on different applied areas. The main pathways available are: Actuarial Science, Applicable Mathematics, Basic Statistics and Business Methods.

Principal Subjects

Actuarial Science, Applicable Mathematics, Applied Statistics, Business Methods.

Univ of MANCHESTER

BA (Econ) Honours Y200

In their first year students enter a broad-based economic and social science degree and take courses in five distinct subject areas. The second year is characterised by an opportunity for increased specialisation. By the third year a student must specialise in one or two areas of study.

BA Combined Studies Y300

An Arts-based degree which draws on the resources of 35 departments from four Faculties. Students are able to follow and develop interests in a number of subjects by combining them in various ways: thus students themselves have considerable control over the degree programme they construct. Students, in each year, choose six modules from two broad study areas (in the proportions four + two or three + three); alternatively, one module may be chosen from a third area consisting of skill modules (eg basic language courses, word-processing etc) thus giving a three + two + one pattern.

MANCHESTER METROPOLITAN Univ

Combined Studies (Foundation) Y108

This course is part of the Faculty of Science and Engineering Foundation Stage. Foundation years are provided for students who do not possess the requirements for many of the courses run by the Faculty. The Foundation Stage is an integral part of the course leading to a degree. Students accepted onto them are enrolled for the full duration of the Degree course (subject to passing the assessments). A Certificate of Credit will be issued to students on completion of the Foundation Stage. Although the content of the foundation years differs according to the course for which they are designed, the following subjects are an integral component: Mathematics, Physics and Information Technology.

Principal Subjects

Applicable Mathematics, Applied Physics, Biology, Business Mathematics, Chemistry, Computing Science, Computer Technology, Electronics, Environmental Studies, Manufacturing, Materials Science, Physics Studies, Polymer Science, Scientific Instrumentation.

Table 72
Course Descriptions

Humanities/Social Studies Y400

The course offers the chance to choose a multidisciplinary programme of three subjects in the first year from Economics, English, History, Languages (French or German or Spanish), Philosophy, Politics, Social and Economic History and Sociology. On this basis students may then specialise to honours level in a single subject (subject to approval) or may combine two or up to three subjects in the second and third years, either through an Equal Subject route, through a Major/Minor route in which one subject is weighted more than the other, or through a Three Subject route. French, German or Spanish may only be taken as part of an Equal Subject, Major/Minor or a Three Subject route. Where a language is taken as an Equal or Major subject students will follow a four year course of study, the third year of which will be completed in a Higher Education Institution in a country of the relevant language. In addition to the proposed single honours and existing joint honours subject programme, students may choose to follow certain Thematic Pathways, such as American Studies, European Studies or Women's Studies in which units from various subject areas can be combined in a structured fashion. Further Pathways are in the process of being developed.

Principal Subjects

Economics, English, French, German, History, Philosophy, Politics, Social & Economic History, Sociology, Spanish.

Interdisciplinary Studies (Options) Y416

The Diploma of Higher Education (Interdisciplinary) caters for highly motivated mature students who often do not possess the formal entry requirements. The course has a strong multidisciplinary foundation in the first year which enables students to make an informed choice of route to complete their studies. Students select units chosen from the 'Area Studies' of Aesthetics, Humanities, Social Science and Technology. On successful completion of the Diploma, most of our students progress immediately to a final year of study at the University, allowing them to graduate on one of the University's degrees.

MIDDLESEX Univ

Joint Honours Degree Programme Y400

The Joint Honours Degree Programme enables students to begin their degree level studies with a combination of subjects and to work within a flexible credit-based modular framework to determine their own balance between Joint Major or Major/Minor. Admissions is to two subjects chosen at application and in the first semester all students also take an elective module from another subject area. In a large number of subjects, Single Honours specialisation is possible from the second year, sometimes depending on performance in the first year assessments but often as a result of the student's own preferences as they develop through experience in the subject. Applicants MUST CHOOSE TWO SUBJECTS and are also advised to select a reserve choice: some combinations cannot be offered because of timetable clashes and details of how to choose a valid programme are given in the UCAS Handbook and the Prospectus. Please telephone us for advice if necessary.

Principal Subjects

Accounting, American Studies, Applied Computing, Art & Design History, Arts Practice in the Community, Asia-Pacific Studies, Biological Sciences, Business Economics, Business Information Systems, Business Policy, Business Studies, Christian Studies, Cognitive Science, Communication Studies, Computer Systems, Criminology, Cultural and Intellectual History, Dance, Drama & Theatre Arts, Economics, Education Design Technology, Education Studies, Electronics, English and Literary Studies, English for Business Communication, English Language and British Culture, Environment and Society, Environmental Science, European Policy Studies, Film Studies, French Studies, Geography, Geology, German,Health Studies, History, Human Resource Management, Information Technology, Italian, Law, Management, Manufacturing Management, Marketing, Mathematics, Mechanical Engineering, Media and Cultural Studies, Music, Pastoral Studies, Philosophy, Physical Geography, Politics and International Studies, Psychology, Social Policy, Social Research Methods, Sociology, Spanish, Statistics, Race and Culture, Teaching English as a Foreign Language, Technology, Telecommunications, Third World Studies, Women's Studies, Work-based Learning Studies, Writing and Publication Studies.

NAPIER Univ

Science with Management Studies Y1N1

This course is designed to give students with a science background a broad education which will prepare them for a wide range of careers in science or management. It allows flexibility because it involves studying a number of science subjects, as well as commerce and management, rather than specialising in a single subject. At the same time, it provides students with the skills and experience necessary to allow them to choose a career area with confidence. The course includes the opportunity of supervised work experience.

Principal Subjects

Business and Management.

Combined Studies (Credit Accumulation and Transfer Framework) Y400

Faculty of Arts and Social Science

Faculty of Engineering and Computing

Faculty of Health Studies

Napier Business School

Faculty of Science

Letts STUDY GUIDES
THE INDEPENDENT

Table 72
Course Descriptions
1603

The Credit Accumulation and Transfer Framework provides an extremely flexible scheme within which an undergraduate programme of study can be designed focused on an individual student's prior learning, personal goals and career development. Rather than follow named routes it is possible to select course units or modules from the University undergraduate provision and to construct a coherent Combined Studies programme which can lead to awards at Certificate, Diploma, Degree and Honours Degree level.

Univ of NEWCASTLE

Combined Studies in Science (BSc) Y100, Y101
Combined Studies in Science permits the study of a wide range of modules from those provided within the various single honours and joint honours degree courses in science. A limited number of modules may be chosen from subject areas outside science. To qualify for honours, 12 modules must be taken in each of the three years and, of these, at least 18 must be beyond stage one and at least 6 must be at stage three. Many of the subjects can be taken without previous experience. Y101 is a four year course which includes a foundation year of study.
Principal Subjects
Chemistry, Computing Science, Mathematics, Physics, Statistics, Surveying and Mapping Science, Astronomy and Astrophysics, Biological Sciences, Psychology.

Combined Studies (BA) Y400
Combined Studies offers a very flexible programme in which students study at least three, but no more than five subjects during the degree. In the first year students take three subjects. In the second and third years students take either two or three subjects in varying combinations. The majority of subjects can be studied without previous experience.
Principal Subjects
Accounting, Ancient History, Archaeology, Biblical Studies, Chinese, Computing Science, East Asian Studies, Education, Economics, English Linguistic Studies, English Literature, English Medieval Studies, Film Studies, French, Geography, German, Greek (Classical), Greek (New Testament), Greek and Roman Culture, Hindu Studies, History, History and Theory of Architecture, History of Art, Japanese, Korean, Latin, Mathematics, Music, Physical Education and Sports Studies, Politics, Portuguese, Psychology, Religious Studies, Sanskrit, Cosmos and Philosophical Traditions, Social Policy, Social Studies, Spanish and Latin America Studies, Education.

Univ of NORTH LONDON

Combined Honours - Science Y100
This scheme offers students the option of specialising in a single subject, OR of studying two subjects in a joint or major/minor pattern. The final award is a named degree whose title reflects the subject(s) studied although intermediate awards of Certificate or Diploma are available. All degree courses can be preceded by a Foundation Year.
Principal Subjects
Biochemistry, Biological Sciences, Business, Chemistry, Communications Engineering, Computer Electronics, Computing, Consumer Studies, Decision Systems, Ecological Sciences, Electronics, Information Systems, Information Technology, Mathematical Sciences, Mathematics, Microbiology, Nutrition, Philosophy, Physics, Polymers, Statistics.

Combined Honours - Humanities Y300
This flexible, unit-based scheme offers students the option of combining any 2 of 16 subjects, in either a joint (equal balance), or major/minor combination. There are opportunities for students to take free units from subjects they are not specialising in. The scheme welcomes mature students - some will have completed Access courses; others will be selected by interview.
Principal Subjects
Caribbean Studies, Classical Civilisation, Critical Theory, Education Studies, English, Film Studies, French, German, History, Humanities, IT, Irish Studies, Philosophy, South Asian Studies, Spanish and Latin American Studies, Theatre Studies, Women's Studies.

Combined Honours - Business Y400
The Combined Business Degree Scheme is designed for students who are interested in studying business subjects in more depth than on conventional business studies degrees. The scheme has a unit based modular structure where students are required to complete 24 units in the 3 year full time programme. Students follow two half degrees and the final degree is named after that combination of two half degrees.
Principal Subjects
Accounting, Arts Management, Business Modelling, Business Economics, Business Operations Management, Human Resource Studies, Hospitality Management, International Business, Law in Business, Economics, Leisure Studies, Marketing, Sports Management, Tourism Studies.

Combined Honours -Applied Social Science Y301
This modular scheme offers students the option of studying two subjects in a joint pattern (equal balance) or major/minor pattern. The final award is a named Honours Degree, reflecting the subject(s) studied, although intermediate awards of Certificate and Diploma are available
Principal Subjects
Applied Psychology, Communication & Cultural Studies, Health Studies, Information Studies, Policy Studies, Politics, Social Research.

Table 72
Course Descriptions

Combined Honours - Interfaculty Y600

The Interfaculty scheme allows students to combine subjects which are not otherwise available within any of the individual faculty modular schemes. On this basis any two subjects in the University may be combined to form joint (equal balance) or major/minor Honours degrees in these subjects depending on the balance between them, although some combinations may not be possible. The Interfaculty Office can advise on the academic viability of combinations. Some popular Interfaculty combinations have been given individual UCAS codes and prospective students should consult the University prospectus for further details.

Univ of NORTHUMBRIA

Combined Honours Y400 Carlisle College

The Combined Honours Programme (CHP) is designed to facilitate a very flexible entry route into the university. It is recognised that many students may wish to begin their study at university in a broader range of subjects than is provided by either single or dual-subject honours degrees. Many people at the point of application are not yet sure of their subject specialism and may wish to defer final choice.
Consequently, the CHP allows students to study in equal depth three subject areas from a broad choice spanning all of the University's five faculties.
The subjects available for CHP students are:
Business Administration, Education Studies, English, Environmental Management, History, Psychology, Sociology, Computing.

NORWICH: City COLL

BSc (Hons) Combined Science Y100

This course enables students to study a range of modules from the single honours fields Environmental Biology and Human Life Sciences. These may be in Equal or in Major/Minor proportions.
Principal Subjects
Biochemistry, Conservation Management, Ecology, Ecosystems, Environmental Physiology, Heredity, Human Physiology, Molecular Biology, Neuropsychology, Population Biology.

BA (Hons) Combined Arts Y300

The Combined Arts Honours programme enables students to study a range of modules from four fields, namely English, History, Sociology and Psychology. The fields each provide a strong subject identity within which students have flexibility to combine modules according to their interests. Programmes of study lead either to a joint honours degree in two subjects equally combined, or to a combined honours degree in two subjects in a major/minor relationship. The scheme also allows students to study modules from other fields within the City College Modular Scheme to complement or contrast with their main academic interests.
Principal Subjects
English Literature, History, Sociology, Psychology.

NOTTINGHAM TRENT Univ

Humanities Y301

Humanities is a well-established, flexible course designed to develop an understanding of people and the human situation. Students take 12 modules each year, six in each semester. Students take two main subjects from the list below and may, in addition, take either a third main subject or a programme of minor studies from the course curriculum. Students specialising in French or German will spend the third year in France or Germany/Austria respectively.
Principal Subjects
English, French, Geography, History, Individual and Society, Media and Cultural Studies, Heritage Studies.

OXFORD Univ

Human Sciences Y400

This course draws on many aspects of the biological and social sciences. It equips the Human Scientist with a new set of approaches to the scientific study of human beings. In addition to studying important aspects of human affairs such as world population growth and the interrelationship between man and his environment, the course includes the consideration of controversial issues of today, which have both a biological and social dimension. Students with a wide variety of educational backgrounds are welcomed and there are no special subject entrance requirements. Willingness to approach the analysis of problems with numbers as well as words is important.
Principal Subjects
Genetics, Evolution, Human Biology, Animal Behaviour, Human Population, Urban/Social Geography, Social Anthropology, Sociology.

Table 72
Course Descriptions

1605

Philosophy, Politics and Economics Y616

The first year, in which Philosophy, Politics and Economics are all studied in parallel, is designed to lay the foundation for the more advanced work of the second and third years. In the second and third years all three subjects can be studied or any two out of three. In each branch the course includes a number of basic subjects of study - the core of the discipline - and a wide range of more specialised subjects.

Principal Subjects

Economics, Philosophy, Politics.

Engineering, Economics and Management Y630

This four-year course offers a broad programme intended to produce engineers with a sound knowledge of modern economics and management techniques. Each subject is taught by specialists in the relevant department. Within certain restrictions, a wide range of options is available to allow students to tailor the course to their own particular interests. Industrial placements are an important feature of the course.

Principal Subjects

Economics, Engineering, Management.

Metallurgy, Economics and Management Y634

This is a broad, four-year degree course which combines a scientific training with sound knowledge of modern economics and management techniques. It is particularly suitable for students who are planning careers in industry or commerce. The first year provides a foundation in the physical sciences, and incorporates a range of option papers in physics, chemistry, mathematics and the principles of metallurgy/materials science. In subsequent years, the study of metallurgy and materials science runs parallel with work on micro- and macro-economics, operations research, organisational behaviour and industrial relations. Two periods are spent in industry, a six-week placement between years two and three, and a six-month management project in the fourth year. The course is accredited at MEng level by the Engineering Council.

Principal Subjects

Economics, Management, Metallurgy.

Psychology, Philosophy and Physiology Y620

PPP allows you to study thought and behaviour from the perspectives of Psychology, Physiology, and Philosophy. It is an extremely flexible course, offering a range of choices across all three branches, as well as the possibility of specialising in one. It also offers a great opportunity to develop an interdisciplinary approach to the study of the mind and the brain. Psychology includes subjects such as social interaction, learning, schizophrenia and artificial intelligence. Physiology introduces mammalian and human physiology from the molecular level to the whole organism. Philosophy is concerned with questions concerning ethics, knowledge, the nature of mind; of special interest to psychologists and physiologists are philosophy's enquiries into the nature of perception, thought and language.

Principal Subjects

Psychology, Philosophy, Physiology.

OXFORD BROOKES Univ

Extended Science Y100

One year foundation stage followed by three year science degree within the Modular Course, for applicants who lack Science A levels. After completing the foundation stage, students follow either joint honours (two subjects from the list below) or single honours (one subject from the list below).

Single Honours (one subject from the following): Applied Geology, Cell and Molecular Biology, Environmental Biology, Geological Sciences, Human Biology, Nutrition and Food Science.

or

Joint Honours (two subjects from the following): Biology, Environmental Biology, Environmental Sciences, Food Science and Nutrition, Geology.

Principal Subjects

Applied Geology, Biology, Cell and Molecular Biology, Electronics, Environmental Biology, Environmental Sciences, Food Science & Nutrition, Geological Sciences, Geology, Human Biology, Microelectronics, Nutrition and Food Science.

International Foundation Y300

One year foundation stage followed by three year arts degree within the Modular Course, for international applicants who do not meet normal UK entry requirements, but have a secondary school leaving certificate that would gain entry to HE in their own country, and who have an English Language qualification at the appropriate level.

Table 72
Course Descriptions

Univ of PAISLEY

Combined Studies (Credit Accumulation & Transfer Scheme) Y400
The scheme gives students more flexibility and choice in terms of the subjects studied, qualifications gained and whether attendance is full or part-time. Existing university courses have been subdivided into a number of units each having an associated number of CATS credit points. Students negotiate their own programme of study to include any of these units and in some cases courses offered at other HE institutions, or through employers' training schemes. On successful completion of units, points are awarded and these accumulated towards a qualification. Students may also receive credit for existing qualifications or relevant work-based learning.
Principal Subjects
Built Environment, Business Administration, Computing, Electronic Technology, Engineering, Mechanical & Manufacturing Technology, Sciences, Social Sciences, Total Quality, Urban and Regional Development, Accounting, Mathematical Sciences, Marketing, Behavioural Sciences, Chemistry, Chemical Engineering, Economics, French, German, Human Resource Management, Information Technology, Language Studies, Spanish.

General Science Y100
Interdisciplinary BSc course available on progression from any year 1 course in the Science and Technology degrees scheme as an alternative to a single subject degree. A great variety of course combinations is possible, however the overall programme is subject to discussion and approval. All students undertake guided self study in a selected interdisciplinary area culminating in the presentation of a substantial written report.

Univ of PLYMOUTH

Extended Science (Foundation Year) Y108
Foundation year for those without normal entry requirements. The extended science programme involves studying basic science subjects in a foundation year and then proceeding to a three year degree - consult University prospectus for details.
Principal Subjects

Agriculture, Biology, Chemistry, Earth Sciences, Environmental Science, Food/Rural Resources, Geology, Management, Marine Science. Art, Social Science,

Science Stage 1 Modules Y400
The University of Plymouth is now collaborating with a number of Partner Colleges in the provision of Stage One degree modules. Applications should be made to the University of Plymouth via UCAS. A variety of these modules is available at the following colleges: Cornwall College, Exeter College, North Devon College, Somerset College of Arts and Technology, South Devon College, St Austell College, Yeovil College. Contact the Partner College direct regarding availability and possible combinations.

QUEEN MARGARET COLL

Combined Studies Y600
Combined Studies has been designed to allow a flexible combination of subjects from within the College's educational provision. The emphasis is on flexibility and student choice of subject combination. The aim is for students to take more responsibility for their learning and design study programmes to suit their particular needs and interests. Three subjects of equal weight are studied in level one. These are selected during application but may be changed at enrolment in exceptional cases. Two of the chosen subjects are normally studied during the remainder of the programme. These can be combined in equal measure for a joint honours award or can be split on a 2:1 ratio for a major/minor honours award. Alternatively modules within the available subjects may be combined in a more flexible way for the award of an honours degree in Combined Studies. Every effort is made to ensure that time-tabling restrictions do not limit choice of subject combinations but this may be a problem in a small number of cases.
Principal Subjects
Applied Sociology & Social Policy, Business Organisation, Consumer Studies, Human and Professional Communication, Information Management, Marketing, Media and Cultural Studies, Psychology, Theatre Studies, Tourism Studies.

Table 72
Course Descriptions

1607

QUEEN MARY & WESTFIELD COLL (Univ of London)

Science and Engineering (4 years with Foundation) Y157
The Science and Engineering Foundation Programme provides a four-year programme of study for students who have non-standard entry qualifications. On completion of the common integral foundation year, students continue towards a BSc degree with honours or BEng degree with honours. A variety of degrees is offered by the following participating departments: Chemistry; Physics; Materials; Aeronautical Engineering; Civil Engineering; Electronic Engineering; Mechanical Engineering; Computer Science.
Students will choose, in conjunction with their personal advisers, the subjects which they wish to study from a range of modules on offer. Additional English Language modules are available which make the Foundation Programme suitable for international students wishing to enter UK higher education.
Principal Subjects
Aeronautical Engineering, Chemistry, Civil Engineering, Electronic Engineering, Materials Engineering, Mechanical Engineering, Physics, Computer Science.

Combined Honours Y158
The Combined Honours code enables students to take any of the courses offered in the science faculty for which they have the necessary background. Students may eventually decide to concentrate on one or two areas of science and will graduate with a degree title reflecting this specialisation. Alternatively, given the flexible structure of the degree and the wide range of course units available, students may choose to follow a more general degree in Science.

ROEHAMPTON INST

Humanities (English History Theology & Religious St) VY93
Humanities provides students with the opportunity to study within three interrelated disciplines - English, History and Theology & Religious Studies. The study of each of the three disciplines complements, facilitates and deepens the study of the others. The Humanities programme involves the study of many of the ways in which humankind has attempted to make sense of the world in which we live. The aim of the programme is that students should be able to analyse, understand and evaluate what is entailed in those human activities.
At Foundation level, students follow modules which are divided equally amongst the three subject areas. At Honours level students may choose between either continuing a balanced study of all three areas, or concentrating more on one or two subject areas for which they have developed a particular interest.
Principal Subjects
English, History, Theology and Religious Studies.

BSc Human Sciences Y200
The course provides a broad study of human activity from a range of viewpoints, by combining fundamental studies in human biology with applied studies in health, sport, consumer science and environmental studies.
Principal Subjects
Biological Sciences.

ROYAL HOLLOWAY, Univ of London

Science Foundation Year Y100
The Science Foundation Year is designed for applicants who do not have the necessary qualifications required for entry to a science degree programme - for those who would like to transfer to science after obtaining non-science A levels, mature students wishing to pursue a science degree, or those with a mixture of vocational experience and qualifications inappropriate for a science degree.
The Foundation Year is the first year of a four-year degree and is taught at one of five further education colleges near to the College. Successful completion of the first year leads to progression to one of a wide range of Royal Holloway science degree programmes - these include single honours programmes, joint honours degrees and `major/minor' combinations; the degrees cover the biological, physical, mathematical and earth sciences.
A brochure describing the scheme is available from the Schools and International Liaison Office, Royal Holloway, University of London, Egham, Surrey TW20 0EX (01784-443957).
Principal Subjects
Applied Physics, Biochemistry, Biology, Botany, Computer Science, Electronics, Environmental Science, Geography, Geology, Mathematics, Molecular Cell Biology, Physics, Physiology, Zoology.

Table 72
Course Descriptions

SCOTTISH AGRICULTURAL COLLEGE

Rural Business Management Y400
A multidisciplinary course combining business management with technology awareness. Study includes a range of arts, social science and science subjects and two periods of industrial placement. After the second year there is a choice of one of four degree programmes broadly representing Agriculture, Food Management, and Rural Enterprise. Applicants are requested to indicate their programme intentions on their application but it is possible to transfer between programmes after entry.
See prospectus for further details.

Univ of SALFORD

Sociology with Cultural Studies L3Y6
See prospectus for further details.

Univ College SCARBOROUGH

Combined Honours
Y-coded courses
See prospectus for further details.

Univ of SHEFFIELD

Foundation Year Course Y100
Most science courses at Sheffield may be taken as four-year courses with a foundation year. These are intended for any students who wish to study science but lack the usual scientific background.
Principal Subjects
Anatomy & Cell Biology, Animal & Plant Biology, Biochemistry, Biological Sciences, Biomedical Science, Biotechnology, Chemical Physics, Chemistry, Computer Science, Ecology, Electronics, Genetics, Mathematics, Medical Biochemistry, Microbiology, Molecular Biology, Neuroscience, Pharmacology, Physics, Plant Sciences, Zoology.

Social and Political Studies Y220
This course enables students to combine four subjects (history, philosophy, politics and sociological studies) in ways that are broader and more varied than a traditional dual honours course. You will major in one subject, which will account for half your modules, and choose the remaining half from the other three subjects.
Principal Subjects
Social History, Philosophy, Politics, Sociological Studies.

Economics with Mathematics and Statistics Y620
A broad-based course enabling economics to be taken along with a range of combinations of mathematics and statistics.
Principal Subjects
Economics, Mathematics, Statistics.

SHEFFIELD HALLAM Univ

Combined Studies Y400
The Combined Studies Programme offers a variety of subject areas with a wide framework of awards. On successful completion of a chosen programme of study, the Combined Studies Programme leads to the award of a DipHE, a BA (Hons) or a BSc (Hons). Students may choose their own degree route which will consist of units drawn from the university's full range of courses, subject to availability. The title of the final award will depend on the choice of units a student makes as she/he progresses through the programme.
Principal Subjects
Accountancy, Architectural Technology, Art, Biomedical Sciences, Business Studies, Catering Systems, Chemistry, Civil Engineering, Communication Studies, Computer Aided Engineering and Design, Computing, Construction, Countryside Management, Design, Education, Electrical Engineering, English, Environmental Engineering, Environmental Management, Environmental Planning, Film Studies, Financial Studies, Food Marketing, Food and Consumer Studies, Health Studies, History, History of Art, Design and Film, Hotel Management, Housing Management, Industrial Studies, Law, Manufacturing Engineering, Materials Engineering, Mathematics, Mechanical and Manufacturing Engineering, Media Studies, Physics, Property Management, Psychology, Public Sector Management, Recreation Management, Science in the Media, Social Policy, Social Studies, Sports Science, Statistics, Surveying, Systems Modelling, Technology (Design Technology), Tourism, Town and Country Planning, Transport Planning, Urban and Regional Geography.

Table 72
Course Descriptions
1609

Combined Studies Y400 & Combined Studies Foundation Programmes Y408 at Partner Colleges Y400 & Y408
These programmes offer a selected range of subjects and are particularly suited to the needs of mature students.

Combined Studies Y400
At Chesterfield College (Campus Code D). First year only - Subject to Approval. Contact College for further information before applying. Principal subjects will cover the Social Sciences and Humanities areas.
At Rother Valley College (Campus Code L). First year only - Subject to Approval. Contact College for further information before applying. Principal subjects will cover the Social Sciences and Humanities areas.
At Northern College (Campus Code K). First year only - Contact College for further information before applying. Principal subjects are Literature, Popular Culture and Media Studies, History, Politics, Psychology, Social Policy, Social Studies, Women's Studies.
At Sheffield College (Campus Code N). First year only - Contact College for further information before applying. Principal subjects are Culture and Visual Studies, English, History, Politics, Psychology, Social Policy, Social Studies, Urban Studies.
At Wakefield College (Campus Code O). Leading to DipHE - Contact College for further information before applying. Principal subjects are English, History, Psychology, Social Policy, Social Studies.

Combined Studies Foundation Programmes Y408
These Foundation Programmes lead to Y400 at Sheffield Hallam University.
At Rother Valley College (Campus Code L). Contact College for further information before applying. Principal subjects are English, Psychology, Social Studies, Urban Studies.
At Sheffield College (Campus Code N). Contact College for further information before applying. Principal subjects are English, History, Psychology, Social Studies. Options include Law, European Studies, World Studies, Gender Issues.

University College of ST MARTIN, LANCASTER AND CUMBRIA

Science, Technology and Society Y100
The STS course will give an insight into the nature of scientific and technological activities, and their impact on society. The course will look at topical issues in science and technology and little previous scientific knowledge is assumed.

Univ of ST ANDREWS

General Degree of BSc Y100
This degree programme, which extends over three years, is modular in nature and typically requires passes in 14 modules, of which four must be taken at second year level. There are many ways to construct this degree based on a wide variety of modules available from those offered in the Faculty of Science.
Principal Subjects
Animal Biology, Applied Mathematics (Science), Astrophysics, Behavioural Biology, Biochemistry, Biology, Cell and Molecular Biology, Chemistry, Computer Science, Economics (Science), Environmental Biology, Experimental Pathology, Genetics, Geochemistry, Geography, Geoscience (38),Logic and Philosophy of Science (59),Management Sciences (Science), Marine and Environmental Biology, Mathematics (Science), Physics, Physics and Electronics, Physiology, Psychology, Pure Mathematics (Science), Statistics (Science), Theoretical Physics.
General Degree of MA Y450
This degree programme, which extends over 3 years, is modular in nature and typically requires passes in 16 modules. There are many ways to construct this degree based on the wide variety of modules available from those offered in the Faculty of Arts, although there is a requirement to choose first level modules from at least three of seven groups of subjects.
Principal Subjects
Ancient History, Applied Mathematics (Arts), Art History, Biblical Studies, Classical Studies, Classics, Economics, English Language and Literature, Geography, Greek, Hebrew, History, International Relations, Latin, Management, Medieval History, Modern History, Modern Languages, Modern Languages (Arabic), Modern Languages (French), Modern Languages (German), Modern Languages (Russian), Modern Languages (Spanish), Philosophy, Psychology, Pure Mathematics (Arts), Scottish History, Social Anthropology, Statistics (Arts), Theology.

European Integration Studies Y602
First level modules in European Integration Studies are normally taken by students who have successfully completed a wide range of relevant courses in the first-year in the University. The class is comprised of two modules. The first module is The Idea of Europe. It examines why states have wanted to join together, and why some of these unions have split apart in the past. The module will focus on case studies from each of Ancient, Medieval and Modern History, such as Greek federations, the Byzantine Empire, the Holy Roman Empire, the nature and fall of Ottoman and Hapsburg Empires and the impact of modern wars. The second module is Politics and Economics. This module takes a more contemporary approach to European Integration. The political questions covered include the rise of the state, nation, sovereignty, interdependence, federalism and integration, NATO, Council of Europe, and European Community/European Union from a comparative perspective. The contemporary economics issues covered include customs unions, common policies such as the Common Agricultural Policy, the EC budget, regional and social policy, the growth development into monetary union.
Principal Subjects
Economics, German, International Relations, Modern History, Philosophy, Russian, French, Spanish.

Table 72
Course Descriptions

Univ of STIRLING

Politics, Philosophy and Economics Y616
The Politics, Philosophy and Economics degree at Stirling (PPE) is the only one of its kind in Scotland and one of only a handful in the United Kingdom. The Stirling degree contains a Scottish option in all three areas of study for those interested. Its focus, clearly, is on the relationship in the 'real world' between these disciplines, and the degree provides an excellent basis for those who wish to understand the way modern British governments and industries operate in the European and World context. It is an ideal degree for those who seek a degree in government or in business management or those who simply want to know what makes things tick in modern Britain.
Principal Subjects
Economics, Philosophy, Politics.

STOCKPORT COLL of F and HE

Science 001Y
This course has been designed in collaboration with local employers. Students can select appropriate modules in Chemistry, Biology or Biochemistry. The course can lead to careers as Senior Laboratory Technicians in industry or the public sector or to full time higher education at University.
Principal Subjects
Biochemistry, Biology, Chemistry.

Univ of STRATHCLYDE

Science Studies (Pass Degree) Y100
All candidates admitted to this BSc Pass course will be allocated to a "parent" department and admission to the course will involve consultation between the student and the Director or Deputy Director. There are several "named" Degrees under the heading Science Studies, for example, BSc Science Studies (Chemistry and Physics). All Science Faculty Departments (and some departments in other faculties) contribute to this Degree. The curriculum of the degree is flexible and gives the student the option of choosing the same curriculum as one of the Honours courses. A good performance provides the student with the possibility of transfer, after one or two years, to certain of the Honours courses.
Principal Subjects
Biology, Biochemistry, Chemistry, Computer Science, Physiology, Horticulture, Mathematics, Microbiology, Physics, Statistics.

BA Degree (Arts and Social Sciences) Y440
This BA offered by the Faculty of Arts and Social Sciences at Strathclyde is distinctive in offering combinations of humanities, social sciences and business subjects to full degree award level. It is a three year course for an ordinary degree, and four for the Honours Degree. Second year entry is sometimes possible. Students take five subjects in the first year, giving them a broad education and a wide choice before specialising in two principal subjects. They also develop computer skills, and receive careers training in each year of their course to enhance career prospects. Students are admitted to the BA Pass (Ordinary) Degree in the first instance and if accepted by the Head(s) of Department(s) concerned may proceed to Single or Joint Honours study once they have qualified with the BA Degree. There are opportunities for study in Europe, the United States and Canada as a recognised part of the BA curriculum. The subjects offered in the BA Pass (Ordinary) Degree are listed below. All but Russian and East European Studies are also offered at Joint Honours level. Subjects marked with an asterisk can be taken at Single Honours level.
Principal Subjects
*English, European Studies, *French, *Geography, *German, *History (Economic and Social), History (Modern), Italian, *Politics, *Psychology, Russian, Russian and East European Studies, Scottish Studies, *Sociology, *Spanish.

UNIVERSITY COLLEGE SUFFOLK

Modular Degree W2Y3,YQ32,YP34
Joint Routes in Media Studies
Literary Studies
Cultural Studies
Each of these routes is offered as a joint option and must, therefore, be combined with another joint route within The Suffolk Modular Degree Programme,
eg Media Studies and Art & Design
Literary Studies and Cultural Studies
Cultural Studies and Media Studies
Media Studies
This route focuses specifically on the mass media forms of film and television. Students will be able to develop their critical understanding of media texts and the relationship between texts and the social and cultural context of their production. The route draws on three underlying themes: media texts, media audiences and media institutions.

Table 72
Course Descriptions
1611

Literary Studies

Study on this route is designed to develop students' critical understanding of a range of literary texts taken mainly from the 19th and 20th centuries. Students will consider how such texts link to the cultural and historical period in which they are produced and read. Texts studied will include novels, poetry, drama, popular literature, experimental writing and various writing from both the UK and Europe.

Cultural Studies

The cultural studies route enables students to explore a broad range of cultural products, processes and contexts. There is an emphasis on interdisciplinary study and on providing an historical perspective to the development of contemporary culture. There are opportunities to develop understanding and practical skills in using local history archives. Study on the route will consider the interrelationships of local culture, national culture and European culture.

Direct entry to Level 3 BA (Hons) Performing Arts

This final year performing arts course is available to students wishing to develop previous study undertaken to second year graduate level. Study focuses on developing practical performance skills and relating these to critical understanding of the context of performance. Students will be able to analyse how actions of drama and dance have been challenged by practitioners working in performance art, multi media and cross cultural areas. Students will produce a balance of practical and written work.

Principal Subjects

Cultural Studies.

Individual Studies Y100,Y400

The Individually Negotiated Learning Route brings together the study of selected modules with individually agreed research activity. The Route is offered on a part or full time basis. Students progressively develop the individual study element of their programme with half the programme at Level 2 and normally all at Level 3 being negotiated between individual students and tutors.

The Philosophy of the Individually Negotiated Learning Route emphasises the learning needs of the individual and is particularly appropriate for mature students wishing to build upon prior experience and for any student who prefers an active mode of learning.

Principal Subjects

Applied Biological Sciences, Early Childhood Studies, Environmental Studies, Human Sciences, Information Technology, Art and Design, Business Studies, Cultural Studies, Media.

Univ of Sunderland

Independent Programme Scheme Y400

The Independent Programmes Scheme operates on a fully modular basis, so subjects can be studied according to interests, abilities and career intentions. BA or BSc degree is awarded depending upon the combination of subject. It is important that each Independent Programmes student has an academically coherent set of modules within their individual programmes of study. Students are therefore required to negotiate and agree with us their planned programme of study. This programme extends beyond the Combined Programmes Scheme, and enables students to select modules from a much wider subject base.

Univ of SUSSEX

Human Sciences (4 Yrs) Y400

The course offers a multidisciplinary and interdisciplinary approach to the study of human beings and the relation between Nature and Culture. It draws upon the differing and often conflicting insights of social and cultural anthropology, biological anthropology, philosophy, psychology, linguistics, biology and cultural studies. Over the first three years, a common core curriculum provides students with a rigorous grounding in some of the central human science disciplines. From the third year onwards, there is the opportunity to pursue an individual programme of study, either specialised or multidisciplinary, according to the student's interests.

Principal Subjects

Human Biological Sciences, Human Culture and Society.

Arts, Humanities and Social Sciences Y200

An integrated four or five year degree taught in conjunction with nearby Lewes Tertiary College. A pass in the first year at Lewes permits continued study on the chosen degree programme. The course is designed for students who have not attained the necessary qualifications for direct entry. Study skills, language preparation and project work are combined with a series of modules in art, humanities and social sciences or, alternatively, one GCE A level or two GCE AS levels.

University of WALES, SWANSEA

Joint Hons in Social Studies with deferred choice of specialisation Y220

In this scheme students choose their two Joint Honours subjects at the end of the first year at university. The choice is made from subjects taken during the first year, and involves any pair of the subjects listed below, timetable permitting. A course in introductory quantitative methods, at first-year level only, is also available.

Principal Subjects

(inc Economic History), (inc Economics), (inc Geography), (inc Philosophy), (inc Politics), (inc Psychology), (inc Social Anthropology), (inc Social History), (inc Social Policy), (inc Sociology).

Table 72
Course Descriptions

SWANSEA INST of HE

Combined Honours Y300
Principal Subjects
English with Drama and Media, English with Studies in Modern Society, European Social and Industrial Studies.

TRINITY COLL Carmarthen

Humanities (Options) Y320
See prospectus for further details.
Principal Subjects
Archaeology, English, Geography, Religious Studies, Theatre Studies, Welsh Studies.

Dyniaethau Y321
See prospectus for further details.
Principal Subjects
History, Religious Studies, Theatre Studies, Welsh.

Univ of ULSTER

Humanities Combined Y320
The course is planned according to the principle of delayed and informed choice, allowing students to acquire a broad foundation in the study of the humanities before choosing specialist subjects. Students take three subjects in Year 1, and in subsequent years they continue with two of these subjects, either as joint or major/minor options.
Principal Subjects
Irish, English, European Studies, French, Geography, German, History, Japanese Studies, Media Studies, Philosophy, Spanish, Theatre Studies.

Modern Studies in the Humanities (3/4 Yrs) Y321
This course offers a study of the humanities by integrating various disciplines. A special feature of the course is an arrangement whereby selected students can spend a year of study at a university in the United States by participating in the international exchange programme. In Year 1 students follow a common programme, which introduces the four 'strands' which form the basis of subsequent study, namely: American studies, the individual and society, literature, culture and society, and the modern state. In the second and final years students concentrate on one of the four strands introduced in year 1.
Principal Subjects
American Studies, Individual and Society, Literature, Culture & Society, The Modern State. Combined Studies in Art and Design.

BA/BSc Hons Combined Studies Y200
The first year of the course provides a foundation in a number of disciplines and in years 2 and 3 students specialise in two of these disciplines. The following discipline areas are available: Politics, History, Public Policy, Management, Informatics, Sociology, Social Policy and Psychology.

UNIVERSITY COLL LONDON (Univ of London)

Physical Sciences Y100 and Y101
An honours degree within the course-unit system for students who seek a broad-based scientific course. The course is suitable for students with various levels of preparation in science, including mature students without A or AS qualifications. First year students follow a mathematics unit plus three units chosen from: astronomy, chemistry, geological sciences, physics, computer science and statistics, biology or psychology. All of these offer introductory courses for entrants who have not studied a subject at sixth-form level. In subsequent years students choose from a wide range of science units and half-units, and may broaden the course further by including a component of economics, a language, philosophy, etc. After a successful first year, there is an option of transferring to a more specialised BSc or MSci degree.
Principal Subjects
Astronomy, Chemistry, Computer Science, Geological Science, Mathematics, Physics, Statistical Science.

Statistics, Computing, Operational Research and Economics Y624
Requiring no previous qualifications in the subjects of its title (SCORE), this programme integrates a training in selected aspects of the applied mathematical disciplines of statistics and operational research, with applications in economics and the development of relevant skills in computer programming. The subjects are designed to reinforce one another so as to produce a coherent and wide-ranging foundation in modern quantitative techniques. The first year covers mathematics, statistics, computing and economics, while second and third year courses introduce, in addition, the techniques of operational research.
Principal Subjects
Computing, Economics, Operational Research, Statistics.

Letts STUDY GUIDES
THE INDEPENDENT

Table 72
Course Descriptions

1613

Statistics, Operational Research and a European Language Y625
Requiring no previous qualifications in the subject of its title (SOREL), this programme integrates a training in selected aspects of the applied mathematical disciplines of statistics and operational research, and provides a thorough training in a modern European language. The mathematical subjects are designed to reinforce one another so as to produce a coherent and wide-ranging foundation in modern quantitative techniques. The first year covers mathematics, statistics, economics and a European language while second and third year courses introduce, in addition, the techniques of operational research.
Principal Subjects
European Language, Operational Research, Statistics.

Human Sciences Y400
Human Sciences looks at the origin of the human species: human anatomy, human physiological and physical functioning, the diversity and the behaviour and distribution of human populations, their relation to the rest of the natural world and to the environment they create.

University College WARRINGTON

Combined Studies (Mature Student Programme) Y400
The BA Combined Honours degree is particularly designed for applicants aged 21 or over at the time of entry. This degree offers the opportunity to select course modules from the widest range with the minimum of restriction. Thus a programme with a strong vocational orientation can be studied by those who wish, or else a programme which provides a broader-based education can be created for those students who might want to make an informed choice about their future plans at a later stage. Programmes can lead towards employment in community related work in the fields of communications, Media, Leisure, Business, Arts and other service industries.

Univ of WARWICK

Maths, Operational Research, Statistics, Economics Y602
See prospectus for further details.
Principal Subjects
Economics, Mathematics, Operational Research, Statistics.

WESTHILL COLL of HE

Humanities - Creative Arts Y4W9
Candidates select three subjects from: Art & Design, Drama, Dance, Music for study over three years. All students also follow the compulsory Interdisciplinary strand for the first two years. Candidates do not need to be equally strong in all three subjects and there are no special subject entrance requirements although a strong interest in, and commitment to, the study should be evident in applications.

Humanities - Childhood Studies Y600
Candidates follow strands in: Education Studies, English, History for three years. All students also follow the compulsory Interdisciplinary strand for the first two years. Childhood is seen as a subject for study from sociological, psychological and educational perspectives. This degree programme will be particularly relevant for students wishing to enter primary teaching through the PACE or for other careers involving children.

Humanities - 19th & 20th Century Studies Y602
Candidates follow strands in: Education Studies, English, History for three years. All students also follow the compulsory Interdisciplinary strand for the first two years. The degree looks at major aesthetic, political and intellectual developments in the 19th & 20th centuries and encourages students to recognise the intellectual and societal links across them.

Humanities - Mathematics, Science and Psychology Y601
Candidates follow strands in: Mathematical Studies, Science, Technology & Society, Psychology. All students also follow the compulsory Interdisciplinary strand for the first two years. The degree studies maths, science & technology and psychology in a human context. Standard college entrance requirements apply. In addition, applicants should preferably have studied mathematics and science beyond GCSE level, but commitment and an aptitude for further study in these areas are the main requirements. Access students will be considered on an individual basis but should have completed some studies at level 3.

Univ of WESTMINSTER

Combined Honours Y200
Applicants may select only 2 of the following half degree subjects to be studied together, or on a major/minor basis: Sociology, Criminology, Socio-legal Studies, Women's Studies, Modern History, Human Geography, Third World Studies, Psychology, Politics, International Relations, European Studies.
All applicants will follow a common level 1 programme, in the course of which the choice of combinations will be finalised. No choice has to be specified on application.

Table 72
Course Descriptions

Univ of WOLVERHAMPTON

Applied Sciences - Modular Scheme Y100

Applied Sciences is an integrated multi-subject Science course. Each student, under the guidance of a personal tutor, selects a programme of study to match his/her own developing academic interests and career aspirations. Programmes may be broad or specialist and are planned from approximately 250 modules in the subjects listed below. Each programme is a highly appropriate professional qualification in the subjects studied. Full time students may choose to include a period in industry in their programme (the 4 year sandwich course).

There are opportunities under current ERASMUS and TEMPUS programmes to study a range of subjects for a limited period at universities in mainland Europe. A wide range of careers in science and technology is available to our graduates as well as careers of a non-specialist nature.

Principal Subjects

Biochemistry, Biology, Biomedical Science, Biotechnology, Business, Chemistry, Computer Aided Design, Computing, Construction Studies, Decision Science, Ecology, Economics, Earth Sciences, Engineering Systems, Environmental Animal Biology, Environmental Management, Environmental Science, Exercise Science, Food Biology, Genetics and Molecular Biology, Health Sciences, Human Biology, Human Physiology, Manufacturing Studies, Materials Technology, Mathematical Sciences, Microbiology, Pharmacology, Plant and Crop Science, Psychology, Public Health.

Applied Sciences (4 Yrs) - Modular Scheme Y110

This is a four year course specifically designed for mature applicants without standard entry qualifications. The first year (foundation year) is spent at Dudley College (subject to approval), Halesowen College, Matthew Boulton College Birmingham, Shrewsbury College of Arts & Technology, Stourbridge College (subject to approval), Sutton Coldfield College of Further Education, Telford College of Arts & Technology, Walsall College of Arts & Technology or Wulfrun College, Wolverhampton.

Students then transfer to BSc (Hons) Applied Sciences, code Y100 at the University of Wolverhampton. Please see the entry for Y100 for details.

Principal Subjects

Biochemistry, Biology, Biomedical Science, Biotechnology, Chemistry, Computer Aided Design, Computing, Construction Studies, Decision Sciences, Earth Sciences, Ecology, Engineering Systems, Environmental Animal Biology, Environmental Management, Environmental Science, Exercise Science, Food Biology, Genetics and Molecular Biology, Human Biology, Human Physiology, Manufacturing Studies, Materials Technology, Mathematical Sciences, Microbiology, Pharmacology, Plant and Crop Science.

Combined Degrees - Modular Scheme Y401

The Scheme provides the opportunity to specialise in one subject or to combine two or three of the ninety one subjects according to the availability listed in the UCAS Handbook. First year programmes are broad based to allow students to experience new subjects and to confirm that their original choice of subjects is appropriate. Applicants are requested to indicate their study intentions at the application stage but it is possible to transfer between study programmes after entry. The decision about the balance of study between subjects can often be left until the start of the final year.

Principal Subjects

Accounting, American Studies, Applied Theology, Art For Society, Biochemistry, Biology, Biomedical Science, Biotechnology, Business, Business Information Management, Business Law, Ceramics, Chemistry, Communication Studies, Computer Aided Design, Computing, Conductive Education, Construction Studies, Dance, Deaf Studies, Decision Sciences, Design and Technology, Design for Floor Covering & Interior Textiles, Design Studies, Earth Science, Ecology, Economics, Education Studies, Education Studies (3 Semesters in Holland), Electronic Media, Engineering Systems, English, English (3 Semesters in Holland), English as a Foreign Language, Environmental Animal Biology, Environmental Law, Environmental Management, Environmental Science, European Cultural Studies, European and International Law, European Studies, Exercise Science, Film Studies, Food Biology, French Studies, Furniture Design, Genetics and Molecular Biology, Geography, Geography - Human, German Studies, Graphic Communication, Health Sciences, History, Human Biology, Human Physiology, Human Resource Management, Illustration, Interactive Multimedia Communication, Italian Studies, Japanese Studies, Latin American Studies, Law, Leisure and Recreation Management, Linguistics, Manufacturing Studies, Marketing, Materials Technology, Mathematical Sciences, Media and Cultural Studies, Microbiology, Music, Music - Popular, Painting, Pharmacology, Philosophy, Photography, Plant and Crop Sciences, Politics, Printmaking, Psychology, Public Health, Quality Management, Religious Studies, Russian Studies, Sculpture, Social Policy, Social Welfare Law, Sociology, Spanish Studies, Special Needs, Sports Studies, Teaching of English for Speakers of Other Languages, Theatre Studies, Tourism, War Studies, Women's Studies, Woods, Metals and Plastics.

Combined Degrees in Art and Design Subjects - Modular Scheme E401

The Scheme offers both specialist and broad-based programmes of study tailored to your individual professional and personal ambitions. You may study one, two or three Art and Design subjects in combination or you may combine study in Art and Design with other subjects in the University Modular Degree and Diploma Scheme. All modules are offered in fully equipped studios and workshops in a purpose built University School of Art and Design.

Principal Subjects

Animation, Art for Society, Ceramics, Design & Technology, Design for Floor Coverings and Interior Textiles, Design Studies, Electronic Media, Furniture Design, Glass, Graphic Communication, Illustration, Interactive Multimedia Communication, Painting, Photography, Printmaking, Sculpture, Woods, Metals and Plastics.

Table 72
Course Descriptions

1615

Univ of YORK

Philosophy, Politics and Economics Y616
An interdisciplinary course which takes an integrated approach to the study of the three subjects. The course contains specially designed joint courses which explore the interrelations between Philosophy, Politics and Economics (Rationality, Morality and Economics, The Democratic Economy, Individual and Community). All students undertake an independent project.
Principal Subjects
Economics, Philosophy, Politics.

NOTES

NOTES

Index

INDEPENDENT
ON SUNDAY

The list of subjects and Course Table numbers is given below as a guide to the division of *UCE:G*. Note that individual course titles can be misleading and may not convey the breadth or focus of the course content nor its structure, which you need to check in individual prospectuses.

A

Accountancy, Accounting 01
Accounting and Finance 01
Acoustics (Engineering) 25
Acoustics (Music) 56
Acoustics 23, 60
Acting 17
Actuarial Science, Studies 01, 52
Administration 12
Advertising (Copywriting, Design and Management) 07, 53
Advertising Management 12
Aerodynamics 20
Aeromechanical Systems Engineering 20
Aeronautical Engineering & Manufacture 20
Aerospace Engineering, Studies 20
African Studies 36
AfroAsian Studies 36
AfroPortuguese 46
Agricultural Biology 02, 09
Agricultural Botany 02
Agricultural Economics 18
Agricultural Engineering 25
Agricultural Management 02, 12, 29
Agriculture, Science 02
Agroforestry 02
Agronomy 02
Air Transport Engineering 20
Amenities Management 66
Alternative Therapies 32
American Arts 03
American Business Studies 12
American Legal Systems 47
American Literature 03, 26
American Management Science 12
American Studies 03
American Studies (History) 03, 33
Amharic Studies 36
Analytical Chemistry Science 13
Anatomy, Anatomical Sciences 04
Ancient Civilisations 05, 33
Ancient Greek 38
Ancient History 33, 38
Anglo Saxon 37
Animal Behaviour 09
Animal Biology 09, 71
Animal Nutrition and Physiology 02, 04, 09
Animal Production, Animal Management 02
Animal Science 02, 09, 71
Animation 07
Anthropology 64
Antiques and Collection Management 12
Applicable Mathematics 52
Applied Arts 07
Applied Social Sciences 64, 65
Aquatic Biology 09
Arabic 43
Arboriculture 02
Archaeology, Archaeological Sciences 05
Architectural Design 06
Architectural Engineering 11, 22
Architectural History 06

Architectural Technology 06, 11
Architecture, Architectural Studies 06, 34
Art 07
Art & Design 07
Art History 34
Artificial Intelligence 15
Arts Therapy, Healing 32
Arts Management 07, 12
Asian Studies, Contemporary 64
Asset Management 01
Astronautics 20
Astronomy 60
Astrophysics 60
Audio and Video Systems 07
Audio and Visual Engineering 07, 23
Audio and Visual Production 14
Audiotechnology 23
Australian Studies 64
Automobile Engineering 25
Automotive Engineering & Design 24, 25
Avionics, Avionic Systems 20, 23

B

Band Studies, Band Musicianship 56
Banking 01
Beauty, Therapy and Sciences 32
Behavioural Biology 09
Behavioural Studies 63, 64
Bengali, Bengali Studies 36
Biblical Studies 68
Biochemical Engineering 21
Biochemistry 08
Biological Chemistry 08, 13
Biological Imaging 07, 09, 51
Biology, Biological Sciences 09
Biomaterials, Biomedical Materials 09, 32, 51
Biomedical Sciences 04, 09, 13, 32, 60, 71
Biometry 09
Biomolecular Chemistry 13
Bio-organic Chemistry 13
Biophysics 08
Bioprocess Engineering 21
Biosciences 09
Biotechnology 02, 08, 09
Bookbinding 07, 53
Botany 10
Brazilian Studies 46
Brewing and Distilling 09
Broadcasting (Engineering) 23
Broadcasting Studies 53
Building Control 11
Building Design 11
Building Management 11
Building Production Engineering 11, 25
Building Services Engineering 11
Building Studies 11
Building Surveying 11
Building Technology 11
Built Environment Studies 11, 12, 27
Burmese, Burmese Studies 36
Business Administration 12
Business, Business Studies 12
Business Computer Systems 12, 15
Business Computing 15
Business Decision Analysis 12, 15
Business Economics 12, 18
Business French 40
Business Information Systems 12, 15
Business Information Technology 15

Index

NOTES

STUDY GUIDES
THE INDEPENDENT

NOTES

List of Course Tables

Course Table Summary Extracts

For full details refer to the Course Table Introduction on pages 164 - 169

Agriculture and Forestry

2

course details	CODE	COURSE
TITLE	NR4C	4FT deg
French (Syllabus B)/Accounting	NR3C	4FT deg
French (Syllabus B)/Banking	NR42	4FT deg
German/Accounting	NR32	4FT deg
German/Banking	N1N4	3FT deg
Management with Accounting	N1N3	3FT deg
Management with Banking, Insurance and Finance	G1N3	3FT deg
Mathematics with Insurance	GN14	3FT deg
Mathematics/Accounting	GN13	3FT deg
Mathematics/Banking	NT49	4FT deg
Modern Languages/Accounting	NT39	4FT deg
Modern Languages/Banking and Insurance	NR48	4FT deg
Russian/Accounting	NR38	4FT deg
Russian/Banking		
BELL COLLEGE OF TECHNOLOGY	004N	2FT HND
Accounting	003N	2FT HND
Financial Services		
Univ of BIRMINGHAM	N400	3FT deg
Accounting & Finance		
Accounting & Finance with French		
Accounting and Finance with German		
Money, Banking		

98 expected requirements

96 entry stats

SUBJECTS	R/AS	NO/C	AGNVQ	IB	SQA(H)	SQA	RATIO R/AS	
E g	18	X	D$^ go	28$	BBBC$	X		
E g	18	X	D$^ go	28$	BBBC$	X		
* g	18	X	D$^ go	28$	BBBC$	X		
* g	18	X	D$^ go	28	BBBC	Ind	7	10/22
* g	18	3M+2D	D$6/^ go	28	BBBC	Ind	4	
* g	18	3M+2D	D$6/^ go	28$	BBBC$	Ind		
* g	CCC	3M+2D$ D$_ go		28$	BBBC$	Ind	8	
M g	CCC	3M+2D D$_ go		28$	BBBC$	Ind	6	
M g	CCC	3M+2D$ D$_ go		28$	BBBC$	X		
M g	18	X	D$_ go	28$	BBBC$	X		
F/G g	18	X	D$_ go	28$	BBBC	Ind		
F/G g	18	3M+3D	D$6/^ go	28	BBBC	Ind		
* g	18	3M+2D	D$6/^ go	28	BBBC	Ind		
* g	DD-D	N $	P$			Ind		
*	DD-D	N $						

A Institutions

B Course Title

C Course Code

D Course

The details here aim to inform you about the nature and duration of the qualification(s) on offer and the type of final award. Key information is given below but remember to check in prospectuses.

Key:

eg 3	Number of years
FT	Full-time course
SW	Sandwich programme or placement
ACC	Accelerated route course
EXT	Extended course built on an initial foundation year
deg	Degree
Dip	Diploma of Higher Education/Institution Diploma
HND	Higher National Diploma

E Expected requirements

F A/AS Subject patterns (Subj's)

Key:

(see table opposite)

G GCE A/AS (A/AS)

The offer may be expressed in terms of a number or range of points, or grades.

To calculate a points score, each grade is given an equivalent value in points.

Key:

A level	Grade A = 10 points, B = 8, C = 6, D = 4, E = 2
AS	Grade A = 5 points, B = 4, C = 3, D = 2, E = 1
eg15	Number of points
ABCDE	Grades required at A level
X	Not sufficient for entry